NEW
AMERICAN
BIBLE

St. Joseph
Medium Size
Edition

OBADIAH	Ob	GENESIS	Gn
JONAH	Jon	EXODUS	Ex
MICAH	Mi	LEVITICUS	Lv
NAHUM	Na	NUMBERS	Nm
HABAKKUK	Hb	DEUTERONOMY	Dt
ZEPHANIAH	Zep	JOSHUA	Jos
HAGGAI	Hg	JUDGES	Jgs
ZECHARIAH	Zec	RUTH	Ru
MALACHI	Mal	1 SAMUEL	1Sm
MATTHEW	Mt	2 SAMUEL	2Sm
MARK	Mk	1 KINGS	1Kgs
LUKE	Lk	2 KINGS	2Kgs
JOHN	Jn	1 CHRONICLES	1Chr
ACTS	Acts	2 CHRONICLES	2Chr
ROMANS	Rom	EZRA	Ez
1 CORINTHIANS	1Cor	NEHEMIAH	Neh
2 CORINTHIANS	2Cor	TOBIT	Tb
		JUDITH	Jdt
GALATIANS	Gal	ESTHER	Est
EPHESIANS	Eph	1 MACCABEES	1Mc
PHILIPPIANS	Phil	2 MACCABEES	2Mc
COLOSSIANS	Col	JOB	Jb
1 THESSALONIANS	1Thes	PSALMS	Ps
2 THESSALONIANS	2Thes	PROVERBS	Prv
1 TIMOTHY	1Tm	ECCLESIASTES	Eccl
2 TIMOTHY	2Tm	SONGS	Sng
TITUS	Ti	WISDOM	Wis
PHILEMON	Phlm	SIRACH	Sir
HEBREWS	Heb	ISAIAH	Is
JAMES	Jas	JEREMIAH	Jer
1 PETER	1Pt	LAMENTATIONS	Lam
2 PETER	2Pt	BARUCH	Bar
1 JOHN	1Jn	EZEKIEL	Ez
2 JOHN	2Jn	DANIEL	Dn
3 JOHN	3Jn	HOSEA	Hos
JUDE	Jude	JOEL	Jl
REVELATION	Rv	AMOS	Am

Saint Joseph Edition of

THE NEW
AMERICAN BIBLE

Translated from the Original Languages
with Critical Use of All the Ancient Sources

INCLUDING
THE REVISED NEW TESTAMENT
AND THE REVISED PSALMS

AUTHORIZED BY THE BOARD OF TRUSTEES
of the
CONFRATERNITY OF CHRISTIAN DOCTRINE

and

APPROVED BY THE ADMINISTRATIVE COMMITTEE/BOARD
of the
NATIONAL CONFERENCE OF CATHOLIC BISHOPS
and the
UNITED STATES CATHOLIC CONFERENCE

WITH MANY HELPS FOR BIBLE READING

Vatican II Constitution on Divine Revelation, How to Read the Bible,
Historical Survey of the Lands of the Bible, Bible Dictionary,
Liturgical Index of Sunday Readings, Doctrinal Bible Index,
and over 50 Photographs and Maps of the Holy Land

SPECIAL EDITION
Available only through
BENZIGER PUBLISHING COMPANY
WOODLAND HILLS, CALIFORNIA

NIHIL OBSTAT: Stephen J. Hartdegen, O.F.M., S.S.L.
        Christian P. Ceroke, O. Carm., S.T.D.

IMPRIMATUR: ✛ Patrick Cardinal O'Boyle, D.D.
         Archbishop of Washington

July 27, 1970

THE REVISED NEW TESTAMENT

NIHIL OBSTAT: Stephen J. Hartdegen, O.F.M., S.S.L.
         Censor Deputatus

IMPRIMATUR: ✛ James A. Hickey, S.T.D., J.C.D.
         Archbishop of Washington

August 27, 1986

THE REVISED PSALMS

IMPRIMATUR: Most Rev. Daniel E. Pilarczyk
         President, National Conference of Catholic Bishops

September 10, 1991

"Let them remember that prayer should accompany the reading of Sacred Scripture, so that God and man may talk together."
(Dogmatic Constitution on Divine Revelation: Second Vatican Council)

Prayer to the Holy Spirit

COME, Holy Spirit, fill the hearts of your faithful and enkindle in them the fire of your love.

Partial Indulgence. *Enchiridion Indulgentiarum,* 1968 edition, no. 62

 A partial indulgence is granted to the faithful who use Sacred Scripture for spiritual reading with the veneration due the word of God. A plenary indulgence is granted if the reading continues for at least one half hour.
(Enchiridion Indulgentiarum, 1968 edition, no. 50)

(T-609)

PREFACE

The increasing interest in and love for the Sacred Scriptures can be attributed to the biblical movement, inaugurated and encouraged by our great modern Pontiffs and given even stronger impetus by the Second Vatican Council. Reminded by them of our duty and privilege, as members of the People of God, to disseminate the inspired Word of God, we have spared no effort to produce this improved New Edition of the Old and New Testaments.

As a sure means of deepening our knowledge of Truth, we have incorporated in this Edition the very latest complete Catholic translation known as "The New American Bible," and produced by members of the Catholic Biblical Association of America under the patronage of the Bishops' Committee of the Confraternity of Christian Doctrine.

We confidently hope that the many distinctive features found in our Edition of this fine modern translation will add greatly to the enjoyment, understanding and appreciation of the Sacred Writings.

Among these features, we might mention: the *Dogmatic Constitution on Divine Revelation* of Vatican II; a helpful section on how to read the Scriptures with more understanding; a valuable panoramic view of the lands, peoples, and major events of the Bible; a special self-indexing feature that enables the reader to find each book of the Bible instantly; a very handy Bible Dictionary; a listing of the new Mass readings for every Sunday of the year; a doctrinal Bible index for quick reference; and an easy-to-read and sight-saving typeface.

Most important of all, we have included a series of 38 self-explaining maps showing key events and areas in the Bible—each placed directly near the text which it concerns. In this way, the reader is kept abreast of the history of salvation without needless turning of pages to some other part of the book.

Finally, the invaluable cross-references and notes at the bottom of each page are all clearly referred to in the text, so that as the reader moves along he is constantly kept aware of the wealth of information provided by the latest biblical scholarship.

May God see fit to make this Edition an instrument of His greater glory and the salvation of souls.

CATHOLIC BOOK PUBLISHING CO.

For the faithful in all English-speaking countries the publication of *The New American Bible* represents a notable achievement. Its pages contain a new Catholic version of the Bible in English, along with illustrations and explanations that facilitate the understanding of the text.

For more than a quarter of a century, members of the Catholic Biblical Association of America, sponsored by the Bishops' Committee of the Confraternity of Christian Doctrine, have labored to create this new translation of the Scriptures from the original languages or from the oldest extant form in which the texts exist.

In so doing, the translators have carried out the directive of our predecessor, Pius XII, in his famous Encyclical *Divino Afflante Spiritu*, and the decree of the Second Vatican Council *(Dei Verbum)*, which prescribed that "up-to-date and appropriate translations be made in the various languages, by preference from the original texts of the sacred books", and that "with the approval of Church authority, these translations may be produced in cooperation with our separated brethren" so that "all Christians may be able to use them".

The holy task of spreading God's word to the widest possible readership has a special urgency today. Despite all his material achievements, man still struggles with the age-old problems of how to order his life for the glory of God, for the welfare of his fellows and the salvation of his soul. Therefore we are gratified to find in this new translation of the Scriptures a new opportunity for men to give themselves to frequent reading of, and meditation on, the living Word of God. In its pages we recognize His voice, we hear a message of deep significance for every one of us. Through the spiritual dynamism and prophetic force of the Bible, the Holy Spirit spreads his light and his warmth over all men, in whatever historical or sociological situation they find themselves.

On all who have contributed to this translation, and all who seek in its pages the sacred teaching and the promise of salvation of Jesus Christ our Lord, we gladly bestow our paternal Apostolic Blessing.

From the Vatican, September 18, 1970

Paulus PP. VI-

CONTENTS

Preface .... [5]
Constitution on Divine Revelation . [8]

How to Read Your Bible .... [17]
The Holy Land .... [26]

THE OLD TESTAMENT

Preface to the New American
Bible—The Old Testament .... [44]

THE PENTATEUCH

The Book of Genesis 2
The Book of Exodus 59
The Book of Leviticus 100
The Book of Numbers 131
The Book of Deuteronomy 174

The Book of Joshua 212
The Book of Judges 236
The Book of Ruth 259

THE HISTORICAL BOOKS

The First Book of Samuel 264
The Second Book of Samuel 296
The First Book of Kings 322
The Second Book of Kings 351
The First Book of Chronicles 380
The Second Book of Chronicles 409
The Book of Ezra 444
The Book of Nehemiah 454
The Book of Tobit 469
The Book of Judith 485
The Book of Esther 500
The First Book of Maccabees 513
The Second Book of Maccabees 546

THE WISDOM BOOKS

The Book of Job 570
The Book of Psalms 603
The Book of Proverbs 701
The Book of Ecclesiastes 733
The Song of Songs 742
The Book of Wisdom 750
The Book of Sirach (Ecclesiasticus) .. 771

THE PROPHETIC BOOKS

The Book of Isaiah 824
The Book of Jeremiah 892
The Book of Lamentations 957
The Book of Baruch 964
The Book of Ezekiel 972
The Book of Daniel 1021
The Book of Hosea 1042
The Book of Joel 1053
The Book of Amos 1057
The Book of Obadiah 1066
The Book of Jonah 1068
The Book of Micah 1071
The Book of Nahum 1077
The Book of Habakkuk 1080
The Book of Zephaniah 1084
The Book of Haggai 1087
The Book of Zechariah 1090
The Book of Malachi 1099

THE NEW TESTAMENT

Preface to the New American Bible—
The New Testament .... [3]

THE GOSPELS

The Gospel according to Matthew 6
The Gospel according to Mark 67
The Gospel according to Luke 95
The Gospel according to John 142

The Acts of the Apostles 179

THE NEW TESTAMENT LETTERS

The Letter to the Romans 221
The First Letter to the Corinthians 242
The Second Letter to the Corinthians . 265
The Letter to the Galatians 283
The Letter to the Ephesians 292
The Letter to the Philippians 300
The Letter to the Colossians 307

The First Letter to the Thessalonians . 313
The Second Letter to the Thessalonians 317
The First Letter to Timothy 321
The Second Letter to Timothy 328
The Letter to Titus 332
The Letter to Philemon 335
The Letter to the Hebrews 337

THE CATHOLIC LETTERS

The Letter of James 356
The First Letter of Peter 362
The Second Letter of Peter 368
The First Letter of John 373
The Second Letter of John 379
The Third Letter of John 380
The Letter of Jude 382
The Book of Revelation 385

APPENDIX

Sponsors, Editors and Translators 410
Bible Dictionary 412

Sunday Readings at Mass 422
Doctrinal Bible Index 428

DOGMATIC CONSTITUTION
ON DIVINE REVELATION

PREFACE

1. Hearing the word of God with reverence and proclaiming it with faith, the sacred Synod takes its direction from these words of St. John: "We announce to you the eternal life which dwelt with the Father and was made visible to us. What we have seen and heard we annouce to you, so that you may have fellowship with us and our common fellowship be with the Father and His Son Jesus Christ" (1 Jn 1, 2-3). Therefore, following in the footsteps of the Council of Trent and of the First Vatican Council, this present Council wishes to set forth authentic doctrine on divine revelation and how it is handed on, so that by hearing the message of salvation the whole world may believe, by believing it may hope, and by hoping it may love.[1]

1. REVELATION ITSELF

2. In His goodness and wisdom God chose to reveal Himself and to make known to us the hidden purpose of His will (see Eph 1, 9) by which through Christ, the Word made flesh, man might in the Holy Spirit have access to the Father and come to share in the divine nature (see Eph 2, 18; 2 Pt 1, 4). Through this revelation, therefore, the invisible God (see Col 1, 15; 1 Tm 1, 17) out of the abundance of His love speaks to men as friends (see Ex 33, 11; Jn 15, 14-15) and lives among them (see Bar 3, 38), so that He may invite and take them into fellowship with Himself. This plan of revelation is realized by deeds and words having an inner unity: the deeds wrought by God in the history of salvation manifest and confirm the teaching and realities signified by the words, while the words proclaim the deeds and clarify the mystery contained in them. By this revelation then, the deepest truth about God and the salvation of man shines out for our sake in Christ, who is both the mediator and the fullness of all revelation.[2]

3. God, who through the Word creates all things (see Jn 1, 3) and keeps them in existence, gives men an enduring witness to Himself in created realities (see Rom 1, 19-20). Planning to make known the way of heavenly salvation, He went further and from the start manifested Himself to our first parents. Then after their fall His promise of redemption aroused in them the hope of being saved (see Gen 3, 15) and from that time on He ceaselessly kept the human race in His care, to give eternal life to those who perseveringly do good in search of salvation (see Rom 2, 6-7). Then, at the time He had appointed He called Abraham in order to make of him a great nation (see Gn 12, 2). Through the patriarchs, and after them through Moses and the prophets, He taught this people to acknowledge Himself the one living and true God, provident father and just judge, and to wait for the Savior promised by Him, and in this manner prepared the way for the Gospel down through the centuries.

4. Then, after speaking in many and varied ways through the prophets, "now at last in these days God has spoken to us in His Son" (Heb 1, 1-2). For He sent His Son, the eternal Word, who enlightens all men, so that He might dwell among men and tell them of the innermost being of God (see Jn 1, 1-18). Jesus Christ, therefore, the Word made flesh, was sent as "a man to men."[3] He "speaks the words of God" (Jn 3, 34), and completes the work of salvation which His Father gave him to do (see Jn 5, 36; 17, 4). To see Jesus is to see His Father (see Jn 14, 9). For this reason

Jesus perfected revelation by fulfilling it through His whole work of making Himself present and manifesting Himself: through His words and deeds, His signs and wonders, but especially through His death and glorious resurrection from the dead and final sending of the Spirit of truth. Moreover He confirmed with divine testimony what revelation proclaimed, that God is with us to free us from the darkness of sin and death, and to raise us up to life eternal.

The Christian dispensation, therefore, as the new and definitive covenant, will never pass away and we now await no further new public revelation before the glorious manifestation of our Lord Jesus Christ (see 1 Tm 6, 14 and Ti 2, 13).

5. "The obedience of faith" (Rom 13, 26; see Rom 1, 5; 2 Cor 10, 5-6) "is to be given to God who reveals, an obedience by which man commits his whole self freely to God, offering the full submission of intellect and will to God who reveals,"[4] and freely assenting to the truth revealed by Him. To make this act of faith, the grace of God and the interior help of the Holy Spirit must precede and assist, moving the heart and turning it to God, opening the eyes of the mind and giving "joy and ease to everyone in assenting to the truth and believing it."[5] To bring about an ever deeper understanding of revelation the same Holy Spirit constantly brings faith to completion by His gifts.

6. Through divine revelation, God chose to show forth and communicate Himself and the eternal decisions of His will regarding the salvation of men. That is to say, He chose to share with them those divine treasures which totally transcend the understanding of the human mind.[6]

As a sacred Synod has affirmed, God, the beginning and end of all things, can be known with certainty from created reality by the light of human reason (see Rom 1, 20); but it teaches that it is through His revelation "that those religious truths which are by their nature accessible to human reason can be known by all men with ease, with solid certitude and with no trace of error, even in this present state of the human race."[7]

2. HANDING ON DIVINE REVELATION

7. In His gracious goodness, God has seen to it that what He had revealed for the salvation of all nations would abide perpetually in its full integrity and be handed on to all generations. Therefore Christ the Lord, in whom the full revelation of the supreme God is brought to completion (see 2 Cor 1, 20; 3, 13; 4, 6), commissioned the Apostles to preach to all men that Gospel which is the source of all saving truth and moral teaching,[1] and to impart to them heavenly gifts. This Gospel had been promised in former times through the prophets, and Christ himself had fulfilled it and promulgated it with His lips. This commission was faithfully fulfilled by the Apostles who, by their oral preaching, by example, and by observances, handed on what they had received from the lips of Christ, from living with Him, and from what He did, or what they had learned through the prompting of the Holy Spirit. The commission was fulfilled, too, by those Apostles and apostolic men who under the inspiration of the same Holy Spirit committed the message of salvation to writing.[2]

But in order to keep the Gospel forever whole and alive within the Church, the Apostles left bishops as their successors, "handing over" to them "the authority to teach in their own place."[3] This sacred tradition, therefore, and Sacred Scripture of both the Old and New Testaments are like a mirror in which the pilgrim Church on earth looks at God, from whom she has received everything, until she is brought finally to see Him as He is, face to face (see 1 Jn 3, 2).

8. And so the apostolic preaching, which is expressed in a special way in the inspired books, was to be preserved by an unending succession of preachers until the end of time. Therefore the Apostles, handing on what they themselves had received, warn the faithful to hold fast to the traditions which they have learned either by word of mouth or by letter (see 2 Thes 2, 15), and to fight in defense of the faith handed on once and for all (see Jude 3).[4] Now what was handed on by the Apostles includes everything which contributes toward the holiness of life and increase in faith of the people of God; and so the Church, in her teaching, life and worship, perpetuates and hands on to all generations all that she herself is, all that she believes.

This tradition which comes from the Apostles develops in the Church with the help of the Holy Spirit.[5] For there is a growth in the understanding of the realities and the words which have been handed down. This happens through the contemplation and study made by believers, who treasure these things in their hearts (see Lk 2, 19. 51), through a penetrating understanding of the spiritual realities which they experience, and through the preaching of those who have received through episcopal succession the sure gift of truth. For as the centuries succeed one another, the Church constantly moves forward toward the fullness of divine truth until the words of God reach their complete fulfillment in her.

The words of the holy Fathers witness to the presence of this living tradition, whose wealth is poured into the practice and life of the believing and praying Church. Through the same tradition the Church's full canon of the sacred books is known, and the sacred writings themselves are more profoundly understood and unceasingly made active in her; and thus God, who spoke of old, uninterruptedly converses with the bride of His beloved Son; and the Holy Spirit, through whom the living voice of the Gospel resounds in the Church, and through her, in the world, leads unto all truth those who believe and makes the word of Christ dwell abundantly in them (see Col 3, 16).

9. Hence there exists a close connection and communication between sacred tradition and Sacred Scripture. For both of them, flowing from the same divine wellspring, in a certain way merge into a unity and tend toward the same end. For Sacred Scripture is the word of God inasmuch as it is consigned to writing under the inspiration of the divine Spirit, while sacred tradition takes the word of God entrusted by Christ the Lord and the Holy Spirit to the Apostles, and hands it on to their successors in its full purity, so that led by the light of the Spirit of truth, they may in proclaiming it preserve this word of God faithfully, explain it, and make it more widely known. Consequently it is not from Sacred Scripture alone that the Church draws her certainty about everything which has been revealed. Therefore both sacred tradition and Sacred Scripture are to be accepted and venerated with the same sense of loyalty and reverence.[6]

10. Sacred tradition and Sacred Scripture form one sacred deposit of the word of God, committed to the Church. Holding fast to this deposit the entire holy people united with their shepherds remain always steadfast in the teaching of the Apostles, in the common life, in the breaking of the bread and in prayers (see Acts 2, 42, Greek text), so that holding to, practicing and professing the heritage of the faith, it becomes on the part of the bishops and faithful a single common effort.[7]

But the task of authentically interpreting the word of God, whether written or handed on,[8] has been entrusted exclusively to the living teaching office of the Church,[9] whose authority is exercised in the name of Jesus Christ. This teaching office is not above the word of God, but serves it, teaching only what has been handed on, listening to it devoutly, guarding it scrupulously and explaining it faithfully in accord with a divine commission, and with the help of the Holy Spirit, it draws from this one deposit of faith everything which it presents for belief as divinely revealed.

It is clear, therefore, that sacred tradition, Sacred Scripture and the teaching authority of the Church, in accord with God's most wise design, are so linked and joined together that one cannot stand without the others, and that all together and each in its own way under the action of the one Holy Spirit contribute effectively to the salvation of souls.

3. SACRED SCRIPTURE, ITS DIVINE INSPIRATION AND INTERPRETATION

11. Those divinely revealed realities which are contained and presented in Sacred Scripture have been committed to writing under the inspiration of the Holy Spirit. For Holy Mother Church, relying on the belief of the Apostles (see Jn 20, 31; 2 Tm 3, 16; 2 Pt 1, 19-20; 3, 15-16), holds that the books of both the Old and New Testaments in their entirety, with all their parts, are sacred and canonical because, written under the inspiration of the Holy Spirit, they have God as their author and have been handed on as such to the Church herself.[1] In composing the sacred books, God chose men and while employed by Him[2] they made use of their powers and abilities, so that with Him acting in them and through them,[3] they, as true authors, consigned to writing everything and only those things which He wanted.[4]

Therefore, since everything asserted by the inspired authors or sacred writers must be held to be asserted by the Holy Spirit, it follows that the books of Scripture must be acknowledged as teaching solidly, faithfully and without error that truth which God wanted put into the sacred writings[5] for the sake of our salvation. Therefore "all Scripture is divinely inspired and has its use for teaching the truth and refuting error, for reformation of manners and discipline in right living, so that the man who belongs to God may be efficient and equipped for good work of every kind" (2 Tm 3, 16-17, Greek text).

12. However, since God speaks in Sacred Scripture through men in human fashion,[6] the interpreter of Sacred Scripture, in order to see clearly what God wanted to communicate to us, should carefully investigate what meaning the sacred writers really intended, and what God wanted to manifest by means of their words.

To search out the intention of the sacred writers, attention should be given, among other things, to "literary forms." For truth is set forth and expressed differently in texts which are variously historical, prophetic, poetic, or of other forms of discourse. The interpreter must investigate what meaning the sacred writer intended to express and actually expressed in particular circumstances by using contemporary literary forms in accordance with the situation of his own time and culture.[7] For the correct understanding of what the sacred author wanted to assert, due attention must be paid to the customary and characteristic styles of feeling, speaking and narrating which prevailed at the time of the sacred writer, and to the patterns men normally employed at that period in their everyday dealings with one another.[8]

But, since holy Scripture must be read and interpreted in the same spirit in which it was written,[9] no less serious attention must be given to the content and unity of the whole of Scripture if the meaning of the sacred texts is to be correctly worked out. The living tradition of the whole Church must be taken into account along with the harmony which exists between elements of the faith. It is the task of exegetes to work according to these rules toward a better understanding and explanation of the meaning of Sacred Scripture, so that through preparatory study the judgment of the Church may mature. For all of what has been said about the way of interpreting Scripture is subject finally to the judgment of the Church, which carries out the divine commission and ministry of guarding and interpreting the word of God.[10]

13. In Sacred Scripture, therefore, while the truth and holiness of God always remains intact, the marvelous "condescension" of eternal wisdom is clearly shown, "that we may learn the gentle kindness of God, which words cannot express, and how far He has gone in adapting His language with thoughtful concern for our weak human nature."[11] For the words of God, expressed in human language, have been made like human discourse, just as the Word of the eternal Father, when He took to Himself the flesh of human weakness, was in every way made like men.

4. THE OLD TESTAMENT

14. In carefully planning and preparing the salvation of the whole human race the God of infinite love, by a special dispensation, chose for Himself a people to whom He would entrust His promises. First He entered into a covenant with Abraham (see Gn 15, 18) and, through Moses, with the people of Israel (see Ex 24, 8). To this people which He had acquired for Himself, He so manifested Himself through words and deeds as the one true and living God that Israel came to know by experience the ways of God with men. Then too, when God Himself spoke to them through the mouth of the prophets, Israel daily gained a deeper and clearer understanding of His ways and made them more widely known among the nations (see Pss 21, 29; 95, 1-3; Is 2, 1-5; Jer 3, 17). The plan of salvation foretold by the sacred authors, recounted and explained by them, is found as the true word of God in the books of the Old Testament: these books, therefore, written under divine inspiration, remain permanently valuable. "For all that was written for our instruction, so that by steadfastness and the encouragement of the Scriptures we might have hope" (Rom 15, 4).

15. The principal purpose to which the plan of the old covenant was directed was to prepare for the coming of Christ, the redeemer of all and of the messianic kingdom, to announce this coming by prophecy (see Lk 24, 44; Jn 5, 39; 1 Pt 1, 10), and to indicate its meaning through various types (see 1 Cor 10, 12). Now the books of the Old Testament, in accordance with the state of mankind before the time of salvation established by Christ, reveal to all men the knowledge of God and of man and the ways in which God, just and merciful, deals with men. These books, though they also contain some things which are incomplete and temporary, nevertheless show us true divine pedagogy.[1] These same books, then, give expression to a lively sense of God, contain a store of sublime teachings about God, sound wisdom about human life, and a wonderful treasury of prayers, and in them the mystery of our salvation is present in a hidden way. Christians should receive them with reverence.

16. God, the inspirer and author of both Testaments, wisely arranged that the New Testament be hidden in the Old and the Old be made manifest in the New.[2] For, though Christ established the new covenant in His blood (see Lk 22, 20; 1 Cor 11, 25), still the books of the Old Testament with all their parts, caught up into the proclamation of the Gospel,[3] acquire and show forth their full meaning in the New Testament (see Mt 5, 17; Lk 24, 27; Rom 16, 25-26; 2 Cor 3, 14. 16) and in turn shed light on it and explain it.

5. THE NEW TESTAMENT

17. The word of God, which is the power of God for the salvation of all who believe (see Rom 1, 16), is set forth and shows its power in a most excellent way in the writings of the New Testament. For when the fullness of time arrived (see Gal 4, 4), the Word was made flesh and dwelt among us in His fullness of graces and truth (see Jn 1, 14). Christ established the kingdom of God on earth, manifested His Father and Himself by deeds and words, and completed His work by His death, resurrection and glorious Ascension and by the sending of the Holy Spirit. Having been lifted up from the earth, He draws all men to Himself (see Jn 12, 32, Greek text), He who alone has the words of eternal life (see Jn 6, 68). This mystery had not been manifested to other generations as it was now revealed to His holy Apostles and prophets in the Holy Spirit (see Eph 3, 4-6, Greek text), so that they might preach the Gospel, stir up faith in Jesus, Christ and Lord, and gather together the Church. Now the writings of the New Testament stand as a perpetural and divine witness to these realities.

18. It is common knowledge that among all the Scriptures, even those of the New Testament, the Gospels have a special preeminence, and rightly so, for they are the principal witness for the life and teaching of the incarnate Word, our Savior.

The Church has always and everywhere held and continues to hold that the four Gospels are of apostolic origin. For what the Apostles preached in fulfillment of the commission of Christ, afterwards they themselves and apostolic men, under the inspiration of the divine Spirit, handed on to us in writing: the foundation of faith, namely, the fourfold Gospel, according to Matthew, Mark, Luke and John.[1]

19. Holy Mother Church has firmly and with absolute constancy held, and continues to hold, that the four Gospels just named, whose historical character the Church unhesitatingly asserts, faithfully hand on what Jesus Christ, while living among men, really did and taught for their eternal salvation until the day He was taken up into heaven (see Acts 1, 1). Indeed, after the Ascension of the Lord the Apostles handed on to their hearers what He had said and done. This they did with that clearer understanding which they enjoyed[3] after they had been instructed by the glorious events of Christ's life and taught by the light of the Spirit of truth.[2] The sacred authors wrote the four Gospels, selecting some things from the many which had been handed on by word of mouth or in writing, reducing some of them to a synthesis, explaining some things in view of the situation of their churches, and preserving the form of proclamation but always in such fashion that they told us the honest truth about Jesus.[4] For their intention in writing was that either from their own memory and recollections, or from the witness of those who "themselves from the beginning were eye-witnesses and ministers of the Word" we might know "the truth" concerning those matters about which we have been instructed (see Lk 1, 2-4).

20. Besides the four Gospels, the canon of the New Testament also contains the epistles of St. Paul and other apostolic writings, composed under the inspiration of the Holy Spirit, by which, according to the wise plan of God, those matters which concern Christ the Lord are confirmed, His true teaching is more and more fully stated, the saving power of the divine work of Christ is preached, the story is told of the beginnings of the Church and its marvelous growth, and its glorious fulfillment is foretold.

For the Lord Jesus was with His Apostles as He had promises (see Mt 28, 20) and sent them the advocate Spirit who would lead them into the fullness of truth (see Jn 16, 13).

6. SACRED SCRIPTURE IN THE LIFE OF THE CHURCH

21. The Church has always venerated the divine Scriptures just as she venerates the body of the Lord, since, especially in the sacred liturgy, she unceasingly receives and offers to the faithful the bread of life from the table both of God's word and of Christ's body. She has always maintained them, and continues to do so, together with sacred tradition, as the supreme rule of faith, since, as inspired by God and committed once and for all to writing, they impart the word of God Himself without change, and make the voice of the Holy Spirit resound in the word of the prophets and Apostles. Therefore, like the Christian religion itself, all the preaching of the Church must be nourished and regulated by Sacred Scripture. For in the sacred books, the Father who is in heaven meets His children with great love and speaks with them; and the force and power in the word of God is so great that it stands as the support and energy of the Church, the strength of faith for her sons, the food of the soul, the pure and everlasting source of spiritual life. Consequently these words are perfectly applicable to Sacred Scripture: "For the word of God is living and active" (Heb 4, 12) and "it has power to build you up and give you your heritage among all those who are sanctified" (Acts 20, 32; see 1 Thes 2, 13).

22. Easy access to Sacred Scripture should be provided for all the Christian faithful. That is why the Church from the very beginning accepted as her own that very ancient Greek translation of the Old Testament which is called the Septuagint; and she has always given a place of honor to other Eastern translations and Latin ones, especially the Latin translation known as the Vulgate. But since the word of God should be accessible at all times, the Church by her authority and with maternal concern sees to it that suitable and correct translations are made into different languages, especially from the original texts of the sacred books. And should the opportunity arise and the Church authorities approve, if these translations are produced in cooperation with the separated brethren as well, all Christians will be able to use them.

23. The bride of the incarnate Word, the Church taught by the Holy Spirit, is concerned to move ahead toward a deeper understanding of the Sacred Scriptures so that she may increasingly feed her sons with the divine words. Therefore, she also encourages the study of the holy Fathers of both East and West and of sacred liturgies. Catholic exegetes then and other students of sacred theology, working diligently together and using appropriate means, should devote their energies, under the watchful care of the sacred teaching office of the Church, to an exploration and exposition of the divine writings. This should be so done that as many ministers of the divine word as possible will be able effectively to provide the nourishment of the Scriptures

for the people of God, to enlighten their minds, strengthen their wills, and set men's hearts on fire with the love of God.[1] The sacred Synod encourages the sons of the Church and Biblical scholars to continue energetically, following the mind of the Church, with the work they have so well begun, with a constant renewal of vigor.[2]

24. Sacred theology rests on the written word of God, together with sacred tradition, as its primary and perpetual foundation. By scrutinizing in the light of faith all truth stored up in the mystery of Christ, theology is most powerfully strengthened and constantly rejuvenated by that word. For the Sacred Scriptures contain the word of God and since they are inspired really are the word of God; and so the study of the sacred page is, as it were, the soul of sacred theology.[3] By the same word of Scripture the ministry of the word also, that is, pastoral preaching, catechetics and all Christian instruction, in which the liturgical homily must hold the foremost place, is nourished in a healthy way and flourishes in a holy way.

25. Therefore, all the clergy must hold fast to the Sacred Scriptures through diligent sacred reading and careful study, especially the priests of Christ and others, such as deacons and catechists who are legitimately active in the ministry of the word. This is to be done so that none of them will become "an empty preacher of the word of God outwardly, who is not a listener to it inwardly"[4] since they must share the abundant wealth of the divine word with the faithful committed to them, especially in the sacred liturgy. The sacred Synod also earnestly and especially urges all the Christian faithful, especially Religious, to learn by frequent reading of the divine Scriptures the "excellent knowledge of Jesus Christ" (Phil 3, 8). "For ignorance of the Scriptures is ignorance of Christ."[5] Therefore, they should gladly put themselves in touch with the sacred text itself, whether it be through the liturgy, rich in the divine word, or through devotional reading, or through instructions suitable for the purpose and other aids which, in our time, with approval and active support of the shepherds of the Church, are commendably spread everywhere. And let them remember that prayer should accompany the reading of Sacred Scripture, so that God and man may talk together; for "we speak to Him when we pray; we hear Him when we read the divine saying."[6]

It devolves on sacred bishops "who have the apostolic teaching"[7] to give the faithful entrusted to them suitable instruction in the right use of the divine books, especially the New Testament and above all the Gospels. This can be done through translations of the sacred texts, which are to be provided with the necessary and really adequate explanations so that the children of the Church may safely and profitably become conversant with the Sacred Scriptures and be penetrated with their spirit.

Furthermore, editions of the Sacred Scriptures, provided with suitable footnotes, should be prepared also for the use of non-Christians and adapted to their situation. Both pastors of souls and Christians generally should see to the wise distribution of these in one way or another.

26. In this way, therefore, through the reading and study of the sacred books "the word of God may spread rapidly and be glorified" (2 Thes 3, 1) and the treasure of revelation, entrusted to the Church, may more and more fill the hearts of men. Just as the life of the Church is strengthened through more frequent celebration of the Eucharistic mystery, similarly we may hope for a new stimulus for the life of the Spirit from a growing reverence for the word of God, which "lasts forever" (Is 40, 8; see 1 Pt 1, 23-25).

NOTES

PREFACE:

Article 1: 1. cf. St. Augustine, "De Catechizandis Rudibus," C.IV 8: PL. 40, 316.

CHAPTER I

Article 2: 2. cf. Matt. 11:27; John 1-14 and 17; 14:6; 17:1-3; 2 Cor. 3:16 and 4, 6; Eph. 1, 3-14.

Article 4: 3. Epistle to Diognetus, c. VII, 4: Funk, Apostolic Fathers, I, p. 403.

Article 5: 4. First Vatican Council, Dogmatic Constitution on the Catholic Faith, Chap. 3, "On Faith:" Denzinger 1789 (3008).

5. Second Council of Orange, Canon 7: Denzinger 180 (377); First Vatican Council, loc. cit.: Denzinger 1791 (3010).

Article 6: 6. First Vatican Council, Dogmatic Constitution on the Catholic Faith, Chap. 2, "On Revelation:" Denzinger 1786 (3005).

7. Ibid: Denzinger 1785 and 1786 (3004 and 3005).

CHAPTER II

Article 7: 1. cf. Matt. 28:19-20, and Mark 16:15; Council of Trent, session IV, Decree on Scriptural Canons: Denzinger 783 (1501).

2. cf. Council of Trent, loc. cit.; First Vatican Council, session III, Dogmatic Constitution on the Catholic Faith, Chap. 2, "On Revelation:" Denzinger 1787 (3005).

3. St. Irenaeus, "Against Heretics" III, 3, 1: PG 7, 848; Harvey, 2, p. 9.

Article 8: 4. cf. Second Council of Nicea: Denzinger 303 (602); Fourth Council of Constance, session X, Canon 1: Denzinger 336 (650-652).

5. cf. First Vatican Council, Dogmatic Constitution on the Catholic Faith, Chap. 4, "On Faith and Reason:" Denzinger 1800 (3020).

Article 9: 6. cf. Council of Trent, session IV, loc. cit.: Denzinger 783 (1501).

Article 10: 7. cf. Pius XII, apostolic constitution, "Munificentissimus Deus," Nov. 1, 1950: A.A.S. 42 (1950) p. 756; Collected Writings of St. Cyprian, Letter 66, 8: Hartel, III, B, p. 733; "The Church [is] people united with the priest and the pastor together with his flock."

8. cf. First Vatican Council, Dogmatic Constitution on the Catholic Faith, Chap. 3 "On Faith:" Denzinger 1792 (3011).

9. cf. Pius XII, encyclical "Humani Generis," Aug. 12, 1950: A.A.S. 42 (1950), pp. 568-69: Denzinger 2314 (3886).

CHAPTER III

Article 11: 1. cf. First Vatican Council, Dogmatic Constitution on the Catholic Faith, Chap. 2 "On Revelation:" Denzinger 1787 (3006); Biblical Commission, Decree of June 18, 1915: Denzinger 2180 (3629): EB 420; Holy Office, Epistle of Dec. 22, 1923: EB 499.

2. cf. Pius XII, encyclical "Divino Afflante Spiritu," Sept. 30, 1943: A. A.S. 35 (1943) p. 314; Enchiridion Biblic. (EB) 556.

3. "In" and "for" man: cf. Heb 1, and 4: 7; ("in"): 2 Sm. 23, 2; Matt. 1:22 and various places; ("for"): First Vatican Council, Schema on Catholic Doctrine, note 9: Coll. Lac. VII, 522.

4. Leo XIII, encyclical "Providentissimus Deus," Nov. 18, 1893: Denzinger 1952 (3293); EB 125.

5. cf. St. Augustine, "Gen. ad Litt." 2, 9, 20: PL 34, 270-271; Epistle 82, 3: PL 33, 277: CSEL 34, 2, p. 354.

St. Thomas, "On Truth," Q. 12, A. 2, C.

Council of Trent, session IV, Scriptural Canons: Denzinger 783 (1501).

Leo XIII, encyclical "Providentissimus Deus:" EB 121, 124, 126-127.

Pius XII, encyclical "Divino Afflante Spiritu:" EB 539.

Article 12: 6. St. Augustine, "City of God," XVII, 6, 2: PL 41, 537: CSEL. XL, 2, 228.

7. St. Augustine, "On Christian Doctrine" III, 18, 26; PL 34, 75-76.

8. Pius XII, loc. cit. Denzinger 2294 (3829-3830); EB 557-562.

9. cf. Benedict XV, encyclical "Spiritus Paraclitus" Sept. 15, 1920; EB 469. St. Jerome, "In Galatians" 5, 19-20: PL 26, 417 A.

10. cf. First Vatican Council, Dogmatic Constitution on the Catholic Faith, Chapter 2, "On Revelation:" Denzinger 1788 (3007).

Article 13: 11. St. John Chrysostom, "In Genesis" 3, 8 (Homily 17, 1): PG 53, 134; "Attemperatio [in English "Suitable adjustment"] in Greek "synkatabasis."

CHAPTER IV

Article 15: 1. Pius XI, encyclical "Mit Brennender Sorge," March 14, 1937: A.A.S. 29 (1937) p. 51.

Article 16: 2. St. Augustine, "Quest. in Hept." 2, 73: PL 34, 623.

3. St. Irenaeus, "Against Heretics" III, 21, 3: PG 7, 950; (Same as 25, 1: Harvey 2, p. 115). St. Cyril of Jerusalem, "Catech." 4, 35; PG 33, 497. Theodore of Mopsuestia, "In Soph." 1, 4-6: PG 66, 452D-453A.

CHAPTER V

Article 18: 1. cf. St. Irenaeus, "Against Heretics" III, 11; 8: PG 7, 885, Sagnard Edition, p. 194.

Article 19: (Due to the necessities of translation, footnote 2 follows footnote 3 in text of Article 19.)

2. cf. John 14:26; 16-13.

3. John 2:22; 12:16; cf. 14:26; 16:12-13; 7:39.

4. cf. instruction "Holy Mother Church" edited by Pontifical Consilium for Promotion of Bible Studies: A.A.S. 56 (1964) p. 715.

CHAPTER VI

Article 23: 1. cf. Pius XII, encyclical "Divino Afflante Spiritu:" EB 551, 553, 567.

Pontifical Biblical Commission, Instruction on Proper Teaching of Sacred Scripture in Seminaries and Religious Colleges, May 13, 1950: A.A.S. 42 (1950) pp. 495-505.

2. cf. Pius XII, ibid: EB 569.

Article 24: 3. cf. Leo XIII, encyclical "Providentissimus Deus:" EB 114; Benedict XV, encyclical "Spiritus Paraclitus:" EB 483.

Article 25: 4. St. Augustine, Sermons, 179, 1: PL 38, 966.

5. St. Jerome, Commentary on Isaiah, Prol.: PL 24, 17.

cf. Benedict XV, encyclical "Spiritus Paraclitus:" EB 475-480; Pius XII, encyclical "Divino Afflante Spiritu:" EB 544.

6. St. Ambrose, On the Duties of Ministers I, 20, 88: PL 16, 50.

7. St. Irenaeus, "Against Heretics" IV, 32, 1: PG 7, 1071; (Same as 49, 2) Harvey, 2, p. 255.

HOW TO READ YOUR BIBLE

1. MOST WIDELY DISSEMINATED BOOK

There is no doubt that the Bible is one of the most widely disseminated books. But "most widely disseminated" does not necessarily mean "most read" and "best understood." The Bible is a compilation of many ancient documents stemming from a time and culture which are rather alien to our own. This brings up the question: Why should I read the Bible? It is so old. Why not leave it alone and read contemporary literature, which is more relevant?

2. WHY THE BIBLE?

a) As Americans, we share a rich Judaeo-Christian civilization. Our language, many of our customs and often our outlook on life, love, good and evil are conditioned by the Judaeo-Christian heritage in which we are rooted. You cannot possibly understand them without knowing the Judaeo-Christian classic: the Bible. A few examples will clearly show this. (1) *Customs and practices:* We observe a seven-day week, take an oath with one hand on the Bible, number years as B.C. or A.D., celebrate Christmas and Easter as holidays, print the words "In God we trust" on our money, regard monogamy as a value and accept woman as a companion equal to man. (2) *Sayings of everyday life:* "The patience of Job," "a doubting Thomas," "a Judas," "as old as Methuselah." (3) *Popular songs:* "Tain't Necessarily So" in *Porgy and Bess,* "Miracle of Miracles" in the Broadway musical *Fiddler on the Roof.* (4) *Negro Spirituals and classic Oratorios:* "Let My People Go," and *The Messiah* by Handel. (5) *Classical literature: Paradise Lost* by Milton, *East of Eden* by Steinbeck. (6) *Plastic art:* Paintings and statues by Rembrandt, El Greco, Rubens, Michelangelo, Rodin. (7) *Movies: The Ten Commandments, The Robe, Samson and Delilah.* None of these is really understandable without an acquaintance with the literature of the Bible. From our roots, we should understand ourselves.

b) However, besides being an American, you are a Christian. For Christians, the Bible is inspired by God. God chose that time (2,000-3,000 years ago), that people (the Jews) and that culture (Hebrew) to reveal Himself. Guided by God, the Hebrew genius interpreted history, war and peace, birth and death, famine and abundance, happiness and frustration, success and failure, in the light of God's presence to His people. And Christians, regarding themselves as descendants of God's chosen people of ancient times, share this interpretation of life. The Bible reflects the restless search for life's meaning, as the Hebrews wrestled with it. As believers see it, this search was guided by God, which is the reason why we take note of it. Believers understand that ultimately God Himself speaks to them in and through Scripture.

3. BIBLICAL INSPIRATION

Artists, philosophers and even scientists speak of inspiration, which is the urge to create a work of beauty (artists), a constructive outlook on reality (philosophers) or a solution to a problem (scientists). How to explain this inspiration?

First of all, inspiration is related to a certain sensitivity which exists in a society at a given time. This sensitivity inspires gifted individuals in that society. These individuals in turn heighten that sensitivity in their fellow citizens. For example, we would never have produced our jazz music, which has captured the whole world, without our Negro communities that are so sensitive to music and rhythm. From such communities we have seen arise such men as Louis Armstrong, Duke Ellington and Ray Charles, who in turn have heightened musical sensitivity in this country and all over the world.

More or less by this same process of mutual influence Hebrew literature came into being. We see in the Hebrew people a highly developed sensitivity for God's presence in their lives. From these pious Hebrew communities we see arise prophets, preachers, writers, who offered their (first spoken) reflections on that shared experience of God's presence with His people. In turn these prophets, preachers and writers heightened that religious sensitivity in their people.

There is a similarity between Hebrew literature and all art. Both are inspired. But Hebrew literature is more than just that. It is inspired (breathed upon) in a very special way by almighty God. This does not mean that God dictated His message as a businessman dictates a letter to a secretary. God takes the author as he is and leaves him free to choose his own means of communication. Isaiah was a great poet and composed beautiful poems to convey his message. Ezekiel was not well-versed in letters and his language is rather poor. Some authors chose existing folktales and even beast fables to bring out their point. *Inspiration is guidance.*

4. INSPIRATION AND REVELATION

God Himself guided (inspired) the Hebrew genius in its searching out of the mysteries of the human condition. This guidance is called *inspiration*. When this restless searching for truth and meaning culminates in unfolding one of God's mysteries, we speak of divine *revelation*. This means that God reveals some aspect of Himself or the human condition in and through man's endeavors to find out. Hence, "everything in the Bible is *inspired*, but not everything is *revealed*" (Pierre Benoit). Sometimes inspired searching for meaning leads to conclusions which cannot be qualified as revelation from God. Think of the "holy wars" of total destruction, fought by the Hebrews when they invaded Palestine. The search for meaning in those wars centuries later was inspired, but the conclusions which attributed all those atrocities to the command of God were imperfect and provisional. See Judges 1, 1-8.

5. A LIBRARY OF BOOKS

Ironically, "The Book" is not just *one* book. It is a library of books, put together in one volume. Look at the contents of your Bible! The authors of these books are mostly unknown. Neither were these books composed at one time. Many centuries elapsed between the oldest traditions and the last book of the Bible. Not even the original language of all these books was the same.

A major disadvantage is that these books are not put together systematically as the books of a modern library. All kinds of literary forms: history, historical novels, parables, allegories, poems, midrash (edifying interpretations of events), and more are often intermingled. Even if you read your Bible in an up-to-date American translation, such as this one, you need guidance. Therefore read the introductions to the Bible books and pay attention to the footnotes! Know that, if you want to understand what God has to tell you through Scripture, you must first understand what the writer wants to say. The Bible is God's word and man's word. One must understand man's word first in order to understand the word of God.

Since this collection of books is of such importance as source book for the humanities and religion (see no. 2), it became known in Western civilization as the "Bible," from the Greek word *biblion* (book); hence, "The Book," which is actually a library of books!

6. LITERARY GENRES OR FORMS

It is very important to know what literary form a writer uses to convey his message. Is it a work of history, a poem, a figure of speech, a parable? If you do not know, you may misunderstand the writer's message. That is why we must pay attention to the literary genres (forms) of the Bible. The following are just a few of them.

a) *The Parable:* A short fictitious narrative from which a moral or spiritual truth is drawn. See Isaiah 5, 1-7 and the parables of the Gospels! Keep in mind that *the point* of the parable (not the details) is God's message to believers.

b) *The Allegory:* A figure story with a *veiled* meaning. Read Genesis 2, 3; 4, 1-16; 6—8; 11, 19. For centuries these chapters have been misunderstood as inspired lessons in science. The Bible does not teach science; it teaches religious values. It uses these folktales to teach a lesson. Again, *the point* of the allegory (not the details) is God's message to you.

c) *The Beast Fable:* See Genesis and Numbers 22, 22-35. (Understand this from Numbers 22, 1-21 and 22, 36-38.) The author chose this literary form to convey his message.

d) *The Short Story and the Historical Novel:* See Genesis 37—50; Judges 13—16; 1 Samuel 17; also Genesis 12—36 and Exodus. The core of these stories is historical, but remember that the author did not intend to write history as we find it in our schoolbooks; he simply uses *traditions* and fashions them to bring out a religious lesson. Bible scholars call this edifying interpretation of the past "midrash."

e) *The Problem Story:* The best-known problem stories in our contemporary literature are those on the race issue. A Hebrew problem story is the Book of Ruth on intermarriage. The point is a plea for tolerance.

f) *The Speech as a Literary Device:* Read 1 Kings 8, 14-21; Acts 17, 22-31. It is not important whether or not King Solomon or Paul delivered these speeches verbatim as related here. It is the inspired author who wants to state something by putting these words into the mouth of a person with authority. This literary form is often used in the Acts of the Apostles. (See also no. 13.)

7. CONDITIONED THOUGHT PATTERNS

Though inspired (guided) by God, the Hebrew authors were free to choose their literary genres to convey the message. As a matter of fact, these literary forms were conditioned by time and culture. Read the well-known poem on creation in Genesis 1. The ancient Hebrews saw the earth as a large plate with a huge vault over it. Above the vault is God's place. This outlook conditioned Genesis 1. Do not be shocked about this! We know that the sun neither rises nor sets; nevertheless we go on speaking of sunset and sunrise, since we did not know better for such a long time.

8. THE BIBLE ON GOD

The sacred writers attribute quite a number of human characteristics to God. In fact the Bible does not offer a philosophy on who the "Ultimate Reality" is in Himself; it is mainly concerned about who God is for us. Speaking of God is necessarily limited by the possibilities of human language and conditioned by time and culture. Read Exodus 19, 16-25 and 20, 1-21; Exodus 13, 20-22; Numbers 9, 15-18. Clouds, angels (blasting trumpets!), smoke, fire, earthquake, lightning, thunder, war, calamities, lies and persecution are biblical figures of speech to describe the the awe-inspiring greatness of God. As a Jew, who was addressing Jews, Jesus of Nazareth adapted Himself to this biblical way of speaking. Read Matthew 25.

9. POEMS IN THE BIBLE

Poetry, like any other meaningful writing, is a communication from the writer to the reader—usually the communication of a feeling as well as of a thought. The poet wants to pack as much meaning as possible in a few lines. That is why he uses figures of speech, since they involve imaginative comparisons. But biblical poems in particular can easily be misunderstood. Read them as poems and not as scientific or historical reports, in which one tries to explain every detail as a revelation from God. See no. 4 and read Psalm 137: "Ballad of the Exiles," paying special attention to verses 8 and 9. The feeling, the thought, the total poem is inspired (guided) by God, though it is not necessarily revealed truth! Read some psalms!

10. THE PROPHETS

Like other nations in the Middle East, Israel had its *nabis* or prophets. These were groups of ecstatic persons, somehow related to a sanctuary. Music and dance heightened their exotic and vaguely religious activities. Read 1 Samuel 9, 1-10. 16; 1 Kings 22 and 18. From the eighth century B.C. on, we encounter the classical prophets, whose oracles and sayings have been preserved in Sacred Scripture. Prophet means "one who speaks for another," especially for God. It does not necessarily mean that he predicts the future!

The classical prophets' concern focused mainly on such values as *monotheism* (one God, with whom Israel considered itself to live in a sacred partnership or covenant) and *morality as related to religion,* which is seldom found in religions of the ancient world. The "gods" of the ancient world were often anything but morally good, and as such they did not offer any reason to their worshipers to do better. Israel was called to be holy in imitation of God Himself!

Another important topic in prophetic preaching is *messianism*. God punishes infidelity to His covenant (partnership). Israel is humiliated for its sins. But at some future date God's kingdom on earth will be restored. God's vicegerent, His Messiah, anointed to royal dignity, will reign in that kingdom. You should pay attention to this messianic expectation in Hebrew literature. This is necessary to understand the literature of the New Testament, which sees the fulfillment of this messianic expectation in Jesus of Nazareth. (See no. 13a.) Read Matthew 23, 33-39; some parts of Amos, Isaiah, Jeremiah.

11. ATONEMENT AND VICARIOUS SUFFERING

In their search for meaning in our human situation, the Hebrews wrestled with the tantalizing problem of evil and guilt, as we see it in and around us. Is there a way out? In the Old Testament we are often confronted with concepts, such as atonement-reconciliation and vicarious satisfaction. Read Isaiah 52, 13-15 and 53. One person could pray, suffer and make up for others. Symbolically, this could be done by "the scapegoat ritual" and other ritual sin-offerings (sacrifices for sin). Read Leviticus 16.

It is important to keep these Old Testament ideas in mind in order to understand the way early theologians of the Church interpreted Jesus' death and resurrection. Who was Jesus of Nazareth? Though innocent, He died a cruel death, but after His death, He was seen by witnesses. What does all this mean? Read how Paul (Philippians 2, 6-11) and the authors of the Epistle to the Hebrews (5, 1-10; 7, 8; 9; 10, 1-18) and the First Epistle of Peter (2, 4-8; 3, 18-22) tried to explain what Jesus of Nazareth means to the new people of God, the Church.

12. HEBREW PHILOSOPHY

Like all peoples, the Hebrews had their sages or philosophers. In the Bible we find their thoughts mainly in the Wisdom Books. This ancient wisdom is a remarkable mixture of philosophy and poetry. Read it as an inspired search for meaning in life. Do not expect too many ready-made answers. See this literature more as a challenge to a faithful searching for meaning in your own human condition!

13. THE GOSPELS

a) New Testament literature reflects the Christian interpretation of the Hebrew Bible (Old Testament). It is based on the astonishing fact that a Jew of Galilee applied "messianism," as it was known in Hebrew literature (see no. 10), to Himself. Read Luke 4, 16-30. Jesus quotes the prophet Isaiah and states, "This text is fulfilled in your hearing." New Testament literature can be understood only in the light of this "fulfillment." In other words, the New Testament movement is the fulfillment of the Hebrew Bible. Jesus of Nazareth proclaims that He is the promised Messiah (anointed) king to come, to establish the kingdom (reign) of God, for which the Old Testament was somehow yearning.

b) *Catechisms*. In no. 6 we mentioned how important it is to know what literary form an author is using. If he chooses to use figurative speech, you should understand it as such. A remarkable fact is that for a long time Christians misunderstood the literary genre of the four Gospels. Until recently they thought that the Gospel writers wanted to present us with a biography of Jesus. After much research, Bible scholars agree that the Gospel writers wanted to write catechisms or digests of Christian teaching concerning the risen Lord Jesus.

c) *Theological Interpretation of History.* Until recently, Catholics learned their religion from the Baltimore Catechism with its questions and answers. Modern catechisms are different. The Gospels are also catechisms, but composed 1,900 years ago. In that time they had their own way of making catechisms. The Gospel writers often used a typically Hebrew way of teaching by reflecting on events of the past (see no. 6d). What did the authors of the Gospels do? In the congregations, mainly in the cities around the Mediterranean, they found scores of narratives about Jesus, the beloved Founder of the Christian faith. The writers took those narratives and frequently even remolded and refashioned them to bring out the lesson they wanted to teach.

d) Read Matthew 1, 1-17. What has the sacred writer done? He used a genealogy, probably made available by the family of Joseph, and took it for what it was. Then the writer refashioned this document to a list of three times fourteen ancestors. (The Hebrews loved to play with sacred numbers: 14 equals 2 times 7.) The lesson: The Messiah is firmly rooted in the Jewish people; he is the son of David.

e) Reading the Gospels, one should distinguish historical facts from theological elaboration. Take the miracle stories. Catholic Bible scholars accept the fact that Jesus worked miracles. However, the miracle accounts of the Gospel are often more than a record of what actually happened; they also contain theological reflections about what happened in order to bring out its meaning for Christian faith. Moreover, some of these accounts may be adaptations of similar ones in the Old Testament in order to bring out the Christian belief in the importance of Jesus' person and mission. We must keep in mind that the Gospel writers did not intend to write history in the scientific sense; rather they were writing theological reflections on existing traditions (accounts of miracles) in order to teach believing Christians the community's faith in Christ and the Church.

f) *Conflict Stories.* An interesting example of literary form is the conflict story. The author lets his characters debate and thus brings out his lesson. In the conflict stories of the Gospels it is usually Jesus who is in conflict with his opponents, those Jews who did not believe in Him. Read Luke 10, 25-37. One may ask: Was Jesus involved in these conversations? Did He answer exactly as related in the Bible? It is not certain. It is true, Jesus was in conflict with the establishment of His country and this conflict caused His death. There were controversies which supplied the background material for the conflict stories of the Gospels. But as these accounts now stand, they are literary forms used by the Gospel writers in their catechisms to bring out what they had to tell the opponents of early Christianity. Read Matthew 9, 10-13; Luke 7, 36-50; John 10, 22-39; Matthew 12, 1-8.

g) *Infancy Narratives.* The first chapters of Matthew and Luke are dedicated to Jesus' infancy. Both authors have used traditions. How did they handle them? (See no. 13c.) For example take Matthew 2, 1-23. Bible scholars tell us that a horoscope of the expected King-Messiah circulated during the time of Jesus' birth. Astrologers (wise men from the East) were watching the sky for the appearance of the Messiah's star. King Herod, superstitious and upset by these people, killing children of two years and under, is extremely probable. Kings could make and break people! People leaving Bethlehem to escape the massacre, is equally acceptable. This would be the historical background of this tradition. The rest is interpretation (no. 13c), elaborated by early Jewish-Christian communities and by the author of Matthew. Its purpose is to show Jesus as the true Israel (God's chosen one!), in whose history the history of the old Israel is recapitulated. Note: Israel was in Egypt! God's dealings with Israel in the past are being reproduced in His dealings with Jesus (the new Israel—the new chosen one!). This is a strange literary device, but the ancient writers loved to work with this kind of figurative speech.

h) *On Communication.* Communication is a complicated thing. It is more than just uttering sound either in English or in Chinese. Often barriers must first be taken away. Emotions, hard feelings, prejudice, ignorance, closed-mindedness must be patiently done away with, and only then communication becomes possible. Which means should God use to communicate with man? He is so entirely different and so much greater than we are. He is so incomprehensible that we cannot possibly develop an adequate concept of Him. "In our time, God has spoken to us by His Son" (Hebrews 1, 2). God speaks to us through Jesus of Nazareth: a child in a crib, a person, His kindness, goodness, justice, honesty, miracles, parables, death and resurrection. It is this very core of New Testament literature which John tries to explain in the introduction of his Gospel version. He uses figures of speech. He calls Jesus God's *word* to those who are ignorant. He calls Him *light* to people who walk in darkness. Jesus of Nazareth, His charming personality, is God's word to man. Prejudice, lack of interest, closed-mindedness prevent understanding. But could God speak a clearer language than He has done through the appealing personality of Jesus of Nazareth? Read John 1, 1-18.

i) *Sayings of Jesus.* Since we do not possess a biography of Jesus (no. 13b), it is difficult to know whether the words or sayings attributed to Him are written exactly as He spoke them. True, the Gospels are based on sound historical facts as related by eyewitnesses, but both deeds and words of Jesus are offered to us in the framework of theological interpretation (no. 13c). The Church was so firmly convinced that the risen Lord who is the Jesus of history lived in her, and taught through her, that she expressed her teaching in the form of Jesus' sayings. The question is: Can we discover at least some words of Jesus that have escaped such elaboration? Bible scholars point to the very short sayings of Jesus, as for example those put together by Matthew in chapter 5, 1-12. Why? Simply because they are short. Early Christians, who had known Jesus, had His words often on their lips: "The Master used to say . . ." Another question is: Did Jesus sit on a hill and recite this list of sayings on the kingdom of heaven? It is the same question as: Did Moses sit on Mount Sinai writing the law? This composition is figurative. The composer of Matthew, a Jew, wrote his catechism for Christians of Jewish background. He draws a parallel between Moses and Jesus. Moses, the ancient lawmaker, is figuratively related to Mount Sinai. Jesus, the new lawmaker, is figuratively related to a mount in Galilee.

j) *Traditions Concerning the Resurrection.* There is no doubt that Jesus died and was seen alive by witnesses. All reports are unanimous on that. But again the New Testament writers chose theological interpretation to teach what the risen Lord means to believers. Jesus' death, His resurrection, His ascension and the communication of the Spirit are actually *one* Christ-event, that of his glorification. The traditions, told in the Gospels, elucidate the four aspects of the one Christ-event, meaningfully celebrated on four different days. Remember the golden rule: keep historical facts distinct from their theological interpretation.

14. APOCALYPTIC LITERATURE

A real problem for Bible readers is the Book of Revelation. This book is a specimen of a special literary form in vogue just before and at the beginning of the Christian era. It is called apocalyptic literature. In the Old Testament, the Book of Daniel is akin to the Book of Revelation. This literary genre is designated as persecution literature. Its purpose is to console the victims of some crisis by holding out to them the assurance of divine intervention in the near future. The problem for the reader is that apocalyptic literature uses mainly a mysterious or symbolical language, understandable only to one who knows all the ins and outs of the situation. It is in a sense underground literature. The writer wants to console his fellows in suffering in a language understandable to them alone. In our literature we possess this literary form in the Negro spirituals. Take "Let My People Go." The slaves sang it in their wooden plantation churches: "Tell ole Pharaoh, To let my people go." The obvious meaning is a longing for freedom from the bondage of sin, Satan, the miseries of life and the hope of a better life hereafter. Obviously genuine biblical piety! But what about "Ole Pharaoh" as the "boss man" of the plantation? Read Revelation 17, 1-8 and 21, 1-4 and see the footnotes for the explanations of the symbolic names used in the text.

15. HOW DO YOU KNOW?

Walking into a modern library, you find all the books neatly arranged under fiction and nonfiction. It is not that simple in the library called the Bible. How does one know whether one deals with history or some form of figurative speech?

To begin with, we should always be disposed to follow the teaching authority of the Church. We should also consult renowned Bible scholars who are experts in Hebrew literature. Sometimes, it is secular science which gives Christians the lead to reconsider their Bible understanding. The discoveries of Copernicus and Galileo made Christians aware that Genesis 1 is not a sacred lesson in science but a poem on creation (no. 7). Most scientists hold that the human species has developed somehow from lower kinds of life. This knowledge helped Christians to understand that Genesis 2 and 3 is not a lesson in Anthropology, but an allegory, teaching us the lesson that sin is the root of all evil (no. 16b).

However, one problem remains: You may hear interpreters of the Bible who are literalists or fundamentalists. They explain the Bible according to the letter: Eve really ate from the apple and Jonah was miraculously kept alive in the belly of the whale. Then there are ultra-liberal scholars (outside the Catholic Church!), who qualify the whole Bible as another book of fairy tales. Catholic Bible scholars follow the sound middle of the road, keeping a balance between fundamentalists and scholars who are too liberal. You may make your own choice as long as it is not contrary to the teaching authority of the Church. The signature of a bishop in your Bible assures you that opinions, expressed in footnotes and introductions, reflect what is generally accepted as sound doctrine in the Catholic tradition.

16. UNDERSTANDING THE SITUATION

We have stated: One must understand man's word in order to understand the word of God in the Bible. That is why some knowledge of the biblical literary forms is necessary. Of great importance also is some knowledge of the situation in which the Bible passage came into being. You understand the Book of Exodus better if you know something about the slavery in Egypt, have seen pictures of monuments, maps and other background material. Jerusalem was threatened by mighty neighbors when Isaiah spoke his oracles. Knowledge of the history of that time will help you to understand Isaiah better. Historical insight into how the Romans colonized other nations contributes highly to the understanding of "messianism" as reflected in the Gospels. Knowing that early Christians mistakenly expected Christ's second coming during their own lifetime helps you to understand 1 and 2 Thessalonians. Reading introductions and footnotes in your Bible is very important.

17. GOD'S WORD TO YOU, NOW!

Reading your Bible, you must keep in mind that the Bible is God's word to you, now! Reading can only be valuable to you if you grow in truth through reading. This does not come from a grammatical insight or from an understanding of the literary forms, nor does it come from a reconstruction of the situation which prompted the text (no. 16).

The past is dead. *We* do not expect Christ's second coming as happening tonight; *we* are not an occupied country (no. 16), nor can we artificially recreate this situation of 2,000 years ago. Yet there is *something in common,* namely, *we* are captives in our odd and sorry human situation (as the Hebrews in Egypt, in Palestine during the Roman occupation); *we* know about God's coming in Christ and wait for a brighter future through Christ's coming (as the early Christians of 1 and 2 Thessalonians did it in their way). This *something in common,* found in any passage of Scripture, is called *existential understanding.* This understanding, related to *your* existence or life-situation, is aided by faithful Bible reading. It is the very reason why a Christian can read the same Bible time and again, since it is *his* book! The Hebrews were restless searchers for meaning in our human condition. Reading their inspired literature should challenge you to go on with a faithful search for meaning in your own situation.

THE HOLY LAND

ST. JEROME, one of the earliest and greatest students of the Holy Scriptures, remarked that as "we have a better understanding of the Greek historians when we have seen Athens . . . [so] we have a better comprehension of Sacred Scripture when we have seen Judea with our own eyes and contemplated the ruins of its ancient cities." These words are verified by every serious student of the Bible who has visited the Holy Land and walked the very places on which our Lord and His disciples stood.

The Sacred Texts come to life under the influence of the Holy Land. The most apparently insignificant details of the human authors are corroborated by visible evidence and take on new meanings. Turns of phrase, expressive but uncommon images and the entire text itself are more easily understood and at times receive different nuances.

Most of all, a unique religious experience is felt. To visit the very places where our Lord was born and lived, to see what he saw and where he went in the mornings, the evenings and the swift days of his earthly life, effectuates a more intimate union with him in all that he said and did. The pilgrim spans the centuries and follows Christ in the eventful days of his life, re-living everything and forgetting nothing. At the end of his pilgrimage, he comes away filled with awe, humility and happiness, with a deeper understanding, and greater faith, hope and love.

However, many persons through no fault of their own never do visit the Holy Places, and thus miss this special experience and love for Scripture that such a pilgrimage imparts. It is for these persons that the following section on the Holy Land is intended. It aims to provide them with the opportunity to view the sacred places at their leisure through the secondary medium of excellent photographs.

To this end, the most up-to-date photographs have been used. Each picture has been carefully selected for its instructive and inspirational content as well as for its photographic quality. In this way, it is hoped that those who cannot journey to the Land of Christ in person will nevertheless be able to visit it in spirit and profit in some way from its salutary influence.

We hope that the magnificent photographs of sacred shrines and traditional sites identifying actual places traversed by the Son of God while on earth will bring the Bible texts to life for all who view them. May these photographs help to inculcate the true spirit of the Scriptures and thus contribute to the magnificent Biblical revival that has made our age truly the Age of the Bible.

BETHLEHEM: TOWN OF CHRIST'S BIRTH — A view from the south of Bethlehem, the city of David, a town five miles southwest of Jerusalem. It rises 2550 feet above sea level, in the hill country of Judea, on the main highway to Hebron and Egypt. In the distance is the belfry of the Church of the Nativity built on the site where Christ was born. (See Mt 2, 1)

JERUSALEM: SCENE OF THE FINDING IN THE TEMPLE — An air view of Jerusalem showing the temple area from the north with the village of Siloam in the distance and the Golden Gate leading to the Kidron Valley on the left. As a twelve-year-old Jesus was taken by his parents to the temple in Jerusalem and found by them there after being lost for three days. (See Lk 2, 41-50)

[27]

THE RIVER JORDAN — The most important river in Palestine measures 135 miles in a straight line, but because of its numerous windings covers a distance of about 250 miles. Its width varies from 80 to 180 feet and its depth from 5 to 12 feet. It was at the Jordan that Jesus was pointed out by John the Baptizer and eventually baptized by him. (See Jn 1, 19-37 and Mt 3, 13)

ANCIENT SYNAGOGUE OF CAPERNAUM — Capernaum was a town on the northwest shore of the Sea of Galilee used by Jesus as his headquarters during his Galilean ministry. Extensive ruins have been unearthed there, including those of the 2nd century synagogue which probably stood on the very site of the one Jesus attended and in which he preached. (See Lk 4, 31-32)

[28]

THE UPPER ROOM — In Jerusalem an "upper room" was frequently built on the roofs of houses and used in summer because it was cooler than the regular living quarters. (Mk 14, 15; Lk 22, 12; Acts 1, 13; 20, 8)

The room above is a medieval structure marking the traditional site in the southwestern corner of the Upper City of Jerusalem where the Last Supper took place as well as the descent of the Holy Spirit on the disciples. (See 14, 14-17; Acts 2, 1-11)

MOUNT OF OLIVES — A range of hills with three peaks rising east of Jerusalem beyond the Kidron Valley. In the foreground is the church of All Nations built in the Garden of Gethsemani; above and to the right of the church of the Agony and in the center on the summit is the tower of the church of the Ascension. This Mount was closely connected with the closing years of our Lord's life and it was here that he retired after the Last Supper. (See Mk 14, 26)

GARDEN OF GETHSEMANI — Close-up of the Garden across the Kidron Valley from Jerusalem; showing the church of All Nations on the left and the city wall with the Golden Gate on the hill beyond. It was in this general area of the Mount of Olives that Christ's Passion began with his agony and arrest. (See Mk 14, 32-52)

[30]

WAY OF THE CROSS (VIA DOLOROSA) — The location of Pilate's judgment hall in which Jesus was sentenced to death is uncertain. Very probably it was in the fortress Antonia at the northwest angle of the temple area.

Pictured above is the street leading from the ruins of the fortress to the traditional site of Calvary in the church of the Holy Sepulchre. In the background is the "fifth station," the little chapel of Simon the Cyrenian who helped Jesus carry the cross. (See Jn 19, 13-18 and Mt 27, 32-34)

R. Kugelman

ANCIENT JEWISH TOMB — The tomb pictured above is located a few miles west of Jerusalem. Note the large circular stone (some stones are said to have weighed one or more tons) used to seal the entrance to the tomb. The tomb in which Jesus was laid was probably similar to this one. (See Jn 19, 42)

Matson Photo Service

TOMB OF OUR LORD — A continuous tradition going back to the time of Constantine identifies Calvary and the tomb of Jesus with the site of the church of the Holy Sepulchre in Jerusalem. The Tomb itself is preceded by a vestibule called the Chapel of the Angel to commemorate the angel who rolled back the stone and announced to the women that Jesus had risen as he had said. (See Jn 20, 1 and Mt 28, 2. 5. 6)

[32]

Matson Photo Service

BETHSAIDA-SEA OF GALILEE — View of the Sea of Galilee (which is an expansion of the Jordan River) with the Plain of Gennesaret and the Mount of Beatitudes in the distance. This might have been the scene of the breakfast that Jesus took with his disciples after his resurrection. (See Jn 21, 1. 15)

Matson Photo Service

MOUNT OF THE ASCENSION — An overall view of the Mount of Olives and surroundings where Jesus led his disciples before his ascension forty days after his resurrection. The Church of the Ascension rises in the background. There is little doubt that though he described the ascension in physical terms, Luke meant to emphasize our Lord's exaltation. (Acts 1, 11)

CHRONOLOGY OF THE HISTORY OF ISRAEL

Year	PALESTINE	NEIGHBORING PEOPLES	MESOPOTAMIA	EGYPT
2000				MIDDLE KINGDOM
1900	THE PATRIARCHS			
1800			Sargon I (Assyria)	
1700			1st Babylonian Dynasty	HYKSOS
1600			HAMMURABI (Babylonia)	
1500		UGARIT		NEW KINGDOM
1400	El Amarna Letters, Incursions of Apiru	Apogee of the Hittite civilization in Syria / Establishment of Edomites	BABYLONIA / ASSHUR — Cassite Dynasty	Amenophis IV (1377-1358), Thoutankamon (1358-1349)
1300	EXODUS / Occupation of Canaan / Arrival of Philistines	Establishment of Moabites / Establishment of Ammonites / Decadence of Hittite Empire	Assyrian Expansion	Ramesses II (1301-1234), Merneptah (1234-1225)
1200	PERIOD OF THE JUDGES	Aramean States / DAMASCUS	Tiglath-Pileser I	Ramesses III (1198-1166)
1100	Samuel - Saul (1030-1010)			
1000	DAVID (1010-970) / SOLOMON (970-931)	Hiram of Tyre		
930	SCHISM			Sheshonk Palestine Campaign
920	ISRAEL: Jeroboam I (931-910), Nadab (910-909), Baasha (909-886)	Ben-Hadad		
910	JUDAH: Rehoboam I (931-913), Abijam (913-911)			

Chronological Chart

Date	PALESTINE	NEIGHBORING PEOPLES	(Assyria / Babylon)	EGYPT
900	Asa (911-870)			Decline of Egypt
890				
880	Elah (886-885) Zimri			
	Omri (885-874) Samaria Founded			
870	Jehoshaphat (870-848)		Rise of Assyria	
860	Ahab (874-853) ELIJAH		Asshurbanipal II	
850	Ahaziah (853-852)	Ben Hadad II	853-Battle of Karkar Shalmaneser III	
	Joram (852-841) ELISHA	Mesha king of Moab		
840	Jehoram (848-841)		Campaign in Syro-Phoenicia	
	Athaliah (841-835)			
830	Jehu (841-814)	Hazad		
820		Ben Hadad III		
810	Joash (835-796)		Adad-Nirari III	
800	Jehoahaz (814-798)			
	Joash (798-783)			
790	Amaziah (796-781)			
780				
770	Jeroboam II (783-743)		Weakness of Assyria	
	Uzziah (781-740)			
760	Zechariah AMOS			
750	Menahem, Shallum(743), Pekahiah, Pekah) HOSEA	Rezin, End of the Kingdom of Damascus		
740	Jotham (749-736)		Tiglath-pileser III	
730	Hoshea (732-724) ISAIAH		Shalmaneser V	
720	Fall Of Samaria (721)		Sargon II captures Samaria	
	Ahaz (736-716) MICAH			
710				
700	Hezekiah (716-687)		SENNACHERIB Campaign in Palestine	
690				
680			Esarhaddon	Assyrian invasion
670			Conquers Lower Egypt	
	Manasseh (687-642) pays tribute to Asshurbanipal		Asshurbanipal Campaign in Higher Egypt	
660				
650				
640	Amon (642-640)			
	Josiah (640-609) religious reform		End of Assyria	Psammeticus I casts out the Assyrians
630				
620	ZEPHANIAH			stops the Scythians
610	Jehoahaz (609) JEREMIAH		NEO-BABYLONIAN EMPIRE Nabopolassar takes Nineveh in 612	Neco goes to the aid of Assyria
600	Jehoiakim (609-598)			
	Jehoiakin(598) Siege of Jerusalem	Siege of Tyre (13 years)		
590	Zedekiah (598-587) EZEKIEL		NEBUCHADNEZZAR takes Jerusalem	Hophra cannot free Jerusalem
580	Fall of Jerusalem in 586			
570	EXILE			
560				

[35]

Year	PALESTINE	NEIGHBORING PEOPLES	MESOPOTAMIA	EGYPT
			CYRUS Capture of Sardis	CYRUS King of Medes and PERSIANS
550				
540				
530	538 Edict of Cyrus (return from the Exile)		Capture of Babylonia	conquers Egypt
520	Zerubbabel		Cambyses (529-522)	
510	Construction of the Temple HAGGAI		Darius I (522-486)	
500	ZECHARIAH			Battle of Marathon
490				
480			Xerxes I (486-465) Ahasuerus	Battle of Salamis
470	MALACHI	GREECE PERICLES		
460		Sophocles	Artaxerxes I (465-423)	
450	Nehemiah	Herodotus		
440	restoration of the walls			
430	Ezra (?)		Darius II (423-404)	
420				
410		Xenophon		
400				Egypt obtains freedom
390				
380			Artaxerxes II Mnemon (403-359)	
370				
360			Artaxerxes III Ochos (358-338)	Reconquest of Egypt
350		Philip the Macedonian		
340		ALEXANDER the Great (336-323)	Darius III Codoman (336-330)	
330				
320			SELEUCIDS in Syria	LAGIDS in Egypt
310				
300	Lagidian Domination		Seleucus I Nicator	Ptolemy I Soter
290				
280			Antiochus I Soter	
270	(translation of Septuagint)			Ptolemy II Philadelphus
260			Antiochus II	
250				
240			Seleucus II	Ptolemy III Euergetes
230				
220				
210			Antiochus III the Great	Ptolemy IV Philopator

Chronological Chart

	PALESTINE	NEIGHBORING PEOPLES	MESOPOTAMIA	EGYPT
B.C.				
160	Seleucid Domination	Progressive Expansion of ROME	Defeat of Panion	
150	Religious Persecution Judas Maccabeus (166-160)		Antiochus IV Epiphanes	
140	Jonathan (160-142)	Macedonia Roman Province	Demetrius I Soter	
130	Simon (145-134)		Antiochus VII	
120	Jewish Autonomy	Province of Asia		
110	John Hyrcanus (134-104)			
100	Aristobulus (104-103)			
90	Alexander Jannaeus (103/76)		Philip II	
80		Aretas III		
70	Alexandra (76-67)			
60	Aristobulus II (67-63)	Pompey, Syria Roman Province		
50	Hyrcanus II (48-37)			
40	Antigonus (40-37)	CAESAR		
30	Herod the Great (37/4)	Antony in the East		
20		Augustus		
10	Birth of Jesus (7/6?)			
0	Herod Antipas — Philip			Egypt Roman Province
A.D.	Archelaus — Judea Roman Province			
10		Tiberius		
20		Caligula		
30	Death of Christ	Claudius		
40	Herod Agrippa I	Nero		
50	Herod Agrippa II			
60				
70	Jewish Revolt — Capture of Jerusalem	Vespasian		
80		Titus		
90		Domitian		
100				
110	Jewish Insurrection	Trajan		
120		Bocra Capital — Creation of the Province of Arabia		
130	Second Jewish Revolt — Jerusalem becomes Aelia Capitolina	Hadrian		

THE EVENTS, THE PERSONAGES, THE IDEAS IN THE BIBLE

FORMATION OF THE PEOPLE OF GOD — FROM 1900 to 1000

PERIODS	MAJOR EVENTS	POLITICS AND SOCIAL LIFE	PERSONAGES	MOVEMENT OF IDEAS
PATRIARCHS **1800 1700**		Coming from Mesopotamia, a family of shepherds leads a nomadic life at the edge of the desert and the cultivated lands of Syro-Palestine	**ABRAHAM** **JACOB**	First ORAL TRADITIONS about the PATRIARCHS (Gn 12—50)—set to writing centuries later, they stress ■ FIDELITY to vocation ■ PROMISE of a posterity and a land ■ FAITH ■ Successive DETACHMENTS (separation from the clan of Terah, separation from Lot, banishment of Ishmael)
	1720 arrival of the HYKSOS in Egypt	The general migration of peoples draws the descendants of Jacob into Egypt	**JOSEPH**	
	1560 departure of the HYKSOS	Silence in the Bible about five centuries of history THE HEBREWS IN EGYPT		
EXODUS **about** **1250 1225**		DELIVERANCE FROM EGYPT. The descendants of Abraham begin to organize themselves into a people ■ Common adventure in the Sinai desert ■ Semi-sedentarization near Kadesh	**MOSES**	ORAL TRADITIONS concerning SINAI (Book of Exodus) set to writing a few centuries later Awareness of a SOLIDARITY: ■ in VOCATION - Conclusion of the Sinai Covenant (Ex 24) ■ in DAILY LIFE - by the observance of the LAW, core of the most ancient legislative collections (ancient cultual laws: Ex 34; *Code of the Covenant*: Ex 21—23; moral Decalogue: Ex 20 and Dt 5) ■ in a COMMON HISTORY -regrouping of the most ancient traditions about the origins of the world and the Patriarchs
INSTALLATION **IN CANAAN** **JUDGES** **__00 1025**		Struggle between the feudal regime in Canaan and the tribes in process of sedentarization The Israelites settle in the mountainous regions (hills of Gilead, mountain of Ephraim, hills of Judah) CONFEDERATION OF THE TWELVE TRIBES, created at the time of the pact of Shechem (Jos 24)	**JOSHUA** **DEBORAH** **JEPHTHAH** **GIDEON** **SAMSON**	The TRADITIONS are preserved around major sanctuaries ■ The proud independence of the nomad jealous of his freedom is opposed to the necessary organization required by the sedentary life which is directed toward royalty ■ Strict Yahwism, the religion of fidelity to a God who guides history confronts the naturalistic religion of the Canaanean Baals, seeking fecundity by means of magical rites
		SEMI-NOMADIC ROYALTY:■ no capital, administration, or professional army ■ the king, simple military chief intervenes only in case of danger	**SAUL SAMUEL**	■ The direct authority of God over his people (Theocracy) and its compatibility with a human royalty These various attitudes are found in the Books of Samuel

YAHWISTIC ROYALTY   1000 to 586

Period	Dates / Events	Description	Kings / Prophets	Literary & Religious Development
UNIFIED MONARCHY 1010 931	Around 1000 CAPTURE OF JERUSALEM	MORE CENTRALIZED ROYALTY than that of Saul. The strong personality of DAVID provisionally unites North and South (Israel and Judah) Capital, mercenary army, administration, taxes; the king rules over the entire population in his territory and no longer only over the tribes of Israel	DAVID NATHAN	Administration gives rise to a class of SCRIBES which is at the origin of the first literary period. Parallel development of royalty and classical PROPHETISM ROYAL IDEOLOGY, foundation of MESSIANISM
		Hypertrophy of the royal organization, great splendor at the court, excessive taxes announcing decadence	SOLOMON	Construction of the temple at Jerusalem, religious capital Apogee of the literary period: ■ *Royal Psalms* ■ Collection of the old traditions *(Yahwist, J)* ■ Beginning of the wisdom literature; *first Proverbs* ■ History of succession to throne (2 Sm 9—20 and 1 Kgs 1—2)
THE TWO KINGDOMS	931 SCHISM	SOUTHERN KINGDOM (JUDAH): dynastic stability Sacred character of royalty Struggle with the North over the establishment of their common frontier, then an alliance		
		NORTHERN KINGDOM (ISRAEL): politically more important than Judah. Dynastic instability (19 kings - 9 dynasties) Search for a capital: Shechem, Penuel, Tirzah (?). Finally Omri founds SAMARIA to foster the opening out to Phoenicia	OMRI; ELIJAH ELISHA	Traditions of the North set to writing *(Elohist, E) The epic of Elijah and Elisha* (1 Kgs 17—2 Kgs 13)
	721 CAPTURE OF SAMARIA by Sargon II	Expansion but social inequality; religion controlled by political system, coalitions with neighboring countries against Assyria	AMOS; HOSEA	SOCIAL JUSTICE Announcement of the Day of Yahweh, day of wrath — LOVE and FIDELITY of Yahweh for his people Struggle against the influence of the religion of the Baals
JUDAH		Series of coalitions against ASSYRIA, then against BABYLONIA	HEZEKIAH ISAIAH; MICAH	ROYALTY - HOLINESS of Yahweh MESSIANISM: a descendant of David will inaugurate a reign of justice. After the trial, a small "remnant" will return to Yahweh — First core of Deuteronomy (19—27), heritage of the Northern tribes Uniting of the Yahwist and Elohist tradition - *Proverbs*
	586 CAPTURE OF JERUSALEM		JOSIAH JEREMIAH	Interior religion, dialogue with God - suffering Announcement of the NEW COVENANT written on man's heart — *Deuteronomy* and Deuteronomic reform; first presentation of Deuteronomic history (Joshua, Judges, Samuel, Kings) completed during the Exile and at the return the codification of the customs of the Priesthood of Jerusalem, core of *Leviticus* (Holiness Code, Lv 17—26)

JUDAISM FROM 586 TO JESUS CHRIST

Period	Event	Description	Figure / Books	Details
PREPARATION OF JUDAISM IN EXILE	586 CAPTURE OF JERUSALEM	Babylonia: the elite of the deported population is fathered into agricultural colonies.		
		Palestine: only the inferior classes remain. The neighbors (Ammon, Edom) infiltrate in to Judah	EZEKIEL	Apocalyptic visions and style - the presence of Yahweh is no longer tied to Zion - personal moral responsibility - grandiose perspectives of restoration after the Exile (demand for purity) Meditation on the past - collection of the *prophetic collections — Priestly History* Constitution of the *prophetic collections — Priestly History* (P) according to the spirit of Ezekiel and the priests of Jerusalem. All this will gradually constitute the "Book of the Word of God" Sacrificial worship is replaced by prayer meetings (beginning of synagogal worship) - insistence on the external marks of belonging to the people of God (sabbath, circumcision, fasting)
	538 EDICT OF CYRUS	Babylonia: The exiles gradually settle down, some enter into administration, others carry on commerce (archives of a bank)	2nd ISAIAH	Confidence in the almighty Word of Yahweh; Universalist overture. Meaning of suffering (songs of the Servant)
ESTABLISHMENT OF JUDAISM Persian period		RETURN TO PALESTINE. Political and Economical difficulties. Religious community directed by priests	ZERUBBABEL HAGGAI MALACHI	End of prophetism - Predominance of SCRIBES and SAGES. End of the work of the Priestly School ■ Bringing together of the traditions of the *Pentateuch* (J-E-D-P) ■ Definitive edition of *Jos - Jgs - 1 and 2 Sm - 1 & 2 kgs*
		Juda is part of a province of the Persian Empire, but the Judeans have a personal juridic statute: for them the "Law of God" is the "law of the king"	EZRA NEHEMIAH	Severe reform which marks the establishing of JUDAISM, but ■ Reprise of a UNIVERSALIST overture: *Jonah* ■ Reprise of the ideas of Dt and return to Messianism: *Chronicles* The Sages: ■ publish their classic teaching: *Proverbs* ■ pose questions: *Ecclesiastes-Job* ■ seek to edify: *Ruth-Esther-Tobit* Religious poems: *Song of Songs* - numerous *Psalms*
SPREAD OF JUDAISM Hellenistic period	333-323 ALEXANDER THE GREAT	The central authority imposes Hellenization. The Jews resist through fidelity to the law		Importance assumed by the Jewish community of Alexandria: ● Translation of the Bible into Greek: the *Septuagint* ● God's wisdom in creation and history: *Sirach*
		Crisis at the time of the persecution of Antiochus IV. The Jewish revolt attains independence. Appearance of politico-religious sects: ■ Sadducees - party of the high priests who admit compromises ■ Pharisees - strictly faithful to the law ■ Political extremists (Zealots) and religious extremists (Essenes) separate themselves from them	The MACCABEES	Resistance to persecution takes various forms: ■ Armed resistance recounted in *1 Maccabees* ■ Hope for divine intervention: *2 Maccabees - Daniel - Judith*
			John HYRCANUS	
	*63 CAPTURE OF JERUSALEM BY THE ROMANS			In the face of persecution a Sage from Alexandria sings of the Wisdom of God who governs the world and saves his people: *Wisdom*

THE NEW TESTAMENT

ROME	DATES	PALESTINE	DATES	SACRED BOOKS
EMPERORS **AUGUSTUS**	31	HEROD THE GREAT	37	**PROBABLE DATES OF RE-DACTION FOR THE PRINCIPAL BOOKS OF THE NEW TESTAMENT**
	6	Birth of Jesus		
	4	Death of Herod the Great Partition of Palestine	4	
		JUDEA GALILEE		
		Tetrarchs:		
		HEROD ARCHELAUS HEROD ANTIPAS	4	
	1		**1**	
	4	ROMAN PROCURATORS		
TIBERIUS	14			
	26	PONTIUS PILATE		
	30	Crucifixion of Jesus		
	35	Martyrdom of Stephen		
CAIUS CALIGULA	37	Conversion of Saul		
CLAUDIUS	41	1st voyage of Paul HEROD AGRIPPA 1st King	41	
		Famine (Acts 11:28)	44	
	49	Council of Jerusalem 2nd voyage of Paul		
			50	1 and 2 Thessalonians
		(Gallio proconsul of Achaia)	52	
			53-54	Galatians
NERO	54	ANTONIUS FELIX		
			56-57	1 Corinthians
			57	2 Corinthians Romans
	58	3rd voyage and arrest of Paul		
		PORCIUS FESTUS	60	Philippians
			62	Colossians Ephesians Gospels of Mark, Matthew and Luke (between 64 and 80)
Burning of Rome	64			
	64-67	Martyrdom of Peter and Paul		
VESPASIAN	67	Jewish Revolt	65-67	Pastoral Epistles
	70	Destruction of the temple of Jerusalem by the Romans	70-80	2nd Epistle of Peter Jude
TITUS	79			
DOMITIAN	81			
TRAJAN	98		90-100	Revelation, Epistles and Gospel of John

ABBREVIATIONS OF BOOKS OF THE BIBLE

Acts—Acts of the Apostles
Am—Amos
Bar—Baruch
1 Chr—1 Chronicles
2 Chr—2 Chronicles
Col—Colossians
1 Cor—1 Corinthians
2 Cor—2 Corinthians
Dn—Daniel
Dt—Deuteronomy
Eccl—Ecclesiastes
Eph—Ephesians
Est—Esther
Ex—Exodus
Ez—Ezekiel
Ezr—Ezra
Gal—Galatians
Gn—Genesis
Hb—Habakkuk
Heb—Hebrews
Hg—Haggai
Hos—Hosea
Is—Isaiah
Jas—James
Jb—Job

Jdt—Judith
Jer—Jeremiah
Jgs—Judges
Jl—Joel
Jn—John
1 Jn—1 John
2 Jn—2 John
3 Jn—3 John
Jon—Jonah
Jos—Joshua
Jude—Jude
1 Kgs—1 Kings
2 Kgs—2 Kings
Lam—Lamentations
Lk—Luke
Lv—Leviticus
Mal—Malachi
1 Mc—1 Maccabees
2 Mc—2 Maccabees
Mi—Micah
Mk—Mark
Mt—Matthew
Na—Nahum
Neh—Nehemiah
Nm—Numbers

Ob—Obadiah
Phil—Philippians
Phlm—Philemon
Prv—Proverbs
Ps(s)—Psalms
1 Pt—1 Peter
2 Pt—2 Peter
Rom—Romans
Ru—Ruth
Rv—Revelation
Sir—Sirach
1 Sm—1 Samuel
2 Sm—2 Samuel
Song(Sg)—Song of Songs
Tb—Tobit
1 Thes—1 Thessalonians
2 Thes—2 Thessalonians
Ti—Titus
1 Tm—1 Timothy
2 Tm—2 Timothy
Wis—Wisdom
Zec—Zechariah
Zep—Zephaniah

NOTE: For greater clarity and convenience, the footnotes and cross-references are printed at the bottom of each page and cross-indexed in the text itself. An *asterisk* (*) in the text indicates that there is a footnote to the text in question. Each footnote is in turn clearly marked with the number of the chapter and verse to which it pertains. Similarly, a *superior letter* (a) in the text indicates that there is a cross-reference to a particular verse. The reference itself is also clearly marked with the same letter. Hence, the reader is always aware of a footnote or a cross-reference simply *by reading the text*.

[ ] Indicates a gloss.
/ = Divides verse
// = Parallel

SIMPLE KEY TO REFERENCES

Gn 1, 1 refers to the Book of Genesis, chapter 1, verse 1.
Gn 1, 1a refers to the Book of Genesis, chapter 1, the first part of verse 1.
Gn 1, 1f refers to the Book of Genesis, chapter 1, verse 1 and the following verse (2).
Gn 1, 1-10 refers to the Book of Genesis, chapter 1, verses 1 to 10 inclusive.
Gn 1, 1-10. 14 refers to the Book of Genesis, chapter 1, verses 1 to 10 inclusive and verse 14.
Gn 1, 1—2, 3 refers to the Book of Genesis, chapter 1, verse 1 to chapter 2, verse 3 inclusive.
Gn 1, 1; 2, 3 refers to the Book of Genesis, chapter 1, verse 1 and chapter 2, verse 3.

Acknowledgments: The section on "How to Read the Bible" has been adapted by John Kersten, S.V.D., from his book *Understanding Hebrew Literature*. The panoramic view of the "The Lands of the Bible" has been adapted with permission from the book *Atlante Biblico* by Giacomo Pesce, C.P. The maps have been adapted with permission from the books *Sagrada Biblia* published by Editorial Regina and *Atlas Historique de l'Ancien Testament* published by Spes.

THE
OLD TESTAMENT

PREFACE TO THE NEW AMERICAN BIBLE
THE OLD TESTAMENT

On September 30, 1943, His Holiness Pope Pius XII issued his now famous encyclical on scripture studies, *Divino afflante Spiritu*. He wrote: "We ought to explain the original text which was written by the inspired author himself and has more authority and greater weight than any, even the very best, translation whether ancient or modern. This can be done all the more easily and fruitfully if to the knowledge of languages be joined a real skill in literary criticism of the same text."

Early in 1944, in conformity with the spirit of the encyclical, and with the encouragement of Archbishop Cicognani, Apostolic Delegate to the United States, the Bishops' Committee of the Confraternity of Christian Doctrine requested members of The Catholic Biblical Association of America to translate the sacred scriptures from the original languages or from the oldest extant form of the text, and to present the sense of the biblical text in as correct a form as possible.

The first English Catholic version of the Bible, the Douay-Rheims (1582-1609/10), and its revision by Bishop Challoner (1750) were based on the Latin Vulgate. In view of the relative certainties more recently attained by textual and higher criticism, it has become increasingly desirable that contemporary translations of the sacred books into English be prepared in which due reverence for the text and strict observance of the rules of criticism would be combined.

The New American Bible has accomplished this in response to the need of the church in America today. It is the achievement of some fifty biblical scholars, the greater number of whom, though not all, are Catholics. In particular, the editors-in-chief have devoted twenty-five years to this work. The collaboration of scholars who are not Catholic fulfills the directive of the Second Vatican Council, not only that "correct translations be made into different languages especially from the original texts of the sacred books," but that, "with the approval of the church authority, these translations be produced in cooperation with separated brothers" so that "all Christians may be able to use them."

The text of the books contained in *The New American Bible* is a completely new translation throughout. From the original and the oldest available texts of the sacred books, it aims to convey as directly as possible the thought and individual style of the inspired writers. The better understanding of Hebrew and Greek, and the steady development of the science of textual criticism, the fruit of patient study since the time of St. Jerome, have allowed the translators and editors in their use of all available materials to approach more closely than ever before the sense of what the sacred authors actually wrote.

The Old Testament

Where the translation supposes the received text—Hebrew, Aramaic, or Greek, as the case may be—ordinarily contained in the best-known editions, as the original or the oldest extant form, no additional remarks are necessary. But for those who are happily able to study the original text of the scriptures at firsthand, a supplementary series of textual notes pertaining to the Old Testament was added originally in an appendix to the typical edition. (It is now obtainable in a separate booklet from The Catholic Biblical Association of America, The Catholic University of America, Washington, DC 20064.) These notes furnish a guide in those cases in which the editorial board judges that the manuscripts in the original language, or the evidence of the ancient versions, or some similar source, furnish the correct reading of a passage, or at least a reading more true to the original than that customarily printed in the available editions.

The Massoretic text of 1 and 2 Samuel as in numerous instances been corrected with the aid of important manuscripts Samuel a, b, and c from Cave 4 of oldest form and its Lucianic recension. Fragments evidence from the Septuagint in both its in Aramaic and in Hebrew, recovered from Cave 4 of Qumran, are in substantial agreement with the Sinaiticus Greek recension used for the translation of this book. The lost original Hebrew text of 1 Maccabees is replaced by its oldest extant form in Greek. Judith, 2 Maccabees, and parts of Esther are also translated from the Greek.

The basic text for the Psalms is not the Massoretic but one which the editors considered closer to the original inspired form, namely the Hebrew text underlying the new Latin Psalter of the Church, the *Liber Psalmorum* (1944^1, 1945^2). Nevertheless they retained full liberty to establish the reading of the original text on sound critical principles.

The translation of Sirach, based on the original Hebrew as far as it is preserved and corrected from the ancient versions, is often interpreted in the light of the traditional Greek text. In the Book of Baruch the basic text is the Greek of the Septuagint, with some readings derived from an underlying Hebrew form no longer extant. In the deuterocanonical sections of Daniel (3, 24-90; 13, 1—14, 42), the basic text is the Greek text of Theodotion, occasionally revised according to the Greek text of the Septuagint.

In some instances in the Book of Job, in Proverbs, Sirach, Isaiah, Jeremiah, Ezekiel, Hosea, Amos, Micah, Nahum, Habakkuk, and Zechariah there is good reason to believe that the original order of lines was accidentally disturbed in the transmission of the text. The verse numbers given in such cases are always those of the current Hebrew text, though the arrangement differs. In these instances the textual notes advise the reader of the difficulty. Cases of exceptional dislocation are called to the reader's attention by footnotes.

The Books of *Genesis to Ruth* were first published in 1952; the Wisdom Books, *Job to Sirach*, in 1955; the Prophetic Books, *Isaiah to Malachi*, in

1961; and the Historical Books, *Samuel to Maccabees*, in 1969. In the present edition of *Genesis to Ruth* there are certain new features: a general introduction to the Pentateuch, a retranslation of the text of Genesis with an introduction, cross-references, and revised textual notes, besides new and expanded exegetical notes which take into consideration the various sources or literary traditions.

The revision of *Job to Sirach* includes changes in strophe division in Job and Proverbs and in titles of principal parts and sections of Wisdom and Ecclesiastes. Corrections in the text of Sirach are made in 39, 27—44, 17 on the basis of the Masada text, and in 51, 13-30 on the basis of the occurrence of this canticle in the Psalms scroll from Qumran Cave 11. In this typical edition, new corrections are reflected in the textual notes of Job, Proverbs, Wisdom, and Sirach. In the Psalms the enumeration found in the Hebrew text is followed instead of the double enumeration according to the Hebrew text and the Latin Vulgate texts, contained in the previous

In the Prophetic Books, *Isaiah to Malachi*, only minor revisions have been made in the structure and wording of the texts, and in the textual notes.

The spelling of proper names in *The New American Bible* follows the customary forms found in most English Bibles since the Authorized Version.

The work of translating the Bible has been characterized as "the sacred and apostolic work of interpreting the word of God and of presenting it to the laity in translations as clear as the difficulty of the matter and the limitations of human knowledge permit" (A. G. Cicognani, Apostolic Delegate, in *The Catholic Biblical Quarterly*, 6, [1944], 389-90). In the appraisal of the present work, it is hoped that the words of the encyclical *Divino afflante Spiritu* will serve as a guide: "Let all the sons of the church bear in mind that the efforts of these resolute laborers in the vineyard of the Lord should be judged not only with equity and justice but also with the greatest charity; all moreover should abhor that intemperate zeal which imagines that whatever is new should for that very reason be opposed or suspected."

Conscious of their personal limitations for the task thus defined, those who have prepared this text cannot expect that it will be considered perfect; but they can hope that it may deepen in its readers "the right understanding of the divinely given Scriptures," and awaken in them "that piety by which it behooves us to be grateful to the God of all providence, who from the throne of his majesty has sent these books as so many personal letters to his own children" *(Divino afflante Spiritu).*

THE PENTATEUCH

The Pentateuch, which consists of the first five books of the Bible (Genesis, Exodus, Leviticus, Numbers, Deuteronomy), enjoys particular prestige among the Jews as the "Law," or "Torah," the concrete expression of God's will in their regard. It is more than a body of legal doctrine, even though such material occupies many chapters, for it contains the story of the formation of the People of God: Abraham and the patriarchs, Moses and the oppressed Hebrews in Egypt, the birth of Israel in the Sinai covenant, the journey to the threshold of the Promised Land, and the "discourses" of Moses.

The grandeur of this historic sweep is the result of a careful and complex joining of several historical traditions, or sources. These are primarily four; the so-called Yahwist, Elohist, Priestly and Deuteronomic strands that run through the Pentateuch. (They are conveniently abbreviated as J, E, P and D.) Each brings to the Torah its own characteristics, its own theological viewpoint—a rich variety of interpretation that the sensitive reader will take pains to appreciate. A superficial difference between two of these sources is responsible for their names: the Yahwist prefers the name *Yahweh* (represented in translation as LORD) by which God revealed himself to Israel; the Elohist prefers the generic name for God, *Elohim*. The Yahwist is concrete, imaginative, using many anthropomorphisms in its theological approach, as seen, e.g., in the narrative of creation in Gn 2, compared with the Priestly version in Gn 1. The Elohist is more sober, moralistic. The Priestly strand, which emphasizes genealogies, is more severely theological in tone. The Deuteronomic approach is characterized by the intense hortatory style of Dt 5—11, and by certain principles from which it works, such as the centralization of worship in the Jerusalem temple.

However, even this analysis of the Pentateuch is an over-simplification, for it is not always possible to distinguish with certainty among the various sources. The fact is that each of these individual traditions incorporates much older material. The Yahwist was himself a collector and adapter. His narrative is made up of many disparate stories that have been reoriented, and given a meaning within the context in which they now stand; e.g., the story of Abraham and Isaac in Gn 22. Within the J and P traditions one has to reckon with many individual units; these had their history and life-setting before they were brought together into the present more or less connected narrative.

This is not to deny the role of Moses in the development of the Pentateuch. It is true we do not conceive of him as the author of the books in the modern sense. But there is no reason to doubt that, in the events described in these traditions, he has a uniquely important role, especially as lawgiver. Even the later laws which have been added in P and D are presented as a Mosaic heritage. Moses is the lawgiver *par excellence,* and all later legislation is conceived in his spirit, and therefore attributed to him. Hence, the reader is not held to undeviating literalness in interpreting the words, "the LORD said to Moses." One must keep in mind that the Pentateuch is the crystallization of Israel's age-old relationship with God.

In presenting the story of the birth of the People of God, the Pentateuch looks back to the promises made to the patriarchs, and forward to the continuing fulfillment of these promises in later books of the Bible. The promises find their classic expression in Gn 12; 1ff. The "God of the Fathers" challenges Abraham to believe: the patriarch is to receive a people, a land, and through him the nations will somehow be blessed.

The mysterious and tortuous way in which this people is brought into being is described: Despite Sarah's sterility, Issac is finally born—to be offered in sacrifice! The promises are renewed to him eventually, and also to the devious Jacob, as if to show that the divine design

1

will be effected, with or without human cunning. The magnificent story of Joseph is high-lighted by the theme of Providence; the promise of a people is taking shape.

Israel is not formed in a vacuum, but amid the age-old civilization of Mesopotamia and the Nile. Oppression in Egypt provokes a striking intervention of God.

Yahweh reveals himself to Moses as a savior, and the epic story of deliverance is told in Exodus. This book also tells of the Sinai covenant, which is rightfully regarded as the key to the Old Testament. Through the covenant Israel becomes Yahweh's people, and Yahweh becomes Israel's God. This act of grace marks the fulfillment of the first promise; that Abraham will be the father of a great nation, God's special possession. The laws in Exodus and Leviticus (P tradition) are both early and late. They spell out the proper relationship of the federation of the Twelve tribes with the LORD. He is a jealous God, demanding exclusive allegiance; he cannot be imaged; he takes vengeance upon the wicked, and shows mercy to the good. Slowly the LORD reveals himself to his people; with remarkable honesty, Israel records the unsteady response—the murmurings and rebellions and infidelities through the desert wanderings up to the plain of Moab.

This sacred history was formed within the bosom of early Israel, guided by the spirit of God. It was sung beside the desert campfires; it was commemorated in the liturgical feasts, such as Passover; it was transmitted by word of mouth from generation to generation—until all was brought together in writing, about the sixth century B.C., when the literary formation of the Pentateuch came to an end.

The Book of Deuteronomy has a history quite peculiar to itself. Its old traditions and law code (12—26) are put forth in the form of "discourses" of Moses before his death. The extraordinary intense and hortatory tone fits the mood of a discourse. The book contains possibly the preaching of the Levites in the northern kingdom of Israel before its fall in 721 B.C. If this book is situated in its proper historical perspective, its true impact is more vividly appreciated. It is the blueprint of the great "Deuteronomic" reform under King Josiah (640-609 B.C.). This was an attempt to galvanize the people into a wholehearted commitment to the covenant ideals, into an obedience motivated by the great commandment of love (Dt 6, 4ff). Israel has yet another chance, if it obeys. The people are poised between life and death; and they are exhorted to choose life—today (26, 16-19; 30, 15-20).

THE BOOK OF GENESIS

Genesis, the first book of the Bible, opens with the Hebrew word bereshit, *which means "in the beginning." The title "Genesis" was given to the Septuagint (Greek) translation of the book, because of its concern with the origin of the world (Gn 1, 1; 2, 4), of the human race, and, in particular, of the Hebrew people.*

Eleven structural units (toledoth), of unequal length and importance, present the unity and purpose of the book in terms of God's universal sovereignty, his dealings with men, and his choice and formation of a special people to be the instrument of his plan of salvation.

The tracing of the direct descendance from Adam to Jacob constitutes the major part of the book, while the genealogical tables of lateral branches are not so developed nor of such interest as those that pertain to the story of the Israelite people. In fact, these lateral branches gradually disappear from the narrative. And with the introduction of Abraham and his covenant with God, the history of humanity as such becomes contracted to the story of the descendants of Abraham through Isaac and Jacob—the chosen people.

Despite its unity of plan and purpose, the book is a complex work, not to be attributed to a single original author. Several sources, or literary traditions, that the final redactor used in his composition are discernible. These are the Yahwist (J), Elohist (E) and Priestly (P) sources, which in turn reflect older oral traditions (see Introduction to the Pentateuch).

In Genesis, the Yahwist source is the most important by reason of its teaching, its antiquity, and the continuity it gives the book. It constitutes a sacred history, continually drawing attention to the working out of God's design through his interventions in the affairs of men. The Elohist source, less well preserved, is found in fragmentary form only, depicting God's manifestations through visions and dreams rather than theophanies. Angels are God's intermediaries with men. Moreover, there is a solicitude for the divine transcendence and greater sensitivity toward the moral order. The Priestly source contains those elements— chronological data, lists, genealogies—that construct the framework of Genesis and bind its contents together. To the J and E sources it adds such legal institutions as the sabbath rest, circumcision and the alliances between God and Noah and God and Abraham.

The interpreter of Genesis will recognize at once the distinct object that sets chapters 1—11 apart: the recounting of the origin of the world and of man (primeval history). To make the truths contained in these chapters intelligible to the Israelite people destined to pre-serve them, they needed to be expressed through elements prevailing among that people at that time. For this reason, the truths themselves must therefore be clearly distinguished from their literary garb.

With the story of the patriarchs Abraham, Isaac and Jacob (Gn 11, 27—50, 26), the character of the narrative changes. While we do not view the account of the patriarchs as history in the strict sense, nevertheless certain of the matters recounted from the time of Abraham onward can be placed in the actual historical and social framework of the Near East in the early part of the second millennium B.C. (2000-1500), and documented by non-biblical sources.

Genesis contains many religious teachings of basic importance: the preexistence and transcendence of God, his wisdom and goodness, his power through which all things are made and on which they all depend; the special creation of man in God's image and likeness, and of woman from the substance of man; the institution of marriage as the union of one man with one woman; man's original state of innocence; man's sin of pride and disobedience, its consequences for the protoparents and their posterity. Despite the severity of their punish-ment, hope of reconciliation is offered by God through the first as well as the subsequent promises of salvation and grace. Abraham is blessed for his faith and obedience, and he is to be a blessing for all nations through his offspring, Isaac, Jacob, and Jacob's sons (Gn 12, 3; 18, 18; 22, 18), of whom the Messiah, mankind's greatest blessing, will eventually be born (Gal 3, 8).

Frequent references to Genesis are found in the New Testament. Christ becomes the antithesis of Adam: sin and death come to mankind through Adam, justification and life through Jesus Christ (Rom 5, 12. 17ff). Noah's ark becomes the symbol of the church, by which men are saved from destruction through the waters of baptism (1 Pt 3, 20ff); Abra-ham's faith is the model for all believers; the sacrifice of his son Isaac typifies the sacrifice of Christ, Son of the Father. The liturgy, too, relates the persons of Abel, Abraham and Mel-chizedek to Christ in his act of sacrifice.

The Book of Genesis is divided as follows: I. The Primeval History (1, 1—11, 26). II. The Patriarch Abraham (11, 27—25, 18). III. The Patriarchs Isaac and Jacob (25, 19—36, 43). IV. Joseph and His Brothers (37, 1—50, 26).

I: THE PRIMEVAL HISTORY

CHAPTER 1

First Story of Creation. * [1] In the beginning, when God created the heavens and the earth,[a] [2] the earth was a formless wasteland, and darkness covered the abyss,* while a mighty wind swept over the waters.[b]

[3] Then God said, "Let there be light," and there was light.[c] [4] God saw how good the light was. God then separated the light from the darkness. [5] God called the light "day," and the darkness he called "night." Thus evening came, and morning followed—the first day.*

[6] Then God said, "Let there be a dome in the middle of the waters, to separate one body of water from the other." And so it happened: [7] God made the dome, and it separated the water above the dome from the water below it.[d] [8] God called the dome "the sky." Evening came, and morning followed—the second day.

[9] Then God said, "Let the water under the sky be gathered into a single basin, so that the dry land may appear." And so it happened: the water under the sky was gathered into its basin, and the dry land appeared.[e] [10] God called the dry land "the earth," and the basin of the water he called "the sea." God saw how good it was. [11] [f] Then God said, "Let the earth bring forth vegetation: every kind of plant that bears seed and every kind of fruit tree on earth that bears fruit with its seed in it." And so it happened: [12] the earth brought forth every kind of plant that bears seed and every kind of fruit tree on earth that bears fruit with its seed in it. God saw how good it was. [13] Evening came, and morning followed—the third day.

[14] Then God said: "Let there be lights in the dome of the sky, to separate day from night. Let them mark the fixed times, the days and the years,[g] [15] and serve as luminaries in the dome of the sky, to shed light upon the earth." And so it happened: [16] God made the two great lights, the greater one to govern the day, and the lesser one to govern the night; and he made the stars.[h] [17] God set them in the dome of the sky, to shed light upon the earth, [18] to govern the day and the night, and to separate the light from the darkness. God saw how good it was. [19] Evening came, and morning followed—the fourth day.

[20] [hh] Then God said, "Let the water teem with an abundance of living creatures, and on the earth let birds fly beneath the dome of the sky." And so it happened: [21] God created the great sea monsters and all kinds of swimming creatures with which the water teems, and all kinds of winged birds. God saw how good it was, [22] and God blessed them, saying, "Be fertile, multiply, and fill the water of the seas; and let the birds multiply on the earth."[i] [23] Evening came, and morning followed—the fifth day.

[24] [j] Then God said, "Let the earth bring forth all kinds of living creatures: cattle, creeping things, and wild animals of all kinds." And so it happened: [25] God made all kinds of wild animals, all kinds of cattle, and all kinds of creeping things of the earth. God saw how good it was. [26] [k] Then God said: "Let us make man in our image, after our likeness. Let them have dominion over the fish of the sea, the birds of the air, and the cattle, and over all the wild animals and all the creatures that crawl on the ground."*

[27] God created man in his image,
     in the divine image he created him;
     male and female he created them.

[28] God blessed them, saying: "Be fertile and multiply; fill the earth and subdue it.

a Gn 2, 1, 4: Jb 38—39; Pss 8, 4; 90, 2; Wis 11, 17; Sir 16, 24; Jer 10, 12; 2 Mc 7, 28; Acts 14, 15; Col 1, 16f; Heb 1, 2f; 3, 4; 11, 3; Rv 4, 11.—b Jer 4, 23.—c 2 Cor 4, 6.—d Prv 8, 27f; 2 Pt 3, 5.—e Jb 38, 8; Ps 33, 7; Jer 5, 22.—f Ps 104, 14.—g Jb 26, 10; Ps 19, 1f; Bar 3, 33.—h Dt 4, 19; Ps 136, 7ff; Wis 13, 2ff; Jer 31, 35.—hh Jb 12, 7-10.—i Gn 8, 17.—j Sir 16, 27f; Bar 3, 32—k 26f: Gn 5, 1. 3; 9, 6; Ps 8, 5f; Wis 2, 23; 10, 2; Sir 17, 1. 3f; Jas 3, 7; 1 Cor 11, 7; Eph 4, 24; Col 3, 10; Mt 19, 4; Mk 10, 6.

1, 1—2, 4a: This section introduces the whole Pentateuch. It shows how God brought an orderly universe out of primordial chaos.

1, 2: *The abyss:* the primordial ocean according to the ancient Semitic cosmogony. After God's creative activity, part of this vast body forms the salt-water seas (vv 9f); part of it is the fresh water under the earth (Ps 33, 7; Ez 31, 4), which wells forth on the earth as springs and fountains (Gn 7, 11; 8, 2; Prv 3, 20). Part of it, "the upper water" (Ps 148, 4; Dn 3, 60), is held up by the dome of the sky (Gn 1, 6f) from which rain descends on the earth (Gn 7, 11; 2 Kgs 7, 2. 19; Ps 104, 13). *A mighty wind:* literally, "a wind of God," or "a spirit of God"; cf Gn 8, 1.

1, 5: In ancient Israel a day was considered to begin at sunset. According to the highly artificial literary structure of Gn 1, 1—2, 4a, God's creative activity is divided into six days to teach the sacredness of the sabbath rest on the seventh day in the Israelite religion (Gn 2, 2f).

1, 26: Man is here presented as the climax of God's creative activity; he resembles God primarily because of the dominion God gives him over the rest of creation.

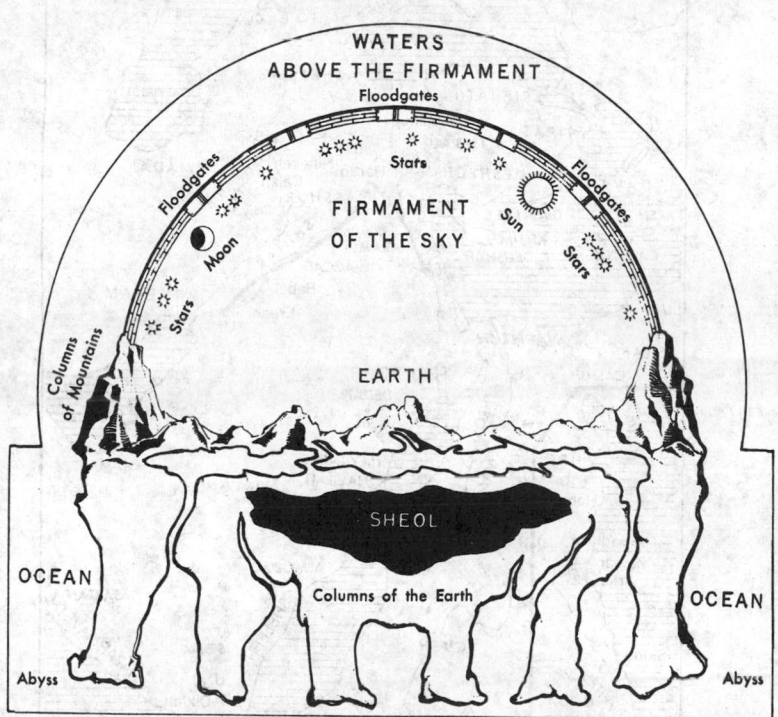

Heavenly Seat of the Divinity

WATERS
ABOVE THE FIRMAMENT
Floodgates

Stars

Floodgates

Floodgates

FIRMAMENT
OF THE SKY

Moon

Sun

Stars

Stars

Columns of Mountains

EARTH

Stars

SHEOL

OCEAN

OCEAN

Columns of the Earth

Abyss

Abyss

THE WORLD OF THE HEBREWS

THE WORLD OF THE HEBREWS — Graphic representation of the Hebrew conception of the world. God's heavenly seat rests above the superior waters. Below these waters lies the firmament or sky which resembles an overturned bowl and is supported by columns. Through the openings (floodgates) in its vault the superior waters fall down upon the earth in the form of rain or snow. The earth is a platform resting on columns and surrounded by waters, the seas. Underneath the columns lie the inferior waters. In the depths of the earth is Sheol, the home of the dead (also called the nether world). This was the same prescientific concept of the universe as that held by the Hebrews' pagan neighbors.

THE PEOPLING OF THE EARTH ACCORDING TO GENESIS 10

THE PEOPLING OF THE EARTH (Gn 10, 1-32; 11, 10-26) — This account, stemming from Israel's monarchical period, represents a remarkable classification of the various peoples known to the ancient Israelites. No similar compilation has so far been found in the literature of any other ancient people. Theologically, the Bible account affirms the unity of the human race and sees the peopling of the earth as the result of the divine blessing (Gn 9, 1); it is a new creation, but now of the nations of the earth. The relationship between the various peoples is based partly on linguistic, partly on geographic, and partly on political grounds. In general, **(a)** the descendants of **Japheth** (10, 2-5) are the peoples of the Indo-European languages to the north and west of **Mesopotamia** and **Syria; (b)** the descendants of **Ham** (10, 6-20) are the Hamitic-speaking people of **northern Africa;** and **(c)** the descendants of **Shem** (10, 21-31) are the Semitic-speaking peoples of **Mesopotamia, Syria,** and **Arabia.** But there are many exceptions to this rule. **(d)** The entire list in Gn 11, 10-26 confirms both the northwestern Mesopotamian origin of Israel's ancestors and the mixed ethnic background suggested by later Israelite traditions.

Have dominion over the fish of the sea, the birds of the air, and all the living things that move on the earth."[l] [29] [m] God also said: "See, I give you every seed-bearing plant all over the earth and every tree that has seed-bearing fruit on it to be your food; [30] and to all the animals of the land, all the birds of the air, and all the living creatures that crawl on the ground, I give all the green plants for food." And so it happened. [31] God looked at everything he had made, and he found it very good. Evening came, and morning followed—the sixth day.[n]

CHAPTER 2

[1] Thus the heavens and the earth and all their array were completed.[o] [2] Since on the seventh day God was finished with the work he had been doing, he rested on the seventh day from all the work he had undertaken.[p] [3] So God blessed the seventh day and made it holy, because on it he rested from all the work he had done in creation.[q]

[4] Such is the story of the heavens and the earth at their creation.

Second Story of Creation.* At the time when the LORD God made the earth and the heavens—[5] while as yet there was no field shrub on earth and no grass of the field had sprouted, for the LORD God had

sent no rain upon the earth and there was no man to till the soil, [6] but a stream was welling up out of the earth and was watering all the surface of the ground—[7] the LORD God formed man out of the clay of the ground* and blew into his nostrils the breath of life, and so man became a living being.[r]

[8] Then the LORD God planted a garden in Eden,* in the east, and he placed there the man whom he had formed.[s] [9] Out of the ground the LORD God made various trees grow that were delightful to look at and good for food, with the tree of life in the middle of the garden and the tree of the knowledge of good and bad.[t]

[10] A river rises* in Eden to water the garden; beyond there it divides and becomes four branches. [11] The name of the first is the Pishon; it is the one that winds through the whole land of Havilah, where there is gold. [12] The gold of that land is excellent; bdellium and lapis lazuli are also there. [13] The name of the second river is the Gihon; it is the one that winds all through the land of Cush.[u] [14] The name of the third river is the Tigris; it is the one that flows east of Asshur. The fourth river is the Euphrates.

[15] The LORD God then took the man and settled him in the garden of Eden, to cultivate and care for it.[v] [16] The LORD God gave man this order: "You are free to eat from any of the trees of the garden[w] [17] except the tree of knowledge of good and bad. From that tree you shall not eat; the moment you eat from it you are surely doomed to die."[x]

[18] The LORD God said: "It is not good for the man to be alone. I will make a suitable partner for him."[y] [19] So the LORD God formed out of the ground various wild animals and various birds of the air, and he brought them to the man to see what he would call them; whatever the man called each of them would be its name. [20] The man gave names to all the cattle, all the birds of the air, and all the wild animals; but none proved to be the suitable partner for the man.

[21] So the LORD God cast a deep sleep on the man, and while he was asleep, he took out one of his ribs and closed up its place with flesh.[z] [22] The LORD God then built up into a woman the rib that he had taken from the man. When he brought her to the man, [23] the man said:

l Gn 8, 17; 9, 1; Pss 8, 6-9; 115, 16; Wis 9, 2.—m 29f: Gn 9, 3; Ps 104, 14f.—n 1 Tm 4, 4.—o Is 45, 12; Jn 1, 3.—p Ex 20, 9ff; 31, 17; Heb 4, 4. 10.—q Ex 20, 11; Dt 5, 14; Neh 9, 14.—r Gn 3, 19; 18, 27; Tb 8, 6; Jb 34, 15; Pss 103, 14; 104, 29; Eccl 3, 20; 12, 7; Wis 7, 1; Sir 33, 10; 1 Cor 15, 45.—s Is 51, 3; Ez 31, 9.—t Gn 3, 22; Prv 3, 18; Rv 2, 7; 22, 2. 14.—u Sir 24, 25.—v Sir 7, 15.—w Ps 104, 14.—x Gn 3, 2f; Rom 6, 23.—y Tb 8, 6; Sir 36, 24; 1 Cor 11, 9; 1 Tm 2, 13.—z Sir 17, 1; 1 Cor 11, 8f; 1 Tm 2, 13.

2, 4b-25: This section is chiefly concerned with the creation of man. It is much older than the narrative of Gn 1, 1—2, 4a. Here God is depicted as creating man before the rest of his creatures, which are made for man's sake.

2, 7: God is portrayed as a potter molding man's body out of clay. There is a play on words in Hebrew between *adam* ("man") and *adama* ("ground"). *Being:* literally, "soul."

2, 8: *Eden:* used here as the name of a region in southern Mesopotamia; the term is derived from the Sumerian word *eden*, "fertile plain." A similar-sounding Hebrew word means "delight"; the *garden in Eden* could therefore be understood as the "garden of delight," so that, through the Greek version, it is now known also as "paradise," literally, a "pleasure park."

2, 10-14: *Rises:* in flood to overflow its banks. *Beyond there:* as one travels upstream. *Branches:* literally, "heads," i.e., upper courses. Eden is near the head of the Persian Gulf, where the Tigris and the Euphrates join with two other streams to form a single river. *The land of Cush* here and in Gn 10, 8, is not Ethiopia (Nubia) as elsewhere, but the region of the Kassites east of Mesopotamia.

"This one, at last, is bone of my bones
　　and flesh of my flesh;
This one shall be called 'woman,'
　　for out of 'her man' this one has been
　　taken."*

24 *a* That is why a man leaves his father
and mother and clings to his wife, and the
two of them become one body.*

25 The man and his wife were both
naked, yet they felt no shame.

CHAPTER 3

The Fall of Man. 1 Now the serpent was
the most cunning of all the animals that
the LORD God had made. The serpent
asked the woman, "Did God really tell you
not to eat from any of the trees in the garden?" 2 The woman answered the serpent:
"We may eat of the fruit of the trees in the
garden; 3 *b* it is only about the fruit of the
tree in the middle of the garden that God
said, 'You shall not eat it or even touch it,
lest you die.' " 4 But the serpent said to the
woman: "You certainly will not die!*c* 5 No,
God knows well that the moment you eat
of it your eyes will be opened and you will
be like gods who know* what is good and
what is bad." 6 The woman saw that the
tree was good for food, pleasing to the
eyes, and desirable for gaining wisdom. So
she took some of its fruit and ate it; and
she also gave some to her husband, who
was with her, and he ate it. *d* 7 Then the
eyes of both of them were opened, and
they realized that they were naked; so they
sewed fig leaves together and made
loincloths for themselves.

8 When they heard the sound of the
LORD God moving about in the garden at
the breezy time of the day,* the man and
his wife hid themselves from the LORD
God among the trees of the garden.*e* 9 The
LORD God then called to the man and
asked him, "Where are you?" 10 He answered, "I heard you in the garden; but I
was afraid, because I was naked, so I hid
myself." 11 Then he asked, "Who told you
that you were naked? You have eaten,
then, from the tree of which I had forbidden you to eat!" 12 The man replied, "The
woman whom you put here with me—she
gave me fruit from the tree, and so I ate
it." 13 The LORD God then asked the
woman, "Why did you do such a thing?"
The woman answered, "The serpent
tricked me into it, so I ate it."*f*

14 Then the LORD God said to the serpent:

"Because you have done this, you shall
　　be banned
　　from all the animals
　　and from all the wild creatures;
On your belly shall you crawl,
　　and dirt shall you eat
　　all the days of your life.*g*

15 I will put enmity between you and the
　　woman,
　　and between your offspring and
　　hers;
He will strike at your head,
　　while you strike at his heel." * *h*

16 To the woman he said:

"I will intensify the pangs of your
　　childbearing;
　　in pain shall you bring forth chil-
　　dren.
Yet your urge shall be for your hus-
　　band,
　　and he shall be your master."*i*

17 To the man he said: "Because you listened to your wife and ate from the tree of
which I had forbidden you to eat,

"Cursed be the ground because of you!
In toil shall you eat its yield
　　all the days of your life.*j*

18 Thorns and thistles shall it bring forth
　　to you,
　　as you eat of the plants of the field.

a Mt 19, 5; Mk 10, 7; 1 Cor 7, 10f; Eph 5, 31.—b Gn 2, 17;
Rom 6, 23.—c 4f: Wis 2, 24; Sir 25, 14; Is 14, 14; Jn 8, 44; 2
Cor 11, 3.—d Gn 3, 22; 1 Tm 2, 14.—e Jer 23, 24.—f 2 Cor 11,
3.—g Is 65, 25; Mi 7, 17; Rv 12, 9.—h Is 7, 14; 9, 5; Rom 16,
20; 1 Jn 3, 8; Rv 12, 17.—i 1 Cor 11, 3; Eph 5, 22f; 1 Tm 2,
12.—j Gn 5, 29; Rom 5, 12; 8, 20; Heb 6, 8.

2, 23: There is a play on the similar-sounding Hebrew words
ishsha ("woman") and *ishah* ("her man, her husband").
2, 24: *One body:* literally "one flesh"; classical Hebrew has
no specific word for "body." The sacred writer stresses the fact
that conjugal union is willed by God.
3, 5: *Like gods who know:* or "like God who knows."
3, 8: *The breezy time of the day:* literally "the wind of the
day." On most days in Palestine a cooling breeze blows from the
sea shortly before sunset.
3, 15: *He will strike . . . at his heel:* since the antecedent
for *he* and *his* is the collective noun *offspring,* i.e., all the descendants of the woman, a more exact rendering of the sacred
writer's words would be, "They will strike . . . at their heels."
However, later theology saw in this passage more than unending
hostility between snakes and men. The serpent was regarded as
the devil (Wis 2, 24; Jn 8, 44; Rv 12, 9; 20, 2), whose eventual
defeat seems implied in the contrast between *head* and *heel.* Because "the Son of God appeared that he might destroy the works
of the devil" (1 Jn 3, 8), the passage can be understood as the
first promise of a Redeemer for fallen mankind. The woman's
offspring then is primarily Jesus Christ.

[19] By the sweat of your face
      shall you get bread to eat,
   Until you return to the ground,
      from which you were taken;
   For you are dirt,
      and to dirt you shall return."[k]

[20] The man called his wife Eve, because she became the mother of all the living.*
[21] For the man and his wife the LORD God made leather garments, with which he clothed them. [22] Then the LORD God said: "See! The man has become like one of us, knowing what is good and what is bad! Therefore, he must not be allowed to put out his hand to take fruit from the tree of life also, and thus eat of it and live forever."[l] [23] The LORD God therefore banished him from the garden of Eden, to till the ground from which he had been taken. [24] When he expelled the man, he settled him east of the garden of Eden; and he stationed the cherubim and the fiery revolving sword, to guard the way to the tree of life.*

CHAPTER 4

Cain and Abel. [1] The man had relations with his wife Eve, and she conceived and bore Cain, saying, "I have produced a man with the help of the LORD."* [2] Next she bore his brother Abel. Abel became a keeper of flocks, and Cain a tiller of the soil. [3] In the course of time Cain brought an offering to the LORD from the fruit of the soil, [4] while Abel, for his part, brought one of the best firstlings of his flock.[m] The LORD looked with favor on Abel and his offering, [5] but on Cain and his offering he did not. Cain greatly resented this and was crestfallen. [6] So the LORD said to Cain: "Why are you so resentful and crestfallen? [7] If you do well, you can hold up your head; but if not, sin is a demon lurking* at the door: his urge is toward you, yet you can be his master."[n]
[8] Cain said to his brother Abel, "Let us go out in the field." When they were in the field, Cain attacked his brother Abel and killed him.[o] [9] Then the LORD asked Cain, "Where is your brother Abel?" He answered, "I do not know. Am I my brother's keeper?" [10] The LORD then said: "What have you done! Listen: Your brother's blood cries out to me from the soil! [11] Therefore you shall be banned from the soil that opened its mouth to receive your brother's blood from your hand.[p] [12] If you till the soil, it shall no longer give you its produce. You shall become a restless wanderer on the earth." [13] Cain said to the LORD: "My punishment is too great to bear. [14] Since you have now banished me from the soil, and I must avoid your presence and become a restless wanderer on the earth, anyone may kill me at sight." [15] "Not so!" the LORD said to him. "If anyone kills Cain, Cain shall be avenged sevenfold." So the LORD put a mark* on Cain, lest anyone should kill him at sight. [16] Cain then left the LORD's presence and settled in the land of Nod,* east of Eden.

Descendants of Cain and Seth. [17] * Cain had relations with his wife, and she conceived and bore Enoch. Cain also became the founder of a city, which he named after his son Enoch. [18] To Enoch was born Irad, and Irad became the father of Mehujael; Mehujael became the father of Methusael, and Methusael became the father of Lamech. [19] Lamech took two wives; the name of the first was Adah, and the name of the second Zillah. [20] Adah gave birth to Jabal, the ancestor of all who dwell in tents and keep cattle. [21] His brother's name was Jubal; he was the ancestor of all who play the lyre and the pipe. [22] Zillah, on her part, gave birth to Tubalcain, the ancestor of all who forge instruments of bronze and iron. The sister of Tubalcain was Naamah.

k Gn 2, 7; Jb 10, 9; 34, 15; Pss 90, 3; 103, 14; Eccl 3, 20; 12, 7; Wis 15, 8; Sir 10, 9; 17, 2; Rom 5, 12; 1 Cor 15, 21; Heb 9, 27.—l Gn 2, 9; Rv 22, 2. 14.—m Ex 34, 19; Heb 11, 4.—n Sir 7, 1; Jude 11.—o Wis 10, 3; Mt 23, 35; Lk 11, 51; 1 Jn 3, 12; Jude 11.—p Dt 27, 24.

3, 20: This verse seems to be out of place; it would fit better after v 24. The Hebrew name *hawwa* ("Eve") is related to the Hebrew word *hay* ("living").

3, 24: The above rendering is based on the ancient Greek version; that of the current Hebrew is, When he expelled the man, he settled east of the garden of Eden, the cherubim.

4, 1: The Hebrew name *qayin* ("Cain") and the term *qaniti* ("I have produced") present another play on words.

4, 7: *Demon lurking:* in Hebrew, *robes,* literally "croucher," is used here, like the similar Akkadian term *rabisu,* to designate a certain kind of evil spirit.

4, 15: *A mark:* probably a tattoo. The use of tattooing for tribal marks has always been common among the nomads of the Near Eastern deserts.

4, 16: *The land of Nod:* not a definite geographic region. The term merely means "the land of nomads."

4, 17-22: In vv 12-16 Cain was presented as the archetype of nomadic peoples. The sacred author in this section follows another ancient tradition that makes Cain the prototype of sedentary peoples with higher material culture.

23 Lamech said to his wives:

"Adah and Zillah, hear my voice;
   wives of Lamech, listen to my utterance:
I have killed a man for wounding me,
   a boy for bruising me.
24 If Cain is avenged sevenfold,
   then Lamech seventy-sevenfold."

25 Adam again had relations with his wife, and she gave birth to a son whom she called Seth. "God has granted* me more offspring in place of Abel," she said, "because Cain slew him." 26 To Seth, in turn, a son was born, and he named him Enosh.

At that time men began to invoke the LORD by name. *q*

CHAPTER 5

Generations: Adam to Noah.* 1 *r* This is the record of the descendants of Adam. When God created man, he made him in the likeness of God; 2 he created them male and female. When they were created, he blessed them and named them "man."

3 *s* Adam was one hundred and thirty years old when he begot a son in his likeness, after his image; and he named him Seth. *t* 4 Adam lived eight hundred years after the birth of Seth, and he had other sons and daughters. 5 The whole lifetime of Adam was nine hundred and thirty years; then he died.

6 When Seth was one hundred and five years old, he became the father of Enosh. 7 Seth lived eight hundred and seven years after the birth of Enosh, and he had other sons and daughters. 8 The whole lifetime of Seth was nine hundred and twelve years; then he died.

9 When Enosh was ninety years old, he became the father of Kenan. 10 Enosh lived eight hundred and fifteen years after the birth of Kenan, and he had other sons and daughters. 11 The whole lifetime of Enosh was nine hundred and five years; then he died.

12 When Kenan was seventy years old, he became the father of Mahalalel, 13 Kenan lived eight hundred and forty years after the birth of Mahalalel, and he had other sons and daughters. 14 The whole lifetime of Kenan was nine hundred and ten years; then he died.

15 When Mahalalel was sixty-five years old, he became the father of Jared.

16 Mahalalel lived eight hundred and thirty years after the birth of Jared, and he had other sons and daughters. 17 The whole lifetime of Mahalalel was eight hundred and ninety-five years; then he died.

18 When Jared was one hundred and sixty-two years old, he became the father of Enoch. 19 Jared lived eight hundred years after the birth of Enoch, and he had other sons and daughters. 20 The whole lifetime of Jared was nine hundred and sixty-two years; then he died.

21 When Enoch was sixty-five years old, he became the father of Methuselah. 22 Enoch lived three hundred years after the birth of Methuselah, and he had other sons and daughters. 23 The whole lifetime of Enoch was three hundred and sixty-five years. 24 Then Enoch walked with God,* and he was no longer here, for God took him. *u*

25 When Methuselah was one hundred and eighty-seven years old, he became the father of Lamech. 26 Methuselah lived seven hundred and eighty-two years after the birth of Lamech, and he had other sons and daughters. 27 The whole lifetime of Methuselah was nine hundred and sixty-nine years; then he died.

28 When Lamech was one hundred and eighty-two years old, he begot a son 29 *v* and named him Noah, saying, "Out of the very ground that the LORD has put under a curse, this one shall bring us relief

---

q 1 Chr 1, 1; Lk 3, 38.—r Gn 1 27; Wis 2, 23; Sir 17, 1; 1 Cor 11, 1; Jas 3, 9.—s Gn 4, 25.—t 3-32: 1 Chr 1, 1-4; Lk 3, 36ff.— u Wis 4, 10f; Sir 44, 16; 49, 14; Heb 11, 5.—v Gn 3, 17ff.

4, 25f: *Has granted:* Hebrew *shat,* a wordplay on the name *shet* ("Seth"). *Enosh:* in Hebrew, a synonym of *adam* ("man"). *At that time . . . name:* men began to call God by his personal name, Yahweh, rendered as "the Lord" in this version of the Bible. The ancient, so-called Yahwist source used here employs the name Yahweh long before the time of Moses. Another ancient source, the Elohist (from its use of the term *Elohim,* "God," instead of *Yahweh,* "Lord," for the pre-Mosaic period), makes Moses the first to use Yahweh as the proper name of Israel's God, previously known by other names as well; cf Ex 3, 13ff.

5, 1-32: Although this chapter, with its highly schematic form, belongs to the relatively late "Priestly document," it is based on very ancient traditions. Together with Gn 11, 10-26, its primary purpose is to bridge the genealogical gap between Adam and Abraham. Adam's line is traced through Seth, but several names in the series are the same as, or similar to, certain names in Cain's line (Gn 4, 17ff). The long lifespans attributed to these ten antediluvian patriarchs have a symbolic rather than a historical value. Babylonian tradition also recorded ten kings with fantastically high ages who reigned successively before the flood.

5, 24: In place of the usual formula, *Then he died,* the change to *Enoch walked with God* clearly implies that he did not die, but like Elijah (2 Kgs 2, 11f) was taken alive to God's abode.

from our work and the toil of our hands."* [30]Lamech lived five hundred and ninety-five years after the birth of Noah, and he had other sons and daughters. [31]The whole lifetime of Lamech was seven hundred and seventy-seven years; then he died.

[32]When Noah was five hundred years old, he became the father of Shem, Ham and Japheth. [w]

CHAPTER 6

Origin of the Nephilim.* [1]When men began to multiply on earth and daughters were born to them, [2]the sons of heaven* saw how beautiful the daughters of man were, and so they took for their wives as many of them as they chose. [x] [3]Then the LORD said: "My spirit* shall not remain in man forever, since he is but flesh. His days shall comprise one hundred and twenty years."

[4]At that time the Nephilim appeared on earth (as well as later*), after the sons of heaven had intercourse with the daughters of man, who bore them sons. They were the heroes of old, the men of renown. [y]

Warning of the Flood. [5]* When the LORD saw how great was man's wickedness on earth, and how no desire that his heart conceived was ever anything but evil, [z] [6]he regretted that he had made man on the earth, and his heart was grieved.

[7]So the LORD said: "I will wipe out

---

w Gn 6, 10; 10, 1.—x Mt 24, 38; Lk 17, 26f.—y Wis 14, 6; Bar 3, 26.—z Ps 14, 2f.—a Wis 10, 4; Sir 44, 17.—b Jb 22, 15ff.—c Ps 14, 2.—d Sir 40, 9f; 44, 17; Mt 24, 37ff.—e Gn 7, 4. 21; 2 Pt 2, 5.

5, 29: There is a similarity in sound between the Hebrew word *noah*, "Noah," and the verbal phrase *yenahamenu*, "he will bring us relief"; this latter refers both to the curse put on the soil because of the fall of man (Gn 3, 17ff) and to Noah's success in agriculture, especially in raising grapes for wine (Gn 9, 20f).

6, 1-4: This is apparently a fragment of an old legend that had borrowed much from ancient mythology. The sacred author incorporates it here, not only in order to account for the prehistoric giants of Palestine, whom the Israelites called *the Nephilim*, but also to introduce the story of the flood with a moral orientation—the constantly increasing wickedness of mankind.

6, 2: *The sons of heaven:* literally "the sons of the gods" or "the sons of God," i.e., the celestial beings of mythology.

6, 3: *My spirit:* the breath of life referred to in Gn 2, 7. *His days . . . years:* probably the time God would still let men live on earth before destroying them with the flood, rather than the maximum span of life God would allot to individual men in the future.

6, 4: *As well as later:* According to Nm 13, 33, when the Israelites invaded Palestine and found there the tall aboriginal Anakim, they likened them to *the Nephilim*; cf Dt 2, 10f. Perhaps the huge megalithic structures in Palestine were thought to have been built by a race of giants, whose superhuman strength was attributed to semi-divine origin. *The heroes of old:* the legendary worthies of ancient mythology.

---

from the earth the men whom I have created, and not only the men, but also the beasts and the creeping things and the birds of the air, for I am sorry that I made them." [8]But Noah found favor with the LORD.

[9]These are the descendants of Noah. Noah, a good man and blameless in that age, [a] [10]for he walked with God, begot three sons: Shem, Ham and Japheth. [11]In the eyes of God the earth was corrupt and full of lawlessness. [b] [12]When God saw how corrupt the earth had become, since all mortals led depraved lives on earth, [c] [13]he said to Noah: "I have decided to put an end to all mortals on earth; the earth is full of lawlessness because of them. So I will destroy them and all life on earth. [d]

Preparation for the Flood. [14]"Make yourself an ark of gopherwood,* put various compartments in it, and cover it inside and out with pitch. [15]This is how you shall build it: the length of the ark shall be three hundred cubits, its width fifty cubits, and its height thirty cubits.* [16]Make an opening for daylight* in the ark, and finish the ark a cubit above it. Put an entrance in the side of the ark, which you shall make with bottom, second and third decks. [17]I, on my part, am about to bring the flood [waters] on the earth, to destroy everywhere all creatures in which there is the breath of life; everything on earth shall perish. [e] [18]But with you I will establish my covenant; you and your sons, your wife

---

6, 5—8, 22: The story of the great flood here recorded is a composite narrative based on two separate sources interwoven into an intricate patchwork. To the Yahwist source, with some later editorial additions, are usually assigned 6, 5-8; 7, 1-5. 7-10. 12. 16b. 17b. 22-23; 8, 2b-3a. 6-12. 13b. 20-22. The other sections come from the "Priestly document." The combination of the two sources produced certain duplications (e.g., 6, 13-22 of the Yahwist source, beside 7, 1-5 of the Priestly source); also certain inconsistencies, such as the number of the various animals taken into the ark (6, 19f; 7, 14f of the Priestly source, beside 7, 2f of the Yahwist source), and the timetable of the flood (8, 3-5. 13f of the Priestly source, beside 7, 4. 10. 12. 17b; 8, 6. 10. 12 of the Yahwist source). Both biblical sources go back ultimately to an ancient Mesopotamian story of a great flood, preserved in the eleventh tablet of the Gilgamesh Epic. The latter account, in some respects remarkably similar to the biblical account, is in others very different from it.

6, 14: *Gopherwood:* an unidentified wood not mentioned elsewhere; *gopher* is merely the Hebrew word for it.

6, 15: The dimensions of Noah's ark were approximately 440 x 73 x 44 feet, a foot and a half to the cubit. The ark of the Babylonian flood story was an exact cube, 120 cubits in length, width, and height.

6, 16: *Opening for daylight:* a conjectural rendering of the Hebrew word *sohar*, occurring only here. The reference is probably to an open space on all sides near the top of the ark to admit light and air. The ark also had a window or hatch, which could be opened and closed (Gn 8, 6).

and your sons' wives, shall go into the ark.*f* ¹⁹Of all other living creatures you shall bring two into the ark, one male and one female, that you may keep them alive with you. ²⁰Of all kinds of birds, of all kinds of beasts, and of all kinds of creeping things, two of each shall come into the ark with you, to stay alive. ²¹Moreover, you are to provide yourself with all the food that is to be eaten, and store it away, that it may serve as provisions for you and for them." ²²This Noah did; he carried out all the commands that God gave him.

CHAPTER 7

¹Then the LORD said to Noah: "Go into the ark, you and all your household, for you alone in this age have I found to be truly just.*g* ²Of every clean animal, take with you seven pairs, a male and its mate; and of the unclean animals, one pair, a male and its mate; ³likewise, of every clean bird of the air, seven pairs, a male and a female, and of all the unclean birds, one pair, a male and a female. Thus you will keep their issue alive over all the earth. ⁴Seven days from now I will bring rain down on the earth for forty days and forty nights, and so I will wipe out from the surface of the earth every moving creature that I have made."*h* ⁵Noah did just as the LORD had commanded him.

The Great Flood. ⁶Noah was six hundred years old when the flood waters came upon the earth. ⁷Together with his sons, his wife, and his sons' wives, Noah went into the ark because of the waters of the flood.*i* ⁸Of the clean animals and the unclean, of the birds, and of everything that creeps on the ground, ⁹[two by two] male and female entered the ark with Noah, just as the LORD had commanded him.*j* ¹⁰As soon as the seven days were over, the waters of the flood came upon the earth.

¹¹In the six hundredth year of Noah's life, in the second month, on the seventeenth day of the month: it was on that day that

    All the fountains of the great abyss*
        burst forth,
        and the floodgates of the sky were
        opened.

¹²For forty days and forty nights heavy rain poured down on the earth.

¹³On the precise day named, Noah and his sons Shem, Ham and Japheth, and

Noah's wife, and the three wives of Noah's sons had entered the ark, ¹⁴together with every kind of wild beast, every kind of domestic animal, every kind of creeping thing of the earth, and every kind of bird. ¹⁵Pairs of all creatures in which there was the breath of life entered the ark with Noah. ¹⁶Those that entered were male and female, and of all species they came, as God had commanded Noah. Then the LORD shut him in.

¹⁷The flood continued upon the earth for forty days. As the waters increased, they lifted the ark, so that it rose above the earth. ¹⁸The swelling waters increased greatly, but the ark floated on the surface of the waters. ¹⁹Higher and higher above the earth rose the waters, until all the highest mountains everywhere were submerged, ²⁰the crest rising fifteen cubits higher than the submerged mountains. ²¹All creatures that stirred on earth perished: birds, cattle, wild animals, and all that swarmed on the earth, as well as all mankind.*k* ²²Everything on dry land with the faintest breath of life in its nostrils died out. ²³The LORD wiped out every living thing on earth: man and cattle, the creeping things and the birds of the air; all were wiped out from the earth. Only Noah and those with him in the ark were left.

CHAPTER 8

²⁴ * The waters maintained their crest over the earth for one hundred and fifty days, ¹and then God remembered Noah and all the animals, wild and tame, that were with him in the ark. So God made a wind sweep over the earth, and the waters began to subside. ²The fountains of the abyss and the floodgates of the sky were closed, and the downpour from the sky was held back. ³Gradually the waters receded from the earth. At the end of one hundred and fifty days, the waters had so diminished ⁴that, in the seventh month, on the seventeenth day of the month, the ark came to rest on the mountains of Ararat.* ⁵The waters continued to

---

f Gn 9, 9; Wis 14, 6; Heb 11, 7; 1 Pt 3, 20.—g Wis 10, 4; Sir 44, 17; 2 Pt 2, 5.—h Gn 6, 17; 2 Pt 2, 5.—i Wis 14, 6; 1 Pt 3, 20; 2 Pt 2, 5.—j Gn 6, 19.—k 21ff: Jb 22, 16; Mt 24, 39; Lk 17, 27; 2 Pt 3, 6.

7, 11: *Abyss:* the subterranean ocean; see note on Gn 1, 2.
8, 24: *The . . . days:* this verse belongs to ch 7.
8, 4: *Ararat:* ancient Urartu, north of the Mesopotamian plain, part of modern Armenia.

diminish until the tenth month, and on the first day of the tenth month the tops of the mountains appeared.

⁶At the end of forty days Noah opened the hatch he had made in the ark,* ⁷and he sent out a raven, to see if the waters had lessened on the earth. It flew back and forth until the waters dried off from the earth. ⁸Then he sent out a dove, to see if the waters had lessened on the earth. ⁹But the dove could find no place to alight and perch, and it returned to him in the ark, for there was water all over the earth. Putting out his hand, he caught the dove and drew it back to him inside the ark. ¹⁰He waited seven days more and again sent the dove out from the ark. ¹¹In the evening the dove came back to him, and there in its bill was a plucked-off olive leaf! So Noah knew that the waters had lessened on the earth. ¹²He waited still another seven days and then released the dove once more; and this time it did not come back.

¹³In the six hundred and first year of Noah's life, in the first month, on the first day of the month, the water began to dry up on the earth. Noah then removed the covering of the ark and saw that the surface of the ground was drying up. ¹⁴In the second month, on the twenty-seventh day of the month, the earth was dry.

¹⁵Then God said to Noah: ¹⁶"Go out of the ark, together with your wife and your sons and your sons' wives. ¹⁷Bring out with you every living thing that is with you—all bodily creatures, be they birds or animals or creeping things of the earth—and let them abound on the earth,

breeding and multiplying on it."ˡ ¹⁸So Noah came out, together with his wife and his sons and his sons' wives; ¹⁹and all the animals, wild and tame, all the birds, and all the creeping creatures of the earth left the ark, one kind after another.

²⁰Then Noah built an altar to the LORD, and choosing from every clean animal and every clean bird, he offered holocausts on the altar. ²¹When the LORD smelled the sweet odor, he said to himself: "Never again will I doom the earth because of man, since the desires of man's heart are evil from the start;* nor will I ever again strike down all living beings, as I have done.ᵐ

²² As long as the earth lasts,
    seedtime and harvest,
    cold and heat,
  Summer and winter,
    and day and night
    shall not cease."ⁿ

CHAPTER 9

Covenant with Noah. ¹God blessed Noah and his sons and said to them: "Be fertile and multiply and fill the earth.ᵒ ²Dread fear of you shall come upon all the animals of the earth and all the birds of the air, upon all the creatures that move about on the ground and all the fishes of the sea; into your power they are delivered. ³ᵖ Every creature that is alive shall be yours to eat; I give them all to you as I did the green plants.* ⁴�q Only flesh with its life-blood still in it you shall not eat.* ⁵For your own lifeblood, too, I will demand an accounting: from every animal I will demand it, and from man in regard to his fellow man I will demand an accounting for human life.ʳ

⁶ If anyone sheds the blood of man,
    by man shall his blood be shed;
  For in the image of God
    has man been made.ˢ

⁷Be fertile, then, and multiply; abound on earth and subdue it."ᵗ

⁸God said to Noah and to his sons with him: ⁹"See, I am now establishing my covenant with you and your descendants after youᵘ ¹⁰and with every living creature that was with you: all the birds, and the various tame and wild animals that were with

---

l Gn 1, 22. 28.—m Sir 44, 18; Is 54, 9; Rom 7, 18.—n Jer 33, 20. 25.—o Gn 1, 22. 28; 8, 17; Jas 3, 7.—p Gn 1, 29f; Dt 12, 15.—q Lv 7, 26f; 17, 4; Dt 12, 16. 23; 1 Sm 14, 33; Acts 15, 20.—r Gn 4, 10f; Ex 21, 12.—s Gn 1, 26f; Lv 24, 17; Nm 35, 33; Jas 3, 9.—t Gn 1, 28; 8, 17; 9, 2.—u Gn 6, 18.

8, 6: In the original Yahwist source, from which this verse is taken, the forty days refer to the full period of the flood itself (cf Gn 7, 4. 17); in the present context, however, they seem to refer to a period following the date just given in v 5 from the Priestly source.

8, 21: *From the start:* literally "from his youth." It is uncertain whether this means from the beginning of the human race or from the early years of the individual.

9, 3: Antediluvian creatures, including man, are depicted as vegetarians (Gn 1, 29f), becoming carnivorous only after the flood.

9, 4: Because a living being dies when it loses most of its blood, the ancients regarded blood as the seat of life, and therefore as sacred. Although in itself the prohibition against eating meat with blood in it is comparable to the ritual laws of the Mosaic code, the Jews considered it binding on all men, because it was given by God to Noah, the new ancestor of all mankind; therefore the early Christian Church retained it for a time (Acts 15, 20. 29).

you and came out of the ark. [11] I will establish my covenant with you, that never again shall all bodily creatures be destroyed by the waters of a flood; there shall not be another flood to devastate the earth."[v] [12] God added: "This is the sign that I am giving for all ages to come, of the covenant between me and you and every living creature with you: [13] [w] I set my bow in the clouds to serve as a sign of the covenant between me and the earth. [14] When I bring clouds over the earth, and the bow appears in the clouds, [15] I will recall the covenant I have made between me and you and all living beings, so that the waters shall never again become a flood to destroy all mortal beings.[x] [16] As the bow appears in the clouds, I will see it and recall the everlasting covenant that I have established between God and all living beings—all mortal creatures that are on earth." [17] God told Noah: "This is the sign of the covenant I have established between me and all mortal creatures that are on earth."

Noah and His Sons. [18] * The sons of Noah who came out of the ark were Shem, Ham and Japheth. (Ham was the father of Canaan.)[y] [19] These three were the sons of Noah, and from them the whole earth was peopled.

[20] Now Noah, a man of the soil, was the first to plant a vineyard. [21] When he drank some of the wine, he became drunk and lay naked inside his tent.[z] [22] Ham, the father of Canaan, saw his father's nakedness, and he told his two brothers outside about it. [23] Shem and Japheth, however, took a robe, and holding it on their backs, they walked backward and covered their father's nakedness; since their faces were turned the other way, they did not see their father's nakedness. [24] When Noah woke up from his drunkenness and learned what his youngest son had done to him, [25] he said:

"Cursed be Canaan!
The lowest of slaves
shall he be to his brothers."[a]

[26] He also said:

"Blessed be the LORD, the God of Shem!*
Let Canaan be his slave.

[27] May God expand Japheth,*
so that he dwells among the tents of Shem;
and let Canaan be his slave."

[28] Noah lived three hundred and fifty years after the flood. [29] The whole lifetime of Noah was nine hundred and fifty years; then he died.

CHAPTER 10

Table of the Nations.* [1] These are the descendants of Noah's sons, Shem, Ham and Japheth, to whom sons were born after the flood.

[2] [b] The descendants of Japheth:
Gomer,* Magog, Madai, Javan, Tubal, Meshech and Tiras.[c]
[3] The descendants of Gomer:
Ashkenaz,* Riphath and Togarmah.
[4] The descendants of Javan:
Elishah,* Tarshish, the Kittim and the Rodanim.

[5] These are the descendants of Japheth, and from them sprang the maritime nations, in their respective lands—each

---

v Sir 44, 18; Is 54, 9.—w Sir 43, 12.—x Is 54, 9.—y Gn 5, 32; 10, 1.—z Lam 4, 21; Heb 2, 15.—a Dt 27, 16; Wis 12, 11.—b 2-8: 1 Chr 1, 5-10.—c Ez 38, 2.

9, 18-27: This story seems to be a composite of two earlier accounts; in the one, Ham was guilty, whereas in the other, it was Canaan. One purpose of the story is to justify the Israelites' enslavement of the Canaanites because of certain indecent sexual practices in the Canaanite religion. Obviously the story offers no justification for enslaving African Negroes, even though Canaan is presented as a "son" of Ham because the land of Canaan belonged to Hamitic Egypt at the time of the Israelite invasion.

9, 26: *Blessed . . . Shem:* perhaps the text read originally, "Blessed of the Lord be Shem," which would be expected in the context.

9, 27: In the Hebrew text there is a play on the words *yapt* ("expand") and *yepet* ("Japheth").

10, 1-32: This chapter presents a remarkably good classification of the various peoples known to the ancient Israelites; it is theologically important as stressing the basic family unity of all men on earth. The relationship between the various peoples is based partly on linguistic, partly on geographic, and partly on political grounds *according to their . . . languages, . . . lands and nations:* v 31). In general, *the descendants of Japheth* (vv 2-5) are the peoples of the Indo-European languages to the north and west of Mesopotamia and Syria; *the descendants of Ham* (vv 6-20) are the Hamitic-speaking peoples of northern Africa; and *the descendants of Shem* (vv 21-31) are the Semitic-speaking peoples of Mesopotamia, Syria and Arabia. But there are many exceptions to this rule; the Semitic-speaking peoples of Canaan, for instance, are considered descendants of Ham, because at the time they were subject to Hamitic Egypt (vv 6. 15-19). This chapter is a composite from the Yahwist source (vv 8-19. 21. 24-30) of about the ninth century B.C., and the Priestly source (vv 1-7. 20. 22f. 31f) of a few centuries later. That is why certain tribes of Arabia are listed under both Ham (v 7) and Shem (vv 26ff).

10, 2: *Gomer:* the Cimmerians; *Madai:* the Medes; *Javan:* the Greeks.

10, 3: *Ashkenaz:* the Scythians.

10, 4: *Elishah:* Cyprus; *the Kittim:* certain inhabitants of Cyprus; *the Rodanim:* the inhabitants of Rhodes.

with its own language—by their clans within their nations.

6 The descendants of Ham:
Cush,* Mizraim, Put and Canaan.
7 The descendants of Cush:
Seba, Havilah, Sabtah, Raamah and Sabteca.
The descendants of Raamah:
Sheba and Dedan.

8 Cush* became the father of Nimrod, who was the first potentate on earth. 9 He was a mighty hunter by the grace of the LORD; hence the saying, "Like Nimrod, a mighty hunter by the grace of the LORD." 10 The chief cities of his kingdom were Babylon, Erech and Accad, all of them in the land of Shinar.* 11 From that land he went forth to Asshur,* where he built Nineveh, Rehoboth-Ir and Calah, 12 as well as Resen, between Nineveh and Calah,* the latter being the principal city.

13 d Mizraim became the father of the Ludim, the Anamim, the Lehabim, the Naphtuhim, 14 the Pathrusim,* the Casluhim, and the Caphtorim from whom the Philistines sprang.

15 Canaan became the father of Sidon, his

---

d 13-18: 1 Chr 1, 11-16.—e 22-29: 1 Chr 1, 17-23.

10, 6: *Cush:* Biblical Ethiopia, modern Nubia. *Mizraim:* Egypt; *Put:* either Punt in East Africa or Libya.
10, 8: *Cush:* here, the Kassites; see note on Gn 2, 10-14. *Nimrod:* probably Tukulti-Ninurta I (thirteenth century B.C.), the first Assyrian conqueror of Babylonia and a famous city-builder at home.
10, 10: *Shinar:* ancient Sumer in southern Mesopotamia, mentioned also in Gn 11, 2: 14, 1.
10, 11: *Asshur:* Assyria. *Rehoboth-Ir:* literally "wide-streets city," was probably not the name of another city, but an epithet of Nineveh; cf Jon 3, 3.
10, 12: *Calah:* Assyrian Kalhu, the capital of Assyria in the ninth century B.C.
10, 14: *The Pathrusim:* the people of upper (southern) Egypt; cf Is 11, 11; Jer 44, 1; Ez 29, 14; 30, 14. *Caphtorim:* Crete; for Caphtor as the place of origin of the Philistines, cf Dt 2, 23; Am 9, 7; Jer 47, 4.
10, 15: *Heth:* the biblical Hittites; see note on Gn 23, 3.
10, 19: *Lasha:* the reading of this name is uncertain; perhaps it should be "Bela"; cf Gn 14, 2.
10, 25: In the Hebrew text there is a play on the name *Peleg* and the word *niplega,* "was divided."
11, 1-9: This story, based on traditions about the temple towers or ziggurats of Babylonia, is used by the sacred writer primarily to illustrate man's increasing wickedness, shown here in his presumptuous effort to create an urban culture apart from God. The secondary motive in the story is to present an imaginative origin of the diversity of the languages among the various peoples inhabiting the earth, as well as an artificial explanation of the name "Babylon."
11, 2: *Shinar:* see note on Gn 10, 10.
11, 4: *Tower with its top in the sky:* a direct reference to the chief ziggurat of Babylon, the *E-sag-ila,* signifying "the house that raises high its head." Babylonian ziggurats were the earliest skyscrapers.

---

first-born, and of Heth;* 16 also of the Jebusites, the Amorites, the Girgashites, 17 the Hivites, the Arkites, the Sinites, 18 the Arvadites, the Zemarites and the Hamathites. Afterward, the clans of the Canaanites spread out, 19 so that the Canaanite borders extended from Sidon all the way to Gerar, near Gaza, and all the way to Sodom, Gomorrah, Admah and Zeboiim, near Lasha.* 20 These are the descendants of Ham, according to their clans and languages, by their lands and nations.

21 To Shem also, Japheth's oldest brother and the ancestor of all the children of Eber, sons were born.

22 e The descendants of Shem:
Elam, Asshur, Arpachshad, Lud and Aram.
23 The descendants of Aram:
Uz, Hul, Gether and Mash.

24 Arpachshad became the father of Shelah, and Shelah became the father of Eber. 25 To Eber two sons were born: the name of the first was Peleg, for in his time the world was divided;* and the name of his brother was Joktan. 26 Joktan became the father of Almodad, Sheleph, Hazarmaveth, Jerah, 27 Hadoram, Uzal, Diklah, 28 Obal, Abimael, Sheba 29 Ophir, Havilah and Jobab. All these were descendants of Joktan. 30 Their settlements extended all the way to Sephar, the eastern hill country.

31 These are the descendants of Shem, according to their clans and languages, by their lands and nations.

32 These are the groupings of Noah's sons, according to their origins and by their nations. From these the other nations of the earth branched out after the flood.

CHAPTER 11

The Tower of Babel.* 1 The whole world spoke the same language, using the same words. 2 While men were migrating in the east, they came upon a valley in the land of Shinar* and settled there. 3 They said to one another, "Come, let us mold bricks and harden them with fire." They used bricks for stone, and bitumen for mortar. 4 Then they said, "Come, let us build ourselves a city and a tower with its top in the sky,* and so make a name for ourselves; otherwise we shall be scattered all over the earth."

⁵The LORD came down to see the city and the tower that the men had built. ⁶Then the LORD said: "If now, while they are one people, all speaking the same language, they have started to do this, nothing will later stop them from doing whatever they presume to do. ⁷Let us then go down and there confuse their language, so that one will not understand what another says." ⁸Thus the LORD scattered them from there all over the earth, and they stopped building the city. ⁹That is why it was called Babel,* because there the LORD confused the speech of all the world. It was from that place that he scattered them all over the earth.

The Line from Shem to Abraham.* ¹⁰ᶠThis is the record of the descendants of Shem. When Shem was one hundred years old, he became the father of Arpachshad, two years after the flood. ¹¹Shem lived five hundred years after the birth of Arpachshad, and he had other sons and daughters.

¹²When Arpachshad was thirty-five years old, he became the father of Shelah.* ¹³Arpachshad lived four hundred and three years after the birth of Shelah, and he had other sons and daughters.

¹⁴When Shelah was thirty years old, he became the father of Eber. ¹⁵Shelah lived four hundred and three years after the birth of Eber, and he had other sons and daughters.

¹⁶When Eber* was thirty-four years old, he became the father of Peleg. ¹⁷Eber lived four hundred and thirty years after the birth of Peleg, and he had other sons and daughters.

¹⁸When Peleg was thirty years old, he became the father of Reu. ¹⁹Peleg lived two hundred and nine years after the birth of Reu, and he had other sons and daughters.

²⁰When Reu was thirty-two years old, he became the father of Serug. ²¹Reu lived two hundred and seven years after the birth of Serug, and he had other sons and daughters.

²²When Serug was thirty years old, he became the father of Nahor. ²³Serug lived two hundred years after the birth of Nahor, and he had other sons and daughters.

²⁴When Nahor was twenty-nine years old, he became the father of Terah. ²⁵Nahor lived one hundred and nineteen years after the birth of Terah, and he had other sons and daughters.

²⁶When Terah was seventy years old, he became the father of Abram, Nahor and Haran.ᵍ

II: THE PATRIARCH ABRAHAM

Terah. ²⁷This is the record of the descendants of Terah. Terah became the father of Abram, Nahor and Haran, and Haran became the father of Lot. ²⁸Haran died before his father Terah, in his native land, in Ur of the Chaldeans.* ²⁹Abram and Nahor took wives; the name of Abram's wife was Sarai, and the name of Nahor's wife was Milcah, daughter of Haran, the father of Milcah and Iscah.ʰ ³⁰Sarai was barren; she had no child.

³¹Terah took his son Abram, his grandson Lot, son of Haran, and his daughter-in-law Sarai, the wife of his son Abram, and brought them out of Ur of the Chaldeans, to go to the land of Canaan.* But when they reached Haran, they settled there.ⁱ ³²The lifetime of Terah was two hundred and five years; then Terah died in Haran.*

CHAPTER 12

Abram's Call and Migration. ¹The LORD said to Abram: "Go forth from the land of

f 10-26: 1 Chr 1, 24-27; Lk 3, 34ff.—g Jos 24, 2; 1 Chr 1, 27.—h Gn 17, 15; 20, 12.—i Jos 24, 3; Neh 9, 7; Jdt 5, 6-9; Acts 7, 4.

11, 9: *Babel:* the Hebrew form of the name "Babylon"; the native name, *Bab-ili,* means "gate of the gods." The Hebrew word *balil,* "he confused," has a similar sound. Apparently the name referred originally only to a certain part of the city, the district near the gate that led to the temple area.

11, 10-26: This section is a continuation of the genealogical record given in Gn 5, 1-32; see note there. Although the ages of the patriarchs in this list are much lower than those of the antediluvian patriarchs, they are still artificial and devoid of historical value. The ages given here are from the current Hebrew text; the Samaritan and Greek texts have divergent sets of numbers in most cases.

11, 12: The Greek text has a certain Kenan (cf Gn 5, 9f) between Arpachshad and Shelah. The text is followed in Lk 3, 36.

11, 16: *Eber:* the eponymous ancestor of the Hebrews, "descendants of Eber" (Gn 10, 21. 24-30); see note on Gn 14, 13.

11, 28: *Ur of the Chaldeans:* Ur was an extremely ancient city of the Sumerians (later, of the Babylonians) in southern Mesopotamia. The Greek text has "the land of the Chaldeans." In either case, the term *Chaldeans* is an anachronism, because the Chaldeans were not known to history until approximately a thousand years after Abraham's time.

11, 31: The Samaritan and Greek texts include Nahor and his wife in Terah's migration to Haran. Although this is probably due to scribal harmonization, Nahor's family actually did migrate to Haran; cf Gn 24, 10; 27, 43.

11, 32: Since Terah was seventy years old when his son Abraham was born (v 26), and Abraham was seventy-five when he left Haran (Gn 12, 4), Terah lived in Haran for sixty years after Abraham's departure. According to the tradition in the Samaritan text, Terah died when he was one hundred and forty-five years old, therefore, in the same year in which Abraham left Haran. This is the tradition followed in St. Stephen's speech: Abraham left Haran "after his father's death" (Acts 7, 4).

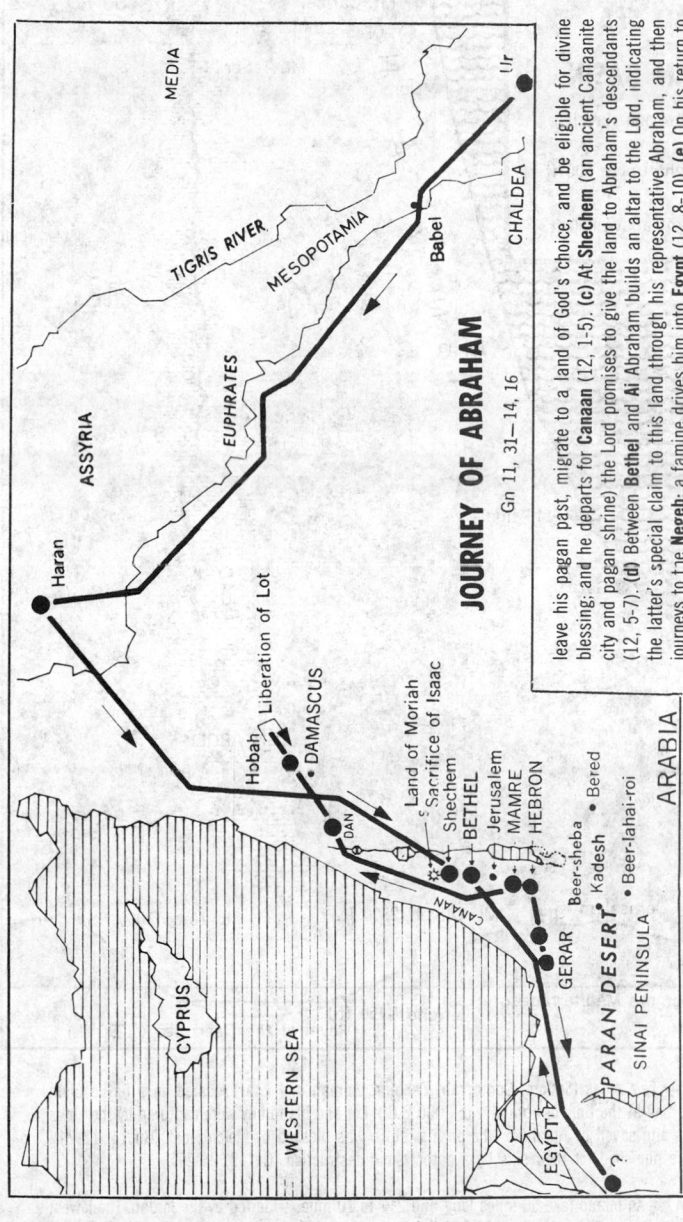

JOURNEY OF ABRAHAM

Gn 11, 31—14, 16

leave his pagan past, migrate to a land of God's choice, and be eligible for divine blessing; and he departs for **Canaan** (12, 1-5). **(c)** At **Shechem** (an ancient Canaanite city and pagan shrine) the Lord promises to give the land to Abraham's descendants (12, 5-7). **(d)** Between **Bethel** and **Ai** Abraham builds an altar to the Lord, indicating the latter's special claim to this land through his representative Abraham, and then journeys to the **Negeb**; a famine drives him into **Egypt** (12, 8-10). **(e)** On his return to **Bethel** he separates himself from Lot who settles near the terebinth of **Mamre**, which is at **Hebron**, and builds an altar to the Lord (13, 1-18). **(f)** When the kings of the **Pentapolis** capture Lot and his household (see Map on next page), Abraham overtakes and defeats them at **Dan** and pursues them as far as **Hobah**, north of **Damascus** (14, 12-16). **(g)** On his triumphant return Abraham is hailed by the king of **Sodom** and blessed by Melchizedek the king of **Salem**, who offers what was probably a covenant meal of bread and wine (14, 17-24).

ABRAHAM'S JOURNEY (Gn 11, 31—14, 16) — **(a)** With his son Abram (later changed to Abraham) and his whole family, Terah departs from **Ur** for **Canaan** but settles in **Haran** (11, 31). (The names Sarai, "princes," and Milcah, "queen," indicate that those who bear them are devoted to Ningal, consort of the moon-god Sin who was worshiped in Ur and Haran.) **(b)** Here Abram receives Yahweh's call to

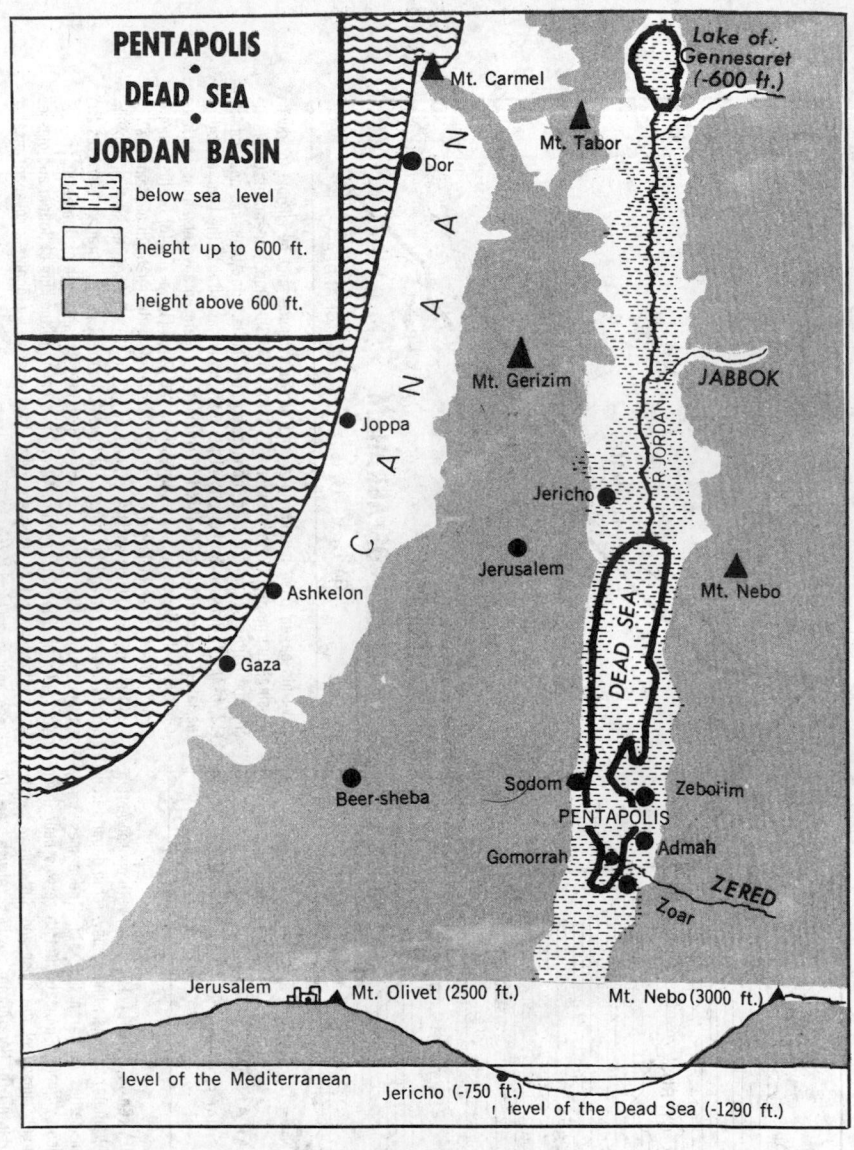

PENTAPOLIS — Five cities **(Sodom, Gomorrah, Zeboiim, Admah and Zoar)** located on a fertile plain near the Dead Sea at the time of Abraham (c 2000 B.C.). Lot and his family were captured by the kings of these cities and saved by Abraham who on his return was blessed by Melchizedek (Gn 14, 12-24). The cities were punished for their sins by a cataclysmic destruction (Gn 19, 24-29).

THE DEAD SEA — An inland lake 53 miles long and 2¾ to 10 miles wide fed by the Jordan. The lowest body of water on the earth's surface, 1290 feet below sea level, it is also called the "Salt Sea" (Gn 14, 3), "Sea of the Arabah" or "Plain" (Dt 3, 17) and "Eastern Sea" (Ez 47, 18).

your kinsfolk and from your father's house to a land that I will show you.*j*

2 "I will make of you a great nation,
and I will bless you;
I will make your name great,
so that you will be a blessing.*k*

3 *l* I will bless those who bless you
and curse those who curse you.
All the communities of the earth
shall find blessing in you."*

4 *m* Abram went as the LORD directed him, and Lot went with him. Abram was seventy-five years old when he left Haran. 5 Abram took his wife Sarai, his brother's son Lot, all the possessions that they had accumulated, and the persons* they had acquired in Haran, and they set out for the land of Canaan. When they came to the land of Canaan, 6 Abram passed through the land as far as the sacred place at Shechem, by the terebinth of Moreh. (The Canaanites were then in the land.) 7 The LORD appeared to Abram and said, "To your descendants I will give this land." So Abram built an altar there to the LORD who had appeared to him.*n* 8 From there he moved on to the hill country east of Bethel, pitching his tent with Bethel to the west and Ai to the east. He built an altar there to the LORD and invoked the

j Acts 7, 3; Heb 11, 8.—k Gn 17, 6; Sir 44, 20; Rom 4, 17-22.—l Gn 18, 18; 22, 18; Acts 3, 25; Gal 3, 8.—m 4f: Gn 11, 31; Jos 24, 3; Acts 7, 4.—n Ex 33, 1; Dt 34, 4; Acts 7, 5.—o Gn 26, 1.—p Gn 20, 12f; 26, 7.—q Ps 105, 14.—r Gn 12, 9.—s Ps 112, 1ff; Prv 10, 22.—t Gn 12, 8.

12, 3: *Shall find blessing in you:* the sense of the Hebrew expression is probably reflexive, "shall bless themselves through you" (i.e., in giving a blessing they shall say, "May you be as blessed as Abraham"), rather than passive, "shall be blessed in you." Since the term is understood in a passive sense in the New Testament (Acts 3, 25; Gal 3, 8), it is considered here by a neutral expression that admits of both meanings. So also in the blessings given by God to Isaac (Gn 26, 4) and Jacob (Gn 28, 14).
12, 5: *Persons:* slaves and retainers that formed the social aggregate under the leadership of Abraham; cf Gn 14, 14.
12, 9: *The Negeb:* the semidesert land of southern Palestine.
12, 13: *You are my sister:* although Abraham's deceit may not be fully defensible, his statement was at least a half-truth; Sarah was indeed his relative, called "a sister" in Hebrew; cf Gn 20, 12. Moreover, the ancient traditions on which this story and the parallel ones in Gn 20, 1-18 and 26, 6-11 are based, probably come from the Hurrian custom of wife-sister marriage. Among the Hurrians, with whom Abraham's clan lived in close contact at Haran, a man could adopt his wife as his sister and thus give her higher status.
12, 16: *Camels:* domesticated camels probably did not come into common use in the ancient Near East until the end of the 2nd millennium B.C. Thus the mention of camels at the time of the patriarchs (Gn 24, 11-64; 30, 43; 31, 17. 34; 32, 8. 16; 37, 25) is seemingly an anachronism.

LORD by name. 9 Then Abram journeyed on by stages to the Negeb.*

Abram and Sarai in Egypt. 10 There was famine in the land; so Abram went down to Egypt to sojourn there, since the famine in the land was severe.*o* 11 When he was about to enter Egypt, he said to his wife Sarai: "I know well how beautiful a woman you are. 12 When the Egyptians see you, they will say, 'She is his wife'; then they will kill me, but let you live. 13 Please say, therefore, that you are my sister,* so that it may go well with me on your account and my life may be spared for your sake."*p* 14 When Abram came to Egypt, the Egyptians saw how beautiful the woman was; 15 and when Pharaoh's courtiers saw her, they praised her to Pharaoh. So she was taken into Pharaoh's palace. 16 On her account it went very well with Abram, and he received flocks and herds, male and female slaves, male and female asses, and camels.*

17 But the LORD struck Pharaoh and his household with severe plagues because of Abram's wife Sarai.*q* 18 Then Pharaoh summoned Abram and said to him: "How could you do this to me! Why didn't you tell me she was your wife? 19 Why did you say, 'She is my sister,' so that I took her for my wife? Here, then, is your wife. Take her and be gone!"

20 Then Pharaoh gave men orders concerning him, and they sent him on his way, with his wife and all that belonged to him.

CHAPTER 13

Abram and Lot Part. 1 From Egypt Abram went up to the Negeb with his wife and all that belonged to him, and Lot accompanied him.*r* 2 Now Abram was very rich in livestock, silver and gold.*s* 3 From the Negeb he traveled by stages toward Bethel, to the place between Bethel and Ai where his tent had formerly stood, 4 the site where he had first built the altar; and there he invoked the LORD by name.*t*

5 Lot, who went with Abram, also had flocks and herds and tents, 6 so that the land could not support them if they stayed together; their possessions were so great that they could not dwell together. 7 There were quarrels between the herdsmen of Abram's livestock and those of Lot's. (At this time the Canaanites and the Perizzites were occupying the land.)

[8] So Abram said to Lot: "Let there be no strife between you and me, or between your herdsmen and mine, for we are kinsmen. [9] Is not the whole land at your disposal? Please separate from me. If you prefer the left, I will go to the right; if you prefer the right, I will go to the left." [10] Lot looked about and saw how well watered the whole Jordan Plain was as far as Zoar, like the LORD's own garden, or like Egypt. (This was before the LORD had destroyed Sodom and Gomorrah.) [11] Lot, therefore, chose for himself the whole Jordan Plain and set out eastward. Thus they separated from each other; [12] Abram stayed in the land of Canaan, while Lot settled among the cities of the Plain, pitching his tents near Sodom. [13] Now the inhabitants of Sodom were very wicked in the sins they committed against the LORD. [u]

[14] After Lot had left, the LORD said to Abram: "Look about you, and from where you are, gaze to the north and south, east and west; [v] [15] all the land that you see I will give to you and your descendants forever. [w] [16] I will make your descendants like the dust of the earth; if anyone could count the dust of the earth, your descendants too might be counted. [x] [17] Set forth and walk about in the land, through its length and breadth, for to you I will give it." [18] Abram moved his tents and went on to settle near the terebinth of Mamre, which is at Hebron. There he built an altar to the LORD. [y]

CHAPTER 14

The Four Kings. [1] In the days of . . . ,* Amraphel king of Shinar, Arioch king of Ellasar, Chedorlaomer king of Elam, and Tidal king of Goiim [2] made war on Bera king of Sodom, Birsha king of Gomorrah, Shinab king of Admah, Shemeber king of Zeboiim, and the king of Bela (that is, Zoar). [3] All the latter kings joined forces in the Valley of Siddim (that is, the Salt Sea*). [4] For twelve years they had been subject to Chedorlaomer, but in the thirteenth year they rebelled. [5] * In the fourteenth year Chedorlaomer and the kings allied with him came and defeated the Rephaim in Ashteroth-karnaim, the Zuzim in Ham, the Emim in Shaveh-kiriathaim, [6] and the Horites in the hill country of Seir, as far

as El-paran, close by the wilderness. [z] [7] They then turned back and came to En-mishpat (that is, Kadesh), and they subdued the whole country both of the Amalekites and of the Amorites who dwelt in Hazazon-tamar. [8] Thereupon the king of Sodom, the king of Gomorrah, the king of Admah, the king of Zeboiim, and the king of Bela (that is, Zoar) marched out, and in the Valley of Siddim they went into battle against them: [9] against Chedorlaomer king of Elam, Tidal king of Goiim, Amraphel king of Shinar, and Arioch king of Ellasar—four kings against five. [10] Now the Valley of Siddim was full of bitumen pits; and as the kings of Sodom and Gomorrah fled, they fell into these, while the rest fled to the mountains. [11] The victors seized all the possessions and food supplies of Sodom and Gomorrah and then went their way, [12] taking with them Abram's nephew Lot, who had been living in Sodom, as well as his possessions. [a]

[13] A fugitive came and brought the news to Abram the Hebrew,* who was camping at the terebinth of Mamre the Amorite, a kinsman of Eshcol and Aner; these were in league with Abram. [14] When Abram heard that his nephew had been captured, he mustered three hundred and eighteen of his retainers, born in his house, and went in pursuit as far as Dan. [15] He and his party deployed against them at night, defeated them, and pursued them as far as Hobah, which is north of Damascus. [16] He recovered all the possessions, besides bringing back his kinsman Lot and his possessions, along with the women and the other captives.

[17] When Abram returned from his victory over Chedorlaomer and the kings who were allied with him, the king of Sodom went

---

u Gn 18, 20; Ez 16, 49; 2 Pt 2, 6ff; Jude 1 7.—v Gn 28, 14.—w Gn 12, 7; Mt 5, 4; Lk 1, 55; Acts 7, 5; Gal 3, 16.—x Gn 22, 17; Nm 23, 10.—y Gn 14. 13.—z Dt 2, 12.—a Gn 13, 10ff.

14, 1: *In the days of . . . :* the personal name by which the event is dated has not been preserved.
14, 3: *The Salt Sea:* now known as the Dead Sea.
14, 5f: The five kings came from north to south through the land east of the Jordan.
14, 13: *Abram the Hebrew:* elsewhere in the Old Testament, until the last pre-Christian centuries, the term "Hebrew" is used only by non-Israelites, or by Israelites in speaking to foreigners, since it evidently had a disparaging connotation—something like "immigrant." The account in this chapter may, therefore, have been taken originally from a non-Israelite source, in which Abraham, a warlike sheik of Palestine, appears as a truly historical figure of profane history.

out to greet him in the Valley of Shaveh (that is, the King's Valley).

[18] Melchizedek, king of Salem,* brought out bread and wine, and being a priest of God Most High, he blessed Abram with these words:[b]

[19] "Blessed be Abram by God Most High,*
    the creator of heaven and earth;
[20] And blessed be God Most High,
    who delivered your foes into your hand."

Then Abram gave him* a tenth of everything.

[21] The king of Sodom said to Abram, "Give me the people; the goods you may keep." [22] But Abram replied to the king of Sodom: "I have sworn to the LORD, God Most High,* the creator of heaven and earth, [23] that I would not take so much as a thread or a sandal strap from anything that is yours, lest you should say, 'I made Abram rich.' [24] Nothing for me except what my servants have used up and the share that is due to the men who joined me— Aner, Eshcol and Mamre; let them take their share."

b Ps 110, 4; Heb 5, 6. 10; 7, 1.—c Gn 17, 16.—d Gn 22, 17: 28, 14; Ex 32, 13; Dt 1, 10; Sir 44, 21; Rom 4, 18; Heb 11, 12.—e 1 Mc 2, 52; Rom 4, 3. 9. 22; Gal 3, 6f; Jas 2, 23.—f Gn 11, 31; 12, 1; Ex 32, 13; Neh 9, 7f; Acts 7, 2f.—g Lv 1, 14.—h Ex 12, 40; Nm 20, 15; Jdt 5, 9f; Is 52, 4; Acts 13, 20; Gal 3, 17.—i Ex 3, 8. 21f.—j 1 Kgs 21, 26.

14, 18: *Salem:* traditionally identified with Jerusalem (Ps 76, 3), but the Hebrew text is not certain; instead of the present *melek shalem* ("king of Salem") the original may have been *melek shelomo* ("a king allied to him"). In Heb 7, 2, "king of Salem" is interpreted as "king of peace" *(shalom).*
14, 19: *God Most High:* in Hebrew, *el-elyon.* In Canaanite texts, each element may occur separately as the name of a specific deity, or they may be applied together to a single deity, as is done here by the Canaanite priest Melchizedek. For the Israelites, *el* became a poetic synonym for *elohim* ("God"); *elyon* ("Most High") became one of the titles of their God Yahweh.
14, 20: *Abram gave him:* literally *"he gave him":* but *Abram* is to be understood as the subject of the sentence, for the *tithes* were the tenth part assigned to priests; cf Heb 7, 4-10.
14, 22: Abraham uses the name of the Canaanite god *el-elyon* ("God, the Most High") in apposition to the name of his God, *yahweh* ("the Lord").
15, 6: Abraham's *faith* in God's promises was regarded as *an act of righteousness,* i.e., as expressing the "right" attitude of man toward God. In turn, God credited this to Abraham, i.e., gave him title to the fulfillment of God's promises. St. Paul (Rom 4, 1-25; Gal 3, 6-9) makes Abraham's faith a model for that of Christians.
15, 9: *Three-year-old:* ritually mature.
15, 16: *Time-span:* the Hebrew term *dor* is commonly rendered as "generation," but it may signify a period of varying length. Neither this passage nor the statement about the four hundred years has any value for determining how long the Israelites were in Egypt.
15, 17: *Brazier:* literally "oven"; a portable one is meant here. The smoke and fire represent God's presence. Although the text does not mention it, Abraham no doubt also walked between the split carcasses. For the meaning of this strange ceremony, see note on Jer 38, 18ff.

CHAPTER 15

The Covenant with Abram. [1] Some time after these events, this word of the LORD came to Abram in a vision:

"Fear not, Abram!
    I am your shield;
    I will make your reward very great."

[2] But Abram said, "O Lord GOD, what good will your gifts be, if I keep on being childless and have as my heir the steward of my house, Eliezer?" [3] Abram continued, "See, you have given me no offspring, and so one of my servants will be my heir." [4] Then the word of the LORD came to him: "No, that one shall not be your heir; your own issue shall be your heir."[c] [5] He took him outside and said, "Look up at the sky and count the stars, if you can. Just so," he added, "shall your descendants be."[d] [6] [e] Abram put his faith in the LORD, who credited it to him as an act of righteousness.*

[7] He then said to him, "I am the LORD who brought you from Ur of the Chaldeans to give you this land as a possession."[f] [8] "O Lord GOD," he asked, "how am I to know that I shall possess it?" [9] He answered him, "Bring me a three-year-old heifer, a three-year-old she-goat, a three-year-old* ram, a turtledove, and a young pigeon."[g] [10] He brought him all these, split them in two, and placed each half opposite the other; but the birds he did not cut up. [11] Birds of prey swooped down on the carcasses, but Abram stayed with them. [12] As the sun was about to set, a trance fell upon Abram, and a deep, terrifying darkness enveloped him.

[13] Then the LORD said to Abram: "Know for certain that your descendants shall be aliens in a land not their own, where they shall be enslaved and oppressed for four hundred years.[h] [14] But I will bring judgment on the nation they must serve, and in the end they will depart with great wealth.[i] [15] You, however, shall join your forefathers in peace; you shall be buried at a contented old age. [16] In the fourth time-span* the others shall come back here; the wickedness of the Amorites will not have reached its full measure until then."[j]

[17] When the sun had set and it was dark, there appeared a smoking brazier* and a flaming torch, which passed between those

pieces. [18] It was on that occasion that the LORD made a covenant* with Abram, saying: "To your descendants I give this land, from the Wadi of Egypt to the Great River [the Euphrates],[k] [19] [l] the land of the Kenites, the Kenizzites, the Kadmonites, [20] the Hittites, the Perizzites, the Rephaim, [21] the Amorites, the Canaanites, the Girgashites, and the Jebusites."

CHAPTER 16

Birth of Ishmael. [1] * Abram's wife Sarai had borne him no children. She had, however, an Egyptian maidservant named Hagar.[m] [2] Sarai said to Abram: "The LORD has kept me from bearing children. Have intercourse, then, with my maid; perhaps I shall have sons through her." Abram heeded Sarai's request.[n] [3] Thus, after Abram had lived ten years in the land of Canaan, his wife Sarai took her maid, Hagar the Egyptian, and gave her to her husband Abram to be his concubine. [4] He had intercourse with her, and she became pregnant. When she became aware of her pregnancy, she looked on her mistress with disdain.[o] [5] [p] So Sarai said to Abram: "You are responsible for this outrage against me. I myself gave my maid to your embrace, but ever since she became aware of her pregnancy, she has been looking on me with disdain. May the LORD decide between you and me!" [6] Abram told Sarai: "Your maid is in your power. Do to her whatever you please." Sarai then abused her so much that Hagar ran away from her.

[7] The LORD's messenger* found her by a spring in the wilderness, the spring on the road to Shur,[q] [8] and he asked, "Hagar, maid of Sarai, where have you come from and where are you going?" She answered, "I am running away from my mistress, Sarai." [9] But the LORD's messenger told her: "Go back to your mistress and submit to her abusive treatment. [10] I will make your descendants so numerous," added the LORD's messenger, "that they will be too many to count.[r] [11] Besides," the LORD's messenger said to her:

"You are now pregnant and shall bear
　a son;
　you shall name him Ishmael,*
For the LORD has heard you,
　God has answered you.

[12] He shall be a wild ass of a man,
　his hand against everyone,
　and everyone's hand against him;
In opposition to all his kin
　shall he encamp."[s]

[13] To the LORD who spoke to her she gave a name, saying, "You are the God of Vision";* she meant, "Have I really seen God and remained alive after my vision?"[t] [14] That is why the well is called Beer-lahairoi.* It is between Kadesh and Bered.

[15] Hagar bore Abram a son, and Abram named the son whom Hagar bore him Ishmael.[u] [16] Abram was eighty-six years old when Hagar bore him Ishmael.

CHAPTER 17

Covenant of Circumcision. [1] When Abram was ninety-nine years old, the LORD appeared to him and said: "I am God the Almighty.* Walk in my presence and be blameless.[v] [2] Between you and me I will establish my covenant, and I will multiply you exceedingly."[w]

[3] When Abram prostrated himself, God continued to speak to him: [4] "My covenant with you is this: you are to become the father of a host of nations.[x] [5] No longer shall you be called Abram; your name shall be Abraham,* for I am making you the father of a host of nations.[y] [6] I will render you exceedingly fertile; I will make nations of you; kings shall stem from you. [7] I will

k Ex 32, 13; Neh 9, 8; Ps 105, 11; Sir 44, 21.—l 19f: Dt 7, 1.—m Gn 11, 30.—n Gn 21, 8f; Gal 4, 22. o 1 Sm 1, 6; Prv 30, 23.—p 5-16: Gn 21, 10-19.—q Ex 15, 22.—r Gn 17, 20; 21, 13. 18; 25, 12-18.—s Gn 21, 20; 25, 18.—t Gn 24, 62.—u Gn 16, 2; Gal 4, 22.—v Gn 35, 11; Ex 6, 3.—w Gn 12, 2; 13, 16; Ex 32, 13.—x Sir 44, 21; Rom 4, 17.—y Neh 9, 7.

15, 18: *Made a covenant:* literally "cut a covenant"; the expression derives from the ceremony of cutting the animals in two.

16, 1-6: Sarah's actions are all in keeping with the laws of the time, as known from ancient extra-biblical sources.

16, 7: *The Lord's messenger:* a manifestation of God in human form; therefore in v 13 the messenger is identified with the Lord himself.

16, 11: *Ishmael:* in Hebrew the name means "God has heard."

16, 13: *The God of Vision:* in Hebrew, *el-roi;* hence the name of the spring. *Remained alive:* for the ancient notion that a person died on seeing God, cf Gn 32, 31; Ex 20, 19; Dt 4, 33; Jgs 13, 22.

16, 14: *Beer-lahai-roi:* probably "the well of living sight," i.e., the well where one can see (God) and yet live.

17, 1: *The Almighty:* traditional but incorrect rendering of the divine title *shaddai,* of uncertain meaning.

17, 5: *Abram* and *Abraham* are merely two forms of the same name, both meaning, "the father is exalted"; another variant form is Abiram (Nm 16, 1; 1 Kgs 16, 34). The additional *-ha-* in the form Abraham is explained by folk etymology as coming from *ab-hamon goyim,* "father of a host of nations."

maintain my covenant with you and your descendants after you throughout the ages as an everlasting pact, to be your God and the God of your descendants after you.[z] [8]I will give to you and to your descendants after you the land in which you are now staying, the whole land of Canaan, as a permanent possession; and I will be their God."[a]

[9]God also said to Abraham: "On your part, you and your descendants after you must keep my covenant throughout the ages. [10]This is my covenant with you and your descendants after you that you must keep: every male among you shall be circumcised.[b] [11]Circumcise the flesh of your foreskin, and that shall be the mark of the covenant between you and me.[c] [12]Throughout the ages, every male among you, when he is eight days old, shall be circumcised, including houseborn slaves and those acquired with money from any foreigner who is not of your blood.[d] [13]Yes, both the houseborn slaves and those acquired with money must be circumcised. Thus my covenant shall be in your flesh as an everlasting pact. [14]If a male is uncircumcised, that is, if the flesh of his foreskin has not been cut away, such a one shall be cut off from his people; he has broken my covenant."

[15]God further said to Abraham: "As for your wife Sarai, do not call her Sarai; her name shall be Sarah.* [16]I will bless her, and I will give you a son by her. Him also will I bless; he shall give rise to nations, and rulers of peoples shall issue from him."[e] [17]Abraham prostrated himself and laughed* as he said to himself, "Can a child be born to man who is a hundred years old? Or can Sarah give birth at ninety?"[f] [18]Then Abraham said to God, "Let but Ishmael live on by your favor!"

[19]God replied: "Nevertheless, your wife Sarah is to bear you a son, and you shall call him Isaac. I will maintain my covenant with him as an everlasting pact, to be his God and the God of his descendants after him.[g] [20]As for Ishmael, I am heeding you: I hereby bless him. I will make him fertile and will multiply him exceedingly. He shall become the father of twelve chieftains, and I will make of him a great nation.[h] [21]But my covenant I will maintain with Isaac, whom Sarah shall bear to you by this time next year."[i] [22]When he had finished speaking with him, God departed from Abraham.

[23]Then Abraham took his son Ishmael and all his slaves, whether born in his house or acquired with his money—every male among the members of Abraham's household—and he circumcised the flesh of their foreskins on that same day, as God had told him to do. [24]Abraham was ninety-nine years old when the flesh of his foreskin was circumcised,[j] [25]and his son Ishmael was thirteen years old when the flesh of his foreskin was circumcised. [26]Thus, on that same day Abraham and his son Ishmael were circumcised; [27]and all the male members of his household, including the slaves born in his house or acquired with his money from foreigners, were circumcised with him.

CHAPTER 18

Abraham's Visitors. [1]The LORD appeared to Abraham by the terebinth of Mamre, as he sat in the entrance of his tent, while the day was growing hot. [2]Looking up, he saw three men standing nearby. When he saw them, he ran from the entrance of the tent to greet them; and bowing to the ground,[k] [3]he said: "Sir,* if I may ask you this favor, please do not go on past your servant. [4]Let some water be brought, that you may bathe your feet, and then rest yourselves under the tree. [5]Now that you have come this close to your servant, let me bring you a little food, that you may refresh yourselves; and afterward you may go on your way." "Very well," they replied, "do as you have said."

[6]Abraham hastened into the tent and told Sarah, "Quick, three seahs* of fine flour! Knead it and make rolls." [7]He ran to the herd, picked out a tender, choice steer, and gave it to a servant, who quickly prepared it. [8]Then he got some

---

z Ps 105, 42; Lk 1, 72f; Gal 3, 16.—a Ex 32, 13; Dt 1, 8; 14, 2; Lk 1, 55; Acts 7, 5.—b Jn 7, 22; Acts 7, 8; Rom 4, 11.—c Sir 44, 21.—d Lv 12, 3; Lk 1, 59; 2, 21.—e Gn 18, 10; Gal 4, 23.—f Rom 4, 19; Heb 11, 11f—g Gn 11, 30; 21, 2; Ex 32, 13; Sir 44, 22.—h Gn 16, 10; 21, 13. 18; 25, 12-16.—i Gn 18, 14; 21, 2; 26, 2-5; Rom 9, 7.—j Gn 17, 10; Rom 4, 11.—k Heb 13, 1f.

17, 15: *Sarai* and *Sarah* are variant forms of the same name, both meaning "princess."

17, 17: *Laughed: yishaq,* which is the Hebrew form of the name "Isaac"; other similar explanations of the name are given in Gn 18, 12 and 21, 6.

18, 3: Abraham addresses the leader of the group, whom he does not yet recognize as Yahweh; in the next two verses he speaks to all *three men.* The other two are later (Gn 19, 1) identified as messengers.

18, 6: *Three seahs:* one ephah, about half a bushel.

curds* and milk, as well as the steer that had been prepared, and set these before them; and he waited on them under the tree while they ate. ⁹"Where is your wife Sarah?" they asked him. "There in the tent," he replied. ¹⁰One of them* said, "I will surely return to you about this time next year, and Sarah will then have a son." Sarah was listening at the entrance of the tent, just behind him.^l ¹¹Now Abraham and Sarah were old, advanced in years, and Sarah had stopped having her womanly periods.^m ¹²So Sarah laughed* to herself and said, "Now that I am so withered and my husband is so old, am I still to have sexual pleasure?" ¹³But the LORD said to Abraham: "Why did Sarah laugh and say, 'Shall I really bear a child, old as I am?' ¹⁴Is anything too marvelous for the LORD to do? At the appointed time, about this time next year, I will return to you, and Sarah will have a son."ⁿ ¹⁵Because she was afraid, Sarah dissembled, saying, "I didn't laugh." But he said, "Yes you did."

Abraham Intercedes for Sodom. ¹⁶The men set out from there and looked down toward Sodom; Abraham was walking with them, to see them on their way. ¹⁷The LORD reflected: "Shall I hide from Abraham what I am about to do, ¹⁸now that he is to become a great and populous nation, and all the nations of the earth are to find blessing in him?^o ¹⁹Indeed, I have singled him out that he may direct his sons and his posterity to keep the way of the LORD by doing what is right and just, so that the LORD may carry into effect for Abraham the promises he made about him." ²⁰ ^p Then the LORD said: "The outcry against Sodom and Gomorrah is so great, and their sin is so grave,* ²¹that I must go down and see whether or not their actions fully correspond to the cry against them that comes to me. I mean to find out."

²²While the two men walked on farther toward Sodom, the LORD remained standing before Abraham. ²³Then Abraham drew nearer to him and said: "Will you sweep away the innocent with the guilty? ²⁴Suppose there were fifty innocent people in the city; would you wipe out the place, rather than spare it for the sake of the fifty innocent people within it? ²⁵Far be it from you to do such a thing, to make the innocent die with the guilty, so that the inno-

cent and the guilty would be treated alike! Should not the judge of all the world act with justice?"^q ²⁶The LORD replied, "If I find fifty innocent people in the city of Sodom, I will spare the whole place for their sake." ²⁷Abraham spoke up again: "See how I am presuming to speak to my Lord, though I am but dust and ashes!^r ²⁸What if there are five less than fifty innocent people? Will you destroy the whole city because of those five?" "I will not destroy it," he answered, "if I find forty-five there." ²⁹But Abraham persisted, saying, "What if only forty are found there?" He replied, "I will forbear doing it for the sake of the forty." ³⁰Then he said, "Let not my Lord grow impatient if I go on. What if only thirty are found there?" He replied, "I will forbear doing it if I can find but thirty there." ³¹Still he went on, "Since I have thus dared to speak to my Lord, what if there are no more than twenty?" "I will not destroy it," he answered, "for the sake of the twenty." ³²But he still persisted, "Please, let not my Lord grow angry if I speak up this last time. What if there are at least ten there?" "For the sake of those ten," he replied, "I will not destroy it."^s

³³The LORD departed as soon as he had finished speaking with Abraham, and Abraham returned home.

CHAPTER 19

Destruction of Sodom and Gomorrah. ¹The two angels reached Sodom in the evening, as Lot was sitting at the gate of Sodom. When Lot saw them, he got up to greet them; and bowing down with his face to the ground, ²he said, "Please, gentle-

---

l Gn 17, 19; 21, 1; 2 Kgs 4, 16; Rom 9, 9.—m Gn 17, 17; Rom 4, 19; Heb 11, 11f.—n Mt 19, 26; Mk 10, 27; Lk 1, 37; 18, 27; Rom 4, 21.—o Lk 1, 55.—p Gn 19, 13; Is 3, 9; Lk 17, 28; Jude 1, 7.—q Dt 32, 4; Jb 8, 3. 20; Wis 12, 15.—r Sir 10, 9; 17, 27.—s Jer 5, 1; Ez 22, 30.

18, 8: *Curds:* a type of soft cheese or yoghurt.

18, 10: *One of them:* i.e., the Lord. Abraham now realizes this for the first time when he hears the prediction of a miraculous birth. *About this time next year:* literally "when the time becomes alive," i.e., at the time when birth is due after the period of gestation; the conception is understood as taking place soon after the prediction.

18, 12: *Sarah laughed:* see note on Gn 17, 17.

18, 20: Israelite tradition was unanimous in ascribing the destruction of Sodom and Gomorrah to the wickedness of these cities, but tradition varied in regard to the nature of this wickedness. According to the present account of the Yahwist, the sin of Sodom was homosexuality (Gn 19, 4f), which is therefore also known as sodomy; but according to Isaiah (1, 9f; 3, 9), it was a lack of social justice; Ezekiel (16, 46-51) described it as a disregard for the poor, whereas Jeremiah (23, 14) saw it as general immorality.

men,* come aside into your servant's house for the night, and bathe your feet; you can get up early to continue your journey." But they replied, "No, we shall pass the night in the town square." *t* ³He urged them so strongly, however, that they turned aside to his place and entered his house. He prepared a meal for them, baking cakes without leaven, and they dined.

4 *u* Before they went to bed, all the townsmen of Sodom, both young and old—all the people to the last man—closed in on the house. ⁵They called to Lot and said to him, "Where are the men who came to your house tonight? Bring them out to us that we may have intimacies with them." ⁶Lot went out to meet them at the entrance. When he had shut the door behind him, ⁷he said, "I beg you, my brothers, not to do this wicked thing. ⁸I have two daughters who have never had intercourse with men. Let me bring them out to you, and you may do to them as you please. But don't do anything to these men, for you know they have come under the shelter of my roof." ⁹They replied, "Stand back! This fellow," they sneered, "came here as an immigrant, and now he dares to give orders! We'll treat you worse than them!" With that, they pressed hard against Lot, moving in closer to break down the door. *v* ¹⁰But his guests put out their hands, pulled Lot inside with them, and closed the door; ¹¹at the same time they struck the men at the entrance of the

house, one and all, with such a blinding light* that they were utterly unable to reach the doorway. ¹²Then the angels said to Lot: "Who else belongs to you here? Your sons [sons-in-law]* and your daughters and all who belong to you in the city—take them away from it! *w* ¹³We are about to destroy this place, for the outcry reaching the LORD against those in the city is so great that he has sent us to destroy it." *x* ¹⁴So Lot went out and spoke to his sons-in-law, who had contracted marriage with his daughters.* "Get up and leave this place," he told them; "the LORD is about to destroy the city." But his sons-in-law thought he was joking.

¹⁵As dawn was breaking, the angels urged Lot on, saying, "On your way! Take with you your wife and your two daughters who are here, or you will be swept away in the punishment of the city." ¹⁶When he hesitated, the men, by the LORD's mercy, seized his hand and the hands of his wife and his two daughters and led them to safety outside the city. ¹⁷As soon as they had been brought outside, he was told: "Flee for your life! Don't look back or stop anywhere on the Plain. Get off to the hills at once, or you will be swept away." *y* ¹⁸"Oh, no, my lord!" replied Lot. ¹⁹"You have already thought enough of your servant to do me the great kindness of intervening to save my life. But I cannot flee to the hills to keep the disaster from overtaking me, and so I shall die. ²⁰Look, this town ahead is near enough to escape to. It's only a small place.* Let me flee there—it's a small place, isn't it?—that my life may be saved." ²¹"Well, then," he replied, "I will also grant you the favor you now ask. I will not overthrow the town you speak of. ²²Hurry, escape there! I cannot do anything until you arrive there." That is why the town is called Zoar. *z*

²³The sun was just rising over the earth as Lot arrived in Zoar; *a* ²⁴at the same time the LORD rained down sulphurous fire upon Sodom and Gomorrah [from the LORD out of heaven]. *b* ²⁵He overthrew* those cities and the whole Plain, together with the inhabitants of the cities and the produce of the soil. *c* ²⁶But Lot's wife looked back, and she was turned into a pillar of salt. *d*

²⁷Early the next morning Abraham went to the place where he had stood in

---

t Wis 10, 6; Sir 16, 8; Ez 16, 50; Heb 13, 1f.—u 4-9: Jgs 19, 22-25; Jude 1, 7.—v Gn 13, 12; 2 Pt 2, 7f.—w 2 Pt 7, 9.—x Is 1, 7. 9; Zep 2, 9; Lk 17, 29.—y Wis 10, 6.—z Wis 10, 6.— a Pss 9, 6; 11, 6; 107, 34.—b Wis 10, 7; Is 1, 9; 13, 19; Lam 4, 6; Lk 17, 29; 2 Pt 2, 6.—c Dt 29, 22; Jer 50, 40; Am 4, 11.—d Wis 10, 7; Lk 17, 32.

19, 2: *Gentlemen:* Lot does not yet know that the distinguished-looking men are God's messengers; cf Gn 18, 3.

19, 11: *Blinding light:* a preternatural flash that temporarily dazed the wicked men and revealed to Lot the true nature of his guests.

19, 12: Since Lot apparently had no *sons*, a glossator interpreted the term to mean *sons-in-law*.

19, 14: It is uncertain whether Lot's *sons-in-law* were fully married to his daughters or only "engaged" to them (Israelite "engagement" was the first part of the marriage ceremony), or even whether the daughters involved were the same as, or different from, the two daughters who were still in their father's house.

19, 20: *A small place:* the Hebrew word *misar*, literally "a little thing," has the same root consonants as the name of the town *Zoar* in v 22.

19, 25: *Overthrew:* the consistent use of this term, literally "turned upside down," to describe the destruction of the Cities of the Plain seems to imply that their upheaval (v 29) was caused primarily by an earthquake; this would naturally be accompanied by a disastrous fire, especially in a region containing bitumen (Gn 14, 10) and its accompanying gases.

the LORD's presence. ²⁸As he looked down toward Sodom and Gomorrah and the whole region of the Plain,* he saw dense smoke over the land rising like fumes from a furnace.ᵉ

²⁹Thus it came to pass: when God destroyed the Cities of the Plain, he was mindful of Abraham by sending Lot away from the upheaval by which God overthrew the cities where Lot had been living.

Moabites and Ammonites.* ³⁰Since Lot was afraid to stay in Zoar, he and his two daughters went up from Zoar and settled in the hill country, where he lived with his two daughters in a cave. ³¹The older one said to the younger: "Our father is getting old, and there is not a man on earth to unite with us as was the custom everywhere. ³²Come, let us ply our father with wine and then lie with him, that we may have offspring by our father." ³³So that night they plied their father with wine, and the older one went in and lay with her father; but he was not aware of her lying down or her getting up. ³⁴Next day the older one said to the younger: "Last night it was I who lay with my father. Let us ply him with wine again tonight, and then you go in and lie with him, that we may both have offspring by our father." ³⁵So that night, too, they plied their father with wine, and then the younger one went in and lay with him; but again he was not aware of her lying down or her getting up.

³⁶Thus both of Lot's daughters became pregnant by their father. ³⁷The older one gave birth to a son whom she named Moab, saying, "From my father."* He is the ancestor of the Moabites of today.ᶠ ³⁸The younger one, too, gave birth to a son, and she named him Ammon, saying, "The son of my kin."* He is the ancestor of the Ammonites of today.ᵍ

CHAPTER 20

Abraham at Gerar. * ¹Abraham journeyed on to the region of the Negeb, where he settled between Kadesh and Shur. While he stayed in Gerar, ²he said of his wife Sarah, "She is my sister." So Abimelech, king of Gerar, sent and took Sarah. ³But God came to Abimelech in a dream one night and said to him, "You are about to die because of the woman you have taken, for she has a husband." ⁴Abimelech, who had not approached

her, said: "O Lord, would you slay a man even though he is innocent? ⁵He himself told me, 'She is my sister,' and she herself also stated, 'He is my brother.' I did it in good faith and with clean hands." ⁶God answered him in the dream: "Yes, I know you did it in good faith. In fact, it was I who kept you from sinning against me; that is why I did not let you touch her. ⁷Therefore, return the man's wife—as a spokesman* he will intercede for you—that your life may be saved. If you do not return her, you can be sure that you and all who are yours will certainly die."

⁸Early the next morning Abimelech called all his court officials and informed them of everything that had happened, and the men were horrified. ⁹Then Abimelech summoned Abraham and said to him: "How could you do this to us! What wrong did I do to you that you should have brought such monstrous guilt on me and my kingdom? You have treated me in an intolerable way. ¹⁰What were you afraid of," he asked him, "that you should have done such a thing?" ¹¹"I was afraid," answered Abraham, "because I thought there would surely be no fear of God in this place, and so they would kill me on account of my wife. ¹²Besides, she is in truth my sister, but only my father's daughter, not my mother's; and so she became my wife.ʰ ¹³When God sent me wandering from my father's house, I asked her: 'Would you do me this favor? In whatever place we come to, say that I am your brother.' "

¹⁴Then Abimelech took flocks and herds and male and female slaves and gave them to Abraham; and after he restored his wife Sarah to him, ¹⁵he said, "Here,

---

e Rv 9, 2; 14, 10f.—f Dt 2, 9.—g Dt 2, 19.—h Gn 12, 13.

19, 28f: From the height east of Hebron, Abraham could easily see the region at the southern end of the Dead Sea, where the *Cities of the Plain* were probably located.

19, 30-38: This Israelite tale about the origin of Israel's neighbors east of the Jordan and the Dead Sea was told partly to ridicule these racially related but rival nations and partly to give folk etymologies for their names.

19, 37: *From my father:* in Hebrew, *meabi,* similar in sound to the name "Moab."

19, 38: *The son of my kin:* in Hebrew, *ben-ammi,* similar in sound to the name "Ammonites."

20, 1-18: This story from the Elohist source (see note on Gn 4, 25) combines elements found in the two very similar but distinct stories of the Yahwist source in Gn 12, 10-20 and 26, 6-11.

20, 7: *Spokesman:* the Hebrew term *nabi* used here is regularly translated as "prophet," but it simply means "one who speaks on behalf of another," whether the latter is God, as in almost all cases, or another man, as in Ex 4, 16.

my land lies at your disposal; settle wherever you please." [16] To Sarah he said: "See, I have given your brother a thousand shekels of silver.* Let that serve you as a vindication before all who are with you; your honor has been preserved with everyone." [17] Abraham then interceded with God, and God restored health to Abimelech, that is, to his wife and his maidservants, so that they could bear children; [18] for God had tightly closed every womb in Abimelech's household on account of Abraham's wife Sarah.

CHAPTER 21

Birth of Isaac. [1] The LORD took note of Sarah as he had said he would; he did for her as he had promised.[i] [2] Sarah became pregnant and bore Abraham a son in his old age, at the set time that God had stated.[j] [3] Abraham gave the name Isaac to this son of his whom Sarah bore him.[k] [4] When his son Isaac was eight days old, Abraham circumcised him, as God had commanded.[l] [5] Abraham was a hundred years old when his son Isaac was born to him. [6] Sarah then said, "God has given me cause to laugh, and all who hear of it will laugh with me.[m] [7] Who would have told Abraham," she added, "that Sarah would nurse children! Yet I have borne him a son in his old age." [8] Isaac grew, and on the day of the child's weaning Abraham held a great feast.

[9] * Sarah noticed the son whom Hagar the Egyptian had borne to Abraham playing with her son Isaac; [10] so she demanded of Abraham: "Drive out that slave and her son! No son of that slave is going to share the inheritance with my son Isaac!"[n] [11] Abraham was greatly distressed, especially on account of his son Ishmael. [12] But God said to Abraham: "Do not be distressed about the boy or about your slave woman. Heed the demands of Sarah, no matter what she is asking of you; for it is through Isaac that descendants shall bear your name.[o] [13] As for the son of the slave woman, I will make a great nation of him also, since he too is your offspring."

[14] Early the next morning Abraham got some bread and a skin of water and gave them to Hagar. Then, placing the child on her back,* he sent her away. As she roamed aimlessly in the wilderness of Beer-sheba, [15] the water in the skin was used up. So she put the child down under a shrub, [16] and then went and sat down opposite him, about a bowshot away; for she said to herself, "Let me not watch to see the child die." As she sat opposite him, he began to cry. [17] God heard the boy's cry, and God's messenger called to Hagar from heaven: "What is the matter, Hagar? Don't be afraid; God has heard the boy's cry in this plight of his.[p] [18] Arise, lift up the boy and hold him by the hand; for I will make of him a great nation." [19] Then God opened her eyes, and she saw a well of water. She went and filled the skin with water, and then let the boy drink.

[20] God was with the boy as he grew up. He lived in the wilderness and became an expert bowman, [21] with his home in the wilderness of Paran. His mother got a wife for him from the land of Egypt.

The Pact at Beer-sheba. [22] About that time Abimelech, accompanied by Phicol, the commander of his army,* said to Abraham: "God is with you in everything you do. [23] Therefore, swear to me by God at this place* that you will not deal falsely with me or with my progeny and posterity, but will act as loyally toward me and the land in which you stay as I have acted toward you." [24] To this Abraham replied, "I so swear."

[25] Abraham, however, reproached Abimelech about a well that Abimelech's

---

i Gn 17, 19; 18, 10.—j Gal 4, 23; Heb 11, 11.—k Mt 1, 2; Lk 3, 34.—l Gn 17, 10ff; Acts 7, 8.—m Gn 17, 17.—n Jgs 11, 2; Gal 4, 30.—o Rom 9, 7; Heb 11, 18.—p Gn 16, 7.

20, 16: *A thousand shekels of silver:* not a gift distinct from that of the animals and the slaves (v 14), but the monetary value of these.

21, 9-19: This story of Hagar's expulsion, in the Elohist source, is in general a duplicate of the one from the Yahwist source in Gn 16, 5-14; but the two stories differ greatly in detail.

21, 14: *Placing the child on her back:* the phrase is translated from an emended form of the Hebrew text. In the current faulty Hebrew text, Abraham put the bread and the waterskin on Hagar's back, while her son apparently walked beside her. This reading seems to be a scribal attempt at harmonizing the present passage with the data of the Priestly source, in which Ishmael would have been at least fourteen years old when Isaac was born; compare Gn 16, 16 with 21, 5; cf 17, 25. But in the present Elohist story Ishmael is obviously a little boy, not much older than Isaac; cf vv 15, 18.

21, 22: Here and in v 32 the Greek text has ". . . Abimelech, accompanied by Ahuzzath, his councilor, and Phicol . . ."; but this is probably a secondary harmonization with Gn 26, 26. Abimelech took Phicol with him in order to intimidate Abraham by a show of strength.

21, 23: *This place:* Beer-sheba (v 31). Abimelech had come from Gerar (Gn 20, 2), about thirty miles west of Beer-sheba.

men had seized by force. 26 "I have no idea who did that," Abimelech replied. "In fact, you never told me about it, nor did I ever hear of it until now." 27 Then Abraham took sheep and cattle and gave them to Abimelech and the two made a pact. 28 Abraham also set apart seven ewe lambs of the flock, 29 and Abimelech asked him, "What is the purpose of these seven ewe lambs that you have set apart?" 30 Abraham answered, "The seven ewe lambs you shall accept from me that thus I may have your acknowledgment that the well was dug by me." 31 This is why the place is called Beer-sheba;* the two of them took an oath there. 32 When they had thus made the pact in Beer-sheba, Abimelech, along with Phicol, the commander of his army, left and returned to the land of the Philistines. 33 Abraham planted a tamarisk at Beer-sheba, and there he invoked by name the LORD, God the Eternal.* 34 Abraham resided in the land of the Philistines for many years.

CHAPTER 22

The Testing of Abraham. 1 Some time after these events, God put Abraham to the test.* He called to him, "Abraham!" "Ready!" he replied.q 2 Then God said: "Take your son Isaac, your only one,* whom you love, and go to the land of Moriah. There you shall offer him up as a holocaust on a height that I will point out to you."r 3 Early the next morning Abraham saddled his donkey, took with him his son Isaac, and two of his servants as well, and with the wood that he had cut for the holocaust, set out for the place of which God had told him. 4 On the third day Abraham got sight of the place from afar. 5 Then he said to his servants: "Both of you stay here with the donkey, while the boy and I go on over yonder. We will worship and then come back to you." 6 Thereupon Abraham took the wood for the holocaust and laid it on his son Isaac's shoulders, while he himself carried the fire and the knife. 7 As the two walked on together, Isaac spoke to his father Abraham: "Father!" he said. "Yes, son," he replied. Isaac continued, "Here are the fire and the wood, but where is the sheep for the holocaust?" 8 "Son," Abra-

ham answered, "God himself will provide the sheep for the holocaust." Then the two continued going forward. 9 When they came to the place of which God had told him, Abraham built an altar there and arranged the wood on it. Next he tied up his son Isaac, and put him on top of the wood on the altar.s 10 Then he reached out and took the knife to slaughter his son.t 11 But the LORD's messenger called to him from heaven, "Abraham, Abraham!" "Yes, Lord," he answered. 12 "Do not lay your hand on the boy," said the messenger. "Do not do the least thing to him. I know now how devoted you are to God, since you did not withhold from me your own beloved son."u 13 As Abraham looked about, he spied a ram caught by its horns in the thicket. So he went and took the ram and offered it up as a holocaust in place of his son. 14 Abraham named the site Yahweh-yireh;* hence people now say, "On the mountain the LORD will see."

15 Again the LORD's messenger called to Abraham from heaven 16 v and said: "I swear by myself, declares the LORD, that because you acted as you did in not withholding from me your beloved son, 17 I will bless you abundantly and make your descendants as countless as the stars of the sky and the sands of the seashore; your descendants shall take possession of the gates of their enemies,w 18 and in your descendants all the nations of the earth shall find blessing—all this because you obeyed my command."x

19 Abraham then returned to his servants, and they set out together for Beer-sheba, where Abraham made his home.

---

q Sir 44, 20.—r 2 Chr 3, 1; 1 Mc 2, 52; Heb 11, 17.—s Jas 2, 21.—t Wis 10, 5.—u Rom 8, 32; 1 Jn 4, 9.—v 16f: Gn 15, 5; Ex 32, 13; Lk 1, 73; Rom 4, 13; Heb 6, 13f; 11, 12,—w Gn 24, 60.—x Gn 12, 3; 18, 18; 26, 4; Sir 44, 21; Acts 3, 25; Gal 3, 16.

21, 31: *Beer-sheba:* the Hebrew name really means "the well of the seven," i.e., the place where there are seven wells, alluded to in the episode of the *seven ewe lambs.* vv 28ff; but it can also be interpreted to mean "the well of the oath."

21, 33: *God the Eternal:* in Hebrew, *el olam,* perhaps the name of the deity of the pre-Israelite sanctuary at Beer-sheba, but used by Abraham merely as a title of Yahweh; cf Is 40, 28.

22, 1: *God put Abraham to the test:* to prove the firmness of Abraham's faith in God's promise that through Isaac all the nations of the earth would find blessing; cf Gn 18, 10. 18; 21, 12.

22, 2: *Only one:* uniquely precious, especially loved; therefore the same term is rendered in vv 12. 17 as "beloved."

22, 14: *Yahweh-yireh:* a Hebrew expression meaning "the Lord will see"; the reference is to the words in v 8, "God himself will see to it."

Nahor's Descendants.* [20] Some time afterward, the news came to Abraham: "Milcah too has borne sons, to your brother Nahor: [21] Uz, his first-born, his brother Buz, Kemuel (the father of Aram), [22] Chesed, Hazo, Pildash, Jidlaph and Bethuel." [23] Bethuel became the father of Rebekah. These eight Milcah bore to Abraham's brother Nahor. [24] His concubine, whose name was Reumah, also bore children: Tebah, Gaham, Tahash and Maacah.

CHAPTER 23

Purchase of a Burial Place. [1] The span of Sarah's life was one hundred and twenty-seven years. [2] She died in Kiriath-arba (that is, Hebron) in the land of Canaan, and Abraham performed the customary mourning rites for her. [3] Then he left the side of his dead one and addressed the Hittites:* [4] "Although I am a resident alien* among you, sell me from your holdings a piece of property for a burial ground, that I may bury my dead wife."[y] [5] The Hittites answered Abraham: "Please, sir, [6] listen to us! You are an elect of God among us. Bury your dead in the choicest of our burial sites. None of us would deny you his burial ground for the burial of your dead." [7] Abraham, however, began to bow

y Gn 33, 19; Acts 7, 16; Heb 11, 9.—z Acts 7, 16.—a 17f: Gn 49, 29f.—b 2f: Gn 47, 29.

22, 20-24: A list of Aramean tribes who lived to the east and northeast of Israel, twelve in number, like the twelve tribes of Israel (Gn 35, 23) and the twelve tribes of Ishmael (Gn 25, 12-16).

23, 3: *The Hittites:* a non-Semitic people in Canaan; their relationship to the well-known Hittites of Asia Minor is uncertain.

23, 4: *A resident alien:* literally "a sojourner and a settler," i.e., a long-term resident alien. Such a one would normally not have the right to own property. The importance of Abraham's purchase of the field in Machpelah, which is worded in technical legal terms, lies in the fact that it gave his descendants their first, though small, land rights in the country that God had promised the patriarch they would one day inherit as their own. Abraham therefore insists on purchasing the field and not receiving it as a gift.

23, 10: *Who sat on his town council:* probable meaning of the literal translation, "who came in at the gate of his city"; so also in v 18.

23, 15: *Four hundred shekels:* probably an exorbitant sum; Jeremiah (32, 9) paid only seventeen shekels for his field in Anathoth, though the Babylonian invasion no doubt helped to reduce the price.

23, 16: *The current market value:* the standard weight called a shekel varied according to time and place.

24, 2: *Put your hand under my thigh:* the symbolism of this act was apparently connected with the Hebrew concept of children issuing from their father's "thigh" (Gn 46, 26; Ex 1, 5). Perhaps the man who took such an oath was thought to bring the curse of sterility on himself if he did not fulfill his sworn promise. Jacob made Joseph swear in the same way (Gn 47, 29). In both these instances, the oath was taken to carry out the last request of a man upon his death.

low before the local citizens, the Hittites, [8] while he appealed to them: "If you will allow me room for burial of my dead, listen to me! Intercede for me with Ephron, son of Zohar, asking him [9] to sell me the cave of Machpelah that he owns; it is at the edge of his field. Let him sell it to me in your presence, at its full price, for a burial place."

[10] Now Ephron was present with the Hittites. So Ephron the Hittite replied to Abraham in the hearing of the Hittites who sat on his town council:* [11] "Please, sir, listen to me! I give you both the field and the cave in it; in the presence of my kinsmen I make this gift. Bury your dead!" [12] But Abraham, after bowing low before the local citizens, addressed Ephron in the hearing of these men: [13] "Ah, if only you would please listen to me! I will pay you the price of the field. Accept it from me, that I may bury my dead there." [14] Ephron replied to Abraham, "Please, [15] sir, listen to me! A piece of land worth four hundred shekels* of silver—what is that between you and me, as long as you can bury your dead?" [16] [z] Abraham accepted Ephron's terms; he weighed out to him the silver that Ephron had stipulated in the hearing of the Hittites, four hundred shekels of silver at the current market value.*

[17] [a] Thus Ephron's field in Machpelah, facing Mamre, together with its cave and all the trees anywhere within its limits, was conveyed [18] to Abraham by purchase in the presence of all the Hittites who sat on Ephron's town council. [19] After this transaction, Abraham buried his wife Sarah in the cave of the field of Machpelah, facing Mamre (that is, Hebron) in the land of Canaan. [20] Thus the field with its cave was transferred from the Hittites to Abraham as a burial place.

CHAPTER 24

Isaac and Rebekah. [1] Abraham had now reached a ripe old age, and the LORD had blessed him in every way. [2] [b] Abraham said to the senior servant of his household, who had charge of all his possessions: "Put your hand under my thigh,* [3] and I will make you swear by the LORD, the God of heaven and the God of earth, that you will not procure a wife for my son from the daughters of the Canaanites among whom

I live,[c] [4]but that you will go to my own land and to my kindred to get a wife for my son Isaac." [5]The servant asked him: "What if the woman is unwilling to follow me to this land? Should I then take your son back to the land from which you migrated?" [6]"Never take my son back there for any reason," Abraham told him. [7]"The LORD, the God of heaven, who took me from my father's house and the land of my kin, and who confirmed by oath the promise he then made to me, 'I will give this land to your descendants'—he will send his messenger before you, and you will obtain a wife for my son there.[d] [8]If the woman is unwilling to follow you, you will be released from this oath. But never take my son back there!" [9]So the servant put his hand under the thigh of his master Abraham and swore to him in this undertaking.

[10]The servant then took ten of his master's camels, and bearing all kinds of gifts from his master, he made his way to the city of Nahor* in Aram Naharaim. [11]Near evening, at the time when women go out to draw water, he made the camels kneel by the well outside the city. [12]Then he prayed: "LORD, God of my master Abraham, let it turn out favorably for me* today and thus deal graciously with my master Abraham. [13]While I stand here at the spring and the daughters of the townsmen are coming out to draw water, [14]if I say to a girl, 'Please lower your jug, that I may drink,' and she answers, 'Take a drink, and let me give water to your camels, too,' let her be the one whom you have decided upon for your servant Isaac. In this way I shall know that you have dealt graciously with my master."

[15] [e] He had scarcely finished these words when Rebekah (who was born to Bethuel, son of Milcah, the wife of Abraham's brother Nahor) came out with a jug on her shoulder. [16]The girl was very beautiful, a virgin, untouched by man. She went down to the spring and filled her jug. As she came up, [17]the servant ran toward her and said, "Please give me a sip of water from your jug." [18]"Take a drink, sir," she replied, and quickly lowering the jug onto her hand, she gave him a drink. [19]When she had let him drink his fill, she said, "I will draw water for your camels, too, until they have drunk their fill." [20]With that, she quickly emptied her jug into the

drinking trough and ran back to the well to draw more water, until she had drawn enough for all the camels. [21]The man watched her the whole time, silently waiting to learn whether or not the LORD had made his errand successful. [22]When the camels had finished drinking, the man took out a gold ring weighing half a shekel, which he fastened on her nose, and two gold bracelets weighing ten shekels, which he put on her wrists. [23]Then he asked her: "Whose daughter are you? Tell me, please. And is there room in your father's house for us to spend the night?" [24]She answered: "I am the daughter of Bethuel the son of Milcah, whom she bore to Nahor. [25]There is plenty of straw and fodder at our place," she added, "and room to spend the night." [26]The man then bowed down in worship to the LORD, [27]saying: "Blessed be the LORD, the God of my master Abraham, who has not let his constant kindness toward my master fail. As for myself also, the LORD has led me straight to the house of my master's brother."

[28]Then the girl ran off and told her mother's household about it. [29] [f] Now Rebekah had a brother named Laban. [30]As soon as he saw the ring and the bracelets on his sister Rebekah and heard her words about what the man had said to her, Laban rushed outside to the man at the spring. When he reached him, he was standing by the camels at the spring. [31]So he said to him: "Come, blessed of the LORD! Why are you staying outside when I have made the house ready for you, as well as a place for the camels?" [32]The man then went inside; and while the camels were being unloaded and provided with straw and fodder, water was brought to bathe his feet and the feet of the men who were with him. [33]But when the table was set for him, he said, "I will not eat until I have told my tale." "Do so," they replied.

[34]"I am Abraham's servant," he began. [35]"The LORD has blessed my master

---

c Gn 24, 37; 28, 1f; Jgs 14, 3; Tb 4, 12.—d Gn 12, 7; Ex 6, 8; Tb 5, 17; Gal 3, 16.—e Gn 22, 23.—f Gn 27, 43.

24, 10: *Nahor:* it is uncertain whether this is to be understood as the name of Abraham's brother (Gn 11, 27), Rebekah's grandfather (Gn 24, 15), or the city of the same name (as known from the Mari documents); *Aram Naharaim,* situated near Haran (Gn 11, 31) in northern Mesopotamia.
24, 12: *Let it turn out favorably for me:* let me have a favorable omen; cf end of v 14.

so abundantly that he has become a wealthy man; he has given him flocks and herds, silver and gold, male and female slaves, and camels and asses. [36] My master's wife Sarah bore a son to my master in her old age, and he has given him everything he owns. [37] My master put me under oath, saying: 'You shall not procure a wife for my son among the daughters of the Canaanites in whose land I live; [38] instead, you shall go to my father's house, to my own relatives, to get a wife for my son.' [39] When I asked my master, 'What if the woman will not follow me?' [40] he replied: 'The LORD, in whose presence I have always walked, will send his messenger with you and make your errand successful, and so you will get a wife for my son from my own kindred of my father's house.[g] [41] Then you shall be released from my ban. If you visit my kindred and they refuse you, then, too, you shall be released from my ban.'

[42] "When I came to the spring today, I prayed: 'LORD, God of my master Abraham, may it be your will to make successful the errand I am engaged on! [43] While I stand here at the spring, if I say to a young woman who comes out to draw water, Please give me a little water from your jug, [44] and she answers, Not only may you have a drink, but I will give water to your camels, too—let her be the woman whom the LORD has decided upon for my master's son.'

[45] "I had scarcely finished saying this prayer to myself when Rebekah came out with a jug on her shoulder. After she went down to the spring and drew water, I said to her, 'Please let me have a drink.' [46] She quickly lowered the jug she was carrying and said, 'Take a drink, and let me bring water for your camels, too.' So I drank, and she watered the camels also. [47] When I asked her, 'Whose daughter are you?' she answered, 'The daughter of Bethuel, son of Nahor, born to Nahor by Milcah.' So I put the ring on her nose and the bracelets on her wrists. [48] Then I bowed down in worship to the LORD, blessing the LORD, the God of my master Abraham, who had led me on the right road to obtain the daughter of my master's kinsman for his

son. [49] If, therefore, you have in mind to show true loyalty to my master, let me know; but if not, let me know that, too. I can then proceed accordingly."

[50] [h] Laban and his household said in reply: "This thing comes from the LORD; we can say nothing to you either for or against it. [51] Here is Rebekah, ready for you; take her with you, that she may become the wife of your master's son, as the LORD has said." [52] When Abraham's servant heard their answer, he bowed to the ground before the LORD. [53] Then he brought out objects of silver and gold and articles of clothing and presented them to Rebekah; he also gave costly presents to her brother and mother. [54] After he and the men with him had eaten and drunk, they spent the night there.

When they were up the next morning, he said, "Give me leave to return to my master."[i] [55] Her brother and mother replied, "Let the girl stay with us a short while, say ten days; after that she may go." [56] But he said to them, "Do not detain me, now that the LORD has made my errand successful; let me go back to my master." [57] They answered, "Let us call the girl and see what she herself has to say about it." [58] So they called Rebekah and asked her, "Do you wish to go with this man?" She answered, "I do." [59] At this they allowed their sister Rebekah and her nurse to take leave, along with Abraham's servant and his men. [60] Invoking a blessing on Rebekah, they said:

"Sister, may you grow
    into thousands of myriads;
And may your descendants gain possession
    of the gates of their enemies!"[j]

[61] Then Rebekah and her maids started out; they mounted their camels and followed the man. So the servant took Rebekah and went on his way.

[62] Meanwhile Isaac had gone from Beerlahai-roi and was living in the region of the Negeb.[k] [63] One day toward evening he went out . . .* in the field, and as he looked around, he noticed that camels were approaching. [64] Rebekah, too, was looking about, and when she saw him, she alighted from her camel [65] and asked the servant, "Who is the man out there, walking through the fields toward us?" "That is

---

g Tb 5, 17; 10, 13.—h 50f: Tb 7, 12.—i Tb 7, 14; 8, 20.—j Gn 22, 17.—k Gn 16, 13f; 25, 11.

24, 63: *He went out:* the meaning of the Hebrew term that follows this is obscure.

my master," replied the servant. Then she covered herself with her veil.

66 The servant recounted to Isaac all the things he had done. 67 Then Isaac took Rebekah into his tent; he married her, and thus she became his wife. In his love for her Isaac found solace after the death of his mother Sarah.

CHAPTER 25

Abraham's Sons by Keturah. 1 *l* * Abraham married another wife, whose name was Keturah. 2 She bore him Zimran, Jokshan, Medan, Midian, Ishbak and Shuah. 3 Jokshan became the father of Sheba and Dedan. The descendants of Dedan were the Asshurim, the Letushim, and the Leummim. *m* 4 The descendants of Midian were Ephah, Epher, Hanoch, Abida and Eldaah. All of these were descendants of Keturah.

5 Abraham deeded everything that he owned to his son Isaac. 6 To his sons by concubinage, however, he made grants while he was still living, as he sent them away eastward, to the land of Kedem,* away from his son Isaac.

Death of Abraham. 7 The whole span of Abraham's life was one hundred and seventy-five years. 8 Then he breathed his last, dying at a ripe old age, grown old after a full life; and he was taken to his kinsmen. 9 *n* His sons Isaac and Ishmael buried him in the cave of Machpelah, in the field of Ephron, son of Zohar the Hittite, which faces Mamre, 10 the field that Abraham had bought from the Hittites; there he was buried next to his wife Sarah. 11 After the death of Abraham, God blessed his son Isaac, who made his home near Beer-lahai-roi.

Descendants of Ishmael. 12 These are the descendants of Abraham's son Ishmael, whom Hagar the Egyptian, Sarah's slave, bore to Abraham. 13 *o* These are the names of Ishmael's sons, listed in the order of their birth: Nebaioth (Ishmael's firstborn), Kedar, Adbeel, Mibsam, *p* 14 Mishma, Dumah, Massa, 15 Hadad, Tema, Jetur, Naphish and Kedemah. 16 These are the sons of Ishmael, their names by their villages and encampments; twelve chieftains of as many tribal groups. *q*

17 The span of Ishmael's life was one hundred and thirty-seven years. After he had breathed his last and died, he was taken to his kinsmen. 18 The Ishmaelites

ranged from Havilah-by-Shur, which is on the border of Egypt, all the way to Asshur; and each of them pitched camp* in opposition to his various kinsmen. *r*

III: THE PATRIARCHS ISAAC AND JACOB

Birth of Esau and Jacob. 19 This is the family history of Isaac, son of Abraham; Abraham had begotten Isaac. 20 Isaac was forty years old when he married Rebekah, the daughter of Bethuel the Aramean of Paddan-aram and the sister of Laban the Aramean. *s* 21 Isaac entreated the LORD on behalf of his wife, since she was sterile. The LORD heard his entreaty, and Rebekah became pregnant. 22 But the children in her womb jostled each other so much that she exclaimed, "If this is to be so, what good will it do me!" She went to consult the LORD, 23 and he answered her:

"Two nations are in your womb,
    two peoples are quarreling while still
        within you;
But one shall surpass the other,
    and the older shall serve the
        younger." *t*

24 When the time of her delivery came, there were twins in her womb. *u* 25 The first to emerge was reddish,* and his whole body was like a hairy mantle; so they named him Esau. 26 His brother came out next, gripping Esau's heel;* so they named

<hr/>

l 1-4: 1 Chr 1, 32f.—m Is 21, 13.—n 9f: Gn 23, 3-20.—o 13-16: 1 Chr 1, 29ff.—p Is 60, 7.—q Gn 17, 20.—r Gn 16, 12.—s Gn 24, 66.—t Gn 27, 29; Nm 24, 18; Mal 1, 2-5; Rom 9, 11f—u Hos 12, 3.

25, 1-11: Though mentioned here, Abraham's marriage to a "concubine," or wife of secondary rank, and his death are not to be understood as happening chronologically after the events narrated in the preceding chapter.

25, 6: *The land of Kedem:* or "the country of the East," the region inhabited by the Kedemites or Easterners (Gn 29, 1; Jgs 6, 3. 33; Jb 1, 3; Is 11, 14). The names mentioned in vv 2ff, as far as they can be identified, are those of tribes in the Arabian desert.

25, 18: *Pitched camp:* literally "fell"; the same Hebrew verb is used in Jgs 7, 12 in regard to the hostile encampment of Bedouin tribes. The present passage shows the fulfillment of the prediction contained in Gn 16, 12.

25, 25: *Reddish:* in Hebrew, *admoni,* a reference to Edom, another name for Esau (v 30; 36, 1). Edom, however, was really the name of the country south of Moab where the descendants of Esau lived. It was called the "red" country because of its reddish sandstone. *Hairy:* in Hebrew, *sear,* a reference to Seir, another name for Edom (Gn 36, 8). One might expect the text to say, "So they named him Seir"; but Esau *(esaw)* also means "hairy."

25, 26: *Esau's heel:* the Hebrew is *baaqeb esaw,* a reference to the name Jacob; cf Gn 27, 36. Probably, however, the name Jacob has no true etymological connection with the Hebrew word for "heel" *(aqeb),* but is instead a shortened form of some such name as *yaaqob-el* ("may God protect").

him Jacob. Isaac was sixty years old when they were born.[v]

[27] As the boys grew up, Esau became a skillful hunter, a man who lived in the open; whereas Jacob was a simple man, who kept to his tents.[w] [28] Isaac preferred Esau, because he was fond of game; but Rebekah preferred Jacob. [29] Once, when Jacob was cooking a stew, Esau came in from the open, famished. [30] He said to Jacob, "Let me gulp down some of that red stuff;* I'm starving." (That is why he was called Edom.) [31] But Jacob replied, "First give me your birthright* in exchange for it."[x] [32] "Look," said Esau, "I'm on the point of dying. What good will any birthright do me?" [33] But Jacob insisted, "Swear to me first!" So he sold Jacob his birthright under oath.[y] [34] Jacob then gave him some bread and the lentil stew; and Esau ate, drank, got up, and went his way. Esau cared little for his birthright.

CHAPTER 26

Isaac and Abimelech. [1] [z] There was a famine in the land (distinct from the earlier one that had occurred in the days of Abraham), and Isaac went down to Abimelech, king of the Philistines in Gerar.[a] [2] The LORD appeared to him and said: "Do not go down to Egypt, but continue to camp wherever in this land I tell you. [3] Stay in this land, and I will be with you and bless you; for to you and your descendants I will give all these lands, in fulfillment of the oath that I swore to your father Abraham.[b] [4] I will make your descendants as numerous as the stars in the

sky and give them all these lands, and in your descendants all the nations of the earth shall find blessing—[c] [5] this because Abraham obeyed me, keeping my mandate (my commandments, my ordinances and my instructions)."

[6] * So Isaac settled in Gerar. [7] When the men of the place asked questions about his wife, he answered, "She is my sister." He was afraid, if he called her his wife, the men of the place would kill him on account of Rebekah, since she was very beautiful. [8] But when he had been there for a long time, Abimelech, king of the Philistines, happened to look out of a window and was surprised to see Isaac fondling his wife Rebekah. [9] He called for Isaac and said: "She must certainly be your wife! How could you have said, 'She is my sister'?" Isaac replied, "I though I might lose my life on her account." [10] "How could you do this to us!" exclaimed Abimelech. "It would have taken very little for one of the men to lie with your wife, and you would have thus brought guilt upon us!" [11] Abimelech therefore gave this warning to all his men: "Anyone who molests this man or his wife shall forthwith be put to death."

[12] * Isaac sowed a crop in that region and reaped a hundredfold the same year. Since the LORD blessed him, [13] [d] he became richer and richer all the time, until he was very wealthy indeed. [14] He acquired such flocks and herds, and so many work animals, that the Philistines became envious of him. ([15] [e] The Philistines had stopped up and filled with dirt all the wells that his father's servants had dug back in the days of his father Abraham.) [16] So Abimelech said to Isaac, "Go away from us; you have become far too numerous for us." [17] Isaac left there and made the Wadi Gerar his regular campsite. ([18] Isaac reopened the wells which his father's servants had dug back in the days of his father Abraham and which the Philistines had stopped up after Abraham's death; he gave them the same names that his father had given them.) [19] But when Isaac's servants dug in the wadi and reached spring water in their well, [20] the shepherds of Gerar quarreled with Isaac's servants, saying, "The water belongs to us!" So the well was called Esek,* because they had challenged him there. [21] Then they dug another well, and they quarreled over that one too; so it was called Sitnah.* [22] When

---

v Mt 1, 2.—w Gn 27, 6f.—x Dt 21, 17.—y Heb 12, 16.—z 1-14: Gn 12, 10-20.—a Gn 12, 1.—b Gn 12, 7; 15, 18; Ex 32, 13; Ps 105, 9; Sir 44, 22; Heb 11, 9.—c Gn 12, 3; 22, 17f; 28, 14; Ex 32, 13.—d 13f: Jb 1, 3.—e 15-24: Gn 21, 25-31.

25, 30: *Red stuff:* in Hebrew, *adom;* another play on the word Edom, the "red" land.

25, 31: *Birthright:* the privilege that entitled the first-born son to a position of honor in the family and to a double share in the possessions inherited from the father.

26, 6-11: The Yahwist's version of the wife-sister episode at Gerar; the Elohist's version (Gn 20, 1-18) is connected with Abraham and Sarah.

26, 12-33: The Yahwist's version of the story about the wells at Beer-sheba; again, the Elohist version (Gn 21, 22f) is connected with Abraham. A redactor joined the two accounts by means of the parenthetical verses 15 and 18.

26, 20: *Esek:* "challenge."

26, 21: *Sitnah:* "opposition"; one might expect the text to be continued by some such words as "because they were in opposition there."

he had moved on from there, he dug still another well; but over this one they did not quarrel. It was called Rehoboth, because he said, "The LORD has now given us ample room, and we shall flourish in the land."

23 From there Isaac went up to Beersheba. 24 The same night the LORD appeared to him and said: "I am the God of your father Abraham. You have no need to fear, since I am with you. I will bless you and multiply your descendants for the sake of my servant Abraham." *f* 25 So he built an altar there and invoked the LORD by name. After he had pitched his tent there, his servants began to dig a well nearby.

26 *g* Abimelech had meanwhile come to him from Gerar, accompanied by Ahuzzath, his councilor, and Phicol, the general of his army. 27 Isaac asked them, "Why have you come to me, seeing that you hate me and have driven me away from you?" 28 They answered: "We are convinced that the LORD is with you, so we propose that there be a sworn agreement between our two sides—between you and us. Let us make a pact with you: 29 you shall not act unkindly toward us, just as we have not molested you, but have always acted kindly toward you and have let you depart in peace. Henceforth, 'The LORD's blessing be upon you!' " 30 Isaac then made a feast for them, and they ate and drank. 31 Early the next morning they exchanged oaths. Then Isaac bade them farewell, and they departed from him in peace.

32 That same day Isaac's servants came and brought him news about the well they had been digging; they told him, "We have reached water!" 33 He called it Shibah;* hence the name of the city, Beersheba, to this day.

34 * When Esau was forty years old, he married Judith, daughter of Beeri the Hittite, and Basemath, daughter of Elon the Hivite. *h* 35 But they became a source of embitterment to Isaac and Rebekah.

CHAPTER 27

Jacob's Deception. * 1 When Isaac was so old that his eyesight had failed him, he called his older son Esau and said to him, "Son!" "Yes, father!" he replied. 2 Isaac then said, "As you can see, I am so old that I may now die at any time. 3 Take your gear, therefore—your quiver and bow—and go out into the country to hunt some game for me. 4 With your catch prepare an appetizing dish for me, such as I like, and bring it to me to eat, so that I may give you my special blessing* before I die."

5 Rebekah had been listening while Isaac was speaking to his son Esau. So when Esau went out into the country to hunt some game for his father, *i* 6 Rebekah said to her son Jacob, "Listen! I overheard your father tell your brother Esau, 7 'Bring me some game and with it prepare an appetizing dish for me to eat, that I may give you my blessing with the LORD's approval before I die.' 8 Now, son, listen carefully to what I tell you. 9 Go to the flock and get me two choice kids. With these I will prepare an appetizing dish for your father, such as he likes. 10 Then bring it to your father to eat, that he may bless you before he dies." 11 "But my brother Esau is a hairy man," said Jacob to his mother Rebekah, "and I am smooth-skinned!*j* 12 Suppose my father feels me? He will think I am making sport of him, and I shall bring on myself a curse instead of a blessing." 13 His mother, however, replied: "Let any curse against you, son, fall on me! Just do as I say. Go and get me the kids."

14 So Jacob went and got them and brought them to his mother; and with them she prepared an appetizing dish, such as his father liked. 15 Rebekah then took the best clothes of her older son Esau that she had in the house, and gave

---

f Gn 46, 3.—g 26-33: Gn 21, 22-31; Prv 16, 7.—h 34f: Gn 27, 46.—i Gn 25, 28.—j Gn 25, 25.

26, 33: *Shibah:* "seven," for the sake of a closer assonance with Beer-sheba; but the present version of the story says nothing about there being seven wells there as implied in Gn 21, 28-31. The Greek version understood the Hebrew text more logically as *shebua,* "oath," in keeping with the present story.

26, 34f: These verses from the Priestly source, which have no logical connection with the preceding stories, serve as an introduction to the following section on Esau's loss of his birthright by suggesting a motivation for this in Isaac's and Rebekah's dislike for Esau's Canaanite wives.

27, 1-45: What Jacob did in deceiving his father and thereby cheating Esau out of Isaac's deathbed blessing is condemned as blameworthy, not only by Hosea (12, 4) and Jeremiah (9, 3), but also, indirectly, by the Yahwist narrator of the present story, who makes the reader sympathize with Esau as the innocent victim of a cruel plot, and shows that Jacob and his mother, the instigator of the plot, paid for it by a lifelong separation from each other. The story was told because it was part of the mystery of God's ways in salvation history—his use of weak, sinful men to achieve his own ultimate purpose.

27, 4: *My special blessing:* "the blessing of my soul." The same expression is used also in vv 19. 25. 31. In the context it must mean something like a solemn deathbed blessing, believed to be especially efficacious.

them to her younger son Jacob to wear; [16]and with the skins of the kids she covered up his hands and the hairless parts of his neck. [17]Then she handed her son Jacob the appetizing dish and the bread she had prepared.

[18]Bringing them to his father, Jacob said, "Father!" "Yes?" replied Isaac. "Which of my sons are you?" [19]Jacob answered his father: "I am Esau, your firstborn. I did as you told me. Please sit up and eat some of my game, so that you may give me your special blessing." [20]But Isaac asked, "How did you succeed so quickly, son?" He answered, "The LORD, your God, let things turn out well with me." [21]Isaac then said to Jacob, "Come closer, son, that I may feel you, to learn whether you really are my son Esau or not." [22]So Jacob moved up closer to his father. When Isaac felt him, he said, "Although the voice is Jacob's, the hands are Esau's." [23](He failed to identify him because his hands were hairy, like those of his brother Esau; so in the end he gave him his blessing.) [24]Again he asked him, "Are you really my son Esau?" "Certainly," he replied. [25]Then Isaac said, "Serve me your game, son, that I may eat of it and then give you my blessing." Jacob served it to him, and Isaac ate; he brought him wine, and he drank. [26]Finally his father Isaac said to him, "Come closer, son, and kiss me." [27]As Jacob went up and kissed him, Isaac smelled the fragrance of his clothes. With that, he blessed him, saying,

"Ah, the fragrance of my son
  is like the fragrance of a field
  that the LORD has blessed![k]

[28] "May God give to you
  of the dew of the heavens
And of the fertility of the earth
  abundance of grain and wine.

[29] *l* "Let peoples serve you,
  and nations pay you homage;
Be master of your brothers,
  and may your mother's sons bow
    down to you.

Cursed be those who curse you,
  and blessed be those who bless you."

[30]Jacob had scarcely left his father, just after Isaac had finished blessing him, when his brother Esau came back from his hunt. [31]Then he too prepared an appetizing dish with his game, and bringing it to his father, he said, "Please, father, eat some of your son's game, that you may then give me your special blessing." [32]"Who are you?" his father Isaac asked him. "I am Esau," he replied, "your firstborn son." [33]With that, Isaac was seized with a fit of uncontrollable trembling. "Who was it, then," he asked, "that hunted game and brought it to me? I finished eating it just before you came, and I blessed him. Now he must remain blessed!" [34]On hearing his father's words, Esau burst into loud, bitter sobbing. "Father, bless me too!" he begged. [35]When Isaac explained, "Your brother came here by a ruse and carried off your blessing," [36]Esau exclaimed, "He has been well named Jacob! He has now supplanted me* twice! First he took away my birthright, and now he has taken away my blessing." Then he pleaded, "Haven't you saved a blessing for me?"*m* [37]Isaac replied: "I have already appointed him your master, and I have assigned to him all his kinsmen as his slaves; besides, I have enriched him with grain and wine. What then can I do for you, son?" [38]But Esau urged his father, "Have you only that one blessing, father? Bless me too!" Isaac, however, made no reply; and Esau wept aloud.*n* [39]Finally Isaac spoke again and said to him:

"Ah, far from the fertile earth
  shall be your dwelling;
  far from the dew of the heavens
    above!*o*

[40] "By your sword you shall live,
  and your brother you shall serve;
But when you became restive,
  you shall throw off his yoke from
    your neck."*p*

[41]Esau bore Jacob a grudge because of the blessing his father had given him. He said to himself, "When the time of mourning for my father comes, I will kill my brother Jacob."*q* [42]When Rebekah got news of what her older son Esau had in mind, she called her younger son Jacob

k Gn 22, 17f; Heb 11, 20.—l Gn 25, 23; 49, 8; Nm 24, 9.—m Gn 25, 26. 29-34; Hos 12, 4.—n Heb 12, 17.—o Heb 11, 20.—p 2 Kgs 8, 20. 22; 2 Chr 21, 8.—q Wis 10, 10; Ob 1, 10.

27, 36: *He has now supplanted me:* in Hebrew, *wayyaqe-beni,* a wordplay on the name Jacob, *yaaqob;* see Jer 9, 3 and note, as well as Gn 25, 26. There is also a play between the He-brew words *bekora* ("birthright") and *beraka* ("blessing").

and said to him: "Listen! Your brother Esau intends to settle accounts with you by killing you. [43]Therefore, son, do what I tell you: flee at once to my brother Laban in Haran, [44]and stay with him a while until your brother's fury subsides [45][until your brother's anger against you subsides] and he forgets what you did to him. Then I will send for you and bring you back. Must I lose both of you in a single day?"

Jacob Sent to Laban. [46]* Rebekah said to Isaac: "I am disgusted with life because of the Hittite women. If Jacob also should marry a Hittite woman, a native of the land, like these women, what good would life be to me?"[r]

CHAPTER 28

[1]Isaac therefore called Jacob, greeted him with a blessing, and charged him: "You shall not marry a Canaanite woman![s] [2]Go now to Paddan-aram, to the home of your mother's father Bethuel, and there choose a wife for yourself from among the daughters of your uncle Laban.[t] [3]May God Almighty bless you and make you fertile, multiply you that you may become an assembly of peoples. [4]May he extend to you and your descendants the blessing he gave to Abraham, so that you may gain possession of the land where you are staying, which he assigned to Abraham."[u] [5]Then Isaac sent Jacob on his way; he went to Paddan-aram, to Laban, son of Bethuel, the Aramean, and brother of Rebekah, the mother of Jacob and Esau.[v]

[6]Esau noted that Isaac had blessed Jacob when he sent him to Paddan-aram to get himself a wife there, charging him, as he gave him his blessing, not to marry a Canaanite woman, [7]and that Jacob had obeyed his father and mother and gone to Paddan-aram. [8]Esau realized how displeasing the Canaanite women were to his father Isaac, [9]so he went to Ishmael, and in addition to the wives he had, married Mahalath, the daughter of Abraham's son Ishmael and sister of Nebaioth.[w]

Jacob's Dream at Bethel. [10]Jacob departed from Beer-sheba and proceeded toward Haran. [11]When he came upon a certain shrine,* as the sun had already set, he stopped there for the night. Taking one of the stones at the shrine, he put it under his head and lay down to sleep at that spot. [12]Then he had a dream: a stairway* rested on the ground, with its top reaching to the

heavens; and God's messengers were going up and down on it.[x] [13]And there was the LORD standing beside him and saying: "I, the LORD, am the God of your forefather Abraham and the God of Isaac; the land on which you are lying I will give to you and your descendants.[y] [14]These shall be as plentiful as the dust of the earth, and through them you shall spread out east and west, north and south. In you and your descendants all the nations of the earth shall find blessing.[z] [15]Know that I am with you; I will protect you wherever you go, and bring you back to this land. I will never leave you until I have done what I promised you."[a]

[16]When Jacob awoke from his sleep, he exclaimed, "Truly, the LORD is in this spot, although I did not know it!" [17]In solemn wonder he cried out: "How awesome is this shrine! This* is nothing else but an abode of God, and that is the gateway to heaven!" [18]Early the next morning Jacob took the stone that he had put under his head, set it up as a memorial stone,* and poured oil on top of it.[b] [19]He called that site Bethel,* whereas the former name of the town had been Luz.[c]

[20]Jacob then made this vow: "If God remains with me, to protect me on this

---

r Gn 26, 34f.—s Gn 24, 3f; 26, 35.—t Gn 22, 22; 17, 1f. 4f.—u Ex 32, 13.—v Jdt 8, 26.—w Gn 36, 2f.—z Jn 1, 51.—y Dt 1, 8; Mi 7, 28.—z Gn 12, 3; 13, 14f; 15, 5f; 18, 18; 22, 17f; 26, 4; Dt 19, 8; Sir 44, 21.—a Gn 31, 3.—b Gn 31, 13; 35, 14f.—c Gn 35, 6; 48, 3; Jos 18, 13; Jgs 1, 23; Hos 12, 4.

27, 46—28, 9: This section, which is from the Priestly source and a direct sequel of Gn 26, 34f, presents a different, though not contradictory, reason for Jacob's going to Paddan-aram: namely, to preserve racial purity among the chosen people. The account of Esau's marriages is given for the purpose of explaining the racial mixture of the Edomites, who were descended in part from tribes related to Israel, in part from older peoples in Edom called Hittites, Horites or Hivites, and in part from the Ishmaelite (Arabian) tribes who later invaded the region.

28, 11: *Shrine:* literally "place," often used specifically of a sacred site. Here the place was Bethel (v 19), a sacred site as early as the time of Abraham (Gn 12, 8).

28, 12: *Stairway:* in Hebrew, *sullam,* traditionally but inaccurately translated as "ladder." The corresponding verb, *salal,* means "to heap up" something, such as dirt for a highway or ramp. The imagery in Jacob's dream is derived from the Babylonian ziggurat or temple tower, *"with its top in the sky"* (Gn 11, 4), and with brick steps leading up to a small temple at the top.

28, 17: *This:* the stone Jacob used as a headrest; cf v 22. *That:* the stairway Jacob saw in his dream.

28, 18: *Memorial stone:* in Hebrew, *masseba,* a stone which might vary in shape and size, set upright and usually intended for some religious purpose. Since the custom of erecting such "sacred pillars" in Palestine went back to its pre-Israelite period, their pagan associations were often retained; therefore, later Israelite religion forbade their erection (Lv 26, 1; Dt 16, 22) and ordered the destruction of those that were associated with paganism (Ex 34, 31; Dt 12, 3).

28, 19: *Bethel:* i.e., "house of God"; the reference is to the abode of God in v 17.

journey I am making and to give me enough bread to eat and clothing to wear, [21] and I come back safe to my father's house, the LORD shall be my God. [22] This stone that I have set up as a memorial stone shall be God's abode. Of everything you give me, I will faithfully return a tenth part to you."

CHAPTER 29

Arrival in Haran. [1] *d* After Jacob resumed his journey, he came to the land of the Easterners.* [2] Looking about, he saw a well in the open country, with three droves of sheep huddled near it, for droves were watered from that well. A large stone covered the mouth of the well.*e* [3] Only when all the shepherds were assembled there could they roll the stone away from the mouth of the well and water the flocks. Then they would put the stone back again over the mouth of the well.

[4] Jacob said to them, "Friends, where are you from?" "We are from Haran," they replied. [5] Then he asked them, "Do you know Laban, son of Nahor?" "We do," they answered.*f* [6] He inquired further, "Is he well?" "He is," they answered; "and here comes his daughter Rachel with his flock." [7] Then he said: "There is still much daylight left; it is hardly the time to bring the animals home. Why don't you water the flocks now, and then continue pasturing them?" [8] "We cannot," they replied, "until all the shepherds are here to roll the stone away from the mouth of the well; only then can we water the flocks."

[9] While he was still talking with them, Rachel arrived with her father's sheep; she was the one who tended them. [10] As soon as Jacob saw Rachel, the daughter of his uncle Laban, with the sheep of his uncle Laban, he went up, rolled the stone away from the mouth of the well, and watered his uncle's sheep. [11] Then Jacob kissed Rachel and burst into tears.* [12] He told her that he was her father's relative, Rebekah's son, and she ran to tell her father. [13] When Laban heard the news about his sister's son Jacob, he hurried out to meet him. After embracing and kissing him, he brought him to his house. Jacob then recounted to Laban all that had happened, [14] and Laban said to him, "You are indeed my flesh and blood." *

Marriage to Leah and Rachel. After Jacob had stayed with him a full month, [15] Laban said to him: "Should you serve me for nothing just because you are a relative of mine? Tell me what your wages should be." [16] Now Laban had two daughters; the older was called Leah, the younger Rachel. [17] Leah had lovely eyes,* but Rachel was well formed and beautiful. [18] Since Jacob had fallen in love with Rachel, he answered Laban, "I will serve you seven years for your younger daughter Rachel."* [19] Laban replied, "I prefer to give her to you rather than to an outsider. Stay with me." [20] So Jacob served seven years for Rachel, yet they seemed to him but a few days because of his love for her.*g*

[21] Then Jacob said to Laban, "Give me my wife, that I may consummate my marriage with her, for my term is now completed." [22] So Laban invited all the local inhabitants and gave a feast. [23] At nightfall he took his daughter Leah and brought her to Jacob, and Jacob consummated the marriage with her. [24] (Laban assigned his slave girl Zilpah to his daughter Leah as her maidservant.) [25] In the morning Jacob was amazed:* it was Leah! So he cried out to Laban: "How could you do this to me! Was it not for Rachel that I served you? Why did you dupe me?" [26] "It is not the custom in our country," Laban replied, "to marry off a younger daughter before an older one. [27] Finish the bridal week* for this one, and then I will give you the other too, in return for another seven years of service with me."*h*

[28] Jacob agreed. He finished the bridal week for Leah, and then Laban gave him his daughter Rachel in marriage. [29] (Laban assigned his slave girl Bilhah to his daughter Rachel as her maidservant.) [30] Jacob then consummated his marriage with

---

d Wis 10, 10.—e Gn 24, 11f.—f Tb 7, 4.—g Hos 12, 13.—h Hos 12, 13.

29, 1: *Easterners:* see note on Gn 25, 6.
29, 11: *Burst into tears:* literally "raised his voice and wept," i.e., for joy.
29, 14: *Flesh and blood:* literally "bone and flesh," i.e., a close relative; on the Hebrew idiom, see Gn 2, 23.
29, 17: *Lovely eyes:* The adjective modifying *eyes* is often translated as "weak," but "lovely" is the more probable word.
29, 18: Jacob offers to render service (Jos 15, 16f; 1 Sm 17, 25; 18, 17) in lieu of the customary bridal price (Ex 22, 16f; Dt 22, 29).
29, 25: *Jacob was amazed:* he had not recognized Leah because a bride was veiled when she was brought to her bridegroom; cf Gn 24, 65.
29, 27: *The bridal week:* an ancient wedding lasted for seven day of festivities; cf Jgs 14, 12.

Rachel also, and he loved her more than Leah. Thus he remained in Laban's service another seven years.[i]

Jacob's Children. [31] When the LORD saw that Leah was unloved, he made her fruitful, while Rachel remained barren. [32] Leah conceived and bore a son, and she named him Reuben;* for she said, "It means, 'The LORD saw my misery; now my husband will love me.' "[j] [33] She conceived again and bore a son, and said, "It means, 'The LORD heard that I was unloved,' and therefore he has given me this one also"; so she named him Simeon.* [34] Again she conceived and bore a son, and she said, "Now at last my husband will become attached to me, since I have now borne him three sons"; that is why she named him Levi.* [35] Once more she conceived and bore a son, and she said, "This time I will give grateful praise to the LORD"; therefore she named him Judah.* Then she stopped bearing children.[k]

CHAPTER 30

[1] When Rachel saw that she failed to bear children to Jacob, she became envious of her sister. She said to Jacob, "Give me children or I shall die!"[l] [2] In anger Jacob retorted, "Can I take the place of God, who has denied you the fruit of the womb?"[m] [3] She replied, "Here is my maidservant Bilhah. Have intercourse with her, and let her give birth on my knees,* so that I too may have offspring, at least through her."[n] [4] So she gave him her maidservant Bilhah as a consort,* and Jacob had intercourse with her. [5] When Bilhah conceived and bore a son, [6] Rachel said, "God has vindicated me; indeed he has heeded my plea and given me a son." Therefore she named him Dan.* [7] Rachel's maidservant Bilhah conceived again and bore a second son, [8] and Rachel said, "I engaged in a fateful struggle with my sister, and I prevailed." So she named him Naphtali.*

[9] When Leah saw that she had ceased to bear children, she gave her maidservant Zilpah to Jacob as a consort. [10] So Jacob had intercourse with Zilpah, and she conceived and bore a son. [11] Leah then said, "What good luck!" So she named him Gad.* [12] Then Leah's maidservant Zilpah bore a second son to Jacob; [13] and Leah said, "What good fortune!"—meaning,

"Women call me fortunate." So she named him Asher.*

[14] One day, during the wheat harvest, when Reuben was out in the field, he came upon some mandrakes* which he brought home to his mother Leah. Rachel asked Leah, "Please let me have some of your son's mandrakes." [15] Leah replied, "Was it not enough for you to take away my husband, that you must now take my son's mandrakes too?" "Very well, then!" Rachel answered. "In exchange for your son's mandrakes, Jacob may lie with you tonight." [16] That evening, when Jacob came home from the fields, Leah went out to meet him. "You are now to come in with me," she told him, "because I have paid for you with my son's mandrakes." So that night he slept with her, [17] and God heard her prayer; she conceived and bore a fifth son to Jacob. [18] Leah then said, "God has given me my reward for having let my husband have my maidservant"; so she named him Issachar.* [19] Leah conceived again and bore a sixth son to Jacob; [20] and

---

i Dt 21, 15ff.—j Gn 49, 3.—k Mt 1, 2; Lk 3, 33.—l Prv 30, 16.—m 2 Kgs 5, 7.—n Gn 16, 2ff.

29, 32: *Reuben:* the literal meaning of the Hebrew name is "look, a son!" But in this case, as also with the names of all the other sons of Jacob, a symbolic rather than an etymological interpretation of the name is given, because the name and the persons were regarded as closely interrelated. The symbolic interpretation of Reuben's name, according to the Yahwist source, is based on the similar-sounding, *raa beonyi,* "he saw my misery." In the Elohist source, the name is explained by the similar-sounding *yeehabani,* "he will love me."

29, 33: *Simeon:* in popular etymology, related to *shama,* "he heard."

29, 34: *Levi:* related to *yillaweh,* "he will become attached."

29, 35: *Judah:* related to *odeh,* "I will give grateful praise."

30, 3: *On my knees:* in the ancient Near East, a father would take a newborn child in his lap to signify that he acknowledged it as his own; Rachel uses this ceremony in order to adopt the child and establish her legal rights to it.

30, 4: *Consort:* the Hebrew word normally means "wife," but here it refers to a wife of secondary rank, who did not have the full legal rights of an ordinary wife.

30, 6: *Dan:* explained by the term *dannanni,* "he has vindicated me."

30, 8: *Naphtali:* explained by the phrase "*naptule elohim niptalti,*" literally, "in a divine wrestling match I have wrestled," perhaps implying the concept of an ordeal; hence the above rendering, *I engaged in a fateful struggle.*

30, 11: *Gad:* explained by the Hebrew term *begad,* literally "in luck," i.e., *what good luck!*

30, 13: *Asher:* explained by the term *beoshri,* literally "in my good fortune," i.e., *what good fortune,* and by the term *ishsheruni,* "they call me fortune."

30, 14: *Mandrakes:* a herb whose root was anciently thought to promote conception. The Hebrew word for mandrakes, *dudaim,* has erotic connotations, since it sounds like the words *daddayim* ("breasts") and *dodim* ("sexual pleasure").

30, 18: *Issachar:* explained by the terms, *sekari,* "my reward," and in v 16, *sakor sekartika,* literally "I have hired you," i.e., I have paid for you.

she said, "God has brought me a precious gift. This time my husband will offer me presents, now that I have borne him six sons"; so she named him Zeubulun.* ²¹ Finally, she gave birth to a daughter, and she named her Dinah.

²² Then God remembered Rachel; he heard her prayer and made her fruitful. ²³ She conceived and bore a son, and she said, "God has removed my disgrace."*ᵒ* ²⁴ So she named him Joseph,* meaning, "May the LORD add another son to this one for me!"

Jacob Outwits Laban. ²⁵ After Rachel gave birth to Joseph, Jacob said to Laban: "Give me leave to go to my homeland. ²⁶ Let me have my wives, for whom I served you, and my children, too, that I may depart. You know very well the service that I have rendered you." ²⁷ Laban answered him: "If you will please. . . .

"I have learned through divination that it is because of you that God has blessed me. ²⁸ So," he continued, "state what wages you want from me, and I will pay them." ²⁹ Jacob replied: "You know what work I did for you and how well your livestock fared under my care; ³⁰ the little you had before I came has grown into very much, since the LORD's blessings came upon you in my company. Therefore I should now do something for my own household as well." ³¹ "What should I pay you?" Laban asked. Jacob answered: "You do not have to pay me anything outright. I will again pasture and tend your flock, if you do this one thing for me: ³² go through your whole flock today and remove from

ᵒ Lk 1, 25.

30, 20: *Zebulun:* related to the Akkadian word *zubullum,* "bridegroom's gift," is explained by the terms, *zebadani . . . zebed tob,* "he has brought me a precious gift," and *yizbeleni,* "he will offer me presents."

30, 24: *Joseph:* explained by the words *yosep,* "may he add," and in v 23, *asap,* "he has removed."

30, 32: *Dark . . . sheep . . . spotted or speckled goats:* in the Near East the normal color of sheep is light gray, whereas that of goats is uniform dark brown or black. Ordinarily, therefore, Jacob would have received but few animals.

30, 35: By giving the abnormally colored animals to his sons, Laban not only deprived Jacob of his first small wages, but he also designed to prevent in this way the future breeding of such animals in the part of his flock entrusted to Jacob.

30, 39–42: Jacob's strategem was based on the widespread notion among simple people that visual stimuli can have prenatal effects on the offspring of breeding animals. Thus, the rods on which Jacob had whittled stripes or bands or chevron marks were thought to cause the female goats that looked at them to bear kids with lighter-colored marks on their dark hair, while the gray ewes were thought to bear lambs with dark marks on them simply by visual cross-breeding with the dark goats.

it every dark animal among the sheep and every spotted or speckled one among the goats.* Only such animals shall be my wages. ³³ In the future, whenever you check on these wages of mine, let my honesty testify against me: any animal in my possession that is not a speckled or spotted goat, or a dark sheep, got there by theft!" ³⁴ "Very well," agreed Laban. "Let it be as you say."

³⁵ That same day Laban removed the streaked and spotted he-goats and all the speckled and spotted she-goats, all those with some white on them, as well as the fully dark-colored sheep; these he left . . . in charge of his sons.* ³⁶ Then he put a three days' journey between himself and Jacob, while Jacob continued to pasture the rest of Laban's flock.

³⁷ Jacob, however, got some fresh shoots of poplar, almond and plane trees, and he made white stripes in them by peeling off the bark down to the white core of the shoots. ³⁸ The rods that he had thus peeled he then set upright in the watering troughs, so that they would be in front of the animals that drank from the troughs. When the animals were in heat as they came to drink, ³⁹ * the goats mated by the rods, and so they brought forth streaked, speckled and spotted kids. ⁴⁰ The sheep, on the other hand, Jacob kept apart, and he set these animals to face the streaked or fully dark-colored animals of Laban. Thus he produced special flocks of his own, which he did not put with Laban's flock. ⁴¹ Moreover, whenever the hardier animals were in heat, Jacob would set the rods in the troughs in full view of these animals, so that they mated by the rods; ⁴² but with the weaker animals he would not put the rods there. So the feeble animals would go to Laban, but the sturdy ones to Jacob. ⁴³ Thus the man grew increasingly prosperous, and he came to own not only large flocks but also male and female servants and camels and asses.

CHAPTER 31

Flight from Laban. ¹ Jacob learned that Laban's sons were saying, "Jacob has taken everything that belonged to our father, and he has accumulated all this wealth of his by using our father's property." ² Jacob perceived, too, that Laban's attitude toward him was not what it had previously been. ³Then the LORD said to Jacob, "Return to the land of your fathers, where you were born, and I will be with you."ᵖ

⁴So Jacob sent for Rachel and Leah to meet him where he was in the field with his flock. ⁵There he said to them: "I have noticed that your father's attitude toward me is not as it was in the past; but the God of my father has been with me. ⁶You well know what effort I put into serving your father; ⁷yet your father cheated me and changed my wages time after time. God, however, did not let him do me any harm.�q ⁸ * Whenever your father said, 'The speckled animals shall be your wages,' the entire flock would bear speckled young; whenever he said, 'The streaked animals shall be your wages,' the entire flock would bear streaked young. ⁹Thus God reclaimed your father's livestock and gave it to me. ¹⁰Once, in the breeding season, I had a dream in which I saw mating he-goats that were streaked, speckled and mottled. ¹¹In the dream God's messenger called to me, 'Jacob!' 'Here!' I replied. ¹²Then he said. 'Note well. All the he-goats in the flock, as they mate, are streaked, speckled and mottled, for I have seen all the things that Laban has been doing to you. ¹³I am the God who appeared to you in Bethel, where you anointed a memorial stone and made a vow to me. Up, then! Leave this land and return to the land of your birth.' "ʳ

¹⁴Rachel and Leah answered him: "Have we still an heir's portion in our father's house? ¹⁵Are we not regarded by him as outsiders?* He not only sold us; he has even used up the money that he got for us! ¹⁶All the wealth that God reclaimed from our father really belongs to us and our children. Therefore, do just as God has told you."ˢ ¹⁷Jacob proceeded to put his children and wives on camels, ¹⁸and he drove off with all his livestock and all the property he had acquired in Paddan-aram, to go to his father Isaac in the land of Canaan.

¹⁹Now Laban had gone away to shear his sheep, and Rachel had meanwhile appropriated her father's household idols.ᵗ * ²⁰Jacob had hoodwinked* Laban the Aramean by not telling him of his intended flight. ²¹Thus he made his escape with all that he had. Once he was across

the Euphrates, he headed for the highlands of Gilead.

²²On the third day, word came to Laban that Jacob had fled. ²³Taking his kinsmen with him, he pursued him for seven days* until he caught up with him in the hill country of Gilead. ²⁴But that night God appeared to Laban the Aramean in a dream and warned him, "Take care not to threaten Jacob with any harm."ᵘ

Jacob and Laban in Gilead. ²⁵When Laban overtook Jacob, Jacob's tents were pitched in the highlands; Laban also pitched his tents there, on Mount Gilead. ²⁶"What do you mean," Laban demanded of Jacob, "by hoodwinking me and carrying off my daughters like war captives?* ²⁷Why did you dupe me by stealing away secretly? You should have told me, and I would have sent you off with merry singing to the sound of tambourines and harps. ²⁸You did not even allow me a parting kiss to my daughters and grandchildren! What you have now done is a senseless thing. ²⁹I have it in my power to harm all of you; but last night the God of your father said to me, 'Take care not to threaten Jacob with any harm!' ³⁰Granted that you had to leave because you were desperately homesick for your father's house, why did you steal my gods?" ³¹"I was frightened," Jacob replied to Laban, "at the thought that you might take your daughters away from me by force. ³²But as for your gods, the one you find them with shall not remain

---

p Gn 26, 3; 28, 15; 32, 10.—q Jdt 8, 26.—r Gn 28, 18.—s Wis 10, 10f.—t Gn 19, 34; 1 Sm 19, 13.—u Wis 10, 12.

31, 8-12: This Elohist account of the miraculous increase in Jacob's flock differs somewhat from the Yahwist account given in Gn 30, 32-42.

31, 15: *Outsiders:* literally "foreign women"; they lacked the favored legal status of native women. *Used up:* literally "eaten, consumed"; the bridal price that a man received for giving his daughter in marriage was legally reserved as her inalienable dowry.

31, 19: *Household idols:* in Hebrew, *terapim,* figurines used in divination (Ez 21, 26; Zec 10, 2). Laban calls them his "gods" (v 30).

31, 20: *Hoodwinked:* literally "stolen the heart of," i.e., lulled the mind of. *Aramean:* the earliest extra-biblical references to the Arameans date from several centuries after the time of Jacob; to call Laban an *Aramean* and to have him speak Aramaic (v 47) would seem to be an anachronism.

31, 23: *For seven days:* literally "a way of seven days," a general term to designate a long distance; it would have taken a camel caravan many more days to travel from Haran to Gilead, the region east of the northern half of the Jordan.

31, 26: *War captives:* literally "women captured by the sword"; the women of a conquered people were treated as part of the victor's booty; cf 1 Sm 30, 2; 2 Kgs 5, 2.

alive! If, with my kinsmen looking on, you identify anything here as belonging to you, take it." Jacob, of course, had no idea that Rachel had stolen the idols.

³³Laban then went in and searched Jacob's tent and Leah's tent, as well as the tents of the two maidservants; but he did not find the idols. Leaving Leah's tent, he went into Rachel's. ³⁴Now Rachel had taken the idols, put them inside a camel cushion, and seated herself upon them. When Laban had rummaged through the rest of her tent without finding them,^v ³⁵Rachel said to her father, "Let not my lord feel offended that I cannot rise in your presence; a woman's period is upon me." So, despite his search, he did not find his idols.

³⁶Jacob, now enraged, upbraided Laban. "What crime or offense have I committed," he demanded, "that you should hound me so fiercely? ³⁷Now that you have ransacked all my things, have you found a single object taken from your belongings? If so, produce it here before your kinsmen and mine, and let them decide between us two.

³⁸"In the twenty years that I was under you, no ewe or she-goat of yours ever miscarried, and I have never feasted on a ram of your flock. ³⁹ ^w I never brought you an animal torn by wild beasts; I made good the loss myself. You held me responsible for anything stolen by day or night.* ⁴⁰How often the scorching heat ravaged me by day, and the frost by night, while sleep fled from my eyes! ⁴¹Of the twenty years that I have now spent in your household, I slaved fourteen years for your two daughters and six years for your flock, while you changed my wages time

after time. ⁴²If my ancestral God, the God of Abraham and the Awesome One of Isaac, had not been on my side, you would now have sent me away empty-handed. But God saw my plight and the fruits of my toil, and last night he gave judgment."^x

⁴³ * Laban replied to Jacob: "The women are mine, their children are mine, and the flocks are mine; everything you see belongs to me. But since these women are my daughters, I will now do something for them and for the children they have borne. ⁴⁴Come, then, we will make a pact, you and I; the LORD shall be a witness between us."

⁴⁵Then Jacob took a stone and set it up as a memorial stone.^y ⁴⁶Jacob said to his kinsmen, "Gather some stones." So they got some stones and made a mound; and they had a meal there at the mound. ⁴⁷Laban called it Jegar-sahadutha,* but Jacob named it Galeed. ⁴⁸"This mound," said Laban, "shall be a witness from now on between you and me." That is why it was named Galeed—⁴⁹and also Mizpah,* for he said: "May the LORD keep watch between you and me when we are out of each other's sight. ⁵⁰If you mistreat my daughters, or take other wives besides my daughters, remember that even though no one else is about, God will be witness between you and me."

⁵¹Laban said further to Jacob: "Here is this mound, and here is the memorial stone that I have set up between you and me. ⁵²This mound shall be witness, and this memorial stone shall be witness, that, with hostile intent, neither may I pass beyond this mound into your territory nor may you pass beyond it into mine. ⁵³May the God of Abraham and the god of Nahor [their ancestral deities] maintain justice between us!" Jacob took the oath by the Awesome One of Isaac. ⁵⁴He then offered a sacrifice on the mountain and invited his kinsmen to share in the meal. When they had eaten, they passed the night on the mountain.

CHAPTER 32

¹Early the next morning, Laban kissed his grandchildren and his daughters goodbye; then he set out on his journey back home, ²while Jacob continued on his own

---

v Gn 31, 19.—w Ex 22, 12.—x Gn 19, 24. 29.—y Gn 28, 18; 35, 14.

31, 39: Laban's actions were contrary to the customs of the ancient Near East, as recorded in the Code of Hammurabi: "If in a sheepfold an act of god has occurred, or a lion has made a kill, the shepherd shall clear himself before the deity, and the owner of the fold must accept the loss" (par. 266); cf Ex 22, 12.

31, 43-54: In this account of the treaty between Laban and Jacob, the Yahwist and Elohist sources are closely interwoven. The *mound* or cairn of stones comes from the Yahwist source, the *memorial stone* or stele comes from the Elohist one.

31, 47: *Jegar-sahadutha:* an Aramaic term meaning "mound of witness." *Galeed:* in Hebrew, *galed,* with the same meaning; also offers an explanation of the regional name Gilead.

31, 49: *Mizpah:* a town in Gilead; cf Jgs 10, 17; 11, 11. 34; Hos 5, 1. The Hebrew name *mispa* ("lookout") is allied to *yisep yhwh* ("may the Lord keep watch"), and also echoes the word *masseba* ("memorial pillar").

way. Then God's messengers encountered Jacob. [3] When he saw them he said, "This is God's encampment." So he named that place Mahanaim.*

Embassy to Esau. [4] Jacob sent messengers ahead to his brother Esau in the land of Seir, the country of Edom,[z] [5] with this message: "Thus shall you say to my lord Esau: 'Your servant Jacob speaks as follows: I have been staying with Laban and have been detained there until now. [6] I own cattle, asses and sheep, as well as male and female servants. I am sending my lord this information in the hope of gaining your favor.' " [7] When the messengers returned to Jacob, they said, "We reached your brother Esau. He is now coming to meet you, accompanied by four hundred men."

[8] Jacob was very much frightened. In his anxiety, he divided the people who were with him, as well as his flocks, herds, and camels, into two camps. [9] "If Esau should attack and overwhelm one camp," he reasoned, "the remaining camp may still survive." [10] Then he prayed, "O God of my father Abraham and God of my father Isaac! You told me, O LORD, 'Go back to the land of your birth, and I will be good to you.'[a] [11] I am unworthy of all the acts of kindness that you have loyally performed for your servant: although I crossed the Jordan here with nothing but my staff, I have now grown into two companies. [12] Save me, I pray, from the hand of my brother Esau! Otherwise I fear that when he comes he will strike me down and slay the mothers and children.[b] [13] You yourself said, 'I will be very good to you, and I will make your descendants like the sands of the sea, which are too numerous to count.' "

[14] After passing the night there, Jacob selected from what he had with him the following presents for his brother Esau: [15] two hundred she-goats and twenty he-goats; two hundred ewes and twenty rams; [16] thirty milch camels and their young; forty cows and ten bulls; twenty she-asses and ten he-asses. [17] He put these animals in charge of his servants, in separate droves, and he told the servants, "Go on ahead of me, but keep a space between one drove and the next." [18] To the servant in the lead he gave this instruction: "When my brother Esau meets you, he may ask

you, 'Whose man are you? Where are you going? To whom do these animals ahead of you belong?' [19] Then you shall answer, 'They belong to your brother Jacob, but they have been sent as a gift to my lord Esau; and Jacob himself is right behind us.' " [20] He gave similar instructions to the second servant and the third and to all the others who followed behind the droves, namely: "Thus and thus shall you say to Esau, when you reach him; [21] and be sure to add, 'Your servant Jacob is right behind us.' " For Jacob reasoned, "If I first appease him with gifts that precede me, then later, when I face him, perhaps he will forgive me." [22] So the gifts went on ahead of him, while he stayed that night in the camp.

Struggle with the Angel. [23] In the course of that night, however, Jacob arose, took his two wives, with the two maidservants and his eleven children, and crossed the ford of the Jabbok. [24] After he had taken them across the stream and had brought over all his possessions, [25] Jacob was left there alone. Then some man* wrestled with him until the break of dawn. [26] When the man saw that he could not prevail over him, he struck Jacob's hip at its socket, so that the hip socket was wrenched as they wrestled.[c] [27] The man then said, "Let me go, for it is daybreak." But Jacob said, "I will not let you go until you bless me." [28] "What is your name?" the man asked. He answered, "Jacob."[d] [29] Then the man said, "You shall no longer be spoken of as Jacob, but as Israel,* because you have contended with divine and human beings and have prevailed." [30] Jacob then asked him, "Do tell me your name, please." He answered, "Why should you want to know my name?" With that he bade him farewell. [31] Jacob named the place

---

z Gn 36, 6.—a Gn 31, 3.—b Gn 28, 14; 48, 16; Ex 32, 13; Heb 11, 12.—c Hos 12, 4.—d Gn 35, 10; 1 Kgs 18, 31; 2 Kgs 17, 34.

32, 3: *Mahanaim:* a town in Gilead (Jos 13, 26. 30; 21, 38; 2 Sm 2, 8; etc.). The Hebrew name means "two camps." There are other allusions to the name in vv 8. 11.

32, 25: *Some man:* a messenger of the Lord in human form, as is clear from vv 29ff.

32, 29: *Israel:* the first part of the Hebrew name *Yisrael* is given a popular explanation in the word *sarita,* "you contended"; the second part is the first syllable of *elohim,* "divine beings." The present incident, with a similar allusion to the name Israel, is referred to in Hos 12, 5, where the mysterious wrestler is explicitly called an angel.

Peniel,* "Because I have seen God face to face," he said, "yet my life has been spared."*e* ³²At sunrise, as he left Penuel, Jacob limped along because of his hip. ³³That is why, to this day, the Israelites do not eat the sciatic muscle that is on the hip socket, inasmuch as Jacob's hip socket was struck at the sciatic muscle.

CHAPTER 33

Jacob and Esau Meet. ¹Jacob looked up and saw Esau coming, accompanied by four hundred men. So he divided his children among Leah, Rachel and the two maidservants, ²putting the maids and their children first, Leah and her children next, and Rachel and Joseph last. ³He himself went on ahead of them, bowing to the ground seven times, until he reached his brother. ⁴Esau ran to meet him, embraced him, and flinging himself on his neck, kissed him as he wept.

⁵When Esau looked about, he saw the women and children. "Who are these with you?" he asked. Jacob answered, "They are the children whom God has graciously bestowed on your servant." ⁶Then the maidservants and their children came forward and bowed low; ⁷next, Leah and her children came forward and bowed low; lastly, Rachel and her children came forward and bowed low. ⁸Then Esau asked, "What did you intend with all those droves that I encountered?" Jacob answered, "It was to gain my lord's favor." ⁹"I have plenty," replied Esau; "you should keep

what is yours, brother." ¹⁰"No, I beg you!" said Jacob. "If you will do me the favor, please accept this gift from me, since to come into your presence is for me like coming into the presence of God, now that you have received me so kindly. ¹¹Do accept the present I have brought you; God has been generous toward me, and I have an abundance." Since he so urged him, Esau accepted.

¹²Then Esau said, "Let us break camp and be on our way; I will travel alongside you." ¹³But Jacob replied: "As my lord can see, the children are frail. Besides, I am encumbered with the flocks and herds, which now have sucklings; if overdriven for a single day, the whole flock will die. ¹⁴Let my lord, then, go on ahead of me, while I proceed more slowly at the pace of the livestock before me and at the pace of my children, until I join my lord in Seir." ¹⁵Esau replied, "Let me at least put at your disposal some of the men who are with me." But Jacob said, "For what reason? Please indulge me in this, my lord." ¹⁶So on the same day that Esau began his journey back to Seir, ¹⁷Jacob journeyed to Succoth. There he built a home for himself and made booths for his livestock. That is why the place was called Succoth.*

¹⁸Having thus come from Paddan-aram, Jacob arrived safely at the city of Shechem, which is in the land of Canaan, and he encamped in sight of the city.*f* ¹⁹The plot of ground on which he had pitched his tent he bought for a hundred pieces of bullion* from the descendants of Hamor, the founder of Shechem.*g* ²⁰He set up a memorial stone there and invoked "El, the God of Israel."*h*

CHAPTER 34

The Rape of Dinah. ¹ * Dinah, the daughter whom Leah had borne to Jacob, went out to visit some of the women of the land. ²When Shechem, son of Hamor the Hivite,* who was chief of the region, saw her, he seized her and lay with her by force. ³Since he was strongly attracted to Dinah, daughter of Jacob, indeed was really in love with the girl, he endeavored to win her affection. ⁴Shechem also asked his father Hamor, "Get me this girl for a wife."

⁵Meanwhile, Jacob heard that Shechem had defiled his daughter Dinah; but since

---

e Jgs 13, 22.—f Gn 12, 6; Jn 4, 6.—g Jos 24, 32; Jn 4, 5; Acts 7, 16.—h Jgs 6, 24.

32, 31: *Peniel:* a variant of the word Penuel (v 32), the name of a town on the north bank of the Jabbok in Gilead (Jgs 8, 8f. 17; 1 Kgs 12, 25). The name is explained as meaning "the face of God," *peni-el.* Yet *my life has been spared:* see note on Gn 16, 13.

33, 17: *Succoth:* an important town near the confluence of the Jabbok and the Jordan (Jos 13, 27; Jgs 8, 5-16; 1 Kgs 7, 46). *Booths:* in Hebrew, *sukkot,* of the same sound as the name of the town.

33, 19: *Pieces of bullion:* in Hebrew, *kesita,* a monetary unit of which the value is now unknown. *Descendants of Hamor:* Hamorites, "the men of Hamor"; cf Jgs 9, 28. Hamor was regarded as the eponymous ancestor of the pre-Israelite inhabitants of Shechem.

34, 1-31: Behind the story of the rape of Dinah and the revenge of Jacob's sons on the men of the city of Shechem there probably lies a dimly recollected historical event connected with an armed conflict between the earliest Israelite tribes invading central Canaan and the Hurrian inhabitants of the Shechem region.

34, 2: *Hivite:* the Greek text has "Horite"; the terms were apparently used indiscriminately to designate the Hurrian or other non-Semitic elements in Palestine.

his sons were out in the fields with his livestock, he held his peace until they came home. [6] Now Hamor, the father of Shechem, went out to discuss the matter with Jacob, [7] just as Jacob's sons were coming in from the fields. When they heard the news, the men were shocked and seethed with indignation. What Shechem had done was an outrage in Israel; such a thing could not be tolerated.[i]

[8] Hamor appealed to them, saying, "My son Shechem has his heart set on your daughter. Please give her to him in marriage. [9] Intermarry with us; give your daughters to us, and take our daughters for yourselves. [10] Thus you can live among us. The land is open before you; you can settle and move about freely in it, and acquire landed property here." [11] Then Shechem, too, appealed to Dinah's father and brothers: "Do me this favor, and I will pay whatever you demand of me. [12] No matter how high you set the bridal price, I will pay you whatever you ask; only give me the maiden in marriage."

Revenge of Jacob's Sons. [13] Jacob's sons replied to Shechem and his father Hamor with guile, speaking as they did because their sister Dinah had been defiled. [14] "We could not do such a thing," they said, "as to give our sister to an uncircumcised man; that would be a disgrace for us. [15] We will agree with you only on this condition, that you become like us by having every male among you circumcised. [16] Then we will give you our daughters and take yours in marriage; we will settle among you and become one kindred people with you. [17] But if you do not comply with our terms regarding circumcision, we will take our daughter and go away."

[18] Their proposal seemed fair to Hamor and his son Shechem. [19] The young man lost no time in acting in the matter, since he was deeply in love with Jacob's daughter. Moreover, he was more highly respected than anyone else in his clan. [20] So Hamor and his son Shechem went to their town counsel and thus presented the matter to their fellow townsmen: [21] "These men are friendly toward us. Let them settle in the land and move about in it freely; there is ample room in the country for them. We can marry their daughters and give our daughters to them in marriage. [22] But the men will agree to live with us and form one kindred people with us only

on this condition, that every male among us be circumcised as they themselves are. [23] Would not the livestock they have acquired—all their animals—then be ours? Let us, therefore, give in to them, so that they may settle among us."

[24] All the able-bodied men of the town* agreed with Hamor and his son Shechem, and all the males, including every able-bodied man in the community, were circumcised. [25] On the third day, while they were still in pain, Dinah's full brothers Simeon and Levi, two of Jacob's sons, took their swords, advanced against the city without any trouble, and massacred all the males.[j] [26] After they had put Hamor and his son Shechem to the sword, they took Dinah from Shechem's house and left.[k] [27] Then the other sons of Jacob followed up the slaughter and sacked the city in reprisal for their sister Dinah's defilement. [28] They seized their flocks, herds and asses, whatever was in the city and in the country around. [29] They carried off all their wealth, their women, and their children, and took for loot whatever was in the houses.[l]

[30] Jacob said to Simeon and Levi: "You have brought trouble upon me by making me loathsome to the inhabitants of the land, the Canaanites and the Perizzites. I have so few men that, if these people unite against me and attack me, I and my family will be wiped out." [31] But they retorted, "Should our sister have been treated like a harlot?"

CHAPTER 35

Bethel Revisited. [1] God said to Jacob: "Go up now to Bethel. Settle there and build an altar there to the God who appeared to you while you were fleeing from your brother Esau."[m] [2] So Jacob told his family and all the others who were with him: "Get rid of the foreign gods* that you have among you; then purify yourselves and put on fresh clothes. [3] We are now to go up to Bethel, and I will build an

---

i 2 Sm 13, 12.—j Gn 49, 6.—k Jdt 9, 2.—l 9, 3f.—m Gn 28, 12f.

34, 24: *Every able-bodied man in the community:* literally "all those who go out at the gate of the city," apparently meaning the men who go out to war. By temporarily crippling them through circumcision, Jacob's sons deprived the city of its defenders.

35, 2: *Foreign gods:* pagan images, including household idols (see note on Gn 31, 19), that Jacob's people brought with them from Paddan-aram.

JACOB'S JOURNEY TO PADDAN-ARAM

CARAVAN OF BEDOUIN NOMADS — Such caravans still cross the desert today, reminiscent of "Jacob's company" in the time of the Patriarchs. This caravan was organized to lead a clan to a new home. (See Gn 31, 17ff)

Matson Photo Service

JACOB'S JOURNEY TO PADDAN-ARAM (Gn 27, 46—35, 29) — **(a)** Jacob sets out from **Beer-sheba** for **Haran** in Paddan-aram (Mesopotamia). He has his vison at **Bethel** (28, 10. 22). **(b)** In Paddan-aram Jacob meets Rachel and remains there fourteen years to be able to marry her; then he prolongs his stay with Laban her father (29—30). **(c)** At the Lord's command Jacob decides to return to **Canaan** with his family (31, 18-21). **(d)** In **Gilead**, Laban overtakes Jacob and the two draw up a peace pact at **Galeed** and **Mizpah** (31, 22—32, 1). **(e)** At **Mahanaim** Jacob encounters God's messengers and sends messengers ahead to Esau in the land of **Seir**, in **Edom** (32, 2-5). **(f)** At the **River Jabbok** Jacob struggles with the Angel (naming the place **Penuel**; he meets Esau and goes on to **Succoth** (32, 23—33, 17). **(g)** At **Shechem** Jacob reaches **Caanan** and sets up a memorial stone to "El, the God of Israel." Dinah is raped and avenged by Jacob's sons (34, 1-31). **(h)** Jacob and his family return to **Bethel,** and build an altar. On the way to **Ephrath** (Bethlehem) Rachel dies. Israel pitches his tent beyond **Migdal-eder.** Jacob arrives home at **Kiriath-arba** (Hebron). Death of Isaac (35, 29).

THE EXODUS FROM EGYPT (c 1230: Ex 12, 37—15, 21) — **(a)** The Israelites set out from **Rameses** for **Succoth** with their livestock (12, 37). **(b)** God does not lead them by way of the Philistines' land, but by the desert near the **Red Sea**. They set out from **Succoth** and encamp at **Etham** on the edge of the desert (13, 17-20). **(c)** Following God's command, the people encamp before **Pi-hahiroth**, between **Migdol** and the sea, in front of **Baal-zephon**. There the Egyptians overtake them (14, 1-9). **(d)** The Lord sweeps the sea with a strong east wind throughout the night and turns it into dry land. The Israelites cross over but when the Egyptians try to follow the waters flow back over them (14, 21-31).

EXODUS

Succoth

Etham

BITTER LAKES

EGYPT

0   10   20
Miles

Pi-hahiroth

Migdol
Baal-zephon

Rameses

Pithom

Succoth

Etham

E G Y P T

M I D I A N

SEA OF REEDS

FLIGHT OF MOSES

HOREB

0   50   100
Miles

THE FLIGHT OF MOSES (Ex 1, 1—12, 36) — **(a)** Oppression of Israel in Egypt; the people build the store-cities of **Pithom** and **Rameses;** birth of Moses and his flight into **Midian** (1, 1—2, 25). **(b)** On the mountain of God, **Horeb,** the Lord appears to Moses, reveals the Divine Name ("I am who am") to him, and gives him the mission of delivering Israel (3, 1—4, 17). **(c)** Moses returns from **Midian,** and at God's command sets out for **Egypt;** at the **mountain of God,** he meets his brother Aaron and both return to **Egypt** (4, 18-31). **(d)** Moses before Pharaoh: the ten plagues; permission to leave Egypt (5, 1—12, 36).

altar there to the God who answered me in my hour of distress and who has been with me wherever I have gone." [4] They therefore handed over to Jacob all the foreign gods in their possession and also the rings* they had in their ears. [5] Then, as they set out, a terror from God fell upon the towns round about, so that no one pursued the sons of Jacob.

[6] Thus Jacob and all the people who were with him arrived in Luz [that is, Bethel] in the land of Canaan. [n] [7] There he built an altar and named the place Bethel, for it was there that God had revealed himself to him when he was fleeing from his brother. [o]

[8] Death came to Rebekah's nurse Deborah; she was buried under the oak below Bethel, and so it was called Allon-bacuth.*

[9] On Jacob's arrival from Paddan-aram, God appeared to him again and blessed him. [10] God said to him:

"You whose name is Jacob
    shall no longer be called Jacob,
but Israel shall be your name." [p]

Thus he was named Israel. [11] God also said to him:

"I am God Almighty;
    be fruitful and multiply.
A nation, indeed an assembly of nations,

n Gn 28, 19; Jos 18, 13; Jgs 1, 22f.—o Gn 28, 12f.—p 1 Kgs 18, 31; 2 Kgs 17, 34.—q Ex 32, 13; Heb 11, 9.—r Gn 28, 18; 31, 45.—s Gn 48, 7; 1 Sm 10, 2; Mi 5, 2.—t Gn 49, 4; 1 Chr 5, 1.

35, 4: *Rings:* earrings were often worn as amulets connected with pagan magic.

35, 8: This verse may have stood originally in some other context. Rebekah's nurse is spoken of without a name, in Gn 24, 59. *Allon-bacuth:* the Hebrew name means "oak of weeping."

35, 18: *Ben-oni:* means either "son of my vigor" or, more likely in the context, "son of affliction." *Benjamin:* "son of the right hand." This may be interpreted to signify a son who is his father's help and support, but more likely its original meaning was "southerner." In the Hebrew idiom, the south lies to one's right hand, and Benjamin was the southernmost of the Rachel tribes.

35, 19: *Bethlehem:* the gloss comes from a later tradition that identified the site with Bethlehem, also called Ephrath or Ephratha (Jos 15, 59; Ru 4, 11; Mi 5, 1). But Rachel's grave was actually near Ramah (Jer 31, 15), a few miles north of Jerusalem, in the territory of Benjamin (1 Sm 10, 2).

35, 24ff: Benjamin is here said to have been born in *Paddanaram,* either because all twelve sons of Jacob are considered as a unit, or because the Priestly source, from which vv 23-29 are taken, follows a tradition different from that of the Elohistic source found in vv 16-20.

36, 2-14: The names of Esau's wives and of their fathers given here differ considerably from those their names cited from other old sources in Gn 26, 34 and 28, 9. *Zibeon the Hivite:* in v 20 he is called a "Horite"; see note on Gn 34, 2.

shall stem from you,
    and kings shall issue from your loins.
[12] The land I once gave
    to Abraham and Isaac
    I now give to you;
And to your descendants after you
    will I give this land." [q]

[13] Then God departed from him. [14] On the site where God had spoken with him, Jacob set up a memorial stone, and upon it he made a libation and poured out oil. [r] [15] Jacob named the site Bethel, because God had spoken with him there.

Jacob's Family. [16] Then they departed from Bethel; but while they still had some distance to go on the way to Ephrath, Rachel began to be in labor and to suffer great distress. [17] When her pangs were most severe, her midwife said to her, "Have no fear! This time, too, you have a son." [18] With her last breath—for she was at the point of death—she called him Benoni;* his father, however, named him Benjamin. [19] [s] Thus Rachel died; and she was buried on the road to Ephrath [that is, Bethlehem].* [20] Jacob set up a memorial stone on her grave, and the same monument marks Rachel's grave to this day.

[21] Israel moved on and pitched his tent beyond Migdal-eder. [22] While Israel was encamped in that region, Reuben went and lay with Bilhah, his father's concubine. When Israel heard of it, he was greatly offended. [t] The sons of Jacob were now twelve. [23] The sons of Leah: Reuben, Jacob's firstborn, Simeon, Levi, Judah, Issachar, and Zebulun; [24] * the sons of Rachel: Joseph and Benjamin; [25] the sons of Rachel's maid Bilhah: Dan and Naphtali; [26] the sons of Leah's maid Zilpah: Gad and Asher. These are the sons of Jacob who were born to him in Paddan-aram.

[27] Jacob went home to his father Isaac at Mamre, in Kiriath-arba [that is, Hebron], where Abraham and Isaac had stayed. [28] The lifetime of Isaac was one hundred and eighty years; [29] then he breathed his last. After a full life, he died as an old man and was taken to his kinsmen. His sons Esau and Jacob buried him.

CHAPTER 36

Edomite Lists. [1] These are the descendants of Esau [that is, Edom]. [2] * Esau took his wives from among the Canaanite women: Adah, daughter of Elon the Hittite; Oholibamah, granddaughter through Anah of Zibeon the Hivite;[u] [3]and Basemath, daughter of Ishmael and sister of Nebaioth. [4]Adah bore Eliphaz to Esau; Basemath bore Reuel;[v] [5]and Oholibamah bore Jeush, Jalam and Korah. These are the sons of Esau who were born to him in the land of Canaan.[w]

[6]Esau took his wives, his sons, his daughters, and all the members of his household, as well as his livestock comprising various animals and all the property he had acquired in the land of Canaan, and went to the land of Seir, out of the way of his brother Jacob.[x] [7]Their possessions had become too great for them to dwell together, and the land in which they were staying could not support them because of their livestock. [8]So Esau settled in the highlands of Seir. [Esau is Edom.][y] [9]These are the descendants of Esau, ancestor of the Edomites, in the highlands of Seir.

[10]These are the names of Esau's sons: Eliphaz, son of Esau's wife Adah; and Reuel, son of Esau's wife Basemath. [11] [z] The sons of Eliphaz were Teman, Omar, Zepho, Gatam and Kenaz. [12](Esau's son Eliphaz had a concubine Timna, and she bore Amalek to Eliphaz.) These are the descendants of Esau's wife Adah. [13]The sons of Reuel were Nahath, Zerah, Shammah and Mizzah. These are the descendants of Esau's wife Basemath.[a] [14]The descendants of Esau's wife Oholibamah—granddaughter through Anah of Zibeon—whom she bore to Esau were Jeush, Jalam and Korah.[b]

[15]The following are the clans of Esau's descendants. The descendants of Eliphaz, Esau's first-born: the clans of Teman, Omar, Zepho, Kenaz, [16]Korah, Gatam and Amalek. These are the clans of Eliphaz in the land of Edom; they are descended from Adah. [17]The descendants of Esau's son Reuel: the clans of Nahath, Zerah, Shammah and Mizzah. These are the clans of Reuel in the land of Edom; they are descended from Esau's wife Basemath. [18]The descendants of Esau's wife Oholibamah: the clans of Jeush, Jalam and Korah. These are the clans of Esau's wife Oholibamah, daughter of Anah. [19]Such are the descendants of Esau [that is, Edom] according to their clans.

[20]The following are the descendants of Seir the Horite,* the original settlers in the land: Lotan, Shobal, Zibeon, Anah,[c] [21]Dishon, Ezer and Dishan; they are the Horite clans descended from Seir, in the land of Edom. [22] [d] Lotan's descendants were Hori and Hemam, and Lotan's sister was Timna. [23]Shobal's descendants were Alvan, Mahanath, Ebal, Shepho and Onam. [24]Zibeon's descendants were Aiah and Anah. (He is the Anah who found water in the desert while he was pasturing the asses of his father Zibeon.) [25]The descendants of Anah were Dishon and Oholibamah, daughter of Anah. [26]The descendants of Dishon were Hemdan, Eshban, Ithran and Cheran. [27]The descendants of Ezer were Bilhan, Zaavan and Akan. [28]The descendants of Dishan were Uz and Aran. [29]These are the Horite clans: the clans of Lotan, Shobal, Zibeon, Anah, [30]Dishon, Ezer and Dishan; they were the clans of the Horites, clan by clan, in the land of Seir.

[31] [e] The following are the kings who reigned in the land of Edom before any king reigned over the Israelites.* [32]Bela, son of Beor, became king in Edom; the name of his city was Dinhabah. [33]When Bela died, Jobab, son of Zerah, from Bozrah, succeeded him as king. [34]When Jobab died, Husham, from the land of the Temanites, succeeded him as king. He defeated the Midianites in the country of Moab; the name of his city was Avith. [35]When Husham died, Hadad, son of Bedad, succeeded him as king. [36]When Hadad died, Samlah, from Masrekah, succeeded him as king. [37]When Samlah died, Shaul, from Rehoboth-on-the-River, succeeded him as king. [38]When Shaul died, Baal-hanan, son of Achbor, succeeded him as king. [39]When Baal-hanan died, Hadar succeeded him as king; the name of his city was Pau. (His wife's name was Mehetabel; she was the daughter of Matred, son of Mezahab.)

[40]The following are the names of the clans of Esau individually according to

---

u Gn 26, 34.—v 1 Chr 1, 35.—w 1 Chr 1, 35.—x Gn 32, 4.—y Dt 2, 4f; Jos 24, 4.—z 11f: 1 Chr 1, 36.—a 1 Chr 1, 37.—b 1 Chr 1, 35.—c 20f: 1 Chr 1, 38.—d 22-28: 1 Chr 1, 39-42.—e 31-43: 1 Chr 1, 43-54.

36, 20: *Seir the Horite:* according to Dt 2, 12, the highlands of Seir were inhabited by Horites before they were occupied by the Edomites.

36, 31: *Before any king reigned over the Israelites:* obviously this statement was written after the time of Saul, Israel's first king.

their subdivisions and localities: the clans of Timna, Alvah, Jetheth, [41] Oholibamah, Elah, Pinon, [42] Kenaz, Teman, Mibzar, [43] Magdiel and Iram. These are the clans of the Edomites, according to their settlements in their territorial holdings. [Esau was the father of the Edomites.]

IV: JOSEPH AND HIS BROTHERS

CHAPTER 37

Joseph Sold into Egypt. [1] Jacob settled in the land where his father had stayed, the land of Canaan. [2] This is his family history. When Joseph was seventeen years old, he was tending the flocks with his brothers; he was an assistant to the sons of his father's wives Bilhah and Zilpah and he brought his father bad reports about them.

[3] Israel loved Joseph best of all his sons, for he was the child of his old age; and he had made him a long tunic. [4] When his brothers saw that their father loved him best of all his sons, they hated him so much that they would not even greet him.

[5] Once Joseph had a dream, which he told to his brothers:[f] [6] "Listen to this dream I had. [7] There we were, binding sheaves in the field, when suddenly my sheaf rose to an upright position, and your sheaves formed a ring around my sheaf and bowed down to it." [8] "Are you really going to make yourself king over us?" his brothers asked him. "Or impose your rule on us?" So they hated him all the more because of his talk about his dreams.[g]

[9] Then he had another dream, and this one, too, he told to his brothers. "I had another dream," he said; "this time, the sun and the moon and eleven stars were bowing down to me." [10] When he also told it to his father, his father reproved him. "What is the meaning of this dream of yours?" he asked. "Can it be that I and your mother and your brothers are to come and bow to the ground before you?" [11] So his brothers were wrought up against him but his father pondered the matter.

[12] One day, when his brothers had gone to pasture their father's flocks at Shechem, [13] Israel said to Joseph, "Your brothers, you know, are tending our flocks at Shechem. Get ready; I will send you to them." "I am ready," Joseph answered. [14] "Go then," he replied; "see if all is well with your brothers and the flocks, and bring back word." So he sent him off from the valley of Hebron. When Joseph reached Shechem, [15] a man met him as he was wandering about in the fields. "What are you looking for?" the man asked him. [16] "I am looking for my brothers," he answered. "Could you please tell me where they are tending the flocks?" [17] The man told him, "They have moved on from here; in fact, I heard them say, 'Let us go on to Dothan.' " So Joseph went after his brothers and caught up with them in Dothan. [18] They noticed him from a distance, and before he came up to them, they plotted to kill him. [19] They said to one another: "Here comes that master dreamer! [20] Come on, let us kill him and throw him into one of the cisterns here; we could say that a wild beast devoured him. We shall then see what comes of his dreams."[h]

[21] * When Reuben heard this, he tried to save him from their hands, saying, "We must not take his life. [22] Instead of shedding blood," he continued, "just throw him into that cistern there in the desert; but don't kill him outright." His purpose was to rescue him from their hands and restore him to his father.[i] [23] So when Joseph came up to them, they stripped him of the long tunic he had on; [24] then they took him and threw him into the cistern, which was empty and dry.

[25] They then sat down to their meal. Looking up, they saw a caravan of Ishmaelites coming from Gilead, their camels laden with gum, balm and resin to be taken down to Egypt.[j] [26] Judah said to his brothers: "What is to be gained by killing our brother and concealing his blood?[k] [27] Rather, let us sell him to these Ishmaelites, instead of doing away with him ourselves. After all, he is our brother, our own flesh." His brothers agreed.

f Gn 42, 9.—g Gn 50, 17.—h Gn 44, 28.—i Gn 42, 22.—j Gn 43, 11.—k Jb 16, 18.

37, 21-36: The chapter thus far is from the Yahwist source, as are also vv 25-28a. But vv 21-24 and 28b-36 are from the Elohist source. In the latter, Reuben tries to rescue Joseph, who is taken in Reuben's absence by certain Midianites; in the Yahwist source, it is Judah who saves Joseph's life by having him sold to certain Ishmaelites. Although the two variant forms in which the story was handed down in early oral tradition differ in these minor points, they agree on the essential fact that Joseph was brought as a slave into Egypt because of the jealousy of his brothers.

[28] They sold Joseph to the Ishmaelites for twenty pieces of silver.*

Some Midianite traders passed by, and they pulled Joseph up out of the cistern and took him to Egypt.[l] [29] When Reuben went back to the cistern and saw that Joseph was not in it, he tore his clothes, [30] and returning to his brothers, he exclaimed: "The boy is gone! And I—where can I turn?" [31] They took Joseph's tunic, and after slaughtering a goat, dipped the tunic in its blood. [32] They then sent someone to bring the long tunic to their father, with the message: "We found this. See whether it is your son's tunic or not." [33] He recognized it and exclaimed: "My son's tunic! A wild beast has devoured him! Joseph has been torn to pieces!"[m] [34] Then Jacob rent his clothes, put sackcloth on his loins, and mourned his son many days. [35] Though his sons and daughters tried to console him, he refused all consolation, saying, "No, I will go down mourning to my son in the nether world." Thus did his father lament him.[n]

[36] The Midianites, meanwhile, sold Joseph in Egypt to Potiphar, a courtier of Pharaoh and his chief steward.[o]

CHAPTER 38*

Judah and Tamar. [1] About that time Judah parted from his brothers and pitched his tent near a certain Adullamite named Hirah. [2] There he met the daughter of a Canaanite named Shua, married her, and had relations with her.[p] [3] She conceived and bore a son, whom she named Er. [4] Again she conceived and bore a son, whom she named Onan. [5] Then she bore still another son, whom she named Shelah. They were in Chezib* when he was born.[q]

[6] Judah got a wife named Tamar for his first-born, Er. [7] But Er, Judah's first-born, greatly offended the LORD; so the LORD took his life.[r] [8][s] Then Judah said to Onan, "Unite with your brother's widow, in fulfillment of your duty as brother-in-law, and thus preserve your brother's line."* [9] Onan, however, knew that the descendants would not be counted as his; so whenever he had relations with his brother's widow, he wasted his seed on the ground, to avoid contributing offspring for his brother. [10] What he did greatly offended the LORD, and the LORD took his life too. [11] Thereupon Judah said to his daughter-in-law Tamar, "Stay as a widow in your father's house until my son Shelah grows up"—for he feared that Shelah also might die like his brothers. So Tamar went to live in her father's house.

[12] Years passed, and Judah's wife, the daughter of Shua, died. After Judah completed the period of mourning, he went up to Timnah for the shearing of his sheep, in company with his friend Hirah the Adullamite. [13] When Tamar was told that her father-in-law was on his way up to Timnah to shear his sheep, [14] she took off her widow's garb, veiled her face by covering herself with a shawl, and sat down at the entrance to Enaim, which is on the way to Timnah; for she was aware that, although Shelah was now grown up, she had not been given to him in marriage.[t] [15] When Judah saw her, he mistook her for a harlot, since she had covered her face. [16] So he went over to her at the roadside, and not realizing that she was his daughter-in-law, he said, "Come, let me have intercourse with you." She replied, "What will you pay me for letting you have intercourse with me?" [17] He answered, "I will send you a kid from the flock." "Very well," she said, "provided you leave a pledge until you send it." [18] Judah asked, "What pledge am I to give you?" She answered, "Your seal and cord,* and the staff you carry." So he gave them to her and had intercourse with her, and she conceived by

---

[l] Ps 105, 17; Wis 10, 13; Acts 7, 9.—[m] Gn 44, 28.—[n] Gn 42, 38.—[o] Ps 105, 17.—[p] 1 Chr 2, 3.—[q] 1 Chr 4, 21.—[r] 1 Chr 2, 3.—[s] Dt 25, 5; Mt 22, 24; Mk 12, 19; Lk 20, 28.—[t] Prv 7, 10.

37, 28: *They sold Joseph . . . silver:* in the Hebrew text, these words occur between *out of the cistern* and *and (they) took him to Egypt* at the end of the verse.

38, 1-30: This chapter, from the Yahwist source, has nothing to do with the Joseph story in which Judah is still living with his father and brothers. The sacred author inserted this independent account from the life of Judah at this place to mark the long lapse of time during which Joseph's family knew nothing of his life in Egypt. This is apparently a personalized history of the early days of the tribe of Judah, which interbred with several Canaanite clans, though some of these soon became extinct.

38, 5: *Chezib:* a variant form of Achzib (Jos 15, 44; Mi 1, 14), a town in the Judean Shephelah.

38, 8: *Preserve your brother's line:* literally, "raise up seed for your brother." The ancient Israelites regarded as very important their law of levirate, or "brother-in-law" marriage; see notes on Dt 25, 5; Ru 2, 20. In the present story, it is primarily Onan's violation of this law, rather than the means he used to circumvent it, that brought on him God's displeasure (vv 9f).

38, 18: *Seal and cord:* the cylinder seal, through which a hole was bored lengthwise so that it could be worn from the neck by a cord, was a distinctive means of identification. Apparently a man's staff was also marked with his name (Nm 17, 16f) or other sign of identification.

him. [19] When she went away, she took off her shawl and put on her widow's garb again.

[20] Judah sent the kid by his friend the Adullamite to recover the pledge from the woman; but he could not find her. [21] So he asked the men of the place, "Where is the temple prostitute,* the one by the roadside in Enaim?" But they answered, "There has never been a temple prostitute here." [22] He went back to Judah and told him, "I could not find her; and besides, the men of the place said there was no temple prostitute there." [23] "Let her keep the things," Judah replied; "otherwise we shall become a laughingstock. After all, I did send her the kid, even though you were unable to find her."

[24] About three months later, Judah was told that his daughter-in-law Tamar had played the harlot and was then with child from her harlotry. "Bring her out," cried Judah; "she shall be burned." [25] But as they were bringing her out, she sent word to her father-in-law, "It is by the man to whom these things belong that I am with child. Please verify," she added, "whose seal and cord and whose staff these are." [26] Judah recognized them and said, "She is more in the right than I am, since I did not give her to my son Shelah." But he had no further relations with her.

[27] When the time of her delivery came, she was found to have twins in her womb. [u] [28] While she was giving birth, one infant put out his hand; and the midwife, taking a crimson thread, tied it on his hand, to note that this one came out first. [29] [v] But as he withdrew his hand, his brother came out; and she said, "What a breach you have made for yourself!" So he was called Perez.* [30] Afterward his brother came out; he was called Zerah. [w] *

CHAPTER 39

Joseph's Temptation. [1] When Joseph was taken down to Egypt, a certain Egyptian (Potiphar, a courtier of Pharaoh and his chief steward*) bought him from the Ishmaelites who had brought him there. [2] [x] But since the LORD was with him, Joseph got on very well and was assigned to the household of his Egyptian master. [3] When his master saw that the LORD was with him and brought him success in whatever he did, [4] he took a liking to Joseph and made him his personal attendant; he put him in charge of his household and entrusted to him all his possessions. [y] [5] From the moment that he put him in charge of his household and all his possessions, the LORD blessed the Egyptian's house for Joseph's sake; in fact, the LORD's blessing was on everything he owned, both inside the house and out. [6] Having left everything he owned in Joseph's charge, he gave no thought, with Joseph there, to anything but the food he ate.

Now Joseph was strikingly handsome in countenance and body. [7] After a time, his master's wife began to look fondly at him and said, "Lie with me." [8] But he refused. "As long as I am here," he told her, "my master does not concern himself with anything in the house, but has entrusted to me all he owns. [9] He wields no more authority in this house than I do, and he has withheld from me nothing but yourself, since you are his wife. How, then, could I commit so great a wrong and thus stand condemned before God?" [10] Although she tried to entice him day after day, he would not agree to lie beside her, or even stay near her. [z]

[11] One such day, when Joseph came into the house to do his work, and none of the household servants were then in the house, [12] she laid hold of him by his cloak, saying, "Lie with me!" But leaving the cloak in her hand, he got away from her and ran outside. [13] When she saw that he had left his cloak in her hand as he fled outside, [14] she screamed for her household servants

u 1 Chr 2, 4.—v Rv 4, 12; Mt 1, 3; Lk 3, 33.—w Nm 26, 20; 1 Chr 2, 4; Mt 1, 3.—x 1 Sm 3, 19; 10, 7; 18, 14; 2 Sm 5, 10; 2 Kgs 18, 7; Acts 7, 9.—y Dn 1, 9.—z 1 Mc 2, 53.

38, 21: *Temple prostitute:* the Hebrew term *qedesha,* literally "consecrated woman," designates a woman who had ritual intercourse with men in pagan fertility rites; cf Dt 23, 18; Hos 4, 14, where the same Hebrew word is used. Hirah the Adullamite uses a word that refers to a higher social class than that designated by the term *zona,* common "harlot," used in vv 15. 24.

38, 29: *He was called Perez:* the Hebrew word means "breach."

38, 30: *He was called Zerah:* a name connected here by popular etymology with a Hebrew verb for the red light of dawn, alluding apparently to the crimson thread.

39, 1: *(Potiphar . . . chief steward):* These words in the text serve to harmonize ch 39 from the Yahwist source, with Gn 37, 36 and 40, 1-23, from the Elohist. In the former, the Ishmaelites who bought Joseph from his brothers (Gn 37, 28) sold him to the unnamed "Egyptian master" of ch 39. In the latter, the Midianites who kidnaped Joseph (Gn 37, 28; 40, 15) sold him to Potiphar, Pharaoh's chief steward (Gn 37, 36), whose house was used as a royal prison (Gn 40, 2f).

and told them, "Look! my husband has brought in a Hebrew slave to make sport of us! He came in here to lie with me, but I cried out as loud as I could. 15 When he heard me scream for help, he left his cloak beside me and ran away outside."

16 She kept the cloak with her until his master came home. 17 Then she told him the same story: "The Hebrew slave whom you brought here broke in on me, to make sport of me. 18 But when I screamed for help, he left his cloak beside me and fled outside." 19 As soon as the master heard his wife's story about how his slave had treated her, he became enraged. 20 He seized Joseph and threw him into the jail where the royal prisoners were confined. *a*

But even while he was in prison, 21 the LORD remained with Joseph; he showed him kindness by making the chief jailer well-disposed toward him. *b* 22 The chief jailer put Joseph in charge of all the prisoners in the jail, and everything that had to be done there was done under his management. 23 The chief jailer did not concern himself with anything at all that was in Joseph's charge, since the LORD was with him and brought success to all he did.

CHAPTER 40

The Dreams Interpreted. 1 Some time afterward, the royal cupbearer and baker gave offense to their lord, the king of Egypt. 2 Pharaoh was angry with his two courtiers, the chief cupbearer and the chief baker, 3 and he put them in custody in the house of the chief steward (the same jail where Joseph was confined). 4 The chief steward assigned Joseph to them, and he became their attendant.

After they had been in custody for some time, 5 the cupbearer and the baker of the king of Egypt who were confined in the jail both had dreams on the same night, each dream with its own meaning. 6 When Joseph came to them in the morning, he noticed that they looked disturbed. 7 So he asked Pharaoh's courtiers who were with him in custody in his master's house, "Why do you look so sad today?" 8 They answered him, "We have had dreams, but there is no one to interpret them for

us." Joseph said to them, "Surely, interpretations come from God. Please tell the dreams to me." *c*

9 Then the chief cupbearer told Joseph his dream. "In my dream," he said, "I saw a vine in front of me, 10 and on the vine were three branches. It had barely budded when its blossoms came out, and its clusters ripened into grapes. 11 Pharaoh's cup was in my hand; so I took the grapes, pressed them out into his cup, and put it in Pharaoh's hand." 12 Joseph said to him: "This is what it means. The three branches are three days; 13 within three days Pharaoh will lift up your head* and restore you to your post. You will be handing Pharaoh his cup as you formerly used to do when you were his cupbearer. 14 So if you will still remember, when all is well with you, that I was here with you, please do me the favor of mentioning me to Pharaoh, to get me out of this place. 15 The truth is that I was kidnaped from the land of the Hebrews, and here I have not done anything for which I should have been put into a dungeon."

16 When the chief baker saw that Joseph had given this favorable interpretation, he said to him: "I too had a dream. In it I had three wicker baskets on my head; 17 in the top one were all kinds of bakery products for Pharaoh, but the birds were pecking at them out of the basket on my head." 18 Joseph said to him in reply: "This is what it means. The three baskets are three days; 19 within three days Pharaoh will lift up your head and have you impaled on a stake, and the birds will be pecking the flesh from your body."

20 And in fact, on the third day, which was Pharaoh's birthday, when he gave a banquet to all his staff, with his courtiers around him, he lifted up the heads of the chief cupbearer and chief baker. 21 He restored the chief cupbearer to his office, so that he again handed the cup to Pharaoh; 22 but the chief baker he impaled—just as Joseph had told them in his interpretation. 23 Yet the chief cupbearer gave no thought to Joseph; he had forgotten him.

---

a Ps 105, 18.—b Acts 7, 9f.—c Gn 41, 16.

40, 13: *Lift up your head:* signifying "pardon you." In v 19 "to lift up the head" means "to behead"; and finally, in v 20, the same expression means "to review the case (of someone)." Joseph couches his interpretation of the dreams in equivocal terms.

CHAPTER 41

Pharaoh's Dream. [1]After a lapse of two years, Pharaoh had a dream. He saw himself standing by the Nile, [2]when up out of the Nile came seven cows, handsome and fat; they grazed in the reed grass. [3]Behind them seven other cows, ugly and gaunt, came up out of the Nile; and standing on the bank of the Nile beside the others, [4]the ugly, gaunt cows ate up the seven handsome, fat cows. Then Pharaoh woke up.

[5]He fell asleep again and had another dream. He saw seven ears of grain, fat and healthy, growing on a single stalk. [6]Behind them sprouted seven ears of grain, thin and blasted by the east wind; [7]and the seven thin ears swallowed up the seven fat, healthy ears. Then Pharaoh woke up, to find it was only a dream.

[8]Next morning his spirit was agitated. So he summoned all the magicians and sages of Egypt and recounted his dreams to them; but no one could interpret his dreams for him. [9]Then the chief cupbearer spoke up and said to Pharaoh: "On this occasion I am reminded of my negligence. [10]Once, when Pharaoh was angry, he put me and the chief baker in custody in the house of the chief steward. [11]Later, we both had dreams on the same night, and each of our dreams had its own meaning. [12]There with us was a Hebrew youth, a slave of the chief steward; and when we told him our dreams, he interpreted them for us and explained for each of us the meaning of his dream.[d] [13]And it turned out just as he had told us: I was restored to my post, but the other man was impaled."

[14]Pharaoh therefore had Joseph summoned, and they hurriedly brought him from the dungeon. After he shaved and changed his clothes, he came into Pharaoh's presence.[e] [15]Pharaoh then said to him: "I had certain dreams that no one can interpret. But I hear it said of you that the moment you are told a dream you can interpret it." [16]"It is not I," Joseph replied to Pharaoh, "but God who will give Pharaoh the right answer."[f]

[17]Then Pharaoh said to Joseph: "In my dream, I was standing on the bank of the Nile, [18]when up from the Nile came seven cows, fat and well-formed; they grazed in the reed grass. [19]Behind them came seven other cows, scrawny, most ill-formed and gaunt. Never have I seen such ugly specimens as these in all the land of Egypt! [20]The gaunt, ugly cows ate up the first seven fat cows. [21]But when they had consumed them, no one could tell that they had done so, because they looked as ugly as before. Then I woke up. [22]In another dream, I saw seven ears of grain, fat and healthy, growing on a single stalk. [23]Behind them sprouted seven ears of grain, shriveled and thin and blasted by the east wind; [24]and the seven thin ears swallowed up the seven healthy ears. I have spoken to the magicians, but none of them can give me an explanation."

[25]Joseph said to Pharaoh: "Both of Pharaoh's dreams have the same meaning. God has thus foretold to Pharaoh what he is about to do. [26]The seven healthy cows are seven years, and the seven healthy ears are seven years—the same in each dream. [27]So also, the seven thin, ugly cows that came up after them are seven years, as are the seven thin, wind-blasted ears; they are seven years of famine. [28]It is just as I told Pharaoh: God has revealed to Pharaoh what he is about to do. [29]Seven years of great abundance are now coming throughout the land of Egypt; [30]but these will be followed by seven years of famine, when all the abundance in the land of Egypt will be forgotten. When the famine has ravaged the land, [31]no trace of the abundance will be found in the land because of the famine that follows it—so utterly severe will that famine be. [32]That Pharaoh had the same dream twice means that the matter has been reaffirmed by God and that God will soon bring it about.

[33]"Therefore, let Pharaoh seek out a wise and discerning man and put him in charge of the land of Egypt. [34]Pharaoh should also take action to appoint overseers, so as to regiment the land during the seven years of abundance. [35]They should husband all the food of the coming good years, collecting the grain under Pharaoh's authority, to be stored in the towns for food. [36]This food will serve as a reserve for the country against the seven years of famine that are to follow in the land of Egypt, so that the land may not perish in the famine."

---

d Dn 1, 17.—e Ps 105, 20.—f Gn 40, 8.

37 This advice pleased Pharaoh and all his officials.[g] 38 "Could we find another like him," Pharaoh asked his officials, "a man so endowed with the spirit of God?" 39 So Pharaoh said to Joseph: "Since God has made all this known to you, no one can be as wise and discerning as you are. 40 You shall be in charge of my palace, and all my people shall dart at your command. Only in respect to the throne shall I outrank you.[h] 41 Herewith," Pharaoh told Joseph, "I place you in charge of the whole land of Egypt." 42 With that, Pharaoh took off his signet ring* and put it on Joseph's finger. He had him dressed in robes of fine linen and put a gold chain about his neck. 43 He then had him ride in the chariot of his vizier, and they shouted "Abrek!"* before him.

Thus was Joseph installed over the whole land of Egypt. 44 "I, Pharaoh, proclaim," he told Joseph, "that without your approval no one shall move hand or foot in all the land of Egypt." 45 Pharaoh also bestowed the name of Zaphenath-peneah* on Joseph, and he gave him in marriage Asenath, the daughter of Potiphera, priest of Heliopolis. 46 Joseph was thirty years old when he entered the service of Pharaoh, king of Egypt.

After Joseph left Pharaoh's presence, he traveled throughout the land of Egypt. 47 During the seven years of plenty, when the land produced abundant crops, 48 he husbanded all the food of these years of plenty that the land of Egypt was enjoying and stored it in the towns, placing in each town the crops of the fields around it. 49 Joseph garnered grain in quantities like the sands of the sea, so vast that at last he stopped measuring it, for it was beyond measure.

50 Before the famine years set in, Joseph became the father of two sons, born to him by Asenath, daughter of Potiphera, priest of Heliopolis.[i] 51 He named his first-born Manasseh,* meaning, "God has made me forget entirely the sufferings I endured at the hands of my family"; 52 and the second he named Ephraim,* meaning, "God has made me fruitful in the land of my affliction."

53 When the seven years of abundance enjoyed by the land of Egypt came to an end, 54 the seven years of famine set in, just as Joseph had predicted. Although there was famine in all the other countries, food was available throughout the land of Egypt.[j] 55 When hunger came to be felt throughout the land of Egypt and the people cried to Pharaoh for bread, Pharaoh directed all the Egyptians to go to Joseph and do whatever he told them. 56 When the famine had spread throughout the land, Joseph opened all the cities that had grain and rationed it to the Egyptians, since the famine had gripped the land of Egypt. 57 In fact, all the world came to Joseph to obtain rations of grain, for famine had gripped the whole world.

CHAPTER 42

The Brothers' First Journey to Egypt.
1 When Jacob learned that grain rations were available in Egypt, he said to his sons: "Why do you keep gaping at one another? 2 I hear," he went on, "that rations of grain are available in Egypt. Go down there and buy some for us, that we may stay alive rather than die of hunger."[k] 3 So ten of Joseph's brothers went down to buy an emergency supply of grain from Egypt. 4 It was only Joseph's full brother Benjamin that Jacob did not send with the rest, for he thought some disaster might befall him. 5 Thus, since there was famine in the land of Canaan also, the sons of Israel were among those who came to procure rations.[l]

6 It was Joseph, as governor of the country, who dispensed the rations to all the people. When Joseph's brothers came and knelt down before him with their faces to

---

g Acts 7, 10.—h Ps 105, 21; Wis 10, 14; 1 Mc 2, 53; Acts 7, 10.—i Gn 46, 20; 48, 5.—j Ps 105, 16; Acts 7, 11.—k Acts 7, 12.—l Jdt 5, 10; Acts 7, 11.

41, 42: *Signet ring:* a finger ring in which was set a stamp seal, different from the cylinder seal such as Judah wore; see note on Gn 38, 18. This is an authentic detail. By receiving Pharaoh's signet ring, Joseph was made vizier of Egypt (v 43); the vizier was known as "seal-bearer of the king of Lower Egypt." Another authentic detail is the *gold chain,* a symbol of high office in ancient Egypt.

41, 43: *Abrek:* apparently a cry of homage, though the word's derivation and actual meaning are uncertain.

41, 45: *Zaphenath-paneah:* a Hebrew transcription of an Egyptian name meaning "the god speaks and he (the new-born child) lives." *Asenath:* means "belonging to (the Egyptian goddess) Neith." *Potiphera:* means "he whom Ra (the Egyptian god) gave"; a shorter form of the same name was borne by Joseph's master (Gn 37, 36). *Heliopolis:* in Hebrew, *On,* a city seven miles northeast of modern Cairo, site of the chief temple of the sun god; it is mentioned also in v 50; Gn 46, 20; Ez 30, 17.

41, 51: *Manasseh:* allusion to this name is in the Hebrew expression, *nishshani,* "he made me forget."

41, 52: *Ephraim:* related to the Hebrew expression *hiphrani,* "(God) has made me fruitful."

the ground,[m] [7] he recognized them as soon as he saw them. But he concealed his own identity from them and spoke sternly to them. "Where do you come from?" he asked them. They answered, "From the land of Canaan, to procure food."

[8] When Joseph recognized his brothers, although they did not recognize him, [9] he was reminded of the dreams he had about them. He said to them: "You are spies.[n] You have come to see the nakedness of the land."* [10] "No, my lord," they replied. "On the contrary, your servants have come to procure food. [11] All of us are sons of the same man. We are honest men; your servants have never been spies." [12] But he answered them: "Not so! You have come to see the nakedness of the land." [13] "We your servants," they said, "were twelve brothers, sons of a certain man in Canaan; but the youngest one is at present with our father, and the other one is gone."[o] [14] "It is just as I said," Joseph persisted; "you are spies. [15] This is how you shall be tested: unless your youngest brother comes here, I swear by the life of Pharaoh that you shall not leave here. [16] So send one of your number to get your brother, while the rest of you stay here under arrest. Thus shall your words be tested for their truth; if they are untrue, as Pharaoh lives, you are spies!" [17] With that, he locked them up in the guardhouse for three days.

[18] On the third day Joseph said to them: "Do this, and you shall live; for I am a God-fearing man. [19] If you have been honest, only one of your brothers need be confined in this prison, while the rest of you may go and take home provisions for your starving families. [20] But you must come back to me with your youngest brother. Your words will thus be verified, and you will not die." To this they agreed.[p] [21] To one another, however, they said: "Alas, we are being punished because of our brother. We saw the anguish of his heart when he pleaded with us, yet we paid no heed;

that is why this anguish has now come upon us."[q] [22] "Didn't I tell you," broke in Reuben, "not to do wrong to the boy? But you wouldn't listen! Now comes the reckoning for his blood."[r] [23] They did not know, of course, that Joseph understood what they said, since he spoke with them through an interpreter. [24] But turning away from them, he wept. When he was able to speak to them again, he had Simeon taken from them and bound before their eyes. [25] Then Joseph gave orders to have their containers filled with grain, their money replaced in each one's sack, and provisions given them for their journey. After this had been done for them, [26] they loaded their donkeys with the rations and departed.

[27] * At the night encampment, when one of them opened his bag to give his donkey some fodder, he was surprised to see his money in the mouth of his bag. [28] "My money has been returned!" he cried out to his brothers. "Here it is in my bag!" At that their hearts sank. Trembling, they asked one another, "What is this that God has done to us?"

[29] When they got back to their father Jacob in the land of Canaan, they told him all that had happened to them. [30] "The man who is lord of the country," they said, "spoke to us sternly and put us in custody as if we were spying on the land. [31] But we said to him: 'We are honest men; we have never been spies. [32] There were twelve of us brothers, sons of the same father; but one is gone, and the youngest one is at present with our father in the land of Canaan.' [33] Then the man who is lord of the country said to us: 'This is how I shall know if you are honest men: leave one of your brothers with me, while the rest of you go home with rations for your starving families. [34] When you come back to me with your youngest brother, and I know that you are honest men and not spies, I will restore your brother to you, and you may move about freely in the land.' "

[35] When they were emptying their sacks, there in each one's sack was his moneybag! At the sight of their moneybags, they and their father were dismayed. [36] Their father Jacob said to them: "Must you make me childless? Joseph is gone, and Simeon is gone, and now you would take away Benjamin! Why must such things always

---

m Ps 105, 21.—n Gn 37, 5.—o Gn 44, 20.—p Gn 43, 5.—q Gn 37, 18-27.—r Gn 37, 22.

42, 9. 12: *The nakedness of the land:* the military weakness of the land, like human nakedness, should not be seen by strangers.

42, 27-28: These two verses are from the Yahwist source, whereas the rest of the chapter is from the Elohist source, in which the men find the money in their sacks (not "bags"—a different Hebrew word) only when they arrive home (v 35); cf Gn 43, 21.

happen to me!" [37] Then Reuben told his father: "Put him in my care, and I will bring him back to you. You may kill my own two sons if I do not return him to you." [38] But Jacob replied: "My son shall not go down with you. Now that his full brother is dead, he is the only one left. If some disaster should befall him on the journey you must make, you would send my white head down to the nether world in grief."[s]

CHAPTER 43*

The Second Journey to Egypt. [1] Now the famine in the land grew more severe. [2] So when they had used up all the rations they had brought from Egypt, their father said to them, "Go back and procure us a little more food." [3] But Judah replied: "The man strictly warned us, 'You shall not appear in my presence unless your brother is with you.'[t] [4] If you are willing to let our brother go with us, we will go down to procure food for you. [5] But if you are not willing, we will not go down, because the man told us, 'You shall not appear in my presence unless your brother is with you.' "[u] [6] Israel demanded, "Why did you bring this trouble on me by telling the man that you had another brother?" [7] They answered: "This man kept asking about ourselves and our family: 'Is your father still living? Do you have another brother?' We had to answer his questions. How could we know that he would say, 'Bring your brother down here'?"

[8] Then Judah urged his father Israel: "Let the boy go with me, that we may be off and on our way if you and we and our children are to keep from starving to death.[v] [9] I myself will stand surety for him. You can hold me responsible for him. If I fail to bring him back, to set him in your presence, you can hold it against me forever.[w] [10] Had we not dillydallied, we could have been there and back twice by now!"

[11] Their father Israel then told them: "If it must be so, then do this: Put some of the land's best products in your baggage and take them down to the man as gifts: some balm and honey, gum and resin, and pistachios and almonds.[x] [12] Also take extra money along, for you must return the amount that was put back in the mouths of your bags; it may have been a mistake.

[13] Take your brother, too, and be off on your way back to the man. [14] May God Almighty dispose the man to be merciful toward you, so that he may let your other brother go, as well as Benjamin. As for me, if I am to suffer bereavement, I shall suffer it."

[15] So the men got the gifts, took double the amount of money with them, and, accompanied by Benjamin, were off on their way down to Egypt to present themselves to Joseph. [16] When Joseph saw Benjamin with them, he told his head steward, "Take these men into the house, and have an animal slaughtered and prepared, for they are to dine with me at noon." [17] Doing as Joseph had ordered, the steward conducted the men to Joseph's house. [18] But on being led to his house, they became apprehensive. "It must be," they thought, "on account of the money put back in our bags the first time, that we are taken inside; they want to use it as a pretext to attack us and take our donkeys and seize us as slaves." [19] So they went up to Joseph's head steward and talked to him at the entrance of the house. [20] "If you please, sir," they said, "we came down here once before to procure food.[y] [21] But when we arrived at a night's encampment and opened our bags, there was each man's money in the mouth of his bag—our money in the full amount! We have now brought it back.[z] [22] We have brought other money to procure food with. We do not know who put the first money in our bags." [23] "Be at ease," he replied; "you have no need to fear. Your God and the God of your father must have put treasures in your bags for you. As for your money, I received it." With that, he led Simeon out to them.

[24] The steward then brought the men inside Joseph's house. He gave them water to bathe their feet, and got fodder for their donkeys. [25] Then they set out their gifts to await Joseph's arrival at noon, for they had heard that they were to dine there. [26] When Joseph came home, they presented him with the gifts they had brought inside, while they bowed down before

---

s Gn 37, 35.—t Gn 44, 23.—u Gn 42, 20.—v Gn 42, 37.—w Gn 44, 32.—x Gn 45, 23.—y Gn 42, 3.—z Gn 42, 27f.

43, 1-34: This chapter and the following one are from the Yahwist source, in which Judah, not Reuben as in the Elohist source, volunteers to go surety for Benjamin.

him to the ground. [27] After inquiring how they were, he asked them, "And how is your aged father, of whom you spoke? Is he still in good health?"[a] [28] "Your servant our father is thriving and still in good health," they said, as they bowed respectfully. [29] When Joseph's eye fell on his full brother Benjamin, he asked, "Is this your youngest brother, of whom you told me?" Then he said to him, "May God be gracious to you, my boy!"[b] [30] With that, Joseph had to hurry out, for he was so overcome with affection for his brother that he was on the verge of tears. He went into a private room and wept there.

[31] After washing his face, he reappeared and, now in control of himself, gave the order, "Serve the meal." [32] It was served separately to him,* to the brothers, and to the Egyptians who partook of his board. (Egyptians may not eat with Hebrews; that is abhorrent to them.) [33] When they were seated by his directions according to their age, from the oldest to the youngest, they looked at one another in amazement; [34] and as portions were brought to them from Joseph's table, Benjamin's portion was five times as large as* anyone else's. So they drank freely and made merry with him.

CHAPTER 44

Final Test. [1] * Then Joseph gave his head steward these instructions: "Fill the men's bags, with as much food as they can carry, and put each man's money in the mouth of his bag. [2] In the mouth of the youngest one's bag put also my silver goblet, together with the money for his rations." The steward carried out Joseph's instructions. [3] At daybreak the men and their

a Tb 7, 4.—b Gn 42, 13.

43, 32: *Separately to him:* that Joseph did not eat with the other Egyptians was apparently a matter of rank.

43, 34: *Five times as large as:* probably an idiomatic expression for "much larger than."

44, 1f: Replacement of the money in the men's bags is probably a redactional addition here, taken from the Yahwist account of the first visit. It is only the goblet in Benjamin's bag, not any replaced money, that plays a part in the rest of the chapter.

44, 5: *Divination:* seeking omens through liquids poured into a cup or bowl was a common practice in the ancient Near East; cf v 15. Even though divination was frowned on in later Israel (Lv 19, 31), it is in this place an authentic touch which the sacred author does not hesitate to ascribe to Joseph, the wisest man in Egypt.

44, 16: *Guilt:* in trying to do away with Joseph when he was young.

44, 19: *My lord . . . your servants:* such frequently repeated expressions in Judah's speech show the formal court style used by a subject in speaking to a high official.

donkeys were sent off. [4] They had not gone far out of the city when Joseph said to his head steward: "Go at once after the men! When you overtake them, say to them, 'Why did you repay good with evil? Why did you steal the silver goblet from me? [5] It is the very one from which my master drinks and which he uses for divination.* What you have done is wrong.' "

[6] When the steward overtook them and repeated these words to them, [7] they remonstrated with him: "How can my lord say such things? Far be it from your servants to do such a thing! [8] We even brought back to you from the land of Canaan the money that we found in the mouths of our bags. Why, then, would we steal silver or gold from your master's house? [9] If any of your servants is found to have the goblet, he shall die, and as for the rest of us, we shall become my lord's slaves." [10] But he replied, "Even though it ought to be as you propose, only the one who is found to have it shall become my slave, and the rest of you shall be exonerated." [11] Then each of them eagerly lowered his bag to the ground and opened it; [12] and when a search was made, starting with the oldest and ending with the youngest, the goblet turned up in Benjamin's bag. [13] At this, they tore their clothes. Then, when each man had reloaded his donkey, they returned to the city.

[14] As Judah and his brothers reentered Joseph's house, he was still there; so they flung themselves on the ground before him. [15] "How could you do such a thing?" Joseph asked them. "You should have known that such a man as I could discover by divination what happened." [16] Judah replied: "What can we say to my lord? How can we plead or how try to prove our innocence? God has uncovered your servant's guilt.* Here we are, then, the slaves of my lord—the rest of us no less than the one in whose possession the goblet was found." [17] "Far be it from me to act thus!" said Joseph. "Only the one in whose possession the goblet was found shall become my slave; the rest of you may go back safe and sound to your father."

[18] Judah then stepped up to him and said: "I beg you, my lord, let your servant speak earnestly to my lord, and do not become angry with your servant, for you are the equal of Pharaoh. [19] * My lord asked

your servants, 'Have you a father, or another brother?' [20]So we said to my lord, 'We have an aged father, and a young brother, the child of his old age. This one's full brother is dead, and since he is the only one by that mother who is left, his father dotes on him.'[c-21]Then you told your servants, 'Bring him down to me that my eyes may look on him.' [22]We replied to my lord, 'The boy cannot leave his father; his father would die if he were to leave him.' [23]But you told your servants, 'Unless your youngest brother comes back with you, you shall not come into my presence again.'[d] [24]When we returned to your servant our father, we reported to him the words of my lord.

[25]"Later, our father told us to come back and buy some food for the family. [26]So we reminded him, 'We cannot go down there; only if our youngest brother is with us can we go, for we may not see the man if our youngest brother is not with us.' [27]Then your servant our father said to us, 'As you know, my wife bore me two sons. [28]One of them, however, disappeared, and I had to conclude that he must have been torn to pieces by wild beasts; I have not seen him since.[e] [29]If you now take this one away from me, too, and some disaster befalls him, you will send my white head down to the nether world in grief.'

[30]"If then the boy is not with us when I go back to your servant my father, whose very life is bound up with his, he will die as soon as he sees that the boy is missing; [31]and your servants will thus send the white head of our father down to the nether world in grief. [32]Besides, I, your servant, got the boy from his father by going surety for him, saying, 'If I fail to bring him back to you, father, you can hold it against me forever.'[f] [33]Let me, your servant, therefore, remain in place of the boy as the slave of my lord, and let the boy go back with his brothers. [34]How could I go back to my father if the boy were not with me? I could not bear to see the anguish that would overcome my father."

CHAPTER 45

The Truth Revealed. [1]Joseph could no longer control himself in the presence of all his attendants, so he cried out, "Have everyone withdraw from me!" Thus no one else was about when he made himself known to his brothers. [2]But his sobs were so loud that the Egyptians heard him, and so the news reached Pharaoh's palace. [3][g] "I am Joseph," he said to his brothers. "Is my father still in good health?" But his brothers could give him no answer, so dumbfounded were they at him.

[4]"Come closer to me," he told his brothers. When they had done so, he said: "I am your brother Joseph, whom you once sold into Egypt. [5]But now do not be distressed, and do not reproach yourselves for having sold me here. It was really for the sake of saving lives that God sent me here ahead of you.[h] [6]For two years now the famine has been in the land, and for five more years tillage will yield no harvest. [7]God, therefore, sent me on ahead of you to ensure for you a remnant on earth and to save your lives in an extraordinary deliverance. [8]So it was not really you but God who had me come here; and he has made of me a father to Pharaoh,* lord of all his household, and ruler over the whole land of Egypt.

[9] * "Hurry back, then, to my father and tell him: 'Thus says your son Joseph: God has made me lord of all Egypt; come to me without delay.[i] [10]You will settle in the region of Goshen, * where you will be near me—you and your children and grandchildren, your flocks and herds, and everything that you own. [11]Since five years of famine still lie ahead, I will provide for you there, so that you and your family and all that are yours may not suffer want.' [12]Surely, you can see for yourselves, and Benjamin can see for himself, that it is I, Joseph, who am speaking to you. [13]Tell my father all about my high position in Egypt and what you have seen. But hurry and bring my father down here." [14]Thereupon he flung himself on the neck of his brother Benjamin and wept, and Benjamin

---

c Gn 42, 13.—d Gn 43, 3.—e Gn 37, 20. 33.—f Gn 43, 9.—g 3f: Acts 7, 13.—h Gn 50, 20; Sir 49, 15.—i Acts 7, 14.

45, 8: *Father to Pharaoh:* a term applied to a vizier in ancient Egypt.

45, 9-15: In these verses, as in Gn 46, 31—47, 5a, all from the Yahwist source, Joseph in his own name invites his father and brothers to come to Egypt. Only after their arrival is Pharaoh informed of the fact. On the other hand, in 45, 16-20 from the Elohist source, it is Pharaoh himself who invites Joseph's kinsmen to migrate to his domain.

45, 10: *The region of Goshen:* modern Wadi Tumilat in the eastern part of the Nile Delta.

wept in his arms. ¹⁵ Joseph then kissed all his brothers, crying over each of them; and only then were his brothers able to talk with him.
¹⁶ When the news reached Pharaoh's palace that Joseph's brothers had come, Pharaoh and his courtiers were pleased. ¹⁷ So Pharaoh told Joseph: "Say to your brothers: 'This is what you shall do: Load up your animals and go without delay to the land of Canaan. ¹⁸ There get your father and your families, and then come back here to me; I will assign you the best land in Egypt, where you will live off the fat of the land.'ʲ ¹⁹ Instruct them further: 'Do this. Take wagons from the land of Egypt for your children and your wives and to transport your father on your way back here. ²⁰ Do not be concerned about your belongings, for the best in the whole land of Egypt shall be yours.' "
²¹ The sons of Israel acted accordingly. Joseph gave them the wagons, as Pharaoh had ordered, and he supplied them with provisions for the journey. ²² He also gave to each of them fresh clothing, but to Benjamin he gave three hundred shekels of silver and five sets of garments. ²³ Moreover, what he sent to his father was ten jackasses loaded with the finest products of Egypt and ten jennies loaded with grain and bread and other provisions for his journey. ²⁴ As he sent his brothers on their way, he told them, "Let there be no recriminations on the way."
²⁵ So they left Egypt and made their way to their father Jacob in the land of Canaan. ²⁶ When they told him, "Joseph is still alive—in fact, it is he who is ruler of all the land of Egypt," he was dumbfounded; he could not believe them. ²⁷ But when they recounted to him all that Joseph had told them, and when he saw the wagons that Joseph had sent for his transport,

the spirit of their father Jacob revived. ²⁸ "It is enough," said Israel. "My son Joseph is still alive! I must go and see him before I die."

CHAPTER 46

Migration to Egypt. ¹ Israel set out with all that was his. When he arrived at Beersheba, he offered sacrifices to the God of his father Isaac. ² There God, speaking to Israel in a vision by night, called, "Jacob! Jacob!" "Here I am," he answered. ³ Then he said: "I am God,* the God of your father. Do not be afraid to go down to Egypt, for there I will make you a great nation. ⁴ Not only will I go down to Egypt with you; I will also bring you back here, after Joseph has closed your eyes."
⁵ So Jacob departed from Beer-sheba, and the sons of Israel put their father and their wives and children on the wagons that Pharaoh had sent for his transport. ⁶ They took with them their livestock and the possessions they had acquired in the land of Canaan. Thus Jacob and all his descendants migrated to Egypt.ᵏ ⁷ His sons and his grandsons, his daughters and his granddaughters—all his descendants—he took with him to Egypt.
⁸ These are the names of the Israelites, Jacob and his descendants, who migrated to Egypt.
Reuben, Jacob's first-born,ˡ ⁹ * and the sons of Reuben: Hanoch, Pallu, Hezron and Carmi.ᵐ ¹⁰ The sons of Simeon: Nemuel, Jamin, Ohad, Jachin, Zohar, and Shaul, son of a Canaanite woman.ⁿ ¹¹ The sons of Levi: Gershon, Kohath and Merari.ᵒ ¹² The sons of Judah: Er, Onan, Shelah, Perez and Zerah—but Er and Onan had died in the land of Canaan; and the sons of Perez were Hezron and Hamul.ᵖ ¹³ The sons of Issachar: Tola, Puah, Jashub and Shimron.q ¹⁴ The sons of Zebulun: Sered, Elon and Jahleel.ʳ ¹⁵ These were the sons whom Leah bore to Jacob in Paddan-aram, along with his daughter Dinah—thirty-three persons in all, male and female.
¹⁶ The sons of Gad: Zephon, Haggi, Shuni, Ezbon, Eri, Arod and Areli.ˢ ¹⁷ The sons of Asher: Imnah, Ishvah, Ishvi and Beriah, with their sister Serah; and the sons of Beriah: Heber and Malchiel.ᵗ ¹⁸ These were the descendants of Zilpah, whom Laban had given to his daughter

---

j Acts 7, 14.—k Ex 1, 1; Jos 24, 4; Jdt 5, 10; Acts 7, 15.—l Ex 1, 2.—m Ex 6, 14; Nm 26, 5; 1 Chr 5, 3.—n Ex 6, 15; Nm 26, 12; 1 Chr 4, 24.—o Ex 6, 16; Nm 3, 17; 26, 57; 1 Chr 6, 1.— p Gn 38, 3-10. 29f; Nm 26, 19; Rv 4, 18-22; 1 Chr 2, 5.—q Nm 26, 23f; 1 Chr 7, 1.—r Nm 26, 26.—s Nm 26, 15f.—t Nm 26, 44; 1 Chr 7, 30f.

46, 3: *I am God:* more precisely according to the Hebrew text, "I am El." "El" is here a divine name, not the common noun "god."

46, 9-27: This genealogical list has here been inserted by a redactor who based it on the clan lists (Nm 26, 5-50) at the time of Moses. Therefore it includes some of Jacob's grandchildren, who would hardly have been born when Joseph was still a relatively young man. The number *fourteen* (v 22) is based on a garbled version of the genealogical list.

Leah; these she bore to Jacob—sixteen persons in all.

¹⁹ The sons of Jacob's wife Rachel: Joseph and Benjamin. ²⁰ In the land of Egypt Joseph became the father of Manasseh and Ephraim, whom Asenath, daughter of Potiphera, priest of Heliopolis, bore to him. ᵘ ²¹ The sons of Benjamin: Bela, Becher, Ashbel, Gera, Naaman, Ahiram, Shupham, Hupham and Ard. ᵛ ²² These were the sons whom Rachel bore to Jacob—fourteen persons in all.

²³ The sons of Dan: Hushim. ʷ ²⁴ The sons of Naphtali: Jahzeel, Guni, Jezer and Shillem. ˣ ²⁵ These were the sons of Bilhah, whom Laban had given to his daughter Rachel: these she bore to Jacob—seven persons in all.

²⁶ Jacob's people who migrated to Egypt—his direct descendants, not counting the wives of Jacob's sons—numbered sixty-six persons in all. ʸ ²⁷ Together with Joseph's sons who were born to him in Egypt—two persons—all the people comprising Jacob's family who had come to Egypt amounted to seventy persons* in all. ᶻ

²⁸ Israel had sent Judah ahead to Joseph, so that he might meet him in Goshen. On his arrival in the region of Goshen, ²⁹ Joseph hitched the horses to his chariot and rode to meet his father Israel in Goshen. As soon as he saw him, he flung himself on his neck and wept a long time in his arms. ³⁰ And Israel said to Joseph, "At last I can die, now that I have seen for myself that Joseph is still alive."

³¹ Joseph then said to his brothers and his father's household: "I will go and inform Pharaoh, telling him: 'My brothers and my father's household, whose home is in the land of Canaan, have come to me. ³² The men are shepherds, having long been keepers of livestock; and they have brought with them their flocks and herds, as well as everything else they own.' ³³ So when Pharaoh summons you and asks what your occupation is, ³⁴ you must answer, 'We your servants, like our ancestors, have been keepers of livestock from the beginning until now,' in order that you may stay in the region of Goshen, since all shepherds are abhorrent to the Egyptians."

CHAPTER 47

Settlement in Goshen. ¹ Joseph went and told Pharaoh, "My father and my brothers have come from the land of Canaan, with their flocks and herds and everything else they own; and they are now in the region of Goshen." ² He then presented to Pharaoh five of his brothers whom he had selected from their full number. ³ When Pharaoh asked them what their occupation was, they answered, "We, your servants, like our ancestors, are shepherds. ⁴ We have come," they continued, "in order to stay in this country, for there is no pasture for your servants' flocks in the land of Canaan, so severe has the famine been there. Please, therefore, let your servants settle in the region of Goshen." ᵃ ⁵ Pharaoh said to Joseph, "They may settle in the region of Goshen; and if you know any of them to be qualified, you may put them in charge of my own livestock."

Thus, when Jacob and his sons came to Joseph in Egypt, and Pharaoh, king of Egypt, heard about it, Pharaoh said to Joseph, "Now that your father and brothers have come to you, ⁶ the land of Egypt is at your disposal; settle your father and brothers in the pick of the land." ⁷ Then Joseph brought his father Jacob and presented him to Pharaoh. After Jacob had paid his respects to Pharaoh, ⁸ Pharaoh asked him, "How many years have you lived?" ⁹ Jacob replied: "The years I have lived as a wayfarer amount to a hundred and thirty. Few and hard have been these years of my life, and they do not compare with the years that my ancestors lived as wayfarers."* ¹⁰ Then Jacob bade Pharaoh farewell and withdrew from his presence.

¹¹ As Pharaoh had ordered, Joseph settled his father and brothers and gave them holdings in Egypt on the pick of the land, in the region of Rameses.* ¹² And Joseph sustained his father and brothers and

---

u Gn 41, 50; Nm 26, 28. 35.—v Nm 26, 38; 1 Chr 7, 6; 8, 1-4.—w Nm 26, 42.—x Nm 26, 48f; 1 Chr 7, 13.—y Ex 1, 5.—z Ex 1, 5; Dt 10, 22; Acts 7, 14.—a Ex 23, 9; Dt 23, 8.

46, 27: *Seventy persons:* either to be understood as a round number, or arrived at by including Jacob and Joseph with the preceding persons, who add up to sixty-eight.

47, 9: *Wayfarer . . . wayfarers:* man is merely a sojourner on earth; cf Ps 39, 13.

47, 11: *The region of Rameses:* same as the region of Goshen; see note on Gn 45, 10. The name Rameses, however, is an anachronism, since this royal name did not come into use before the end of the fourteenth century B.C., long after the time of Joseph.

his father's whole household, down to the youngest, with food.

Joseph's Land Policy. 13 Since there was no food in any country because of the extreme severity of the famine, and the lands of Egypt and Canaan were languishing from hunger, 14 Joseph gathered in, as payment for the rations that were being dispensed, all the money that was to be found in Egypt and Canaan, and he put it in Pharaoh's palace. 15 When all the money in Egypt and Canaan was spent, all the Egyptians came to Joseph, pleading, "Give us food or we shall perish under your eyes; for our money is gone." 16 "Since your money is gone," replied Joseph, "give me your livestock, and I will sell you bread in return for your livestock." 17 So they brought their livestock to Joseph, and he sold them food in return for their horses, their flocks of sheep and herds of cattle, and their donkeys. Thus he got them through that year with bread in exchange for all their livestock. 18 When that year ended, they came to him in the following one and said: "We cannot hide from my lord that, with our money spent and our livestock made over to my lord, there is nothing left to put at my lord's disposal except our bodies and our farm land. 19 Why should we and our land perish before your very eyes? Take us and our land in exchange for food, and we will become Pharaoh's slaves and our land his property; only give us seed, that we may survive and not perish, and that our land may not turn into a waste."

20 Thus Joseph acquired all the farm land of Egypt for Pharaoh, since with the famine too much for them to bear, every Egyptian sold his field; so the land passed over to Pharaoh, 21 and the people were reduced to slavery, from one end of Egypt's territory to the other. 22 Only the priests' lands Joseph did not take over. Since the priests had a fixed allowance from Pharaoh and lived off the allowance Pharaoh had granted them, they did not have to sell their land.

23 Joseph told the people: "Now that I have acquired you and your land for Pharaoh, here is your seed for sowing the land. 24 But when the harvest is in, you must give a fifth of it to Pharaoh, while you keep four-fifths as seed for your fields, and as food for yourselves and your families [and as food for your children]." 25 "You have saved our lives!" they answered. "We are grateful to my lord that we can be Pharaoh's slaves." 26 Thus Joseph made it a law for the land in Egypt, which is still in force, that a fifth of its produce should go to Pharaoh. Only the land of the priests did not pass over to Pharaoh.

Jacob Blesses Ephraim and Manasseh. 27 Thus Israel settled in the land of Egypt, in the region of Goshen. There they acquired property, were fertile, and increased greatly.[b] 28 Jacob lived in the land of Egypt for seventeen years; the span of his life came to a hundred and forty-seven years. 29 When the time approached for Israel to die, he called his son Joseph and said to him: "If you really wish to please me, put your hand under my thigh as a sign of your constant loyalty to me; do not let me be buried in Egypt. 30 When I lie down with my ancestors, have me taken out of Egypt and buried in their burial place."[c] 31 "I will do as you say," he replied. But his father demanded, "Swear it to me!" So Joseph swore to him. Then Israel bowed at the head of the bed.*

CHAPTER 48

1 Some time afterward, Joseph was informed, "Your father is failing." So he took along with him his two sons, Manasseh and Ephraim. 2 When Jacob was told, "Your son Joseph has come to you," he rallied his strength and sat up in bed.

3 [d] Jacob then said to Joseph: "God Almighty appeared to me at Luz* in the land of Canaan, and blessing me, 4 he said, 'I will make you fertile and numerous and raise you into an assembly of tribes, and I will give this land to your descendants after you as a permanent possession.' 5 Your two sons, therefore, who were born to you in the land of Egypt before I joined you here, shall be mine; Ephraim and Manasseh shall be mine as much as Reuben and Simeon are mine. 6 Progeny born to you after them shall remain yours; but their heritage shall be recorded in the

---

b Ex 1, 7.—c Gn 50, 5.—d 3f: Gn 28, 12-15; 35, 6.

47, 31: *Israel bowed at the head of the bed:* meaning perhaps that he gave a nod of assent and appreciation as he lay on his bed. By reading with different vowels the Hebrew word for "bed," the Greek version translated it as "staff," and understood the phrase to mean that he bowed in worship, leaning on the top of his staff; it is thus quoted in Heb 11, 21.

48, 3: *Luz:* an older name of Bethel (Gn 28, 19).

names of their two brothers. [7] *e* I do this because, when I was returning from Paddan, your mother Rachel died, to my sorrow, during the journey in Canaan, while we were still a short distance from Ephrath; and I buried her there on the way to Ephrath [that is, Bethlehem]."*

[8] When Israel saw Joseph's sons, he asked, "Who are these?" [9] "They are my sons," Joseph answered his father, "whom God has given me here." "Bring them to me," said his father, "that I may bless them." [10] (Now Israel's eyes were dim from age, and he could not see well.) When Joseph brought his sons close to him, he kissed and embraced them. [11] Then Israel said to Joseph, "I never expected to see your face again, and now God has allowed me to see your descendants as well!"

[12] Joseph removed them from his father's knees and bowed down before him with his face to the ground. [13] Then Joseph took the two, Ephraim with his right hand, to Israel's left, and Manasseh with his left hand, to Israel's right, and led them to him. [14] But Israel, crossing his hands, put out his right hand and laid it on the head of Ephraim, although he was the younger, and his left hand on the head of Manasseh, although he was the first-born. [15] Then he blessed them with these words:

"May the God in whose ways
    my fathers Abraham and Isaac
    walked,
The God who has been my shepherd
    from my birth to this day, *f*
[16] The Angel who has delivered me from
    all harm,
    bless these boys
That in them my name be recalled,
    and the names of my fathers, Abraham and Isaac,
And they may become teeming multitudes
    upon the earth!"

[17] When Joseph saw that his father had laid his right hand on Ephraim's head, this seemed wrong to him; so he took hold of his father's hand, to remove it from Ephraim's head to Manasseh's, [18] saying, "That is not right, father; the other one is the first-born; lay your right hand on his head!" [19] But his father resisted. "I know it, son," he said, "I know. That one too

shall become a tribe, and he too shall be great. Nevertheless, his younger brother shall surpass him, and his descendants shall become a multitude of nations." [20] So when he blessed them that day and said, "By you shall the people of Israel pronounce blessings; may they say, 'God make you like Ephraim and Manasseh,' " he placed Ephraim before Manasseh. *g*

[21] Then Israel said to Joseph: "I am about to die. But God will be with you and will restore you to the land of your fathers. [22] *h* As for me, I give to you, as to the one above his brothers, Shechem, which I captured from the Amorites with my sword and bow."*

CHAPTER 49

Jacob's Testament. [1] Jacob called his sons and said: "Gather around, that I may tell you what is to happen to you in days to come.

[2] "Assemble and listen, sons of Jacob,
    listen to Israel, your father.

[3] "You, Reuben, my first-born,
    my strength and the first fruit of my
        manhood,
    excelling in rank and excelling in
        power!
[4] Unruly as water, you shall no longer
        excel,
    for you climbed into your father's
        bed
    and defiled my couch to my sorrow. *i*

[5] "Simeon and Levi, brothers indeed,
    weapons of violence are their
        knives.*
[6] Let not my soul enter their council,
    or my spirit be joined with their company;
    For in their fury they slew men,

---

e Gn 35, 19.—f Heb 11, 21.—g Heb 11, 21.—h Jos 17, 14.
17f; Jn 4, 5.—i Gn 35, 22; 1 Chr 5, 1f.

48, 7: Since her early death prevented Rachel from bearing more than two sons, Jacob feels justified in treating her two grandsons as if they were her own offspring.
48, 22: Both the meaning of the Hebrew and the historical reference in this verse are obscure. By taking the Hebrew word for Shechem as a common noun meaning shoulder or mountain slope, some translators render the verse, "I give you one portion more than your brothers, which I captured . . ." The reference may be to the capture of Shechem by the sons of Jacob (Gn 34, 24-29). Shechem lay near the border separating the tribal territory of Manasseh from that of Ephraim (Jos 16, 4-9; 17, 1f. 7).
49, 5: *Knives:* if this is the meaning of the obscure Hebrew word here, the reference may be to the knives used in circumcising the men of Shechem (Gn 34, 24; cf Jos 5, 2).

in their willfulness they maimed oxen.*j*

7 Cursed be their fury so fierce,
  and their rage so cruel!
  I will scatter them in Jacob,
  disperse them throughout Israel.

8 "You, Judah, shall your brothers praise
  —your hand on the neck of your enemies;
  the sons of your father shall bow down to you.

9 Judah, like a lion's whelp,
  you have grown up on prey, my son.
  He crouches like a lion recumbent,
  the king of beasts—who would dare rouse him?*k*

10 The scepter shall never depart from Judah,
  or the mace from between his legs,
  While tribute is brought to him,*
  and he receives the peoples' homage.

11 He tethers his donkey to the vine,
  his purebred ass to the choicest stem.
  In wine he washes his garments,
  his robe in the blood of grapes.*

12 His eyes are darker than wine,
  and his teeth are whiter than milk.

13 "Zebulun shall dwell by the seashore
  [This means a shore for ships],
  and his flank shall be based on Sidon.

14 "Issachar is a rawboned ass,
  crouching between the saddlebags.

15 When he saw how good a settled life was,
  and how pleasant the country,
  He bent his shoulder to the burden
  and became a toiling serf.

16 "Dan shall achieve justice* for his kindred
  like any other tribe of Israel.

17 Let Dan be a serpent by the roadside,

---

a horned viper by the path,
That bites the horse's heel,
  so that the rider tumbles backward.

18 "[I long for your deliverance, O LORD!]

19 "Gad shall be raided by raiders,
  but he shall raid at their heels.*

20 "Asher's produce is rich,
  and he shall furnish dainties for kings.

21 "Naphtali is a hind let loose,
  which brings forth lovely fawns.

22 "Joseph is a wild colt,
  a wild colt by a spring,
  a wild ass on a hillside.

23 Harrying and attacking,
  the archers opposed him;

24 But each one's bow remained stiff,
  as their arms were unsteady,
  By the power of the Mighty One of Jacob,
  because of the Shepherd, the Rock of Israel,

25 The God of your father, who helps you,*
  God Almighty, who blesses you,
  With the blessings of the heavens above,
  the blessings of the abyss that crouches below,
  The blessings of breasts and womb,

26 the blessings of fresh grain and blossoms,
  The blessings of the everlasting mountains,
  the delights of the eternal hills.
  May they rest on the head of Joseph,
  on the brow of the prince among his brothers.

27 "Benjamin is a ravenous wolf;
  mornings he devours the prey,
  and evenings he distributes the spoils."

Farewell and Death. 28 All these are the twelve tribes of Israel, and this is what their father said about them, as he bade them farewell and gave to each of them an appropriate message. 29 Then he gave them this charge: "Since I am about to be taken to my kindred, bury me with my fathers in the cave that lies in the field of Ephron the Hittite, 30 the cave in the field of Machpelah, facing on Mamre, in the land of Canaan, the field that Abraham bought from Ephron the Hittite for a burial ground.*l* 31 There Abraham and his wife Sarah are buried, and so are Isaac and his

---

j Gn 34, 25.—k 1 Chr 5, 2.—l Gn 23, 17.

49, 10: *While tribute is brought to him:* this translation is based on a slight change in the Hebrew text, which, as it stands, would seem to mean, "until he comes to Shiloh." A somewhat different reading of the Hebrew text would be, "until he comes to whom it belongs." This last has been traditionally understood in a Messianic sense. In any case, the passage foretells the supremacy of the tribe of Judah, which found its fulfillment in the Davidic dynasty and ultimately in the Messianic Son of David, Jesus Christ.

49, 11: *In wine . . . the blood of grapes:* Judah's clothes are poetically pictured as soaked with grape juice from trampling in the wine press, the rich vintage of his land; cf Is 63, 2.

49, 16: In Hebrew the verb for *achieve justice* is from the same root as the name *Dan.*

49, 19: In Hebrew there is a certain assonance between the name *Gad* and the words for "raided," "raiders" and "raid."

49, 25f: A very similar description of the agricultural riches of the tribal land of Joseph is given in Dt 33, 13-16.

wife Rebekah, and there, too, I buried Leah—³²the field and the cave in it that had been purchased from the Hittites."

³³When Jacob had finished giving these instructions to his sons, he drew his feet into the bed, breathed his last, and was taken to his kindred.

CHAPTER 50

Jacob's Funeral. ¹Joseph threw himself on his father's face and wept over him as he kissed him. ²Then he ordered the physicians in his service to embalm his father. When they embalmed Israel, ³they spent forty days at it, for that is the full period of embalming; and the Egyptians mourned him for seventy days. ⁴When that period of mourning was over, Joseph spoke to Pharaoh's courtiers. "Please do me this favor," he said, "and convey to Pharaoh this request of mine. ⁵Since my father, at the point of death, made me promise on oath to bury him in the tomb that he had prepared for himself in the land of Canaan, may I go up there to bury my father and then come back?"ᵐ ⁶Pharaoh replied, "Go and bury your father, as he made you promise on oath."

⁷So Joseph left to bury his father; and with him went all of Pharaoh's officials who were senior members of his court and all the other dignitaries of Egypt, ⁸as well as Joseph's whole household, his brothers, and his father's household; only their children and their flocks and herds were left in the region of Goshen. ⁹Chariots, too, and charioteers went up with him; it was a very large retinue.

¹⁰When they arrived at Goren-ha-atad,* which is beyond the Jordan, they held there a very great and solemn memorial service; and Joseph observed seven days of mourning for his father. ¹¹When the Canaanites who inhabited the land saw the mourning at Goren-ha-atad, they said, "This is a solemn funeral the Egyptians are having." That is why the place was named Abel-mizraim. It is beyond the Jordan.

¹²Thus Jacob's sons did for him as he had instructed them. ¹³They carried him to the land of Canaan and buried him in the cave in the field of Machpelah, facing on Mamre, the field that Abraham had bought for a burial ground from Ephron the Hittite.ⁿ

¹⁴After Joseph had buried his father he returned to Egypt, together with his brothers and all who had gone up with him for the burial of his father.

Plea for Forgiveness. ¹⁵Now that their father was dead, Joseph's brothers became fearful and thought, "Suppose Joseph has been nursing a grudge against us and now plans to pay us back in full for all the wrong we did him!" ¹⁶So they approached Joseph and said: "Before your father died, he gave us these instructions: ¹⁷'You shall say to Joseph, Jacob begs you to forgive the criminal wrongdoing of your brothers, who treated you so cruelly.' Please, therefore, forgive the crime that we, the servants of your father's God, committed." When they spoke these words to him, Joseph broke into tears. ¹⁸Then his brothers proceeded to fling themselves down before him and said, "Let us be your slaves!" ¹⁹But Joseph replied to them: "Have no fear. Can I take the place of God? ²⁰Even though you meant harm to me, God meant it for good, to achieve his present end, the survival of many people.ᵒ ²¹Therefore have no fear. I will provide for you and for your children." By thus speaking kindly to them, he reassured them.ᵖ

²²Joseph remained in Egypt, together with his father's family. He lived a hundred and ten years. ²³He saw Ephraim's children to the third generation, and the children of Manasseh's son Machir were also born on Joseph's knees.�q

Death of Joseph. ²⁴Joseph said to his brothers: "I am about to die. God will surely take care of you and lead you out of this land to the land that he promised on oath to Abraham, Isaac and Jacob."ʳ ²⁵Then, putting the sons of Israel under oath, he continued, "When God thus takes care of you, you must bring my bones up with you from this place."ˢ ²⁶Joseph died at the age of a hundred and ten. He was embalmed and laid to rest in a coffin in Egypt.ᵗ

---

m Gn 47, 30.—n Gn 23, 16; Acts 7, 16.—o Gn 45, 5; Sir 49, 15.—p Gn 47, 12.—q Nm 32, 39; Jos 17, 1.—r Ex 3, 8; Jos 24, 32; Heb 11, 22.—s Ex 13, 19; Heb 11, 22.—t Sir 49, 15.

50, 10f: *Goren-ha-atad:* "Threshing Floor of the Brambles." *Abel-mizraim:* although the name really means "watercourse of the Egyptians," it is understood here, by a play on the first part of the term, to mean "mourning of the Egyptians." The site has not been identified through either reading of the name. But it is difficult to see why the mourning rites should have been held in the land *beyond the Jordan* when the burial was at Hebron. Perhaps an earlier form of the story placed the mourning rites beyond the Wadi of Egypt, the traditional boundary between Canaan and Egypt (Nm 34, 5; Jos 15, 4. 47).

THE BOOK OF EXODUS

The second book of the Pentateuch is called Exodus from the Greek word for "departure," because the central event narrated in it is the departure of the Israelites from Egypt. It continues the history of the chosen people from the point where the Book of Genesis leaves off. It recounts the oppression by the Egyptians of the ever-increasing descendants of Jacob and their miraculous deliverance by God through Moses, who led them across the Red Sea to Mount Sinai where they entered into a special covenant with the Lord.

These events were of prime importance to the chosen people, for they became thereby an independent nation and enjoyed a unique relationship with God. Through Moses God gave to the Israelites at Mount Sinai the "law": the moral, civil and ritual legislation by which they were to become a holy people, in whom the promise of a Savior for all mankind would be fulfilled.

The principal divisions of Exodus are: I. The Israelites in Egypt (Ex 1, 1—12, 36). II. The Exodus from Egypt and the Journey to Sinai (Ex 12, 37—18, 27). III. The Covenant at Mount Sinai (Ex 19, 1—24, 18). IV. The Dwelling and Its Furnishings (Ex 25, 1—40, 38).

I: THE ISRAELITES IN EGYPT

CHAPTER 1

Jacob's Descendants in Egypt. [1] These are the names of the sons of Israel* who, accompanied by their households, migrated with Jacob into Egypt: [2]* Reuben, Simeon, Levi and Judah; [3] Issachar, Zebulun and Benjamin; [4] Dan and Naphtali; Gad and Asher. [5] The total number of the direct descendants* of Jacob was seventy.[a] Joseph was already in Egypt. [6] Now Joseph and all his brothers and that whole generation died.[b] [7] But the Israelites were fruitful and prolific. They became so numerous and strong that the land was filled with them.

The Oppression. [8] Then a new king, who knew nothing of Joseph,* came to power in Egypt.[c] [9] He said to his subjects, "Look how numerous and powerful the Israelite people are growing, more so than we ourselves! [10] Come, let us deal shrewdly with them to stop their increase; otherwise, in time of war they too may join our enemies to fight against us, and so leave our country."

[11] Accordingly, taskmasters were set over the Israelites to oppress them with forced labor.[d] Thus they had to build for Pharaoh* the supply cities of Pithom and Raamses. [12] Yet the more they were oppressed, the more they multiplied and spread. The Egyptians, then, dreaded the Israelites [13] and reduced them to cruel slavery, [14] making life bitter for them with hard work in mortar* and brick and all kinds of field work—the whole cruel fate of slaves.

Command to the Midwives. [15] The king of Egypt told the Hebrew midwives, one of whom was called Shiphrah and the other Puah, [16] "When you act as midwives for the Hebrew women and see them giving birth,* if it is a boy, kill him; but if it is a girl, she may live." [17] The midwives, however, feared God; they did not do as the king of Egypt had ordered them, but let the boys live. [18] So the king summoned the midwives and asked them, "Why have you acted thus, allowing the boys to live?" [19] The midwives answered Pharaoh, "The Hebrew women are not like the Egyptian women. They are robust and give birth before the midwife arrives." [20] Therefore God dealt well with the midwives. The people, too, increased and grew strong. [21] And because the midwives feared God, he built up

---

a Gn 46, 27; Dt 10, 22; Acts 7, 14.—b Gn 50, 26.—c 8ff: Acts 7, 18.—d Dt 26, 6.

1, 1: *Sons of Israel:* here literally the first-generation sons of Jacob. Cf v 5. However, beginning with Ex 1, 7 the same Hebrew phrase refers to the more remote descendants of Jacob; hence, from there on, it is ordinarily rendered as "the Israelites." *Households:* the family in its fullest sense, including wives, children and servants.

1, 2: The sons of Jacob are listed here according to the respective mothers. Cf Gn 29, 31; 30, 20; 35, 16-26.

1, 5: *Direct descendants:* literally, persons coming from the loins of Jacob; hence, wives and servants are here excluded. Cf Gn 46, 26.

1, 8: *Who knew nothing of Joseph:* this king ignored the services that Joseph had rendered to Egypt.

1, 11: *Pharaoh:* not a personal name, but a title common to all the kings of Egypt.

1, 14: *Mortar:* either the wet clay with which the bricks were made, as in Na 3, 14, or the cement used between the bricks in building, as in Gn 11, 3.

1, 16: *And see them giving birth:* the Hebrew text is uncertain.

families for them. [22]Pharaoh then commanded all his subjects, "Throw into the river* every boy that is born to the Hebrews,[e] but you may let all the girls live."

CHAPTER 2

Birth and Adoption of Moses. [1]Now a certain man of the house of Levi married a Levite woman,[f] [2]who conceived and bore a son. Seeing that he was a goodly child, she hid him for three months.[g] [3]When she could hide him no longer, she took a papyrus basket,* daubed it with bitumen and pitch, and putting the child in it, placed it among the reeds on the river bank. [4]His sister stationed herself at a distance to find out what would happen to him.

[5]Pharaoh's daughter came down to the river to bathe, while her maids walked along the river bank. Noticing the basket among the reeds, she sent her handmaid to fetch it. [6]On opening it, she looked, and lo, there was a baby boy, crying! She was moved with pity for him and said, "It is one of the Hebrews' children." [7]Then his sister asked Pharaoh's daughter, "Shall I go and call one of the Hebrew women to nurse the child for you?" [8]"Yes, do so," she answered. So the maiden went and called the child's own mother. [9]Pharaoh's daughter said to her, "Take this child and nurse it for me, and I will repay you." The woman therefore took the child and nursed it. [10]When the child grew,* she brought him to Pharaoh's daughter, who adopted him as her son[h] and called him Moses; for she said, "I drew him out of the water."

Moses' Flight to Midian. [11]On one occasion, after Moses had grown up,* when he visited his kinsmen[i] and witnessed their forced labor, he saw an Egyptian striking a Hebrew, one of his own kinsmen. [12]Looking about and seeing no one, he slew the Egyptian and hid him in the sand. [13]The next day he went out again, and now two Hebrews were fighting! So he asked the culprit, "Why are you striking your fellow Hebrew?" [14]But he replied, "Who has appointed you ruler and judge over us? Are you thinking of killing me as you killed the Egyptian?" Then Moses became afraid and thought, "The affair must certainly be known."

[15]Pharaoh, too, heard of the affair and sought to put him to death. But Moses fled

from him and stayed in the land of Midian.[j] As he was seated there by a well, [16]seven daughters of a priest of Midian came to draw water and fill the troughs to water their father's flock. [17]But some shepherds came and drove them away. Then Moses got up and defended them and watered their flock. [18]When they returned to their father Reuel,* he said to them, "How is it you have returned so soon today?" [19]They answered, "An Egyptian* saved us from the interference of the shepherds. He even drew water for us and watered the flock!" [20]"Where is the man?" he asked his daughters. "Why did you leave him there? Invite him to have something to eat." [21]Moses agreed to live with him, and the man gave him his daughter Zipporah in marriage. [22]She bore him a son, whom he named Gershom;* for he said, "I am a stranger in a foreign land."[k]

The Burning Bush. [23]A long time passed, during which the king of Egypt died. Still the Israelites groaned and cried out because of their slavery. As their cry for release went up to God,[l] [24]he heard their groaning and was mindful of his covenant[m] with Abraham, Isaac and Jacob. [25]He saw the Israelites and knew. . . .

CHAPTER 3

[1]Meanwhile Moses was tending the flock of his father-in-law Jethro, the priest of Midian. Leading the flock across the desert, he came to Horeb, the mountain of

---

e Acts 7, 19.—f Ex 6, 20; Nm 26, 59.—g Acts 7, 20; Heb 11, 23.—h Acts 7, 21, Heb 11, 24.—i 11-14: Acts 7, 23-28.—j Acts 7, 29; Heb 11, 27.—k Ex 18, 3.—l Ex 3, 7. 9; Dt 26, 7.—m Ex 6, 5; Pss 105, 8f; 106, 44f.

1, 22: *The river:* the Nile, which was "the" river for the Egyptians.

2, 3: *Basket:* literally, "chest" or "ark"; the same Hebrew word is used in Gn 6, 14 for Noah's ark. Here, however, the chest was made of papyrus stalks.

2, 10: *When the child grew:* probably when he was weaned or a little later. *Moses:* in Hebrew, *Mosheh;* the Hebrew word for "draw out" is *mashah.* This explanation of the name is not intended as a scientific etymology but as a play on words. The name is probably derived from an Egyptian word for "has been born," referring the birth to a god thought to be its sponsor.

2, 11: *After Moses has grown up:* Acts 7, 23 indicates that this was after an interval of nearly forty years. Cf Ex 7, 7. *Striking:* probably in the sense of "flogging"; according to some, "slaying."

2, 18: *Reuel:* he was also called Jethro. Cf. Ex 3, 1; 4, 18; 18, 1.

2, 19: *An Egyptian:* Moses was probably wearing Egyptian dress, or spoke Egyptian to Reuel's daughters.

2, 22: *Gershom:* the name is explained as if it came from the Hebrew word *ger,* "stranger," joined to the Hebrew word *sham,* "there." Some Greek and Latin manuscripts add here a passage taken from Ex 18, 4.

God.* ²There an angel of the LORD* appeared to him in fire flaming out of a bush.ⁿ As he looked on, he was surprised to see that the bush, though on fire, was not consumed. ³So Moses decided, "I must go over to look at this remarkable sight, and see why the bush is not burned."

The Call of Moses. ⁴When the LORD saw him coming over to look at it more closely, God called out to him from the bush, "Moses! Moses!" He answered, "Here I am." ⁵God said, "Come no nearer!ᵒ Remove the sandals from your feet, for the place where you stand is holy ground. ⁶ ᵖ I am the God of your father," he continued, "the God of Abraham, the God of Isaac, the God of Jacob."* Moses hid his face, for he was afraid to look at God. ⁷But the LORD said, "I have witnessed the affliction of my people in Egypt and have heard their cry of complaint against their slave drivers, so I know well what they are suffering. ⁸Therefore I have come down* to rescue them from the hands of the Egyptians and lead them out of that land into a good and spacious land, a land flowing with milk and honey, the country of the Canaanites, Hittites, Amorites, Perizzites, Hivites and Jebusites.�q ⁹So indeed the cry of the Israelites has reached me, and I have truly noted that the Egyptians are oppressing them. ¹⁰Come, now! I will send you to Pharaoh to lead my people, the Israelites, out of Egypt."

¹¹But Moses said to God, "Who am I* that I should go to Pharaoh and lead the Israelites out of Egypt?" ¹²He answered, "I will be with you; and this shall be your proof that it is I who have sent you: when you bring my people out of Egypt, you will worship God on this very mountain." ¹³"But," said Moses to God, "when I go to the Israelites and say to them, 'The God of your fathers has sent me to you,' if they ask me, 'What is his name?' what am I to tell them?" ¹⁴God replied, "I am who am."* Then he added, "This is what you shall tell the Israelites: I AM sent me to you."

¹⁵God spoke further to Moses, "Thus shall you say to the Israelites: The LORD, the God of your fathers, the God of Abraham, the God of Isaac, the God of Jacob, has sent me to you.

"This is my name forever,ʳ
this is my title for all generations.

¹⁶"Go and assemble the elders* of the Israelites, and tell them: The LORD, the God of your fathers, the God of Abraham, Isaac and Jacob, has appeared to me and said: I am concerned about you and about the way you are being treated in Egypt; ¹⁷so I have decided to lead you up out of the misery of Egypt into the land of the Canaanites, Hittites, Amorites, Perizzites, Hivites and Jebusites, a land flowing with milk and honey.

¹⁸"Thus they will heed your message. Then you and the elders of Israel shall go to the king of Egypt and say to him: ˢ The LORD, the God of the Hebrews, has sent us word. Permit us, then, to go a three days' journey in the desert, that we may offer sacrifice to the LORD, our God. ¹⁹"Yet I know that the king of Egypt will not allow you to go unless he is forced. ²⁰I will stretch out my hand, therefore, and smite Egypt by doing all kinds of wondrous deeds there. After that he will send you away. ²¹I will even make the Egyptians so well-disposed toward this people that, when you leave, you will not go empty-handed. ²² ᵗ Every woman shall ask her neighbor and her house guest for silver

---

n 2-10; Acts 7, 30-35.—o Jos 5, 15.—p Ex 4, 5; Mt 22, 32; Mk 12, 36; Lk 20, 37.—q 8f: Gn 15, 19ff.—r Ps 135, 13.—s Ex 5, 3.—t 21f: Ex 11, 2f; 12, 35f.

3, 1: *The mountain of God:* probably given this designation because of the divine apparitions which took place there, such as on this occasion and when the Israelites were there after the departure from Egypt.

3, 2: *An angel of the Lord:* the visual form under which God appeared and spoke to men is referred to indifferently in some Old Testament texts either as God's angel or as God himself. Cf Gn 16, 7. 11-13; Ex 14, 19. 24f; Nm 22, 22-35; Jgs 6, 11-18.

3, 6: The appearance of God caused fear of death, since it was believed that no one could see God and live; cf Gn 32, 30. *The God of Abraham . . . Jacob:* cited by Christ in proof of the resurrection since the patriarchs, long dead, live on in God who is the God of the living. Cf Mt 22, 32; Mk 12, 26; Lk 20, 37.

3, 8: *I have come down:* a figure of speech signifying an extraordinary divine intervention in human affairs. Cf Gn 11, 5. 7. *Flowing with milk and honey:* an expression denoting agricultural prosperity, which seems to have been proverbial in its application to Palestine. Cf Ex 13, 5; Nm 13, 27; Jos 5, 6; Jer 11, 5; 32, 22; Ez 20, 6. 15.

3, 11: *Who am I:* besides naturally shrinking from such a tremendous undertaking, Moses realized that, as a fugitive from Pharaoh, he could hardly hope to carry out a mission to him. Perhaps he also recalled that on one occasion even his own kinsmen questioned his authority. Cf Ex 2, 14.

3, 14: *I am who am:* apparently this utterance is the source of the word *Yahweh*, the proper personal name of the God of Israel. It is commonly explained in reference to God as the absolute and necessary Being. It may be understood of God as the Source of all created beings. Out of reverence for this name, the term *Adonai,* "my Lord," was later used as a substitute. The word Lord in the present version represents this traditional usage. The word "Jehovah" arose from a false reading of this name as it is written in the current Hebrew text.

3, 16: *Elders:* the Israelite leaders, who were usually older men. They were representatives of the people.

and gold articles* and for clothing to put on your sons and daughters. Thus you will despoil the Egyptians."

CHAPTER 4

Confirmation of Moses' Mission. [1] "But," objected Moses, "suppose they will not believe me, nor listen to my plea? For they may say, 'The LORD did not appear to you.' " [2] The LORD therefore asked him, "What is that in your hand?" "A staff," he answered. [3] The LORD then said, "Throw it on the ground." When he threw it on the ground it was changed into a serpent,[u] and Moses shied away from it. [4] "Now, put out your hand," the LORD said to him, "and take hold of its tail." So he put out his hand and laid hold of it, and it became a staff in his hand. [5] "This will take place so that they may believe," he continued, "that the LORD, the God of their fathers, the God of Abraham, the God of Isaac, the God of Jacob, did appear to you."

[6] Again the LORD said to him, "Put your hand in your bosom." He put it in his bosom, and when he withdrew it, to his surprise his hand was leprous, like snow. [7] The LORD then said, "Now, put your hand back in your bosom." Moses put his hand back in his bosom, and when he withdrew it, to his surprise it was again like the rest of his body. [8] "If they will not believe you, nor heed the message of the first sign, they should believe the message of the second. [9] And if they will not believe even these two signs, nor heed your plea, take some water from the river and pour it on the dry land. The water you take from the river will become blood on the dry land."[v]

Aaron's Office as Assistant. [10] Moses, however, said to the LORD, "If you please, LORD, I have never been eloquent, neither in the past, nor recently, nor now that you have spoken to your servant; but I am slow of speech and tongue."[w] [11] The LORD said to him, "Who gives one man speech and makes another deaf and dumb? Or who gives sight to one and makes another blind? Is it not I, the LORD? [12] Go, then! It is I who will assist you in speaking and will teach you what you are to say." [13] Yet he insisted, "If you please, LORD, send someone else!"* [14] Then the LORD became angry with Moses and said, "Have you not your brother, Aaron the Levite? I know that he is an eloquent speaker. Besides, he is now on his way to meet you. [15] When he sees you, his heart will be glad. You are to speak to him,

then, and put the words in his mouth. I will assist both you and him in speaking and will teach the two of you what you are to do. [16] He shall speak to the people for you: he shall be your spokesman,* and you shall be as God to him.[x] [17] Take this staff* in your hand; with it you are to perform the signs."

Moses' Return to Egypt. [18] After this Moses returned to his father-in-law Jethro and said to him, "Let me go back, please, to my kinsmen in Egypt, to see whether they are still living." Jethro replied, "Go in peace."* [19] In Midian[y] the LORD said to Moses, "Go back to Egypt, for all the men who sought your life are dead." [20] So Moses took his wife and his sons, and started back to the land of Egypt, with them riding the ass. The staff of God he carried with him. [21] The LORD said to him, "On your return to Egypt, see that you perform before Pharaoh all the wonders I have put in your power. I will make him obstinate,* however, so that he will not let the people go. [22] [z] So you shall say to Pharaoh: Thus says the LORD: Israel is my son, my first-born. [23] Hence I tell you: Let my son go, that he may serve me. If you refuse to let him go, I warn you, I will kill your son, your first-born."[a]

[24] * On the journey, at a place where they spent the night, the LORD came upon Moses and would have killed him. [25] [b] But Zipporah took a piece of flint and cut off her son's foreskin and, touching his person, she said, "You are a spouse of blood to me." [26] Then God let Moses go. At that time she said, "A spouse of blood," in regard to the circumcision.

---

u Ex 7, 10.—v Ex 7, 17. 19f.—w Ex 6, 12.—x 15f: Ex 7, 1.—y Ex 2, 15. 23.—z Sir 36, 11.—a Ex 11, 5; 12, 29.—b Is 6, 2; 7, 20.

3, 22: *Articles:* probably jewelry. *Despoil:* this was permissible, that the Israelites might compensate themselves for their many years of servitude; besides, the Egyptians would give these things willingly. Cf Ex 12, 33-36.

4, 13: *Send someone else:* literally, "Send by means of him whom you will send," that is, "Send whom you will."

4, 16: *Spokesman:* literally, "mouth"; Aaron was to serve as a mouthpiece for Moses, as a prophet does for God; hence the relation between Moses and Aaron is compared to that between God and his prophet. Cf Ex 7, 1.

4, 17: *This staff:* probably the same as that of vv 2ff; but some understand it here of a new staff now given by God to Moses.

4, 18: Moses did not tell his father-in-law his main reason for returning to Egypt, but this secondary motive which he offered was also true.

4, 21: *Make him obstinate:* literally, "harden his heart." God permitted Pharaoh to be stubborn in his opposition to the departure of the Israelites. Cf Rom 9, 17f.

4, 24ff: Apparently God was angry with Moses for having failed to keep the divine command given to Abraham in Gn 17, 10ff. Moses' life is spared when his wife circumcises their son.

²⁷ The LORD said to Aaron, "Go into the desert to meet Moses." So he went, and when they met at the mountain of God, Aaron kissed him. ²⁸ Moses informed him of all the LORD had said in sending him, and of the various signs he had enjoined upon him. ²⁹ Then Moses and Aaron went and assembled all the elders of the Israelites. ³⁰ Aaron told them everything the LORD had said to Moses, and he performed the signs before the people. ³¹ The people believed, and when they heard that the LORD was concerned about them and had seen their affliction, they bowed down in worship.

CHAPTER 5

Pharaoh's Obduracy. ¹ After that, Moses and Aaron went to Pharaoh and said, "Thus says the LORD, the God of Israel: Let my people go, that they may celebrate a feast to me in the desert." ² Pharaoh answered, "Who is the LORD, that I should heed his plea to let Israel go? I do not know the LORD; even if I did, I would not let Israel go." ³ They replied, "The God of the Hebrews has sent us word. Let us go a three days' journey in the desert, that we may offer sacrifice to the LORD, our God;ᶜ otherwise he will punish us with pestilence or the sword."

⁴ The king of Egypt answered them, "What do you mean, Moses and Aaron, by taking the people away from their work? Off to your labor! ⁵ Look how numerous the people of the land are already," continued Pharaoh, "and yet you would give them rest from their labor!"

⁶ That very day Pharaoh gave the taskmasters and foremen* of the people this order: ⁷ "You shall no longer supply the people with straw for their brickmaking* as you have previously done. Let them go and gather straw themselves! ⁸ Yet you shall levy upon them the same quota of bricks as they have previously made. Do not reduce it. They are lazy; that is why they are crying, 'Let us go to offer sacrifice to our God.' ⁹ Increase the work for the men, so that they keep their mind on it and pay no attention to lying words."

¹⁰ So the taskmasters and foremen of the

c Ex 3, 18.—d Gn 17, 1; 35, 11.

5, 6: *The taskmasters and foremen:* the former were higher officials and probably Egyptians; the latter were lower officials, chosen from the Israelites themselves. Cf v 14.
5, 7: Straw was mixed with the clay to give the sun-dried bricks greater consistency.

people went out and told them, "Thus says **Ex** Pharaoh: I will not provide you with straw. ¹¹ Go and gather the straw yourselves, wherever you can find it. Yet there must not be the slightest reduction in your work." ¹² The people, then, scattered throughout the land of Egypt to gather stubble for straw, ¹³ while the taskmasters kept driving them on, saying, "Finish your work, the same daily amount as when your straw was supplied."

Complaint of the Foremen. ¹⁴ The foremen of the Israelites, whom the taskmasters of Pharaoh had placed over them, were beaten, and were asked, "Why have you not completed your prescribed amount of bricks yesterday and today, as before?"

¹⁵ Then the Israelite foremen came and made this appeal to Pharaoh: "Why do you treat your servants in this manner? ¹⁶ No straw is supplied to your servants, and still we are told to make bricks. Look how your servants are beaten! It is you who are at fault." ¹⁷ Pharaoh answered, "It is just because you are lazy that you keep saying, 'Let us go and offer sacrifice to the LORD.' ¹⁸ Off to work, then! Straw shall not be provided for you, but you must still deliver your quota of bricks."

¹⁹ The Israelite foremen knew they were in a sorry plight, having been told not to reduce the daily amount of bricks. ²⁰ When, therefore, they left Pharaoh and came upon Moses and Aaron, who were waiting to meet them, ²¹ they said to them, "The LORD look upon you and judge! You have brought us into bad odor with Pharaoh and his servants and have put a sword in their hands to slay us."

Renewal of God's Promise. ²² Moses again had recourse to the LORD and said, "Lord, why do you treat this people so badly? And why did you send me on such a mission? ²³ Ever since I went to Pharaoh to speak in your name, he has maltreated this people of yours, and you have done nothing to rescue them."

CHAPTER 6

¹ Then the LORD answered Moses, "Now you shall see what I will do to Pharaoh. Forced by my mighty hand, he will send them away; compelled by my outstretched arm, he will drive them from his land."

² God also said to Moses, "I am the LORD. ³ As God the Almighty I appearedᵈ to Abraham, Isaac and Jacob, but my name,

LORD, I did not make known to them. [4]I also established my covenant with them, to give them the land of Canaan, the land in which they were living as aliens.[e] [5]And now that I have heard the groaning of the Israelites, whom the Egyptians are treating as slaves, I am mindful of my covenant.[f] [6]Therefore, say to the Israelites: I am the LORD. I will free you from the forced labor of the Egyptians and will deliver you from their slavery. I will rescue you by my outstretched arm and with mighty acts of judgment. [7]I will take you as my own people, and you shall have me as your God.[g] You will know that I, the LORD, am your God when I free you from the labor of the Egyptians [8]and bring you into the land which I swore to give to Abraham, Isaac and Jacob. I will give it to you as your own possession—I, the LORD!" [9]But when Moses told this to the Israelites, they would not listen to him because of their dejection and hard slavery.

[10]Then the LORD said to Moses, [11]"Go and tell Pharaoh, king of Egypt, to let the Israelites leave his land." [12]But Moses protested to the LORD, "If the Israelites would not listen to me, how can it be that Pharaoh will listen to me, poor speaker[h] that I am!" [13]Still, the LORD, to bring the Israelites out of Egypt, spoke to Moses and Aaron and gave them his orders regarding both the Israelites and Pharaoh, the king of Egypt.

Genealogy of Moses and Aaron. [14]These are the heads of the ancestral houses.* The sons of Reuben,[i] the first-born of Israel, were Hanoch, Pallu, Hezron and Carmi; these are the clans of Reuben. [15]The sons of Simeon[j] were Jemuel, Jamin, Ohad, Jachin, Zohar and Shaul, who was the son of a Canaanite woman; these are the clans of Simeon. [16]The names of the sons of Levi,[k] in their genealogical order, are Gershon, Kohath and Merari. Levi lived one hundred and thirty-seven years.

[17]The sons of Gershon,[l] as heads of clans, were Libni and Shimei. [18]The sons of Kohath[m] were Amram, Izhar, Hebron and Uzziel. Kohath lived one hundred and thirty-three years. [19]The sons of Merari[n] were Mahli and Mushi. These are the clans of Levi in their genealogical order. [20]Amram married his aunt* Jochebed,[o] who bore him Aaron, Moses and Miriam. Amram lived one hundred and thirty-seven years. [21]The sons of Izhar were Korah,

Nepheg and Zichri. [22]The sons of Uzziel were Mishael, Elzaphan and Sithri. [23]Aaron married Amminadab's[p] daughter, Elisheba, the sister of Nahshon; she bore him Nadab, Abihu, Eleazar and Ithamar. [24]The sons of Korah were Assir, Elkanah and Abiasaph. These are the clans of the Korahites. [25]Aaron's son, Eleazar, married one of Putiel's daughters, who bore him Phinehas. These are the heads of the ancestral clans of the Levites. [26]This is the Aaron and this the Moses to whom the LORD said, "Lead the Israelites from the land of Egypt, company by company." [27]These are the ones who spoke to Pharaoh, king of Egypt, to bring the Israelites out of Egypt—the same Moses and Aaron.

Moses and Aaron before Pharaoh. [28]On the day the LORD spoke to Moses in Egypt [29]he said, "I am the LORD. Repeat to Pharaoh, king of Egypt, all that I tell you." [30]But Moses protested to the LORD, "Since I am a poor speaker,[q] how can it be that Pharaoh will listen to me?"

CHAPTER 7

[1]The LORD answered him, "See! I have made you as God to Pharaoh,[r] and Aaron your brother shall act as your prophet.* [2]You shall tell him all that I command you. In turn, your brother Aaron shall tell Pharaoh to let the Israelites leave his land. [3]Yet I will make Pharaoh so obstinate that, despite the many signs and wonders that I will work in the land of Egypt, [4]he will not listen to you. Therefore I will lay my hand on Egypt and by great acts of judgment I will bring the hosts of my people, the Israelites, out of the land of Egypt, [5]so that the Egyptians may learn that I am the LORD, as I stretch out my hand against Egypt and lead the Israelites out of their midst."

[6]Moses and Aaron did as the LORD had commanded them. [7]Moses was eighty

---

e Gn 15, 18; 17, 4-8.—f Ex 2, 24.—g Lv 26, 12.—h Ex 6, 30.—i Nm 26, 5f; 1 Chr 5, 3.—j Nm 26, 12; 1 Chr 4, 24.—k Nm 3, 17; 1 Chr 6, 1. 16; 23, 6.—l Nm 3, 21; 1 Chr 6, 17; 23, 7.—m Nm 3, 27; 1 Chr 6, 2. 18.—n Nm 3, 20; 1 Chr 6, 19; 23, 21.—o Nm 26, 59.—p Ru 4, 19f; 1 Chr 2, 10.—q Ex 6, 12.—r Ex 4, 15f.

6, 14: The purpose of the genealogy here is to give the line from which Moses and Aaron sprang. Reuben and Simeon are first mentioned because, as older brothers of Levi, their names occur before his in the genealogy.

6, 20: *His aunt:* more exactly, "his father's sister." Later on such a marriage was forbidden. Cf Lv 18, 12. Hence, the Greek and Latin versions render here, "his cousin."

7, 1: Just as God had his prophets to speak to men in his name, so Moses had Aaron as his "prophet" to speak to Pharaoh. Cf Ex 4, 16.

years old and Aaron eighty-three when they spoke to Pharaoh.

The Staff Turned into a Snake. [8] The LORD told Moses and Aaron, [9] "If Pharaoh demands that you work a sign or wonder, you shall say to Aaron: Take your staff and throw it down before Pharaoh, and it will be changed into a snake." [s] [10] Then Moses and Aaron went to Pharaoh and did as the LORD had commanded. Aaron threw his staff down before Pharaoh and his servants, and it was changed into a snake. [11] Pharaoh, in turn, summoned wise men and sorcerers, and they also, the magicians[t] of Egypt, did likewise by their magic arts. [12] Each one threw down his staff, and it was changed into a snake. But Aaron's staff swallowed their staffs. [13] Pharaoh, however, was obstinate and would not listen to them, just as the LORD had foretold.

First Plague: Water Turned into Blood. [14] * Then the LORD said to Moses, "Pharaoh is obdurate in refusing to let the people go. [15] Tomorrow morning, when he sets out for the water, go and present yourself by the river bank, holding in your hand the staff that turned into a serpent. [16] Say to him: The LORD, the God of the Hebrews, sent me to you with the message: Let my people go to worship me in the desert. But as yet you have not listened. [17] The LORD now says: This is how you shall know that I am the LORD. I will strike the water of the river with the staff I hold, and it shall be changed into blood.[u] [18] The fish in the river shall die, and the river itself shall become so polluted that the Egyptians will be unable to drink its water."

[19] The LORD then said to Moses, "Say to Aaron: Take your staff and stretch out your hand over the waters of Egypt—their streams and canals and pools, all their supplies of water—that they may become blood. Throughout the land of Egypt there shall be blood, even in the wooden pails and stone jars."

[20] Moses and Aaron did as the LORD had commanded. Aaron raised his staff and struck the waters of the river in full view of Pharaoh and his servants, and all the water of the river was changed into blood. [21] The fish in the river died, and the river itself became so polluted that the Egyptians could not drink its water. There was blood throughout the land of Egypt. [22] But the Egyptian magicians did the same by their magic arts. So Pharaoh remained obstinate and would not listen to Moses and Aaron, just as the LORD had foretold. [23] He turned away and went into his house, with no concern even for this. [24] All the Egyptians had to dig in the neighborhood of the river for drinking water, since they could not drink the river water.

Second Plague: the Frogs. [25] Seven days passed after the LORD had struck the river. [26] * Then the LORD said to Moses, "Go to Pharaoh and tell him:[v] Thus says the LORD: Let my people go to worship me. [27] If you refuse to let them go, I warn you, I will send a plague of frogs over all your territory. [28] The river will teem with frogs. They will come up into your palace and into your bedroom and onto your bed, into the houses of your servants, too, and your subjects, even into your ovens and your kneading bowls. [29] The frogs will swarm all over you and your subjects and your servants."

CHAPTER 8

[1] The LORD then told Moses, "Say to Aaron: Stretch out your hand and your staff over the streams and canals and pools, to make frogs overrun the land of Egypt." [2] Aaron stretched out his hand over the waters of Egypt, and the frogs came up and covered the land of Egypt. [3] But the magicians did the same by their magic arts. They, too, made frogs overrun the land of Egypt.

[4] Then Pharaoh summoned Moses and Aaron and said, "Pray the LORD to remove the frogs from me and my subjects, and I will let the people go to offer sacrifice to the LORD." [5] Moses answered Pharaoh, "Do me the favor of appointing the time when I am to pray for you and your servants and your subjects, that the frogs may be taken away from you and your houses and be left only in the river." [6] "Tomorrow," said Pharaoh. Then Moses replied, "It shall be as you have said, so that you may learn that there is none like the LORD, our God. [7] The frogs shall leave you and your houses, your servants and your subjects; only in the river shall they be left."

---

s Ex 4, 3.—t 2 Tm 3, 8.—u 17-21: Ex 4, 9; Pss 78, 44; 105, 29: Wis 11, 5-7.—v 26-29: Pss 78, 45; 105, 30.

7, 14: Most of the ten plagues of Egypt seem to be similar to certain natural phenomena of that country; but they are represented as supernatural at least in their greater intensity and in their occurring exactly according to Moses' commands.

7, 26—8, 28: This is Ex 8, 1-32 in the verse enumeration of the Vulgate.

⁸After Moses and Aaron left Pharaoh's presence, Moses implored the LORD to fulfill the promise he had made to Pharaoh about the frogs; ⁹and the LORD did as Moses had asked. The frogs in the houses and courtyards* and fields died off. ¹⁰Heaps and heaps of them were gathered up, and there was a stench in the land. ¹¹But when Pharaoh saw that there was a respite, he became obdurate and would not listen to them, just as the LORD had foretold.

Third Plague: the Gnats. ¹²Thereupon the LORD said to Moses, "Tell Aaron to stretch out his staff and strike the dust of the earth, that it may be turned into gnats*ʷ* throughout the land of Egypt."* ¹³They did so. Aaron stretched out his hand, and with his staff he struck the dust of the earth, and gnats came upon man and beast. The dust of the earth was turned into gnats throughout the land of Egypt. ¹⁴Though the magicians tried to bring forth gnats by their magic arts, they could not do so.*ˣ* As the gnats infested man and beast, ¹⁵the magicians said to Pharaoh, "This is the finger of God."* Yet Pharaoh remained obstinate and would not listen to them, just as the LORD had foretold.

Fourth Plague: the Flies. ¹⁶Again the LORD told Moses, "Early tomorrow morning present yourself to Pharaoh when he goes forth to the water, and say to him: Thus says the LORD: Let my people go to worship me. ¹⁷If you will not let my people go, I warn you, I will loose swarms of flies upon you and your servants and your subjects and your houses. The houses of the Egyptians and the very ground on which they stand shall be filled with swarms of flies. ¹⁸But on that day I will make an exception of the land of Goshen: there shall be no flies where my people dwell, that you may know that I am the LORD in the midst of the earth. ¹⁹I will make this distinction between my people and your people. This sign shall take place tomorrow." ²⁰This the LORD did. Thick swarms of flies entered the house of Pharaoh and the houses of his servants; throughout Egypt the land was infested with flies.*ʸ*

²¹Then Pharaoh summoned Moses and Aaron and said to them, "Go and offer sacrifice to your God in this land." ²²But Moses replied, "It is not right to do so, for the sacrifices we offer to the LORD, our God, are an abomination to the Egyptians.* If before their very eyes we offer sacrifices which are an abomination to them, will not the Egyptians stone us? ²³We must go a three days' journey in the desert to offer sacrifice to the LORD, our God, as he commands us." ²⁴"Well, then," said Pharaoh, "I will let you go to offer sacrifice to the LORD, your God, in the desert, provided that you do not go too far away and that you pray for me." ²⁵Moses answered, "As soon as I leave your presence I will pray to the LORD that the flies may depart tomorrow from Pharaoh and his servants and his subjects. Pharaoh, however, must not play false again by refusing to let the people go to offer sacrifice to the LORD." ²⁶When Moses left Pharaoh's presence, he prayed to the LORD; ²⁷and the LORD did as Moses had asked. He removed the flies from Pharaoh and his servants and subjects. Not one remained. ²⁸But once more Pharaoh became obdurate and would not let the people go.

CHAPTER 9

Fifth Plague: the Pestilence. ¹Then the LORD said to Moses, "Go to Pharaoh and tell him: Thus says the LORD, the God of the Hebrews: Let my people go to worship me. ²If you refuse to let them go and persist in holding them, ³I warn you, the LORD will afflict all your livestock in the field—your horses, asses, camels, herds and flocks—with a very severe pestilence. ⁴But the LORD will distinguish between the livestock of Israel and that of Egypt, so that none belonging to the Israelites will die." ⁵And setting a definite time, the LORD added, "Tomorrow the LORD shall do this in the land." ⁶And on the next day the LORD did so. All the livestock of the Egyptians died,*ᶻ* but not one beast belonging to the Israelites. ⁷But though Pharaoh's messengers informed him that not even one beast belonging to the Israelites had died, he still remained obdurate and would not let the people go.

---

w 12f: Ps 105, 31.—x Wis 17, 7.—y Pss 78, 45; 105, 31; Wis 16, 9.—z Ps 78, 48.

8, 9: *Courtyards:* some render "farmhouses."
8, 12. 17: *Gnats, flies:* it is uncertain what species of troublesome insects are here meant.
8, 15: *The finger of God:* understood by the magicians as the staff mentioned in Ex 8, 13. Cf Lk 11, 20.
8, 22: The Egyptians would fiercely resent the sacrifice of any animal they considered sacred. Certain animals were worshiped in Egypt, at least as the symbols of various deities.

Sixth Plague: the Boils. [8] Then the LORD said to Moses and Aaron, "Take a double handful of soot from a furnace, and in the presence of Pharaoh let Moses scatter it toward the sky. [9] It will then turn into fine dust over the whole land of Egypt and cause festering boils on man and beast throughout the land."

[10] So they took soot from a furnace and stood in the presence of Pharaoh. Moses scattered it toward the sky, and it caused festering boils on man and beast. [11] The magicians could not stand in Moses' presence, for there were boils on the magicians no less than on the rest of the Egyptians. [12] But the LORD made Pharaoh obstinate, and he would not listen to them, just as the LORD had foretold to Moses.

Seventh Plague: the Hail. [13] Then the LORD told Moses, "Early tomorrow morning present yourself to Pharaoh and say to him: Thus says the LORD, the God of the Hebrews: Let my people go to worship me, [14] or this time I will hurl all my blows upon you and your servants and your subjects, that you may know that there is none like me anywhere on earth. [15] For by now I would have stretched out my hand and struck you and your subjects with such pestilence as would wipe you from the earth. [16] But this is why I have spared you: to show you* my power and to make my name resound throughout the earth![a] [17] Will you still block the way for my people by refusing to let them go? [18] I warn you, then, tomorrow at this hour I will rain down such fierce hail as there has never been in Egypt from the day the nation was founded up to the present. [19] Therefore, order all your livestock and whatever else you have in the open fields to be brought to a place of safety. Whatever man or beast remains in the fields and is not brought to shelter shall die when the hail comes upon them." [20] Some of Pharaoh's servants feared the warning of the LORD and hurried their servants and livestock off to shelter. [21] Others, however, did not take the warning of the LORD to heart and left their servants and livestock in the fields.

[22] The LORD then said to Moses, "Stretch out your hand toward the sky,

a Rom 9, 17.—b 23f; Pss 78, 47; 105, 32f.—c Dt 6, 20ff.

9, 16: *To show you:* some ancient versions read, "to show through you." Cf Rom 9, 17.

that hail may fall upon the entire land of Egypt, on man and beast and every growing thing in the land of Egypt." [23] When Moses stretched out his staff toward the sky, the LORD sent forth hail[b] and peals of thunder. Lightning flashed toward the earth, and the LORD rained down hail upon the land of Egypt; [24] and lightning constantly flashed through the hail, such fierce hail as had never been seen in the land since Egypt became a nation. [25] It struck down every man and beast that was in the open throughout the land of Egypt; it beat down every growing thing and splintered every tree in the fields. [26] Only in the land of Goshen, where the Israelites dwelt, was there no hail.

[27] Then Pharaoh summoned Moses and Aaron and said to them, "I have sinnned again! The LORD is just; it is I and my subjects who are at fault. [28] Pray to the LORD, for we have had enough of God's thunder and hail. Then I will let you go; you need stay no longer." [29] Moses replied, "As soon as I leave the city I will extend my hands to the LORD; the thunder will cease, and there will be no more hail. Thus you shall learn that the earth is the LORD's. [30] But you and your servants, I know, do not yet fear the LORD God."

[31] Now the flax and the barley were ruined, because the barley was in ear and the flax in bud. [32] But the wheat and the spelt were not ruined, for they grow later. [33] When Moses had left Pharaoh's presence and had gone out of the city, he extended his hands to the LORD. Then the thunder and the hail ceased, and the rain no longer poured down upon the earth. [34] But Pharaoh, seeing that the rain and hail and thunder had ceased, sinned again: he with his servants became obdurate, [35] and in his obstinacy he would not let the Israelites go, as the LORD had foretold through Moses.

CHAPTER 10

Eighth Plague: the Locusts. [1] Then the LORD said to Moses, "Go to Pharaoh, for I have made him and his servants obdurate in order that I may perform these signs of mine among them [2] and that you may recount to your son and grandson how ruthlessly I dealt with the Egyptians and what signs I wrought among them, so that you may know that I am the LORD."[c]

³ So Moses and Aaron went to Pharaoh and told him, "Thus says the LORD, the God of the Hebrews: How long will you refuse to submit to me? Let my people go to worship me. ⁴ If you refuse to let my people go, I warn you, tomorrow I will bring locusts into your country. ⁵ They shall cover the ground, so that the ground itself will not be visible. They shall eat up the remnant you saved unhurt from the hail, as well as all the foliage that has since sprouted in your fields. ⁶ They shall fill your houses and the houses of your servants and of all the Egyptians; such a sight your fathers or grandfathers have not seen from the day they first settled on this soil up to the present day." With that he turned and left Pharaoh.

⁷ But Pharaoh's servants said to him, "How long must he be a menace to us? Let the men go to worship the LORD, their God. Do you not yet realize that Egypt is being destroyed?" ⁸ So Moses and Aaron were brought back to Pharaoh, who said to them, "You may go and worship the LORD, your God. But how many of you will go?" ⁹ "Young and old must go with us," Moses answered, "our sons and daughters as well as our flocks and herds must accompany us. That is what a feast of the LORD means to us." ¹⁰ "The LORD help you,"* Pharaoh replied, "if I ever let your little ones go with you! Clearly, you have some evil in mind. ¹¹ No, no! Just you men can go and worship the LORD.* After all, that is what you want." With that they were driven from Pharaoh's presence.

¹² The LORD then said to Moses, "Stretch out your hand over the land of Egypt, that locusts*ᵈ* may swarm over it and eat up all the vegetation and whatever the hail has left." ¹³ So Moses stretched out his staff over the land of Egypt, and the LORD sent an east wind* blowing over the land all that day and all that night. At dawn the east wind brought the locusts. ¹⁴ They swarmed over the whole land of Egypt and settled down on every part of it. Never before had there been such a fierce swarm of locusts, nor will there ever be. ¹⁵ They covered the surface of the whole land, till it was black with them. They ate up all the vegetation in the land and the fruit of whatever trees the hail had spared. Nothing green was left on any tree or plant throughout the land of Egypt.

¹⁶ Hastily Pharaoh summoned Moses and Aaron and said, "I have sinned against the LORD, your God, and against you. ¹⁷ But now, do forgive me my sin once more, and pray the LORD, your God, to take at least this deadly pest from me." ¹⁸ When Moses left the presence of Pharaoh, he prayed to the LORD, ¹⁹ and the LORD changed the wind to a very strong west wind, which took up the locusts and hurled them into the Red Sea.* But though not a single locust remained within the confines of Egypt, ²⁰ the LORD made Pharaoh obstinate, and he would not let the Israelites go.

Ninth Plague: the Darkness. ²¹ Then the LORD said to Moses, "Stretch out your hand toward the sky, that over the land of Egypt there may be such intense darkness* that one can feel it." ²² So Moses stretched out his hand toward the sky, and there was dense darkness*ᵉ* throughout the land of Egypt for three days. ²³ Men could not see one another, nor could they move from where they were, for three days. But all the Israelites had light where they dwelt.

²⁴ Pharaoh then summoned Moses and Aaron and said, "Go and worship the LORD. Your little ones, too, may go with you. But your flocks and herds must remain." ²⁵ Moses replied, "You must also grant us sacrifices and holocausts to offer up the LORD, our God. ²⁶ Hence, our livestock also must go with us. Not an animal must be left behind. Some of them we must sacrifice to the LORD, our God, but we ourselves shall not know which ones we must sacrifice to him until we arrive at the place itself." ²⁷ But the LORD made Pharaoh obstinate, and he would not let them go. ²⁸ "Leave my presence," Pharaoh said to him, "and see to it that you do not

---

d 12ff: Pss 78, 46; 105, 34f.—e Ps 105, 28.

10, 10: *The Lord help you . . . :* literally, "May the LORD be with you in the same way as I let you . . ."; a sarcastic blessing intended as a curse.

10, 11: Pharaoh realized that if the men alone went they would have to return to their families. He suspected that the Hebrews had no intention of returning.

10, 13: *East wind:* coming across the desert from Arabia, the strong east wind brings Egypt the burning sirocco and, at times, locusts. Cf Ex 14, 21.

10, 19: *The Red Sea:* according to the traditional translation, but the Hebrew is literally, "the Reed Sea"; hence the Red Sea of Exodus was probably a body of shallow water somewhat to the north of the present deep Red Sea.

10, 21: *Darkness:* at times a storm from the south, called the *khamsin*, blackens the sky of Egypt with sand from the Sahara; the dust in the air is then so thick that the darkness can, in a sense, "be felt."

appear before me again! The day you appear before me you shall die!" ²⁹ Moses replied, "Well said! I will never appear before you again."

CHAPTER 11

Tenth Plague: the Death of the First-born. ¹ Then the LORD told Moses, "One more plague will I bring upon Pharaoh and upon Egypt. After that he will let you depart. In fact, he will not merely let you go; he will drive you away. ² Instruct your people that every man is to ask his neighbor, and every woman her neighbor, for silver and gold articles and for clothing."*ᶠ* ³ The LORD indeed made the Egyptians well-disposed toward the people; Moses himself was very highly regarded by Pharaoh's servants and the people in the land of Egypt.

⁴ Moses then said, "Thus says the LORD: At midnight I will go forth through Egypt.*ᵍ* ⁵ Every first-born in this land shall die,*ʰ* from the first-born of Pharaoh on the throne to the first-born of the slave-girl at the handmill, as well as all the first-born of the animals. ⁶ Then there shall be loud wailing throughout the land of Egypt, such as has never been, nor will ever be again. ⁷ But among the Israelites and their animals not even a dog shall growl, so that you may know how the LORD distinguishes between the Egyptians and the Israelites. ⁸ ⁱ All these servants of yours shall then come down to me, and prostrate before me, they shall beg me, 'Leave us, you and all your followers!' Only then will I depart." With that he left Pharaoh's presence in hot anger.

⁹ The LORD said to Moses, "Pharaoh refuses to listen to you that my wonders may be multiplied in the land of Egypt." ¹⁰ Thus, although Moses and Aaron performed these various wonders in Pharaoh's

presence, the LORD made Pharaoh obstinate, and he would not let the Israelites leave his land.

CHAPTER 12

The Passover Ritual Prescribed. ¹ The LORD said to Moses and Aaron in the land of Egypt, ² "This month* shall stand at the head of your calendar; you shall reckon it the first month of the year.*ʲ* ³ Tell the whole community of Israel: On the tenth of this month every one of your families must procure for itself a lamb, one apiece for each household. ⁴ If a family is too small for a whole lamb, it shall join the nearest household in procuring one and shall share in the lamb* in proportion to the number of persons who partake of it. ⁵ The lamb must be a year-old male and without blemish. You may take it from either the sheep or the goats. ⁶ You shall keep it until the fourteenth day of this month, and then, with the whole assembly of Israel present, it shall be slaughtered during the evening twilight. ⁷ They shall take some of its blood and apply it to the two doorposts and the lintel of every house in which they partake of the lamb. ⁸ That same night they shall eat its roasted flesh with unleavened bread and bitter herbs. ⁹ It shall not be eaten raw or boiled, but roasted whole, with its head and shanks and inner organs. ¹⁰ None of it must be kept beyond the next morning; whatever is left over in the morning shall be burned up.

¹¹ "This is how you are to eat it: with your loins girt, sandals on your feet and your staff in hand, you shall eat like those who are in flight. It is the Passover* of the LORD. ¹² For on this same night I will go through Egypt, striking down every first-born of the land, both man and beast, and executing judgment on all the gods of Egypt—I, the LORD! ¹³ But the blood will mark the houses where you are. Seeing the blood, I will pass over you; thus, when I strike the land of Egypt, no destructive blow will come upon you.*ᵏ*

¹⁴ "This day shall be a memorial feast for you, which all your generations shall celebrate with pilgrimage to the LORD, as a perpetual institution. ¹⁵ For seven days you must eat unleavened bread. From the very first day you shall have your houses clear of all leaven. Whoever eats leavened bread from the first day to the seventh shall be cut off from Israel. ¹⁶ On the first

f 2f: Ex 3, 21f; 12, 35f.—g Ex 12, 12.—h 5f: Ex 12, 29f.—i Ex 12, 31ff.—j 2-20: Lv 23, 5-8; Nm 9, 2-5; 28, 16ff; Dt 16, 1-8.—k Heb 11, 28.

12, 2: *This month:* Abib, the month of "ripe grain." Cf Ex 13, 4; 23, 15; 34, 18; Dt 16, 1. It occurred near the vernal equinox, March-April. Later it was known by the Babylonian name of Nisan. Cf Neh 2, 1; Est 3, 7.

12, 4: *Share in the lamb:* probably, in the expenses of its purchase. Some explain, "reckon for the lamb the number of persons required to eat it." Cf Ex 12, 10.

12, 11: *Passover:* in Hebrew, *pesach,* in Aramaic, *pascha.* In the following verses the same root is used in the verb "to pass over." The word may be originally Egyptian, *pesach,* "the blow," i.e., the final plague which destroyed the Egyptian first-born.

day you shall hold a sacred assembly, and likewise on the seventh. On these days you shall not do any sort of work, except to prepare the food that everyone needs. [17]"Keep, then, this custom of the unleavened bread.[1] Since it was on this very day that I brought your ranks out of the land of Egypt, you must celebrate this day throughout your generations as a perpetual institution. [18]From the evening of the fourteenth day of the first month until the evening of the twenty-first day of this month you shall eat unleavened bread. [19]For seven days no leaven may be found in your houses. Anyone, be he a resident alien or a native, who eats leavened food shall be cut off from the community of Israel. [20]Nothing leavened may you eat; wherever you dwell you may eat only unleavened bread."

Promulgation of the Passover. [21]Moses called all the elders of Israel and said to them, "Go and procure lambs for your families, and slaughter them as Passover victims. [22]Then take a bunch of hyssop,* and dipping it in the blood that is in the basin, sprinkle the lintel and the two doorposts with this blood.[m] But none of you shall go outdoors until morning. [23]For the LORD will go by, striking down the Egyptians. Seeing the blood on the lintel and the two doorposts, the LORD will pass over that door and not let the destroyer come into your houses to strike you down.

[24]"You shall observe this as a perpetual ordinance for yourselves and your descendants. [25]Thus, you must also observe this rite when you have entered the land which the LORD will give you as he promised. [26]When your children ask you, 'What does this rite of yours mean?'[n] [27]you shall reply, 'This is the Passover sacrifice of the LORD, who passed over the houses of the Israelites in Egypt; when he struck down the Egyptians, he spared our houses.' "

Then the people bowed down in worship, [28]and the Israelites went and did as the LORD had commanded Moses and Aaron.

Death of the First-born. [29]At midnight the LORD slew every first-born in the land of Egypt,[o] from the first-born of Pharaoh on the throne to the first-born of the prisoner in the dungeon, as well as all the first-born of the animals. [30]Pharaoh arose in the night, he and all his servants and all the Egyptians; and there was loud wailing throughout Egypt, for there was not a house without its dead.

Permission to Depart. [31]During the night Pharaoh summoned Moses and Aaron and said, "Leave my people at once, you and the Israelites with you! Go and worship the LORD as you said. [32]Take your flocks, too, and your herds, as you demanded, and be-gone; and you will be doing me a favor."

[33]The Egyptians likewise urged the people on, to hasten their departure from the land; they thought that otherwise they would all die. [34]The people, therefore, took their dough before it was leavened, in their kneading bowls wrapped in their cloaks on their shoulders. [35]The Israelites did as Moses had commanded: they asked the Egyptians for articles of silver and gold and for clothing.[p] [36]The LORD indeed had made the Egyptians so well disposed toward the people that they let them have whatever they asked for. Thus did they despoil the Egyptians.

II: THE EXODUS FROM EGYPT AND THE JOURNEY TO SINAI

Departure from Egypt. [37]The Israelites set out from Rameses[q] for Succoth, about six hundred thousand men on foot, not counting the children. [38]A crowd of mixed ancestry* also went up with them, besides their livestock, very numerous flocks and herds. [39]Since the dough they had brought out of Egypt was not leavened, they baked it into unleavened loaves. They had been rushed out of Egypt and had no opportunity even to prepare food for the journey. [40]The time the Israelites had stayed in Egypt* was four hundred and thirty years.[r] [41]At the end of four hundred and thirty years, all the hosts of the LORD left the land of Egypt on this very date. [42]This was a night of vigil for the LORD, as he led them out of the land of Egypt; so on this same night all the Israelites must keep a vigil for the LORD throughout their generations.

Passover Regulations. [43]The LORD said to Moses and Aaron, "These are the regulations for the Passover. No foreigner may

---

[1] Ex 13, 3.—m 22f: Ex 12, 7. 13.—n 26f: Ex 13, 8. 14; Dt 6, 20f.—o 29f: Ex 11, 4ff; Pss 78, 51; 105, 36; 136; 10; Wis 18, 10-16.—p 35f: Ex 3, 21f; 11, 2f; Ps 105, 37f.—q Nm 33, 3ff.—r Gn 15, 13; Acts 7, 6; Gal 3, 17.

12, 22: *Hyssop:* a plant with many woody branchlets that made a convenient sprinkler.
12, 38: *Mixed ancestry:* half-Hebrew and half-Egyptian. Cf Nm 11, 4; Lv 24, 10f.
12, 40: *In Egypt:* according to some ancient sources, "in Canaan and Egypt," thus reckoning from the time of Abraham. Cf Gal 3, 17.

partake of it. [44]However, any slave who has been bought for money may partake of it, provided you have first circumcised him. [45]But no transient alien or hired servant may partake of it. [46]It must be eaten in one and the same house; you may not take any of its flesh outside the house.[s] You shall not break any of its bones.[*] [47]The whole community of Israel must keep this feast. [48]If any aliens[t] living among you wish to celebrate the Passover of the LORD, all the males among them must first be circumcised, and then they may join in its observance just like the natives. But no man who is uncircumcised may partake of it. [49]The law shall be the same for the resident alien as for the native."

[50]All the Israelites did just as the LORD had commanded Moses and Aaron. [51]On that same day the LORD brought the Israelites out of Egypt company by company.

CHAPTER 13

Consecration of First-born. [1]The LORD spoke to Moses and said, [2]"Consecrate to me every first-born that opens the womb among the Israelites,[u] both of man and beast, for it belongs to me."

[3]Moses said to the people, "Remember this day on which you came out of Egypt, that place of slavery.[v] It was with a strong hand that the LORD brought you away. Nothing made with leaven must be eaten. [4]This day of your departure is in the month of Abib. [5]Therefore, it is in this month that you must celebrate this rite, after the LORD, your God, has brought you into the land of the Canaanites, Hittites, Amorites, Hivites and Jebusites, which he swore to your fathers he would give you, a land flowing with milk and honey. [6]For seven days you shall eat unleavened bread, and the seventh day shall also be a festival to the LORD. [7]Only un-

leavened bread may be eaten during the seven days; no leaven and nothing leavened may be found in all your territory. [8]On this day you shall explain to your son, 'This is because of what the LORD did for me when I came out of Egypt.' [9]It shall be as a sign on your hand and as a reminder on your forehead;[w] thus the law of the LORD will ever be on your lips, because with a strong hand the LORD brought you out of Egypt. [10]Therefore, you shall keep this prescribed rite at its appointed time from year to year.

[11]"When the LORD, your God, has brought you into the land of the Canaanites, which he swore to you and your fathers he would give you, [12]you shall dedicate to the LORD every son that opens the womb;[x] and all the male firstlings of your animals shall belong to the LORD. [13]Every first-born of an ass you shall redeem with a sheep. If you do not redeem it, you shall break its neck. Every first-born son you must redeem. [14]If your son should ask you later on, 'What does this mean?' you shall tell him, 'With a strong hand the LORD brought us out of Egypt, that place of slavery. [15]When Pharaoh stubbornly refused to let us go, the LORD killed every first-born in the land of Egypt, every first-born of man and of beast. That is why I sacrifice to the LORD everything of the male sex that opens the womb, and why I redeem every first-born of my sons.' [16]Let this, then, be as a sign on your hand and as a pendant on your forehead: with a strong hand the LORD brought us out of Egypt."[y]

Toward the Red Sea. [17]Now, when Pharaoh let the people go, God did not lead them by way of the Philistines' land,[*] though this was the nearest; for he thought, should the people see that they would have to fight, they might change their minds and return to Egypt. [18]Instead, he rerouted them toward the Red Sea by way of the desert road. In battle array the Israelites marched out of Egypt. [19]Moses also took Joseph's bones[z] along, for Joseph had made the Israelites swear solemnly that, when God should come to them, they would carry his bones away with them.

[20]Setting out from Succoth, they camped at Etham[a] near the edge of the desert.

[21]The Lord preceded them, in the daytime by means of a column of cloud[*] to show them the way, and at night by means

---

[s] Nm 9, 12; Jn 19, 36.—[t] 47f: Nm 9, 14.—[u] Ex 13, 12-15.—[v] 3-10: Ex 12, 2-20.—[w] Ex 13, 16; Dt 6, 8; 11, 18.—[x] 12-15: Ex 13, 2; 22, 29f; 34, 19f; Nm 3, 12f; 8, 16; 18, 15; Dt 15, 19.—[y] Ex 13, 9.—[z] Gn 50, 25; Jos 24, 32.—[a] Nm 33, 6.

12, 46: *You shall not break any of its bones:* the application of these words to our Lord on the cross shows that the Paschal lamb was a prophetic type of Christ, immolated to free men from the bondage of sin. Cf also 1 Cor 5, 7; 1 Pt 1, 19.

13, 17: *By way of the Philistines' land:* the most direct route from Egypt to Palestine, along the shore of the Mediterranean.

13, 21: *A column of cloud . . . a column of fire:* probably one and the same preternatural phenomenon, a central nucleus of fire surrounded by smoke; only at night was its luminous nature visible. Cf Ex 40, 38.

of a column of fire to give them light.[b] Thus they could travel both day and night. [22] Neither the column of cloud by day nor the column of fire by night ever left its place in front of the people.

CHAPTER 14

[1] Then the LORD said to Moses, [2] * "Tell the Israelites to turn about and camp before Pi-hahiroth, between Migdol and the sea.[c] You shall camp in front of Baal-zephon, just opposite, by the sea. [3] Pharaoh will then say, 'The Israelites are wandering about aimlessly in the land. The desert has closed in on them.' [4] Thus will I make Pharaoh so obstinate that he will pursue them. Then I will receive glory through Pharaoh and all his army, and the Egyptians will know that I am the LORD." This the Israelites did. [5] When it was reported to the king of Egypt that the people had fled, Pharaoh and his servants changed their minds about them. "What have we done!" they exclaimed. "Why, we have released Israel from our service!" [6] So Pharaoh made his chariots ready and mustered his soldiers—[7] six hundred first-class chariots and all the other chariots of Egypt, with warriors on them all. [8] So obstinate had the LORD made Pharaoh that he pursued[d] the Israelites even while they were marching away in triumph. [9] The Egyptians, then, pursued them; Pharaoh's whole army, his horses, chariots and charioteers, caught up with them as they lay encamped by the sea, at Pi-hahiroth, in front of Baal-zephon.

Crossing of the Red Sea. [10] Pharaoh was already near when the Israelites looked up and saw that the Egyptians were on the march in pursuit of them. In great fright they cried out to the LORD. [11] And they complained to Moses, "Were there no burial places in Egypt that you had to bring us out here to die in the desert? Why did you do this to us? Why did you bring us out of Egypt? [12] Did we not tell you this in Egypt, when we said, 'Leave us alone. Let us serve the Egyptians'? Far better for us to be the slaves of the Egyptians than to die in the desert." [13] But Moses answered the people, "Fear not! Stand your ground, and you will see the victory the LORD will win for you today. These Egyptians whom you see today you will never see again. [14] The LORD himself will fight for you; you have only to keep still."

[15] Then the LORD said to Moses, "Why are you crying out to me? Tell the Israelites to go forward. [16] And you, lift up your staff and, with hand outstretched over the sea, split the sea in two, that the Israelites may pass through it on dry land. [17] But I will make the Egyptians so obstinate that they will go in after them. Then I will receive glory through Pharaoh and all his army, his chariots and charioteers. [18] The Egyptians shall know that I am the LORD, when I receive glory through Pharaoh and his chariots and charioteers."

[19] The angel of God, who had been leading Israel's camp, now moved and went around behind them. The column of cloud also, leaving the front, took up its place behind them, [20] so that it came between the camp of the Egyptians and that of Israel. But the cloud now became dark,* and thus the night passed without the rival camps coming any closer together all night long. [21] Then Moses stretched out his hand over the sea, and the LORD swept the sea with a strong east wind throughout the night and so turned it into dry land.[e] When the water was thus divided, [22] the Israelites marched into the midst of the sea on dry land, with the water like a wall to their right and to their left.

Destruction of the Egyptians. [23] The Egyptians followed in pursuit; all Pharaoh's horses and chariots and charioteers went after them right into the midst of the sea. [24] In the night watch just before dawn the LORD cast through the column of the fiery cloud upon the Egyptian force a glance that threw it into a panic; [25] and he so clogged their chariot wheels that they could hardly drive. With that the Egyptians sounded the retreat before Israel, because the LORD was fighting for them against the Egyptians.

[26] Then the LORD told Moses, "Stretch out your hand over the sea, that the water may flow back upon the Egyptians, upon

b 21f: Ex 40, 38; Nm 9, 15-22; Dt 1, 33; Neh 9, 19; Pss 78, 14; 105, 39; Wis 10, 17.—c Nm 33, 7f.—d 5-8: Wis 19, 3; 1 Mc 4, 9.—e 21f: Ex 15, 19; Pss 66, 6; 78, 13; 136, 13f; Wis 10, 18; 19, 7f; Is 63, 12f; Heb 11, 29.

14, 2: These places have not been definitively identified. Even the relative position of *Pi-hahiroth* and *Baal-zephon* is not clear; perhaps the former was on the west shore of the sea, where the Israelites were, and the latter on the opposite shore.
14, 20: *The cloud now became dark:* the light which it ordinarily cast at night would now have been a help to the Egyptians; its present obscurity serves as a shield for the Israelites. However, the reading of the original text here is not quite certain.

their chariots and their charioteers." ²⁷So Moses stretched out his hand over the sea, and at dawn the sea flowed back to its normal depth. The Egyptians were fleeing head on toward the sea, when the LORD hurled them into its midst. ²⁸As the water flowed back, it covered the chariots and the charioteers of Pharaoh's whole army*f* which had followed the Israelites into the sea. Not a single one of them escaped. ²⁹But the Israelites had marched on dry land through the midst of the sea, with the water like a wall to their right and to their left. ³⁰Thus the LORD saved Israel on that day from the power of the Egyptians. When Israel saw the Egyptians lying dead on the seashore ³¹and beheld the great power that the LORD had shown against the Egyptians, they feared the LORD and believed in him*g* and in his servant Moses.

CHAPTER 15

¹Then Moses and the Israelites sang*h* this song to the LORD:*

I will sing to the LORD, for he is gloriously triumphant;
    horse and chariot he has cast into the sea.
²My strength and my courage is the LORD,
    and he has been my savior.
He is my God, I praise him;
    the God of my father, I extol him.*i*

³The LORD is a warrior,
    LORD is his name!
⁴Pharaoh's chariots and army he hurled into the sea;
    the elite of his officers were submerged in the Red Sea.
⁵The flood waters covered them,
    they sank into the depths like a stone.*j*

⁶Your right hand, O LORD, magnificent in power,
    your right hand, O LORD, has shattered the enemy.
⁷In your great majesty you overthrew your adversaries;
    you loosed your wrath to consume them like stubble.

⁸At a breath of your anger the waters piled up,
    the flowing waters stood like a mound,
    the flood waters congealed in the midst of the sea.
⁹The enemy boasted, "I will pursue and overtake them;
    I will divide the spoils and have my fill of them;
    I will draw my sword; my hand shall despoil them!"
¹⁰When your wind blew, the sea covered them;
    like lead they sank in the mighty waters.
¹¹Who is like to you among the gods, O LORD?
    Who is like to you, magnificent in holiness?
    O terrible in renown, worker of wonders,
¹²   when you stretched out your right hand, the earth swallowed them!
¹³In your mercy you led the people you redeemed;
    in your strength you guided them to your holy dwelling.
¹⁴The nations heard and quaked:
    anguish gripped the dwellers in Philistia.
¹⁵Then were the princes of Edom dismayed;
    trembling seized the chieftains of Moab;
    All the dwellers in Canaan melted away;
¹⁶   terror and dread fell upon them.*k*
    By the might of your arm they were frozen like stone,
    while your people, O LORD, passed over,
    while the people you had made your own passed over.
¹⁷And you brought them in and planted them on the mountain of your inheritance—
    the place where you made your seat, O LORD,
    the sanctuary, O LORD, which your hands established.
¹⁸The LORD shall reign forever and ever.

¹⁹They sang thus because Pharaoh's horses and chariots and charioteers had gone into the sea, and the LORD made the waters of the sea flow back upon them, though the Israelites had marched on dry

---

f 28f: Dt 11, 4; Ps 106, 11.—g 31f: Ps 106, 12; Wis 10, 20.—h Ex 15, 21.—i Ps 118, 14; Is 12, 2.—j Neh 9, 11.—k 16f: Ps 78, 53ff.

15, 1-21: This canticle (used in Christian liturgy) celebrates God's saving power, miraculously delivering his people from their enemies, and leading them to the victorious conquest of the Promised Land.

land through the midst of the sea.[l] [20]The prophetess Miriam, Aaron's sister, took a tambourine in her hand, while all the women went out after her with tambourines, dancing; [21]and she led them* in the refrain:

> Sing to the LORD, for he is gloriously triumphant;
> horse and chariot he has cast into the sea.[m]

At Marah and Elim. [22] [n] Then Moses led Israel forward from the Red Sea, and they marched out to the desert of Shur. After traveling for three days through the desert without finding water, [23]they arrived at Marah, where they could not drink the water, because it was too bitter. Hence this place was called Marah. [24]As the people grumbled against Moses, saying, "What are we to drink?" [25]he appealed to the LORD, who pointed out to him a certain piece of wood. When he threw this into the water, the water became fresh.[o]

It was here that the LORD, in making rules and regulations for them, put them to the test. [26]"If you really listen to the voice of the LORD, your God," he told them, "and do what is right in his eyes: if you heed his commandments and keep all his precepts, I will not afflict you with any of the diseases with which I afflicted the Egyptians;[p] for I, the LORD, am your healer."

[27]Then they came to Elim, where there were twelve springs of water and seventy palm trees, and they camped there near the water.[q]

CHAPTER 16

The Desert of Sin. [1]Having set out from Elim, the whole Israelite community came into the desert of Sin, which is between Elim and Sinai, on the fifteenth day of the second month* after their departure from the land of Egypt. [2]Here in the desert the whole Israelite community grumbled against Moses and Aaron. [3]The Israelites said to them, "Would that we had died at the LORD's hand in the land of Egypt, as we sat by our fleshpots and ate our fill of bread! But you had to lead us into this desert to make the whole community die of famine!"

The Quail and Manna. [4]Then the LORD said to Moses,[r] "I will now rain down bread from heaven* for you. Each day the people are to go out and gather their daily

portion; thus will I test them, to see whether they follow my instructions or not. [5]On the sixth day, however, when they prepare what they bring in, let it be twice as much as they gather on the other days." [6]So Moses and Aaron told all the Israelites, "At evening you will know that it was the LORD who brought you out of the land of Egypt; [7]and in the morning you will see the glory of the LORD, as he heeds your grumbling against him.[s] But what are we that you should grumble against us? [8]When the LORD gives you flesh to eat in the evening," continued Moses, "and in the morning your fill of bread, as he heeds the grumbling you utter against him, what then are we? Your grumbling is not against us, but against the LORD."

[9]Then Moses said to Aaron, "Tell the whole Israelite community: Present yourselves before the LORD, for he has heard your grumbling." [10]When Aaron announced this to the whole Israelite community, they turned toward the desert, and lo, the glory of the LORD appeared in the cloud! [11]The LORD spoke to Moses and said, [12]"I have heard the grumbling of the Israelites. Tell them: In the evening twilight you shall eat flesh, and in the morning you shall have your fill of bread, so that you may know that I, the LORD, am your God."

[13]In the evening quail[t] came up and covered the camp. In the morning a dew lay all about the camp, [14]and when the dew evaporated, there on the surface of the desert were fine flakes like hoarfrost on the ground. [15]On seeing it, the Israelites asked one another, "What is this?"* for they did not know what it was. But Moses told them,

---

l Ex 14, 21-29.—m Ex 15, 1.—n 22f: Nm 33, 8.—o Sir 38, 5.—p Dt 7, 15.—q Nm 33, 9.—r Pss 78, 24f; 105, 40; Jn 6, 31f; 1 Cor 10, 3.—s 6f: Ex 16, 12.—t Nm 11, 31; Ps 78, 27f.

15, 21: *She led them:* Miriam's refrain re-echoes the first verse of this song and was probably sung as an antiphon after each verse.

16, 1: *On the fifteenth day of the second month:* just one full month after their departure from Egypt. Cf Ex 12, 2. 51; Nm 33, 3f. They encamped in the desert of Sin on a Friday; the murmuring (vv 2f) occurred on the sabbath, the arrival of the quail (v 13) the evening before Sunday, followed by six mornings (vv 14-27) of collecting manna before the next sabbath.

16, 4: *Bread from heaven:* as a gift from God, the manna is said to come down from the sky. Cf Ps 78, 25; Wis 16, 20. Perhaps it was similar to a natural substance that is still found in small quantities on the Sinai peninsula, but here it is, at least in part, clearly miraculous. Our Lord referred to the manna as a type of the Blessed Eucharist. Cf Jn 6, 32. 49-52.

16, 15: *What is this:* the original *man hu* is thus rendered by the ancient versions, which understood the phrase as a popular etymology of the Hebrew word *man.* "manna"; some render, "This is manna."

"This is the bread which the LORD has given you to eat."[u]

Regulations Regarding the Manna. [16]"Now, this is what the LORD has commanded. So gather it that everyone has enough to eat, an omer for each person, as many of you as there are, each man providing for those of his own tent." [17]The Israelites did so. Some gathered a large and some a small amount. [18] * But when they measured it out by the omer, he who had gathered a large amount did not have too much, and he who had gathered a small amount did not have too little.[v] They so gathered that everyone had enough to eat. [19]Moses also told them, "Let no one keep any of it over until tomorrow morning." [20]But they would not listen to him. When some kept a part of it over until the following morning, it became wormy and rotten. Therefore Moses was displeased with them.

[21]Morning after morning they gathered it, till each had enough to eat; but when the sun grew hot, the manna melted away. [22]On the sixth day they gathered twice as much food, two omers for each person. When all the leaders of the community came and reported this to Moses, [23]he told them, "That is what the LORD prescribed. Tomorrow is a day of complete rest, the sabbath, sacred to the LORD. You may either bake or boil the manna, as you please; but whatever is left put away and keep for the morrow." [24]When they put it away for the morrow, as Moses commanded, it did not become rotten or wormy. [25]Moses then said, "Eat it today, for today is the sabbath of the LORD. On this day you will not find any of it on the ground. [26]On the other six days you can gather it, but on the seventh day, the sabbath, none of it will be there." [27]Still, on the seventh day some of the people went out to gather it, although they did not find any. [28]Then the LORD said to Moses,

"How long will you refuse to keep my commandments and laws? [29]Take note! The LORD has given you the sabbath. That is why on the sixth day he gives you food for two days. On the seventh day everyone is to stay home and no one is to go out." [30]After that the people rested on the seventh day.

[31]The Israelites called this food manna.[w] It was like coriander seed,* but white, and it tasted like wafers made with honey. [32]Moses said, "This is what the LORD has commanded. Keep an omerful of manna for your descendants, that they may see what food I gave you to eat in the desert when I brought you out of the land of Egypt." [33]Moses then told Aaron, "Take an urn* and put an omer of manna in it. Then place it before the LORD in safekeeping for your descendants."[x] [34]So Aaron placed it in front of the commandments* for safekeeping, as the LORD had commanded Moses.

[35]The Israelites ate this manna for forty years, until they came to settled land;[y] they ate manna until they reached the borders of Canaan. [36][An omer is one tenth of an ephah.]

CHAPTER 17

Water from the Rock. [1]From the desert of Sin the whole Israelite community journeyed by stages, as the LORD directed, and encamped at Rephidim.[z]

Here there was no water for the people to drink. [2]They quarreled, therefore, with Moses and said, "Give us water to drink."[a] Moses replied, "Why do you quarrel with me? Why do you put the LORD to a test?" [3]Here, then, in their thirst for water, the people grumbled against Moses, saying, "Why did you ever make us leave Egypt? Was it just to have us die here of thirst with our children and our livestock?" [4]So Moses cried out to the LORD, "What shall I do with this people? A little more and they will stone me!" [5]The LORD answered Moses, "Go over there in front of the people, along with some of the elders of Israel, holding in your hand, as you go, the staff with which you struck the river. [6]I will be standing there in front of you on the rock in Horeb. Strike the rock, and the water will flow from it for the people to drink."[b] This Moses did, in the presence of the

---

u Dt 8, 3.—v 2 Cor 8, 15.—w Nm 11, 7.—x Heb 9, 4.—y Jos 5, 12.—z Nm 33, 12ff.—a 2-7: Nm 20, 2-13.—b 5f: Dt 8, 15; Pss 78, 15f; 105, 41; Wis 11, 4; Is 43, 20; 48, 21.

16, 18: St. Paul cites this passage as an example of equitable sharing. Cf 2 Cor 8, 15.

16, 31: *Coriander seed:* small, round, aromatic seeds of bright brown color; the comparison, therefore, refers merely to the size and shape, not to the taste or color of the manna.

16, 33: *Urn:* according to the Greek translation, which is followed in Heb 9, 4, this was a golden vessel.

16, 34: *The commandments:* the two tablets of the ten commandments, which were kept in the ark. Cf Ex 25, 16. 21f.

elders of Israel. ⁷The place was called Massah and Meribah,* because the Israelites quarreled there and tested the LORD, saying, "Is the LORD in our midst or not?"ᶜ

Battle with Amalek. ⁸At Rephidim, Amalek* came and waged war against Israel.ᵈ ⁹Moses, therefore, said to Joshua, "Pick out certain men, and tomorrow go out and engage Amalek in battle. I will be standing on top of the hill with the staff of God in my hand." ¹⁰So Joshua did as Moses told him: he engaged Amalek in battle after Moses had climbed to the top of the hill with Aaron and Hur. ¹¹As long as Moses kept his hands raised up, Israel had the better of the fight, but when he let his hands rest, Amalek had the better of the fight. ¹²Moses' hands, however, grew tired; so they put a rock in place for him to sit on. Meanwhile Aaron and Hur supported his hands, one on one side and one on the other, so that his hands remained steady till sunset. ¹³And Joshua mowed down Amalek and his people with the edge of the sword.

¹⁴Then the LORD said to Moses, "Write this down in a document as something to be remembered, and recite it in the ears of Joshua.ᵉ I will completely blot out the memory of Amalek from under the heavens." ¹⁵Moses also built an altar there, which he called Yahweh-nissi;* ¹⁶ for he said, "The LORD takes in hand his banner; the LORD will war against Amalek through the centuries."

CHAPTER 18

Meeting with Jethro. ¹Now Moses' father-in-law Jethro, the priest of Midian, heard of all that God had done for Moses and for his people Israel: how the LORD had brought Israel out of Egypt. ²So his father-in-law Jethro took along Zipporah, Moses' wife, whom Moses had sent back to him, ³and her two sons. One of these was called Gershom;ᶠ for he said, "I am a stranger in a foreign land." ⁴The other was called Eliezer; for he said, "My father's God is my helper; he has rescued me from Pharaoh's sword." ⁵Together with Moses' wife and sons, then, his father-in-law Jethro came to him in the desert where he was encamped near the mountain of God, ⁶and he sent word to Moses, "I, Jethro, your father-in-law, am coming to you, along with your wife and her two sons."

⁷Moses went out to meet his father-in-law, bowed down before him, and kissed him. Having greeted each other, they went into the tent. ⁸Moses then told his father-in-law of all that the LORD had done to Pharaoh and the Egyptians for the sake of Israel, and of all the hardships they had had to endure on their journey, and how the LORD had come to their rescue. ⁹Jethro rejoiced over all the goodness that the LORD had shown Israel in rescuing them from the hands of the Egyptians. ¹⁰"Blessed be the LORD," he said, "who has rescued his people from the hands of Pharaoh and the Egyptians. ¹¹Now I know that the LORD is a deity great beyond any other; for he took occasion of their being dealt with insolently to deliver the people from the power of the Egyptians." ¹²Then Jethro, the father-in-law of Moses, brought a holocaust and other sacrifices to God, and Aaron came with all the elders of Israel to participate with Moses' father-in-law in the meal before God.

Appointment of Minor Judges. ¹³The next day Moses sat in judgment for the people, who waited about him from morning until evening. ¹⁴When his father-in-law saw all that he was doing for the people, he inquired, "What sort of thing is this that you are doing for the people? Why do you sit alone while all the people have to stand about you from morning till evening?" ¹⁵Moses answered his father-in-law, "The people come to me to consult God. ¹⁶Whenever they have a disagreement, they come to me to have me settle the matter between them and make known to them God's decisions and regulations."

¹⁷"You are not acting wisely," his father-in-law replied. ¹⁸"You will surely wear yourself out, and not only yourself but also these people with you. The task is too heavy for you;ᵍ you cannot do it alone. ¹⁹Now, listen to me, and I will give you some advice, that God may be with you. Act as the people's representative before God, bringing to him whatever they have to say. ²⁰Enlighten them in regard to the decisions and regulations, showing them

---

c Ps 95, 8f.—d Dt 25, 17; 1 Sm 15, 2.—e Nm 24, 20; 1 Sm 15, 3. 20.—f Ex 2, 22.—g Nm 11, 14.

17, 7: *Massah . . . Meribah:* Hebrew words meaning respectively, "the (place of the) test," and "the (place of the) quarreling."

17, 8: *Amalek:* the Amalekites were an aboriginal people of southern Palestine and the Sinai peninsula. Cf Nm 24, 20.

17, 15: *Yahweh-nissi:* meaning, "the LORD is my banner."

how they are to live and what they are to do. [21] But you should also look among all the people for able and God-fearing men, trustworthy men who hate dishonest gain, and set them as officers over groups of thousands, of hundreds, of fifties, and of tens.[h] [22] Let these men render decisions for the people in all ordinary cases. More important cases they should refer to you, but all the lesser cases they can settle themselves. Thus, your burden will be lightened, since they will bear it with you. [23] If you do this, when God gives you orders you will be able to stand the strain, and all these people will go home satisfied."

[24] Moses followed the advice of his father-in-law and did all that he had suggested. [25] He picked out able men from all Israel and put them in charge of the people as officers over groups of thousands, of hundreds, of fifties, and of tens. [26] They rendered decisions for the people in all ordinary cases. The more difficult cases they referred to Moses, but all the lesser cases they settled themselves. [27] Then Moses bade farewell to his father-in-law, who went off to his own country.

III. THE COVENANT AT MOUNT SINAI

CHAPTER 19

Arrival at Sinai. [1] [i] In the third month after their departure from the land of Egypt, on its first day, the Israelites came to the desert of Sinai. [2] After the journey from Rephidim to the desert of Sinai, they pitched camp.

While Israel was encamped here in front of the mountain, [3] Moses went up the mountain to God. Then the LORD called to him and said, "Thus shall you say to the house of Jacob; [4] tell the Israelites: You have seen for yourselves how I treated the

Egyptians and how I bore you up on eagle wings and brought you here to myself.[j] [5] Therefore, if you hearken to my voice and keep my covenant, you shall be my special possession, dearer to me than all other people,[k] though all the earth is mine. [6] You shall be to me a kingdom of priests,* a holy nation.[l] That is what you must tell the Israelites." [7] So Moses went and summoned the elders of the people. When he set before them all that the LORD had ordered him to tell them, [8] the people all answered together, "Everything the LORD has said, we will do." Then Moses brought back to the LORD the response of the people.

[9] The LORD also told him, "I am coming to you in a dense cloud,[m] so that when the people hear me speaking with you, they may always have faith in you also." When Moses, then, had reported to the LORD the response of the people, [10] the LORD added, "Go to the people and have them sanctify themselves today and tomorrow. Make them wash their garments [11] and be ready for the third day; for on the third day the LORD will come down on Mount Sinai before the eyes of all the people. [12] Set limits for the people all around the mountain,[n] and tell them: Take care not to go up the mountain, or even to touch its base. If anyone touches the mountain he must be put to death. [13] No hand shall touch him; he must be stoned to death or killed with arrows. Such a one, man or beast, must not be allowed to live. Only when the ram's horn resounds may they go up to the mountain." [14] Then Moses came down from the mountain to the people and had them sanctify themselves and wash their garments. [15] He warned them, "Be ready for the third day. Have no intercourse with any woman."

The Great Theophany. [16] On the morning of the third day there were peals of thunder and lightning, and a heavy cloud over the mountain, and a very loud trumpet blast, so that all the people in the camp trembled. [17] But Moses led the people out of the camp to meet God, and they stationed themselves at the foot of the mountain.[o] [18] Mount Sinai was all wrapped in smoke, for the LORD came down upon it in fire. The smoke rose from it as though from a furnace, and the whole mountain trembled violently. [19] The trumpet blast grew louder and louder, while Moses was

---

h 21. 25: Dt 1, 15; 16, 18.—i 1f: Nm 33, 15.—j Dt 32, 11.—k Dt 7, 6; 14, 2; 26, 18f; 32, 8f.—l 1 Pt 2, 9.—m Ex 20, 21; 24, 15-18.—n 12f: Ex 34, 3; Heb 12, 18f.—o 16ff: Dt 4, 10ff.

19, 6: *Kingdom of priests:* inasmuch as the whole Israelite nation was consecrated to God in a special way, it formed a race of royal priests who participated in the liturgical sacrifices, even though the actual offering of the sacrifices was the exclusive prerogative of the Aaronic priesthood. The same condition exists in the New Dispensation as regards the whole Christian people and the Christian priesthood in the strict sense. Cf Is 61, 6; 1 Pt 2, 5. 9.

speaking and God answering him with thunder.

²⁰When the LORD came down to the top of Mount Sinai, he summoned Moses to the top of the mountain, and Moses went up to him. ²¹Then the LORD told Moses, "Go down and warn the people not to break through toward the LORD in order to see him; otherwise many of them will be struck down. ²²The priests, too, who approach the LORD must sanctify themselves; else he will vent his anger upon them." ²³Moses said to the LORD, "The people cannot go up to Mount Sinai, for you yourself warned us to set limits around the mountain to make it sacred." ²⁴The LORD repeated, "Go down now! Then come up again along with Aaron. But the priests and the people must not break through to come up to the LORD; else he will vent his anger upon them." ²⁵So Moses went down to the people and told them this.

CHAPTER 20

The Ten Commandments. ¹Then God delivered all these commandments:*

² ᵖ "I, the LORD, am your God, who brought you out of the land of Egypt,�q that place of slavery. ³You shall not have other gods besides me. ⁴You shall not carve idolsʳ for yourselves in the shape of anything in the sky above or on the earth below or in the waters beneath the earth; ⁵you shall not bow down before them or worship them.ˢ For I, the LORD, your God, am a jealous* God, inflicting punishment for their fathers' wickedness on the children of those who hate me, down to the third and fourth generation; ⁶but bestowing mercy down to the thousandth generation, on the children of those who love me and keep my commandments.

⁷"You shall not take the name of the LORD, your God, in vain.ᵗ For the LORD will not leave unpunished him who takes his name in vain.

⁸"Remember to keep holy the sabbath day. ⁹Six days you may labor and do all your work, ¹⁰but the seventh day is the sabbath of the LORD, your God.ᵘ No work may be done then either by you, or your son or daughter, or your male or female slave, or your beast, or by the alien who lives with you. ¹¹In six days the LORD made the heavens and the earth, the sea and all that is in them; but on the seventh

day he rested.ᵛ That is why the LORD has blessed the sabbath day and made it holy.

¹² ʷ "Honor your father and your mother, that you may have a long life in the land which the Lord, your God, is giving you.ˣ

¹³"You shall not kill.ʸ

¹⁴"You shall not commit adultery.ᶻ

¹⁵"You shall not steal.ᵃ

¹⁶"You shall not bear false witness against your neighbor.ᵇ

¹⁷"You shall not covet your neighbor's house. You shall not covet your neighbor's wife, nor his male or female slave, nor his ox or ass, nor anything else that belongs to him."ᶜ

The Fear of God. ¹⁸When the people witnessed the thunder and lightning, the trumpet blast and the mountain smoking, they all feared and trembled.ᵈ So they took up a position much farther away ¹⁹and said to Moses, "You speak to us, and we will listen; but let not God speak to us, or we shall die." ²⁰Moses answered the people, "Do not be afraid, for God has come to you only to test you and put his fear upon you, lest you should sin." ²¹Still the people remained at a distance, while Moses approached the cloud where God was.

²²The LORD told Moses, "Thus shall you speak to the Israelites: You have seen for yourselves that I have spoken to you from heaven. ²³Do not make anything to rank with me; neither gods of silver nor gods of gold shall you make for yourselves.ᵉ

²⁴ ᶠ "An altar of earth you shall make for me, and upon it you shall sacrifice your holocausts and peace offerings, your sheep and your oxen. In whatever place I choose for the remembrance of my name* I

---

p 2-17: Dt 5, 6-21.—q Lv 26, 13; Ps 81, 10; Hos 13, 4.—r Ex 34, 17; Lv 26, 1; Dt 4, 15-19; 27, 15.—s Ex 34, 7. 14; Nm 14, 18; Dt 4, 24; 6, 15.—t Lv 19, 12; 24, 16.—u 8ff: Ex 23, 12; 31, 13-16: 34, 21; 35, 2; Lv 23, 3.—v Ex 31, 17; Gn 2, 2f.—w 12-16: Mt 19, 18f; Mk 10, 19; Lk 18, 20; Rom 13, 9.—x Mt 15, 4; Mk 7, 10; Eph 6, 2f.—y Mt 5, 21.—z Lv 18, 20; 20, 10; Dt 22, 22; Mt 5, 27.—a Lv 19, 11.—b Ex 23, 1; Dt 19, 16ff; Prv 19, 5. 9; 24, 28.—c Rom 7, 7.—d 18-21: Dt 4, 11; 5, 22-27; 18, 16; Heb 12, 18f.—e Ex 20, 3f.—f Dt 12, 5. 11; 14, 23; 16, 6.

20, 1-17: The precise division of these precepts into "ten commandments" is somewhat uncertain. Traditionally among Catholics vv 1-6 are considered as only one commandment, and v 17 as two. Cf Dt 5, 6-21.

20, 5: *Jealous:* demanding exclusive allegiance, such as a wife must have for her husband.

20, 24: *I choose for the remembrance of my name:* literally, "where I make my name to be remembered": at the sacred site where God wishes to be worshiped and his name revered.

come to you and bless you. 25 If you make an altar of stone for me,^{g} do not build it of cut stone, for by putting a tool to it you desecrate it. 26 You shall not go up by steps to my altar, on which you must not be indecently uncovered.

CHAPTER 21

Laws Regarding Slaves. 1 "These are the rules* you shall lay before them. 2 ^{h} When you purchase a Hebrew slave, he is to serve you for six years, but in the seventh year he shall be given his freedom without cost. 3 If he comes into service alone, he shall leave alone; if he comes with a wife, his wife shall leave with him. 4 But if his master gives him a wife and she bears him sons or daughters, the woman and her children shall remain the master's property and the man shall leave alone. 5 If, however, the slave declares, 'I am devoted to my master and my wife and children; I will not go free,' 6 his master shall bring him to God* and there, at the door or doorpost, he shall pierce his ear with an awl, thus keeping him as his slave forever.

7 "When a man sells his daughter as a slave, she shall not go free as male slaves do. 8 But if her master, who had destined her* for himself, dislikes her, he shall let her be redeemed. He has no right to sell her to a foreigner, since he has broken faith with her. 9 If he destines her for his son, he shall treat her like a daughter. 10 If he takes another wife, he shall not withhold her food, her clothing, or her conjugal rights. 11 If he does not grant her these three things, she shall be given her freedom absolutely, without cost to her.

g Dt 27, 5; Jos 8, 31.—h 2-6: Lv 25, 39ff; Dt 15, 12-18; Jer 34, 14.—i 12ff Lv 24, 17; Nm 35, 15-29; Dt 4, 41f; 19, 2-5.—j Dt 24, 7.—k Lv 20, 9; Prv 20, 20; Mt 15, 4; Mk 7, 10.—l 22-25: Lv 24, 18-21; Dt 19, 21; Mt 5, 38.

21, 1: *Rules:* judicial precedents to be used in settling questions of law and custom. This introductory phrase serves as the title of the following collection of civil and religious laws (chapters 21-23) which is called in Ex 24, 7, *the book of the covenant.*

21, 6: *To God:* to the sanctuary; or perhaps the phrase is to be rendered, "to the gods," in the sense of "to the judges." Cf Ps 82, 1. Since the expression "to have an open ear" meant "to obey," a pierced earlobe was an ancient symbol of obedience. Cf Ps 40, 7.

21, 8: *Destined her:* intended her as a wife of second rank.

21, 23ff: This section is known as the *lex talionis,* the law of tit for tat. The purpose of this law was not merely the enforcement of rigorous justice, but also the prevention of greater penalties than would be just. Christ refers to this passage when he exhorts Christians to cede their lawful rights for the sake of charity. Cf Mt 5, 38ff.

Personal Injury. 12 "Whoever strikes a man a mortal blow must be put to death.^{i} 13 He, however, who did not hunt a man down, but caused his death by an act of God, may flee to a place which I will set apart for this purpose. 14 But when a man kills another after maliciously scheming to do so, you must take him even from my altar and put him to death. 15 Whoever strikes his father or mother shall be put to death.

16 "A kidnaper, whether he sells his victim or still has him when caught, shall be put to death.^{j}

17 "Whoever curses his father or mother shall be put to death.^{k}

18 "When men quarrel and one strikes the other with a stone or with his fist, not mortally, but enough to put him in bed, 19 the one who struck the blow shall be acquitted, provided the other can get up and walk around with the help of his staff. Still, he must compensate him for his enforced idleness and provide for his complete cure.

20 "When a man strikes his male or female slave with a rod so hard that the slave dies under his hand, he shall be punished. 21 If, however, the slave survives for a day or two, he is not to be punished, since the slave is his own property.

22 "When men have a fight and hurt a pregnant woman, so that she suffers a miscarriage, but no further injury, the guilty one shall be fined as much as the woman's husband demands of him, and he shall pay in the presence of the judges.^{l} 23 * But if injury ensues, you shall give life for life, 24 eye for eye, tooth for tooth, hand for hand, foot for foot, 25 burn for burn, wound for wound, stripe for stripe.

26 "When a man strikes his male or female slave in the eye and destroys the use of the eye, he shall let the slave go free in compensation for the eye. 27 If he knocks out a tooth of his male or female slave, he shall let the slave go free in compensation for the tooth.

28 "When an ox gores a man or a woman to death, the ox must be stoned; its flesh may not be eaten. The owner of the ox, however, shall go unpunished. 29 But if an ox was previously in the habit of goring people and its owner, though warned, would not keep it in; should it then kill a man or a woman, not only must the ox be stoned, but its owner also must be put to

death. [30] If, however, a fine is imposed on him, he must pay in ransom for his life whatever amount is imposed on him. [31] This law applies if it is a boy or a girl that the ox gores. [32] But if it is a male or a female slave that it gores, he must pay the owner of the slave thirty shekels of silver, and the ox must be stoned.

Property Damage. [33] "When a man uncovers or digs a cistern and does not cover it over again, should an ox or an ass fall into it, [34] the owner of the cistern must make good by restoring the value of the animal to its owner; the dead animal, however, he may keep.

[35] "When one man's ox hurts another's ox so badly that it dies, they shall sell the live ox and divide this money as well as the dead animal equally between them. [36] But if it was known that the ox was previously in the habit of goring and its owner would not keep it in, he must make full restitution, an ox for an ox; but the dead animal he may keep.

[37] * "When a man steals an ox or a sheep and slaughters or sells it, he shall restore five oxen for the one ox, and four sheep for the one sheep. [m]

CHAPTER 22

[1] "[If a thief is caught* in the act of housebreaking and beaten to death, there is no bloodguilt involved. [2] But if after sunrise he is thus beaten, there is bloodguilt.] He must make full restitution. If he has nothing, he shall be sold to pay for his theft. [3] If what he stole is found alive in his possession, be it an ox, an ass or a sheep, he shall restore two animals for each one stolen.

[4] * "When a man is burning over a field or a vineyard, if he lets the fire spread so that it burns in another's field, he must make restitution with the best produce of his own field or vineyard. [5] If the fire spreads further, and catches on to thorn bushes, so that shocked grain or standing grain or the field itself is burned up, the one who started the fire must make full restitution.

Trusts and Loans. [6] "When a man gives money or any article to another for safekeeping and it is stolen from the latter's house, the thief, if caught, must make twofold restitution. [7] If the thief is not caught, the owner of the house shall

be brought to God,* to swear that he himself did not lay hands on his neighbor's property. [8] In every question of dishonest appropriation, whether it be about an ox, or an ass, or a sheep, or a garment, or anything else that has disappeared, where another claims that the thing is his, both parties shall present their case before God; the one whom God convicts must make twofold restitution to the other.

[9] "When a man gives an ass, or an ox, or a sheep, or any other animal to another for safekeeping, if it dies, or is maimed or snatched away, without anyone witnessing the fact, [10] the custodian shall swear by the Lord that he did not lay hands on his neighbor's property; the owner must accept the oath, and no restitution is to be made. [11] But if the custodian is really guilty of theft, he must make restitution to the owner. [12] If it has been killed by a wild beast, let him bring it as evidence, and he need not make restitution for the mangled animal. [n]

[13] "When a man borrows an animal from his neighbor, if it is maimed or dies while the owner is not present, the man must make restitution. [14] But if the owner is present, he need not make restitution. If it was hired, this was covered by the price of its hire.

Social Laws. [15] "When a man seduces a virgin who is not betrothed, and lies with her, he shall pay her marriage price and marry her. [o] [16] If her father refuses to give her to him, he must still pay him the customary marriage price for virgins.*

[17] "You shall not let a sorceress live. [p]

[18] "Anyone who lies with an animal shall be put to death. [q]

[19] "Whoever sacrifices to any god, except to the Lord alone, shall be doomed. [r]

---

m 2 Sm 12, 6.—n Gn 31, 39.—o 15f: Dt 22, 28f.—p Lv 19, 26. 31; 20, 6. 27; Dt 18, 10f.—q Lv 18, 23; Dt 27, 21.—r Dt 13; 17, 2-7.

21, 37—22, 30: In the Vulgate, 22, 1-31.

22, 1f: *If a thief is caught:* this seems to be a fragment of what was once a longer law on housebreaking, which has been inserted here into the middle of a law on stealing animals. At night the householder would be justified in killing a burglar outright, but not so in the daytime, when the burglar could more easily be caught alive. *He must make full restitution:* this stood originally immediately after 21, 37.

22, 4: The Greek and Latin versions understood this verse as a prohibition against allowing one's cattle to graze in the field of another.

22, 7: *Brought to God:* see note on Ex 21, 6. Cf also Ex 22, 10.

22, 16: *The customary marriage price for virgins:* fifty shekels according to Dt 22, 29.

20 "You shall not molest or oppress an alien, for you were once aliens yourselves in the land of Egypt.ˢ ²¹ You shall not wrong any widow or orphan. ²² If ever you wrong them and they cry out to me, I will surely hear their cry. ²³ My wrath will flare up, and I will kill you with the sword; then your own wives will be widows, and your children orphans.

²⁴ ᵗ "If you lend money to one of your poor neighbors among my people, you shall not act like an extortioner toward him by demanding interest from him. ²⁵ If you take your neighbor's cloak as a pledge, you shall return it to him before sunset; ²⁶ for this cloak of his is the only covering he has for his body. What else has he to sleep in? If he cries out to me, I will hear him; for I am compassionate.

²⁷ "You shall not revile God,* nor curse a prince of your people.ᵘ

²⁸ "You shall not delay the offering of your harvest and your press. You shall give me the first-born of your sons. ²⁹ You must do the same with your oxen and your sheep; for seven days the firstling may stay with its mother, but on the eighth day you must give it to me.ᵛ

³⁰ "You shall be men sacred to me. Flesh torn to pieces in the field you shall not eat; throw it to the dogs.ʷ

CHAPTER 23

¹ "You shall not repeat a false report. Do not join the wicked in putting your hand, as an unjust witness, upon anyone.ˣ ² Neither shall you allege the example of the many as an excuse for doing wrong, nor shall you, when testifying in a lawsuit, side with the many in perverting justice. ³ You shall not favor a poor man in his lawsuit.ʸ

---

s 20-23: Ex 23, 9; Lv 19, 33f; Dt 10, 18f; 24, 17f; 27, 19; Zec 7, 10.—t 24-26: Lv 25, 35-38; Dt 23, 19f; 24, 10-13; Ez 18, 7f. 17f.—u Acts 23, 5.—v Ex 13, 2; 34, 19; Lv 22, 27; Dt 15, 19.— w Lv 17, 24; 17, 15; 22, 8.—x 1f: Dt 19, 16ff.—y Lv 19, 15.—z Dt 22, 1ff.—a Dt 16, 19; 27, 25; Sir 20, 28.—b Ex 22, 21.—c 10f: Lv 25, 3-7.—d Ex 20, 8.—e 14-17: Ex 34, 18. 22ff; Lv 23; Dt 16, 1-17.—f 18f: Ex 34, 25f.

22, 27: *God:* or perhaps "the gods," in the sense of "the judges," as the parallel with *a prince of your people* suggests.

23, 14: These three feasts are elsewhere called the Passover, Pentecost and Booths. Cf Ex 34, 18-26; Lv 23; Dt 16.

23, 15: *Appear before me:* the original expression was "see my face"; so also in several other places, as Ex 23, 17; 34, 23f; Dt 16, 16; 31, 11.

23, 19: *Boil a kid in its mother's milk:* this was part of a Canaanite ritual; hence it is forbidden here as a pagan ceremony.

⁴ "When you come upon your enemy's ox or ass going astray, see to it that it is returned to him.ᶻ ⁵ When you notice the ass of one who hates you lying prostrate under its burden, by no means desert him; help him, rather, to raise it up.

⁶ "You shall not deny one of your needy fellow men his rights in his lawsuit. ⁷ You shall keep away from anything dishonest. The innocent and the just you shall not put to death, nor shall you acquit the guilty. ⁸ Never take a bribe, for a bribe blinds even the most clear-sighted and twists the words even of the just.ᵃ ⁹ You shall not oppress an alien; you well know how it feels to be an alien, since you were once aliens yourselves in the land of Egypt.ᵇ

Religious Laws. ¹⁰ ᶜ "For six years you may sow your land and gather in its produce. ¹¹ But the seventh year you shall let the land lie untilled and unharvested, that the poor among you may eat of it and the beasts of the field may eat what the poor leave. So also shall you do in regard to your vineyard and your olive grove.

¹² "For six days you may do your work, but on the seventh day you must rest,ᵈ that your ox and your ass may also have rest, and that the son of your maidservant and the alien may be refreshed. ¹³ Give heed to all that I have told you.

"Never mention the name of any other god; it shall not be heard from your lips.

¹⁴ ᵉ "Three times a year you shall celebrate a pilgrim feast to me.* ¹⁵ You shall keep the feast of Unleavened Bread. As I have commanded you, you must eat unleavened bread for seven days at the prescribed time in the month of Abib, for it was then that you came out of Egypt. No one shall appear before me* empty-handed. ¹⁶ You shall also keep the feast of the grain harvest with the first of the crop that you have sown in the field; and finally, the feast at the fruit harvest at the end of the year, when you gather in the produce from the fields. ¹⁷ Thrice a year shall all your men appear before the Lᴏʀᴅ God.

¹⁸ "You shall not offer the blood of my sacrifice with leavened bread;ᶠ nor shall the fat of my feast be kept overnight till the next day. ¹⁹ The choicest first fruits of your soil you shall bring to the house of the Lᴏʀᴅ, your God.

"You shall not boil a kid in its mother's milk.*

Reward of Fidelity. [20]"See, I am sending an angel[g] before you, to guard you on the way and bring you to the place I have prepared. [21]Be attentive to him and heed his voice. Do not rebel against him, for he will not forgive your sin. My authority resides in him.* [22]If you heed his voice and carry out all I tell you, I will be an enemy to your enemies and a foe to your foes.

[23]"My angel will go before you and bring you to the Amorites, Hittites, Perizzites, Canaanites, Hivites and Jebusites; and I will wipe them out. [24]Therefore, you shall not bow down in worship before their gods, nor shall you make anything like them;* rather, you must demolish them and smash their sacred pillars.[h] [25]The LORD, your God, you shall worship; then I will bless your food and drink, and I will remove all sickness from your midst; [26]no woman in your land will be barren or miscarry; and I will give you a full span of life.

[27]"I will have the fear of me precede you, so that I will throw into panic every nation you reach.[i] I will make all your enemies turn from you in flight, [28]and ahead of you I will send hornets* to drive the Hivites, Canaanites and Hittites out of your way. [29]But not in one year will I drive them all out before you; else the land will become so desolate that the wild beasts will multiply against you. [30]Instead, I will drive them out little by little before you, until you have grown numerous enough to take possession of the land. [31][j] I will set your boundaries from the Red Sea to the sea of the Philistines,* and from the desert to the River; all who dwell in this land I will hand over to you to be driven out of your way. [32]You shall not make a covenant with them or their gods. [33]They must not abide in your land, lest they make you sin against me by ensnaring you into worshiping their gods."[k]

CHAPTER 24

Ratification of the Covenant. [1]Moses himself was told, "Come up to the LORD, you and Aaron, with Nadab, Abihu, and seventy of the elders of Israel. You shall all worship at some distance, [2]but Moses alone is to come close to the LORD; the others shall not come too near, and the people shall not come up at all with Moses."

[3]When Moses came to the people and related all the words and ordinances of the LORD, they all answered with one voice, "We will do everything that the LORD has told us."[l] [4]Moses then wrote down all the words of the LORD and, rising early the next day, he erected at the foot of the mountain an altar and twelve pillars* for the twelve tribes of Israel. [5]Then, having sent certain young men of the Israelites to offer holocausts and sacrifice young bulls as peace offerings to the LORD, [6]Moses took half of the blood and put it in large bowls; the other half he splashed on the altar. [7]Taking the book of the covenant, he read it aloud to the people, who answered, "All that the LORD has said, we will heed and do." [8]Then he took the blood and sprinkled it on the people, saying, "This is the blood of the covenant which the LORD has made with you in accordance with all these words of his."[m]

[9]Moses then went up with Aaron, Nadab, Abihu, and seventy elders of Israel, [10]and they beheld the God of Israel. Under his feet there appeared to be sapphire tilework, as clear as the sky itself. [11]Yet he did not smite these chosen Israelites. After gazing on God,* they could still eat and drink.

Moses on the Mountain. [12]The LORD said to Moses, "Come up to me on the mountain and, while you are there, I will give you the stone tablets[n] on which I have written the commandments intended for their instruction." [13]So Moses set out with Joshua, his aide, and went up to the mountain of God. [14]The elders, however, had

---

g Ex 14, 19; 32, 34; 33, 2.—h 23f: Ex 34, 10-16; Nm 33, 51f; Dt 7, 24ff.—i 27ff: Dt 2, 25; 7, 20ff.—j Gn 15, 18; Dt 11, 24; Jos 1, 4.—k 32f: Ex 34, 12-16; Dt 7, 2ff.—l Ex 19, 8.—m 5-8: Heb 9, 18ff.—n Ex 31, 18; 32, 15f; Dt 5, 22.

23, 21: *My authority resides in him:* literally, "My name is within him."

23, 24: *Make anything like them:* some render, "act according to their conduct." *Sacred pillars:* objects of religious veneration at Canaanite sanctuaries.

23, 28: *Hornets:* some understand this figuratively of various troublesome afflictions; others translate the Hebrew word as "leprosy." Cf Dt 7, 20; Jos 24, 12; Wis 12, 8.

23, 31: *The sea of the Philistines:* the Mediterranean. *The River:* the Euphrates. Only in the time of David and Solomon did the territory of Israel come near to reaching such distant borders.

24, 4: *Pillars:* stone shafts or slabs, erected as symbols of the fact that each of the twelve tribes had entered into this covenant with God; not idolatrous as in Ex 23, 24, although the same Hebrew word is used in both passages. See note on Gn 28, 18.

24, 11: *After gazing on God:* the ancients thought that the sight of God would bring instantaneous death. Cf Ex 33, 20; Gn 16, 13; 32, 31; Jgs 6, 22f; 13, 22. *Eat and drink:* partake of the sacrificial meal.

been told by him, "Wait here for us until we return to you. Aaron and Hur are staying with you. If anyone has a complaint, let him refer the matter to them." [15] After Moses had gone up, a cloud covered the mountain. [16] The glory of the LORD settled upon Mount Sinai. The cloud covered it for six days, and on the seventh day he called to Moses from the midst of the cloud.[o] [17] To the Israelites the glory of the LORD was seen as a consuming fire on the mountaintop.[p] [18] But Moses passed into the midst of the cloud as he went up on the mountain; and there he stayed for forty days and forty nights.[q]

IV: THE DWELLING AND ITS FURNISHINGS

CHAPTER 25

Collection of Materials. [1] This is what the LORD then said to Moses:[r] [2] "Tell the Israelites to take up a collection for me. From every man you shall accept the contribution that his heart prompts him to give me. [3] These are the contributions you shall accept from them: gold, silver and bronze;[s] [4] violet, purple and scarlet yarn; fine linen and goat hair; [5] rams' skins dyed red, and tahash* skins; acacia wood; [6] oil for the light; spices for the anointing oil and for the fragrant incense; [7] onyx stones and other gems for mounting on the ephod and the breastpiece.

[8] "They shall make a sanctuary for me, that I may dwell in their midst.[t] [9] This

---

o Sir 45, 4.—p Ex 19, 18; Heb 12, 18.—q Ex 34, 28; Dt 9, 9.—r 1-7: Ex 35, 4-9. 20-29.—s Ex 35, 4-9.—t 8f: Ex 26, 1-30; 36, 8-38.—u Acts 7, 44.—v 10-22: Ex 37, 1-9; Heb 9, 1-5.—w 23-30: Ex 37, 10-16.—x Lv 24, 5ff.

25, 5: *Tahash:* perhaps the name of a marine animal, such as the dugong or the porpoise. The Greek and Latin versions took it for the color hyacinth.

25, 17: *Propitiatory:* this traditional rendering of the Hebrew term, which may mean merely "cover," is derived from its connection with the ceremony of the Day of Atonement whereby God was rendered "propitious." Cf Lv 16, 14ff.

25, 18ff: *Cherubim:* probably in the form of human-headed winged lions. The cherubim over the ark formed the throne for the invisible Lord. Cf Ps 80, 2. For a more detailed description of the somewhat different cherubim in the temple of Solomon, see 1 Kgs 6, 23-28; 2 Chr 3, 10-13.

25, 25: *A frame:* probably placed near the bottom of the legs to keep them steady. The golden table of Herod's temple is pictured thus on the Arch of Titus.

25, 29f: The *plates* held the showbread, that is, the holy bread which was placed upon the table every sabbath as an offering to God, and was later eaten by the priests. The *cups* held the incense which was strewn upon the bread. Cf Lv 24, 5-9. The libation wine was poured from the *pitchers* into the *bowls*. All these vessels were kept on the golden table.

Dwelling and all its furnishings you shall make exactly according to the pattern that I will now show you.[u]

Plan of the Ark. [10] "You shall make an ark of acacia wood,[v] two and a half cubits long, one and a half cubits wide, and one and a half cubits high. [11] Plate it inside and outside with pure gold, and put a molding of gold around the top of it. [12] Cast four gold rings and fasten them on the four supports of the ark, two rings on one side and two on the opposite side. [13] Then make poles of acacia wood and plate them with gold. [14] These poles you are to put through the rings on the sides of the ark, for carrying it; [15] they must remain in the rings of the ark and never be withdrawn. [16] In the ark you are to put the commandments which I will give you.

[17] "You shall then make a propitiatory* of pure gold, two cubits and a half long, and one and a half cubits wide. [18] Make two cherubim* of beaten gold for the two ends of the propitiatory, [19] fastening them so that one cherub springs direct from each end. [20] The cherubim shall have their wings spread out above, covering the propitiatory with them; they shall be turned toward each other, but with their faces looking toward the propitiatory. [21] This propitiatory you shall then place on top of the ark. In the ark itself you are to put the commandments which I will give you. [22] There I will meet you and there, from above the propitiatory, between the two cherubim on the ark of the commandments, I will tell you all the commands that I wish to give to the Israelites.

The Table. [23] "You shall also make a table of acacia[w] wood, two cubits long, a cubit wide, and a cubit and a half high. [24] Plate it with pure gold and make a molding of gold around it. [25] Surround it with a frame,* a handbreadth high, with a molding of gold around the frame. [26] You shall also make four rings of gold for it and fasten them at the four corners, one at each leg, [27] on two opposite sides of the frame as holders for the poles to carry the table. [28] These poles for carrying the table you shall make of acacia wood and plate with gold. [29] Of pure gold you shall make its plates* and cups, as well as its pitchers and bowls for pouring libations. [30] On the table you shall always keep showbread set before me.[x]

The Lampstand. [31]"You shall make a lampstand of pure beaten gold[y]—its shaft and branches—with its cups and knobs and petals springing directly from it. [32]Six branches are to extend from the sides of the lampstand, three branches on one side, and three on the other. [33] * On one branch there are to be three cups, shaped like almond blossoms, each with its knob and petals; on the opposite branch there are to be three cups, shaped like almond blossoms, each with its knob and petals; and so for the six branches that extend from the lampstand. [34]On the shaft there are to be four cups,* shaped like almond blossoms, with their knobs and petals, [35]including a knob below each of the three pairs of branches that extend from the lampstand. [36]Their knobs and branches shall so spring from it that the whole will form but a single piece of pure beaten gold. [37] * You shall then make seven lamps[z] for it and so set up the lamps that they shed their light on the space in front of the lampstand. [38]These, as well as the trimming shears and trays,* must be of pure gold. [39]Use a talent of pure gold for the lampstand and all its appurtenances. [40]See that you make them according to the pattern shown you on the mountain.[a]

CHAPTER 26

The Tent Cloth. [1]"The Dwelling itself you shall make out of sheets* woven of fine linen twined and of violet, purple and scarlet yarn, with cherubim embroidered on them.[b] [2]The length of each shall be twenty-eight cubits, and the width four cubits; all the sheets shall be of the same size. [3]Five of the sheets are to be sewed together, edge to edge; and the same for the other five. [4]Make loops of violet yarn along the edge of the end sheet in one set, and the same along the edge of the end sheet in the other set. [5]There are to be fifty loops along the edge of the end sheet in one set, and fifty loops along the edge of the corresponding sheet in the second set, and so placed that the loops are directly opposite each other. [6]Then make fifty clasps of gold, with which to join the two sets of sheets, so that the Dwelling forms one whole.

[7]"Also make sheets woven of goat hair, to be used as a tent covering* over the Dwelling. [8]Eleven such sheets are to be made; the length of each shall be thirty cubits, and the width four cubits: all eleven sheets shall be of the same size. [9]Sew five of the sheets, edge to edge, into one set, and the other six sheets into another set. Use the sixth sheet double at the front of the tent.* [10]Make fifty loops along the edge of the end sheet in one set, and fifty loops along the edge of the end sheet in the second set. [11]Also make fifty bronze clasps and put them into the loops, to join the tent into one whole. [12]There will be an extra half sheet of tent covering, which will be allowed to hang down over the rear of the Dwelling. [13]Likewise, the sheets of the tent will have an extra cubit's length to be left hanging down on either side of the Dwelling to protect it. [14]Over the tent itself you shall make a covering of rams' skins dyed red, and above that, a covering of tahash skins.

The Wooden Walls. [15] [c] "You shall make boards of acacia wood as walls for the Dwelling. [16]The length of each board is to be ten cubits, and its width one and a half cubits. [17]Each board shall have two arms* that shall serve to fasten the boards in line. In this way all the boards of the Dwelling are to be made. [18]Set up the boards of the Dwelling as follows: twenty boards on the south side, [19]with forty silver pedestals under the twenty boards, so that there are two pedestals under each board, at its two arms; [20]twenty boards on the other side of the Dwelling, the north side, [21]with their forty silver pedestals, two under each

---

y 31-40: Ex 37, 17-24.—z Lv 24, 2ff; Nm 8, 2.—a Heb 8, 5.— b 1-14: Ex 36, 8-19.—c 15-30: Ex 36, 20-34.

25, 33: In keeping with the arrangement of the ornaments on the shaft, the three sets of ornaments on each branch were probably so placed that one was at the top and the other two equally spaced along the length of the branch. *Knob:* the cup-shaped seed capsule at the base of a flower.

25, 34f: Of the four ornaments on the shaft, one was at the top and one was below each of the three sets of side branches.

25, 37: The lamps were probably shaped like small boats, with the wick at one end; the end with the wick was turned toward the front of the lampstand.

25, 38: *Trays:* small receptacles for the burnt-out wicks.

26, 1: *Sheets:* strips of tapestry, woven of white linen, the colored threads being used for the cherubim which were embroidered on them. These sheets were stretched across the top of the Dwelling to form a roof, their free ends hanging down inside the boards which formed walls.

26, 7: *Tent covering:* the cloth made of sheets of goat hair to cover the Dwelling.

26, 9: Half the width of the end strip was folded back at the front of the Dwelling, thus leaving another half-strip to hang down at the rear. Cf v 12.

26, 17: *Arms:* literally, "hands." According to some, they served as "tongue and groove" to mortise the boards together; according to others, they were pegs at the bottom of the boards and fitted into sockets in the pedestals.

board; ²² six boards for the rear of the Dwelling, to the west; ²³ and two boards for the corners at the rear of the Dwelling. ²⁴ These two shall be double at the bottom, and likewise double at the top, to the first ring. That is how both boards in the corners are to be made. ²⁵ Thus, there shall be in the rear eight boards, with their sixteen silver pedestals, two pedestals under each board. ²⁶ Also make bars of acacia wood: five for the boards on one side of the Dwelling, ²⁷ five for those on the other side, and five for those at the rear, toward the west. ²⁸ The center bar, at the middle of the boards, shall reach across from end to end. ²⁹ Plate the boards with gold, and make gold rings on them as holders for the bars, which are also to be plated with gold. ³⁰ You shall erect the Dwelling according to the pattern shown you on the mountain.

The Veils. ³¹ "You shall have a veil woven of violet, purple and scarlet yarn,^d and of fine linen twined, with cherubim embroidered on it.^e ³² It is to be hung on four gold-plated columns of acacia wood, which shall have hooks* of gold and shall rest on four silver pedestals. ³³ Hang the veil from clasps. The ark of the commandments you shall bring inside, behind this veil which divides the holy place from the holy of holies. ³⁴ Set the propitiatory on the ark of the commandments in the holy of holies.

³⁵ "Outside the veil you shall place the table and the lampstand, the latter on the south side of the Dwelling, opposite the table which is to be put on the north side. ³⁶ For the entrance of the tent make a variegated* curtain of violet, purple and scarlet yarn and of fine linen twined. ³⁷ Make five columns of acacia wood for this curtain; have them plated with gold, with their hooks of gold; and cast five bronze pedestals for them.

d 2 Chr 3, 14.—e 31-37: Ex 36, 35-38.—f 1-8: Ex 38, 1-7.—g 9-19: Ex 38, 9-20.

26, 32: *Hooks:* probably placed near the tops of the columns, to hold the rope from which the veils and curtains hung.
26, 36: *Variegated:* without definite designs such as the cherubim on the inner veil.
27, 4: *Grating:* it is not clear whether this was flush with the altar or at some small distance from it; in the latter case the space between the altar and the grating would be filled with stones and serve as a platform around the altar, which would otherwise be too high for the priest to reach conveniently.
27, 8: *Hollow:* probably filled with earth or stones when in use. Cf Ex 20, 24f.

CHAPTER 27

The Altar of Holocausts. ¹ "You shall make an altar^f of acacia wood, on a square, five cubits long and five cubits wide; it shall be three cubits high. ² At the four corners there are to be two horns, so made that they spring directly from the altar. You shall then plate it with bronze. ³ Make pots for removing the ashes, as well as shovels, basins, forks and fire pans, all of which shall be of bronze. ⁴ Make a grating* of bronze network for it; this to have four bronze rings, one at each of its four corners. ⁵ Put it down around the altar, on the ground. This network is to be half as high as the altar. ⁶ You shall also make poles of acacia wood for the altar, and plate them with bronze. ⁷ These poles are to be put through the rings, so that they are on either side of the altar when it is carried. ⁸ Make the altar itself in the form of a hollow * box, just as it was shown you on the mountain.

Court of the Dwelling. ⁹ ^g "You shall also make a court for the Dwelling. On the south side the court shall have hangings a hundred cubits long, woven of fine linen twined, ¹⁰ with twenty columns and twenty pedestals of bronze; the hooks and bands on the columns shall be of silver. ¹¹ On the north side there shall be similar hangings, a hundred cubits long, with twenty columns and twenty pedestals of bronze; the hooks and bands on the columns shall be of silver. ¹² On the west side, across the width of the court, there shall be hangings, fifty cubits long, with ten columns and ten pedestals. ¹³ The width of the court on the east side shall be fifty cubits. ¹⁴ On one side there shall be hangings to the extent of fifteen cubits, with three columns and three pedestals; ¹⁵ on the other side there shall be hangings to the extent of fifteen cubits, with three columns and three pedestals.

¹⁶ "At the entrance of the court there shall be a variegated curtain, twenty cubits long, woven of violet, purple and scarlet yarn and of fine linen twined. It shall have four columns and four pedestals.

¹⁷ "All the columns around the court shall have bands and hooks of silver, and pedestals of bronze. ¹⁸ The enclosure of the court is to be one hundred cubits long, fifty cubits wide, and five cubits

high. Fine linen twined must be used, and the pedestals must be of bronze. [19] All the fittings of the Dwelling, whatever be their use, as well as all its tent pegs and all the tent pegs in the court, must be of bronze.

Oil for the Lamps. [20] "You shall order the Israelites to bring you clear oil of crushed olives, to be used for the light, so that you may keep lamps burning regularly. [h] [21] From evening to morning Aaron and his sons shall maintain them before the LORD in the meeting tent, outside the veil which hangs in front of the commandments. This shall be a perpetual ordinance for the Israelites throughout their generations.

CHAPTER 28

The Priestly Vestments. [1] [i] "From among the Israelites have your brother Aaron, together with his sons Nadab, Abihu, Eleazar and Ithamar, brought to you, that they may be my priests. [2] For the glorious adornment of your brother Aaron you shall have sacred vestments made. [3] Therefore, to the various expert workmen whom I have endowed with skill, you shall give instructions to make such vestments for Aaron as will set him apart for his sacred service as my priest. [4] These are the vestments they shall make: a breastpiece, an ephod, a robe, a brocaded tunic, a miter and a sash. In making these sacred vestments which your brother Aaron and his sons are to wear in serving as my priests, [5] they shall use gold, violet, purple and scarlet yarn and fine linen.

The Ephod and Breastpiece. [6] "The ephod* they shall make of gold thread and of violet, purple and scarlet yarn, embroidered on cloth of fine linen twined. [j] [7] It shall have a pair of shoulder straps joined to its two upper ends. [8] The embroidered belt on the ephod shall extend out from it and, like it, be made of gold thread, of violet, purple and scarlet yarn, and of fine linen twined.

[9] "Get two onyx stones and engrave on them the names of the sons of Israel: [10] six of their names on one stone, and the other six on the other stone, in the order of their birth. [11] As a gem-cutter engraves a seal, so shall you have the two stones engraved with the names of the

sons of Israel and then mounted in gold filigree work. [12] Set these two stones on the shoulder straps of the ephod as memorial stones of the sons of Israel. Thus Aaron shall bear their names on his shoulders as a reminder before the LORD. [13] Make filigree rosettes of gold, [k] [14] as well as two chains of pure gold, twisted like cords, and fasten the cord-like chains to the filigree rosettes.

[15] [l] "The breastpiece* of decision you shall also have made, embroidered like the ephod with gold thread and violet, purple and scarlet yarn on cloth of fine linen twined. [16] It is to be square when folded double, a span high and a span wide. [17] * On it you shall mount four rows of precious stones: in the first row, a carnelian, a topaz and an emerald; [18] in the second row, a garnet, a sapphire and a beryl; [19] in the third row, a jacinth, an agate and an amethyst; [20] in the fourth row, a chrysolite, an onyx and a jasper. These stones are to be mounted in gold filigree work, [21] twelve of them to match the names of the sons of Israel, each stone engraved like a seal with the name of one of the twelve tribes.

[22] "When the chains of pure gold, twisted like cords, have been made for the breastpiece, [23] you shall then make two rings of gold for it and fasten them to the two upper ends of the breastpiece. [24] The gold cords are then to be fastened to the two rings at the upper ends of the breastpiece, [25] the other two ends of the cords being fastened in front to the two filigree rosettes which are attached to the shoulder straps of the ephod. [26] Make two other rings of gold and put them on the two lower ends of the breastpiece, on its edge that faces the ephod. [27] Then make two more rings of gold and fasten them to

---

h 20f: Lv 24, 1-4.—i 1-5: Ex 39, 1; Sir 45, 7.—j 6-12: Ex 39, 2-7; Sir 45, 8-14.—k 13f: Ex 28, 22. 25; 39, 15, 18.—l 15-21: Ex 39, 15-21.

28, 6: *Ephod:* this Hebrew word is retained in the translation because it is the technical term for a peculiar piece of the priestly vestments, the exact nature of which is uncertain. It seems to have been a sort of apron that hung from the shoulders of the priest by *shoulder straps* (v 7) and was tied around his waist by the loose ends of the attached belt (v 8).

28, 15-30: *Breastpiece:* in shape like a modern altar burse, it was a pocketlike receptacle for holding the *Urim* and *Thummim* (v 30), and formed an integral part of the ephod, to which it was attached by an elaborate system of rings and chains. Both the ephod and its breastpiece were made of brocaded linen.

28, 17-20: The translation of the Hebrew names of some of these gems is quite conjectural.

the bottom of the shoulder straps next to where they join the ephod in front, just above its embroidered belt. [28] Violet ribbons shall bind the rings of the breastpiece to the rings of the ephod, so that the breastpiece will stay right above the embroidered belt of the ephod and not swing loose from it.

[29] "Whenever Aaron enters the sanctuary, he will thus bear the names of the sons of Israel on the breastpiece of decision over his heart as a constant reminder before the LORD. [30] In this breastpiece of decision[m] you shall put the Urim and Thummim,* that they may be over Aaron's heart whenever he enters the presence of the LORD. Thus he shall always bear the decisions for the Israelites over his heart in the LORD's presence.

Other Vestments. [31] "The robe of the ephod[n] you shall make entirely of violet material. [32] It shall have an opening for the head in the center, and around this opening there shall be a selvage, woven as at the opening of a shirt, to keep it from being torn. [33] All around the hem at the bottom you shall make pomegranates, woven of violet, purple and scarlet yarn and fine linen twined, with gold bells between them; [34] first a gold bell, then a pomegranate, and thus alternating all around the hem of the robe. [35] Aaron shall wear it when ministering, that its tinkling may be heard as he enters and leaves the LORD's presence in the sanctuary; else he will die.

[36] "You shall also make a plate of pure gold and engrave on it, as on a seal engraving, 'Sacred to the LORD.' [37] This plate is to be tied over the miter with a violet ribbon in such a way that it rests on the front of the miter,[o] [38] over Aaron's forehead. Since Aaron bears whatever guilt the Israelites may incur in consecrating any of their sacred gifts, this plate must always be over his forehead, so that they may find favor with the LORD.

---

m Lv 8, 8; Sir 45, 11.—n 31-35: Ex 39, 20ff; Lv 8, 9; Sir 45, 10.—o Ex 39, 31; Lv 8, 9.—p 39-43: Ex 39, 27ff.—q Ez 44, 18.—r 1-8: Lv 8, 1-9.—s Lv 8, 13.—t 10-26: Lv 8, 14-30.

28, 30: *Urim and Thummim:* both the meaning of these Hebrew words and the exact nature of the objects so designated are uncertain. They were apparently lots of some kind which were drawn or cast by the priest to ascertain God's decision in doubtful matters. Hence, the burse in which they were kept was called "the breastpiece of decision."

28, 41: *Ordain them:* literally, "fill their hands," a technical expression used solely for the installation of priests. The phrase probably originated in the custom of placing in the priests' hands the instruments or other symbols of the sacerdotal office.

---

[39] *p* "The tunic of fine linen shall be brocaded. The miter shall be made of fine linen. The sash shall be of variegated work.

[40] "Likewise, for the glorious adornment of Aaron's sons you shall have tunics and sashes and turbans made. [41] With these you shall clothe your brother Aaron and his sons. Anoint and ordain them,* consecrating them as my priests. [42] You must also make linen drawers for them, to cover their naked flesh from their loins to their thighs.[q] [43] Aaron and his sons shall wear them whenever they go into the meeting tent or approach the altar to minister in the sanctuary, lest they incur guilt and die. This shall be a perpetual ordinance for him and for his descendants.

CHAPTER 29

Consecration of the Priests. [1] "This is the rite you shall perform in consecrating them as my priests.[r] Procure a young bull and two unblemished rams. [2] With fine wheat flour make unleavened cakes mixed with oil, and unleavened wafers spread with oil, [3] and put them in a basket. Take the basket of them along with the bullock and the two rams. [4] Aaron and his sons you shall also bring to the entrance of the meeting tent, and there wash them with water. [5] Take the vestments and clothe Aaron with the tunic, the robe of the ephod, the ephod itself, and the breastpiece, fastening the embroidered belt of the ephod around him. [6] Put the miter on his head, the sacred diadem on the miter. [7] Then take the anointing oil and anoint him with it, pouring it on his head. [8] Bring forward his sons also and clothe them with the tunics, [9] gird them with the sashes, and tie the turbans on them.[s] Thus shall the priesthood be theirs by perpetual law, and thus shall you ordain Aaron and his sons.

Ordination Sacrifices. [10] *t* "Now bring forward the bullock in front of the meeting tent. There Aaron and his sons shall lay their hands on his head. [11] Then slaughter the bullock before the LORD, at the entrance of the meeting tent. [12] Take some of its blood and with your finger put it on the horns of the altar. All the rest of the blood you shall pour out at the base of the altar. [13] All the fat that covers its inner organs, as well as the lobe of its liver and its two kidneys, together with the fat that is on them, you shall take and burn on the altar. ¹⁴ But the flesh and hide and offal of the bullock you must burn up outside the camp, since this is a sin offering.ᵘ

¹⁵ "Then take one of the rams, and after Aaron and his sons have laid their hands on its head, ¹⁶ slaughter it. The blood you shall take and splash on all the sides of the altar. ¹⁷ Cut the ram into pieces; its inner organs and shanks you shall first wash, and then put them with the pieces and with the head. ¹⁸ The entire ram shall then be burned on the altar, since it is a holocaust, a sweet-smelling oblation to the LORD.

¹⁹ "After this take the other ram, and when Aaron and his sons have laid their hands on its head, ²⁰ slaughter it. Some of its blood you shall take and put on the tip of Aaron's right ear and on the tips of his sons' right ears and on the thumbs of their right hands and the great toes of their right feet. Splash the rest of the blood on all the sides of the altar. ²¹ Then take some of the blood that is on the altar, together with some of the anointing oil, and sprinkle this on Aaron and his vestments, as well as on his sons and their vestments, that his sons and their vestments may be sacred.

²² "Now, from this ram you shall take its fat: its fatty tail,* the fat that covers its inner organs, the lobe of its liver, its two kidneys with the fat that is on them, and its right thigh, since this is the ordination ram; ²³ then, out of the basket of unleavened food that you have set before the LORD, you shall take one of the loaves of bread, one of the cakes made with oil, and one of the wafers. ²⁴ All these things you shall put into the hands of Aaron and his sons, so that they may wave them as a wave offering* before the LORD. ²⁵ After you have received them back from their hands, you shall burn them on top of the holocaust on the altar as a sweet-smelling oblation to the LORD. ²⁶ Finally, take the breast of Aaron's ordination ram and wave it as a wave offering before the LORD; this is to be your own portion.

²⁷ * "Thus shall you set aside the breast of whatever wave offering is waved,ᵛ as well as the thigh of whatever raised offering is raised up, whether this be the ordination ram or anything else belonging to Aaron or his sons. ²⁸ Such things are due to Aaron and his sons from the Israelites by a perpetual ordinance as a contribution. From their peace offerings, too, the Israelites shall make a contribution, their contribution to the LORD.

²⁹ "The sacred vestmentsʷ of Aaron shall be passed down to his descendants, that in them they may be anointed and ordained. ³⁰ The descendant who succeeds him as priest and who is to enter the meeting tent to minister in the sanctuary shall be clothed with them for seven days.

³¹ ˣ "You shall take the flesh of the ordination ram and boil it in a holy place. ³² At the entrance of the meeting tent Aaron and his sons shall eat the flesh of the ram and the bread that is in the basket. ³³ They themselves are to eat of these things by which atonement was made at their ordination and consecration; but no layman may eat of them, since they are sacred. ³⁴ If some of the flesh of the ordination sacrifice or some of the bread remains over on the next day, this remnant must be burned up; it is not to be eaten, since it is sacred. ³⁵ Carry out all of these orders in regard to Aaron and his sons just as I have given them to you.ʸ

"Seven days you shall spend in ordaining them, ³⁶ ᶻ sacrificing a bullock each day as a sin offering, to make atonement. Thus also shall you purge the altar* in making atonement for it; you shall anoint it in order to consecrate it. ³⁷ Seven days you shall spend in making atonement for the altar and in consecrating it. Then the altar will be most sacred, and whatever touches it will become sacred.

³⁸ * "Now this is what you shall offer on the altar: two yearling lambsᵃ as the sacrifice established for each day; ³⁹ one

---

u Heb 13, 11.—v 27f: Lv 7, 31-34; 10, 14f; Nm 18, 18f; Dt 18, 3.—w Nm 20, 26. 28.—x 31-34: Lv 8, 31f.—y Lv 8, 36.—z 36f: Lv 8, 33ff.—a 38-42: Nm 28, 3-8.

29, 22: *Fatty tail:* the thick layer of fat surrounding the tails of sheep and rams bred in Palestine even today. It is regarded as a choice food. Cf Lv 3, 9.

29, 24-26: *Wave offering:* the portions of a peace offering, breast and right thigh, which the officiating priest moved to and fro (waved) in the presence of the Lord. They were reserved for Aaron and his sons.

29, 27-30: These verses are a parenthetical interruption of the ordination ritual; v 31 belongs logically immediately after v 26.

29, 36f: *Purge the altar:* the construction of an altar by profane hands rendered it impure. The anointing and consecration of the altar purified it and made it sacred.

29, 38-42: A parenthesis inserted into the rubrics for consecrating the altar; v 43 belongs directly after v 37.

lamb in the morning and the other lamb at the evening twilight. [40] With the first lamb there shall be a tenth of an ephah of fine flour mixed with a fourth of a hin of oil of crushed olives and, as its libation, a fourth of a hin of wine. [41] The other lamb you shall offer at the evening twilight, with the same cereal offering and libation as in the morning. You shall offer this as a sweet-smelling oblation to the LORD. [42] Throughout your generations this established holocaust shall be offered before the LORD at the entrance of the meeting tent, where I will meet you and speak to you.

[43] "There, at the altar, I will meet the Israelites; hence, it will be made sacred by my glory.[b] [44] Thus I will consecrate the meeting tent and the altar, just as I also consecrate Aaron and his sons to be my priests. [45] I will dwell in the midst of the Israelites and will be their God. [46] They shall know that I, the LORD, am their God who brought them out of the land of Egypt, so that I, the LORD, their God, might dwell among them.

CHAPTER 30

Altar of Incense. [1] "For burning incense you shall make an altar of acacia wood,[c] [2] with a square surface, a cubit long, a cubit wide, and two cubits high, with horns that spring directly from it. [3] Its grate on top, its walls on all four sides, and its horns you shall plate with pure gold. Put a gold molding around it. [4] Underneath the molding you shall put gold rings, two on one side and two on the opposite side, as holders for the poles used in carrying it. [5] Make the poles, too, of acacia wood and plate them with gold. [6] This altar you are to place in front of the veil that hangs before the ark of the commandments where I will meet you.[d]

[7] "On it Aaron shall burn fragrant incense. Morning after morning, when he prepares the lamps, [8] and again in the evening twilight, when he lights the lamps, he shall burn incense. Throughout your generations this shall be the established incense offering before the LORD. [9] On this altar you shall not offer up any profane incense, or any holocaust or cereal

offering; nor shall you pour out a libation upon it. [10] Once a year Aaron shall perform the atonement rite on its horns.[e] Throughout your generations this atonement is to be made once a year with the blood of the atoning sin offering. This altar is most sacred to the LORD."

Census Tax. [11] The LORD also said to Moses, [12] "When you take a census[f] of the Israelites who are to be registered, each one, as he is enrolled, shall give the LORD a forfeit for his life, so that no plague may come upon them for being registered. [13] Everyone who enters the registered group must pay a half-shekel, according to the standard of the sanctuary shekel, twenty gerahs to the shekel. This payment of a half-shekel is a contribution to the LORD.[g] [14] Everyone of twenty years or more who enters the registered group must give this contribution to the LORD. [15] The rich need not give more, nor shall the poor give less, than a half-shekel in this contribution to the LORD to pay the forfeit for their lives. [16] [h] When you receive this forfeit money from the Israelites, you shall donate it to the service of the meeting tent, that there it may be the Israelites' reminder, before the LORD, of the forfeit paid for their lives."

The Laver. [17] The LORD said to Moses, [18] "For ablutions you shall make a bronze laver with a bronze base. Place it between the meeting tent and the altar, and put water in it.[i] [19] Aaron and his sons shall use it in washing their hands and feet.[j] [20] When they are about to enter the meeting tent, they must wash with water, lest they die. Likewise when they approach the altar in their ministry, to offer an oblation to the LORD, [21] they must wash their hands and feet, lest they die. This shall be a perpetual ordinance for him and his descendants throughout their generations."

The Anointing Oil. [22] The LORD said to Moses, [23] "Take the finest spices: five hundred shekels of free-flowing myrrh; half that amount, that is, two hundred and fifty shekels, of fragrant cinnamon; two hundred and fifty shekels of fragrant cane; [24] five hundred shekels of cassia—all according to the standard of the sanctuary shekel; together with a hin of olive oil; [25] and blend them into sacred anointing oil,[k] perfumed ointment expertly prepared. [26] [l] With this sacred anointing oil

---

b Ex 25, 22.—c 1-5: Ex 37, 25-28.—d Ex 40, 26.—e Lv 16, 18.—f Nm 1, 2f; 26, 2.—g Mt 17, 24-27.—h Ex 38, 25.—i Ex 38, 8; 40, 7. 30.—j 19ff: Ex 40, 31f.—k Ex 37, 29.—l 26-29: Ex 40, 9ff; Lv 8, 10; Nm 7, 1.

you shall anoint the meeting tent and the ark of the commandments, [27] the table and all its appurtenances, the lampstand and its appurtenances, the altar of incense [28] and the altar of holocausts with all its appurtenances, and the laver with its base. [29] When you have consecrated them, they shall be most sacred; whatever touches them shall be sacred. [30] Aaron and his sons you shall also anoint and consecrate as my priests. [m] [31] To the Israelites you shall say: As sacred anointing oil this shall belong to me throughout your generations. [32] It may not be used in any ordinary anointing of the body, nor may you make any other oil of a like mixture. It is sacred, and shall be treated as sacred by you. [33] Whoever prepares a perfume like this, or whoever puts any of this on a layman, shall be cut off from his kinsmen."

The Incense. [34] [n] The LORD told Moses, "Take these aromatic substances: storax and onycha and galbanum, these and pure frankincense in equal parts; [35] and blend them into incense. This fragrant powder, expertly prepared, is to be salted and so kept pure and sacred. [36] Grind some of it into fine dust and put this before the commandments in the meeting tent where I will meet you. This incense shall be treated as most sacred by you. [37] You may not make incense of a like mixture for yourselves; you must treat it as sacred to the LORD. [38] Whoever makes an incense like this for his own enjoyment of its fragrance, shall be cut off from his kinsmen."

CHAPTER 31

Choice of Artisans. [1] [o] The LORD said to Moses, [2] "See, I have chosen Bezalel, son of Uri, son of Hur, of the tribe of Judah, [3] and I have filled him with a divine spirit of skill and understanding and knowledge in every craft: [4] in the production of embroidery, in making things of gold, silver or bronze, [5] in cutting and mounting precious stones, in carving wood, and in every other craft. [6] As his assistant I have appointed Oholiab, son of Ahisamach, of the tribe of Dan. I have also endowed all the experts with the necessary skill to make all the things I have ordered you to make: [7] [p] the meeting tent, the ark of the commandments with the propitiatory on top of it, all the furnishings of the tent, [8] the table with its appurtenances, the pure

gold lampstand with all its appurtenances, the altar of incense, [9] the altar of holocausts with all its appurtenances, the laver with its base, [10] the service cloths,* the sacred vestments for Aaron the priest, the vestments for his sons in their ministry, [11] the anointing oil, and the fragrant incense for the sanctuary. All these things they shall make just as I have commanded you."

Sabbath Laws. [12] [q] The LORD said to Moses, [13] "You must also tell the Israelites: Take care to keep my sabbaths, for that is to be the token between you and me throughout the generations, to show that it is I, the LORD, who make you holy. [14] Therefore, you must keep the sabbath as something sacred. Whoever desecrates it shall be put to death. If anyone does work on that day, he must be rooted out of his people. [15] Six days there are for doing work, but the seventh day is the sabbath of complete rest, sacred to the LORD. Anyone who does work on the sabbath day shall be put to death. [16] So shall the Israelites observe the sabbath, keeping it throughout their generations as a perpetual covenant. [17] Between me and the Israelites it is to be an everlasting token; for in six days the LORD made the heavens and the earth, but on the seventh day he rested at his ease."

[18] When the LORD had finished speaking to Moses on Mount Sinai, he gave him the two tablets of the commandments, the stone tablets inscribed by God's own finger. [r]

CHAPTER 32

The Golden Calf. [1] When the people became aware of Moses' delay in coming down from the mountain, they gathered around Aaron and said to him, "Come, make us a god who will be our leader; as for the man Moses who brought us out of the land of Egypt, we do not know what has happened to him." [s] [2] Aaron replied, "Have your wives and sons and daughters take off the golden earrings they are wearing, and bring them to me." [3] So all the people took off their earrings and brought

---

m Ex 29, 7; Lv 8, 12.—n 34ff: Ex 25, 6; 37, 29.—o 1-6: Ex 35, 30-35.—p 7-11: Ex 35, 10-19.—q 12-17: Ex 20, 8-11; 35, 1-3.—r Ex 24, 12; 32, 15f; Dt 5, 22.—s Ex 32, 23; Acts 7, 40.

31, 10: *The service cloths:* so the Greek. They were perhaps the colored cloths mentioned in Nm 4, 4-15.

them to Aaron, [4] who accepted their offering, and fashioning this gold with a graving tool, made a molten calf. Then they cried out, "This is your God, O Israel, who brought you out of the land of Egypt." [t] [5] On seeing this, Aaron built an altar before the calf and proclaimed, "Tomorrow is a feast of the LORD." [*] [6] Early the next day the people offered holocausts and brought peace offerings. Then they sat down to eat and drink, and rose up to revel. [u]

[7] With that, the LORD said to Moses, "Go down at once to your people, whom you brought out of the land of Egypt, for they have become depraved. [8] [v] They have soon turned aside from the way I pointed out to them, making for themselves a molten calf and worshiping it, sacrificing to it and crying out, 'This is your God, O Israel, who brought you out of the land of Egypt!' [w] [9] I see how stiff-necked this people is," continued the LORD to Moses. [10] "Let me alone, then, that my wrath may blaze up against them to consume them. Then I will make of you a great nation."

[11] But Moses implored the LORD, his God, saying, [x] "Why, O LORD, should your wrath blaze up against your own people, whom you brought out of the land of Egypt with such great power and with so strong a hand? [12] Why should the Egyptians say, 'With evil intent he brought them out, that he might kill them in the mountains and exterminate them from the face of the earth'? Let your blazing wrath die down; relent in punishing your people. [13] Remember your servants Abraham, Isaac and Israel, and how you swore to them by your own self, saying, [y] 'I will make your descendants as numerous as the stars in the sky; and all this land that I

promised, I will give your descendants as their perpetual heritage.' " [14] So the LORD relented in the punishment he had threatened to inflict on his people.

[15] Moses then turned and came down the mountain with the two tablets of the commandments in his hands, [z] tablets that were written on both sides, front and back; [16] tablets that were made by God, having inscriptions on them that were engraved by God himself. [a] [17] Now, when Joshua heard the noise of the people shouting, he said to Moses, "That sounds like a battle in the camp." [18] But Moses answered, "It does not sound like cries of victory, nor does it sound like cries of defeat; the sounds that I hear are cries of revelry." [19] As he drew near the camp, he saw the calf and the dancing. With that, Moses' wrath flared up, so that he threw the tablets down and broke them on the base of the mountain. [b] [20] Taking the calf they had made, he fused it in the fire and then ground it down to powder, which he scattered on the water* and made the Israelites drink. [c]

[21] Moses asked Aaron, "What did this people ever do to you that you should lead them into so grave a sin?" Aaron replied, "Let not my lord be angry. [22] You know well enough how prone the people are to evil. [23] They said to me, 'Make us a god to be our leader; as for the man Moses who brought us out of the land of Egypt, we do not know what has happened to him.' [24] So I told them, 'Let anyone who has gold jewelry take it off.' They gave it to me, and I threw it into the fire, and this calf came out."

[25] When Moses realized that, to the scornful joy of their foes, Aaron had let the people run wild, [26] he stood at the gate of the camp and cried, "Whoever is for the Lord, let him come to me!" All the Levites [d] then rallied to him, [27] and he told them, "Thus says the LORD, the God of Israel: Put your sword on your hip, every one of you! Now go up and down the camp, from gate to gate, and slay your own kinsmen,* your friends and neighbors!" [28] The Levites carried out the command of Moses, and that day there fell about three thousand of the people. [29] Then Moses said, "Today you have been dedicated to the LORD,* for you were against your own sons and kinsmen, to bring a blessing upon yourselves this day."

---

t Ex 32, 8; 1 Kgs 12, 28.—u 1 Cor 10, 7.—v 7f: Dt 9, 12. 16.— w 9f: Dt 9, 13; Ps 106, 23.—x 11f: Nm 14, 13ff; Dt 9, 28.—y Gn 22, 16f.—z Dt 9, 15.—a Ex 31, 18.—b Dt 9, 16f.—c Dt 9, 21.—d 26-29: Dt 33, 8f.

32, 5: *The calf . . . a feast of the Lord:* from this it is clear that the golden calf was intended as an image, not of a false god, but of the Lord himself, his strength being symbolized by the strength of a young bull. The Israelites, however, had been forbidden to represent the Lord under any visible form. Cf Ex 20, 4.

32, 20: *The water:* the stream that flowed down Mount Sinai. Cf Dt 9, 21.

32, 27: *Slay your own kinsmen:* those who were especially guilty of the idolatry.

32, 29: *Dedicated to the Lord:* because of their zeal for the true worship of the Lord, the Levites were chosen to be special ministers of the ritual service. However, the meaning of the Hebrew here is somewhat disputed.

The Atonement. [30] On the next day Moses said to the people,[e] "You have committed a grave sin. I will go up to the LORD, then; perhaps I may be able to make atonement for your sin." [31] So Moses went back to the LORD and said, "Ah, this people has indeed committed a grave sin in making a god of gold for themselves! [32] If you would only forgive their sin! If you will not, then strike me out of the book that you have written."* [33] The LORD answered, "Him only who has sinned against me will I strike out of my book. [34] Now, go and lead the people whither I have told you. My angel will go before you. When it is time for me to punish, I will punish them for their sin."

[35] Thus the LORD smote the people for having had Aaron make the calf for them.

CHAPTER 33

[1] The LORD told Moses, "You and the people whom you have brought up from the land of Egypt are to go up from here to the land which I swore to Abraham, Isaac and Jacob I would give to their descendants.[f] [2] Driving out the Canaanites, Amorites, Hittites, Perizzites, Hivites and Jebusites, I will send an angel before you[g] [3] to the land flowing with milk and honey. But I myself will not go up in your company, because you are a stiff-necked people; otherwise I might exterminate you on the way." [4] When the people heard this bad news, they went into mourning, and no one wore his ornaments.

[5] The LORD said to Moses, "Tell the Israelites: You are a stiff-necked people. Were I to go up in your company even for a moment, I would exterminate you. Take off your ornaments, therefore; I will then see what I am to do with you." [6] So, from Mount Horeb onward, the Israelites laid aside their ornaments.

Moses' Intimacy with God. [7] The tent,[h] which was called the meeting tent,* Moses used to pitch at some distance away, outside the camp. Anyone who wished to consult the LORD would go to this meeting tent outside the camp. [8] Whenever Moses went out to the tent, the people would all rise and stand at the entrance of their own tents, watching Moses until he entered the tent. [9] As Moses entered the tent, the

column of cloud would come down and stand at its entrance while the LORD spoke with Moses. [10] On seeing the column of cloud stand at the entrance of the tent, all the people would rise and worship at the entrance of their own tents. [11] The LORD used to speak to Moses face to face,[i] as one man speaks to another. Moses would then return to the camp, but his young assistant, Joshua, son of Nun, would not move out of the tent.

[12] Moses said to the LORD, "You, indeed, are telling me to lead this people on;[j] but you have not let me know whom you will send with me. Yet you have said, 'You are my intimate friend,' and also, 'You have found favor with me.' [13] Now, if I have found favor with you, do let me know your ways so that, in knowing you, I may continue to find favor with you. Then, too, this nation is, after all, your own people." [14] "I myself,"* the LORD answered, "will go along, to give you rest." [15] Moses replied, "If you are not going yourself, do not make us go up from here. [16] For how can it be known that we, your people and I, have found favor with you, except by your going with us? Then we, your people and I, will be singled out from every other people on the earth." [17] The LORD said to Moses, "This request, too, which you have just made, I will carry out, because you have found favor with me and you are my intimate friend."

[18] Then Moses said, "Do let me see your glory!" [19] He answered, "I will make all my beauty pass before you, and in your presence I will pronounce my name, 'LORD'; I who show favors to whom I will, I who grant mercy to whom I will.[k] [20] But my face you cannot see,[l] for no man sees me and still lives. [21] Here," continued the LORD, "is a place near me where you shall station yourself on the rock. [22] When my glory passes I will set you in the hollow of the rock and will cover you with

---

e 30-34: Dt 9, 18ff.—f Gn 12, 7.—g Ex 23, 23.—h Ex 29, 42f.—i Nm 12, 8; Dt 34, 10; Sir 45, 4-6.—j Ex 32, 34.—k Rom 9, 15.—l Jn 1, 18; 1 Tm 6, 16.

32, 32: *The book that you have written:* the list of God's intimate friends. In a similar sense St. Paul wished to be anathema from Christ for the sake of his brethren. Cf Rom 9, 3.

33, 7-11: *The meeting tent* is mentioned here by anticipation; its actual construction is described in the following chapters.

33, 14: *I myself:* literally, "my face," that is, "my presence." *To give you rest:* in the Promised Land; some understand, "to put your mind at rest"; others, by a slight emendation in the text, render, "to lead you."

my hand until I have passed by. [23] Then I will remove my hand, so that you may see my back;* but my face is not to be seen." .

CHAPTER 34

Renewal of the Tablets. [1] The LORD said to Moses, "Cut two stone tablets like the former,[m] that I may write on them the commandments which were on the former tablets that you broke. [2] Get ready for tomorrow morning, when you are to go up Mount Sinai and there present yourself to me on the top of the mountain. [3] No one shall come up with you, and no one is even to be seen on any part of the mountain;[n] even the flocks and the herds are not to go grazing toward this mountain." [4] Moses then cut two stone tablets like the former, and early the next morning he went up Mount Sinai as the LORD had commanded him, taking along the two stone tablets.

[5] Having come down in a cloud, the LORD stood with him there and proclaimed his name, "LORD." [6] Thus the LORD passed before him and cried out, "The LORD, the LORD, a merciful and gracious God, slow to anger and rich in kindness and fidelity, [7] continuing his kindness for a thousand generations, and forgiving wickedness and crime and sin; yet not declaring the guilty guiltless, but punishing children and grandchildren to the third and fourth generation for their fathers' wickedness!"[o] [8] Moses at once bowed down to the ground in worship. [9] Then he said, "If I find favor with you, O LORD, do come along in our company. This is indeed a stiff-necked people; yet pardon our wickedness and sins, and receive us as your own."

m Dt 10, 1f.—n Ex 19, 12f. 21.—o 6f: Ex 20, 5f; Nm 14, 18; Dt 5, 9f; Jer 32, 18.—p Ex 13, 5; 33, 2.—q 12-16: Ex 23, 32f; Dt 7, 1-5; 12, 2f.—r Lv 19, 4; 5, 8f.—s Ex 12, 15ff; 13, 3f.—t 19f: Ex 13, 2. 12f; 23, 15.—u Ex 20, 9f.—v 22f: Ex 23, 16f; Dt 16, 10. 13. 16.

33, 23: *You may see my back:* man can see God's glory as reflected in creation, but his "face," that is, God as he is in himself, mortal man cannot behold. Cf 1 Cor 13, 12.

34, 13: *Sacred poles:* "Ashera" was the name of a Canaanite goddess. in her honor wooden poles *(asherot)* were erected, just as stone pillars *(massebot)* were erected in honor of the god Baal. Both were placed near the altar in a Canaanite shrine.

34, 14: *The Lord is "the Jealous One":* see note on Ex 20, 5. Some, by a slight emendation, render, "The LORD is jealous for his name." Cf Ez 39, 25.

34, 22: *Feast of Weeks:* the festival of thanksgiving for the harvest, celebrated seven weeks or fifty days after the beginning of the harvest. It was also called Pentecost (fiftieth) and coincided with the giving of the law on Mount Sinai, fifty days after the offering of the first fruits; cf Lv 23, 10f; Dt 16, 9.

Religious Laws. [10] "Here, then," said the LORD, "is the covenant I will make. Before the eyes of all your people I will work such marvels as have never been wrought in any nation anywhere on earth, so that this people among whom you live may see how awe-inspiring are the deeds which I, the LORD, will do at your side. [11] But you, on your part, must keep the commandments I am giving you today.[p]

"I will drive out before you the Amorites, Canaanites, Hittites, Perizzites, Hivites, and Jebusites. [12] [q] Take care, therefore, not to make a covenant with these inhabitants of the land that you are to enter; else they will become a snare among you. [13] Tear down their altars; smash their sacred pillars, and cut down their sacred poles.* [14] You shall not worship any other god, for the LORD is 'the Jealous One';* a jealous God is he. [15] Do not make a covenant with the inhabitants of that land; else, when they render their wanton worship to their gods and sacrifice to them, one of them may invite you and you may partake of his sacrifice. [16] Neither shall you take their daughters as wives for your sons; otherwise, when their daughters render their wanton worship to their gods, they will make your sons do the same.

[17] "You shall not make for yourselves molten gods.[r]

[18] "You shall keep the feast of Unleavened Bread.[s] For seven days at the prescribed time in the month of Abib you are to eat unleavened bread, as I commanded you; for in the month of Abib you came out of Egypt.

[19] "To me belongs every first-born male that opens the womb among all your livestock, whether in the herd or in the flock.[t] [20] The firstling of an ass you shall redeem with one of the flock; if you do not redeem it, you must break its neck. The first-born among your sons you shall redeem.

"No one shall appear before me empty-handed.

[21] "For six days you may work,[u] but on the seventh day you shall rest; on that day you must rest even during the seasons of plowing and harvesting.

[22] [v] "You shall keep the feast of Weeks* with the first of the wheat harvest; likewise, the feast at the fruit harvest at the close of the year. [23] Three times a year all your men shall appear before the Lord,

the LORD, God of Israel. [24] Since I will drive out the nations before you to give you a large territory, there will be no one to covet your land when you go up three times a year to appear before the LORD, your God.

[25] "You shall not offer me the blood of sacrifice with leavened bread, nor shall the sacrifice of the Passover feast be kept overnight for the next day.

[26] "The choicest first fruits of your soil you shall bring to the house of the LORD, your God.

"You shall not boil a kid in its mother's milk."[w]

Radiance of Moses' Face. [27] Then the LORD said to Moses, "Write down these words, for in accordance with them I have made a covenant with you and with Israel." [28] So Moses stayed there with the LORD for forty days and forty nights,[x] without eating any food or drinking any water, and he wrote on the tablets the words of the covenant, the ten commandments.

[29] As Moses came down from Mount Sinai with the two tablets of the commandments in his hands, he did not know that the skin of his face had become radiant while he conversed with the LORD. [30] When Aaron, then, and the other Israelites saw Moses and noticed how radiant the skin of his face had become, they were afraid to come near him. [31] Only after Moses called to them did Aaron and all the rulers of the community come back to him. Moses then spoke to them. [32] Later on, all the Israelites came up to him, and he enjoined on them all that the LORD had told him on Mount Sinai. [33] When he finished speaking with them, he put a veil over his face.* [34] Whenever Moses entered the presence of the LORD to converse with him, he removed the veil until he came out again.[y] On coming out, he would tell the Israelites all that had been commanded. [35] Then the Israelites would see that the skin of Moses' face was radiant; so he would again put the veil over his face until he went in to converse with the LORD.

CHAPTER 35

Sabbath Regulations. [1] Moses assembled the whole Israelite community and said to them,[z] "This is what the LORD has com-

manded to be done. [2] On six days work may be done, but the seventh day shall be sacred to you as the sabbath of complete rest to the LORD. Anyone who does work on that day shall be put to death. [3] You shall not even light a fire in any of your dwellings on the sabbath day."

Collection of Materials. [4] Moses told the whole Israelite community, "This is what the LORD has commanded: [5] [a] Take up among you a collection for the LORD. Everyone, as his heart prompts him, shall bring, as a contribution to the LORD, gold, silver and bronze; [6] violet, purple and scarlet yarn; fine linen and goat hair; [7] rams' skins dyed red, and tahash skins; acacia wood; [8] oil for the light; spices for the anointing oil and for the fragrant incense; [9] onyx stones and other gems for mounting on the ephod and on the breastpiece.

Call for Artisans. [10] [b] "Let every expert among you come and make all that the LORD has commanded: [11] the Dwelling, with its tent, its covering, its clasps, its boards, its bars, its columns and its pedestals; [12] the ark, with its poles, the propitiatory, and the curtain veil; [13] the table, with its poles and all its appurtenances, and the showbread; [14] the lampstand, with its appurtenances, the lamps, and the oil for the light; [15] the altar of incense, with its poles; the anointing oil, and the fragrant incense; the entrance curtain for the entrance of the Dwelling; [16] the altar of holocausts, with its bronze grating, its poles, and all its appurtenances; the laver, with its base; [17] the hangings of the court, with their columns and pedestals; the curtain for the entrance of the court; [18] the tent pegs for the Dwelling and for the court, with their ropes; [19] the service cloths for use in the sanctuary; the sacred vestments for Aaron, the priest; and the vestments worn by his sons in their ministry."

The Contribution. [20] When the whole Israelite community left Moses' presence, [21] everyone, as his heart suggested and his spirit prompted, brought a contribution

w 25f: Ex 23, 18f.—x Ex 24, 18; Dt 9, 9. 18; 10, 2. 4.—y 33f: 2 Cor 3, 13. 16.—z 1-3: Ex 31, 13-17.—a 5-9: Ex 25, 2-7.—b 10-19: Ex 31, 6-11.

34, 33: *He put a veil over his face:* St. Paul sees in this a symbol of the failure of the Jews to recognize Jesus as the promised Messiah. The true spiritual meaning of the writings of Moses and the prophets is still veiled from the unbelieving Jews. Cf 2 Cor 3, 7-18.

to the LORD for the construction of the meeting tent, for all its services, and for the sacred vestments. [22]Both the men and the women, all as their hearts prompted them, brought brooches, earrings, rings, necklaces and various other gold articles.[c] Everyone who could presented an offering of gold to the LORD. [23]Everyone who happened to have violet, purple or scarlet yarn, fine linen or goat hair, rams' skins dyed red or tahash skins, brought them. [24]Whoever could make a contribution of silver or bronze offered it to the LORD; and everyone who happened to have acacia wood for any part of the work, brought it. [25]All the women who were expert spinners brought hand-spun violet, purple and scarlet yarn and fine linen thread. [26]All the women who possessed the skill, spun goat hair. [27]The princes brought onyx stones and other gems for mounting on the ephod and on the breastpiece; [28]as well as spices, and oil for the light, anointing oil, and fragrant incense. [29]Every Israelite man and woman brought to the LORD such voluntary offerings as they thought best, for the various kinds of work which the LORD had commanded Moses to have done.

The Artisans. [30]Moses said to the Israelites, [d] "See, the LORD has chosen Bezalel, son of Uri, son of Hur, of the tribe of Judah, [31]and has filled him with a divine spirit of skill and understanding and knowledge in every craft: [32]in the production of embroidery, in making things of gold, silver or bronze, [33]in cutting and mounting precious stones, in carving wood, and in every other craft. [34]He has also given both him and Oholiab, son of Ahisamach, of the tribe of Dan, the ability to teach others. [35]He has endowed them with skill to execute all types of work: engraving, embroidering, the making of variegated cloth of violet, purple and scarlet yarn and fine linen thread, weaving, and all other arts and crafts.

CHAPTER 36

[1]"Bezalel, therefore, will set to work with Oholiab and with all the experts whom the LORD has endowed with skill and understanding in knowing how to execute all the work for the service of the sanctuary, just as the LORD has commanded."[e]

c 22-28: Ex 25, 3-7.—d 30-35: Ex 31, 1-6.—e 1f: Ex 31, 1. 6.—f 8-19: Ex 26, 1-14.

[2]Moses then called Bezalel and Oholiab and all the other experts whom the LORD had endowed with skill, men whose hearts moved them to come and take part in the work. [3]They received from Moses all the contributions which the Israelites had brought for establishing the service of the sanctuary. Still, morning after morning the people continued to bring their voluntary offerings to Moses. [4]Thereupon the experts who were executing the various kinds of work for the sanctuary, all left the work they were doing, [5]and told Moses, "The people are bringing much more than is needed to carry out the work which the LORD has commanded us to do." [6]Moses, therefore, ordered a proclamation to be made throughout the camp: "Let neither man nor woman make any more contributions for the sanctuary." So the people stopped bringing their offerings; [7]there was already enough at hand, in fact, more than enough, to complete the work to be done.

The Tent Cloth and Coverings. [8] [f] The various experts who were executing the work, made the Dwelling with its ten sheets woven of fine linen twined, having cherubim embroidered on them with violet, purple and scarlet yarn. [9]The length of each sheet was twenty-eight cubits, and the width four cubits; all the sheets were of the same size. [10]Five of the sheets were sewed together, edge to edge; and the same for the other five. [11]Loops of violet yarn were made along the edge of the end sheet in the first set, and the same along the edge of the end sheet in the second set. [12]Fifty loops were thus put on one inner sheet, and fifty loops on the inner sheet in the other set, with the loops directly opposite each other. [13]Then fifty clasps of gold were made, with which the sheets were joined so that the Dwelling formed one whole.

[14]Sheets of goat hair were also woven as a tent over the Dwelling. Eleven such sheets were made. [15]The length of each sheet was thirty cubits and the width four cubits; all eleven sheets were of the same size. [16]Five of these sheets were sewed edge to edge into one set; and the other six sheets into another set. [17]Fifty loops were made along the edge of the end sheet in one set, and fifty loops along the edge of the corresponding sheet in the other set. [18]Fifty bronze clasps were made with

which the tent was joined so that it formed one whole. ¹⁹ A covering for the tent was made of rams' skins dyed red, and above that, a covering of tahash skins.

The Boards. ²⁰ ᵍ Boards of acacia wood were made as walls for the Dwelling. ²¹ The length of each board was ten cubits, and the width one and a half cubits. ²² Each board had two arms, fastening them in line. In this way all the boards of the Dwelling were made. ²³ They were set up as follows: twenty boards on the south side, ²⁴ with forty silver pedestals under the twenty boards, so that there were two pedestals under each board, at its two arms; ²⁵ twenty boards on the other side of the Dwelling, the north side, ²⁶ with their forty silver pedestals, two under each board; ²⁷ six boards at the rear of the Dwelling, to the west; ²⁸ and two boards at the corners in the rear of the Dwelling. ²⁹ These were double at the bottom, and likewise double at the top, to the first ring. That is how both boards in the corners were made. ³⁰ Thus, there were in the rear eight boards, with their sixteen silver pedestals, two pedestals under each board. ³¹ Bars of acacia wood were also made, five for the boards on one side of the Dwelling, ³² five for those on the other side, and five for those at the rear, to the west. ³³ The center bar, at the middle of the boards, was made to reach across from end to end. ³⁴ The boards were plated with gold, and gold rings were made on them as holders for the bars, which were also plated with gold.

The Veil. ³⁵ ʰ The veil was woven of violet, purple and scarlet yarn, and of fine linen twined, with cherubim embroidered on it. ³⁶ Four gold-plated columns of acacia wood, with gold hooks, were made for it, and four silver pedestals were cast for them.

³⁷ The curtain for the entrance of the tent was made of violet, purple and scarlet yarn, and of fine linen twined, woven in a variegated manner. ³⁸ Its five columns, with their hooks as well as their capitals and bands, were plated with gold; their five pedestals were of bronze.

CHAPTER 37

The Ark. ¹ Bezalel made the ark of acacia wood, two and a half cubits long, one and a half cubits wide, and one and a half cubits high. ² The inside and outside were plated with gold, and a molding of gold was put around it. ³ Four gold rings were cast and put on its four supports, two rings for one side and two for the opposite side. ⁴ Poles of acacia wood were made and plated with gold; ⁵ these were put through the rings on the sides of the ark, for carrying it.

⁶ The propitiatory was made of pure gold, two and a half cubits long and one and a half cubits wide. ⁷ Two cherubim of beaten gold were made for the two ends of the propitiatory, ⁸ one cherub fastened at one end, the other at the other end, springing directly from the propitiatory at its two ends. ⁹ The cherubim had their wings spread out above, covering the propitiatory with them. They were turned toward each other, but with their faces looking toward the propitiatory.ʲ

The Table. ¹⁰ ⁱ The table was made of acacia wood, two cubits long, one cubit wide, and one and a half cubits high. ¹¹ It was plated with pure gold, and a molding of gold was put around it. ¹² A frame a handbreadth high was also put around it, with a molding of gold around the frame. ¹³ Four rings of gold were cast for it and fastened, one at each of the four corners. ¹⁴ The rings were alongside the frame as holders for the poles to carry the table. ¹⁵ These poles were made of acacia wood and plated with gold. ¹⁶ The vessels that were set on the table, its plates and cups, as well as its pitchers and bowls for pouring libations, were of pure gold.

The Lampstand. ¹⁷ ᵏ The lampstand was made of pure beaten gold—its shaft and branches as well as its cups and knobs and petals springing directly from it. ¹⁸ Six branches extended from its sides, three branches on one side and three on the other. ¹⁹ On one branch there were three cups, shaped like almond blossoms, each with its knob and petals; on the opposite branch there were three cups, shaped like almond blossoms, each with its knob and petals; and so for the six branches that extended from the lampstand. ²⁰ On the shaft there were four cups, shaped like almond blossoms, with their knobs and petals, ²¹ including a knob below each of the

g 20-34: Ex 26, 15-29.—h 35-38: Ex 26, 31-37.—i 1-9: Ex 25, 10-22.—j 10-16: Ex 25, 23-30.—k 17-24: Ex 25, 31-39.

three pairs of branches that extended from the lampstand. [22] The knobs and branches sprang so directly from it that the whole formed but a single piece of pure beaten gold. [23] Its seven lamps, as well as its trimming shears and trays, were made of pure gold. [24] A talent of pure gold was used for the lampstand and its various appurtenances.

The Altar of Incense. [25] *l* The altar of incense was made of acacia wood, on a square, a cubit long, a cubit wide, and two cubits high, having horns that sprang directly from it. [26] Its grate on top, its walls on all four sides, and its horns were plated with pure gold; and a molding of gold was put around it. [27] Underneath the molding gold rings were placed, two on one side and two on the opposite side, as holders for the poles to carry it. [28] The poles, too, were made of acacia wood and plated with gold.

[29] The sacred anointing oil and the fragrant incense were prepared in their pure form by a perfumer. *m*

CHAPTER 38

The Altar of Holocausts. [1] The altar of holocausts *n* was made of acacia wood, on a square, five cubits long and five cubits wide; its height was three cubits. [2] At the four corners horns were made that sprang directly from the altar. The whole was plated with bronze. [3] All the utensils of the altar, the pots, shovels, basins, forks and fire pans, were likewise made of bronze. [4] A grating of bronze network was made for the altar and placed round it, on the ground, half as high as the altar itself. [5] Four rings were cast for the four corners of the bronze grating, as holders for the poles, [6] which were made of acacia wood and plated with bronze. [7] The poles were put through the rings on the sides of the altar for carrying it. The altar was made in the form of a hollow box.

[8] The bronze laver, *o* with its bronze base, was made from the mirrors of the women who served* at the entrance of the meeting tent.

---

1 25-28: Ex 30, 1-5.—m Ex 30, 23ff. 34ff.—n 1-7: Ex 27, 1-8; 2 Chr 1, 5.—o Ex 30, 18-21.—p 9-20: Ex 27, 9-19.—q 22f: Ex 31, 2. 6; 35, 30. 34; 36, 1.

38, 8: The reflecting surface of ancient mirrors was usually of polished bronze. *The women who served:* cf 1 Sm 2, 22.

The Court. [9] *p* The court was made as follows. On the south side of the court there were hangings, woven of fine linen twined, a hundred cubits long, [10] with twenty columns and twenty pedestals of bronze, the hooks and bands of the columns being of silver. [11] On the north side there were similar hangings, one hundred cubits long, with twenty columns and twenty pedestals of bronze, the hooks and bands of the columns being of silver. [12] On the west side there were hangings, fifty cubits long, with ten columns and ten pedestals, the hooks and bands of the columns being of silver. [13] On the east side the court was fifty cubits long. [14] Toward one side there were hangings to the extent of fifteen cubits, with three columns and three pedestals; [15] toward the other side, beyond the entrance of the court, there were likewise hangings to the extent of fifteen cubits, with three columns and three pedestals. [16] The hangings on all sides of the court were woven of fine linen twined. [17] The pedestals of the columns were of bronze, while the hooks and bands of the columns were of silver; the capitals were silverplated, and all the columns of the court were banded with silver.

[18] At the entrance of the court there was a variegated curtain, woven of violet, purple and scarlet yarn and of fine linen twined, twenty cubits long and five cubits wide, in keeping with the hangings of the court. [19] There were four columns and four pedestals of bronze for it, while their hooks were of silver. [20] All the tent pegs for the Dwelling and for the court around it were of bronze.

Amount of Metal Used. [21] The following is an account of the various amounts used on the Dwelling, the Dwelling of the commandments, drawn up at the command of Moses by the Levites under the direction of Ithamar, son of Aaron the priest. [22] However, it was Bezalel, son of Uri, *q* son of Hur, of the tribe of Judah, who made all that the Lord commanded Moses, [23] and he was assisted by Oholiab, son of Ahisamach, of the tribe of Dan, who was an engraver, an embroiderer, and a weaver of variegated cloth of violet, purple and scarlet yarn and of fine linen. [24] All the gold used in the entire construction of the sanctuary, having previously been given as an offering, amounted to twenty-nine talents and seven hundred and thirty shekels, according to the standard of the sanctuary shekel. ²⁵ The amount of the silver received from the community was one hundred talents and one thousand seven hundred and seventy-five shekels, according to the standard of the sanctuary shekel; ²⁶ one bekah apiece, that is, a half-shekel apiece, according to the standard of the sanctuary shekel, was received from every man of twenty years or more who entered the registered group; the number of these was six hundred and three thousand five hundred and fifty men.ʳ ²⁷ One hundred talents of silver were used for casting the pedestals of the sanctuary and the pedestals of the veil, one talent for each pedestal, or one hundred talents for the one hundred pedestals. ²⁸ The remaining one thousand seven hundred and seventy-five shekels were used for making the hooks on the columns, for plating the capitals, and for banding them with silver. ²⁹ The bronze, given as an offering, amounted to seventy talents and two thousand four hundred shekels. ³⁰ With this were made the pedestals at the entrance of the meeting tent, the bronze altar with its bronze gratings and all the appurtenances of the altar, ³¹ the pedestals around the court, the pedestals at the entrance of the court, and all the tent pegs for the Dwelling and for the court around it.

CHAPTER 39

The Vestments. ¹ With violet, purple and scarlet yarn were woven the service cloths for use in the sanctuary, as well as the sacred vestments ˢ for Aaron, as the LORD had commanded Moses.
² ᵗ The ephod was woven of gold thread and of violet, purple and scarlet yarn and of fine linen twined. ³ Gold was first hammered into gold leaf and then cut up into threads, which were woven with the violet, purple and scarlet yarn into an embroidered pattern on the fine linen. ⁴ Shoulder straps were made for it and joined to its two upper ends. ⁵ The embroidered belt on the ephod extended out from it, and like it, was made of gold thread, of violet, purple and scarlet yarn, and of fine linen twined, as the LORD had commanded Moses. ⁶ The onyx stones were prepared and mounted in gold filigree work; they were engraved like seal engravings with the names of the sons of Israel. ⁷ These stones were set on the shoulder straps of the ephod as memorial stones of the sons of Israel, just as the LORD had commanded Moses.

⁸ ᵘ The breastpiece was embroidered like the ephod, with gold thread and violet, purple and scarlet yarn on cloth of fine linen twined. ⁹ It was square and folded double, a span high and a span wide in its folded form. ¹⁰ Four rows of precious stones were mounted on it: in the first row a carnelian, a topaz and an emerald; ¹¹ in the second row, a garnet, a sapphire and a beryl; ¹² in the third row a jacinth, an agate and an amethyst; ¹³ in the fourth row a chrysolite, an onyx and a jasper. They were mounted in gold filigree work. ¹⁴ These stones were twelve, to match the names of the sons of Israel, and each stone was engraved like a seal with the name of one of the twelve tribes.

¹⁵ ᵛ Chains of pure gold, twisted like cords, were made for the breastpiece, ¹⁶ together with two gold filigree rosettes and two gold rings. The two rings were fastened to the two upper ends of the breastpiece. ¹⁷ The two gold chains were then fastened to the two rings at the ends of the breastpiece. ¹⁸ The other two ends of the two chains were fastened in front to the two filigree rosettes, which were attached to the shoulder straps of the ephod. ¹⁹ Two other gold rings were made and put on the two lower ends of the breastpiece, on the edge facing the ephod. ²⁰ Two more gold rings were made and fastened to the bottom of the two shoulder straps next to where they joined the ephod in front, just above its embroidered belt. ²¹ Violet ribbons bound the rings of the breastpiece to the rings of the ephod, so that the breastpiece stayed right above the embroidered belt of the ephod and did not swing loose from it. All this was just as the LORD had commanded Moses.

The Other Vestments. ²² The robe of the ephod was woven entirely of violet yarn, ²³ with an opening in its center like the opening of a shirt, with selvage around the opening to keep it from being torn. ²⁴ At the hem of the robe pomegranates were made of violet, purple and scarlet yarn and of fine linen twined; ²⁵ bells of pure gold

---

r Nm 1, 46.—s Ex 31, 10.—t 2-10: Ex 28, 6-12.—u 8-14: Ex 28, 15-21.—v 15-21: Ex 28, 31-35.

were also made and put between the pomegranates all around the hem of the robe: [26] first a bell, then a pomegranate, and thus alternating all around the hem of the robe which was to be worn in performing the ministry—all this, just as the LORD had commanded Moses.

[27] For Aaron and his sons there were also woven tunics of fine linen; [w] [28] the miter of fine linen; the ornate turbans of fine linen; drawers of linen [of fine linen twined]; [29] and sashes of variegated work made of fine linen twined and of violet, purple and scarlet yarn, as the LORD had commanded Moses. [30] The plate of the sacred diadem was made of pure gold [x] and inscribed, as on a seal engraving: "Sacred to the LORD." [31] It was tied over the miter with a violet ribbon, as the LORD had commanded Moses.

Presentation of the Work to Moses. [32] Thus the entire work of the Dwelling of the meeting tent was completed. The Israelites did the work just as the LORD had commanded Moses. [33] They then brought to Moses the Dwelling, the tent with all its appurtenances, the clasps, the boards, the bars, the columns, the pedestals, [34] the covering of rams' skins dyed red, the covering of tahash skins, the curtain veil; [35] the ark of the commandments with its poles, the propitiatory, [36] the table with all its appurtenances and the showbread, [37] the pure gold lampstand with its lamps set up on it and with all its appurtenances, the oil for the light, [38] the golden altar, the anointing oil, the fragrant incense; the curtain for the entrance of the tent, [39] the altar of bronze with its bronze grating, its poles and all its appurtenances, the laver with its base, [40] the hangings of the court with their columns and pedestals, the curtain for the entrance of the court with its ropes and tent pegs, all the equipment for the service of the Dwelling of the meeting tent; [41] the service cloths for use in the sanctuary, the sacred vestments for Aaron the priest, and the vestments to be worn by his sons in their ministry. [42] The Israelites had carried out all the work just as the LORD had commanded Moses. [43] So

when Moses saw that all the work was done just as the LORD had commanded, he blessed them.

CHAPTER 40

Erection of the Dwelling. [1] Then the LORD said to Moses, [2] [y] "On the first day of the first month* you shall erect the Dwelling of the meeting tent. [z] [3] Put the ark of the commandments in it, and screen off the ark with the veil. [a] [4] Bring in the table and set it. Then bring in the lampstand and set up the lamps on it. [5] Put the golden altar of incense in front of the ark of the commandments, and hang the curtain at the entrance of the Dwelling. [6] Put the altar of holocausts in front of the entrance of the Dwelling of the meeting tent. [7] Place the laver between the meeting tent and the altar, and put water in it. [8] Set up the court round about, and put the curtain at the entrance of the court.

[9] [b] "Take the anointing oil and anoint the Dwelling and everything in it, consecrating it and all its furnishings, so that it will be sacred. [10] Anoint the altar of holocausts and all its appurtenances, consecrating it, so that it will be most sacred. [11] Likewise, anoint the laver with its base, and thus consecrate it.

[12] [c] "Then bring Aaron and his sons to the entrance of the meeting tent, and there wash them with water. [13] Clothe Aaron with the sacred vestments and anoint him, thus consecrating him as my priest. [14] Bring forward his sons also, and clothe them with the tunics. [15] As you have anointed their father, anoint them also as my priests. Thus, by being anointed, they shall receive a perpetual priesthood throughout all future generations."

[16] Moses did exactly as the LORD had commanded him. [17] On the first day of the first month of the second year the Dwelling was erected. [18] It was Moses who erected the Dwelling. He placed its pedestals, set up its boards, put in its bars, and set up its columns. [19] He spread the tent over the Dwelling and put the covering on top of the tent, as the LORD had commanded him. [20] [d] He took the commandments and put them in the ark; he placed poles alongside the ark and set the propitiatory upon it. [21] He brought the ark into the Dwelling and hung the curtain veil, thus screening off the ark of the command-

---

w 27ff: Ex 28, 39-42.—x 30f: Ex 28, 36f.—y 2-8: Ex 40, 16-33.—z Ex 26, 30.—a 3ff: Ex 26, 33ff.—b 9ff: Ex 30, 26-29.—c 12-15: Ex 28, 41; 29, 4-9; Lv 8, 1-13.—d 20ff: Ex 25, 16. 21; 26, 33ff.

40, 2: *On the first day of the first month:* almost a year after the departure of the Israelites from Egypt. Cf v 17.

ments, as the LORD had commanded him. [22] He put the table in the meeting tent, on the north side of the Dwelling, outside the veil, [23] and arranged the bread on it before the LORD, as the LORD had commanded him.[e] [24] He placed the lampstand in the meeting tent, opposite the table, on the south side of the Dwelling, [25] and he set up the lamps before the LORD, as the LORD had commanded him. [26] He placed the golden altar in the meeting tent, in front of the veil, [27] and on it he burned fragrant incense, as the LORD had commanded him. [28] He hung the curtain at the entrance of the Dwelling. [29] He put the altar of holocausts in front of the entrance of the Dwelling of the meeting tent, and offered holocausts and cereal offerings on it, as the LORD had commanded him. [30] [f] He placed the laver between the meeting tent and the altar, and put water in it for washing. [31] Moses and Aaron and his sons used to wash their hands and feet there, [32] for they washed themselves whenever they went into the meeting tent or approached the altar, as the LORD had commanded Moses. [33] Finally, he set up the court around the Dwelling and the altar and hung the curtain at the entrance of the court. Thus Moses finished all the work.

God's Presence in the Dwelling. [34] [g] Then the cloud covered the meeting tent, and the glory of the LORD filled the Dwelling. [35] Moses could not enter the meeting tent, because the cloud settled down upon it and the glory of the LORD filled the Dwelling. [36] Whenever the cloud rose from the Dwelling, the Israelites would set out on their journey. [37] But if the cloud did not lift, they would not go forward; only when it lifted did they go forward. [38] In the daytime the cloud of the LORD was seen over the Dwelling; whereas at night, fire was seen in the cloud by the whole house of Israel in all the stages of their journey.

e Ex 25, 30.—f 30ff: Ex 30, 18ff.—g 34-38: Nm 9, 15-22.

THE BOOK OF LEVITICUS

The name "Leviticus" was bestowed on the third book of the Pentateuch by the ancient Greek translators because a good part of this book consists of sacrificial and other ritual laws prescribed for the priests of the tribe of Levi.

Continuing the legislation given by God to Moses at Mount Sinai, Leviticus is almost entirely legislative in character; the rare narrative portions are subordinate to the main legislative theme. Generally speaking, the laws contained in this book serve to teach the Israelites that they should always keep themselves in a state of legal purity, or external sanctity, as a sign of their intimate union with the Lord. Accordingly, the central idea of Leviticus is contained in its oft-repeated injunction: "You shall be holy, because I, the LORD, am holy."

The main divisions of Leviticus are: I. Ritual of Sacrifices (Lv 1—7). II. Ceremony of Ordination (Lv 8—10). III. Laws regarding Legal Purity (Lv 11—16). IV. Code of Legal Holiness (Lv 17—26). V. Redemption of Offerings (Lv 27).

I: RITUAL OF SACRIFICES

CHAPTER 1

Holocausts. [1] The LORD called Moses, and from the meeting tent gave him this message: [2] [a] "Speak to the Israelites and tell them: When any one of you wishes to bring an animal offering to the LORD, such an offering must be from the herd or from the flock.*

[3] "If his holocaust* offering is from the herd, it must be a male without blemish.[b] To find favor with the LORD, he shall bring it to the entrance of the meeting tent [4] and there lay his hand on the head of the holocaust, so that it may be acceptable to make atonement for him.[c] [5] He shall then slaughter the bull before the LORD,

a Lv 22, 18. 19.—b Ex 12, 5.—c Lv 3, 2. 8. 13; 4, 15; 8, 14. 22; 16, 21; Ex 29, 10. 15.

1, 2: *From the herd or from the flock:* the only animals which could be used as sacrificial victims were either of the bovine class (bulls, cows and calves) or the ovine class (sheep and lambs, goats and kids). Excluded, therefore, were not only all wild animals, but also such "unclean" domestic animals as the camel and the ass. See note on Lv 11, 1ff.

1, 3: *Holocaust:* from the Greek word meaning "wholly burned," this is the technical term for the special type of sacrifice in which an entire animal except its hide was consumed in the fire on the altar. The primary purpose of this complete gift was to render glory and praise to God.

but Aaron's sons, the priests, shall offer up its blood by splashing it on the sides of the altar which is at the entrance of the meeting tent.*d* ⁶Then he shall skin the holocaust and cut it up into pieces. ⁷After Aaron's sons, the priests, have put some burning embers on the altar and laid some wood on them, ⁸they shall lay the pieces of meat, together with the head and the suet, on top of the wood and embers on the altar. ⁹The inner organs and the shanks, however, the offerer shall first wash with water. The priest shall then burn the whole offering on the altar as a holocaust, a sweet-smelling oblation to the LORD.*e*

¹⁰"If his holocaust offering is from the flock, that is, a sheep or a goat, he must bring a male without blemish. ¹¹This he shall slaughter before the LORD at the north side of the altar. Then Aaron's sons, the priests, shall splash its blood on the sides of the altar. ¹²When the offerer has cut it up into pieces, the priest shall lay these, together with the head and suet, on top of the wood and the fire on the altar. ¹³The inner organs and the shanks, however, the offerer shall first wash with water. The priest shall offer them up and then burn the whole offering on the altar as a holocaust, a sweet-smelling oblation to the LORD.

¹⁴"If he offers a bird as a holocaust to the LORD, he shall choose a turtledove or a pigeon as his offering.*f* ¹⁵Having brought it to the altar where it is to be burned, the priest shall snap its head loose and squeeze out its blood against the side of the altar.*g* ¹⁶Its crop and feathers shall be removed and thrown on the ash heap at the east side of the altar. ¹⁷Then, having split the bird down the middle without separating the halves, the priest shall burn it on the altar, over the wood on the fire, as a holocaust, a sweet-smelling oblation to the LORD.

---

d Lv 3, 8.—e Lv 3, 5. 16; Ex 29, 18.—f Lv 5, 7; 12, 8; Lk 2, 24.—g Lv 5, 8.—h Nm 15, 4.—i Lv 6, 15.—j Lv 7, 9f; Sir 7, 31; 1 Cor 9, 13.—k 1 Chr 23, 29.—l Lv 6, 16f; Mt 16, 12; Mk 8, 15; Lk 12, 1; 1 Cor 5, 7; Gal 5, 9.—m Ez 43, 24.

2, 2: *Token offering:* literally, "reminder." Instead of burning the whole cereal offering, they burned only this part of it on the altar; it thus corresponded to the fat of the peace offering. See note on Lv 3, 1.

2, 13: *The salt of the covenant of your God:* the partaking in common of salt by those seated together at table was an ancient symbol of friendship and alliance. Cf Mk 9, 49 and Col 4, 6; and see note on Nm 18, 19.

CHAPTER 2

Cereal Offerings. ¹"When anyone wishes to bring a cereal offering to the LORD, his offering must consist of fine flour. He shall pour oil on it and put frankincense over it.*h* ²When he has brought it to Aaron's sons, the priests, one of them shall take a handful of this fine flour and oil, together with all the frankincense, and this he shall burn on the altar as a token offering,* a sweet-smelling oblation to the LORD.*i* ³The rest of the cereal offering belongs to Aaron and his sons. It is a most sacred oblation to the LORD.*j*

⁴"When the cereal offering you present is baked in an oven, it must be in the form of unleavened cakes made of fine flour mixed with oil, or of unleavened wafers spread with oil. ⁵If you present a cereal offering that is fried on a griddle, it must be of fine flour mixed with oil and unleavened.*k* ⁶Such a cereal offering must be broken into pieces, and oil must be poured over it. ⁷If you present a cereal offering that is prepared in a pot, it must be of fine flour, deep-fried in oil. ⁸A cereal offering that is made in any of these ways you shall bring to the LORD, offering it to the priest, who shall take it to the altar. ⁹Its token offering the priest shall then lift from the cereal offering and burn on the altar as a sweet-smelling oblation to the LORD. ¹⁰The rest of the cereal offering belongs to Aaron and his sons. It is a most sacred oblation to the LORD.

¹¹"Every cereal offering that you present to the LORD shall be unleavened, for you shall not burn any leaven or honey as an oblation to the LORD.*l* ¹²Such you may indeed present to the LORD in the offering of first fruits, but they are not to be placed on the altar for a pleasing odor. ¹³However, every cereal offering that you present to the LORD shall be seasoned with salt.*m* Do not let the salt of the covenant of your God* be lacking from your cereal offering. On every offering you shall offer salt.

¹⁴"If you present a cereal offering of first fruits to the LORD, you shall offer it in the form of fresh grits of new ears of grain, roasted by fire. ¹⁵On this cereal offering you shall put oil and frankincense. ¹⁶For its token offering the priest shall then burn some of the grits and oil, together with all the frankincense, as an oblation to the LORD.

CHAPTER 3

Peace Offerings. [1]"If someone in presenting a peace offering* makes his offering from the herd, he may offer before the LORD either a male or a female animal, but it must be without blemish.[n] [2]He shall lay his hand on the head of his offering,[o] and then slaughter it at the entrance of the meeting tent; but Aaron's sons, the priests, shall splash its blood on the sides of the altar. [3]From the peace offering he shall offer as an oblation to the LORD the fatty membrane over the inner organs, and all the fat that adheres to them,[p] [4]as well as the two kidneys, with the fat on them near the loins, and the lobe of the liver,* which he shall sever above the kidneys. [5]All this Aaron's sons shall then burn on the altar with the holocaust,[q] on the wood over the fire, as a sweet-smelling oblation to the LORD.

[6]"If the peace offering he presents to the LORD is from the flock, he may offer either a male or a female animal, but it must be without blemish. [7]If he presents a lamb as his offering, he shall bring it before the LORD, [8]and after laying his hand on the head of his offering, he shall slaughter it before the meeting tent; but Aaron's sons shall splash its blood on the sides of the altar. [9]As an oblation to the LORD he shall present the fat of the peace offering: the whole fatty tail,* which he must sever close to the spine, the fatty membrane over the inner organs, and all the fat that adheres to them,[r] [10]as well as the two kidneys, with the fat on them near the loins, and the lobe of the liver, which he must sever above the kidneys. [11]All this the priest shall burn on the altar as the food of the LORD's oblation.

[12]"If he presents a goat, he shall bring it before the LORD, [13]and after laying his hand on its head, he shall slaughter it before the meeting tent; but Aaron's sons shall splash its blood on the sides of the altar. [14]From it he shall offer as an oblation to the LORD the fatty membrane over the inner organs, and all the fat that adheres to them, [15]as well as the two kidneys, with the fat on them near the loins, and the lobe of the liver, which he must sever above the kidneys. [16]All this the priest shall burn on the altar as the food of the sweet-smelling oblation. All the fat belongs to the LORD. [17]This shall be a perpetual ordinance for your descendants wherever they may dwell. You shall not partake of any fat* or any blood."[s]

CHAPTER 4

Sin Offerings: For Priests. [1]The LORD said to Moses, [2]"Tell the Israelites: When a person inadvertently commits a sin* against some command of the LORD by doing one of the forbidden things,[t] [3]if it is the anointed priest* who thus sins and thereby makes the people also become guilty, he shall present to the LORD a young, unblemished bull as a sin offering for the sin he committed.[u] [4]Bringing the bullock to the entrance of the meeting tent, before the LORD, he shall lay his hand on its head and slaughter it before the LORD.[v] [5]The anointed priest shall then take some of the bullock's blood and bring it into the meeting tent, [6]where, dipping his finger in the blood, he shall sprinkle it seven times before the LORD, toward the veil of the sanctuary.[w] [7]The priest shall also put some of the blood on the horns of the altar[x] of fragrant incense which is before the LORD in the meeting tent. The rest of the bullock's blood he shall pour out at the base of the altar of holocausts which is at the entrance of the meeting tent. [8]From the sin-offering bullock he shall remove all the fat: the fatty membrane over the inner organs, and all the fat that adheres to them, [9]as well as the two kidneys, with the fat on them near the loins, and the lobe of the liver, which he must sever above the kidneys. [10]This is the same as is removed from the ox of the peace offering; and the priest shall burn it on the altar of holocausts. [11]The hide of

n Lv 22, 21.—o Lv 1, 4.—p Ex 29, 13. 22.—q Lv 6, 12.—r Lv 9, 19.—s Lv 17, 10-14; Gn 9, 4; Dt 12, 16. 23; 15, 23.—t Lv 5, 15. 17; Nm 15, 22-29.—u Heb 7, 27.—v Lv 1, 3f.—w Lv 8, 11.— x Lv 8, 15; 9, 9; 16, 18; Ex 29, 12.

3, 1: *Peace offering:* thus the ancient versions have rendered the Hebrew word, which perhaps means more exactly, "fulfillment sacrifice," offered up in fulfillment of a vow. Cf Prv 7, 14. Its characteristic feature was the sacred banquet at which the offerer and his guests partook of the meat of the sacrificed animal. Cf Lv 7, 11-21.
3, 4: *The lobe of the liver:* some render, "the fatty covering of the liver."
3, 9: *The whole fatty tail:* see note on Ex 29, 22.
3, 17: *Any fat:* only the fat mentioned in vv 9f. 14f is meant; other fat could be eaten by the Israelites.
4, 2: *A sin:* not necessarily a moral fault; included are all the cases of ritual uncleanness which people necessarily incurred in certain unavoidable circumstances.
4, 3: *The anointed priest:* his violation of the ceremonial law brought a sort of collective guilt on all the people whom he represented before God. *Sin offering:* more exactly, "sacrifice for remitting sin"; sin is here understood as explained above.

the bullock and all its flesh, with its head, legs, inner organs and offal,[y] [12] in short, the whole bullock, shall be brought outside the camp to a clean place where the ashes are deposited and there be burned up in a wood fire. At the place of the ash heap, there it must be burned.

For the Community. [13] "If the whole community of Israel inadvertently and without even being aware of it does something that the LORD has forbidden and thus makes itself guilty,[z] [14] should it later on become known that the sin was committed, the community shall present a young bull as a sin offering. They shall bring it before the meeting tent, [15] and here, before the LORD, the elders of the community shall lay their hands on the bullock's head.[a] When the bullock has been slaughtered before the LORD, [16] the anointed priest shall bring some of its blood into the meeting tent, [17] and dipping his finger in the blood, he shall sprinkle it seven times before the LORD, toward the veil. [18] He shall also put some of the blood on the horns of the altar of fragrant incense which is before the LORD in the meeting tent. The rest of the blood he shall pour out at the base of the altar of holocausts which is at the entrance of the meeting tent. [19] All of its fat he shall take from it and burn on the altar, [20] doing with this bullock just as he did with the other sin-offering bullock. Thus the priest shall make atonement for them, and they will be forgiven. [21] This bullock must also be brought outside the camp and burned, just as has been prescribed for the other one. This is the sin offering for the community.

For the Princes. [22] "Should a prince commit a sin inadvertently by doing one of the things which are forbidden by some commandment of the LORD, his God, and thus become guilty, [23] if later on he learns of the sin he committed, he shall bring as his offering an unblemished male goat. [24] Having laid his hands on its head, he shall slaughter the goat as a sin offering before the LORD, in the place where the holocausts are slaughtered. [25] The priest shall then take some of the blood of the sin offering on his finger and put it on the horns of the altar of holocausts. The rest

of the blood he shall pour out at the base of this altar. [26] All of the fat he shall burn on the altar like the fat of the peace offering.[b] Thus the priest shall make atonement for the prince's sin, and it will be forgiven.

For Private Persons. [27] "If a private person commits a sin inadvertently[c] by doing one of the things which are forbidden by the commandments of the LORD, and thus becomes guilty, [28] should he later on learn of the sin he committed, he shall bring an unblemished she-goat as the offering for his sin. [29] Having laid his hand on the head of the sin offering,[d] he shall slaughter it at the place of the holocausts. [30] The priest shall then take some of its blood on his finger and put it on the horns of the altar of holocausts. The rest of the blood he shall pour out at the base of the altar. [31] All the fat shall be removed, just as the fat is removed from the peace offering, and the priest shall burn it on the altar for an odor pleasing to the LORD.[e] Thus the priest shall make atonement for him, and he will be forgiven.

[32] "If, however, for his sin offering he presents a lamb, he shall bring an unblemished female. [33] Having laid his hand on its head, he shall slaughter this sin offering in the place where the holocausts are slaughtered. [34] The priest shall then take some of the blood of the sin offering on his finger and put it on the horns of the altar of holocausts. The rest of the blood he shall pour out at the base of the altar. [35] All the fat shall be removed, just as the fat is removed from the peace-offering lamb,[f] and the priest shall burn it on the altar with the other oblations of the LORD. Thus the priest shall make atonement for the man's sin, and it will be forgiven.

CHAPTER 5

For Special Cases. [1] "If any person refuses to give the information which, as a witness of something he has seen or learned, he has been adjured to give, and thus commits a sin and has guilt to bear;[g] [2] or if someone, without being aware of it, touches any unclean thing, as the carcass of an unclean wild animal, or that of an unclean domestic animal,[h] or that of an unclean swarming creature, and thus becomes unclean and guilty; [3] or if someone, without being aware of it, touches some human uncleanness, whatever kind of un-

---

y Lv 8, 17; 9, 11; Ex 29, 14; Nm 19, 5.—z Lv 5, 2-4; Nm 15, 24-26.—a Lv 1, 4.—b Lv 3, 3-5.—c Nm 15, 27.—d Lv 1, 4.—e Lv 1, 9; 3, 3-5.—f Lv 3, 3. 9.—g Prv 29, 24.—h Lv 11, 24. 31. 39; 12; 13; 15.

cleanness this may be, and then recognizes his guilt; [4] or if someone, without being aware of it, rashly utters an oath[i] to do good or evil, such as men are accustomed to utter rashly, and then recognizes that he is guilty of such an oath; [5] then whoever is guilty in any of these cases shall confess the sin he has incurred,[j] [6] and as his sin offering for the sin he has committed he shall bring to the LORD a female animal from the flock, a ewe lamb or a she-goat. The priest shall then make atonement for his sin.

[7] "If, however, he cannot afford an animal of the flock, he shall bring to the LORD as the sin offering for his sin two turtledoves or two pigeons, one for a sin offering and the other for a holocaust.[k] [8] He shall bring them to the priest, who shall offer the one for the sin offering first. Snapping its head loose at the neck, yet without breaking it off completely,[l] [9] he shall sprinkle some of the blood of the sin offering against the side of the altar.[m] The rest of the blood shall be squeezed out against the base of the altar. Such is the offering for sin. [10] The other bird shall be offered as a holocaust in the usual way. Thus the priest shall make atonement for the sin the man committed, and it will be forgiven.

[11] "If he is unable to afford even two turtledoves or two pigeons, he shall present as a sin offering for his sin one tenth of an ephah of fine flour. He shall not put oil or frankincense on it, because it is a sin offering. [12] When he has brought it to the priest, the latter shall take a handful of this flour as a token offering, and this he shall burn as a sin offering on the altar with the other oblations of the LORD. [13] Thus the priest shall make atonement for the sin that the man committed in any of the above cases, and it will be forgiven.[n] The rest of the flour, like the cereal offerings, shall belong to the priest."

Guilt Offerings. [14] The LORD said to Moses, [15] "If someone commits a sin by inadvertently cheating* in the LORD's sacred dues, he shall bring to the LORD as his guilt offering an unblemished ram from the flock, valued at two silver shekels according to the standard of the sanctuary shekel. [16] He shall also restore what he has sinfully withheld from the sanctuary, adding to it a fifth of its value.[o] This is to be given to the priest, who shall then make atonement for him with the guilt-offering ram, and he will be forgiven.

[17] [p] "If someone, without being aware of it,* commits such a sin by doing one of the things which are forbidden by some commandment of the LORD, that he incurs guilt for which he must answer, [18] he shall bring as a guilt offering to the priest an unblemished ram of the flock of the established value. The priest shall then make atonement for the fault which was unwittingly committed, and it will be forgiven. [19] Such is the offering for guilt; the penalty of the guilt must be paid to the LORD."

[20] The LORD said to Moses, [21] "If someone commits a sin of dishonesty against the LORD by denying his neighbor a deposit or a pledge for a stolen article, or by otherwise retaining his neighbor's goods unjustly, [22] or if, having found a lost article, he denies the fact and swears falsely about it with any of the sinful oaths that men make in such cases, [23] he shall therefore, since he has incurred guilt by his sin, restore the thing that was stolen or unjustly retained by him or the deposit left with him or the lost article he found [24] or whatever else he swore falsely about; on the day of his guilt offering he shall make full restitution of the thing itself, and in addition, give the owner one fifth of its value. [25] As his guilt offering he shall bring to the LORD an unblemished ram of the flock of the established value. When he has presented this as his guilt offering to the priest, [26] the latter shall make atonement for him before the LORD, and he will be forgiven whatever guilt he may have incurred."

CHAPTER 6

The Daily Holocaust. [1] The LORD said to Moses, [2] "Give Aaron and his sons the following command: This is the ritual* for

---

i Jgs 11, 30f; 1 Sm 14, 24; Mk 6, 23; Acts 23, 12.—j Lv 26, 40; Nm 5, 7.—k Lv 12, 8; Lk 2, 24.—l Lv 1, 15. 17.—m Lv 1, 15.—n Lv 4, 26. 35.—o Lv 22, 14.—p Lv 4, 2.

5, 15: *Cheating:* not offering the full amount in tithes, first fruits, etc. *Guilt offering:* its characteristic was a certain additional penalty imposed as reparation for the injustice involved in the fault which was atoned for by this sacrifice. However, in certain passages, e.g., Lv 14, 12f; Nm 6, 12; Ezr 10, 19, the term "guilt offering" is used for more important cases of "sin offerings" where no apparent injustice is involved.

5, 17: *Without being aware of it:* the case naturally presupposes that later on the offender learns of his mistake. Cf Lv 4, 13f.

6, 2: *Ritual:* literally, "law, instruction." Here, and in the following paragraphs, are given additional prescriptions for various kinds of sacrifices which were, in part, treated of in the preceding chapters.

holocausts. The holocaust is to remain on the hearth of the altar all night until the next morning, and the fire is to be kept burning on the altar. ³ The priest, clothed in his linen robe and wearing linen drawers on his body, shall take away the ashes to which the fire has reduced the holocaust on the altar, and lay them at the side of the altar. ⁴ Then, having taken off these garments and put on other garments, he shall carry the ashes to a clean place outside the camp. ⁵ The fire on the altar is to be kept burning; it must not go out. Every morning the priest shall put firewood on it. On this he shall lay out the holocaust and burn the fat of the peace offerings. ⁶ The fire is to be kept burning continuously on the altar; it must not go out.

Daily Cereal Offering. ⁷ "This is the ritual of the cereal offering. One of Aaron's sons shall first present it before the LORD, in front of the altar. ⁸ Then he shall take from it a handful of its fine flour and oil, together with all the frankincense that is on it, and this he shall burn on the altar as its token offering, a sweet-smelling oblation to the LORD. ⁹ The rest of it Aaron and his sons may eat; but it must be eaten in the form of unleavened cakes and in a sacred place: in the court of the meeting tent they shall eat it. ¹⁰ It shall not be baked with leaven. I have given it to them as their portion from the oblations of the LORD; it is most sacred, like the sin offering and the guilt offering. ¹¹ All the male descendants of Aaron may partake of it as their rightful share in the oblations of the LORD perpetually throughout your generations. Whatever touches the oblations becomes sacred."

¹² * The LORD said to Moses, ¹³ "This is the offering that Aaron and his sons shall present to the LORD [on the day he is anointed]: one tenth of an ephah of fine flour for the established cereal offering, half in the morning and half in the evening. ¹⁴ It shall be well kneaded and fried in oil on a griddle when you bring it in. Having broken the offering into pieces,

you shall present it as a sweet-smelling oblation to the LORD. ¹⁵ Aaron's descendant who succeeds him as the anointed priest shall do likewise. This is a perpetual ordinance: for the LORD the whole offering shall be burned. ¹⁶ Every cereal offering of a priest shall be a whole burnt offering; it may not be eaten."

Sin Offerings. ¹⁷ The LORD said to Moses, ¹⁸ "Tell Aaron and his sons: This is the ritual for sin offerings. At the place where holocausts are slaughtered, there also, before the LORD, shall the sin offering be slaughtered.�q It is most sacred. ¹⁹ The priest who presents the sin offering may partake of it; but it must be eaten in a sacred place,ʳ in the court of the meeting tent. ²⁰ Whatever touches its flesh shall become sacred. If any of its blood is spilled on a garment, the stained part must be washed in a sacred place. ²¹ A clay vessel in which it has been cooked shall thereafter be broken;ˢ if it is cooked in a bronze vessel, this shall be scoured afterward and rinsed with water. ²² All the males of the priestly line may partake of the sin offering, since it is most sacred.ᵗ ²³ But no one may partake of any sin offering of which some blood has been brought into the meeting tentᵘ to make atonement in the sanctuary; such an offering must be burned up in the fire.

CHAPTER 7

Guilt Offerings. ¹ "This is the ritual for guilt offerings, which are most sacred. ² At the place where the holocausts are slaughtered, there also shall the guilt offering be slaughtered.ᵛ Its blood shall be splashed on the sides of the altar. ³ ʷ All of its fat shall be taken from it and offered up: the fatty tail, the fatty membrane over the inner organs, ⁴ as well as the two kidneys with the fat on them near the loins, and the lobe of the liver, which must be severed above the kidneys. ⁵ All this the priest shall burn on the altar as an oblation to the LORD. This is the guilt offering. ⁶ All the males of the priestly line may partake of it; but it must be eaten in a sacred place, since it is most sacred.ˣ

⁷ "Because the sin offering and the guilt offering are alike, both having the same ritual, the guilt offering likewise belongs

---

q Lv 7, 2.—r Lv 10, 17.—s Lv 11, 33; 15, 12.—t Lv 7, 6; Nm 18, 10.—u Lv 4, 5; Heb 13, 11.—v Lv 6, 18.—w 3-5: Lv 3, 4. 9f. 14-16; 4, 8f.—x Lv 6, 22.

6, 12-16: This is another law about the daily or "established" cereal offering. It differs in some respects from the preceding law (vv 7-11) and also from the law in Ex 29, 38-42. Hence, the words *on the day he is anointed* were probably added by some later scribe in order to avoid the difficulty of harmonizing this law with the other two laws on the same matter.

to the priest who makes atonement with it. [8] Similarly, the priest who offers a holocaust for someone may keep for himself the hide of the holocaust that he has offered. [9] *y* Also, every cereal offering that is baked in an oven or deep-fried in a pot or fried on a griddle shall belong to the priest who offers it, [10] whereas all cereal offerings*z* that are offered up dry or mixed with oil shall belong to all of Aaron's sons without distinction.

Peace Offerings. [11] "This is the ritual for the peace offerings that are presented to the LORD. [12] When anyone makes a peace offering in thanksgiving, together with his thanksgiving sacrifice he shall offer unleavened cakes mixed with oil, unleavened wafers spread with oil, and cakes made of fine flour mixed with oil and well kneaded. [13] His offering shall also include loaves of leavened bread* along with the victim of his peace offering for thanksgiving. [14] From each of his offerings he shall present one portion as a contribution to the LORD; this shall belong to the priest who splashes the blood of the peace offering.

[15] *a* "The flesh of the thanksgiving sacrifice shall be eaten on the day it is offered; none of it may be kept till the next day. [16] However, if the sacrifice is a votive or a free-will offering, it should indeed be eaten on the day the sacrifice is offered, but what is left over may be eaten on the next day. [17] Should any flesh from the sacrifice be left over on the third day, it must be burned up in the fire. [18] If, therefore, any of the flesh of the peace offering is eaten on the third day, it shall not win favor for him nor shall it be reckoned to his credit; rather, it shall be considered as refuse, and anyone who eats of it shall have his guilt to bear. [19] Should the flesh touch anything unclean, it may not be eaten, but shall be burned up in the fire.

"All who are clean may partake of this flesh. [20] If, however, someone while in a state of uncleanness eats any of the flesh of a peace offering belonging to the LORD, that person shall be cut off from his people. [21] Likewise, if someone touches anything unclean, whether the uncleanness be of human or of animal origin or from some loathsome crawling creature, and then eats of a peace offering belonging to the LORD, that person, too, shall be cut off from his people."

Prohibition against Blood and Fat. [22] The LORD said to Moses, [23] "Tell the Israelites: You shall not eat the fat* of any ox or sheep or goat.*b* [24] Although the fat of an animal that has died a natural death or has been killed by wild beasts may be put to any other use, you may not eat it.*c* [25] If anyone eats the fat of an animal from which an oblation is made to the LORD, such a one shall be cut off from his people. [26] Wherever you dwell, you shall not partake of any blood, be it of bird or of animal. [27] Every person who partakes of any blood shall be cut off from his people."*d*

The Portions for Priests. [28] The LORD said to Moses, [29] "Tell the Israelites: He who presents a peace offering to the LORD shall bring a part of it as his special offering to him, [30] carrying in with his own hands the oblations to the LORD. The fat is to be brought in, together with the breast, which is to be waved as a wave offering * before the LORD. [31] The priest shall burn the fat on the altar,*e* but the breast belongs to Aaron and his sons. [32] Moreover, from your peace offering you shall give to the priest the right leg as a raised offering. [33] The descendant of Aaron who offers up the blood and fat of the peace offering shall have the right leg as his portion, [34] for from the peace offerings of the Israelites I have taken the breast that is waved and the leg that is raised up, and I have given them to Aaron, the priest, and to his sons by a perpetual ordinance as a contribution from the Israelites."*f*

[35] This is the priestly share* from the oblations of the LORD, allotted to Aaron and his sons on the day he called them to be the priests of the LORD; [36] on the day he anointed them the LORD ordered the Israelites to give them this share by a

---

y Lv 2, 3-10; Nm 18, 9; Ez 44, 29.—z Lv 2, 14f.—a 15-18: Lv 19, 6f.—b Lv 3, 17.—c Lv 22, 8.—d Lv 17, 10.—e Lv 3, 11. 16.—f Ex 29, 27f.

7, 13: *Leavened bread:* these loaves were not burned on the altar (cf Lv 2, 11), but were eaten at the "communion" meal which followed the sacrifice. See note on Lv 3, 1.

7, 23: *The fat:* only the particular portions specified in Lv 3, 9f. 14f are meant. *Ox or sheep or goat:* such animals as could be sacrificed; the fat of other clean animals could be eaten.

7, 30-34: *A wave offering . . . a raised offering:* these ceremonies are described in Ex 29, 24-28. The Hebrew word for "raised offering" is also rendered, in certain contexts, as "contribution."

7, 35: *The priestly share:* literally, "the anointed part."

perpetual ordinance throughout their generations. ³⁷This is the ritual for holocausts, cereal offerings, sin offerings, guilt offerings, [ordination offerings] and peace offerings, ³⁸which the LORD enjoined on Moses at Mount Sinai at the time when he commanded the Israelites in the wilderness of Sinai to bring their offerings to the LORD.

II: CEREMONY OF ORDINATION

CHAPTER 8

Ordination of Aaron and His Sons. ¹The LORD*ᵍ* said to Moses.* ²"Take Aaron and his sons, together with the vestments,* the anointing oil, the bullock for a sin offering, the two rams, and the basket of unleavened food. ³Then assemble the whole community at the entrance of the meeting tent." ⁴And Moses did as the LORD had commanded. When the community had assembled at the entrance of the meeting tent, ⁵Moses told them what the LORD had ordered to be done. ⁶Bringing forward Aaron and his sons, he first washed them with water.*ʰ* ⁷Then he put the tunic on Aaron,*ⁱ* girded him with the sash, clothed him with the robe, placed the ephod on him, and girded him with the embroidered belt of the ephod, fastening it around him. ⁸*ʲ* He then set the breastpiece on him, with the Urim and Thummim* in it, ⁹*ᵏ* and put the miter on his head, attaching the gold plate, the sacred diadem, over the front of the miter, at his forehead, as the LORD had commanded him to do.

¹⁰Taking the anointing oil, Moses anointed and consecrated the Dwelling, with all that was in it.*ˡ* ¹¹Then he sprinkled some of this oil seven times on the altar, and anointed the altar, with all its appurtenances, and the laver, with its base, thus consecrating them. ¹²He also poured some of the anointing oil on Aaron's head, thus consecrating him.*ᵐ* ¹³Moses likewise brought forward Aaron's sons, clothed them with tunics, girded them with sashes, and put turbans on them, as the LORD had commanded him to do.

---

g 1-36: cf Ex 29.—*h* 6f: Ex 40, 12f.—*i* 7ff: Sir 45, 8-13.—*j* Ex 28, 30.—*k* Ex 28, 36.—*l* Ex 30, 26.—*m* Sir 45, 15.—*n* Lv 4, 7; Heb 9, 22.—*o* 16f: Lv 3, 4; 4, 8-11.—*p* Lv 14, 14.

8, 1—9, 21: Though presented in the form of a narrative, this description of Aaron's ordination was intended to serve as a guide for all future ordinations.
8, 2: *The vestments, etc.:* already described in Ex 28—29.
8, 8: *The Urim and Thummim:* see note on Ex 28, 30.

Ordination Sacrifices. ¹⁴When he had brought forward the bullock for a sin offering, Aaron and his sons laid their hands on its head. ¹⁵Then Moses slaughtered it, and taking some of its blood, with his finger he put it on the horns around the altar, thus purifying the altar. He also made atonement for the altar by pouring out the blood at its base when he consecrated it.*ⁿ* ¹⁶Taking all the fat that was over the inner organs, as well as the lobe of the liver and the two kidneys with their fat,*ᵒ* Moses burned them on the altar. ¹⁷The bullock, however, with its hide and flesh and offal he burned in the fire outside the camp, as the LORD had commanded him to do.

¹⁸He next brought forward the holocaust ram, and Aaron and his sons laid their hands on its head. ¹⁹When he had slaughtered it, Moses splashed its blood on all sides of the altar. ²⁰After cutting up the ram into pieces, he burned the head, the cut-up pieces and the suet; ²¹then, having washed the inner organs and the shanks with water, he also burned these remaining parts of the ram on the altar as a holocaust, a sweet-smelling oblation to the LORD, as the LORD had commanded him to do.

²²Then he brought forward the second ram, the ordination ram, and Aaron and his sons laid their hands on its head. ²³When he had slaughtered it, Moses took some of its blood and put it on the tip of Aaron's right ear, on the thumb of his right hand, and on the big toe of his right foot.*ᵖ* ²⁴Moses had the sons of Aaron also come forward, and he put some of the blood on the tips of their right ears, on the thumbs of their right hands, and on the big toes of their right feet. The rest of the blood he splashed on the sides of the altar. ²⁵He then took the fat: the fatty tail and all the fat over the inner organs, the lobe of the liver and the two kidneys with their fat, and likewise the right leg; ²⁶from the basket of unleavened food that was set before the LORD he took one unleavened cake, one loaf of bread made with oil, and one wafer; these he placed on top of the portions of fat and the right leg. ²⁷He then put all these things into the hands of Aaron and his sons, whom he had wave them as a wave offering before the LORD. ²⁸When he had received them back, Moses burned them with the holocaust on the altar as the ordination offering, a sweet-smelling obla-

tion to the LORD. ²⁹He then took the breast and waved it as a wave offering before the LORD; this was Moses' own portion of the ordination ram. All this was in keeping with the LORD's command to Moses. ³⁰Taking some of the anointing oil and some of the blood that was on the altar, Moses sprinkled with it Aaron and his vestments, as well as his sons and their vestments, thus consecrating both Aaron and his vestments and his sons and their vestments.

³¹Finally, Moses said to Aaron and his sons, "Boil the flesh at the entrance of the meeting tent, and there eat it with the bread that is in the basket of the ordination offering, in keeping with the command I have received: 'Aaron and his sons shall eat of it.' ³²What is left over of the flesh and the bread you shall burn up in the fire. ³³Moreover, you are not to depart from the entrance of the meeting tent for seven days, until the days of your ordination are completed; for your ordination is to last for seven days. ³⁴ * The LORD has commanded that what has been done today be done to make atonement for you. ³⁵Hence you must remain at the entrance of the meeting tent day and night for seven days, carrying out the prescriptions of the LORD; otherwise you shall die; for this is the command I have received." ³⁶So Aaron and his sons did all that the LORD had commanded through Moses.

CHAPTER 9

Octave of the Ordination. ¹On the eighth day Moses summoned Aaron and his sons, together with the elders of Israel, ²and said to Aaron, "Take a calf for a sin offering and a ram for a holocaust, both without blemish, and offer them before the LORD. ³Tell the elders of Israel, too: Take a he-goat for a sin offering, a calf and a lamb, both umblemished yearlings, for a holocaust, ⁴and an ox and a ram for a peace offering, to sacrifice them before the LORD, along with a cereal offering mixed with oil; for today the LORD will reveal himself to you." ⁵So they brought what Moses had ordered. When the whole community had come forward and stood before the LORD, ⁶Moses said, "This is what the LORD orders you to do, that the glory of the LORD may be revealed to you.

⁷Come up to the altar," Moses then told Aaron, "and offer your sin offering and your holocaust in atonement for yourself and for your family; then present the offering of the people in atonement for them, as the LORD has commanded."

⁸Going up to the altar, Aaron first slaughtered the calf that was his own sin offering. ⁹When his sons presented the blood to him, he dipped his finger in the blood and put it on the horns of the altar. The rest of the blood he poured out at the base of the altar. ¹⁰He then burned on the altar the fat, the kidneys and the lobe of the liver that were taken from the sin offering, as the LORD had commanded Moses; ¹¹but the flesh and the hide he burned up in the fire outside the camp. ¹²Then Aaron slaughtered his holocaust. When his sons brought him the blood, he splashed it on all sides of the altar. ¹³They then brought him the pieces and the head of the holocaust, and he burned them on the altar. ¹⁴Having washed the inner organs and the shanks, he burned these also with the holocaust on the altar.

¹⁵Thereupon he had the people's offering brought up. Taking the goat that was for the people's sin offering, he slaughtered it and offered it up for sin as before. ¹⁶Then he brought forward the holocaust, other than the morning holocaust, and offered it in the usual manner. ¹⁷He then presented the cereal offering; taking a handful of it, he burned it on the altar. ¹⁸Finally he slaughtered the ox and the ram, the peace offering of the people. When his sons brought him the blood, Aaron splashed it on all sides of the altar. ¹⁹The portions of fat from the ox and from the ram, the fatty tail, the fatty membrane over the inner organs, the two kidneys, with the fat that is on them, and the lobe of the liver,�q ²⁰he placed on top of the breasts and burned them on the altar, ²¹ ʳ having first waved the breasts and the right legs as a wave offering before the LORD, in keeping with the LORD's command to Moses.

---

q 19f: Lv 3, 3ff.—r Lv 7, 31f.

8, 34: The sense is not quite clear. Either the verse gives merely the reason why God ordered this ceremony, or it contains God's command that the same ceremony be used in all future ordinations, or it decrees a repetition of the entire ceremony on each of the seven days. At least a sin offering for atonement was made on each of these days. Cf Ex 29, 29-36.

Revelation of the Lord's Glory. ²²Aaron then raised his hands over the people and blessed them. When he came down from offering the sin offering and holocaust and peace offering, ²³Moses and Aaron went into the meeting tent.ˢ On coming out they again blessed the people. Then the glory of the LORD was revealed to all the people. ²⁴Fire came forth from the LORD's presenceᵗ and consumed the holocaust and the remnants of the fat on the altar. Seeing this, all the people cried out and fell prostrate.

CHAPTER 10

Nadab and Abihu. ¹During this time Aaron's sons Nadab and Abihu* took their censers and, strewing incense on the fire they had put in them,ᵘ they offered up before the LORD profane fire, such as he had not authorized. ²Fire* therefore came forth from the LORD's presence and consumed them,ᵛ so that they died in his presence. ³Moses then said to Aaron, "This is as the LORD said:

Through those who approach me I will manifest my sacredness;*
In the sight of all the people I will reveal my glory."ʷ

But Aaron said nothing. ⁴Then Moses summoned Mishael and Elzaphan, the sons of Aaron's uncle Uzziel, with the order, "Come, remove your kinsmen from the sanctuary and carry them to a place outside the camp." ⁵So they went in and took them, in their tunics,* outside the camp, as Moses had commanded.

s Nm 6, 23-26.—t 1 Kgs 18, 38; 2 Chr 7, 1.—u Lv 16, 1; Nm 3, 4; 26, 61; 1 Chr 24, 2.—v Nm 16, 35.—w Lv 21, 17. 21.—x Lv 21, 10.—y Ez 44, 21.—z Lv 11, 47; 20, 25; Ez 22, 26; 44, 23.—a Sir 45, 16.—b Lv 6, 16.—c 14f: Lv 7, 34.—d Lv 6, 18f.

10, 1: *Nadab and Abihu:* the older sons of Aaron. Cf Ex 6, 23f.

10, 2: *Fire:* perhaps after the manner of lightning.

10, 3: *I will manifest my sacredness:* the presence of God is so sacred that it strikes dead those who approach him without the proper holiness. Cf Nm 20, 13; Ez 28, 22.

10, 5: *In their tunics:* they were buried just as they were, with no shroud or funeral solemnities.

10, 6: *Bare your heads:* go without the customary head covering, as a sign of mourning. Some interpreters, however, understand it as the cutting off of one's hair, which ordinarily all the Israelites, men as well as women, let grow long. Cf Is 15, 2; Jer 7, 29. Still others understand the verb to mean "to let one's hair hang loose and wild." Cf Lv 13, 45; 21, 10, where the same phrase is used.

10, 16-19: *Eleazar and Ithamar* burned the entire goat of the sin offering (Lv 9, 15) instead of eating it in a sacred place (Lv 6, 19) to bear the guilt of the community. Aaron defends this action of his sons against Moses' displeasure by implying that they did not have sufficient sanctity to eat the flesh of the victim and thus perform the expiation of the people. They themselves still labored under the blow of the divine anger which struck their brothers Nadab and Abihu.

Conduct of the Priests. ⁶Moses said to Aaron and his sons Eleazar and Ithamar, "Do not bare your heads* or tear your garments,ˣ lest you bring not only death on yourselves but God's wrath also on the whole community. Your kinsmen, the rest of the house of Israel, shall mourn for those whom the LORD's fire has smitten; ⁷but do not you go beyond the entry of the meeting tent, else you shall die; for the anointing oil of the LORD is upon you." So they did as Moses told them.

⁸The LORD said to Aaron, ⁹"When you are to go to the meeting tent, you and your sons are forbidden under pain of death, by a perpetual ordinance throughout your generations, to drink any wine or strong drink.ʸ ¹⁰You must be able to distinguish between what is sacred and what is profane, between what is clean and what is unclean;ᶻ ¹¹you must teach the Israelites all the laws that the LORD has given them through Moses."ᵃ

The Eating of the Priestly Portions. ¹²Moses said to Aaron and his surviving sons, Eleazar and Ithamar, "Take the cereal offering left over from the oblations of the LORD, and eat it beside the altar in the form of unleavened cakes.ᵇ Since it is most sacred, ¹³you must eat it in a sacred place. This is your due from the oblations of the LORD, and that of your sons; such is the command I have received. ¹⁴ ᶜ With your sons and daughters you shall also eat the breast of the wave offering and the leg of the raised offering, in a clean place; for these have been assigned to you and your children as your due from the peace offerings of the Israelites. ¹⁵The leg of the raised offering and the breast of the wave offering shall first be brought in with the oblations, the fatty portions, that are to be waved as a wave offering before the LORD. Then they shall belong to you and your children by a perpetual ordinance, as the LORD has commanded."

¹⁶ * When Moses inquired about the goat of the sin offering, he discovered that it had all been burned. So he was angry with the surviving sons of Aaron, Eleazar and Ithamar, and said, ¹⁷ ᵈ "Why did you not eat the sin offering in the sacred place, since it is most sacred? It has been given to you that you might bear the guilt of the community and make atonement for them before the LORD. ¹⁸If its blood was not brought into the inmost part of the sanc-

tuary, you should certainly have eaten the offering in the sanctuary, in keeping with the command I had received." [19] Aaron answered Moses, "Even though they presented their sin offering and holocaust before the LORD today, yet this misfortune has befallen me. Had I then eaten of the sin offering today, would it have been pleasing to the LORD?" [20] On hearing this, Moses was satisfied.

III: LAWS REGARDING LEGAL PURITY

CHAPTER 11

Clean and Unclean Food. [1] The LORD said to Moses and Aaron,* [2] "Speak to the Israelites and tell them: Of all land animals these are the ones you may eat: [3] any animal that has hoofs you may eat, provided it is cloven-footed and chews the cud. [4] But you shall not eat any of the following that only chew the cud or only have hoofs: the camel, which indeed chews the cud, but does not have hoofs and is therefore unclean for you; [5] the rock badger,* which indeed chews the cud, but does not have hoofs and is therefore unclean for you; [6] the hare, which indeed chews the cud, but does not have hoofs and is therefore unclean for you; and the pig, [7] which does indeed have hoofs and is cloven-footed, but does not chew the cud and is therefore unclean for you. [8] Their flesh you shall not eat, and their dead bodies you shall not touch; they are unclean for you.

[9] "Of the various creatures that live in the water, you may eat the following: whatever in the seas or in river waters has both fins and scales you may eat. [10] But of the various creatures that crawl or swim in the water, whether in the sea or in the rivers, all those that lack either fins or scales are loathsome for you, [11] and you shall treat them as loathsome. Their flesh you shall not eat, and their dead bodies you shall loathe. [12] Every water creature that lacks fins or scales is loathsome for you.

[13] "Of the birds, these you shall loathe and, as loathsome, they shall not be eaten:* the eagle, the vulture, the osprey, [14] the kite, the various species of falcons, [15] the various species of crows, [16] the ostrich, the nightjar, the gull, the various species of hawks, [17] the owl, the cormorant, the screech owl, [18] the barn owl, the

desert owl, the buzzard, [19] the stork, the various species of herons, the hoopoe, and the bat.*
[20] "The various winged insects that walk on all fours are loathsome for you. [21] But of the various winged insects that walk on all fours you may eat those that have jointed legs for leaping on the ground; [22] hence of these you may eat the following: the various kinds of locusts,* the various kinds of grasshoppers, the various kinds of katydids, and the various kinds of crickets. [23] All other winged insects that have four legs are loathsome for you.

[24] * "Such is the uncleanness that you contract, that everyone who touches their dead bodies shall be unclean until evening, [25] and everyone who picks up any part of their dead bodies shall wash his garments and be unclean until evening. [26] All hoofed animals that are not cloven-footed* or do not chew the cud are unclean for you; everyone who touches them becomes unclean. [27] Of the various quadrupeds, all those that walk on paws* are unclean for you; everyone who touches their dead bodies shall be unclean until evening, [28] and everyone who picks up their dead bodies shall wash his garments and be unclean until evening. Such is their uncleanness for you.

[29] "Of the creatures that swarm on the ground, the following are unclean for you: the rat, the mouse, the various kinds of lizards, [30] the gecko, the chameleon, the agama, the skink, and the mole. [31] Among the various swarming creatures, these are unclean for you. Everyone who touches them when they are dead shall be un-

11, 1ff: These distinctions between edible and inedible meats were probably based on traditional ideas of hygiene, but they are here given a moral, religious basis: the inedible varieties are classified as "unclean" to remind the Israelites that they are to be a pure and holy people, dedicated to the Lord.

11, 5f: According to modern zoology, *the rock badger* (hyrax Syriacus) is classified as an ungulate, and *the hare* as a rodent; neither is a ruminant. They appear to chew their food as the true ruminants do, and it is upon this appearance that the classification in the text is based.

11, 13-19. 30: The identification of the various Hebrew names for these birds and reptiles is in many cases uncertain.

11, 19: *The bat:* actually a mammal, but listed here with birds because of its wings.

11, 22: The Hebrew distinguishes four classes of edible locust-like insects, but the difference between them is quite uncertain. Cf Mt 3, 4.

11, 24-28: This paragraph sharpens the prohibition against unclean animals: not only is their meat unfit for food, but contact with their dead bodies makes a person ritually unclean.

11, 26: *All hoofed animals that are not cloven-footed:* such as the horse and the ass.

11, 27: *All those that walk on paws:* such as dogs and cats.

clean until evening. ³² Everything on which one of them falls when dead becomes unclean. Any such article that men use, whether it be an article of wood, cloth, leather or goat hair, must be put in water and remain unclean until evening, when it again becomes clean. ³³ Should any of these creatures fall into a clay vessel, everything in it becomes unclean, and the vessel itself you must break. ³⁴ Any solid food that was in contact with water, and any liquid that men drink, in any such vessel become unclean. ³⁵ Any object on which one of their dead bodies falls becomes unclean; if it is an oven or a jar-stand, this must be broken to pieces; they are unclean and shall be treated as unclean by you. ³⁶ However, a spring or a cistern for collecting water remains clean; but whoever touches the dead body* becomes unclean. ³⁷ Any sort of cultivated grain remains clean even though one of their dead bodies falls on it; ³⁸ but if the grain has become moistened, it becomes unclean when one of these falls on it.

³⁹ "When one of the animals that you could otherwise eat, dies of itself, anyone who touches its dead body shall be unclean until evening; ⁴⁰ and anyone who eats of its dead body shall wash his garments and be unclean until evening;ᵉ so also, anyone who removes its dead body shall wash his garments and be unclean until evening.

⁴¹ "All the creatures that swarm on the ground are loathsome and shall not be eaten. ⁴² Whether it crawls on its belly, goes on all fours, or has many legs, you shall eat no swarming creature: they are loathsome. ⁴³ Do not make yourselves loathsome or unclean with any swarm-

ing creature through being contaminated by them.ᶠ ⁴⁴ For I, the LORD, am your God; and you shall make and keep yourselves holy, because I am holy.ᵍ You shall not make yourselves unclean, then, by any swarming creature that crawls on the ground. ⁴⁵ Since I, the LORD, brought you up from the land of Egypt that I might be your God, you shall be holy, because I am holy.

⁴⁶ "This is the law for animals and birds and for all the creatures that move about in the water or swarm on the ground, ⁴⁷ that you may distinguish between the clean and the unclean, between creatures that may be eaten and those that may not be eaten."ʰ

CHAPTER 12

Uncleanness of Childbirth. ¹ The LORD said to Moses, ² "Tell the Israelites: When a woman has conceived and gives birth to a boy, she shall be unclean* for seven days, with the same uncleanness as at her menstrual period.ⁱ ³ On the eighth day, the flesh of the boy's foreskin shall be circumcised,ʲ ⁴ and then she shall spend thirty-three days more in becoming purified of her blood; she shall not touch anything sacred nor enter the sanctuary till the days of her purification are fulfilled. ⁵ If she gives birth to a girl, for fourteen days she shall be as unclean as at her menstruation, after which she shall spend sixty-six days in becoming purified of her blood.

⁶ "When the days of her purification for a son or for a daughter are fulfilled,ᵏ she shall bring to the priest at the entrance of the meeting tent a yearling lamb for a holocaust and a pigeon or a turtledove for a sin offering. ⁷ The priest shall offer them up before the LORD to make atonement for her, and thus she will be clean again after her flow of blood. Such is the law for the woman who gives birth to a boy or a girl child. ⁸ * If, however, she cannot afford a lamb, she may take two turtledoves or two pigeons,ˡ the one for a holocaust and the other for a sin offering. The priest shall make atonement for her, and thus she will again be clean."

CHAPTER 13

Leprosy. ¹ The LORD said to Moses and Aaron, ² ᵐ "If someone has on his skin* a scab or pustule or blotch which appears

e Lv 17, 15; 22, 8.—f 43f: Lv 20, 25f.—g Lv 19, 2; 20 7. 26; Mt 5, 48; 1 Pt 1, 16.—h Lv 10, 10.—i Lv 15, 19.—j Gn 17, 12; Jn 7, 22.—k Lk 2, 22.—l Lv 1, 14; Lk 2, 24.—m Dt 24, 8.

11, 36: *Whoever touches the dead body:* to remove the dead insect from the water supply.

12, 2f: The uncleanness of the woman was more serious during the first period, the seven days after the birth of a boy or the fourteen days after the birth of a girl; only during this period would the rules given in Lv 15, 19-24 apply.

12, 8: Forty days after the birth of Jesus, his Virgin Mother made this offering of the poor (Lk 2, 22. 24); since the holocaust was offered in thanksgiving for the birth of the child, this was most fittingly offered by Mary. However, because of her miraculous delivery, she was not really obliged to make the sin offering of purification.

13, 2ff: Various kinds of skin blemishes are treated here which were not contagious but simply disqualified their subjects from association with others, especially in public worship, until they were declared ritually clean. The Hebrew term used does not refer to Hansen's disease, currently called leprosy.

to be the sore of leprosy, he shall be brought to Aaron, the priest, or to one of the priests among his descendants, [3] who shall examine the sore on his skin. If the hair on the sore has turned white and the sore itself shows that it has penetrated below the skin, it is indeed the sore of leprosy; the priest, on seeing this, shall declare the man unclean. [4] If, however, the blotch on the skin is white, but does not seem to have penetrated below the skin, nor has the hair turned white, the priest shall quarantine the stricken man for seven days. [5] On the seventh day the priest shall again examine him. If he judges that the sore has remained unchanged and has not spread on the skin, the priest shall quarantine him for another seven days, [6] and once more examine him on the seventh day. If the sore is now dying out and has not spread on the skin, the priest shall declare the man clean; it was merely eczema. The man shall wash his garments and so become clean. [7] But if, after he has shown himself to the priest to be declared clean, the eczema spreads at all on his skin, he shall once more show himself to the priest. [8] Should the priest, on examining it, find that the eczema has indeed spread on the skin, he shall declare the man unclean; it is leprosy.

[9] "When someone is stricken with leprosy, he shall be brought to the priest. [10] Should the priest, on examining him, find that there is a white scab on the skin which has turned the hair white and that there is raw flesh in it, [11] it is skin leprosy that has long developed. The priest shall declare the man unclean without first quarantining him, since he is certainly unclean. [12] If leprosy breaks out on the skin* and, as far as the priest can see, covers all the skin of the stricken man from head to foot, [13] should the priest then, on examining him, find that the leprosy does cover his whole body, he shall declare the stricken man clean; since it has all turned white, the man is clean. [14] But as soon as raw flesh appears on him, he is unclean; [15] on observing the raw flesh, the priest shall declare him unclean, because raw flesh is unclean; it is leprosy. [16] If, however, the raw flesh again turns white, he shall return to the priest; [17] should the latter, on examining him, find that the sore has indeed turned

white, he shall declare the stricken man clean, and thus he will be clean.

[18] "If a man who had a boil on his skin which later healed, [19] should now in the place of the boil have a white scab or a pink blotch, he shall show himself to the priest. [20] If the latter, on examination, sees that it is deeper than the skin and that the hair has turned white, he shall declare the man unclean: it is the sore of leprosy that has broken out in the boil. [21] But if the priest, on examining him, finds that there is no white hair in it and that it is not deeper than the skin and is already dying out, the priest shall quarantine him for seven days. [22] If it has then spread on the skin, the priest shall declare him unclean; the man is stricken. [23] But if the blotch remains in its place without spreading, it is merely the scar of the boil; the priest shall therefore declare him clean.

[24] "If a man had a burn on his skin, and the proud flesh of the burn now becomes a pink or a white blotch, [25] the priest shall examine it. If the hair has turned white on the blotch and this seems to have penetrated below the skin, it is leprosy that has broken out in the burn; the priest shall therefore declare him unclean and stricken with leprosy. [26] But if the priest, on examining it, finds that there is no white hair on the blotch and that this is not deeper than the skin and is already dying out, the priest shall quarantine him for seven days. [27] Should the priest, when examining it on the seventh day, find that it has spread at all on the skin, he shall declare the man unclean and stricken with leprosy. [28] But if the blotch remains in its place without spreading on the skin and is already dying out, it is merely the scab of the burn; the priest shall therefore declare the man clean, since it is only the scar of the burn.

[29] "When a man or a woman has a sore on the head or cheek, [30] should the priest, on examining it, find that the sore has penetrated below the skin and that there is fine yellow hair on it, the priest shall declare the person unclean, for this is scall,* a leprous disease of the head or cheek.

13, 12ff: *If leprosy breaks out on the skin:* the symptoms described here point to a form of skin disease which is merely on the surface and therefore easily cured.

13, 30: *Scall:* a scabby or scaly eruption of the scalp. According to some, "ringworm."

[31] But if the priest, on examining the scall sore, finds that it has not penetrated below the skin, though the hair on it may not be black, the priest shall quarantine the person with scall sore for seven days, [32] and on the seventh day again examine the sore. If the scall has not spread and has no yellow hair on it and does not seem to have penetrated below the skin, [33] the man shall shave himself, but not on the diseased spot. Then the priest shall quarantine him for another seven days. [34] If the priest, when examining the scall on the seventh day, finds that it has not spread on the skin and that it has not penetrated below the skin, he shall declare the man clean; the latter shall wash his garments, and thus he will be clean. [35] But if the scall spreads at all on his skin after he has been declared clean, [36] the priest shall again examine it. If the scall has indeed spread on the skin, he need not look for yellow hair; the man is surely unclean. [37] If, however, he judges that the scall has remained in its place and that black hair has grown on it, the disease has been healed; the man is clean, and the priest shall declare him clean.

[38] "When the skin of a man or a woman is spotted with white blotches, [39] the priest shall make an examination. If the blotches on the skin are white and already dying out, it is only tetter* that has broken out on the skin, and the person therefore is clean.

[40] "When a man loses the hair of his head, he is not unclean merely because of his bald crown. [41] So too, if he loses the hair on the front of his head, he is not unclean merely because of his bald forehead. [42] But when there is a pink sore on his bald crown or bald forehead, it is leprosy that is breaking out there. [43] The priest shall examine him; and if the scab on the sore of the bald spot has the same pink appearance as that of skin leprosy of the fleshy part of the body, [44] the man is leprous and unclean, and the priest shall declare him unclean by reason of the sore on his head.

[45] "The one who bears the sore of leprosy shall keep his garments rent and his head bare, and shall muffle his beard; he shall cry out, 'Unclean, unclean!' [46] As long as the sore is on him he shall declare himself unclean, since he is in fact unclean.[n] He shall dwell apart, making his abode outside the camp.

Leprosy of Clothes. [47] "When a leprous infection* is on a garment of wool or of linen, [48] or on woven or knitted material of linen or wool, or on a hide or anything made of leather, [49] if the infection on the garment or hide, or on the woven or knitted material, or on any leather article is greenish or reddish, the thing is indeed infected with leprosy and must be shown to the priest. [50] Having examined the infection, the priest shall quarantine the infected article for seven days.

[51] "On the seventh day the priest shall again examine the infection. If it has spread on the garment, or on the woven or knitted material, or on the leather, whatever be its use, the infection is malignant leprosy, and the article is unclean. [52] He shall therefore burn up the garment, or the woven or knitted material of wool or linen, or the leather article, whatever it may be, which is infected; since it has malignant leprosy, it must be destroyed by fire. [53] But if the priest, on examining the infection, finds that it has not spread on the garment, or on the woven or knitted material, or on the leather article, [54] he shall give orders to have the infected article washed and then quarantined for another seven days. [55] "Then the priest shall again examine the infected article after it has been washed. If the infection has not changed its appearance, even though it may not have spread, the article is unclean and shall be destroyed by fire. [56] But if the priest, on examining the infection, finds that it is dying out after the washing, he shall tear the infected part out of the garment, or the leather, or the woven or knitted material. [57] If, however, the infection again appears on the garment, or on the woven or knitted material, or on the leather article, it is still virulent and the thing infected shall be destroyed by fire. [58] But if, after the washing, the infection has left the garment, or the woven or knitted material, or the leather article, the thing shall be washed a second time, and thus it will be clean. [59] This is the law for leprous infection[o] on a garment of wool or linen, or on woven or knitted material, or

---

n Nm 5, 2; 12, 14f; 2 Kgs 15, 5; Lk 17, 12.—o Lv 14, 54.

13, 39: *Tetter:* vitiligo, a harmless form of skin disease.
13, 47: *A leprous infection:* some mold or fungus growth resembling human leprosy.

on any leather article, to determine whether it is clean or unclean."

CHAPTER 14

Purification after Leprosy. [1]The LORD said to Moses, [2] *p* "This is the law for the victim of leprosy at the time of his purification. He shall be brought to the priest, [3]who is to go outside the camp to examine him. If the priest finds that the sore of leprosy has healed in the leper, [4]he shall order the man who is to be purified, to get two live, clean birds, as well as some cedar wood, scarlet yarn,* and hyssop. [5]The priest shall then order him to slay one of the birds over an earthen vessel with spring water* in it. [6]Taking the living bird with the cedar wood, the scarlet yarn and the hyssop, the priest shall dip them all in the blood of the bird that was slain over the spring water, [7]and then sprinkle seven times the man to be purified from his leprosy. When he has thus purified him, he shall let the living bird fly away over the countryside. [8]The man being purified shall then wash his garments and shave off all his hair and bathe in water; only when he is thus made clean may he come inside the camp; but he shall still remain outside his tent for seven days. [9]On the seventh day he shall again shave off all the hair of his head, his beard, his eyebrows, and any other hair he may have, and also wash his garments and bathe his body in water; and so he will be clean.

Purification Sacrifices. [10]"On the eighth day he shall take two unblemished male lambs, one unblemished yearling ewe lamb, three tenths of an ephah of fine flour mixed with oil for a cereal offering, and one log of oil. [11]The priest who performs the purification ceremony shall place the man who is being purified, as well as all these offerings, before the LORD at the entrance of the meeting tent. [12]Taking one of the male lambs, the priest shall present it as a guilt offering, along with the log of oil, waving them as a wave offering before the LORD. [13](This lamb he shall slaughter in the sacred place where the sin offering and the holocaust are slaughtered; because, like the sin offering, the guilt offering belongs to the priest and is most sacred.) [14]Then the priest shall take some of the blood of the guilt offering and put it on the tip of the man's right ear, the thumb

of his right hand, and the big toe of his right foot. *q* [15]The priest shall also take the log of oil and pour some of it into the palm of his own left hand; [16]then, dipping his right forefinger in it, he shall sprinkle it seven times before the LORD. [17]Of the oil left in his hand the priest shall put some on the tip of the man's right ear, the thumb of his right hand, and the big toe of his right foot, over the blood of the guilt offering. [18]The rest of the oil in his hand the priest shall put on the head of the man being purified. Thus shall the priest make atonement for him before the LORD. [19]Only after he has offered the sin offering in atonement for the man's uncleanness shall the priest slaughter the holocaust [20]and offer it, together with the cereal offering, on the altar before the LORD. When the priest has thus made atonement for him, the man will be clean.

Poor Leper's Sacrifice. [21]"If a man is poor and cannot afford so much, he shall take one male lamb for a guilt offering, to be used as a wave offering in atonement for himself, one tenth of an ephah of fine flour mixed with oil for a cereal offering, a log of oil, [22]and two turtledoves* or pigeons, which he can more easily afford, the one as a sin offering and the other as a holocaust. [23]On the eighth day of his purification he shall bring them to the priest, at the entrance of the meeting tent before the LORD. [24]Taking the guilt-offering lamb, along with the log of oil, the priest shall wave them as a wave offering before the LORD. [25]When he has slaughtered the guilt-offering lamb, he shall take some of its blood, and put it on the tip of the right ear of the man being purified, on the thumb of his right hand, and on the big toe of his right foot. [26]The priest shall then pour some of the oil into the palm of his own left hand [27]and with his right forefinger sprinkle it seven times before the LORD. [28]Some of the oil in his hand the priest shall also put on the tip of the man's right ear, the thumb of his right hand, and the big toe of his right foot, over the blood

---

p Mt 8, 4; Mk 1, 44; Lk 5, 14.—q Lv 8, 23f.

14, 4: *Scarlet yarn:* probably used for tying the hyssop sprig to the cedar branchlet.
14, 5: *Spring water:* literally, "living water," taken from some source of running water, not from a cistern.
14, 22: *Two turtledoves:* substitutes for the two additional lambs, similar to the offering of a poor woman after childbirth. Cf Lv 12, 8.

of the guilt offering. ²⁹ The rest of the oil in his hand the priest shall put on the man's head. Thus shall he make atonement for him before the LORD. ³⁰ Then, of the turtledoves or pigeons, such as the man can afford, ³¹ the priest shall offer up one as a sin offering and the other as a holocaust, along with the cereal offering. Thus shall the priest make atonement before the LORD for the man who is to be purified. ³² This is the law for one afflicted with leprosy who has insufficient means for his purification."

Leprosy of Houses. ³³ The LORD said to Moses and Aaron, ³⁴ "When you come into the land of Canaan, which I am giving you to possess, if I put a leprous infection on any house of the land you occupy, ³⁵ the owner of the house shall come and report to the priest, 'It looks to me as if my house were infected.' ³⁶ The priest shall then order the house to be cleared out before he goes in to examine the infection, lest everything in the house become unclean. Only after this is he to go in to examine the house. ³⁷ If the priest, on examining it, finds that the infection on the walls of the house consists of greenish or reddish depressions which seem to go deeper than the surface of the wall, ³⁸ he shall close the door of the house behind him and quarantine the house for seven days. ³⁹ On the seventh day the priest shall return to examine the house again. If he finds that the infection has spread on the walls, ⁴⁰ he shall order the infected stones to be pulled out and cast in an unclean place outside the city. ⁴¹ The whole inside of the house shall then be scraped, and the mortar that has been scraped off shall be dumped in an unclean place outside the city. ⁴² Then new stones shall be brought and put in the place of the old stones, and new mortar shall be made and plastered on the house.

⁴³ "If the infection breaks out once more after the stones have been pulled out and the house has been scraped and replastered, ⁴⁴ the priest shall come again; and if he finds that the infection has spread in the house, it is corrosive leprosy, and the house is unclean. ⁴⁵ It shall be pulled down, and all its stones, beams and mortar shall be hauled away to an unclean place outside the city. ⁴⁶ Whoever enters a house

while it is quarantined shall be unclean until evening. ⁴⁷ Whoever sleeps or eats in such a house shall also wash his garments. ⁴⁸ If the priest finds, when he comes to examine the house, that the infection has in fact not spread after the plastering, he shall declare the house clean, since the infection has been healed. ⁴⁹ To purify the house, he shall take two birds, as well as cedar wood, scarlet yarn, and hyssop. ⁵⁰ One of the birds he shall slay over an earthen vessel with spring water in it. ⁵¹ Then, taking the cedar wood, the hyssop and the scarlet yarn, together with the living bird, he shall dip them all in the blood of the slain bird and the spring water, and sprinkle the house seven times. ⁵² Thus shall he purify the house with the bird's blood and the spring water, along with the living bird, the cedar wood, the hyssop, and the scarlet yarn. ⁵³ He shall then let the living bird fly away over the countryside outside the city. When he has thus made atonement for it, the house will be clean.

⁵⁴ "This is the law for every kind of human leprosy and scall, ⁵⁵ ʳ for leprosy of garments and houses, ⁵⁶ as well as for scabs, pustules and blotches, ⁵⁷ so that it may be manifest when there is a state of uncleanness and when a state of cleanness. This is the law for leprosy."

CHAPTER 15

Personal Uncleanness. ¹ The LORD said to Moses and Aaron, ² "Speak to the Israelites and tell them: Every man who is afflicted with a chronic flow from his private parts is thereby unclean.ˢ ³ Such is his uncleanness from this flow that it makes no difference whether the flow drains off or is blocked up; his uncleanness remains. ⁴ Any bed on which the man afflicted with the flow lies, is unclean, and any piece of furniture on which he sits, is unclean. ⁵ Anyone who touches his bed shall wash his garments, bathe in water, and be unclean until evening. ⁶ Whoever sits on a piece of furniture on which the afflicted man was sitting, shall wash his garments, bathe in water, and be unclean until evening. ⁷ Whoever touches the body of the afflicted man shall wash his garments, bathe in water, and be unclean until evening. ⁸ If the afflicted man spits on a clean man, the latter shall wash his gar-

---

ments, bathe in water, and be unclean until evening. [9] Any saddle on which the afflicted man rides, is unclean. [10] Whoever touches anything that was under him shall be unclean until evening; whoever lifts up any such thing shall wash his garments, bathe in water, and be unclean until evening. [11] Anyone whom the afflicted man touches with unrinsed hands shall wash his garments, bathe in water, and be unclean until evening. [12] Earthenware touched by the afflicted man shall be broken; and every wooden article shall be rinsed with water.

[13] "When a man who has been afflicted with a flow becomes free of his affliction, he shall wait seven days for his purification. Then he shall wash his garments and bathe his body in fresh water, and so he will be clean. [14] On the eighth day he shall take two turtledoves or two pigeons, and going before the LORD, to the entrance of the meeting tent, he shall give them to the priest, [15] who shall offer them up, the one as a sin offering and the other as a holocaust. Thus shall the priest make atonement before the LORD for the man's flow.

[16] "When a man has an emission of seed, he shall bathe his whole body in water and be unclean until evening. [17] Any piece of cloth or leather with seed on it shall be washed with water and be unclean until evening.

[18] "If a man lies carnally with a woman, they shall both bathe in water and be unclean until evening.

[19] "When a woman has her menstrual flow, she shall be in a state of impurity for seven days.[t] Anyone who touches her shall be unclean until evening. [20] Anything on which she lies or sits during her impurity shall be unclean. [21] Anyone who touches her bed shall wash his garments, bathe in water, and be unclean until evening. [22] Whoever touches any article of furniture on which she was sitting, shall wash his garments, bathe in water, and be unclean until evening. [23] * But if she is on the bed or on the seat when he touches it, he shall be unclean until evening. [24] If a man dares to lie with her, he contracts her impurity and shall be unclean for seven days;[u] every bed on which he then lies also becomes unclean.

[25] "When a woman is afflicted with a flow of blood for several days outside her menstrual period, or when her flow continues beyond the ordinary period,[v] as long as she suffers this unclean flow she shall be unclean, just as during her menstrual period. [26] Any bed on which she lies during such a flow becomes unclean, as it would during her menstruation, and any article of furniture on which she sits becomes unclean just as during her menstruation. [27] Anyone who touches them becomes unclean; he shall wash his garments, bathe in water, and be unclean until evening.

[28] "If she becomes freed from her affliction, she shall wait seven days, and only then is she to be purified. [29] On the eighth day she shall take two turtledoves or two pigeons and bring them to the priest at the entrance of the meeting tent. [30] The priest shall offer up one of them as a sin offering and the other as a holocaust. Thus shall the priest make atonement before the LORD for her unclean flow.

[31] "You shall warn the Israelites of their uncleanness, lest by defiling my Dwelling, which is in their midst, their uncleanness be the cause of their death.

[32] "This is the law for the man who is afflicted with a chronic flow, or who has an emission of seed, and thereby becomes unclean; [33] as well as for the woman who has her menstrual period, or who is afflicted with a chronic flow; the law for male and female; and also for the man who lies with an unclean woman."

CHAPTER 16

The Day of Atonement. [1] After the death of Aaron's two sons, who died when they approached the LORD's presence, the LORD spoke to Moses [2] and said to him,[w] "Tell your brother Aaron that he is not to come whenever he pleases into the sanctuary, inside the veil,* in front of the propitiatory on the ark; otherwise, when I reveal myself in a cloud above the propitiatory, he will die. [3] Only in this way

t Lv 12, 2. 5.—u Lv 18, 19.—v Mt 9, 20; Mk 5, 25; Lk 8, 43.— w Heb 9, 6-12.

15, 23: What is added to the legislation by this verse is uncertain in both the Hebrew and the Greek.
16, 2: *The sanctuary, inside the veil:* the innermost part of the sanctuary, known also as "the holy of holies." Cf Ex 26, 33f. Here the high priest was allowed to enter only once a year, on *Yom Kippur,* the Day of Atonement. In Heb 9, 3-12 this ceremony is applied to Christ's single act of Redemption, whereby he won for us an everlasting atonement. *Propitiatory:* see note on Ex 25, 17.

may Aaron enter the sanctuary. He shall bring a young bullock for a sin offering and a ram for a holocaust. [4] He shall wear the sacred linen tunic, with the linen drawers next his flesh, gird himself with the linen sash and put on the linen miter. But since these vestments are sacred, he shall not put them on until he has first bathed his body in water. [5] From the Israelite community he shall receive two male goats for a sin offering and one ram for a holocaust. [x]

[6] "Aaron shall bring in the bullock, his sin offering to atone for himself and for his household. [7] Taking the two male goats, and setting them before the LORD at the entrance of the meeting tent, [8] he shall cast lots to determine which one is for the LORD and which for Azazel.* [9] The goat that is determined by lot for the LORD, Aaron shall bring in and offer up as a sin offering. [10] But the goat determined by lot for Azazel he shall set alive before the LORD, so that with it he may make atonement by sending it off to Azazel in the desert.

[11] "Thus shall Aaron offer up the bullock, his sin offering, to atone for himself and for his family. When he has slaughtered it, [12] he shall take a censer full of glowing embers from the altar before the LORD, as well as a double handful of finely ground fragrant incense, and bringing them inside the veil, [13] there before the LORD he shall put incense on the fire, so that a cloud of incense may cover the propitiatory over the commandments; else he will die. * [14] Taking some of the bullock's blood, he shall sprinkle it with his finger on the fore part of the propitiatory and likewise sprinkle some of the blood with his finger seven times in front of the propitiatory.[y]

[15] "Then he shall slaughter the people's sin-offering goat, and bringing its blood inside the veil, he shall do with it as he did with the bullock's blood, sprinkling it on the propitiatory and before it.[z] [16] Thus he shall make atonement for the sanctuary because of all the sinful defilements and faults of the Israelites. He shall do the same for the meeting tent, which is set up among them in the midst of their uncleanness. [17] No one else may be in the meeting tent from the time he enters the sanctuary to make atonement until he departs. When he has made atonement for himself and his household, as well as for the whole Israelite community, [18] he shall come out to the altar before the LORD and make atonement for it also. Taking some of the bullock's and the goat's blood, he shall put it on the horns around the altar,[a] [19] and with his finger sprinkle some of the blood on it seven times. Thus he shall render it clean and holy, purged of the defilements of the Israelites.

The Scapegoat. [20] "When he has completed the atonement rite for the sanctuary, the meeting tent and the altar, Aaron shall bring forward the live goat. [21] Laying both hands on its head, he shall confess over it all the sinful faults and transgressions of the Israelites, and so put them on the goat's head.[b] He shall then have it led into the desert by an attendant. [22] Since the goat is to carry off their iniquities to an isolated region, it must be sent away into the desert.[c]

[23] * "After Aaron has again gone into the meeting tent, he shall strip off and leave in the sanctuary the linen vestments he had put on when he entered there. [24] After bathing his body with water in a sacred place, he shall put on his vestments, and then come out and offer his own and the people's holocaust, in atonement for himself and for the people, [25] and also burn the fat of the sin offering on the altar.

[26] "The man who has led away the goat for Azazel shall wash his garments and bathe his body in water; only then may he enter the camp. [27] The sin-offering bullock and goat whose blood was brought into the sanctuary to make atonement, shall be taken outside the camp,[d] where their hides and flesh and offal shall be burned up in the fire. [28] The one who burns them shall wash his garments and bathe his body in water; only then may he enter the camp.

The Fast. [29] [e] "This shall be an everlasting ordinance for you: on the tenth day of the seventh month every one of you,

---

x Nm 29, 11.—y Heb 9, 13. 25.—z Heb 5, 1; 6, 19.—a Ex 30, 12.—b Is 53, 6; 2 Cor 5, 21.—c Is 53, 11. 12; Jn 1, 29; 1 Pt 2, 24.—d Heb 13, 11.—e Lv 23, 27. 32; Nm 29, 7.

16, 8: *Azazel:* perhaps a name of Satan, used only in this chapter. The ancient versions translated this word as "the escaping goat," whence the English word "scapegoat."

16, 13: *Else he will die:* the smoke is to conceal the resplendent majesty of God, the sight of which would strike any man dead.

16, 23: This verse is best read after v 25. According to later Jewish practice the high priest again went into the holy of holies to remove the censer.

whether a native or a resident alien, shall mortify himself* and shall do no work. 30 Since on this day atonement is made for you to make you clean, so that you may cleansed of all your sins before the LORD, 31 by everlasting ordinance it shall be a most solemn sabbath for you, on which you must mortify yourselves.

32 "This atonement is to be made by the priest who has been anointed and ordained to the priesthood in succession to his father. He shall wear the linen garments, the sacred vestments, 33 and make atonement for the sacred sanctuary, the meeting tent and the altar, as well as for the priests and all the people of the community. 34 This, then, shall be an everlasting ordinance for you: once a year atonement shall be made for all the sins of the Israelites."*f*

Thus was it done, as the LORD had commanded Moses.

IV: CODE OF LEGAL HOLINESS

CHAPTER 17

Sacredness of Blood. 1 The LORD said to Moses, 2 "Speak to Aaron and his sons, as well as to all the Israelites, and tell them: This is what the LORD has commanded. 3 * Any Israelite who slaughters an ox or a sheep or a goat, whether in the camp or outside of it, 4 without first bringing it to the entrance of the meeting tent to present it as an offering to the LORD in front of his Dwelling, shall be judged guilty of bloodshed; and for this, such a man shall be cut off from among his people. 5 Therefore, such sacrifices as they used to offer up in the open field the Israelites shall henceforth offer to the LORD, bringing them to the priest at the entrance of the meeting tent and sacrificing them there as peace offerings to the LORD. 6 The priest shall splash the blood on the altar of the LORD at the entrance of the meeting tent and there burn the fat for an odor pleasing to the LORD. 7 No longer shall they offer their sacrifices to the satyrs to whom they used to render their wanton worship.*g* This shall be an everlasting ordinance for them and their descendants.

8 "Tell them, therefore: Anyone, whether of the house of Israel or of the aliens residing among them, who offers a holocaust or sacrifice 9 without bringing it to the entrance of the meeting tent to offer it to the LORD, shall be cut off from his kinsmen. 10 And if anyone, whether of the house of Israel or of the aliens residing among them, partakes of any blood, I will set myself against that one who partakes of blood and will cut him off from among his people.*h* 11 *i* Since the life of a living body is in its blood, I have made you put it on the altar, so that atonement may thereby be made for your own lives,* because it is the blood, as the seat of life, that makes atonement. 12 That is why I have told the Israelites: No one among you, not even a resident alien, may partake of blood.

13 "Anyone hunting, whether of the Israelites or of the aliens residing among them, who catches an animal or a bird that may be eaten, shall pour out its blood and cover it with earth. 14 Since the life of every living body is its blood, I have told the Israelites: You shall not partake of the blood of any meat.*j* Since the life of every living body is its blood, anyone who partakes of it shall be cut off.

15 *k* "Everyone, whether a native or an alien, who eats of an animal that died of itself or was killed by a wild beast, shall wash his garments, bathe in water, and be unclean until evening, and then he will be clean. 16 If he does not wash or does not bathe his body, he shall have the guilt to bear."

CHAPTER 18

The Sanctity of Sex. 1 The LORD said to Moses, 2 "Speak to the Israelites and tell them: I, the LORD, am your God. 3 You shall not do as they do in the land of Egypt, where you once lived, nor shall you do as they do in the land of Canaan,

---

f Heb 9, 7. 25.—g Ex 34, 15; Dt 32, 17; 2 Chr 11, 15; 1 Cor 10, 20.—h Lv 3, 17.—i Gn 9, 4.—j Lv 7, 26f.—k Lv 11, 39f; 22, 8.

16, 29: *Mortify himself:* literally, "afflict his soul"; traditionally understood by the Jews as signifying abstinence from all food. This is the only fast day prescribed in the Mosaic law.

17, 3ff: The ancients considered blood the seat and sign of life, and therefore something sacred, even in animals. Cf Gn 9, 4f. Hence, even the ordinary butchering of an animal for meat was looked upon as having a sacrificial character, so that it should be performed at the sanctuary. This law, however, could not be carried out without great difficulty when the Israelites were scattered throughout Palestine, and so was modified in Dt 12, 20ff.

17, 11: *That atonement may thereby be made for your own lives:* hence, the sacrifice of an animal was a symbolic act which substituted the victim's life for the life of the offerer, who thus acknowledged that he deserved God's punishments for his sins. This idea of sacrifice is applied in Heb 9—10 to the death of Christ, inasmuch as "without the shedding of blood there is no forgiveness" (Heb 9, 22).

where I am bringing you; do not conform to their customs. [4]My decrees you shall carry out, and my statutes you shall take care to follow. I, the LORD, am your God. [5]Keep, then, my statutes and decrees, for the man who carries them out will find life through them. I am the LORD.[l]

[6] * "None of you shall approach a close relative to have sexual intercourse with her. I am the LORD. [7] [m] You shall not disgrace your father by having intercourse with your mother. Besides, since she is your own mother, you shall not have intercourse with her. [8]You shall not have intercourse with your father's wife,[n] for that would be a disgrace to your father. [9]You shall not have intercourse with your sister, your father's daughter or your mother's daughter, whether she was born in your own household or born elsewhere. [10]You shall not have intercourse with your son's daughter or with your daughter's daughter, for that would be a disgrace to your own family. [11]You shall not have intercourse with the daughter whom your father's wife bore to him, since she, too, is your sister. [12] [o] You shall not have intercourse with your father's sister, since she is your father's relative. [13]You shall not have intercourse with your mother's sister, since she is your mother's relative. [14]You shall not disgrace your father's brother by being intimate with his wife,[p] since she, too, is your aunt. [15]You shall not have intercourse with your daughter-in-law; she is your son's wife, and therefore you shall not disgrace her. [16]You shall not have intercourse with your brother's wife,* for that would be a disgrace to your brother.[q] [17]You shall not have intercourse with a woman and also with her daughter, nor

shall you marry and have intercourse with her son's daughter or her daughter's daughter; this would be shameful, because they are related to her. [18]While your wife is still living you shall not marry her sister as her rival; for thus you would disgrace your first wife.

[19]"You shall not approach a woman to have intercourse with her while she is unclean from menstruation. [20]You shall not have carnal relations with your neighbor's wife, defiling yourself with her. [21] [r] You shall not offer any of your offspring to be immolated to Molech,* thus profaning the name of your God. I am the LORD. [22]You shall not lie with a male as with a woman; such a thing is an abomination.[s] [23]You shall not have carnal relations with an animal, defiling yourself with it; nor shall a woman set herself in front of an animal to mate with it; such things are abhorrent.[t]

[24]"Do not defile yourselves by any of these things by which the nations whom I am driving out of your way have defiled themselves. [25]Because their land has become defiled, I am punishing it for its wickedness, by making it vomit out its inhabitants. [26]You, however, whether natives or resident aliens, must keep my statutes and decrees forbidding all such abominations [27]by which the previous inhabitants defiled the land; [28]otherwise the land will vomit you out also for having defiled it, just as it vomited out the nations before you. [29]Everyone who does any of these abominations shall be cut off from among his people. [30]Heed my charge, then, not to defile yourselves by observing the abominable customs that have been observed before you.[u] I, the LORD, am your God."

CHAPTER 19

Various Rules of Conduct. [1]The LORD said to Moses, [2]"Speak to the whole Israelite community and tell them: Be holy, for I, the LORD, your God, am holy.[v] [3]Revere your mother and father,[w] and keep my sabbaths. I, the LORD, am your God.

[4]"Do not turn aside to idols, nor make molten gods for yourselves.[x] I, the LORD, am your God.

[5]"When you sacrifice your peace offering to the LORD, if you wish it to be acceptable, [6]it must be eaten on the very

---

l Gal 3, 12.—m 7-16: Lv 20, 11-21.—n Dt 23, 1; 27, 20; 1 Cor 5, 1.—o 12f: Lv 20, 19.—p Lv 20, 20.—q Lv 20, 21; Mt 14, 3f; Mk 6, 18.—r Lv 20, 2-5; Dt 18, 10; 2 Kgs 16, 3; 21, 6.—s Lv 20, 13; Rom 1, 27; 1 Cor 6, 9f.—t Lv 20, 15f; Ex 22, 18.—u Lv 20, 23; Dt 18, 9.—v Lv 11, 44; Mt 5, 48; 1 Pt 1, 16.—w Ex 20, 12.—x Lv 26, 1; Ex 20, 3-5; 34, 17; Dt 27, 15.

18, 6-18: These laws are formulated as directed to the male Israelites only, but naturally the same norms of consanguinity and affinity would apply to the women as well. Marriage, as well as casual intercourse, is here forbidden between men and women of the specified degrees of relationship.

18, 16: *With your brother's wife:* it was the violation of this law which aroused the wrath of John the Baptist against Herod Antipas. Cf Mk 6, 18. An exception to this law is made in Dt 25, 5.

18, 21: *Immolated to Molech:* the reference is to the Canaanite custom of sacrificing children to the god Molech. The little victims were first slain and then cremated. Cf Ez 16, 20ff; 20, 26. 31; 23, 37.

day of your sacrifice or on the following day. Whatever is left over until the third day shall be burned up in the fire. [7] If any of it is eaten on the third day, the sacrifice will be unacceptable as refuse;[y] [8] whoever eats of it then shall pay the penalty for having profaned what is sacred to the LORD. Such a one shall be cut off from his people.

[9] "When you reap the harvest of your land, you shall not be so thorough that you reap the field to its very edge, nor shall you glean the stray ears of grain.[z] [10] Likewise, you shall not pick your vineyard bare, nor gather up the grapes that have fallen. These things you shall leave for the poor and the alien. I, the LORD, am your God.

[11] "You shall not steal. You shall not lie or speak falsely to one another.[a] [12] You shall not swear falsely by my name, thus profaning the name of your God.[b] I am the LORD.

[13] "You shall not defraud or rob your neighbor. You shall not withhold overnight the wages of your day laborer.[c] [14] You shall not curse the deaf, or put a stumbling block in front of the blind, but you shall fear your God. I am the LORD.

[15] "You shall not act dishonestly in rendering judgment. Show neither partiality to the weak nor deference to the mighty, but judge your fellow men justly.[d] [16] You shall not go about spreading slander among your kinsmen; nor shall you stand by idly when your neighbor's life is at stake. I am the LORD.

[17] "You shall not bear hatred for your brother in your heart.[e] Though you may have to reprove your fellow man, do not incur sin because of him. [18] Take no revenge and cherish no grudge against your fellow countrymen. You shall love your neighbor as yourself.* I am the LORD.[f]

[19] "Keep my statutes: do not breed any of your domestic animals with others of a different species; do not sow a field of yours with two different kinds of seed; and do not put on a garment woven with two different kinds of thread.

[20] * "If a man has carnal relations with a female slave who has already been living with another man but has not yet been redeemed or given her freedom, they shall be punished but not put to death, because she is not free. [21] The man, moreover, shall bring to the entrance of the meeting tent a ram as his guilt offering to the

LORD. [22] With this ram the priest shall make atonement before the LORD for the sin he has committed, and it will be forgiven him.

[23] "When you come into the land and plant any fruit tree there, first look upon its fruit as if it were uncircumcised. For three years, while its fruit remains uncircumcised,* it may not be eaten. [24] In the fourth year, however, all of its fruit shall be sacred to the LORD as a thanksgiving feast to him. [25] Not until the fifth year may you eat its fruit. Thus it will continue its yield for you. I, the LORD, am your God.

[26] "Do not eat meat with the blood still in it.[g] Do not practice divination or soothsaying. [27] * Do not clip your hair at the temples, nor trim the edges of your beard.[h] [28] Do not lacerate your bodies for the dead, and do not tattoo yourselves. I am the LORD.

[29] "You shall not degrade your daughter by making a prostitute of her; else the land will become corrupt and full of lewdness. [30] Keep my sabbaths, and reverence my sanctuary.[i] I am the LORD.

[31] "Do not go to mediums or consult fortune-tellers, for you will be defiled by them.[j] I, the LORD, am your God.

[32] "Stand up in the presence of the aged, and show respect for the old; thus shall you fear your God. I am the LORD.

[33] "When an alien resides with you in your land, do not molest him.[k] [34] You shall treat the alien who resides with you no differently than the natives born among you; have the same love for him as for yourself; for you too were once aliens in the land of Egypt.[l] I, the LORD, am your God.

19, 18: *You shall love your neighbor as yourself:* cited by our Lord as the second of the two most important commandments of God. Cf Mt 22, 39; Mk 12, 31. Although in the present context the word "neighbor" is restricted to "fellow countrymen," in Lk 10, 29-37 Christ extends its meaning to embrace all men, even enemies. Cf also Mt 5, 43ff.

19, 20ff: This law seems out of its proper context here; perhaps it stood originally after Lv 20, 12. *Female slave . . . given her freedom:* reference is to the case treated of in Ex 21, 7-11.

19, 23ff: *Uncircumcised:* by analogy with a newborn boy, the newly planted tree was considered impure until "circumcised" by offering to the Lord all the fruit it bore in the fourth year.

19, 27: See note on Lv 21, 5.

35 "Do not act dishonestly in using measures of length or weight or capacity. 36 You shall have a true scale and true weights, an honest ephah and an honest hin.*m* I, the LORD, am your God, who brought you out of the land of Egypt. 37 Be careful, then, to observe all my statutes and decrees. I am the LORD."

CHAPTER 20

Penalties for Various Sins. 1 The LORD said to Moses, 2 "Tell the Israelites: Anyone, whether an Israelite or an alien residing in Israel, who gives any of his offspring to Molech shall be put to death.*n* Let his fellow citizens stone him. 3 *o* I myself will turn against such a man and cut him off from the body of his people; for in giving his offspring to Molech, he has defiled my sanctuary and profaned my holy name. 4 Even if his fellow citizens connive at such a man's crime of giving his offspring to Molech, and fail to put him to death, 5 I myself will set my face against that man and his family and will cut off from their people both him and all who join him in his wanton worship of Molech. 6 Should anyone turn to mediums and fortune-tellers and follow their wanton ways,*p* I will turn against such a one and cut him off from his people. 7 Sanctify yourselves, then, and be holy; for I, the LORD, your God, am holy.*q* 8 Be careful, therefore, to observe what I, the LORD, who make you holy, have prescribed.

9 "Anyone who curses his father or mother shall be put to death;*r* since he has cursed his father or mother, he has forfeited his life. 10 If a man commits adultery with his neighbor's wife, both the adulterer and the adulteress shall be put to death.*s* 11 If a man disgraces his father*t* by lying with his father's wife, both the man and his stepmother shall be put to death; they have forfeited their lives. 12 If a man lies with his daughter-in-law,*u* both of them shall be put to death; since they have committed an abhorrent deed, they have forfeited their lives. 13 If a man lies with a

male as with a woman,*v* both of them shall be put to death for their abominable deed; they have forfeited their lives. 14 If a man marries a woman and her mother also,*w* the man and the two women as well shall be burned to death for their shameful conduct, so that such shamefulness may not be found among you. 15 If a man has carnal relations with an animal, the man shall be put to death,*x* and the animal shall be slain. 16 If a woman goes up to any animal to mate with it,*y* the woman and the animal shall be slain; let them both be put to death; their lives are forfeit. 17 If a man consummates marriage with his sister or his half-sister,*z* they shall be publicly cut off from their people for this shameful deed; the man shall pay the penalty of having had intercourse with his own sister. 18 If a man lies in sexual intercourse with a woman during her menstrual period,*a* both of them shall be cut off from their people, because they have laid bare the flowing fountain of her blood. 19 You shall not have intercourse with your mother's sister or your father's sister;*b* whoever does so shall pay the penalty of incest. 20 If a man disgraces his uncle by having intercourse with his uncle's wife, the man and his aunt shall pay the penalty by dying childless. 21 If a man marries his brother's wife and thus disgraces his brother, they shall be childless because of this incest.

22 "Be careful to observe all my statutes and all my decrees; otherwise the land where I am bringing you to dwell will vomit you out. 23 Do not conform, therefore, to the customs of the nations*c* whom I am driving out of your way, because all these things that they have done have filled me with disgust for them. 24 But to you I have said: *d* Their land shall be your possession, a land flowing with milk and honey. I am giving it to you as your own, I, the LORD, your God, who have set you apart from the other nations. 25 *e* You, too, must set apart, then, the clean animals from the unclean, and the clean birds from the unclean, so that you may not be contaminated with the uncleanness of any beast or bird or of any swarming creature in the land that I have set apart for you. 26 To me, therefore, you shall be sacred; for I, the LORD, am sacred,*f* I, who have set you apart from the other nations to be my own.

m Dt 25, 13. 15; Prv 11, 1; 16, 11; 20, 10; Ez 45, 10.—n Lv 18, 21.—o Ez 23, 39.—p Lv 19, 31.—q Lv 11, 44; 19, 2; 1 Pt 1, 16.—r Ex 21, 17; Prv 20, 20; Mt 15, 4; Mk 7, 10.—s Lv 18, 20; Dt 22, 22; Jn 8, 5.—t Lv 18, 7f.—u Lv 18, 15.—v Lv 18, 22.—w Lv 18, 17; Dt 27, 23.—x Ex 22, 28; Dt 27, 21.—y Lv 18, 23.—z Lv 18, 9; Dt 27, 22.—a Lv 18, 19.—b Lv 18, 12f.—c Lv 18, 30.—d Ex 3, 8. 17; 6, 8.—e Lv 11, 2-47; Dt 14, 4-20.—f Lv 11, 44; Ex 19, 6; 1 Pt 1, 16.

²⁷ * "A man or a woman who acts as a medium or fortune-teller*g* shall be put to death by stoning; they have no one but themselves to blame for their death."

CHAPTER 21

Sanctity of the Priesthood. ¹The LORD said to Moses, "Speak to Aaron's sons, the priests, and tell them: None of you shall make himself unclean for any dead person* among his people,*h* ²except for his nearest relatives, his mother or father, his son or daughter, his brother ³or his maiden sister, who is of his own family while she remains unmarried; for these he may make himself unclean ⁴But for a sister who has married out of his family he shall not make himself unclean; this would be a profanation.

⁵ * "The priests shall not make bare the crown of the head, nor shave the edges of the beard,*i* nor lacerate the body. ⁶To their God they shall be sacred,* and not profane his name; since they offer up the oblations of the LORD, the food of their God, they must be holy.

⁷"A priest shall not marry a woman who has been a prostitute or has lost her honor, nor a woman who has been divorced by her husband; for the priest is sacred to his God.*j* ⁸Honor him as sacred who offers up the food of your God; treat him as sacred, because I, the LORD, who have consecrated him, am sacred.

⁹"A priest's daughter who loses her honor by committing fornication and thereby dishonors her father also, shall be burned to death.

¹⁰"The most exalted of the priests, upon whose head the anointing oil has been poured and who has been ordained to wear the special vestments, shall not bare his head* or rend his garments, ¹¹nor shall he go near any dead person. Not even for his father or mother may he thus become unclean ¹²or leave the sanctuary;*k* otherwise he will profane the sanctuary of his God, for with the anointing oil upon him, he is dedicated to his God, to me, the LORD.

¹³"The priest shall marry a virgin. ¹⁴Not a widow or a woman who has been divorced or a woman who has lost her honor as a prostitute, but a virgin, taken from his own people, shall he marry;*l* ¹⁵otherwise he will have base offspring among his people. I, the LORD, have made him sacred."

Irregularities. ¹⁶The LORD said to Moses, ¹⁷"Speak to Aaron and tell him: None of your descendants, of whatever generation, who has any defect shall come forward to offer up the food of his God. ¹⁸Therefore, he who has any of the following defects may not come forward: he who is blind, or lame, or who has any disfigurement or malformation, ¹⁹or a crippled foot or hand, ²⁰or who is humpbacked or weakly or walleyed, or who is afflicted with eczema, ringworm or hernia. ²¹No descendant of Aaron the priest who has any such defect may draw near to offer up the oblations of the LORD; on account of his defect he may not draw near to offer up the food of his God. ²²He may, however, partake of the food of his God: of what is most sacred as well as of what is sacred. ²³Only, he may not approach the veil nor go up to the altar on account of his defect; he shall not profane these things that are sacred to me, for it is I, the LORD, who make them sacred."

²⁴Moses, therefore, told this to Aaron and his sons and to all the Israelites.

CHAPTER 22

Sacrificial Banquets. ¹The LORD said to Moses, ²"Tell Aaron and his sons to respect the sacred offerings which the Israelites consecrate to me; else they will profane my holy name. I am the LORD.

³"Tell them: If any one of you, or of your descendants in any future generation, dares, while he is in a state of uncleanness, to draw near the sacred offerings which the Israelites consecrate to the LORD, such a one shall be cut off from my presence. I am the LORD.

⁴"No descendant of Aaron who is stricken with leprosy, or who suffers from a flow, may eat of these sacred offerings,

---

g Lv 19, 31; Ex 22, 17; Dt 18, 11.—h Ez 44, 25.—i Ez 44, 20.—j Ez 44, 22.—k Lv 10, 7.—l Ez 44, 22.

20, 27: This verse is best read immediately after v 6.
21, 1: *Unclean for any dead person:* by preparing the corpse for burial. Cf Nm 6, 6; 19, 11-19.
21, 5: Such mourning customs of the Canaanites were forbidden to all the Israelites, but especially to the priests. Cf Lv 19, 27f.
21, 6: *Sacred:* the same Hebrew word has both the active meaning of "holy," that is, keeping oneself free from profane impurities, and the passive meaning of "sacred," that is, set apart from what is profane and therefore treated with religious reverence.
21, 10: *Bare his head:* see note on Lv 10, 6.

unless he again becomes clean.^m Moreover, if anyone touches a person who has become unclean by contact with a corpse, or if anyone has had an emission of seed, ⁵or if anyone touchesⁿ any swarming creature or any man whose uncleanness, of whatever kind it may be, is contagious, ⁶the one who touches such as these shall be unclean until evening and may not eat of the sacred portions until he has first bathed his body in water;^o ⁷then, when the sun sets, he again becomes clean. Only then may he eat of the sacred offerings, which are his food. ⁸He shall not make himself unclean by eating of any animal that has died of itself or has been killed by wild beasts.^p I am the LORD.

⁹"They shall keep my charge and not do wrong in this matter; else they will die for their profanation. I am the LORD who have consecrated them.

¹⁰"Neither a lay person nor a priest's tenant or hired servant may eat of any sacred offering.^q ¹¹But a slave whom a priest acquires by purchase or who is born in his house may eat of his food. ¹²A priest's daughter who is married to a layman may not eat of the sacred contributions. ¹³But if a priest's daughter is widowed or divorced and, having no children, returns to her father's house, she may then eat of her father's food as in her youth. No layman, however, may eat of it. ^{14 r} If such a one eats of a sacred offering through inadvertence, he shall make restitution to the priest for the sacred offering, with an increment of one fifth of the amount. ¹⁵The sacred offerings which the Israelites contribute to the LORD the priests shall not allow to be profaned^s ¹⁶nor in the eating of the sacred offering shall they bring down guilt that must be punished; it is I, the LORD, who make them sacred."

Unacceptable Victims. ¹⁷The LORD said to Moses, ¹⁸"Speak to Aaron and his sons and to all the Israelites, and tell them: When anyone of the house of Israel, or any alien residing in Israel, who wishes to offer a sacrifice, brings a holocaust as a votive offering or as a free-will offering to the LORD, ¹⁹if it is to be acceptable, the ox or sheep or goat that he offers must be an unblemished male.^t ²⁰You shall not offer one that has any defect, for such a one would not be acceptable for you.^u ²¹When anyone presents a peace offering^v to the LORD from the herd or the flock in fulfillment of a vow, or as a free-will offfering, if it is to find acceptance, it must be unblemished; it shall not have any defect. ²²One that is blind or crippled or maimed, or one that has a running sore or mange or ringworm, you shall not offer to the LORD; do not put such an animal on the altar as an oblation to the LORD. ²³An ox or a sheep that is in any way ill-proportioned or stunted you may indeed present as a free-will offering, but it will not be acceptable as a votive offering. ²⁴One that has its testicles bruised or crushed or torn out or cut off you shall not offer to the LORD. You shall neither do this in your own land ²⁵nor receive from a foreigner any such animals to offer up as the food of your God; since they are deformed or defective,^w they will not be acceptable for you."

²⁶The LORD said to Moses, ²⁷"When an ox or a lamb or a goat is born, it shall remain with its mother for seven days; only from the eighth day onward will it be acceptable, to be offered as an oblation to the LORD.^x ²⁸You shall not slaughter an ox or a sheep on one and the same day with its young. ²⁹Whenever you offer a thanksgiving sacrifice to the LORD, so offer it that it may be acceptable for you; ³⁰it must, therefore, be eaten on the same day; none of it shall be left over until the next day.^y I am the LORD.

³¹"Be careful to observe the commandments which I, the LORD, give you, ³²and do not profane my holy name; in the midst of the Israelites I, the LORD, must be held as sacred. It is I who made you sacred ³³and led you out of the land of Egypt, that I, the LORD, might be your God."

CHAPTER 23

Holy Days. ¹The LORD said to Moses, ²"Speak to the Israelites and tell them: The following are the festivals of the LORD, my feast days, which you shall celebrate with a sacred assembly. ³"For six days work may be done; but the seventh day is the sabbath rest, a day for sacred assembly, on which you shall

m Lv 7, 20; 15, 16.—n Lv 11, 24. 43.—o Heb 10, 22.—p Lv 17, 15; Dt 14, 21; Ez 44, 31.—q 1 Sm 21, 6; Mt 12, 4.—r Lv 5, 16; 27, 13. 15. 19.—s Lv 19, 8; Nm 18, 32.—t Lv 1, 3. 10.—u Dt 15, 21; 17, 1; Mal 1, 8. 14.—v Lv 3, 1. 6.—w Mal 1, 14.—x Ex 22, 29.—y Lv 7, 15.

do no work. The sabbath shall belong to the LORD wherever you dwell.[z]

Passover. [4]"These, then, are the festivals of the LORD which you shall celebrate at their proper time with a sacred assembly.[a] [5]The Passover of the LORD falls on the fourteenth day of the first month, at the evening twilight.[b] [6]The fifteenth day of this month is the LORD's feast of Unleavened Bread.[c] For seven days you shall eat unleavened bread. [7]On the first of these days you shall hold a sacred assembly and do no sort of work.[d] [8]On each of the seven days you shall offer an oblation to the LORD. Then on the seventh day you shall again hold a sacred assembly and do no sort of work."

[9]The LORD said to Moses, [10]"Speak to the Israelites and tell them: When you come into the land which I am giving you, and reap your harvest, you shall bring a sheaf of the first fruits of your harvest to the priest, [11]who shall wave the sheaf before the LORD that it may be acceptable for you. On the day after the sabbath* the priest shall do this. [12]On this day, when your sheaf is waved, you shall offer to the LORD for a holocaust an unblemished yearling lamb. [13]Its cereal offering shall be two tenths of an ephah of fine flour mixed with oil, as a sweet-smelling oblation to the LORD; and its libation shall be a fourth of a hin of wine. [14]Until this day, when you bring your God this offering, you shall not eat any bread* or roasted grain or fresh kernels. This shall be a perpetual statute for you and your descendants wherever you dwell.

Pentecost. [15]"Beginning with the day after the sabbath, the day on which you bring the wave-offering sheaf, you shall count seven full weeks,[e] [16]and then on the day after the seventh week, the fiftieth* day,[f] you shall present the new cereal offering to the LORD. [17]For the wave offering of your first fruits to the LORD, you shall bring with you from wherever you live two loaves of bread made of two tenths of an ephah of fine flour and baked with leaven. [18]Besides the bread, you shall offer to the LORD a holocaust of seven unblemished yearling lambs, one young bull, and two rams, along with their cereal offering and libations, as a sweet-smelling oblation to the LORD. [19]One male goat shall be sacrificed as a sin offering, and two yearling lambs as a peace offering.[g]

[20]The priest shall wave the bread of the first fruits and the two lambs as a wave offering before the LORD; these shall be sacred to the LORD and belong to the priest. [21]On this same day you shall by proclamation have a sacred assembly, and no sort of work may be done. This shall be a perpetual statute for you and your descendants wherever you dwell.

[22]"When you reap the harvest of your land, you shall not be so thorough that you reap the field to its very edge, nor shall you glean the stray ears of your grain. These things you shall leave for the poor and the alien. I, the LORD, am your God."

New Year's Day. [23]The LORD said to Moses, [24]"Tell the Israelites: On the first day of the seventh month you shall keep a sabbath rest, with a sacred assembly and with the trumpet blasts as a reminder; [25]you shall then do no sort of work, and you shall offer an oblation to the LORD."

The Day of Atonement. [26] [h] The LORD said to Moses, [27]"The tenth of this seventh month is the Day of Atonement,[i] when you shall hold a sacred assembly and mortify yourselves and offer an oblation to the LORD. [28]On this day you shall not do any work, because it is the Day of Atonement, when atonement is made for you before the LORD, your God. [29]Anyone who does not mortify himself on this day shall be cut off from his people; [30]and if anyone does any work on this day, I will remove him from the midst of his people. [31]This is a perpetual statute for you and your descendants wherever you dwell: you shall do no work, [32]but shall keep a sabbath of complete rest and mortify yourselves. Beginning on the evening of the ninth of the

---

z Ex 20, 8-11, 23, 12; 31, 14f; 34, 21; Dt 5, 12-15; Lk 13, 14.—a Ex 23, 14-19.—b Nm 9, 2f; 28, 16.—c Ex 12, 18; 13, 3. 10; 23, 15; 34, 18.—d Ex 12, 15; Nm 28, 18. 25.—e Ex 34, 22; Nm 28, 26; Dt 16, 9.—f Acts 2, 1.—g Nm 28, 30.—h Lv 25, 9.—i Lv 16, 29f; Nm 29, 7.

23, 11: *The sabbath:* according to the Jewish tradition this was the feast day itself, the fifteenth of Nisan, which was a special day of rest. Cf v 7. However, some understand here the Saturday of the Passover week, or even the Saturday following it; cf Jn 19, 31.

23, 14: *Any bread:* made from the new grain. The harvest had first to be sanctified for man's use by this offering to God.

23, 16: *The fiftieth:* from the Greek word for this we have the name "Pentecost." Cf 2 Mc 12, 31; Acts 2, 1. It was also called "the feast of the Seven Weeks," or simply "the feast of Weeks" (Nm 28, 26; Dt 16, 10; Tb 2, 1). *The new cereal offering:* of flour made from the new grain. Pentecost was the thanksgiving feast at the end of the grain harvest, which began after Passover. Later tradition made it a commemoration of the giving of the law at Sinai.

month, you shall keep this sabbath of yours from evening to evening."

The Feast of Booths. [33] The LORD said to Moses, [34] "Tell the Israelites: The fifteenth day of this seventh month[j] is the LORD's feast of Booths,* which shall continue for seven days. [35] On the first day there shall be a sacred assembly, and you shall do no sort of work. [36] For seven days you shall offer an oblation to the LORD, and on the eighth day you shall again hold a sacred assembly and offer an oblation to the LORD. On that solemn closing you shall do no sort of work.

[37] "These, therefore, are the festivals of the LORD on which you shall proclaim a sacred assembly, and offer as an oblation to the LORD holocausts and cereal offerings, sacrifices and libations, as prescribed for each day, [38] in addition to those of the LORD's sabbaths, your donations, your various votive offerings and the free-will offerings that you present to the LORD.

[39] "On the fifteenth day, then, of the seventh month, when you have gathered in the produce of the land,[k] you shall celebrate a pilgrim feast of the LORD for a whole week. The first and the eighth day shall be days of complete rest. [40] On the first day you shall gather foliage* from majestic trees, branches of palms and boughs of myrtles and of valley poplars, and then for a week you shall make merry before the LORD, your God. [41] By perpetual statute for you and your descendants you shall keep this pilgrim feast of the LORD for one whole week[l] in the seventh month of the year. [42] During this week every native Israelite among you shall dwell in booths, [43] that your descendants[m] may realize that, when I led the

Israelites out of the land of Egypt, I made them dwell in booths. I, the LORD, am your God."

[44] Thus did Moses announce to the Israelites the festivals of the LORD.

CHAPTER 24

The Sanctuary Light. [1] The LORD said to Moses, [2] "Order the Israelites to bring you clear oil of crushed olives for the light, so that you may keep lamps burning regularly.[n] [3] In the meeting tent, outside the veil that hangs in front of the commandments, Aaron shall set up the lamps to burn before the LORD regularly, from evening till morning. Thus, by a perpetual statute for you and your descendants, [4] the lamps shall be set up on the pure gold lampstand,[o] to burn regularly before the LORD.

The Showbread. [5] "You shall take fine flour and bake it[p] into twelve cakes, using two tenths of an ephah of flour for each cake. [6] These you shall place in two piles, six in each pile, on the pure gold table before the LORD. [7] On each pile put some pure frankincense, which shall serve as an oblation to the LORD, a token offering for the bread. [8] Regularly on each sabbath day this bread shall be set out afresh [q] before the LORD, offered on the part of the Israelites by an everlasting agreement. [9] It shall belong to Aaron and his sons, who must eat it in a sacred place, since, as something most sacred among the various oblations to the LORD, it is his by perpetual right."

Punishment of Blasphemy. [10] Among the Israelites there was a man born of an Israelite mother (Shelomith, daughter of Dibri, of the tribe of Dan) and an Egyptian father. [11] This man quarreled publicly with another Israelite and cursed and blasphemed the LORD's name. So the people brought him to Moses, [12] who kept him in custody till a decision from the LORD should settle the case for them. [13] The LORD then said to Moses, [14] "Take the blasphemer outside the camp, and when all who heard him have laid their hands on his head, let the whole community stone him. [15] Tell the Israelites: Anyone who curses his God shall bear the penalty of his sin; [16] whoever blasphemes the name of the LORD shall be put to death.[r] The whole community shall stone

---

j Nm 29, 12; Dt 16, 13; 2 Mc 1, 9. 18; Jn 7, 2.—k Ex 23, 16; Dt 16, 13.—l Nm 29, 12-38.—m Dt 31, 10-13.—n Ex 27. 20f.—o Ex 25, 31.—p Ex 25, 30; 1 Kgs 7, 48; 2 Chr 4, 19; 13, 11; Heb 9, 2.—q 1 Chr 9, 32.—r 1 Kgs 21, 10. 13; Mt 26, 65f; Jn 10, 33.

23, 34: *Feast of Booths:* the joyful observance of the vintage and fruit harvest. Cf Dt 16, 13. During the seven days of the feast the Israelites camped in booths of branches erected on the roofs of their houses or in the streets in commemoration of their wanderings in the desert, where they dwelt in booths.

23, 40: *Foliage:* literally, "fruit," but here probably used in the general sense of "produce, growth." These branches were used for constructing the "booths" or huts in which the people lived during the feast. Cf Neh 8, 15. However, from about the time of Christ on, the Jews have understood this of "fruit" in the strict sense; hence, branches of lemons and oranges were carried with the other branches in joyous procession.

him; alien and native alike must be put to death for blaspheming the LORD's name. [17] "Whoever takes the life of any human being shall be put to death;[s] [18] whoever takes the life of an animal shall make restitution of another animal. A life for a life![t] [19] Anyone who inflicts an injury on his neighbor shall receive the same in return. [20] Limb for limb, eye for eye, tooth for tooth! The same injury that a man gives another shall be inflicted on him in return.[u] [21] Whoever slays an animal shall make restitution, but whoever slays a man shall be put to death. [22] You shall have but one rule, for alien and native alike.[v] I, the LORD, am your God."

[23] When Moses told this to the Israelites, they took the blasphemer outside the camp and stoned him;[w] they carried out the command that the LORD had given Moses.

CHAPTER 25

The Sabbatical Year. [1] The LORD said to Moses on Mount Sinai, [2] "Speak to the Israelites and tell them: When you enter the land that I am giving you, let the land, too, keep a sabbath for the LORD. [3] For six years you may sow your field, and for six years prune your vineyard, gathering in their produce.[x] [4] But during the seventh year the land shall have a complete rest, a sabbath for the LORD,[y] when you may neither sow your field nor prune your vineyard. [5] * The aftergrowth of your harvest you shall not reap, nor shall you pick the grapes of your untrimmed vines in this year of sabbath rest for the land. [6] While the land has its sabbath, all its produce will be food equally for you yourself and for your male and female slaves, for your hired help and the tenants who live with you, [7] and likewise for your livestock and for the wild animals on your land.

The Jubilee Year. [8] "Seven weeks of years shall you count—seven times seven years—so that the seven cycles amount to forty-nine years. [9] Then, on the tenth day of the seventh month let the trumpet resound; on this, the Day of Atonement, the trumpet blast shall re-echo throughout your land. [10] This fiftieth year* you shall make sacred by proclaiming liberty in the land for all its inhabitants.[z] It shall be a jubilee for you, when every one of you shall return to his own property, every one to his own family estate. [11] In this

fiftieth year, your year of jubilee, you shall not sow, nor shall you reap the aftergrowth or pick the grapes from the untrimmed vines. [12] Since this is the jubilee, which shall be sacred for you, you may not eat of its produce, except as taken directly from the field.

[13] "In this year of jubilee, then, every one of you shall return to his own property. [14] Therefore, when you sell any land to your neighbor or buy any from him, do not deal unfairly. [15] On the basis of the number of years since the last jubilee shall you purchase the land from him;[a] and so also, on the basis of the number of years for crops, shall he sell it to you. [16] When the years are many, the price shall be so much the more; when the years are few, the price shall be so much the less. For it is really the number of crops that he sells you. [17] Do not deal unfairly, then; but stand in fear of your God. I, the LORD, am your God.

[18] "Observe my precepts and be careful to keep my regulations, for then you will dwell securely in the land. [19] The land will yield its fruit and you will have food in abundance, so that you may live there without worry.[b] [20] Therefore, do not say, 'What shall we eat in the seventh year, if we do not then sow or reap our crop?'[c] [21] I will bestow such blessings on you in the sixth year that there will then be crop enough for three years. [22] When you sow in the eighth year, you will continue to eat from the old crop; and even into the ninth year, when the crop comes in, you will still have the old to eat from.[d]

Redemption of Property. [23] [e] "The land shall not be sold in perpetuity; for the land is mine, and you are but aliens who have become my tenants. [24] Therefore, in every part of the country that you occupy,

s Gn 9, 5f; Ex 21, 12; Nm 35, 31; Dt 19, 11f.—t Ex 21, 33f.— u Dt 19, 21; Mt 5, 38.—v Lv 19, 34; Ex 12, 49; Nm 15, 16.—w Acts 7, 57f.—x Ex 23, 10f.—y 1 Mc 6, 49. 53.—z Nm 36, 4; Is 61, 2; Ez 46, 17; Lk 4, 19.—a Lv 27, 18. 23.—b Lv 26, 5.—c Mt 6, 25. 31; Lk 12, 22. 29.—d Lv 26, 10.—e 1 Pt 2, 11.

25, 5ff: As long as the produce of the sabbatical year remains on the field, it remains available to everyone; cf v 12. In Ex 23, 10f the poor and the wild beasts that have no other source of nourishment are alone mentioned.

25, 10: *Fiftieth year:* to arrive at this number, the preceding year of jubilee is included in the count, and therefore this is more exactly the forty-ninth year, the seventh sabbatical year. *Liberty:* Israelite slaves were set free (v 50) and landed property was returned to its original owner (v 13): two important laws for preserving the social and economic equilibrium. *Jubilee:* derived from the Hebrew word *yobel,* "ram's horn," which was blown on this occasion.

you must permit the land to be redeemed. ²⁵When one of your countrymen is reduced to poverty and has to sell some of his property, his closest relative, who has the right to redeem it, may go and buy back what his kinsman has sold.ᶠ ²⁶If, however, the man has no relative to redeem his land, but later on acquires sufficient means to buy it back in his own name, ²⁷he shall make a deduction from the price in proportion to the number of years since the sale, and then pay back the balance to the one to whom he sold it, so that he may thus regain his own property. ²⁸But if he does not acquire sufficient means to buy back his land, what he has sold shall remain in the possession of the purchaser until the jubilee, when it must be released and returned to its original owner.ᵍ

²⁹"When someone sells a dwelling in a walled town, he has the right to buy it back during the time of one full year from its sale. ³⁰But if such a house in a walled town has not been redeemed at the end of a full year, it shall belong in perpetuity to the purchaser and his descendants; nor shall it be released in the jubilee. ³¹However, houses in villages that are not encircled by walls shall be considered as belonging to the surrounding farm land; they may be redeemed at any time, and in the jubilee they must be released.

³²"In levitical cities the Levites shall always have the right to redeem the town houses that are their property. ³³Any town house of the Levites in their cities that had been sold and not redeemed, shall be released in the jubilee; for the town houses of the Levites are their hereditary property in the midst of the Israelites. ³⁴Moreover, the pasture land belonging to their cities shall not be sold at all;ʰ it must always remain their hereditary property.

³⁵"When one of your fellow countrymen is reduced to poverty and is unable to hold out beside you, extend to him the privileges of an alien or a tenant, so that he may continue to live with you.ⁱ ³⁶Do not exact interest from your countryman either in money or in kind, but out of fear of God let him live with you. ³⁷ʲYou are to lend him neither money at interest nor food at a profit. ³⁸I, the LORD, am your God, who

brought you out of the land of Egypt to give you the land of Canaan and to be your God.

³⁹"When, then, your countryman becomes so impoverished beside you that he sells you his services, do not make him work as a slave.ᵏ ⁴⁰Rather, let him be like a hired servant or like your tenant, working with you until the jubilee year, ⁴¹when he, together with his children, shall be released from your service and return to his kindred and to the property of his ancestors. ⁴²Since those whom I brought out of the land of Egypt are servants of mine, they shall not be sold as slaves to any man. ⁴³Do not lord it over them harshly, but stand in fear of your God.

⁴⁴"Slaves, male and female, you may indeed possess, provided you buy them from among the neighboring nations. ⁴⁵You may also buy them from among the aliens who reside with you and from their children who are born and reared in your land. Such slaves you may own as chattels, ⁴⁶and leave to your sons as their hereditary property, making them perpetual slaves. But you shall not lord it harshly over any of the Israelites, your kinsmen.ˡ

⁴⁷"When one of your countrymen is reduced to such poverty that he sells himself to a wealthy alien who has a permanent or a temporary residence among you, or to one of the descendants of an immigrant family, ⁴⁸even after he has thus sold his services he still has the right of redemption; he may be redeemed by one of his own brothers, ⁴⁹or by his uncle or cousin, or by some other relative or fellow clansman; or, if he acquires the means, he may redeem himself. ⁵⁰With his purchaser he shall compute the years from the sale to the jubilee, distributing the sale price over these years as though he had been hired as a day laborer. ⁵¹The more such years there are, the more of the sale price he shall pay back as ransom; ⁵²the fewer years there are left before the jubilee year, the more he has to his credit; in proportion to his years of service shall he pay his ransom. ⁵³The alien shall treat him as a servant hired on an annual basis, and he shall not lord it over him harshly under your very eyes. ⁵⁴If he is not thus redeemed, he shall nevertheless be released, together with his children, in the

f Ru 2, 20; 4, 4. 6; Jer 32, 7f.—g Lv 27, 24.—h Nm 35, 3.—i Dt 15, 7. 8.—j Dt 23, 19.—k 1 Kgs 9, 22.—l Is 14, 1f.

jubilee year.[m] [55]For to me the Israelites belong as servants; they are servants of mine, because I brought them out of the land of Egypt, I, the LORD, your God.

CHAPTER 26

The Reward of Obedience. [1]"Do not make false gods for yourselves. You shall not erect an idol or a sacred pillar for yourselves, nor shall you set up a stone figure for worship in your land;[n] for I, the LORD, am your God. [2]Keep my sabbaths, [o] and reverence my sanctuary. I am the LORD.

[3] * "If you live in accordance with my precepts and are careful to observe my commandments, [4]I will give you rain in due season, so that the land will bear its crops, and the trees their fruit;[p] [5]your threshing will last till vintage time, and your vintage till the time for sowing, and you will have food to eat in abundance, so that you may dwell securely in your land. [6]I will establish peace in the land, that you may lie down to rest without anxiety. I will rid the country of ravenous beasts, and keep the sword of war from sweeping across your land. [7]You will rout your enemies and lay them low with your sword. [8]Five of you will put a hundred of your foes to flight, and a hundred of you will chase ten thousand of them, till they are cut down by your sword. [9]I will look with favor upon you, and make you fruitful and numerous, as I carry out my covenant with you. [10]So much of the old crops will you have stored up for food that you will have to discard them to make room for the new.[q] [11] [r] I will set my Dwelling among you, and will not disdain you. [12]Ever present in your midst, I will be your God, and you will be my people; [13]for it is I, the LORD, your God, who brought you out of the land of the Egyptians and freed you from their slavery, breaking the yoke they had laid upon you and letting you walk erect.

Punishment of Disobedience. [14]"But if you do not heed me and do not keep all these commandments, [15]if you reject my precepts and spurn my decrees, refusing to obey all my commandments and breaking my covenant, [16]then I, in turn, will give you your deserts. I will punish you with terrible woes—with wasting and fever to dim the eyes and sap the life. You will sow your seed in vain, for your enemies will

consume the crop. [17]I will turn against you, till you are beaten down before your enemies and lorded over by your foes. You will take to flight though no one pursues you.[s]

[18]"If even after this you do not obey me, I will increase the chastisement for your sins sevenfold, [19]to break your haughty confidence. I will make the sky above you as hard as iron, and your soil as hard as bronze, [20]so that your strength will be spent in vain; your land will bear no crops, and its trees no fruit.

[21]"If then you become defiant in your unwillingness to obey me, I will multiply my blows another sevenfold, as your sins deserve. [22]I will unleash the wild beasts against you, to rob you of your children and wipe out your livestock, till your population dwindles away and your roads become deserted.

[23]"If, with all this, you still refuse to be chastened by me and continue to defy me, [24]I, too, will defy you and will smite you for your sins seven times harder than before.[t] [25]I will make the sword, the avenger of my covenant, sweep over you. Though you then huddle together in your walled cities, I will send in pestilence among you, till you are forced to surrender to the enemy. [26]And as I cut off your supply of bread, ten women will need but one oven for baking all the bread they dole out to you in rations[u]—not enough food to still your hunger.

[27]"If, despite all this, you still persist in disobeying and defying me, [28]I, also, will meet you with fiery defiance and will chastise you with sevenfold fiercer punishment for your sins, [29] [uu] till you begin to eat the flesh of your own sons and daughters.* [30]I will demolish your high places,[v] overthrow your incense stands, and cast your corpses on those of your idols. In my abhorrence of you, [31]I will lay waste your cities and

---

m Ex 21, 2f.—n Lv 19, 4; Ex 20, 4; Nm 33, 52; Dt 5, 8.—o Ex 20, 8.—p Ps 85, 13.—q Lv 25, 22.—r 11f: Ex 29, 45; Ez 37, 26ff; 2 Cor 6, 16.—s Dt 28, 25.—t 24f: Jer 2, 30; Ez 5, 17; 14, 17.—u Is 9, 19; Ez 4, 16; 5, 16; 14, 13; Mi 6, 14.—uu Is 9, 18.—v 2 Chr 14, 5; 34, 3. 4. 7; Ez 6, 3-6.

26, 3-45: Since God's covenant was with the Israelite nation as a whole, these promises and threats are made primarily to the entire community. The rewards and punishments are of a temporal nature because the community as such exists only here on earth, not in the hereafter.

26, 29: *Eat the flesh of your own sons and daughters:* extreme famine in cities under siege often forced their inhabitants to such dire means of subsistence. Cf Dt 28, 53; Jer 19, 9; Ez 5, 10; 2 Kgs 6, 28f.

devastate your sanctuaries, refusing to accept your sweet-smelling offerings. [32]So devastated will I leave the land that your very enemies who come to live there will stand aghast at the sight of it.[w] [33]You yourselves I will scatter among the nations[x] at the point of my drawn sword, leaving your countryside desolate and your cities deserted. [34]Then shall the land retrieve its lost sabbaths during all the time it lies waste, while you are in the land of your enemies; then shall the land have rest and make up for its sabbaths[y] [35]during all the time that it lies desolate, enjoying the rest that you would not let it have on the sabbaths when you lived there.

[36]"Those of you who survive in the lands of their enemies I will make so faint-hearted that, if leaves rustle behind them, they will flee headlong, as if from the sword, though no one pursues them; [37]stumbling over one another as if to escape a weapon, while no one is after them—so helpless will you be to take a stand against your foes! [38]You will be lost among the Gentiles, swallowed up in your enemies' country. [39]Those of you who survive in the lands of their enemies will waste away for their own and their fathers' guilt.[z]

[40]"Thus they will have to confess that they and their fathers were guilty of having rebelled against me and of having defied me, [41]so that I, too, had to defy them and bring them into their enemies' land. Then, when their uncircumcised hearts are humbled and they make amends for their guilt, [42]I will remember my covenant with Jacob, my covenant with Isaac, and my covenant with Abraham;[a] and of the land, too, I will be mindful. [43]But the land must first be rid of them, that in its desolation it may make up its lost sabbaths, and that they, too, may make good the debt of their guilt for having spurned my precepts and abhorred my statutes. [44]Yet even so, even

<hr>

w 1 Kgs 9, 8; Jer 9, 11; 18, 16; 19, 8; 25, 18; Ez 5, 15.—x Jer 9, 16; Zec 7, 14.—y Lv 25, 2; 2 Chr 36, 21.—z Ez 4, 17; 24, 23; 33, 10.—a Ex 6, 5; 2 Kgs 13, 23; Ps 106, 45; Ez 16, 60.—b Ex 12, 51.

<hr>

26, 46: The Book of Leviticus seems originally to have ended here; the following chapter is an appendix.

27, 12: *Determine its value:* fix the price at which the animal may be sold to someone else. Only the original owner must pay the twenty percent tax, as a penalty for buying back what he had vowed to God. So also for houses and fields that are vowed to the Lord, as treated of in the following verses. The money from the sale or from the redemption of such vowed property naturally goes to the sanctuary.

while they are in their enemies' land, I will not reject or spurn them, lest, by wiping them out, I make void my covenant with them; for I, the LORD, am their God. [45]I will remember them because of the covenant I made with their forefathers, whom I brought out of the land of Egypt under the very eyes of the Gentiles,[b] that I, the LORD, might be their God."

[46] * These are the precepts, decrees and laws which the LORD had Moses promulgate on Mount Sinai in the pact between himself and the Israelites.

V: REDEMPTION OF OFFERINGS

CHAPTER 27

Redemption of Votive Offerings. [1]The LORD said to Moses, [2]"Speak to the Israelites and tell them: When anyone fulfills a vow of offering one or more persons to the LORD, who are to be ransomed at a fixed sum of money, [3]for persons between the ages of twenty and sixty, the fixed sum, in sanctuary shekels, shall be fifty silver shekels for a man, [4]and thirty shekels for a woman; [5]for persons between the ages of five and twenty, the fixed sum shall be twenty shekels for a youth, and ten for a maiden; [6]for persons between the ages of one month and five years, the fixed sum shall be five silver shekels for a boy, and three for a girl; [7]for persons of sixty or more, the fixed sum shall be fifteen shekels for a man, and ten for a woman. [8]However, if the one who took the vow is too poor to meet the fixed sum, the person must be set before the priest, who shall determine the sum for his ransom in keeping with the means of the one who made the vow.

[9]"If the offering vowed to the LORD is an animal that may be sacrificed, every such animal, when vowed to the LORD, becomes sacred. [10]The offerer shall not present a substitute for it by exchanging either a better for a worse one or a worse for a better one. If he attempts to offer one animal in place of another, both the original and its substitute shall be treated as sacred. [11]If the animal vowed to the LORD is unclean and therefore unfit for sacrifice, it must be set before the priest, [12]who shall determine its value* in keeping with its good or bad qualities, and the value set by the priest shall stand. [13]If the offerer

wishes to redeem the animal, he shall pay one fifth more than this valuation.[c]

14 "When someone dedicates his house as sacred to the LORD, the priest shall determine its value in keeping with its good or bad points, and the value set by the priest shall stand. 15 If the one who dedicated his house wishes to redeem it, he shall pay one fifth more than the price thus established, and then it will again be his.

16 "If the object which someone dedicates to the LORD is a piece of his hereditary land, its valuation shall be made according to the amount of seed required to sow it, the acreage sown with a homer of barley seed being valued at fifty silver shekels. 17 If the dedication of a field is made at the beginning of a jubilee period, the full valuation shall hold; 18 but if it is some time after this, the priest shall estimate its money value according to the number of years left until the next jubilee year, with a corresponding rebate on the valuation.[d] 19 If the one who dedicated his field wishes to redeem it, he shall pay one fifth more than the price thus established, and so reclaim it. 20 If, instead of redeeming such a field, he sells it to someone else, it may no longer be redeemed; 21 but at the jubilee it shall be released as sacred to the LORD; like a field that is doomed, it shall become priestly property.

22 "If the field that some man dedicates to the LORD is one he had purchased and not a part of his hereditary property, 23 the priest shall compute its value in proportion to the number of years until the next jubilee, and on the same day the price thus established shall be given as sacred to the LORD; 24 at the jubilee,[e] however, the field shall revert to the hereditary owner of this land from whom it had been purchased.

25 "Every valuation shall be made according to the standard of the sanctuary shekel. There are twenty gerahs to the shekel.

Offerings Not To Be Redeemed. 26 "Note that a first-born animal,[f] which as such already belongs to the LORD, may not be dedicated by vow to him. If it is an ox or a sheep, it shall be ceded to the LORD; 27 but if it is an unclean animal,* it may be redeemed by paying one fifth more than its fixed value. If it is not redeemed, it shall be sold at its fixed value.

28 "Note, also, that any one of his possessions which a man vows as doomed to the LORD, whether it is a human being or an animal or a hereditary field, shall be neither sold nor ransomed; everything that is thus doomed becomes most sacred to the LORD.[g] 29 All human beings that are doomed* lose the right to be redeemed; they must be put to death.

30 "All tithes of the land, whether in grain from the fields or in fruit from the trees, belong to the LORD, as sacred to him.[h] 31 If someone wishes to buy back any of his tithes, he shall pay one fifth more than their value. 32 The tithes of the herd and the flock shall be determined by ceding to the LORD as sacred every tenth animal as they are counted by the herdsman's rod. 33 It shall not matter whether good ones or bad ones are thus chosen, and no exchange may be made. If any exchange is attempted, both the original animal and its substitute shall be treated as sacred, without the right of being bought back."

34 These are the commandments which the LORD gave Moses on Mount Sinai for the Israelites.

c Lv 22, 14.—d Lv 25, 15f.—e Lv 25, 10. 28. 41.—f Ex 13, 2.—g 1 Sm 15, 21.—h Nm 18, 21. 24; 2 Chr 31, 5f. 12; Mal 3, 8. 10.

27, 27: *An unclean animal:* such as the first-born of an ass, which was unfit for sacrifice. According to Ex 13, 13; 34, 20, a first-born ass was to be redeemed by offering a sheep in its stead, or was to have its neck broken. The present law is probably a later modification of the earlier one.

27, 29: *All human beings that are doomed:* according to some interpreters, this signifies the idolatrous Canaanites, who were doomed to destruction by divine authority; according to others, this drastic law was enacted for the purpose of discouraging private persons from rashly vowing their slaves or other dependents as offerings to God. Cf Ex 22, 19; Dt 13, 13-19.

THE BOOK OF NUMBERS

The Book of Numbers derives its name from the account of the two censuses of the Hebrew people taken, one near the beginning and the other toward the end of the journey in the desert (chapters 1 and 26). It continues the story of that journey, begun in Exodus, and describes briefly the experiences of the Israelites for a period of thirty-eight years, from the end of their encampment at Sinai to their arrival at the border of the Promised Land. Numerous legal ordinances are interspersed in the account, making the book a combination of law and history.

The various events described clearly indicate the action of God, who punishes the murmuring of the people by prolonging their stay in the desert, at the same time preparing them by this discipline to be his witnesses among the nations.

In the New Testament Christ and the Apostles derive useful lessons from such events in the Book of Numbers as the brazen serpent (Jn 3, 14f), the sedition of Korah and its consequences (1 Cor 10, 10), the prophecies of Balaam (2 Pt 2, 15f), and the water gushing from the rock (1 Cor 10, 4).

The chief divisions of the Book of Numbers are as follows: I. Preparation for the Departure from Sinai (Nm 1, 1—10, 10). II. From Sinai to the Plains of Moab (Nm 10, 11—22, 1). III. On the Plains of Moab (Nm 22, 2—36, 13).

I: PREPARATION FOR THE DEPARTURE FROM SINAI

CHAPTER 1

The Census. [1] In the year following that of the Israelites' departure from the land of Egypt, on the first day of the second month, the LORD said to Moses in the meeting tent in the desert of Sinai: [2] * "Take a census of the whole community of the Israelites,[a] by clans and ancestral houses, registering each male individually. [3] You and Aaron shall enroll in companies all the men in Israel of twenty years or more who are fit for military service.

Moses' Assistants. [4] "To assist you there shall be a man from each tribe, the head of his ancestral house. [5] [b] These are the names of those who are to assist you:

from Reuben: Elizur, son of Shedeur;
[6] from Simeon: Shelumiel, son of Zurishaddai;
[7] from Judah: Nahshon, son of Amminadab;
[8] from Issachar: Nethanel, son of Zuar;
[9] from Zebulun: Eliab, son of Helon;
[10] from Ephraim: Elishama, son of Ammihud, and

from Manasseh: Gamaliel, son of Pedahzur, for the descendants of Joseph;
[11] from Benjamin: Abidan, son of Gideoni;
[12] from Dan: Ahiezer, son of Ammishaddai;
[13] from Asher: Pagiel, son of Ochran;
[14] from Gad: Eliasaph, son of Reuel;
[15] from Naphtali: Ahira, son of Enan."

[16] [c] These were councilors of the community, princes of their ancestral tribes, chiefs of the troops* of Israel. [17] So Moses and Aaron took these men who had been designated, [18] and assembled the whole community on the first day of the second month. Every man of twenty years or more then declared his name and lineage according to clan and ancestral house, [19] as the LORD had commanded Moses.

Count of the Twelve Tribes. This is their census as taken in the desert of Sinai. [20] Of the descendants of Reuben, the first-born of Israel, registered by lineage in clans and ancestral houses: when all the males of twenty years or more who were fit for military service were polled, [21] forty-six thousand five hundred were enrolled in the tribe of Reuben.

[22] Of the descendants of Simeon, registered by lineage in clans and ancestral houses: when all the males of twenty years or more who were fit for military service were polled, [23] fifty-nine thousand three hundred were enrolled in the tribe of Simeon.

---

a 2f: Nm 14, 29; 26, 2-51.—b 5-15: Nm 10, 14-27.—c Ex 18, 21. 25.

1, 2: All Israel was divided into tribes, each tribe into clans, and each clan into ancestral houses.

1, 16: *Troops:* literally "thousands"; this division of the Israelites, with its subdivisions of "hundreds, fifties and tens," was primarily for military and judicial purposes. Cf Ex 18, 21; 2 Sm 18, 1.

²⁴Of the descendants of Gad, registered by lineage in clans and ancestral houses: when all the males of twenty years or more who were fit for military service were polled, ²⁵forty-five thousand six hundred and fifty were enrolled in the tribe of Gad.

²⁶Of the descendants of Judah, registered by lineage in clans and ancestral houses: when all the males of twenty years or more who were fit for military service were polled, ²⁷seventy-four thousand six hundred were enrolled in the tribe of Judah.

²⁸Of the descendants of Issachar, registered by lineage in clans and ancestral houses: when all the males of twenty years or more who were fit for military service were polled, ²⁹fifty-four thousand four hundred were enrolled in the tribe of Issachar.

³⁰Of the descendants of Zebulun, registered by lineage in clans and ancestral houses: when all the males of twenty years or more who were fit for military service were polled, ³¹fifty-seven thousand four hundred were enrolled in the tribe of Zebulun.

³²Of the descendants of Joseph—

Of the descendants of Ephraim, registered by lineage in clans and ancestral houses: when all the males of twenty years or more who were fit for military service were polled, ³³forty thousand five hundred were enrolled in the tribe of Ephraim.

³⁴Of the descendants of Manasseh, registered by lineage in clans and ancestral houses: when all the males of twenty years or more who were fit for military service were polled, ³⁵thirty-two thousand two hundred were enrolled in the tribe of Manasseh.

³⁶Of the descendants of Benjamin, registered by lineage in clans and ancestral houses: when all the males of twenty years or more who were fit for military service were polled, ³⁷thirty-five thousand four hundred were enrolled in the tribe of Benjamin.

³⁸Of the descendants of Dan, registered by lineage in clans and ancestal houses: when all the males of twenty years or more who were fit for military service were polled, ³⁹sixty-two thousand seven hundred were enrolled in the tribe of Dan.

⁴⁰Of the descendants of Asher, registered by lineage in clans and ancestral houses: when all the males of twenty years or more who were fit for military service were polled, ⁴¹forty-one thousand five hundred were enrolled in the tribe of Asher.

⁴²Of the descendants of Naphtali, registered by lineage in clans and ancestral houses: when all the males of twenty years or more who were fit for military service were polled, ⁴³fifty-three thousand four hundred were enrolled in the tribe of Naphtali.

⁴⁴It was these who were registered, each according to his ancestral house, in the census taken by Moses and Aaron and the twelve princes of Israel. ⁴⁵The total number of the Israelites of twenty years or more who were fit for military service, registered by ancestral houses, ⁴⁶was six hundred and three thousand five hundred and fifty.

Levites Omitted in the Census. ⁴⁷The Levites, however, were not registered*ᵈ* by ancestral tribe with the others.* ⁴⁸For the LORD had told Moses, ⁴⁹"The tribe of Levi alone you shall not enroll nor include in the census along with the other Israelites. ⁵⁰You are to give the Levites charge of the Dwelling of the commandments with all its equipment and all that belongs to it. It is they who shall carry the Dwelling with all its equipment and who shall be its ministers.*ᵉ* They shall therefore camp around the Dwelling. ⁵¹When the Dwelling is to move on, the Levites shall take it down; when the Dwelling is to be pitched, it is the Levites who shall set it up.*ᶠ* Any layman who comes near it shall be put to death. ⁵²While the other Israelites shall camp by companies, each in his own division of the camp,*ᵍ* ⁵³the Levites shall camp around the Dwelling of the commandments.*ʰ* Otherwise God's wrath will strike the Israelite community. The Levites, then, shall have charge of the Dwelling of the commandments." ⁵⁴All this the Israelites fulfilled as the LORD had commanded Moses.

CHAPTER 2

Arrangement of the Tribes. ¹The LORD said to Moses and Aaron: ²"The Israelites

---

d Nm 2, 33; 3, 14-39; 26 57-62.—e Nm 3, 7f; 4, 2-49; 1 Chr 6, 48.—f Nm 3, 10. 38; 18, 7; 2 Sm 6, 6f; 1 Chr 13, 10.—g Nm 2, 2. 34.—h Nm 3, 7f. 38; 8, 19; 18, 4f.

1, 47: The Levites were not enrolled in this census, which was principally for military purposes, but a separate census was made of them. Cf Nm 3, 15f. 39.

shall camp, each in his own division, under the ensigns of their ancestral houses.[i] They shall camp around the meeting tent, but at some distance from it.

3 * "Encamped on the east side, toward the sunrise, shall be the divisional camp of Judah, arranged in companies. [The prince of the Judahites was Nahshon, son of Amminadab, [4] and his soldiers amounted in the census to seventy-four thousand six hundred.] [5] With Judah shall camp the tribe of Issachar [their prince was Nethanel, son of Zuar, [6] and his soldiers amounted in the census to fifty-four thousand four hundred] [7] and the tribe of Zebulun. [Their prince was Eliab, son of Helon, [8] and his soldiers amounted in the census to fifty-seven thousand four hundred. [9] The total number of those registered by companies in the camp of Judah was one hundred and eighty-six thousand four hundred.] These shall be first on the march.

[10] "On the south side shall be the divisional camp of Reuben, arranged in companies. [Their prince was Elizur, son of Shedeur, [11] and his soldiers amounted in the census to forty-six thousand five hundred.] [12] Beside them shall camp the tribe of Simeon [their prince was Shelumiel, son of Zurishaddai, [13] and his soldiers amounted in the census to fifty-nine thousand three hundred] [14] and next the tribe of Gad. [Their prince was Eliasaph, son of Reuel, [15] and his soldiers amounted in the census to forty-five thousand six hundred and fifty. [16] The total number of those registered by companies in the camp of Reuben was one hundred and fifty-one thousand four hundred and fifty.] These shall be second on the march.

[17] "Then the meeting tent and the camp of the Levites shall set out in the middle of the line. As in camp, so also on the march, every man shall be in his proper place, with his own division.

[18] "On the west side shall be the divisional camp of Ephraim, arranged in companies. [Their prince was Elishama, son of Ammihud, [19] and his soldiers amounted in the census to forty thousand five hundred.] [20] Beside them shall camp the tribe of Manasseh [their prince was

Gamaliel, son of Pedahzur, [21] and his soldiers amounted in the census to thirty-two thousand two hundred] [22] and the tribe of Benjamin. [Their prince was Abidan, son of Gideoni, [23] and his soldiers amounted in the census to thirty-five thousand four hundred. [24] The total number of those registered by companies in the camp of Ephraim was one hundred and eight thousand one hundred.] These shall be third on the march.

[25] "On the north side shall be the divisional camp of Dan, arranged in companies. [Their prince was Ahiezer, son of Ammishaddai, [26] and his soldiers amounted in the census to sixty-two thousand seven hundred.] [27] Beside them shall camp the tribe of Asher [their prince was Pagiel, son of Ochran, [28] and his soldiers amounted in the census to forty-one thousand five hundred] [29] and next the tribe of Naphtali. [Their prince was Ahira, son of Enan, [30] and his soldiers amounted in the census to fifty-three thousand four hundred. [31] The total number of those registered by companies in the camp of Dan was one hundred and fifty-seven thousand six hundred.] These shall be the last of the divisions on the march."

[32] [j] This was the census of the Israelites taken by ancestral houses. The total number of those registered by companies in the camps was six hundred and three thousand five hundred and fifty. [33] The Levites, however, were not registered with the other Israelites, for so the LORD had commanded Moses. [34] The Israelites did just as the LORD had commanded Moses; both in camp and on the march they were in their own divisions, every man according to his clan and his ancestral house.

CHAPTER 3

The Sons of Aaron. [1] The following were the descendants of Aaron and Moses at the time that the LORD spoke to Moses on Mount Sinai. [2] The sons of Aaron were Nadab his first-born, Abihu, Eleazar, and Ithamar.[k] [3] These are the names of the sons of Aaron, the anointed priests who were ordained to exercise the priesthood. [4] But when Nadab and Abihu offered profane fire before the LORD in the desert of Sinai, they met death[l] in the presence of the LORD, and left no sons. Thereafter only Eleazar and Ithamar performed the

---

i Nm 1, 52.—j 32-33: Nm 1, 46-49.—k Ex 6, 23.—l Nm 26, 61; Lv 10, 1f; 1 Chr 24, 2.

2, 3-31: A similar arrangement of the tribes around the central sanctuary in the ideal Israelite state is given in Ez 48.

priestly functions under the direction of their father Aaron.

Levites in Place of the First-born. [5] Now the LORD said to Moses: [6] "Summon the tribe of Levi and present them to Aaron the priest, as his assistants.[m] [7] They shall discharge his obligations and those of the whole community before the meeting tent[n] by serving at the Dwelling. [8] They shall have custody of all the furnishings of the meeting tent and discharge the duties of the Israelites in the service of the Dwelling. [9] You shall give the Levites to Aaron and his sons;[o] they have been set aside from among the Israelites as dedicated to me. [10] But only Aaron and his descendants shall you appoint to have charge of the priestly functions.[p] Any layman who comes near shall be put to death."

[11] The LORD said to Moses, [12] "It is I who have chosen the Levites from the Israelites in place of every first-born that opens the womb among the Israelites.[q] The Levites, therefore, are mine, [13] because every first-born is mine. When I slew all the first-born in the land of Egypt, I made all the first-born in Israel sacred to me, both of man and of beast. They belong to me; I am the LORD."

Census of the Levites. [14] The LORD said to Moses in the desert of Sinai, [15] "Take a census of the Levites by ancestral houses and clans, registering every male of a month or more."[r] [16] Moses, therefore, took their census in accordance with the command the LORD had given him.

[17] [s] The sons of Levi were named Gershon, Kohath and Merari. [18] The descendants of Gershon, by clans, were named Libni and Shimei. [19] The descendants of Kohath, by clans, were Amram, Izhar, Hebron and Uziel. [20] The descendants of Merari, by clans, were Mahli and Mushi. These were the clans of the Levites by ancestral houses.

Duties of the Levitical Clans. [21] To Gershon belonged the clan of the Libnites and the clan of the Shimeites; these were the clans of the Gershonites. [22] When all their males of a month or more were registered, they numbered seven thousand five hundred. [23] The clans of the Gershonites camped behind the Dwelling, to the west. [24] The prince of their ancestral house was Eliasaph, son of Lael. [25] [t] At the meeting tent they had charge of whatever pertained to the Dwelling,* the tent and its cover-

ing, the curtain at the entrance of the meeting tent, [26] the hangings of the court, the curtain at the entrance of the court enclosing both the Dwelling and the altar, and the ropes.

[27] To Kohath belonged the clans of the Amramites, the Izharites, the Hebronites, and the Uzzielites; these were the clans of the Kohathites. [28] When all their males of a month or more were registered, they numbered eight thousand three hundred. They had charge of the sanctuary. [29] The clans of the Kohathites camped at the south side of the Dwelling. [30] The prince of their ancestral house was Elizaphan, son of Uzziel. [31] They had charge of whatever pertained to the ark, the table, the lampstand, the altars, the utensils with which the ministry of the sanctuary was exercised, and the veil.* [32] The chief prince of the Levites, however, was Eleazar, son of Aaron the priest; he was supervisor over those who had charge of the sanctuary.

[33] To Merari belonged the clans of the Mahlites and the Mushites; these were the clans of Merari. [34] When all their males of a month or more were registered, they numbered six thousand two hundred. [35] The prince of the ancestral house of the clans of Merari was Zuriel, son of Abihail. They camped at the north side of the Dwelling. [36] * The Merarites were charged with the care of whatever pertained to the boards of the Dwelling, its bars, columns, pedestals, and all its fittings, [37] as well as the columns of the surrounding court with their pedestals, pegs and ropes.

[38] East of the Dwelling, that is, in front of the meeting tent, toward the sunrise, were camped Moses and Aaron and the latter's sons. They discharged the obligations

m Nm 18, 2.—n Nm 8, 24.—o Nm 8, 19.—p Nm 1, 51; 18, 7.—q 12f: Nm 3, 41; 8, 16f; Ex 13, 2. 12. 15.—r Nm 3, 39; 26, 62.—s 17-20: Nm 26, 57; Gn 46, 11; Ex 6, 16-19; 1 Chr 6, 1f. 16-19.—t 25-26: Ex 26, 7. 14. 36; 36, 14.

3, 25f: The Gershonites had two wagons for transporting these things; cf Nm 7, 7. For a description of *the Dwelling,* see Ex 26, 1-6; *the tent,* Ex 26, 7-13; *its covering,* Ex 26, 14; *the curtain at the entrance,* Ex 26, 36; *the hangings of the court,* Ex 27, 9-15; *the curtain at the entrance of the court,* Ex 27, 16; *the ropes of the Dwelling,* Ex 35, 18.

3, 31: The Kohathites had to carry these sacred objects on their shoulders; cf Nm 7, 9. For a description of *the ark,* see Ex 25, 10-22; *the table,* Ex 25, 23-30; *the lampstand,* Ex 25, 31-40; *the altars,* Ex 27, 1-8; 30, 1-10.

3, 36f: The Merarites had four wagons for transporting this heavy material; cf Nm 7, 8. For a description of *the boards, bars, etc., of the Dwelling,* see Ex 26, 15-30; *the columns, pedestals, etc., of the court,* Ex 27, 9-19.

of the sanctuary for the Israelites. Any layman who came near was to be put to death. [39] The total number of male Levites a month old or more whom Moses had registered by clans in keeping with the LORD's command, was twenty-two thousand.

Census and Ransom of First-born. [40] The LORD then said to Moses, "Take a census of all the first-born males of the Israelites a month old or more, and compute their total number. [41] Then assign the Levites to me, the LORD, in place of all the first-born of the Israelites, as well as their cattle in place of all the first-born among the cattle of the Israelites." [42] So Moses took a census of all the first-born of the Israelites, as the LORD had commanded him. [43] When all the first-born males of a month or more were registered, they numbered twenty-two thousand two hundred and seventy-three.

[44] The LORD said to Moses: [45] "Take the Levites in place of all the first-born of the Israelites, and the Levites' cattle in place of their cattle, that the Levites may belong to me. I am the LORD. [46] As ransom for the two hundred and seventy-three first-born of the Israelites who outnumber the Levites, [47] you shall take five shekels for each individual, according to the standard of the sanctuary shekel, twenty gerahs to the shekel. [u] [48] Give this silver to Aaron and his sons as ransom for the extra number." [49] So Moses took the silver as ransom from those who were left when the rest had been redeemed by the Levites. [50] From the first-born of the Israelites he received in silver one thousand three hundred and sixty-five shekels according to the sanctuary standard. [51] He then gave this ransom silver to Aaron and his sons, as the LORD had commanded him.

CHAPTER 4

Duties Further Defined. [1] The LORD said to Moses and Aaron: [2] "Among the Le-

u Nm 18, 16; Ex 30, 13; Lv 27, 25; Ez 45, 12.—v Nm 8, 24; 1 Chr 23, 24-27.—w 2 Sm 6, 6f; 1 Chr 13, 9f.

4, 3: *Thirty:* at a later period the Levites began to serve when they were twenty-five (Nm 8, 24) or even only twenty years old (1 Chr 23, 24. 27; 2 Chr 31, 17; Ezr 3, 8; but cf 1 Chr 23, 3).
4, 5: *The screening curtain:* the veil between the inner and the outer rooms of the sanctuary. Cf Ex 26, 31-33.
4, 11: *The golden altar:* the altar of incense. Cf Ex 30, 1-6.
4, 13: *The altar:* the bronze altar of holocausts. Cf Ex 27, 1-8.
4, 14: *Forks:* used in turning over the sacrificed animal on the fire of the altar. *Basins:* to receive the sacrificial blood; cf Zec 9, 15.

vites take a total of the Kohathites, by clans and ancestral houses, all the men of the Kohathites [3] between thirty* and fifty years of age; these are to undertake obligatory tasks in the meeting tent. [v] [4] "The service of the Kohathites concerns the most sacred objects. [5] In breaking camp, Aaron and his sons shall go in and take down the screening curtain* and cover the ark of the commandments with it. [6] Over these they shall put a cover of tahash skin, and on top of this spread an all-violet cloth. They shall then put the poles in place. [7] On the table of the Presence they shall spread a violet cloth and put on it the plates and cups, as well as the bowls and pitchers for libations; the established bread offering shall remain on the table. [8] Over these they shall spread a scarlet cloth and cover all this with tahash skin. They shall then put the poles in place. [9] They shall use a violet cloth to cover the lampstand with its lamps, trimming shears, and trays, as well as the various containers of oil from which it is supplied. [10] The lampstand with all its utensils they shall then enclose in a covering of tahash skin, and place on a litter. [11] Over the golden altar* they shall spread a violet cloth, and cover this also with a covering of tahash skin. They shall then put the poles in place. [12] Taking the utensils of the sanctuary service, they shall wrap them all in violet cloth and cover them with tahash skin. They shall then place them on a litter. [13] After cleansing the altar* of its ashes, they shall spread a purple cloth over it. [14] On this they shall put all the utensils with which it is served: the fire pans, forks,* shovels, basins, and all the utensils of the altar. They shall then spread a covering of tahash skin over this, and put the poles in place."

[15] "Only after Aaron and his sons have finished covering the sacred objects and all their utensils on breaking camp, shall the Kohathites enter to carry them. But they shall not touch the sacred objects; if they do they will die. [w] These, then, are the objects in the meeting tent that the Kohathites shall carry.

[16] "Eleazar, son of Aaron the priest, shall be in charge of the oil for the light, the fragrant incense, the established cereal offering, and the anointing oil. He shall be in charge of the whole Dwelling with

all the sacred objects and utensils that are in it."

17 The LORD said to Moses and Aaron: 18 "Do not let the group of Kohathite clans perish from the body of the Levites. 19 That they may live and not die when they approach the most sacred objects, this is what you shall do for them: Aaron and his sons shall go in and assign to each of them his task and what he must carry; 20 but the Kohathites shall not go in to look upon the sacred objects, even for an instant; if they do, they will die."x

21 The LORD said to Moses, 22 "Take a total among the Gershonites also, by ancestral houses and clans, 23 of all the men between thirty and fifty years of age; these are to undertake obligatory tasks in the meeting tent. 24 This is the task of the clans of the Gershonites, what they must do and what they must carry: 25 they shall carry the sheets of the Dwelling, the meeting tent with its covering and the outer wrapping of tahash skin, the curtain at the entrance of the meeting tent, 26 the hangings of the court, the curtain at the entrance of the court that encloses both the Dwelling and the altar, together with their ropes and all other objects necessary in their use. Whatever is to be done with these things shall be their task. 27 The service of the Gershonites shall be entirely under the direction of Aaron and his sons, with regard to what they must do and what they must carry; you shall make each man of them responsible for what he is to carry. 28 This, then, is the task of the Gershonites in the meeting tent; and they shall be under the supervision of Ithamar, son of Aaron the priest.

29 "Among the Merarites, too, you shall enroll by clans and ancestral houses 30 all their men between thirty and fifty years of age; these are to undertake obligatory tasks in the meeting tent. 31 y This is what they shall be responsible for carrying, all the years of their service in the meeting tent: the boards of the Dwelling with its bars, columns and pedestals, 32 and the columns of the surrounding court with their pedestals, pegs and ropes. You shall designate for each man of them all the objects connected with his service, which he shall be responsible for carrying. 33 This, then, is the task of the clans of the Merarites during all their service in the meeting tent under the super-

vision of Ithamar, son of Aaron the priest."

Number of Adult Levites. 34 So Moses and Aaron and the princes of the community made a registration among the Kohathites, by clans and ancestral houses, 35 of all the men between thirty and fifty years of age. These were to undertake obligatory tasks in the meeting tent; 36 as registered by clans, they numbered two thousand seven hundred and fifty. 37 Such was the census of all the men of the Kohathite clans who were to serve in the meeting tent, which Moses took, together with Aaron, as the LORD bade him.

38 The registration was then made among the Gershonites, by clans and ancestral houses, 39 of all the men between thirty and fifty years of age. These were to undertake obligatory tasks in the meeting tent; 40 as registered by clans and ancestral houses, they numbered two thousand six hundred and thirty. 41 Such was the census of all the men of the Gershonite clans who were to serve in the meeting tent, which Moses took, together with Aaron, at the LORD's bidding.

42 Then the registration was made among the Merarites, by clans and ancestral houses, 43 of all the men from thirty up to fifty years of age. These were to undertake obligatory tasks in the meeting tent; 44 as registered by clans, they numbered three thousand two hundred. 45 Such was the census of the men of the Merarite clans which Moses took, together with Aaron, as the LORD bade him.

46 Therefore, when Moses and Aaron and the Israelite princes had completed the registration among the Levites, by clans and ancestral houses, 47 of all the men between thirty and fifty years of age who were to undertake tasks of service or transport of the meeting tent, the total number registered was eight thousand five hundred and eighty. 48 According to the LORD's bidding to Moses, they gave them their individual assignments for service and for transport; so the LORD had commanded Moses.

CHAPTER 5

The Unclean Expelled. 1 The LORD said to Moses: 2 "Order the Israelites to expel from camp every leper, and everyone suffering from a discharge, and everyone who

x 1 Sm 6, 19.—y Nm 3, 36f.

has become unclean by contact with a corpse.* ᶻ ³Male and female alike, you shall compel them to go out of the camp; they are not to defile the camp in which I dwell."ᵃ ⁴The Israelites obeyed the command that the LORD had given Moses; they expelled them from the camp.

Unjust Possession. ⁵ * The LORD said to Moses, ⁶ ᵇ "Tell the Israelites: If a man (or woman) commits a fault against his fellow man and wrongs him, thus breaking faith with the LORD, ⁷he shall confess the wrong he has done, restore his ill-gotten goods in full, and in addition give one fifth of their value to the one he has wronged. ⁸However, if the latter has no next of kin* to whom restoration of the ill-gotten goods can be made, the goods to be restored shall be the LORD's and shall fall to the priest; this is apart from the atonement ram with which the priest makes amends for the guilty man. ⁹Likewise, every sacred contribution that the Israelites are bound to make shall fall to the priest.ᶜ ¹⁰Each Israelite man may dispose of his own sacred contributions; they become the property of the priest to whom he gives them."ᵈ

Ordeal for a Suspected Adulteress. ¹¹The LORD said to Moses, ¹²"Speak to the Israelites and tell them: If a man's wife goes astray and becomes unfaithful to him ¹³by having intercourse with another man,ᵉ though her husband has not sufficient evidence of the fact, so that her impurity remains unproved for lack of a witness who might have caught her in the act; ¹⁴or if a

man is overcome by a feeling of jealousy that makes him suspect his wife, whether she was actually impure or not: ¹⁵he shall bring his wife to the priest and shall take Nm along as an offering for her a tenth of an ephah of barley meal. However, he shall not pour oil on it nor put frankincense over it, since it is a cereal offering of jealousy, a cereal offering for an appeal in a question of guilt.

¹⁶"The priest shall first have the woman come forward and stand before the LORD. ¹⁷In an earthen vessel he shall meanwhile put some holy water,* as well as some dust that he has taken from the floor of the Dwelling.ᶠ ¹⁸Then, as the woman stands before the LORD, the priest shall uncover her head and place in her hands the cereal offering of her appeal,* that is, the cereal offering of jealousy, while he himself shall hold the bitter water that brings a curse. ¹⁹Then he shall adjure the woman, saying to her, 'If no other man has had intercourse with you, and you have not gone astray by impurity while under the authority of your husband, be immune to the curse brought by this bitter water. ²⁰But if you have gone astray while under the authority of your husband and have acted impurely by letting a man other than your husband have intercourse with you'—²¹so shall the priest adjure the woman with this oath of imprecation— 'may the LORD make you an example of malediction and imprecation* among your people by causing your thighs to waste away and your belly to swell! ²²May this water, then, that brings a curse, enter your body to make your belly swell and your thighs waste away!'ᵍ And the woman shall say, 'Amen, amen!'* ²³The priest shall put these imprecations in writing and shall then wash them off into the bitter water, ²⁴which he is to have the woman drink, so that it may go into her with all its bitter curse. ²⁵But first he shall take the cereal offering of jealousy from the woman's hand, and having waved this offering before the LORD, shall put it near the altar,ʰ ²⁶where he shall take a handful of the cereal offering as its token offering and burn it on the altar. Only then shall he have the woman drink the water. ²⁷Once she has done so, if she has been impure and unfaithful to her husband, this bitter water that brings a curse will go into her, and her belly will swell and her thighs will

z Nm 19, 11. 13; Lv 13, 46; 21, 1; 22, 4.—a Nm 35, 34.—b 6ff: Lv 5, 21-25.—c Dt 18, 3f; Ez 44, 29f.—d Lv 10, 12-15.—e Lv 18, 20; Jn 8, 4.—f Nm 19, 17.—g Ps 109, 18.—h Lv 5, 12.

5, 2: For the laws regarding victims of leprosy, see Lv 13—14; those *suffering from a discharge,* Lv 15; the *unclean by contact with a corpse,* Nm 19, 11—12; Lv 21, 1-4.

5, 5-10: The basic law on unjust possession is given in Lv 5, 14-26. The new item here concerns the case where the injured party has died and left no heirs, in which case the restitution must be made to the priest.

5, 8: *Next of kin:* literally, "redeemer," a technical term denoting the nearest relative, upon whom devolved the obligation of "redeeming" the family property, in order to keep it within the family. Cf Lv 25, 25; Ru 4, 1-6.

5, 17: *Holy water:* water from the laver that stood in the court of the Dwelling.

5, 18: *Appeal:* by which she invokes the Lord and refers her case to his decision.

5, 21: *An example of malediction and imprecation:* the woman's name would be used in curses and oaths to invoke a similar misfortune on another person or on oneself. Cf Is 65, 15; Jer 29, 22.

5, 22: *Amen:* a Hebrew word meaning, "certainly, truly," used to give assent to a statement, a curse, a blessing, a prayer, or the like; in this sense of "so be it," the Christian liturgy also uses it after prayers and blessings.

waste away, so that she will become an example of imprecation among her people. [28] If, however, the woman has not defiled herself, but is still pure, she will be immune and will still be able to bear children.

[29] "This, then, is the law for jealousy: When a woman goes astray while under the authority of her husband and acts impurely, [30] or when such a feeling of jealousy comes over a man that he becomes suspicious of his wife, he shall have her stand before the LORD, and the priest shall apply this law in full to her. [31] The man shall be free from guilt,* but the woman shall bear such guilt as she may have."

CHAPTER 6

Laws Concerning Nazirites. [1] The LORD said to Moses: [2] "Speak to the Israelites and tell them: When a man (or a woman) solemnly takes the nazirite* vow to dedicate himself to the LORD, [3] he shall abstain from wine and strong drink;[i] he may neither drink wine vinegar, other vinegar, or any kind of grape juice, nor eat either fresh or dried grapes. [4] As long as he is a nazirite he shall not eat anything of the produce of the vine, not even unripe grapes or grapeskins. [5] While he is under the nazirite vow, no razor shall touch his hair.[j] Until the period of his dedication to the LORD is over, he shall be sacred, and shall let the hair of his head grow freely. [6] As long as he is dedicated to the LORD, he shall not enter where a dead person is.[k] [7] Not even for his father or mother, his sister or brother, should they die, may he become unclean, since his head bears his dedication to God. [8] As long as he is a nazirite he is sacred to the LORD.

[9] "If someone dies very suddenly in his presence, so that his dedicated head becomes unclean, he shall shave his head on the day of his purification, that is, on the seventh day. [10] On the eighth day he shall bring two turtledoves or two pigeons to the priest at the entrance of the meeting tent. [11] The priest shall offer up the one as a sin offering and the other as a holocaust, thus making atonement for him for the sin he has committed by reason of the dead person. On the same day he shall reconsecrate his head [12] and begin anew the period of his dedication to the LORD as a nazirite,

bringing a yearling lamb as a guilt offering. The previous period is not valid, because his dedicated head became unclean.

[13] "This is the ritual for the nazirite:[l] On the day he completes the period of his dedication he shall go to the entrance of the meeting tent, [14] bringing as his offering to the LORD one unblemished yearling lamb for a holocaust, one unblemished yearling ewe lamb for a sin offering, one unblemished ram as a peace offering, along with their cereal offerings and libations, [15] and a basket of unleavened cakes of fine flour mixed with oil and of unleavened wafers spread with oil. [16] The priest shall present them before the LORD, and shall offer up the sin offering and the holocaust for him. [17] He shall then offer up the ram as a peace offering to the LORD, with its cereal offering and libation, and the basket of unleavened cakes. [18] Then at the entrance of the meeting tent the nazirite shall shave his dedicated head,[m] collect the hair, and put it in the fire that is under the peace offering. [19] After the nazirite has shaved off his dedicated hair, the priest shall take a boiled shoulder of the ram, as well as one unleavened cake and one unleavened wafer from the basket, and shall place them in the hands of the nazirite. [20] The priest shall then wave them as a wave offering before the LORD. They become sacred and shall belong to the priest, along with the breast of the wave offering and the leg of the raised offering. Only after this may the nazirite drink wine.

[21] "This, then, is the law for the nazirite; this is the offering to the LORD which is included in his vow of dedication apart from anything else which his means may allow. Thus shall he carry out the law of his dedication in keeping with the vow he has taken."

---

i 3f: Jgs 13, 7. 14.—j Jgs 13, 5; 16, 17; 1 Sm 1, 11.—k Nm 19, 11. 16; Lv 21, 11.—l Acts 21, 24. 26.—m Acts 18, 18; 21, 24.

5, 31: *Free from guilt:* by fulfilling his obligation of obtaining a decision in the matter.

6, 1ff: *Nazirite:* from the Hebrew word *nazir,* meaning "set apart as sacred, dedicated, vowed." The nazirite vow could be either for a limited period or for life. Those bound by this vow had to abstain from all the products of the grapevine, from cutting or shaving their hair, and from contact with a corpse. They were regarded as men of God like the prophets; cf Am 2, 11f. Examples of lifelong nazirites were Samson (Jgs 13, 4f. 7; 16, 17), Samuel (1 Sm 1, 11), and John the Baptizer (Lk 1, 15). At the time of Christ the practice of taking the nazirite vow for a limited period seems to have been quite common, even among the early Christians; cf Acts 18, 18; 21, 23f. 26.

The Priestly Blessing. [22] The LORD said to Moses: [23] "Speak to Aaron and his sons and tell them: This is how you shall bless the Israelites. Say to them:

[24] The LORD bless you and keep you!
[25] The LORD let his face shine* upon you, and be gracious to you!
[26] The LORD look upon you kindly and give you peace!*

[27] So shall they invoke my name upon the Israelites, and I will bless them."

CHAPTER 7

Offerings of Princes. [1] Now, when Moses had completed the erection of the Dwelling and had anointed and consecrated it with all its equipment[n] (as well as the altar with all its equipment), [2] an offering was made by the princes of Israel, who were heads of ancestral houses; the same princes of the tribes who supervised the census. [3] The offering they brought before the LORD consisted of six baggage wagons and twelve oxen, that is, a wagon for every two princes, and an ox for every prince. These they presented as their offering before the Dwelling.

[4] The LORD then said to Moses, [5] "Accept their offering, that these things may be put to use in the service of the meeting tent. Assign them to the Levites, to each group in proportion to its duties." [6] So Moses accepted the wagons and oxen, and assigned them to the Levites. [7] He gave two wagons and four oxen to the Gershonites[o] in proportion to their duties, [8] and four wagons and eight oxen to the Merarites in proportion to their duties, under the supervision of Ithamar, son of Aaron the priest. [9] He gave none to the Kohathites, because they had to carry on their shoulders the sacred objects which were their charge.[p]

[10] For the dedication of the altar also, the princes brought offerings before the altar on the day it was anointed.[q] [11] But the LORD said to Moses, "Let one prince a day present his offering for the dedication of the altar."

[12] * The one who presented his offering on the first day was Nahshon, son of Amminadab, prince of the tribe of Judah. [13] His offering consisted of one silver plate weighing a hundred and thirty shekels according to the sanctuary standard and one silver basin weighing seventy shekels, both filled with fine flour mixed with oil for a cereal offering; [14] one gold cup of ten shekels' weight filled with incense; [15] one young bull, one ram, and one yearling lamb for a holocaust; [16] one goat for a sin offering; [17] and two oxen, five rams, five goats, and five yearling lambs for a peace offering. This was the offering of Nahshon, son of Amminadab.

[18] On the second day Nethanel, son of Zuar, prince of Issachar, made his offering. [19] He presented as his offering one silver plate weighing a hundred and thirty shekels according to the sanctuary standard and one silver basin weighing seventy shekels, both filled with fine flour mixed with oil for a cereal offering; [20] one gold cup of ten shekels' weight filled with incense; [21] one young bull, one ram, and one yearling lamb for a holocaust; [22] one goat for a sin offering; [23] and two oxen, five rams, five goats, and five yearling lambs for a peace offering. This was the offering of Nethanel, son of Zuar.

[24] On the third day it was the turn of Eliab, son of Helon, prince of the Zebulunites. [25] His offering consisted of one silver plate weighing a hundred and thirty shekels according to the sanctuary standard and one silver basin weighing seventy shekels, both filled with fine flour mixed with oil for a cereal offering; [26] one gold cup of ten shekels' weight filled with incense; [27] one young bull, one ram, and one yearling lamb for a holocaust; [28] one goat for a sin offering; [29] and two oxen, five rams, five goats, and five yearling lambs for a peace offering. This was the offering of Eliab, son of Helon.

[30] On the fourth day it was the turn of Elizur, son of Shedeur, prince of the Reubenites. [31] His offering consisted of one silver plate weighing a hundred and thirty shekels according to the sanctuary standard and one silver basin weighing seventy shekels, both filled with fine flour mixed with oil for a cereal offering; [32] one gold cup of ten shekels' weight filled with incense; [33] one young bull, one ram, and one yearling lamb for a holocaust; [34] one goat for a sin offering; [35] and two oxen, five rams, five goats, and five yearling

---

n Ex 40, 17.—o 7f: Nm 4, 24-33.—p Nm 3, 31; 4, 4-15.—q Nm 7, 84.

6, 25: *Let his face shine:* a Hebrew idiom for "smile."
6, 26: *Peace:* the Hebrew word includes the idea of "prosperity, happiness."
7, 12-88: The repetitious account of the same offerings brought by each of the twelve tribal princes and the summary of them are characteristic of an official registration.

lambs for a peace offering. This was the offering of Elizur, son of Shedeur.
³⁶ On the fifth day it was the turn of Shelumiel, son of Zurishaddai, prince of the Simeonites. ³⁷ His offering consisted of one silver plate weighing a hundred and thirty shekels according to the sanctuary standard and one silver basin weighing seventy shekels, both filled with fine flour mixed with oil for a cereal offering; ³⁸ one gold cup of ten shekels' weight filled with incense; ³⁹ one young bull, one ram, and one yearling lamb for a holocaust; ⁴⁰ one goat for a sin offering; ⁴¹ and two oxen, five rams, five goats, and five yearling lambs for a peace offering. This was the offering of Shelumiel, son of Zurishaddai.

⁴² On the sixth day it was the turn of Eliasaph, son of Reuel, prince of the Gadites. ⁴³ His offering consisted of one silver plate weighing a hundred and thirty shekels according to the sanctuary standard and one silver basin weighing seventy shekels, both filled with fine flour mixed with oil for a cereal offering; ⁴⁴ one gold cup of ten shekels' weight filled with incense; ⁴⁵ one young bull, one ram, and one yearling lamb for a holocaust; ⁴⁶ one goat for a sin offering; ⁴⁷ and two oxen, five rams, five goats, and five yearling lambs for a peace offering. This was the offering of Eliasaph, son of Reuel.

⁴⁸ On the seventh day it was the turn of Elishama, son of Ammihud, prince of the Ephraimites. ⁴⁹ His offering consisted of one silver plate weighing a hundred and thirty shekels according to the sanctuary standard and one silver basin weighing seventy shekels, both filled with fine flour mixed with oil for a cereal offering; ⁵⁰ one gold cup of ten shekels' weight filled with incense; ⁵¹ one young bull, one ram, and one yearling lamb for a holocaust; ⁵² one goat for a sin offering; ⁵³ and two oxen, five rams, five goats, and five yearling lambs for a peace offering. This was the offering of Elishama, son of Ammihud.

⁵⁴ On the eighth day it was the turn of Gamaliel, son of Pedahzur, prince of the Manassehites. ⁵⁵ His offering consisted of one silver plate weighing a hundred and thirty shekels according to the sanctuary standard and one silver basin weighing seventy shekels, both filled with fine flour mixed with oil for a cereal offering; ⁵⁶ one gold cup of ten shekels' weight filled with

incense; ⁵⁷ one young bull, one ram, and one yearling lamb for a holocaust; ⁵⁸ one goat for a sin offering; ⁵⁹ and two oxen, five rams, five goats, and five yearling lambs for a peace offering. This was the offering of Gamaliel, son of Pedahzur.

⁶⁰ On the ninth day it was the turn of Abidan, son of Gideoni, prince of the Benjaminites. ⁶¹ His offering consisted of one silver plate weighing a hundred and thirty shekels according to the sanctuary standard and one silver basin weighing seventy shekels, both filled with fine flour mixed with oil for a cereal offering; ⁶² one gold cup of ten shekels' weight filled with incense; ⁶³ one young bull, one ram, and one yearling lamb for a holocaust; ⁶⁴ one goat for a sin offering; ⁶⁵ and two oxen, five rams, five goats, and five yearling lambs for a peace offering. This was the offering of Abidan, son of Gideoni.

⁶⁶ On the tenth day it was the turn of Ahiezer, son of Ammishaddai, prince of the Danites. ⁶⁷ His offering consisted of one silver plate weighing a hundred and thirty shekels according to the sanctuary standard and one silver basin weighing seventy shekels, both filled with fine flour mixed with oil for a cereal offering; ⁶⁸ one gold cup of ten shekels' weight filled with incense; ⁶⁹ one young bull, one ram, and one yearling lamb for a holocaust; ⁷⁰ one goat for a sin offering; ⁷¹ and two oxen, five rams, five goats, and five yearling lambs for a peace offering. This was the offering of Ahiezer, son of Ammishaddai.

⁷² On the eleventh day it was the turn of Pagiel, son of Ochran, prince of the Asherites. ⁷³ His offering consisted of one silver plate weighing a hundred and thirty shekels according to the sanctuary standard and one silver basin weighing seventy shekels, both filled with fine flour mixed with oil for a cereal offering; ⁷⁴ one gold cup of ten shekels' weight filled with incense; ⁷⁵ one young bull, one ram, and one yearling lamb for a holocaust; ⁷⁶ one goat for a sin offering; ⁷⁷ and two oxen, five rams, five goats, and five yearling lambs for a peace offering. This was the offering of Pagiel, son of Ochran.

⁷⁸ On the twelfth day it was the turn of Ahira, son of Enan, prince of the Naphtalites. ⁷⁹ His offering consisted of one silver plate weighing a hundred and thirty shekels according to the sanctuary standard and one silver basin weighing seventy

shekels, both filled with fine flour mixed with oil for a cereal offering; [80] one gold cup of ten shekels' weight filled with incense; [81] one young bull, one ram, and one yearling lamb for a holocaust; [82] one goat for a sin offering; [83] and two oxen, five rams, five goats, and five yearling lambs for a peace offering. This was the offering of Ahira, son of Enan.

[84] These were the offerings for the dedication of the altar, given by the princes of Israel on the occasion of its anointing: twelve silver plates, twelve silver basins, and twelve gold cups. [85] Each silver plate weighed a hundred and thirty shekels, and each silver basin seventy, so that all the silver of these vessels amounted to two thousand four hundred shekels, according to the sanctuary standard. [86] The twelve gold cups that were filled with incense weighed ten shekels apiece, according to the sanctuary standard, so that all the gold of the cups amounted to one hundred and twenty shekels. [87] The animals for the holocausts were, in all, twelve young bulls, twelve rams, and twelve yearling lambs, with their cereal offerings; those for the sin offerings were twelve goats. [88] The animals for the peace offerings were, in all, twenty-four oxen, sixty rams, sixty goats, and sixty yearling lambs. These, then, were the offerings for the dedication of the altar after it was anointed.

The Voice. [89] When Moses entered the meeting tent to speak with him, he heard the voice addressing him from above the propitiatory[r] on the ark of the commandments, from between the two cherubim; and it spoke to him. . . .

CHAPTER 8

The Lamps Set Up. [1] The LORD spoke to Moses, and said, [2] "Give Aaron this command: When you set up the seven lamps,[s] have them throw their light toward the front of the lampstand." [3] Aaron did so,

setting up the lamps to face toward the front of the lampstand, just as the LORD had commanded Moses. [4] The lampstand was made of beaten gold[t] in both its shaft and its branches, according to the pattern which the LORD had shown Moses.

Purification of the Levites. [5] The LORD said to Moses: [6] "Take the Levites from among the Israelites and purify them.* [7] This is what you shall do to them to purify them. Sprinkle them with the water of remission;* then have them shave their whole bodies and wash their clothes, and so purify themselves. [8] They shall take a young bull, along with its cereal offering of fine flour mixed with oil; you shall take another young bull for a sin offering. [9] Then have the Levites come forward in front of the meeting tent, where you shall assemble also the whole community of the Israelites. [10] While the Levites are present before the LORD, the Israelites shall lay their hands upon them. [11] Let Aaron then offer the Levites before the LORD as a wave offering from the Israelites, thus devoting them to the service of the LORD. [12] The Levites in turn shall lay their hands on the heads of the bullocks, which shall then be immolated, the one as a sin offering and the other as a holocaust to the LORD, in atonement for the Levites. [13] Thus, then, shall you have the Levites stand before Aaron and his sons, to be offered as a wave offering to the LORD; [14] and thus shall you set aside the Levites from the rest of the Israelites, that they may be mine.[u]

[15] "Only then shall the Levites enter upon their service in the meeting tent. You shall purify them and offer them as a wave offering; [16] because they, among the Israelites, are strictly dedicated to me; I have taken them for myself in place of every first-born that opens the womb among the Israelites.[v] [17] Indeed, all the first-born among the Israelites, both of man and of beast, belong to me; I consecrated them to myself on the day I slew all the first-born in the land of Egypt.[w] [18] But in place of all the first-born Israelites I have taken the Levites; [19] and I have given these dedicated Israelites to Aaron and his sons[x] to discharge the duties of the Israelites in the meeting tent and to make atonement for them, so that no plague may strike among the Israelites should they come near the sanctuary."

. r Ex 25, 22.—s Ex 25, 37.—t Ex 25, 31. 40.—u Nm 3, 45.—v Nm 3, 12. 45.—w Nm 3, 13; 13, 2; Lk 2, 23.—x Nm 3, 9f.

8, 6: *Purify them:* in the language of the Pentateuch only the priests were "consecrated," that is, made sacred or set aside for the Lord, in an elaborate ceremony described in Ex 29; Lv 8. The Levites were merely "purified," that is, made ritually clean for their special work.

8, 7: *Water of remission:* literally, "water of sin," that is, for the remission of sin.

20 Thus, then, did Moses and Aaron and the whole community of the Israelites deal with the Levites, carrying out exactly the command which the LORD had given Moses concerning them. 21 When the Levites had cleansed themselves of sin* and washed their clothes, Aaron offered them as a wave offering before the LORD, and made atonement for them to purify them. 22 Only then did they enter upon their service in the meeting tent under the supervision of Aaron and his sons. The command which the LORD had given Moses concerning the Levites was carried out.

Age Limits for Levitical Service. 23 The LORD said to Moses: 24 "This is the rule for the Levites. Each from his twenty-fifth year onward shall perform the required service in the meeting tent.*y* 25 When he is fifty years old, he shall retire from the required service and work no longer. 26 His service with his fellow Levites shall consist in sharing their responsibilities in the meeting tent, but he shall not do the work. This, then, is how you are to regulate the duties of the Levites."

CHAPTER 9

Second Passover. 1 In the first month of the year following their departure from the land of Egypt, the LORD said to Moses in the desert of Sinai, 2 "Tell the Israelites to celebrate the Passover at the prescribed time. 3 The evening twilight of the fourteenth day of this month *z* is the prescribed time when you shall celebrate it, observing all its rules and regulations." 4 Moses, therefore, told the Israelites to celebrate the Passover. 5 And they did so, celebrating the Passover in the desert of Sinai during the evening twilight of the fourteenth day of the first month, just as the LORD had commanded Moses.

6 There were some, however, who were unclean because of a human corpse and so could not keep the Passover that day. These men came up to Moses and Aaron that same day 7 and said, "Although we are unclean because of a corpse, why should we be deprived of presenting the LORD's offering at its proper time along with the other Israelites?" 8 Moses answered them, "Wait until I learn what the LORD will command in your regard."

9 The LORD then said to Moses: 10 "Speak to the Israelites and say: If any one of you or of your descendants is unclean because of a corpse, or if he is absent on a journey, he may still keep the LORD's Passover. 11 But he shall keep it in the second month,*a* during the evening twilight of the fourteenth day of that month, eating it with unleavened bread and bitter herbs, 12 and not leaving any of it over till morning, nor breaking any of its bones,*b* but observing all the rules of the Passover. 13 However, anyone who is clean and not away on a journey, who yet fails to keep the Passover, shall be cut off from his people, because he did not present the LORD's offering at the prescribed time. That man shall bear the consequences of his sin.

14 "If an alien* who lives among you wishes to keep the LORD's Passover, he too shall observe the rules and regulations for the Passover. You shall have the same law for the resident alien as for the native of the land."*c*

The Fiery Cloud. 15 On the day when the Dwelling was erected, the cloud* covered the Dwelling, the tent of the commandments; but from evening until morning it took on the appearance of fire over the Dwelling.*d* 16 It was always so: during the day the Dwelling was covered by the cloud, which at night had the appearance of fire. 17 Whenever the cloud rose from the tent, the Israelites would break camp; wherever the cloud came to rest, they would pitch camp.*e* 18 At the bidding of the LORD the Israelites moved on, and at his bidding they encamped.*f* As long as the cloud stayed over the Dwelling, they remained in camp.

19 Even when the cloud tarried many days over the Dwelling, the Israelites obeyed the LORD and would not move on; 20 yet sometimes the cloud was over the Dwelling only for a few days. It was at the bidding of the LORD that they stayed in camp, and it was at his bidding that they departed. 21 Sometimes the cloud remained there only from evening until morning; and when it rose in the morning,

---

y Nm 4, 3. 23.—z Ex 12, 6; Lv 23, 5.— a 2 Chr 30, 2-15.—b Ex 12, 46; Jn 19, 36.—c Ex 12, 48f.—d Ex 13, 21.—e Wis 18, 3.—f 1 Cor 10, 1.

8, 21: *Cleansed themselves of sin:* by having the "water of remission" sprinkled on them as prescribed in v 7.

9, 14: *An alien:* this passage presupposes that he is already circumcised as prescribed in Ex 12, 48.

9, 15: *The cloud:* already mentioned at the departure from Egypt; cf Ex 13, 21f.

they would depart. Or if the cloud lifted during the day, or even at night, they would then set out. [22] Whether the cloud tarried over the Dwelling for two days or for a month or longer, the Israelites remained in camp and did not depart; but when it lifted, they moved on. [23] Thus, it was always at the bidding of the LORD that they encamped, and at his bidding that they set out; ever heeding the charge of the LORD, as he had bidden them through Moses.

CHAPTER 10

The Silver Trumpets. [1] The LORD said to Moses: [2] "Make two trumpets of beaten silver, which you shall use in assembling the community and in breaking camp. [3] When both are blown, the whole community shall gather round you at the entrance of the meeting tent; [4] but when one of them is blown, only the princes, the chiefs of the troops of Israel, shall gather round you. [5] When you sound the first alarm, those encamped on the east side shall set out; [6] when you sound the second alarm, those encamped on the south side shall set out; when you sound the third alarm, those encamped on the west side shall set out; when you sound the fourth alarm, those encamped on the north side shall set out. Thus shall the alarm be sounded for them to depart. [7] But in calling forth an assembly you are to blow an ordinary blast, without sounding the alarm.

[8] "It is the sons of Aaron, the priests, who shall blow the trumpets; and the use of them is prescribed by perpetual statute for you and your descendants. [9] g When in your own land you go to war against an enemy that is attacking you, you shall sound the alarm on the trumpets, and the LORD, your God, will remember you and save you from your foes. [10] On your days of celebration,* your festivals, and your new-moon feasts, you shall blow the trumpets over your holocausts and your peace offerings; h this will serve as a reminder of you before your God. I, the LORD, am your God."

g 2 Chr 13, 14.—h Nm 29, 1; 2 Chr 29, 26ff.—i 14ff: Nm 2, 3. 5. 7.

10, 10: *Days of celebration:* special holidays, such as the occasion of a victory. *Festivals:* the great annual feasts of the Passover, Pentecost and Booths described in Lv 23; Nm 28—29.
10, 30ff: Hobab wished to be coaxed before granting the favor. From Jgs 1, 16 it seems probable that he did accede to Moses' request.

II: FROM SINAI TO THE PLAINS OF MOAB

Departure from Sinai. [11] In the second year, on the twentieth day of the second month, the cloud rose from the Dwelling of the commandments. [12] The Israelites moved on from the desert of Sinai by stages, until the cloud came to rest in the desert of Paran.

[13] The first time that they broke camp at the bidding of the LORD through Moses, [14] i the camp of the Judahites, under its own standard and arranged in companies, was the first to set out. Nahshon, son of Amminadab, was over their host, [15] and Nethanel, son of Zuar, over the host of the tribe of Issachar, [16] and Eliab, son of Helon, over the host of the tribe of Zebulun. [17] Then, after the Dwelling was dismantled, the clans of Gershon and Merari set out, carrying the Dwelling. [18] The camp of the Reubenites, under its own standard and arranged in companies, was the next to set out, with Elizur, son of Shedeur, over their hosts, [19] and Shelumiel, son of Zurishaddai, over the host of the tribe of Simeon, [20] and Eliasaph, son of Reuel, over the host of the tribe of Gad. [21] The clan of Kohath then set out, carrying the sacred objects for the Dwelling, which was to be erected before their arrival. [22] The camp of the Ephraimites next set out, under its own standard and arranged in companies, with Elishama, son of Ammihud, over their host, [23] and Gamaliel, son of Pedahzur, over the host of the tribe of Manasseh, [24] and Abidan, son of Gideoni, over the host of the tribe of Benjamin. [25] Finally, as rear guard for all the camps, the camp of the Danites set out, under its own standard and arranged in companies, with Ahiezer, son of Ammishaddai, over their host, [26] and Pagiel, son of Ochran, over the host of the tribe of Asher, [27] and Ahira, son of Enan, over the host of the tribe of Naphtali. [28] This was the order of departure for the Israelites, company by company.

Hobab as Guide. As they were setting out, [29] Moses said to his brother-in-law Hobab, son of Reuel the Midianite, "We are setting out for the place which the LORD has promised to give us. Come with us, and we will be generous toward you, for the LORD has promised prosperity to Israel." [30] * But he answered, "No, I will not come. I am going instead to my own country and to my own kindred." [31] Moses said, "Please, do not leave us; you know where we can camp in the desert, and you will serve as eyes for us. [32] If you come with us, we will share with you the prosperity the LORD will bestow on us."

Into the Desert. [33] *j* They moved on from the mountain of the LORD,* a three days' journey, and the ark of the covenant of the LORD which was to seek out their resting place went the three days' journey with them. [34] And when they set out from camp, the cloud of the LORD was over them by day.

[35] Whenever the ark set out, Moses would say,

"Arise, O LORD, that your enemies
    may be scattered,
and those who hate you may flee before you."

[36] And when it came to rest, he would say,

"Return, O LORD, you who ride upon
    the clouds,
to the troops of Israel."

CHAPTER 11

Discontent of the People. [1] Now the people complained in the hearing of the LORD;[k] and when he heard it his wrath flared up so that the fire of the LORD burned among them and consumed the outskirts of the camp. [2] But when the people cried out to Moses, he prayed to the LORD and the fire died out. [3] Hence that place was called Taberah,* because there the fire of the LORD burned among them.

[4] The foreign elements among them were so greedy for meat that even the Israelites lamented again,[l] "Would that we had meat for food! [5] We remember the fish we used to eat without cost in Egypt, and the cucumbers, the melons, the leeks, the onions, and the garlic. [6] But now we are famished; we see nothing before us but this manna."[m]

[7] *n* Manna was like coriander seed* and had the appearance of bdellium. [8] When they had gone about and gathered it up, the people would grind it between millstones or pound it in a mortar, then cook it in a pot and make it into loaves, which tasted like cakes made with oil. [9] At night, when the dew fell upon the camp, the manna also fell.[o]

[10] When Moses heard the people, family after family, crying at the entrance of their tents, so that the LORD became very angry, he was grieved. [11] "Why do you treat your servant so badly?" Moses asked the LORD. "Why are you so displeased with me that you burden me with all this people? [12] Was it I who conceived all this people? or was it I who gave them birth, that you tell me to carry them at my bosom, like a foster father carrying an infant, to the land you have promised under oath to their fathers? [13] Where can I get meat to give to all this people? For they are crying to me, 'Give us meat for our food.' [14] I cannot carry all this people by myself, for they are too heavy for me. [15] If this is the way you will deal with me, then please do me the favor of killing me at once, so that I need no longer face this distress."

The Seventy Elders. [16] Then the LORD said to Moses, "Assemble for me seventy of the elders of Israel, men you know for true elders and authorities among the people, and bring them to the meeting tent. When they are in place beside you, [17] I will come down and speak with you there. I will also take some of the spirit that is on you and will bestow it on them, that they may share the burden of the people with you. You will then not have to bear it by yourself.

[18] "To the people, however, you shall say: Sanctify yourselves for tomorrow, when you shall have meat to eat. For in the hearing of the LORD you have cried, 'Would that we had meat for food! Oh, how well off we were in Egypt!' Therefore the LORD will give you meat for food, [19] and you will eat it, not for one day, or two days, or five, or ten, or twenty days, [20] but for a whole month—until it comes out of your very nostrils and becomes loathsome to you. For you have spurned the LORD who is in your midst, and in his presence you have wailed, 'Why did we ever leave Egypt?' "

[21] But Moses said, "The people around me include six hundred thousand soldiers;

---

j Dt 1, 33; Ps 68, 2.—k Dt 9, 22.—l Ps 78, 18.—m 5f: Nm 21, 5; Ex 16, 3; Acts 7, 39.—n 7f: Ex 16, 14f. 31; Ps 78, 24; Wis 16, 20; Jn 6, 31.—o Ex 16, 14f.

10, 33: *The mountain of the Lord:* Sinai (Horeb), elsewhere always called "the mountain of God."
11, 3: *Taberah:* means "the burning."
11, 7: *Coriander seed:* see note on Ex 16, 31. *Bdellium:* a transparent, amber-colored gum resin, which is also mentioned in Gn 2, 12.

yet you say, 'I will give them meat to eat for a whole month.' [22]Can enough sheep and cattle be slaughtered for them? If all the fish of the sea were caught for them, would they have enough?" [23]The LORD answered Moses, "Is this beyond the LORD's reach? You shall see now whether or not what I have promised you takes place."

The Spirit on the Elders. [24]So Moses went out and told the people what the LORD had said. Gathering seventy elders of the people, he had them stand around the tent. [25]The LORD then came down in the cloud and spoke to him. Taking some of the spirit that was on Moses, he bestowed it on the seventy elders; and as the spirit came to rest on them, they prophesied.[*]

[26]Now two men, one named Eldad and the other Medad, were not in the gathering but had been left in the camp. They too had been on the list, but had not gone out to the tent; yet the spirit came to rest on them also, and they prophesied in the camp. [27]So, when a young man quickly told Moses, "Eldad and Medad are prophesying in the camp," [28]Joshua, son of Nun, who from his youth had been Moses' aide, said, "Moses, my lord, stop them." [29]But Moses answered him, "Are you jealous for my sake? Would that all the people of the LORD were prophets! Would that the LORD might bestow his spirit on them all!" [30]Then Moses retired to the camp, along with the elders of Israel.

The Quail. [31]There arose a wind[p] sent by the LORD, that drove in quail from the sea and brought them down over the camp site at a height of two cubits from the ground[*] for the distance of a day's journey all around the camp. [32] [q] All that day, all night, and all the next day the people gathered in the quail. Even the one who got the least gathered ten homers of them. Then they spread them out[*] all around the camp. [33]But while the meat was still between their teeth, before it could be consumed, the LORD's wrath flared up against the people, and he struck them with a very great plague. [34]So that place was named Kibroth-hattaavah,[*] because it was there that the greedy people were buried.

[35]From Kibroth-hattaavah the people set out for Hazeroth.

CHAPTER 12

Jealousy of Aaron and Miriam. While they were in Hazeroth, [1]Miriam and Aaron spoke against Moses on the pretext of the marriage he had contracted with a Cushite woman.[*] [2]They complained, [*] "Is it through Moses alone that the LORD speaks? Does he not speak through us also?" And the LORD heard this. [3] [r] Now, Moses himself was by far the meekest man on the face of the earth. [4]So at once the LORD said to Moses and Aaron and Miriam, "Come out, you three, to the meeting tent." And the three of them went. [5]Then the LORD came down in the column of cloud, and standing at the entrance of the tent, called Aaron and Miriam. When both came forward, [6]he said, "Now listen to the words of the LORD:

> Should there be a prophet among you,
>   in visions will I reveal myself to him,
>   in dreams will I speak to him;
> [7] Not so with my servant Moses!
> Throughout my house he bears my trust:[s]
> [8]   face to face I speak to him,[t]
>   plainly and not in riddles.
> The presence of the LORD he beholds.

Why, then, did you not fear to speak against my servant Moses?"

Miriam's Leprosy. [9]So angry was the LORD against them that when he departed, [10]and the cloud withdrew from the tent, there was Miriam,[u] a snow-white leper![*] When Aaron turned and saw her a leper, [11]"Ah, my lord!" he said to Moses, "please do not charge us with the sin that we have

---

p Ps 78, 26ff.—q 32f; Ps 78, 26-31; 1 Cor 10, 6-7.—r Sir 45, 1f.—s Sir 45, 3; Heb 3, 2. 5.—t Ex 33, 11; Dt 34, 10.—u Dt 24, 9.

11, 25: *They prophesied:* in the sense, not of foretelling the future, but of speaking in enraptured enthusiasm. Such manifestations of mystic exaltation occurred in the early days of Hebrew prophecy (1 Sm 10, 10ff; 19, 20ff) and in the first years of the Church (Acts 2, 6-11. 17; 19, 6; 1 Cor 12—14).

11, 31: *At a height of two cubits from the ground:* exhausted by the storm, the quail could take but short, low flights, so that they were easily captured. To give food to the hungry people, God may have used the natural phenomenon of the annual migration of quail across the Sinai Peninsula. In the spring large flocks of these birds cross the Gulf of Aqabah flying toward the west; in the fall they fly eastward from the Mediterranean. *The sea* mentioned here probably refers to the former body of water.

11, 32: *They spread them out:* to cure by drying.

11, 34: *Kibroth-hattaavah:* means "graves of greed."

12, 1: *Cushite woman:* apparently Zipporah, the Midianitess, is meant; cf Ex 2, 21. Perhaps the term is used here merely in the sense of "despised foreigner."

12, 2: The real reason for Miriam's quarrel with her brother Moses was her jealousy of his superior position; his Cushite wife served only as an occasion for the dispute. Aaron merely followed his sister in her rebellion; hence she alone was punished.

12, 10: *A snow-white leper:* afflicted with "white leprosy," a skin disease that generally is not serious or of long duration. Cf Lv 13, 3-6.

foolishly committed! ¹²Let her not thus be like the stillborn babe that comes forth from its mother's womb with its flesh half consumed." ¹³Then Moses cried to the LORD, "Please, not this! Pray, heal her!" ¹⁴But the LORD answered Moses, "Suppose her father had spit in her face, would she not hide in shame for seven days? Let her be confined outside the camp for seven days; only then may she be brought back." ¹⁵So Miriam was confined outside the camp for seven days, and the people did not start out again until she was brought back.

¹⁶After that the people set out from Hazeroth and encamped in the desert of Paran.

CHAPTER 13

The Twelve Scouts. ¹The LORD said to Moses, ²"Send men to reconnoiter the land of Canaan, which I am giving the Israelites. You shall send one man from each ancestral tribe, all of them princes." ³ᵛ So Moses dispatched them from the desert of Paran, as the LORD had ordered. All of them were leaders among the Israelites; ⁴by name they were:

Shammua, son of Zaccur, of the tribe of Reuben;
⁵ Shaphat, son of Hori, of the tribe of Simeon;
⁶ Caleb, son of Jephunneh, of the tribe of Judah;
⁷ Igal [son of Joseph] of the tribe of Issachar;
¹⁰ Gaddiel, son of Sodi, of the tribe of Zebulun;
¹¹ Gaddi, son of Susi, of the tribe of Manasseh, for the Josephites, with
⁸ Hoshea, son of Nun, of the tribe of Ephraim;
⁹ Palti, son of Raphu, of the tribe of Benjamin;
¹² Ammiel, son of Gemalli, of the tribe of Dan;
¹³ Sethur, son of Michael, of the tribe of Asher;
¹⁴ Nahbi, son of Vophsi, of the tribe of Naphtali;
¹⁵ Geuel, son of Machi, of the tribe of Gad.

¹⁶These are the names of the men whom Moses sent out to reconnoiter the land. But Hoshea, son of Nun, Moses called Joshua.*

¹⁷In sending them to reconnoiter the land of Canaan, Moses said to them, "Go up here in the Negeb, up into the highlands, ¹⁸and see what kind of land it is. Are the people living there strong or weak, few or many? ¹⁹Is the country in which they live good or bad? Are the towns in which they dwell open or fortified? ²⁰Is the soil fertile or barren, wooded or clear? And do your best to get some of the fruit of the land." It was then the season for early grapes.

²¹So they went up and reconnoitered the land from the desert of Zin * as far as where Rehob adjoins Labo of Hamath. ²² ʷ Going up by way of the Negeb, they reached Hebron, where Ahiman, Sheshai and Talmai, descendants of the Anakim,* were living. [Hebron had been built seven years before Zoan in Egypt.] ²³They also reached the Wadi Eshcol,* where they cut down a branch with a single cluster of grapes on it, which two of them carried on a pole, as well as some pomegranates and figs. ²⁴It was because of the cluster the Israelites cut there that they call the place Wadi Eshcol.ˣ

Their Return. ²⁵After reconnoitering the land for forty days they returned, ²⁶ ʸ met Moses and Aaron and the whole community of the Israelites in the desert of Paran at Kadesh, made a report to them all, and showed them the fruit of the country. ²⁷They told Moses: "We went into the land to which you sent us. It does indeed flow with milk and honey, and here is its fruit. ²⁸However, the people who are living in the land are fierce, and the towns are fortified and very strong.ᶻ Besides, we saw descendants of the Anakim there. ²⁹Amalekites live in the region of the Negeb; Hittites, Jebusites and Amorites dwell in the highlands, and Canaanites along the seacoast and the banks of the Jordan."

---

v 3-33: Dt 1, 22-28.—w Jos 11, 21f.—x Nm 32, 9; Dt 1, 24f.—y 26f: Ex 3, 8. 17.—z 28f: Dt 9, 1f.

13, 16: *Joshua:* in Hebrew, "Jehoshua," which was later modified to "Joshua," the Hebrew pronunciation of the name "Jesus." Hoshea and Joshua are variants of one original name meaning "the LORD saves." Cf Mt 1, 21.
13, 21: *The desert of Zin:* north of Paran and southwest of the Dead Sea. It is quite distinct from "the desert of Sin" near the border of Egypt (Ex 16, 1; 17, 1; Nm 33, 11). *Labo of Hamath:* a town near Riblah (Jer 39, 5f) at the southern border of *Hamath,* an independent kingdom in southern Syria. David's conquests extended as far as *Hamath* (2 Sm 8, 9ff), and Labo thus formed the northern border of the ideal extent of Israel's possessions (Nm 34, 7ff; Ez 47, 15; 48, 1). Some commentators think that this verse is a later addition to the text; cf Dt 1, 24.
13, 22. 28: *Anakim:* an aboriginal race in southern Palestine, largely absorbed by the Canaanites before the Israelite invasion. Either because of their tall stature or because of the massive stone structures left by them the Israelites regarded them as giants.
13, 23: *Eshcol:* means "cluster."

³⁰Caleb, however, to quiet the people toward Moses, said, "We ought to go up and seize the land, for we can certainly do so." ³¹But the men who had gone up with him said, "We cannot attack these people; they are too strong for us." ³²So they spread discouraging reports*ᵃ* among the Israelites about the land they had scouted, saying, "The land that we explored is a country that consumes its inhabitants. And all the people we saw there are huge men, ³³ *ᵇ* veritable giants* [the Anakim were a race of giants]; we felt like mere grasshoppers, and so we must have seemed to them."

CHAPTER 14

Threats of Revolt. ¹At this, the whole community broke out with loud cries, and even in the night the people wailed. ² *ᶜ* All the Israelites grumbled against Moses and Aaron, the whole community saying to them, "Would that we had died in the land of Egypt, or that here in the desert we were dead! ³ Why is the LORD bringing us into this land only to have us fall by the sword? Our wives and little ones will be taken as booty. Would it not be better for us to return to Egypt?" ⁴So they said to one another, "Let us appoint a leader and go back to Egypt."

⁵But Moses and Aaron fell prostrate before the whole assembled community of the Israelites; ⁶while Joshua, son of Nun, and Caleb, son of Jephunneh, who had been in the party that scouted the land, tore their garments ⁷and said to the whole community of the Israelites,*ᵈ* "The country which we went through and explored is a fine, rich land. ⁸If the LORD is pleased with us, he will bring us in and give us that land, a land flowing with milk and honey. ⁹ *ᵉ* But do not rebel against the LORD! You need not be afraid of the people of that land; they are but food for us!* Their defense has left them, but the LORD is with us. Therefore, do not be afraid of

them." ¹⁰In answer, the whole community threatened to stone them.

The Lord's Sentence. But then the glory of the LORD appeared at the meeting tent to all the Israelites. ¹¹And the LORD said to Moses, "How long will this people spurn me? How long will they refuse to believe in me, despite all the signs I have performed among them?*ᶠ* ¹²I will strike them with pestilence and wipe them out. Then I will make of you a nation greater and mightier than they."*ᵍ*

¹³ *ʰ* But Moses said to the LORD: "Are the Egyptians to hear of this? For by your power you brought out this people from among them. ¹⁴And are they to tell of it to the inhabitants of this land? It has been heard that you, O LORD, are in the midst of this people; you, LORD, who plainly reveal yourself! Your cloud stands over them, and you go before them by day in a column of cloud and by night in a column of fire.*ⁱ* ¹⁵If now you slay this whole people, the nations who have heard such reports of you will say, ¹⁶"The LORD was not able to bring this people into the land he swore to give them; that is why he slaughtered them in the desert.'*ʲ* ¹⁷Now then, let the power of my Lord be displayed in its greatness, even as you have said, ¹⁸ *ᵏ* 'The LORD is slow to anger and rich in kindness, forgiving wickedness and crime; yet not declaring the guiltless guilty, but punishing children to the third and fourth generation for their fathers' wickedness.' ¹⁹Pardon, then, the wickedness of this people in keeping with your great kindness, even as you have forgiven them from Egypt until now."*ˡ*

²⁰The LORD answered: "I pardon them as you have asked. ²¹Yet, by my life and the LORD's glory that fills the whole earth, ²²of all the men who have seen my glory and the signs I worked in Egypt and in the desert,*ᵐ* and who nevertheless have put me to the test ten times already and have failed to heed my voice, ²³not one shall see the land which I promised on oath to their fathers. None of these who have spurned me shall see it. ²⁴But because my servant Caleb has a different spirit and follows me unreservedly,*ⁿ* I will bring him into the land where he has just been, and his descendants shall possess it. ²⁵But now, since the Amalekites and Canaanites are living in the valleys,* turn away tomorrow and set out in the desert on the Red Sea road."

---

a Nm 32, 9; Jos 14, 8.—b Dt 2, 10.—c Ex 16, 3; Ps 106, 25.—d 7f: Dt 1, 25.—e Dt 7, 18.—f Ps 78, 22. 32.—g Ex 32, 10.—h 13-16: Ex 32, 12; Dt 9, 26ff; Ps 106, 23.—i Ex 13, 21; Jos 2, 9f.—j Ex 32, 12; Dt 9, 28.—k Ex 20, 5; 34, 6f; Pss 103, 8; 145, 8.—l Ps 78, 38.—m 22f: Dt 1, 35.—n Jos 14, 8f.

13, 33: *Giants:* in Hebrew, "nephilim." Cf Gn 6, 4.

14, 9: *They are but food for us:* that is, "we can easily consume and destroy them." This is the answer to the pessimistic report that this land "consumes its inhabitants" (Nm 13, 32).

14, 25: *The valleys:* the low-lying plains in the Negeb and along the seacoast and in the Jordan depression, as well as the higher valleys in the mountains farther north; cf Nm 14, 45.

²⁶The LORD also said to Moses and Aaron: ²⁷"How long will this wicked community grumble against me?ᵒ I have heard the grumblings of the Israelites against me. ²⁸Tell them: * By my life, says the LORD, I will do to you just what I have heard you say. ²⁹Here in the desertᵖ shall your dead bodies fall. Of all your men of twenty years or more, registered in the census, who grumbled against me, ³⁰not one shall enter the land where I solemnly swore to settle you, except Caleb, son of Jephunneh, and Joshua, son of Nun. ³¹Your little ones, however, who you said would be taken as booty, I will bring in, and they shall appreciate the land you spurned.�q ³²But as for you, your bodies shall fall here in the desert, ³³here where your children must wander for forty years, suffering for your faithlessness, till the last of you lies dead in the desert.ʳ ³⁴Forty days you spent in scouting the land; forty years shall you suffer for your crimes: one year for each day. Thus you will realize what it means to oppose me. ³⁵I, the LORD, have sworn to do this to all this wicked community that conspired against me: here in the desert they shall die to the last man."

³⁶And so it happened to the men whom Moses had sent to reconnoiter the landˢ and who on returning had set the whole community grumbling against him by spreading discouraging reports about the land; ³⁷these men who had given out the bad report about the land were struck down by the LORD and died. ³⁸Of all the men who had gone to reconnoiter the land, only Joshua, son of Nun, and Caleb, son of Jephunneh, survived.ᵗ

Unsuccessful Invasion. ³⁹When Moses repeated these words to all the Israelites, the people felt great remorse. ⁴⁰Early the next morning they started up into the foothills, saying, "Here we are, ready to go up to the place that the LORD spoke of:ᵘ for we were indeed doing wrong." ⁴¹But Moses said, "Why are you again disobeying the LORD's orders? This cannot succeed. ⁴²Do not go up, because the LORD is not in your midst; if you go, you will be beaten down before your enemies.ᵛ ⁴³For there the Amalekites and Canaanites face you, and you will fall by the sword. You have turned back from following the LORD; therefore the LORD will not be with you."

⁴⁴Yet they dared to go up into the foothills,ʷ even though neither the ark of the covenant of the LORD nor Moses left the camp. ⁴⁵And the Amalekites and Canaanites who dwelt in that hill country came down and defeated them, beating them back as far as Hormah.*

CHAPTER 15

Secondary Offerings. ¹The LORD said to Moses, ² * "Give the Israelites these instructions: When you have entered the land that I will give you for your homesteads, ³if you make to the LORD a sweet-smelling oblation from the herd or from the flock, in holocaust, in fulfillment of a vow, or as a freewill offering, or for one of your festivals, ⁴whoever does so shall also present to the LORD a cereal offering consisting of a tenth of an ephah of fine flour mixed with a fourth of a hin of oil, ⁵as well as a libation of a fourth of a hin of wine, with each lamb sacrificed in holocaust or otherwise. ⁶With each sacrifice of a ram you shall present a cereal offering of two tenths of an ephah of fine flour mixed with a third of a hin of oil, ⁷and a libation of a third of a hin of wine, thus making a sweet-smelling offering to the LORD. ⁸When you sacrifice an ox as a holocaust, or in fulfillment of a vow, or as a peace offering to the LORD, ⁹with it you shall present a cereal offering of three tenths of an ephah of fine flour mixed with half a hin of oil, ¹⁰and a libation of half a hin of wine, as a sweet-smelling oblation to the LORD. ¹¹The same is to be done for each ox, ram, lamb or goat. ¹²Whatever the number you offer, do the same for each of them.

¹³"All the native-born shall make these offerings in the same way, whenever they present a sweet-smelling oblation to the LORD. ¹⁴Likewise, in any future generation, any alien residing with you permanently or for a time, who presents a sweet-

---

o Ex 16, 7. 12.—p Dt 1, 35; Heb 3, 17.—q Dt 1, 39.—r 33f: Nm 13, 26; 32, 13; Ps 95, 10; Ez 4, 6.—s 36f: Nm 13, 17. 32f; 1 Cor 10, 10.—t Nm 26, 65.—u Nm 13, 18; Dt 1, 41.—v Dt 1, 42.—w Dt 1, 43.

14, 28f: God punished the malcontents by giving them their wish; cf v 2. Their lack of faith and of confidence in God is cited in 1 Cor 10, 10, and Heb 3, 12-18, as a warning for Christians.

14, 45: Hormah: one of the Canaanite royal cities in southern Judea (Jos 12, 14), known at this time as "Zephath"; the origin of the later name is told in Nm 21, 3; Jgs 1, 17.

15, 2-16: These laws on sacrifice are complementary to those of Lv 1—3. Since the food of the Israelites consisted not only of meat but also of bread, oil and wine, so, besides the animal oblations, they offered flour, wine and oil in sacrifice to the Lord.

smelling oblation to the LORD, shall do as you do. ¹⁵There is but one rule for you and for the resident alien, a perpetual rule for all your descendants. Before the LORD you and the alien are alike, ¹⁶with the same law and the same application of it for the alien residing among you as for yourselves."

¹⁷The LORD said to Moses, ¹⁸"Speak to the Israelites and tell them: When you enter the land into which I will bring you ¹⁹and begin to eat of the food of that land, you shall offer the LORD a contribution ²⁰consisting of a cake of your first batch of dough.* You shall offer it just as you offer a contribution from the threshing floor.ˣ ²¹Throughout your generations you shall give a contribution to the LORD from your first batch of dough.

Sin Offerings. ²² * "When through inadvertence you fail to carry out any of these commandments which the LORD gives to Moses,ʸ ²³and through Moses to you, from the time the LORD first issues the commandment down through your generations: ²⁴if the community itself unwittingly becomes guilty of the fault of inadvertence, the whole community shall offer the holocaust of one young bull as a sweetsmelling oblation pleasing to the LORD, along with its prescribed cereal offering and libation, as well as one he-goat as a sin offering. ²⁵ ᶻ Then the priest shall make

x 19-20: Ez 44, 30.—y 22f: Lv 4, 13f.—z Lv 4, 20.—a 27f: Lv 4, 27f.—b Dt 17, 12.—c Prv 13, 13.—d Lv 24, 12.—e Dt 22, 12.—f Lv 22, 32f.

15, 20: *Dough:* some render, "barley grits." This word is used elsewhere only in Ez 44, 30 and Neh 10, 33; a related Hebrew word is used in Lv 2, 14.

15, 22ff: Although no moral guilt is incurred by an inadvertent violation of God's commandments, the sanctity of the law can require some reparation even for such violations.

15, 34: *No clear decision:* they already knew that a willful violation of the sabbath was a capital offense, but they did not yet know how the death penalty was to be inflicted.

15, 38: *Tassels:* at the time of Christ these tassels were worn by all pious Jews, including our Lord (Mt 9, 20f; Mk 6, 56); the Pharisees wore very large ones in ostentation of their zeal for the law (Mt 23, 5).

16, 1ff: The evidence seems to show that there were two distinct rebellions: one of Korah and his band (Nm 27, 3) and the other of Dathan and Abiram (Dt 11, 6); cf Ps 106. The present account combines both events into one narrative; but even here it is rather easy to separate the two, once certain proper names (vv 1. 6. 24. 32. 35) have been identified as glosses. The rebellion of the Reubenites, Dathan and Abiram, was of a political nature, against Moses alone as the civil leader; these rebels were punished by being swallowed alive in an earthquake. The rebellion of Korah was of a religious nature, against the religious leadership of both Moses and Aaron; about two hundred and fifty malcontents joined Korah's band; they were punished by fire. The parts of the present section which refer to the rebellion of Dathan and Abiram are vv 12-15 and vv 25-34 of chapter 16; the rest of chapter 16 and all of chapter 17 concern the rebellion of Korah.

atonement for the whole Israelite community; thus they will be forgiven the inadvertence for which they have brought their holocaust as an oblation to the LORD. ²⁶Not only the whole Israelite community, but also the aliens residing among you, shall be forgiven, since the fault of inadvertence affects all the people.

²⁷"However, if it is an individual who sins inadvertently,ᵃ he shall bring a yearling she-goat as a sin offering, ²⁸and the priest shall make atonement before the LORD for him who sinned inadvertently; when atonement has been made for him, he will be forgiven. ²⁹You shall have but one law for him who sins inadvertently, whether he be a native Israelite or an alien residing with you.

³⁰"But anyone who sins defiantly,ᵇ whether he be a native or an alien, insults the LORD, and shall be cut off from among his people. ³¹ ᶜ Since he has despised the word of the LORD and has broken his commandment, he must be cut off. He has only himself to blame."

The Sabbath-breaker. ³²While the Israelites were in the desert, a man was discovered gathering wood on the sabbath day. ³³Those who caught him at it brought him to Moses and Aaron and the whole assembly. ³⁴But they kept him in custody, for there was no clear decision* as to what should be done with him.ᵈ ³⁵Then the LORD said to Moses, "This man shall be put to death; let the whole community stone him outside the camp." ³⁶So the whole community led him outside the camp and stoned him to death, as the LORD had commanded Moses.

Tassels on the Cloak. ³⁷The LORD said to Moses, ³⁸"Speak to the Israelites and tell them that they and their descendants must put tassels* on the corners of their garments, fastening each corner tassel with a violet cord.ᵉ ³⁹When you use these tassels, let the sight of them remind you to keep all the commandments of the LORD, without going wantonly astray after the desires of your hearts and eyes. ⁴⁰Thus you will remember to keep all my commandments and be holy to your God. ⁴¹I, the LORD, am your God who, as God, brought you out of Egypt that I, the LORD, may be your God."ᶠ

CHAPTER 16

Rebellion of Korah. ¹Korah, son of Izhar, son of Kohath, son of Levi,* [and

Dathan and Abiram, sons of Eliab, son of Pallu, son of Reuben] took [2] two hundred and fifty Israelites who were leaders in the community, members of the council and men of note. They stood before Moses, [3] and held an assembly against Moses and Aaron, to whom they said,[g] "Enough from you! The whole community, all of them, are holy; the LORD is in their midst. Why then should you set yourselves over the LORD's congregation?"

[4] When Moses heard this, he fell prostrate. [5] Then he said to Korah and to all his band, "May the LORD make known tomorrow morning who belongs to him and who is the holy one and whom he will have draw near to him! Whom he chooses, he will have draw near him. [6] Do this: take your censers [Korah and all his band] [7] and put fire in them and place incense in them before the LORD tomorrow. He whom the LORD then chooses is the holy one. Enough from you Levites!"

[8] Moses also said to Korah, "Listen to me, you Levites! [9] [h] Is it too little for you that the God of Israel has singled you out from the community of Israel, to have you draw near him for the service of the LORD's Dwelling and to stand before the community to minister for them? [10] He has allowed you and your kinsmen, the descendants of Levi, to approach him, and yet you now seek the priesthood too. [11] It is therefore against the LORD that you and all your band are conspiring. For what has Aaron done that you should grumble against him?"

Rebellion of Dathan and Abiram. [12] Moses summoned Dathan and Abiram, sons of Eliab, but they answered, "We will not go.* [13] Are you not satisfied with having led us here away from a land flowing with milk and honey, to make us perish in the desert, that you must now lord it over us? [14] Far from bringing us to a land flowing with milk and honey, or giving us fields and vineyards for our inheritance, will you also gouge out our eyes?* No, we will not go."

[15] Then Moses became very angry and said to the LORD, "Pay no heed to their offering. I have never taken a single ass from them, nor have I wronged any one of them."[i]

Korah. [16] Moses said to Korah, "You and all your band shall appear before the LORD tomorrow—you and they and Aaron

too. [17] Then each of your two hundred and fifty followers shall take his own censer, put incense in it, and offer it to the LORD; and you and Aaron, each with his own censer, shall do the same." [18] So they all took their censers, and laying incense on the fire they had put in them, they took their stand by the entrance of the meeting tent along with Moses and Aaron. [19] Then, when Korah had assembled all his band against them at the entrance of the meeting tent, the glory of the LORD appeared to the entire community, [20] and the LORD said to Moses and Aaron, [21] "Stand apart from this band, that I may consume them at once." [22] But they fell prostrate and cried out, "O God, God of the spirits of all mankind, will one man's sin make you angry with the whole community?" [23] The LORD answered Moses, [24] "Speak to the community and tell them: Withdraw from the space around the Dwelling" [of Korah, Dathan and Abiram].

Punishment of Dathan and Abiram. [25] Moses, followed by the elders of Israel, arose and went to Dathan and Abiram.* [26] Then he warned the community, "Keep away from the tents of these wicked men and do not touch anything that is theirs: otherwise you too will be swept away because of all their sins." [27] When Dathan and Abiram had come out and were standing at the entrance of their tents with their wives and sons and little ones, [28] Moses said, "This is how you shall know that it was the LORD who sent me to do all I have done, and that it was not I who planned it: [29] if these men die an ordinary death, merely suffering the fate common to all mankind, then it was not the LORD who sent me. [30] But if the LORD does something entirely new, and the ground opens its mouth and swallows them alive down into the nether world, with all belonging to them, then you will know that these men have defied the LORD." [31] [j] No sooner had he finished saying all this than the ground beneath them split open, [32] and the earth opened its mouth and swallowed them

---

g Ps 106, 16ff; Sir 45, 19; 1 Cor 10, 10.—h Dt 10, 8.—i 1 Sm 12, 3.—j 31ff: Nm 26, 10; Lv 10, 2; Dt 11, 6; Ps 106, 7f.

16, 12: *We will not go:* to appear before Moses' tribunal.
16, 14: *Gouge out our eyes:* blind us to the real state of affairs.
16, 25: Since Dathan and Abiram had refused to go to Moses (vv 12ff), he, with the elders as witnesses, was obliged to go to their tent.

and their families [and all of Korah's men] and all their possessions. 33 They went down alive to the nether world with all belonging to them; the earth closed over them, and they perished from the community. 34 But all the Israelites near them fled at their shrieks, saying, "The earth might swallow us too!"

Punishment of Korah. 35 So they withdrew from the space around the Dwelling [of Korah,* Dathan and Abiram]. And fire from the LORD came forth which consumed the two hundred and fifty men who were offering the incense.

CHAPTER 17

1 The LORD said to Moses, 2 "Tell Eleazar, son of Aaron the priest, to remove the censers from the embers; and scatter the fire some distance away, 3 * for these sinners have consecrated the censers at the cost of their lives. Have them hammered into plates to cover the altar, because in being presented before the LORD they have become sacred. In this way they shall serve as a sign to the Israelites." 4 So Eleazar the priest had the bronze censers of those burned during the offering hammered into a covering for the altar, 5 in keeping with the orders which the LORD had given him through Moses. This cover was to be a reminder to the Israelites that no layman, no one who was not a descendant of Aaron, should approach the altar to offer incense before the LORD, lest he meet the fate of Korah and his band.

6 The next day the whole Israelite community grumbled against Moses and Aaron, saying, "It is you who have slain the LORD's people." 7 But while the community was deliberating against them, Moses and Aaron turned toward the meeting tent, and the cloud now covered it and the glory of the LORD appeared. 8 Then Moses and Aaron came to the front of the meeting tent, 9 and the LORD said to Moses and Aaron, 10 "Depart from this community, that I may consume them at once." But they fell prostrate.

11 Then Moses said to Aaron, "Take your censer, put fire from the altar in it, lay incense on it, and bring it quickly to the community to make atonement for them; for wrath has come forth from the LORD and the blow is falling."k 12 Obeying the orders of Moses, Aaron took his censer and ran in among the community, where the blow was already falling on the people. Then, as he offered the incense and made atonement for the people, 13 standing there between the living and the dead, the scourge was checked. 14 Yet fourteen thousand seven hundred died from the scourge, in addition to those who died because of Korah. 15 When the scourge had been checked, Aaron returned to Moses at the entrance of the meeting tent.

Aaron's Staff. 16 The LORD now said to Moses, 17 "Speak to the Israelites and get one staff* from them for each ancestral house, twelve tribal staffs in all, one from each of their tribal princes. Mark each man's name on his staff; 18 and mark Aaron's name on Levi's staff,* for the head of Levi's ancestral house shall also have a staff. 19 Then lay them down in the meeting tent, in front of the commandments, where I meet you. 20 There the staff of the man of my choice shall sprout. Thus will I suppress from my presence the Israelites' grumbling against you."

21 So Moses spoke to the Israelites, and their princes gave him staffs, twelve in all, one from each tribal prince; and Aaron's staff was with them. 22 Then Moses laid the staffs down before the LORD in the tent of the commandments. 23 The next day, when Moses entered the tent, Aaron's staff, representing the house of Levi, had sprouted and put forth not only shoots, but blossoms as well, and even bore ripe almonds! 24 Moses thereupon brought out all the staffs from the LORD's presence to the Israelites. After each prince identified his own staff and

k Wis 18, 20f.

16, 35: This verse continues v 24; the first sentence is transposed from v 27.

17, 3: Whatever was brought into intimate contact with something sacred shared in its sacredness. See note on Nm 19, 20.

17, 17: The staff was not merely an article of practical use, but also a symbol of authority; cf Gn 49, 10; Nm 24, 17; Jer 48, 17. Hence, the staff of a leader of a tribe was considered the emblem of his tribe; in fact, certain Hebrew words for "staff" also mean "tribe." Perhaps for this reason, to avoid confusion, the author here uses the term "ancestral house" instead of the ordinary word for "tribe."

17, 18: *Levi's staff:* it is not clear whether this is considered as one of the twelve mentioned in the preceding verse, or as a thirteenth staff. Sometimes Levi is reckoned as one of the twelve tribes (e.g., Dt 27, 12f), but more often the number twelve is arrived at by counting the two sub-tribes of Joseph, i.e., Ephraim and Manasseh, as distinct tribes. In this passage also it seems probable that the tribe of Levi is considered apart from the other twelve.

took it, [25] the LORD said to Moses, "Put back Aaron's staff in front of the commandments, to be kept there as a warning to the rebellious, so that their grumbling may cease before me; if it does not, they will die." [26] And Moses did as the LORD had commanded him.

Charge of the Sacred Things. [27] * Then the Israelites cried out to Moses, "We are perishing; we are lost, we are all lost! [28] Every time anyone approaches the Dwelling of the LORD, he dies! Are we to perish to the last man?"

CHAPTER 18

[1] The LORD said to Aaron,* "You and your sons as well as the other members of your ancestral house shall be responsible for the sanctuary; but the responsibility of the priesthood shall rest on you and your sons alone. [2] Bring with you also your other kinsmen of the tribe of Levi, your ancestral tribe, as your associates* and assistants, while you and your sons are in front of the tent of the commandments. [3] They shall look after your persons and the whole tent; however, they shall not come near the sacred vessels or the altar, lest both they and you die. [4] As your associates they shall have charge of all the work connected with the meeting tent. But no layman* shall come near you. [5] You shall have charge of the sanctuary and of the altar, that wrath may not fall again upon the Israelites.

[6] "Remember, it is I who have taken your kinsmen, the Levites, from the body of the Israelites; they are a gift to you,[l] dedicated to the LORD for the service of the meeting tent. [7] [m] But only you and your sons are to have charge of performing the priestly functions in whatever concerns the altar and the room within the veil.* I give you the priesthood as a gift. Any layman who draws near shall be put to death."

The Priests' Share of the Sacrifices. [8] The LORD said to Aaron,* "I myself have given you charge of the contributions made to me in the various sacred offerings of the Israelites;[n] by perpetual ordinance I have assigned them to you and to your sons as your priestly share. [9] You shall have the right to share in the oblations that are most sacred, in whatever they offer me as cereal offerings or sin offerings or guilt offerings;

these shares shall accrue to you and to your sons. [10] In eating them you shall treat them as most sacred; every male among you may partake of them. As sacred, they belong to you.

[11] "You shall also have what is removed from the gift in every wave offering* of the Israelites; by perpetual ordinance I have assigned it to you and to your sons and daughters.[o] All in your family who are clean may partake of it. [12] I have also assigned to you all the best[p] of the new oil and of the new wine and grain that they give to the LORD as their first fruits; [13] and likewise, of whatever grows on their land, the first products that they bring in to the LORD shall be yours; all of your family who are clean may partake of them. [14] Whatever is doomed* in Israel shall be yours. [15] Every living thing that opens the womb, whether of man or of beast, such as are to be offered to the LORD, shall be yours;[q] but you must let the first-born of man, as well as of unclean animals, be redeemed. [16] The ransom for a boy is to be paid when he is a month old; it is fixed at five silver shekels according to the sanctuary standard, twenty gerahs to the shekel. [17] But the first-born of cattle, sheep or goats shall not be redeemed; they are sacred. Their blood you must splash on the altar and their fat you must burn as a sweet-smelling oblation to the LORD. [18] [r] Their meat, however, shall be yours, just as the breast and the right leg of the wave offering belong to you. [19] By perpetual ordi-

---

l Nm 3, 9; 8, 19.—m Nm 3, 10.—n Nm 5, 9.—o Ex 29, 27f; Lv 7, 34; 10, 14.—p 12f: Dt 18, 4; 26, 2.—q Ex 13, 2.—r Lv 7, 31-34.

17, 27f: Logically these two verses belong immediately after Nm 16, 35.

18, 1ff: This law, which kept unqualified persons from contact with sacred things, is the answer to the Israelites' cry in Nm 17, 28. It is followed by other laws concerning priests and Levites.

18, 2: *Associates:* in Hebrew this word alludes to the popular etymology of the name "Levi." Cf Gn 29, 34.

18, 4: *Layman:* here, "one who is not a Levite"; in v 7, "one who is not a priest."

18, 7: *Veil:* the outer veil, or "curtain," is probably meant.

18, 8ff: Two classes of offerings are here distinguished: the *most sacred* offering, which only the male members of the priestly families could eat (vv 8ff) and the other offerings, which even the women of the priestly families could eat (vv 11-19).

18, 11: *Wave offering:* this included the breast and right leg (v 18), the shoulder of the peace offering (Lv 7, 30-34), and portions of the nazirite sacrifice (Nm 6, 19f).

18, 14: *Doomed:* in Hebrew, *herem,* which means here "set aside from profane use and made sacred to the Lord." Cf Lv 27, 21. 28.

nance I have assigned to you and to your sons and daughters all the contributions from the sacred gifts which the Israelites make to the LORD; this is an inviolable covenant* to last forever before the LORD, for you and for your descendants." [20] [s] Then the LORD said to Aaron,* "You shall not have any heritage in the land of the Israelites nor hold any portion among them; I will be your portion and your heritage among them.

Tithes Due the Levites. [21] "To the Levites, however, I hereby assign all tithes in Israel as their heritage in recompense for the service they perform in the meeting tent.[t] [22] The Israelites may no longer approach the meeting tent; else they will incur guilt deserving death. [23] Only the Levites are to perform the service of the meeting tent, and they alone shall be held responsible; this is a perpetual ordinance for all your generations. The Levites, therefore, shall not have any heritage among the Israelites, [24] for I have assigned to them as their heritage the tithes which the Israelites give as a contribution to the LORD. That is why I have ordered that they are not to have any heritage among the Israelites."

Tithes Paid by the Levites. [25] The LORD said to Moses, [26] "Give the Levites these instructions: When you receive from the Israelites the tithes I have assigned you from them as your heritage, you are to make a contribution from them to the LORD, a tithe of the tithes; [27] and your contribution will be credited to you as if it were grain from the threshing floor or new wine from the press. [28] Thus you too shall make a contribution from all the tithes you receive from the Israelites, handing over

---

[s] Dt 10, 9; 18, 1f; Jos 13, 33; Ez 44, 28.—[t] Heb 7, 5

18, 19: *An inviolable covenant:* literally, "a covenant of salt." Cf 2 Chr 13, 5. The reference may perhaps be to the preservative power of salt (cf Mt 5, 13); but more likely the phrase refers to the custom of partaking of the same salt in common to render a contract unbreakable. See note on Lv 2, 13.
18, 20: The priests and Levites were forbidden to own hereditary land such as the other Israelites possessed; therefore in the allotment of the land they were not to receive any portion of it. Certain cities, however, were assigned to them for their residence; cf Nm 35, 1-8.
19, 3: *Outside the camp:* several Fathers of the Church saw in this a prefiguring of the sacrificial death of Christ outside the walls of Jerusalem; cf Jn 19, 20; Heb 13, 12; in the purifying water, into which the ashes of the red heifer were put, they saw a type of the water of Baptism.
19, 4: *Toward the front of the meeting tent:* since the tabernacle faced the east (Ex 26, 15-30), the killing of the heifer took place east of the camp; in later times it was done on the Mount of Olives, east of the Temple.

---

to Aaron the priest the part to be contributed to the LORD. [29] From all the gifts that you receive, and from the best parts, you are to consecrate to the LORD your own full contribution.

[30] "Tell them also: Once you have made your contribution from the best part, the rest of the tithes will be credited to you Levites as if it were produce of the threshing floor or of the wine press. [31] Your families, as well as you, may eat them anywhere, since they are your recompense for service at the meeting tent. [32] You will incur no guilt so long as you make a contribution of the best part. Do not profane the sacred gifts of the Israelites and so bring death on yourselves."

CHAPTER 19

Ashes of the Red Heifer. [1] The LORD said to Moses and Aaron: [2] "This is the regulation which the law of the LORD prescribes. Tell the Israelites to procure for you a red heifer that is free from every blemish and defect and on which no yoke has ever been laid. [3] This is to be given to Eleazar the priest, to be led outside the camp* and slaughtered in his presence. [4] Eleazar the priest shall take some of its blood on his finger and sprinkle it seven times toward the front of the meeting tent.* [5] Then the heifer shall be burned in his sight, with its hide and flesh, its blood and offal; [6] and the priest shall take some cedar wood, hyssop and scarlet yarn and throw them into the fire in which the heifer is being burned. [7] The priest shall then wash his garments and bathe his body in water. He remains unclean until the evening, and only afterward may he return to the camp. [8] Likewise, he who burned the heifer shall wash his garments, bathe his body in water, and be unclean until evening. [9] Finally, a man who is clean shall gather up the ashes of the heifer and deposit them in a clean place outside the camp. There they are to be kept for preparing lustral water for the Israelite community. The heifer is a sin offering. [10] He who has gathered up the ashes of the heifer shall also wash his garments and be unclean until evening. This is a perpetual ordinance, both for the Israelites and for the aliens residing among them.

Use of the Ashes. [11] "Whoever touches the dead body of any human being shall be unclean for seven days; [12] he shall purify himself with the water on the third and on the seventh day, and then he will be clean again. But if he fails to purify himself on the third and on the seventh day, he will not become clean. [13] *u* Everyone who fails to purify himself after touching the body of any deceased person, defiles the Dwelling of the LORD and shall be cut off from Israel. Since the lustral water has not been splashed over him, he remains unclean; his uncleanness still clings to him.

[14] "This is the law: When a man dies in a tent, everyone who enters the tent, as well as everyone already in it, shall be unclean for seven days; [15] likewise, every vessel that is open, or with its lid unfastened, shall be unclean. [16] Moreover, everyone who in the open country touches a dead person, whether he was slain by the sword or died naturally, or who touches a human bone or a grave, shall be unclean for seven days. [17] * For anyone who is thus unclean, ashes from the sin offering shall be put in a vessel, and spring water shall be poured on them. [18] Then a man who is clean shall take some hyssop, dip it in this water, and sprinkle it on the tent and on all the vessels and persons that were in it, or on him who touched a bone, a slain person or other dead body, or a grave. [19] The clean man shall sprinkle the unclean on the third and on the seventh day; thus purified on the seventh day, he shall wash his garments and bathe his body in water, and in the evening he will be clean again. [20] * Any unclean man who fails to have himself purified shall be cut off from the community, because he defiles the sanctuary of the LORD. As long as the lustral water has not been splashed over him, he remains unclean. [21] This shall be a perpetual ordinance for you.

"One who sprinkles the lustral water shall wash his garments, and anyone who comes in contact with this water shall be unclean until evening. [22] Moreover, whatever the unclean person touches becomes unclean itself, and anyone who touches it becomes unclean until evening."

CHAPTER 20

Death of Miriam. [1] The whole Israelite community arrived in the desert of Zin in the first month,* and the people settled at Kadesh. It was here that Miriam died, and here that she was buried.

Water Famine at Kadesh. [2] As the community had no water, they held a council against Moses and Aaron. [3] The people contended with Moses, exclaiming, "Would that we too had perished with our kinsmen in the LORD's presence! [4] Why have you brought the LORD's community into this desert where we and our livestock are dying? [5] Why did you lead us out of Egypt, only to bring us to this wretched place which has neither grain nor figs nor vines nor pomegranates? Here there is not even water to drink!" [6] But Moses and Aaron went away from the assembly to the entrance of the meeting tent, where they fell prostrate.

Sin of Moses and Aaron. Then the glory of the LORD appeared to them, [7] and the LORD said to Moses, [8] "Take the staff and assemble the community, you and your brother Aaron, and in their presence order the rock to yield its waters. From the rock you shall bring forth water for the community and their livestock to drink." [9] So Moses took the staff from its place before the LORD, as he was ordered. [10] He and Aaron assembled the community in front of the rock, where he said to them, *v* "Listen to me, you rebels! Are we to bring water for you out of this rock?" [11] *w* Then, raising his hand, Moses struck the rock twice* with his staff, and water gushed out in abundance for the community and their livestock to drink. [12] * But the LORD said to Moses and Aaron, "Because you were not faithful to me in showing forth my sanctity before the Israelites, you shall

u Lv 15, 31.—v Ex 17, 5f.—w Ps 78, 15f; Wis 11, 4; 1 Cor 10, 4.

19, 17ff: "If . . . the sprinkled ashes of a heifer sanctify the unclean unto the cleansing of the flesh, how much more will the blood of Christ . . . cleanse your conscience from dead works?" (Heb 9, 13f).

19, 20: Ritual uncleanness is, as it were, contagious; so also sacredness; see note on Nm 17, 3.

20, 1: *The first month:* we would expect the mention also of the day and of the year (after the exodus) when this took place; cf similar dates in Nm 1, 1; 10, 11; 33, 38; Dt 1, 3. Here the full date seems to have been lost. Probably the Israelites arrived in Kadesh in the third year after the exodus. Cf Dt 1, 46. *The desert of Zin:* a barren region with a few good oases, southwest of the Dead Sea. See note on Nm 13, 21.

20, 11: *Twice:* perhaps because he had not sufficient faith to work the miracle with the first blow. Cf v 12.

20, 12f: The sin of Moses and Aaron consisted in doubting God's mercy toward the ever-rebellious people. *In showing forth my sanctity:* God's sacred power and glory: an allusion to the name of the place, *Kadesh,* which means "sanctified, sacred." *Meribah* means "contention." Cf Ex 17, 7.

not lead this community into the land I will give them."
¹³ These are the waters of Meribah,ˣ where the Israelites contended against the LORD, and where he revealed his sanctity among them.

Edom's Refusal. ¹⁴ From Kadesh Moses sent men to the king of Edom with the message: "Your brother Israel* has this to say: You know of all the hardships that have befallen us, ¹⁵ how our fathers went down to Egypt, where we stayed a long time, how the Egyptians maltreated us and our fathers, ¹⁶ and how, when we cried to the LORD,ʸ he heard our cry and sent an angel who led us out of Egypt. Now here we are at the town of Kadesh at the edge of your territory. ¹⁷ Kindly let us pass through your country. We will not cross any fields or vineyards, nor drink any well water, but we will go straight along the royal road* without turning to the right or to the left, until we have passed through your territory."
¹⁸ But Edom answered him, "You shall not pass through here; if you do, I will advance against you with the sword." ¹⁹ The Israelites insisted, "We want only to go up along the highway. If we or our livestock drink any of your water, we will pay for it. Surely there is no harm in merely letting us march through." ²⁰ But Edom still said, "No, you shall not pass through,"ᶻ and advanced against them with a large and

heavily armed force. ²¹ Therefore, since Edom refused to let them pass through their territory, Israel detoured around them.

Death of Aaron. ²² ᵃ Setting out from Kadesh, the whole Israelite community came to Mount Hor.* ²³ There at Mount Hor, on the border of the land of Edom, the LORD said to Moses and Aaron, ²⁴ "Aaron is about to be taken to his people; he shall not enter the land I am giving to the Israelites, because you both rebelled against my commandment at the waters of Meribah. ²⁵ Take Aaron and his son Eleazar and bring them up on Mount Hor.ᵇ ²⁶ Then strip Aaron of his garments and put them on his son Eleazar; for there Aaron shall be taken in death."
²⁷ Moses did as the LORD commanded. When they had climbed Mount Hor in view of the whole community, ²⁸ Moses stripped Aaron of his garments and put them on his son Eleazar. Then Aaron died there on top of the mountain.ᶜ When Moses and Eleazar came down from the mountain, ²⁹ all the community understood that Aaron had passed away; and for thirty days the whole house of Israel mourned him.

CHAPTER 21

Victory over Arad. ¹ When the Canaanite king of Arad,* who lived in the Negeb,ᵈ heard that the Israelites were coming along the way of Atharim, he engaged them in battle and took some of them captive. ² Israel then made this vow to the LORD: "If you deliver this people into my hand, I will doom their cities."ᵉ ³ Later, when the LORD heeded Israel's prayer and delivered up the Canaanites,ᶠ they doomed them and their cities. Hence that place was named Hormah.*

The Bronze Serpent. ⁴ From Mount Hor they set out on the Red Sea road, to bypass the land of Edom. But with their patience worn out by the journey, ⁵ the people complainedᵍ against God and Moses, "Why have you brought us up from Egypt to die in this desert, where there is no food or water? We are disgusted with this wretched food!"*
⁶ In punishment the LORD sent among the people saraph* serpents, which bitʰ the people so that many of them died.

---

x Nm 27, 14: Ex 17, 7.—y Ex 2, 23.—z Jgs 11, 17.—a 21f: Nm 33, 37.—b 25f: Dt 32, 50.—c Nm 33, 38.—d Nm 33, 40.—e Jos 6, 17; Jgs 1, 17.—f Nm 14, 45.—g Nm 11, 6; Ex 16, 3.—h Dt 8, 15; Wis 16, 5; 1 Cor 10, 9.

20, 14: *Your brother Israel:* the Edomites were descended from Esau, the brother of Jacob. Their country, to the southeast of the Dead Sea, was also known as Seir; cf Gn 25, 24ff; 36, 1. 8f.

20, 17: *The royal road:* an important highway, running north and south along the plateau east of the Dead Sea. In ancient times it was much used by caravans and armies; later it was improved by the Romans, and large stretches of it are still clearly recognizable.

20, 22: *Mount Hor:* not definitively identified, but probably to be sought in the vicinity of Kadesh. According to Dt 10, 6, Aaron died at Moserah (cf "Moseroth" in Nm 33, 30f), which is apparently the name of the region in which Mount Hor is situated.

21, 1-3: The account of this episode seems to be a later insertion here, for Nm 21, 4, belongs logically immediately after Nm 20, 29. Perhaps this is the same event as that mentioned in Jgs 1, 16f.

21, 3: *Hormah:* related to the Hebrew word *herem,* meaning "doomed." See notes on Nm 14, 45; 18, 14.

21, 5: *This wretched food:* apparently the manna is meant.

21, 6: *Saraph:* the Hebrew name for a certain species of venomous snakes; the word probably signifies "the fiery one," these snakes being so called from the burning effect of their poisonous bite.

⁷Then the people came to Moses and said, "We have sinned in complaining against the LORD and you. Pray the LORD to take the serpents from us." So Moses prayed for the people, ⁸and the LORD said to Moses, "Make a saraph and mount it on a pole, and if anyone who has been bitten looks at it, he will recover." * ⁹Moses accordingly made a bronze serpent* and mounted it on a pole, and whenever anyone who had been bitten by a serpent looked at the bronze serpent, he recovered.ⁱ

Journey around Moab. ¹⁰The Israelites moved on and encamped in Oboth.ʲ ¹¹Setting out from Oboth, they encamped in Iye-abarim* in the desert fronting Moab on the east. ¹²Setting out from there, they encamped in the Wadi Zered. ¹³Setting out from there, they encamped on the other side of the Arnon, in the desert that extends from the territory of the Amorites; for the Arnon forms Moab's boundary with the Amorites. ¹⁴Hence it is said in the "Book of the Wars of the LORD"*:

"Waheb in Suphah and the wadies,
¹⁵ Arnon and the wadi gorges
That reach back toward the site of Ar
and slant to the border of Moab."

¹⁶From there they went to Beer,* where there was the well of which the LORD said to Moses, "Bring the people together, and I will give them water." ¹⁷Then it was that Israel sang this song:

"Spring up, O well!—so sing to it—
¹⁸ The well that the princes sank,
that the nobles of the people dug,
with their scepters and their staffs."

From Beer they went to Mattanah, ¹⁹from Mattanah to Nahaliel, from Nahaliel to Bamoth, ²⁰from Bamoth to the cleft in the plateau of Moab at the headland of Pisgah that overlooks Jeshimon.*

Victory over Sihon. ²¹Now Israel sent men to Sihon, king of the Amorites, with the message, ²²"Let us pass through your country. We will not turn aside into any field or vineyard, nor will we drink any well water, but we will go straight along the royal road until we have passed through your territory." ²³Sihon,ᵏ however, would not let Israel pass through his territory, but mustered all his forces and advanced into the desert against Israel. When he reached Jahaz, he engaged

Israel in battle. ²⁴But Israel defeated him at the point of the sword, and took possession of his land from the Arnon to the Jabbok and as far as the country of the Ammonites, whose boundary was at Jazer. ²⁵ ˡ Israel seized all the towns here and settled in these towns of the Amorites, in Heshbon and all its dependencies. ²⁶Now Heshbon was the capital of Sihon, king of the Amorites, who had fought against the former king of Moab and had seized all his land from Jazer to the Arnon. ²⁷That is why the poets say:

"Come to Heshbon, let it be rebuilt,
let Sihon's capital be firmly constructed.
²⁸ For fire went forth from Heshbon
and a blaze from the city of Sihon;
It consumed the cities of Moab
and swallowed up the high places of the Arnon.

²⁹ Woe to you, O Moab!
You are ruined, O people of Chemosh!*
He let his sons become fugitives
and his daughters be taken captive
by the Amorite king Sihon.
³⁰ Their plowland is ruined from Heshbon to Dibon;
Ar is laid waste; fires blaze as far as Medeba."

³¹When Israel had settled in the land of the Amorites, ³²Moses sent spies to Jazer; Israel then captured it with its dependen-

---

i Wis 16, 6f. 10; Jn 3, 14f.—j Nm 33, 43f.—k Dt 2, 32; Jgs 11, 20.—l 25f: Jos 21, 39; Jgs 11, 26.

21, 8: *If anyone who has been bitten looks at it, he will recover:* "and as Moses lifted up the serpent in the desert, even so must the Son of Man be lifted up, that those who believe in him may not perish, but may have life everlasting" (Jn 3, 14f).

21, 9: King Hezekiah, in his efforts to abolish idolatry, "smashed the bronze serpent which Moses had made" (2 Kgs 18, 4).

21, 11: *Iye-abarim:* probably means "the ruins in the Abarim (Mountains)." See note on Nm 27, 12.

21, 14: *The "Book of the Wars of the Lord":* an ancient collection of Israelite songs, now lost. *Waheb in Suphah:* since neither place is mentioned elsewhere, it is quite uncertain whether these dubious Hebrew words are even to be considered as place names; some Hebrew words apparently lost must have preceded this phrase.

21, 16: *Beer:* means a well.

21, 20: *Jeshimon:* "the wasteland"; in 1 Sm 23, 19. 24, and 26, 1. 3, this is the desert of Judah, on the western side of the Dead Sea, but here and in Nm 23, 28, it seems to refer to the southern end of the Jordan valley where Beth-jeshimoth was situated.

21, 29: *Chemosh:* the chief god of the Moabites, and mentioned as such in the famous inscription of Mesha, king of Moab, who was the contemporary of the dynasty of Omri in Israel. Cf 1 Kgs 11, 7. 33; 2 Kgs 23, 13; Jer 48, 7. 13.

cies and dispossessed the Amorites who were there.

Victory over Og. [33] [m] Then they turned and went up along the road to Bashan. But Og, king of Bashan, advanced against them with all his people to give battle at Edrei. [34] The LORD, however, said to Moses, "Do not be afraid of him; for into your hand I will deliver him with all his people and his land. Do to him as you did to Sihon, king of the Amorites, who lived in Heshbon." [n] [35] So they struck him down with his sons and all his people, until not a survivor was left to him, and they took possession of his land.

CHAPTER 22

[1] Then the Israelites moved on and encamped in the plains of Moab* on the other side of the Jericho stretch of the Jordan.

III: ON THE PLAINS OF MOAB

Balaam Summoned. [2] Now Balak, son of Zippor, saw all that Israel did to the Amorites. [3] Indeed, Moab feared the Israelites greatly because of their numbers, and detested them. [4] So Moab said to the elders of Midian, "Soon this horde will devour all the country around us as an ox devours the grass of the field." And Balak, Zippor's son, who was king of Moab at that time, [5] sent messengers to Balaam, son of Beor, at Pethor on the Euphrates, in the land of the Amawites, summoning him with these words, "A people has come here from Egypt who now cover the face of the earth and are settling down opposite us! [6] Please come and curse this people for us;* they are stronger than we are. We may then be able to defeat them and drive them out of the country. For I know that whoever you bless is blessed and whoever you curse is

---

m Dt 3, 1ff.—n Ps 136, 17ff.—o Nm 24, 13.

22, 1: *The plains of Moab:* the lowlands to the northeast of the Dead Sea, between the Jordan and the foothills below Mount Nebo. Here the Israelites remained until they crossed the Jordan, as told in Jos 1—4. *Jericho* lay to the west of the Jordan.

22, 6: *Curse this people for us:* Balak believed that if Balaam forecast an evil omen for Israel, this evil would come to pass, as if by magic. Balaam was a soothsayer or foreteller; cf Jos 13, 22.

22, 22: *The anger of God flared up:* not merely because Balaam was going to Balak, for he had God's permission for the journey (v 20), but perhaps because he was tempted by avarice to curse Israel against God's command. "They have followed the way of Balaam, son of Bosor, who loved the wages of wrongdoing" (2 Pt 2, 15); "and have rushed on thoughtlessly into the error of Balaam for the sake of gain" (Jude 11). Cf v 32 and compare Ex 4, 18-26.

---

cursed." [7] Then the elders of Moab and of Midian left with the divination fee in hand and went to Balaam. When they had given him Balak's message, [8] he said to them in reply, "Stay here overnight, and I will give you whatever answer the LORD gives me." So the princes of Moab lodged with Balaam.

[9] Then God came to Balaam and said, "Who are these men visiting you?" [10] Balaam answered God, "Balak, son of Zippor, king of Moab, sent me the message: [11] 'This people that came here from Egypt now cover the face of the earth. Please come and lay a curse on them for us; we may then be able to give them battle and drive them out.' " [12] But God said to Balaam, "Do not go with them and do not curse this people, for they are blessed." [13] The next morning Balaam arose and told the princes of Balak, "Go back to your own country, for the LORD has refused to let me go with you." [14] So the princes of Moab went back to Balak with the report, "Balaam refused to come with us."

Second Appeal to Balaam. [15] Balak again sent princes, who were more numerous and more distinguished than the others. [16] On coming to Balaam they told him, "This is what Balak, son of Zippor, has to say: Please do not refuse to come to me. [17] I will reward you very handsomely and will do anything you ask of me. Please come and lay a curse on this people for me." [18] [o] But Balaam replied to Balak's officials, "Even if Balak gave me his house full of silver and gold, I could not do anything, small or great, contrary to the command of the LORD, my God. [19] But, you too shall stay here overnight, till I learn what else the LORD may tell me."

[20] That night God came to Balaam and said to him, "If these men have come to summon you, you may go with them; yet only on the condition that you do exactly as I tell you." [21] So the next morning when Balaam arose, he saddled his ass, and went off with the princes of Moab.

The Talking Ass. [22] But now the anger of God flared up* at him for going, and the angel of the LORD stationed himself on the road to hinder him as he was riding along on his ass, accompanied by two of his servants. [23] When the ass saw the angel of the LORD standing on the road with sword drawn, she turned off the road and went into the field, and Balaam had to beat her to bring her back on the road. ²⁴Then the angel of the LORD took his stand in a narrow lane between vineyards with a stone wall on each side. ²⁵When the ass saw the angel of the LORD there, she shrank against the wall; and since she squeezed Balaam's leg against it, he beat her again. ²⁶The angel of the LORD then went ahead, and stopped next in a passage so narrow that there was no room to move either to the right or to the left. ²⁷When the ass saw the angel of the LORD there, she cowered under Balaam. So, in anger, he again beat the ass with his stick.

²⁸ ᵖ But now the LORD opened the mouth of the ass, and she asked Balaam, "What have I done to you that you should beat me these three times?" ²⁹"You have acted so willfully against me," said Balaam to the ass, "that if I but had a sword at hand, I would kill you here and now." ³⁰But the ass said to Balaam, "Am I not your own beast, and have you not always ridden upon me until now? Have I been in the habit of treating you this way before?" "No," replied Balaam.

³¹Then the LORD removed the veil from Balaam's eyes, so that he too saw the angel of the LORD standing on the road with sword drawn; and he fell on his knees and bowed to the ground. ³²But the angel of the LORD said to him, "Why have you beaten your ass these three times? It is I who have come armed to hinder you because this rash journey of yours is directly opposed to me. ³³When the ass saw me, she turned away from me these three times. If she had not turned away from me, I would have killed you; her I would have spared." ³⁴Then Balaam said to the angel of the LORD, "I have sinned. Yet I did not know that you stood against me to oppose my journey. Since it has displeased you, I will go back home." ³⁵But the angel of the LORD said to Balaam, "Go with the men; but you may say only what I tell you." So Balaam went on with the princes of Balak.

³⁶When Balak heard that Balaam was coming, he went out to meet him at the boundary city Ir-moab on the Arnon at the end of the Moabite territory. ³⁷And he said to Balaam, "I sent an urgent summons to you! Why did you not come to me? Did you think I could not reward you?" ³⁸Balaam answered him, "Well, I have

come to you after all. But what power have I to say anything? I can speak only what God puts in my mouth." ³⁹Then Balaam went with Balak, and they came to Kiriath-huzoth. ⁴⁰Here Balak slaughtered oxen and sheep, and sent portions to Balaam and to the princes who were with him.

The First Oracle. ⁴¹The next morning Balak took Balaam up on Bamoth-baal, and from there he saw some of the clans.

CHAPTER 23

¹Then Balaam said to Balak, "Build me seven altars, and prepare seven bullocks and seven rams for me here." ²So he did as Balaam had ordered, offering a bullock and a ram on each altar. And Balak said to him, "I have erected the seven altars, and have offered a bullock and a ram on each." ³Balaam then said to him, "Stand here by your holocaust while I go over there. Perhaps the LORD will meet me, and then I will tell you whatever he lets me see." He went out on the barren height, ⁴and God met him. ⁵When he had put an utterance in Balaam's mouth, the LORD said to him, "Go back to Balak, and speak accordingly." ⁶So he went back to Balak, who was still standing by his holocaust together with all the princes of Moab. ⁷Then Balaam gave voice to his oracle:

> From Aram* has Balak brought me here,
> Moab's king, from the Eastern Mountains:�q
> "Come and lay a curse for me on Jacob come and denounce Israel."
> ⁸ How can I curse whom God has not cursed?
> How denounce whom the LORD has not denounced?
> ⁹ For from the top of the crags I see him, from the heights I behold him.
> Here is a people that lives apart* and does not reckon itself among the nations.
> ¹⁰Who has ever counted the dust of Jacob,

p 2 Pt 2, 16.—q Nm 22, 6.

23, 7: *Aram:* the ancient name of the region later known as Syria. *The Eastern Mountains:* the low ranges in the Syrian desert near the Euphrates and Balaam's town of Pethor; cf Nm 22, 5.

23, 9: *A people that lives apart:* Israel, as the chosen people of God, occupied a unique place among the nations, from which they kept themselves aloof.

or numbered Israel's wind-borne
particles?*
May I die the death of the just,
may my descendants be as many as
theirs!

11 "What have you done to me?" cried
Balak to Balaam. "It was to curse my foes
that I brought you here; instead, you have
even blessed them." 12 Balaam replied, "Is
it not what the LORD puts in my mouth
that I must repeat with care?"
The Second Oracle. 13 Then Balak said to
him, "Please come with me to another
place* from which you can see only some
and not all of them, and from there curse
them for me." 14 So he brought him to the
lookout field on the top of Pisgah, where
he built seven altars and offered a bullock
and a ram on each of them. 15 Balaam then
said to Balak, "Stand here by your holocaust, while I seek a meeting over there."
16 Then the LORD met Balaam, and having
put an utterance in his mouth, he said to
him, "Go back to Balak, and speak accordingly." 17 So he went back to Balak, who
was still standing by his holocaust together
with the princes of Moab. When Balak
asked him, "What did the LORD say?"
18 Balaam gave voice to his oracle:

Be aroused, O Balak, and hearken;
    give ear to my testimony, O son of
        Zippor!
19 God is not man that he should speak
        falsely,
    nor human, that he should change
        his mind.
Is he one to speak and not act,
    to decree and not fulfill?
20 It is a blessing I have been given to pro-
        nounce;
    a blessing which I cannot restrain.
21 Misfortune is not observed in Jacob,
    nor misery* seen in Israel.
The LORD, his God, is with him;
    with him is the triumph of his King.

r Nm 24, 8.—s Nm 24, 9; Gn 49, 9.

23, 10: *The dust of Jacob . . . Israel's wind-borne particles:* the Israelites will be as numerous as dust in a desert
sandstorm. *May I . . . as many as theirs:* a formula by which
Balaam swears he is speaking the truth; he sees the reward of virtue in having numerous descendants.
23, 13: *To another place:* Balak thought that if Balaam
would view Israel from a different site, he could forecast a different kind of omen.
23, 21: *Misfortune . . . misery:* Balaam admits that he is unable to predict any evils for Israel.
23, 22: *A wild bull of towering might:* the reference is to
Israel, rather than to God.

22 It is God who brought him out of
    Egypt,r
    a wild bull of towering might.*
23 No, there is no sorcery against Jacob,
    nor omen against Israel.
It shall yet be said of Jacob,
    and of Israel, "Behold what God has
        wrought!"
24 Here is a people that springs up like a
        lioness,
    and stalks forth like a lion;
It rests not till it has devoured its prey
    and has drunk the blood of the slain.s

25 "Even though you cannot curse
them," said Balak to Balaam, "at least do
not bless them." 26 But Balaam answered
Balak, "Did I not warn you that I must do
all that the LORD tells me?"
The Third Oracle. 27 Then Balak said to
Balaam, "Come, let me bring you to another place; perhaps God will approve of
your cursing them for me from there."
28 So he took Balaam to the top of Peor,
that overlooks Jeshimon. 29 Balaam then
said to him, "Here build me seven altars;
and here prepare for me seven bullocks
and seven rams." 30 And Balak did as
Balaam had ordered, offering a bullock
and a ram on each altar.

CHAPTER 24

1 Balaam, however, perceiving that the
LORD was pleased to bless Israel, did not
go aside as before to seek omens, but
turned his gaze toward the desert. 2 When
he raised his eyes and saw Israel encamped, tribe by tribe, the spirit of God
came upon him, 3 and he gave voice to his
oracle:

The utterance of Balaam, son of Beor,
    the utterance of the man whose eye is
        true,
4 The utterance of one who hears what
        God says,
    and knows what the Most High
        knows,
Of one who sees what the Almighty
        sees,
    enraptured, and with eyes unveiled:
5 How goodly are your tents, O Jacob;
    your encampments, O Israel!
6 They are like gardens beside a stream,
    like the cedars planted by the LORD.
7 His wells shall yield free-flowing wa-
        ters,

he shall have the sea within reach;
His king shall rise higher than. . . .
    and his royalty shall be exalted.
8 It is God who brought him out of
    Egypt,
    a wild bull of towering might.
He shall devour the nations like grass,
    their bones he shall strip bare.[t]
9 He lies crouching like a lion,
    or like a lioness; who shall arouse
    him?
Blessed is he who blesses you,
    and cursed is he who curses you![u]

10 Balak beat his palms* together in a blaze of anger at Balaam and said to him, "It was to curse my foes that I summoned you here; yet three times now you have even blessed them instead![v] 11 Be off at once, then, to your home. I promised to reward you richly, but the LORD has withheld the reward from you!" 12 Balaam replied to Balak, "Did I not warn the very messengers whom you sent to me, 13 'Even if Balak gave me his house full of silver and gold, I could not of my own accord do anything, good or evil, contrary to the command of the LORD'? Whatever the LORD says I must repeat.[w]

The Fourth Oracle. 14 "But now that I am about to go to my own people, let me first warn you what this people will do to your people in the days to come." 15 Then Balaam gave voice to his oracle:

The utterance of Balaam, son of Beor,
    the utterance of the man whose eye is
    true,
16 The utterance of one who hears what
    God says,
    and knows what the Most High
    knows,
Of one who sees what the Almighty
    sees,
    enraptured and with eyes unveiled.
17 I see him, though not now;
    I behold him, though not near:
A star shall advance from Jacob,
    and a staff* shall rise from Israel,
That shall smite the brows of Moab,[x]
    and the skulls of all the Shuthites,
18 Till Edom is dispossessed,
    and no fugitive is left in Seir.
Israel shall do valiantly,
19   and Jacob shall overcome his foes.

20 Upon seeing Amalek, Balaam gave voice to his oracle:

First* of the peoples was Amalek,
    but his end is to perish forever.[y]
21 Upon seeing the Kenites,* he gave voice to his oracle:

Your abode is enduring, O smith,
    and your nest is set on a cliff;
22 Yet destined for burning—
    even as I watch—are your inhabitants.

23 Upon seeing. . . . he gave voice to his oracle:

    * Alas, who shall survive of Ishmael,
24   to deliver his people from the hands
    of the Kittim?
When they have conquered Asshur and
    conquered Eber,
He too shall perish forever.

25 Then Balaam set out on his journey home; and Balak also went his way.

CHAPTER 25

Worship of Baal of Peor. 1 While Israel was living at Shittim,* the people degraded themselves by having illicit relations with the Moabite women.[z] 2 These then invited the people to the sacrifices of their god, and the people ate of the sacrifices[a] and worshiped their god. 3 When Israel thus submitted to the rites of Baal of Peor,[b] the LORD's anger flared up against Israel, 4 [c] and he said to Moses, "Gather

t Nm 23, 22.—u Nm 23, 24; Gn 12, 3; 27, 29; 49, 9.—v Nm 23, 11.—w Nm 22, 18.—x 2 Sm 8, 2.—y Ex 17, 14; 1 Sm 15, 3.—z Nm 31, 16.—a Ex 34, 15f.—b Ps 106, 28; Hos 9, 10.—c Dt 4, 3.

24, 10: *Balak beat his palms:* a sign of disclaiming any responsibility for paying the promised reward.

24, 17: *A star . . . a staff:* many of the Fathers have understood this as a Messianic prophecy, although it is not referred to anywhere in the New Testament; in this sense the *star* is Christ himself, just as he is the *staff from Israel;* cf Is 11, 1. But it is doubtful whether this passage is to be connected with the "star of the Magi" in Mt 2, 1-12. *The Shuthites:* mentioned in other documents of this period as nomads on the border of Palestine.

24, 20: *First:* literally "the beginning." Amalek was an aboriginal people in Palestine and therefore considered as of great antiquity. There is a deliberate contrast here between the words *first* and *end.*

24, 21: *The Kenites* lived in high strongholds in the mountains of southern Palestine and the Sinai Peninsula, and were skilled in working the various metals found in their territory. Their name is connected, at least by popular etymology, with the Hebrew word for "smith"; of similar sound is the Hebrew word for "nest"—hence the play on words in the present passage.

24, 23f: The translation of this short oracle is based on a reconstructed text and is rather uncertain. *Ishmael:* the survival of Ishmael is indicated in Gn 17, 20; 21, 13. 18.

25, 1: *Shittim:* the full name was Abel-shittim, a locality at the foot of the mountains in the northeastern corner of *the plains of Moab* (Nm 33, 49). *Illicit relations:* perhaps as part of the licentious worship of Baal of Peor.

all the leaders of the people, and hold a public execution* of the guilty ones before the LORD, that his blazing wrath may be turned away from Israel." [5] So Moses told the Israelite judges, "Each of you shall kill those of his men who have submitted to the rites of Baal of Peor."

Zeal of Phinehas. [6] Yet a certain Israelite came and brought in a Midianite woman* to his clansmen in the view of Moses and of the whole Israelite community, while they were weeping at the entrance of the meeting tent. [7] [d] When Phinehas, son of Eleazar, son of Aaron the priest, saw this, he left the assembly, and taking a lance in hand, [8] followed the Israelite into his retreat where he pierced the pair of them, the Israelite and the woman. Thus the slaughter of Israelites was checked; [9] but only after twenty-four thousand had died.

[10] Then the LORD said to Moses, [11] "Phinehas, son of Eleazar, son of Aaron the priest, has turned my anger from the Israelites by his zeal for my honor* among them; that is why I did not put an end to the Israelites for the offense to my honor. [12] [e] Announce, therefore, that I hereby give him my pledge of friendship, [13] which shall be for him and for his descendants after him the pledge of an everlasting priesthood, because he was zealous on behalf of his God and thus made amends for the Israelites."

[14] * The Israelite slain with the Midianite woman was Zimri, son of Salu, prince of an ancestral house of the Simeonites. [15] The slain Midianite woman was Cozbi,

d Ps 106, 30.—e 12f: Sir 45, 23f; Ps 106, 31; 1 Mc 2, 26. 54.—f 17f: Nm 31, 2-12.—g Nm 1, 2f.—h 5f: 1 Chr 5, 3.—i 9f: Nm 16, 1. 32.

25, 4: *Hold a public execution:* the same phrase occurs in 2 Sm 21, 6-14, where the context shows that at least a part of the penalty consisted in being denied honorable burial. In both passages, dismemberment as a punishment for the breaking of covenant pledges is a current understanding of the phrase.

25, 6: *Midianite woman:* at this time the Midianites were leagued with the Moabites in opposing Israel; cf Nm 22, 4. 7. Balaam had induced both the Midianites (Nm 31, 16) and the Moabites (Rv 2, 14) to lure the Israelites to the obscene rites of Baal of Peor. *They were weeping:* on account of the plague that had struck them; cf v 8.

25, 11: *For my honor:* by taking vengeance on those who had made Baal of Peor a rival of the Lord.

25, 14f: The nobility of the slain couple is mentioned in order to stress the courage of Phinehas in punishing them. The zeal of Phinehas became proverbial; cf Ps 106, 30; Sir 45, 23; 1 Mc 2, 26. 54.

25, 16ff: The account of the execution of this command is given in Nm 31, 1-18.

26, 19: This is the last verse of Ch 25.

26, 12: *Nemuel:* so also in Gn 46, 10; 1 Chr 4, 24. In Ex 6, 15, the same man is called "Jemuel"; it is uncertain which form is correct.

daughter of Zur, who was head of a clan, an ancestral house, in Midian.

Vengeance on the Midianites. [16] * The LORD then said to Moses, [17] [f] "Treat the Midianites as enemies and crush them, [18] for they have been your enemies by their wily dealings with you as regards Peor and as regards their kinswoman Cozbi, the daughter of the Midianite prince, who was killed at the time of the slaughter because of Peor."

CHAPTER 26

The Second Census. [19] After the slaughter* [1] the LORD said to Moses and Eleazar, son of Aaron the priest, [2] "Take a census, by ancestral houses, throughout the community of the Israelites of all those of twenty years or more who are fit for military service in Israel." [g] [3] So on the plains of Moab along the Jericho stretch of the Jordan, Moses and the priest Eleazar registered [4] those of twenty years or more, as the LORD had commanded Moses.

The Israelites who came out of the land of Egypt were as follows:

[5] [h] Of Reuben, the first-born of Israel, the Reubenites by clans were: through Hanoch the clan of the Hanochites, through Pallu the clan of the Palluites, [6] through Hezron the clan of the Hezronites, through Carmi the clan of the Carmites. [7] These were the clans of the Reubenites, of whom forty-three thousand seven hundred and thirty men were registered.

[8] From Pallu descended Eliab, [9] and the descendants of Eliab were Dathan and Abiram[i]—the same Dathan and Abiram, councilors of the community, who revolted against Moses and Aaron [like Korah's band when it rebelled against the LORD]. [10] The earth opened its mouth and swallowed them as a warning [Korah too and the band that died when the fire consumed two hundred and fifty men. [11] The descendants of Korah, however, did not die out].

[12] The Simeonites by clans were: through Nemuel* the clan of the Nemuelites, through Jamin the clan of the Jaminites, through Jachin the clan of the Jachinites, [13] through Sohar the clan of the Soharites, through Shaul the clan of the Shaulites. [14] These were the clans of the Simeonites, of whom twenty-two thousand two hundred men were registered.

[15] The Gadites by clans were: through Zephon the clan of the Zephonites,

through Haggi the clan of the Haggites, through Shuni the clan of the Shunites, 16 through Ozni the clan of the Oznites, through Eri the clan of the Erites, 17 through Arod the clan of the Arodites, through Areli the clan of the Arelites. 18 These were the clans of the Gadites, of whom forty thousand five hundred men were registered.

19 The sons of Judah who died in the land of Canaan were Er and Onan.*j* 20 The Judahites by clans were: through Shelah the clan of the Shelahites, through Perez the clan of the Perezites, through Zerah the clan of the Zerahites. 21 The Perezites were: through Hezron the clan of the Hezronites, through Hamul the clan of the Hamulites. 22 These were the clans of Judah, of whom seventy-six thousand five hundred men were registered.

23 The Issacharites by clans were: through Tola the clan of the Tolaites, through Puvah the clan of the Puvahites, 24 through Jashub the clan of the Jashubites, through Shimron the clan of the Shimronites. 25 These were the clans of Issachar, of whom sixty-four thousand three hundred men were registered.

26 The Zebulunites by clans were: through Sered the clan of the Seredites, through Elon the clan of the Elonites, through Jahleel the clan of the Jahleelites. 27 These were the clans of the Zebulunites, of whom sixty thousand five hundred men were registered.

28 The sons of Joseph were Manasseh and Ephraim. 29 The Manassehites by clans were: through Machir the clan of the Machirites, through Gilead, a descendant of Machir, the clan of the Gileadites. 30 The Gileadites were: through Abiezer the clan of the Abiezrites, through Helek the clan of the Helekites, 31 through Asriel the clan of the Asrielites, through Shechem the clan of the Shechemites, 32 through Shemida the clan of the Shemidaites, through Hepher the clan of the Hepherites. 33 *k* Zelophehad, son of Hepher, had no sons, but only daughters, whose names were Mahlah, Noah, Hoglah, Milcah and Tirzah. 34 These were the clans of Manasseh, of whom fifty-two thousand seven hundred men were registered.

35 The Ephraimites by clans were: through Shuthelah the clan of the Shuthelahites, through Becher the clan of the Bechrites, through Tahan the clan of the Tahanites. 36 The Shuthelahites were: through Eran the clan of the Eranites. 37 These were the clans of the Ephraimites, of whom thirty-two thousand five hundred men were registered.

These were the descendants of Joseph by clans.

38 The Benjaminites by clans were: through Bela the clan of the Belaites, through Ashbel the clan of the Ashbelites, through Ahiram the clan of the Ahiramites, 39 through Shupham the clan of the Shuphamites, through Hupham the clan of the Huphamites. 40 The descendants of Bela were Arad and Naaman: through Arad the clan of the Aradites, through Naaman the clan of the Naamanites. 41 These were the Benjaminites by clans, of whom forty-five thousand six hundred men were registered.

42 The Danites by clans were: through Shuham the clan of the Shuhamites. These were the clans of Dan, 43 of whom sixty-four thousand four hundred men were registered.

44 The Asherites by clans were: through Imnah the clan of the Imnites, through Ishvi the clan of the Ishvites, through Beriah the clan of the Beriites, 45 through Heber the clan of the Heberites, through Malchiel the clan of the Malchielites. 46 The name of Asher's daughter was Serah. 47 These were the clans of Asher, of whom fifty-three thousand four hundred men were registered.

48 The Naphtalites by clans were: through Jahzeel the clan of the Jahzeelites, through Guni the clan of the Gunites, 49 through Jezer the clan of the Jezerites, through Shillem the clan of the Shillemites. 50 These were the clans of Naphtali, of whom forty-five thousand four hundred men were registered.

51 These six hundred and one thousand seven hundred and thirty were the Israelites who registered.

Allotment of the Land. 52 * The LORD said to Moses, 53 *l* "Among these groups

---

j Gn 38, 7. 10; 46, 12; 1 Chr 2, 3.—k Nm 27, 1; 36, 11; Jos 17, 3.—l Jos 11, 23.

26, 52-56: The division of Canaan among the various tribes and clans and families was determined partly by the size of each group and partly by lot. Perhaps the lots determined the respective locality of each tribal land and the section reserved for each clan, while the relative size of the allotted locality and section depended on the numerical strength of each group. The Hebrews considered the outcome of the drawing of lots as an expression of God's will; cf Acts 1, 23-26.

the land shall be divided as their heritage in keeping with the number of individuals in each group. [54] *m* To a large group you shall assign a large heritage, to a small group a small heritage, each group receiving its heritage in proportion to the number of men registered in it. [55] But the land shall be divided by lot, as the heritage of the various ancestral tribes. [56] As the lot falls shall each group, large or small, be assigned its heritage."

Census of the Levites. [57] The Levites registered by clans were: through Gershon the clans of the Gershonites, through Kohath the clan of the Kohathites, through Merari the clans of the Merarites. [58] These also were clans of Levi: the clan of the Libnites, the clan of the Hebronites, the clan of the Mahlites, the clan of the Mushites, the clan of the Korahites.

Among the descendants of Kohath was Amram, [59] whose wife was named Jochebed. She also was of the tribe of Levi, born to the tribe in Egypt. To Amram she bore Aaron and Moses and their sister Miriam. [60] To Aaron were born Nadab and Abihu, Eleazar and Ithamar. [61] But Nadab and Abihu died when they offered profane fire before the LORD.

[62] The total number of male Levites one month or more of age, who were registered, was twenty-three thousand. *n* They were not registered with the other Israelites, however, for no heritage was given them among the Israelites.

[63] These, then, were the men registered by Moses and the priest Eleazar in the census of the Israelites taken on the plains of Moab along the Jericho stretch of the Jordan. [64] Among them there was not a man of those who had been registered by Moses

---

m Nm 33, 54; 35, 8.—*n* Nm 3, 39.—*o* Nm 14, 22ff. 29.—*p* Nm 26, 33; Jos 17, 3.—*q* Jer 32, 6-9.—*r* Dt 3, 27; 32, 49; 34, 1.—*s* 13f: Nm 20, 12. 24.—*t* Dt 32, 51.

27, 3: *He did not join . . . against the Lord:* had he done so, he and his heirs could have rightly been deprived of the privilege of receiving a portion in the Promised Land.

27, 5-11: The purpose of this law, as also that of the related laws in Nm 36, 2-10 (heiresses to marry within the same tribe), Dt 25, 5-10 (levirate marriage), and Lv 25, 10 (return of property in the jubilee year), was to keep the landed property within the proper domain of each tribe.

27, 12: *The Abarim Mountains:* the range on the eastern side of the Dead Sea.

27, 16: *The God of the spirits of all mankind:* the sense is either that God knows the character and abilities of all men and therefore knows best whom to appoint (cf Acts 1, 24), or, more probably, that God is Master of life and death and therefore can call Moses from this world whenever he wishes; cf the same phrase in Nm 16, 22, where "spirit" evidently means "the life principle."

---

and the priest Aaron in the census of the Israelites taken in the desert of Sinai. [65] *o* For the LORD had told them that they would surely die in the desert, and not one of them was left except Caleb, son of Jephunneh, and Joshua, son of Nun.

CHAPTER 27

Zelophehad's Daughters. [1] Zelophehad, son of Hepher, son of Gilead, son of Machir, son of Manasseh, son of Joseph, had daughters named Mahlah, Noah, Hoglah, Milcah and Tirzah,*p* They came forward, [2] and standing in the presence of Moses, the priest Eleazar, the princes, and the whole community at the entrance of the meeting tent, said: [3] "Our father died in the desert. Although he did not join those who banded together against the LORD* [in Korah's band], he died for his own sin without leaving any sons. [4] But why should our father's name be withdrawn from his clan merely because he had no son? Let us, therefore, have property among our father's kinsmen."

Laws Concerning Heiresses. [5] * When Moses laid their case before the LORD, [6] the LORD said to him, [7] "The plea of Zelophehad's daughters is just; you shall give them hereditary property among their father's kinsmen, letting their father's heritage pass on to them. [8] Therefore, tell the Israelites: If a man dies without leaving a son, you shall let his heritage pass on to his daughter; [9] if he has no daughter, you shall give his heritage to his brothers; [10] if he has no brothers, you shall give his heritage to his father's brothers; [11] if his father had no brothers, you shall give his heritage to his nearest relative in his clan, who shall then take possession of it." This is the legal norm for the Israelites, as the LORD commanded Moses.*q*

Joshua To Succeed Moses. [12] The LORD said to Moses, "Go up here into the Abarim Mountains* and view the land that I am giving to the Israelites.*r* [13] When you have viewed it, you too shall be taken to your people, as was your brother Aaron,*s* [14] because in the rebellion of the community in the desert of Zin you both rebelled against my order to manifest my sanctity to them by means of the water."*t* [This is the water of Meribah of Kadesh in the desert of Zin.]

[15] Then Moses said to the LORD, [16] "May the LORD, the God of the spirits of all mankind,* set over the community a

man [17] who shall act as their leader in all things, to guide them in all their actions; that the LORD's community may not be like sheep without a shepherd." [18] And the LORD replied to Moses, "Take Joshua, son of Nun,[u] a man of spirit,* and lay your hand upon him. [19] Have him stand in the presence of the priest Eleazar and of the whole community, and commission him before their eyes. [20] Invest him with some of your own dignity, that the whole Israelite community may obey him. [21] He shall present himself to the priest Eleazar, to have him seek out for him the decisions of the Urim* in the LORD's presence; and as he directs, Joshua, all the Israelites with him, and the community as a whole shall perform all their actions."

[22] Moses did as the LORD had commanded him. Taking Joshua and having him stand in the presence of the priest Eleazar and of the whole community, [23] he laid his hands on him and gave him his commission, as the LORD had directed through Moses.

CHAPTER 28

General Sacrifices. [1] The LORD said to Moses, [2] "Give the Israelites this commandment: At the times I have appointed, you shall be careful to present to me the food offerings that are offered to me as sweet-smelling oblations.

Each Morning and Evening. [3] [v] "You shall tell them therefore: This is the oblation which you shall offer to the LORD: two unblemished yearling lambs each day as the established holocaust,* [4] offering one lamb in the morning and the other during the evening twilight, [5] each with a cereal offering of one tenth of an ephah of fine flour mixed with a fourth of a hin of oil of crushed olives.* [6] This is the established holocaust that was offered at Mount Sinai as a sweet-smelling oblation to the LORD. [7] And as the libation for the first lamb, you shall pour out to the LORD in the sanctuary* a fourth of a hin of wine. [8] The other lamb, to be offered during the evening twilight, you shall offer with the same cereal offering and the same libation as in the morning, as a sweet-smelling oblation to the LORD.

On the Sabbath. [9] "On the sabbath day you shall offer two unblemished yearling lambs, with their cereal offering, two tenths of an ephah of fine flour mixed with

oil, and with their libations. [10] Each sabbath there shall be the sabbath holocaust in addition to the established holocaust and its libation.

At the New Moon Feast. [11] "On the first of each month* you shall offer as a holocaust to the LORD two bullocks, one ram, and seven unblemished yearling lambs, [12] with three tenths of an ephah of fine flour mixed with oil as the cereal offering for each bullock, two tenths of an ephah of fine flour mixed with oil as the cereal offering for the ram, [13] and one tenth of an ephah of fine flour mixed with oil as the cereal offering for each lamb, that the holocaust may be a sweet-smelling oblation to the LORD. [14] Their libations shall be half a hin of wine for each bullock, a third of a hin for the ram, and a fourth of a hin for each lamb. This is the new moon holocaust for every new moon of the year. [15] Moreover, one goat shall be sacrificed as a sin offering to the LORD. These are to be offered in addition to the established holocaust and its libation.

At the Passover. [16] "On the fourteenth day* of the first month falls the Passover of the LORD,[w] [17] and the fifteenth day of this month is the pilgrimage feast. For seven days unleavened bread is to be eaten. [18] On the first of these days you shall hold a sacred assembly, and do no sort of work.[x] [19] As an oblation you shall offer a holocaust to the LORD, which shall consist of two bullocks, one ram, and seven yearling lambs that you are sure are unblemished, [20] with their cereal offerings of fine flour mixed with oil, offering three tenths of an ephah for each bullock, two tenths for the

u Dt 34, 9.—v 3-8: Ex 29, 38-42.—w Ex 12, 18; Lv 23, 5; Dt 16, 1.—x Ex 12, 16; Lv 23, 7.

27, 18: *A man of spirit:* literally, "a man in whom there is spirit": one who has the qualities of a good leader—courage, prudence, and strength of will. Cf Gn 41, 38; Dt 34, 9.

27, 21: *The Urim:* certain sacred objects which the Hebrew priests employed to ascertain the divine will, probably by obtaining a positive or negative answer to a given question. The full expression was "the Urim and Thummim"; cf Ex 28, 30; Lv 8, 8; Dt 33, 8; Ezr 2, 63; Neh 7, 65. Joshua was ordinarily not to receive direct revelations from God as Moses had received them.

28, 3: *The established holocaust:* "the tamid holocaust," the technical term for the daily sacrifice.

28, 5: *Oil of crushed olives:* this oil, made in a mortar, was purer and more expensive than oil extracted in the olive press.

28, 7: *In the sanctuary:* according to Sir 50, 15, it was at the base of the altar.

28, 11: *On the first of each month:* literally, "at the new moons"; beginning on the evening when the crescent of the new moon first appeared.

28, 16: *On the fourteenth day:* toward evening at the end of this day; cf Ex 12, 6. 18.

ram, [21] and one tenth for each of the seven lambs; [22] and offer one goat as a sin offering in atonement for yourselves. [23] These offerings you shall make in addition to the established morning holocaust: [24] you shall make exactly the same offerings each day for seven days as food offerings, in addition to the established holocaust with its libation, for a sweet-smelling oblation to the LORD. [25] On the seventh day you shall hold a sacred assembly, and do no sort of work.[y]

At Pentecost. [26] "On the day of first fruits,* on your feast of Weeks,[z] when you present to the LORD the new cereal offering, you shall hold a sacred assembly, and do no sort of work. [27] You shall offer as a sweet-smelling holocaust to the LORD two bullocks, one ram, and seven yearling lambs that you are sure are unblemished, [28] with their cereal offerings of fine flour mixed with oil; offering three tenths of an ephah for each bullock, two tenths for the ram, [29] and one tenth for each of the seven lambs. [30] Moreover, one goat shall be offered as a sin offering in atonement for yourselves. [31] You shall make these offerings, together with their libations, in addition to the established holocaust with its cereal offering.

CHAPTER 29

On New Year's Day. [1] "On the first day of the seventh month* you shall hold a sacred assembly, and do no sort of work; it shall be a day on which you sound the trumpet.[a] [2] You shall offer as a sweet-smelling holocaust to the LORD one bullock, one

ram, and seven unblemished yearling lambs, [3] with their cereal offerings of fine flour mixed with oil; offering three tenths of an ephah for the bullock, two tenths for the ram, [4] and one tenth for each of the seven lambs. [5] Moreover, one goat shall be offered as a sin offering in atonement for yourselves. [6] These are to be offered in addition to the ordinary new moon holocaust with its cereal offering, and in addition to the established holocaust with its cereal offering, together with the libations prescribed for them, as a sweet-smelling oblation to the LORD.

On the Day of Atonement. [7] "On the tenth day of this seventh month* you shall hold a sacred assembly, and mortify yourselves, and do no sort of work.[b] [8] You shall offer as a sweet-smelling holocaust to the LORD one bullock, one ram, and seven yearling lambs that you are sure are unblemished, [9] with their cereal offerings of fine flour mixed with oil; offering three tenths of an ephah for the bullock, two tenths for the ram, [10] and one tenth for each of the seven lambs. [11] Moreover, one goat shall be sacrificed as a sin offering. These are to be offered in addition to the atonement sin offering,* the established holocaust with its cereal offering, and their libations.

On the Feast of Booths.* [12] "On the fifteenth day of the seventh month you shall hold a sacred assembly,[c] and do no sort of work; then, for seven days following, you shall celebrate a pilgrimage feast to the LORD. [13] You shall offer as a sweet-smelling holocaust to the LORD thirteen bullocks,* two rams, and fourteen yearling lambs that are unblemished, [14] with their cereal offerings of fine flour mixed with oil; offering three tenths of an ephah for each of the thirteen bullocks, two tenths for each of the two rams, [15] and one tenth for each of the fourteen lambs. [16] Moreover, one goat shall be sacrificed as a sin offering. These are to be offered in addition to the established holocaust with its cereal offering and libation.

[17] "On the second day you shall offer twelve bullocks, two rams, and fourteen unblemished yearling lambs, [18] with their cereal offerings and libations as prescribed for the bullocks, rams and lambs in proportion to their number, [19] as well as one goat for a sin offering, besides the established holocaust with its cereal offering and libation.

---

y Ex 12, 16; 13, 6; Lv 23, 8.—z Ex 34, 22.—a Nm 10, 10; Lv 23, 24.—b Lv 16, 29; 23, 27f. 32.—c Lv 23, 34f.

28, 26: *The day of first fruits:* a unique term for this feast, which is usually called "the feast of Weeks"; it was celebrated as a thanksgiving for the wheat harvest seven weeks after the barley harvest (Passover). In the time of Christ it was commonly known by the Greek word "Pentecost," that is, "fiftieth" (day after the Passover); see note on Lv 23, 16.

29, 1: *The first day of the seventh month:* (about September-October) is now the Jewish New Year's Day. In the older calendar the year began with the first of Nisan (March-April); cf Ex 12, 2.

29, 7: *The tenth day of this seventh month:* the Day of Atonement. *Mortify yourselves:* literally, "afflict your souls," that is, with fasting.

29, 11: *The atonement sin offering:* the bullock prescribed in Lv 16, 11f.

29, 12: This feast of Booths celebrating the vintage harvest was the most popular of all and therefore had the most elaborate ritual. See note on Lv 23, 34.

29, 13: *Thirteen bullocks:* the number of bullocks sacrificed before the octave day was seventy, arranged on a descending scale so that the number on the seventh day was the sacred number seven.

20 "On the third day you shall offer eleven bullocks, two rams, and fourteen unblemished yearling lambs, 21 with their cereal offerings and libations as prescribed for the bullocks, rams and lambs in proportion to their number, 22 as well as one goat for a sin offering, besides the established holocaust with its cereal offering and libation.

23 "On the fourth day you shall offer ten bullocks, two rams, and fourteen unblemished yearling lambs, 24 with their cereal offerings and libations as prescribed for the bullocks, rams and lambs in proportion to their number, 25 as well as one goat for a sin offering, besides the established holocaust with its cereal offering and libation.

26 "On the fifth day you shall offer nine bullocks, two rams, and fourteen unblemished yearling lambs, 27 *d* with their cereal offerings and libations as prescribed for the bullocks, rams and lambs in proportion to their number, 28 as well as one goat for a sin offering, besides the established holocaust with its cereal offering and libation.

29 "On the sixth day you shall offer eight bullocks, two rams, and fourteen unblemished yearling lambs, 30 with their cereal offerings and libations as prescribed for the bullocks, rams and lambs in proportion to their number, 31 as well as one goat for a sin offering, besides the established holocaust with its cereal offering and libation.

32 "On the seventh day you shall offer seven bullocks, two rams, and fourteen unblemished yearling lambs, 33 with their cereal offerings and libations as prescribed for the bullocks, rams and lambs in proportion to their number, 34 as well as one goat for a sin offering, besides the established holocaust with its cereal offering and libation.

35 "On the eighth day *e* you shall hold a solemn meeting,* and do no sort of work. 36 You shall offer up in holocaust as a sweet-smelling oblation to the LORD one bullock, one ram, and seven unblemished yearling lambs, 37 with their cereal offerings and libations as prescribed for the bullocks, rams and lambs in proportion to their number, 38 as well as one goat for a sin offering, besides the established holocaust with its cereal offering and libation.

39 "These are the offerings you shall make to the LORD on your festivals, besides whatever holocausts, cereal offerings, libations, and peace offerings you present as your votive or free-will offerings."

CHAPTER 30

1 Moses then gave the Israelites these instructions, just as the LORD had ordered him.

Validity and Annulment of Vows. 2 Moses said to the heads of the Israelite tribes, "This is what the LORD has commanded: 3 When a man makes a vow to the LORD or binds himself under oath to a pledge* of abstinence, he shall not violate his word, but must fulfill exactly the promise he has uttered. *f*

4 "When a woman, while still a maiden in her father's house, makes a vow to the LORD, or binds herself to a pledge, 5 if her father learns of her vow or the pledge to which she bound herself and says nothing to her about it, then any vow or any pledge she has made remains valid. 6 But if on the day he learns of it her father expresses to her his disapproval, then any vow or any pledge she has made becomes null and void; and the LORD releases her from it, since her father has expressed to her his disapproval.

7 "If she marries while under a vow or under a rash pledge to which she bound herself, 8 and her husband learns of it, yet says nothing to her that day about it, then the vow or pledge she had made remains valid. 9 But if on the day he learns of it her husband expresses to her his disapproval, he thereby annuls the vow she had made or the rash pledge to which she had bound herself, and the LORD releases her from it. 10 The vow of a widow or of a divorced woman, or any pledge to which such a woman binds herself, is valid.

11 "If it is in her husband's house* that she makes a vow or binds herself under oath to a pledge, 12 and her husband learns

d Nm 29, 30. 37.—e Lv 23, 36; Jn 7, 37.—f Dt 23, 22; Eccl 5, 3f.

29, 35: *A solemn meeting:* the Hebrew word is the technical term for the closing celebration of the three major feasts of the Passover, Pentecost and Booths, or of other special feasts that lasted for a week. Cf Lv 23, 36; Dt 16, 8; 2 Chr 7, 9; Neh 8, 18.

30, 3: *A vow . . . a pledge:* here the former signifies the doing of some positive good deed, in particular the offering of some sacrifice; the latter signifies the abstaining from some otherwise licit action or pleasure; cf v 14.

30, 11: *In her husband's house:* after her marriage. This contrasts with the case given in vv 7ff.

of it yet says nothing to express to her his disapproval, then any vow or any pledge she has made remains valid. ¹³But if on the day he learns of them her husband annuls them, then whatever she has expressly promised in her vow or in her pledge becomes null and void; since her husband has annulled them, the LORD releases her from them.

¹⁴"Any vow or any pledge that she makes under oath to mortify herself, her husband can either allow to remain valid or render null and void. ¹⁵But if her husband, day after day, says nothing at all to her about them, he thereby allows as valid any vow or any pledge she has made; he has allowed them to remain valid, because on the day he learned of them he said nothing to her about them. ¹⁶If, however, he countermands them* some time after he first learned of them, he is responsible for her guilt."

¹⁷These are the statutes which the LORD prescribed through Moses concerning the relationship between a husband and his wife, as well as between a father and his daughter while she is still a maiden in her father's house.

CHAPTER 31

Extermination of the Midianites. ¹The LORD said to Moses,* ²"Avenge the Israelites on the Midianites, and then you shall be taken to your people." ³So Moses told the people, "Select men from your midst and arm them for war, to attack the Midianites and execute the LORD's vengeance on them. ⁴From each of the tribes of Israel you shall send a band of one thousand men to war." ⁵From the clans of Israel, therefore, a thousand men of each tribe were levied, so that there were twelve thousand men armed for war. ⁶Moses sent them out on the campaign, a thousand from each tribe, with Phinehas, son of

g 2 Pt 2, 15; Rv 2, 14.

30, 16: *He countermands them:* he prevents their fulfillment. Since he has first allowed the vows to remain valid, he can no longer annul them.

31, 1ff: The narrative of Israel's relations with Midian, which was interrupted after Nm 25, 18, is now resumed.

31, 8: *The five Midianite kings:* they are called "Midianite princes, Sihon's vassals" in Jos 13, 21.

31, 17: There are later references to Midian in Jgs 6—8; 1 Kgs 11, 18; Is 60, 6. The present raid was only against those Midianites who were dwelling at this time near the encampment of the Israelites.

31, 23: *Lustral water:* water mixed with the ashes of the red heifer as prescribed in Nm 19, 9.

Eleazar, the priest for the campaign, who had with him the sacred vessels and the trumpets for sounding the alarm. ⁷They waged war against the Midianites, as the LORD had commanded Moses, and killed every male among them. ⁸Besides those slain in battle, they killed the five Midianite kings:* Evi, Rekem, Zur, Hur and Reba; and they also executed Balaam, son of Beor, with the sword. ⁹But the Israelites kept the women of the Midianites with their little ones as captives, and all their herds and flocks and wealth as spoil, ¹⁰while they set on fire all the towns where they had settled and all their encampments. ¹¹Then they took all the booty, with the people and beasts they had captured, and brought the captives, together with the spoils and booty, ¹²to Moses and the priest Eleazar and to the Israelite community at their camp on the plains of Moab, along the Jericho stretch of the Jordan.

Treatment of the Captives. ¹³When Moses and the priest Eleazar, with all the princes of the community, went outside the camp to meet them, ¹⁴Moses became angry with the officers of the army, the clan and company commanders, who were returning from combat. ¹⁵"So you have spared all the women!" he exclaimed. ¹⁶"Why, they are the very ones who on Balaam's advice prompted the unfaithfulness of the Israelites toward the LORD in the Peor affair,g which began the slaughter of the LORD's community. ¹⁷ * Slay, therefore, every male child and every woman who has had intercourse with a man. ¹⁸But you may spare and keep for yourselves all girls who had no intercourse with a man.

Purification after Combat. ¹⁹"Moreover, you shall stay outside the camp for seven days, and those of you who have slain anyone or touched anyone slain in battle shall purify yourselves on the third and on the seventh day. This applies both to you and to your captives. ²⁰You shall also purify every article of cloth, leather, goats' hair, or wood."

²¹Eleazar the priest told the soldiers who had returned from combat: "This is what the law, as prescribed by the LORD to Moses, ordains: ²²Whatever can stand fire, such as gold, silver, bronze, iron, tin and lead, ²³you shall put into the fire, that it may become clean; however, it must also be purified with lustral water.* But what-

ever cannot stand fire you shall put into the water. [24] On the seventh day you shall wash your clothes, and then you will again be clean. After that you may enter the camp."

Division of the Booty. [25] The LORD said to Moses: [26] "With the help of the priest Eleazar and of the heads of the ancestral houses, count up all the human captives and the beasts that have been taken; [27] then divide them evenly,* giving half to those who took active part in the war by going out to combat, and half to the rest of the community. [28] You shall levy a tax for the LORD on the warriors who went out to combat: one out of every five hundred persons, oxen, asses and sheep [29] in their half of the spoil you shall turn over to the priest Eleazar as a contribution to the LORD. [30] From the Israelites' half you shall take one out of every fifty persons, and the same from the different beasts, oxen, asses and sheep, and give them to the Levites, who have charge of the LORD's Dwelling." [31] So Moses and the priest Eleazar did this, as the LORD had commanded Moses.

Amount of Booty. [32] This booty, what was left of the loot which the soldiers had taken, amounted to six hundred and seventy-five thousand sheep, [33] seventy-two thousand oxen, [34] sixty-one thousand asses, [35] and thirty-two thousand girls who were still virgins.

[36] The half that fell to those who had gone out to combat was: three hundred and thirty-seven thousand five hundred sheep, [37] of which six hundred and seventy-five fell as tax to the LORD; [38] thirty-six thousand oxen, of which seventy-two fell as tax to the LORD; [39] thirty thousand five hundred asses, of which sixty-one fell as tax to the LORD; [40] and sixteen thousand persons, of whom thirty-two fell as tax to the LORD. [41] The taxes contributed to the LORD, Moses gave to the priest Eleazar, as the LORD had commanded him.

[42] The half for the other Israelites, which fell to the community when Moses had taken it from the soldiers, was: [43] three hundred and thirty-seven thousand five hundred sheep, [44] thirty-six thousand oxen, [45] thirty thousand five hundred asses, [46] and sixteen thousand persons. [47] From this, the Israelites' share, Moses, as the LORD had ordered, took one out of every fifty, both of persons and of beasts, and gave them to the Levites, who had charge of the LORD's Dwelling.

Gifts of the Officers. [48] Then the officers who had been clan and company commanders of the army came up to Moses [49] and said to him, "Your servants have counted up the soldiers under our command, and not one is missing. [50] * So, to make atonement for ourselves before the LORD, each of us will bring as an offering to the LORD some gold article he has picked up, such as an anklet, a bracelet, a ring, an earring, or a necklace." [51] Moses and the priest Eleazar accepted this gold from them, all of it in well-wrought articles. [52] The gold that they gave as a contribution to the LORD amounted in all to sixteen thousand seven hundred and fifty shekels. This was from the clan and company commanders; [53] what the common soldiers had looted each one kept for himself. [54] Moses, then, and the priest Eleazar accepted the gold from the clan and company commanders, and put it in the meeting tent as a memorial for the Israelites before the LORD.

CHAPTER 32

Request of Gad and Reuben. [1] Now the Reubenites and Gadites had a very large number of livestock. Noticing that the land of Jazer and of Gilead* was grazing country, [2] they came to Moses and the priest Eleazar and to the princes of the community and said, [3] * "The region of Ataroth, Dibon, Jazer, Nimrah, Heshbon, Elealeh, Sebam, Nebo and Baal-meon, [4] which the LORD has laid low before the community of Israel, is grazing country. Now, since your servants have livestock," [5] they continued, "if we find favor with you, let this land be given to your servants as their property. Do not make us cross the Jordan."

Moses' Rebuke. [6] But Moses answered the Gadites and Reubenites: "Are your kinsmen, then, to engage in war, while

---

31, 27: *Divide them evenly:* for a similar division of the booty into two equal parts, between those who engaged in the fray and those who stayed with the baggage, cf 1 Sm 30, 24. But note that here the tax on the booty of the non-combatants is ten times as much as that on the soldier's booty.

31, 50: The precise nature and use of some of these articles of gold is not certain.

32, 1: *Gilead:* the name of the western part of the plateau east of the Jordan, sometimes signifying the whole region from the Yarmuk to the Jordan, sometimes only the northern part of this region, and sometimes, as here, only its southern part. *Jazer* lay to the east of southern Gilead.

32, 3: The places named in this verse, as well as the additional ones given in vv 34-38, were all in the former kingdom of Sihon, that is, in the region between the Jabbok and the Arnon. Cf Nm 21, 23f; Jos 13, 19-21. 24-27.

you remain here? [7] Why do you wish to discourage the Israelites from crossing to the land the LORD has given them? [8] That is just what your fathers did when I sent them from Kadesh-barnea to reconnoiter the land.[h] [9] They went up to the Wadi Eshcol and reconnoitered the land, then so discouraged the Israelites that they would not enter the land the LORD had given them. [10] [i] At that time the wrath of the LORD flared up, and he swore, [11] 'Because they have not followed me unreservedly, none of these men of twenty years or more who have come up from Egypt shall ever see this country I promised under oath to Abraham and Isaac and Jacob, [12] [j] except the Kenizzite* Caleb, son of Jephunneh, and Joshua, son of Nun, who have followed the LORD unreservedly.' [13] So in his anger with the Israelites the LORD made them wander in the desert forty years, until the whole generation that had done evil in the sight of the LORD had died out. [14] And now here you are, a brood of sinners, rising up in your fathers' place to add still more to the LORD's blazing wrath against the Israelites. [15] If you turn away from following him, he will make them stay still longer in the desert, and so you will bring about the ruin of this whole nation."

Counter Proposal. [16] But they were insistent with him: "We wish only to build sheepfolds here for our flocks, and towns for our families; [17] but we ourselves will march as troops in the van of the Israelites,[k] until we have led them to their destination. Meanwhile our families can remain here in the fortified towns, safe from attack by the natives. [18] We will not return to our homes until every one of the Israelites has taken possession of his heritage, [19] [l] and will not claim any heritage with them once we cross the Jordan, so long as we re-

ceive a heritage for ourselves on this eastern side of the Jordan."

Agreement Reached. [20] * Moses said to them in reply: "If you keep your word to march as troops in the LORD's vanguard [21] and to cross the Jordan in full force before the LORD until he has driven his enemies out of his way [22] and the land is subdued before him, then you may return here, quit of every obligation to the LORD and to Israel, and this region shall be your possession before the LORD.[m] [23] But if you do not do this, you will sin against the LORD, and you can be sure that you will not escape the consequences of your sin. [24] Build the towns, then, for your families, and the folds for your flocks, but also fulfill your express promise."

[25] The Gadites and Reubenites answered Moses, "Your servants will do as you command, my lord. [26] [n] While our wives and children, our herds and other livestock remain in the towns of Gilead, [27] all your servants will go across as armed troops to battle before the LORD, just as your lordship says."

[28] Moses, therefore, gave this order in their regard to the priest Eleazar, to Joshua, son of Nun, and to the heads of the ancestral tribes of the Israelites: [29] "If all the Gadites and Reubenites cross the Jordan with you as combat troops before the LORD, you shall give them Gilead as their property when the land has been subdued before you. [30] But if they will not go across with you as combat troops before the LORD, you shall bring their wives and children and livestock across before you into Canaan, and they shall have their property with you in the land of Canaan."

[31] To this the Gadites and Reubenites replied, "We will do what the LORD has commanded us, your servants. [32] We ourselves will go across into the land of Canaan as troops before the LORD, but we will retain our hereditary property on this side of the Jordan." [33] So Moses gave them [*the Gadites and Reubenites, as well as half the tribe of Manasseh, son of Joseph, the kingdom of Sihon, king of the Amorites, and the kingdom of Og, king of Bashan,] the land with its towns and the districts that surrounded them.[o]

[34] The Gadites rebuilt the fortified towns of Dibon, Ataroth, Aroer, [35] Atroth-shophan, Jazer, Jogbehah, [36] Beth-nimrah and Beth-haran, and they built sheepfolds.

---

h 8f: Nm 13, 31ff; Dt 1, 22.—i 10f: Dt 1, 34f.—j Nm 14, 24; Dt 1, 36.—k Jos 4, 12f.—l Jos 13, 8.—m Jos 1, 15.—n Jos 1, 14.—o Dt 3, 12; 29, 7; Jos 12, 6; 13, 8.

32, 12: *Kenizzite:* a member of the clan of Kenaz, which, according to Gn 36, 11. 15. 42, was Edomitic; hence, although Caleb belonged to the tribe of Judah (Nm 13, 6; 34, 19), he must have had Edomite blood in his veins; cf also Jos 14, 6. 14.

32, 20ff: Since the oath of the Lord was borne into battle with the Israelite army, the vanguard was said to march *before the Lord.*

32, 33: The preceding is concerned solely with the two tribes of Gad and Reuben and with the land of the former kingdom of Sihon; hence it seems probable that the sudden reference here to the half-tribe of Manasseh and to their territory in Bashan, the former kingdom of Og, is a later addition to the text.

37 The Reubenites rebuilt Heshbon, Elealeh, Kiriathaim, 38 Nebo, Baal-meon [names to be changed!], * and Sibmah. These towns, which they rebuilt, they called by their old names.

Other Conquests. 39 The descendants of Machir, son of Manasseh, invaded Gilead and captured it, driving out the Amorites who were there. 40 [Moses gave Gilead to Machir,*p* son of Manasseh, and he settled there.] 41 Jair,*q* a Manassehite clan, campaigned against the tent villages, captured them and called them Havvoth-jair. 42 Nobah also campaigned against Kenath, captured it with its dependencies and called it Nobah after his own name.

CHAPTER 33

Stages on the Journey. 1 The following are the stages by which the Israelites journeyed up by companies from the land of Egypt under the guidance of Moses and Aaron.* 2 By the LORD's command Moses recorded the starting places of the various stages. The starting places of the successive stages were:

3 * They set out from Rameses in the first month,
     on the fifteenth day of the first month.
On the Passover morrow the Israelites went forth
     in triumph, in view of all Egypt,
4 While the Egyptians buried their first-born
     all of whom the LORD had struck down;
     on their gods, too, the LORD executed judgments.*r*

From Egypt to Sinai. 5 Setting out from Rameses, the Israelites camped at Succoth. 6 Setting out from Succoth, they camped at Etham near the edge of the desert. 7 Setting out from Etham, they turned back to Pi-hahiroth, which is opposite Baal-zephon, and they camped opposite Migdol.*s* 8 Setting out from Pi-hahiroth, they crossed over through the sea into the desert,*t* and after a three days' journey in the desert of Etham, they camped at Marah. 9 Setting out from Marah, they came to Elim, where there were twelve springs of water and seventy palm trees, and they camped there.*u* 10 Setting out from Elim, they camped beside the Red Sea. 11 Setting out from the Red Sea, they camped in the desert of Sin. 12 Setting out from the desert

of Sin, they camped at Dophkah. 13 Setting out from Dophkah, they camped at Alush. 14 Setting out from Alush, they camped at Rephidim, where there was no water for the people to drink.*v* 15 Setting out from Rephidim, they camped in the desert of Sinai.*w*

From Sinai to Kadesh. 16 Setting out from the desert of Sinai, they camped at Kibroth-hattaavah. 17 Setting out from Kibroth-hattaavah, they camped at Hazeroth.*x* 18 Setting out from Hazeroth, they camped at Rithmah. 19 Setting out from Rithmah, they camped at Rimmon-perez. 20 Setting out from Rimmon-perez, they camped at Libnah. 21 Setting out from Libnah, they camped at Rissah. 22 Setting out from Rissah, they camped at Kehelathah. 23 Setting out from Kehelathah, they camped at Mount Shepher. 24 Setting out from Mount Shepher, they camped at Haradah. 25 Setting out from Haradah, they camped at Makheloth. 26 Setting out from Makheloth, they camped at Tahath. 27 Setting out from Tahath, they camped at Terah. 28 Setting out from Terah, they camped at Mithkah. 29 Setting out from Mithkah, they camped at Hashmonah. 30 * Setting out from Hashmonah, —

From Mount Hor to Ezion-geber. They camped at Moseroth. 31 Setting out from Moseroth, they camped at Bene-jaakan. 32 Setting out from Bene-jaakan, they camped at Mount Gidgad. 33 Setting out from Mount Gidgad, they camped at Jotbathah. 34 Setting out from Jotbathah, they camped at Abronah. 35 Setting out from

p Dt 3, 15.—q Dt 3, 14.—r 4f: Ex 12, 12. 29. 37.—s Ex 14, 2.—t Ex 15, 22.—u Ex 15, 27.—v Ex 17, 1.—w Ex 19, 2.—x 17f: Nm 11, 34f.

32, 38: The phrase in brackets is a gloss, warning the reader either to change the order of the preceding names, or, more probably, to read some other word, such as *bosheth,* "shame," for *Baal. They called by their old names:* literally, "they called by their names" (see Textual Notes); however, some understand the current Hebrew text to mean, "they called by new names."

33, 1ff: This list of camping sites was drawn up by Moses, as v 2 expressly states. However, in its present form it probably includes some glosses. Moreover, a comparison with the more detailed accounts of the journey as given elsewhere shows that this is not complete. It records just forty camping sites, not counting the starting place, Rameses, and the terminus, the plains of Moab. This number, which corresponds exactly to the forty years of wandering in the desert, is probably a schematic device. Besides, it seems that in its present form the order of some of these names has been disturbed. Several names listed here are not recorded elsewhere.

33, 3f: These two verses were probably borrowed from some ancient song celebrating the exodus from Egypt.

33, 30-36: Moseroth is mentioned in Dt 10, 6 (in the form of "Moserah"), as the place where Aaron died. It must therefore have been close to Mount Hor; cf Nm 20, 22ff. It seems very probable that the section vv 36b-41a stood originally immediately after v 30a.

ROUTE OF THE EXODUS (Nm 33, 1-49) — **(a) From Egypt to Sinai:** Departure from Rameses. Encampments at Succoth, Etham (Pi-hahiroth opposite Baal-zephon), Migdol, Marah, Elim, stopping place near the Red Sea, in the desert of Sin, Dophkah, Alush, Rephidim, Sinai desert (Nm 33, 11-15). **(b) From Sinai to Kadesh:** Encampments at Kibroth-hattaavah, Hazeroth, Rithmah, Rimmon-perez, Libnah, Rissah, Kehelathah, Mount Shepher, Haradah, Makheloth, Tahath, Terah, Mithkah, Hashmonah; they encamp in the desert of Zin, that is, Kadesh (Nm 33, 16-30). **(c) Near Kadesh:** Encampments at Moseroth, Bene-jaakan, Mount Hor (Dt 10, 6: Bene-jaakan, Moserah) where Aaron dies (Nm 33, 30-38). **(d) From Kadesh to the frontier of Moab:** Hor-haggidgad (Dt 10, 6 Gudgodah), Jotbathah, Abronah, Ezion-geber, Zalmonah, Punon, Oboth, Iye-abarim (Nm 33, 37-44). **(e) From the frontier of Moab to the Jordan:** Starting from Iye-abarim they encamp at Dibon-gad, Almon-diblathaim, in the Abarim Mountains, and on the plains of Moab, near the Jordan at Jericho, between Beth-jeshimoth and Abel-shittim in the plains of Moab (Nm 33, 45-49). **(f) Order of encampment:** Cf. schema. **(g) Order of march:** army of Judah — Gershon and Merari with the tabernacle. — Army of Reuben — Kohathites with the holy things — army of Ephraim — army of Dan.

ENTRANCE INTO CANAAN
(Jos 1, 1-8, 35)

Kartan

ÉBAL
Shechem
GERIZIM

JABBOK

Adam

Bethel
Ai
Beeroth
Jericho
Gilgal
Shittim

Gibeon
Chephirah
Kiriath-jearim

VALLEY OF ACHOR

JORDAN

SEA OF THE ARABAH

0   10
Miles

ENTRANCE INTO CANAAN (between 1220 and 1200: Jos 1, 1—8, 35 — (a) At Shittim Joshua makes plans for passage across the **Jordan.** He sends spies to **Jericho** (1, 1—2, 4). **(b) At the Jordan:** the entry into the Promised Land marks the end of the Exodus. Joshua leaves **Shittim** with all the Israelites and crosses the Jordan opposite **Jericho** and camps at **Gilgal,** to the east of **Jericho** where the people celebrate the Passover (3, 1—4, 19). **(c) At Jericho,** the town is taken after seven days of siege (5, 13—6, 27). **At Ai,** the Israelites are defeated by the people of Ai and driven back from the city. Violation of the anathema by Achan, who is stoned in the **Valley of Achor.** Joshua captures **Ai** by an ambush between **Bethel** and **Ai,** to the west of the town (7, 2—8, 28) **(e) At Shechem,** confirmation of the covenant takes place (8, 30-35).

Abronah, they camped at Ezion-geber. [36] Setting out from Ezion-geber, —

From Kadesh to Mount Hor. They camped in the desert of Zin, at Kadesh.[y] [37] Setting out from Kadesh, they camped at Mount Hor on the border of the land of Edom. [38] [Aaron the priest ascended Mount Hor[z] at the LORD's command, and there he died in the fortieth year from the departure of the Israelites from the land of Egypt, on the first day of the fifth month. [39] Aaron was a hundred and twenty-three years old when he died on Mount Hor. [40] * Now, when the Canaanite king of Arad, who lived in the Negeb in the land of Canaan, heard that the Israelites were coming. . . .] [41] Setting out from Mount Hor, —

From Ezion-geber to the Plains of Moab.* They camped at Zalmonah. [42] Setting out from Zalmonah, they camped at Punon. [43] Setting out from Punon, they camped at Oboth. [44] Setting out from Oboth, they camped at Iye-abarim on the border of Moab. [45] Setting out from Iye-abarim, they camped at Dibon-gad. [46] Setting out from Dibon-gad they camped at Almon-diblathaim. [47] Setting out from Almon-diblathaim, they camped in the Abarim Mountains opposite Nebo. [48] Setting out from the Abarim Mountains, they camped on the plains of Moab along the Jericho stretch of the Jordan. [49] Their camp along the Jordan on the plains of Moab extended from Beth-jeshimoth to Abel-shittim.

Conquest and Division of Canaan. [50] The LORD spoke to Moses on the plains of Moab beside the Jericho stretch of the Jordan and said to him: [51] "Tell the Israelites: When you go across the Jordan into the land of Canaan, [52] drive out all the inhabitants of the land before you; destroy all their stone figures and molten images, and demolish all their high places.[a]

[53] "You shall take possession of the land and settle in it, for I have given you the land as your property. [54] You shall apportion the land among yourselves by lot, clan by clan, assigning a large heritage to a

large group and a small heritage to a small group.[b] Wherever anyone's lot falls, there shall his property be within the heritage of his ancestral tribe.

[55] "But if you do not drive out the inhabitants of the land before you, those whom you allow to remain will become as barbs in your eyes and thorns in your sides, and they will harass you in the country where you live,[c] [56] and I will treat you as I had intended to treat them."

CHAPTER 34

The Boundaries. [1] The LORD said to Moses, [2] "Give the Israelites this order: When you enter the land of Canaan, this is the territory that shall fall to you as your heritage—the land of Canaan with its boundaries:

[3] "Your southern boundary shall be at the desert of Zin along the border of Edom;[d] on the east it shall begin at the end of the Salt Sea, [4] and turning south of the Akrabbim Pass, it shall cross Zin, and extend south of Kadesh-barnea to Hazaraddar; thence it shall cross to Azmon,[e] [5] and turning from Azmon to the Wadi of Egypt, shall terminate at the Sea.[f]

[6] "For your western boundary you shall have the Great Sea* with its coast; this shall be your western boundary.

[7] "The following shall be your boundary on the north: from the Great Sea you shall draw a line to Mount Hor,* [8] and shall continue it from Mount Hor to Labo in the land of Hamath, with the boundary extending through Zedad. [9] Thence the boundary shall reach to Ziphron and terminate at Hazar-enan. This shall be your northern boundary.

[10] "For your eastern boundary you shall draw a line from Hazar-enan to Shepham. [11] From Shepham the boundary shall go down to Ar-Baal, east of Ain, and descending further, shall strike the ridge on the east side of the Sea of Chinnereth; [12] thence the boundary shall continue along the Jordan and terminate with the Salt Sea.

"This is the land that shall be yours, with the boundaries that surround it."

[13] Moses also gave this order to the Israelites: "This is the land, to be apportioned among you by lot, which the LORD has commanded to be given to the nine and one half tribes. [14] For all the ancestral houses of the tribe of Reuben, and the ancestral houses of the tribe of Gad, as well

y 36f: Nm 20, 1. 22.—z Nm 20, 25; Dt 32, 50.—a Ex 23, 31; 34, 13; Dt 7, 5; 12, 3.—b Nm 26, 53ff.—c Jos 23, 13; Jgs 2, 3.—d Jos 15, 1f.—e Jos 15, 3.—f Jos 15, 4.

33, 40: The verse begins the same account of the victory over Arad as is given in Nm 21, 1ff, where it also follows the account of Aaron's death.

33, 41b-49: It seems that this section stood originally immediately after v 36a.

34, 6: The Great Sea: the Mediterranean.

34, 7f: Mount Hor: different from the one where Aaron died; cf Nm 20, 22; 33, 37f.

as half of the tribe of Manasseh, have already received their heritage; [15] these two and one half tribes have received their heritage on the eastern side of the Jericho stretch of the Jordan, toward the sunrise."

Supervisors of the Allotment. [16] The LORD said to Moses, [17] "These are the names of the men who shall apportion the land among you: Eleazar the priest, and Joshua, son of Nun, [18] [g] and one prince from each of the tribes whom you shall designate for this task. [19] These shall be as follows:

from the tribe of Judah: Caleb, son of Jephunneh;
[20] from the tribe of Simeon: Samuel, son of Ammihud;
[21] from the tribe of Benjamin: Elidad, son of Chislon;
[22] from the tribe of Dan: Bukki, son of Jogli;
[23] from the tribe of Manasseh: Hanniel, son of Ephod; and
[24] from the tribe of Ephraim: Kemuel, son of Shiphtan, for the descendants of Joseph;
[25] from the tribe of Zebulun: Elizaphan, son of Parnach;
[26] from the tribe of Issachar: Paltiel, son of Azzan;
[27] from the tribe of Asher: Ahihud, son of Shelomi;
[28] from the tribe of Naphtali: Pedahel, son of Ammihud."

[29] These are they whom the LORD commanded to assign the Israelites their heritage in the land of Canaan.

CHAPTER 35

Cities for the Levites. [1] The LORD gave these instructions to Moses on the plains of Moab beside the Jericho stretch of the Jordan: [2] [h] "Tell the Israelites that out of their hereditary property they shall give the Levites cities for homes, as well as pasture lands around the cities. [3] The cities shall serve them to dwell in, and the pasture lands shall serve their herds and flocks and other animals. [4] The pasture lands of the cities to be assigned the Levites shall extend a thousand cubits from the city walls in each direction. [5] Thus you shall measure out two thousand cubits outside the city along each side—east, south, west and north—with the city lying in the center. This shall serve them as the pasture lands of their cities.

[6] [i] "Now these are the cities you shall give to the Levites: the six cities of asylum which you must establish as places where a homicide can take refuge, and in addition forty-two other cities—[7] a total of forty-eight cities with their pasture lands to be assigned the Levites. [8] * In assigning the cities from the property of the Israelites, take more from a larger group and fewer from a smaller one, so that each group will cede cities to the Levites in proportion to its own heritage."

Cities of Asylum. [9] The LORD said to Moses, [10] "Tell the Israelites: When you go across the Jordan into the land of Canaan, [11] select for yourselves cities[j] to serve as cities of asylum, where a homicide who has killed someone unintentionally may take refuge. [12] These cities shall serve you as places of asylum from the avenger of blood,* so that a homicide shall not be put to death unless he is first tried before the community. [13] Six cities of asylum shall you assign: [14] three beyond the Jordan, and three in the land of Canaan. [15] These six cities of asylum shall serve not only the Israelites but all the resident or transient aliens among them, so that anyone who has killed another unintentionally may take refuge there.

Murder and Manslaughter. [16] * "If a man strikes another with an iron instrument and causes his death, he is a murderer and shall be put to death.[k] [17] If a man strikes another with a death-dealing stone in his hand and causes his death, he is a murderer and shall be put to death. [18] If a man strikes another with a death-dealing club in his hand and causes his death, he is a murderer and shall be put to death. [19] The avenger of blood may execute the murderer, putting him to death on sight.

[20] "If a man pushes another out of hatred, or after lying in wait for him throws something at him, and causes his death,[l] [21] or if he strikes another out of enmity and causes his death, he shall be put to death as a murderer. The avenger of blood may execute the murderer on sight.

[22] [m] "However, if a man pushes another

---

g Nm 1, 4.—h Jos 14, 3f; 21, 2.—i Dt 4, 41f; Jos 20, 2.—j 10ff: Dt 19, 2; Jos 20, 2ff.—k Ex 21, 12; Lv 24, 17.—l Ex 21, 14; Dt 19, 11.—m Jos 20, 3.

35, 8: This provision was hardly observed in the actual assignment of the levitical cities as narrated in Jos 21.

35, 12: *The avenger of blood:* one of the close relatives of the slain (2 Sm 14, 7) who, as executor of public justice, had the right and duty to take the life of the murderer; cf Dt 19, 6. 12; Jos 20, 3. 5. 9.

35, 16-25: Here, as also in Dt 19, 1-13, there is a casuistic development of the original law as stated in Ex 21, 12ff.

accidentally and not out of enmity, or if without lying in wait for him he throws some object at him, [23] or without seeing him throws a death-dealing stone which strikes him and causes his death, although he was not his enemy nor seeking to harm him: [24] then the community, deciding the case between the slayer and the avenger of blood in accordance with these norms, [25] shall free the homicide from the avenger of blood and shall remand him to the city of asylum where he took refuge;[n] and he shall stay there until the death of the high priest who has been anointed with sacred oil. [26] If the homicide of his own accord leaves the bounds of the city of asylum where he has taken refuge, [27] and the avenger of blood finds him beyond these bounds and kills him, the avenger incurs no blood-guilt; [28] the homicide was bound to stay in his city of asylum until the death of the high priest. Only after the death of the high priest may the homicide return to his own district.

[29] "These shall be norms for you and all your descendants, wherever you live, for rendering judgment.

Witnesses. [30] "Whenever someone kills another, the evidence of witnesses is required for the execution of the murderer.[o] The evidence of a single witness is not sufficient for putting a person to death.

No Indemnity. [31] "You shall not accept indemnity in place of the life of a murderer who deserves the death penalty; he must be put to death. [32] Nor shall you accept indemnity to allow a refugee to leave his city of asylum and again dwell elsewhere in the land before the death of the high priest. [33] You shall not desecrate the land where you live. Since bloodshed desecrates the land, the land can have no atonement for the blood shed on it except through the blood of him who shed it. [34] Do not defile the land in which you live and in the midst of which I dwell;[p] for I am the LORD who dwells in the midst of the Israelites."

CHAPTER 36

Property of Heiresses. [1] The heads of the ancestral houses in the clan of descendants of Gilead, son of Machir, son of Manasseh—one of the Josephite clans—came up and laid this plea before Moses and the priest Eleazar and before the princes who were the heads of the ancestral houses of the other Israelites. [2] They said: "The LORD commanded you, my lord, to apportion the land by lot among the Israelites;[q] and you, my lord, were also commanded by the LORD to give the heritage of our kinsman Zelophehad to his daughters. [3] But if they marry into one of the other Israelite tribes, their heritage will be withdrawn from our ancestral heritage and will be added to that of the tribe into which they marry; thus the heritage that fell to us by lot will be diminished. [4] When the Israelites celebrate the jubilee year,* the heritage of these women will be permanently added to that of the tribe into which they marry and will be withdrawn from that of our ancestral tribe."

[5] * So Moses gave this regulation to the Israelites according to the instructions of the LORD: "The tribe of the Josephites are right in what they say. [6] This is what the LORD commands with regard to the daughters of Zelophehad: They may marry anyone they please, provided they marry into a clan of their ancestral tribe, [7] so that no heritage of the Israelites will pass from one tribe to another, but all the Israelites will retain their own ancestral heritage. [8] Therefore, every daughter who inherits property in any of the Israelite tribes shall marry someone belonging to a clan of her own ancestral tribe, in order that all the Israelites may remain in possession of their own ancestral heritage. [9] Thus, no heritage can pass from one tribe to another, but all the Israelite tribes will retain their own ancestral heritage."

[10] The daughters of Zelophehad obeyed the command which the LORD had given to Moses. [11] Mahlah, Tirzah, Hoglah, Milcah and Noah, Zelophehad's daughters, married relatives on their father's side [12] within the clans of the descendants of Manasseh, son of Joseph; hence their heritage remained in the tribe of their father's clan.

Conclusion. [13] These are the commandments and decisions which the LORD prescribed for the Israelites through Moses, on the plains of Moab beside the Jericho stretch of the Jordan.

---

n Jos 20, 6.—o Dt 17, 6; 19, 15; Jn 8, 17; 2 Cor 13, 1; 1 Tm 5, 19.—p Ex 29, 45.—q Nm 26, 55; 27, 6; Jos 17, 3f.

36, 4: Before the jubilee year various circumstances, such as divorce, could make such property revert to its original tribal owners; but in the jubilee year it became irrevocably attached to its new owners.

36, 5-9: This is a supplement to the law given in Nm 27, 5-11.

THE BOOK OF DEUTERONOMY

*The fifth and last book of the Pentateuch is called Deuteronomy, meaning "second law."
In reality, what it contains is not a new law but a partial repetition, completion and explanation
of the law proclaimed on Mount Sinai. The historical portions of the book are also a résumé
of what is related elsewhere in the Pentateuch.*

*The chief characteristic of this book is its vigorous oratorical style. In a series of eloquent
discourses Moses presents the theme of covenant renewal in a vital religious framework. He
exhorts, corrects and threatens his people, appealing to their past glory, their historic mission
and the promise of future triumph. His aim is to enforce among the Israelites the Lord's claim
to their obedience, loyalty and love.*

*The events contained in the Book of Deuteronomy took place in the plains of Moab (Dt 1,
5) between the end of the wanderings in the desert (Dt 1, 3) and the crossing of the Jordan
River (Jos 4, 19), a period of no more than forty days.*

*The Book of Deuteronomy, written after the Israelites had for centuries been resident in
the Land of Promise, takes the form of a testament of Moses, the great leader and legislator,
to his people on the eve of his death. At the time of our Lord's coming, it shared with the
Psalms a preeminent religious influence among the Old Testament books.*

*The Savior quoted passages of Deuteronomy in overcoming the threefold temptation of
Satan in the desert (Mt 4; Dt 6, 13. 16; 8, 3; 10, 20), and in explaining to the lawyer the first
and greatest commandment (Mt 22, 35-39; Dt 6, 4). The book is divided as follows: I. Historical Review and Exhortation (Dt 1, 1—4, 43). II. God and His Covenant (Dt 4, 44—11, 32).
III. Exposition of the Law (Dt 12, 1—26, 19). IV. Final Words of Moses (Dt 27, 1—34, 12).*

I: HISTORICAL REVIEW AND EXHORTATION

CHAPTER 1

Introduction. ¹ These are the words which
Moses spoke to all Israel beyond the Jordan [* in the desert, in the Arabah, opposite Suph, between Paran and Tophel, Laban, Hazeroth and Dizahab; ² it is a journey of eleven days from Horeb to Kadeshbarnea by way of the highlands of Seir].

³ In the fortieth year, on the first day of
the eleventh month, Moses spoke to the Israelites all the commands that the LORD
had given him in their regard. ⁴ After he
had defeated Sihon, king of the Amorites,
who lived in Heshbon,ᵃ and Og, king of
Bashan, who lived in Ashtaroth and in
Edrei, ⁵ Moses began to explain the law in
the land of Moab beyond the Jordan, as
follows:

Departure from Horeb. ⁶ "The LORD, our
God, said to us at Horeb, 'You have stayed
long enough at this mountain. ⁷ * Leave
here and go to the hill country of the Amorites and to all the surrounding regions,ᵇ
the land of the Canaanites in the Arabah,
the mountains, the foothills, the Negeb
and the seacoast; to Lebanon, and as far as
the Great River [the Euphrates]. ⁸ I have
given that land over to you.ᶜ Go now and
occupy the land I swore to your fathers,
Abraham, Isaac and Jacob, I would give to
them and to their descendants.'

Appointment of Elders. ⁹ "At that time I
said to you, 'Alone, I am unable to carry
you.* ¹⁰ The LORD, your God, has so multiplied you that you are now as numerous
as the stars in the sky.ᵈ ¹¹ May the LORD,
the God of your fathers, increase you a
thousand times over, and bless you as he
promised! ¹² But how can I alone bear the
crushing burden that you are, along with
your bickering? ¹³ ᵉ Choose wise, intelligent and experienced men from each of
your tribes, that I may appoint them as
your leaders.' ¹⁴ You answered me, 'We
agree to do as you have proposed.' ¹⁵ So I
took outstanding men of your tribes, wise
and experienced, and made them your
leaders as officials over thousands, over
hundreds, over fifties and over tens, and
other tribal officers. ¹⁶ I charged your
judges at that time, 'Listen to complaints
among your kinsmen, and administer true
justice to both parties even if one of them
is an alien.ᶠ ¹⁷ In rendering judgment, do

---

a Dt 3, 2; Nm 21, 21-35.—b Nm 13, 29.—c Gn 12, 7; 15, 18;
17, 7f; 28, 13f.—d Dt 10, 22; Gn 15, 5.—e 13ff: Ex 18, 21-
25.—f 16f: Ex 18, 26; 2 Chr 19, 6f; Prv 24, 23; Jn 7, 24; Jas 2, 9.

1, 1: The local setting of all these discourses is *in the land of
Moab beyond the Jordan* (cf v 5), also known as *the plains of
Moab* (Nm 36, 13).
1, 7: The Amorites and the Canaanites formed the principal
part of the pre-Israelite population of Palestine. *The foothills:*
the hills on the western slope of the Judean mountain range. *The
Arabah:* the valley of the Jordan and the depression south of the
Dead Sea. *The Negeb:* the arid land in southern Palestine.
1, 9: *Carry you:* cf v 31.

not consider who a person is; give ear to the lowly and to the great alike, fearing no man, for judgment is God's. Refer to me any case that is too hard for you and I will hear it.' [18] Thereupon I gave you all the commands you were to fulfill.

The Twelve Scouts. [19] "Then, in obedience to the command of the LORD, our God, we set out from Horeb and journeyed through the whole desert, vast and fearful as you have seen,[g] in the direction of the hill country of the Amorites. We had reached Kadesh-barnea [20] when I said to you, 'You have come to the hill country of the Amorites, which the LORD, our God, is giving us. [21] The LORD, your God, has given this land over to you. Go up and occupy it, as the LORD, the God of your fathers, commands you. Do not fear or lose heart.' [22][h] Then all of you came up to me and said, 'Let us send men ahead to reconnoiter the land for us and report to us on the road we must follow and the cities we must take.' [23] Agreeing with the proposal, I chose twelve men from your number, one from each tribe. [24] They set out into the hill country as far as the Wadi Eshcol, and explored it. [25] Then, taking along some of the fruit of the land, they brought it down to us and reported, 'The land which the LORD, our God, gives us is good.'

Threats of Revolt. [26] "But you refused to go up,[i] and after defying the command of the LORD, your God, [27] you set to murmuring in your tents,* 'Out of hatred for us the LORD has brought us up out of the land of Egypt,[j] to deliver us into the hands of the Amorites and destroy us. [28] What shall we meet with up there? Our kinsmen have made us fainthearted by reporting that the people are stronger and taller than we, and their cities are large and fortified to the sky; besides, they saw the Anakim there.'[k]

[29] "But I said to you, 'Have no dread or fear of them. [30] The LORD, your God, who goes before you, will himself fight for you, just as he took your part before your very

eyes in Egypt, [31] as well as in the desert, where you saw how the LORD, your God, carried you, as a man carries his child, all along your journey until you arrived at this place.' [32] Despite this, you would not trust the LORD, your God, [33] who journeys before you to find you a resting place—by day in the cloud, and by night in the fire, to show the way you must go.[l] [34] When the LORD heard your words, he was angry; [35] and he swore, 'Not one man of this evil generation shall look upon the good land I swore to give to your fathers,[m] [36] except Caleb,* son of Jephunneh; he shall see it. For to him and to his sons I will give the land he trod upon, because he has followed the LORD unreservedly.'

[37] "The LORD was angered against me also on your account, and said, 'Not even you shall enter there,[n] [38] but your aide Joshua,[o] son of Nun, shall enter. Encourage him, for he is to give Israel its heritage. [39] Your little ones, who you said would become booty, and your children, who as yet do not know good from bad—they shall enter; to them I will give it, and they shall occupy it.[p] [40] But as for yourselves: turn about and proceed into the desert on the Red Sea road.'

Unsuccessful Invasion. [41][q] "In reply you said to me, 'We have sinned against the LORD. We will go up ourselves and fight, just as the LORD, our God, commanded us.' And each of you girded on his weapons, making light of going up into the hill country. [42] But the LORD said to me, 'Warn them: Do not go up and fight, lest you be beaten down before your enemies, for I will not be in your midst.' [43] I gave you this warning but you would not listen. In defiance of the LORD's command you arrogantly marched off into the hill country. [44] Then the Amorites living there came out against you and, like bees, chased you, cutting you down in Seir as far as Hormah. [45] On your return you wept before the LORD, but he did not listen to your cry or give ear to you. [46] That is why you had to stay as long as you did at Kadesh.

CHAPTER 2

Northward along Edom. [1] "When we did turn and proceed into the desert on the Red Sea road,[r] as the LORD had commanded me, we circled around the highlands of Seir for a long time. [2] Finally the LORD said to me, [3] 'You have wandered

---

g Dt 8, 15; 32, 10.—h 22-28: Nm 13, 2-34.—i Dt 9, 23.—j Dt 9, 28; Nm 14, 1-4; Ps 106, 25.—k Dt 9, 1f.—l Ex 13, 21; Nm 10, 33f; 14, 14.—m 34ff: Nm 14, 22f. 28-38; Jos 14, 9.—n Dt 4, 21; 34, 4; Nm 20, 12—o Dt 31, 3. 7; Nm 27, 18ff; 34, 17.—p 39f: Nm 14, 31.—q 41-45: Nm 14, 40. 42-45.—r Dt 1, 40; Nm 14, 25; 21, 4.

1, 27: *In your tents:* among yourselves.
1, 36: *Except Caleb:* Joshua also was allowed to enter, but he is not referred to here because special mention is made of him in v 38 as the successor of Moses.

round these highlands long enough; turn and go north. [4] Give this order to the people: You are now about to pass through the territory of your kinsmen, the descendants of Esau, who live in Seir. Though they are afraid of you, be very careful [5] not to come in conflict with them, for I will not give you so much as a foot of their land, since I have already given Esau possession of the highlands of Seir. [6] You shall purchase from them with silver the food you eat and the well water you drink. [7] The LORD, your God, has blessed you in all your undertakings; he has been concerned about your journey through this vast desert. It is now forty years that he has been with you, and you have never been in want.'[s]

Along Moab. [8] "Then we left behind us the Arabah route, Elath, Ezion-geber, and Seir, where our kinsmen, the descendants of Esau, live; and we went on toward the desert of Moab.[t] [9] And the LORD said to me, 'Do not show hostility to the Moabites or engage them in battle, for I will not give you possession of any of their land, since I have given Ar to the descendants of Lot as their own.[u] [10] [Formerly the Emim lived there, a people strong and numerous and tall like the Anakim;[v] [11] like them they were considered Rephaim. It was the Moabites who called them Emim. [12] In Seir, however, the former inhabitants were the Horites;[w] the descendants of Esau dispossesed them, clearing them out of the way and taking their place, just as the Israelites have done in the land of their heritage which the LORD has given them.] [13] Get ready, then, to cross the Wadi Zered.'[x] So we crossed it. [14] Thirty-eight years had elapsed between our departure from Kadesh-barnea and that crossing; in the meantime the whole generation of soldiers had perished from the camp, as the LORD had sworn they should.[y] [15] For it was the LORD's hand that was against them, till he wiped them out of the camp completely.

Along Ammon. [16] "When at length death had put an end to all the soldiers among the people, [17] the LORD said to me, [18] 'You are now about to leave Ar and the territory of Moab behind. [19] As you come opposite the Ammonites,[z] do not show hostility or come in conflict with them, for I will not give you possession of any land of the Ammonites, since I have given it to the descendants of Lot as their own. [20] [This also was considered a country of the Rephaim

from its former inhabitants, whom the Ammonites called Zamzummim, [21] a people strong and numerous and tall like the Anakim. But these, too, the LORD cleared out of the way for the Ammonites, who ousted them and took their place. [22] He had done the same for the descendants of Esau, who dwell in Seir, by clearing the Horites out of their way, so that the descendants of Esau have taken their place down to the present. [23] So also the Caphtorim,* migrating from Caphtor, cleared away the Avvim, who once dwelt in villages as far as Gaza, and took their place.]

Defeat of Sihon. [24] " 'Advance now across the Wadi Arnon.[a] I now deliver into your hands Sihon, the Amorite king of Heshbon, and his land. Begin the occupation; engage him in battle. [25] This day I will begin to put a fear and dread of you into every nation under the heavens, so that at the mention of your name they will quake and tremble before you.'

[26] "So I sent messengers from the desert of Kedemoth to Sihon, king of Heshbon, with this offer of peace: [27] 'Let me pass through your country by the highway; I will go along it without turning aside to the right or to the left. [28] For the food I eat which you will supply, and for the water you give me to drink, you shall be paid in silver. Only let me march through, [29] as the descendants of Esau who dwell in Seir[b] and the Moabites who dwell in Ar have done, until I cross the Jordan into the land which the LORD, our God, is about to give us.' [30] But Sihon, king of Heshbon, refused to let us pass through his land, because the LORD, your God, made him stubborn in mind and obstinate in heart that he might deliver him up to you, as indeed he has now done.

[31] "Then the LORD said to me, 'Now that I have already begun to hand over to you Sihon and his land, begin the actual occupation.' [32] So Sihon and all his people advanced against us to join battle at Jahaz; [33] but since the LORD, our God, had delivered him to us, we defeated him and his sons and all his people.[c] [34] At that time we

2, 23: *The Caphtorim:* members of one of the groups of sea peoples who invaded the coast of Egypt and the southern part of Palestine about 1200 B.C. *Caphtor:* the ancient name of the island of Crete. Cf Am 9, 7.

seized all his cities and doomed* them all, with their men, women and children; we left no survivor. *d* 35 Our only booty was the livestock and the loot of the captured cities. 36 From Aroer on the edge of the Wadi Arnon and from the city in the wadi itself, as far as Gilead, *e* no city was too well fortified for us to whom the LORD had delivered them up. 37 However, in obedience to the command of the LORD, our God, you did not encroach upon any of the Ammonite land, neither the region bordering on the Wadi Jabbok, nor the cities of the highlands. *f*

CHAPTER 3

Defeat of Og. 1 "Then we turned and proceeded toward Bashan. But Og, king of Bashan, *g* advanced against us with all his people to give battle at Edrei. 2 The LORD, however, said to me, *h* 'Do not be afraid of him, for I have delivered him into your hand with all his people and his land. Do to him as you did to Sihon, king of the Amorites, who lived in Heshbon.' 3 And thus the LORD, our God, delivered into our hands Og, king of Bashan, with all his people. We defeated him so completely that we left him no survivor. 4 At that time we captured all his cities, none of them eluding our grasp, the whole region of Argob, the kingdom of Og in Bashan: sixty cities in all, 5 to say nothing of the great number of unwalled towns. All the cities were fortified with high walls and gates and bars. 6 *i* As we had done to Sihon, king of Heshbon, so also here we doomed all the cities, with their men, women and children; 7 but all the livestock and the loot of each city we took as booty for ourselves.

8 "And so at that time we took from the two kings of the Amorites beyond the Jordan the territory from the Wadi Arnon to Mount Hermon 9 [which is called Sirion by the Sidonians and Senir by the Amorites], 10 comprising all the cities of the plateau and all Gilead and all the cities of the kingdom of Og in Bashan including Salecah and Edrei. 11 [Og, king of Bashan, was the

last remaining survivor of the Rephaim. He had a bed of iron,* nine regular cubits long and four wide, which is still preserved in Rabbah of the Ammonites.]

Allotment of the Conquered Lands. 12 *j* "When we occupied the land at that time, I gave Reuben and Gad the territory from Aroer, on the edge of the Wadi Arnon, halfway up into the highlands of Gilead, with the cities therein. 13 The rest of Gilead and all of Bashan, the kingdom of Og, the whole Argob region, I gave to the half-tribe of Manasseh. [All this region of Bashan was once called a land of the Rephaim. 14 Jair, a Manassehite clan, *k* took all the region of Argob as far as the border of the Geshurites and Maacathites, and called it after his own name Bashan Havvoth-jair, the name it bears today.] 15 To Machir I gave Gilead, 16 and to Reuben and Gad the territory from Gilead to the Wadi Arnon—including the wadi bed and its banks—and to the Wadi Jabbock, which is the border of the Ammonites, 17 as well as the Arabah with the Jordan and its eastern banks from Chinnereth to the Salt Sea of the Arabah, under the slopes of Pisgah. *l*

18 "At that time I charged them* as follows: 'The LORD, your God, has given you this land as your own. But all you troops equipped for battle must cross over in the vanguard of your brother Israelites. *m* 19 Only your wives and children, as well as your livestock, of which I know you have a large number, shall remain behind in the towns I have given you, *n* 20 until the LORD has settled your kinsmen as well, and they too possess the land which the LORD, your God, will give them on the other side of the Jordan. *o* Then you may all return to the possessions I have given you.'

21 "It was then that I instructed Joshua, 'Your eyes have seen all that the LORD, your God, has done to both these kings; so, too, will the LORD do to all the kingdoms which you will encounter over there. 22 Fear them not, for the LORD, your God, will fight for you.'

Refusal to Moses. 23 "And it was then that I besought the LORD, 24 'O LORD God, you have begun to show to your servant your greatness and might. For what god in heaven or on earth can perform deeds as mighty as yours? 25 Ah, let me cross over and see this good land beyond the Jordan, this fine hill country, and the Lebanon!' 26 But the LORD was angry with

d Dt 3, 6; 29, 7f.—e Dt 3, 12; Jos 13, 9. 16; Jgs 11, 26.—f Nm 21, 24; Jos 12, 2.—g Dt 29, 6; Nm 21, 33.—h 2f: Nm 21, 34f.—i Ps 135, 10ff.—j 12f: Nm 32, 29. 32f; Jos 13, 8. 29.—k Nm 32, 41; Jos 13, 11. 13.—l Dt 4, 49; Jos 12, 3.—m Jos 1, 14; 4, 12.— n Nm 32, 1. 4; Jos 1, 14.—o Jos 22, 4.

2, 34: *Doomed:* see notes on Nm 18, 14; 21, 3.
3, 11: *Bed of iron:* some translate, "a sarcophagus of basalt."
3, 18: *I charged them:* the words which follow were spoken to the men of Reuben and Gad (cf Nm 32).

me on your account and would not hear me.[p] 'Enough!' the LORD said to me. 'Speak to me no more of this. [27]Go up to the top of Pisgah and look out to the west, and to the north, and to the south, and to the east. Look well, for you shall not cross this Jordan.[q] [28]Commission Joshua,[r] and encourage and strengthen him, for he shall cross at the head of this people and shall put them in possession of the land you are to see.' [29]This was while we were in the ravine opposite Beth-peor.

CHAPTER 4

Advantages of Fidelity. [1]"Now, Israel, hear the statutes and decrees which I am teaching you to observe, that you may live, and may enter in and take possession of the land which the LORD, the God of your fathers, is giving you. [2]In your observance of the commandments of the LORD, your God,[s] which I enjoin upon you, you shall not add to what I command you nor subtract from it. [3]You have seen with your own eyes what the LORD did at Baal-peor:[t] the LORD, your God, destroyed from your midst everyone that followed the Baal of Peor; [4]but you, who clung to the LORD your God, are all alive today. [5]Therefore, I teach you the statutes and decrees as the LORD, my God, has commanded me, that you may observe them in the land you are entering to occupy. [6]Observe them carefully, for thus will you give evidence of your wisdom and intelligence to the nations, who will hear of all these statutes and say, 'This great nation is truly a wise and intelligent people.' [7] [u] For what great nation is there that has gods so close to it as the LORD, our God, is to us whenever we call upon him? [8]Or what great nation has statutes and decrees that are as just as this whole law which I am setting before you today?

Revelation at Horeb. [9]"However, take care and be earnestly on your guard not to forget the things which your own eyes have seen, nor let them slip from your memory as long as you live, but teach them to your children[v] and to your children's children: [10] * There was the day on which you stood before the LORD, your God, at Horeb, and he said to me,[w] 'Assemble the people for me; I will have them hear my words, that they may learn to fear me as long as they live in the land and may so teach their children.' [11]You came near

and stood at the foot of the mountain,[x] which blazed to the very sky with fire and was enveloped in a dense black cloud. [12]Then the LORD spoke to you from the midst of the fire.[y] You heard the sound of the words, but saw no form; there was only a voice. [13]He proclaimed to you his covenant, which he commanded you to keep: the ten commandments, which he wrote on two tablets of stone. [14]The LORD charged me at that time to teach you the statutes and decrees which you are to observe over in the land you will occupy.

Danger of Idolatry. [15]"You saw no form at all on the day the LORD spoke to you at Horeb from the midst of the fire.[z] Be strictly on your guard, therefore, [16]not to degrade yourselves by fashioning an idol to represent any figure, whether it be the form of a man or of a woman,[a] [17]of any animal on the earth or of any bird that flies in the sky, [18]of anything that crawls on the ground or of any fish in the waters under the earth. [19]And when you look up to the heavens and behold the sun or the moon or any star among the heavenly hosts, do not be led astray into adoring them and serving them.[b] These the LORD, your God, has let fall to the lot of all other nations under the heavens; [20]but you he has taken and led out of that iron foundry,* Egypt, that you might be his very own people, as you are today.[c] [21]Since the LORD was angered against me on your account[d] and swore that I should not cross the Jordan nor enter the good land which he is giving you as a heritage, [22]I myself shall die in this country without crossing the Jordan; but you will cross over and take possession of that good land.[e] [23]Take heed, therefore, lest, forgetting the covenant which the LORD, your God, has made with you, you fashion for yourselves against his command an idol in any form whatsoever.[f] [24]For the LORD, your God, is a consuming fire, a jealous God.

---

p Dt 4, 21.—q Dt 34, 4; Nm 27, 12f.—r Dt 1, 38; 31, 7; Nm 27, 22f.—s Dt 13, 1.—t Nm 25, 3-9.—u 2 Sm 7, 23.—v Dt 11, 19; Ps 78, 3-6.—w Heb 12, 18f.—x Ex 19, 17f.—y Dt 4, 33. 36; 5, 4.—z Ex 24, 12; 31, 18; 34, 28.—a Dt 5, 8; Ex 20, 4.—b Dt 17, 3; Jb 31, 26ff.—c 1 Kgs 8, 51; Jer 11, 4.—d Dt 1, 37; 3, 26.—e Dt 3, 27.—f Dt 4, 16.

4, 10: Beginning here and continuing on for several verses (at least to the end of v 14) is the "reminiscence," the account of the things that the Israelites should recall and teach their children.

4, 20: Egypt is called an *iron foundry*, or furnace for smelting iron, because God allowed the Israelites to be afflicted there for the sake of their spiritual purification; the same expression for Egypt occurs also in 1 Kgs 8, 51; Jer 11, 4; compare the expression, "the furnace of affliction," in Is 48, 10.

God's Fidelity. ²⁵"When you have children and grandchildren, and have grown old* in the land, should you then degrade yourselves by fashioning an idol in any form and by this evil done in his sight provoke the LORD, your God, ²⁶I call heaven and earth this day to witness against you, that you shall all quickly perish from the land which you will occupy when you cross the Jordan. You shall not live in it for any length of time but shall be promptly wiped out. ²⁷The LORD will scatter you among the nations, and there shall remain but a handful of you among the nations to which the LORD will lead you.ᵍ ²⁸There you shall serve gods fashioned by the hands of man out of wood and stone, gods which can neither see nor hear, neither eat nor smell.ʰ ²⁹Yet there too you shall seek the LORD, your God; and you shall indeed find him when you search after him with your whole heart and your whole soul.ⁱ ³⁰In your distress, when all these things shall have come upon you, you shall finally return to the LORD, your God, and heed his voice. ³¹Since the LORD, your God, is a merciful God, he will not abandon and destroy you, nor forget the covenant which under oath he made with your fathers.ʲ

Proofs of God's Love. ³²"Ask now of the days of old, before your time, ever since God created man upon the earth; ask from one end of the sky to the other: Did anything so great ever happen before? Was it ever heard of? ³³Did a people ever hear the voice of God speaking from the midst of fire, as you did, and live?ᵏ ³⁴Or did any god venture to go and take a nation for himself from the midst of another nation, by testings,* by signs and wonders,ˡ by war, with his strong hand and outstretched arm, and by great terrors, all of which the LORD, your God, did for you in Egypt before your very eyes? ³⁵All this you were allowed to see that you might know the LORD is God and there is no other. ³⁶Out

of the heavens he let you hear his voice to discipline you; on earth he let you see his great fire, and you heard him speaking out of the fire. ³⁷For love of your fathers he chose their descendants and personally led you out of Egypt by his great power, ³⁸driving out of your way nations greater and mightier than you, so as to bring you in and to make their land your heritage, as it is today. ³⁹This is why you must now know, and fix in your heart, that the LORD is God in the heavens above and on earth below, and that there is no other.ᵐ ⁴⁰You must keep his statutes and commandments which I enjoin on you today, that you and your children after you may prosper, and that you may have long life on the land which the LORD, your God, is giving you forever."ⁿ

Cities of Refuge. ⁴¹ ᵒ Then Moses set apart three cities in the region east of the Jordan, ⁴²that a homicide might take refuge there if he unwittingly killed his neighbor to whom he had previously borne no malice, and that he might save his life by fleeing to one of these cities: ⁴³Bezer in the desert, in the region of the plateau, for the Reubenites; Ramoth in Gilead for the Gadites; and Golan in Bashan for the Manassehites.

II: GOD AND HIS COVENANT

Introduction. ⁴⁴This is the law which Moses set before the Israelites. ⁴⁵These are the ordinances, statutes and decrees which he proclaimed to them when they had come out of Egypt ⁴⁶and were beyond the Jordan in the ravine opposite Beth-peor, in the land of Sihon, king of the Amorites, who dwelt in Heshbon and whom Moses and the Israelites defeated after coming out of Egypt. ⁴⁷They occupied his land and the land of Og, king of Bashan, as well—the land of these two kings of the Amorites in the region east of the Jordan: ⁴⁸from Aroer on the edge of the Wadi Arnon to Mount Sion* (that is, Hermon) ⁴⁹and all the Arabah east of the Jordan, as far as the Arabah Sea under the slopes of Pisgah.ᵖ

CHAPTER 5

The Covenant at Horeb. ¹Moses summoned all Israel and said to them, "Hear, O Israel, the statutes and decrees which I proclaim in your hearing this day, that you may learn them and take care to observe

---

g 27f: Dt 28, 36. 62. 64.—h Ps 135, 15ff; Is 44, 9.—i Jer 29, 13.—j Dt 31, 8.—k Dt 4, 36; 5, 24. 26; Ex 20, 19.—l Dt 7, 19; 26, 8; 29, 2; Ex 7, 3; 15, 3-10; Jer 32, 21.—m Dt 4, 35.—n Dt 6, 2f; 12, 28.—o 41ff: Dt 19, 2-13; Nm 35, 6-29; Jos 20, 8; 21, 27. 36f; 1 Chr 6, 71. 80.—p Dt 3, 17.

4, 25: *Grown old:* Israel will lose the freshness of its youthful fervor.

4, 34: *Testings:* the demonstrations of God's power as in the ten great plagues of Egypt; cf Dt 7, 19; 29, 2.

4, 48: *Sion:* another name for Mount Hermon, besides those mentioned in Dt 3, 9.

them. [2]The LORD, our God, made a covenant with us at Horeb;[q] [3]not with our fathers did he make this covenant, but with us, all of us who are alive here this day. [4]The LORD spoke with you face to face on the mountain from the midst of the fire. [5] [r] Since you were afraid of the fire and would not go up the mountain, I stood between the LORD and you at that time, to announce to you these words of the LORD:

The Decalogue. [6] [s] 'I, the LORD, am your God, who brought you out of the land of Egypt,[t] that place of slavery. [7] [u] You shall not have other gods besides me. [8]You shall not carve idols for yourselves[v] in the shape of anything in the sky above or on the earth below or in the waters beneath the earth; [9] * you shall not bow down before them or worship them. For I, the LORD, your God, am a jealous God,[w] inflicting punishments for their fathers' wickedness on the children of those who hate me, down to the third and fourth generation [10]but bestowing mercy, down to the thousandth generation,[x] on the children of those who love me and keep my commandments.

[11]'You shall not take the name of the LORD, your God, in vain.[y] For the LORD will not leave unpunished him who takes his name in vain.

[12]'Take care to keep holy the sabbath day as the LORD, your God, commanded you. [13]Six days you may labor and do all your work; [14]but the seventh day is the sabbath of the LORD, your God. [z] No work may be done then, whether by you, or your son or daughter, or your male or female slave, or your ox or ass or any of your beasts, or the alien who lives with you. Your male and female slave should rest as you do. [15]For remember that you too were once slaves in Egypt,[a] and the LORD, your God, brought you from there with his strong hand and outstretched arm. That is why the LORD, your God, has commanded you to observe the sabbath day.

[16] [b] 'Honor your father and your mother, as the LORD, your God, has commanded you, that you may have a long life and prosperity in the land which the LORD, your God, is giving you.

[17] [c] 'You shall not kill.

[18]'You shall not commit adultery.

[19]'You shall not steal.

[20]'You shall not bear dishonest witness against your neighbor.

[21]'You shall not covet your neighbor's wife.

'You shall not desire your neighbor's house or field, nor his male or female slave, nor his ox or ass, nor anything that belongs to him.'

Moses as Mediator. [22]"These words, and nothing more, the LORD spoke with a loud voice to your entire assembly on the mountain from the midst of the fire and the dense cloud. He wrote them upon two tablets of stone and gave them to me. [23]But when you heard the voice from the midst of the darkness, while the mountain was ablaze with fire, you came to me in the person of all your tribal heads and elders, [24]and said, 'The LORD, our God, has indeed let us see his glory and his majesty! We have heard his voice from the midst of the fire[d] and have found out today that a man can still live after God has spoken with him. [25]But why should we die now? Surely this great fire will consume us. If we hear the voice of the LORD, our God, any more, we shall die.[e] [26]For what mortal has heard, as we have, the voice of the living God speaking from the midst of fire, and survived? [27]Go closer, you, and hear all that the LORD, our God, will say, and then tell us what the LORD, our God, tells you; we will listen and obey.'[f]

[28]"The LORD heard your words as you were speaking to me and said to me, 'I have heard the words these people have spoken to you, which are all well said.[g] [29]Would that they might always be of such a mind, to fear me and to keep all my commandments! Then they and their descendants would prosper forever. [30]Go, tell them to return to their tents. [31]Then you wait here near me and I will give you all the commandments, the statutes and decrees you must teach them, that they may observe them in the land which I am giving them to possess.'

q Dt 28, 69.—r Ex 24, 2.—s 6-21: Ex 20, 2-17.—t Ps 81, 11.—u Ps 81, 10.—v Dt 27, 15; Lv 26, 1; Ps 97, 7.—w Ex 34, 14.—x Dt 7, 9; Ex 20, 6.—y Mt 5, 33.—z Gn 2, 2; Ex 20, 8; 23, 12; Heb 4, 4.—a Dt 15, 15; 16, 12; 24, 18. 22.—b Sir 3, 2-16; Mt 15, 4; Mk 7, 10; Lk 18, 20; Eph 6, 2.—c 17-20: Mt 5, 21. 27; Lk 18, 20; Jas 2, 11.—d Dt 4, 33.—e Dt 18, 16.—f Ex 20, 19.—g Dt 18, 17.

5, 9f: God does not punish us for another's sins, but because of the solidarity of human society, the good or evil deeds of one generation may make their effects felt even in later generations. Yet note how God's mercy allows the good effects of virtue to last much longer than the bad effects of vice: a thousand generations compared to three or four.

³²"Be careful, therefore, to do as the LORD, your God, has commanded you, not turning aside to the right or to the left, ³³but following exactly the way prescribed for you by the LORD, your God, that you may live and prosper, and may have long life in the land which you are to occupy.^h

CHAPTER 6

¹"These then are the commandments, the statutes and decreesⁱ which the LORD, your God, has ordered that you be taught to observe in the land into which you are crossing for conquest, ²so that you and your son and your grandson may fear the LORD, your God, and keep, throughout the days of your lives, all his statutes and commandments^j which I enjoin on you, and thus have long life. ³Hear then, Israel, and be careful to observe them, that you may grow and prosper the more, in keeping with the promise of the LORD, the God of your fathers, to give you a land flowing with milk and honey.

The Great Commandment. ⁴*"Hear, O Israel! The LORD is our God, the LORD alone!^k ⁵Therefore, you shall love the LORD, your God, with all your heart, and with all your soul, and with all your strength.^l ⁶Take to heart these words which I enjoin on you today. ⁷Drill them into your children.^m Speak of them at home and abroad, whether you are busy or at rest. ⁸Bind them at your wrist as a sign* and let them be as a pendant on your forehead.ⁿ ⁹Write them on the doorposts of your houses and on your gates.^o

Fidelity in Prosperity. ¹⁰"When the LORD, your God, brings you into the land which he swore to your fathers, Abraham,

---

h Dt 4, 40.—i Dt 4, 1; 5, 31; 12, 1.—j Dt 4, 40; 5, 29; 10, 12f.—k Mk 12, 29.—l Dt 10, 12; 11, 13; Mt 22, 37; Mk 12, 30; Lk 10, 27.—m 6f: Dt 4, 9; 11, 18; 32, 46.—n Dt 11, 18; Ex 13, 9. 16; Mt 23, 5.—o Dt 11, 20.—p 10f: Jos 24, 13.—q Dt 5, 6.—r Dt 10, 20; Mt 4, 10; Lk 4, 8.—s 14f: Dt 8, 19: 11, 16. 28.—t Nm 20, 1-13.—u Ex 23, 27; 34, 11.—v Ex 12, 26; 13, 14.—w Ex 20, 2.

6, 4f: This passage contains the basic principle of the whole Mosaic law, the keynote of the Book of Deuteronomy: since the Lord alone is God, we must love him with an undivided heart. Christ cited these words as "the greatest and the first commandment," embracing in itself the whole law of God (Mt 22, 37f and parallels).

6, 8: *Bind them . . . as a sign:* these injunctions were probably meant merely in a figurative sense; cf Ex 13, 9. 16. However, the later Jews understood them literally, and tied on their wrists and foreheads "phylacteries," boxes containing strips of parchment on which the words were inscribed; cf Mt 23, 5.

6, 13: *Him shall you serve:* here, to "serve" God means especially to "worship" him; in this sense it is quoted by our Lord (Mt 4, 10) as an argument against worshiping the devil.

Isaac and Jacob, that he would give you, a land with fine, large cities that you did not build,^p ¹¹with houses full of goods of all sorts that you did not garner, with cisterns that you did not dig, with vineyards and olive groves that you did not plant; and when, therefore, you eat your fill, ¹²*q* take care not to forget the LORD, who brought you out of the land of Egypt, that place of slavery. ¹³*r* The LORD, your God, shall you fear; him shall you serve,* and by his name shall you swear. ¹⁴You shall not follow other gods, such as those of the surrounding nations, ¹⁵lest the wrath of the LORD, your God, flare up against you and he destroy you from the face of the land;^s for the LORD, your God, who is in your midst, is a jealous God.

¹⁶ *t* "You shall not put the LORD, your God, to the test, as you did at Massah. ¹⁷But keep the commandments of the LORD, your God, and the ordinances and statutes he has enjoined on you. ¹⁸Do what is right and good in the sight of the LORD, that you may, according to his word, prosper, and may enter in and possess the good land which the LORD promised on oath to your fathers, ¹⁹thrusting all your enemies out of your way.^u

Instruction to Children. ²⁰"Later on, when your son asks you what these ordinances, statutes and decrees mean^v which the LORD, our God, has enjoined on you, ²¹you shall say to your son, 'We were once slaves of Pharaoh in Egypt, but the LORD brought us out of Egypt with his strong hand^w ²²and wrought before our eyes signs and wonders, great and dire, against Egypt and against Pharaoh and his whole house. ²³He brought us from there to lead us into the land he promised on oath to our fathers, and to give it to us. ²⁴Therefore, the LORD commanded us to observe all these statutes in fear of the LORD, our God, that we may always have as prosperous and happy a life as we have today; ²⁵and our justice before the LORD, our God, is to consist in carefully observing all these commandments he has enjoined on us.'

CHAPTER 7

Destruction of Pagans. ¹"When the LORD, your God, brings you into the land which you are to enter and occupy, and dislodges great nations before you—the Hittites, Girgashites, Amorites, Canaanites, Perizzites, Hivites and Jebusites:[x] seven nations more numerous and powerful than you—[2]and when the LORD, your God, delivers them up to you and you defeat them, you shall doom them. Make no covenant with them[y] and show them no mercy. [3]You shall not intermarry with them, neither giving your daughters to their sons nor taking their daughters for your sons.[z] [4]For they would turn your sons from following me to serving other gods, and then the wrath of the LORD would flare up against you and quickly destroy you.

[5]"But this is how you must deal with them:[a] Tear down their altars, smash their sacred pillars, chop down their sacred poles,* and destroy their idols by fire. [6]For you are a people sacred to the LORD, your God; he has chosen you from all the nations on the face of the earth to be a people peculiarly his own.[b] [7]It was not because you are the largest of all nations that the LORD set his heart on you and chose you, for you are really the smallest of all nations. [8]It was because the LORD loved you and because of his fidelity to the oath he had sworn to your fathers, that he brought you out with his strong hand from the place of slavery, and ransomed you from the hand of Pharaoh, king of Egypt. [9] [c] Understand, then, that the LORD, your God, is God indeed, the faithful God who keeps his merciful covenant down to the thousandth generation toward those who love him and keep his commandments, [10]but who repays with destruction the person who hates him; he does not dally with such a one, but makes him personally pay for it. [11]You shall therefore carefully observe the commandments, the statutes and the decrees which I enjoin on you today.

Blessings of Obedience. [12] [d] "As your reward for heeding these decrees and observing them carefully, the LORD, your God, will keep with you the merciful covenant which he promised on oath to your fathers. [13]He will love and bless and multiply you; he will bless the fruit of your womb and the produce of your soil, your grain and wine and oil, the issue of your herds and the young of your flocks, in the land which he swore to your fathers he would give you.[e] [14]You

will be blessed above all peoples; no man or woman among you shall be childless nor shall your livestock be barren. [15]The LORD will remove all sickness from you; he will not afflict you with any of the malignant diseases that you know from Egypt, but will leave them with all your enemies.

[16]"You shall consume all the nations which the LORD, your God, will deliver up to you. You are not to look on them with pity, lest you be ensnared into serving their gods. [17]Perhaps you will say to yourselves,[f] 'These nations are greater than we. How can we dispossess them?' [18]But do not be afraid of them. Rather, call to mind what the LORD, your God, did to Pharaoh and to all Egypt: [19]the great testings which your own eyes have seen, the signs and wonders, his strong hand and outstretched arm with which the LORD, your God, brought you out.[g] The same also will he do to all the nations of whom you are now afraid. [20]Moreover, the LORD, your God, will send hornets among them, until the survivors who have hidden from you are destroyed.[h] [21]Therefore, do not be terrified by them, for the LORD, your God, who is in your midst, is a great and awesome God. [22]He will dislodge these nations before you little by little. You cannot exterminate them all at once, lest the wild beasts become too numerous for you.[i] [23]The LORD, your God, will deliver them up to you and will rout them utterly until they are annihilated.[j] [24]He will deliver their kings into your hand, that you may make their names perish from under the heavens. No man will be able to stand up against you,[k] till you have put an end to them. [25]The images of their gods you shall destroy by fire. Do not covet the silver or gold on them, nor take it for yourselves, lest you be ensnared by it; for it is an abomination to the LORD, your God. [26]You shall not bring any abominable thing into your house, lest you be doomed with it; loathe and abhor it utterly as a thing that is doomed.

---

x Ex 23, 23; 33, 2.—y Ex 34, 12.—z 3f: Ex 34, 16; 1 Kgs 11, 1f.—a Dt 12, 3; Ex 34, 13.—b Dt 14, 2; 26, 18; Ex 19, 6.—c 9f: Dt 5, 9f.—d 12-16: Dt 28, 1-14; Ex 23, 22-26; Lv 26, 3-13.—e Dt 30, 9.—f 17f: Dt 1, 28ff.—g Dt 4, 34.—h Ex 23, 28ff.—i Ex 23, 29f.—j Dt 7, 2.—k Dt 11, 25.

7, 5: *Sacred pillars . . . poles:* see note on Ex 34, 13.

CHAPTER 8

God's Care. [1]"Be careful to observe all the commandments[*l*] I enjoin on you today, that you may live and increase, and may enter in and possess the land which the LORD promised on oath to your fathers. [2]Remember how for forty years now the LORD, your God, has directed all your journeying in the desert,[*m*] so as to test you by affliction and find out whether or not it was your intention to keep his commandments. [3]He therefore let you be afflicted with hunger, and then fed you with manna,[*n*] a food unknown to you and your fathers, in order to show you that not by bread alone[*] does man live, but by every word that comes forth from the mouth of the LORD. [4]The clothing did not fall from you in tatters, nor did your feet swell these forty years.[*o*] [5]So you must realize that the LORD, your God, disciplines you even as a man disciplines his son.

Danger of Prosperity. [6]"Therefore, keep the commandments of the LORD, your God, by walking in his ways and fearing him. [7]For the LORD, your God, is bringing you into a good country,[*p*] a land with streams of water, with springs and fountains welling up in the hills and valleys, [8]a land of wheat and barley, of vines and fig trees and pomegranates, of olive trees and of honey, [9]a land where you can eat bread without stint and where you will lack nothing, a land whose stones contain iron and in whose hills you can mine copper. [10]But when you have eaten your fill, you must bless the LORD, your God, for the good country he has given you. [11]Be careful not to forget the LORD, your God, by neglecting his commandments and decrees and statutes which I enjoin on you today: [12]lest, when you have eaten your fill, and have built fine houses and lived in them, [13]and have increased your herds and flocks, your silver and gold, and all your property, [14]you then become haughty of heart and unmindful of the LORD, your God, who brought you out of the land

of Egypt, that place of slavery; [15]who guided you through the vast and terrible desert with its saraph serpents and scorpions, its parched and waterless ground; who brought forth water for you from the flinty rock[*q*] [16]and fed you in the desert with manna, a food unknown to your fathers, that he might afflict you and test you, but also make you prosperous in the end. [17]Otherwise, you might say to yourselves,[*r*] 'It is my own power and the strength of my own hand that has obtained for me this wealth.' [18]Remember then, it is the LORD, your God, who gives you the power to acquire wealth, by fulfilling, as he has now done, the covenant which he swore to your fathers. [19]But if you forget the LORD, your God, and follow other gods, serving and worshiping them,[*s*] I forewarn you this day that you will perish utterly. [20]Like the nations which the LORD destroys before you, so shall you too perish for not heeding the voice of the LORD, your God.

CHAPTER 9

Unmerited Success. [1]"Hear, O Israel! You are now about to cross the Jordan to enter in and dispossess nations greater and stronger than yourselves, having large cities fortified to the sky,[*t*] [2]the Anakim, a people great and tall.[*u*] You know of them and have heard it said of them, 'Who can stand up against the Anakim?' [3]Understand, then, today that it is the LORD, your God, who will cross over before you as a consuming fire; he it is who will reduce them to nothing and subdue them before you, so that you can drive them out and destroy them quickly, as the LORD promised you.[*v*] [4]After the LORD, your God, has thrust them out of your way, do not say to yourselves, 'It is because of my merits that the LORD has brought me in to possess this land';[*w*] for it is really because of the wickedness of these nations that the LORD is driving them out before you. [5]No, it is not because of your merits or the integrity of your heart that you are going in to take possession of their land; but the LORD, your God, is driving these nations out before you on account of their wickedness and in order to keep the promise which he made on oath to your fathers, Abraham, Isaac and Jacob. [6]Understand this, therefore: it is not because of your

---

l Dt 4, 1; 6, 1.—m Dt 2, 7; 29, 4; Am 2, 10.—n Ex 16, 12-15. 35; Nm 11, 6-9; Mt 4, 4; Lk 4, 4.—o Dt 29, 4; Neh 9, 21.—p Dt 11, 10ff.—q Wis 11, 4.—r Dt 9, 4.—s Dt 4, 25f; 30, 18.—t Dt 1, 28; 4, 38.—u Nm 13, 33.—v Dt 31, 3; Ex 23, 27.—w Dt 8, 17.

8, 3: *Not by bread alone,* etc.: quoted by our Lord in Mt 4, 4. The sense is: God takes care of those who love him even when natural means seem to fail them.

merits that the LORD, your God, is giving you this good land to possess, for you are a stiff-necked people.

The Golden Calf. 7 "Bear in mind and do not forget how you angered the LORD, your God, in the desert. From the day you left the land of Egypt until you arrived in this place, you have been rebellious toward the LORD.ˣ 8 At Horeb you so provoked the LORD that he was angry enough to destroy you,ʸ 9 when I had gone up the mountain to receive the stone tablets of the covenant which the LORD made with you.ᶻ Meanwhile I stayed on the mountain forty days and forty nights without eating or drinking, 10 till the LORD gave me the two tablets of stone inscribed, by God's own finger,ᵃ with a copy of all the words that the LORD spoke to you on the mountain from the midst of the fire on the day of the assembly. 11 Then, at the end of the forty days and forty nights, when the LORD had given me the two stone tablets of the covenant, 12 he said to me,ᵇ 'Go down from here now, quickly, for your people whom you have brought out of Egypt have become depraved; they have already turned aside from the way I pointed out to them and have made for themselves a molten idol. 13 I have seen now how stiff-necked this people is,' the LORD said to me. 14 'Let me be, that I may destroy them and blot out their name from under the heavens. I will then make of you a nation mightier and greater than they.'

15 "When I had come down again from the blazing, fiery mountain, with the two tablets of the covenant in both my hands,ᶜ 16 I saw how you had sinned against the LORD, your God: you had already turned aside from the way which the LORD had pointed out to you by making for yourselves a molten calf! 17 Raising the two tablets with both hands I threw them from me and broke them before your eyes.ᵈ 18 Then, as before, I lay prostrate before the LORD for forty days and forty nights without eating or drinking, because of all the sin you had committed in the sight of the LORD and the evil you had done to provoke him.ᵉ 19 For I dreaded the fierce anger of the LORD against you: his wrath would destroy you.ᶠ Yet once again the LORD listened to me. 20 With Aaron, too, the LORD was deeply angry, and would

have killed him had I not prayed for him also at that time. 21 Then, taking the calf, the sinful object you had made, and fusing it with fire, I ground it down to powder as fine as dust, which I threw into the wadi that went down the mountainside.ᵍ

22 "At Taberah, at Massah, and at Kibroth-hattaavah likewise, you provoked the LORD to anger.ʰ 23 And when he sent you up from Kadesh-barnea to take possession of the land he was giving you, you rebelled against this command of the LORD, your God, and would not trust or obey him.ⁱ 24 Ever since I have known you, you have been rebels against the LORD.

25 "Those forty days, then, and forty nights, I lay prostrate before the LORD, because he had threatened to destroy you. 26 This was my prayer to him: O Lord GOD, destroy not your people, the heritage which your majesty has ransomed and brought out of Egypt with your strong hand. 27 Remember your servants, Abraham, Isaac and Jacob. Look not upon the stubbornness of this people nor upon their wickedness and sin, 28 lest the people from whose land you have brought us say, 'The LORD was not able to bring them into the land he promised them'; or 'Out of hatred for them, he brought them out to slay them in the desert.'ʲ 29 They are, after all, your people and your heritage, whom you have brought out by your great power and with your outstretched arm.ᵏ

CHAPTER 10

1 "At that time the LORD said to me, 'Cut two tablets of stone like the former;ˡ then come up the mountain to me. Also make an ark of wood. 2 I will write upon the tablets the commandments that were on the former tablets that you broke, and you shall place them in the ark.' 3 So I made an ark of acacia wood, and cut two tablets of stone like the former, and went up the mountain carrying the two tablets.ᵐ 4 ⁿ The LORD then wrote on them, as he had written before, the ten commandments which he spoke to you on the moun-

x Dt 31, 27; Ex 14, 11; Nm 14, 11.—y Ex 32, 4; Ps 106, 19.—z Ex 24, 12. 18; Ex 34, 28.—a Ex 31, 18.—b 12ff: Ex 32, 7-10.—c Ex 32, 15.—d 16f: Ex 32, 19.—e Ex 32, 31; 34, 28.—f Dt 10, 10; Ex 32, 10.—g Ex 32, 20.—h Ex 17, 7; Nm 11, 1ff. 34.—i Nm 14, 1-4; Ps 106, 24f.—j Nm 14, 14ff.—k Dt 4, 20; Ex 6, 6f.—l Ex 34, 1.—m Ex 34, 4.—n Ex 20, 1-17; 34, 28.

tain from the midst of the fire on the day of the assembly. After the LORD had given them to me, [5] I turned and came down the mountain, and placed the tablets in the ark I had made.[o] There they have remained, in keeping with the command the LORD gave me.

[6] [The Israelites set out from Beeroth Bene-jaakan;[p] for Moserah, where Aaron died and was buried, his son Eleazar succeeding him in the priestly office. [7] From there they set out for Gudgodah, and from Gudgodah for Jotbathah,[q] a region where there is water in the wadies.]

[8] "At that time the LORD set apart the tribe of Levi to carry the ark of the covenant of the LORD,[r] to be in attendance before the LORD and minister to him, and to give blessings in his name, as they have done to this day. [9] For this reason, Levi has no share in the heritage with his brothers;[s] the LORD himself is his heritage, as the LORD, your God, has told him.

[10] "After I had spent these other forty days and forty nights on the mountain, and the LORD had once again heard me and decided not to destroy you, [11] he said to me, 'Go now and set out at the head of your people,[t] that they may enter in and occupy the land which I swore to their fathers I would give them.'

The Lord's Majesty. [12] "And now, Israel, what does the LORD, your God, ask of you but to fear the LORD, your God, and follow his ways exactly, to love and serve the LORD, your God, with all your heart and all your soul,[u] [13] to keep the commandments and statutes of the LORD which I enjoin on you today for your own good? [14] Think! The heavens, even the highest heavens,* belong to the LORD, your God, as well as the earth and everything on it.[v] [15] Yet in his love for your fathers the LORD was so attached to them as to choose you,

their descendants, in preference to all other peoples, as indeed he has now done.[w] [16] Circumcise your hearts,* therefore, and be no longer stiff-necked. [17] For the LORD, your God, is the God of gods, the LORD of lords, the great God, mighty and awesome. who has no favorites, accepts no bribes;[x] [18] who executes justice for the orphan and the widow, and befriends the alien, feeding and clothing him. [19] So you too must befriend the alien, for you were once aliens yourselves in the land of Egypt.[y] [20] The LORD, your God, shall you fear, and him shall you serve; hold fast to him and swear by his name.[z] [21] He is your glory, he, your God, who has done for you those great and terrible things which your own eyes have seen. [22] Your ancestors went down to Egypt seventy strong,[a] and now the LORD, your God, has made you as numerous as the stars of the sky.

CHAPTER 11

The Wonders of the Lord. [1] "Love the LORD, your God, therefore, and always heed his charge: his statutes, decrees and commandments. [2] It is not your children, who have not known it from experience, but you yourselves who must now understand the discipline of the LORD, your God; his majesty, his strong hand and outstretched arm; [3] the signs and deeds he wrought among the Egyptians, on Pharaoh, king of Egypt, and on all his land;[b] [4] what he did to the Egyptian army and to their horses and chariots, engulfing them in the water of the Red Sea as they pursued you,[c] and bringing ruin upon them even to this day; [5] what he did for you in the desert until you arrived in this place; [6] and what he did to the Reubenites Dathan and Abiram, sons of Eliab, when the ground opened its mouth and swallowed them up out of the midst of Israel, with their families and tents and every living thing that belonged to them.[d] [7] With your own eyes you have seen all these great deeds that the LORD has done. [8] Keep all the commandments, then, which I enjoin on you today, that you may be strong enough to enter in and take possession of the land into which you are crossing, [9] and that you may have long life on the land which the LORD swore to your fathers he would give to them and their descendants, a land flowing with milk and honey.

---

o Ex 40, 20; 1 Kgs 8, 9.—p Nm 33, 31.—q Nm 33, 32f.—r Nm 3, 6; 6, 23-27; 16, 9.—s Nm 18, 20.—t Ex 32, 34; 33, 1.—u Dt 6, 2. 5.—v Neh 9, 6.—w Dt 7, 6ff.—x 2 Chr 19, 7; Jb 34, 19; Wis 6, 7; Acts 10, 34; Rom 2, 11; Gal 2, 6.—y Ex 22, 21; 23, 9; Lv 19, 33f.—z Dt 6, 13; Mt 4, 10; Lk 4, 8.—a Gn 46, 27; Ex 1, 5; Acts 7, 14.—b Dt 6, 22; Ps 78, 42-51.—c Ex 14, 26ff; 15, 9; Pss 78, 53; 106, 11.—d Nm 16, 31ff.

10, 14: *Even the highest heavens:* literally, "and the heavens of the heavens"; compare the phrase, "the third heaven," in 2 Cor 12, 2.

10, 16: *Circumcise your hearts:* cf Dt 30, 6; Jer 4, 4; Rom 2, 29. The "uncircumcised heart" (Lv 26, 41; Jer 9, 25; Ez 44, 7. 9) is closed and unreceptive to divine grace and guidance, just as "uncircumcised ears" (Jer 6, 10) are closed to sound, and "uncircumcised lips" (Ex 6, 12. 30) do not open well in speech.

The Gift of Rain. [10]"For the land which you are to enter and occupy is not like the land of Egypt from which you have come, where you would sow your seed and then water it by hand, as in a vegetable garden. [11] *e* No, the land into which you are crossing for conquest is a land of hills and valleys that drinks in rain from the heavens, [12] a land which the LORD, your God, looks after; his eyes are upon it continually from the beginning of the year to the end. [13] * If, then, you truly heed my commandments which I enjoin on you today, loving and serving the LORD, your God, with all your heart and all your soul,*f* [14] I will give the seasonal rain to your land, the early rain* and the late rain, that you may have your grain, wine and oil to gather in; [15] and I will bring forth grass in your fields for your animals.*g* Thus you may eat your fill. [16] But be careful lest your heart be so lured away that you serve other gods and worship them.*h* [17] For then the wrath of the LORD will flare up against you and he will close up the heavens, so that no rain will fall, and the soil will not yield its crops, and you will soon perish from the good land he is giving you.

Reward of Fidelity. [18] *i* "Therefore, take these words of mine into your heart and soul. Bind them at your wrist as a sign, and let them be a pendant on your forehead. [19] Teach them to your children, speaking of them at home and abroad, whether you are busy or at rest. [20] And write them on the doorposts of your houses and on your gates, [21] so that, as long as the heavens are above the earth, you and your children may live on in the land which the LORD swore to your fathers he would give them.

[22] "For if you are careful to observe all these commandments I enjoin on you, loving the LORD, your God, and following his ways exactly, and holding fast to him, [23] the LORD will drive all these nations out of your way,*j* and you will dispossess nations greater and mightier than yourselves. [24] *k* Every place where you set foot shall be yours: from the desert and from Lebanon, from the Euphrates River to the Western Sea,* shall be your territory. [25] None shall stand up against you; the LORD, your God, will spread the fear and dread of you through any land where you set foot, as he promised you.*l*

A Blessing and a Curse. [26] *m* "I set before you here, this day, a blessing and a curse: [27] a blessing for obeying the commandments of the LORD, your God, which I enjoin on you today; [28] a curse if you do not obey the commandments of the LORD, your God, but turn aside from the way I ordain for you today, to follow other gods, whom you have not known. [29] When the LORD, your God, brings you into the land which you are to enter and occupy, then you shall pronounce the blessing on Mount Gerizim,*n* the curse* on Mount Ebal. [30] [Are they not beyond the Jordan, on the other side of the western road in the country of the Canaanites who live in the Arabah, opposite the Gilgal beside the terebinth of Moreh?] [31] For you are about to cross the Jordan to enter and occupy the land which the LORD, your God, is giving you. When, therefore, you take possession of it and settle there, [32] be careful to observe all the statutes and decrees that I set before you today.

III: EXPOSITION OF THE LAW

CHAPTER 12

One Sanctuary. [1] "These are the statutes and decrees which you must be careful to observe in the land which the LORD, the God of your fathers, has given you to occupy, as long as you live on its soil. [2] Destroy without fail every place on the high mountains, on the hills, and under every leafy tree where the nations you are to dispossess worship their gods.*o* [3] Tear down their altars, smash their sacred pillars, destroy by fire their sacred poles, and shatter the idols of their gods, that you may stamp out the remembrance of them in any such place.

e 11f: Dt 8, 7f.—f 13f: Dt 10, 12; Lv 26, 4.—g Ps 104, 14.—h 16f: Dt 4, 25f; 6, 14.—i 18-21: Dt 6, 6-9.—j Dt 7, 1; 9, 1.—k Ex 23, 31.—l Dt 2, 25; 7, 24; Ex 23, 27.—m 26ff: Dt 28, 2-45; 30, 1. 15. 19.—n Dt 27, 12f.—o 2f: Dt 7, 5; Ex 23, 24; 34, 13.

11, 13ff: As often in the Prophets, the discourse passes into the words of God himself. Cf Dt 7, 4; 17, 3; 28, 20; 29, 4f.

11, 14: *The early rain:* the rains which begin in October or November and continue intermittently throughout the winter. *The late rain:* the heavy showers of March and April. In Palestine the crops are sown in the autumn and reaped in the spring.

11, 24: *The Western Sea:* the Mediterranean.

11, 29: *You shall pronounce the blessing . . . the curse:* for the full ceremony, see chapters 27 and 28. *Gerizim . . . Ebal:* adjacent mountains in Samaria with a deep ravine between them. Their summits command an excellent view of the entire country.

⁴"That is not how you are to worship the LORD, your God. ⁵Instead,ᵖ you shall resort to the place which the LORD, your God, chooses out of all your tribes and designates as his dwelling ⁶and there you shall bring your holocausts and sacrifices, your tithes and personal contributions, your votive and freewill offerings, and the firstlings of your herds and flocks. ⁷There, too, before the LORD, your God, you and your families shall eat and make merry over all your undertakings, because the LORD, your God, has blessed you. ⁸You shall not do as we are now doing; here, everyone does what seems right to himself, ⁹since you have not yet reached your resting place, the heritage which the LORD, your God, will give you. ¹⁰But after you have crossed the Jordan and dwell in the land which the LORD, your God, is giving you as a heritage, when he has given you rest from all your enemies round about and you live there in security, ¹¹then to the place which the LORD, your God, chooses as the dwelling place for his name you shall bring all the offerings I command you: your holocausts and sacrifices, your tithes and personal contributions, and every special offering you have vowed to the LORD. ¹²You shall make merry before the LORD, your God, with your sons and daughters, your male and female slaves, as well as with the Levite who belongs to your community but has no share of his own in your heritage. ¹³Take care not to offer up your holocausts in any place you fancy, ¹⁴but offer them up in the place which the LORD chooses from among your tribes; there you shall make whatever offerings I enjoin upon you.

Profane and Sacred Meals. ¹⁵"However, in any of your communities you may slaughter and eat to your heart's desire as much meat as the LORD, your God, has blessed you with; and the unclean as well as the clean may eat it, as they do the gazelle or the deer. ¹⁶Only, you shall not partake of the blood, but must pour it out on the ground like water.q ¹⁷Moreover, you shall not, in your own communities, partake of your tithe of grain or wine or oil, of the first-born of your herd or flock,

of any offering you have vowed, of your freewill offerings, or of your personal contributions. ¹⁸These you must eat before the LORD, your God, in the place he chooses, along with your son and daughter, your male and female slave, and the Levite who belongs to your community; and there, before the LORD, you shall make merry over all your undertakings. ¹⁹Take care, also, that you do not neglect the Levite as long as you live in the land.r

²⁰"After the LORD, your God, has enlarged your territory, as he promised you,ˢ when you wish meat for food,* you may eat it at will, to your heart's desire; ²¹and if the place which the LORD, your God, chooses for the abode of his name is too far, you may slaughter in the manner I have told you any of your herd or flock that the LORD has given you, and eat it to your heart's desire in your own community. ²²You may eat it as you would the gazelle or the deer: the unclean and the clean eating it alike. ²³But make sure that you do not partake of the blood; for blood is life, and you shall not consume this seat of life with the flesh. ²⁴Do not partake of the blood, therefore, but pour it out on the ground like water. ²⁵Abstain from it, that you and your children after you may prosper for doing what is right in the sight of the LORD. ²⁶However, any sacred gifts or votive offerings that you may have, you shall bring with you to the place which the LORD chooses, ²⁷and there you must offer both the flesh and the blood of your holocausts on the altar of the LORD, your God; of your other sacrifices the blood indeed must be poured out against the altar of the LORD, your God,ᵗ but their flesh may be eaten. ²⁸Be careful to heed all these commandments I enjoin on you, that you and your descendants may always prosper for doing what is good and right in the sight of the LORD, your God.

Pagan Rites. ²⁹"When the LORD, your God, removes the nations from your way as you advance to dispossess them, be on your guard! Otherwise, once they have been wiped out before you and you have replaced them and are settled in their land, ³⁰you will be lured into following them. Do not inquire regarding their gods, 'How did these nations worship their gods? I, too, would do the same.'

---

p 5-7. 11f: Dt 14, 22-26; 15, 19f; 16, 2. 10f. 14f; 26, 2.—q Dt 15, 23; Gn 9, 4: Lv 3, 17.—r Dt 14, 27.—s Dt 19, 8; Gn 28, 14; Ex 34, 24.—t Lv 17, 11.

12, 20: *Meat for food:* as on special feasts. Meat was not eaten every day in Israel, even by the wealthy.

[31] You shall not thus worship the LORD, your God, because they offered to their gods every abomination that the LORD detests, even burning their sons and daughters to their gods.[u]

CHAPTER 13

Penalties for Idolatry. [1] "Every command that I enjoin on you, you shall be careful to observe, neither adding to it nor subtracting from it.

[2] "If there arises among you a prophet or a dreamer* who promises you a sign or wonder, [3] urging you to follow other gods, whom you have not known, and to serve them: even though the sign or wonder he has foretold you comes to pass, [4] pay no attention to the words of that prophet or that dreamer; for the LORD, your God, is testing you to learn whether you really love him with all your heart and with all your soul. [5] The LORD, your God, shall you follow, and him shall you fear; his commandment shall you observe, and his voice shall you heed, serving him and holding fast to him alone. [6] [v] But that prophet or that dreamer shall be put to death, because, in order to lead you astray from the way which the LORD, your God, has directed you to take, he has preached apostasy from the LORD, your God, who brought you out of the land of Egypt and ransomed you from that place of slavery. Thus shall you purge the evil from your midst.

[7] "If your own full brother, or your son or daughter, or your beloved wife, or your intimate friend, entices you secretly to serve other gods, whom you and your fathers have not known, [8] gods of any other nation, near at hand or far away, from one end of the earth to the other: [9] do not yield to him or listen to him, nor look with pity upon him, to spare or shield him, [10] but kill him. Your hand shall be the first raised to slay him; the rest of the people shall join in with you. [11] You shall stone him to death, because he sought to lead you astray from the LORD, your God, who brought you out of the land of Egypt, that place of slavery. [12] And all Israel, hearing of it, shall fear and never again do such evil as this in your midst.

[13] "If, in any of the cities which the LORD, your God, gives you to dwell in, you hear it said [14] that certain scoundrels have sprung up among you and have led astray the inhabitants of their city to serve other gods whom you have not known, [15] you must inquire carefully into the matter and investigate it thoroughly. If you find that it is true and an established fact that this abomination has been committed in your midst, [16] [w] you shall put the inhabitants of that city to the sword, dooming the city and all life that is in it, even its cattle, to the sword. [17] Having heaped up all its spoils in the middle of its square, you shall burn the city with all its spoils as a whole burnt offering to the LORD, your God. Let it be a heap of ruins forever, never to be rebuilt. [18] You shall not retain anything that is doomed, that the blazing wrath of the LORD may die down and he may show you mercy and in his mercy for you may multiply you as he promised your fathers on oath; [19] because you have heeded the voice of the LORD, your God, keeping all his commandments which I enjoin on you today, doing what is right in his sight.

CHAPTER 14

Pagan Mourning Rites. [1] "You are children of the LORD, your God. You shall not gash yourselves nor shave the hair above your foreheads for the dead.[x] [2] For you are a people sacred to the LORD, your God, who has chosen you from all the nations on the face of the earth to be a people peculiarly his own.[y]

Clean and Unclean Animals. [3] "You shall not eat any abominable thing.[z] [4] [a] These are the animals you may eat: the ox, the sheep, the goat, [5] the red deer, the gazelle, the roe deer, the ibex, the addax, the oryx,* and the mountain sheep. [6] Any animal that has hoofs you may eat, provided it is cloven-footed and chews the cud. [7] But you shall not eat any of the following that only chew the cud or only have cloven hoofs: the camel, the hare and the rock badger, which indeed chew

---

u Lv 18, 21: Jer 7, 31.—v 6-10. 14: Dt 6, 14; 17, 2-7.—w 16f: Jos 6, 18. 24; 7, 26; 8, 28.—x Lv 19, 28.—y Dt 7, 6.—z Ez 4, 14; Acts 10, 14.—a 4-20: Lv 11, 2-23.

13, 2. 4. 6: *Dreamer:* a false prophet who pretended to have received revelations from God in his dreams; cf Jer 23, 25-32; Zec 10, 2. But dreams could also be a channel of true prophecy (Nm 12, 6; Jl 3, 1) and of genuine revelations (Gn 20, 3. 6; 31, 10. 24; 37, 5. 9; Mt 1, 20; 2, 12f. 19; etc.).

14, 5: *The gazelle, the addax, the oryx:* species of antelopes. *The ibex:* a species of wild goat.

the cud, but do not have hoofs and are therefore unclean for you; [8] and the pig, which indeed has hoofs and is cloven-footed, but does not chew the cud and is therefore unclean for you. Their flesh you shall not eat, and their dead bodies you shall not touch.[b]

[9] "Of the various creatures that live in the water, whatever has both fins and scales you may eat, [10] but all those that lack either fins or scales you shall not eat; they are unclean for you.

[11] "You may eat all clean birds. [12] But you shall not eat any of the following: the eagle, the vulture, the osprey, [13] the various kites and falcons, [14] all the various species of crows, [15] the ostrich, the nightjar, the gull, the various species of hawks, [16] the owl, the screech owl, the ibis, [17] the desert owl, the buzzard, the cormorant, [18] the stork, the various species of herons, the hoopoe, and the bat. [19] * All winged insects, too, are unclean for you and shall not be eaten. [20] But you may eat any clean winged creatures.

[21] "You must not eat any animal that has died of itself, for you are a people sacred to the LORD, your God.[c] But you may give it to an alien who belongs to your community, and he may eat it, or you may sell it to a foreigner.

"You shall not boil a kid in its mother's milk.*

Tithes. [22] "Each year you shall tithe all the produce that grows in the field you have sown;[d] [23] then in the place which the LORD, your God, chooses as the dwelling place of his name[e] you shall eat in his presence your tithe of the grain, wine and oil, as well as the firstlings of your herd and flock, that you may learn always to fear the LORD, your God. [24] If, however, the journey is too much for you and you are not able to bring your tithe, because the place which the LORD, your God, chooses for the abode of his name is too far for you, considering how the LORD has blessed you,* [25] you may exchange the tithe for money and, with the purse of money in hand, go to the place which the LORD, your God, chooses. [26] You may then exchange the money for whatever you desire, oxen or sheep, wine or strong drink, or anything else you would enjoy, and there before the LORD, your God, you shall partake of it and make merry with your family. [27] But do not neglect the Levite who belongs to your community, for he has no share in the heritage with you.[f]

[28] "At the end of every third year you shall bring out all the tithes of your produce for that year and deposit them in community stores, [29] that the Levite who has no share in the heritage with you, and also the alien, the orphan and the widow who belong to your community, may come and eat their fill;[g] so that the LORD, your God, may bless you in all that you undertake.

CHAPTER 15

Debts and the Poor. [1] "At the end of every seven-year period* you shall have a relaxation of debts,[h] [2] which shall be observed as follows. Every creditor shall relax his claim on what he has loaned his neighbor; he must not press his neighbor, his kinsman, because a relaxation in honor of the LORD has been proclaimed. [3] You may press a foreigner, but you shall relax the claim on your kinsman for what is yours.[i] [4] Nay, more! since the LORD, your God, will bless you abundantly in the land he will give you to occupy as your heritage, there should be no one of you in need. [5] If you but heed the voice of the LORD, your God, and carefully observe all these commandments which I enjoin on you today, [6] you will lend to many nations, and borrow from none;[j] you will rule over many nations, and none will rule over you, since the LORD, your God, will bless you as he promised. [7] If one of your kinsmen in any community is in need in the land which the LORD, your

---

b Lv 11, 26.—c Ex 22, 30; 23, 19; 34, 26.—d Lv 27, 30.—e 23f: Dt 12, 5ff.—f Dt 12, 12. 19.—g 28f: Dt 26, 12.—h Neh 10, 31.—i Dt 23, 20.—j Dt 28, 12f.

14, 19f: The apparent contradiction is to be resolved in the light of Lv 11, 20-23; the *unclean winged insects* are those that walk on the ground; the *clean winged creatures* are those that leap on the ground, such as certain species of locusts.

14, 21: *Boil a kid in its mother's milk:* see note on Ex 23, 19.

14, 24: *Considering how the Lord has blessed you:* should the Israelite farmer be blessed with an abundant harvest, a tenth of this would be too much to transport for a great distance.

15, 1: *At the end of every seven-year period:* in every seventh, or sabbatical, year. Cf Dt 15, 9; 31, 10; and compare Jer 34, 14 with Dt 15, 12. *A relaxation of debts:* it is uncertain whether a full cancellation of debts is meant, or merely a suspension of payment on them or on their interest among the Israelites. Cf Ex 23, 11 where the same Hebrew root is used of a field that is "let lie fallow" in the sabbatical year.

God, is giving you, you shall not harden your heart nor close your hand to him in his need. [8] Instead, you shall open your hand to him and freely lend him enough to meet his need.[k] [9] Be on your guard lest, entertaining the mean thought that the seventh year, the year of relaxation, is near, you grudge help to your needy kinsman and give him nothing; else he will cry to the LORD against you and you will be held guilty. [10] When you give to him, give freely and not with ill will; for the LORD, your God, will bless you for this in all your works and undertakings. [11] The needy will never be lacking* in the land; that is why I command you to open your hand to your poor and needy kinsman in your country.[l]

Hebrew Slaves [12] "If your kinsman, a Hebrew man or woman, sells himself to you, he is to serve you for six years, but in the seventh year you shall dismiss him from your service, a free man.[m] [13] When you do so, you shall not send him away empty-handed, [14] but shall weight him down with gifts from your flock and threshing floor and wine press, in proportion to the blessing of the LORD, your God, has bestowed on you. [15] For remember that you too were once slaves in the land of Egypt, and the LORD, your God, ransomed you. That is why I am giving you this command today.[n] [16] If, however, he tells you that he does not wish to leave you, because he is devoted to you and your household, since he fares well with you, [17] you shall take an awl and thrust it through his ear* into the door, and he shall then be your slave forever.[o] Your female slave, also, you shall treat in the same way. [18] You must not be reluctant to let your slave go free, since the service he has given you for six years was worth twice a hired man's salary; then also the LORD, your God, will bless you in everything you do.

Firstlings. [19] [p] "You shall consecrate to the LORD, your God, all the male firstlings of your herd and of your flock. You shall not work the firstlings of your cattle, nor shear the firstlings of your flock. [20] Year after year you and your family shall eat them before the LORD, your God, in the place he chooses.[q] [21] If, however, a firstling is lame or blind or has any other serious defect, you shall not sacrifice it to the LORD, your God, [22] but

in your own communities you may eat it, the unclean and the clean eating it alike, as you would a gazelle or a deer. [23] Only, you shall not partake of its blood, which must be poured out on the ground like water.[r]

CHAPTER 16

Feast of the Passover. [1] "Observe the month of Abib* by keeping the Passover of the LORD, your God,[s] since it was in the month of Abib that he brought you by night out of Egypt. [2] You shall offer the Passover sacrifice from your flock or your herd to the LORD, your God, in the place which he chooses as the dwelling place of his name. [3] [t] You shall not eat leavened bread with it. For seven days you shall eat with it only unleavened bread, the bread of affliction, that you may remember as long as you live the day of your departure from the land of Egypt; for in frightened haste you left the land of Egypt. [4] Nothing leavened may be found in all your territory for seven days, and none of the meat which you sacrificed on the evening of the first day shall be kept overnight for the next day.

[5] "You may not sacrifice the Passover in any of the communities which the LORD, your God, gives you; [6] only at the place which he chooses as the dwelling place of his name, and in the evening at sunset, on the anniversary of your departure from Egypt, shall you sacrifice the Passover. [7] You shall cook and eat it at the place the LORD, your God, chooses; then in the morning you may return to your tents. [8] For six days you shall eat unleavened bread, and on the seventh there shall be a solemn meeting in honor of the LORD, your God; on that day you shall not do any sort of work.

Feast of Weeks. [9] [u] "You shall count off seven weeks, computing them from the day when the sickle is first put to the

---

k Lv 25, 35; Sir 29, 1f; Mt 5, 42.—l Dt 15, 8; Sir 29, 12.—m Ex 21, 2; Jer 34, 14.—n Dt 5, 15.—o 16f: Ex 21, 5f.—p Ex 13, 11.—q Dt 14, 23.—r 21ff: Dt 12, 15f; Lv 22, 20.—s 1-8: Ex 12, 2-20; 23, 15; Nm 28, 16ff. 24f.—t 3f: Ex 13, 6f; 34, 18.—u 9-12: Lv 23, 15-21.

15, 11: *The needy will never be lacking:* compare the words of Christ, "The poor you have always with you" (Mt 26, 11).

15, 17: *His ear:* cf Ex 21, 6 and the note there.

16, 1: *Abib:* ear of grain, ripe grain," the name of the month in which the barley harvest fell, corresponding to our March and April; at a later period this month received the Babylonian name of "Nisan."

standing grain. [10] You shall then keep the feast of Weeks* in honor of the LORD, your God, and the measure of your own freewill offering shall be in proportion to the blessing the LORD, your God, has bestowed on you. [11] In the place which the LORD, your God, chooses as the dwelling place of his name,[v] you shall make merry in his presence together with your son and daughter, your male and female slave, and the Levite who belongs to your community, as well as the alien, the orphan and the widow among you. [12] Remember that you too were once slaves in Egypt, and carry out these statutes carefully.

Feast of Booths. [13] [w] "You shall celebrate the feast of Booths for seven days, when you have gathered in the produce from your threshing floor and wine press.* [14] You shall make merry at your feast,[x] together with your son and daughter, your male and female slave, and also the Levite, the alien, the orphan and the widow who belong to your community. [15] For seven days you shall celebrate this pilgrim feast in honor of the LORD, your God, in the place which he chooses; since the LORD, your God, has blessed you in all your crops and in all your undertakings, you shall do naught but make merry.

[16] "Three times a year,[y] then, every male among you shall appear before the LORD, your God, in the place which he chooses: at the feast of Unleavened Bread, at the feast of Weeks, and at the feast of Booths. No one shall appear before the LORD empty-handed, [17] but each of you with as much as he can give, in proportion to the blessings which the LORD, your God, has bestowed on you.

Judges. [18] "You shall appoint judges and officials throughout your tribes to administer true justice for the people in all the

---

v Dt 12, 5. 7. 12. 18.—w 13-15: Ex 23, 16; Lv 23, 34-43; Nm 29, 12-38.—x Dt 16, 11.—y Ex 23, 14f. 17; 34, 23; 2 Chr 8, 13.—z Dt 1, 17; Ex 23, 8.—a 1 Kgs 14, 15; 2 Chr 33, 3.—b Lv 22, 20.—c 2-7: Dt 13, 6-15.—d Dt 4, 19.—e Dt 19, 15; Nm 35, 30; Mt 18, 16; Jn 8, 17; 2 Cor 13, 1.—f Dt 13, 10.—g Dt 21, 5; 2 Chr 19, 8.

16, 10: *Feast of Weeks:* later known more commonly as "Pentecost."
16, 13: See note on Lv 23, 34.
16, 21—17, 7: This section seems to be out of its proper place, since it interrupts the natural sequence of the laws for the judges (Dt 16, 18-20 and 17, 8-13). It probably belongs to the similar section, Dt 12, 29—14, 2.
16, 21f: *Sacred pole . . . sacred pillar;* see note on Ex 34, 13.
17, 5: *Out to your city gates:* outside the gates in an unclean place; cf Lv 24, 14; Nm 15, 36; Acts 7, 58; Heb 13, 12.

---

communities which the LORD, your God, is giving you. [19] You shall not distort justice; you must be impartial.[z] You shall not take a bribe; for a bribe blinds the eyes even of the wise and twists the words even of the just. [20] Justice and justice alone shall be your aim, that you may have life and may possess the land which the LORD, your God, is giving you.

Pagan Worship. [21] * "You shall not plant a sacred pole of any kind of wood beside the altar of the LORD, your God, which you will build;[a] [22] nor shall you erect a sacred pillar,* such as the LORD, your God, detests.

CHAPTER 17

[1] "You shall not sacrifice to the LORD, your God, from the herd or from the flock an animal with any serious defect;[b] that would be an abomination to the LORD, your God.

[2] [c] "If there is found among you, in any one of the communities which the LORD, your God, gives you, a man or a woman who does evil in the sight of the LORD, and transgresses his covenant, [3] by serving other gods, or by worshiping the sun or the moon or any of the host of the sky, against my command;[d] [4] and if, on being informed of it, you find by careful investigation that it is true and an established fact that this abomination has been committed in Israel: [5] you shall bring the man (or woman) who has done the evil deed out to your city gates* and stone him to death. [6] The testimony of two or three witnesses is required for putting a person to death;[e] no one shall be put to death on the testimony of only one witness. [7] At the execution, the witnesses are to be the first to raise their hands against him; afterward all the people are to join in.[f] Thus shall you purge the evil from your midst.

Judges. [8] "If in your own community there is a case at issue which proves too complicated for you to decide, in a matter of bloodshed or of civil rights or of personal injury, you shall then go up to the place which the LORD, your God, chooses, [9] to the levitical priests or to the judge who is in office at that time. They shall study the case and then hand down to you their decision.[g] [10] According to this decision that they give you in the place which the LORD chooses, you shall act, being careful to do exactly as they direct. [11] You shall

[11] carry out the directions they give you and the verdict they pronounce for you, without turning aside to the right or to the left from the decision they hand down to you. [12] Any man who has the insolence to refuse to listen to the priest* who officiates there in the ministry of the LORD, your God, or to the judge, shall die. Thus shall you purge the evil from your midst. [13] And all the people, on hearing of it, shall fear, and never again be so insolent.

The King. [14] "When you have come to the land which the LORD, your God, is giving you, and have occupied it and settled in it, should you then decide to have a king over you like all the surrounding nations,[h] [15] you shall set that man over you as your king whom the LORD, your God, chooses.[i] He whom you set over you as king must be your kinsman; a foreigner, who is no kin of yours, you may not set over you. [16] But he shall not have a great number of horses;* nor shall he make his people go back again to Egypt to acquire them, against the LORD's warning that you must never go back that way again.[j] [17] Neither shall he have a great number of wives, lest his heart be estranged,[k] nor shall he accumulate a vast amount of silver and gold. [18] When he is enthroned in his kingdom, he shall have a copy of this law made from the scroll that is in the custody of the levitical priests.[l] [19] He shall keep it with him and read it all the days of his life that he may learn to fear the LORD, his God, and to heed and fulfill all the words of this law and these statutes. [20] Let him not become estranged from his countrymen through pride, nor turn aside to the right or to the left from these commandments. Then he and his descendants will enjoy a long reign in Israel.

CHAPTER 18

Priests. [1] "The whole priestly tribe of Levi shall have no share in the heritage with Israel; they shall live on the oblations of the LORD and the portions due to him.[m] [2] Levi shall have no heritage among his brothers; the LORD himself is his heritage, as he has told him. [3] The priests shall have ⸢ight to the following things from the ⸢: from those who are offering a sac-⸢⸢ether the victim is from the herd ⸢flock, the priest shall receive

the shoulder, the jowls and the stomach. [4] You shall also give him the first fruits of your grain and wine and oil,[n] as well as the first fruits of the shearing of your flock; [5] for the LORD, your God, has chosen him and his sons out of all your tribes to be always in attendance to minister in the name of the LORD.

[6] "When a Levite goes from one of your communities anywhere in Israel in which he ordinarily resides, to visit, as his heart may desire, the place which the LORD chooses, [7] he may minister there in the name of the LORD, his God, like all his fellow Levites who are in attendance there before the LORD. [8] He shall then receive the same portions to eat as the rest, along with his monetary offerings and heirlooms.

Prophets. [9] "When you come into the land which the LORD, your God, is giving you, you shall not learn to imitate the abominations of the peoples there.[o] [10] Let there not be found among you anyone who immolates his son or daughter[p] in the fire,* nor a fortune-teller, soothsayer, charmer, diviner, [11] or caster of spells, nor one who consults ghosts and spirits or seeks oracles from the dead. [12] Anyone who does such things is an abomination to the LORD, and because of such abominations the LORD, your God, is driving these nations out of your way.[q] [13] You, however, must be altogether sincere toward the LORD, your God. [14] Though these nations whom you are to dispossess listen to their soothsayers and fortune-tellers,

---

h 1 Sm 8, 5. 19f.—i 1 Sm 9, 16; 10, 24; 16, 12.—j Dt 28, 68; 1 Kgs 4, 26; 10, 26.—k 1 Kgs 11; 3f; Neh 13, 26.—l Dt 31, 9. 26.—m Nm 18, 8f. 20-24; 1 Cor 9, 13.—n Nm 18, 12; 2 Chr 31, 5.—o Dt 12, 29ff; Lv 18, 26-30.—p 10f: Lv 18, 21; 19, 31; 20, 27; 1 Sm 28, 7; 2 Kgs 17, 17; 21, 6.—q Dt 9, 4.

17, 12: *The priest:* the high priest; *the judge:* a layman. The former presided over the court in cases which directly concerned religion, the latter in cases of a more secular nature; cf 2 Chr 19, 8-11.

17, 16: *Horses:* chariotry for war. *The Lord's warning:* the same warning is also referred to in Dt 28, 68, although it is not mentioned explicitly elsewhere in the Pentateuch. We know from other sources that Egypt used to export war horses to Palestine. The danger envisioned here is that some king might make Israel a vassal of Egypt for the sake of such military aid.

18, 10f: *Immolates his son or daughter in the fire:* to Molech. See note on Lv 18, 21. Such human sacrifices are classed here with other pagan superstitions because they were believed to possess magical powers for averting a calamity; cf 2 Kgs 3, 27. Three other forms of superstition are listed here: augury (by a *fortune-teller,* a *soothsayer* or a *diviner);* black magic (by a *charmer . . . or caster of spells);* and necromancy (by *one who consults ghosts and spirits or seeks oracles from the dead).*

the LORD, your God, will not permit you to do so.

[15] "A prophet like me* will the LORD, your God, raise up for you from among your own kinsmen; to him you shall listen.[r] [16] This is exactly what you requested of the LORD, your God, at Horeb on the day of the assembly, when you said, 'Let us not again hear the voice of the LORD, our God, nor see this great fire any more, lest we die.'[s] [17] And the LORD said to me, 'This was well said. [18] I will raise up for them a prophet like you from among their kinsmen, and will put my words into his mouth; he shall tell them all that I command him. [19] If any man will not listen to my words which he speaks in my name, I myself will make him answer for it.[t] [20] But if a prophet presumes to speak in my name[u] an oracle that I have not commanded him to speak, or speaks in the name of other gods, he shall die.'

[21] "If you say to yourselves, 'How can we recognize an oracle which the LORD has spoken?', [22] know that, even though a prophet speaks in the name of the LORD, if his oracle is not fulfilled or verified, it is an oracle which the LORD did not speak. The prophet has spoken it presumptuously, and you shall have no fear of him.

CHAPTER 19

Cities of Refuge. [1] "When the LORD, your God, removes the nations whose land he is giving you, and you have taken their place and are settled in their cities and houses, [2] [v] you shall set apart three cities* in the land which the LORD, your God, is

---

r Jn 1, 45; 6, 14; Acts 3, 22; 7, 37.—s Ex 20, 19.—t Acts 3, 23.—u 20. 22: Dt 13, 2ff.—v Dt 4, 41ff; Ex 21, 13; Nm 35, 10-15; Jos 20, 2. 8.—w Dt 4, 42; Nm 35, 15; Jos 20, 3. 5.—x Gn 15, 18-21; 28, 14; Ex 23, 31; 34, 24.—y 11ff: Ex 21, 12. 14; Nm 35, 20f.—z Dt 27, 17; Prv 23, 10; Hos 5, 10.

18, 15: *A prophet like me:* from the context (opposition to the pagan soothsayers) it seems that Moses is referring in general to all the true prophets who were to succeed him. But since Christ is the Great Prophet in whom the prophetic office finds its fulfillment and completion, this passage was understood in a special Messianic sense both by the Jews (Jn 6, 14; 7, 40) and by the Apostles (Acts 3, 22; 7, 37).

19, 2: *Set apart three cities:* the Israelites were to have at least six cities of refuge, three in the land east of the Jordan and three in the land of Canaan west of the Jordan (Nm 35, 9-34); but since the three cities east of the Jordan had now been appointed (Dt 4, 41-43), reference is made here only to the three west of the Jordan. The execution of this command is narrated in Jos 20.

19, 6: *The avenger of blood:* see note on Nm 35, 12.

---

giving you to occupy. [3] You shall thereby divide into three regions the land which the LORD, your God, will give you as a heritage, and so arrange the routes that every homicide will be able to find a refuge.

[4] "It is in the following case that a homicide may take refuge in such a place to save his life: when someone unwittingly kills his neighbor to whom he had previously borne no malice.[w] [5] For example, if he goes with his neighbor to a forest to cut wood, and as he swings his ax to fell a tree, its head flies off the handle and hits his neighbor a mortal blow, he may take refuge in one of these cities to save his life. [6] Should the distance be too great, the avenger of blood* may in the heat of his anger pursue the homicide and overtake him and strike him dead, even though he does not merit death since he had previously borne the slain man no malice. [7] That is why I order you to set apart three cities.

[8] [x] "But if the LORD, your God, enlarges your territory, as he swore to your fathers, and gives you all the land he promised your fathers he would give [9] in the event that you carefully observe all these commandments which I enjoin on you today, loving the LORD, your God, and ever walking in his ways: then add three cities to these three. [10] Thus, in the land which the LORD, your God, is giving you as a heritage, innocent blood will not be shed and you will not become guilty of bloodshed.

[11] [y] "However, if someone lies in wait for his neighbor out of hatred for him, and rising up against him, strikes him mortally, and then takes refuge in one of these cities, [12] the elders of his own city shall send for him and have him taken from there, and shall hand him over to be slain by the avenger of blood. [13] Do not look on him with pity, but purge from Israel the stain of shedding innocent blood, that you may prosper.

Removal of Landmarks. [14] "You shall not move your neighbor's landmarks erected by your forefathers in the heritage you receive in the land which the LORD, your God, is giving you to occupy.[z]

False Witnesses. [15] "One witness alone shall not take the stand against a man in regard to any crime or any offense of which he may be guilty; a judicial fact shall be established only on the testimony of two or three witnesses.[a]

16 "If an unjust witness takes the stand against a man to accuse him of a defection from the law, 17 the two parties in the dispute shall appear before the LORD in the presence of the priests or judges in office at that time;[b] 18 and if after a thorough investigation the judges find that the witness is a false witness and has accused his kinsman falsely, 19 you shall do to him as he planned to do to his kinsman.[c] Thus shall you purge the evil from your midst. 20 The rest, on hearing of it, shall fear, and never again do a thing so evil among you. 21 Do not look on such a man with pity. Life for life, eye for eye, tooth for tooth, hand for hand, and foot for foot![d]

CHAPTER 20

Courage in War. 1 "When you go out to war against your enemies and you see horses and chariots and an army greater than your own, do not be afraid of them, for the LORD, your God, who brought you up from the land of Egypt, will be with you. 2 "When you are about to go into battle, the priest shall come forward and say to the soldiers: 3 'Hear, O Israel! Today you are going into battle against your enemies. Be not weakhearted or afraid; be neither alarmed nor frightened by them. 4 For it is the LORD, your God, who goes with you to fight for you against your enemies and give you victory.'[e] 5 "Then the officials shall say to the soldiers,[f] 'Is there anyone who has built a new house and not yet had the housewarming? Let him return home, lest he die in battle and another dedicate it. 6 Is there anyone who has planted a vineyard and never yet enjoyed its fruits? Let him return home, lest he die in battle and another enjoy its fruits in his stead. 7 Is there anyone who has betrothed a woman and not yet taken her as his wife? Let him return home, lest he die in battle and another take her to wife.'[g] 8 In fine, the officials shall say to the soldiers, 'Is there anyone who is afraid and weakhearted?[h] Let him return home, lest he make his fellows fainthearted as himself.' When the officials have finished the soldiers, military officers pointed over the army.

Cities of the Enemy. 10 "When you march up to attack a city, first offer it terms of peace. 11 If it agrees to your terms of peace and opens its gates to you, all the people to be found in it shall serve you in forced labor. 12 But if it refuses to make peace with you and instead offers you battle, lay siege to it, 13 and when the LORD, your God, delivers it into your hand, put every male in it to the sword; 14 but the women and children and livestock and all else in it that is worth plundering you may take as your booty, and you may use this plunder of your enemies which the LORD, your God, has given you.[i] 15 "That is how you shall deal with any city at a considerable distance from you which does not belong to the peoples of this land. 16 But in the cities of those nations which the LORD, your God, is giving you as your heritage, you shall not leave a single soul alive. 17 You must doom them all—the Hittites, Amorites, Canaanites, Perizzites, Hivites and Jebusites[j]—as the LORD, your God, has commanded you, 18 lest they teach you to make any such abominable offerings as they make to their gods, and you thus sin against the LORD, your God.

Trees of a Besieged City. 19 "When you are at war with a city and have to lay siege to it for a long time before you capture it, you shall not destroy its trees by putting an ax to them. You may eat their fruit, but you must not cut down the trees. After all, are the trees of the field men, that they should be included in your siege? 20 However, those trees which you know are not fruit trees you may destroy, cutting them down to build siegeworks with which to reduce the city that is resisting you.

CHAPTER 21

Expiation of Untraced Murder. 1 "If the corpse of a slain man* is found lying in the open on the land which the LORD, your God, is giving you to occupy, and it is

---

a Dt 17, 6; Nm 35, 30; Mt 18, 16; Jn 8, 17; 2 Cor 13, 1.—b Dt 17, 8f.—c 18f: Dn 13, 61f.—d Ex 21, 23f; Lv 24, 20; Mt 5, 38.—e Dt 1, 30; 3, 22; Jos 23, 10.—f 5ff: 1 Mc 3, 56.—g Dt 24, 5.—h Jgs 7, 3.—i 13f: Nm 31, 7. 9. 11; Jos 22, 8.—j 16f: Dt 7, 1f; Jos 10, 40; 11, 14.

21, 1-9: This paragraph is best read immediately after Dt 19, 21. The *slain man* may not necessarily have been murdered; he may have been killed by a wild beast. But the blood of the slain cries out to God from the soil where it was shed; cf Gn 4, 10. Therefore a religious ceremony of propitiation is here prescribed in order to avert God's anger on the community.

not known who killed him, [2] your elders and judges shall go out and measure the distances to the cities that are in the neighborhood of the corpse. [3] When it is established which city is nearest the corpse, the elders of that city shall take a heifer that has never been put to work as a draft animal under a yoke, [4] and bringing it down to a wadi with an ever-flowing stream at a place that has not been plowed or sown, they shall cut the heifer's throat there in the wadi.* [5] The priests, the descendants of Levi, shall also be present, for the LORD, your God, has chosen them to minister to him and to give blessings in his name, and every case of dispute or violence must be settled by their decision.[k] [6] Then all the elders of that city nearest the corpse shall wash their hands* over the heifer whose throat was cut in the wadi, [7] and shall declare, 'Our hands did not shed this blood,* and our eyes did not see the deed. [8] Absolve, O LORD, your people Israel, whom you have ransomed, and let not the guilt of shedding innocent blood remain in the midst of your people Israel.' Thus they shall be absolved from the guilt of bloodshed, [9] and you shall purge from your midst the guilt of innocent blood, that you may prosper for doing what is right in the sight of the LORD.

Marriage with a Female Captive. [10] "When you go out to war against your enemies and the LORD, your God, delivers them into your hand, so that you take captives, [11] if you see a comely woman among the captives and become so enamored of her that you wish to have her as wife, [12] you may take her home to your house. But before she may live there, she must shave her head* and pare her nails [13] and lay aside her captive's garb. After she has mourned her father and mother for a full month, you may have relations with her, and you shall be her husband and she shall be your wife. [14] However, if later on you lose your liking for her, you shall give her her freedom, if she wishes it; but you shall not sell her or enslave her, since she was married to you under compulsion.

Rights of the First-born. [15] "If a man with two wives loves one and dislikes the other; and if both bear him sons, but the first-born is of her whom he dislikes: [16] when he comes to bequeath his property to his sons he may not consider as his first-born the son of the wife he loves, in preference to his true first-born, the son of the wife whom he dislikes. [17] On the contrary, he shall recognize as his first-born the son of her whom he dislikes, giving him a double share of whatever he happens to own, since he is the first fruits of his manhood, and to him belong the rights of the first-born.

The Incorrigible Son. [18] "If a man has a stubborn and unruly son who will not listen to his father or mother, and will not obey them even though they chastise him, [19] his father and mother shall have him apprehended and brought out to the elders at the gate* of his home city, [20] where they shall say to those city elders, 'This son of ours is a stubborn and unruly fellow who will not listen to us; he is a glutton and a drunkard.' [21] Then all his fellow citizens shall stone him to death. Thus shall you purge the evil from your midst, and all Israel, on hearing of it, shall fear.

Corpse of a Criminal. [22] "If a man guilty of a capital offense is put to death and his corpse hung on a tree,* [23] it shall not remain on the tree overnight.[l] You shall bury it the same day; otherwise, since God's curse rests on him who hangs on a tree,* you will defile the land which the LORD, your God, is giving you as an inheritance.

CHAPTER 22

Care for Lost Animals. [1] "You shall not see your kinsman's ox or sheep driven

---

k Dt 19, 17.—l Gal 3, 13.

21, 4: *They shall cut the heifer's throat there in the wadi:* its blood is to be carried away by the stream, signifying thereby the removal of the human blood from the soil. This is not a sacrifice but a symbolic action; the priests are present merely as official witnesses.

21, 6: *Wash their hands:* a symbolic gesture in protestation of one's own innocence when human blood is unjustly shed; cf Mt 27, 24.

21, 7: *This blood:* the blood of the slain man as symbolized by the heifer's blood.

21, 12f: *Shave her head . . .:* these symbolic actions are meant to signify the purification of the woman from her pagan defilement or perhaps the end of her period of mourning for her previous husband.

21, 19: *The gate:* in the city walls. This open space served as the forum for the administration of justice. Cf Dt 22, 15; 25, 7; Ru 4, 1f. 11; Is 29, 21; Am 5, 10. 12. 15.

21, 22: *Hung on a tree:* some understand, "impaled on a stake." In any case the hanging or impaling was not the means used to execute the criminal; he was first put to death by the ordinary means, stoning, and his corpse was then exposed on high as a salutary warning for others. Cf Jos 8, 29; 10, 26; 1 Sm 31, 10; 2 Sm 21, 9.

21, 23: *God's curse rests on him who hangs on a tree:* St. Paul quotes these words in Gal 3, 13, where he applies them to the crucified Savior, who "redeemed us from the curse of the law, becoming a curse for us."

astray without showing concern about it; see to it that it is returned to your kinsman.*m* [2]If this kinsman does not live near you, or you do not know who he may be, take it to your own place and keep it with you until he claims it; then give it back to him. [3]You shall do the same with his ass, or his garment, or anything else which your kinsman loses and you happen to find; you may not be unconcerned about them. [4]You shall not see your kinsman's ass or ox foundering on the road without showing concern about it; see to it that you help him lift it up.

Various Precepts. [5]"A woman shall not wear an article proper to a man, nor shall a man put on a woman's dress; for anyone who does such things is an abomination to the LORD, your God.

[6]"If, while walking along, you chance upon a bird's nest with young birds or eggs in it, in any tree or on the ground, and the mother bird is sitting on them, you shall not take away the mother bird along with her brood; [7]you shall let her go, although you may take her brood away. It is thus that you shall have prosperity and a long life.

[8]"When you build a new house, put a parapet around the roof; otherwise, if someone falls off, you will bring bloodguilt upon your house.

[9] *n* "You shall not sow your vineyard with two different kinds of seed; if you do, its produce shall become forfeit,* both the crop you have sown and the yield of the vineyard. [10]You shall not plow with an ox and an ass harnessed together. [11]You shall not wear cloth of two different kinds of thread, wool and linen, woven together.

[12]"You shall put twisted cords* on the four corners of the cloak that you wrap around you.*o*

Crimes against Marriage. [13]"If a man, after marrying a woman and having relations with her, comes to dislike her, [14]and makes monstrous charges against her and defames her by saying, 'I married this woman, but when I first had relations with her I did not find her a virgin,' [15]the father and mother of the girl shall take the evidence of her virginity* and bring it to the elders at the city gate. [16]There the father of the girl shall say to the elders, 'I gave my daughter to this man

in marriage, but he has come to dislike her, [17]and now brings monstrous charges against her, saying: I did not find your daughter a virgin. But here is the evidence of my daughter's virginity!' And they shall spread out the cloth before the elders of the city. [18]Then these city elders shall take the man and chastise him,* [19]besides fining him one hundred silver shekels, which they shall give to the girl's father, because the man defamed a virgin in Israel. Moreover, she shall remain his wife, and he may not divorce her as long as he lives.

[20]"But if this charge is true, and evidence of the girl's virginity is not found, [21]they shall bring the girl to the entrance of her father's house and there her townsmen shall stone her to death, because she committed a crime against Israel by her unchasteness in her father's house. Thus shall you purge the evil from your midst.

[22]"If a man is discovered having relations with a woman who is married to another, both the man and the woman with whom he has had relations shall die.*p* Thus shall you purge the evil from your midst.

[23]"If within the city a man comes upon a maiden who is betrothed,* and has relations with her, [24]you shall bring them both out to the gate of the city and there stone them to death: the girl because she did not cry out for help though she was in the city, and the man because he violated his neighbor's wife. Thus shall you purge the evil from your midst.

[25]"If, however, it is in the open fields that a man comes upon such a betrothed maiden, seizes her and has relations with her, the man alone shall die. [26]You shall do nothing to the maiden, since she is not guilty of a capital offense. This case is like that of a man who rises up against his neighbor and murders him: [27]it was in the

---

m 1-4: Ex 23, 4f.—n 9. 11: Lv 19, 19.—o Nm 15, 38; Mt 23, 5.—p Lv 20, 10; Jn 8, 4f.

22, 9: *Become forfeit:* to the sanctuary; cf Lv 19, 19; Jos 6, 19.

22, 12: *Twisted cords:* referred to as "tassels" on "violet cords" in Nm 15, 38. See note there.

22, 15: *The evidence of her virginity:* the bridal garment or sheet stained with a little blood from the first nuptial relations.

22, 18: *Chastise him:* flog him, as prescribed in Dt 25, 1-3.

22, 23: *A maiden who is betrothed:* a girl who is married but not yet brought to her husband's home and whose marriage is therefore still unconsummated.

open fields that he came upon her, and though the betrothed maiden may have cried out for help, there was no one to come to her aid. [28] *q* "If a man comes upon a maiden that is not betrothed, takes her and has relations with her, and their deed is discovered, [29] the man who had relations with her shall pay the girl's father fifty silver shekels and take her as his wife, because he has deflowered her. Moreover, he may not divorce her as long as he lives.

CHAPTER 23

[1] "A man shall not marry his father's wife,* nor shall he dishonor his father's bed.

Membership in the Community. [2] "No one whose testicles have been crushed or whose penis has been cut off, may be admitted into the community of the LORD. [3] No child of an incestuous union may be admitted into the community of the LORD, nor any descendant of his even to the tenth generation. [4] *r* No Ammonite or Moabite may ever be admitted into the community of the LORD, nor any descendants of theirs even to the tenth generation, [5] *s* because they would not succor you with food and water on your journey after you left Egypt, and because Moab hired Balaam, son of Beor, from Pethor in Aram Naharaim, to curse you; [6] though the LORD, your God, would not listen to Balaam and turned his curse into a blessing for you, because he loves you. [7] Never promote their peace and prosperity as long as you live. [8] *t* But do not abhor the Edomite, since he is your brother, nor the Egyptian, since you were an alien in his country. [9] Children born to them may in the third generation be admitted into the community of the LORD.

Cleanliness in Camp. [10] "When you are in camp during an expedition against your enemies, you shall keep yourselves from everything offensive. [11] If one of you becomes unclean because of a nocturnal emission, he shall go outside the camp, and not return until, [12] toward evening, he has bathed in water; then, when the sun has set, he may come back into the camp. [13] Outside the camp you shall have a place set aside to be used as a latrine. [14] You shall also keep a trowel in your equipment and with it, when you go outside to ease nature, you shall first dig a hole and afterward cover up your excrement. [15] Since the LORD, your God, journeys along within your camp to defend you and to put your enemies at your mercy, your camp must be holy; otherwise, if he sees anything indecent in your midst, he will leave your company.

Various Precepts. [16] "You shall not hand over to his master a slave who has taken refuge from him with you. [17] Let him live with you wherever he chooses, in any one of your communities* that pleases him. Do not molest him.

[18] * "There shall be no temple harlot among the Israelite women, nor a temple prostitute among the Israelite men. *u* [19] You shall not offer a harlot's fee or a dog's price as any kind of votive offering in the house of the LORD, your God; both these things are an abomination to the LORD, your God.

[20] "You shall not demand interest from your countrymen on a loan of money or of food or of anything else on which interest is usually demanded. *v* [21] You may demand interest from a foreigner, but not from your countryman, so that the LORD, your God, may bless you in all your undertakings on the land you are to enter and occupy.

[22] "When you make a vow to the LORD, your God, you shall not delay in fulfilling it; otherwise you will be held guilty, for the LORD, your God, is strict in requiring it of you. [23] Should you refrain from making a vow, you will not be held guilty. [24] But you must keep your solemn word and fulfill the votive offering you have freely promised to the LORD.

[25] "When you go through your neighbor's vineyard, you may eat as many grapes as you wish, but do not put them in your basket. [26] When you go through your neighbor's grainfield, you may pluck some of the ears with your hand,

---

q 28f: Ex 22, 16.—r Neh 13, 1f.—s Nm 24, 10.—t Gn 25, 24ff.—u 1 Kgs 14, 24; 22, 46; 2 Kgs 23, 7.—v Ex 22, 25; Lv 25, 37; Lk 6, 34f.

23, 1: *Father's wife:* stepmother. *Dishonor:* cf Dt 27, 20.
23, 17: *In any one of your communities:* from this it would seem that the slave in question is a fugitive from a foreign country.
23, 18f: The pagans believed that they could enter into special relationship with their gods and goddesses by having sexual relations with the pagan priests and priestesses who prostituted themselves for this purpose. The money paid for this was considered a sort of votive offering made to the pagan sanctuary. Such abominations were naturally forbidden in Israel. *A dog's price:* the money paid the pagan priest for his indecent service.

but do not put a sickle to your neighbor's grain.

CHAPTER 24

Marriage Laws. [1]"When a man,* after marrying a woman and having relations with her, is later displeased with her because he finds in her something indecent,* and therefore he writes out a bill of divorce and hands it to her, thus dismissing her from his house: [2]if on leaving his house she goes and becomes the wife of another man, [3]and the second husband, too, comes to dislike her and dismisses her from his house by handing her a written bill of divorce; [4]or if this second man who has married her, dies; then her former husband, who dismissed her, may not again take her as his wife after she has become defiled. That would be an abomination before the LORD, and you shall not bring such guilt upon the land which the LORD, your God, is giving you as a heritage.

[5] *w* "When a man is newly wed, he need not go out on a military expedition, nor shall any public duty be imposed on him. He shall be exempt for one year for the sake of his family, to bring joy to the wife he has married.

Justice, Equity and Charity. [6] * "No one shall take a hand mill or even its upper stone as a pledge for debt, for he would be taking the debtor's sustenance as a pledge.

[7]"If any man is caught kidnaping a fellow Israelite in order to enslave him and sell him, the kidnaper shall be put to death. *x* Thus shall you purge the evil from your midst.

[8] *y* "In an attack of leprosy you shall be careful to observe exactly and to carry out all the directions of the levitical priests. Take care to act in accordance with the instructions I have given them. [9] *z* Remember what the LORD, your God, did to Miriam on the journey after you left Egypt.

[10] * "When you make a loan of any kind to your neighbor, you shall not enter his house to receive a pledge from him, [11]but shall wait outside until the man to whom you are making the loan brings his pledge outside to you. [12]If he is a poor man, you shall not sleep in the mantle he gives as a pledge, [13]but shall return it

to him at sunset that he himself may sleep in it. *a* Then he will bless you, and it will be a good deed of yours before the LORD, your God.

[14]"You shall not defraud a poor and needy hired servant, whether he be one of your own countrymen or one of the aliens who live in your communities. [15]You shall pay him each day's wages before sundown on the day itself, since he is poor and looks forward to them. *b* Otherwise he will cry to the LORD against you, and you will be held guilty.

[16]"Fathers shall not be put to death for their children, nor children for their fathers; only for his own guilt shall a man be put to death. *c*

[17]"You shall not violate the rights of the alien or of the orphan, nor take the clothing of a widow as a pledge. *d* [18]For, remember, you were once slaves in Egypt, and the LORD, your God, ransomed you from there; that is why I command you to observe this rule.

[19] *e* "When you reap the harvest in your field and overlook a sheaf there, you shall not go back to get it; let it be for the alien, the orphan or the widow, that the LORD, your God, may bless you in all your undertakings. [20]When you knock down the fruit of your olive trees, you shall not go over the branches a second time; let what remains be for the alien, the orphan and the widow. [21]When you pick your grapes, you shall not go over the vineyard a second time; let what remains be for the alien, the orphan, and the widow. [22]For remember that you

w Dt 20, 7.—x Ex 21, 16.—y Lv 13, 1-14.—z Nm 12, 10-15.— a Ex 22, 26.—b 14f: Lv 19, 13; Tb 4, 15; Sir 34, 25f; Jer 22, 13.—c 2 Kgs 14, 6; 2 Chr 25, 4; Ez 18, 20.—d Ex 22, 22; 23, 9.—e 19ff: Lv 19, 9f; 23, 22.

24, 1-4: This law is directly concerned only with forbidding divorced couples to remarry each other, and indirectly with checking hasty divorces, by demanding sufficient cause and certain legal formalities. Divorce itself is taken for granted and tolerated as an existing custom whose evils this law seeks to lessen. Cf Dt 22, 19. 29; Mal 2, 14ff. Christ gave the authentic interpretation of this law: "Moses, by reason of the hardness of your heart, permitted you to put away your wives; but it was not so from the beginning" (Mt 19, 8f).

24, 1: *Something indecent:* a rather indefinite phrase, meaning perhaps "immodest conduct." At the time of Christ the rabbis differed in opinion concerning the sufficient grounds for divorce; cf Mt 19, 3.

24, 6: Since the Israelites ground their grain into flour only in sufficient quantity for their current need, to deprive a debtor of his hand mill was virtually equivalent to condemning him to starve to death.

24, 10f: The debtor had the right to select the pledge that the creditor demanded as a guarantee for his loan.

were once slaves in Egypt; that is why I command you to observe this rule.

CHAPTER 25

[1] "When men have a dispute and bring it to court, and a decision is handed down to them acquitting the innocent party and condemning the guilty party, [2] if the latter deserves stripes, the judge shall have him lie down and in his presence receive the number of stripes his guilt deserves. [3] Forty stripes* may be given him, but no more;[f] lest, if he were beaten with more stripes than these, your kinsman should be looked upon as disgraced because of the severity of the beating.

[4] * "You shall not muzzle an ox when it is treading out grain.[g]

Levirate Marriage. [5] "When brothers live together* and one of them dies without a son, the widow of the deceased shall not marry anyone outside the family; but her husband's brother shall go to her and perform the duty of a brother-in-law by marrying her.[h] [6] [i] The first-born son she bears shall continue the line of the deceased brother, that his name may not be blotted out from Israel. [7] If, however, a man does not care to marry his brother's wife, she shall go up to the elders at the gate and declare, 'My brother-in-law does not intend to perform his duty toward me and refuses to perpetuate his brother's name in Israel.' [8] Thereupon the elders

of his city shall summon him and admonish him. If he persists in saying, 'I am not willing to marry her,' [9] * his sister-in-law, in the presence of the elders, shall go up to him and strip his sandal from his foot and spit in his face, saying publicly, 'This is how one should be treated who will not build up his brother's family!' [10] And his lineage shall be spoken of in Israel as 'the family of the man stripped of his sandal.'

Various Precepts. [11] "When two men are fighting and the wife of one intervenes to save her husband from the blows of his opponent, if she stretches out her hand and seizes the latter by his private parts, [12] you shall chop off her hand without pity.

[13] "You shall not keep two differing weights in your bag, one large and the other small;[j] [14] nor shall you keep two different measures in your house, one large and the other small. [15] But use a true and just weight, and a true and just measure, that you may have a long life on the land which the LORD, your God, is giving you. [16] Everyone who is dishonest in any of these matters is an abomination to the LORD, your God.

[17] * "Bear in mind what Amalek did to you on the journey after you left Egypt,[k] [18] how without fear of any god he harassed you along the way, weak and weary as you were, and cut off at the rear all those who lagged behind. [19] Therefore, when the LORD, your God, gives you rest from all your enemies round about in the land which he is giving you to occupy as your heritage, you shall blot out the memory of Amalek from under the heavens.[l] Do not forget!

CHAPTER 26

Thanksgiving for the Harvest. [1] "When you have come into the land which the LORD, your God, is giving you as a heritage, and have occupied it and settled in it, [2] you shall take some first fruits[m] of the various products of the soil which you harvest from the land which the LORD, your God, gives you, and putting them in a basket, you shall go to the place which the LORD, your God, chooses for the dwelling place of his name. [3] There you shall go to the priest in office at that time and say to him, 'Today I acknowledge to the LORD, my

f 2 Cor 11, 24.—g 1 Cor 9, 9; 1 Tm 5, 18.—h Mt 22, 24; Mk 12, 19; Lk 20, 28.—i 6-9: Ru 4, 5-10.—j 13ff: Lv 19, 35f; Prv 16, 11; Ez 45, 10; Mi 6, 11.—k Ex 17, 8.—l Ex 17, 14; 1 Sm 15, 2f.—m Ex 23, 19; 34, 26.

25, 3: *Forty stripes:* a relatively mild punishment in ancient times. Later Jewish practice limited the number to thirty-nine; cf 2 Cor 11, 24.

25, 4: St. Paul argues from this verse that a laborer has the right to live on the fruits of his labor; cf 1 Cor 9, 9; 1 Tm 5, 18.

25, 5: *When brothers live together:* when relatives of the same clan, though married, hold their property in common. It was only in this case that the present law was to be observed, since one of its purposes was to keep the property of the deceased within the same clan. Such a marriage of a widow with her brother-in-law is known as a "levirate" marriage from the Latin word *levir,* meaning "a husband's brother."

25, 9f: The penalty decreed for a man who refuses to comply with this law of family loyalty is public disgrace (the widow is to *spit in his face*) and the curse of poverty; sandals were proverbially a man's cheapest possession (cf Am 2, 6; 8, 6), and therefore "a man without sandals" was the poorest of the poor. Some commentators, however, connect this symbolic act with the ceremony mentioned in Ru 4, 7f.

25, 17-19: This attack on Israel by Amalek is not mentioned elsewhere in the Old Testament, although it probably was connected with the battle mentioned in Ex 17, 8. A campaign against Amalek was carried out by Saul; cf 1 Sm 15.

God, that I have indeed come into the land which he swore to our fathers he would give us.' [4] The priest shall then receive the basket from you and shall set it in front of the altar of the LORD, your God. [5] Then you shall declare before the LORD, your God, 'My father was a wandering Aramean* who went down to Egypt with a small household and lived there as an alien.[n] But there he became a nation great, strong and numerous. [6] [o] When the Egyptians maltreated and oppressed us, imposing hard labor upon us, [7] we cried to the LORD, the God of our fathers, and he heard our cry and saw our affliction, our toil and our oppression. [8] He brought us out of Egypt with his strong hand and outstretched arm, with terrifying power, with signs and wonders;[p] [9] and bringing us into this country, he gave us this land flowing with milk and honey.[q] [10] Therefore, I have now brought you the first fruits of the products of the soil which you, O LORD, have given me.' And having set them before the LORD, your God, you shall bow down in his presence. [11] Then you and your family, together with the Levite and the aliens who live among you, shall make merry over all these good things which the LORD, your God, has given you.[r]

Prayer with the Tithes. [12] "When you have finished setting aside all the tithes of your produce in the third year,[s] the year of the tithes, and you have given them to the Levite,* the alien, the orphan and the widow, that they may eat their fill in your own community, [13] you shall declare before the LORD, your God, 'I have purged my house of the sacred portion and I have given it to the Levite, the alien, the orphan and the widow, just as you have commanded me. In this I have not broken or forgotten any of your commandments: [14] * I have not eaten any of the tithe as a mourner; I have not brought any of it out as one unclean; I have not offered any of it to the dead. I have thus hearkened to the voice of the LORD, my God, doing just as you have commanded me. [15] Look down, then, from heaven, your holy abode, and bless your people Israel and the soil you have given us in the land flowing with milk and honey which you promised on oath to our fathers.'

The Covenant. [16] "This day the LORD, your God, commands you to observe these statutes and decrees. Be careful, then, to observe them with all your heart and with all your soul. [17] Today you are making this agreement with the LORD: he is to be your God and you are to walk in his ways and observe his statutes, commandments and decrees, and to hearken to his voice.[t] [18] And today the LORD is making this agreement with you: you are to be a people peculiarly his own,[u] as he promised you; and provided you keep all his commandments, [19] he will then raise you high in praise and renown and glory above all other nations he has made, and you will be a people sacred to the LORD, your God, as he promised."

IV: FINAL WORDS OF MOSES

CHAPTER 27

Ceremonies. [1] Then Moses, with the elders of Israel, gave the people this order: "Keep all these commandments which I enjoin on you today. [2] On the day you cross the Jordan into the land which the LORD, your God, is giving you, set up some large stones and coat them with plaster. [3] Also write on them,[v] at the time you cross, all the words of this law, that you may thus enter into the land flowing with milk and honey, which the LORD, your God, and the God of your fathers, is giving you as he promised you. [4] When, moreover, you have crossed the Jordan, besides setting up on Mount Ebal these stones concerning which I command you today, and coating them with plaster, [5] you shall also build to the LORD, your God, an altar made of stones that no iron tool has touched.[w] [6] You shall make this altar of the LORD, your God, with undressed stones, and shall offer on it holocausts to the LORD, your God. [7] You shall also sacrifice peace offerings and eat them there, making merry before the LORD, your God. [8] On the stones* you shall inscribe all the words of this law very clearly."

---

n Gn 46, 6f; Acts 7, 14f.—o 6f: Ex 1, 8-22; 2, 23ff; 3, 9; Nm 20, 15f.—p Ex 12, 51.—q Ex 3, 8.—r Dt 12, 7. 12.—s Dt 14, 28f.—t Ex 24, 7.—u 18f: Dt 7, 6; 14, 2; 28, 1; Ex 19, 5.—v Jos 8, 32.—w Ex 20, 25; Jos 8, 31.

26, 5: *Aramean:* either in reference to the origin of the patriarchs from Aram Naharaim (cf Gn 24, 10; 25, 20; 28, 5; 31, 20. 24), or merely in the sense of "nomad," in the same way as "Arab" was later used; cf Jer 3, 2.

26, 12: *And you have given them to the Levite . . .:* as prescribed in Dt 14, 28f.

26, 14: These are allusions to pagan religious practices.

27, 8: *On the stones:* cf vv 3f; not the stones of the altar.

[9]Moses, with the levitical priests, then said to all Israel: "Be silent, O Israel, and listen! This day you have become the people of the LORD, your God.[x] [10]You shall therefore hearken to the voice of the LORD, your God, and keep his commandments and statutes which I enjoin on you today."

[11]That same day Moses gave the people this order: [12]"When you cross the Jordan, Simeon, Levi, Judah, Issachar, Joseph and Benjamin shall stand on Mount Gerizim[y] to pronounce blessings over the people, [13]while Reuben, Gad, Asher, Zebulun, Dan and Naphtali shall stand on Mount Ebal to pronounce curses.

The Twelve Curses. [14]"The Levites shall proclaim aloud to all the men of Israel: [15]'Cursed be the man who makes a carved or molten idol[z]—an abomination to the LORD, the product of a craftsman's hands—and sets it up in secret!' And all the people shall answer, 'Amen!'*

[16]'Cursed be he who dishonors his father or his mother!'[a] And all the people shall answer, 'Amen!'

[17]'Cursed be he who moves his neighbor's landmarks!'[b] And all the people shall answer, 'Amen!'

[18]'Cursed be he who misleads a blind man on his way!'[c] And all the people shall answer, 'Amen!'

[19]'Cursed be he who violates the rights of the alien, the orphan or the widow!'[d] And all the people shall answer, 'Amen!'

[20]'Cursed be he who has relations with his father's wife, for he dishonors his father's bed!'[e] And all the people shall answer, 'Amen!'

[21]'Cursed be he who has relations with any animal!'[f] And all the people shall answer, 'Amen!'

[22]'Cursed be he who has relations with his sister or his half-sister!'[g] And all the people shall answer, 'Amen!'

[23]'Cursed be he who has relations with his mother-in-law!'[h] And all the people shall answer, 'Amen!'

[24]'Cursed be he who slays his neighbor in secret!'[i] And all the people shall answer, 'Amen!'

[25]'Cursed be he who accepts payment for slaying an innocent man!' And all the people shall answer, 'Amen!'

[26]'Cursed be he who fails to fulfill any of the provisions of this law!' [j] And all the people shall answer, 'Amen!'

Dt

CHAPTER 28*

Blessings for Obedience. [1]"Thus, then,[k] shall it be:[l] if you continue to heed the voice of the LORD, your God, and are careful to observe all his commandments which I enjoin on you today, the LORD, your God, will raise you high above all the nations of the earth.[m] [2]When you hearken to the voice of the LORD, your God, all these blessings will come upon you and overwhelm you:

[3] "May you be blessed in the city,
   and blessed in the country!
[4] "Blessed be the fruit of your womb,
      the produce of your soil and the offspring of your livestock,
      the issue of your herds and the young of your flocks![n]
[5] "Blessed be your grain bin and your kneading bowl!
[6] "May you be blessed in your coming in,
   and blessed in your going out!*

Victory and Prosperity. [7]"The LORD will beat down before you the enemies that rise up against you; though they come out against you from but one direction, they will flee before you in seven.* [8]The LORD will affirm his blessing upon you, on your barns and on all your undertakings, blessing you in the land that the LORD, your God, gives you. [9]Provided that you keep the commandments of the LORD, your God, and walk in his ways, he will establish you as a people sacred to himself, as he swore to you;[o] [10]so that, when all the nations of the earth see you bearing the name of the LORD,* they will stand in awe of you.[p] [11]The LORD will increase in more than goodly measure the fruit of your

---

x Dt 26, 17ff.—y 12f: Dt 11, 29; Jos 8, 33f.—z Ex 20, 4. 23; Lv 19, 4; Wis 14, 8.—a Dt 21, 18-21; Ex 21, 17; Lv 20, 9.—b Dt 19, 14.—c Lv 19, 14.—d Dt 24, 17; Ex 22, 21f.—e Dt 22; 23, 1; Lv 18, 8; 20, 11.—f Ex 22, 18; Lv 18, 23; 20, 15.—g Lv 18, 9; 20, 17.—h Lv 18, 17; 20, 14.—i Ex 20, 13; 21, 12; Nm 35, 20f.—j Gal 3, 10.—k 1-68: Lv 26, 1-45.—l 1-14: Dt 7, 12-16.—m Dt 26, 19.—n Dt 7, 13; 30, 9.—o Dt 26, 18; Ex 19, 5f.—p Dt 2, 25; 11, 25.

27, 15-26: *Amen:* see note on Nm 5, 22.
28, 1-69: This chapter would read better immediately after chapter 26.
28, 6: *In your coming in . . . in your going out:* at the beginning and end of every action, or in all actions in general.
28, 7. 25: *From but one direction . . . in seven:* in one compact mass, contrasted with many scattered groups.
28, 10: *You bearing the name of the LORD:* literally, "The LORD's name is called over you," an expression signifying ownership and protection. Cf 2 Sm 12, 28; 1 Kgs 8, 43; Is 4, 1; 63, 19; Jer 7, 10f; 14, 9; 15, 16; 25, 29; Am 9, 12.

womb, the offspring of your livestock, and the produce of your soil, in the land which he swore to your fathers he would give you. [12] The LORD will open up for you his rich treasure house of the heavens, to give your land rain in due season, blessing all your undertakings, so that you will lend to many nations and borrow from none.[q] [13] The LORD will make you the head, not the tail,* and you will always mount higher and not decline, as long as you obey the commandments of the LORD, your God, which I order you today to observe carefully; [14] not turning aside to the right or to the left from any of the commandments which I now give you, in order to follow other gods and serve them.

Curses for Disobedience. [15] "But if you do not hearken to the voice of the LORD, your God,[r] and are not careful to observe all his commandments which I enjoin on you today, all these curses shall come upon you and overwhelm you:

[16] "May you be cursed in the city,
    and cursed in the country!
[17] "Cursed be your grain bin and your
    kneading bowl!
[18] "Cursed be the fruit of your womb,
    the produce of your soil and the
      offspring of your livestock,
    the issue of your herds and the young
      of your flocks!
[19] "May you be cursed in your coming in,
    and cursed in your going out!

Sickness and Defeat. [20] "The LORD will put a curse on you, defeat and frustration in every enterprise you undertake, until you are speedily destroyed and perish for the evil you have done in forsaking me. [21] The LORD will bring a pestilence upon you that will persist until he has exterminated you from the land you are entering to occupy. [22] The LORD will strike you with wasting and fever, with scorching, fiery drought, with blight and searing wind, that will plague you until you perish. [23] The sky over your heads will be like bronze and the earth under your feet like iron.[s] [24] For rain the LORD will give your land powdery dust, which will come down upon you from the sky until you are destroyed. [25] The LORD will let you be beaten down before your enemies; though you advance against them from one direction, you will flee before them in seven, so that you will become a terrifying example

to all the kingdoms of the earth.[t] [26] Your carcasses will become food for all the birds of the air and for the beasts of the field, with no one to frighten them off. [27] The LORD will strike you with Egyptian boils[u] and with tumors, eczema and the itch, until you cannot be cured. [28] And the LORD will strike you with madness, blindness and panic, [29] so that even at midday you will grope like a blind man in the dark, unable to find your way.

Despoilment. "You will be oppressed and robbed continually, with no one to come to your aid. [30] Though you betroth a wife, another man will have her. Though you build a house, you will not live in it. Though you plant a vineyard, you will not enjoy its fruits. [31] Your ox will be slaughtered before your eyes, and you will not eat of its flesh. Your ass will be stolen in your presence, but you will not recover it. Your flocks will be given to your enemies, with no one to come to your aid. [32] Your sons and daughters will be given to a foreign nation while you look on and grieve for them in constant helplessness. [33] A people whom you do not know will consume the fruit of your soil and of all your labor, and you will be oppressed and crushed at all times without surcease, [34] until you are driven mad by what your eyes must look upon. [35] * The LORD will strike you with malignant boils of which you cannot be cured, on your knees and legs, and from the soles of your feet to the crown of your head.

Exile. [36] [v] "The LORD will bring you, and your king whom you have set over you, to a nation which you and your fathers have not known, and there you will serve strange gods of wood and stone, [37] and will call forth amazement, reproach and barbed scorn from all the nations to which the LORD will lead you.

Fruitless Labors. [38] "Though you spend much seed on your field, you will harvest but little, for the locusts will devour the crop.[w] [39] Though you plant and cultivate vineyards, you will not drink or store up the wine, for the grubs will eat the vines clean.[x] [40] Though you have olive trees

q Dt 15, 6.—r Bar 1, 20; Dn 9, 11; Mal 2, 2.—s 22f: Lv 26, 19.—t Lv 26, 17. 37.—u Ex 9, 9ff.—v 1 Kgs 9, 7ff; 2 Chr 7, 20ff; 33, 11; 36, 6. 20.—w Mi 6, 15; Hg 1, 6.—x Zep 1, 13.

28, 13: *The head, not the tail:* in the honorable position as leader. Cf Is 9, 14; 19, 15.
28, 35: This verse is best read with v 27.

throughout your country, you will have no oil for ointment, for your olives will drop off unripe.[y] [41] Though you beget sons and daughters, they will not remain with you, but will go into captivity.[z] [42] Buzzing insects will infest all your trees and the crops of your soil. [43] The alien residing among you will rise higher and higher above you, while you sink lower and lower. [44] He will lend to you, not you to him. He will become the head, you the tail.

[45] "All these curses will come upon you, pursuing you and overwhelming you, until you are destroyed, because you would not hearken to the voice of the LORD, your God, nor keep the commandments and statutes he gave you. [46] They will light on you and your descendants as a sign and a wonder* for all time. [47] Since you would not serve the LORD, your God, with joy and gratitude for abundance of every kind, [48] therefore in hunger and thirst, in nakedness and utter poverty, you will serve the enemies whom the LORD will send against you. He will put an iron yoke on your neck, until he destroys you.

Invasion and Siege. [49] [a] "The LORD will raise up against you a nation from afar, from the end of the earth, that swoops down like an eagle, a nation whose tongue you do not understand, [50] a nation of stern visage, that shows neither respect for the aged nor pity for the young. [51] They will consume the offspring of your livestock and the produce of your soil, until you are destroyed; they will leave you no grain or wine or oil, no issue of your herds or young of your flocks, until they have brought about your ruin. [52] They will besiege you in each of your communities, until the great, unscalable walls you trust in come tumbling down all over your land. They will so besiege you in every community throughout the land which the LORD, your God, has given you, [53] that in the distress of the siege to which your enemy

subjects you, you will eat the fruit of your womb, the flesh of your own sons and daughters[b] whom the LORD, your God, has given you. [54] The most refined and fastidious man among you will begrudge his brother and his beloved wife and his surviving children [55] any share in the flesh of his children that he himself is using for food when nothing else is left him in the straits of the siege to which your enemy will subject you in all your communities. [56] The most refined and delicate woman among you, so delicate and refined that she would not venture to set the sole of her foot on the ground, will begrudge her beloved husband and her son and daughter [57] the afterbirth that issues from her womb and the infant she brings forth when she secretly uses them for food for want of anything else, in the straits of the siege to which your enemy will subject you in your communities.

Plagues. [58] "If you are not careful to observe every word of the law which is written in this book, and to revere the glorious and awesome name of the LORD, your God, [59] he will smite you and your descendants with severe and constant blows, malignant and lasting maladies. [60] He will again afflict you with all the diseases of Egypt* which you dread, and they will persist among you.[c] [61] Should there be any kind of sickness or calamity not mentioned in this book of the law, that too the LORD will bring upon you until you are destroyed. [62] Of you who were numerous as the stars in the sky,[d] only a few will be left, because you would not hearken to the voice of the LORD, your God.

Exile. [63] "Just as the LORD once took delight in making you grow and prosper,[e] so will he now take delight in ruining and destroying you, and you will be plucked out of the land you are now entering to occupy. [64] The LORD will scatter you among all the nations from one end of the the earth to the other,[f] and there you will serve strange gods of wood and stone, such as you and your fathers have not known. [65] Among these nations you will find no repose, not a foot of ground to stand upon, for there the LORD will give you an anguished heart and wasted eyes* and a dismayed spirit. [66] You will live in constant suspense and stand in dread both day

y Mi 6, 15.—z Lam 1, 5.—a 49-52: Jer 5, 15ff; Bar 4, 15f.—b Lv 26, 29: 2 Kgs 6, 28f; Jer 19, 9; Lam 4, 10; Bar 2, 3.—c Dt 28, 27.—d Dt 1, 10; Jer 42, 2.—e Dt 30, 9.—f Lv 26, 33.

28, 46: *A sign and a wonder:* an ominous example, attracting attention; cf Dt 29, 21-28.

28, 60: *He will again afflict you with all the diseases of Egypt:* such as the Lord had promised to remove from his people; cf Dt 7, 15.

28, 65: *Wasted eyes:* worn out and disappointed in their longing gaze.

and night, never sure of your existence. [67] In the morning you will say, 'Would that it were evening!' and in the evening you will say, 'Would that it were morning!' for the dread that your heart must feel and the sight that your eyes must see. [68] The LORD will send you back in galleys* to Egypt, to the region I told you that you were never to see again;[g] and there you will offer yourselves for sale to your enemies as male and female slaves, but there will be no buyer."

[69] These are the words of the covenant which the LORD ordered Moses to make with the Israelites in the land of Moab, in addition to the covenant which he made with them at Horeb.

CHAPTER 29

Past Favors Recalled. [1] Moses summoned all Israel and said to them, "You have seen all that the LORD did in the land of Egypt before your very eyes to Pharaoh and all his servants and to all his land; [2] the great testings your own eyes have seen, and those great signs and wonders.[h] [3] But not even at the present day has the LORD yet given you a mind to understand, or eyes to see, or ears to hear.* [4] I led you for forty years in the desert.[i] Your clothes did not fall from you in tatters nor your sandals from your feet; [5] bread was not your food, nor wine or beer your drink. Thus you should know that I, the LORD, am your God.' [6] [j] When we came to this place, Sihon, king of Heshbon, and Og, king of Bashan, came out to engage us in battle, but we defeated them [7] and took over their land, which we then gave as a heritage to the Reubenites, Gadites, and half the tribe of Manasseh.[k] [8] Keep the terms of this covenant, therefore, and fulfill them, that you may succeed in whatever you do.

All Israel Bound to the Covenant. [9] "You are all now standing before the LORD, your God—your chiefs and judges, your elders and officials, and all of the men of Israel, [10] together with your wives and children and the aliens who live in your camp, down to those who hew wood and draw water for you—[11] that you may enter into the covenant of the LORD, your God, which he concluded with you today under this sanction of a curse;* [12] so that he may

now establish you as his people and he may be your God, as he promised you and as he swore to your fathers Abraham, Isaac and Jacob. [13] But it is not with you alone that I am making this covenant, under this sanction of a curse; [14] it is just as much with those who are not here among us* today as it is with those of us who are now here present before the LORD, our God.

Warning against Idolatry. [15] "You know in what surroundings we lived in the land of Egypt and what we passed by in the nations we traversed, [16] and you saw the loathsome idols of wood and stone, of gold and silver, that they possess. [17] Let there be, then, no man or woman, no clan or tribe among you, who would now turn away their hearts from the LORD, our God, to go and serve these pagan gods! Let there be no root that would bear such poison and wormwood among you! [18] If any such person, upon hearing the words of this curse, should beguile himself into thinking that he can safely persist in his stubbornness of heart, as though to sweep away both the watered soil and the parched ground,* [19] the LORD will never consent to pardon him. Instead, the LORD's wrath and jealousy will flare up against that man, and every curse mentioned in this book will alight on him. The LORD will blot out his name from under the heavens [20] and will single him out from all the tribes of Israel for doom, in keeping with all the curses of the covenant inscribed in this book of the law.

Punishment for Infidelity. [21] "Future generations, your own descendants who will rise up after you, as well as the foreigners who will come here from far-off lands, when they see the calamities of this land and the ills with which the LORD has smitten it—[22] all its soil being nothing but

---

g Hos 8, 13; 9, 3.—h Dt 4, 34; Ex 19, 4.—i Dt 8, 2. 4.—j Dt 2, 24. 32; 3, 1; Nm 21, 33ff.—k Dt 3, 16; Nm 32, 33.

28, 68: *In galleys:* in the ships of the Phoenician slave traders (Ez 27, 13; Jl 4, 6; Am 1, 9), who also dealt with Egypt (Is 23, 3).

29, 3: *Eyes to see . . . ears to hear:* with inner, spiritual discernment. Cf Mt 13, 43.

29, 11: *Sanction of a curse:* the present pact binds under penalty of the curses mentioned in this book. Cf v 20.

29, 14: *Not here among us:* this includes their descendants.

29, 18: *To sweep away both the watered soil and the parched ground:* apparently a proverb signifying that such an unfaithful Israelite will cause God to punish the good with the wicked, to root out the good plants growing in irrigated soil, together with the worthless plants growing in the dry ground.

sulphur and salt, a burnt-out waste, un-sown and unfruitful, without a blade of grass, destroyed like Sodom and Gomor-rah,[1] Admah and Zeboiim, which the LORD overthrew in his furious wrath— [23] they and all the nations will ask, 'Why has the LORD dealt thus with this land? Why this fierce outburst of wrath?'[m] [24] And the answer will be, 'Because they forsook the covenant which the LORD, the God of their fathers, had made with them when he brought them out of the land of Egypt, [25] and they went and served other gods and adored them, gods whom they did not know and whom he had not let fall to their lot: [26] that is why the LORD was angry with this land and brought on it all the imprecations listed in this book; [27] in his furious wrath and tremendous anger the LORD uprooted them from their soil and cast them out into a strange land,[n] where they are today.' [28] [Both what is still hidden* and what has already been re-vealed concern us and our descendants for-ever, that we may carry out all the words of this law.]

CHAPTER 30

Mercy for the Repentant. [1] "When all these things which I have set before you, the blessings and the curses, are fulfilled in you,[o] and from among whatever nations the LORD, your God, may have dispersed you, you ponder them in your heart: [2] then, provided that you and your chil-dren return to the LORD, your God, and heed his voice with all your heart and all your soul,[p] just as I now command you, [3] the LORD, your God, will change your lot; and taking pity on you, he will again gather you from all the nations wherein he has scattered you. [4] Though you may have

---

1 Gn 14, 10f; 19, 24f.—m 23f: 1 Kgs 9, 8f; Jer 22, 8f.—n Dn 9, 11-14.—o Dt 11, 26ff.—p 2f: Neh 1, 9.—q Dt 6, 5.—r Dt 28, 11.

29, 28: *What is still hidden:* the events of the future. *What has already been revealed:* God's law and the punishments in store for those who break it. Leave the future to God; our busi-ness is to keep his law.

30, 6: *Circumcise your hearts:* see note on Dt 10, 16.

30, 11-14: God has revealed his will so clearly that ignorance of his law can be no excuse. St. Paul in Rom 10, 6-10, applies these words to the ease with which we can come to faith and sal-vation in Christ.

30, 14: *In your mouths:* that you may readily talk about it; cf Dt 6, 7; 11, 19. *And in your hearts:* that you may easily re-member it; cf Dt 6, 6; 11, 18.

been driven to the farthest corner of the world, even from there will the LORD, your God, gather you; even from there will he bring you back. [5] The LORD, your God, will then bring you into the land which your fathers once occupied, that you too may occupy it, and he will make you more prosperous and numerous than your fathers. [6] The LORD, your God, will cir-cumcise your hearts* and the hearts of your descendants,[q] that you may love the LORD, your God, with all your heart and all your soul, and so may live. [7] But all those curses the LORD, your God, will as-sign to your enemies and the foes who persecuted you. [8] You, however, must again heed the LORD's voice and carry out all his commandments which I now enjoin on you. [9] Then the LORD, your God, will increase in more than goodly measure the returns from all your labors, the fruit of your womb, the offspring of your live-stock, and the produce of your soil;[r] for the LORD, your God, will again take de-light in your prosperity, even as he took delight in your fathers', [10] if only you heed the voice of the LORD, your God, and keep his commandments and statutes that are written in this book of the law, when you return to the LORD, your God, with all your heart and all your soul.

God's Command Clear. [11] * "For this command which I enjoin on you today is not too mysterious and remote for you. [12] It is not up in the sky, that you should say, 'Who will go up in the sky to get it for us and tell us of it, that we may carry it out?' [13] Nor is it across the sea, that you should say, 'Who will cross the sea to get it for us and tell us of it, that we may carry it out?' [14] No, it is something very near to you, already in your mouths* and in your hearts; you have only to carry it out.

The Choice before Israel. [15] "Here, then, I have today set before you life and pros-perity, death and doom. [16] If you obey the commandments of the LORD, your God, which I enjoin on you today, loving him, and walking in his ways, and keeping his commandments, statutes and decrees, you will live and grow numerous, and the LORD, your God, will bless you in the land you are entering to occupy. [17] If, however, you turn away your hearts and will not listen, but are led astray and adore and serve other gods, [18] I tell you now that you will certainly perish; you will not have a long life on the land which you are crossing the Jordan to enter and occupy. [19] I call heaven and earth today to witness against you:[s] I have set before you life and death, the blessing and the curse.[t] Choose life, then, that you and your descendants may live, [20] by loving the LORD, your God, heeding his voice, and holding fast to him. For that will mean life for you, a long life for you to live on the land which the LORD swore he would give to your fathers Abraham, Isaac and Jacob."

CHAPTER 31

The Lord's Leadership. [1] When Moses had finished speaking these words to all Israel, [2] he said to them, "I am now one hundred and twenty years old[u] and am no longer able to move about freely; besides, the LORD has told me that I shall not cross this Jordan. [3] It is the LORD, your God, who will cross before you; he will destroy these nations before you, that you may supplant them.[v] [It is Joshua who will cross before you, as the LORD promised.] [4] [w] The LORD will deal with them just as he dealt with Sihon and Og, the kings of the Amorites whom he destroyed, and with their country. [5] When, therefore, the LORD delivers them up to you, you must deal with them exactly as I have ordered you.[x] [6] Be brave and steadfast; have no fear or dread of them, for it is the LORD, your God, who marches with you; he will never fail you or forsake you."[y]

Call of Joshua. [7] Then Moses summoned Joshua and in the presence of all Israel said to him,[z] "Be brave and steadfast, for you must bring this people into the land which the LORD swore to their fathers he would give them; you must put them in possession of their heritage. [8] It is the LORD who marches before you; he will be with you and will never fail you or forsake you. So do not fear or be dismayed."

The Reading of the Law. [9] When Moses had written down this law, he entrusted it to the levitical priests who carry the ark of the covenant of the LORD, and to all the elders of Israel, [10] giving them this order: "On the feast of Booths,[a] at the prescribed time in the year of relaxation* which comes at the end of every seven-year period, [11] when all Israel goes to appear before the LORD, your God, in the place

which he chooses, you shall read this law* aloud in the presence of all Israel. [12] Assemble the people—men, women and children, as well as the aliens who live in your communities—that they may hear it and learn it, and so fear the LORD, your God, and carefully observe all the words of this law. [13] Their children also, who do not know it yet, must hear it and learn it, that they too may fear the LORD, your God, as long as you live on the land which you will cross the Jordan to occupy."

Commission of Joshua. [14] The LORD said to Moses, "The time is now approaching for you to die. Summon Joshua, and present yourselves at the meeting tent that I may give him his commission." So Moses and Joshua went and presented themselves at the meeting tent.* [15] And the LORD appeared at the tent in a column of cloud, which stood still at the entrance of the tent.

A Command to Moses. [16] The LORD said to Moses, "Soon you will be at rest with your fathers, and then this people will take to rendering wanton worship to the strange gods among whom they will live in the land they are about to enter.[b] They will forsake me and break the covenant which I have made with them. [17] At that time my anger will flare up against them; I will forsake them and hide my face from them, so that they will become a prey to be devoured, and many evils and troubles will befall them. At that time they will indeed say, 'Is it not because our God is not among us that these evils have befallen us?' [18] Yet I will be hiding my face from them at that time only because of all the evil they have done in turning to other gods. [19] Write out this song,[c] then, for yourselves. Teach it to the Israelites and have them recite it, so that this song may be a witness for me against the Israelites. [20] For when I have brought them into the land flowing with milk and honey which I promised on oath to their fathers, and they have eaten their fill and grown fat,

---

s Dt 4, 26.—t Dt 11, 26ff; 28, 2. 15.—u Dt 34, 7; Nm 20, 12.—v Dt 9, 3.—w Nm 21, 21-35.—x Dt 7, 2.—y Dt 20, 3f.—z 7f; Jos 1, 6f. 9.—a 10f: Dt 16, 13ff.—b Jgs 2, 12. 17.—c Dt 31, 21; 32, 1-43.

31, 10: *The year of relaxation:* cf Dt 15, 1ff and the note there.

31, 11ff: Reading the law not only instructed the people but also consoled them by the assurance of the divine goodness.

31, 14f. 23: V 23 is best read immediately after v 15; perhaps the original order was vv 7-8. 14-15. 23.

if they turn to other gods and serve them, despising me and breaking my covenant; [21] then, when many evils and troubles befall them, this song, which their descendants will not have forgotten to recite, will bear witness against them. For I know what they are inclined to do even at the present time, before I have brought them into the land which I promised on oath to their fathers." [22] So Moses wrote this song that same day, and he taught it to the Israelites.

Commission of Joshua. [23] Then the LORD commissioned Joshua, son of Nun, and said to him, "Be brave and steadfast, for it is you who must bring the Israelites into the land which I promised them on oath.[d] I myself will be with you."

The Law Placed in the Ark. [24] When Moses had finished writing out on a scroll the words of the law in their entirety, [25] he gave the Levites[e] who carry the ark of the covenant of the LORD this order: [26] "Take this scroll of the law and put it beside the ark of the covenant of the LORD, your God, that there it may be a witness against you. [27] For I already know how rebellious and stiff-necked you will be. Why, even now, while I am alive among you, you have been rebels against the LORD! How much more, then, after I am dead! [28] f Therefore, assemble all your tribal elders and your officials before me, that I may speak these words for them to hear, and so may call heaven and earth to witness against them. [29] g For I know that after my death you are sure to become corrupt and to turn aside from the way along which I directed you, so that evil will befall you in some future age because you have done evil in the LORD's sight, and provoked him by your deeds."

---

d Dt 31, 7f; Jos 1, 5ff.—e 24f: Dt 31, 9.—f Dt 32, 1-43.—g Jgs 2, 19.—h Ps 92, 15; Rv 15, 3.—i Dt 31, 29; Ps 78, 8; Lk 9, 41.—j Ex 4, 22; Is 63, 16; 64, 8; Jer 31, 9.—k Dt 4, 32; Ps 44, 2.—l Gn 10, 1-32; Acts 17, 26.—m Ex 19, 5; Ps 33, 12.—n Dt 8, 15; Jer 2, 6; Zec 2, 8.

32, 1-43: In the style of the great prophets, the speaker is often God himself. The whole song is a poetic sermon, having for its theme God's benefits to Israel (vv 1-14) and Israel's ingratitude and idolatry in turning to the gods of the pagans, which sins will be punished by the pagans themselves (vv 15-29); in turn, the foolish pride of the pagans will be punished, and the Lord's honor will be vindicated (vv 30-43).
32, 8: *The sons of God:* the angels; cf Jb 1, 6; 2, 1; 38, 7; Ps 89, 7f. Here the various nations are portrayed as having their respective guardian angels. Cf Dn 10, 20f; 12, 1.

The Song of Moses. [30] Then Moses recited the words of this song from beginning to end, for the whole assembly of Israel to hear:

Dt

CHAPTER 32

A

[1] Give ear, O heavens, while I speak;*
  let the earth hearken to the words of
    my mouth!
[2] May my instruction soak in like the
    rain,
  and my discourse permeate like the
    dew,
  Like a downpour upon the grass,
    like a shower upon the crops:

[3] For I will sing the LORD's renown.
  Oh, proclaim the greatness of our
    God!
[4] The Rock—how faultless are his deeds,
    how right all his ways!
  A faithful God, without deceit,
    how just and upright he is![h]

[5] Yet basely has he been treated by his
    degenerate children,
  a perverse and crooked race![i]
[6] Is the LORD to be thus repaid by you,
    O stupid and foolish people?
  Is he not your father who created you?
  Has he not made you and established
    you?[j]

[7] Think back on the days of old,
  reflect on the years of age upon age.
  Ask your father and he will inform you,
    ask your elders and they will tell
    you:[k]
[8] When the Most High assigned the nations their heritage,
  when he parceled out the descendants
    of Adam,[l]
  He set up the boundaries of the peoples
    after the number of the sons of God;*
[9] While the LORD's own portion was
    Jacob,
  his hereditary share was Israel.[m]

[10] He found them in a wilderness,
  a wasteland of howling desert.
  He shielded them and cared for them,
    guarding them as the apple of his
    eye.[n]

[11] As an eagle incites its nestlings forth
    by hovering over its brood,

So he spread his wings to receive them
and bore them up on his pinions. [o]

12 The LORD alone was their leader,
no strange god was with him.
13 He had them ride triumphant over the
summits of the land*
and live off the products of its fields,
Giving them honey to suck from its
rocks
and olive oil from its hard, stony
ground;
14 Butter from its cows and milk from its
sheep,
with the fat of its lambs and rams;
Its Bashan* bulls and its goats,
with the cream of its finest wheat;
and the foaming blood of its grapes
you drank.

B

15 [So Jacob ate his fill,]
the darling* grew fat and frisky;
you became fat and gross and
gorged.
They spurned the God who made them
and scorned their saving Rock. [p]
16 They provoked him with strange gods
and angered him with abominable
idols. [q]
17 They offered sacrifice to demons, to
"no-gods,"
to gods whom they had not known
before,
To newcomers just arrived,
of whom their fathers had never
stood in awe.
18 You were unmindful of the Rock that
begot you,
you forgot the God who gave you
birth. [r]
19 When the LORD saw this, he was filled
with loathing
and anger toward his sons and
daughters.
20 "I will hide my face from them," he
said,
"and see what will then become of
them.
What a fickle race they are,
sons with no loyalty in them! [s]
21 "Since they have provoked me with
their 'no-god'
and angered me with their vain idols,
I will provoke them with a 'no-people';
with a foolish nation I will anger
them. [t]

22 "For by my wrath a fire is enkindled
that shall rage to the depths of the
nether world,
Consuming the earth with its yield,
and licking with flames the roots of
the mountains. [u]
23 I will spend on them woe upon woe
and exhaust all my arrows against
them:
24 "Emaciating hunger and consuming
fever
and bitter pestilence,
And the teeth of wild beasts I will send
among them,
with the venom of reptiles gliding in
the dust.
25 "Snatched away by the sword in the
street
and by sheer terror at home
Shall be the youth and the maiden
alike,
the nursing babe as well as the hoary
old man. [v]
26 "I would have said, 'I will make an end
of them
and blot out their name from men's
memories,'
27 Had I not feared the insolence of their
enemies,
feared that these foes would mistakenly boast,
'Our own hand won the victory;
the LORD had nothing to do with
it.' "
28 For they are a people devoid of reason,*
having no understanding.
29 If they had insight they would realize
what happened,
they would understand their future
and say,

C

30 "How could one man rout a thousand,
or two men put ten thousand to
flight,
Unless it was because their Rock sold
them
and the LORD delivered them up?"

---

o Ex 19, 4.—p Dt 31, 20.—q Nm 25, 2f; Ps 78, 58.—r Jer 2,
32.—s Dt 31, 17.—t Rom 10, 19.—u Lam 4, 11.—v Lv 26, 25.

32, 13: *The land:* Canaan.
32, 14: *Bashan:* a fertile grazing land east of the Jordan, famous for its strong cattle. Cf Ps 22, 13; Ex 39, 18; Am 4, 1.
32, 15: *The darling:* a probable meaning of the Hebrew word
yeshurun, a term of endearment for "Israel." Cf Dt 33, 5. 26;
Is 44, 2.
32, 28-35: The reference is to the pagan nations, not to
Israel.

³¹ Indeed, their "rock" is not like our
Rock,
and our foes are under condemnation.
³² They are a branch of Sodom's vine-
stock,
from the vineyards of Gomorrah.

Poisonous are their grapes.
and bitter their clusters.
³³ Their wine is the venom of dragons
and the cruel poison of cobras.

³⁴ "Is not this preserved in my treasury,
sealed up in my storehouse,
³⁵ Against the day of vengeance and requital,
against the time they lose their footing?"

Close at hand is the day of their disaster,
and their doom is rushing upon
them!
³⁶ Surely, the LORD shall do justice for his
people;
on his servants he shall have pity.
When he sees their strength failing,
and their protected and unprotected*
alike disappearing,ʷ
³⁷ He will say, "Where are their godsˣ
whom they relied on as their 'rock'?
³⁸ Let those who ate the fat of your sacrifices
and drank the wine of your libations
Rise up now and help you!
Let them be your protection!

³⁹ "Learn then that I, I alone, am God,
and there is no god besides me.
It is I who bring both death and life,
I who inflict wounds and heal them,
and from my hand there is no res-
cue.ʸ

⁴⁰ "To the heavens I raise my hand and
swear:
As surely as I live forever,
⁴¹ I will sharpen my flashing sword,

---

w 2 Mc 7, 6.—x 37f: Jgs 10, 14; Jer 2, 28.—y Dt 4, 35; Tb 13,
2; Wis 16, 13.—z Dt 4, 9.—a Nm 27, 12; 33, 47f.—b Nm 20,
24ff. 28; 27, 13; 33, 38.—c Nm 20, 12; 27, 14.—d Dt 3, 27; 34,
4.

32, 36: *Their protected and unprotected:* the meaning of
the Hebrew is uncertain; according to some, the idea is "slaves
and freemen."
33, 2-5. 26-29: These verses seem to form an independent
hymn describing, in the form of a theophany, the conquest of Canaan. The first section of this hymn (vv 2-5) serves here as an introduction to the various "blessings"; the second section (vv 26-
29), as their conclusion.

---

and my hand shall lay hold of my
quiver.
"With vengeance I will repay my foes
and requite those who hate me.
⁴² I will make my arrows drunk with
blood,
and my sword shall gorge itself with
flesh—
With the blood of the slain and the captured,
flesh from the heads of the enemy
leaders."

⁴³ Exult with him, you heavens,
glorify him, all you angels of God;
For he avenges the blood of his servants
and purges his people's land.

⁴⁴ So Moses, together with Joshua, son
of Nun, went and recited all the words of
this song for the people to hear.

Final Appeal. ⁴⁵ When Moses had finished
speaking all these words to all Israel, ⁴⁶ he
said,ᶻ "Take to heart all the warning which
I have now given you and which you must
impress on your children, that you may
carry out carefully every word of this law.
⁴⁷ For this is no trivial matter for you;
rather, it means your very life, since it is
by this means that you are to enjoy a long
life on the land which you will cross the
Jordan to occupy."

Moses to View Canaan. ⁴⁸ On that very
day the LORD said to Moses, ⁴⁹ "Go up on
Mount Nebo, here in the Abarim Mountains [it is in the land of Moab facing
Jericho], and view the land of Canaan,
which I am giving to the Israelites as their
possession.ᵃ ⁵⁰ Then you shall die on the
mountain you have climbed, and shall be
taken to your people, just as your brother
Aaron died on Mount Hor and there was
taken to his people;ᵇ ⁵¹ because both of you
broke faith with me among the Israelites at
the waters of Meribath-kadesh in the desert of Zin by failing to manifest my sanctity among the Israelites.ᶜ ⁵² You may indeed view the land at a distance, but you
shall not enter that land which I am giving
to the Israelites."ᵈ

CHAPTER 33

Blessing upon the Tribes. ¹ This is the
blessing which Moses, the man of God,
pronounced upon the Israelites before he
died. ² He said:
"The LORD came from Sinai*
and dawned on his people from Seir;

He shone forth from Mount Paran
  and advanced from Meribath-
  kadesh,
While at his right hand a fire blazed
  forth
  and his wrath devastated the nations.[e]
3 But all his holy ones were in his hand;*
  they followed at his feet
  and he bore them up on his pinions.
4 A law he gave to us;
  he made the community of Jacob his
  domain,[f]
5 and he became king of his darling,*
  When the chiefs of the people assembled
  and the tribes of Israel came together.

6 "May Reuben live and not die out,[g]
  but let his men be few."*

7 The following is for Judah. He said:
  "The LORD hears the cry of Judah;
  you will bring him to his people.*
  His own hands defend his cause
  and you will be his help against his
  foes."[h]

8 Of Levi he said:
  "To Levi belong your Thummim,
  to the man of your favor your Urim;*
  For you put him to the test at Massah
  and you contended with him at the
  waters of Meribah.[i]
9 He said of his father, 'I regard him not';
  his brothers he would not acknowledge,
  and his own children he refused to
  recognize.
  Thus the Levites keep your words,
  and your covenant they uphold.*
10 They promulgate your decisions to
  Jacob
  and your law to Israel.
  They bring the smoke of sacrifice to
  your nostrils,
  and burnt offerings to your altar.[j]
11 Bless, O LORD, his possessions
  and accept the ministry of his hands.
  Break the backs of his adversaries
  and of his foes, that they may not
  rise."

12 Of Benjamin he said:
  "Benjamin is the beloved of the LORD,
  who shelters him all the day,
  while he abides securely at his
  breast."[k]

13 Of Joseph he said:[l]
  "Blessed by the LORD is his land
  with the best of the skies above
  and of the abyss crouching beneath;
14 With the best of the produce of the
  year,
  and the choicest sheaves of the
  months;
15 With the finest gifts of the age-old
  mountains
  and the best from the timeless hills;
16 With the best of the earth and its fullness,
  and the favor of him who dwells in
  the bush.*
  These shall come upon the head of
  Joseph
  and upon the brow of the prince
  among his brothers,
17 The majestic bull, his father's first-
  born,
  whose horns are those of the wild ox
  With which to gore the nations,
  even those at the ends of the earth."
  [These are the myriads of Ephraim,
  and these the thousands of Manasseh.]

18 Of Zebulun he said:[m]
  "Rejoice, O Zebulun, in your pursuits,
  and you, Issachar, in your tents!
19 You who invite the tribes to the mountains
  where feasts are duly held,
  Because you suck up the abundance of
  the seas*
  and the hidden treasures of the
  sand."

---

e Ex 19, 18. 20; Jgs 5, 4f.—f Jn 1, 17; 7, 19.—g Gn 49, 3f.—h
Gn 49, 8-12.—i Gn 49, 5; Ex 17, 7; 28, 30; Nm 20, 13.—j Ex
30, 7f.—k Gn 49, 27.—l 13-17: Gn 49, 22-26.—m 18f: Gn 49,
13ff.

33, 3: *His holy ones were in his hand:* the Israelites were
protected by the Lord.
33, 5. 26: *The darling:* see note on Dt 32, 15.
33, 6: In keeping with the other blessings, probably this verse
was once introduced by the phrase, "Of Reuben he said." It is to
be noted that there is no blessing here for Simeon.
33, 7: *Bring him to his people:* this probably refers to the
isolated position of the tribe of Judah during the conquest of the
Promised Land (cf Jgs 1, 17-19); according to some commentators the reference is to the divided kingdom.
33, 8: *Thummim . . . Urim:* see note on Ex 28, 30.
33, 9: The reference is probably to the Levites' slaughter of
their brethren after the affair of the golden calf in the desert; cf
Ex 32, 27-29.
33, 16: *Him who dwells in the bush:* a title given to the
Lord because of his appearance to Moses in the burning bush; cf
Ex 3.
33, 19: *The abundance of the seas:* perhaps the wealth that
comes from sea-borne trade or from fishing. *The hidden trea-*

20 Of Gad he said:[n]
"Blessed be he who has made Gad so
vast!
He lies there like a lion
that has seized the arm and head of
the prey.
21 He saw that the best should be his
when the princely portion* was assigned,
while the heads of the people were
gathered.
He carried out the justice of the LORD
and his decrees respecting Israel."[o]

22 Of Dan he said:
"Dan is a lion's whelp,[p]
that springs forth from Bashan!"*

23 Of Naphtali he said:
"Naphtali is enriched with favors
and filled with the blessings of the
LORD;
The lake* and south of it are his posses-
sion!"[q]

24 Of Asher he said:[r]
"More blessed than the other sons be
Asher!
May he be the favorite among his
brothers,
as the oil of his olive trees runs over
his feet!*
25 May your bolts be of iron and bronze;
may your strength endure through all
your days!"

26 "There is no god like the God of the
darling,
who rides the heavens in his power,
and rides the skies in his majesty;
27 He spread out the primeval tent;
he extended the ancient canopy.
He drove the enemy out of your way
and the Amorite he destroyed,

28 Israel has dwelt securely,
and the fountain of Jacob has been
undisturbed,
In a land of grain and wine,
where the heavens drip with dew.[s]
29 How fortunate you are, O Israel!
Where else is a nation victorious in
the LORD?
The LORD is your saving shield,
and his sword is your glory.
Your enemies fawn upon you,
as you stride upon their heights."[t]

CHAPTER 34

Death and Burial of Moses. [1]Then Moses
went up from the plains of Moab to Mount
Nebo,[u] the headland of Pisgah which faces
Jericho, and the LORD showed him all the
land—Gilead, and as far as Dan, [2]all
Naphtali, the land of Ephraim and Manasseh, all the land of Judah as far as the
Western Sea, [3]the Negeb, the circuit of
the Jordan with the lowlands at Jericho,
city of palms, and as far as Zoar. [4]The
LORD then said to him, "This is the land[v]
which I swore to Abraham, Isaac and
Jacob that I would give to their descendants. I have let you feast your eyes upon
it, but you shall not cross over." [5]So there,
in the land of Moab, Moses, the servant of
the LORD, died[w] as the LORD had said;
[6]and he was buried in the ravine opposite
Beth-peor in the land of Moab, but to this
day no one knows the place of his burial.
[7]Moses was one hundred and twenty years
old[x] when he died, yet his eyes were undimmed and his vigor unabated. [8]For
thirty days the Israelites wept for Moses in
the plains of Moab, till they had completed
the period of grief and mourning for
Moses.
[9]Now Joshua, son of Nun,[y] was filled
with the spirit of wisdom, since Moses had
laid his hands upon him; and so the Israelites gave him their obedience, thus carrying out the LORD's command to Moses.
[10] [z] Since then no prophet has arisen in
Israel like Moses, whom the LORD knew
face to face. [11] [a] He had no equal in all the
signs and wonders the LORD sent him to
perform in the land of Egypt against
Pharaoh and all his servants and against all
his land, [12]and for the might and the terrifying power that Moses exhibited in the
sight of all Israel.

---

n 20f: Gn 49, 19.—o Nm 32, 1. 5. 16-19. 31f; Jos 1, 12-15;
1 Chr 5, 18-22.—p Gn 49, 16f.—q Gn 49, 21; Jos 19, 32-39.—r
24f: Gn 49, 20.—s Gn 27, 28.—t Dt 4, 7f.—u Dt 3, 27.—v Dt 3,
27; 32, 52; Gn 12, 7; 15, 18.—w Dt 32, 50.—x Dt 31, 2.—y Nm
27, 18. 23; Jos 1, 17.—z Ex 33, 11.—a Dt 4, 34.

---

sures of the sand: possibly an allusion to the valuable purple
dye extracted from certain marine shells found on the coast of
northern Palestine.
33, 21: *The princely portion:* Moses gave the tribe of Gad
their land on the east of the Jordan only on condition that they
would help other tribes conquer the land west of the river; cf Nm
32; Jos 22.
33, 22: The sense is, "May he leap up like a lion of Bashan";
the heavily wooded hills of Bashan were notorious for their lions,
but the tribe of Dan was not settled in this region.
33, 23: *The lake:* the Lake of Gennesaret on which the land
of this tribe bordered.
33, 24: The land of the tribe of Asher was covered with olive
groves.

THE BOOK OF JOSHUA

The Book of Joshua derives its name from the successor of Moses, with whose deeds it is principally concerned. The purpose of the book is to demonstrate God's fidelity in giving to the Israelites the land he had promised them for an inheritance (Gn 15, 18ff; Jos 1, 2ff; 21, 41ff; 23, 14ff).

Their occupation of the country is begun with the crossing of the Jordan and the conquest of Jericho (ch 1—6), in both of which the Lord intervenes on their behalf. This is followed by a first foothold on the Palestinian mountain range, at Ai, Bethel and Gibeon (ch 7—9), and two sweeping campaigns against the city states in the south of the country (ch 10) and in the north (ch 11), with a summary in ch 12. The broad claim to total sovereignty thus established is spelled out by a combined list of tribal boundaries and of the towns contained within each area or administrative district (ch 13—19), including cities of asylum and cities for the Levites (ch 20, 21). The book closes with a narrative about the tribes east of the Jordan (ch 22), a warning speech by Joshua (ch 23), and a renewal at Shechem (ch 24) of the covenant with the Lord, already affirmed there near the beginning (8, 30-35) of the conquest.

Like the books which precede it, the Book of Joshua was built up by a long and complex process of editing traditional materials. Both Jewish and Christian believers have always regarded it as inspired.

The entire history of the conquest of the Promised Land is a prophecy of the spiritual conquest of the world through the church under the leadership of Jesus the Messiah.

The Book of Joshua may be divided as follows: I. Conquest of Canaan (Jos 1, 1—12, 24). II. Division of the Land (Jos 13, 1—21, 45). III. Return of the Transjordan Tribes and Joshua's Farewell (Jos 22, 1—24, 33).

I: CONQUEST OF CANAAN

CHAPTER 1

Divine Promise of Assistance. [1] After Moses, the servant of the LORD, had died, the LORD said to Moses' aide Joshua, son of Nun: [2] "My servant Moses is dead. So prepare to cross the Jordan here, with all the people, into the land I will give the Israelites. [3] As I promised Moses, I will deliver to you every place where you set foot. [4] * Your domain is to be all the land of the Hittites, from the desert and from Lebanon east to the great river Euphrates and west to the Great Sea.[a] [5] No one can withstand you while you live. I will be with you as I was with Moses:[b] I will not leave you nor forsake you. [6] Be firm and steadfast, so that you may give this people possession of the land which I swore to their fathers I would give them. [7] Above all, be firm and steadfast, taking care to observe the entire law which my servant Moses enjoined on you. Do not swerve from it either to the right or to the left, that you may succeed wherever you go. [8] Keep this book of the law on your lips. Recite it by day and by night, that you may observe carefully all that is written in it; then you will successfully attain your goal. [9] I command you: be firm and steadfast! Do not fear nor be dismayed, for the LORD, your God, is with you wherever you go."[c]

[10] So Joshua commanded the officers of the people: [11] "Go through the camp and instruct the people, 'Prepare your provisions, for three days from now you shall

a 3f: Jos 14, 9; Gn 15, 18; Dt 11, 24.—b Dt 31, 8; Heb 13, 5.—c Dt 31, 7f.

1, 4: The ideal frontiers are given: in the south *the desert* of Sinai, in the north the *Lebanon* range, in the east the *Euphrates,* and in the west *the Great Sea,* the Mediterranean.

212

cross the Jordan here, to march in and take possession of the land which the LORD, your God, is giving you.' "*d*

The Transjordan Tribes. ¹²Joshua reminded the Reubenites, the Gadites, and the half-tribe of Manasseh: ¹³"Remember what Moses, the servant of the LORD, commanded you when he said,*c* 'The LORD, your God, will permit you to settle in this land.' ¹⁴Your wives, your children, and your livestock shall remain in the land Moses gave you here beyond the Jordan.*e* But all the warriors among you must cross over armed ahead of your kinsmen and you must help them ¹⁵until the LORD has settled your kinsmen, and they like you possess the land which the LORD, your God, is giving them. Afterward you may return and occupy your own land, which Moses, the servant of the LORD, has given you east of the Jordan."*f* ¹⁶"We will do all you have commanded us," they answered Joshua, "and we will go wherever you send us. We will obey you as completely as we obeyed Moses. ¹⁷But may the LORD, your God, be with you as he was with Moses. ¹⁸If anyone rebels against your orders and does not obey every command you give him, he shall be put to death. But be firm and steadfast."

CHAPTER 2

Spies Saved by Rahab. ¹Then Joshua, son of Nun, secretly sent out two spies from Shittim, saying, "Go, reconnoiter the land and Jericho." When the two reached Jericho, they went into the house of a harlot* named Rahab,*g* where they lodged. ²But a report was brought to the king of Jericho that some Israelites had come there that night to spy out the land. ³So the

---

d Dt 11, 31.—e Nm 32, 26.—f Jos 22, 4; Dt 3, 20.—g Mt 1, 5; Jas 2, 25.—h Jos 6, 17.—i Ex 15, 15f; 23, 27.—j Jos 4, 23; Ex 14, 21; Nm 21, 23-26. 33ff.—k Dt 4, 39.—l Jos 2, 18; 6, 23. 25.

2, 1: *Harlot:* this is the regular equivalent of the Hebrew word, but perhaps it is used here of Rahab in the broader sense of a woman who kept a public house. Joshua's spies hoped to remain undetected at such an inn.

2, 6: *Stalks of flax spread out:* to dry in the sun, after they had been soaked in water, according to the ancient process of preparing flax for linen-making. In the Near East the flax harvest occurs near the time of the feast of the Passover (Jos 4, 19; 5, 10); cf Ex 9, 31.

2, 8-11: Rahab's faith and good works are praised in the New Testament; cf Heb 11, 31; Jas 2, 25.

2, 15: *A house built into the city wall:* such houses, which used the city wall for their own inner walls, have been found at ancient sites. The upper story of Rahab's house was evidently higher than the city wall. It was through the window of such a house that St. Paul escaped from Damascus; cf Acts 9, 25; 2 Cor 11, 33.

---

king of Jericho sent Rahab the order, "Put out the visitors who have entered your house, for they have come to spy out the entire land." ⁴The woman*h* had taken the two men and hidden them, so she said, "True, the men you speak of came to me, but I did not know where they came from. ⁵At dark, when it was time for the gate to be shut, they left, and I do not know where they went. You will have to pursue them immediately to overtake them." ⁶Now, she had led them to the roof, and hidden them among her stalks of flax spread out* there. ⁷But the pursuers set out along the way to the fords of the Jordan, and once they had left, the gate was shut.

⁸Before the spies fell asleep, Rahab* came to them on the roof ⁹and said: "I know that the LORD has given you the land, that a dread of you has come upon us, and that all the inhabitants of the land are overcome with fear of you.*i* ¹⁰For we have heard how the LORD dried up the waters of the Red Sea before you when you came out of Egypt,*j* and how you dealt with Sihon and Og, the two kings of the Amorites beyond the Jordan, whom you doomed to destruction. ¹¹At these reports, we are disheartened; everyone is discouraged because of you, since the LORD, your God, is God in heaven above and on earth below.*k* ¹²Now then, swear to me by the LORD that, since I am showing kindness to you, you in turn will show kindness to my family;*l* and give me an unmistakable token ¹³that you are to spare my father and mother, brothers and sisters, and all their kin, and save us from death." ¹⁴"We pledge our lives for yours," the men answered her. "If you do not betray this errand of ours, we will be faithful in showing kindness to you when the LORD gives us the land."

¹⁵Then she let them down through the window with a rope; for she lived in a house built into the city wall.* ¹⁶"Go up into the hill country," she suggested to them, "that your pursuers may not find you. Hide there for three days, until they return; then you may proceed on your way." ¹⁷The men answered her, "This is how we will fulfill the oath you made us take: ¹⁸When we come into the land, tie this scarlet cord in the window through which you are letting us down; and gather your father and mother, your brothers

and all your family into your house. [19]Should any of them pass outside the doors of your house, he will be responsible for his own death, and we shall be guiltless. But we shall be responsible if anyone in the house with you is harmed. [20]If, however, you betray this errand of ours, we shall be quit of the oath you have made us take." [21]"Let it be as you say," she replied, and bade them farewell. When they were gone, she tied the scarlet cord in the window.

[22]They went up into the hills, where they stayed three days until their pursuers, who had sought them all along the road without finding them, returned. [23]Then the two came back down from the hills, crossed the Jordan to Joshua, son of Nun, and reported all that had befallen them. [24]They assured Joshua, "The LORD has delivered all this land into our power; indeed, all the inhabitants of the land are overcome with fear of us."

CHAPTER 3

Preparations for Crossing the Jordan. [1]Early the next morning, Joshua[m] moved with all the Israelites from Shittim to the Jordan, where they lodged before crossing over. [2]Three days later the officers went through the camp [3]and issued these instructions to the people: "When you see the ark of the covenant of the LORD, your God, which the levitical priests will carry, you must also break camp and follow it, [4]that you may know the way to take, for you have not gone over this road before. But let there be a space of two thousand cubits between you and the ark. Do not come nearer to it." [5]Joshua also said to the people, "Sanctify yourselves, for tomorrow the LORD will perform wonders among you." [6]And he directed the priests to take up the ark of the covenant and go on ahead of the people; and they did so.

[7]Then the LORD said to Joshua, "Today I will begin to exalt you in the sight of all Israel, that they may know I am with you, as I was with Moses.[n] [8]Now command the priests carrying the ark of the covenant to come to a halt in the Jordan when they reach the edge of the waters."

[9]So Joshua said to the Israelites, "Come here and listen to the words of the LORD, your God." [10]He continued: "This is how you will know that there is a living God in your midst, who at your approach will dispossess the Canaanites, Hittites, Hi-

vites, Perizzites, Girgashites, Amorites and Jebusites.[o] [11]The ark of the covenant of the LORD of the whole earth will precede you into the Jordan. [12][Now choose twelve men,[p] one from each of the tribes of Israel.] [13]When the soles of the feet of the priests carrying the ark of the LORD, the Lord of the whole earth, touch the water of the Jordan, it will cease to flow; for the water flowing down from upstream will halt in a solid bank."

The Crossing Begun. [14]The people struck their tents to cross the Jordan, with the priests carrying the ark of the covenant ahead of them. [15]No sooner had these priestly bearers of the ark waded into the waters at the edge of the Jordan, which overflows all its banks during the entire season of the harvest,* [16]than the waters flowing from upstream halted, backing up in a solid mass[q] for a very great distance indeed, from Adam, a city in the direction of Zarethan; while those flowing downstream toward the Salt Sea of the Arabah disappeared entirely.* Thus the people crossed over opposite Jericho. [17]While all Israel crossed over on dry ground, the priests carrying the ark of the covenant of the LORD remained motionless on dry ground in the bed of the Jordan[r] until the whole nation had completed the passage.

CHAPTER 4

Memorial Stones. [1]After the entire nation had crossed the Jordan, the LORD said to Joshua, [2]"Choose twelve men[s] from the people, one from each tribe, [3]and instruct them to take up twelve stones from this spot in the bed of the Jordan where the priests have been standing motionless.[t] Carry them over with you, and place them where you are to stay tonight."

---

m Jos 2, 1.—n Jos 1, 5; 4, 14.—o Ex 33, 2; Dt 7, 1.—p Jos 4, 2. 4.—q Ps 114, 3.—r Jos 4, 7. 22.—s Jos 3, 12.—t Jos 3, 13; 4, 8f; Dt 27, 2.

3, 15: *Season of the harvest:* toward the end of March and the beginning of April, when the grain and other crops that grew during the rainy season of winter were reaped. The crossing took place "on the tenth day of the first month" of the Hebrew year, which began with the first new moon after the spring equinox; cf Jos 4, 19. At this time of the year the Jordan would be swollen as a result of the winter rains and the melting snow of Mount Hermon.

3, 16: The sudden damming of the river could have been caused by a landslide, as has happened on other occasions. The miraculous character of this event would not thereby be removed because God, who foretold it (Jos 3, 13), also caused it to take place at precisely the right moment (Jos 3, 15), whether or not he used natural forces to accomplish his will.

⁴Summoning the twelve men whom he had selected from among the Israelites, one from each tribe, ⁵Joshua said to them: "Go to the bed of the Jordan in front of the ark of the LORD, your God; lift to your shoulders one stone apiece, so that they will equal in number the tribes of the Israelites. ⁶In the future, these are to be a sign among you. When your children ask you what these stones mean to you, ⁷you shall answer them, 'The waters of the Jordan ceased to flow before the ark of the covenant of the LORD when it crossed the Jordan.'ᵘ Thus these stones are to serve as a perpetual memorial to the Israelites." ⁸The twelve Israelites did as Joshua had commanded: they took up as many stones from the bed of the Jordan as there were tribes of the Israelites, and carried them along to the camp site, where they placed them, according to the LORD's direction. ⁹Joshua also had twelve stones set up in the bed of the Jordan on the spot where the priests stood who were carrying the ark of the covenant. They are there to this day.

¹⁰ * The priests carrying the ark remained in the bed of the Jordan until everything had been done that the LORD had commanded Joshua to tell the people. The people crossed over quickly, ¹¹and when all had reached the other side, the ark of the LORD, borne by the priests, also crossed to its place in front of them. ¹²The Reubenites, Gadites, and half-tribe of Manasseh, armed, marched in the vanguard of the Israelites, as Moses had ordered.ᵛ ¹³About forty thousand troops equipped for battle passed over before the LORD to the plains of Jericho.

¹⁴That day the LORD exalted Joshua in the sight of all Israel,ʷ and thenceforth during his whole life they respected him as they had respected Moses.

¹⁵Then the LORD said to Joshua, ¹⁶"Command the priests carrying the ark of the commandments to come up from the Jordan."ˣ ¹⁷Joshua did so, ¹⁸and when

the priests carrying the ark of the covenant of the LORD had come up from the bed of the Jordan, as the soles of their feet regained the dry ground, the waters of the Jordan resumed their course and as before overflowed all its banks.

¹⁹The people came up from the Jordan on the tenth day of the first month, and camped in Gilgal on the eastern limits of Jericho. ²⁰At Gilgal Joshua set up the twelve stones which had been taken from the Jordan, ²¹saying to the Israelites, "In the future, when the children among you ask their fathers what these stones mean, ²²you shall inform them, 'Israel crossed the Jordan here on dry ground.' ²³For the LORD, your God, dried up the waters of the Jordan in front of you until you crossed over, just as the LORD, your God, had done at the Red Sea, which he dried up in front of us until we crossed over;ʸ ²⁴in order that all the peoples of the earth may learn that the hand of the LORD is mighty, and that you may fear the LORD, your God, forever."

CHAPTER 5

Rites at Gilgal. ¹When all the kings of the Amorites to the west of the Jordan and all the kings of the Canaanites by the sea heard that the LORD had dried up the waters of the Jordan before the Israelites until they crossed over, they were disheartened and lost courage at their approach.

²On this occasion the LORD said to Joshua, "Make flint knives and circumcise the Israelite nation for the second time." ³So Joshua made flint knives and circumcised the Israelites at Gibeath-haaraloth,* ⁴under these circumstances: Of all the people who came out of Egypt, every man of military age had died in the desertᶻ during the journey after they left Egypt. ⁵Though all the men who came out were circumcised, none of those born in the desert during the journey after the departure from Egypt were circumcised. ⁶Now the Israelites had wandered forty years in the desert, until all the warriors among the people that came forth from Egypt died off because they had not obeyed the command of the LORD.ᵃ For the LORD sw>swore<ᵇ that he would not let them see the land flowing with milk and honey which he had promised their

---

u Jos 3, 13, 16.—v Dt 3, 18.—w Jos 3, 7.—x Jos 3, 6.—y Ex 14, 21.—z Nm 14, 29; 26, 64f; Dt 2, 16; Ps 106, 26; 1 Cor 10, 5.—a Nm 14, 29.—b Heb 3, 11. 17.

4, 10-18: After the digression about the two sets of memorial stones, the author resumes the narrative by briefly repeating the story of the crossing, which he had already told in Jos 3, 14-17.

5, 3: *Gibeath-haaraloth:* "Hill of the Foreskins."

fathers he would give us. [7] *c* It was the children whom he raised up in their stead whom Joshua circumcised, for these were yet with foreskins, not having been circumcised on the journey. [8] When the rite had been performed, the whole nation remained in camp where they were, until they recovered. [9] Then the LORD said to Joshua, "Today I have removed the reproach of Egypt from you."*d* Therefore the place is called Gilgal* to the present day.

[10] *e* While the Israelites were encamped at Gilgal on the plains of Jericho, they celebrated the Passover on the evening of the fourteenth of the month.* [11] On the day after the Passover they ate of the produce of the land in the form of unleavened cakes and parched grain. On that same day [12] after the Passover on which they ate of the produce of the land, the manna ceased. No longer was there manna for the Israelites, who that year ate of the yield of the land of Canaan.*f*

Siege at Jericho. [13] * While Joshua was near Jericho, he raised his eyes and saw one who stood facing him, drawn sword in hand.*g* Joshua went up to him and asked, "Are you one of us or of our enemies?" [14] He replied, "Neither. I am the captain of the host of the LORD and I have just arrived." Then Joshua fell prostrate to the ground in worship, and said to him, "What has my lord to say to his servant?" [15] The captain of the host of the LORD replied to Joshua, "Remove your sandals from your feet, for the place on which you are standing is holy."*h* And Joshua obeyed.

CHAPTER 6

[1] Now Jericho was in a state of siege because of the presence of the Israelites, so that no one left or entered. [2] And to Joshua the LORD said, "I have delivered Jericho and its king into your power. [3] Have all the soldiers circle the city, marching once around it. Do this for six days, [4] *i* with seven priests carrying ram's horns ahead of the ark. On the seventh day march around the city seven times, and have the priests blow the horns. [5] When they give a long blast on the ram's horns and you hear that signal, all the people shall shout aloud. The wall of the city will collapse, and they will be able to make a frontal attack."

[6] Summoning the priests, Joshua, son of Nun, then ordered them to take up the ark of the covenant with seven of the priests carrying ram's horns in front of the ark of the LORD. [7] And he ordered the people to proceed in a circle around the city, with the picked troops marching ahead of the ark of the LORD. [8] At this order they proceeded, with the seven priests who carried the ram's horns before the LORD blowing their horns, and the ark of the covenant of the LORD following them. [9] In front of the priests with the horns marched the picked troops; the rear guard followed the ark, and the blowing of horns was kept up continually as they marched. [10] But the people had been commanded by Joshua not to shout or make any noise or outcry until he gave the word: only then were they to shout. [11] So he had the ark of the LORD circle the city, going once around it, after which they returned to camp for the night.

[12] Early the next morning, Joshua had the priests take up the ark of the LORD. [13] The seven priests bearing the ram's horns marched in front of the ark of the LORD, blowing their horns. Ahead of these marched the picked troops, while the rear guard followed the ark of the LORD, and the blowing of horns was kept up continually. [14] On this second day they again marched around the city once before returning to camp; and for six days in all they did the same.

[15] On the seventh day, beginning at daybreak, they marched around the city seven times in the same manner; on that day only did they march around the city seven times. [16] The seventh time around, the priests blew the horns and Joshua said to the people, "Now shout, for the LORD has given you the city [17] and everything

---

c Dt 1, 39.—d Jos 4, 19.—e Ex 12, 6; Lv 23, 5; Nm 9, 3-5.—f Ex 16, 35.—g Ex 23, 20.—h Ex 3, 5; Acts 7, 33.—i Nm 10, 8f.

5, 9: *The place is called Gilgal:* by popular etymology, because of the similarity of sound with the Hebrew word *gallothi,* "I have removed." Gilgal probably means "(the place of) the circle of standing stones." Cf Jos 4, 4-8.

5, 10: *The month:* the first month of the year, later called Nisan; see note on Jos 3, 15. The crossing of the Jordan occurred, therefore, about the same time of the year as did the equally miraculous crossing of the Red Sea; cf Ex 12—14.

5, 13—6, 26: The account of the siege of Jericho embraces: (1) the command of the Lord, through his angel, to Joshua (Jos 5, 13—6, 5); (2) Joshua's instructions to the Israelites, with a brief summary of how these orders were carried out (Jos 6, 6-11); (3) a description of the action on each of the first six days (Jos 6, 12-14); (4) the events on the seventh day (Jos 6, 15-26).

in it.^j It is under the LORD's ban. Only the harlot Rahab and all who are in the house with her are to be spared, because she hid the messengers we sent. ^18 ^k But be careful not to take, in your greed, anything that is under the ban;* else you will bring upon the camp of Israel this ban and the misery of it. ^19 All silver and gold, and the articles of bronze or iron, are sacred to the LORD. They shall be put in the treasury of the LORD."

The Fall of Jericho. ^20 As the horns blew, the people began to shout. When they heard the signal horn, they raised a tremendous shout. The wall collapsed,* and the people stormed the city in a frontal attack and took it.^l ^21 They observed the ban by putting to the sword all living creatures^m in the city: men and women, young and old, as well as oxen, sheep and asses.

^22 Joshua directed the two men who had spied out the land, "Go into the harlot's house and bring out the woman with all her kin, as you swore to her you would do."^n ^23 The spies entered and brought out Rahab, with her father, mother, brothers, and all her kin.^o Her entire family they led forth and placed them outside the camp of Israel. ^24 The city itself they burned with all that was in it,^p except the silver, gold, and articles of bronze and iron, which were placed in the treasury of the house of the LORD. ^25 * Because Rahab the harlot had hidden the messengers whom Joshua had sent to reconnoiter Jericho, Joshua spared her with her family and all her kin, who continue in the midst of Israel to this day.

^26 ^q On that occasion Joshua imposed the oath: Cursed before the LORD be the man who attempts to rebuild this city,

Jericho. He shall lose his first-born when he lays its foundation, and he shall lose his youngest son when he sets up its gates.*

^27 Thus the LORD was with Joshua so that his fame spread throughout the land.^r

CHAPTER 7

Defeat at Ai. ^1 But the Israelites violated the ban; Achan, son of Carmi, son of Zerah, son of Zara of the tribe of Judah, took goods that were under the ban,^s and the anger of the LORD flared up against the Israelites.

^2 Joshua next sent men from Jericho to Ai, which is near Bethel on its eastern side, with instructions to go up and reconnoiter the land. When they had explored Ai, ^3 they returned to Joshua and advised, "Do not send all the people up; if only about two or three thousand go up, they can overcome Ai. The enemy there are few; you need not call for an effort from all the people." ^4 About three thousand of the people made the attack, but they were defeated by those at Ai, ^5 who killed some thirty-six of them. They pressed them back across the clearing in front of the city gate till they broke ranks, and defeated them finally on the descent, so that the confidence of the people melted away like water.

^6 Joshua, together with the elders of Israel, rent his garments and lay prostrate before the ark of the LORD until evening; and they threw dust on their heads. ^7 "Alas, O Lord GOD," Joshua prayed, "why did you ever allow this people to pass over the Jordan, delivering us into the power of the Amorites, that they might destroy us? Would that we had been content to dwell on the other side of the Jordan. ^8 Pray, Lord, what can I say, now that Israel has turned its back to its enemies? ^9 When the Canaanites and the other inhabitants of the land hear of it, they will close in around us and efface our name from the earth. What will you do for your great name?"

^10 The LORD replied to Joshua: "Stand up. Why are you lying prostrate? ^11 ^t Israel has sinned: they have violated the covenant which I enjoined on them. They have stealthily taken goods subject to the ban, and have deceitfully put them in their baggage. ^12 If the Israelites cannot stand up to their enemies, but must turn their

---

j Jos 2, 4; Dt 20, 17; Heb 11, 31.—k Jos 7, 12. 25; Dt 13, 18.—l 2 Mc 12, 15; Heb 11, 30.—m Dt 7, 2.—n Jos 2, 14.—o Jos 2, 13; Heb 11, 31.—p Jos 8, 2.—q 1 Kgs 16, 34.—r Jos 1, 5.—s Jos 6, 18; 22, 20; 1 Chr 2, 7.—t Jos 6, 17-19.

6, 18: *That is under the ban:* that is doomed to destruction; see notes on Lv 27, 29; Nm 18, 14; 21, 3.

6, 20: *The wall collapsed:* by the miraculous intervention of God. The blowing of the horns and the shouting of the people were a customary feature of ancient warfare, here intended by God as a test of the people's obedience and of their faith in his promise; cf Heb 11, 30.

6, 25: From Mt 1, 5, we learn that Rahab married Salmon of the tribe of Judah and thus became the great-great-grandmother of David, Christ's ancestor; cf Ru 4, 18-22.

6, 26: *He shall lose his first-born . . . its gates:* this curse was fulfilled when Hiel rebuilt Jericho as a fortified city during the reign of Ahab, king of Israel; cf 1 Kgs 16, 34. Till then Jericho was merely an unwalled village; cf Jos 18, 12. 21; Jgs 3, 13; 2 Sm 10, 5.

back to them, it is because they are under the ban.^{u} I will not remain with you unless you remove from among you whoever has incurred the ban. ^{13}Rise, sanctify the people.^{v} Tell them to sanctify themselves before tomorrow, for the LORD, the God of Israel, says: You are under the ban, O Israel. You cannot stand up to your enemies until you remove from among you whoever has incurred the ban. ^{14}In the morning you must present yourselves by tribes. The tribe which the LORD designates shall come forward by clans; the clan which the LORD designates shall come forward by families; the family which the LORD designates shall come forward one by one. ^{15}He who is designated as having incurred the ban shall be destroyed by fire, with all that is his, because he has violated the covenant of the LORD and has committed a shameful crime in Israel."

Achan's Guilt and Punishment. ^{16}Early the next morning Joshua had Israel come forward by tribes, and the tribe of Judah was designated.* ^{17}Then he had the clans of Judah come forward, and the clan of Zerah was designated. He had the clan of Zerah^w come forward by families, and Zabdi was designated. ^{18}Finally he had that family come forward one by one and Achan, son of Carmi, son of Zabdi, son of Zerah of the tribe of Judah, was designated. ^{19}Joshua said to Achan, "My son, give to the LORD, the God of Israel, glory and honor by telling me what you have done; do not hide it from me." ^{20}Achan answered Joshua, "I have indeed sinned against the LORD, the God of Israel. This is what I have done: ^{21}Among the spoils, I saw a beautiful Babylonian mantle, two hundred shekels of silver, and a bar of gold fifty shekels in weight; in my greed I took them. They are now hidden in the ground inside my tent, with the silver underneath." ^{22}The messengers whom Joshua sent hastened to the tent and found them hidden there, with the silver underneath. ^{23}They took them from the tent, brought them to Joshua and all the Israelites, and spread them out before the LORD.

^{24}Then Joshua and all Israel took Achan, son of Zerah, with the silver, the mantle, and the bar of gold, and with his sons and daughters, his ox, his ass and his sheep, his tent, and all his possessions, and led them off to the Valley of Achor. ^{25}Joshua said, "The LORD bring upon you today the misery with which you have afflicted us!"^{x} And all Israel stoned him to death ^{26}and piled a great heap of stones over him, which remains to the present day.^{y} Then the anger of the LORD relented. That is why the place is called the Valley of Achor* to this day.

CHAPTER 8

Capture of Ai. ^{1}The LORD then said to Joshua, "Do not be afraid or dismayed. Take all the army with you and prepare to attack Ai.^{z} I have delivered the king of Ai into your power, with his people, city, and land. ^{2}Do to Ai and its king what you did to Jericho and its king; except that you may take its spoil and livestock as booty.^{a} Set an ambush behind the city." ^{3}So Joshua and all the soldiers prepared to attack Ai. Picking out thirty thousand warriors,* Joshua sent them off by night ^{4}with these orders: "See that you ambush the city from the rear, at no great distance; then all of you be on the watch. ^{5}The rest of the people and I will come up to the city, and when they make a sortie against us as they did the last time, we will flee from them. ^{6}They will keep coming out after us until we have drawn them away from the city, for they will think we are fleeing from them as we did the last time. When this occurs, ^{7}rise from ambush and take possession of the city, which the LORD, your God, will deliver into your power. ^{8}When you have taken the city, set it afire in obedience to the LORD's command. These are my orders to you." ^{9}Then Joshua sent them away. They went to the place of ambush, taking up their position to the west of Ai, toward Bethel. Joshua, however, spent that night in the plain.

^{10}Early the next morning Joshua mustered the army and went up to Ai at its head, with the elders of Israel. ^{11}When all

---

u Jos 6, 18.—v Jos 3, 5; Lv 20, 7; 1 Sm 16, 5.—w Nm 26, 20.—x Jos 6, 18; 22, 20; 1 Chr 2, 7.—y Jos 8, 29.—z Jos 2, 24.—a Jos 6, 21. 24; Dt 20, 14.

7, 16ff: *Was designated:* probably by means of the Urim and Thummim; cf 1 Sm 14, 38-42. See note on Ex 28, 30.

7, 26: *Achor:* "misery, affliction." The reference is to the saying of Joshua in v 25, with an allusion also to the similar-sounding name of Achan.

8, 3: *Thirty thousand warriors:* this figure of the Hebrew text, which seems extremely high, may be due to a copyist's error; some manuscripts of the Septuagint have "three thousand," which is the number of the whole army in the first, unsuccessful attack (Jos 7, 4); the variant reading in v 12 mentions "five thousand."

the troops he led were drawn up in position before the city, they pitched camp north of Ai, on the other side of the ravine. ¹²[He took about five thousand men and set them in ambush between Bethel and Ai, west of the city.] ¹³Thus the people took up their stations, with the main body north of the city and the ambush west of it, and Joshua waited overnight among his troops. ¹⁴The king of Ai saw this, and he and all his army came out very early in the morning to engage Israel in battle at the descent toward the Arabah, not knowing that there was an ambush behind the city. ¹⁵Joshua and the main body of the Israelites fled in seeming defeat toward the desert, ¹⁶till the last of the soldiers in the city had been called out to pursue them. ¹⁷Since they were drawn away from the city, with every man engaged in this pursuit of Joshua and the Israelites, not a soldier remained in Ai [or Bethel], and the city was open and unprotected.

¹⁸Then the LORD directed Joshua, "Stretch out the javelin in your hand toward Ai, for I will deliver it into your power." Joshua stretched out the javelin in his hand toward the city, ¹⁹and as soon as he did so, the men in ambush rose from their post, rushed in, captured the city, and immediately set it on fire. ²⁰By the time the men of Ai looked back, the smoke from the city was already sky-high. Escape in any direction was impossible, because the Israelites retreating toward the desert now turned on their pursuers; ²¹for when Joshua and the main body of Israelites saw that the city had been taken from ambush and was going up in smoke, they struck back at the men of Ai. ²²Since those in the city came out to intercept them, the men of Ai were hemmed in by Israelites on either side, who cut them down without any fugitives or survivors[b] ²³except the king, whom they took alive and brought to Joshua.

²⁴All the inhabitants of Ai who had pursued the Israelites into the desert were slain by the sword there in the open, down to the last man. Then all Israel returned and put to the sword those inside the city. ²⁵There fell that day a total of twelve thousand men and women, the entire population of Ai. ²⁶ᶜJoshua kept the javelin in his hand stretched out until he had fulfilled the doom on all the inhabitants of Ai. ²⁷However, the Israelites took for themselves as booty the livestock and the spoil of that city, according to the command of the LORD issued to Joshua. ²⁸Then Joshua destroyed the place by fire, reducing it to an everlasting mound of ruins, as it remains today.[d] ²⁹He had the king of Ai hanged on a tree until evening;[e] then at sunset Joshua ordered the body removed from the tree and cast at the entrance of the city gate, where a great heap of stones was piled up over it, which remains to the present day.

Altar on Mount Ebal. ³⁰ * Later Joshua built an altar to the LORD, the God of Israel, on Mount Ebal, ³¹of unhewn stones on which no iron tool had been used,[f] in keeping with the command to the Israelites of Moses, the servant of the LORD, as recorded in the book of the law. On this altar they offered holocausts and peace offerings to the LORD. ³²There, in the presence of the Israelites, Joshua inscribed upon the stones a copy of the law written by Moses.[g] ³³And all Israel, stranger and native alike, with their elders, officers and judges, stood on either side of the ark facing the levitical priests who were carrying the ark of the covenant of the LORD.[h] Half of them were facing Mount Gerizim and half Mount Ebal, thus carrying out the instructions of Moses, the servant of the LORD, for the blessing of the people of Israel on this first occasion. ³⁴ⁱThen were read aloud all the words of the law, the blessings and the curses, exactly as written in the book of the law. ³⁵ʲEvery single word that Moses had commanded, Joshua read aloud to the entire community, including the women and children, and the strangers who had accompanied Israel.

CHAPTER 9

Confederacy against Israel. ¹When the news reached the kings west of the Jordan, in the mountain regions and in the foothills, and all along the coast of the Great Sea as far as Lebanon: Hittites, Amorites, Canaanites, Perizzites, Hivites and Jebusites,[k] ²they all formed an alliance to

---

b Dt 7, 2.—c Ex 17, 11ff.—d Dt 13, 16.—e Jos 10, 26f; Dt 21, 22f; Jn 19, 31.—f Ex 20, 24f; Dt 27, 5f.—g Dt 27, 2. 8.—h Jos 3, 3; Dt 11, 27; 27, 12; 31, 9. 12.—i Dt 28, 2-68; 30, 19; 31, 11; Neh 8, 2f.—j Dt 31, 12.—k Jos 3, 10; Ex 3, 8. 17; 23, 23; Dt 1, 7.

8, 30-35: These ceremonies were prescribed in Dt 11, 29, and Dt 27, 2-26. See notes on those passages.

launch a common attack against Joshua and Israel.

The Gibeonite Deception. [3] On learning what Joshua had done to Jericho and Ai, the inhabitants of Gibeon[l] [4] put into effect a device of their own. They chose provisions for a journey, making use of old sacks for their asses, and old wineskins, torn and mended. [5] They wore old, patched sandals and shabby garments; and all the bread they took was dry and crumbly. [6] Thus they journeyed to Joshua in the camp at Gilgal, where they said to him and to the men of Israel, "We have come from a distant land to propose that you make an alliance with us."[m] [7] But the men of Israel replied to the Hivites,* "You may be living in land that is ours. How, then, can we make an alliance with you?" [8] But they answered Joshua, "We are your servants." Then Joshua asked them, "Who are you? Where do you come from?" [9] They answered him, "Your servants have come from a far-off land, because of the fame of the LORD, your God. For we have heard reports of all that he did in Egypt[n] [10] and all that he did to the two kings of the Amorites beyond the Jordan,[o] Sihon, king of Heshbon, and Og, king of Bashan, who lived in Ashtaroth. [11] So our elders and all the inhabitants of our country said to us, 'Take along provisions for the journey and go to meet them. Say to them: We are your servants; we propose that you make an alliance with us.' [12] This bread of ours was still warm when we brought it from home as provisions the day we left to come to you, but now it is dry and crumbled. [13] Here are our wineskins, which were new when we filled them, but now they are torn. Look at our garments and sandals, which are worn out from the very long journey." [14] Then the Israelite princes partook of their provisions, without seeking the advice of the LORD.[p] [15] So Joshua made an alliance with them and entered into an agreement to spare them,[q] which the princes of the community sealed with an oath.

Gibeonites Made Vassals. [16] Three days after the agreement was entered into, the Israelites learned that these people were from nearby, and would be living in Israel. [17] The third day on the road, the Israelites came to their cities of Gibeon, Chephirah, Beeroth and Kiriath-jearim, [18] but did not attack them, because the princes of the community had sworn to them by the LORD, the God of Israel. When the entire community grumbled against the princes, [19] these all remonstrated with the people, "We have sworn to them by the LORD, God of Israel, and so we cannot harm them. [20] Let us therefore spare their lives and so deal with them that we shall not be punished for the oath we have sworn to them." [21] Thus the princes recommended that they be let live, as hewers of wood and drawers of water* for the entire community; and the community did as the princes advised them.

[22] Joshua summoned the Gibeonites and said to them, "Why did you lie to us and say that you lived at a great distance from us, when you will be living in our very midst? [23] For this are you accursed: every one of you shall always be a slave [hewers of wood and drawers of water] for the house of my God." [24] They answered Joshua, "Your servants were fully informed of how the LORD, your God, commanded his servant Moses that you be given the entire land and that all its inhabitants be destroyed before you. Since, therefore, at your advance, we were in great fear for our lives, we acted as we did.[r] [25] And now that we are in your power, do with us what you think fit and right." [26] * Joshua did what he had decided: while he saved them from being killed by the Israelites, [27] at the same time he made them, as they still are, hewers of wood and drawers of water for the community and for the altar of the LORD, in the place of the LORD's choice.[s]

CHAPTER 10

The Siege of Gibeon. [1] Now Adonizedek, king of Jerusalem, heard that, in the capture and destruction of Ai, Joshua had done to that city and its king as he had done to Jericho and its king.[t] He heard

---

l Jos 6, 21. 24; 11, 19.—m Ex 23, 32; Dt 7, 2.—n Jos 2, 10.— o Nm 21, 25. 33.—p Nm 27, 21.—q Jos 11, 19; 2 Sm 21, 2.—r Ex 23, 27f; Dt 7, 1f.—s Dt 12, 5.—t Jos 9, 15; 6, 21. 24; 8, 26-29.

9, 7: *The Hivites:* apparently the Gibeonites belonged to this larger ethnic group (cf also Jos 11, 19), although in 2 Sm 21, 2 they are classed as Amorites; both groups are listed among the *seven nations* in Canaan whom the Israelites were to exterminate; cf Dt 7, 1f.

9, 21: *Hewers of wood and drawers of water:* proverbial terms for the lowest social class in the Israelite community; cf Dt 29, 10f.

9, 26f: Later on, Saul violated the immunity of the Gibeonites, but David vindicated it; cf 2 Sm 21, 1-9.

DEFEAT OF THE AMORITE KINGS (Jos 9, 1—10, 14) — **(a)** At **Gilgal** the Gibeonites trick Joshua into an alliance. Their cities of **Gibeon, Chephirah, Beeroth** and **Kiriath-jearim** are spared (9, 1-27). **(b)** The five kings of the Amorites, the kings of **Jerusalem, Hebron, Jarmuth, Lachish** and **Eglon,** lay siege to **Gibeon** which asks Joshua for help (10, 1-6). **(c)** From **Gilgal** Joshua goes to **Gibeon** and in the famous battle of the "sun standing still" slaughters the Amorites, chasing them by the way of ascent of **Beth-horon** and as far as **Azekah** and **Makkedah** (10, 7-14).

CONQUEST OF SOUTHERN CANAAN (Jos 10, 15-43) — **(a) From Gilgal to Lachish:** Joshua returns to **Gilgal,** then goes back to capture the kings who had hidden in the caves of **Makkedah.** Joshua takes **Makkedah, Libnah, Lachish,** and defeats the king of **Gezer** who had gone to the aid of Lachish. Then he takes **Eglon, Hebron** and **Debir** (10, 15-43).

CANAAN AS DIVIDED BY JOSHUA FOR THE TWELVE TRIBES (Jos 13—19) — **(a) Judah** consists of about eighty towns in the south (15, 1-12). **(b)** Southward of it in the **Negeb** is **Simeon** with seventeen towns (19, 1-9). **(c)** North of Judah lies **Benjamin** with twenty-six towns (18, 11-28). **(d) Dan** is at first north of Judah and west of Benjamin but later part of the tribe migrates northward and settles near Leshem, henceforth called **Dan** (19, 40-48; Jgs 18). **(e) Ephraim** occupies the center of the country (16, 5-9). **(f)** Half of **Manasseh** lies north of Ephraim (17, 1-13) and the other half in the northern part of the country east of the Jordan (13, 29-31). **(g)** Around the plain of Esdraelon lies **Issachar** (19, 17-23). **(h)** West of the Lake of Tiberias belongs to **Zebulun** (19, 10-16). **(i) Asher** lies along the maritime plain of Galilee (19, 24-31). **(j) Naphtali** occupies the northernmost part of the country (19, 32-39). **(k)** South of the district east of Jordan dwells **Reuben** (13, 15-23). **(l)** North of Reuben lies **Gad** (13, 24-28).

also that the inhabitants of Gibeon had made their peace with Israel, remaining among them, [2] and that there was great fear abroad, because Gibeon was large enough for a royal city, larger even than the city of Ai, and all its men were brave. [3] So Adonizedek, king of Jerusalem, sent for Hoham, king of Hebron, Piram, king of Jarmuth, Japhia, king of Lachish, and Debir, king of Eglon, [4] to come to his aid for an attack on Gibeon, since it had concluded peace with Joshua and the Israelites.[u] [5] The five Amorite kings, of Jerusalem, Hebron, Jarmuth, Lachish and Eglon,* united all their forces and marched against Gibeon, where they took up siege positions. [6] Thereupon, the men of Gibeon sent an appeal to Joshua in his camp at Gilgal: "Do not abandon your servants. Come up here quickly and save us. Help us, because all the Amorite kings of the mountain country have joined forces against us."[v]

Joshua's Victory. [7] So Joshua marched up from Gilgal with his picked troops and the rest of his soldiers. [8] Meanwhile the LORD said to Joshua, "Do not fear them, for I have delivered them into your power. Not one of them will be able to withstand you." [9] And when Joshua made his surprise attack upon them after an all-night march from Gilgal, [10] the LORD threw them into disorder before him. The Israelites inflicted a great slaughter on them at Gibeon and pursued them down the Beth-horon slope, harassing them as far as Azekah and Makkedah. [11] While they fled before Israel along the descent from Beth-horon, the LORD hurled great stones from the sky* above them all the way to Azekah, killing many.[w] More died from these hailstones than the Israelites slew with the sword.

---

u Jos 9, 15.—v Jos 9, 6.—w Jb 38, 22.—x Sir 46, 4; Is 28, 21; Heb 3, 11.—y 26f: Jos 8, 29; Dt 21, 22f.

10, 5: *Hebron . . . Eglon:* these four cities were to the south and southwest of Jerusalem.
10, 11: *Great stones from the sky:* the hailstones mentioned in the next sentence.
10, 13: *Is this not recorded:* the reference is to the preceding, poetic passage. Evidently the *Book of Jashar,* like the *Book of the Wars of the Lord* (Nm 21, 14), recounted in epic style the exploits of Israel's early heroes. *The sun halted:* though it is widely supposed that this passage describes in popular language and according to external appearances a miraculous lengthening of the day, it is equally probable that Joshua's prayer was rather for an abrupt obscuration of the sun, which would impede his enemies in their flight homeward and also prevent them from rallying their forces; this request would have been answered by the hailstorm (cf Sir 46, 5) and by a darkness relieved only twenty-four hours later, well into the next day.

[12] On this day, when the LORD delivered up the Amorites to the Israelites,

Joshua prayed to the LORD,
and said in the presence of Israel:
Stand still, O sun, at Gibeon,
O moon, in the valley of Aijalon!
[13] And the sun stood still,
and the moon stayed,
while the nation took vengeance on
its foes.[x]

Is this not recorded* in the Book of Jashar? The sun halted in the middle of the sky; not for a whole day did it resume its swift course. [14] Never before or since was there a day like this, when the LORD obeyed the voice of a man; for the LORD fought for Israel. [15] [Then Joshua and all Israel returned to the camp at Gilgal.]

Execution of Amorite Kings. [16] Meanwhile the five kings who had fled, hid in a cave at Makkedah. [17] When Joshua was told that the five kings had been discovered hiding in a cave at Makkedah, [18] he said, "Roll large stones to the mouth of the cave and post men over it to guard them. [19] But do not remain there yourselves. Pursue your enemies, and harry them in the rear. Do not allow them to escape to their cities, for the LORD, your God, has delivered them into your power."

[20] Once Joshua and the Israelites had finally inflicted the last blows in this very great slaughter, and the survivors had escaped from them into the fortified cities, [21] all the army returned safely to Joshua and the camp at Makkedah, no man uttering a sound against the Israelites. [22] Then Joshua said, "Open the mouth of the cave and bring out those five kings to me." [23] Obediently, they brought out to him from the cave the five kings, of Jerusalem, Hebron, Jarmuth, Lachish and Eglon. [24] When they had done so, Joshua summoned all the men of Israel and said to the commanders of the soldiers who had marched with him, "Come forward and put your feet on the necks of these kings." They came forward and put their feet upon their necks. [25] Then Joshua said to them, "Do not be afraid or dismayed, be firm and steadfast. This is what the LORD will do to all the enemies against whom you fight." [26] [y] Thereupon Joshua struck and killed them, and hanged them on five trees, where they remained hanging until evening. [27] At sunset they were removed

from the trees at the command of Joshua and cast into the cave where they had hidden; over the mouth of the cave large stones were placed, which remain until this very day. **Conquest of Southern Canaan.** [28] z Makkedah, too, Joshua captured and put to the sword at that time. He fulfilled the doom on the city, on its king, and on every person in it, leaving no survivors. Thus he did to the king of Makkedah what he had done to the king of Jericho. [29] Joshua then passed on with all Israel from Makkedah to Libnah, which he attacked. [30] Libnah also, with its king, the LORD delivered into the power of Israel. He put it to the sword with every person there, leaving no survivors. Thus he did to its king what he had done to the king of Jericho. [31] Joshua next passed on with all Israel from Libnah to Lachish, where they set up a camp during the attack. [32] The LORD delivered Lachish into the power of Israel, so that on the second day Joshua captured it and put it to the sword with every person in it, just as he had done to Libnah. [33] At that time Horam, king of Gezer, came up to help Lachish, but Joshua defeated him and his people, leaving him no survivors. [34] From Lachish, Joshua passed on with all Israel to Eglon; encamping near it, they attacked it [35] and captured it the same day, putting it to the sword. He fulfilled the doom that day on every person in it, just as he had done at Lachish. [36] From Eglon, Joshua went up with all Israel to Hebron, which they attacked [37] and captured. They put it to the sword with its king, all its towns, and every person there, leaving no survivors, just as Joshua had done to Eglon. He fulfilled the doom on it and on every person there. [38] Then Joshua and all Israel turned back to Debir and attacked it, [39] capturing it with its king and all its towns. They put them to the sword and fulfilled the doom on every person there, leaving no survivors. Thus was done to Debir and its king what had been done to Hebron, as well as to Libnah and its king.

[40] a Joshua conquered the entire country; the mountain regions, the Negeb, the foothills, and the mountain slopes, with all their kings. He left no survivors, but fulfilled the doom on all who lived there, just as the LORD, the God of Israel, had commanded. [41] Joshua conquered from Kadesh-barnea to Gaza, and all the land of Goshen* to Gibeon. [42] All these kings and their lands Joshua captured in a single campaign, for the LORD, the God of Israel, fought for Israel. [43] Thereupon Joshua with all Israel returned to the camp at Gilgal.

CHAPTER 11

Northern Confederacy. [1] When Jabin, king of Hazor,* learned of this, he sent a message to Jobab, king of Madon, to the king of Shimron, to the king of Achshaph, [2] and to the northern kings in the mountain regions and in the Arabah near Chinneroth, in the foothills, and in Naphath-dor to the west. b [3] These were Canaanites to the east and west, Amorites, Hittites, Perizzites and Jebusites in the mountain regions, and Hivites at the foot of Hermon in the land of Mizpah. [4] They came out with all their troops, an army numerous as the sands on the seashore, and with a multitude of horses and chariots. [5] All these kings joined forces and marched to the waters of Merom,* where they encamped together to fight against Israel.

[6] The LORD said to Joshua, "Do not fear them, for by this time tomorrow I will stretch them slain before Israel. You must hamstring their horses and burn their chariots." [7] Joshua with his whole army came upon them at the waters of Merom in a surprise attack. [8] The LORD delivered them into the power of the Israelites, who defeated them and pursued them to Greater Sidon, to Misrephoth-maim, c and eastward to the valley of Mizpeh. They struck them all down, leaving no survivors. [9] Joshua did to them as the LORD had commanded: he hamstrung their horses and burned their chariots. **Conquest of Northern Canaan.** [10] At that time Joshua, turning back, captured Hazor and slew its king with the sword; for Hazor formerly was the chief of all those kingdoms. [11] He also fulfilled the

---

z Jos 6, 21.—a Dt 20, 16f.—b Jos 12, 3; Jgs 1, 27.—c Jos 13, 6.

10, 41: *Goshen:* a town and its surrounding district at the southern end of the Judean mountains (cf Jos 11, 16; 15, 51); not to be confused with the *land of Goshen* in northeastern Egypt (Gen 45, 10), although in the current Hebrew Bible both names are spelled the same.

11, 1ff: *Hazor, Madon, Shimron,* and *Chinneroth:* cities and their surrounding districts in eastern Galilee. *Achshaph* and *Naphath-dor:* southwest of Galilee. *The mountain regions:* in central and northern Galilee.

11, 5: *The waters of Merom:* a stream in central Galilee that flows southeast to water the fertile Arabah, or plain of Chinneroth on the western shore of the lake of Gennesaret.

doom by putting every person there to the sword, till none was left alive. Hazor itself he burned. ¹²Joshua thus captured all those kings with their cities and put them to the sword, fulfilling the doom on them, as Moses, the servant of the LORD, had commanded.*d* ¹³However, Israel did not destroy by fire any of the cities built on raised sites, except Hazor, which Joshua burned. ¹⁴The Israelites took all the spoil and livestock of these cities as their booty; but the people they put to the sword, until they had exterminated the last of them, leaving none alive. ¹⁵As the LORD had commanded his servant Moses, so Moses commanded Joshua, and Joshua acted accordingly.*e* He left nothing undone that the LORD had commanded Moses should be done.

Survey of the Conquest. ¹⁶So Joshua captured all this land: the mountain regions, the entire Negeb, all the land of Goshen, the foothills, the Arabah, as well as the mountain regions and foothills of Israel,*f* ¹⁷from Mount Halak that rises toward Seir*g* as far as Baal-gad in the Lebanon valley at the foot of Mount Hermon. All their kings he captured and put to death. ¹⁸Joshua waged war against all these kings for a long time. ¹⁹With the exception of the Hivites who lived in Gibeon, no city made peace with the Israelites; all were taken in battle.*h* ²⁰For it was the design of the LORD to encourage them to wage war against Israel, that they might be doomed to destruction and thus receive no mercy, but be exterminated, as the LORD had commanded Moses.*i*

²¹ * At that time Joshua penetrated the mountain regions and exterminated the Anakim in Hebron,*j* Debir, Anab, the en-

---

d Dt 7, 2; 20, 16f.—*e* Dt 7, 2.—*f* Jos 10, 41; 12, 8.—*g* Jos 12, 7; Dt 7, 24.—*h* Jos 9, 3. 7. 15.—*i* Dt 2, 30; 20, 16f.—*j* Jos 15, 13f; Nm 13, 22; Dt 1, 28.—*k* Jos 14, 1—19, 51; Nm 34, 2-12.— *l* 2-5: Nm 21, 21-26. 33ff.—*m* Jos 13, 20.—*n* Jos 13, 11f.—*o* Nm 32, 33; Dt 3, 12f.—*p* Jos 6, 2; 8, 23.—*q* 10f: Jos 10, 23.—*r* Jos 10, 23. 33.—*s* Jos 10, 38f; 15, 36.—*t* Jos 10, 29f; 15, 35.

11, 21ff: Most of the land assigned to the tribe of Judah was not conquered by it till the early period of the Judges. See note on Jgs 1, 1-36.

11, 23: *The land enjoyed peace:* of a limited and temporary nature. Many of the individual tribes had still to fight against the remaining Canaanites; cf Jos 15, 13-17; 17, 12f. This verse forms the conclusion to the first part of the book. Cf note on Jos 12, 1-24.

12, 1-24: This chapter, inserted between the two principal parts of the book (chapters 1-11 and 13-21), resembles the lists of conquered cities which are inscribed on monuments of the Egyptian and Assyrian monarchs. Perhaps it was copied here from some such public Israelite record.

tire mountain region of Judah, and the entire mountain region of Israel. Joshua fulfilled the doom on them and on their cities, ²²so that no Anakim were left in the land of the Israelites. However, some survived in Gaza, in Gath, and in Ashdod. ²³*k* Thus Joshua captured the whole country, just as the LORD had foretold to Moses. Joshua gave it to Israel as their heritage, apportioning it among the tribes. And the land enjoyed peace.*

CHAPTER 12*

Lists of Conquered Kings. ¹The kings of the land east of the Jordan, from the River Arnon to Mount Hermon, including all the eastern section of the Arabah, whom the Israelites conquered and whose lands they occupied, were: ²*l* First, Sihon, king of the Amorites, who lived in Heshbon. His domain extended from Aroer, which is on the bank of the Wadi Arnon, to include the wadi itself, and the land northward through half of Gilead to the Wadi Jabbok, ³as well as the Arabah from the eastern side of the Sea of Chinnereth, as far south as the eastern side of the Salt Sea of the Arabah in the direction of Beth-jeshimoth,*m* to a point under the slopes of Pisgah. ⁴Secondly, Og, king of Bashan, a survivor of the Rephaim, who lived at Ashtaroth and Edrei.*n* ⁵He ruled over Mount Hermon, Salecah, and all Bashan as far as the boundary of the Geshurites and Maacathites, and over half of Gilead as far as the territory of Sihon, king of Heshbon. ⁶After Moses, the servant of the LORD, and the Israelites conquered them, he assigned their land to the Reubenites, the Gadites, and the half-tribe of Manasseh, as their property.*o*

⁷This is a list of the kings whom Joshua and the Israelites conquered west of the Jordan and whose land, from Baal-gad in the Lebanon valley to Mount Halak which rises toward Seir, Joshua apportioned to the tribes of Israel. ⁸It included the mountain regions and foothills, the Arabah, the slopes, the desert, and the Negeb, belonging to the Hittites, Amorites, Canaanites, Perizzites, Hivites and Jebusites. ⁹They were the kings of Jericho,*p* Ai (which is near Bethel), ¹⁰Jerusalem, Hebron, ¹¹Jarmuth, Lachish,*q* ¹²Eglon, Gezer,*r* ¹³Debir, Geder,*s* ¹⁴Hormah, Arad, ¹⁵Libnah, Adullam,*t* ¹⁶Makkedah, Beth-

el,[u] [17]Tappuah, Hepher,[v] [18]Aphek, Lasharon,[w] [19]Madon, Hazor,[x] [20]Shimron, Achshaph,[y] [21]Taanach, Megiddo,[z] [22]Kedesh, Jokneam (at Carmel),[a] [23]and Dor (in Naphath-dor), the foreign king at Gilgal,[b] [24]and the king of Tirzah, thirty-one kings in all.

II: DIVISION OF THE LAND

CHAPTER 13

Division of Land Commanded. [1]When Joshua was old and advanced in years, the LORD said to him:[c] "Though now you are old and advanced in years, a very large part of the land still remains to be conquered. [2]This additional land includes all Geshur* and all the districts of the Philistines [3](from the stream adjoining Egypt to the boundary of Ekron in the north is reckoned Canaanite territory, though held by the five lords of the Philistines in Gaza, Ashdod, Ashkelon, Gath and Ekron); also where the Avvim are in the south;[d] [4]all the land of the Canaanites from Mearah of the Sidonians to Aphek, and the boundaries of the Amorites; [5]and the Gebalite territory; and all the Lebanon on the east, from Baal-gad at the foot of Mount Hermon to Labo in the land of Hamath. [6]At the advance of the Israelites I will drive out all the Sidonian inhabitants of the mountain regions between Lebanon and Misrephoth-maim;[e] at least include these areas in the division of the Israelite heritage, just as I have commanded you. [7]Now, therefore, apportion among the nine tribes and the half-tribe of Manasseh the land which is to be their heritage."

The Eastern Tribes. [8] [f] Now the other half of the tribe of Manasseh, as well as the Reubenites and Gadites, had received their heritage which Moses, the servant of the LORD, had given them east of the Jordan: [9]from Aroer on the bank of the Wadi Arnon and the city in the wadi itself, through the tableland of Medeba and Dibon, [10]with the rest of the cities of Sihon, king of the Amorites, who reigned in Heshbon, to the boundary of the Ammonites; [11]also Gilead and the territory of the Geshurites and Maacathites, all Mount Hermon, and all Bashan as far as Salecah, [12]the entire kingdom in Bashan of Og, a survivor of the Rephaim, who reigned at Ashtaroth and Edrei. Though Moses conquered and occupied these territories,

[13]the Israelites did not dislodge the Geshurites and Maacathites, so that Geshur and Maacath survive in the midst of Israel to this day. [14] [g] However, to the tribe of Levi Moses assigned no heritage since, as the LORD had promised them, the LORD, the God of Israel, is their heritage.

Reuben. [15] [h] What Moses gave to the Reubenite clans:[i] [16]Their territory reached from Aroer, on the bank of the Wadi Arnon, and the city in the wadi itself, through the tableland about Medeba, [17]to include Heshbon and all its towns which are on the tableland, Dibon, Bamoth-baal, Beth-baal-meon, [18]Jahaz, Kedemoth, Mephaath, [19]Kiriathaim, Sibmah, Zereth-shahar on the knoll within the valley, [20]Beth-peor, the slopes of Pisgah, Beth-jeshimoth, [21]and the other cities of the tableland and, generally, of the kingdom of Sihon. This Amorite king, who reigned in Heshbon, Moses had killed, with his vassals, the princes of Midian, who were settled in the land: Evi, Rekem, Zur, Hur and Reba;[j] [22]and among their slain followers the Israelites put to the sword also the soothsayer Balaam, son of Beor.[k] [23]The boundary of the Reubenites was the bank of the Jordan. These cities and their villages were the heritage of the clans of the Reubenites.

Gad. [24] [l] What Moses gave to the Gadite clans: [25]Their territory included Jazer, all the cities of Gilead, and half the land of the Ammonites as far as Aroer, toward Rabbah [26](that is, from Heshbon to Ramath-mizpeh and Betonim, and from Mahanaim to the boundary of Lodebar); [27]and in the Jordan valley: Beth-haram, Beth-nimrah, Succoth, Zaphon, the other part of the kingdom of Sihon, king of Heshbon, with the bank of the Jordan to the southeastern tip of the Sea of Chinnereth. [28]These cities and their villages were the heritage of the clans of the Gadites.

Manasseh. [29] [m] What Moses gave to the clans of the half-tribe of Manasseh:

---

u Jos 8, 17; 10, 28.—v Jos 15, 34.—w Jos 15, 53.—x Jos 11, 1. 10.—y Jos 11, 1.—z Jos 17, 11.—a Jos 19, 37.—b Jos 11, 2.—c Jos 23, 1.—d Jgs 3, 3.—e Jos 11, 8.—f Jos 12, 6; Nm 32, 33.—g Jos 14, 3f; Nm 18, 20-24.—h 15-31: Dt 3, 12-17.—i 15-23: Nm 21, 25-31; 32, 37f.—j Nm 21, 24; 31, 8; Dt 3, 10.—k Nm 31, 8.—l 24-28: Nm 32, 34ff.—m 29-31: Nm 32, 39ff.

13, 2: *Geshur:* not to be confused with the large Aramaean district of the same name in Bashan (vv 11-13; Dt 3, 14); here it is a region to the south of the Philistine country, since vv 2-5 list the unconquered lands along the coast from south to north; cf also 1 Sm 27, 8.

30 Their territory included Mahanaim, all of Bashan, the entire kingdom of Og, king of Bashan, and all the villages of Jair, which are sixty cities in Bashan[n] 31 Half of Gilead, with Ashtaroth and Edrei, once the royal cities of Og in Bashan, fell to the descendants of Machir, son of Manasseh, for half the clans descended from Machir.

32 These are the portions which Moses gave when he was in the plains of Moab, beyond the Jordan east of Jericho. 33 However, Moses gave no heritage to the tribe of Levi, since the LORD himself, the God of Israel, is their heritage, as he promised.[o]

CHAPTER 14

The Western Tribes. 1 Here follow the portions which the Israelites received in the land of Canaan.[p] Eleazar the priest, Joshua, son of Nun, and the heads of families in the tribes of the Israelites determined 2 their heritage by lot, in accordance with the instructions the LORD had given through Moses concerning the remaining nine and a half tribes.[q] 3 For to two and a half tribes Moses had already given a heritage beyond the Jordan; and though the Levites were given no heritage among the tribes,[r] 4 the descendants of Joseph formed two tribes, Manasseh and Ephraim. The Levites themselves received no share of the land except cities to live in, with their pasture lands for the cattle and flocks.[s]

5 Thus, in apportioning the land, did the Israelites carry out the instructions of the LORD to Moses.

Caleb's Portion. 6 [t] When the Judahites came up to Joshua in Gilgal, the Kenizzite Caleb, son of Jephunneh, said to him: "You know what the LORD said to the man of God, Moses, about you and me in Kadesh-barnea. 7 [u] I was forty years old when the servant of the LORD, Moses, sent me from Kadesh-barnea to reconnoiter the land; and I brought back to him a conscientious report. 8 [v] My fellow scouts who went up with me discouraged the people, but I was completely loyal to the LORD, my God. 9 On that occasion Moses swore this oath, 'The land where you have

set foot shall become your heritage and that of your descendants forever, because you have been completely loyal to the LORD, my God.' 10 Now, as he promised, the LORD has preserved me while Israel was journeying through the desert, for the forty-five years since the LORD spoke thus to Moses; and although I am now eighty-five years old,[w] 11 I am still as strong today as I was the day Moses sent me forth, with no less vigor whether for war or for ordinary tasks.[x] 12 Give me, therefore, this mountain region which the LORD promised me that day, as you yourself heard. True, the Anakim are there, with large fortified cities, but if the LORD is with me I shall be able to drive them out, as the LORD promised."[y] 13 Joshua blessed Caleb, son of Jephunneh, and gave him Hebron as his heritage.[z] 14 Therefore Hebron remains the heritage of the Kenizzite Caleb, son of Jephunneh, to the present day, because he was completely loyal to the LORD, the God of Israel. 15 Hebron was formerly called Kiriath-arba, for Arba, the greatest among the Anakim.[a] And the land enjoyed peace.

CHAPTER 15

Boundaries of Judah. 1 The lot for the clans of the Judahite tribe fell in the extreme south toward the boundary of Edom, the desert of Zin in the Negeb.[b] [2] [c] The boundary there ran from the bay that forms the southern end of the Salt Sea, 3 southward below the pass of Akrabbim, across through Zin, up to a point south of Kadesh-barnea, across to Hezron, and up to Addar; from there, looping around Karka, 4 it crossed to Azmon and then joined the Wadi of Egypt before coming out at the sea. [This is your southern boundary.] 5 The eastern boundary was the Salt Sea as far as the mouth of the Jordan.

6 [d] The northern boundary climbed from the bay where the Jordan meets the sea, up to Beth-hoglah, and ran north of Beth-arabah, up to Eben-Bohan-ben-Reuben. 7 Thence it climbed to Debir, north of the vale of Achor,[e] in the direction of the Gilgal that faces the pass of Adummim, on the south side of the wadi; from there it crossed to the waters of En-shemesh and emerged at En-rogel. 8 Climbing again to the Valley of Ben-

n Nm 32, 41.—o Jos 18, 7; Nm 18, 20.—p Jos 17, 4; 21, 1; Nm 34. 17f.—q Nm 26, 55; 33, 54; 34, 13.—r Jos 13, 8. 14. 33.—s Jos 21, 3-40; Gn 48, 5.—t Nm 14, 24. 30; 32, 12; Dt 1, 36. 38.—u Nm 14, 6-9.—v Nm 13, 31ff; 14, 24; 32, 12; Dt 1, 36.—w Nm 14, 30.—x Sir 46, 1ff.—y Jos 11, 21.—z Jos 10, 36f; 15, 13-19; 21, 11f.—a Jgs 1, 10.—b Nm 34, 3.—c 2-4: Nm 34, 3ff.—d Jos 18, 18f. 22.—e Jos 7, 26; 18, 16ff: 2 Sm 17, 17.

hinnom* on the southern flank of the Jebusites [that is, Jerusalem], the boundary rose to the top of the mountain at the northern end of the Valley of Rephaim,ᶠ which bounds the Valley of Hinnom on the west. ⁹From the top of the mountain it ran to the fountain of waters of Nephtoah,ᵍ extended to the cities of Mount Ephron, and continued to Baalah, or Kiriath-jearim. ¹⁰From Baalah the boundary curved westward to Mount Seir and passed north of the ridge of Mount Jearim (that is, Chesalon); thence it descended to Beth-shemesh, and ran across to Timnah. ¹¹It then extended along the northern flank of Ekron, continued through Shikkeron, and across to Mount Baalah, thence to include Jabneel, before it came out at the sea. ¹²The western boundary was the Great Sea and its coast. This was the complete boundary of the clans of the Judahites.

Conquest by Caleb. ¹³ ʰ As the LORD had commanded, Joshua gave Caleb, son of Jephunneh,ⁱ a portion among the Judahites, namely, Kiriath-arba (Arba was the father of Anak), that is, Hebron. ¹⁴ ʲ And Caleb drove out from there the three Anakim, the descendants of Anak: Sheshai, Ahiman and Talmai. ¹⁵From there he marched up against the inhabitants of Debir,ᵏ which was formerly called Kiriath-sepher. ¹⁶Caleb said, "I will give my daughter Achsah in marriage to the one who attacks Kiriath-sepher and captures it." ¹⁷ * Othniel, son of Caleb's brother Kenaz, captured it, and so Caleb gave him his daughter Achsah in marriage. ¹⁸On the day of her marriage to Othniel, she induced him to ask her father for some land. Then, as she alighted from the ass, Caleb asked her, "What is troubling you?" ¹⁹She answered, "Give me an additional gift! Since you have assigned to me land in the Negeb, give me also pools of water." So he gave her the upper and the lower pools.

Cities of Judah. ²⁰ * This is the heritage of the clans of the tribe of Judahites: ²¹The cities of the tribe of the Judahites in the extreme southern district toward Edom were: Kabzeel, Eder, Jagur, ²²Kinah, Dimonah, Adadah, ²³Kedesh, Hazor and Ithnan; ²⁴Ziph, Telem, Bealoth, ²⁵Hazor-hadattah, and Kerioth-hezron (that is, Hazor); ²⁶Amam, Shema, Moladah, ²⁷Hazar-gaddah, Heshmon, Beth-pelet, ²⁸Hazar-shual, Beer-sheba,

and Biziothiah, ²⁹Baalah, Iim, Ezem, ³⁰Eltolad, Chesil, Hormah, ³¹Ziklag,ˡ Madmannah, Sansannah, ³²Lebaoth, Shilhim and En-rimmon; a total of twenty-nine cities with their villages.

³³In the foothills:* Eshtaol, Zorah, Ashnah, ³⁴Zanoah, Engannim, Tappuah, Enam, ³⁵Jarmuth, Adullam, Socoh, Azekah, ³⁶Shaaraim, Adithaim, Gederah, and Gederothaim; fourteen cities and their villages. ³⁷Zenan, Hadashah, Migdal-gad, ³⁸Dilean, Mizpeh, Joktheel, ³⁹Lachish, Bozkath, Eglon, ⁴⁰Cabbon, Lahmam, Chitlish, ⁴¹Gederoth, Beth-dagon, Naamah and Makkedah; sixteen cities and their villages. ⁴²Libnah, Ether, Ashan, ⁴³Iphtah, Ashnah, Nezib, ⁴⁴Keilah, Achzib and Mareshah; nine cities and their villages. ⁴⁵Ekron and its towns and villages; ⁴⁶from Ekron to the sea, all the towns that lie alongside Ashdod and their villages; ⁴⁷Ashdod and its towns and villages; Gaza and its towns and villages, as far as the Wadi of Egypt and the coast of the Great Sea.

⁴⁸In the mountain regions: Shamir, Jattir, Socoh, ⁴⁹Dannah, Kiriath-sannah (that is, Debir), ⁵⁰Anab, Eshtemoh, Anim, ⁵¹Goshen, Holon and Giloh; eleven cities and their villages. ⁵²Arab, Dumah, Eshan, ⁵³Janim, Beth-tappuah, Aphekah, ⁵⁴Humtah, Kiriath-arba (that is, Hebron), and Zior; nine cities and their villages. ⁵⁵Maon, Carmel, Ziph, Juttah, ⁵⁶Jezreel, Jokdeam, Zanoah, ⁵⁷Kain, Gibbeah and Timnah; ten cities and their villages. ⁵⁸Halhul, Beth-zur, Gedor, ⁵⁹Maarath, Beth-anoth and Eltekon; six cities and their villages. Tekoa, Ephrathah (that is, Bethlehem), Peor, Etam, Kulom, Tatam, Zores, Karim, Gallim, Bether and Manoko; eleven cities and their villages.

---

f Jos 18. 16.—g Jos 18, 15.—h 13-19: Jgs 1, 10-15.—i Jos 14, 13ff.—j Nm 13, 22; Jgs 1, 20.—k Jos 10, 38.—l 1 Sm 27, 6.

15, 8: *The Valley of Ben-hinnom:* the southern limit of Jerusalem. *Ben-hinnom* means "son of Hinnom." The place was also called *Valley of Hinnom,* in Hebrew *ge-hinnom,* whence the word "Gehenna" is derived.

15, 17-19: The story of Othniel is told again in Jgs 1, 13-15; cf also Jgs 3, 9-11.

15, 20-62: This elaborate list of the cities of Judah was probably taken from a document made originally for administrative purposes; the cities are divided into four provincial districts, some of which have further subdivisions. For similar lists of the cities of Judah, cf Jos 19, 2-7; 1 Chr 4, 28-32; Neh 11, 25-30. This list has suffered in transmission, so that the totals given in vv 32 and 36 are not exact, and some of the names are probably misspelled; many of the cities cannot be identified.

15, 33: *In the foothills:* see note on Dt 1, 7.

[60] Kiriath-baal (that is, Kiriath-jearim) and Rabbah: two cities and their villages.[m]

[61] In the desert:* Beth-arabah, Middin, Secacah, [62] Nibshan, Ir-hamelah and Engedi; six cities and their villages. [63] [But the Jebusites who lived in Jerusalem the Judahites could not drive out; so the Jebusites dwell in Jerusalem beside the Judahites to the present day.[n]]

CHAPTER 16

The Joseph Tribes. [1] The lot that fell to the Josephites* extended from the Jordan at Jericho to the waters of Jericho east of the desert; then the boundary went up from Jericho to the heights at Bethel.* [2] Leaving Bethel for Luz, it crossed the ridge to the border of the Archites at Ataroth, [3] and descended westward to the border of the Japhletites, to that of Lower Beth-horon, and to Gezer, ending thence at the sea.[o]

Ephraim. [4] Within the heritage of Manasseh and Ephraim, sons of Joseph, [5] the dividing line* for the heritage of the clans of the Ephraimites ran from east of Atarothaddar to Upper Beth-horon[p] [6] and thence to the sea. From Michmethath[q] on the north, their boundary curved eastward around Taanath-shiloh, and continued east of it to Janoah; [7] from there it descended to Ataroth and Naarah, and skirting Jericho, it ended at the Jordan. [8] From Tappuah[r] the boundary ran westward to the Wadi Kanah and ended at the sea. This was the heritage of the clans of the Ephraimites, [9] including the villages that belonged to each city set aside for the Ephraimites within the territory of the Manassehites.[s]

[10] But they did not drive out the Canaanites living in Gezer,[t] who live on within Ephraim to the present day, though they have been impressed as laborers.

CHAPTER 17

Manasseh. [1] Now as for the lot that fell to the tribe of Manasseh[u] as the first-born of Joseph: since his eldest son, Machir, the father of Gilead, was a warrior, who had already obtained Gilead and Bashan, [2] [v] the allotment was now made to the other descendants of Manasseh, the clans of Abiezer, Helek, Asriel, Shechem, Hepher and Shemida, the other male children of Manasseh, son of Joseph.

[3] Futhermore, Zelophedad, son of Hepher,[w] son of Gilead, son of Machir, son of Manasseh, had had no sons, but only daughters, whose names were Mahlah, Noah, Hoglah, Milcah, and Tirzah. [4] These presented themselves to Eleazar the priest, to Joshua, son of Nun, and to the princes, saying, "The LORD commanded Moses to give us a heritage among our kinsmen." So in obedience to the command of the LORD a heritage was given to each of them among their father's kinsmen.[x] [5] Thus ten shares fell to Manasseh apart from the land of Gilead and Bashan beyond the Jordan,[y] [6] since these female descendants of Manasseh received each a portion among his sons. The land of Gilead fell to the rest of the Manassehites.

[7] Manasseh bordered on Asher.* From Michmethath, near Shechem, another boundary ran southward to include the natives of En-Tappuah, [8] because the district of Tappuah belonged to Manasseh, although Tappuah itself was an Ephraimite city on the border of Manasseh. [9] This same boundary continued down to the Wadi Kanah.[z] The cities that belonged to Ephraim from among the cities of Manasseh were those to the south of the wadi; thus the territory of Manasseh ran north of the wadi and ended at the sea. [10] The land on the south belonged to Ephraim and that on the north to Manasseh; with the sea as their common boundary, they reached Asher on the north and Issachar on the east.

[11] [a] Moreover, in Issachar and in Asher Manasseh was awarded Beth-shean[b] and its towns, Ibleam and its towns, Dor and its towns and the natives there, Endor and

---

m Jos 18, 14.—n Jgs 1, 21; 2 Sm 5, 6.—o Jos 10, 10. 33.—p Jos 18, 13.—q Jos 17, 7.—r Jos 17, 7.—s Jos 17, 9.—t Jgs 1, 29.—u Gn 41, 51; 46, 20; 48, 18; 50, 23; Nm 26, 29; Dt 3, 13. 15.—v Nm 26, 29-32.—w Nm 26, 33; 27, 1; 36, 2.—x Nm 27, 6f; 36, 2.—y Jos 13, 30f.—z Jos 16, 8f.—a 1 Chr 7, 29.—b 11ff: Jgs 1, 27f.

15, 61: *In the desert:* in the Jordan rift near the Dead Sea.

16, 1—17, 18: The boundaries and cities of Judah, the most important tribe, having been given, the land of the next most important group, the two Josephite tribes of Ephraim and Manasseh, is now described, though it was separated from Judah by the territories of Benjamin (Jos 18, 11-20) and Dan (Jos 19, 40-48).

16, 1-3: This line formed the southern boundary of Ephraim and the northern boundaries of Benjamin and of Dan.

16, 5: *The dividing line:* separating Ephraim from Manasseh. Ephraim's northern border (v 5) is given in an east-to-west direction; its eastern border (v 6f) in a north-to-south direction.

17, 7: *Manasseh bordered on Asher:* only at the extreme northwestern section of Manasseh's territory. The boundary given in the following sentences (vv 7-10) is a more detailed description of the one already mentioned in Jos 16, 5ff, as separating Manasseh from Ephraim.

its towns and natives, Taanach and its towns and natives, and Megiddo and its towns and natives [the third is Naphath-dor]. [12] Since the Manassehites could not conquer these cities, the Canaanites persisted in this region. [13] When the Israelites grew stronger they impressed the Canaanites as laborers, but they did not drive them out.

Protest of Joseph Tribes. [14] The descendants of Joseph said to Joshua, "Why have you given us only one lot and one share as our heritage?[c] Our people are too many, because of the extent to which the LORD has blessed us." [15] Joshua answered them, "If you are too many, go up to the forest and clear out a place for yourselves there in the land of the Perizzites and Rephaim, since the mountain regions of Ephraim are so narrow." [16] For the Josephites said, "Our mountain regions are not enough for us; on the other hand, the Canaanites living in the valley region all have iron chariots, in particular those in Beth-shean and its towns, and those in the valley of Jezreel."[d] [17] Joshua therefore said to Ephraim and Manasseh, the house of Joseph, "You are a numerous people and very strong. You shall have not merely one share, [18] for the mountain region which is now forest shall be yours when you clear it. Its adjacent land shall also be yours if, despite their strength and iron chariots, you drive out the Canaanites."

CHAPTER 18

[1] After they had subdued the land, the whole community of the Israelites assembled at Shiloh, where they set up the meeting tent.[e]

The Seven Remaining Portions. [2] Seven tribes among the Israelites had not yet received their heritage. [3] Joshua therefore said to the Israelites, "How much longer will you put off taking steps to possess the land which the LORD, the God of your fathers, has given you? [4] Choose three men from each of your tribes; I will commission them to begin a survey of the land, which they shall describe for purposes of inheritance. When they return to me, [5] you shall divide it into seven parts. Judah is to retain its territory in the south,[f] and the house of Joseph its territory in the north. [6] You shall bring here to me the description

of the land in seven sections. I will then cast lots for you here before the LORD, our God. [7] For the Levites have no share among you,[g] because the priesthood of the LORD is their heritage; while Gad, Reuben, and the half-tribe of Manasseh have already received the heritage east of the Jordan which Moses, the servant of the LORD, gave them."

[8] When those who were to map out the land were ready for the journey, Joshua instructed them to survey the land, prepare a description of it, and return to him; then he would cast lots for them there before the LORD in Shiloh. [9] So they went through the land, listed its cities in writing in seven sections, and returned to Joshua in the camp at Shiloh. [10] Joshua then divided up the land for the Israelites into their separate shares, casting lots for them before the LORD in Shiloh.

Benjamin. [11] One lot fell to the clans of the tribe of Benjaminites. The territory allotted them lay between the descendants of Judah and those of Joseph. [12] [h] Their northern boundary* began at the Jordan and went over the northern flank of Jericho, up westward into the mountains, till it reached the desert of Beth-aven. [13] From there it crossed over to the southern flank of Luz (that is, Bethel). Then it ran down to Ataroth-addar, on the mountaintop south of Lower Beth-horon.[i] [14] For the western border, the boundary line swung south from the mountaintop opposite Beth-horon till it reached Kiriath-baal (that is, Kiriath-jearim), which city belonged to the Judahites. This was the western boundary. [15] The southern boundary began at the limits of Kiriath-jearim and projected to the spring at Nephtoah. [16] It went down to the edge of the mountain on the north of the Valley of Rephaim, where it faces the Valley of Ben-hinnom; and continuing down the Valley of Hinnom along the southern flank of the Jebusites, reached En-rogel.[j] [17] Inclining to the north, it extended to En-shemesh, and thence to Geliloth, opposite the pass

---

c Jos 16, 4; Gn 48, 19f. 22.—d Jgs 6, 33.—e Jos 19, 51.—f Jos 15, 1—17, 18.—g Jos 13, 8. 33.—h Jos 16, 1.—i Jos 16, 2f. 5; Gn 28, 19.—j Jos 15, 7f.

18, 12-20: Benjamin's *northern boundary* (vv 12f) corresponded to part of the southern boundary of Ephraim (Jos 16, 1f). Their *western border* (v 14) was the eastern border of Dan (cf Jos 19, 40-47). Their *southern boundary* (vv 15-19) corresponded to part of the northern boundary of Judah (Jos 15, 6-9).

of Adummim. Then it dropped to Eben-Bohan-ben-Reuben, [18]across the northern flank of the Arabah overlook, down into the Arabah.[k] [19]From there the boundary continued across the northern flank of Beth-hoglah and extended to the northern tip of the Salt Sea, at the southern end of the Jordan. This was the southern boundary. [20]The Jordan bounded it on the east. This was how the heritage of the clans of the Benjaminites was bounded on all sides.

[21]Now the cities belonging to the clans of the tribe of the Benjaminites were: Jericho, Beth-hoglah, Emek-keziz, [22]Beth-arabah, Zemaraim, Bethel, [23]Avvim, Parah, Ophra, [24]Chephar-ammoni, Ophni and Geba; twelve cities and their villages. [25]Also Gibeon, Ramah, Beeroth, [26]Mizpeh, Chephirah, Mozah, [27]Rekem, Irpeel, Taralah, [28]Zela, Haeleph, the Jebusite city (that is, Jerusalem), Gibeah and Kiriath; fourteen cities and their villages. This was the heritage of the clans of Benjaminites.

CHAPTER 19

Simeon. [1]The second lot fell to Simeon. The heritage of the clans of the tribe of Simeonites lay within that of the Judahites. [2] [l] For their heritage they received Beer-sheba, Shema, Moladah, [3]Hazar-shual, Balah, Ezem, [4]Eltolad, Bethul, Hormah, [5]Ziklag, Bethmar-caboth, Hazar-susah, [6]Beth-lebaoth and Sharuhen; thirteen cities and their villages. [7]Also En-rimmon, Ether and Ashan; four cities and their villages, [8]besides all the

villages around these cities as far as Baalath-beer (that is, Ramoth-negeb). This was the heritage of the clans of the tribe of the Simeonites. [9]This heritage of the Simeonites was within the confines of the Judahites; for since the portion of the latter was too large for them, the Simeonites obtained their heritage within it.

Zebulun. [10] * The third lot fell to the clans of the Zebulunites. The limit of their heritage was at Sarid. [11]Their boundary went up west . . . and through Mareal, reaching Dabbesheth and the wadi that is near Jokneam. [12]From Sarid eastward it ran to the district of Chisloth-tabor, on to Daberath, and up to Japhia. [13]From there it continued eastward to Gath-hepher and to Eth-kazin, extended to Rimmon, and turned to Neah. [14]Skirting north of Hannathon, the boundary ended at the valley of Iphtahel. [15]Thus, with Kattath, Nahalal, Shimron, Idalah and Bethlehem, there were twelve cities and their villages [16]to comprise the heritage of the clans of the Zebulunites.

Issachar. [17] * The fourth lot fell to Issachar. The territory of the clans of the Issacharites [18]included Jezreel Chesulloth, Shunem, [19]Hapharaim, Shion, Anaharath, [20]Rabbith, Kishion, Ebez, [21]Remeth, En-gannim, En-haddah and Beth-pazzez. [22]The boundary reached Tabor, Shahazumah and Beth-shemesh, ending at the Jordan. These sixteen cities and their villages [23]were the heritage of the clans of the Issacharites.

Asher. [24] * The fifth lot fell to the clans of the tribe of the Asherites. [25]Their territory included Helkath, Hali, Beten, Achshaph, [26]Allammelech, Amad and Mishal, and reached Carmel on the west, and Shihor-libnath. [27]In the other direction, it ran eastward of Beth-dagon, reached Zebulun and the valley of Iphtahel; then north of Beth-emek and Neiel, it extended to Cabul, [28]Mishal, Abdon, Rehob,[m] Hammon and Kanah, near Greater Sidon. [29]Then the boundary turned back to Ramah and to the fortress city of Tyre; thence it cut back to Hosah and ended at the sea. Thus, with Mahalab, Achzib, [30]Ummah, Acco, Aphek and Rehob, there were twenty-two cities and their villages [31]to comprise the heritage of the clans of the tribe of the Asherites.

Naphtali. [32] * The sixth lot fell to the Naphtalites. The boundary of the clans of

---

k Jos 15, 6.—l 2-8: 1 Chr 4, 28-33.—m 28f: Jgs 1, 31.

19, 10-16: Zebulun's territory was in the central section of the Plain of Esdraelon and of southern Galilee; it was bounded on the south by Manasseh, on the southeast by Issachar, on the northeast and north by Naphtali, and on the west by Asher. The site of the later city of Nazareth was within its borders. *Bethlehem* of Zebulun was, of course, distinct from the city of the same name in Judah. *Twelve cities:* apparently seven of the names are missing from v 15, unless some of the places mentioned in vv 12-14 are to be included in the number.

19, 17-23: Issachar's land was on the eastern watershed of the Plain of Esdraelon, but also included the southeastern end of the Galilean mountains. It was surrounded by Manasseh on the south and east, by Naphtali on the north, and by Zebulun on the west. *Jezreel* (v 18) dominated the plain to which it gave its name, the later form of which was Esdraelon.

19, 24-31: Asher inherited the western slope of the Galilean hills as far as the sea, with Manasseh to the south, Zebulun and Naphtali to the east, and Phoenicia to the north.

19, 32-39: Naphtali received eastern Galilee; Asher was to the west and Zebulun and Issachar were to the south, while the upper Jordan and Mount Hermon formed the eastern border. Part of the tribe of Dan later on occupied the northern extremity of Naphtali's lands, at the sources of the Jordan (v 47).

the Naphtalites [33] extended from Heleph, from the oak at Zaanannim to Lakkum, including Adami-nekeb and Jabneel, and ended at the Jordan. [34] In the opposite direction, westerly, it ran through Aznoth-tabor and from there extended to Hukkok; it touched Zebulun on the south, Asher on the west, and the Jordan on the east. [35] The fortified cities were Ziddim, Zer, Hammath, Rakkath, Chinnereth, [36] Adamah, Ramah, Hazor, [37] Kedesh, Edrei, En-hazor, [38] Yiron, Migdal-el, Horem, Beth-anath and Beth-shemesh;[n] nineteen cities and their villages, [39] to comprise the heritage of the clans of the tribe of the Naphtalites.

Dan. [40] * The seventh lot fell to the clans of the tribe of Danites. [41] Their heritage was the territory of Zorah, Eshtaol, Ir-shemesh, [42] Shaalabbin, Aijalon, Ithlah,[o] [43] Elon, Timnah, Ekron, [44] El-tekoh, Gibbethon, Baalath, [45] Jehud, Bene-berak, Gath-rimmon, [46] Me-jarkon and Rakkon, with the coast at Joppa. [47] [p] But the territory of the Danites was too small for them; so the Danites marched up and attacked Leshem,* which they captured and put to the sword. Once they had taken possession of Leshem, they renamed the settlement after their ancestor Dan. [48] These cities and their villages were the heritage of the clans of the tribe of the Danites.

Joshua's City. [49] When the last of them had received the portions of the land they were to inherit, the Israelites assigned a heritage in their midst to Joshua, son of Nun. [50] In obedience to the command of the LORD, they gave him the city which he requested, Timnah-serah[q] in the mountain region of Ephraim. He rebuilt the city and made it his home.

[51] These are the final portions into which Eleazar the priest, Joshua, son of Nun, and the heads of families in the tribes of the Israelites divided the land by lot in the presence of the LORD, at the door of the meeting tent in Shiloh.

CHAPTER 20

Cities of Asylum. [1] The LORD said to Joshua:* [2] "Tell the Israelites to designate the cities of which I spoke to them through Moses,[r] [3] to which one guilty of accidental and unintended homicide may flee for asylum from the avenger of blood. [4] To one of these cities the killer shall flee, and standing at the entrance of the city gate, he shall plead his case before the elders, who must receive him and assign him a place in which to live among them. [5] Though the avenger of blood pursues him, they are not to deliver up the homicide who slew his fellow man unintentionally and not out of previous hatred. [6] Once he has stood judgment before the community, he shall live on in that city till the death of the high priest who is in office at the time. Then the killer may go back home to his own city from which he fled."[s]

List of Cities. [7] So they set apart Kedesh in Galilee in the mountain region of Naphtali, Shechem in the mountain region of Ephraim, and Kiriath-arba (that is, Hebron) in the mountain region of Judah.[t] [8] And beyond the Jordan east of Jericho they designated Bezer on the open tableland in the tribe of Reuben, Ramoth in Gilead in the tribe of Gad, and Golan in Bashan in the tribe of Manasseh.[u] [9] These were the designated cities[v] to which any Israelite or stranger living among them who had killed a person accidentally might flee to escape death at the hand of the avenger of blood, until he could appear before the community.

CHAPTER 21

Levitical Cities. [1] The heads of the Levite families* came up to Eleazar the priest, to Joshua, son of Nun, and to the heads of families of the other tribes of the Israelites[w] [2] at Shiloh in the land of Canaan, and said to them, "The LORD com-

---

n Jgs 1, 33.—o Jgs 1, 35.—p Jgs 18, 27-29.—q Jos 24, 30; Jgs 2, 9.—r Ex 21, 13; Nm 35, 10-14; Dt 4, 41-43; 19, 2-9.—s Nm 35, 12. 24f.—t Jos 15, 13; 19, 37; 21, 21.—u Jos 21, 27. 36f.—v Nm 35, 15.—w Ex 6, 16-19; Nm 3, 17-20.

19, 40-46: The original territory of Dan was a small enclave between Judah, Benjamin, Ephraim and the Philistines.

19, 47: *Leshem:* called Laish in Jgs 18, where the story of the migration of the Danites is told at greater length.

20, 1-9: The laws concerning the cities of refuge are given in Nm 35, 9-28; Dt 19, 1-13; see notes on Nm 35, 16-25; Dt 19, 2.

21, 1: The order to establish special cities for the Levites is given in Nm 35, 1-8. The forty-eight cities listed here were hardly the exclusive possession of the Levites; at least the more important of them, such as Hebron, Shechem and Ramoth in Gilead, were certainly peopled for the most part by the tribe in whose territory they were situated. But in all these cities the Levites had special property rights which they did not possess in other cities; cf Lv 25, 32ff.

manded, through Moses, that cities be given us to dwell in, with pasture lands for our livestock."ˣ ³Out of their own heritage, in obedience to this command of the LORD, the Israelites gave the Levites the following cities with their pasture lands.

⁴When the first lot among the Levites fell to the clans of the Kohathites, the descendants of Aaron the priest obtained thirteen cities by lot from the tribes of Judah, Simeon and Benjamin. ⁵The rest of the Kohathites obtained ten cities by lot from the clans of the tribe of Ephraim, from the tribe of Dan, and from the half-tribe of Manasseh. ⁶The Gershonites obtained thirteen cities by lot from the clans of the tribe of Issachar, from the tribe of Asher, from the tribe of Naphtali, and from the half-tribe of Manasseh. ⁷The clans of the Merarites obtained twelve cities from the tribes of Reuben, Gad and Zebulun. ⁸These cities with their pasture lands the Israelites allotted to the Levites in obedience to the LORD's command through Moses.ʸ

Cities of the Priests. ⁹ ᶻ From the tribes of the Judahites and Simeonites they designated the following cities, ¹⁰and assigned them to the descendants of Aaron in the Kohathite clan of the Levites, since the first lot fell to them: ¹¹first, Kiriath-arba (Arba was the father of Anak), that is, Hebron, in the mountain region of Judah, with the adjacent pasture lands, ¹²although the open country and villages belonging to the city had been given to Caleb, son of Jephunneh, as his property.ᵃ ¹³Thus to the descendants of Aaron the priest were given the city of asylum for homicides at Hebron, with its pasture lands; also, Libnah with its pasture lands, ¹⁴Jattir with its pasture lands, Eshtemoa with its pasture lands, ¹⁵Holon with its pasture lands, Debir with its pasture lands, ¹⁶Ashan with its pasture lands, Juttah with its pasture lands, and Bethshemesh with its pasture lands: nine cities from the two tribes mentioned. ¹⁷From the tribe of Benjamin they obtained the four cities of Gibeon with its pasture lands, Geba with its pasture lands, ¹⁸Anathothᵇ with its pasture lands, and Almon with its pasture lands. ¹⁹These cities which with

their pasture lands belonged to the priestly descendants of Aaron, were thirteen in all.

Cities of the Other Kohathites. ²⁰ ᶜ The rest of the Kohathite clans among the Levites obtained by lot, from the tribe of Ephraim, four cities. ²¹They were assigned, with its pasture lands, the city of asylum for homicides at Shechem in the mountain region of Ephraim; also Gezer with its pasture lands, ²²Kibzaim with its pasture lands, and Beth-horon with its pasture lands. ²³From the tribe of Dan they obtained the four cities of Elteke with its pasture lands, Gibbethon with its pasture lands, ²⁴Aijalon with its pasture lands, and Gath-rimmon with its pasture lands; ²⁵and from the half-tribe of Manasseh the two cities of Taanach with its pasture lands and Ibleam with its pasture lands. ²⁶These cities which with their pasture lands belonged to the rest of the Kohathite clans were ten in all.

Cities of the Gershonites. ²⁷ ᵈ The Gershonite clan of the Levites received from the half-tribe of Manasseh two cities: the city of asylum for homicides at Golan with its pasture lands; and also Beth-Astharoth with its pasture lands. ²⁸From the tribe of Issachar they obtained the four cities of Kishion with its pasture lands, Daberath with its pasture lands, ²⁹Jarmuth with its pasture lands, and En-gannim with its pasture lands; ³⁰from the tribe of Asher, the four cities of Mishal with its pasture lands, Abdon with its pasture lands, ³¹Helkath with its pasture lands, and Rehob with its pasture lands; ³²and from the tribe of Naphtali, three cities: the city of asylum for homicides at Kedesh in Galilee, with its pasture lands; also Hammath with its pasture lands, and Rakkath with its pasture lands. ³³These cities which with their pasture lands belonged to the Gershonite clans were thirteen in all.

Cities of the Merarites. ³⁴ ᵉ The Merarite clans, the last of the Levites, received from the tribe of Zebulun the four cities of Jokneam with its pasture lands, Kartah with its pasture lands, ³⁵Rimmon with its pasture lands, and Nahalal with its pasture lands; ³⁶also, across the Jordan, from the tribe of Reuben, four cities: the city of asylum for homicides at Bezer with its pasture lands, Jahaz with its pasture lands, ³⁷Kedemoth with its pasture lands, and Mephaath with its pasture lands; ³⁸and

x Nm 35, 2.—y Nm 35, 2.—z 9-19: 1 Chr 6, 54-60.—a Jos 14, 14; 15, 13.—b Jer 1, 1.—c 20-26: 1 Chr 6, 66-70.—d 27-33: 1 Chr 6, 71-76.—e 34-38: 1 Chr 6, 77-81.

from the tribe of Gad a total of four cities: the city of asylum for homicides at Ramoth in Gilead with its pasture lands, also Mahanaim with its pasture lands, ³⁹ Heshbon with its pasture lands, and Jazer with its pasture lands. ⁴⁰The cities which were allotted to the Merarite clans, the last of the Levites, were therefore twelve in all. ⁴¹Thus the total number of cities*f* within the territory of the Israelites which, with their pasture lands, belonged to the Levites, was forty-eight. ⁴²With each and every one of these cities went the pasture lands round about it.

⁴³And so the LORD gave Israel all the land he had sworn to their fathers he would give them.*g* Once they had conquered and occupied it, ⁴⁴the LORD gave them peace on every side, just as he had promised their fathers. Not one of their enemies could withstand them; the LORD brought all their enemies under their power. ⁴⁵Not a single promise*h* that the LORD made to the house of Israel was broken; every one was fulfilled.

III: RETURN OF THE TRANSJORDAN TRIBES AND JOSHUA'S FAREWELL

CHAPTER 22

The Eastern Tribes Dismissed. ¹At that time Joshua summoned the Reubenites, the Gadites, and the half-tribe of Manasseh ²and said to them:*i* "You have done all that Moses, the servant of the LORD, commanded you, and have obeyed every command I gave you. ³For many years now you have not once abandoned your kinsmen, but have faithfully carried out the commands of the LORD, your God. ⁴Since, therefore, the LORD, your God, has settled your kinsmen as he promised them, you may now return to your tents beyond the Jordan; to your own land, which Moses, the servant of the LORD, gave you.*j* ⁵But be very careful to observe the precept and law which Moses, the servant of the LORD, enjoined upon you: love the LORD, your God;*k* follow him faithfully; keep his commandments; remain loyal to him; and serve him with your whole heart and soul." ⁶Joshua then blessed them and sent them away to their own tents.

⁷(For, to half the tribe of Manasseh Moses had assigned land in Bashan;*l* and to the other half Joshua had given a portion along with their kinsmen west of the Jordan.) What Joshua said to them when he sent them off to their tents with his blessing was, ⁸"Now that you are returning to your own tents with great wealth, with very numerous livestock, with silver, gold, bronze and iron, and with a very large supply of clothing, divide these spoils of your enemies with your kinsmen there."*m* ⁹So the Reubenites, the Gadites, and the half-tribe of Manasseh left the other Israelites at Shiloh in the land of Canaan and returned to the land of Gilead, their own property, which they had received according to the LORD's command through Moses.*n*

The Altar beside the Jordan. ¹⁰When the Reubenites, the Gadites, and the half-tribe of Manasseh came to the region of the Jordan in the land of Canaan, they built there at the Jordan a conspicuously large altar. ¹¹The other Israelites heard the report*o* that the Reubenites, the Gadites, and the half-tribe of Manasseh had built an altar in the region of the Jordan facing the land of Canaan,* across from them, ¹²and therefore they assembled their whole community at Shiloh to declare war on them.*

Accusation of the Western Tribes. ¹³First, however, they sent to the Reubenites, the Gadites, and the half-tribe of Manasseh in the land of Gilead an embassy consisting of Phinehas, son of Eleazar the priest,*p* ¹⁴and ten princes, one from every tribe of Israel, each one being both prince and military leader of his ancestral house. ¹⁵When these came to the Reubenites, the Gadites, and the half-tribe of Manasseh in the land of Gilead, they said to them: ¹⁶*q* "The whole community of the LORD sends this message: What act of treachery is this you have committed against the God of

f Nm 35, 7.—g Gn 12, 7; 13, 15; 15, 18; 26, 3; 28, 4. 13.—h Jos 23, 14f.—i Jos 1, 16f; Nm 32, 20ff; Dt 3, 18ff.—j Jos 1, 13; 13, 8; Nm 32, 33.—k Dt 6, 5f. 17; 10, 12; 11, 1. 13. 22.—l Jos 17, 5.—m Nm 31, 27.—n Jos 18, 1; Nm 32, 1. 26. 29.—o Dt 13, 13ff.—p Ex 6, 25; Sir 45, 28.—q Lv 17, 8f.

22, 11: *In the region of the Jordan facing the land of Canaan:* on the eastern side of the Jordan valley. The river itself formed the boundary between these eastern tribes and the rest of the tribes who lived in what was formerly Canaan—though the term *Canaan* could also be used of both sides of the Jordan valley (cf v 10). The Transjordan tribes naturally built their altar in their own territory.

22, 12: *To declare war on them:* the western Israelites considered this altar, which seemed to violate the customary unity of the sanctuary (cf Lv 17, 1-9; Dt 12, 4-14), as a sign of secession and dangerous to national unity. The motives for the war were political as well as religious.

Israel? You have seceded from the LORD this day, and rebelled against him by building an altar of your own! [17] For the sin of Peor, a plague came upon the community of the LORD.[r] [18] We are still not free of that; must you now add to it? You are rebelling against the LORD today and by tomorrow he will be angry with the whole community of Israel! [19] If you consider the land you now possess unclean,* cross over to the land the LORD possesses, where the Dwelling of the LORD stands,[s] and share that with us. But do not rebel against the LORD, nor involve us in rebellion, by building an altar of your own in addition to the altar of the LORD, our God. [20] When Achan, son of Zerah,[t] violated the ban, did not wrath fall upon the entire community of Israel? Though he was but a single man, he did not perish alone* for his guilt!"

Reply of the Eastern Tribes. [21] The Reubenites, the Gadites, and the half-tribe of Manasseh replied to the military leaders of the Israelites: "The LORD is the God of gods. [22] The LORD, the God of gods,* knows and Israel shall know. If now we have acted out of rebellion or treachery against the LORD, our God, [23] and if we have built an altar of our own to secede from the LORD, or to offer holocausts, grain offerings or peace offerings upon it, the LORD himself will exact the penalty. [24] We did it rather out of our anxious concern lest in the future your children should say to our children: 'What have you to do with the LORD, the God of Israel? [25] For the LORD has placed the Jordan as a boundary between you and us. You descendants of Reuben and Gad have no share in the LORD.' Thus your children would prevent ours from revering the

LORD. [26] So we decided to guard our interests by building this altar of our own: not for holocausts or for sacrifices, [27] [u] but as evidence for you on behalf of ourselves and our descendants, that we have the right to worship the LORD in his presence with our holocausts, sacrifices, and peace offerings. Now in the future your children cannot say to our children, 'You have no share in the LORD.' [28] Our thought was, that if in the future they should speak thus to us or to our descendants, we could answer: 'Look at the model of the altar of the LORD which our fathers made, not for holocausts or for sacrifices, but to witness* between you and us.' [29] Far be it from us to rebel against the LORD or to secede now from the LORD by building an altar for holocaust, grain offering, or sacrifice in addition to the altar of the LORD, our God, which stands before his Dwelling."

[30] When Phinehas the priest and the princes of the community, the military leaders of the Israelites, heard what the Reubenites, the Gadites and the Manassehites had to say, they were satisfied. [31] Phinehas, son of Eleazar the priest, said to the Reubenites, the Gadites and the Manassehites, "Now we know that the LORD is with us. Since you have not committed this act of treachery against the LORD, you have kept the Israelites free from punishment by the LORD." [32] Phinehas, son of Eleazar the priest, and the princes returned from the Reubenites and the Gadites in the land of Gilead to the Israelites in the land of Canaan, and reported the matter to them. [33] The report satisfied the Israelites, who blessed God and decided against declaring war on the Reubenites and Gadites or ravaging the land they occupied. [34] The Reubenites and the Gadites gave the altar its name* as a witness among them that the LORD is God.

---

r Nm 25, 3f; Dt 4, 3.—s Jos 18, 1.—t Jos 7, 1. 5.—u Dt 12, 5f. 17f.—v Jos 13, 1.

22, 19: *Unclean:* not sanctified by the Dwelling of the Lord.
22, 20: *Achan . . . did not perish alone:* his guilt caused the failure of the first attack on Ai (Jos 7, 4-23); this fact is adduced as an argument for the solidarity and mutual responsibility of all the Israelites.
22, 22: *The LORD, the God of gods:* the Hebrew, which cannot be adequately rendered in English here, adds to the divine name Yahweh ("the LORD") two synonymous words for "God," *el* and *elohim.* The repetition of these three sacred words adds force to the protestations of fidelity and innocence.
22, 28: *To witness:* far from being destined to form a rival sanctuary, the model of the altar was intended by the eastern tribes solely as a means of teaching their children to be faithful to the one true sanctuary beyond the Jordan.
22, 34: The name of this altar was the Hebrew word for "witness," *c ed.*

CHAPTER 23

Joshua's Final Plea. [1] Many years later, after the LORD had given the Israelites rest from all their enemies round about them, and when Joshua was old and advanced in years,[v] [2] he summoned all Israel (including their elders, leaders, judges and officers) and said to them: "I am old and advanced in years. [3] You have seen all that the LORD, your God, has done for you against all these nations; for it has been the LORD, your God, himself who fought for you. [4] *w* Bear in mind that I have apportioned among your tribes as their heritage the nations that survive [as well as those I destroyed] between the Jordan and the Great Sea in the west. [5] The LORD, your God, will drive them out and dislodge them at your approach, so that you will take possession of their land as the LORD, your God, promised you. [6] Therefore strive hard to observe and carry out all that is written in the book of the law of Moses, not straying from it in any way, *x* [7] or mingling with these nations while they survive among you. You must not invoke their gods, or swear by them, or serve them, or worship them, *y* [8] but you must remain loyal to the LORD, your God, as you have been to this day. [9] At your approach the LORD has driven out large and strong nations, and to this day no one has withstood you. [10] One of you puts to flight a thousand, because it is the LORD, your God, himself who fights for you, *z* as he promised you. [11] Take great care, however, to love the LORD, your God. [12] For if you ever abandon him and ally yourselves with the remnant of these nations while they survive among you, by intermarrying and intermingling with them, *a* [13] know for certain that the LORD, your God, will no longer drive these nations out of your way. Instead they will be a snare and a trap for you, a scourge for your sides and thorns for your eyes, until you perish from this good land which the LORD, your God, has given you.

[14] "Today, as you see, I am going the way of all men.* So now acknowledge with your whole heart and soul that not one of all the promises the LORD, your God, made to you has remained unfulfilled. Every promise has been fulfilled for you, with not one single exception. [15] *b* But just as every promise the LORD, your God, made to you has been fulfilled for you, so will he fulfill every threat,* even so far as to exterminate you from this good land which the LORD, your God, has given you. [16] If you transgress the covenant of the LORD, your God, which he enjoined on you, serve other gods and worship them, the anger of the LORD will flare up against you and you will quickly perish from the good land which he has given you."

CHAPTER 24

Reminder of the Divine Goodness. [1] Joshua gathered together all the tribes of Israel at Shechem, summoning their elders, their leaders, their judges and their officers. When they stood in ranks before God, [2] Joshua addressed all the people: "Thus says the LORD, the God of Israel: In times past your fathers, down to Terah, *c* father of Abraham and Nahor, dwelt beyond the River* and served other gods. [3] But I brought your father Abraham from the region beyond the River and led him through the entire land of Canaan. *d* I made his descendants numerous, and gave him Isaac. [4] To Isaac I gave Jacob and Esau. *e* To Esau I assigned the mountain region of Seir in which to settle, while Jacob and his children went down to Egypt.

[5] "Then I sent Moses and Aaron, and smote Egypt with the prodigies which I wrought in her midst. *f* [6] Afterward I led you out of Egypt, and when you reached the sea, the Egyptians pursued your fathers to the Red Sea with chariots and horsemen. *g* [7] Because they cried out to the LORD, *h* he put darkness between your people and the Egyptians, upon whom he brought the sea so that it engulfed them. After you witnessed what I did to Egypt, and dwelt a long time in the desert, [8] *i* I brought you into the land of the Amorites who lived east of the Jordan. They fought against you, but I delivered them into your power. You took possession of their land, and I destroyed them [the two kings of the Amorites] before you. [9] *j* Then Balak, son of Zippor, king of Moab, prepared to war against Israel. He summoned Balaam, son of Beor, to curse you; [10] *k* but I would not listen to Balaam. On the contrary, he had to bless you, and I saved you from him. [11] Once you crossed the Jordan *l* and came to Jericho, the

w Jos 13, 2-7; 14, 2; 18, 10; Ps 78, 55.—x Jos 1, 7.—y Dt 7, 2ff.—z Ex 14, 14; Lv 26, 8; Dt 3, 22.—a Ex 34, 16; Dt 7, 3.—b Lv 26, 14-39; Dt 28, 15-68.—c Gn 11, 26. 31; 31, 53.—d Gn 12, 1; Acts 7, 2-4.—e Gn 25, 24ff; 36, 8; 46, 1. 6; Acts 7, 15.—f Ex 3, 10; 7, 14—12, 30.—g Ex 12, 37. 51; 14, 9.—h Ex 14, 10. 20. 27f.—i Nm 21, 21-35.—j Nm 22, 2-5.—k Nm 23, 1—24, 25.—l Jos 3, 14; 6, 1.

23, 14: *Going the way of all men:* drawing near to death, the inevitable goal of all; cf 1 Kgs 2, 1f.
23, 15: *Every threat:* mentioned especially in Dt 28, 15-68.
24, 2: *Beyond the River:* east of the Euphrates; cf Gn 11, 28-31.

men of Jericho fought against you, but I delivered them also into your power. [12] And I sent the hornets* ahead of you which drove them [the Amorites, Perizzites, Canaanites, Hittites, Girgashites, Hivites and Jebusites] out of your way; it was not your sword or your bow.*m*

[13] "I gave you a land which you had not tilled and cities which you had not built, to dwell in; you have eaten of vineyards and olive groves which you did not plant.*n*

[14] *o* "Now, therefore, fear the LORD and serve him completely and sincerely. Cast out the gods your fathers served beyond the River and in Egypt, and serve the LORD. [15] *p* If it does not please you to serve the LORD, decide today whom you will serve, the gods your fathers served* beyond the River or the gods of the Amorites in whose country you are dwelling. As for me and my household, we will serve the LORD."

Renewal of the Covenant. [16] But the people answered, "Far be it from us to forsake the LORD for the service of other gods. [17] For it was the LORD, our God, who brought us and our fathers up out of the land of Egypt, out of a state of slavery. He performed those great miracles before our very eyes and protected us along our entire journey and among all the peoples through whom we passed. [18] At our approach the LORD drove out [all the peoples, including] the Amorites who dwelt in the land. Therefore we also will serve the LORD, for he is our God."

[19] Joshua in turn said to the people,

---

m Jos 11, 20; Ex 23, 28; Dt 7, 20.—n Dt 6, 10f.—o Dt 10, 12; 1 Sm 7, 3; 12, 24; Tb 14, 9.—p Dt 30, 15-19.—q Ex 20, 5; 23, 21; 34, 14; Lv 19, 2.—r Gn 28, 18; 31, 45; Jgs 9, 6.—s Gn 31, 48. 52; Dt 31, 19. 21. 26.—t Jgs 2, 6.—u 29ff: Jgs 2, 7ff.—y Jos 19, 50; Jgs 2, 9.—w Gn 33, 19; 50, 24; Ex 13, 19.—x Jos 22, 13.

24, 12: *The hornets:* see note on Ex 23, 28.

24, 15: *The gods your fathers served:* Abraham's ancestors were polytheists.

24, 19: *You may not be able:* fidelity to God's service is not easy, and therefore those who take such solemn obligations on themselves must be ever vigilant against human weakness.

24, 32: *The bones of Joseph:* the mummified body of Joseph (Gn 50, 25f), which the Israelites took with them as they left Egypt (Ex 13, 19), was fittingly buried at the ancient city of Shechem, near the border between the two Josephite tribes of Ephraim and Manasseh.

"You may not be able* to serve the LORD, for he is a holy God; he is a jealous God*q* who will not forgive your transgressions or your sins. [20] If, after the good he has done for you, you forsake the LORD and serve strange gods, he will do evil to you and destroy you."

[21] But the people answered Joshua, "We will still serve the LORD." [22] Joshua therefore said to the people, "You are your own witnesses that you have chosen to serve the LORD." They replied, "We are, indeed!" [23] "Now, therefore, put away the strange gods that are among you and turn your hearts to the LORD, the God of Israel." [24] Then the people promised Joshua, "We will serve the LORD, our God, and obey his voice."

[25] So Joshua made a covenant with the people that day and made statutes and ordinances for them at Shechem, [26] which he recorded in the book of the law of God. Then he took a large stone and set it up there under the oak that was in the sanctuary of the LORD.*r* [27] And Joshua said to all the people, "This stone shall be our witness,*s* for it has heard all the words which the LORD spoke to us. It shall be a witness against you, should you wish to deny your God." [28] Then Joshua dismissed the people, each to his own heritage.*t*

Death of Joshua. [29] *u* After these events, Joshua, son of Nun, servant of the LORD, died at the age of a hundred and ten. [30] He was buried within the limits of his heritage at Timnath-serah*v* in the mountain region of Ephraim north of Mount Gaash. [31] Israel served the LORD during the entire lifetime of Joshua and that of the elders who outlived Joshua and knew all that the LORD had done for Israel. [32] *w* The bones of Joseph,* which the Israelites had brought up from Egypt, were buried in Shechem in the plot of ground Jacob had bought from the sons of Hamor, father of Shechem, for a hundred pieces of money. This was a heritage of the descendants of Joseph. [33] When Eleazar, son of Aaron, also died, he was buried on the hill which had been given to his son Phinehas*x* in the mountain region of Ephraim.

THE BOOK OF JUDGES

The Book of Judges derives its title from the twelve heroes of Israel whose deeds it records. They were not magistrates, but military leaders sent by God to aid and to relieve his people in time of external danger. They exercised their activities in the interval of time between the death of Joshua and the institution of the monarchy in Israel. Six of them—Othniel, Ehud, Barak, Gideon, Jephthah and Samson—are treated in some detail and have accordingly been styled the Major Judges. The other six, of whose activities this book preserves but a summary record, are called the Minor Judges. There were two other judges, whose judgeships are described in 1 Samuel—Eli and Samuel, who seem to have ruled the entire nation of Israel just before the institution of the monarchy. The twelve judges of the present book, however, very probably exercised their authority, sometimes simultaneously, over one or another tribe of Israel, never over the entire nation.

The purpose of the book is to show that the fortunes of Israel depended upon the obedience or disobedience of the people to God's law. Whenever they rebelled against him, they were oppressed by pagan nations; when they repented, he raised up judges to deliver them (cf Jgs 2, 10-23).

The accounts of various events, whether written shortly after their occurrence or orally transmitted, were later skillfully unified according to the moral purpose of the redactor sometime during the Israelite monarchy.

The book is divided as follows: I. Palestine after the Death of Joshua (Jgs 1, 1—3, 6). II. Stories of the Judges (Jgs 3, 7—16, 31), III. The Tribes of Dan and Benjamin in the Days of the Judges (Jgs 17, 1—21, 25).

I: PALESTINE AFTER THE DEATH OF JOSHUA

CHAPTER 1

Pagan Survivors in Palestine. ¹After the death of Joshua* the Israelites consulted the LORD, asking, "Who shall be first among us to attack the Canaanites and to do battle with them?"ᵃ ²The LORD answered, "Judah shall attack: I have delivered the land into his power." ³Judah then said to his brother Simeon, "Come up with me into the territory allotted to me, and let us engage the Canaanites in battle. I will likewise accompany you into the territory allotted to you." So Simeon went with him.

⁴When the forces of Judah attacked, the LORD delivered the Canaanites and Perizzites into their power, and they slew ten thousand of them in Bezek. ⁵It was in Bezek that they came upon Adonibezek and fought against him. When they defeated the Canaanites and Perizzites, ⁶Adonibezek fled. They set out in pursuit, and when they caught him, cut off his thumbs and his big toes. ⁷At this Adonibezek said, "Seventy kings, with their thumbs and big toes cut off, used to pick up scraps under my table. As I have done, so has God repaid me." He was brought to Jerusalem, and there he died. ⁸[The Judahites fought against Jerusalem and captured it, putting it to the sword; then they destroyed the city by fire.]

⁹ ᵇ Afterward the Judahites went down to fight against the Canaanites who lived in the mountain region, in the Negeb, and in the foothills. ¹⁰ ᶜ Judah also marched against the Canaanites who dwelt in Hebron, which was formerly called Kiriath-arba, and defeated Sheshai, Ahiman and Talmai.ᵈ ¹¹From there they marched against the inhabitants of Debir, which was formerly called Kiriath-sepher. ¹²And Caleb said, "I will give my daughter Achsah in marriage to the one who attacks Kiriath-sepher and captures it." ¹³ ᵉ Othniel, son of Caleb's younger brother Kenaz, captured it; so Caleb gave him his daughter Achsah in marriage. ¹⁴On the day of her marriage to Othniel she induced him to ask her father for some land. Then, as she alighted from the ass, Caleb asked her, "What is troubling you?" ¹⁵"Give me an additional gift," she answered. "Since you have assigned land in the Negeb to me, give me also pools of water." So Caleb gave her the upper and the lower pool. ¹⁶The descendants of the Kenite, Moses' father-in-law,* came up with the Judahites

a Jgs 20, 18.—Nm 27, 21.—b Jos 10, 40; 11, 16; 12, 8.—c Jos 15, 13-19.—d Nm 13, 22; Jos 14, 15.—e Jgs 3, 9.

1, 1-36: This chapter summarizes events most of which occurred shortly after the death of Joshua. Perhaps because they were planned and inaugurated by him, they are also attributed to him in the last half of the preceding book (Jos 14—22).

1, 16: *Moses' father-in-law:* Reuel; cf Nm 10, 29-32 and note. *City of palms:* Jericho (cf Dt 34, 3) or a town in the Negeb.

236

from the city of palms to the desert at Arad [which is in the Negeb]. But they later left and settled among the Amalekites.ᶠ
17 ᵍ Judah then went with his brother Simeon, and they defeated the Canaanites who dwelt in Zephath. After having doomed the city to destruction, they renamed it Hormah. 18 ʰ Judah, however, did not occupy Gaza with its territory, Ashkelon with its territory, or Ekron with its territory. 19 ⁱ Since the LORD was with Judah, he gained possession of the mountain region. Yet he could not dislodge those who lived on the plain, because they had iron chariots. 20 As Moses had commanded, Hebron was given to Caleb, who then drove from it the three sons of Anak.ʲ
21 * The Benjaminites did not dislodge the Jebusites who dwelt in Jerusalem, with the result that the Jebusites live in Jerusalem beside the Benjaminites to the present day.ᵏ
22 The house of Joseph, too, marched up against Bethel, and the LORD was with them. 23 The house of Joseph had a reconnaissance made of Bethel, which formerly was called Luz.ˡ 24 The scouts saw a man coming out of the city and said to him, "Show us a way into the city, and we will spare you." 25 He showed them a way into the city, which they then put to the sword; but they let the man and his whole clan go free. 26 He then went to the land of the Hittites, where he built a city and called it Luz, as it is still called.
27 Manasseh did not take possession of Beth-shean with its towns or of Taanach with its towns. Neither did he dislodge the inhabitants of Dor and its towns, those of Ibleam and its towns, or those of Megiddo and its towns.ᵐ The Canaanites kept their hold in this district. 28 When the Israelites grew stronger, they impressed the Canaanites as laborers, but did not drive them out. 29 Similarly, the Ephraimites did not drive out the Canaanites living in Gezer, and so the Canaanites live in Gezer in their midst.ⁿ

30 Zebulun did not dislodge the inhabitants of Kitron or those of Nahalol; the Canaanites live among them, but have become forced laborers.
31 ᵒ Nor did Asher drive out the inhabitants of Acco or those of Sidon, or take possession of Mahaleb, Achzib, Helbah, Aphik or Rehob. 32 The Asherites live among the Canaanite natives of the land, whom they have not dislodged.
33 ᵖ Naphtali did not drive out the inhabitants of Beth-shemesh or those of Beth-anath, and so they live among the Canaanite natives of the land. However, the inhabitants of Beth-shemesh and Beth-anath have become forced laborers for them.
34 The Amorites hemmed in the Danites in the mountain region, not permitting them to go down into the plain.�q 35 The Amorites had a firm hold in Harheres, Aijalon and Shaalbim, but as the house of Joseph gained the upper hand, they were impressed as laborers.
36 The territory of the Amorites extended from the Akrabbim pass to Sela and beyond.

CHAPTER 2

Infidelities of the Israelites. 1 ʳ An angel of the LORD went up from Gilgal to Bochim and said, "It was I who brought you up from Egypt and led you into the land which I promised on oath to your fathers. I said that I would never break my covenant with you, 2 but that you were not to make a pact with the inhabitants of this land, and you were to pull down their altars. Yet you have not obeyed me.ˢ What did you mean by this? 3 For now I tell you, I will not clear them out of your way; they shall oppose you and their gods shall become a snare for you."ᵗ
4 When the angel of the LORD had made these threats to all the Israelites, the people wept aloud; 5 and so that place came to be called Bochim.* They offered sacrifice there to the LORD.
6 ᵘ When Joshua dismissed the people, each Israelite went to take possession of his own hereditary land. 7 The people served the LORD during the entire lifetime of Joshua, and of those elders who outlived Joshua and who had seen all the great work which the LORD had done for Israel. 8 Joshua, son of Nun, the servant of the LORD, was a hundred and ten years old when he died; 9 and they buried him

Jgs

---

f Jgs 4, 11; Nm 10, 29-32.—g Nm 21, 3.—h Jos 11, 22.—i Jos 17, 16ff.—j Jos 14, 9. 13; 15, 14.—k Jos 15, 63.—l Gn 28, 19; 35, 6; 48, 3; Jos 18, 13.—m 27f: Jos 17, 11ff.—n Jos 16, 10.—o 31f: Jos 19, 24-31.—p Jos 19, 32-39.—q Jos 19, 47f.—r 1ff: Jgs 6, 8ff.—s Ex 34, 12f. 15; Dt 7, 2. 5; 12, 2f.—t Nm 33, 55; Jos 23, 13.—u 6-9: Jos 24, 28-31.

1, 21: According to Jos 18, 16, Jerusalem was assigned to the tribe of Benjamin. But it was not actually taken from the Jebusites until David captured it (2 Sm 5, 6-9) and made it his capital, outside the tribal organization.

2, 5: *Bochim:* the Hebrew word for "weepers."

within the borders of his heritage at Timnath-heres in the mountain region of Ephraim north of Mount Gaash.[v]

10 But once the rest of that generation were gathered to their fathers, and a later generation arose that did not know the LORD, or what he had done for Israel, 11 the Israelites offended the LORD by serving the Baals.*[w] 12 Abandoning the LORD, the God of their fathers, who had led them out of the land of Egypt, they followed the other gods of the various nations around them, and by their worship of these gods provoked the LORD. 13 Because they had thus abandoned him and served Baal and the Ashtaroth,* 14 the anger of the LORD flared up against Israel, and he delivered them over to plunderers who despoiled them. He allowed them to fall into the power of their enemies round about whom they were no longer able to withstand. 15 Whatever they undertook, the LORD turned into disaster for them, as in his warning he had sworn he would do, till they were in great distress.[x] 16 Even when the LORD raised up judges to deliver them from the power of their despoilers, 17 they did not listen to their judges, but abandoned themselves to the worship of other gods. They were quick to stray from the way their fathers had taken, and did not follow their example of obedience to the commandments of the LORD. 18 Whenever the LORD raised up judges for them, he would be with the judge and save them from the power of their enemies as long as the judge lived; it was thus the LORD took pity on their distressful cries of affliction under their oppressors. 19 But when the judge died, they would relapse and do worse than their fathers, following other gods in service and worship, relinquishing none of their evil practices or stubborn conduct.[y]

20 [z] In his anger toward Israel the LORD said, "Inasmuch as this nation has violated my covenant which I enjoined on their fathers, and has disobeyed me, 21 I for my part will not clear away for them any more of the nations which Joshua left when he died." 22 Through these nations the Israelites were to be made to prove whether or not they would keep to the way of the LORD and continue in it as their fathers had done; 23 therefore the LORD allowed them to remain instead of expelling them immediately, or delivering them into the power of Israel.

CHAPTER 3

1 The following are the nations which the LORD allowed to remain, so that through them he might try all those Israelites who had no experience of the battles with Canaan 2 [just to instruct, by training them in battle, those generations only of the Israelites who would not have had that previous experience]: 3 [a] the five lords of the Philistines;* and all the Canaanites, the Sidonians, and the Hivites who dwell in the mountain region of Lebanon between Baal-hermon and the entrance to Hamath. 4 These served to put Israel to the test, to determine whether they would obey the commandments the LORD had enjoined on their fathers through Moses. 5 Besides, the Israelites were living among the Canaanites, Hittites, Amorites, Perizzites, Hivites and Jebusites. 6 In fact, they took their daughters in marriage, and gave their own daughters to their sons in marriage, and served their gods.

II: STORIES OF THE JUDGES

Othniel. 7 [b] Because the Israelites had offended the LORD by forgetting the LORD, their God, and serving the Baals and the Asherahs,* 8 the anger of the LORD flared up against them, and he allowed them to fall into the power of Cushan-rishathaim, king of Aram Naharaim, whom they served for eight years. 9 But when the Israelites cried out to the LORD, he raised up for them a savior, Othniel, son of Caleb's younger brother Kenaz, who rescued them. 10 The spirit of the LORD came upon him, and he judged Israel.[c] When he went out to war, the LORD delivered Cushan-rishathaim, king of Aram, into his power, so that he made him subject.

v Jos 19, 50.—w 11. 14: Jgs 3, 7f; 4, 1f; 6, 1; 10, 6f; 13, 1.—x Dt 28, 15-68.—y Jgs 3, 12; 4, 1; 6, 1; 8, 33.—z 20f: Jos 23, 16.—a Jos 13, 2-6.—b Jgs 2, 11ff.—c Jgs 6, 34; 11, 29; 13, 25; 14, 6. 19; 15, 14.

2, 11: *Baals:* the chief god of the Canaanites and the Phoenicians was called "Baal," a word meaning "lord." He was honored by various titles, hence the plural form here, equivalent to "the pagan gods."

2, 13: *Ashtaroth:* the Canaanite Phoenician goddess of love and fertility was Astarte. The plural form used here refers to her various titles and images and is equivalent to "goddesses."

3, 3: *The Philistines:* non-Semitic invaders, who gave their name to all Palestine, although they occupied only its southwestern plains. Their confederation embraced the five leading cities of Gaza, Ashkelon, Ashdod, Gath and Ekron.

3, 7: *Asherahs:* elsewhere rendered "sacred poles." See note on Ex 34, 13 and on Dt 7, 5. Here the word seems to mean "goddesses."

¹¹ The land then was at rest for forty years,*d* until Othniel, son of Kenaz, died.

Ehud. ¹² Again the Israelites offended the LORD, who because of this offense strengthened Eglon, king of Moab, against Israel. ¹³ In alliance with the Ammonites and Amalekites, he attacked and defeated Israel, taking possession of the city of palms. ¹⁴ The Israelites then served Eglon, king of Moab, for eighteen years.

¹⁵ But when the Israelites cried out to the LORD, he raised up for them a savior, the Benjaminite Ehud, son of Gera, who was left-handed. It was by him that the Israelites sent their tribute to Eglon, king of Moab. ¹⁶ Ehud made himself a two-edged dagger a foot long, and wore it under his clothes over his right thigh. ¹⁷ He presented the tribute to Eglon, king of Moab, who was very fat, ¹⁸ and after the presentation went off with the tribute bearers. ¹⁹ He returned, however, from where the idols are, near Gilgal, and said, "I have a private message for you, O king." And the king said, "Silence!" Then when all his attendants had left his presence, ²⁰ and Ehud went in to him where he sat alone in his cool upper room, Ehud said, "I have a message from God for you." So the king rose from his chair, ²¹ and then Ehud with his left hand drew the dagger from his right thigh, and thrust it into Eglon's belly. ²² The hilt also went in after the blade, and the fat closed over the blade because he did not withdraw the dagger from his body.

²³ Then Ehud went out into the hall, shutting the doors of the upper room on him and locking them. ²⁴ When Ehud had left and the servants came, they saw that the doors of the upper room were locked, and thought, "He must be easing himself in the cool chamber." ²⁵ They waited until they finally grew suspicious. Since he did not open the doors of the upper room, they took the key and opened them. There on the floor, dead, lay their lord!

²⁶ During their delay Ehud made good his escape and, passing the idols, took refuge in Seirah. ²⁷ On his arrival he sounded the horn in the mountain region of Ephraim, and the Israelites went down from the mountains with him as their leader. ²⁸ "Follow me," he said to them, "for the LORD has delivered your enemies the Moabites into your power." So they followed him down and seized the fords of the Jordan leading to Moab, permitting no one to cross. *e* ²⁹ On that occasion they slew about ten thousand Moabites, all of them strong and valiant men. Not a man escaped. ³⁰ Thus was Moab brought under the power of Israel at that time; and the land had rest for eighty years.

Shamgar. ³¹ After him there was Shamgar, son of Anath, who slew six hundred Philistines with an oxgoad. He, too, rescued Israel.

CHAPTER 4

Deborah and Barak. ¹ After Ehud's death, however, the Israelites again offended the LORD. ² So the LORD allowed them to fall into the power of the Canaanite king, Jabin, who reigned in Hazor.*f* The general of his army was Sisera, who dwelt in Harosheth-ha-goiim. ³ But the Israelites cried out to the LORD; for with his nine hundred iron chariots he sorely oppressed the Israelites for twenty years.

⁴ At this time the prophetess Deborah, wife of Lappidoth, was judging Israel. ⁵ She used to sit under Deborah's palm tree, situated between Ramah and Bethel in the mountain region of Ephraim, and there the Israelites came up to her for judgment. ⁶ She sent and summoned Barak, son of Abinoam,*g* from Kedesh of Naphtali. "This is what the LORD, the God of Israel, commands," she said to him; "go, march on Mount Tabor, and take with you ten thousand Naphtalites and Zebulunites. ⁷ I will lead Sisera, the general of Jabin's army, out to you at the Wadi Kishon,*h* together with his chariots and troops, and will deliver them into your power." ⁸ But Barak answered her, "If you come with me, I will go; if you do not come with me, I will not go." ⁹ "I will certainly go with you," she replied, "but you shall not gain the glory in the expedition on which you are setting out, for the LORD will have Sisera fall into the power of a woman." So Deborah joined Barak and journeyed with him to Kedesh.

¹⁰ Barak summoned Zebulun and Naphtali to Kedesh, and ten thousand men followed him. Deborah also went up with him.*i* ¹¹ * Now the Kenite Heber had de-

---

d Jgs 5, 31; 8, 28.—e Jgs 4, 7. 14; 7, 9. 15.—f Jos 11, 1. 10; Ps 83, 10; 1 Sm 12, 9.—g Heb 11, 32.—h Jgs 5, 21; Ps 83, 10.— i Jgs 5, 18.

4, 11: Most of the Kenites occupied a district in the southern part of Judah (Jgs 1, 16). A group of them, however, had detached themselves and settled in lower Galilee.

Jgs

tached himself from his own people, the descendants of Hobab, Moses' brother-in-law,[j] and had pitched his tent by the terebinth of Zaanannim, which was near Kedesh. [12] It was reported to Sisera that Barak, son of Abinoam, had gone up to Mount Tabor. [13] So Sisera assembled from Harosheth-ha-goiim at the Wadi Kishon all nine hundred of his iron chariots and all his forces. [14] Deborah then said to Barak, "Be off, for this is the day on which the LORD has delivered Sisera into your power. The LORD marches before you." So Barak went down Mount Tabor, followed by his ten thousand men. [15] And the LORD put Sisera[k] and all his chariots and all his forces to rout before Barak. Sisera himself dismounted from his chariot and fled on foot. [16] Barak, however, pursued the chariots and the army as far as Harosheth-ha-goiim. The entire army of Sisera fell beneath the sword, not even one man surviving.

[17] * Sisera, in the meantime, had fled on foot to the tent of Jael, wife of the Kenite Heber, since Jabin, king of Hazor, and the family of the Kenite Heber were at peace with one another. [18] Jael went out to meet Sisera and said to him, "Come in, my lord, come in with me; do not be afraid." So he went into her tent, and she covered him with a rug. [19] He said to her, "Please give me a little water to drink. I am thirsty." But she opened a jug of milk for him to drink, and then covered him over.[l] [20] "Stand at the entrance of the tent," he said to her. "If anyone comes and asks, 'Is there someone here?' say, 'No!' " [21] Instead Jael, wife of Heber, got a tent peg and took a mallet in her hand. While Sisera was sound asleep, she stealthily approached him and drove the peg through his temple down into the ground, so that he perished in death.[m] [22] Then when Barak came in pursuit of Sisera, Jael went out to meet him and said to him, "Come, I will show you the man you seek." So he went in with her, and there lay Sisera dead, with the tent peg through his temple.

[23] Thus on that day God humbled the Canaanite king, Jabin, before the Israelites; [24] their power weighed ever heavier upon him, till at length they destroyed the Canaanite king, Jabin.

CHAPTER 5

Canticle of Deborah. [1] On that day Deborah [and Barak, son of Abinoam] sang this song:

[2] Of chiefs who took the lead in Israel,*
     of noble deeds by the people who
         bless the LORD,
[3] Hear, O kings! Give ear, O princes!
     I to the LORD will sing my song,
     my hymn to the LORD, the God of
         Israel.
[4] O LORD, when you went out from Seir,
     when you marched from the land of
         Edom,
     The earth quaked and the heavens were
         shaken,
     while the clouds sent down showers.
[5] Mountains trembled
     in the presence of the LORD, the One
         of Sinai,[n]
     in the presence of the LORD, the God
         of Israel.[o]
[6] In the days of Shamgar, son of Anath,[p]
     in the days of slavery caravans ceased;
     Those who traveled the roads
     went by roundabout paths.
[7] Gone was freedom beyond the walls,
     gone indeed from Israel.
     When I, Deborah, rose,
     when I rose, a mother in Israel,
[8] New gods* were their choice;
     then the war was at their gates.
     Not a shield could be seen, nor a lance,
     among forty thousand in Israel!
[9] My heart is with the leaders of Israel,
     nobles of the people who bless the
         LORD;
[10] They who ride on white asses,
     seated on saddlecloths as they go
         their way;
[11] Sing of them to the strains of the harpers at the wells,
     where men recount the just deeds of
         the LORD,
     his just deeds that brought freedom
         to Israel.

j Nm 10, 29.—k Ps 83, 10.—l Jgs 5, 25.—m Jgs 5, 26.—n Dt 33, 2; 2 Sm 22, 8; Pss 18, 8; 68, 9.—o Ex 19, 16; Dt 4, 11; Ps 97, 5.—p Jgs 5, 31.

4, 17-22: It is to be noted that the sacred author merely records the fact of the murder of Sisera. We must not construe this as approval of Jael's action.

5, 2-31: This canticle is an excellent example of early Hebrew poetry, even though some of its verses are now obscure.

5, 8: *New gods:* pagan deities; cf Dt 32, 16-18. God punished the idolatry of the Israelites by leaving them relatively unarmed before the attacks of their enemies, who had better weapons, made of iron; cf 1 Sm 13, 19-22.

¹² Awake, awake, Deborah!
    awake, awake, strike up a song.
  Strength! arise, Barak,
    make despoilers your spoil, son of
    Abinoam.
¹³ Then down came the fugitives with the
    mighty,
    the people of the LORD came down
    for me as warriors.
¹⁴ From Ephraim, princes were in the val-
    ley;*
    behind you was Benjamin, among
    your troops.
  From Machir came down commanders,
    from Zebulun wielders of the mar-
    shal's staff.
¹⁵ With Deborah were the princes of Is-
    sachar;
    Barak, too, was in the valley, his
    course unchecked.
  Among the clans of Reuben
    great were the searchings of heart.[q]
¹⁶ Why do you stay beside your hearths
    listening to the lowing of the herds?
  Among the clans of Reuben
    great were the searchings of heart!
¹⁷ Gilead, beyond the Jordan, rests;
    why does Dan spend his time in ships?
  Asher, who dwells along the shore,
    is resting in his coves.
¹⁸ Zebulun is the people defying death;
    Naphtali, too, on the open heights![r]
¹⁹ The kings came and fought;
    then they fought, those kings of Ca-
    naan,
  At Taanach by the waters of Megiddo;
    no silver booty did they take.[s]
²⁰ From the heavens the stars, too,
    fought;*
    from their courses they fought
    against Sisera.[t]
²¹ The Wadi Kishon swept them away;
    a wadi . . . , the Kishon.[u]
²² Then the hoofs of the horses pounded,
    with the dashing, dashing of his
    steeds.

---

q Jgs 4, 14.—r Jgs 4, 10.—s Jgs 1, 27; Jos 17, 11.—t Jgs 4,
15; Jos 10, 14.—u Jgs 4, 7. 13.—v Jgs 4, 17; Jdt 13, 17; Lk 1,
28. 42.—w 25f: Jgs 4, 19. 21.—x Ps 83, 10-19.—y 3f: Jgs 7, 12;
Dt 28, 30ff.

5, 14-22: Praise for the tribes which formed the Israelite
league against Sisera: Ephraim, Benjamin, Manasseh (represented by Machir), Zebulun, Issachar, and Naphtali (led by
Barak). The tribes of Reuben, Gad (Gilead), Dan, and Asher are
chided for their lack of cooperation. The more distant tribes of
Judah and Simeon are not mentioned.

5, 20f: It would seem that nature aided the Hebrews in some
way. Perhaps the torrential rains swelled the waters of Kishon,
which then overwhelmed the Canaanites.

5, 23: *Meroz:* an unknown locality in which Hebrews probably
resided, since its inhabitants are cursed for their failure to proffer
aid.

²³ "Curse Meroz,"* says the LORD,
    "hurl a curse at its inhabitants!
  For they came not to my help,
    as warriors to the help of the LORD."
²⁴ Blessed among women be Jael,
    blessed among tent-dwelling women.[v]
²⁵ He asked for water, she gave him
    milk;[w]
    in a princely bowl she offered curds.
²⁶ With her left hand she reached for the
    peg,
    with her right, for the workman's
    mallet.
  She hammered Sisera, crushed his
    head;
    she smashed, stove in his temple.
²⁷ At her feet he sank down, fell, lay still;
    down at her feet he sank and fell;
    where he sank down, there he fell,
    slain.
²⁸ From the window peered down and
    wailed
    the mother of Sisera, from the lat-
    tice:
  "Why is his chariot so long in coming?
    why are the hoofbeats of his chariots
    delayed?"
²⁹ The wisest of her princesses answers
    her,
    and she, too, keeps answering her-
    self:
³⁰ "They must be dividing the spoil they
    took:
    there must be a damsel or two for
    each man,
  Spoils of dyed cloth as Sisera's spoil,
    an ornate shawl or two for me in the
    spoil."
³¹ May all your enemies perish thus, O
    LORD![x]
    but your friends be as the sun rising
    in its might!*

  And the land was at rest for forty years.

CHAPTER 6

The Call of Gideon. ¹The Israelites offended the LORD, who therefore delivered
them into the power of Midian for seven
years, ²so that Midian held Israel subject.
For fear of Midian the Israelites established the fire signals on the mountains,
the caves for refuge, and the strongholds.
³And it used to be that when the Israelites
had completed their sowing, Midian,
Amalek and the Kedemites would come
up,[y] ⁴encamp opposite them, and destroy
the produce of the land as far as the out-

skirts of Gaza, leaving no sustenance in Israel, nor sheep, oxen or asses. ⁵For they would come up with their livestock, and their tents would become as numerous as locusts; and neither they nor their camels could be numbered, when they came into the land to lay it waste. ⁶Thus was Israel reduced to misery by Midian, and so the Israelites cried out to the LORD.

⁷When Israel cried out to the LORD because of Midian, ⁸ ᶻ he sent a prophet to the Israelites who said to them, "The LORD, the God of Israel, says: I led you up from Egypt; I brought you out of the place of slavery. ⁹I rescued you from the power of Egypt and of all your other oppressors. I drove them out before you and gave you their land. ¹⁰And I said to you: I, the LORD, am your God; you shall not venerate the gods of the Amorites in whose land you are dwelling. But you did not obey me."

¹¹Then the angel of the LORD came and sat under the terebinth in Ophrah that belonged to Joash the Abiezrite. While his son Gideon was beating out wheat in the wine press to save it from the Midianites, ¹²the angel of the LORD appeared to him and said, "The LORD is with you, O champion!" ¹³"My lord," Gideon said to him, "if the LORD is with us, why has all this happened to us? Where are his wondrous deeds of which our fathers told us when they said, 'Did not the LORD bring us up from Egypt?' For now the LORD has abandoned us and has delivered us into the power of Midian." ¹⁴The LORD turned to him and said, "Go with the strength you have and save Israel from the power of Midian. It is I who send you." ¹⁵But he answered him, "Please, my lord, how can I save Israel? My family is the meanest in Manasseh, and I am the most insignificant in my father's house." ¹⁶"I shall be with you," the LORD said to him, "and you will cut down Midian to the last man." ¹⁷He answered him, "If I find favor with you, give me a sign that you are speaking with me. ¹⁸Do not depart from here, I pray you, until I come back to you and bring out my offering and set it before you." He answered, "I will await your return."

¹⁹So Gideon went off and prepared a kid and an ephah of flour in the form of unleavened cakes. Putting the meat in a basket and the broth in a pot, he brought them out to him under the terebinth and presented them. ²⁰The angel of God said to him, "Take the meat and unleavened cakes and lay them on this rock; then pour out the broth."ᵃ When he had done so, ²¹the angel of the LORD stretched out the tip of the staff he held, and touched the meat and unleavened cakes. Thereupon a fire came up from the rock which consumed the meat and unleavened cakes, and the angel of the LORD disappeared from sight. ²² ᵇ Gideon, now aware that it had been the angel of the LORD, said, "Alas, Lord GOD, that I have seen the angel of the LORD face to face!" ²³The LORD answered him, "Be calm, do not fear. You shall not die." ²⁴So Gideon built there an altar to the LORD and called it Yahweh-shalom.* To this day it is still in Ophrah of the Abiezrites.

²⁵That same night the LORD said to him, "Take the seven-year-old spare bullock and destroy your father's altar to Baal and cut down the sacred pole* that is by it. ²⁶You shall build, instead, the proper kind of altar to the LORD, your God, on top of this stronghold. Then take the spare bullock and offer it as a holocaust on the wood from the sacred pole you have cut down." ²⁷So Gideon took ten of his servants and did as the LORD had commanded him. But through fear of his family and of the townspeople, he would not do it by day, but did it at night. ²⁸Early the next morning the townspeople found that the altar of Baal had been destroyed, the sacred pole near it cut down, and the spare bullock offered on the altar that was built. ²⁹They asked one another, "Who did this?" Their inquiry led them to the conclusion that Gideon, son of Joash, had done it. ³⁰So the townspeople said to Joash, "Bring out your son that he may die, for he has destroyed the altar of Baal and has cut down the sacred pole that was near it." ³¹But Joash replied to all who were standing around him, "Do you intend to act in Baal's stead, or be his champion? If anyone acts for him, he shall be put to death by morning. If he whose altar has been destroyed is a god, let him act for himself!" ³²So on that day Gideon was called Jerubbaal,* because of the words,

---

z 8ff: Jgs 2, 1f; 10, 11-14.—a Jgs 13, 19.—b 22f: Gn 32, 31; Dt 5, 24ff.

6, 24: *Yahweh-shalom:* Hebrew for "the LORD is peace," a reference to the Lord's words, "Be calm," literally, "Peace be to you!"

6, 25: *The sacred pole:* see note on Ex 34, 13.

6, 32: *Jerubbaal:* similar in sound to the Hebrew words meaning, "Let Baal take action."

"Let Baal take action against him, since he destroyed his altar."[c]

[33] Then all Midian and Amalek and the Kedemites mustered and crossed over into the valley of Jezreel, where they encamped. [34] The spirit of the Lord enveloped Gideon; he blew the horn that summoned Abiezer to follow him. [35] He sent messengers, too, throughout Manasseh, which also obeyed his summons; through Asher, Zebulun and Naphtali, likewise, he sent messengers and these tribes advanced to meet the others. [36] Gideon said to God, "If indeed you are going to save Israel through me, as you promised, [37] I am putting this woolen fleece on the threshing floor. If dew comes on the fleece alone, while all the ground is dry, I shall know that you will save Israel through me, as you promised." [38] That is what took place. Early the next morning he wrung the dew from the fleece, squeezing out of it a bowlful of water. [39] Gideon then said to God, "Do not be angry with me if I speak once more. Let me make just one more test with the fleece. Let the fleece alone be dry, but let there be dew on all the ground." [40] That night God did so; the fleece alone was dry, but there was dew on all the ground.

CHAPTER 7

Defeat of Midian. [1] Early the next morning Jerubbaal[d] (that is, Gideon) encamped by En-harod with all his soldiers. The camp of Midian was in the valley north of Gibeath-hammoreh. [2] The LORD said to Gideon, "You have too many soldiers with you for me to deliver Midian into their power, lest Israel vaunt itself against me and say, 'My own power brought me the victory.' [3] Now proclaim to all the soldiers, 'If anyone is afraid or fearful, let him leave.' "[e] When Gideon put them to this test on the mountain, twenty-two thousand of the soldiers left, but ten thousand remained. [4] The LORD said to Gideon, "There are still too many soldiers. Lead them down to the

---

c 1 Sm 12, 11.—d Jgs 6, 32.—e Dt 20, 8.

7, 5: The Lord desired not numerous but reliable soldiers. Those who drank from their hands were alert, standing ready to resist attack, whereas the others were careless and undependable. The cowardly soldiers had already been dismissed (v 3); cf Dt 20, 8.

7, 13: The barley loaf represents the agricultural Hebrews while the tent refers to the nomadic Midianites. The overthrow of the tent indicates the victory of the Hebrews over their Midianite oppressors.

water and I will test them for you there. If I tell you that a certain man is to go with you, he must go with you. But no one is to go if I tell you he must not." [5] * When Gideon led the soldiers down to the water, the LORD said to him, "You shall set to one side everyone who laps up the water as a dog does with its tongue; to the other, everyone who kneels down to drink." [6] Those who lapped up the water raised to their mouths by hand numbered three hundred, but all the rest of the soldiers knelt down to drink the water. [7] The LORD said to Gideon, "By means of the three hundred who lapped up the water I will save you and will deliver Midian into your power. So let all the other soldiers go home." [8] Their horns, and such supplies as the soldiers had with them, were taken up, and Gideon ordered the rest of the Israelites to their tents, but kept the three hundred men. Now the camp of Midian was beneath him in the valley.

[9] That night the LORD said to Gideon, "Go, descend on the camp, for I have delivered it up to you. [10] If you are afraid to attack, go down to the camp with your aide Purah. [11] When you hear what they are saying, you will have the courage to descend on the camp." So he went down with his aide Purah to the outposts of the camp. [12] The Midianites, Amalekites, and all the Kedemites lay in the valley, as numerous as locusts. Nor could their camels be counted, for these were as many as the sands on the seashore. [13] * When Gideon arrived, one man was telling another about a dream. "I had a dream," he said, "that a round loaf of barley bread was rolling into the camp of Midian. It came to our tent and struck it, and as it fell it turned the tent upside down." [14] "This can only be the sword of the Israelite Gideon, son of Joash," the other replied. "God has delivered Midian and all the camp into his power." [15] When Gideon heard the description and explanation of the dream, he prostrated himself. Then returning to the camp of Israel, he said, "Arise, for the LORD has delivered the camp of Midian into your power."

[16] He divided the three hundred men into three companies, and provided them all with horns and with empty jars and torches inside the jars. [17] "Watch me and follow my lead," he told them. "I shall go to the edge of the camp, and as I do, you

must do also. [18] When I and those with me blow horns, you too must blow horns all around the camp and cry out, 'For the LORD and for Gideon!' " [19] So Gideon and the hundred men who were with him came to the edge of the camp at the beginning of the middle watch,* just after the posting of the guards. They blew the horns and broke the jars they were holding. [20] All three companies blew horns and broke their jars. They held the torches in their left hands, and in their right the horns they were blowing, and cried out, "A sword for the LORD and Gideon!" [21] They all remained standing in place around the camp, while the whole camp fell to running and shouting and fleeing. [22] But the three hundred men kept blowing the horns, and throughout the camp the LORD set the sword of one against another.*f* The army fled as far as Beth-shittah in the direction of Zarethan, near the border of Abel-meholah at Tabbath.

[23] The Israelites were called to arms from Naphtali, from Asher, and from all Manasseh, and they pursued Midian. [24] Gideon also sent messengers throughout the mountain region of Ephraim to say, "Go down to confront Midian, and seize the water courses against them as far as Beth-barah, as well as the Jordan." So all the Ephraimites were called to arms, and they seized the water courses as far as Beth-barah, and the Jordan as well. [25] *g* They captured the two princes of Midian, Oreb and Zeeb, killing Oreb at the rock of Oreb and Zeeb at the wine press of Zeeb. Then they pursued Midian and carried the heads of Oreb and Zeeb to Gideon beyond the Jordan.

CHAPTER 8

[1] But the Ephraimites said to him, "What have you done to us, not calling us when you went to fight against Midian?" And they quarreled bitterly with him. [2] "What have I accomplished now in comparison with you?" he answered them. "Is not the gleaning of Ephraim better than the vintage of Abiezer?*h* [3] Into your power God delivered the princes of Midian, Oreb and Zeeb. What have I been able to do in comparison with you?" When he said this, their anger against him subsided.

[4] When Gideon reached the Jordan and crossed it with his three hundred men, they were exhausted and famished. [5] So he said to the men of Succoth, "Will you give my followers some loaves of bread? They are exhausted, and I am pursuing Zebah and Zalmunna, kings of Midian." [6] But the princes of Succoth replied, "Are the hands of Zebah and Zalmunna already in your possession, that we should give food to your army?"* [7] Gideon said, "Very well; when the LORD has delivered Zebah and Zalmunna into my power, I will grind your flesh in with the thorns and briers of the desert." [8] He went up from there to Penuel and made the same request of them, but the men of Penuel answered him as had the men of Succoth. [9] So to the men of Penuel, too, he said, "When I return in triumph, I will demolish this tower."

[10] Now Zebah and Zalmunna were in Karkor with their force of about fifteen thousand men; these were all who were left of the whole Kedemite army, a hundred and twenty thousand swordsmen having fallen. [11] Gideon went up by the route of the nomads east of Nobah and Jogbehah, and attacked the camp when it felt secure. [12] Zebah and Zalmunna fled. He pursued them and took the two kings of Midian, Zebah and Zalmunna, captive, throwing the entire army into panic.

[13] Then Gideon, son of Joash, returned from battle by the pass of Heres. [14] He captured a young man of Succoth, who upon being questioned listed for him the seventy-seven princes and elders of Succoth. [15] So he went to the men of Succoth and said, "Here are Zebah and Zalmunna, with whom you taunted me, 'Are the hands of Zebah and Zalmunna already in your possession, that we should give food to your weary followers?' " [16] He took the elders of the city, and thorns and briers of the desert, and ground these men of Succoth into them. [17] He also demolished the tower of Penuel and slew the men of the city.

[18] Then he said to Zebah and Zalmunna, "Where now are the men you killed at Tabor?" "They all resembled you," they

---

f 22f: Ps 83, 10; Is 9, 4.—g Jgs 8, 3; Ps 83, 12; Is 10, 26.—h Jgs 6, 34.

7, 19: *At the beginning of the middle watch:* about two hours before midnight. The ancient Hebrews divided the night into three watches of about four hours each. At the beginning of a watch the sentinels were changed.

8, 6: *Are the hands . . . in your possession . . . ?* : i.e., can you already boast of victory? The hands as well as the heads of slain enemies were cut off and counted as trophies; cf 2 Sm 4, 8; 2 Kgs 10, 7f; and the Ugaritic Anath Epic, V AB, II 10ff.

replied. "They appeared to be princes."
¹⁹"They were my brothers, my mother's sons," he said. "As the LORD lives, if you had spared their lives, I should not kill you." ²⁰Then he said to his first-born, Jether, "Go, kill them." Since Jether was still a boy, he was afraid and did not draw his sword. ²¹Zebah and Zalmunna said, "Come, kill us yourself, for a man's strength is like the man." So Gideon stepped forward and killed Zebah and Zalmunna. He also took the crescents that were on the necks of their camels.
²²The Israelites then said to Gideon, "Rule over us—you, your son, and your son's son—for you rescued us from the power of Midian." ²³But Gideon answered them, "I will not rule over you, nor shall my son rule over you. The LORD must rule over you."
²⁴Gideon went on to say, "I should like to make a request of you. Will each of you give me a ring from his booty?" (For being Ishmaelites,* the enemy had gold rings.) ²⁵"We will gladly give them," they replied, and spread out a cloak into which everyone threw a ring from his booty. ²⁶The gold rings that he requested weighed seventeen hundred gold shekels, in addition to the crescents and pendants, the purple garments worn by the kings of Midian, and the trappings that were on the necks of their camels. ²⁷Gideon made an ephod out of the gold and placed it in his city Ophrah. However, all Israel paid idolatrous homage to it there, and caused the ruin of Gideon and his family.
²⁸Thus was Midian brought into subjection by the Israelites; no longer did they hold their heads high. And the land had rest for forty years, during the lifetime of Gideon.

Gideon's Son Abimelech. ²⁹Then Jerubbaal, son of Joash, went back home to stay. ³⁰ *i* Now Gideon had seventy sons, his direct descendants, for he had many wives. ³¹His concubine* who lived in Shechem also bore him a son, whom he

---

i Jgs 9, 2. 5.—j Jgs 8, 31.—k Jgs 8, 22f.

8, 24: *Ishmaelites:* here as in Gn 37, 25-28, the designation is not ethnic; it refers rather to their status as nomads.
8, 31: *Concubine:* cf Gn 25, 1-11 and note.
8, 33: *Baal of Berith:* one of the titles of Baal as worshiped by the Canaanites of Shechem, meaning "the lord of the covenant."
9, 9: *Whereby men and gods are honored:* oil was used in the worship both of the true God and of false gods; it was prescribed in the worship of Yahweh (Lv 2, 1. 6. 15; 24, 2). It was also used to consecrate prophets, priests and kings (Ex 30, 25. 30; 1 Sm 10, 1; 16, 13).

named Abimelech. ³²At a good old age Gideon, son of Joash, died and was buried in the tomb of his father Joash in Ophrah of the Abiezrites. ³³But after Gideon was dead, the Israelites again abandoned themselves to the Baals, making Baal of Berith* their god ³⁴and forgetting the LORD, their God, who had delivered them from the power of their enemies all around them. ³⁵Nor were they grateful to the family of Jerubbaal [Gideon] for all the good he had done for Israel.

CHAPTER 9

¹Abimelech, son of Jerubbaal, went to his mother's kinsmen in Shechem,ʲ and said to them and to the whole clan to which his mother's family belonged, ²"Put this question to all the citizens of Shechem: 'Which is better for you: that seventy men, or all Jerubbaal's sons, rule over you, or that one man rule over you?' You must remember that I am your own flesh and bone." ³When his mother's kin repeated these words to them on his behalf, all the citizens of Shechem sympathized with Abimelech, thinking, "He is our kinsman." ⁴They also gave him seventy silver shekels from the temple of Baal of Berith, with which Abimelech hired shiftless men and ruffians as his followers. ⁵He then went to his ancestral house in Ophrah, and slew his brothers, the seventy sons of Jerubbaal, on one stone. Only the youngest son of Jerubbaal, Jotham, escaped, for he was hidden. ⁶Then all the citizens of Shechem and all Beth-millo came together and proceeded to make Abimelech king by the terebinth at the memorial pillar in Shechem.

⁷When this was reported to him, Jotham went to the top of Mount Gerizim, and standing there, cried out to them in a loud voice: "Hear me, citizens of Shechem, that God may then hear you! ⁸Once the trees went to anoint a king over themselves. So they said to the olive tree, 'Reign over us.'ᵏ ⁹But the olive tree answered them, 'Must I give up my rich oil, whereby men and gods are honored,* and go to wave over the trees?' ¹⁰Then the trees said to the fig tree, 'Come; you reign over us!' ¹¹But the fig tree answered them, 'Must I give up my sweetness and my good fruit, and go to wave over the trees?' ¹²Then the trees said to the vine, 'Come you, and reign over us.' ¹³But the vine

Jgs

answered them, 'Must I give up my wine that cheers gods* and men, and go to wave over the trees?' [14] Then all the trees said to the buckthorn, 'Come; you reign over us!' [15] But the buckthorn replied to the trees, 'If you wish to anoint me king over you in good faith, come and take refuge in my shadow. Otherwise, let fire come from the buckthorn and devour the cedars of Lebanon.'

[16] * "Now then, if you have acted in good faith and honorably in appointing Abimelech your king, if you have dealt well with Jerubbaal and with his family, and if you have treated him as he deserved—[17] for my father fought for you at the risk of his life when he saved you from the power of Midian; [18] but you have risen against his family this day and have killed his seventy sons upon one stone, and have made Abimelech, the son of his handmaid,[l] king over the citizens of Shechem, because he is your kinsman—[19] if, then, you have acted in good faith and with honor toward Jerubbaal and his family this day, rejoice in Abimelech and may he in turn rejoice in you. [20] But if not, let fire come forth from Abimelech to devour the citizens of Shechem and Beth-millo, and let fire come forth from the citizens and from Beth-millo to devour Abimelech." [21] Then Jotham went in flight to Beer, where he remained for fear of his brother Abimelech.

[22] When Abimelech had ruled Israel for three years, [23] God put bad feelings between Abimelech and the citizens of Shechem, who rebelled against Abimelech. [24] This was to repay the violence done to the seventy sons of Jerubbaal and to avenge their blood upon their brother Abimelech, who killed them, and upon the citizens of Shechem, who encouraged him to kill his brothers. [25] The citizens of Shechem then set men in ambush for him on the mountaintops, and these robbed all who passed them on the road. But it was reported to Abimelech.

[26] Now Gaal, son of Ebed, came over to Shechem with his kinsmen. The citizens of Shechem put their trust in him, [27] and went out into the fields, harvested their grapes and trod them out. Then they held a festival and went to the temple of their god, where they ate and drank and cursed Abimelech. [28] Gaal, son of Ebed, said, "Who is Abimelech? And why should we

of Shechem serve him? Were not the son of Jerubbaal and his lieutenant Zebul once subject to the men of Hamor, father of Shechem?[m] Why should we serve him? [29] Would that this people were entrusted to my command! I would depose Abimelech. I would say to Abimelech, 'Get a larger army and come out!' "

[30] At the news of what Gaal, son of Ebed, had said, Zebul, the ruler of the city, was angry [31] and sent messengers to Abimelech in Arumah with the information: "Gaal, son of Ebed, and his kinsmen have come to Shechem and are stirring up the city against you. [32] Now rouse yourself; set an ambush tonight in the fields, you and the men who are with you. [33] Promptly at sunrise tomorrow morning, make a raid on the city. When he and his followers come out against you, deal with him as best you can."

[34] During the night Abimelech advanced with all his soldiers and set up an ambush for Shechem in four companies. [35] Gaal, son of Ebed, went out and stood at the entrance of the city gate. When Abimelech and his soldiers rose from their place of ambush, [36] Gaal saw them and said to Zebul, "There are men coming down from the hilltops!" But Zebul answered him, "You see the shadow of the hills as men." [37] But Gaal went on to say, "Men are coming down from the region of Tabbur-Haares, and one company is coming by way of Elon-Meonenim." [38] Zebul said to him, "Where now is the boast you uttered, 'Who is Abimelech that we should serve him?' Are these not the men for whom you expressed contempt? Go out now and fight with them." [39] So Gaal went out at the head of the citizens of Shechem and fought against Abimelech. [40] But Abimelech routed him, and he fled before him; and many fell slain right up to the entrance of the gate. [41] Abimelech returned to Arumah, but Zebul drove Gaal and his kinsmen from Shechem, which they had occupied.

[42] The next day, when the people were taking the field, it was reported to Abime-

---

l Jgs 8, 31.—m Gn 34, 2. 6.

9, 13: *Cheers gods:* wine was used in the libations both of the Temple of Jerusalem and of pagan temples.

9, 16: Just as the noble trees refused the honor of royalty and were made subject to a mean plant, so did Abimelech of less noble birth than the seventy sons of Gideon now tyrannize over the people.

lech, [43] who divided the men he had into three companies, and set up an ambush in the fields. He watched till he saw the people leave the city, and then rose against them for the attack. [44] Abimelech and the company with him dashed in and stood by the entrance of the city gate, while the other two companies rushed upon all who were in the field and attacked them. [45] That entire day Abimelech fought against the city, and captured it. He then killed its inhabitants and demolished the city, sowing the site with salt.*

[46] When they heard of this, all the citizens of Migdal-shechem went into the crypt of the temple of El-berith. [47] It was reported to Abimelech that all the citizens of Migdal-shechem were gathered together. [48] So he went up Mount Zalmon with all his soldiers, took his ax in his hand, and cut down some brushwood. This he lifted to his shoulder, then said to the men with him, "Hurry! Do just as you have seen me do." [49] So all the men likewise cut down brushwood, and following Abimelech, placed it against the crypt. Then they set the crypt on fire over their heads, so that every one of the citizens of Migdal-shechem, about a thousand men and women, perished.

[50] Abimelech proceeded to Thebez, which he invested and captured. [51] Now there was a strong tower in the middle of the city, and all the men and women, in a word all the citizens of the city, fled there, shutting themselves in and going up to the roof of the tower. [52] Abimelech came up to the tower and fought against it, advancing to the very entrance of the tower to set it on fire. [53] But a certain woman cast the upper part of a millstone down on Abimelech's head, and it fractured his skull.[n] [54] He immediately called his armorbearer and said to him, "Draw your sword and dispatch me, lest they say of me that a woman killed me."[o] So his attendant ran him through and he died. [55] When the Israelites saw that Abimelech was dead, they all left for their homes.

[56] Thus did God requite the evil Abimelech had done to his father in killing his seventy brothers. [57] God also brought all their wickedness home to the Shechemites, for the curse of Jotham, son of Jerubbaal, overtook them.

CHAPTER 10

Tola. [1] After Abimelech there rose to save Israel the Issacharite Tola, son of Puah, son of Dodo, a resident of Shamir in the mountain region of Ephraim. [2] When he had judged Israel twenty-three years, he died and was buried in Shamir.

Jair. [3] Jair the Gileadite came after him and judged Israel twenty-two years. [4] He had thirty sons who rode on thirty saddle-asses* and possessed thirty cities in the land of Gilead; these are called Havvoth-jair to the present day.[p] [5] Jair died and was buried in Kamon.

Oppression by the Ammonites. [6] The Israelites again offended the LORD, serving the Baals and Ashtaroths, the gods of Aram, the gods of Sidon, the gods of Moab, the gods of the Ammonites, and the gods of the Philistines. Since they had abandoned the LORD and would not serve him, [7] the Lord became angry with Israel and allowed them to fall into the power of [the Philistines and] the Ammonites. [8] For eighteen years they afflicted and oppressed the Israelites in Bashan, and all the Israelites in the Amorite land beyond the Jordan in Gilead. [9] The Ammonites also crossed the Jordan to fight against Judah, Benjamin, and the house of Ephraim, so that Israel was in great distress.

[10] Then the Israelites cried out to the LORD, "We have sinned against you; we have forsaken our God and have served the Baals." [11] [q] The LORD answered the Israelites: "Did not the Egyptians, the Amorites,[r] the Ammonites, the Philistines, [12] the Sidonians, the Amalekites, and the Midianites oppress you?[s] Yet when you cried out to me, and I saved you from their grasp, [13] you still forsook me and worshiped other gods. Therefore I will save you no more. [14] Go and cry out to the gods you have chosen; let them save you now that you are in distress." [15] But the Israelites said to the LORD, "We have sinned. Do to us whatever you please. Only save us this day." [16] And they cast out the foreign gods from their midst and served the LORD, so that he grieved over the misery of Israel.

---

n 2 Sm 11, 21.—o 1 Sm 31, 4; 1 Chr 10, 4.—p Dt 3, 14.—q 11-14: Jgs 2, 1ff; 6, 8ff.—r Nm 21, 21-32.—s Jgs 6, 3.

9, 45: *Sowing the site with salt:* a severe measure, which was a symbol of desolation, and even more, since it actually rendered the ground barren and useless.

10, 4: *Saddle-asses:* a sign of rank and wealth; cf Jgs 5, 10; 12, 14.

[17] The Ammonites had gathered for war and encamped in Gilead, while the Israelites assembled and encamped in Mizpah.[t] [18] And among the people the princes of Gilead said to one another, "The one who begins the war against the Ammonites shall be leader of all the inhabitants of Gilead."[u]

CHAPTER 11

Jephthah. [1] There was a chieftain, the Gileadite Jephthah, born to Gilead of a harlot. [2] Gilead's wife had also borne him sons, and on growing up the sons of the wife had driven Jephthah away, saying to him, "You shall inherit nothing in our family, for you are the son of another woman." [3] So Jephthah had fled from his brothers and had taken up residence in the land of Tob. A rabble had joined company with him, and went out with him on raids.

[4] Some time later, the Ammonites warred on Israel. [5] When this occurred the elders of Gilead went to bring Jephthah from the land of Tob. [6] "Come," they said to Jephthah, "be our commander that we may be able to fight the Ammonites." [7] "Are you not the ones who hated me and drove me from my father's house?" Jephthah replied to the elders of Gilead. "Why do you come to me now, when you are in distress?" [8] The elders of Gilead said to Jephthah, "In any case, we have now come back to you; if you go with us to fight against the Ammonites, you shall be the leader of all of us who dwell in Gilead." [9] Jephthah answered the elders of Gilead, "If you bring me back to fight against the Ammonites and the LORD delivers them up to me, I shall be your leader." [10] The elders of Gilead said to Jephthah, "The LORD is witness between us that we will do as you say."

[11] So Jephthah went with the elders of Gilead, and the people made him their leader and commander.[v] In Mizpah, Jephthah settled all his affairs before the LORD. [12] Then he sent messengers to the king of the Ammonites to say, "What have you against me that you come to fight with me in my land?" [13] He answered the messengers of Jephthah, "Israel took away my land from the Arnon

to the Jabbok and the Jordan when they came up from Egypt.[w] Now restore the same peaceably."

[14] Again Jephthah sent messengers to the king of the Ammonites, [15] saying to him, "This is what Jephthah says: Israel did not take the land of Moab or the land of the Ammonites.[x] [16] For when they came up from Egypt, Israel went through the desert to the Red Sea and came to Kadesh. [17] Israel then sent messengers to the king of Edom saying, 'Let me pass through your land.' But the king of Edom did not give consent. They also sent to the king of Moab, but he too was unwilling. So Israel remained in Kadesh.[y] [18] Then they went through the desert, and bypassing the land of Edom and the land of Moab, went east of the land of Moab and encamped across the Arnon.[z] Thus they did not go through the territory of Moab, for the Arnon is the boundary of Moab. [19] [a] Then Israel sent messengers to Sihon, king of the Amorites, king of Heshbon. Israel said to him, 'Let me pass through your land to my own place.' [20] But Sihon refused to let Israel pass through his territory. On the contrary, he gathered all his soldiers, who encamped at Jahaz and fought Israel. [21] But the LORD, the God of Israel, delivered Sihon and all his men into the power of Israel, who defeated them and occupied all the land of the Amorites dwelling in that region, [22] the whole territory from the Arnon to the Jabbok, from the desert to the Jordan. [23] If now the LORD, the God of Israel, has cleared the Amorites out of the way of his people, are you to dislodge Israel? [24] Should you not possess that which your god Chemosh* gave you to possess, and should we not possess all that the LORD, our God, has cleared out for us?[b] [25] Again, are you any better than Balak, son of Zippor, king of Moab? Did he ever quarrel with Israel, or did he war against

---

t Jgs 11, 29.—u Jgs 11, 5-11.—v Jgs 10, 18.—w Nm 21, 13. 24ff.—x Dt 2, 9. 19.—y Nm 20, 1. 14. 18-21; Dt 1, 46.—z Nm 21, 4. 11. 13; 22, 36; Dt 2, 8.—a 19-22: Nm 21, 21-26; Dt 2, 26-36.—b Nm 21, 29; 1 Kgs 11, 7.

11, 24: *Chemosh:* the chief god of the Moabites—not of the Ammonites, whose leading deity was called Molech or Milcom; cf Nm 21, 29; 1 Kgs 11, 7; 2 Kgs 23, 13. The error is probably due to an ancient copyist. Jephthah argues from the viewpoint of his adversaries, the Ammonites, that they were entitled to all the land they had conquered with the aid of their god. It does not necessarily follow that Jephthah himself believed in the actual existence of this pagan god.

them[c] [26]when Israel occupied Heshbon and its villages, Aroer and its villages, and all the cities on the banks of the Arnon?[d] Three hundred years have passed; why did you not recover them during that time? [27]I have not sinned against you, but you wrong me by warring against me. Let the LORD, who is judge, decide this day between the Israelites and the Ammonites!" [28]But the king of the Ammonites paid no heed to the message Jephthah sent him.

Jephthah's Vow. [29]The spirit of the LORD came upon Jephthah. He passed through Gilead and Manasseh, and through Mizpah-Gilead as well, and from there he went on to the Ammonites. [30] * Jephthah made a vow to the LORD. "If you deliver the Ammonites into my power," he said, [31]"whoever comes out of the doors of my house to meet me when I return in triumph from the Ammonites shall belong to the LORD. I shall offer him up as a holocaust."

[32]Jephthah then went on to the Ammonites to fight against them, and the LORD delivered them into his power, [33]so that he inflicted a severe defeat on them, from Aroer to the approach of Minnith (twenty cities in all) and as far as Abel-keramim. Thus were the Ammonites brought into subjection by the Israelites. [34]When Jephthah returned to his house in Mizpah, it was his daughter who came forth, playing the tambourines and dancing. She was an only child: he had neither son nor daughter besides her. [35]When he saw her, he rent his garments and said, "Alas, daughter, you have struck me down and brought calamity upon me. For I have made a vow to the LORD and I cannot retract."[e] [36]"Father," she replied, "you have made a vow to the LORD. Do with me as you have vowed, because the LORD has wrought vengeance for you on

---

c Nm 22, 2; Jos 24, 9; Mi 6, 5.—d Nm 21, 25; Dt 2, 36.—e Nm 30, 3.—f Jgs 8, 1.

11, 30-40: The text clearly implies that Jephthah vowed a human sacrifice, according to the custom of his pagan neighbors; cf 2 Kgs 3, 27. The inspired author merely records the fact; he does not approve of the action.

11, 37: *Mourn my virginity:* to bear children was woman's greatest pride; to be childless was regarded as a great misfortune. Hence Jephthah's daughter asks permission to mourn the fact that she will be put to death before she can bear children.

12, 6: *Shibboleth:* "an ear of grain." But this Hebrew word can also mean "flood water" as in Ps 69, 3. 16. Apparently the Gileadites engaged the Ephraimites in conversation about the "flood water" of the Jordan. Differences in enunciating the initial sibilant of the Hebrew word betrayed different tribal affinities.

your enemies the Ammonites." [37]Then she said to her father, "Let me have this favor. Spare me for two months, that I may go off down the mountains to mourn my virginity* with my companions." [38]"Go," he replied, and sent her away for two months. So she departed with her companions and mourned her virginity on the mountains. [39]At the end of the two months she returned to her father, who did to her as he had vowed. She had not been intimate with man. It then became a custom in Israel [40]for Israelite women to go yearly to mourn the daughter of Jephthah the Gileadite for four days of the year.

CHAPTER 12

The Shibboleth Incident. [1]The men of Ephraim gathered together and crossed over to Zaphon. They said to Jephthah, "Why do you go on to fight with the Ammonites without calling us to go with you? We will burn your house over you."[f] [2]Jephthah answered them, "My soldiers and I were engaged in a critical contest with the Ammonites. I summoned you, but you did not rescue me from their power. [3]When I saw that you would not effect a rescue, I took my life in my own hand and went on to the Ammonites, and the LORD delivered them into my power. Why, then, do you come up against me this day to fight with me?"

[4]Then Jephthah called together all the men of Gilead and fought against Ephraim, whom they defeated; for the Ephraimites had said, "You of Gilead are Ephraimite fugitives in territory belonging to Ephraim and Manasseh." [5]The Gileadites took the fords of the Jordan toward Ephraim. When any of the fleeing Ephraimites said, "Let me pass," the men of Gilead would say to him, "Are you an Ephraimite?" If he answered, "No!" [6]they would ask him to say "Shibboleth."* If he said "Sibboleth," not being able to give the proper pronunciation, they would seize him and kill him at the fords of the Jordan. Thus forty-two thousand Ephraimites fell at that time.

[7]After having judged Israel for six years, Jephthah the Gileadite died and was buried in his city in Gilead.

Ibzan. [8]After him Ibzan of Bethlehem judged Israel. [9]He had thirty sons. He also had thirty daughters married outside the family, and he brought in as wives for his sons thirty young women from outside the family. After having judged Israel for seven years, [10] Ibzan died and was buried in Bethlehem.

Elon. [11] After him the Zebulunite Elon judged Israel. When he had judged Israel for ten years, [12] the Zebulunite Elon died and was buried in Elon in the land of Zebulun.

Abdon. [13] After him the Pirathonite Abdon, son of Hillel, judged Israel. [14] He had forty sons and thirty grandsons who rode on seventy saddle-asses. After having judged Israel for eight years, [15] the Pirathonite Abdon, son of Hillel, died and was buried in Pirathon in the land of Ephraim on the mountain of the Amalekites.

CHAPTER 13

The Birth of Samson. [1] The Israelites again offended the LORD, who therefore delivered them into the power of the Philistines for forty years.[g]

[2] There was a certain man from Zorah, of the clan of the Danites, whose name was Manoah. His wife was barren and had borne no children. [3] An angel of the LORD appeared to the woman and said to her, "Though you are barren and have had no children, yet you will conceive and bear a son.[h] [4] Now, then, be careful to take no wine or strong drink and to eat nothing unclean. [5] As for the son you will conceive and bear, no razor shall touch his head,[i] for this boy is to be consecrated* to God from the womb. It is he who will begin the deliverance of Israel from the power of the Philistines."

[6] The woman went and told her husband, "A man of God came to me; he had the appearance of an angel of God, terrible indeed. I did not ask him where he came from, nor did he tell me his name. [7] But he said to me, 'You will be with child and will bear a son. So take neither wine nor strong drink, and eat nothing unclean. For the boy shall be consecrated to God from the womb, until the day of his death.' " [8] Manoah then prayed to the LORD. "O LORD, I beseech you," he said, "may the man of God whom you sent, return to us to teach us what to do for the boy who will be born."

[9] God heard the prayer of Manoah, and the angel of God came again to the woman as she was sitting in the field. Since her husband Manoah was not with her, [10] the woman ran in haste and told her husband. "The man who came to me the other day has appeared to me," she said to him; [11] so Manoah got up and followed his wife. When he reached the man, he said to him, "Are you the one who spoke to my wife?" "Yes," he answered. [12] Then Manoah asked, "Now, when that which you say comes true, what are we expected to do for the boy?" [13] The angel of the LORD answered Manoah, "Your wife is to abstain from all the things of which I spoke to her. [14] She must not eat anything that comes from the vine, nor take wine or strong drink, nor eat anything unclean. Let her observe all that I have commanded her."

[15] Then Manoah said to the angel of the LORD, "Can we persuade you to stay, while we prepare a kid for you?" [16] But the angel of the LORD answered Manoah, "Although you press me, I will not partake of your food. But if you will, you may offer a holocaust to the LORD." Not knowing that it was the angel of the LORD, [17] Manoah said to him, "What is your name, that we may honor you when your words come true?" [18] The angel of the LORD answered him,[j] "Why do you ask my name, which is mysterious?"* [19] [k] Then Manoah took the kid with a cereal offering and offered it on the rock to the LORD, whose works are mysteries. While Manoah and his wife were looking on, [20] as the flame rose to the sky from the altar, the angel of the LORD ascended in the flame of the altar. When Manoah and his wife saw this, they fell prostrate to the ground; [21] but the angel of the LORD was seen no more by Manoah and his wife. Then Manoah, realizing that it was the angel of the LORD, [22] said to his wife, "We will certainly die, for we have seen God."[l] [23] But his wife pointed out to him, "If the LORD had meant to kill us, he would not have accepted a holocaust and cereal offering from our hands! Nor would he have let us see all this just now, or hear what we have heard."

---

g Jgs 10, 6.—h 3f: 1 Sm 1, 20; Lk 1, 31.—i Nm 6, 5.—j Gn 32, 29.—k 19f: Jgs 6, 19ff.—l 21f: Jgs 6, 22f.

13, 5: *Consecrated:* in Hebrew, *nazir.* Samson therefore was for life to be under the nazirite vow, which obliged him to abstain from drinking wine or having his hair cut; cf Nm 6, 2-8.

13, 18: *Mysterious:* incomprehensible, above human understanding. Hence, the angel speaks in the name of the Lord himself, to whom Manoah at once offers a sacrifice.

24 The woman bore a son and named him Samson. *m* The boy grew up and the LORD blessed him; 25 the spirit of the LORD first stirred him in Mahaneh-dan, which is between Zorah and Eshtaol.

CHAPTER 14

Marriage of Samson. 1 Samson went down to Timnah and saw there one of the Philistine women.* 2 On his return he told his father and mother, "There is a Philistine woman I saw in Timnah whom I wish you to get as a wife for me." 3 His father and mother said to him, "Can you find no wife among your kinsfolk or among all our people, that you must go and take a wife from the uncircumcised Philistines?" But Samson answered his father, "Get her for me, for she pleases me." 4 *n* Now his father and mother did not know that this had been brought about by the LORD, who was providing an opportunity against the Philistines; for at that time they had dominion over Israel.

5 * So Samson went down to Timnah with his father and mother. When they had come to the vineyards of Timnah, a young lion came roaring to meet him. 6 But the spirit of the LORD came upon Samson, and although he had no weapons, he tore the lion in pieces as one tears a kid. 7 However, on the journey to speak for the woman, he did not mention to his father or mother what he had done. 8 Later, when he returned to marry the woman who pleased him, he stepped aside to look at the remains of the lion and found a swarm of bees and honey in the lion's carcass. 9 So he scooped the honey out into his palms and ate it as he went along. When he came to his father and mother, he gave them some to eat, without telling them that he had scooped the honey from the lion's carcass.

10 His father also went down to the woman, and Samson gave a banquet there, since it was customary for the young men to do this. 11 When they met him, they brought thirty men to be his companions.* 12 Samson said to them, "Let me propose a riddle to you. If within the seven days of the feast you solve it for me successfully, I will give you thirty linen tunics and thirty sets of garments. 13 But if you cannot answer it for me, you must give me thirty tunics and thirty sets of garments." "Propose your riddle," they responded; "we will listen to it." 14 So he said to them,

"Out of the eater came forth food,
   and out of the strong came forth sweetness."

After three days' failure to answer the riddle, 15 they said on the fourth day to Samson's wife, "Coax your husband to answer the riddle for us, or we will burn you and your family. Did you invite us here to reduce us to poverty?" 16 At Samson's side, his wife wept and said, "You must hate me; you do not love me, for you have proposed a riddle to my countrymen, but have not told me the answer." He said to her, "If I have not told it even to my father or my mother, must I tell it to you?" 17 But she wept beside him during the seven days the feast lasted. On the seventh day, since she importuned him, he told her the answer, and she explained the riddle to her countrymen.

18 On the seventh day, before the sun set, the men of the city said to him,

"What is sweeter than honey,
   and what is stronger than a lion?"

He replied to them,

"If you had not plowed with my heifer,
   you would not have solved my riddle."

19 The spirit of the LORD came upon him, and he went down to Ashkelon, where he killed thirty of their men and despoiled them; he gave their garments to those who had answered the riddle. Then he went off to his own family in anger, 20 and Samson's wife was married to the one who had been best man at his wedding. *o*

---

m Heb 11, 32.—n Jgs 15, 11.—o Jgs 15, 2. 6.

14, 1-3: Marriages were arranged by the parents of the bridegroom as well as of the bride; cf Gn 24, 2-8; 34, 3-6. The Mosaic law specified only seven pagan nations, not including the Philistines, in the prohibition against mixed marriages; cf Dt 7, 1-4. But national and religious sentiment was against any marriage with a non-Israelite; cf Gn 28, 1f; 1 Kgs 11, 1-10.

14, 5ff: Although Samson was accompanied by his parents on the journey to Timnah, v 7 implies that he was not near them when *he tore the lion in pieces.*

14, 11: *Companions:* known at a later period as "the friends of the bridegroom" (1 Mc 9, 39; Mk 2, 19), the best man and his fellows. Here they are Philistines (v 16), appointed by the family of the bride, who would also have several bridesmaids; cf Mt 25, 1-13.

CHAPTER 15

Samson Defeats the Philistines. [1] After some time, in the season of the wheat harvest, Samson visited his wife, bringing a kid. But when he said, "Let me be with my wife in private," her father would not let him enter, [2] saying, "I thought it certain you wished to repudiate her; so I gave her to your best man. Her younger sister is more beautiful than she; you may have her instead." [3] Samson said to them, "This time the Philistines cannot blame me if I harm them." [4] So Samson left and caught three hundred foxes. Turning them tail to tail, he tied between each pair of tails one of the torches he had at hand. [5] He then kindled the torches and set the foxes loose in the standing grain of the Philistines, thus burning both the shocks and the standing grain, and the vineyards and olive orchards as well.

[6] *p* When the Philistines asked who had done this, they were told, "Samson, the son-in-law of the Timnite, because his wife was taken and given to his best man." So the Philistines went up and destroyed her and her family by fire. [7] Samson said to them, "If this is how you act, I will not stop until I have taken revenge on you." [8] And with repeated blows, he inflicted a great slaughter on them. Then he went down and remained in a cavern of the cliff of Etam.

[9] The Philistines went up and, from a camp in Judah, deployed against Lehi. [10] When the men of Judah asked, "Why have you come up against us?" they answered, "To take Samson prisoner; to do to him as he has done to us." [11] Three thousand men of Judah went down to the cavern in the cliff of Etam and said to Samson, "Do you not know that the Philistines are our rulers? Why, then, have you done this to us?" He answered them, "As they have done to me, so have I done to them." [12] They said to him, "We have come to take you prisoner, to deliver you over to the Philistines." Samson said to them, "Swear to me that you will not kill me yourselves." [13] "No," they replied, "we will certainly not kill you but will only bind you and deliver you over to them." *q* So they bound him with two new ropes and brought him up from the cliff. [14] When he reached Lehi, and the Philistines came shouting to meet him, the spirit of the LORD came upon him: the ropes around his arms became as flax that is consumed by fire and his bonds melted away from his hands. [15] Near him was the fresh jawbone of an ass; he reached out, grasped it, and with it killed a thousand men. [16] Then Samson said,

"With the jawbone of an ass
    I have piled them in a heap;
With the jawbone of an ass
    I have slain a thousand men."

[17] As he finished speaking he threw the jawbone from him; and so that place was named Ramath-lehi.* [18] Being very thirsty, he cried to the LORD and said, "You have granted this great victory by the hand of your servant. Must I now die of thirst or fall into the hands of the uncircumcised?" [19] Then God split the cavity in Lehi, and water issued from it, which Samson drank till his spirit returned and he revived. Hence that spring in Lehi is called En-hakkore* to this day.

[20] Samson judged Israel for twenty years in the days of the Philistines. *r*

CHAPTER 16

[1] Once Samson went to Gaza, where he saw a harlot and visited her. [2] Informed that Samson had come there, the men of Gaza surrounded him with an ambush at the city gate all night long. And all the night they waited, saying, "Tomorrow morning we will kill him." [3] Samson rested there until midnight. Then he rose, seized the doors of the city gate and the two gateposts, and tore them loose, bar and all. He hoisted them on his shoulders and carried them to the top of the ridge opposite Hebron.

Samson and Delilah. [4] After that he fell in love with a woman in the Wadi Sorek whose name was Delilah. [5] The lords of the Philistines came to her and said, "Beguile him and find out the secret of his great strength, and how we may overcome and bind him so as to keep him helpless. We will each give you eleven hundred shekels of silver." [6] So Delilah said to Samson, "Tell me the secret of your great strength and how

---

p Jgs 14, 20.—q Jgs 16, 11f.—r Jgs 16, 31.

15, 17: *Ramath-lehi:* "heights of the jawbone."
15, 19: *En-hakkore:* "the spring of him who cries out," an allusion to Samson's cry in v 18.

you may be bound so as to be kept helpless." ⁷"If they bind me with seven fresh bowstrings which have not dried," Samson answered her, "I shall be as weak as any other man." ⁸So the lords of the Philistines brought her seven fresh bowstrings which had not dried, and she bound him with them. ⁹She had men lying in wait in the chamber and so she said to him, "The Philistines are upon you, Samson!" But he snapped the strings as a thread of tow is severed by a whiff of flame;ˢ and the secret of his strength remained unknown.

¹⁰Delilah said to Samson, "You have mocked me and told me lies. Now tell me how you may be bound." ¹¹"If they bind me tight with new ropes, with which no work has been done," he answered her, "I shall be as weak as any other man."ᵗ ¹²So Delilah took new ropes and bound him with them. Then she said to him, "The Philistines are upon you, Samson!" For there were men lying in wait in the chamber. But he snapped them off his arms like thread.

¹³Delilah said to Samson again, "Up to now you have mocked me and told me lies. Tell me how you may be bound." He said to her, "If you weave my seven locks of hair into the web and fasten them with the pin, I shall be as weak as any other man." ¹⁴So while he slept, Delilah wove his seven locks of hair into the web, and fastened them in with the pin. Then she said, "The Philistines are upon you, Samson!" Awakening from his sleep, he pulled out both the weaver's pin and the web.

¹⁵Then she said to him, "How can you say that you love me when you do not confide in me? Three times already you have mocked me, and not told me the secret of your great strength!" ¹⁶She importuned him continually and vexed him with her complaints till he was deathly weary of them. ¹⁷So he took her completely into his confidence and told her, "No razor has touched my head,ᵘ for I have been consecrated to God from my mother's womb. If I am shaved, my strength will leave me, and I shall be as weak as any other man!" ¹⁸When Delilah saw that he had taken her completely into his confidence, she summoned the lords of the Philistines, say-

ing, "Come up this time, for he has opened his heart to me." So the lords of the Philistines came and brought up the money with them. ¹⁹She had him sleep on her lap, and called for a man who shaved off his seven locks of hair. Then she began to mistreat him, for his strength had left him. ²⁰When she said, "The Philistines are upon you, Samson!", and he woke from his sleep, he thought he could make good his escape as he had done time and again, for he did not realize that the LORD had left him. ²¹But the Philistines seized him and gouged out his eyes. Then they brought him down to Gaza and bound him with bronze fetters, and he was put to grinding in the prison. ²²But the hair of his head began to grow as soon as it was shaved off.

The Death of Samson. ²³ᵛ The lords of the Philistines assembled to offer a great sacrifice to their god Dagon* and to make merry. They said,

> "Our god has delivered into our power
>   Samson our enemy."

²⁵When their spirits were high, they said, "Call Samson that he may amuse us." So they called Samson from the prison, and he played the buffoon before them. ²⁴When the people saw him, they praised their god. For they said,

> "Our god has delivered into our power
>   our enemy, the ravager of our land,
>   the one who has multiplied our
>   slain."

Then they stationed him between the columns. ²⁶Samson said to the attendant who was holding his hand, "Put me where I may touch the columns that support the temple and may rest against them." ²⁷The temple was full of men and women: all the lords of the Philistines were there, and from the roof about three thousand men and women looked on as Samson provided amusement. ²⁸Samson cried out to the LORD and said, "O Lord GOD, remember me! Strengthen me, O God, this last time that for my two eyes I may avenge myself once and for all on the Philistines." ²⁹Samson grasped the two middle columns on which the temple rested and braced himself against them, one at his right hand, the other at his left. ³⁰And Samson said, "Let me die with the Philistines!" He

---

s Jgs 15, 14.—t Jgs 15, 13.—u Jgs 13, 5.—v 1 Sm 5, 2-5.

16, 23: Dagon was originally a Mesopotamian deity, whom the Philistines came to worship as their own god of grain.

pushed hard, and the temple fell upon the lords and all the people who were in it. Those he killed at his death were more than those he had killed during his lifetime. [31] All his family and kinsmen went down and bore him up for burial in the grave of his father Manoah between Zorah and Eshtaol. He had judged Israel for twenty years.[w]

III: THE TRIBES OF DAN AND BENJAMIN
IN THE DAYS OF THE JUDGES

CHAPTER 17

Micah and the Levite. [1] There was a man in the mountain region of Ephraim whose name was Micah. [2] He said to his mother, "The eleven hundred shekels of silver over which you pronounced a curse in my hearing when they were taken from you, are in my possession. It was I who took them; so now I will restore them to you." [3] When he restored the eleven hundred shekels of silver to his mother, she took two hundred of them and gave them to the silversmith, who made of them a carved idol* overlaid with silver.[x] [4] Then his mother said, "May the LORD bless my son! I have consecrated the silver to the LORD as my gift in favor of my son, by making a carved idol overlaid with silver." It remained in the house of Micah. [5] Thus the layman Micah had a sanctuary. He also made an ephod and household idols,[y] and consecrated one of his sons, who became his priest. [6] In those days there was no king in Israel; everyone did what he thought best.[z]

[7] There was a young Levite who had resided within the tribe of Judah at Bethlehem of Judah. [8] From that city he set out to find another place of residence. On his journey he came to the house of Micah in the mountain region of Ephraim. [9] Micah said to him, "Where do you come from?" He answered him, "I am a Levite from Bethlehem in Judah, and am on my way to find some other place of residence." [10] "Stay with me," Micah said to him. "Be father and priest to me,[a] and I will give you ten silver shekels a year, a set of garments, and your food." [11] So the young Levite decided to stay with the man, to whom he became as one of his own sons. [12] * Micah consecrated the young Levite, who became

his priest, remaining in his house. [13] Therefore Micah said, "Now I know that the LORD will prosper me, since the Levite has become my priest."

CHAPTER 18

Migration of the Danites. [1] At that time there was no king in Israel.[b] Moreover the tribe of Danites were in search of a district to dwell in, for up to that time they had received no heritage among the tribes of Israel.*

[2] So the Danites sent from their clan a detail of five valiant men of Zorah and Eshtaol, to reconnoiter the land and scout it. With their instructions to go and scout the land, they traveled as far as the house of Micah in the mountain region of Ephraim, where they passed the night. [3] Near the house of Micah, they recognized the voice* of the young Levite[c] and turned in that direction. "Who brought you here and what are you doing here?" they asked him. "What is your interest here?" [4] "This is how Micah treats me," he replied to them. "He pays me a salary and I am his priest."[d] [5] They said to him, "Consult God, that we may know whether the undertaking we are engaged in will succeed." [6] The priest said to them, "Go and prosper: the LORD is favorable to the undertaking you are engaged in."

[7] So the five men went on and came to Laish. They saw that the people dwelling there lived securely after the manner of the Sidonians, quiet and trusting, with no lack of any natural resources. They were distant from the Sidonians and had no contact with other people. [8] When the five returned to their kinsmen in Zorah and Eshtaol and were asked for a report, [9] they replied, "Come, let us attack them, for we have seen the land and it is very good. Are you

---

w Jgs 15, 20.—x Ex 20, 4; Lv 19, 4.—y Jgs 18, 14. 17.—z Jgs 18, 1; 21, 25.—a Jgs 18, 19.—b Jos 19, 40-48.—c Jgs 17, 7.—d Jgs 17, 10.

17, 3: *Idol:* an image, not of a pagan god, but of the Lord. The Mosaic law forbade the making of an image even of the true God.

17, 12f: According to Nm 18, 1-7 only those Levites who were descended from Aaron could be consecrated as priests.

18, 1: The tribe of Dan had been assigned a territory with definite limits in central Palestine. However they were unable to gain possession of the better portion of their land (Jgs 1, 34). So they now seek territory elsewhere in Palestine.

18, 3: *Recognized the voice:* perhaps they noticed the peculiar pronunciation of his south Hebrew dialect.

MIGRATION OF THE DANITES
(Jgs 17, 1—18, 31)

Labels on map: Tyre, Mahaleb, Beth-rehob, Dan, ARAM, PHOENICIA, MAACHAH, Achzib, Beth-anath, GESHUR, Rehob, Sea-of-Chinnereth, Aphek, Harosheth-ha-goiim, Nahalol, THEKELS, Kattath, Beth-shemesh, Dor, Megiddo, Jezreel, Taanach, Beth-shean, Plain of SHARON, Ibleam, MEDITERRANEAN SEA (GREAT SEA), Jordan, Jabbok, Shechem, AMMON, Shiloh, Rabbah, Beeroth, Gezer, Shaalbim, Gibeon, Aijalon, Chephirah, Ekron, Zorah, Kiriath-jearim, Acco, Eshtaol, Jerusalem, Beth-shemesh, Ashkelon, PHILISTINES, Gath, Gaza, Hebron, DEAD SEA, CELEBITES, Arnon, NEGEB, Beer-sheba, KENITES, MOAB

0 10 20 30
Miles

OBSTACLES TO NATIONAL UNITY DURING THE ERA OF THE JUDGES (Jgs 1—4); MIGRATION OF THE DANITES (Jgs 7, 1—18, 31). — After the Israelite conquest some Canaanite towns as well as other strongholds of the enemy remain intact. **(a) Around the Plain of Jezreel:** Beth-shean, Taanach, Ibleam, Megiddo, Kitron (Kattath), Nahalol, Beth-shemesh of Naphtali, Beth-anath, Harosheth-ha-goiim. **(b) To the south of Ephraim:** Gibeon, Chephirah, Beeroth, Kiriath-jearim, Gezer, Har-heres (Beth-shemesh of Dan), Aijalon, Shaalbim, Jerusalem. The **Danites** find proximity to the Philistines difficult, so they set out from **Zorah** and **Eshtaol**, encamp at **Kiriath-jearim** in Judah, then cross the **mountain of Ephraim,** taking with them a priest of the house of Micah. They conquer **Laish** and change its name to **Dan. (c) Along the Great Sea: The Phoenicians:** at Gebal, Sidon, Tyre, Rehob, Acco, Ahlab, Achzib, Aphik. **The Thekels (related to the Philistines):** at Dor and the Plain of Sharon. **The Philistines:** at Ekron, Gath, Ashdod, Ashkelon, Gaza. **(d) In the south: Amalek:** to the north of the Sinai Peninsula. **Edom:** to the south of the Zered brook between the Dead Sea and Elath. **The Calebites, Kenites, Jerahmeelites:** in the Negeb of judah. **The Midianites:** beyond Edom, toward Arabia. **(e) In the east: Moab:** between the Zered brook and the Arnon River. **Ammon:** on the upper basin of the Jabbok river, capital: Rabbah, Geshur and Maacah: **Aramean peoples:** to the east of the sea of Chinnereth and lake Merom. **In the north: The Arameans** of Beth-rehob, of Zobah on both sides of the Hermon. **The Hittites of Hamath:** on the Orontes River.

THE PEOPLE OF ISRAEL
PALESTINE IN THE TIME OF SAMUEL AND SAUL
(1 SAMUEL)
Transferal of the Ark of the Covenant

Tabor
Endor
GILBOA
Shunem
Beth-shan

WESTERN SEA

Land of Shaalim and Benjamin
Bezek
EPHRAIM
GILEAD
Aphek
Tomb of Rachel (?)
Land of Zuph
Shalishah
Jabesh-gilead
Ebenezer
Shiloh
Beth-horon
Beth-car
Beth-aven
Ophrah
Bethel
Ekron
Mizpah
Valley of the Hyenas
BENJAMIN
Aijalon
AMMON
Beth-shemesh
Nob
Gibeah
Gilgal
GAD
Ashdod
Ha-Yebusi
Azekah
Kiriath-jearim
Socoh
Bethlehem
Ashkelon
Vale of the Terebinth
Mizpah of Moab
Gath
Adullam
Hereth
MOAB
Ephes-dammim
Keilah
Ziph
Hill of Hachilah
Gaza
Hormah
Horsa
Carmel
DEAD SEA
MOAB
Negeb of Judah
JUDAH
Eshtemoa
Maon
En-gedi
Ziklag
Jattir
Borashan
NEGEB
Transferal of the Ark of the Covenant
Beer-sheba
Negeb of the Kenites
SHUR
Athach
Negeb of Yerahmeel
Aroer
AMORITES
GESHURITES
Wadi Besor
AMALEKITES
HAVILAH
Arabah

R. Jordan
PHILISTINES

PALESTINE IN THE TIME OF SAMUEL AND SAUL (1 Sm 1—13) — (a) The period of the Judges ends with the fall of the sanctuary at **Shiloh** and the capture of the ark of the covenant under the onslaught of the Philistine invasions (c 1050-1020). **(b)** Self-supporting states emerge, each under the authority of its king similar to the Canaanite kings found in **Ammon,** and **Moab** in Transjordan and among the **Arameans** in Syria. **(c)** To ward off the **Philistines** or "People of the Sea" who settle on the coastal plain of **Canaan** and set up a confederation of city-states **(Ashdod, Ashkelon, Gaza, Gath** and **Ekron),** the ark is moved from **Shiloh** to lead the Hebrew armies. The Israelites are defeated and the ark is captured (4, 1-11). **(d)** The Philistines transfer the ark in turn to **Ebenezer** to **Ashdod, Gath, Ekron** and then return it at **Beth-shemesh.** From there it is taken to **Kiriath-jearim** with rejoicing (5, 1—7, 1). **(e)** The priestly prophet Samuel then anoints Saul as king of Israel (7, 2—12, 25).

going to hesitate? Do not be slothful about beginning your expedition to possess the land. ¹⁰ Those against whom you go are a trusting people, and the land is ample. God has indeed given it into your power: a place where no natural resource is lacking."
¹¹ So six hundred men of the clan of the Danites, fully armed with weapons of war, set out from where they were in Zorah and Eshtaol, ¹² and camped in Judah, up near Kiriath-jearim; hence to this day the place, which lies west of Kiriath-jearim, is called Mahaneh-dan.^e
¹³ From there they went on to the mountain region of Ephraim and came to the house of Micah. ¹⁴ The five men who had gone to reconnoiter the land of Laish said to their kinsmen, "Do you know that in these houses there are an ephod, household idols, and a carved idol overlaid with silver?^f Now decide what you must do!"
¹⁵ So turning in that direction, they went to the house of the young Levite at the home of Micah and greeted him. ¹⁶ The six hundred men girt with weapons of war, who were Danites, stood by the entrance of the gate, and the priest stood there also. ¹⁷ Meanwhile the five men who had gone to reconnoiter the land went up and entered the house of Micah. ¹⁸ When they had gone in and taken the ephod, the household idols, and the carved idol overlaid with silver, the priest said to them, "What are you doing?" ¹⁹ They said to him, "Be still: put your hand over your mouth. Come with us and be our father and priest.^g Is it better for you to be priest for the family of one man or to be priest for a tribe and a clan in Israel?" ²⁰ The priest, agreeing, took the ephod, household idols, and carved idol and went off in the midst of the band. ²¹ As they turned to depart, they placed their little ones, their livestock, and their goods at the head of the column.
²² The Danites had already gone some distance, when those in the houses near that of Micah took up arms and overtook them. ²³ They called to the Danites, who turned about and said to Micah, "What do you want, that you have taken up arms?"

²⁴ "You have taken my god, which I made, and have gone off with my priest as well," he answered. "What is left for me? How, then, can you ask me what I want?" ²⁵ The Danites said to him, "Let us hear no further sound from you, lest fierce men fall upon you and you and your family lose your lives." ²⁶ The Danites then went on their way, and Micah, seeing that they were stronger than he, returned home.
²⁷ Having taken what Micah had made, and the priest he had had, they attacked Laish, a quiet and trusting people; they put them to the sword and destroyed their city by fire. ²⁸ No one came to their aid, since the city was far from Sidon and they had no contact with other people. The Danites then rebuilt the city, which was in the valley that belongs to Beth-rehob, and lived there. ²⁹ They named it Dan after their ancestor Dan, son of Israel. However, the name of the city was formerly Laish. ³⁰ The Danites set up the carved idol for themselves, and Jonathan, son of Gershom, son of Moses, and his descendants were priests for the tribe of the Danites until the time of the captivity of the land.* ³¹ They maintained the carved idol Micah had made as long as the house of God was in Shiloh.

CHAPTER 19

The Levite from Ephraim. ¹ At that time, when there was no king in Israel,^h there was a Levite residing in remote parts of the mountain region of Ephraim who had taken for himself a concubine from Bethlehem of Judah. ² His concubine was unfaithful to him and left him for her father's house in Bethlehem of Judah, where she stayed for some four months. ³ Her husband then set out with his servant and a pair of asses, and went after her to forgive her and take her back. She brought him into her father's house, and on seeing him, the girl's father joyfully made him welcome. ⁴ He was detained by the girl's father, and so he spent three days with this father-in-law of his, eating and drinking and passing the night there. ⁵ * On the fourth day they rose early in the morning and he prepared to go. But the girl's father said to his son-in-law, "Fortify yourself

---

e Jgs 13, 25.—f Jgs 17, 4f.—g Jgs 17, 10.—h Jgs 17, 6.

18, 30: *Until . . . land:* about the year 734 B.C., when the Assyrian emperor Tiglath-pileser III subjected northern Palestine.
19, 5-9: Such importuning of guests to prolong their stay at the home of their host is characteristic of Oriental hospitality.

with a little food; you can go later on." [6]So they stayed and the two men ate and drank together. Then the girl's father said to the husband, "Why not decide to spend the night here and enjoy yourself?" [7]The man still made a move to go, but when his father-in-law pressed him he went back and spent the night there.

[8]On the fifth morning he rose early to depart, but the girl's father said, "Fortify yourself and tarry until the afternoon." When he and his father-in-law had eaten, [9]and the husband was ready to go with his concubine and servant, the girl's father said to him, "It is already growing dusk. Stay for the night. See, the day is coming to an end. Spend the night here and enjoy yourself. Early tomorrow you can start your journey home." [10]The man, however, refused to stay another night; he and his concubine set out with a pair of saddled asses, and traveled till they came opposite Jebus, which is Jerusalem. [11]Since they were near Jebus with the day far gone, the servant said to his master, "Come, let us turn off to this city of the Jebusites and spend the night in it." [12]But his master said to him, "We will not turn off to a city of foreigners, who are not Israelites, but will go on to Gibeah.[i] [13]Come," he said to his servant, "let us make for some other place, either Gibeah or Ramah, to spend the night."[j] [14]So they continued on their way till the sun set on them when they were abreast of Gibeah of Benjamin.

[15] * There they turned off to enter Gibeah for the night.[k] The man waited in the public square of the city he had entered, but no one offered them the shelter of his home for the nght. [16]In the evening, however, an old man came from his work in the field; he was from the mountain region of Ephraim, though he lived among the Benjaminite townspeople of Gibeah. [17]When he noticed the traveler in the public square of the city, the old man asked where he was going, and whence he had come. [18]He said to him, "We are traveling from Bethlehem of Judah far up into the mountain region of Ephraim, where I belong. I have been to Bethlehem of Judah and am now going back home; but no one has offered us the shelter of his house. [19]We have straw and fodder for our asses, and bread and wine for the woman and myself and for our servant; there is nothing

else we need." [20]"You are welcome," the old man said to him, "but let me provide for all your needs, and do not spend the night in the public square." [21]So he led them to his house and provided fodder for the asses. Then they washed their feet, and ate and drank.[l]

The Outrage at Gibeah. [22] [m] While they were enjoying themselves, the men of the city, who were corrupt,* surrounded the house and beat on the door. They said to the old man whose house it was, "Bring out your guest, that we may abuse him." [23]The owner of the house went out to them and said, "No, my brothers; do not be so wicked. Since this man is my guest, do not commit this crime. [24]Rather let me bring out my maiden daughter or his concubine. Ravish them, or do whatever you want with them; but against the man you must not commit this wanton crime." [25]When the men would not listen to his host, the husband seized his concubine and thrust her outside to them. They had relations with her and abused her all night until the following dawn, when they let her go. [26]Then at daybreak the woman came and collapsed at the entrance of the house in which her husband was a guest, where she lay until the morning. [27]When her husband rose that day and opened the door of the house to start out again on his journey, there lay the woman, his concubine, at the entrance of the house with her hands on the threshold. [28]He said to her, "Come, let us go"; but there was no answer. So the man placed her on an ass and started out again for home.

[29] * On reaching home, he took a knife to the body of his concubine, cut her into twelve pieces, and sent them throughout the territory of Israel. [30] [n] Everyone who saw this said, "Nothing like this has been done or seen from the day the Israelites came up from the land of Egypt to this day. Take note of it, and state what you propose to do."

---

i Jgs 1, 21.—j Jos 18, 25.—k Jgs 20, 4.—l Gn 18, 4; 24, 32; 43, 24.—m 22-25: Gn 19, 4-9.—n Hos 9, 9; 10, 9.

19, 15: Private hospitality was the customary means of providing comfort to travelers where public facilities were so rare.

19, 22: *Who were corrupt:* literally "sons of Belial," indicating extreme perversion; cf Gn 19, 4-8. This crime and its punishment made the name *Gibeah* proverbial as a place of shameful wickedness; cf Hos 9, 9; 10, 9.

19, 29: A drastic means for arousing the tribes to avenge the unheard of crime of the Benjaminites.

CHAPTER 20

Assembly of Israelites. [1] So all the Israelites came out as one man: from Dan to Beer-sheba,* and from the land of Gilead, the community was gathered to the LORD at Mizpah. [2] The leaders of all the people and all the tribesmen of Israel, four hundred thousand foot soldiers who were swordsmen, presented themselves in the assembly of the people of God. [3] Meanwhile, the Benjaminites heard that the Israelites had gone up to Mizpah. The Israelites asked to be told how the crime had taken place, [4] and the Levite, the husband of the murdered woman, testified: "My concubine and I went into Gibeah of Benjamin[o] for the night. [5] [p] But the citizens of Gibeah rose up against me by night and surrounded the house in which I was. Me they attempted to kill, and my concubine they abused so that she died. [6] [q] So I took my concubine and cut her up and sent her through every part of the territory of Israel, because of the monstrous crime they had committed in Israel. [7] * Now that you are all here, O Israelites, state what you propose to do."[r] [8] All the people rose as one man to say, "None of us is to leave for his tent or return to his home. [9] Now as for Gibeah, this is what we will do: We will proceed against it by lot, [10] taking from all the tribes of Israel ten men for every hundred, a hundred for every thousand, a thousand for every ten thousand, and procuring supplies for the soldiers who will go to deal fully and suitably with Gibeah of Benjamin for the crime it committed in Israel."

[11] When, therefore, all the men of Israel without exception were leagued together

o Jgs 19, 14f.—p Jgs 19, 22-27.—q Jgs 19, 29.—r Jgs 19, 30.—s Jgs 1, 1f.—t 1 Sm 4, 3f.

20, 1: *From Dan to Beer-sheba:* from north to south. *The land of Gilead:* all the territory east of the Jordan.

20, 7: The Israelites were asked to decide at once what action to take concerning this crime: cf 2 Sm 16, 20. The Levite undoubtedly addressed the tribal heads who would speak in behalf of the multitude.

20, 12: Before the crime at Gibeah was punished, the Benjaminites were invited to join their brethren, the Israelites, in punishing the crime. Since they failed to respond, special messengers were sent asking them to deliver up the guilty ones. They replied by gathering their forces for combat.

20, 18: *Judah shall go first:* the same response as in Jgs 1, 1f, but without the assurance of immediate success. Only after the Israelites were punished at the hands of the Benjaminites for their own grossness, and had performed penance, did they succeed in punishing the latter for their part in the crime of rape and murder, by gaining the victory over them.

against the city, [12] * the tribes of Israel sent men throughout the tribe of Benjamin to say, "What is this evil which has occurred among you? [13] Now give up these corrupt men of Gibeah, that we may put them to death and thus purge the evil from Israel." But the Benjaminites refused to accede to the demand of their brothers, the Israelites. [14] Instead, the Benjaminites assembled from their other cities to Gibeah, to do battle with the Israelites. [15] The number of the Benjaminite swordsmen from the other cities on that occasion was twenty-six thousand, in addition to the inhabitants of Gibeah. [16] Included in this total were seven hundred picked men who were left-handed, every one of them able to sling a stone at a hair without missing. [17] Meanwhile the other Israelites who, without Benjamin, mustered four hundred thousand swordsmen ready for battle, [18] moved on to Bethel and consulted God. When the Israelites asked who should go first in the attack on the Benjaminites,[s] the LORD said, "Judah shall go first."* [19] The next day the Israelites advanced on Gibeah with their forces.

War with Benjamin. [20] On the day the Israelites drew up in battle array at Gibeah for the combat with Benjamin, [21] the Benjaminites came out of the city and felled twenty-two thousand men of Israel. [23] Then the Israelites went up and wept before the LORD until evening. "Shall I again engage my brother Benjamin in battle?" they asked the LORD; and the LORD answered that they should. [22] But though the Israelite soldiers took courage and again drew up for combat in the same place as on the previous day, [24] when they met the Benjaminites for the second time, [25] once again the Benjaminites who came out of Gibeah against them felled eighteen thousand Israelites, all of them swordsmen. [26] So the entire Israelite army went up to Bethel, where they wept and remained fasting before the LORD until evening of that day, besides offering holocausts and peace offerings before the LORD. [27] [t] When the Israelites consulted the LORD (for the ark of the covenant of God was there in those days, [28] and Phinehas, son of Eleazar, son of Aaron, was ministering to him in those days), and asked, "Shall I go out again to battle with Benjamin, my brother, or shall I desist?" the LORD said, "Attack! for tomorrow I will deliver him into your power." [29] [u] So Israel set men in ambush around Gibeah.*

[30] The Israelites went up against the Benjaminites for the third time and formed their line of battle at Gibeah as on other occasions. [31] The Benjaminites went out to meet them, and in the beginning they killed off about thirty of the Israelite soldiers in the open field, just as on the other occasions. [32] Therefore the Benjaminites thought, "We are defeating them as before"; not realizing that disaster was about to overtake them. The Israelites, however, had planned the flight so as to draw them away from the city onto the highways. They were drawn away from the city onto the highways, of which the one led to Bethel, the other to Gibeon. [33] And then all the men of Israel rose from their places. They re-formed their ranks at Baal-tamar, and the Israelites in ambush rushed from their place west of Gibeah, [34] ten thousand picked men from all Israel, and advanced against the city itself. In a fierce battle, [35] the LORD defeated Benjamin before Israel; and on that day the Israelites killed twenty-five thousand one hundred men of Benjamin, all of them swordsmen.

[36] To the Benjaminites it had looked as though the enemy were defeated, for the men of Israel gave ground to Benjamin, trusting in the ambush they had set at Gibeah. [37] But then the men in ambush made a sudden dash into Gibeah, overran it, and put the whole city to the sword. [38] Now, the other Israelites had agreed with the men in ambush on a smoke signal they were to send up from the city. [39] And though the men of Benjamin had begun by killing off some thirty of the men of Israel, under the impression that they were defeating them as surely as in the earlier fighting, the Israelites wheeled about to resist [40] as the smoke of the signal column began to rise up from the city. It was when Benjamin looked back and saw the whole city in flames against the sky [41] that the men of Israel wheeled about. Therefore the men of Benjamin were thrown into confusion, for they realized the disaster that had overtaken them. [42] They retreated before the men of Israel in the direction of the desert, with the fight being pressed against them. In their very midst, meanwhile, those who had been in the city were spreading destruction. [43] The men of Benjamin had been surrounded, and were

now pursued to a point east of Gibeah, [44] while eighteen thousand of them fell, warriors to a man. [45] The rest turned and fled through the desert to the rock Rimmon. [v] But on the highways the Israelites picked off five thousand men among them, and chasing them up to Gidom, killed another two thousand of them there. [46] Those of Benjamin who fell on that day were in all twenty-five thousand swordsmen, warriors to a man. [47] But six hundred others who turned and fled through the desert reached the rock Rimmon, where they remained for four months.

[48] The men of Israel withdrew through the territory of the Benjaminites, putting to the sword the inhabitants of the cities, the livestock, and all they chanced upon. Moreover they destroyed by fire all the cities they came upon.

CHAPTER 21

Wives for the Survivors. [1] Now the men of Israel* had sworn at Mizpah that none of them would give his daughter in marriage to anyone from Benjamin. [2] So the people went to Bethel and remained there before God until evening, raising their voices in bitter lament. [w] [3] They said, "LORD, God of Israel, why has it come to pass in Israel that today one tribe of Israel should be lacking?" [4] Early the next day the people built an altar there and offered holocausts and peace offerings. [5] Then the Israelites asked, "Are there any among all the tribes of Israel who did not come up to the LORD for the assembly?" For they had taken a solemn oath that anyone who did not go up to the LORD at Mizpah should be put to death without fail. [x]

[6] * The Israelites were disconsolate over their brother Benjamin and said, "Today one of the tribes of Israel has been cut off. [7] What can we do about wives for the survivors, since we have sworn by the LORD

---

u 29-46: Jos 8, 4-24.—v Jgs 21, 13.—w Jgs 20, 26.—x Jgs 20, 8ff.

20, 29-46: This stratagem proved more useful to the Israelites than force, as in the siege of Ai (Jos 8, 3-21). In the parallel accounts the first (vv 29-35) is a summary of the second (vv 36-46).
21, 1-3: The anger of the Israelites led them to destroy their brethren, the Benjaminites. Having realized their goal, however, they were soon filled with dismay, and sought to restore the tribe they had all but exterminated.
21, 6-9: This account is summarized in the parallel passage in vv 2-5.

not to give them any of our daughters in marriage?" [8] And when they asked whether anyone among the tribes of Israel had not come up to the LORD in Mizpah, they found that none of the men of Jabesh-gilead had come to the encampment for the assembly. [9] A roll call of the army established that none of the inhabitants of that city were present. [10] The community, therefore, sent twelve thousand warriors with orders to go to Jabesh-gilead and put those who lived there to the sword, including the women and children. [11] They were told to include under the ban* all males and every woman who was not still a virgin.[y] [12] Finding among the inhabitants of Jabesh-gilead four hundred young virgins, who had had no relations with men, they brought them to the camp at Shiloh in the land of Canaan. [13] [z] Then the whole community sent a message to the Benjaminites at the rock Rimmon, offering them peace. [14] When Benjamin returned at that time, they gave them as wives the women of Jabesh-gilead whom they had spared; but these proved to be not enough for them.

---

y Nm 31, 17.—z Jgs 20, 47.—a Jgs 17, 6; 18, 1; 19, 1.

21, 11: *Under the ban:* see note on Nm 21, 3.
21, 15: *Had made a breach:* what is here attributed to God was in reality the free and deliberate act of the Israelites and happened only by the permissive will of God. The ancients attributed to the first primary cause what is more directly due to secondary causes.
21, 18: Regardless of the serious consequences of their vow, the Israelites considered themselves obliged to fulfill it; cf Jgs 11, 31. 35f. 39.
21, 25: Cf Jgs 17, 6; 18, 1; 19, 1. The verse gives the reason why the lawlessness of the period of judges, and the events described herein, were possible.

[15] The people were still disconsolate over Benjamin because the LORD had made a breach* among the tribes of Israel. [16] And the elders of the community said, "What shall we do for wives for the survivors? For every woman in Benjamin has been put to death." [17] They said, "Those of Benjamin who survive must have heirs, else one of the Israelite tribes will be wiped out. [18] * Yet we cannot give them any of our daughters in marriage, because the Israelites have sworn, 'Cursed be he who gives a woman to Benjamin!' " [19] Then they thought of the yearly feast of the LORD at Shiloh, north of Bethel, east of the highway that goes up from Bethel to Shechem, and south of Lebonah. [20] And they instructed the Benjaminites, "Go and lie in wait in the vineyards. [21] When you see the girls of Shiloh come out to do their dancing, leave the vineyards and each of you seize one of the girls of Shiloh for a wife, and go to the land of Benjamin. [22] When their fathers or their brothers come to complain to us, we shall say to them, 'Release them to us as a kindness, since we did not take a woman apiece in the war. Had you yourselves given them these wives, you would now be guilty.' "

[23] The Benjaminites did this; they carried off a wife for each of them from their raid on the dancers, and went back to their own territory, where they rebuilt and occupied the cities. [24] Also at that time the Israelites dispersed; each of them left for his own heritage in his own clan and tribe.

[25] * In those days there was no king in Israel; everyone did what he thought best. [a]

◆

THE BOOK OF RUTH

The Book of Ruth is named after the Moabite woman who was joined to the Israelite people by her marriage with the influential Boaz of Bethlehem.

The book contains a beautiful example of filial piety, pleasing to the Hebrews especially because of its connection with King David, and useful both to Hebrews and to Gentiles. Its aim is to demonstrate the divine reward for such piety even when practiced by a stranger. Ruth's piety (Ru 2, 11), her spirit of self-sacrifice, and her moral integrity were favored by God with the gift of faith and an illustrious marriage whereby she became the ancestress of David and of Christ. In this, the universality of the messianic salvation is foreshadowed.

In the Greek and Latin canons the Book of Ruth is placed just after Judges, to which it is closely related because of the time of its action, and just before Samuel, for which it is an excellent introduction, since it traces the ancestry of the Davidic dynasty. One might characterize the literary form of this book as dramatic, since about two-thirds of it is in dialogue. Yet there is every indication that, as tradition has always held, it contains true history.

There is no certainty about the author of the book. It was written long after the events had passed (Ru 4, 7), which took place "in the time of the judges" (Ru 1, 1).

CHAPTER 1

Naomi in Moab. ¹Once in the time of the judges* there was a famine in the land; so a man from Bethlehem of Judah departed with his wife and two sons to reside on the plateau of Moab. ²The man was named Elimelech, his wife Naomi, and his sons Mahlon and Chilion; they were Ephrathites from Bethlehem of Judah. Some time after their arrival on the Moabite plateau, ³Elimelech, the husband of Naomi, died, and she was left with her two sons, ⁴who married Moabite women, one named Orpah, the other Ruth. When they had lived there about ten years, ⁵both Mahlon and Chilion died also, and the woman was left with neither her two sons nor her husband. ⁶She then made ready to go back from the plateau of Moab because word reached her there that the LORD had visited his people and given them food.

⁷She and her two daughters-in-law left the place where they had been living. Then as they were on the road back to the land of Judah, ⁸Naomi said to her two daughters-in-law, "Go back, each of you, to your mother's house!* May the LORD be kind to you as you were to the departed and to me! ⁹May the LORD grant each of you a husband and a home in which you will find rest." She kissed them good-bye, but they wept with loud sobs, ¹⁰and told her they would return with her to her people. ¹¹"Go back, my daughters!" said Naomi. "Why should you come with me? Have I other sons in my womb who may become your husbands?* ¹²Go back, my daughters! Go, for I am too old to marry again. And even if I could offer any hopes, or if tonight I had a husband or had borne sons, ¹³would you then wait and deprive yourselves of husbands until those sons grew up? No, my daughters! my lot is too

bitter for you, because the LORD has extended his hand against me." ¹⁴Again they sobbed aloud and wept; and Orpah kissed her mother-in-law good-bye, but Ruth stayed with her.

¹⁵"See now!" she said, "your sister-in-law has gone back to her people and her god. Go back after your sister-in-law!" ¹⁶ * But Ruth said, "Do not ask me to abandon or forsake you! for wherever you go I will go, wherever you lodge I will lodge, your people shall be my people, and your God my God. ¹⁷Wherever you die I will die, and there be buried. May the LORD do so and so to me, and more besides, if aught but death separates me from you!" ¹⁸Naomi then ceased to urge her, for she saw she was determined to go with her.

The Return to Bethlehem. ¹⁹So they went on together till they reached Bethlehem. On their arrival there, the whole city was astir over them, and the women asked, "Can this be Naomi?" ²⁰ *a* But she said to them, "Do not call me Naomi.* Call me Mara, for the Almighty has made it

---

a Ex 15, 23.

1, 1f: *In the time of the judges:* three generations before the end of the period of Judges; cf Ru 4, 21f. *Bethlehem of Judah:* to distinguish it from the town of the same name in the tribe of Zebulun (Jos 19, 15). *Ephrathites from Bethlehem:* belonging to a Judean clan which settled in Bethlehem; cf 1 Sm 17, 12; 1 Chr 2, 50f; 4, 4.

1, 8: *Mother's house:* the women's part of the dwelling; cf Jgs 4, 17; Song 3, 4.

1, 11: *Have I other sons . . . husbands?:* Naomi insisted that her daughters-in-law remain in their own country only for the sake of posterity. If she had had other sons, the levirate law would have obliged them to marry the widows of her deceased sons to perpetuate the names of the deceased; cf Gn 38, 8; Dt 25, 5f.

1, 16f: An example of heroic fidelity and piety. Ruth's decision, confirmed with an oath, to adhere to her mother-in-law impelled her to abandon her country and its pagan worship.

1, 20f: *Naomi:* means "amiable" or "pleasant," suggesting God's favor toward her. *The Almighty has brought evil upon me:* the ancients regarded adversity as a punishment from God for personal sin, as if good and evil were always repaid in a temporal and material manner.

very bitter for me. [21] I went away with an abundance, but the LORD has brought me back destitute. Why should you call me Naomi, since the LORD has pronounced against me and the Almighty has brought evil upon me?" [22] Thus it was that Naomi returned with the Moabite daughter-in-law, Ruth, who accompanied her back from the plateau of Moab. They arrived in Bethlehem at the beginning of the barley harvest.*

CHAPTER 2

The Meeting. [1] Naomi had a prominent kinsman named Boaz,[b] of the clan of her husband Elimelech. [2] Ruth the Moabite said to Naomi, "Let me go and glean ears of grain* in the field of anyone who will allow me that favor."[c] Naomi said to her, "Go, my daughter," [3] and she went. The field she entered to glean after the harvesters happened to be the section belonging to Boaz of the clan of Elimelech. [4] Boaz himself came from Bethlehem and said to the harvesters, "The LORD be with you!"* and they replied, "The LORD bless you!" [5] Boaz asked the overseer of his harvesters, "Whose girl is this?" [6] The overseer of the harvesters answered, "She is the Moabite girl who returned from the plateau of Moab with Naomi.[d] [7] She asked leave to gather the gleanings into sheaves after the harvesters; and ever since she came this morning she has remained here until now, with scarcely a moment's rest."

[8] Boaz said to Ruth, "Listen, my daughter! Do not go to glean in anyone else's field; you are not to leave here. Stay here with my women servants. [9] Watch to see which field is to be harvested, and follow them; I have commanded the young men to do you no harm. When you are thirsty, you may go and drink from the vessels

the young men have filled." [10] Casting herself prostrate upon the ground, she said to him, "Why should I, a foreigner, be favored with your notice?" [11] [e] Boaz answered her: "I have had a complete account of what you have done for your mother-in-law after your husband's death; you have left your father and your mother and the land of your birth, and have come to a people whom you did not know previously. [12] May the LORD reward what you have done! May you receive a full reward from the LORD, the God of Israel, under whose wings you have come for refuge." [13] She said, "May I prove worthy of your kindness, my lord: you have comforted me, your servant, with your consoling words; would indeed that I were a servant of yours!" [14] At mealtime Boaz said to her, "Come here and have some food; dip your bread in the sauce." Then as she sat near the reapers, he handed her some roasted grain and she ate her fill and had some left over. [15] She rose to glean, and Boaz instructed his servants to let her glean among the sheaves themselves without scolding her, [16] and even to let drop some handfuls and leave them for her to glean without being rebuked.

[17] She gleaned in the field until evening, and when she beat out what she had gleaned it came to about an ephah of barley, [18] which she took into the city and showed to her mother-in-law. Next she brought out and gave her what she had left over from lunch, [19] So her mother-in-law said to her, "Where did you glean today? Where did you go to work? May he who took notice of you be blessed!" Then she told her mother-in-law with whom she had worked. "The man at whose place I worked today is named Boaz," she said. [20] [f] "May he be blessed by the LORD who is ever merciful to the living and to the dead," Naomi exclaimed to her daughter-in-law; and she continued, "He is a relative of ours, one of our next of kin."* [21] "He even told me," added Ruth the Moabite, "that I should stay with his servants until they complete his entire harvest." [22] "You would do well, my dear," Naomi rejoined, "to go out with his servants; for in someone else's field you might be insulted." [23] So she stayed gleaning with the servants of Boaz until the end of the barley and wheat harvests.

Ru

---

b Ru 3, 2. 12; 4, 21; Mt 1, 5.—c Dt 24, 19.—d Ru 1, 22.—e Ru 1, 14-17.—f Ru 3, 9.

1, 22: *Barley harvest:* early April. This circumstance favored the events of the narrative that follow.

2, 2: *Let me go and glean . . . grain:* even the poor, the widow, the stranger, and the orphan had a right to glean at harvest time; cf Lv 19, 9f; 23, 22; Dt 24, 19-22.

2, 4: *The Lord be with you:* courtesy and religious feeling characterize the salutations of the Hebrews. This greeting is used in the Christian liturgy.

2, 20: *One of our next of kin:* literally "our redeemer," a near relative of the same clan who had the right and duty to restore the land which an impoverished kinsman had alienated (Lv 25, 25-28), and to marry the widow of a relative who had died without male offspring so as to raise up posterity to his name (Dt 25, 5-10).

CHAPTER 3

Ruth Again Presents Herself. When she was back with her mother-in-law, [1]Naomi said to her, "My daughter, I must seek a home for you that will please you. [2] g Now is not Boaz, with whose servants you were, a relative of ours? This evening he will be winnowing barley at the threshing floor. [3]So bathe and anoint yourself; then put on your best attire and go down to the threshing floor. Do not make yourself known to the man before he has finished eating and drinking. [4]But when he lies down, take note of the place where he does so. Then go, uncover a place at his feet,* and lie down. He will tell you what to do." [5]"I will do whatever you advise," Ruth replied. [6]So she went down to the threshing floor and did just as her mother-in-law had instructed her.

[7]Boaz ate and drank to his heart's content. Then when he went and lay down at the edge of the sheaves, she stole up, uncovered a place at his feet, and lay down. [8]In the middle of the night, however, the man gave a start and turned around to find a woman lying at his feet. [9]He asked, "Who are you?" And she replied, "I am your servant Ruth. Spread the corner of your cloak over me,* for you are my next of kin." [10]He said, "May the LORD bless you, my daughter! You have been even more loyal now than before in not going after the young men, whether poor or rich. h [11]So be assured, daughter, I will do for you whatever you say; all my townspeople know you for a worthy woman. [12] i Now, though indeed I am closely related to you, you have another relative still closer.* [13]Stay as you are for tonight, and tomorrow, if he wishes to claim you, good! let him do so. But if he does not wish to claim you, as the LORD lives, I will claim you myself. Lie there until morning." j [14]So she lay at his feet until morning, but rose before men could recognize one another. Boaz said, "Let it not be known that this woman came to the threshing floor." [15]Then he said to her, "Take off your cloak and hold it out." When she did so, he poured out six measures of barley, helped her lift the bundle, k and left for the city.

[16]Ruth went home to her mother-in-law, who asked, "How have you fared,

my daughter?" So she told her all the man had done for her, [17]and concluded, "He gave me these six measures of barley because he did not wish me to come back to my mother-in-law empty-handed!" [18]Naomi then said, "Wait here, my daughter, until you learn what happens, for the man will not rest, but will settle the matter today."

CHAPTER 4

Boaz Marries Ruth. [1]Boaz went and took a seat at the gate;* and when he saw the closer relative l of whom he had spoken come along, he called to him by name, "Come and sit beside me!" And he did so. [2]Then Boaz picked out ten of the elders* of the city and asked them to sit nearby. When they had done this, [3]he said to the near relative: "Naomi, who has come back from the Moabite plateau, is putting up for sale the piece of land that belonged to our kinsman Elimelech. [4] * So I thought I would inform you, bidding you before those here present, including the elders of my people, to put in your claim for it if you wish to acquire it as next of kin. m But if you do not wish to claim it, tell me so, that I may be guided accordingly, for no one has a prior claim to yours, and mine is next." He answered, "I will put in my claim."

[5] * Boaz continued, "Once you acquire the field from Naomi, you must take also

g Ru 1.—h Dt 25, 5.—i Ru 4, 1.—j Ru 4, 5; Dt 25, 5.—k Ru 2, 17.—l Ru 3, 12.—m Lv 25, 25.

3, 4: *Uncover a place at his feet . . . :* confident of the virtue of Ruth and Boaz, Naomi advises this unusual expedient to her daughter-in-law for the purpose of introducing her claim.
3, 9: *Spread the corner of your cloak over me:* be my protector by marrying me according to the duty of a near kinsman; cf Dt 25, 5; Ez 16, 8.
3, 12: *Relative still closer:* who had a prior right and duty to marry Ruth.
4, 1: *Took a seat at the gate:* i.e., of the city, where business affairs were settled.
4, 2: *Ten of the elders:* to serve as judges in legal matters as well as witnesses of the settlement of business affairs; cf Dt 25, 7-9.
4, 4: Poverty had obliged Naomi to sell the land of her deceased husband. The law permitted the nearest kinsman to redeem the land and thus preserve the family patrimony; cf Lv 25, 25.
4, 5f: The heir of Elimelech's field had died without children (Ru 1, 5). The nearest of kin could now redeem the land but he must also take Ruth, *the widow of the late heir,* to wife to perpetuate the family of the deceased; cf Dt 25, 5f. The first male child of such a marriage would be the legal son of Mahlon and grandson of Elimelech.

Ruth the Moabite,[n] the widow of the late heir, and raise up a family for the departed on his estate." [6] The near relative replied, "I cannot exercise my claim lest I depreciate my own estate. Put in a claim yourself in my stead, for I cannot exercise my claim." [7] Now it used to be the custom in Israel that, to make binding a contract of redemption or exchange, one party would take off his sandal* and give it to the other. This was the form of attestation in Israel. [8] So the near relative, in saying to Boaz, "Acquire it for yourself," drew off his sandal. [9] Boaz then said to the elders and to all the people, "You are witnesses today that I have acquired from Naomi all the holdings of Elimelech, Chilion and Mahlon. [10] I also take Ruth the Moabite, the widow of Mahlon, as my wife, in order to raise up a family for her late husband on his estate, so that the name of the departed may not perish among his kinsmen and fellow citizens. Do you witness this to-

n Ru 3, 13; Dt 25, 5.—o Gn 29, 31—30, 24; 35, 19.—p Gn 38, 29.—q Lk 1, 58.—r 18-22: 1 Chr 2, 4-15; Mk 1, 3-6.—s Gn 46, 12; 1 Chr 4, 1.—t Ex 6, 23; Nm 1, 7.—u 1 Sm 16, 10-13.

4, 7: *Take off his sandal. . . . :* by this act the near relative renounced his legal right, both to the field of Elimelech and to the marriage with Ruth. The custom mentioned in Dt 25, 6 is somewhat different.

4, 12: *Perez, whom Tamar bore to Judah:* the right which Judah unwittingly satisfied for his daughter-in-law Tamar (Gn 38), Boaz willingly rendered to Ruth.

4, 16: *Placed him on her lap:* took him as her own; cf Gn 30, 3; 48, 12; Nm 11, 12.

4, 17: *The father of Jesse, the father of David:* indicating the place of Obed, Jesse and David in the line of Judah and the ancestry of Christ, the Messiah; cf Mt 1, 5f.

day?" [11] [o] All those at the gate, including the elders, said, "We do so. May the LORD make this wife come into your house like Rachel and Leah, who between them built up the house of Israel. May you do well in Ephrathah and win fame in Bethlehem. [12] [p] With the offspring the LORD will give you from this girl, may your house become like the house of Perez, whom Tamar bore to Judah."*

[13] Boaz took Ruth. When they came together as man and wife, the LORD enabled her to conceive and she bore a son. [14] Then the women said to Naomi, "Blessed is the LORD who has not failed to provide you today with an heir! May he become famous in Israel! [15] He will be your comfort and the support of your old age, for his mother is the daughter-in-law who loves you. She is worth more to you than seven sons!" [16] Naomi took the child, placed him on her lap,* and became his nurse. [17] And the neighbor women gave him his name,[q] at the news that a grandson had been born to Naomi. They called him Obed. He was the father of Jesse, the father of David.*

[18] [r] These are the descendants of Perez: Perez was the father of Hezron,[s] [19] Hezron was the father of Ram, Ram was the father of Amminadab, [20] [t] Amminadab was the father of Nahshon, Nahshon was the father of Salmon, [21] Salmon was the father of Boaz, Boaz was the father of Obed, [22] [u] Obed was the father of Jesse, and Jesse became the father of David.

Ru

THE HISTORICAL BOOKS

The historical books include 1 and 2 Samuel, 1 and 2 Kings, 1 and 2 Chronicles, Ezra, Nehemiah, 1 and 2 Maccabees. To these are added the special literary group of Tobit, Judith and Esther.

The books of Tobit, Judith, and 1 and 2 Maccabees, as well as parts of Esther, are called deuterocanonical: they are not contained in the Hebrew canon but have been accepted by the Catholic Church as canonical and inspired.

By means of a series of episodes involving the persons of Samuel, Saul, and David, a century of history unfolds in 1 and 2 Samuel from the close of the period of Judges to the rise and establishment of the monarchy in Israel. Most important is God's promise to David of a lasting dynasty (2 Sm 7), from which royal messianism in the Bible developed.

In 1 and 2 Kings the religious history of Israel extends another four centuries, from the last days of David to the Babylonian captivity and the destruction of Jerusalem (587 B.C.). The various sources for these books are woven into a uniform pattern based on the principle of fidelity to Yahweh for rulers and people alike. The sequence of regnal chronicles in both books is interrupted by a cycle of traditions surrounding the prophets Elijah (1 Kgs) and Elisha (2 Kgs).

Chronicles, Ezra and Nehemiah form a historical work, uniform in style and basic ideas. Chronicles records the long period from the reign of Saul to the return from exile, not so much with exactitude of detail as with concern for the meaning of the facts which demonstrate God's intervention in history. The Ezra-Nehemiah chronicle constitutes the most important source for the formation of the Jewish religious community after the Babylonian exile; the two persons most responsible for the reorganization of Jewish life were Ezra and Nehemiah

1 and 2 Maccabees contain independent accounts of partially identical events which accompanied the attempted suppression of Judaism in Palestine in the second century B.C. Vigorous reaction to this attempt established for a time the religious and political independence of the Jews. 1 Maccabees portrays God as the eternal benefactor of the Jews and their unfailing source of help. The people are required to be devoted to his exclusive worship and to observe exactly the law he has given them. 2 Maccabees, besides supplementing the former volume, gives a theological interpretation of the history of the period and contains teaching on the resurrection from the dead, intercession of the saints, and suffrages for the dead.

Tobit, Judith, and Esther are examples of free composition—the religious novel used for purposes of edification and instruction. Interest in whatever historical data these books may contain is merely intensified by the addition of vivid details. Judith is a lesson in Providence: a pious reflection on the annual Passover observance to convey the reassurance that God is still the master of history who saves Israel from her enemies. Esther's purpose is the glorification of the Jewish people and the explanation of the origin, significance, and date of the feast of Purim. It is a literary development of the principle of reversal of fortune through punishment of the prosperous rich and reward for the virtuous who are oppressed.

Samuel to Maccabees demonstrates that before as well as during the millennium of history with which it is concerned, Israel was a covenanted people, bound to Yahweh, Lord of the universe, by the ties of faith and obedience. This required observance of the law and worship in his temple, the consequent rewards of which were divine favor and protection. In this way these books anticipate and prepare for the coming of him who would bring type and prophecy to fulfillment, history to term, and holiness to perfection: Christ, the Son of David and the promised Messiah.

THE BOOKS OF SAMUEL

Originally but one book, the scroll of Samuel was early divided into two. The Greek translators called these the first and second Books of Kingdoms, a title St. Jerome later modified to "Kings." The Hebrew title, "Samuel," alludes to the leading figure in the first book, who was responsible for the enthronement of David. It is David's history that the second book recounts.

This sacred work thus comprises the history of about a century, describing the close of the age of the Judges and the beginnings of monarchy in Israel under Saul and David. It is not a complete and continuous history, nor a systematic account of the period, but rather a series of episodes centered around the persons of Samuel, Saul and David, the principal figures leading up to the establishment of the royal dynasty of David.

The final editor is unknown, nor are we certain of the time at which the various strands of the narrative were put together, though one may think of the period, perhaps late in the seventh century B.C., when the other volumes of the "Former Prophets," from Joshua through Kings, were built into a more or less continuous historical corpus. The Samuel-Saul-David narratives clearly depend on several written sources: a Samuel cycle, two sets of stories about Saul and David, and a family history of David. This last part (2 Sm 9—20; 1 Kgs 1—2), one of the most vivid historical narratives surviving from ancient times, probably originated early in the reign of Solomon.

One of the most significant theological contributions of the Old Testament is found in 2 Samuel 7, the oracle of Nathan. David is here promised an eternal dynasty, and this becomes the basis for the development of royal messianism throughout the Bible. With this promise to David one should compare 2 Chr 17; Pss 89, 20-38 and 132, 11ff; Acts 2, 30; and Heb 1, 5.

The contents of this work may be divided as follows: I. History of the Last Judges, Eli and Samuel (1 Sm 1—7, 17). II. Establishment of the Monarchy in Israel (1 Sm 8, 1—12, 25). III. Saul and David (1 Sm 13, 1—2 Sm 2, 7). IV. The Reign of David (2 Sm 2, 8—20, 26). V. Appendixes (2 Sm 21, 1—24, 25).

THE FIRST BOOK OF SAMUEL

I: HISTORY OF THE LAST JUDGES, ELI AND SAMUEL

CHAPTER 1

Elkanah and His Family at Shiloh. ¹There was a certain man from Ramathaim, Elkanah by name, a Zuphite from the hill country of Ephraim. He was the son of Jeroham, son of Elihu, son of Tohu, son of Zuph, an Ephraimite.ᵃ ²He had two wives, one named Hannah, the other Peninnah; Peninnah had children, but Hannah was childless. ³This man regularly went on pilgrimage from his city to worship the LORD of hosts and to sacrifice to him at Shiloh, where the two sons of Eli, Hophni and Phinehas, were ministering as priests of the LORD.ᵇ ⁴When the day came for Elkanah to offer sacrifice, he used to give a portion each to his wife Peninnah and to all her sons and daughters, ⁵but a double portion to Hannah because he loved her, though the LORD had made her barren.ᶜ ⁶Her rival, to upset her, turned it into a constant reproach to her that the LORD had left her barren.ᵈ ⁷This went on year after year; each time they made their pilgrimage to the sanctuary of the LORD, Peninnah would approach her, and Hannah would weep and refuse to eat. ⁸Her husband Elkanah used to ask her: "Hannah, why do you weep, and why do you refuse to eat? Why do you grieve? Am I not more to you than ten sons?"ᵉ

Hannah's Prayer. ⁹Hannah rose after one such meal at Shiloh, and presented herself before the LORD; at the time, Eli the priest was sitting on a chair near the doorpost of the LORD's temple. ¹⁰In her bitterness she prayed to the LORD, weeping copiously,

a 1 Chr 6, 19f.—b Ex 23, 14-17; 34, 23; Dt 16, 16; Jgs 21, 19.—c Dt 21, 15ff.—d Gn 16, 4f.—e Ru 4, 15.

[11] and she made a vow, promising: "O LORD of hosts, if you look with pity on the misery of your handmaid, if you remember me and do not forget me, if you give your handmaid a male child, I will give him to the LORD* for as long as he lives; neither wine nor liquor shall he drink, and no razor shall ever touch his head."[f] [12] As she remained long at prayer before the LORD, Eli watched her mouth, [13] for Hannah was praying silently; though her lips were moving, her voice could not be heard. Eli, thinking her drunk, [14] said to her, "How long will you make a drunken show of yourself? Sober up from your wine!" [15] "It isn't that, my lord," Hannah answered. "I am an unhappy woman. I have had neither wine nor liquor; I was only pouring out my troubles to the LORD. [16] Do not think your handmaid a ne'er-do-well; my prayer has been prompted by my deep sorrow and misery." [17] Eli said, "Go in peace, and may the God of Israel grant you what you have asked of him." [18] She replied, "Think kindly of your maidservant," and left. She went to her quarters, ate and drank with her husband, and no longer appeared downcast. [19] Early the next morning they worshiped before the LORD, and then returned to their home in Ramah.

Hannah Bears a Son. When Elkanah had relations with his wife Hannah, the LORD remembered her. [20] She conceived, and at the end of her term bore a son whom she called Samuel, since she had asked* the LORD for him. [21] The next time her husband Elkanah was going up with the rest of his household to offer the customary sacrifice to the LORD and

to fulfill his vows, [22] Hannah did not go, explaining to her husband, "Once the child is weaned, I will take him to appear before the LORD and to remain there forever; I will offer him as a perpetual nazirite." [23] Her husband Elkanah answered her: "Do what you think best; wait until you have weaned him. Only, may the LORD bring your resolve to fulfillment!" And so she remained at home and nursed her son until she had weaned him.

Samuel Is Offered to God. [24] Once he was weaned, she brought him up with her, along with a three-year-old bull, an ephah* of flour, and a skin of wine, and presented him at the temple of the LORD in Shiloh. [25] After the boy's father had sacrificed the young bull, Hannah, his mother, approached Eli [26] and said: "Pardon, my lord! As you live, my lord, I am the woman who stood near you here, praying to the LORD. [27] I prayed for this child, and the LORD granted my request. [28] Now I, in turn, give him to the LORD; as long as he lives, he shall be dedicated to the LORD." She left him there; [1] * and as she worshiped the LORD, she said:

CHAPTER 2

"My heart exults in the LORD,*
  my horn* is exalted in my God.
I have swallowed up my enemies;
  I rejoice in my victory.[g]
[2] There is no Holy One like the LORD;
  there is no Rock like our God.[h]

[3] "Speak boastfully no longer,
  nor let arrogance issue from your mouths.*
For an all-knowing God is the LORD,
  a God who judges deeds.[i]
[4] The bows of the mighty are broken,
  while the tottering gird on strength.[j]
[5] The well-fed hire themselves out for bread,
  while the hungry batten on spoil.
The barren wife bears seven sons,
  while the mother of many languishes.

[6] "The LORD puts to death and gives life;
  he casts down to the nether world;
  he raises up again.[k]
[7] The LORD makes poor and makes rich,
  he humbles, he also exalts.

---

f Nm 6, 1-5; Jgs 13, 2-5; 16, 17; Lk 1, 15.—g Dt 33, 17; 2 Sm 22, 3; Ps 18, 2; Is 61, 10; Lk 1, 47. 69.—h 2 Sm 22, 3; Ps 18, 2.—i Ps 75, 4.—j Is 40, 29.—k Dt 32, 39; Tb 4, 19; Jb 5, 11; Ps 30, 4; Wis 16, 13; Lk 1, 52.

1, 11: *Give him to the Lord:* some ancient texts call Samuel a *nazir* in this context; see note on Nm 6, 1ff.

1, 20: *Since she had asked:* this explanation would be more directly appropriate for the name Saul, which means "asked"; Samuel means "name of God."

1, 24: *An ephah:* a little more than a bushel.

1, 1: *And . . . said:* this belongs to ch 2.

2, 1-10: A hymn attributed to Hannah, the mother of Samuel, as her thanksgiving to God because she has borne a son despite her previous sterility. She praises God as the helper of the weak (1ff), who casts down the mighty and raises up the lowly (3ff), and who alone is the source of true strength (8ff); the hymn ends with a prayer for the king (v 10). This canticle has several points of resemblance with our Lady's *Magnificat*.

2, 1: *Horn:* the symbol of strength; cf Pss 18, 3; 75, 5; 89, 18; 112, 9.

2, 3: *Speak . . . mouths:* addressed to the *enemies* mentioned in v 1.

8 He raises the needy from the dust;
   from the ash heap he lifts up the
   poor,
To seat them with nobles
   and make a glorious throne their
   heritage.*l*
He gives to the vower his vow,
   and blesses the sleep of the just.

"For the pillars of the earth are the
   LORD's,
   and he has set the world upon them.
9 He will guard the footsteps of his faithful ones,
   but the wicked shall perish in the
   darkness.
   For not by strength does man prevail;
10   the LORD's foes shall be shattered.
The Most High in heaven thunders;
   the LORD judges the ends of the
   earth.
Now may he give strength to his king
   and exalt the horn of his anointed!"*m*

11 When Elkanah returned home to
Ramah, the child remained in the service
of the LORD under the priest Eli.

Wickedness of Eli's Sons. 12 Now the sons
of Eli were wicked; they had respect
neither for the LORD 13 nor for the priests'
duties toward the people. When someone
offered a sacrifice, the priest's servant
would come with a three-pronged fork,
while the meat was still boiling,*n* 14 and
would thrust it into the basin, kettle, caldron, or pot. Whatever the fork brought
up, the priest would keep. That is how all
the Israelites were treated who came to the
sanctuary at Shiloh. 15 In fact, even before
the fat was burned, the priest's servant
would come and say to the man offering
the sacrifice, "Give me some meat to roast
for the priest. He will not accept boiled
meat from you, only raw meat." 16 And if
the man protested to him, "Let the fat be
burned first as is the custom, then take
whatever you wish," he would reply, "No,
give it to me now, or else I will take it by
force."*o* 17 Thus the young men sinned
grievously in the presence of the LORD;
they treated the offerings to the LORD with
disdain.

The Lord Rewards Hannah. 18 Meanwhile
the boy Samuel, girt with a linen apron,*
was serving in the presence of the LORD.
19 His mother used to make a little garment
for him, which she would bring him each
time she went up with her husband to

offer the customary sacrifice. 20 And Eli
would bless Elkanah and his wife, as they
were leaving for home. He would say,
"May the LORD repay you with children
from this woman for the gift she has made
to the LORD!" 21 The LORD favored Hannah so that she conceived and gave birth to
three more sons and two daughters, while
young Samuel grew up in the service of the
LORD.*p*

Eli's Futile Rebuke. 22 When Eli was very
old, he heard repeatedly how his sons were
treating all Israel [and that they were having relations with the women serving at the
entry of the meeting tent.]* 23 So he said to
them: "Why are you doing such things?
24 No, my sons, you must not do these
things! It is not a good report that I hear
the people of the LORD spreading about
you. 25 If a man sins against another man,
one can intercede for him with the LORD;
but if a man sins against the LORD, who
can intercede for him?" But they disregarded their father's warning, since
LORD had decided on their death. 26 Meanwhile, young Samuel was growing in stature and in worth in the estimation of the
LORD and of men.*q*

Doom of Eli's House. * 27 A man of God
came to Eli and said to him: "This is what
the LORD says: 'I went so far as to reveal
myself to your father's family when they
were in Egypt as slaves to the house of
Pharaoh. 28 I chose them out of all the
tribes of Israel to be my priests, to go up to
my altar, to burn incense, and to wear the
ephod* before me; and I assigned all the

---

l Jb 9, 6; 38, 6; Ps 104, 5; 121, 3.—m Ps 98, 9.—n 13-15: Ex
29, 27f; Lv 7, 29-36; Dt 18, 3.—o Lv 3, 3ff.—p 1 Sm 3, 19.—q
Lk 2, 52.

2, 18: *Linen apron:* called in Hebrew "ephod," but not the
same as the high priest's ephod (Ex 28, 6-14) or the ephod used
in divination (v 28). Samuel wore a simple apron such as was
worn by the priests (1 Sm 22, 18), and on one occasion also by
David (2 Sm 6, 14).
2, 22: The bracketed words, which recall Ex 38, 8, are a gloss
in the received text; they are lacking in the oldest Greek translation, and in a Hebrew manuscript from Qumran.
2, 27-36: These verses propose the punishment of Eli from a
point of view contemporary with the reform of Josiah (2 Kgs 23,
9; cf v 36); they hint at the events recorded in 1 Sm 22, 18-23
and 1 Kgs 2, 27. The older story of this divine warning is that in
1 Sm 3, 11-14.
2, 28: *Ephod:* a portable container, presumably of cloth, for
the lots used in ritual consultation of God during the days of the
Judges (Jgs 17, 5; 18, 14-15) and down into the time of David (1
Sm 14, 3ff; 23, 6ff; 30, 7f). The ephod of the high priest described in Ex 28, 6ff becomes a garment upon which a
breastpiece of decision symbolizes, but no longer serves for,
such consultation. The Exodus text codifies a later form of the
tradition.

oblations of the Israelites to your father's family.*r* *29*Why do you keep a greedy eye on my sacrifices and on the offerings which I have prescribed? And why do you honor your sons in preference to me, fattening yourselves with the choicest part of every offering of my people Israel?' *30* *s* This, therefore, is the oracle of the LORD, the God of Israel: 'I said in the past that your family and your father's family should minister in my presence forever. But now,' the LORD declares, 'away with this! for I will honor those who honor me, but those who spurn me shall be accursed. *31*Yes, the time is coming when I will break your strength and the strength of your father's family, so that no man in your family shall reach old age. *32*You shall witness as a disappointed rival all the benefits enjoyed by Israel, but there shall never be an old man in your family. *33*I will permit some of your family to remain at my altar, to wear out their eyes in consuming greed; but the rest of the men of your family shall die by the sword. *34*You shall have a sign in what will happen to your two sons, Hophni and Phinehas: both shall die on the same day.*t* *35*I will choose a faithful priest who shall do what I have in heart and mind. I will establish a lasting house for him which shall function in the presence of my anointed forever. *36*Then whoever is left of your family will come to grovel before him for a piece of silver or a loaf of bread, and will say: Appoint me, I beg you, to a priestly function, that I may have a morsel of bread to eat.' "*u*

CHAPTER 3

Revelation to Samuel. *1*During the time young Samuel was minister to the LORD under Eli, a revelation of the LORD was uncommon* and vision infrequent. *2*One day Eli was asleep in his usual place. His eyes had lately grown so weak that he could not see. *3*The lamp of God was not yet extinguished, and Samuel was sleep-

ing in the temple of the LORD where the ark of God was.*v* *4*The LORD called to Samuel, who answered, "Here I am." *5*He ran to Eli and said, "Here I am. You called me." "I did not call you," Eli said. "Go back to sleep." So he went back to sleep. *6*Again the LORD called Samuel, who rose and went to Eli. "Here I am," he said. "You called me." But he answered, "I did not call you, my son. Go back to sleep."

*7*At that time Samuel was not familiar with the LORD, because the LORD had not revealed anything to him as yet. *8*The LORD called Samuel again, for the third time. Getting up and going to Eli, he said, "Here I am. You called me." Then Eli understood that the LORD was calling the youth. *9*So he said to Samuel, "Go to sleep, and if you are called, reply, 'Speak, LORD, for your servant is listening.' " When Samuel went to sleep in his place, *10*the LORD came and revealed his presence, calling out as before, "Samuel, Samuel!" Samuel answered, "Speak, for your servant is listening." *11*The LORD said to Samuel: "I am about to do something in Israel that will cause the ears of everyone who hears it to ring. *12*On that day I will carry out in full against Eli everything I threatened against his family. *13*I announce to him that I am condemning his family once and for all, because of this crime: though he knew his sons were blaspheming God, he did not reprove them.*w* *14*Therefore, I swear to the family of Eli that no sacrifice or offering will ever expiate its crime." *15*Samuel then slept until morning, when he got up early and opened the doors of the temple of the LORD. He feared to tell Eli the vision, *16*but Eli called to him, "Samuel, my son!" He replied, "Here I am." *17*Then Eli asked, "What did he say to you? Hide nothing from me! May God do thus and so to you* if you hide a single thing he told you." *18*So Samuel told him everything, and held nothing back. Eli answered, "He is the LORD. He will do what he judges best."

Samuel Acknowledged as Prophet. *19*Samuel grew up, and the LORD was with him, not permitting any word of his to be without effect.*x* *20* *y* Thus all Israel from Dan to Beer-sheba came to know that Samuel was an accredited prophet of the LORD. *21*The LORD continued to ap-

1Sm

---

r 1 Sm 23, 9; 30, 7f; Jgs 17, 5.—s 30f: 2 Sm 22, 26; 1 Kgs 2, 27; Ps 18, 25.—t 1 Sm 4, 11.—u 2 Kgs 23, 9.—v Ex 25, 22; 27, 20f; Lv 24, 2. 4; 2 Chr 13, 11.—w 1 Sm 2, 27-36.—x 1 Sm 2, 21.—y Jgs 20, 1.

3, 1: *Uncommon:* prophetic communications from God were almost unknown.

3, 17: *May God do thus and so to you:* the Biblical writers avoid repeating for us the specific terms of a curse as the speaker would have uttered it.

pear at Shiloh; he manifested himself to Samuel at Shiloh through his word, [1] * and Samuel spoke to all Israel.

CHAPTER 4

Defeat of the Israelites. At that time, the Philistines gathered for an attack on Israel. Israel went out to engage them in battle and camped at Ebenezer, while the Philistines camped at Aphek. [2] The Philistines then drew up in battle formation against Israel. After a fierce struggle Israel was defeated by the Philistines, who slew about four thousand men on the battlefield. [3] When the troops retired to the camp, the elders of Israel said, "Why has the LORD permitted us to be defeated today by the Philistines? Let us fetch the ark of the LORD from Shiloh that it may go into battle among us and save us from the grasp of our enemies."

Loss of the Ark. [4] So the people sent to Shiloh and brought from there the ark of the LORD of hosts, who is enthroned upon the cherubim.* The two sons of Eli, Hophni and Phinehas, were with the ark of God.[z] [5] When the ark of the LORD arrived in the camp, all Israel shouted so loudly that the earth resounded. [6] The Philistines, hearing the noise of shouting, asked, "What can this loud shouting in the camp of the Hebrews mean?" On learning that the ark of the LORD had come into the camp, [7] the Philistines were frightened. They said, "Gods have come to their camp." They said also, "Woe to us! This has never happened before. [8] Woe to us! Who can deliver us from the power of these mighty gods?* These are the gods that struck the Egyptians with various plagues and with pestilence. [9] Take courage and be manly, Philistines; otherwise you will become slaves to the Hebrews, as they were your slaves. So fight manfully!" [10] The Philistines fought and Israel was defeated; every man fled to his own tent. It was a disastrous defeat, in which Israel lost thirty thousand foot soldiers.[a] [11] The ark of God was captured, and Eli's two sons, Hophni and Phinehas, were among the dead.[b]

Death of Eli. [12] A Benjaminite fled from the battlefield and reached Shiloh that same day, with his clothes torn and his head covered with dirt.[c] [13] When he arrived, Eli was sitting in his chair beside the gate, watching the road, for he was troubled at heart about the ark of God. The man, however, went into the city to divulge his news, which put the whole city in an uproar. [14] Hearing the outcry of the men standing near him, Eli inquired, "What does this commotion mean?" [15] (Eli was ninety-eight years old, and his eyes would not focus, so that he could not see.) [16] The man quickly came up to Eli and said, "It is I who have come from the battlefield; I fled from there today." He asked, "What happened, my son?" [17] And the messenger answered: "Israel fled from the Philistines; in fact, the troops suffered heavy losses. Your two sons, Hophni and Phinehas, are among the dead, and the ark of God has been captured." [18] At this mention of the ark of God, Eli fell backward from his chair into the gateway; since he was an old man and heavy, he died of a broken neck. He had judged Israel for forty years.

[19] His daughter-in-law, the wife of Phinehas, was with child and at the point of giving birth. When she heard the news concerning the capture of the ark and the deaths of her father-in-law and her husband, she was seized with the pangs of labor, and gave birth. [20] She was about to die when the women standing around her said to her, "Never fear! You have given birth to a son." Yet she neither answered nor paid any attention.[d] [21] [She named the child Ichabod, saying, "Gone is the glory from Israel," with reference to the capture of the ark of God and to her father-in-law and her husband.] [22] She said, "Gone is the glory from Israel," because the ark of God had been captured.[e]

CHAPTER 5

The Ark in the Temple of Dagon. [1][f] The Philistines, having captured the ark of God, transferred it from Ebenezer to Ashdod. [2] They then took the ark of God and brought it into the temple of Dagon,

z Ex 25, 22.—a Ps 78, 61.—b 1 Sm 2, 34.—c Jos 7, 6; 2 Sm 1, 2; Jer 7, 12.—d 1 Sm 14, 3; Gn 35, 16ff.—e Ps 78, 61.—f 1-5: Jgs 16, 23-30; Is 45, 5f. 20f.

3, 1: *And . . . Israel:* this belongs to ch 4.

4, 4: *Enthroned upon the cherubim:* this title of the Lord seems to have originated in the sanctuary at Shiloh; it represents the divine Majesty as seated upon a throne on which he can be borne through the heavens by winged creatures somewhat as in the visions of Ez 1 and 10.

4, 8: *These mighty gods:* the Philistines, who were polytheists, are represented as supposing the Israelites honored several gods.

placing it beside Dagon. ³When the people of Ashdod rose early the next morning, Dagon was lying prone on the ground before the ark of the LORD. So they picked Dagon up and replaced him. ⁴But the next morning early, when they arose, Dagon lay prone on the ground before the ark of the LORD, his head and hands broken off and lying on the threshold, his trunk alone intact. ⁵For this reason, neither the priests of Dagon nor any others who enter the temple of Dagon tread on the threshold of Dagon in Ashdod to this very day; they always step over it.

The Ark Is Carried About. ⁶Now the LORD dealt severely with the people of Ashdod. He ravaged and afflicted the city and its vicinity with hemorrhoids; he brought upon the city a great and deadly plague of mice* that swarmed in their ships and overran their fields.ᵍ ⁷On seeing how matters stood, the men of Ashdod decided, "The ark of the God of Israel must not remain with us, for he is handling us and our god Dagon severely." ⁸So they summoned all the Philistine lords and inquired of them, "What shall we do with the ark of the God of Israel?" The men of Gath replied, "Let them move the ark of the God of Israel on to us." ⁹So they moved the ark of the God of Israel to Gath! But after it had been brought there, the LORD threw the city into utter turmoil: he afflicted its inhabitants, young and old, and hemorrhoids broke out on them. ¹⁰The ark of God was next sent to Ekron; but as it entered that city, the people there cried out, "Why have they brought the ark of the God of Israel here to kill us and our kindred?" ¹¹Then they, too, sent a summons to all the Philistine lords and pleaded: "Send away the ark of the God of Israel. Let it return to its own place, that it may not kill us and our kindred." A deadly panic had seized the whole city, since the hand of God had been very heavy upon it. ¹²Those who escaped death were afflicted with hemorrhoids, and the outcry from the city went up to the heavens.

---

g Ps 78, 66.—h Ex 7, 14; 8, 15; 9, 34.—i Nm 19, 2; Dt 21, 3; 2 Sm 6, 3.

5, 6: *Hemorrhoids . . . mice:* a double calamity fell upon them—a plague of mice or rats, and a severe epidemic of pestilential tumors, probably the bubonic plague.

6, 3: *A guilt offering:* a propitiatory offering customary after unwitting transgression of the ordinances of God regarding holy things or property rights; cf Lv 6, 1ff.

CHAPTER 6

The Ark To Be Returned. ¹The ark of the LORD had been in the land of the Philistines seven months ²when they summoned priests and fortune-tellers to ask "What shall we do with the ark of the LORD? Tell us what we should send back with it." ³They replied: "If you intend to send away the ark of the God of Israel, you must not send it alone, but must, by all means, make amends to him through a guilt offering.* Then you will be healed, and will learn why he continues to afflict you." ⁴When asked further, "What guilt offering should be our amends to him?", they replied:

"Five golden hemorrhoids and five golden mice to correspond to the number of Philistine lords, since the same plague has struck all of you and your lords. ⁵Therefore, make images of the hemorrhoids and of the mice that are infesting your land and give them as a tribute to the God of Israel. Perhaps then he will cease to afflict you, your gods, and your land. ⁶Why should you become stubborn, as the Egyptians and Pharaoh were stubborn? Was it not after he had dealt ruthlessly with them that the Israelites were released and departed?ʰ ⁷So now set to work and make a new cart. Then take two milch cows that have not borne the yoke; hitch them to the cart, but drive their calves indoors away from them.ⁱ ⁸You shall next take the ark of the LORD and place it on the cart, putting in a box beside it the golden articles that you are offering, as amends for your guilt. Start it on its way, and let it go. ⁹Then watch! If it goes up to Beth-shemesh along the route to his own territory, he has brought this great calamity upon us; if not, we will know it was not he who struck us, but that an accident happened to us."

The Ark in Beth-shemesh. ¹⁰They acted upon this advice. Taking two milch cows, they hitched them to the cart but shut up their calves indoors. ¹¹Then they placed the ark of the LORD on the cart, along with the box containing the golden mice and the images of the hemorrhoids. ¹²The cows went straight for the route to Beth-shemesh and continued along this road, mooing as they went, without turning right or left. The Philistine lords followed them as far as the border of Beth-shemesh.

¹³The people of Beth-shemesh were harvesting the wheat in the valley. When they looked up and spied the ark, they greeted it with rejoicing. ¹⁴The cart came to the field of Joshua the Beth-shemite and stopped there. At a large stone in the field, the wood of the cart was split up and the cows were offered as a holocaust to the LORD.ʲ ¹⁵The Levites, meanwhile, had taken down the ark of God and the box beside it, in which the golden articles were, and had placed them on the great stone. The men of Beth-shemesh also offered other holocausts and sacrifices to the LORD that day. ¹⁶After witnessing this, the five Philistine lords returned to Ekron the same day.

Guilt Offering. ¹⁷The golden hemorrhoids the Philistines sent back as a guilt offering to the LORD were as follows: one for Ashdod, one for Gaza, one for Ashkelon, one for Gath, and one for Ekron. ¹⁸The golden mice, however, corresponded to the number of all the cities of the Philistines belonging to the five lords, including fortified cities and open villages. The large stone on which the ark of the LORD was placed is still in the field of Joshua the Beth-shemite at the present time.

Penalty for Irreverence. ¹⁹The descendants of Jeconiah did not join in the celebration with the inhabitants of Bethshemesh when they greeted the ark of the LORD, and seventy of them were struck down. The people went into mourning at this great calamity with which the LORD had afflicted them. ²⁰The men of Bethshemesh asked, "Who can stand in the presence of this Holy One? To whom shall he go from us?" ²¹They then sent messengers to the inhabitants of Kiriath-jearim, saying, "The Philistines have returned the ark of the LORD; come down and get it."

CHAPTER 7

¹So the inhabitants of Kiriath-jearim came for the ark of the LORD and brought it into the house of Abinadab on the hill, appointing his son Eleazar as guardian of the ark of the LORD.

Religious Reform. ²From the day the ark came to rest in Kiriath-jearim a long time, twenty years, elapsed, and the whole Israelite population turned to the LORD. ³Samuel said to them: "If you wish with your whole heart to return to the LORD, put away your foreign gods and your Ashtaroth, devote yourselves to the LORD, and worship him alone. Then he will deliver you from the power of the Philistines."ᵏ ⁴So the Israelites put away their Baals and Ashtaroth, and worshiped the LORD alone. ⁵Samuel then gave orders, "Gather all Israel to Mizpah, that I may pray to the LORD for you."ˡ ⁶When they were gathered at Mizpah, they drew water and poured it out on the ground* before the LORD, and they fasted that day, confessing, "We have sinned against the LORD." It was at Mizpah that Samuel began to judge the Israelites.ᵐ

Rout of the Philistines. ⁷When the Philistines heard that the Israelites had gathered at Mizpah, their lords went up against Israel. Hearing this, the Israelites became afraid of the Philistines ⁸and said to Samuel, "Implore the LORD our God unceasingly for us, to save us from the clutches of the Philistines."ⁿ ⁹Samuel therefore took an unweaned lamb and offered it entire as a holocaust to the LORD.ᵒ He implored the LORD for Israel, and the LORD heard him. ¹⁰While Samuel was offering the holocaust, the Philistines advanced to join battle with Israel. That day, however, the LORD thundered loudly against the Philistines, and threw them into such confusion that they were defeated by Israel. ¹¹Thereupon the Israelites sallied forth from Mizpah and pursued the Philistines, harrying them down beyond Beth-car. ¹²Samuel then took a stone and placed it between Mizpah and Jeshanah; he named it Ebenezer,* explaining, "To this point has the LORD helped us." ¹³Thus were the Philistines subdued, never again to enter the territory of Israel, for the LORD was severe with them as long as Samuel lived.ᵖ ¹⁴The cities from Ekron to Gath which the Philistines had taken from Israel were restored to them. Israel also freed the territory of these cities from the dominion of the Philistines. Moreover there was peace between Israel and the Amorites.

¹⁵Samuel judged Israel as long as he lived. ¹⁶He made a yearly journey, passing

---

j 2 Sm 24, 21ff.—k 1 Sm 12, 10. 20. 24; Jos 24, 23; Jgs 6, 6-10; 10, 10-16.—l 1 Sm 10, 17; Jgs 20, 1.—m Jgs 20, 26; Ps 22, 14; Lam 2, 19.—n Ex 17, 9-13.—o 9f: 2 Sm 22, 14f; Sir 46, 16ff.—p Jgs 3, 30; 8, 28; 11, 33.

7, 6: *Poured it out on the ground:* for the symbolism, cf 2 Sm 14, 14.

7, 12: *Ebenezer:* or *eben ha-ezer,* means "stone of help."

through Bethel, Gilgal and Mizpah and judging Israel at each of these sanctuaries. [17] Then he used to return to Ramah, for that was his home. There, too, he judged Israel and built an altar to the LORD. [q]

II: ESTABLISHMENT OF THE MONARCHY IN ISRAEL

CHAPTER 8 *

Request for a King. [1] In his old age Samuel appointed his sons judges over Israel. [2] His first-born was named Joel, his second son, Abijah; they judged at Beersheba. [3] His sons did not follow his example but sought illicit gain and accepted bribes, perverting justice. [r] [4] Therefore all the elders of Israel came in a body to Samuel at Ramah [5] and said to him, "Now that you are old, and your sons do not follow your example, appoint a king over us, as other nations have, to judge us." [s]

God Grants the Request. [6] Samuel was displeased when they asked for a king to judge them. He prayed to the LORD, however, [7] who said in answer: "Grant the people's every request. It is not you they reject, they are rejecting me as their king. [t] [8] As they have treated me constantly from the day I brought them up from Egypt to this day, deserting me and worshiping strange gods, so do they treat you too. [9] Now grant their request; but at the same time, warn them solemnly and inform them of the rights of the king who will rule them."

The Rights of a King. [10] Samuel delivered the message of the LORD in full to those who were asking him for a king. [11] He told them: "The rights of the king who will rule you will be as follows: He will take your sons and assign them to his chariots and horses, and they will run before his

chariot. [u] [12] He will also appoint from among them his commanders of groups of a thousand and of a hundred soldiers. He will set them to do his plowing and his harvesting, and to make his implements of war and the equipment of his chariots. [v] [13] He will use your daughters as ointment-makers, as cooks, and as bakers. [14] He will take the best of your fields, vineyards, and olive groves, and give them to his officials. [w] [15] He will tithe your crops and your vineyards, and give the revenue to his eunuchs and his slaves. [16] He will take your male and female servants, as well as your best oxen and your asses, and use them to do his work. [17] He will tithe your flocks and you yourselves will become his slaves. [x] [18] When this takes place, you will complain against the king whom you have chosen, but on that day the LORD will not answer you."

Persistent Demand. [19] The people, however, refused to listen to Samuel's warning and said, "Not so! There must be a king over us. [y] [20] We too must be like other nations, with a king to rule us and to lead us in warfare and fight our battles." [21] When Samuel had listened to all the people had to say, he repeated it to the LORD, [22] who then said to him, "Grant their request and appoint a king to rule them." Samuel thereupon said to the men of Israel, "Each of you go to his own city."

CHAPER 9

[1] There was a stalwart man from Benjamin named Kish, who was the son of Abiel, son of Zeror, son of Becorath, son of Aphiah, a Benjaminite. [z] [2] He had a son named Saul, who was a handsome young man. There was no other Israelite handsomer than Saul; he stood head and shoulders above the people. [a]

The Lost Asses. [3] Now the asses of Saul's father, Kish, had wandered off. Kish said to his son Saul, "Take one of the servants with you and go out and hunt for the asses." [4] Accordingly they went through the hill country of Ephraim, and through the land of Shalishah. Not finding them there, they continued through the land of Shaalim without success. They also went through the land of Benjamin, but they failed to find the animals. [5] When they came to the land of Zuph, Saul said to the servant who was with him, "Come, let us turn back, lest my father forget about the

---

q 1 Sm 9, 12; 14, 35.—r Ex 23, 8; Dt 16, 19; Prv 17, 23.—s 5f: Dt 17, 14f; Hos 13, 10; Acts 13, 21.—t 7f: 1 Sm 12, 1. 12f; Jgs 8, 22f; 10, 13; 1 Kgs 9, 9.—u 1 Sm 10, 25; Dt 17, 14-20; 1 Kgs 12.—v 2 Sm 15, 1; 1 Kgs 1, 5.—w 1 Sm 22, 7; 1 Kgs 21, 1-24; Ez 46, 18.—x 1 Kgs 12, 4.—y 1 Sm 10, 19.—z 1 Sm 14, 51; 1 Chr 8, 33.—a 1 Sm 10, 23.

8, 1: From this chapter on, the First Book of Samuel gives us two and sometimes three viewpoints on most of the events with which it is concerned, such as the appointment of Saul as king, the reasons for his downfall, his relationship with David, and the circumstances of Saul's death (1 Sm 31; 2 Sm 1). The choice of Saul as king is seen, in ch 8, followed by 10, 17-24 and ch 12, as motivated by the people's defection from the proper service of God; this later editorial approach incorporates not only narratives with which it is consistent, but also early traditions (9, 1-10. 16; ch 11) which portray the events and their motivation quite differently.

asses and become anxious about us." [6]The servant replied, "Listen! There is a man of God in this city, a man held in high esteem; all that he says is sure to come true. Let us go there now! Perhaps he can tell us how to accomplish our errand." [7] [b] But Saul said to his servant, "If we go, what can we offer the man? There is no bread in our bags, and we have no present to give the man of God. What have we?" [8]Again the servant answered Saul, "I have a quarter of a silver shekel.* If I give that to the man of God, he will tell us our way." [10]Saul then said to his servant, "Well said! Come on, let us go!" And they went to the city where the man of God lived.

Quest for Samuel's Aid. [11] [c] As they were going up the ascent to the city, they met some girls coming out to draw water and inquired of them, "Is the seer in town?" [9] [d] (In former times in Israel, anyone who went to consult God used to say, "Come, let us go to the seer." For he who is now called prophet was formerly called seer.)* [12] [e] The girls answered, "Yes, there— straight ahead. Hurry now; just today he came to the city, because the people have a sacrifice today on the high place.* [13]When you enter the city, you may reach him before he goes up to the high place to eat. The people will not eat until he arrives; only after he blesses the sacrifice will the invited guests eat. Go up immediately, for you should find him right now."

Samuel's Revelation about Saul. [14]So they went up to the city. As they entered it, Samuel was coming toward them on his way to the high place. [15]The day before Saul's arrival, the LORD had given Samuel the revelation:[f] [16]"At this time tomorrow I will send you a man from the land of Benjamin whom you are to anoint as commander of my people Israel. He shall save my people from the clutches of the Philistines, for I have witnessed their misery and accepted their cry for help."[g] [17]When Samuel caught sight of Saul, the LORD assured him, "This is the man of whom I told you; he is to govern my people." [18]Saul met Samuel in the gateway and said, "Please tell me where the seer lives." [19]Samuel answered Saul: "I am the seer. Go up ahead of me to the high place and eat with me today. In the morning, before dismissing you, I will tell you whatever you wish. [20]As for the asses you lost three days ago, do not worry about them, for

they have been found. Whom does Israel desire ardently if not you and your father's family?" [21]Saul replied: "Am I not a Benjaminite, of one of the smallest tribes of Israel, and is not my clan the least among the clans of the tribe of Benjamin? Why say such things to me?"[h] [22]Samuel then took Saul and his servant and brought them to the room, where he placed them at the head of the guests, of whom there were about thirty. [23]He said to the cook, "Bring the portion I gave you and told you to put aside." [24]So the cook took up the leg and what went with it,* and placed it before Saul. Samuel said: "This is a reserved portion that has been set before you. Eat, for it was kept for you until your arrival; I explained that I was inviting some guests." Thus Saul dined with Samuel that day. [25]When they came down from the high place into the city, a mattress was spread for Saul on the roof, [26]and he slept there.

Saul's Anointing. At daybreak Samuel called to Saul on the roof, "Get up, and I will start you on your journey." Saul rose, and he and Samuel went outside the city together. [27]As they were approaching the edge of the town, Samuel said to Saul, "Tell the servant to go on ahead of us, but stay here yourself for the moment, that I may give you a message from God."

CHAPTER 10

[1]Then, from a flask he had with him, Samuel poured oil on Saul's head; he also kissed him, saying: "The LORD anoints you commander over his heritage. You are to govern the LORD's people Israel, and

b 7f: Nm 22, 7; 1 Kgs 14, 3; 2 Kgs 4, 42; 5, 15; 8, 8f.—c Gn 24, 11ff; Ex 2, 16.—d Sir 46, 15.—e 1 Sm 7, 17; 16, 2. 5; 20, 6. 29; Dt 12, 13; 1 Kgs 3, 2. 4.—f Acts 13, 21.—g 1 Sm 10, 1.— h 1 Sm 15, 17.

9, 8: *A quarter of a silver shekel:* about a tenth of an ounce of silver.
9, 9: This verse is a later explanation of the term *seer,* first used in the text in 1 Sm 9, 11.
9, 12: *On the high place:* the local sanctuary on the top of a hill, where the sacrifice was offered and the sacrificial meal eaten.
9, 24: *And what went with it:* a slight change would give "and the fatty tail" as perhaps the original reading. Sheep in the Near East are exceptionally fat-tailed, and such a portion would be thought a special delicacy by the Hebrews. However, the ritual legislation as we know it (Lv 3, 9) would require that the fat tail be burned on the altar. If this general rule was later than the time of Samuel, the present text may have been retouched so as not to seem to contravene it. A Qumran text has "the festive (leg)" here.

to save them from the grasp of their enemies roundabout.[i]

"This will be the sign for you that the LORD has anointed you commander over his heritage: [2]When you leave me today, you will meet two men near Rachel's tomb* at Zelzah in the territory of Benjamin, who will say to you, 'The asses you went to look for have been found. Your father is no longer worried about the asses, but is anxious about you and says, What shall I do about my son?'[j] [3]Farther on, when you arrive at the terebinth of Tabor, you will be met by three men going up to God at Bethel; one will be bringing three kids, another three loaves of bread, and the third a skin of wine. [4]They will greet you and offer you two wave offerings of bread, which you will take from them. [5] [k] After that you will come to Gibeathelohim, where there is a garrison of the Philistines.* As you enter that city, you will meet a band of prophets, in a prophetic state, coming down from the high place preceded by lyres, tambourines, flutes and harps. [6]The spirit of the Lord will rush upon you, and you will join them in their prophetic state and will be changed into another man.[l] [7]When you see these signs fulfilled, do whatever you judge feasible, because God is with you. [8] [m] Now go down ahead of me to Gilgal, for I shall come down to you, to offer holocausts and to sacrifice peace offerings. Wait seven days until I come to you; I shall then tell you what you must do."*

Fulfillment of the Signs. [9]As Saul turned to leave Samuel, God gave him another

heart. That very day all these signs came to pass. . . . [10] * When they were going from there to Gibeah, a band of prophets met him, and the spirit of God rushed upon him, so that he joined them in their prophetic state.[n] [11]When all who had known him previously saw him in a prophetic state among the prophets, they said to one another, "What has happened to the son of Kish? Is Saul also among the prophets?"[o] [12]And someone from that district added, "And who is their father?" Thus the proverb arose, "Is Saul also among the prophets?" [13]When he came out of the prophetic state, he went home.

Silence about the Kingship. [14]Saul's uncle inquired of him and his servant, "Where have you been?" Saul replied, "To look for the asses. When we could not find them, we went to Samuel." [15]Then Saul's uncle said, "Tell me, then, what Samuel said to you." [16]Saul said to his uncle, "He assured us that the asses had been found." But he mentioned nothing to him of what Samuel had said about the kingship.

Saul Chosen King by Lot. [17]Samuel called the people together to the LORD at Mizpah[p] [18]and addressed the Israelites: "Thus says the LORD, the God of Israel, 'It was I who brought Israel up from Egypt and delivered you from the power of the Egyptians and from the power of all the kingdoms that oppressed you.'[q] [19]But today you have rejected your God, who delivers you from all your evils and calamities, by saying to him, 'Not so, but you must appoint a king over us.' Now, therefore, take your stand before the LORD according to tribes and families."[r] [20]So Samuel had all the tribes of Israel come forward, and the tribe of Benjamin was chosen. [21]Next he had the tribe of Benjamin come forward in clans, and the clan of Matri was chosen, and finally Saul, son of Kish, was chosen. But they looked for him in vain. [22] [s] Again they consulted the LORD, "Has he come here?" The LORD answered, "He is hiding among the baggage." [23]They ran to bring him from there; and when he stood among the people, he was head and shoulders above all the crowd.[t] [24]Samuel said to all the people, "Do you see the man whom the LORD has chosen? There is none like him among all the people!" Then all the people shouted, "Long live the king!"[u] [25]Samuel next explained to the people

---

i 1 Sm 9, 16f; 24 7; Jgs 9, 9; 1 Kgs 1, 39; Acts 13, 21.—j Jer 31, 15; Mk 14, 13.—k 5f: 1 Sm 13, 3; 16, 13; 19, 20f.—l 1 Sm 11, 6; 16, 13; Jgs 14, 6. 19; 15, 14; 2 Kgs 3, 15.—m 1 Sm 13, 8; Lv 3, 1.—n 1 Sm 19, 20-24; Nm 11, 25.—o 1 Sm 19, 24.—p 1 Sm 7, 5.—q Ex 20, 2; Lv 11, 45; 25, 38; Nm 15, 41; Dt 5, 6; Jgs 6, 8f.—r 1 Sm 8, 19.—s 1 Sm 30, 24.—t 1 Sm 9, 2; 16, 7.— u 2 Sm 16, 16; 1 Kgs 1, 25; 2 Kgs 11, 12.

10, 2: Here, as in Jer 31, 15, Rachel's tomb is placed north of Jerusalem. Later tradition understood Gn 35, 19f in the sense given by Mt 2, 16ff, and placed the tomb at Bethlehem, farther south.

10, 5: *A garrison of the Philistines:* the Hebrew word for "garrison" has been explained alternatively to mean a pillar erected to mark the Philistine occupation, or an inspector or officer for the collection of taxes. *In a prophetic state:* in an ecstatic condition due to strong feelings of religious enthusiasm, induced by a communal observance, possibly accompanied by music and dancing.

10, 8: By inserting this verse, with its *seven days,* an editor has prepared for one narrative of the rejection of Saul (1 Sm 13, 8-15) in the very context of Saul's anointing.

10, 10: The story has here been abridged by omitting the fulfillment of the first two signs given by Samuel (1 Sm 10, 2ff).

the law of royalty* and wrote it in a book, which he placed in the presence of the LORD. This done, Samuel dismissed the people, each to his own place.*v* *26* Saul also went home to Gibeah, accompanied by warriors whose hearts the LORD had touched. *27* But certain worthless men said, "How can this fellow save us?" They despised him and brought him no present.*w*

CHAPTER 11

Defeat of the Ammonites. *1* About a month later,* Nahash the Ammonite went up and laid siege to Jabesh-gilead. All the men of Jabesh begged Nahash, "Make a treaty with us, and we will be your subjects."*x* *2* But Nahash the Ammonite replied, "This is my condition for a treaty with you: I must gouge out every man's right eye, that I may thus bring ignominy on all Israel." *3* The elders of Jabesh said to him: "Give us seven days to send messengers throughout the territory of Israel. If no one rescues us, we will surrender to you." *4* When the messengers arrived at Gibeah of Saul, they related the news to the people, all of whom wept aloud. *5* Just then Saul came in from the field, behind his oxen. "Why are the people weeping?" he asked. The message of the inhabitants of Jabesh was repeated to him. *6* As he listened to this report, the spirit of God rushed upon him and he became very angry.*y* *7* Taking a yoke of oxen, he cut them into pieces, which he sent throughout the territory of Israel by couriers with the message, "If anyone does not come out to follow Saul [and Samuel], the same as this will be done to his oxen!" In dread of the LORD, the people turned out to a man.*z* *8* When he reviewed them in Bezek, there were three hundred thousand Israelites and seventy thousand Judahites.

9 To the messengers who had come he said, "Tell the inhabitants of Jabesh-gilead that tomorrow, while the sun is hot, they will be rescued." The messengers came and reported this to the inhabitants of Jabesh, who were jubilant, *10* and said to Nahash, "Tomorrow we will surrender to you, and you may do whatever you please with us." *11* On the appointed day, Saul arranged his troops in three companies and invaded the camp during the dawn watch. They slaughtered Ammonites until the heat of the day; by then the survivors

were so scattered that no two were left together.

Saul Accepted as King. *12* * The people then said to Samuel: "Who questioned whether Saul should rule over us? Hand over the men and we will put them to death."*a* *13* But Saul broke in to say, "No man is to be put to death this day, for today the LORD has saved Israel."*b* *14* Samuel said to the people, "Come, let us go to Gilgal to inaugurate the kingdom there." *15* So all the people went to Gilgal, where, in the presence of the LORD, they made Saul king. They also sacrificed peace offerings there before the LORD, and Saul and all the Israelites celebrated the occasion with great joy.

CHAPTER 12

Samuel's Integrity. *1* Samuel addressed all Israel: "I have granted your request in every respect," he said. "I have set a king over you*c* *2* and now the king is your leader. As for me, I am old and gray, and have sons among you. I have lived with you from my youth to the present day. *3* Here I stand! Answer me in the presence of the LORD and of his anointed. Whose ox have I taken? Whose ass have I taken? Whom have I cheated? Whom have I oppressed? From whom have I accepted a bribe and overlooked his guilt? I will make restitution to you."*d* *4* They replied, "You have neither cheated us, nor oppressed us, nor accepted anything from anyone." *5* So he said to them, "The LORD is witness against you this day, and his anointed as well, that you have found nothing in my possession." "He is witness," they agreed.

Samuel Upbraids the People. *6* Continuing, Samuel said to the people: "The LORD is witness, who appointed Moses and Aaron, and who brought your fathers up from the land of Egypt.*e* *7* Now,

---

v 1 Sm 8, 11; Dt 17, 14-20.—w 1 Sm 11, 12.—x 1 Sm 12, 12; 31, 11.—y 1 Sm 16, 13; Jgs 14, 6. 19.—z 1 Kgs 11, 30; 2 Kgs 13, 18.—a 1 Sm 10, 27.—b 2 Sm 19, 23.—c 1 Sm 8, 7. 9. 22.— d Ex 20, 17; 23, 8; Nm 16, 15; Dt 16, 19; Sir 46, 19.—e Mi 6, 4.

10, 25: *The law of royalty:* the charter defining the rights of the king.

11, 1: *About a month later:* there is ancient evidence for a longer introduction to this campaign. The time indication here may refer to its earlier stages rather than to the events of ch 10.

11, 12-14: With these verses, an editor has harmonized the account of the acknowledgment of Saul as king at Mizpah (1 Sm 10, 17-24) with the public acclamation at Gilgal (1 Sm 11, 15) after the defeat of the Ammonites (1 Sm 11, 1-11). The Greek text of 1 Sm 11, 15 reads "and Samuel anointed Saul as king," instead of *they made Saul king.*

therefore, take your stand, and I shall arraign you before the LORD, and shall recount for you all the acts of mercy the LORD has done for you and your fathers. [8]When Jacob and his sons went to Egypt and the Egyptians oppressed them, your fathers appealed to the LORD, who sent Moses and Aaron to bring them out of Egypt, and he gave them this place to live in.[f] [9]But they forgot the LORD their God; and he allowed them to fall into the clutches of Sisera, the captain of the army of Jabin, king of Hazor, into the grasp of the Philistines, and into the grip of the king of Moab, who made war against them.[g] [10]Each time they appealed to the LORD and said, 'We have sinned in forsaking the LORD and worshiping Baals and Ashtaroth; but deliver us now from the power of our enemies, and we will worship you.'[h] [11]Accordingly, the LORD sent Jerubbaal, Barak, Jephthah, and Samson; he delivered you from the power of your enemies on every side, so that you were able to live in security.[i] [12]Yet, when you saw Nahash, king of the Ammonites, advancing against you, you said to me, 'Not so, but a king must rule us,' even though the LORD your God is your king.[j]

Warnings for People and King. [13]"Now you have the king you want, a king the LORD has given you.[k] [14]If you fear the LORD and worship him, if you are obedient to him and do not rebel against the LORD's command, if both you and the king who rules you follow the LORD your God—well and good. [15]But if you do not obey the LORD and if you rebel against his command, the LORD will deal severely with you and your king, and destroy you. [16]Now then, stand ready to witness the great marvel the LORD is about to accomplish before your eyes. [17]Are we not in the harvest time for wheat? Yet I shall call to the LORD, and he will send thunder and rain. Thus you will see and understand how greatly the LORD is displeased that you have asked for a king."[l] [18]Samuel then called to the LORD, and the LORD sent thunder and rain that day.

Assistance Promised. As a result, all the people dreaded the LORD and Samuel. [19]They said to Samuel, "Pray to the LORD your God for us, your servants, that we may not die for having added to all our other sins the evil of asking for a king." [20]"Do not fear," Samuel answered them. "It is true you have committed all this evil; still, you must not turn from the LORD, but must worship him with your whole heart. [21]Do not turn to meaningless idols which can neither profit nor save; they are nothing.[m] [22]For the sake of his own great name the LORD will not abandon his people, since the LORD himself chose to make you his people.[n] [23]As for me, far be it from me to sin against the LORD by ceasing to pray for you and to teach you the good and right way.[o] [24]But you must fear the LORD and worship him faithfully with your whole heart; keep in mind the great things he has done among you. [25]If instead you continue to do evil, both you and your king shall perish."

III: SAUL AND DAVID

CHAPTER 13

[1][Saul was . . . years old when he became king and he reigned . . . (two) years over Israel.]*

Saul Offers Sacrifice. [2]Saul chose three thousand men of Israel, of whom two thousand remained with him in Michmash and in the hill country of Bethel, and one thousand were with Jonathan in Gibeah of Benjamin. He sent the rest of the people back to their tents. [3]Now Jonathan overcame the Philistine garrison* which was in Gibeah, and the Philistines got word of it. Then Saul sounded the horn throughout the land, with a proclamation, "Let the Hebrews hear!"[p] [4]Thus all Israel learned that Saul had overcome the garrison of the Philistines and that Israel had brought disgrace upon the Philistines; and the soldiers were called up to Saul in Gilgal. [5]The Philistines also assembled for battle, with three thousand chariots, six thousand horsemen, and foot soldiers as numerous as the sands of the seashore. Moving up

---

f Gn 46, 5; Ex 1, 11; 2, 23ff.—g Jgs 3, 12ff; 4, 2f; 10, 7; 13, 1.—h 1 Sm 7, 3f.—i Jgs 6, 14. 32; 11, 1.—j 1 Sm 8, 6f. 19; 11, 1f; Jgs 8, 23.—k 1 Sm 8, 7.—l Ex 9, 23. 28ff; 1 Kgs 18, 1.—m Dt 32, 37ff.—n Jer 14, 21; Ex 20, 9; Dn 3, 34.—o Ex 32, 11.—p 1 Sm 14, 1-15; Jgs 3, 27; 6, 34; 2 Sm 20, 1f.

13, 1: A formula like that of 2 Sm 5, 4 was introduced here at some time; but the age of Saul when he became king remains a blank, and the *two years* assigned for his reign in the received text cannot be correct. Tradition (Acts 13, 21) offers the round number, "forty years."
13, 3-4: *The Philistine garrison:* see note on 1 Sm 10, 5. *Let the Hebrews hear:* a different reading of these verses, based on the Greek, would yield: "And the Philistines heard that the Hebrews (or: the slaves) had revolted. Saul in the meantime sounded the trumpet throughout all the land (v 4), and all Israel heard that Saul. . . ."

against Israel, they encamped in Michmash, east of Beth-aven. ⁶Some Israelites, aware of the danger and of the difficult situation, hid themselves in caves, in thickets, among rocks, in caverns, and in cisterns,*q* ⁷and other Hebrews passed over the Jordan into the land of Gad and Gilead. Saul, however, held out at Gilgal, although all his followers were seized with fear.* ⁸He waited seven days—the time Samuel had determined. When Samuel did not arrive at Gilgal, the men began to slip away from Saul.*r* ⁹He then said, "Bring me the holocaust and peace offerings," and he offered up the holocaust.

King Saul Reproved. ¹⁰He had just finished this offering when Samuel arrived. Saul went out to greet him, ¹¹and Samuel asked him, "What have you done?" Saul replied: "When I saw that the men were slipping away from me, since you had not come by the specified time, and with the Philistines assembled at Michmash, ¹²I said to myself, 'Now the Philistines will come down against me at Gilgal, and I have not yet sought the LORD's blessing.' So in my anxiety I offered up the holocaust." ¹³Samuel's response was: "You have been foolish! Had you kept the command the LORD your God gave you, the LORD would now establish your kingship in Israel as lasting; ¹⁴but as things are, your kingdom shall not endure. The LORD has sought out a man after his own heart and has appointed him commander of his people, because you broke the LORD's command."*s*

Philistine Invasion. ¹⁵Then Samuel set out from Gilgal and went his own way; but the rest of the people went up after Saul to meet the soldiers, going from Gilgal to Gibeah of Benjamin. Saul then numbered the soldiers he had with him, who were about six hundred.*t* ¹⁶Saul, his son Jonathan, and the soldiers they had with them were now occupying Geba of Benjamin, and the Philistines were encamped at Michmash. ¹⁷Meanwhile, raiders left the camp of the Philistines in three bands.*u* One band took the Ophrah road toward the district of Shual; ¹⁸another turned in the direction of Beth-horon; and the third took the road for Geba that overlooks the Valley of the Hyenas toward the desert.

Disarmament of Israel. ¹⁹Not a single smith was to be found in the whole land of Israel, for the Philistines had said, "Otherwise the Hebrews will make swords or spears."*v* ²⁰All Israel, therefore, had to go down to the Philistines to sharpen their plowshares, mattocks, axes, and sickles. ²¹The price for the plowshares and mattocks was two-thirds of a shekel, and a third of a shekel for sharpening the axes and for setting the ox-goads. ²²And so on the day of battle neither sword nor spear could be found in the possession of any of the soldiers with Saul or Jonathan. Only Saul and his son Jonathan had them.

Jonathan's Exploit. ²³An outpost of the Philistines had pushed forward to the pass of Michmash.*w*

CHAPTER 14

¹One day Jonathan, son of Saul, said to his armor-bearer, "Come, let us go over to the Philistine outpost on the other side." But he did not inform his father.*x* ²(Saul's command post was under the pomegranate tree near the threshing floor on the outskirts of Geba; those with him numbered about six hundred men. ³Ahijah, son of Ahitub, brother of Ichabod, who was the son of Phinehas, son of Eli, the priest of the LORD at Shiloh, was wearing the ephod.) Nor did the soldiers know that Jonathan had gone.*y* ⁴Flanking the ravine through which Jonathan intended to get over to the Philistine outpost there was a rocky crag on each side, one called Bozez, the other Seneh. ⁵One crag was to the north, toward Michmash, the other to the south, toward Geba. ⁶Jonathan said to his armor-bearer: "Come, let us go over to that outpost of the uncircumcised. Perhaps the LORD will help us, because it is no more difficult for the LORD to grant victory through a few than through many."*z* ⁷His armor-bearer replied, "Do whatever you are inclined to do; I will match your resolve." ⁸Jonathan continued: "We shall go over to those men and show ourselves to them. ⁹If they say to us, 'Stay there until we can come to you,' we shall stop where

13, 7-15: These verses, like 1 Sm 10, 8, anticipate the rejection of Saul; a different occasion and motivation for this are given in ch 15, resumed in 1 Sm 28, 17f.

we are; we shall not go up to them. [10]But if they say, 'Come up to us,' we shall go up, because the LORD has delivered them into our grasp. That will be our sign." [11]Accordingly, the two of them appeared before the outpost of the Philistines, who said, "Look, some Hebrews are coming out of the holes where they have been hiding." [12]The men of the outpost called to Jonathan and his armor-bearer. "Come up here," they said, "and we will teach you a lesson." So Jonathan said to his armor-bearer, "Climb up after me, for the LORD has delivered them into the grasp of Israel." [13]Jonathan clambered up with his armor-bearer behind him; as the Philistines turned to flee him, he cut them down, and his armor-bearer followed him and finished them off. [14]In this first exploit Jonathan and his armor-bearer slew about twenty men within half a furlong. [15]Then panic spread to the army and to the countryside, and all the soldiers, including the outpost and the raiding parties, were terror-stricken. The earth also shook, so that the panic was beyond human endurance.

Rout of the Philistines. [16]The lookouts of Saul in Geba of Benjamin saw that the enemy camp had scattered and were running about in all directions. [17]Saul said to those around him, "Count the troops and find out if any of us are missing." When they had investigated, they found Jonathan and his armor-bearer missing. [18]Saul then said to Ahijah, "Bring the ephod* here." (Ahijah was wearing the ephod in front of the Israelites at that time.) [19]While Saul was speaking to the priest, the tumult in the Philistine camp kept increasing. So he said to the priest, "Withdraw your hand." [20]And Saul and all his men shouted and rushed into the fight, where the Philistines, wholly confused, were thrusting swords at one another.[a] [21]In addition, the Hebrews who had previously sided with the Philistines and had gone up with them to the camp, turned to join the Israelites under Saul and

a Jgs 7, 22.—b 1 Sm 29, 4.—c 1 Sm 13, 6.—d 1 Sm 15, 19. 21; Lv 3, 17; 7, 26f; 17, 10-14; Acts 15, 20. 29.

14, 18: *Ephod:* to be used in consulting God; see note on v 41, and that on 1 Sm 2, 28 above.

14, 23: *Past Beth-horon:* this is a textual correction influenced by 1 Sm 13, 18; the received Hebrew text refers to Bethel (Beth-aven), but the effect of the victory would seem to have been that the main ridge of mountains in the territories of Benjamin and Ephraim was cleared of Philistines.

Jonathan.[b] [22]Likewise, all the Israelites who were hiding in the hill country of Ephraim, on hearing that the Philistines were fleeing, pursued them in the rout.[c] [23]Thus the LORD saved Israel that day.

Saul's Oath. The battle continued past Beth-horon;* [24]the whole people, about ten thousand combatants, were with Saul, and there was scattered fighting in every town in the hill country of Ephraim. And Saul swore a very rash oath that day, putting the people under this ban: "Cursed be the man who takes food before evening, before I am able to avenge myself on my enemies." So none of the people tasted food. [25]Indeed, there was a honeycomb lying on the ground, [26]and when the soldiers came to the comb the swarm had left it; yet no one would raise a hand to his mouth from it, because the people feared the oath.

Violation of the Oath. [27]Jonathan, who had not heard that his father had put the people under oath, thrust out the end of the staff he was holding and dipped it into the honey. Then he raised it to his mouth and his eyes lit up. [28]At this one of the soldiers spoke up: "Your father put the people under a strict oath, saying, 'Cursed be the man who takes food this day!' As a result the people are weak." [29]Jonathan replied: "My father brings trouble to the land. Look how bright my eyes are from this small taste of honey I have had. [30]What is more, if the people had eaten freely today of their enemy's booty when they came across it, would not the slaughter of the Philistines by now have been the greater for it?"

Use of Flesh with Blood Forbidden. [31]After the Philistines were routed that day from Michmash to Aijalon, the people were completely exhausted. [32]So they pounced upon the spoil and took sheep, oxen and calves, slaughtering them on the ground and eating the flesh with blood.[d] [33]Informed that the people were sinning against the LORD by eating the flesh with blood, Saul said: "You have broken faith. Roll a large stone here for me." [34]He continued: "Mingle with the people and tell each of them to bring his ox or his sheep to me. Slaughter it here and then eat, but you must not sin against the LORD by eating the flesh with blood." So everyone brought to the LORD whatever ox he had seized, and they slaughtered them there; [35] and Saul built an altar to the LORD—this was the first time he built an altar to the LORD.[e]

Jonathan in Danger of Death. [36] Then Saul said, "Let us go down in pursuit of the Philistines by night, to plunder among them until daybreak and to kill them all off." They replied, "Do what you think best." But the priest said, "Let us consult God." [37] So Saul inquired of God: "Shall I go down in pursuit of the Philistines? Will you deliver them into the power of Israel?" But he received no answer on this occasion.[f] [38] Saul then said, "Come here, all officers of the army. We must investigate and find out how this sin was committed today. [39] As the LORD lives who has given victory to Israel, even if my son Jonathan has committed it, he shall surely die!" But none of the people answered him. [40] So he said to all Israel, "Stand on one side, and I and my son Jonathan will stand on the other." The people responded, "Do what you think best."[g] [41] And Saul said to the LORD, the God of Israel: "Why did you not answer your servant this time? If the blame for this resides in me or my son Jonathan, LORD, God of Israel, respond with Urim; but if this guilt is in your people Israel, respond with Thummim."[*] Jonathan and Saul were designated, and the people went free.[h] [42] Saul then said, "Cast lots between me and my son Jonathan." And Jonathan was designated. [43] Saul said to Jonathan, "Tell me what you have done." Jonathan replied, "I only tasted a little honey from the end of the staff I was holding. Am I to die for this?" [44] Saul said, "May God do thus and so to me if you do not indeed die, Jonathan!"[i]

Rescue of Jonathan. [45] But the army said to Saul: "Is Jonathan to die, though it was he who brought Israel this great victory? This must not be! As the LORD lives, not a single hair of his head shall fall to the ground, for God was with him in what he did today!" Thus the soldiers were able to rescue* Jonathan from death.[j] [46] After that Saul gave up the pursuit of the Philistines, who returned to their own territory.

Wars and Victories. [47] After taking over the kingship of Israel, Saul waged war on all their surrounding enemies—Moab,

the Ammonites, Aram, Beth-rehob, the king of Zobah, and the Philistines. Wherever he turned, he was successful[k] [48] and fought bravely. He defeated Amalek and delivered Israel from the hands of those who were plundering them.

Saul's Family. [49] The sons of Saul were Jonathan, Ishvi,* and Malchishua; his two daughters were named, the elder, Merob, and the younger, Michal.[l] [50] Saul's wife, who was named Ahinoam, was the daughter of Ahimaaz. The name of his general was Abner, son of Saul's uncle, Ner; [51] Kish, Saul's father, and Ner, Abner's father, were sons of Abiel.[m]

[52] An unremitting war was waged against the Philistines during Saul's lifetime. When Saul saw any strong or brave man, he took him into his service.

CHAPTER 15

[1] Samuel said to Saul: "It was I the LORD sent to anoint you king over his people Israel. Now, therefore, listen to the message of the LORD. [2] This is what the LORD of hosts has to say: 'I will punish what Amalek did to Israel when he barred his way as he was coming up from Egypt.[n] [3] Go, now, attack Amalek, and deal with him and all that he has under the ban.* Do not spare him, but kill men and women, children and infants, oxen and sheep, camels and asses.' "[o]

Disobedience of Saul. [4] Saul alerted the soldiers, and at Telaim reviewed two hundred thousand foot soldiers and ten thousand men of Judah.* [5] Saul went to

e 1 Sm 7, 17; Jgs 6, 24.—f 1 Sm 28, 6. 15.—g Jos 7, 13ff.—h 1 Sm 28, 6; Ex 28, 30; Dt 33, 8.—i 1 Sm 3, 17; Ru 1, 17.—j 2 Sm 14, 11; 1 Kgs 1, 52.—k 2 Sm 1, 22; 8, 2-5.—l 1 Sm 18, 20. 25; 31, 2; 1 Chr 8, 33; 9, 39; 10, 2.—m 1 Sm 9, 1.—n Ex 17, 8-10. 16; Dt 25, 17ff.—o 1 Sm 27, 8; 30, 17; Ex 17, 16; Nm 24, 20.

14, 41: The *Urim* and *Thummim*, or sacred lots, were a device for ascertaining the will of God; they ceased to be used after the time of David. The material and the shape of these objects, and the manner in which they were used, are unknown. They gave a "yes" or "no" answer to specific questions.

14, 45: *Rescue:* the Hebrew word used is that for the "redemption" of the first-born (Ex 13, 13ff).

14, 49: *Ishvi:* known also as Ishbaal, in 2 Sm 2, 8 and elsewhere. The name may once have read "Ishyo" here.

15, 3: *Under the ban:* in such wars of extermination, all things (men, cities, beasts, etc.) were to be blotted out; nothing could be reserved for private use. The interpretation of God's will here attributed to Samuel is in keeping with the abhorrent practices of blood revenge prevalent among pastoral, seminomadic peoples such as the Hebrews had recently been. The slaughter of the innocent has never been in conformity with the will of God.

15, 4: The numbers here are not realistic; compare 1 Sm 14, 24 above.

THE WARS OF SAUL (1 Sm 14, 47—15, 35) — **(a)** Saul becomes king of Israel and defeats all its surrounding enemies: **Moab, the Ammonites, Edom, Beth-rehob,** the king of **Zobah,** the **Philistines,** and the **Amalekites** (14, 47). **(b)** Saul is told to strike **Amalek** and destroy everything and everybody in it. After reviewing his troops at **Telaim** he goes to the city of **Amalek** and prepares an ambush in the wadi. He defeats the **Amalekites** from **Havilah** as far as **Shur** but fails to carry out the ban (15, 1-9). **(c)** At **Carmel** Saul raises a trophy in his honor (15, 21). **(d)** At **Gilgal** Samuel reproaches Saul for disobeying the Lord, and Saul asks for pardon. After executing Agag, king of Amalek, Samuel goes to **Ramah** and Saul to **Gibeah**—and the two never meet again (15, 13-15).

DAVID AND GOLIATH (1 Sm 16—17, 58) — **(a)** At **Bethlehem** Samuel anoints David (16, 13). **(b)** At the **Vale of the Terebinth** the Philistines encamp between **Socoh** and **Azekah** at **Ephes-dammim;** the Israelites on the opposite side. Individual battle between David and Goliath. The Israelites pursue the Philistines to the approaches of **Gath** and the gates of **Ekron** (17, 1-54).

FLIGHT OF DAVID (1 Sm 18, 1—27, 12). — **(a)** Break between Saul and David, but David keeps the friendship of Jonathan (18, 1—19, 17). **(b)** At **Ramah** David, fleeing, takes refuge near Samuel in the strongholds of the wilderness. Saul pursues him there unsuccessfully (19, 18-24). **(c)** At **Nob** Ahimelech gives the holy bread and the sword of Goliath to David (21, 1-10). **(d)** At **Gath** David simulates madness before Achish, king of Gath (21, 11-16). **(e)** At the **Cave of Adullam** David surrounds himself with 400 men (22, 1-2). **(f)** In **Moab** David puts his family for safety at **Mizpeh.** Vengeance of Saul on the priests of Nob. David returns to Judah and hides in the forest of **Hereth** (22, 3-23). **(g)** At **Keilah** David defeats the Philistines there, and then sets out at random with 600 men (23, 1-13). **(h)** In the **desert of Ziph** Saul pursues David, hidden in the forest, on the **hill of Hachilah.** David renews the alliance with Jonathan, and withdraws to the **desert of Maon.** Saul then goes to battle with the Philistines. **(i)** In the **Cave of Engedi** David spares Saul. Death of Samuel (24, 1—25, 1). **(j)** At **Carmel** David seeks food from Nabal, and is insulted by him (25, 2-43). **(k)** In the **desert of Ziph** and at the **hill of Hachilah** David goes to the tent of Saul during the night and spares him. Saul returns to **Gibeah** (26, 1-25). **(l)** **Among the Philistines** Achish, king of **Gath,** gives **Ziklag** to David. From there David makes excursions against the **Geshurites** and the **Amalekites,** and pretends that he has plundered the **Negeb** of Judah, of **Jerahmeel** and of the **Kenites** (27, 1-12).

the city of Amalek, and after setting an ambush in the wadi, [6] [p] warned the Kenites: "Come! Leave Amalek and withdraw, that I may not have to destroy you with them, for you were kind to the Israelites when they came up from Egypt." After the Kenites left, [7] Saul routed Amalek from Havilah to the approaches of Shur, on the frontier of Egypt.[q] [8] He took Agag, king of Amalek, alive, but on the rest of the people he put into effect the ban of destruction by the sword. [9] He and his troops spared Agag and the best of the fat sheep and oxen, and the lambs. They refused to carry out the doom on anything that was worthwhile, dooming only what was worthless and of no account.

Saul Is Reproved. [10] Then the LORD spoke to Samuel: [11] "I regret* having made Saul king, for he has turned from me and has not kept my command." At this Samuel grew angry and cried out to the LORD all night. [12] Early in the morning he went to meet Saul, but was informed that Saul had gone to Carmel, where he erected a trophy in his own honor, and that on his return he had passed on and gone down to Gilgal. [13] When Samuel came to him, Saul greeted him: "The LORD bless you! I have kept the command of the LORD." [14] But Samuel asked, "What, then, is the meaning of this bleating of sheep that comes to my ears, and the lowing of oxen that I hear?" [15] Saul replied: "They were brought from Amalek. The men spared the best sheep and oxen to sacrifice to the LORD, your God; but we have carried out the ban on the rest." [16] Samuel said to Saul: "Stop! Let me tell you what the LORD said to me last night." "Speak!" he replied. [17] Samuel then said: "Though little in your own esteem, are you not leader of the tribes of Israel? The LORD anointed you king of Israel[r] [18] and sent you on a mission, saying, 'Go and put the sinful Amalekites under a ban of destruction. Fight against them until you have exterminated them.'[s]

---

p Nm 24, 21.—q 1 Sm 27, 8.—r 1 Sm 9, 21.—s 1 Sm 28, 18.—t 1 Sm 14, 32.—u Lv 27, 28.—v Prv 21, 3; Hos 6, 6; Am 5, 21-25; Zec 10, 2; Mt 9, 13; 12, 7; Heb 10, 9.—w 1 Sm 26, 21.—x 1 Kgs 11, 11. 30f.—y 1 Sm 24, 6.—z 1 Sm 28, 17; 2 Sm 7, 15f.—a Nm 23, 19.

15, 11: *I regret:* God manifests "regret" when, offended by men, he takes away his benefits, graces and favors. It is not God, but men, who change, to their own detriment.

15, 22: Samuel is disapproving, not of sacrifices in general, but of merely external sacrifices offered in defiance of God's commandment and without heartfelt obedience.

[19] Why then have you disobeyed the LORD? You have pounced on the spoil, thus displeasing the LORD."[t] [20] Saul answered Samuel: "I did indeed obey the LORD and fulfill the mission on which the LORD sent me. I have brought back Agag, and I have destroyed Amalek under the ban. [21] But from the spoil the men took sheep and oxen, the best of what had been banned, to sacrifice to the LORD their God in Gilgal."[u] [22] [v] But Samuel said:

"Does the LORD so delight in
    holocausts and sacrifices
  as in obedience to the command of
    the LORD?
Obedience is better than sacrifice,
  and submission than the fat of
    rams.*
[23] For a sin like divination is rebellion,
  and presumption is the crime of
    idolatry.
Because you have rejected the command of the LORD,
  he, too, has rejected you as ruler."

Saul Asks Forgiveness. [24] Saul replied to Samuel: "I have sinned, for I have disobeyed the command of the LORD and your instructions. In my fear of the people, I did what they said.[w] [25] Now forgive my sin, and return with me, that I may worship the LORD." [26] But Samuel said to Saul, "I will not return with you, because you rejected the command of the LORD and the LORD rejects you as king of Israel."[x] [27] As Samuel turned to go, Saul seized a loose end of his mantle, and it tore off.[y] [28] So Samuel said to him: "The LORD has torn the kingdom of Israel from you this day, and has given it to a neighbor of yours, who is better than you.[z] [29] The Glory of Israel neither retracts nor repents, for he is not man that he should repent."[a] [30] But he answered: "I have sinned, yet honor me now before the elders of my people and before Israel. Return with me that I may worship the LORD your God." [31] And so Samuel returned with him, and Saul worshiped the LORD.

Agag Is Cut Down. [32] Afterward Samuel commanded, "Bring Agag, king of Amalek, to me." Agag came to him struggling and saying, "So it is bitter death!" [33] And Samuel said,

"As your sword has made women child-
    less,

so shall your mother be childless among women."

Then he cut Agag down before the LORD in Gilgal.*b*

34 Samuel departed for Ramah, while Saul went up to his home in Gibeah of Saul. 35 Never again, as long as he lived, did Samuel see Saul. Yet he grieved over Saul, because the LORD regretted having made him king of Israel.*c*

CHAPTER 16

Samuel Sent to Bethlehem. 1 *d* The LORD said to Samuel: "How long will you grieve for Saul, whom I have rejected as king of Israel? Fill your horn with oil, and be on your way. I am sending you to Jesse of Bethlehem, for I have chosen my king from among his sons."* 2 But Samuel replied: "How can I go? Saul will hear of it and kill me." To this the LORD answered: "Take a heifer along and say, 'I have come to sacrifice to the LORD.' 3 Invite Jesse to the sacrifice, and I myself will tell you what to do; you are to anoint for me the one I point out to you."

4 Samuel did as the LORD had commanded him. When he entered Bethlehem, the elders of the city came trembling to meet him and inquired, "Is your visit peaceful, O seer?" 5 He replied: "Yes! I have come to sacrifice to the LORD. So cleanse yourselves and join me today for the banquet." He also had Jesse and his sons cleanse themselves and invited them to the sacrifice.*e* 6 As they came, he looked at Eliab and thought, "Surely the LORD's anointed is here before him." 7 But the LORD said to Samuel: "Do not judge from his appearance or from his lofty stature, because I have rejected him. Not as man sees does God see, because man sees the appearance but the LORD looks into the heart."*f* 8 *g* Then Jesse called Abinadab and presented him before Samuel, who said, "The LORD has not chosen him." 9 Next Jesse presented Shammah, but Samuel said, "The LORD has not chosen this one either." 10 In the same way Jesse presented seven sons before Samuel, but Samuel said to Jesse, "The LORD has not chosen any one of these." 11 Then Samuel asked Jesse, "Are these all the sons you have?" Jesse replied, "There is still the youngest, who is tending the sheep."

Samuel said to Jesse, "Send for him; we will not begin the sacrificial banquet until he arrives here."*h* 12 Jesse sent and had the young man brought to them. He was ruddy, a youth handsome to behold and making a splendid appearance. The LORD said, "There—anoint him, for this is he!"*i* 13 Then Samuel, with the horn of oil in hand, anointed him in the midst of his brothers; and from that day on, the spirit of the LORD rushed upon David. When Samuel took his leave, he went to Ramah.*j*

Saul's Spirit of Melancholy. 14 *k* The spirit of the LORD had departed from Saul, and he was tormented by an evil spirit sent by the LORD.* 15 So the servants of Saul said to him: "Please! An evil spirit from God is tormenting you. 16 If your lordship will order it, we, your servants here in attendance on you, will look for a man skilled in playing the harp. When the evil spirit from God comes over you, he will play and you will feel better." 17 Saul then told his servants, "Find me a skillful harpist and bring him to me." 18 *l* A servant spoke up to say: "I have observed that one of the sons of Jesse of Bethlehem is a skillful harpist. He is also a stalwart soldier, besides being an able speaker, and handsome. Moreover, the LORD is with him."*

David Made Armor-Bearer. 19 Accordingly, Saul dispatched messengers to ask Jesse to send him his son David, who was with the flock. 20 Then Jesse took five loaves of bread, a skin of wine, and a kid, and sent them to Saul by his son David.*m* 21 Thus David came to Saul and entered his service. Saul became very fond of him,

---

b Ex 21, 23.—c Gn 6, 6.—d 1 Kgs 1, 39; Ru 4, 17-22; 1 Chr 11, 3; Is 11, 1; Lk 2, 4.—e 1 Sm 9, 12f; 20, 26; Ex 19, 10; Jb 1, 5.—f 1 Sm 10, 23f; 1 Chr 28, 9; Prv 15, 11; Jer 17, 10; 20, 12; Lk 16, 15; Acts 1, 24.—g 8ff: 1 Sm 17, 12f; 1 Chr 2, 13ff.—h 1 Sm 17, 15. 28, 34; 2 Sm 7, 8.—i 1 Sm 9, 2.—j 1 Sm 10, 6; 11, 6; Jgs 3, 10; 9, 9; Sir 46, 13.—k 1 Sm 18, 10f.—l 2 Sm 17, 8.—m 1 Sm 9, 7f; 10, 4. 27; 16, 1; 17, 27ff.

16, 1: The anointing here prepared for is unknown to David's brother Eliab in the next chapter (1 Sm 17, 28), and David is twice anointed after Saul's death (2 Sm 2, 4; 5, 3).

16, 14: *An evil spirit sent by the Lord:* the Lord permitted Saul to be tormented with violent fits of rage.

16, 18: Of the two traditions which describe the coming of David into Saul's service, the oldest Greek translation retains only the one comprised in 1 Sm 16, 14-23; 17, 1-11. 32-54. This effort at consistency is not in accord with the character of the rest of the book; see note on 1 Sm 8, 1. Though square brackets are used in this edition to indicate the passages lacking in the oldest translation, this is meant only to help the reader follow one account at a time. Both are equally a part of the inspired text, as are also the various amplifications and retouchings of the narrative given within brackets in chs 18 and 19.

made him his armor-bearer,[n] [22] and sent Jesse the message, "Allow David to remain in my service, for he meets with my approval." [23] Whenever the spirit from God seized Saul, David would take the harp and play, and Saul would be relieved and feel better, for the evil spirit would leave him.

CHAPTER 17

The Challenge of Goliath. [1] The Philistines rallied their forces for battle at Socoh in Judah and camped between Socoh and Azekah at Ephes-dammim. [2] Saul and the Israelites also gathered and camped in the Vale of the Terebinth, drawing up their battle line to meet the Philistines. [3] The Philistines were stationed on one hill and the Israelites on an opposite hill, with a valley between them.

[4] A champion named Goliath of Gath came out from the Philistine camp; he was six and a half feet tall. [5] He had a bronze helmet on his head and wore a bronze corselet of scale armor weighing five thousand shekels, [6] and bronze greaves, and had a bronze scimitar* slung from a baldric. [7] The shaft of his javelin was like a weaver's heddle-bar, and its iron head weighed six hundred shekels.* His shield-bearer went before him.[o] [8] He stood and shouted to the ranks of Israel: "Why come out in battle formation? I am a Philistine, and you are Saul's servants. Choose one of your men, and have him come down to me. [9] If he beats me in combat and kills me, we will be your vassals; but if I beat him and kill him, you shall be our vassels and serve us." [10] The Philistine continued: "I defy the ranks of Israel today. Give me a man and let us fight together." [11] Saul and all the men of Israel, when they heard this challenge of the Philistine, were dismayed and terror-stricken.

David Comes to the Camp.* [12] [David was the son of an Ephrathite named Jesse,

---

n 1 Sm 18, 2.—o 2 Sm 21, 19; 1 Chr 11, 23; 20, 5.—p 1 Sm 16, 1. 10; Ru 1, 2.—q 1 Sm 18, 2; 2 Sm 7, 8.—r 1 Sm 26, 5.—s 1 Sm 25, 13.—t 1 Sm 18, 17; Jos 15, 16.—u 1 Sm 18, 25; Jgs 15, 18; 2 Kgs 19, 4; Is 37, 4.

17, 6: *Scimitar:* the Hebrew word for this is rather rare, and the nature of the weapon was in doubt until recent years. It is not the same as the *sword* of v 45.

17, 7: *Six hundred shekels:* over 15 pounds.

17, 12-31: An alternative account of how David came to undertake the combat with the Philistine is here inserted; it is continued in 1 Sm 17, 55—18, 6. See note on 1 Sm 16, 18.

---

who was from Bethlehem in Judah. He had eight sons, and in the days of Saul was old and well on in years.[p] [13] The three oldest sons of Jesse had followed Saul to war; these three sons who had gone off to war were named, the first-born Eliab, the second son Abinadab, and the third Shammah. [14] David was the youngest. While the three oldest had joined Saul, [15] David would go and come from Saul to tend his father's sheep at Bethlehem.[q]

[16] [Meanwhile the Philistine came forward and took his stand morning and evening for forty days.

[17] [Now Jesse said to his son David: "Take this ephah of roasted grain and these ten loaves for your brothers, and bring them quickly to your brothers in the camp. [18] Also take these ten cheeses for the field officer. Greet your brothers and bring home some token from them. [19] Saul, and they, and all Israel are fighting against the Philistines in the Vale of the Terebinth." [20] Early the next morning, having left the flock with a shepherd, David set out on his errand, as Jesse had commanded him. He reached the barricade of the camp just as the army, on their way to the battleground, were shouting their battle cry.[r] [21] The Israelites and the Philistines drew up opposite each other in battle array. [22] David entrusted what he had brought to the keeper of the baggage and hastened to the battle line where he greeted his brothers.[s] [23] While he was talking with them, the Philistine champion, by name Goliath of Gath, came up from the ranks of the Philistines and spoke as before, and David listened. [24] When the Israelites saw the man, they all retreated before him, very much afraid. [25] The Israelites had been saying: "Do you see this man coming up? He comes up to insult Israel. If anyone should kill him, the king would give him great wealth, and his daughter as well, and would grant exemption to his father's family in Israel."[t] [26] David now said to the men standing by: "What will be done for the man who kills this Philistine and frees Israel of the disgrace? Who is this uncircumcised Philistine in any case, that he should insult the armies of the living God?"[u] [27] They repeated the same words to him and said, "That is how the man who kills him will be rewarded." [28] When

1Sm

Eliab, his oldest brother, heard him speaking with the men, he grew angry with David and said: "Why did you come down? With whom have you left those sheep in the desert meanwhile? I know your arrogance and your evil intent. You came down to enjoy the battle!" 29 David replied, "What have I done now?—I was only talking." 30 Yet he turned from him to another and asked the same question; and everyone gave him the same answer as before. 31 The words that David had spoken were overheard and reported to Saul, who sent for him.]

David Fights Goliath. 32 Then David spoke to Saul: "Let your majesty not lose courage. I am at your service to go and fight this Philistine." 33 But Saul answered David, "You cannot go up against this Philistine and fight with him, for you are only a youth, while he has been a warrior from his youth." 34 *v* Then David told Saul: "Your servant used to tend his father's sheep, and whenever a lion or bear came to carry off a sheep from the flock, 35 I would go after it and attack it and rescue the prey from its mouth. If it attacked me, I would seize it by the jaw, strike it, and kill it. 36 Your servant has killed both a lion and a bear, and this uncircumcised Philistine will be as one of them, because he has insulted the armies of the living God." 37 David continued: "The LORD, who delivered me from the claws of the lion and the bear, will also keep me safe from the clutches of this Philistine." Saul answered David, "Go! the LORD will be with you." *w*

Preparation for the Encounter. 38 Then Saul clothed David in his own tunic, putting a bronze helmet on his head and arming him with a coat of mail. 39 David also girded himself with Saul's sword over the tunic. He walked with difficulty, however, since he had never tried armor before. He said to Saul, "I cannot go in these, because I have never tried them before." So he took them off. 40 Then, staff in hand, David selected five smooth stones from the wadi and put them in the pocket of his shepherd's bag. With his sling also ready to hand, he approached the Philistine.

David's Victory. 41 With his shield-bearer marching before him, the Philistine also advanced closer and closer to David.

42 When he had sized David up, and seen that he was youthful, and ruddy, and handsome in appearance, he held him in contempt. 43 The Philistine said to David, "Am I a dog that you come against me with a staff?" Then the Philistine cursed David by his gods 44 and said to him, "Come here to me, and I will leave your flesh for the birds of the air and the beasts of the field." *x* 45 David answered him: "You come against me with sword and spear and scimitar, but I come against you in the name of the LORD of hosts, the God of the armies of Israel that you have insulted. 46 Today the LORD shall deliver you into my hand; I will strike you down and cut off your head. This very day I will leave your corpse and the corpses of the Philistine army for the birds of the air and the beasts of the field; thus the whole land shall learn that Israel has a God. 47 All this multitude, too, shall learn that it is not by sword or spear that the LORD saves. For the battle is the LORD's, and he shall deliver you into our hands." *y*

48 The Philistine then moved to meet David at close quarters, while David ran quickly toward the battle line in the direction of the Philistine. 49 David put his hand into the bag and took out a stone, hurled it with the sling, and struck the Philistine on the forehead. The stone embedded itself in his brow, and he fell prostrate on the ground. 50 [Thus David overcame the Philistine with sling and stone; he struck the Philistine mortally, and did it without a sword.] *z* 51 Then David ran and stood over him; with the Philistine's own sword [which he drew from its sheath] he dispatched him and cut off his head. *a*

Flight of the Philistines. When they saw that their hero was dead, the Philistines took to flight. 52 Then the men of Israel and Judah, with loud shouts, went in pursuit of the Philistines to the approaches of Gath and to the gates of Ekron, and Philistines fell wounded along the road from Sha-araim as far as Gath and Ekron. 53 On their return from the pursuit of the Philistines, the Israelites looted their camp. 54 *b* David took the head of the Philistine and brought it to Jerusa-

---

v 34f: Jgs 14, 6; Sir 47, 3.—w Prv 28, 1.—x Dt 28, 26; Is 18, 6; Jer 15, 3.—y 1 Sm 14, 6; Ps 33, 16.—z Sir 47, 4; 1 Mc 4, 30.—a 1 Sm 21, 10.—b 1 Sm 31, 9.

lem; but he kept Goliath's armor in his own tent.*

David Presented to Saul. [55] [When Saul saw David go out to meet the Philistine, he asked his general Abner, "Abner, whose son is that youth?" Abner replied, "As truly as your majesty is alive, I have no idea." [56] And the king said, "Find out whose son the lad is." [57] So when David returned from slaying the Philistine, Abner took him and presented him to Saul. David was still holding the Philistine's head. [58] Saul then asked him, "Whose son are you, young man?" David replied, "I am the son of your servant Jesse of Bethlehem."

CHAPTER 18

David and Jonathan. [1] [By the time David finished speaking with Saul, Jonathan had become as fond of David as if his life depended on him; he loved him as he loved himself.[c] [2] Saul laid claim to David that day and did not allow him to return to his father's house.[d] [3] And Jonathan entered into a bond with David, because he loved him as himself. [4] Jonathan divested himself of the mantle he was wearing and gave it to David, along with his military dress, and his sword, his bow and his belt.[e] [5] David then carried out successfully every mision on which Saul sent him. So Saul put him in charge of his soldiers, and this was agreeable to the whole army, even to Saul's own officers.]

Saul's Jealousy. [6] At the approach of Saul and David (on David's return after slaying the Philistine), women came out from each of the cities of Israel to meet King Saul, singing and dancing, with tambourines, joyful songs, and sistrums.[f] [7] The women played and sang:

"Saul has slain his thousands,
    and David his ten thousands."[g]

[8] Saul was very angry and resentful of the song, for he thought: "They give David ten thousands, but only thousands to me.

c 1 Sm 19, 1-7; 20, 17; 23, 16; 2 Sm 1, 26; 9, 1.—d 1 Sm 16, 21; 17, 15.—e 2 Sm 1, 22.—f Ex 15, 20f; Jgs 11, 34; Jdt 15, 12.—g 1 Sm 21, 12; 29, 5; Sir 47, 6f.—h 10f: 1 Sm 16, 14; 19, 9f; 20, 33; 22, 6; 26, 8.—i 2 Sm 5, 2.—j 1 Sm 14, 49; 17, 25.— k 1 Sm 21, 8; 24, 16.—l 1 Sm 14, 49; 25, 44; 26, 23; 2 Sm 3, 13.

17, 54: At the time supposed by this narrative, Jerusalem was still Jebusite, and David had no military tent of his own; the verse is a later gloss.

All that remains for him is the kingship." [9] [And from that day on, Saul was jealous of David.

[10] [[h] The next day an evil spirit from God came over Saul, and he raged in his house. David was in attendance, playing the harp as at other times, while Saul was holding his spear. [11] Saul poised the spear, thinking to nail David to the wall, but twice David escaped him.] [12] Saul then began to fear David, [because the LORD was with him, but had departed from Saul himself.] [13] Accordingly, Saul removed him from his presence by appointing him a field officer. So David led the people on their military expeditions, [14] and prospered in all his enterprises, for the LORD was with him. [15] Seeing how successful he was, Saul conceived a fear of David; [16] on the other hand, all Israel and Judah loved him, since he led them on their expeditions.[i]

[17] [Saul said to David, "There is my older daughter, Merob, whom I will give you in marriage if you become my champion and fight the battles of the LORD." Saul had in mind, "I shall not touch him; let the Philistines strike him."[j] [18] But David answered Saul: "Who am I? And who are my kin or my father's clan in Israel that I should become the king's son-in-law?" [19] However, when it was time for Saul's daughter Merob to be given to David, she was given in marriage to Adriel the Meholathite instead.][k]

[20] Now Saul's daughter Michal loved David, and it was reported to Saul, who was pleased at this,[l] [21] for he thought, "I will offer her to him to become a snare for him, so that the Philistines may strike him." [Thus for the second time Saul said to David, "You shall become my son-in-law today."] [22] Saul then ordered his servants to speak to David privately and to say: "The king is fond of you, and all his officers love you. You should become the king's son-in-law." [23] But when Saul's servants mentioned this to David, he said: "Do you think it easy to become the king's son-in-law? I am poor and insignificant." [24] When his servants reported to him the nature of David's answer, [25] Saul commanded them to say this to David: "The king desires no other price for the bride than the foreskins of one hundred Philistines, that he may thus take vengeance on his enemies." Saul intended in this way to bring about David's death through

1Sm

the Philistines.*ᵐ* 26 When the servants reported this offer to David, he was pleased with the prospect of becoming the king's son-in-law. [Before the year was up,] 27 David made preparations and sallied forth with his men and slew two hundred Philistines. He brought back their foreskins and counted them out before the king, that he might thus become the king's son-in-law. So Saul gave him his daughter Michal in marriage. 28 Saul thus came to recognize that the LORD was with David; besides, his own daughter Michal loved David. 29 Therefore Saul feared David all the more [and was his enemy ever after].

30 [The Philistine chiefs continued to make forays, but each time they took the field, David was more successful against them than any other of Saul's officers, and as a result acquired great fame.]

CHAPTER 19

Persecution of David. 1 Saul discussed his intention of killing David with his son Jonathan and with all his servants. But Saul's son Jonathan, who was very fond of David,*ⁿ* 2 told him: "My father Saul is trying to kill you. Therefore, please be on your guard tomorrow morning; get out of sight and remain in hiding. 3 I, however, will go out and stand beside my father in the countryside where you are, and will speak to him about you. If I learn anything, I will let you know."

4 Jonathan then spoke well of David to his father Saul, saying to him: "Let not your majesty sin against his servant David, for he has committed no offense against you, but has helped you very much by his deeds. 5 When he took his life in his hands and slew the Philistine, and the LORD brought about a great victory for all Israel through him, you were glad to see it. Why, then, should you become guilty of shedding innocent blood by killing David without cause?"*ᵒ* 6 Saul heeded Jonathan's plea and swore, "As the LORD lives, he shall not be killed." 7 So Jonathan summoned David and repeated the whole conversation to him. Jonathan then brought David to Saul, and David served him as before.

8 When war broke out again, David went out to fight against the Philistines and inflicted a great defeat upon them, putting them to flight. 9 *ᵖ* Then an evil spirit from the LORD came upon Saul as he was sitting in his house with spear in hand and David was playing the harp nearby. 10 Saul tried to nail David to the wall with the spear, but David eluded Saul, so that the spear struck only the wall, and David got away safe.

11 The same night, Saul sent messengers to David's house to guard it, that he might kill him in the morning. David's wife Michal informed him, "Unless you save yourself tonight, tomorrow you will be killed."* 12 Then Michal let David down through a window, and he made his escape in safety.*ᵍ* 13 Michal took the household idol and laid it in the bed, putting a net of goat's hair at its head and covering it with a spread.*ʳ* 14 When Saul sent messengers to arrest David, she said, "He is sick." 15 Saul, however, sent the messengers back to see David and commanded them, "Bring him up to me in the bed, that I may kill him." 16 But when the messengers entered, they found the household idol in the bed, with the net of goat's hair at its head. 17 Saul therefore asked Michal: "Why did you play this trick on me? You have helped my enemy to get away!" Michal answered Saul: "He threatened me, 'Let me go or I will kill you.' "

David and Samuel in Ramah. 18 Thus David got safely away; he went to Samuel in Ramah, informing him of all that Saul had done to him. Then he and Samuel went to stay in the sheds. 19 When Saul was told that David was in the sheds near Ramah, 20 he sent messengers to arrest David. But when they saw the band of prophets, presided over by Samuel, in a prophetic frenzy, they too fell into the prophetic state.*ˢ* 21 Informed of this, Saul sent other messengers, who also fell into the prophetic state. For the third time Saul sent messengers, but they too fell into the prophetic state.

Saul among the Prophets. 22 Saul then went to Ramah himself. Arriving at the cistern of the threshing floor on the bare hilltop, he inquired, "Where are Samuel and David?", and was told, "At the sheds near Ramah." 23 As he set out from the

---

m 1 Sm 17, 26; Gn 34, 12.—n 1 Sm 18, 1; 20, 1ff.—o Dt 19, 10; Ps 119, 109.—p 9f: 1 Sm 16, 14; 18, 10f.—q Jos 2, 15; Acts 9, 25; 2 Cor 11, 33.—r Gn 31, 19; Jgs 17, 5; 18, 14. 18. 20.—s 1 Sm 10, 5f. 10; Nm 11, 25.

19, 11: This story in all probability originally followed 1 Sm 18, 29, placing the episode of David's escape on the night of his marriage with Michal.

hilltop toward the sheds, the spirit of God came upon him also, and he continued on in a prophetic condition until he reached the spot. At the sheds near Ramah [24] he, too, stripped himself of his garments and he, too, remained in the prophetic state in the presence of Samuel; all that day and night he lay naked. That is why they say, "Is Saul also among the prophets?"[t]

CHAPTER 20

David Consults with Jonathan. [1] David fled from the sheds near Ramah, and went to Jonathan. "What have I done?" he asked him. "What crime or what offense does your father hold against me that he seeks my life?"[u] [2] Jonathan answered him: "Heaven forbid that you should die! My father does nothing, great or small, without disclosing it to me. Why, then, should my father conceal this from me? This cannot be so!" [3] But David replied: "Your father is well aware that I am favored with your friendship, so he has decided, 'Jonathan must not know of this lest he be grieved.' Nevertheless, as the LORD lives and as you live, there is but a step between me and death." [4] Jonathan then said to David, "I will do whatever you wish." [5] David answered: "Tomorrow is the new moon, when I should in fact dine with the king. Let me go and hide in the open country until evening.[v] [6] If it turns out that your father misses me, say, 'David urged me to let him go on short notice to his city Bethlehem, because his whole clan is holding its seasonal sacrifice there.' [7] If he says, 'Very well,' your servant is safe. But if he becomes quite angry, you can be sure he has planned some harm. [8] [w] Do this kindness for your servant because of the LORD's bond between us, into which you brought me: if I am guilty, kill me yourself! Why should you give me up to your father?" [9] But Jonathan answered: "Not I! If ever I find out that my father is determined to inflict injury upon you, I will certainly let you know." [10] David

then asked Jonathan, "Who will tell me if your father gives you a harsh answer?"
Mutual Agreement. [11] [Jonathan replied to David, "Come, let us go out into the field." When they were out in the open country together, [12] Jonathan said to David: "As the LORD, the God of Israel, lives, I will sound out my father about this time tomorrow. Whether he is well disposed toward David or not, I will send you the information. [13] [x] Should it please my father to bring any injury upon you, may the LORD do thus and so to Jonathan if I do not apprise you of it and send you on your way in peace. May the LORD be with you even as he was with my father. [14] Only this: if I am still alive, may you show me the kindness of the LORD. But if I die, [15] never withdraw your kindness from my house. And when the LORD exterminates all the enemies of David from the surface of the earth, [16] the name of Jonathan must never be allowed by the family of David to die out from among you, or the LORD will make you answer for it." [17] And in his love for David, Jonathan renewed his oath to him, because he loved him as his very self.]

[18] Jonathan then said to him: "Tomorrow is the new moon; and you will be missed, since your place will be vacant. [19] On the following day you will be missed all the more. Go to the spot where you hid on the other occasion and wait near the mound there.[y] [20] On the third day of the month I will shoot arrows, as though aiming at a target. [21] I will then send my attendant to go and recover the arrows. If in fact I say to him, 'Look, the arrow is this side of you; pick it up,' come, for you are safe. As the LORD lives, there will be nothing to fear. [22] But if I say to the boy, 'Look, the arrow is beyond you,' go, for the LORD sends you away. [23] However, in the matter which you and I have discussed, the LORD shall be between you and me forever." [24] So David hid in the open country.

On the day of the new moon, when the king sat at table to dine, [25] taking his usual place against the wall, Jonathan sat facing him, while Abner sat at the king's side, and David's place was vacant. [26] [z] Saul, however, said nothing that day, for he thought, "He must have become unclean by accident, and not yet have been cleansed."[*] [27] On the next day, the second

---

t 1 Sm 10, 10ff.—u 1 Sm 19, 1-7. 11-17.—v Nm 10, 10; 28, 11-15.—w 8f: 1 Sm 23, 17f.—x 13-16; 1 Sm 24, 22f; 2 Sm 9, 1-13; 21, 7.—y 1 Sm 19, 1-7.—z 1 Sm 16, 5; Lv 7, 20f; 15, 1ff.

20, 26: The meal on the first day of the month would have religious overtones, and a ritual impurity (Lv 15, 16; Dt 23, 10ff) would bar David from sharing in it.

1Sm

day of the month, David's place was vacant. Saul inquired of his son Jonathan, "Why has the son of Jesse not come to table yesterday or today?" [28] Jonathan answered Saul: "David urgently asked me to let him go to his city, Bethlehem. [29] 'Please let me go,' he begged, 'for we are to have a clan sacrifice in our city, and my brothers insist on my presence. Now, therefore, if you think well of me, give me leave to visit my brothers.' That is why he has not come to the king's table." [30] But Saul was extremely angry with Jonathan and said to him: "Son of a rebellious woman, do I not know that, to your own shame and to the disclosure of your mother's shame, you are the companion of Jesse's son? [31] Why, as long as the son of Jesse lives upon the earth, you cannot make good your claim to the kingship! So send for him, and bring him to me, for he is doomed."[a] [32] But Jonathan asked his father Saul: "Why should he die? What has he done?" [33] At this Saul brandished his spear to strike him, and thus Jonathan learned that his father was resolved to kill David.[b] [34] Jonathan sprang up from the table in great anger and took no food that second day of the month, for he was grieved on David's account, since his father had railed against him.

Jonathan's Farewell. [35] The next morning Jonathan went out into the field with a little boy for his appointment with David. [36] There he said to the boy, "Run and fetch the arrow." And as the boy ran, he shot an arrow beyond him in the direction of the city. [37] When the boy made for the spot where Jonathan had shot the arrow, Jonathan called after him, "The arrow is farther on!" [38] Again he called to his lad, "Hurry, be quick, don't delay!" Jonathan's boy picked up the arrow and brought it to his master. [39] The boy knew nothing; only Jonathan and David knew what was meant. [40] Then Jonathan gave his weapons to this boy of his and said to him, "Go, take them to the city." [41] When the boy had left, David rose from beside the mound and prostrated himself on the ground three times before Jonathan in homage. They kissed each other and wept aloud together. [42] [c] At length Jonathan said to David, "Go in peace, in keeping with what we two have sworn by the name of the LORD: 'The LORD shall be between

you and me, and between your posterity and mine forever.'"

CHAPTER 21

[1] Then David departed on his way, while Jonathan went back into the city.

The Holy Bread. [2] David went to Ahimelech, the priest of Nob, who came trembling to meet him and asked, "Why are you alone? Is there no one with you?"[d] [3] David answered the priest: "The king gave me a commission and told me to let no one know anything about the business on which he sent me or the commission he gave me. For that reason I have arranged a meeting place with my men. [4] [e] Now what have you on hand? Give me five loaves, or whatever you can find." [5] But the priest replied to David, "I have no ordinary bread on hand, only holy bread; if the men have abstained from women, you may eat some of that."* [6] David answered the priest: "We have indeed been segregated from women as on previous occasions. Whenever I go on a journey, all the young men are consecrated—even for a secular journey. All the more so today, when they are consecrated at arms!" [7] So the priest gave him holy bread, for no other bread was on hand except the showbread which had been removed from the LORD's presence and replaced by fresh bread when it was taken away.[f] [8] One of Saul's servants was there that day, detained before the LORD; his name was Doeg the Edomite, and he was Saul's chief henchman.

The Sword of Goliath. [9] David then asked Ahimelech: "Do you have a spear or a sword on hand? I brought along neither my sword nor my weapons, because the king's business was urgent." [10] The priest replied: "The sword of Goliath the Philistine, whom you killed in the Vale of the Terebinth, is here [wrapped in a mantle] behind an ephod. If you wish to take that, take it; there is no sword here except that one." David said: "There is none to match it. Give it to me!"[g]

a 2 Sm 12, 5.—b 1 Sm 18, 11.—c 2 Sm 9, 1; 21, 7.—d Is 10, 32; Mk 2, 26.—e Lv 24, 5. 9.—f 1 Sm 22, 9; Lv 24, 5-9; Mt 12, 3f; Mk 2, 26; Lk 6, 3ff.—g 1 Sm 17, 51. 54.

21, 5f: *From women:* the high priest, willing to distribute the holy bread to David and his men, requires that they be free from ritual uncleanness, associated in Old Testament times (Lv 15, 18) with the marriage act. David's answer supposes the discipline of a military campaign under the conditions of "holy war" (Dt 23, 10).

David a Fugitive. [11]That same day David took to flight from Saul, going to Achish, king of Gath.[h] [12]But the servants of Achish said, "Is this not David, the king of the land? During their dances do they not sing,

'Saul has slain his thousands,
but David his ten thousands'?"[i]

[13]David took note of these remarks and became very much afraid of Achish, king of Gath. [14]So, as they watched, he feigned insanity and acted like a madman in their hands, drumming on the doors of the gate and drooling onto his beard. [15]Finally Achish said to his servants: "You see the man is mad. Why did you bring him to me? [16]Do I not have enough madmen, that you bring in this one to carry on in my presence? Should this fellow come into my house?"

CHAPTER 22

[1]David left Gath and escaped to the cave of Adullam. When his brothers and the rest of his family heard about it, they came down to him there.[j] [2]He was joined by all those who were in difficulties or in debt, or who were embittered, and he became their leader. About four hundred men were with him.

[3]From there David went to Mizpeh of Moab and said to the king of Moab, "Let my father and mother stay with you, until I learn what God will do for me." [4]He left them with the king of Moab, and they stayed with him as long as David remained in the refuge.*

[5]But the prophet Gad said to David: "Do not remain in the refuge. Leave, and go to the land of Judah." And so David left and went to the forest of Hereth.

Doeg Betrays Ahimelech. [6]Now Saul heard that David and his men had been located. At the time he was sitting in Gibeah under a tamarisk tree on the high place, holding his spear, while all his servants were standing by.[k] [7]So he said to them: "Listen, men of Benjamin! Will the son of Jesse give all of you fields and vineyards? Will he make each of you an officer over

a thousand or a hundred men,[l] [8]that you have all conspired against me and no one tells me that my son has made an agreement with the son of Jesse? None of you shows sympathy for me or discloses to me that my son has stirred up my servant to be an enemy against me, as is the case today." [9] [m] Then Doeg the Edomite, who was standing with the officers of Saul, spoke up: "I saw the son of Jesse come to Ahimelech, son of Ahitub, in Nob. [10]He consulted the LORD for him and gave him supplies, and the sword of Goliath the Philistine as well."

Slaughter of the Priests. [11]At this the king sent a summons to Ahimelech the priest, son of Ahitub, and to all his family who were priests in Nob; and they all came to the king. [12]Then Saul said, "Listen, son of Ahitub!" He replied, "Yes, my lord." [13]Saul asked him, "Why did you conspire against me with the son of Jesse by giving him food and a sword and by consulting God for him, that he might rebel against me and become my enemy, as is the case today?" [14]Ahimelech answered the king: "And who among all your servants is as loyal as David, the king's son-in-law, captain of your bodyguard, and honored in your own house? [15]Is this the first time I have consulted God for him? No indeed! Let not the king accuse his servant or anyone in my family of such a thing. Your servant knows nothing at all, great or small, about the whole matter." [16]But the king said, "You shall die, Ahimelech, with all your family." [17]The king then commanded his henchmen standing by: "Make the rounds and kill the priests of the LORD, for they assisted David. They knew he was a fugitive and yet failed to inform me." But the king's servants refused to lift a hand to strike the priests of the LORD.[n]

[18]The king therefore commanded Doeg, "You make the rounds and kill the priests!" So Doeg the Edomite went from one to the next and killed the priests himself, slaying on that day eighty-five who wore the linen ephod. [19]Saul also put the priestly city of Nob to the sword, including men and women, children and infants, and oxen, asses and sheep.

Abiathar Escapes. [20]One son of Ahimelech, son of Ahitub, named Abiathar, escaped and fled to David.[o] [21]When Abiathar told David that Saul had slain the priests of the LORD, [22]David said

1Sm

h 1 Sm 27, 2; 29, 5.—i 1 Sm 18, 7; 29, 5.—j 2 Sm 23, 13; Ps 63; Mi 1, 15.—k Ps 52.—l 1 Sm 8, 14.—m 9f: 1 Sm 21, 2-10.— n 1 Sm 2, 31. 33; 21, 7.—o 1 Sm 23, 6; 30, 7; 1 Kgs 2, 26f.

22, 4-5: *Refuge:* seemingly connected with the cave complex spoken of in v 1.

to him: "I knew that day, when Doeg the Edomite was there, that he would surely tell Saul. I am responsible for the death of all your family. ²³Stay with me. Fear nothing; he that seeks your life must seek my life also. You are under my protection."

CHAPTER 23

Keilah Liberated. ¹David received information that the Philistines were attacking Keilah and plundering the threshing floors.ᵖ ²So he consulted the LORD, inquiring, "Shall I go and defeat these Philistines?" The LORD answered, "Go, for you will defeat the Philistines and rescue Keilah."�q ³But David's men said to him: "We are afraid here in Judah. How much more so if we go to Keilah against the forces of the Philistines!" ⁴Again David consulted the LORD, who answered, "Go down to Keilah, for I will deliver the Philistines into your power." ⁵David then went with his men to Keilah and fought with the Philistines. He drove off their cattle and inflicted a severe defeat on them, and thus rescued the inhabitants of Keilah.

⁶Abiathar, son of Ahimelech, who had fled to David, went down with David to Keilah, taking the ephod with him.ʳ

Flight from Keilah. ⁷When Saul was told that David had entered Keilah, he said: "God has put him in my grip. Now he has shut himself in, for he has entered a city with gates and bars." ⁸Saul then called all the people to war, in order to go down to Keilah and besiege David and his men. ⁹When David found out that Saul was planning to harm him, he said to the priest Abiathar, "Bring forward the ephod."ˢ ¹⁰David then said: "O LORD God of Israel, your servant has heard a report that Saul plans to come to Keilah, to destroy the city on my account. ¹¹Will they hand me over? And now: will Saul come down as your servant has heard? O LORD God of Israel, tell your servant." The LORD answered, "He will come down." ¹²David then asked, "Will the citizens of Keilah deliver me and my men into the grasp of Saul?" And the LORD answered, "Yes." ¹³So David and his men, about six hundred in number, left Keilah and wandered from place to place. When Saul was informed that David had escaped from Keilah, he abandoned the expedition.

David and Jonathan in Horesh. ¹⁴David now lived in the refuges in the desert, or in the barren hill country near Ziph. Though Saul sought him continually, the LORD did not deliver David into his grasp. ¹⁵David was apprehensive because Saul had come out to seek his life; but while he was at Horesh in the barrens near Ziph, ¹⁶Saul's son, Jonathan, came down there to David and strengthened his resolve in the LORD.ᵗ ¹⁷He said to him: "Have no fear, my father Saul shall not lay a hand to you. You shall be king of Israel and I shall be second to you. Even my father Saul knows this." ¹⁸They made a joint agreement before the LORD in Horesh, where David remained, while Jonathan returned to his home.ᵘ

Treachery of the Ziphites. ¹⁹Some of the Ziphites went up to Saul in Gibeah and said, "David is hiding among us, now in the refuges, and again at Horesh, or on the hill of Hachilah, south of the wasteland.ᵛ ²⁰Therefore, whenever the king wishes to come down, let him do so. It will be our task to deliver him into the king's grasp." ²¹Saul replied: "The LORD bless you for your sympathy toward me.ʷ ²²Go now and make sure once more! Take note of the place where he sets foot" (for he thought, perhaps they are playing some trick on me). ²³"Look around and learn in which of all the various hiding places he is holding out. Then come back to me with sure information, and I will go with you. If he is in the region, I will search him out among all the families of Judah." ²⁴So they went off to Ziph ahead of Saul. At this time David and his men were in the desert below Maon, in the Arabah south of the wasteland.ˣ

Escape from Saul. ²⁵When Saul and his men came looking for him, David got word of it and went down to the gorge in the desert below Maon. Saul heard of this and pursued David into the desert below Maon. ²⁶As Saul moved along one rim of the gorge, David and his men took to the other. David was in anxious flight to escape Saul, and Saul and his men were attempting to outflank David and his men in order to capture them, ²⁷when a messenger came to Saul, saying, "Come

p Jos 15, 44.—q 1 Sm 28, 6.—r 1 Sm 22, 20; 30, 7.—s 1 Sm 2, 28.—t 1 Sm 18, 1.—u 1 Sm 18, 3; 20, 8.—v 1 Sm 26, 1-3; Ps 54.—w 2 Sm 2, 5.—x 1 Sm 25, 2.

quickly, because the Philistines have invaded the land." [28] Saul interrupted his pursuit of David and went to meet the Philistines. This is how that place came to be called the Gorge of Divisions.

CHAPTER 24

David Spares Saul. [1] David then went up from there and stayed in the refuges behind Engedi. [2] And when Saul returned from the pursuit of the Philistines, he was told that David was in the desert near Engedi. [3] So Saul took three thousand picked men from all Israel and went in search of David and his men in the direction of the wild goat crags. [4] When he came to the sheepfolds along the way, he found a cave, which he entered to ease nature. David and his men were occupying the inmost recesses of the cave.[y]

[5] David's servants said to him, "This is the day of which the LORD said to you, 'I will deliver your enemy into your grasp; do with him as you see fit.' " So David moved up and stealthily cut off an end of Saul's mantle. [6] Afterward, however, David regretted that he had cut off an end of Saul's mantle.[z] [7] He said to his men, "The LORD forbid that I should do such a thing to my master, the LORD's anointed, as to lay a hand on him, for he is the LORD's anointed."[a] [8] With these words David restrained his men and would not permit them to attack Saul. Saul then left the cave and went on his way. [9] David also stepped out of the cave, calling to Saul, "My lord the king!" When Saul looked back, David bowed to the ground in homage [10] and asked Saul: "Why do you listen to those who say, 'David is trying to harm you'? [11] You see for yourself today that the LORD just now delivered you into my grasp in the cave. I had some thought of killing you, but I took pity on you instead. I decided, 'I will not raise a hand against my lord, for he is the LORD's anointed and a father to me.' [12] Look here at this end of your mantle which I hold. Since I cut off an end of your mantle and did not kill you, see and be convinced that I plan no harm and no rebellion. I have done you no wrong, though you are hunting me down

to take my life.[b] [13] The LORD will judge between me and you, and the LORD will exact justice from you in my case. I shall not touch you. [14] The old proverb says, 'From the wicked comes forth wickedness.' So I will take no action against you. [15] Against whom are you on campaign, O king of Israel? Whom are you pursuing? A dead dog, or a single flea! [16] The LORD will be the judge; he will decide between me and you. May he see this, and take my part, and grant me justice beyond your reach!"[c]

Saul's Remorse. [17] When David finished saying these things to Saul, Saul answered, "Is that your voice, my son David?" And he wept aloud. [18] Saul then said to David: "You are in the right rather than I; you have treated me generously, while I have done you harm. [19] Great is the generosity you showed me today, when the LORD delivered me into your grasp and you did not kill me. [20] For if a man meets his enemy, does he send him away unharmed? May the LORD reward you generously for what you have done this day. [21] And now, since I know that you shall surely be king and that sovereignty over Israel shall come into your possession,[d] [22] swear to me by the LORD that you will not destroy my descendants and that you will not blot out my name and family."[e] [23] David gave Saul his oath and Saul returned home, while David and his men went up to the refuge.

CHAPTER 25

Death of Samuel. [1] Samuel died, and all Israel gathered to mourn him; they buried him at his home in Ramah.[f]

Nabal and Abigail. [2] Then David went down to the desert of Maon. There was a man of Maon who had property in Carmel; he was very wealthy, owning three thousand sheep and a thousand goats. At this time he was present for the shearing of his flock in Carmel.[g] [3] The man was named Nabal, his wife, Abigail. The woman was intelligent and attractive, but Nabal himself, a Calebite, was harsh and ungenerous in his behavior.[h] [4] When David heard in the desert that Nabal was shearing his flock, [5] he sent ten young men, instructing them: "Go up to Carmel. Pay Nabal a visit and greet him in my name. [6] Say to him, 'Peace be with you, my brother, and with your family, and with all who belong

y Ps 57.—z 1 Sm 15, 27.—a 1 Sm 10, 1; 31, 4; 2 Sm 1, 14.—b Rom 12, 19.—c 1 Sm 18, 19. 31; 26, 19; Pss 35, 1ff; 43, 1.—d 1 Sm 26, 25.—e 2 Sm 9, 1ff.—f 1 Sm 28, 3; Sir 46, 13-20.—g 1 Sm 23, 24; Jos 15, 55.—h 1 Sm 27, 3; Jos 14, 6; 1 Chr 2, 42. 45.

to you. ⁷I have just heard that shearers are with you. Now, when your shepherds were with us, we did them no injury, neither did they miss anything all the while they were in Carmel. ⁸Ask your servants and they will tell you so. Look kindly on these young men, since we come at a festival time. Please give your servants and your son David whatever you can manage.' "

⁹When David's young men arrived, they delivered this message fully to Nabal in David's name, and then waited. ¹⁰But Nabal answered the servants of David: "Who is David? Who is the son of Jesse? Nowadays there are many servants who run away from their masters. ¹¹Must I take my bread, my wine, my meat that I have slaughtered for my own shearers, and give them to men who come from I know not where?" ¹²So David's young men retraced their steps and on their return reported to him all that had been said. ¹³Thereupon David said to his men, "Let everyone gird on his sword." And so everyone, David included, girded on his sword. About four hundred men went up after David, while two hundred remained with the baggage.

¹⁴But Nabal's wife Abigail was informed of this by one of the servants, who said: "David sent messengers from the desert to greet our master, but he flew at them screaming. ¹⁵Yet these men were very good to us. We were done no injury, neither did we miss anything all the while we were living among them during our stay in the open country. ¹⁶For us they were like a rampart night and day the whole time we were pasturing the sheep near them. ¹⁷Now, see what you can do, for you must realize that otherwise evil is in store for our master and for his whole family. He is so mean that no one can talk to him." ¹⁸Abigail quickly got together two hundred loaves, two skins of wine, five dressed sheep, five seahs of roasted grain, a hundred cakes of pressed raisins, and two hundred cakes of pressed figs, and loaded them on asses. ¹⁹She then said to her servants. "Go on ahead; I will follow you." But she did not tell her husband Nabal.

²⁰As she came down through a mountain defile riding on an ass, David and his men were also coming down from the opposite direction. When she met them,

²¹David had just been saying: "Indeed, it was in vain that I guarded all this man's possessions in the desert, so that he missed nothing. He has repaid good with evil. ²²May God do thus and so to David, if by morning I leave a single male alive among all those who belong to him."ⁱ ²³As soon as Abigail saw David, she dismounted quickly from the ass and, falling prostrate on the ground before David, did him homage. ²⁴As she fell at his feet she said:

"My lord, let the blame be mine. Please let your handmaid speak to you, and listen to the words of your handmaid. ²⁵Let not my lord pay attention to that worthless man Nabal, for he is just like his name. Fool is his name,* and he acts the fool. I, your handmaid, did not see the young men whom my lord sent. ²⁶Now, therefore, my lord, as the LORD lives, and as you live, it is the LORD who has kept you from shedding blood and from avenging yourself personally. May your enemies and those who seek to harm my lord become as Nabal!* ²⁷Accept this present, then, which your maidservant has brought for my lord, and let it be given to the young men who follow my lord. ²⁸Please forgive the transgression of your handmaid, for the LORD shall certainly establish a lasting dynasty for my lord, because your lordship is fighting the battles of the LORD, and there is no evil to be found in you your whole life long. ²⁹If anyone rises to pursue you and to seek your life, may the life of my lord be bound in the bundle of the living* in the care of the LORD your God; but may he hurl out the lives of your enemies as from the hollow of a sling.ʲ ³⁰And when the LORD carries out for my lord the promise of success he has made concerning you, and appoints you as commander over Israel,ᵏ ³¹you shall not have this as a qualm or burden on your conscience, my lord, for having shed innocent blood or for having avenged yourself personally. When

---

i 1 Kgs 16, 11; 21, 21; 2 Kgs 9, 8.—j Ps 69, 28.—k 1 Sm 13, 14; 2 Sm 3, 10.

25, 25: *Fool is his name:* Nabal in Hebrew means "a fool."
25, 26: Abigail anticipates that some misfortune will shortly overtake Nabal, as in fact it does (vv 37-38).
25, 29: *The bundle of the living:* the figure is perhaps taken from the practice of tying up valuables in a kerchief or bag for safekeeping. Abigail desires that David enjoy permanent peace and security, but that his enemies be subject to constant agitation and humiliation like a stone whirled about, cast out of the sling, and thereafter disregarded.

the LORD confers this benefit on your lordship, remember your handmaid." [32] David said to Abigail: "Blessed be the LORD, the God of Israel, who sent you to meet me today. [33] Blessed be your good judgment and blessed be you yourself, who this day have prevented me from shedding blood and from avenging myself personally. [34] Otherwise, as the LORD, the God of Israel, lives, who has restrained me from harming you, if you had not come so promptly to meet me, by dawn Nabal would not have had a single man or boy left alive." [35] David then took from her what she had brought him and said to her: "Go up to your home in peace! See, I have granted your request as a personal favor."

Nabal's Death. [36] When Abigail came to Nabal, there was a drinking party in his house like that of a king, and Nabal was merry because he was very drunk. So she told him nothing at all before daybreak the next morning. [37] But then, when Nabal had become sober, his wife told him what had happened. At this his courage died within him, and he became, like a stone. [38] About ten days later the LORD struck him and he died. [39] On hearing that Nabal was dead, David said: "Blessed be the LORD, who has requited the insult I received at the hand of Nabal, and who restrained his servant from doing evil, but has punished Nabal for his own evil deeds."

David Marries Abigail and Ahinoam. David then sent a proposal of marriage to Abigail. [40] When David's servants came to Abigail in Carmel, they said to her, "David has sent us to you that he may take you as his wife." [41] Rising and bowing to the ground, she answered, "Your handmaid would become a slave to wash the feet of my lord's servants." [42] She got up immediately, mounted an ass, and followed David's messengers, with her five maids following in attendance upon her. She became his wife, [43] *l* and David also married Ahinoam of Jezreel. Thus both of them were his wives; but Saul gave David's wife Michal, Saul's own daughter, to Palti, son of Laish, who was from Gallim. *m*

CHAPTER 26

Saul's Life Again Spared. [1] *n* Men from Ziph came to Saul in Gibeah, reporting

---

1 1 Sm 27, 3.—m 1 Sm 18, 20; 27, 3; 30, 5; 2 Sm 3, 2. 13ff; 1 Chr 3, 1.—n 1f: 1 Sm 23, 19f; Ps 54.—o 1 Sm 17, 20.—p 1 Chr 2, 16.—q 1 Sm 18, 11; 19, 10.

that David was hiding on the hill of Hachilah at the edge of the wasteland. [2] So Saul went off down to the desert of Ziph with three thousand picked men of Israel, to search for David in the desert of Ziph. [3] Saul camped beside the road on the hill of Hachilah, at the edge of the wasteland. David, who was living in the desert, saw that Saul had come into the desert after him [4] and sent out scouts, who confirmed Saul's arrival. [5] David himself then went to the place where Saul was encamped and examined the spot where Saul and Abner, son of Ner, the general, had their sleeping quarters. Saul's were within the barricade, and all his soldiers were camped around him. *o* [6] David asked Ahimelech the Hittite, and Abishai, son of Zeruiah and brother of Joab, "Who will go down into the camp with me to Saul?" Abishai replied, "I will." *p* [7] So David and Abishai went among Saul's soldiers by night and found Saul lying asleep within the barricade, with his spear thrust into the ground at his head and Abner and his men sleeping around him.

[8] Abishai whispered to David: "God has delivered your enemy into your grasp this day. Let me nail him to the ground with one thrust of the spear; I will not need a second thrust!" *q* [9] But David said to Abishai, "Do not harm him, for who can lay hands on the LORD's anointed and remain unpunished? [10] As the LORD lives," David continued, "it must be the LORD himself who will strike him, whether the time comes for him to die, or he goes out and perishes in battle. [11] But the LORD forbid that I touch his anointed! Now take the spear which is at his head and the water jug, and let us be on our way." [12] So David took the spear and the water jug from their place at Saul's head, and they got away without anyone's seeing or knowing or awakening. All remained asleep, because the LORD had put them into a deep slumber.

David Taunts Abner. [13] Going across to an opposite slope, David stood on a remote hilltop at a great distance from Abner, son of Ner, and the troops. [14] He then shouted, "Will you not answer, Abner?" And Abner answered, "Who is it that calls me?" [15] David said to Abner: "Are you not a man whose like does not exist in Israel? Why, then, have you not guarded your lord the king when one of his subjects went to kill the king, your lord? [16] This is no creditable service you have performed. As the LORD lives, you people deserve death because you have not guarded your lord, the LORD's anointed. Go, look: where are the king's spear and the water jug that was at his head?"

Saul Admits His Guilt. [17] Saul recognized David's voice and asked, "Is that your voice, my son David?" David answered, "Yes, my lord the king." [18] He continued: "Why does my lord pursue his servant? What have I done? What evil do I plan? [19] Please, now, let my lord the king listen to the words of his servant. If the LORD has incited you against me, let an offering appease him; but if men, may they be cursed before the LORD, because they have exiled me so that this day I have no share in the LORD's inheritance,* but am told: 'Go, serve other gods!'[r] [20] Do not let my blood flow to the ground far from the presence of the LORD. For the king of Israel has come out to seek a single flea as if he were hunting partridge in the mountains." [21] Then Saul said: "I have done wrong. Come back, my son David, I will not harm you again, because you have held my life precious today. Indeed, I have been a fool and have made a serious mistake." [22] But David answered: "Here is the king's spear. Let an attendant come over to get it. [23] The LORD will reward each man for his justice and faithfulness. Today, though the LORD delivered you into my grasp, I would not harm the LORD's anointed.[s] [24] As I valued your life highly today, so may the LORD value my life highly and deliver me from all difficulties." [25] Then Saul said to David: "Blessed are you, my son David! You shall certainly succeed in whatever you undertake." David went his way, and Saul returned to his home.[t]

CHAPTER 27

Refuge among Philistines. [1] But David said to himself: "I shall perish some day at the hand of Saul. I have no choice but to escape to the land of the Philistines; then Saul will give up his continuous search for me throughout the land of Israel, and I shall be out of his reach." [2] Accordingly, David departed with his six hundred men and went over to Achish, son of Maoch, king of Gath.[u] [3] David and his men lived in Gath with Achish; each one had his family, and David had his two wives, Ahinoam

from Jezreel and Abigail, the widow of Nabal from Carmel.[v] [4] When Saul was told that David had fled to Gath, he no longer searched for him.

In Ziklag. [5] David said to Achish: "If I meet with your approval, let me have a place to live in one of the country towns. Why should your servant live with you in the royal city?" [6] That same day Achish gave him Ziklag, which has, therefore, belonged to the kings of Judah* up to the present time.[w] [7] In all, David lived a year and four months in the country of the Philistines.[x]

Raids on Israel's Foes. [8] David and his men went up and made raids on the Geshurites, Girzites, and Amalekites—peoples living in the land between Telam, on the approach to Shur, and the land of Egypt.[y] [9] In attacking the land David would not leave a man or woman alive, but would carry off sheep, oxen, asses, camels, and clothes. On his return he brought these to Achish, [10] who asked, "Whom did you raid this time?" And David answered, "The Negeb of Judah," or "The Negeb of Jerahmeel," or "The Negeb of the Kenites."[z] [11] But David would not leave a man or woman alive to be brought to Gath, fearing that they would betray him by saying, "This is what David did." This was his custom as long as he lived in the country of the Philistines. [12] And Achish trusted David, thinking, "He must certainly be detested by his people Israel. I shall have him as my vassal forever."

CHAPTER 28

[1] In those days the Philistines mustered their military forces to fight against Israel. So Achish said to David, "You realize, of course, that you and your men must go out on campaign with me to Jezreel." [2] David answered Achish, "Good! Now you shall learn what your servant can do." Then Achish said to David, "I shall appoint you my permanent bodyguard."

---

r 1 Sm 24, 16.—s 1 Sm 18, 20.—t 1 Sm 24, 21.—u 1 Sm 21, 11-16.—v 1 Sm 25, 3. 44; 30, 3ff; 2 Sm 2, 3.—w 1 Sm 30, 1.—x 1 Sm 29, 3.—y 1 Sm 15, 3. 7.—z 1 Sm 30, 14. 29; 1 Chr 2, 9. 25. 42.

26, 19: *The Lord's inheritance:* the land of Israel (Dt 32, 8f), under the Lord's special protection, where he could be freely worshiped.

27, 6: *Has . . . belonged to the kings of Judah:* as a personal holding, outside the system of tribal lands; Jerusalem, when taken by David, had a similar status (2 Sm 5, 7-9).

[3] Now Samuel had died and, after being mourned by all Israel, was buried in his city, Ramah. Meanwhile Saul had driven mediums and fortune-tellers out of the land.[a]

Saul in Dismay. [4] The Philistine levies advanced to Shunem and encamped. Saul, too, mustered all Israel; they camped on Gilboa. [5] When Saul saw the camp of the Philistines, he was dismayed and lost heart completely. [6] He therefore consulted the LORD; but the LORD gave no answer, whether in dreams or by the Urim or through prophets.[b] [7] Then Saul said to his servants, "Find me a woman who is a medium, to whom I can go to seek counsel through her." His servants answered him, "There is a woman in Endor who is a medium."[c]

The Witch of Endor. [8] So he disguised himself, putting on other clothes, and set out with two companions. They came to the woman by night, and Saul said to her, "Tell my fortune through a ghost; conjure up for me the one I ask you to."[d] [9] But the woman answered him, "You are surely aware of what Saul has done, in driving the mediums and fortune-tellers out of the land. Why, then, are you laying snares for my life, to have me killed?" [10] But Saul swore to her by the LORD, "As the LORD lives, you shall incur no blame for this." [11] Then the woman asked him, "Whom do you want me to conjure up?" and he answered, "Samuel."

Samuel Appears. [12] When the woman saw Samuel, she shrieked at the top of her voice and said to Saul, "Why have you deceived me? You are Saul!"[*] [13] But the king said to her, "Have no fear. What do you see?" The woman answered Saul, "I see a preternatural being rising from the earth." [14] "What does he look like?" asked Saul. And she replied, "It is an old man who is rising, clothed in a mantle." Saul knew that it was Samuel,

and so he bowed face to the ground in homage.

Saul's Doom. [15] Samuel then said to Saul, "Why do you disturb me by conjuring me up?" Saul replied: "I am in great straits, for the Philistines are waging war against me and God has abandoned me. Since he no longer answers me through prophets or in dreams, I have called you to tell me what I should do."[e] [16] To this Samuel said: "But why do you ask me, if the LORD has abandoned you and is with your neighbor?[f] [17] The LORD has done to you what he foretold through me: he has torn the kingdom from your grasp and has given it to your neighbor David.

[18] "Because you disobeyed the LORD's directive and would not carry out his fierce anger against Amalek, the LORD has done this to you today.[g] [19] Moreover, the LORD will deliver Israel, and you as well, into the clutches of the Philistines. By tomorrow you and your sons will be with me, and the LORD will have delivered the army of Israel into the hands of the Philistines."[h]

Saul's Despair. [20] Immediately Saul fell full length on the ground, for he was badly shaken by Samuel's message. Moreover, he had no bodily strength left, since he had eaten nothing all that day and night. [21] Then the woman came to Saul, and seeing that he was quite terror-stricken, said to him: "Remember, your maidservant obeyed you: I took my life in my hands and fulfilled the request you made of me. [22] Now you, in turn, please listen to your maidservant. Let me set something before you to eat, so that you may have strength when you go on your way." [23] But he refused, saying, "I will not eat." However, when his servants joined the woman in urging him, he listened to their entreaties, got up from the ground, and sat on a couch. [24] The woman had a stall-fed calf in the house, which she now quickly slaughtered. Then taking flour, she kneaded it and baked unleavened bread. [25] She set the meal before Saul and his servants, and they ate. Then they stood up and left the same night.

---

a 1 Sm 25, 1; Sir 46, 20.—b 1 Sm 14, 37. 41; Ex 28, 30; Lv 8, 8.—c Lv 19, 31; 20, 27; Dt 18, 10ff; 1 Chr 10, 13f; Acts 16, 16.—d 1 Kgs 14, 2.—e Sir 46, 20.—f 1 Sm 15, 27f.—g 1 Sm 15, 18f. 26.—h 1 Sm 31, 2-6; Sir 46, 20.—i 1 Sm 4, 1.

28, 12: Human beings cannot communicate at will with the souls of the dead. God may, however, permit a departed soul to appear to the living and even to disclose things unknown to them. Saul's own prohibition of necromancy and divination (v 3) was in keeping with the consistent teaching of the Old Testament. If we are to credit the reality of the apparition to Saul, it was due, not to the summons of the witch, but to God's will; the woman merely furnished the occasion.

CHAPTER 29

David's Aid Rejected. [1] Now the Philistines had mustered all their forces in Aphek, and the Israelites were encamped at the spring of Harod near Jezreel.[i] [2] As the Philistine lords were marching their groups of a hundred and a thousand, David and his men were marching in the rear guard with Achish. ³The Philistine chiefs asked, "What are those Hebrews doing here?" And Achish answered them: "Why, that is David, the officer of Saul, king of Israel. He has been with me now for a year or two, and I have no fault to find with him from the day he came over to me until the present."ʲ ⁴But the Philistine chiefs were angered at this and said to him: "Send that man back! Let him return to the place you picked out for him. He must not go down into battle with us, lest during the battle he become our enemy. For how else can he win back his master's favor, if not with the heads of these men of ours?ᵏ ⁵Is this not the David of whom they sing during their dances,

'Saul has slain his thousands,
  but David his ten thousands'?"ˡ

⁶So Achish summoned David and said to him: "As the LORD lives, you are honest, and I should be pleased to have you active with me in the camp, for I have found nothing wrong with you from the day of your arrival to this day. But you are not welcome to the lords. ⁷Withdraw peaceably, now, and do nothing that might displease the Philistine lords." ⁸But David said to Achish: "What have I done? Or what have you against your servant from the first day I have been with you to this day, that I cannot go to fight against the enemies of my lord the king?" ⁹"You know," Achish answered David, "that you are acceptable to me. But the Philistine chiefs have determined you are not to go up with us to battle. ¹⁰So the first thing tomorrow, you and your lord's servants who came with you, go to the place I picked out for you. Do not decide to take umbrage at this; you are as acceptable to me as an angel of God. But make an early morning start, as soon as it grows light, and be on your way." ¹¹So David and his men left early in the morning to return to the land of the Philistines. The Philistines, however, went on up to Jezreel.

CHAPTER 30

Ziklag in Ruins. ¹Before David and his men reached Ziklag on the third day, the Amalekites had raided the Negeb and Ziklag, had stormed the city, and had set it on fire.ᵐ ²They had taken captive the women and all who were in the city, young and old, killing no one; they had carried them off when they left. ³David and his men arrived at the city to find it burned to the ground and their wives, sons and daughters taken captive. ⁴Then David and those who were with him wept aloud until they could weep no more. ⁵David's two wives, Ahinoam of Jezreel and Abigail, the widow of Nabal from Carmel, had also been carried off with the rest.ⁿ ⁶Now David found himself in great difficulty, for the men spoke of stoning him, so bitter were they over the fate of their sons and daughters. But with renewed trust in the LORD his God, ⁷ᵒ David said to Abiathar, the priest, son of Ahimelech, "Bring me the ephod!" When Abiathar brought him the ephod, ⁸David inquired of the LORD, "Shall I pursue these raiders? Can I overtake them?" The LORD answered him, "Go in pursuit, for you shall surely overtake them and effect a rescue."

Raid of the Amalekites. ⁹So David went off with his six hundred men and came as far as the Wadi Besor, where those who were to remain behind halted. ¹⁰David continued the pursuit with four hundred men, but two hundred were too exhausted to cross the Wadi Besor and remained behind. ¹¹An Egyptian was found in the open country and brought to David. He was provided with food, which he ate, and given water to drink; ¹²a cake of pressed figs and two cakes of pressed raisins were also offered to him. When he had eaten, he revived; he had not taken food nor drunk water for three days and three nights. ¹³Then David asked him, "To whom do you belong, and where do you come from?" He replied: "I am an Egyptian, the slave of an Amalekite. My master abandoned me because I fell sick three days ago today. ¹⁴We raided the Negeb of the Cherethites, the territory of Judah, and the Negeb of Caleb; and we set Ziklag on fire."ᵖ ¹⁵David then asked him, "Will you lead me down to this raiding party?" He answered, "Swear to me by God that you will not kill me or deliver me to my master, and I will lead you to the raiding party." ¹⁶He did lead them, and there were the Amalekites scattered all over the

---

j 1 Sm 27, 7.—k 1 Chr 12, 19f.—l 1 Sm 18, 6f; 21, 11.—m 1 Sm 27, 6. 10; 1 Chr 12, 21.—n 1 Sm 25, 42; 27, 3; 30, 5.—o 7f: 1 Sm 2, 28; 23, 6; Ex 28, 30.—p 1 Sm 27, 10; Ez 25, 16.

ground, eating, drinking, and in a festive mood because of all the rich booty they had taken from the land of the Philistines and from the land of Judah.
The Booty Recovered. [17] From dawn to sundown David attacked them, putting them under the ban so that none escaped except four hundred young men, who mounted their camels and fled.[q] [18] David recovered everything the Amalekites had taken, and rescued his two wives. [19] Nothing was missing, small or great, booty or sons or daughters, of all that the Amalekites had taken. David brought back everything. [20] Moreover, David took all the sheep and oxen, and as they drove them before him, they shouted, "This is David's spoil."
Division of the Spoils. [21] When David came to the two hundred men who had been too exhausted to follow him, and whom he had left behind at the Wadi Besor, they came out to meet David and the men with him. On nearing them David greeted them. [22] But all the stingy and worthless men among those who had accompanied David spoke up to say, "Since they did not accompany us, we will not give them anything from the booty, except to each man his wife and children. Let them take those along and be on their way." [23] But David said: "You must not do this, my brothers, after what the LORD has given us. He has protected us and delivered into our grip the band that came against us. [24] Who could agree with this proposal of yours? Rather, the share of the one who goes down to battle and that of the one who remains with the baggage shall be the same; they shall share alike."[r] [25] And from that day forward he made it a law and a custom in Israel, as it still is today.[s]
David's Gifts to Judah. [26] When David came to Ziklag, he sent part of the spoil to the elders of Judah, city by city, saying, "This is a gift to you from the spoil of the enemies of the LORD": [27] to those in

Bethel, to those in Ramoth-negeb, to those in Jattir, [28] to those in Aroer, to those in Siphmoth, to those in Eshtemoa, [29] to those in Racal, to those in the Jerahmeelite cities, to those in the Kenite cities,[t] [30] to those in Hormah, to those in Borashan, to those in Athach, [31] to those in Hebron, and to all the places frequented by David and his men.

CHAPTER 31

Death of Saul and His Sons. [1] [u] As they pressed their attack on Israel, with the Israelites fleeing before them and falling mortally wounded on Mount Gilboa, [2] the Philistines pursued Saul and his sons closely, and slew Jonathan, Abinadab, and Malchishua, sons of Saul.[v] [3] The battle raged around Saul, and the archers hit him; he was pierced through the abdomen. [4] Then Saul said to his armor-bearer, "Draw your sword and run me through, lest these uncircumcised come and make sport of me." But his armor-bearer, badly frightened, refused to do it. So Saul took his own sword and fell upon it.[w] [5] [x] When the armor-bearer saw that Saul was dead, he too fell upon his sword and died with him.* [6] Thus Saul, his three sons, and his armor-bearer died together on that same day.
[7] When the Israelites on the slope of the valley and those along the Jordan saw that the men of Israel had fled and that Saul and his sons were dead, they too abandoned their cities and fled. Then the Philistines came and lived in those cities.
[8] The day after the battle the Philistines came to strip the slain, and found Saul and his three sons lying on Mount Gilboa. [9] They cut off Saul's head and stripped him of his armor, and then sent the good news throughout the land of the Philistines to their idols and to the people.[y] [10] They put his armor in the temple of Astarte, but impaled his body on the wall of Bethshan.
Burial of Saul. [11] [z] When the inhabitants of Jabesh-gilead heard what the Philistines had done to Saul, [12] all their warriors set out, and after marching throughout the night, removed the bodies of Saul and his sons from the wall of Beth-shan, and brought them to Jabesh, where they cremated them.* [13] Then they took their bones and buried them under the tamarisk tree in Jabesh, and fasted for seven days.

q 1 Sm 15, 3; Jos 6, 17; Jgs 7, 12.—r 1 Sm 17, 22; 25, 13.—s Nm 31, 27.—t 1 Sm 27, 10.—u 1-13: 1 Chr 10, 1-12; 2 Sm 1, 1-16; 4, 4.—v 1 Sm 14, 49; 28, 19; 1 Chr 10, 2f.—w 1 Sm 24, 7; Jgs 9, 54; 1 Chr 10, 4.—x 1 Sm 10, 1; 26, 9; 2 Mc 14, 42.—y 1 Sm 17, 54; 2 Sm 1, 20; 2 Mc 15, 35.—z 11ff: 1 Sm 11, 1-11; 2 Sm 2, 4-7.

31, 5: This report of the suicidal act of Saul is presented as a part of his downfall, to be judged accordingly.
31, 12: *Cremated them:* cremation was not normally practiced in Israel, though it was known in the country from pre-Israelite times.

1Sm

THE SECOND BOOK OF SAMUEL

CHAPTER 1

Report of Saul's Death. ¹After the death of Saul, David returned from his defeat of the Amalekites and spent two days in Ziklag.ᵃ ²On the third day a man came from Saul's camp, with his clothes torn and dirt on his head. Going to David, he fell to the ground in homage. ³David asked him, "Where do you come from?" He replied, "I have escaped from the Israelite camp." ⁴"Tell me what happened," David bade him. He answered that the soldiers had fled the battle and that many of them had fallen and were dead, among them Saul and his son Jonathan. ⁵Then David said to the youth who was reporting to him, "How do you know that Saul and his son Jonathan are dead?" ⁶ᵇ The youthful informant replied: "It was by chance that I found myself on Mount Gilboa and saw Saul leaning on his spear, with chariots and horsemen closing in on him. ⁷He turned around and, seeing me, called me to him. When I said, 'Here I am,' ⁸he asked me, 'Who are you?' and I replied, 'An Amalekite.' ⁹Then he said to me, 'Stand up to me, please, and finish me off, for I am in great suffering, yet fully alive.' ¹⁰So I stood up to him and dispatched him, for I knew that he could not survive his wound. I removed the crown from his head and the armlet from his arm and brought them here to my lord."

¹¹David seized his garments and rent them, and all the men who were with him did likewise.ᶜ ¹²They mourned and wept and fasted until evening for Saul and his son Jonathan, and for the soldiers of the LORD of the clans of Israel, because they had fallen by the sword.ᵈ ¹³Then David said to the young man who had brought him the information, "Where are you from?" He replied, "I am the son of an Amalekite immigrant." ¹⁴David said to him, "How is it that you were not afraid to put forth your hand to desecrate the LORD's anointed?"ᵉ ¹⁵David then called one of the attendants and said to him, "Come, strike him down"; and the youth struck him a mortal blow. ¹⁶Meanwhile David said to him, "You are responsible for your own death, for you testified against yourself when you said, 'I dispatched the LORD's anointed.' "

Elegy for Saul and Jonathan. ¹⁷Then David chanted this elegy for Saul and his son Jonathan, ¹⁸which is recorded in the Book of Jashar to be taught to the Judahites. He sang:ᶠ

¹⁹ "Alas! the glory of Israel, Saul,
    slain upon the heights;
    how can the warriors have fallen!

²⁰ "Tell it not in Gath,
    herald it not in the streets of Ashkelon,
    Lest the Philistine maidens rejoice,
    lest the daughters of the strangers exult!ᵍ

²¹ Mountains of Gilboa,
    may there be neither dew nor rain upon you,
    nor upsurgings of the deeps!*
    Upon you lie begrimed the warriors' shields,
    the shield of Saul, no longer anointed with oil.ʰ

²² "From the blood of the slain,
    from the bodies of the valiant,
    The bow of Jonathan did not turn back,
    or the sword of Saul return unstained.ⁱ

²³ Saul and Jonathan, beloved and cherished,
    separated neither in life nor in death,
    swifter than eagles, stronger than lions!

²⁴ Women of Israel, weep over Saul,
    who clothed you in scarlet and in finery,
    who decked your attire with ornaments of gold.

---

a 1 Sm 30, 17-20; 31, 1-13.—b 6-10: 2 Sm 4, 10; 1 Sm 31, 1-4; 1 Chr 10, 1-4.—c 2 Sm 13, 31.—d 1 Sm 31, 13.—e 1 Sm 10, 1; 24, 7; Ps 105, 15.—f Jos 10, 13.—g Jgs 16, 23; 1 Sm 31, 9; Mi 1, 10.—h Gn 27, 28.—i 1 Sm 14, 47.

1, 21: *Upsurgings of the deeps:* this reading attempts to recover from an unintelligible Hebrew phrase the poetic parallel to dew and rain. The sense would be a wish that the mountain should have neither moisture from above nor water from springs or wells.

25 "How can the warriors have fallen—
in the thick of the battle,
slain upon your heights!
26 "I grieve for you, Jonathan my brother!
most dear have you been to me;
More precious have I held love for you
than love for women.*j*
27 "How can the warriors have fallen,
the weapons of war have perished!"

CHAPTER 2

David Anointed King. [1] After this David inquired of the LORD, "Shall I go up into one of the cities of Judah?" The LORD replied to him, "Yes." Then David asked, "Where shall I go?" He replied, "To Hebron." [2] So David went up there accompanied by his two wives, Ahinoam of Jezreel and Abigail, the widow of Nabal of Carmel.*k* [3] David also brought up his men with their families, and they dwelt in the cities near Hebron. [4] Then the men of Judah came there and anointed David king of the Judahites.*l*

A report reached David that the men of Jabesh-gilead had buried Saul. [5] So David sent messengers to the men of Jabeshgilead and said to them: "May you be blessed by the LORD for having done this kindness to your lord Saul in burying him. [6] And now may the LORD be kind and faithful to you. I, too, will be generous to you for having done this. [7] Take courage, therefore, and prove yourselves valiant men, for though your lord Saul is dead, the Judahites have anointed me their king."

IV: THE REIGN OF DAVID

Ishbaal King of Israel. [8] Abner, son of Ner, Saul's general, took Ishbaal, son of Saul, and brought him over to Mahanaim,*m* [9] where he made him king over Gilead, the Ashurites, Jezreel, Ephraim, Benjamin, and the rest of Israel. [10] Ishbaal, son of Saul, was forty years old when he became king over Israel, and he reigned for two years. The Judahites alone followed David. [11] In all, David spent seven years and six months in Hebron as king of the Judahites.*n*

Combat near Gibeon. [12] Now Abner, son of Ner, and the servants of Ishbaal, Saul's son, left Mahanaim for Gibeon. [13] Joab, son of Zeruiah, and David's servants also set out and met them at the pool of Gibeon. And they sat down, one group on one side of the pool and the other on the opposite side. [14] Then Abner said to Joab, "Let the young men rise and perform for us." Joab replied, "All right!" [15] So they rose and were counted off: twelve of the Benjaminites of Ishbaal, son of Saul, and twelve of David's servants. [16] Then each one grasped his opponent's head and thrust his sword into his opponent's side, and all fell down together.* And so that place, which is in Gibeon, was named the Field of the Sides.

Death of Asahel. [17] After a very fierce battle that day, Abner and the men of Israel were defeated by David's servants. [18] The three sons of Zeruiah were there—Joab, Abishai, and Asahel. Asahel, who was as fleet of foot as a gazelle in the open field,*o* [19] set out after Abner, turning neither right nor left in his pursuit.*p* [20] Abner turned around and said, "Is that you, Asahel?" He replied, "Yes." [21] Abner said to him, "Turn right or left; seize one of the young men and take what you can strip from him." But Asahel would not desist from his pursuit. [22] Once more Abner said to Asahel: "Stop pursuing me! Why must I strike you to the ground? How could I face your brother Joab?"*q* [23] Still he refused to stop. So Abner struck him in the abdomen with the heel of his javelin, and the weapon protruded from his back. He fell there and died on the spot. And all who came to the place where Asahel had fallen and died, came to a halt. [24] Joab and Abishai, however, continued the pursuit of Abner. The sun had gone down when they came to the hill of Ammah which lies east of the valley toward the desert near Geba.

Truce between Joab and Abner. [25] Here the Benjaminites rallied around Abner, forming a single group, and made a stand on the hilltop. [26] Then Abner called to Joab and said: "Must the sword destroy to the utmost? Do you not know that afterward there will be bitterness? How much longer will you refrain from ordering the people to stop the pursuit of their brothers?" [27] Joab replied, "As God lives, if you had not spoken, the soldiers

j 1 Sm 18, 1; 1 Mc 9, 21.—k 1 Sm 25, 42f.—l 1 Sm 31, 11ff.—m 1 Sm 14, 50.—n 2 Sm 5, 5; 1 Kgs 2, 11.—o 2 Sm 23, 24; 1 Chr 2, 16.—p 1 Chr 27, 7.—q 2 Sm 3, 27f. 30.

2, 16: The nature of this gruesome game is not clear, and the place name is variously given in the older texts.

would not have been withdrawn from the pursuit of their brothers until morning." [28] Joab then sounded the horn, and all the soldiers came to a halt, pursuing Israel no farther and fighting no more. [29] Abner and his men marched all night long through the Arabah, crossed the Jordan, marched all through the morning, and came to Mahanaim. [30] Joab, after interrupting the pursuit of Abner, assembled all the men. Besides Asahel, nineteen other servants of David were missing. [31] But David's servants had fatally wounded three hundred and sixty men of Benjamin, followers of Abner. [32] They took up Asahel and buried him in his father's tomb in Bethlehem. Joab and his men made an all-night march, and dawn found them in Hebron.

CHAPTER 3

[1] There followed a long war between the house of Saul and that of David, in which David grew stronger, but the house of Saul weaker.

Sons Born in Hebron. [2] [r] Sons were born to David in Hebron: his first-born, Amnon, of Ahinoam from Jezreel; [3] the second, Chileab, of Abigail the widow of Nabal of Carmel; the third, Absalom, son of Maacah the daughter of Talmai, king of Geshur; [s] [4] the fourth, Adonijah, son of Haggith; the fifth, Shephatiah, son of Abital; [t] [5] and the sixth, Ithream, of David's wife Eglah. These were born to David in Hebron.

Ishbaal and Abner Quarrel. [6] During the war between the house of Saul and that of David, Abner was gaining power in the house of Saul. [7] Now Saul had had a concubine, Rizpah, the daughter of Aiah. And Ishbaal, son of Saul, said to Abner, "Why have you been intimate with my father's concubine?" [u] [8] Enraged at the words of Ishbaal, Abner said, "Am I a dog's head in Judah? At present I am doing a kindness to the house of your father Saul, to his brothers and his friends, by keeping you out of David's clutches; yet this day you charge me with a crime involving a woman! [9] May God do thus and so to Abner if I do not carry out for David what the LORD swore to him [v]—[10] that is, take away the kingdom from the house of Saul and establish the throne of David over Israel and over Judah from Dan to Beer-

sheba." [w] [11] In his fear of Abner, Ishbaal was no longer able to say a word to him.

Abner and David Reconciled. [12] Then Abner sent messengers to David in Telam, where he was at the moment, to say, "Make an agreement with me, and I will aid you by bringing all Israel over to you." [13] He replied, "Very well, I will make an agreement with you. But one thing I require of you. You must not appear before me unless you bring back Michal, Saul's daughter, when you come to present yourself to me." [x] [14] At the same time David sent messengers to Ishbaal, son of Saul, to say, "Give me my wife Michal, whom I espoused by paying a hundred Philistine foreskins." [15] Ishbaal sent for her and took her away from her husband Paltiel, son of Laish, [y] [16] who followed her weeping as far as Bahurim. But Abner said to him, "Go back!" And he turned back.

[17] Abner then said in discussion with the elders of Israel: "For a long time you have been seeking David as your king. [18] Now take action, for the LORD has said of David, 'By my servant David I will save my people Israel from the grasp of the Philistines and from the grasp of all their enemies.' " [19] Abner also spoke personally to Benjamin, and then went to make his own report to David in Hebron concerning all that would be agreeable to Israel and to the whole house of Benjamin. [20] When Abner, accompanied by twenty men, came to David in Hebron, David prepared a feast for Abner and for the men who were with him. [21] Then Abner said to David, "I will now go to assemble all Israel for my lord the king, that they may make an agreement with you; you will then be king over all whom you wish to rule." So David bade Abner farewell, and he went away in peace.

Death of Abner. [22] Just then David's servants and Joab were coming in from an expedition, bringing much plunder with them. Abner, having been dismissed by David, was no longer with him in Hebron but had gone his way in peace. [23] When Joab and the whole force he had with him arrived, he was informed, "Abner, son of Ner, came to David; he has been sent on his way in peace." [24] So Joab went to the king and said:

---

r 2-5: 1 Chr 3, 14.—s 2 Sm 13, 37; 15, 8.—t 1 Kgs 1, 5.—
u 2 Sm 21, 8ff.—v Ru 1, 17.—w 2 Sm 5, 2; 1 Sm 25, 30.—x
1 Sm 18, 20-27.—y 1 Sm 25, 44.

"What have you done? Abner came to you. Why did you let him go peacefully on his way? [25] Are you not aware that Abner came to deceive you and to learn the ins and outs of all that you are doing?" [26] Joab then left David, and without David's knowledge sent messengers after Abner, who brought him back from the cistern of Sirah. [27] When Abner returned to Hebron, Joab took him aside within the city gate as though to speak with him privately. There he stabbed him in the abdomen, and he died in revenge for the killing of Joab's brother Asahel. [z] [28] Later David heard of it and said: "Before the LORD, I and my kingdom are forever innocent. [a] [29] May the full responsibility for the death of Abner, son of Ner, be laid to Joab and to all his family. May the men of Joab's family never be without one suffering from a discharge, or a leper, or one unmanly, one falling by the sword, or one in need of bread!" [30] [Joab and his brother Abishai had lain in wait for Abner because he killed their brother Asahel in battle at Gibeon.]

David Mourns Abner. [31] Then David said to Joab and to all the people who were with him, "Rend your garments, gird yourselves with sackcloth, and mourn over Abner." King David himself followed the bier. [b] [32] When they had buried Abner in Hebron, the king wept aloud at the grave of Abner, and the people also wept. [33] And the king sang this elegy over Abner:

"Would Abner have died like a fool?
[34] Your hands were not bound with chains,
    nor your feet placed in fetters;
As men fall before the wicked, you fell."

And all the people continued to weep for him. [35] Then they went to console David with food while it was still day. But David swore, "May God do thus and so to me if I eat bread or anything else before sunset." [c] [36] All the people noted this with approval, just as they were pleased with everything that the king did. [37] So on that day all the people and all Israel came to know that the king had no part in the killing of Abner, son of Ner. [38] The king then said to his servants: "You must recognize that a great general has fallen today in Israel. [39] Although I am the anointed king, I am weak this day, and these men, the sons of Zeruiah, are too ruthless for me. May the LORD requite the evildoer in accordance with his evil deed." [d]

CHAPTER 4

Death of Ishbaal. [1] When Ishbaal, son of Saul, heard that Abner had died in Hebron, he ceased to resist and all Israel was alarmed. [2] Ishbaal, son of Saul, had two company leaders named Baanah and Rechab, sons of Rimmon the Beerothite, of the tribe of Benjamin. [Beeroth, too, was ascribed to Benjamin: [e] [3] the Beerothites fled to Gittaim, where they have been resident aliens to this day. [f] [4] Jonathan, son of Saul, had a son named Meribbaal* with crippled feet. He was five years old when the news about Saul and Jonathan came from Jezreel, and his nurse took him up and fled. But in their hasty flight, he fell and became lame.] [g] [5] The sons of Rimmon the Beerothite, Rechab and Baanah, came into the house of Ishbaal during the heat of the day, while he was taking his siesta. [6] The portress of the house had dozed off while sifting wheat, and was asleep. So Rechab and his brother Baanah slipped past [7] and entered the house while Ishbaal was lying asleep in his bedroom. They struck and killed him, and cut off his head. Then, taking the head, they traveled on the Arabah road all night long.

The Murder Avenged. [8] They brought the head of Ishbaal to David in Hebron and said to the king: "This is the head of Ishbaal, son of your enemy Saul, who sought your life. Thus has the LORD this day avenged my lord the king on Saul and his posterity." [9] But David replied to Rechab and his brother Baanah, sons of Rimmon the Beerothite: "As the LORD lives, who rescued me from all difficulty, [10] in Ziklag I seized and put to death the man who informed me of Saul's death, thinking himself the bearer of good news for which I ought to give him a reward. [h] [11] How much more now, when wicked men have slain an innocent man in bed at home, must I hold

---

z 1 Kgs 2, 5. 32.—a 28. 30: 2 Sm 2, 22f.—b 2 Sm 21, 10.—c Ru 1, 17.—d Ps 28, 4; Is 3, 11.—e 2 Sm 9, 3; Jos 9, 17f.—f Jos 18, 25.—g 2 Sm 9, 3; 19, 25.—h 2 Sm 1, 6-10. 14. 16.

4, 4: Saul's grandson Meribbaal is the subject of ch 9 below. The text of this verse may owe its present place to the fact that pre-Christian copies of the Books of Samuel tended to confuse his name with that of his uncle Ishbaal, Saul's son and successor, a principal figure in chapters 2—4.

2Sm

you responsible for his death and destroy you from the earth!" [12] So at a command from David, the young men killed them and cut off their hands and feet, hanging them up near the pool in Hebron. But he took the head of Ishbaal and buried it in Abner's grave in Hebron.[i]

CHAPTER 5

David King of Israel. [1] [j] All the tribes of Israel came to David in Hebron and said: "Here we are, your bone and your flesh. [2] In days past, when Saul was our king, it was you who led the Israelites out and brought them back. And the LORD said to you, 'You shall shepherd my people Israel and shall be commander of Israel.' "[k] [3] When all the elders of Israel came to David in Hebron, King David made an agreement with them there before the LORD, and they anointed him king of Israel. [4] David was thirty years old when he became king, and he reigned for forty years: [5] seven years and six months in Hebron over Judah, and thirty-three years in Jerusalem over all Israel and Judah.[l]

Capture of Zion.* [6] [m] Then the king and his men set out for Jerusalem against the Jebusites who inhabited the region. David was told, "You cannot enter here: the blind and the lame will drive you away!" which was their way of saying, "David cannot enter here."[n] [7] But David did take the stronghold of Zion, which is the City of David. [8] On that day David said: "All who wish to attack the Jebusites must strike at them through the water shaft. The lame and the blind shall be the personal enemies of David." That is why it is said, "The blind and the lame shall not enter the palace."[o] [9] David then dwelt in the stronghold, which was called the City of David; he built up the area from Millo to the palace.[p] [10] David grew steadily more powerful, for the LORD of hosts was with him.[q] [11] [r] Hiram, king of Tyre, sent ambassadors to David; he furnished cedar wood, as well as carpenters and masons, who built a palace for David.[s] [12] And David knew that the LORD had established him as king of Israel and had exalted his rule for the sake of his people Israel.

David's Family in Jerusalem. [13] [t] David took more concubines and wives in Jerusalem after he had come from Hebron, and more sons and daughters were born to him in Jerusalem. [14] These are the names of those who were born to him in Jerusalem: Shammua, Shobab, Nathan, Solomon, [15] Ibhar, Elishua, Nepheg, Japhia, [16] Elishama, Baaliada, and Eliphelet.

Rout of the Philistines. [17] When the Philistines heard that David had been anointed king of Israel, they all took the field in search of him. On hearing this, David went down to the refuge.* [18] The Philistines came and overran the valley of Rephaim.* [19] David inquired of the LORD, "Shall I attack the Philistines—will you deliver them into my grip?" The LORD replied to David, "Attack, for I will surely deliver the Philistines into your grip." [20] David then went to Baal-perazim,* where he defeated them. He said, "The LORD has scattered my enemies before me like waters that have broken free." That is why the place is called Baal-perazim. [21] They abandoned their gods there, and David and his men carried them away. [22] But the Philistines came up again and overran the valley of Rephaim. [23] So David inquired of the LORD, who replied: "You must not attack frontally, but circle their rear and meet them before the mastic trees. [24] When you hear a sound of marching* in the tops of the mastic trees, act decisively, for the LORD will have gone forth before you to attack the camp of the Philistines." [25] David obeyed the LORD's command and routed the Philistines from Gibeon as far as Gezer.

CHAPTER 6

The Ark Brought to Jerusalem. [1] [u] David again assembled all the picked men of

---

i Dt 21, 22f; 1 Sm 31, 10.—j 1ff: 1 Chr 11, 1ff.—k 2 Sm 3, 10; Dt 17, 15; 1 Sm 18, 16.—l 2 Sm 2, 11; 1 Kgs 2, 11; 1 Chr 3, 4.—m 6-10: 1 Chr 11, 4-9.—n Jos 15, 63; Jgs 1, 19. 21; Is 29, 3.—o Lv 21, 18; Mt 21, 14f.—p 1 Kgs 3, 1; 11, 27.—q Pss 78, 70ff. 89; 132, 13.—r 11-25: 1 Chr 14, 1-16.—s 1 Kgs 5, 15; 1 Chr 14, 1f.—t 13-16: 1 Chr 3, 5-8; 14, 3-7.—u 1-11: 1 Chr 13, 1-14.

5, 6-12: David's most important military exploit, the taking of Jerusalem, is here presented before his battles with the Philistines, vv 17-25, which were earlier in time. The sense of vv 6 and 8 is in doubt.

5, 17: *Refuge:* probably near Adullam (1 Sm 22, 1-5).

5, 18-25: The successive defeats of the Philistines in the *valley of Rephaim* southwest of Jerusalem had the effect of blocking their access to the mountain ridge near *Gibeon,* and confining them to their holdings on the coast and in the foothills beyond Gezer to the west and south.

5, 20: *Baal-perazim:* means approximately "the lord of scatterings."

5, 24: *Sound of marching:* the wind in the treetops suggestive of the Lord's footsteps.

Israel, thirty thousand in number. ² Then David and all the people who were with him set out for Baala of Judah to bring up from there the ark of God, which bears the name of the LORD of hosts enthroned above the cherubim.ᵛ ³ The ark of God was placed on a new cart and taken away from the house of Abinadab on the hill. Uzzah and Ahio, sons of Abinadab, guided the cart,ʷ ⁴ with Ahio walking before it, ⁵ while David and all the Israelites made merry before the LORD with all their strength, with singing and with citharas, harps, tambourines, sistrums and cymbals.ˣ ⁶ When they came to the threshing floor of Nodan, Uzzah reached out his hand to the ark of God and steadied it, for the oxen were making it tip. ⁷ But the LORD was angry with Uzzah; God struck him on that spot, and he died there before God. ⁸ David was disturbed because the LORD had vented his anger on Uzzah. (The place has been called Perez-uzzah down to the present day.)ʸ ⁹ David feared the LORD that day and said, "How can the ark of the LORD come to me?" ¹⁰ So David would not have the ark of the LORD brought to him in the City of David, but diverted it to the house of Obededom the Gittite. ¹¹ The ark of the LORD remained in the house of Obededom the Gittite for three months, and the LORD blessed Obededom and his whole house.ᶻ ¹² ᵃ When it was reported to King David that the LORD had blessed the family of Obededom and all that belonged to him, David went to bring up the ark of God from the house of Obededom into the City of David amid festivities. ¹³ As soon as the bearers of the ark of the LORD had advanced six steps, he sacrificed an ox and a fatling. ¹⁴ Then David, girt with a linen apron, came dancing before the LORD with abandon,ᵇ ¹⁵ as he and all the Israelites were bringing up the ark of the LORD with shouts of joy and to the sound of the horn. ¹⁶ As the ark of the LORD was entering the City of David, Saul's daughter Michal looked down through the window and saw King David leaping and dancing before the LORD, and

she despised him in her heart. ¹⁷ ᶜ The ark of the LORD was brought in and set in its place within the tent David had pitched for it. Then David offered holocausts and peace offerings before the LORD. ¹⁸ When he finished making these offerings, he blessed the people in the name of the LORD of hosts. ¹⁹ He then distributed among all the people, to each man and each woman in the entire multitude of Israel, a loaf of bread, a cut of roast meat, and a raisin cake. With this, all the people left for their homes.

²⁰ When David returned to bless his own family, Saul's daughter Michal came out to meet him and said, "How the king of Israel has honored himself today, exposing himself to the view of the slave girls of his followers, as a commoner might do!"ᵈ ²¹ But David replied to Michal: "I was dancing before the LORD. As the LORD lives, who preferred me to your father and his whole family when he appointed me commander of the LORD's people, Israel, not only will I make merry before the LORD,ᵉ ²² but I will demean myself even more. I will be lowly in your esteem, but in the esteem of the slaves girls you spoke of I will be honored." ²³ And so Saul's daughter Michal was childless to the day of her death.

CHAPTER 7

David's Concern for the Ark. ¹ ᶠ When King David was settled in his palace, and the LORD had given him rest from his enemies on every side,ᵍ ² he said to Nathan the prophet, "Here I am living in a house of cedar, while the ark of God dwells in a tent!"ʰ ³ Nathan answered the king, "Go, do whatever you have in mind, for the LORD is with you."ⁱ ⁴ But that night the LORD spoke to Nathan and said: ⁵ "Go, tell my servant David, 'Thus says the LORD: Should you build me a house to dwell in?ʲ ⁶ I have not dwelt in a house from the day on which I led the Israelites out of Egypt to the present, but I have been going about in a tent under cloth. ⁷ In all my wanderings everywhere among the Israelites, did I ever utter a word to any one of the judges whom I charged to tend my people Israel, to ask: Why have you not built me a house of cedar?'

The Lord's Promises. ⁸ "Now then, speak thus to my servant David, 'The LORD of

v Ex 25, 10; Jos 15, 9; Ps 132, 8ff; 1 Chr 1, 4.—w 1 Sm 4, 3f; 6, 7f; 7, 1; Dn 3, 55.—x Pss 68, 25f; 150, 3. 5.—y 1 Kgs 8, 1.—z 1 Chr 26, 4.—a 12-23: 1 Chr 15, 1-29; Ps 24, 7-10.—b 1 Sm 2, 18.—c 17ff: Lv 1, 1-17; 3, 1-17; 1 Chr 16, 1ff.—d 1 Chr 16, 43.—e 1 Sm 13, 14; 15, 28.—f 1-29: 1 Chr 17, 1-27.—g 1 Kgs 5, 4.—h Dt 12, 10; 25, 19.—i Ps 132, 1-5.—j 1 Kgs 5, 17; 8, 16. 27; 1 Chr 22, 8; 28, 3; Is 66, 1; Acts 7, 48.

hosts has this to say:* It was I who took you from the pasture and from the care of the flock to be commander of my people Israel.[k] [9]I have been with you wherever you went, and I have destroyed all your enemies before you. And I will make you famous like the great ones of the earth.[l] [10]I will fix a place for my people Israel; I will plant them so that they may dwell in their place without further disturbance. Neither shall the wicked continue to afflict them as they did of old, [11]since the time I first appointed judges over my people Israel. I will give you rest from all your enemies. The LORD also reveals to you that he will establish a house for you.[m] [12] [n] And when your time comes and you rest with your ancestors, I will raise up your heir after you, sprung from your loins, and I will make his kingdom firm. [13]It is he who shall build a house for my name. And I will make his royal throne firm forever. [14]I will be a father to him, and he shall be a son to me. And if he does wrong, I will correct him with the rod of men and with human chastisements; [15]but I will not withdraw my favor from him as I withdrew it from your predecessor Saul, whom I removed from my presence.[o] [16]Your house and your kingdom shall endure forever before me; your throne shall stand firm forever.' "[p] [17]Nathan reported all these words and this entire vision to David.

King David's Prayer. [18]Then King David went in and sat before the LORD and said, "Who am I, Lord GOD, and who are the members of my house, that you have brought me to this point?[q] [19]Yet even this you see as too little, Lord GOD; you have also spoken of the house of your servant for a long time to come: this too you have shown to man,* Lord GOD! [20]What more can David say to you? You know your servant, Lord GOD! [21]For your servant's sake and as you have had at heart, you have brought about this entire magnificent disclosure to your servant. [22]And so—

"Great are you, Lord GOD! There is none like you and there is no God but you, just as we have heard it told.[r] [23]What other nation on earth is there like your people Israel, which God has led, redeeming it as his people; so that you have made yourself renowned by doing this magnificent deed, and by doing awe-inspiring things as you have cleared nations and

their gods out of the way of your people, which you redeemed for yourself from Egypt?[s] [24] [t] You have established for yourself your people Israel as yours forever, and you, LORD, have become their God. [25]And now, LORD God, confirm for all time the prophecy you have made concerning your servant and his house, and do as you have promised. [26]Your name will be forever great, when men say, 'The LORD of hosts is God of Israel,' and the house of your servant David stands firm before you. [27]It is you, LORD of hosts, God of Israel, who said in a revelation to your servant, 'I will build a house for you.' Therefore your servant now finds the courage to make this prayer to you. [28]And now, Lord GOD, you are God and your words are truth; you have made this generous promise to your servant.[u] [29]Do, then, bless the house of your servant that it may be before you forever; for you, Lord GOD, have promised, and by your blessing the house of your servant shall be blessed forever."

CHAPTER 8

Summary of David's Wars. [1][v] After this David attacked the Philistines and conquered them, wresting . . .* from the Philistines. [2]He also defeated Moab and then measured them with a line, making them lie down on the ground. He told off two lengths* of line for execution, and a full

k 1 Sm 16, 13; 17, 15-20; Ps 78, 70f; Am 7, 14.—l Ps 89, 27.—m 2 Sm 23, 5; 1 Kgs 2, 4-24.—n 12ff: 1 Kgs 5, 19; 8, 19; 1 Chr 22, 10; 2 Chr 7, 18; Ps 89, 5. 27f. 30. 37f; Lk 1, 32; Heb 1, 5.—o 2 Sm 23, 5; 1 Sm 13, 14; 15, 26. 28; 2 Kgs 19, 34; 1 Chr 17, 11-14; Ps 89, 34.—p 2 Sm 23, 5; Dn 2, 45; 1 Mc 2, 57; Mk 11, 10; Lk 1, 32f; Heb 1, 8.—q 1 Chr 17, 16.—r Ex 15, 11; Is 45, 5.—s Dt 4, 7. 34.—t 24f: Ex 6, 7; Dt 7, 6; 26, 17; 29, 12.—u Nm 23, 19; Jn 17, 17.—v 1-18: 1 Chr 18, 1-17.

7, 8-16: The prophecy to David contained in these verses is cited again, in poetic form, in Ps 89, 20-38, and alluded to in Ps 132. The promise regarding the people of Israel, vv 10-11, is a part of the promise to David at least as old as the composition of this chapter of Samuel, where it is anticipated in vv 6-7, and alluded to in David's thanksgiving, vv 23-24; it applies to the people an expression used of David in Ps 89, 23. The prophecy to David is the basis for Jewish expectation of a messiah, son of David, which Jesus Christ fulfilled in a transcendent way; cf Acts 2, 30; Heb 1, 5.

7, 19: *This too you have shown to man:* the text as transmitted has, rather, "and this is instruction for (or: the law of) mankind." The author of Chronicles (1 Chr 17, 17) saw approximately the same phrase, which he endeavored to fit into the context in a quite different sense. The above is conjectural; cf Dt 5, 24.

8, 1: *Wresting . . . :* the Hebrew text here gives "the bridle of the cubit"; 1 Chr 18, 1 understood "Gath and its dependent villages"; others implausibly read "dominion of the capital city."

8, 2: *Two lengths . . . a full length:* usually taken to mean that two-thirds of them were executed; but it could mean that two-thirds were spared, if the line was used full length in their case but doubled on itself to make "two lines" for those to be put to death.

WARS OF DAVID
(2 Sm 5, 17—12, 13;
1 Chr 14—20)

Berothai

Damascus
BETH-REHOB

Tyre

Maachah

GESHUR

Helam

GILEAD

Land of
TOB

Thebez

PHILISTINES

AMMÔN
Rabbah

Gittaim
Gibeon
Gezer
Kiriath-jearim
Baal-perazim
JÉRUSALEM
Adullam
Medeba
Gath
Hebron

Beer-sheba

Valley of
SALT

0   10   20   30
Miles

E D O M

MOAB

DAVID AND ISHBAAL (2 Sm 8—5, 16) — **(a)**
At **Mahanaim** Abner, leader of Saul's army,
establishes Ishbaal, son of Saul, as king over
Gilead, the **Asshurites, Jezreel, Ephraim,
Benjamin** and all **Israel** (2, 8-11). **(b)** At **Gib-
eon,** the servants of Ishbaal and those of
David battle near the pool. Joab pursues
Abner to the hill of **Ammah** which lies east of
the valley toward the desert near **Geba** (2, 11-
24). **(c)** At **Mahanaim** Abner retakes the city
through the **valley of the Jordan.** Later he is
reconciled with David and killed by Joab.
Death of Ishbaal (2, 25—4, 8). **(d)** At **Hebron**
David is acknowledged as king by all Israel.
He captures **Jerusalem** and makes it his
capital (5, 1-16).

2Sm

**DAVID AND
ISHBAAL**
(2 Sm 2, 8—5, 16)

Jezreel

Jabesh

Mahanaim

E P H R A Ï M

Beeroth

Gibeon   Géba

JÉRUSALEM

Bethlehem

Gath

Hebron

Gilgal

WARS OF DAVID (2 Sm 5, 17—8, 4; 10, 1—12, 13; 1 Chr 14—20) — **(a)** David makes war against
the **Philistines.** From **Adullam** David routs the Philistines twice in the **Valley of Rephaim,** first at **Baal-
perazim,** and secondly from **Gibeon** to **Gezer.** Transferal of the ark of the covenant from **Kiriath-jearim**
to **Jerusalem** (5, 17—7, 29). **(b)** David makes the Moabites pay tribute (8, 1-2). **(c)** David defeats
Hadadezer, king of **Zobah** and the **Arameans** of Damascus who had come to his aid. He carries away
a great quantity of bronze from **Tebah** and **Berothai.** The king of Hamath sends a message of friendship
to David (8, 3-12). **(d)** Defeated in the **Valley of Salt,** the **Edomites** become subjects of David (8, 13-14).
(e) In a first campaign, the Ammonites hire the Arameans of **Beth-rehob** and **Zobah,** the king of
Maacah and his men, and the people of **Tob.** Joab divides his army in two and successively defeats the
Arameans before **Medeba** and the Ammonites who hastened to return to their city. Joab spares **Rabbah,**
capital of the Ammonites. David's sin and repentance (10, 1—12, 31). **(f)** Second campaign against
Hadadezer, between the two Ammonite campaigns. David rallies all Israel, crosses the **Jordan** and de-
feats the army of Hadadezer at **Helam** (1, 15-19).

GILEAD

DAVID AND ABSALOM

(2 Sm 13, 1—19, 44)

o Shechem

JORDAN

o Mahanaim

Baal-hazor o

o Ephraim

Rabbah

Gilgal

Bahurim

JÉRUSALEM o ▲ MT. OF OLIVES

Kedron

JUDAH

Gilo o

o Tekoa

DEAD SEA

| 0 | 10 | 20 |

Miles

DAVID AND ABSALOM (2 Sm 13, 1—19, 44) — **(a)** At **Baal-hazor,** near **Ephraim,** Absalom has Amnon put to death, and for three years takes refuge with the king of Geshur. Subsequently he passes two years of disgrace in Jerusalem (13—14). **(b)** At **Hebron** four years later, Absalom proclaims himself king. He sends for Ahithophel the Gilonite, David's counselor (15, 1-12). **(c)** At **Jerusalem** David, knowing himself to be in great danger, flees in the direction of the Jordan, accompanied by Cherethites, Pelethites, and by Ittai and the Gittites come from **Gath** (15, 13-22). **(d)** At the **Kidron brook** David sends Zadok the priest back to **Jerusalem** with the ark (15, 25-29). **(e)** At the **Mount of Olives** he sends Hushai to Absalom to frustrate the projects of Ahithophel. After having mounted to the summit, David receives provisions from Ziba, servant of Meribbaal (15, 30—16, 4). **(f)** At **Bahurim** Shimei insults David (16, 5-14). **(g)** At **Jerusalem** Hushai pretends to be on the side of Absalom and fights the proposition of Ahithophel who wishes to pursue David immediately. He causes David to avoid danger. The emissaries leave **En-rogel** and for a time hide themselves at **Bahurim** (16, 15—17, 23). **(h)** At **Mahanaim** supporters from **Rabbah** and **Lodebar** bring provisions and furniture to David, who musters the army but himself remains behind. The battle takes place in the forest near **Mahanaim.** Defeat and death of Absalom (17, 24—18, 15). **(i)** At **Gilgal** the people of Judah come to meet the king who has come back from **Mahanaim.** David pardons Shimei. Meeting with Meribbaal. The king continues his journey with Chimham, son of Barzillai the Gileadite (18, 6—19, 44).

length to be spared. Thus the Moabites became tributary to David. [3] [w] Next David defeated Hadadezer, son of Rehob, king of Zobah, when he went to reestablish his dominion at the Euphrates River.[x] [4] David captured from him one thousand seven hundred horsemen and twenty thousand foot soldiers. And he hamstrung all the chariot horses, preserving only enough for a hundred chariots.[y] [5] When the Arameans of Damascus came to the aid of Hadadezer, king of Zobah, David slew twenty-two thousand of them. [6] David then placed garrisons in Aram of Damascus, and the Arameans became subjects, tributary to David. The LORD brought David victory in all his undertakings. [7] David also took away the golden shields used by Hadadezer's servants and brought them to Jerusalem. [These Shishak, king of Egypt, took away when he came to Jerusalem in the days of Rehoboam, son of Solomon.] [8] From Tebah and Berothai, towns of Hadadezer, King David removed a very large quantity of bronze. [9] When Toi, king of Hamath, heard that David had defeated all the forces of Hadadezer, [10] he sent his son Hadoram to King David to greet him and to congratulate him for his victory over Hadadezer in battle, because Toi had been in many battles with Hadadezer. Hadoram also brought with him articles of silver, gold, and bronze. [11] These, too, King David consecrated to the LORD, together with the silver and gold he had taken from every nation he had conquered: [12] from Edom and Moab, from the Ammonites, from the Philistines, from the Amalekites, and from the plunder of Hadadezer, son of Rehob, king of Zobah.

[13] On his return,* David became famous for having slain eighteen thousand Edomites in the Salt Valley;[z] [14] after which he placed garrisons in Edom. Thus all the Edomites became David's subjects, and the LORD brought David victory in all his undertakings.

David's Officials. [15] [a] David reigned over all Israel, judging and administering justice to all his people. [16] Joab, son of

Zeruiah, was in command of the army. Jehoshaphat, son of Ahilud, was chancellor. [17] Zadok, son of Ahitub, and Ahimelech, son of Abiathar, were priests. Shawsha was scribe. [18] Benaiah, son of Jehoiada, was in command of the Cherethites and Pelethites. And David's sons were priests.[b]

CHAPTER 9

David and Meribbaal. [1] David asked, "Is there any survivor of Saul's house to whom I may show kindness for the sake of Jonathan?"[c] [2] Now there was a servant of the family of Saul named Ziba. He was summoned to David, and the king asked him, "Are you Ziba?" He replied, "Your servant."[d] [3] Then the king inquired, "Is there any survivor of Saul's house to whom I may show God's kindness?" Ziba answered the king, "There is still Jonathan's son, whose feet are crippled."[e] [4] The king said to him, "Where is he?" and Ziba answered, "He is in the house of Machir, son of Ammiel, in Lodebar."[f] [5] So King David sent for him and had him brought from the house of Machir, son of Ammiel, in Lodebar. [6] When Meribbaal, son of Jonathan, son of Saul, came to David, he fell prostrate in homage. David said, "Meribbaal," and he answered, "Your servant." [7] "Fear not," David said to him, "I will surely be kind to you for the sake of your father Jonathan. I will restore to you all the lands of your grandfather Saul, and you shall always eat at my table." [8] Bowing low, he answered, "What is your servant that you should pay attention to a dead dog like me?"[g] [9] The king then called Ziba, Saul's attendant, and said to him: "I am giving your lord's son all that belonged to Saul and to all his family. [10] You and your sons and servants must till the land for him. You shall bring in the produce, which shall be food for your lord's family to eat. But Meribbaal, your lord's son, shall always eat at my table." Ziba, who had fifteen sons and twenty servants, [11] said to the king, "Your servant shall do just as my lord the king has commanded him." And so Meribbaal ate at David's table like one of the king's sons.[h] [12] Meribbaal had a young son whose name was Mica; and all the tenants of Ziba's family worked for Meribbaal.[i] [13] But Meribbaal lived in Jerusalem, because he always ate at the king's table. He was lame in both feet.[j]

---

w 3-8: 2 Sm 10, 15-19.—x 2 Sm 10, 6; 1 Kgs 11, 23.—y Jos 11, 6. 9.—z 2 Kgs 14, 7.—a 15-18: 2 Sm 20, 23-26; 1 Kgs 4, 1-6; 1 Chr 18, 14-17.—b 2 Sm 15, 18; 20, 7. 23; 23, 20.—c 2 Sm 21, 7; 1 Sm 18, 1-4; 20, 8ff. 15f. 42.—d 2 Sm 16, 1-4; 19, 27.—e 2 Sm 4, 4.—f 2 Sm 17, 27.—g 1 Sm 24, 15.—h 2 Sm 19, 29.—i 1 Chr 8, 34.—j 2 Sm 21, 7.

8, 13: *On his return:* possibly to Jerusalem, after the revolt of Absalom, a circumstance which this catalogue of victories would avoid mentioning. 1 Chr 18, 13 attributes the defeat of the Edomites to Abishai.

CHAPTER 10

Insult of the Ammonites. [1] [k] Some time later* the king of the Ammonites died, and his son Hanun succeeded him as king. [2] David thought, "I will be kind to Hanun, son of Nahash, as his father was kind to me." So David sent his servants with condolences to Hanun for the loss of his father. But when David's servants entered the country of the Ammonites, [3] the Ammonite princes said to their lord Hanun: "Do you think that David is honoring your father by sending men with condolences? Is it not rather to explore the city, to spy on it, and to overthrow it, that David has sent his messengers to you?" [4] Hanun, therefore, seized David's servants and, after shaving off half their beards and cutting away the lower halves of their garments at the buttocks, sent them away. [l] [5] When he was told of it, King David sent out word to them, since the men were quite ashamed. "Stay in Jericho until your beards grow," he said, "and then come back."

Ammonites Defeated. [6] * In view of the offense they had given to David, the Ammonites sent for and hired twenty thousand Aramean foot soldiers from Beth-rehob and Zobah, as well as the king of Maacah with one thousand men, and twelve thousand men from Tob. [m] [7] On learning this, David sent out Joab with the entire levy of trained soldiers. [n] [8] The Ammonites came out and drew up in battle formation at the entrance of their city gate, while the Arameans of Zobah and Rehob and the men of Tob and Maacah remained apart in the open country. [9] When Joab saw the battle lines drawn up against him, both front and rear, he made a selection from all the picked troops of Israel and arrayed them against the Arameans. [10] He placed the rest of the soldiers under the command of his brother Abishai, who arrayed them against the Ammonites. [11] Joab said, "If the Arameans are stronger than I, you shall help me. But if the Ammonites are stronger than you, I will come to help you. [12] Be brave; let us prove our valor for the sake of our people and the cities of our God; the LORD will do what he judges best." [13] When Joab and the soldiers who were with him approached the Arameans for battle, they fled before him. [14] The Ammonites, seeing that the Arameans had fled, also fled from Abishai and with-

drew into the city. Joab then ceased his attack on the Ammonites and returned to Jerusalem.

Arameans Defeated. [15] [o] Then the Arameans responded to their defeat by Israel with a full mustering of troops; [16] Hadadezer sent for and enlisted Arameans from beyond the Euphrates. They came to Helam, with Shobach, general of Hadadezer's army, at their head. [17] On receiving this news, David assembled all Israel, crossed the Jordan, and went to Helam. The Arameans drew up in formation against David and fought with him. [18] But the Arameans gave way before Israel, and David's men killed seven hundred charioteers and forty thousand of the Aramean foot soldiers. Shobach, general of the army, was struck down and died on the field. [19] All of Hadadezer's vassal kings, in view of their defeat by Israel, then made peace with the Israelites and became their subjects. And the Arameans were afraid to give further aid to the Ammonites.

CHAPTER 11

David's Sin. [1] At the turn of the year,* when kings go out on campaign, David sent out Joab along with his officers and the army of Israel, and they ravaged the Ammonites and besieged Rabbah. David, however, remained in Jerusalem. [p] [2] One evening David rose from his siesta and strolled about on the roof of the palace. From the roof he saw a woman bathing, who was very beautiful. [3] David had inquiries made about the woman and was told, "She is Bathsheba, daughter of Eliam, and wife of [Joab's armor-bearer] Uriah the Hittite." [q] [4] Then David sent messengers and took her. When she came to him, he had relations with her, at a time when she was just purified after her monthly period. She then returned to her house. [r] [5] But the woman had conceived, and sent the information to David, "I am with child."

k 1-19: 1 Chr 19, 1-19.—l Is 20, 4.—m 2 Sm 8, 3; 1 Sm 14, 47.—n 2 Sm 11, 1.—o 15-19: 2 Sm 8, 3-8; 1 Chr 9, 16-19.—p 2 Sm 10, 7; 1 Chr 20, 1.—q 2 Sm 23, 39.—r Lv 15, 19.

10, 1: *Some time later:* early in the reign of David, since Hanun's father had been ruling in Ammon at the beginning of Saul's reign (1 Sm 11) and Solomon was as yet unborn (2 Sm 11, 1; 12, 24).

10, 6-9: A Hebrew text from Qumran (4Q Sam ᵃ) comes closer in these verses to what is given in 1 Chr 19, 6-9. The scene of the conflict is more likely Rabbath-Ammon, with Josephus (Ant., vii, 123), than Madeba, as in 1 Chr; compare ch 11.

11, 1: *At the turn of the year:* in the spring.

⁶David therefore sent a message to Joab, "Send me Uriah the Hittite." So Joab sent Uriah to David. ⁷When he came, David questioned him about Joab, the soldiers, and how the war was going, and Uriah answered that all was well. ⁸David then said to Uriah, "Go down to your house and bathe your feet." Uriah left the palace, and a portion was sent out after him from the king's table. ⁹But Uriah slept at the entrance of the royal palace with the other officers of his lord, and did not go down to his own house. ¹⁰David was told that Uriah had not gone home. So he said to Uriah, "Have you not come from a journey? Why, then, did you not go down to your house?" ¹¹Uriah answered David, "The ark and Israel and Judah are lodged in tents, and my lord Joab and your majesty's servants are encamped in the open field. Can I go home to eat and to drink and to sleep with my wife? As the LORD lives and as you live, I will do no such thing."ˢ ¹²Then David said to Uriah, "Stay here today also, I shall dismiss you tomorrow." So Uriah remained in Jerusalem that day. On the day following, ¹³David summoned him, and he ate and drank with David, who made him drunk. But in the evening he went out to sleep on his bed among his lord's servants, and did not go down to his home. ¹⁴The next morning David wrote a letter to Joab which he sent by Uriah. ¹⁵In it he directed: "Place Uriah up front, where the fighting is fierce. Then pull back and leave him to be struck down dead." ¹⁶So while Joab was besieging the city, he assigned Uriah to a place where he knew the defenders were strong. ¹⁷When the men of the city made a sortie against Joab, some officers of David's army fell, and among them Uriah the Hittite died.

¹⁸Then Joab sent David a report of all the details of the battle, ¹⁹instructing the messenger, "When you have finished giving the king all the details of the battle, ²⁰the king may become angry and say to you: 'Why did you go near the city to fight? Did you not know that they would shoot from the wall above? ²¹Who killed Abimelech, son of Jerubbaal? Was it not a woman who threw a millstone down on him from the wall above, so that he died in Thebez? Why did you go near the wall?' Then you in turn shall say, 'Your servant Uriah the Hittite is also dead.' "ᵗ ²²The messenger set out, and on his arrival he relayed to David all the details as Joab had instructed him.* ²³He told David: "The men had us at a disadvantage and came out into the open against us, but we pushed them back to the entrance of the city gate. ²⁴Then the archers shot at your servants from the wall above, and some of the king's servants died, among them your servant Uriah." ²⁵David said to the messenger: "This is what you shall convey to Joab: 'Do not be chagrined at this, for the sword devours now here and now there. Strengthen your attack on the city and destroy it.' Encourage him."

²⁶When the wife of Uriah heard that her husband had died, she mourned her lord. ²⁷But once the mourning was over, David sent for her and brought her into his house. She became his wife and bore him a son. But the LORD was displeased with what David had done.

CHAPTER 12

Nathan's Parable. ¹ * The LORD sent Nathan to David, and when he came to him, he said: "Judge this case for me! In a certain town there were two men, one rich, the other poor.ᵘ ²The rich man had flocks and herds in great numbers. ³But the poor man had nothing at all except one little ewe lamb that he had bought. He nourished her, and she grew up with him and his children. She shared the little food he had and drank from his cup and slept in his bosom. She was like a daughter to him. ⁴Now, the rich man received a visitor, but he would not take from his own flocks and herds to prepare a meal for the wayfarer who had come to him. Instead he took the poor man's ewe lamb and made a meal of it for his visitor." ⁵David grew very angry with that man and said to Nathan: "As the LORD lives, the man who has done this merits death! ⁶He shall restore the ewe lamb fourfold because he has done this and has had no pity."ᵛ

David's Punishment. ⁷Then Nathan said to David: "You are the man! Thus says the LORD God of Israel: 'I anointed you

---

s 1 Sm 4, 3f.—t Jgs 9, 50-54.—u Sir 47, 1.—v Ex 21, 37; Lk 19, 8.

11, 22: After this verse, the Greek text, which is here the older form, has David, angry with Joab, repeat exactly the questions Joab had foreseen in vv 20ff. In v 24 of our oldest Greek text, the messenger specifies that about eighteen men were killed.

12, 1-4: This utterance of Nathan is in regular lines in Hebrew, resembling English blank verse.

king of Israel. I rescued you from the hand of Saul.[w] [8]I gave you your lord's house and your lord's wives for your own. I gave you the house of Israel and of Judah. And if this were not enough, I could count up for you still more. [9]Why have you spurned the LORD and done evil in his sight? You have cut down Uriah the Hittite with the sword; you took his wife as your own, and him you killed with the sword of the Ammonites. [10]Now, therefore, the sword shall never depart from your house, because you have despised me and have taken the wife of Uriah to be your wife.'[x] [11]Thus says the LORD: 'I will bring evil upon you out of your own house. I will take your wives while you live to see it, and will give them to your neighbor. He shall lie with your wives in broad daylight.[y] [12]You have done this deed in secret, but I will bring it about in the presence of all Israel, and with the sun looking down.'"

David's Repentance. [13]Then David said to Nathan, "I have sinned against the LORD." Nathan answered David: "The LORD on his part his forgiven your sin: you shall not die.[z] [14]But since you have utterly spurned the LORD by this deed, the child born to you must surely die." [15]Then Nathan returned to his house.

The LORD struck the child that the wife of Uriah had borne to David, and it became desperately ill. [16]David besought God for the child. He kept a fast, retiring for the night to lie on the ground clothed in sackcloth. [17]The elders of his house stood beside him urging him to rise from the ground; but he would not, nor would he take food with them. [18]On the seventh day, the child died. David's servants, however, were afraid to tell him that the child was dead, for they said: "When the child was alive, we spoke to him, but he would not listen to what we said. How can we tell him the child is dead? He may do some harm!" [19]But David noticed his servants whispering among themselves and realized that the child was dead. He asked his servants, "Is the child dead?" They replied, "Yes, he is." [20]Rising from the ground, David washed and anointed himself, and changed his clothes. Then he went to the house of the LORD and worshiped. He returned to his own house, where at his request food was set before him, and he ate. [21]His servants said to him: "What is this

you are doing? While the child was living, you fasted and wept and kept vigil; now that the child is dead, you rise and take food." [22]He replied: "While the child was living, I fasted and wept, thinking, 'Perhaps the LORD will grant me the child's life.' [23]But now he is dead. Why should I fast? Can I bring him back again? I shall go to him, but he will not return to me."[a] [24]Then David comforted his wife Bathsheba. He went and slept with her; and she conceived and bore him a son, who was named Solomon. The LORD loved him [25]and sent the prophet Nathan to name him Jedidiah, on behalf of the LORD.

Ammonite War Ends. [26] [b] Joab fought against Rabbah of the Ammonites and captured this royal city. [27]He sent messengers to David with the word: "I have fought against Rabbah and have taken the water-city. [28]Therefore, assemble the rest of the soldiers, join the siege against the city and capture it, lest it be I that capture the city and it be credited to me." [29]So David assembled the rest of the soldiers and went to Rabbah. When he had fought against it and captured it, [30]he took the crown from Milcom's head. It weighed a talent,* of gold and precious stones; it was placed on David's head. He brought out immense booty from the city, [31]and also led away the inhabitants, whom he assigned to work with saws, iron picks, and iron axes, or put to work at the brickmold. This is what he did to all the Ammonite cities. David and all the soldiers then returned to Jerusalem.

CHAPTER 13

The Crime of Amnon. [1]Some time later the following incident occurred. David's son Absalom had a beautiful sister named Tamar, and David's son Amnon loved her.[c] [2]He was in such straits over his sister Tamar that he became sick; since she was a virgin, Amnon thought it impossible to carry out his designs toward her. [3]Now Amnon had a friend named Jonadab, son of David's brother Shimeah, who was very

---

w 1 Sm 16, 13.—x 2 Sm 13, 28f; 18, 14.—y 2 Sm 16, 11. 22.—z 1 Kgs 21, 29; Pss 32, 5; 50, 6; Sir 47, 11.—a Jb 7, 9.—b 26-31: 1 Chr 20, 1-3.—c 2 Sm 3, 2f; 1 Chr 3, 9.

12, 30: *Weighed a talent:* since this would be more than 75 pounds, some commentators picture the idol's crown as displaying a single precious stone of large size, which David took to wear; but the text does not say this.

clever.*ᵈ* *⁴*He asked him, "Prince, why are you so dejected morning after morning? Why not tell me?" So Amnon said to him, "I am in love with Tamar, my brother Absalom's sister." *⁵*Then Jonadab replied, "Lie down on your bed and pretend to be sick. When your father comes to visit you, say to him, 'Please let my sister Tamar come and encourage me to take food. If she prepares something appetizing in my presence, for me to see, I will eat it from her hand.'" *⁶*So Amnon lay down and pretended to be sick. When the king came to visit him, Amnon said to the king, "Please let my sister Tamar come and prepare some fried cakes before my eyes, that I may take nourishment from her hand."

*⁷*David then sent home a message to Tamar, "Please go to the house of your brother Amnon and prepare some nourishment for him." *⁸*Tamar went to the house of her brother Amnon, who was in bed. Taking dough and kneading it, she twisted it into cakes before his eyes and fried the cakes. *⁹*Then she took the pan and set out the cakes before him. But Amnon would not eat; he said, "Have everyone leave me." When they had all left him, *¹⁰*Amnon said to Tamar, "Bring the nourishment into the bedroom, that I may have it from your hand." So Tamar picked up the cakes she had prepared and brought them to her brother Amnon in the bedroom. *¹¹*But when she brought them to him to eat, he seized her and said to her, "Come! Lie with me, my sister!" *¹²*But she answered him, "No, my brother! Do not shame me! That is an intolerable crime in Israel. Do not commit this insensate deed.*ᵉ* *¹³*Where would I take my shame? And you would be a discredited man in Israel. So please, speak to the king; he will not keep me from you."*ᶠ*

*¹⁴*Not heeding her plea, he overpowered her; he shamed her and had relations with her. *¹⁵*Then Amnon conceived an intense hatred for her, which far surpassed the love he had had for her. "Get up and leave," he said to her. *¹⁶*She replied, "No, brother, because to drive me out would be far worse than the first injury you have done me." He would not listen to her, *¹⁷*but called the youth who was his attendant and said, "Put her outside, away from me, and bar

the door after her." *¹⁸*Now she had on a long tunic, for that is how maiden princesses dressed in olden days. When his attendant put her out and barred the door after her, *¹⁹*Tamar put ashes on her head and tore the long tunic in which she was clothed. Then, putting her hands to her head, she went away crying out loudly. *²⁰*Her brother Absalom said to her: "Has your brother Amnon been with you? Be still now, my sister; he is your brother. Do not take this affair to heart." But Tamar remained grief-stricken and forlorn in the house of her brother Absalom. *²¹*King David, who got word of the whole affair, became very angry. He did not, however, spark the resentment of his son Amnon, whom he favored because he was his firstborn. *²²*Absalom, moreover, said nothing at all to Amnon, although he hated him for having shamed his sister Tamar.

Absalom's Plot. *²³*After a period of two years Absalom had shearers in Baal-hazor near Ephraim, and he invited all the princes. *²⁴*Absalom went to the king and said: "Your servant is having shearers. Please, your majesty, come with all your retainers to your servant." *²⁵*But the king said to Absalom, "No, my son, all of us should not go lest we be a burden to you." And though Absalom urged him, he refused to go and began to bid him goodbye. *²⁶*Absalom then said, "If you will not come yourself, please let my brother Amnon come to us." The king asked him, "Why should he go to you?" *²⁷*At Absalom's urging, however, he sent Amnon and all the other princes with him. Absalom prepared a banquet fit for royalty. *²⁸* *ᵍ*But he had instructed his servants: "Now watch! When Amnon is merry with wine and I say to you, 'Kill Amnon,' put him to death. Do not be afraid, for it is I who order you to do it. Be resolute and act manfully."

Death of Amnon. *²⁹*When the servants did to Amnon as Absalom had commanded, all the other princes rose, mounted their mules, and fled. *³⁰*While they were still on the road, a report reached David that Absalom had killed all the princes and that not one of them had survived. *³¹*The king stood up, rent his garments, and then lay on the ground. All his servants standing by him also rent their garments.*ʰ* *³²*But Jonadab, son of David's brother Shimeah, spoke up: "Let not

---

d 2 Sm 21, 21.—e Lv 18, 9; 20, 17; Dt 27, 22.—f Gn 34, 7.—g 28f: 2 Sm 12, 10.—h 2 Sm 1, 11.

my lord think that all the young princes have been killed! Amnon alone is dead, for Absalom was determined on this ever since Amnon shamed his sister Tamar. [33] So let not my lord the king put faith in the report that all the princes are dead. Amnon alone is dead." [34] Meanwhile, Absalom had taken flight. Then the servant on watch looked about and saw a large group coming down the slope from the direction of Bahurim. He came in and reported this, telling the king that he had seen some men coming down the mountainside from the direction of Bahurim. [35] So Jonadab said to the king: "There! The princes have come. It is as your servant said." [36] No sooner had he finished speaking than the princes came in, weeping aloud. The king, too, and all his servants wept bitterly. [37] But Absalom, who had taken flight, went to Talmai, son of Ammihud, king of Geshur,[i] [38] and stayed in Geshur for three years.

Efforts for Absalom's Return. [39] The king continued during all that time to mourn over his son; but his longing reached out for Absalom as he became reconciled to the death of Amnon.

CHAPTER 14

[1] When Joab, son of Zeruiah, observed how the king felt toward Absalom, [2] he sent to Tekoa and brought from there a gifted woman, to whom he said: "Pretend to be in mourning. Put on mourning apparel and do not anoint yourself with oil, that you may appear to be a woman who has been long in mourning for a departed one. [3] Then go to the king and speak to him in this manner." And Joab instructed her what to say.

[4] So the woman of Tekoa went to the king and fell prostrate to the ground in homage, saying, "Help, your majesty!" [5] [j] The king said to her, "What do you want?" She replied: "Alas, I am a widow; my husband is dead. [6] Your servant had two sons, who quarreled in the field. There being no one to part them, one of them struck his brother and killed him. [7] Then the whole clan confronted your servant and demanded: 'Give up the one who killed his brother. We must put him to death for the life of his brother whom he has slain; we must extinguish the heir also.' Thus they will quench my remaining hope* and leave my husband neither name

nor posterity upon the earth."[k] [8] The king then said to the woman: "Go home. I will issue a command on your behalf." [9] The woman of Tekoa answered him, "Let me and my family be to blame, my lord king; you and your throne are innocent." [10] Then the king said, "If anyone says a word to you, have him brought to me, and he shall not touch you again." [11] But she went on to say, "Please, your majesty, keep in mind the LORD your God, that the avenger of blood may not go too far in destruction and that my son may not be done away with." He replied, "As the LORD lives, not a hair of your son shall fall to the ground."

[12] The woman continued, "Please let your servant say still another word to my lord the king." He replied, "Speak." [13] So the woman said: "Why, then, do you think of this same kind of thing against the people of God? In pronouncing as he has, the king shows himself guilty, for not bringing back his own banished son. [14] We must all die; we are then like water that is poured out on the ground and cannot be gathered up. Yet, though God does not bring back life, he does take thought how not to banish* anyone from him.[l] [15] And now, if I have presumed to speak of this matter to your majesty, it is because the people have given me cause to fear. And so your servant thought: 'Let me speak to the king. Perhaps he will grant the petition of his maidservant. [16] For the king must surely consent to free his servant from the grasp of one who would seek to destroy me and my son as well from God's inheritance.'" [17] And the woman concluded: "Let the word of my lord the king provide a resting place;* indeed, my lord the king is like an angel of God, evaluating good and bad. The LORD your God be with you."[m]

[18] The king answered the woman, "Now do not conceal from me anything I may ask you!" The woman said, "Let my lord the king speak." [19] So the king asked, "Is Joab

i 2 Sm 3, 3; 15, 8.—j 5f: 2 Kgs 6, 26f.—k Nm 35, 19.—l Jb 7, 9; 14, 7-12; Ps 88, 5. 11ff.—m 17. 20: 1 Sm 29, 9.

14, 7: *Hope:* literally, "glowing coal." The image is similar to that of the lighted lamp, e.g., Ps 89, 17, to keep alive the ancestral name.
14, 14: *How not to banish:* a possible allusion to the religious institution of cities of refuge for involuntary murderers; see Nm 35, 9-15.
14, 17: *A resting place:* cf Ps 95, 11; Heb 3, 7—4, 11. The reference here is to a return home for Absalom to Israel.

involved with you in all this?" And the woman answered: "As you live, my lord the king, it is just as your majesty has said, and not otherwise. It was your servant Joab who instructed me and told your servant all these things she was to say. [20] Your servant Joab did this to come at the issue in a roundabout way. But my lord is as wise as an angel of God, so that he knows all things on earth."

Absalom's Return. [21] Then the king said to Joab: "I hereby grant this request. Go, therefore, and bring back young Absalom." [22] Falling prostrate to the ground in homage and blessing the king, Joab said, "This day I know that I am in good favor with you, my lord the king, since the king has granted the request of his servant." [23] Joab then went off to Geshur and brought Absalom to Jerusalem. [24] But the king said, "Let him go to his own house; he shall not appear before me." So Absalom went off to his house and did not appear before the king.

[25] In all Israel there was not a man who could so be praised for his beauty as Absalom, who was without blemish from the sole of his foot to the crown of his head. [26] When he shaved his head—which he used to do at the end of every year, because his hair became too heavy for him— the hair weighed two hundred shekels according to the royal standard. [27] Absalom had three sons born to him, besides a daughter named Tamar, who was a beautiful woman.[n]

Absalom Is Pardoned. [28] Absalom lived in Jerusalem for two years without appearing before the king. [29] Then he summoned Joab to send him to the king, but Joab would not come to him. Although he summoned him a second time, Joab refused to come. [30] He therefore instructed his servants: "You see Joab's field that borders mine, on which he has barley. Go, set it on fire." And so Absalom's servants set the field on fire.[o] Joab's farmhands came to him with torn garments and reported to him what had been done. [31] At this, Joab went to Absalom in his house and asked him, "Why have your servants set my field on fire?" [32] Absalom answered Joab: "I was summoning you to come here, that I may send you to the king to say: 'Why did I come back from Geshur? I would be bet-

ter off if I were still there!' Now, let me appear before the king. If I am guilty, let him put me to death." [33] Joab went to the king and reported this. This king then called Absalom, who came to him and in homage fell on his face to the ground before the king. Then the king kissed him.

CHAPTER 15

Absalom's Plot. [1] After this Absalom provided himself with chariots, horses, and fifty henchmen.[p] [2] Moreover, Absalom used to rise early and stand alongside the road leading to the gate. If someone had a lawsuit to be decided by the king, Absalom would call to him and say, "From what city are you?" And when he replied, "Your servant is of such and such a tribe of Israel," [3] Absalom would say to him, "Your suit is good and just, but there is no one to hear you in the king's name." [4] And he would continue: "If only I could be appointed judge in the land! Then everyone who has a lawsuit to be decided might come to me and I would render him justice." [5] Whenever a man approached him to show homage, he would extend his hand, hold him, and kiss him. [6] By behaving in this way toward all the Israelites who came to the king for judgment, Absalom was stealing away the loyalties of the men of Israel.

Conspiracy in Hebron. [7] After a period of four years, Absalom said to the king: "Allow me to go to Hebron and fulfill a vow I made to the LORD. [8] For while living in Geshur in Aram, your servant made this vow: 'If the LORD ever brings me back to Jerusalem, I will worship him in Hebron.' "[q] [9] The king wished him a safe journey, and he went off to Hebron. [10] Then Absalom sent spies throughout the tribes of Israel to say, "When you hear the sound of the horn, declare Absalom king in Hebron." [11] Two hundred men had accompanied Absalom from Jerusalem. They had been invited and went in good faith, knowing nothing of the plan. [12] Absalom also sent to Ahithophel the Gilonite, David's counselor, an invitation to come from his town, Giloh, for the sacrifices he was about to offer. So the conspiracy gained strength, and the people with Absalom increased in numbers.[r]

David Flees Jerusalem. [13] An informant came to David with the report, "The Israelites have transferred their loyalty to

n 2 Sm 18, 18.—o Jgs 15, 4f.—p 1 Sm 8, 11; 1 Kgs 1, 5.—q 2 Sm 3, 3; 13, 37.—r 2 Sm 16, 23.

2Sm

Absalom."[s] [14]At this, David said to all his servants who were with him in Jerusalem: "Up! Let us take flight, or none of us will escape from Absalom. Leave quickly, lest he hurry and overtake us, then visit disaster upon us and put the city to the sword." [15]The king's officers answered him, "Your servants are ready, whatever our lord the king chooses to do." [16]Then the king set out, accompanied by his entire household, except for ten concubines whom he left behind to take care of the palace.[t] [17]As the king left the city, with all his officers accompanying him, they halted opposite the ascent of the Mount of Olives, at a distance, [18]while the whole army marched past him.[u]

David and Ittai. As all the Cherethites and Pelethites, and the six hundred men of Gath who had accompanied him from that city, were passing in review before the king, [19]he said to Ittai the Gittite: "Why should you also go with us? Go back and stay with the king, for you are a foreigner and you, too, are an exile from your own country. [20]You came only yesterday, and shall I have you wander about with us today, wherever I have to go? Return and take your brothers with you, and may the LORD be kind and faithful to you." [21]But Ittai answered the king, "As the LORD lives, and as my lord the king lives, your servant shall be wherever my lord the king may be, whether for death or for life."[v] [22]So the king said to Ittai, "Go, then, march on." And Ittai the Gittite, with all his men and all the dependents that were with him, marched on. [23]Everyone in the countryside wept aloud as the last of the soldiers went by, and the king crossed the Kidron Valley with all the soldiers moving on ahead of him by way of the Mount of Olives, toward the desert.

David and the Priests. [24]Zadok, too [with all the Levite bearers of the ark of the covenant of God], and Abiathar brought the ark of God to a halt until the soldiers had marched out of the city. [25]Then the king said to Zadok: "Take the ark of God back to the city. If I find favor with the LORD, he will bring me back and permit me to see it and its lodging. [26]But if he should say, 'I am not pleased with you,' I am ready; let him do to me as he sees fit."[w] [27]The king also said to the priest Zadok: "See to it that you and Abiathar return to the city in peace, and both your sons with you, your own son Ahimaaz, and Abiathar's son

Jonathan. [28]Remember, I shall be waiting at the fords near the desert until I receive information from you." [29]So Zadok and Abiathar took the ark of God back to Jerusalem and remained there.

[30]As David went up the Mount of Olives, he wept without ceasing. His head was covered, and he was walking barefoot. All those who were with him also had their heads covered and were weeping as they went.[x] [31]When David was informed that Ahithophel was among the conspirators with Absalom, he said, "O LORD, turn the counsel of Ahithophel to folly!"[y]

David and Hushai. [32]When David reached the top, where men used to worship God, Hushai the Archite was there to meet him, with rent garments and dirt upon his head.[z] [33]David said to him: "If you come with me, you will be a burden to me. [34]But if you return to the city and say to Absalom, 'Let me be your servant, O king; I was formerly your father's servant, but now I will be yours,' you will undo for me the counsel of Ahithophel.[a] [35]You will have the priests Zadok and Abiathar there with you. If you hear anything from the royal palace, you shall report it to the priests Zadok and Abiathar, [36]who have there with them both Zadok's son Ahimaaz and Abiathar's son Jonathan. Through them you shall send on to me whatever you hear." [37]So David's friend Hushai went into the city of Jerusalem as Absalom was about to enter it.

CHAPTER 16

David and Ziba. [1]David had gone a little beyond the top when Ziba, the servant of Meribbaal, met him with saddled asses laden with two hundred loaves of bread, an ephah of cakes of pressed raisins, an ephah of summer fruits, and a skin of wine.[b] [2]The king said to Ziba, "What do you plan to do with these?" Ziba replied: "The asses are for the king's household to ride on. The bread and summer fruits are for your servants to eat, and the wine for those to drink who are weary in the desert." [3]Then the king said, "And where is your lord's son?" Ziba answered the king, "He is staying in Jerusalem, for he said, 'Now the Israelites will restore to me my father's kingdom.'[c] [4]The king therefore

s Ps 3.—t 2 Sm 16, 21f; 20, 3.—u 2 Sm 8, 18.—v Ru 1, 16.— w 2 Sm 16, 10.—x 2 Sm 19, 5; Mi 1, 8.—y 2 Sm 16, 23; 17, 14. 23.—z 2 Sm 16, 16.—a 2 Sm 16, 19.—b 2 Sm 4, 4; 9, 1-13; 19, 18. 25.—c 2 Sm 19, 26f.

said to Ziba, "So! Everything Meribbaal had is yours." Then Ziba said: "I pay you homage, my lord the king. May I find favor with you!"*d*
David and Shimei. *5*As David was approaching Bahurim, a man named Shimei, the son of Gera of the same clan as Saul's family, was coming out of the place, cursing as he came.*e* *6*He threw stones at David and at all the king's officers, even though all the soldiers, including the royal guard, were on David's right and on his left. *7*Shimei was saying as he cursed: "Away, away, you murderous and wicked man! *8*The LORD has requited you for all the bloodshed in the family of Saul,* in whose stead you became king, and the LORD has given over the kingdom to your son Absalom. And now you suffer ruin because you are a murderer." *9*Abishai, son of Zeruiah, said to the king: "Why should this dead dog curse my lord the king? Let me go over, please, and lop off his head."*f* *10*But the king replied: "What business is it of mine or of yours, sons of Zeruiah, that he curses? Suppose the LORD has told him to curse David; who then will dare to say, 'Why are you doing this?' "*g* *11*Then the king said to Abishai and to all his servants: "If my own son, who came forth from my loins, is seeking my life, how much more might this Benjaminite do so? Let him alone and let him curse, for the LORD has told him to.*h* *12*Perhaps the LORD will look upon my affliction and make it up to me with benefits for the curses he is uttering this day." *13*David and his men continued on the road, while Shimei kept abreast of them on the hillside, all the while cursing and throwing stones and dirt as he went.*i* *14*The king and all the soldiers with him arrived at the Jordan tired out, and stopped there for a rest.
Absalom's Counselors. *15*In the meantime Absalom, accompanied by Ahithophel, entered Jerusalem with all the Israelites. *16*When David's friend Hushai the Archite came to Absalom, he said to him: "Long live the king! Long live the king!"*j* *17*But Absalom asked Hushai: "Is this your devotion to your friend? Why did

you not go with your friend?" *18*Hushai replied to Absalom: "On the contrary, I am his whom the LORD and all this people and all Israel have chosen, and with him I will stay. *19*Furthermore, as I was in attendance upon your father, so will I be before you. Whom should I serve, if not his son?"*k* *20*Then Absalom said to Ahithophel, "Offer your counsel on what we should do." *21*Ahithophel replied to Absalom: "Have relations with your father's concubines, whom he left behind to take care of the palace. When all Israel hears how odious you have made yourself to your father, all your partisans will take courage."*l* *22*So a tent was pitched on the roof for Absalom, and he visited his father's concubines in view of all Israel.*m*
Counsel of Ahithophel. *23*Now the counsel given by Ahithophel at that time was as though one had sought divine revelation. Such was all his counsel both to David and to Absalom.*n*

CHAPTER 17

*1*Ahithophel went on to say to Absalom: "Please let me choose twelve thousand men, and be off in pursuit of David tonight. *2*If I come upon him when he is weary and discouraged, I shall cause him to panic. When all the people with him flee, I shall strike down the king alone. *3*Then I can bring back the rest of the people to you, as a bride returns to her husband. It is the death of only one man you are seeking; then all the people will be at peace." *4*This plan was agreeable to Absalom and to all the elders of Israel.
Counsel of Hushai. *5*Then Absalom said, "Now call Hushai the Archite also; let us hear what he too has to say." *6*When Hushai came to Absalom, Absalom said to him: "This is what Ahithophel proposed. Shall we follow his proposal? If not, speak up." *7*Hushai replied to Absalom, "This time Ahithophel has not given good counsel." *8*And he went on to say: "You know that your father and his men are warriors, and that they are as fierce as a bear in the wild robbed of her cubs. Moreover, since your father is skilled in warfare, he will not spend the night with the people.*o* *9*Even now he lies hidden in one of the caves or in some other place. And if some of our soldiers should fall at the first attack, whoever hears of it will say, 'Absalom's followers have been slaughtered.' *10*Then even

d 2 Sm 19, 30.—e 2 Sm 3, 16; 19, 17. 22f; 1 Kgs 2, 8.—f 2 Sm 19, 23. 29; 1 Sm 24, 15; 26, 6.—g 2 Sm 15, 25f; 19, 23.—h 2 Sm 12, 11.—i 2 Sm 19, 19-24.—j 2 Sm 15, 32-37.—k 2 Sm 15, 34.—l 2 Sm 15, 16; 20, 3.—m 2 Sm 12, 11f.—n 2 Sm 15, 12. 31; 17, 23.—o Hos 13, 8.

16, 8: *Bloodshed . . . Saul:* refers to the episode recounted in 2 Sm 21, 1-14.

2Sm

the brave man with the heart of a lion will lose courage. For all Israel knows that your father is a warrior and that those who are with him are brave. [11] "This is what I counsel: Let all Israel from Dan to Beer-sheba, who are as numerous as the sands by the sea, be called up for combat; and go with them yourself. [12] We can then attack him wherever we find him, settling down upon him as dew alights on the ground. None shall survive—neither he nor any of his followers. [13] And if he retires into a city, all Israel shall bring ropes to that city and we can drag it into the gorge, so that not even a pebble of it can be found." [14] Then Absalom and all the Israelites pronounced the counsel of Hushai the Archite better than that of Ahithophel. For the LORD had decided to undo Ahithophel's good counsel, in order thus to bring Absalom to ruin.[p]

David Told of the Plan. [15] Then Hushai said to the priests Zadok and Abiathar: "This is the counsel Ahithophel gave Absalom and the elders of Israel, and this is what I counseled. [16] So send a warning to David immediately, not to spend the night at the fords near the desert, but to cross over without fail. Otherwise the king and all the people with him will be destroyed." [17] Now Jonathan and Ahimaaz were staying at En-rogel, since they could not risk being seen entering the city. A maidservant was to come with information for them, and they in turn were to go and report to King David. [18] But an attendant saw them and informed Absalom. They sped on their way and reached the house of a man in Bahurim who had a cistern in his courtyard. They let themselves down into this, [19] and the housewife took the cover and spread it over the cistern, strewing ground grain on the cover so that nothing could be noticed. [20] When Absalom's servants came to the woman at the house, they asked, "Where are Ahimaaz and Jonathan?" The woman replied, "They went by a short while ago toward the water." They searched, but found no one, and so returned to Jerusalem. [21] As soon as they left, Ahimaaz and Jonathan came up out of the cistern and went on to inform King David. They said to him: "Leave! Cross the water at once, for Ahithophel has given the following coun-

sel in regard to you." [22] So David and all his people moved on and crossed the Jordan. By daybreak, there was no one left who had not crossed.

[23] When Ahithophel saw that his counsel was not acted upon, he saddled his ass and departed, going to his home in his own city. Then, having left orders concerning his family, he hanged himself. And so he died and was buried in his father's tomb.[q]

[24] Now David had gone to Mahanaim when Absalom crossed the Jordan accompanied by all the Israelites. [25] Absalom had put Amasa in command of the army in Joab's place. Amasa was the son of an Ishmaelite named Ithra, who had married Abigail, daughter of Jesse and sister of Joab's mother Zeruiah.[r] [26] Israel and Absalom encamped in the territory of Gilead.

[27] When David came to Mahanaim, Shobi, son of Nahash from Rabbah of the Ammonites, Machir, son of Ammiel from Lodebar, and Barzillai, the Gileadite from Rogelim,[s] [28] brought couches, coverlets, basins and earthenware, as well as wheat, barley, flour, roasted grain, beans, lentils,[t] [29] honey, butter and cheese from the flocks and herds, for David and those who were with him to eat; for they said, "The people have been hungry and tired and thirsty in the desert."

CHAPTER 18

Preparation for Battle. [1] After mustering the troops he had with him, David placed officers in command of groups of a thousand and groups of a hundred. [2] David then put a third part of the soldiers under Joab's command, a third under the command of Abishai, son of Zeruiah and brother of Joab, and a third under command of Ittai the Gittite. The king then said to the soldiers, "I intend to go out with you myself." [3] But they replied: "You must not come out with us. For if we should flee, we shall not count; even if half of us should die, we shall not count. You are equal to ten thousand of us. Therefore it is better that we have you to help us from the city." [4] So the king said to them, "I will do what you think best"; and he stood by the gate as all the soldiers marched out in units of a hundred and of a

p 2 Sm 15, 31.—q 2 Sm 15, 31; 16, 23.—r 2 Sm 19, 14; 20, 4-13.—s 2 Sm 9, 4; 19, 32; 1 Kgs 2, 7.—t 2 Sm 19, 32; Ezr 2, 61.

thousand. [5] But the king gave this command to Joab, Abishai and Ittai: "Be gentle with young Absalom for my sake." All the soldiers heard the king instruct the various leaders with regard to Absalom.

Defeat of Absalom. [6] David's army then took the field against Israel, and a battle was fought in the forest near Mahanaim. [7] The forces of Israel were defeated by David's servants, and the casualties there that day were heavy—twenty thousand men. [8] The battle spread out over that entire region, and the thickets consumed more combatants that day than did the sword.

Death of Absalom. [9] Absalom unexpectedly came up against David's servants. He was mounted on a mule, and, as the mule passed under the branches of a large terebinth, his hair caught fast in the tree. He hung between heaven and earth while the mule he had been riding ran off. [10] Someone saw this and reported to Joab that he had seen Absalom hanging from a terebinth. [11] Joab said to his informant: "If you saw him, why did you not strike him to the ground on the spot? Then it would have been my duty to give you fifty pieces of silver and a belt." [12] But the man replied to Joab: "Even if I already held a thousand pieces of silver in my two hands, I would not harm the king's son, for the king charged you and Abishai and Ittai in our hearing to protect the youth Absalom for his sake. [13] Had I been disloyal and killed him, the whole matter would have come to the attention of the king, and you would stand aloof." [14] Joab replied, "I will not waste time with you in this way." And taking three pikes in hand, he thrust for the heart of Absalom, still hanging from the tree alive. [u] [15] Next, ten of Joab's young armor-bearers closed in on Absalom, and killed him with further blows. [16] Joab then sounded the horn, and the soldiers turned back from the pursuit of the Israelites, because Joab called on them to halt. [v] [17] Absalom was taken up and cast into a deep pit in the forest, and a very large mound of stones was erected over him. And all the Israelites fled to their own tents. [w]

[18] During his lifetime Absalom had taken a pillar and erected it for himself in the King's Valley, for he said, "I have no son to perpetuate my name." The pillar which he named for himself is called Yad-absalom to the present day. [x]

David Told of Absalom's Death. [19] Then Ahimaaz, son of Zadok, said, "Let me run to take the good news to the king that the LORD has set him free from the grasp of his enemies." [20] But Joab said to him: "You are not the man to bring the news today. On some other day you may take the good news, but today you would not be bringing good news, for in fact the king's son is dead." [21] Then Joab said to a Cushite, "Go, tell the king what you have seen." The Cushite bowed to Joab and sped away. [22] But Ahimaaz, son of Zadok, said to Joab again, "Come what may, permit me also to run after the Cushite." Joab replied: "Why do you want to run, my son? You will receive no reward." [23] But he insisted, "Come what may, I want to run." Joab said to him, "Very well." Ahimaaz sped off by way of the Jordan plain and outran the Cushite.

[24] Now David was sitting between the two gates, and a lookout mounted to the roof of the gate above the city wall, where he looked about and saw a man running all alone. [25] The lookout shouted to inform the king, who said, "If he is alone, he has good news to report." As he kept coming nearer, [26] the lookout spied another runner. From his place atop the gate he cried out, "There is another man running by himself." And the king responded, "He, too, is bringing good news." [27] Then the lookout said, "I notice that the first one runs like Ahimaaz, son of Zadok." The king replied, "He is a good man; he comes with good news." [y] [28] Then Ahimaaz called out and greeted the king. With face to the ground he paid homage to the king and said, "Blessed be the LORD your God, who has delivered up the men who rebelled against my lord the king." [29] But the king asked, "Is the youth Absalom safe?" And Ahimaaz replied, "I saw a great disturbance when the king's servant Joab sent your servant on, but I do not know what it was." [30] The king said, "Step aside and remain in attendance here." So he stepped aside and remained there. [31] When the Cushite came in, he said, "Let my lord the king receive the good news that this day the LORD has taken your part, freeing you from the grasp of all who rebelled against you."

2Sm

u 2 Sm 12, 10; 13, 28f.—v 2 Sm 20, 23-26.—w Jos 7, 26; 8, 29; 10, 27.—x 2 Sm 14, 27.—y 2 Kgs 9, 20.

[32] But the king asked the Cushite, "Is young Absalom safe?" The Cushite replied, "May the enemies of my lord the king and all who rebel against you with evil intent be as that young man!"

CHAPTER 19

[1] The king was shaken, and went up to the room over the city gate to weep. He said as he wept, "My son Absalom! My son, my son Absalom! If only I had died instead of you, Absalom, my son, my son!"

Joab Reproves David. [2] Joab was told that the king was weeping and mourning for Absalom; [3] and that day's victory was turned into mourning for the whole army when they heard that the king was grieving for his son. [4] The soldiers stole into the city that day like men shamed by flight in battle. [5] Meanwhile the king covered his face and cried out in a loud voice, "My son Absalom! Absalom! My son, my son!"[z] [6] Then Joab went to his residence and said: "Though they saved your life and your sons' and daughters' lives, also the lives of your wives and those of your concubines, you have put all your servants to shame today [7] by loving those who hate you and hating those who love you. For you have shown today that officers and servants mean nothing to you. Indeed I am now certain that if Absalom were alive today and all of us dead, you would think that more suitable. [8] Now then, get up! Go out and speak kindly to your servants. I swear by the LORD that if you do not go out, not a single man will remain with you overnight, and this will be a far greater disaster for you than any that has afflicted you from your youth until now." [9] So the king stepped out and sat at the gate. When all the people were informed that the king was sitting at the gate, they came into his presence.

The Reconciliation. Now the Israelites had fled to their separate tents, [10] but throughout the tribes of Israel all the people were arguing among themselves, saying to one another: "The king delivered us from the clutches of our enemies, and it was he who rescued us from the grip of the Philistines. But now he has fled from the country before Absalom, [11] and Absalom, whom we anointed over us, died in battle. Why, then, should you remain silent about

restoring the king to his palace?" When the talk of all Israel reached the king, [12] David sent word to the priests Zadok and Abiathar: "Say to the elders of Judah: 'Why should you be last to restore the king to his palace? [13] You are my brothers, you are my bone and flesh. Why should you be the last to restore the king?' [14] Also say to Amasa: 'Are you not my bone and flesh? May God do thus and so to me, if you do not become my general permanently in place of Joab.' "[a] [15] He won over all the Judahites as one man, and so they summoned the king to return, with all his servants.

David and Shimei. [16] When the king, on his return, reached the Jordan, Judah had come to Gilgal to meet him and to escort him across the Jordan. [17] Shimei, son of Gera, the Benjaminite from Bahurim, hurried down with the Judahites to meet King David,[b] [18] accompanied by a thousand men from Benjamin. Ziba, too, the servant of the house of Saul, accompanied by his fifteen sons and twenty servants, hastened to the Jordan before the king.[c] [19][d] They crossed over the ford to bring the king's household over and to do whatever he wished. When Shimei, son of Gera, crossed the Jordan, he fell down before the king [20] and said to him: "May my lord not hold me guilty, and may he not remember and take to heart the wrong that your servant did the day my lord the king left Jerusalem. [21] For your servant knows that he has done wrong. Yet realize that I have been the first of the whole house of Joseph to come down today to meet my lord the king." [22] But Abishai, son of Zeruiah, countered: "Shimei must be put to death for this. He cursed the LORD's anointed." [23] David replied: "What has come between you and me, sons of Zeruiah, that you would create enmity for me this day? Should anyone die today in Israel? Am I not aware that today I am king of Israel?"[e] [24] Then the king said to Shimei, "You shall not die." And the king gave him his oath.

David and Meribbaal. [25] Meribbaal, son of Saul, also went down to meet the king. He had not washed his feet nor trimmed his mustache nor washed his clothes from the day the king left until he returned safely. [26] When he came from Jerusalem to meet

z 2 Sm 15, 30.—a 2 Sm 17, 25; 20, 4.—b 2 Sm 16, 5-13.—c
2 Sm 16, 1-4; 19, 25-31.—d 19ff: 2 Sm 16, 13; Ex 22, 27; 1 Kgs
2, 8.—e 2 Sm 16, 9f; 1 Sm 11, 13; 1 Kgs 2, 8. 38. 46.

the king, the king asked him, "Why did you not go with me, Meribbaal?"*f* 27 He replied: "My lord the king, my servant betrayed me. For your servant, who is lame, said to him, 'Saddle the ass for me, that I may ride on it and go with the king.'*g* 28 But he slandered your servant before my lord the king. But my lord the king is like an angel of God. Do what you judge best. 29 For though my father's entire house deserved only death from my lord the king, yet you placed your servant among the guests at your table. What right do I still have to make further appeal to the king?"*h* 30 But the king said to him: "Why do you go on talking? I say, 'You and Ziba shall divide the property.' "*i* 31 Meribbaal answered the king, "Indeed let him have it all, now that my lord the king has returned safely to his palace."

David and Barzillai. 32 Barzillai the Gileadite also came down from Rogelim and escorted the king to the Jordan for his crossing, taking leave of him there.*j* 33 It was Barzillai, a very old man of eighty and very wealthy besides, who had provisioned the king during his stay in Mahanaim. 34 The king said to Barzillai, "Cross over with me, and I will provide for your old age as my guest in Jerusalem." 35 But Barzillai answered the king: "How much longer have I to live, that I should go up to Jerusalem with the king? 36 I am now eighty years old. Can I distinguish between good and bad? Can your servant taste what he eats and drinks, or still appreciate the voices of singers and songstresses? Why should your servant be any further burden to my lord the king? 37 In escorting the king across the Jordan, your servant is doing little enough! Why should the king give me this reward? 38 Please let your servant go back to die in his own city by the tomb of his father and mother. Here is your servant Chimham. Let him cross over with my lord the king. Do for him whatever you will." 39 Then the king said to him, "Chimham shall come over with me, and I will do for him as you would wish. And anything else you would like me to do for you, I will do." 40 Then all the people crossed over the Jordan, but the king remained; he kissed Barzillai and bade

him Godspeed as he returned to his own district. 41 Finally the king crossed over to Gilgal, accompanied by Chimham.

Israel and Judah Quarrel. All the people of Judah and half of the people of Israel had escorted the king across. 42 But all these Israelites began coming to the king and saying, "Why did our brothers the Judahites steal you away and escort the king and his household across the Jordan, along with all David's men?" 43 All the Judahites replied to the men of Israel: "Because the king is our relative. Why are you angry over this affair? Have we had anything to eat at the king's expense? Or have portions from his table been given to us?" 44 The Israelites answered the Judahites: "We have ten shares in the king. Also, we are the first-born rather than you. Why do you slight us? Were we not first to speak of restoring the king?" Then the Judahites in turn spoke even more fiercely than the Israelites.*k*

CHAPTER 20

Sheba's Rebellion. 1 Now a rebellious individual from Benjamin named Sheba, the son of Bichri, happened to be there. He sounded the horn and cried out,

"We have no portion in David,
   nor any share in the son of Jesse.
Every man to his tent, O Israel!"*l*

2 So all the Israelites left David for Sheba, son of Bichri. But from the Jordan to Jerusalem the Judahites remained loyal to their king. 3 When King David came to his palace in Jerusalem, he took the ten concubines whom he had left behind to take care of the palace and placed them in confinement. He provided for them, but had no further relations with them. And so they remained in confinement to the day of their death, lifelong widows.*m*

Amasa's Death. 4 Then the king said to Amasa: "Summon the Judahites for me within three days. Then present yourself here."*n* 5 Accordingly Amasa set out to summon Judah, but delayed beyond the time set for him by David. 6 Then David said to Abishai: "Sheba, son of Bichri, may now do us more harm than Absalom did. Take your lord's servants and pursue him, lest he find fortified cities and take shelter while we look on." 7 So Joab and the Cherethites and Pelethites and all

2Sm

f 2 Sm 16, 3.—g 2 Sm 9, 2-13; Dt 21, 12f.—h 2 Sm 9, 9ff.—i 2 Sm 16, 4.—j 2 Sm 17, 27ff; 19, 32ff.—k 1 Kgs 11, 31.—l 1 Kgs 12, 16.—m 2 Sm 15, 16; 16, 20ff.—n 2 Sm 17, 25; 19, 14.

the warriors marched out behind Abishai from Jerusalem to campaign in pursuit of Sheba, son of Bichri.o 8 * They were at the great stone in Gibeon when Amasa met them. Now Joab had a belt over his tunic, from which was slung, in its sheath near his thigh, a sword that could be drawn with a downward movement.p 9 And Joab asked Amasa, "How are you, my brother?" With his right hand Joab held Amasa's beard as if to kiss him. 10 And since Amasa was not on his guard against the sword in Joab's other hand, Joab stabbed him in the abdomen with it, so that his entrails burst forth to the ground, and he died without receiving a second thrust. Then Joab and his brother Abishai pursued Sheba, son of Bichri.q 11 One of Joab's attendants stood by Amasa and said, "Let him who favors Joab and is for David follow Joab." 12 Amasa lay covered with blood in the middle of the highroad, and the man noticed that all the soldiers were stopping. So he removed Amasa from the road to the field and placed a garment over him, because all who came up to him were stopping. 13 When he had been removed from the road, everyone went on after Joab in pursuit of Sheba, son of Bichri.

Joab Pursues Sheba. 14 Sheba passed through all the tribes of Israel to Abel Beth-maacah. Then all the Bichrites assembled and they too entered the city after him. 15 So David's servants came and besieged him in Abel Beth-maacah. They threw up a mound against the city, and all the soldiers who were with Joab began battering the wall to throw it down. 16 Then a wise woman from the city stood on the outworks and called out, "Listen, listen! Tell Joab to come here, that I may speak with him." 17 When Joab had come near her, the woman said, "Are you Joab?" And he replied, "Yes." She said to him, "Listen to what your maidservant has to say." He replied, "I am listening." 18 Then she went on to say: "There is an ancient saying,* 'Let them ask if they will in Abel^r 19 or in Dan whether loyalty is finished or ended in Israel.' You are seeking to beat down a city that is a mother in Israel. Why do you wish to destroy the inheritance of the LORD?" 20 Joab answered, "Not at all, not at all! I do not wish to destroy or to ruin anything. 21 That is not the case at all. A man named Sheba, son of Bichri, from

the hill country of Ephraim has rebelled against King David. Surrender him alone, and I will withdraw from the city." Then the woman said to Joab, "His head shall be thrown to you across the wall." 22 She went to all the people with her advice, and they cut off the head of Sheba, son of Bichri, and threw it out to Joab. He then sounded the horn, and they scattered from the city to their own tents, while Joab returned to Jerusalem to the king.

David's Officials. 23 Joab was in command of the whole army of Israel. Banaiah, son of Jehoiada, was in command of the Cherethites and Pelethites.s 24 Adoram was in charge of the forced labor. Jehoshaphat, son of Ahilud, was the chancellor. 25 Shawsha was the scribe. Zadok and Abiathar were priests.t 26 Ira the Jairite was also David's priest.

V: APPENDIXES
CHAPTER 21

Gibeonite Vengeance. 1 During David's reign there was a famine for three successive years. David had recourse to the LORD, who said, "There is bloodguilt on Saul and his family because he put the Gibeonites to death."u 2 So the king called the Gibeonites and spoke to them. (Now the Gibeonites were not Israelites, but survivors of the Amorites; and although the Israelites had given them their oath, Saul had attempted to kill them off in his zeal for the men of Israel and Judah.)v 3 David said to the Gibeonites, "What must I do for you and how must I make atonement, that you may bless the inheritance of the LORD?" 4 The Gibeonites answered him, "We have no claim against Saul and his house for silver or gold, nor is it our place to put any man to death in Israel." Then he said, "I will do for you whatever you propose." 5 They said to the king, "As for the man who was exterminating us and who intended to destroy us that we might have no place in all the territory of Israel, 6 let seven men from among his descendants be given to us, that we may dismember them before the LORD in Gibeon,

---

o 2 Sm 8, 18.—p 2 Sm 2, 13.—q 1 Kgs 2, 5.—r Gn 49, 16.—s 2 Sm 8, 16ff; 23, 20.—t 2 Sm 8, 17f.—u 2 Sm 24, 13.—v Jos 9, 3-27.

20, 8: The text of this verse is quite uncertain.

20, 18f: The proverbial expression here has been poorly transmitted, and its sense is doubtful.

on the LORD's mountain." The king replied, "I will give them up." [7] The king, however, spared Meribbaal, son of Jonathan, son of Saul, because of the LORD's oath that formed a bond between David and Saul's son Jonathan. [w] [8] But the king took Armoni and Meribbaal, the two sons that Aiah's daughter Rizpah had borne to Saul, and the five sons of Saul's daughter Merob that she had borne to Adriel, son of Barzillai the Meholathite, [x] [9] and surrendered them to the Gibeonites. They then dismembered them on the mountain before the LORD. The seven fell at the one time; they were put to death during the first days of the harvest—that is, at the beginning of the barley harvest.

[10] Then Rizpah, Aiah's daughter, took sackcloth and spread it out for herself on the rock from the beginning of the harvest until rain came down on them from the sky, fending off the birds of the sky from settling on them by day, and the wild animals by night. [y] [11] When David was informed of what Rizpah, Aiah's daughter, the concubine of Saul, had done, [12] he went and obtained the bones of Saul and of his son Jonathan from the citizens of Jabesh-gilead, who had carried them off secretly from the public square of Beth-shan, where the Philistines had hanged them at the time they killed Saul on Gilboa. [z] [13] When he had brought up from there the bones of Saul and of his son Jonathan, the bones of those who had been dismembered were also gathered up. [14] Then the bones of Saul and of his son Jonathan were buried in the tomb of his father Kish at Zela in the territory of Benjamin. After all that the king commanded had been carried out, God granted relief to the land. [a]

---

w 2 Sm 9, 13; 1 Sm 18, 3; 20, 8ff. 15f. 42.—x 2 Sm 3, 7.—y 2 Sm 3, 31; 12, 16.—z 1 Sm 31, 10-13.—a 2 Sm 24, 25.—b 1 Kgs 11, 36; 15, 4; 2 Kgs 8, 19.—c 18-22: 1 Chr 20, 4-8.—d 2 Sm 23, 27.—e 19f: 1 Sm 17, 4. 7.—f 2 Sm 13, 3.—g Ps 18, 1.—h 2-51: Ps 18, 3-51.—i 1 Sm 2, 1f.

22, 1-51: This song of thanksgiving is also given, with a few small variants, in Ps 18. In both places it is attributed to David. Two main sections can be distinguished. In the first part, after an introductory stanza of praise to God (2-4), David describes the peril he was in (5-7), and then poetically depicts, under the form of a theophany, God's intervention in his behalf (8-20), concluding with an acknowledgment of God's justice (21-31). In the second part, God is praised for having prepared the psalmist for war (32-35), given him victory over his enemies (36-39), whom he put to flight (40-43), and bestowed on him dominion over many peoples (44-46). The entire song ends with a paean of grateful praise (47-51).

22, 3: *The horn of my salvation:* my strong savior. The horn, the dreadful weapon of an enraged bull, was a symbol of strength; cf Lk 1, 69.

22, 5f: These verses are to be understood figuratively.

Exploits in Philistine Wars. [15] There was another battle between the Philistines and Israel. David went down with his servants and fought the Philistines, but David grew tired. [16] Dadu, one of the Rephaim, whose bronze spear weighed three hundred shekels, was about to take him captive. Dadu was girt with a new sword and planned to kill David, [17] but Abishai, son of Zeruiah, came to his assistance and struck and killed the Philistine. Then David's men swore to him, "You must not go out to battle with us again, lest you quench the lamp of Israel." [b]

[18] [c] After this there was another battle with the Philistines in Gob. On that occasion Sibbecai, from Husha, killed Saph, one of the Rephaim. [d] [19] [e] There was another battle with the Philistines in Gob, in which Elhanan, son of Jair from Bethlehem, killed Goliath of Gath, who had a spear with a shaft like a weaver's heddle-bar. [20] There was another battle at Gath in which there was a man of large stature with six fingers on each hand and six toes on each foot—twenty-four in all. He too was one of the Rephaim. [21] And when he insulted Israel, Jonathan, son of David's brother Shimei, killed him. [f] [22] These four were Rephaim in Gath, and they fell at the hands of David and his servants.

CHAPTER 22

Song of Thanksgiving. [*] [1] David sang the words of this song to the LORD when the LORD had rescued him from the grasp of all his enemies and from the hand of Saul. [g] [2] This is what he sang: [h]

A

I

"O LORD, my rock, my fortress, my
　deliverer,
[3] 　my God, my rock of refuge!
My shield, the horn of my salvation, [*]
　my stronghold, my refuge,
　my savior, from violence you keep
　me safe. [i]
[4] 'Praised be the LORD,' I exclaim,
　and I am safe from my enemies.

II

[5] "The breakers of death surged round
　about me, [*]
　the floods of perdition overwhelmed
　me;

6 The cords of the nether world en-
meshed me,
the snares of death overtook me.
7 In my distress I called upon the LORD
and cried out to my God;
From his temple* he heard my voice,
and my cry reached his ears.

III

8 "The earth swayed and quaked;*
the foundations of the heavens trembled
and shook when his wrath flared up.
9 Smoke rose from his nostrils,
and a devouring fire from his mouth;
he kindled coals into flame.
10 He inclined the heavens and came
down,
with dark clouds under his feet.[j]
11 He mounted a cherub* and flew,
borne on the wings of the wind.[k]
12 He made darkness the shelter about
him,
with spattering rain and thickening
clouds.
13 From the brightness of his presence
coals were kindled to flame.

14 "The LORD thundered from heaven;
the Most High gave forth his voice.
15 He sent forth arrows to put them to
flight;
he flashed lightning and routed
them.[l]
16 Then the wellsprings of the sea appeared,
the foundations of the earth were laid
bare,
At the rebuke of the LORD,
at the blast of the wind of his wrath.

17 "He reached out from on high and
grasped me;
he drew me out of the deep waters.[m]
18 He rescued me from my mighty enemy,
from my foes, who were too powerful
for me.
19 They attacked me on my day of calamity,
but the LORD came to my support.
20 He set me free in the open,
and rescued me, because he loves
me.

IV

21 "The LORD rewarded me according to
my justice;
according to the cleanness of my
hands he requited me.
22 For I kept the ways of the LORD
and was not disloyal to my God.
23 For his ordinances were all present to
me,
and his statutes I put not from me;
24 But I was wholehearted toward him,
and I was on my guard against guilt.
25 And the LORD requited me according to
my justice,
according to my innocence in his
sight.

26 [n] "Toward the faithful you are faithful;*
toward the wholehearted you are
wholehearted;
27 Toward the sincere you are sincere;
but toward the crooked you are as-
tute.
28 You save lowly people,
though on the lofty your eyes look
down.
29 You are my lamp,* O LORD!
O my God, you brighten the darkness about me.
30 For with your aid I run against an
armed band,
and by the help of my God I leap
over a wall.
31 God's way is unerring;
the promise of the LORD is fire-tried;
he is a shield to all who take refuge in
him."[o]

B

I

32 "For who is God except the LORD?
Who is a rock save our God?

j Ps 144, 5.—k Ex 25, 18.—l Ps 144, 6.—m Ps 144, 7.—n
26f: 1 Sm 2, 30.—o Prv 30, 5.

22, 7: *His temple:* his heavenly abode.
22, 8ff: God's intervention is graphically portrayed under the
figures of an earthquake (vv 8. 16) and a thunderstorm (vv 9-15);
cf Jgs 5, 4f; Pss 29; 97, 2-6; Hb 3.
22, 11: *He mounted a cherub:* since God makes the winds
his messengers, or "angels" (Ps 104, 4), he is spoken of poetically as riding on the clouds, or on the angelic creatures called
"cherubim." His earthly throne above the ark of the covenant was
likewise associated with two winged cherubim; cf Ex 37, 7ff. In
both senses the Lord is enthroned upon the cherubim; cf Pss 79,
2; 99, 1.
22, 26f: Men are treated by God in the same way they treat
him and their fellow men.
22, 29: *My lamp:* a figure of life and happiness; cf 1 Kgs 11,
36.

33 The God who girded me with strength
  and kept my way unerring;
34 Who made my feet swift as those of
  hinds
  and set me on the heights;*
35 Who trained my hands for war
  till my arms could bend a bow of
  brass.

II

36 "You have given me your saving shield;
  and your help has made me great.
37 You made room for my steps;
  unwavering was my stride.
38 I pursued my enemies and destroyed
  them,
  nor did I turn again till I made an
  end of them.
39 I smote them and they did not rise;
  they fell beneath my feet.

III

40 "You girded me with strength for war;
  you subdued my adversaries beneath
  me.
41 My enemies you put to flight before me
  and those who hated me I destroyed.
42 They cried for help—but no one saved
  them;
  to the LORD—but he answered them
  not.
43 I ground them fine as the dust of the
  earth;
  like the mud in the streets I trampled
  them down.

IV

44 "You rescued me from the strife of my
  people;
  you made me head over nations.
  A people I had not known became my
  slaves;
45 as soon as they heard me, they
  obeyed.
46 The foreigners fawned and cringed before me;
  they staggered forth from their fortresses."

C

47 "The LORD live! And blessed be my
  Rock!
  Extolled be my God, Rock of my salvation.
48 O God, who granted me vengeance,
  who made peoples subject to me
49 and helped me escape from my
  enemies,
  Above my adversaries you exalt me
  and from the violent man you rescue
  me.
50 Therefore will I proclaim you, O LORD,
  among the nations,
  and I will sing praise to your name,*p*
51 You who gave great victories to your
  king
  and showed kindness to your
  anointed,
  to David and his posterity forever."

CHAPTER 23

The Last Words of David*

1 These are the last words of David:
  "The utterance of David, son of Jesse;
  the utterance of the man God raised
  up,
  Anointed of the God of Jacob,
  favorite of the Mighty One of Israel. *q*
2 The spirit of the LORD spoke through
  me;
  his word was on my tongue. *r*
3 The God of Israel spoke;
  of me the Rock of Israel said,
  'He that rules over men in justice,
  that rules in the fear of God, *s*
4 Is like the morning light at sunrise
  on a cloudless morning,
  making the greensward sparkle after
  rain.' *t*
5 Is not my house firm before God?
  He has made an eternal covenant
  with me,
  set forth in detail and secured. *u*
  Will he not bring to fruition
  all my salvation and my every desire?
6 But the wicked are all like thorns to be
  cast away;
  they cannot be taken up by hand. *v*
7 He who wishes to touch them
  must arm himself with iron and the
  shaft of a spear,
  and they must be consumed by fire."

David's Warriors. **8** These are the names
of David's warriors.* Ishbaal, son of
Hachamoni, was the first of the Three. It

p Ps 22, 23; Rom 15, 9.—q 1 Kgs 2, 3-9; Sir 47, 8.—r Is 59,
21; Jer 1, 9.—s Ps 72, 1-4.—t Jgs 5, 31; Ps 72, 6.—u 2 Sm 7,
11. 15f; Ps 89, 30; Is 55, 3.—v Dt 13, 14.

22, 34: *The heights:* a natural stronghold safe from attack; cf
Ps 62, 3; Hb 3, 19.

23, 1-7: The text of this short composition in the spirit of the
wisdom writers (Prv 30, 1-6) is difficult in places; it views
David's career in retrospect.

23, 8ff: There are thirty-seven warriors in all mentioned in this
list. First there are the Three warriors most noted for singlehanded
exploits (vv 8-12). Then comes the story of a daring adventure by
three unnamed members of the larger group (vv 13-17). Next come
the commanders of the king's bodyguard, Abishai (vv 18-19) and
Benaiah (vv 20-23), with whom must be counted Asahel (v 24) and
Joab (vv 18. 24. 37), and finally the group of the Thirty (vv 24-39).

was he who brandished his battle-ax over eight hundred slain in a single encounter.[w] [9]Next to him, among the Three warriors, was Eleazar, son of Dodo the Ahohite. He was with David at Ephes-dammim when the Philistines assembled there for battle. The Israelites had retreated,[x] [10]but he stood his ground and fought the Philistines until his hand grew tired and became cramped, holding fast to the sword. The LORD brought about a great victory on that day; the soldiers turned back after Eleazar, but only to strip the slain. [11]Next to him was Shammah, son of Agee the Hararite. The Philistines had assembled at Lehi, where there was a plot of land full of lentils. When the soldiers fled from the Philistines,[y] [12]he took his stand in the middle of the plot and defended it. He slew the Philistines, and the LORD brought about a great victory. Such were the deeds of the Three warriors.

[13]During the harvest three of the Thirty went down to David in the cave of Adullam, while a Philistine clan was encamped in the Vale of Rephaim.[z] [14]At that time David was in the refuge, and there was a garrison of Philistines in Bethlehem. [15]Now David had a strong craving and said, "Oh, that someone would give me a drink of water from the cistern that is by the gate of Bethlehem!" [16]So the Three warriors broke through the Philistine camp and drew water from the cistern that is by the gate of Bethlehem. But when they brought it to David he refused to drink it, and instead poured it out to the LORD, [17]saying: "The LORD forbid that I do this! Can I drink the blood of these men who went at the risk of their lives?" So he refused to drink it.

[18]Abishai, brother of Joab, son of Zeruiah, was at the head of the Thirty. It was he who brandished his spear over three hundred slain. He was listed among the Thirty [19]and commanded greater respect than the Thirty, becoming their leader. However, he did not attain to the Three.

[20]Benaiah, son of Jehoiada, a stalwart from Kabzeel, was a man of great achievements. It was he who slew the two lions in Moab. He also went down and killed the lion in the cistern at the time of the snow.[a] [21]It was he, too, who slew an Egyptian of large stature. Although the Egyptian was armed with a spear, he went against him with a club and wrested the spear from the Egyptian's hand, then killed him with his own spear. [22]Such were the deeds performed by Benaiah, son of Jehoiada. He was listed among the Thirty warriors [23]and commanded greater respect than the Thirty. However, he did not attain to the Three. David put him in command of his bodyguard.[b] [24]Asahel,* brother of Joab. . . .[c]

Among the Thirty were: Elhanan, son of Dodo, from Bethlehem; [25]Shammah from En-harod; Elika from En-harod; [26]Helez from Beth-pelet; Ira, son of Ikkesh, from Tekoa; [27]Abiezer from Anathoth; Sibbekai from Hushah;[d] [28]Zalmon from Ahoh; Maharai from Netophah; [29]Heled, son of Baanath, from Netophah; Ittai, son of Ribai, from Gibeah of the Benjaminites; [30]Benaiah from Pirathon; Hiddai from Nahalegaash; [31]Abibaal from Beth-arabah; Azmaveth from Bahurim; [32]Eliahba from Shaalbon; Jashen the Gunite; Jonathan, [33]son of Shammah the Hararite; Ahiam, son of Sharar the Hararite; [34]Eliphelet, son of Ahasbai, from Beth-maacah; Eliam, son of Ahithophel, from Gilo; [35]Hezrai from Carmel; Paarai the Arbite; [36]Igal, son of Nathan, from Zobah; Bani the Gadite; [37]Zelek the Ammonite; Naharai from Beeroth, armorbearer of Joab, son of Zeruiah; [38]Ira from Jattir; Gareb from Jattir; [39]Uriah the Hittite—thirty-seven in all.[e]

CHAPTER 24

Census of the People. [1] * The LORD's anger against Israel flared again,[f] and he incited David against the Israelites by prompting him to number Israel and Judah. [2]Accordingly the king said to Joab and the leaders of the army who were with him, "Tour all the tribes in Israel from Dan to Beer-sheba and register the people, that I may know their number." [3]But Joab said to the king: "May the LORD your God increase the number of people a hundredfold for your royal majesty to see it with

---

w 8-39: 1 Chr 11, 41; 27, 1-15.—x 1 Sm 17, 1.—y Jgs 15, 9.— z 1 Sm 22, 1; Mi 1, 15.—a 2 Sm 8, 18; 20, 23; Jgs 14, 6; 1 Kgs 2, 29f.—b 1 Sm 22, 14.—c 2 Sm 2, 18-23.—d 2 Sm 21, 18.—e 2 Sm 11, 3f.—f 1-25: 1 Chr 21, 1-27.

23, 24: A more complete notice about Asahel, who died early in his career (2 Sm 2, 16-23), is to be presumed lost at this point. Elhanan is the first of the Thirty.

24, 1ff: This story was probably joined at one time to 2 Sm 21, 1-14.

his own eyes. But why does it please my lord the king to order a thing of this kind?" [4] The king, however, overruled Joab and the leaders of the army, so they left the king's presence in order to register the people of Israel. [5] Crossing the Jordan, they began near Aroer, south of the city in the wadi, and went in the direction of Gad, toward Jazer. [6] They continued on to Gilead and to the district below Mount Hermon. Then they proceeded to Dan; from there they turned toward Sidon, [7] going to the fortress of Tyre and to all the cities of the Hivites and Canaanites, and ending up at Beer-sheba in the Negeb of Judah. [8] Thus they toured the whole country, reaching Jerusalem again after nine months and twenty days. [9] Joab then reported to the king the number of people registered: in Israel, eight hundred thousand men fit for military service; in Judah, five hundred thousand.

The Pestilence. [10] Afterward, however, David regretted having numbered the people, and said to the LORD: "I have sinned grievously in what I have done.[g] But now, LORD, forgive the guilt of your servant, for I have been very foolish."* [11] When David rose in the morning, the LORD had spoken to the prophet Gad, David's seer, saying: [12] "Go and say to David, 'This is what the LORD says: I offer you three alternatives; choose one of them, and I will inflict it on you.'" [13] Gad then went to David to inform him. He asked: "Do you want a three years' famine to come upon your land, or to flee from your enemy three months while he pursues you, or to have a three days' pestilence in your land? Now consider and decide what I must reply to him who sent me."[h] [14] David answered Gad: "I am in very serious difficulty. Let us fall by the hand of God, for he is most merciful; but let me not fall by the hand of man." [15] Thus David chose the pestilence. Now

it was the time of the wheat harvest when the plague broke out among the people. [The LORD then sent a pestilence over Israel from morning until the time appointed, and seventy thousand of the people from Dan to Beer-sheba died.] [16] But when the angel stretched forth his hand toward Jerusalem to destroy it, the LORD regretted the calamity and said to the angel causing the destruction among the people, "Enough now! Stay your hand." The angel of the LORD was then standing at the threshing floor of Araunah the Jebusite.[i] [17] When David saw the angel who was striking the people, he said to the LORD: "It is I who have sinned; it is I, the shepherd, who have done wrong. But these are sheep; what have they done? Punish me and my kindred."*

Sacrifice of Atonement. [18] On the same day Gad went up to David and said to him, "Go up and build an altar to the LORD on the threshing floor of Araunah the Jebusite." [19] Following Gad's bidding, David went up as the LORD had commanded. [20] Now Araunah looked down and noticed the king and his servants coming toward him while he was threshing wheat. So he went out and paid homage to the king, with face to the ground. [21] Then Araunah asked, "Why does my lord the king come to his servant?" David replied, "To buy the threshing floor from you, to build an altar to the LORD, that the plague may be checked among the people." [22] [j] But Araunah said to David: "Let my lord the king take and offer up whatever he may wish. Here are oxen for holocausts, and threshing sledges and the yokes of the oxen for wood. [23] All this does Araunah give to the king." Araunah then said to the king, "May the LORD your God accept your offering." [24] The king, however, replied to Araunah, "No, I must pay you for it, for I cannot offer to the LORD my God holocausts that cost nothing." So David bought the threshing floor and the oxen for fifty silver shekels. [25] Then David built an altar there to the LORD, and offered holocausts and peace offerings. The LORD granted relief to the country, and the plague was checked in Israel.

2Sm

---

g 1 Sm 24, 6; 1 Chr 21, 7.—h 2 Sm 21, 1.—i Ex 12, 23; 2 Kgs 19, 35.—j 22f: 1 Sm 6, 14; 1 Kgs 19, 21.

24, 10: The narrative supposes that since the people belonged to the Lord rather than to the king, only the Lord should know their exact number.

24, 17: Before this verse a Qumram manuscript (4Q Sam ᵃ) gives the fuller text of 1 Chr 21, 16, an alternative to the words *When David saw the angel who was striking the people.*

THE BOOKS OF KINGS

The two Books of Kings were originally, like 1 and 2 Samuel, a single historical work. In conjunction with the Books of Samuel, they extend the consecutive history of Israel from the birth of Samuel to the destruction of Jerusalem in 587 B.C. This combined work is designed as a religious history; hence in Kings the temple, which is the chosen site for the worship of Yahweh, occupies the center of attention.

The Books of Kings show clearly the theological bent of a Deuteronomic editor. In them, as already in Judges, material from various sources, such as the "book of the acts of Solomon" (1 Kgs 11, 41) and the "book of the chronicles of the kings of Israel" (1 Kgs 14, 19), is forged into structural unity by an editor whose principal interest is in the fidelity to Yahweh of rulers and people. The reigns of individual kings are adapted to an editorial framework consisting of a presentation and an obituary notice for each, in stereotyped formulas. In between, the achievements of the king are reported—above all, his fidelity or lack of fidelity to Yahweh. The faithful prosper; the unfaithful pay for their defections. Since this is basically a narrative of sin and retribution, it would not be inappropriate to entitle the Books of Kings "The Rise and Fall of the Israelite Monarchy."

Without minimizing the complexity of the process by which this material was transmitted for many centuries, one may speak of two editions of the Books: the first at some time between 621 B.C. and 597 B.C., and the second, final edition during the Exile; probably shortly after Johoiachin was released from his Babylonian prison (561 B.C.).

1 Kings carries the history of Israel from the last days and death of David to the accession in Samaria of Ahaziah, son of Ahab, near the end of the reign of Jehoshaphat, king of Judah. Judgment is passed on Ahaziah's reign but the details are given only later, in 2 Kings. We should note the two large cycles of traditions which grew up around the great prophetic figures of Elijah and Elisha, the former in 1 Kings and the latter chiefly in 2 Kings. These cycles, which interrupt the sequence of regnal chronicles, were very probably preserved and transmitted by the prophetic communities to which there are references in the same traditions. The Elijah cycle is the more important since it dramatically underscores Israel's critical struggle with the religion of Canaan.

The principal divisions of the Books of Kings are: I. The Reign of Solomon (1 Kgs 1, 1—11, 43). II. Judah and Israel to the Time of Ahab (1 Kgs 12, 1—16, 34). III. Stories of the Prophets (1 Kgs 17, 1—22, 54). IV. The Kingdoms of Israel and Judah (2 Kgs 1, 1—17, 41). V. The Kingdom of Judah after 721 B.C. (2 Kgs 18, 1—25, 30).

THE FIRST BOOK OF KINGS

I: THE REIGN OF SOLOMON

CHAPTER 1

¹When King David was old and advanced in years, though they spread covers over him he could not keep warm. ²His servants therefore said to him, "Let a young virgin be sought to attend you, lord king, and to nurse you. If she sleeps with your royal majesty, you will be kept warm." ³So they sought for a beautiful girl throughout the territory of Israel, and found Abishag the Shunamite, whom they brought to the king. ⁴The maiden, who was very beautiful, nursed the king and cared for him, but the king did not have relations with her.

Ambition of Adonijah. ⁵Adonijah, son of Haggith, began to display his ambition to be king. He acquired chariots, drivers, and fifty henchmen. ⁶Yet his father never rebuked him or asked why he was doing this. Adonijah was also very handsome, and next in age to Absalom by the same mother. ⁷He conferred with Joab, son of Zeruiah, and with Abiathar the priest,

DAVID
1010-970
CENSUS
(2 Sm 5, 1—24, 25)
(1 Kgs 1, 1—2, 1)

TRIBUTARIES

END OF THE REIGN OF DAVID (2 Sm 20—24; 1 Kgs 1, 1—2, 11; 1 Chr 21—29) — **(a)** In the last years of his reign David combats the revolt of Sheba the Benjaminite (20, 1-22) and the conspiracy of his son Adonijah (1 Kgs 1—2). (2 Sm 20—24 and 1 Chr 21—29 here add other narratives of uncertain date: David expiates an injustice done to the Gibeonites by Saul. The brave men of David. Songs of David. Preparation for the construction of the Temple.) **(b)** The king tells Joab and the rulers of the army to take a **census** from **Dan** to **Beer-sheba.** Crossing the Jordan, they begin near **Aroer,** and go toward **Gad** and on to **Jazer.** They continue on to **Gilead** and to **Kadesh** in the land of the **Hittites;** they come to **Dan,** and turn to **Sidon,** going to the fortress of **Tyre** and to all cities of the **Hivites** and **Canaanites;** and ending up in the **Negeb of Judah** at **Beer-sheba.** They come to **Jerusalem** at the end of nine months and twenty days (24, 1-9). **(d)** David's old age. Conspiracy of Adonijah. Solomon is solemnly crowned. Death of David after reigning for forty years: seven years at **Hebron** and thirty-three years at **Jerusalem** (2 Sm 24, 10-25; 1 Kgs 1, 1—2, 11).

SOLOMON
THE 12 DISTRICTS
970-931
(1 Kgs 2, 12—11, 43)
[2 Chr 1, 1—9, 31]

INTERIOR POLITICS (1 Kgs 2, 12—4, 19; 2 Chr 1, 1-18) — Solomon consolidates his power through the deaths of Adonijah, Joab and Shimei, and the exile of Abiathar of Anathoth. The dream at Gibeon. He reorganizes the administration of the kingdom by establishing **twelve districts and commissaries:** (1) In the hill country of Ephraim. (2) At Makaz, Shaalbim, Beth-shemesh, Elon and Beth-hanan. (3) At Arubboth, Socoh, and the whole region of Hepher. (4) All the Naphath-dor. (5) Taanach and Megiddo, and beyond Jokmeam, and in all Beth-shean, and in the country around Zarethan below Jezreel from Beth-shean to Abel-meholah. (6) Ramoth-gilead, the villages of Jair, the district of Argob, which is in Bashan, sixty cities. (7) Mahanaim. (8) Naphtali. (9) Asher and along the rocky coast. (10) Issachar. (11) Benjamin. (12) The land of Gilead, the land of Sihon, king of the Amorites, and of Og, king of Bashan. Besides, there was one prefect in the king's own land (Judah) (4, 8-19).

EXTERIOR POLITICS (1 Kgs 4, 20—11, 43; 2 Chr 1, 18—9, 31). — **(a)** Solomon's rule extends from **Tiphsah** on the Euphrates to **Gaza** and the border of **Egypt.** He builds the temple, fortifies **Jerusalem, Hazor, Megiddo, Gezer, Beth-horon** the lower, **Baalath,** and **Tamar** in the wilderness (4, 20—9, 25). **(b)** At **Ezion-geber** near **Elath** he arms a fleet of ships which proceed to **Ophir** and bring back precious cargoes (9, 26-28). **(c)** The Queen of Sheba pays him a visit for a treaty of commerce; Egypt's Pharaoh gives him his daughter in marriage (10, 1-13; 9, 16). **(d)** Hiram of Tyre, in exchange for his alliance, acquires an important part of the 9th district, twenty towns of the "Land of Galilee" (1 Kgs 9, 10-14). Hadad, Rezon and Jeroboam rise up against Solomon (11, 14-40).

and they supported him. [8] However, Zadok the priest, Benaiah, son of Jehoiada, Nathan the prophet, and Shimei and his companions, the pick of David's army, did not side with Adonijah. [9] When he slaughtered sheep, oxen, and fatlings at the stone Zoheleth, near En-rogel,* Adonijah invited all his brothers, the king's sons, and all the royal officials of Judah. [10] But he did not invite the prophet Nathan, or Benaiah, or the pick of the army, or his brother Solomon.

Solomon Proclaimed King. [11] Then Nathan said to Bathsheba, Solomon's mother: "Have you not heard that Adonijah, son of Haggith, has become king without the knowledge of our lord David? [12] Come now, let me advise you so that you may save your life and that of your son Solomon. [13] Go, visit King David, and say to him, 'Did you not, lord king, swear to your handmaid: Your son Solomon shall be king after me and shall sit upon my throne? Why, then, has Adonijah become king?' [14] And while you are still there speaking to the king, I will come in after you and confirm what you have said."

[15] So Bathsheba visited the king in his room, while Abishag the Shunamite was attending him because of his advanced age. [16] Bathsheba bowed in homage to the king, who said to her, "What do you wish?" [17] She answered him: "My lord, you swore to me your handmaid by the LORD, your God, that my son Solomon should reign after you and sit upon your throne. [18] But now Adonijah has become king, and you, my lord king, do not know it. [19] He has slaughtered oxen, fatlings, and sheep in great numbers; he has invited all the king's sons, Abiathar the priest, and Joab, the general of the army, but not your servant Solomon. [20] Now, my lord king, all Israel is waiting for you to make known to them who is to sit on the throne after your royal majesty.* [21] If this is not done, when my lord the king sleeps with his fathers, I and my son Solomon will be considered criminals."

[22] While she was still speaking to the king, the prophet Nathan came in. [23] When he had been announced, the prophet entered the king's presence and, bowing to the floor, did him homage. [24] Then Nathan said: "Have you decided, my lord king, that Adonijah is to reign after you and sit on your throne? [25] He went down today and slaughtered oxen, fatlings, and sheep in great numbers; he invited all the king's sons, the commanders of the army, and Abiathar the priest, and they are eating and drinking in his company and saying, 'Long live King Adonijah!' [26] But me, your servant, he did not invite; nor Zadok the priest, nor Benaiah, son of Jehoiada, nor your servant Solomon. [27] Was this done by my royal master's order without my being told who was to succeed to your majesty's kingly throne?"

[28] King David answered, "Call Bathsheba here." When she re-entered the king's presence and stood before him, [29] the king swore, "As the LORD lives, who has delivered me from all distress, [30] this very day I will fulfill the oath I swore to you by the LORD, the God of Israel, that your son Solomon should reign after me and should sit upon my throne in my place." [31] Bowing to the floor in homage to the king, Bathsheba said, "May my lord, King David, live forever!" [32] Then King David summoned Zadok the priest, Nathan the prophet, and Benaiah, son of Jehoiada. When they had entered the king's presence, [33] he said to them: "Take with you the royal attendants. Mount my son Solomon upon my own mule and escort him down to Gihon. [34] There Zadok the priest and Nathan the prophet are to anoint him king of Israel, and you shall blow the horn and cry, 'Long live King Solomon!' [35] When you come back in his train, he is to go in and sit upon my throne and reign in my place. I designate him ruler of Israel and of Judah." [36] In answer to the king, Benaiah, son of Jehoiada, said: "So be it! May the LORD, the God of my lord the king, so decree! [37] As the LORD has been with your royal majesty, so may he be with Solomon, and exalt his throne even more than that of my lord, King David!"

[38] So Zadok the priest, Nathan the prophet, Benaiah, son of Jehoiada, and the

1 Kgs

1, 9: *En-rogel:* the modern Job's Well southeast of Jerusalem. It marked the ancient boundary between the tribes of Benjamin and Judah (Jos 15, 7; 18, 16). Here David's men sought information about Absalom's revolt (2 Sm 17, 17).

1, 20: At this time, neither law nor the right of primogeniture, but the will of the ruling monarch, determined succession to the throne.

Cherethites and Pelethites* went down, and mounting Solomon on King David's mule, escorted him to Gihon. ³⁹Then Zadok the priest took the horn of oil from the tent and anointed Solomon. They blew the horn and all the people shouted, "Long live King Solomon!" ⁴⁰Then all the people went up after him, playing flutes and rejoicing so much as to split open the earth with their shouting.

⁴¹Adonijah and all the guests who were with him heard it, just as they ended their banquet. When Joab heard the sound of the horn, he asked, "What does this uproar in the city mean?" ⁴²As he was speaking, Jonathan, son of Abiathar the priest, arrived. "Come," said Adonijah, "you are a man of worth and must bring good news." ⁴³"On the contrary!" Jonathan answered him. "Our lord, King David, has made Solomon king. ⁴⁴The king sent with him Zadok the priest, Nathan the prophet, Benaiah, son of Jehoiada, and the Cherethites and Pelethites, and they mounted him upon the king's own mule. ⁴⁵Zadok the priest and Nathan the prophet anointed him king at Gihon, and they went up from there rejoicing, so that the city is in an uproar. That is the noise you heard. ⁴⁶Besides, Solomon took his seat on the royal throne, ⁴⁷and the king's servants went in and paid their respects to our lord, King David, saying, 'May God make Solomon more famous than you and exalt his throne more than your own!' And the king in his bed worshiped God, ⁴⁸and this is what he said: 'Blessed be the LORD, the God of Israel, who has this day seated one of my sons upon my throne, so that I see it with my own eyes.'"

⁴⁹All the guests of Adonijah left in terror, each going his own way. ⁵⁰Adonijah, in fear of Solomon, also left; he went and seized the horns of the altar.* ⁵¹It was reported to Solomon that Adonijah, in his fear of King Solomon, had seized the horns of the altar and said, "Let King Solomon first swear that he will not kill me, his servant, with the sword." ⁵²Solomon answered, "If he proves himself worthy, not a hair shall fall from his head. But if he is found guilty of crime, he shall die." ⁵³King Solomon sent to have him brought down from the altar, and he came and paid homage to the king. Solomon then said to him, "Go to your home."

CHAPTER 2

David's Last Instructions and Death. ¹When the time of David's death drew near,* he gave these instructions to his son Solomon: ²"I am going the way of all mankind. Take courage and be a man. ³Keep the mandate of the LORD, your God, following his ways and observing his statutes, commands, ordinances, and decrees as they are written in the law of Moses, that you may succeed in whatever you do, wherever you turn,ᵃ ⁴and the LORD may fulfill the promise he made on my behalf when he said, 'If your sons so conduct themselves that they remain faithful to me with their whole heart and with their whole soul, you shall always have someone of your line on the throne of Israel.'ᵇ ⁵You yourself know what Joab, son of Zeruiah, did to me when he slew the two generals of Israel's armies, Abner, son of Ner, and Amasa, son of Jether. He took revenge for the blood of war in a time of peace, and put blood shed without provocation on the belt about my waist and on the sandal on my foot.ᶜ ⁶Act with the wisdom you possess; you must not allow him to go down to the grave in peaceful old age.

⁷"But be kind to the sons of Barzillai the Gileadite, and have them eat at your table. For they received me kindly when I was fleeing your brother Absalom.ᵈ

⁸"You also have with you Shimei, son of Gera, the Benjaminite of Bahurim, who cursed me balefully when I was going to Mahanaim. Because he came down to meet me at the Jordan, I swore to him by the LORD that I would not put him to the sword.ᵉ ⁹But you must not let him go unpunished. You are a prudent man and will know how to deal with

---

a Dt 17, 19.—b 2 Sm 7, 11-16; Ps 132, 11f.—c 2 Sm 3, 27; 20, 10.—d 2 Sm 19, 33ff.—e 2 Sm 16, 5; 19, 19.

1, 38: *Cherethites and Pelethites:* mercenaries in David's bodyguard. They became part of his retinue after he defeated the Philistines and established himself in Jerusalem; cf 2 Sm 8, 18; 15, 18; 20, 23.

1, 50: *Horns of the altar:* the protuberances on each of the four corners of the altar were surrounded with a special degree of holiness (Ex 27, 2; 29, 12), and constituted a place of asylum for transgressors of the law (Ex 21, 13f; 1 Kgs 2, 28).

2, 1-6. 8-9: Solomon is expected to remove from his father's family the imputation of blood guilt brought upon it by Joab in the unwarranted killings of Abner (2 Sm 3, 27-29) and Amasa (2 Sm 19, 9-10); and likewise to punish Shimei for his curse, the effects of which David had pledged himself not to avenge in person (2 Sm 19, 21-23). The standards of morality presumed in these verses are far from the Christian ones.

him to send down his hoary head in blood to the grave."

10 David rested with his ancestors and was buried in the City of David. f 11 The length of David's reign over Israel was forty years: he reigned seven years in Hebron and thirty-three years in Jerusalem. g

The Kingdom Made Secure. 12 When Solomon was seated on the throne of his father David, with his sovereignty firmly established, 13 Adonijah, son of Haggith, went to Bathsheba, the mother of Solomon. "Do you come as a friend?" she asked. "Yes," he answered, 14 and added, "I have something to say to you." She replied, "Say it." 15 So he said: "You know that the kingdom was mine, and all Israel expected me to be king. But the kingdom escaped me and became my brother's, for the LORD gave it to him. 16 But now there is one favor I would ask of you. Do not refuse me." And she said, "Speak on." 17 He said, "Please ask King Solomon, who will not refuse you, to give me Abishag the Shunamite for my wife."* 18 "Very well," replied Bathsheba, "I will speak to the king for you."

19 Then Bathsheba went to King Solomon to speak to him for Adonijah, and the king stood up to meet her and paid her homage. Then he sat down upon his throne, and a throne was provided for the king's mother, who sat at his right. 20 "There is one small favor I would ask of you," she said. "Do not refuse me." "Ask it, my mother," the king said to her, "for I will not refuse you." 21 So she said, "Let Abishag the Shunamite be given to your brother Adonijah for his wife." 22 "And why do you ask Abishag the Shunamite for Adonijah?" King Solomon answered his mother. "Ask the kingdom for him as well, for he is my elder brother and has with him Abiathar the priest and Joab, son of Zeruiah." 23 And King Solomon swore by the LORD: "May God do thus and so to me, and more besides, if Adonijah has not proposed this at the cost of his life.

f Acts 2, 29.—g 1 Chr 29, 27.—h 1 Sm 2, 31—i 2 Sm 3, 27; 20, 10.

2, 17. 22-25: *Abishag* had been the concubine of King David (1 Kgs 1, 4). His successor, Solomon, inherited his father's harem. When Adonijah requested Abishag as his wife, he was subtly undermining the security of Solomon's throne and exposing himself to the suspicion of insurrection that would cost him his life; cf 2 Sm 3, 6-11; 16, 22.

24 And now, as the LORD lives, who has seated me firmly on the throne of my father David and made of me a dynasty as he promised, this day shall Adonijah be put to death." 25 Then King Solomon sent Benaiah, son of Jehoiada, who struck him dead.

26 The king said to Abiathar the priest: "Go to your land in Anathoth. Though you deserve to die, I will not put you to death this time, because you carried the ark of the Lord GOD before my father David and shared in all the hardships my father endured." 27 So Solomon deposed Abiathar from his office of priest of the LORD, thus fulfilling the prophecy which the LORD had made in Shiloh about the house of Eli. h

28 When the news came to Joab, who had sided with Adonijah, though not with Absalom, he fled to the tent of the LORD and seized the horns of the altar. 29 King Solomon was told that Joab had fled to the tent of the LORD and was at the altar. He sent Benaiah, son of Jehoiada, with the order, "Go, strike him down." 30 Benaiah went to the tent of the LORD and said to him, "The king says, 'Come out.' " But he answered, "No! I will die here." Benaiah reported to the king, "This is what Joab said to me in reply." 31 The king answered him: "Do as he has said. Strike him down and bury him, and you will remove from me and from my family the blood which Joab shed without provocation. 32 The LORD will hold him responsible for his own blood, because he struck down two men better and more just than himself, and slew them with the sword without my father David's knowledge: Abner, son of Ner, general of Israel's army, and Amasa, son of Jether, general of Judah's army. i 33 Joab and his descendants shall be responsible forever for their blood. But there shall be the peace of the LORD forever for David, and his descendants, and his house, and his throne." 34 Benaiah, son of Jehoiada, went back, struck him down and killed him; he was buried in his house in the desert. 35 The king appointed Benaiah, son of Jehoiada, over the army in his place, and put Zadok the priest in place of Abiathar.

36 Then the king summoned Shimei and said to him: "Build yourself a house in Jerusalem and live there. Do not go anywhere else. 37 For if you leave, and cross

1 Kg

the Kidron Valley, be certain you shall die without fail. You shall be responsible for your own blood." [38] Shimei answered the king: "I accept. Your servant will do just as the king's majesty has said." So Shimei stayed in Jerusalem for a long time. [39] But three years later, two of Shimei's servants ran away to Achish, son of Maacah, king of Gath, and Shimei was informed that his servants were in Gath. [40] So Shimei rose, saddled his ass, and went to Achish in Gath in search of his servants, whom he brought back. [41] When Solomon was informed that Shimei had gone from Jerusalem to Gath, and had returned, [42] the king summoned Shimei and said to him: "Did I not have you swear by the LORD to your clear understanding of my warning that, if you left and went anywhere else, you should die without fail? And you answered, 'I accept and obey.' [43] Why, then, have you not kept the oath of the LORD and the command that I gave you?" [44] And the king said to Shimei: "You know in your heart the evil that you did to my father David. Now the LORD requites you for your own wickedness. [45] But King Solomon shall be blessed, and David's throne shall endure before the LORD forever." [46] The king then gave the order to Benaiah, son of Jehoiada, who struck him dead as he left.

CHAPTER 3

Wisdom of Solomon. [1] With the royal power firmly in his grasp, Solomon allied himself by marriage with Pharaoh, king of Egypt. The daughter of Pharaoh, whom he married, he brought to the City of David, until he should finish building his palace, and the temple of the LORD, and the wall around Jerusalem.[j]

[2] However, the people were sacrificing on the high places, for up to that time no temple had been built to the name of the LORD. [3] Solomon loved the LORD, and obeyed the statutes of his father David; yet he offered sacrifice and burned incense on the high places.

[4] The king went to Gibeon to sacrifice there, because that was the most renowned high place. Upon its altar Solomon offered a thousand holocausts. [5] In Gibeon the LORD appeared to Solomon in a dream at night. God said, "Ask something of me and I will give it to you." [6] Solomon

answered: "You have shown great favor to your servant, my father David, because he behaved faithfully toward you, with justice and an upright heart; and you have continued this great favor toward him, even today, seating a son of his on his throne. [7] O LORD, my God, you have made me, your servant, king to succeed my father David; but I am a mere youth, not knowing at all how to act. [8] I serve you in the midst of the people whom you have chosen, a people so vast that it cannot be numbered or counted. [9] Give your servant, therefore, an understanding heart to judge your people and to distinguish right from wrong. For who is able to govern this vast people of yours?"[k]

[10] The LORD was pleased that Solomon made this request. [11] So God said to him: "Because you have asked for this—not for a long life for yourself, nor for riches, nor for the life of your enemies, but for understanding so that you may know what is right—[12] I do as you requested. I give you a heart so wise and understanding that there has never been anyone like you up to now, and after you there will come no one to equal you. [13] In addition, I give you what you have not asked for, such riches and glory that among kings there is not your like.[l] [14] And if you follow me by keeping my statutes and commandments, as your father David did, I will give you a long life."

[15] When Solomon awoke from his dream, he went to Jerusalem, stood before the ark of the covenant of the LORD, offered holocausts and peace offerings, and gave a banquet for all his servants. **Solomon's Judgment.** [16] Later, two harlots came to the king and stood before him. [17] One woman said: "By your leave, my lord, this woman and I live in the same house, and I gave birth in the house while she was present. [18] On the third day after I gave birth, this woman also gave birth. We were alone in the house; there was no one there but us two. [19] This woman's son died during the night; she smothered him by lying on him. [20] Later that night she got up and took my son from my side, as I, your handmaid, was sleeping. Then she laid him in her bosom, after she had laid her dead child in my bosom. [21] I rose in the

---

j 1 Kgs 7, 8; 2 Chr 1, 1.—k 2 Chr 1, 10.—l Wis 7, 11; Mt 6, 29.

morning to nurse my child, and I found him dead. But when I examined him in the morning light, I saw it was not the son whom I had borne."
²² The other woman answered, "It is not so! The living one is my son, the dead one is yours." But the first kept saying, "No, the dead one is your child, the living one is mine!" Thus they argued before the king.
²³ Then the king said: "One woman claims, 'This, the living one, is my child, and the dead one is yours.' The other answers, 'No! The dead one is your child; the living one is mine.' " ²⁴ The king continued, "Get me a sword." When they brought the sword before him, ²⁵ he said, "Cut the living child in two, and give half to one woman and half to the other."
²⁶ The woman whose son it was, in the anguish she felt for it, said to the king, "Please, my lord, give her the living child—please do not kill it!" The other, however, said, "It shall be neither mine nor yours. Divide it!" ²⁷ The king then answered, "Give the first one the living child! By no means kill it, for she is the mother."
²⁸ When all Israel heard the judgment the king had given, they were in awe of him, because they saw that the king had in him the wisdom of God for giving judgment.

CHAPTER 4

Chief Officers of the Kingdom. ¹ Solomon was king over all Israel, ² and these were the officials he had in his service:

Azariah, son of Zadok, priest;
³ Elihoreph and Ahijah, sons of Shisha, scribes;
Jehoshaphat, son of Ahilud, chancellor;
⁴ [Benaiah, son of Jehoiada, commander of the army;
Zadok and Abiathar, priests;]
⁵ Azariah, son of Nathan, chief of the commissaries;
Zabud, son of Nathan, companion to the king;
⁶ Ahishar, major-domo of the palace; and

Adoniram, son of Abda, superintendent of the forced labor.
Solomon's Royal State. ⁷ * Solomon had twelve commissaries for all Israel who supplied food for the king and his household, each having to provide for one month in the year. ⁸ Their names were:

the son of Hur in the hill country of Ephraim;
⁹ the son of Deker in Makaz, Shaalbim, Beth-shemesh, Elon and Beth-hanan;
¹⁰ the son of Hesed in Arubboth, as well as in Socoh and the whole region of Hepher;
¹¹ the son of Abinadab, who was married to Solomon's daughter Taphath, in all the Naphath-dor;
¹² Baana, son of Ahilud, in Taanach and Megiddo, and beyond Jokmeam, and in all Beth-shean, and in the country around Zarethan below Jezreel from Beth-shean to Abel-meholah;
¹³ the son of Geber in Ramoth-Gilead, having charge of the villages of Jair, son of Manasseh, in Gilead; and of the district of Argob in Bashan—sixty large walled cities with gates barred with bronze;
¹⁴ Ahinadab, son of Iddo, in Mahanaim;
¹⁵ Ahimaaz, who was married to Basemath, another daughter of Solomon, in Naphtali;
¹⁶ Baana, son of Hushai, in Asher and along the rocky coast;
¹⁷ Jehoshaphat, son of Paruah, in Issachar;
¹⁸ Shimei, son of Ela, in Benjamin;
¹⁹ Geber, son of Uri, in the land of Gilead, the land of Sihon, king of the Amorites, and of Og, king of Bashan.

There was one prefect besides, in the king's own land.*

CHAPTER 5

⁷ These commissaries, one for each month, provided food for King Solomon and for all the guests at the royal table. They left nothing unprovided. ⁸ For the chariot horses and draft animals also, each brought his quota of barley and straw to the required place.
²⁰ * Judah and Israel were as numerous as the sands by the sea; they ate and drank

4, 7-19: The administration of the kingdom thus initiated by Solomon continued in its main features for the duration of the monarchy in Israel and Judah.
4, 19: *One prefect . . . in the king's own land:* the royal territory of Judah had its own peculiar administration different from that of the twelve districts which had to supply the king and his household with a month's provisions of food each year (v 7).
5, 20: This verse belongs to ch 4.

and made merry. ¹Solomon ruled over all the kingdoms from the River to the land of the Philistines, down to the border of Egypt; they paid Solomon tribute and were his vassals as long as he lived.ᵐ

²Solomon's supplies for each day were thirty kors of fine flour, sixty kors of meal, ³ten fatted oxen, twenty pasture-fed oxen, and a hundred sheep, not counting harts, gazelles, roebucks, and fatted fowl. ⁴He ruled over all the land west of the Euphrates, from Tiphsah to Gaza, and over all its kings, and he had peace on all his borders round about. ⁵Thus Judah and Israel lived in security, every man under his vine or under his fig tree from Dan to Beer-sheba, as long as Solomon lived.

⁶Solomon had four thousand stalls for his twelve thousand chariot horses.ⁿ

⁹ ᵒ Moreover, God gave Solomon wisdom and exceptional understanding and knowledge, as vast as the sand on the seashore. ¹⁰Solomon surpassed all the Cedemites and all the Egyptians in wisdom. ¹¹He was wiser than all other men—than Ethan the Ezrahite, or Heman, Chalcol, and Darda, the musicians—and his fame spread throughout the neighboring nations. ¹²Solomon also uttered three thousand proverbs, and his songs numbered a thousand and five.ᵖ ¹³He discussed plants, from the cedar on Lebanon to the hyssop growing out of the wall, and he spoke about beasts, birds, reptiles, and fishes. ¹⁴Men came to hear Solomon's wisdom from all nations, sent by all the kings of the earth who had heard of his wisdom.

Preparations for the Temple. ¹⁵When Hiram, king of Tyre, heard that Solomon had been anointed king in place of his father, he sent an embassy to him; for Hiram had always been David's friend. ¹⁶Solomon sent back this message to Hiram: ¹⁷"You know that my father David, because of the enemies surrounding him on all sides, could not build a temple in honor of the LORD, his God, until such a time as the LORD should put these enemies under the soles of his feet. ¹⁸But now the LORD, my God, has given me peace on all sides. There is no enemy or threat of danger. ¹⁹So I propose to build a temple in honor of the LORD, my God, as the LORD predicted to my father

David when he said: 'It is your son whom I will put upon your throne in your place who shall build the temple in my honor.'�q ²⁰Give orders, then, to have cedars from the Lebanon cut down for me. My servants shall accompany yours, since you know that there is no one among us who is skilled in cutting timber like the Sidonians, and I will pay you whatever you say for your servants' salary."

²¹When he had heard the words of Solomon, Hiram was pleased and said, "Blessed be the LORD this day, who has given David a wise son to rule this numerous people." ²²Hiram then sent word to Solomon, "I agree to the proposal you sent me, and I will provide all the cedars and fir trees you wish. ²³My servants shall bring them down from the Lebanon to the sea, and I will arrange them into rafts in the sea and bring them wherever you say. There I will break up the rafts, and you shall take the lumber. You, for your part, shall furnish the provisions I desire for my household."

²⁴So Hiram continued to provide Solomon with all the cedars and fir trees he wished; ²⁵while Solomon every year gave Hiram twenty thousand kors of wheat to provide for his household, and twenty thousand measures of pure oil. ²⁶The LORD, moreover, gave Solomon wisdom as he promised him, and there was peace between Hiram and Solomon, since they were parties to a treaty.

²⁷King Solomon conscripted thirty thousand workmen from all Israel. ²⁸He sent them to the Lebanon each month in relays of ten thousand, so that they spent one month in the Lebanon and two months at home. Adoniram was in charge of the draft. ²⁹Solomon had seventy thousand carriers and eighty thousand stonecutters in the mountain, ³⁰in addition to three thousand three hundred overseers, answerable to Solomon's prefects for the work, directing the people engaged in the work. ³¹By order of the king, fine, large blocks were quarried to give the temple a foundation of hewn stone. ³²Solomon's and Hiram's builders, along with the Gebalites, hewed them out, and prepared the wood and stones for building the temple.

m Sir 47, 15f; 2 Chr 9, 26.—n 2 Chr 9, 25f.—o 9-14: Sir 47, 16f.—p 1 Kgs 3, 12.—q 2 Sm 7, 13; 1 Chr 22, 10.

CHAPTER 6

Building of the Temple. [1] In the four hundred and eightieth year from the departure of the Israelites from the land of Egypt, in the fourth year of Solomon's reign over Israel, in the month of Ziv, which is the second month, the construction of the temple of the LORD* was begun.[r]

[2] The temple which King Solomon built for the LORD was sixty cubits long, twenty wide, and twenty-five high. [3] The porch in front of the temple was twenty cubits from side to side, along the width of the nave, and ten cubits deep in front of the temple. [4] Splayed windows with trellises were made for the temple, [5] and adjoining the wall of the temple, which enclosed the nave and the sanctuary, an annex of several stories was built. [6] Its lowest story was five cubits wide, the middle one six cubits wide, the third seven cubits wide, because there were offsets along the outside of the temple so that the beams would not be fastened into the walls of the temple. [7] (The temple was built of stone dressed at the quarry, so that no hammer, axe, or iron tool was to be heard in the temple during its construction.) [8] The entrance to the lowest floor of the annex was at the right side of the temple, and stairs with intermediate landings led up to the middle story and from the middle story to the third. [9] When the temple was built to its full height, it was roofed in with rafters and boards of cedar. [10] The annex, with its lowest story five cubits high, was built all along the outside of the temple, to which it was joined by cedar beams.

[11] This word of the LORD* came to Solomon: [12] "As to this temple you are building—if you observe my statutes, carry out my ordinances, keep and obey all my commands, I will fulfill toward you the promise I made to your father David.[s] [13] I will dwell in the midst of the Israelites and will not forsake my people Israel."

[14] When Solomon finished building the temple, [15] its walls were lined from floor to ceiling beams with cedar paneling, and its floor was laid with fir planking. [16] At the rear of the temple a space of twenty cubits was set off by cedar partitions from the floor to the rafters, enclosing the sanctuary, the holy of holies. [17] The nave, or part of the temple in front of the sanctuary, was forty cubits long. [18] The cedar in the interior of the temple was carved in the form of gourds and open flowers; all was of cedar, and no stone was to be seen.

[19] In the innermost part of the temple* was located the sanctuary to house the ark of the LORD's covenant, [20] twenty cubits long, twenty wide, and twenty high.* [21] Solomon overlaid the interior of the temple with pure gold. He made in front of the sanctuary a cedar altar, overlaid it with gold, and looped it with golden chains. [22] The entire temple was overlaid with gold so that it was completely covered with it; the whole altar before the sanctuary was also overlaid with gold. [23] In the sanctuary were two cherubim, each ten cubits high, made of olive wood. [24] Each wing of a cherub measured five cubits so that the space from wing tip to wing tip of each was ten cubits. [25] The cherubim were identical in size and shape, [26] and each was exactly ten cubits high. [27] The cherubim were placed in the inmost part of the temple, with their wings spread wide, so that one wing of each cherub touched a side wall while the other wing, pointing toward the middle of the room, touched the corresponding wing of the second cherub. [28] The cherubim, too, were overlaid with gold.

[29] The walls on all sides of both the inner and the outer rooms had carved figures of cherubim, palm trees, and open flowers. [30] The floor of both the inner and the outer rooms was overlaid with gold. [31] At the

---

r 2 Chr 3, 1.—s 2 Sm 7, 13.—t 1 Chr 22, 9f.

6, 1: *Construction of the temple of the Lord* is here paralleled in importance with the founding of the nation after the departure from Egypt. In both, God is the central figure who chose Israel as his people, and now chooses the place where his temple should be built (Dt 12, 4-18. 26). The year is given in a round number, 480, which corresponds to twelve generations. *The fourth year of Solomon's reign:* c. 968 B.C.

6, 11ff: *The word of the Lord . . . my people Israel:* the oracle, which came as a climax at the completion of the work, was an expression of God's acceptance and approval. Nevertheless the fulfillment of God's promises to David and his royal descendants will depend on their observance of his ordinances and commands.

6, 19: *The innermost part of the temple:* the sanctuary or holy of holies reserved exclusively for the Lord. Here through his presence he dwelt as on a throne between the cherubim above the ark of the covenant (2 Kgs 6, 23-28; 2 Chr 3, 10-13). See note on Ex 25, 18ff.

6, 20: *Twenty (cubits) high:* it is usually supposed that the holy of holies was of this height because it had a raised floor, five cubits above the floor level of the nave, rather than a dropped ceiling. The building was twenty-five cubits high (v 2) according to the reading here followed.

entrance of the sanctuary, doors of olive wood were made; the doorframes had beveled posts. [32]The two doors were of olive wood, with carved figures of cherubim, palm trees, and open flowers. The doors were overlaid with gold, which was also molded to the cherubim and the palm trees. [33]The same was done at the entrance to the nave, where the doorposts of olive wood were rectangular. [34]The two doors were of fir wood; each door was banded by a metal strap, front and back, [35]and had carved cherubim, palm trees, and open flowers, over which gold was evenly applied.

[36]The inner court was walled off by means of three courses of hewn stones and one course of cedar beams.

[37]The foundations of the LORD's temple were laid in the month of Ziv [38]in the fourth year, and it was completed in all particulars, exactly according to plan, in the month of Bul, the eighth month, in the eleventh year. Thus it took Solomon seven years to build it.

CHAPTER 7

Building of the Palace. [1]His own palace Solomon completed after thirteen years of construction.[u] [2]He built the hall called the Forest of Lebanon one hundred cubits long, fifty wide, and thirty high; it was supported by four rows of cedar columns, with cedar capitals upon the columns. [3]Moreover, it had a ceiling of cedar above the beams resting on the columns; these beams numbered forty-five, fifteen to a row. [4]There were three window frames at either end, with windows in strict alignment. [5]The posts of all the doorways were rectangular, and the doorways faced each other, three at either end. [6]The porch of the columned hall he made fifty cubits long and thirty wide. The porch extended the width of the columned hall, and there was a canopy in front. [7]He also built the vestibule of the throne where he gave judgment—that is, the tribunal; it was paneled with cedar from floor to ceiling beams. [8]His living quarters were in another court, set in deeper than the tribunal and of the same construction. A palace like this tribunal was built for Pharaoh's daughter, whom Solomon had married.[v]

[9]All these buildings were of fine stones, hewn to size and trimmed front and back

with a saw, from the foundation to the bonding course. [10](The foundation was made of fine, large blocks, some ten cubits and some eight cubits. [11]Above were fine stones hewn to size, and cedar wood.) [12]The great court was enclosed by three courses of hewn stones and a bonding course of cedar beams. So also were the inner court of the temple of the LORD and the temple porch.

Furnishing of the Temple. [13]King Solomon had Hiram brought from Tyre. [14]He was a bronze worker, the son of a widow from the tribe of Naphtali; his father had been from Tyre. He was endowed with skill, understanding, and knowledge of how to produce any work in bronze. He came to King Solomon and did all his metal work.

[15]Two hollow bronze columns* were cast, each eighteen cubits high and twelve cubits in circumference; their metal was of four fingers' thickness.[w] [16]There were also two capitals cast in bronze, to place on top of the columns, each of them five cubits high. [17]Two pieces of network with a chainlike mesh were made to cover the (nodes of the) capitals on top of the columns, one for each capital. [18]Four hundred pomegranates were also cast; two hundred of them in a double row encircled the piece of network on each of the two capitals. [19]The capitals on top of the columns were finished wholly in a lotus pattern [20]above the level of the nodes and their enveloping network. [21]The columns were then erected adjacent to the porch of the temple, one to the right, called Jachin, and the other to the left, called Boaz. [22]Thus the work on the columns was completed.

[23]The sea was then cast; it was made with a circular rim, and measured ten cubits across, five in height, and thirty in circumference.[x] [24]Under the brim, gourds encircled it, ten to the cubit all the way around; the gourds were in two rows and were cast in one mold with the sea. [25]This rested on twelve oxen,* three facing

u 1 Kgs 9, 10.—v 1 Kgs 3, 1.—w Jer 52, 21.—x 2 Chr 4, 2.

7, 15-21: The *two hollow bronze columns,* Jachin and Boaz (2 Chr 3, 17), stood free to the right and left of the temple porch. The names are related to God's power *(Boaz)* founding *(Jachin)* the temple and his people.

7, 23-26: *The sea . . rested on twelve oxen:* this was a large circular tank containing about twelve thousand gallons of water.

north, three facing west, three facing south, and three facing east, with their haunches all toward the center, where the sea was set upon them. [26]It was a hand-breadth thick, and its brim resembled that of a cup, being lily-shaped. Its capacity was two thousand measures.

[27]Ten stands were also made of bronze, each four cubits long, four wide, and three high. [28]When these stands were constructed, panels were set within the framework. [29]On the panels between the frames there were lions, oxen, and cherubim; and on the frames likewise, above and below the lions and oxen, there were wreaths in relief.

[30]Each stand had four bronze wheels and bronze axles. [32]The four wheels were below the paneling, and the axletrees of the wheels and the stand were of one piece. Each wheel was a cubit and a half high. [33]The wheels were constructed like chariot wheels; their axles, fellies, spokes, and hubs were all cast.

The four legs of each stand had cast braces, which were under the basin; they had wreaths on each side. [34]These four braces, extending to the corners of each stand, were of one piece with the stand. [35]On top of the stand there was a raised collar half a cubit high, with supports and panels which were of one piece with the top of the stand. [31]This was surmounted by a crown one cubit high within which was a rounded opening to provide a receptacle a cubit and a half in depth. There was carved work at the opening, on panels that were angular, not curved. [36]On the surfaces of the supports and on the panels, wherever there was a clear space, cherubim, lions, and palm trees were carved, as well as wreaths all around. [37]This was how the ten stands were made, all of the same casting, the same size, the same shape. [38]Ten bronze basins were then made, each four cubits in diameter with a capacity of forty measures, one basin for the top of each of the ten stands. [39]The stands were placed, five on the south side of the temple and five on the north. The sea was placed off to the southeast from the south side of the temple.

[40]When Hiram made the pots, shovels, and bowls, he therewith completed all his work for King Solomon in the temple

of the LORD: [41]two columns, two nodes for the capitals on top of the columns, two pieces of network covering the nodes for the capitals on top of the columns, [42]four hundred pomegranates in double rows on both pieces of network that covered the two nodes of the capitals where they met the columns, [43]ten stands, ten basins on the stands, [44]one sea, twelve oxen supporting the sea, [45]pots, shovels, and bowls. All these articles which Hiram made for King Solomon in the temple of the LORD were of burnished bronze. [46]The king had them cast in the neighborhood of the Jordan, in the clayey ground between Succoth and Zarethan. [47]Solomon did not weigh all the articles because they were so numerous; the weight of the bronze, therefore, was not determined.

[48]Solomon had all the articles made for the interior of the temple of the LORD: the golden altar; the golden table on which the showbread lay; [49]the lampstands of pure gold, five to the right and five to the left before the sanctuary, with their flowers, lamps, and tongs of gold; [50]basins, snuffers, bowls, cups, and fire pans of pure gold; and hinges of gold for the doors of the inner room, or holy of holies, and for the doors of the outer room, the nave.

[51]When all the work undertaken by King Solomon in the temple of the LORD was completed, he brought in the dedicated offerings of his father David, putting the silver, gold, and other articles in the treasuries of the temple of the LORD.[y]

CHAPTER 8

Dedication of the Temple. [1]At the order of Solomon, the elders of Israel and all the leaders of the tribes, the princes in the ancestral houses of the Israelites, came to King Solomon in Jerusalem, to bring up the ark of the LORD's covenant from the City of David [which is Zion].[z] [2]All the men of Israel assembled before King Solomon during the festival in the month of Ethanim (the seventh month). [3]When all the elders of Israel had arrived, the priests took up the ark; [4]they carried the ark of the LORD and the meeting tent with all the sacred vessels that were in the tent. (The priests and Levites carried them.) [5]King Solomon and the entire community of Israel present for the occasion

y 2 Chr 5, 1.—z 2 Chr 5, 2.

sacrificed before the ark sheep and oxen too many to number or count. 6 * The priests brought the ark of the covenant of the LORD to its place beneath the wings of the cherubim in the sanctuary, the holy of holies of the temple. 7 The cherubim had their wings spread out over the place of the ark, sheltering the ark and its poles from above. 8 The poles were so long that their ends could be seen from that part of the holy place adjoining the sanctuary; however, they could not be seen beyond. (They have remained there to this day.) 9 There was nothing in the ark but the two stone tablets which Moses had put there at Horeb, when the LORD made a covenant with the Israelites at their departure from the land of Egypt.[a]

10 When the priests left the holy place, the cloud filled the temple of the LORD 11 so that the priests could no longer minister because of the cloud, since the LORD's glory had filled the temple of the LORD. 12 Then Solomon said, "The LORD intends to dwell in the dark cloud;[b] 13 I have truly built you a princely house, a dwelling where you may abide forever."

14 The king turned and greeted the whole community of Israel as they stood. 15 He said to them: "Blessed be the LORD, the God of Israel, who with his own mouth made a promise to my father David and by his hand has brought it to fulfillment. It was he who said, 16 'Since the day I brought my people Israel out of Egypt, I have not chosen a city out of any tribe of Israel for the building of a temple to my honor; but I choose David to rule my people Israel.' 17 When my father David wished to build a temple to the honor of the LORD, the God of Israel,[c] 18 the LORD said to him, 'In wishing to build a temple to my honor, you do well. 19 It will not be you, however, who will build the temple; but the son who will spring from you, he shall build the temple to my honor.' 20 And now the LORD has fulfilled the promise that he made: I have succeeded my father David and sit on the throne of Israel, as the LORD foretold, and I have built this temple to honor the LORD, the God of Israel. 21 I have provided in it a place for the ark in which is the covenant of the LORD, which he made with our fathers when he brought them out of the land of Egypt."

Solomon's Prayer. 22 Solomon stood before the altar of the LORD in the presence of the whole community of Israel, and stretching forth his hands toward heaven, 23 he said, "LORD, God of Israel, there is no God like you in heaven above or on earth below; you keep your covenant of kindness with your servants who are faithful to you with their whole heart. 24 You have kept the promise you made to my father David, your servant. You who spoke that promise, have this day, by your own power, brought it to fulfillment. 25 Now, therefore, LORD, God of Israel, keep the further promise you made to my father David, your servant, saying, 'You shall always have someone from your line to sit before me on the throne of Israel, provided only that your descendants look to their conduct so that they live in my presence, as you have lived in my presence.'[d] 26 Now, LORD, God of Israel, may this promise which you made to my father David, your servant, be confirmed. 27 "Can it indeed be that God dwells among men on earth? If the heavens and the highest heavens cannot contain you, how much less this temple which I have built! 28 Look kindly on the prayer and petition of your servant, O LORD, my God, and listen to the cry of supplication which I, your servant, utter before you this day. 29 May your eyes watch night and day over this temple, the place where you have decreed you shall be honored; may you heed the prayer which I, your servant, offer in this place. 30 Listen to the petitions of your servant and of your people Israel which they offer in this place. Listen from your heavenly dwelling and grant pardon.

31 "If a man sins against his neighbor and is required to take an oath sanctioned by a curse, when he comes and takes the oath before your altar in this temple, 32 listen in heaven; take action and pass judgment on your servants. Condemn the wicked and punish him for his conduct, but acquit the just and establish his innocence.

---

a Ex 34, 27; Heb 9, 4.—b 2 Chr 6, 1.—c 2 Sm 7, 5.—d 2 Sm 7, 12.

8, 6-9: The transfer of the ark of the covenant into the newly constructed temple building, and the oracle of God's acceptance (1 Kgs 9, 3-9), and his act of possession (1 Kgs 8, 10-13), constituted the temple's solemn dedication, and made of it the abiding dwelling of God among his people for which David had hoped (2 Sm 6, 12-15; 7, 1-3). The concurrence of the feast of Booths marks an appropriate transition of God's dwelling among nomadic tribes to his permanent abode among a settled people.

³³ * "If your people Israel sin against you and are defeated by an enemy, and if then they return to you, praise your name, pray to you, and entreat you in this temple, ³⁴ listen in heaven and forgive the sin of your people Israel, and bring them back to the land you gave their fathers.

³⁵ "If the sky is closed, so that there is no rain, because they have sinned against you and you afflict them, and if then they repent of their sin, and pray, and praise your name in this place, ³⁶ listen in heaven and forgive the sin of your servant and of your people Israel, teaching them the right way to live and sending rain upon this land of yours which you have given to your people as their heritage.

³⁷ "If there is famine in the land or pestilence; or if blight comes, or mildew, or a locust swarm, or devouring insects; if an enemy of your people besieges them in one of their cities; whatever plague or sickness there may be, ³⁸ if then any one [of your entire people Israel] has remorse of conscience and offers some prayer or petition, stretching out his hands toward this temple, ³⁹ listen from your heavenly dwelling place and forgive. You who alone know the hearts of all men, render to each one of them according to his conduct; knowing their hearts, so treat them ⁴⁰ that they may fear you as long as they live on the land you gave our fathers.

⁴¹ "To the foreigner, likewise, who is not of your people Israel, but comes from a distant land to honor you ⁴² (since men will learn of your great name and your mighty hand and your outstretched arm), when he comes and prays toward this temple, ⁴³ listen from your heavenly dwelling. Do all that the foreigner asks of you, that all the peoples of the earth may know your name, may fear you as do your people Israel, and may acknowledge that this temple which I have built is dedicated to your honor.

⁴⁴ "Whatever the direction in which you may send your people forth to war against their enemies, if they pray to you, O Lord, toward the city you have chosen and the temple I have built in your

honor, ⁴⁵ listen in heaven to their prayer and petition, and defend their cause.

⁴⁶ "When they sin against you (for there is no man who does not sin), and in your anger against them you deliver them to the enemy, so that their captors deport them to a hostile land, far or near,ᵉ ⁴⁷ may they repent in the land of their captivity and be converted. If then they entreat you in the land of their captors and say, 'We have sinned and done wrong; we have been wicked'; ⁴⁸ if with their whole heart and soul they turn back to you in the land of the enemies who took them captive, pray to you toward the land you gave their fathers, the city you have chosen, and the temple I have built in your honor, ⁴⁹ listen from your heavenly dwelling. ⁵⁰ Forgive your people their sins and all the offenses they have committed against you, and grant them mercy before their captors, so that these will be merciful to them. ⁵¹ For they are your people and your inheritance, whom you brought out of Egypt, from the midst of an iron furnace.

⁵² "Thus may your eyes be open to the petition of your servant and to the petition of your people Israel. Hear them whenever they call upon you, ⁵³ because you have set them apart among all the peoples of the earth for your inheritance, as you declared through your servant Moses when you brought our fathers out of Egypt, O Lord God."

⁵⁴ When Solomon finished offering this entire prayer of petition to the Lord, he rose from before the altar of the Lord, where he had been kneeling with his hands outstretched toward heaven. ⁵⁵ He stood and blessed the whole community of Israel, saying in a loud voice: ⁵⁶ "Blessed be the Lord who has given rest to his people Israel, just as he promised. Not a single word has gone unfulfilled of the entire generous promise he made through his servant Moses. ⁵⁷ May the Lord, our God, be with us as he was with our fathers and may he not forsake us nor cast us off. ⁵⁸ May he draw our hearts to himself, that we may follow him in everything and keep the commands, statutes, and ordinances which he enjoined on our fathers. ⁵⁹ May this prayer I have offered to the Lord, our God, be present to him day and night, that he may uphold the cause of his ser-

e 2 Chr 6, 36; Eccl 7, 20; 1 Jn 1, 8.

8, 33-34. 46-53: These references to deportation of Israelites to *a hostile land* are an expansion of Solomon's prayer dating from the Babylonian exile four centuries later.

vant and of his people Israel as each day requires, 60 that all the peoples of the earth may know the LORD is God and there is no other. 61 You must be wholly devoted to the LORD, our God, observing his statutes and keeping his commandments, as on this day."

62 The king and all Israel with him offered sacrifices before the LORD. 63 Solomon offered as peace offerings to the LORD twenty-two thousand oxen and one hundred twenty thousand sheep. Thus the king and all the Israelites dedicated the temple of the LORD. 64 On that day the king consecrated the middle of the court facing the temple of the LORD; he offered there the holocausts, the cereal offerings, and the fat of the peace offerings, because the bronze altar before the LORD was too small to hold these offerings.

65 On this occasion Solomon and all the Israelites, who had assembled in large numbers from Labo of Hamath to the wadi of Egypt, celebrated the festival before the LORD, our God, for seven days. 66 On the eighth day he dismissed the people, who bade the king farewell and went to their homes, rejoicing and happy over all the blessings the LORD had given to his servant David and to his people Israel.

CHAPTER 9

Promise and Warning to Solomon. 1 After Solomon finished building the temple of the LORD, the royal palace, and everything else that he had planned, 2 the LORD appeared to him a second time, as he had appeared to him in Gibeon.*f* 3 The LORD said to him: "I have heard the prayer of petition which you offered in my presence. I have consecrated this temple which you have built; I confer my name upon it forever, and my eyes and my heart shall be there always. 4 As for you, if you live in my presence as your father David lived, sincerely and uprightly, doing just as I have commanded you, keeping my statutes and decrees, 5 I will establish your throne of sovereignty over Israel forever, as I promised your father David when I said, 'You shall always have someone from your line on the throne of Israel.'*g* 6 But if you and your descendants ever withdraw from me, fail to keep the commandments and statutes which I set before you, and proceed to venerate and worship strange gods, 7 I will

cut off Israel from the land I gave them and repudiate the temple I have consecrated to my honor. Israel shall become a proverb and a byword among all nations, 8 and this temple shall become a heap of ruins. Every passerby shall catch his breath in amazement, and ask, 'Why has the LORD done this to the land and to this temple?'*h* 9 Men will answer: 'They forsook the LORD, their God, who brought their fathers out of the land of Egypt; they adopted strange gods which they worshiped and served. That is why the LORD has brought down upon them all this evil.' "

Other Acts of the King. 10 After the twenty years during which Solomon built the two houses, the temple of the LORD and the palace of the king—11 Hiram, king of Tyre, supplying Solomon with all the cedar wood, fir wood, and gold he wished—King Solomon gave Hiram twenty cities in the land of Galilee. 12 Hiram left Tyre to see the cities Solomon had given him, but was not satisfied with them. 13 So he said, "What are these cities you have given me, my brother?" And he called them the land of Cabul, as they are called to this day. 14 Hiram, however, had sent King Solomon one hundred and twenty talents of gold.*

15 This is an account of the forced labor which King Solomon levied in order to build the temple of the LORD, his palace, Millo,* the wall of Jerusalem, Hazor, Megiddo, Gezer 16 (Pharaoh, king of Egypt, had come up and taken Gezer and, after destroying it by fire and slaying all the Canaanites living in the city, had given it as dowry to his daughter, Solomon's wife; 17 Solomon then rebuilt Gezer), Lower Beth-horon, 18 Baalath, Tamar in the desert of Judah, 19 all his cities for supplies, cities for chariots and for horses, and whatever else Solomon decided should be built in Jerusalem, in Lebanon, and in the entire land under his dominion. 20 All the non-Israelite people who remained in the land, descendants of the Amorites, Hittites, Perizzites, Hivites, and Jebusites 21 whose doom the Israelites had been unable to accom-

---

f 1 Kgs 3, 5; 11, 9; 2 Chr 7, 12.—g 2 Sm 7, 12-16.—h Dt 29, 23; Jer 22, 8.

9, 14: *One hundred and twenty talents of gold:* approximately three million six hundred thousand dollars.

9, 15: *Millo:* probably means a filling, and may refer to an artificial earthwork or platform of stamped ground south of the temple area. It was begun by David (2 Sm 5, 9); cf 1 Kgs 9, 24; 11, 27.

plish, Solomon conscripted as forced laborers, as they are to this day. [22] But Solomon enslaved none of the Israelites, for they were his fighting force, his ministers, commanders, adjutants, chariot officers, and charioteers. [23] The supervisors of Solomon's works who policed the people engaged in the work numbered five hundred and fifty.

[24] As soon as Pharaoh's daughter went up from the City of David to her palace, which he had built for her, Solomon built Millo.

[25] Three times a year Solomon used to offer holocausts and peace offerings on the altar which he had built to the LORD, and to burn incense before the LORD; and he kept the temple in repair.

[26] King Solomon also built a fleet at Ezion-geber, which is near Elath on the shore of the Red Sea in the land of Edom.* [27] In this fleet Hiram placed his own expert seamen with the servants of Solomon. [28] They went to Ophir, and brought back four hundred and twenty talents of gold to King Solomon.

CHAPTER 10

Visit of the Queen of Sheba. [1] The queen of Sheba,* having heard of Solomon's fame, came to test him with subtle questions.[i] [2] She arrived in Jerusalem with a very numerous retinue, and with camels bearing spices, a large amount of gold, and precious stones. She came to Solomon and questioned him on every subject in which she was interested. [3] King Solomon explained everything she asked about, and there remained nothing hidden from him that he could not explain to her.

[4] When the queen of Sheba witnessed Solomon's great wisdom, the palace he had built, [5] the food at his table, the seating of his ministers, the attendance and garb of his waiters, his banquet service, and the holocausts he offered in the temple of the LORD, she was breathless. [6] "The report I heard in my country about your deeds and

your wisdom is true," she told the king. [7] "Though I did not believe the report until I came and saw with my own eyes, I have discovered that they were not telling me the half. Your wisdom and prosperity surpass the report I heard. [8] Happy are your men, happy these servants of yours, who stand before you always and listen to your wisdom. [9] Blessed be the LORD, your God, whom it has pleased to place you on the throne of Israel. In his enduring love for Israel, the LORD has made you king to carry out judgment and justice." [10] Then she gave the king one hundred and twenty gold talents, a very large quantity of spices, and precious stones. Never again did anyone bring such an abundance of spices as the queen of Sheba gave to King Solomon.

[11] Hiram's fleet, which used to bring gold from Ophir, also brought from there a large quantity of cabinet* wood and precious stones. [12] With the wood the king made supports for the temple of the LORD and for the palace of the king, and harps and lyres for the chanters. No more such wood was brought or seen to the present day.

[13] King Solomon gave the queen of Sheba everything she desired and asked for, besides such presents as were given her from Solomon's royal bounty. Then she returned with her servants to her own country.

Solomon's Wealth. [14] The gold that Solomon received every year weighed six hundred and sixty-six gold talents, [15] in addition to what came from the Tarshish fleet, from the traffic of merchants, and from all the kings of Arabia and the governors of the country. [16] Moreover, King Solomon made two hundred shields of beaten gold (six hundred gold shekels went into each shield)[j] [17] and three hundred bucklers of beaten gold (three minas of gold went into each buckler); and he put them in the hall of the Forest of Lebanon. [18] The king also had a large ivory throne made, and overlaid it with refined gold. [19] The throne had six steps, a back with a round top, and an arm on each side of the seat. Next to each arm stood a lion; [20] and twelve other lions stood on the steps, two to a step, one on either side of each step. Nothing like this was produced in any other kingdom. [21] In addition, all King Solomon's drinking vessels were of gold, and all the utensils in the

---

i 2 Chr 9, 1; Mt 12, 42; Lk 11, 31.—j 1 Kgs 14, 26.

9, 26: *Ezion-geber . . . Edom:* the first mention of maritime commerce in the Israelite kingdom (to which the land of Edom was subject after its conquest by King David; cf 2 Sm 8, 14).

10, 1: *Queen of Sheba:* women rulers among the Arabs are recorded in eighth-century-B.C. Assyrian inscriptions. Sheba was for centuries the leading principality in what is now the Yemen.

10, 11f: *Cabinet:* an unknown wood, probably fragrant.

hall of the Forest of Lebanon were of pure gold. There was no silver, for in Solomon's time it was considered worthless. 22 The king had a fleet of Tarshish ships* at sea with Hiram's fleet. Once every three years the fleet of Tarshish ships would come with a cargo of gold, silver, ivory, apes, and monkeys. 23 Thus King Solomon surpassed in riches and wisdom all the kings of the earth. 24 And the whole world sought audience with Solomon, to hear from him the wisdom which God had put in his heart. 25 Each one brought his yearly tribute: silver or gold articles, garments, weapons, spices, horses and mules.

26 Solomon collected chariots and drivers; he had one thousand four hundred chariots and twelve thousand drivers; these he allocated among the chariot cities and to the king's service in Jerusalem.*k* 27 The king made silver as common in Jerusalem as stones, and cedars as numerous as the sycamores of the foothills. 28 Solomon's horses were imported from Cilicia, where the king's agents purchased them. 29 A chariot imported from Egypt cost six hundred shekels, a horse one hundred and fifty shekels; they were exported at these rates to all the Hittite and Aramean kings.

CHAPTER 11

The Sins of Solomon. 1 * King Solomon loved many foreign women besides the daughter of Pharaoh (Moabites, Ammonites, Edomites, Sidonians, and Hittites),*l* 2 from nations with which the LORD had forbidden the Israelites to intermarry, "because," he said, "they will turn your hearts to their gods."*m* 3 But Solomon fell in love with them. He had seven hundred wives of princely rank and three hundred concubines, and his wives turned his heart.

4 When Solomon was old his wives had turned his heart to strange gods, and his heart was not entirely with the LORD, his God, as the heart of his father David had been. 5 By adoring Astarte, the goddess of the Sidonians, and Milcom, the idol of the Ammonites, 6 Solomon did evil in the sight of the LORD; he did not follow him unreservedly as his father David had done. 7 Solomon then built a high place to Chemosh, the idol of Moab, and to Molech, the idol of the Ammonites, on the hill opposite Jerusalem. 8 He did the

same for all his foreign wives who burned incense and sacrificed to their gods. 9 The LORD, therefore, became angry with Solomon, because his heart was turned away from the LORD, the God of Israel, who had appeared to him twice*n* 10 (for though the LORD had forbidden him this very act of following strange gods, Solomon had not obeyed him).

11 So the LORD said to Solomon: "Since this is what you want, and you have not kept my covenant and my statutes which I enjoined on you, I will deprive you of the kingdom and give it to your servant. 12 I will not do this during your lifetime, however, for the sake of your father David; it is your son whom I will deprive.*o* 13 Nor will I take away the whole kingdom. I will leave your son one tribe for the sake of my servant David and of Jerusalem, which I have chosen."

14 The LORD then raised up an adversary to Solomon: Hadad the Edomite, who was of the royal line in Edom. 15 Earlier, when David had conquered Edom, Joab, the general of the army, while going to bury the slain, put to death every male in Edom.*p* 16 Joab and all Israel remained there six months until they had killed off every male in Edom. 17 Meanwhile, Hadad, who was only a boy, fled toward Egypt with some Edomite servants of his father. 18 They left Midian and passing through Paran, where they picked up additional men, they went into Egypt to Pharaoh, king of Egypt, who gave Hadad a house, appointed him rations, and assigned him land.

19 Hadad won great favor with Pharaoh, so that he gave him in marriage the sister of Queen Tahpenes, his own wife. 20 Tah-

---

k 2 Chr 1, 14.—l Dt 17, 17; Sir 47, 19f.—m Ex 34, 16.—n 1 Kgs 9, 2.—o 1 Kgs 12, 15.—p 2 Sm 8, 14.

10, 22: *Tarshish ships:* large, strong vessels for long voyages. *Tarshish* was the ancient Tartessus, a Phoenician colony in southern Spain, the name of which denotes a center for smelting metallic ore.
11, 1-3. 7: The glorious rise of Solomon, his piety and wisdom, administrative skill and wealth, the extension of his kingdom, his prestige among neighboring rulers, his reign of peace, above all his friendship with God—these are now eclipsed by his sins of intermarriage with great numbers of pagan wives and the consequent forbidden worship of their gods (Ex 34, 11-16; Dt 7, 1-5). His construction of temples in their honor merited the punishment of loss of a united kingdom to his posterity, and the opposition of adversaries to himself (vv 14. 23-27). Hadad the Edomite rebelled against Solomon at the beginning of his reign (v 25). Rezon of Syria established a new kingdom in Damascus; Jeroboam of Israel constituted the greatest threat because of his revolt from within. This threefold threat culminated in the breakup of Solomon's kingdom.

penes' sister bore Hadad a son, Genubath. After his weaning, the queen kept him in Pharaoh's palace, where he then lived with Pharaoh's own sons. [21] When Hadad in Egypt heard that David rested with his ancestors and that Joab, the general of the army, was dead, he said to Pharaoh, "Give me leave to return to my own country." [22] Pharaoh said to him, "What do you lack with me, that you are seeking to return to your own country?" "Nothing," he said, "but please let me go!"

[23] God raised up against Solomon another adversary, in Rezon, the son of Eliada, who had fled from his lord, Hadadezer, king of Zobah, [24] when David defeated them with slaughter. Rezon gathered men about him and became leader of a band, went to Damascus, settled there, and became king in Damascus. [25] He was an enemy of Israel as long as Solomon lived; this added to the harm done by Hadad, who made a rift in Israel by becoming king over Edom.

[26] Solomon's servant Jeroboam, son of Nebat, an Ephraimite from Zeredah with a widowed mother, Zeruah, also rebelled against the king.[q] [27] This is why he rebelled. King Solomon was building Millo, closing up the breach of his father's City of David. [28] Jeroboam was a man of means, and when Solomon saw that he was also an industrious young man, he put him in charge of the entire labor force of the house of Joseph. [29] At that time Jeroboam left Jerusalem, and the prophet Ahijah the Shilonite met him on the road. The two were alone in the area, and the prophet was wearing a new cloak.[r] [30] Ahijah took off his new cloak, tore it into twelve pieces, [31] and said to Jeroboam:

"Take ten pieces for yourself; the LORD, the God of Israel, says: 'I will tear away the kingdom from Solomon's grasp and will give you ten of the tribes.[s] [32] One tribe shall remain to him for the sake of David my servant, and of Jerusalem, the city I have chosen out of all the tribes of Israel. [33] The ten I will give you because he has forsaken me and has worshiped Astarte, goddess of the Sidonians, Chemosh, god

of Moab, and Milcom, god of the Ammonites; he has not followed my ways or done what is pleasing to me according to my statutes and my decrees, as his father David did. [34] Yet I will not take any of the kingdom from Solomon himself, but will keep him a prince as long as he lives for the sake of my servant David, whom I chose, who kept my commandments and statutes. [35] But I will take the kingdom from his son and will give it to you—that is, the ten tribes. [36] I will give his son one tribe, that my servant David may always have a lamp before me in Jerusalem, the city in which I choose to be honored. [37] I will take you; you shall reign over all that you desire and shall become king of Israel. [38] If, then, you heed all that I command you, follow my ways, and please me by keeping my statutes and my commandments like my servant David, I will be with you. I will establish for you, as I did for David, a lasting dynasty; I will give Israel to you. [39] I will punish David's line for this, but not forever.'"

[40] When Solomon tried to have Jeroboam killed for his rebellion, he escaped to King Shishak, in Egypt, where he remained until Solomon's death.

[41] The rest of the acts of Solomon, with all his deeds and all his wisdom, are recorded in the book of the chronicles of Solomon. [42] The time that Solomon reigned in Jerusalem over all Israel was forty years. [43] Solomon rested with his ancestors; he was buried in his father's City of David, and his son Rehoboam succeeded him as king.

II: JUDAH AND ISRAEL TO THE TIME OF AHAB

CHAPTER 12

Secession of Israel. [1] Rehoboam went to Shechem,* where all Israel had come to proclaim him king.[t] [3] They said to Rehoboam: [4] "Your father put on us a heavy yoke. If you now lighten the harsh service and the heavy yoke your father imposed on us, we will serve you." [5] "Come back to me in three days," he answered them. When the people had departed, [6] King Rehoboam consulted the elders who had been in his father's service while he was alive, and asked, "What answer do you advise me to give this people?" [7] They replied, "If today you will be the servant of this people

---

q 2 Chr 13, 6.—r 1 Kgs 14, 2; 2 Chr 10, 15.—s 1 Kgs 12, 15.—t 2 Chr 10, 1.

12, 1: *Shechem:* chief city of the northern tribes, where a covenant of fidelity had previously been made between the Lord and his people and a stone of witness had been erected in memory of the event (Jos 24, 25ff).

and submit to them, giving them a favorable answer, they will be your servants forever." [8]But he ignored the advice the elders had given him, and consulted the young men who had grown up with him and were in his service. [9]He said to them, "What answer do you advise me to give this people, who have asked me to lighten the yoke my father imposed on them?" [10]The young men who had grown up with him replied, "This is what you must say to this people who have asked you to lighten the yoke your father put on them: 'My little finger is thicker than my father's body. [11]Whereas my father put a heavy yoke on you, I will make it heavier. My father beat you with whips, but I will beat you with scorpions.' "

[12]On the third day all Israel came back to King Rehoboam, as he had instructed them to do. [13]Ignoring the advice the elders had given him, the king gave the people a harsh answer. [14]He said to them, as the young men had advised: "My father put on you a heavy yoke, but I will make it heavier. My father beat you with whips, but I will beat you with scorpions." [15]The king did not listen to the people, for the LORD brought this about to fulfill the prophecy he had uttered to Jeroboam, son of Nebat, through Ahijah the Shilonite.[u]

[16]When all Israel saw that the king did not listen to them, the people answered the king:

"What share have we in David?[*]
We have no heritage in the son of Jesse.
To your tents, O Israel!
Now look to your own house, David."

So Israel went off to their tents, [17]but Rehoboam reigned over the Israelites who lived in the cities of Judah. [18]King Rehoboam then sent out Adoram, superintendent of the forced labor, but all Israel stoned him to death. Rehoboam managed to mount his chariot to flee to Jerusalem, [19]and Israel went into rebellion against David's house to this day. [2]Jeroboam, son of Nebat, who was still in Egypt, where he had fled from King Solomon, returned from Egypt as soon as he learned this. [20]When all Israel heard that Jeroboam had returned, they summoned him to an assembly and made him king over all Israel. None remained loyal to David's house except the tribe of Judah alone.

[21]On his arrival in Jerusalem, Rehoboam gathered together all the house of Judah and the tribe of Benjamin—one hundred eighty thousand seasoned warriors—to fight against the house of Israel, to restore the kingdom to Rehoboam, son of Solomon. [22] [v] However, the LORD spoke to Shemaiah, a man of God: [23]"Say to Rehoboam, son of Solomon, king of Judah, and to the house of Judah and to Benjamin, and to the rest of the people: [24]'Thus says the LORD: You must not march out to fight against your brother Israelites. Let every man return home, for I have brought this about.' " They accepted this message of the LORD and gave up the expedition accordingly.

[25]Jeroboam built up Shechem in the hill country of Ephraim and lived there. Then he left it and built up Penuel.

Religious Rebellion.[*] [26]Jeroboam thought to himself: "The kingdom will return to David's house. [27]If now this people go up to offer sacrifices in the temple of the LORD in Jerusalem, the hearts of this people will return to their master, Rehoboam, king of Judah, and they will kill me." [28]After taking counsel, the king made two calves of gold and said to the people: "You have been going up to Jerusalem long enough. Here is your God, O Israel, who brought you up from the land of Egypt."[w] [29]And he put one in Bethel, the other in Dan.[*] [30]This led to sin, because the people frequented these calves in Bethel and in Dan. [31]He also built temples on the high places and made priests from among the people who were not Levites.[x] [32]Jeroboam established a feast in the eighth month on the fifteenth day

---

u 1 Kgs 11, 12. 31.—v 22-24: 2 Chr 11, 2ff.—w Tb 1, 5; Ex 32, 8.—x 2 Chr 11, 15.

12, 16: *What share have we in David:* even in David's time the northern tribes seemed ready to withdraw from Judah (2 Sm 20, 1). The unreasonable attitude of Rehoboam toward them intensified the discontent caused by the oppression of Solomon (v 4) and thus precipitated the establishment of a rival monarchy (v 20).

12, 26-32: *Jeroboam* feared reunification of the divided kingdom through worship in the single temple in Jerusalem. To prevent this he encouraged shrines on the high places, and appointed false priests to supplement those of levitical descent. The golden bullocks he installed in two of his sanctuaries, though probably intended as bearers of the invisible Divine Majesty, quickly became occasions for idolatry. Thus Jeroboam caused Israel to sin, and sealed his doom and that of his royal house (1 Kgs 13, 34; 14, 7-14).

12, 29: *Bethel* and *Dan:* at the southern and northern boundaries of the separate kingdom of Israel, where sanctuaries had existed in the past (Gn 12, 8; 13, 3; 18, 10-22; 25, 1-16; Jgs 18, 1-31).

THE SCHISM
About 931

ABIJAH	——————
JEROBOAM	‒ ‒ ‒
SHISHAK	••••••

(1 Kgs 12, 1—15, 8;
2 Chr 10, 1—13, 22)

THE KINGDOM OF JUDAH

1. REHOBOAM (931-913)

1 Kgs 12, 1—14, 30; 2 Chr 10, 1—12, 16

THE KINGDOM OF ISRAEL

1. JEROBOAM (931-910)

1 Kgs 12, 20—14, 18

At **Shechem**, convocation of the people and revolt of the northern tribes.

(a) Rehoboam reigns over Judah and Benjamin. The prophet Shemaiah advises against any attempt at forced reunification (12, 17-24). Rehoboam builds fortified cities: **Bethlehem, Etam, Tekoa, Beth-zur, Soco, Adullam, Gath, Mareshah, Ziph, Adoraim, Lachish, Azekah, Zorah, Aijalon, Hebron** (2 Chr 11, 5-12). **(b)** Persecuted by Jeroboam, the priests, scattered in Israel, come to Jerusalem (2 Chr 11, 13-17), **(c)** However, Sheshonk (Shishak), king of Egypt, invades Judah, pillages the temple and the royal palace (1 Kgs 14, 25-27).

(a) Returning from Egypt, Jeroboam is crowned king of Israel by the people of the dissident tribes (12, 1-16). **(b)** He fortifies **Shechem** and **Penuel**; he institutes idolatrous worship at **Bethel** and **Dan** (12, 25-32). A prophet from Judah condemns the altar at **Bethel**. The prophet Ahijah of **Shiloh** predicts the death of Abijah, son of Jeroboam (12, 32—13, 34).

2. ABIJAH (913-911)

1 Kgs 15, 1-8; 2 Chr 13

War between Abijah and Jeroboam. The latter is defeated at **Mount Zemaraim,** in the highlands of Ephraim. Abijah annexes **Bethel, Jeshanah, Ephron** (2 Chr 13, 1-21).

THE PROPHET ELIJAH
IN THE TIME OF AHAB
(874-853)
(1 Kgs 16, 29—19, 21
2 Kgs 1, 1—2, 13)

Zarephath

ARAM

Kishon

Jezreel

GILEAD

Cherith

oTishbe

Abel-meholan

o SAMARIA

I S R A E L

Jordan

Gilgal

Bethel

Jericho

J U D A H

Beer-sheba

Toward HOREB

THE PROPHET ELIJAH (1 Kgs 16, 29—2 Kgs 2, 18 — (a) Elijah practices his ministry in Israel during the reigns of Ahab (874-853) and Ahaziah (853-852). **(b)** In **Samaria** Ahab marries Jezebel, daughter of the king of the Sidonians, and builds a temple to Baal. Elijah predicts a drought (1 Kgs 16, 29—17, 1). **(c)** At **Cherith** Elijah hides himself by the brook (17, 2-6) following the command of the Lord. **(d)** The brook dries up, and Elijah receives orders to go to **Zarephath** which belongs to **Sidon.** Miracles of the multiplication of the meal and of the raising of the widow's son (17, 7-24). **(e)** Elijah goes to meet Ahab at **Carmel** in the third year. He defies the prophets of Baal and proves them false before all the people; he has them killed and thrown into the brook **Kishon** (18, 1-40). **(f)** Having predicted rain, Elijah leaves for **Jezreel** with Ahab. Threatened by Jezebel, he flees to **Beer-sheba,** and from there to **Mount Horeb.** An angel comforts him (18, 41—19, 7). **(g)** At **Mount Horeb** the Lord commands Elijah to go to the desert near **Damascus.** Elijah is told to anoint Hazael as king of **Aram,** Jehu as king of **Israel,** and Elisha of **Abel-meholah** as prophet in his place (19, 8-18). **(h)** At **Abel-meholah** he throws his cloak over Elisha (19, 19-21). **(i)** At **Jezreel** Elijah reprimands Ahab concerning the vineyard of Naboth (21, 1-29). **(j)** "On a hilltop" Elijah receives the officers sent by Ahaziah (2 Kgs 1, 9-21). **(k)** On his way from **Gilgal,** Elijah, accompanied by Elisha, passes through **Bethel** and **Jericho,** crosses the **Jordan,** and then is taken up into heaven (2 Kgs 2, 1-12).

of the month to duplicate in Bethel the pilgrimage feast of Judah, with sacrifices to the calves he had made; and he stationed in Bethel priests of the high places he had built.

Message of the Prophet from Judah.
[33] Jeroboam ascended the altar he built in Bethel on the fifteenth day of the eighth month, the month in which he arbitrarily chose to establish a feast for the Israelites; he was going to offer sacrifice.

CHAPTER 13

[1] A man of God came from Judah to Bethel by the word of the LORD, while Jeroboam was standing at the altar to offer sacrifice. [2] He cried out against the altar the word of the LORD: "O altar, altar, the LORD says, 'A child shall be born to the house of David, Josiah by name, who shall slaughter upon you the priests of the high places who offer sacrifice upon you, and he shall burn human bones upon you.' "[y] [3] He gave a sign that same day and said: "This is the sign that the LORD has spoken: The altar shall break up and the ashes on it shall be strewn about."

[4] When King Jeroboam heard what the man of God was crying out against the altar, he stretched forth his hand from the altar and said, "Seize him!" But the hand he stretched forth against him withered, so that he could not draw it back. [5] Moreover, the altar broke up and the ashes from it were strewn about—the sign the man of God had given as the word of the LORD. [6] Then the king appealed to the man of God. "Entreat the LORD, your God," he said, "and intercede for me that I may be able to withdraw my hand." So the man of God entreated the LORD, and the king recovered the normal use of his hand. [7] "Come home with me for some refreshment," the king invited the man of God, "and I will give you a present." [8] "If you gave me half your kingdom," the man of God said to the king, "I would not go with you, nor eat bread or drink water in this place. [9] For I was instructed by the word of the LORD not to eat bread or drink water and not to return by the way I came." [10] So he departed by another road and did not go back the way he had come to Bethel.

[11] There was an old prophet living in the city, whose sons came and told him all that the man of God had done that day in Bethel. When they repeated to their father the words he had spoken to the king, [12] the father asked them, "Which way did he go?" And his sons pointed out to him the road taken by the man of God who had come from Judah. [13] Then he said to his sons, "Saddle the ass for me." When they had saddled it, he mounted [14] and followed the man of God, whom he found seated under a terebinth. When he asked him, "Are you the man of God who came from Judah?" he answered, "Yes." [15] Then he said, "Come home with me and have some bread." [16] "I cannot go back with you, and I cannot eat bread or drink water with you in this place," he answered, [17] "for I was told by the word of the LORD neither to eat bread nor drink water here, and not to go back the way I came." [18] But he said to him, "I, too, am a prophet like you, and an angel told me in the word of the LORD to bring you back with me to my house and to have you eat bread and drink water." He was lying to him, however.

[19] So he went back with him, and ate bread and drank water in his house. [20] But while they were sitting at table, the LORD spoke to the prophet who had brought him back, [21] and he cried out to the man of God who had come from Judah: "The LORD says, 'Because you rebelled against the command of the LORD and did not keep the command which the LORD, your God, gave you, [22] but returned and ate bread and drank water in the place where he told you to do neither, your corpse shall not be brought to the grave of your ancestors.' "

[23] After he had eaten bread and drunk water, the ass was saddled for him, and he again [24] set out. But a lion met him on the road, and killed him. His corpse lay sprawled on the road, and the ass remained standing by it, and so did the lion. [25] Some passersby saw the body lying in the road, with the lion standing beside it, and carried the news to the city where the old prophet lived. [26] On hearing it, the prophet who had brought him back from his journey said: "It is the man of God who rebelled against the command of the LORD. He has delivered him to a lion, which mangled and killed him, as the LORD predicted to him." [27] Then he said to his sons, "Saddle the ass for me."

y 2 Kgs 23, 16.

When they had saddled it, ²⁸he went off and found the body lying in the road with the ass and the lion standing beside it. The lion had not eaten the body nor had it harmed the ass. ²⁹The prophet lifted up the body of the man of God and put it on the ass, and brought it back to the city to mourn over it and to bury it. ³⁰He laid the man's body in his own grave, and they mourned over it: "Alas, my brother!" ³¹After he had buried him, he said to his sons, "When I die, bury me in the grave where the man of God is buried. Lay my remains beside his. ³²For the word of the LORD which he proclaimed against the altar in Bethel and against all the shrines on the high places in the cities of Samaria shall certainly come to pass."

³³Jeroboam did not give up his evil ways after this event, but again made priests for the high places from among the common people. Whoever desired it was consecrated and became a priest of the high places. ³⁴This was a sin on the part of the house of Jeroboam for which it was to be cut off and destroyed from the earth.

CHAPTER 14

Death of Abijah. ¹At that time Abijah, son of Jeroboam, took sick. ²So Jeroboam said to his wife, "Get ready and disguise yourself so that none will recognize you as Jeroboam's wife. Then go to Shiloh, where you will find the prophet Ahijah. It is he who predicted my reign over this people.ᶻ ³Take along ten loaves, some cakes, and a jar of preserves, and go to him. He will tell you what will happen to the child." ⁴The wife of Jeroboam obeyed. She made the journey to Shiloh and entered the house of Ahijah who could not see because age had dimmed his sight.

⁵The LORD had said to Ahijah: "Jeroboam's wife is coming to consult you about her son, for he is sick. This is what you must tell her. When she comes, she will be in disguise." ⁶So Ahijah, hearing the sound of her footsteps as she entered the door, said, "Come in, wife of Jeroboam. Why are you in disguise? I have been commissioned to give you bitter news. ⁷Go, tell Jeroboam, 'This is what the LORD, the God of Israel, says: I exalted you from among the people and made you ruler of my people Israel. ⁸I

deprived the house of David of the kingdom and gave it to you. Yet you have not been like my servant David, who kept my commandments and followed me with his whole heart, doing only what pleased me. ⁹You have done worse than all who preceded you: you have gone and made for yourself strange gods and molten images to provoke me; but me you have cast behind your back. ¹⁰Therefore, I am bringing evil upon the house of Jeroboam: I will cut off every male in Jeroboam's line, whether slave or freeman in Israel, and will burn up the house of Jeroboam completely, as though dung were being burned.ᵃ ¹¹When one of Jeroboam's line dies in the city, dogs will devour him; when one of them dies in the field, he will be devoured by the birds of the sky. For the LORD has spoken!'ᵇ ¹²So leave; go home! As you step inside the city, the child will die, ¹³and all Israel will mourn him and bury him, for he alone of Jeroboam's line will be laid in the grave, since in him alone of Jeroboam's house has something pleasing to the LORD, the God of Israel, been found. ¹⁴Today, at this very moment, the LORD will raise up for himself a king of Israel who will destroy the house of Jeroboam. ¹⁵The LORD will strike Israel like a reed tossed about in the water and will pluck out Israel from this good land which he gave their fathers, scattering them beyond the River, because they made sacred poles for themselves and thus provoked the LORD. ¹⁶He will give up Israel because of the sins Jeroboam has committed and caused Israel to commit."

¹⁷So Jeroboam's wife started back; when she reached Tirzah and crossed the threshold of her house, the child died. ¹⁸He was buried with all Israel mourning him, as the LORD had prophesied through his servant the prophet Ahijah.

¹⁹The rest of the acts of Jeroboam, with his warfare and his reign, are recorded in the book of the chronicles of the kings of Israel. ²⁰The length of Jeroboam's reign was twenty-two years. He rested with his ancestors, and his son Nadab succeeded him as king.

Reign of Rehoboam. ²¹Rehoboam, son of Solomon, reigned in Judah. He was forty-one years old when he became king, and he reigned seventeen years in Jerusa-

z 1 Kgs 11, 29.—a 1 Kgs 15, 29.—b 1 Kgs 16, 4.

lem, the city in which, out of all the tribes of Israel, the LORD chose to be honored. His mother was the Ammonite named Naamah. *c*
²²Judah did evil in the sight of the LORD, and by their sins angered him even more than their fathers had done. ²³They, too, built for themselves high places, pillars, and sacred poles, upon every high hill and under every green tree. ²⁴There were also cult prostitutes in the land. Judah imitated all the abominable practices of the nations whom the LORD had cleared out of the Israelites' way.
²⁵In the fifth year of King Rehoboam, Shishak, king of Egypt, attacked Jerusalem.* ²⁶He took everything, including the treasures of the temple of the LORD and those of the royal palace, as well as all the gold shields made under Solomon. *d* ²⁷To replace them, King Rehoboam had bronze shields made, which he entrusted to the officers of the guard on duty at the entrance of the royal palace. ²⁸Whenever the king visited the temple of the LORD, those on duty would carry the shields, and then return them to the guardroom.
²⁹The rest of the acts of Rehoboam, with all that he did, are recorded in the book of the chronicles of the kings of Judah. ³⁰There was constant warfare between Rehoboam and Jeroboam. ³¹Rehoboam rested with his ancestors; he was buried with them in the City of David. His mother was the Ammonite named Naamah. His son Abijam succeeded him as king.

CHAPTER 15

Reign of Abijam. ¹In the eighteenth year of King Jeroboam, son of Nebat, Abijam became king of Judah; *e* ²he reigned three years in Jerusalem. His mother's name was

c 2 Chr 12, 13.—d 1 Kgs 10, 16.— 2 Chr 13, 1f.—f 2 Sm 1, 4.—g 2 Chr 13, 2.—h 2 Chr 16, 1.

14, 25: *In the fifth year . . . Shishak, king of Egypt, attacked Jerusalem:* c. 926 B.C. According to 2 Chr 12, 1-12, the repentance of King Rehoboam and of the princes of Israel after the warning of the prophet Shemaiah diverted the actual attack on Jerusalem. Shishak, however, *carried off the treasures of the temple of the Lord and of the king's palace* (2 Chr 12, 9). A bas-relief of this Pharaoh in the temple of Aman at Karnak commemorates his conquest of some hundred and fifty Palestinian and Trans-Jordanian cities and towns.

15, 18: *Ben-hadad . . . king of Aram:* Ben-hadad I, third successor of Rezon, who had thrown off the yoke of the Israelites during the reign of Solomon and become king of Aram (11, 23f).

Maacah, daughter of Abishalom. ³He imitated all the sins his father had committed before him, and his heart was not entirely with the LORD, his God, like the heart of his grandfather David. ⁴Yet for David's sake the LORD, his God, gave him a lamp in Jerusalem, raising up his son after him and permitting Jerusalem to endure; ⁵because David had pleased the LORD and did not disobey any of his commands as long as he lived, except in the case of Uriah the Hittite. *f*
⁷The rest of Abijam's acts, with all that he did, are written in the book of the chronicles of the kings of Judah. *g* ⁶There was war between Abijam and Jeroboam. ⁸Abijam rested with his ancestors; he was buried in the City of David, and his son Asa succeeded him as king.
Reign of Asa. ⁹In the twentieth year of Jeroboam, king of Israel, Asa, king of Judah, began to reign; ¹⁰he reigned forty-one years in Jerusalem. His grandmother's name was Maacah, daughter of Abishalom. ¹¹Asa pleased the LORD like his forefather David, ¹²banishing the temple prostitutes from the land and removing all the idols his father had made. ¹³He also deposed his grandmother Maacah from her position as queen mother, because she had made an outrageous object for Asherah. Asa cut down this object and burned it in the Kidron Valley. ¹⁴The high places did not disappear; yet Asa's heart was entirely with the LORD as long as he lived. ¹⁵He brought into the temple of the LORD his father's and his own votive offerings of silver, gold, and various utensils.
¹⁶There was war between Asa and Baasha, king of Israel, as long as they both reigned. ¹⁷Baasha, king of Israel, attacked Judah and fortified Ramah to prevent communication with Asa, king of Judah. *h* ¹⁸Asa then took all the silver and gold remaining in the treasuries of the temple of the LORD and of the royal palace. Entrusting them to his ministers, King Asa sent them to Ben-hadad, son of Tabrimmon, son of Hezion, king of Aram,* resident in Damascus. He said: ¹⁹"There is a treaty between you and me, as there was between your father and my father. I am sending you a present of silver and gold. Go, break your treaty with Baasha, king of Israel, that he may withdraw from me." ²⁰Ben-hadad agreed

1Kgs

with King Asa and sent the leaders of his troops against the cities of Israel. They attacked Ijon, Dan, Abel-beth-maacah, and all Chinnereth, besides all the land of Naphtali. ²¹When Baasha heard of it, he left off fortifying Ramah, and stayed in Tirzah. ²²Then King Asa summoned all Judah without exception, and they carried away the stones and beams with which Baasha was fortifying Ramah. With them King Asa built Geba of Benjamin and Mizpeh.

²³The rest of the acts of Asa, with all his valor and accomplishments, and the cities he built, are written in the book of the chronicles of the kings of Judah. In his old age, Asa had an infirmity in his feet. ²⁴He rested with his ancestors; he was buried in his forefather's City of David, and his son Jehoshaphat succeeded him as king.ⁱ

Reign of Nadab. ²⁵In the second year of Asa, king of Judah, Nadab, son of Jeroboam, became king of Israel; he reigned over Israel two years. ²⁶He did evil in the LORD's sight, imitating his father's conduct and the sin which he had caused Israel to commit. ²⁷Baasha, son of Ahijah, of the house of Issachar, plotted against him and struck him down at Gibbethon of the Philistines, which Nadab and all Israel were besieging. ²⁸Baasha killed him in the third year of Asa, king of Judah, and reigned in his stead. ²⁹Once he was king, he killed off the entire house of Jeroboam, not leaving a single soul to Jeroboam but destroying him utterly, according to the warning which the LORD had pronounced through his servant, Ahijah the Shilonite,ʲ ³⁰because of the sins Jeroboam committed and caused Israel to commit, by which he provoked the LORD, the God of Israel, to anger.

³¹The rest of the acts of Nadab, with all that he did, are written in the book of the chronicles of the kings of Israel. ³²[There was war between Asa and Baasha, king of Israel, as long as they lived.]

Reign of Baasha. ³³In the third year of Asa, king of Judah, Baasha, son of Ahijah, began his twenty-four-year reign over Israel in Tirzah. ³⁴He did evil in the LORD's sight, imitating the conduct of Jeroboam and the sin he had caused Israel to commit.

CHAPTER 16

¹The LORD spoke against Baasha to Jehu, son of Hanani, and said: ²"Inasmuch as I lifted you up from the dust and made you ruler of my people Israel, but you have imitated the conduct of Jeroboam and have caused my people Israel to sin, provoking me to anger by their sins, ³I will destroy you, Baasha, and your house;ᵏ ⁴I will make your house like that of Jeroboam, son of Nebat. If anyone of Baasha's line dies in the city, dogs shall devour him; if he dies in the field, he shall be devoured by the birds of the sky."ˡ

⁵The rest of the acts of Baasha, with all his valor and accomplishments, are written in the book of the chronicles of the kings of Israel.ᵐ ⁶Baasha rested with his ancestors; he was buried in Tirzah, and his son Elah succeeded him as king. ⁷[Through the prophet Jehu, son of Hanani, the LORD had threatened Baasha and his house, because of all the evil Baasha did in the sight of the LORD, provoking him to anger by his evil deeds, so that he became like the house of Jeroboam; and because he killed Nadab.]

Reign of Elah. ⁸In the twenty-sixth year of Asa, king of Judah, Elah, son of Baasha, began his two-year reign over Israel in Tirzah. ⁹His servant Zimri, commander of half his chariots, plotted against him. As he was in Tirzah, drinking to excess in the house of Arza, superintendent of his palace in Tirzah, ¹⁰Zimri entered; he struck and killed him in the twenty-seventh year of Asa, king of Judah, and reigned in his place.ⁿ ¹¹Once he was seated on the royal throne, he killed off the whole house of Baasha, not sparing a single male relative or friend of his. ¹²Zimri destroyed the entire house of Baasha, as the LORD had prophesied to Baasha through the prophet Jehu, ¹³because of all the sins which Baasha and his son Elah committed and caused Israel to commit, provoking the LORD, the God of Israel, to anger by their idols.

¹⁴The rest of the acts of Elah, with all that he did, are written in the book of the chronicles of the kings of Israel.

Reign of Zimri. ¹⁵In the twenty-seventh year of Asa, king of Judah, Zimri

---

i 2 Chr 17, 1.—j 1 Kgs 14, 10; 21, 22.—k 1 Kgs 21, 22.—l 1 Kgs 14, 11.—m 2 Chr 16, 1.—n 2 Kgs 9, 31.

reigned seven days in Tirzah. The army was besieging Gibbethon of the Philistines [16]when they heard that Zimri had formed a conspiracy and had killed the king. So that day in the camp all Israel proclaimed Omri, general of the army, king of Israel. [17]Omri marched up from Gibbethon, accompanied by all Israel, and laid siege to Tirzah. [18]When Zimri saw the city was captured, he entered the citadel of the royal palace and burned down the palace over him. He died [19]because of the sins he had committed, doing evil in the sight of the LORD by imitating the sinful conduct of Jeroboam, thus causing Israel to sin. [20]The rest of the acts of Zimri, with the conspiracy he carried out, are written in the book of the chronicles of the kings of Israel.

[21]At that time the people of Israel were divided, half following Tibni, son of Ginath, to make him king, and half for Omri. [22]The partisans of Omri prevailed over those of Tibni, son of Ginath. Tibni died and Omri became king.

Reign of Omri. [23]In the thirty-first year of Asa, king of Judah, Omri became king; he reigned over Israel twelve years, the first six of them in Tirzah. [24]He then bought the hill of Samaria from Shemer for two silver talents and built upon the hill, naming the city he built Samaria after Shemer, the former owner. [25]But Omri did evil in the LORD's sight beyond any of his predecessors. [26]He closely imitated the sinful conduct of Jeroboam, son of Nebat, causing Israel to sin and to provoke the LORD, the God of Israel, to anger by their idols. [27]The rest of the acts of Omri, with all his valor and accomplishments, are written in the book of the chronicles of the kings of Israel. [28]Omri rested with his ancestors; he was buried in Samaria, and his son Ahab succeeded him as king.

Reign of Ahab. [29]In the thirty-eighth year of Asa, king of Judah, Ahab, son of Omri, became king of Israel; he reigned over

---

o Jos 6, 26.—p Sir 48, 3; Jas 5, 17.—q Lk 4, 26.

17, 1: *Elijah the Tishbite:* one of the most important figures in Old Testament history. As his name indicates ("Yahweh is my God"), Elijah was the successful leader in the struggle to preserve the knowledge and worship of Yahweh against the encroaching worship of Baal introduced into Israel by Jezebel, the Tyrian wife of Ahab. The Elijah cycle of narratives includes, besides the above struggle, miracle stories, denunciations of kings, and a preparation for the prophet's role as eschatological forerunner of the "great day of the Lord"; cf Mal 3, 23-24; Mt 17, 10-13; Lk 1, 17.

Israel in Samaria for twenty-two years. [30]Ahab, son of Omri, did evil in the sight of the LORD more than any of his predecessors. [31]It was not enough for him to imitate the sins of Jeroboam, son of Nebat. He even married Jezebel, daughter of Ethbaal, king of the Sidonians, and went over to the veneration and worship of Baal. [32]Ahab erected an altar to Baal in the temple of Baal which he built in Samaria, [33]and also made a sacred pole. He did more to anger the LORD, the God of Israel, than any of the kings of Israel before him. [34]*o* During his reign, Hiel from Bethel rebuilt Jericho. He lost his first-born son, Abiram, when he laid the foundation, and his youngest son, Segub, when he set up the gates, as the LORD had foretold through Joshua, son of Nun.

III: STORIES OF THE PROPHETS

CHAPTER 17

Drought Predicted by Elijah. [1]Elijah the Tishbite,* from Tishbe in Gilead, said to Ahab: "As the LORD, the God of Israel, lives, whom I serve, during these years there shall be no dew or rain except at my word."*p* [2]The LORD then said to Elijah: [3]"Leave here, go east and hide in the Wadi Cherith, east of the Jordan. [4]You shall drink of the stream, and I have commanded ravens to feed you there." [5]So he left and did as the LORD had commanded. He went and remained by the Wadi Cherith, east of the Jordan. [6]Ravens brought him bread and meat in the morning, and bread and meat in the evening, and he drank from the stream.

Elijah and the Widow. [7]After some time, however, the brook ran dry, because no rain had fallen in the land. [8]So the LORD said to him: [9]"Move on to Zarephath of Sidon and stay there. I have designated a widow there to provide for you." [10]He left and went to Zarephath. As he arrived at the entrance of the city, a widow was gathering sticks there; he called out to her, "Please bring me a small cupful of water to drink."*q* [11]She left to get it, and he called out after her, "Please bring along a bit of bread." [12]"As the LORD, your God, lives," she answered, "I have nothing baked; there is only a handful of flour in my jar and a little oil in my jug. Just now I was

1Kgs

collecting a couple of sticks, to go in and prepare something for myself and my son; when we have eaten it, we shall die." [13]"Do not be afraid," Elijah said to her. "Go and do as you propose. But first make me a little cake and bring it to me. Then you can prepare something for yourself and your son. [14]For the LORD, the God of Israel, says, 'The jar of flour shall not go empty, nor the jug of oil run dry, until the day when the LORD sends rain upon the earth.'" [15]She left and did as Elijah had said. She was able to eat for a year, and he and her son as well; [16]the jar of flour did not go empty, nor the jug of oil run dry, as the LORD had foretold through Elijah.

[17]Some time later the son of the mistress of the house fell sick, and his sickness grew more severe until he stopped breathing. [18]So she said to Elijah, "Why have you done this to me, O man of God? Have you come to me to call attention to my guilt and to kill my son?" [19]"Give me your son," Elijah said to her. Taking him from her lap, he carried him to the upper room where he was staying, and laid him on his own bed. [20]He called out to the LORD: "O LORD, my God, will you afflict even the widow with whom I am staying by killing her son?" [21]Then he stretched himself out upon the child three times and called out to the LORD: "O LORD, my God, let the life breath return to the body of this child." [22]The LORD heard the prayer of Elijah; the life breath returned to the child's body and he revived. [23]Taking the child, Elijah brought him down into the house from the upper room and gave him to his mother. "See!" Elijah said to her, "your son is alive." [24]"Now indeed I know that you are a man of God," the woman replied to Elijah. "The word of the LORD comes truly from your mouth."

CHAPTER 18

Elijah and the Prophets of Baal. [1]Long afterward, in the third year, the LORD spoke to Elijah. "Go, present yourself to Ahab," he said, "that I may send rain upon the earth." [2]So Elijah went to present himself to Ahab.

[3]Now the famine in Samaria was bitter, [4]and Ahab had summoned Obadiah, his vizier, who was a zealous follower of the LORD. When Jezebel was murdering the prophets of the LORD, Obadiah took

a hundred prophets, hid them away fifty each in two caves, and supplied them with food and drink. [5]Ahab said to Obadiah, "Come, let us go through the land to all sources of water and to all the streams. We may find grass and save the horses and mules, so that we shall not have to slaughter any of the beasts." [6]Dividing the land to explore between them, Ahab went one way by himself, Obadiah another way by himself.

[7]As Obadiah was on his way, Elijah met him. Recognizing him, Obadiah fell prostrate and asked, "Is it you, my lord Elijah?" [8]"Yes," he answered. "Go tell your master, 'Elijah is here!'" [9]But Obadiah said, "What sin have I committed, that you are handing me over to Ahab to have me killed? [10]As the LORD, your God, lives, there is no nation or kingdom where my master has not sent in search of you. When they replied, 'He is not here,' he made each kingdom and nation swear they could not find you. [11]And now you say, 'Go tell your master: Elijah is here!' [12]After I leave you, the spirit of the LORD will carry you to some place I do not know, and when I go to inform Ahab and he does not find you, he will kill me. Your servant has revered the LORD from his youth. [13]Have you not been told, my lord, what I did when Jezebel was murdering the prophets of the LORD—that I hid a hundred of the prophets of the LORD, fifty each in two caves, and supplied them with food and drink? [14]And now you say, 'Go tell your master: Elijah is here!' He will kill me!" [15]Elijah answered, "As the LORD of hosts lives, whom I serve, I will present myself to him today."

[16]So Obadiah went to meet Ahab and informed him. Ahab came to meet Elijah, [17]and when he saw Elijah, said to him, "Is it you, you disturber of Israel?" [18]"It is not I who disturb Israel," he answered, "but you and your family, by forsaking the commands of the LORD and following the Baals. [19]Now summon all Israel to me on Mount Carmel, as well as the four hundred and fifty prophets of Baal and the four hundred prophets of Asherah who eat at Jezebel's table." [20]So Ahab sent to all the Israelites and had the prophets assemble on Mount Carmel.

[21]Elijah appealed to all the people and said, "How long will you straddle the issue? If the LORD is God, follow him; if

Baal, follow him." The people, however, did not answer him. ²²So Elijah said to the people, "I am the only surviving prophet of the LORD, and there are four hundred and fifty prophets of Baal. ²³Give us two young bulls. Let them choose one, cut it into pieces, and place it on the wood, but start no fire. I shall prepare the other and place it on the wood, but shall start no fire. ²⁴You shall call on your gods, and I will call on the LORD. The God who answers with fire is God." All the people answered, "Agreed!"

²⁵Elijah then said to the prophets of Baal, "Choose one young bull and prepare it first, for there are more of you. Call upon your gods, but do not start the fire." ²⁶Taking the young bull that was turned over to them, they prepared it and called on Baal from morning to noon, saying, "Answer us, Baal!" But there was no sound, and no one answering. And they hopped around the altar they had prepared. ²⁷When it was noon, Elijah taunted them: "Call louder, for he is a god and may be meditating, or may have retired, or may be on a journey. Perhaps he is asleep and must be awakened." ²⁸They called out louder and slashed themselves with swords and spears, as was their custom, until blood gushed over them. ²⁹Noon passed and they remained in a prophetic state until the time for offering sacrifice. But there was not a sound; no one answered, and no one was listening.

³⁰Then Elijah said to all the people, "Come here to me." When they had done so, he repaired the altar of the LORD which had been destroyed. ³¹He took twelve stones, for the number of tribes of the sons of Jacob, to whom the LORD had said, "Your name shall be Israel." ³²He built an altar in honor of the LORD with the stones, and made a trench around the altar large enough for two seahs of grain. ³³When he had arranged the wood, he cut up the young bull and laid it on the wood. ³⁴"Fill four jars with water," he said, "and pour it over the holocaust and over the wood." "Do it again," he said, and they did it again. "Do it a third time," he said, and they did it a third time. ³⁵The water flowed around the altar, and the trench was filled with the water.

³⁶At the time for offering sacrifice, the prophet Elijah came forward and said, "LORD, God of Abraham, Isaac, and Israel, let it be known this day that you are God in Israel and that I am your servant and have done all these things by your command. ³⁷Answer me, LORD! Answer me, that this people may know that you, LORD, are God and that you have brought them back to their senses." ³⁸The LORD's fire came down and consumed the holocaust, wood, stones, and dust, and it lapped up the water in the trench. ³⁹Seeing this, all the people fell prostrate and said, "The LORD is God! The LORD is God!" ⁴⁰Then Elijah said to them, "Seize the prophets of Baal. Let none of them escape!" They were seized, and Elijah had them brought down to the brook Kishon and there he slit their throats.

⁴¹Elijah then said to Ahab, "Go up, eat and drink, for there is the sound of a heavy rain." ⁴²So Ahab went up to eat and drink, while Elijah climbed to the top of Carmel, crouched down to the earth, and put his head between his knees. ⁴³"Climb up and look out to sea," he directed his servant, who went up and looked, but reported, "There is nothing." Seven times he said, "Go, look again!" ⁴⁴And the seventh time the youth reported, "There is a cloud as small as a man's hand rising from the sea." Elijah said, "Go and say to Ahab, 'Harness up and leave the mountain before the rain stops you.' " ⁴⁵In a trice, the sky grew dark with clouds and wind, and a heavy rain fell. Ahab mounted his chariot and made for Jezreel. ⁴⁶But the hand of the LORD was on Elijah, who girded up his clothing and ran before Ahab as far as the approaches to Jezreel.

CHAPTER 19

Flight to Horeb. ¹Ahab told Jezebel all that Elijah had done—that he had put all the prophets to the sword. ²Jezebel then sent a messenger to Elijah and said, "May the gods do thus and so to me if by this time tomorrow I have not done with your life what was done to each of them." ³Elijah was afraid and fled for his life, going to Beer-sheba of Judah. He left his servant there ⁴and went a day's journey into the desert, until he came to a broom tree and sat beneath it. He prayed for death: "This is enough,

O LORD! Take my life, for I am no better than my fathers." ⁵He lay down and fell asleep under the broom tree, but then an angel touched him and ordered him to get up and eat. ⁶He looked and there at his head was a hearth cake and a jug of water. After he ate and drank, he lay down again, ⁷but the angel of the LORD came back a second time, touched him, and ordered, "Get up and eat, else the journey will be too long for you!" ⁸He got up, ate and drank; then strengthened by that food, he walked forty days and forty nights to the mountain of God, Horeb.
⁹There he came to a cave, where he took shelter. But the word of the LORD came to him, "Why are you here, Elijah?" ¹⁰He answered: "I have been most zealous for the LORD, the God of hosts, but the Israelites have forsaken your covenant, torn down your altars, and put your prophets to the sword. I alone am left, and they seek to take my life." ¹¹ * Then the LORD said, "Go outside and stand on the mountain before the LORD; the LORD will be passing by." A strong and heavy wind was rending the mountains and crushing rocks before the LORD—but the LORD was not in the wind. After the wind there was an earthquake—but the LORD was not in the earthquake. ¹²After the earthquake there was fire—but the LORD was not in the fire. After the fire there was a tiny whispering sound. ¹³When he heard this, Elijah hid his face in his cloak and went and stood at the entrance of the cave. A voice said to him, "Elijah, why are you here?" ¹⁴He replied, "I have been most zealous for the LORD, the God of hosts. But the Israelites have forsaken your covenant, torn down your altars, and put your prophets to the sword. I alone am left, and they seek to take my life."ʳ ¹⁵ * "Go, take the road back to the desert near Damascus," the LORD said to him. "When you arrive, you shall anoint Hazael as king of Aram. ¹⁶Then you shall anoint Jehu, son of Nimshi, as king of Israel, and Elisha, son of Shaphat of Abelmeholah, as prophet to succeed you.ˢ ¹⁷If anyone escapes the sword of Hazael, Jehu will kill him. If he escapes the sword of Jehu, Elisha will kill him. ¹⁸Yet I will leave seven thousand men in Israel—all those who have not knelt to Baal or kissed him."ᵗ

Call of Elisha.* ¹⁹Elijah set out, and came upon Elisha, son of Shaphat, as he was plowing with twelve yoke of oxen; he was following the twelfth. Elijah went over to him and threw his cloak over him. ²⁰Elisha left the oxen, ran after Elijah, and said, "Please, let me kiss my father and mother goodbye, and I will follow you." "Go back!" Elijah answered. "Have I done anything to you?" ²¹Elisha left him and, taking the yoke of oxen, slaughtered them; he used the plowing equipment for fuel to boil their flesh, and gave it to his people to eat. Then he left and followed Elijah as his attendant.

CHAPTER 20

Ahab's Victories over Ben-hadad. ¹Benhadad, king of Aram, gathered all his forces, and accompanied by thirty-two kings with horses and chariotry, proceeded to invest and attack Samaria. ²He sent couriers to Ahab, king of Israel, within the city, ³and said to him, "This is Benhadad's message: 'Your silver and gold are mine, and your wives and your promising sons are mine.' " ⁴The king of Israel answered, "As you say, my lord king, I and all I have are yours." ⁵But the couriers came again and said, "This is Ben-hadad's message: 'I sent you word to give me your silver and gold, your wives and your sons. ⁶Now, however, at this time tomorrow I will send my servants to you, and they shall ransack your house and the houses of your servants. They shall seize and take away whatever they consider valuable.' "
⁷The king of Israel then summoned all the elders of the land and said: "Under-

---

r Rom 11, 3.—s 2 Kgs 9, 2.—t Rom 11, 4.

19, 11ff: Compare these divine manifestations to Elijah with those to Moses (Ex 19, 1-23; 33, 21ff; 34, 5) on the same Mount Horeb (Sinai) (Dt 4, 10-15). Though various phenomena, such as wind, storms, earthquakes, fire (Ex 19, 18f), herald the divine presence, they do not constitute the presence itself which, like the *tiny whispering sound*, is imperceptible and bespeaks the spirituality of God. It was fitting that Elijah, whose mission it was to reestablish the covenant and restore the pure faith, should have returned to Horeb where the covenant was revealed to Moses and through him to the Israelite people (Ex 3, 1-4. 17; 33, 18—34, 9). Moses and Elijah appeared with Christ at the time of his transfiguration (Mt 17, 1-9; Mk 9, 1-7; Lk 9, 28-36).
19, 15-17: Elijah himself carried out only the third of the commissions entrusted to him (vv 19-21); Elisha was deputed to perform the first in person (2 Kgs 8, 7-19), and the second through one of his followers (2 Kgs 9, 1-10).
19, 19-21: Elijah's act of throwing his mantle over the shoulders of Elisha expressed the divine call to share the prophetic mission. Elisha's prompt response through destruction of his plow and oxen is an example of total obedience and detachment from his former manner of living in order to promote the glory of God.

stand clearly that this man wants to ruin us. When he sent to me for my wives and sons, my silver and my gold, I did not refuse him." [8]All the elders and all the people said to him, "Do not listen. Do not give in." [9]Accordingly he directed the couriers of Ben-hadad, "Say to my lord the king, 'I will do all that you demanded of your servant the first time. But this I cannot do.' " The couriers left and reported this. [10]Ben-hadad then sent him the message, "May the gods do thus and so to me if there is enough dust in Samaria to make handfuls for all my followers." [11]The king of Israel replied, "Tell him, 'It is not for the man who is buckling his armor to boast as though he were taking it off.' " [12]Ben-hadad was drinking in the pavilions with the kings when he heard this reply. "Prepare the assault," he commanded his servants; and they made ready to storm the city.

[13]Then a prophet came up to Ahab, king of Israel, and said: "The LORD says, 'Do you see all this huge army? When I deliver it up to you today, you will know that I am the LORD.' " [14]But Ahab asked, "Through whom will it be delivered up?" He answered, "The LORD says, 'Through the retainers of the governors of the provinces.' " Then Ahab asked, "Who is to attack?" He replied, "You are." [15]So Ahab called up the retainers of the governors of the provinces, two hundred thirty-two of them. Behind them he mustered all the Israelite soldiery, who numbered seven thousand. [16]They marched out at noon, while Ben-hadad was drinking heavily in the pavilions with the thirty-two kings who were his allies. [17]When the retainers of the governors of the provinces marched out first, Ben-hadad received word that some men had marched out of Samaria. [18]He answered, "Whether they have come out for peace or for war, in any case take them alive." [19]But when these had come out of the city—the soldiers of the governors of the provinces with the army following them—[20]each of them struck down his man. The Arameans fled with Israel pursuing them, while Ben-hadad, king of Aram, escaped on a chariot steed. [21]The king of Israel went out, took the horses and chariots, and inflicted a severe defeat on Aram.

[22]Then the prophet went up to the king of Israel and said to him: "Go, regroup your forces. Mark well what you do, for at the beginning of the year* the king of Aram will attack you." [23]On the other hand, the servants of the king of Aram said to him: "Their gods are gods of mountains. That is why they defeated us. But if we fight them on level ground, we shall be sure to defeat them. [24]This is what you must do: Take the kings from their posts and put prefects in their places. [25]Mobilize an army as large as the army that has deserted you, horse for horse, chariot for chariot. Let us fight them on level ground, and we shall surely defeat them." He took their advice and did this.

[26]At the beginning of the year, Ben-hadad mobilized Aram and went up to Aphek to fight against Israel. [27]The Israelites, too, were called to arms and supplied with provisions; then they went out to engage the foe. The Israelites, encamped opposite them, seemed like a couple of small flocks of goats, while Aram covered the countryside. [28]A man of God came up and said to the king of Israel: "The LORD says, 'Because Aram has said the LORD is a god of mountains, not a god of plains, I will deliver up to you all this large army, that you may know I am the LORD.' " [29]They were encamped opposite each other for seven days. On the seventh day battle was joined, and the Israelites struck down one hundred thousand foot soldiers of Aram in one day. [30]The survivors, twenty-seven thousand of them, fled into the city of Aphek, and there the wall collapsed. Ben-hadad, too, fled, and took refuge within the city, in an inside room.

[31]His servants said to him: "We have heard that the kings of the land of Israel are merciful kings. Allow us, therefore, to garb ourselves in sackcloth, with cords around our heads, and go out to the king of Israel. Perhaps he will spare your life." [32]So they dressed in sackcloth girded at the waist, and wearing cords around their heads, they went to the king of Israel. "Your servant Ben-hadad pleads for his life," they said. "Is he still alive?" the king asked. "He is my brother." [33]Hearing this as a good omen, the men quickly took him at his word and said, "Ben-hadad is your brother." He answered, "Go and get him." When Ben-hadad came out to him, the king had him mount his chariot. [34]Ben-

---

20, 22: *At the beginning of the year:* in the spring.

hadad said to him, "I will restore the cities which my father took from your father, and you may make yourself bazaars in Damascus, as my father did in Samaria." "On these terms," Ahab replied, "I will set you free." So he made an agreement with him and then set him free.

35 One of the guild prophets was prompted by the LORD to say to his companion, "Strike me." But he refused to strike him. 36 Then he said to him, "Since you did not obey the voice of the LORD, a lion will kill you when you leave me." When they parted company, a lion came upon him and killed him. 37 The prophet met another man and said, "Strike me." The man struck him a blow and wounded him. 38 The prophet went on and waited for the king on the road, having disguised himself with a bandage over his eyes. 39 As the king was passing, he called out to the king and said, "Your servant went into the thick of the battle, and suddenly someone turned and brought me a man and said, 'Guard this man. If he is missing, you shall have to pay for his life with your life or pay out a talent of silver.' 40 But while your servant was looking here and there, the man disappeared." The king of Israel said to him, "That is your sentence. You have decided it yourself." 41 He immediately removed the bandage from his eyes, and the king of Israel recognized him as one of the prophets. 42 He said to him: "The LORD says, 'Because you have set free the man I doomed to destruction, your life shall pay for his life, your people for his people.'" Disturbed and angry, the king of Israel went off homeward and entered Samaria. *u*

CHAPTER 21

Seizure of Naboth's Vineyard. 1 Some time after this, as Naboth the Jezreelite had a vineyard in Jezreel next to the palace of Ahab, king of Samaria, 2 Ahab said to Naboth, "Give me your vineyard to be my vegetable garden, since it is close by, next to my house. I will give you a better vineyard in exchange, or, if you prefer, I will give you its value in money." 3 "The LORD forbid," Naboth answered him, "that I should give you my ancestral heritage." 4 Ahab went home disturbed and angry at the answer Naboth the Jezreelite had made to him:

"I will not give you my ancestral heritage." Lying down on his bed, he turned away from food and would not eat.

5 His wife Jezebel came to him and said to him, "Why are you so angry that you will not eat?" 6 He answered her, "Because I spoke to Naboth the Jezreelite and said to him, 'Sell me your vineyard, or, if you prefer, I will give you a vineyard in exchange.' But he refused to let me have his vineyard." 7 "A fine ruler over Israel you are indeed!" his wife Jezebel said to him. "Get up. Eat and be cheerful. I will obtain the vineyard of Naboth the Jezreelite for you."

8 So she wrote letters in Ahab's name and, having sealed them with his seal, sent them to the elders and to the nobles who lived in the same city with Naboth. 9 This is what she wrote in the letters: "Proclaim a fast and set Naboth at the head of the people. 10 Next, get two scoundrels to face him and accuse him of having cursed God and king. Then take him out and stone him to death." 11 His fellow citizens—the elders and the nobles who dwelt in his city—did as Jezebel had ordered them in writing, through the letters she had sent them. 12 They proclaimed a fast and placed Naboth at the head of the people. 13 Two scoundrels came in and confronted him with the accusation, "Naboth has cursed God and king." And they led him out of the city and stoned him to death. 14 Then they sent the information to Jezebel that Naboth had been stoned to death.

15 When Jezebel learned that Naboth had been stoned to death, she said to Ahab, "Go on, take possession of the vineyard of Naboth the Jezreelite which he refused to sell you, because Naboth is not alive, but dead." 16 On hearing that Naboth was dead, Ahab started off on his way down to the vineyard of Naboth the Jezreelite, to take possession of it.

17 But the LORD said to Elijah the Tishbite: 18 "Start down to meet Ahab, king of Israel, who rules in Samaria. He will be in the vineyard of Naboth, of which he has come to take possession. 19 * *v* This is what you shall tell him, 'The LORD says: After murdering, do you also take posses-

---

u 1 Kgs 22, 35.—v 1 Kgs 22, 38.

21, 19: The response of Ahab to this divine judgment is described in v 27, and the consequences are given in vv 28-29, and in 2 Kgs 9, 21-26.

sion? For this, the Lord says: In the place where the dogs licked up the blood of Naboth, the dogs shall lick up your blood, too.' " [20] * "Have you found me out, my enemy?" Ahab said to Elijah. "Yes," he answered. "Because you have given yourself up to doing evil in the LORD's sight, [21] I am bringing evil upon you: I will destroy you and will cut off every male in Ahab's line, whether slave or freeman, in Israel.[w] [22] I will make your house like that of Jeroboam, son of Nebat, and like that of Baasha, son of Ahijah, because of how you have provoked me by leading Israel into sin."[x] [23] (Against Jezebel, too, the LORD declared, "The dogs shall devour Jezebel in the district of Jezreel.")[y] [24] "When one of Ahab's line dies in the city, dogs will devour him; when one of them dies in the field, the birds of the sky will devour him." [25] Indeed, no one gave himself up to the doing of evil in the sight of the LORD as did Ahab, urged on by his wife Jezebel. [26] He became completely abominable by following idols, just as the Amorites had done, whom the LORD drove out before the Israelites. [27] When Ahab heard these words, he tore his garments and put on sackcloth over his bare flesh. He fasted, slept in the sackcloth, and went about subdued. [28] Then the LORD said to Elijah the Tishbite, [29] "Have you seen that Ahab has humbled himself before me? Since he has humbled himself before me, I will not bring the evil in his time. I will bring the evil upon his house during the reign of his son."[z]

CHAPTER 22

Campaign against Ramoth-gilead. [1] Three years passed without war between Aram and Israel.[a] [2] In the third year, however, King Jehoshaphat of Judah came down to

---

w 2 Kgs 9, 8.—x 1 Kgs 15, 29; 16, 3.—y 2 Kgs 9, 36.—z 2 Kgs 9, 26.—a 2 Chr 18, 1.

21, 20-26: In these verses the Judean editor of the Books of Kings substitutes, for the message of Elijah prepared for in v 19, a sweeping and definitive judgment against the whole family of Ahab in the same terms as were used against the families of Jeroboam I (1 Kgs 14, 9-11) and Baasha (1 Kgs 16, 2-4). This judgment is the fruit of later theological reflection; it is not occasioned directly by the crime against Naboth, but by the idolatry of Ahab and Jezebel. The judgment on Jezebel herself (v 23) may have been uttered by Elijah during the Naboth episode; it finds its fulfillment in 2 Kgs 9, 36-37. Still another theological explanation for the death of Ahab is given by the north Israelite writer of 1 Kgs 20, 35-42 above.

the king of Israel, [3] who said to his servants, "Do you not know that Ramoth-gilead is ours and we are doing nothing to take it from the king of Aram?" [4] He asked Jehoshaphat, "Will you come with me to fight against Ramoth-gilead?" Jehoshaphat answered the king of Israel, "You and I are as one, and your people and my people, your horses and my horses as well." [5] Jehoshaphat also said to the king of Israel, "Seek the word of the LORD at once."

[6] The king of Israel gathered together the prophets, about four hundred of them, and asked, "Shall I go to attack Ramoth-gilead or shall I refrain?" "Go up," they answered. "The Lord will deliver it over to the king." [7] But Jehoshaphat said, "Is there no other prophet of the Lord here whom we may consult?" [8] The king of Israel answered, "There is one other through whom we might consult the Lord, Micaiah, son of Imlah; but I hate him because he prophesies not good but evil about me." Jehoshaphat said, "Let not your majesty speak of evil against you."

[9] So the king of Israel called an official and said to him, "Get Micaiah, son of Imlah, at once." [10] The king of Israel and King Jehoshaphat of Judah were seated, each on his throne, clothed in their robes of state on a threshing floor at the entrance of the gate of Samaria, and all the prophets were prophesying before them. [11] Zedekiah, son of Chenaanah, made himself horns of iron and said, "The Lord says, 'With these you shall gore Aram until you have destroyed them.' " [12] The other prophets prophesied in a similar vein, saying: "Go up to Ramoth-gilead; you shall succeed. The Lord will deliver it over to the king."

[13] The messenger who had gone to call Micaiah said to him, "Look now, the prophets are unanimously predicting good for the king. Let your word be the same as any of theirs; predict good." [14] "As the Lord lives," Micaiah answered, "I shall say whatever the Lord tells me."

[15] When he came to the king, the king said to him, "Micaiah, shall we go to fight against Ramoth-gilead, or shall we refrain?" "Go up," he answered, "you shall succeed! The Lord will deliver it over to the king." [16] But the king answered him, "How many times must I adjure you to tell

1Kgs

me nothing but the truth in the name of the Lord?" [17]So Micaiah said:

"I see all Israel
scattered on the mountains,
like sheep without a shepherd,
and the LORD saying, 'These have no
    master!
Let each of them go back home in
    peace.' "

[18]The king of Israel said to Jehoshaphat, "Did I not tell you he prophesies not good but evil about me?" [19] * Micaiah continued: "Therefore hear the word of the LORD: I saw the LORD seated on his throne, with the whole host of heaven standing by to his right and to his left. [20]The LORD asked, 'Who will deceive Ahab, so that he will go up and fall at Ramoth-gilead?' And one said this, another that, [21]until one of the spirits came forth and presented himself to the LORD, saying, 'I will deceive him.' The LORD asked, 'How?' [22]He answered, 'I will go forth and become a lying spirit in the mouths of all his prophets.' The LORD replied, 'You shall succeed in deceiving him. Go forth and do this.' [23]So now, the LORD has put a lying spirit in the mouths of all these prophets of yours, but the LORD himself has decreed evil against you."

[24]Thereupon Zedekiah, son of Chenaanah, came up and slapped Micaiah on the cheek, saying, "Has the spirit of the LORD, then, left me to speak with you?" [25]"You shall find out," Micaiah replied, "on that day when you retreat into an inside room to hide." [26]The king of Israel then said, "Seize Micaiah and take him back to Amon, prefect of the city, and to Joash, the king's son, [27]and say, 'This is the king's order: Put this man in prison and feed him scanty rations of bread and water until I return in safety.' " [28]But Micaiah said, "If ever you return in safety, the LORD has not spoken through me."*

[29]The king of Israel and King Jehoshaphat of Judah went up to Ramoth-gilead, [30]and the king of Israel said to Jehoshaphat, "I will disguise myself and go into battle, but you put on your own clothes." So the king of Israel disguised himself and entered the fray. [31]In the meantime the king of Aram had given his thirty-two chariot commanders the order, "Do not fight with anyone at all except the king of Israel." [32]When the chariot commanders saw Jehoshaphat, they cried out, "That must be the king of Israel!" and shifted to fight him. But Jehoshaphat shouted his battle cry, [33]and the chariot commanders, aware that he was not the king of Israel, gave up pursuit of him. [34]Someone, however, drew his bow at random, and hit the king of Israel between the joints of his breastplate. He ordered his charioteer, "Rein about and take me out of the ranks, for I am disabled." [35]The battle grew fierce during the day, and the king, who was propped up in his chariot facing the Arameans, died in the evening. The blood from his wound flowed to the bottom of the chariot. *b* [36]At sunset a cry went through the army, "Every man to his city, every man to his land, [37]for the king is dead!" So they went to Samaria, where they buried the king. [38]When the chariot was washed at the pool of Samaria, the dogs licked up his blood and harlots bathed there, as the LORD had prophesied. *c*

[39]The rest of the acts of Ahab, with all that he did, including the ivory palace and all the cities he built, are recorded in the book of the chronicles of the kings of Israel. [40]Ahab rested with his ancestors, and his son Ahaziah succeeded him as king.

Reign of Jehoshaphat. [41]Jehoshaphat, son of Asa, began to reign over Judah in the fourth year of Ahab, king of Israel. [42]Jehoshaphat was thirty-five years old when he began to reign, and he reigned twenty-five years in Jerusalem. His mother's name was Azubah, daughter of Shilhi. [43]He followed all the ways of his father Asa unswervingly, doing what was right in the LORD's sight. [44]Nevertheless, the high places did not disappear, and the people continued to sacrifice and to burn incense on the high places. [45]Jehoshaphat also made peace with the king of Israel. [46]The rest of the acts of Jehoshaphat, with his prowess, what he did and how he fought, are recorded in the book of the chronicles of the kings of Judah.

---

b 1 Kgs 20, 42.—c 1 Kgs 21, 19.

22, 19-23: The prophet Micaiah uses as a last resort to deter Ahab from his foolhardy design of fighting against Ramoth-gilead the literary device of describing false prophets as messengers of a lying spirit which God, after holding counsel with his angels, permits to deceive them.
22, 28: A note in the Hebrew text after this verse attributes to Micaiah ben Imlah the first words of the book of a different Micaiah, the minor prophet of Moresheth.

⁴⁷He removed from the land the rest of the cult prostitutes who had remained in the reign of his father Asa. ⁴⁸There was no king in Edom, but an appointed regent. ⁴⁹Jehoshaphat made Tarshish ships to go to Ophir for gold; but in fact the ships did not go, because they were wrecked at Ezion-geber. ⁵⁰Then Ahaziah, son of Ahab, said to Jehoshaphat, "Let my servants accompany your servants in the ships." But Jehoshaphat would not agree.

22, 52: *Seventeeth year:* so the present Hebrew text. More consistent with 2 Kgs 1, 17 would be a date in the twenty-fourth year of Jehoshaphat for Ahab's death; see note on 2 Kgs 1, 1.

⁵¹Jehoshaphat rested with his ancestors; he was buried in his forefathers' City of David. His son Jehoram succeeded him as king.

Reign of Ahaziah. ⁵²Ahaziah, son of Ahab, began to reign over Israel in Samaria in the seventeenth year* of Jehoshaphat, king of Judah; he reigned two years over Israel. ⁵³He did evil in the sight of the LORD, behaving like his father, his mother, and Jeroboam, son of Nebat, who caused Israel to sin. ⁵⁴He served and worshiped Baal, thus provoking the LORD, the God of Israel, just as his father had done.

2Kgs

THE SECOND BOOK OF KINGS

IV: THE KINGDOMS OF ISRAEL AND JUDAH

CHAPTER 1

Ahaziah Consults Baalzebub. ¹After Ahab's death, Moab rebelled against Israel.ᵃ ²Ahaziah had fallen through the lattice of his roof terrace at Samaria and had been injured. So he sent out messengers with the instructions: "Go and inquire of Baalzebub,* the god of Ekron, whether I shall recover from this injury."

³Meanwhile, the angel of the LORD said to Elijah the Tishbite: "Go, intercept the messengers of Samaria's king, and ask them, 'Is it because there is no God in Israel that you are going to inquire of Baalzebub, the god of Ekron?' ⁴For this, the LORD says: 'You shall not leave the bed upon which you lie; instead, you shall die.' " And with that, Elijah departed. ⁵The messengers then returned to Ahaziah, who asked them, "Why have you

a 2 Kgs 3, 4-27.—b Zec 13, 4.—c Lv 10, 2; Sir 48, 3f; Lk 9, 54f.

1, 2: *Baalzebub:* in this form, "Baal of flies." The name in the Hebrew text is a derisive alteration of Baalzebul, "Prince Baal." The best New Testament evidence supports the latter form in Mt 10, 25; Lk 11, 15. Later associations with Aramaic *beeldebaba,* "enemy," gave the ancient name its connotation of "devil."

1, 8: *Hairy garment:* a sign of ascetical and prophetic calling, imitated by John the Baptizer; see Mt 3, 4; Mk 1, 6.

1, 12: *Divine fire:* literally, "fire of God," which in Hebrew sounds quite like *man of God.* The play on words is the basis for Elijah's alleged retort. This story was told among the people to enhance the dignity of the prophet and to reflect the power of God whom he served. The mercy which God extends even to the wicked is described in Wis 11, 17—12, 22, and the prophet Elijah was well aware of it (1 Kgs 21, 28f).

returned?" ⁶"A man came up to us," they answered, "who said to us, 'Go back to the king who sent you and tell him: The LORD says, Is it because there is no God in Israel that you are sending to inquire of Baalzebub, the god of Ekron? For this you shall not leave the bed upon which you lie; instead, you shall die.' " ⁷The king asked them, "What was the man like who came up to you and said these things to you?" ⁸"Wearing a hairy garment,"* they replied, "with a leather girdle about his loins." "It is Elijah the Tishbite!" he exclaimed.ᵇ

Death of Two Captains. ⁹Then the king sent a captain with his company of fifty men after Elijah. The prophet was seated on a hilltop when he found him. "Man of God," he ordered, "the king commands you to come down." ¹⁰"If I am a man of God," Elijah answered the captain, "may fire come down from heaven and consume you and your fifty men." And fire came down from heaven and consumed him and his fifty men.ᶜ ¹¹Ahaziah sent another captain with his company of fifty men after Elijah. "Man of God," he called out to Elijah, "the king commands you to come down immediately." ¹²"If I am a man of God," Elijah answered him, "may fire come down from heaven and consume you and your fifty men." And divine fire* came down from heaven, consuming him and his fifty men.

Death of the King. ¹³Again, for the third time, Ahaziah sent a captain with his company of fifty men. When the third captain arrived, he fell to his knees before Elijah, pleading with him. "Man of God," he implored him, "let my life and the lives of these fifty men, your servants, count for something in your sight! ¹⁴ Already fire has come down from heaven, consuming two captains with their companies of fifty men. But now, let my life mean something to you!" ¹⁵ Then the angel of the LORD said to Elijah, "Go down with him; you need not be afraid of him."

¹⁶ So Elijah left and went down with him and stated to the king: "Thus says the LORD: 'Because you sent messengers to inquire of Baalzebub, the god of Ekron, you shall not leave the bed upon which you lie; instead you shall die.' "*d*

¹⁷ Ahaziah died in fulfillment of the prophecy of the LORD spoken by Elijah. Since he had no son, his brother Joram* succeeded him as king, in the second year of Jehoram, son of Jehoshaphat, king of Judah. ¹⁸ The rest of the acts of Ahaziah are recorded in the book of chronicles of the kings of Israel.

CHAPTER 2

Elijah and Elisha. ¹ When the LORD was about to take Elijah up to heaven in a whirlwind, he and Elisha were on their way from Gilgal.* ² "Stay here, please," Elijah said to Elisha. "The LORD has sent me on to Bethel." "As the LORD lives, and as you yourself live," Elisha replied, "I will not leave you." So they went down to Bethel, ³ where the guild prophets went out to Elisha and asked him, "Do you know that the LORD will take your master from over you today?" "Yes, I know it," he replied. "Keep still."

⁴ Then Elijah said to him, "Stay here, please, Elisha, for the LORD has sent me on to Jericho." "As the LORD lives, and as you yourself live," Elisha replied, "I will not leave you." ⁵ They went on to Jericho, where the guild prophets approached Elisha and asked him, "Do you know that the LORD will take your master from over you today?" "Yes, I know it," he replied. "Keep still."

⁶ Elijah said to Elisha, "Please stay here; the LORD has sent me on to the Jordan." "As the LORD lives, and as you yourself live," Elisha replied, "I will not leave you." And so the two went on together.

⁷ Fifty of the guild prophets followed, and when the two stopped at the Jordan, stood facing them at a distance. ⁸ Elijah took his mantle, rolled it up and struck the water, which divided, and both crossed over on dry ground.*e*

Elisha Succeeds Elijah. ⁹ When they had crossed over, Elijah said to Elisha, "Ask for whatever I may do for you, before I am taken from you." Elisha answered, "May I receive a double portion of your spirit."* ¹⁰ "You have asked something that is not easy," he replied. "Still, if you see me taken up from you, your wish will be granted; otherwise not."*f* ¹¹ As they walked on conversing, a flaming chariot and flaming horses came between them, and Elijah went up to heaven in a whirlwind.*g* ¹² When Elisha saw it happen he cried out, "My father!* my father! Israel's chariots and drivers!" But when he could no longer see him, Elisha gripped his own garment and tore it in two.*h*

¹³ Then he picked up Elijah's mantle which had fallen from him, and went back and stood at the bank of the Jordan.*i* ¹⁴ Wielding the mantle which had fallen from Elijah, he struck the water in his turn and said, "Where is the LORD, the God of Elijah?" When Elisha struck the water it divided and he crossed over.

¹⁵ The guild prophets in Jericho, who were on the other side, saw him and said "The spirit of Elijah rests on Elisha." They went to meet him, bowing to the ground before him. ¹⁶ "Among your ser-

---

d Sir 48, 6.—e Ex 14, 16. 22.—f Nm 11, 17. 25.—g Gn 5, 24; 1 Mc 2, 58; Acts 1, 9.—h 2 Kgs 13, 14; Sir 48, 9. 12.—i 1 Kgs 19, 19.

1, 17: *Joram:* in the Second Book of Kings the name Joram *(yoram),* alternately Jehoram *(yehoram),* appears in numerous passages to designate both the king of Judah, son and successor of Jehoshaphat (848-841 B.C.), and the contemporary king of Israel, son of Ahab (852-841 B.C.). For the convenience of the reader in distinguishing these two kings, the longer form, Jehoram, is used to designate the king of Judah and the shorter form, Joram, to designate the king of Israel. See note on 2 Kgs 3, 1.

2, 1: *Gilgal:* commonly identified with Jiljulieh, about seven miles north of Bethel, and different from the Gilgal in Dt 11, 30 near Shechem, and that in Jos 4 and 5, passim, near Jericho.

2, 9: *Double portion of your spirit:* as the first-born son inherited a double portion of his father's property (Dt 21, 17), so Elisha asks to inherit from Elijah his spirit of prophecy in the degree befitting his principal disciple. In Nm 11, 17. 25, God bestows some of the spirit of Moses on others.

2, 12: *My father:* a religious title accorded prophetic leaders; cf 2 Kgs 6, 21; 8, 9. *Israel's chariots and drivers:* Elijah was worth more than a whole army in defending Israel and the true religion. King Joash of Israel uses the same phrase of Elisha himself (2 Kgs 13, 14).

vants are fifty brave men," they said. "Let them go in search of your master. Perhaps the spirit of the LORD has carried him away to some mountain or some valley." "Do not send them," he answered.[j] [17]However, they kept urging him, until he was embarrassed and said, "Send them." So they sent the fifty men, who searched for three days without finding him. [18]When they returned to Elisha in Jericho, where he was staying, he said to them, "Did I not tell you not to go?"

Healing of the Water. [19]Once the inhabitants of the city complained to Elisha, "The site of the city is fine indeed, as my lord can see, but the water is bad and the land unfruitful." [20]"Bring me a new bowl," Elisha said, "and put salt into it." When they had brought it to him, [21]he went out to the spring and threw salt into it, saying, "Thus says the LORD, 'I have purified this water. Never again shall death or miscarriage spring from it.'" [22]And the water has stayed pure even to this day, just as Elisha prophesied.

The Prophet's Curse. [23] * From there Elisha went up to Bethel. While he was on the way, some small boys came out of the city and jeered at him. "Go up, baldhead," they shouted, "go up, baldhead!" [24]The prophet turned and saw them, and he cursed them in the name of the LORD. Then two she-bears came out of the

j 1 Kgs 18, 12.—k 1 Kgs 22, 4.—l 1 Kgs 22, 7.

2, 23f: This story, like the one about Elijah and the captains (ch 1), is preserved for us in Scripture to convey a popular understanding of the dignity of the prophet. Told in popular vein, it becomes a caricature, in which neither Elisha nor the bears behave in character. See note on 2 Kgs 1, 12 and the contrasting narrative in ch 4.

3, 1: The sequence of the reigns between Ahab and Jehu of Israel may be reconstructed as follows: Jehoshaphat of Judah outlived Ahab by a short time, so that Ahaziah of Israel was his contemporary. Jehoram of Judah succeeded his father Jehoshaphat while Ahaziah of Israel was still alive. Jehoram (Joram) of Israel became king, following his brother Ahaziah, in the second year of Jehoram of Judah (2 Kgs 1, 17); this is one datum on which the earliest Greek evidence and the standard Hebrew text are in agreement.

The two Jehorams were contemporary for much of their reigns; Jehoram of Judah was succeeded by Ahaziah something more than a year before Jehu did away with the rulers of both kingdoms (2 Kgs 9, 1-29).

The Moabite campaign of 2 Kgs 3, 4-27 is thus best placed under the two Kings Jehoram, before the Edomite rebellion mentioned in 2 Kgs 8, 20. In the received Hebrew text, Jehoshaphat has been made the Judahite protagonist in the campaign against Moab as a tribute to his piety; this assimilates the story of 2 Kgs 3 to that of 1 Kgs 22, but creates difficulties in the chronology which the extant data leave partly unresolved. An older practice for stories of the Israelite kings was to leave them and their fellow kings without identification by name; cf 2 Kgs 6, 8—7, 20. The name of Jehoshaphat has been omitted from a number of places in 2 Kgs 3—8, in this translation; cf 1 Kgs 22, 51.

of the woods and tore forty-two of the children to pieces. [25]From there he went to Mount Carmel, and thence he returned to Samaria.

CHAPTER 3

Campaign of Joram against Moab. [1]Joram, son of Ahab, became king of Israel in Samaria [in the eighteenth year of Jehoshaphat, king of Judah, and he reigned for twelve years].* [2]He did evil in the LORD's sight, though not as much as his father and mother. He did away with the pillar of Baal, which his father had made, [3]but he still clung to the sin to which Jeroboam, son of Nebat, had lured Israel; this he did not give up.

[4]Now Mesha, king of Moab, who raised sheep, used to pay the king of Israel as tribute a hundred thousand lambs and the wool of a hundred thousand rams. [5]But when Ahab died, the king of Moab had rebelled against the king of Israel. [6]Joram as king mustered all Israel, and when he set out on a campaign from Samaria, [7]he sent the king of Judah the message: "The king of Moab is in rebellion against me. Will you join me in battle against Moab?" "I will," he replied. "You and I shall be as one, your people and mine, and your horses and mine as well."[k] [8]They discussed the route for their attack, and settled upon the route through the desert of Edom.

[9]So the king of Israel set out, accompanied by the king of Judah and the king of Edom. After their roundabout journey of seven days the water gave out for the army and for the animals with them. [10]"Alas!" exclaimed the king of Israel. "The LORD has called together these three kings to put them in the grasp of Moab." [11]But the king of Judah asked, "Is there no prophet of the LORD here through whom we may inquire of the LORD?" One of the officers of the king of Israel replied, "Elisha, son of Shaphat, who poured water on the hands of Elijah, is here."[l] [12]"He has the word of the LORD," the king of Judah agreed. So the kings of Israel, Judah, and Edom went down to Elisha. [13]"What do you want with me?" Elisha asked the king of Israel. "Go to the prophets of your father and to the prophets of your mother." "No," the king of Israel replied. "The LORD has called these three kings together to put them in the grasp

of Moab." ¹⁴Then Elisha said, "As the LORD of hosts lives, whom I serve, were it not that I respect the king of Judah, I should neither look at you nor notice you at all.*ᵐ* ¹⁵Now get me a minstrel."

When the minstrel played, the power of the LORD came upon Elisha ¹⁶and he announced: "Thus says the LORD, 'Provide many catch basins in this wadi.' ¹⁷For the LORD says, 'Though you will see neither wind nor rain, yet this wadi will be filled with water for you, your livestock, and your pack animals to drink.' ¹⁸And since the LORD does not consider this enough, he will also deliver Moab into your grasp. ¹⁹You shall destroy every fortified city, fell every fruit tree, stop up all the springs, and ruin every fertile field with stones."*ⁿ*

²⁰In the morning, at the time of the sacrifice, water came from the direction of Edom and filled the land.*ᵒ* ²¹Meanwhile, all Moab heard that the kings had come to give them battle; every man capable of bearing arms was called up and stationed at the border. ²²Early that morning, when the sun shone on the water, the Moabites saw the water at a distance as red as blood.* ²³"This is blood!" they exclaimed. "The kings have fought among themselves and killed one another. Quick! To the spoils, Moabites!" ²⁴But when they reached the camp of Israel, the Israelites rose up and attacked the Moabites, who fled from them. They ranged through the countryside striking down the Moabites, and ²⁵destroying the cities; each of them cast stones onto every fertile field till they had loaded it down; all the springs they stopped up and every useful tree they felled. Finally only Kir-hareseth* was left behind its stone walls, and the slingers had surrounded it and were attacking it.*ᵖ* ²⁶When he saw that he was losing the battle, the king of Moab took seven hundred swordsmen to break through to the king of Aram, but he failed. ²⁷So he took his firstborn, his heir apparent, and offered him as a holocaust upon the wall. The wrath against Israel* was so great that they gave up the siege and returned to their own land.*q*

CHAPTER 4

The Widow's Oil. ¹ *ʳ* A certain woman, the widow of one of the guild prophets, complained to Elisha: "My husband, your servant, is dead. You know that he was a

God-fearing man, yet now his creditor has come to take my two children as his slaves."* ²"How can I help you?" Elisha answered her. "Tell me what you have in the house." "This servant of yours has nothing in the house but a jug of oil," she replied. ³"Go out," he said, "borrow vessels from all your neighbors—as many empty vessels as you can. ⁴Then come back and close the door on yourself and your children; pour the oil into all the vessels, and as each is filled, set it aside." ⁵She went and did so, closing the door on herself and her children. As they handed her the vessels, she would pour in oil. ⁶When all the vessels were filled, she said to her son, "Bring me another vessel." "There is none left," he answered her. And then the oil stopped. ⁷She went and told the man of God, who said, "Go and sell the oil to pay off your creditor; with what remains, you and your children can live."

Elisha and the Shunammite. ⁸One day Elisha came to Shunem, where there was a woman of influence, who urged him to dine with her. Afterward, whenever he passed by, he used to stop there to dine. ⁹So she said to her husband, "I know that he is a holy man of God. Since he visits us often, ¹⁰let us arrange a little room on the roof and furnish it for him with a bed, table, chair, and lamp, so that when he comes to us he can stay there." ¹¹Some time later Elisha arrived and stayed in the room overnight. ¹²Then he said to his servant Gehazi, "Call this Shunammite woman." He did so, and when she stood before Elisha, ¹³he told Gehazi, "Say to her, 'You have lavished all this care on us; what can we do for you? Can we say a good word for you to the king or to the commander of the army?'" She replied, "I am living among my own people." ¹⁴Later Elisha asked, "Can something be done for her?" "Yes!" Gehazi answered. "She has no son, and her husband is getting on

m 1 Kgs 18, 15.—n Dt 20, 19.—o 1 Kgs 18, 29.—p Jb 5, 23.— q Jgs 11, 30f.—r 1 Kgs 17, 8-16.

3, 22: *Red as blood:* possibly caused by the red sandstone of the Wadi Zered (Dt 2, 13), south of Moab.

3, 25: *Kir-hareseth:* modern Kerak, east of the Dead Sea; cf Is 16, 7. 11; Jer 48, 31. 36.

3, 27: *The wrath against Israel:* probably the wrath of Chemosh, the Moabite god to whom the child was offered. He was feared by the Israelites who lost heart on foreign soil.

4, 1: *His creditor . . . slaves:* Hebrew law permitted the selling of wife and children as chattels for debt; cf Ex 21, 7; Am 2, 6; 8, 6; Is 50.

in years." ¹⁵"Call her," said Elisha. When she had been called, and stood at the door, ¹⁶Elisha promised, "This time next year you will be fondling a baby son." "Please, my lord," she protested, "you are a man of God; do not deceive your servant."ˢ ¹⁷Yet the woman conceived, and by the same time the following year she had given birth to a son, as Elisha had promised.

¹⁸The day came when the child was old enough to go out to his father among the reapers.ᵗ ¹⁹"My head hurts!" he complained to his father. "Carry him to his mother," the father said to a servant. ²⁰The servant picked him up and carried him to his mother; he stayed with her until noon, when he died in her lap. ²¹The mother took him upstairs and laid him on the bed of the man of God. Closing the door on him, she went out ²²and called to her husband, "Let me have a servant and a donkey. I must go quickly to the man of God, and I will be back." ²³"Why are you going to him today?" he asked. "It is neither the new moon nor the sabbath." But she bade him good-bye, ²⁴and when the donkey was saddled, said to her servant: "Lead on! Do not stop my donkey unless I tell you to." ²⁵She kept going till she reached the man of God on Mount Carmel. When he spied her at a distance, the man of God said to his servant Gehazi: "There is the Shunammite! ²⁶Hurry to meet her, and ask if all is well with her, with her husband, and with the boy." "Greetings,"* she replied. ²⁷But when she reached the man of God on the mountain, she clasped his feet. Gehazi came near to push her away, but the man of God said: "Let her alone, she is in bitter anguish; the LORD hid it from me and did not let me know." ²⁸"Did I ask my lord for a son?" she cried out. "Did I not beg you not to deceive me?" ²⁹"Gird your loins," Elisha said to Gehazi, "take my staff with you and be off; if you meet anyone, do not greet him,* and if anyone greets you, do not answer. Lay my staff upon the boy." ³⁰But the boy's mother cried out: "As the LORD

lives and as you yourself live, I will not release you." So he started to go back with her.

³¹ ᵘ Meanwhile, Gehazi had gone on ahead and had laid the staff upon the boy, but there was no sound or sign of life. He returned to meet Elisha and informed him that the boy had not awakened. ³²When Elisha reached the house, he found the boy lying dead. ³³He went in, closed the door on them both, and prayed to the LORD.ᵛ ³⁴Then he lay upon the child on the bed, placing his mouth upon the child's mouth, his eyes upon the eyes, and his hands upon the hands. As Elisha stretched himself over the child, the body became warm. ³⁵He arose, paced up and down the room, and then once more lay down upon the boy, who now sneezed seven times and opened his eyes.ʷ ³⁶Elisha summoned Gehazi and said, "Call the Shunammite." She came at his call, and Elisha said to her, "Take your son." ³⁷She came in and fell at his feet in gratitude; then she took her son and left the room.

The Poisoned Stew. ³⁸When Elisha returned to Gilgal, there was a famine in the land. Once, when the guild prophets were seated before him, he said to his servant, "Put the large pot on, and make some vegetable stew for the guild prophets." ³⁹Someone went out into the field to gather herbs and found a wild vine, from which he picked a clothful of wild gourds. On his return he cut them up into the pot of vegetable stew without anybody's knowing it. ⁴⁰The stew was poured out for the men to eat, but when they began to eat it, they exclaimed, "Man of God, there is poison in the pot!" And they could not eat it. ⁴¹"Bring some meal," Elisha said. He threw it into the pot and said, "Serve it to the people to eat." And there was no longer anything harmful in the pot.

Multiplication of Loaves. ⁴²A man came from Baal-shalishah bringing the man of God twenty barley loaves made from the first-fruits, and fresh grain in the ear. "Give it to the people to eat," Elisha said. ⁴³But his servant objected, "How can I set this before a hundred men?" "Give it to the people to eat," Elisha insisted. "For thus says the LORD, 'They shall eat and there shall be some left over.'" ⁴⁴And when they had eaten, there was some left over, as the LORD had said.

2Kgs

---

s Gn 18, 10.—t 1 Kgs 17, 17-24.—u 31-36: Acts 20, 10ff.—v 1 Kgs 17, 21-23.—w Heb 11, 35.

4, 26: *Greetings:* the conventional answer to Gehazi's question, which tells him nothing.

4, 29: *Do not greet him:* the profuse exchange of compliments among Orientals meeting and greeting one another consumed time. Urgency necessitated their omission, as our Lord counseled his disciples (Lk 10, 4).

CHAPTER 5

Cure of Naaman. ¹Naaman, the army commander of the king of Aram, was highly esteemed and respected by his master, for through him the LORD had brought victory to Aram. But valiant as he was, the man was a leper. ²Now the Arameans had captured from the land of Israel in a raid a little girl, who became the servant of Naaman's wife. ³"If only my master would present himself to the prophet in Samaria," she said to her mistress, "he would cure him of his leprosy." ⁴Naaman went and told his lord just what the slave girl from the land of Israel had said. ⁵"Go," said the king of Aram. "I will send along a letter to the king of Israel." So Naaman set out, taking along ten silver talents, six thousand gold pieces, and ten festal garments. ⁶To the king of Israel he brought the letter, which read: "With this letter I am sending my servant Naaman to you, that you may cure him of his leprosy."

⁷When he read the letter, the king of Israel tore his garments and exclaimed: "Am I a god with power over life and death, that this man should send someone to me to be cured of leprosy? Take note! You can see he is only looking for a quarrel with me!"ˣ ⁸When Elisha, the man of God, heard that the king of Israel had torn his garments, he sent word to the king: "Why have you torn your garments? Let him come to me and find out that there is a prophet in Israel."

⁹Naaman came with his horses and chariots and stopped at the door of Elisha's house. ¹⁰The prophet sent him the message: "Go and wash seven times in the Jordan, and your flesh will heal, and you will be clean."ʸ ¹¹But Naaman went away angry, saying, "I thought that he would surely come out and stand there to invoke the LORD his God, and would move his hand over the spot, and thus cure the leprosy. ¹²Are not the rivers of Damascus, the Abana and the Pharpar, better than all the waters of Israel? Could I not wash in them and be cleansed?"* With this, he turned about in anger and left.

¹³But his servants came up and reasoned with him. "My father," they said, "if the prophet had told you to do something extraordinary, would you not have done it? All the more now, since he said to you,

'Wash and be clean,' should you do as he said." ¹⁴So Naaman went down and plunged into the Jordan seven times at the word of the man of God. His flesh became again like the flesh of a little child, and he was clean.ᶻ

¹⁵He returned with his whole retinue to the man of God. On his arrival he stood before him and said, "Now I know that there is no God in all the earth, except in Israel. Please accept a gift from your servant."

¹⁶"As the LORD lives whom I serve, I will not take it," Elisha replied; and despite Naaman's urging, he still refused. ¹⁷Naaman said: "If you will not accept, please let me, your servant, have two mule-loads of earth,* for I will no longer offer holocaust or sacrifice to any other god except to the LORD. ¹⁸But I trust the LORD will forgive your servant this: when my master enters the temple of Rimmon to worship there, then I, too, as his adjutant, must bow down in the temple of Rimmon. May the LORD forgive your servant this." ¹⁹"Go in peace,"* Elisha said to him.

²⁰Naaman had gone some distance when Gehazi, the servant of Elisha, the man of God, thought to himself: "My master was too easy with this Aramean Naaman, not accepting what he brought. As the LORD lives, I will run after him and get something out of him." ²¹So Gehazi hurried after Naaman. Aware that someone was running after him, Naaman alighted from his chariot to wait for him. "Is everything all right?" he asked. ²²"Yes," Gehazi replied, "but my master sent me to say, 'Two young men have just come to me, guild prophets from the hill country of Ephraim. Please give them a talent of silver and two festal garments.'" ²³"Please take two talents," Naaman said, and pressed them upon him. He tied up these silver talents in bags and gave them, with the two festal garments, to two of his servants, who carried them before Gehazi.

---

x Gn 30, 2; 1 Sm 2, 6; Jn 5, 21.—y Jn 9, 7.—z Lk 4, 27.

5, 12: *Wash in them and be cleansed:* typical of the ambiguity in ritual healing or cleanliness. The muddy waters of the Jordan are no match hygienically for the mountain spring waters of Damascus; ritually, it is the other way around.

5, 17: *Two mule-loads of earth:* Israelite earth on which to erect in Aram an altar to the God of Israel.

5, 19: *Go in peace:* Elisha understands and approves the situation of Naaman who, though a proselyte as regards belief in and worship of the God of Israel, is required by his office to assist his master, the king, worshiping in the pagan temple of Rimmon.

24 When they reached the hill, Gehazi took what they had, carried it into the house, and sent the men on their way.
25 He went in and stood before Elisha his master, who asked him, "Where have you been, Gehazi?" He answered, "Your servant has not gone anywhere." 26 But Elisha said to him: "Was I not present in spirit when the man alighted from his chariot to wait for you? Is this a time to take money or to take garments, olive orchards or vineyards, sheep or cattle, male or female servants? 27 The leprosy of Naaman shall cling to you and your descendants forever." And Gehazi left Elisha, a leper white as snow.ᵃ

CHAPTER 6

Recovery of the Lost Ax. 1 The guild prophets once said to Elisha: "There is not enough room for us to continue to live here with you. 2 Let us go to the Jordan, where by getting one beam apiece we can build ourselves a place to live." "Go," Elisha said. 3 "Please agree to accompany your servants," one of them requested. "Yes, I will come," he replied.
4 So he went with them, and when they arrived at the Jordan they began to fell trees. 5 While one of them was felling a tree trunk, the iron axhead slipped into the water. "O master," he cried out, "it was borrowed!" 6 "Where did it fall?" asked the man of God. When he pointed out the spot, Elisha cut off a stick, threw it into the water, and brought the iron to the surface. 7 "Pick it up," he said. And the man reached down and grasped it.
Aramean Ambush. 8 When the king of Aram was waging war on Israel, he would make plans with his servants to attack a particular place. 9 But the man of God would send word to the king of Israel, "Be careful! Do not pass by this place, for Aram will attack there." 10 So the king of Israel would send word to the place which the man of God had indicated, and alert it; then they would be on guard. This happened several times.
11 Greatly disturbed over this, the king

of Aram called together his officers. "Will you not tell me," he asked them, "who among us is for the king of Israel?" 12 "No one, my lord king," answered one of the officers. "The Israelite prophet Elisha can tell the king of Israel the very words you speak in your bedroom." 13 "Go, find out where he is," he said, "so that I may take him captive."
Blinded Aramean Soldiers. Informed that Elisha was in Dothan, 14 he sent there a strong force with horses and chariots. They arrived by night and surrounded the city. 15 Early the next morning, when the attendant of the man of God arose and went out, he saw the force with its horses and chariots surrounding the city. "Alas!" he said to Elisha. "What shall we do, my lord?" 16 "Do not be afraid," Elisha answered. "Our side outnumbers theirs." 17 Then he prayed, "O LORD, open his eyes, that he may see." And the LORD opened the eyes of the servant, so that he saw the mountainside filled with horses and fiery chariots around Elisha.ᵇ
18 When the Arameans came down to get him, Elisha prayed to the LORD, "Strike this people blind, I pray you." And in answer to the prophet's prayer the LORD struck them blind. 19 Then Elisha said to them: "This is the wrong road, and this is the wrong city. Follow me! I will take you to the man you want." And he led them to Samaria.
20 When they entered Samaria, Elisha prayed, "O LORD, open their eyes that they may see." The LORD opened their eyes, and they saw that they were inside Samaria. 21 When the king of Israel saw them, he asked, "Shall I kill them, my father?" 22 "You must not kill them," replied Elisha. "Do you slay those whom you have taken captive with your sword or bow?* Serve them bread and water. Let them eat and drink, and then go back to their master." 23 The king spread a great feast for them. When they had eaten and drunk he sent them away, and they went back to their master. No more Aramean raiders came into the land of Israel.
Siege of Samaria. 24 After this, Benhadad, king of Aram, mustered his whole army and laid siege to Samaria. 25 Because of the siege the famine in Samaria was so severe that an ass's head sold for eighty pieces of silver, and a fourth of a kab of wild onion for five pieces of silver.

---

a Ex 4, 6; Nm 12, 10.—b 2 Kgs 7, 6; Ps 67, 18.

6, 22: *With your sword or bow:* since the king would not slay prisoners who had surrendered to his power, much less should he slay prisoners captured by God's power. By Oriental custom they became guests within Samaria's walls.

²⁶One day, as the king of Israel was walking on the city wall, a woman cried out to him, "Help, my lord king!" ²⁷"No," he replied, "the LORD help you! Where could I find help for you: from the threshing floor or the winepress?" ²⁸Then the king asked her, "What is your trouble?" She replied: "This woman said to me, 'Give up your son that we may eat him today; then tomorrow we will eat my son.'ᶜ ²⁹So we boiled my son and ate him. The next day I said to her, 'Now give up your son that we may eat him.' But she hid her son." ³⁰When the king heard the woman's words, he tore his garments. And as he was walking on the wall, the people saw that he was wearing sackcloth underneath, next to his skin.ᵈ ³¹"May God do thus and so to me," the king exclaimed, "if the head of Elisha, son of Shaphat, stays on him today!" ³²Meanwhile, Elisha was sitting in his house in conference with the elders. The king had sent a man ahead before he himself should come to him. Elisha had said to the elders: "Do you know that this son of a murderer is sending someone to cut off my head? When the messenger comes, see that you close the door and hold it fast against him. His master's footsteps are echoing behind him." ³³While Elisha was still speaking, the king came down to him and said, "This evil is from the LORD. Why should I trust in the LORD any longer?"

CHAPTER 7

¹Elisha said: "Hear the word of the LORD! Thus says the LORD, 'At this time tomorrow a seah of fine flour will sell for a shekel, and two seahs of barley for a shekel, in the market* of Samaria.' " ²But the adjutant on whose arm the king leaned, answered the man of God, "Even if the LORD were to make windows in heaven, how could this happen?" "You shall see it with your own eyes," Elisha said, "but you shall not eat of it."ᵉ

The Lepers at the Gate. ³At the city gate were four lepers who were deliberating, "Why should we sit here until we die?ᶠ ⁴If we decide to go into the city, we shall die there, for there is famine in the city. If we remain here, we shall die too. Come, let us desert to the camp of the Arameans. If they spare us, we live; if they kill us, we die." ⁵At twilight they left for the Ara-

means, but when they reached the edge of the camp, no one was there. ⁶ᵍThe LORD had caused the army of the Arameans to hear the sound of chariots and horses, the din of a large army, and they had reasoned among themselves, "The king of Israel has hired the kings of the Hittites and the kings of the borderlands* to fight us." ⁷Then in the twilight they fled, abandoning their tents, their horses, and their asses, the whole camp just as it was, and fleeing for their lives.

⁸After the lepers reached the edge of the camp, they went first into one tent, ate and drank, and took silver, gold, and clothing from it, and went out and hid them. Back they came into another tent, took things from it, and again went out and hid them. ⁹Then they said to one another: "We are not doing right. This is a day of good news, and we are keeping silent. If we wait until morning breaks, we shall be blamed. Come, let us go and inform the palace."

¹⁰They came and summoned the city gatekeepers. "We went to the camp of the Arameans," they said, "but no one was there—not a human voice, only the horses and asses tethered, and the tents just as they were left." ¹¹The gatekeepers announced this and it was reported within the palace. ¹²Though it was night, the king got up; he said to his servants: "Let me tell you what the Arameans have done to us. Knowing that we are in famine, they have left their camp to hide in the field, hoping to take us alive and enter our city when we leave it." ¹³One of his servants, however, suggested: "Since those who are left in the city are no better off than all the throng that has perished, let some of us take five of the abandoned horses and send scouts to investigate."

End of the Siege. ¹⁴They took two chariots, and horses, and the king sent them to reconnoiter the Aramean army. "Go and find out," he ordered. ¹⁵They followed the Arameans as far as the Jordan, and the whole route was strewn with garments and other objects that the Arameans

---

c Dt 28, 53-57.—d 1 Kgs 20, 31; 21, 27.—e 2 Kgs 7, 17; Ps 78, 23; Is 24, 18.—f Lv 13, 46.—g 6f: 2 Kgs 6, 17; 19, 35f; 2 Sm 5. 24.

7, 1: *Market:* literally "gate," the principal place of trading in ancient walled cities in time of peace.

7, 6: *Kings of the borderlands:* from Musur in Anatolia rather than Egypt.

had thrown away in their haste. The messengers returned and told the king. [16]The people went out and plundered the camp of the Arameans; and then a seah of fine flour sold for a shekel and two seahs of barley for a shekel, as the LORD had said. [17]The king put in charge of the gate the officer who was his adjutant; but the people trampled him to death at the gate, just as the man of God had predicted when the king visited him. [18]Thus was fulfilled the prophecy of the man of God to the king, "Two seahs of barley will sell for a shekel, and one seah of fine flour for a shekel at this time tomorrow at the gate of Samaria." [19]The adjutant had answered the man of God, "Even if the LORD were to make windows in heaven, how could this happen?" And Elisha had replied, "You shall see it with your own eyes, but you shall not eat of it." [20]And that is what happened to him, for the people trampled him to death at the gate.

CHAPTER 8

Prediction of Famine. [1]Elisha once said to the woman whose son he had restored to life: "Get ready! Leave with your family and settle wherever you can, because the LORD has decreed a seven-year famine which is coming upon the land."[h] [2]The woman got ready and did as the man of God said, setting out with her family and settling in the land of the Philistines for seven years. [3]At the end of the seven years, the woman returned from the land of the Philistines and went out to the king to claim her house and her field. [4]The king was talking with Gehazi, the servant of the man of God. "Tell me," he said, "all the great things that Elisha has done." [5]Just as he was relating to the king how his master had restored a dead person to life, the very woman whose son Elisha had restored to life came to the king to claim her house and field. "My lord king," Gehazi said,

h 2 Kgs 4, 36.—i 2 Kgs 13, 7.—j 2 Kgs 15, 16; 1 Kgs 19, 15.—k 17ff: 2 Chr 21, 5ff.

8, 6: *An official:* literally "eunuch," and perhaps actually so in this instance.
8, 13: *A dog . . . your servant:* Hazael feigns humility (1 Sm 24, 14; 2 Sm 9, 8), without attending to the crimes he would commit after usurping the royal power as the prophet predicts. *Anything so important:* literally "a great deed" for a patriotic Syrian.
8, 16: *Jehoram* of Judah succeeded his father Jehoshaphat during the reign of Ahaziah of Israel. See note on 2 Kgs 3, 1.

"this is the woman, and this is that son of hers whom Elisha restored to life." [6]The king questioned the woman, and she told him her story. With that the king placed an official* at her disposal, saying, "Restore all her property to her, with all that the field produced from the day she left the land until now."

Death of Ben-hadad Foretold. [7]Elisha came to Damascus at a time when Ben-hadad, king of Aram, lay sick. When he was told that the man of God had come there, [8]the king said to Hazael, "Take a gift with you and go call on the man of God. Have him consult the LORD as to whether I shall recover from this sickness." [9]Hazael went to visit him, carrying a present, and with forty camel loads of the best goods of Damascus. On his arrival, he stood before the prophet and said, "Your son Ben-hadad, king of Aram, has sent me to ask you whether he will recover from his sickness." [10]"Go and tell him," Elisha answered, "that he will surely recover. However, the LORD has showed me that he will in fact die." [11]Then he stared him down until Hazael became ill at ease. The man of God wept, [12]and Hazael asked, "Why are you weeping, my lord?" Elisha replied, "Because I know the evil that you will inflict upon the Israelites. You will burn their fortresses, you will slay their youth with the sword, you will dash their little children to pieces, you will rip open their pregnant women."[i] [13]Hazael exclaimed, "How can a dog like me, your servant,* do anything so important?" "The LORD has showed you to me as king over Aram," replied Elisha.[j] [14]Hazael left Elisha and returned to his master. "What did Elisha tell you?" asked Ben-hadad. "He told me that you would surely recover," replied Hazael. [15]The next day, however, Hazael took a cloth, dipped it in water, and spread it over the king's face, so that he died. And Hazael reigned in his stead.

Reign of Jehoram of Judah. [16]In the fifth year of Joram, son of Ahab, king of Israel, Jehoram,* son of Jehosaphat, king of Judah, became king. [17][k] He was thirty-two years old when he began to reign, and he reigned eight years in Jerusalem. [18]He conducted himself like the kings of Israel of the line of Ahab, since the sister of Ahab was his wife; and he did evil in the LORD's sight. [19]Even so, the LORD was unwilling to destroy Judah, because of his servant David. For he had promised David that he would leave him a lamp in the LORD's presence for all time.*l* [20]During Jehoram's reign, Edom revolted against the sovereignty of Judah and chose a king of its own. [21]Thereupon Jehoram with all his chariots crossed over to Zair. He arose by night and broke through the Edomites when they had surrounded him and the commanders of his chariots. Then his army fled homeward. [22]To this day Edom has been in revolt against the rule of Judah. Libnah also revolted at that time.*m* [23]The rest of the acts of Jehoram, with all that he did, are recorded in the book of the chronicles of the kings of Judah. [24]Jehoram rested with his ancestors and was buried with them in the City of David. His son Ahaziah succeeded him as king.

Accession of Ahaziah. [25]Ahaziah, son of Jehoram, king of Judah, became king in the twelfth year of Joram,* son of Ahab, king of Israel. [26]He was twenty-two years old when he began his reign, and he reigned one year in Jerusalem. His mother's name was Athaliah; she was the daughter of Omri, king of Israel. [27]He conducted himself like the house of Ahab, doing evil in the LORD's sight as they did, since he was related to them by marriage. [28]He joined Joram, son of Ahab, in battle against Hazael, king of Aram, at Ramoth-gilead, where the Arameans wounded Joram.*n* [29]King Joram returned to Jezreel to be healed of the wounds which the Arameans had inflicted on him at Ramah in his battle against Hazael, king of Aram. Then Ahaziah, son of Jehoram, king of Judah, went down to Jezreel to visit him there in his illness.

CHAPTER 9

Anointing of Jehu. [1]The prophet Elisha called one of the guild prophets and said to him: "Gird your loins, take this flask of oil with you, and go to Ramoth-gilead.*o* [2]When you get there, look for Jehu, son of Jehoshaphat, son of Nimshi. Enter and take him away from his companions into an inner chamber.*p* [3]From the flask you have, pour oil on his head, and say, 'Thus says the LORD: I anoint you king over Israel.' Then open the door and flee without delay."*q* [4]The

young man (the guild prophet) went to Ramoth-gilead. [5]When he arrived, the commanders of the army were in session. "I have a message for you, commander," he said. "For which one of us?" asked Jehu. "For you, commander," he answered. [6]Jehu got up and went into the house. Then the young man poured the oil on his head and said, "Thus says the LORD, the God of Israel: 'I anoint you king over the people of the LORD, over Israel. [7] * You shall destroy the house of Ahab your master; thus will I avenge the blood of my servants the prophets, and the blood of all the other servants of the LORD shed by Jezebel, [8] *r* and by all the rest of the family of Ahab. I will cut off every male in Ahab's line, whether slave or freeman in Israel. [9]I will deal with the house of Ahab as I dealt with the house of Jeroboam, son of Nebat, and with the house of Baasha, son of Ahijah. [10]Dogs shall devour Jezebel at the confines of Jezreel, so that no one can bury her.' " Then he opened the door and fled.

[11]When Jehu rejoined his master's servants, they asked him, "Is all well? Why did that madman come to you?" "You know that kind of man and his talk," he replied. [12]But they said, "Not at all! Come, tell us." So he told them what the young man had said to him, and finally, "Thus says the LORD: 'I anoint you king over Israel.' " [13]At once each took his garment, spread it under Jehu on the bare steps, blew the trumpet, and cried out, "Jehu is king!"*s*

[14] *t* Thus Jehu, son of Jehoshaphat, son of Nimshi, formed a conspiracy against Joram. Joram, with all Israel, had been besieging Ramoth-gilead against Hazael, king of Aram, [15]but had returned to Jezreel to be healed of the wounds the Arameans had inflicted on him in the battle against Hazael, king of Aram.

Murder of Joram. "If you are truly with me," Jehu said, "see that no one escapes

---

1 2 Sm 7, 11-16; 21, 17; 1 Kgs 11, 36; 15, 4; 2 Chr 21, 7.—m Gn 27, 40; 2 Chr 21, 8ff.—n 2 Kgs 9, 14f.—o 1 Kgs 21, 29; Hos 1, 4.—p 1 Kgs 19, 16.—q 1 Kgs 19, 16.—r 8ff: 1 Kgs 14, 10f; 16, 3f; 21, 21-24.—s Mt 21, 8.—t 14f: 2 Kgs 8, 28f; 1 Kgs 22, 3f.

8, 25: *Twelfth year of Joram:* i.e., of Israel, who probably reigned only eight years.

9, 7-10: The editors of the Books of Kings have here added to the prophet's message the same type of indictment and sanctions against the *family of Ahab* as were invoked against the dynasties of *Jeroboam* (1 Kgs 14, 10f), *Baasha* (1 Kgs 16, 3f), and *Ahab* on a previous occasion (1 Kgs 21, 21-24).

from the city to report in Jezreel."
¹⁶Then Jehu mounted his chariot and
drove to Jezreel, where Joram lay ill and
Ahaziah, king of Judah, had come to
visit him.
¹⁷The watchman standing on the tower
in Jezreel saw the troop of Jehu coming
and reported, "I see chariots." "Get a
driver," Joram said, "and send him to
meet them and to ask whether all is
well." ¹⁸So a driver went out to meet
him and said, "The king asks whether all
is well." "What does it matter to you
how things are?" Jehu said. "Get behind
me." The watchman reported to the
king, "The messenger has reached them,
but is not returning."
¹⁹Joram sent a second driver, who
went to them and said, "The king asks
whether all is well." "What does it matter to you how things are?" Jehu replied.
"Get behind me."
²⁰The watchman reported, "The mes-
senger has reached them, but is not returning. The driving is like that of Jehu,
son of Nimshi, in its fury." ²¹"Prepare
my chariot," said Joram. When they had
done so, Joram, king of Israel, and
Ahaziah, king of Judah, set out, each in
his own chariot, to meet Jehu. They
reached him near the field of Naboth the
Jezreelite. ²²When Joram recognized
Jehu, he asked, "Is all well, Jehu?"
"How can all be well," Jehu replied, "as
long as the many fornications and witchcrafts* of your mother Jezebel continue?"
²³Joram reined about and fled, crying to
Ahaziah, "Treason, Ahaziah!" ²⁴But Jehu
drew his bow and shot Joram between
the shoulders, so that the arrow went
through his heart and he collapsed in his
chariot. ²⁵ ^u Then Jehu said to his adjutant Bidkar, "Take him and throw him
into the field of Naboth the Jezreelite.
For I remember that when we were driving teams behind his father Ahab, the
LORD delivered this oracle against him:
²⁶'As surely as I saw yesterday the blood
of Naboth and the blood of his sons,'
says the LORD, 'I will repay you for it in
that very plot of ground, says the LORD.'
So now take him into this plot of ground,
in keeping with the word of the LORD."

u 25f: 1 Kgs 21, 9-16.—v 27ff: 2 Chr 22, 7ff.—w 1 Kgs 16,
9ff.—x 1 Kgs 21, 23.—y Jgs 9, 5; 1 Kgs 15, 29; 16, 11.

9, 22: *Fornications and witchcrafts:* the worship of foreign gods.

Death of Ahaziah. ²⁷ ^v Seeing what was
happening, Ahaziah, king of Judah, fled
toward Beth-haggan. Jehu pursued him,
shouting, "Kill him too!" And they
pierced him as he rode through the pass of
Gur near Ibleam. He continued his flight
as far as Megiddo and died there. ²⁸His
servants brought him in a chariot to Jerusalem and buried him in the tomb of his
ancestors in the City of David. ²⁹Ahaziah
had become king of Judah in the eleventh
year of Joram, son of Ahab.
Death of Jezebel. ³⁰When Jezebel
learned that Jehu had arrived in Jezreel,
she shadowed her eyes, adorned her hair,
and looked down from her window. ³¹As
Jehu came through the gate, she cried out,
"Is all well, Zimri, murderer of your mas-
ter?" ^w ³²Jehu looked up to the window
and shouted, "Who is on my side? Any-
one?" At this, two or three eunuchs looked
down toward him. ³³"Throw her down,"
he ordered. They threw her down, and
some of her blood spurted against the wall
and against the horses. Jehu rode in over
her body ³⁴and, after eating and drinking,
he said: "Attend to that accursed woman
and bury her; after all, she was a king's
daughter." ³⁵But when they went to bury
her, they found nothing of her but the
skull, the feet, and the hands. ³⁶They returned to Jehu, and when they told him,
he said, "This is the sentence which the
LORD pronounced through his servant
Elijah the Tishbite: 'In the confines of Jezreel dogs shall eat the flesh of Jezebel. ^x
³⁷The corpse of Jezebel shall be like dung
in the field in the confines of Jezreel, so
that no one can say: This was Jezebel.'"

CHAPTER 10

Killing of Ahab's Descendants. ¹Ahab had
seventy descendants in Samaria. Jehu prepared letters and sent them to the city rulers, to the elders, and to the guardians of
Ahab's descendants in Samaria.^y ²"Since
your master's sons are with you," he
wrote, "and you have the chariots, the
horses, a fortified city, and the weapons,
when this letter reaches you ³decide which
is the best and the fittest of your master's
offspring, place him on his father's throne,
and fight for your master's house." ⁴They
were overcome with fright and said, "If
two kings could not withstand him, how

can we?" ⁵So the vizier and the ruler of the city, along with the elders and the guardians, sent this message to Jehu: "We are your servants, and we will do everything you tell us. We will proclaim no one king; do whatever you think best." ⁶So Jehu wrote them a second letter: "If you are on my side and will obey me, count the heads of your master's sons and come to me in Jezreel at this time tomorrow." [The seventy princes were in the care of prominent men of the city, who were rearing them.]

⁷When the letter arrived, they took the princes and slew all seventy of them, put their heads in baskets, and sent them to Jehu in Jezreel. ⁸"They have brought the heads of the princes," a messenger came in and told him. "Pile them in two heaps at the entrance of the city until morning," he ordered. ⁹Going out in the morning, he stopped and said to all the people: "You are not responsible, and although I conspired against my lord and slew him, yet who killed all these? ¹⁰Know that not a single word which the LORD has spoken against the house of Ahab shall go unfulfilled. The LORD has accomplished all that he foretold through his servant Elijah."ᶻ ¹¹Thereupon Jehu slew all who were left of the family of Ahab in Jezreel, as well as all his powerful supporters, intimates, and priests, leaving him no survivor.ᵃ

Ahaziah's Kinsmen. ¹² ᵇ Then he set out for Samaria, and at Beth-eked-haroim on the way, ¹³he came across kinsmen of Ahaziah, king of Judah. "Who are you?" he asked. "We are kinsmen of Ahaziah," they replied. "We are going down to visit the princes and the family of the queen mother." ¹⁴"Take them alive," Jehu ordered. They were taken alive, forty-two in number, then slain at the pit of Beth-eked. Not one of them was spared.

Jehu in Samaria. ¹⁵When he had left there, Jehu met Jehonadab, son of Rechab, on the road. He greeted him and asked, "Are you sincerely disposed toward me, as I am toward you?" "Yes," replied Jehonadab. "If you are," continued Jehu, "give me your hand." Jehonadab gave him his hand, and Jehu drew him up into his chariot.ᶜ ¹⁶"Come with me," he said, "and see my zeal for the LORD." And he took him along in his own chariot.

¹⁷When he arrived in Samaria, Jehu slew all who remained there of Ahab's line, doing away with them completely and thus fulfilling the prophecy which the LORD had spoken to Elijah.

Baal's Temple Destroyed. ¹⁸Jehu gathered all the people together and said to them: "Ahab served Baal to some extent, but Jehu will serve him yet more.ᵈ ¹⁹Now summon for me all Baal's prophets, all his worshipers, and all his priests. See that no one is absent, for I have a great sacrifice for Baal. Whoever is absent shall not live." This Jehu did as a ruse, so that he might destroy the worshipers of Baal. ²⁰Jehu said further, "Proclaim a solemn assembly in honor of Baal." They did so, ²¹and Jehu sent word of it throughout the land of Israel. All the worshipers of Baal without exception came into the temple of Baal, which was filled to capacity. ²²Then Jehu said to the custodian of the wardrobe, "Bring out the garments for all the worshipers of Baal." When he had brought out the garments for them,ᵉ ²³Jehu, with Jehonadab, son of Rechab, entered the temple of Baal and said to the worshipers of Baal, "Search and be sure that there is no worshiper of the LORD here with you, but only worshipers of Baal." ²⁴Then they proceeded to offer sacrifices and holocausts. Now Jehu had stationed eighty men outside with this warning, "If one of you lets anyone escape of those whom I shall deliver into your hands, he shall pay life for life." ²⁵As soon as he finished offering the holocaust, Jehu said to the guards and officers, "Go in and slay them. Let no one escape." So the guards and officers put them to the sword and cast them out. Afterward they went into the inner shrine of the temple of Baal, ²⁶took out the stele of Baal, and burned the shrine. ²⁷Then they smashed the stele of Baal, tore down the building, and turned it into a latrine, as it remains today.

²⁸Thus Jehu rooted out the worship of Baal from Israel. ²⁹However, he did not desist from the sins which Jeroboam, son of Nebat, had caused Israel to commit, as regards the golden calves at Bethel and at Dan.ᶠ ³⁰The LORD said to Jehu, "Because you have done well what I deem right, and have treated the house of Ahab as I

z 1 Kgs 21, 17-24. 29.—a Hos 1, 4.—b 12ff: 2 Chr 22, 8f.—c 1 Chr 2, 55; Jer 35, 1-11.—d 1 Kgs 16, 30ff.—e 1 Kgs 16, 32.—f 1 Kgs 12, 28f.

desire, your sons to the fourth generation shall sit upon the throne of Israel."g 31 But Jehu was not careful to observe wholeheartedly the law of the LORD, the God of Israel, since he did not desist from the sins which Jeroboam caused Israel to commit. 32 h At that time the LORD began to dismember Israel. Hazael defeated the Israelites throughout their territory 33 east of the Jordan (all the land of Gilead, of the Gadites, Reubenites and Manassehites), from Aroer on the river Arnon up through Gilead and Bashan.

34 The rest of the acts of Jehu, his valor and all his accomplishments, are written in the book of the chronicles of the kings of Israel. 35 Jehu rested with his ancestors and was buried in Samaria. His son Jehoahaz succeeded him as king. 36 The length of Jehu's reign over Israel in Samaria was twenty-eight years.

CHAPTER 11

Rule of Athaliah. 1 When Athaliah, the mother of Ahaziah, saw that her son was dead, she began to kill off the whole royal family.i 2 But Jehosheba,* daughter of King Jehoram and sister of Ahaziah, took Joash, his son, and spirited him away, along with his nurse, from the bedroom where the princes were about to be slain. She concealed him from Athaliah, and so he did not die. 3 For six years he remained hidden in the temple of the LORD, while Athaliah ruled the land.

4 j But in the seventh year, Jehoiada summoned the captains of the Carians and of the guards. He had them come to him in the temple of the LORD, exacted from them a sworn commitment, and then showed them the king's son. 5 He gave them these orders: "This is what you must do: the third of you who come on duty on the sabbath shall guard the king's palace; 6 another third shall be at the gate Sur; and the last third shall be at the gate behind the guards. 7 The two of your divisions who are going off duty that week shall keep guard over the temple of the LORD for the king. 8 You shall surround the king, each with drawn weapons, and if anyone tries to approach the cordon, kill him; stay with the king, whatever he may do."

9 k The captains did just as Jehoiada the priest commanded. Each one with his men, both those going on duty for the sabbath and those going off duty that week, came to Jehoiada the priest. 10 l He gave the captains King David's spears and shields, which were in the temple of the LORD. 11 And the guards, with drawn weapons, lined up from the southern to the northern limit of the enclosure, surrounding the altar and the temple on the king's behalf. 12 Then Jehoiada led out the king's son and put the crown and the insignia upon him. They proclaimed him king and anointed him, clapping their hands and shouting, "Long live the king!"m

13 n Athaliah heard the noise made by the people, and appeared before them in the temple of the LORD. 14 When she saw the king standing by the pillar,* as was the custom, and the captains and trumpeters near him, with all the people of the land rejoicing and blowing trumpets, she tore her garments and cried out, "Treason, treason!" 15 Then Jehoiada the priest instructed the captains in command of the force: "Bring her outside through the ranks. If anyone follows her," he added, "let him die by the sword." He had given orders that she should not be slain in the temple of the LORD. 16 She was led out forcibly to the horse gate of the royal palace, where she was put to death.

17 o Then Jehoiada made a covenant between the LORD as one party and the king and the people as the other, by which they would be the LORD's people; and another covenant, between the king and the people. 18 Thereupon all the people of the land went to the temple of Baal and demolished it. They shattered its altars and images completely, and slew Mattan, the priest of Baal, before the altars. After appointing a detachment for the temple of the LORD, Jehoiada 19 with the captains, the Carians, the guards, and all the people of the land, led the king down from the temple of the LORD through the guards' gate to the palace, where Joash took his seat on the royal throne. 20 All the people of the land rejoiced and the city was quiet, now that Athaliah had been slain with the sword at the royal palace.

2Kgs

---

g 2 Kgs 15, 12ff.—h Am 1, 3.—i Jgs 9, 5.—j 4-8: 2 Chr 23, 1-7.—k 9-12: 2 Chr 23, 8-11.—l 10ff: 2 Sm 8, 7; 1 Kgs 1, 33f.—m 2 Sm 1, 10.—n 13-16: 2 Chr 23, 12-15.—o 17-20: 2 Chr 23, 16-21.

11, 2: *Jehosheba* was the wife of Jehoiada, the high priest; cf 2 Chr 22, 11.
11, 14: *By the pillar:* see note on 2 Chr 23, 13.

CHAPTER 12

Reign of Joash. [1] Joash was seven years old when he became king.[p] [2] Joash began to reign in the seventh year of Jehu, and he reigned forty years in Jerusalem. His mother, who was named Zibiah, was from Beer-sheba. [3] Joash did what was pleasing to the LORD as long as he lived, because the priest Jehoiada guided him. [4] Still, the high places did not disappear; the people continued to sacrifice and to burn incense there.

[5] [q] For the priests Joash made this rule: "All the funds for sacred purposes that are brought to the temple of the LORD—the census tax, personal redemption money, and whatever funds are freely brought to the temple of the LORD—[6] the priests may take for themselves, each from his own clients. However, they must make whatever repairs on the temple may prove necessary." [7] Nevertheless, as late as the twenty-third year of the reign of King Joash, the priests had not made needed repairs on the temple. [8] Accordingly, King Joash summoned the priest Johoiada and the other priests. "Why do you not repair the temple?" he asked them. "You must no longer take funds from your clients, but you shall turn them over for the repairs." [9] [r] So the priests agreed that they would neither take funds from the people nor make the repairs on the temple.

[10] The priest Jehoiada then took a chest, bored a hole in its lid, and set it beside the stele, on the right as one entered the temple of the LORD. The priests who guarded the entry would put into it all the funds that were brought to the temple of the LORD. [11] When they noticed that there was a large amount of silver in the chest, the royal scribe [and the priest] would come up, and they would melt down all the funds that were in the temple of the LORD, and weigh them. [12] The amount thus realized they turned over to the master workmen in the temple of the LORD. They in turn would give it to the carpenters and builders working in the temple of the LORD, [13] and to the lumbermen and stone cutters, and for the purchase of the wood and hewn stone used in repairing the breaches, and for any other expenses that were necessary to repair the temple. [14] None of the funds brought to the temple of the LORD were used there to make silver

cups, snuffers, basins, trumpets, or any gold or silver article. [15] Instead, they were given to the workmen, and with them they repaired the temple of the LORD. [16] Moreover, no reckoning was asked of the men who were provided with the funds to give to the workmen, because they held positions of trust. [17] The funds from guilt-offerings and from sin-offerings, however, were not brought to the temple of the LORD; they belonged to the priests.

[18] [s] Then King Hazael of Aram mounted a siege against Gath. When he had taken it, Hazael decided to go on to attack Jerusalem.[t] [19] But King Jehoash of Judah took all the dedicated offerings presented by his forebears, Jehoshaphat, Jehoram, and Ahaziah, kings of Judah, as well as his own, and all the gold there was in the treasuries of the temple and the palace, and sent them to King Hazael of Aram, who then led his forces away from Jerusalem. [20] The rest of the acts of Joash, with all that he did, are recorded in the book of the chronicles of the kings of Judah. [21] Certain of his officials entered into a plot against him and killed him at Beth-millo. [22] Jozacar, son of Shimeath, and Jehozabad, son of Shomer, were the officials who killed him. He was buried in his forefathers' City of David, and his son Amaziah succeeded him as king.

CHAPTER 13

Reign of Jehoahaz of Israel. [1] In the twenty-third year of Joash, son of Ahaziah, king of Judah, Jehoahaz, son of Jehu, began his seventeen-year reign over Israel in Samaria. [2] He did evil in the LORD's sight, conducting himself like Jeroboam, son of Nebat, and not renouncing the sin he had caused Israel to commit. [3] The LORD was angry with Israel and for a long time left them in the power of Hazael, king of Aram, and of Ben-hadad, son of Hazael. [4] Then Jehoahaz entreated the LORD, who heard him, since he saw the oppression to which the king of Aram had subjected Israel.[u] [5] So the LORD gave Israel a savior,* and the Israelites, freed from the power of Aram, dwelt in their

---

p 1f: 2 Chr 24, 1f.—q 5-8: 2 Chr 24, 5-10.—r 9-16: 2 Chr 24, 11-14.—s 2 Kgs 8, 12.—t 18-22: 2 Chr 24, 23-27.—u 2 Kgs 14, 26f.

13, 5: *A savior:* by this language, typical of the Book of Judges (Jgs 3, 9. 15), Jeroboam II of Israel is meant; cf 2 Kgs 14, 27.

own homes as formerly. [6]Nevertheless, they did not desist from the sins which the house of Jeroboam had caused Israel to commit, but persisted in them. The sacred pole* also remained standing in Samaria.[v] [7]No soldiers were left to Jehoahaz, except fifty horsemen with ten chariots and ten thousand foot soldiers, since the king of Aram had destroyed them and trampled them like dust. [8]The rest of the acts of Jehoahaz, with all his valor and accomplishments, are recorded in the book of the chronicles of the kings of Israel. [9]Jehoahaz rested with his ancestors and was buried in Samaria. His son Joash succeeded him as king.

Reign of Joash of Israel. [10]In the thirty-seventh year of Joash, king of Judah, Jehoash, son of Jehoahaz, began his sixteen-year reign over Israel in Samaria. [11]He did evil in the sight of the LORD; he did not desist from any of the sins which Jeroboam, son of Nebat, had caused Israel to commit, but persisted in them. [12] * [The rest of the acts of Joash, the valor with which he fought against Amaziah, king of Judah, and all his accomplishments, are recorded in the book of the chronicles of the kings of Israel.[w] [13]Joash rested with his ancestors, and Jeroboam occupied the throne. Joash was buried with the kings of Israel in Samaria.] [14]When Elisha was suffering from the sickness of which he was to die, King Joash of Israel went down to visit him. "My father, my father!" * he exclaimed, weeping over him. "Israel's chariots and horsemen!"[x] [15]"Take a bow and some arrows," Elisha said to him. When he had done so, [16] * Elisha said to the king of Israel, "Put your hand on the bow."

v Ex 34, 13.—w 2 Kgs 14, 8-16.—x 2 Kgs 2, 12.—y Sir 48, 14.—z Dt 9, 27.—a 2f: 2 Chr 25, 1f.—b 5f: 2 Chr 25, 3f.

13, 6: *Sacred pole:* see note on Ex 34, 13.
13, 12f: The conclusion to the reign of Joash is given again in 2 Kgs 14, 15f, where it is more appropriate.
13, 14: *My father, my father:* the king expresses here the same sentiments as those with which Elisha addressed Elijah.
13, 16-19: Symbolic acts similar to these are seen in Ex 17, 8ff; Jos 8, 18ff; Ez 4, 1ff.
14, 1f: *In the second year . . . twenty-nine years in Jerusalem:* the reigns of the kings of Judah between Athaliah and Ahaz are assigned too many years in all to correspond to the reigns in Israel from Jehu to the fall of Samaria. It seems probable that Amaziah was murdered as soon as his son Azariah was old enough to rule, and that Amaziah's reign was nearer nineteen than twenty-nine years. The correlation, in 2 Kgs 15, 1, of the beginning of Azariah's reign with the 27th year of Jeroboam II can hardly be correct; and the sixteen-year reign of Jotham of Judah (2 Kgs 15, 33) consisted for the most part of a regency during the illness of his father (2 Kgs 15, 5).

As the king held the bow, Elisha placed his hands over the king's hands [17]and said, "Open the window toward the east." He opened it, Elisha said, "Shoot," and he shot. The prophet exclaimed, "The LORD's arrow of victory! The arrow of victory over Aram! You will completely conquer Aram at Aphec." [18]Then he said to the king of Israel, "Take the arrows," which he did. Elisha said to him, "Strike the ground!" He struck the ground three times and stopped. [19]Angry with him, the man of God said: "You should have struck five or six times; you would have defeated Aram completely. Now, you will defeat Aram only three times." [20]Elisha died and was buried. At the time, bands of Moabites used to raid the land each year. [21]Once some people were burying a man, when suddenly they spied such a raiding band. So they cast the dead man into the grave of Elisha, and everyone went off. But when the man came in contact with the bones of Elisha, he came back to life and rose to his feet.[y] [22]King Hazael of Aram oppressed Israel during the entire reign of Jehoahaz. [23]But the LORD was merciful with Israel and looked on them with compassion because of his covenant with Abraham, Isaac, and Jacob. He was unwilling to destroy them or to cast them out from his presence.[z] [24]So when King Hazael of Aram died and his son Ben-hadad succeeded him as king, [25]Joash, son of Jehoahaz, took back from Ben-hadad, son of Hazael, the cities which Hazael had taken in battle from his father Jehoahaz. Joash defeated Ben-hadad three times, and thus recovered the cities of Israel.

CHAPTER 14

Amaziah of Judah. * [1]In the second year of Joash, son of Jehoahaz, king of Israel, Amaziah, son of Joash, king of Judah, began to reign. [2] [a] He was twenty-five years old when he became king, and he reigned twenty-nine years in Jerusalem. His mother, whose name was Jehoaddin, was from Jerusalem. [3]He pleased the LORD, yet not like his forefather David, since he did just as his father Joash had done. [4]Thus the high places did not disappear, but the people continued to sacrifice and to burn incense on them. [5] [b] When

Amaziah had the kingdom firmly in hand, he slew the officials who had murdered the king, his father. 6 But the children of the murderers he did not put to death, obeying the LORD's command written in the book of the law of Moses, "Fathers shall not be put to death for their children, nor shall children be put to death for their fathers; each one shall die for his own sin."*c*
7 Amaziah slew ten thousand Edomites in the Salt Valley, and took Sela in battle. He renamed it Joktheel, the name it has to this day.*d*
8 Then Amaziah sent messengers to Jehoash, son of Jehoahaz, son of Jehu, king of Israel, with this challenge, "Come, let us meet face to face."*e* 9 King Jehoash of Israel sent this reply to the king of Judah: "The thistle of Lebanon sent word to the cedar of Lebanon, 'Give your daughter to my son in marriage,' but an animal of Lebanon passed by and trampled the thistle underfoot. 10 You have indeed conquered Edom, and you have become ambitious. Enjoy your glory, but stay at home! Why involve yourself and Judah with you in misfortune and failure?"
11 But Amaziah would not listen. King Jehoash of Israel then advanced, and he and King Amaziah of Judah met in battle at Beth-shemesh of Judah. 12 Judah was defeated by Israel, and all the Judean soldiery fled homeward. 13 King Jehoash of Israel captured Amaziah, son of Jehoash, son of Ahaziah, king of Judah, at Beth-shemesh. He went on to Jerusalem where he tore down four hundred cubits of the city wall, from the Gate of Ephraim to the Corner Gate. 14 He took all the gold and silver and all the utensils there were in the temple of the LORD and in the treasuries of the palace, and hostages as well. Then he returned to Samaria. 15 The rest of the acts of Jehoash, his valor, and how he fought Amaziah, king of Judah, are recorded in the book of the chronicles of the kings of Israel.*f* 16 Jehoash rested with his ancestors; he was buried in Samaria with the kings of Israel. His son Jeroboam succeeded him as king.
17 Amaziah, son of Joash, king of Judah, survived Jehoash, son of Jehoahaz, king of Israel, by fifteen years.* 18 The rest of the acts of Amaziah are written in the book of the chronicles of the kings of Judah. 19 When a conspiracy was formed against him in Jerusalem, he fled to Lachish. But

he was pursued to Lachish and killed there. 20 He was brought back on horses and buried with his ancestors in the City of David in Jerusalem. 21 Thereupon all the people of Judah took the sixteen-year-old Azariah* and proclaimed him king to succeed his father Amaziah.*g* 22 It was Azariah who rebuilt Elath and restored it to Judah, after King Amaziah rested with his ancestors.

Jeroboam II of Israel. 23 In the fifteenth year of Amaziah, son of Joash, king of Judah, Jeroboam, son of Joash, king of Israel, began his forty-one-year reign in Samaria. 24 He did evil in the sight of the LORD; he did not desist from any of the sins which Jeroboam, son of Nebat, had caused Israel to commit. 25 He restored the boundaries of Israel from Labo-of-Hamath to the sea of the Arabah,* just as the LORD, the God of Israel, had prophesied through his servant, the prophet Jonah, son of Amittai, from Gath-hepher. 26 For the LORD saw the very bitter affliction of Israel, where there was neither slave nor freeman, no one at all to help Israel.*h* 27 Since the LORD had not determined to blot out the name of Israel from under the heavens, he saved them through Jeroboam, son of Joash. 28 The rest of the acts of Jeroboam, his valor and all his accomplishments, how he fought with Damascus and turned back Hamath from Israel, are recorded in the book of chronicles of the kings of Israel. 29 Jeroboam rested with his ancestors, the kings of Israel, and his son Zechariah succeeded him as king.

CHAPTER 15

Azariah of Judah. 1 *i* Azariah, son of Amaziah, king of Judah, became king in the twenty-seventh year* of Jeroboam, king of Israel. 2 He was sixteen years old when he began to reign, and he reigned fifty-two years in Jerusalem. His mother, whose name was Jecholiah, was from Jerusalem. 3 He pleased the LORD just as his father Amaziah had done. 4 Yet the

---

c Dt 24, 16; Ez 18, 20.—d 2 Sm 8, 13f; 2 Chr 25, 11.—e 2 Kgs 13, 12; Jgs 9, 8-15.—f 2 Kgs 13, 12f.—g 2 Chr 26, 1f.—h 2 Kgs 13, 4f; 1 Kgs 14, 10.—i 1ff: 2 Chr 26, 3f.

14, 17: See note on 2 Kgs 14, 1f.
14, 21: *Azariah:* also called Uzziah in many texts.
14, 25: *Sea of the Arabah:* the Dead Sea. *Jonah:* see note on Jon 1, 1.
15, 1: *Twenty-seventh year:* see note on 2 Kgs 14, 1f.

high places did not disappear; the people continued to sacrifice and to burn incense on them. ⁵ *ʲ* The LORD afflicted the king, and he was a leper to the day of his death. He lived in a house apart, while Jotham, the king's son, was vizier and regent for the people of the land. ⁶The rest of the acts of Azariah, and all his accomplishments, are recorded in the book of the chronicles of the kings of Judah. ⁷Azariah rested with his ancestors, and was buried with them in the City of David. His son Jotham succeeded him as king.

Zechariah of Israel. ⁸In the thirty-eighth year of Azariah, king of Judah, Zechariah, son of Jeroboam, was king of Israel in Samaria for six months. ⁹He did evil in the sight of the LORD as his fathers had done, and did not desist from the sins which Jeroboam, son of Nebat, had caused Israel to commit. ¹⁰Shallum, son of Jabesh, conspired against Zechariah, attacked and killed him at Ibleam, and reigned in his place. ¹¹The rest of the acts of Zechariah are recorded in the book of the chronicles of the kings of Israel. ¹²Thus the LORD's promise to Jehu, "Your descendants shall sit upon the throne of Israel," was fulfilled.*ᵏ*

Shallum of Israel. ¹³Shallum, son of Jabesh, became king in the thirty-ninth year of Uzziah, king of Judah; he reigned one month in Samaria. ¹⁴Menahem, son of Gadi, came up from Tirzah to Samaria, where he attacked and killed Shallum, son of Jabesh, and reigned in his place. ¹⁵The rest of the acts of Shallum, and the fact of his conspiracy, are recorded in the book of the chronicles of the kings of Israel. ¹⁶At that time, Menahem punished Tappuah, all the inhabitants of the town and of its whole district, because on his way from Tirzah they did not let him in. He punished them even to ripping open all the pregnant women.

Menahem of Israel. ¹⁷In the thirty-ninth year of Azariah, king of Judah, Mena-

hem, son of Gadi, began his ten-year reign over Samaria. ¹⁸He did evil in the sight of the LORD, not desisting from the sins which Jeroboam, son of Nebat, had caused Israel to commit. During his reign, ¹⁹Pul,* king of Assyria, invaded the land, and Menahem gave him a thousand talents of silver to have his assistance in strengthening his hold on the kingdom. ²⁰Menahem secured the money to give to the king of Assyria by exacting it from all the men of substance in the country, fifty silver shekels from each. The king of Assyria did not remain in the country but withdrew. ²¹The rest of the acts of Menahem, and all his accomplishments, are recorded in the book of the chronicles of the kings of Israel. ²²Menahem rested with his ancestors, and his son Pekahiah succeeded him as king.

2Kgs

Pekahiah of Israel. ²³In the fiftieth year of Azariah, king of Judah, Pekahiah, son of Menahem, began his two-year reign over Israel in Samaria. ²⁴He did evil in the sight of the LORD, not desisting from the sins which Jeroboam, son of Nebat, had caused Israel to commit. ²⁵His adjutant Pekah, son of Remaliah, who had with him fifty men from Gilead, conspired against him, killed him within the palace stronghold in Samaria, and reigned in his place. ²⁶The rest of the acts of Pekahiah, and all his accomplishments, are recorded in the book of the chronicles of the kings of Israel.

Pekah of Israel. ²⁷In the fifty-second year of Azariah, king of Judah, Pekah, son of Remaliah, began his twenty-year reign over Israel in Samaria.* ²⁸He did evil in the sight of the LORD, not desisting from the sins which Jeroboam, son of Nebat, had caused Israel to commit. ²⁹During the reign of Pekah, king of Israel, Tiglath-pileser, king of Assyria, came and took Ijon, Abel-beth-maacah, Janoah, Kedesh, Hazor, all the territory of Naphtali, Gilead, and Galilee, deporting the inhabitants to Assyria. ³⁰Hoshea, son of Elah, conspired against Pekah, son of Remaliah; he attacked and killed him, and reigned in his place [in the twentieth year of Jotham, son of Uzziah]. ³¹The rest of the acts of Pekah, and all his accomplishments, are recorded in the book of the chronicles of the kings of Israel.

Jotham of Judah. ³² *ˡ* In the second year of Pekah, son of Remaliah, king of Israel,

j 5ff: 2 Chr 26, 21ff.—k 2 Kgs 10, 30.—l 32-38: 2 Chr 27, 1-4. 7-9.

15, 19: *Pul:* the Babylonian throne name of the Assyrian Tiglath-pileser III; cf 2 Kgs 15, 29.

15, 27: The twenty years here ascribed to Pekah are an impossibility; the calculation which made his reign, of five years at most, appear so long may have been based on the attempt to give Jotham of Judah a full sixteen-year reign independently of his regency. See 2 Kgs 16, 1 and the note on 2 Kgs 14, 1f.

Jotham, son of Uzziah, king of Judah, began to reign. [33] He was twenty-five years old when he became king, and he reigned sixteen years in Jerusalem. His mother's name was Jerusha, daughter of Zadok. [34] He pleased the LORD, just as his father Uzziah had done. [35] Nevertheless the high places did not disappear and the people continued to sacrifice and to burn incense on them. It was he who built the Upper Gate* of the temple of the LORD. [36] The rest of the acts of Jotham, and all his accomplishments, are recorded in the book of the chronicles of the kings of Judah. [37] It was at that time that the LORD first loosed Rezin, king of Aram, and Pekah, son of Remaliah, against Judah. [38] Jotham rested with his ancestors and was buried with them in his forefather's City of David. His son Ahaz succeeded him as king.

CHAPTER 16

Ahaz of Judah. [1] *m* In the seventeenth year of Pekah, son of Remaliah, Ahaz, son of Jotham, king of Judah, began to reign. [2] Ahaz was twenty years old when he became king, and he reigned sixteen years in Jerusalem. He did not please the LORD, his God, like his forefather David, [3] but conducted himself like the kings of Israel, and even immolated his son by fire, in accordance with the abominable practice of the nations whom the LORD had cleared out of the way of the Israelites. *n* [4] Further, he sacrificed and burned incense on the high places, on hills, and under every leafy tree. *o*

[5] Then Rezin, king of Aram, and Pekah, son of Remaliah, king of Israel, came up to Jerusalem to attack it. Although they besieged Ahaz, they were unable to conquer him. *p* [6] At the same time the king of Edom recovered Elath for Edom, driving the Judeans out of it. The Edomites then entered Elath, which they have occupied until the present. *q*

[7] Meanwhile, Ahaz sent messengers to Tiglath-pileser, king of Assyria, with the plea: "I am your servant and your son. Come up and rescue me from the clutches of the king of Aram and the king of Israel, who are attacking me." *r* [8] Ahaz took the silver and gold that were in the temple of the LORD and in the

palace treasuries and sent them as a present to the king of Assyria, *s* [9] who listened to him and moved against Damascus, which he captured. He deported its inhabitants to Kir and put Rezin to death.*

[10] King Ahaz went to Damascus to meet Tiglath-pileser, king of Assyria. When he saw the altar in Damascus, King Ahaz sent to Uriah the priest a model of the altar and a detailed design of its construction. [11] Uriah the priest built an altar according to the plans which King Ahaz sent him from Damascus, and had it completed by the time the king returned home. [12] On his arrival from Damascus, the king inspected this altar, then went up to it and offered sacrifice on it, [13] burning his holocaust and cereal-offering, pouring out his libation, and sprinkling the blood of his peace-offerings on the altar. *t* [14] The bronze altar that stood before the LORD he brought from the front of the temple—that is, from the space between the new altar and the temple of the LORD—and set it on the north side of his altar. [15] *u* "Upon the large altar," King Ahaz commanded Uriah the priest, "burn the morning holocaust and the evening cereal-offering, the royal holocaust and cereal-offering, as well as the holocausts, cereal-offerings, and libations of the people. You must also sprinkle on it all the blood of holocausts and sacrifices. But the old bronze altar shall be mine for consultation."* [16] Uriah the priest did just as King Ahaz had commanded. [17] King Ahaz

---

m 1-4: 2 Chr 28, 1-4.—n Lv 18, 21.—o Dt 12, 2.—p 2 Chr 28, 5f.—q 2 Chr 28, 17.—r 2 Chr 28, 16.—s 2 Chr 28, 21.—t 2 Chr 28, 23.—u Ex 29, 38f; Nm 28, 3f.

15, 35: *The Upper Gate:* also the Gate of Benjamin; cf Jer 20, 2; Ez 9, 2.

16, 9: Firmly dated events bearing on chapters 16 through 20 are: the fall of Damascus (16, 9) in 732 B.C., the fall of Samaria (18, 9-11) in 721 B.C., and Sennacherib's invasion of Judah (18, 3) in 701 B.C., which is equated both in Kgs and in Is 36, 1 with the 14th year of Hezekiah. These data made it necessary to credit Ahaz with at least a twenty-year reign, between 735 and c. 715 B.C., and to exclude the correlations between Hoshea of Israel and Hezekiah in chapter 18.

If the 14th-year correspondence for 701 B.C. is given up, other arrangements are possible. The alleged ages of Jotham (15, 33), Ahaz (16, 2), and Hezekiah (18, 2) at their successive accessions to the throne do not argue for an early date for Hezekiah; but one or more of these may be artificial. Azariah (15, 1-7; Is 6, 1) was still on the throne of Judah in 743 B.C.

16, 15: *For consultation:* perhaps the introduction into Judah of the Babylonian practice of omen sacrifices; cf Ez 21, 16.

JUDAH & ISRAEL
733-721

REZIN OF ARAM •-•-•-•

PHILISTINES-EDOM •••••

SHALMANESER V ━ ━ ━

2 Kgs 15, 30—17, 5; 2 Chr 28, 5-37

DAMASCUS

A R A M

I S R A E L

SAMARIA ○

Gimzo ○   Jericho
Gederoth ○   Aijalon ○
B-Shemesh   JERUSALEM
Timna ○
Soco ○

PHILISTINES

Gaza ○   J U D A H

○ Hebron

Beer-sheba

E D O M

0 10 20 30 km.

JUDAH AND ISRAEL (733-721) (2 Kgs 15, 30—17, 5) — **(a)** Rezin, king of **Aram,** and Pekah, king of **Israel,** join forces to make war against **Judah,** they besiege **Jerusalem** but fail to conquer it; they succeed in carrying away a large number of captives who are mistreated until the prophet Oded obtains their release (2 Kgs 16, 1-4; 2 Chr 28, 9-15). **(b)** Ahaz of Judah obtains the intervention of the king of Assyria, Tiglath-pileser II, who conquers **Damascus** in 733-32 and destroys the kingdom of **Aram;** the captives are taken to **Kir** (2 Kgs 16, 7-9). **(c)** In 732, the Edomites profit from the circumstances to retake **Elath** and invade **Judah** (2 Chr 28, 17). **(d)** In 724, the Philistines raid the cities of the foothills and the **Negeb** of Judah, capturing **Beth-shemesh, Aijalon, Gederoth, Soco,** and **Gimzo** (2 Chr 28, 18). **(e)** At the same time Shalmaneser V, king of Assyria, advances against Hoshea of Israel who becomes his vassal and pays tribute; however, Hoshea appeals to the king of Egypt and is imprisoned by the Assyrians (2 Kgs 17, 3-5). **(f)** Shalmaneser V then occupies the whole land and lays siege to Samaria (2 Kgs 17, 5).

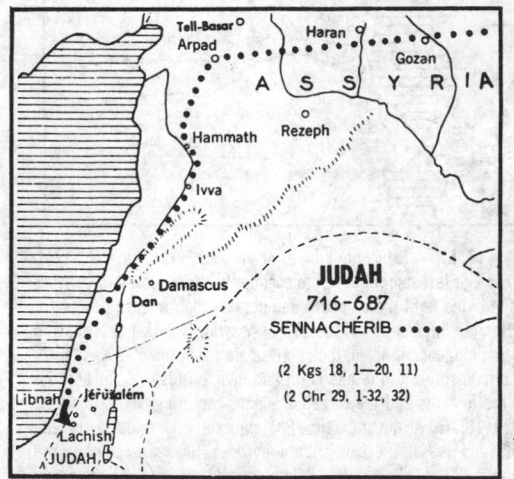

THE EXILE OF ISRAEL
721
(2 Kgs 17, 6; 18, 9-11)

0   500
miles

THE EXILE OF THE KINGDOM OF ISRAEL (721) (2 Kgs 17, 6; 18, 9-11) — **(a)** After suffering siege for three years, the city of **Samaria** is finally captured by Sargon II, son of Shalmaneser V, in 721 (17, 5-6). **(b)** The Israelites are deported to **Halah** at the **Habor**, a river **Gozan**, and to the cities of **Media** (17, 6). **(c)** In a non-biblical inscription in which Sargon II takes credit for capturing Israel, he lists 22,290 Israelites deported; with the aid of statistics given in 2 Kgs 15, 6, scholars calculate that these captives constituted one-tenth to one-twentieth of the population—taken mostly from the influential classes in order to discourage rebellion among those who remained.

JUDAH
716-687
SENNACHÉRIB ••••

(2 Kgs 18, 1—20, 11)
(2 Chr 29, 1-32, 32)

JUDAH UNDER SIEGE (2 Kgs 18, 1—20, 11; Is 36-37; 2 Chr 29-32) — **(a)** After purifying the temple and defeating the Philistines at **Gaza**, Hezekiah is attacked by Sennacherib fresh from victories in Hamath at **Arpah, Sepharvaim, Hena, Ivva,** and **Samaria** on his campaign throughout Palestine (2 Kgs 18, 8-27). **(b)** The Lord sends "an exterminating angel" driving Sennacherib to **Nineveh** (19, 35-37) where he is killed by his sons and succeeded by his son Esarhaddon (681). **(c)** Assyrian records give accounts of the campaign Sennacherib was waging in Palestine at the same time that he was attacking Jerusalem in 701; in them he boasts that he "shut up Hezekiah like a bird in a cage" but significantly says nothing about capturing Jerusalem, thus corroborating the biblical account.

detached the frames from the bases and removed the lavers from them; he also took down the bronze sea from the bronze oxen that supported it, and set it on a stone pavement.*v* *18* In deference to the king of Assyria he removed from the temple of the LORD the emplacement which had been built in the temple for a throne, and the outer entrance for the king.* *19* The rest of the acts of Ahaz are recorded in the book of the chronicles of the kings of Judah.*w* *20* Ahaz rested with his ancestors and was buried with them in the City of David. His son Hezekiah succeeded him as king.

CHAPTER 17

Hoshea of Israel. *1* In the twelfth year of Ahaz, king of Judah, Hoshea, son of Elah, began his nine-year reign over Israel in Samaria. *2* He did evil in the sight of the LORD, yet not to the extent of the kings of Israel before him. *3* Shalmaneser,* king of Assyria, advanced against him, and Hoshea became his vassal and paid him tribute.*x* *4* But the king of Assyria found Hoshea guilty of conspiracy for sending envoys to the king of Egypt at Sais, and for failure to pay the annual tribute to his Assyrian overlord. *5* For this the king of Assyria arrested and imprisoned Hoshea; he then occupied the whole land and attacked Samaria, which he besieged for three years. *6* In the ninth year of Hoshea, the king of Assyria* took Samaria, and deported the Israelites to Assyria, settling them in Halah, at the Habor, a river of Gozan, and in the cities of the Medes.*y*

7 This came about because the Israelites sinned against the LORD, their God, who had brought them up from the land of Egypt, from under the domination of Pharaoh, king of Egypt, and because they venerated other gods. *8* They followed the rites of the nations whom the LORD had cleared out of the way of the Israelites [and the kings of Israel whom they set up]. *9* They adopted unlawful practices toward the LORD, their God. They built high

places in all their settlements, the watchtowers as well as the walled cities. *10* They set up pillars and sacred poles for themselves on every high hill and under every leafy tree.*z* *11* There, on all the high places, they burned incense like the nations whom the LORD had sent into exile at their coming. They did evil things that provoked the LORD, *12* and served idols, although the LORD had told them, "You must not do this."

13 And though the LORD warned Israel and Judah by every prophet and seer, "Give up your evil ways and keep my commandments and statutes, in accordance with the entire law which I enjoined on your fathers and which I sent you by my servants the prophets," *14* *a* they did not listen, but were as stiffnecked as their fathers, who had not believed in the LORD, their God. *15* They rejected his statutes, the covenant which he had made with their fathers, and the warnings which he had given them. The vanity they pursued, they themselves became: they followed the surrounding nations whom the LORD had commanded them not to imitate.*b* *16* They disregarded all the commandments of the LORD, their God, and made for themselves two molten calves; they also made a sacred pole and worshiped all the host of heaven, and served Baal.*c* *17* *d* They immolated their sons and daughters by fire, practiced fortune-telling and divination, and sold themselves into evildoing in the LORD's sight, provoking him *18* till, in his great anger against Israel, the LORD put them away out of his sight. Only the tribe of Judah was left.

19 Even the people of Judah, however, did not keep the commandments of the LORD, their God, but followed the rites practiced by Israel. *20* So the LORD rejected the whole race of Israel. He afflicted them and delivered them over to plunderers, finally casting them out from before him. *21* When he tore Israel away from the house of David, they made Jeroboam, son of Nebat, king: he drove the Israelites away from the LORD, causing them to commit a great sin.*e* *22* The Israelites imitated Jeroboam in all the sins he committed, nor would they desist from them. *23* Finally, the LORD put Israel away out of his sight as he had foretold through all his servants, the

---

v 2 Chr 28, 24.—w 2 Chr 28, 26f.—x 2 Kgs 18, 9; Tb 1, 2.—y 2 Kgs 18, 10f.—z Ex 23, 24; 34, 13; Dt 12, 2.—a Jer 25, 5; Dt 9, 13.—b Jer 2, 5.—c 1 Kgs 12, 28; Ex 34, 13; Dt 4, 19; 17, 2f.—d Lv 18, 21; Dt 18, 10.—e 1 Kgs 12, 19f; 12, 26-33.

16, 18: *Emplacement . . . for a throne, and the outer entrance for the king:* signs of sovereignty for the Hebrew kings.

17, 3: *Shalmaneser:* son and successor of Tiglath-pileser.

17, 6: *The king of Assyria:* Shalmaneser's successor and usurper, Sargon II.

prophets; and Israel went into exile from their native soil to Assyria, an exile lasting to the present.*f*

²⁴The king of Assyria brought people from Babylon, Cuthah, Avva, Hamath, and Sepharvaim, and settled them in the cities of Samaria in place of the Israelites. They took possession of Samaria and dwelt in its cities. ²⁵When they first settled there, they did not venerate the LORD, so he sent lions among them that killed some of their number. ²⁶A report reached the king of Assyria: "The nations whom you deported and settled in the cities of Samaria do not know how to worship the God of the land, and he has sent lions among them that are killing them, since they do not know how to worship the God of the land." ²⁷The king of Assyria gave the order, "Send back one of the priests whom I deported, to go there and settle, to teach them how to worship the God of the land." ²⁸So one of the priests who had been deported from Samaria returned and settled in Bethel, and taught them how to venerate the LORD.

²⁹But these peoples began to make their own gods in the various cities in which they were living; in the shrines on the high places which the Samaritans had made, each people set up gods.*g* ³⁰Thus the Babylonians made Marduk and his consort; the men of Cuth made Nergal; the men of Hamath made Ashima; ³¹the men of Avva made Nibhaz and Tartak; and the men of Sepharvaim immolated their children by fire to their city gods, King Hadad and his consort Anath. ³²They also venerated the LORD, choosing from their number priests for the high places, who officiated for them in the shrines on the high places.*h* ³³But, while venerating the LORD, they served their own gods, following the worship of the nations from among whom they had been deported.

³⁴To this day they worship according to their ancient rites.* [They did not venerate the LORD nor observe the statutes and regulations, the law and commandments, which the LORD enjoined on the descendants of Jacob, whom he had named Israel.*i* ³⁵When he made a covenant with them, he commanded them: "You must not venerate other gods, nor worship them, nor serve them, nor offer sacrifice to them.*j* ³⁶The LORD, who brought you up from the land of Egypt with great power

and outstretched arm: him shall you venerate, him shall you worship, and to him shall you sacrifice. ³⁷You must be careful to observe forever the statutes and regulations, the law and commandments, which he wrote for you, and you must not venerate other gods. ³⁸The covenant which I made with you, you must not forget; you must not venerate other gods. ³⁹But the LORD, your God, you must venerate; it is he who will deliver you from the power of all your enemies." ⁴⁰They did not listen, however, but continued in their earlier manner.] ⁴¹Thus these nations venerated the LORD, but also served their idols. And their sons and grandsons, to this day, are doing as their fathers did.

V: THE KINGDOM OF JUDAH AFTER 721 B.C.

CHAPTER 18

Hezekiah. ¹*k* In the third year of Hoshea, son of Elah, king of Israel, Hezekiah, son of Ahaz, king of Judah, began to reign. ²He was twenty-five years old when he became king, and he reigned twenty-nine years in Jerusalem. His mother's name was Abi, daughter of Zechariah. ³He pleased the LORD, just as his forefather David had done. ⁴It was he who removed the high places, shattered the pillars, and cut down the sacred poles. He smashed the bronze serpent called Nehushtan which Moses had made, because up to that time the Israelites were burning incense to it.*l* ⁵He put his trust in the LORD, the God of Israel; and neither before him nor after him was there anyone like him among all the kings of Judah. ⁶Loyal to the LORD, Hezekiah never turned away from him, but observed the commandments which the LORD had given Moses. ⁷The LORD was with him, and he prospered in all that he set out to do. He rebelled against the king of Assyria and did not serve him. ⁸He also subjugated the watchtowers and walled cities of the Philistines, all the way to Gaza and its territory.

---

f Jer 25, 9.—g Jn 4, 9.—h 1 Kgs 12, 31.—i Gn 32, 29.—j Ex 20, 3ff.—k 1ff: 2 Chr 28, 27; 29, 1f.—l Ex 23, 24; 34, 13; Nm 21, 9; Dt 12, 2; 2 Chr 31, 1; Wis 16, 6; Jn 3, 14.

17, 34-40: *They did not . . . earlier manner:* this passage is an adaptation of language denouncing the Israelites to make it applicable to the later Samaritan sect of post-exilic times. The original bearing of the discourse (vv 13-15) can be seen by reading it between vv 22 and 23. Cf also 2 Kgs 18, 12.

⁹ In the fourth year of King Hezekiah, which was the seventh year of Hoshea, son of Elah, king of Israel, Shalmaneser, king of Assyria, attacked Samaria, laid siege to it,* ¹⁰ *m* and after three years captured it. In the sixth year of Hezekiah, the ninth year of Hoshea, king of Israel, Samaria was taken. ¹¹ The king of Assyria then deported the Israelites to Assyria and settled them in Halah, at the Habor, a river of Gozan, and in the cities of the Medes. ¹² This came about because they had not heeded the warning of the LORD, their God, but violated his covenant, not heeding and not fulfilling the commandments of Moses, the servant of the LORD. *ⁿ*

Invasion of Sennacherib. ¹³ * In the fourteenth year of King Hezekiah, Sennacherib,* king of Assyria, went on an expedition against all the fortified cities of Judah and captured them.*ᵒ* ¹⁴ Hezekiah, king of Judah, sent this message to the king of Assyria at Lachish: "I have done wrong. Leave me, and I will pay whatever tribute you impose on me." The king of Assyria exacted three hundred talents of silver and thirty talents of gold from Hezekiah, king of Judah. ¹⁵ Hezekiah paid him all the funds there were in the temple of the LORD and in the palace treasuries. ¹⁶ He broke up the door panels and the uprights of the temple of the LORD which he himself had ordered to be overlaid with gold, and gave the gold to the king of Assyria.*ᵖ*

¹⁷ The king of Assyria sent the general, the lord chamberlain, and the commander* from Lachish with a great army to King Hezekiah at Jerusalem. They went up, and on their arrival in Jerusalem, stopped at the conduit of the upper pool on the highway of the fuller's field.*q* ¹⁸ They called for the king, who sent out to them Eliakim, son of Hilkiah, the master of the the palace; Shebnah the scribe; and the herald Joah, son of Asaph.*r* ¹⁹ The commander said to them, "Tell Hezekiah, 'Thus says the great king, the king of Assyria: On what do you base this confidence of yours? ²⁰ Do you think mere words substitute for strategy and might in war? On whom, then, do you rely, that you rebel against me? ²¹ This Egypt, the staff on which you rely, is in fact a broken reed which pierces the hand of anyone who leans on it. That is what Pharaoh, king of Egypt, is to all who rely on him.*s* ²² But if you say to me, We rely on the LORD, our God, is not he the one whose high places and altars Hezekiah has removed, commanding Judah and Jerusalem to worship before this altar in Jerusalem?'

²³ "Now, make a wager with my lord, the king of Assyria: I will give you two thousand horses if you can put riders on them. ²⁴ How then can you repulse even one of the least servants of my lord, relying as you do on Egypt for chariots and horsemen? ²⁵ Was it without the LORD's will that I have come up to destroy this place? The LORD said to me, 'Go up and destroy that land!' "

²⁶ Then Eliakim, son of Hilkiah, and Shebnah and Joah said to the commander: "Please speak to your servants in Aramaic; we understand it. Do not speak to us in Judean within earshot of the people who are on the wall."

²⁷ But the commander replied: "Was it to your master and to you that my lord sent me to speak these words? Was it not rather to the men sitting on the wall, who, with you, will have to eat their own excrement and drink their urine?" ²⁸ Then the commander stepped forward and cried out in a loud voice in Judean, "Listen to the words of the great king, the king of Assyria. ²⁹ Thus says the king: 'Do not let Hezekiah deceive you, since he cannot deliver you out of my hand. ³⁰ Let not Hezekiah induce you to rely on the LORD, saying, The LORD will surely save us; this city will not be handed over to the king of Assyria. ³¹ Do not listen to Hezekiah, for the king of Assyria says: Make peace with me and surrender! Then each of you will eat of his own vine and of his own fig-tree, and drink the water of his own cistern, ³² until I come to take you to a land like your own, a land of grain and wine, of bread and orchards, of olives, oil and fruit syrup. Choose life, not death. Do not listen

m 1Of: 2 Kgs 17, 6; Tb 1, 2.—n 2 Kgs 17, 7-18.—o 2 Chr 32, 1ff; Sir 48, 18; Is 36, 1.—p 1 Kgs 6, 20-22.—q 2 Chr 32, 9; Is 36, 1ff.—r Is 22, 13-25.—s Is 30, 1-7; 31, 1-3; Ez 29, 6-7.

18, 9: See note on 2 Kgs 16, 9.

18, 13—20, 11: Duplication of Is 36, 1—38, 8. 21. 22.

18, 13: *Sennacherib* succeeded Sargon II as king of Assyria. His Judean campaign was waged in 701 B.C. See note on 2 Kgs 16, 9.

18, 17: *General, the lord chamberlain . . . commander:* the text lists three major functionaries by their Assyrian titles, of which only the first, more nearly "lord lieutenant," is military in origin; the *commander* was technically the king's chief butler.

2Kgs

to Hezekiah when he would seduce you by saying, The LORD will rescue us. ³³Has any of the gods of the nations ever rescued his land from the hand of the king of Assyria? ³⁴Where are the gods of Hamath and Arpad? Where are the gods of Sepharvaim, Hena, and Avva? Where are the gods of the land of Samaria?ᵗ ³⁵Which of the gods for all these lands ever rescued his land from my hand? Will the LORD then rescue Jerusalem from my hand?' " ³⁶But the people remained silent and did not answer him one word, for the king had ordered them not to answer him.

³⁷Then the master of the palace, Eliakim, son of Hilkiah, Shebnah the scribe, and the herald Joah, son of Asaph, came to Hezekiah with their garments torn, and reported to him what the commander had said.

CHAPTER 19

Hezekiah and Isaiah. ¹ ᵘ When King Hezekiah heard this, he tore his garments, wrapped himself in sackcloth, and went into the temple of the LORD. ²He sent Eliakim, the master of the palace, Shebnah the scribe, and the elders of the priests, wrapped in sackcloth, to tell the prophet Isaiah, son of Amoz, ³"Thus says Hezekiah: 'This is a day of distress, of rebuke, and of disgrace. Children are at the point of birth, but there is no strength to bring them forth.* ⁴Perhaps the LORD, your God, will hear all the words of the commander, whom his master, the king of Assyria, sent to taunt the living God, and will rebuke him for the words which the LORD, your God, has heard. So send up a prayer for the remnant that is here.' " ⁵When the servants of King Hezekiah had come to Isaiah, ⁶he said to them, "Tell this to your master: 'Thus says the LORD: Do not be frightened by the words you have heard, with which the servants of the king of Assyria have blasphemed me.ᵛ ⁷I am about to put in him such a spirit that, when he hears a certain report, he will return to his own land, and there I will cause him to fall by the sword.' "

⁸When the commander, on his return, heard that the king of Assyria had withdrawn from Lachish, he found him besieging Libnah. ⁹The king of Assyria heard a report that Tirhakah, king of Ethiopia, had come out to fight against him. Again

he sent envoys to Hezekiah with this message: ¹⁰"Thus shall you say to Hezekiah, king of Judah: 'Do not let your God on whom you rely deceive you by saying that Jerusalem will not be handed over to the king of Assyria. ¹¹You have heard what the kings of Assyria have done to all other countries: they doomed them! Will you, then, be saved? ¹²Did the gods of the nations whom my fathers destroyed save them? Gozan, Haran, Rezeph, or the Edenites in Telassar?ʷ ¹³Where are the king of Hamath, the king of Arpad, or the kings of the cities Sepharvaim, Hena and Avva?"ˣ

¹⁴ ʸ Hezekiah took the letter from the hand of the messengers and read it; then he went up to the temple of the LORD, and spreading it out before him, ¹⁵he prayed in the LORD's presence: "O LORD, God of Israel, enthroned upon the cherubim! You alone are God over all the kingdoms of the earth. You have made the heavens and the earth.ᶻ ¹⁶Incline your ear, O LORD, and listen! Open your eyes, O LORD, and see! Hear the words of Sennacherib which he sent to taunt the living God. ¹⁷Truly, O LORD, the kings of Assyria have laid waste the nations and their lands, ¹⁸and cast their gods into the fire; they destroyed them because they were not gods, but the work of human hands, wood and stone.ᵃ ¹⁹Therefore, O LORD, our God, save us from the power of this man, that all the kingdoms of the earth may know that you alone, O LORD, are God."ᵇ

Punishment of Sennacherib. ²⁰Then Isaiah, son of Amoz, sent this message to Hezekiah: "Thus says the LORD, the God of Israel, in answer to your prayer for help against Sennacherib, king of Assyria: I have listened! ²¹This is the word the LORD has spoken concerning him:*

" 'She despises you, laughs you to scorn
    the virgin daughter of Zion.
Behind you she wags her head,
    daughter Jerusalem.
²²Whom have you insulted and blasphemed,

---

t 2 Kgs 17, 24.—u 1-7: Is 37, 1-7.—v Is 10, 5-19.—w 2 Kgs 17, 6.—x 2 Kgs 18, 34.—y 14-19: 2 Chr 32, 20; Is 37, 14-20.—z Ex 25, 18.—a Jer 10, 3.—b 1 Kgs 18, 24.

19, 3: See note on Is 37, 3.
19, 21-31: Vv 21-28 are addressed to Sennacherib, vv 29-31 to Judah.

against whom have you raised your
voice
And lifted up your eyes on high?
Against the Holy One of Israel!
²³ Through your servants you have insulted the LORD.
You said: With my many chariots
I climbed the mountain heights,
the recesses of Lebanon;
I cut down its lofty cedars,
its choice cypresses;
I reached the remotest heights,
its forest park.
²⁴ I dug wells and drank water in foreign
lands;
I dried up with the soles of my feet
all the rivers of Egypt.

²⁵ " 'Have you not heard?
Long ago I prepared it,
From days of old I planned it.
Now I have brought it to pass:
That you should reduce fortified cities
into heaps of ruins,
²⁶ While their inhabitants, shorn of
power,
are dismayed and ashamed,
Becoming like the plants of the field,
like the green growth,
like the scorched grass on the housetops.
²⁷ I am aware whether you stand or sit;
I know whether you come or go,ᶜ
²⁸   and also your rage against me.
Because of your rage against me
and your fury which has reached my
ears,
I will put my hook in your nose
and my bit in your mouth,
and make you return the way you
came.

²⁹ " 'This shall be a sign for you:
this year you shall eat the aftergrowth,
next year, what grows of itself;
But in the third year, sow and reap,
plant vineyards and eat their fruit!
³⁰ The remaining survivors of the house of
Judah
shall again strike root below
and bear fruit above.
³¹ For out of Jerusalem shall come a remnant,

and from Mount Zion, survivors.
The zeal of the LORD of hosts shall do
this.'

³² "Therefore, thus says the LORD concerning the king of Assyria: 'He shall not
reach this city, nor shoot an arrow at it,
nor come before it with a shield, nor cast
up siege-works against it. ³³ He shall return by the same way he came, without entering the city, says the LORD. ³⁴ I will
shield and save this city for my own sake,
and for the sake of my servant David.' "ᵈ
³⁵ That night the angel of the LORD went
forth and struck down one hundred and
eighty-five thousand men in the Assyrian
camp. Early the next morning, there they
were, all the corpses of the dead.ᵉ ³⁶ So
Sennacherib, the king of Assyria, broke
camp, and went back home to Nineveh.
³⁷ When he was worshiping in the temple of his god Nisroch, his sons Adrammelech and Sharezer slew him with the
sword and fled into the land of Ararat.
His son Esar-haddon reigned in his
stead.

CHAPTER 20

Hezekiah's Illness. ¹ ᶠ In those days,
when Hezekiah was mortally ill, the
prophet Isaiah, son of Amoz, came and
said to him: "Thus says the LORD: 'Put
your house in order, for you are about
to die; you shall not recover.' " ²He
turned his face to the wall and prayed to
the LORD: ³ "O LORD, remember how
faithfully and wholeheartedly I conducted myself in your presence, doing
what was pleasing to you!" And
Hezekiah wept bitterly.
⁴ Before Isaiah had left the central
courtyard, the word of the LORD came
to him: ⁵ "Go back and tell Hezekiah,
the leader of my people: 'Thus says the
LORD, the God of your forefather David:
I have heard your prayer and seen your
tears. I will heal you. In three days you
shall go up to the LORD's temple; ⁶ I will
add fifteen years to your life. I will rescue you and this city from the hand of
the king of Assyria; I will be a shield to
this city for my own sake, and for the
sake of my servant David.' "
⁷ Isaiah then ordered a poultice of figs
to be brought and applied to the boil,
that he might recover. ⁸ Then Hezekiah

c Ps 139, 2f.—d 2 Sm 7, 12; Hos 1, 7.—e Sir 48, 21; 2 Chr 32,
21f; Is 37, 36-38; 1 Mc 7, 41; 2 Mc 8, 19.—f 1-9: 2 Chr 32, 24;
Is 38, 1-8.

asked Isaiah, "What is the sign that the LORD will heal me and that I shall go up to the temple of the LORD on the third day?" 9 Isaiah replied, "This will be the sign for you from the LORD that he will do what he has promised: Shall the shadow go forward or back ten steps?" 10 "It is easy for the shadow to advance ten steps," Hezekiah answered. "Rather, let it go back ten steps." 11 So the prophet Isaiah invoked the LORD, who made the shadow retreat the ten steps it had descended on the staircase to the terrace of Ahaz.

12 * At that time, when Merodach-baladan, son of Baladan, king of Babylon, heard that Hezekiah had been ill, he sent letters and gifts to him.*g* 13 Hezekiah was pleased at this, and therefore showed the messengers his whole treasury, his silver, gold, spices and fine oil, his armory, and all that was in his storerooms; there was nothing in his house or in all his realm that Hezekiah did not show them.

14 Then Isaiah the prophet came to King Hezekiah and asked him: "What did these men say to you? Where did they come from?" "They came from a distant land, from Babylon," replied Hezekiah. 15 "What did they see in your house?" the prophet asked. "They saw everything in my house," answered Hezekiah. "There is nothing in my storerooms that I did not show them." 16 Then Isaiah said to Hezekiah: "Hear the word of the LORD: 17 The time is coming when all that is in your house, and everything that your fathers have stored up until this day, shall be carried off to Babylon; nothing shall be left, says the LORD. 18 Some of your own bodily descendants shall be taken and made servants in the palace of the king of Babylon."

19 Hezekiah replied to Isaiah, "The word of the LORD which you have spoken is favorable." For he thought, "There will be peace and security in my lifetime."

20 The rest of the acts of Hezekiah, all his valor, and his construction of the pool and conduit* by which water was brought into the city, are written in the book of the chronicles of the kings of Judah.*h* 21 Hezekiah rested with his ancestors and his son Manasseh succeeded him as king.

CHAPTER 21

Reign of Manasseh. 1 *i* Manasseh was twelve years old when he began to reign, and he reigned fifty-five years in Jerusalem. His mother's name was Hephzibah. 2 He did evil in the sight of the LORD, following the abominable practices of the nations whom the LORD had cleared out of the way of the Israelites. 3 He rebuilt the high places which his father Hezekiah had destroyed. He erected altars to Baal, and also set up a sacred pole, as Ahab, king of Israel, had done. He worshiped and served the whole host of heaven.*j* 4 He built altars in the temple of the LORD, about which the LORD had said, "I will establish my name in Jerusalem"—5 altars for the whole host of heaven, in the two courts of the temple.*k*

6 He immolated his son by fire. He practiced soothsaying and divination, and reintroduced the consulting of ghosts and spirits. He did much evil in the LORD's sight and provoked him to anger.

7 The Asherah idol he had made, he set up in the temple, of which the LORD had said to David and to his son Solomon: "In this temple and in Jerusalem, which I have chosen out of all the tribes of Israel, I shall place my name forever.*l* 8 I will not in future allow Israel to be driven off the land I gave their fathers, provided that they are careful to observe all I have commanded them, the entire law which my servant Moses enjoined upon them." 9 But they did not listen, and Manasseh misled them into doing even greater evil than the nations whom the LORD had destroyed at the coming of the Israelites.

10 Then the LORD spoke through his servants the prophets: 11 "Because Manasseh, king of Judah, has practiced these abominations and has done greater evil than all that was done by the Amorites before him, and has led Judah into sin by his idols,*m* 12 therefore thus says the LORD, the God of Israel: 'I will bring such evil on Jerusalem and Judah that, whenever anyone hears of it, his ears shall ring. 13 I will measure Jerusalem with the same cord as I did

---

g 12f: Is 39, 1f; 2 Chr 32, 27ff.—h 2 Chr 32, 30; Sir 48, 17.—i 1-10: 2 Chr 33, 1-10.—j 2 Kgs 17 16; 1 Kgs 18, 4; 16, 32f.—k Lv 18, 21.—l 2 Sm 7, 13; 1 Kgs 8, 16; 9, 3.—m 1 Kgs 21, 26; Jer 15, 4.

20, 12-19: Duplication of Is 39, 1-8.
20, 20: *Pool and conduit:* Hezekiah's tunnel; cf 2 Chr 32, 30.

Samaria, and with the plummet I used for the house of Ahab. I will wipe Jerusalem clean as one wipes a dish, wiping it inside and out.[n] [14] I will cast off the survivors of my inheritance and deliver them into enemy hands, to become a prey and a booty for all their enemies, [15] because they have done evil in my sight and provoked me from the day their fathers came forth from Egypt until today.' "

[16] In addition to the sin which he caused Judah to commit, Manasseh did evil in the sight of the LORD, shedding so much innocent blood as to fill the length and breadth of Jerusalem. [17] The rest of the acts of Manasseh, the sin he committed and all that he did, are written in the book of the chronicles of the kings of Judah.[o] [18] Manasseh rested with his ancestors and was buried in his palace garden, the garden of Uzza. His son Amon succeeded him as king.

Reign of Amon. [19] [p] Amon was twenty-two years old when he began to reign, and he reigned two years in Jerusalem. His mother's name was Meshullemeth, daughter of Haruz of Jotbah. [20] He did evil in the sight of the LORD, as his father Manasseh had done. [21] He followed exactly the path his father had trod, serving and worshiping the idols his father had served. [22] He abandoned the LORD, the God of his fathers, and did not follow the path of the LORD. [23] Subjects of Amon conspired against him and slew the king in his palace, [24] but the people of the land then slew all who had conspired against King Amon, and proclaimed his son Josiah king in his stead. [25] The rest of the acts that Amon did are written in the book of the chronicles of the kings of Judah. [26] He was buried in his own grave in the garden of Uzza, and his son Josiah succeeded him as king.

CHAPTER 22

Reign of Josiah. [1] [q] Josiah was eight years old when he began to reign, and he reigned thirty-one years in Jerusalem. His mother's name was Jedidah, daughter of

Adaiah of Bozkath. [2] He pleased the LORD and conducted himself unswervingly just as his ancestor David had done.

[3] [r] In his eighteenth year, King Josiah sent the scribe Shaphan,* son of Azaliah, son of Meshullam, to the temple of the LORD with orders to [4] [s] go to the high priest Hilkiah and have him smelt down the precious metals that had been donated to the temple of the LORD, which the doorkeepers had collected from the people. [5] They were to be consigned to the master workmen in the temple of the LORD, who should then pay them out to the carpenters, builders, and lumbermen making repairs on the temple, [6] and for the purchase of wood and hewn stone for the temple repairs. [7] No reckoning was asked of them regarding the funds consigned to them, because they held positions of trust.

The Book of the Law. [8] The high priest Hilkiah informed the scribe Shaphan, "I have found the book of the law in the temple of the LORD." Hilkiah gave the book to Shaphan, who read it. [9] Then the scribe Shaphan went to the king and reported, "Your servants have smelted down the metals available in the temple and have consigned them to the master workmen in the temple of the LORD." [10] The scribe Shaphan also informed the king that the priest Hilkiah had given him a book, and then read it aloud to the king. [11] When the king had heard the contents of the book of the law, he tore his garments[t] [12] and issued this command to Hilkiah the priest, Ahikam, son of Shaphan, Achbor, son of Micaiah, the scribe Shaphan, and the king's servant Asaiah: [13] "Go, consult the LORD for me, for the people, for all Judah, about the stipulations of this book that has been found, for the anger of the LORD has been set furiously ablaze against us, because our fathers did not obey the stipulations of this book, nor fulfill our written obligations."

[14] So Hilkiah the priest, Ahikam, Achbor, Shaphan, and Asaiah betook themselves to the Second Quarter in Jerusalem, where the prophetess Huldah resided. She was the wife of Shallum, son of Tikvah, son of Harhas, keeper of the wardrobe. When they had spoken to her, [15] she said to them, "Thus says the LORD, the God of Israel: 'Say to the man who sent you to me, [16] Thus says the LORD: I will bring upon this place and upon its in-

22, 3: *Shaphan:* head of a prominent family in the reign of Josiah, secretary to the king, bearer and reader of the newfound book of the law (vv 3-13; 2 Chr 34, 8f. 15-20). He and his sons favored the reform of King Josiah and supported the prophet Jeremiah; cf Jer 26, 24.

habitants all the evil that is threatened in the book which the king of Judah has read. [17] Because they have forsaken me and have burned incense to other gods, provoking me by everything to which they turn their hands, my anger is ablaze against this place and it cannot be extinguished.'

[18] "But to the king of Judah who sent you to consult the LORD, give this response: 'Thus says the LORD, the God of Israel: As for the threats you have heard, [19] because you were heartsick and have humbled yourself before the LORD when you heard my threats that this place and its inhabitants would become a desolation and a curse; because you tore your garments and wept before me; I in turn have listened, says the LORD. [20] I will therefore gather you to your ancestors; you shall go to your grave in peace, and your eyes shall not see all the evil I will bring upon this place.'" This they reported to the king.

CHAPTER 23

[1] [u] The king then had all the elders of Judah and of Jerusalem summoned together before him. [2] The king went up to the temple of the LORD with all the men of Judah and all the inhabitants of Jerusalem: priests, prophets, and all the people, small and great. He had the entire contents of the book of the covenant that had been found in the temple of the LORD read out to them. [3] Standing by the column, the king made a covenant before the LORD that they would follow him and observe his ordinances, statutes and decrees with their whole hearts and souls, thus reviving the terms of the covenant which were written in this book. And all the people stood as participants in the covenant.

[4] Then the king commanded the high priest Hilkiah, his vicar, and the doorkeepers to remove from the temple of the LORD all the objects that had been made for Baal, Asherah, and the whole host of heaven. He had these burned outside Jerusalem on the slopes of the Kidron and their ashes carried to Bethel. [v] [5] He also put an end to the pseudo-priests whom the kings of Judah had appointed to burn incense on the high places in the cities of Judah and in the vicinity of Jerusalem, as well as those who burned incense to Baal, to the sun, moon, and signs of the Zodiac, and to

the whole host of heaven. [w] [6] From the temple of the LORD he also removed the sacred pole, to the Kidron Valley, outside Jerusalem; there he had it burned and beaten to dust, which was then scattered over the common graveyard. [x] [7] He tore down the apartments of the cult prostitutes* which were in the temple of the LORD, and in which the women wove garments for the Asherah. [y]

[8] He brought in all the priests from the cities of Judah, and then defiled, from Geba to Beer-sheba, the high places where they had offered incense. He also tore down the high place of the satyrs, which was at the entrance of the Gate of Joshua, governor of the city, to the left as one enters the city gate. [z] [9] The priests of the high places could not function at the altar of the LORD in Jerusalem; but they, along with their relatives, ate the unleavened bread.

[10] The king also defiled Topheth in the Valley of Ben-hinnom, so that there would no longer be any immolation of sons or daughters by fire* in honor of Molech. [a] [11] He did away with the horses which the kings of Judah had dedicated to the sun; these were at the entrance of the temple of the LORD, near the chamber of Nathanmelech the eunuch, which was in the large building.* The chariots of the sun he destroyed by fire. [12] He also demolished the altars made by the kings of Judah on the roof (the roof terrace of Ahaz), and the altars made by Manasseh in the two courts of the temple of the LORD. He pulverized them and threw the dust into the Kidron Valley. [b] [13] The king defiled the high places east of Jerusalem, south of the Mount of Misconduct,* which Solomon, king of Israel, had built in honor of Astarte, the Sidonian horror, of Chemosh, the Moabite horror, and of Milcom, the idol of the Ammonites. [c] [14] He broke to pieces the pillars,

---

u 1-5: 2 Chr 34, 29-33.—v 2 Chr 34, 3-5; Sir 49, 3.—w Dt 17, 3ff.—x Dt 16, 21; 1 Kgs 14, 23.—y 1 Kgs 14, 24; Dt 23, 18f.—z Dt 12, 2f.—a Lv 18, 21.—b 2 Kgs 21, 5.—c 1 Kgs 11, 7.

23, 7: *Cult prostitutes:* of both sexes; cf 1 Kgs 14, 24.
23, 10: *Topheth . . . by fire:* condemned by Deuteronomic law and denounced by Jeremiah (Dt 12, 31; Jer 7, 29ff; Jer 19).
23, 11: *Large building:* to the west of the temple area (1 Chr 26, 18), named in the Hebrew by an Egyptian name for a similar construction.
23, 13: *Mount of Misconduct:* a paranomasia on "Mount of Olives" (in Hebrew *Maschit/mishcheh*) as suggested by the Targum. Cf Vulgate, "Mount of Offense." *Horror . . . idol:* in all three phrases here the Hebrew uses a pejorative designation meaning "abomination."

cut down the sacred poles, and filled the places where they had been with human bones.*d* **15** Likewise the altar which was at Bethel, the high place built by Jeroboam, son of Nebat, who caused Israel to sin— this same altar and high place he tore down, breaking up the stones and grinding them to powder, and burning the Asherah.*e*

16 When Josiah turned and saw the graves there on the mountainside, he ordered the bones taken from the graves and burned on the altar, and thus defiled it in fulfillment of the word of the LORD which the man of God had proclaimed as Jeroboam was standing by the altar on the feast day. When the king looked up and saw the grave of the man of God who had proclaimed these words, **17** he asked, "What is that tombstone I see?" The men of the city replied, "It is the grave of the man of God who came from Judah and predicted the very things you have done to the altar of Bethel." **18** *f* "Let him be," he said, "let no one move his bones." So they left his bones undisturbed together with the bones of the prophet who had come from Samaria.*

19 Josiah also removed all the shrines on the high places near the cities of Samaria which the kings of Israel had erected, thereby provoking the LORD; he did the very same to them as he had done in Bethel.*g* **20** He slaughtered upon the altars all the priests of the high places that were at the shrines, and burned human bones upon them. Then he returned to Jerusalem.

21 The king issued a command to all the people to observe the Passover of the LORD, their God, as it was prescribed in that book of the covenant.*h* **22** No Passover such as this had been observed during the period when the Judges ruled Israel, or during the entire period of the kings of Israel and the kings of Judah, **23** until the

eighteenth year of King Josiah, when this Passover of the LORD was kept in Jerusalem.

24 Further, Josiah did away with the consultation of ghosts and spirits, with the household gods, idols,* and all the other horrors to be seen in the land of Judah and in Jerusalem, so that he might carry out the stipulations of the law written in the book that the priest Hilkiah had found in the temple of the LORD.*i*

25 Before him there had been no king who turned to the LORD as he did, with his whole heart, his whole soul, and his whole strength, in accord with the entire law of Moses; nor could any after him compare with him.*j*

26 Yet, because of all the provocations that Manasseh had given, the LORD did not desist from his fiercely burning anger against Judah. **27** The LORD said: "Even Judah will I put out of my sight as I did Israel. I will reject this city, Jerusalem, which I chose, and the temple of which I said, 'There shall my name be.' "*k*

28 The rest of the acts of Josiah, with all that he did, are written in the book of the chronicles of the kings of Judah.*l* **29** In his time Pharaoh Neco, king of Egypt, went up toward the river Euphrates to the king of Assyria. King Josiah set out to confront him, but was slain at Megiddo at the first encounter.*m* **30** His servants brought his body on a chariot from Megiddo to Jerusalem, where they buried him in his own grave. Then the people of the land* took Jehoahaz, son of Josiah, anointed him, and proclaimed him king to succeed his father.

Reign of Jehoahaz. **31** Jehoahaz was twenty-three years old when he began to reign, and he reigned three months in Jerusalem. His mother, whose name was Hamutal, daughter of Jeremiah, was from Libnah.*n* **32** He did evil in the sight of the LORD, just as his forebears had done. **33** Pharaoh Neco took him prisoner at Riblah in the land of Hamath, thus ending his reign in Jerusalem. He imposed a fine upon the land of a hundred talents of silver and a talent of gold.* **34** Pharaoh Neco then appointed Eliakim, son of Josiah, king in place of his father Josiah; he changed his name to Jehoiakim. Jehoahaz he took away with him to Egypt, where he died. **35** Jehoiakim gave the silver and gold to Pharaoh, but taxed the land to raise the

2Kgs

---

d Dt 16, 21f; 1 Kgs 14, 23.—e 1 Kgs 12, 31f; 13, 32.—f 1 Kgs 13, 31.—g 2 Chr 34, 6f.—h Dt 16, 1-8; 2 Chr 35, 1ff. 18f.—i 2 Kgs 21, 6; Gn 31, 19; Dt 18, 11; Jgs 18, 14.—j Dt 6, 5.—k 2 Kgs 24, 2.—l 2 Chr 35, 26f.—m 2 Chr 35, 20-24.—n 2 Chr 36, 2f.

23, 18: *From Samaria:* more narrowly, from Bethel; cf 1 Kgs 13, 31f.

23, 24: *Household gods . . . idols:* teraphim. See note on Gn 31, 19.

23, 30. 35: *People of the land:* in this period, the phrase referred to "landed gentry"; in later times it meant "the poor." Cf 2 Kgs 24, 14.

23, 33: *A talent of gold:* some manuscripts of the Greek and Syriac texts have "ten talents."

amount Pharaoh demanded. He exacted the silver and gold from the people of the land, from each proportionately, to pay Pharaoh Neco.

Reign of Jehoiakim. [36] *o* Jehoiakim was twenty-five years old when he began to reign, and he reigned eleven years in Jerusalem. His mother's name was Zebidah, daughter of Pedaiah, from Rumah. [37] He did evil in the sight of the LORD, just as his forebears had done.

CHAPTER 24

[1] *p* During his reign Nebuchadnezzar, king of Babylon, moved against him, and Jehoiakim became his vassal for three years. Then Jehoiakim turned and rebelled against him. [2] The LORD loosed against him bands of Chaldeans, Arameans, Moabites, and Ammonites; he loosed them against Judah to destroy it, as the LORD had threatened through his servants the prophets. *q* [3] This befell Judah because the LORD had stated that he would inexorably put them out of his sight for the sins Manasseh had committed in all that he did; [4] and especially because of the innocent blood he shed, with which he filled Jerusalem, the LORD would not forgive. *r*

[5] The rest of the acts of Jehoiakim, with all that he did, are written in the book of the chronicles of the kings of Judah. *s* [6] Jehoiakim rested with his ancestors, and his son Jehoiachin succeeded him as king. [7] The king of Egypt did not again leave his own land, for the king of Babylon had taken all that belonged to the king of Egypt from the wadi of Egypt to the Euphrates River.

Reign of Jehoiachin. [8] Jehoiachin was eighteen years old when he began to reign, and he reigned three months* in Jerusalem. His mother's name was Nehushta, daughter of Elnathan of Jerusalem. [9] He did evil in the sight of the LORD, just as his forebears had done.

[10] At that time the officials of Nebuchadnezzar, king of Babylon, attacked Jerusalem, and the city came under siege. *t* [11] Nebuchadnezzar, king of Babylon, himself arrived at the city while his servants were besieging it. [12] Then Jehoiachin, king of Judah, together with his mother, his ministers, officers, and functionaries, surrendered to the king of Babylon, who, in the eighth year of his reign, took him captive. [13] He carried off all the treasures of the temple of the LORD and those of the

palace, and broke up all the gold utensils that Solomon, king of Israel, had provided in the temple of the LORD, as the LORD had foretold. *u* [14] He deported all Jerusalem: all the officers and men of the army, ten thousand in number, and all the craftsmen and smiths. None were left among the people of the land except the poor. [15] He deported Jehoiachin to Babylon, and also led captive from Jerusalem to Babylon the king's mother and wives, his functionaries, and the chief men of the land. *v* [16] The king of Babylon also led captive to Babylon all seven thousand men of the army, and a thousand craftsmen and smiths, all of them trained soldiers. [17] In place of Jehoiachin, the king of Babylon appointed his uncle Mattaniah king, and changed his name to Zedekiah.

Reign of Zedekiah. [18] Zedekiah was twenty-one years old when he became king, and he reigned eleven years in Jerusalem. His mother's name was Hamutal, daughter of Jeremiah of Libnah. *w* [19] He also did evil in the sight of the LORD, just as Jehoiakim had done. [20] The LORD's anger befell Jerusalem and Judah till he cast them out from his presence. Thus Zedekiah rebelled against the king of Babylon. *x*

CHAPTER 25

[1] * *y* In the tenth month of the ninth year of Zedekiah's reign, on the tenth day of the month, Nebuchadnezzar, king of Babylon, and his whole army advanced against Jerusalem, encamped around it, and built siege walls on every side. [2] The siege of the city continued until the eleventh year of Zedekiah. [3] On the ninth day of the fourth month, when famine had gripped the city, and the people had no more bread, [4] the city walls were breached. Then the king and all the soldiers left the city by night through the gate between the two walls which was near the king's garden. Since the Chaldeans had the city surrounded, they went in the direction of the Arabah. [5] But the Chaldean army pursued the king and overtook him in the desert near Jericho, abandoned by his whole army.

---

o 36f: 2 Chr 36, 4f.—p 1-5: 2 Chr 36, 6ff.—q 2 Kgs 23, 27.—r 2 Kgs 21, 16.—s 2 Chr 36, 8.—t 2 Chr 36, 10; Dn 1, 1f.—u 2 Kgs 20, 17; Is 39, 6.—v Est A, 3; 2, 6.—w 2 Chr 36, 9; Jer 37, 1f; 52, 1ff.—x 2 Kgs 22, 17; 23, 27.—y 1-21: Jer 39, 1-10; 52, 4-28.

24, 8: *He reigned three months:* in the year 597 B.C.
25, 1-30: This chapter parallels Jer 39 and 52; see notes to those parts of Jeremiah.

JUDAH UNDER JOSIAH (640-609) (2 Kgs 22, 1—23, 30; 2 Chr 34—35) — **(a)** Reign of justice. Discovery of the book of the law. Josiah orders the destruction of the idolatrous temples of **Bethel,** of the high places of **Samaria, Manasseh, Ephraim, Simeon, Naphtali.** Solemn celebrations of the Passover, and renewal of the covenant (22, 1—23, 27). **(b)** Neco, king of Egypt, crosses Palestine to come to the aid of the king of Assyria (Ashurbanipal) against the king of Babylon. Josiah confronts him on the plain of **Megiddo** and is killed there (23, 28-30). **(c)** Jehoahaz succeeds Josiah and reigns only three months. Neco captures him at **Riblah,** puts him in exile in Egypt, and replaces him by Eliakim, to whom he gives the name of Jehoiakim (23, 31-34). **(d)** In 605 the battle of **Carchemish** takes place in which Nebuchadnezzar defeats the Egyptians (Neco) and drives them back to **Hamath.**

JUDAH INVADED (609-598) (2 Kgs 23, 36—24, 6; Jer 26, 36; 2 Chr 36, 5-8) — **(a)** Jehoiakim submits to Nebuchadnezzar and remains subjugated for three years (24, 1). **(b)** Jeremiah prophesies the ruin of Jerusalem (Jer 26). **(c)** Jehoiakim attempts a revolt. But he sees his country invaded by the Chaldeans, the Syrians, the Moabites and the Ammonites, encouraged by Nebuchadnezzar who is occupied elsewhere (24, 2-3). **(d)** In 598 Jehoiachin becomes king and the first siege of Jerusalem by Nebuchadnezzar takes place. Jehoiachin goes there with all his family; he is deported into Babylon. His uncle Mattaniah is established as king under the name Zedekiah (24, 8-17).

FALL OF JUDAH (587) (2 Kgs 24, 18—5, 21; 2 Chr 36, 11-21) — **(a)** In 588 Zedekiah, counting on help from Hophra, king of Egypt, revolts against Assyria (24, 18-20). Nebuchadnezzar once again comes down from Babylon and besieges Jerusalem. He lifts the siege temporarily while he goes off to defeat Hophra but returns and defeats Zedekiah at **Jericho**. He returns to Jerusalem and takes the city in 587, tears down its walls and carries off thousands of people into exile into **Babylon** (25, 1-21). **(b)** The Jews in exile are comforted by the prophets Deutero-Isaiah, and Ezekiel. **(c)** In 538 Cyrus the Mede captures Babylon and allows the exiles to start back for home under Zerubbabel (Ezr 1, 1—2, 10). **(d)** Over the next two hundred years the Jewish commonwealth is reestablished (as part of the generally benevolent Persian Empire) with the aid especially of Nehemiah the court official and Ezra the scribe.

⁶The king was therefore arrested and brought to Riblah to the king of Babylon, who pronounced sentence on him. ⁷He had Zedekiah's sons slain before his eyes. Then he blinded Zedekiah, bound him with fetters, and had him brought to Babylon.

⁸On the seventh day of the fifth month (this was in the nineteenth year of Nebuchadnezzar, king of Babylon), Nebuzaradan, captain of the bodyguard, came to Jerusalem as the representative of the king of Babylon. ⁹He burned the house of the LORD, the palace of the king, and all the houses of Jerusalem; every large building was destroyed by fire.ᶻ ¹⁰Then the Chaldean troops who were with the captain of the guard tore down the walls that surrounded Jerusalem.

¹¹Then Nebuzaradan, captain of the guard, led into exile the last of the people remaining in the city, and those who had deserted* to the king of Babylon, and the last of the artisans. ¹²But some of the country's poor, Nebuzaradan, captain of the guard, left behind as vinedressers and farmers.

¹³The bronze pillars that belonged to the house of the LORD, and the wheeled carts and the bronze sea in the house of the LORD, the Chaldeans broke into pieces; they carried away the bronze to Babylon.ᵃ ¹⁴They took also the pots, the shovels, the snuffers, the bowls, the pans and all the bronze vessels used for service.ᵇ ¹⁵The fire-holders and the bowls which were of gold or silver the captain of the guard also carried off. ¹⁶The weight in bronze of the two pillars, the bronze sea, and the wheeled carts, all of them furnishings which Solomon had made for the house of the LORD, was never calculated. ¹⁷Each of the pillars was eighteen cubits high; a bronze capital five cubits high surmounted each pillar, and a network with pomegranates encircled the capital, all of bronze; and so for the other pillar, as regards the network.ᶜ ¹⁸The captain of the guard also took

Seraiah the high priest, Zephaniah the second priest, and the three keepers of the entry. ¹⁹And from the city he took one courtier, a commander of soldiers, five men in the personal service of the king who were still in the city, the scribe of the army commander, who mustered the people of the land, and sixty of the common people still remaining in the city. ²⁰The captain of the guard, Nebuzaradan, arrested these and brought them to the king of Babylon at Riblah; ²¹the king had them struck down and put to death in Riblah, in the land of Hamath. Thus was Judah exiled from her land.

Governorship of Gedaliah. ²² ᵈ As for the people whom he had allowed to remain in the land of Judah, Nebuchadnezzar, king of Babylon, appointed as their governor Gedaliah, son of Ahikam, son of Shaphan. ²³Hearing that the king of Babylon had appointed Gedaliah governor, all the army commanders with their men came to him at Mizpah: Ishmael, son of Nethaniah, Johanan, son of Kareah, Seraiah, son of Tanhumeth the Netophathite, and Jaazaniah, from Beth-maacah. ²⁴Gedaliah gave the commanders and their men his oath. "Do not be afraid of the Chaldean officials," he said to them. "Remain in the country and serve the king of Babylon, and all will be well with you."

²⁵But in the seventh month Ishmael, son of Nethaniah, son of Elishama, of royal descent, came with ten men, attacked Gedaliah and killed him, along with the Jews and Chaldeans who were in Mizpah with him. ²⁶Then all the people, great and small, left with the army commanders and went to Egypt for fear of the Chaldeans.

Release of Jehoiachin. ²⁷ ᵉ In the thirty-seventh year of the exile of Jehoiachin, king of Judah, on the twenty-seventh day of the twelfth month, Evil-merodach, king of Babylon, in the inaugural year of his own reign, raised up Jehoiachin, king of Judah, from prison. ²⁸He spoke kindly to him and gave him a throne higher than that of the other kings who were with him in Babylon. ²⁹Jehoiachin took off his prison garb and ate at the king's table as long as he lived. ³⁰The allowance granted him by the king was a perpetual allowance, in fixed daily amounts, for as long as he lived.

---

z 2 Chr 36, 19; Ps 74, 7.—a 2 Kgs 16, 17; 1 Kgs 7, 15-39; 2 Chr 3, 15; 36, 18; Jer 27, 19.—b 1 Kgs 7, 48ff.—c 1 Kgs 7, 15; Jer 52, 21ff.—d 22-26: Jer 40, 5. 7—41, 1-3.—e 27-30: Jer 52, 31-34.

25, 11: *Those who had deserted:* perhaps on the advice of Jeremiah; cf Jer 38, 2f.

THE FIRST BOOK OF CHRONICLES

Originally the two books of Chronicles formed, with the Books of Ezra and Nehemiah, a single historical work, uniform in style and basic ideas. The Greek title, paraleipomena, *means "things omitted, or passed over (in Samuel and Kings)." The Books of Chronicles, however, are more than a supplement to Samuel and Kings; a comparison of the two histories discloses striking differences in scope and purpose. The Books of Chronicles record in some detail the lengthy span from the reign of Saul to the return from the Exile. Unlike the exact science of history today, wherein factual accuracy and impartiality of judgment are the standards for estimating what is of permanent worth, ancient biblical history, with rare exceptions, was less concerned with reporting in precise detail all the facts of a situation than with explaining the meaning of those facts. Such history was primarily interpretative and, in the Old Testament, its purpose was to disclose the action of the living God in the affairs of men. For this reason we speak of it as "sacred history"; its writer's first concern was to bring out the divine or supernatural dimension in history.*

This is apparent when we examine the primary objective of the Chronicler in compiling his work. In view of the situation which confronted the Jewish people at this time (the end of the fifth century B.C.), the Chronicler realized that Israel's political greatness was a thing of the past. It would be a people under God, or nothing. Yet Israel's past held the key to her future. The Chronicler proposed to establish and defend the legitimate claims of the Davidic monarchy in Israel's history, and to underscore the place of Jerusalem and its divinely established temple worship as the center of religious life for the Jewish community of his day. If Judaism was to survive and prosper, it would have to heed the lessons of the past and devoutly serve Yahweh in the place where he had chosen to dwell, the temple of Jerusalem. From the Chronicler's point of view, David's reign was the ideal to which all subsequent rule in Judah must aspire.

The Chronicler was much more interested in David's religious and cultic influence than in his political power. There is little of royal messianism in his book. He apparently regarded as something of the distant past the prophet Zechariah's abortive attempt to have the Davidic kingdom reestablished in the time of Zerubbabel at the end of the sixth century B.C. (Zec 6, 9-15). He saw David's primary importance as deriving from the establishment of Jerusalem and its temple as the center of the true worship of the Lord. Furthermore, he presented David as the one who had authorized the elaborate ritual (which, in point of fact, only gradually evolved in the temple built by Zerubbabel) and who had also appointed Levites to supervise the liturgical services there.

There are good reasons for believing that originally the Books of Ezra and Nehemiah formed the last part of a single literary work that began with 1 and 2 Chronicles. Some authors even regard Ezra himself as having been the anonymous Chronicler. In any case, the Chronicler's Hebrew as well as his religious and political outlook points to c. 400 B.C. as the time of composition of this work.

The Chronicler used sources in writing his history. Besides the canonical Books of Genesis, Exodus, Numbers, Joshua and Ruth, and especially the Books of Samuel and Kings, he cites the titles of many other works no longer extant. "The books of the kings of Israel," or "the books of the kings of Israel and Judah," "the history of Samuel the seer," "the history of Nathan the prophet," "the history of Gad the seer," "the commentary on the Books of Kings," are some of the documents mentioned as historical sources.

In addition, the Chronicler's work contains early preexilic material not found in the Books of Kings. At one time scholars discounted the value of this material, but modern research has shown that, even though the Chronicler may have at times treated the material rather freely, he derived it from authentic and reliable sources.

The principal divisions of 1 Chronicles are as follows: I. Genealogical Tables (1, 1—9, 34). II. The History of David (9, 35—29, 30).

I: GENEALOGICAL TABLES

CHAPTER 1

From Adam to Abraham. [1] *a* * Adam, Seth, Enosh, [2] *b* Kenan, Mahalalel, Jared, [3] Enoch, Methuselah, Lamech,*c* [4] Noah, Shem, Ham, and Japheth.*d* [5] *e* The descendants of Japheth were Gomer, Magog, Madai, Javan, Tubal, Meshech, and Tiras. [6] The descendants of Gomer were Ashkenaz, Riphath, and Togarmah. [7] The descendants of Javan were Elishah, Tarshish, the Kittim, and the Rodanim.
[8] *f* The descendants of Ham were Cush, Mesraim, Put, and Canaan. [9] The descendants of Cush were Seba, Havilah, Sabta, Raama, and Sabteca. The descendants of Raama were Sheba and Dedan. [10] Cush became the father of Nimrod, who was the first to be a conqueror on the earth. [11] *g* Mesraim became the father of the Ludim, Anamim, Lehabim, Naphtuhim, [12] Pathrusim, Casluhim, and Caphtorim, from whom the Philistines sprang. [13] Canaan became the father of Sidon, his first-born, and Heth, [14] and the Jebusite, the Amorite, the Girgashite, [15] the Hivite, the Arkite, the Sinite, [16] the Arvadite, the Zemarite, and the Hamathite.
[17] *h* The descendants of Shem were Elam, Asshur, Arpachshad, Lud, and Aram. The descendants of Aram were Uz, Hul, Gether, and Mash. [18] Arpachshad became the father of Shelah, and Shelah became the father of Eber. [19] Two sons were born to Eber; the first was named Peleg (for in his time the world was divided), and his brother was Joktan. [20] Joktan became the father of Al-

a 1 Chr 4, 25f; Gn 5, 3. 6. 9.—b 2ff: Gn 5, 9-32; 10, 2ff.—c Gn 4, 25.—d Gn 5, 32; 6, 10; 9, 18.—e 5ff: Gn 10, 2ff.—f Gn 10, 8.—g 11-16: Gn 10, 13-18.—h 17-23: Gn 10, 22-29; 11, 10-18.—i 24-27: Gn 11, 10-26; Lk 3, 34ff.—j Gn 17, 5; Neh 9, 7.—k Gn 16, 11. 15; 21, 2f; Gal 4, 22f; Heb 11, 11.—l 29ff: Gn 25, 13-16.—m 32f: Gn 25, 1-4.—n Gn 21, 2f; 25, 19. 25f: 32, 28f; Mt 1, 2; Lk 3, 34.—o 35ff: Gn 36, 4f. 10-13. 15ff.—p 38-42: Gn 36, 20-28.—q 43-54: Gn 36, 31-43.—r Is 34, 6; 63, 1; Jer 49, 13. 22.—s Gn 36, 11; Jb 2, 11; Jer 49, 7. 20.

1, 1–9, 34: The Chronicler set as his task the retelling, from his particular viewpoint, of the story of God's people from the beginning to his own day. Since his primary interest was the history of David and the Davidic dynasty of Judah, he presents through mere genealogical lists a summary of what preceded the reign of Saul, David's predecessor in the kingdom. The sources for these genealogies are mostly the canonical Hebrew Scriptures that were already in their present form in his time. The cross references in this book indicate in each case the scriptural sources used.

1, 38: *Seir:* another name for *Esau* (v 35) or *Edom* (v 43).

modad, Sheleph, Hazarmaveth, Jerah, [21] Hadoram, Uzal, Diklah, [22] Ebal, Abimael, Sheba, [23] Ophir, Havilah, and Jobab; all these were the sons of Joktan.
[24] *i* Shem, Arpachshad, Shelah, [25] Eber, Peleg, Reu, [26] Serug, Nahor, Terah, [27] Abram, who was Abraham.*j*
From Abraham to Jacob. [28] The sons of Abraham were Isaac and Ishmael.*k* [29] These were their descendants:*l*
Nebaioth, the first-born of Ishmael, then Kedar, Adbeel, Mibsam, [30] Mishma, Dumah, Massa, Hadad, Tema, [31] Jetur, Naphish, and Kedemah. These were the descendants of Ishmael.
[32] *m* The descendants of Keturah, Abraham's concubine: she bore Zimran, Jokshan, Medan, Midian, Ishbak, and Shuah. The sons of Jokshan were Sheba and Dedan. [33] The descendants of Midian were Ephah, Epher, Hanoch, Abida, and Eldaah. All these were the descendants of Keturah.
[34] Abraham became the father of Isaac. The sons of Isaac were Esau and Israel.*n*
[35] *o* The sons of Esau were Eliphaz, Reuel, Jeush, Jalam, and Korah. [36] The sons of Eliphaz were Teman, Omar, Zephi, Gatam, Kenaz, [Timna,] and Amalek. [37] The sons of Reuel were Nahath, Zerah, Shammah, and Mizzah.
[38] *p* The descendants of Seir* were Lotan, Shobal, Zibeon, Anah, Dishon, Ezer, and Dishan. [39] The sons of Lotan were Hori and Homam; Timna was the sister of Lotan. [40] The sons of Shobal were Alian, Manahath, Ebal, Shephi, and Onam. The sons of Zibeon were Aiah and Anah. [41] The sons of Anah: Dishon. The sons of Dishon were Hemdan, Eshban, Ithran, and Cheran. [42] The sons of Ezer were Bilhan, Zaavan, and Jaakan. The sons of Dishan were Uz and Aran.
[43] *q* The kings who reigned in the land of Edom before they had Israelite kings were the following: Bela, son of Beor, the name of whose city was Ninhabah. [44] When Bela died, Jobab, son of Zerah, from Bozrah, succeeded him.*r* [45] When Jobab died, Husham, from the land of the Temanites, succeeded him.*s* [46] Husham died and Hadad, son of Bedad, succeeded him. He overthrew the Midianites on the Moabite plateau, and the name of his city was Avith. [47] Hadad

1Chr

died and Samlah of Masrekah succeeded him. [48] Samlah died and Shaul from Rehoboth-han-nahar succeeded him. [49] When Shaul died, Baalhanan, son of Achbor, succeeded him. [50] Baalhanan died and Hadad succeeded him. The name of his city was Pai, and his wife's name was Mehetabel. She was the daughter of Matred, who was the daughter of Mezahab. [51] *t* After Hadad died. . . .

These were the chiefs of Edom: the chiefs of Timna, Aliah, Jetheth, [52] Oholibamah, Elah, Pinon, [53] Kenaz, Teman, Mibzar, [54] Magdiel, and Iram were the chiefs of Edom.

CHAPTER 2

[1] These were the sons of Israel: Reuben, Simeon, Levi, Judah, Issachar, Zebulun, *u* [2] Dan, Joseph, Benjamin, Naphtali, Gad, and Asher. *v*

Judah. [3] The sons of Judah* were: Er, Onan, and Shelah; these three were born to him of Bathshua, a Canaanite woman. But Judah's first-born, Er, was wicked in the sight of the LORD, so he killed him. *w* [4] Judah's daughter-in-law Tamar bore him Perez and Zerah, so that he had five sons in all. *x* [5] The sons of Perez were Hezron and Hamul. *y* [6] The sons of Zerah were Zimri, Ethan, Heman, Calcol, and Darda—five in all. *z* [7] The sons of Zimri: Carmi. The sons of Carmi: Achar, who brought trouble upon Israel by violating the ban. *a* [8] The sons of Ethan: Azariah. [9] The sons born to Hezron were Jerahmeel, Ram, and Chelubai. *b* *

[10] * Ram became the father of Amminadab, and Amminadab became the father of Nahshon, a prince of the Judahites. *c* [11] *d* Nahshon became the father of Salma. Salma became the father of Boaz. [12] Boaz became the father of Obed. Obed became the father of Jesse. [13] *e* Jesse became the father of Eliab, his first-born, of Abinadab, the second son, Shimea, the third, *f* [14] Nethanel, the fourth, Raddai, the fifth, [15] Ozem, the sixth, and David, the seventh. [16] Their sisters were Zeruiah and Abigail. Zeruiah had three sons: Abishai, Joab, and Asahel. *g* [17] Abigail bore Amasa, whose father was Jether the Ishmaelite. *h*

[18] * By his wife Azubah, Caleb, son of Hezron, became the father of a daughter, Jerioth. Her sons were Jesher, Shobab, and Ardon. *i* [19] When Azubah died, Caleb married Ephrath, who bore him Hur. *j* [20] Hur became the father of Uri, and Uri became the father of Bezalel. *k* [21] Then Hezron had relations with the daughter of Machir, the father of Gilead, having married her when he was sixty years old. She bore him Segub. *l* [22] Segub became the father of Jair, *m* who possessed twenty-three cities in the land of Gilead. [23] Geshur and Aram took from them the villages of Jair, that is, Kenath and its towns, sixty cities in all, which had belonged to the sons of Machir, the father of Gilead. *n* [24] After the death of Hezron, Caleb had relations with Ephrathah, the widow of his father Hezron, and she bore him Ashhur, the father of Tekoa. *o*

[25] The sons of Jerahmeel,* the first-born of Hezron, were Ram, the first-born, then Bunah, Oren, and Ozem, his brothers. *p* [26] Jerahmeel also had another wife, Atarah by name, who was the mother of Onam. [27] The sons of Ram, the first-born of Jerahmeel, were Maaz, Jamin, and Eker. [28] The sons of Onam were Shammai and Jada. The sons of Shammai were Nadab and Abishur. [29] Abishur's wife, who was named Abihail, bore him Ahban and Molid. [30] The sons of Nadab were Seled and Appaim. Seled died without sons. [31] The sons of Appaim: Ishi. The sons of Ishi: Sheshan. The sons of Sheshan: Ahlai. *q* [32] The sons of Jada, the brother

t 51-54: Gn 36, 40-43.—u Gn 29, 32-35; 30, 18. 20; 35, 23.—v Gn 30, 6. 8. 11. 13. 24; 35, 18. 24ff.—w 1 Chr 4, 21; Gn 38, 1-5; 46, 12.—x Gn 38, 7. 13-30; 46, 12; Rv 4, 12. 18; Mt 1, 3.—y Gn 46, 12.—z 1 Kgs 5, 11.—a Jos 7, 1. 18ff. 24f; 22, 20.—b Rv 4, 19; Mt 1, 3.—c Rv 4, 19; Mt 1, 4.—d 11f: Nm 1, 7; Rv 4, 20f; Mt 1, 4f.—e 13ff: 1 Sm 16, 6-13; 17, 13f.—f 2 Chr 11, 18.—g 2 Sm 2, 18.—h 2 Sm 17, 25; 19, 14; 20, 4-13.—i 1 Chr 2, 24.—j 1 Chr 2, 24.—k Ex 24, 14; 31, 2; 35, 30; 2 Chr 1, 5.—l Nm 26, 29; 27, 1; 32, 39; Jos 13, 31; Jgs 5, 14.—m Nm 32, 41; 1 Kgs 4, 13.—n Dt 3, 14; Jos 13, 30; Jgs 10, 4.—o 1 Chr 2, 19; 2 Sm 14, 2; 2 Chr 11, 6.—p 1 Sm 27, 10; 30, 29; Jb 32, 2.—q 1 Chr 4, 20.

2, 3–4, 23: For two reasons, the Chronicler places the genealogy of the tribe of Judah before that of the other tribes, giving it also at greater length than the others: because of his interest in David and because in the Chronicler's time the people of God were almost exclusively Jews. Both David and the Jews were of the tribe of Judah.

2, 9: *Chelubai:* a variant form of the name *Caleb* (vv 18. 42), distinct from *Chelub* of 1 Chr 4, 11.

2, 10-17: Immediate ancestors of David. A similar list is given in Ru 4, 19-22; each list, independent of the other, derives from a common source.

2, 18-24: Descendants of Caleb. In 1 Chr 4, 15, as is often the case in the Pentateuch (Nm 13, 6; 14, 6. 30; 26, 65; etc.), Caleb is called *son of Jephunneh.* Here he is called *son of Hezron,* perhaps because the Calebites were reckoned as part of the clan of the Hezronites.

2, 25-41: The Jerahmeelites were a clan in the Negeb of Judah.

of Shammai, were Jether and Jonathan. Jether died without sons. [33] The sons of Jonathan were Peleth and Zaza. These were the descendants of Jerahmeel. [34] Sheshan, who had no sons, only daughters, had an Egyptian slave named Jarha. [35] Sheshan gave his daughter in marriage to his slave Jarha, and she bore him Attai. [36] Attai became the father of Nathan. Nathan became the father of Zabad. [37] Zabad became the father of Ephlal. Ephlal became the father of Obed. [38] Obed became the father of Jehu. Jehu became the father of Azariah. [39] Azariah became the father of Helez. Helez became the father of Eleasah. [40] Eleasah became the father of Sismai. Sismai became the father of Shallum. [41] Shallum became the father of Jekamiah. Jekamiah became the father of Elishama.

[42] The descendants of Caleb,* the brother of Jerahmeel: [Mesha] his first-born, who was the father of Ziph. Then the sons of Mareshah, who was the father of Hebron. [43] The sons of Hebron were Korah, Tappuah, Rekem, and Shema. [44] Shema became the father of Raham, who was the father of Jorkeam. Rekem became the father of Shammai. [45] The sons of Shammai: Maon, who was the father of Beth-zur. [46] Ephah, Caleb's concubine, bore Haran, Moza, and Gazez. Haran became the father of Gazez. [47] The sons of Jahdai were Regem, Jotham, Geshan, Pelet, Ephah, and Shaaph. [48] Maacah, Caleb's concubine, bore Sheber and Tirhanah. [49] She also bore Shaaph, the father of Madmannah, Sheva, the father of Machbenah, and the father of Gibea. Achsah was Caleb's daughter.[r]

---

r Jos 15, 16; Jgs 1, 12.—s Jgs 18, 2.—t Nm 24, 21; Jgs 1, 16; 4, 11; 1 Sm 15, 6.—u 1-4: 2 Sm 3, 2.-5.—v 2 Sm 2, 11; 5, 5.—w 5-8: 2 Sm 5, 14ff.—x 2 Sm 5, 5.—y 2 Sm 13, 1f.—z 10-17: Mt 1, 7-12.—a 1 Kgs 11, 43; 14, 31; 15, 1. 8. 24; 2 Chr 9, 31; 12, 16; 13, 23; 17, 1.—b 1 Kgs 22, 51; 2 Chr 21, 1; 22, 1; 24, 1. 27.—c 2 Kgs 12, 21; 14, 21; 15, 7; 2 Chr 25, 1; 26, 1. 23; 27, 1.—d 2 Kgs 15, 38; 16, 20; 20, 21; 2 Chr 28, 1. 27; 32, 33.—e 2 Kgs 21, 18. 26; 2 Chr 33, 20. 25.—f 2 Kgs 23, 34; 24, 17; 2 Chr 36, 4. 10.—g 2 Kgs 24, 6. 17; 2 Chr 36, 8. 10.

2, 42-49: Another list, dating from preexilic times, of the Calebites, a clan that inhabited the south of Judah.
2, 50-55: The Hurites, a clan dwelling to the south and west of Jerusalem and related to the Calebites.
3, 1-9: David's sons.
3, 1: *Daniel:* called *Chileab* in 2 Sm 3, 3.
3, 5: *Shimea:* called *Shammua* in 2 Sm 5, 14. *Ammiel:* called *Eliam* in 2 Sm 11, 3.
3, 10-16: The kings of Judah from Solomon to the destruction of Jerusalem by the Babylonians.
3, 15: *Shallum:* the same as Jehoahaz, Josiah's successor; cf Jer 22, 11.

[50] These were descendants of Caleb, sons of Hur,* the first-born of Ephrathah: Shobal, the father of Kiriath-jearim, [51] Salma, the father of Bethlehem, and Hareph, the father of Bethgader. [52] The sons of Shobal, the father of Kiriath-jearim, were Reaiah, half the Manahathites, [53] and the clans of Kiriath-jearim: the Ithrites, the Puthites, the Shumathites, and the Mishraites. From these the people of Zorah and the Eshtaolites derived.[s] [54] The descendants of Salma were Bethlehem, the Netophathites, Atrothbeth-Joab, half the Manahathites, and the Zorites. [55] [t] The clans of the Sopherim dwelling in Jabez were the Tirathites, the Shimeathites, and the Sucathites. They were the Kenites, who came from Hammath of the ancestor of the Rechabites.

CHAPTER 3

[1] [u] The following* were the sons of David who were born to him in Hebron: the first-born, Amnon, by Ahinoam of Jezreel; the second, Daniel,* by Abigail of Carmel; [2] the third, Absalom, son of Maacah, who was the daughter of Talmai, king of Geshur; the fourth, Adonijah, son of Haggith; [3] the fifth, Shephatiah, by Abital; the sixth, Ithream, by his wife Eglah. [4] Six in all were born to him in Hebron, where he reigned seven years and six months. Then he reigned thirty-three years in Jerusalem,[v] [5] [w] where the following were born to him: Shimea,* Shobab, Nathan, Solomon—four by Bathsheba, the daughter of Ammiel;[x] [6] Ibhar, Elishua, Eliphelet, [7] Nogah, Nepheg, Japhia, [8] Elishama, Eliada, and Eliphelet—nine. [9] All these were sons of David, in addition to other sons by concubines; and Tamar was their sister.[y]

[10] [z] * The son of Solomon was Rehoboam, whose son was Abijah, whose son was Asa, whose son was Jehoshaphat,[a] [11] whose son was Joram, whose son was Ahaziah, whose son was Joash,[b] [12] whose son was Amaziah, whose son was Azariah, whose son was Jotham,[c] [13] whose son was Ahaz, whose son was Hezekiah, whose son was Manasseh,[d] [14] whose son was Amon, whose son was Josiah.[e] [15] The sons of Josiah were: the first-born, Johanan; the second, Jehoiakim; the third, Zedekiah; the fourth, Shallum.* [f] [16] The sons of Jehoiakim were: Jeconiah, his son; Zedekiah, his son.[g]

1Chr

17 The sons of Jeconiah* the captive were: Shealtiel,*h* 18 Malchiram, Pedaiah, Shenazzar,* Jekamiah, Shama, and Nedabiah. 19 The sons of Pedaiah were Zerubbabel* and Shimei. The sons of Zerubbabel were Meshullam and Hananiah; Shelomith was their sister. 20 The sons of Meshullam were Hashubah, Ohel, Berechiah, Hasadiah, Jushab-hesed—five. 21 The sons of Hananiah were Pelatiah, Jeshaiah, Rephaiah, Aranan, Obadiah, and Shecaniah. 22 *i* The sons of Shecaniah were Shemiah, Hattush, Igal, Bariah, Neariah, Shaphat—six. 23 The sons of Neariah were Elioenai, Hizkiah, and Azrikam—three. 24 The sons of Elioenai were Hodaviah, Eliashib, Pelaiah, Akkub, Johanan, Delaiah, and Anani—seven.

CHAPTER 4

1 * The descendants of Judah were: Perez, Hezron, Carmi, Hur, and Shobal.*j* 2 Reaiah, the son of Shobal, became the father of Jahath, and Jahath became the father of Ahumai and Lahad. These were the clans of the Zorathites.

3 These were the descendants of Hareph, the father of Etam: Jezreel, Ishma, and Idbash; their sister was named Hazzelelponi. 4 Penuel was the father of Gedor, and Ezer the father of Hushah. These were the descendants of Hur, the first-born of Ephrathah, the father of Bethlehem.

5 Ashhur, the father of Tekoa, had two wives, Helah and Naarah.*k* 6 Naarah bore him Ahuzzam, Hepher, the Temenites and the Ahashtarites. These were the descendants of Naarah. 7 The sons of Helah were Zereth, Izhar, Ethnan, and Koz. 8 Koz became the father of Anub and Zobebah, as well as of the clans of Aharhel, son of Harum. 9 Jabez was the most distinguished of the brothers. His mother had named him Jabez, saying, "I bore him with pain." 10 Jabez prayed to the God of Israel: "Oh, that you may truly bless me and extend my boundaries! Help me and make me free of misfortune, without pain!" And God granted his prayer.

11 Chelub, the brother of Shuhah, became the father of Mehir, who was the father of Eshton. 12 Eshton became the father of Bethrapha, Paseah, and Tehinnah, the father of the city of Nahas. These were the men of Recah.

13 The sons of Kenaz were Othniel and Seraiah. The sons of Othniel were Hathath and Meonothai;*l* 14 Meonothai became the father of Ophrah. Seraiah became the father of Joab, the father of Geharashim, so called because they were craftsmen. 15 The sons of Caleb, son of Jephunneh, were Ir, Elah, and Naam. The sons of Elah were . . . and Kenaz.*m* 16 The sons of Jehallelel were Ziph, Ziphah, Tiria, and Asarel. 17 The sons of Ezrah were Jether, Mered, Epher, and Jalon. Jether became the father of Miriam, Shammai, and Ishbah, the father of Eshtemoa. [. . . . . .]*n* 18 His (Mered's) Egyptian wife bore Jared, the father of Gedor, Heber, the father of Soco, and Jekuthiel, the father of Zanoah. These were the sons of Bithiah, the daughter of Pharaoh, whom Mered married. 19 The sons of his Jewish wife, the sister of Naham, the father of Keilah, were Shimon the Garmite and Ishi the Maacathite. 20 The sons of Shimon were Amnon, Rinnah, Benhanan, and Tilon. The son of Ishi was Zoheth and the son of Zoheth. . . .

21 The descendants of Shelah, son of Judah, were: Er, the father of Lecah; Laadah, the father of Mareshah; the clans of the linen weavers' guild in Bethashbea;*o* 22 Jokim; the men of Cozeba; and Joash and Saraph, who held property in Moab, but returned to Bethlehem. [These are events of old.] 23 They were potters and inhabitants of Netaim and Gederah, where they lived in the king's service.

Simeon. 24 The sons of Simeon were Nemuel, Jamin, Jachin, Zerah, and Shaul,*p* 25 whose son was Mibsam, whose

h 17. 19: Ezr 2, 2; 3, 2. 8; 5, 2; Sir 49, 11; Hg 1, 1. 12. 14; Mt 1, 12f; Lk 3, 27.—i Neh 3, 29.—j 1 Chr 2, 4f. 7. 9. 50; Gn 38, 29; 46, 12; Mt 1, 3.—k 1 Chr 2, 24.—l Jos 15, 17; Jgs 1, 13; 3, 9. 11.—m Nm 13, 6; 14, 6; 32, 12; Jgs 14, 6. 14.—n 1 Sm 30, 28.—o 1 Chr 2, 3; Gn 38, 5; 46, 12; Nm 26, 20.—p Gn 46, 10; Ex 6, 15; Nm 26, 12f.

3, 17-24: The descendants of King *Jeconiah* up to the time of the Chronicler. If twenty-five years are allowed to each generation, the ten generations between *Jeconiah* and *Anani* (the last name on the list) would bring the birth of the latter to about 405 B.C.—an important item in establishing the approximate date of the Chronicler.

3, 18: *Shenazzar:* presumably the same as *Sheshbazzar* of Ezr 1, 8. 11; 5, 14ff, the prince of Judah who was the first Jewish governor of Judah after the exile. Both forms of the name probably go back to the Babylonian name Sin-ab-ussar signifying, "O [god] Sin, protect [our] father!"

3, 19: *Zerubbabel:* here called the son of *Pedaiah,* though elsewhere (Hg 1, 12. 14; 2, 2. 23; Ezr 3, 2. 8; 5, 2; Neh 12, 1) called *son of Shealtiel.* The latter term may merely mean that Zerubbabel succeeded Shealtiel as head of the house of David.

4, 1-43: The southern tribes.

son was Mishma. [26] The descendants of Mishma were his son Hammuel, whose son was Zaccur, whose son was Shimei. [27] Shimei had sixteen sons and six daughters. His brothers, however, did not have many sons, and as a result all their clans did not equal the number of the Judahites.

[28] *q* They dwelt in Beer-sheba, Moladah, Hazar-shual, [29] Bilhah, Ezem, Tolad, [30] Bethuel, Hormah, Ziklag, [31] Bethmarcaboth, Hazar-susim, Bethbiri, and Shaaraim. Until David came to reign, these were their cities [32] and their villages. Etam, also, and Ain, Rimmon, Tochen, and Ashan—five cities, [33] together with all their outlying villages as far as Baal. Here is where they dwelt, and so it was inscribed of them in their family records.

[34] Meshobab, Jamlech, Joshah, son of Amaziah, [35] Joel, Jehu, son of Joshibiah, son of Seraiah, son of Asiel, [36] Elioenai, Jaakobath, Jeshohaiah, Asaiah, Adiel, Jesimiel, Benaiah, [37] Ziza, son of Shiphi, son of Allon, son of Jedaiah, son of Shimri, son of Shemaiah—[38] these just named were princes in their clans, and their ancestral houses spread out to such an extent[r] [39] that they went to the approaches of Gedor,* east of the valley, seeking pasture for their flocks. [40] They found abundant and good pastures, and the land was spacious, quiet, and peaceful. [41] They who have just been listed by name set out during the reign of Hezekiah, king of Judah, and attacked the tents of Ham (for Hamites dwelt there formerly) and also the Meunites who were there. They pronounced against them the ban that is still in force and dwelt in their place because they found pasture there for their flocks.[s]

[42] Five hundred of them (the Simeonites) went to Mount Seir under the leadership of Pelatiah, Neariah, Rephaiah, and Uzziel, sons of Ishi. [43] They attacked the surviving Amalekites who had escaped, and have resided there to the present day.[t]

q 28-32: Jos 19, 2-8.—r Nm 1, 2.—s 2 Kgs 18, 1f; 2 Chr 29, 1.—t Ex 17, 8. 14; Dt 25, 17ff; 1 Sm 14, 48; 15, 3. 7f; 2 Sm 8, 12.—u Gn 35, 22; 48, 5. 15-22; 49, 3f; Dt 33, 6.—v 1 Chr 28, 4; Gn 49, 8ff.—w Gn 46, 9; Ex 6, 14; Nm 26, 5f.—x 2 Kgs 15, 29.—y Jos 13, 9. 16f; Nm 32, 3. 38.—z Jos 22, 9.—a Ps 83, 6.—b Jos 13, 11. 24-28.—c Gn 46, 16.

4, 39: *Gedor:* in the Greek, Gerar, no doubt correct.
5, 1-26: The Transjordan tribes.

CHAPTER 5

Reuben. [1] * The sons of Reuben, the first-born of Israel. (He was indeed the first-born, but because he disgraced the couch of his father his birthright was given to the sons of Joseph, son of Israel, so that he is not listed in the family records according to birthright.[u] [2] Judah, in fact, became powerful among his brothers, so that the ruler came from him, though the birthright had been Joseph's.)[v] [3] The sons of Reuben, the first-born of Israel, were Hanoch, Pallu, Hezron, and Carmi.[w] [4] His son was Joel, whose son was Shemaiah, whose son was Gog, whose son was Shimei, [5] whose son was Micah, whose son was Reaiah, whose son was Baal, [6] whose son was Beerah, whom Tiglath-pileser, the king of Assyria, took into exile; he was a prince of the Reubenites.[x] [7] His brothers who belonged to his clans, when they were listed in the family records according to their descendants, were: Jeiel, the chief, and Zechariah, [8] and Bela, son of Azaz, son of Shema, son of Joel. The Reubenites lived in Aroer and as far as Nebo and Baal-meon;[y] [9] toward the east they dwelt as far as the desert which extends from the Euphrates River, for they had much livestock in the land of Gilead.[z] [10] During the reign of Saul they waged war with the Hagrites, and when they had defeated them they occupied their tents throughout the region east of Gilead.[a]

Gad. [11] The Gadites lived alongside them in the land of Bashan as far as Salecah.[b] [12] Joel was chief, Shapham was second in command, and Janai was judge in Bashan.[c] [13] Their brothers, corresponding to their ancestral houses, were: Michael, Meshullam, Sheba, Jorai, Jacan, Zia, and Eber—seven. [14] These were the sons of Abihail, son of Huri, son of Jaroah, son of Gilead, son of Michael, son of Jeshishai, son of Jahdo, son of Buz. [15] Ahi, son of Abdiel, son of Guni, was the head of their ancestral houses. [16] They dwelt in Gilead, in Bashan and its towns, and in all the pasture lands of Sirion to the borders. [17] All were listed in the family records in the time of Jotham, king of Judah, and of Jeroboam, king of Israel.

[18] The Reubenites, Gadites, and half-tribe of Manasseh were warriors, men who bore shield and sword and who drew

the bow, trained in warfare—forty-four thousand seven hundred and sixty men fit for military service. ¹⁹When they waged war against the Hagrites and against Jetur, Naphish, and Nodab,ᵈ ²⁰they received help so that they mastered the Hagrites and all who were with them. For during the battle they called on God, and he heard them because they had put their trust in him.ᵉ ²¹Along with one hundred thousand men they also captured their livestock: fifty thousand camels, two hundred fifty thousand sheep, and two thousand asses. ²²Many had fallen in battle, for victory is from God; and they took over their dwelling place until the time of the exile.ᶠ

East Manasseh. ²³The numerous members of the half-tribe of Manasseh lived in the land of Bashan as far as Baal-hermon, Senir, and Mount Hermon. ²⁴The following were the heads of their ancestral houses: Epher, Ishi, Eliel, Azriel, Jeremiah, Hodaviah, and Jahdiel—men who were warriors, famous men, and heads over their ancestral houses.

²⁵However, they offended the God of their fathers by lusting after the gods of the natives of the land, whom God had cleared out of their way.ᵍ ²⁶Therefore the God of Israel incited against them the anger of Pul,* king of Assyria, and of Tiglath-pileser, king of Assyria, who deported the Reubenites, the Gadites, and the half-tribe of Manasseh and brought them to Halah, Habor, and Hara, and to the river Gozan, where they have remained to this day.ʰ

Levi. ²⁷ * The sons of Levi were Gershon, Kohath, and Merari.ⁱ ²⁸The sons of Kohath were Amram, Izhar, Hebron, and Uzziel.ʲ ²⁹The children of Amram were Aaron, Moses, and Miriam. The sons of Aaron were Nadab, Abihu, Eleazar, and Ithamar.ᵏ ³⁰ * Eleazar became the father of Phinehas. Phinehas became the father of Abishua. ³¹Abishua became the father of Bukki. Bukki became the father of Uzzi. ³²Uzzi became the father of Zerahiah. Zerahiah became the father of Meraioth. ³³Meraioth became the father of Amariah. Amariah became the father of Ahitub. ³⁴Ahitub became the father of Zadok. Zadok became the father of Ahimaaz. ³⁵Ahimaaz became the father of Azariah. Azariah became the father of Johanan. ³⁶Johanan became the father of Azariah,

who served as priest in the temple Solomon built in Jerusalem. ³⁷Azariah became the father of Amariah. Amariah became the father of Ahitub. ³⁸Ahitub became the father of Zadok. Zadok became the father of Shallum. ³⁹Shallum became the father of Hilkiah. Hilkiah became the father of Azariah. ⁴⁰Azariah became the father of Seraiah. Seraiah became the father of Jehozadak. ⁴¹Jehozadak was one of those who went into the exile which the LORD inflicted on Judah and Jerusalem through Nebuchadnezzar.

CHAPTER 6

¹The sons of Levi were Gershon, Kohath, and Merari.ˡ ²The sons of Gershon were named Libni and Shimei.ᵐ ³The sons of Kohath were Amram, Izhar, Hebron, and Uzziel.ⁿ ⁴ ᵒ The sons of Merari were Mahli and Mushi.

The following were the clans of Levi, distributed according to their ancestors: ⁵of Gershon: his son Libni, whose son was Jahath, whose son was Zimmah, ⁶whose son was Joah, whose son was Iddo, whose son was Zerah, whose son was Jetherai.

⁷The descendants of Kohath were: his son Amminadab, whose son was Korah, whose son was Assir, ⁸whose son was Elkanah, whose son was Ebiasaph, whose son was Assir, ⁹whose son was Tahath, whose son was Uriel, whose son was Uzziah, whose son was Shaul. ¹⁰The sons of Elkanah were Amasai and Ahimoth, ¹¹whose son was Elkanah, whose son was Zophai, whose son was Nahath, ¹²whose son was Eliab, whose son was Jeroham, whose son was Elkanah, whose son was Samuel. ¹³The sons of Samuel were Joel, the first-born, and Abijah, the second.

d 1 Chr 1, 31; 5, 10; Gn 25, 15; Ps 83, 6.—e Dt 33, 20f.—f Nm 32, 39; Dt 3, 8ff; Jgs 3, 3.—g Ex 34, 14ff; 2 Kgs 17, 7.—h 2 Kgs 15, 9. 29; 17, 6.—i 1 Chr 6, 1; 23, 6; Gn 46, 11; Ex 6, 16; Nm 26, 57.—j 1 Chr 6, 3; Ex 6, 18.—k Ex 6, 20; Nm 26, 59f.—l 1 Chr 5, 27; 23, 6; Gn 46, 11; Ex 6, 16; Nm 26, 57.—m Ex 6, 17.—n Ex 6, 18; Nm 3, 19; 26, 59.—o 1 Chr 6, 14; Ex 6, 19; Nm 3, 20; 26, 58.

5, 26: *Pul:* the name which the Assyrian king *Tiglath-pileser* III (745-727 B.C.) took as king of Babylon.

5, 27—6, 66: The tribe of Levi. The list gives special prominence to Levi's son *Kohath,* from whom were descended both the Aaronite priests (1 Chr 5, 28-41) and the leading group of temple singers (1 Chr 6, 18-23).

5, 30-41: The line of preexilic priests. The list seems to be confused in vv 36ff, which repeat the names, mostly in inverse order, that occur in vv 34f. A similar but shorter list is given, with variations, in Ezr 7, 1-5.

14 The descendants of Merari were Mahli, whose son was Libni, whose son was Shimei, whose son was Uzzah,^{p} 15 whose son was Shimea, whose son was Haggiah, whose son was Asaiah.

16 The following were entrusted by David with the choir services* in the LORD's house from the time when the ark had obtained a permanent resting place. 17 They served as singers before the Dwelling of the meeting tent until Solomon built the temple of the LORD in Jerusalem, and they performed their services in an order prescribed for them. 18 Those who so performed are the following, together with their descendants.

Among the Kohathites: Heman, the chanter, son of Joel, son of Samuel, 19 son of Elkanah, son of Jeroham, son of Eliel, son of Toah, 20 son of Zuth, son of Elkanah, son of Mahath, son of Amasi, 21 son of Elkanah, son of Joel, son of Azariah, son of Zephaniah, 22 son of Tahath, son of Assir, son of Ebiasaph, son of Korah,^{q} 23 son of Izhar, son of Kohath, son of Levi, son of Israel.

24 His brother Asaph stood at his right hand. Asaph was the son of Berechiah, son of Shimea, 25 son of Michael, son of Baaseiah, son of Malchijah, 26 son of Ethni, son of Zerah, son of Adaiah, 27 son of Ethan, son of Zimmah,^{r} son of Shimei, 28 son of Jahath, son of Gershon, son of Levi.

29 Their brothers, the Merarites, stood at the left: Ethan, son of Kishi, son of Abdi, son of Malluch, 30 son of Hashabiah, son of Amaziah, son of Hilkiah, 31 son of Amzi, son of Bani, son of Shemer, 32 son of Mahli, son of Mushi, son of Merari, son of Levi.^{s}

33 Their brother Levites were appointed to all other services of the Dwelling of the house of God.^{t} 34 However, it was Aaron and his descendants who burnt the offerings on the altar of holocausts and on the altar of incense; they alone had charge of the holy of holies and of making atonement for Israel, as Moses, the servant of God, had ordained.^{u}

p 1 Chr 6, 4; Ex 6, 19; Nm 3, 20; 26, 58.—q Ex 6, 24.—r 1 Chr 6, 2. 5.—s Ex 6, 19; Nm 26, 58.—t 1 Chr 15, 17. 19; 16, 41f; 2 Chr 5, 12.—u 1 Chr 16, 39f.

6, 16-32: The origin of the *choir services* performed by the levitical families in the postexilic temple at the time of the Chronicler is here attributed to David, somewhat as all the laws in the Pentateuch are attributed to Moses.

6, 39-66: Regarding the nature of the rights of Levites in the cities assigned to them, see note on Jos 21. 1.

35 These were the descendants of Aaron: his son Eleazar, whose son was Phinehas, whose son was Abishua, 36 whose son was Bukki, whose son was Uzzi, whose son was Zerahiah, 37 whose son was Meraioth, whose son was Amariah, whose son was Ahitub, 38 whose son was Zadok, whose son was Ahimaaz.

39 * The following were their dwelling places to which their encampment was limited. To the descendants of Aaron who belonged to the clan of the Kohathites, since the first lot fell to them, 40 was assigned Hebron with its adjacent pasture lands in the land of Judah, 41 although the open country and the villages belonging to the city had been given to Caleb, the son of Jephunneh. 42 There were assigned to the descendants of Aaron: Hebron, a city of asylum, Libnah with its pasture lands, Jattir with its pasture lands, Eshtemoa with its pasture lands, 43 Holon with its pasture lands, Debir with its pasture lands, 44 Ashan with its pasture lands, Jetta with its pasture lands, and Beth-shemesh with its pasture lands. 45 Also from the tribe of Benjamin: Gibeon with its pasture lands, Geba with its pasture lands, Almon with its pasture lands, Anathoth with its pasture lands. In all, they had thirteen cities with their pasture lands. 49 The Israelites assigned these cities with their pasture lands to the Levites, 50 designating them by name and assigning them by lot from the tribes of the Judahites, Simeonites, and Benjaminites.

46 The other Kohathites obtained ten cities by lot for their clans from the tribe of Ephraim, from the tribe of Dan, and from the half-tribe of Manasseh. 47 The clans of the Gershonites obtained thirteen cities from the tribes of Issachar, Asher, and Naphtali, and from the half-tribe of Manasseh in Bashan. 48 The clans of the Merarites obtained twelve cities by lot from the tribes of Reuben, Gad, and Zebulun.

51 The clans of the Kohathites obtained cities by lot from the tribe of Ephraim. 52 They were assigned: Shechem in the mountain region of Ephraim, a city of asylum, with its pasture lands, Gezer with its pasture lands, 53 Kibzaim with its pasture lands, and Beth-horon with its pasture lands. 54 From the tribe of Dan: Elteke with its pasture lands, Gibbethon

with its pasture lands, Aijalon with its pasture lands, and Gath-rimmon with its pasture lands. [55] From the half-tribe of Manasseh: Taanach with its pasture lands and Ibleam with its pasture lands. These belonged to the rest of the Kohathite clan.

[56] The clans of the Gershonites received from the half-tribe of Manasseh: Golan in Bashan with its pasture lands and Ashtaroth with its pasture lands. [57] From the tribe of Issachar: Kedesh with its pasture lands, Daberath with its pasture lands, [58] Ramoth with its pasture lands, and Engannim with its pasture lands. [59] From the tribe of Asher: Mashal with its pasture lands, Abdon with its pasture lands, [60] Hilkath with its pasture lands, and Rehob with its pasture lands. [61] From the tribe of Naphtali: Kedesh in Galilee with its pasture lands, Hammon with its pasture lands, and Kiriathaim with its pasture lands.

[62] The rest of the Merarites received from the tribe of Zebulun: Jokneam with its pasture lands, Kartah with its pasture lands, Rimmon with its pasture lands, and Tabor with its pasture lands. [63] Across the Jordan at Jericho [that is, east of the Jordan] they received from the tribe of Reuben: Bezer in the desert with its pasture lands, Jahzah with its pasture lands, [64] Kedemoth with its pasture lands, and Mephaath with its pasture lands. [65] From the tribe of Gad: Ramoth in Gilead with its pasture lands, Mahanaim with its pasture lands, [66] Heshbon with its pasture lands, and Jazer with its pasture lands.

CHAPTER 7

Issachar.[*] [1] The sons of Issachar were Tola, Puah, Jashub, and Shimron: four.[v] [2] The sons of Tola were Uzzi, Rephaiah, Jeriel, Jahmai, Ibsam, and Shemuel, warrior heads of the ancestral houses of Tola. Their kindred numbered twenty-two thousand six hundred in the time of David.[w] [3] The sons of Uzzi: Izarahiah. The sons of Izarahiah were Michael, Obadiah, Joel and Isshiah. All five of these were chiefs. [4] Their kindred, by ancestral houses, numbered thirty-six thousand men in organized military troops, since they had more wives and sons [5] than their fellow tribesmen. In all the clans of Issachar there was a total of eighty-

seven thousand warriors in their family records.

Benjamin. [6] The sons of Benjamin were Bela, Becher, and Jediael—three.[x] [7] The sons of Bela were Ezbon, Uzzi, Uzziel, Jerimoth, and Iri—five. They were heads of their ancestral houses and warriors. Their family records listed twenty-two thousand and thirty-four. [8] The sons of Becher were Zemirah, Joash, Eliezer, Elioenai, Omri, Jeremoth, Abijah, Anathoth, and Alemeth—all these were sons of Becher.[y] [9] Their family records listed twenty thousand two hundred of their kindred who were heads of their ancestral houses and warriors. [10] The sons of Jediael: Bilhan. The sons of Bilhan were Jeush, Benjamin, Ehud, Chenaanah, Zethan, Tarshish, and Ahishahar. [11] All these were descendants of Jediael, heads of ancestral houses and warriors. They numbered seventeen thousand two hundred men fit for military service . . . Shupham and Hupham.[z]

Dan, Naphtali and Manasseh. [12] [a] The sons of Dan: Hushim. [13] The sons of Naphtali were Jahziel, Guni, Jezer, and Shallum. These were descendants of Bilhah. [14] The sons of Manasseh, whom his Aramean concubine bore:[b] she bore Machir, the father of Gilead.[c] [15] Machir took a wife whose name was Maacah; his sister's name was Molecheth. Manasseh's second son was named Zelophehad, but to Zelophehad only daughters were born.[d] [16] Maacah, Machir's wife, bore a son whom she named Peresh. He had a brother named Sheresh, whose sons were Ulam and Rakem. [17] The sons of Ulam: Bedan. These were the descendants of Gilead, the son of Machir, the son of Manasseh. [18] His sister Molecheth bore Ishhod, Abiezer, and Mahlah. [19] The sons of Shemida were Ahian, Shechem, Likhi, and Aniam.

Ephraim. [20] [e] The sons of Ephraim: Shuthelah, whose son was Bered, whose son was Tahath, whose son was Eleadah, whose son was Tahath, [21] whose son was Zabad. Ephraim's son Shuthelah, and Ezer and Elead, who were born in the

---

v Gn 46, 13.—w Nm 26, 23f; Jgs 10, 1.—x 1 Chr 7, 6; Gn 46, 21: Nm 26, 38.—y 1 Chr 7, 8.—z Nm 26, 39.—a 12f: Gn 46, 24; Nm 26, 48f.—b 14-19: Nm 26, 29-32.—c Nm 26, 29; Jos 17, 1.—d Nm 26, 33; Jos 17, 3.—e Nm 26, 35.

7, 1-40: The northern tribes.

land, were slain by the inhabitants of Gath because they had gone down to take away their livestock. ²²Their father Ephraim mourned a long time, but after his kinsmen had come and comforted him, ²³he visited his wife, who conceived and bore a son whom he named Beriah, since evil had befallen his house.^f ²⁴He had a daughter, Sheerah, who built lower and upper Beth-horon and Uzzen-sheerah. ²⁵Zabad's son was Rephah, whose son was Resheph, whose son was Telah, whose son was Tahan, ²⁶whose son was Ladan, whose son was Ammihud, whose son was Elishama,^g ²⁷whose son was Nun, whose son was Joshua.

²⁸Their property and their dwellings were in Bethel and its towns, Naaran to the east, Gezer and its towns to the west, and also Shechem and its towns as far as Ayyah and its towns.^h ²⁹Manasseh, however, had possession of Beth-shean and its towns, Taanach and its towns, Megiddo and its towns, and Dor and its towns. In these dwelt the descendants of Joseph, the son of Israel.ⁱ

Asher. ³⁰The sons of Asher were Imnah, Iishvah, Ishvi, and Beriah; their sister was Serah.^j ³¹Beriah's sons were Heber and Malchiel, who was the father of Birzaith. ³²Heber became the father of Japhlet, Shomer, Hotham, and their sister Shua. ³³The sons of Japhlet were Pasach, Bimhal, and Ashvath; these were the sons of Japhlet. ³⁴The sons of Shomer were Ahi, Rohgah, Jehubbah, and Aram. ³⁵The sons of his brother Hotham were Zophah, Imna, Shelesh, and Amal. ³⁶The sons of Zophah were Suah, Harnepher, Shual, Beri, Imrah, ³⁷Bezer, Hod, Shamma, Shilshah, Ithran, and Beera. ³⁸The sons of Jether were Jephunneh, Pispa, and Ara. ³⁹The sons of Ulla were Arah, Hanniel, and Rizia. ⁴⁰All these were descendants of Asher, heads of ancestral houses, distinguished men, warriors, and chiefs among the princes. Their family records numbered twenty-six thousand men fit for military service.

f 1 Chr 8, 13.—g Nm 1, 10; 2, 18; 7, 48; 10, 22.—h Gn 12, 8; 1 Kgs 9, 16.—i Jos 17, 11.—j Gn 46, 17; Nm 26, 44ff.—k 1 Chr 7, 6; Gn 46, 21; Nm 26, 38ff.—l Jgs 3, 15.—m Neh 11, 35.—n 29-32: 1 Chr 9, 35-38.—o 33-38: 1 Chr 9, 39-44.—p 1 Chr 10, 2; 1 Sm 9, 1; 14, 49. 51; 31, 2.

8, 1-40: A second, variant list of the Benjaminites, with special prominence given to Saul's family (vv 33-40).

CHAPTER 8

Benjamin. * ¹Benjamin became the father of Bela, his first-born, Ashbel, the second son, Aharah, the third,^k ²Nohah, the fourth, and Rapha, the fifth. ³The sons of Bela were Addar and Gera, the father of Ehud. ⁴The sons of Ehud were Abishua, Naaman, Ahoah,^l ⁵Gera, Shephuphan, and Huram. ⁶These were the sons of Ehud, family heads over those who dwelt in Geba and were deported to Manahath. ⁷Also Naaman, Ahijah, and Gera. The last, who led them into exile, became the father of Uzza and Ahihud. ⁸Shaharaim became a father on the Moabite plateau after he had put away his wives Hushim and Baara. ⁹By his wife Hodesh he became the father of Jobab, Zibia, Mesha, Malcam, ¹⁰Jeuz, Sachia, and Mirmah. These were his sons, family heads. ¹¹By Hushim he became the father of Abitub and Elpaal. ¹²The sons of Elpaal were Eber, Misham, Shemed, who built Ono and Lod with its nearby towns,^m ¹³Beriah, and Shema. They were family heads of those who dwelt in Aijalon, and they put the inhabitants of Gath to flight. ¹⁴Their brethren were Elpaal, Shashak, and Jeremoth. ¹⁵Zebadiah, Arad, Eder, ¹⁶Michael, Ishpah, and Joha were the sons of Beriah. ¹⁷Zebadiah, Meshullam, Hizki, Heber, ¹⁸Ishmerai, Izliah, and Jobab were the sons of Elpaal. ¹⁹Jakim, Zichri, Zabdi, ²⁰Elienai, Zillethai, Eliel, ²¹Adaiah, Beraiah, and Shimrath were the sons of Shimei. ²²Ishpan, Eber, Eliel, ²³Abdon, Zichri, Hanan, ²⁴Hananiah, Elam, Anthothijah, ²⁵Iphdeiah, and Penuel were the sons of Shashak. ²⁶Shamsherai, Shehariah, Athaliah, ²⁷Jaareshiah, Elijah, and Zichri were the sons of Jeroham. ²⁸These were family heads over their kindred, chiefs who dwelt in Jerusalem.

²⁹ ⁿ In Gibeon dwelt Jeiel, the founder of Gibeon, whose wife's name was Maacah; ³⁰also his first-born son, Abdon, and Zur, Kish, Baal, Ner, Nadab, ³¹Gedor, Ahio, Zecher, and Mikloth. ³²Mikloth became the father of Shimeah. These, too, dwelt with their relatives in Jerusalem, opposite their fellow tribesmen. ³³ ^o Ner became the father of Kish, and Kish became the father of Saul. Saul became the father of Jonathan, Malchishua, Abinadab, and Eshbaal.^p ³⁴The son of Jonathan was Meribbaal, and

Meribbaal became the father of Micah.�q ³⁵The sons of Micah were Pithon, Melech, Tarea, and Ahaz. ³⁶Ahaz became the father of Jehoaddah, and Jehoaddah became the father of Alemeth, Azmaveth, and Zimri. Zimri became the father of Moza.ʳ ³⁷Moza became the father of Binea, whose son was Raphah, whose son was Eleasah, whose son was Azel.ˢ ³⁸Azel had six sons, whose names were Azrikam, his first-born, Ishmael, Sheariah, Azariah, Obadiah, and Hanan; all these were the sons of Azel. ³⁹The sons of Eshek, his brother, were Ulam, his first-born, Jeush, the second son, and Eliphelet, the third. ⁴⁰The sons of Ulam were combat archers, and many were their sons and grandsons: one hundred and fifty. All these were the descendants of Benjamin.

CHAPTER 9

¹Thus all Israel was inscribed in its family records which are recorded in the book of the kings of Israel.ᵗ

Now Judah had been carried in captivity to Babylon because of its rebellion. ²ᵘ* The first to settle again in their cities and dwell there were certain lay Israelites, the priests, the Levites, and the temple slaves.ᵛ

Jerusalemites. ³In Jerusalem lived Judahites and Benjaminites; also Ephraimites and Manassehites. ⁴Among the Judahites was Uthai, son of Ammihud, son of Omri, son of Imri, son of Bani, one of the descendants of Perez, son of Judah. ⁵Among the Shelanites were Asaiah, the first-born, and his sons. ⁶Among the Zerahites were Jeuel and six hundred and ninety of their brethren. ⁷Among the Benjaminites were Sallu, son of Meshullam, son of Hodaviah, son of Hassenuah; ⁸Ibneiah, son of Jeroham; Elah, son of Uzzi, son of Michri; Meshullam, son of Shephatiah, son of Reuel, son of Ibnijah. ⁹Their kindred of various families were nine hundred and fifty-six. All those named were heads of their ancestral houses.

¹⁰Among the priests were Jedaiah; Jehoiarib; Jachin; ¹¹Azariah, son of Hilkiah, son of Meshullam, son of Zadok, son of Meraioth, son of Ahitub, the ruler of the house of God; ¹²Adaiah, son of Jeroham, son of Pashhur, son of Malchijah; Maasai, son of Adiel, son of Jahzerah, son of Meshullam, son of

Meshillemith, son of Immer. ¹³Their brethren, heads of their ancestral houses, were one thousand seven hundred and sixty, valiant for the work of the service of the house of God.

¹⁴Among the Levites were Shemaiah, son of Hasshub, son of Azrikam, son of Hashabiah, one of the descendants of Merari; ¹⁵Bakbakkar; Heresh; Galal; Mattaniah, son of Mica, son of Zichri, a descendant of Asaph; ¹⁶Obadiah, son of Shemaiah, son of Galal, a descendant of Jeduthun; and Berechiah, son of Asa, son of Elkanah, whose family lived in the villages of the Netophathites.

¹⁷The gatekeepers were Shallum, Akkub, Talmon, Ahiman, and their brethren; Shallum was the chief. ¹⁸Previously they had stood guard at the king's gate on the east side; now they became gatekeepers for the encampments of the Levites. ¹⁹Shallum, son of Kore, son of Ebiasaph, a descendant of Korah, and his brethren of the same ancestral house of the Korahites had as their assigned task the guarding of the threshold of the tent, just as their fathers had guarded the entrance to the encampment of the Lᴏʀᴅ. ²⁰Phinehas, son of Eleazar, had been their chief in times past—the Lᴏʀᴅ be with him!ʷ ²¹Zechariah, son of Meshelemiah, guarded the gate of the meeting tent.ˣ ²²In all, those who were chosen for gatekeepers at the threshold were two hundred and twelve. They were inscribed in the family records of their villages. David and Samuel the seer had established them in their position of trust. ²³Thus they and their sons kept guard over the gates of the house of the Lᴏʀᴅ, the house which was then a tent. ²⁴The gatekeepers were stationed at the four sides, to the east, the west, the north, and the south.ʸ ²⁵Their kinsmen who lived in their own villages took turns in assisting them for seven-day periods,ᶻ ²⁶while the four chief gatekeepers were on constant duty. These were the Levites who also had charge of the chambers and treasures of the house of God. ²⁷At night they lodged about the house of

q 2 Sm 4, 4; 9, 6. 10. 12.—r 1 Chr 9, 42.—s 1 Chr 9, 43.—t 2 Chr 16, 11; 20, 34; 25, 26; 27, 7; 33, 18; 36, 8.—u 2-22: Neh 11, 3-19.—v Ezr 2, 70; 7, 7; Neh 11, 3.—w Ex 6, 25; Nm 25, 7. 11; Jgs 20, 28.—x 1 Chr 26, 2. 14.—y 1 Chr 26, 13.—z 2 Chr 23, 4f.

9, 2-34: The inhabitants of Jerusalem after the exile. A similar list, with many variants in the names, is given in Neh 11, 3-24.

God, for it was in their charge and they had the duty of opening it each morning. [28] Some of them had charge of the liturgical equipment, tallying it as it was brought in and taken out. [29] Others were appointed to take care of the utensils and all the sacred vessels, as well as the fine flour, the wine, the oil, the frankincense, and the spices. [30] It was the sons of priests, however, who mixed the spiced ointments.*a* [31] *b* Mattithiah, one of the Levites, the first-born of Shallum the Koreite, was entrusted with preparing the cakes. [32] Benaiah the Kohathite, one of their brethren, was in charge of setting out the showbread each sabbath.*c*

[33] These were the chanters and the gatekeepers, family heads over the Levites. They stayed in the chambers when free of duty, for day and night they had to be ready for service. [34] These were the levitical family heads over their kindred, chiefs who dwelt in Jerusalem.

II: THE HISTORY OF DAVID

Genealogy of Saul. [35] *d* In Gibeon dwelt Jeiel, the founder of Gibeon, whose wife's name was Maacah. [36] His first-born son was Abdon; then came Zur, Kish, Baal, Ner, Nadab, [37] Gedor, Ahio, Zechariah, and Mikloth. [38] Mikloth became the father of Shimeam. These, too, with their brethren, dwelt opposite their brethren in Jerusalem. [39] Ner became the father of Kish, and Kish became the father of Saul. Saul became the father of Jonathan, Malchishua, Abinadab, and Eshbaal. [40] The son of Jonathan was Meribbaal, and Meribbaal became the father of Micah. [41] The sons of Micah were Pithon, Melech, Tahrea, and Ahaz. [42] Ahaz became the father of Jehoaddah, and Jehoaddah became the father of Alemeth, Azmaveth, and Zimri. Zimri became the father of Moza. [43] Moza became the father of Binea, whose son was Rephaiah, whose son was Eleasah, whose son was Azel. [44] Azel had

six sons, whose names were Azrikam, his first-born, Ishmael, Sheariah, Azariah, Obadiah, and Hanan; these were the sons of Azel.

CHAPTER 10

His Death and Burial. [1] *e* Now the Philistines were at war with Israel; the Israelites fled before the Philistines, and a number of them fell, slain on Mount Gilboa. [2] The Philistines pressed hard after Saul and his sons. When the Philistines had killed Jonathan, Abinadab, and Malchishua, sons of Saul, [3] the whole fury of the battle descended upon Saul. Then the archers found him, and wounded him with their arrows.

[4] Saul said to his armor-bearer, "Draw your sword and thrust me through with it, that these uncircumcised may not come and maltreat me." But the armor-bearer, in great fear, refused. So Saul took his own sword and fell on it; [5] and seeing him dead, the armor-bearer also fell on his sword and died. [6] Thus, with Saul and his three sons, his whole house died at one time. [7] When all the Israelites who were in the valley saw that Saul and his sons had died in the rout, they left their cities and fled; thereupon the Philistines came and occupied them.

[8] On the following day, when the Philistines came to strip the slain, they found Saul and his sons where they had fallen on Mount Gilboa. [9] They stripped him, cut off his head, and took his armor; these they sent throughout the land of the Philistines to convey the good news to their idols and their people. [10] His armor they put in the house of their gods, but his skull they impaled on the temple of Dagon.

[11] When all the inhabitants of Jabesh-gilead had heard what the Philistines had done to Saul, [12] its warriors rose to a man, recovered the bodies of Saul and his sons, and brought them to Jabesh. They buried their bones under the oak of Jabesh, and fasted seven days.*f*

[13] * Thus Saul died because of his rebellion against the LORD in disobeying his command, and also because he had sought counsel of a necromancer,*g* [14] and had not rather inquired of the LORD. Therefore the LORD slew him, and transferred his kingdom to David, the son of Jesse.*h*

---

a Ex 30, 22-33.—b 31f: 1 Chr 23, 29; Lv 2, 1ff; 6, 13ff; 7, 11.—c Ex 25, 30; Lv 24, 5-8.—d 35-44: 1 Chr 8, 29-38.—e 1-12: 1 Sm 31, 1-13.—f 2 Sm 2, 5.—g Dt 18, 10ff; 1 Sm 13, 13f; 15, 3. 11. 26.—h 1 Sm 15, 28; 2 Sm 3, 9f.

10, 13f: The Chronicler's comment on why Saul met his tragic end: he had disobeyed the Lord's command given through the prophet Samuel (1 Sm 15, 3-9), and *had sought counsel of a necromancer* (1 Sm 28, 6-19), contrary to the Mosaic law against necromancy (Dt 18, 10f).

CHAPTER 11

David Is Made King. [1] *i* Then all Israel gathered about David in Hebron, and they said: "Surely, we are of the same bone and flesh as you. [2] Even formerly, when Saul was still the king, it was you who led Israel in all its battles. And now the LORD, your God, has said to you, 'You shall shepherd my people Israel and be ruler over them.'" *j* [3] Then all the elders of Israel came to the king at Hebron, and there David made a covenant with them in the presence of the LORD; and they anointed him king over Israel, in accordance with the word of the LORD as revealed through Samuel. *k*

Jerusalem Captured. [4] Then David and all Israel went to Jerusalem, that is, Jebus, where the natives of the land were called Jebusites. *l* [5] The inhabitants of Jebus said to David, "You shall not enter here." David nevertheless captured the fortress of Sion, which is the City of David. [6] David said, "Whoever strikes the Jebusites first shall be made the chief commander." Joab, the son of Zeruiah, was the first to go up; and so he became chief. *m* [7] David took up his residence in the fortress, which thenceforth was called the City of David. [8] He rebuilt the city on all sides, from the Millo all the way around, while Joab restored the rest of the city. *n* [9] David became more and more powerful, for the LORD of hosts was with him.

David's Warriors. [10] *o* These were David's chief warriors who, together with all Israel, supported him in his reign in order to make him true king, even as the LORD had commanded concerning Israel. [11] Here is the list of David's warriors:

Ishbaal, the son of Hachamoni, chief of the Three.* He brandished his spear against three hundred, whom he slew in a single encounter.

[12] Next to him Eleazar, the son of Dodo the Ahohite, one of the Three warriors. *p* [13] He was with David at Pasdammim, where the Philistines had massed for battle. The plowland was fully planted with barley, but its defenders were retreating before the Philistines. *q* [14] He made a stand on the sown ground, kept it safe, and cut down the Philistines. Thus the LORD brought about a great victory.

[15] Three of the Thirty chiefs went down to the rock, to David, who was in the cave of Adullam while the Philistines were encamped in the valley of Rephaim. *r* [16] David was then in the stronghold, and a Philistine garrison was at Bethlehem. [17] David expressed a desire: "Oh, that someone would give me a drink from the cistern that is by the gate at Bethlehem!" [18] Thereupon the Three broke through the encampment of the Philistines, drew water from the cistern by the gate at Bethlehem, and carried it back to David. But David refused to drink it. Instead, he poured it out as a libation to the LORD, [19] saying, "God forbid that I should do such a thing! Could I drink the blood of these men who risked their lives?" For at the risk of their lives they brought it; and so he refused to drink it. Such deeds as these the Three warriors performed.

[20] *s* Abishai, the brother of Joab. He was the chief of the Thirty;* he brandished his spear against three hundred, and slew them. Thus he had a reputation like that of the Three. *t* [21] He was twice as famous as any of the Thirty and became their commander, but he did not attain to the Three.

[22] Benaiah, the son of Jehoiada, a valiant man of mighty deeds, from Kabzeel. He killed the two sons of Ariel of Moab, and also, on a snowy day, he went down and killed the lion in the cistern. [23] He likewise slew the Egyptian, a huge man five cubits tall. The Egyptian carried a spear that was like a weaver's heddle-bar, but he came against him with a staff, wrested the spear from the Egyptian's hand, and killed him with his own spear. [24] Such deeds as these of Benaiah, the son of Jehoiada, gave him a reputation like that of the Three. [25] He was more famous than any of the Thirty, but he did not attain to the Three. David put him in charge of his bodyguard. *u*

[26] Also these warriors: Asahel, the brother of Joab; Elhanan, son of Dodo,

i 1-9: 2 Sm 5, 1-10.—j 1 Sm 18, 5. 13-16. 30; 19, 8.—k 1 Sm 16, 1. 13; 2 Sm 2, 4.—l Jos 15, 8; Jgs 1, 21; 19, 10f.—m 2 Sm 2, 13ff; 8, 16.—n 1 Kgs 9, 15. 24; 11, 27; 2 Chr 32, 5.—o 10-41: 2 Sm 23, 8-39.—p 1 Chr 27, 4.—q 1 Sm 17, 1.—r 1 Chr 14, 9; 2 Sm 5, 18. 22.—s 20f: 2 Sm 23, 18f.—t 1 Chr 18, 12; 1 Sm 26, 6ff; 2 Sm 16, 9; 18, 2; 21, 17.—u 2 Sm 8, 18; 20, 23.

11, 11f: *The Three:* the Chronicler names only two of them: *Ishbaal* and *Eleazar.* According to 2 Sm 23, 8-12, the Three were *Ishbaal, Eleazar,* and *Shammah.*

11, 20: *The Thirty:* listed by name in vv 26-47. The list given in 2 Sm 23, 8-39 often differs in names and spellings; for the numbers, see the note there.

from Bethlehem;[v] [27] Shammoth, from En-harod; Helez, from Palti; [28] Ira, son of Ik-kesh, from Tekoa; Abiezer, from Anathoth; [29] Sibbecai, from Husha; Ilai, from Ahoh;[w] [30] Maharai, from Netophah; Heled, son of Baanah, from Netophah;[x] [31] Ithai, son of Ribai, from Gibeah of Benjamin; Benaiah, from Pirathon;[y] [32] Hurai, from the valley of Gaash; Abiel, from Betharabah; [33] Azmaveth, from Bahurim; Eliahba, from Shaalbon; [34] Jashen the Gunite; Jonathan, son of Shagee, from Enharod; [35] Ahiam, son of Sachar, from Enharod; Elipheleth, son of [36] Ahasabi, from Beth-maacah; Ahijah, from Gilo; [37] Hezro, from Carmel; Naarai, the son of Ezbai; [38] Joel, brother of Nathan, from Rehob, the Gadite; [39] Zelek the Ammonite; Naharai, from Beeroth, the armor-bearer of Joab, son of Zeruiah; [40] Ira, from Jattir; Gareb, from Jattir; [41] Uriah the Hittite; Zabad, son of Ahlai, [42] and, in addition to the Thirty, Adina, son of Shiza, the Reubenite, chief of the tribe of Reuben; [43] Hanan, from Beth-maacah; Joshaphat the Mithnite; [44] Uzzia, from Ashterath; Shama and Jeiel, sons of Hotham, from Aroer; [45] Jediael, son of Shimri, and Joha, his brother, the Tizite; [46] Eliel the Mahavite; Jeribai and Joshaviah, sons of Elnaam; Ithmah, from Moab; [47] Eliel, Obed, and Jaasiel the Mezobian.

CHAPTER 12

David's Early Followers. [1] The following men came to David in Ziklag while he was still under banishment from Saul, son of Kish; they, too, were among the warriors who helped him in his battles.[z] [2] They were archers who could use either the right or the left hand, both in slinging stones and in shooting arrows with the bow. They were some of Saul's kinsmen, from Benjamin. [3] Ahiezer was their chief, along with Joash, both sons of Shemaah of Gibeah; also Jeziel and Pelet, sons of Azmaveth; Beracah; Jehu, from Anathoth;[a] [4] Ishmaiah the Gibeonite, a warrior on the level of the Thirty, and in addition to their number: [5] Jeremiah; Jahaziel; Johanan; Jozabad, from Gederah; [6] Eluzai; Jerimoth; Bealiah; Shemariah; Shephatiah the Haruphite; [7] Elkanah, Isshiah, Azarel, Joezer, and Ishbaal, who were

Korahites; [8] Joelah, finally, and Zebadiah, sons of Jeroham, from Gedor.

[9] Some of the Gadites also went over to David when he was at the stronghold in the wilderness. They were valiant warriors, experienced soldiers equipped with shield and spear, who bore themselves like lions, and were as swift as the gazelles on the mountains.[b] [10] Ezer was their chief, Obadiah was second, Eliab third, [11] Mishmannah fourth, Jeremiah fifth, [12] Attai sixth, Eliel seventh, [13] Johanan eighth, Elzabad ninth, [14] Jeremiah tenth, and Machbannai eleventh. [15] These Gadites were army commanders, the lesser placed over hundreds and the greater over thousands. [16] It was they who crossed over the Jordan when it was overflowing both its banks in the first month, and dispersed all who were in the valleys to the east and to the west.

[17] Some Benjaminites and Judahites also came to David at the stronghold. [18] David went out to meet them and addressed them in these words: "If you come peacefully, to help me, I am of a mind to have you join me. But if you have come to betray me to my enemies though my hands have done no wrong, may the God of our fathers see and punish you."

[19] Then spirit enveloped Amasai, the chief of the Thirty, who spoke:

"We are yours, O David,
we are with you, O son of Jesse.
Peace, peace to you,
and peace to him who helps you;
your God it is who helps you."

So David received them and placed them among the leaders of his troops.

[20] Men from Manasseh also deserted to David when he came with the Philistines to battle against Saul. However, he did not help the Philistines, for their lords took counsel and sent him home, saying, "At the cost of our heads he will desert to his master Saul." [21] As he was returning to Ziklag, therefore, these deserted to him from Manasseh: Adnah, Jozabad, Jediael, Michael, Jozabad, Elihu, and Zillethai, chiefs of thousands of Manasseh. [22] They helped David by taking charge of his troops, for they were all warriors and became commanders of his army. [23] And from day to day men kept coming to David's help until there was a vast encampment, like an encampment of angels.

v 1 Chr 2, 16; 27, 7.—w 1 Chr 27, 11.—x 1 Chr 27, 13.—y 1 Chr 27, 14.—z 1 Sm 27, 1-7.—a 1 Chr 27, 12.—b Dt 33, 20.

The Assembly at Hebron. ²⁴This is the muster of the detachments of armed troops that came to David at Hebron to transfer to him Saul's kingdom, as the LORD had ordained. ²⁵ * Judahites bearing shields and spears: six thousand eight hundred armed troops. ²⁶Of the Simeonites, warriors fit for battle: seven thousand one hundred. ²⁷Of the Levites: four thousand six hundred, ²⁸along with Jehoiada, leader of the line of Aaron, with another three thousand seven hundred, ²⁹and Zadok, a young warrior, with twenty-two princes of his father's house. ³⁰Of the Benjaminites, the brethren of Saul: three thousand— until this time, most of them had held their allegiance to the house of Saul. ³¹Of the Ephraimites: twenty thousand eight hundred warriors, men renowned in their ancestral houses. ³²Of the half-tribe of Manasseh: eighteen thousand, designated by name to come and make David king. ³³Of the Issacharites, their chiefs who were endowed with an understanding of the times and who knew what Israel had to do: two hundred chiefs, together with all their brethren under their command. ³⁴From Zebulun, men fit for military service, set in battle array with every kind of weapon for war: fifty thousand men rallying with a single purpose. ³⁵From Naphtali: one thousand captains, and with them, armed with shield and lance, thirty-seven thousand men. ³⁶Of the Danites, set in battle array: twenty-eight thousand six hundred. ³⁷From Asher, fit for military service and set in battle array: forty thousand. ³⁸From the other side of the Jordan, of the Reubenites, Gadites, and the half-tribe of Manasseh, men equipped with every kind of weapon of war: one hundred and twenty thousand.

³⁹All these soldiers, drawn up in battle order, came to Hebron with the resolute intention of making David king over all Israel. The rest of Israel was likewise of one mind to make David king. ⁴⁰They remained with David for three days, feasting and drinking, for their brethren had prepared for them. ⁴¹Moreover, their neighbors from as far as Issachar, Zebulun, and Naphtali came bringing food on asses, camels, mules, and oxen—provisions in great quantity of meal, pressed figs, raisins, wine, oil, oxen, and sheep. For there was rejoicing in Israel.

CHAPTER 13

Transfer of the Ark. ¹ ^c After David had taken counsel with his commanders of thousands and of hundreds, that is to say, with every one of his leaders, ²he said to the whole assembly of Israel: "If it seems good to you, and is so decreed by the LORD our God, let us summon the rest of our brethren from all the districts of Israel, and also the priests and the Levites from their cities with pasture lands, that they may join us;^d ³and let us bring the ark of our God here among us, for in the days of Saul we did not visit it." ⁴And the whole assembly agreed to do this, for the idea was pleasing to all the people.

⁵Then David assembled all Israel, from Shihor of Egypt* to Labo of Hamath, to bring the ark of God from Kiriath-jearim.^e ⁶David and all Israel went up to Baalah, that is, to Kiriath-jearim, of Judah, to bring back the ark of God, which was known by the name "LORD enthroned upon the cherubim."^f ⁷They transported the ark of God on a new cart from the house of Abinadab; Uzzah and Ahio were guiding the cart, ⁸while David and all Israel danced before God with great enthusiasm, amid songs and music on lyres, harps, tambourines, cymbals, and trumpets.

⁹As they reached the threshing floor of Chidon,* Uzzah stretched out his hand to steady the ark, for the oxen were upsetting it. ¹⁰Then the LORD became angry with Uzzah and struck him; he died there in God's presence, because he had laid his hand on the ark. ¹¹David was disturbed because the LORD's anger had broken out against Uzzah. Therefore that place has been called Perez-uzza* even to this day.

---

c 1-14: 2 Sm 6, 1-11.—d Nm 35, 1ff; Jos 14, 4; 21, 2ff.—e 1 Chr 15, 3; Jos 13, 3. 5; 1 Sm 6, 21; 7, 1f; 2 Sm 6, 1-11.—f Jos 15, 9; 18, 14; 1 Sm 4, 4; 7, 1.

12, 25-38: The Chronicler fills out the pageantry of joyous occasions in keeping with his much later appreciation of the significance of the event in the history of God's people: the numbers in attendance at David's crowning in Hebron (cf 2 Sm 5, 1ff) are recounted in the same spirit of enthusiasm which in v 23 compares David's band of desert freebooters to a numerous encampment of angels.

13, 5: *Shihor of Egypt:* the eastern branch of the Nile delta. *Labo of Hamath:* in southern Syria.

13, 9: *Chidon:* in 2 Sm 6, 6, *Nodan.*

13, 11: *Perez-uzza:* a Hebrew term meaning "the breaking out against Uzza."

[12] David was now afraid of God, and he said, "How can I bring the ark of God with me?" [13] Therefore he did not take the ark back with him to the City of David, but he took it instead to the house of Obed-edom the Gittite. [14] The ark of God remained in the house of Obed-edom with his family for three months, and the LORD blessed Obed-edom's household and all that he possessed.[g]

CHAPTER 14

David in Jerusalem. [1] [h] Hiram, king of Tyre, sent envoys to David along with masons and carpenters, and cedar wood to build him a house.[i] [2] David now understood that the LORD had truly confirmed him as king over Israel, for his kingdom was greatly exalted for the sake of his people Israel. [3] [j] David took other wives in Jerusalem and became the father of more sons and daughters. [4] These are the names of those who were born to him in Jerusalem: Shammua, Shobab, Nathan, Solomon, [5] Ibhar, Elishua, Elpelet, [6] Nogah, Nepheg, Japhia, [7] Elishama, Beeliada, and Eliphelet.

The Philistine Wars. [8] When the Philistines had heard that David was anointed king over all Israel, they went up in unison to seek him out. But when David heard of this, he marched out against them. [9] Meanwhile the Philistines had come and raided the valley of Rephaim.[k] [10] David inquired of God, "Shall I advance against the Philistines, and will you deliver them into my power?" The LORD answered him, "Advance, for I will deliver them into your power." [11] They advanced, therefore, to Baal-perazim, and David defeated them there. Then David said, "God has used me to break through my enemies just as water breaks through a dam." Therefore that place was called Baal-perazim. [12] The Philistines had left their gods there, and David ordered them to be burnt.[l]

[13] Once again the Philistines raided the valley, [14] and again David inquired of God. But God answered him: "Do not try to pursue them, but go around them and come upon them from the direction of the

mastic trees. [15] When you hear the sound of marching in the tops of the mastic trees, then go forth to battle, for God has already gone before you to strike the army of the Philistines." [16] David did as God commanded him, and they routed the Philistine army from Gibeon to Gezer.

[17] Thus David's fame was spread abroad through every land, and the LORD made all the nations fear him.

CHAPTER 15

The Ark Brought to Jerusalem. [1] David built houses for himself in the City of David and prepared a place for the ark of God, pitching a tent for it there. [2] At that time he said, "No one may carry the ark of God except the Levites, for the LORD chose them to carry the ark of the LORD and to minister to him forever."[m] [3] Then David assembled all Israel in Jerusalem to bring the ark of the LORD to the place which he had prepared for it.[n] [4] David also called together the sons of Aaron and the Levites: [5] of the sons of Kohath, Uriel, their chief, and one hundred and twenty of his brethren; [6] of the sons of Merari, Asaiah, their chief, and two hundred and twenty of his brethren; [7] of the sons of Gershon, Joel, their chief, and one hundred and thirty of his brethren; [8] of the sons of Elizaphan, Shemaiah, their chief, and two hundred of his brethren; [9] of the sons of Hebron, Eliel, their chief, and eighty of his brethren; [10] of the sons of Uzziel, Amminadab, their chief, and one hundred and twelve of his brethren.

[11] David summoned the priests Zadok and Abiathar, and the Levites Uriel, Asaiah, Joel, Shemaiah, Eliel, and Amminadab,[o] [12] and said to them: "You, the heads of the levitical families, must sanctify yourselves along with your brethren and bring the ark of the LORD, the God of Israel, to the place which I have prepared for it.[p] [13] Because you were not with us the first time, the wrath of the LORD our God burst upon us, for we did not seek him aright."[q] [14] Accordingly, the priests and the Levites sanctified themselves to bring up the ark of the LORD, the God of Israel. [15] The Levites bore the ark of God on their shoulders with poles, as Moses had ordained according to the word of the LORD.[r]

g 1 Chr 26, 4f.—h 1-16: 2 Sm 5, 11-25.—i 1 Kgs 5, 1; 2 Chr 2, 3.—j 3-7: 1 Chr 3, 5-8; 2 Sm 5, 13-16.—k 1 Chr 11, 15.—l Dt 7, 5. 25.—m Nm 1, 50; 7, 9; Dt 10, 8; 31, 25; 1 Sm 6, 15; Jos 3, 8.—n 1 Chr 13, 5; 2 Sm 6, 15. 17.—o 1 Chr 16, 39; 2 Sm 8, 17; 15, 29. 35.—p 2 Chr 29, 5. 15. 34; 30, 3. 15. 24.—q 1 Chr 13, 3.—r Ex 25, 13ff; Nm 1, 50; 7, 9; 2 Chr 35, 3.

1Chr

16 David commanded the chiefs of the Levites to appoint their brethren as chanters, to play on musical instruments, harps, lyres, and cymbals, to make a loud sound of rejoicing. *s* 17 Therefore the Levites appointed Heman, son of Joel, and, among his brethren, Asaph, son of Berechiah; and among the sons of Merari, their brethren, Ethan, son of Kushaiah;*t* 18 and, together with these, their brethren of the second rank: the gatekeepers Zechariah, Uzziel, Shemiramoth, Jehiel, Unni, Eliab, Benaiah, Maaseiah, Mattithiah, Eliphelehu, Mikneiah, Obed-edom, and Jeiel. 19 The chanters, Heman, Asaph, and Ethan, sounded brass cymbals. 20 Zechariah, Uzziel, Shemiramoth, Jehiel, Unni, Eliab, Maaseiah, and Benaiah played on harps set to "Alamoth."* 21 But Mattithiah, Eliphelehu, Mikneiah, Obed-edom, and Jeiel led the chant on lyres set to "the eighth." 22 Chenaniah was the chief of the Levites in the chanting; he directed the chanting, for he was skillful.*u* 23 Berechiah and Elkanah were gatekeepers before the ark. 24 The priests, Shebaniah, Joshaphat, Nethanel, Amasai, Zechariah, Benaiah, and Eliezer, sounded the trumpets before the ark of God. Obed-edom and Jeiel were also gatekeepers before the ark.*v*

25 *w* Thus David, the elders of Israel, and the commanders of thousands went to bring up the ark of the covenant of the LORD with joy from the house of Obed-edom. 26 While the Levites, with God's help, were bearing the ark of the covenant of the LORD, seven bulls and seven rams were sacrificed.*x* 27 David was clothed in a robe of fine linen, as were all the Levites who carried the ark, the singers, and Chenaniah, the leader of the chant; David was also wearing a linen ephod.*y* 28 Thus all Israel brought back the ark of the covenant of the LORD with joyful shouting, and to the sound of horns, trumpets, and cymbals, and the music of harps and lyres. 29 But as the ark of the covenant of the LORD was entering the City of David, Michal, daughter of Saul, looked down from her window, and when she saw King David leaping and dancing, she despised him in her heart.*z*

CHAPTER 16

1 *a* They brought in the ark of God and set it within the tent which David had pitched for it. Then they offered up holocausts and peace offerings to God.*b* 2 When David had finished offering up the holocausts and peace offerings, he blessed the people in the name of the LORD, 3 and distributed to every Israelite, to every man and to every woman, a loaf of bread, a piece of meat, and a raisin cake.

The Ministering Levites. 4 He now appointed certain Levites to minister before the ark of the LORD, to celebrate, thank, and praise the LORD, the God of Israel.*c* 5 Asaph was their chief, and second to him were Zechariah, Uzziel, Shemiramoth, Jehiel, Mattithiah, Eliab, Benaiah, Obededom, and Jeiel. These were to play on harps and lyres, while Asaph was to sound the cymbals, 6 and the priests Benaiah and Jahaziel were to be the regular trumpeters before the ark of the covenant of God. 7 Then, on that same day, David appointed Asaph and his brethren to sing for the first time these praises of the LORD:

8 * Give thanks to the LORD, invoke his name;*d*
  make known among the nations his deeds.
9 Sing to him, sing his praise,
  proclaim all his wondrous deeds.
10 Glory in his holy name;
  rejoice, O hearts that seek the LORD!
11 Look to the LORD in his strength;
  seek to serve him constantly.
12 Recall the wondrous deeds that he has wrought,
  his portents, and the judgments he has uttered,
13 You descendants of Israel, his servants,
  sons of Jacob, his chosen ones!

s 1 Chr 13, 8; 16, 5; 2 Chr 5, 12; 29, 25; Neh 12, 27.—t 1 Chr 6, 31-47; 25, 1-8.—u 1 Chr 26, 29.—v Nm 10, 8; Jos 6, 4ff.—w 25-29: 2 Sm 6, 12-16.—x 2 Sm 6, 13; 2 Chr 29, 21.—y 1 Sm 2, 18; 2 Sm 6, 14.—z 2 Sm 6, 20ff.—a 1-3: 2 Sm 6, 17ff.—b 1 Sm 15, 1.—c Sir 47, 9.—d 8-22: Ps 105, 1-15.

15, 20: *Alamoth:* a musical term (literally, "young women") of uncertain meaning, occurring also in Ps 46, 1, where it is rendered as virgins. Perhaps it may mean something like "soprano," whereas the term "eighth" (Hebrew *sheminith*, v 21) may then mean "bass"; cf Pss 6, 1; 12, 1.

16, 8-36: A hymn composed of parts, with textual variants, from several Psalms; vv 8-22 = Ps 105, 1-15; vv 23-33 = Ps 96, 1-13; vv 34-36 = Ps 106, 1. 47f.

14 He, the LORD, is our God;
    throughout the earth his judgments
        prevail.
15 He remembers forever his covenant
    which he made binding for a
        thousand generations—
16 Which he entered into with Abraham
    and by his oath to Isaac;
17 Which he established for Jacob by stat-
    ute,
    for Israel as an everlasting covenant,
18 Saying, "To you will I give the land of
    Canaan
    as your allotted inheritance."

19 When they were few in number,
    a handful, and strangers there,
20 Wandering from nation to nation,
    from one kingdom to another people,
21 He let no one oppress them,
    and for their sake he rebuked kings:
22 "Touch not my anointed,
    and to my prophets do no harm."

23 *e* Sing to the LORD, all the earth,
    announce his salvation, day after
        day.
24 Tell his glory among the nations;
    among all peoples, his wondrous
        deeds.
25 For great is the LORD and highly to be
    praised;
    and awesome is he, beyond all gods.
26 For all the gods of the nations are things
    of nought,
    but the LORD made the heavens.
27 Splendor and majesty go before him;
    praise and joy are in his holy place.

28 Give to the LORD, you families of na-
    tions,
    give to the LORD glory and praise;
29 Give to the LORD the glory due his
    name!
    Bring gifts, and enter his presence;
    worship the LORD in holy attire.
30 Tremble before him, all the earth;
    he has made the world firm, not to be
        moved.

31 Let the heavens be glad and the earth
    rejoice;
    let them say among the nations: The
        LORD is king.

32 Let the sea and what fills it resound;
    let the plains rejoice and all that is in
        them!
33 Then shall all the trees of the forest
    exult
    before the LORD, for he comes:
    he comes to rule the earth.

34 *f* Give thanks to the LORD, for he is
    good,
    for his kindness endures forever;
35 And say, "Save us, O God, our savior,
    gather us and deliver us from the na-
        tions,
    That we may give thanks to your holy
        name
    and glory in praising you."

36 Blessed be the LORD, the God of Israel,
    through all eternity!
    Let all the people say, Amen! Alleluia.

37 Then David left Asaph and his brethren there before the ark of the covenant of
the LORD to minister before the ark regularly according to the daily ritual; 38 he also
left there Obed-edom and sixty-eight of his
brethren, including Obed-edom, son of
Jeduthun, and Hosah, to be gatekeepers. *g*
39 But the priest Zadok and his priestly
brethren he left before the Dwelling of the
LORD on the high place at Gibeon, *h* 40 to
offer holocausts to the LORD on the altar of
holocausts regularly, morning and evening, and to do all that is written in the law
of the LORD which he has decreed for Israel. *i* 41 With them were Heman and
Jeduthun and the others who were chosen
and designated by name to give thanks to
the LORD, "because his kindness endures
forever," *j* 42 with trumpets and cymbals
for accompaniment, and instruments for
the sacred chant. The sons of Jeduthun
kept the gate. *k*
43 Then all the people departed, each to
his own home, and David returned to bless
his household. *l*

CHAPTER 17

The Oracle of Nathan. 1 *m* After David had
taken up residence in his house, he said to
Nathan the prophet, "See, I am living in a
house of cedar, but the ark of the covenant
of the LORD dwells under tentcloth." *n*
2 Nathan replied to David, "Do, therefore,
whatever you desire, for God is with you."

---

e 23-33: Ps 96, 1-13.—f 34ff: Ps 106, 1. 47f.—g 1 Chr 15,
24.—h 1 Kgs 3, 4.—i Ex 29, 38-42; Lv 6, 9; Nm 28, 3. 6; 2 Chr
13, 11.—j 2 Chr 5, 12; 7, 3. 6; 20, 21; Ezr 3, 11.—k 2 Chr 29,
27.—l 2 Sm 6, 19f.—m 1-27: 2 Sm 7, 1-29.—n 1 Chr 15, 1; 2
Sm 5, 11.

3 But that same night the word of God came to Nathan: 4 "Go and tell my servant David, Thus says the LORD: It is not you who are to build a house for me to dwell in.*o* 5 For I have never dwelt in a house, from the time when I led Israel onward, even to this day, but I have been lodging in tent or pavilion 6 as long as I have wandered about with all of Israel. Did I ever say a word to any of the judges of Israel whom I commanded to guide my people, such as, 'Why have you not built me a house of cedar?' 7 Therefore, tell my servant David, Thus says the LORD of hosts: I took you from the pasture, from following the sheep, that you might become ruler over my people Israel.*p* 8 I was with you wherever you went, and I cut down all your enemies before you. I will make your name great like that of the greatest on the earth. 9 I will assign a place for my people Israel and I will plant them in it to dwell there henceforth undisturbed; nor shall wicked men ever again oppress them, as they did at first, 10 and during all the time when I appointed judges over my people Israel. And I will subdue all your enemies. Moreover, I declare to you that I, the LORD, will build you a house; 11 so that when your days have been completed and you must join your fathers, I will raise up your offspring after you who will be one of your own sons, and I will establish his kingdom.*q* 12 He it is who shall build me a house, and I will establish his throne forever.*r* 13 I will be a father to him, and he shall be a son to me, and I will not withdraw my favor from him as I withdrew it from him who preceded you;*s* 14 but I will maintain him in my house and in my kingdom forever, and his throne shall be firmly established forever."

15 All these words and this whole vision Nathan related exactly to David.

David's Thanksgiving. 16 Then David came in and sat in the LORD's presence, saying: "Who am I, O LORD God, and what is my family, that you should have brought me as far as I have come? 17 And yet, even this you now consider too little, O God! For you have made a promise regarding your servant's family reaching into the distant future, and you have looked on me as henceforth the most notable of men, O LORD God.*t* 18 What more can David say to you? You know your servant. 19 O LORD, for your servant's sake and in keeping with your purpose, you have done this great thing. 20 O LORD, there is no one like you and there is no God but you, just as we have always understood.*u*

21 "Is there, like your people Israel, whom you redeemed from Egypt, another nation on earth whom a god went to redeem as his people? You won for yourself a name for great and awesome deeds by driving out the nations before your people.*v* 22 You made your people Israel your own forever, and you, O LORD, became their God. 23 Therefore, O LORD, may the promise that you have uttered concerning your servant and his house remain firm forever. Bring about what you have promised, 24 that your renown as LORD of hosts, God of Israel, may be great and abide forever, while the house of David, your servant, is established in your presence.

25 "Because you, O my God, have revealed to your servant that you will build him a house, your servant has made bold to pray before you.*w* 26 Since you, O LORD, are truly God and have promised this good thing to your servant, 27 and since you have deigned to bless the house of your servant, so that it will remain forever—since it is you, O LORD, who blessed it, it is blessed forever."*x*

CHAPTER 18

David's Victories. 1 *y* After this, David defeated the Philistines and subdued them; and he took Gath and its towns away from the control of the Philistines. 2 He also defeated Moab, and the Moabites became his subjects, paying tribute.

3 David then defeated Hadadezer, king of Zobah toward Hamath, when the latter was on his way to set up his victory stele at the river Euphrates. 4 David took from him twenty thousand foot soldiers, one thousand chariots, and seven thousand horsemen. Of the chariot horses, David hamstrung all but one hundred.*z* 5 The Arameans of Damascus came to the aid of Hadadezer, king of Zobah, but David also slew twenty-two thousand of their men. 6 Then David set up garrisons in the

Damascus region of Aram, and the Arameans became his subjects, paying tribute. Thus the LORD made David victorious in all his campaigns.

[7] David took the golden shields that were carried by Hadadezer's attendants and brought them to Jerusalem. [8] He likewise took away from Tibhath and Cun, cities of Hadadezer, large quantities of bronze, which Solomon later used to make the bronze sea and the pillars and the vessels of bronze.[a]

[9] When Tou, king of Hamath, heard that David had defeated the entire army of Hadadezer, king of Zobah, [10] he sent his son Hadoram to wish King David well and to congratulate him on having waged a victorious war against Hadadezer; for Hadadezer had been at war with Tou. He also sent David gold, silver and bronze utensils of every sort.[b] [11] These also King David consecrated to the LORD along with all the silver and gold that he had taken from the nations: from Edom, Moab, the Ammonites, the Philistines, and Amalek.

[12] Abishai, the son of Zeruiah, also slew eighteen thousand Edomites in the Valley of Salt.[c] [13] He set up garrisons in Edom, and all the Edomites became David's subjects. Thus the LORD made David victorious in all his campaigns.

David's Officials. [14] [d] David reigned over all Israel and dispensed justice and right to all his people. [15] Joab, son of Zeruiah, was in command of the army; Jehoshaphat, son of Ahilud, was herald;[e] [16] Zadok, son of Ahitub, and Ahimelech, son of Abiathar, were priests;* Shavsha was scribe;[f] [17] Benaiah, son of Jehoiada, in command of the Cherethites and the Pelethites; and David's sons were the chief assistants to the king.*[g]

CHAPTER 19

Campaigns against Ammon. [1] [h] Afterward Nahash, king of the Ammonites, died and his son succeeded him as king. [2] David said, "I will show kindness to Hanun, the son of Nahash, for his father treated me with kindness." Therefore he sent envoys to him to comfort him over the death of his father. But when David's servants had entered the land of the Ammonites to comfort Hanun, [3] the Ammonite princes said to Hanun, "Do you think David is doing this—sending you these consolers—to honor your father? Have not his servants rather come to you to explore the land, spying it out for its overthrow?" [4] Thereupon Hanun seized David's servants and had them shaved and their garments cut off half-way at the hips. Then he sent them away. [5] When David was informed of what had happened to his men, he sent messengers to meet them, for the men had been greatly disgraced. "Remain at Jericho," the king told them, "until your beards have grown again; and then you may come back here."

[6] When the Ammonites realized that they had put themselves in bad odor with David, Hanun and the Ammonites sent a thousand talents of silver to hire chariots and horsemen from Aram Naharaim, from Aram-maacah, and from Zobah. [7] They hired thirty-two thousand chariots along with the king of Maacah and his army, who came and encamped before Medeba. The Ammonites also assembled from their cities and came out for war.

[8] When David heard of this, he sent Joab and his whole army of warriors against them. [9] The Ammonites marched out and lined up for battle at the gate of the city, while the kings who had come to their help remained apart in the open field. [10] When Joab saw that there was a battle line both in front of and behind him, he chose some of the best fighters among the Israelites and set them in array against the Arameans;[i] [11] the rest of the army, which he placed under the command of his brother Abishai, then lined up to oppose the Ammonites.[j] [12] And he said: "If the Arameans prove too strong for me, you must come to my help; and if the Am-

---

a 2 Sm 8, 8; 1 Kgs 7, 15. 23. 27.—b 2 Sm 8, 10.—c 2 Sm 8, 13; 2 Kgs 14, 7.—d 14-17: 2 Sm 8, 15-18.—e 1 Chr 11, 6; 2 Sm 8, 16; 1 Kgs 4, 3.—f 1 Chr 24, 3. 6. 31; 2 Sm 8, 17.—g 1 Chr 11, 22; 2 Sm 8, 18; 1 Kgs 1, 38. 44.—h 1-19: 2 Sm 10, 1-19.—i 1 Chr 20, 23; 1 Kgs 2, 28. 34.—j 1 Chr 23, 18f.

18, 16: Zadok . . . and Ahimelech, son of Abiathar, were priests: as in the Chronicler's source, 2 Sm 8, 17. But according to 2 Sm 15, 24. 29. 35; 17, 15; 19, 11; 20, 25, and even 1 Chr 15, 11, it was Abiathar who shared the priestly office with Zadok, and he remained in this office even during the early years of Solomon's reign (1 Kgs 2, 26; 4, 4). Moreover, according to 1 Sm 22, 20; 23, 6; 30, 7, Ahimelech was the father, not the son, of Abiathar. If the text Ahimelech, son of Abiathar, is not due to a scribal change, one must assume that Abiathar had a son who was named after his grandfather and who shared the priestly office with his father during the last years of David's reign.

18, 17: David's sons were the chief assistants to the king: in the parallel passage, 2 Sm 8, 18, which was the Chronicler's source, David's sons were priests. The change is characteristic of the Chronicler, for whom only Aaron's descendants could be priests.

monites prove too strong for you, I will save you. [13] Hold steadfast and let us show ourselves courageous for the sake of our people and the cities of our God; then may the LORD do what seems best to him." [14] Joab therefore advanced with his men to engage the Arameans in battle; but they fled before him. [15] And when the Ammonites saw that the Arameans had fled, they also took to flight before his brother Abishai, and reentered the city. Joab then returned to Jerusalem.

[16] Seeing themselves vanquished by Israel, the Arameans sent messengers to bring out the Arameans from the other side of the River, with Shophach, the general of Hadadezer's army, at their head. [17] When this was reported to David, he gathered all Israel together, crossed the Jordan, and met them. With the army of David drawn up to fight the Arameans, they gave battle. [18] But the Arameans fled before Israel, and David slew seven thousand of their chariot fighters and forty thousand of their foot soldiers; he also killed Shophach, the general of the army. [19] When the vassals of Hadadezer saw themselves vanquished by Israel, they made peace with David and became his subjects. After this, the Arameans refused to come to the aid of the Ammonites.

CHAPTER 20

[1] At the beginning of the following year, the time when kings go to war, Joab led the army out in force, laid waste the land of the Ammonites, and went on to besiege Rabbah, while David himself remained in Jerusalem. When Joab had attacked Rabbah and destroyed it, [2] [k] David took the crown of Milcom from the idol's head. It was found to weigh a talent of gold; and it contained precious stones, which David wore on his own head. He also brought out a great amount of booty from the city. [3] He deported the people of the city and set them to work with saws, iron picks, and axes. Thus David dealt with all the cities of the Ammonites. Then he and his whole army returned to Jerusalem.

Victories over the Philistines. [4] [l] Afterward there was another battle with the Philistines, at Gezer. At that time, Sibbecai the Hushathite slew Sippai, one of the descendants of the Raphaim, and the Philistines were subdued. [m] [5] Once again

there was war with the Philistines, and Elhanan, the son of Jair, slew Lahmi, the brother of Goliath* of Gath, whose spear shaft was like a weaver's heddle-bar. [n] [6] In still another battle, at Gath, they encountered a giant, also a descendant of the Raphaim, who had six fingers to each hand and six toes to each foot; twenty-four in all. [7] He defied Israel, and Jonathan, the son of Shimea, David's brother, slew him. [8] These were the descendants of the Raphaim of Gath who died at the hands of David and his servants.

CHAPTER 21

David's Census; the Plague. [1] [o] A satan* rose up against Israel, and he enticed David into taking a census of Israel. [p] [2] David therefore said to Joab and to the other generals of the army, "Go, find out the number of the Israelites from Beersheba to Dan, and report back to me that I may know their number." [3] But Joab replied: "May the LORD increase his people a hundredfold! My lord king, are not all of them my lord's subjects? Why does my lord seek to do this thing? Why will he bring guilt upon Israel?" [4] However, the king's command prevailed over Joab, who departed and traversed all of Israel, and then returned to Jerusalem. [5] Joab reported the result of the census to David: of men capable of wielding a sword, there were in all Israel one million one hundred thousand, and in Judah four hundred and seventy thousand. [6] Levi and Benjamin, however, he did not include in the census, for the king's command was repugnant to Joab. [q] [7] This command displeased God, who began to punish Israel. [8] Then David said to God, "I have sinned greatly in doing this thing. Take away your servant's guilt, for I have acted very foolishly."

---

k 2f: 2 Sm 12, 30f.—l 4-8: 2 Sm 21, 18-22.—m 1 Chr 11, 29; 27, 11.—n 1 Chr 11, 26; 1 Sm 17, 4. 23.—o 1-7: 2 Sm 24, 1-25.—p Zec 3, 1f.—q 1 Chr 27, 24; Nm 1, 49.

20, 5: *Elhanan . . . slew Lahmi, the brother of Goliath:* the Chronicler thus solves the difficulty of the apparent contradiction between 1 Sm 17, 49ff (David killed Goliath) and 2 Sm 21, 19 *(Elhanan killed Goliath).*

21, 1: *A satan:* in the parallel passage of 2 Sm 24, 1, *the Lord's anger,* The change in the term reflects the changed theological outlook of postexilic Israel, when evil could no longer be attributed directly to God. At an earlier period the Hebrew word *satan* ("adversary," or, especially in a court of law, "accuser"), when not used of men, designated an angel who accused men before God (Jb 1, 6-12; 2, 1-7; Zec 3, 1f). Here, as in later Judaism (Wis 2, 24) and in the New Testament, *satan,* or the "devil" (from the Greek translation of the word), designates an evil spirit who tempts men to wrongdoing.

⁹Then the LORD spoke to Gad, David's seer, in these words:ʳ ¹⁰"Go, tell David: Thus says the LORD: I offer you three alternatives; choose one of them, and I will inflict it on you." ¹¹Accordingly, Gad went to David and said to him: "Thus says the LORD: Decide now—¹²will it be three years of famine; or three months of fleeing your enemies, with the sword of your foes ever at your back; or three days of the LORD's own sword, a pestilence in the land, with the LORD's destroying angel in every part of Israel? Therefore choose: What answer am I to give him who sent me?" ¹³Then David said to Gad: "I am in dire straits. But I prefer to fall into the hand of the LORD, whose mercy is very great, than into the hands of men."

¹⁴Therefore the LORD sent pestilence upon Israel, and seventy thousand men of Israel died. ¹⁵God also sent an angel to destroy Jerusalem; but as he was on the point of destroying it, the LORD saw and decided against the calamity, and said to the destroying angel, "Enough now! Stay your hand!"ˢ

Ornan's Threshing Floor. The angel of the LORD was then standing by the threshing floor of Ornan the Jebusite. ¹⁶When David raised his eyes, he saw the angel of the LORD standing between earth and heaven, with a naked sword in his hand stretched out against Jerusalem. David and the elders, clothed in sackcloth, prostrated themselves face to the ground, ¹⁷and David prayed to God: "Was it not I who ordered the census of the people? I am the one who sinned, I did this wicked thing. But these sheep, what have they done? O LORD, my God, strike me and my father's family, but do not afflict your people with this plague!"

¹⁸Then the angel of the LORD commanded Gad to tell David to go up and erect an altar to the LORD on the threshing floor of Ornan the Jebusite.ᵗ ¹⁹David went up at Gad's command, given in the name of the LORD. ²⁰While Ornan was threshing wheat, he turned around and saw the king, and his four sons who were with him, without recognizing them. ²¹But as David came on toward him, he looked up and saw that it was David. Then he left the threshing floor and bowed down before David, his face to the ground. ²²David said to Ornan: "Sell me the ground of this threshing floor, that I may build on it an altar to the LORD. Sell it to me at its full price, that the plague may be stayed from the people." ²³But Ornan said to David: "Take it as your own, and let my lord the king do what seems best to him. See, I also give you the oxen for the holocausts, the threshing sledges for the wood, and the wheat for the cereal offering. I give it all to you." ²⁴But King David replied to Ornan: "No! I will buy it from you properly, at its full price. I will not take what is yours for the LORD, nor offer up holocausts that cost me nothing." ²⁵So David paid Ornan six hundred shekels of gold* for the place.

Altar of Holocausts. ²⁶David then built an altar there to the LORD, and offered up holocausts and peace offerings. When he called upon the LORD, he answered him by sending down fire from heaven upon the altar of holocausts.ᵘ ²⁷Then the LORD gave orders to the angel to return his sword to its sheath.

²⁸Once David saw that the LORD had heard him on the threshing floor of Ornan the Jebusite, he continued to offer sacrifices there. ²⁹The Dwelling of the LORD, which Moses had built in the desert, and the altar of holocausts were at that time on the high place at Gibeon.ᵛ ³⁰But David could not go there to worship God, for he was fearful of the sword of the angel of the LORD. ¹Therefore David said, "This is the house of the LORD God, and this is the altar of holocausts for Israel."*ʷ

r 1 Chr 29, 29; 1 Sm 9, 9; 2 Chr 29, 25.—s Gn 6, 6; Ex 32, 14; 2 Sm 24, 16; Jon 3, 10.—t 2 Chr 3, 1.—u Lv 9, 24; Jgs 6, 21; 1 Kgs 18. 38; 2 Chr 7, 1; 2 Mc 2, 10ff.—v 1 Chr 16, 39; 1 Kgs 8, 4; 2 Chr 1, 8.—w 1 Chr 21, 18. 26. 28; 2 Chr 3, 1.—x 1 Kgs 5, 31f; 9, 20f; 2 Chr 2, 16f.

21, 25: *Six hundred shekels of gold:* about 10,000 dollars. According to 2 Sm 24, 24, David paid 50 shekels of silver, about 20 dollars, for Ornan's threshing floor; but for the Chronicler the site of the temple was much more precious than that.

21, 1: This belongs to ch 22.

22, 2ff: According to 1 Kgs 5, 15-32, it was Solomon who made the material preparations for building the temple, even though David had wished to do so (1 Kgs 5, 17ff). The Chronicler, however, sought to have David, who was Israel's ideal king, more closely connected with Israel's most sacred sanctuary, the temple of Jerusalem.

CHAPTER 22

Material for the Temple. ² * David then ordered that all the aliens who lived in the land of Israel be brought together, and he appointed them stonecutters to hew out stone blocks for building the house of God.ˣ ³He also laid up large stores of iron to make nails for the doors of the gates, and clamps, together with so much bronze that it could not be weighed,*y* [4] and cedar trees without number. The Sidonians and Tyrians brought great stores of cedar logs to David,*z* [5] who said: "My son Solomon is young and immature; but the house that is to be built for the LORD must be made so magnificent that it will be renowned and glorious in all countries. Therefore I will make preparations for it." Thus before his death David laid up materials in abundance.*a*

Charge to Solomon. [6] Then he called for his son Solomon and commanded him to build a house for the LORD, the God of Israel. [7] *b* David said to Solomon: "My son, it was my purpose to build a house myself for the honor of the LORD, my God. [8] But this word of the LORD came to me: 'You have shed much blood, and you have waged great wars. You may not build a house in my honor, because you have shed too much blood upon the earth in my sight. [9] However, a son is to be born to you. He will be a peaceful man, and I will give him rest from all his enemies on every side. For Solomon shall be his name, and in his time I will bestow peace* and tranquility on Israel.*c* [10] It is he who shall build a house in my honor; he shall be a son to me, and I will be a father to him, and I will establish the throne of his kingship over Israel forever.'*d* [11] Now, my son, the LORD be with you, and may you succeed in building the house of the LORD your God, as he has said you shall. [12] May the LORD give you prudence and discernment when he brings you to rule over Israel, so that you keep the law of the LORD, your God. [13] Only then shall you succeed, if you are careful to observe the precepts and decrees which the LORD gave Moses for Israel. Be brave and steadfast; do not fear or lose heart.*e* [14] See, with great effort I have laid up for the house of the LORD a hundred thousand talents of gold,* a million talents of silver, and bronze and iron in such great quantities that they cannot be weighed. I have also stored up wood and stones, to which you must add.*f* [15] Moreover, you have available an unlimited supply of workmen, stonecutters, masons, carpenters, and every kind of craftsman [16] skilled in gold, silver, bronze, and iron. Set to work, therefore, and the LORD be with you!"

Charge to the Leaders. [17] David also commanded all of Israel's leaders to help his son Solomon: [18] "Is not the LORD your God with you? Has he not given you rest on every side? Indeed, he has delivered the occupants of the land into my power, and the land is subdued before the LORD and his people.*g* [19] Therefore, devote your hearts and souls to seeking the LORD your God. Proceed to build the sanctuary of the LORD God, that the ark of the covenant of the LORD and God's sacred vessels may be brought into the house built in honor of the LORD."*h*

CHAPTER 23

The Levitical Classes. [1] When David had grown old and was near the end of his days, he made his son Solomon king over Israel.*i* [2] He then gathered together all the leaders of Israel, together with the priests and the Levites.

[3] The Levites thirty years old and above were counted, and their total number was found to be thirty-eight thousand men.*j* [4] Of these, twenty-four thousand were to direct the service of the house of the LORD, six thousand were to be officials and judges, [5] four thousand were to be gatekeepers, and four thousand were to praise the LORD with the instruments which David had devised for praise.*k* [6] David divided them into classes according to the sons of Levi: Gershon, Kohath, and Merari.*l*

[7] To the Gershonites belonged Ladan and Shimei. [8] The sons of Ladan: Jehiel the chief, then Zethan and Joel; three in all.*m* [9] The sons of Shimei were Shelomoth, Haziel, and Haran; three. These were

y 1 Chr 18, 8; 1 Kgs 7, 47.—z 1 Chr 10, 27; Ezr 3, 7.—a 1 Chr 29, 1.—b 7-10: 1 Chr 17, 1-14; 28, 2-7; 2 Sm 7, 1-16; 1 Kgs 5, 3ff; 8, 17-21.—c 2 Sm 12, 24.—d Heb 1, 5.—e 1 Chr 28, 7. 20; Dt 31, 6. 23; Jos 1; 6f. 9; 1 Kgs 2, 2f.—f 1 Chr 29, 2ff.—g 1 Chr 23, 25; Jos 21, 44; 23, 1; 2 Sm 7, 1.—h 1 Kgs 8, 6. 21; 2 Chr 5, 7; 6, 11.—i 1 Chr 28, 5; 1 Kgs 1, 30.—j Nm 4, 3. 23. 30. 35. 39. 43. 47; 8, 23-26; 2 Chr 31, 17.—k 1 Chr 9, 22.—l 1 Chr 6, 1. 16-30; 26, 1-19; Ex 6, 16; Nm 3, 17; 26, 57.—m 1 Chr 26, 21f; 29, 8.

22, 9: The Hebrew word for peace, *shalom*, is reflected in the name Solomon, in Hebrew, *Shelomo*. A contrast is drawn here between Solomon, the *peaceful man*, and David, who *waged great wars* (v 8). David was prevented from building the temple, not only because all his time was taken up in waging war (1 Kgs 5, 17), but also because he *shed much blood* (v 8), and in the eyes of the Chronicler this made him ritually unfit for the task.
22, 14: *A hundred thousand talents of gold:* about 3,775 tons of gold. *A million talents of silver:* about 37,750 tons of silver. The fantastically exaggerated figures are intended merely to stress the inestimable value of the temple as the center of Israelite worship. More modest figures are given in 1 Kgs 9, 14. 28; 10, 10. 14.

the heads of the families of Ladan. [10]The sons of Shimei were Jahath, Zizah, Jeush, and Beriah; these were the sons of Shimei, four in all. [11]Jahath was the chief and Zizah was second to him; but Jeush and Beriah had not many sons, and therefore they were classed as a single family, fulfilling a single office. [12]The sons of Kohath: Amram, Izhar, Hebron, and Uzziel; four in all.[n] [13]The sons of Amram were Aaron and Moses. Aaron was set apart to be consecrated as most holy, he and his sons forever, to offer sacrifice before the LORD, to minister to him, and to bless his name forever.[o] [14]As for Moses, however, the man of God, his sons were counted as part of the tribe of Levi. [15]The sons of Moses were Gershon and Eliezer.[p] [16]The sons of Gershon: Shubael the chief.[q] [17]The sons of Eliezer were Rehabiah the chief—Eliezer had no other sons, but the sons of Rehabiah were very numerous. [18]The sons of Izhar: Shelomith the chief. [19]The sons of Hebron: Jeriah, the chief, Amariah, the second, Jahaziel, the third, and Jekameam, the fourth.[r] [20]The sons of Uzziel: Micah, the chief, and Isshiah, the second.[s]

[21]The sons of Merari: Mahli and Mushi. The sons of Mahli: Eleazar and Kish.[t] [22]Eleazar died leaving no sons, only daughters; the sons of Kish, their kinsmen, married them.[u] [23]The sons of Mushi: Mahli, Eder, and Jeremoth; three in all.[v]

[24]These were the sons of Levi according to their ancestral houses, the family heads as they were enrolled one by one according to their names. They performed the work of the service of the house of the LORD from twenty years of age upward,[w] [27]for David's final orders were to enlist the Levites from the time they were twenty years old. [25]David said: "The LORD, the God of Israel, has given rest to his people, and has taken up his dwelling in Jerusalem.[x]

[26]Henceforth the Levites need not carry the Dwelling or any of its furnishings or equipment.[y] [28]Rather, their duty shall be to assist the sons of Aaron in the service of the house of the LORD, having charge of the courts, the chambers, and the preservation of everything holy: they shall take part in the service of the house of God. [29]They shall also have charge of the showbread, of the fine flour for the cereal offering, of the wafers of unleavened bread, and of the baking and mixing, and of all measures of quantity and size.[z] [30]They must be present every morning to offer thanks and to praise the LORD, and likewise in the evening;[a] [31]and at every offering of holocausts to the LORD on sabbaths, new moons, and feast days, in such numbers as are prescribed, they must always be present before the LORD.[b] [32]They shall observe what is prescribed for them concerning the meeting tent, the sanctuary, and the sons of Aaron, their brethren, in the service of the house of the LORD."[c]

CHAPTER 24

The Priestly Classes. [1]The descendants of Aaron also were divided into classes. The sons of Aaron were Nadab, Abihu, Eleazar, and Ithamar.[d] [2]Nadab and Abihu died before their father, leaving no sons; therefore only Eleazar and Ithamar served as priests.[e] [3]David, with Zadok, a descendant of Eleazar, and Ahimelech, a descendant of Ithamar, assigned the functions for the priestly service.[f] [4]But since the descendants of Eleazar were found to be more numerous than those of Ithamar, the former were divided into sixteen groups, and the latter into eight groups, each under its family head. [5]Their functions were assigned impartially by lot, for there were officers of the holy place, and officers of the divine presence, descended both from Eleazar and from Ithamar. [6]The scribe Shemaiah, son of Nethanel, a Levite, made a record of it in the presence of the king, and of the leaders, of Zadok the priest, and of Ahimelech, son of Abiathar,* and of the heads of the ancestral houses of the priests and of the Levites, listing two successive family groups from Eleazar before each one from Ithamar.[g]

[7][h] The first lot fell to Jehoiarib, the second to Jedaiah, [8]the third to Harim, the fourth to Seorim, [9]the fifth to Malchijah,

---

n 1 Chr 26, 23; Ex 6, 18; Nm 3, 19; 26, 23ff.—o 1 Chr 6, 49; Ex 6, 20; 28, 1; Nm 6, 23.—p Ex 2, 22; 18, 3f.—q 1 Chr 26, 24.— r 1 Chr 24, 23.—s 1 Chr 24, 24f.—t 1 Chr 6, 29; 24, 26. 28f; Ex 6, 19; Nm 3. 20. 33.—u 1 Chr 24, 28f.—v 1 Chr 6, 47; 24, 30.—w 2 Chr 31, 17; Ezr 3, 8.—x 1 Chr 22, 18; Ps 132, 13.—y 1 Chr 15, 15; 2 Chr 35, 3.—z 1 Chr 9, 29. 31f; Lv 2, 1. 4f; 24, 5-8.—a Nm 28, 3-8.—b Nm 28, 2-29. 39.—c Nm 3, 6-9; 18, 2-5.—d Ex 6, 23; Nm 3, 2ff; 26, 60.—e Lv 10, 1-7. 12; Nm 3, 2. 4.—f 1 Chr 18, 16; 2 Sm 8, 17; 2 Chr 8, 14.—g 1 Chr 18, 16; 2 Sm 8, 17.—h 7-10: 1 Chr 9, 10ff; Ezr 2, 36ff; Neh 7, 39ff: 11, 10ff.

24, 6: *Ahimelech, son of Abiathar:* see note on 1 Chr 18, 16.

the sixth to Mijamin, [10] the seventh to Hakkoz, the eighth to Abijah,[i] [11] the ninth to Jeshua, the tenth to Shecaniah, [12] the eleventh to Eliashib, the twelfth to Jakim, [13] the thirteenth to Huppah, the fourteenth to Ishbaal, [14] the fifteenth to Bilgah, the sixteenth to Immer, [15] the seventeenth to Hezir, the eighteenth to Happizzez, [16] the nineteenth to Pethahiah, the twentieth to Jehezkel, [17] the twenty-first to Jachin, the twenty-second to Gamul, [18] the twenty-third to Delaiah, the twenty-fourth to Maaziah. [19] This was the appointed order of their service when they functioned in the house of the LORD in keeping with the precepts given them by Aaron, their father, as the LORD, the God of Israel, had commanded him.[j]

Other Levites. [20] [k] Of the remaining Levites, there were Shubael, of the descendants of Amram, and Jehdeiah, of the descendants of Shubael; [21] Isshiah, the chief, of the descendants of Rehabiah; [22] Shelomith of the Izharites, and Jahath of the descendants of Shelomith. [23] The descendants of Hebron were Jeriah, the chief, Amariah, the second, Jahaziel, the third, Jekameam, the fourth. [24] The descendants of Uzziel were Micah; Shamir, of the descendants of Micah; [25] Isshiah, the brother of Micah; and Zechariah, a descendant of Isshiah. [26] The descendants of Merari were Mahli, Mushi, and the descendants of his son Uzziah. [27] The descendants of Merari through his son Uzziah: Shoham, Zaccur, and Ibri. [28] Descendants of Mahli were Eleazar, who had no sons, [29] and Jerahmeel, of the descendants of Kish. [30] The descendants of Mushi were Mahli, Eder, and Jerimoth.

These were the descendants of the Levites according to their ancestral houses. [31] They too, in the same manner as their relatives, the descendants of Aaron, cast lots in the presence of King David, Zadok, Ahimelech, and the heads of the priestly and levitical families; the more important family did so in the same way as the less important one.[l]

CHAPTER 25

The Singers. [1] David and the leaders of the liturgical cult set apart for service the descendants of Asaph, Heman, and Jeduthun, as singers of inspired song to the accompaniment of lyres and harps and cymbals.[m]

This is the list of those who performed this service: [2] * Of the sons of Asaph: Zaccur, Joseph, Nethaniah, and Asharelah, sons of Asaph, under the direction of Asaph, who sang inspired songs under the guidance of the king. [3] Of Jeduthun, these sons of Jeduthun: Gedaliah, Zeri, Jeshaiah, Shimei, Hashabiah, and Mattithiah; six, under the direction of their father Jeduthun, who sang inspired songs to the accompaniment of a lyre, to give thanks and praise to the LORD. [4] Of Heman, these sons of Heman: Bukkiah, Mattaniah, Uzziel, Shubael, and Jerimoth; Hananiah, Hanani, Eliathah, Giddalti, Romamti-ezer, Joshbekashah, Mallothi, Hothir, and Mahazioth. [5] All these were the sons of Heman, the king's seer in divine matters; to enhance his prestige, God gave Heman fourteen sons and three daughters.[n] [6] All these, whether of Asaph, Jeduthun, or Heman, were under their fathers' direction in the singing in the house of the LORD to the accompaniment of cymbals, harps and lyres, serving in the house of God, under the guidance of the king.[o] [7] Their number, together with that of their brethren who were trained in singing to the LORD, all of them skilled men, was two hundred and eighty-eight. [8] They cast lots for their functions equally, young and old, master and pupil alike.[p]

[9] The first lot fell to Asaph, the family of Joseph; he and his sons and his brethren were twelve. Gedaliah was the second; he and his brethren and his sons were twelve. [10] The third was Zaccur, his sons, and his brethren: twelve. [11] The fourth fell to Izri, his sons, and his brethren: twelve. [12] The fifth was Nethaniah, his sons, and his brethren: twelve. [13] The sixth was Bukkiah, his sons, and his brethren: twelve. [14] The seventh was Jesarelah, his sons, and his brethren: twelve.

i Lk 1, 5.—j 2 Chr 23, 8.—k 20-31: 1 Chr 23, 7-23.—l 1 Chr 25, 8; 26, 13.—m 1 Chr 6, 31ff; 15, 16f. 19; 16, 37; 2 Chr 5, 12; 35, 15; Neh 12, 27. 45.—n 2 Chr 35, 15.—o 1 Chr 15, 16.—p 1 Chr 24, 31.

25, 2-31: This list of twenty-four classes of temple singers balances the list of the twenty-four classes of priests (1 Chr 24, 4-19). The last nine names in 1 Chr 25, 4, which seem to form a special group, appear to have been originally fragments or *incipits* of hymns. With some slight changes in the vocalization, the names would mean: "Have mercy on me, O Lord," "Have mercy on me," "You are my God," "I magnify," "I extol the help of . . . ," "Sitting in adversity," "I have fulfilled," "He made abundant," and "Visions."

¹⁵The eighth was Jeshaiah, his sons, and his brethren: twelve. ¹⁶The ninth was Mattaniah, his sons, and his brethren: twelve. ¹⁷The tenth was Shimei, his sons, and his brethren: twelve. ¹⁸The eleventh was Uzziel, his sons, and his brethren: twelve. ¹⁹The twelfth fell to Hashabiah, his sons, and his brethren: twelve. ²⁰The thirteenth was Shubael, his sons, and his brethren: twelve. ²¹The fourteenth was Mattithiah, his sons, and his brethren: twelve. ²²The fifteenth fell to Jeremoth, his sons, and his brethren: twelve. ²³The sixteenth fell to Hananiah, his sons, and his brethren: twelve. ²⁴The seventeenth fell to Joshbekashah, his sons, and his brethren: twelve. ²⁵The eighteenth fell to Hanani, his sons, and his brethren: twelve. ²⁶The nineteenth fell to Mallothi, his sons, and his brethren: twelve. ²⁷The twentieth fell to Eliathah, his sons, and his brethren: twelve. ²⁸The twenty-first fell to Hothir, his sons, and his brethren: twelve. ²⁹The twenty-second fell to Giddalti, his sons, and his brethren: twelve. ³⁰The twenty-third fell to Mahazioth, his sons, and his brethren: twelve. ³¹The twenty-fourth fell to Romamti-ezer, his sons, and his brethren: twelve.

CHAPTER 26

Classes of Gatekeepers. ¹ *q* As for the classes of gatekeepers. Of the Korahites was Meshelemiah, the son of Kore, one of the sons of Abiasaph. ²Meshelemiah's sons: Zechariah, the first-born, Jediael, the second son, Zebadiah, the third, Jathniel, the fourth, ³Elam, the fifth, Jehohanan, the sixth, Eliehoenai, the seventh. ⁴Obed-edom's sons: Shemaiah, the first-born, Jehozabad, a second son, Joah, the third, Sachar, the fourth, Nethanel, the fifth, ⁵Ammiel, the sixth, Issachar, the seventh, Peullethai, the eighth, for God blessed him. ⁶To his son Shemaiah were born sons who ruled over their family, for they were warriors. ⁷The sons of Shemaiah were Othni, Rephael, Obed, and Elzabad; also his brethren who were men of might, Elihu and Semachiah. ⁸All these were of the sons of Obed-edom, who, together with their sons and their

brethren, were mighty men, fit for the service. Of Obed-edom, sixty-two. ⁹Of Meshelemiah, eighteen sons and brethren, mighty men.

¹⁰Hosah, a descendant of Merari, had these sons: Shimri, the chief (for though he was not the first-born, his father made him chief),^r ¹¹Hilkiah, the second son, Tebaliah, the third, Zechariah, the fourth. All the sons and brethren of Hosah were thirteen.

¹²To these classes of gatekeepers, under their chief men, were assigned watches in the service of the house of the LORD, for each group in the same way. ¹³They cast lots for each gate, the small and the large families alike. ¹⁴When the lot was cast for the east side, it fell to Meshelemiah. Then they cast lots for his son Zechariah, a prudent counselor, and the north side fell to his lot.^s ¹⁵To Obed-edom fell the south side, and to his sons the storehouse. ¹⁶To Hosah fell the west side with the Shallecheth gate at the ascending highway. For each family, watches were established. ¹⁷On the east, six watched each day, on the north, four each day, on the south, four each day, and at the storehouse they were two and two; ¹⁸as for the large building* on the west, there were four at the highway and two at the large building. ¹⁹These were the classes of the gatekeepers, descendants of Kore and Merari.

Treasurers. ²⁰Their brother Levites superintended the stores for the house of God and the stores of votive offerings.^t ²¹Among the descendants of Ladan the Gershonite, the family heads were descendants of Jehiel: the descendants of Jehiel,^u ²² *v* Zetham and his brother Joel, who superintended the treasures of the house of the LORD. ²³From the Amramites, Izharites, Hebronites, and Uzzielites, ²⁴Shubael, son of Gershon, son of Moses, was chief superintendent over the treasures. ²⁵ *w* His associate pertained to Eliezer, whose son was Rehabiah, whose son was Jeshaiah, whose son was Joram, whose son was Zichri, whose son was Shelomith. ²⁶This Shelomith and his brethren superintended all the stores of the votive offerings dedicated by King David, the heads of the families, the commanders of thousands and of hundreds, and the commanders of the army,^x ²⁷from the booty they had taken in the wars, for the enhancement of the house of the LORD.

---

q 1 Chr 9, 19; 2 Chr 8, 14; 23, 19; 35, 15; Neh 12, 45.—r 1 Chr 16, 38.—s 1 Chr 9, 24.—t 1 Chr 28, 12; 1 Kgs 7, 51.—u 1 Chr 23, 7f; 29, 8.—v 22ff: 1 Chr 23, 8. 12. 16.—w 1 Chr 23, 17f; 24, 21.—x 2 Sm 8, 11.

26, 18: *The large building* (in the Hebrew text *Parbar*): see note on 2 Kgs 23, 11.

28 Also, whatever Samuel the seer, Saul, son of Kish, Abner, son of Ner, Joab, son of Zeruiah, and all others had consecrated, was under the charge of Shelomith and his brethren.

Magistrates. 29 Among the Izharites, Chananiah and his sons were in charge of Israel's civil affairs as officials and judges.*y* 30 Among the Hebronites, Hashabiah and his brethren, one thousand seven hundred police officers, had the administration of Israel on the western side of the Jordan in all the work of the LORD and in the service of the king.*z* 31 Among the Hebronites, Jerijah was their chief according to their family records. In the fortieth year of David's reign search was made, and there were found among them outstanding officers at Jazer of Gilead.*a* 32 His brethren were also police officers, two thousand seven hundred heads of families. King David appointed them to the administration of the Reubenites, the Gadites, and the half-tribe of Manasseh in everything pertaining to God and to the king.

CHAPTER 27

Army Commanders.* 1 This is the list of the Israelite family heads, commanders of thousands and of hundreds, and other officers who served the king in all that pertained to the divisions, of twenty-four thousand men each, that came and went month by month throughout the year.

2 Over the first division for the first month was Ishbaal, son of Zabdiel, and in his division were twenty-four thousand men; 3 a descendant of Perez, he was chief over all the commanders of the army for the first month. 4 Over the division of the second month was Eleazar, son of Dodo, from Ahoh, and in his division were twenty-four thousand men.*b* 5 *c* The third army commander, chief for the third month, was Benaiah, son of Jehoiada the priest, and in his division were twenty-four thousand men. 6 This Benaiah was a warrior among the Thirty and over the Thirty. His son Ammizabad was over his division. 7 Fourth, for the fourth month, was Asahel, brother of Joab, and after him his son Zebadiah, and in his division were twenty-four thousand men.*d* 8 Fifth, for the fifth month, was the commander Shamhuth, a descendant of Zerah, and in his division were twenty-four thousand men. 9 Sixth, for the sixth month, was

Ira, son of Ikkesh, from Tekoa, and in his division were twenty-four thousand men. 10 Seventh, for the seventh month, was Helles, from Beth-pheleth, of the sons of Ephraim, and in his divison were twenty-four thousand men. 11 Eighth, for the eighth month, was Sibbecai the Hushathite, a descendant of Zerah, and in his division were twenty-four thousand men.*e* 12 Ninth, for the ninth month, was Abiezer from Anathoth, of Benjamin, and in his division were twenty-four thousand men. 13 Tenth, for the tenth month, was Maharai from Netophah, a descendant of Zerah, and in his division were twenty-four thousand men. 14 Eleventh, for the eleventh month, was Benaiah the Pirathonite, of Ephraim, and in his division were twenty-four thousand men. 15 Twelfth, for the twelfth month, was Heldai the Netophathite, of the family of Othniel, and in his division were twenty-four thousand men.

Tribal Heads. 16 Over the tribes of Israel, for the Reubenites the leader was Eliezer, son of Zichri; for the Simeonites, Shephatiah, son of Maacah; 17 for Levi, Hashabiah, son of Kemuel; for Aaron, Zadok; 18 for Judah, Eliab, one of David's brothers; for Issachar, Omri, son of Michael;*f* 19 for Zebulun, Ishmaiah, son of Obadiah; for Naphtali, Jeremoth, son of Azriel; 20 for the sons of Ephraim, Hoshea, son of Azaziah; for the half-tribe of Manasseh, Joel, son of Pedaiah; 21 for the half-tribe of Manasseh in Gilead, Iddo, son of Zechariah; for Benjamin, Jaasiel, son of Abner; 22 for Dan, Azarel, son of Jeroham. These were the commanders of the tribes of Israel.

23 David did not count those who were twenty years of age or younger, for the LORD had promised to multiply Israel like the stars of the heavens.*g* 24 Joab, son of Zeruiah, began to take the census, but he did not complete it, for because of it wrath fell upon Israel. Therefore the number did not enter into the book of the chronicles of King David.*h*

y 1 Chr 23, 4.—z 1 Chr 27, 17; Neh 11, 15f.—a 1 Chr 23, 19; 29, 27; Jos 13, 25.—b 1 Chr 9, 37; 11, 12; 2 Sm 23, 9.—c 5f: 1 Chr 11, 22ff; 18, 17; 2 Sm 23, 20ff.—d 2 Sm 2, 18; 23, 24.—e 1 Chr 11, 29; 20, 4; 2 Sm 21, 18.—f 1 Chr 2, 13.—g 1 Chr 22, 17.—h 2 Sm 24, 10.

27, 1-15: This list of army commanders is similar to, but distinct from, the list of David's warriors as given in 1 Chr 11, 10-47. The schematic enumeration of the soldiers as presented here is, no doubt, artificial and grossly exaggerated (12 x 24,000 = 288,000 men!), unless the Hebrew word *(eleph)* for *thousand* is understood as designating a military unit of much smaller size; see note on 1 Chr 12, 25-38.

Overseers. [25] Over the treasures of the king was Azmaveth, the son of Adiel. Over the stores in the country, the cities, the villages, and the towers was Jonathan, son of Uzziah.[i] [26] Over the farm workers who tilled the soil was Ezri, son of Chelub. [27] Over the vineyards was Shimei from Ramah, and over their produce for the wine cellars was Zabdi the Shiphmite. [28] Over the olive trees and sycamores of the foothills was Baalhanan the Gederite, and over the stores of oil was Joash. [29] Over the cattle that grazed in Sharon was Shitrai the Sharonite, and over the cattle in the valleys was Shaphat, the son of Adlai; [30] over the camels was Obil the Ishmaelite; over the she-asses was Jehdeiah the Meronothite; [31] and over the flocks was Jaziz the Hagrite. All these were the overseers of King David's possessions.

David's Court. [32] Jonathan, David's uncle and a man of intelligence, was counselor and scribe; he and Jehiel, the son of Hachmoni, were tutors of the king's sons. [33] Ahithophel was also the king's counselor, and Hushai the Archite was the king's confidant.[j] [34] After Ahithophel* came Jehoiada, the son of Benaiah, and Abiathar. The commander of the king's army was Joab.

CHAPTER 28

The Assembly at Jerusalem. [1] David assembled at Jerusalem all the leaders of Israel, the heads of the tribes, the commanders of the divisions who were in the service of the king, the commanders of thousands and of hundreds, the overseers of all the king's estates and possessions, and his sons, together with the courtiers, the warriors, and every important man.[k] [2] [l] King David rose to his feet and said: "Hear

i 2 Sm 23, 31.—j 2 Sm 15, 12. 32-37; 16, 16-19. 23; 17, 5-16. 23.—k 1 Chr 27, 2-22. 25-31; 11, 10ff.—l 2f: 1 Chr 17, 4; 22, 7ff; 2 Sm 7, 5; 1 Kgs 5, 3; Ps 132, 3-7.—m 1 Chr 17, 23; Gn 49, 8ff; 1 Sm 16, 6-13.—n 1 Chr 3, 1-9; 14, 3-7; 22, 9; 23, 1; Wis 9, 7.—o 1 Chr 17, 11ff; 22, 9f; 2 Sm 7, 12f.—p Dt 4, 5.—q 1 Chr 29, 17; 2 Chr 15, 2; 1 Kgs 8, 61.—r Ex 25, 9. 40; 26, 30.

27, 34: *After Ahithophel:* after his suicide (2 Sm 17, 23). Jehoiada then succeeded him as the king's counselor. *Abiathar:* the priest. The Chronicler does not mention his office because he regards only the Zadokites as legitimate high priests.

28, 2: *The ark . . . the footstool . . . of our God:* the Lord, who was invisibly enthroned upon the cherubim that were associated with the ark of the covenant at Shiloh and later in the Jerusalem temple, had the ark as his footstool; cf Pss 99, 5; 132, 7. The *propitiatory* (1 Chr 28, 11) and the *chariot throne* (1 Chr 28, 18) reflect the different circumstances of the postexilic community, for whom only the place of the ark was a focal point of worship, though the ark itself was no longer present.

me, my brethren and my people. It was my purpose to build a house of repose myself for the ark of the covenant of the LORD, the footstool for the feet of our God;* and I was preparing to build it. [3] But God said to me, 'You may not build a house in my honor, for you are a man who fought wars and shed blood.' [4] However, the LORD, the God of Israel, chose me from all my father's family to be king over Israel forever. For he chose Judah as leader, then one family of Judah, that of my father; and finally, among all the sons of my father, it pleased him to make me king over all Israel.[m] [5] And of all my sons—for the LORD has given me many sons—he has chosen my son Solomon to sit on the LORD's royal throne over Israel.[n] [6] For he said to me: 'It is your son Solomon who shall build my house and my courts, for I have chosen him for my son, and I will be a father to him.[o] [7] I will establish his kingdom forever, if he perseveres in keeping my commandments and decrees as he keeps them now.' [8] Therefore in the presence of all Israel, the assembly of the LORD, and in the hearing of our God, I exhort you to keep and to carry out all the commandments of the LORD, your God, that you may continue to possess this good land and afterward leave it as an inheritance to your children forever.[p]

[9] "As for you, Solomon, my son, know the God of your father and serve him with a perfect heart and a willing soul, for the LORD searches all hearts and understands all the mind's thoughts. If you seek him, he will let himself be found by you; but if you abandon him, he will cast you off forever.[q] [10] See, then! The LORD has chosen you to build a house as his sanctuary. Take courage and set to work."

Temple Plans Given to Solomon. [11] Then David gave to his son Solomon the pattern of the portico and of the building itself, with its storerooms, its upper rooms and inner chambers, and the room with the propitiatory.[r] [12] He provided also the pattern for all else that he had in mind by way of courts for the house of the LORD, with the surrounding compartments for the stores for the house of God and the stores of the votive offerings, [13] as well as for the divisions of the priests and Levites, for all the work of the service of the house of the LORD, and for all the liturgical vessels of the house of the LORD. [14] He specified the weight of gold to be used in the golden vessels for the various services and the weight of silver to be used in the silver vessels for the various services; [15] likewise for the golden lampstands and their lamps he specified the weight of gold for each lampstand and its lamps, and for the silver lampstands he specified the weight of silver for each lampstand and its lamps, depending on the use to which each lampstand was to be put. [s] [16] He specified the weight of gold for each table to hold the showbread, and the silver for the silver tables; [17] the pure gold to be used for the forks and pitchers; the amount of gold for each golden bowl and the silver for each silver bowl; [18] the refined gold, and its weight, to be used for the altar of incense; and, finally, gold for what would suggest a chariot throne:* the cherubim that spread their wings and covered the ark of the covenant of the LORD. [t] [19] He had successfully committed to writing the exact specifications of the pattern, because the hand of the LORD was upon him.

[20] Then David said to his son Solomon: "Be firm and steadfast; go to work without fear or discouragement, for the LORD God, my God, is with you. He will not fail you or abandon you before you have completed all the work for the service of the house of the LORD. [u] [21] The classes of the priests and Levites are ready for all the service of the house of God; they will help you in all your work with all those who are eager to show their skill in every kind of craftsmanship. Also the leaders and all the people will do everything that you command." [v]

CHAPTER 29

Offerings for the Temple. [1] King David then said to the whole assembly: "My son Solomon, whom alone God has chosen, is still young and immature; the work, however, is great, for this castle is not intended for man, but for the LORD God. [w] [2] For this reason I have stored up for the house of my God, as far as I was able, gold for what will be made of gold, silver for what will be made of silver, bronze for what will be made of bronze, iron for what will be made of iron, wood for what will be made of wood, onyx stones and settings for them, carnelian and mosaic stones, every other kind of precious stone, and great quantities of marble. [x] [3] But now, because of the

delight I take in the house of my God, in addition to all that I stored up for the holy house, I give to the house of my God my personal fortune in gold and silver: [4] three thousand talents of Ophir gold, and seven thousand talents of refined silver, for overlaying the walls of the rooms, [y] [5] for the various utensils to be made of gold and silver, and for every work that is to be done by artisans. Now, who else is willing to contribute generously this day to the LORD?" [z]

[6] Then the heads of the families, the leaders of the tribes of Israel, the commanders of thousands and of hundreds, and the overseers of the king's affairs came forward willingly [a] [7] and contributed for the service of the house of God five thousand talents and ten thousand darics of gold, ten thousand talents of silver, eighteen thousand talents of bronze, and one hundred thousand talents of iron. [b] [8] Those who had precious stones gave them into the keeping of Jehiel the Gershonite for the treasury of the house of the LORD. [c] [9] The people rejoiced over these free-will offerings, which had been contributed to the LORD wholeheartedly. King David also rejoiced greatly. [d]

David's Prayer. [10] Then David blessed the LORD in the presence of the whole assembly, praying in these words:

"Blessed may you be, O LORD,
   God of Israel our father,
   from eternity to eternity.
[11] "Yours, O LORD, are grandeur and
   power,
   majesty, splendor, and glory.
For all in heaven and on earth is yours;
   yours, O LORD, is the sovereignty;
   you are exalted as head over all.
[12] "Riches and honor are from you,
   and you have dominion over all.
In your hand are power and might;
   it is yours to give grandeur and
   strength to all. [e]
[13] Therefore, our God, we give you thanks
   and we praise the majesty of your
   name.

---

s Ex 25, 31-37.—t Ex 25, 18-22; 30, 1-10; 1 Kgs 6, 23-28.—u 1 Chr 22, 13. 16; Jos 1, 5.—v Ex 36, 1-5.—w 1 Chr 22, 5; 28, 5.—x 1 Chr 22, 14.—y 2 Chr 9, 10; 1 Kgs 9, 28; 10, 11.—z Ex 25, 2; 35, 5f.—a 1 Chr 22, 1. 25-31; 28, 1.—b Ezr 2, 69; 8, 27; Neh 7, 70ff.—c 1 Chr 23, 8; 26, 21.—d 2 Kgs 12, 4.—e 2 Chr 20, 6; Wis 6, 3.

28, 18: *Chariot throne:* probably suggested by Ez 1, 4-24; 10, 1-22.

14 "But who am I, and who are my people, that we should have the means to contribute so freely? For everything is from you, and we only give you what we have received from you. 15 For we stand before you as aliens: we are only your guests, like all our fathers. Our life on earth is like a shadow that does not abide.*f* 16 O LORD our God, all this wealth that we have brought together to build you a house in honor of your holy name comes from you and is entirely yours. 17 I know, O my God, that you put hearts to the test and that you take pleasure in uprightness. With a sincere heart I have willingly given all these things, and now with joy I have seen your people here present also giving to you generously. 18 O LORD, God of our fathers Abraham, Isaac, and Israel, keep such thoughts in the hearts and minds of your people forever, and direct their hearts toward you.*g* 19 Give to my son Solomon a wholehearted desire to keep your commandments, precepts, and statutes, that he may carry out all these plans and build the castle for which I have made preparation."

20 Then David besought the whole assembly, "Now bless the LORD your God!" And the whole assembly blessed the LORD, the God of their fathers, bowing down and prostrating themselves before

---

f Lv 25, 23; Wis 2, 5; 5, 9.—g Ex 3, 6. 15f; 4, 5; 1 Kgs 18, 36.—h 1 Chr 28, 5; 2 Chr 9, 8; 1 Kgs 2, 10ff.—i 2 Chr 1, 12; 1 Kgs 3, 13.—j 2 Sm 5, 5; 1 Kgs 2, 11.—k 1 Chr 23, 1.—l 1 Chr 21, 9; 1 Sm 22, 5.

29, 22: *For a second time:* the first time is referred to in 1 Chr 23, 1. Here there is a solemn public ratification of David's earlier appointment of Solomon as his successor.

---

the LORD and before the king. 21 On the following day they offered sacrifices and holocausts to the LORD, a thousand bulls, a thousand rams, and a thousand lambs, together with their libations and many other sacrifices for all Israel; 22 and on that day they ate and drank in the LORD's presence with great rejoicing.

Solomon Anointed. Then for a second time* they proclaimed David's son Solomon king, and they anointed him as the LORD's prince, and Zadok as priest. 23 Thereafter Solomon sat on the throne of the LORD as king in place of his father David; he prospered, and all Israel obeyed him.*h* 24 All the leaders and warriors, and also all the other sons of King David, swore allegiance to King Solomon. 25 And the LORD exalted Solomon greatly in the eyes of all Israel, giving him a glorious reign such as had not been enjoyed by any king over Israel before him.*i*

Death of David. 26 Thus David, the son of Jesse, had reigned over all Israel. 27 The time that he reigned over Israel was forty years: in Hebron he reigned seven years, and in Jerusalem thirty-three.*j* 28 He died at a ripe old age, rich in years and wealth and glory, and his son Solomon succeeded him as king.*k*

29 Now the deeds of King David, first and last, can be found written in the history of Samuel the seer, the history of Nathan the prophet, and the history of Gad the seer,*l* 30 together with the particulars of his reign and valor, and of the events that affected him and all Israel and all the kingdoms of the surrounding lands.

THE SECOND BOOK OF CHRONICLES

The Second Book of Chronicles takes up the history of the monarchy where the First Book breaks off. It begins with the account of the reign of Solomon from the special viewpoint of the Chronicler. The portrait of Solomon is an idealized one; he appears as second only to David. The great achievement of the building of the temple and the magnificence of Solomon's court are described in detail while the serious defects of his reign are passed over without comment. All this is in keeping with the Chronicler's purpose of stressing the supreme importance of the temple and its worship. He wishes to impress on his readers the splendor of God's dwelling and the magnificence of the liturgy of sacrifice, prayer and praise offered there. Judah's kings are judged by their attitude toward the temple and its cult. To this ideal of one people, united in the worship of the one true God at the temple of Jerusalem founded by David and Solomon, the restored community would have to conform.

In treating the period of divided monarchy, the Chronicler gives practically all his attention to the kingdom of Judah. His omission of the northern Israelite kings is significant. In his view, the northern tribes of Israel were in religious schism as long as they worshiped Yahweh in a place other than the temple of Jerusalem. The Chronicler makes no mention of the important sanctuaries of Yahweh at Dan and Bethel—as though they had never existed. Nevertheless he retains the ancient ideal of "all Israel" (a phrase occurring forty-one times in Chronicles) as the people of God. The condition he places for a united people is that "the whole congregation of Israel" worship the Lord only in his temple at Jerusalem. This explains his praise of Kings Hezekiah and Josiah for striving, after the fall of Samaria, to unite the remnants of the northern tribes of Israel into the kingdom of Judah.

At the end of the fifth century B.C., during the Chronicler's own time, "the people of the land" were the descendants of the people of all the tribes (including Judah) who had not gone into exile. These had become intermingled with aliens and had evolved a religion of Yahweh very different from the Judaism that developed during the Babylonian exile. Thus, religious and political cooperation between the returned exiles and these "people of the land" was out of the question for the Chronicler. This he clearly shows in the last part of his work, the Books of Ezra and Nehemiah.

The Second Book of Chronicles is divided as follows: I. The Reign of Solomon (1, 1—9, 31). II. The Monarchy before Hezekiah (10, 1—27, 9). III. Reforms of Hezekiah and Josiah (28, 1—36, 1). IV. End of the Kingdom (36, 2-23).

I: THE REIGN OF SOLOMON

CHAPTER 1

Solomon at Gibeon. [1] Solomon, son of David, strengthened his hold on the kingdom, for the LORD, his God, was with him, constantly making him more renowned. [2] He sent a summons to all Israel, to the commanders of thousands and of hundreds, the judges, the princes of all Israel, and the family heads; [3] [a] and, accompanied by the whole assembly, he went to the high place at Gibeon, because the meeting tent of God, made in the desert by Moses, the LORD's servant, was there. [4] (The ark of God, however, David had brought up from Kiriath-jearim to Jerusalem, where he had provided a place and pitched a tent for it.) [5] The bronze altar made by Bezalel, son of Uri, son of Hur, he put in front of the LORD's Dwelling* on the high place. There Solomon and the assembly consulted the LORD; [b] [6] and Solomon offered sacrifice in the LORD's presence on the bronze altar at the meeting tent; he offered a thousand holocausts upon it.

[7] That night God appeared to Solomon and said to him, "Make a request of me, and I will grant it to you." [8] Solomon answered God: "You have shown great favor to my father David, and you have allowed me to succeed him as king. [9] Now, LORD God, may your promise to my father David be fulfilled, for you have made me king

over a people as numerous as the dust of the earth. [10] Give me, therefore, wisdom and knowledge to lead this people, for otherwise who could rule this great people of yours?" [11] God then replied to Solomon: "Since this has been your wish and you have not asked for riches, treasures and glory, nor for the life of those who hate you, nor even for a long life for yourself, but have asked for wisdom and knowledge in order to rule my people over whom I have made you king, [12] wisdom and knowledge are given you; but I will also give you riches, treasures and glory, such as kings before you never had, nor will those have them who come after you."

Solomon's Wealth. [13] Solomon returned to Jerusalem from the high place at Gibeon, from the meeting tent, and became king over Israel. [14] He gathered together chariots and drivers, so that he had one thousand four hundred chariots and twelve thousand drivers he could station in the chariot cities and with the king in Jerusalem. [c] [15] The king made silver and gold as

a 3-12: 1 Kgs 3, 4-15; 1 Chr 21, 29.—b Ex 27, 1f; 31, 2; 1 Chr 2, 20.—c 2 Chr 9, 25; 10-26-29.

1, 5: *The bronze altar . . . the Lord's Dwelling:* the Chronicler justifies Solomon's worship at the high place of Gibeon. He pictures *the Lord's Dwelling,* i.e., the Mosaic meeting tent, and *the bronze altar* made at Moses' command (Ex 31, 1-9) as still at Gibeon after David had removed the ark of the covenant from there to a new tent in Jerusalem (1 Chr 15, 1. 25; 16, 1). The altar made by Bezalel is described as being of acacia wood plated with bronze (Ex 27, 1f). Solomon later made an all-bronze altar for the temple in Jerusalem (2 Chr 4, 1).

common in Jerusalem as stones, while cedars became as numerous as the sycamores of the foothills.*d* [16] Solomon also imported horses from Egypt and Cilicia.*e* The king's agents would acquire them by purchase from Cilicia,* [17] and would then bring up chariots from Egypt and export them at six hundred silver shekels, with the horses going for a hundred and fifty shekels. At these rates they served as middlemen for all the Hittite and Aramean kings.*f*

Preparations for the Temple. [18] Solomon gave orders for the building of a house to honor the LORD and also of a house for his own royal estate.

CHAPTER 2

[1] He conscripted seventy thousand men to carry stone and eighty thousand to cut the stone in the mountains, and over these he placed three thousand six hundred overseers.*g* [2] *h* Moreover, Solomon sent this mesage to Huram, king of Tyre: "As you dealt with my father David, sending him cedars to build a house for his dwelling, so deal with me. [3] I intend to build a house for the honor of the LORD, my God, and to consecrate it to him, for the burning of fragrant incense in his presence, for the perpetual display of the showbread, for holocausts morning and evening, and for the sabbaths, new moons, and festivals of the LORD, our God: such is Israel's perpetual obligation.*i* [4] And the house I intend to build must be large, for our God is greater than all other gods. [5] Yet who is really able to build him a house, since the heavens and even the highest heavens cannot contain him? And who am I that I should build him a house, unless it be to offer incense in his presence?*j* [6] Now,

send me men skilled at work in gold, silver, bronze and iron, in purple, crimson, and violet fabrics, and who know how to do engraved work, to join the craftsmen who are with me in Judah and Jerusalem, whom my father David appointed. [7] Also send me boards of cedar, cypress and cabinet wood from Lebanon, for I realize that your servants know how to cut the wood of the Lebanon. My servants will labor with yours [8] in order to prepare for me a great quantity of wood, since the house I intend to build must be lofty and wonderful. [9] I will furnish as food for your servants, the hewers who cut the wood, twenty thousand kors of wheat, twenty thousand kors of barley, twenty thousand measures of wine, and twenty thousand measures of oil."*k*

[10] Huram, king of Tyre, wrote an answer which he sent to Solomon: "Because the LORD loves his people, he has placed you over them as king." [11] He added: "Blessed be the LORD, the God of Israel, who made heaven and earth, for having given King David a wise son of intelligence and understanding, who will build a house for the LORD and also a house for his royal estate.*l* [12] I am now sending you a craftsman of great skill, Huram-abi,*m* [13] son of a Danite woman* and of a father from Tyre; he knows how to work with gold, silver, bronze and iron, with stone and wood, with purple, violet, fine linen and crimson, and also how to do all kinds of engraved work and to devise every type of artistic work that may be given him and your craftsmen and the craftsmen of my lord David your father. [14] *n* And now, let my lord send to his servants the wheat, barley, oil and wine which he has promised. [15] For our part, we will cut trees on Lebanon, as many as you need, and float them down to you at the port of Joppa, whence you may take them up to Jerusalem."*o*

[16] *p* Thereupon Solomon took a census of all the alien men who were in the land of Israel (following the census David his father had taken of them), who were found to number one hundred fifty-three thousand six hundred. [17] Of these he made seventy thousand carriers and eighty thousand cutters in the mountains, and three thousand six hundred overseers to keep the people working.*q*

---

d 1 Kgs 10, 27.—e 1 Kgs 10, 28.—f 1 Kgs 10, 29.—g 2 Chr 2, 17; 5, 29f.—h 2-9: 1 Kgs 5, 15-20; 1 Chr 14, 1.—i Lv 24, 5-8; Nm 28—29.—j 2 Chr 6, 18.—k 1 Kgs 5, 25; Ezr 3, 7.—l 1 Kgs 5, 21.—m 12f: 1 Kgs 7, 13f; Ex 31, 1-5.—n 14f: 1 Kgs 5, 22-26.—o Ezr 3, 7.—p 16f: 1 Chr 22, 2.—q 2 Chr 2, 1.

1, 16f: *Egypt . . . Cilicia:* it seems likely that the horses came from Cilicia and the chariots from Egypt. Some read the source of these data in 1 Kgs 10, 28f as containing the name (Musur) of a mountain district north of Cilicia, rather than of Egypt; but the author of Chronicles surely understood *Egypt;* cf 2 Chr 9, 28.

2, 13: *A Danite woman:* a widow of the tribe of Naphtali (1 Kgs 7, 14). The Danites had settled in the northern section of Naphtali's territory (Jgs 18, 27ff). Bezalel's fellow craftsman was of the tribe of Dan (Ex 31, 6).

2Chr

CHAPTER 3

Building of the Temple. [1r] Then Solomon began to build the house of the LORD in Jerusalem on Mount Moriah,* which had been pointed out to his father David, on the spot which David had selected, the threshing floor of Ornan the Jebusite. [2] He began to build in the second month of the fourth year of his reign. [3] These were the specifications laid down by Solomon for building the house of God: the length was sixty cubits according to the old measure, and the width was twenty cubits;[s] [4] the porch which lay before the nave along the width of the house was also twenty cubits, and it was twenty cubits high.* He overlaid its interior with pure gold.[t] [5] The nave he overlaid with cypress wood which he covered with fine gold, embossing on it palms and chains.[u] [6] He also decorated the building with precious stones. [7] The house, its beams and thresholds, as well as its walls and its doors, he overlaid with gold, and he engraved cherubim upon the walls. (The gold was from Parvaim.) [8] He also made the room of the holy of holies. Its length corresponded to the width of the house, twenty cubits, and its width was also twenty cubits. He overlaid it with fine gold to the amount of six hundred talents.[v] [9] The weight of the nails was fifty gold shekels. The upper chambers he likewise covered with gold.

[10] [w] For the room of the holy of holies he made two cherubim of carved workmanship, which were then overlaid with gold. [11] The wings of the cherubim spanned twenty cubits: [12] one wing of each cherub, five cubits in length, extended to a wall of the building, while the other wing, also five cubits in length, touched the corresponding wing of the second cherub. [13] The combined wingspread of the two cherubim was thus twenty cubits. They stood upon their own feet, facing toward the nave. [14] He made the veil* of violet, purple, crimson and fine linen, and had cherubim embroidered upon it.[x]

[15] [y] In front of the building he set two columns thirty-five cubits high; the capital topping each was of five cubits. [16] He worked out chains in the form of a collar with which he encircled the capitals of the columns, and he made a hundred pomegranates which he set on the chains. [17] He set up the columns to correspond with the nave, one for the right side and the other for the left, and he called the one to the right Jachin and the one to the left Boaz.

CHAPTER 4

[1] Then he made a bronze altar twenty cubits long, twenty cubits wide and ten cubits high.[z] [2] [a] He also made the molten sea. It was perfectly round, ten cubits in diameter, five in depth, and thirty in circumference; [3] below the rim a ring of figures of oxen* encircled the sea, ten to the cubit, all the way around; there were two rows of these cast in the same mold with the sea. [4] It rested on twelve oxen, three facing north, three west, three south, and three east, with their haunches all toward the center; the sea rested on their backs. [5] It was a handbreadth thick, and its brim was made like that of a cup, being lily-shaped. It had a capacity of three thousand measures.*

[6] Then he made ten basins for washing, placing five of them to the right and five to the left. Here were cleansed the victims for the holocausts; but the sea was for the priests to wash in.[b]

[7] He made the lampstands of gold, ten of them as was prescribed, and placed them in the nave, five to the right and five to the left.[c] [8] He made ten tables and had them set in the nave, five to the right and five to the left; and he made a hundred golden bowls.[d] [9] He made the court

r 1f: Gn 22, 2; 1 Kgs 6, 1; 1 Chr 21, 22-26.—s 1 Kgs 6, 2; Ez 40, 5.—t 1 Kgs 6, 3; Ez 40, 48.—u 1 Kgs 6, 15; Ez 41, 1.—v 1 Kgs 6, 16f. 20; Ez 41, 3.—w 10-13: 1 Kgs 6, 23-27.—x Mt 27, 51.—y 15ff: 1 Kgs 7, 15-22; Ez 40, 49.—z Ez 43, 13-17.—a 2-5: 1 Kgs 7, 23-26; Ez 43, 13.—b 1 Kgs 7, 38f; Ez 40, 38.—c 1 Kgs 7, 49.—d 1 Kgs 7, 50; 1 Chr 28, 16.

3, 1: *Mount Moriah:* the *height* in *the land of Moriah* (Gn 22, 2). This is the only place in the Bible where the temple mount is identified with the site where Abraham was to sacrifice Isaac.

3, 4: *The porch . . . twenty cubits high:* this measurement, not given in the Books of Kings, is here based on a variant Greek text that may be a later revision. The received Hebrew text says, "one hundred and twenty cubits high." The height of the two freestanding columns adjacent to the porch (1 Kgs 7, 15-16) is nearly doubled by the Chronicler (2 Chr 3, 15).

3, 14: *The veil:* at the entrance of the holy of holies, as also in the Mosaic meeting tent (Ex 26, 31f). Solomon's temple had doors at this place (1 Kgs 6, 31). Apparently there was a veil here in the temple of the Chronicler's time as there was also in Herod's temple (Mt 27, 51; Mk 15, 38; Lk 23, 45).

4, 3: *Oxen:* in 1 Kgs 7, 24 this double row of ornaments is described as being gourds. The text of Kings available to the Chronicler may have been faulty on this point as the words are similar in sound. In 2 Chr 4, 16 the *forks* correspond in a similar way to *bowls* in the text of 1 Kings (7, 40).

4, 5: *Three thousand measures:* according to 1 Kgs 7, 26, *two thousand measures.*

of the priests and the great courtyard and the gates of the courtyard; the gates he overlaid with bronze.[e] [10]The sea was placed off to the southeast from the right side of the temple.[f]

[11] [g] Huram also made the pots, the shovels and the bowls. Huram thus completed the work he had to do for King Solomon in the house of God: [12]two columns, two nodes for the capitals topping these two columns, and two networks covering the nodes of the capitals topping the columns; [13]also four hundred pomegranates for the two networks, with two rows of pomegranates to each network, to cover the two nodes of the capitals topping the columns. [14]He made the stands, and the basins on the stands; [15]one sea, and the twelve oxen under it; [16]likewise the pots, the shovels and the forks. Huram-abi made all these articles for King Solomon from polished bronze for the house of the LORD. [17]The king had them cast in the Jordan region, in the clayey ground between Succoth and Zeredah. [18]Solomon made all these vessels, so many in number that the weight of the bronze was not ascertained.

[19]Solomon had all these articles made for the house of God: the golden altar, the tables on which the showbread lay, [20]the lampstands and their lamps of pure gold which were to burn according to prescription before the sanctuary, [21]flowers, lamps and gold tongs [this was the purest gold], [22]snuffers, bowls, cups and firepans of pure gold. As for the entry to the house, its inner doors to the holy of holies, as well as the doors to the nave, were of gold.

CHAPTER 5

Dedication of the Temple. [1] [h] When all the work undertaken by Solomon for the temple of the LORD had been completed, he brought in the dedicated offerings of his father David, putting the silver, the gold and all the other articles in the treasuries of the house of God. [2]At Solomon's order the

elders of Israel and all the leaders of the tribes, the princes of the Israelite ancestral houses, came to Jerusalem to bring up the ark of the LORD's covenant from the City of David (which is Zion). [3]All the men of Israel assembled before the king during the festival of the seventh month. [4] [i] When all the elders of Israel had arrived, the Levites* took up the ark, [5]and they carried the ark and the meeting tent with all the sacred vessels that were in the tent; it was the levitical priests who carried them.

[6]King Solomon and the entire community of Israel gathered about him before the ark were sacrificing sheep and oxen so numerous that they could not be counted or numbered. [7]The priests brought the ark of the covenant of the LORD to its place beneath the wings of the cherubim in the sanctuary, the holy of holies of the temple. [8]The cherubim had their wings spread out over the place of the ark, sheltering the ark and its poles from above. [9]The poles were long enough so that their ends could be seen from that part of the holy place nearest the sanctuary; however, they could not be seen beyond. The ark has remained there to this day.* [10]There was nothing in it but the two tablets which Moses put there on Horeb, the tablets of the covenant which the LORD made with the Israelites at their departure from Egypt.

[11]When the priests came out of the holy place (all the priests who were present had purified themselves without reference to the rotation of their various classes), [12]the Levites who were singers, all who belonged to Asaph, Heman, Jeduthun, and their sons and brothers, clothed in fine linen, with cymbals, harps and lyres, stood east of the altar, and with them a hundred and twenty priests blowing trumpets. [13]When the trumpeters and singers were heard as a single voice praising and giving thanks to the LORD, and when they raised the sound of the trumpets, cymbals and other musical instruments to "give thanks to the LORD, for he is good, for his mercy endures forever," the building of the LORD's temple was filled with a cloud. [14]The priests could not continue to minister because of the cloud, since the LORD's glory filled the house of God.[j]

e 1 Kgs 7, 12.—f 1 Kgs 7, 39.—g 11-22; 1 Kgs 7, 40-51.—h 1-14: 1 Kgs 7, 51—8, 13.—i 4f: 2 Chr 35, 3.—j 2 Chr 7, 2; 1 Kgs 8, 10f.

5, 4: *The Levites:* The parallel passage in 1 Kgs 8, 3 has *the priests;* but see 2 Chr 5, 5, where the Deuteronomic term *levitical priests* is used, as also in 2 Chr 23, 18; 30, 27.

5, 9: *The ark has remained there to this day:* the Chronicler must have copied this from his source (1 Kgs 8, 8) without reflecting that the ark was lost in the Babylonian destruction of Jerusalem; cf 2 Mc 2, 4-8.

CHAPTER 6

1 *k* Then Solomon said: "The LORD intends to dwell in the dark cloud. 2 I have truly built you a princely house and dwelling, where you may abide forever." 3 *l* Turning about, the king greeted the whole community of Israel as they stood. 4 He said: "Blessed be the LORD, the God of Israel, who with his own mouth made a promise to my father David and by his own hands brought it to fulfillment. He said: 5 'Since the day I brought my people out of the land of Egypt, I have not chosen any city from among all the tribes of Israel for the building of a temple to my honor, nor have I chosen any man to be commander of my people Israel; 6 but now I choose Jerusalem, where I shall be honored, and I choose David to rule my people Israel.' 7 My father David wished to build a temple to the honor of the LORD, the God of Israel, 8 but the LORD said to him: 'In wishing to build a temple to my honor, you do well. 9 However, you shall not build the temple; rather, your son whom you will beget shall build the temple to my honor.'

10 "Now the LORD has fulfilled the promise that he made. I have succeeded my father David and have taken my seat on the throne of Israel, as the LORD foretold, and I have built the temple to the honor of the LORD, the God of Israel. 11 And I have placed there the ark, in which abides the covenant of the LORD which he made with the Israelites."

Solomon's Prayer. 12 *m* Solomon then took his place before the altar of the LORD in the presence of the whole community of Israel and stretched forth his hands. 13 He had made a bronze platform five cubits long, five cubits wide, and three cubits high, which he had placed in the middle of the courtyard. Having ascended it, Solomon knelt in the presence of the whole of Israel and stretched forth his hands toward heaven.* 14 Thus he prayed: "LORD, God of Israel, there is no god like you in heaven or on earth; you keep your covenant and show kindness to your servants who are wholeheartedly faithful to you. 15 You have kept the promise you made to my father David, your servant. With your own mouth you spoke it, and by your own hand you have brought it to fulfillment this day. 16 Now,

therefore, LORD, God of Israel, keep the further promise you made to my father David, your servant, when you said, 'You shall always have someone from your line to sit before me on the throne of Israel, provided only that your descendants look to their conduct so as always to live according to my law, even as you have lived in my presence.' 17 Now, LORD, God of Israel, may this promise which you made to your servant David be confirmed.

18 "Can it indeed be that God dwells with mankind on earth? If the heavens and the highest heavens cannot contain you, how much less this temple which I have built! 19 Look kindly on the prayer and petition of your servant, O LORD, my God, and listen to the cry of supplication your servant makes before you. 20 May your eyes watch day and night over this temple, the place where you have decreed you shall be honored; may you heed the prayer which I your servant offer toward this place. 21 Listen to the petitions of your servant and of your people Israel which they direct toward this place. Listen from your heavenly dwelling, and when you have heard, pardon.

22 "When any man sins against his neighbor and is required to take an oath of execration against himself, and when he comes for the oath before your altar in this temple, 23 listen from heaven: take action and pass judgment on your servants, requiting the wicked man and holding him responsible for his conduct, but absolving the innocent and rewarding him according to his virtue. 24 When your people Israel have sinned against you and are defeated by the enemy, but afterward they return and praise your name, and they pray to you and entreat you in this temple, 25 listen from heaven and forgive the sin of your people Israel, and bring them back to the land which you gave them and their fathers. 26 When the sky is closed so that there is no rain, because they have sinned against you, but then they pray toward this place and praise

k 1f: 1 Kgs 8, 12f.—l 3-11: 1 Kgs 8, 14-21.—m 12-41: 1 Kgs 8, 22-53.

6, 13: This verse is not found in the Chronicler's source; cf 1 Kgs 8, 22f. He has Solomon praying on *a bronze platform . . . in the middle of the courtyard* because at the time of the Chronicler only the priests prayed before the altar.

your name, and they withdraw from sin because you afflict them, [27] listen in heaven and forgive the sin of your servants and of your people Israel. But teach them the right way to live, and send rain upon your land which you gave your people as their heritage. [28] When there is famine in the land, when there is pestilence, or blight, or mildew, or locusts, or caterpillars; when their enemies besiege them at any of their gates; whenever there is a plague or sickness of any kind; [29] when any Israelite of all your people offers a prayer or petition of any kind, and in awareness of his affliction and pain, stretches out his hands toward this temple, [30] listen from your heavenly dwelling place, and forgive. Knowing his heart, render to everyone according to his conduct, for you alone know the hearts of men. [31] So may they fear you and walk in your ways as long as they live on the land you gave our fathers.

[32] "For the foreigner, too, who is not of your people Israel, when he comes from a distant land to honor your great name, your mighty power, and your outstretched arm, when they come in prayer to this temple, [33] listen from your heavenly dwelling place, and do whatever the foreigner entreats you, that all the peoples of the earth may know your name, fearing you as do your people Israel, and knowing that this house which I have built is dedicated to your honor.

[34] "When your people go forth to war against their enemies, wherever you send them, and pray to you in the direction of this city and of the house I have built to your honor, [35] listen from heaven to their prayer and petition, and defend their cause. [36] When they sin against you (for there is no man who does not sin), and in your anger against them you deliver them to the enemy, so that their captors deport them to another land, far or near, [37] when they repent in the land where they are captive and are converted, when they entreat you in the land of their captivity and say, 'We have sinned and done wrong; we have been wicked,' [38] and with their whole heart and with their whole soul they turn back to you in the land of those who hold them captive, when

n 1-10: 1 Kgs 8, 54-66; Jgs 6, 21; 1 Chr 21, 26; 2 Mc 2, 10.—o 2 Chr 5, 14; Ex 24, 16; 1 Kgs 8, 10f.—p 2 Chr 5, 13; 1 Kgs 8, 62; Ps 136, 1.—q 1 Kgs 8, 62f.—r Nm 10, 8. 10; Ps 136, 1.

they pray in the direction of their land which you gave their fathers, and of the city you have chosen, and of the house which I have built to your honor, [39] listen from your heavenly dwelling place, hear their prayer and petitions, and uphold their cause. Forgive your people who have sinned against you. [40] My God, may your eyes be open and your ears attentive to the prayer of this place. [41] And now,

"Advance, LORD God, to your resting place,
 you and the ark of your majesty.
May your priests, LORD God, be clothed with salvation,
 may your faithful ones rejoice in good things.
[42] LORD God, reject not the plea of your anointed,
 remember the devotion of David, your servant."

CHAPTER 7

[1] [n] When Solomon had ended his prayer, fire came down from heaven and consumed the holocaust and the sacrifices, and the glory of the LORD filled the house. [2] But the priests could not enter the house of the LORD, for the glory of the LORD had filled the house of the LORD. [o] [3] All the Israelites looked on while the fire came down and the glory of the LORD was upon the house, and they fell down upon the pavement with their faces to the earth and adored, praising the LORD, "for he is good, for his mercy endures forever." [4] The king and all the people were offering sacrifices before the LORD. [p] [5] King Solomon offered as sacrifice twenty-two thousand oxen, and one hundred twenty thousand sheep. [q]

End of the Dedication. [6] Thus the king and all the people dedicated the house of God. The priests were standing at their stations, as were the Levites, with the musical instruments of the LORD which King David had made for "praising the LORD, for his mercy endures forever," when David used them to accompany the hymns. Across from them the priests blew the trumpets and all Israel stood. [r]

7 Then Solomon consecrated the middle part of the court which lay before the house of the LORD; there he offered the holocausts and the fat of the peace offerings, since the bronze altar which Solomon had made could not hold the holocausts, the cereal offerings and the fat.[s]

8 On this occasion Solomon and with him all Israel, who had assembled in very large numbers from Labo of Hamath to the Wadi of Egypt, celebrated the festival for seven days.[t] 9 [u] On the eighth day they held a special meeting, for they had celebrated the dedication of the altar for seven days and the feast* for seven days. 10 On the twenty-third day of the seventh month he sent the people back to their tents, rejoicing and glad at heart at the good things the LORD had done for David, for Solomon, and for his people Israel. 11 [v] Solomon completed the house of the LORD and the royal palace; he successfully accomplished everything he had planned to do in regard to the house of the LORD and his own house.

God's Promise to Solomon. 12 The LORD appeared to Solomon during the night and said to him: "I have heard your prayer, and I have chosen this place for my house of sacrifice. 13 If I close heaven so that there is no rain, if I command the locust to devour the land, if I send pestilence among my people, 14 and if my people, upon whom my name has been pronounced, humble themselves and pray, and seek my presence and turn from their evil ways, I will hear them from heaven and pardon their sins and revive their land. 15 Now my eyes shall be open and my ears attentive to the prayer of this place. 16 And now I have chosen and consecrated this house that my name may be there forever; my eyes and my heart also shall be there always.

17 "As for you, if you live in my presence as your father David did, doing all that I have commanded you and keeping my statutes and ordinances, 18 I will establish your royal throne as I covenanted with your father David when I said, 'There shall never be lacking someone of yours as ruler in Israel.' 19 But if you turn away and forsake my statutes and commands which I placed before you, if you proceed to venerate and worship strange gods, 20 then I will uproot the people from the land I gave them; I will cast from my sight this house which I have consecrated to my honor, and I will make it a proverb and a byword among all peoples. 21 This temple which is so exalted—everyone passing by it will be amazed and ask: 'Why has the LORD done this to this land and to this house?' 22 And men will answer: 'They forsook the LORD, the God of their fathers, who brought them out of the land of Egypt, and they adopted strange gods and worshiped them and served them. That is why he has brought down upon them all this evil.' "

CHAPTER 8

Public Works. 1 [w] After the twenty years during which Solomon built the house of the LORD and his own house, 2 he built up the cities which Huram had given him,* and settled Israelites there. 3 Then Solomon went to Hamath of Zoba and conquered it. 4 He built Tadmor* in the desert region and all the supply cities, which he built in Hamath. 5 [x] He built Upper Bethhoron and Lower Beth-horon, fortified cities with walls, gates and bars; 6 also Baalath, all the supply cities belonging to Solomon, and all the cities for the chariots, the cities for the horsemen, and whatever else Solomon decided should be built in Jerusalem, in the Lebanon, and in the entire land under his dominion. 7 All the people that remained of the Hittites, Amorites, Perizzites, Hivites, and Jebusites, who were not of Israel— 8 that is, their descendants remaining in the land, whom the Israelites had not destroyed—Solomon subjected to forced labor, as they continue to this day. 9 But Solomon did not enslave

s 1 Kgs 8, 64.—t 1 Kgs 8, 65.—u 9f: 1 Kgs 8, 66.—v 11-22: 1 Kgs 9, 1-9.—w 1f: 1 Kgs 9, 10f.—x 5-12: 1 Kgs 9, 18-25.

7, 9f: *The feast:* of Booths, celebrated on the fifteenth day of the seventh month and followed by a solemn octave lasting through the twenty-second day (Lv 23, 33-36, Nm 29, 12-35); the people are therefore sent home on the twenty-third day (v 10). The festival (v 8) for *the dedication of the altar* and of the temple lasted for seven days before the feast of Booths, from the seventh to the fourteenth day. According to 1 Kgs 8, 65f, the people are dismissed at the end of these seven days.

8, 2: *The cities which Huram had given him:* according to 1 Kgs 9, 10-14, Solomon had ceded the cities as payment for the timber and gold received from Tyre. But since Huram was dissatisfied, he may have returned the cities to Solomon.

8, 4: *Tadmor:* later known as Palmyra, an important caravan city in the Syrian desert. The parallel passage in 1 Kgs 9, 18 has *Tamar,* in southern Judah; cf Ez 47, 19; 48, 28. But Solomon may well have fortified Tadmor against the Arameans.

the Israelites for his works. They became soldiers, commanders of his warriors, and commanders of his chariots and his horsemen. [10] They were also King Solomon's two hundred and fifty overseers who had charge of the people.

Solomon's Piety. [11] Solomon brought the daughter of Pharaoh up from the City of David to the palace which he had built for her, for he said, "No wife of mine shall dwell in the house of David, king of Israel, for the places where the ark of the LORD has come are holy."

[12] In those times Solomon offered holocausts to the LORD upon the altar of the LORD which he had built in front of the porch, [13] as was required day by day according to the command of Moses, and in particular on the sabbaths, at the new moons, and on the fixed festivals three times a year: on the feast of the Unleavened Bread, the feast of Weeks and the feast of Booths.[y]

[14] And according to the ordinance of his father David he appointed the various classes of the priests for their service, and the Levites according to their functions of praise and ministry alongside the priests, as the daily duty required. The gatekeepers of the various classes stood guard at each gate, since such was the command of David, the man of God.[z] [15] There was no deviation from the king's command in any respect relating to the priests and Levites or the treasuries. [16] All of Solomon's work was carried out successfully from the day the foundation of the house of the LORD was laid until the house of the LORD had been completed in every detail.

Glories of the Court. [17] In those times Solomon went to Ezion-geber and to Elath on the seashore of the land of Edom.[a] [18] Huram, through his servants, sent him ships and crewmen acquainted with the sea, who accompanied Solomon's servants to Ophir and brought back from there four hundred and fifty talents of gold to King Solomon.[b]

CHAPTER 9

[1] When the queen of Sheba heard of Solomon's fame, she came to Jerusalem to test

him with subtle questions, accompanied by a very numerous retinue and by camels bearing spices, much gold, and precious stones. She came to Solomon and questioned him on every subject in which she was interested.[c] [2] Solomon explained to her everything she asked about, and there remained nothing hidden from Solomon that he could not explain to her.

[3] When the queen of Sheba witnessed Solomon's wisdom, the palace he had built, [4] the food at his table, the seating of his ministers, the attendance of his servants and their dress, his cupbearers and their dress, and the holocausts he offered in the house of the LORD, it took her breath away. [5] "The account I heard in my country about your deeds and your wisdom is true," she told the king. [6] "Yet I did not believe the report until I came and saw with my own eyes. I have discovered that they did not tell me the half of your great wisdom; you have surpassed the stories I heard. [7] Happy are your men, happy these servants of yours, who stand before you always and listen to your wisdom. [8] Blessed be the LORD, your God, who has been so pleased with you as to place you on his throne as king for the LORD, your God. Because your God has so loved Israel as to will to make it last forever, he has appointed you over them as king to administer right and justice." [9] Then she gave the king one hundred and twenty gold talents and a very large quantity of spices, as well as precious stones. There was no other spice like that which the queen of Sheba gave to King Solomon.

[10] The servants of Huram and of Solomon who brought gold from Ophir also brought cabinet wood and precious stones. [11] With the cabinet wood the king made stairs for the temple of the LORD and the palace of the king; also lyres and harps for the chanters. The like of these had not been seen before in the land of Judah.

[12] King Solomon gave the queen of Sheba everything she desired and asked him for, more than she had brought to the king. Then she returned to her own country with her servants.

[13] [d] The gold that Solomon received each year weighed six hundred and sixty-six gold talents, [14] in addition to what was collected from travelers and what the merchants brought. All the kings of Arabia

y 1 Kgs 9, 25; Ex 23, 14; Nm 28—29.—z 1 Chr 23—26; Neh 12, 46.—a 1 Kgs 9, 26; Mt 12, 42; Lk 11, 31.—b 1 Kgs 9, 27f.— c 1 Kgs 10, 1f; Mt 12, 42; Lk 11, 31.—d 13-28: 1 Kgs 10, 14-28.

also, and the governors of the country, brought gold and silver to Solomon.

15 Moreover, King Solomon made two hundred large shields of beaten gold, six hundred shekels of beaten gold going into each shield, 16 and three hundred bucklers of beaten gold, three hundred shekels of gold going into each buckler; these the king put in the hall of the Forest of Lebanon.

17 King Solomon also made a large ivory throne which he overlaid with fine gold. 18 The throne had six steps; a footstool of gold was fastened to it, and there was an arm on each side of the seat, with two lions standing beside the arms. 19 Twelve other lions also stood there, one on either side of each step. Nothing like this had ever been produced in any other kingdom. 20 Furthermore, all of King Solomon's drinking vessels were of gold, and all the utensils in the hall of the Forest of Lebanon were of pure gold; silver was not considered of value in Solomon's time. 21 For the king had ships that went to Tarshish with the servants of Huram. Once every three years the fleet of Tarshish would return with a cargo of gold and silver, ivory, apes and monkeys. 22 Thus King Solomon surpassed all the other kings of the earth in riches as well as in wisdom.

23 All the kings of the earth sought audience with Solomon, to hear from him the wisdom which God had put in his heart. 24 Year in and year out, each one would bring his tribute—silver and gold articles, garments, weapons, spices, horses and mules. 25 Solomon also had four thousand stalls of horses, chariots, and twelve thousand horsemen, which he assigned to the chariot cities and to the king in Jerusalem. 26 He was ruler over all the kings from the River to the land of the Philistines and down to the border of Egypt. 27 The king made silver as common in Jerusalem as stones, while cedars became as numerous as the sycamores of the foothills. 28 Horses were imported for Solomon from Egypt and from all the lands.*

The Death of Solomon. 29 *e* The rest of the acts of Solomon, first and last, are written, as is well known, in the acts of Nathan the prophet, in the prophecy of Ahijah the Shilonite, and in the visions of Iddo the seer which concern Jeroboam, son of Nebat. 30 Solomon reigned in Jerusalem over all Israel for forty years. 31 He rested with his ancestors; he was buried in his father's City of David, and his son Rehoboam succeeded him as king.

II: THE MONARCHY BEFORE HEZEKIAH

CHAPTER 10

Division of the Kingdom. 1 *f* Rehoboam went to Shechem, for all Israel* had come to Shechem to proclaim him king. 2 When Jeroboam, son of Nebat, heard of this in Egypt where he had fled from King Solomon, he returned from Egypt. 3 Jeroboam was summoned to the assembly, and he and all Israel said to Rehoboam: 4 "Your father laid a heavy yoke upon us. If you now lighten the harsh service and the heavy yoke that your father imposed on us, we will serve you." 5 "In three days," he answered them, "come back to me."

When the people had departed, 6 King Rehoboam consulted the elders who had been in the service of his father during Solomon's lifetime, asking, "What answer do you advise me to give this people?" 7 They replied, "If you will deal kindly with this people and give in to them, acceding to their request, they will be your servants forever." 8 But he ignored the advice the elders had given him and consulted the young men who had grown up with him and were in his service. 9 He said to them, "What answer do you advise me to give this people, who have asked me to lighten the yoke my father imposed on them?" 10 The young men who had grown up with him replied: "This is the answer you should give to this people who have said to you, 'Your father laid a heavy yoke upon us, but do you lighten our yoke'; this you should say to them: 'My little finger is thicker than my father's body. 11 Whereas my father put a heavy yoke on you, I will make it heavier!

e 29ff: 1 Kgs 11, 41ff.—f 1-14: 1 Kgs 12, 1-14.

9, 28: See note on 2 Chr 1, 16f.

10, 1: *All Israel:* as in the original source (1 Kgs 12, 1), the northern tribes, distinct from Judah and Benjamin. Contrast the Chronicler's own terms, *those Israelites who lived in the cities of Judah* (v 17), and *all the Israelites* [literally, all Israel] *in Judah and Benjamin* (2 Chr 11, 3).

My father beat you with whips, but I will beat you with scorpions!' "
¹²On the third day, Jeroboam and all the people came back to King Rehoboam as he had instructed them to do. ¹³Ignoring the advice the elders had given him, the king gave them a harsh answer, ¹⁴speaking to them according to the advice of the young men: "My father laid a heavy yoke on you, but I will make it heavier. My father beat you with whips, but I will beat you with scorpions." ¹⁵The king would not listen to the people, for this turn of events was divinely ordained to fulfill the prophecy the LORD had uttered to Jeroboam, the son of Nebat, through Ahijah the Shilonite. ᵍ

¹⁶ ʰ When all Israel saw that the king would not listen to them, the people answered the king,

"What share have we in David?
   We have no heritage in the son of Jesse.
Everyone to your tents, O Israel!
   Now look to your own house, David!"

So all Israel went off to their tents. ¹⁷Rehoboam, therefore, reigned over only those Israelites who lived in the cities of Judah. ¹⁸King Rehoboam then sent out Hadoram, who was superintendent of the forced labor, but the Israelites stoned him to death. Rehoboam himself managed to mount his chariot and flee to Jerusalem. ¹⁹Thus Israel has been in rebellion against David's house to this day.

CHAPTER 11

¹ ⁱ On his arrival in Jerusalem Rehoboam gathered together the house of Judah and Benjamin, a hundred and eighty thousand seasoned warriors, to have them fight against Israel and restore the kingdom to him. ²However, the word of the LORD came to Shemaiah, a man of God: ³"Say to Rehoboam, son of Solomon, king of Judah, and to all the Israelites in Judah and Benjamin: ⁴'Thus says the LORD: You must not march out to fight against your brothers. Let every man

return home, for what has occurred I have brought about.' " They obeyed this message of the LORD and gave up the expedition against Jeroboam.

Rehoboam's Works. * ⁵Rehoboam took up residence in Jerusalem and built fortified cities in Judah. ⁶He built up Bethlehem, Etam, Tekoa, ⁷Beth-zur, Soco, Adullam, ⁸Gath, Mareshah, Ziph, ⁹Adoraim, Lachish, Azekah, ¹⁰Zorah, Aijalon, and Hebron; these were fortified cities in Judah and Benjamin. ¹¹Then he strengthened the fortifications and put commanders in them, with supplies of food, oil and wine. ¹²In every city were shields and spears, and he made them very strong. Thus Judah and Benjamin remained his.

Refugees from the North. ¹³Now the priests and Levites throughout Israel presented themselves to him from all parts of their land, ¹⁴for the Levites left their assigned pasture lands and their holdings and came to Judah and Jerusalem, because Jeroboam and his sons repudiated them as priests of the LORD. ʲ ¹⁵In their place, he himself appointed priests for the high places and satyrs and calves he had made. ᵏ ¹⁶After them, all those of the Israelite tribes who firmly desired to seek the LORD, the God of Israel, came to Jerusalem to sacrifice to the LORD, the God of their fathers. ¹⁷Thus they strengthened the kingdom of Judah and made Rehoboam, son of Solomon, prevail for three years; for they walked in the way of David and Solomon three years.

Rehoboam's Family. ¹⁸Rehoboam took to himself as wife Mahalath, daughter of Jerimoth, son of David and of Abihail, daughter of Eliab, son of Jesse. ¹⁹She bore him sons: Jehush, Shemariah and Zaham. ²⁰After her, he married Maacah, daughter of Absalom, who bore him Abijah, Attai, Ziza and Shelomith. ˡ ²¹Rehoboam loved Maacah, daughter of Absalom, more than all his other wives and concubines; he had taken eighteen wives and sixty concubines, and he fathered twenty-eight sons and sixty daughters. ²²Rehoboam constituted Abijah, son of Maacah, commander among his brothers, for he intended to make him king. ²³He acted prudently, distributing various of his sons throughout all the districts of Judah and Benjamin, in all the fortified cities; and he furnished them with

2Chr

---

g 1 Kgs 11, 29-39; 12, 15.—h 16-19: 1 Kgs 12, 16-19.—i 1-4: 1 Kgs 12, 21-24.—j 1 Kgs 12, 32.—k 1 Kgs 12, 32; Lv 17, 7.—l 1 Kgs 15, 2.

11, 5-12: These verses, though not found in 1 Kgs, are apparently based on a reliable, ancient source.

copious provisions and sought an abundance of wives for them.

CHAPTER 12

His Apostasy. [1] After Rehoboam had consolidated his rule and had become powerful, he abandoned the law of the LORD, he and all Israel with him.[m] [2] Thus it happened that in the fifth year of King Rehoboam, Shishak, king of Egypt, attacked Jerusalem, for they had been unfaithful to the LORD.[n] [3] He came up with twelve hundred chariots and sixty thousand horsemen, and there was no counting the army that came with him from Egypt—Libyans, Sukkites* and Ethiopians. [4] They captured the fortified cities of Judah and came as far as Jerusalem. [5] Then Shemaiah the prophet came to Rehoboam and the commanders of Judah who had gathered at Jerusalem because of Shishak, and said to them: "Thus says the LORD: 'You have abandoned me, and therefore I have abandoned you to the power of Shishak.'"[o]

[6] However, the commanders of Israel and the king humbled themselves, saying, "The LORD is just." [7] When the LORD saw that they had humbled themselves, the word of the LORD came to Shemaiah: "Because they have humbled themselves, I will not destroy them; I will give them some deliverance, and my wrath shall not be poured out upon Jerusalem through Shishak. [8] But they shall be his servants, that they may know what it is to serve me and what it is to serve earthly kingdoms."

[9] [p] Therefore Shishak, king of Egypt, attacked Jerusalem and carried off the treasures of the temple of the LORD and of the king's palace. He took everything, including the gold bucklers that Solomon had made. [10] (To replace them, King Rehoboam made bronze bucklers, which he entrusted to the officers of the guard on duty at the entrance of the royal palace. [11] Whenever the king visited the temple of the LORD, the troops would come bearing them, and then they would return them to the guardroom.) [12] Because he had humbled himself, the anger of the LORD turned from him so that it did not destroy him completely; and in Judah, moreover, good deeds were found.

[13] King Rehoboam consolidated his power in Jerusalem and continued to rule; he was forty-one years old when he became king, and he reigned seventeen years in Jerusalem, the city in which, out of all the tribes of Israel, the LORD chose to be honored. Rehoboam's mother was named Naamah, an Ammonite.[q] [14] He did evil, for he had not truly resolved to seek the LORD. [15] [r] The acts of Rehoboam, first and last, are written, as is well known, in the history of Shemaiah the prophet and of Iddo the seer [his family record]. There was war continually between Rehoboam and Jeroboam. [16] Rehoboam rested with his ancestors; he was buried in the City of David. His son Abijah succeeded him as king.

CHAPTER 13

War between Abijah and Jeroboam. [1] [s] In the eighteenth year of King Jeroboam, Abijah became king of Judah; [2] he reigned three years in Jerusalem. His mother was named Michaiah, daughter of Uriel of Gibeah. There was war between Abijah and Jeroboam.

[3] Abijah joined battle with a force of four hundred thousand picked warriors, while Jeroboam lined up against him in battle with eight hundred thousand picked and valiant warriors. [4] * Abijah stood on Mount Zemaraim, which is in the highlands of Ephraim, and said: "Listen to me, Jeroboam and all Israel! [5] Do you not know that the LORD, the God of Israel, has given the kingdom of Israel to David forever, to him and to his sons, by a covenant made in salt? [6] Yet Jeroboam, son of Nebat, the servant of Solomon, son of David, has stood up and rebelled against his lord![t] [7] Worthless men, scoundrels, joined him and overcame Rehoboam, son of Solomon, when Rehoboam was young and unthinking, and no match for them. [8] But now, do you think you are a match for the kingdom of the LORD commanded by the sons of David, simply because you are a huge multitude and have with you the golden calves which Jeroboam made you for gods?

[9] "Have you not expelled the priests of the LORD, the sons of Aaron, and the

---

m 1 Kgs 11, 4; 14, 22.—n 1 Kgs 14, 25.—o 2 Chr 11, 2.—p 9ff: 1 Kgs 14, 25-28.—q 1 Kgs 14, 21.—r 15f: 1 Kgs 14, 29ff.— s 1f: 1 Kgs 15, 1f.—t 1 Kgs 11, 26.

12, 3: *Sukkites:* foreign mercenaries in the Egyptian army.
13, 4-12: This is a free composition of the Chronicler to show that this was a religious, rather than a political, war.

Levites, and made for yourselves priests like the people of foreign lands? Everyone who comes to consecrate himself with a young bull and seven rams becomes a priest of no-gods. ¹⁰But as for us, the LORD is our God, and we have not forsaken him. The priests ministering to the LORD are sons of Aaron, and the Levites also have their offices. ¹¹They burn holocausts to the LORD and fragrant incense morning after morning and evening after evening; they display the showbread on the pure table, and the lamps of the golden lampstand burn evening after evening; for we observe our duties to the LORD, our God, but you have abandoned him. ¹²See, God is with us, at our head, and his priests are here with trumpets to sound the attack against you. Do not battle against the LORD, the God of your fathers, O Israelites, for you will not succeed!"

¹³But Jeroboam had an ambush go around them to come at them from the rear; so that while his army faced Judah, his ambush lay behind them. ¹⁴When Judah turned and saw that they had to battle on both fronts, they cried out to the LORD and the priests sounded the trumpets. ¹⁵Then the men of Judah shouted; and when they did so, God defeated Jeroboam and all Israel before Abijah and Judah. ¹⁶The Israelites fled before Judah, and God delivered them into their hands. ¹⁷Abijah and his people inflicted a severe defeat upon them; five hundred thousand picked men of Israel fell slain. ¹⁸The Israelites were subdued on that occasion and the Judahites were victorious because they relied on the LORD, the God of their fathers. ¹⁹Abijah pursued Jeroboam and took cities from him: Bethel and its dependencies, Jeshanah and its dependencies, and Ephron and its dependencies. ²⁰Jeroboam did not regain power during the time of Abijah; the LORD struck him down and he died, ²¹while Abijah continued to grow stronger. He took to himself fourteen wives and fathered twenty-two sons and sixteen daughters.

u 22f: 2 Chr 12, 15; 1 Kgs 7ff.—v 1f: 2 Chr 33, 15; Ex 23, 24; 34, 13; 1 Kgs 15, 11f.—w 2 Chr 16, 8.—x 2 Chr 32, 8.—y Pss 20, 7f; 60, 11f.

14, 7-14: An Ethiopian invasion of Judah is mentioned only in 1 Chronicles. This account may be a legend contrived to show how the pious King Asa was rewarded through divine assistance. There may, however, have been an incursion of nomads from the Negeb at this time; cf vv 13f.

Death of Abijah. ²² ᵘ The rest of Abijah's acts, his deeds and his words, are written in the midrash of the prophet Iddo. ²³Abijah rested with his ancestors; they buried him in the City of David. His son Asa succeeded him as king. During his time, ten years of peace began in the land.

CHAPTER 14

Asa the Reformer. ¹ ᵛ Asa did what was good and pleasing to the LORD, his God, ²removing the heathen altars and the high places, breaking to pieces the sacred pillars, and cutting down the sacred poles. ³He commanded Judah to seek the LORD, the God of their fathers, and to observe the law and its commands. ⁴He removed the high places and incense stands from all the cities of Judah, and under him the kingdom had peace. ⁵He built fortified cities in Judah, for the land had peace and no war was waged against him during these years, because the LORD had given him peace. ⁶He said to Judah: "Let us build these cities and surround them with walls, towers, gates and bars. The land is still ours, for we have sought the LORD, our God; we sought him, and he has given us rest on every side." So they built and prospered.

The Ethiopian Invasion.* ⁷Asa had an army of three hundred thousand shield- and lance-bearers from Judah, and two hundred and eighty thousand from Benjamin who carried bucklers and were archers, all of them valiant warriors. ⁸Zerah the Ethiopian moved against them with a force of one million men and three hundred chariots, and he came as far as Mareshah.ʷ ⁹Asa went out to meet him and set himself in battle array in the valley of Zephathah, near Mareshah. ¹⁰Asa called upon the LORD, his God, praying: "O LORD, there is none like you to help the powerless against the strong. Help us, O LORD, our God, for we rely on you, and in your name we have come against this multitude. You are the LORD, our God; let no man prevail against you."ˣ ¹¹And so the LORD defeated the Ethiopians before Asa and Judah, and they fled.ʸ ¹²Asa and those with him pursued them as far as Gerar, and the Ethiopians fell until there were no survivors, for they were crushed before the LORD and his army, which carried away enormous spoils. [13] Then the Judahites conquered all the cities around Gerar, for the fear of the LORD was upon them; they despoiled all the cities, for there was much booty in them. [14] They attacked also the tents of the cattle-herders and carried off a great number of sheep and camels. Then they returned to Jerusalem.

CHAPTER 15

Cult Reform. [1] Upon Azariah, son of Oded, came the spirit of God. [2] He went forth to meet Asa and said to him: "Hear me, Asa and all Judah and Benjamin! The LORD is with you when you are with him, and if you seek him he will be present to you; but if you abandon him, he will abandon you. [z] [3] For a long time Israel had no true God, no priest-teacher and no law, [4] but when in their distress they turned to the LORD, the God of Israel, and sought him, he was present to them. [a] [5] In that former time there was no place for anyone to go or come, but there were many terrors upon the inhabitants of the lands. [6] Nation crushed nation and city crushed city, for God destroyed them by every kind of adversity. [b] [7] But as for you, be strong and do not relax, for your work shall be rewarded." [c]

[8] When Asa heard these words and the prophecy [Oded the prophet], he was encouraged to remove the detestable idols from the whole land of Judah and Benjamin and from the cities he had taken in the highlands of Ephraim, and to restore the altar of the LORD, which was before the vestibule of the LORD. [9] Then he convened all Judah and Benjamin, together with those of Ephraim, Manasseh and Simeon who sojourned with them; for many had fled to him from Israel when they saw that the LORD, his God, was with him. [10] * They gathered at Jerusalem in the third month of the fifteenth year of Asa's reign, [11] and sacrificed to the LORD at that time seven hundred oxen and seven thousand sheep of the booty they had brought. [12] They entered into a covenant to seek the LORD, the God of their fathers, with all their heart and soul; [13] and everyone who would not seek the LORD, the God of Israel, was to be put to death, whether small or great, whether man or woman. [d] [14] They swore to the LORD with a loud voice, with shouting and with trumpets and horns.

[15] All Judah rejoiced over the oath, for they had sworn with their whole heart and sought him with complete desire, so that he was present to them. And the LORD gave them rest on every side. [e]

[16] [f] Maacah, the mother of King Asa, he deposed as queen mother because she had made an outrageous object for Asherah; Asa cut this down, smashed it, and burnt it in the Kidron Valley. [17] Although the high places did not disappear from Israel, yet Asa's heart was undivided as long as he lived. [18] He brought into the house of God his father's votive offerings and his own: silver, gold, and various utensils. [19] There was no war until the thirty-fifth year of Asa's reign.

CHAPTER 16

Asa's Infidelity. [1] [g] In the thirty-sixth year of Asa's reign, Baasha, king of Israel, attacked Judah and fortified Ramah to prevent any communication with Asa, king of Judah. [2] Asa then brought out silver and gold from the treasuries of the temple of the LORD and of the royal palace and sent them to Ben-hadad, king of Aram, who lived in Damascus, with this message: [3] "There is a treaty between you and me, as there was between your father and my father. See, I am sending you silver and gold. Go, break your treaty with Baasha, king of Israel, that he may withdraw from me." [4] Ben-hadad agreed to King Asa's request and sent the leaders of his troops against the cities of Israel. They attacked Ijon, Dan, Abel-maim, and all the store cities of Naphtali. [5] When Baasha heard of it, he left off fortifying Ramah; he stopped his work. [6] Then King Asa commandeered all of Judah to carry away the stone and wood with which Baasha had been fortifying Ramah, and with them he fortified Geba and Mizpah.

[7] At that time Hanani the seer came to Asa, king of Judah, and said to him: "Because you relied on the king of Aram and did not rely on the LORD, your God, the

---

z Jer 29, 13f; Hos 3, 4f.—a Dt 4, 29f.—b Is 19, 2.—c Is 7, 4; Jer 31, 16.—d Neh 10, 30.—e Dt 4, 29.—f 16ff: 1 Kgs 15, 13ff.—g 1-6: 1 Kgs 15, 16-21.

15, 10ff: With this description of a covenant ceremony in the *third month* of a year beginning in the spring, the Chronicler lays a foundation for celebrating the ancient feast of Pentecost (Weeks) as the time for a solemn renewal of the people's covenant with God on Mount Sinai; see Ex 19, 1ff; Lv 23, 16 and the note there. This is also the background for Pentecost as the "birthday of the Church."

army of the king of Aram has escaped*
your hand. [8] Were not the Ethiopians and
Libyans a vast army, with great numbers
of chariots and drivers? And yet, because
you relied on the LORD, he delivered them
into your power.[h] [9] The eyes of the LORD
roam over the whole earth, to encourage
those who are devoted to him wholeheartedly. You have acted foolishly in this
matter, for from now on you will have
wars."[i] [10] But Asa became angry with the
seer and imprisoned him in the stocks, so
greatly was he enraged at him over this.
Asa also oppressed some of his people at
this time.
[11] [j] Now the acts of Asa, first and last,
can be found recorded in the book of the
kings of Judah and Israel. [12] In the thirty-
ninth year of his reign, Asa contracted a
serious disease in his feet. But even in his
sickness he did not seek the LORD, but
only the physicians. [13] Asa rested with his
ancestors; he died in the forty-first year of
his reign. [14] They buried him in the tomb
he had hewn for himself in the City of
David, having laid him upon a couch
which was filled with spices and various
kinds of aromatics compounded into an
ointment. They also burned a very great
funeral pyre for him.

CHAPTER 17

Zeal of Jehoshaphat for the Law. [1] His son
Jehoshaphat succeeded him as king and
strengthened his hold against Israel.[k] [2] He
placed armed forces in all the fortified
cities of Judah, and put garrisons in the
land of Judah and in the cities of Ephraim
which his father Asa had taken. [3] The
LORD was with Jehoshaphat,* for he
walked in the ways his father had pursued
in the beginning, and he did not consult
the Baals. [4] Rather, he sought the God of
his father and observed his commands,
and not the practices of Israel. [5] As a result, the LORD made his kingdom secure,
and all Judah gave Jehoshaphat gifts, so
that he enjoyed great wealth and glory.
[6] Thus he was encouraged to follow the
LORD's ways, and again he removed the
high places and the sacred poles from
Judah.[l]
[7] In the third year of his reign he sent his
leading men, Ben-hail, Obadiah, Zechariah, Nethanel and Micaiah, to teach in the
cities of Judah. [8] With them he sent the
Levites Shemaiah, Nethaniah, Zebadiah,
Asahel,   Shemiramoth,   Jehonathan,
Adonijah and Tobijah, together with the
priests Elishama and Jehoram.[m] [9] They
taught in Judah, having with them the
book containing the law of the LORD; they
traveled through all the cities of Judah and
taught among the people.[n]

His Power. [10] Now the fear of the LORD
was upon all the kingdoms of the countries
surrounding Judah, so that they did not
war against Jehoshaphat. [11] Some of the
Philistines brought Jehoshaphat gifts and a
tribute of silver; and the Arabs also
brought him a flock of seven thousand
seven hundred rams and seven thousand
seven hundred he-goats.
[12] Jehoshaphat grew steadily greater. He
built strongholds and store cities in Judah.
[13] He carried out many works in the cities
of Judah, and he had soldiers, valiant warriors, in Jerusalem. [14] This was their mustering according to their ancestral houses.
Of Judah, the commanders of thousands:
Adnah the commander, and with him
three hundred thousand valiant warriors.
[15] Next to him, Jehohanan the commander, and with him two hundred eighty
thousand. [16] Next to him, Amasiah, son of
Zichri, who offered himself to the LORD,
and with him two hundred thousand valiant warriors. [17] From Benjamin: Eliada, a
valiant warrior, and with him two hundred
thousand armed with bow and buckler.
[18] Next to him, Jozabad, and with him one
hundred and eighty thousand equipped for
war. [19] These were at the service of the
king; in addition were those whom the
king had placed in the fortified cities
throughout all Judah.

CHAPTER 18

Alliance with Israel. [1] [o] Jehoshaphat therefore had wealth and glory in abundance;
but he became related to Ahab by marriage. [2] After some years he went down to
Ahab at Samaria; Ahab offered numerous
sheep and oxen for him and the people
with him, and persuaded him to go up
against Ramoth-gilead. [3] Ahab, king of

---

h 2 Chr 14, 8-14.—i Ps 33, 13ff.—j 11-14: 1 Kgs 15, 23f.—k
1 Kgs 15, 24.—l 2 Chr 20, 33; Ex 34, 13.—m 2 Chr 19, 8.—n
Ezr 7, 25.—o 1-34: 1 Kgs 22, 1-35.

16, 7: *The king of Aram . . . escaped:* according to the
Lucianic recension, "the king of Israel escaped": this may well be
the original reading; Asa was friendly with Aram.
17, 3: *The Lord was with Jehoshaphat:* along with
Hezekiah and Josiah, Jehoshaphat was one of the Chronicler's favorite kings.

Israel, asked Jehoshaphat, king of Judah, "Will you come with me to Ramoth-gilead?" "You and I are as one," was his answer; "your people and my people as well. We will be with you in the battle." ⁴But Jehoshaphat also said to the king of Israel, "Seek the word of the LORD at once."

The Prophets. ⁵The king of Israel gathered his prophets, four hundred in number, and asked them, "Shall we go to attack Ramoth-gilead, or shall I refrain?" "Go up," they answered. "God will deliver it over to the king." ⁶But Jehoshaphat said, "Is there no other prophet of the LORD here whom we may consult?" ⁷The king of Israel answered Jehoshaphat, "There is still another through whom we may consult the LORD, but I hate him, for he prophesies not good but always evil about me. That is Micaiah, son of Imlah." Jehoshaphat said, "Let not your Majesty speak of evil against you." ⁸So the king of Israel called an official, to whom he said, "Get Micaiah, son of Imlah, at once." ⁹The king of Israel and King Jehoshaphat of Judah were seated each on his throne, clothed in their robes of state on a threshing floor at the entrance of the gate of Samaria, and all the prophets were prophesying before them.

¹⁰Zedekiah, son of Chenaanah, made iron horns for himself and said: "The LORD says, 'With these you shall gore Aram until you have destroyed them.'" ¹¹The other prophets prophesied in the same vein, saying: "Go up to Ramoth-gilead. You shall succeed; the LORD will deliver it over to the king." ¹² * The messenger who had gone to call Micaiah said to him: "Look now, the prophets unanimously predict good for the king. Let your word, like each of theirs, predict good." ¹³"As the LORD lives," Micaiah answered, "I will say what my God tells me."

¹⁴When he came to the king, the king said to him, "Micaiah, shall we go to fight against Ramoth-gilead, or shall I refrain?" "Go up," he answered, "and succeed; they will be delivered into your power." ¹⁵But the king said to him, "How many times must I adjure you to tell me nothing but the truth in the name of the LORD?" ¹⁶Then Micaiah answered:

"I see all Israel
    scattered on the mountains,

Like sheep without a shepherd,
    and the LORD saying, 'These have no
        master!
Let each of them go back home in
    peace.'"

¹⁷The king of Israel said to Jehoshaphat, "Did I not tell you that he prophesies no good about me, but only evil?" ¹⁸But Micaiah continued: "Therefore hear the word of the LORD: I saw the LORD seated on his throne, with the whole host of heaven standing by to his right and to his left. ¹⁹The LORD asked, 'Who will deceive Ahab, king of Israel, so that he will go up and fall at Ramoth-gilead?' And one said this, another that, ²⁰until a spirit came forward and presented himself to the LORD, saying, 'I will deceive him.' The LORD asked, 'How?' ²¹He answered, 'I will go forth and become a lying spirit in the mouths of all his prophets.' The LORD agreed: 'You shall succeed in deceiving him. Go forth and do this.' ²²So now the LORD has put a lying spirit in the mouths of these your prophets, but the LORD himself has decreed evil against you."

²³Thereupon Zedekiah, son of Chenaanah, came up and slapped Micaiah on the cheek, saying, "Which way did the spirit of the LORD go when he left me to speak to you?" ²⁴"You shall find out," Micaiah replied, "on that day when you enter an innermost chamber to hide." ²⁵The king of Israel then said: "Seize Micaiah and take him back to Amon, prefect of the city, and to Joash the king's son, ²⁶and say, 'This is the king's order: Put this man in prison and feed him scanty rations of bread and water until I return in safety!'" ²⁷But Micaiah said, "If ever you return in safety, the LORD has not spoken through me." And he said, "Hear, O peoples, all of you!"*

Ahab's Death. ²⁸The king of Israel and King Jehoshaphat of Judah went up to Ramoth-gilead ²⁹and the king of Israel said to Jehoshaphat, "I will go into battle disguised, but you put on your own clothes." So the king of Israel disguised himself and they entered the fray. ³⁰Meanwhile, the king of Aram had given his

---

18, 12-22: See note on 1 Kgs 22, 19-23.
18, 27: *"Hear, O peoples, all of you!"*: this quotation, which appears in some texts of 1 Kgs 22, 28, ascribes to the prophet Micaiah ben Imlan the opening words of the prophetic utterance of Micah of Moresheth (Mi 1, 2), a century later.

chariot commanders the order, "Fight with no one, small or great, except the king of Israel." [31] When the commanders saw Jehoshaphat, they exclaimed, "That must be the king of Israel!" and shifted to fight him. But Jehoshaphat cried out and the LORD helped him; God induced them to leave him. [32] The chariot commanders became aware that he was not the king of Israel and gave up their pursuit of him. [33] Someone, however, drew his bow at random and hit the king of Israel between the joints of his breastplate. He ordered his charioteer, "Rein about and take me out of the ranks, for I am disabled."[p] [34] The battle grew fierce during the day, and the king of Israel braced himself up on his chariot facing the Arameans until evening. He died as the sun was setting.

CHAPTER 19

Jehoshaphat Rebuked. [1] King Jehoshaphat of Judah returned in safety to his house in Jerusalem. [2] Jehu the seer, son of Hanani,* met King Jehoshaphat and said to him: "Should you help the wicked and love those who hate the LORD? For this reason, wrath is upon you from the LORD. [3] Yet some good things are to be found in you, since you have removed the sacred poles from the land and have been determined to seek God."

Judges Appointed. [4] Jehoshaphat dwelt in Jerusalem; but he went out again among the people from Beer-sheba to the highlands of Ephraim and brought them back to the LORD, the God of their fathers. [5] He appointed judges in the land, in all the fortified cities of Judah, city by city, [6] and he said to them: "Take care what you do, for you are judging, not on behalf of man, but on behalf of the LORD; he judges with you.[q] [7] And now, let the fear of the LORD be upon you. Act carefully, for with the LORD, our God, there is no injustice, no

partiality, no bribe-taking."[r] [8] In Jerusalem also, Jehoshaphat appointed some Levites and priests and some of the family heads of Israel to judge in the name of the LORD and to settle quarrels among the inhabitants of Jerusalem.[s] [9] He gave them this command: "You shall act faithfully and wholeheartedly in the fear of the LORD. [10] And in every dispute that your brethren living in their cities bring to you, whether it concerns bloodguilt or questions of law, command, statutes, or judgments, warn them lest they become guilty before the LORD and his wrath come upon you and your brethren. Do that and you shall be guiltless.[t] [11] See now, Amariah is high priest over you in everything that pertains to the LORD, and Zebadiah, son of Ishmael, is leader of the house of Judah in all that pertains to the king; and the Levites will be your officials. Act firmly, and the LORD will be with the good."

CHAPTER 20

Invasion from Edom.* [1] After this the Moabites, the Ammonites, and with them some Meunites came to fight against Jehoshaphat. [2] The message was brought to Jehoshaphat: "A great multitude is coming against you from across the sea, from Edom; they are already in Hazazon-tamar" (which is En-gedi). [3] Jehoshaphat was frightened, and he hastened to consult the LORD. He proclaimed a fast for all Judah. [4] Then Judah gathered to seek help from the LORD; from every one of the cities of Judah they came to seek the LORD.[u]

Prayer of Jehoshaphat. [5] Jehoshaphat stood up in the assembly of Judah and Jerusalem in the house of the LORD before the new court, [6] and he said: "LORD, God of our fathers, are you not the God in heaven, and do you not rule over all the kingdoms of the nations? In your hand is power and might, and no one can withstand you.[v] [7] Was it not you, our God, who drove out the inhabitants of this land before your people Israel and gave it forever to the descendants of Abraham, your friend?[w] [8] They have dwelt in it and they built in it a sanctuary to your honor, saying, [9] "When evil comes upon us, the sword of judgment, or pestilence, or famine, we will stand before this house and before you, for your name is in this

2Chr

---

p 2 Chr 35, 23; 1 Kgs 22, 34.—q Dt 1, 16ff; 16, 19f.—r Dt 10, 17.—s 2 Chr 17, 8f; Dt 17, 8-13; Ps 122, 3ff.—t Nm 35, 19.—u Jer 36, 6; Jb 1, 14.—v 2 Chr 32, 7; Dt 4, 39.—w Dn 3, 35.

19, 2: *Jehu the seer, son of Hanani:* hardly the same seer as Jehu, son of Hanani, who prophesied against Baasha almost 50 years earlier (1 Kgs 16, 1).

20, 1-30: Although the account here seems to be a free composition of the Chronicler, there is probably a basis in fact for it; there could well have been a raid of nomads against Judah in the reign of Jehoshaphat, similar to Zerah's attack on Asa (2 Chr 14, 8-14). The story may also, in some way, be connected with the campaign of Israel and Judah against Moab through the territory of Edom (2 Kgs 3, 4-27).

house, and we will cry out to you in our affliction, and you will hear and save!' [10]And now, see the Ammonites, Moabites, and those of Mount Seir whom you did not allow Israel to invade when they came from the land of Egypt, but instead they passed them by and did not destroy them.[x] [11]See how they are now repaying us by coming to drive us out of the possession you have given us. [12]O our God, will you not pass judgment on them? We are powerless before this vast multitude that comes against us. We are at a loss what to do, hence our eyes are turned toward you."

Victory Prophesied. [13]All Judah was standing before the LORD, with their little ones, their wives, and their young sons. [14]And the spirit of the LORD came upon Jahaziel, son of Zechariah, son of Benaiah, son of Jeiel, son of Mattaniah, a Levite of the clan of Asaph, in the midst of the assembly, [15]and he said: "Listen, all of Judah, inhabitants of Jerusalem, and King Jehoshaphat! The LORD says to you: 'Do not fear or lose heart at the sight of this vast multitude, for the battle is not yours but God's. [16]Go down against them tomorrow. You will see them coming up by the ascent of Ziz, and you will come upon them at the end of the wadi which opens on the wilderness of Jeruel. [17]You will not have to fight in this encounter. Take your places, stand firm, and see how the LORD will be with you to deliver you, Judah and Jerusalem. Do not fear or lose heart. Tomorrow go out to meet them, and the LORD will be with you.' "[y] [18]Then Jehoshaphat knelt down with his face to the ground, and all Judah and the inhabitants of Jerusalem fell down before the LORD in worship. [19]Levites from among the Kohathites and Korahites rose to sing the praises of the LORD, the God of Israel, in a resounding chorus.

The Invaders Destroyed. [20]In the early morning they hastened out to the wilderness of Tekoa. As they were going out, Jehoshaphat halted and said: "Listen to me, Judah and inhabitants of Jerusalem! Trust in the LORD, your God, and you will be found firm. Trust in his prophets and you will succeed."[z] [21]After consulting with the people, he appointed some to sing to the LORD and some to praise the holy Appearance* as it went forth at the head

of the army. They sang: "Give thanks to the LORD, for his mercy endures forever."[a] [22]At the moment they began their jubilant hymn, the LORD laid an ambush against the Ammonites, Moabites, and those of Mount Seir who were coming against Judah, so that they were vanquished. [23]For the Ammonites and Moabites set upon the inhabitants of Mount Seir and completely exterminated them. And when they had finished with the inhabitants of Seir, they began to destroy each other.[b]

[24]When Judah came to the watchtower of the desert and looked toward the throng, they saw only corpses fallen on the ground, with no survivors. [25]Jehoshaphat and his people came to take plunder, and they found an abundance of cattle and personal property, garments and precious vessels. They took so much that they were unable to carry it all; they were three days taking the spoil, so great was it. [26]On the fourth day they held an assembly in the Valley of Beracah—for there they blessed the LORD; therefore that place has ever since been called the Valley of Beracah.* [27]Then all the men of Judah and Jerusalem, with Jehoshaphat at their head, turned back toward Jerusalem celebrating the joyful victory the LORD had given them over their enemies. [28]They came to Jerusalem, to the house of the LORD, with harps, lyres and trumpets. [29]And the fear of God came upon all the kingdoms of the surrounding lands when they heard how the LORD had fought against the enemies of Israel. [30]Thereafter Jehoshaphat's kingdom enjoyed peace, for his God gave him rest on every side.

Jehoshaphat's Other Deeds. [31] [c] Thus Jehoshaphat reigned over Judah. He was thirty-five years old when he became king, and he reigned twenty-five years in Jerusalem. His mother was named Azubah, daughter of Shilhi. [32]He followed the path of his father Asa unswervingly, doing what was right in the LORD's sight. [33]But the high places were not removed, nor as yet had the people fixed their hearts on the God of their fathers.

x Dt 2, 4f. 9f. 18f.—y Is 8, 10.—z Is 7, 9.—a Ps 136, 1.—b Jos 6, 17; Ez 38, 21.—c 31-34: 1 Kgs 22, 41-45.

20, 21: *Holy Appearance:* the Lord, who is with the Israelite army (v 17), manifests himself (the same language is in Ps 29, 2) in bringing Israel the victory (Ex 14, 14. 24).
20, 26: *Beracah:* the Hebrew word for "blessing."

³⁴The rest of the acts of Jehoshaphat, first and last, can be found written in the chronicle of Jehu, son of Hanani, which is inserted in the book of the kings of Israel. ³⁵After this, King Jehoshaphat of Judah allied himself with King Ahaziah of Israel, who did evil. ³⁶ *d* He joined with him in building ships to sail to Tarshish; the fleet was built at Ezion-geber. ³⁷But Eliezer, son of Dodavahu from Mareshah, prophesied against Jehoshaphat, saying, "Because you have joined with Ahaziah, the LORD will shatter your work." And the ships were wrecked and were unable to sail to Tarshish.

CHAPTER 21

¹Jehoshaphat rested with his ancestors; he was buried with them in the City of David. Jehoram, his son, succeeded him as king.*e* ²His brothers, sons of Jehoshaphat, were Azariah, Jehiel, Zechariah, Azariah, Michael and Shephatiah; all these were sons of King Jehoshaphat of Judah. ³Their father gave them numerous gifts of silver, gold and precious objects, together with fortified cities in Judah, but the kingship he gave to Jehoram because he was the first-born.

Evil Deeds of Jehoram. ⁴When Jehoram had come into his father's kingdom and had consolidated his power, he put to the sword all his brothers and also some of the princes of Israel. ⁵ *f* Jehoram was thirty-two years old when he became king, and he reigned eight years in Jerusalem. ⁶He conducted himself like the kings of Israel of the line of Ahab, because one of Ahab's daughters* was his wife. He did evil in the sight of the LORD, ⁷but the LORD would not destroy the house of David because of the covenant he had made with David and because of his promise to give him and his sons a lamp for all time.*g* ⁸ *h* During his time Edom revolted against the sovereignty of Judah; they chose a king of their own. ⁹Thereupon

---

d 36f: 1 Kgs 22, 48f.—e 1 Kgs 22, 51.—f 5ff: 2 Kgs 8, 17ff.—g 1 Kgs 11, 36; 2 Kgs 8, 19.—h 8ff: Gn 27, 40; 2 Kgs 8, 20ff.—i 2 Kgs 8, 24.—j 1-6: 2 Kgs 8, 24-29.

21, 6: *One of Ahab's daughters:* Athaliah. In 2 Chr 22, 2 (and its source, 2 Kgs 8, 26) she is called Omri's daughter; but this should probably be understood in the sense of granddaughter.
21, 12: *Elijah:* the only mention by the Chronicler of this prophet of the northern kingdom of Israel. It is doubtful that Elijah was still living in the reign of Jehoram of Judah; in any case, the attribution of the letter to him is most likely an imaginative filling out of the narration.

Jehoram crossed over with his officers and all the chariots he had. He arose by night and broke through the Edomites when they had surrounded him and the commanders of his chariots. ¹⁰However, Edom has continued in revolt against the sovereignty of Judah down to the present time. Libnah also revolted at that time against Jehoram's sovereignty because he had forsaken the LORD, the God of his fathers. ¹¹He also set up high places in the mountains of Judah; he led the inhabitants of Jerusalem into idolatry and seduced Judah.

Retribution. ¹²He received a letter from the prophet Elijah* with this message: "Thus says the LORD, the God of your ancestor David: 'Because you have not followed the path of your father Jehoshaphat, nor of Asa, king of Judah, ¹³but instead have walked in the way of the kings of Israel and have led Judah and the inhabitants of Jerusalem into idolatry, as did the house of Ahab, and also because you have murdered your brothers of your father's house who were better than you, ¹⁴the LORD will strike your people, your children, your wives, and all that is yours with a great plague; ¹⁵and you shall have severe pains from a disease in your bowels, while your bowels issue forth because of the disease, day after day.' "

¹⁶Then the LORD stirred up against Jehoram the animosity of the Philistines and of the Arabs who bordered on the Ethiopians. ¹⁷They came up against Judah, invaded it, and carried away all the wealth found in the king's palace, along with his sons and his wives; there was left to him only one son, Jehoahaz, his youngest. ¹⁸After these events, the LORD afflicted him with an incurable disease of the bowels. ¹⁹As time went on until a period of two years had elapsed, his bowels issued forth because of the disease and he died in great pain. His people did not make a pyre for him like that of his fathers. ²⁰He was thirty-two years old when he became king, and he reigned eight years in Jerusalem. He departed unloved and was buried in the City of David, but not in the tombs of the kings.*i*

CHAPTER 22

Ahaziah. ¹ *j* Then the inhabitants of Jerusalem made Ahaziah, his youngest son, king in his stead, since all the older sons had been slain by the band that had come into the fort with the Arabs. Thus Ahaziah, son of Jehoram, reigned as king of Judah. [2] He was twenty-two years old when he became king, and he reigned one year in Jerusalem. His mother was named Athaliah, daughter of Omri. [3] He, too, followed the ways of the house of Ahab, because his mother counseled him to act sinfully. [4] To his own destruction, he did evil in the sight of the LORD, as did the house of Ahab, since they were his counselors after the death of his father.

[5] He was also following their counsel when he accompanied Jehoram, son of Ahab, king of Israel, to battle against Hazael, king of Aram, at Ramoth-gilead. There Jehoram was wounded by the Arameans. [6] He returned to Jezreel to be healed of the wounds he had received at Rama in his battle against Hazael, king of Aram. Because of this illness, Ahaziah, son of Jehoram, king of Judah, went down to visit Jehoram, son of Ahab, in Jezreel. [7] Now it was willed by God for Ahaziah's downfall that he should join Jehoram, for after his arrival he rode out with Jehoram to Jehu, son of Nimshi, whom the LORD had anointed to cut down the house of Ahab.[k] [8] While Jehu was executing judgment on the house of Ahab, he also encountered the princes of Judah and the nephews of Ahaziah who were his attendants, and he slew them.[l] [9] Then he looked for Ahaziah himself. They caught him where he was hiding in Samaria and brought him to Jehu, who put him to death. They buried him, for they said, "He was the grandson of Jehoshaphat, who sought the LORD with his whole heart."[m] There remained in Ahaziah's house no one powerful enough to wield the kingship.*

Usurpation of Athaliah. [10] [n] When Athaliah, mother of Ahaziah, learned that her son was dead, she proceeded to kill off all the royal offspring of the house of Judah. [11] But Jehosheba, a royal princess, secretly took Ahaziah's son Joash from among the king's sons who were about to be slain, and put him and his nurse in a bedroom. In this way Jehosheba, who was the daughter of King Jehoram, a sister of Ahaziah, and wife of Jehoiada the priest, hid the child from Athaliah's sight, so that she did not put him to death. [12] For six years he remained hidden with them

in the house of God, while Athaliah ruled over the land.

CHAPTER 23

Athaliah Overthrown. [1] [o] In the seventh year, Jehoiada took courage and entered a conspiracy with certain captains: Azariah, son of Jehoram; Ishmael, son of Jehohanan; Azariah, son of Obed; Masseiah, son of Adaiah; and Elishaphat, son of Zichri. [2] They journeyed about Judah, gathering the Levites from all the cities of Judah and also the heads of the Israelite families. When they had come to Jerusalem, [3] the whole assembly made a covenant with the king in the house of God. Jehoiada said to them: "Here is the king's son who must reign, as the LORD promised concerning the sons of David. [4] This is what you must do: a third of your number, both priests and Levites, who come in on the sabbath must guard the thresholds, [5] another third must be at the king's palace, and the final third at the Foundation Gate, when all the people will be in the courts of the LORD's temple. [6] Let no one enter the LORD's house except the priests and those Levites who are ministering. They may enter because they are holy; but all the other people must observe the prescriptions of the LORD. [7] The Levites shall surround the king on all sides, each with his weapon drawn. Whoever tries to enter the house must be slain. Stay with the king wherever he goes."

[8] The Levites and all Judah did just as Jehoiada the priest commanded. Each brought his men, those who were to come in on the sabbath as well as those who were to depart on the sabbath, since Jehoiada the priest had not dismissed any of the divisions.[p] [9] Jehoiada the priest gave the captains the spears, shields and bucklers of King David which were in the house of God. [10] He stationed all the people, each with his spear in hand, from the southern to the northern extremity of the enclosure, around the altar and the temple on the king's behalf. [11] Then they brought out the king's son, set the crown and the insignia upon him, and made him king. Jehoiada

---

k 2 Kgs 9, 21; 10, 12ff.—l 2 Kgs 10, 12ff.—m 2 Kgs 9, 27f.—n 10ff: 2 Kgs 11, 1ff.—o 1-17. 19ff: 2 Kgs 11, 4-20.—p 2 Kgs 11, 9; 1 Chr 24, 19.

22, 9: This account of the death of Ahaziah of Judah is not derived from 2 Kgs 9, 27f, with which it is at variance.

and his sons anointed him, and they cried, "Long live the king!" 12 When Athaliah heard the din of the people running and acclaiming the king, she went to the people in the temple of the LORD. 13 She looked, and there was the king standing beside his pillar* at the entrance, the officers and the trumpeters around him, and all the people of the land rejoicing and blowing trumpets, while the singers with their musical instruments were leading the acclaim. Athaliah tore her garments and cried out, "Treason! treason!" 14 Then Jehoiada the priest sent out the captains who were in command of the army; he said to them: "Take her outside through the ranks, and if anyone tries to follow her, let him die by the sword. For," the priest continued, "you must not put her to death in the LORD's temple." 15 So they seized her, and when she arrived at the entrance to the Horse Gate of the palace, they put her to death there.

16 Then Jehoiada made a covenant between himself and all the people and the king, that they should be the LORD's people. 17 And all the people went to the temple of Baal and tore it down. They smashed its altars and images, and they slew Mattan, the priest of Baal, before the altars. 18 Then Jehoiada gave the charge of the LORD's temple into the hands of the levitical priests, to whom David had assigned turns in the temple for offering the holocausts of the LORD, as is written in the law of Moses, with rejoicing and song, as David had provided.*q* 19 Moreover, he stationed guards at the gates of the LORD's temple, so that no one unclean in any respect might enter. 20 Then he took the captains, the nobles, the rulers among the people, and all the people of the land, and led the king out of the LORD's house. When they had come within the upper gate of the king's house, they seated

the king upon the royal throne. 21 All the people of the land rejoiced and the city was quiet, now that Athaliah had been put to death by the sword.

CHAPTER 24

The Temple Restored. 1 *r* Joash was seven years old when he became king, and he reigned forty years in Jerusalem. His mother, named Zibiah, was from Beersheba. 2 Joash did what was pleasing to the LORD as long as Jehoiada the priest lived. 3 Jehoiada provided him with two wives, and he became the father of sons and daughters.

4 After some time, Joash decided to restore the LORD's temple. 5 He called together the priests and Levites and said to them: "Go out to all the cities of Judah and collect money* from all Israel that you may repair the house of your God over the years. You must hasten this affair." But the Levites did not hasten. 6 Then the king summoned Jehoiada, who was in charge, and said to him: "Why have you not required the Levites to bring in from Judah and Jerusalem the tax levied by Moses, the servant of the LORD, and by the assembly of Israel, for the tent of the testimony?"*s* 7 For the wicked Athaliah and her sons had damaged the house of God and had even turned over to the Baals the dedicated resources of the LORD's temple.

8 At the king's command, therefore, they made a chest, which they put outside the gate of the LORD's temple.*t* 9 They had it proclaimed throughout Judah and Jerusalem that the tax which Moses, the servant of God, had imposed on Israel in the desert should be brought to the LORD.*u* 10 All the princes and the people rejoiced; they brought what was asked and cast it into the chest until it was filled. 11 Whenever the chest was brought to the royal officials by the Levites and they saw that it contained much money, the royal scribe and an overseer for the high priest came, emptied the chest, then took it back and returned it to its place. This they did day after day until they had collected a large sum of money. 12 Then the king and Jehoiada gave it to the workmen in charge of the labor on the LORD's temple, who hired masons and carpenters to restore the temple, and also iron- and bronze-smiths

---

q 1 Chr 23, 13.—r 1-14: 2 Kgs 12, 1-13.—s Ex 25, 1-9; Neh 10, 33.—t 2 Chr 34, 9.—u Ex 30, 13.

23, 13: *Beside his pillar:* the king had a special place in the eastern gateway of the temple court that contained the altar of holocausts. He occupied this place on feasts and sabbaths at the time of the statutory offerings, or when he made freewill offerings of his own; cf 2 Kgs 11, 4 and also Ez 46, 1-8 for a later reflection of this.

24, 5: *Collect money:* according to 2 Kgs 12, 5, the people themselves brought the money to the temple; it consisted, at least in part, of voluntary contributions. At the time of the Chronicler (see Neh 10, 32) there was a fixed head tax for the upkeep of the temple (2 Chr 34, 9), based on Ex 30, 12-16. This was still in force in New Testament times (Mt 17, 24f).

2Chr

to repair it. [13]The workmen labored, and the task of restoration progressed under their hands. They restored the house of God according to its original form, and reinforced it. [14]After they had finished, they brought the rest of the money to the king and to Jehoiada, who had it made into utensils for the LORD's temple, utensils for the service and the holocausts, and basins and other gold and silver utensils. They offered holocausts in the LORD's temple continually throughout the lifetime of Jehoiada. [15]Jehoiada lived to a ripe old age; he was a hundred and thirty years old when he died. [16]He was buried in the City of David with the kings, because he had done good in Israel, in particular with respect to God and his temple.

Apostasy of King Joash. [17]After the death of Jehoiada, the princes of Judah came and paid homage to the king, and the king then listened to them. [18]They forsook the temple of the LORD, the God of their fathers, and began to serve the sacred poles and the idols; and because of this crime of theirs, wrath came upon Judah and Jerusalem.[v] [19]Although prophets were sent to them to convert them to the LORD, the people would not listen to their warnings. [20]Then the spirit of God possessed Zechariah, son of Jehoiada the priest. He took his stand above the people and said to them: "God says, 'Why are you transgressing the LORD's commands, so that you cannot prosper? Because you have abandoned the LORD, he has abandoned you.'" [21]But they conspired against him, and at the king's order they stoned him to death in the court of the LORD's temple. [22]Thus King Joash was unmindful of the devotion shown him by Jehoiada, Zechariah's father, and slew his son. And as he was dying, he said, "May the LORD see and avenge."

Retribution. [23]At the turn of the year a force of Arameans came up against Joash. They invaded Judah and Jerusalem, did away with all the princes of the people, and sent all their spoil to the king of Damascus.[w] [24]Though the Aramean force came with few men, the LORD surrendered a very large force into their power, because Judah had abandoned the LORD, the God of their fathers. So punishment was meted out

to Joash.[x] [25][y]After the Arameans had departed from him, leaving him in grievous suffering, his servants conspired against him because of the murder of the son of Jehoiada the priest. They killed him on his sickbed. He was buried in the City of David, but not in the tombs of the kings. [26]These conspired against him: Zabad, son of Shimeath from Ammon, and Jehozabad, son of Shimrith from Moab. [27]Of his sons, and the great tribute imposed on him, and of his rebuilding of the house of God, there is a written account in the midrash of the book of the kings. His son Amaziah succeeded him as king.[z]

CHAPTER 25

Campaign in Edom. [1][a]Amaziah was twenty-five years old when he became king, and he reigned twenty-nine years in Jerusalem. His mother, named Jehoaddan, was from Jerusalem. [2]He did what was pleasing in the sight of the LORD, though not wholeheartedly. [3]After he had strengthened his hold on the kingdom, he slew those of his servants who had killed the king, his father; [4]but he did not put their children to death, for he acted according to what is written in the law, in the Book of Moses, as the LORD commanded: "Fathers shall not be put to death for their children, nor children for their fathers; but only for his own guilt shall a man be put to death."[b]

[5]Amaziah mustered Judah and placed them, out of all Judah and Benjamin according to their ancestral houses, under leaders of thousands and of hundreds. When he had counted those of twenty years and over, he found them to be three hundred thousand picked men fit for war, capable of handling lance and shield. [6]He also hired a hundred thousand valiant warriors from Israel for a hundred talents of silver. [7]But a man of God came to him and said: "O king, let not the army of Israel go with you, for the LORD is not with Israel, with any Ephraimite. [8]Instead, go on your own, strongly prepared for the conflict; otherwise the LORD will defeat you in the face of the enemy. It is God who has the power to reinforce or to defeat." [9]Amaziah

v Ex 34, 13.—w 2 Kgs 12, 17f.—x Dt 32, 30.—y 25f: 2 Kgs 12, 21f.—z 2 Kgs 12, 19. 22.—a 1-4: 2 Kgs 14, 1-6.—b Dt 24, 16; 2 Kgs 14, 5f; Ez 18, 20.

answered the man of God, "But what is to be done about the hundred talents that I paid for the troops of Israel?" The man of God replied, "The LORD can give you much more than that." [10] Amaziah then disbanded the troops that had come to him from Ephraim, and sent them home. They, however, became furiously angry with Judah, and returned home blazing with resentment.

[11] Amaziah now assumed command of his army. They proceeded to the Valley of Salt, and there they killed ten thousand men of Seir.[c] [12] The Judahites also brought back another ten thousand alive, whom they led to the summit of the Rock and then cast down, so that they were all crushed. [13] Meanwhile, the mercenaries whom Amaziah had dismissed from battle service with him raided the cities of Judah from Samaria to Beth-horon. They killed three thousand of the inhabitants and took away much booty.

Infidelity of Amaziah. [14] When Amaziah returned from his conquest of the Edomites he brought back with him the gods of the people of Seir, which he set up as his own gods; he bowed down before them and offered sacrifice to them. [15] Then the anger of the LORD blazed out against Amaziah, and he sent a prophet to him who said: "Why have you had recourse to this people's gods that could not save their own people from your hand?" [16] While he was still speaking, however, the king said to him: "Have you been made the king's counselor? Be silent! Why should it be necessary to kill you?" Therefore the prophet desisted. "I know, however," he said, "that God has let you take counsel to your own destruction, because you have done this thing and have refused to hear my counsel."

Retribution. [17] [d] Having taken counsel, King Amaziah of Judah sent messengers to Joash, son of Jehoahaz, son of Jehu, the king of Israel, saying, "Come, let us meet each other face to face." [18] King Joash of Israel sent this reply to King Amaziah of

Judah: "The thistle of the Lebanon sent a message to the cedar of the Lebanon, saying, 'Give your daughter to my son for his wife.' But the wild beasts of the Lebanon passed by and trampled the thistle down.[e] [19] You are thinking, 'See, I have beaten Edom!', and thus ambition makes you proud. Remain at home. Why involve yourself, and Judah with you, in misfortune and failure?" [20] But Amaziah would not listen, for God had determined to hand them over because they had had recourse to the gods of Edom.

[21] Therefore King Joash of Israel advanced and he and King Amaziah met in battle at Beth-shemesh of Judah. [22] There Judah was defeated by Israel, and all the Judean soldiers fled homeward. [23] King Joash of Israel captured Amaziah, king of Judah, son of Joash, son of Jehoahaz, at Beth-shemesh and brought him to Jerusalem. Then he tore down the wall of Jerusalem from the Ephraim Gate to the Corner Gate, a distance of four hundred cubits. [24] He took away all the gold and silver and all the vessels he found in the house of God with Obed-edom,* together with the treasures of the palace, and hostages as well. Then he returned to Samaria.

[25] [f] Amaziah, son of Joash, king of Judah, survived Joash, son of Jehoahaz, king of Israel, by fifteen years. [26] The rest of the acts of Amaziah, first and last, can be found written, as is well known, in the book of the kings of Judah and Israel. [27] Now from the time that Amaziah ceased to follow the LORD, a conspiracy was formed against him in Jerusalem; hence he fled to Lachish. But they pursued him to Lachish and put him to death there. [28] They brought him back on horses and buried him with his ancestors in the City of Judah.*

CHAPTER 26

The Works of Uzziah. [1] [g] All the people of Judah chose Uzziah, though he was but sixteen years of age, and proclaimed him king to succeed his father Amaziah. [2] He rebuilt Elath and restored it to Judah; this was after King Amaziah had gone to rest with his ancestors. [3] Uzziah was sixteen years old when he became king, and he reigned fifty-two years in Jerusalem. His mother, named Jecoliah, was from Jerusa-

---

c 2 Kgs 14, 7.—d 17-24: 2 Kgs 14, 8-14.—e Jgs 9, 7-15; 2 Kgs 14, 9.—f 25-28: 2 Kgs 14, 17-20.—g 1-4: 2 Kgs 14, 21f; 15, 1ff.

25, 24: *With Obed-edom:* possibly a reference to the priest of an Edomite false worship (cf v 14), if not to a levitical family of gatekeepers; cf 1 Chr 15, 18; 26, 12-15.

25, 28: *The City of Judah:* in the parallel passage of 2 Kgs 14, 20, *the City of David.* The Chronicler is referring, by this term, to the capital of Judah, Jerusalem.

lem. [4] He pleased the LORD, just as his father Amaziah had done.

[5] He was prepared to seek God as long as Zechariah* lived, who taught him to fear God; and as long as he sought the LORD, God made him prosper.[h] [6] He went out and fought the Philistines and razed the walls of Gath, Jabneh and Ashdod [and built cities in the district of Ashdod and in Philistia].[i] [7] God helped him against the Philistines, against the Arabs who dwelt in Gurbaal, and against the Meunites. [8] The Ammonites paid tribute to Uzziah and his fame spread as far as Egypt, for he grew stronger and stronger. [9] Moreover, Uzziah built towers in Jerusalem at the Corner Gate, at the Valley Gate, and at the Angle, and he fortified them. [10] He built towers in the desert and dug numerous cisterns, for he had many cattle. He had plowmen in the foothills and the plains, and vinedressers in the highlands and the garden land. He was a lover of the soil.

[11] Uzziah also had a standing army of fit soldiers divided into bands according to the number in which they were mustered by Jeiel the scribe and Maaseiah the recorder, under the command of Hananiah, one of the king's officials. [12] The entire number of family heads over these valiant warriors was two thousand six hundred, [13] and at their disposal was a mighty army of three hundred seven thousand five hundred fighting men of great valor to help the king against his enemies. [14] Uzziah provided for them— for the entire army—bucklers, lances, helmets, breastplates, bows and slingstones. [15] He also built machines in Jerusalem, devices contrived to stand on the towers and at the angles of the walls to shoot arrows and cast large stones. His fame spread far and wide, and his power was ascribed to the marvelous help he had received.

Pride and Fall. [16] But after he had become strong, he became proud to his own destruction and broke faith with the LORD, his God. He entered the temple of the LORD to make an offering on the altar of incense. [17] But Azariah the priest, and with him eighty other priests of the LORD, courageous men, followed him. [18] They opposed King Uzziah, saying to him: "It is not for you, Uzziah, to burn incense to the LORD, but for the priests,

the sons of Aaron, who have been consecrated for this purpose. Leave the sanctuary, for you have broken faith and no longer have a part in the glory that comes from the LORD God."[j] [19] Uzziah, who was holding a censer for burning the incense, became angry, but at the moment he showed his anger to the priests, while they were looking at him in the house of the LORD beside the altar of incense, leprosy broke out on his forehead.[k] [20] Azariah the chief priest and all the other priests examined him, and when they saw that his forehead was leprous, they expelled him from the temple. He himself fled willingly, for the LORD had afflicted him. [21] [l] King Uzziah remained a leper to the day of his death. As a leper he dwelt in a segregated house, for he was excluded from the house of the LORD. Therefore his son Jotham was regent of the palace and ruled the people of the land.

[22] The prophet Isaiah, son of Amos, wrote the rest of the acts of Uzziah, first and last. [23] Uzziah rested with his ancestors; he was buried with them in the field adjoining the royal cemetery, for they said, "He was a leper." His son Jotham succeeded him as king.

CHAPTER 27

Jotham. [1] [m] Jotham was twenty-five years old when he became king, and he reigned sixteen years in Jerusalem. His mother was named Jerusa, daughter of Zadok. [2] He pleased the LORD just as his father Uzziah had done, though he did not enter the temple of the LORD; the people, however, continued to act sinfully.

[3] He built the upper gate of the LORD's house and had much construction done on the wall of Ophel. [4] Moreover, he built cities in the hill country of Judah, and in the forest land he set up fortresses and towers. [5] He fought with the king of the Ammonites and conquered them. That year the Ammonites paid him one hundred talents of silver, together with ten thousand kors of wheat and ten thousand of barley. They brought the same to him

h 2 Chr 24, 2.—i Am 1, 8.—j Ex 30, 7.—k Nm 12, 10.—l 21ff: 2 Kgs 15, 5ff; Lv 13, 46; Nm 19, 20.—m 1-3: 2 Kgs 15, 32-35.

26, 5: *Zechariah:* this person, not otherwise identified, is referred to in language suggesting a pious layman rather than a priest or prophet; cf 2 Chr 29, 1.

also in the second and in the third year. ⁶Thus Jotham continued to grow strong because he lived resolutely in the presence of the LORD, his God. ⁷ *n* The rest of the acts of Jotham, his wars and his activities, can be found written in the book of the kings of Israel and Judah. ⁸He was twenty-five years old when he became king, and he reigned sixteen years in Jerusalem. ⁹Jotham rested with his ancestors and was buried in the City of David, and his son Ahaz succeeded him as king.

III: REFORMS OF HEZEKIAH AND JOSIAH

CHAPTER 28

Impiety of Ahaz. ¹ *o* Ahaz was twenty years old when he became king, and he reigned sixteen years in Jerusalem. He did not please the LORD as his forefather David had done, ²but conducted himself like the kings of Israel and even made molten idols of the Baals. ³Moreover, he offered sacrifice in the Valley of Ben-hinnom, and immolated his sons by fire according to the abominable practice of the nations which the LORD had cleared out before the Israelites. *p* ⁴He offered sacrifice and incense on the high places, on hills, and under every leafy tree.

Retribution. ⁵Therefore the LORD, his God, delivered him into the power of the king of Aram. The Arameans defeated him and carried away captive a large number of his people, whom they brought to Damascus. He was also delivered into the power of the king of Israel, who defeated him with great slaughter. *q* ⁶For Pekah, son of Remaliah, slew one hundred and twenty thousand of Judah in a single day, all of them valiant men, because they had abandoned the LORD, the God of their fathers. ⁷Zichri, an Ephraimite warrior, killed Maaseiah, the king's son, and Azrikam, the master of the palace, and also Elkanah, who was second to the king. ⁸The Israelites took away as captives two hundred thousand of their brethren's wives, sons and daughters; they also took from them

much plunder, which they brought to Samaria.

The Prophecy of Oded. ⁹In Samaria there was a prophet of the LORD by the name of Oded. He went out to meet the army returning to Samaria and said to them: "It was because the LORD, the God of your fathers, was angry with Judah that he delivered them into your hands. You, however, have slaughtered them with a fury that has reached up to heaven. ¹⁰And now you are planning to make the children of Judah and Jerusalem your slaves and bondwomen. Are not you yourselves, therefore, guilty of a crime against the LORD your God? ¹¹Now listen to me: send back the captives you have carried off from among your brethren, for the burning anger of the LORD is upon you." ¹²At this, some of the Ephraimite leaders, Azariah, son of Johanan, Berechiah, son of Meshillemoth, Jehizkiah, son of Shallum, and Amasa, son of Hadlai, themselves stood up in opposition to those who had returned from the war. ¹³They said to them: "Do not bring the captives here, for what you propose will make us guilty before the LORD and increase our sins and our guilt. Our guilt is already great, and there is a burning anger upon Israel." ¹⁴Therefore the soldiers left their captives and the plunder before the princes and the whole assembly. ¹⁵Then the men just named proceeded to help the captives. All of them who were naked they clothed from the booty; they clothed them, put sandals on their feet, gave them food and drink, anointed them, and all who were weak they set on asses. They brought them to Jericho, the city of palms, to their brethren. Then they returned to Samaria. *r*

Further Sins of Ahaz. ¹⁶At that time King Ahaz sent an appeal for help to the kings of Assyria. *s* ¹⁷The Edomites had returned, attacked Judah, and carried off captives. *t* ¹⁸The Philistines too had raided the cities of the foothills and the Negeb of Judah; they captured Bethshemesh, Aijalon, Gederoth, Soco and its dependencies, Timnah and its dependencies, and Gimzo and its dependencies, and occupied them. ¹⁹For the LORD had brought Judah low because of Ahaz, king of Israel,* who let Judah go its own way and proved utterly faithless to the

2Chr

---

n 7-9: 2 Kgs 15, 36ff.—o 1-4: 2 Kgs 16, 1-4.—p 2 Kgs 16, 3; Lv 18, 21.—q 2 Kgs 16, 5; Is 7, 1-9.—r Lk 10, 25-37.—s 2 Kgs 16, 7.—t 2 Kgs 16, 6.

28, 19: *Ahaz, king of Israel:* in the period of the divided kingdom the term *king of Israel* would elsewhere mean "king of the northern Kingdom of Israel."

LORD. ²⁰Tilgath-pilneser, king of Assyria, did indeed come to him, but to oppress him rather than to help him.ᵘ ²¹Though Ahaz plundered the LORD's house and the houses of the king and the princes to make payment to the king of Assyria, it availed him nothing.ᵛ ²²While he was already in distress, the same King Ahaz became even more unfaithful to the LORD. ²³He sacrificed to the gods of Damascus who had defeated him, saying, "Since it was the gods of the kings of Aram who helped them, I will sacrifice to them that they may help me also." However, they only caused further disaster to him and to all Israel.ʷ ²⁴Ahaz gathered up the utensils of God's house and broke them in pieces. He closed the doors of the LORD's house and had altars made for himself in every corner of Jerusalem.ˣ ²⁵In every city throughout Judah he set up high places to offer sacrifice to other gods. Thus he angered the LORD, the God of his fathers. ²⁶ʸ The rest of his deeds and his activities, first and last, can be found written in the book of the kings of Judah and Israel. ²⁷Ahaz rested with his ancestors and was buried in Jerusalem—in the city, for they did not bring him to the tombs of the kings of Israel. His son Hezekiah succeeded him as king.

CHAPTER 29

Reforms of Hezekiah. ¹ ᶻ Hezekiah was twenty-five years old when he became king, and he reigned twenty-nine years in Jerusalem. His mother was named Abia, daughter of Zechariah. ²He pleased the LORD just as his forefather David had done. ³It was he who, in the first month of the first year of his reign, opened the doors of the LORD's house and repaired them.ᵃ ⁴He summoned the priests and Levites, gathered them in the open space to the east, ⁵and said to them: "Listen to me, you Levites! Sanctify yourselves now and sanctify the house of the LORD, the God of your fathers, and clean out the filth from the sanctuary. ⁶Our fathers acted faithlessly and did evil in the eyes of the LORD, our God. They abandoned him, turned away their faces from the LORD's dwelling, and turned their backs on him. ⁷They also closed the doors of the vestibule, extin-

guished the lamps, and refused to burn incense and offer holocausts in the sanctuary to the honor of the God of Israel.ᵇ ⁸ ᶜ Therefore the anger of the LORD has come upon Judah and Jerusalem; he has made them an object of terror, astonishment and mockery, as you see with your own eyes. ⁹For our fathers, as you know, fell by the sword, and our sons, our daughters and our wives have been taken captive because of this. ¹⁰Now, I intend to make a covenant with the LORD, the God of Israel, that his burning anger may withdraw from us. ¹¹My sons, be not negligent any longer, for it is you whom the LORD has chosen to stand before him, to minister to him, to be his ministers and to offer incense."

¹²Then the Levites arose: Mahath, son of Amasai, and Joel, son of Azariah, descendants of the Kohathites; of the sons of Merari: Kish, son of Abdi, and Azariah, son of Jehallel; of the Gershonites: Joah, son of Zimmah, and Eden, son of Joah; ¹³of the sons of Elizaphan: Shimri and Jeuel; of the sons of Asaph: Zechariah and Mattaniah; ¹⁴of the sons of Heman: Jehuel and Shimei; of the sons of Jeduthun: Shemiah and Uzziel. ¹⁵They gathered their brethren together and sanctified themselves; then they came as the king had ordered, to cleanse the LORD's house in keeping with his words.

¹⁶The priests entered the interior of the LORD's house to cleanse it; and whatever they found in the LORD's temple that was unclean they brought out to the court of the LORD's house, where the Levites took it from them and carried it out to the Kidron Valley. ¹⁷They began the work of consecration on the first day of the first month, and on the eighth day of the month they arrived at the vestibule of the LORD; they consecrated the LORD's house during eight days, and on the sixteenth day of the first month, they had finished. ¹⁸Then they went inside to King Hezekiah and said: "We have cleansed the entire house of the LORD, the altar of holocausts with all its utensils, and the table for the showbread with all its utensils. ¹⁹All the articles which King Ahaz during his reign had thrown away because

u 2 Kgs 16, 10; Is 7, 17-20; 8, 5-8.—v 2 Kgs 16, 8.—w 2 Kgs 16, 12f; Is 10, 20.—x 2 Chr 29, 3; 30, 14; 2 Kgs 16, 17.—y 26f: 2 Kgs 16, 19f.—z 1ff: 2 Kgs 18, 1ff.—a 2 Chr 28, 24.—b 2 Kgs 16, 15.—c 8f: Lv 26, 32f; Dt 28, 25; Jer 25, 18.

of his apostasy, we have restored and consecrated, and they are now before the LORD's altar."

The Rite of Expiation. ²⁰Then King Hezekiah hastened to convoke the princes of the city and went up to the LORD's house. ²¹Seven bulls, seven rams, seven lambs and seven he-goats were brought for a sin offering for the kingdom, for the sanctuary, and for Judah, and he ordered the sons of Aaron, the priests, to offer them on the altar of the LORD. ²²They slaughtered the bulls, and the priests collected the blood and cast it on the altar. Then they slaughtered the rams and cast the blood on the altar; then they slaughtered the lambs and cast the blood on the altar. ²³Then the he-goats for the sin offering were led before the king and the assembly, who laid their hands upon them. ²⁴The priests then slaughtered them and offered their blood on the altar to atone for the sin of all Israel; for "The holocaust and the sin offering," the king had said, "is for all Israel."

²⁵He stationed the Levites in the LORD's house with cymbals, harps and lyres according to the prescriptions of David, of Gad the king's seer, and of Nathan the prophet; for the prescriptions were from the LORD though his prophets. ²⁶The Levites were stationed with the instruments of David, and the priests with the trumpets. ²⁷Then Hezekiah ordered the holocaust to be sacrificed on the altar, and in the same instant that the holocaust began, they also began the song of the LORD, to the accompaniment of the trumpets and the instruments of David, king of Israel. ²⁸The entire assembly prostrated itself, and they continued to sing the song and to sound the trumpets until the holocaust had been completed. ²⁹As the holocaust was completed, the king and all who were with him knelt and prostrated themselves. ³⁰King Hezekiah and the princes then commanded the Levites to sing the praises of the LORD in the words of David and of Asaph the seer. They sang praises till their joy was full, then fell down and prostrated themselves.

³¹Hezekiah now spoke out this command: "You have undertaken a work for the LORD. Approach, and bring forward the sacrifices and thank offerings for the

house of the LORD." Then the assembly brought forward the sacrifices and thank offerings and all the holocausts which were free-will offerings. ³²The number of holocausts that the assembly brought forward was seventy oxen, one hundred rams, and two hundred lambs: all of these as a holocaust to the LORD. ³³As consecrated gifts there were six hundred oxen and three thousand sheep. ³⁴Since the priests were too few in number to be able to skin all the victims for the holocausts, their brethren the Levites assisted them until the task was completed and the priests had sanctified themselves; the Levites, in fact, were more willing than the priests to sanctify themselves. *d* ³⁵Also, the holocausts were many, along with the fat of the peace offerings and the libations for the holocausts. Thus the service of the house of the LORD was reestablished. ³⁶Hezekiah and all the people rejoiced over what God had reestablished for the people, and at how suddenly this had been done.

CHAPTER 30

Invitation to the Passover. ¹Hezekiah sent a message to all Israel and Judah, and even wrote letters to Ephraim and Manasseh saying that they should come to the house of the LORD in Jerusalem to celebrate the Passover in honor of the LORD, the God of Israel. *e* ² *f* The king, his princes, and the entire assembly in Jerusalem had agreed to celebrate the Passover during the second month, ³for they could not celebrate it at the time of the restoration: the priests had not sanctified themselves in sufficient numbers, and the people were not gathered at Jerusalem. ⁴When this proposal had been approved by the king and the entire assembly, ⁵they issued a decree to be proclaimed throughout all Israel from Beer-sheba to Dan, that everyone should come to Jerusalem to celebrate the Passover in honor of the LORD, the God of Israel; for not many had kept it in the manner prescribed. ⁶Accordingly, the couriers, with the letters written by the king and his princes, traversed all Israel and Judah, and at the king's command they said: "Israelites, return to the LORD, the God of Abraham, Isaac and Israel, that he may return to you, the remnant left from the hands of

---

d 1 Chr 15, 12.—e Ex 12, 1-28.—f 2ff: Nm 9, 6-13.

the Assyrian kings. ⁷Be not like your fathers and your brethren who proved faithless to the LORD, the God of their fathers, so that he delivered them over to desolation, as you yourselves now see.ᵍ ⁸Be not obstinate, as your fathers were; extend your hands to the LORD and come to his sanctuary that he has consecrated forever, and serve the LORD, your God, that he may turn away his burning anger from you. ⁹For when you return to the LORD, your brethren and your children will find mercy with their captors and return to this land; for merciful and compassionate is the LORD, your God, and he will not turn away his face from you if you return to him."ʰ

¹⁰So the couriers passed from city to city in the land of Ephraim and Manasseh and as far as Zebulun, but they were derided and scofffed at. ¹¹Nevertheless, some from Asher, Manasseh and Zebulun humbled themselves and came to Jerusalem. ¹²In Judah, however, the power of God brought it about that the people were of one mind to carry out the command of the king and the princes in accordance with the word of the LORD. ¹³Thus many people gathered in Jerusalem to celebrate the feast of Unleavened Bread in the second month; it was a very great assembly.

The Passover Celebrated. ¹⁴They proceeded to take down the altars that were in Jerusalem; also they removed all the altars of incense and cast them into the Kidron Valley.ⁱ ¹⁵They slaughtered the Passover on the fourteenth day of the second month. The priests and Levites, touched with shame, sanctified themselves and brought holocausts into the house of the LORD. ¹⁶They stood in the places prescribed for them according to the law of Moses, the man of God. The priests sprinkled the blood given them by the Levites; ¹⁷for many in the assembly had not sanctified themselves, and the Levites were in charge of slaughtering the Passover victims for all who were unclean and therefore could not consecrate them to the LORD.ʲ ¹⁸The greater part of the people, in fact, chiefly from Ephraim, Manasseh, Issachar and Zebulun, had not cleansed themselves. Nevertheless they ate the Passover, contrary to the prescription; for Hezekiah prayed for them, saying, "May the LORD, who is good, grant pardon to

¹⁹everyone who has resolved to seek God, the LORD, the God of his fathers, though he be not clean as holiness requires." ²⁰The LORD heard Hezekiah and spared the people.

²¹Thus the Israelites who were in Jerusalem celebrated the feast of Unleavened Bread with great rejoicing for seven days, and the Levites and the priests sang the praises of the LORD day after day with all their strength. ²²Hezekiah spoke encouragingly to all the Levites who had shown themselves well skilled in the service of the LORD. And when they had completed the seven days of festival, slaying peace offerings and singing praises to the LORD, the God of their fathers, ²³the whole assembly agreed to celebrate another seven days. With joy, therefore, they continued the festivity seven days longer. ²⁴King Hezekiah of Judah had contributed a thousand bulls and seven thousand sheep to the assembly, and the princes had contributed to the assembly a thousand bulls and ten thousand sheep. The priests sanctified themselves in great numbers, ²⁵and the whole assembly of Judah rejoiced, together with the priests and Levites and the rest of the assembly that had come from Israel, as well as the sojourners from the land of Israel and those that lived in Judah. ²⁶There was great rejoicing in Jerusalem, for since the days of Solomon, son of David, king of Israel, there had not been the like in the city. ²⁷Then the levitical priests rose and blessed the people; their voice was heard and their prayer reached heaven, God's holy dwelling.

CHAPTER 31

Liturgical Reform. ¹After all this was over, those Israelites who had been present went forth to the cities of Judah and smashed the sacred pillars, cut down the sacred poles, and tore down the high places and altars throughout Judah, Benjamin, Ephraim and Manasseh, until all were destroyed. Then the Israelites returned to their various cities, each to his own possession.ᵏ

²Hezekiah reestablished the classes of the priests and the Levites according to their former classification, assigning to each priest and Levite his proper service

g Acts 7, 51.—h 1 Kgs 8, 50.—i 2 Chr 28, 42f.—j 2 Chr 35, 6.—k 2 Chr 34, 3f; 2 Kgs 18, 4.

whether in regard to holocausts or peace offerings, thanksgiving or praise, or ministering in the gates of the encampment of the LORD. [3] From his own wealth the king allotted a portion for holocausts, those of morning and evening and those on sabbaths, new moons and festivals, as prescribed in the law of the LORD.[l] [4] He also commanded the people living in Jerusalem to provide the support of the priests and Levites, that they might devote themselves entirely to the law of the LORD.

[5] As soon as the order was promulgated, the Israelites brought, in great quantities, the best of their grain, wine, oil and honey, and all the produce of the fields; they gave a generous tithe of everything.[m] [6] Israelites and Judahites living in other cities of Judah also brought in tithes of oxen, sheep, and things that had been consecrated to the LORD, their God; these they brought in and set out in heaps.[n] [7] It was in the third month that they began to establish these heaps, and they completed them in the seventh month.* [8] When Hezekiah and the princes had come and seen the heaps, they blessed the LORD and his people Israel. [9] Then Hezekiah questioned the priests and the Levites concerning the heaps, [10] and the priest Azariah, head of the house of Zadoc, answered him, "Since they began to bring the offerings to the house of the LORD, we have eaten to the full and have had much left over, for the LORD has blessed his people. This great supply is what was left over."[o] [11] Hezekiah then gave orders that chambers should be constructed in the house of the LORD. When this had been done, [12] the offerings, tithes and consecrated things were deposited there in safekeeping. The overseer of these things was Conaniah the Levite, and his brother Shimei was second in charge. [13] Jehiel, Azaziah, Nathan, Asahel, Jerimoth, Jozabad, Eliel, Ismachiah, Mahath and Benaiah were supervisors subject to Conaniah and his brother Shimei by appointment of King Hezekiah and of Azariah, the prefect of the house of

God. [14] Kore, the son of Imnah, a Levite and the keeper of the eastern gate, was in charge of the free-will gifts made to God; he distributed the offerings made to the LORD and the most holy of the consecrated things. [15] Under him in the priestly cities were Eden, Miniamin, Jeshua, Shemaiah, Amariah and Shecaniah, who faithfully made the distribution to their brethren, great and small alike, according to their classes.

[16] There was also a register by ancestral houses of males thirty years of age and over, for all priests who were eligible to enter the house of the LORD according to the daily rule to fulfill their service in the order of their classes.[p] [17] The priests were inscribed in their family records according to their ancestral houses, and the Levites of twenty years and over according to their various offices and classes.[q] [18] A distribution was also made to all who were inscribed in the family records, for their little ones, wives, sons and daughters—thus for the entire assembly, since they were to sanctify themselves by sharing faithfully in the consecrated things. [19] The sons of Aaron, the priests who lived on the lands attached to their cities, had in every city men designated by name to distribute portions to every male among the priests and to every Levite listed in the family records. [20] This Hezekiah did in all Judah. He did what was good, upright and faithful before the LORD, his God. [21] Everything that he undertook, for the service of the house of God or for the law and the commandments, was to do the will of his God. He did this wholeheartedly, and he prospered.[r]

CHAPTER 32

Invasion of Sennacherib. [1] But after he had proved his fidelity by such deeds, Sennacherib, king of Assyria, came. He invaded Judah, besieged the fortified cities, and proposed to take them by storm.[s] [2] When Hezekiah saw that Sennacherib was coming with the intention of attacking Jerusalem, [3] he decided in counsel with his princes and warriors to stop the waters of the springs outside the city. When they had pledged him their support, [4] [t] a large crowd was gathered which stopped all the springs and also the running stream in the valley nearby. For they

---

l 1 Chr 29, 3; Ez 45, 17; Nm 28—29.—m Nm 18, 8-24; Dt 14, 22f.—n Nm 12, 44-47; 13, 10-13.—o Lv 25, 19-22.—p 1 Chr 23, 3f.—q 1 Chr 23, 6-24.—r Ps 119, 2f.—s 2 Kgs 18, 13.—t Is 22, 9. 11.

31, 7: *Third month . . . seventh month:* between the feast of Pentecost and that of Booths, an interval without rain in Palestine, at the end of which the problem of storage (v 11) would become more urgent.

said, "Why should the kings of Assyria come and find an abundance of water?" [5] He then looked to his defenses: he rebuilt the wall where it was broken down, raised towers upon it, and built another wall outside. He strengthened the Millo of the City of David and had a great number of spears and shields prepared. [u] [6] Then he appointed army commanders over the people. He gathered them together in his presence in the open space at the gate of the city and encouraged them with these words: [7] "Be brave and steadfast; do not be afraid or dismayed because of the king of Assyria and all the throng that is coming with him, for there is more with us than with him. [v] [8] For he has only an arm of flesh, but we have the LORD, our God, to help us and to fight our battles." And the people took confidence from the words of King Hezekiah of Judah. [w]

Threat of Sennacherib. [9] [x] After this, while Sennacherib, king of Assyria, himself remained at Lachish with all his forces, he sent his officials to Jerusalem with this message for King Hezekiah of Judah, and all the Judahites who were in Jerusalem: [10] "King Sennacherib of Assyria has this to say: On what are you relying, while you remain under siege in Jerusalem? [11] Has not Hezekiah deceived you, delivering you over to a death of famine and thirst, by his claim that 'the LORD, our God, will save us from the grasp of the king of Assyria'? [12] Has not this same Hezekiah removed his high places and altars and commanded Judah and Jerusalem, 'You shall prostrate yourselves before one altar only, and on it alone you shall offer incense'? [13] Do you not know what my fathers and I have done to all the peoples of other lands? Were the gods of the nations in those lands able to save their lands from my hand? [14] Who among all the gods of those nations which my fathers put under the ban was able to save his people from my hand? Will your god, then, be able to save you from my hand? [15] Let not Hezekiah mislead you further and deceive you in any such way. Do not believe him! Since no other god of any other nation or kingdom has been able to save his people from my hand or the hands of my fathers, how much the less shall your god save you from my hand!"

[16] His officials said still more against the LORD God and against his servant Hezekiah, [17] for he had written letters to deride the LORD, the God of Israel, speaking of him in these terms: "As the gods of the nations in other lands have not saved their people from my hand, neither shall Hezekiah's god save his people from my hand." [y] [18] In a loud voice they shouted in the Judean language to the people of Jerusalem who were on the wall, to frighten and terrify them so that they might capture their city. [19] They spoke of the God of Israel as though he were one of the gods of the other peoples of the earth, a work of human hands. [20] But because of this, King Hezekiah and the prophet Isaiah, son of Amos, prayed and called out to heaven. [z]

Defeat of Sennacherib. [21] Then the LORD sent an angel, who destroyed every valiant warrior, leader and commander in the camp of the Assyrian king, so that he had to return shamefaced to his own country. And when he entered the temple of his god, some of his own offspring struck him down there with the sword. [a] [22] Thus the LORD saved Hezekiah and the inhabitants of Jerusalem from the hand of Sennacherib, king of Assyria, as from every other power; he gave them rest on every side. [23] Many brought gifts for the LORD to Jerusalem and costly objects for King Hezekiah of Judah, who thereafter was exalted in the eyes of all the nations. [b]

Hezekiah's Other Deeds. [24] In those days Hezekiah became mortally ill. He prayed to the LORD, who answered him by giving him a sign. [c] [25] Hezekiah, however, did not then discharge his debt of gratitude, for he had become proud. Therefore anger descended upon him and upon Judah and Jerusalem. [26] [d] But then Hezekiah humbled himself for his pride—both he and the inhabitants of Jerusalem; and therefore the LORD did not vent his anger on them during the time of Hezekiah.

[27] [e] Hezekiah possessed very great wealth and glory. He had treasuries made for his silver, gold, precious stones, spices,

u Neh 2, 17f.—v 2 Chr 14, 10; 20, 6-12.—w Is 31, 3.—x 9-20: 2 Kgs 18, 17-37; Is 36, 1-22.—y 2 Kgs 19, 9-13; Is 37, 9-13.—z 2 Kgs 19, 14-19; Is 37, 14-20.—a 2 Kgs 19, 35ff; Is 37, 36ff.—b 2 Chr 14, 6.—c 2 Kgs 20, 1-11; Is 38, 1-8.—d 26. 31: 2 Kgs 20, 12-19; Is 39, 1-8.—e 27f: 2 Kgs 20, 13; Is 39, 2.

jewels, and other precious things of all kinds; 28 also storehouses for the harvest of grain, for wine and oil, and barns for the various kinds of cattle and for the flocks. 29 He built cities for himself, and he acquired sheep and oxen in great numbers, for God gave him very great riches. 30 This same Hezekiah stopped the upper outflow of water from Gihon and led it underground westward to the City of David. Hezekiah prospered in all his undertakings.*f* 31 Nevertheless, in respect to the ambassadors [princes] sent to him from Babylon to investigate the sign that had occurred in the land, God forsook him to test him, that he might know all that was in his heart.

32 The rest of Hezekiah's acts, including his pious works, can be found written in the Vision of the Prophet Isaiah, son of Amos, and in the book of the kings of Judah and Israel. 33 Hezekiah rested with his ancestors; he was buried at the approach to the tombs* of the descendants of David. All Judah and the inhabitants of Jerusalem paid him honor at his death. His son Manasseh succeeded him as king.

CHAPTER 33

Impiety of Manasseh. 1 *g* Manasseh was twelve years old when he became king, and he reigned fifty-five years in Jerusalem. 2 He did evil in the sight of the LORD, following the abominable practices of the nations whom the LORD had cleared out of the way of the Israelites. 3 He rebuilt the high places which his father Hezekiah had torn down, erected altars for the Baals, made sacred poles, and prostrated himself before the whole host of heaven and worshiped them. 4 He even built altars in the temple of the

LORD, of which the LORD had said, "In Jerusalem shall my name be forever": 5 he built altars to the whole host of heaven in the two courts of the LORD's house. 6 It was he, too, who immolated his sons by fire in the Valley of Ben-hinnom. He practiced augury, divination and magic, and appointed necromancers and diviners of spirits, so that he provoked the LORD with the great evil that he did in his sight. 7 He placed an idol that he had carved in the house of God, of which God had said to David and his son Solomon: "In this house and in Jerusalem which I have chosen from all the tribes of Israel I shall place my name forever. 8 I will not again allow Israel's feet to leave the land which I assigned to your fathers, provided they are careful to observe all that I commanded them, keeping the whole law and the statutes and the ordinances given by Moses." 9 Manasseh misled Judah and the inhabitants of Jerusalem into doing even greater evil than the nations which the LORD had destroyed at the coming of the Israelites. 10 The LORD spoke to Manasseh and his people, but they paid no attention.

His Conversion. 11 *h* Therefore the LORD brought against them the army commanders of the Assyrian king; they took Manasseh with hooks, shackled him with chains, and transported him to Babylon.* 12 In this distress, he began to appease the LORD, his God. He humbled himself abjectly before the God of his fathers 13 and prayed to him.* The LORD let himself be won over: he heard his prayer and restored him to his kingdom in Jerusalem. Then Manasseh understood that the LORD is indeed God.

14 Afterward he built an outer wall for the City of David to the west of Gihon in the valley, extending to the Fish Gate and encircling Ophel; he built it very high. He stationed army officers in all the fortified cities of Judah. 15 He removed the foreign gods and the idol from the LORD's house and all the altars he had built on the mount of the LORD's house and in Jerusalem, and he cast them outside the city.*i* 16 He restored the altar of the LORD, and sacrificed on it peace offerings and thank offerings, and commanded Judah to serve the LORD, the God of Israel. 17 Though the people con-

---

f 2 Kgs 20, 20f.—g 1-10: 2 Kgs 21, 1-9.—h Jb 36, 7f; Ez 19, 9.—i 2 Chr 14, 2.

32, 33: *The approach to the tombs:* literally, "the ascent of the tombs," which may mean "the upper section of the tombs," their most prominent and honored place.

33, 11: There is no evidence elsewhere for an imprisonment of King Manasseh in Babylon. However, according to the Assyrian inscriptions, he paid tribute to the Assyrian kings Esarhaddon (680-669 B.C.) and Asshurbanipal (668-627 B.C.). He may well have been obliged to go to Nineveh to take the oath of allegiance as vassal to the king of Assyria.

33, 13: *And prayed to him:* these words led an unknown writer to compose the apocryphal "Prayer of Manasseh," which is added as an appendix to many editions of the Vulgate Bible and is used in the public prayers of the church.

tinued to sacrifice on the high places, they now did so to the LORD, their God.

[18] *j* The rest of the acts of Manasseh, his prayer to his God, and the words of the seers who spoke to him in the name of the LORD, the God of Israel, can be found written in the chronicles of the kings of Israel. [19] His prayer and how his supplication was heard, all his sins and his infidelity, the sites where he built high places and erected sacred poles and carved images before he humbled himself, all can be found written down in the history of his seers. [20] Manasseh rested with his ancestors and was buried in his own palace. His son Amon succeeded him as king.

Amon. [21] *k* Amon was twenty-two years old when he became king, and he reigned two years in Jerusalem. [22] He did evil in the sight of the LORD, just as his father Manasseh had done. Amon offered sacrifice to all the idols which his father Manasseh had made, and worshiped them. [23] Moreover, he did not humble himself before the LORD as his father Manasseh had done; on the contrary, Amon only increased his guilt. [24] His servants conspired against him and put him to death in his own house. [25] But the people of the land slew all those who had conspired against King Amon, and then they, the people of the land, made his son Josiah king in his stead.

CHAPTER 34

Reforms of Josiah. [1] *l* Josiah was eight years old when he became king, and he reigned thirty-one years in Jerusalem. [2] He pleased the LORD, following the path of his ancestor David. [3] *m* In the eighth year of his reign, while he was still a youth, he began to seek after the God of his forefather David, and in his twelfth year* he began to purge Judah and Jerusalem of the high places, the sacred poles and the carved and molten images. [4] In his presence, the altars of the Baals were destroyed; the incense stands erected above them were torn down; the sacred poles and the carved and molten images were shattered and beaten into dust, which was strewn over the tombs of those who had sacrificed to them; [5] and the bones of the priests he burned upon their altars. Thus he purged Judah and Jerusalem. [6] He did

likewise in the cities of Manasseh, Ephraim, Simeon, and in the ruined villages of the surrounding country as far as Naphtali; [7] he destroyed the altars, broke up the sacred poles and carved images and beat them into dust, and tore down the incense stands throughout the land of Israel. Then he returned to Jerusalem.

The Temple Restored. [8] *n* In the eighteenth year of his reign, in order to cleanse the temple as well as the land, he sent Shaphan, son of Azaliah, Maaseiah, the ruler of the city, and Joah, son of Joahaz, the chamberlain, to restore the house of the LORD, his God. [9] They came to Hilkiah the high priest and turned over the money brought to the house of God which the Levites, the guardians of the threshold, had collected from Manasseh, Ephraim, and all the remnant of Israel, as well as from all of Judah, Benjamin, and the inhabitants of Jerusalem. *o* [10] They turned it over to the master workmen in the house of the LORD, and these in turn used it to pay the workmen in the LORD's house who were restoring and repairing the temple. [11] They also gave it to the carpenters and the masons to buy hewn stone and timber for the tie beams and rafters of the buildings which the kings of Judah had allowed to fall into ruin. [12] The men worked faithfully at their tasks; their overseers were Jahath and Obadiah, Levites of the line of Merari, and Zechariah and Meshullam, of the Kohathites, who directed them. All those Levites who were skillful with musical instruments [13] were in charge of the men who carried the burdens, and they directed all the workers in every kind of labor. Some of the other Levites were scribes, officials and gatekeepers.

The Finding of the Law. [14] *p* When they brought out the money that had been deposited in the house of the LORD, Hilkiah the priest found the book of the law of

---

j 18. 20: 2 Kgs 21, 17f.—k 21-25: 2 Kgs 21, 19-26.—l 1f: 2 Kgs 22, 1f.—m 3-7: 2 Chr 14, 1-4; 31, 1; 2 Kgs 23, 4-20.—n 8-13: 2 Kgs 22, 3-7.—o 2 Chr 24, 8f.—p 14-28: 2 Kgs 22, 8-20.

34, 3: *In his twelfth year:* c. 628 B.C., the year after Asshurbanipal's death, when Judah could free itself from Assyrian domination. From 2 Kgs 22, 1—23, 25 alone, one might think that Josiah's reform began only after the discovery of the book of the law in the temple, in the eighteenth year of his reign. But the Chronicler is no doubt right in placing the beginning of the reform at an earlier period. The very repair of the temple, which led to the finding of the book of the law, must have been occasioned by a cultic reform.

the LORD given through Moses. [15] He reported this to Shaphan the scribe, saying, "I have found the book of the law in the house of the LORD." Hilkiah gave the book to Shaphan, [16] who brought it to the king at the same time that he was making his report to him. He said, "Your servants are doing everything that has been entrusted to them; [17] they have turned into bullion the metals deposited in the LORD's house and have handed it over to the overseers and the workmen." [18] Then Shaphan the scribe announced to the king, "Hilkiah the priest has given me a book." And Shaphan read from it before the king.

[19] When the king heard the words of the law, he tore his garments [20] and issued this command to Hilkiah, to Ahikam, son of Shaphan, to Abdon, son of Michah, to Shaphan the scribe, and to Asaiah, the king's servant: [21] "On behalf of myself and those who are left in Israel and Judah, go, consult the LORD concerning the words of the book that has been found. For the anger of the LORD has been set furiously ablaze against us, since our fathers have not kept the word of the LORD and have not done all that is written in this book." [22] Then Hilkiah and the other men from the king went to the prophetess Huldah, the wife of Shallum, son of Tokhath, son of Hasrah, the guardian of the wardrobe; she dwelt in Jerusalem, in the new quarter. They spoke to her as they had been instructed, [23] and she said to them: "Thus says the LORD, the God of Israel: 'Tell the one who sent you to me, [24] The LORD says: I am prepared to bring evil upon this place and upon its inhabitants, all the curses written in the book that has been read before the king of Judah. [25] Because they have abandoned me and have offered incense to other gods, provoking me by every deed that they have performed, my anger is ablaze against this place and cannot be extinguished.'

[26] "But to the king of Judah who sent you to consult the LORD, give this response: 'Thus says the LORD, the God of Israel, concerning the threats you have heard: [27] Because you were heartsick and have humbled yourself before God on

hearing his words spoken against this place and its inhabitants; because you have humbled yourself before me, have torn your garments, and have wept before me, I in turn have listened—so declares the LORD. [28] I will gather you to your ancestors and you shall be taken to your grave in peace. Your eyes shall not see all the evil I will bring upon this place and upon its inhabitants.' "

They brought back this message to the king.

Renewal of the Covenant. [29] *q* The king now convened all the elders of Judah and Jerusalem. [30] He went up to the house of the LORD with all the men of Judah and the inhabitants of Jerusalem, the priests, the Levites, and all the people, great and small; and he had read aloud to them the entire text of the book of the covenant that had been found in the house of the LORD. [31] Standing at his post,* the king made a covenant before the LORD to follow the LORD and to keep his commandments, decrees, and statutes with his whole heart and soul, thus observing the terms of the covenant written in this book. [32] He thereby committed all who were of Jerusalem and Benjamin, and the inhabitants of Jerusalem conformed themselves to the covenant of God, the God of their fathers. [33] Josiah removed every abominable thing from all the territory belonging to the Israelites, and he obliged all who were in Israel to serve the LORD, their God. During his lifetime they did not desert the LORD, the God of their fathers. *r*

CHAPTER 35

The Passover. [1] *s* Josiah celebrated in Jerusalem a Passover to honor the LORD; the Passover sacrifice was slaughtered on the fourteenth day of the first month. *t* [2] He reappointed the priests to their duties and encouraged them in the service of the LORD's house. [3] He said to the Levites who were to instruct all Israel, and who were consecrated to the LORD: "Put the holy ark in the house built by Solomon, son of David, king of Israel. It shall no longer be a burden on your shoulders. Serve now the LORD, your God, and his people Israel. *u* [4] Prepare yourselves in your ancestral houses and your classes according to the prescriptions of King David of Israel and

q 29-32: 2 Kgs 23, 1ff.—r 2 Kgs 23, 4-20.—s 1-19: 2 Kgs 23, 21ff.—t Ex 12, 1-28; 2 Kgs 23, 21.—u 2 Chr 5, 4; 1 Chr 15, 12. 15.

34, 31: *Standing at his post:* see note on 2 Chr 23, 13.

2Chr

his son Solomon. ⁵ Stand in the sanctuary according to the divisions of the ancestral houses of your brethren, the common people, so that the distribution of the Levites and the families may be the same.ᵛ ⁶ Slay the Passover sacrifice, sanctify yourselves, and be at the disposition of your brethren, that all may be carried out according to the word of the LORD given through Moses."ʷ

⁷ Josiah contributed to the common people a flock of lambs and kids, thirty thousand in number, each to serve as a Passover victim for any who were present, and also three thousand oxen; these were from the king's property.ˣ ⁸ His princes also gave a free-will gift to the people, the priests and the Levites. Hilkiah, Zechariah and Jehiel, prefects of the house of God, gave to the priests two thousand six hundred Passover victims together with three hundred oxen.ʸ ⁹ Conaniah and his brothers Shemaiah, Nethanel, Hashabiah, Jehiel and Jozabad, the rulers of the Levites, contributed to the Levites five thousand Passover victims, together with five hundred oxen.

¹⁰ When the service had been arranged, the priests took their places, as did the Levites in their classes according to the king's command. ¹¹ The Passover sacrifice was slaughtered, whereupon the priests sprinkled some of the blood and the Levites proceeded to the skinning. ¹² They separated what was destined for the holocaust and gave it to various groups of the ancestral houses of the common people to offer to the LORD, as is prescribed in the book of Moses. They did the same with the oxen. ¹³ They cooked the Passover on the fire as prescribed, and also cooked the sacred meals in pots, cauldrons and pans, then brought them quickly to all the common people.ᶻ ¹⁴ Afterward they prepared the Passover for themselves and for the priests. Indeed the priests, the sons of Aaron, were busy offering holocausts and the fatty portions until night; therefore the Levites prepared for themselves and for the priests, the sons of Aaron. ¹⁵ The singers, the sons of Asaph, were at their posts as prescribed by David: Asaph, Heman and Jeduthun, the king's seer. The gatekeepers were at every gate; there was no need for them to leave their stations, for their brethren, the Levites, prepared for them. ¹⁶ Thus the entire service of the LORD was arranged that day so that the Passover could be celebrated and the holocausts offered on the altar of the LORD, as King Josiah had commanded. ¹⁷ The Israelites who were present on that occasion kept the Passover and the feast of the Unleavened Bread for seven days. ¹⁸ ᵃ No such Passover had been observed in Israel since the time of the prophet Samuel, nor had any king of Israel kept a Passover like that of Josiah, the priests and Levites, all of Judah and Israel that were present, and the inhabitants of Jerusalem. ¹⁹ It was in the eighteenth year of Josiah's reign that this Passover was observed.

Josiah's Reign Ends. ²⁰ After Josiah had done all this to restore the temple, Neco, king of Egypt, came up to fight at Carchemish on the Euphrates, and Josiah went out to intercept him. ²¹ Neco sent messengers to him, saying: "What quarrel is between us, king of Judah? I have not come against you this day, for my war is with another kingdom, and God has told me to hasten. Do not interfere with God who is with me, as otherwise he will destroy you." ²² But Josiah would not withdraw from him, for he had sought a pretext for fighting with him. Therefore he would not listen to the words of Neco that came from the mouth of God, but went out to fight in the plain of Megiddo. ²³ Then the archers shot King Josiah, who said to his servants, "Take me away, for I am seriously wounded."ᵇ ²⁴ His servants removed him from his own chariot, placed him in another he had in reserve, and brought him to Jerusalem, where he died. He was buried in the tombs of his ancestors, and all Judah and Jerusalem mourned him. ²⁵ Jeremiah also composed a lamentation over Josiah,* which is recited to this day by all the male and female singers in their lamentations over Josiah. These have been made obligatory for Israel, and can be found written in the Lamentations.

²⁶ ᶜ The rest of the chronicle of Josiah, his pious deeds in regard to what is written in the law of the LORD, and his acts, first and last, can be found written in the book of the kings of Israel and Judah.

v 1 Chr 24—26.—w 2 Chr 30, 17.—x Ex 12, 5.—y Nm 7, 1-83.—z Nm 12, 8f.—a 18f: 2 Kgs 23, 22f.—b 2 Chr 18, 33f.—c 2 Kgs 23, 28.

35, 25: The reference to a *lamentation over Josiah* composed by Jeremiah is not found either in 2 Kgs or Jer; but see note on Zec 12, 11. *Their lamentations:* probably a reference to the canonical Book of Lamentations.

CHAPTER 36

[1] The people of the land took Jehoahaz, son of Josiah, and made him king in Jerusalem in his father's stead.

IV: END OF THE KINGDOM

Jehoahaz. [2] Jehoahaz was twenty-three years old when he became king, and he reigned three months in Jerusalem. [3] The king of Egypt deposed him in Jerusalem and fined the land one hundred talents of silver and a talent of gold. [4] Then the king of Egypt made his brother Eliakim king over Judah and Jerusalem, and changed his name to Jehoiakim. Neco took his brother Jehoahaz away and brought him to Egypt.

Jehoiakim. [5] Jehoiakim was twenty-five years old when he became king, and he reigned eleven years in Jerusalem. He did evil in the sight of the LORD, his God.[e] [6] Nebuchadnezzar, king of Babylon, came up against him and bound him with chains to take him to Babylon.[*] [7] Nebuchadnezzar also carried away to Babylon some of the vessels of the house of the LORD and put them in his palace in Babylon. [8] The rest of the acts of Jehoiakim, the abominable things that he did, and what therefore happened to him, can be found written in the book of the kings of Israel and Judah. His son Jehoiachin succeeded him as king.[g]

Jehoiachin. [9] Jehoiachin was eighteen years old when he became king, and he reigned three months [and ten days] in

d 1-4: 2 Kgs 23, 30-34; 1 Chr 3, 15f.—e 2 Kgs 23, 36f; Jer 22, 18f.—f 2 Kgs 24, 1f.—g 2 Kgs 24, 5.—h 2 Kgs 24, 8f.—i 2 Kgs 24, 10-16.—j 2 Kgs 24, 18ff; Jer 52, 1ff.—k Jer 37, 1ff.—l 2 Kgs 25, 1; Jer 52, 4; Ez 17, 13-16.—m Jer 7, 25; Heb 1, 1.—n Mt 23, 34ff.—o Lam 1, 15; 5, 11-14.—p 2 Kgs 25, 14f.—q 2 Kgs 25, 9f; Lam 2, 8.

36, 6:*Nebuchadnezzar . . . bound him with chains to take him to Babylon:* the Chronicler does not say that Jehoiakim was actually taken to Babylon. According to 2 Kgs 24, 1-6, Jehoiakim revolted after being Nebuchadnezzar's vassal for three years; he died in Jerusalem before the Babylonian king could reach the city. However, Dn 1, 1f, apparently based on 2 Chr 36, 6f, speaks of Jehoiakim's deportation to Babylon.

36, 10: *His brother Zedekiah:* Zedekiah was actually the brother of Jehoiakim and the uncle of *Jehoiachin* (2 Kgs 24, 17; Jer 37, 1), though scarcely older than his nephew (2 Kgs 24, 8. 18; 2 Chr 36, 9. 11).

36, 22f: The words of these verses are identical with those of Ezr 1, 1-3a. Originally Ezra-Nehemiah formed the last part of the single work of the Chronicler, of which 1 and 2 Chronicles formed the first part. But when Ezra-Nehemiah was regarded as a natural sequence to the Books of Samuel and of Kings, it was separated from 1 and 2 Chronicles and placed before them. Thus, 1 and 2 Chronicles became the last part of the Hebrew Bible. To prevent this work from ending on a note of doom, Ezr 1, 1-3a was repeated as 2 Chr 36, 22f.

Jerusalem. He did evil in the sight of the LORD.[b] [10] At the turn of the year, King Nebuchadnezzar sent for him and had him brought to Babylon, along with precious vessels from the temple of the LORD. He made his brother Zedekiah[*] king over Judah and Jerusalem.[i]

Zedekiah. [11] Zedekiah was twenty-one years old when he became king, and he reigned eleven years in Jerusalem.[j] [12] He did evil in the sight of the LORD, his God, and he did not humble himself before the prophet Jeremiah, who spoke the word of the LORD.[k] [13] He also rebelled against King Nebuchadnezzar, who had made him swear by God. He became stiffnecked and hardened his heart rather than return to the LORD, the God of Israel.[l] [14] Likewise all the princes of Judah, the priests and the people added infidelity to infidelity, practicing all the abominations of the nations and polluting the LORD's temple which he had consecrated in Jerusalem.

2Chr

Dissolution of Judah. [15] Early and often did the LORD, the God of their fathers, send his messengers to them, for he had compassion on his people and his dwelling place.[m] [16] But they mocked the messengers of God, despised his warnings, and scoffed at his prophets, until the anger of the LORD against his people was so inflamed that there was no remedy.[n] [17] Then he brought up against them the king of the Chaldeans, who slew their young men in their own sanctuary building, sparing neither young man nor maiden, neither the aged nor the decrepit; he delivered all of them over into his grip.[o] [18] All the utensils of the house of God, the large and the small, and the treasures of the LORD's house and of the king and his princes, all these he brought to Babylon.[p] [19] They burnt the house of God, tore down the walls of Jerusalem, set all its palaces afire, and destroyed all its precious objects.[q] [20] Those who escaped the sword he carried captive to Babylon, where they became his and his sons' servants until the kingdom of the Persians came to power. [21] All this was to fulfill the word of the LORD spoken by Jeremiah: "Until the land has retrieved its lost sabbaths, during all the time it lies waste it shall have rest while seventy years are fulfilled."

Decree of Cyrus. [22] * In the first year of Cyrus, king of Persia, in order to fulfill the word of the LORD spoken by Jeremiah, the LORD inspired King Cyrus of Persia to issue this proclamation throughout his kingdom, both by word of mouth and in writing:[r] [23]"Thus says Cyrus, king of Persia: 'All the kingdoms of the earth the LORD, the God of heaven, has given to me, and he has also charged me to build him a house in Jerusalem, which is in Judah. Whoever, therefore, among you belongs to any part of his people, let him go up, and may his God be with him!' "

r Ezr 1, 1ff.

THE BOOK OF EZRA

The last four books of the Hebrew canon are Ezra, Nehemiah, 1 and 2 Chronicles, in that order. Originally, however, Ezra and Nehemiah followed the Books of Chronicles, and formed with them a unified historical work so homogeneous in spirit that one usually speaks of a single author for the four books. He is called "the Chronicler." The treatment of Ezra-Nehemiah as a single book by the earliest chroniclers was undoubtedly due to the fact that in ancient times the two books were put under the one name—Ezra. The combined work Ezra-Nehemiah is our most important literary source for the formation of the Jewish religious community after the Babylonian exile. This is known as the period of the Restoration, and the two men most responsible for the reorganization of Jewish life at this time were Ezra and Nehemiah.

In the present state of the Ezra-Nehemiah text, there are several dislocations of large sections so that the chronological or logical sequence is disrupted. The major instances are pointed out in the footnotes. Although Ezra appears before Nehemiah in this work, it seems probable that Nehemiah's activity preceded his.

What is known of Ezra and his work is due almost exclusively to Ezra 7—10 (the "Ezra Memoirs") and to Neh 8—9. Strictly speaking, the term "Ezra Memoirs" should be used only of that section in which Ezra speaks in the first person, i.e., 7, 27—9, 15. Compare the "Nehemiah Memoirs" in Neh 1, 1—7, 72a; 11, 1f; 12, 27-43; 13, 4-31. The Chronicler combined this material with other sources at his disposal. The personality of Ezra is less known than that of Nehemiah. Ben Sirach, in his praise of the fathers, makes no mention of Ezra. The genealogy of Ezra (7, 1-5) traces his priesthood back to Aaron, brother of Moses. This was the accepted way of establishing the legality of one's priestly office. He is also called a scribe, well-versed in the law of Moses (7, 6), indicating Ezra's dedication to the study of the Torah, which he sought to make the basic rule of life in the restored community. It was in religious and cultic reform rather than in political affairs that Ezra made his mark as a postexilic leader. Jewish tradition holds him in great honor; the Talmud even regards him as a second Moses, claiming that the Torah would have been given to Israel through Ezra had not Moses preceded him

Ezra is sometimes accused of having been a mere legalist who gave excessive attention to the letter of the law. His work, however, should be seen and judged within a specific historical context. He gave to his people a cohesion and spiritual unity which prevented the disintegration of the small Jewish community. Had it not been for the intransigence of Ezra and of those who adopted his ideal, it is doubtful that Judaism would have so effectively resisted Hellenism, then or in later centuries. Ezra set the tone of the postexilic community, and it was characterized by fidelity to the Torah, Judaism's authentic way of life. It is in this light that we can judge most fairly the work of Ezra during the Restoration.

The Book of Ezra is divided as follows: I. The Return from Exile (1, 1—6, 22). II. The Deeds of Ezra (7, 1—10, 44).

The following list of the kings of Persia, with the dates of their reigns, will be useful for dating the events mentioned in Ezra-Nehemiah:

Cyrus	538-529 B.C.	Darius II	423-404 B.C.
Cambyses	529-521 B.C.	Artaxerxes II	404-358 B.C.
Darius I	521-485 B.C.	Artaxerxes III	358-337 B.C.
Xerxes	485-464 B.C.	End of the Persian Empire	
Artaxerxes I	464-423 B.C.	(Defeat of Darius III)	331 B.C.

PERSIAN EMPIRE

(DARIUS (521-485))

THE EXILE AND THE PERSIAN EMPIRE — **(a)** Cyrus, a petty prince of **Anshan,** a small district of **Elam,** rebels against Astyges his overlord and becomes king of the Medes in 550 B.C.; a few years later, Cyrus marches into Asia Minor and conquers Croesus, the fabulously wealthy king of Lydia (546). **(b)** At this point, Deutero-Isaiah points to Cyrus as the instrument of Yahweh who will enable his people to return home and rebuild Jerusalem. **(c)** In 538 this hope is justified as Cyrus captures Babylon without waging a battle, overturns the Babylonian Empire, and reverses the policy of mass deportations by allowing the captives, including the Jews, to return to their lands and rebuild their temples. **(d)** Some of the exiles start immediately back for home under Zerubbabel (Ezr 1, 1—2, 10) but many elect to remain in Babylon, continuing to practice their religion without sacrificial ritual and taking advantage of the opportunity for trade and amassing riches instead of coping with the sterile soil of their fathers.

PALESTINE UNDER PERSIAN RULE

WESTERN SEA

PARDES

Sidon
Damascus

Tyre
Paneas
Kadesh
L. Huleh
Acco
L. Gennesaret
KARNAIM
GALILEE

Dor
GILEAD
DOR
Samaria
SAMARIA
R. Jordan
AMMON
Joppa
Rabbah

Jerusalem
Ashdod
JUDEA
ASHDOD
Ashkalon
Lachish
Dead Sea
MOAB
IDUMEA

THE PERIOD OF RESTORATION UNDER PERSIAN DOMINATION (538-333 B.C.) — **(a)** During these next two hundred years the Jewish commonwealth is established as part of the generally benevolent Persian Empire. A new community is formed out of a combination of the Judean peasants who had remained in Palestine and kept up their religion in an ignorant and superstitious way (Jer 41, 5ff) and the more intelligent of the religious devotees who had returned from the Exile where they had cherished the laws of the past and framed codes for the future. **(b)** In 538-515 the Jewish colony which occupies but a small territory about Jerusalem under Zerubbabel begins to construct the temple prompted by the leadership and inspiration of the prophets **Haggai** and **Zechariah**. **(c)** About 445, **Nehemiah** a court official of Artaxerxes I, secures the governorship of Judah and rebuilds the walls of the holy city; he reorganizes the Jewish community as distinct from the Samaritans (Neh 13, 28ff). **(d)** In 398 Ezra arrives in Jerusalem and establishes the observance of the Mosaic law (Neh 8) and the renewal of the Covenant (Neh 9—10).

I: THE RETURN FROM EXILE

CHAPTER 1

The Decree of Cyrus. [1] [a] In the first
year of Cyrus,* king of Persia, in order to
fulfill the word of the LORD spoken by
Jeremiah, the LORD inspired King Cyrus
of Persia to issue this proclamation
throughout his kingdom, both by word of
mouth and in writing: [2] "Thus says Cyrus,
king of Persia: 'All the kingdoms of the
earth the LORD, the God of heaven, has
given to me, and he has also charged me
to build him a house in Jerusalem, which
is in Judah. [3] Whoever, therefore, among
you belongs to any part of his people, let
him go up, and may his God be with him!
[4] Let everyone who has survived, in whatever place he may have dwelt, be assisted
by the people of that place with silver,
gold, goods, and cattle, together with
free-will offerings for the house of God in
Jerusalem.' "
[5] Then the family heads of Judah and
Benjamin and the priests and Levites—
everyone, that is, whom God had inspired
to do so—prepared to go up to build the
house of the LORD in Jerusalem. [6] All their
neighbors gave them help in every way,
with silver, gold, goods, and cattle, and
with many precious gifts besides all their
free-will offerings.[b] [7] King Cyrus, too, had
the utensils of the house of the LORD
brought forth which Nebuchadnezzar had
taken away from Jerusalem and placed in
the house of his god. [8] Cyrus, king of Persia, had them brought forth by the treasurer Mithredath, and counted out to
Sheshbazzar,* the prince of Judah. [9] This
was the inventory: sacks of goldware,
thirty; sacks of silverware, one thousand
and twenty-nine; [10] golden bowls, thirty;
silver bowls, four hundred and ten;

---

a 1ff: 2 Chr 36, 22f; Jer 25, 11f; 29, 10: Zec 1, 12.—b Ex 3, 22; 11, 2; 12, 35.—c Neh 7, 6-67.

1, 1: *In the first year of Cyrus:* as sovereign over the world empire which began with his conquest of Babylon; that is, 538 B.C.

1, 8: *Sheshbazzar:* very probably the fourth son of Jehoiachin, king of Judah, taken captive to Babylon in 598 B.C., listed in 1 Chr 3, 18 as Senneser; if so, he was the uncle of Zerub-babel (Ezr 3, 2ff); see note on 1 Chr 3, 18.

1, 11: *Total . . . five thousand four hundred pieces:* either this figure or the figures given for one or more of the items listed (vv 9f) have been corrupted in the transmission of the text.

2, 1-67: As it now stands, this list is an expanded form of the lists of returned captives from the sixth century B.C.; see Neh 7, 6-72, where it reappears.

---

other ware, one thousand pieces. [11] Total
of the gold- and silverware: five thousand
four hundred pieces.* All these Sheshbazzar took with him when the exiles were
brought back from Babylon to Jerusalem.

CHAPTER 2

Census of the Province. [1] * These are the
inhabitants of the province who returned
from the captivity of the exiles, whom
Nebuchadnezzar, king of Babylon, had
carried away to Babylon,[c] and who came
back to Jerusalem and Judah, each man in
his own city* [2] (those who returned with
Zerubbabel, Jeshua, Nehemiah, Seraiah,
Reelaiah, Mordecai, Bilshan, Mispereth,
Bigvai, Rehum, and Baanah):
The census of the men of Israel: [3] sons of
Parosh, two thousand one hundred and
seventy-two; [4] sons of Shephatiah, three
hundred and seventy-two; [5] sons of Arah,
seven hundred and seventy-five; [6] sons of
Pahath-moab, who were sons of Jeshua
and Joab, two thousand eight hundred and
twelve; [7] sons of Elam, one thousand two
hundred and fifty-four; [8] sons of Zattu,
nine hundred and forty-five; [9] sons of Zaccai, seven hundred and sixty; [10] sons of
Bani, six hundred and forty-two; [11] sons of
Bebai, six hundred and twenty-three;
[12] sons of Azgad, one thousand two hundred and twenty-two; [13] sons of Adonikam, six hundred and sixty-six; [14] sons of
Bigvai, two thousand and fifty-six; [15] sons
of Adin, four hundred and fifty-four;
[16] sons of Ater, who were sons of
Hezekiah, ninety-eight; [17] sons of Bezai,
three hundred and twenty-three; [18] sons of
Jorah, one hundred and twelve; [19] sons of
Hashum, two hundred and twenty-three;
[20] sons of Gibeon, ninety-five; [21] sons of
Bethlehem, one hundred and twenty-
three; [22] men of Netophah, fifty-six; [23] men
of Anathoth, one hundred and twenty-
eight; [24] men of Beth-azmaveth, forty-two;
[25] men of Kiriath-jearim, Chephirah, and
Beeroth, seven hundred and forty-three;
[26] men of Ramah and Geba, six hundred
and twenty-one; [27] men of Michmas, one
hundred and twenty-two; [28] men of Bethel
and Ai, two hundred and twenty-three;
[29] sons of Nebo, fifty-two; [30] sons of Mag-
bish, one hundred and fifty-six; [31] sons of
the other Elam, one thousand two hundred and fifty-four; [32] sons of Harim, three

hundred and twenty; [33]sons of Lod, Hadid, and Ono, seven hundred and twenty-five; [34]sons of Jericho, three hundred and forty-five; [35]sons of Senaah, three thousand six hundred and thirty.

[36]The priests: sons of Jedaiah, who were of the house of Jeshua, nine hundred and seventy-three; [37]sons of Immer, one thousand and fifty-two; [38]sons of Pashhur, one thousand two hundred and forty-seven; [39]sons of Harim, one thousand and seventeen.

[40]The Levites: sons of Jeshua, Kadmiel, Binnui, and Hodaviah, seventy-four.[d]

[41]The singers: sons of Asaph, one hundred and twenty-eight.

[42]The gatekeepers: sons of Shallum, sons of Ater, sons of Talmon, sons of Akkub, sons of Hatita, sons of Shobai, one hundred and thirty-nine in all.

[43]The temple slaves: sons of Ziha, sons of Hasupha, sons of Tabbaoth, [44]sons of Keros, sons of Siaha, sons of Padon, [45]sons of Lebanah, sons of Hagabah, sons of Akkub, [46]sons of Hagab, sons of Shamlai, sons of Hanan, [47]sons of Giddel, sons of Gahar, sons of Reaiah, [48]sons of Rezin, sons of Nekoda, sons of Gazzam, [49]sons of Uzza, sons of Paseah, sons of Besai, [50]sons of Asnah, sons of the Meunites, sons of the Nephusites, [51]sons of Bakbuk, sons of Hakupha, sons of Harhur, [52]sons of Bazluth, sons of Mehida, sons of Harsha, [53]sons of Barkos, sons of Sisera, sons of Temah, [54]sons of Neziah, sons of Hatipha.

[55]Descendants of the slaves of Solomon: sons of Sotai, sons of Hassophereth, sons of Peruda, [56]sons of Jaalah, sons of Darkon, sons of Giddel, [57]sons of Shephatiah, sons of Hattil, sons of Pochereth-hazzebaim, sons of Ami. [58]The total of the temple slaves and the descendants of the slaves of Solomon was three hundred and ninety-two.

[59]The following who returned from Telmelah, Tel-harsha, Cherub, Addan, and Immer were unable to prove that their ancestral houses and their descent were Israelite: [60]sons of Delaiah, sons of Tobiah, sons of Nekoda, six hundred and fifty-two. [61]Also, of the priests: sons of Habaiah, sons of Hakkoz, sons of Barzillai (he had married one of the daughters of Barzillai the Gileadite and became known by his name).[e] [62]These men searched their family records, but their names could not be found written there; hence they were degraded from the priesthood, [63]and His Excellency* ordered them not to partake of the most holy foods until there should be a priest bearing the Urim and Thummim.

[64]The entire assembly taken together came to forty-two thousand three hundred and sixty, [65]not counting their male and female slaves, who were seven thousand three hundred and thirty-seven. They also had two hundred male and female singers. [66]Their horses were seven hundred and thirty-six, their mules two hundred and forty-five, [67]their camels four hundred and thirty-five, their asses six thousand seven hundred and twenty.

[68]When they arrived at the house of the LORD in Jerusalem, some of the family heads made free-will offerings for the house of God, to rebuild it in its place. [69]According to their means they contributed to the treasury for the temple service: sixty-one thousand drachmas of gold, five thousand minas of silver, and one hundred garments for the priests. [70]The priests, the Levites, and some of the common people took up residence in Jerusalem; but the singers, the gatekeepers, and the temple slaves dwelt in their cities. Thus all the Israelites dwelt in their cities.

CHAPTER 3

Restoration of the Altar. [1]Now when the seventh month* came, after the Israelites had settled in their cities, the people gathered at Jerusalem as one man.[f] [2]Then Jeshua, son of Jozadak, together with his brethren the priests, and Zerubbabel,

d Neh 12, 24.—e 2 Sm 17, 27; 19, 32f; 1 Kgs 2, 7.—f Neh 7, 73—8, 1.

2, 63: *His Excellency:* the deputy of the Persian government; from the context, he was one of the Jewish exile leaders. Nehemiah as governor receives the same title (Neh 8, 9; 10, 2). *Urim and Thummim:* see note on Ex 28, 30.

3, 1f: *The seventh month:* Tishri (September-October), apparently of 538 B.C.; cf Ezr 1, 1; 4, 5. In this case, it was Sheshbazzar who erected the first altar, since he began the work on the foundations of the temple in Jerusalem; cf Ezr 5, 16. It was in the second year of Darius I, i.e., in 520 B.C., that *Jeshua* and *Zerubbabel* resumed the work on the temple that had been temporarily interrupted (Ezr 4, 24—5, 1; Hg 1, 1; 2, 1). The Chronicler or a later editor of the text here attributes to them the beginning of the work which, in reality, they merely completed. *Shealtiel:* the oldest son of King Jehoiachin of Judah and the brother of Sheshbazzar (1 Chr 3, 18f); Zerubbabel was therefore the grandson of Jehoiachin; see note on Ezr 1, 8.

son of Shealtiel, together with his brethren, set about rebuilding the altar of the God of Israel in order to offer on it the holocausts prescribed in the law of Moses, the man of God. ³Despite their fear of the peoples of the land, they replaced the altar on its foundations and offered holocausts to the LORD on it, both morning and evening.^g ⁴They also kept the feast of Booths in the manner prescribed, and they offered the daily holocausts in the proper number required for each day.^h ⁵Thereafter they offered the established holocaust, the sacrifices prescribed for the new moons and all the festivals sacred to the LORD, and those which anyone might offer as a freewill gift to the LORD. ⁶From the first day of the seventh month they began to offer holocausts to the LORD, though the foundation of the temple of the LORD had not yet been laid.

Founding of the Temple. ⁷Then they hired stonecutters and carpenters, and sent food and drink and oil to the Sidonians and Tyrians that they might ship cedar trees from the Lebanon to the port of Joppa, as Cyrus, king of Persia, had authorized.ⁱ ⁸In the year after their coming to the house of God in Jerusalem, in the second month, Zerubbabel, son of Shealtiel, and Jeshua, son of Jozadak, together with the rest of their brethren, the priests and Levites and all who had come from the captivity to Jerusalem, began by appointing the Levites twenty years of age and over to supervise the work on the house of the LORD. ⁹Jeshua and his sons and brethren, with Kadmiel and Binnui, son of Henadad, and their sons and their brethren, the Levites, stood as one man to supervise those who were engaged in the work on the house of God. ¹⁰When the builders had laid the foundation of the LORD's temple, the vested priests with the trumpets and the Levites, sons of Asaph,

were stationed there with the cymbals to praise the LORD in the manner laid down by David, king of Israel.^j ¹¹They alternated in songs of praise and thanksgiving to the LORD, "for he is good, for his kindness to Israel endures forever"; and all the people raised a great shout of joy, praising the LORD because the foundation of the LORD's house had been laid.^k ¹²Many of the priests, Levites, and family heads, the old men who had seen the former house, cried out in sorrow as they watched the foundation of the present house being laid.^l Many others, however, lifted up their voices in shouts of joy, ¹³and no one could distinguish the sound of the joyful shouting from the sound of those who were weeping; for the people raised a mighty clamor which was heard afar off.^m

Ezr

CHAPTER 4

Samaritan Interference. ¹When the enemies of Judah and Benjamin heard that the exiles were building a temple for the LORD, the God of Israel, ²they approached Zerubbabel and the family heads and said to them, "Let us build with you, for we seek your God just as you do, and we have sacrificed to him since the days of Esarhaddon, king of Assyria, who had us brought here." ³But Zerubbabel, Jeshua, and the rest of the family heads of Israel answered them, "It is not your responsibility to build with us a house for our God, but we alone must build it for the LORD, the God of Israel, as King Cyrus of Persia has commanded us." ⁴Thereupon the people of the land set out to intimidate and dishearten the people of Judah so as to keep them from building. ⁵They also suborned counselors to work against them and thwart their plans during the remaining years of Cyrus, king of Persia, and until the reign of Darius,* king of Persia.

Later Hostility. ⁶Also at the beginning of the reign of Ahasuerus they prepared a written accusation against the inhabitants of Judah and Jerusalem.

⁷Again, in the time of Artaxerxes, Mithredath wrote in concert with Tabeel and the rest of his fellow officials to Artaxerxes, king of Persia. The document was written in Aramaic* and was accompanied by a translation. [Aramaic:]

---

g 1 Kgs 8, 64; Dn 9, 25.—h Ex 23, 16; Nm 28, 3-8.—i 1 Chr 22, 4; 2 Chr 2, 9.—j Ezr 2, 41.—k Pss 100, 5; 136; Jer 33, 11.—l Hg 2, 3.—m Tb 14, 5.

4, 5: *Darius:* Darius I (521-485 B.C.). The temple-building narrative continues in Ezr 4, 24. In between (Ezr 4, 6-23) is a series of notes about the opposition to the returned exiles voiced at the Persian court in the early fifth century B.C., after the temple had been reestablished.

4, 7: *Aramaic:* this word in the original text seems to be a note indicating a change of language from Hebrew to Aramaic, which in fact takes place here. The Aramaic section ends with Ezr 6, 18, but again in Ezr 7, 12-26 a royal letter is cited in Aramaic.

8 * Then Rehum, the governor, and Shimshai, the scribe, wrote the following letter against Jerusalem to King Artaxerxes: 9 "Rehum, the governor, Shimshai, the scribe, and their fellow judges, officials, and agents from among the Persian, Urukian, Babylonian, Susian (that is, Elamite), 10 and the other peoples whom the great and illustrious Assurbanipal transported and settled in the city of Samaria and elsewhere in the province West-of-Euphrates, as follows. . . ." 11 This is a copy of the letter that they sent to him:

"To King Artaxerxes, your servants, the men of West-of-Euphrates, as follows: 12 Let it be known to the king that the Jews who came up from you to us have arrived at Jerusalem and are now rebuilding this rebellious and evil city. They are raising up its walls, and the foundations have already been laid. 13 Now let it be known to the king that if this city is rebuilt and its walls are raised up again, they will no longer pay taxes, tributes, or tolls; thus it can only result in harm to the throne. 14 Now, since we partake of the salt of the palace, we ought not simply to look on while the king is being dishonored. Therefore we have sent this message to inform you, O king, 15 so that inquiry may be made in the historical records of your fathers. In the historical records you can discover and verify that this city is a rebellious city which has proved fatal to kings and provinces, and that sedition has been fostered there since ancient times. For that reason this city was destroyed. 16 We inform you, O king, that if this city is rebuilt and its walls are raised up again, by that very fact you will no longer own any part of West-of-Euphrates."

17 The king sent this answer: "To Rehum, the governor, Shimshai, the scribe, and their fellow officials living in Samaria and elsewhere in the province West-of-Euphrates, greetings and the following: 18 The communication which you sent us has been read plainly in my presence. 19 When at my command inquiry was made, it was verified that from ancient times this city has risen up against kings and that rebellion and sedition have been fostered there. 20 Powerful kings were once in Jerusalem who ruled over all West-of-Euphrates, and taxes, tributes, and tolls were paid to them. 21 Give orders, there-

fore, that will stop the work of these men. This city may not be rebuilt until a further decree has been issued by me. 22 Take care that you do not neglect this matter, lest the evil grow to the detriment of the throne."

23 As soon as a copy of King Artaxerxes' letter had been read before Rehum, the governor, Shimshai, the scribe, and their fellow officals, they went in all haste to the Jews in Jerusalem and stopped their work by force of arms.[n]

Rebuilding of the Temple. 24 Thus it was that the work on the house of God in Jerusalem was halted. This inaction lasted until the second year of the reign of Darius,* king of Persia.

CHAPTER 5

1 Then the prophets Haggai and Zechariah,* son of Iddo, began to prophesy to the Jews in Judah and Jerusalem in the name of the God of Israel.[o] 2 Thereupon Zerubbabel, son of Shealtiel, and Jeshua, son of Jozadak, began again to build the house of God in Jerusalem, with the prophets of God giving them support. 3 At that time there came to them Tattenai, governor of West-of-Euphrates, and Shethar-bozenai, and their fellow officials, who asked of them: "Who issued the decree for you to build this house and raise this edifice? 4 What are the names of the men who are building this structure?" 5 But their God watched over the elders of the Jews so that they were not hindered, until a report could go to Darius and then a written order be sent back concerning this matter.

6 A copy of the letter sent to King Darius by Tattenai, governor of West-of-Euphrates, and Shethar-bozenai, and their fellow officials from West-of-Euphrates; 7 they sent him a report in which was written the following:

"To King Darius, all good wishes! 8 Let

n Neh 1, 3.—o Hg 1, 14—2, 9; Zec 4, 9.

4, 8-23: The central question here is the rebuilding of the fortification walls of Jerusalem, not the building of the temple. The interruption of work on the city wall some time before 445 B.C. was the occasion for the coming of Nehemiah to Palestine (Neh 1, 1-4; 2, 1-5). *Artaxerxes:* Artaxerxes I (464-423 B.C.).

4, 24: *The second year . . . of Darius:* 520 B.C.; it marks the beginning of the successful restoration of the temple, which was accomplished within the five years following (Ezr 5, 1—6, 18).

5, 1: *The prophets Haggai and Zechariah:* two of the Minor Prophets, whose books record their role in the encouragement of this work.

it be known to the king that we have visited the province of Judah and the house of the great God: it is being rebuilt of cut stone and the walls are being reinforced with timber; the work is being carried on diligently and is making good progress under their hands. ⁹We then questioned the elders, addressing to them the following words: 'Who issued the decree for you to build this house and raise this edifice?' ¹⁰We also asked them their names, to report them to you in a list of the men who are their leaders. ¹¹This was their answer to us: 'We are the servants of the God of heaven and earth, and we are rebuilding the house built here long years ago, which a great king of Israel built and finished. ¹²But because our fathers provoked the wrath of the God of heaven, he delivered them into the power of the Chaldean, Nebuchadnezzar, king of Babylon, who destroyed this house and led the people captive to Babylon. ¹³However, in the first year of Cyrus, king of Babylon, King Cyrus issued a decree for the rebuilding of this house of God. ¹⁴Moreover, the gold and silver utensils of the house of God which Nebuchadnezzar had taken from the temple in Jerusalem and carried off to the temple in Babylon, King Cyrus ordered to be removed from the temple in Babylon and consigned to a certain Sheshbazzar, whom he named governor. ¹⁵And he commanded him: Take these utensils and deposit them in the temple of Jerusalem, and let the house of God be rebuilt on its former site. ¹⁶Then this same Sheshbazzar came and laid the foundations of the house of God in Jerusalem. Since that time the building has been going on, and it is not yet completed.' ¹⁷Now, if it please the king, let a search be made in the royal archives of Babylon to discover whether a decree really was issued by King Cyrus for the rebuilding of this house of God in Jerusalem. And may the king's pleasure in this matter be communicated to us."

CHAPTER 6

The Decree of Darius. ¹Thereupon King Darius issued an order to search the archives in which the Babylonian records were stored away; ² ᵖ and in Ecbatana, the

stronghold in the province of Media, a scroll was found containing the following text: "Memorandum. ³In the first year of King Cyrus, King Cyrus issued a decree: The house of God in Jerusalem. The house is to be rebuilt as a place for offering sacrifices and bringing burnt offerings. Its height is to be sixty cubits and its width sixty cubits. ⁴It shall have three courses of cut stone for each one of timber. The costs are to be borne by the royal palace. ⁵Also, the gold and silver utensils of the house of God which Nebuchadnezzar took from the temple of Jerusalem and brought to Babylon are to be sent back: to be returned to their place in the temple of Jerusalem and deposited in the house of God.

⁶"Now, therefore, Tattenai, governor of West-of-Euphrates, and Shethar-bozenai, and you, their fellow officials in West-of-Euphrates, do not interfere in that place. ⁷Let the governor and the elders of the Jews continue the work on that house of God; they are to rebuild it on its former site. ⁸I also issue this decree concerning your dealing with these elders of the Jews in the rebuilding of that house of God: From the royal revenue, the taxes of West-of-Euphrates, let these men be repaid for their expenses, in full and without delay. ⁹Whatever else is required—young bulls, rams, and lambs for holocausts to the God of heaven, wheat, salt, wine, and oil, according to the requirements of the priests who are in Jerusalem—is to be delivered to them day by day without fail, ¹⁰that they may continue to offer sacrifices of pleasing odor to the God of heaven and pray for the life of the king and his sons. ¹¹I also issue this decree: If any man violates this edict, a beam is to be taken from his house, and he is to be lifted up and impaled on it; and his house is to be reduced to rubble for this offense. ¹²And may the God who causes his name to dwell there overthrow every king or people who may undertake to alter this or to destroy this house of God in Jerusalem. I, Darius, have issued this decree; let it be carefully executed."

¹³Then Tattenai, the governor of West-of-Euphrates, and Shethar-bozenai, and their fellow officials carried out fully the instructions King Darius had sent them. ¹⁴The elders of the Jews continued to make progress in the building, sup-

ported by the message of the prophets, Haggai and Zechariah, son of Iddo. They finished the building according to the command of the God of Israel and the decrees of Cyrus and Darius [and of Artaxerxes, king of Persia]. ¹⁵ They completed this house on the third day of the month Adar, in the sixth year of the reign of King Darius. ¹⁶ The Israelites—priests, Levites, and the other returned exiles—celebrated the dedication of this house of God with joy. ¹⁷ For the dedication of this house of God, they offered one hundred bulls, two hundred rams, and four hundred lambs, together with twelve he-goats as a sin-offering for all Israel, in keeping with the number of the tribes of Israel. ¹⁸ Finally, they set up the priests in their classes and the Levites in their divisions for the service of God in Jerusalem, as is prescribed in the book of Moses.

The Passover. ¹⁹ *q* The exiles kept the Passover on the fourteenth day of the first month. ²⁰ The Levites, every one of whom had purified himself for the occasion, sacrificed the Passover for the rest of the exiles, for their brethren the priests, and for themselves. ²¹ The Israelites who had returned from the exile partook of it together with all those who had separated themselves from the uncleanness of the peoples of the land to join them in seeking the LORD, the God of Israel.*r* ²² They joyfully kept the feast of Unleavened Bread for seven days, for the LORD had filled them with joy by making the king of Assyria* favorable to them, so that he gave them help in their work on the house of God, the God of Israel.

II: THE DEEDS OF EZRA

CHAPTER 7

Ezra the Scribe. ¹ After these events,* during the reign of Artaxerxes, king of Persia, Ezra, son of Seraiah, son of Azariah, son of Hilkiah, ² son of Shallum, son of Zadok, son of Ahitub, ³ son of Amariah, son of Azariah, son of Meraioth, ⁴ son of Zerahiah, son of Uzzi, son of Bukki, ⁵ son of Abishua, son of Phinehas, son of Eleazar, son of the high priest Aaron—⁶ this Ezra came up from Babylon. He was a scribe, well-versed in the law of Moses which was given by the LORD, the God of Israel. Because the

hand of the LORD, his God, was upon him, the king granted him all that he requested.*s*

⁷ Some of the Israelites and some priests, Levites, singers, gatekeepers, and temple slaves also came up to Jerusalem in the seventh year of King Artaxerxes. ⁸ Ezra came to Jerusalem in the fifth month of that seventh year of the king. ⁹ On the first day of the first month he resolved on the journey up from Babylon, and on the first day of the fifth month he arrived at Jerusalem, for the favoring hand of his God was upon him. ¹⁰ Ezra had set his heart on the study and practice of the law of the LORD and on teaching statutes and ordinances in Israel.*t*

The Decree of Artaxerxes. ¹¹ This is a copy of the rescript which King Artaxerxes gave to Ezra the priest-scribe, the scribe of the text of the LORD's commandments and statutes for Israel:

¹² *u* "Artaxerxes, king of kings, to Ezra the priest, scribe of the law of the God of heaven (then, after greetings): ¹³ I have issued this decree, that anyone in my kingdom belonging to the people of Israel, its priests or Levites, who is minded to go up to Jerusalem with you, may do so. ¹⁴ You are the envoy from the king and his seven counselors to supervise Judah and Jerusalem in respect of the law of your God which is in your possession, ¹⁵ and to bring with you the silver and gold which the king and his counselors have freely contributed to the God of Israel, whose dwelling is in Jerusalem, ¹⁶ as well as all the silver and gold which you may receive throughout the province of Babylon, together with the free-will offerings which the people and priests freely contribute for the house of their God in Jerusalem. ¹⁷ You must take care, therefore, to use this money to buy bulls, rams, lambs, and the cereal offerings and libations proper to

q 19-22: Ex 12, 1-20.—r Ps 47, 9.—s Ezr 7, 28; 8, 18; Neh 2, 8. 18.—t Ps 119, 45.—u 12-17: Ezr 1, 2ff.

6, 22: *Assyria:* used here in a broad sense for the Persian Empire.

7, 1-8: The date of Ezra's journey to Palestine is not known with certainty. The *seventh year* of King Artaxerxes I would be 458 B.C., and the present order of the text suggests that date. The narratives of Ezra and Nehemiah make it seem to many, however, that the arrival of Nehemiah in 445 B.C. should precede that of Ezra. If so, Ezra may be thought to have come in 398 B.C., the seventh year of King Artaxerxes II. Others argue for the thirty-seventh year of Artaxerxes I, that is, 428 B.C.; this would suppose that the date given in the text has suffered in transmission.

these, and offer them on the altar of the house of your God in Jerusalem. [18] You and your brethren may do whatever seems best to you with the remainder of the silver and gold, conformably to the will of your God. [19] The utensils consigned to you for the service of the house of your God you are to deposit before the God of Jerusalem. [20] Whatever else you may be required to supply for the needs of the house of your God, you may draw from the royal treasury. [21] I, Artaxerxes the king, issue this decree to all the treasurers of West-of-Euphrates: Whatever Ezra the priest, scribe of the law of the God of heaven, requests of you, dispense to him accurately, [22] within these limits: silver, one hundred talents; wheat, one hundred kors; wine, one hundred baths; oil, one hundred baths; salt, without limit. [23] Let everything that is ordered by the God of heaven be carried out exactly for the house of the God of heaven, that wrath may not come upon the realm of the king and his sons. [24] We also inform you that it is not permitted to impose taxes, tributes, or tolls on any priest, Levite, singer, gatekeeper, temple slave, or any other servant of that house of God.

[25] "As for you, Ezra, in accordance with the wisdom of your God* which is in your possession, appoint magistrates and judges to administer justice to all the people in West-of-Euphrates, to all, that is, who know the laws of your God. Instruct those who do not know these laws.[v] [26] Whoever does not obey the law of your God and the law of the king, let strict judgment be executed upon him, whether death, or corporal punishment, or a fine on his goods, or imprisonment."

Ezra and His Companions. [27] Blessed be the LORD, the God of our fathers, who thus disposed the mind of the king to glorify the house of the LORD in Jerusalem, [28] and who let me find favor with the king, with his counselors, and with all the most influential royal officials. I therefore took courage and, with the hand of the LORD, my God, upon me, I gathered together Israelite family heads to make the return journey with me.[w]

---

v 2 Chr 17, 9.—w Ezr 7, 6.—x Ezr 7, 6.

7, 25: *The wisdom of your God:* the Mosaic law; cf vv 6, 14.
8, 15: *Ahava:* a town at an unidentified site in Babylonia. The river that flowed toward it was probably a branch or canal of the Euphrates.

CHAPTER 8

[1] This is the list of the family heads who returned with me from Babylon during the reign of King Artaxerxes: [2] Of the sons of Phinehas, Gershon; of the sons of Ithamar, Daniel; of the sons of David, Hattush, [3] son of Shecaniah; of the sons of Parosh, Zechariah, and with him one hundred and fifty males were enrolled; [4] of the sons of Pahath-moab, Eliehoenai, son of Zerahiah, and with him two hundred males; [5] of the sons of Zattu, Shecaniah, son of Jahaziel, and with him three hundred males; [6] of the sons of Adin, Ebed, son of Jonathan, and with him fifty males; [7] of the sons of Elam, Jeshaiah, son of Athaliah, and with him seventy males; [8] of the sons of Shephatiah, Zebadiah, son of Michael, and with him eighty males; [9] of the sons of Joab, Obadiah, son of Jehiel, and with him two hundred and eighteen males; [10] of the sons of Bani, Shelomith, son of Josiphiah, and with him one hundred and sixty males; [11] of the sons of Bebai, Zechariah, son of Bebai, and with him twenty-eight males; [12] of the sons of Azgad, Johanan, son of Hakkatan, and with him one hundred and ten males; [13] of the sons of Adonikam, younger sons, whose names were Eliphelet, Jeiel, and Shemaiah, and with them sixty males; [14] of the sons of Bigvai, Uthai, son of Zakkur, and with him seventy males.

The Journey to Jerusalem. [15] I had them assemble by the river that flows toward Ahava,* where we made camp for three days. There I perceived that both laymen and priests were present, but I could not discover a single Levite. [16] Therefore I sent Eliezer, Ariel, Shemaiah, Jarib, Elnathan, Nathan, Zechariah, and Meshullam, wise leaders, [17] with a command for Iddo, the leader in the place Casiphia, instructing them what to say to Iddo and his brethren, and to the temple slaves in Casiphia, in order to procure for us ministers for the house of our God. [18] They sent to us—for the favoring hand of our God was upon us—a well-instructed man, one of the sons of Mahli, son of Levi, son of Israel, namely Sherebiah, with his sons and brethren, eighteen men.[x] [19] They also sent us Hashabiah, and with him Jeshaiah, sons of Merari, and their brethren and their sons, twenty men. [20] Of the temple slaves (those whom David and the princes appointed to serve the Levites) there were two hundred and twenty. All these men were enrolled by name.[y]

[21] Then I proclaimed a fast, there by the river of Ahava, that we might humble ourselves before our God to petition from him a safe journey for ourselves, our children, and all our possessions. [22] For I would have been ashamed to ask the king for troops and horsemen to protect us against enemies along the way, since we had said to the king, "The favoring hand of our God is upon all who seek him, but his mighty wrath is against all who forsake him."[z] [23] So we fasted, and prayed to our God for this, and our petition was granted. [24] Next I selected twelve of the priestly leaders along with Sherebiah, Hashabiah, and ten of their brethren, [25] and I weighed out before them the silver and the gold and the utensils offered for the house of our God by the king, his counselors, his officials, and all the Israelites of that region. I consigned it to them in these amounts: [26] silver, six hundred and fifty talents; silver utensils, one hundred; gold, one hundred talents; [27] twenty golden bowls valued at a thousand darics; two vases of excellent polished bronze, as precious as gold. [28] I addressed them in these words: "You are consecrated to the LORD, and the utensils are also consecrated; the silver and the gold are a free-will offering to the LORD, the God of your fathers. [29] Keep good watch over them till you weigh them out in Jerusalem in the presence of the chief priests and Levites and the family leaders of Israel, in the chambers of the house of the LORD." [30] The priests and the Levites then took over the silver, the gold, and the utensils that had been weighed out, to bring them to Jerusalem, to the house of our God.

[31] We set out for Jerusalem from the river of Ahava on the twelfth day of the first month. The hand of our God remained upon us, and he protected us from enemies and bandits along the way. [32] Thus we arrived at Jerusalem, where we first rested for three days. [33] On the fourth day, the silver, the gold, and the utensils were weighed out in the house of our God and consigned to the priest Meremoth, son of Uriah, who was assisted by Eleazar, son of Phinehas; they were assisted by the Levites Jozabad, son of Jeshua, and Noadiah, son of Binnui. [34] Everything was in order as to number and weight, and the total weight was registered. At that same time, [35] those who had returned from the captivity, the exiles, offered as holocausts to the God of Israel twelve bulls for all Israel, ninety-six rams, seventy-seven lambs, and twelve goats as sin-offerings: all these as a holocaust to the LORD. [36] Finally, the orders of the king were presented to the king's satraps and to the governors in West-of-Euphrates, who gave their support to the people and to the house of God.*

CHAPTER 9

Denunciation of Mixed Marriages. [1] [a] When these matters had been concluded, the leaders approached me with this report: "Neither the Israelite laymen nor the priests nor the Levites have kept themselves aloof from the peoples of the land and their abominations [Canaanites, Hittites, Perizzites, Jebusites, Ammonites, Moabites, Egyptians, and Amorites]; [2] for they have taken some of their daughters as wives for themselves and their sons, and thus they have desecrated the holy race with the peoples of the land. Furthermore, the leaders and rulers have taken a leading part in this apostasy!"

Ezra's Exhortation. [3] When I had heard this thing, I tore my cloak and my mantle, plucked hair from my head and beard, and sat there stupefied. [b] [4] Around me gathered all who were in dread of the sentence of the God of Israel on this apostasy of the exiles, while I remained motionless until the evening sacrifice. [c] [5] Then, at the time of the evening sacrifice, I rose in my wretchedness, and with cloak and mantle torn I fell on my knees, stretching out my hands to the LORD, my God.

[6] I said: "My God, I am too ashamed and confounded to raise my face to you, O my God, for our wicked deeds are heaped up above our heads and our guilt reaches up to heaven.[d] [7] * From the time of our fathers even to this day great has been

---

y Ezr 2, 43.—z Neh 2, 9.—a 1f: Dt 7, 1; Neh 9, 2.—b Ps 119, 136.—c Is 66, 2.—d Ps 38, 4.

8, 36: The story of Ezra's mission is seemingly continued from this point by Neh 7, 72b—8, 18, which may be read before Ezr 9, 1.

9, 7: After this verse, the next part of the prayer attributed to Ezra is perhaps to be found in Neh 9, 6-37, which may be read as leading up to Ezr 9, 8-15.

our guilt, and for our wicked deeds we have been delivered over, we and our kings and our priests, to the will of the kings of foreign lands, to the sword, to captivity, to pillage, and to disgrace, as is the case today.

⁸"And now, but a short time ago, mercy came to us from the LORD, our God, who left us a remnant and gave us a stake in his holy place; thus our God has brightened our eyes and given us relief in our servitude.ᵉ ⁹For slaves we are, but in our servitude our God has not abandoned us; rather, he has turned the good will of the kings of Persia toward us. Thus he has given us new life to raise again the house of our God and restore its ruins, and has granted us a fence in Judah and Jerusalem.ᶠ ¹⁰But now, O our God, what can we say after all this? For we have abandoned your commandments, ¹¹which you gave through your servants the prophets: the land which you are entering to take as your possession is a land unclean with the filth of the peoples of the land, with the abominations with which they have filled it from one end to the other in their uncleanness.ᵍ ¹²Do not, then, give your daughters to their sons in marriage, and do not take their daughters for your sons. Never promote their peace and prosperity; thus you will grow strong, enjoy the produce of the land, and leave it as an inheritance to your children forever.ʰ

¹³"After all that has come upon us for our evil deeds and our great guilt—though you, our God, have made less of our sinfulness than it deserved and have allowed us to survive as we do—¹⁴shall we again violate your commandments by intermarrying with these abominable peoples? Would you not become so angered with us as to destroy us without remnant or survivor? ¹⁵O LORD, God of Israel, you are just; yet we have been spared, the remnant we are

today. Here we are before you in our sins. Because of all this, we can no longer stand in your presence."

CHAPTER 10

The People's Response. ¹While Ezra prayed and acknowledged their guilt, weeping and prostrate before the house of God, a very large assembly of Israelites gathered about him, men, women, and children; and the people wept profusely. ²Then Shecaniah, the son of Jeheil, one of the sons of Elam, made this appeal to Ezra: "We have indeed betrayed our God by taking as wives foreign women of the peoples of the land. Yet even now there remains a hope for Israel. ³Let us therefore enter into a covenant before our God to dismiss all our foreign wives and the children born of them, in keeping with what you, my lord, advise, and those who fear the commandments of our God. Let the law be observed! ⁴Rise, then, for this is your duty! We will stand by you, so have courage and take action!"

⁵Ezra rose to his feet and demanded an oath from the chiefs of the priests, from the Levites and from all Israel that they would do as had been proposed; and they swore it. ⁶Then Ezra retired from his place before the house of God and entered the chamber of Johanan, son of Eliashib,* where he spent the night neither eating food nor drinking water, for he was in mourning over the betrayal by the exiles. ⁷A proclamation was made throughout Judah and Jerusalem that all the exiles should gather together in Jerusalem, ⁸and that whoever failed to appear within three days would, according to the judgment of the leaders and elders, suffer the confiscation of all his possessions, and himself be excluded from the assembly of the exiles.

⁹All the men of Judah and Benjamin gathered together in Jerusalem within the three-day period: it was in the ninth month,* on the twentieth day of the month. All the people, standing in the open place before the house of God, were trembling both over the matter at hand and because it was raining. ¹⁰Then Ezra, the priest, stood up and said to them: "Your unfaithfulness in taking foreign women as wives has added to Israel's guilt. ¹¹But now, give praise to the LORD, the God of your fathers, and do his will:

Ezr

---

e Is 4, 3.—f Ps 106, 46.—g Lv 18, 24f; Ez 36, 17.—h Dt 7, 3.

10, 6: *Johanan, son of Eliashib:* actually, the grandson of Eliashib; the father of Johanan was Eliashib's son Joiada (Neh 12, 10f. 22). Since Eliashib was high priest at the time of Nehemiah (Neh 3, 1. 20f; 13, 4. 7) and Johanan, if not yet high priest, was at least old enough to have his own separate quarters *(chamber)* in the temple at the time of Ezra, it is practically certain that Nehemiah's activity in Jerusalem must have preceded that of Ezra.

10, 9: *Ninth month:* Chislev (November-December), during the "early rains" in Palestine. Since the assembly took place *in the open . . . all the people . . . were trembling . . . because it was raining.*

separate yourselves from the peoples of the land and from these foreign women."*i* [12] In answer, the whole assembly cried out with a loud voice: "Yes, it is our duty to do as you say! [13] But the people are numerous and it is the rainy season, so that we cannot remain out-of-doors; besides, this is not a task that can be performed in a single day or even two, for those of us who have sinned in this regard are many. [14] Let our leaders represent the whole assembly; then let all those in our cities who have taken foreign women for wives appear at appointed times, accompanied by the elders and magistrates of each city in question, till we have turned away from us our God's burning anger over this affair." [15] Only Jonathan, son of Ashael, and Jahzeiah, son of Tikvah, were against this proposal, with Meshullam and Shabbethai the Levite supporting them.

The Guilty. [16] * The exiles did as agreed. Ezra appointed as his assistants men who were family heads, one for each family, all of them designated by name. They held sessions to examine the matter, beginning with the first day of the tenth month. [17] By the first day of the first month they had passed judgment on all the men who had taken foreign women for wives.

[18] Among the priests, the following were found to have taken foreign women for wives: Of the sons of Jeshua, son of Jozadak, and his brethren: Maaseiah, Eliezer, Jarib, and Gedaliah. [19] They pledged themselves to dismiss their wives, and as a guilt-offering for their guilt they gave a ram from the flock. [20] Of the sons of Immer: Hanani and Zebadiah; [21] of the sons of Harim: Maaseiah, Elijah, Shemaiah, Jehiel, and Uzziah; [22] of the sons of Pashhur: Elioenai, Maaseiah, Ishmael, Nethanel, Jozabad, and Elasah. [23] Of the Levites: Jozabad, Shemei,

Kelaiah (also called Kelita), Pethahiah, Judah, and Eliezer.*j* [24] Of the singers: Eliashib and Zakkur; of the gatekeepers: Shallum, Telem, and Uri. [25] Among the other Israelites: Of the sons of Parosh: Ramiah, Izziah, Malchijah, Mijamin, Eleazar, Malchijah, and Benaiah; [26] of the sons of Elam: Mattaniah, Zechariah, Jehiel, Abdi, Jeremoth, and Elijah; [27] of the sons of Zattu: Elioenai, Eliashib, Mattaniah, Jeremoth, Zabad, and Aziza; [28] of the sons of Bebai: Jehohanan, Hananiah, Zabbai, and Athlai; [29] of the sons of Bani: Meshullam, Malluch, Adaiah, Jashub, Sheal, and Jeremoth; [30] of the sons of Pahath-moab: Adna, Chelal, Benaiah, Maaseiah, Mattaniah, Bezalel, Binnui, and Manasseh; [31] of the sons of Harim: Eliezer, Isshijah, Malchijah, Shemaiah, Shimeon, [32] Benjamin, Malluch, Shemariah; [33] of the sons of Hashum: Mattenai, Mattattah, Zabad, Eliphelet, Jeremai, Manasseh, Shimei; [34] of the sons of Begui: Maadai, Amram, Uel, [35] Benaiah, Bedeiah, Cheluhi, [36] Vaniah, Meremoth, Eliashib, [37] Mattaniah, Mattenai, and Jassu; [38] of the sons of Binnui: Shimei, [39] Shelemiah, Nathan, and Adaiah; [40] of the sons of Zachai: Shashai, Sharai, [41] Azarel, Shelemiah, Shemariah, [42] Shallum, Amariah, Joseph; [43] of the sons of Nebo: Jeiel, Mattithiah, Zabad, Zebina, Jaddai, Joel, Benaiah. [44] All these had taken foreign wives; but they sent them away, both the women and their children.*

i Neh 9, 2.—j Neh 8, 7; 10, 11.

10, 16f: The work of the committee lasted three months, from *the first day of the tenth month,* Tebet (December-January), to *the first day of the first month,* Nisan (March-April), of the following Jewish year.

10, 44: The account of the problem of mixed marriages at the time of Ezra is continued in Neh 9, 1-5; this may be read immediately after Ezr 10, 44, though the date given in Neh 9, 1 fits more precisely after Ezr 10, 15; cf Hg 2, 10-14.

THE BOOK OF NEHEMIAH

Problems common to the combined Books Ezra-Nehemiah have been pointed out in the Introduction to the Book of Ezra. The achievements of the two men were complementary; each helped to make it possible for Judaism to maintain its identity during the difficult days of the Restoration. Nehemiah was the man of action who rebuilt the walls of Jerusalem and introduced necessary administrative reforms. Ezra in turn was the great religious reformer who succeeded in establishing the Torah as the constitution of the returned community.

The biblical sources for Nehemiah's life and work are the autobiographical portions scattered through the book. They are called the "Memoirs of Nehemiah," and have been used more extensively and effectively by "the Chronicler" than the "Memoirs of Ezra." No competent scholar questions the authenticity of Nehemiah's memoirs. From these and other sources, the picture emerges of a man dedicated to the single purpose of the welfare of his people. Despite temperamental shortcomings, Nehemiah was a man of good practical sense combined with deep faith in God. In view of his selfless service to a community capable of severely testing any leader, we can be indulgent toward his numerous appeals to God to credit him with the work he had done. Nehemiah was a layman, and his generous dedication of talents to the service of God and of God's people remains an example of undiminished force for laymen today.

The Book of Nehemiah is divided as follows: I. The Deeds of Nehemiah (1, 1—7, 72). II. Promulgation of the Law (8, 1—13, 31).

I: THE DEEDS OF NEHEMIAH

CHAPTER 1

Nehemiah's Vocation. ¹The words of Nehemiah, the son of Hacaliah.*

In the month Chislev of the twentieth year, I was in the citadel of Susa ²when Hanani, one of my brothers, came with other men from Judah. I asked them about the Jews, the remnant preserved after the captivity, and about Jerusalem, ³and they answered me: "The survivors of the captivity there in the province are in great distress and under reproach. Also, the wall of Jerusalem lies breached, and its gates have been gutted with fire." ⁴When I heard this report, I began to weep and continued mourning for several days; I fasted and prayed before the God of heaven.

⁵I prayed: "O LORD, God of heaven, great and awesome God, you who preserve your covenant of mercy toward those who love you and keep your commandments,ᵃ ⁶may your ear be attentive, and your eyes open, to heed the prayer which I, your servant, now offer in your presence day and night for your servants the Israelites, confessing the sins which we of Israel have committed against you, I and my father's house included.ᵇ ⁷Grievously have we offended you, not keeping the command-

ments, the statutes, and the ordinances which you committed to your servant Moses.ᶜ ⁸But remember, I pray, the promise which you gave through Moses, your servant, when you said:ᵈ 'Should you prove faithless, I will scatter you among the nations; ⁹but should you return to me and carefully keep my commandments, even though your outcasts have been driven to the farthest corner of the world, I will gather them from there, and bring them back to the place which I have chosen as the dwelling place for my name.' ¹⁰They are your servants, your people, whom you freed by your great might and your strong hand.ᵉ ¹¹O LORD, may your ear be attentive to my prayer and that of all your willing servants who revere your name. Grant success to your servant this day, and let him find favor with this man"—for I was cupbearer to the king.*ᶠ

CHAPTER 2

Appointment by the King. ¹In the month Nisan of the twentieth year of King Artaxerxes, when the wine was in my charge, I took some and offered it to the king. As I had never before been sad in his presence, ²the king asked me, "Why do you look sad? If you are not sick, you must be sad at heart." Though I was seized with great fear, ³I answered the king: "May the king live forever! How could I not look sad when the city where my ancestors are buried lies in ruins, and its gates have been eaten out by fire?" ⁴The king asked me, "What is it, then, that you wish?" I prayed to the God of heaven ⁵and then answered the king: "If it please the king, and if your servant is deserving of your favor, send

---

a Dt 7, 9, 12; Dn 9, 4.—b 2 Chr 6, 40.—c Dn 3, 29f.—d 8f: Dt 30, 1-5.—e Dt 9, 29.—f Ps 118, 25.

1, 1: The first mission of Nehemiah, from the *twentieth year* of Artaxerxes I, lasted from the spring (Neh 2, 1) of 445 B.C. until 433 B.C. (Neh 5, 14). It is recounted in Neh 1, 1—6, 15; 12, 27-43; 6, 16—7, 5; 11, 1-21, which may be read in that order.

1, 11: *Cupbearer to the king:* an important official in the royal household. Because Nehemiah could appear in the queen's presence (Neh 2, 6), it is commonly presumed that he was a eunuch; but this is not necessarily so.

me to Judah, to the city of my ancestors' graves, to rebuild it." [6] Then the king, and the queen seated beside him, asked me how long my journey would take and when I would return. I set a date that was acceptable to him, and the king agreed that I might go.

[7] I asked the king further: "If it please the king, let letters be given to me for the governors of West-of-Euphrates, that they may afford me safe-conduct till I arrive in Judah; [8] also a letter for Asaph, the keeper of the royal park, that he may give me wood for timbering the gates of the temple-citadel and for the city wall and the house that I shall occupy." The king granted my requests, for the favoring hand of my God was upon me.[g] [9] Thus I proceeded to the governors of West-of-Euphrates and presented the king's letters to them. The king also sent with me army officers and cavalry.[h]

[10] When Sanballat the Horonite* and Tobiah the Ammonite slave had heard of this, they were very much displeased that someone had come to seek the welfare of the Israelites.

Circuit of the City. [11] When I had arrived in Jerusalem, I first rested there for three days. [12] Then I set out by night with only a few other men (for I had not told anyone what my God had inspired me to do for Jerusalem) and with no other animals but my own mount. [13] * I rode out at night by the Valley Gate, passed by the Dragon Spring, and came to the Dung Gate, observing how the walls of Jerusalem lay in ruins and its gates had been eaten out by fire. [14] Then I passed over to the Spring Gate and to the King's Pool. Since there was no room here for my mount to pass with me astride, [15] I continued on foot up the wadi by night, inspecting the wall all the while till I once more reached the Valley Gate, by which I went back in. [16] The magistrates knew nothing of where I had gone or what I was doing, for as yet I had disclosed nothing to the Jews, neither to the priests, nor to the nobles, nor to the magistrates, nor to the others who would be concerned about the matter.

Rebuilding Jerusalem's Walls. [17] Afterward I said to them: "You see the evil plight in which we stand: how Jerusalem lies in ruins and its gates have been gutted by fire. Come, let us rebuild the wall of Jerusalem, so that we may no longer be an object of derision!" [18] Then I explained to them how the favoring hand of my God had rested upon me, and what the king had said to me. They replied, "Let us be up and building!" And they undertook the good work with vigor.[i]

[19] On hearing of this, Sanballat the Horonite, Tobiah the Ammonite slave, and Geshem the Arab mocked us and ridiculed us. "What is this that you are about?" they asked. "Are you rebelling against the king?" [20] My answer to them was this: "It is the God of heaven who will grant us success. We, his servants, shall set about the rebuilding; but for you there is to be neither share nor claim nor memorial* in Jerusalem."

CHAPTER 3

List of Workers.* [1] Eliashib the high priest and his priestly brethren took up the task of rebuilding the Sheep Gate. They timbered it and set up its doors, its bolts, and its bars, then continued the rebuilding to the Tower of Hananel.[j] [2] At their side the men of Jericho were rebuilding, and next to them was Zaccur, son of Imri.

g Ezr 7, 6.—h Ezr 8, 22.—i Ezr 7, 6.— j Jer 31, 38.

2, 10: *Sanballat the Horonite:* the governor of the province of Samaria (Neh 3, 33f), apparently a native of one of the Bethhorons. A letter from the Jews living at Elephantine in southern Egypt, dated 408-407 B.C., mentions "Delayah and Shelemyah, the sons of Sanballat, the governor of Samaria." Although his own name was Babylonian — *Sin-uballit,* i.e., "Sin (the moon god) has given life"—two sons had names referring to Yahweh. *Tobiah, the Ammonite slave:* the governor of the province of Ammon in Transjordan. His honorary title, "servant" (in Hebrew, *ebed),* i.e., of the king, could also be understood as *slave,* and Nehemiah no doubt meant it in this derogatory sense. The Tobiads remained a powerful family even in Maccabean times (2 Mc 3, 11). Sanballat and Tobiah together with Geshem the Arab (Neh 2, 19; 6, 1f), who was probably in charge of Edom and the regions to the south and southeast of Judah, opposed the rebuilding of Jerusalem's walls on political grounds; the city was the capital of a rival province.

2, 13ff: Nehemiah left Jerusalem by *the Valley Gate* near the northwestern end of the old City of David and went south down the Tyropoean Valley toward *the Dragon Spring* (or the Enrogel of Jos 15, 7; 18, 16; 2 Sm 17, 17; 1 Kgs 1, 9, now known as Job's Well) at the juncture of the Valley of Hinnom and the Kidron Valley; he then turned north at *the Dung Gate* (or *the Potsherd Gate* of Jer 19, 2) at the southern end of the city and proceeded up the *wadi,* that is, the Kidron Valley, passing *the Spring Gate* (at the Spring of Gihon) and *the King's Pool* (unidentified); finally he turned west and then south to his starting point.

2, 20: *Neither share nor claim nor memorial:* although Sanballat and Tobiah were Yahwist, Nehemiah would not let them participate in any of the rights of the religious community in Jerusalem.

3, 1-32: The construction work on the gates and walls of the city is described in counterclockwise direction, beginning and ending at *the Sheep Gate* (to the north of the temple). The exact sites of many of the topographical points mentioned are uncertain.

³The Fish Gate was rebuilt by the sons of Hassenaah; they timbered it and set up its doors, its bolts, and its bars.*ᵏ* ⁴At their side Meremoth, son of Uriah, son of Hakkoz, carried out the work of repair; next to him was Meshullam, son of Berechiah, son of Meshezabel; and next to him was Zadok, son of Baana. ⁵Next to him the Tekoites carried out the work of repair; however, some of their outstanding men would not submit to the labor asked by their lords. ⁶The New City Gate was repaired by Joiada, son of Paseah; and Meshullam, son of Besodeiah; they timbered it and set up its doors, its bolts, and its bars. ⁷At their side were Melatiah the Gibeonite, Jadon the Meronothite, and the men of Gibeon and of Mizpah, who were under the jurisdiction of the governor of West-of-Euphrates. ⁸Next to them the work of repair was carried out by Uzziel, son of Harhaiah, a member of the goldsmiths' guild, and at his side was Hananiah, one of the perfumers' guild. They restored Jerusalem as far as the wall of the public square.* ⁹Next to them the work of repair was carried out by Rephaiah, son of Hur, leader of half the district of Jerusalem, ¹⁰and at his side was Jedaiah, son of Harumaph, who repaired opposite his own house. Next to him Hattush, son of Hashabneiah, carried out the work of repair. ¹¹The adjoining sector, as far as the Oven Tower, was repaired by Malchijah, son of Harim, and Hasshub, of Pahathmoab. ¹²At their side the work of repair was carried out by Shallum, son of Hallohesh, leader of half the district of Jerusalem, by himself and his daughters. ¹³The Valley Gate was repaired by Hanun and the inhabitants of Zanoah; they rebuilt it and set up its doors, its bolts, and its bars. They also repaired a thousand cubits of the wall up to the Dung Gate. ¹⁴The Dung Gate was repaired by Malchijah, son of Rechab, leader of the district of Beth-haccherem; he rebuilt it and set up its doors, its bolts, and its bars. ¹⁵The Spring Gate was repaired by Shallum, son of Colhozeh, leader of the district of Mizpah; he rebuilt it, roofed it over, and set up its doors, its bolts, and its bars. He also repaired the

wall of the Aqueduct Pool near the king's garden as far as the steps that lead down from the City of David. ¹⁶After him, the work of repair was carried out by Nehemiah, son of Azbuk, leader of half the district of Beth-zur, to a place opposite the tombs of David, as far as the artificial pool and the barracks. ¹⁷After him, the Levites carried out the work of repair: Rehum, son of Bani. Next to him, for his own district, was Hashabiah, leader of half the district of Keilah. ¹⁸After him, their brethren carried out the work of repair: Binnui, son of Henadad, leader of half the district of Keilah; ¹⁹next to him Ezer, son of Jeshua, leader of Mizpah, who repaired the adjoining sector, the Corner, opposite the ascent to the arsenal. ²⁰After him, Baruch, son of Zabbai, repaired the adjoining sector from the Corner to the entrance of the house of Eliashib, the high priest. ²¹After him, Meremoth, son of Uriah, son of Hakkoz, repaired the adjoining sector from the entrance of Eliashib's house to the end of the house. ²²After him, the work of repair was carried out by the priests, men of the surrounding country. ²³After them, Benjamin and Hasshub carried out the repair in front of their houses; after them, Azariah, son of Maaseiah, son of Ananiah, made the repairs alongside his house. ²⁴After him, Binnui, son of Henadad, repaired the adjoining sector from the house of Azariah to the Corner [that is, to the Angle]. ²⁵After him, Palal, son of Uzai, carried out the work of repair opposite the Corner and the tower projecting from the Upper Palace at the quarters of the guard. After him, Pedaiah, son of Parosh, carried out the work of repair ²⁶to a point opposite the Water Gate on the east, and the projecting tower. ²⁷After him, the Tekoites repaired the adjoining sector opposite the great projecting tower, to the wall of Ophel [the temple slaves were dwelling on Ophel]. ²⁸Above the Horse Gate the priests carried out the work of repair, each before his own house. ²⁹After them Zadok, son of Immer, carried out the repair before his house, and after him the repair was carried out by Shemaiah, son of Shecaniah, keeper of the East Gate.*ˡ* ³⁰After him, Hananiah, son of Shelemiah, and Hanun, the sixth son of Zalaph, repaired the adjoining sector; after them, Meshullam, son of Bere-

---

k Ezr 2, 35; Zep 1, 10.—l Ezr 40, 6.

3, 8: *Wall of the public square:* that is, the section of wall bounding the place of assembly outside the Gate of Ephraim, or New City Gate; cf Neh 3, 6; 8, 16.

chiah, repaired the place opposite his own lodging. [31] After him, Malchijah, a member of the goldsmiths' guild, carried out the work of repair as far as the quarters of the temple slaves and the merchants, before the Gate of Inspection and as far as the upper chamber of the Angle. [32] Between the upper chamber of the Angle and the Sheep Gate, the goldsmiths and the merchants carried out the work of repair.

Opposition from Judah's Foes. [33] When Sanballat heard that we were rebuilding the wall, it roused his anger and he became very much incensed. He ridiculed the Jews, [34] saying in the presence of his brethren and the troops of Samaria: "What are these miserable Jews trying to do? Will they complete their restoration in a single day? Will they recover these stones, burnt as they are, from the heaps of dust?" [35] Tobiah the Ammonite was beside him, and he said: "It is a rubble heap they are building. Any fox that attacked it would breach their wall of stones!" [36] Take note, O our God, how we were mocked! Turn back their derision upon their own heads and let them be carried away to a land of captivity! [37] Hide not their crime and let not their sin be blotted out in your sight, for they insulted the builders to their face![m] [38] We, however, continued to build the wall, which was soon filled in and completed up to half its height. The people worked with a will.

CHAPTER 4

[1] When Sanballat, Tobiah, the Arabs, the Ammonites, and the Ashdodites heard that the restoration of the walls of Jerusalem was progressing—for the gaps were beginning to be closed up—they became extremely angry. [2] Thereupon they all plotted together to come and fight against Jerusalem and thus to throw us into confusion. [3] We prayed to our God and posted a watch against them day and night for fear of what they might do. [4] Meanwhile the Judahites were saying:

"Slackened is the bearers' strength,
    there is no end to the rubbish;
Never shall we be able
    the wall to rebuild."

[5] Our enemies thought, "Before they are aware of it or see us, we shall come into their midst, kill them, and put an end to the work."

[6] When the Jews who lived near them had come to us from one place after another, and had told us ten times over that they were about to attack us, [7] I stationed guards down below, behind the wall, near the exposed points, assigning them by family groups with their swords, their spears, and their bows. [8] I made an inspection, then addressed these words to the nobles, the magistrates, and the rest of the people: "Have no fear of them! Keep in mind the LORD, who is great and to be feared, and fight for your brethren, your sons and daughters, your wives and your homes." [9] When our enemies became aware that we had been warned and that God had upset their plan, we all went back, each to his own task at the wall.

[10] From that time on, however, only half my able men took a hand in the work, while the other half, armed with spears, bucklers, bows, and breastplates, stood guard behind the whole house of Judah[n] [11] as they rebuilt the wall. The load carriers, too, were armed; each did his work with one hand and held a weapon with the other. [12] Every builder, while he worked, had his sword girt at his side. Also, a trumpeter stood beside me, [13] for I had said to the nobles, the magistrates, and the rest of the people: "Our work is scattered and extensive, and we are widely separated from one another along the wall; [14] wherever you hear the trumpet sound, join us there; our God will fight with us." [15] Thus we went on with the work, half of the men with spears at the ready, from daybreak till the stars came out.

[16] At the same time I told the people to spend the nights inside Jerusalem, each man with his own attendant, so that they might serve as a guard by night and a working force by day. [17] Neither I, nor my kinsmen, nor any of my attendants, nor any of the bodyguard that accompanied me took off his clothes; everyone kept his weapon at his right hand.

CHAPTER 5

Antisocial Conduct. [1] [o] Then there rose a great outcry of the common people and their wives against certain of their fellow Jews. [2] Some said: "We are forced to pawn our sons and daughters in order to get grain to eat that we may live." [3] Others

---

m Jer 18, 23.—n Ps 149, 6.—o 1f: Jer 34, 8-22.

said: "We are forced to pawn our fields, our vineyards, and our houses, that we may have grain during the famine." [4] Still others said: "To pay the king's tax we have borrowed money on our fields and our vineyards. [5] And though these are our own kinsmen and our children are as good as theirs, we have had to reduce our sons and daughters to slavery, and violence has been done to some of our daughters! Yet we can do nothing about it, for our fields and our vineyards belong to others." [p]

Nehemiah's Action. [6] I was extremely angry when I heard the reasons they had for complaint. [7] After some deliberation, I called the nobles and magistrates to account, saying to them, "You are exacting interest from your own kinsmen!"[*] I then rebuked them severely, [8] saying to them: "As far as we were able, we bought back our fellow Jews who had been sold to Gentiles; you, however, are selling your own brothers, to have them bought back by us." They remained silent, for they could find no answer. [q] [9] I continued: "What you are doing is not good. Should you not walk in the fear of our God, and put an end to the derision of our Gentile enemies? [10] I myself, my kinsmen, and my attendants have lent the people money and grain without charge. Let us put an end to this usury! [11] I ask that you return to them this very day their fields, their vineyards, their olive groves, and their houses, together with the interest on the money, the grain, the wine, and the oil that you have lent them." [12] They answered: "We will return everything and exact nothing further from them. We will do just what you ask." Then I called for the priests and had them administer an oath to these men that they would do as they had promised. [13] I also shook out the folds of my garment, saying, "Thus may God shake from his home and his fortune every man who fails to keep this promise, and may he thus be shaken out and emptied!" And the whole assembly answered, "Amen," and praised the LORD. Then the people did as they had promised.

Nehemiah's Lack of Self-Interest. [14] Moreover, from the time that King Artaxerxes appointed me governor in the land of Judah, from his twentieth to his thirty-second year—during these twelve years neither I nor my brethren lived from the governor's allowance. [15] The earlier governors, my predecessors, had laid a heavy burden on the people, taking from them each day forty silver shekels for their food; then too, their men oppressed the people. But I, because I feared God, did not act thus. [16] Moreover, though I had acquired no land of my own, I did my part in this work on the wall, and all my men were gathered there for the work. [17] Though I set my table for a hundred and fifty persons, Jews and magistrates, as well as those who came to us from the nations round about, [18] and though the daily preparations were made at my expense—one beef, six choice muttons, poultry—besides all kinds of wine in abundance every ten days, despite this I did not claim the governor's allowance, for the labor lay heavy upon this people. [19] Keep in mind, O my God, in my favor all that I did for this people.

CHAPTER 6

Plots against Nehemiah. [1] When it had been reported to Sanballat, Tobiah, Geshem the Arab, and our other enemies that I had rebuilt the wall and that there was no breach left in it (though up to that time I had not yet set up the doors in the gates), [2] Sanballat and Geshem sent me this message: "Come, let us hold council together at Caphirim in the plain of Ono." They were planning to do me harm. [3] However, I sent messengers to them with this reply: "I am engaged in a great enterprise and am unable to come down; why should the work stop, while I leave it to come down to you?" [4] Four times they sent me this same proposal, and each time I gave the same reply. [5] Then, the fifth time, Sanballat sent me the same message by one of his servants, who bore an unsealed letter [6] containing this text: "Among the nations it has been reported—Geshem is witness to this—that you and the Jews are planning a rebellion; that for this reason you are rebuilding the wall; and that you are to be their king"—and so on. [7] "Also, that you have set up prophets in Jerusalem to

---

p Ex 21, 7; Lv 25, 39.—q Lv 25, 48.

5, 7: *You are exacting interest from your own kinsmen!:* contrary to the Mosaic law (Dt 23, 20).

proclaim you king of Judah. Now, since matters like these must reach the ear of the king, come, let us hold council together." [8] I sent him this answer: "Nothing of what you report has taken place; rather, it is the invention of your own mind." [9] They were all trying to frighten us, thinking, "Their hands will slacken in the work, and it will never be completed." But instead, I now redoubled my efforts.

[10] I went to the house of Shemaiah, son of Delaiah, son of Mehetabel, who was unable to go about, and he said:

"Let us meet in the house of God,
    inside the temple building;
    let us lock the doors of the temple.
For men are coming to kill you;
    by night they are coming to kill
      you."

[11] My answer was: "A man like me take flight? Can a man like me enter the temple to save his life? I will not go!" [12] For on consideration it was plain to me that God had not sent him; rather, because Tobiah and Sanballat had bribed him, he voiced this prophecy concerning me [13] that I might act on it out of fear and commit this sin. Then they would have had a shameful story with which to discredit me. [14] Keep in mind Tobiah and Sanballat, O my God, because of these things they did; keep in mind as well Noadiah the prophetess and the other prophets who were trying to frighten me.[r]

Conclusion of the Work. [15] The wall was finished on the twenty-fifth day of Elul;* it had taken fifty-two days. [16] When all our enemies had heard of this, and all the nations round about had taken note of it, our enemies lost much face in the eyes of the nations, for they knew that it was with our God's help that this work had been completed.[s] [17] * At that same time, however, many letters were going to Tobiah from the nobles of Judah, and Tobiah's letters were reaching them, [18] for many in Judah were in league with him, since he was the son-in-law of Shecaniah, son of Arah, and his son Jehohanan had married the daughter of Meshullam, son of Berechiah. [19] Thus they would praise his good deeds in my presence and relate to him whatever I said; and Tobiah sent letters trying to frighten me.

CHAPTER 7

[1] When the wall had been rebuilt, I had the doors set up, and the gatekeepers [and the singers and the Levites] were put in charge of them. [2] Over Jerusalem I placed Hanani, my brother, and Hananiah, the commander of the citadel, who was a more trustworthy and God-fearing man than most. [3] I said to them: "The gates of Jerusalem are not to be opened until the sun is hot, and while the sun is still shining they shall shut and bar the doors. Appoint as watchmen the inhabitants of Jerusalem, some at their watch posts, and others before their own houses."

Census of the Province. [4] Now the city was quite wide and spacious, but its population was small, and none of the houses had been rebuilt. [5] When my God had put it into my mind to gather together the nobles, the magistrates, and the common people, and to examine their family records, I came upon the family list of those who had returned in the earliest period. There I found the following written:

[6] *t* * These are the inhabitants of the province who returned from the captivity of the exiles whom Nebuchadnezzar, king of Babylon, had carried away, and who came back to Jerusalem and Judah, each man to his own city [7] (those who returned with Zerubbabel, Jeshua, Nehemiah, Azariah, Raamiah, Nahamani, Mordecai, Bilshan, Mispereth, Bigvai, Nehum, and Baanah).

The census of the men of Israel: [8] sons of Parosh, two thousand one hundred and seventy-two; [9] sons of Shephatiah, three hundred and seventy-two; [10] sons of Arah, six hundred and fifty-two; [11] sons of Pahath-moab who were sons of Jeshua and Joab, two thousand eight hundred and eighteen; [12] sons of Elam, one thousand two hundred and fifty-four; [13] sons of Zattu, eight hundred and forty-five; [14] sons of Zaccai, seven hundred and sixty; [15] sons of Binnui, six hundred and forty-eight; [16] sons of Bebai, six hundred and

---

r Jer 23, 9-40; Zec 13, 3.—s Ps 118, 22f; 127, 1.—t 6-72: Ezr 2, 1-70.

6, 15: *Elul:* the sixth month (August-September). *Fifty-two days:* according to Josephus (*Antiquities* XI, v 8), the rebuilding of the walls of Jerusalem by Nehemiah took two years and four months, which seems more probable.
6, 17ff: These verses should be read immediately after v 14.
7, 6-72a: See note on Ezr 2, 1-67.

twenty-eight; [17]sons of Azgad, two thousand three hundred and twenty-two; [18]sons of Adonikam, six hundred and sixty-seven; [19]sons of Bigvai, two thousand and sixty-seven; [20]sons of Adin, six hundred and fifty-five; [21]sons of Ater who were sons of Hezekiah, ninety-eight; [22]sons of Hashum, three hundred and twenty-eight; [23]sons of Bezai, three hundred and twenty-four; [24]sons of Hariph, one hundred and twelve; [25]sons of Gibeon, ninety-five; [26]men of Bethlehem and Netophah, one hundred and eighty-eight; [27]men of Anathoth, one hundred and twenty-eight; [28]men of Beth-azmaveth, forty-two; [29]men of Kiriath-jearim, Chephirah, and Beeroth, seven hundred and forty-three; [30]men of Ramah and Geba, six hundred and twenty-one; [31]men of Michmas, one hundred and twenty-two; [32]men of Bethel and Ai, one hundred and twenty-three; [33]men of Nebo, fifty-two; [34]sons of another Elam, one thousand two hundred and fifty-four; [35]sons of Harim, three hundred and twenty; [36]sons of Jericho, three hundred and forty-five; [37]sons of Lod, Hadid, and Ono, seven hundred and twenty-one; [38]sons of Senaah, three thousand nine hundred and thirty.

[39]The priests: sons of Jedaiah who were of the house of Jeshua, nine hundred and seventy-three; [40]sons of Immer, one thousand and fifty-two; [41]sons of Pashhur, one thousand two hundred and forty-seven; [42]sons of Harim, one thousand and seventeen.

[43]The Levites: sons of Jeshua, Kadmiel, Binnui, Hodeviah, seventy-four.

[44]The singers: sons of Asaph, one hundred and forty-eight.

[45]The gatekeepers: sons of Shallum, sons of Ater, sons of Talmon, sons of Akkub, sons of Hatita, sons of Shobai, one hundred and thirty-eight.

[46]The temple slaves: sons of Ziha, sons of Hasupha, sons of Tabbaoth, [47]sons of Keros, sons of Sia, sons of Padon, [48]sons of Lebana, sons of Hagaba, sons of Shalmai, [49]sons of Hanan, sons of Giddel, sons of Gahar, [50]sons of Reaiah, sons of Rezin, sons of Nekoda, [51]sons of Gazzam, sons of Uzza, sons of Paseah, [52]sons of Besai, sons of the Meunites, sons of the Nephusites, [53]sons of Bakbuk,

sons of Hakupha, sons of Harhur, [54]sons of Bazlith, son of Mehida, sons of Harsha, [55]sons of Barkos, sons of Sisera, sons of Temah, [56]sons of Neziah, sons of Hatipha.

[57]Descendants of the slaves of Solomon: sons of Sotai, sons of Sophereth, sons of Perida, [58]sons of Jaala, sons of Darkon, sons of Giddel, [59]sons of Shephatiah, sons of Hattil, sons of Pochereth-hazzebaim, sons of Amon. [60]The total of the temple slaves and the descendants of the slaves of Solomon was three hundred and ninety-two.

[61]The following who returned from Telmelah, Tel-harsha, Cherub, Addon, and Immer were unable to prove that their ancestral houses and their descent were Israelite: [62]sons of Delaiah, sons of Tobiah, sons of Nekoda, six hundred and forty-two. [63]Also, of the priests: sons of Hobaiah, sons of Hakkoz, sons of Barzillai (he had married one of the daughters of Barzillai the Gileadite and became known by his name). [64]These men searched their family records, but their names could not be found written there; hence they were degraded from the priesthood, [65]and His Excellency* ordered them not to partake of the most holy foods until there should be a priest bearing the Urim and Thummim.

[66]The entire assembly taken together came to forty-two thousand three hundred and sixty, [67]not counting their male and female slaves, who were seven thousand three hundred and thirty-seven. They also had two hundred male and female singers. Their horses were seven hundred and thirty-six, their mules two hundred and forty-five, [68]their camels four hundred and thirty-five, their asses six thousand seven hundred and twenty.

[69]Certain of the family heads contributed to the service. His Excellency put into the treasury one thousand drachmas of gold, fifty basins, thirty garments for priests, and five hundred minas of silver. [70]Some of the family heads contributed to the treasury for the temple service: twenty thousand drachmas of gold and two thousand two hundred minas of silver. [71]The contributions of the rest of the people amounted to twenty thousand drachmas of gold, two thousand minas of silver, and sixty-seven garments for priests.

Neh

7, 65. 69: *His Excellency:* see note on Ezr 2, 63.

72 The priests, the Levites, the gatekeepers, the singers, the temple slaves, and all Israel took up residence in their cities.

II: PROMULGATION OF THE LAW

CHAPTER 8

Ezra Reads the Law.* Now when the seventh month came, ¹ the whole people gathered as one man in the open space before the Water Gate, and they called upon Ezra the scribe to bring forth the book of the law of Moses which the LORD prescribed for Israel.ᵘ ² On the first day of the seventh month, therefore, Ezra the priest brought the law before the assembly, which consisted of men, women, and those children old enough to understand. ³ Standing at one end of the open place that was before the Water Gate, he read out of the book from daybreak till midday, in the presence of the men, the women, and those children old enough to understand; and all the people listened attentively to the book of the law. ⁴ Ezra the scribe stood on a wooden platform that had been made for the occasion; at his right side stood Mattithiah, Shema, Anaiah, Uriah, Hilkiah, and Masseiah, and on his left Pedaiah, Mishael, Malchijah, Hashum, Hashbaddanah, Zechariah, Meshullam. ⁵ Ezra opened the scroll so that all the people might see it (for he was standing higher up than any of the people); and, as he opened it, all the people rose. ⁶ Ezra blessed the LORD, the great God, and all the people, their hands raised high, answered, "Amen, amen!" Then they bowed down and prostrated themselves before the LORD, their faces to the ground. ⁷ [The Levites Jeshua, Bani, Sherebiah, Jamin, Akkub, Shabbethai, Hodiah, Maaseiah, Kelita, Azariah, Jozabad, Hanan, and Pelaiah explained the law to the people, who remained in their places.]ᵛ ⁸ Ezra read plainly from the book of the law of God, interpreting it so that all could understand what was read.ʷ ⁹ Then [Nehemiah, that is, His Excellency, and] Ezra the priest-scribe [and the Levites who were instructing the people] said to all the people: "Today is holy to the LORD your God. Do not be sad, and do not weep"—for all the people were weeping as they heard the words of the law. ¹⁰ He said further: "Go, eat rich foods and drink sweet drinks, and allot portions to those who had nothing

prepared; for today is holy to our LORD. Do not be saddened this day, for rejoicing in the LORD must be your strength!"ˣ ¹¹ [And the Levites quieted all the people, saying, "Hush, for today is holy, and you must not be saddened."] ¹² Then all the people went to eat and drink, to distribute portions, and to celebrate with great joy, for they understood the words that had been expounded to them.

The Feast of Booths. ¹³ On the second day, the family heads of the whole people and also the priests and the Levites gathered around Ezra the scribe and examined the words of the law more closely. ¹⁴ They found it written in the law prescribed by the LORD through Moses that the Israelites must dwell in booths during the feast of the seventh month;ʸ ¹⁵ and that they should have this proclamation made throughout their cities and in Jerusalem: "Go out into the hill country and bring in branches of olive trees, oleasters, myrtle, palm, and other leafy trees, to make booths, as the law prescribes."ᶻ ¹⁶ The people went out and brought in branches with which they made booths for themselves, on the roofs of their houses, in their courtyards, in the courts of the house of God, and in the open spaces of the Water Gate and the Gate of Ephraim. ¹⁷ Thus the entire assembly of the returned exiles made booths and dwelt in them. Now the Israelites had done nothing of this sort from the days of Jeshua, son of Nun, until this occasion; therefore there was very great joy. ¹⁸ Ezra read from the book of the law of God day after day, from the first day to the last. They kept the feast for seven days, and the solemn assembly on the eighth day, as was required.

CHAPTER 9

Confession of the People. ¹ ᵃ * On the twenty-fourth day of this month, the Israelites gathered together fasting and in sackcloth, their heads covered with dust.

---

u Ezr 3, 1.—v Neh 10, 11.—w Ezr 7, 6.—x Est 9, 19.—y Ex 23, 14; Lv 23, 33-36.—z Ps 118, 27.—a Dn 9, 3.

7, 72b—8, 18: To be read after Ezr 8, 36. The gloss mentioning *Nehemiah* in v 9 was inserted in this Ezra section after the dislocation of several parts of Ezra-Nehemiah had occurred. There is no clear evidence of a simultaneous presence of Nehemiah and Ezra in Jerusalem; Neh 12, 26 and 12, 36 are also scribal glosses.

9, 1-5: This is a continuation of the account concerning the problem of mixed marriages at the time of Ezra; it should be read immediately after Ezr 10, 44.

2 Those of Israelite descent separated themselves from all who were of foreign extraction, then stood forward and confessed their sins and the guilty deeds of their fathers. *b* 3 When they had taken their places, they read from the book of the law of the LORD their God, for a fourth part of the day, and during another fourth part they made their confession and prostrated themselves before the LORD their God. 4 Standing on the platform of the Levites were Jeshua, Binnui, Kadmiel, Shebaniah, Bunni, Sherebiah, Bani, and Chenani, who cried out to the LORD their God with a loud voice. 5 The Levites Jeshua, Kadmiel, Bani, Hashabneiah, Sherebiah, Hodiah, Shebaniah, and Pethahiah said,

"Arise, bless the LORD, your God, from eternity to eternity!"

The Israelites answered with the blessing,

"Blessed is your glorious name, and exalted above all blessing and praise." *c*

6 * Then Ezra said: "It is you, O LORD, you are the only one; you made the heavens, the highest heavens and all their host, the earth and all that is upon it, the seas and all that is in them. To all of them you give life, and the heavenly hosts bow down before you.

7 "You, O LORD, are the God who chose Abram, who brought him out from Ur of the Chaldees, and named him Abraham. *d* 8 When you had found his heart faithful in your sight, you made the covenant with him to give to him and his posterity the land of the Canaanites, Hittites, Amorites, Perizzites, Jebusites, and Girgashites. These promises of yours you fulfilled, for you are just. *e*

9 "You saw the affliction of our fathers in Egypt, you heard their cry by the Red Sea; *f*
10 You worked signs and wonders against Pharaoh, against all his servants and the people of his land, Because you knew of their insolence toward them;

thus you made for yourself a name even to this day. *g*
11 The sea you divided before them, on dry ground they passed through the midst of the sea; Their pursuers you hurled into the depths, like a stone into the mighty waters. *h*
12 With a column of cloud you led them by day, and by night with a column of fire, To light the way of their journey, the way in which they must travel. *i*
13 On Mount Sinai you came down, you spoke with them from heaven; You gave them just ordinances, firm laws, good statutes, and commandments; *j*
14 Your holy sabbath you made known to them, commandments, statutes, and law you prescribed for them, by the hand of Moses your servant. *k*
15 Food from heaven you gave them in their hunger, water from a rock you sent them in their thirst. You bade them enter and occupy the land which you had sworn with upraised hand to give them. *l*

16 "But they, our fathers, proved to be insolent; they held their necks stiff and would not obey your commandments. 17 They refused to obey and no longer remembered the miracles you had worked for them. They stiffened their necks and turned their heads to return to their slavery in Egypt. But you are a God of pardons, gracious and compassionate, slow to anger and rich in mercy; you did not forsake them. *m* 18 Though they made for themselves a molten calf, and proclaimed, 'Here is your God who brought you up out of Egypt,' and were guilty of great effronteries, *n* 19 yet in your great mercy you did not forsake them in the desert. The column of cloud did not cease to lead them by day on their journey, nor did the column of fire by night cease to light for them the way by which they were to travel.

20 "Your good spirit you bestowed on them, to give them understanding; your manna you did not withhold from their mouths, and you gave them water in their thirst. *o* 21 Forty years in the desert you

b Ezr 9, 1f; 10, 11.—c Dn 2, 20; 3, 52.—d Gn 12, 1; 17, 5.—e Gn 15, 18f.—f Ex 2, 23f.—g Ex 7—11; 14.—h Ex 15, 5. 10.—i Ex 13, 21f.—j Ex 19—20.—k Ex 20, 8.—l Ex 16, 4; 17, 1f.—m Nm 14, 1-4; Ex 34, 6; Dn 9, 9.—n Ex 32, 4.—o Dt 2, 7.

9, 6-37: The prayer of Ezra which began in Ezr 9, 6f is here continued; see note on Ezr 9, 7.

sustained them: they did not want; their garments did not become worn, and their feet did not become swollen.ᵖ ²² You gave them kingdoms and peoples, which you divided up among them as border lands. They possessed the land of Sihon, king of Heshbon, and the land of Og, king of Bashan.�q

²³ "You made their children as numerous as the stars of the heavens, and you brought them into the land which you had commanded their fathers to enter and possess.ʳ ²⁴ The sons went in to take possession of the land, and you humbled before them the Canaanite inhabitants of the land and delivered them over into their power, their kings as well as the peoples of the land, to do with them as they would. ²⁵ They captured fortified cities and fertile land; they took possession of houses filled with all good things, cisterns already dug, vineyards, olive groves, and fruit trees in abundance. They could eat and have their fill, fatten and feast themselves on your immense good gifts.ˢ

²⁶ "But they were contemptuous and rebellious: they cast your law behind their backs; they slew your prophets who bore witness against them in order to bring them back to you, and they were guilty of great effronteries.ᵗ ²⁷ Therefore you delivered them into the power of their enemies, who oppressed them. But in the time of their oppression they would cry out to you, and you would hear them from heaven, and according to your great mercy give them saviors to deliver them from the power of their enemies.ᵘ

²⁸ "As soon as they had relief, they would go back to doing evil in your sight. Then again you abandoned them to the power of their enemies, who crushed them. Then they cried out to you, and you heard them from heaven and delivered them according to your mercy, many times over. ²⁹ You bore witness against them, in order to bring them back to your law. But they were insolent and would not obey your commandments; they sinned against your ordinances, from which men draw life when they practice them. They turned stubborn backs, stiffened their necks, and would not obey.ᵛ ³⁰ You were patient with them for many years, bearing witness against them through your spirit, by

means of your prophets; still they would not listen. Thus you delivered them over into the power of the peoples of the lands. ³¹ Yet in your great mercy you did not completely destroy them and you did not forsake them, for you are a kind and merciful God.

³² "Now, therefore, O our God, great, mighty, and awesome God, you who in your mercy preserve the covenant, take into account all the disasters that have befallen us, our kings, our princes, our priests, our prophets, our fathers, and your entire people, from the time of the kings of Assyria until this day!ʷ ³³ In all that has come upon us you have been just, for you kept faith while we have done evil.ˣ ³⁴ Yes, our kings, our princes, our priests, and our fathers have not kept your law; they paid no attention to your commandments and the obligations of which you reminded them. ³⁵ While they were yet in their kingdom, in the midst of the many good things that you had given them and in the wide and fertile land that you had spread out before them, they did not serve you nor did they turn away from their evil deeds. ³⁶ But, see, we today are slaves; and as for the land which you gave our fathers that they might eat its fruits and good things—see, we have become slaves upon it! ³⁷ Its rich produce goes to the kings whom you set over us because of our sins, who rule over our bodies and our cattle as they please. We are in great distress!"

CHAPTER 10

Agreement of the People. ¹ * In view of all this, we are entering into a firm pact, which we are putting into writing. On the sealed document appear the names of our princes, our Levites, and our priests.ʸ

² On the sealed document: His Excellency Nehemiah, son of Hacaliah, and Zedekiah.

³ Seraiah, Azariah, Jeremiah, ⁴ Pashhur, Amariah, Malchijah, ⁵ Hattush, Sheba-

---

p Dt 8, 4.—q Nm 21, 21-35; Dt 1, 4; 2, 26—3, 11.—r Dt 1, 10.—s Dt 3, 5; 6, 10f; 11, 11; 32, 15.—t Wis 2, 10-20.—u Dn 9, 19.—v Lv 18, 5; Dt 11, 21; 30, 16; 32, 47.—w Lam 5.—x Dn 3, 27; 9, 14.—y Neh 12, 12-26.

10, 1-40: This section belongs to the Nehemiah narrative rather than to that of Ezra. It is best read after Neh 13, 31. *In view of all this:* considering the situation described in Neh 13, 4-31.

niah, Malluch, ⁶Harim, Meremoth, Obadiah, ⁷Daniel, Ginnethon, Baruch, ⁸Meshullam, Abijah, Mijamin, ⁹Maaziah, Bilgai, Shemaiah: these are the priests. ¹⁰The Levites: Jeshua, son of Azaniah; Binnui, of the sons of Henadad; Kadmiel; ¹¹and their brethren Shebaniah, Hodiah, Kelita, Pelaiah, Hanan,ᶻ ¹²Mica, Rehob, Hashabiah, ¹³Zaccur, Sherebiah, Shebaniah, ¹⁴Hodiah, Bani, Beninu.

¹⁵The leaders of the people: Parosh, Pahath-moab, Elam, Zattu, Bani, ¹⁶Bunni, Azgad, Bebai, ¹⁷Adonijah, Bigvai, Adin, ¹⁸Ater, Hezekiah, Azzur, ¹⁹Hodiah, Hashum, Bezai, ²⁰Hariph, Anathoth, Nebai, ²¹Magpiash, Meshullam, Hazir, ²²Meshezabel, Zadok, Jaddua, ²³Pelatiah, Hanan, Anaiah, ²⁴Hoshea, Hananiah, Hasshub, ²⁵Hallohesh, Pilha, Shobek, ²⁶Rehum, Hashabnah, Maaseiah, ²⁷Ahiah, Hanan, Anan, ²⁸Malluch, Harim, Baanah.

Provisions of the Pact. ²⁹The rest of the people, priests, Levites, gatekeepers, singers, temple slaves, and all others who have separated themselves from the peoples of the lands in favor of the law of God, with their wives, their sons, their daughters, all who are of the age of discretion, ³⁰join with their brethren who are their princes, and with the sanction of a curse take this oath to follow the law of God which was given through Moses, the servant of God, and to observe carefully all the commandments of the LORD, our Lord, his ordinances and his statutes.ᵃ

³¹Agreed, that we will not marry our daughters to the peoples of the land, and that we will not take their daughters for our sons.ᵇ

³²When the peoples of the land bring in merchandise or any kind of grain for sale on the sabbath day, we will not buy from them on the sabbath or on any other holyday. We will forgo the seventh year, as well as every kind of debt.ᶜ

³³We impose these commandments on ourselves: to give a third of a shekel each year for the service of the house of

our God,ᵈ ³⁴for the showbread, for the daily cereal offering, for the daily holocaust, for the sabbaths, new moons, and festivals, for the holy offerings, for sin offerings to make atonement for Israel, and for every service of the house of our God. ³⁵We, priests, Levites, and people, have determined by lot concerning the procurement of wood: it is to be brought to the house of our God by each of our family houses at stated times each year, to be burnt on the altar of the LORD, our God, as the law prescribes.ᵉ ³⁶ ᶠWe have agreed to bring each year to the house of the LORD the first fruits of our fields and of our fruit trees, of whatever kind; ³⁷also, as is prescribed in the law, to bring to the house of our God, to the priests who serve in the house of our God, the first-born of our children and our animals, including the first-born of our flocks and herds. ³⁸The first batch of our dough, and our offerings of the fruit of every tree, of wine and of oil, we will bring to the priests, to the chambers of the house of our God. The tithe of our fields we will bring to the Levites; they, the Levites, shall take the tithe in all the cities of our service.ᵍ ³⁹An Aaronite priest shall be with the Levites when they take the tithe, and the Levites shall bring the tithe of the tithes to the house of our God, to the chambers of the treasury. ⁴⁰For to these chambers the Israelites and Levites bring the offerings of grain, wine, and oil; there also are housed the utensils of the sanctuary, and the ministering priests, the gatekeepers, and the singers. We will not neglect the house of our God.

CHAPTER 11

Repeopling of Jerusalem. ¹ * The leaders of the people took up residence in Jerusalem, and the rest of the people cast lots to bring one man in ten to reside in Jerusalem, the holy city, while the other nine would remain in the other cities.ʰ ²The people applauded all those men who willingly agreed to take up residence in Jerusalem.

The Residents of Jerusalem. ³ ⁱ These are the heads of the province who took up residence in Jerusalem. (In the cities of Judah dwelt lay Israelites, priests, Levites, temple slaves, and the descendants of the slaves of Solomon, each man on the property he owned in his own city.)

z Ezr 10, 23.—a Neh 13, 23-27.—b Neh 13, 15-22.—c Neh 5, 1-13; Ex 20, 8; Lv 25, 2-7.—d 2 Chr 24, 6. 9f; Lv 24, 5-9.—e Neh 13, 31.—f 36f: Ex 13, 1. 11ff; Dt 26, 1.—g Neh 13, 10-14; Nm 18, 21. 24ff.—h Neh 7, 4.—i 3-19: 1 Chr 9, 2-34.

11, 1-19: This list of the family heads who lived in Jerusalem at the time of Nehemiah is best read after Neh 7, 72a. It is basically the same as that given in 1 Chr 9, 2-17, but there are many differences between the two lists.

⁴In Jerusalem dwelt both Judahites and Benjaminites. Of the Judahites: Athaiah, son of Uzziah, son of Zechariah, son of Amariah, son of Shephatiah, son of Mehallalel, of the sons of Perez; ⁵Maaseiah, son of Baruch, son of Colhozeh, son of Hazaiah, son of Adaiah, son of Joiarib, son of Zechariah, a son of the Shelanites. ⁶The total of the sons of Perez who dwelt in Jerusalem was four hundred and sixty-eight valiant men.

⁷These were the Benjaminites: Sallu, son of Meshullam, son of Joed, son of Pedaiah, son of Kolaiah, son of Maaseiah, son of Ithiel, son of Jeshaiah, ⁸and his brethren, warriors, nine hundred and twenty-eight in number. ⁹Joel, son of Zichri, was their commander, and Judah, son of Hassenuah, was second in charge of the city.

¹⁰Among the priests were: Jedaiah; Joiarib; Jachin; ¹¹Seraiah, son of Hilkiah, son of Meshullam, son of Zadok, son of Meraioth, son of Ahitub, the ruler of the house of God, ¹²and their brethren who carried out the temple service, eight hundred and twenty-two; Adaiah, son of Jeroham, son of Pelaliah, son of Amzi, son of Zechariah, son of Pashhur, son of Malchijah, ¹³and his brethren, family heads, two hundred and forty-two; and Amasai, son of Azarel, son of Ahzai, son of Meshillemoth, son of Immer, ¹⁴and his brethren, warriors, one hundred and twenty-eight. Their commander was Zabdiel, son of Haggadol.

¹⁵Among the Levites were Shemaiah, son of Hasshub, son of Azrikam, son of Hashabiah, son of Bunni; ¹⁶Shabbethai and Jozabad, levitical chiefs who were placed over the external affairs of the house of God; ¹⁷Mattaniah, son of Micah, son of Zabdi, son of Asaph, director of the psalms, who led the thanksgiving at prayer; Bakbukiah, second in rank among his brethren; and Abda, son of Shammua, son of Galal, son of Jeduthun. ¹⁸The total of the Levites in the holy city was two hundred and eighty-four.

¹⁹The gatekeepers were Akkub, Talmon, and their brethren, who kept watch over the gates; one hundred and seventy-two in number.

²⁰The rest of Israel, including priests and Levites, were in all the other cities of Judah, each man in his inheritance.

²¹The temple slaves lived on Ophel. Ziha and Gishpa were in charge of the temple slaves.

²²The prefect of the Levites in Jerusalem was Uzzi, son of Bani, son of Hashabiah, son of Mattaniah, son of Mica; he was one of the sons of Asaph, the singers appointed to the service of the house of Godʲ—²³for they had been appointed by royal decree, and there was a fixed schedule for the singers assigning them their daily duties.

²⁴Pethahiah, son of Meshezabel, a descendant of Zerah, son of Judah, was royal deputy in all affairs that concerned the people.

The Other Cities. ²⁵As concerns their villages in the country: Judahites lived in Kiriath-arba and its dependencies, in Dibon and its dependencies, in Jekabzeel and its villages, ²⁶in Jeshua, Moladah, Beth-pelet, ²⁷in Hazar-shual, in Beersheba and its dependencies, ²⁸in Ziklag, in Meconah and its dependencies, ²⁹in En-rimmon, Zorah, Jarmuth, ³⁰Zanoah, Adullam, and their villages, Lachish and its countryside, Azekah and its dependencies. They were settled from Beer-sheba to Ge-hinnom.

³¹Benjaminites were in Geba, Michmash, Aija, Bethel and its dependencies, ³²Anathoth, Nob, Ananiah, ³³Hazor, Ramah, Gittaim, ³⁴Hadid, Zeboim, Neballat, ³⁵Lod, Ono, and the Valley of the Artisans.

³⁶Some sections of the Levites from Judah settled in Benjamin.

CHAPTER 12

Priests and Levites under Zerubbabel. ¹ ᵏThe following are the priests and Levites who returned with Zerubbabel, son of Shealtiel, and Jeshua: Seraiah, Jeremiah, Ezra, ²Amariah, Malluch, Hattush, ³Shecaniah, Rehum, Meremoth, ⁴Iddo, Ginnethon, Abijah, ⁵Mijamin, Maadiah, Bilgah, ⁶Shemaiah, and Joiarib, Jedaiah, ⁷Sallu, Amok, Hilkiah, Jedaiah. These were the priestly heads and their brethren in the days of Jeshua.

⁸The Levites were Jeshua, Binnui, Kadmiel, Sherebiah, Judah, Mattaniah; the last-mentioned, together with his brethren, was in charge of the hymns, ⁹while Bakbukiah and Unno and their brethren ministered opposite them by turns.

j 2 Chr 20, 14.—k 1-6: Neh 12, 12-22.

High Priests.* [10]Jeshua became the father of Joiakim, Joiakim became the father of Eliashib, and Eliashib became the father of Joiada. [11]Joiada became the father of Johanan, and Johanan became the father of Jaddua.

Priests and Levites under Joiakim. [12] *l* In the days of Joiakim these were the priestly family heads: for Seraiah, Meraiah; for Jeremiah, Hananiah; [13]for Ezra, Meshullam; for Amariah, Jehohanan; [14]for Malluch, Jonathan; for Shebaniah, Joseph; [15]for Harim, Adna; for Meremoth, Helkai; [16]for Iddo, Zechariah; for Ginnethon, Meshullam; [17]for Abijah, Zichri; for Miamin, . . . ; for Maadiah, Piltai; [18]for Bilgah, Shammua; for Shemaiah, Jehonathan; [19]and for Joiarib, Mattenai; for Jedaiah, Uzzi; [20]for Sallu, Kallai; for Amok, Eber; [21]for Hilkiah, Hashabiah; for Jedaiah, Nethanel.

[22]In the time of Eliashib, Joiada, Johanan, and Jaddua, the family heads of the priests were written down in the Book of Chronicles, up until the reign of Darius the Persian. [23]The sons of Levi: the family heads were written down in the Book of Chronicles, up until the time of Johanan, the son of Eliashib.

[24]The heads of the Levites were Hashabiah, Sherebiah, Jeshua, Binnui, Kadmiel. Their brethren who stood opposite them to sing praises and thanksgiving in fulfillment of the command of David, the man of God, one section opposite the other,*m* [25]were Mattaniah, Bakbukiah, Obadiah.

Meshullam, Talmon, and Akkub were gatekeepers. They kept watch over the storerooms at the gates.*n*

---

l 12-22: Neh 10, 3-9; 12, 1-6.—m Ezr 2, 40.—n Neh 11, 17.

12, 10f: *Jeshua,* the high priest when Zerubbabel was governor, i.e., the last decades of the sixth century B.C. (Hg 1, 1. 12. 14; 2, 2. 4). He was the grandfather of *Eliashib,* the high priest at least in the early period of Nehemiah's governorship, i.e., 445-433 B.C. (Ezr 10, 6; Neh 3, 1. 20f; 13, 4. 7). Eliashib, in turn, was the grandfather of *Johanan,* a grown man, if not yet a high priest, at the time of Ezra, i.e., c. 400 B.C. (Ezr 10, 6, and note). According to Josephus *(Antiquities* XI, v) whose testimony here is doubtful, *Jaddua,* son of Johanan, died as an old man about the same time that Alexander the Great died, i.e., 323 B.C. If this list of the postexilic high priests, at least as far as Johanan, comes, as seems probable (cf v 23), from the Chronicler himself and not from a later scribe, it is of prime importance for dating the Chronicler's work in the first decades of the fourth century B.C.

12, 27-43: *The dedication of the wall of Jerusalem* took place, no doubt, soon after the restoration of the wall and its gates had been completed. Therefore, this section is best read after Neh 6, 15.

[26]All these lived in the time of Joiakim, son of Jeshua, son of Jozadak [and in the time of Nehemiah the governor and of Ezra the priest-scribe].

Dedication of the City Wall. [27] * At the dedication of the wall of Jerusalem, the Levites were sought out wherever they lived and were brought to Jerusalem to celebrate a joyful dedication with thanksgiving hymns and the music of cymbals, harps, and lyres. [28]The levitical singers gathered together from the region about Jerusalem, from the villages of the Netophathites, [29]from Beth-gilgal, and from the plains of Geba and Azmaveth (for the singers had built themselves settlements about Jerusalem). [30]The priests and Levites first purified themselves, then they purified the people, the gates, and the wall.

[31]I had the princes of Judah mount the wall, and I arranged two great choirs. The first of these proceeded to the right, along the top of the wall, in the direction of the Dung Gate, [32]followed by Hoshaiah and half the princes of Judah, [33]along with Azariah, Ezra, Meshullam, [34]Judah, Benjamin, Shemaiah, and Jeremiah, [35]priests with the trumpets, and also Zechariah, son of Jonathan, son of Shemaiah, son of Mattaniah, son of Micaiah, son of Zaccur, son of Asaph, [36]and his brethren Shemaiah, Azarel, Milalai, Gilalai, Maai, Nethanel, Judah, and Hanani, with the musical instruments of David, the man of God. [Ezra the scribe was at their head.] [37]At the Spring Gate they went straight up by the steps of the City of David and continued along the top of the wall above the house of David until they came to the Water Gate on the east.

[38]The second choir proceeded to the left, followed by myself and the other half of the princes of the people, along the top of the wall past the Oven Tower as far as the Broad Wall, [39]then past the Ephraim Gate [the New City Gate], the Fish Gate, the Tower of Hananel, and the Hundred Tower, as far as the Sheep Gate [and they came to a halt at the Prison Gate].

[40]The two choirs took up a position in the house of God; I, too, who had with me half the magistrates, [41]the priests Eliakim, Maaseiah, Minjamin, Micaiah, Elioenai, Zechariah, Hananiah, with the trumpets, [42]and Maaseiah, Shemaiah, Eleazar,

Uzzi, Jehohanan, Malchijah, Elam, and Ezer. The singers were heard under the leadership of Jezrahiah. [43] Great sacrifices were offered on that day, and there was rejoicing over the great feast of the LORD in which they shared. The women and the children joined in, and the rejoicing at Jerusalem could be heard from afar off.

Offerings for Priests and Levites.* [44] o At that time men were appointed over the chambers set aside for stores, offerings, first fruits, and tithes; in them they were to collect from the fields of the various cities the portions legally assigned to the priests and Levites. For Judah rejoiced in its appointed priests and Levites [45] who carried out the ministry of their God and the ministry of purification (as did the singers and the gatekeepers) in accordance with the prescriptions of David and of Solomon, his son. [46] For the heads of the families of the singers and the hymns of praise and thanksgiving to God came down from the days of David and Asaph in times of old.[p] [47] Thus all Israel, in the days of Zerubbabel [and in the days of Nehemiah], gave the singers and the gatekeepers their portions, according to their daily needs. They made their consecrated offering to the Levites, and the Levites made theirs to the sons of Aaron.[q]

CHAPTER 13

Separation from Aliens. [1] r * At that time, when there was reading from the book of Moses in the hearing of the people, it was found written there that "no Ammonite or Moabite may ever be admitted into the assembly of God; [2] for they would not succor the Israelites with food and water, but they hired Balaam to curse them, though our God turned the curse into a blessing."[s] [3] When they had heard the law, they separated from Israel every foreign element.[t]

Reform in the Temple. [4] * Before this, the priest Eliashib, who had been placed in charge of the chambers of the house of our God and who was an associate of Tobiah, [5] had set aside for the latter's use a large chamber in which had previously been stored the cereal offerings, incense and utensils, the tithes in grain, wine, and oil allotted to the Levites, singers, and gatekeepers, and the offerings due the priests.[u] [6] During all this time I had

not been in Jerusalem, for in the thirty-second year of Artaxerxes, king of Babylon, I had gone back to the king. After due time,* however, I asked leave of the king [7] and returned to Jerusalem, where I discovered the evil thing that Eliashib had done for Tobiah, in setting aside for him a chamber in the courts of the house of God. [8] This displeased me very much, and I had all of Tobiah's household goods thrown outside the chamber. [9] Then I gave orders to purify the chambers, and I had them replace there the utensils of the house of God, the cereal offerings, and the incense.

[10] I learned, too, that the portions due the Levites were no longer being given, so that the Levites and the singers who should have been carrying out the services had deserted, each man to his own field. [11] I took the magistrates to task, demanding, "Why is the house of God abandoned?" Then I brought the Levites together and had them resume their stations. [12] All Judah once more brought in the tithes of grain, wine, and oil to the storerooms;[v] [13] and in charge of the storerooms I appointed the priest Shelemiah, Zadok the scribe, and Pedaiah, one of the Levites, together with Hanan, son of Zaccur, son of Mattaniah, as their assistant; for these men were held to be trustworthy. It was their duty to make the distribution to their brethren. [14] Remember this to my credit, O my God! Let not the devotion which I showed for the house of my God and its services be forgotten!

Sabbath Observance. [15] In those days I perceived that men in Judah were treading the winepresses on the sabbath; that

---

o 44f: 1 Chr 23—26; 2 Chr 8, 14.—p 2 Chr 29, 30; 35. 15.—q Neh 13, 10f; 10, 39; Nm 18, 26.—r 1ff: Dt 23, 3-6.—s Nm 22—24.—t Neh 13, 23-28.—u Neh 12, 44.—v Neh 10, 38f; 12, 44f. 47; 2 Chr 31, 6.

12, 44-47: This account of the provisions made for the temple services is apparently a composition of the Chronicler. *At that time:* a mere connective; no particular time is meant, but the account fits best after that of the restoration of the temple (Ezr 6, 13-18) in the days of Zerubbabel (v 47). The gloss mentioning Nehemiah is not in the ancient Greek version.

13, 1ff: These verses were composed by the Chronicler to serve as an introduction to the reforms that Nehemiah instituted during his second mission in Jerusalem (vv 4-31). The part of *the book of Moses* read to the people is freely quoted here from Dt 23, 3-6.

13, 4-31: This is part of the "Memoirs of Nehemiah"; it is continued in Neh 10, 1-40.

13, 6: *After due time:* it is not known when Nehemiah returned to Jerusalem or how long his second period of activity there lasted, but it probably ended before Ezra came to Palestine; see note on Ezr 7, 1-8.

they were bringing in sheaves of grain, loading them on their asses, together with wine, grapes, figs, and every other kind of burden, and bringing them to Jerusalem on the sabbath day. I warned them to sell none of these victuals.*w* [16]In Jerusalem itself the Tyrians who were resident there were importing fish and every other kind of merchandise and selling it to the Judahites on the sabbath. [17]I took the nobles of Judah to task, demanding of them: "What is this evil thing that you are doing, profaning the sabbath day? [18]Did not your fathers act in this same way, with the result that our God has brought all this evil upon us and upon this city? Would you add to the wrath against Israel by once more profaning the sabbath?"

[19]When the shadows were falling on the gates of Jerusalem before the sabbath, I ordered the doors to be closed and forbade them to be reopened till after the sabbath. I posted some of my own men at the gates so that no burden might enter on the sabbath day. [20]The merchants and sellers of various kinds of merchandise spent the night once or twice outside Jerusalem, [21]but then I warned them, saying to them: "Why do you spend the night alongside the wall? If you keep this up, I will lay hands on you!" From that time on, they did not return on the sabbath. [22]Then I ordered the Levites to purify themselves and to go and watch the gates, so that the sabbath day might be kept holy. This, too,

w Neh 10, 32; Ex 20, 8.—x Neh 10, 31; 13, 1ff; Dt 23, 3.—y 1 Kgs 11, 1-13.—z Neh 2, 10; 13, 4f. 7ff.—a Neh 10, 35f.

13, 24: *Ashdodite:* the language spoken at Ashdod, more likely an Aramaic rather than a Philistine dialect. *Jewish:* Hebrew as spoken in postexilic Judah.

remember in my favor, O my God, and have mercy on me in accordance with your great mercy!

Mixed Marriages. [23]Also in those days I saw Jews who had married Ashdodite, Ammonite, or Moabite wives.*x* [24]Of their children, half spoke Ashdodite,* and none of them knew how to speak Jewish; and so it was in regard to the languages of the various other peoples. [25]I took them to task and cursed them; I had some of them beaten and their hair pulled out; and I adjured them by God: "You shall not marry your daughters to their sons not take any of their daughters for your sons or for yourselves! [26]Did not Solomon, the king of Israel, sin because of them? Though among the many nations there was no king like him, and though he was beloved of his God and God had made him king over all Israel, yet even he was made to sin by foreign women.*y* [27]Must it also be heard of you that you have done this same very great evil, betraying our God by marrying foreign women?"

[28]One of the sons of Joiada, son of Eliashib the high priest, was the son-in-law of Sanballat the Horonite! I drove him from my presence.*z* [29]Remember against them, O my God, how they defiled the priesthood and the covenant of the priesthood and the Levites!

[30]Thus I cleansed them of all foreign contamination. I established the various functions for the priests and Levites, so that each had his appointed task. [31]I also provided for the procurement of wood at stated times and for the first fruits. Remember this in my favor, O my God!*a*

Tb

THE BOOK OF TOBIT

The Book of Tobit, named after its principal hero, combines specifically Jewish piety and morality with oriental folklore in a fascinating story that has enjoyed wide popularity in both Jewish and Christian circles. Prayers, psalms, and words of wisdom, as well as the skillfully constructed story itself, provide valuable insights into the faith and the religious milieu of its unknown author. The book was probably written early in the second century B.C.; it is not known where.

Tobit, a devout and wealthy Israelite living among the captives deported to Nineveh from the northern kingdom of Israel in 721 B.C., suffers severe reverses and is finally blinded. Because of his misfortunes he begs the Lord to let him die. But recalling the large sum he had formerly deposited in far-off Media, he sends his son Tobiah there to bring back the money. In Media, at this same time, a young woman, Sarah, also prays for death, be-

cause she has lost seven husbands, each killed in turn on his wedding night by the demon Asmodeus. God hears the prayers of Tobit and Sarah, and sends the angel Raphael in disguise to aid them both.

Raphael makes the trip to Media with Tobiah. When Tobiah is attacked by a large fish as he bathes, Raphael orders him to seize it and to remove its gall, heart, and liver because they make "useful medicines." Later, at Raphael's urging, Tobiah marries Sarah, and uses the fish's heart and liver to drive Asmodeus from the bridal chamber. Returning to Nineveh with his wife and his father's money, Tobiah rubs the fish's gall into his father's eyes and cures them. Finally, Raphael reveals his true identity and returns to heaven. Tobit then utters his beautiful hymn of praise. Before dying, Tobit tells his son to leave Nineveh because God will destroy that wicked city. After Tobiah buries his father and mother, he and his family depart for Media, where he later learns that the destruction of Nineveh has taken place.

The inspired author of the book used the literary form of religious novel (as in Jonah and Judith) for the purpose of instruction and edification. There may have been a historical nucleus around which the story was composed, but this possibility has nothing to do with the teaching of the book. The seemingly historical data—names of kings, cities, etc.—are used merely as vivid details to create interest and charm.

Although the Book of Tobit is usually listed with the historical books, it more correctly stands midway between them and the wisdom literature. It contains numerous maxims like those found in the wisdom books (cf 4, 3-19. 21; 12, 6-10; 14, 7. 9) as well as the customary sapiential themes: fidelity to the law, the intercessory function of angels, piety toward parents, the purity of marriage, reverence for the dead, and the value of almsgiving, prayer, and fasting. The book makes Tobit a relative of Ahiqar, a hero of ancient Near Eastern folklore.

Written in Aramaic, the original of the book was lost for centuries. The Greek translation, existing in three different recensions, is our primary source. In 1955, fragments of the book in Aramaic and in Hebrew were recovered from Cave IV at Qumran. These texts are in substantial agreement with the Greek recension that has served as the basis for the present translation.

The divisions of the Book of Tobit are: I. Tobit's Ordeals (1, 3—3, 6). II. Sarah's Plight (3, 7-17). III. Tobiah's Journey and Marriage to Sarah (4, 1—9, 6). IV. Tobiah's Return; Cure of Tobit's Blindness (10, 1—11, 18). V. Raphael Reveals His Identity (12, 1-22). VI. Tobit's Song of Praise (13, 1-18). VII. Epilogue (14, 1-15).

CHAPTER 1

Tobit. ¹This book tells the story of Tobit,* son of Tobiel, son of Hananiel, son of Aduel, son of Gabael of the family of Asiel, of the tribe of Naphtali, ²who during the reign of Shalmaneser,* king of Assyria, was taken captive from Thisbe, which is south of Kedesh Naphtali in upper Galilee, above and to the west of Asser, north of Phogor.ᵃ

I: TOBIT'S ORDEALS

His Virtue. ³I, Tobit, have walked all the days of my life on the paths of truth and righteousness. I performed many charitable works for my kinsmen and my people who had been deported with me to Nineveh, in Assyria. ⁴When I lived as a

young man in my own country, Israel, the entire tribe of my forefather Naphtali had broken away from the house of David and from Jerusalem. This city had been singled out of all Israel's tribes, so that they all might offer sacrifice in the place where the temple, God's dwelling, had been built and consecrated for all generations to come. ⁵ ᵇ All my kinsmen, like the

a 2 Kgs 17, 3; 18, 9ff.—b 1 Kgs 12, 26-32.

1, 1: *Tobit:* in the fragments of the book found at Qumran, is given as *Tobi,* an abbreviated form of *Tobiyah* (v 9; Ezr 2, 60) or of *Tobiyahu* (2 Chr 17, 8), a name which means "Yahweh is good." *Tobiel,* "God is good"; *Hananiel,* "God is merciful." The book abounds in theophoric names.
1, 2: *Shalmaneser* V (727-722 B.C): began the siege of Samaria; the inhabitants of the northern kingdom were taken into captivity by his successor, Sargon II (722-705). *Thisbe* and *Phogor:* towns of Galilee that have not been identified; Thisbe in Gilead was perhaps the birthplace of Elijah. *Kedesh:* cf Jos 20, 7. *Asser:* Hazor (Jos 11, 1).

rest of the tribe of my forefather Naphtali, used to offer sacrifice on all the mountains of Galilee as well as to the young bull which Jeroboam, king of Israel, had made in Dan.*

⁶ *c* I, for my part, would often make the pilgrimage alone to Jerusalem for the festivals, as is prescribed for all Israel by perpetual decree.* Bringing with me the first fruits of the field and the firstlings of the flock, together with a tenth of my income and the first shearings of the sheep,*d* I would hasten to Jerusalem ⁷ *e* and present them to the priests, Aaron's sons, at the altar. To the Levites who were doing service in Jerusalem I would give the tithe of grain, wine, olive oil, pomegranates, figs, and other fruits. And except for sabbatical years, I used to give a second tithe in money, which each year I would go and disburse in Jerusalem. ⁸ The third tithe I gave to orphans and widows, and to converts who were living with the Israelites. Every third year I would bring them this offering, and we ate it in keeping with the decree of the Mosaic law and the commands of Deborah, the mother of my father Tobiel; for when my father died, he left me an orphan.

⁹ When I reached manhood, I married Anna, a woman of our own lineage. By her

---

c Ex 23, 14f. 17; 34, 23.—d Dt 16, 16.—e 7f: Nm 18, 12f. 24; Dt 14, 22-29; 18, 4f.—f Lv 11; Dt 14, 3-21; Acts 15, 29; 1 Cor 8, 7ff.—g Dn 2, 48f.—h Jb 31, 16-20.—i 2 Kgs 19, 37; 2, Chr 32, 21; Sir 48, 21; Is 37, 38; 2 Mc 8, 19.

1, 5: Jeroboam established sanctuaries in Dan and Bethel so that the people would no longer go to Jerusalem for the festivals. The gold statues of bulls which he placed in the sanctuaries were considered the throne of Yahweh; but the people soon came to worship the images themselves. Jeroboam also encouraged the high places or hilltop shrines (1 Kgs 12, 26-33).

1, 6ff: *Perpetual decree:* Dt 12, 11. 13-14. Refusing to worship at Jeroboam's shrines, the faithful Tobit continued to bring his offerings to Jerusalem; see 2 Chr 11, 16. For the various tithes, cf Nm 18, 20-32; 2 Chr 31, 4-6; Dt 14, 22-29; 26, 12f.

1, 14: *A great sum of money:* literally, "ten silver talents," about ten thousand dollars. *Rages:* modern Rai, about five miles southeast of Teheran. *Media:* the northwestern part of modern Iran.

1, 15: *Sennacherib* (705-681 B.C.): the son of Sargon (722-705 B.C.); neither was descended from Shalmaneser. Inconsistencies such as this point to the fact that the Book of Tobit is a religious novel (see Introduction; also notes on Tb 5, 6 and 14, 15).

1, 17-18: Tobit risked his own life to bury the dead. Deprivation of burial was viewed with horror by the Jews. Cf Tb 4, 3-4; 6, 15; 14, 12-13.

1, 21: *Esarhaddon:* 681-669 B.C. *Ahiqar:* a hero of ancient folklore, known for his outstanding wisdom. The *Story (or Wisdom) of Ahiqar* was very popular in antiquity and is extant in many different forms: Aramaic, Syriac, Armenian, Arabic (*Arabian Nights*), Greek (*Aesop's Fables*), Slavonic, Ethiopic, and Romanian. The sacred author makes Tobit the uncle of the famous Ahiqar in order to enhance Tobit's own prestige. See note on Tb 14, 10.

I had a son whom I named Tobiah. ¹⁰ Now after I had been deported to Nineveh, all my brothers and relatives ate the food of heathens,*f* ¹¹ but I refrained from eating that kind of food. ¹² Because of this wholehearted service of God, ¹³ the Most High granted me favor and status with Shalmaneser, so that I became purchasing agent for all his needs.*g* ¹⁴ Every now and then until his death I would go to Media to buy goods for him. I also deposited several pouches containing a great sum of money* with my kinsman Gabael, son of Gabri, who lived at Rages, in Media. ¹⁵ But when Shalmaneser died and his son Sennacherib* succeeded him as king, the roads to Media became unsafe, so I could no longer go there.

Courage in Burying the Dead. ¹⁶ During Shalmaneser's reign I performed many charitable works for my kinsmen and my people. ¹⁷ *h* I would give my bread to the hungry and my clothing to the naked. If I saw one of my people who had died and been thrown outside the walls of Nineveh, I would bury him.* ¹⁸ I also buried anyone whom Sennacherib slew when he returned as a fugitive from Judea during the days of judgment decreed against him by the heavenly King because of the blasphemies he had uttered. In his rage he killed many Israelites, but I used to take their bodies by stealth and bury them; so when Sennacherib looked for them, he could not find them. ¹⁹ But a certain citizen of Nineveh informed the king that it was I who buried the dead. When I found out that the king knew all about me and wanted to put me to death, I went into hiding; then in my fear I took to flight. ²⁰ Afterward, all my property was confiscated; I was left with nothing. All that I had was taken to the king's palace, except for my wife Anna and my son Tobiah.

²¹ But less than forty days later the king was assassinated by two of his sons, who then escaped into the mountains of Ararat. His son Esarhaddon,* who succeeded him as king, placed Ahiqar, my brother Anael's son, in charge of all the accounts of his kingdom, so that he took control over the entire administration. *i* ²² Then Ahiqar interceded on my behalf, and I was able to return to Nineveh. For under Sennacherib, king of Assyria, Ahiqar had been

Tb

chief cupbearer, keeper of the seal, administrator, and treasurer; and Esarhaddon reappointed him. He was a close relative—in fact, my nephew.

CHAPTER 2

[1] Thus under King Esarhaddon I returned to my home, and my wife Anna and my son Tobiah were restored to me. Then on our festival of Pentecost, the feast of Weeks,* a fine dinner was prepared for me, and I reclined to eat.*j* [2] The table was set for me, and when many different dishes were placed before me, I said to my son Tobiah: "My son, go out and try to find a poor man from among our kinsmen exiled here in Nineveh. If he is a sincere worshiper of God, bring him back with you, so that he can share this meal with me. Indeed, son, I shall wait for you to come back."*

[3] Tobiah went out to look for some poor kinsman of ours. When he returned he exclaimed, "Father!" I said to him, "What is it, son?" He answered, "Father, one of our people has been murdered! His body lies in the market place where he was just strangled!" [4] I sprang to my feet, leaving the dinner untouched; and I carried the dead man from the street and put him in one of the rooms, so that I might bury him after sunset. [5] Returning to my own own quarters, I washed myself* and ate my food in sorrow.*k* [6] I was reminded of the oracle pronounced by the prophet Amos against Bethel:*l*

"Your festivals shall be turned into mourning,
And all your songs into lamentation."

[7] And I wept. Then at sunset I went out, dug a grave, and buried him.

[8] The neighbors mocked me, saying to one another: "Will this man never learn! Once before he was hunted down for execution because of this very thing; yet now that he has escaped, here he is again burying the dead!"

Tobit's Blindness. [9] That same night I bathed, and went to sleep next to the wall of my courtyard. Because of the heat I left my face uncovered. [10] I did not know there were birds perched on the wall above me, till their warm droppings settled in my eyes, causing cataracts.* I went to see some doctors for a cure, but the more they anointed my eyes with various salves, the

worse the cataracts became, until I could see no more. For four years I was deprived of eyesight, and all my kinsmen were grieved at my condition. Ahiqar, however, took care of me for two years, until he left for Elymais.

[11] At that time my wife Anna worked for hire at weaving cloth, the kind of work women do. [12] When she sent back the goods to their owners, they would pay her. Late in winter* she finished the cloth and sent it back to the owners. They paid her the full salary, and also gave her a young goat for the table. [13] On entering my house the goat began to bleat. I called to my wife and said: "Where did this goat come from? Perhaps it was stolen! Give it back to its owners; we have no right to eat stolen food!" [14] *m* But she said to me, "It was given to me as a bonus over and above my wages." Yet I would not believe her, and told her to give it back to its owners. I became very angry with her over this. So she retorted: "Where are your charitable deeds now? Where are your virtuous acts? See! Your true character is finally showing itself!"*

CHAPTER 3

[1] Grief-stricken in spirit, I groaned and wept aloud. Then with sobs I began to pray:

Tobit's Prayer for Death

[2] "You are righteous, O Lord,
    and all your deeds are just;
All your ways are mercy and truth;
    you are the judge of the world.*n*
[3] And now, O Lord, may you be mindful of me,
    and look with favor upon me.

---

j Lv 23, 15-21; Nm 28, 26-31; Dt 16, 9-12.—k Nm 19, 11-22.—l Am 8, 10; 1 Mc 1, 39.—m Jb 2, 9.—n Pss 25, 10; 119, 137; Dn 3, 27.

2, 1: *The feast of Weeks:* also called by its Greek name *Pentecost,* was celebrated fifty days after the Passover. Cf Lv 23, 15-21; Dt 16, 9-12.

2, 2: Almsgiving and charity to the poor are important virtues taught by the book (Tb 4, 7-11. 16f; 12, 8f; 14, 10f).

2, 5: *I washed myself:* because of ritual defilement from touching a corpse (Nm 19, 11-13).

2, 10: *Cataracts:* literally, "white scales, or films." *Elymais:* the Greek name of ancient Elam, a district northeast of the head of the Persian Gulf.

2, 12: *Late in winter:* literally, "seventh of Dystros," the Macedonian month which corresponds to the Jewish month of Shebat (January-February). *For the table:* literally, "for the hearth"; the gift had probably been made in view of some springtime festival like the Jewish Purim.

2, 14: Anna's sharp rebuke calls to mind the words of Job's wife (Jb 2, 9).

Punish me not for my sins,
  nor for my inadvertent offenses,
  nor for those of my fathers.*o*

"They sinned against you,
4   and disobeyed your commandments.
So you handed us over to plundering,
  exile, and death,
    till we were an object lesson, a
    byword, a reproach
  in all the nations among whom you
    scattered us.*p*

5 "Yes, your judgments are many and
  true
  in dealing with me as my sins
  and those of my fathers deserve.
For we have not kept your commandments,
  nor have we trodden the paths of
  truth before you.

6 "So now, deal with me as you please,
  and command my life breath to be
  taken from me,
  that I may go from the face of the
  earth into dust.
It is better for me to die than to live,*
  because I have heard insulting
  calumnies,
  and I am overwhelmed with grief.*q*

"Lord, command me to be delivered
  from such anguish;
let me go to the everlasting abode;
Lord, refuse me not.
For it is better for me to die
  than to endure so much misery in
  life,
  and to hear these insults!"

---

o Ex 34, 7.—p Dt 28, 15; Bar 1, 16-22; 2, 4f; 3, 8; Dn 9, 5f.—
q Nm 11, 15; 1 Kgs 19, 4; Jb 7, 15; Jon 4, 3. 8.—r Tb 6, 15; Gn
37, 35; 42, 38; 44, 29. 31.—s 1 Kgs 8, 44. 48; Pss 28, 2; 134,
2; Dn 6, 11.

3, 6: *It is better for me to die than to live:* in his distress
Tobit uses the words of the petulant Jonah (Jon 4, 3. 8), who
wished to die because God did not destroy the hated Ninevites. In
similar circumstances, Moses (Nm 11, 15), Elijah (1 Kgs 19, 4),
and Job (Jb 7, 15) also prayed for death. *Everlasting abode:* a
reference to Sheol, the dismal abode of the dead from which no
one returns (Jb 7, 9-10; 14, 12; Is 26, 14). The revelation of a
blessed immortality had not yet been made. See note on Tb 4, 6.
3, 7: From here on, the story is told in the third person. V 7 relates one of the several marvelous coincidences which the
storyteller uses to heighten interest; see also vv 16. 17; 4, 1; 5,
4. *Ecbatana: Hamadan* in modern Iran; this was the capital of
ancient Media. *Raguel:* "friend of God."
3, 8: *Asmodeus:* in Persian *aeshma daeva,* "demon of
wrath," adopted into Aramaic with the sense of "the Destroyer."
He will be subdued (Tb 8, 3) by Raphael (v 17), "God heals."
3, 11: *Facing the window:* that is, looking toward Jerusalem; cf Dn 6, 11. *Blessed are you* and "Blessed be God" are
traditional openings of Jewish prayers (Tb 8, 5. 15; 11, 14; 13,
1).

II: SARAH'S PLIGHT

Sarah Falsely Accused. 7 * On the same
day, at Ecbatana in Media, it so happened
that Raguel's daughter Sarah also had to
listen to abuse, from one of her father's
maids. 8 For she had been married to seven
husbands, but the wicked demon Asmodeus* killed them off before they could
have intercourse with her, as it is prescribed for wives. So the maid said to her:
"You are the one who strangles your husbands! Look at you! You have already
been married seven times, but you have
had no joy with any one of your husbands.
9 Why do you beat us? Because your husbands are dead? Then why not join them!
May we never see a son or daughter of
yours!"

10 That day she was deeply grieved in
spirit. She went in tears to an upstairs
room in her father's house with the intention of hanging herself. But she reconsid-
ered, saying to herself: "No! People would
level this insult against my father: 'You
had only one beloved daughter, but she
hanged herself because of ill fortune!' And
thus would I cause my father in his old age
to go down to the nether world laden with
sorrow. It is far better for me not to hang
myself, but to beg the Lord to have me
die, so that I need no longer live to hear
such insults."*r*

11 At that time, then, she spread out her
hands, and facing the window,* poured
out this prayer:

Sarah's Prayer for Death

"Blessed are you, O Lord, merciful
  God!
Forever blessed and honored is your
  holy name;
  may all your works forever bless
  you.*s*
12 And now, O Lord, to you I turn my
  face
  and raise my eyes.
13 Bid me to depart from the earth,
  never again to hear such insults.
14 "You know, O Master, that I am innocent
  of any impure act with a man,
15 And that I have never defiled my own
  name
  or my father's name in the land of my
  exile.

"I am my father's only daughter,
and he has no other child to make his
heir,
Nor does he have a close kinsman or
other relative
whom I might bide my time to
marry.
I have already lost seven husbands;
why then should I live any longer?
But if it please you, Lord, not to slay
me,
look favorably upon me and have
pity on me;
never again let me hear these insults!"

An Answer to Prayer. ¹⁶At that very
time, the prayer of these two suppliants
was heard in the glorious presence of Almighty God. ¹⁷ *t* So Raphael was sent to
heal them both: to remove the cataracts
from Tobit's eyes, so that he might again
see God's sunlight; and to marry Raguel's
daughter Sarah to Tobit's son Tobiah, and
then drive the wicked demon Asmodeus
from her. For Tobiah had the right* to
claim her before any other who might wish
to marry her.

In the very moment that Tobit returned
from the courtyard to his house, Raguel's
daughter Sarah came downstairs from her
room.

III: TOBIAH'S JOURNEY AND MARRIAGE TO SARAH

CHAPTER 4

A Father's Instruction. ¹That same day
Tobit remembered the money he had deposited with Gabael at Rages in Media,
and he thought, ²"Now that I have asked
for death, why should I not call my son
Tobiah and let him know about this
money before I die?" ³So he called his son
Tobiah; and when he came, he said to
him:* "My son, when I die, give me a decent burial. Honor your mother, and do
not abandon her as long as she lives. Do
whatever pleases her, and do not grieve
her spirit in any way.ᵘ ⁴Remember, my
son, that she went through many trials for
your sake while you were in her womb.
And when she dies, bury her in the same
grave with me.

⁵"Through all your days, my son, keep
the Lord in mind, and suppress every desire to sin or to break his commandments.
Perform good works all the days of your

life, and do not tread the paths of wrongdoing. ⁶ *v* For if you are steadfast in your
service, your good works will bring success, not only to you, but also to all those
who live uprightly.*

⁷"Give alms from your possessions. Do
not turn your face away from any of the
poor, and God's face will not be turned
away from you.ʷ ⁸Son, give alms in proportion to what you own. If you have great
wealth, give alms out of your abundance;
if you have but little, distribute even some
of that. But do not hesitate to give alms;
⁹you will be storing up a goodly treasure
for yourself against the day of adversity.ˣ
¹⁰Almsgiving frees one from death, and
keeps one from going into the dark abode.
¹¹Alms are a worthy offering in the sight
of the Most High for all who give them.ʸ

¹²"Be on your guard, son, against every
form of immorality, and above all, marry a
woman of the lineage of your forefathers.
Do not marry a stranger who is not of your
father's tribe, because we are sons of the
prophets. My boy, keep in mind Noah,
Abraham, Isaac, and Jacob, our fathers
from of old: all of them took wives from
among their own kinsmen and were
blessed in their children. Remember that
their posterity shall inherit the land.ᶻ
¹³Therefore, my son, love your kinsmen.
Do not be so proud-hearted toward your
kinsmen, the sons and daughters of your
people, as to refuse to take a wife for yourself from among them. For in such arrogance there is ruin and great disorder.
Likewise, in worthlessness there is decay
and dire poverty, for worthlessness is the
mother of famine.
¹⁴"Do not keep with you overnight the
wages of any man who works for you,

---

t Tb 4, 12f; 6, 12f; Gn 24, 3f.—u Ex 20, 12; Prv 23, 22; Sir
7, 27.—v Tb 13, 6; Jn 3, 21; Eph 4, 15.—w 7f: Tb 12, 8ff; Dt 15,
7f. 11; Prv 19, 17; Sir 4, 1-6; 14, 13; Lk 14, 13; 1 Jn 3, 17.—x
Mt 6, 20f.—y Sir 3, 30; 29, 12.—z Tb 3, 15. 17; 6, 12; Gn 11,
29. 31; 25, 20; 28, 1-4; 29, 15-30; Ex 34, 16; Dt 7, 3; Jgs 14, 3.

3, 17: *Tobiah had the right:* according to the patriarchal
custom of marriage within the family group. Tobiah was Sarah's
closest eligible relative (Tb 6, 12). Cf Tb 4, 12-13; Gn 24.
4, 3-19: A collection of maxims which parallel those in the
wisdom literature, especially Prv and Sir (see Introduction):
duties toward parents (3-4); cf also Tb 14, 13; perseverance in
virtue and avoidance of evil (5-6. 14b); necessity and value of
almsgiving and charity (7-11. 16-17); marriage to a kinsman (12-
13a); industry (13b); prompt payment of wages (14a); the golden
rule (15a); temperance (15b); docility (18); prayer (19).
4, 6: Before the revelation of retribution for all men in the afterlife—a doctrine taught in the Book of Wisdom—Old Testament man believed that virtue guaranteed earthly prosperity, and
sin earthly disaster (cf Dt 28).

but pay him immediately. If you thus behave as God's servant, you will receive your reward. Keep a close watch on yourself, my son, in everything you do, and discipline yourself in all your conduct.*a* ¹⁵ Do to no one what you yourself dislike. Do not drink wine till you become drunk, nor let drunkenness accompany you on your way.*b* ¹⁶ *c* "Give to the hungry some of your bread, and to the naked some of your clothing. Whatever you have left over, give away as alms; and do not begrudge the alms you give. ¹⁷ *d* Be lavish with your bread and wine at the burial of the virtuous, but do not share them with sinners.* ¹⁸ "Seek counsel from every wise man, and do not think lightly of any advice that can be useful. ¹⁹ *e* At all times bless the Lord God, and ask him to make all your paths straight and to grant success to all your endeavors and plans. For no pagan nation possesses good counsel, but the Lord himself gives all good things. If the Lord chooses, he raises a man up; but if he should decide otherwise, he casts him down to the deepest recesses of the nether world. So now, my son, keep in mind my commandments, and never let them be erased from your heart.* ²⁰ "And now, son, I wish to inform you that I have deposited a great sum of money with Gabri's son Gabael at Rages in Media. ²¹ Do not be discouraged, my child, because of our poverty. You will be a rich man if you fear God, avoid all sin, and

do what is right before the Lord your God."*f*

CHAPTER 5

The Angel Raphael. ¹ Then Tobiah replied to his father Tobit: "Everything that you have commanded me, father, I will do. ² But how shall I be able to obtain the money from him, since he does not know me nor do I know him? What can I show him to make him recognize me and trust me, so that he will give me the money? I do not even know which roads to take for the journey into Media!" ³ Tobit answered his son Tobiah: "We exchanged signatures on a document* written in duplicate; I divided it into two parts, and each of us kept one; his copy I put with the money. Think of it, twenty years have already passed since I deposited that money! So now, my son, find yourself a trustworthy man who will make the journey with you. We will, of course, give him a salary when you return; but get back that money from Gabael." Tb

⁴ Tobiah went to look for someone acquainted with the roads who would travel with him to Media. As soon as he went out, he found the angel Raphael standing before him, though he did not know* that this was an angel of God.*g* ⁵ Tobiah said to him, "Who are you, young man?" He replied, "I am an Israelite, one of your kinsmen. I have come here to work." Tobiah said, "Do you know the way to Media?" ⁶ The other replied: "Yes, I have been there many times. I know the place well and I know all the routes. I have often traveled to Media; I used to stay with our kinsman Gabael, who lives at Rages in Media. It is a good two days' travel from Ecbatana to Rages,* for Rages is situated at the mountains, Ecbatana out on the plateau." ⁷ Tobiah said to him, "Wait for me, young man, till I go back and tell my father; for I need you to make the journey with me. I will, of course, pay you."*h* ⁸ Raphael replied, "Very well, I will wait for you; but do not be long."

⁹ Tobiah went back to tell his father Tobit what had happened. He said to him, "I have just found a man who is one of our own Israelite kinsmen!" Tobit said, "Call the man, so that I may find out what family and tribe he comes from, and whether he is trustworthy enough to

---

a Lv 19, 13; Dt 24, 15.—b Mt 7, 12; Lk 6, 31.—c Dt 15, 10; Is 58, 7; Mt 25, 35f; 2 Cor 9, 7.—d Jer 16, 7; Lk 14, 13.—e Dt 4, 6; Ps 119, 10.—f 1 Tm 6, 6ff.—g Heb 13, 2.—h Tb 12, 2.

4, 17: Tobit counsels his son either to give alms in honor of the dead, or, more probably, to give the "bread of consolation" to the family of the deceased. Cf Jer 16, 7; Ez 24, 17.

4, 19: Prayer is the foundation of a moral life.

5, 3: *Document:* in Greek *cheirographon.* In the Middle Ages, notably in England, a deed and its duplicate were written on one piece of parchment, with the Latin word *chirographum* inscribed across the top of the sheet or between the two copies of the text. The document was then cut in two in either a straight or a wavy line, the parts being given to the persons concerned. Perhaps this procedure derived from the present verse of Tobit. Duplicate documents, usually one open and the other sealed, are well known from the ancient Near East.

5, 4: *He did not know:* the theme of an angel in disguise occurs frequently in folklore as well as in the Old Testament (Gn 18; cf Heb 13, 2).

5, 6: *It is a good two days' travel from Ecbatana to Rages:* Alexander's army took eleven days in forced marches to cover this distance, about 180 miles. The author is merely using popular impressions about faraway places; he is not teaching geography. (See notes on Tb 1, 15; 3, 7 and Introduction.)

travel with you, son." Tobiah went out to summon the man saying, "Young man, my father would like to see you." ¹⁰When Raphael entered the house, Tobit greeted him first. Raphael said, "Hearty greetings* to you!" Tobit replied: "What joy is left for me any more? Here I am, a blind man who cannot see God's sunlight, but must remain in darkness, like the dead who no longer see the light! Though alive, I am among the dead. I can hear a man's voice, but I cannot see him." Raphael said, "Take courage! God has healing in store for you; so take courage!" Tobit then said: "My son Tobiah wants to go to Media. Can you go with him to show him the way? I will of course pay you, brother." Raphael answered: "Yes, I can go with him, for I know all the routes. I have often traveled to Media and crossed all its plains and mountains; so I know every road well." ¹¹Tobit asked, "Brother, tell me, please, what family and tribe are you from?" ¹²Raphael said: "Why? Do you need a tribe and a family? Or are you looking for a hired man to travel with your son?" Tobit replied, "I wish to know truthfully whose son you are, brother, and what your name is."ⁱ

¹³Raphael answered, "I am Azariah,* son of Hananiah the elder, one of your own kinsmen." ¹⁴Tobit exclaimed: "Welcome! God save you, brother! Do not be provoked with me, brother, for wanting to learn the truth about your family. So it turns out that you are a kinsman, and from a noble and good line! I knew Hananiah and Nathaniah, the two sons of Shemaiah the elder; with me they used to make the pilgrimage to Jerusalem, where we would worship together. No, they did not stray from the right path; your kinsmen are good men. You are certainly of good lineage, and welcome!" ¹⁵Then he added: "For each day you are away I will give you the normal wages,* plus expenses for you and for my son. If you go with my son, ¹⁶I will even add a bonus to your wages!" Raphael replied: "I will go with him; have no fear. In good health we shall leave you, and in good health we shall return to you, for the way is safe." ¹⁷Tobit said, "God bless you, brother." Then he called his son and said to him: "My son, prepare whatever you need for the journey, and set

out with your kinsman. May God in heaven protect you on the way and bring you back to me safe and sound; and may his angel accompany you for safety, my son."

Before setting out on his journey, Tobiah kissed his father and mother. Tobit said to him, "Have a safe journey." ¹⁸But his mother began to weep. She said to Tobit: "Why have you decided to send my child away? Is he not the staff to which we cling, ever there with us in all that we do? ¹⁹I hope more money is not your chief concern! Rather let it be a ransom for our son! ²⁰What the Lord has given us to live on is certainly enough for us." ²¹Tobit reassured her: "Have no such thought. Our son will leave in good health and come back to us in good health. Your own eyes will see the day when he returns to you safe and sound. ²²So, no such thought; do not worry about them, my love.* For a good angel will go with him, his journey will be successful, and he will return unharmed." ¹Then she stopped weeping.*

CHAPTER 6

Journey to Rages. ²When the boy left home, accompanied by the angel, the dog followed Tobiah out of the house and went with them. The travelers walked till nightfall, and made camp beside the Tigris River. ³Now when the boy went down to wash his feet in the river, a large fish suddenly leaped out of the water and tried to swallow his foot. He shouted in alarm. ⁴But the angel said to him, "Take hold of the fish and don't let it get away!" The boy seized the fish and hauled it up on the shore. ⁵The angel then told him: "Cut the fish open and take out its gall,

---

i Jgs 13, 17f.

5, 10: *Hearty greetings* and *what joy* form a wordplay on the Greek verb *chairein,* "to greet" and "to be joyful."

5, 13-14: *Azariah,* "Yahweh helps"; *Hananiah,* "Yahweh is merciful"; *Nathaniah,* "Yahweh gives"; *Shemaiah,* "Yahweh hears."

5, 15: *The normal wages:* literally, "a drachma," about seventeen cents, a day's wage for a workingman.

5, 22: *My love:* literally, "sister," a term of endearment applied to one's wife; cf Tb 7, 11. 15; 8, 4. 21; 10, 6. 13; Song 4, 9. 10. 12; 5, 1f. *A good angel:* a reference to the guardian angel, though Tobit does not know, of course, that Raphael himself, disguised as Azariah, is the good angel in this case.

5, 1: *Then . . . weeping:* this verse belongs to ch 6.

heart, and liver, and keep them with you; but throw away the entrails. Its gall, heart, and liver make useful medicines."* ⁶After the lad had cut the fish open, he put aside the gall, heart, and liver. Then he broiled and ate part of the fish; the rest he salted and kept for the journey.

Raphael's Instructions. ⁷Afterward they traveled on together till they were near Media. The boy asked the angel this question: "Brother Azariah, what medicinal value is there in the fish's heart, liver, and gall?" ⁸He answered: "As regards the fish's heart and liver, if you burn them so that the smoke surrounds a man or a woman who is afflicted by a demon or evil spirit, the affliction will leave him completely, and no demons will ever return to him again. ⁹And as for the gall, if you rub it on the eyes of a man who has cataracts, blowing into his eyes right on the cataracts, his sight will be restored."

¹⁰When they had entered Media and were getting close to Ecbatana, ¹¹Raphael said to the boy, "Brother Tobiah!" He answered, "Yes, what is it?" Raphael continued: "Tonight we must stay with Raguel, who is a relative of yours. He has a daughter named Sarah, ¹²but no other child. Since you are Sarah's closest relative, you before all other men have the right to marry her. Also, her father's estate is rightfully yours to inherit. Now the girl is sensible, courageous, and very beautiful; and her father loves her dearly."ʲ ¹³He continued: "Since you have the right to marry her, listen to me, brother. Tonight I will ask the girl's father to let us have her as your bride. When we return from Rages, we will hold the wedding feast for her. I know that Raguel cannot keep her from you or let her become engaged to another man; that would be a capital crime according to the decree in the Book of Moses,* and he knows that it is your right, before all other men, to marry his daughter. So heed my words, brother; tonight we must speak for the girl, so that we may have her engaged to you. And when

we return from Rages, we will take her and bring her back with us to your house."

¹⁴Tobiah objected, however: "Brother Azariah, I have heard that this woman has already been married seven times, and that her husbands died in their bridal chambers. On the very night they approached her, they dropped dead. And I have heard it said that it was a demon who killed them. ¹⁵So now I too am afraid of this demon. Because he loves her, he does not harm her; but he does slay any man who wishes to come close to her. I am my father's only child. If I should die, I would bring my father and mother down to their grave in sorrow over me. And they have no other son to bury them!"ᵏ

¹⁶Raphael said to him: "Do you not remember your father's orders? He commanded you to marry a woman from your own family. So now listen to me, brother; do not give another thought to this demon, but marry Sarah. I know that tonight you shall have her for your wife! ¹⁷When you go into the bridal chamber, take the fish's liver and heart, and place them on the embers for the incense. ¹⁸As soon as the demon smells the odor they give off, he will flee and never again show himself near her. Then when you are about to have intercourse with her, both of you first rise up to pray.* Beg the Lord of heaven to show you mercy and grant you deliverance. But do not be afraid, for she was set apart for you before the world existed. You will save her, and she will go with you. And I suppose that you will have children by her, who will take the place of brothers for you. So do not worry."

When Tobiah heard Raphael say that she was his kinswoman, of his own family's lineage, he fell deeply in love with her, and his heart became set on her.

CHAPTER 7

At the House of Raguel. ¹When they entered Ecbatana, Tobiah said, "Brother Azariah, lead me straight to our kinsman Raguel." So he brought him to the house of Raguel, whom they found seated by his courtyard gate. They greeted him first. He said to them, "Greetings to you too, brothers! Good health to you, and welcome!" When he brought them into his home, ²he said to his wife Edna, "This

---

j Tb 4, 12f; Nm 36, 8.—k Tb 3, 10.

6, 5: *Its gall . . . medicines:* belief in the healing power of these organs was common among even the physicians of antiquity.
6, 13: *Raguel . . . Book of Moses:* Nm 36, 6-8 prescribed marriage within the ancestral tribe, but no death penalty is mentioned.
6, 18: *Rise up to pray:* prayer is needed to drive out the demon.

Tb

young man looks just like my kinsman Tobit!" [3] So Edna asked them, "Who are you, brothers?" They answered, "We are of the exiles from Naphtali at Nineveh." [4] She said, "Do you know our kinsman Tobit?" They answered, "Indeed we do!" She asked, "Is he well?" [5] They answered, "Yes, he is alive and well." Then Tobiah exclaimed, "He is my father!" [6] Raguel sprang up and kissed him, shedding tears of joy. [7] But when he heard that Tobit had lost his eyesight, he was grieved and wept aloud. He said to Tobiah: "My child, God bless you! You are the son of a noble and good father. But what a terrible misfortune that such a righteous and charitable man should be afflicted with blindness!" He continued to weep in the arms of his kinsman Tobiah. [8] His wife Edna also wept for Tobit; and even their daughter Sarah began to weep.

Marriage of Tobiah and Sarah. [9] Afterward, Raguel slaughtered a ram from the flock and gave them a cordial reception. When they had bathed and reclined to eat, Tobiah said to Raphael, "Brother Azariah, ask Raguel to let me marry my kinswoman Sarah." [10] Raguel overheard the words; so he said to the boy: "Eat and drink and be merry tonight, for no man is more entitled to marry my daughter Sarah than you, brother. Besides, not even I have the right to give her to anyone but you, because you are my closest relative. But I will explain the situation to you very frankly. [11] I have given her in marriage to seven men, all of whom were kinsmen of ours, and all died on the very night they approached her. But now, son, eat and drink. I am sure the Lord will look after you both." Tobiah answered, "I will eat or drink nothing until you set aside what belongs to me."

Raguel said to him: "I will do it. She is yours according to the decree of the Book of Moses. Your marriage to her has been decided in heaven! Take your kinswoman; from now on you are her love, and she is your beloved. She is yours today and ever after. And tonight, son, may the Lord of heaven prosper you both. May he grant you mercy and peace." [12] Then Raguel called his daughter Sarah, and she came to him. He took her by the hand and gave her to Tobiah with the words: "Take her according to the law. According to the decree written in the Book of Moses she is your wife. Take her and bring her back

safely to your father. And may the God of heaven grant both of you peace and prosperity."[l] [13] He then called her mother and told her to bring a scroll, so that he might draw up a marriage contract stating that he gave Sarah to Tobiah as his wife according to the decree of the Mosaic law. Her mother brought the scroll, and he drew up the contract, to which they affixed their seals.[m]

[14] Afterward they began to eat and drink. [15] Later Raguel called his wife Edna and said, "My love, prepare the other bedroom and bring the girl there." [16] She went and made the bed in the room, as she was told, and brought the girl there. After she had cried over her, she wiped away the tears and said: [17] "Be brave, my daughter. May the Lord of heaven grant you joy in place of your grief. Courage, my daughter." Then she left.

CHAPTER 8

Expulsion of the Demon. [1] When they had finished eating and drinking, the girl's parents wanted to retire. They brought the young man out of the dining room and led him into the bedroom. [2] At this point Tobiah, mindful of Raphael's instructions, took the fish's liver and heart from the bag which he had with him, and placed them on the embers for the incense.* [3] The demon, repelled by the odor of the fish, fled into Upper Egypt;* Raphael pursued him there and bound him hand and foot. Then Raphael returned immediately.

[4] When the girl's parents left the bedroom and closed the door behind them, Tobiah arose from bed and said to his wife, "My love, get up. Let us pray and beg our Lord to have mercy on us and to grant us deliverance." [5] She got up, and they started to pray and beg that deliverance might be theirs. He began with these words:

---

l Gn 24, 50f.—m Tb 6, 12.

8, 2f: The manner of coping with demonic influences among the ancients seems quaint to us. However, the fish here is part of the story, and not a recipe for exorcism. It is clear that the author places primary emphasis on the value of prayer to God (Tb 6, 18; 8, 4-8), on the role of the angel as God's agent, and on the pious dispositions of Tobiah.

8, 3: *Into Upper Egypt:* to the desert there. The desert was considered the dwelling place of demons. Cf Is 13, 21; 34, 14; Mt 4, 1; 12, 43.

"Blessed are you, O God of our fathers;
praised be your name forever and
ever.
Let the heavens and all your creation
praise you forever.[n]
[6] You made Adam and you gave him his
wife Eve
to be his help and support;
and from these two the human race
descended.
You said, 'It is not good for the man to
be alone;
let us make him a partner like himself.'[o]
[7] Now, Lord, you know that I take this
wife of mine
not because of lust,
but for a noble purpose.
Call down your mercy on me and on
her,
and allow us to live together to a
happy old age."

[8] They said together, "Amen, amen," [9] and
went to bed for the night.

But Raguel got up and summoned his
servants. With him they went out to dig a
grave, [10] for he said, "I must do this, because if Tobiah should die, we would be
subjected to ridicule and insult." [11] When
they had finished digging the grave,
Raguel went back into the house and
called his wife, [12] saying, "Send one of the
maids in to see whether Tobiah is alive or
dead, so that if necessary we may bury him
without anyone's knowing about it." [13] She
sent the maid, who lit a lamp, opened the
bedroom door, went in, and found them
sound asleep together. [14] The maid went
out and told the girl's parents that Tobiah
was alive, and that there was nothing
wrong. [15] Then Raguel praised the God of
heaven in these words:

"Blessed are you, O God, with every
holy and pure blessing!
Let all your chosen ones praise you;
let them bless you forever!
[16] Blessed are you, who have made me
glad;
what I feared did not happen.

Rather you have dealt with us
according to your great mercy.
[17] Blessed are you, for you were merciful
toward two only children.
Grant them, Master, mercy and deliverance,
and bring their lives to fulfillment
with happiness and mercy."

[18] Then he told his servants to fill in the
grave before dawn.

Wedding Feast. [19] He asked his wife to
bake many loaves of bread; he himself
went out to the herd and picked out two
steers and four rams which he ordered to
be slaughtered. So the servants begain to
prepare the feast. [20] He summoned Tobiah and made an oath in his presence,
saying: "For fourteen days* you shall not
stir from here, but shall remain here eating and drinking with me; and you shall
bring joy to my daughter's sorrowing
spirit. [21] Take, to begin with, half of
whatever I own when you go back in
good health to your father; the other half
will be yours when I and my wife die. Be
of good cheer, my son! I am your father,
and Edna is your mother; and we belong
to you and to your beloved now and forever. So be happy, son!"

CHAPTER 9

The Money Recovered. [1] Then Tobiah
called Raphael and said to him: [2] "Brother
Azariah, take along with you four servants
and two camels and travel to Rages. Go to
Gabael's house and give him this bond.
Get the money and then bring him along
with you to the wedding celebration. [4] For
you know that my father is counting the
days. If I should delay my return by a
single day, I would cause him intense
grief. [3] You witnessed the oath that Raguel
has sworn; I cannot violate his oath." [5] So
Raphael, together with the four servants
and two camels, traveled to Rages in
Media, where they stayed at Gabael's
house. Raphael gave Gabael his bond and
told him about Tobit's son Tobiah, and
that he had married and was inviting him
to the wedding celebration. Gabael
promptly checked over the sealed moneybags, and they placed them on the camels.
[6] The following morning they got an
early start and traveled to the wedding

---

n Dn 3, 26.—o Gn 2, 18-23.

8, 20: *For fourteen days:* because of the happy, and unexpected, turn of events, Raguel doubles the time of the wedding
feast. When Tobiah returns home, the usual seven-day feast is
held (Tb 11, 18). Cf Jgs 14, 12.

celebration. When they entered Raguel's house, they found Tobiah reclining at table. He sprang up and greeted Gabael, who wept and blessed him, exclaiming: "O noble and good child, son of a noble and good, upright and charitable man, may the Lord grant heavenly blessing to you and to your wife, and to your wife's father and mother. Blessed be God, because I have seen the very image of my cousin Tobit!"

IV: TOBIAH'S RETURN; CURE OF TOBIT'S BLINDNESS

CHAPTER 10

Anxiety of the Parents. [1] Meanwhile, day by day, Tobit was keeping track of the time Tobiah would need to go and to return. When the number of days was reached and his son did not appear, [2] he said, "I wonder what has happened. Perhaps he has been detained there; or perhaps Gabael is dead, and there is no one to give him the money." [3] And he began to worry. [4] His wife Anna said, "My son has perished and is no longer among the living!" And she began to weep aloud and to wail over her son: [5] "Alas, my child, light of my eyes, that I let you make this journey!" [6] But Tobit kept telling her: "Hush, do not think about it, my love; he is safe! Probably they have to take care of some unexpected business there. The man who is traveling with him is trustworthy, and is one of our own kinsmen. So do not worry over him, my love. He will be here soon." [7] But she retorted, "Stop it, and do not lie to me! My child has perished!" She would go out and keep watch all day at the road her son had taken, and she ate nothing. At sunset she would go back home to wail and cry the whole night through, getting no sleep at all. *p*

Departure from Ecbatana. Now at the end of the fourteen-day wedding celebration which Raguel had sworn to hold for his daughter, Tobiah went to him and said: "Please let me go, for I know that my father and mother do not believe they will ever see me again. So I beg you, father, let me go back to my father. I have already told you how I left him." [8] Raguel said to Tobiah: "Stay, my child, stay with me. I am sending messengers to your father Tobit, and they will give him news

of you." [9] But Tobiah insisted, "No, I beg you to let me go back to my father."

[10] Raguel then promptly handed over to Tobiah Sarah his wife, together with half of all his property: male and female slaves, oxen and sheep, asses and camels, clothing, money, and household goods. [11] Bidding them farewell, he let them go. He embraced Tobiah and said to him: "Goodbye, my son. Have a safe journey. May the Lord of heaven grant prosperity to you and to your wife Sarah. And may I see children of yours before I die!" [12] Then he kissed his daughter Sarah and said to her: "My daughter, honor your father-in-law and your mother-in-law, because from now on they are as much your parents as the ones who brought you into the world. Go in peace, my daughter; let me hear good reports about you as long as I live." Finally he said good-bye to them and sent them away.

[13] Then Edna said to Tobiah: "My child and beloved kinsman, may the Lord bring you back safely, and may I live long enough to see children of you and of my daughter Sarah before I die. Before the Lord, I entrust my daughter to your care. Never cause her grief at any time in your life. Go in peace, my child. From now on I am your mother, and Sarah is your beloved. May all of us be prosperous all the days of our lives." She kissed them both and sent them away in peace.

[14] When Tobiah left Raguel, he was full of happiness and joy, and he blessed the Lord of heaven and earth, the King of all, for making his journey so successful. Finally he said good-bye to Raguel and his wife Edna, and added, "May I honor you all the days of my life!"

CHAPTER 11

Homeward Journey. [1] Then they left and began their return journey. When they were near Kaserin, just before Nineveh, [2] Raphael said: "You know how we left your father. [3] Let us hurry on ahead of your wife to prepare the house while the rest of the party are still on the way." [4] So they both went on ahead and Raphael said to Tobiah, "Have the gall in your hand!" And the dog ran along behind them.

p Gn 45, 26.

⁵Meanwhile, Anna sat watching the road by which her son was to come. ⁶When she saw him coming, she exclaimed to his father, "Tobit, your son is coming, and the man who traveled with him!"

⁷Raphael said to Tobiah before he reached his father: "I am certain that his eyes will be opened. ⁸Smear the fish gall on them. This medicine will make the cataracts shrink and peel off from his eyes; then your father will again be able to see the light of day."

Sight Restored. ⁹Then Anna ran up to her son, threw her arms around him, and said to him, "Now that I have seen you again, son, I am ready to die!" And she sobbed aloud.�q ¹⁰Tobit got up and stumbled out through the courtyard gate. Tobiah went up to him ¹¹with the fish gall in his hand, and holding him firmly, blew into his eyes. "Courage, father," he said. ¹²Next he smeared the medicine on his eyes, ¹³and it made them smart. Then, beginning at the corners of Tobit's eyes, Tobiah used both hands to peel off the cataracts. When Tobit saw his son, he threw his arms around him ¹⁴and wept. He exclaimed, "I can see you, son, the light of my eyes!" Then he said:

"Blessed be God,
  and praised be his great name,
  and blessed be all his holy angels.
May his holy name be praised
  throughout all the ages,
¹⁵ Because it was he who scourged me,
  and it is he who has had mercy on
  me.
Behold, I now see my son Tobiah!"

Then Tobit went back in, rejoicing and praising God with full voice. Tobiah told his father that his journey had been a success; that he had brought back the money; and that he had married Raguel's daughter Sarah, who would arrive shortly, for she was approaching the gate of Nineveh.ʳ

¹⁶Rejoicing and praising God, Tobit went out to the gate of Nineveh to meet his daughter-in-law. When the people of Nineveh saw him walking along briskly, with no one leading him by the hand, they were amazed. ¹⁷Before them all Tobit proclaimed how God had mercifully restored sight to his eyes. When Tobit reached Sarah, the wife of his son Tobiah, he greeted her: "Welcome, my daughter! Blessed be your God for bringing you to us, daughter! Blessed are your father and your mother. Blessed is my son Tobiah, and blessed are you, daughter! Welcome to your home with blessing and joy. Come in, daughter!" That day there was joy for all the Jews who lived in Nineveh. ¹⁸Ahiqar and his nephew Nadab also came to rejoice with Tobit. They celebrated Tobiah's wedding feast for seven happy days, and he received many gifts.

V: RAPHAEL REVEALS HIS IDENTITY

CHAPTER 12

Raphael's Wages.* ¹When the wedding celebration came to an end, Tobit called his son Tobiah and said to him, "Son, see to it that you give what is due to the man who made the journey with you; give him a bonus too." ²Tobiah said: "Father, how much shall I pay him? It would not hurt me at all to give him half of all the wealth he brought back with me.ˢ ³He led me back safe and sound; he cured my wife; he brought the money back with me; and he cured you. How much of a bonus should I give him?" ⁴Tobit answered, "It is only fair, son, that he should receive half of all that he brought back." ⁵So Tobiah called Raphael and said, "Take as your wages half of all that you have brought back, and go in peace."

Exhortation.* ⁶Raphael called the two men aside privately and said to them: "Thank God! Give him the praise and the glory. Before all the living, acknowledge the many good things he has done for you, by blessing and extolling his name in song. Before all men, honor and proclaim God's deeds, and do not be slack in praising him.* ⁷A king's secret it is prudent to keep, but the works of God are to be declared and made known. Praise them with due honor. Do good, and evil will not find its way to you. ⁸Prayer and fasting are good, but better than either is almsgiving accompanied by

---

q Gn 33, 4; 45, 14; 46, 29f; Lk 15, 20.—r Tb 13, 2; Dt 32, 39; 1 Sm 2, 6.—s Tb 5, 3. 7. 15f.

12, 1-5: Tobit and his son generously agree to give Azariah far more than the wages agreed upon in Tb 5, 15-16.

12, 6-10: In the fashion of a wisdom teacher, Raphael gives the two men a short exhortation similar to the one Tobit gave his son in Tb 4, 3-19.

12, 6f: The Jews considered the duty of praising God their most esteemed privilege. Without praise of God, life was meaningless. Cf Is 38, 16-20.

righteousness.* A little with righteousness is better than abundance with wickedness. It is better to give alms than to store up gold;[t] [9]for almsgiving saves one from death and expiates every sin. Those who regularly give alms shall enjoy a full life;[u] [10]but those habitually guilty of sin are their own worst enemies.

Raphael's Identity. [11]"I will now tell you the whole truth; I will conceal nothing at all from you. I have already said to you, 'A king's secret it is prudent to keep, but the works of God are to be made known with due honor.' [12] [v] I can now tell you that when you, Tobit, and Sarah prayed, it was I who presented and read the record of your prayer before the Glory of the Lord; and I did the same thing when you used to bury the dead.* [13]When you did not hesitate to get up and leave your dinner in order to go and bury the dead, [14]I was sent to put you to the test.* At the same time, however, God commissioned me to heal you and your daughter-in-law Sarah. [15]I am Raphael, one of the seven angels who enter and serve before the Glory of the Lord."[w]

[16]Stricken with fear, the two men fell to the ground. [17]But Raphael said to them: "No need to fear; you are safe. Thank God now and forever. [18]As for me, when I came to you it was not out of any favor on my part, but because it was God's will. So continue to thank him every day; praise him with song. [19]Even though you watched me eat and drink, I did not really do so; what you were seeing was a vision. [20]So now get up from the ground and praise God. Behold, I am about to ascend to him who sent me; write down all these things that have happened to you."[x] [21]When Raphael ascended, they rose to their feet and could no longer see him. [22]They kept thanking God and singing his praises; and they continued to acknowledge these marvelous deeds which he had done when the angel of God appeared to them.

VI: TOBIT'S SONG OF PRAISE

CHAPTER 13

[1]Then Tobit composed this joyful prayer:*

Blessed be God who lives forever,
  because his kingdom lasts for all ages.[y]

[2] For he scourges and then has mercy;
  he casts down to the depths of the nether world,
  and he brings up from the great abyss.
No one can escape his hand.[z]
[3] Praise him, you Israelites, before the Gentiles,
  for though he has scattered you among them,
[4]   he has shown you his greatness even there.

Exalt him before every living being,
  because he is the Lord our God,
  our Father and God forever.
[5] He scourged you for your iniquities,
  but will again have mercy on you all.
He will gather you from all the Gentiles
  among whom you have been scattered.[a]
[6] When you turn back to him with all your heart,
  to do what is right before him,
Then he will turn back to you,
  and no longer hide his face from you.[b]
So now consider what he has done for you,
  and praise him with full voice.
Bless the Lord of righteousness,
  and exalt the King of the ages.
In the land of exile I praise him,
  and show his power and majesty to a sinful nation.

"Turn back, you sinners! do the right before him:
  perhaps he may look with favor upon you
  and show you mercy.

---

t Tb 4, 7-11; Sir 29, 8-13.—u Dn 4, 24.—v Jb 33, 23f; Acts 10, 4; Rv 8, 3f.—w Lk 1, 19; Rv 8, 2.—x Jgs 13, 20.—y Tb 3, 11; 8, 5. 15; 1 Chr 29, 10; Dn 3, 26.—z Tb 11, 15; 13, 9; Dt 32, 39; 1 Sm 2, 6; Wis 16, 13.—a Dt 30, 3; Neh 1, 9.—b Dt 30, 2.

12, 8: *Prayer . . . fasting . . . almsgiving . . . righteousness:* these, together with the proper attitude toward wealth, are treated in great detail by Christ our Lord in the Sermon on the Mount (Mt 6).

12, 12. 15: Raphael is one of the seven specially designated intercessors who present man's prayers to God. Angelology was developing in this period. The names of two other angels are given in the Bible: Gabriel (Dn 8, 16; 9, 21; Lk 1, 19. 26) and Michael (Dn 10, 13. 21; 12, 1; Jude 9; Rv 12, 7).

12, 14: *I was sent . . . test:* God often sends trials to purify his faithful servants further. Cf Jb 1—2.

13, 1-18: Tobit's hymn of praise (cf Ex 15, 1-18; Jdt 16, 1-17) is divided into two parts. The first part (vv 1-8) is a song of praise that echoes themes from the hymns and psalms of the kingdom; the second (vv 9-18) is addressed to Jerusalem in the style of the prophets who spoke of a new and ideal Jerusalem (Is 60); cf Rv 21.

7 "As for me, I exalt my God,
and my spirit rejoices in the King of
heaven.
8 Let all men speak of his majesty,
and sing his praises in Jerusalem."

9 O Jerusalem, holy city,
he scourged you for the works of
your hands,*
but will again pity the children of the
righteous. *c*
10 Praise the Lord for his goodness,
and bless the King of the ages,
so that his tent may be rebuilt in you
with joy.
May he gladden within you all who
were captives;
all who were ravaged may he cherish
within you
for all generations to come. *d*
11 A bright light will shine to all parts of
the earth;
many nations shall come to you from
afar,
And the inhabitants of all the limits of
the earth,
drawn to you by the name of the
Lord God,
Bearing in their hands their gifts
for the King of heaven.
Every generation shall give joyful
praise in you,
and shall call you the chosen one,
through all ages forever. *e*
12 Accursed are all who speak a harsh
word against you;
accursed are all who destroy you
and pull down your walls,
And all who overthrow your towers
and set fire to your homes;
but forever blessed are all those who
build you up. *f*
13 Go, then, rejoice over the children of
the righteous,

who shall all be gathered together
and shall bless the Lord of the ages.
14 Happy are those who love you,
and happy those who rejoice in your
prosperity.
Happy are all the men who shall grieve
over you,
over all your chastisements,
For they shall rejoice in you
as they behold all your joy forever. *g*
15 My spirit blesses the Lord, the great
King;
16 Jerusalem shall be rebuilt as his home
forever.
Happy for me if a remnant of my offspring survive
to see your glory and to praise the
King of heaven!
The gates of Jerusalem shall be built
with sapphire and emerald,
and all your walls with precious
stones.
The towers of Jerusalem shall be built
with gold,
and their battlements with pure
gold. *h*
17 The streets of Jerusalem shall be paved
with rubies and stones of Ophir;
18 The gates of Jerusalem shall sing hymns
of gladness,
and all her houses shall cry out, "Alleluia!"
"Blessed be God who has raised you
up!
may he be blessed for all ages!"
For in you they shall praise his holy
name forever.
The end of Tobit's hymn of praise

VII: EPILOGUE

CHAPTER 14

Parting Advice. 1 Tobit died peacefully at
the age of a hundred and twelve, and received an honorable burial in Nineveh.
2 He was sixty-two years old when he lost
his eyesight, and after he recovered it he
lived in prosperity, giving alms and continually blessing God and praising the divine Majesty.
3 Just before he died, he called his son
Tobiah and Tobiah's seven sons, and gave
him this command: "Son, take your children[i] 4 and flee into Media, for I believe
God's word which was spoken by Nahum*

---

c Tb 11, 15; Mi 7, 19; Rv 21.—d Is 44, 26. 28; Am 9, 11; Zec
1, 16.—e Is 2, 3f; 9, 1; 49, 6; 60, 1; Mi 4, 2; Zec 8, 22.—f Bar
4, 31f.—g Ps 122, 6; Is 66, 10.—h Tb 14, 5; Is 54, 11-13; 62,
2; Rv 21, 10-21.—i Gn 47, 29f.

13, 9: *Works of your hands:* idols.
14, 4f: *Nahum:* one of the minor prophets, whose book contains oracles of doom against Nineveh. Here, in keeping with the
period to which he assigns his story, the sacred author makes
Tobit speak as if the punishment of Nineveh, the destruction of
Jerusalem (587 B.C.), the exile from Judah and the return, would
all take place in the future. The technique of using the facts of
past history as seemingly future predictions, is a frequent device
of apocalyptic writers. *The Good Land:* a favorite name for the
promised land. Cf Dt 1, 35; 3, 25; 4, 21. 22.

against Nineveh. It shall all happen, and shall overtake Assyria and Nineveh; indeed, whatever was said by Israel's prophets, whom God commissioned, shall occur. Not one of the oracles shall remain unfulfilled, but everything shall take place in the time appointed for it. So it will be safer in Media than in Assyria or Babylon. For I know and believe that whatever God has spoken will be accomplished. It shall happen, and not a single word of the prophecies shall prove false.

"As for our kinsmen who dwell in Israel, they shall all be scattered and led away into exile from the Good Land. The entire country of Israel shall become desolate; even Samaria and Jerusalem shall become desolate! God's temple there shall be burnt to the ground and shall be desolate for a while.*j* 5 But God will again have mercy on them and bring them back to the land of Israel. They shall rebuild the temple, but it will not be like the first one, until the era when the appointed times shall be completed.* Afterward all of them shall return from their exile, and they shall rebuild Jerusalem with splendor. In her the temple of God shall also be rebuilt; yes, it will be rebuilt for all generations to come, just as the prophets of Israel said of her.*k* 6 *l* All the nations of the world shall be converted and shall offer God true worship; all shall abandon their idols which have deceitfully led them into error,* 7 and shall bless the God of the ages in righteousness. Because all the Israelites who are to be saved in those days will truly be mindful of God, they shall be gathered together and go to Jerusalem; in security shall they dwell forever in the land of Abraham, which will be given over to them. Those who sincerely love God shall rejoice, but those who become guilty of sin shall completely disappear from the land.*m*

9 "Now, children, I give you this command: serve God faithfully and do what is right before him; you must tell your children to do what is upright and to give alms, to be mindful of God and at all times to bless his name sincerely and with all their strength.

8 "Now, as for you, my son, depart from Nineveh; do not remain here. 10 The day you bury your mother next to me, do not even stay overnight within the confines of the city. For I see that people here

shamelessly commit all sorts of wickedness and treachery. Think, my son, of all that Nadab* did to Ahiqar, the very one who brought him up: Ahiqar went down alive into the earth! Yet God made Nadab's disgraceful crime rebound against him. Ahiqar came out again into the light, but Nadab went into the everlasting darkness, for he had tried to kill Ahiqar. Because Ahiqar had given alms to me, he escaped from the deadly trap Nadab had set for him. But Nadab himself fell into the deadly trap, and it destroyed him.*n* 11 So, my children, note well what almsgiving does, and also what wickedness does—it kills! But now my spirit is about to leave me."

Death of Tobit and Tobiah. 12 They placed him on his bed and he died; and he received an honorable burial. When Tobiah's mother died, he buried her next to his father. He then departed with his wife and children for Media, where he settled in Ecbatana with his father-in-law Raguel.*o* 13 He took respectful care of his aging father-in-law and mother-in-law; and he buried them at Ecbatana in Media. Then he inherited Raguel's estate as well as that of his father Tobit. 14 He died at the venerable age of a hundred and seventeen. 15 But before he died, he heard of the destruction of Nineveh and saw its effects. He witnessed the exile of the city's inhabitants when Cyaxares,* king of Media, led them captive into Media. Tobiah praised God for all that he had done against the citizens of Nineveh and Assyria. Before dying he rejoiced over Nineveh's destruction, and he blessed the Lord God forever and ever. Amen.

---

j Na 2, 2—3, 19.—k Neh 12, 27; Jer 31, 38.—l Tb 45, 14; Is 60, 1-4.—m Is 60, 21; Jer 32, 37; Ez 34, 28; 37, 25; 39, 26.—n Tb 1, 21f.—o Tb 4, 4.

14, 5: *Until the era . . . completed:* a reference to the advent of messianic times, in which a new, more perfect temple was to be expected. Cf Heb 9, 1-14.

14, 6: Conversion of the Gentiles is also to come in the messianic era.

14, 10: *Nadab:* In the *Story of Ahiqar,* the hero Ahiqar, chancellor under the Assyrian kings Sennacherib and Esarhaddon, adopts his nephew Nadab and prepares him to become his successor. But Nadab treacherously plots to have his uncle put to death. Ahiqar hides in a friend's house, and is finally vindicated *(came out again into the light)* when Nadab's scheme is discovered. Thereupon Nadab is thrown into a dungeon where he dies *(went into everlasting darkness).* It was Ahiqar's almsgiving that delivered him from death; see note on Tb 2, 2.

14, 15: *Cyaxares:* Nabopolassar, king of Babylon, and Cyaxares conquered and destroyed Nineveh in 612 B.C.; see note on Tb 1, 15.

THE BOOK OF JUDITH

The Book of Judith is a vivid story relating how, in a grave crisis, God delivered the Jewish people through the instrumentality of a woman. The unknown author composed this edifying narrative of divine providence at the end of the second or the beginning of the first century B.C. The original was almost certainly written in Hebrew, but the Greek text shows so much freedom in adapting from the Septuagint the language of older biblical books that it must be regarded as having a literary character of its own. It is this Greek form of the book, accepted as canonical by the Catholic Church, which is translated here. St. Jerome, who prepared (with some reluctance) a Latin text of Judith, based his work on a secondary Aramaic text available to him in Palestine, combined with an older Latin rendering from the Greek. The long hymn of chapter 16 he took in its entirety from that earlier Latin text.

Since it is no longer possible to determine with any precision the underlying events which may have given rise to this narrative, it is enough to note that the author sought to strengthen the faith of his people in God's abiding presence among them. The Book of Judith is a tract for difficult times; the reader, it was hoped, would take to heart the lesson that God was still the Master of history, who could save Israel from her enemies. Note the parallel with the time of the Exodus: as God had delivered his people by the hand of Moses, so he could deliver them by the hand of the pious widow Judith (see note on 2, 12).

The story can be divided into two parts. In the first (cc 1—7), Holofernes, commander-in-chief of the armies of Nebuchadnezzar, leads an overwhelming Assyrian force in a punitive campaign against the vassals who refused to help in the Assyrian war against the Medes. The Jewish people stubbornly resist the enemy at Bethulia, guarding the route of access to Jerusalem. Despite the warning of Achior that the Jews cannot be conquered unless they sin against God, the proud general lays siege to the town and cuts off its water supply. After a siege of thirty-four days, the exhausted defenders are desperate and ready to surrender.

At this point, the climax of the story, Judith (the name means "Jewess") appears and promises to defeat the Assyrians. The rest of the story is too well known to repeat in detail. Having fasted and prayed, Judith dresses in her finest garments and proceeds to the Assyrian camp, where she succeeds in killing Holofernes while he lies in a drunken stupor. The Assyrians panic when they discover this, and the Jews are able to rout and slaughter them. The beautiful hymn of the people honoring Judith (15, 9-10) is often applied to Mary in the liturgy.

Any attempt to read the book directly against the backdrop of Jewish history in relation to the empires of the ancient world is bound to fail. The story was written as a pious reflection on the meaning of the yearly Passover observance. It draws its inspiration from the Exodus narrative (especially Ex 14, 31) and from the texts of Isaiah and the Psalms portraying the special intervention of God for the preservation of Jerusalem. The theme of God's hand as the agent of this providential activity, reflected of old in the hand of Moses and now in the hand of Judith, is again exemplified at a later time in Jewish synagogue art. God's hand reaching down from heaven appears as part of the scene at Dura-Europos (before A.D. 256) in paintings of the Exodus, of the sacrifice of Isaac (Gn 22), and of Ezekiel's valley of dry bones (Ez 37).

The Book of Judith is divided as follows: I. Peril of the Jews (1, 1—7, 32). II. Deliverance of the Jews (8, 1—14, 10). III. Victory (14, 11—16, 25).

I: PERIL OF THE JEWS

CHAPTER 1

War against the Medes. [1] It was the twelfth year of the reign of Nebuchadnezzar, king of the Assyrians in the great city of Nineveh. At that time Arphaxad ruled over the Medes in Ecbatana. [2] Around this city he built a wall of blocks of stone, each three cubits in height and six in length. He made the wall seventy cubits high and fifty thick. [3] At the gates he raised towers of a hundred cubits, with a thickness of sixty cubits at the base. [4] The gateway he built to a height of seventy cubits, with an opening forty cubits wide for the passage of his chariot forces and the marshaling of his infantry. [5] Then King Nebuchadnezzar waged war against King Arphaxad in the vast plain, in the district of Ragae. [6] To him there rallied all the inhabitants of the mountain region, all who dwelt along the Euphrates, the Tigris, and the Hydaspes, and King Arioch of the Elamites, in the plain. Thus many nations came together to resist the people of Cheleoud.*

Ultimatum to the West. [7] Now Nebuchadnezzar, king of the Assyrians, sent messengers to all the inhabitants of Persia, and to all those who dwelt in the West: to the inhabitants of Cilicia and Damascus, Lebanon and Anti-Lebanon, to all who dwelt along the seacoast, [8] to the peoples of Carmel, Gilead, Upper Galilee, and the vast plain of Esdraelon, [9] to all those in Samaria and its cities, and west of the Jordan as far as Jerusalem, Bethany, Chelous, Kadesh, and the River of Egypt; to Tahpanhes, Raamses, all the land of Goshen, [10] Tanis, Memphis and beyond, and to all the inhabitants of Egypt as far as the borders of Ethiopia.

[11] But the inhabitants of all that land disregarded the summons of Nebuchadnezzar, king of the Assyrians, and would not go with him to the war. They were not afraid of him but regarded him as a lone individual opposed to them, and turned away his envoys empty-handed, in disgrace. [12] Then Nebuchadnezzar fell into a violent rage against all that land, and swore by his throne and his kingdom that he would avenge himself on all the territories of Cilicia and Damascus and Syria, and also destroy with his sword all the inhabitants of Moab, Ammon, the whole of Judea, and those living anywhere in Egypt as far as the borders of the two seas.*

Defeat of Arphaxad. [13] In the seventeenth year he proceeded with his army against King Arphaxad, and was victorious in his campaign. He routed the whole force of Arphaxad, his entire cavalry and all his chariots, [14] and took possession of his cities. He pressed on to Ecbatana and took its towers, sacked its marketplaces, and turned its glory into shame. [15] Arphaxad himself he overtook in the mountains of Ragae, ran him through with spears, and utterly destroyed him. [16] Then he returned home with all his numerous, motley horde of warriors; and there he and his army relaxed and feasted for a hundred and twenty days.[a]

CHAPTER 2

Council of War against the West. [1] In the eighteenth year, on the twenty-second day of the first month, there was a discusssion in the palace of Nebuchadnezzar, king of the Assyrians, about taking revenge on the whole world, as he had threatened. [2] He summoned all his ministers and nobles, laid before them his secret plan, and urged the total destruction of those countries. [3] They decided to do away with all those who had refused to comply with the order he had issued.

[4] When he had completed his plan, Nebuchadnezzar, king of the Assyrians, summoned Holofernes, general in chief of his forces, second to himself in command, and said to him: [5] [b] "Thus says the great king, the lord of all the earth: Go forth from my presence, take with you men of proven valor, a hundred and twenty thousand infantry and twelve thousand cavalry, [6] and proceed against all the land of the West, because they did not comply with the order I issued. [7] Tell them to have earth and water* ready, for I will come against them in my wrath; I will cover all the land with the feet of my soldiers, to whom I will deliver them as spoils. [8] Their

---

a Est 1, 3f.—b 5f: Est 3, 8f.

1, 6: *Cheleoud:* probably the Chaldeans are meant.
1, 12: *The two seas:* the ancient rulers in Mesopotamia often designated the limits of their realm as extending from the Upper Sea (the Mediterranean) to the Lower Sea (the Persian Gulf).
2, 7: *Earth and water:* in the Persian period, the offering of these to a conqueror was a symbolic gesture of unconditional surrender.

slain shall fill their ravines and wadies, the swelling torrent shall be choked with their dead; [9] and I will deport them as exiles to the very ends of the earth. [10] "You go before me and take possession of all their territories for me. If they surrender to you, guard them for me till the day of their punishment. [11] As for those who resist, show them no quarter, but deliver them up to slaughter and plunder in each country you occupy. [12] For as I live,* and by the strength of my kingdom, what I have spoken I will accomplish by my power. [13] Do not disobey a single one of the orders of your lord; fulfill them exactly as I have commanded you, and do it without delay."

Campaign of Holofernes. [14] So Holofernes left the presence of his lord, and summoned all the princes, and the generals and officers of the Assyrian army. [15] He mustered a hundred and twenty thousand picked troops, as his lord had commanded, and twelve thousand mounted archers, [16] and grouped them into a complete combat force. [17] He took along a very large number of camels, asses, and mules for their baggage; innumerable sheep, cattle, and goats for their food supply; [18] abundant provisions for each man, and much gold and silver from the royal palace. [19] Then he and his whole army proceeded on their expedition in advance of King Nebuchadnezzar, to cover all the western region with their chariots and cavalry and regular infantry. [20] A huge, irregular force, too many to count, like locusts or the dust of the earth, went along with them. [c]

[21] After a three-day march from Nineveh, they reached the plain of Bectileth, and from Bectileth they next encamped near the mountains to the north of Upper Cilicia. [22] From there Holofernes took his whole force, the infantry, cavalry,

and chariots, and marched into the mountain region. [23] He devastated Put and Lud,* and plundered all the Rassisites and the Ishmaelites on the border of the desert toward the south of Chaldea.

[24] Then, following the Euphrates, he went through Mesopotamia, and battered down every fortified city along the Wadi Abron, until he reached the sea. [25] He seized the territory of Cilicia, and cut down everyone who resisted him. Then he proceeded to the southern borders of Japheth, toward Arabia. [26] He surrounded all the Midianites, burned their tents, and plundered their sheepfolds. [27] Descending to the plain of Damascus at the time of the wheat harvest, he set fire to all their fields, destroyed their flocks and herds, despoiled their cities, devastated their plains, and put all their youths to the sword.

[28] The fear and dread of him fell upon all the inhabitants of the coastland, upon those in Sidon and Tyre, and those who dwelt in Sur and Ocina, and the inhabitants of Jamnia. Those in Azotus and Ascalon also feared him greatly.

CHAPTER 3

Submission of the West. [1] They therefore sent messengers to him to sue for peace in these words: [2] "We, the servants of Nebuchadnezzar the great king, lie prostrate before you; do with us as you will. [3] Our dwellings and all our wheat fields, our flocks and herds, and all our encampments are at your disposal; make use of them as you please. [4] Our cities and their inhabitants are also at your service; come and deal with them as you see fit."

[5] After the spokesmen had reached Holofernes and given him this message, [6] he went down with his army to the seacoast, and stationed garrisons in the fortified cities; from them he impressed picked troops as auxiliaries. [7] The people of these cities and all the inhabitants of the countryside received him with garlands and dancing to the sound of timbrels. [8] Nevertheless, he devastated their whole territory and cut down their sacred groves, for he had been commissioned to destroy all the gods of the earth, so that every nation might worship Nebuchadnezzar alone, and every people and tribe invoke him as a god. [d] [9] At length Holofernes reached Esdraelon in the neighborhood of

---

c Jgs 7, 12.—d Ex 34, 13.

2, 12: *As I live:* in the Old Testament, an oath proper to divinity; cf Dt 32, 40. Nebuchadnezzar is making himself equal to God; see Jdt 6, 2. *By my power:* literally "by my hand." The hand of Nebuchadnezzar raised in opposition to God and to his people is the occasion for Judith's intervention *by a woman's hand;* cf Jdt 9, 9f; Is 10, 5-14.
2, 23: *Put and Lud:* the same as the "Put and Lud" mentioned in Ez 30, 5 as allies of Egypt, and in Ez 27, 10 as supplying mercenary soldiers to Tyre. Here they seem inserted to embellish the narrative with assonance and prophetic associations rather than to indicate definite localities.

Dothan, the approach to the main ridge of the Judean mountains; ¹⁰he set up his camp between Geba* and Scythopolis, and stayed there a whole month to refurbish all the equipment of his army.

CHAPTER 4

Israelite Defense. ¹When the Israelites who dwelt in Judea heard of all that Holofernes, commander in chief of Nebuchadnezzar, king of the Assyrians, had done to the nations, and how he had despoiled all their temples and destroyed them, ²they were in extreme dread of him, and greatly alarmed for Jerusalem and the temple of the LORD, their God. ³Now, they had lately returned from exile, and only recently had all the people of Judea been gathered together, and the vessels, the altar, and the temple been purified from profanation.* ⁴So they sent word to the whole region of Samaria, to Kona, Beth-horon, Belmain, and Jericho, to Choba and Aesora, and to the valley of Salem. ⁵The people there posted guards on all the summits of the high mountains, fortified their villages, and since their fields had recently been harvested, stored up provisions in preparation for war.

⁶Joakim, who was high priest* in Jerusalem in those days, wrote to the inhabitants of Bethulia [and Betomesthaim], which is on the way to Esdraelon, facing the plain near Dothan, ⁷and instructed them to keep firm hold of the mountain passes, since these offered access to Judea. It would be easy to ward off the attacking forces, as the defile was only wide enough for two abreast. ⁸The Israelites carried out the orders given them by Joakim, the high priest, and the senate of the whole people of Israel, which met in Jerusalem.*

Prayer and Penance. ⁹All the men of Israel cried to God with great fervor and did penance—¹⁰ ᵉ they, along with their wives, and children, and domestic animals.* All their resident aliens, hired laborers, and slaves also girded themselves with sackcloth. ¹¹And all the Israelite men, women, and children who lived in Jerusalem prostrated themselves in front of the temple building,* with ashes strewn on their heads, displaying their sackcloth covering before the LORD. ¹²The altar, too, they draped in sackcloth; and with one accord they cried out fervently to the God of Israel not to allow their children to

be seized, their wives to be taken captive, the cities of their inheritance to be ruined, or the sanctuary to be profaned and mocked for the nations to gloat over.ᶠ ¹³The LORD heard their cry and had regard for their distress. For the people observed a fast of many days' duration throughout Judea, and before the sanctuary of the LORD Almighty in Jerusalem.ᵍ ¹⁴The high priest Joakim, and all the priests in attendance on the LORD who served his altar, were also girded with sackcloth as they offered the daily holocaust, the votive offerings, and the free-will offerings of the people. ¹⁵With ashes upon their turbans, they cried to the LORD with all their strength to look with favor on the whole house of Israel.

CHAPTER 5

Council against the Israelites. ¹It was reported to Holofernes, commander in chief of the Assyrian army, that the Israelites were ready for battle, and had blocked the mountain passes, fortified the summits of all the higher peaks, and placed roadblocks in the plains. ²In great anger he summoned all the rulers of the Moabites, the generals of the Ammonites, and all the satraps of the seacoast ³and said to them: "Now tell me, you Canaanites, what sort of people is this that dwells in the mountains? Which cities do they inhabit? How large is their army? In what does their power and strength consist? Who has set himself up as their king and the leader of their army? ⁴Why have they refused to come out to meet me along with all the other inhabitants of the West?"

Achior's Speech. ⁵Then Achior, the leader of all the Ammonites, said to him:

e 10f: Jon 3, 7f.—f Est 4, 1f.—g Est 4, 16.

3, 10: *Geba:* perhaps originally "Gelboe," the mountain range near the eastern end of which lay *Scythopolis,* the Greek name for ancient Beth-shean (Jos 17, 11).

4, 3: *Returned from exile . . . profanation:* these allusions are variously attributed—to the Persian period (538-323 B.C.), or even to a condition in the days of Antiochus Epiphanes (175-164 B.C.).

4, 6: *Joakim, who was high priest:* see Bar 1, 7 and the footnote on Bar 1, 8f; this name for a high priest cannot be used in dating the events in Jdt.

4, 8: The organization of the Jewish nation as subject to a *high priest* and a *senate,* or council of elders, was proper to the Greek period (after 323 B.C.), and is reflected in the coinage of John Hyrcanus (135-104 B.C.).

4, 10: *Domestic animals:* see note on Jon 3, 8.

4, 11: *Prostrated themselves in front of the temple building:* for a parallel to this ceremony of entreaty, see Jl 1, 13f; 2, 15ff, and the note on Jl 2, 17.

"My lord, hear this account from your servant; I will tell you the truth about this people that lives near you [that inhabits this mountain region]; no lie shall escape your servant's lips. [h]
6 * "These people are descendants of the Chaldeans. [7] They formerly dwelt in Mesopotamia, for they did not wish to follow the gods of their forefathers who were born in the land of the Chaldeans. [i] [8] Since they abandoned the way of their ancestors, and acknowledged with divine worship the God of heaven, their forefathers expelled them from the presence of their gods. So they fled to Mesopotamia and dwelt there a long time. [9] Their God bade them leave their abode and proceed to the land of Canaan. Here they settled, and grew very rich in gold, silver, and a great abundance of livestock. [j] [10] Later, when famine had gripped the whole land of Canaan, they went down into Egypt. They stayed there as long as they found sustenance, and grew into such a great multitude that the number of their race could not be counted. [k] [11] [l] The king of Egypt, however, rose up against them, shrewdly forced them to labor at brickmaking, oppressed them and enslaved them. [12] But they cried to their God, and he struck the land of Egypt with plagues for which there was no remedy. When the Egyptians expelled them, [13] [m] God dried up the Red Sea before them, [14] and led them along the route to Sinai and Kadesh-barnea. First they drove out all the inhabitants of the desert; [15] then they settled in the land of the Amorites, destroyed all the Heshbonites by main force, crossed the Jordan, and took possession of the whole mountain region. [n] [16] They expelled the Canaanites, the Perizzites, the Jebusites, the Shechemites, and all the Gergesites; and they lived in these mountains a long time. [o]
[17] [p] "As long as the Israelites did not sin in the sight of their God, they prospered, for their God, who hates wickedness,

was with them. [18] But when they deviated from the way he prescribed for them, they were ground down steadily, more and more, by frequent wars, and finally taken as captives into foreign lands. The temple of their God was razed to the ground, and their cities were occupied by their enemies. [q] [19] But now that they have returned to their God, they have come back from the Dispersion wherein they were scattered, and have repossessed Jerusalem, where their sanctuary is, and have settled again in the mountain region which was unoccupied.
[20] [r] "So now, my lord and master, if these people are at fault, and is sinning against their God, and if we verify this offense of theirs, then we shall be able to go up and conquer them. [21] But it they are not a guilty nation, then your lordship should keep his distance; otherwise their LORD and God will shield them, and we shall become the laughingstock of the whole world."
[22] Now when Achior had concluded his recommendation, all the people standing round about the tent murmured; and the officers of Holofernes and all the inhabitants of the seacoast and of Moab alike said he should be cut to pieces. [23] "We are not afraid of the Israelites," they said, "for they are a powerless people, incapable of a strong defense. [24] Let us therefore attack them; your great army, Lord Holofernes, will swallow them up." [s]

CHAPTER 6

Holofernes' Answer. [1] When the noise of the crowd surrounding the council had subsided, Holofernes, commander in chief of the Assyrian army, said to Achior, in the presence of the whole throng of coastland peoples, of the Moabites, and of the Ammonite mercenaries: [2] "Who are you, Achior, to prophesy among us as you have done today, and to tell us not to fight against the Israelites because their God protects them? What god is there beside Nebuchadnezzar? He will send his force and destroy them from the face of the earth. Their God will not save them; [t] [3] but we, the servants of Nebuchadnezzar, will strike them down as one man, for they will be unable to withstand the force of our cavalry. [u] [4] We shall overwhelm them with it, and the mountains shall be drunk with

h Jdt 11, 9-19.—i Gn 11, 31.—j Gn 11, 31—12, 5.—k Gn 42, 1-5; 46, 1-7; Ex 1, 7.—l 11f: Ex 5, 4-21; 7, 1-9.—m 13f: Ex 14, 21f. 29.—n Nm 21, 21-32; Jos 2, 10.—o Dt 7, 1.—p 17f: Dt 28—30; Ps 106, 40-46; Is 59, 7.—q 2 Kgs 25.—r 20f: Jdt 8, 18ff; 11, 10.—s Jdt 6, 2; 9, 7; 16, 2.—t Jdt 3, 8; 9, 7.—u Is 36, 18ff.

5, 6-9: Achior outlines the early history of the Hebrews, whose forefather, Abraham, first lived in Ur of the *Chaldeans* (Gn 11, 28) and then migrated to Haran (Gn 11, 31) in Aram Naharaim (Gn 24, 10), which was called *Mesopotamia* by the Greeks. *The gods of their forefathers* were the pagan deities worshiped by Abraham's relatives (Jos 24, 2).

their blood, and their plains filled with their corpses. Not a trace of them shall survive our attack: they shall utterly perish, says King Nebuchadnezzar, lord of all the earth; for he has spoken, and his words shall not remain unfulfilled.[v] [5]As for you, Achior, you Ammonite mercenary, for saying these things in a moment of perversity you shall not see my face after today, until I have taken revenge on this race of people from Egypt. [6]Then at my return, the sword of my army or the spear of my servants will pierce your sides, and you shall fall among their slain.[w] [7]My servants will now conduct you to the mountain region, and leave you at one of the towns along the ascent. [8]You shall not die till you are destroyed together with them. [9]If you still cherish the hope that they will not be taken, then there is no need for you to be downcast. I have spoken, and my words shall not prove false in any respect."

Achior in Bethulia. [10]Then Holofernes ordered the servants who were standing by in his tent to seize Achior, conduct him to Bethulia, and hand him over to the Israelites. [11]So the servants took him in custody and brought him out of the camp into the plain. From there they led him into the mountain region till they reached the springs below Bethulia. [12]When the men of the city saw them, they seized their weapons and ran out of the city to the crest of the ridge; and all the slingers blocked the ascent of Holofernes' servants by hurling stones upon them. [13]So they took cover below the mountain, where they bound Achior and left him lying at the foot of the mountain; then they returned to their lord.

[14]The Israelites came down to him from their city, loosed him, and brought him into Bethulia. They haled him before the rulers of the city, [15]who in those days were Uzziah, son of Micah of the tribe of Simeon, Chabris, son of Gothoniel, and Charmis, son of Melchiel. [16]They then convened all the elders of the city; and all their young men, as well as the women, gathered in haste at the place of assembly. They placed Achior in the center of the throng, and Uzziah questioned him about what had happened. [17]He replied by giving them an account of what was said in the council of Holofernes, and of all his own words among the Assyrian officers, and of all the boasting threats of Holofernes against the house of Israel. [18]At this the people fell prostrate and worshiped God; and they cried out: [19]"LORD, God of heaven, behold their arrogance! Have pity on the lowliness of our people, and look with favor this day on those who are consecrated to you."* [20]Then they reassured Achior and praised him highly. [21]Uzziah brought him from the assembly to his home, where he gave a banquet for the elders. That whole night they called upon the God of Israel for help.

CHAPTER 7

Siege of Bethulia. [1]The following day Holofernes ordered his whole army, and all the allied troops that had come to his support, to move against Bethulia, seize the mountain passes, and engage the Israelites in battle. [2]That same day all their fighting men went into action. Their forces numbered a hundred and seventy thousand infantry and twelve thousand horsemen, not counting the baggage train or the men who accompanied it on foot—a very great army. [3]They encamped at the spring in the valley near Bethulia, and spread out in breadth toward Dothan as far as Balbaim, and in length from Bethulia to Cyamon, which faces Esdraelon.

[4]When the Israelites saw how many there were, they said to one another in great dismay: "Soon they will devour the whole country. Neither the high mountains nor the valleys and hills can support the mass of them." [5]Yet they all seized their weapons, lighted fires on their bastions,* and kept watch throughout the night.

[6]On the second day Holofernes led out all his cavalry in the sight of the Israelites who were in Bethulia. [7]He reconnoitered the approaches to their city and located their sources of water; these he seized,

---

v Jdt 6, 17.—w Jdt 5, 22.

6, 19: The Latin Vulgate (6, 15) has a longer form of this prayer: "Lord, God of heaven and earth, behold their arrogance; regard our lowliness and look with favor on your holy ones; show that you do not abandon those who trust in you, but that you humble those who trust in themselves and glory in their own strength."

7, 5: *Lighted fires on their bastions:* to serve as signals for alerting the neighboring towns. Reference to fire signals in time of siege is made in the Lachish ostraca at the beginning of the sixth century B.C. *Kept watch throughout the night:* to prevent a surprise attack.

stationing armed detachments around them, while he himself returned to his troops.

⁸All the commanders of the Edomites and all the leaders of the Ammonites, together with the generals of the seacoast, came to Holofernes and said: ⁹"Sir, listen to what we have to say, that there may be no losses among your troops. ¹⁰These Israelites do not rely on their spears, but on the height of the mountains where they dwell; it is not easy to reach the summit of their mountains.ˣ ¹¹Therefore, sir, do not attack them in regular formation; thus not a single one of your troops will fall. ¹²Stay in your camp, and spare all your soldiers. Have some of your servants keep control of the source of water that flows out at the base of the mountain, ¹³for that is where the inhabitants of Bethulia get their water. Then thirst will begin to carry them off, and they will surrender their city. Meanwhile, we and our men will go up to the summits of the nearby mountains, and encamp there to guard against anyone's leaving the city.ʸ ¹⁴They and their wives and children will languish with hunger, and even before the sword strikes them they will be laid low in the streets of their city. ¹⁵Thus you will render them dire punishment for their rebellion and their refusal to meet you peacefully."

¹⁶Their words pleased Holofernes and all his ministers, and he ordered their proposal to be carried out. ¹⁷Thereupon the Moabites moved camp, together with five thousand Assyrians. They encamped in the valley, and held the water supply and the springs of the Israelites. ¹⁸The Edomites and the Ammonites went up and encamped in the mountain region opposite Dothan; and they sent some of their men to the south and to the east opposite Egrebel, near Chusi, which is on Wadi Mochmur. The rest of the Assyrian army was encamped in the plain, covering the whole countryside. Their enormous store of tents and equipment was spread out in profusion everywhere.

¹⁹The Israelites cried to the LORD, their God, for they were disheartened, since all their enemies had them surrounded, and there was no way of slipping through their lines.ᶻ ²⁰The whole Assyrian camp, infantry, chariots, and cavalry, kept them thus surrounded for thirty-four days. All the reservoirs of water failed the inhabitants of Bethulia, ²¹and the cisterns ran dry, so that on no day did they have enough to drink, but their drinking water was rationed. ²²Their children fainted away, and the women and youths were consumed with thirst and were collapsing in the streets and gateways of the city, with no strength left in them.

²³All the people, therefore, including youths, women, and children, went in a crowd to Uzziah and the rulers of the city. They set up a great clamor and said before the elders: ²⁴"God judge between you and us! You have done us grave injustice in not making peace with the Assyrians. ²⁵There is no help for us now! Instead, God has sold us into their power by laying us prostrate before them in thirst and utter exhaustion. ²⁶Therefore, summon them and deliver the whole city as booty to the troops of Holofernes and to all his forces; ²⁷we would be better off to become their prey. We should indeed be made slaves, but at least we should live, and not have to behold our little ones dying before our eyes and our wives and children breathing out their souls. ²⁸We adjure you by heaven and earth, and by our God, the LORD of our forefathers, who is punishing us for our sins and those of our forefathers, to do as we have proposed, this very day."

²⁹All in the assembly with one accord broke into shrill wailing and loud cries to the LORD their God. ³⁰But Uzziah said to them, "Courage, my brothers! Let us wait five days more for the LORD our God, to show his mercy toward us; he will not utterly forsake us. ³¹But if those days pass without help coming to us, I will do as you say." ³²Then he dispersed the men to their posts, and they returned to the walls and towers of the city; the women and children he sent to their homes. Throughout the city they were in great misery.

II: DELIVERANCE OF THE JEWS

CHAPTER 8

Judith. ¹Now in those days Judith, daughter of Merari, son of Joseph, son of Oziel, son of Elkiah, son of Ananias, son of Gideon, son of Raphain, son of Ahitob, son of Elijah, son of Hilkiah, son of Eliab,

x 1 Kgs 20, 23. 28.—y Ex 5, 21.—z Ps 106, 6.

son of Nathanael, son of Salamiel, son of Sarasadai,* son of Simeon, son of Israel, heard of this. [2] Her husband, Manasseh, of her own tribe and clan, had died at the time of the barley harvest. [3] While he was in the field supervising those who bound the sheaves, he suffered sunstroke; and he died of this illness in Bethulia, his native city. He was buried with his forefathers in the field between Dothan and Balamon. [4] The widowed Judith remained three years and four months at home, [5] where she set up a tent* for herself on the roof of her house. She put sackcloth about her loins and wore widow's weeds. [6] She fasted all the days of her widowhood, except sabbath eves and sabbaths, new moon eves and new moons, feastdays and holidays of the house of Israel.[a] [7] She was beautifully formed and lovely to behold. Her husband, Manasseh, had left her gold and silver, servants and maids, livestock and fields, which she was maintaining. [8] No one had a bad word to say about her, for she was a very God-fearing woman.

Her Words to the Elders. [9] When Judith, therefore, heard of the harsh words which the people, discouraged by their lack of water, had spoken against their rulers, and of all that Uzziah had said to them in reply, swearing that he would hand over the city to the Assyrians at the end of five days, [10] she sent the maid who was in charge of all her things to ask Uzziah, Chabris, and Charmis, the elders of the city, to visit her. [11] When they came, she said to them: "Listen to me, you rulers of the people of Bethulia. What you said to the people today is not proper. When you promised to hand over the city to our enemies at the end of five days unless within that time the LORD comes to our aid, you interposed between God and yourselves this oath which you took. [12] Who are you, then, that you should have put God to the test this day, setting yourselves in the place of God in human affairs?[b] [13] It is the LORD Almighty for whom you are laying down conditions; will you never understand anything? [14] You cannot plumb the depths of the human heart or grasp the workings of the human mind; how then can you fathom God, who has made all these things, discern his mind, and understand his plan?[c]

"No, my brothers, do not anger the LORD our God. [15] For if he does not wish to come to our aid within the five days, he has it equally within his power to protect us at such time as he pleases, or to destroy us in the face of our enemies. [16] It is not for you to make the LORD our God give surety for his plans.

"God is not man that he should be
  moved by threats,
nor human, that he may be given an ultimatum.

[17] "So while we wait for the salvation that comes from him, let us call upon him to help us, and he will hear our cry if it is his good pleasure. [18] For there has not risen among us in recent generations, nor does there exist today, any tribe, or clan, or town, or city of ours that worships gods made by hands, as happened in former days.[d] [19] It was for such conduct that our forefathers were handed over to the sword and to pillage, and fell with great destruction before our enemies.[e] [20] But since we acknowledge no other god but the LORD, we hope that he will not disdain us or any of our people. [21] If we are taken, all Judea will fall, our sanctuary will be plundered, and God will make us pay for its profanation with our life's blood. [22] For the slaughter of our kinsmen, for the taking of exiles from the land, and for the devastation of our inheritance, he will lay the guilt on our heads. Wherever we shall be enslaved among the nations, we shall be a mockery and a reproach in the eyes of our masters. [23] Our enslavement will not be turned to our benefit, but the LORD our God will maintain it to our disgrace.

[24] "Therefore, my brothers, let us set an example for our kinsmen. Their lives depend on us, and the defense of the sanctuary, the temple, and the altar rests with us. [25] f Besides all this, we should be grateful to the LORD our God, for putting us to the test, as he did our forefathers. [26] Recall how he dealt with Abraham, and how he tried Isaac, and all that happened

a Lk 2, 37.—b Jb 38, 2; 40, 2. 7f; 42, 3.—c Jb 41, 3; Prv 14, 10; Wis 9, 13; Is 40, 13; Rom 11, 33f; 1 Cor 2, 11.—d Jdt 5, 20f; 11, 10.—e Pss 78, 56f; 106, 13f; Jer 7, 16-20; 14, 7.—f 25f: Gn 22, 1-12; 29, 22-30.

8, 1: *Salamiel, son of Sarasadai:* head of the tribe of *Simeon* during the wanderings of the Israelites in the desert (Nm 1, 6).
8, 5: *A tent:* erected by Judith on the roof of her house (v 5); it was here that the elders came to confer with her (v 11).

to Jacob in Syrian Mesopotamia while he was tending the flocks of Laban, his mother's brother. [27]Not for vengeance did the LORD put them in the crucible to try their hearts, nor has he done so with us. It is by way of admonition that he chastises those who are close to him."[g]

Uzziah's Response. [28]Then Uzziah said to her: "All that you have said was spoken with good sense, and no one can gainsay your words. [29]Not today only is your wisdom made evident, but from your earliest years all the people have recognized your prudence, which corresponds to the worthy dispositions of your heart. [30]The people, however, were so tortured with thirst that they forced us to speak to them as we did, and to bind ourselves by an oath that we cannot break. [31]But now, God-fearing woman that you are, pray for us that the LORD may send rain to fill up our cisterns, lest we be weakened still further."

[32]Then Judith said to them: "Listen to me! I will do something that will go down from generation to generation among the descendants of our race. [33]Stand at the gate tonight to let me pass through with my maid; and within the days you have specified before you will surrender the city to our enemies, the LORD will rescue Israel by my hand. [34]You must not inquire into what I am doing, for I will not tell you until my plan has been accomplished." [35]Uzziah and the rulers said to her, "Go in peace, and may the LORD God go before you to take vengeance upon our enemies!" [36]Then they withdrew from the tent and returned to their posts.

CHAPTER 9

The Prayer of Judith. [1]Judith threw herself down prostrate, with ashes strewn upon her head, and wearing nothing over the sackcloth. While the incense was being offered in the temple of God in Jerusalem that evening, Judith prayed to the LORD with a loud voice:[h] [2]"LORD, God of my

forefather Simeon! You put a sword into his hand to take revenge upon the foreigners who had immodestly loosened the maiden's* girdle, shamefully exposed her thighs, and disgracefully violated her body. This they did, though you forbade it.[i] [3]Therefore you had their rulers slaughtered; and you covered with their blood the bed in which they lay deceived, the same bed that had felt the shame of their own deceiving. You smote the slaves together with their princes, and the princes together with their servants.* [4]Their wives you handed over to plunder, and their daughters to captivity; and all the spoils you divided among your favored sons, who burned with zeal for you, and in their abhorrence of the defilement of their kinswoman, called on you for help.

[5]"O God, my God, hear me also, a widow. It is you who were the author of those events and of what preceded and followed them. The present, also, and the future you have planned. Whatever you devise comes into being;[j] [6]the things you decide on come forward and say, 'Here we are!' All your ways are in readiness, and your judgment is made with foreknowledge.[k]

[7]l "Here are the Assyrians, a vast force, priding themselves on horse and rider, boasting of the power of their infantry, trusting in shield and spear, bow and sling. They do not know that

[8]" 'You, the LORD, crush warfare;
  Lord is your name.'

"Shatter their strength in your might, and crush their force in your wrath; for they have resolved to profane your sanctuary, to defile the tent where your glorious name resides, and to overthrow with iron the horns of your altar. [9]See their pride, and send forth your wrath upon their heads. Give me, a widow, the strong hand to execute my plan.[m] [10]With the guile of my lips, smite the slave together with the ruler, the ruler together with his servant; crush their pride by the hand of a woman.

[11]"Your strength is not in numbers, nor does your power depend upon stalwart men; but you are the God of the lowly, the helper of the oppressed, the supporter of the weak, the protector of the forsaken, the savior of those without hope.

g Dt 4, 7.—h Ex 30, 7f; Ps 141, 2.—i Gn 34.—j Is 44, 7.—k Jb 38, 35; Is 46, 9-13; Bar 3, 35.—l 7f: Jdt 5, 23; 6, 2; 16, 2.— m Ps 33, 16.

9, 2: *The maiden:* Dinah, Jacob's daughter, who was violated by Shechem, the Hivite (Gn 34, 2).

9, 3: Because Shechem had deceived and violated Dinah, her brothers, Simeon and Levi, tricked Shechem and the men of his city into being circumcised, and then slew them while they were confined to bed from the circumcision; cf Gn 34, 13-29.

12 "Please, please, God of my forefather, God of the heritage of Israel, LORD of heaven and earth, Creator of the waters, King of all you have created, hear my prayer! 13 Let my guileful speech bring wound and wale on those who have planned dire things against your covenant, your holy temple, Mount Zion, and the homes your children have inherited.ⁿ 14 Let your whole nation and all the tribes know clearly that you are the God of all power and might, and that there is no other who protects the people of Israel but you alone."

CHAPTER 10

Judith's Departure. ¹ As soon as Judith had thus concluded, and ceased her invocation to the God of Israel, ² she rose from the ground. She called her maid and they went down into the house, which she used only on sabbaths and feast days. ³ She took off the sackcloth she had on, laid aside the garments of her widowhood, washed her body with water, and anointed it with rich ointment. She arranged her hair and bound it with a fillet, and put on the festive attire she had worn while her husband, Manasseh, was living.ᵒ ⁴ She chose sandals for her feet, and put on her anklets, bracelets, rings, earrings, and all her other jewelry. Thus she made herself very beautiful, to captivate the eyes of all the men who should see her.ᵖ

⁵ She gave her maid a leather flask of wine and a cruse of oil. She filled a bag with roasted grain, fig cakes, bread and cheese; all these provisions she wrapped up and gave to the maid to carry.�q

⁶ Then they went to the gate of the city of Bethulia and found Uzziah and the elders of the city, Chabris and Charmis, standing there. ⁷ When these men saw Judith transformed in looks and differently dressed, they were very much astounded at her beauty and said to her, ⁸ "May the God of our fathers bring you to favor, and make your undertaking a success, for the glory of the Israelites and the exaltation of Jerusalem."

Judith bowed down to God. Then she said to them, ⁹ "Order the gate of the city opened for me, that I may go to carry out the business we discussed." So they ordered the youths to open the gate for her as she requested. ¹⁰ When they did so, Judith and her maid went out. The men of the city kept her in view as she went down the mountain and crossed the valley; then they lost sight of her.

Judith Captured. ¹¹ As Judith and her maid walked directly across the valley, they encountered the Assyrian outpost. ¹² The men took her in custody and asked her, "To what people do you belong? Where do you come from, and where are you going?" She replied: "I am a daughter of the Hebrews, and I am fleeing from them, because they are about to be delivered up to you as prey.* ¹³ I have come to see Holofernes, the general in chief of your forces, to give him a trustworthy report; I will show him the route by which he can ascend and take possession of the whole mountain district without a single one of his men suffering injury or loss of life."ʳ

¹⁴ When the men heard her words and gazed upon her face, which appeared wondrously beautiful to them, they said to her, ¹⁵ "By coming down thus promptly to see our master, you have saved your life. Now go to his tent; some of our men will accompany you to present you to him. ¹⁶ When you stand before him, have no fear in your heart; give him the report you speak of, and he will treat you well." ¹⁷ So they detailed a hundred of their men as an escort for her and her maid, and these conducted them to the tent of Holofernes.

¹⁸ When the news of her arrival spread among the tents, a crowd gathered in the camp. They came and stood around her as she waited outside the tent of Holofernes, while he was being informed about her. ¹⁹ They marveled at her beauty, regarding the Israelites with wonder because of her, and they said to one another, "Who can despise this people that has such women among them? It is not wise to leave one man of them alive, for if any were to be spared they could beguile the whole world."

Judith Meets Holofernes. ²⁰ The guard of Holofernes and all his servants came out and ushered her into the tent. ²¹ Now Holofernes was reclining on his bed under a canopy with a netting of crimson and gold, emeralds and other precious stones.

n Jdt 10, 4; 11, 20. 23; 16, 6. 9.—o Jdt 8, 6ff.—p Jdt 9, 13.— q Jdt 12, 2.—r Jdt 11, 5f.

10, 12f: The deceitful means used by Judith against Holofernes, here and in Jdt 11, 5-19, are to be judged in the light of the moral concepts of Old Testament times; cf Gn 27, 1-25; 34, 13-29; 37, 32ff; Jos 2, 1-7; Jgs 4, 17-22.

[22] When they announced her to him, he came out to the antechamber, preceded by silver lamps; [23] and when Holofernes and his servants beheld Judith, they all marveled at the beauty of her face. She threw herself down prostrate before him, but his servants raised her up.

CHAPTER 11

[1] Then Holofernes said to her: "Take courage, lady; have no fear in your heart! Never have I harmed anyone who chose to serve Nebuchadnezzar, king of all the earth. [2] Nor would I have raised my spear against your people who dwell in the mountain region, had they not despised me and brought this upon themselves. [3] But now tell me why you fled from them and came to us. In any case, you have come to safety. Take courage! Your life is spared tonight and for the future. [4] No one at all will harm you. Rather, you will be well treated, as are all the servants of my lord, King Nebuchadnezzar."

[5] *s* Judith answered him: "Listen to the words of your servant, and let your handmaid speak in your presence! I will tell no lie to my lord this night, [6] and if you follow out the words of your handmaid, God will give you complete success, and my lord will not fail in any of his undertakings. [7] By the life of Nebuchadnezzar, king of all the earth, and by the power of him who has sent you to set all creatures aright! not only do men serve him through you; but even the wild beasts and the cattle and the birds of the air, because of your strength, will live for Nebuchadnezzar and his whole house. *t* [8] Indeed, we have heard of your wisdom and sagacity, and all the world is aware that throughout the kingdom you alone are competent, rich in experience, and distinguished in military strategy.

[9] *u* "As for Achior's speech in your council, we have heard of it. When the men of Bethulia spared him, he told them all he had said to you. [10] So then, my lord and master, do not disregard his word, but bear it in mind, for it is true. For our people are not punished, nor does the sword prevail against them, except when they sin against their God. *v* [11] But now their guilt has caught up with them by which they bring the wrath of their God upon them whenever they do wrong; so that my lord will not be repulsed and fail, but death will overtake them. [12] Since their food gave out and all their water ran low, they decided to kill their animals, and determined to consume all the things which God in his laws forbade them to eat. [13] They decreed that they would use up the first fruits of grain and the tithes of wine and oil which had sanctified and reserved for the priests who minister in the presence of our God in Jerusalem: things which no layman should even touch with his hands. [14] They have sent messengers to Jerusalem to bring back to them authorization from the council of the elders; for the inhabitants there have also done these things. [15] On the very day when the response reaches them and they act upon it, they will be handed over to you for destruction.

[16] "As soon as I, your handmaid, learned all this, I fled from them. God has sent me to perform with you such deeds that people throughout the world will be astonished on hearing of them. [17] Your handmaid is, indeed, a God-fearing woman, serving the God of heaven night and day. Now I will remain with you, my lord; but each night your handmaid will go out to the ravine and pray to God. He will tell me when the Israelites have committed their crimes. [18] Then I will come and let you know, so that you may go out with your whole force, and not one of them will be able to withstand you. [19] I will lead you through Judea, till you come to Jerusalem, and there I will set up your judgment seat. You will drive them like sheep that have no shepherd, and not even a dog will growl at you. This was told me, and announced to me in advance, and I in turn have been sent to tell you."

[20] Her words pleased Holofernes and all his servants; they marveled at her wisdom and exclaimed, *w* [21] "No other woman from one end of the world to the other looks so beautiful and speaks so wisely!" [22] Then Holofernes said to her: "God has done well in sending you ahead of your people, to bring victory to our arms, and destruction to those who have despised my lord. [23] You are fair to behold, and your words are well spoken. If you do as you

s 5f: Jdt 10, 13.—t Jer 27, 6; Bar 3, 16f; Dn 2, 38.—u 9f: Jdt 5, 5.—v Jdt 5, 21; 8, 18.—w Jdt 9, 13.

have said, your God will be my God; you shall dwell in the palace of King Nebuchadnezzar, and shall be renowned throughout the earth."[x]

CHAPTER 12

Judith's Conduct. [1] Then he ordered them to lead her into the room where his silverware was kept, and bade them set a table for her with his own delicacies to eat and his own wine to drink. [2] But Judith said, "I will not partake of them, lest it be an occasion of sin; but I shall be amply supplied from the things I brought with me."[y] [3] Holofernes asked her: "But if your provisions give out, where shall we get more of the same to provide for you? None of your people are with us." [4] Judith answered him, "As surely as you, my lord, live, your handmaid will not use up her supplies till the LORD accomplishes by my hand what he has determined."

[5] Then the servants of Holofernes led her into the tent, where she slept till midnight. In the night watch just before dawn, she rose [6] and sent this message to Holofernes, "Give orders, my lord, to let your handmaid go out for prayer." [7] So Holofernes ordered his bodyguard not to hinder her. Thus she stayed in the camp three days. Each night she went out to the ravine of Bethulia, where she washed herself at the spring of the camp. [8] After bathing, she besought the LORD, the God of Israel, to direct her way for the triumph of his people. [9] Then she returned purified to the tent, and remained there until her food was brought to her toward evening.

Holofernes' Banquet. [10] On the fourth day Holofernes gave a banquet for his servants alone, to which he did not invite any of the officers.* [11] And he said to Bagoas, the eunuch in charge of his household: "Go and persuade this Hebrew woman in your care to come and to eat and drink with us. [12] It would be a disgrace for us to have such a woman with us without enjoying her company. If we do not entice her, she will laugh us to scorn."

[13] So Bagoas left the presence of Holofernes, and came to Judith and said, "So fair a maiden should not be reluctant to come to my lord to be honored by him, to enjoy drinking wine with us, and to be like one of the Assyrian women who live in the palace of Nebuchadnezzar." [14] She replied, "Who am I to refuse my lord? Whatever is pleasing to him I will promptly do. This will be a joy for me till the day of my death."

[15] Thereupon she proceeded to put on her festive garments and all her feminine adornments. Meanwhile her maid went ahead and spread out on the ground for her in front of Holofernes the fleece Bagoas had furnished for her daily use in reclining at her dinner. [16] Then Judith came in and reclined on it. The heart of Holofernes was in rapture over her, and his spirit was shaken. He was burning with the desire to possess her, for he had been biding his time to seduce her from the day he saw her. [17] Holofernes said to her, "Drink and be merry with us!" [18] Judith replied, "I will gladly drink, my lord, for at no time since I was born have I ever enjoyed life as much as I do today." [19] She then took the things her maid had prepared, and ate and drank in his presence. [20] Holofernes, charmed by her, drank a great quantity of wine, more than he had ever drunk on one single day in his life.

CHAPTER 13

[1] When it grew late, his servants quickly withdrew. Bagoas closed the tent from the outside and excluded the attendants from their master's presence. They went off to their beds, for they were all tired from the prolonged banquet. [2] Judith was left alone in the tent with Holofernes, who lay prostrate on his bed, for he was sodden with wine. [3] She had ordered her maid to stand outside the bedroom and wait, as on the other days, for her to come out; she said she would be going out for her prayer. To Bagoas she had said this also.

Beheading of Holofernes. [4] When all had departed, and no one, small or great, was left in the bedroom, Judith stood by Holofernes' bed and said within herself: "O LORD, God of all might, in this hour look graciously on my undertaking for the exaltation of Jerusalem; [5] now is the time for aiding your heritage and for carrying

x Jdt 9, 13.—y Jdt 10, 5; Dn 1, 8.

12, 10: *Banquet for his servants alone . . . officers:* Holofernes invited the officials of his household, but not the officers of his army who were needed for military duty.

out my design to shatter the enemies who have risen against us." ⁶She went to the bedpost near the head of Holofernes, and taking his sword from it, ⁷drew close to the bed, grasped the hair of his head, and said, "Strengthen me this day, O God of Israel!" ⁸Then with all her might she struck him twice in the neck and cut off his head.ᶻ ⁹She rolled his body off the bed and took the canopy from its supports. Soon afterward, she came out and handed over the head of Holofernes to her maid, ¹⁰who put it into her food pouch; and the two went off together as they were accustomed to do for prayer.

The Return to Bethulia. They passed through the camp, and skirting the ravine, reached Bethulia on the mountain. As they approached its gates, ¹¹Judith shouted to the guards from a distance: "Open! Open the gate! God, our God, is with us. Once more he has made manifest his strength in Israel and his power against our enemies; he has done it this very day." ¹²When the citizens heard her voice, they quickly descended to their city gate and summoned the city elders. ¹³All the people, from the least to the greatest, hurriedly assembled, for her return seemed unbelievable. They opened the gate and welcomed the two women. They made a fire for light; and when they gathered around the two, ¹⁴Judith urged them with a loud voice: "Praise God, praise him! Praise God, who has not withdrawn his mercy from the house of Israel, but has shattered our enemies by my hand this very night." ¹⁵Then she took the head out of the pouch, showed it to them, and said: "Here is the head of Holofernes, general in charge of the Assyrian army, and here is the canopy under which he lay in his drunkenness. The LORD struck him down by the hand of a woman.ᵃ ¹⁶As the LORD lives, who has protected me in the path I have followed, I swear that it was my face that seduced Holofernes to his ruin, and that he did not sin with me to my defilement or disgrace."

¹⁷All the people were greatly astonished. They bowed down and wor-

shiped God, saying with one accord, "Blessed are you, our God, who today have brought to nought the enemies of your people." ¹⁸Then Uzziah said to her: "Blessed are you, daughter, by the Most High God, above all the women on earth; and blessed be the LORD God, the creator of heaven and earth, who guided your blow at the head of the chief of our enemies.ᵇ ¹⁹Your deed of hope will never be forgotten by those who tell of the might of God. ²⁰May God make this redound to your everlasting honor, rewarding you with blessings, because you risked your life when your people were oppressed, and you averted our disaster, walking uprightly before our God." And all the people answered, "Amen! Amen!"

CHAPTER 14

Judith's Counsel. ¹Then Judith said to them: "Listen to me, my brothers. Take this head and hang it on the parapet of your wall. ²At daybreak, when the sun rises on the earth, let each of you seize his weapons, and let all the able-bodied men rush out of the city under command of a captain, as if about to go down into the plain against the advance guard of the Assyrians, but without going down. ³They will seize their armor and hurry to their camp to awaken the generals of the Assyrian army. When they run to the tent of Holofernes and do not find him, panic will seize them, and they will flee before you. ⁴Then you and all the other inhabitants of the whole territory of Israel will pursue them and strike them down in their tracks. ⁵But before doing this, summon for me Achior the Ammonite, that he may see and recognize the one who despised the house of Israel and sent him here to meet his death."

Achior Summoned.* ⁶So they called Achior from the house of Uzziah. When he came and saw the head of Holofernes in the hand of one of the men in the assembly of the people, he fell forward in a faint. ⁷Then, after they lifted him up, he threw himself at the feet of Judith in homage, saying: "Blessed are you in every tent of Judah; and in every foreign nation, all who hear of you will be struck with terror. ⁸But now, tell me all that you did during these days." So Judith told him, in the presence of the people, all that she had been doing

---

z Jgs 4, 21.—a Jdt 14, 18.—b Jgs 5, 24; Lk 1, 28. 42.

14, 6-10: In recognizing the head of Holofernes, whom he had known personally, Achior was so overcome with the evidence of the Lord's power exerted through a woman that he believed in the God of Israel.

from the day she left till the time she began speaking to them. ⁹When she finished her account, the people cheered loudly, and their city resounded with shouts of joy. ¹⁰Now Achior, seeing all that the God of Israel had done, believed firmly in him. He had the flesh of his foreskin circumcised, and he has been united with the house of Israel to the present day.

III: VICTORY

Consternation in the Camp. ¹¹At daybreak they hung the head of Holofernes on the wall. Then all the Israelite men took up their arms and went to the slopes of the mountain. ¹²When the Assyrians saw them, they notified their captains; these, in turn, went to the generals and division leaders and all their other commanders. ¹³They came to the tent of Holofernes and said to the one in charge of all his things, "Waken our master, for the slaves have dared come down to give us battle, to their utter destruction." ¹⁴Bagoas went in, and knocked at the entry of the tent, presuming that he was sleeping with Judith. ¹⁵As no one answered, he parted the curtains, entered the bedroom, and found him lying on the floor, a headless corpse. ¹⁶He broke into a loud clamor of weeping, groaning, and howling, and rent his garments. ¹⁷Then he entered the tent where Judith had her quarters; and, not finding her, he rushed out to the troops and cried: ¹⁸"The slaves have duped us! A single Hebrew woman has brought disgrace on the house of King Nebuchadnezzar. Here is Holofernes headless on the ground!"*c*

¹⁹When the commanders of the Assyrian army heard these words, they rent their tunics and were seized with consternation. Loud screaming and howling arose in the camp.

CHAPTER 15

¹On hearing what happened, those still in their tents were amazed, ²and overcome with fear and trembling. No one kept ranks any longer; they scattered in all directions, and fled along every road, both through the valley and in the mountains. ³Those also who were stationed in the mountain district around Bethulia took to flight. Then all the Israelite warriors overwhelmed them.

Pursuit. ⁴Uzziah sent messengers to Betomasthaim, to Choba and Kona, and to the whole country of Israel to report what had happened, that all might fall upon the enemy and destroy them. ⁵On hearing this, all the Israelites, with one accord, attacked them and cut them down as far as Choba. Even those from Jerusalem and the rest of the mountain region took part in this, for they too had been notified of the happenings in the camp of their enemies. The Gileadites and the Galileans struck the enemy's flanks with great slaughter, even beyond Damascus and its territory. ⁶The remaining inhabitants of Bethulia swept down on the camp of the Assyrians, plundered it, and acquired great riches. ⁷The Israelites who returned from the slaughter took possession of what was left, till the towns and villages in the mountains and on the plain were crammed with the enormous quantity of booty they had seized.*d*

⁸The high priest Joakim and the elders of the Israelites, who dwelt in Jerusalem, came to see for themselves the good things that the LORD had done for Israel, and to meet and congratulate Judith.*e* ⁹When they had visited her, all with one accord blessed her, saying:

"You are the glory of Jerusalem,
   the surpassing joy of Israel;
   you are the splendid boast of our people.*
¹⁰ With your own hand you have done all this;
   you have done good to Israel,
   and God is pleased with what you have wrought.
May you be blessed by the LORD Almighty
   forever and ever!"

And all the people answered, "Amen!"
¹¹For thirty days the whole populace plundered the camp, giving Judith the tent of Holofernes, with all his silver, his couches, his dishes, and all his furniture, which she accepted. She harnessed her mules, hitched her wagons to them, and loaded these things on them.
¹²All the women of Israel gathered to see her; and they blessed her and performed a dance in her honor. She took

---

e Jdt 13, 15; 16, 5-9; Jgs 9, 54.—d Est 9, 5. 16.—e Est 9, 10.

15, 9: *You are the glory of Jerusalem, the surpassing joy of Israel; you are the splendid boast of our people:* these words are used in the liturgy of the Church in regard to the Blessed Virgin Mary.

branches in her hands and distributed them to the women around her,*f* ¹³ and she and the other women crowned themselves with garlands of olive leaves. At the head of all the people, she led the women in the dance, while the men of Israel followed in their armor, wearing garlands and singing hymns.

Hymn of Praise. ¹⁴ Judith led all Israel in this song of thanksgiving, and the people swelled this hymn of praise:

CHAPTER 16

¹ "Strike up the instruments,
    a song to my God with timbrels,
    chant to the LORD with cymbals;
Sing to him a new song,
    exalt and acclaim his name.*g*
² For the LORD is God; he crushes warfare,
    and sets his encampment among his people;
he snatched me from the hands of my persecutors.*h*
³ "The Assyrian came from the mountains of the north,
    with the myriads of his forces he came;
Their numbers blocked the torrents,
    their horses covered the hills.
⁴ He threatened to burn my land,
    put my youths to the sword,
Dash my babes to the ground,
    make my children a prey,
    and seize my virgins as spoil.
⁵ "But the LORD Almighty thwarted them,
    by a woman's hand he confounded them.*i*
⁶ Not by youths was their mighty one struck down,
    nor did titans bring him low,
    nor huge giants attack him;
But Judith, the daughter of Merari,
    by the beauty of her countenance disabled him.*j*
⁷ She took off her widow's garb
    to raise up the afflicted in Israel.
She anointed her face with fragrant oil,

⁸ with a fillet she fastened her tresses
    and put on a linen robe to beguile him.
⁹ Her sandals caught his eyes,
    and her beauty captured his mind.
    The sword cut through his neck.*k*
¹⁰ "The Persians were dismayed at her daring,
    the Medes appalled at her boldness.
¹¹ When my lowly ones shouted, they were terrified;
    when my weaklings cried out, they trembled;
    at the sound of their war cry, they took to flight.
¹² The sons of slave girls pierced them through;
    the supposed sons of rebel mothers cut them down;
    they perished before the ranks of my LORD.
¹³ "A new hymn I will sing to my God.
    O LORD, great are you and glorious,
    wonderful in power and unsurpassable.*l*
¹⁴ Let your every creature serve you;
    for you spoke, and they were made,
You sent forth your spirit, and they were created;
    no one can resist your word.*m*
¹⁵ The mountains to their bases, and the seas, are shaken;
    the rocks, like wax, melt before your glance.*n*

"But to those who fear you,
    you are very merciful.
¹⁶ Though the sweet odor of every sacrifice is a trifle,
    and the fat of all holocausts but little in your sight,
one who fears the LORD is forever great.*o*
¹⁷ "Woe to the nations that rise against my people!
    the LORD Almighty will requite them;
in the day of judgment he will punish them:
He will send fire and worms into their flesh,*
    and they shall burn and suffer forever."*p*

Thanksgiving. ¹⁸ The people then went to Jerusalem to worship God; when they were purified, they offered their holo-

Jdt

---

f Ex 15, 20f; Jgs 11. 34; 1 Sm 18, 6; Jer 31, 4. 13.—g Pss 81, 2f; 135, 1ff; 149, 1ff.—h Jdt 5, 23; 6, 2; 9; 7f; Ex 15, 3; Ps 46, 10.—i Jdt 14, 8.—j Jdt 9, 13.—k Jdt 9, 13.—l Ps 144, 9.—m Pss 33, 9; 104, 30; 148, 5.—n Jgs 5, 5; Ps 97, 5.—o Ps 86, 11; Sir 34, 13-17.—p Is 66, 24.

16, 17: *Fire and worms into their flesh:* see footnote on Is 66, 24.

causts, free-will offerings, and gifts. [19] Judith dedicated, as a votive offering to God, all the things of Holofernes that the people had given her, as well as the canopy that she herself had taken from his bedroom.[q] [20] For three months the people continued their celebration in Jerusalem before the sanctuary, and Judith remained with them.

Judith's Renown. [21] When those days were over, each one returned to his inheritance. Judith went back to Bethulia and remained on her estate. For the rest of her life she was renowned throughout the land. [22] Many wished to marry her, but she gave herself to no man all the days of her life from the time of the death and burial of her husband, Manasseh. [23] She lived to be very old in the house of her husband,

reaching the advanced age of a hundred and five. She died in Bethulia, where they buried her in the tomb of her husband, Manasseh;[r] [24] and the house of Israel mourned her for seven days. Before she died, she distributed her goods to the relatives of her husband, Manasseh, and to her own relatives; and to the maid she gave her freedom.

[25] [s] During the life of Judith and for a long time after her death, no one again disturbed the Israelites.*

q Nm 31, 48-54; Dt 13, 13-18; Jos 6, 18f.—r Gn 23, 19; 49, 29-32.—s Jgs 3, 11. 30; 5, 31; 8, 28.

16, 25; The Vulgate adds: "The feast day of this victory was adopted by the Hebrews into the calendar of their holy days, and has been celebrated by the Jews from that time to the present." However, there is no other evidence of such a festivity; and it is the ancient feast of Passover to which the narrative is especially suited.

THE BOOK OF ESTHER

    The Book of Esther is named after its Jewish heroine. It tells the story of the plot of Haman the Agagite, jealous and powerful vizier of King Xerxes (Ahasuerus) of Persia (485-464 B.C.), to destroy in a single day all the Jews living in the Persian Empire. He is moved to this out of hatred for the Jewish servant Mordecai, who for religious motives refuses to render him homage. The day of the proposed massacre is determined by lot. Meanwhile Esther, niece and adopted daughter of Mordecai, is chosen queen by King Xerxes in place of Vashti. She averts the pogrom planned against her people and has the royal decree of extermination reversed against Haman and the enemies of the Jews. Mordecai replaces Haman, and together with Esther, works for the welfare of their people. The event is celebrated with feasting and great joy, and the memory of it is to be perpetuated by the annual observance of the feast of Purim (lots), when the lot of destruction for the Jews was reversed for one of deliverance and triumph by Queen Esther and her uncle Mordecai.

    The purpose of the book is didactic: the glorification of the Jewish people and the explanation of the origin, significance and date of the feast of Purim on the fourteenth and fifteenth of Adar (February-March). The book was intended as a consolation for Israel, a reminder that God's providence continually watches over them, never abandoning them when they serve him faithfully or turn to him in sincere repentance. There is no justification for interpreting the story in mythological or cultic terms, as though Mordecai and Esther represented Marduk and Ishtar in their mythological triumph over two Elamite deities.

    The Hebrew text of Esther is found in the Hebrew Bible, where it is the last of the five megilloth (scrolls) read on special feasts of the Jewish liturgical year.

    The book is a free composition—not a historical document, despite the Achaemenian coloring of the narrative. Its time of composition may well have been at the end of the Persian Empire, toward the close of the fourth century B.C. The author shows skill in developing his story and in using the art of contrast for instruction and edification. The solution to the difficulties of the book is to be found in its literary presentation rather than in a forced attempt to square detailed data of the narrative with facts. The evident literary motif of the reversal of fortune of the prosperous wicked and the oppressed virtuous through eventual punishment of the former and triumph of the latter finds parallels in the story of Joseph (Gn 37; 39—45) and of Judith (8—16). The book is vindictive, but it should be remembered that the precept of love of enemies had not yet been taught by the word and example of Christ.

The text of Esther, written originally in Hebrew, was transmitted in two forms: a short Hebrew form and a longer Greek version. The latter contains 107 additional verses, inserted at appropriate places within the Hebrew form of the text. A few of these seem to have a Hebrew origin while the rest are Greek in original composition. It is possible that the Hebrew form of the text is original throughout. If it systematically omits reference to God and his Providence over Israel, this is perhaps due to fear of irreverent response (see note on 4, 14). The Greek text with the above-mentioned additions is probably a later literary paraphrase in which the author seeks to have the reader share his sentiments. This standard Greek text is pre-Christian in origin. The church has accepted the additions as equally inspired with the rest of the book.

In the present translation, the portions preceded by the letters A through F indicate the underlying Greek additions referred to above. The regular chapter numbers apply to the Hebrew text.

The book may be divided as follows: I. Prologue (A, 1-17). II. Elevation of Esther (1, 1—2, 23). III. Haman's Plot against the Jews (3, 1-13; B, 1-7; 3, 14—4, 8; B, 8; 4, 9-16; C, 1—D, 16; 5, 1-14). IV. Vindication of the Jews (6, 1—8, 12; E, 1-24; 8, 13—10, 3). V. Epilogue (F, 1-11).

The order of the Vulgate text in relation to the order of the Greek text is as follows:

Vulg. 11, 2—12, 6 = A, 1-17 at the beginning of the book.

13, 1-7 = B, 1-7 after 3, 13.
13, 8—15, 3-19 = C, 1—D, 16 after 4, 16.
15, 1-2 = B, 8. 9 after 4, 8.
16, 1-24 = E, 1-24 after 8, 12.
10, 4—10, 13 = F, 1-10 after 10, 3.

Est

I: PROLOGUE

CHAPTER A

Dream of Mordecai. ¹In the second year of the reign of the great King Ahasuerus,* on the first day of Nisan, Mordecai, son of Jair, son of Shemei, son of Kish, of the tribe of Benjamin, had a dream.*ᵃ ²He was a Jew residing in the city of Susa, a prominent man who served at the king's court,

---

a Est 2, 5.—b Est 2, 6; 2 Kgs 24, 15; 2 Chr 36, 9f; Jer 22, 24ff; 24, 1; 29, 1f.—c 4ff: Est F, 2. 4ff.—d 9f: Est F, 3.

A, 1: *King Ahasuerus:* Xerxes I (485-464 B.C.). *Mordecai:* a Babylonian name, after the god Marduk. The genealogy of Mordecai is designed to reflect opposition to Israel's enemy, as narrated in 1 Sm 15, 7ff, where Saul (whose father's name was *Kish, of the tribe of Benjamin*) conquered Agag the Amalekite; in A, 17 Haman is said to be the son of an Agagite. Further emphasis on the Benjaminite-Agagite opposition can be seen in *Shimei,* the Benjaminite who reviled David (2 Sm 16, 5ff). Jair appears to be the minor Judge, a Transjordan Manassehite (Jgs 10, 3). The chronology of the book would make Mordecai well over one hundred years old, since he was deported with Jehoiachin about 598 B.C.; cf Est 2, 5f.
A, 4: The interpretation of this dream is given in Est F, 1-6.

³and one of the captives whom Nebuchadnezzar, king of Babylon, had taken from Jerusalem with Jeconiah, king of Judah.ᵇ ⁴ᶜ This was his dream.* There was noise and tumult, thunder and earthquake—confusion upon the earth. ⁵Two great dragons came on, both poised for combat. They uttered a mighty cry, ⁶and at their cry every nation prepared for war, to fight against the race of the just. ⁷It was a dark and gloomy day. Tribulation and distress, evil and great confusion, lay upon the earth. ⁸The whole race of the just were dismayed with fear of the evils to come upon them, and were at the point of destruction. ⁹ᵈ Then they cried out to God, and as they cried, there appeared to come forth a great river, a flood of water from a little spring. ¹⁰The light of the sun broke forth; the lowly were exalted and they devoured the nobles.

¹¹Having seen this dream and what God intended to do, Mordecai awoke. He kept

it in mind, and tried in every way, until night, to understand its meaning.
The Plot Discovered. [12] [e] Mordecai lodged at the court with Bagathan and Thares, two eunuchs of the king who were court guards. [13] He overheard them plotting, investigated their plans, and discovered that they were preparing to lay hands on King Ahasuerus. So he informed the king about them, [14] and the king had the two eunuchs questioned and, upon their confession, put to death. [15] Then the king had these things recorded; Mordecai, too, put them into writing. [16] The king also appointed Mordecai to serve at the court, and rewarded him* for his actions. [f]

[17] Haman, however, son of Hammedatha the Agagite,* who was in high honor with the king, sought to harm Mordecai and his people because of the two eunuchs of the king. [g]

II: ELEVATION OF ESTHER

CHAPTER 1

The Banquet of Ahasuerus. [1] During the reign of Ahasuerus—this was the Ahasuerus who ruled over a hundred and twenty-seven provinces from India to Ethiopia*—[2] while he was occupying the royal throne in the stronghold of Susa,* [3] in the third year of his reign, he presided over a feast for all his officers and ministers: the Persian and Median aristocracy, the nobles, and the governors of the provinces. [h] [4] For as many as a hundred and eighty days, he displayed the glorious riches of his kingdom and the resplendent wealth of his royal estate.

[5] At the end of this time the king gave a feast of seven days in the garden court of the royal palace for all the people, great and small, who were in the stronghold of Susa. [6] There were white cotton draperies and violet hangings, held by cords of crimson byssus from silver rings on marble pillars. Gold and silver couches were on the pavement, which was of porphyry, marble, mother-of-pearl, and colored stones. [7] Liquor was served in a variety of golden cups, and the royal wine flowed freely, as befitted the king's munificence. [8] By ordinance of the king the drinking was unstinted, for he had instructed all the stewards of his household to comply with the good pleasure of everyone.

[9] Queen Vashti* also gave a feast for the women inside the royal palace of King Ahasuerus.
Deposal of Vashti. [10] On the seventh day, when the king was merry with wine, he instructed Mehuman, Biztha, Harbona, Bigtha, Abagtha, Zethar, and Carkas, the seven eunuchs who attended King Ahasuerus, [i] [11] to bring Queen Vashti into his presence wearing the royal crown, that he might display her beauty to the populace and the officials, for she was lovely to behold. [12] But Queen Vashti refused to come at the royal order issued through the eunuchs. At this the king's wrath flared up, and he burned with fury. [13] He conferred with the wise men versed in the law, because the king's business was conducted in general consultation with lawyers and jurists. [14] He summoned Carshena, Shethar, Admatha, Tarshish, Meres, Marsena and Memucan, the seven Persian and Median officials who were in the king's personal service and held first rank in the realm, [j] [15] and asked them, "What is to be done by law with Queen Vashti for disobeying the order of King Ahasuerus issued through the eunuchs?"

[16] In the presence of the king and of the officials, Memucan answered: "Queen Vashti has not wronged the king alone, but all the officials and the populace throughout the provinces of King Ahasuerus. [17] For the queen's conduct will become known to all the women, and they will look with disdain upon their husbands when it is reported, 'King Ahasuerus commanded that Queen Vashti be ushered into his presence, but she would not come.' [18] This very day the Persian and Median ladies who hear of the queen's conduct will rebel against all the royal officials, with

---

e 12-15: Est 2, 21ff; 6, 1ff.—f Est 6, 3.—g Est 3, 1-15; B, 1-7; E, 13.—h Jdt 1, 16.—i Dn 5, 1.—j Ezr 7, 14.

A, 16: *Rewarded him:* this reward comes only later; see the sequence of events from the Hebrew text of Esther at 2, 22f, and 6, 3, below.

A, 17: *Haman . . . the Agagite:* opposed Mordecai the Benjaminite, by whom, however, he was overcome (Est 7, 9f), just as King Agag, the Amalekite, was conquered by King Saul, ancestor of Mordecai (1 Sm 15, 7ff).

1, 1: *From India to Ethiopia:* from western India to Upper Egypt, the greatest extent of the Persian Empire achieved under Darius the Great, father of Ahasuerus.

1, 2: *Susa:* ancient capital of Elam (Gn 14, 1); under the Achamenid kings, one of the two capitals of the Persian Empire. The other was Persepolis, the summer palace of the kings.

1, 9: *Queen Vashti:* Herodotus (*Histories* 7, 61) relates that the wife of Ahasuerus was Amestris.

corresponding disdain and rancor. [19] If it please the king, let an irrevocable royal decree* be issued by him and inscribed among the laws of the Persians and Medes, forbidding Vashti to come into the presence of King Ahasuerus and authorizing the king to give her royal dignity to one more worthy than she.[k] [20] Thus, when the decree which the king will issue is published throughout his realm, vast as it is, all wives will honor their husbands, from the greatest to the least."

[21] This proposal found acceptance with the king and the officials, and the king acted on the advice of Memucan. [22] He sent letters to all the royal provinces, to each province in its own script and to each people in its own language,* to the effect that every man should be lord in his own home.

CHAPTER 2

Esther Made Queen. [1] After this, when King Ahasuerus' wrath had cooled, he thought over what Vashti had done and what had been decreed against her. [2] Then the king's personal attendants suggested: "Let beautiful young virgins be sought for the king. [3] Let the king appoint commissaries in all the provinces of his realm to bring together all beautiful young virgins to the harem in the stronghold of Susa. Under the care of the royal eunuch Hegai, custodian of the women, let cosmetics be given them. [4] Then the girl who pleases the king shall reign in place of Vashti." This suggestion pleased the king, and he acted accordingly.

[5] There was in the stronghold of Susa a certain Jew named Mordecai, son of Jair, son of Shimei, son of Kish, a Benjaminite, [6] who had been exiled from Jerusalem with the captives taken with Jeconiah, king of

k Est 8, 5. 8; Dn 6, 8f.—l Est A, 3; 2 Kgs 24, 15; 2 Chr 36, 9f; Jer 22, 24ff; 24, 1; 29, 1f.—m Est 2, 15.—n Est 2, 19f; 4, 11. 16.

1, 19: *Irrevocable royal decree:* the historian Siculus indicates that such a concept of *irrevocable* laws existed in the time of Darius III (335-331 B.C.), the last of the Persian kings; cf Est 8, 8.

1, 22: *To each province . . . script and to each people . . . language:* many languages were spoken in the Persian Empire, the principal ones being Persian, Elamite, Babylonian, Aramaic, Phoenician, Egyptian, and Greek. Each of them had its own script.

2, 7: *Hadassah* (the feminine form of *hadas*, myrtle) was the name by which this woman would be known among her Jewish compatriots. *Esther* is a variant of the name of the Babylonian goddess Ishtar.

Judah, whom Nebuchadnezzar, king of Babylon, had deported.[l] [7] He was foster father to Hadassah,* that is, Esther, his cousin; for she had lost both father and mother. The girl was beautifully formed and lovely to behold. On the death of her father and mother, Mordecai had taken her as his own daugher.[m]

[8] When the king's order and decree had been obeyed and many maidens brought together to the stronghold of Susa under the care of Hegai, Esther also was brought into the royal palace under the care of Hegai, custodian of the women. [9] The girl pleased him and won his favor. So he promptly furnished her with cosmetics and provisions. Then picking out seven maids for her from the royal palace, he transferred both her and her maids to the best place in the harem. [10] Esther did not reveal her nationality or family, for Mordecai had commanded her not to do so.

[11] Day by day Mordecai would walk about in front of the court of the harem, to learn how Esther was faring and what was to become of her.

[12] Each girl went in turn to visit King Ahasuerus after the twelve months' preparation decreed for the women. Of this period of beautifying treatment, six months were spent wth oil of myrrh, and the other six months with perfumes and cosmetics. [13] Then, when the girl was to visit the king, she was allowed to take with her from the harem to the royal palace whatever she chose. [14] She would go in the evening and return in the morning to a second harem under the care of the royal eunuch Shaashgaz, custodian of the concubines. She could not return to the king unless he was pleased with her and had her summoned by name.[n]

[15] As for Esther, daughter of Abihail and adopted daughter of his nephew Mordecai, when her turn came to visit the king, she did not ask for anything but what the royal eunuch Hegai, custodian of the women, suggested. Yet she won the admiration of all who saw her. [16] Esther was led to King Ahasuerus in his palace in the tenth month, Tebeth, in the seventh year of his reign. [17] The king loved Esther more than all other women, and of all the virgins she won his favor and benevolence. So he placed the royal diadem on her head and made her queen in place of Vashti.

Est

18 Then the king gave a great feast in honor of Esther to all his officials and ministers, granting a holiday* to the provinces and bestowing gifts with royal bounty.

The Plot Discovered.* 19 *o* [To resume: From the time the virgins had been brought together, and while Mordecai was passing his time at the king's gate, 20 Esther had not revealed her family or nationality, because Mordecai had told her not to; and Esther continued to follow Mordecai's instructions, just as she had when she was being brought up by him. 21 *p* And during the time that Mordecai spent at the king's gate,* Bagathan and Thares, two of the royal eunuchs who guarded the entrance, had plotted in anger to lay hands on King Ahasuerus. 22 When the plot became known to Mordecai, he told Queen Esther, who in turn informed the king for Mordecai. 23 The matter was investigated and verified, and both of them were hanged on a gibbet.* This was written in the annals for the king's use.]

III: HAMAN'S PLOT AGAINST THE JEWS

CHAPTER 3

Mordecai Refuses to Honor Haman. 1 After these events King Ahasuerus raised Haman, son of Hammedatha the Agagite, to high rank, seating him above all his fellow officials.*q* 2 All the king's servants who were at the royal gate would kneel and bow down to Haman, for that is what the king had ordered in his regard.*r* Mordecai, however, would not kneel and bow down.* 3 The king's servants who were at the royal gate said to Mordecai, "Why do you disobey the king's order?"*s* 4 When they had reminded him day after day and he would not listen to them, they informed Haman, to see whether Mordecai's explanation was acceptable, since he had told them that he was a Jew.

Haman's Reprisal. 5 When Haman observed that Mordecai would not kneel and bow down to him, he was filled with anger. 6 Moreover, he thought it was not enough to lay hands on Mordecai alone. Since they had told Haman of Mordecai's nationality, he sought to destroy all the Jews, Mordecai's people, throughout the realm of King Ahasuerus. 7 In the first month, Nisan, in the twelfth year of King Ahasuerus, the *pur,** or lot, was cast in Haman's presence, to determine the day and the month for the destruction of Mordecai's people on a single day, and the lot fell on the thirteenth day of the twelfth month, Adar.*t*

Decree against the Jews. 8 Then Haman said to King Ahasuerus: "Dispersed among the nations throughout the provinces of your kingdom, there is a certain people living apart, with laws differing from those of every other people. They do not obey the laws of the king, and so it is not proper for the king to tolerate them.*u* 9 If it please the king, let a decree be issued to destroy them; and I will deliver to the procurators ten thousand silver talents for deposit in the royal treasury."*v* 10 The king took the signet ring* from his hand and gave it to Haman, son of Hammedatha the Agagite, the enemy of the Jews.*w* 11 "The silver you may keep," the king said to Haman, "but as for this people, do with them whatever you please."

12 So the royal scribes were summoned; and on the thirteenth day of the first month they wrote, at the dictation of Haman, an order to the royal satraps, the governors of every province, and the officials of every people, to each province in its own script and to each people in its own language. It was written in the name of King Ahasuerus and sealed with the royal signet ring. 13 Letters were sent by couriers to all the royal provinces, that all the Jews, young and old, including women and children, should be killed, destroyed, wiped out in one day, the thirteenth day of

---

o 19f: Est 2, 14.—p 21ff: Est A, 12-15; 6, 1ff.—q Est B, 3; 5, 11; E, 11.—r Est C, 5; 5, 9. 13; 6, 10. 12.—s Est 4, 16.—t Est 9, 24ff; F, 10.—u Est 3, 13; B, 4; E, 24; Dn 3, 8-12; Wis 2, 14f.—v Est 7, 4.—w Gn 41, 42.

2, 18: *A holiday:* or perhaps, "a remission of taxes."
2, 19-23: This is a resumption, in a slightly different form, of the story already told in Est A, 12-15.
2, 21: *Mordecai . . . at the king's gate:* to exercise watchful care for Esther. Some understand this to mean that Mordecai was stationed at the gate to render royal service; cf Est A, 2.
2, 23: *Hanged on a gibbet:* impaled, perhaps, after the Babylonian manner.
3, 2: *Mordecai . . . would not kneel and bow down:* in order not to render to man the homage which he regarded as belonging to God alone; cf Est C, 5ff.
3, 7: *Pur:* a Babylonian word which the Hebrew translates as *goral,* "lot." This word is preserved in the text because its plural, *purim,* became the name of the feast of Purim commemorating the deliverance of the Jews; cf Est 9, 24. 26.
3, 10: *Signet ring:* a ring containing a seal which was impressed on documents to authenticate them. By giving this ring to Haman, the king bestowed on him the power to authenticate royal decrees.

the twelfth month, Adar, and that their goods should be seized as spoil.*ˣ*

CHAPTER B

¹This is a copy of the letter:
"The great King Ahasuerus writes to the satraps of the hundred and twenty-seven provinces from India to Ethiopia, and the governors subordinate to them, as follows: ²When I came to rule many peoples and to hold sway over the whole world, I determined not to be carried away with the sense of power, but always to deal fairly and with clemency; to provide for my subjects a life of complete tranquillity; and by making my government humane and effective as far as the borders, to restore the peace desired by all men.*ʸ* ³When I consulted my counselors as to how this might be accomplished, Haman, who excels among us in wisdom, who is outstanding for constant devotion and steadfast loyalty, and who has gained the second rank in the kingdom,*ᶻ* ⁴brought it to our attention that, mixed in with all the races throughout the world, there is one people of bad will, which by its laws is opposed to every other people and continually disregards the decrees of kings, so that the unity of empire blamelessly designed by us cannot be established.*ᵃ*

⁵"Having noted, therefore, that this most singular people is continually at variance with all men, lives by divergent and alien laws, is inimical to our interests, and commits the worst crimes, so that stability of government cannot be obtained, ⁶we hereby decree that all those who are indicated to you in the letters of Haman, who is in charge of the administration and is a second father to us, shall, together with their wives and children, be utterly destroyed by the swords of their enemies, without any pity or mercy, on the fourteenth day* of the twelfth month, Adar, of the current year;*ᵇ* ⁷so that when these people, whose present ill will is of long standing, have gone down into the nether world by a violent death on one same day,

they may at last leave our affairs stable and undisturbed for the future."

(CHAPTER 3)

¹⁴A copy of the decree to be promulgated as law in every province was published to all the peoples, that they might be prepared for that day. ¹⁵The couriers set out in haste at the king's command; meanwhile, the decree was promulgated in the stronghold of Susa. The king and Haman then sat down to feast, but the city of Susa was thrown into confusion.

CHAPTER 4

Esther's Aid Sought by Mordecai. ¹When Mordecai learned all that was happening, he tore his garments, put on sackcloth and ashes, and walked through the city, crying out loudly and bitterly,*ᶜ* ²till he came before the royal gate, which no one clothed in sackcloth might enter. ³(Likewise in each of the provinces, wherever the king's legal enactment reached, the Jews went into deep mourning, with fasting, weeping, and lament; they all slept on sackcloth and ashes.)

⁴Queen Esther's maids and eunuchs came and told her. Overwhelmed with anguish, she sent garments for Mordecai to put on, so that he might take off his sackcloth; but he refused. ⁵Esther then summoned Hathach, one of the king's eunuchs whom he had placed at her service, and commanded him to find out what this action of Mordecai meant and the reason for it. ⁶So Hathach went out to Mordecai in the public square in front of the royal gate, ⁷and Mordecai told him all that had happened, as well as the exact amount of silver Haman had promised to pay to the royal treasury for the slaughter of the Jews. ⁸He also gave him a copy of the written decree for their destruction which had been promulgated in Susa, to show and explain to Esther. He was to instruct her to go to the king; she was to plead and intercede with him in behalf of her people. ⁸ * "Remember the days of your lowly estate," Mordecai had him say, "when you were brought up in my charge; for Haman, who is second to the king, has asked for our death. ⁹Invoke the LORD and speak to the king for us; save us from death."

Hathach returned to Esther and told her what Mordecai had said. [10] Then Esther replied to Hathach and gave him this message for Mordecai: [11] "All the servants of the king and the people of his provinces know that any man or woman who goes to the king in the inner court without being summoned, suffers the automatic penalty of death, unless the king extends to him the golden scepter, thus sparing his life. Now as for me, I have not been summoned to the king for thirty days."[d]

[12] When Esther's words were reported to Mordecai, [13] he had this reply brought to her: "Do not imagine that because you are in the king's palace, you alone of all the Jews will escape. [14] Even if you now remain silent, relief and deliverance will come to the Jews from another source;* but you and your father's house will perish. Who knows but that it was for a time like this that you obtained the royal dignity?"

[15] Esther sent back to Mordecai the response: [16] "Go and assemble all the Jews who are in Susa; fast on my behalf, all of you, not eating or drinking, night or day, for three days. I and my maids will also fast in the same way. Thus prepared, I will go to the king, contrary to the law. If I perish, I perish!" [e]

CHAPTER C

Prayer of Mordecai. Mordecai went away and did exactly as Esther had commanded. [1] Recalling all that the LORD had done, he prayed to him [2] and said: "O Lord God, almighty King, all things are in your power, and there is no one to oppose you in your will to save Israel. [3] You made heaven and earth and every wonderful thing under the heavens. [4] You are LORD of all, and there is no one who can resist you, LORD. [5] [f] You know all things. You know, O LORD, that it was not out of insolence or pride or desire for fame that I acted thus in not bowing down to the proud Haman. [6] Gladly would I have kissed the soles of his feet for the salvation of Israel. [7] But I acted as I did so as not to place the honor of man above that of God. I will not bow down to anyone but you, my LORD. It is not out of pride that I am acting thus. [8] And now, LORD God, King, God of Abraham, spare your people, for our enemies plan our ruin and are bent upon

destroying the inheritance that was yours from the beginning. [9] Do not spurn your portion, which you redeemed for yourself out of Egypt. [10] Hear my prayer; have pity on your inheritance and turn our sorrow into joy: thus we shall live to sing praise to your name, O LORD. Do not silence those who praise you."

[11] All Israel, too, cried out with all their strength, for death was staring them in the face.

Prayer of Esther. [12] [g] Queen Esther, seized with mortal anguish, likewise had recourse to the LORD. [13] Taking off her splendid garments, she put on garments of distress and mourning. In place of her precious ointments she covered her head with dirt and ashes. She afflicted her body severely; all her festive adornments were put aside, and her hair was wholly disheveled.

[14] Then she prayed to the LORD, the God of Israel, saying: "My LORD, our King, you alone are God. Help me, who am alone and have no help but you, [15] for I am taking my life in my hand. [h] [16] As a child I was wont to hear from the people of the land of my forefathers that you, O LORD, chose Israel from among all peoples, and our fathers from among all their ancestors, as a lasting heritage, and that you fulfilled all your promises to them. [i] [17] But now we have sinned in your sight, and you have delivered us into the hands of our enemies, [18] because we worshiped their gods. You are just, O LORD. [19] But now they are not satisfied with our bitter servitude, but have undertaken [20] to do away with the decree you have pronounced, and to destroy your heritage; to close the mouths of those who praise you, and to extinguish the glory of your temple and your altar; [21] to open the mouths of the heathen to acclaim their false gods, and to extol an earthly king forever.

[22] "O Lord, do not relinquish your scepter to those that are nought. Let them not gloat over our ruin, but turn their own counsel against them and make an example of our chief enemy. [23] Be mindful of us, O LORD. Manifest yourself in the time of our distress and give me courage, King of gods

d Est 2, 14; 4, 12; D, 12.—e Est C, 12f.—f 5ff: Est 3, 2; 5, 9.—g 12f: Est 4, 16.—h Est 4, 16.—i Dt 4, 20; 7, 6; 9, 29; 14, 2; 26, 18; 32, 9.

4, 14: *From another source:* very probably Mordecai refers to divine aid; the Greek additions (C) are explicit about this.

and Ruler of every power. ²⁴Put in my mouth persuasive words in the presence of the lion and turn his heart to hatred for our enemy, so that he and those who are in league with him may perish. ²⁵Save us by your power, and help me, who am alone and have no one but you, O LORD.

"You know all things. ²⁶You know that I hate the glory of the pagans, and abhor the bed of the uncircumcised or of any foreigner. ²⁷You know that I am under constraint, that I abhor the sign of grandeur which rests on my head when I appear in public; abhor it like a polluted rag, and do not wear it in private. ²⁸I, your handmaid, have never eaten at the table of Haman, nor have I graced the banquet of the king or drunk the wine of libations.* ²⁹From the day I was brought here till now, your handmaid has had no joy except in you, O LORD, God of Abraham. ³⁰O God, more powerful than all, hear the voice of those in despair. Save us from the power of the wicked, and deliver me from my fear."

CHAPTER D

Esther Is Received by the King. ¹On the third day, putting an end to her prayers, she took off her penitential garments and arrayed herself in her royal attire. ²In making her state appearance, after invoking the all-seeing God and savior, she took with her two maids; ³on the one she leaned gently for support, ⁴while the other followed her, bearing her train. ⁵She glowed with the perfection of her beauty and her countenance was as joyous as it was lovely, though her heart was shrunk with fear. ⁶She passed through all the portals till she stood face to face with the king, who was seated on his royal throne, clothed in full robes of state, and covered with gold and precious stones, so that he inspired great awe. ⁷As he looked up, his features ablaze with the height of majestic anger, the queen staggered, changed color, and leaned weakly against the head of the maid in front of her. ⁸But God changed the king's anger to gentleness. In great anxiety he sprang from his throne, held her in his arms until she recovered, and comforted

her with reassuring words. ⁹"What is it, Esther?" he said to her. "I am your brother. Take courage! ¹⁰You shall not die because of this general decree of ours. ¹¹Come near!" ¹²Raising the golden scepter, he touched her neck with it, embraced her, and said, "Speak to me."ʲ

¹³She replied: "I saw you, my lord, as an angel of God, and my heart was troubled with fear of your majesty. ¹⁴For you are awesome, my lord, though your glance is full of kindness." ¹⁵As she said this, she fainted. ¹⁶The king became troubled and all his attendants tried to revive her.

CHAPTER 5

¹ * [Now on the third day, Esther put on her royal garments and stood in the inner courtyard, looking toward the royal palace, while the king was seated on his royal throne in the audience chamber, facing the palace doorway. ²He saw Queen Esther standing in the courtyard, and made her welcome by extending toward her the golden staff which he held. She came up to him, and touched the top of the staff.]

³Then the king said to her, "What is it, Queen Esther? What is your request? Even if it is half of my kingdom, it shall be granted you."ᵏ ⁴"If it please your majesty," Esther replied, "come today with Haman to a banquet I have prepared." ⁵And the king ordered, "Have Haman make haste to fulfill the wish of Esther."

First Banquet of Esther. So the king went with Haman to the banquet Esther had prepared. ⁶During the drinking of the wine, the king said to Esther, "Whatever you ask for shall be granted, and whatever request you make shall be honored, even if it is for half of my kingdom."ˡ ⁷Esther replied: "This is my petition and request: ⁸if I have found favor with the king and if it pleases your majesty to grant my petition and honor my request, come with Haman tomorrow to a banquet which I shall prepare for you; and then I will do as you ask."

Haman's Plot against Mordecai. ⁹That day Haman left happy and in good spirits. But when he saw that Mordecai at the royal gate did not rise, and showed no fear of him, he was filled with anger toward him.ᵐ ¹⁰Haman restrained himself, how-

---

j Est 4, 11.—k Est 5, 6; 7, 2; 9, 12.—l Est 5, 3.—m Est 3, 2f; C, 5ff; 6, 10. 12.

C, 28: *Wine of libations:* offered in sacrifice to the gods.
5, 1f: The Hebrew text here translated is a short form of the account already given in Greek.

ever, and went home, where he summoned his friends and his wife Zeresh. [11]He recounted the greatness of his riches, the large number of his sons, and just how the king had promoted him and placed him above the officials and royal servants.[n] [12]"Moreover," Haman added, "Queen Esther invited no one but me to the banquet with the king; again tomorrow I am to be her guest, with the king. [13]Yet none of this satisfies me as long as I continue to see the Jew Mordecai sitting at the royal gate."[o] [14]His wife Zeresh and all his friends said to him, "Have a gibbet set up, fifty cubits in height, and in the morning ask the king to have Mordecai hanged on it. Then go to the banquet with the king in good cheer." This suggestion pleased Haman, and he had the gibbet erected.[p]

IV: VINDICATION OF THE JEWS

CHAPTER 6

Mordecai's Reward from the King. [1]That night the king, unable to sleep, asked that the chronicle of notable events be brought in. While this was being read to him, [2]the passage occurred in which Mordecai reported Bagathan and Teresh, two of the royal eunuchs who guarded the entrance, for seeking to lay hands on King Ahasuerus.[q] [3]The king asked, "What was done to reward and honor Mordecai for this?" The king's attendants replied, "Nothing was done for him."[r]

[4]"Who is in the court?" the king asked. Now Haman had entered the outer court of the king's palace to suggest to the king that Mordecai should be hanged on the gibbet he had raised for him.[s] [5]The king's servants answered him, "Haman is waiting in the court." "Let him come in," the king said. [6]When Haman entered, the king said to him, "What should be done for the man whom the king wishes to reward?" Now Haman thought to himself, "Whom would the king more probably wish to reward than me?" [7]So he replied to the king: "For the man whom the king wishes to reward [8]there should be brought the royal robe which the king wore and the horse on which the king rode when the royal crown was placed on his head. [9]The robe and the horse should be consigned to one of the noblest of the king's officials, who must clothe the man the king wishes to reward, have him ride on the horse in the public

square of the city, and cry out before him, 'This is what is done for the man whom the king wishes to reward.' "[t] [10]Then the king said to Haman: "Hurry! Take the robe and horse as you have proposed, and do this for the Jew Mordecai, who is sitting at the royal gate. Do not omit anything you proposed."[u] [11]So Haman took the robe and horse, clothed Mordecai, had him ride in the public square of the city, and cried out before him, "This is what is done for the man whom the king wishes to reward."

[12]Mordecai then returned to the royal gate, while Haman hurried home, his head covered in grief.[v] [13]When he told his wife Zeresh and all his friends everything that had happened to him, his advisers and his wife Zeresh said to him, "If Mordecai, before whom you are beginning to decline, is of the Jewish race, you will not prevail against him, but will surely be defeated by him."

Esther's Second Banquet. [14]While they were speaking with him, the king's eunuchs arrived and hurried Haman off to the banquet Esther had prepared.

CHAPTER 7

[1]So the king and Haman went to the banquet with Queen Esther. [2]Again, on this second day, during the drinking of the wine, the king said to Esther, "Whatever you ask, Queen Esther, shall be granted you. Whatever request you make shall be honored, even for half the kingdom."[w] [3]Queen Esther replied: "If I have found favor with you, O king, and if it pleases your majesty, I ask that my life be spared, and I beg that you spare the lives of my people. [4]For my people and I have been delivered to destruction, slaughter, and extinction. If we were to be sold into slavery I would remain silent, but as it is, the enemy will be unable to compensate for the harm done to the king."[x] [5]"Who and where," said King Ahasuerus to Queen Esther, "is the man who has dared to do this?"[y] [6]Esther replied, "The enemy oppressing us is this wicked Haman." At this, Haman was seized with dread of the king and queen.

n Est 3, 1; B, 3; E, 11; 9, 6-10.—o Est 3, 2f; 6, 10, 12.—p Est 6, 4; 7, 9f.—q Est A, 12ff; 2, 21ff.—r Est A, 16.—s Est 5, 14; 7, 9f.—t Gn 41, 42f; 1 Kgs 1, 33; Dn 5, 29.—u Est 2, 21; 3, 2f; 5, 9. 13.—v Est 2, 21; 3, 2f; 5, 9. 13.—w Est 5, 3.—x Est 3, 13; B, 6.—y Est 3, 8f.

⁷The king left the banquet in anger and went into the garden of the palace, but Haman stayed to beg Queen Esther for his life, since he saw that the king had decided on his doom. ⁸When the king returned from the garden of the palace to the banquet hall, Haman had thrown himself on the couch on which Esther was reclining; and the king exclaimed, "Will he also violate the queen while she is with me in my own house!" Scarely had the king spoken, when the face of Haman was covered over.

Punishment of Haman. ⁹ ᶻ Harbona, one of the eunuchs who attended the king, said, "At the house of Haman stands a gibbet fifty cubits high. Haman prepared it for Mordecai, who gave the report that benefited the king." The king answered, "Hang him on it." ¹⁰So they hanged Haman on the gibbet which he had made ready for Mordecai, and the anger of the king abated.

CHAPTER 8

¹That day King Ahasuerus gave the house of Haman, enemy of the Jews, to Queen Esther; and Mordecai was admitted to the king's presence, for Esther had revealed his relationship to her.ᵃ ²The king removed his signet ring from Haman, and transferred it into the keeping of Mordecai; and Esther put Mordecai in charge of the house of Haman.ᵇ

The Second Royal Decree. ³In another audience with the king, Esther fell at his feet and tearfully implored him to revoke the harm done by Haman the Agagite, and the plan he had devised against the Jews. ⁴The king stretched forth the golden scepter to Esther. So she rose and, standing in his presence, ⁵said: "If it pleases your majesty and seems proper to you, and if I have found favor with you and you love me, let a document be issued to revoke the letters which that schemer Haman, son of Hammedatha the Agagite, wrote for the destruction of the Jews in all the royal provinces.ᶜ ⁶For how can I witness the evil that is to befall my people, and how can I behold the destruction of my race?"

⁷King Ahasuerus then said to Queen Esther and to the Jew Mordecai: "Now that I have given Esther the house of Haman, and they have hanged him on the gibbet because he attacked the Jews, 8 ᵈ you in turn may write in the king's name what you see fit concerning the Jews and seal the letter with the royal signet ring." For whatever is written in the name of the king and sealed with the royal signet ring cannot be revoked.*

⁹At that time, on the twenty-third day of the third month, Sivan, the royal scribes were summoned. Exactly as Mordecai dictated, they wrote to the Jews and to the satraps, governors, and officials of the hundred and twenty-seven provinces from India to Ethiopia: to each province in its own script and to each people in its own language, and to the Jews in their own script and language. ¹⁰These letters, which he wrote in the name of King Ahasuerus and sealed with the royal signet ring, he sent by mounted couriers riding thoroughbred royal steeds. 11 ᵉ In these letters the king authorized the Jews in each ⟨Est⟩ and every city to group together and defend their lives, and to kill, destroy, wipe out, along with their wives and children, every armed group of any nation or province which should attack them, and to seize their goods as spoil ¹²throughout the provinces of King Ahasuerus, on a single day, the thirteenth of the twelfth month, Adar.

CHAPTER E

¹The following is a copy of the letter: "King Ahasuerus the Great to the governors of the provinces in the hundred and twenty-seven satrapies from India to Ethiopia, and to those responsible for our interests: Greetings! ²"Many have become the more ambitious the more they were showered with honors through the bountiful generosity of their patrons. ³Not only do they seek to do harm to our subjects; incapable of bearing such greatness, they even begin plotting against their own benefactors. ⁴Not only do they drive out gratitude from among men; with the arrogant boastfulness of those to whom goodness has no meaning, they suppose they will escape the vindictive judgment of the all-seeing God.

---

z 9f: Est 5, 14; 6, 4.—a Est 9, 1; Prv 11, 8; 26, 27; Mt 7, 2.— b Prv 13, 22; Dn 2, 48f.—c Est 1, 19.—d Est 1, 19.—e 11f: Est 9, 1-4.

8, 8: *Whatever is written . . . cannot be revoked:* the king cannot directly grant Esther's request (v 5) to revoke the previous decree against the Jews because of the irrevocable character of the laws of the Medes and Persians (Est 1, 19; Dn 6, 9); but he empowers Esther to issue a new decree in his name which renders the earlier decree without effect; cf Est 3, 12f.

[5] "Often, too, the fair speech of friends entrusted with the administration of affairs has induced many placed in authority to become accomplices in the shedding of innocent blood, and has involved them in irreparable calamities [6] by deceiving with malicious slander the sincere good will of rulers. [7] This can be verified in the ancient stories that have been handed down to us, but more fully when one considers the wicked deeds perpetrated in your midst by the pestilential influence of those undeserving of authority. [8] *f* We must provide for the future, so as to render the kingdom undisturbed and peaceful for all men, [9] taking advantage of changing conditions and deciding always with equitable treatment matters coming to our attention.

[10] "For instance, Haman, son of Hammedatha, a Macedonian,* certainly not of Persian blood, and very different from us in generosity, was hospitably received by us. [11] He so far enjoyed the good will which we have toward all peoples that he was proclaimed 'father of the king,' before whom everyone was to bow down; he attained the rank second to the royal throne. *g* [12] But, unequal to this dignity, he strove to deprive us of kingdom and of life; [13] and by weaving intricate webs of deceit, he demanded the destruction of Mordecai, our savior and constant benefactor, and of Esther, our blameless royal consort, together with their whole race. *h* [14] For by such measures he hoped to catch us defenseless and to transfer the rule of the Persians to the Macedonians. [15] But we find that the Jews, who were doomed to extinction by this archcriminal, are not evildoers, but rather are governed by very just laws [16] and are the children of the Most High, the living God of majesty, who has maintained the kingdom in a flourishing condition for us and for our forebears.

[17] "You will do well, then, to ignore the letter sent by Haman, son of Hammedatha, [18] for he who composed it has been hanged, together with his entire household, before the gates of Susa. Thus swiftly has God, who governs all, brought just punishment upon him. *i*

[19] "You shall exhibit a copy of this letter publicly in every place, to certify that the Jews may follow their own laws, [20] and that you may help them on the day set for their ruin, the thirteenth day of the twelfth month, Adar, to defend themselves against those who attack them. [21] For God, the ruler of all, has turned that day for them from one of destruction of the chosen race into one of joy. [22] Therefore, you too must celebrate this memorable day among your designated feasts with all rejoicing, [23] so that both now and in the future it may be, for us and for loyal Persians, a celebration of victory, and for those who plot against us a reminder of destruction.

[24] "Every city and province, without exception, that does not observe this decree shall be ruthlessly destroyed with fire and sword, so that it will be left not merely untrodden by men, but even shunned by wild beasts and birds forever." *j*

(CHAPTER 8)

[13] A copy of the letter to be promulgated as law in each and every province was published among all the peoples, so that the Jews might be prepared on that day to avenge themselves on their enemies.* [14] Couriers mounted on royal steeds sped forth in haste at the king's order, and the decree was promulgated in the stronghold of Susa.

[15] Mordecai left the king's presence clothed in a royal robe of violet and of white cotton, with a large crown of gold and a cloak of crimson byssus. The city of Susa shouted with joy, *k* [16] and there was splendor and merriment for the Jews, exultation and triumph. [17] In each and every province and in each and every city, wherever the king's order arrived, there was merriment and exultation, banqueting and feasting for the Jews. And many of the peoples of the land embraced Judaism, for they were seized with a fear of the Jews. *l*

CHAPTER 9

Victory of the Jews. [1] *m* When the day arrived on which the order decreed by the king was to be carried out, the thirteenth day of the twelfth month, Adar, on which

---

f 8f: Est B, 2.—g Est B, 3. 6.—h Est A, 17.—i Est 7, 10; 9, 14.—j Est 3, 8f; B, 4.—k Dn 5, 7.—l Est 9, 27.—m 1f: Est 8, 11f.

E, 10: *Macedonian:* a redactor of the book in the Hellenistic period used the designation *Macedonian,* here and in v 14, to express, after Macedonia's conquest of Persia, the most odious kind of man that a Persian ruler could be supposed to think of; the Hebrew text, for a similar reason, called Haman an Agagite. See note on Est A, 17.

8, 13: *Avenge themselves on their enemies:* partly in self-defense (Est E, 20), and partly to express the fact that the extreme cruelty designed against the Jews by their enemies now recoiled upon the latter as a punishment. Cf 9, 1f.

the enemies of the Jews had expected to become masters of them, the situation was reversed: the Jews became masters of their enemies. [2]The Jews mustered in their cities throughout the provinces of King Ahasuerus to attack those who sought to do them harm, and no one could withstand them, but all peoples were seized with a fear of them. [3]Moreover, all the officials of the provinces, the satraps, governors, and royal procurators supported the Jews from fear of Mordecai; [4]for Mordecai was powerful in the royal palace, and the report was spreading through all the provinces that he was continually growing in power.

[5]The Jews struck down all their enemies with the sword, killing and destroying them; they did to their enemies as they pleased.[n] [6][o] In the stronghold of Susa, the Jews killed and destroyed five hundred men. [7]They also killed Parshandatha, Dalphon, Aspatha, [8]Porathai, Adalia, Aridatha, [9]Parmashta, Arisai, Aridai, and Vaizatha, [10][p] the ten sons of Haman, son of Hammedatha, the foe of the Jews. However, they did not engage in plundering.[*]

[11]On the same day, when the number of those killed in the stronghold of Susa was reported to the king, [12]he said to Queen Esther: "In the stronghold of Susa the Jews have killed and destroyed five hundred men, as well as the ten sons of Haman. What must they have done in the other royal provinces! You shall again be granted whatever you ask, and whatever you request shall be honored." [13]So Esther said, "If it pleases your majesty, let the Jews in Susa be permitted again tomorrow to act according to today's decree, and let the ten sons of Haman be hanged on gibbets." [14]The king then gave an order to this effect, and the decree was published in Susa. So the ten sons of Haman were hanged,[q] [15]and the Jews in Susa mustered again on the fourteenth of the month of Adar and killed three hundred men in Susa.[*] However, they did not engage in plundering.[r]

[16]The other Jews, who dwelt in the royal provinces, also mustered and defended themselves, and obtained rest from their enemies. They killed seventy-five thousand[*] of their foes, without engaging in plunder,[s] [17]on the thirteenth day of the month of Adar. On the fourteenth of the month they rested, and made it a day of feasting and rejoicing.

[18](The Jews in Susa, however, mustered on the thirteenth and fourteenth of the month. But on the fifteenth they rested, and made it a day of feasting and rejoicing.) [19]That is why the rural Jews, who dwell in villages, celebrate the fourteenth of the month of Adar as a day of rejoicing and feasting, a holiday on which they send gifts of food to one another.

The Feast of Purim. [20]Mordecai recorded these events and sent letters to all the Jews, both near and far, in all the provinces of King Ahasuerus. [21]He ordered them to celebrate every year both the fourteenth and the fifteenth of the month of Adar [22]as the day on which the Jews obtained rest from their enemies and as the month which was turned for them from sorrow into joy, from mourning into festivity. They were to observe these days with feasting and gladness, sending food to one another and gifts to the poor. [23]The Jews took upon themselves for the future this observance which they instituted at the written direction of Mordecai.[t]

[24][u] Haman, son of Hammedatha the Agagite, the foe of all the Jews, had planned to destroy them and had cast the *pur*, or lot, for the time of their defeat and destruction. [25]Yet, when Esther entered the royal presence, the king ordered in writing that the wicked plan Haman had devised against the Jews should instead be turned against Haman and that he and his sons should be hanged on gibbets.[v] [26]And so these days have been named Purim after the word *pur*.

Thus, because of all that was contained in this letter, and because of what they had witnessed and experienced in this affair, [27]the Jews established and took upon themselves, their descendants, and all who should join them, the inviolable obligation of celebrating these two days every year in the manner prescribed by this letter, and at the time appointed.[w] [28]These days were to be commemorated and kept in every

n Jdt 15, 6.—o 6-10; Est 5, 11; B, 3; E, 11.—p Est 9, 15; Jdt 15, 7. 11.—q Est 7, 10; E, 18.—r Est 9, 10.—s Jdt 15, 6.—t Est 9, 29.—u 24ff: Est 3, 7; F, 10.—v Est 6, 5-13.—w Est 8, 12. 17.

9, 10: *They did not engage in plundering:* in contrast to the Israelites who fought Agag (1 Sm 15, 9); cf also vv 15f.

9, 15: This second slaughter explains the two dates (13th and 14th) of the Purim celebration by Jews in Susa (v 18).

9, 16: *Seventy-five thousand:* according to the Greek text this number was fifteen thousand.

generation, by every clan, in every province, and in every city. These days of Purim were never to fall into disuse among the Jews, nor into oblivion among their descendants. [29] Queen Esther, daughter of Abihail and of Mordecai* the Jew, wrote to confirm with full authority this second letter about Purim, [30] when Mordecai sent documents concerning peace and security to all the Jews in the hundred and twenty-seven provinces of Ahasuerus' kingdom.ˣ [31] Thus were established, for their appointed time, these days of Purim which Mordecai the Jew and Queen Esther had designated for the Jews, just as they had previously enjoined upon themselves and upon their race the duty of fasting and supplication.* [32] The command of Esther confirmed these prescriptions for Purim and was recorded in the book.

CHAPTER 10

[1] King Ahasuerus laid tribute on the land and on the islands of the sea. [2] All the acts of his power and valor, as well as a detailed account of the greatness of Mordecai, whom the king promoted, are recorded in the chronicles of the kings of Media and Persia. [3] The Jew Mordecai was next in rank to King Ahasuerus, in high standing among the Jews, and was regarded with favor by his many brethren, as the promoter of his people's welfare and the herald of peace for his whole race.ʸ

V: EPILOGUE

CHAPTER F

Mordecai's Dream Fulfilled. [1] ᶻ Then Mordecai said: "This is the work of God. [2] I recall the dream I had about these very things, and not a single detail has been left unfulfilled—[3] the tiny spring that grew into a river, the light of the sun, the many waters. The river is Esther, whom the king married and made queen. [4] The two dragons are myself and Haman. [5] The nations are those who assembled to destroy the name of the Jews, [6] but my people is Israel, who cried to God and was saved.

"The LORD saved his people and delivered us from all these evils. God worked signs and great wonders, such as have not occurred among the nations. [7] For this purpose he arranged two lots:* one for the people of God, the second for all the other nations. [8] These two lots were fulfilled in the hour, the time, and the day of judgment before God and among all the nations. [9] God remembered his people and rendered justice to his inheritance.

[10] ᵃ "Gathering together with joy and happiness before God, they shall celebrate these days on the fourteenth and fifteenth of the month Adar throughout all future generations of his people Israel."*

x Est 9, 23-26.—y 2 Mc 15, 14.—z 1-6: Est A, 4-10.—a Est 3, 7; 9, 17f. 21. 24-28.

9, 29: *Queen Esther, daughter of Abihail and of Mordecai:* the natural offspring of Abihail and adopted daughter of Mordecai; cf Est 2, 15. *This second letter:* for the burden of this letter see Est 9, 20ff. It was endorsed by Queen Esther. The first letter, written in the king's name, is referred to in Est 8, 9.

9, 31: *Fasting and supplication:* as the Jews had previously undertaken the duty of fasting and supplication to prevent the impending disaster, they now observe days of festival to commemorate their deliverance—in both cases (cf Est 4, 3. 15f) at the request of Mordecai and Esther.

F, 7: *Two lots:* in this passage of the Greek text, which gives a more religious interpretation of the feast, the *two lots* are drawn by God to determine, respectively, the destiny of Israel and that of the nations. In Est 3, 7 above, translated from the Hebrew text, the feast is called *Purim* because of the lots which Aman cast to determine the day for the extinction of the Jews.

F, 10: The Greek text of Esther contains a postscript as follows: *In the fourth year of the reign of Ptolemy and Cleopatra, Dositheus, who said he was a priest and Levite, and his son Ptolemy brought the present letter of Purim, saying that it was genuine and that Lysimachus, son of Ptolemy, of the community of Jerusalem, had translated it.* The date referred to in this postscript is most probably 78-77 B.C., in the reign of Ptolemy XII and Cleopatra V.

THE FIRST BOOK OF MACCABEES

The name Maccabee, probably meaning "hammer," is actually applied in the Books of Maccabees to only one man, Judas, third son of the priest Mattathias and first leader of the revolt against the Seleucid kings who persecuted the Jews (1 Mc 2, 4. 66; 2 Mc 8, 5. 16; 10, 1. 16). Traditionally the name has come to be applied to the brothers of Judas, his supporters, and even to other Jewish heroes of the period, such as the seven brothers (2 Mc 7).

The two Books of Maccabees, placed last in the Douai version of the Old Testament, contain independent accounts of events in part identical which accompanied the attempted suppression of Judaism in Palestine in the second century B.C. The vigorous reaction to this attempt established for a time the religious and political independence of the Jews.

1 Maccabees was written about 100 B.C., in Hebrew, but the original has not come down to us. Instead, we have an early, pre-Christian, Greek translation full of Hebrew idioms. The author, probably a Palestinian Jew, is unknown. He was familiar with the traditions and sacred books of his people and had access to much reliable information on their recent history (from 175 to 134 B.C.). He may well have played some part in it himself in his youth. His purpose in writing is to record the salvation of Israel which God worked through the family of Mattathias (5, 62)—especially through his three sons, Judas, Jonathan, and Simon, and his grandson, John Hyrcanus. Implicitly the writer compares their virtues and their exploits with those of the ancient heroes, the Judges, Samuel, and David.

There are seven poetic sections in the book which imitate the style of classical Hebrew poetry: four laments (1, 25-28. 36-40; 2, 8-13; 3, 45), and three hymns of praise of "our fathers" (2, 51-64), of Judas (3, 3-9), and of Simon (14, 4-15).

The doctrine expressed in the book is the customary belief of Israel, without the new developments which appear in 2 Maccabees and Daniel. The people of Israel have been specially chosen by the one true God as his covenant-partner, and they alone are privileged to know him and worship him. He is their eternal benefactor and their unfailing source of help. The people, in turn, must be loyal to his exclusive worship and must observe exactly the precepts of the law he has given them.

1Mc

There is no doctrine of individual immortality except in the survival of one's name and fame, nor does the book express any messianic expectation, though messianic images are applied historically to "the days of Simon" (14, 4-17). In true deuteronomic tradition, the author insists on fidelity to the law as the expression of Israel's love for God. The contest which he describes is a struggle, not simply between Jew and Gentile, but between those who would uphold the law and those, Jews or Gentiles, who would destroy it. His severest condemnation goes, not to the Seleucid politicians, but to the lawless apostates among his own people, adversaries of Judas and his brothers, who are models of faith and loyalty.

1 Maccabees has importance also for the New Testament. Salvation is paralleled with Jewish national aspirations (1 Mc 4, 46—14, 41), in contrast to the universal reign of God taught by Christ in the Gospel (Mt 13, 47-50; 22, 1-14). Also, destruction of the wall of the temple separating Jew from Gentile is an act of desecration in 1 Mc 9, 54, but in Eph 2, 14, an act of redemption and unification of both through Christ. On the other hand, association, in 1 Mc 2, 52, of Abraham's offering up of Isaac (Gn 22) with his justification by God (Gn 15, 6) is reflected in Jn 2, 21f, just as the Scriptures are regarded as a source of consolation in 1 Mc 12, 9 and in Rom 15, 4.

The Books of Maccabees, though regarded by Jews and Protestants as apocryphal, i.e., not inspired Scripture, because not contained in the Palestinian Canon or list of books drawn up at the end of the first century A.D., have nevertheless always been accepted by the Catholic Church as inspired, on the basis of apostolic tradition.

1 Maccabees is divided as follows: I. Introduction: Hellenism in Asia Minor (1, 1-9). II. The Maccabean Revolt (1, 10—2, 70). III. Leadership of Judas Maccabeus (3, 1—9, 22). IV. Leadership of Jonathan (9, 23—12, 54). V. Simon, High Priest and Ethnarch (13, 1—16, 24).

I: INTRODUCTION: HELLENISM IN ASIA MINOR

CHAPTER 1

Conquests and Death of Alexander. [1] [a] After Alexander the Macedonian, Philip's son, who came from the land of Kittim,* had defeated Darius, king of the Persians and Medes, he became king in his place, having first ruled in Greece. [2] He fought many campaigns, captured fortresses, and put kings to death. [3] He advanced to the ends of the earth, gathering plunder from many nations; the earth fell silent before him, and his heart became proud and arrogant. [4] He collected a very strong army and conquered provinces, nations, and rulers, and they became his tributaries. [5] But after all this he took to his bed, realizing that he was going to die. [6] He therefore summoned his officers, the nobles, who had been brought up with him from his youth, to divide his kingdom among them while he was still alive. [7] Alexander had reigned twelve years* when he died.

[8] So his officers took over his kingdom, each in his own territory, [9] and after his death they all put on royal crowns, and so did their sons after them for many years, causing much distress over the earth.

II: THE MACCABEAN REVOLT

Pact between Jews and Gentiles. [10] There sprang from these a sinful offshoot, Antiochus Epiphanes, son of King Antiochus, once a hostage at Rome. He became king in the year one hundred and thirty-seven* of the kingdom of the Greeks. [b]

[11] In those days there appeared in Israel men who were breakers of the law, and they seduced many people, saying: "Let us go and make an alliance with the Gentiles all around us; since we separated from them, many evils have come upon us." [c] [12] The proposal was agreeable; [13] [d] some from among the people promptly went to the king, and he authorized them to introduce the way of living of the Gentiles. [14] Thereupon they built a gymnasium* in Jerusalem according to the Gentile custom. [15] They covered over the mark of their circumcision and abandoned the holy covenant; they allied themselves with the Gentiles and sold themselves to wrongdoing. [e]

Egyptian Campaign of Antiochus. [16] When his kingdom seemed secure, Antiochus proposed to become king of Egypt, so as to rule over both kingdoms. [17] He invaded Egypt with a strong force, with chariots and elephants,* and with a large fleet, [f] [18] to make war on Ptolemy, king of Egypt. Ptolemy was frightened at his presence and fled, leaving many casualties. [19] The fortified cities in the land of Egypt were captured, and Antiochus plundered the land of Egypt.

Persecution of the Jews. [20] [g] After Antiochus had defeated Egypt in the year one hundred and forty-three,* he returned and went up to Israel and to Jeru-

a 1-10: Dn 8, 20ff; 11, 3f. 21.—b 2 Mc 4, 7.—c 2 Mc 4, 9-17.—d 13ff: 2 Mc 4, 7-17.—e 1 Cor 7, 18.—f 2 Mc 5, 1; Dn 11, 25-28.—g 20-24: 2 Mc 5, 11-21.

1, 1: *Land of Kittim:* Greece. The name referred originally to inhabitants of Kiti, capital of the isle of Cyprus, then to any Cypriots (Is 23, 1; Jer 2, 10), later to Greeks in general, and finally even to Romans. See note on Dn 11, 30. *Darius:* Darius III, Codoman (336-331 B.C.).

1, 7: *Twelve years:* 336-323 B.C.

1, 10: *The year one hundred and thirty-seven:* Antiochus IV seized the throne in September, 175 B.C. Dates are given in this book according to the Seleucid era, which however was reckoned in two different ways. Antiochians considered this date to be October, 312 B.C. (Syrian calendar), while Babylonians and Jewish priests accepted April, 311 B.C. as the commencement of the era (temple calendar). The author of 1 Mc dates political events by the Syrian calendar but religious events by the temple calendar. Accordingly, the civil New Year occurred variously in September or October, the religious New Year in March or April.

1, 14: *Gymnasium:* symbol and center of athletic and intellectual life, it was the chief instrument of Hellenistic propaganda. Jewish youth were attracted by sports and encouraged to join youth clubs. They received training in military skills and in the duties of citizens. Through participation in the intellectual life, many were gradually won over to paganism.

1, 17: *Elephants:* an important part of Seleucid armament. About 300 B.C. Seleucus I, founder of the dynasty, procured five hundred of them from India; cf 1 Mc 6, 34-37.

1, 20: *Defeated Egypt in the year one hundred and forty-three:* 169 B.C. No mention is made in 1 Mc of the second expedition to Egypt a year later, described in 2 Mc 5, 1. 11. Dn 11, 25. 29 records both.

PALESTINE AND SYRIA IN THE TIME OF THE MACCABEES

1Mc

PALESTINE AND SYRIA IN THE TIME OF THE MACCABEES (166-63) (1 Mc 1—16; 2 Mc 8—15) — (a)
With their defeat by Alexander the Great at the battle of Arbela (331), the Persians lose not only their empire but also control over Palestine. After the death of Alexander, the Jews are ruled benevolently by the Egyptian Ptolemies for over one hundred years (323-198). **(b)** The Seleucids, who have inherited the greater part of Alexander's empire, bring the Jews under their dominion again (198), and Antiochus IV Epiphanes determines to compel the Jews to adopt the Greek religion and converts the temple to the worship of the Olympian Zeus (168) (1 Mc 1). **(c)** The sons of the priest Mattathias (from **Modein**) organize a revolt under the leader Judas (called Maccabeus or "the Hammerer"). Judas cleanses the temple in 165, an event commemorated in the Jewish festival of Dedication (Hanukkah) before being killed in battle in 160 (1 Mc 3, 1—9, 22). **(d)** He is succeeded first by his brothers, Jonathan (160-142) and then Simon (142-134) who gains Jewish independence and establishes the Hasmonean dynasty, holding the high priesthood and the civil power (1 Mc 9, 23—16, 16). **(e)** John Hyrcanus I (134-104) wins complete independence for the Jews and enlarges their territory to include **Samaria** and the **Moabite region** beyond the Jordan. **(f)** In 63 the Romans end Jewish independence, but allow the last two Hasmoneans to govern: Hyrcanus II (63-40) and Antigonus (40-36).

ROMAN EMPIRE

AT THE TIME OF CHRIST

(Map labels, roughly top to bottom / left to right:)

ATLANTIC OCEAN — ENGLISH CHANNEL — BELGICA — M. CANTABRICUM — ASTURES — Lutetia — Treverorum — LUGDUNENSIS — GAUL — Lugdunum — AQUITANIA — Massilia — NARBONENSIS — Narbo — Ilerda — Tarraco — LUSITANIA — SPAIN — Emerita — Caesar Augusta — Toletum — TARRACONENSIS — BETICA — Hispalis — Carthago Nova — IBERIAN SEA — Balearic Islands — Corsica — Sardinia — Mediolanum — RECIA — NORICUM — PANNONIA — ITALY — ROME — TYRRHENIAN SEA — Sicily — Carthage — AFRICA — Melitus — DALMATIA — ILLYRICUM — ADRIATIC SEA — MACEDONIA — GREECE — IONIAN SEA — M. IONICUM — Athens — AEGEAN SEA — MARE INTERNUM — TRIPOLITANIA — CYRENAICA — Cyrene — BLACK SEA — PAPHLAGONIA — ASIA MINOR — MYSIA — PHRYGIA — Pergamum — LYDIA — PAMPHYLIA — Miletus — CILICIA — LYCIA — Rhodes — Crete — Cyprus — Antioch — SYRIA — Damascus — Tyre — PALESTINE — Jerusalem — EGYPT — Alexandria

---

THE ROMAN WORLD AT THE BEGINNING OF THE CHRISTIAN ERA — **(a)** Historically, the "Pax Romana" ("Peace of Rome") inaugurates a new period for the Mediterranean world; the era of conflicts is over: from the **Rhone to the Indus,** Rome acts as the guarantor of public order and unity. **(b)** Economically, this world enjoys a considerable prosperity over the past, though it continues to retain privileged groups: transportation and commerce are facilitated by fast sea lanes and a vast network of roads linking interior places with the principal ports. **(c)** Socially, the two extremes of the ladder (the rich and the poor) preserve their traditional status but the intervening rungs consisting of free men by birth or enfranchisement enjoy more benefits than ever. **(d)** Culturally, there is at least a surface unity as a result of the Hellenization process brought about by Alexander the Great (336-323) through his conquests and by the dynasties that succeeded him. **(e)** Religiously, the Jewish piety offers what neither the civic nor the oriental religions nor the various philosophies can give: the discovery of a unique God, creator of the world and Lord of history, a light for the moral eye and wisdom for the mind—above all, a God who listens to the poor, dispenses justice and mercy, and holds out the hope of a definitive salvation.

salem with a strong force. ²¹ He insolently invaded the sanctuary and took away the golden altar, the lampstand for the light with all its fixtures, ²² the offering table, the cups and the bowls, the golden censers, the curtain, the crowns, and the golden ornament on the façade of the temple. He stripped off everything, ²³ and took away the gold and silver and the precious vessels; he also took all the hidden treasures he could find. ²⁴ Taking all this, he went back to his own country, after he had spoken with great arrogance and shed much blood.

25 And there was great mourning for Israel, in every place where they dwelt,
26   and the rulers and the elders groaned.
Virgins and young men languished,
and the beauty of the women was disfigured.
27 Every bridegroom took up lamentation,
she who sat in the bridal chamber mourned,
28 And the land was shaken on account of its inhabitants,
and all the house of Jacob was covered with shame.

29 ʰ Two years later, the king sent the Mysian commander to the cities of Judah, and he came to Jerusalem with a strong force. ³⁰ He spoke to them deceitfully in peaceful terms, and won their trust. Then he attacked the city suddenly, in a great onslaught, and destroyed many of the people in Israel. ³¹ He plundered the city and set fire to it, demolished its houses and its surrounding walls, ³² took captive the women and children, and seized the cattle. ³³ Then they built up the City of David* with a high, massive wall and strong towers, and it became their citadel.ⁱ ³⁴ There they installed a sinful race, perverse men, who fortified themselves inside it, ³⁵ storing up weapons and provisions, and depositing there the plunder they had col-

lected from Jerusalem. And they became a great threat.

36 The citadel became an ambush against the sanctuary,
and a wicked adversary to Israel at all times.
37 And they shed innocent blood around the sanctuary;
they defiled the sanctuary.
38 Because of them the inhabitants of Jerusalem fled away,
and she became the abode of strangers.
She became a stranger to her own offspring,
and her children forsook her.
39 Her sanctuary was as desolate as a wilderness;ʲ
her feasts were turned into mourning,
Her sabbaths to shame,
her honor to contempt.
40 Her dishonor was as great as her glory had been,
and her exaltation was turned into mourning.

Prohibitions against Religion. ⁴¹ Then the king wrote to his whole kingdom that all should be one people, ⁴² each abandoning his particular customs. All the Gentiles conformed to the command of the king, ⁴³ and many Israelites were in favor of his religion; they sacrificed to idols and profaned the sabbath.

44 ᵏ The king sent messengers with letters to Jerusalem and to the cities of Judah, ordering them to follow customs foreign to their land: ⁴⁵ to prohibit holocausts, sacrifices, and libations in the sanctuary, to profane the sabbaths and feast days, ⁴⁶ ˡ to desecrate the sanctuary and the sacred ministers, to build pagan altars and temples and shrines, ⁴⁷ to sacrifice swine and unclean animals, ⁴⁸ to leave their sons uncircumcised, and to let themselves be defiled with every kind of impurity and abomination, ⁴⁹ so that they might forget the law and change all their observances. ⁵⁰ Whoever refused to act according to the command of the king should be put to death.ᵐ

51 Such were the orders he published throughout his kingdom. He appointed inspectors over all the people, and he ordered the cities of Judah to offer sacrifices, each city in turn. ⁵² Many of the people,

---

h 29-32: 2 Mc 5, 24ff.—i 1 Mc 6, 18.—j 39f: Tb 2, 6; Am 8, 10.—k 44-63: 2 Mc 6, 1-11.—l 2 Mc 6, 2; Dn 9, 27.—m 2 Mc 6, 18—7, 41.

1, 33: *City of David:* not Mount Zion on the eastern hill of Jerusalem, which David captured from the Jebusites (2 Sm 5, 7), but a new fortress built on the western hill and overlooking the temple and its courts on Mount Zion. It was occupied for twenty-six years by the Syro-Macedonian garrison, together with apostate Jews, and was a continual threat to the temple and the Jewish people (v 36); cf 1 Mc 13, 49ff.

those who abandoned the law, joined them and committed evil in the land. [53] Israel was driven into hiding, wherever places of refuge could be found.

[54] On the fifteenth day of the month Chislev, in the year one hundred and forty-five,* the king erected the horrible abomination upon the altar of holocausts, and in the surrounding cities of Judah they built pagan altars.[n] [55] They also burnt incense at the doors of houses and in the streets. [56] Any scrolls of the law* which they found they tore up and burnt. [57] Whoever was found with a scroll of the covenant, and whoever observed the law, was condemned to death by royal decree.[o] [58] So they used their power against Israel, against those who were caught, each month, in the cities. [59] On the twenty-fifth day of each month they sacrificed on the altar erected over the altar of holocausts. [60] [p] Women who had had their children circumcised were put to death, in keeping with the decree, [61] with the babies hung from their necks; their families also and those who had circumcised them were killed. [62] But many in Israel were determined and resolved in their hearts not to eat anything unclean; [63] they preferred to die rather than to be defiled with unclean food or to profane the holy covenant; and they did die. Terrible affliction was upon Israel.[q]

CHAPTER 2

Mattathias and His Sons. [1] In those days Mattathias, son of John, son of Simeon, a priest of the family of Joarib, left Jerusalem and settled in Modein.* [2] He had five sons: John, who was called Gaddi;[r] [3] Simon, who was called Thassi; [4] Judas, who was called Maccabeus; [5] Eleazar, who was called Avaran; and Jonathan, who was called Apphus. [6] When he saw the sacrileges that were being committed in Judah and in Jerusalem, [7] he said: "Woe is me! Why was I born to see the ruin of my people and the ruin of the holy city, and to sit idle while it is given into the hands of enemies, and the sanctuary into the hands of strangers?

[8] "Her temple has become like a man disgraced,

[9] her glorious ornaments have been carried off as spoils,

Her infants have been murdered in her streets,
her young men by the sword of the enemy.[s]

[10] What nation has not taken its share of her realm,
and laid its hand on her possessions?

[11] All her adornment has been taken away. From being free, she has become a slave.

[12] We see our sanctuary and our beauty and our glory laid waste,
And the Gentiles have defiled them!

[13] Why are we still alive?"

[14] Then Mattathias and his sons tore their garments, put on sackcloth, and mourned bitterly.

Pagan Worship Refused. [15] The officers of the king in charge of enforcing the apostasy came to the city of Modein to organize the sacrifices. [16] Many of Israel joined them, but Mattathias and his sons gathered in a group apart. [17] Then the officers of the king addressed Mattathias: "You are a leader, an honorable and great man in this city, supported by sons and kinsmen. [18] Come now, be the first to obey the king's command, as all the Gentiles and the men of Judah and those who are left in Jerusalem have done. Then you and your sons shall be numbered among the King's Friends,* and shall be enriched with silver and gold and many gifts." [19] But Mattathias answered in a loud voice: "Although all the Gentiles in the king's realm obey him, so that each forsakes the religion of his fathers and consents to the king's orders, [20] yet I and my sons and my kinsmen will keep to the covenant of our fathers. [21] God forbid that we should forsake the law and the commandments. [22] We will not obey the words of the king nor depart from our religion in the slightest degree."

---

n 1 Mc 6, 7; Dn 9, 27; 11, 31.—o 2 Mc 2, 14.—p 60f: 2 Mc 6, 10.—q 2 Mc 6, 10.—r 1 Chr 24, 7.—s Lam 2, 11. 21.

1, 54: *Fifteenth day of the month Chislev in the year one hundred and forty-five:* early December, 167 B.C. *Horrible abomination:* in the original Hebrew, a contemptuous pun on the title "Lord of heaven" given to the god Zeus Olympios, to whom an image or perhaps an altar was erected *upon the altar of holocausts* in the temple of Jerusalem; cf Dn 9, 27; 11, 31.

1, 56f: *Scrolls of the law:* one or more of the first five books of the Old Testament.

2, 1: *Modein:* a village twenty miles northwest of Jerusalem.

2, 18: *The King's Friends:* a regular order of nobility at Hellenistic courts. The various grades are frequently mentioned in this book: Friends, Chief Friends, Kinsmen.

23 As he finished saying these words, a certain Jew came forward in the sight of all to offer sacrifice on the altar in Modein according to the king's order. 24 When Mattathias saw him, he was filled with zeal; his heart was moved and his just fury was aroused; he sprang forward and killed him upon the altar. 25 At the same time, he also killed the messenger of the king who was forcing them to sacrifice, and he tore down the altar. 26 Thus he showed his zeal for the law, just as Phinehas did with Zimri, son of Salu.*t*

27 Then Mattathias went through the city shouting, "Let everyone who is zealous for the law and who stands by the covenant follow after me!" 28 Thereupon he fled to the mountains with his sons, leaving behind in the city all their possessions.*u* 29 Many who sought to live according to righteousness and religious custom went out into the desert* to settle there, 30 they and their sons, their wives and their cattle, because misfortunes pressed so hard on them.

31 It was reported to the officers and soldiers of the king who were in the City of David, in Jerusalem, that certain men who had flouted the king's order had gone out to the hiding places in the desert. 32 *v* Many hurried out after them, and having caught up with them, camped opposite and prepared to attack them on the sabbath. 33 "Enough of this!" the pursuers said to them. "Come out and obey the king's command, and your lives will be spared." 34 But they replied, "We will not come out, nor will we obey the king's command to profane the sabbath." 35 Then the enemy attacked them at once; 36 but they did not retaliate; they neither threw stones, nor blocked up their own hiding places. 37 They said, "Let us all die without reproach; heaven and earth are our witnesses that you destroy us unjustly." 38 So the officers and soldiers attacked

them on the sabbath, and they died with their wives, their children and their cattle, to the number of a thousand persons.

39 When Mattathias and his friends heard of it, they mourned deeply for them. 40 "If we all do as our kinsmen have done," they said to one another, "and do not fight against the Gentiles for our lives and our traditions, they will soon destroy us from the earth." 41 On that day they came to this decision: "Let us fight against anyone who attacks us on the sabbath, so that we may not all die as our kinsmen died in the hiding places."

42 Then they were joined by a group of Hasideans,* valiant Israelites, all of them devout followers of the law. 43 And all those who were fleeing from the disaster joined them and supported them. 44 They gathered an army and struck down sinners in their anger and law-breakers in their wrath, and the survivors fled to the Gentiles for safety.*w* 45 Mattathias and his friends went about and tore down the pagan altars; 46 they also forcibly circumcised any uncircumcised boys whom they found in the territory of Israel. 47 They put to flight the arrogant, and the work prospered in their hands. 48 They saved the law from the hands of the Gentiles and of the kings and did not let the sinner triumph.

Death of Mattathias. 49 When the time came for Mattathias to die, he said to his sons: "Arrogance and scorn have now grown strong; it is a time of disaster and violent anger. 50 Therefore, my sons, be zealous for the law and give your lives for the covenant of our fathers.

51 "Remember the deeds that our fathers
    did in their times,
  and you shall win great glory and an
    everlasting name.
52 Was not Abraham found faithful in
    trial,
  and it was reputed to him as uprightness?*x*
53 Joseph, when in distress, kept the
    commandment,
  and he became master of Egypt.*y*
54 Phinehas our father, for his burning
    zeal,
  received the covenant of an everlasting priesthood.*z*

---

t 1 Mc 2, 54; Nm 25, 6-14.—u 2 Mc 5, 27.—v 32-38: 2 Mc 6, 11.—w Is 63, 3.—x Gn 15, 6; 22, 1ff.—y Gn 39, 7-10; 41, 39-43.—z Nm 25, 10-13; Sir 45, 28ff.

2, 29: *The desert:* the sparsely inhabited mountain country southward from Jerusalem and west of the Dead Sea. It was an arid region with some perennial springs and a fair amount of rain in winter.

2, 42: *Hasideans:* in Hebrew *hasidim,* "pious ones," a religious group devoted to the strict observance of the law. They were the forerunners of both the Pharisees and the Essenes. They first supported the Maccabean movement, but subsequently opposed it, regarding it as too political.

1Mc

⁵⁵ Joshua, for executing his commission,
    became a judge in Israel.ᵃ
⁵⁶ Caleb, for bearing witness before the assembly,
    received an inheritance in the land.ᵇ
⁵⁷ David, for his piety,
    received as a heritage a throne of
    everlasting royalty.ᶜ
⁵⁸ Elijah, for his burning zeal for the law,
    was taken up to heaven.ᵈ
⁵⁹ Hananiah, Azariah and Mishael, for
    their faith,
    were saved from the fire.ᵉ
⁶⁰ Daniel, for his innocence,
    was delivered from the jaws of lions.ᶠ
⁶¹ And so, consider this from generation
    to generation,
    that none who hope in him shall fail
    in strength.
⁶² Do not fear the words of a sinful man,
    for his glory ends in corruption and
    worms.
⁶³ Today he is exalted, and tomorrow he is
    not to be found,
    because he has returned to his dust,
    and his schemes have perished.
⁶⁴ Children! be courageous and strong in
    keeping the law,
    for by it you shall be glorified.

⁶⁵ "Here is your brother Simeon who I know is a wise man; listen to him always, and he will be a father to you. ⁶⁶ And Judas Maccabeus, a warrior from his youth, shall be the leader of your army and direct the war against the nations. ⁶⁷ You shall also gather about you all who observe the law, and you shall avenge the wrongs of your people. ⁶⁸ Pay back the Gentiles what they deserve, and observe the precepts of the law."

⁶⁹ Then he blessed them, and he was united with his fathers. ⁷⁰ He died in the year one hundred and forty-six,* and was buried in the tombs of his fathers in Modein, and all Israel mourned him greatly.

III: LEADERSHIP OF JUDAS MACCABEUS

CHAPTER 3

Defeat of Apollonius and Seron. ¹ Then his son Judas, who was called Maccabeus, took his place. ² All his brothers and all who had joined his father supported him, and they carried on Israel's war joyfully.

³ He spread abroad the glory of his people,
    and put on his breastplate like a
    giant.
He armed himself with weapons of war;
    he planned battles and protected the
    camp with his sword.ᵍ
⁴ In his actions he was like a lion,
    like a young lion roaring for prey.
⁵ He pursued the wicked, hunting them
    out,
    and those who troubled his people he
    destroyed by fire.
⁶ The lawbreakers were cowed by fear of
    him,
    and all evildoers were dismayed.
By his hand redemption was happily
    achieved,
⁷ and he afflicted many kings;
He made Jacob glad by his deeds,
    and his memory is blessed forever.
⁸ He went about the cities of Judah
    destroying the impious there.
He turned away wrath from Israel
⁹ and was renowned to the ends of the
    earth;
    he gathered together those who were
    perishing.

¹⁰ Then Apollonius* gathered the Gentiles, together with a large army from Samaria, to fight against Israel. ¹¹ When Judas learned of it, he went out to meet him and defeated and killed him. Many fell wounded, and the rest fled. ¹² Their possessions were seized and the sword of Apollonius was taken by Judas, who fought with it the rest of his life.

¹³ But Seron, commander of the Syrian army, heard that Judas had gathered many about him, an assembly of faithful men ready for war. ¹⁴ So he said, "I will make a name for myself and win glory in the kingdom by defeating Judas and his followers, who have despised the king's command." ¹⁵ And again a large company of renegades advanced with him to help him take revenge on the Israelites.

---

a Jos 1, 2. 5.—b Nm 13, 30; 14, 6-9. 24; Jos 14, 14.—c 2 Sm 2, 4; 7, 16.—d 1 Kgs 19, 10. 14; 2 Kgs 2, 11.—e Dn 3, 50.—f Dn 6, 23; 14, 31-42.—g 2 Mc 8, 5.

2, 70: *In the year one hundred and forty-six:* 166 B.C.
3, 10: *Apollonius:* the Mysian commander mentioned in 1 Mc 1, 29 and in 2 Mc 5, 24.

16 When he reached the ascent of Beth-horon,* Judas went out to meet him with a few men. 17 But when they saw the army coming against them, they said to Judas: "How can we, few as we are, fight such a mighty host as this? Besides, we are weak today from fasting." 18 But Judas said: "It is easy for many to be overcome by a few; in the sight of Heaven there is no difference between deliverance by many or by few; 19 for victory in war does not depend upon the size of the army, but on strength that comes from Heaven. *h* 20 With great presumption and lawlessness they come against us to destroy us and our wives and children and to despoil us; 21 but we are fighting for our lives and our laws. 22 He himself* will crush them before us; so do not be afraid of them." 23 When he finished speaking, he rushed suddenly upon Seron and his army, who were crushed before him. 24 He pursued Seron down the descent of Beth-horon into the plain. About eight hundred* of their men fell, and the rest fled to the country of the Philistines. *i* 25 Then Judas and his brothers began to be feared, and dread fell upon the Gentiles about them. 26 His fame reached the king, and all the Gentiles talked about the battles of Judas.

Regency of Lysias. 27 When Antiochus heard about these events, he was angry; so he ordered a muster of all the forces of his kingdom, a very strong army. 28 He opened his treasure chests, gave his soldiers a year's pay, and commanded them to be prepared for anything. 29 He then found that this exhausted the money in his treasury; moreover the income from the

province was small, because of the dissension and distress he had brought upon the land by abolishing the laws which had been in effect from of old. 30 He feared that, as had happened more than once, he would not have enough for his expenses and for the gifts that he had previously given with a more liberal hand than the preceding kings. 31 Greatly perplexed, he decided to go to Persia and levy tribute on those provinces, and so raise a large sum of money. 32 He left Lysias, a nobleman of royal blood, in charge of the king's affairs from the Euphrates River to the frontier of Egypt, 33 and commissioned him to take care of his son Antiochus until his own return. 34 He entrusted to him half of the army, and the elephants, and gave him instructions concerning everything he wanted done. As for the inhabitants of Judea and Jerusalem, 35 Lysias was to send an army against them to crush and destroy the power of Israel and the remnant of Jerusalem and efface their memory from the land. 36 He was to settle foreigners in all their territory and distribute their land by lot.

37 The king took the remaining half of the army and set out from Antioch, his capital, in the year one hundred and forty-seven; he crossed the Euphrates River and advanced inland.*

The Victories of Judas. 38 *j* Lysias chose Ptolemy, son of Dorymenes, and Nicanor* and Gorgias, capable men among the King's Friends, *k* 39 and with them he sent forty thousand men and seven thousand cavalry to invade the land of Judah and ravage it according to the king's orders. 40 Setting out with all their forces, they came and pitched their camp near Emmaus* in the plain. 41 When the merchants of the country heard of their fame, they came to the camp, bringing fetters and a large sum of silver and gold, to buy the Israelites as slaves. A force from Idumea and from Philistia joined with them.

42 Judas and his brothers saw that the situation had become critical now that armies were encamped within their territory; they knew of the orders which the king had given to destroy and utterly wipe out the people. 43 So they said to one another, "Let us restore our people from their ruined estate, and fight for our people and our sanctuary!"

1Mc

---

h 1 Sm 14, 6.—i Jos 10, 10.—j 38-44: 2 Mc 8, 8-15.—k 38f: 1 Mc 7, 26; 2 Mc 4, 45; 8, 8f; 10, 14.

3, 16: *Beth-horon:* the famous pass leading up from the coastal plain to the Judean hill country. Here Joshua won an important battle (Jos 10, 10f), and in 66 A.D. a Roman force under Cestius was trapped and massacred.
3, 22: *He himself:* out of reverence for God, the author of 1 Mc prefers to use this and other expressions, such as "Heaven," instead of the divine name. Cf 1 Mc 3, 50.
3, 24: *About eight hundred:* the figures given in this book for strength of armies and number of casualties are not to be taken literally. In accordance with biblical usage, they indicate rather the importance of the battle described or the greatness of the victory.
3, 37: This expedition, in the spring of 165 B.C., resulted in failure; cf ch 6.
3, 38: *Nicanor:* the leader of another attack against the Jews four years later. He was finally killed by Judas; cf 1 Mc 7, 26-46.
3, 40: *Emmaus:* probably not the village mentioned in Lk 24, 13, but a settlement about twenty miles west of Jerusalem at the edge of the hill country.

⁴⁴The assembly gathered together to prepare for battle and to pray and implore mercy and compassion.

⁴⁵ Jerusalem was uninhabited, like a desert;
> not one of her children entered or came out.
> The sanctuary was trampled on,
> and foreigners were in the citadel;
> it was a habitation of Gentiles.
> Joy had disappeared from Jacob,
> and the flute and the harp were silent.

⁴⁶ *l* Thus they assembled and went to Mizpah near Jerusalem, because there was formerly at Mizpah a place of prayer for Israel.* ⁴⁷That day they fasted and wore sackcloth; they sprinkled ashes on their heads and tore their clothes. ⁴⁸They unrolled the scroll of the law, to learn about the things for which the Gentiles consulted the images of their idols.* ⁴⁹They brought with them the priestly vestments, the first fruits, and the tithes; and they brought forward the nazirites* who had completed the time of their vows. *m* ⁵⁰And they cried aloud to Heaven: "What shall we do with these men, and where shall we take them? ⁵¹For your sanctuary has been trampled on and profaned, and your priests are in mourning and humiliation. ⁵²Now the Gentiles are gathered together against us to destroy us. You know what they plot against us. ⁵³How shall we be able to resist them unless you help us?" ⁵⁴Then they blew the trumpets and cried out loudly.

⁵⁵After this Judas appointed officers among the people, over thousands, over hundreds, over fifties, and over tens. ⁵⁶He proclaimed that those who were building houses, or were just married, or were planting vineyards, and those who were afraid, could each return to his home, according to the law. *n* ⁵⁷Then the army moved off, and they camped to the south of Emmaus. ⁵⁸Judas said: "Arm yourselves and be brave; in the morning be ready to fight these Gentiles who have assembled against us to destroy us and our sanctuary. ⁵⁹It is better for us to die in battle than to witness the ruin of our nation and our sanctuary. Whatever Heaven wills, he will do." *o*

CHAPTER 4

¹Now Gorgias took five thousand infantry and a thousand picked cavalry, and this detachment set out at night ²in order to attack the camp of the Jews and take them by surprise. Some men from the citadel were their guides. ³Judas heard of it, and himself set out with his soldiers to attack the king's army at Emmaus, ⁴while the latter's forces were still scattered away from the camp. ⁵During the night Gorgias came into the camp of Judas, and found no one there; so he began to hunt for them in the mountains, saying, "They are fleeing from us."

⁶But at daybreak Judas appeared in the plain with three thousand men, who lacked such armor and swords as they would have wished. ⁷They saw the army of the Gentiles, strong and breastplated, flanked with cavalry, and made up of expert soldiers. ⁸Judas said to the men with him: "Do not be afraid of their numbers or dread their attack. ⁹Remember how our fathers were saved in the Red Sea, when Pharaoh pursued them with an army. *p* ¹⁰So now let us cry to Heaven in the hope that he will favor us, remember his covenant with our fathers, and destroy this army before us today. *q* ¹¹All the Gentiles shall know that there is One who redeems and delivers Israel."

¹²When the foreigners looked up and saw them marching toward them, ¹³they came out of their camp for battle, and the men with Judas blew the trumpet. ¹⁴The battle was joined and the Gentiles were defeated and fled toward the plain. ¹⁵Their whole rearguard fell by the sword, and they were pursued as far as Gazara* and the plains of Judea, to Azotus and Jamnia. About three thousand of their men fell.

¹⁶When Judas and the army returned

---

l 46ff: 1 Sm 7, 5f; 2 Mc 8, 16-23.—m Nm 6, 2-5.—n Dt 20, 5-8; Jgs 7, 3.—o 1 Mc 2, 21f.—p Ex 14, 21ff.—q 1 Mc 2, 21.

3, 46: . . . *Mizpah a place of prayer for Israel:* a holy place established of old eight miles north and slightly west of Jerusalem. It was here that Samuel began to judge the Israelites (1 Sm 7, 5-11; 10, 17).

3, 48: *To learn . . . idols:* favorable omens for the coming battle. A contrast is intended between the idol worship of the pagans and the consultation of the word of God by the Jews; cf 2 Mc 8, 23.

3, 49: *Nazirites:* see note on Nm 6, 1ff.

4, 15: *Gazara:* Gezer of the Hebrew Bible, five miles northwest of Emmaus; *Azotus,* Hebrew *Ashdod,* lay to the southwest; and *Jamnia,* Hebrew *Jabneel* (Jos 15, 11) or *Jabneh* (2 Chr 26, 6), to the west of Gazara.

from the pursuit, [17]he said to the people: "Do not be greedy for the plunder, for there is a fight ahead of us, [18]and Gorgias and his army are near us on the mountain. But now stand firm against our enemies and overthrow them. Afterward you can freely take the plunder."

[19]As Judas was finishing this speech, a detachment appeared, looking down from the mountain. [20]They saw that their army had been put to flight and their camp was being burned. The smoke that could be seen indicated what had happened. [21]When they realized this, they were terrified; and when they also saw the army of Judas in the plain ready to attack, [22]they all fled to Philistine territory.*

[23]Then Judas went back to plunder the camp, and his men collected much gold and silver, violet and crimson cloth, and great treasure. [24]As they returned, they were singing hymns and glorifying Heaven, "for he is good, for his mercy endures forever."[r] [25]Thus Israel had a great deliverance that day.

Victory over Lysias. [26] [s] But those of the foreigners who had escaped went and told Lysias all that had occurred. [27]When he heard it he was disturbed and discouraged, because things in Israel had not turned out as he intended and as the king had ordered.

[28]So the following year he gathered together sixty thousand picked men and five thousand cavalry, to subdue them. [29]They came into Idumea and camped at Bethzur,* and Judas met them with ten thousand men. [30]Seeing that the army was strong, he prayed thus:

"Blessed are you, O Savior of Israel, who broke the rush of the mighty one by the hand of your servant David and delivered the camp of the Philistines into the hand of Jonathan, the son of Saul, and his armor-bearer.[t] [31]Give this army into

the hands of your people Israel; make them ashamed of their troops and their cavalry. [32]Strike them with fear, weaken the boldness of their strength, and let them tremble at their own destruction. [33]Strike them down by the sword of those who love you, that all who know your name may hymn your praise."

[34]Then they engaged in battle, and about five thousand of Lysias' men fell in hand-to-hand fighting. [35]When Lysias saw his ranks beginning to give way, and the increased boldness of Judas, whose men were ready either to live or to die bravely, he withdrew to Antioch and began to recruit mercenaries so as to return to Judea with greater numbers.*

Purification of the Temple. [36] [u] Then Judas and his brothers said, "Now that our enemies have been crushed, let us go up to purify the sanctuary* and rededicate it." [37]So the whole army assembled, and went up to Mount Zion. [38]They found the sanctuary desolate, the altar desecrated, the gates burnt, weeds growing in the courts as in a forest or on some mountain, and the priests' chambers demolished.[v] [39]Then they tore their clothes and made great lamentation; they sprinkled their heads with ashes [40]and fell with their faces to the ground. And when the signal was given with trumpets, they cried out to Heaven.

[41]Judas appointed men to attack those in the citadel, while he purified the sanctuary. [42]He chose blameless priests, devoted to the law; [43]these purified the sanctuary and carried away the stones of the Abomination to an unclean place. [44]They deliberated what ought to be done with the altar of holocausts that had been desecrated.[w] [45]The happy thought came to them to tear it down, lest it be a lasting shame to them that the Gentiles had defiled it; so they tore down the altar.[x] [46]They stored the stones in a suitable place on the temple hill, until a prophet should come and decide what to do with them. [47]Then they took uncut stones, according to the law, and built a new altar like the former one.[y] [48]They also repaired the sanctuary and the interior of the temple and purified the courts. [49]They made new sacred vessels and brought the lampstand, the altar of incense, and the table into the temple.[z]

r Ps 118, 1ff. 29.—s 26-35: 2 Mc 11, 1-12.—t 1 Sm 17, 48ff.—u 36-59: 2 Mc 10, 1-8.—v Ps 74, 2-7.—w 1 Kgs 8, 64.—x 1 Mc 6, 7.—y Ex 20, 25.—z Ex 25, 23-39; 30, 1-6.

4, 22: *Philistine territory:* the coastal cities of southern Palestine, traditionally hostile to Jerusalem. Jamnia in particular was an important base for the Seleucid power.

4, 29: *Beth-zur:* an important frontier city in the mountain area, fifteen miles southwest of Jerusalem. Its inhabitants were sympathetic to the Maccabees and refused to receive Lysias.

4, 35: According to 2 Mc 11, 13-15, peace negotiations followed between Lysias and Judas.

4, 36: *The sanctuary:* the whole temple area with its walls, courts and outbuildings, to be distinguished from the temple proper, the oblong edifice with porch, main room and inner shrine.

⁵⁰Then they burned incense on the altar and lighted the lamps on the lampstand, and these illuminated the temple. ᵃ ⁵¹They also put loaves on the table and hung up the curtains. Thus they finished all the work they had undertaken.

⁵²Early in the morning on the twenty-fifth day of the ninth month, that is, the month of Chislev, in the year one hundred and forty-eight,* ⁵³they arose and offered sacrifice according to the law on the new altar of holocausts that they had made. ᵇ ⁵⁴On the anniversary of the day on which the Gentiles had defiled it, on that very day it was reconsecrated with songs, harps, flutes, and cymbals. ⁵⁵All the people prostrated themselves and adored and praised Heaven, who had given them success.

⁵⁶For eight days they celebrated the dedication of the altar and joyfully offered holocausts and sacrifices of deliverance and praise. ⁵⁷They ornamented the façade of the temple with gold crowns and shields; they repaired the gates and the priests' chambers and furnished them with doors. ⁵⁸There was great joy among the people now that the disgrace of the Gentiles was removed. ⁵⁹Then Judas and his brothers and the entire congregation of Israel decreed that the days of the dedication* of the altar should be observed with joy and gladness on the anniversary every year for eight days, from the twenty-fifth day of the month Chislev. ᶜ

⁶⁰At that time they built high walls and strong towers around Mount Zion, to prevent the Gentiles from coming and trampling over it as they had done before. ⁶¹Judas also placed a garrison there to protect it, and likewise fortified Beth-zur, that the people might have a stronghold facing Idumea.

CHAPTER 5*

Punishment of Hostile Acts. ¹ ᵈ When the Gentiles round about heard that the altar had been rebuilt and the sanctuary consecrated as before, they were very angry. ²So they decided to destroy the descendants of Jacob who were among them, and they began to massacre and persecute the people. ³ ᵉ Then Judas attacked the sons of Esau at Akrabattene* in Idumea, because they were blockading Israel; he defeated them heavily, overcame and de-

spoiled them. ⁴He also remembered the malice of the sons of Baean,* who had become a snare and a stumbling block to the people by ambushing them along the roads. ⁵He forced them to take refuge in towers, which he besieged; he vowed their annihilation and burned down the towers along with all the persons in them. ⁶ * Then he crossed over to the Ammonites, where he found a strong army and a large body of people with Timothy as their leader. ⁷He fought many battles with them, routed them, and struck them down. ⁸After seizing Jazer and its villages, he returned to Judea.

Liberation of Galilean Jews. ⁹The Gentiles in Gilead assembled to attack and destroy the Israelites who were in their territory; these then fled to the stronghold of Dathema. ¹⁰They sent a letter to Judas and his brothers saying: "The Gentiles around us have combined against us to destroy us, ¹¹and they are preparing to come and seize this stronghold to which we have fled. Timothy is the leader of their army. ¹²Come at once and rescue us from them, for many of us have fallen. ¹³All our kinsmen who were among the Tobiads have been killed; the Gentiles have carried away their wives and children and their goods, and they have slain there about a thousand men." ᶠ

¹⁴While they were reading this letter, suddenly other messengers, in torn clothes, arrived from Galilee to deliver a similar message: ¹⁵that the inhabitants of Ptolemais,* Tyre, and Sidon, and the whole of Gentile Galilee had joined forces to destroy them. ¹⁶When Judas and the people heard this, a great assembly con-

---

a Ex 30, 7ff.—b 53. 56: Ex 30, 10; Ez 43, 18-27.—c Jn 10, 22.—d 1f: 1 Mc 13, 6.—e 3ff: 2 Mc 10, 15-23.—f 2 Mc 12, 17.

4, 52: *Twenty-fifth day of the ninth month . . . in the year one hundred and forty-eight:* December 14, 164 B.C.

4, 59: *Days of the dedication . . . Chislev:* institution of the feast of Hanukkah, also called the feast of Dedication (Jn 10, 22). Josephus Flavius calls it the feast of Lights.

5, 1: The events of this chapter occurred within the year 163 B.C.

5, 3: *Akrabattene:* a district southwest of the Dead Sea.

5, 4: *Sons of Baean:* 2 Mc 10, 15-23 calls them simply Idumeans.

5, 6ff: This summary anticipates the order of events and would fit better between vv 36 and 37. It corresponds to 2 Mc 12, 17-23. The action was probably a reprisal for the massacre referred to in v 13. Timothy was the Seleucid governor of Transjordan. *Jazer:* a town on the road from the Jordan to Amman.

5, 15: *Ptolemais:* Hebrew Acco (Jgs 1, 31), modern Acre, on the coast north of Haifa.

vened to consider what they should do for their unfortunate kinsmen who were being attacked by enemies. [17] Judas said to his brother Simon: "Choose men for yourself, and go, rescue your kinsmen in Galilee; I and my brother Jonathan will go to Gilead." [18] In Judea he left Joseph, son of Zechariah, and Azariah, leader of the people, with the rest of the army to guard it. [19] "Take charge of these people," he commanded them, "but do not fight against the Gentiles until we return." [20] Three thousand men were allotted to Simon, to go into Galilee, and eight thousand men to Judas, for Gilead. [21] Simon went into Galilee and fought many battles with the Gentiles. They were crushed before him, [22] and he pursued them to the very gate of Ptolemais. About three thousand men of the Gentiles fell, and he gathered their spoils. [23] He took with him the Jews who were in Galilee and in Arbatta, with their wives and children and all that they had, and brought them to Judea with great rejoicing.

Rescue in Gilead. [24] [g] Judas Maccabeus and his brother Jonathan crossed the Jordan and marched for three days through the desert. [25] There they met some Nabateans,* who received them peacefully and told them all that had happened to the Jews in Gilead: [26] "Many of them have been imprisoned in Bozrah, in Bosor near Alema, in Chaspho, Maked, and Carnaim" all of these are large fortified cities—[27] "and some have been imprisoned in the other cities of Gilead. Tomorrow their enemies plan to attack the strongholds and to seize and destroy all these people in one day."

[28] Thereupon Judas suddenly changed direction with his army, marched across the desert to Bozrah, and captured the city. He slaughtered all the male population, took all their possessions, and set fire to the city. [29] He led his army from that place by night, and they marched toward the stronghold of Dathema. [30] When

morning came, they looked ahead and saw a countless multitude of people, with ladders and devices for capturing the stronghold, and beginning to attack the people within. [31] When Judas perceived that the struggle had begun and that the noise of the battle was resounding to heaven with trumpet blasts and loud shouting, [32] he said to the men of his army, "Fight for our kinsmen today."

[33] He came up behind them with three columns blowing their trumpets and shouting in prayer. [34] When the army of Timothy realized that it was Maccabeus, they fell back before him, and he inflicted on them a crushing defeat. About eight thousand of their men fell that day. [35] Then he turned toward Alema and attacked and captured it; he killed all the male population, plundered the place, and burned it down. [36] From there he moved on and took Chaspho, Maked, Bosor, and the other cities of Gilead.

[37] [h] After these events Timothy assembled another army and camped opposite Raphon, on the other side of the stream. [38] Judas sent men to spy on the camp, and they reported to him: "All the Gentiles around us have rallied to him, making a very large force; [39] they have also hired Arabs to help them, and have camped beyond the stream, ready to attack you." So Judas went forward to attack them.

[40] As Judas and his army were approaching the running stream, Timothy said to the officers of his army: "If he crosses over to us first, we shall not be able to resist him; he will certainly defeat us. [i] [41] But if he is afraid and camps on the other side of the river, we will cross over to him and defeat him."

[42] But when Judas reached the running stream, he stationed the officers of the people beside the stream and gave them this order: "Do not allow any man to pitch a tent; all must go into battle." [43] He was the first to cross to the attack, with all the people behind him, and the Gentiles were crushed before them; they threw away their arms and fled to the temple enclosure at Carnaim. [44] The Jews captured that city and burnt the enclosure with all who were in it. So Carnaim was subdued, and Judas met with no more resistance. [j]

[45] Then he assembled all the Israelites, great and small, who were in Gilead, with

---

g 24-36: 2 Mc 12, 10ff.—h 37-44: 2 Mc 12, 20-26.—i 1 Sm 14, 9f.—j 2 Mc 12, 21.

5, 25: *Nabateans:* an Arab people who acquired wealth and power as caravan merchants in the final two centuries B.C. They settled down, established Petra as their capital, and for a time controlled all of Transjordan, even as far as Damascus. It was from a Nabatean governor that St. Paul escaped about 38 A.D. (2 Cor 11, 32f).

their wives and children and their goods, a great crowd of people, to go into the land of Judah. [46] *k* When they reached Ephron,* a large and strongly fortified city along the way, they found it impossible to encircle it on either the right or the left; they would have to march right through it. [47] But the men in the city shut them out and blocked up the gates with stones.[l] [48] Then Judas sent them this peaceful message: "We wish to cross your territory in order to reach our own; no one will harm you; we will only march through." But they would not open to him.

[49] So Judas ordered a proclamation to be made in the camp that everyone make an attack from the place where he was. [50] When the men of the army took up their positions, he assaulted the city all that day and night, and it was delivered to him. [51] He slaughtered every male, razed and plundered the city, and passed through it over the slain.

[52] Then they crossed the Jordan to the great plain in front of Beth-shan; [53] and Judas kept rounding up the stragglers and encouraging the people the whole way, until he reached the land of Judah. [54] They ascended Mount Zion in joy and gladness and offered holocausts, because not one of them had fallen; they returned in safety.

Joseph and Azariah Defeated. [55] During the time that Judas and Jonathan were in the land of Gilead, and Simon his brother was in Galilee opposite Ptolemais, [56] Joseph, son of Zechariah, and Azariah, the leaders of the army, heard about the brave deeds and the fighting that they were doing. [57] They said, "Let us also make a name for ourselves by going out and fighting against the Gentiles around us."

[58] They gave orders to the men of their army who were with them, and marched toward Jamnia. [59] But Gorgias and his men came out of the city to meet them in battle. [60] Joseph and Azariah were beaten, and were pursued to the frontiers of Judea, and about two thousand Israelites fell that day. [61] It was a bad defeat for the people, because they had not obeyed Judas and his brothers, thinking that they would do brave deeds. [62] But they did not belong to the family of those men to whom it was granted to achieve Israel's salvation. [63] The valiant Judas and his brothers were greatly renowned in all Israel and among all the Gentiles, wherever their name was heard; [64] and men gathered about them and praised them.

[65] Then Judas and his brothers went out and attacked the sons of Esau* in the country toward the south; he took Hebron and its villages, and he destroyed its strongholds and burned the towers around it. [66] He then set out for the land of the Philistines and passed through Marisa. [67] At that time some priests fell in battle who had gone out rashly to fight in their desire to distinguish themselves. [68] Judas then turned toward Azotus in the land of the Philistines. He destroyed their altars and burned the statues of their gods; and after plundering their cities he returned to the land of Judah.

CHAPTER 6

Defeat and Death of Antiochus IV. [1] *m* As King Antiochus was traversing the inland provinces, he heard that in Persia there was a city called Elymais,* famous for its wealth in silver and gold, [2] and that its temple was very rich, containing gold helmets, breastplates, and weapons left there by Alexander, son of Philip, king of Macedon, the first king of the Greeks. [3] He went therefore and tried to capture and pillage the city. But he could not do so, because his plan became known to the people of the city [4] who rose up in battle against him. So he retreated and in great dismay withdrew from there to return to Babylon.

[5] While he was in Persia, a messenger brought him news that the armies sent into the land of Judah had been put to flight; [6] that Lysias had gone at first with a strong army and been driven back by the Israelites; that they had grown strong by reason of the arms, men, and abundant possessions taken from the armies they had destroyed; [7] that they had pulled down the

---

k 46-54: 2 Mc 12, 27-31.—l Nm 20, 17-21; 21, 21-25.—m 1-13: 2 Mc 1, 12-17; 9, 1-29.

5, 46: *Ephron:* a city in Trans-Jordan opposite Beth-shan, about five miles east of the Jordan River. Situated on a height, it dominated the valleys of the two tributaries of the Jordan.
5, 65: *Sons of Esau:* Idumeans.
6, 1: *Elymais:* the mountainous region of Elam, north of the Persian Gulf. This section continues the story from 1 Mc 3, 37 and pertains to events preceding those in 1 Mc 4, 37ff.

Abomination which he had built upon the altar in Jerusalem; and that they had surrounded with high walls both the sanctuary, as it had been before, and his city of Beth-zur.[n]

[8] When the king heard this news, he was struck with fear and very much shaken. Sick with grief because his designs had failed, he took to his bed. [9] There he remained many days, overwhelmed with sorrow, for he knew he was going to die.

[10] So he called in all his Friends and said to them: "Sleep has departed from my eyes, for my heart is sinking with anxiety. [11] I said to myself: 'Into what tribulation have I come, and in what floods of sorrow am I now! [12] Yet I was kindly and beloved in my rule.' But I now recall the evils I did in Jerusalem, when I carried away all the vessels of gold and silver that were in it, and for no cause gave orders that the inhabitants of Judah be destroyed. [13] I know that this is why these evils have overtaken me; and now I am dying, in bitter grief, in a foreign land."

[14] Then he summoned Philip, one of his Friends, and put him in charge of his whole kingdom. [15] He gave him his crown, his robe, and his signet ring, so that he might guide the king's son Antiochus and bring him up to be king. [16] King Antiochus died in Persia in the year one hundred and forty-nine.[*]

The Citadel Besieged. [17] When Lysias learned that the king was dead, he set up the king's son Antiochus,[*] whom he had reared as a child, to be king in his place; and he gave him the title Eupator.[o]

[18] The men in the citadel were hemming in Israel around the sanctuary, continually trying to harm them and to strengthen the Gentiles.[p] [19] But Judas planned to destroy them, and called all the people together to

besiege them. [20] So in the year one hundred and fifty[*] they assembled and stormed the citadel, for which purpose he constructed catapults and other devices. [21] Some of the besieged escaped, joined by impious Israelites; [22] they went to the king and said:

"How long will you fail to do justice and avenge our kinsmen? [23] We agreed to serve your father and to follow his orders and obey his edicts. [24] And for this the sons of our people have become our enemies; they have put to death as many of us as they could find and have plundered our estates. [25] They have acted aggressively not only against us, but throughout their whole territory. [26] Look! They have now besieged the citadel in Jerusalem in order to capture it, and they have fortified the sanctuary and Beth-zur. [27] Unless you quickly forestall them, they will do even worse things than these, and you will not be able to stop them."

Campaign against Judas. [28] [q] When the king heard this he was angry, and he called together all his Friends, the officers of his army, and the commanders of the cavalry.[r] [29] Mercenary forces also came to him from other kingdoms and from the islands of the seas. [30] His army numbered a hundred thousand foot-soldiers, twenty thousand cavalry, and thirty-two elephants trained for war. [31] They passed through Idumea and camped before Beth-zur. For many days they attacked it; they constructed siege-devices, but the besieged made a sortie and burned these, and they fought bravely.

[32] Then Judas marched away from the citadel and moved his camp to Bethzechariah, on the way to the king's camp. [33] The king, rising before dawn, moved his force hastily along the road to Bethzechariah; and the armies prepared for battle, while the trumpets sounded. [34] They made the elephants drunk on grape and mulberry wine to provoke them to fight. [35] The beasts were distributed along the phalanxes, each elephant having assigned to it a thousand men in coats of mail, with bronze helmets, and five hundred picked cavalry. [36] These anticipated the beast wherever it was; and wherever it moved, they moved too and never left it. [37] A strong wooden tower covering each elephant, and fastened to it by a

---

n 1 Mc 1, 54; 4, 41ff. 60f.—o 2 Mc 10, 10f.—p 1 Mc 1, 33ff.—q 28-54: 2 Mc 13, 1-23.—r 28ff: 2 Mc 13, 1f.

6, 16: *The year one hundred and forty-nine:* September 22, 164, to October 9, 163 B.C. A Babylonian list of the Seleucid kings indicates that Antiochus died in November or early December of 164.

6, 17: *The king's son Antiochus:* Antiochus V Eupator, then about nine years old. He was in Antioch, still in the charge of Lysias, who proceeded to govern and wage wars in his name. Both were put to death two years later, when Demetrius, brother of Antiochus IV, arrived to claim the kingship; cf 1 Mc 7, 1ff.

6, 20: *The year one hundred and fifty:* October, 163, to September, 162 B.C.

harness, held, besides the Indian mahout, three soldiers who fought from it. [38] The remaining cavalry were stationed on one or the other of the two flanks of the army, to harass the enemy and to be protected from the phalanxes. [39] When the sun shone on the gold and bronze shields, the mountains gleamed with their brightness and blazed like flaming torches. [40] Part of the king's army extended over the heights, while some were on low ground, but they marched forward steadily and in good order. [41] All who heard the noise of their numbers, the tramp of their marching, and the clashing of the arms, trembled; for the army was very great and strong.

[42] Judas with his army advanced to fight, and six hundred men of the king's army fell. [43] Eleazar, called Avaran, saw one of the beasts bigger than any of the others and covered with royal armor, and he thought the king must be on it. [s] [44] So he gave up his life to save his people and win an everlasting name for himself. [45] He dashed up to it in the middle of the phalanx, killing men right and left, so that they fell back from him on both sides. [46] He ran right under the elephant and stabbed it in the belly, killing it. The beast fell to the ground on top of him, and he died there.

[47] When the Jews saw the strength of the royal army and the ardor of its forces, they retreated from them. [48] [t] A part of the king's army went up to Jerusalem to attack them, and the king established camps in Judea and at Mount Zion. [49] [u] He made peace with the men of Beth-zur, and they evacuated the city, because they had no food there to enable them to stand a siege, for that was a sabbath year in the land.* [50] The king took Beth-zur and stationed a garrison there to hold it. [51] For many days he besieged the sanctuary, setting up artillery and machines, fire-throwers, catapults and mechanical bows for shooting arrows and slingstones. [52] The Jews countered by setting up machines of their own, and kept up the fight a long time. [53] But there were no provisions in the storerooms, because it was the seventh year, and the tide-over provisions had been eaten up by those who had been rescued from the Gentiles and brought to Judea. [54] Few men remained in the sanctuary; the rest scattered, each to

his own home, for the famine was too much for them.

Peace Treaty. [55] [n] Lysias heard that Philip, whom King Antiochus, before his death, had appointed to train his son Antiochus to be king, [56] had returned from Persia and Media with the army that accompanied the king, and that he was seeking to take over the government. [57] So he hastily resolved to withdraw. He said to the king, the leaders of the army, and the soldiers: "We are growing weaker every day, our provisions are scanty, the place we are besieging is strong, and it is our duty to take care of the affairs of the kingdom. [w] [58] Therefore let us now come to terms with these men, and make peace with them and all their nation. [59] Let us grant them freedom to live according to their own laws as formerly; it was on account of their laws, which we abolished, that they became angry and did all these things."

[60] The proposal found favor with the king and the leaders; he sent peace terms to the Jews, and they accepted. [61] So the king and the leaders swore an oath to them, and on these terms they evacuated the fortification. [62] But when the king entered Mount Zion and saw how the place was fortified, he broke the oath he had sworn and gave orders for the encircling wall to be destroyed. [63] Then he departed in haste and returned to Antioch, where he found Philip in possession of the city. He fought against him and took the city by force.

CHAPTER 7

Expedition of Bacchides and Alcimus. [1] [x] In the year one hundred and fifty-one,* Demetrius, son of Seleucus, set out from Rome, arrived with a few men in a city on the seacoast, and began to rule there. [2] As he was preparing to enter the royal

---

s 2 Mc 13, 15.—t 48f: 2 Mc 13, 22-23.—u Lv 25, 2.—v 55-63: 2 Mc 13, 23-26.—w 2 Mc 11, 13ff.—x 1-7: 2 Mc 14, 1-11.

6, 49: *A sabbath year in the land:* when sowing and reaping were prohibited (Ex 23, 10f; Lv 25, 2-7). The year without a harvest (autumn of 164 to autumn of 163) was followed by a food shortage.

7, 1ff: *The year one hundred and fifty-one:* the spring of 161 B.C. *Demetrius,* son of Seleucus, was the lawful heir to the kingdom; but when only nine years old, he was taken as a hostage at Rome in place of his uncle, who ruled as Antiochus IV Epiphanes. At the age of twenty-five Demetrius fled secretly from Rome and, with the support of the Syrians, overcame his rival Antiochus V and put him to death. *The royal palace:* at Antioch.

palace of his ancestors, the soldiers seized Antiochus and Lysias to bring them to him. ³ When he was informed of this, he said, "Do not show me their faces." ⁴ So the soldiers killed them, and Demetrius sat on the royal throne.

⁵ Then all the lawless and impious men of Israel came to him. They were led by Alcimus,* who desired to be high priest. ⁶ They made this accusation to the king against the people: "Judas and his brothers have destroyed all your friends and have driven us out of our country. ⁷ So now, send a man whom you trust to go and see all the havoc Judas has done to us and to the king's land, and let him punish them and all their supporters."

⁸ Then the king chose Bacchides, one of the King's Friends, governor of West-of-Euphrates, a great man in the kingdom, and faithful to the king. ⁹ ^y He sent him and the impious Alcimus, to whom he granted the high priesthood, with orders to take revenge on the Israelites. ¹⁰ They set out and, on arriving in the land of Judah with a great army, sent messengers who spoke deceitfully to Judas and his brothers in peaceful terms. ¹¹ But these paid no attention to their words, seeing that they had come with a great army. ¹² A group of scribes, however, gathered about Alcimus and Bacchides to ask for a just agreement. ¹³ ^z The Hasideans were the first among the Israelites to seek peace with them, ¹⁴ for they said, "A priest of the line of Aaron has come with the army, and he will not do us any wrong." ¹⁵ He spoke with them peacefully and swore to them, "We will not try to injure you or your friends." ¹⁶ So they trusted him. But he arrested sixty of them and killed them in one day, according to the text of Scripture:

y 9ff: 2 Mc 14, 46.—z 13f: 1 Mc 2, 42.—a Ps 79, 1ff.—b 26f: 1 Mc 3, 38; 2 Mc 8, 9; 14, 12f.—c 2 Mc 14, 30.

7, 5f: *Alcimus:* a regenade Jew hostile to the Maccabees, who became high priest after the death of Menelaus (2 Mc 14, 3). He received confirmation in his office from the new King Demetrius (v 9), and brought malicious charges against *Judas and his brothers* and the people (v 6). He wrought more evils on the Israelites than the Gentiles had done (v 23).

7, 19: *Beth-zaith:* about three miles north of Beth-zur and twelve miles south of Jerusalem.

7, 27: *Nicanor . . . deceitfully sent to Judas:* a more favorable picture of Nicanor, as an honest man who became a personal friend of Judas, is given in 2 Mc 14, 17-25. Their friendship was broken by the intrigues of Alcimus (2 Mc 14, 26-30).

7, 31: *Caphar-salama:* a village seven miles north-northwest of Jerusalem, on the road leading to Beth-horon.

¹⁷ "The flesh of your saints they have strewn,
and their blood they have shed round about Jerusalem,
and there was no one to bury them."^a

¹⁸ Then fear and dread of them came upon all the people, who said: "There is no truth or justice among them; they violated the agreement and the oath that they swore."

¹⁹ Bacchides withdrew from Jerusalem and pitched his camp in Beth-zaith.* He had many of the men arrested who deserted to him, throwing them into the great pit. ²⁰ He handed the province over to Alcimus, leaving troops to help him, while he himself returned to the king. ²¹ Alcimus spared no pains to maintain his high priesthood, ²² and all those who were disturbing their people gathered about him. They took possession of the land of Judah and caused great distress in Israel. ²³ When Judas saw all the evils that Alcimus and his men were bringing upon the Israelites, more than even the Gentiles had done, ²⁴ he went about all the borders of Judea and took revenge on the men who had deserted, preventing them from going out into the country. ²⁵ But when Alcimus saw that Judas and his followers were gaining strength and realized that he could not oppose them, he returned to the king and accused them of grave crimes.

Defeat of Nicanor. ²⁶ ^b Then the king sent Nicanor, one of his famous officers, who was a bitter enemy of Israel, with orders to destroy the people. ²⁷ Nicanor came to Jerusalem with a large force and deceitfully sent to Judas* and his brothers this peaceable message: ²⁸ "Let there be no fight between me and you. I will come with a few men to meet you peaceably."

²⁹ So he came to Judas, and they greeted one another peaceably. But Judas' enemies were prepared to seize him. ³⁰ When he became aware that Nicanor had come to him with treachery in mind, Judas was afraid and would not meet him again.^c ³¹ When Nicanor saw that his plan had been discovered, he went out to fight Judas near Caphar-salama.* ³² About five hundred men of Nicanor's army fell; the rest fled to the City of David.

33 *d* After this, Nicanor went up to Mount Zion. Some of the priests from the sanctuary and some of the elders of the people came out to greet him peaceably and to show him the holocaust that was being offered for the king. 34 But he mocked and ridiculed them, defiled them,* and spoke disdainfully. 35 In a rage he swore: "If Judas and his army are not delivered to me at once, when I return victorious I will burn this temple down." He went away in great anger. 36 The priests, however, went in and stood before the altar and the sanctuary.*e* They wept and said: 37 "You have chosen this house to bear your name, to be a house of prayer and petition for your people. 38 Take revenge on this man and his army, and let them fall by the sword. Remember their blasphemies, and do not let them continue."

39 Nicanor left Jerusalem and pitched his camp at Beth-horon, where the Syrian army joined him. 40 But Judas camped in Adasa* with three thousand men. Here Judas uttered this prayer: 41 "When they who were sent by the king blasphemed, your angel went out and killed a hundred and eighty-five thousand of them.*f* 42 In the same way, crush this army before us today, and let the rest know that Nicanor spoke wickedly against your sanctuary; judge him according to his wickedness."*g*

43 The armies met in battle on the thirteenth day of the month Adar. Nicanor's army was crushed, and he himself was the first to fall in the battle.*h* 44 When his army saw that Nicanor was dead, they threw down their arms and fled. 45 The Jews pursued them a day's journey, from Adasa to near Gazara, blowing the trumpets behind them as signals. 46 From all the surrounding villages of Judea people came out and closed in on them. They hemmed them in, and all the enemies fell by the sword; not a single one escaped.

47 Then the Jews collected the spoils and the booty; they cut off Nicanor's head and his right arm, which he had lifted up so arrogantly. These they brought to Jerusalem and displayed there. 48 The people rejoiced greatly, and observed that day as a great festival. 49 They decreed that it should be observed every year on the thirteenth of Adar.* 50 And for a short time* the land of Judah was quiet.

CHAPTER 8

Treaty with the Romans.* 1 Judas had heard of the reputation of the Romans. They were valiant fighters and acted amiably to all who took their side. They established a friendly alliance with all who applied to them. 2 He was also told of their battles and the brave deeds that they had performed against the Gauls,* conquering them and forcing them to pay tribute. 3 They had gotten possession of the silver and gold mines in Spain, 4 and by planning and persistence had conquered the whole country, although it was very remote from their own. They had crushed the kings who had come against them from the far corners of the earth and had inflicted on them severe defeat, and the rest paid tribute to them every year. 5 Philip* and Perseus, king of the Macedonians, and the others who opposed them in battle had been overwhelmed and subjugated. 6 Antiochus* the Great, king of Asia, who

---

d 33-38: 2 Mc 14, 31-36.—e Jl 2, 17.—f 41f: 2 Mc 8, 19; 15, 22ff.—g Is 37, 36ff.—h 2 Mc 15, 25-35.

7, 34: *Defiled them:* spitting on the priests caused them to become legally defiled.

7, 40: *Adasa:* a village southeast of Caphar-salama.

7, 49: *The thirteenth of Adar:* March 27, 160 B.C. This day in the Jewish calendar was called the "Day of Nicanor" (2 Mc 15, 36), but it was not long celebrated by the Jews.

7, 50: *A short time:* about one month following the death of Nicanor. After that began the attack of Bacchides resulting in the death of Judas (1 Mc 9, 1-18).

8, 1: This chapter contains the account of the embassy which Judas sent to Rome, probably before the death of Nicanor, to conclude a treaty of alliance between Rome and the Jewish nation. Without precise chronology, the pertinent data are gathered into a unified theme.

The image of the Roman Republic greatly impressed the smaller Eastern peoples seeking support against their overlords (1-16), because of Roman success in war (2-11) and effective aid to their allies (12-13). Numerous interventions by Rome in the politics of the Near East bear witness to its power and prestige in the second century B.C. Cf 1 Mc 1, 10; 7, 2; 12, 3; 15, 15-24; 2 Mc 11, 34. With the Roman control of Palestine in 63 B.C., the Republic and later the Empire became heartily detested. The eulogy of Rome in this chapter is one of the reasons why 1 Maccabees was not preserved by the Palestinian Jews of the century that followed.

8, 2: *Gauls:* probably the Celts of northern Italy and southern France, subdued by the Romans in 222 B.C., and again in 200-191 B.C.; but perhaps also those in Asia Minor (the Galatians), whom the Romans defeated in 189 B.C.

8, 5: *Philip:* Philip V of Macedonia, defeated by a Graeco-Roman alliance at Cynoscephalae in 197 B.C. *Perseus,* his son, was defeated at Pydna in 168 B.C., and died a prisoner. With this, the kingdom of Macedonia came to an end.

8, 6: *Antiochus:* Antiochus III, greatest of the Seleucid kings. He was defeated at Magnesia in 190 B.C. By the Treaty of Apamea in 189, he was obliged to pay Rome a crushing indemnity of 15,000 talents. It was the weakening of Antiochene power and the growing military and economic influence of Rome that led Antiochus IV to adopt the policy of political, religious and cultural unification of Syria and Palestine.

had fought against them with a hundred and twenty elephants and with cavalry and chariots and a very great army, had been defeated by them. [7]They had taken him alive and obliged him and the kings who succeeded him to pay a heavy tribute, to give hostages and a section of [8]Lycia, Mysia,* and Lydia from among their best provinces. The Romans took these from him and gave them to King Eumenes. [9] * When the men of Greece had planned to come and destroy them, [10]the Romans discovered it, and sent against the Greeks a single general who made war on them. Many were wounded and fell, and the Romans took their wives and children captive. They plundered them, took possession of their land, tore down their strongholds and reduced them to slavery even to this day. [11]All the other kingdoms and islands that had ever opposed them they destroyed and enslaved; [12]with their friends, however, and those who relied on them, they maintained friendship. They had conquered kings both far and near, and all who heard of their fame were afraid of them. [13]In truth, those whom they desired to help to a kingdom became kings, and those whom they wished to depose they deposed; and they were greatly exalted. [14]Yet with all this, none of them put on a crown or wore purple as a display of grandeur. [15]They had made for themselves a senate house, and every day three hundred and twenty men took counsel, deliberating on all that concerned the people and their well-being. [16]They

i 1 Mc 12, 1f; 15, 15-22.—j 1 Mc 14, 18.

8, 8: *Lycia, Mysia:* regions in western Asia Minor. These names are restored here by conjectural emendation; the Greek text has "India, Media," most likely through scribal error. *Eumenes:* Eumenes II (197-158), king of Pergamum, an ally of Rome who benefited greatly from Antiochus' losses.
8, 9f: The revolt of the Achaean League, inserted here, occurred in 146 B.C., after Judas' time. It was crushed by the Roman consul Lucius Mummius and marked the end of Greek independence. The author regards all Greeks as the enemies of God.
8, 16: *They entrusted their government to one man:* actually the Roman Republic always had two consuls as joint heads of the government. Presumably, a single one dealt with embassies and answered letters, hence the impression the Jews received; cf 1 Mc 15, 16.
8, 22: *The reply . . . on bronze tablets and sent to Jerusalem:* the decree of the Senate would be inscribed on bronze and kept in the Roman Capitol, with only a copy in letter form sent to Jerusalem. The translation of the decree into Hebrew and then into Greek, as found here in 1 Mc, may have occasioned this error.

entrusted their government to one man* every year, to rule over their entire country, and they all obeyed that one, and there was no envy or jealousy among them.
[17]So Judas chose Eupolemus, son of John, son of Accos, and Jason, son of Eleazar, and sent them to Rome to establish an alliance of friendship with them.[i] [18]He did this to get rid of the yoke, for it was obvious that the kingdom of the Greeks was subjecting Israel to slavery. [19]After making a very long journey to Rome, the envoys entered the senate and spoke as follows: [20]"Judas, called Maccabeus, and his brothers, with the Jewish people, have sent us to you to make a peaceful alliance with you, and to enroll ourselves among your allies and friends." [21]The proposal pleased the Romans, [22]and this is a copy of the reply they inscribed on bronze tablets and sent to Jerusalem,* to remain there with the Jews as a record of peace and alliance:[j]
[23]"May it be well with the Romans and the Jewish nation at sea and on land forever; may sword and enemy be far from them. [24]But if war is first made on Rome, or any of its allies in any of their dominions, [25]the Jewish nation will help them wholeheartedly, as the occasion shall demand; [26]and to those who wage war they shall not give nor provide grain, arms, money or ships; this is Rome's decision. They shall fulfill their obligations without receiving any recompense. [27]In the same way, if war is made first on the Jewish nation, the Romans will help them willingly, as the occasion shall demand, [28]and to those who are attacking them there shall not be given grain, arms, money, or ships; this is Rome's decision. They shall fulfill their obligations without deception. [29]On these terms the Romans have made an agreement with the Jewish people. [30]But if both parties hereafter decide to add or take away anything, they shall do as they choose, and whatever they shall add or take away shall be valid.
[31]"Moreover, concerning the wrongs that King Demetrius has done to them, we have written to him thus: 'Why have you made your yoke heavy upon our friends and allies the Jews? [32]If they complain about you again, we will do them justice and make war on you by land and sea.' "

1Mc

CHAPTER 9

Invasion of Judah. [1]When Demetrius heard that Nicanor and his army had fallen in battle, he again sent Bacchides and Alcimus into the land of Judah, along with the right wing of his army. [2]They took the road to Galilee, and camping opposite the ascent at Arbela, they captured it* and killed many people. [3]In the first month of the year one hundred and fifty-two,* they encamped against Jerusalem. [4]Then they set out for Berea with twenty thousand men and two thousand cavalry. [5]Judas, with three thousand picked men, had camped at Elasa. [6]When his men saw the great number of the troops, they were very much afraid, and many slipped away from the camp, until only eight hundred men remained.

[7]As Judas saw that his army was melting away just when the battle was imminent, he was panic-stricken, because he had no time to gather them together. [8]But in spite of his discouragement, he said to those who remained: "Let us go forward to meet our enemies; perhaps we can put up a good fight against them." [9]They tried to dissuade him, saying: "We certainly cannot. Let us save our lives now, and come back with our kinsmen, and then fight against them. Now we are too few." [10]But Judas said: "Far be it from me to do such a thing as to flee from them! If our time has come, let us die bravely for our kinsmen and not leave a stain upon our glory!"

Death of Judas. [11]Then the army of Bacchides moved out of camp and took its position for combat. The cavalry were divided into two squadrons, and the slingers and the archers came on ahead of the army, and all the valiant men were in the front line. [12]Bacchides was on the right wing. Flanked by the two squadrons, the phalanx attacked as they blew their trumpets. Those who were on Judas' side also blew their trumpets. [13]The earth shook with the noise of the armies, and the battle raged from morning until evening. [14]Seeing that Bacchides was on the right, with the main force of his army, Judas, with all the most stouthearted rallying to him, [15]drove back the right wing and pursued them as far as the mountain slopes.* [16]But when the men on the left wing saw that the right wing was driven back, they turned and followed Judas and his men, taking them in the rear. [17]The battle was fought desperately, and many on both sides fell wounded. [18]Then Judas fell, and the rest fled.

[19]Jonathan and Simon took their brother Judas and buried him in the tomb of their fathers at Modein. [20]All Israel bewailed him in great grief. They mourned for him many days, and they said, [21]"How the mighty one has fallen, the savior of Israel!"[k] [22]The other acts of Judas, his battles, the brave deeds he performed, and his greatness have not been recorded; but they were very many.

IV: LEADERSHIP OF JONATHAN

Bacchides and Jonathan. [23]After the death of Judas, the transgressors of the law raised their heads in every part of Israel, and all kinds of evildoers appeared. [24]In those days there was a very great famine, and the country deserted to them. [25]Bacchides chose impious men and made them masters of the country. [26]These sought out and hunted down the friends of Judas and brought them to Bacchides, who punished and derided them. [27]There had not been such great distress in Israel since the time prophets ceased to appear among the people.

[28]Then all the friends of Judas came together and said to Jonathan: [29]"Since your brother Judas died, there has been no one like him to oppose our enemies, Bacchides and those who are hostile to our nation. [30]Now therefore we have chosen you today to be our ruler and leader in his place, and to fight our battle."

---

k 2 Sm 1, 27.

9, 2: *They took the road . . . Arbela, they captured it:* this passage is restored, in part, by conjectural emendation. The present Greek text could be translated, "They took the road to Gilgal, and camping opposite Mesaloth at Arbela, they captured it." But Arbela (modern Khirbet Irbid) was in Galilee—on a high hill overlooking the western shore of the Sea of Galilee. Gilgal, on the contrary, was in the Jordan valley near Jericho. "Mesaloth" is probably a corrupt form of a Hebrew word meaning "steps, ascent."

9, 3: *The first month of the year one hundred and fifty-two:* April/May 160 B.C., by the temple calendar.

9, 15: *As far as the mountain slopes:* conjectural emendation. The Greek text has "as far as Mount Azotus"; this is most unlikely. Apparently the Greek translator mistook the Hebrew word *ashdot*, "slopes," for *asdod*, "Azotus."

31 From that moment Jonathan accepted the leadership, and took the place of Judas his brother. 32 When Bacchides learned of it, he sought to kill him. 33 But Jonathan and his brother Simon and all the men with him discovered this, and they fled to the desert of Tekoa* and camped by the waters of the pool of Asphar.* 35 Jonathan sent his brother* as leader of the convoy to ask permission of his friends, the Nabateans, to deposit with them their great quantity of baggage.*l* 36 But the sons of Jambri from Medaba* made a raid and seized and carried off John and everything he had. 37 After this, word was brought to Jonathan and his brother Simon: "The sons of Jambri are celebrating a great wedding, and with a large escort they are bringing the bride, the daughter of one of the great princes of Canaan, from Nadabath." 38 Remembering the blood of John their brother, they went up and hid themselves under cover of the mountain. 39 They watched, and suddenly saw a noisy crowd with baggage; the bridegroom and his friends and kinsmen had come out to meet the bride's party with tambourines and musicians and much equipment. 40 The Jews rose up against them from their ambush and killed them. Many fell wounded, and after the survivors fled toward the mountain, all their spoils were taken. 41 Thus the wedding was turned into mourning, and the sound of music into lamentation. 42 Having taken their revenge for the blood of their brother, the Jews returned to the marshes of the Jordan.

43 When Bacchides heard of it, he came on the sabbath to the banks of the Jordan with a large force. 44 Then Jonathan said to his companions, "Let us get up now and fight for our lives, for today is not like yesterday and the day before. 45 The battle is before us, and behind us are the waters of the Jordan on one side, marsh and thickets on the other, and there is no way of escape.* 46 Cry out now to Heaven for deliverance from our enemies." 47 When they joined battle, Jonathan raised his arm to strike Bacchides, but Bacchides backed away from him. 48 Jonathan and his men jumped into the Jordan and swam across to the other side, but the enemy did not pursue them across the Jordan. 49 A thousand men on Bacchides' side fell that day.

50 On returning to Jerusalem, Bacchides built strongholds in Judea: the Jericho fortress, as well as Emmaus, Beth-horon, Bethel, Timnath, Pharathon, and Tephon, with high walls and gates and bars.* 51 In each he put a garrison to oppose Israel. 52 He fortified the city of Beth-zur, Gazara and the citadel, and put soldiers in them and stores of provisions. 53 He took as hostages the sons of the leaders of the country and put them in custody in the citadel at Jerusalem.*m*

54 In the year one hundred and fifty-three, in the second month,* Alcimus ordered the wall of the inner court of the sanctuary to be torn down, thus destroying the work of the prophets. But he only began to tear it down. 55 Just at that time he had a stroke, and his work was interrupted; his mouth was closed and he was paralyzed, so that he could no longer utter a word to give orders concerning his house. 56 Finally he died in great agony. 57 Seeing that Alcimus was dead, Bacchides returned to the king, and the land of Judah was quiet for two years.

58 Then all the transgressors of the law held a council and said: "Jonathan and his companions are living in peace and security. Now then, let us have Bacchides return, and he will capture all of them in a single night." 59 So they went and took counsel with him. 60 When Bacchides was setting out with a large force, he sent letters secretly to all his allies in Judea, telling them to seize Jonathan and his companions. They were not able to do this, however, because their plot became known. 61 In fact, Jonathan's men seized about fifty of the men of the country who were ringleaders in the mischief and put them to death. 62 Then Jonathan and Simon and their companions withdrew to Bethbasi* in the desert; they rebuilt and

---

l 1 Mc 5, 25.—m 1 Mc 10, 9.

9, 33: *Tekoa:* home of the prophet Amos in the wild country above the Dead Sea, southeast of Jerusalem.
9, 34: Omitted, it is a dittography of verse 43.
9, 35: *Jonathan sent his brother:* this was John who was called Gaddi (1 Mc 2, 2; cf 9, 36. 38).
9, 36: *Medaba:* northeast of the Dead Sea.
9, 45: Jonathan's force was apparently trapped in one of the many oxbows of the lower Jordan. Bacchides had crossed and caught them still on the east bank.
9, 50: These sites constitute a ring on the edges of the province of Judea.
9, 54: *In the year . . . second month:* May 159 B.C.
9, 62: *Bethbasi:* two miles east of Bethlehem, and six miles north of Tekoa.

strengthened its fortifications that had been demolished. [63] When Bacchides learned of this, he gathered together his whole force and sent word to those who were in Judea. [64] He came and pitched his camp before Bethbasi, and constructing siege-machines, he fought against it for many days.

[65] Leaving his brother Simon in the city, Jonathan, accompanied by a small group of men, went out into the field. [66] He struck down Odomera and his kinsmen and the sons of Phasiron in their encampment; these men had set out to go up to the siege with their forces. [67] Simon and his men then sallied forth from the city and set fire to the machines. [68] They fought against Bacchides, and he was beaten. This caused him great distress. Because the enterprise he had planned came to naught, [69] he was angry with the lawless men who had advised him to invade the province. He killed many of them and resolved to return to his own country.

[70] Jonathan learned of this and sent ambassadors to make peace with him and to obtain the release of the prisoners. [71] He agreed to do as Jonathan had asked. He swore an oath to him that he would never try to injure him for the rest of his life; [72] and he released the prisoners he had previously taken from the land of Judah. He returned to his own country and never came into their territory again.

[73] Then the sword ceased in Israel. Jonathan settled in Michmash; he began to judge* the people, and he destroyed the impious in Israel.

CHAPTER 10

Revolt of Alexander. [1] In the year one hundred and sixty,* Alexander, who was called Epiphanes, son of Antiochus, came up and took Ptolemais. He was accepted and began to reign there. [2] When King Demetrius heard of it, he mustered a very large army and marched out to engage him in combat. [3] Demetrius sent a letter to Jonathan written in peaceful terms, to pay him honor; [4] for he said: "Let us be the first to make peace with him, before he makes peace with Alexander against us, [5] since he will remember all the wrongs we have done to him, his brothers, and his nation."

[6] So Demetrius authorized Jonathan, as his ally, to gather an army and procure arms; and he ordered that the hostages in the citadel be released to him. [7] Accordingly Jonathan went up to Jerusalem and read the letter to all the people. The men in the citadel [8] were struck with fear when they heard that the king had given him authority to gather an army. [9] They released the hostages to Jonathan, and he gave them back to their parents.[n] [10] Thereafter Jonathan dwelt in Jerusalem, and began to build and restore the city. [11] He ordered the workmen to build the walls and encircle Mount Zion with square stones for its fortification, which they did. [12] The foreigners in the strongholds that Bacchides had built, took flight; [13] each one of them left his place and returned to his own country. [14] Only in Beth-zur did some remain of those who had abandoned the law and the commandments, for they used it as a place of refuge.

Jonathan Supports Alexander. [15] King Alexander heard of the promises that Demetrius had made to Jonathan; he was also told of the battles and valiant deeds of Jonathan and his brothers and the troubles that they had endured. [16] He said, "Shall we ever find another man like him? Let us now make him our friend and ally." [17] So he sent Jonathan a letter written in these terms: [18] "King Alexander sends greetings to his brother Jonathan. [19] We have heard of you, that you are a mighty warrior and worthy to be our friend. [20] We have therefore appointed you today to be high priest of your nation; you are to be called the King's Friend, and you are to look after our interests and preserve amity with us." He also sent him a purple robe and a crown of gold.[o]

[21] Jonathan put on the sacred vestments in the seventh month of the year one hundred and sixty at the feast of Booths*

---

n 1 Mc 9, 53.—o 1 Mc 2, 18.

9, 73: *Began to judge:* exercise the governing authority as in the book of Judges. With Jerusalem and the garrison towns (v 50) firmly in Seleucid hands, Jonathan's freedom of action was greatly restricted. *Michmash,* southeast of Bethel, famous for the exploit of the former Jonathan, son of Saul; cf 1 Sm 14.

10, 1: *The year one hundred and sixty:* 152 B.C. *Alexander . . . Antiochus:* Alexander Balas claimed to be a son of Antiochus IV. He had the backing of the Romans, who had never forgiven Demetrius for becoming king without their permission. The latter meanwhile had become unpopular with his own people as well as with the Jews.

and he gathered an army and procured many arms. [22] When Demetrius heard of these things, he was distressed and said: [23] "Why have we allowed Alexander to get ahead of us by gaining the friendship of the Jews and thus strengthening himself? [24] I too will write them conciliatory words and offer dignities and gifts, so that they may be an aid to me."

[25] So he sent them this message: "King Demetrius sends greetings to the Jewish nation. [26] We have heard how you have kept the treaty with us and continued in our friendship and not gone over to our enemies, and we are glad. [27] Continue, therefore, to keep faith with us, and we will reward you with favors in return for what you do in our behalf. [28] We will grant you many exemptions and will bestow gifts on you.

[29] "I now free you, as I also exempt all the Jews, from the tribute, the salt tax, and the crown levies.*p* [30] Instead of collecting the third of the grain and the half of the fruit of the trees that should be my share, I renounce the right from this day forward. Neither now nor in the future will I collect them from the land of Judah or from the three districts annexed from Samaria.* [31] Let Jerusalem and her territory, her tithes and her tolls, be sacred and free from tax. [32] I also yield my authority over the citadel in Jerusalem, and I transfer it to the high priest, that he may put in it such men as he shall choose to guard it. [33] Every one of the Jews who has been carried into captivity from the land of Judah into any part of my kingdom I set at liberty without ransom; and let all their taxes, even those on their cattle, be canceled. [34] Let all feast days, sabbaths, new moon festivals, appointed days, and the three days that precede each feast day, and the three days that follow, be days of immunity and exemption for every Jew in my

kingdom. [35] Let no man have authority to exact payment from them or to molest any of them in any matter.

[36] "Let thirty thousand Jews be enrolled in the king's army and allowances be given them, as is due to all the king's soldiers. [37] Let some of them be stationed in the king's principal strongholds, and of these let some be given positions of trust in the affairs of the kingdom. Let their superiors and their rulers be taken from among them, and let them follow their own laws, as the king has commanded in the land of Judah.

[38] "Let the three districts that have been added to Judea from the province of Samaria be incorporated with Judea so that they may be under one man and obey no other authority than the high priest. [39] Ptolemais and its confines I give as a present to the sanctuary in Jerusalem for the necessary expenses of the sanctuary. [40] I make a yearly personal grant of fifteen thousand silver shekels out of the royal revenues, from appropriate places. [41] All the additional funds that the officials did not hand over as they had done in the first years, shall henceforth be handed over for the services of the temple. [42] Moreover, the dues of five thousand silver shekels that used to be taken from the revenue of the sanctuary every year shall be canceled, since these funds belong to the priests who perform the services. [43] Whoever takes refuge in the temple of Jerusalem or in any of its precincts, because of money he owes the king, or because of any other debt, shall be released, together with all the goods he possesses in my kingdom. [44] The cost of rebuilding and restoring the structures of the sanctuary shall be covered out of the royal revenue. [45] Likewise the cost of building the walls of Jerusalem and fortifying it all around, and of building walls in Judea, shall be donated from the royal revenue."

[46] When Jonathan and the people heard these words, they neither believed nor accepted them, for they remembered the great evil that Demetrius had done in Israel, and how sorely he had afflicted them. [47] They therefore decided in favor of Alexander, for he had been the first to address them peaceably, and they remained his allies for the rest of his life.

---

p 1 Mc 11, 28f. 35.—q 1 Mc 11, 28. 34.

10, 21: *Jonathan . . . feast of Booths:* Jonathan began to discharge the office of high priest October 23-30, 152 B.C. For seven years after the death of Alcimus there had been no high priest in Jerusalem. It was taken for granted that the king, though a Gentile, had the power to appoint one. The Maccabees, though a priestly family, were not of the line of Zadok, and some in Israel regarded Jonathan's tenure as a usurpation.

10, 30: *The three districts annexed from Samaria:* mentioned by name in 1 Mc 11, 34. The present Greek text, by a scribal error, has added "and Galilee" after "Samaria."

⁴⁸King Alexander gathered together a large army and encamped opposite Demetrius. ⁴⁹The two kings joined battle, and when the army of Demetrius fled, Alexander pursued him, and overpowered his soldiers. ⁵⁰He pressed the battle hard until sunset, and Demetrius fell that day.

Treaty of Ptolemy and Alexander.
⁵¹Alexander sent ambassadors to Ptolemy, king of Egypt, with this message: ⁵²"Now that I have returned to my realm, taken my seat on the throne of my fathers, and established my rule by crushing Demetrius and gaining control of my country—⁵³for I engaged him in battle, defeated him and his army, and recovered the royal throne—⁵⁴let us now establish friendship with each other. Give me your daughter for my wife; and as your son-in-law, I will give to you and to her gifts worthy of you."

⁵⁵King Ptolemy answered in these words: "Happy the day on which you returned to the land of your fathers and took your seat on their royal throne! ⁵⁶I will do for you what you have written; but meet me in Ptolemais, so that we may see each other, and I will become your father-in-law as you have proposed."

⁵⁷So Ptolemy with his daughter Cleopatra* set out from Egypt and came to Ptolemais in the year one hundred and sixty-two. ⁵⁸There King Alexander met him, and Ptolemy gave him his daughter Cleopatra in marriage. Their wedding was celebrated at Ptolemais with great splendor according to the custom of kings.

⁵⁹King Alexander also wrote to Jonathan to come and meet him. ⁶⁰So he went with pomp to Ptolemais, where he met the two kings and gave them and their friends silver and gold and many gifts and thus won their favor.ʳ ⁶¹Some pestilent Israelites, transgressors of the law, united against him to accuse him, but the king paid no heed to them. ⁶²He ordered Jonathan to be divested of his ordinary garments and to be clothed in royal purple; and so it was done. ⁶³The king also had him seated at his side. He said to his magistrates: "Go with him to the center of the city and make a proclamation that no one is to bring charges against him on any grounds or be troublesome to him in any way."

⁶⁴ ˢ When his accusers saw the honor paid to him in the proclamation, and the purple with which he was clothed, they all fled. ⁶⁵The king also honored him by numbering him among his Chief Friends and made him military commander and governor of the province. ⁶⁶So Jonathan returned in peace and happiness to Jerusalem.

Victory over Apollonius. ⁶⁷In the year one hundred and sixty-five,* Demetrius, son of Demetrius, came from Crete to the land of his fathers. ⁶⁸When King Alexander heard of it he was greatly troubled, and returned to Antioch. ⁶⁹Demetrius appointed Apollonius governor of Coelesyria. Having gathered a large army, Apollonius pitched his camp at Jamnia. From there he sent this message to Jonathan the high priest: ⁷⁰"You are the only one who resists us. I am laughed at and put to shame on your account. Why are you displaying power against us in the mountains? ⁷¹If you have confidence in your forces, come down now to us in the plain, and let us test each other's strength there; the city forces are on my side. ⁷²Inquire and learn who I am and who the others are who are helping me. Men say that you cannot make a stand against us because your fathers were twice put to flight in their own land. ⁷³Now you too will be unable to withstand our cavalry and such a force as this in the plain, where there is not a stone or a pebble or a place to flee."

⁷⁴When Jonathan heard the message of Apollonius, he was roused. Choosing ten thousand men, he set out from Jerusalem, and Simon his brother joined him to help him. ⁷⁵He pitched camp near Joppa, but the men in the city shut him out because Apollonius had a garrison there. When the Jews besieged it, ⁷⁶the men of the city became afraid and

---

r 1 Mc 2, 18.—s 64f: 1 Mc 2, 18; 11, 27.

10, 57: *Cleopatra:* Cleopatra Thea, then about fifteen years old. She later married Demetrius II, and later still, his brother Antiochus VII. *The year one hundred and sixty-two:* 151/150 B.C.
10, 67: *The year one hundred and sixty-five:* 147 B.C. *Demetrius:* Demetrius II Nicator.

opened the gates, and so Jonathan took possession of Joppa.*

77 When Apollonius heard of it, he drew up three thousand horsemen and an innumerable infantry. He marched on Azotus as though he were going on through the country, but at the same time he advanced into the plain, because he had such a large number of horsemen to rely on. 78 Jonathan followed him to Azotus, and they engaged in battle. 79 Apollonius, however, had left a thousand cavalry in hiding behind them. 80 When Jonathan discovered that there was an ambush behind him, his army was surrounded. From morning until evening they showered his men with arrows. 81 But his men held their ground, as Jonathan had commanded, whereas the enemy's horses became tired out. 82 When the horsemen were exhausted, Simon attacked the phalanx, overwhelmed it and put it to flight. 83 The horsemen too were scattered over the plain. The enemy fled to Azotus and entered Beth-dagon, the temple of their idol, to save themselves. 84 But Jonathan burned and plundered Azotus with its neighboring towns, and destroyed by fire both the temple of Dagon and the men who had taken refuge in it.[l] 85 Those who fell by the sword, together with those who were burned alive, came to about eight thousand men. 86 Then Jonathan left there and pitched his camp at Ashkalon, and the people of that city came out to meet him with great pomp. 87 He and his men then returned to Jerusalem, laden with much booty. 88 When King Alexander heard of these events, he accorded new honors to Jonathan. 89 He sent him a gold buckle, such as is usually given to King's Kinsmen;* he also gave him Ekron and all its territory as a possession.

---

t 1 Mc 11, 4; 1 Sm 5, 2-5.—u 1 Mc 10, 84.

10, 76: *Joppa:* about forty miles northwest of Jerusalem. For the first time the Maccabees took possession of a seaport; nominally it was on behalf of King Alexander.

10, 89: *Kinsmen:* a class higher than Chief Friends.

11, 7: *Eleutherus:* modern Nahr el-Kebir, the northern border of modern Lebanon; in the second century B.C. the northern limit of Coelesyria.

11, 8: *Seleucia-by-the-Sea:* at the mouth of the Orontes, the port city of Antioch.

11, 10: *I regret . . . to kill me:* according to Josephus, Ammonius, a friend of Alexander, had tried to assassinate Ptolemy, and the latter claimed that Alexander was the instigator, thus calumniating him to gain his kingdom (v 11).

CHAPTER 11

Alliance of Demetrius and Ptolemy. 1 The king of Egypt gathered his forces, as numerous as the sands of the seashore, and many ships; and he sought by deceit to take Alexander's kingdom and add it to his own. 2 He entered Syria with peaceful words, and the people in the cities opened their gates to welcome him, as King Alexander had ordered them to do, since Ptolemy was his father-in-law. 3 But when Ptolemy entered the cities, he stationed garrison troops in each one. 4 When he reached Azotus, he was shown the temple of Dagon destroyed by fire, Azotus and its suburbs demolished, corpses lying about, and the charred bodies of those burned by Jonathan in the war and stacked up along his route.[u] 5 To prejudice the king against Jonathan, he was told what the latter had done; but the king said nothing. 6 Jonathan met the king with pomp at Joppa, and they greeted each other and spent the night there. 7 Jonathan accompanied the king as far as the river called Eleutherus* and then returned to Jerusalem.

8 Plotting evil against Alexander, King Ptolemy took possession of the cities along the seacoast as far as Seleucia-by-the-Sea.* 9 He sent ambassadors to King Demetrius, saying: "Come, let us make a pact with each other; I will give you my daughter whom Alexander has married, and you shall reign over your father's kingdom. 10 I regret that I gave him my daughter, for he has sought to kill me."* 11 His real reason for accusing Alexander, however, was that he coveted Alexander's kingdom. 12 After taking his daughter away and giving her to Demetrius, Ptolemy broke with Alexander; their enmity became open. 13 Then Ptolemy entered Antioch and assumed the crown of Asia; he thus wore two crowns on his head, that of Egypt and that of Asia.

Deaths of Alexander and Ptolemy. 14 King Alexander was in Cilicia at that time, because the people of that region had revolted. 15 When Alexander heard the news, he came to challenge Ptolemy in battle. Ptolemy marched out and met him with a strong force and put him to flight. 16 Alexander fled to Arabia to seek protection. King Ptolemy's triumph was complete 17 when the Arab Zabdiel cut off Alex-

1Mc

ander's head and sent it to Ptolemy. [18] But three days later King Ptolemy himself died, and his men in the fortified cities were killed by the inhabitants of the strongholds. [19] Thus Demetrius became king in the year one hundred and sixty-seven.*

Pact with Demetrius. [20] At that time Jonathan gathered together the men of Judea to attack the citadel in Jerusalem, and they set up many machines against it. [21] Some transgressors of the law, enemies of their own nation, went to the king and informed him that Jonathan was besieging the citadel. [22] When Demetrius heard this, he was furious, and set out immediately for Ptolemais. He wrote to Jonathan to discontinue the siege and to meet him for a conference at Ptolemais as soon as possible.

[23] On hearing this, Jonathan ordered the siege to continue. He selected some elders and priests of Israel and exposed himself to danger [24] by going to the king at Ptolemais. He brought with him silver, gold apparel, and many other presents, and found favor with the king. [25] Although some impious men of his own nation brought charges against him, [26] the king treated him just as his predecessors had done and showed him great honor in the presence of all his Friends. [27] He confirmed him in the high priesthood and in all the honors he had previously held, and had him enrolled among his Chief Friends.

[28] Jonathan asked the king to exempt Judea and the three districts of Samaria from tribute, promising him in return three hundred talents.[v] [29] The king agreed and wrote the following letter to Jonathan about all these matters:

[30] [w] "King Demetrius sends greetings to his brother* Jonathan and to the Jewish nation. [31] We are sending you, for your information, a copy of the letter that we wrote to Lasthenes* our kinsman concerning you. [32] 'King Demetrius sends greetings to his father Lasthenes. [33] Because of the good will they show us, we have decided to bestow benefits on the Jewish nation, who are our friends and who observe their obligations to us. [34] [x] Therefore we confirm their possession, not only of the territory of Judea, but also of the three districts of Aphairema,* Lydda, and Rama-

thaim. These districts, together with all their dependencies, were transferred from Samaria to Judea in favor of all those who offer sacrifices for us in Jerusalem instead of paying the royal taxes that formerly the king received from them each year from the produce of the soil and the fruit of the trees. [35] From this day on we grant them release from payment of all other things that would henceforth be due to us, that is, of tithes and tribute and of the tax on the salt pans and the crown tax. [36] Henceforth none of these provisions shall ever be revoked. [37] Be sure, therefore, to have a copy of these instructions made and given to Jonathan, that it may be displayed in a conspicuous place on the holy hill.' "

The Intrigue of Trypho. [38] When King Demetrius saw that the land was peaceful under his rule and that he had no opposition, he dismissed his entire army, every man to his home, except the foreign troops which he had hired from the islands of the nations. So all the soldiers who had served under his predecessors hated him. [39] When a certain Trypho, who had previously belonged to Alexander's party, saw that all the troops were grumbling at Demetrius, he went to Imalkue the Arab, who was bringing up Alexander's young son Antiochus.[y] [40] Trypho kept urging Imalkue to hand over the boy to him, that he might make him king in his father's place. During his stay there of many days, he told him of all that Demetrius had done and of the hatred that his soldiers had for him.

Jonathan Aids Demetrius. [41] Meanwhile Jonathan sent the request to King Demetrius to withdraw his troops from the

---

v 1 Mc 10, 29; 11, 34.—w 30-37: 1 Mc 10, 26-45.—x 34f: 1 Mc 10, 29; 11, 28.—y 1 Mc 12, 39.

11, 19: *The year one hundred and sixty-seven:* 146/145 B.C. The two deaths (vv 17-18) occurred in the summer of 145 B.C.

11, 30: *Brother:* this title and *father* in v 32 are honorific titles used of the Kinsmen.

11, 31: *Lasthenes:* leader of the mercenary troops who had come with Demetrius from Crete. He was now the young king's chief minister and was apparently responsible for the disastrous policy (v 38) of disbanding the national army.

11, 34: *Aphairema:* the Ophrah of Jos 18, 23; 1 Sm 23, 6; the Ephron of 2 Chr 13, 19; and the Ephraim of Jn 11, 54—modern et-Taiyibeh, five miles northeast of Bethel. *Lydda:* the Lod of the postexilic Jews (Ez 2, 33; Neh 11, 35) and the hometown of Aeneas, who was cured by Peter (Acts 9, 32ff). It is ten miles southeast of Joppa. *Ramathaim:* the Ramathaim-zophim of 1 Sm 1, 1, and the Arimathea of Mt 27, 57—modern Rentis, nine miles northeast of Lydda.

citadel of Jerusalem and from the other strongholds, for they were constantly hostile to Israel. [42] Demetrius, in turn, sent this word to Jonathan: "I will not only do this for you and your nation, but I will greatly honor you and your nation when I find the opportunity. [43] Do me the favor, therefore, of sending men to fight for me, because all my troops have revolted."

[44] So Jonathan sent three thousand good fighting men to him at Antioch. When they came to the king, he was delighted over their arrival, [45] for the populace, one hundred and twenty thousand strong, had massed in the center of the city in an attempt to kill him. [46] But he took refuge in the palace, while the populace gained control of the main streets and began to fight. [47] So the king called the Jews to his aid. They all rallied around him and spread out through the city. On that day they killed about a hundred thousand men in the city, [48] which, at the same time, they set on fire and plundered on a large scale. Thus they saved the king's life. [49] When the populace saw that the Jews held the city at their mercy, they lost courage and cried out to the king in supplication, [50] "Give us your terms and let the Jews stop attacking us and our city." So they threw down their arms and made peace. [51] The Jews thus gained glory in the eyes of the king and all his subjects, and they became renowned throughout his kingdom. Finally they returned to Jerusalem with much spoil. [52] But when King Demetrius was sure of his royal throne, and the land was peaceful under his rule, [53] he broke all his promises and became estranged from Jonathan. Instead of rewarding Jonathan for all the favors he had received from him, he caused him much trouble.

Alliance with Trypho. [54] After this, Trypho returned and brought with him the young boy Antiochus, who became

king and wore the royal crown.[z] [55] All the soldiers whom Demetrius had discharged rallied around Antiochus and fought against Demetrius, who was routed and fled. [56] Trypho captured the elephants and occupied Antioch. [57] Then young Antiochus wrote to Jonathan: "I confirm you in the high priesthood and appoint you ruler over the four districts and wish you to be one of the King's Friends." [58] He also sent him gold dishes and a dinner service, gave him the right to drink from gold cups, to dress in royal purple, and to wear a gold buckle.[a] [59] Likewise, he made Jonathan's brother Simon governor of the region from the Ladder of Tyre* to the frontier of Egypt.

[60] Jonathan set out and traveled through West-of-Euphrates* and its cities, and all the forces of Syria espoused his cause as allies. When he arrived at Ashkalon, the citizens welcomed him with pomp. [61] But when he set out for Gaza, the people of Gaza locked their gates against him. So he besieged it and burned and plundered its suburbs. [62] Then the people of Gaza appealed to him for mercy, and he granted them peace. He took the sons of their chief men as hostages and sent them to Jerusalem. He then traveled on through the province as far as Damascus.

War with Demetrius. [63] Jonathan heard that the generals of Demetrius had come with a strong force to Kadesh in Galilee, intending to remove him from office. [64] So he went to meet them, leaving his brother Simon in the province. [65] Simon besieged Beth-zur, attacked it for many days, and blockaded the inhabitants. [66] When they sued for peace, he granted it to them. He expelled them from the city, took possession of it, and put a garrison there.

[67] Meanwhile, Jonathan and his army pitched their camp near the waters of Gennesaret, and at daybreak they went to the plain of Hazor.* [68] There, in front of him on the plain, was the army of the foreigners. This army attacked him in the open, having first detached an ambush against him in the mountains. [69] Then the men in ambush rose out of their places and joined in the battle. [70] All of Jonathan's men fled; no one stayed except the army commanders Mattathias, son of Absalom, and Judas, son of Chalphi. [71] Jonathan tore his

---

z 1 Mc 11, 39; 12, 39.—a 1 Mc 2, 18.

11, 59: *Ladder of Tyre:* modern Ras en-Naquurah, on the border between Lebanon and Israel, where the mountains reach the sea, so that the coastal road must ascend in a series of steps.

11, 60: *West-of-Euphrates:* refers here to the territory of Palestine and Coelesyria, but not Upper Syria; cf 1 Mc 3, 32; 7, 8.

11, 67: *Plain of Hazor:* the site of the ancient Canaanite city (Jos 11, 10), ten miles north of the Lake of Gennesaret.

clothes, threw earth on his head, and prayed. [72] Then he went back to the combat and so overwhelmed the enemy that they took to flight. [73] Those of his men who were running away saw it and returned to him; and with him they pursued the enemy as far as their camp in Kadesh, where they pitched their own camp. [74] Three thousand of the foreign troops fell on that day. Then Jonathan returned to Jerusalem.

CHAPTER 12

Alliances with Rome and Sparta. [1] When Jonathan saw that the times favored him, he sent selected men to Rome to confirm and renew his friendship with the Romans.[b] [2] He also sent letters to Sparta and other places for the same purpose. [3] After reaching Rome, the men entered the senate chamber and said, "The high priest Jonathan and the Jewish people have sent us to renew the earlier friendship and alliance between you and them." [4] The Romans gave them letters addressed to the authorities in the various places, requesting them to provide the envoys with safe conduct to the land of Judah.

[5] This is a copy of the letter that Jonathan wrote to the Spartans: [6] "Jonathan the high priest, the senate of the nation, the priests, and the rest of the Jewish people send greetings to their brothers the Spartans. [7] Long ago a letter was sent to the high priest Onias* from Arius, who then reigned over you, stating that you are our brothers, as the attached copy shows.[c] [8] Onias welcomed the envoy with honor and received the letter, which clearly referred to alliance and friendship. [9] [d] Though we have no need of these things, since we have for our encouragement the sacred books that are in our possession,* [10] we have ventured to send word to you for the renewal of brotherhood and friendship, so as not to become strangers to you altogether; a long time has passed since your mission to us. [11] We, on our part, have never ceased to remember you in the sacrifices and prayers that we offer on our feasts and other appropriate days, as it is right and proper to remember brothers. [12] We likewise rejoice in your renown. [13] But many hardships and wars have beset us, and the kings around us have attacked us. [14] We did not wish to be troublesome to you and to the rest of our allies and friends in these wars; [15] with the help of Heaven for our support, we have been saved from our enemies, and they have been humbled. [16] So we have chosen Numenius, son of Antiochus, and Antipater, son of Jason, and we have sent them to the Romans to renew our former friendship and alliance with them.[e] [17] We have also ordered them to come to you and greet you, and to deliver to you our letter about the renewal of our brotherhood. [18] Therefore kindly send us an answer on this matter."

[19] This is a copy of the letter that was sent to Onias: [20] [f] "Arius, king of the Spartans, sends greetings to Onias the high priest. [21] A document has been found stating that the Spartans and the Jews are brothers; both nations descended from Abraham. [22] Now that we have learned this, kindly write to us about your welfare. [23] We, on our part, are informing you that your cattle and your possessions are ours, and ours are yours. We have, therefore, given orders that you should be told of this."

Demetrius Repelled. [24] Jonathan heard that the generals of Demetrius had returned to attack him with a stronger army than before. [25] He set out from Jerusalem and went into the country of Hamath* to meet them, giving them no time to enter his province. [26] The spies he had sent into their camp came back and reported that the enemy had made ready to attack the Jews that very night. [27] Therefore, when the sun set, Jonathan ordered his men to be on guard and to remain armed, ready for combat, throughout the night. He also set outposts all around the camp. [28] When the enemy heard that Jonathan and his men were ready for battle, their hearts sank with fear and dread. They lighted fires and then withdrew. [29] But because Jonathan and his men were watching the lights burning, they did not know what

---

b 1 Mc 8, 17.—c 1 Mc 12, 20-23.—d Rom 15, 4.—e 1 Mc 14, 22; 15, 15.—f 20-23: 1 Mc 12, 6f.

12, 7: *Onias:* Onias I, high priest from 323-300 or 290 B.C. *Arius:* Arius I, king from 309 to 265 B.C. The letter was sent *long ago,* i.e., a century and a half before.

12, 9: *The sacred books . . . in our possession:* a reference to "the law, the prophets and other books," as mentioned in the Prologue to Sirach (v 1), after 132 B.C.

12, 25: *Country of Hamath:* the Seleucid territory of Upper Syria northeast of Coelesyria and separated from it by the Eleutherus River. The latter territory was under the command of Jonathan (1 Mc 11, 59f).

had happened until morning. ³⁰Then Jonathan pursued them, but he could not overtake them, for they had crossed the river Eleutherus. ³¹So Jonathan turned aside against the Arabs who are called Zabadeans, overwhelming and plundering them. ³²Then he marched on to Damascus and traversed that whole region.

³³Simon also set out and went as far as Ashkalon and its neighboring strongholds. He then turned to Joppa and occupied it, ³⁴for he heard that its men had intended to hand over this stronghold to the supporters of Demetrius. He left a garrison there to guard it.

³⁵When Jonathan returned, he assembled the elders of the people, and with them he made plans for building strongholds in Judea, ³⁶for making the walls of Jerusalem still higher, and for erecting a high barrier between the citadel and the city, that would isolate the citadel and so prevent its garrison from commerce with the city. ³⁷The people therefore worked together on building up the city, for part of the east wall above the ravine had collapsed. The quarter called Chaphenatha was also repaired. ³⁸Simon likewise built up Adida in the Shephelah, and strengthened its fortifications by providing them with gates and bars.

Capture of Jonathan. ³⁹Trypho was determined to become king of Asia, assume the crown, and do away with King Antiochus.ᵍ ⁴⁰But he was afraid that Jonathan would not permit him, but would fight against him. Looking for a way to seize and kill him, he set out and reached Beth-shan. ⁴¹Jonathan marched out against him with forty thousand picked fighting men and came to Beth-shan. ⁴²But when Trypho saw that Jonathan had arrived with a large army, he was afraid to offer him violence. ⁴³Instead, he received him with honor, introduced him to all his friends, and gave him presents. He also ordered his friends and soldiers to obey him as they would himself. ⁴⁴Then he said to Jonathan: "Why have you put all your soldiers to so much trouble when we are not at war? ⁴⁵Pick out a few men to stay with you, send the rest back home, and then come with me

to Ptolemais. I will hand it over to you together with other strongholds and their garrisons, as well as the officials, then I will leave and go home. That is why I came here."

⁴⁶Jonathan believed him and did as he said. He dismissed his troops, and they returned to the land of Judah. ⁴⁷But he kept with him three thousand men, of whom he sent two thousand to Galilee while one thousand accompanied him. ⁴⁸Then as soon as Jonathan had entered Ptolemais, the men of the city closed the gates and seized him; all who had entered with him, they killed with the sword.

⁴⁹Trypho sent soldiers and cavalry to Galilee and the Great Plain* to destroy all Jonathan's men. ⁵⁰These, upon learning that Jonathan had been captured and his companions killed, encouraged one another and went out in compact body ready to fight. ⁵¹As their pursuers saw that they were ready to fight for their lives, they turned back. ⁵²Thus all these men of Jonathan came safely into the land of Judah. They mourned over Jonathan and his men, and were in great fear, and all Israel fell into deep mourning.

⁵³All the nations round about sought to destroy them. They said, "Now that they have no leader to help them, let us make war on them, and wipe out their memory from among men."ʰ

V: SIMON, HIGH PRIEST AND ETHNARCH

CHAPTER 13

Simon, Leader of the Jews. ¹When Simon heard that Trypho was gathering a large army to invade and ravage the land of Judah, ²and saw that the people were in dread and terror, he went up to Jerusalem. There he assembled the people ³and exhorted them in these words: "You know what I, my brothers, and my father's house have done for the laws and the sanctuary; what battles and disasters we have been through. ⁴It was for the sake of these, for the sake of Israel, that all my brothers have perished, and I alone am left. ⁵Far be it from me, then, to save my own life in any time of distress, for I am not better than my brothers. ⁶Rather will I avenge my nation and the sanctuary, as well as your wives and children, for all the nations out of hatred have united to destroy us."ⁱ

---

g 1 Mc 11, 39f. 54f.—h 1 Mc 5, 2; 13, 6.—i 1 Mc 5, 2; 12, 53.

12, 49: *The Great Plain:* of Beth-shan (v 41), where Jonathan's disbanded troops remained.

⁷As the people heard these words, their spirit was rekindled. ⁸They shouted in reply: "You are our leader in place of your brothers Judas and Jonathan. ⁹Fight our battles, and we will do everything that you tell us." ¹⁰So Simon mustered all the men able to fight, and quickly completing the walls of Jerusalem, fortified it on every side. ¹¹He sent Jonathan, son of Absalom, to Joppa with a large force; Jonathan drove out the occupants and remained there.

Deceit and Treachery of Trypho. ¹²Then Trypho moved from Ptolemais with a large army to invade the land of Judah, bringing Jonathan with him as prisoner. ¹³But Simon pitched his camp at Adida, facing the plain. ¹⁴When Trypho learned that Simon had succeeded his brother Jonathan, and that he intended to fight him, he sent envoys to him with this message: ¹⁵"We have detained your brother Jonathan on account of the money that he owed the royal treasury in connection with the offices that he held. ¹⁶Therefore, if you send us a hundred talents of silver, and two of his sons as hostages to guarantee that when he is set free he will not revolt against us, we will release him."

¹⁷Although Simon knew that they were speaking deceitfully to him, he gave orders to get the money and the boys for fear of provoking much hostility among the people, who might say ¹⁸that Jonathan perished because Simon would not send Trypho the money and the boys. ¹⁹So he sent the boys and the hundred talents; but Trypho broke his promise and would not let Jonathan go. ²⁰ * Next he began to invade and ravage the country. His troops went around by the road that leads to Adora, but Simon and his army moved along opposite him everywhere he went. ²¹The men in the citadel sent messengers to Trypho, urging him to come to them by way of the desert, and to send them provisions. ²²Although Trypho got all his cavalry ready to go, there was a heavy fall of snow that night, and he could not go. So he left for Gilead. ²³When he was approaching Baskama,* he had Jonathan killed and buried there. ²⁴Then Trypho returned to his own country.

Jonathan's Tomb. ²⁵Simon sent for the remains of his brother Jonathan, and buried him in Modein, the city of his fathers. ²⁶All Israel bewailed him with solemn lamentation, mourning over him for many days. ²⁷Then Simon erected over the tomb of his father and his brothers a monument of stones, polished front and back, and raised high enough to be seen at a distance. ²⁸He set up seven pyramids facing one another for his father and his mother and his four brothers. ²⁹For the pyramids he devised a setting of big columns, on which he carved suits of armor as a perpetual memorial, and next to the armor he placed carved ships, which could be seen by all who sailed the sea. ³⁰This tomb which he built at Modein is there to the present day.

Pact between Simon and Demetrius. ³¹Trypho dealt treacherously with the young King Antiochus. He killed him ³²and assumed the kingship in his place, putting on the crown of Asia. Thus he brought much evil on the land. ³³Simon, on his part, built up the strongholds of Judea, strengthening their fortifications with high towers, thick walls, and gates with bars, and he stored up provisions in the fortresses. ³⁴Simon also sent chosen men to King Demetrius with the request that he grant the land a release from taxation, for all that Trypho did was to plunder the land. ³⁵In reply, King Demetrius sent him the following letter:

³⁶"King Demetrius sends greetings to Simon the high priest, the friend of kings, and to the elders and the Jewish people. ³⁷We have received the gold crown and the palm branch that you sent. We are willing to be on most peaceful terms with you and to write to our official to grant you release from tribute. ³⁸Whatever we have guaranteed to you remains in force, and the strongholds that you have built shall remain yours. ³⁹We remit any oversights and defaults incurred up to now, as well as the crown tax that you owe. Any other tax that may have been collected in Jerusalem shall no longer be collected there. ⁴⁰If any of you are qualified for enrollment in our service, let them be enrolled. Let there be peace between us."

⁴¹Thus in the year one hundred and

13, 20f: The invaders made a wide flanking movement to invade Judea from the south. *Adora* was a few miles southwest of Beth-zur. They would avoid Beth-zur itself and other strongholds of the Maccabees by following the *way of the desert.*
13, 23: *Baskama:* northeast of the Sea of Galilee.

seventy,* the yoke of the Gentiles was removed from Israel, ⁴² and the people began to write in their records and contracts, "In the first year of Simon, high priest, governor, and leader of the Jews."

Capture of Gazara and the Citadel. ⁴³ In those days Simon besieged Gazara* and surrounded it with troops. He made a siege machine, pushed it up against the city, and attacked and captured one of the towers.*j* ⁴⁴ The men who had been on the siege machine jumped down into the city and caused a great tumult there. ⁴⁵ The men of the city, joined by their wives and children, went up on the wall, with their garments rent, and cried out in loud voices, begging Simon to grant them peace. ⁴⁶ "Do not treat us according to our evil deeds," they said, "but according to your mercy."

⁴⁷ So Simon came to terms with them and did not destroy them. He made them leave the city, however, and he purified the houses in which there were idols. Then he entered the city with hymns and songs of praise. ⁴⁸ After removing from it everything that was impure, he settled there men who observed the law. He improved its fortifications and built himself a residence.

⁴⁹ The men in the citadel in Jerusalem were prevented from going out into the country and back for the purchase of food; they suffered greatly from hunger, and many of them died of starvation. ⁵⁰ They finally cried out to Simon for peace, and he gave them peace. He expelled them from the citadel and cleansed it of impurities. ⁵¹ On the twenty-third day of the second month,* in the year one hundred and seventy-one, the Jews entered the citadel with shouts of jubilation, waving of palm branches, the music of harps and cymbals

and lyres, and the singing of hymns and canticles, because a great enemy of Israel had been destroyed.*k* ⁵² Simon decreed that this day should be celebrated every year with rejoicing. He also strengthened the fortifications of the temple hill alongside the citadel, and he and his companions dwelt there. ⁵³ Seeing that his son John* was now a grown man, Simon made him commander of all his soldiers, with his residence in Gazara.

CHAPTER 14

Capture of Demetrius. ¹ In the year one hundred and seventy-two,* King Demetrius assembled his army and marched into Media to obtain help so that he could fight Trypho. ² When Arsaces,* king of Persia and Media, heard that Demetrius had invaded his territory, he sent one of his generals to take him alive. ³ The general went forth and defeated the army of Demetrius; he captured him and brought him to Arsaces, who put him in prison.

Glory of Simon

⁴ The land was at rest all the days of
Simon,
  who sought the good of his nation.
His people were delighted with his
power
  and his magnificence throughout his
reign.*l*
⁵ As his crowning glory he captured the
port of Joppa
  and made it a gateway to the isles of
the sea.
⁶ He enlarged the borders of his nation
  and gained control of the country.*m*
⁷ He took many enemies prisoners of war
  and made himself master of Gazara,
Beth-zur, and the citadel.
He cleansed the citadel of its impurities;
  there was no one to withstand him.
⁸ The people cultivated their land in
peace;
  the land yielded its produce
  and the trees of the field their fruit.*n*
⁹ Old men sat in the squares,
  all talking about the good times,
  while the young men wore the glorious apparel of war.*o*
¹⁰ He supplied the cities with food

---

j 2 Mc 10, 32-38.—k 1 Mc 1, 36.—l 1 Mc 3, 3-9.—m Ex 34, 24.—n Zec 8, 12.—o Zec 8, 4f.

13, 41: *The year one hundred and seventy:* March, 142, to April, 141 B.C., by the temple calendar.
13, 43: *Gazara:* a key position in the Shephelah, fortified by Bacchides in 160 B.C.; cf 1 Mc 9, 52.
13, 51: *The twenty-third day of the second month:* June 3, 141 B.C.
13, 53: *John:* John Hyrcanus, who was to succeed his father as ruler and high priest; cf 1 Mc 16, 23f.
14, 1: *The year one hundred and seventy-two:* 141-140 B.C. The expedition began most probably in the spring of 140.
14, 2: *Arsaces:* Arsaces VI, also called Mithridates I, the Parthian king (171-138 B.C.). Parthians had overrun Persia and now held Babylonia, both of which had hitherto belonged to the Seleucid empire. The Greeks and Macedonians in these countries had appealed to Demetrius for help.

and equipped them with means of
defense,
till his glorious name reached the
ends of the earth.
11 He brought peace to the land,
and Israel was filled with happiness.ᴾ
12 Every man sat under his vine and his fig
tree,
with no one to disturb him.�q
13 No one was left to attack them in their
land;
the kings in those days were crushed.
14 He strengthened all the lowly among his
people
and was zealous for the law;
he suppressed all the lawless and the
wicked.
15 He made the temple splendid
and enriched its equipment.

Alliance with Rome and Sparta. 16When
people heard in Rome and even in Sparta
that Jonathan had died, they were deeply
grieved.* 17But when the Romans heard
that his brother Simon had been made
high priest in his place and was master of
the country and the cities, 18they sent him
inscribed tablets of bronze to renew with
him the friendship and alliance that they
had established with his brothers Judas
and Jonathan.ʳ 19These were read before
the assembly in Jerusalem.

20This is a copy of the letter that the
Spartans sent: "The rulers and the citizens
of Sparta send greetings to Simon the high
priest, the elders, the priests, and the rest
of the Jewish people, our brothers. 21The
envoys you sent to our people have informed us of your glory and fame, and we
were happy that they came. 22In accordance with what they said we have recorded the following in the public decrees:
Since Numenius, son of Antiochus, and
Antipater, son of Jason, envoys of the
Jews, have come to us to renew their
friendship with us,ˢ 23the people have
voted to receive the men with honor, and
to deposit a copy of their words in the public archives, so that the people of Sparta
may have a record of them. A copy of this
decree has been made for Simon the high
priest."

24After this, Simon sent Numenius to
Rome with a great gold shield weighing a
thousand minas, to confirm the alliance
with the Romans.ᵗ

Decree of Honor. 25When the people
heard of these things, they said, "How can
we thank Simon and his sons? 26He and
his brothers and his father's house have
stood firm and repulsed Israel's enemies.
They have thus preserved its liberty." So
they made an inscription on bronze tablets, which they affixed to pillars on
Mount Zion. 27The following is a copy of
the inscription:
"On the eighteenth day of Elul,* in the
year one hundred and seventy-two, that is,
the third year under Simon the high priest
in Asaramel, 28in a great assembly of
priests, people, rulers of the nations, and
elders of the country, the following proclamation was made:
29" 'Since there have often been wars in
our country, Simon, son of the priest Mattathias, descendant of Joarib, and his
brothers have put themselves in danger
and resisted the enemies of their nation, so
that their sanctuary and law might be
maintained, and they have thus brought
great glory to their nation. 30After
Jonathan had rallied his nation and become their high priest, he was gathered to
his kinsmen. 31When the enemies of the
Jews sought to invade and devastate their
country and to lay hands on their temple,
32Simon rose up and fought for his nation,
spending large sums of his own money to
equip the men of his nation's armed forces
and giving them their pay. 33He fortified
the cities of Judea, especially the frontier
city of Beth-zur, where he stationed a garrison of Jewish soldiers, and where previously the enemy's arms had been stored.
34He also fortified Joppa by the sea and
Gazara on the border of Azotus, a place
previously occupied by the enemy; these
cities he resettled with Jews, and furnished
them with all that was necessary for their
restoration. 35When the Jewish people saw
Simon's loyalty and the glory he planned
to bring to his nation, they made him their
leader and high priest because of all he had
accomplished and the loyalty and justice

---

p Lv 26, 6.—q Mi 4, 4; Zec 3, 10.—r 1 Mc 8, 22.—s 1 Mc 12,
16; 15, 15.—t 1 Mc 12, 16; 15, 15.

14, 16: The embassy to Rome and Sparta was sent soon after
Simon's accession to power, and the replies were received before
Demetrius' expedition (vv 1-3)—probably in 142 B.C.
14, 27: *Eighteenth day of Elul:* September 13, 140 B.C.
Asaramel: a Hebrew name meaning "court of the people of
God."

he had shown his nation. In every way he sought to exalt his people.

36 " 'In his time and under his guidance they succeeded in driving the Gentiles out of their country, especially those in the City of David in Jerusalem, who had built for themselves a citadel from which they used to sally forth to defile the environs of the temple and inflict grave injury on its purity. 37 In this citadel he stationed Jewish soldiers, and he strengthened its fortifications for the defense of the land and the city, while he also raised the wall of Jerusalem to a greater height. 38 Consequently, King Demetrius confirmed him in the high priesthood, 39 *u* made him one of his Friends, and conferred the highest honors on him. 40 He had indeed heard that the Romans had addressed the Jews as friends, allies, and brothers and that they had received Simon's envoys with honor.

41 " 'The Jewish people and their priest have, therefore, made the following decisions. Simon shall be their permanent leader and high priest until a true prophet arises. 42 He shall act as governor general over them, and shall have charge of the temple, to make regulations concerning its functions and concerning the country, its weapons and strongholds; 43 he shall be obeyed by all. All contracts made in the country shall be dated by his name. He shall have the right to wear royal purple and gold ornaments. 44 It shall not be lawful for any of the people or priests to nullify any of these decisions, or to contradict the orders given by him, or to convene an assembly in the country without his consent, to be clothed in royal purple or wear an official gold brooch. 45 Whoever acts otherwise or violates any of these prescriptions shall be liable to punishment.

46 " 'All the people approved of granting Simon the right to act in accord with these decisions, 47 and Simon accepted

and agreed to act as high priest, governor general, and ethnarch* of the Jewish people and priests and to exercise supreme authority over all.' "

48 It was decreed that this inscription should be engraved on bronze tablets, to be set up in a conspicuous place in the precincts of the temple, 49 and that copies of it should be deposited in the treasury, where they would be available to Simon and his sons.

CHAPTER 15

Letter of Antiochus. 1 Antiochus,* son of King Demetrius, sent a letter from the islands of the sea to Simon, the priest and ethnarch of the Jews, and to all the nation, 2 which read as follows:

"King Antiochus sends greetings to Simon, the priest and ethnarch, and to the Jewish nation. 3 Whereas certain villains have gained control of the kingdom of my ancestors, I intend to reclaim it, that I may restore it to its former state. I have recruited a large number of mercenary troops and equipped warships 4 to make a landing in my country and take revenge on those who have ruined it and laid waste many cities in my realm.

5 "Now, therefore, I confirm to you all the tax exemptions that the kings before me granted you and whatever other privileges they conferred on you. 6 I authorize you to coin your own money, as legal tender in your country. 7 Jerusalem and its temple shall be free. All the weapons you have prepared and all the strongholds you have built and now occupy shall remain in your possession. 8 All debts, present or future, due to the royal treasury shall be canceled for you, now and for all time. 9 When we recover our kingdom, we will greatly honor you and your nation and the temple, so that your glory will be manifest in all the earth."

10 In the year one hundred and seventy-four,* Antiochus invaded the land of his ancestors, and all the troops rallied to him, so that few were left with Trypho. 11 Pursued by Antiochus, Trypho fled to Dor, by the sea,* 12 realizing what a mass of troubles had come upon him now that his soldiers had deserted him. 13 Antiochus encamped before Dor with a hundred and twenty thousand infantry and eight thousand horsemen. 14 While he invested

1Mc

---

u 39f: 1 Mc 2, 18.

14, 47: *Ethnarch:* a subaltern ruler over a racial group whose office needed confirmation by a higher authority within the empire.

15, 1: *Antiochus:* Antiochus VII Sidetes, son of Demetrius I, and younger brother of Demetrius II, now a prisoner of the Parthians. At the age of twenty he set out from the island of Rhodes to take his brother's place and drive out the usurper Trypho.

15, 10: *The year one hundred and seventy-four:* 138 B.C.

15, 11: *Dor, by the sea:* a fortress on the Palestinian coast, fifteen miles south of Carmel.

the city, his ships closed in along the coast, so that he blockaded it by land and sea and let no one go in or out.

Roman Alliance Renewed. [15] Meanwhile, Numenius and his companions left Rome with letters such as this addressed to various kings and countries:[v]

[16] "Lucius,* Consul of the Romans, sends greetings to King Ptolemy. [17] Certain envoys of the Jews, our friends and allies, have come to us to renew their earlier alliance of friendship. They had been sent by Simon the high priest and the Jewish people, [18] and they brought with them a gold shield worth a thousand minas.[w] [19] Therefore we have decided to write to various kings and countries, that they are not to harm them, or wage war against them or their cities or their country, and are not to assist those who fight against them. [20] We have also decided to accept the shield from them. [21] If, then, any troublemakers from their country take refuge with you, hand them over to Simon the high priest, so that he may punish them according to their law."

[22] The consul sent similar letters to Kings Demetrius, Attalus,* Ariarthes and Arsaces; [23] to all the countries—Sampsames, Sparta, Delos, Myndos, Sicyon, Caria, Samos, Pamphlia, Lycia, Halicarnassus, Rhodes, Phaselis, Cos, Side, Aradus, Gortyna, Cnidus, Cyprus, and Cyrene. [24] A copy of the letter was also sent to Simon the high priest.

Hostility of Antiochus. [25] When King Antiochus was encamped before Dor, he assaulted it continuously both with troops and with the siege machines he had made. He blockaded Trypho by preventing anyone from going in or out. [26] Simon sent to Antiochus' support two thousand elite troops, together with gold and silver and much equipment. [27] But he refused to accept the aid; in fact, he broke all the agreements he had previously made with Simon and became hostile toward him.

[28] He sent Athenobius, one of his Friends, to confer with Simon and say: "You are occupying Joppa and Gazara and the citadel of Jerusalem; these are cities of my kingdom. [29] You have laid waste their territories, done great harm to the land, and taken possession of many districts in my realm. [30] Therefore, give up the cities you have seized and the tribute money of the districts outside the territory of Judea of which you have taken possession; [31] or instead, pay me five hundred talents of silver for the devastation you have caused and five hundred talents more for the tribute money of the cities. If you do not do this, we will come and make war on you."

[32] So Athenobius, the king's Friend, came to Jerusalem, and on seeing the splendor of Simon's court, the gold and silver plate on the sideboard, and the rest of his rich display, he was amazed. When he gave him the king's message, [33] Simon said to him in reply:

"We have not seized any foreign land; what we took is not the property of others, but our ancestral heritage which for a time had been unjustly held by our enemies. [34] Now that we have the opportunity, we are holding on to the heritage of our ancestors. [35] As for Joppa and Gazara, which you demand, the men of these cities were doing great harm to our people and laying waste our country; however, we are willing to pay you a hundred talents for these cities."

[36] Athenobius made no reply, but returned to the king in anger. When he told him of Simon's words, of his splendor, and of all he had seen, the king fell into a violent rage.

Victory over Cendebeus. [37] Trypho had gotten aboard a ship and escaped to Orthosia.* [38] Then the king appointed Cendebeus commander in chief of the seacoast, and gave him infantry and cavalry forces. [39] He ordered him to move his troops against Judea and to fortify Kedron* and strengthen its gates, so that he could launch attacks against the Jewish people. Meanwhile the king went in pursuit of Trypho. [40] When Cendebeus came to Jamnia, he began to harass the people and to make incursions into Judea,

---

v 1 Mc 8, 17; 12, 16; 14, 22. 24.—w 1 Mc 14, 24.

15, 16: *Lucius:* perhaps Lucius Caecilius Metellus, consul in 142 B.C., or Lucius Calpurnicus Piso, consul in 140-139 B.C. This document pertains to Simon's first year as leader.

15, 22: *Attalus:* Attalus II of Pergamum, reigned 159-138 B.C. *Ariarthes:* Ariarthes V of Cappadocia, reigned 162-130 B.C. *Arsaces:* see notes on 1 Mc 14, 2.

15, 37: *Orthosia:* a port between Tripoli and the Eleutherus River.

15, 39: *Kedron:* a few miles southeast of Jamnia and facing the fortress of Gazara held by John Hyrcanus.

where he took people captive or massacred them. [41] As the king ordered, he fortified Kedron and stationed horsemen and infantry there, so that they could go out and patrol the roads of Judea.

CHAPTER 16

[1] John then went up from Gazara and told his father Simon what Cendebeus was doing. [2] Simon called his two oldest sons, Judas and John, and said to them: "I and my brothers and my father's house have fought the battles of Israel from our youth until today, and many times we succeeded in saving Israel. [3] I have now grown old, but you, by the mercy of Heaven, have come to man's estate. Take my place and my brother's, and go out and fight for our nation; and may the help of Heaven be with you!"

[4] John then mustered in the land twenty thousand warriors and horsemen. Setting out against Cendebeus, they spent the night at Modein, [5] rose early, and marched into the plain. There, facing them, was an immense army of foot soldiers and horsemen, and between the two armies was a stream. [6] John and his men took their position against the enemy. Seeing that his men were afraid to cross the stream, John crossed first. When his men saw this, they crossed over after him. [7] Then he divided his infantry into two corps and put his cavalry between them, for the enemy's horsemen were very numerous. [8] They blew the trumpets, and Cendebeus and his army were put to flight; many of them fell wounded, and the rest fled toward the stronghold. [9] It was then that John's brother Judas fell wounded; but John pursued them until Cendebeus reached Kedron, which he had fortified. [10] Some took refuge in the towers on the plain of Azotus, but John set fire to these, and

16, 14: *In the year one hundred and seventy-seven, in the eleventh month:* January-February, 134 B.C., by the temple calendar.

16, 15: *Dok:* a fortress built on a cliff three miles northwest of Jericho, near modern Ain Duq.

16, 23f: John Hyrcanus was ruler and high priest from 134 B.C. till his death in 104 B.C. These verses suggest that the book was written, or at least completed, only after he died.

about two thousand of the enemy perished. He then returned to Judea in peace.

Murder of Simon and His Sons. [11] Ptolemy, son of Abubus, had been appointed governor of the plain of Jericho, and he had much silver and gold, [12] being the son-in-law of the high priest. [13] But he became ambitious and sought to get control of the country. So he made treacherous plans to do away with Simon and his sons. [14] As Simon was inspecting the cities of the country and providing for their needs, he and his sons Mattathias and Judas went down to Jericho in the year one hundred and seventy-seven, in the eleventh month* (that is, the month Shebat). [15] The son of Abubus gave them a deceitful welcome in the little stronghold called Dok* which he had built. While serving them a sumptuous banquet, he had his men hidden there. [16] Then, when Simon and his sons had drunk freely, Ptolemy and his men sprang up, weapons in hand, rushed upon Simon in the banquet hall, and killed him, his two sons, and some of his servants. [17] By this vicious act of treason he repaid good with evil.

[18] Then Ptolemy wrote an account of this and sent it to the king, asking that troops be sent to help him and that the country be turned over to him. [19] He sent other men to Gazara to do away with John. To the army officers he sent letters inviting them to come to him so that he might present them with silver, gold, and gifts. [20] He also sent others to seize Jerusalem and the mount of the temple. [21] But someone ran ahead and brought word to John at Gazara that his father and his brothers had perished, and that Ptolemy had sent men to kill him also. [22] On hearing this, John was utterly astounded. When the men came to kill him, he had them arrested and put to death, for he knew what they meant to do. [23] * Now the rest of the history of John, his wars and the brave deeds he performed, his rebuilding of the walls, and his other achievements—[24] these things are recorded in the chronicle of his pontificate, from the time that he succeeded his father as high priest.

THE SECOND BOOK OF MACCABEES

Although this book, like the preceding one, receives its title from its protagonist, Judas Maccabee (or Maccabeus), it is not a sequel to 1 Maccabees. The two differ in many respects. Whereas the first covers the period from the beginning of the reign of Antiochus IV (175 B.C.) to the accession of John Hyrcanus I (134 B.C.), this present book treats of the events in Jewish history from the time of the high priest Onias III and King Seleucus IV (c. 180 B.C.) to the defeat of Nicanor's army (161 B.C.).

The author of 2 Maccabees states (2, 23) that his one-volume work is an abridgment of a certain five-volume work by Jason of Cyrene; but since this latter has not survived, it is difficult to determine its relationship to the present epitome. One does not know how freely the anonymous epitomizer may have rewritten his shorter composition, or how closely he may have followed the wording of the original in the excerpts he made. Some parts of the text here, clearly not derived from Jason's work, are the Preface (2, 19-32), the Epilogue (15, 37-39), and probably also certain moralizing reflections (e.g., 5, 17-20; 6, 12-17). It is certain, however, that both works were written in Greek, which explains why the Second Book of Maccabees was not included in the canon of the Hebrew Bible.

The book is not without genuine historical value in supplementing 1 Maccabees, and it contains some apparently authentic documents (11, 16-38). Its purpose, whether intended by Jason himself or read into it by the compiler, is to give a theological interpretation to the history of the period. There is less interest, therefore, in the actual exploits of Judas Maccabeus than in God's marvelous interventions. These direct the course of events, both to punish the sacrilegious and blasphemous pagans, and to purify God's holy temple and restore it to his faithful people. The author sometimes effects his purpose by transferring events from their proper chronological order, and giving exaggerated figures for the size of armies and the numbers killed in battle; he also places long, edifying discourses and prayers in the mouths of his heroes, and inclines to elaborate descriptions of celestial apparitions (3, 24-34; 5, 2ff; 10, 29f; 15, 11-16). He is the earliest known composer of stories that glorify God's holy martyrs (6, 18—7, 42; 14, 37-46).

Of theological importance are the author's teachings on the resurrection of the just on the last day (7, 9. 11. 14. 23; 14, 46), the intercession of the saints in heaven for people living on earth (15, 11-16), and the power of the living to offer prayers and sacrifices for the dead (12, 39-46).

The beginning of 2 Maccabees consists of two letters sent by the Jews of Jerusalem to their coreligionists in Egypt. They deal with the observance of the feast commemorating the central event of the book, the purification of the temple. It is uncertain whether the author or a later scribe prefixed these letters to the narrative proper. If the author is responsible for their insertion, he must have written his book some time after 124 B.C., the date of the more recent of the two letters. In any case, Jason's five-volume work very likely continued the history of the Jews well into the Hasmonean period, so that 2 Maccabees would probably not have been produced much before the end of the second century B.C.

The main divisions of 2 Maccabees are: I. Letters to the Jews in Egypt (1, 1—2, 18). II. Author's Preface (2, 19-32). III. Heliodorus' Attempt To Profane the Temple (3, 1-40). IV. Profanation and Persecution (4, 1—7, 42). V. Victories of Judas and Purification of the Temple (8, 1—10, 8). VI. Renewed Persecution (10, 9—15, 36). VII. Epilogue (15, 37-39).

I: LETTERS TO THE JEWS IN EGYPT

CHAPTER 1

First Letter 124 B.C. [1] The Jews in Jerusalem and in the land of Judea send greetings to their brethren, the Jews in Egypt, and wish them true peace! [2] May God bless you and remember his covenant with his faithful servants, Abraham, Isaac and Jacob. [3] May he give to all of you a heart to worship him and to do his will readily and generously. [4] May he open your heart to his law and his commandments and grant you peace. [5] May he hear your prayers, and be reconciled to you, and never forsake you in time of adversity. [6] Even now we are praying for you here.

[7] In the reign of Demetrius,* the year one hundred and sixty-nine, we Jews wrote to you during the trouble and violence that overtook us in those years after Jason and his followers had revolted against the holy land and the kingdom,[a] [8] setting fire to the gatehouse and shedding innocent blood. But we prayed to the LORD, and our prayer was heard;* we offered sacrifices and fine flour; we lighted the lamps and set out the loaves of bread.[b] [9] We are now reminding you to celebrate the feast of Booths in the month of Chislev.* [10] Dated in the year one hundred and eighty-eight.*

Festival Letter 164 B.C. The people of Jerusalem and Judea, the senate, and Judas send greetings and good wishes to Aristobulus, counselor of King Ptolemy and member of the family of the anointed priests, and to the Jews in Egypt. [11] Since we have been saved by God from grave dangers, we give him great thanks for having fought on our side against the king;* [12] [c] it was he who drove out those who fought against the holy city. [13] When their leader arrived in Persia with his seemingly irresistible army, they were cut to pieces in the temple of the goddess Nanea* through a deceitful stratagem employed by Nanea's priests. [14] * On the pretext of marrying the goddess, Antiochus with his Friends had come to the place to get its great treasures by way of dowry. [15] When the priests of the Nanaeon had displayed the treasures, Antiochus with a few attendants came to the temple precincts. As soon as he entered the temple, the priests locked the doors. [16] Then they opened a hidden trapdoor in the ceiling, hurled stones at the leader and his companions and struck them down. They dismembered the bodies, cut off their heads and tossed them to the people outside. [17] Forever blessed be our God, who has thus punished the wicked!

[18] * We shall be celebrating the purification of the temple on the twenty-fifth day of the month Chislev, so we thought it right to inform you that you too may celebrate the feast of Booths and of the fire that appeared when Nehemiah, the rebuilder of the temple* and the altar, offered sacrifices. [19] When our fathers were being exiled to Persia,* devout priests of the time took some of the fire from the altar and hid it secretly in the hollow of a dry cistern, making sure that the place would be unknown to anyone. [20] Many years later, when it so pleased God, Nehemiah, commissioned by the king of Persia, sent the descendants of the priests who had hidden the fire to look for it. [21] When they informed us that they could

2Mc

---

a 2 Mc 4, 7-20.—b 1 Mc 4, 38.—c 12-17: 2 Mc 9, 1-29; 1 Mc 6, 1-13.

1, 7: *Demetrius:* Demetrius II, king of Syria (145-139, 129-125 B.C.). *The year one hundred and sixty-nine* of the Seleucid era, 143 B.C. Regarding the dates in 1 and 2 Mc, see note on 1 Mc 1, 10. On the troubles caused by *Jason* and his revolt against *the kingdom,* i.e., the rule of the legitimate high priest, see 2 Mc 4, 7-22.

1, 8: *Our prayer was heard:* in the ultimate victory of the Maccabees.

1, 9: *Feast of Booths in the month of Chislev:* really the feast of the Dedication of the temple (2 Mc 10, 1-8), celebrated on the twenty-fifth of Chislev (Nov.-Dec.). Its solemnity resembles that of the true feast of Booths (Lv 23, 33-43), celebrated on the fifteenth of Tishri (Sept.-Oct.); cf 2 Mc 1, 18.

1, 10: 124 B.C. The date pertains to the preceding, not the following letter. *King Ptolemy:* Ptolemy VI Philometor, ruler of Egypt from 180 to 145 B.C.; he is mentioned also in 1 Mc 1, 18; 10, 51-59.

1, 11f: *The king:* Antiochus IV of Syria, the bitter persecutor of the Jews, who, as *leader* of the Syrian army that invaded Persia, perished there in 164 B.C.

1, 13: *Nanea:* an oriental goddess comparable to Artemis of the Greeks.

1, 14-17: A different account of the death of Antiochus IV is given in 2 Mc 9, 1-29, and another variant account in 1 Mc 6, 1-16. The writer of this letter had probably heard a distorted rumor of the king's death. This fact and other indications show that the letter was written very soon after Antiochus IV died, hence in 164 B.C.

1, 18-36: This purely legendary account of Nehemiah's miraculous fire is incorporated in the letter because of its connection with the temple and its rededication.

1, 18: *Nehemiah, the rebuilder of the temple:* he rebuilt the walls of Jerusalem, but the temple had been rebuilt by Zerubbabel almost a century before.

1, 19: *Persia:* actually Babylonia, which later became part of the Persian Empire.

not find any fire, but only muddy water, he ordered them to scoop some out and bring it. After the material for the sacrifices had been prepared, Nchcmiah ordered the priests to sprinkle with the water the wood and what lay on it. [22] When this was done and in time the sun, which had been clouded over, began to shine, a great fire blazed up, so that everyone marveled. [23] While the sacrifice was being burned, the priests recited a prayer, and all present joined in with them, Jonathan leading and the rest responding with Nehemiah.

[24] The prayer was as follows: "Lord, Lord God, creator of all things, awesome and strong, just and merciful, the only king and benefactor, [25] who alone are gracious, just, almighty, and eternal, Israel's savior from all evil, who chose our forefathers and sanctified them: [26] accept this sacrifice on behalf of all your people Israel and guard and sanctify your heritage. [27] Gather together our scattered people, free those who are the slaves of the Gentiles, look kindly on those who are despised and detested, and let the Gentiles know that you are our God. [28] Punish those who tyrannize over us and arrogantly mistreat us. [29] Plant your people in your holy place, as Moses promised." [d]

[30] Then the priests began to sing hymns. [31] After the sacrifice was burned, Nehemiah ordered the rest of the liquid to be poured upon large stones. [32] As soon as this was done, a flame blazed up, but its light was lost in the brilliance cast from a light on the altar. [33] When the event became known and the king of the Persians was told that, in the very place where the exiled priests had hidden the fire, a liquid was found with which Nehemiah and his people had burned the sacrifices, [34] the king, after verifying the fact, fenced the place off and declared it sacred. [35] To those on whom the king wished to bestow favors he distributed the large revenues he received there. [36] Nehemiah and his companions called the liquid nephthar, meaning purification, but most people name it naphtha.*

CHAPTER 2

[1] * You will find in the records, not only that Jeremiah the prophet ordered the deportees to take some of the aforementioned fire with them, [2] but also that the prophet, in giving them the law, admonished them not to forget the commandments of the LORD or be led astray in their thoughts, when seeing the gold and silver idols and their ornaments. [e] [3] With other similar words he urged them not to let the law depart from their hearts. [4] [f] The same document also tells how the prophet, following a divine revelation, ordered that the tent and the ark should accompany him and how he went off to the mountain* which Moses climbed to see God's inheritance. [5] When Jeremiah arrived there, he found a room in a cave in which he put the tent, the ark, and the altar of incense; then he blocked up the entrance. [6] Some of those who followed him came up intending to mark the path, but they could not find it. [7] When Jeremiah heard of this, he reproved them: "The place is to remain unknown until God gathers his people together again and shows them mercy. [8] Then the LORD will disclose these things, and the glory of the LORD will be seen in the cloud, just as it appeared in the time of Moses and when Solomon prayed that the Place* might be gloriously sanctified." [g]

[9] It is also related how Solomon in his wisdom offered a sacrifice at the dedication and the completion of the temple. [10] Just as Moses prayed to the LORD and fire descended from the sky and consumed the sacrifices, so Solomon also prayed and fire came down and burned up the holocausts. [h] [11] Moses had said, [i] "Because it had not been eaten, the sin offering was burned up."* [12] Solomon also celebrated the feast in the same way for eight days.

[13] Besides these things, it is also told in the records and in Nehemiah's Memoirs* how he collected the books about the kings, the writings of the prophets and of David, and the royal letters about sacred

d 2 Mc 2, 18; Dt 30, 3ff.—e Bar 6, 3-72.—f 4f: Dt 32, 49; 34, 1; Rv 11, 19.—g 1 Kgs 8, 11.—h Lv 9, 23f; 2 Chr 7, 1.—i Lv 10, 16-20.

1, 36: By a play on words, the Greek term *naphtha* (petroleum) is assimilated to some Semitic word, perhaps *nephthar*, meaning "loosened."

2, 1-8: This legendary account of how Jeremiah hid the sacred tent (which was not mentioned after the time of Solomon!), the ark, and the altar is given for the purpose of explaining why the postexilic temple was the legitimate place of worship even without these sacred objects.

2, 4: *The mountain:* Nebo; cf Dt 34, 1.

2, 8: *The Place:* the temple of Jerusalem.

2, 11: The statement attributed here to Moses seems to be based on Lv 10, 16-20.

2, 13: *Nehemiah's Memoirs:* a lost apocryphal work.

offerings. [14] In like manner Judas also collected for us the books that had been scattered because of the war, and we now have them in our possession.[j] [15] If you need them, send messengers to get them for you.

[16] As we are about to celebrate the feast of the purification of the temple, we are writing to you requesting you also to please celebrate the feast. [17] It is God who has saved all his people and has restored to all of them their heritage, the kingdom, the priesthood, and the sacred rites, [18] as he promised through the law. We trust in God, that he will soon have mercy on us and gather us together from everywhere under the heavens to his holy Place, for he has rescued us from great perils and has purified his Place.[k]

II: AUTHOR'S PREFACE

[19] This is the story of Judas Maccabeus and his brothers, of the purification of the great temple, the dedication of the altar, [20] the campaigns against Antiochus Epiphanes and his son Eupator,* [21] and of the heavenly manifestations accorded to the heroes who fought bravely for Judaism, so that, few as they were, they seized the whole land, put to flight the barbarian hordes, [22] regained possession of the world-famous temple, liberated the city, and reestablished the laws that were in danger of being abolished, while the LORD favored them with all his generous assistance. [23] All this, which Jason of Cyrene set forth in detail in five volumes, we will try to condense into a single book.

Purpose and Method. [24] In view of the flood of statistics, and the difficulties encountered by those who wish to plunge into historical narratives where the material is abundant, [25] we have aimed to please those who prefer simple reading, as well as to make it easy for the studious who wish to commit things to memory, and to be helpful to all. [26] For us who have taken upon ourselves the labor of making this digest, the task, far from being easy, is one of sweat and of sleepless nights, [27] just as the preparation of a festive banquet is no light matter for one who thus seeks to give enjoyment to others. Similarly, to win the gratitude of many we will gladly endure these inconveniences, [28] while we leave the responsibility for exact details to the original author, and confine our efforts to giving only a summary outline. [29] As the architect of a new house must give his attention to the whole structure, while the man who undertakes the decoration and the frescoes has only to concern himself with what is needed for ornamentation, so I think it is with us. [30] To enter into questions and examine them thoroughly from all sides is the task of the professional historian; [31] but the man who is making an adaptation should be allowed to aim at brevity of expression and to omit detailed treatment of the matter. [32] Here, then, we shall begin our account without further ado; it would be nonsense to write a long preface to a story and then abbreviate the story itself.

III: HELIODORUS' ATTEMPT TO PROFANE THE TEMPLE*

CHAPTER 3

Treachery of Simon. [1] [l] While the holy city lived in perfect peace and the laws were strictly observed because of the piety of the high priest Onias* and his hatred of evil, [2] the kings themselves honored the Place and glorified the temple with the most magnificent gifts. [3] Thus Seleucus,* king of Asia, defrayed from his own revenues all the expenses necessary for the sacrificial services. [4] But a certain Simon, of the priestly course of Bilgah,* who had been appointed superintendent of the temple, had a quarrel with the high priest about the supervision of the city market.[m] [5] Since he could not prevail against Onias, he went to Apollonius of Tarsus, who at that time was governor of Coelesyria and Phoenicia, [6] and reported to him that the treasury in Jerusalem was so full of untold riches that the total sum of money was

---

j 1 Mc 1, 57.—k Dt 30, 3ff.—l 1ff: 2 Mc 5, 19f; 15, 12.—m 2 Mc 4, 23.

2, 20: For the account of *the campaigns against Antiochus IV Epiphanes,* see 2 Mc 4, 7—10, 9; and for the account of those against *his son* Antiochus V *Eupator,* see 2 Mc 10, 10—13, 26.

3, 1-40: This legendary episode about Heliodorus is recounted here for the purpose of stressing the inviolability of the temple of Jerusalem; its later profanation was allowed by God because of the people's sins; cf 2 Mc 5, 17f.

3, 1: *The high priest Onias:* Onias III, who was priest from 196 to 175 B.C., and died in 171 B.C. He was the son of Simon, whose praises are sung in Sir 50, 1-21.

3, 3: *Seleucus:* Seleucus IV Philopator, who reigned from 187 to 175 B.C.

3, 4: *Bilgah:* a priestly family mentioned in Neh 12, 5. 18.

incalculable and out of all proportion to the cost of the sacrifices, and that it would be possible to bring it all under the control of the king. **Mission of Heliodorus.** [7] When Apollonius had an audience with the king, he informed him about the riches that had been reported to him. The king chose his minister Heliodorus and sent him with instructions to expropriate the aforesaid wealth. [8] So Heliodorus immediately set out on his journey, ostensibly to visit the cities of Coelesyria and Phoenicia, but in reality to carry out the king's purpose. [9] When he arrived in Jerusalem and had been graciously received by the high priest of the city, he told him about the information that had been given, and explained the reason for his presence, and he asked if these things were really true. [10] The high priest explained that part of the money was a care fund for widows and orphans,[n] [11] and a part was the property of Hyrcanus, son of Tobias,* a man who occupied a very high position. Contrary to the calumnies of the impious Simon, the total amounted to four hundred talents of silver and two hundred of gold. [12] He added that it was utterly unthinkable to defraud those who had placed their trust in the sanctity of the Place and in the sacred inviolability of a temple venerated all over the world. [13] But because of the orders he had from the king, Heliodorus said that in any case the money must be confiscated for the royal treasury. [14] So on the day he had set he went in to take an inventory of the funds. **Anguish of the Faithful.** There was great distress throughout the city. [15] Priests prostrated themselves in their priestly robes before the altar, and loudly begged him in heaven who had given the law about deposits to keep the deposits safe for those who had made them. [16] Whoever saw the appearance of the high priest was pierced to the heart, for the changed color of his face manifested the anguish of his soul. [17] The terror and bodily trembling that had come over the man clearly showed those who saw him the pain that lodged in his heart. [18] People rushed out of their houses in crowds to make public supplication, because the Place was in danger of being profaned. [19] Women, girded with sackcloth below their breasts, filled the streets; maidens secluded indoors ran together, some to the gates, some to the

walls, others peered through the windows, [20] all of them with hands raised toward heaven, making supplication. [21] It was pitiful to see the populace variously prostrated in prayer and the high priest full of dread and anguish. **Divine Intervention.** [22] While they were imploring the almighty LORD to keep the deposits safe and secure for those who had placed them in trust, [23] Heliodorus went on with his plan. [24] But just as he was approaching the treasury with his bodyguards, the LORD of spirits who holds all power manifested himself in so striking a way that those who had been bold enough to follow Heliodorus were panic-stricken at God's power and fainted away in terror. [25] There appeared to them a richly caparisoned horse, mounted by a dreadful rider. Charging furiously, the horse attacked Heliodorus with its front hoofs. The rider was seen to be wearing golden armor. [26] Then two other young men, remarkably strong, strikingly beautiful, and splendidly attired, appeared before him. Standing on each side of him, they flogged him unceasingly until they had given him innumerable blows. [27] Suddenly he fell to the ground, enveloped in great darkness. Men picked him up and laid him on a stretcher. [28] The man who a moment before had entered that treasury with a great retinue and his whole bodyguard was carried away helpless, having dearly experienced the sovereign power of God. [29] While he lay speechless and deprived of all hope of aid, due to an act of God's power, [30] the Jews praised the LORD who had marvelously glorified his holy Place; and the temple, charged so shortly before with fear and commotion, was filled with joy and gladness, now that the almighty LORD had manifested himself.

[31] Soon some of the companions of Heliodorus begged Onias to invoke the Most High, praying that the life of the man who was about to expire might be spared. [32] Fearing that the king might think that Heliodorus had suffered some foul play at the hands of the Jews, the high priest offered a sacrifice for the man's recovery. [33] While the high priest was offer-

---

n Dt 14, 29.

3, 11: *Son of Tobias:* a member of the Tobiad family of Transjordan (Neh 2, 10; 6, 17ff; 13, 4-8). Hyrcanus' father was Joseph, whose mother was the sister of the high priest Onias II.

ing the sacrifice of atonement, the same young men in the same clothing again appeared and stood before Heliodorus. "Be very grateful to the high priest Onias," they told him. "It is for his sake that the LORD has spared your life. ³⁴ Since you have been scourged by Heaven, proclaim to all men the majesty of God's power." When they had said this, they disappeared.

Testimony of Heliodorus. ³⁵ After Heliodorus had offered a sacrifice to the LORD and made most solemn vows to him who had spared his life, he bade Onias farewell, and returned with his soldiers to the king. ³⁶ Before all men he gave witness to the deeds of the most high God that he had seen with his own eyes. ³⁷ When the king asked Heliodorus who would be a suitable man to be sent to Jerusalem next, he answered: ³⁸ "If you have an enemy or a plotter against the government, send him there, and you will receive him back well-flogged, if indeed he survives at all; for there is certainly some special divine power about the Place. ³⁹ He who has his dwelling in heaven watches over that Place and protects it, and he strikes down and destroys those who come to harm it." ⁴⁰ This was how the matter concerning Heliodorus and the preservation of the treasury turned out.

IV: PROFANATION AND PERSECUTION

CHAPTER 4

Onias Appeals to the King. ¹ The Simon mentioned above as the informer about the funds against his own country, made false accusations that it was Onias who threatened Heliodorus and instigated the

---

o 2 Mc 1, 7; 1 Mc 1, 10.—p 1 Mc 8, 17.—q 1 Mc 1, 14.

4, 7: *Seleucus died:* he was murdered by Heliodorus. *Antiochus Epiphanes* was his younger brother. Onias' brother showed his love for the Greek way of life (v 10) by changing his Hebrew name Joshua, or Jesus, to the Greek name *Jason.*

4, 9: *Youth club:* an educational institution in which young men were trained both in Greek intellectual culture and in physical fitness. *Antiochians:* honorary citizens of Antioch, a Hellenistic city of the Seleucid Kingdom that had a corporation of such Antiochians, who enjoyed certain political and commercial privileges.

4, 11: *Eupolemus:* one of the two envoys sent to Rome by Judas Maccabeus (1 Mc 8, 17).

4, 12: Since the *gymnasium*, where the youth exercised naked (Greek *gymnos)*, lay in the Tyropoeon Valley to the east of the citadel, it was directly next to the temple on its eastern side. *The Greek hat:* a wide-brimmed hat, traditional headgear of Hermes, the patron god of athletic contests; it formed part of the distinctive costume of the members of the "youth club."

whole miserable affair. ² He dared to brand as a plotter against the government the man who was a benefactor of the city, a protector of his compatriots, and a zealous defender of the laws. ³ When Simon's hostility reached such a point that murders were being committed by one of his henchmen, ⁴ Onias saw that the opposition was serious and that Apollonius, son of Menestheus, the governor of Coelesyria and Phoenicia, was abetting Simon's wickedness. ⁵ So he had recourse to the king, not as an accuser of his countrymen, but as a man looking to the general and particular good of all the people. ⁶ He saw that, unless the king intervened, it would be impossible to have a peaceful government, and that Simon would not desist from his folly.

Jews Led by Jason To Apostatize. ⁷ But Seleucus died,* and when Antiochus surnamed Epiphanes succeeded him on the throne, Onias' brother Jason obtained the high priesthood by corrupt means:* ⁸ in an interview, he promised the king three hundred and sixty talents of silver, as well as eighty talents from another source of income. ⁹ Besides this he agreed to pay a hundred and fifty more, if he were given authority to establish a gymnasium and a youth club* for it and to enroll men in Jerusalem as Antiochians.

¹⁰ When Jason received the king's approval and came into office, he immediately initiated his countrymen into the Greek way of life. ¹¹ He set aside the royal concessions granted to the Jews through the mediation of John, father of Eupolemus* (that Eupolemus who would later go on an embassy to the Romans to establish a treaty of friendship with them); he abrogated the lawful institutions and introduced customs contrary to the law.*
¹² He quickly established a gymnasium* at the very foot of the acropolis, where he induced the noblest young men to wear the Greek hat.*
¹³ The craze for Hellenism and foreign customs reached such a pitch, through the outrageous wickedness of the ungodly pseudo-high-priest Jason, ¹⁴ that the priests no longer cared about the service of the altar. Disdaining the temple and neglecting the sacrifices, they hastened, at the signal for the discus-throwing, to take part in the unlawful exercises on the athletic field. ¹⁵ They despised what their ancestors had regarded as honors,

2Mc

while they highly prized what the Greeks esteemed as glory. [16] Precisely because of this, they found themselves in serious trouble: the very people whose manner of life they emulated, and whom they desired to imitate in everything, became their enemies and oppressors. [17] It is no light matter to flout the laws of God, as the following period will show.

[18] When the quinquennial games were held at Tyre in the presence of the king, [19] the vile Jason sent envoys as representatives of the Antiochians of Jerusalem, to bring there three hundred silver drachmas for the sacrifice to Hercules. But the bearers themselves decided that the money should not be spent on a sacrifice, as that was not right, but should be used for some other purpose. [20] So the contribution destined by the sender for the sacrifice to Hercules was in fact applied, by those who brought it, to the construction of triremes.*

[21] When Apollonius, son of Menestheus, was sent to Egypt for the coronation of King Philometor,* Antiochus learned that the king was opposed to his policies; so he took measures for his own security. [22] After going to Joppa, he proceeded to Jerusalem. There he was received with great pomp by Jason and the people of the city, who escorted him with torchlights and acclamations; following this, he led his army into Phoenicia.

Menelaus Supplants Jason. [23] Three years later Jason sent Menelaus,* brother of the aforementioned Simon, to deliver the money to the king, and to obtain decisions on some important matters. [24] When he had been introduced to the king, he flattered him with such an air of authority that he secured the high priesthood for himself, outbidding Jason by three hundred talents of silver. [25] He returned with the royal commission, but with nothing that made him worthy of the high priesthood; he had the temper of a cruel tyrant and the rage of a wild beast. [26] Then Jason, who had cheated his own brother and now saw himself cheated by another man, was driven out as a fugitive to the country of the Ammonites.

[27] Although Menelaus had obtained the office, he did not make any payments of the money he had promised to the king, [28] in spite of the demand of Sostratus, the commandant of the citadel, whose duty it was to collect the taxes. For this reason, both were summoned before the king. [29] Menelaus left his brother Lysimachus as his substitute in the high priesthood, while Sostratus left Crates, commander of the Cypriots, as his substitute.

Murder of Onias. [30] While these things were taking place, the people of Tarsus and Mallus* rose in revolt, because their cities had been given as a gift to Antiochis, the king's mistress. [31] The king, therefore, went off in haste to settle the affair, leaving Andronicus, one of his nobles, as his deputy. [32] Then Menelaus, thinking this a good opportunity, stole some gold vessels from the temple and presented them to Andronicus; he had already sold some other vessels in Tyre and in the neighboring cities. [33] When Onias had clear evidence of the facts, he made a public protest, after withdrawing to the inviolable sanctuary at Daphne, near Antioch. [34] Thereupon Menelaus approached Andronicus privately and asked him to lay hands on Onias. So Andronicus went to Onias, and by treacherously reassuring him through sworn pledges with right hands joined, persuaded him, in spite of his suspicions, to leave the sanctuary. Then, without any regard for justice, he immediately put him to death.

[35] As a result, not only the Jews, but many people of other nations as well, were indignant and angry over the unjust murder of the man. [36] When the king returned from the region of Cilicia, the Jews of the city,* together with the Greeks who detested the crime, went to see him about the murder of Onias. [37] Antiochus was deeply grieved and full of pity; he wept as he recalled the prudence and noble conduct of the deceased. [38] Inflamed with anger, he immediately stripped Andronicus of his purple robe, tore off his other garments, and had him led through the whole city to the very place where he had committed the outrage against Onias; and there he put the murderer to death. Thus the LORD rendered him the punishment he deserved.

4, 20: *Triremes:* war vessels with three banks of oars.

4, 21: *Philometor:* Ptolemy VI, king of Egypt, c. 172 to c. 145 B.C.

4, 23: *Menelaus:* Jewish high priest from c. 172 to his execution in 162 B.C. (2 Mc 13, 3-8).

4, 30: *Mallus:* a city of Cilicia (v 36) in southeastern Asia Minor, about thirty miles east of *Tarsus.*

4, 36: *The city:* Antioch. But some understand the Greek to mean "each city."

Riot against Lysimachus. [39]Many sacrilegious thefts had been committed by Lysimachus in the city* with the connivance of Menelaus. When word was spread that a large number of gold vessels had been stolen, the people assembled in protest against Lysimachus. [40]As the crowds, now thoroughly enraged, began to riot, Lysimachus launched an unjustified attack against them with about three thousand armed men under the leadership of Auranus, a man as advanced in folly as he was in years. [41]Reacting against Lysimachus' attack, the people picked up stones or pieces of wood or handfuls of the ashes lying there and threw them in wild confusion at Lysimachus and his men. [42]As a result, they wounded many of them and even killed a few, while they put all the rest to flight. The sacrilegious thief himself they slew near the treasury.

[43]Charges about this affair were brought against Menelaus. [44]When the king came to Tyre, three men sent by the senate* presented to him the justice of their cause. [45]But Menelaus, seeing himself on the losing side, promised Ptolemy, son of Dorymenes, a substantial sum of money if he would win the king over.[r] [46]So Ptolemy retired with the king under a colonnade, as if to get some fresh air, and persuaded him to change his mind. [47]Menelaus, who was the cause of all the trouble, the king acquitted of the charges, while he condemned to death those poor men who would have been declared innocent even if they had pleaded their case before Scythians. [48]Thus, those who had prosecuted the case for the city, for the people, and for the sacred vessels, quickly suffered unjust punishment. [49]For this reason, even some Tyrians were indignant over the

crime and provided sumptuously for their burial. [50]But Menelaus, thanks to the covetousness of the men in power, remained in office, where he grew in wickedness and became the chief plotter against his fellow citizens.

CHAPTER 5

Sedition and Death of Jason. [1]About this time Antiochus sent his second expedition* into Egypt.[s] [2][t] It then happened that all over the city, for nearly forty days, there appeared horsemen charging in midair, clad in garments interwoven with gold—companies fully armed with lances [3]and drawn swords; squadrons of cavalry in battle array, charges and countercharges on this side and that, with brandished shields and bristling spears, flights of arrows and flashes of gold ornaments, together with armor of every sort. [4]Therefore all prayed that this vision might be a good omen.

[5]But when a false rumor circulated that Antiochus was dead, Jason* gathered fully a thousand men and suddenly attacked the city. As the defenders on the walls were forced back and the city was finally being taken, Menelaus took refuge in the citadel. [6]Jason then slaughtered his fellow citizens without mercy, not realizing that triumph over one's own kindred was the greatest failure, but imagining that he was winning a victory over his enemies, not his fellow countrymen. [7]Even so, he did not gain control of the government, but in the end received only disgrace for his treachery, and once again took refuge in the country of the Ammonites. [8]At length he met a miserable end. Called to account before Aretas,* king of the Arabs, he fled from city to city, hunted by all men, hated as a transgressor of the laws, abhorred as the butcher of his country and his countrymen. After being driven into Egypt, [9]he crossed the sea to the Spartans, among whom he hoped to find protection because of his relations with them. There he who had exiled so many from their country perished in exile; [10]and he who had cast out so many to lie unburied went unmourned himself with no funeral of any kind or any place in the tomb of his ancestors.

The City Ravaged. [11][u] When these happenings were reported to the king, he

r 2 Mc 8, 8; 1 Mc 3, 38.—s 1 Mc 1, 17.—t 2f: 2 Mc 3, 24ff; 10, 29f; 11, 8.—u 11-21: 1 Mc 1, 20-24.

4, 39: *The city:* Jerusalem. *Menelaus* was still in Syria.
4, 44: *The senate:* the council of Jewish elders at Jerusalem; cf 1 Mc 12, 6.
5, 1: *Second expedition:* the first invasion of Egypt by Antiochus in 169 B.C. (1 Mc 1, 16-20) is not mentioned in 2 Mc, unless the coming of the Syrian army to Palestine (2 Mc 4, 21f) is regarded as the first invasion. The author of 2 Mc apparently combines the first pillage of Jerusalem in 169 B.C. after Antiochus' first invasion of Egypt (1 Mc 1, 20-28; cf 2 Mc 5, 5ff) with the second pillage of the city two years later (167 B.C.), following the king's second invasion of Egypt in 168 B.C. (1 Mc 1, 29-35; cf 2 Mc 5, 24ff).
5, 5: *Jason:* brother of Onias III, claimant of the high priesthood (2 Mc 4, 7-10). Later he was supplanted by Menelaus who drove him into Transjordan (2 Mc 4, 26).
5, 8: *Aretas:* King Aretas I of the Nabateans; cf 1 Mc 5, 25.

thought that Judea was in revolt. Raging like a wild animal, he set out from Egypt and took Jerusalem by storm. [12] He ordered his soldiers to cut down without mercy those whom they met and to slay those who took refuge in their houses. [13] There was a massacre of young and old, a killing of women and children, a slaughter of virgins and infants. [14] In the space of three days, eighty thousand were lost, forty thousand meeting a violent death, and the same number being sold into slavery. [15] Not satisfied with this, the king dared to enter the holiest temple in the world; Menelaus, that traitor both to the laws and to his country, served as guide. [16] He laid his impure hands on the sacred vessels and gathered up with profane hands the votive offerings made by other kings for the advancement, the glory, and the honor of the Place. [17] Puffed up in spirit, Antiochus did not realize that it was because of the sins of the city's inhabitants that the LORD was angry for a little while and hence disregarded the holy Place.[v] [18] If they had not become entangled in so many sins, this man, like Heliodorus, who was sent by King Seleucus to inspect the treasury, would have been flogged and turned back from his presumptuous action as soon as he approached. [19][w] The LORD, however, had not chosen the people for the sake of the Place, but the Place for the sake of the people.[*] [20] Therefore, the Place itself, having shared in the people's misfortunes, afterward participated in their good fortune; and what the Almighty had forsaken in his anger was restored in all its glory, once the great Sovereign became reconciled.

[21] Antiochus carried off eighteen hundred talents from the temple, and hurried back to Antioch. In his arrogance he planned to make the land navigable and the sea passable on foot, so carried away was he with pride.[x] [22] But he left governors to harass the nation: at Jerusalem, Philip, a Phrygian by birth,[*] and in character more cruel than the man who appointed him; [23] at Mount Gerizim,[*] Andronicus; and besides these, Menelaus, who lorded it over his fellow citizens worse than the others did. Out of hatred for the Jewish citizens, [24][y] the king sent Apollonius,[*] commander of the Mysians, at the head of an army of twenty-two thousand men, with orders to kill all the grown men

and sell the women and young men into slavery. [25] When this man arrived in Jerusalem, he pretended to be peacefully disposed and waited until the holy day of the sabbath; then, finding the Jews refraining from work, he ordered his men to parade fully armed. [26] All those who came out to watch, he massacred, and running through the city with armed men, he cut down a large number of people.

[27] But Judas Maccabeus with about nine others withdrew to the wilderness where he and his companions lived like wild animals in the hills, continuing to eat what grew wild to avoid sharing the defilement.[z]

CHAPTER 6

The Temple Desecrated. [1][a] Not long after this the king sent an Athenian senator to force the Jews to abandon the customs of their ancestors and live no longer by the laws of God; [2] also to profane the temple of Jerusalem and dedicate it to Olympian Zeus,[*] and that on Mount Gerizim to Zeus the Hospitable, as the inhabitants of the place requested.[b] [3] This intensified the evil in an intolerable and utterly disgusting way. [4] The Gentiles filled the temple with debauchery and revelry; they amused themselves with prostitutes[*] and had intercourse with women even in the sacred court. They also brought into the temple things that were forbidden, [5] so that the altar was covered with abominable offerings prohibited by the laws.

Abolition of the Law. [6] A man could not keep the sabbath or celebrate the traditional feasts, nor even admit that he was a

---

v 2 Mc 6, 12-16; 7, 16-19. 32-38.—w 19ff: 2 Mc 3, 1ff; 1 Chr 17, 9; Mk 2, 27.—x 1 Mc 1, 23f.—y 24ff: 1 Mc 1, 29f.—z 1 Mc 2, 28.—a 1-11: 1 Mc 1, 44-63.—b 1 Mc 1, 46; Dn 9, 27.

5, 19: Man is more important than even the most sacred institutions; cf Mk 2, 27.

5, 22: *Philip, a Phrygian by birth:* the Philip of 2 Mc 6, 11 and 8, 8, but probably not the same as Philip the regent of 2 Mc 9, 29 and 1 Mc 6, 14.

5, 23: *Mount Gerizim:* the sacred mountain of the Samaritans at Shechem; cf 2 Mc 6, 2.

5, 24: *Apollonius:* the *Mysian commander* of 1 Mc 1, 29; mentioned also in 2 Mc 3, 5; 4, 4.

6, 2: *Olympian Zeus:* equated with the Syrian Baal shomem ("the lord of the heavens"), a term which the Jews rendered as *"Shiqqus shomem," horrible abomination* (Dn 9, 27; 11, 31; 12, 11; 1 Mc 1, 54).

6, 4: *Amused themselves with prostitutes:* as in the fertility cults of the ancient Near East; see notes on Bar 6, 10. 42f.

Jew. [7] Moreover, at the monthly celebration of the king's birthday the Jews had, from bitter necessity, to partake of the sacrifices, and when the festival of Dionysus* was celebrated, they were compelled to march in his procession, wearing wreaths of ivy.

[8] At the suggestion of the citizens of Ptolemais, a decree was issued ordering the neighboring Greek cities to act in the same way against the Jews: oblige them to partake of the sacrifices, [9] and put to death those who would not consent to adopt the customs of the Greeks. It was obvious, therefore, that disaster impended. [10] Thus, two women who were arrested for having circumcised their children were publicly paraded about the city with their babies hanging at their breasts and then thrown down from the top of the city wall.[c] [11] Others, who had assembled in nearby caves to observe the sabbath in secret, were betrayed to Philip and all burned to death. In their respect for the holiness of that day, they had scruples about defending themselves.[d]

Purpose of Divine Judgment. [12] [e] Now I beg those who read this book not to be disheartened by these misfortunes, but to consider that these chastisements were meant not for the ruin but for the correction of our nation. [13] It is, in fact, a sign of great kindness to punish sinners promptly instead of letting them go for long. [14] [f] Thus, in dealing with other nations, the LORD patiently waits until they reach the full measure of their sins before he punishes them; but with us he has decided to deal differently, [15] in order that he may not have to punish us more severely later, when our sins have reached their fullness. [16] He never withdraws his mercy from us. Although he disciplines us with misfortunes, he does not abandon his own people. [17] Let these words suffice for recalling this truth. Without further ado we must go on with our story.

---

c 1 Mc 1, 60f.—d 1 Mc 2, 32-38.—e 12-16: 2 Mc 5, 17; 7, 16-19. 32-38.—f Wis 11, 9f; 12, 2. 22.—g Lv 11, 7f; Heb 11, 35.

6, 7: *Dionysus:* called also Bacchus the god of the grape harvest and of wine; *ivy* was one of his symbols.
6, 18—7, 42: The stories of Eleazar and of the mother and her seven sons, among the earliest models of "martyrology," were understandably popular among the Christians of the early centuries. Written originally to encourage God's people in times of persecution, they add gruesome details to the record of tortures, and place long speeches in the mouths of the martyrs.

Martyrdom of Eleazar.* [18] Eleazar, one of the foremost scribes, a man of advanced age and noble appearance, was being forced to open his mouth to eat pork.[g] [19] But preferring a glorious death to a life of defilement, he spat out the meat, and went forward of his own accord to the instrument of torture, [20] as men ought to do who have the courage to reject the food which it is unlawful to taste even for love of life. [21] Those in charge of that unlawful ritual meal took the man aside privately, because of their long acquaintance with him, and urged him to bring meat of his own providing, such as he could legitimately eat, and to pretend to be eating some of the meat of the sacrifice prescribed by the king; [22] in this way he would escape the death penalty, and be treated kindly because of their old friendship with him. [23] But he made up his mind in a noble manner, worthy of his years, the dignity of his advanced age, and the merited distinction of his gray hair, and of the admirable life he had lived from childhood; and so he declared that above all he would be loyal to the holy laws given by God.

He told them to send him at once to the abode of the dead, explaining: [24] "At our age it would be unbecoming to make such a pretense; many young men would think the ninety-year-old Eleazar had gone over to an alien religion. [25] Should I thus dissimulate for the sake of a brief moment of life, they would be led astray by me, while I would bring shame and dishonor on my old age. [26] Even if, for the time being, I avoid the punishment of men, I shall never, whether alive or dead, escape the hands of the Almighty. [27] Therefore, by manfully giving up my life now, I will prove myself worthy of my old age, [28] and I will leave to the young a noble example of how to die willingly and generously for the revered and holy laws."

He spoke thus, and went immediately to the instrument of torture. [29] Those who shortly before had been kindly disposed now became hostile toward him because what he had said seemed to them utter madness. [30] When he was about to die under the blows, he groaned and said: "The LORD in his holy knowledge knows full well that, although I could have escaped death, I am not only enduring terrible pain in my body from this scourging, but also suffering it with joy in my soul because of my devotion to him." ³¹This is how he died, leaving in his death a model of courage and an unforgettable example of virtue not only for the young but for the whole nation.

CHAPTER 7

Martyrdom of a Mother and Her Sons. ¹It also happened that seven brothers with their mother were arrested and tortured with whips and scourges by the king, to force them to eat pork in violation of God's law.ʰ ²One of the brothers, speaking for the others, said: "What do you expect to achieve by questioning us? We are ready to die rather than transgress the laws of our ancestors." ³At that the king, in a fury, gave orders to have pans and caldrons heated. ⁴While they were being quickly heated, he commanded his executioners to cut out the tongue of the one who had spoken for the others, to scalp him and cut off his hands and feet, while the rest of his brothers and his mother looked on. ⁵When he was completely maimed but still breathing, the king ordered them to carry him to the fire and fry him. As a cloud of smoke spread from the pan, the brothers and their mother encouraged one another to die bravely, saying such words as these: ⁶"The LORD God is looking on, and he truly has compassion on us, as Moses declared in his canticle, when he protested openly with the words, 'And he will have pity on his servants.' "ⁱ

⁷When the first brother had died in this manner, they brought the second to be made sport of. After tearing off the skin and hair of his head, they asked him, "Will you eat the pork rather than have your body tortured limb by limb?" ⁸Answering in the language of his forefathers, he said, "Never!" So he too in turn suffered the same tortures as the first. ⁹At the point of death he said: "You accursed fiend, you are depriving us of this present life, but the King of the world will raise us up* to live again forever. It is for his laws that we are dying."ʲ

¹⁰After him the third suffered their cruel sport. He put out his tongue at once when told to do so, and bravely held out his hands, ¹¹as he spoke these noble words: "It was from Heaven that I received these; for the sake of his laws I disdain them; from him I hope to receive

them again."ᵏ ¹²Even the king and his attendants marveled at the young man's courage, because he regarded his sufferings as nothing.

¹³After he had died, they tortured and maltreated the fourth brother in the same way. ¹⁴When he was near death, he said, "It is my choice to die at the hands of men with the God-given hope of being restored to life by him; but for you, there will be no resurrection to life."

¹⁵They next brought forward the fifth brother and maltreated him. ¹⁶Looking at the king, he said:ˡ "Since you have power among men, mortal though you are, do what you please. But do not think that our nation is forsaken by God. ¹⁷Only wait, and you will see how his great power will torment you and your descendants."

¹⁸After him they brought the sixth brother. When he was about to die, he said: "Have no vain illusions. We suffer these things on our own account, because we have sinned against our God; that is why such astonishing things have happened to us. ¹⁹Do not think, then, that you will go unpunished for having dared to fight against God."ᵐ

²⁰Most admirable and worthy of everlasting remembrance was the mother, who saw her seven sons perish in a single day, yet bore it courageously because of her hope in the LORD. ²¹Filled with a noble spirit that stirred her womanly heart with manly courage, she exhorted each of them in the language of their forefathers with these words: ²²"I do not know how you came into existence in my womb; it was not I who gave you the breath of life, nor was it I who set in order the elements of which each of you is composed. ²³Therefore, since it is the Creator of the universe who shapes each man's beginning, as he brings about the origin of everything, he, in his mercy, will give you back both breath and life, because you now disregard yourselves for the sake of his law."

²⁴Antiochus, suspecting insult in her words, thought he was being ridiculed. As the youngest brother was still alive, the king appealed to him, not with mere

h Jer 15, 9.—i Dt 32, 36.—j 2 Mc 12, 44; 14, 46.—k 2 Mc 12, 43ff.—l 16-19: 2 Mc 5, 17; 6, 12-16.—m Acts 5, 39.

7, 9: *The King of the world will raise us up:* here, and in vv 11. 14. 23. 29. 36, belief in the future resurrection of the body, at least for the just, is clearly stated; cf also 2 Mc 12, 44; 14, 46; Dn 12, 2.

words, but with promises on oath, to make him rich and happy if he would abandon his ancestral customs: he would make him his Friend and entrust him with high office. ²⁵When the youth paid no attention to him at all, the king appealed to the mother, urging her to advise her boy to save his life. ²⁶After he had urged her for a long time, she went through the motions of persuading her son. ²⁷In derision of the cruel tyrant, she leaned over close to her son and said in their native language: "Son, have pity on me, who carried you in my womb for nine months, nursed you for three years, brought you up, educated and supported you to your present age. ²⁸I beg you, child, to look at the heavens and the earth and see all that is in them; then you will know that God did not make them out of existing things;* and in the same way the human race came into existence. ²⁹Do not be afraid of this executioner, but be worthy of your brothers and accept death, so that in the time of mercy I may receive you again with them."

³⁰She had scarcely finished speaking when the youth said: "What are you waiting for? I will not obey the king's command. I obey the command of the law given to our forefathers through Moses. ³¹But you, who have contrived every kind of affliction for the Hebrews, will not escape the hands of God. ³² ⁿ We, indeed, are suffering because of our sins. ³³Though our living LORD treats us harshly for a little while to correct us with chastisements, he will again be reconciled with his servants. ³⁴But you, wretch, vilest of all men! do not, in your insolence, concern yourself with unfounded hopes, as you raise your hand against the children of Heaven. ³⁵You have not yet escaped the judgment of the almighty and all-seeing God. ³⁶My brothers, after enduring brief pain, have drunk of never-failing life, under God's covenant, but you, by the judgment of God, shall receive just punishments for your arrogance. ³⁷Like

my brothers, I offer up my body and my life for our ancestral laws, imploring God to show mercy soon to our nation, and by afflictions and blows to make you confess that he alone is God. ³⁸Through me and my brothers, may there be an end to the wrath of the Almighty that has justly fallen on our whole nation." ³⁹At that, the king became enraged and treated him even worse than the others, since he bitterly resented the boy's contempt. ⁴⁰ ᵒ Thus he too died undefiled, putting all his trust in the LORD. ⁴¹The mother was last to die, after her sons.

⁴²Enough has been said about the sacrificial meals and the excessive cruelties.

V: VICTORIES OF JUDAS AND PURIFICATION OF THE TEMPLE

CHAPTER 8

Judas Maccabeus. ¹ ᵖ Judas Maccabeus and his companions entered the villages secretly, summoned their kinsmen, and by also enlisting others who remained faithful to Judaism, assembled about six thousand men. ²They implored the LORD to look kindly upon his people, who were being oppressed on all sides; to have pity on the temple, which was profaned by godless men; ³to have mercy on the city, which was being destroyed and about to be leveled to the ground; to hearken to the blood that cried out to him; ⁴to remember the criminal slaughter of innocent children and the blasphemies uttered against his name; and to manifest his hatred of evil. ⁵ ᵍ Once Maccabeus got his men organized, the Gentiles could not withstand him, for the LORD's wrath had now changed to mercy. ⁶Coming unexpectedly upon towns and villages, he would set them on fire. He captured strategic positions, and put to flight a large number of the enemy. ⁷He preferred the nights as being especially helpful for such attacks. Soon the fame of his valor spread everywhere.

First Victory over Nicanor.* ⁸When Philip saw that Judas was gaining ground little by little and that his successful advances were becoming more frequent, he wrote to Ptolemy, governor of Coelesyria and Phoenicia, to come to the aid of the king's government.ʳ ⁹Ptolemy promptly selected Nicanor, son of Patroclus, one of the Chief

2Mc

---

n 32. 38: 2 Mc 5, 17; 6, 12-16; 17, 16-19.—o 40f: Heb 11, 35.—p 1-7: 2 Mc 5, 27; 1 Mc 3, 10-26.—q 5ff: 1 Mc 3, 3-9.—r 2 Mc 4, 45; 1 Mc 3, 38.

7, 28: *God did not make them out of existing things:* that is, God made all things solely by his omnipotent will and his creative word; cf Heb 11, 3.

8, 8-29. 34ff: This account of the campaign of Nicanor and Gorgias against Judas is paralleled, with certain differences, in 1 Mc 3, 38—4, 24.

Friends, and sent him at the head of at least twenty thousand armed men of various nations to wipe out the entire Jewish race. With him he associated Gorgias, a professional military commander, well-versed in the art of war.*s* ¹⁰Nicanor planned to raise the two thousand talents of tribute owed by the king to the Romans by selling captured Jews into slavery. ¹¹So he immediately sent word to the coastal cities, inviting them to buy Jewish slaves and promising to deliver ninety slaves for a talent— little did he dream of the punishment that was to fall upon him from the Almighty.

¹²When Judas learned of Nicanor's advance and informed his companions about the approach of the army, ¹³the cowardly and those who lacked faith in God's justice deserted and got away. ¹⁴But the others sold everything they had left, and at the same time besought the LORD to deliver those whom the ungodly Nicanor had sold before even meeting them. ¹⁵They begged the LORD to do this, if not for their sake, at least for the sake of the covenants made with their forefathers, and because they themselves bore his holy, glorious name. ¹⁶Maccabeus assembled his men, six thousand strong, and exhorted them not to be panic-stricken before the enemy, nor to fear the large number of the Gentiles attacking them unjustly, but to fight courageously, ¹⁷keeping before their eyes the lawless outrage perpetrated by the Gentiles against the holy Place and the affliction of the humiliated city, as well as the subversion of their ancestral way of life. ¹⁸"They trust in weapons and acts of daring," he said, "but we trust in almighty God, who can by a mere nod destroy not only those who attack us, but the whole world." ¹⁹He went on to tell them of the times when help had been given their ancestors: both the time of Sennacherib, when a hundred and eighty-five thousand of his men were destroyed,*t* ²⁰and the time of the battle in Babylonia against the Galatians, when only eight thousand Jews fought along with four thousand Macedonians; yet when the Macedonians were hard pressed, the eight thousand routed one hundred and twenty thousand and took a great quantity of booty, because of the help they received from Heaven. ²¹With such words he encouraged them and made them ready to die for their laws and their country.

Then Judas divided his army into four, ²²placing his brothers, Simon, Joseph,* and Jonathan, each over a division, assigning to each fifteen hundred men. ²³(There was also Eleazar.) After reading to them from the holy book and giving them the watchword, "The Help of God," he himself took charge of the first division and joined in battle with Nicanor.*u* ²⁴With the Almighty as their ally, they killed more than nine thousand of the enemy, wounded and disabled the greater part of Nicanor's army, and put all of them to flight. ²⁵They also seized the money of those who had come to buy them as slaves. When they had pursued the enemy for some time, ²⁶they were obliged to return by reason of the late hour. It was the day before the sabbath, and for that reason they could not continue the pursuit. ²⁷They collected the enemy's arms and stripped them of their spoils, and then observed the sabbath with fervent praise and thanks to the LORD who kept them safe for that day on which he let descend on them the first dew of his mercy. ²⁸After the sabbath, they gave a share of the booty to the persecuted and to widows and orphans; the rest they divided among themselves and their children. ²⁹When this was done, they made supplication in common, imploring the merciful LORD to be completely reconciled with his servants.

Timothy and Bacchides Defeated. ³⁰They also challenged the forces of Timothy and Bacchides, killed more than twenty thousand of them, and captured some very high fortresses. They divided the enormous plunder, allotting half to themselves and the rest to the persecuted, to orphans, widows, and the aged. ³¹They collected the enemies' weapons and carefully stored them in suitable places; the rest of the spoils they carried to Jerusalem. ³²They also killed the commander of Timothy's forces, a most wicked man, who had done great harm to the Jews. ³³While celebrating the victory in their ancestral city, they burned both those who had set fire to the

---

s 1 Mc 7, 26.—t 2 Mc 15, 22; 2 Kgs 19, 35; Is 37, 36.—u 1 Mc 3, 48.

8, 22: *Joseph:* called John in 1 Mc 2, 2; 9, 36. 38. This paragraph interrupts the story of Nicanor's defeat, which is resumed in v 34. The purpose of the author apparently is to group together the defeats suffered by the Syrians on various occasions. Battles against Timothy are recounted in 1 Mc 5, 37-44 and 2 Mc 12, 10-25; against Bacchides in 1 Mc 7, 8-20.

sacred gates and Callisthenes, who had taken refuge in a little house; so he received the reward his wicked deeds deserved.

Humiliation of Nicanor. [34] [v] The accursed Nicanor, who had brought the thousand slave dealers to buy the Jews, [35] after being humbled through the LORD's help by those whom he had thought of no account, laid aside his fine clothes and fled alone across country like a runaway slave, until he reached Antioch. He was eminently successful in destroying his own army. [36] So he who had promised to provide tribute for the Romans by the capture of the people of Jerusalem testified that the Jews had a champion, and that they were invulnerable for the very reason that they followed the laws laid down by him.

CHAPTER 9

Punishment and Death of Antiochus.* [1] [w] About that time Antiochus retreated in disgrace from the region of Persia. [2] He had entered the city called Persepolis and attempted to rob the temple and gain control of the city. Thereupon the people had swift recourse to arms, and Antiochus' men were routed, so that in the end Antiochus was put to flight by the natives and forced to beat a shameful retreat. [3] On his arrival in Ecbatana, he learned what had happened to Nicanor and to Timothy's forces. [4] Overcome with anger, he planned to make the Jews suffer for the injury done by those who had put him to flight. Therefore he ordered his charioteer to drive without stopping until he finished the journey.

Yet the condemnation of Heaven rode with him, since he said in his arrogance, "I will make Jerusalem the common graveyard of the Jews as soon as I arrive there." [5] So the all-seeing LORD, the God of Israel, struck him down with an unseen but incurable blow; for scarcely had he uttered those words when he was seized with ex-

cruciating pains in his bowels and sharp internal torment, [x] [6] a fit punishment for him who had tortured the bowels of others with many barbarous torments. [7] Far from giving up his insolence, he was all the more filled with arrogance. Breathing fire in his rage against the Jews, he gave orders to drive even faster. As a result he hurtled from the dashing chariot, and every part of his body was racked by the violent fall. [8] [y] Thus he who previously, in his superhuman presumption, thought he could command the waves of the sea, and imagined he could weigh the mountaintops in his scales, was now thrown to the ground and had to be carried on a litter, clearly manifesting to all the power of God. [9] [z] The body of this impious man swarmed with worms, and while he was still alive in hideous torments, his flesh rotted off, so that the entire army was sickened by the stench of his corruption. [10] Shortly before, he had thought that he could reach the stars of heaven, and now, no one could endure to transport the man because of this intolerable stench.

[11] At last, broken in spirit, he began to give up his excessive arrogance, and to gain some understanding, under the scourge of God, for he was racked with pain unceasingly. [12] When he could no longer bear his own stench, he said, "It is right to be subject to God, and not to think one's mortal self divine." [13] Then this vile man vowed to the LORD, who would no longer have mercy on him, [14] that he would set free the holy city, toward which he had been hurrying with the intention of leveling it to the ground and making it a common graveyard; [15] he would put on perfect equality with the Athenians all the Jews, whom he had judged not even worthy of burial, but fit only to be thrown out with their children to be eaten by vultures and wild animals; [16] he would adorn with the finest offerings the holy temple which he had previously despoiled; he would restore all the sacred vessels many times over; and would provide from his own revenues the expenses required for the sacrifices. [17] Besides all this, he would become a Jew himself and visit every inhabited place to proclaim there the power of God. [18] But since God's punishment had justly come upon him, his sufferings were not lessened, so he lost hope for himself and wrote the following letter

2Mc

---

v 34f: 2 Mc 8, 23f; 1 Mc 7, 26.—w 1-29: 2 Mc 1, 12-17; 1 Mc 6, 1-13.—x Acts 12, 20-23.—y Jb 38, 8-11; Ps 65, 6f; Is 40, 12.—z Acts 12, 23.

9, 1-28: In order to keep together the various accounts of God's punishment of the persecutors of his people, the author places here the stories of Antiochus' illness and death (in actuality the king died only after the purification of the temple; cf 1 Mc 4, 36-59; 6, 1-16; 2 Mc 10, 1-8); of Judas' campaigns in Idumea and Transjordan (cf 1 Mc 5, 1-51; 2 Mc 10, 14-38); and of the first expedition of Lysias (1 Mc 4, 26-35; 2 Mc 11, 1-15).

to the Jews in the form of a supplication. It read thus:

19 * "To my esteemed Jewish citizens, Antiochus, their king and general, sends hearty greetings and best wishes for their health and happiness. 20 If you and your children are well and your affairs are going as you wish, I thank God very much, for my hopes are in heaven. 21 Now that I am ill, I recall with affection the esteem and good will you bear me. On returning from the regions of Persia, I fell victim to a troublesome illness; so I thought it necessary to form plans for the general welfare of all. 22 Actually, I do not despair about my health, since I have great hopes of recovering from my illness. 23 Nevertheless, I know that my father, whenever he went on campaigns in the hinterland, would name his successor, 24 so that, if anything unexpected happened or any unwelcome news came, the people throughout the realm would know to whom the government had been entrusted, and so not be disturbed. 25 I am also bearing in mind that the neighboring rulers, especially those on the borders of our kingdom, are on the watch for opportunities and waiting to see what will happen. I have therefore appointed as king my son Antiochus, whom I have often before entrusted and commended to most of you, when I made hurried visits to the outlying provinces. I have written to him the letter copied below.* 26 Therefore I beg and entreat each of you to remember the general and individual benefits you have received, and to continue to show good will toward me and my son. 27 I am confident that, following my policy, he will treat you with mildness and kindness in his relations with you."

28 So this murderer and blasphemer, after extreme sufferings, such as he had inflicted on others, died a miserable death in the mountains of a foreign land. 29 His foster brother Philip brought the body home; but fearing Antiochus' son, he later withdrew into Egypt, to Ptolemy Philometor.

CHAPTER 10

Purification of Temple and City. 1 *a* When Maccabeus and his companions, under the LORD's leadership, had recovered the temple and the city, 2 they destroyed the altars erected by the Gentiles in the marketplace and the sacred enclosures. 3 After purifying the temple, they made a new altar. Then, with fire struck from flint, they offered sacrifice for the first time in two years,* burned incense, and lighted lamps. They also set out the showbread. 4 When they had done this, they prostrated themselves and begged the LORD that they might never again fall into such misfortunes, and that if they should sin at any time, he might chastise them with moderation and not hand them over to blasphemous and barbarous Gentiles. 5 On the anniversary of the day on which the temple had been profaned by the Gentiles, that is, the twenty-fifth of the same month Chislev, the purification of the temple took place. 6 The Jews celebrated joyfully for eight days as on the feast of Booths, remembering how, a little while before, they had spent the feast of Booths living like wild animals in caves on the mountains. 7 Carrying rods entwined with leaves, green branches and palms, they sang hymns of grateful praise to him who had brought about the purification of his own Place. 8 By public edict and decree they prescribed that the whole Jewish nation should celebrate these days every year.

VI: RENEWED PERSECUTION

Death of Ptolemy. 9 Such was the end of Antiochus surnamed Epiphanes.*b* 10 Now we shall relate what happened under Antiochus Eupator, the son of that godless man, and shall give a summary of the chief evils caused by the wars. 11 When Eupator succeeded to the kingdom, he put a certain Lysias in charge of the government as commander in chief of Coelesyria and Phoenicia. 12 Ptolemy, surnamed Macron,* had taken the lead in treating the Jews fairly because of the previous injustice that had been done them, and he en-

---

a 1-8: 1 Mc 4, 36-59.—b 2 Mc 2, 21; 1 Mc 6, 17.

9, 19-27: Despite the statement in v 18, this letter is not really a *supplication*. It is rather a notification to all the king's subjects of the appointment of his son as his successor and a request that they be loyal to the new king. Apparently the same letter, which has every appearance of being authentic, was sent to the various peoples throughout the kingdom, with only a few words of address changed for each group.

9, 25: *The letter copied below:* not included in the text of 2 Mc.

10, 3: *Two years:* three years according to 1 Mc 1, 54 and 4, 52.

10, 12: *Ptolemy Macron:* son of Dorymenes (2 Mc 4, 45), was formerly hostile to the Jews (2 Mc 6, 8).

deavored to have peaceful relations with them. [13] As a result, he was accused before Eupator by the King's Friends. In fact, on all sides he heard himself called a traitor for having abandoned Cyprus, which Philometor had entrusted to him, and for having gone over to Antiochus Epiphanes. Since he could not command the respect due to his high office, he ended his life by taking poison.

Victory over the Idumeans.* [14] When Gorgias became governor of the region, he employed foreign troops and used every opportunity to attack the Jews. [15] *c* At the same time the Idumeans, who held some important strongholds, were harassing the Jews; they welcomed fugitives from Jerusalem and endeavored to continue the war. [16] Maccabeus and his companions, after public prayers asking God to be their ally, moved quickly against the strongholds of the Idumeans. [17] Attacking vigorously, they gained control of the places, drove back all who manned the walls, and cut down those who opposed them, killing as many as twenty thousand men. [18] When at least nine thousand took refuge in two very strong towers, containing everything necessary to sustain a siege, [19] Maccabeus left Simon and Joseph, along with Zacchaeus and his men, in sufficient numbers to besiege them, while he himself went off to places where he was more urgently needed. [20] But some of the men in Simon's force who were money lovers let themselves be bribed by some of the men in the towers; on receiving seventy thousand drachmas, they allowed a number of them to escape. [21] When Maccabeus was told what had happened, he assembled the rulers of the people and accused those men of having sold their kinsmen for money by setting their enemies free to fight against them. [22] So he put them to death as traitors, and without delay captured the two towers. [23] As he was successful at arms in all his undertakings,

he destroyed more than twenty thousand men in the two strongholds.

Victory over Timothy. [24] Timothy, who had previously been defeated by the Jews,* gathered a tremendous force of foreign troops and collected a large number of cavalry from Asia; then he appeared in Judea, ready to conquer it by force. [25] At his approach, Maccabeus and his men made supplication to God, sprinkling earth upon their heads and girding their loins in sackcloth. [26] Lying prostrate at the foot of the altar, they begged him to be gracious to them, and to be an enemy to their enemies, and a foe to their foes, as the law declares. *d*

[27] After the prayer, they took up their arms and advanced a considerable distance from the city, halting when they were close to the enemy. [28] As soon as dawn broke,* the armies joined battle, the one having as pledge of success and victory not only their valor but also their reliance on the LORD, and the other taking fury as their leader in the fight.

[29] *e* In the midst of the fierce battle, there appeared to the enemy from the heavens five majestic men riding on golden-bridled horses, who led the Jews on. [30] They surrounded Maccabeus, and shielding him with their own armor, kept him from being wounded. They shot arrows and hurled thunderbolts at the enemy, who were bewildered and blinded, thrown into confusion and routed. [31] Twenty-five hundred of their foot soldiers and six hundred of their horsemen were slain. [32] Timothy, however, fled to a well-fortified stronghold called Gazara, where Chaereas was in command. *f* [33] For four days Maccabeus and his men eagerly besieged the fortress. [34] Those inside, relying on the strength of the place, kept repeating outrageous blasphemies and uttering abominable words. [35] When the fifth day dawned, twenty young men in the army of Maccabeus, angered over such blasphemies, bravely stormed the wall and with savage fury cut down everyone they encountered. [36] Others who climbed up the same way swung around on the defenders, taking the besieged in the rear; they put the towers to the torch, spread the fire and burned the blasphemers alive. Still others broke down the gates and let in the rest of the troops, who took possession of the city. [37] Timothy had hidden in a cistern, but they killed* him, along with his brother

c 15-23: 1 Mc 5, 3ff.—d Ex 23, 22.—e 29f: 2 Mc 3, 24ff; 5, 2f; 10, 29f; 11, 8.—f 1 Mc 13, 43-48.

10, 14-23: Probably the same campaign of Judas against the Idumeans that is mentioned in 1 Mc 5, 1-3.

10, 24: *Timothy . . . previously . . . defeated by the Jews:* as recounted in 2 Mc 8, 30ff.

10, 28: *As soon as dawn broke:* the same battle at dawn as in 1 Mc 5, 30-34.

10, 37: *Timothy . . . they killed.* apparently, the same Timothy is still alive in 2 Mc 12, 2. 18-25. The present passage is not in chronological order; Gazara, v 32 (Gezer), was not captured by the Jews until much later (cf 1 Mc 9, 50ff; 13, 53).

Chaereas, and Apollophanes. [38] On completing these exploits, they blessed, with hymns of grateful praise, the LORD who shows great kindness to Israel and grants them victory.

CHAPTER 11

Defeat of Lysias.* [1] [g] Very soon afterward, Lysias, guardian and kinsman of the king and head of the government, being greatly displeased at what had happened, [2] mustered about eighty thousand infantry and all his cavalry and marched against the Jews. His plan was to make Jerusalem a Greek settlement; [3] to levy tribute on the temple, as he did on the sanctuaries of the other nations; and to put the high priesthood up for sale every year. [4] He did not take God's power into account at all, but felt exultant confidence in his myriads of foot soldiers, his thousands of horsemen, and his eighty elephants. [5] So he invaded Judea, and when he reached Beth-zur, a fortified place about twenty miles from Jerusalem, launched a strong attack against it. [6] When Maccabeus and his men learned that Lysias was besieging the strongholds, they and all the people begged the LORD with lamentations and tears to send a good angel to save Israel. [h] [7] Maccabeus himself was the first to take up arms, and he exhorted the others to join him in risking their lives to help their kinsmen. Then they resolutely set out together. [8] Suddenly, while they were still near Jerusalem, a horseman appeared at their head, clothed in white garments and brandishing gold weapons. [i] [9] Then all of them together thanked God for his mercy, and their hearts were filled with such courage that they were ready to assault not only men, but the most savage beasts, yes, even walls of iron. [10] Now that the LORD had shown his mercy toward them, they advanced in battle order with the aid of their heavenly ally. [11] Hurling themselves upon the enemy like lions, they laid low eleven thousand foot soldiers and sixteen hundred horsemen, and put all the rest to flight. [12] Most of those who got away were wounded and stripped of their arms, while Lysias himself escaped only by shameful flight.

Peace with the Syrians. [13] [j] But Lysias was not a stupid man. He reflected on the defeat he had suffered, and came to realize that the Hebrews were invincible because the mighty God was their ally. He therefore sent a message [14] persuading them to settle everything on just terms, and promising to persuade the king also, and to induce him to become their friend. [15] Maccabeus, solicitous for the common good, agreed to all that Lysias proposed; and the king, on his part, granted in behalf of the Jews all the written requests of Maccabeus to Lysias.

Official Letters. [16] These are the terms of the letter which Lysias wrote to the Jews: "Lysias sends greetings to the Jewish people. [17] John and Absalom, your envoys, have presented your signed communication and asked about the matters contained in it. [18] Whatever had to be referred to the king I called to his attention, and the things that were acceptable he has granted. [19] If you maintain your loyalty to the government, I will endeavor to further your interests in the future. [20] On the details of these matters I have authorized my representatives, as well as your envoys, to confer with you. [21] Farewell." The year one hundred and forty-eight,* the twenty-fourth of Dioscorinthius.

[22] The king's letter read thus: "King Antiochus sends greetings to his brother Lysias. [23] Now that our father has taken his place among the gods, we wish the subjects of our kingdom to be undisturbed in conducting their own affairs. [24] We understand that the Jews do not agree with our father's policy concerning Greek customs but prefer their own way of life. They are petitioning us to let them retain their own customs. [25] Since we desire that this people too should be undisturbed, our decision is that their temple be restored to them and that they live in keeping with the customs of their ancestors. [26] Accordingly, please send them messengers to give them our assurances of friendship, so that, when they learn of our decision, they may have nothing to worry about but may contentedly go about their own business."

[27] The king's letter to the people was as follows: "King Antiochus sends greetings

---

g 1-12: 1 Mc 4, 26-35.—h Ex 23, 20.—i 2 Mc 3, 24ff; 5, 2f; 10, 29f.—j 13-33: 1 Mc 6, 57-61.

11, 1-12: The defeat of Lysias at Beth-zur probably occurred before the purification of the temple; cf 1 Mc 4, 26-35.

11, 21: *The year one hundred and forty-eight:* 164 B.C. The reading of the name of the month and its position in the calendar are uncertain.

to the Jewish senate and to the rest of the Jews. ²⁸If you are well, it is what we desire. We too are in good health. ²⁹Menelaus has told us of your wish to return home and attend to your own affairs. ³⁰Therefore, those who return by the thirtieth of Xanthicus will have our assurance of full permission ³¹to observe their dietary laws and other laws, just as before, and none of the Jews shall be molested in any way for faults committed through ignorance. ³²I have also sent Menelaus to reassure you. ³³Farewell." In the year one hundred and forty-eight, the fifteenth of Xanthicus.*

³⁴The Romans also sent them a letter as follows: "Quintus Memmius and Titus Manius, legates of the Romans, send greetings to the Jewish people. ³⁵Whatever Lysias, kinsman of the king, has granted you, we also approve. ³⁶But the matters on which he passed judgment should be submitted to the king. As soon as you have considered them, send someone to us with your decisions so that we may present them to your advantage, for we are on our way to Antioch. ³⁷Make haste, then, to send us those who can inform us of your intentions. ³⁸Farewell." In the year one hundred and forty-eight, the fifteenth of Xanthicus.*

CHAPTER 12

Persecution Renewed. ¹After these agreements were made, Lysias returned to the king, and the Jews went about their farming. ²But some of the local governors, Timothy and Apollonius, son of Gennaeus,* as also Hieronymus and Demophon, to say nothing of Nicanor, the commander of the Cyprians, would not allow them to live in peace.

³Some people of Joppa also committed this outrage: they invited the Jews who lived among them, together with their wives and children, to embark on boats which they had provided. There was no hint of enmity toward them; ⁴this was done by public vote of the city. When the Jews, not suspecting treachery and wishing to live on friendly terms, accepted the invitation, the people of Joppa took them out to sea and drowned at least two hundred of them.

Activity of Judas. ⁵As soon as Judas heard of the barbarous deed perpetrated against his countrymen, he summoned his men; ⁶and after calling upon God, the just judge, he marched against the murderers of his kinsmen. In a night attack he set the harbor on fire, burnt the boats, and put to the sword those who had taken refuge there. ⁷When the gates of the town were shut, he withdrew, intending to come back later and wipe out the entire population of Joppa.

⁸On hearing that the men of Jamnia planned to give like treatment to the Jews who lived among them, ⁹he attacked the Jamnian populace by night, setting fire to the harbor and the fleet, so that the glow of the flames was visible as far as Jerusalem, thirty miles away.

¹⁰ *k* When the Jews had gone about a mile from there* in the campaign against Timothy, they were attacked by Arabs numbering at least five thousand foot soldiers, and five hundred horsemen. ¹¹After a hard fight, Judas and his companions, with God's help, were victorious. The defeated nomads begged Judas to make friends with them and promised to supply the Jews with cattle and to help them in every other way. ¹²Realizing that they could indeed be useful in many respects, Judas agreed to make peace with them. After the pledge of friendship had been exchanged, the Arabs withdrew to their tents.

¹³He also attacked a certain city called Caspin, fortified with earthworks and ramparts and inhabited by a mixed population of Gentiles. ¹⁴Relying on the strength of their walls and their supply of provisions, the besieged treated Judas and his men with contempt, insulting them and even uttering blasphemies and profanity. ¹⁵But Judas and his men invoked the aid of the great Sovereign of the world, who, in the

2Mc

---

k 10-16: 1 Mc 5, 24-36.

11, 33: The date, which is the same as the date of the Romans' letter (v 38), cannot be correct. The king's letter must be connected with the peace treaty of the year 149 of the Seleucid era, i.e., 163 B.C. Perhaps the mention of the month of Xanthicus in the body of the letter (v 30) caused the date of the Romans' letter to be transferred to this one.

11, 38: The date is April 12, 164 B.C.

12, 2: *Apollonius, son of Gennaeus:* not the Apollonius who was the son of Menestheus (2 Mc 4, 21). *Nicanor:* probably distinct from the Nicanor of 2 Mc 14, 2.

12, 10: *From there:* not from the aforesaid Jamnia (vv 8f) or Joppa (vv 3-7), but from a place in Transjordan; vv 10-26 parallel the account given in 1 Mc 5, 9-13. 24-54 of Judas' campaign in northern Transjordan.

day of Joshua, overthrew Jericho without battering-ram or siege machine; then they furiously stormed the ramparts.[l] [16]Capturing the city by the will of God, they inflicted such indescribable slaughter on it that the adjacent pool, which was about a quarter of a mile wide, seemed to be filled with the blood that flowed into it.

[17] [m] When they had gone on some ninety miles, they reached Charax,[n] where there were certain Jews known as Toubiani.* [18]But they did not find Timothy in that region, for he had already departed from there without having done anything except to leave behind in one place a very strong garrison. [19]But Dositheus and Sosipater, two of Maccabeus' captains, marched out and destroyed the force of more than ten thousand men that Timothy had left in the stronghold. [20]Meanwhile, Maccabeus divided his army into cohorts, with a commander over each cohort, and went in pursuit of Timothy, who had a force of a hundred and twenty thousand foot soldiers and twenty-five hundred horsemen. [21]When Timothy learned of the approach of Judas, he sent on ahead of him the women and children, as well as the baggage, to a place called Karnion, which was hard to besiege and even hard to reach because of the difficult terrain of that region. [22]But when Judas' first cohort appeared, the enemy was overwhelmed with fear and terror at the manifestation of the All-seeing. Scattering in every direction, they rushed away in such headlong flight that in many cases they wounded one another, pierced by the swords of their own men. [23]Judas pressed the pursuit vigorously, putting the sinners to the sword and destroying as many as thirty thousand men.

[24]Timothy himself fell into the hands of the men under Dositheus and Sosipater; but with great cunning, he asked them to spare his life and let him go, because he had in his power the parents and relatives of many of them, and could make these suffer. [25]When he had fully confirmed his solemn pledge to restore them unharmed, they let him go for the sake of saving their brethren.

Further Successes. [26]Judas then marched to Karnion and the shrine of Atargatis,* where he killed twenty-five thousand people. [27] [o] After the defeat and destruction of these, he moved his army to Ephron, a fortified city inhabited by people of many nationalities. Robust young men took up their posts in defense of the walls, from which they fought valiantly; inside were large supplies of machines and missiles. [28]But the Jews, invoking the Sovereign who forcibly shatters the might of his enemies, got possession of the city and slaughtered twenty-five thousand of the people in it. [29]Then they set out from there and hastened on to Scythopolis,* seventy-five miles from Jerusalem. [30]But when the Jews who lived there testified to the good will shown by the Scythopolitans and to their kind treatment even in times of adversity, [31]Judas and his men thanked them and exhorted them to be well disposed to their race in the future also. Finally they arrived in Jerusalem, shortly before the feast of Weeks.

[32]After this feast called Pentecost, they lost no time in marching against Gorgias, governor of Idumea, [33]who opposed them with three thousand foot soldiers and four hundred horsemen. [34]In the ensuing battle, a few of the Jews were slain. [35]A man called Dositheus, a powerful horseman and one of Bacenor's men,* caught hold of Gorgias, grasped his military cloak and dragged him along by main strength, intending to capture the vile wretch alive, when a Thracian horseman attacked Dositheus and cut off his arm at the shoulder. Then Gorgias fled to Marisa. [36]After Esdris and his men had been fighting for a long time and were weary, Judas called upon the LORD to show himself their ally and leader in the battle. [37]Then, raising a battle cry in his ancestral language, and with songs, he charged Gorgias' men when they were not expecting it and put them to flight.

Expiation for the Dead. [38]Judas rallied his army and went to the city of Adullam. As the week was ending, they purified themselves according to custom and kept the sabbath there. [39]On the following day, since the task had now become urgent,

---

l Jos 6, 1-21.—m 17-26: 1 Mc 5, 37-44.—n 1 Mc 5, 13.—o 27-31: 2 Mc 5, 45-54.

12, 17: *Certain Jews known as Toubiani:* because they lived "in the land of Tob" (1 Mc 5, 13).
12, 26: *Atargatis:* a Syrian goddess, represented by the body of a fish.
12, 29: *Scythopolis:* the Greek name of the city of Beth-shan; cf 1 Mc 5, 52.
12, 35: *One of Bacenor's men:* certain ancient witnesses to the text have "one of the Toubiani"; cf v 17.

Judas and his men went to gather up the bodies of the slain and bury them with their kinsmen in their ancestral tombs. [40] But under the tunic of each of the dead they found amulets sacred to the idols of Jamnia, which the law forbids the Jews to wear. So it was clear to all that this was why these men had been slain.[p] [41] They all therefore praised the ways of the LORD, the just judge who brings to light the things that are hidden. [42] * Turning to supplication, they prayed that the sinful deed might be fully blotted out. The noble Judas warned the soldiers to keep themselves free from sin, for they had seen with their own eyes what had happened because of the sin of those who had fallen. [43] He then took up a collection among all his soldiers, amounting to two thousand silver drachmas, which he sent to Jerusalem to provide for an expiatory sacrifice. In doing this he acted in a very excellent and noble way, inasmuch as he had the resurrection of the dead in view; [44] for if he were not expecting the fallen to rise again, it would have been useless and foolish to pray for them in death. [45] But if he did this with a view to the splendid reward that awaits those who had gone to rest in godliness, it was a holy and pious thought. [46] Thus he made atonement for the dead that they might be freed from this sin.

CHAPTER 13

The Syrians Invade Judea. [1] In the year one hundred and forty-nine,* Judas and his men learned that Antiochus Eupator was invading Judea with a large force, [2] and that with him was Lysias, his guardian, who was in charge of the government.

p Dt 7, 25.—q 1 Mc 6, 30.—r 1 Tm 6, 15; Rv 17, 14; 19, 16.

12, 42-46: This is the earliest statement of the doctrine that prayers (v 42) and sacrifices (v 43) for the dead are beneficial. The statement is made here, however, only for the purpose of proving that Judas believed in the resurrection of the just (2 Mc 7, 9. 14. 23. 36). That is, he believed that expiation could be made for certain sins of otherwise good men—soldiers who had given their lives for God's cause. Thus, they could share in the resurrection. His belief was similar to, but not quite the same as, the Catholic doctrine of purgatory.
13, 1: *In the year one hundred and forty-nine:* 163-162 B.C.
13, 2: *They led:* the Greek means literally "Each (of them) led," but it is unlikely that the author meant the already immense numbers to be doubled; the numbers are similar to those in 1 Mc 6, 30.
13, 4: *Beroea:* the Greek name of Aleppo.
13, 5: *Ashes:* probably smoldering ashes; the *tower* resembles the ancient Persian fire towers.

They led* a Greek army of one hundred and ten thousand foot soldiers, fifty-three hundred horsemen, twenty-two elephants, and three hundred chariots armed with scythes.[q] **Death of Menelaus.** [3] Menelaus also joined them, and with great duplicity kept urging Antiochus on, not for the welfare of his country, but in the hope of being established in office. [4] But the King of kings aroused the anger of Antiochus against the scoundrel. When the king was shown by Lysias that Menelaus was to blame for all the trouble, he ordered him to be taken to Beroea* and executed there in the customary local method.[r] [5] There is at that place a tower seventy-five feet high, full of ashes,* with a circular rim sloping down steeply on all sides toward the ashes. [6] A man guilty of sacrilege or notorious for certain other crimes is brought up there and then hurled down to destruction. [7] In such a manner was Menelaus, the transgressor of the law, fated to die; he was deprived even of decent burial. [8] It was altogether just that he who had committed so many sins against the altar with its pure fire and ashes should meet his death in ashes. **Skirmish near Modein.** [9] The king was advancing, his mind full of savage plans for inflicting on the Jews worse things than those they suffered in his father's time. [10] When Judas learned of this, he urged the people to call upon the LORD night and day, to help them now, if ever, [11] when they were about to be deprived of their law, their country, and their holy temple; and not to allow this nation, which had just begun to revive, to be subjected again to blasphemous Gentiles. [12] When they had all joined in doing this, and had implored the merciful LORD continuously with weeping and fasting and prostrations for three days, Judas encouraged them and told them to stand ready. [13] After a private meeting with the elders, he decided that, before the king's army could invade Judea and take possession of the city, the Jews should march out and settle the matter with God's help. [14] Leaving the outcome to the Creator of the world, and exhorting his followers to fight nobly to death for the laws, the temple, the city, the country, and the government, he pitched his camp near Modein. [15] Giving his men the battle cry "God's Victory," he made a night attack on the king's pavilion with a picked force of the bravest young men and killed about two thousand in the camp. They also slew* the lead elephant and its rider.ˢ ¹⁶Finally they withdrew in triumph,* having filled the camp with terror and confusion. ¹⁷Day was just breaking when this was accomplished with the help and protection of the LORD.

Treaty with Antiochus V. ¹⁸ ᵗ The king, having had a taste of the Jews' daring, tried to take their positions by a stratagem. ¹⁹So he marched against Beth-zur, a strong fortress of the Jews; but he was driven back, checked, and defeated. ²⁰Judas then sent supplies to the men inside, ²¹but Rhodocus, of the Jewish army, betrayed military secrets* to the enemy. He was found out, arrested, and imprisoned. ²²The king made a second attempt by negotiating with the men of Beth-zur. After giving them his pledge and receiving theirs, he withdrew ²³and attacked Judas and his men. But he was defeated. Next he heard that Philip, who was left in charge of the government in Antioch, had rebelled. Dismayed, he parleyed with the Jews, submitted to their terms, and swore to observe their rights. Having come to this agreement, he offered a sacrifice, and honored the temple with a generous donation. ²⁴He approved of Maccabeus and left him as military and civil governor of the territory from Ptolemais to the region of the Gerrenes.* ²⁵When he came to Ptolemais, the people of that city were angered by the peace treaty; in fact they were so indignant that they wanted to annul its provisions. ²⁶But Lysias took the platform, defended the treaty as well as he could, and won them over by persuasion. After calming them and gaining their good will, he returned to Antioch.

That is how the king's attack and withdrawal went.

CHAPTER 14

Antagonism of Alcimus. ¹ ᵘ Three years later,* Judas and his men learned that Demetrius, son of Seleucus, had sailed into the port of Tripolis with a powerful army and a fleet, ²and that he had occupied the country, after doing away with Antiochus and his guardian Lysias.

³A certain Alcimus, a former high priest, who had willfully incurred defile-

ment at the time of the revolt, realized that there was no way for him to salvage his position and regain access to the holy altar. ⁴So he went to King Demetrius in the year one hundred and fifty-one and presented him with a gold crown and a palm branch, as well as some of the customary olive branches from the temple. On that occasion he kept quiet.ᵛ ⁵But he found an opportunity to further his mad scheme when he was invited to the council by Demetrius and questioned about the dispositions and intentions of the Jews. He replied: ⁶"Those Jews called Hasideans, led by Judas Maccabeus, are warmongers, who stir up sedition and keep the kingdom from enjoying peace and quiet. ⁷For this reason, now that I am deprived of my ancestral dignity, that is to say, the high priesthood, I have come here—⁸first, out of my genuine concern for the king's interests, and secondly, out of consideration for my own countrymen, since our entire nation is suffering great affliction from the unreasonable conduct of the people just mentioned. ⁹When you have informed yourself in detail on these matters, O king, act in the interest of our country and its hard-pressed people with the same gracious consideration that you show toward all. ¹⁰As long as Judas is around, it is impossible for the state to enjoy peace." ¹¹When he had said this, the other Friends who were hostile to Judas quickly added fuel to Demetrius' indignation.

Dealings with Nicanor. ¹² ʷ The king immediately chose Nicanor, who had been in command of the elephants, and appointed him governor of Judea. He sent him off ¹³with orders to put Judas to death, to disperse his followers, and to set up Alcimus as high priest of the great temple. ¹⁴The Gentiles from Judea, who would have

---

s 1 Mc 6, 43-46.—t 18-23: 1 Mc 6, 48-53.—u 1-11: 1 Mc 7, 1-7.—v 1 Mc 7, 7. 25.—w 12f: 2 Mc 8, 9; 1 Mc 3, 38f.

13, 15: *Slew:* literally "stabbed"; the deed was done by Eleazar (1 Mc 6, 43-46).

13, 16: *They withdrew in triumph:* according to 1 Mc 6, 47 they fled.

13, 21: *Military secrets:* probably about the lack of provisions in the besieged city; cf 1 Mc 6, 49.

13, 24: The Greek text is uncertain and may be rendered: "He approved of Maccabeus, then left Hegemonides as governor of the territory . . ." *Gerrenes:* probably the inhabitants of Gerar, southeast of Gaza.

14, 1: *Three years later:* actually, *Demetrius* (I Soter), *son of Seleucus* (IV), landed at *Tripolis* in the year 151 of the Seleucid era (v 4), i.e., 162-161 B.C.; cf 1 Mc 7, 1-7.

banished Judas,* came flocking to Nicanor, thinking that the misfortunes and calamities of the Jews would mean prosperity for themselves. [15] ˣ When the Jews heard of Nicanor's coming, and that the Gentiles were rallying to him, they sprinkled themselves with earth and prayed to him who established his people forever, and who always comes to the aid of his heritage. [16] At their leader's command, they set out at once and came upon the enemy at the village of Adasa. [17] Judas' brother Simon had engaged Nicanor, but because of the sudden appearance of the enemy suffered a slight repulse. [18] However, when Nicanor heard of the valor of Judas and his men, and the great courage with which they fought for their country, he shrank from deciding the issue by bloodshed. [19] So he sent Posidonius, Theodotus and Mattathias to arrange an agreement. [20] After a long discussion of the terms, each leader communicated them to his troops; and when general agreement was expressed, they assented to the treaty. [21] A day was set on which the leaders would meet by themselves. From each side a chariot came forward and thrones were set in place. [22] Judas had posted armed men in readiness at suitable points for fear that the enemy might suddenly carry out some treacherous plan. But the conference was held in the proper way. [23] Nicanor stayed on in Jerusalem, where he did nothing out of place. He got rid of the throngs of ordinary people who gathered around him; [24] but he always kept Judas in his company, for he had a cordial affection for the man. [25] He urged him to marry and have children; so Judas married, settled down, and shared the common life.

Threats against Judas. [26] When Alcimus saw their friendship for each other, he took the treaty that had been made, went to Demetrius, and said that Nicanor was plotting against the state, and that he had appointed Judas, the conspirator against the kingdom, to be his successor. [27] Stirred up by the villain's calumnies, the king became enraged. He wrote to Nicanor,

stating that he was displeased with the treaty, and ordering him to send Maccabeus as a prisoner to Antioch without delay. [28] When this message reached Nicanor he was dismayed, for he hated to break his agreement with a man who had done no wrong. [29] However, there was no way of opposing the king, so he watched for an opportunity to carry out this order by a stratagem. [30] But Maccabeus noticed that Nicanor was becoming cool in his dealings with him, and acting with unaccustomed rudeness when they met; he concluded that this coldness betokened no good. So he gathered together a large number of his men, and went into hiding from Nicanor.

[31] ʸ When Nicanor realized that he had been disgracefully outwitted by the man, he went to the great and holy temple, at a time when the priests were offering the customary sacrifices, and ordered them to surrender Judas. [32] As they declared under oath that they did not know where the wanted man was, [33] he raised his right hand toward the temple and swore this oath: "If you do not hand Judas over to me as prisoner, I will level this shrine of God to the ground; I will tear down the altar, and erect here a splendid temple to Dionysus." [34] With these words he went away. The priests stretched out their hands toward heaven, calling upon the unfailing defender of our nation in these words: [35] "LORD of all, though you are in need of nothing, you have approved of a temple for your dwelling place among us. ᶻ [36] Therefore, O holy One, LORD of all holiness, preserve forever undefiled this house, which has been so recently purified."

The Story of Razis.* [37] A certain Razis, one of the elders of Jerusalem, was denounced to Nicanor as a patriot. A man highly regarded, he was called a father of the Jews because of his love for them. [38] In the early days of the revolt, he had been convicted of Judaism, and had risked body and life in his ardent zeal for it. [39] Nicanor, to show his detestation of the Jews, sent more than five hundred soldiers to arrest him. [40] He thought that by arresting such a man he would deal the Jews a hard blow. [41] But when these troops, on the point of capturing the tower, were forcing the outer gate and calling for fire to set the door ablaze, Razis, now caught on all

2Mc

---

x 15-19: 1 Mc 7, 26-32.—y 31-36: 1 Mc 7, 33-38.—z Acts 17, 25.

14, 14: *Who would have banished Judas:* the meaning of the Greek is uncertain; some render it: "who had fled before Judas."
14, 37-46: The story of *Razis* belongs to the "martyrology" class of literature; it is similar to the stories in 2 Mc 6, 18—7, 42.

sides, turned his sword against himself, [42] preferring to die nobly rather than fall into the hands of vile men and suffer outrages unworthy of his noble birth. [43] In the excitement of the struggle he failed to strike exactly. So while the troops rushed in through the doors, he gallantly ran up to the top of the wall and with manly courage threw himself down into the crowd. [44] But as they quickly drew back and left an opening, he fell into the middle of the empty space. [45] Still breathing, and inflamed with anger, he got up and ran through the crowd, with blood gushing from his frightful wounds. [46] Then, standing on a steep rock, as he lost the last of his blood, he tore out his entrails and flung them with both hands into the crowd, calling upon the LORD of life and of spirit to give these back to him again. Such was the manner of his death. [a]

CHAPTER 15

Nicanor's Blasphemy. [1] When Nicanor learned that Judas and his companions were in the territory of Samaria, he decided to attack them in all safety on the day of rest. [2] The Jews who were forced to follow him pleaded, "Do not massacre them in that way, like a savage barbarian, but show respect for the day which the All-seeing has exalted with holiness above all other days." [3] At this the thrice-sinful wretch asked if there was a ruler in heaven who prescribed the keeping of the sabbath day. [b] [4] When they replied that there was indeed such a ruler in heaven, the living LORD himself, who commanded the observance of the sabbath day, [5] he said, "I, on my part, am ruler on earth, and my orders are that you take up arms and carry out the king's business." Nevertheless he did not succeed in carrying out his cruel plan.

Fresh Hope. [6] In his utter boastfulness and arrogance Nicanor had determined to erect a public monument of victory* over Judas and his men. [7] But Maccabeus remained confident, fully convinced that he would receive help from the LORD. [8] He urged his men not to fear the enemy, but mindful of the help they had received from Heaven in the past, to expect that now, too, victory would be given them by the Almighty. [9] By encouraging them with words from the law and the prophets,* and

by reminding them of the battles they had already won, he filled them with fresh enthusiasm. [10] Having stirred up their courage, he gave his orders and pointed out at the same time the perfidy of the Gentiles and their violation of oaths. [11] When he had armed each of them, not so much with the safety of shield and spear as with the encouragement of noble words, he cheered them all by relating a dream, a kind of vision, worthy of belief.

[12] What he saw was this: Onias, the former high priest,* a good and virtuous man, modest in appearance, gentle in manners, distinguished in speech, and trained from childhood in every virtuous practice, was praying with outstretched arms for the whole Jewish community. [c] [13] Then in the same way another man appeared, distinguished by his white hair and dignity, and with an air about him of extraordinary, majestic authority. [14] Onias then said of him, "This is God's prophet Jeremiah,* who loves his brethren and fervently prays for his people and their holy city." [15] Stretching out his right hand, Jeremiah presented a gold sword to Judas. As he gave it to him he said, [16] "Accept this holy sword as a gift from God; with it you shall crush your adversaries."

Defeat and Death of Nicanor. [17] Encouraged by Judas' noble words, which had power to instill valor and stir young hearts to courage, the Jews determined not to delay, but to charge gallantly and decide the issue by hand-to-hand combat with the utmost courage, since their city and its temple with the sacred vessels were in danger. [18] They were not so much concerned about their wives and children or their brothers and kinsmen; their first and foremost fear was for the consecrated sanctuary. [d] [19] Those who remained in the city suffered a like agony, anxious as they were about the battle in the open country.

---

a 2 Mc 7, 9ff.—b 1 Mc 7, 34.—c 2 Mc 3, 1ff.—d 1 Mc 4, 36.

15, 6: *Public monument of victory:* a heap of stones covered with the arms and armor of the fallen enemy.
15, 9: *The law and the prophets:* the first of the three parts of the Hebrew Scriptures, called the *sacred books* (1 Mc 12, 9).
15, 12: *Onias, the former high priest:* Onias III (2 Mc 3, 1-40). Evidently the author believed that the departed just were in some way alive even before the resurrection.
15, 14: *Jeremiah:* regarded by the postexilic Jews as one of the greatest figures in their history; cf 2 Mc 2, 1; Mt 16, 14. *Who . . . prays for his people:* a clear belief in the intercession of the saints.

20 Everyone now awaited the decisive moment. The enemy were already drawing near with their troops drawn up in battle line, their elephants placed in strategic positions, and their cavalry stationed on the flanks. 21 Maccabeus, contemplating the hosts before him, their elaborate equipment, and the fierceness of their elephants, stretched out his hands toward heaven and called upon the LORD who works miracles; for he knew that it is not through arms but through the LORD's decision that victory is won by those who deserve it. 22 *e* He prayed to him thus: "You, O LORD, sent your angel in the days of King Hezekiah of Judea, and he slew a hundred and eighty-five thousand men of Sennacherib's army. 23 Sovereign of the heavens, send a good angel now to spread fear and dread before us. 24 By the might of your arm may those be struck down who have blasphemously come against your holy people!" With this he ended his prayer.

25 *f* Nicanor and his men advanced to the sound of trumpets and battle songs. 26 But Judas and his men met the army with supplication and prayers. 27 Fighting with their hands and praying to God with their hearts, they laid low at least thirty-five thousand, and rejoiced greatly over this manifestation of God's power. 28 When the battle was over and they were joyfully departing, they discovered Nicanor lying there in all his armor; 29 so they raised tumultuous shouts in their native tongue in praise of the divine Sovereign.

30 Then Judas, who was ever in body and soul the chief defender of his fellow citizens, and had maintained from youth his affection for his countrymen, ordered Nicanor's head and whole right arm to be cut off and taken to Jerusalem. 31 When he arrived there, he assembled his countrymen, stationed the priests before the altar, and sent for those in the citadel.* 32 He showed them the vile Nicanor's head and the wretched blasphemer's arm that had been boastfully stretched out against the holy dwelling of the Almighty. 33 He cut out the tongue of the godless Nicanor, saying he would feed it piecemeal to the birds and would hang up the other wages of his folly opposite the temple. 34 At this, everyone looked toward heaven and praised the LORD who manifests his divine power, saying, "Blessed be he who has kept his own Place undefiled!"

35 Judas hung up Nicanor's head on the wall of the citadel, a clear and evident proof to all of the LORD's help. *g* 36 By public vote it was unanimously decreed never to let this day pass unobserved, *h* but to celebrate it on the thirteenth day of the twelfth month, called Adar in Aramaic, the eve of Mordecai's Day.*

VII: EPILOGUE

Author's Apology. 37 Since Nicanor's doings ended in this way, with the city remaining in possession of the Hebrews from that time on, I will bring my own story to an end here too. 38 If it is well written and to the point, that is what I wanted; if it is poorly done and mediocre, that is the best I could do. 39 Just as it is harmful to drink wine alone or water alone, whereas mixing wine with water makes a more pleasant drink that increases delight, so a skillfully composed story delights the ears of those who read the work. Let this, then, be the end.

---

e 22f: 2 Mc 8, 19; 2 Kgs 19, 35; Is 37, 36; 1 Mc 7, 40f.—f 25-36: 2 Mc 8, 39-50.—g 1 Sm 31, 9f.—h 1 Mc 7, 49.

15, 31: *Those in the citadel:* presumably Jewish soldiers; actually, the citadel was still in the possession of the Syrians.
15, 36: *Mordecai's Day:* the feast of Purim, celebrated on the fourteenth and fifteenth days of Adar (Est 9, 17-22).

2Mc

THE WISDOM BOOKS

The Books of Job, Psalms, Proverbs, Ecclesiastes, the Song of Songs, Wisdom, and Sirach, are all versified by the skillful use of parallelism, that is, of the balanced and symmetrical phrases peculiar to Hebrew poetry. With the exception of the Psalms, the majority of which are devotional lyrics, and the Song of Songs, a nuptial hymn, these books belong to the general class of wisdom or didactic literature, strictly so called because their chief purpose is instruction.

The wisdom literature of the Bible is the fruit of a movement among ancient oriental people to gather, preserve and express, usually in aphoristic style, the results of human experience as an aid toward understanding and solving the problems of life. In Israel especially, the movement concerned itself with such basic and vital problems as man's origin and destiny, his quest for happiness, the problem of suffering, of good and evil in human conduct, of death, and the state beyond the grave. Originating with oral tradition, these formulations found their way into the historical books of the Old Testament in the shape of proverbs, odes, chants, epigrams, and also into those psalms intended for instruction.

The developed compositions of this literature form the sapiential books. The Book of Proverbs is a collection of sentences or practical norms for moral conduct. The Book of Job is an artistic dialogue skillfully handling the problem of suffering though only from the standpoint of temporal life. Ecclesiastes examines a wide range of human experience only to conclude that all things are vanity except the fear of the Lord and observance of his commandments, and that God requites man in his own good time. Sirach gathers and presents the fruits of past experience, thus preparing for the Book of Wisdom, which sees for the just man seeking happiness the full hope of immortality (Wis 3, 4).

Those who cultivated wisdom were called sages. Men of letters, scribes, skilled in the affairs of government, and counselors to rulers, they were instructors of the people, especially of youth (Sir 51, 13-30). In times of crisis they guided the people by revaluating tradition, thus helping to preserve unity, peace and good will. The most illustrious of the sages, and the originator of wisdom literature in Israel, was Solomon. Because of his fame, some of the wisdom books of which he was not the author bear his name.

Despite numerous resemblances, sometimes exaggerated, between the sapiential literature of pagan nations and the wisdom books of the Bible, the former are often replete with vagaries and abound in polytheistic conceptions; the latter remained profoundly human, universal, fundamentally moral, and essentially religious and monotheistic. Under the influence of the law and the prophets, wisdom became piety and virtue; impiety and vice were folly. The teachers of wisdom were regarded as men of God, and their books were placed beside the law and the prophets. The highest wisdom became identified with the spirit of God through which the world was created and preserved (Prv 8, 22-31), and mankind was enlightened.

The limitations of Old Testament wisdom served to crystallize the problems of human life and destiny, thus preparing for their solution through New Testament revelation. Ecclesiastes' vain search for success and happiness on earth ends when the Savior assures these things to his followers, not in this world but in the bliss of heaven. The anxiety in the Book of Job over reconciling God's justice and wisdom with the suffering of the innocent is relieved by the account of the crucified and risen Redeemer in the gospel. By fulfilling all that the Psalms foretold concerning him, Jesus makes the Psalter his prayer book and that of the church for all time. The love of God for the chosen people which underlies the Song of Songs is perfected in the union of Christ with his church. The personification of the wisdom of Proverbs, Wisdom and Sirach shines forth in resplendent reality in the Word who was with God, and who was God, and who became incarnate to dwell among us; cf Jn 1, 2. 14.

THE BOOK OF JOB

The Book of Job, named after its protagonist, is an exquisite dramatic poem which treats of the problem of the suffering of the innocent, and of retribution. The contents of the book, together with its artistic structure and elegant style, place it among the literary masterpieces of all time.

Job, an oriental chieftain, pious and upright, richly endowed in his own person and in domestic prosperity, suffers a sudden and complete reversal of fortune. He loses his property and his children; a loathsome disease afflicts his body; and sorrow oppresses his soul. Nevertheless, Job does not complain against God. When some friends visit him to condole with him, Job protests his innocence and does not understand why he is afflicted. He curses the day of his birth and longs for death to bring an end to his sufferings. The debate which ensues consists of three cycles of speeches. Job's friends insist that his plight can only be a punishment for personal wrongdoing and an invitation from God to repentance. Job rejects their inadequate explanation and calls for a response from God himself. At this point the speeches of a youth named Elihu (ch 32—37) interrupt the development.

In response to Job's plea that he be allowed to see God and hear from him the cause of his suffering, God answers, not by justifying his action before men, but by referring to his own omniscience and almighty power. Job is content with this. He recovers his attitude of humility and trust in God, which is deepened now and strengthened by his experience of suffering.

The author of the book is not known; it was composed some time between the 7th and 5th centuries B.C. Its literary form, with speeches, prologue and epilogue disposed according to a studied plan, indicates that the purpose of the writing is didactic. The lesson is that even the just may suffer here, and their sufferings are a test of their fidelity. They shall be rewarded in the end. Man's finite mind cannot probe the depths of the divine omniscience that governs the world. The problems we encounter can be solved by a broader and deeper awareness of God's power, presence (42, 5) and wisdom.

The divisions of the Book of Job are as follows: I. Prologue (1, 1—2, 13). II. First Cycle of Speeches (3, 1—14, 22). III. Second Cycle of Speeches (15, 1—21, 34). IV. Third Cycle of Speeches (22, 1—28, 28). V. Job's Final Summary of His Cause (29, 1—31, 37). VI. Elihu's Speeches (32, 1—37, 24). VII. The Lord's Speech (38, 1—42, 6). VIII. Epilogue (42, 7-17).

I: PROLOGUE

CHAPTER 1

Job's Wealth and Piety. ¹ In the land of Uz* there was a blameless and upright man named Job,*a* who feared God and avoided evil. ² * Seven sons and three daughters were born to him; ³ and he had seven thousand sheep, three thousand camels, five hundred yoke of oxen, five hundred she-asses, and a great number of work animals, so that he was greater than any of the men of the East.* ⁴ His sons used to take turns giving feasts, sending invitations to their three sisters to eat and drink with them. ⁵ And when each feast had run its course, Job would send for them and sanctify them, rising early and offering holocausts for every one of them. For Job said, "It may be that my sons have sinned and blasphemed God in their hearts." This Job did habitually.

⁶ *b* One day, when the sons of God* came to present themselves before the LORD, Satan also came among them.*c* ⁷ And the LORD said to Satan, "Whence do you come?" Then Satan answered the LORD and said,*d* "From roaming the earth and patrolling it." ⁸ And the LORD said to Satan, "Have you noticed my servant Job, and that there is no one on earth like him, blameless and upright, fearing God and avoiding evil?" ⁹ But Satan answered the LORD and said, "Is it for nothing that Job is God-fearing? ¹⁰ Have you not surrounded him and his family and all that he has with your protection? You have blessed the work of his hands, and his livestock are spread over the land. ¹¹ *e* But now put forth your hand and touch anything that he has, and surely he will blaspheme you to your face." ¹² And the LORD said to Satan, "Behold, all that he has is in your power; only do not lay a hand upon his person." So Satan went forth from the presence of the LORD.

The First Trial. ¹³ And so one day, while his sons and his daughters were eating and drinking wine in the house of their eldest brother, ¹⁴ a messenger came to Job and said, "The oxen were plowing and the

a Jb 2, 3.—b 6ff: Jb 2, 1ff.—c Gn 6, 2. 4; Zec 3, 1; Lk 22, 31; Rv 12, 9.—d 1 Pt 5, 8.—e Jb 2, 5.

1, 1: *Uz:* somewhere in Edom or Arabia. *Job:* a not uncommon name in ancient Semitic circles; its original meaning was "enemy."

1, 2f: The numbers mentioned here indicate Job's great wealth and happiness, external proof of God's friendship.

1, 3: *Men of the East:* that is, east of Palestine.

1, 6: *Sons of God:* angels. *Satan:* literally, "adversary."

asses grazing beside them, [15] and the Sabeans* carried them off in a raid. They put the herdsmen to the sword, and I alone have escaped to tell you." [16] While he was yet speaking, another came and said, "Lightning* has fallen from heaven and struck the sheep and their shepherds and consumed them; and I alone have escaped to tell you." [17] While he was yet speaking, another came and said, "The Chaldeans formed three columns, seized the camels, carried them off, and put those tending them to the sword, and I alone have escaped to tell you." [18] While he was yet speaking, another came and said, "Your sons and daughters were eating and drinking wine in the house of their eldest brother, [19] when suddenly a great wind came across the desert and smote the four corners of the house. It fell upon the young people and they are dead; and I alone have escaped to tell you." [20] Then Job began to tear his cloak and cut off his hair. He cast himself prostrate upon the ground, [21] and said,

"Naked I came forth from my mother's womb,[f]
and naked shall I go back again.*
The LORD gave and the LORD has taken away;
blessed be the name of the LORD!"

[22] In all this Job did not sin,[g] nor did he say anything disrespectful of God.

CHAPTER 2

The Second Trial. [1] Once again the sons of God[h] came to present themselves before the LORD, and Satan also came with them. [2] And the LORD said to Satan, "Whence do you come?" and Satan answered the LORD and said, "From roaming the earth and patrolling it." [3] And the LORD said to Satan, "Have you noticed my servant Job, and that there is no one on earth like him,

---

f Eccl 5, 14; 1 Tm 6, 7.—g Jb 2, 10; Jas 5, 11.—h Jb 1, 6.—i Jb 1, 1.—j Jb 1, 11.—k Jb 19, 17.—l Jb 1, 22; Sir 2, 4; Jas 5, 11.—m Jer 20, 14.

1, 15: *Sabeans:* from southern Arabia.
1, 16: *Lightning:* literally, "God's fire."
1, 21: *Go back again:* to the earth; cf Gn 2, 7; Sir 40, 1.
2, 4: *Skin for skin:* an expression which, as applied to Job, means that he has borne his suffering patiently thus far only because he seeks to avoid greater suffering and to receive greater favors from God.
2, 9: *Curse God and die:* you have nothing to hope for from God and therefore nothing to live for.
2, 11: The names of Job's friends suggest Edomite origin. The Edomites (Ob 8f) and more specifically the Temanites (Jer 49, 7) enjoyed a reputation for wisdom.

---

faultless and upright, fearing God and avoiding evil?[i] He still holds fast to his innocence although you incited me against him to ruin him without cause." [4] And Satan answered the LORD and said, "Skin for skin!* All that a man has will he give for his life. [5] [j] But now put forth your hand and touch his bone and his flesh, and surely he will blaspheme you to your face." [6] And the LORD said to Satan, "He is in your power; only spare his life." [7] So Satan went forth from the presence of the LORD and smote Job with severe boils from the soles of his feet to the crown of his head. [8] And he took a potsherd to scrape himself, as he sat among the ashes. [9] Then his wife said to him,[k] "Are you still holding to your innocence? Curse God and die."* [10] But he said to her, "Are even you going to speak as senseless women do? We accept good things from God; and should we not accept evil?" Through all this, Job said nothing sinful.[l]

Job's Three Friends. [11] Now when three of Job's friends heard of all the misfortune that had come upon him, they set out each one from his own place: Eliphaz from Teman, Bildad from Shuh, and Zophar from Naamath.* They met and journeyed together to give him sympathy and comfort. [12] But when, at a distance, they lifted up their eyes and did not recognize him, they began to weep aloud; they tore their cloaks and threw dust upon their heads. [13] Then they sat down upon the ground with him seven days and seven nights, but none of them spoke a word to him; for they saw how great was his suffering.

II: FIRST CYCLE OF SPEECHES

CHAPTER 3

Job's Plaint. [1] After this, Job opened his mouth and cursed his day. [2] Job spoke out and said:

[3] Perish the day on which I was born,[m]
     the night when they said, "The child is a boy!"
[4] May that day be darkness:
     let not God above call for it,
     nor light shine upon it!
[5] May darkness and gloom claim it,
     clouds settle upon it,
     the blackness of night affright it!
[6] May obscurity seize that day;
     let it not occur among the days of the year,

nor enter into the count of the months!

7 May that night be barren;
let no joyful outcry greet it!
8 Let them curse it who curse the sea,
the appointed disturbers of Leviathan!*
9 May the stars of its twilight be darkened;
may it look for daylight, but have none,
nor gaze on the eyes of the dawn,
10 Because it kept not shut the doors of the womb
to shield my eyes from trouble!

11 Why did I not perish at birth,[n]
come forth from the womb and expire?
16 Or why was I not buried away like an untimely birth,*
like babes that have never seen the light?
12 Wherefore did the knees receive me?
or why did I suck at the breasts?

13 For then I should have lain down and been tranquil;
had I slept, I should then have been at rest
14 With kings and counselors of the earth
who built where now there are ruins
15 Or with princes who had gold
and filled their houses with silver.

17 There* the wicked cease from troubling,
there the weary are at rest.
18 There the captives are at ease together,
and hear not the voice of the slave driver.
19 Small and great are there the same,
and the servant is free from his master.
20 Why is light given to the toilers,
and life to the bitter in spirit?
21 They wait for death and it comes not;
they search for it rather than for hidden treasures,
22 Rejoice in it exultingly,
and are glad when they reach the grave:
23 Men whose path is hidden from them,
and whom God has hemmed in!
24 For sighing comes more readily to me than food,
and my groans well forth like water.
25 For what I fear overtakes me,

and what I shrink from comes upon me.
26 I have no peace nor ease;
I have no rest, for trouble comes!

CHAPTER 4

Eliphaz's First Speech. 1 Then spoke Eliphaz the Temanite, who said:

2 If someone attempts a word with you, will you mind?
For how can anyone refrain from speaking?
3 Behold, you have instructed many,
and have made firm their feeble hands.
4 Your words have upheld the stumbler;
you have strengthened his faltering knees.
5 But now that it comes to you, you are impatient;
when it touches yourself, you are dismayed.
6 Is not your piety a source of confidence,
and your integrity of life your hope?
7 Reflect now, what innocent person perishes?[o]
Since when are the upright destroyed?
8 As I see it, those who plow for mischief
and sow trouble, reap the same.
9 By the breath of God they perish,[p]
and by the blast of his wrath they are consumed.
10 Though the lion* roars, though the king of beasts cries out,
yet the teeth of the young lions are broken;
11 The old lion perishes for lack of prey,
and the cubs of the lioness are scattered.

---

n Jb 10, 18f.—o Ps 37, 25.—p Ps 18, 16; Is 11, 4; 2 Thes 2, 8.

3, 8: *Leviathan:* in Jb 40, 25, the crocodile; here the reference is probably to a mythological sea monster symbolizing primeval chaos. Cf Jb 9, 13; 26, 13; Pss 74, 13f; 104, 26; Is 27, 1.

3, 16: This verse has been placed between vv 11 and 12 where it probably stood originally. There is reason to believe that here, as well as in several other places in Job, the original order of the poetic lines was accidentally disturbed in the early transmission of the text; so in chapters 12-15; 19-21; 24-31; 34; 36; 38-42. The verse numbers given in such cases are always those of the current Hebrew text, though the arrangement may differ. The footnotes will advise the reader of the difficulties and provide him with further indications for following the progress of thought in the book.

3, 17: *There:* in death.

4, 10: *The lion:* used figuratively here for the violent, rapacious sinner who cannot prevail against God.

¹² For a word was stealthily brought to
   me,*
   and my ear caught a whisper of it.
¹³ In my thoughts during visions of the
   night,*q*
   when deep sleep falls on men,
¹⁴ Fear came upon me, and shuddering,
   that terrified me to the bones.
¹⁵ Then a spirit passed before me,
   and the hair of my flesh stood up.
¹⁶ It paused, but its likeness I could not
   discern;
   a figure was before my eyes, and I
   heard a still voice:
¹⁷ "Can a man be righteous as against
   God?*r*
   Can a mortal be blameless against his
   Maker?
¹⁸ Lo, he puts no trust in his servants,*s*
   and with his angels he can find fault.
¹⁹ How much more with those that dwell
   in houses of clay,
   whose foundation is in the dust,
   who are crushed more easily than the
   moth!
²⁰ Morning or evening they may be shattered;
   with no heed paid to it, they perish
   forever.
²¹ The pegs of their tent are plucked up;
   they die without knowing wisdom."

CHAPTER 5

¹ Call now! Will anyone respond to you?
   To which of the holy ones will you
   appeal?
² Nay, impatience kills the fool
   and indignation slays the simpleton.
³ I have seen a fool spreading his roots,*t*
   but his household suddenly decayed.
⁴ His children shall be far from safety;
   they shall be crushed at the gate*
   without a rescuer.
⁵ What they have reaped the hungry shall
   eat up;

[or God shall take it away by blight;]
   and the thirsty shall swallow their
   substance.
⁶ For mischief comes not out of the earth,
   nor does trouble spring out of the
   ground;
⁷ But man himself begets mischief,
   as sparks* fly upward.

⁸ In your place, I would appeal to God,
   and to God I would state my plea.*
¹⁰ He gives rain upon the earth
   and sends water upon the fields;
¹¹ *u* He sets up on high the lowly,
   and those who mourn he exalts to
   safety.

¹² He frustrates the plans of the cunning,
   so that their hands achieve no success;
¹³ He catches the wise in their own ruses,*v*
   and the designs of the crafty are
   routed.

¹⁴ They meet with darkness in the daytime,
   and at noonday they grope as though
   it were night.
¹⁵ But the poor from the edge of the sword
   and from the hand of the mighty, he
   saves.
¹⁶ Thus the unfortunate have hope,
   and iniquity closes her mouth.

¹⁷ Happy is the man whom God reproves!
   The Almighty's chastening do not reject.
¹⁸ For he wounds, but he binds up;*vv*
   he smites, but his hands give healing.
¹⁹ Out of six troubles he will deliver you,
   and at the seventh* no evil shall
   touch you.
²⁰ In famine he will deliver you from
   death,
   and in war from the threat of the
   sword;
²¹ From the scourge of the tongue you
   shall be hidden,
   and shall not fear approaching ruin.

²² At destruction and want you shall
   laugh;
   the beasts of the earth you need not
   dread.
²³ You shall be in league with the stones of
   the field,
   and the wild beasts shall be at peace
   with you.

q Jb 33, 15.—r Jb 9, 2; 15, 14ff; 25, 4; Pss 130, 3; 143, 2.—s
Jb 15, 15; 2 Pt 2, 4; Jude 6.—t Ps 37, 35f.—u 1 Sm 2, 7f; Ps
113, 7; Lk 1, 52.—v 1 Cor 3, 19.—vv Hos 6, 1f.

4, 12-21: A dramatic presentation of the idea of man's nothingness in contrast to God's greatness.
   5, 4: *At the gate:* of the city, where justice was administered.
   5, 7: *Sparks:* in Hebrew, "sons of resheph," which the ancient
versions took as the name of a bird.
   5, 9: Omitted here; it is a duplicate of Jb 9, 10.
   5, 19: *Six . . . the seventh:* proverbial expression for any
large number; cf Prv 24, 16; Lk 17, 4.

24 And you shall know that your tent is secure;
taking stock of your household, you shall miss nothing.
25 You shall know that your descendants are many,
and your offspring as the grass of the earth.
26 You shall approach the grave in full vigor,
as a shock of grain comes in at its season.
27 Lo, this we have searched out; so it is!
This we have heard, and you should know.

CHAPTER 6

Job's First Reply. 1 Then Job answered and said:

2 Ah, could my anguish but be measured
and my calamity laid with it in the scales,
3 They would now outweigh the sands of the sea!
Because of this I speak without restraint.
4 For the arrows of the Almighty pierce me,^{w}
and my spirit drinks in their poison;
the terrors of God are arrayed against me.
5 Does the wild ass bray when he has grass?*
Does the ox low over his fodder?
6 Can a thing insipid be eaten without salt?
Is there flavor in the white of an egg?
7 I refuse to touch them;
they are loathsome food to me.

8 Oh, that I might have my request,
and that God would grant what I long for:
9 Even that God would decide to crush me,
that he would put forth his hand and cut me off!
10 Then I should still have consolation
and could exult through unremitting pain,
because I have not transgressed the commands of the Holy One.
11 What strength have I that I should endure,
and what is my limit that I should be patient?

12 Have I the strength of stones,
or is my flesh of bronze?
13 Have I no helper,^{x}
and has advice deserted me?
14 A friend owes kindness to one in despair,
though he have forsaken the fear of the Almighty.

15 My brethren are undependable as a brook,
as watercourses that run dry in the wadies;
16 Though they may be black with ice,
and with snow heaped upon them,
17 Yet once they flow, they cease to be;
in the heat, they disappear from their place.
18 Caravans turn aside from their routes;
they go into the desert and perish.
19 The caravans of Tema* search,
the companies of Sheba have hopes;
20 They are disappointed, though they were confident;
they come there and are frustrated.
21 It is thus that you have now become for me;
you see a terrifying thing and are afraid.
22 Have I asked you to give me anything,
to offer a gift for me from your possessions,
23 Or to deliver me from the enemy,
or to redeem me from oppressors?
24 Teach me, and I will be silent;
prove to me wherein I have erred.
25 How agreeable are honest words;
yet how unconvincing is your argument!
26 Do you consider your words as proof,
but the sayings of a desperate man as wind?
27 You would even cast lots for the orphan,
and would barter away your friend!
28 Come, now, give me your attention;
surely I will not lie to your face.
29 Think it over; let there be no injustice.
Think it over; I still am right.
30 Is there insincerity on my tongue,
or cannot my taste discern falsehood?

---

w Ps 88, 17.—x Jb 19, 14f.

6, 5f: Job would not complain if his life were as pleasant to him as fodder to a hungry animal; but his life is as disagreeable as insipid food. *White of an egg:* thus the obscure Hebrew has been understood in Jewish tradition; some render it "mallow juice."
6, 19: *Tema:* in northwest Arabia. *Sheba:* see note on Jb 1, 15.

CHAPTER 7

¹ ʸ Is not man's life on earth a drudgery?*
   Are not his days those of a hireling?
² He is a slave who longs for the shade,
   a hireling who waits for his wages.
³ So I have been assigned months of misery,
   and troubled nights have been told off for me.
⁴ If in bed I say, "When shall I arise?"
   then the night drags on;
   I am filled with restlessness until the dawn.
⁵ My flesh is clothed with worms and scabs;ᶻ
   my skin cracks and festers;
⁶ My days are swifter than a weaver's shuttle;
   they come to an end without hope.
⁷ Remember that my life is like the wind;ᵃ
   I shall not see happiness again.
⁸ The eye that now sees me shall no more behold me;
   as you look at me, I shall be gone.
⁹ As a cloud dissolves and vanishes,ᵇ
   so he who goes down to the nether world shall come up no more.
¹⁰ He shall not again return to his house;
   his place shall know him no more.
¹¹ My own utterance I will not restrain;
   I will speak in the anguish of my spirit;
   I will complain in the bitterness of my soul.
¹² * Am I the sea, or a monster of the deep,
   that you place a watch over me?*
   Why have you set me up as an object of attack?
   or why should I be a target for you?
¹³ When I say, "My bed shall comfort me,
   my couch shall ease my complaint,"
¹⁴ Then you affright me with dreams
   and with visions terrify me,
¹⁵ So that I should prefer choking
   and death rather than my pains.

¹⁶ I waste away: I cannot live forever;ᶜ
   let me alone, for my days are but a breath.
¹⁷ What is man, that you make much of him,
   or pay him any heed?
¹⁸ You observe him with each new dayᵈ
   and try him at every moment!
¹⁹ How long will it be before you look away from me,
   and let me alone long enough to swallow my spittle?
²⁰ Though I have sinned, what can I do to you,
   O watcher of men?
²¹ Why do you not pardon my offense,
   or take away my guilt?
   For soon I shall lie down in the dust;
   and should you seek me I shall then be gone.

CHAPTER 8

Bildad's First Speech. ¹Bildad the Shuhite spoke out and said:

² How long will you utter such things?
   The words from your mouth are like a mighty wind!
³ Does God pervert judgment,ᵉ
   and does the Almighty distort justice?
⁴ If your children have sinned against him
   and he has left them in the grip of their guilt,
⁵ Still, if you yourself have recourse to God
   and make supplication to the Almighty,
⁶ Should you be blameless and upright,
   surely now he will awake for you
   and restore your rightful domain;
⁷ Your former state will be of little moment,
   for in time to come you will flourish indeed.
⁸ If you inquire of the former generations,
   and give heed to the experience of the fathersᶠ
⁹ (As we are but of yesterday and have no knowledge,
   because our days on earth are but a shadow),ᵍ
¹⁰ Will they not teach you and tell you
   and utter their words of understanding?

---

y Jb 14, 14.—z Jb 2, 7f.—a Pss 8, 5; 144, 3.—b 9f: Jb 10, 21;
14, 10ff; 2 Sm 12, 23; 14, 14; Wis 2, 1.—c Jb 14, 1ff. 5.—d Ps
17, 3.—e Jb 34, 10ff.—f Dt 4, 32; 32, 7.—g Jb 14, 2; Pss 102,
12; 109, 23; 144, 4; Wis 2, 5.

7, 1: *Drudgery:* taken by some to refer to military service; cf
also Jb 14, 14.
7, 12: An allusion in poetic imagery to primeval chaos as a
monstrous ocean vanquished by God at the world's creation.
7, 12-21: Job now speaks, not to his friends, but to God.

11 Can the papyrus grow up without mire?*
    Can the reed grass flourish without
        water?
12 While it is yet green and uncut,
    it withers quicker than any grass.
13 So is the end of everyone who forgets
        God,
    and so shall the hope of the godless
        man perish.
14 His confidence is but a gossamer thread
    and his trust is a spider's web.
15 He shall rely upon his family, but it
        shall not last;
    he shall cling to it, but it shall not en-
        dure.
16 He is full of sap before sunrise,
    and beyond his garden his shoots go
        forth;
17 About a heap of stones are his roots en-
        twined;
    among the rocks he takes hold.
18 Yet if one tears him from his place,
    it will disown him: "I have never seen
        you!"
19 There he lies rotting beside the road,
    and out of the soil another sprouts.
20 Behold, God will not cast away the up-
        right;
    neither will he take the hand of the
        wicked.
21 Once more will he fill your mouth with
        laughter,
    and your lips with rejoicing.
22 They that hate you shall be clothed with
        shame,
    and the tent of the wicked shall be no
        more.

CHAPTER 9

Job's Second Reply. [1] Then Job answered
and said:

2 I know well that it is so;
    but how can a man be justified before
        God?
3 Should one wish to contend with him,
    he could not answer him once in a
        thousand times.
4 God is wise in heart and mighty in
        strength;
    who has withstood him and remained
        unscathed?
5 He removes the mountains before they
        know it;
    he overturns them in his anger.
6 He shakes the earth out of its place, *h*
    and the pillars beneath it tremble.

7 He commands the sun, and it rises not;
    he seals up the stars.
8 He alone stretches out the heavens*i*
    and treads upon the crests of the sea.
9 He made the Bear and Orion,
    the Pleiades and the constellations of
        the south;
10 He does great things past finding out,
    marvelous things beyond reckoning.
11 Should he come near me, I see him not;
    should he pass by, I am not aware of
        him;
12 Should he seize me forcibly, who can
        say him nay?
    Who can say to him, "What are you
        doing?"
13 He is God and he does not relent;
    the helpers of Rahab* bow beneath
        him.
14 How much less shall I give him any an-
        swer,
    or choose out arguments against him!
15 Even though I were right, I could not
        answer him,*j*
    but should rather beg for what was
        due me.
16 If I appealed to him and he answered
        my call,
    I could not believe that he would
        hearken to my words;
17 With a tempest he might overwhelm
        me,
    and multiply my wounds without
        cause;
18 He need not suffer me to draw breath,
    but might fill me with bitter griefs.
19 If it be a question of strength, he is
        mighty;
    and if of judgment, who will call him
        to account?
20 Though I were right, my own mouth
        might condemn me;*k*
    were I innocent, he might put me in
        the wrong.
21 Though I am innocent, I myself cannot
        know it;
    I despise my life.
22 It is all one! therefore I say:

h Jb 26, 11.—i Ps 104, 2; Is 40, 22.— j Jb 10, 15.—k Jb 15,
6.

8, 11ff: As marsh plants need water, so man needs God. These
verses are taken by some as a quotation from the teaching of the
forefathers; cf v 10.
9, 13: *Rahab:* cf Jb 26, 12. See note on Ps 89, 11.

Both the innocent and the wicked he
destroys.[l]

23 When the scourge slays suddenly,
he laughs at the despair of the innocent.

24 The earth is given into the hands of the
wicked;
he covers the faces of its judges.
If it is not he, who then is it?

25 My days are swifter than a runner,
they flee away; they see no happiness;[m]

26 They shoot by like skiffs of reed,
like an eagle swooping upon its prey.

27 If I say: I will forget my complaining,
I will lay aside my sadness and be of
good cheer,

28 Then I am in dread of all my pains;
I know that you* will not hold me innocent.

29 If I must be accounted guilty,
why then should I strive in vain?

30 If I should wash myself with snow
and cleanse my hands with lye,

31 Yet you would plunge me in the ditch,
so that my garments would abhor me.

32 For he is not a man like myself, that I
should answer him,
that we should come together in judgment.

33 Would that there were an arbiter between us,
who could lay his hand upon us both

34 and withdraw his rod from me.
Would that his terrors did not frighten
me;

35 that I might speak without being
afraid of him.
Since this is not the case with me,

1 * I loathe my life.[n]

CHAPTER 10

I will give myself up to complaint;
I will speak from the bitterness of my
soul.

2 I will say to God: Do not put me in the
wrong!
Let me know why you oppose me.

3 Is it a pleasure for you to oppress,
to spurn the work of your hands,
and smile on the plan of the wicked?

4 Have you eyes of flesh?
Do you see as man sees?

5 Are your days as the days of a mortal,[o]
and are your years as a man's
lifetime,

6 That you seek for guilt in me
and search after my sins,

7 Even though you know that I am not
wicked,[p]
and that none can deliver me out of
your hand?

8 Your hands have formed me and
fashioned me;
will you then turn and destroy me?

9 Oh, remember that you fashioned me
from clay?[q]
Will you then bring me down to dust
again?

10 Did you not pour me out as milk,
and thicken me like cheese?

11 With skin and flesh you clothed me,
with bones and sinews knit me together.

12 Grace and favor you granted me,
and your providence has preserved
my spirit.

13 Yet these things you have hidden in
your heart;
I know that they are your purpose:

14 If I should sin, you would keep a watch
against me,
and from my guilt you would not absolve me.

15 If I should be wicked, alas for me!
if righteous, I dare not hold up my
head,
filled with ignominy and sodden with
affliction!

16 Should it lift up, you hunt me like a
lion:
repeatedly you show your wondrous
power against me,

17 You renew your attack upon me
and multiply your harassment of me;
in waves your troops come against me.

18 Why then did you bring me forth from
the womb?[r]
I should have died and no eye have
seen me.

19 I should be as though I had never lived;
I should have been taken from the
womb to the grave.

20 Are not the days of my life few?
Let me alone, that I may recover a little

Jb

---

l Eccl 9, 2.—m Jb 7, 6.—n Jb 9, 21.—o Jb 36, 26.—p Jb 2, 3.
9; Dt 32, 39; Wis 16, 15.—q Jb 4, 19; 33, 6; Gn 2, 7; 3, 19; Ps
146, 4.—r Jb 3, 3. 11.

9, 28-31: *You:* refers to God.
10, 1: *I loathe my life:* this is the first verse of ch 10.

21 Before I go whence I shall not return,*s*
　　to the land of darkness and of gloom,
22 The black, disordered land
　　where darkness is the only light.

CHAPTER 11

Zophar's First Speech. ¹And Zophar the Naamathite spoke out and said:

2 Should not the man of many words be answered,
　　or must the garrulous man necessarily be right?
3 Shall your babblings keep men silent,
　　and shall you deride and no one give rebuke?
4 Shall you say: "My teaching is pure,
　　and I am clean in your sight"?
5 But oh, that God would speak,
　　and open his lips against you,
6 And tell you that the secrets of wisdom
　　are twice as effective:
　So you might learn that God
　　will make you answer for your guilt.

7 Can you penetrate the designs of God?*t*
　　Dare you vie with the perfection of the Almighty?
8 It is higher than the heavens; what can you do?
　　It is deeper than the nether world; what can you know?
9 It is longer than the earth in measure,
　　and broader than the sea.
10 If he seize and imprison
　　or call to judgment, who then can say him nay?
11 For he knows the worthlessness of men
　　and sees iniquity; will he then ignore it?
12 Will empty man then gain understanding,
　　and the wild jackass*u* be made docile?

13 If you set your heart aright
　　and stretch out your hands toward him,
14 If you remove all iniquity from your conduct,
　　and let not injustice dwell in your tent,
15 Surely then you may lift up your face in innocence;
　　you may stand firm and unafraid.
16 For then you shall forget your misery,
　　or recall it like waters that have ebbed away.

17 Then your life shall be brighter than the noonday;
　　its gloom shall become as the morning,
18 And you shall be secure, because there is hope;
　　you shall look round you and lie down in safety,*v*
19 and you shall take your rest with none to disturb.

　Many shall entreat your favor,
20 but the wicked, looking on, shall be consumed with envy.
　Escape shall be cut off from them,
　　they shall wait to expire.

CHAPTER 12

Job's Third Reply. ¹Then Job replied and said:

2 No doubt you are the intelligent folk,
　　and with you wisdom shall die!
3 But I have intelligence as well as you; *w*
　　for who does not know such things as these?
4 I have become the sport of my neighbors:*
　"The one whom God answers when he calls upon him,
　　the just, the perfect man," is a laughingstock;*x*
5 The undisturbed esteem my downfall a disgrace
　　such as awaits unsteady feet;
6 Yet the tents of robbers are prosperous,
　　and those who provoke God are secure.

7 But now ask the beasts to teach you,
　　and the birds of the air to tell you;
8 Or the reptiles on earth to instruct you,
　　and the fish of the sea to inform you.
9 Which of all these does not know
　　that the hand of God has done this?
10 In his hand is the soul of every living thing,*y*
　　and the life breath of all mankind.
11 Does not the ear judge words
　　as the mouth tastes food?*z*
12 So with old age is wisdom,*a*
　　and with length of days understanding.

---

s Jb 7, 9f; 16, 22.—t Rom 11, 33.—u Jb 39, 5-8.—v Lv 26, 6; Ps 4, 9.—w Jb 13, 2; 15, 9.—x Jb 21, 3; 30, 1.—y Acts 17, 28.—z Jb 34, 3.—a Jb 32, 7.

12, 4f: The Hebrew is somewhat obscure, but the general sense is that the wicked mock at the pious when the latter appear to be abandoned by God; cf Ps 22, 7ff; Mt 27, 39-43.

13 With him are wisdom and might;
  his are counsel and understanding.
14 If he breaks a thing down, there is no
    rebuilding;[b]
  if he imprisons a man, there is no re-
    lease.
15 He holds back the waters and there is
    drought;[c]
  he sends them forth and they over-
    whelm the land.
18 He loosens the bonds imposed by kings
  and leaves but a waistcloth to bind
    the king's own loins.*
21 He breaks down the barriers of the
    streams
19 and lets their never-failing waters
    flow away.
16 With him are strength and prudence;
  the misled and the misleaders are his.
17 He sends counselors away barefoot,
  and of judges he makes fools.
20 He silences the trusted adviser,
  and takes discretion from the aged.
22 The recesses of the darkness he dis-
    closes,
  and brings the gloom forth to the
    light.
23 He makes nations great and he destroys
    them;
  he spreads peoples abroad and he
    abandons them.
24 He takes understanding from the lead-
    ers of the land,
25 till they grope in the darkness with-
    out light;
  he makes them stagger like drunken
    men.

CHAPTER 13

1 Lo, all this my eye has seen;
  my ear has heard and perceived it.
2 What you know, I also know;[d]
  I fall not short of you.
3 But I would speak with the Almighty; [e]
  I wish to reason with God.
4 You are glossing over falsehoods

and offering vain remedies, every one
  of you!
5 Oh, that you would be altogether silent!
  This for you would be wisdom.
6 Hear now the rebuke I shall utter
  and listen to the reproof from my lips.
7 Is it for God that you speak falsehood?
  Is it for him that you utter deceit?
8 Is it for him that you show partiality?
  Do you play advocate on behalf of
    God?
9 Will it be well when he shall search you
    out?
  Would you impose on him as one
    does on men?
10 He will openly rebuke you
  if even in secret you show partiality.
11 Surely will his majesty affright you
  and the dread of him fall upon you.
12 Your reminders are ashy maxims,
  your fabrications are mounds of clay.
13 Be silent, let me alone! that I may speak
  and give vent to my feelings.
14 I will carry my flesh between my teeth,
  and take my life in my hand.*
15 Slay me though he might,[f] I will wait
    for him;
  I will defend my conduct before him.
16 And this shall be my salvation,
  that no impious man can come into
    his presence.
17 Pay careful heed to my speech,
  and give my statement a hearing.
18 Behold, I have prepared my case,[g]
  I know that I am in the right.
19 If anyone can make a case against me,
  then I shall be silent and die.
20 These things only do not use against
    me,*
  then from your presence I need not
    hide:
21 Withdraw your hand far from me,
  and let not the terror of you frighten
    me.
22 Then call me, and I will respond;
  or let me speak first, and answer me.
23 What are my faults and my sins?
  My misdeeds and my sins make
    known to me!
24 Why do you hide your face[h]
  and consider me your enemy?
25 Will you harass a wind-driven leaf,
  or pursue a withered straw?
26 For you draw up bitter indictments
    against me,

---

b Rv 3, 7.—c Gn 7, 11-24.—d Jb 12, 3; 15, 9.—e Jb 23, 4.—f
Jb 27, 5.—g Jb 33, 9.—h Jb 19, 11; 33, 10.

12, 18: *Waistcloth . . . loins:* he reduces kings to the condition of slaves, who wear only a cloth wrapped about the waist.
13, 14: The second half of the verse is a common biblical expression for risking one's life; cf Jgs 12, 3; 1 Sm 19, 5; 28, 21;
Ps 119, 109; the first half of the verse must have a similar meaning. Job is so confident of his innocence that he is willing to risk
his life by going to judgment with God.
13, 20: From here to the end of chapter 14, Job pleads his
case, addressing God rather than his three friends.

Jb

and punish in me the faults of my
youth.
27 You put my feet in the stocks;
you watch all my paths
and trace out all my footsteps.

CHAPTER 14

1 Man born of woman
is short-lived and full of trouble,*i*
2 Like a flower that springs up and
fades,*j*
swift as a shadow that does not abide.
3 Upon such a one will you cast your eyes
so as to bring him into judgment before you,
28 Though he wears out like a leather bot-
tle,
like a garment that the moth has consumed?*
4 Can a man be found who is clean of defilement?*k*
There is none, 5however short his
days.
You know the number of his months;
you have fixed the limit which he
cannot pass.
6 Look away from him and let him be,
while, like a hireling, he completes
his day.
7 For a tree there is hope,
if it be cut down, that it will sprout
again
and that its tender shoots will not
cease.
8 Even though its root grow old in the
earth,
and its stump die in the dust,
9 Yet at the first whiff of water it may
flourish again
and put forth branches like a young
plant.
10 But when a man dies, all vigor leaves
him;*l*
when man expires, where then is he?
11 As when the waters of a lake fail,
or a stream grows dry and parches,
12 So men lie down and rise not again.
Till the heavens are no more, they
shall not awake,
nor be roused out of their sleep.*m*
13 Oh, that you would hide me in the
nether world
and keep me sheltered till your wrath
is past;
would fix a time for me, and then remember me!

14 When a man has died, were he to live
again,
all the days of my drudgery I would
wait,*n*
until my relief should come.
15 You would call, and I would answer
you;
you would esteem the work of your
hands.
16 Surely then you would count my steps,*o*
and not keep watch for sin in me.
17 My misdeeds would be sealed up in a
pouch*
and you would cover over my guilt.
18 But as a mountain falls at last
and its rock is moved from its place,
19 As waters wear away the stones
and floods wash away the soil of the
land
so you destroy the hope of man.
20 You prevail once for all against him and
he passes on;
with changed appearance you send
him away.
21 If his sons are honored, he is not aware
of it;
if they are in disgrace, he does not
know about them.
22 Only his own flesh pains him,
and his soul grieves for him.

III: SECOND CYCLE OF SPEECHES

CHAPTER 15

Second Speech of Eliphaz. 1 Then Eliphaz
the Temanite spoke and said:

2 Should a wise man answer with airy
opinions,
or puff himself up with wind?
3 Should he argue in speech which does
not avail,
and in words which are to no profit?
4 You in fact do away with piety,
and you lessen devotion toward God,
5 Because your wickedness instructs your
mouth,
and you choose to speak like the
crafty.

---

i Jb 10, 20; 15, 14; Pss 39, 5f; 89, 46; Wis 2, 1.—j Jb 8, 9;
Pss 90, 6; 102, 12; 103, 15; 109, 23; 144, 4; Is 40, 6f; Jas 1,
10.—k Ps 51, 4. 7.—l Jb 20, 7.—m Jb 7, 10.—n Jb 7, 1.—o Jb
31, 4; 34, 21.

14, 28: This verse has been transposed from ch 13.
14, 17: *Sealed up in a pouch:* hidden away and forgotten.

6 Your own mouth condemns you, not I;*p*
  your own lips refute you.
7 Are you indeed the first-born of mankind,
  or were you brought forth before the
  hills?
8 Are you privy to the counsels of God,*q*
  and do you restrict wisdom to yourself?
9 What do you know that we do not
  know?*r*
  What intelligence have you which we
  have not?
10 There are gray-haired old men among us
  more advanced in years than your
  father.
11 Are the consolations of God not enough
  for you,
  and speech that deals gently with you?
12 Why do your notions carry you away,
  and why do your eyes blink,
13 So that you turn your anger against God
  and let such words escape your
  mouth!
14 What is a man that he should be blameless,*s*
  one born of woman that he should be
  righteous?*t*
15 If in his holy ones God places no confidence,*u*
  and if the heavens are not clean in his
  sight,
16 How much less so is the abominable,
  the corrupt:
  man, who drinks in iniquity like
  water!
17 I will show you, if you listen to me;
  what I have seen I will tell—
18 What wise men relate
  and have not contradicted since the
  days of their fathers,
19 To whom alone the land was given,
  when no foreigner moved among
  them.
20 The wicked man is in torment all his
  days,
  and limited years are in store for the
  tyrant;
21 The sound of terrors is in his ears;
  when all is prosperous, the spoiler
  comes upon him.

22 He despairs of escaping the darkness,
  and looks ever for the sword;
23 A wanderer, food for the vultures,
  he knows that his destruction is imminent.
24 By day the darkness fills him with
  dread;
  distress and anguish overpower him.
25 Because he has stretched out his hand
  against God
  and bade defiance to the Almighty,
26 One shall rush sternly upon him
  with the stout bosses of his shield,
  like a king prepared for the charge.
27 Because he has blinded himself with his
  crassness,
  padding his loins with fat,
28 He shall dwell in ruinous cities,
  in houses that are deserted,
  That are crumbling into clay
29 with no shadow to lengthen over the
  ground.
  He shall not be rich, and his possessions
  shall not endure;
31 for vain shall be his bartering.
30 A flame shall wither him up in his early
  growth,
  and with the wind his blossoms shall
  disappear.
32 His stalk shall wither before its time,
  and his branches shall be green no
  more.
33 He shall be like a vine that sheds its
  grapes unripened,
  and like an olive tree casting off its
  bloom.
34 For the breed of the impious shall be
  sterile,*v*
  and fire shall consume the tents of ex-
  tortioners.
35 They conceive malice and bring forth
  emptiness;*w*
  they give birth to failure.*

CHAPTER 16

Job's Fourth Reply. 1 Then Job answered
and said:
2 I have heard this sort of thing many
  times.*x*
  Wearisome comforters are you all!
3 Is there no end to windy words?
  Or what sickness have you that you
  speak on?
4 I also could talk as you do,
  were you in my place.

p Jb 9, 20.—q Jb 11, 7; Wis 9, 13; Jer 23, 18; Rom 11, 34; 1
Cor 2, 11. 16.—r Jb 12, 3; 13, 2.—s 14ff: Jb 25, 4ff.—t Jb 14, 4.—
u Jb 4, 18f.—v Wis 3, 11. 18.—w Ps 7, 15; Is 59, 4.—x Jb 12, 3.

15, 35: *They give birth to failure:* their wicked plans yield
nothing but futile results. Cf Ps 7, 15; Is 59, 4.

I could declaim over you,
or wag my head at you;
5 I could strengthen you with talk,
or shake my head with silent lips.
6 If I speak, this pain I have will not be
checked;
if I leave off, it will not depart from
me.

7 But now that I am exhausted and
stunned,
all my company has closed in on me.
8 As a witness there rises up
my traducer, speaking openly against
me;
9 I am the prey his wrath assails,
he gnashes his teeth against me.
My enemies lord it over me;
10 their mouths are agape to bite me.
They smite me on the cheek insultingly;
they are all enlisted against me.
11 God has given me over to the impious;
into the clutches of the wicked he has
cast me.
12 I was in peace, but he dislodged me;
he seized me by the neck and dashed
me to pieces.

He has set me up for a target;
13 his arrows strike me from all directions,
He pierces my sides without mercy,
he pours out my gall upon the
ground.
14 He pierces me with thrust upon thrust;
he attacks me like a warrior.
15 I have fastened sackcloth over my skin,
and have laid my brow in the dust.
16 My face is inflamed with weeping
and there is darkness over my eyes,
17 Although my hands are free from violence,
and my prayer is sincere.

18 O earth, cover not my blood,
nor let my outcry come to rest!*
19 Even now, behold, my witness* is in
heaven,
and my spokesman is on high.
20 My friends it is who wrong me;
before God my eyes drop tears,
21 That he may do justice for a mortal in
his presence
and decide between a man and his
neighbor.
22 For my years are numbered now,
and I am on a journey from which I
shall not return.

CHAPTER 17

1 My spirit is broken, my lamp of life extinguished;
my burial is at hand.
2 I am indeed mocked,
and, as their provocation mounts, my
eyes grow dim.
3 Grant me one to offer you a pledge on
my behalf:*
who is there that will give surety for
me?
4 You darken their minds to knowledge;
therefore they do not understand.
5 My lot is described as evil,
6 and I am made a byword of the people;*y*
their object lesson I have become.
7 My eye has grown blind with anguish,
and all my frame is shrunken to a
shadow.
8 Upright men are astonished at this,
and the innocent aroused against the
wicked.
9 Yet the righteous shall hold to his way,
and he who has clean hands increase
in strength.
10 But turn now, and come on again;
for I shall not find a wise man among
you!
11 My days are passed away, my plans are
at an end,
the cherished purposes of my heart.
12 Such men change the night into day;
where there is darkness they talk of
approaching light.
13 If I look for the nether world as my
dwelling,
if I spread my couch in the darkness,
14 If I must call corruption "my father,"
and the maggot "my mother" and
"my sister,"
15 Where then is my hope,
and my prosperity, who shall see?
16 Will they descend with me into the
nether world?
Shall we go down together into the
dust?

CHAPTER 18

Bildad's Second Speech. 1 Then Bildad
the Shuhite replied and said:

y Jb 30, 9.

16, 18: As the blood of those who were unjustly slain cries to
heaven for vengeance (Gn 4, 10; Ez 24, 6-9), so Job's sufferings
demand redress.
16, 19: *Witness:* refers either to God or, more probably, to
Job's prayer.
17, 3: Addressed to God; v 10 to Job's friends.

2 When will you put an end to words?
    Reflect, and then we can have discussion.

3 Why are we accounted like the beasts,
    their equals in your sight?

4 You who tear yourself in your anger,*
    shall the earth be neglected on your account
    [or the rock be moved out of its place]?

5 Truly, the light of the wicked is extinguished;
    no flame brightens his hearth.

6 The light is darkened in his tent;
    in spite of him, his lamp goes out.*z*

7 His vigorous steps are hemmed in,
    and his own counsel casts him down.

8 For he rushes headlong into a net,
    and he wanders into a pitfall.

9 A trap seizes him by the heel,
    and a snare lays hold of him.

10 A noose for him is hid on the ground,
    and the toils for him on the way.

11 On every side terrors affright him;*a*
    they harry him at each step.

12 Disaster is ready at his side,
13   the first-born of death* consumes his limbs.

14 Fiery destruction lodges in his tent,
    and marches him off to the king of terrors.*
    He is plucked from the security of his tent;
15   over his abode brimstone is scattered.

16 Below, his roots dry up,
    and above, his branches wither.

17 His memory perishes from the land,*b*
    and he has no name on the earth.

18 He is driven from light into darkness,
    and banished out of the world.

19 He has neither son nor grandson among his people,
    nor any survivor where once he dwelt.

20 They who come after shall be appalled at his fate;

they who went before are struck with horror.

21 So is it then with the dwelling of the impious man,
    and such is the place of him who knows not God!

CHAPTER 19

Job's Fifth Reply. [1]Then Job answered and said:

2 How long will you vex my soul,
    grind me down with words?

3 These ten times you have reviled me,
    have assailed me without shame!

4 Be it indeed that I am at fault
    and that my fault remains with me.

5 Even so, if you would vaunt yourselves against me
    and cast up to me my reproach,

6 Know then that God has dealt unfairly with me,
    and compassed me round with his net.

7 If I cry out "Injustice!" I am not heard.*c*
    I cry for help, but there is no redress.

8 He has barred my way and I cannot pass;
    he has veiled my path in darkness;

9 He has stripped me of my glory,
    and taken the diadem from my brow.

10 He breaks me down on every side, and I am gone;
    my hope he has uprooted like a tree.

11 His wrath he has kindled against me;
    he counts me among his enemies.*d*

12 His troops advance as one man;
    they build up their road to attack me,
    and they encamp around my tent.

13 My brethren have withdrawn from me,*e*
    and my friends are wholly estranged.

14 My kinsfolk and companions neglect me,
    and my guests have forgotten me.

15 Even my handmaids treat me as a stranger;
    I am an alien in their sight.

16 I call my servant, but he gives no answer,
    though in my speech I plead with him.

17 My breath is abhorred by my wife;*f*
    I am loathsome to the men of my family.

18 The young children, too, despise me;
    when I appear, they speak against me.

19 All my intimate friends hold me in horror;
    those whom I loved have turned against me!*g*

Jb

---

z Jb 21, 17; Prv 13, 9; 24, 20.—a Jb 15, 20-24; 27, 20.—b Ps
34, 17; Prv 2, 22; 10, 7.—c Jb 30, 20.—d Jb 13, 24; 33, 10.—e
Jb 6, 13.—f Jb 2, 9.—g Sir 6, 8.

18, 4: Job himself is portrayed as having the heedless rage of
wild beasts, despite which God does not forsake the usual course
of Divine Providence.
18, 13: *First-born of death:* that is, disease, plague.
18, 14: *The king of terrors:* of the nether world, death; however, the Hebrew is obscure.

20 My bones cleave to my skin,
   and I have escaped with my flesh between my teeth.*
21 Pity me, pity me, O you my friends,
   for the hand of God has struck me!
22 Why do you hound me as though you
   were divine,*
   and insatiably prey upon me?

23 Oh, would that my words were written
   down!ʰ
   Would that they were inscribed in a
   record:*
24 That with an iron chisel and with lead
   they were cut in the rock forever!
25 But as for me, I know that my Vindicator lives,*
   and that he will at last stand forth
   upon the dust;ⁱ
27 Whom I myself shall see:
   my own eyes, not another's, shall behold him,
26 And from my flesh I shall see God;
   my inmost being is consumed with
   longing.

28 But you who say, "How shall we persecute him,
   seeing that the root of the matter is
   found in him?"
29 Be afraid of the sword for yourselves,
   for these crimes deserve the sword;
   that you may know that there is a
   judgment.

CHAPTER 20

Zophar's Second Speech. ¹ Then Zophar
the Naamathite spoke and said:
3 A rebuke which puts me to shame I
   hear,
2 and because of this I am disturbed.
   So now my thoughts provide me with
   an answer,
   and from my understanding a spirit
   gives me a reply.
4 Do you not know this from olden time,
   since man was placed upon the earth,
5 That the triumph of the wicked is short
   and the joy of the impious but for a
   moment?ʲ
6 Though his pride mount up to the
   heavens
   and his head reach to the clouds,
7 Yet he perishes forever like the fuel of
   his fire,
   and the onlookers say, "Where is
   he?"ᵏ

8 Like a dream he takes flight and is not
   found again;
   he fades away like a vision of the
   night.
9 The eye which saw him does so no more;
   nor shall his dwelling again behold
   him.
11 Though his frame is full of youthful
   vigor,
   this shall lie with him in the dust.
12 Though wickedness is sweet in his
   mouth,
   and he hides it under his tongue,
13 Though he retains it and will not let it go
   but keeps it still within his mouth,
14 Yet in his stomach the food shall turn;
   it shall be venom of asps inside him.
15 The riches he swallowed he shall disgorge;
   God shall compel his belly to disown
   them.
16 The poison of asps he shall drink in;
   the viper's fangs shall slay him.
17 He shall see no streams of oil,*
   no torrents of honey or milk.
18 Restoring his gains, he shall not enjoy
   them;
   though his wealth increases, he shall
   not rejoice.
19 Because he has oppressed the poor,
   and stolen a patrimony he had not
   built up,
21 Therefore his prosperity shall not endure,
10 and his hands shall yield up his
   riches.ˡ
20 Though he has known no quiet in his
   greed,
   his treasures shall not save him.ᵐ
22 ⁿ When he abounds to overflowing, he

h Jb 31, 35.—i 25ff:Phil 3, 20; Ti 2, 13.—j Jb 21, 13; Ps 37,
35f.—k Jb 14, 10; Ps 37, 10. 36.—l Jb 27, 14.—m Eccl 5, 9; Lk
12, 20.—n Jb 15, 20-35.

19, 20: *With my flesh between my teeth:* meaning perhaps
that Job has been reduced to such an extremity that he scarcely
has thin lips over his teeth. But the current Hebrew text of this
line is probably corrupt.
19, 22: *Divine:* possessing God's attributes of judgment and
authority to punish.
19, 23f: Job regards what he is about to say as so important
that he wishes it recorded in a permanent manner.
19, 25. 27: The meaning of this passage is obscure because
the original text has been poorly preserved and the ancient versions do not agree among themselves. It is certain that Job expresses his belief in a future vindication by God (called here in the
Hebrew "Goel"), but the time and manner of this vindication are
undefined. In the Vulgate Job is made to indicate a belief in physical resurrection after death, but the Hebrew and the other ancient versions are less specific.
20, 17: *Oil:* olive oil, one of the main agricultural products of
Palestine, a land proverbially rich in *honey* and *milk.*

shall be brought into straits,
and nought shall be left of his goods.

23 God shall send against him the fury of
his wrath
and rain down his missiles of war
upon him.

24 Should he escape the iron weapon,
the bow of bronze shall pierce him
through;

25 The dart shall come out of his back;
terrors shall fall upon him.

26 Complete darkness is in store for him;
the fire which shall consume him
needs not to be fanned.ᵒ

27 The heavens shall reveal his guilt,
and the earth shall rise up against him.

28 The flood shall sweep away his house
with the waters that run off in the day
of God's anger.

29 This is the portion of a wicked man,
and the heritage appointed him by
God.ᵖ

CHAPTER 21

Job's Sixth Reply. ¹Then Job said in
reply:

2 At least listen to my words,�q
and let that be the consolation you
offer.

3 Bear with me while I speak;
and after I have spoken, you can
mock!

4 Is my complaint toward man?
And why should I not be impatient?

5 Look at me and be astonished,
put your hands over your mouths.

6 When I think of it, I am dismayed,
and horror takes hold on my flesh.

7 Why do the wicked survive,
grow old, become mighty in power?ʳ

8 Their progeny is secure in their sight;
they see before them their kinsfolk
and their offspring.

9 Their homes are safe and without fear,
nor is the scourge of God upon them.

10 Their bulls gender without fail;
their cows calve and do not miscarry.

11 These folks have infants numerous as
lambs,
and their children dance.

12 They sing to the timbrel and harp,
and make merry to the sound of the
flute.

13 They live out their days in prosperity,
and tranquilly go down to the nether
world.ˢ

14 Yet they say to God, "Depart from us,ᵗ
for we have no wish to learn your
ways!

15 What is the Almighty that we should
serve him?
And what gain shall we have if we
pray to him?"ᵘ

16 If their happiness is not in their own
hands
and if the counsel of the wicked is repulsive to God,ᵛ

17 How often is the lamp of the wicked put
out?
How often does destruction come
upon them,
the portion he allots in his anger?

18 Let them be like straw before the wind,
and like chaff which the storm
snatches away!

19 May God not store up the man's misery
for his children;
let him requite the man himself so
that he feels it,

20 Let his own eyes see the calamity,
and the wrath of the Almighty let him
drink!

21 For what interest has he in his family
after him,
when the number of his months is
finished?

23 One dies in his full vigor,
wholly at ease and content;

24 His figure is full and nourished,
and his bones are rich in marrow.

25 Another dies in bitterness of soul,
having never tasted happiness.

26 Alike they lie down in the dust,
and worms cover them both.

27 Behold, I know your thoughts,
and the arguments you rehearse
against me.

28 For you say, "Where is the house of the
magnate,
and where the dwelling place of the
wicked?"

29 Have you not asked the wayfarers
and do you not recognize their monuments?

30 Nay, the evil man is spared calamity
when it comes;

32 and on the day he is carried to the
grave

31 Who will charge him with his conduct
to his face,

Jb

---

o Dt 32, 22.—p Jb 27, 13.—q Jb 13, 17.—r Jb 12, 6; Pss 37,
35; 73, 3; Eccl 8, 14; Jer 12, 1f; Mal 3, 14f.—s Jb 34, 20.—t Jb
22, 17.—u Mal 3, 14.—v Jb 22, 18.

and for what he has done who will repay him?

33 Sweet to him are the clods of the valley,
and over him the funeral mound keeps watch,
While all the line of mankind follows him,
and the countless others who have gone before.

34 How then can you offer me vain comfort,
while in your answers perfidy remains?

IV: THIRD CYCLE OF SPEECHES

CHAPTER 22

Eliphaz's Third Speech. [1] Then Eliphaz the Temanite answered and said:

2 Can a man be profitable to God?[w]
Though to himself a wise man be profitable!

22 Can anyone teach God knowledge,
seeing that he judges those on high?[*]

3 Is it of advantage to the Almighty if you are just?[x]
Or is it a gain to him if you make your ways perfect?

4 Is it because of your piety that he reproves you—
that he enters with you into judgment?

5 Is not your wickedness manifold?
Are not your iniquities endless?

6 You have unjustly kept your kinsmen's goods in pawn,[*]
left them stripped naked of their clothing.[y]

7 To the thirsty you have given no water to drink,
and from the hungry you have withheld bread;

8 As if the land belonged to the man of might,
and only the privileged were to dwell in it.

9 You have sent widows away empty-handed,
and the resources of orphans you have destroyed.[z]

10 Therefore snares are round about you,[a]
and a sudden terror causes you dismay,

11 Or darkness, in which you cannot see;
a deluge of waters covers you.

12 Does not God, in the heights of the heavens,[b]
behold the stars, high though they are?

13 Yet you say, "What does God know?[c]
Can he judge through the thick darkness?

14 Clouds hide him so that he cannot see;
he walks upon the vault of the heavens!"

15 Do you indeed keep to the ancient way
trodden by worthless men,

16 Who were snatched away before their time;
whose foundations a flood swept away?

17 These men said to God, "Depart from us!"
and, "What can the Almighty do to us?"

18 [Yet he had filled their houses with good things![d]
But far be from me the mind of the impious!][*]

19 The just look on and are gladdened,
and the innocent deride them:[e]

20 "Truly these have been destroyed where they stood,
and such as were left, fire has consumed!"

21 Come to terms with him to be at peace.
In this shall good come to you:

22 Receive instruction from his mouth,
and lay up his words in your heart.

23 If you return to the Almighty, you will be restored;
if you put iniquity far from your tent,

24 And treat raw gold like dust,
and the fine gold of Ophir[*] as pebbles from the brook,

25 Then the Almighty himself shall be your gold
and your sparkling silver.

26 For then you shall delight in the Almighty
and you shall lift up your face toward God.

---

w Jb 9, 2.—x Jb 35, 7.—y Jb 24, 3; Dt 24, 6. 17; Ez 18, 12. 16.—z Dt 24, 17; 27, 19.—a Jb 18, 8ff.—b Jb 11, 8.—c 13f: Pss 10, 11; 73, 11; 94, 7; Is 29, 15; Ez 8, 12; 9, 9.—d Jb 21, 16.—e Ps 107, 42.

22, 22: *Those on high:* the angels. (This verse has been transposed from ch 21.)

22, 6ff: This criticism of Job by Eliphaz is altogether untrue, but it is made to dramatize the latter's argument that God always acts justly when he causes someone to suffer. Verse 8 is misplaced.

22, 18: A gloss, taken partly from Jb 21, 16.

22, 24: *Ophir:* cf note to Ps 45, 10.

27 You shall entreat him and he will hear
you,*f*
and your vows you shall fulfill.
28 When you make a decision, it shall succeed for you,
and upon your ways the light shall
shine.
29 For he brings down the pride of the
haughty,
but the man of humble mien he
saves.*g*
30 God delivers him who is innocent;
you shall be delivered through cleanness of hands. *h*

CHAPTER 23

Job's Seventh Reply. ¹Again Job answered and said:

2 Though I know my complaint is bitter,
his hand is heavy upon me in my
groanings.
3 Oh, that today I might find him,
that I might come to his judgment
seat!
4 I would set out my cause before him,
and fill my mouth with arguments;
5 I would learn the words with which he
would answer,
and understand what he would reply
to me.
6 Even should he contend against me
with his great power,
yet, would that he himself might
heed me!
7 There the upright man might reason
with him,
and I should once and for all preserve
my rights.

8 But if I go to the east, he is not there;
or to the west, I cannot perceive him;
9 Where the north enfolds him, I behold
him not;
by the south he is veiled, and I see
him not.
10 Yet he knows my way;
if he proved me, I should come forth
as gold. *i*

11 My foot has always walked in his steps;
his way I have kept and have not
turned aside.
12 From the commands of his lips I have
not departed;
the words of his mouth I have treasured in my heart.
13 But he has decided, and who can say
him nay?
What he desires, that he does.*j*
14 For he will carry out what is appointed
for me;
and many such things may yet be in
his mind.
15 Therefore am I dismayed before him;
when I take thought, I fear him.
16 Indeed God has made my courage fail;
the Almighty has put me in dismay.
17 Yes, would that I had vanished in darkness,
and that thick gloom were before me
to conceal me.

CHAPTER 24

1 Why are not times set by the Almighty,
and why do his friends not see his
days?*
2 The wicked remove landmarks;
they steal away herds and pasture
them.
3 The asses of orphans they drive away;
they take the widow's ox for a pledge.
4 They force the needy off the road;
all the poor of the land are driven into
hiding.
5 Like wild asses in the desert, these go
forth
to their task of seeking food;
The steppe provides food for the young
among them;
6 they harvest at night in the untilled
land.
7 They pass the night naked, without
clothing,
for they have no covering against the
cold;
8 They are drenched with the rain of the
mountains,
and for want of shelter they cling to
the rock.
11 Between the rows they press out the oil;
they glean in the vineyard of the
wicked.
They tread the wine presses, yet suffer
thirst,

f Jb 33, 26.—g Ps 138, 6; Prv 29, 23; Mt 23, 12; Lk 1, 52; Jas
4, 10; 1 Pt 5, 5.—h Jb 17, 9; Ps 18, 21. 25.—i Ps 66, 10; Prv
17, 3; Mal 3, 3; 1 Pt 1, 7.—j Jb 42, 2; Pss 115, 3; 135, 6.

24, 1: Why does not God favor his friends by the speedy
punishment of his enemies? (The text and order of verses in this
chapter are not certain; note the omission of v 9 which duplicates
words of vv 2-4.)

10 and famished are those who carry the
sheaves.

12 From the dust the dying groan,
and the souls of the wounded cry out
[yet God does not treat it as un-
seemly].

13 There are those who are rebels against
the light;[k]
they know not its ways;
they abide not in its paths.

14 When there is no light the murderer
rises,
to kill the poor and needy.

15 The eye of the adulterer watches for the
twilight;[l]
he says, "No eye will see me."
In the night the thief roams about,
and he puts a mask over his face;

16 in the dark he breaks into houses.
By day they shut themselves in;
none of them know the light,

17 for daylight they regard as darkness.*

* * *

18 Their portion in the land is accursed,

20 and wickedness is splintered like
wood.

19. 21. ....

22 To him who rises without assurance of
his life

23 he gives safety and support.
He sustains the mighty by his strength,
and his eyes are on their ways.

24 They are exalted for a while, and then
they are gone;
they are laid low and, like all others,
are gathered up;
like ears of grain they shrivel.

* * *

25 If this be not so, who will confute me,
and reduce my argument to nought?

CHAPTER 25

Bildad's Third Speech. [1] Then Bildad the
Shuhite answered and said:

2 Dominion and awesomeness are his
who brings about harmony in his
heavens.

3 Is there any numbering of his troops?*
Yet to which of them does not his
light extend?

4 How can a man be just in God's sight,[m]
or how can any woman's child be innocent?

5 Behold, even the moon is not bright
and the stars are not clear in his sight.

6 How much less man, who is but a maggot,
the son of man, who is only a worm?[n]

CHAPTER 26

Job's Reply. [1] Then Job spoke again and
said:*

2 What help you give to the powerless,
what strength to the feeble arm!

3 How you counsel, as though he had no
wisdom;
how profuse is the advice you offer!

4 With whose help have you uttered those
words,
and whose is the breath that comes
forth from you?[o]

5 The shades* beneath writhe in terror,[p]
the waters, and their inhabitants.

6 Naked before him is the nether world,*
and Abaddon has no covering.[q]

7 He stretches out the North* over empty
space,
and suspends the earth over nothing
at all;

8 He binds up the waters in his clouds,
yet the cloud is not rent by their
weight;

9 He holds back the appearance of the full
moon
by spreading his clouds before it.

10 He has marked out a circle* on the surface of the deep[r]
as the boundary of light and darkness.

k Jn 3, 19f.—l Prv 7, 9f.—m Jb 4, 17ff; 9, 2.—n Jb 4, 19; 15,
16.—o Gn 2, 7.—p Prv 9, 18.—q Ps 139, 7-12.—r Jb 38, 8-11;
Prv 8, 29.

24, 17: The asterisks which follow this verse mark off a passage
(vv 18-24) which cannot be ascribed to Job with certainty. Vv 17-24
are in general poorly preserved; and much of vv 18-21 has not been
translated because these verses are obscure. St. Jerome renders
them as follows: "(18) He is light upon the face of the water, cursed
be his portion on the earth; let him not walk by the way of vineyards.
(19) Let him pass from the snow waters to excessive heat, and his
sin even to hell. (20) Let mercy forget him; may worms be his
sweetness; let him be remembered no more, but be broken in pieces
as an unfruitful tree. (21) For he has fed the barren that bears not,
and to the widow he has done no good."
25, 3: *His troops:* the heavenly hosts, the stars or the angels.
His light: compare the wording in Jb 24, 13: *those who are
rebels against the light.*
26, 1-14: Probably to be read as Job's reply to Bildad's short
speech. Some, however, would make it the reply to Zophar (Jb
27, 13-21); it would thus lead up to the poem of ch 28.
26, 5: *Shades:* the dead in Sheol, the nether world; cf Pss 6,
6; 88, 11.
26, 6: *Nether world:* cf note to Ps 6, 6. *Abaddon:* Hebrew
for "(place of) destruction," a synonym for *nether world;* cf Jb
28, 22; Rv 9, 11.
26, 7: *The North:* used here as a synonym for the firmament,
the heavens; cf Is 14, 13.
26, 10: *Circle:* the horizon of the ocean which serves as the
boundary for the activity of light and darkness.

11 The pillars of the heavens tremble[s]
and are stunned at his thunderous rebuke;

12 By his power he stirs up the sea,
and by his might he crushes Rahab;*

13 With his angry breath he scatters the
water,
and he hurls the lightning against it
relentlessly;
His hand pierces the fugitive dragon*
as from his hand it strives to flee.[t]

14 Lo, these are but the outlines of his
ways,
and how faint is the word we hear!

CHAPTER 27

Job's Reply

11 I will teach you the manner of God's
dealings,
and the way of the Almighty I will
not conceal.

2 As God lives,* who withholds my deserts,[u]
the Almighty, who has made bitter
my soul,

3 So long as I still have life in me
and the breath of God is in my nostrils,

4 My lips shall not speak falsehood,
nor my tongue utter deceit!

5 Far be it from me to account you right;
till I die I will not renounce my innocence.[v]

6 My justice I maintain and I will not relinquish it;
my heart does not reproach me for
any of my days.

s Jb 9, 6.—t Is 27, 1.—u Jb 34, 5.—v Jb 2, 3. 9; 13, 15; 33,
9.—w Jb 20, 4-29.—x Pss 49, 18; 76, 6.

26, 12: *Rahab:* cf Jb 9, 13; see note on Ps 89, 11.
26, 13: *The fugitive dragon:* the same term occurs in Is 27,
1 in apposition to Leviathan; see note on Jb 3, 8. This is actually
Jb 27, 22.
27, 2-12: This is probably to be read as Job's reply to Zophar's
speech of Jb 27, 13-21. In the current Hebrew text the heading
for this chapter (Jb 27, 1, here omitted) is identical with Jb 29,
1; we should expect rather such a heading as in Jb 21, 1; 23, 1;
26, 1.
27, 13-21: This is probably to be read as Zophar's third
speech. The asterisks are present to indicate it is not likely that
the sacred writer intended these words to be ascribed to Job.
27, 21: The Hebrew has two more verses: v 22 (read above
with Jb 26, 13); and v 23, which is a variant form of v 21.
28, 1-28: Note the changed order of verses; v 4 is uncertain.
This chapter contains a beautifully vivid description of that
Wisdom which is beyond the attainment of creatures; known only
to God, it is reflected in the order and majesty of his creation.
Man, however, can, in a way, participate in this Wisdom by fearing the Lord and avoiding evil. Scholars are not agreed regarding
the authorship of this poem, though it is altogether worthy of the
author of the Book of Job. Used here as a counterpoise to ch 3 at
the beginning of the dialogue, it may have been first conceived as
an independent poem.

7 Let my enemy be as the wicked
and my adversary as the unjust!

8 For what can the impious man expect
when he is cut off,
when God requires his life?

9 Will God then attend to his cry
when calamity comes upon him?

10 Will he then delight in the Almighty
and call upon him constantly?

12 Behold, you yourselves have all seen it;
why then do you spend yourselves in
idle words!

* * *

13 * This is the portion of a wicked man
from God,
the inheritance an oppressor receives
from the Almighty:[w]

14 Though his children be many, the
sword is their destiny.
His offspring shall not be filled with
bread.

15 His survivors, when they die, shall have
no burial,
and their widows shall not be
mourned.

16 Though he heap up silver like dust
and store away mounds of clothing,

17 What he has stored the just man shall
wear,
and the innocent shall divide the
silver.

18 He builds his house as of cobwebs,
or like a booth put up by the vine-
keeper.

19 He lies down a rich man, one last time;
he opens his eyes and nothing remains to him.[x]

20 Terrors rush upon him by day;
at night the tempest carries him off.

21 The storm wind seizes him and he disappears;
it sweeps him out of his place.*

* * *

CHAPTER 28

The Inaccessibility of Wisdom

1 There is indeed a mine for silver,*
and a place for gold which men refine.

2 Iron is taken from the earth,
and copper is melted out of stone.

4 . . . .

5 The earth, though out of it comes forth
bread,
is in fiery upheaval underneath.

Jb

6 Its stones are the source of sapphires,
and there is gold in its dust.

12 But whence can wisdom be obtained,
and where is the place of understanding?[y]

13 Man knows nothing to equal it,
not is it to be had in the land of the living.

15 Solid gold cannot purchase it,
not can its price be paid with silver.[z]

16 It cannot be bought with gold of Ophir,*
with the precious onyx or the sapphire.

17 Gold or crystal cannot equal it,
nor can golden vessels reach its worth.

18 Neither coral nor jasper should be thought of;
it surpasses pearls and 19 Arabian topaz.

20 Whence, then, comes wisdom,
and where is the place of understanding?

21 It is hid from the eyes of any beast;
from the birds of the air it is concealed.

7 The path to it no bird of prey knows,
nor has the hawk's eye seen that path.

8 The proud beasts have not trodden it,
nor has the lion gone that way.

14 The abyss declares, "It is not in me";
and the sea says, "I have it not."

22 Abaddon* and Death say,
"Only by rumor have we heard of it."

23 God knows the way to it;[a]
it is he who is familiar with its place.[b]

24 For he beholds the ends of the earth
and sees all that is under the heavens.

3 He has set a boundary for the darkness;
to the farthest confines he penetrates.

9 He sets his hand to the flinty rock,
and overturns the mountains at their foundations.

10 He splits channels in the rocks;
his eyes behold all that is precious.

11 He probes the wellsprings of the streams,
and brings hidden things to light.

25 He has weighed out the wind,
and fixed the scope of the waters;

26 When he made rules for the rain
and a path for the thunderbolts,[c]

27 Then he saw wisdom and appraised it,
gave it its setting, knew it through and through.

28 And to man he said:
Behold, the fear of the LORD is wisdom;
and avoiding evil is understanding.[d]

V: JOB'S FINAL SUMMARY OF HIS CAUSE

CHAPTER 29

1 Job took up his theme anew and said:

2 Oh, that I were as in the months past!
as in the days when God watched over me,[e]

3 While he kept his lamp shining above my head,
and by his light I walked through darkness;

4 As I was in my flourishing days,
when God sheltered my tent;

5 When the Almighty was yet with me,
and my children were round about me;

6 When my footsteps were bathed in milk,
and the rock flowed with streams of oil;*

7 When I went forth to the gate of the city
and set up my seat in the square—

8 Then the young men saw me and withdrew,
while the elders rose up and stood;

9 The chief men refrained from speaking
and covered their mouths with their hands;[f]

10 The voice of the princes was silenced,
and their tongues stuck to the roofs of their mouths.

21 For me they listened and waited;
they were silent for my counsel.

22 Once I spoke, they said no more,
but received my pronouncement drop by drop.

23 They waited for me as for the rain;
they drank in my words like the spring rains.

24 When I smiled on them they were reassured;

---

y Eccl 7, 24f; Bar 3, 14f. 29-33.—z Prv 3, 14; 8, 10f. 19; 16, 16; Wis 7, 7-11.—a 23-27: Prv 8, 22-31.—b Prv 2, 6; Sir 1, 1; Jas 1, 5.—c Jb 38, 25; Prv 3, 20.—d Ps 111, 10; Prv 1, 7; 9, 10; Sir 1, 16.—e Jb 1, 10.—f Wis 8, 10ff.

28, 16: *Ophir:* cf note to Ps 45, 10.
28, 22: *Abaddon:* cf note to Jb 26, 6.
29, 6: Hyperbole to express abundance; see note on Jb 20, 17.

25 mourners took comfort from my cheerful glance.
I chose out their way and presided;
I took a king's place in the armed forces.

11 Whoever heard of me blessed me;
those who saw me commended me.

12 For I rescued the poor who cried out for help,
the orphans, and the unassisted;

13 The blessing of those in extremity came upon me,
and the heart of the widow I made joyful.

14 I wore my honesty like a garment;
justice was my robe and my turban.

15 I was eyes to the blind,
and feet to the lame was I;

16 I was a father to the needy;
the rights of the stranger I studied,

17 And I broke the jaws of the wicked man;
from his teeth I forced the prey.

18 Then I said: "In my own nest I shall grow old;
I shall multiply years like the phoenix.*

19 My root is spread out to the waters;
the dew rests by night on my branches.

20 My glory is fresh within me,
and my bow is renewed in my hand!"

CHAPTER 30

1 But now they hold me in derision
who are younger in years than I;[g]
Whose fathers I should have disdained
to rank with the dogs of my flock.

2 Such strength as they had, to me meant nought;
they were utterly destitute.

3 In want and hunger was their lot,[h]
they who fled to the parched wastelands:

---

g Jb 12, 4; 19, 18.—h 3-8: Jb 24, 5f.—i Jb 17, 6.—j Jb 19, 7.—k Heb 9, 27.

29, 18: *Phoenix:* a legendary bird which, after several centuries of life, consumed itself in fire, then rose from its ashes in youthful freshness. This meaning, originally intended in the Greek, later came to mean "palm tree." Some render the Hebrew as "sand."

30, 4: *Saltwort:* found in salt marshes and very sour to the taste; eaten by the extremely poor as a cooked vegetable. *Broom plant:* the juniper or brushwood; cf Ps 120, 4; a figure of bitterness and poverty, because of its bitter-tasting roots which are practically inedible.

30, 18-23: Job here refers to God's stern treatment of him.

---

4 They plucked saltwort* and shrubs;
the roots of the broom plant were their food.

5 They were banished from among men,
with an outcry like that against a thief—

6 To dwell on the slopes of the wadies,
in caves of sand and stone;

7 Among the bushes they raised their raucous cry;
under the nettles they huddled together.

8 Irresponsible, nameless men,
they were driven out of the land.

9 Yet now they sing of me in mockery;
I am become a byword among them.[i]

10 They abhor me, they stand aloof from me,
they do not hesitate to spit in my face!

11 Indeed, they have loosed their bonds; they lord it over me,
and have thrown off restraint in my presence.

12 To subvert my paths they rise up;
they build their approaches for my ruin.

13 To destroy me, they attack with none to stay them;

14 as through a wide breach they advance.
Amid the uproar they come on in waves.

15 over me rolls the terror.
My dignity is borne off on the wind,
and my welfare vanishes like a cloud.

18 One with great power lays hold of my clothing;*
by the collar of my tunic he seizes me:

19 He has cast me into the mire;
I am leveled with the dust and ashes.

20 I cry to you, but you do not answer me;[j]
you stand off and look at me,

21 Then you turn upon me without mercy
and with your strong hand you buffet me.

22 You raise me up and drive me before the wind;
I am tossed about by the tempest.

23 Indeed I know you will turn me back in death
to the destined place of everyone alive.[k]

24 Yet should not a hand be held out
to help a wretched man in his calamity?
25 Or have I not wept for the hardships of others;
was not my soul grieved for the destitute?[1]
26 Yet when I looked for good, then evil came;
when I expected light, then came darkness.
16 My soul ebbs away from me;
27 days of affliction have overtaken me.
17 My frame takes no rest by night;
my inward parts seethe and will not be stilled.
28 I go about in gloom, without the sun;
I rise up in public to voice my grief.
29 I have become the brother of jackals,
companion to the ostrich.
30 My blackened skin falls away from me;
the heat scorches my very frame.
31 My harp is turned to mourning,
and my reed pipe to sounds of weeping.

CHAPTER 31

2 But what is man's lot from God above,
his inheritance from the Almighty on high?
3 Is it not calamity for the unrighteous,
and woe for evildoers?
4 Does he not see my ways,
and number all my steps?[m]
6 Let God weigh me in the scales of justice;
thus will he know my innocence![n]
5 If I have walked in falsehood*
and my foot has hastened to deceit;
7 If my steps have turned out of the way,
and my heart has followed my eyes,
or any stain clings to my hands,
8 Then may I sow, but another eat of it,
or may my planting be rooted up!
38 If my land has cried out against me
till its very furrows complained;
39 If I have eaten its produce without payment
and grieved the hearts of its tenants;
40 Then let the thistles grow instead of wheat
and noxious weeds instead of barley!
1 If I have made an agreement with my eyes*

and entertained any thoughts against a maiden;
9 If my heart has been enticed toward a woman,
and I have lain in wait at my neighbor's door;
10 Then may my wife grind for another,
and may others cohabit with her!
11 For that would be heinous,
a crime to be condemned;[o]
12 A fire that should burn down to the abyss
till it consumed all my possessions to the roots.[p]
13 Had I refused justice to my manservant
or to my maid, when they had a claim against me,
14 What then should I do when God rose up;
what could I answer when he demanded an account?
15 Did not he who made me in the womb make him?
Did not the same One fashion us before our birth?
16 If I have denied anything to the poor,[q]
or allowed the eyes of the widow to languish
17 While I ate my portion alone,
with no share in it for the fatherless,
18 Though like a father God has reared me from my youth,
guiding me even from my mother's womb—
19 If I have seen a wanderer without clothing,
or a poor man without covering,
20 Whose limbs have not blessed me
when warmed with the fleece of my sheep;
21 If I have raised my hand against the innocent
because I saw that I had supporters at the gate—*
22 Then may my arm fall from the shoulder,
my forearm be broken at the elbow!
23 For the dread of God will be upon me,
and his majesty will overpower me.

---

l Jb 29, 12-16.—m Jb 14, 16; 34, 21; Ps 139, 3; Prv 5, 21.—n Jb 23, 10.—o Ex 20, 14; Lv 20, 10; Dt 22, 22.—p Sir 9, 8f.—q 16-23: Jb 29, 12-16.

31, 5-34: Job's final protestation of his innocence.
31, 1. 9: Note the gradation: avoidance of sinful glances and thoughts against a maiden; desire for another's wife.
31, 21: *Gate:* cf notes on Jb 5, 4; Ru 4, 1.

24 Had I put my trust in gold
   or called fine gold my security;
25 Or had I rejoiced that my wealth was
   great,
   or that my hand had acquired abundance—
26 Had I looked upon the sun as it shone,*r*
   or the moon in the splendor of its
   progress,*
27 And had my heart been secretly enticed
   to waft them a kiss with my hand;
28 This too would be a crime for condemnation;
   for I should have denied God above.*s*

29 Had I rejoiced at the destruction of my
   enemy
   or exulted when evil fell upon him,*t*
30 Even though I had not suffered my
   mouth to sin
   by uttering a curse against his life—

31 Had not the men of my tent exclaimed,
   "Who has not been fed with his
   meat!"*
32 Because no stranger lodged in the
   street,
   but I opened my door to wayfarers—

33 Had I, out of human weakness, hidden
   my sins
   and buried my guilt in my bosom*
34 Because I feared the noisy multitude
   and the scorn of the tribes terrified
   me—
   then I should have remained silent,
   and not come out of doors!

35 Oh, that I had one to hear my case,

and that my accuser would write out
   his indictment!*u*
36 Surely, I should wear it on my shoulder*
   or put it on me like a diadem;
37 Of all my steps I should give him an account;
   like a prince* I should present myself
   before him.

This is my final plea; let the Almighty
answer me!

The words of Job are ended.

VI: ELIHU'S SPEECHES

CHAPTER 32

¹ Then the three men ceased to answer
Job, because he was righteous*v* in his own
eyes. ² *w* But the anger of Elihu,* son of
Barachel the Buzite, of the family of Ram,
was kindled. He was angry with Job for
considering himself rather than God to be
in the right. ³ *x* He was angry also with the
three friends because they had not found a
good answer and had not condemned Job.
⁴ But since these men were older than he,
Elihu bided his time before addressing
Job. ⁵ When, however, Elihu saw that
there was no reply in the mouths of the
three men, his wrath was inflamed. ⁶ So
Elihu, son of Barachel the Buzite, spoke
out and said:

I am young and you are very old;
   therefore I held back and was afraid
   to declare to you my knowledge.
7 Days should speak, I thought,
   and many years teach wisdom!*y*
8 But it is a spirit in man,*z*
   the breath of the Almighty, that gives
   him understanding.
9 It is not those of many days who are
   wise,
   nor the aged who understand the
   right.
10 Therefore I say, hearken to me;
   let me too set forth my knowledge!

11 Behold, I have waited for your discourses,
   and have given ear to your arguments.
12 Yes, I followed you attentively
   as you searched out what to say;
   And behold, there is none who has convicted Job,
   not one of you could refute his statements.

---

r 26f: Dt 4, 19.—s Dt 17, 2-7.—t Prv 24, 17.—u Jb 19, 23;
23, 3-7.—v Jb 33, 9.—w Jb 13, 18; 27, 6; 34, 5; 35, 2.—x Jb 22,
5.—y Jb 12, 12.—z Jb 33, 4.

31, 26ff: Job never sinned by worshiping the sun or the moon;
waft them a kiss: an act of idolatrous worship.
31, 31: The members of his household will testify to his hospitality.
31, 33f: Job's present protest is made, not in spite of hidden
sins which he had been unwilling to disclose, but out of genuine
innocence.
31, 36: *On my shoulder:* i.e., boldly, proudly.
31, 37: *Like a prince:* not as a frightened criminal. *Final
plea:* literally, "tau," the last letter of the Hebrew alphabet; in
the current Hebrew text this line is in v 35, while the following
one ends v 40.
32, 2: *Elihu* means "My God is he." This speaker was from
Buz, which, according to Jer 25, 23, was near Tema and Dedan.
A young man, he impetuously and impatiently upbraids Job for his
boldness toward God, and the three friends for not successfully
answering Job. He undertakes to defend God's absolute justice
and to explain more clearly why there is suffering. While fundamentally his position is the same as that of the three friends, he
does locate more definitely, though not perfectly, the place of suffering in the divine plan.

13 Yet do not say, "We have met wisdom.*
   God may vanquish him but not man!"
14 For had he addressed his words to me,
   I should not then have answered him
   as you have done.
15 They are dismayed, they make no more
   reply;
   words fail them.
16 Must I wait? Now that they speak no
   more,
   and have ceased to make reply,
17 I too will speak my part;
   I also will show my knowledge!
18 For I am full of matters to utter;
   the spirit within me compels me.
19 Like a new wineskin with wine under
   pressure,
   my bosom is ready to burst.
20 Let me speak and obtain relief;
   let me open my lips, and make reply.
21 I would not be partial to anyone,
   nor give flattering titles to any.
22 For I know nought of flattery;
   if I did, my Maker would soon take
   me away.

CHAPTER 33

1 Therefore, O Job, hear my discourse,
   and hearken to all my words.
2 Behold, now I open my mouth;
   my tongue and my voice form words.
3 I will state directly what is in my mind,
   my lips shall utter knowledge sincerely;
4 For the spirit of God has made me,
   the breath of the Almighty keeps me
   alive.ᵃ
5 If you are able, refute me;
   draw up your arguments and stand
   forth.
6 Behold I, like yourself, have been taken
   from the same clay by God.ᵇ
7 Therefore no fear of me should dismay
   you,
   nor should my presence weigh heavily upon you.
8 But you have said in my hearing,
   as I listened to the sound of your
   words:
9 "I am clean and without transgression;
   I am innocent; there is no guilt in
   me.ᶜ
10 Yet he invents pretexts against me
   and reckons me as his enemy.ᵈ
11 He puts my feet in the stocks;
   he watches all my ways!"ᵉ

12 In this you are not just, let me tell you;
   for God is greater than man.
13 Why, then, do you make complaint
   against him
   that he gives no account of his doings?ᶠ
14 For God does speak, perhaps once,
   or even twice, though one perceive it
   not.
15 In a dream, in a vision of the night,
   [when deep sleep falls upon men]
   as they slumber in their beds,
16 It is then he opens the ears of men
   and as a warning to them, terrifies
   them;
17 By turning man from evil
   and keeping pride away from him,
18 He withholds his soul from the pit
   and his life from passing to the grave.
19 Or a man is chastened on his bed by
   pain
   and unceasing suffering within his
   frame,
20 So that to his appetite food becomes repulsive,
   and his senses reject the choicest
   nourishment.ᵍ
21 His flesh is wasted so that it cannot be
   seen,
   and his bones, once invisible, appear;
22 His soul draws near to the pit,
   his life to the place of the dead.
23 If then there be for him an angel,*
   one out of a thousand, a mediator,
   To show him what is right for him
   and bring the man back to justice,
24 He will take pity on him and say,
   "Deliver him from going down to the
   pit;
   I have found him a ransom."
25 Then his flesh shall become soft as a
   boy's;
   he shall be again as in the days of his
   youth.
26 He shall pray and God will favor him;
   he shall see God's face with rejoic-
   ing.ʰ
27 He shall sing before men and say,

---

a Jb 32, 8.—b Jb 31, 15.—c Jb 10, 7; 13, 18; 27, 5f; 29, 14;
32, 1; 34, 5.—d Jb 13, 24; 19, 11.—e Jb 13, 27; 31, 4.—f Jb 31,
35.—g Jb 6, 7.—h Jb 22, 26-29.

32, 13: *Met wisdom:* in Job's arguments.
33, 23: *Angel:* one of the thousands who stand between God
and man as intermediaries, reminding man of his duties and giving God an account of their fulfillment.

"I sinned and did wrong,
yet he has not punished me accordingly.

28 He delivered my soul from passing to
the pit,
and I behold the light of life."

29 Lo, all these things God does,
twice, or thrice, for a man,

30 Bringing back his soul from the pit
to the light, in the land of the living.

31 Be attentive, O Job; listen to me!
Be silent and I will speak.

32 If you have aught to say, then answer
me.
Speak out! I should like to see you
justified.

33 If not, then do you listen to me;
be silent while I teach you wisdom.

CHAPTER 34

1 Then Elihu continued and said:

2 Hear, O wise men, my discourse,
and you that have knowledge, hear
me!

3 For the ear tests words,
as the taste does food.*i*

4 Let us discern for ourselves what is
right;
let us learn between us what is good.

5 For Job has said, "I am innocent,
but God has taken what is my due.*j*

6 Notwithstanding my right I am set at
nought;
in my wound the arrow rankles, sinless though I am."*k*

7 What man is like Job?
He drinks in blasphemies like water,

8 Keeps company with evildoers
and goes along with wicked men,

9 When he says, "It profits a man nought
that he is pleasing to God."*l*

10 Therefore, men of understanding, hearken to me:
far be it from God to do wickedness;
far from the Almighty to do wrong!*m*

11 Rather, he requites men for their conduct,

and brings home to a man his way of
life.*n*

12 Surely, God cannot act wickedly,
the Almighty cannot violate justice.*o*

13 Who gave him government over the
earth,
or who else set all the land in its
place?*p*

14 If he were to take back his spirit to himself,
withdraw to himself his breath,

15 All flesh would perish together,
and man would return to the dust.*q*

16 Now, do you, O Job, hear this!
Hearken to the words I speak!

17 Can an enemy of justice indeed be in
control,
or will you condemn the supreme
Just One,

18 Who says to a king, "You are worthless!"
and to nobles, "You are wicked!"

19 Who neither favors the person of
princes,
nor respects the rich more than the
poor?
For they are all the work of his hands;*r*

20 in a moment they die, even at midnight.*s*
He brings on nobles, and takes them
away,
removing the powerful without lifting
a hand;

21 For his eyes are upon the ways of man,
and he beholds all his steps.

22 There is no darkness so dense
that evildoers can hide in it.

25 Therefore he discerns their works;
he turns at night and crushes them.

23 For he forewarns no man of his time
to come before God in judgment.

24 Without a trial he breaks the mighty,*t*
and sets others in their stead,

27 Because they turned away from him
and heeded none of his ways,

28 But caused the cries of the poor to reach
him,
so that he heard the plea of the
afflicted.

29 If he remains tranquil, who then can
condemn?*
If he hides his face, who then can behold him?

30 ....

31 When anyone says to God,
"I was misguided; I will offend no
more.

---

i Jb 12, 11.—j Jb 33, 9f.—k Jb 9, 20.—l Jb 9, 22f. 30f; 21,
15; 35, 3.—m Jb 36, 23.—n Ps 62, 13; Prv 24, 12; Mt 16, 27;
Rom 2, 6; 2 Cor 5, 10; Rv 22, 12.—o Jb 8, 3.—p Jb 38, 4-7.—q
Jb 10, 9.—r Dt 10, 17; 2 Chr 19, 7; Wis 6, 7; Acts 10, 34; Rom
2, 11; Eph 6, 9; Col 3, 25; 1 Pt 1, 17.—s Jb 21, 3.—t Ps 2, 9.

34, 26. 29f: The extant Hebrew text of these verses contains
several added phrases which either represent duplication or are
very obscure.

Jb

32 Teach me wherein I have sinned;
    if I have done wrong, I will do so no
    more,"
33 Would you then say that God must
    punish,
    since you reject what he is doing?
It is you who must choose, not I;
    speak, therefore, what you know.
34 Men of understanding will say to me,
    every wise man who hears my views:
35 "Job speaks without intelligence,
    and his words are without sense."*u*
36 Let Job be tried to the limit,
    since his answers are those of the im-
    pious;
37 For he is adding rebellion to his sin
    by brushing off our arguments
    and addressing many words to God.

CHAPTER 35

1 Then Elihu proceeded and said:

2 Do you think it right to say,
    "I am just rather than God"?*v*
3 To say, "What does it profit me;
    what advantage have I more than if I
    had sinned?"*w*
4 I have words for a reply to you*
    and your three companions as well.
5 Look up to the skies and behold;
    regard the heavens high above you.
6 If you sin, what injury do you do to God?
    Even if your offenses are many, how
    do you hurt him?
7 If you are righteous, what do you give
    him,
    or what does he receive from your
    hand?*x*
8 Your wickedness can affect only a man
    like yourself;
    and your justice only a fellow human
    being.
9 In great oppression men cry out;
    they call for help because of the
    power of the mighty,
10 Saying, "Where is God, my Maker,
    who has given visions in the night,
11 Taught us rather than the beasts of the
    earth,
    and made us wise rather than the
    birds of the heavens?"
12 Though thus they cry out, he answers
    not
    against the pride of the wicked.
13 But it is idle to say God does not hear
    or that the Almighty does not take
    notice.

14 Even though you say that you see him
    not,*
    the case is before him; with trembling
    should you wait upon him.
15 But now that you have done otherwise,
    God's anger punishes,
    nor does he show concern that a man
    will die.
16 Yet Job to no purpose opens his mouth,
    and without knowledge multiplies
    words.*y*

CHAPTER 36

1 Elihu proceeded further and said:

2 Wait yet a little and I will instruct you,
    for there are still words to be said on
    God's behalf.
3 I will bring my knowledge from afar,
    and to my Maker I will accord the
    right.
4 For indeed, my theme cannot fail me:
    the one perfect in knowledge I set be-
    fore you.
5 Behold, God rejects the obstinate in
    heart,*
    he preserves not the life of the wick-
    ed,
6 He withholds not the just man's rights,
    but grants vindication to the op-
    pressed*z*
7 And with kings upon thrones
    he sets them, exalted forever.*a*
8 Or if they are bound with fetters
    and held fast by bonds of affliction,
9 Then he makes known to them what
    they have done
    and their sins of boastful pride.
10 He opens their ears to correction
    and exhorts them to turn back from
    evil.
11 If they obey and serve him,
    they spend their days in prosperity,
    their years in happiness.

---

u Jb 35, 16; 38, 2; 42, 3.—v Jb 32, 2.—w Jb 34, 9.—x Jb 22,
3; 41, 2; Lk 17, 10; Rom 11, 35.—y Jb 34, 35; 38, 2; 42, 3.—z
Ps 72, 4. 12f.—a Ps 113, 7f.

35, 4: *A reply to you:* Elihu refers to Job's statement that the
innocent suffer as much as the wicked, and especially to Eliphaz's
words in Jb 22, 2f.
35, 14f: The text here is uncertain. It seems to indicate that
Job should have realized God's indifference is only apparent, and
that, because he has not done so, God will punish him.
36, 5-21: Perhaps this section should be read between vv 6
and 7 of chapter 34.

¹² But if they obey not, they perish;
  they die for lack of knowledge.*

¹³ The impious in heart lay up anger for
  themselves;
  they cry not for help when he en-
  chains them;
¹⁴ Therefore they expire in youth,
  and perish among the reprobate.*
¹⁵ But he saves the unfortunate through
  their affliction,
  and instructs them through distress.
¹⁶⁻²⁰ .... *
²¹ Take heed, turn not to evil;
  for you have preferred carousal to
  affliction.

²² Behold, God is sublime in his power.
  What teacher is there like him?
²³ Who prescribes for him his conduct,
  or who can say, "You have done
  wrong"?ᵇ
²⁴ Remember, you should extol his work,
  which men have praised in song.
²⁵ All men contemplate it;
  man beholds it from afar.

²⁶ Lo, God is great beyond our knowledge;
  the number of his years is past
  searching out.
²⁷ He holds in check the waterdrops
  that filter in rain through his mists,
²⁸ Till the skies run with them
  and the showers rain down on mankind.
³¹ For by these* he nourishes the nations,
  and gives them food in abundance.

---

b Jb 34, 10; Is 40, 13.—c Ps 148, 17.

36, 12: *Knowledge:* practical wisdom in serving God, which
they lack because they refused it when warned (cf v 10).
36, 14: *Reprobate:* cf Dt 23, 18f.
36, 16-20: The Hebrew text here is in disorder. The Vulgate
has: "(16) Therefore he will give you most ample salvation from
the narrow mouth which has no foundations beneath it; but the repose of your table will be filled with fatness. (17) Your case has
been judged as that of the wicked; case and judgment you will receive. (18) Let no wrath, then, overcome you, that you oppress
anyone; nor let numerous gifts mislead you. (19) Lay down your
greatness without tribulation, and all who are mighty in strength.
(20) Do not draw out the night, that people may go in place of
them."
36, 31: *These:* refers to *the showers* of v 28, if the verse
order indicated above is correct.
36, 29f: Because of the uncertainty of the text, no translation
of these verses has received unanimous approval from exegetes.
37, 2: *Voice:* the thunder.
37, 9: *Chamber:* where it was popularly believed storms were
kept enclosed.
37, 12: *Their rounds:* of *rain* (Jb 36, 27), of *clouds* (Jb 36,
29f), of *lightning* and *thunder* (Jb 36, 32f), of *snow* (Jb 37,
6), of *winds* (Jb 37, 9).

²⁹·³⁰ Lo! he spreads the clouds in layers
  as the carpeting of his tent.*
³² In his hands he holds the lightning,
  and he commands it to strike the
  mark.
³³ His thunder speaks for him
  and incites the fury of the storm.

CHAPTER 37

¹ At this my heart trembles
  and leaps out of its place,
² To hear his angry voice*
  as it rumbles forth from his mouth!
³ Everywhere under the heavens he sends
  it,
  with his lightning, to the ends of the
  earth.
⁴ Again his voice roars—
  the majestic sound of his thunder.
⁵ He does great things beyond our knowing;
  wonders past our searching out.
⁶ For he says to the snow, "Fall to the
  earth";
  likewise to his heavy, drenching rain.
⁷ He shuts up all mankind indoors;
⁸ the wild beasts take to cover
  and remain quietly in their dens.

⁹ Out of its chamber* comes forth the
  tempest;
  from the north winds, the cold.
¹⁰ With his breath God brings the frost,
  and the broad waters become con-
  gealed.ᶜ
¹¹ With hail, also, the clouds are laden,
  and they scatter their flashes of light.
¹² He it is who changes their rounds,* according to his plans,
  in their task upon the surface of the
  earth,
¹³ whether for punishment or mercy, as
  he commands.

¹⁴ Hearken to this, O Job!
  Stand and consider the wondrous
  works of God!
¹⁵ Do you know how God lays his commands upon them,
  and makes the light shine forth from
  his clouds?
¹⁶ Do you know how the clouds are
  banked,
  the wondrous work of him who is
  perfect in knowledge?
¹⁷ You, whom the streams of water fail
  when a calm from the south comes
  over the land,

18 Do you spread out with him the firmament of the skies,
hard as a brazen mirror?*
19 Teach us then what we shall say to him;
we cannot, for the darkness, make our plea.
20 Will he be told about it when I speak,
or when a man says he is being destroyed?*
21 Nay, rather, it is as the light which men see not
while it is obscured among the clouds,
till the wind comes by and sweeps the clouds away.*
22 From the North the splendor comes,*
surrounding God's awesome majesty!
23 The Almighty! we cannot discover him,
pre-eminent in power and judgment;
his great justice owes no one an accounting.
24 Therefore men revere him,
though none can see him, however wise their hearts.

VII: THE LORD'S SPEECH

CHAPTER 38

1 Then the LORD* addressed Job out of the storm and said:
2 Who is this that obscures divine plans with words of ignorance?
3 Gird up your loins* now, like a man;
I will question you, and you tell me the answers!*d*
4 Where were you when I founded the earth?
Tell me, if you have understanding.
5 Who determined its size; do you know?
Who stretched out the measuring line for it?
6 Into what were its pedestals sunk,
and who laid the cornerstone,
7 While the morning stars sang in chorus
and all the sons of God* shouted for joy?

8 And who shut within doors the sea,
when it burst forth from the womb;*e*
9 When I made the clouds its garment
and thick darkness its swaddling bands?
10 When I set limits for it
and fastened the bar of its door,
11 And said: Thus far shall you come but no farther,

and here shall your proud waves be stilled!
12 Have you ever in your lifetime commanded the morning
and shown the dawn its place
13 For taking hold of the ends of the earth,
till the wicked are shaken from its surface?
14 The earth is changed as is clay by the seal,
and dyed as though it were a garment;
15 But from the wicked the light is withheld,
and the arm of pride is shattered.

16 Have you entered into the sources of the sea,
or walked about in the depths of the abyss?
17 Have the gates of death been shown to you,
or have you seen the gates of darkness?
18 Have you comprehended the breadth of the earth?
Tell me, if you know all:
19 Which is the way to the dwelling place of light,
and where is the abode of darkness,
20 That you may take them to their boundaries
and set them on their homeward paths?
21 You know, because you were born before them,
and the number of your years is great!*

---

d Jb 40, 2.—e Gn 1, 9.

37, 18: *The firmament . . . mirror:* the ancients thought of the sky as a ceiling above which were the "upper waters" (cf Gn 1, 6f; 7, 11); when this ceiling became as hard as metal, the usual rain failed to fall on the earth (cf Lv 26, 19; Dt 28, 23).

37, 20: Will an angel bring this to God's attention?

37, 21: Even though God seems not to know our circumstances, he does know them, just as surely as the sun shines, unseen by man, behind the clouds.

37, 22: Now the storms of doubt and ignorance disappear, and *from the North,* used here as a symbol for God's mysterious abode, comes *the splendor* of the manifestation of God's majestic ways.

38, 1: Now the Lord enters the debate and addresses two discourses (38—39 and 40—41) to Job, in which he speaks of his wisdom and power, which are altogether beyond the capacity of Job, who therefore should never dare to demand a reason for the divine actions. *Out of the storm:* frequently the background of the appearances of the Lord in the Old Testament; cf Pss 18; 50; Na 1, 3; Hb 3.

38, 3: *Gird up your loins:* prepare for combat—figuratively, be ready to defend yourself in debate.

38, 7: *Sons of God:* angels; cf Jb 1, 6.

38, 21: Divine irony.

22 Have you entered the storehouse of the
snow,
and seen the treasury of the hail
23 Which I have reserved for times of
stress,
for the days of war* and of battle?
24 Which way to the parting of the winds,
whence the east wind spreads over
the earth?

25 Who has laid out a channel for the
downpour
and for the thunderstorm a path
26 To bring rain to no man's land,
the unpeopled wilderness;
27 To enrich the waste and desolate
ground
till the desert blooms with verdure?

28 Has the rain a father;
or who has begotten the drops of
dew?
29 Out of whose womb comes the ice,
and who gives the hoarfrost its birth
in the skies,
30 When the waters lie covered as though
with stone
that holds captive the surface of the
deep?

31 Have you fitted a curb to the Pleiades,*
or loosened the bonds of Orion?
32 Can you bring forth the Mazzaroth in
their season,
or guide the Bear with its train?
33 Do you know the ordinances of the
heavens;
can you put into effect their plan on
the earth?

34 Can you raise your voice among the
clouds,
or veil yourself in the waters of the
storm?*
35 Can you send forth the lightnings on
their way,
or will they say to you, "Here we
are"?*

37 Who counts the clouds in his wisdom?
Or who tilts the water jars of heaven
38 So that the dust of earth is fused into a
mass
and its clods made solid?

39 Do you hunt the prey for the lioness
or appease the hunger of her cubs
40 While they crouch in their dens,
or lie in wait in the thicket?
36 Who puts wisdom in the heart,
and gives the cock its understanding?*
41 Who provides nourishment for the ravens
when their young ones cry out to
God,*f*
and they rove abroad without food?

CHAPTER 39

1 Do you know about the birth of the
mountain goats,
watch for the birth pangs of the
hinds,
2 Number the months that they must fulfill,
and fix the time of their bringing
forth?
3 They crouch down and bear their
young;
they deliver their progeny in the desert.
4 When their offspring thrive and grow,
they leave and do not return.

5 Who has given the wild ass his freedom,
and who has loosed him from bonds?
6 I have made the wilderness his home
and the salt flats his dwelling.
7 He scoffs at the uproar of the city,
and hears no shouts of a driver.
8 He ranges the mountains for pasture,
and seeks out every patch of green.

9 Will the wild ox consent to serve you,
and to pass the nights by your manger?
10 Will a rope bind him in the furrow,
and will he harrow the valleys after
you?
11 Will you trust him for his great strength
and leave to him the fruits of your
toil?
12 Can you rely on him to thresh out your
grain
and gather in the yield of your threshing floor?

---

f Ps 147, 9.

38, 22f: *Hail . . . of war:* thus God used a hailstorm to rout
Joshua's foes in the battle of Gibeon; cf Jos 10, 11; Sir 46, 5.
38, 31f: *Pleiades . . . Orion . . . Bear:* cf Jb 9, 9. *Mazzaroth:* it is uncertain what astronomical group is meant by this
Hebrew word; perhaps a southern constellation (cf Jb 9, 9).
38, 34: *Veil yourself . . . storm:* wrap yourself in a cloud, as
God comes in a theophany; cf Ps 18, 12.
38, 35: *Here we are:* at your service.
38, 36: *Understanding:* the reflection of divine Wisdom discernible in the created animal instincts of the *cock.*

13 The wings of the ostrich* beat idly;
   her plumage is lacking in pinions.
14 When she leaves her eggs on the
      ground*
   and deposits them in the sand,
15 Unmindful that a foot may crush them,
   that the wild beasts may trample
      them,
16 She cruelly disowns her young
   and ruthlessly makes nought of her
      brood;
17 For God has withheld wisdom from her
   and has given her no share in under-
      standing.
18 Yet in her swiftness of foot
   she makes sport of the horse and his
      rider.

19 Do you give the horse his strength,*
   and endow his neck with splendor?
20 Do you make the steed to quiver
      while   his   thunderous   snorting
      spreads terror?
21 He jubilantly paws the plain
   and rushes in his might against the
      weapons.
22 He laughs at fear and cannot be de-
      terred;
   he turns not back from the sword.
23 Around him rattles the quiver,
   flashes the spear and the javelin.
24 Frenzied and trembling he devours the
      ground;
   he holds not back at the sound of the
      trumpet,
25   but at each blast he cries, "Aha!"
   Even from afar he scents the battle,
   the roar of the chiefs and the shout-
      ing.

26 Is it by your discernment that the hawk
      soars,
   that he spreads his wings toward the
      south?
27 Does the eagle fly up at your command
   to build his nest aloft?
28 On the cliff he dwells and spends the
      night,
   on a spur of the cliff or the fortress.
29 From thence he watches for his prey;
   his eyes behold it afar off.
30 His young ones greedily drink blood;
   where the slain are, there is he.g

CHAPTER 40

1 The LORD then said to Job:

2 Will we have arguing with the Almighty
   by the critic?

Let him who would correct God give
   answer!h

3 Then Job answered the LORD and said:

4 Behold, I am of little account; what can
      I answer you?
   I put my hand over my mouth.
5 Though I have spoken once, I will not
      do so again;
   though twice, I will do so no more.

6 Then the LORD addressed Job out of
the storm and said:

7 Gird up your loins now, like a man.
   I will question you, and you tell me
      the answers!
8 Would you refuse to acknowledge my
      right?
   Would you condemn me that you
      may be justified?
9 Have you an arm like that of God,
   or can you thunder with a voice like
      his?
10 Adorn   yourself   with   grandeur   and
      majesty,
   and array yourself with glory and
      splendor.
11 Let loose the fury of your wrath;
12   tear down the wicked and shatter
      them.
   Bring down the haughty with a glance;
13   bury them in the dust together;
   in the hidden world imprison them.
14 Then will I too acknowledge
   that your own right hand can save
      you.

15 See, besides you I made Behemoth,*
   that feeds on grass like an ox.
16 Behold the strength in his loins,
   and his vigor in the sinews of his
      belly.
17 He carries his tail like a cedar;
   the sinews of his thighs are like ca-
      bles.
18 His bones are like tubes of bronze;
   his frame is like iron rods.

19 He came at the beginning of God's
      ways,

---

g Mt 24, 28; Lk 17, 37.—h Jb 38, 3.

39, 13: *The wings of the ostrich* cannot raise her from the
ground, but they help her to run swiftly.
39, 14ff: It was popularly believed that, because the ostrich
laid her eggs on the sand, she was thereby cruelly abandoning
them; cf Lam 4, 3.
39, 19-25: The famous description of a war horse.
40, 15: *Behemoth:* the hippopotamus.

and was made the taskmaster of his
fellows;

20 For the produce of the mountains is
brought to him,
and of all wild animals he makes
sport.

21 Under the lotus trees he lies,
in coverts of the reedy swamp.

22 The lotus trees cover him with their
shade;
all about him are the poplars on the
bank.

23 If the river grows violent, he is not disturbed;
he is tranquil though the torrent
surges about his mouth.

24 Who can capture him by his eyes,
or pierce his nose* with a trap?

25 Can you lead about Leviathan* with a
hook,
or curb his tongue with a bit?

26 Can you put a rope into his nose,
or pierce through his cheek with a
gaff?

27 Will he then plead with you, time after
time,
or address you with tender words?

28 Will he make an agreement with you
that you may have him as a slave forever?

29 Can you play with him, as with a bird?
Can you put him in leash for your
maidens?

30 Will the traders bargain for him?
Will the merchants* divide him up?

31 Can you fill his hide with barbs,
or his head with fish spears?

32 Once you but lay a hand upon him,
no need to recall any other conflict!

CHAPTER 41

2 Is he not relentless when aroused;
who then dares stand before him?*

1 Whoever might vainly hope to do so
need only see him to be overthrown.

3 Who has assailed him and come off
safe—
who under all the heavens?

40, 24: *Eyes . . . nose:* the only exposed parts of the submerged beast.
40, 25: *Leviathan* here is the crocodile. But cf Jb 3, 8.
40, 30: *Merchants:* literally, "Canaanites," whose reputation
for trading was so widespread that their name came to be used
for merchants; cf Prv 31, 24. The meaning of this verse is that the
crocodile is too powerful a creature to be sold like common fish.
41, 2: *Before him:* some read, "before me," i.e., God; also in
v 3.
41, 17: The text here is uncertain.

4 I need hardly mention his limbs,
his strength, and the fitness of his
armor.

5 Who can strip off his outer garment,
or penetrate his double corselet?

6 Who can force open the doors of his
mouth,
close to his terrible teeth?

7 Rows of scales are on his back,
tightly sealed together;

8 They are fitted each so close to the next
that no space intervenes;

9 So joined one to another
that they hold fast and cannot be
parted.

10 When he sneezes, light flashes forth;
his eyes are like those of the dawn.

11 Out of his mouth go forth firebrands;
sparks of fire leap forth.

12 From his nostrils issues steam,
as from a seething pot or bowl.

13 His breath sets coals afire;
a flame pours from his mouth.

14 Strength abides in his neck,
and terror leaps before him.

15.16 His heart is hard as stone:
his flesh, as the lower millstone.

17 When he rises up, the mighty are
afraid;
the waves of the sea fall back.*

18 Should the sword reach him, it will not
avail;
nor will the spear, nor the dart, nor
the javelin.

19 He regards iron as straw,
and bronze as rotten wood.

20 The arrow will not put him to flight;
slingstones used against him are but
straws.

21 Clubs he esteems as splinters;
he laughs at the crash of the spear.

22 His belly is sharp as pottery fragments;
he spreads like a threshing sledge
upon the mire.

23 He makes the depths boil like a pot;
the sea he churns like perfume in a
kettle.

24 Behind him he leaves a shining path;
you would think the deep had the
hoary head of age.

25 Upon the earth there is not his like,
intrepid he was made.

26 All, however lofty, fear him;
he is king over all proud beasts.

CHAPTER 42

¹ Then Job answered the LORD and said:

² I know that you can do all things,*
and that no purpose of yours can be
hindered.

³ I have dealt with great things that I do
not understand;
things too wonderful for me, which I
cannot know.ⁱ

⁵ I had heard of you by word of mouth,
but now my eye has seen you.

⁶ Therefore I disown what I have said,
and repent in dust and ashes.

VIII: EPILOGUE

Job's Restoration. ⁷ And it came to pass
after the LORD had spoken these words to
Job, that the LORD said to Eliphaz the
Temanite, "I am angry with you and with
your two friends;* for you have not spoken
rightly concerning me, as has my servant
Job. ⁸ Now, therefore, take seven bullocks
and seven rams, and go to my servant Job,
and offer up a holocaust for yourselves;
and let my servant Job pray for you;* for
his prayer I will accept, not to punish you
severely. For you have not spoken rightly
concerning me, as has my servant Job."
⁹ Then Eliphaz the Temanite, and Bildad
the Shuhite, and Zophar the Naamathite,
went and did as the LORD had commanded
them. And the LORD accepted the intercession of Job.

¹⁰ Also, the LORD restored the prosperity of Job, after he had prayed for his
friends; the LORD even gave to Job twice
as much as he had before. ¹¹ Then all his
brethren and his sisters came to him, and

all his former acquaintances, and they
dined with him in his house. They con-
doled with him and comforted him for all
the evil which the LORD had brought upon
him; and each one gave him a piece of
money* and a gold ring.

¹² ʲ Thus the LORD blessed the latter
days of Job more than his earlier ones. For
he had fourteen thousand sheep, six
thousand camels, a thousand yoke of oxen,
and a thousand she-asses. ¹³ And he had
seven sons and three daughters, ¹⁴ of
whom* he called the first Jemimah, the
second Keziah, and the third Keren-happuch. ¹⁵ In all the land no other women
were as beautiful as the daughters of Job;
and their father gave them an inheritance*
among their brethren. ¹⁶ After this, Job
lived a hundred and forty years;* and he
saw his children, his grandchildren, and
even his great-grandchildren.ᵏ ¹⁷ Then Job
died, old and full of years.

---

i Jb 34, 35; 35, 16; 38, 2.—j Jb 1, 3.—k Jb 5, 25f.

42, 2-6: In the current Hebrew text, this final utterance of Job
is interrupted by words ascribed to God (vv 3f) which are in large
part a duplication of Jb 38, 2f.

42, 7: The three friends of Job (Elihu is ignored in the Epilogue) are criticized by the Lord because they had (even though
in good faith) leveled false charges against him.

42, 8: Job becomes the intercessor for his friends, as were
other great Old Testament characters, e.g., Abraham and Moses,
and as our Lord would be, whom he prefigured. *Seven:* a symbolic number.

42, 11: *A piece of money:* the term is the same as that used
in Gn 33, 19; Jos 24, 32. *Gold ring:* for the nose or ear.

42, 14: Job's daughters had names symbolic of their charms:
Jemimah, dove; *Keziah,* precious perfume (cf Ps 45, 9);
Keren-happuch, cosmetic jar—more precisely, a container for
a black powder that was used like modern mascara.

42, 15: Ordinarily daughters did not inherit property unless
there were no sons; cf Nm 27, 1-11.

42, 16: As his other rewards were *twice as much as he had
before* (v 10), so Job's *hundred and forty years* were double
the expected span of human life; cf Ps 90, 10.

THE BOOK OF PSALMS

The Hebrew Psalter numbers 150 songs. The corresponding number in the LXX differs because of a different division of certain psalms. Hence the numbering in the Greek Psalter (which was followed by the Latin Vulgate) is usually one digit behind the Hebrew. In The New American Bible the numbering of the verses follows the Hebrew numbering; many of the traditional English translations are often a verse number behind the Hebrew because they do not count the superscriptions as a verse.

The superscriptions derive from pre-Christian Jewish tradition, and they contain technical terms, many of them apparently liturgical, which are no longer known to us. Seventy-three psalms are attributed to David, but there is no sure way of dating any psalm. Some are preexilic (before 587), and others are postexilic (after 539), but not as late as the Maccabean period (ca. 165). The psalms are the product of many individual collections (e.g., Songs of Ascents, Pss 120—134), which were eventually combined into the present work in which one can detect five "books," because of the doxologies which occur at 41:14; 72:18-19; 89:53; 106:48.

Two important features of the psalms deserve special notice. First, the majority were composed originally precisely for liturgical worship. This is shown by the frequent indication of liturgical leaders interacting with the community (e.g., 118:1-4). Secondly, they follow certain distinct patterns or literary forms. Thus, the hymn is a song of praise, in which a community is urged joyfully to sing out the praise of God. Various reasons are given for this praise (often introduced by "for" or "because"): the divine work of creation and sustenance (Pss 8, 104), or the divine acts in Israel's favor (Pss 135:1-12; 136). Some of the hymns have received a more specific classification, based on content. The "Songs of Zion" are so called because they exalt Zion, the city in which God dwells among the people (Pss 46, 48). Others are termed "enthronement" psalms because they re-enact or re-present in the liturgy the kingship of the Lord (Pss 47; 96—99). Characteristic of the songs of praise is the joyful summons to get involved in the activity; Ps 104 is an exception to this, although it remains universal in its thrust.

Another type of psalm is similar to the hymn: the thanksgiving psalm. This too is a song of praise acknowledging the Lord as the rescuer of the psalmist from a desperate situation. Very often the psalmist will give a flash-back, recounting the past distress, and the plea that was uttered (Pss 30; 116). The setting for such prayers seems to have been the offering of a todah (a "praise" sacrifice) with friends in the temple.

There are more psalms of lament than of any other type. They may be individual (e.g., Pss 3—7; 22) or communal (e.g., Ps 44). Although they usually begin with a cry for help, they develop in various ways. The description of the distress is couched in the broad imagery typical of the Bible (one is in Sheol, the Pit, or is afflicted by enemies or wild beasts, etc.)—in such a way that one cannot pinpoint the exact nature of the psalmist's plight. However, Ps 51 (cf also Ps 130) seems to refer clearly to deliverance from sin. Several laments end on a note of certainty that the Lord has heard the prayer (cf Ps 7, but contrast Ps 88), and the Psalter has been characterized as a movement from lament to praise. If this is somewhat of an exaggeration, it serves at least to emphasize the frequent expressions of trust which characterize the lament. In some cases it would seem as if the theme of trust has been lifted out to form a literary type all its own; cf Pss 23, 62, 91. Among the communal laments can be counted Pss 74 and 79. They complain to the Lord about some national disaster, and try to motivate God to intervene in favor of the suffering people.

Other psalms are clearly classified on account of content, and they may be in themselves laments or psalms of thanksgiving. Among the "royal" psalms, that deal directly with the currently reigning king, are Pss 20, 21, and 72. Many of the royal psalms were given a messianic interpretation by Christians. In Jewish tradition they were preserved, even after kingship had disappeared, because they were read in the light of the Davidic covenant re-

ported in 2 Samuel 7. Certain psalms are called wisdom psalms because they seem to betray the influence of the concerns of the sages (cf Pss 37, 49), but there is no general agreement as to the number of these prayers. Somewhat related to the wisdom psalms are the "torah" psalms, in which the torah (instruction or law) of the Lord is glorified (Pss 1; 19:8-14; 119). Pss 78, 105 and 106 can be considered as "historical" psalms. Although the majority of the psalms have a liturgical setting, there are certain prayers that may be termed "liturgies," so clearly does their structure reflect a liturgical incident (e.g., Pss 15, 24).

It is obvious that not all of the psalms can be pigeon-holed into neat classifications, but even a brief sketch of these types helps us to catch the structure and spirit of the psalms we read. It has been rightly said that the psalms are "a school of prayer." They not only provide us with models to follow, but inspire us to voice our own deepest feelings and aspirations.

FIRST BOOK—PSALMS 1–41

PSALM 1*

True Happiness in God's Law

I

1 Happy those* who do not follow
    the counsel of the wicked,
  Nor go the way* of sinners,
    nor sit in company with scoffers. *a*
2 Rather, the law of the LORD* is their
    joy;
  God's law they study day and night. *b*
3 They are like a tree *c*
    planted near streams of water,
    that yields its fruit in season;
  Its leaves never wither;
    whatever they do prospers.

II

4 But not the wicked!*
    They are like chaff driven by the
    wind. *d*
5 Therefore the wicked will not survive
    judgment,
  nor will sinners in the assembly of the
    just.
6 The LORD watches over the way of the
    just, *e*
  but the way of the wicked leads to
    ruin.

PSALM 2*

A Psalm for a Royal Coronation

1 Why do the nations protest
    and the peoples grumble in vain? *f*
2 Kings on earth rise up
    and princes plot together
    against the LORD and his anointed:* *g*
3 "Let us break their shackles
    and cast off their chains!" *h*

4 The one enthroned in heaven laughs;
    the Lord derides them, *i*
5 Then speaks to them in anger,
    terrifies them in wrath:
6 "I myself have installed my king
    on Zion, my holy mountain."
7 I will proclaim the decree of the LORD,
    who said to me, "You are my son;
    today I am your father. *j*
8 Only ask it of me,
    and I will make your inheritance the
    nations,
  your possession the ends of the earth.
9 With an iron rod you shall shepherd
    them,
  like a clay pot you will shatter
    them." *k*

---

a Pss 26, 4-5; 40, 5.—b Jos 1, 8; Ps 119; Sir 39, 1.—c Pss 52, 10; 92, 13-15; Jer 17, 8.—d Pss 35, 5; 83, 14-16; Jb 21, 18.—e Ps 37, 18.—f Rv 11, 18.—g Ps 83, 6.—h Ps 149, 8.—i Pss 37, 13; 59, 9; Wis 4, 18.—j Pss 89, 27; 110, 2-3; Is 49, 1.—k Rv 2, 27; 12, 5; 19, 15.

Ps 1: A preface to the whole Book of Psalms, contrasting with striking similes the destiny of the good and the wicked. The psalm views life as activity, as choosing either the good or the bad. Each "way" brings its inevitable consequences. The wise through their good actions will experience rootedness and life, and the wicked, rootlessness and death.

1, 1: *Those:* literally, "the man." That word is used here and in many of the Psalms as typical, and therefore is translated "they." *The way:* a common biblical term for manner of living or moral conduct (Pss 32, 8; 101, 2. 6; Prv 2, 20; 1 Kgs 8, 36).

1, 2: *The law of the LORD:* either the Torah, the first five books of the Bible, or, more probably, divine teaching or instruction.

1, 4: *The wicked:* those who by their actions distance themselves from God's life-giving presence.

Ps 2: A royal psalm. To rebellious kings (1-3) God responds vigorously (4-6). A speaker proclaims the divine decree (in the legal adoption language of the day), making the Israelite king the earthly representative of God (7-9) and warning kings to obey (10-11). The psalm has a messianic meaning for the Church; the New Testament understands it of Christ (Acts 4, 25-27; 13, 33; Heb 1, 5).

2, 2: *Anointed:* in Hebrew *mashiah,* "anointed"; in Greek *christos,* whence English Messiah and Christ. In Israel kings (Jgs 9, 8; 1 Sm 9, 16; 16, 12-13) and high priests (Lv 8, 12; Nm 3, 3) received the power of their office through anointing.

10 And now, kings, give heed;
    take warning, rulers on earth.
11 Serve the LORD with fear;
    with trembling bow down in homage,
    Lest God be angry and you perish from
      the way
    in a sudden blaze of anger.
    Happy are all who take refuge in God!*l*

PSALM 3*

Threatened but Trusting

1 A psalm of David,* when he fled from his
son Absalom.*m*

I
2 How many are my foes, LORD!
    How many rise against me!
3 How many say of me,
    "God will not save that one."*n* *Selah**
4 But you, LORD, are a shield around
      me;
    my glory, you keep my head high.*o*

II
5 Whenever I cried out to the LORD,
    I was answered from the holy moun-
      tain. *Selah*
6 Whenever I lay down and slept,
    the LORD preserved me to rise
      again.*p*
7 I do not fear, then, thousands of people
    arrayed against me on every side.

---

l Pss 34, 9; 146, 5; Prv 16, 20.—m 2 Sm 15, 13ff.—n Ps 71,
11.—o Pss 7, 11; 18, 3; 62, 7-8; Dt 33, 29; Is 60, 19.—p Ps 4,
9; Prv 3, 24.—q Ps 58, 7.—r Ps 28, 9; Jon 2, 10.—s Ps 118,
5.—t Ps 62, 4.—u Eph 4, 26.—v Ps 51, 19.—w Pss 31, 17; 44,
4; 67, 1; 80, 4; Jb 13, 24; Nm 6, 25; Dn 9, 17.—x Ps 3, 6.—y
Pss 86, 6; 130, 1-2.—z Wis 16, 28.

Ps 3: An individual lament complaining of enemies who deny
that God will come to the rescue (2-3). Despite such taunts the
psalmist hopes for God's protection even in sleep (4-7). The
psalm prays for an end to the enemies' power to speak maliciously
(8) and closes peacefully with an expression of trust (9).
3, 1: The superscription, added later, relates the psalm to an
incident in the life of David.
3, 3. 5. 9: *Selah:* the term is generally considered a direction
to the cantor or musicians but its exact meaning is not known. It
occurs 71 times in 39 psalms.
Ps 4: An individual lament emphasizing trust in God. The petition is based upon the psalmist's vivid experience of God as
savior (2). That experience of God is the basis for the warning to
the wicked: revere God who intervenes on the side of the faithful
(3-6). The faithful psalmist exemplifies the blessings given to the
just (7- 9).
4, 1: *For the leader:* many psalm headings contain this rubric.
Its exact meaning is unknown but may signify that such psalms
once stood together in a collection of "the choirmaster." Cf 1 Chr
15, 21.
4, 5: *Tremble:* be moved deeply with religious awe. The
Greek translation understood the emotion to be anger, and it is so
cited in Eph 4, 26.
Ps 5: A lament contrasting the security of the house of God (8-
9. 12-13) with the danger of the company of evildoers (5-7. 10-
11). The psalmist therefore prays that God will hear (2-4) and
grant the protection and joy of the temple.

III
8 Arise, LORD! Save me, my God!
    You will shatter the jaws of all my
      foes;
    you will break the teeth of the wick-
      ed.*q*
9 Safety comes from the LORD!
    Your blessing for your people!*r*
                                    Selah

PSALM 4*

Trust in God

1 For the leader;* with stringed instruments. A
psalm of David.
I
2 Answer when I call, my saving God.
    In my troubles, you cleared a way;
    show me favor; hear my prayer.*s*
II
3 How long will you people mock my
      honor,
    love what is worthless, chase after
      lies?*t* *Selah*
4 Know that the LORD works wonders for
      the faithful;
    the LORD hears when I call out.
5 Tremble* and do not sin;
    upon your beds ponder in silence.*u*
6 Offer fitting sacrifice
    and trust in the LORD.*v*
III
7 Many say, "May we see better times!
    LORD, show us the light of your
      face!"*w* *Selah*
8 But you have given my heart more joy
    than they have when grain and wine
      abound.
9 In peace I shall both lie down and
      sleep,*x*
    for you alone, LORD, make me se-
      cure.

PSALM 5*

Prayer for Divine Help

1 For the leader; with wind instruments. A
psalm of David.
I
2 Hear my words, O LORD;
    listen to my sighing.*y*
3 Hear my cry for help,
    my king, my God!
    To you I pray, O LORD;
4   at dawn you will hear my cry;
    at dawn I will plead before you and
      wait.*z*

II

5 You are not a god who delights in evil;
    no wicked person finds refuge with
      you;
6   the arrogant cannot stand before you.
You hate all who do evil;
7   you destroy all who speak falsely.*a*
Murderers and deceivers
    the LORD abhors.

III

8 But I can enter your house
    because of your great love.
I can worship in your holy temple
    because of my reverence for you,
    LORD.*b*
9 Guide me in your justice because of my
    foes;
    make straight your way before me.*c*

IV

10 For there is no sincerity in their mouths;
    their hearts are corrupt.
Their throats* are open graves;*d*
    on their tongues are subtle lies.
11 Declare them guilty, God;
    make them fall by their own devices.*e*
Drive them out for their many sins;
    they have rebelled against you.

V

12 Then all who take refuge in you will be
    glad
    and forever shout for joy.*f*
Protect them that you may be the joy
    of those who love your name.
13 For you, LORD, bless the just;
    you surround them with favor like a
    shield.

PSALM 6*

Prayer in Distress

1 For the leader; with stringed instruments,
"upon the eighth."* A psalm of David.

I

2 Do not reprove me in your anger, LORD,
    nor punish me in your wrath.*g*
3 Have pity on me, LORD, for I am weak;
    heal me, LORD, for my bones are
    trembling.*h*
4 In utter terror is my soul—
    and you, LORD, how long . . . ?*i*
5 Turn, LORD, save my life;
    in your mercy* rescue me.
6 For who among the dead remembers
    you?*
Who praises you in Sheol?*j*

II

7 I am wearied with sighing;
    all night long tears drench my bed;
    my couch is soaked with weeping.
8 My eyes are dimmed with sorrow,
    worn out because of all my foes.*k*

III

9 Away from me, all who do evil!*l*
    The LORD has heard my weeping.
10 The LORD has heard my prayer;
    the LORD takes up my plea.
11 My foes will be terrified and disgraced;
    all will fall back in sudden shame.*m*

PSALM 7*

God the Vindicator

1 A plaintive song of David, which he sang to
the LORD concerning Cush, the Benjaminite.

I

2 LORD my God, in you I take refuge;
    rescue me; save me from all who pur-
    sue me,*n*
3 Lest they maul me like lions,
    tear me to pieces with none to save.

II

4 LORD my God, if I am at fault in this,*
    if there is guilt on my hands,

---

a Ps 101, 7; Wis 14, 9; Hb 1, 13.—b Ps 138, 2; Jon 2, 5.—c
Ps 23, 3; Prv 4, 11; Is 26, 7.—d Rom 3, 13.—e Ps 141, 10.—f
Ps 64, 11.—g Ps 38, 2.—h Jer 17, 14-15.—i Pss 13, 2-3; 74,
10; 89, 47.—j Pss 30, 10; 88, 11; 115, 17; Is 38, 18.—k Pss
31, 10; 38, 11; 40, 13.—l Ps 119, 115; Mt 7, 23; Lk 13, 27.—m
Pss 35, 4. 26; 40, 15; 71, 13.—n Pss 6, 5; 22, 21.

5, 10: *Their throats:* their speech brings harm to their hearers
(cf Jer 5, 16). The verse mentions four parts of the body, each a
source of evil to the innocent.

Ps 6: The first of the seven Penitential Psalms (Pss 6, 32, 38,
51, 102, 130, 143), a designation dating from the seventh century
A.D. for psalms suitable to express repentance. The psalmist does
not, as in many laments, claim to be innocent but appeals to God's
mercy (5). Sin here, as often in the Bible, is both the sinful act
and its injurious consequences; here it is physical sickness (3-4.
7-8) and the attacks of enemies (8. 9. 11). The psalmist prays
that the effects of personal and social sin be taken away.

6, 1: *Upon the eighth:* apparently a musical notation, now lost.

6, 4: *How long?:* elliptical for "How long will it be before
you answer my prayer?" Cf Ps 13, 2-3.

6, 5: *Mercy:* Hebrew *hesed*, translated as "mercy" or "love,"
describes God's affectionate fidelity to human beings, which is
rooted in divine and not human integrity.

6, 6: A motive for God to preserve the psalmist from death: in
the shadowy world of the dead no one offers you praise. Sheol is
the biblical term for the underworld where the insubstantial souls
of dead human beings dwelt. It was similar to the Hades of Greek
and Latin literature. In the second century B.C., biblical books begin
to speak positively of life with God after death (Dn 12, 1-3; Wis 3).

Ps 7: An individual lament. The psalmist flees to God's presence
in the sanctuary for justice and protection (2-3) and takes an oath
that only the innocent can swear (4-6). The innocent psalmist can
thus hope for the just God's protection (7-14) and be confident
that the actions of the wicked will come back upon their own
heads (15-17). The justice of God leads the psalmist to praise (18).

7, 4: *At fault in this:* in the accusation the enemies have made
against the psalmist.

5 If I have repaid my friend with evil—
   I spared even those who hated me
     without cause—
6 Then let my enemy pursue and overtake
   me,
   trample my life to the ground,
   and leave me dishonored in the
     dust.[o]   *Selah*

III
7 Rise up, LORD, in your anger;
   rise against the fury of my foes.[p]
   Wake to judge as you have de-
     creed.
8 Have the assembly of the peoples gather
   about you;
   sit on your throne high above them,
9 O LORD, judge of the nations.
   Grant me justice, LORD, for I am blame-
     less,
   free of any guilt.
10 Bring the malice of the wicked to an
   end;
   uphold the innocent,
   O God of justice,
   who tries hearts and minds.[q]

IV
11 A shield before me is God
   who saves the honest heart.[r]
12 God is a just judge,
   who rebukes in anger every day.

---

o Ps 143, 3.—p Pss 9, 4; 19, 20.—q Pss 17, 3; 26, 2; 35, 24;
43, 1; 139, 23; Jer 17, 10; 20, 12.—r Ps 3, 4.—s Ps 11, 2.—t
Is 50, 11.—u Jb 15, 35; Is 59, 4.—v Pss 9, 16; 35, 8; 57, 7; Prv
26, 27; Eccl 10, 8; Sir 27, 26.—w Pss 18, 50; 30, 5; 135, 3;
146, 2.—x Mt 21, 16; Wis 10, 21.—y Ps 144, 3; Jb 7, 17.—z
Heb 2, 6ff.—a 7ff: Gn 1, 26. 28; Wis 9, 2; 1 Cor 15, 27.

Ps 8: While marveling at the limitless grandeur of God (2-3),
the psalmist is struck first by the smallness of human beings in
creation (4-5), and then by the royal dignity and power that God
has graciously bestowed upon them (6-10).
8, 1: *Upon the gittith:* probably the title of the melody to
which the psalm was to be sung or a musical instrument.
8, 3: *Babes and infants:* the text is obscure. Some join this
line to the last line of 2 (itself obscure) to read: "[you] whose
majesty is exalted above the heavens / by the mouths of babes
and infants." *Drawn a defense:* some prefer the Septuagint's
"fashioned praise," which is quoted in Mt 21, 16. *Enemy and
avenger:* probably cosmic enemies. The primeval powers of
watery chaos are often personified in poetic texts (Pss 74, 13-14;
89, 11; Jb 9, 13; 26, 12-13; Is 51, 9).
8, 5: *Humans. . . mere mortals:* literally, "[mortal] person"
. . . "son of man [in the sense of a human being, Hebrew *'adam*]."
The emphasis is on the fragility and mortality of human beings to
whom God has given great dignity.
8, 6: *Little less than a god:* Hebrew *'elohim*, the ordinary
word for "God" or "the gods" or members of the heavenly court.
The Greek version translated *'elohim* by "angel, messenger";
several ancient and modern versions so translate. The meaning
seems to be that God created human beings almost at the level
of the beings in the heavenly world. Heb 2, 9 finds the eminent
fulfillment of this verse in Jesus Christ, who was humbled before
being glorified. Cf also 1 Cor 15, 27, where St. Paul applies to
Christ the closing words of v 7.

13 If sinners do not repent,
   God sharpens his sword,
   strings and readies the bow,[s]
14 Prepares his deadly shafts,
   makes arrows blazing thunderbolts.[t]

V
15 Sinners conceive iniquity;
   pregnant with mischief,
   they give birth to failure.[u]
16 They open a hole and dig it deep,
   but fall into the pit they have dug.[v]
17 Their mischief comes back upon themselves;
   their violence falls on their own heads.

VI
18 I praise the justice of the LORD;
   I celebrate the name of the LORD Most
   High.[w]

PSALM 8*

Divine Majesty and Human Dignity

1 For the leader; "upon the *gittith*."* A psalm
of David.

2 O LORD, our Lord,
   how awesome is your name through
   all the earth!
   You have set your majesty above the
   heavens!
3 Out of the mouths of babes[x] and infants*
   you have drawn a defense against your
   foes,
   to silence enemy and avenger.
4 When I see your heavens, the work of
   your fingers,
   the moon and stars that you set in
   place—
5 What are humans that you are mindful
   of them,[y]
   mere mortals* that you care for
   them?[z]
6 Yet you have made them little less than
   a god,*
   crowned them with glory and honor.
7 You have given them rule over the works
   of your hands,[a]
   put all things at their feet:
8 All sheep and oxen,
   even the beasts of the field,
9 The birds of the air, the fish of the sea,
   and whatever swims the paths of the
   seas.
10 O LORD, our Lord,
   how awesome is your name through
   all the earth!

Ps

PSALMS 9—10*

Thanksgiving for Victory and Prayer for Justice

[1] For the leader; according to *Muth Labben*.* A psalm of David.

A

I

[2] I will praise you, LORD, with all my heart;
  I will declare all your wondrous deeds.
[3] I will delight and rejoice in you;
  I will sing hymns to your name, Most High.
[4] For my enemies turn back;
  they stumble and perish before you.

II

[5] You upheld my right and my cause,
  seated on your throne, judging justly.
[6] You rebuked the nations, you destroyed the wicked;
  their name you blotted out for all time.[b]
[7] The enemies have been ruined forever;
  you destroyed their cities;
  their memory has perished.

III

[8] The LORD rules forever,
  has set up a throne for judgment.
[9] It is God who governs the world with justice,[c]
  who judges the peoples with fairness.
[10] The LORD is a stronghold for the oppressed,
  a stronghold in times of trouble.[d]
[11] Those who honor your name trust in you;
  you never forsake those who seek you, LORD.

IV

[12] Sing hymns to the LORD enthroned on Zion;
  proclaim God's deeds among the nations!
[13] For the avenger of bloodshed remembers,
  does not forget the cry of the afflicted.[e]

V

[14] Have mercy on me, LORD;
  see how my foes afflict me!
  You alone can raise me from the gates of death.[f]
[15] Then I will declare all your praises,
  sing joyously of your salvation
  in the gates of daughter Zion.*

VI

[16] The nations fall into the pit they dig;
  in the snare they hide, their own foot is caught.
[17] The LORD is revealed in this divine rule:*
  by the deeds they do the wicked are trapped.[g]   *Higgaion. Selah*

VII

[18] To Sheol the wicked will depart,
  all the nations that forget God.
[19] The needy will never be forgotten,
  nor will the hope of the afflicted ever fade.[h]
[20] Arise, LORD, let no mortal prevail;
  let the nations be judged in your presence.
[21] Strike them with terror, LORD;
  show the nations they are mere mortals.   *Selah*

B

I

[1] Why, LORD, do you stand at a distance
  and pay no heed to these troubled times?
[2] Arrogant scoundrels pursue the poor;
  they trap them by their cunning schemes.[i]

II

[3] The wicked even boast of their greed;
  these robbers curse and scorn the LORD.[j]
[4] In their insolence the wicked boast:
  "God doesn't care, doesn't even exist."[k]
[5] Yet their affairs always succeed;
  they ignore your judgment on high;
  they sneer at all who oppose them.
[6] They say in their hearts, "We will never fall;
  never will we see misfortune."

---

b Jb 18, 17.—c Pss 96, 10; 98, 9.—d Ps 37, 39; Is 25, 4.—e Jb 16, 18.—f Wis 16, 13.—g Sir 27, 26.—h Prv 23, 18.—i Is 32, 7.—j Ps 36, 2.—k Ps 14, 1; Jb 22, 13; Is 29, 15; Jer 5, 12; Zep 1, 12.

Pss 9—10: Pss 9 and 10 in the Hebrew text have been transmitted as separate poems but they actually form a single acrostic poem and are so transmitted in the Greek and Latin tradition. Each verse of the two psalms begins with a successive letter of the Hebrew alphabet (though several letters have no corresponding stanza). The psalm states loosely connected themes: the rescue of the helpless poor from their enemies, God's worldwide judgment and rule over the nations, the psalmist's own concern for rescue (14-15).

9, 1: *Muth Labben:* probably the melodic accompaniment of the psalm, now lost.

9, 15: *Daughter Zion:* an ancient Near Eastern city could sometimes be personified as a woman or a queen, the spouse of the god of the city.

9, 17: *The LORD is revealed in this divine rule:* God has so made the universe that the wicked are punished by the very actions they perform.

7 Their mouths are full of oaths, violence,
and lies;
    discord and evil are under their
    tongues.[l]
8 They wait in ambush near towns;
    their eyes watch for the helpless,
    to murder the innocent in secret.[m]
9 They lurk in ambush like lions in a
thicket,
    hide there to trap the poor,
    snare them and close the net.[n]
10 The helpless are crushed, laid low;
    they fall into the power of the wicked,
11 Who say in their hearts, "God pays no
attention,
    shows no concern, never bothers to
    look."[o]

III

12 Rise up, LORD God! Raise your arm!
    Do not forget the poor!
13 Why should the wicked scorn God,
    say in their hearts, "God doesn't
    care"?
14 But you do see;
    you do observe this misery and sorrow;[p]
    you take the matter in hand.
To you the helpless can entrust their
cause;
    you are the defender of orphans.[q]
15 Break the arms of the wicked and depraved;
    make them account for their crimes;
    let none of them survive.

---

l Is 32, 7; Rom 3, 14.—m Ps 11, 2; Jb 24, 14.—n Ps 17, 12;
Prv 1, 11; Jer 5, 26.—o Pss 44, 25; 64, 6; 73, 11; 94, 7; Ez 9,
9.—p Pss 31, 8; 56, 9; 2 Kgs 20, 5; Is 25, 8; Rv 7, 17.—q Ex 22,
21-22.—r Ps 145, 13; Jer 10, 10.—s Dt 10, 18.—t Pss 55, 7;
91, 4.—u Pss 7, 13; 37, 14; 57, 5; 64, 4.—v Pss 14, 2; 102, 20;
Hb 2, 20; Dt 26, 15; Is 66, 1; Mt 5, 34.—w Pss 120, 4; 140, 11;
Prv 16, 27; Ez 38, 22; Rv 8, 5; 20, 10.—x Pss 14, 3; 116, 11;
Is 59, 15; Mi 7, 2.—y Pss 28, 3; 55, 22; Is 59, 3-4; Jer 9, 7.—z
Sir 5, 3.

Ps 11: A song of trust. Though friends counsel flight to the
mountain country (a traditional hideout) to escape trouble (1-3),
the innocent psalmist reaffirms confidence in God, who protects
those who seek asylum in the temple (4-7).

11, 3: *Foundations:* usually understood of public order. Cf Ps
82, 5.

11, 6: *Their allotted cup:* the cup that God gives people to
drink is a common figure for their destiny. Cf Pss 16, 5; 75, 9; Mt
20, 22; 26, 39; Rv 14, 10.

Ps 12: A lament. The psalmist, thrown into a world where
lying and violent people persecute the just (2-3), prays that the
wicked be punished (4-5). The prayer is not simply for vengeance
but arises from a desire to see God's justice appear on earth. V 6
preserves the word of assurance spoken by the priest to the lamenter; it is not usually transmitted in such psalms. In vv 7-9 the
psalmist affirms the intention to live by the word of assurance.

IV

16 The LORD is king forever;[r]
    the nations have vanished from God's
    land.
17 You listen, LORD, to the needs of the
poor;
    you encourage them and hear their
    prayers.
18 You win justice for the orphaned and oppressed;[s]
    no one on earth will cause terror again.

PSALM 11*

Confidence in the Presence of God

1 For the leader. Of David.

I

In the LORD I take refuge;
    how can you say to me,
    "Flee like a bird to the mountains!"[t]
2 See how the wicked string their bows,
    fit their arrows to the string
    to shoot from the shadows at the upright.[u]
3 When foundations* are being destroyed,
    what can the upright do?

II

4 The LORD is in his holy temple;
    the LORD's throne is in heaven.[v]
God's eyes keep careful watch;
    they test all peoples.
5 The LORD tests the good and the bad,
    hates those who love violence,
6 And rains upon the wicked
    fiery coals and brimstone,
    a scorching wind their allotted cup.*[w]
7 The LORD is just and loves just deeds;
    the upright shall see his face.

PSALM 12*

Prayer against Evil Tongues

1 For the leader; "upon the eighth." A psalm of
David.

I

2 Help, LORD, for no one loyal remains;
    the faithful have vanished from the
    human race.[x]
3 Those who tell lies to one another
    speak with deceiving lips and a double
    heart.[y]

II

4 May the LORD cut off all deceiving lips,
    and every boastful tongue,
5 Those who say, "By our tongues we prevail;
    when our lips speak, who can lord it
    over us?"[z]

Ps

III

6 "Because they rob the weak, and the
needy groan,
I will now arise," says the LORD;
"I will grant safety to whoever longs
for it."*a*

IV

7 The promises of the LORD are sure,
silver refined in a crucible,*
silver purified seven times.*b*

8 LORD, protect us always;
preserve us from this generation.

9 On every side the wicked strut;
the shameless are extolled by all.

PSALM 13*

Prayer in Time of Illness

1 For the leader. A psalm of David.

I

2 How long, LORD? Will you utterly
forget me?
How long will you hide your face
from me?*c*

3 How long must I carry sorrow in my
soul,
grief in my heart day after day?
How long will my enemy triumph
over me?

II

4 Look upon me, answer me, LORD, my
God!
Give light to my eyes lest I sleep in
death,

5 Lest my enemy say, "I have prevailed,"
lest my foes rejoice at my downfall.*d*

III

6 I trust in your faithfulness.
Grant my heart joy in your help,
That I may sing of the LORD,
"How good our God has been to
me!"*e*

PSALM 14*

A Lament over Widespread Corruption

1 For the leader. Of David.

I

Fools* say in their hearts,
"There is no God."*f*
Their deeds are loathsome and corrupt;
not one does what is right.

2 The LORD looks down from heaven
upon the human race,*g*
To see if even one is wise,*h*
if even one seeks God.

3 All have gone astray;
all alike are perverse.

Not one does what is right,
not even one.*i*

II

4 Will these evildoers never learn?
They devour my people as they devour bread;*j*
they do not call upon the LORD.*k*

5 They have good reason, then, to fear;
God is with the company of the just.

6 They would crush the hopes of the
poor,
but the poor have the LORD as their
refuge.

III

7 Oh, that from Zion might come
the deliverance of Israel,
That Jacob may rejoice, and Israel be
glad
when the LORD restores his people!*l*

PSALM 15*

The Righteous Israelite

1 A psalm of David.

I

LORD, who may abide in your tent?
Who may dwell on your holy mountain?*m*

II

2 Whoever walks without blame,*n*
doing what is right,
speaking truth from the heart;

---

a Is 33, 10.—b Pss 18, 31; 19, 8; Prv 30, 5.—c Pss 6, 4; 44, 25; 77, 8; 79, 5; 89, 47; 94, 3; Lam 5, 20.—d Ps 38, 17.—e Ps 116, 7.—f Pss 10, 4; 36, 2; Is 32, 6; Jer 5, 12.—g Pss 11, 4; 102, 20.—h 2b-3: Rom 3, 11-12.—i Ps 12, 1.—j Ps 27, 2; Is 9, 11.—k Ps 79, 6.—l Ps 85, 2.—m Is 56, 7.—n Ps 119, 1.

12, 7: *A crucible:* literally, "in a crucible in the ground." The crucible was placed in the ground for support.

Ps 13: A lament in which the psalmist, seriously ill (4), expresses fear that enemies will interpret his or her death as a divine judgment. Hence the heartfelt prayer (2-3) is for healing that will signal to those enemies that the psalmist enjoys God's favor (4-5). The poem ends with a confession of trust in God and a statement of praise (6).

Ps 14: The lament (duplicated in Ps 53) depicts the world as consisting of two types of people: "the fools" (= the wicked, 1-3) and "the company of the just" (4-6; also called "my people," and "the poor"). The wicked persecute the just, but the psalm expresses the hope that God will punish the wicked and reward the good.

14, 1: *Fools:* literally, "the fool." The singular is used typically, hence the plural translation.

14, 7: *Israel . . . Jacob . . . his people:* the righteous poor are identified with God's people.

Ps 15: The psalm records a liturgical scrutiny at the entrance to the temple court (cf Ps 24, 3-6; Is 33, 14b-16). The Israelite wishing to be admitted had to ask the temple official what conduct was appropriate to God's precincts. Note the emphasis on virtues relating to one's neighbor.

15, 1: *Your tent . . . your holy mountain:* the temple could be referred to as "tent" (Ps 61, 5; Is 33, 20), a reference to the tent of the wilderness period and the tent of David (2 Sm 6, 17; 7, 2), predecessors of the temple. *Holy mountain:* a venerable designation of the divine abode (Pss 2, 6; 3, 5; 43, 3; 48, 2, etc.).

³ Who does not slander a neighbor,
  does no harm to another,
  never defames a friend;
⁴ Who disdains the wicked,
  but honors those who fear the LORD;
  Who keeps an oath despite the cost,
⁵ lends no money at interest,*
  accepts no bribe against the inno-
  cent.ᵒ
III
Whoever acts like this
  shall never be shaken.

PSALM 16*
God the Supreme Good
¹ A miktam* of David.
I
Keep me safe, O God;
  in you I take refuge.ᵖ
² I say to the LORD,
  you are my Lord,
  you are my only good.
³ Worthless are all the false gods of the
  land.
  Accursed are all who delight in them.
⁴ They multiply their sorrows
  who court other gods.

---

o Ex 22, 24; 23, 8.—p Ps 25, 20.—q Pss 23, 5; 73, 26; Nm
18, 20; Lam 3, 24.—r Pss 73, 23; 121, 5. 8-12; Acts 2, 25-28.—
s Pss 28, 1; 30, 4; 49, 16; 86, 13; Jon 2, 7; Acts 13, 35.—t Pss
26, 2; 139, 23.—u Ps 18, 36; Jb 23, 11-12.—v Pss 36, 8; 57, 2;
61, 5; 63, 8; 91, 4; Dt 32, 10; Ru 2, 12; Zec 2, 12; Mt 23, 37.

15, 5: *Lends no money at interest:* lending money in the Old
Testament was often seen as assistance to the poor in their distress, not as an investment; making money off the poor by charging interest was thus forbidden (Ex 22, 24; Lv 25, 36-37; Dt 23,
20).

Ps 16: In the first section, the psalmist rejects the futile worship of false gods (2-5), preferring Israel's God (1), the giver of
the land (6). The second section reflects on the wise and life-giving presence of God (7-11).

16, 1: *Miktam:* a term occurring six times in psalm
superscriptions, always with "David." Its meaning is unknown.

16, 4: *Take their names:* to use the gods' names in oaths and
hence to affirm them as one's own gods.

16, 6: *Pleasant places were measured out for me:* the
psalmist is pleased with the plot of land measured out to the family, which was to be passed on to succeeding generations ("my inheritance").

16, 10: *Nor let your faithful servant see the pit:* Hebrew
shahath means here the pit, a synonym for Sheol, the underworld. The Greek translation derives the word here and elsewhere from the verb *shahath,* "to be corrupt." On the basis of
the Greek, Acts 2, 25-32 and 13, 35-37 apply the verse to
Christ's resurrection, "Nor will you suffer your holy one to see
corruption."

Ps 17: A lament of an individual unjustly attacked who has
taken refuge in the temple. Confident of being found innocent, the
psalmist cries out for God's just judgment (1-5) and requests divine help against enemies (6-9a). Those ravenous lions (9b-12)
should be punished (13-14). The psalm ends with a serene statement of praise (15). The Hebrew text of vv 3-4 and 14 is uncertain.

17, 8: *Apple of your eye . . . shadow of your wings:* images of God's special care. Cf Dt 32, 10; Prv 7, 2; Is 49, 2.

Blood libations to them I will not pour
  out,
  nor will I take their names* upon my
  lips.
⁵ LORD, my allotted portion and my cup,
  you have made my destiny secure.�q
⁶ Pleasant places were measured out for
  me;*
  fair to me indeed is my inheritance.
II
⁷ I bless the LORD who counsels me;
  even at night my heart exhorts me.
⁸ I keep the LORD always before me;
  with the Lord at my right, I shall
  never be shaken.ʳ
⁹ Therefore my heart is glad, my soul rejoices;
  my body also dwells secure,
¹⁰ For you will not abandon me to Sheol,
  nor let your faithful servant see the
  pit.*ˢ
¹¹ You will show me the path to life,
  abounding joy in your presence,
  the delights at your right hand forever.

PSALM 17*
Prayer for Rescue from Persecutors
¹ A prayer of David.
I
Hear, LORD, my plea for justice;
  pay heed to my cry;
Listen to my prayer
  spoken without guile.
² From you let my vindication come;
  your eyes see what is right.
³ You have tested my heart,
  searched it in the night.ᵗ
You have tried me by fire,
  but find no malice in me.
My mouth has not transgressed
⁴ as humans often do.
As your lips have instructed me,
  I have kept the way of the law.
⁵ My steps have kept to your paths;
  my feet have not faltered.ᵘ
II
⁶ I call upon you; answer me, O God.
  Turn your ear to me; hear my prayer.
⁷ Show your wonderful love,
  you who deliver with your right arm
  those who seek refuge from their
  foes.
⁸ Keep me as the apple of your eye;
  hide me in the shadow of your wings*
⁹ from the violence of the wicked.ᵛ

Ps

III

My ravenous enemies press upon me;[w]
10   they close their hearts,*
    fill their mouths with proud roaring.
11 Their steps even now encircle me;
    they watch closely, keeping low to
    the ground,
12 Like lions eager for prey,
    like young lions lurking in ambush.
13 Rise, O LORD, confront and cast them
    down;
    rescue me so from the wicked.
14 Slay them with your sword;
    with your hand, LORD, slay them;
    snatch them from the world in their
    prime.
    Their bellies are being filled with your
    friends;
    their children are satisfied too,
    for they share what is left with their
    young.
15 I am just—let me see your face;
    when I awake,* let me be filled with
    your presence.[x]

PSALM 18*

A King's Thanksgiving for Victory

[1] For the leader. Of David, the servant of the
LORD, who sang to the LORD the words of this
song after the LORD had rescued him from the
clutches of all his enemies and from the hand of
Saul. [2] He said:

I

I love you, LORD, my strength,
3   LORD, my rock, my fortress, my de-
    liverer,[y]
My God, my rock of refuge,
    my shield, my saving horn,* my
    stronghold![z]
4 Praised be the LORD, I exclaim!
    I have been delivered from my
    enemies.

II

5 The breakers of death surged round
    about me;
    the menacing floods terrified me.
6 The cords* of Sheol tightened;
    the snares of death lay in wait for
    me.[a]
7 In my distress I called out: LORD!
    I cried out to my God.[b]
From his temple* he heard my voice;
    my cry to him reached his ears.

8 The earth rocked and shook;*
    the foundations of the mountains
    trembled;
    they shook as his wrath flared up.[c]
9 Smoke rose in his nostrils,
    a devouring fire poured from his
    mouth;
    it kindled coals into flame.
10 He parted the heavens and came down,
    a dark cloud under his feet.[d]
11 Mounted on a cherub* he flew,
    borne along on the wings of the
    wind.
12 He made darkness the cover about
    him;
    his canopy, heavy thunderheads.
13 Before him scudded his clouds,
    hail and lightning too.[e]
14 The LORD thundered from heaven;
    the Most High made his voice re-
    sound.[f]
15 He let fly his arrows* and scattered
    them;
    shot his lightning bolts and dispersed
    them.[g]

w 9b-12: Pss 10, 9; 22, 14. 22; 35, 17; 58, 7; Jb 4, 10-11.—x
Pss 4, 7; 31, 17; 67, 2; 80, 4; Nm 6, 25; Dn 9, 17.—y 2-51: 2
Sm 22, 2-51.—z Pss 3, 4; 31, 3-4; 42, 10; Gn 49, 24; Dt 32,
4.—a Pss 88, 8; 93, 3-4; 116, 3-4.—b Jon 2, 3.—c Pss 97, 3-4;
99, 1; Jgs 5, 4-5; Is 64, 1; Hab 3, 9-11.—d Pss 104, 3; 144, 5;
Is 63, 19.—e Ex 13, 21; 19, 16.—f Pss 29; 77, 19; Ex 19, 19;
Jb 37, 3-4.—g Ps 144, 6; Wis 5, 21.

17, 10-12. 14: An extended metaphor: the enemies are lions.
  17, 15: *When I awake:* probably the psalmist has spent the
night in the sanctuary (cf 3) and hopes to wake to an oracle assuring God's protective presence.
  Ps 18: A royal thanksgiving for a military victory, duplicated in
2 Sm 22. Thanksgiving psalms are in essence reports of divine
rescue. The psalm has two parallel reports of rescue, the first told
from a heavenly perspective (5-20), and the second from an
earthly perspective (36-46). The first report adapts old mythic
language of a cosmic battle between sea and rainstorm in order
to depict God's rescue of the Israelite king from his enemies.
Each report has a short hymnic introduction (2-4. 32-35) and
conclusion (21-31. 47-51).
  18, 3: *My saving horn:* my strong savior. The horn referred
to is the weapon of a bull and the symbol of fertility. Cf 1 Sm 2,
10; Ps 132, 17; Lk 1, 69.
  18, 6: *Cords:* hunting imagery, the cords of a snare.
  18, 7: *His temple:* his heavenly abode.
  18, 8-16: God appears in the storm, which in Palestine comes
from the west. The introduction to the theophany (vv 8-9) is probably a description of a violent, hot, and dry east-wind storm. In
the fall transition period from the rainless summer to the rainy
winter such storms regularly precede the rains. Cf Ex 14, 21-22.
  18, 11: *Cherub:* a winged creature, derived from myth, in the
service of the deity (Gn 3, 24; Ex 25, 18-20; 37, 6-9). Cherubim
were the throne bearers of the deity (Pss 80, 2; 99, 1; 1 Kgs 6,
23-28; 8, 6-8).
  18, 15: *Arrows:* lightning.

16 Then the bed of the sea appeared;
   the world's foundations lay bare,[h]
At the roar of the LORD,
   at the storming breath of his nostrils.
17 He reached down from on high and
   seized me;
   drew me out of the deep waters.[i]
18 He rescued me from my mighty enemy,
   from foes too powerful for me.
19 They attacked me on a day of distress,
   but the LORD came to my support.
20 He set me free in the open;
   he rescued me because he loves me.

III

21 The LORD acknowledged my righteousness,
   rewarded my clean hands.[j]
22 For I kept the ways of the LORD;
   I was not disloyal to my God.
23 His laws were all before me,
   his decrees I did not cast aside.
24 I was honest toward him;
   I was on guard against sin.
25 So the LORD rewarded my righteousness,
   the cleanness of my hands in his
   sight.
26 Toward the faithful you are faithful;
   to the honest you are honest;[k]
27 Toward the sincere, sincere;
   but to the perverse you are devious.
28 Humble people you save;
   haughty eyes you bring low.[l]
29 You, LORD, give light to my lamp;
   my God brightens the darkness about
   me.[m]
30 With you I can rush an armed band,
   with my God to help I can leap a wall.
31 God's way is unerring;
   the LORD's promise is tried and true;
   he is a shield for all who trust in
   him.[n]

IV

32 Truly, who is God except the LORD?
   Who but our God is the rock?[o]
33 This God who girded me with might,
   kept my way unerring,

34 Who made my feet swift as a deer's,
   set me safe on the heights,[p]
35 Who trained my hands for war,
   my arms to bend even a bow of
   bronze.*[q]

V

36 You have given me your protecting
   shield;
   your right hand has upheld me;
   you stooped to make me great.
37 You gave me room to stride;
   my feet never stumbled.[r]
38 I pursued my enemies and overtook
   them;
   I did not turn back till I destroyed
   them.
39 I struck them down; they could not
   rise;
   they fell dead at my feet.
40 You girded me with strength for war,
   subdued adversaries at my feet.
41 My foes you put to flight before me;
   those who hated me I destroyed.
42 They cried for help, but no one saved
   them,
   cried to the LORD but got no answer.
43 I ground them fine as dust in the wind;
   like mud in the streets I trampled
   them down.
44 You rescued me from the strife of peoples;
   you made me head over nations.
   A people I had not known became my
   slaves;
45 as soon as they heard of me they
   obeyed.
   Foreigners cringed before me;
46   their courage failed;
   they came trembling from their fortresses.[s]

VI

47 The LORD lives! Blessed be my rock![t]
   Exalted be God, my savior!
48 O God who granted me vindication,
   made peoples subject to me,[u]
49 and preserved me from my enemies,
   Truly you have exalted me above my
   adversaries,
   from the violent you have rescued
   me.
50 Thus I will proclaim you, LORD, among
   the nations;
   I will sing the praises of your name.[v]
51 You have given great victories to your
   king,
   and shown kindness to your anointed,
   to David and his posterity forever.[w]

---

h Ps 77, 17; Zec 9, 14.—i Ps 144, 7.—j Ps 26; 1 Sm 26, 23.—
k Ps 125, 4.—l Jb 22, 29; Prv 3, 34.—m Pss 27, 1; 36, 10; 43,
3; 119, 105; Jb 29, 3; Mi 7, 8.—n Pss 12, 6; 77, 13; Prv 30,
5.—o Is 44, 8; 45, 21.—p Hb 3, 19.—q Ps 144, 1.—r Ps 17, 5.—
s Mi 7, 17.—t Ps 144, 1.—u Ps 144, 2.—v Ps 7, 18; 30, 5; 57,
9; 135, 3; 146, 2; Rom 15, 9.—w Pss 89, 28-37; 144, 10; 1 Sm
2, 10.

18, 35: *Bow of bronze:* hyperbole for a bow difficult to bend
and therefore capable of propelling an arrow with great force.

PSALM 19*

God's Glory in the Heavens and in the Law

¹ For the leader. A psalm of David.

I

² The heavens declare the glory of God;
  the sky proclaims its builder's craft. ˣ
³ One day to the next conveys that message;
  one night to the next imparts that knowledge.
⁴ There is no word or sound;*
  no voice is heard;
⁵ Yet their report goes forth through all the earth,
  their message, to the ends of the world.
God has pitched a tent there for the sun;*
⁶ it comes forth like a bridegroom from his chamber,
  and like an athlete joyfully runs its course.
⁷ From one end of the heavens it comes forth;
  its course runs through to the other;
  nothing escapes its heat.

II

⁸ The law of the LORD is perfect,
  refreshing the soul.
The decree of the LORD is trustworthy,
  giving wisdom to the simple.ʸ
⁹ The precepts of the LORD are right,
  rejoicing the heart.
The command of the LORD is clear,
  enlightening the eye.
¹⁰ The fear of the LORD is pure,
  enduring forever.
The statutes of the LORD are true,
  all of them just;
¹¹ More desirable than gold,
  than a hoard of purest gold,
Sweeter also than honey
  or drippings from the comb. ᶻ
¹² By them your servant is instructed;*
  obeying them brings much reward.

III

¹³ Who can detect heedless failings?
  Cleanse me from my unknown faults.
¹⁴ But from willful sins keep your servant;
  let them never control me.
Then shall I be blameless,
  innocent of grave sin.

¹⁵ Let the words of my mouth meet with your favor,
  keep the thoughts of my heart before you,
LORD, my rock and my redeemer.

PSALM 20*

Prayer for the King in Time of War

¹ For the leader. A psalm of David.

I

² The LORD answer you in time of distress;
  the name of the God of Jacob defend you!
³ May God send you help from the temple,
  from Zion be your support. ᵃ
⁴ May God remember* your every offering,
  graciously accept your holocaust,
                                          Selah
⁵ Grant what is in your heart,
  fulfill your every plan.
⁶ May we shout for joy at your victory,*
  raise the banners in the name of our God.
The LORD grant your every prayer!

---

x Pss 8, 1; 50, 6; 97, 6.—y Pss 12, 7; 119.—z Sir 24, 19.—a Pss 128, 5; 134, 3.

Ps 19: The heavenly elements of the world, now beautifully arranged, bespeak the power and wisdom of their creator (2-7). The creator's wisdom is available to human beings in the law (8-11), toward which the psalmist prays to be open (12-15). The themes of light and speech unify the poem.

19, 4: *No word or sound:* the regular functioning of the heavens and the alternation of day and night inform humans without words of the creator's power and wisdom.

19, 5: *The sun:* in other religious literature the sun is a judge and lawgiver since it sees all in its daily course; 5b-7 form a transition to the law in 8-11. The six synonyms for God's revelation (8-11) are applied to the sun in comparable literature.

19, 12: *Instructed:* the Hebrew verb means both to shine and to teach. Cf Dn 12, 3.

Ps 20: The people pray for the king before battle. The people ask for divine help (2-6) and express confidence that such help will be given (7-10). A solemn assurance of divine help may well have been given between the two sections in the liturgy, something like the promises of Pss 12, 6 and 21, 9-13. The final verse (10) echoes the opening verse.

20, 4: *Remember:* God's remembering implies readiness to act. Cf Gn 8, 1; Ex 2, 24.

20, 6: *Victory:* the Hebrew root is often translated "salvation," "to save," but in military contexts it can have the specific meaning of "victory."

II

7 Now I know victory is given
  to the anointed of the LORD.[b]
God will answer him from the holy
    heavens
  with a strong arm that brings vic-
    tory.
8 Some rely on chariots, others on horses,
  but we on the name of the LORD our
    God.[c]
9 They collapse and fall,
  but we stand strong and firm.[d]
10 LORD, grant victory to the king;
  answer when we call upon you.

PSALM 21*

Thanksgiving and Assurances
for the King

1 For the leader. A psalm of David.

I

2 LORD, the king finds joy in your
    power;[e]
  in your victory how greatly he re-
    joices!
3 You have granted him his heart's de-
    sire;
  you did not refuse the prayer of his
    lips.   *Selah*
4 For you welcomed him with goodly
    blessings;

---

b Pss 18, 51; 144, 10; 1 Sm 2, 10.—c Ps 147, 10-11; 2 Chr
14, 10; Prv 21, 31; 1 Sm 17, 45; Is 31, 1; 36, 9.—d Is 40, 30.—
e Ps 63, 12.—f 1 Kgs 3, 14.—g Nm 10, 35.—h Is 49, 14; 54, 7;
Mt 27, 46; Mk 15, 34.—i Sir 2, 10.—j Is 6, 3.

Ps 21: The first part of this royal psalm is a thanksgiving (2-
8), and the second is a promise that the king will triumph over his
enemies (9-14). The king's confident prayer (3. 5) and trust in
God (8) enable him to receive the divine gifts of vitality, peace,
and military success. V 14 reprises v 1. When kings ceased in Israel after the sixth century B.C., the psalm was sung of a future
Davidic king.

Ps 22: A lament unusual in structure and in intensity of feeling. The psalmist's present distress is contrasted with God's past
mercy in vv 2-12. In vv 13-22 enemies surround the psalmist. The
last third is an invitation to praise God (23-27), becoming a universal chorus of praise (28-32). The psalm is important in the
New Testament. Its opening words occur on the lips of the
crucified Jesus (Mk 15, 34; Mt 27, 46), and several other verses
are quoted, or at least alluded to, in the accounts of Jesus' passion
(Mt 27, 35. 43; Jn 19, 24).

22, 1: *The deer of the dawn:* apparently the title of the
melody.

---

you placed on his head a crown of
    pure gold.
5 He asked life of you;
  you gave it to him,
  length of days forever.[f]
6 Great is his glory in your victory;
  majesty and splendor you confer
    upon him.
7 You make him the pattern of blessings
    forever,
  you gladden him with the joy of your
    presence.
8 For the king trusts in the LORD,
  stands firm through the love of the
    Most High.

II

9 Your hand will reach all your enemies;
  your right hand will reach your foes!
10 At the time of your coming
  you will drive them into a furnace.
Then the LORD's anger will consume
    them,
  devour them with fire.
11 Even their descendants you will wipe
    out from the earth,
  their offspring from the human race.
12 Though they intend evil against you,
  devising plots, they will not succeed,
13 For you will put them to flight;
  you will aim at them with your bow.

III

14 Arise, LORD, in your power![g]
  We will sing and chant the praise of
    your might.

PSALM 22*

The Prayer of an Innocent Person

1 For the leader; according to "The deer of the
dawn."* A psalm of David.

I

2 My God, my God, why have you aban-
    doned me?
  Why so far from my call for help,
    from my cries of anguish?[h]
3 My God, I call by day, but you do not
    answer;
  by night, but I have no relief.[i]
4 Yet you are enthroned as the Holy One;
  you are the glory of Israel.[j]
5 In you our ancestors trusted;
  they trusted and you rescued them.

6 To you they cried out and they escaped;
  in you they trusted and were not disappointed.[k]
7 But I am a worm, hardly human,*
  scorned by everyone, despised by the
  people.[l]
8 All who see me mock me;
  they curl their lips and jeer;
  they shake their heads at me:[m]
9 "You relied on the LORD—let him deliver you;
  if he loves you, let him rescue you."[n]
10 Yet you drew me forth from the womb,
  made me safe at my mother's breast.
11 Upon you I was thrust from the womb;
  since birth you are my God.[o]
12 Do not stay far from me,
  for trouble is near,
  and there is no one to help.[p]

II
13 Many bulls* surround me;
  fierce bulls of Bashan encircle me.
14 They open their mouths against me,
  lions that rend and roar.[q]
15 Like water my life drains away;
  all my bones grow soft.
  My heart has become like wax,
  it melts away within me.
16 As dry as a potsherd is my throat;
  my tongue sticks to my palate;
  you lay me in the dust of death.*
17 Many dogs surround me;
  a pack of evildoers closes in on me.
  So wasted are my hands and feet
18 that I can count all my bones.[r]
  They stare at me and gloat;
19 they divide my garments among them;
  for my clothing they cast lots.[s]
20 But you, LORD, do not stay far off;
  my strength, come quickly to help
  me.
21 Deliver me from the sword,
  my forlorn life from the teeth of the
  dog.
22 Save me from the lion's mouth,
  my poor life from the horns of wild
  bulls.[t]

III
23 Then I will proclaim your name to the
  assembly;
  in the community I will praise you:*[u]
24 "You who fear the LORD, give praise!
  All descendants of Jacob, give honor;
  show reverence, all descendants of Israel!
25 For God has not spurned or disdained
  the misery of this poor wretch,
  Did not turn away* from me,
  but heard me when I cried out.
26 I will offer praise in the great assembly;
  my vows I will fulfill before those who
  fear him.
27 The poor* will eat their fill;
  those who seek the LORD will offer
  praise.
  May your hearts enjoy life forever!"[v]

IV
28 All the ends of the earth
  will worship and turn to the LORD;
  All the families of nations
  will bow low before you.[w]
29 For kingship belongs to the LORD,
  the ruler over the nations.[x]
30 All who sleep in the earth
  will bow low before God;
  All who have gone down into the dust*
  will kneel in homage.
31 And I will live for the LORD;
  my descendants will serve you.
32 The generation to come will be told of
  the Lord,
  that they may proclaim to a people yet
  unborn
  the deliverance you have brought.[y]

---

k Ps 25, 3; Is 49, 23; Dn 3, 40.—l Is 53, 3.—m Ps 109, 25;
Mt 27, 39; Mk 15, 29; Lk 23, 35.—n Ps 71, 11; Wis 2, 18-20;
Mt 27, 43.—o Ps 71, 6; Is 44, 2; 46, 3.—p Pss 35, 22; 38, 22;
71, 12.—q Ps 17, 12; Jb 4, 10; 1 Pt 5, 8.—r Ps 109, 24.—s Mt
27, 35; Mk 15, 24; Lk 23, 34; Jn 19, 24.—t Pss 7, 2-3; 17, 12;
35, 17; 57, 5; 58, 7; 2 Tm 4, 17.—u Pss 26, 12; 35, 18; 40, 10;
109, 30; 149, 1; 2 Sm 22, 50; Heb 2, 12.—v Pss 23, 5; 69,
33.—w Ps 86, 9; Tb 13, 11; Is 45, 22; 52, 10; Zec 14, 16.—x
Ps 103, 19; Ob 21; Zec 14, 9.—y Pss 48, 14-15; 71, 18; 78, 6;
102, 19; Is 53, 10.

22, 7: *I am a worm, hardly human:* the psalmist's sense of
isolation and dehumanization, an important motif of Ps 22, is
vividly portrayed here.
22, 13-14: *Bulls:* the enemies of the psalmist are also portrayed in less-than-human form, as wild animals (cf 17. 21-22).
Bashan: a grazing land east of the Jordan, famed for its cattle.
Cf Dt 32, 14; Ez 39, 18; Am 4, 1.
22, 16: *The dust of death:* the netherworld, the domain of
the dead.
22, 23: *In the community I will praise you:* the person who
offered a thanksgiving sacrifice in the temple recounted to the
other worshipers the favor received from God and invited them
to share in the sacrificial banquet. The final section (24-32) may
be a summary or a citation of the psalmist's poem of praise.
22, 25: *Turn away:* literally, "hides his face from me," an
important metaphor for God withdrawing from someone, e.g., Mi
3, 4; Is 8, 17; Pss 27, 9; 69, 18; 88, 15.
22, 27: *The poor:* originally the poor, who were dependent
on God; the term ('*anawim*) came to include the religious sense
of "humble, pious, devout."
22, 30: Hebrew unclear. The translation assumes that all on
earth (28-29) and under the earth (30) will worship God.

PSALM 23*

The Lord, Shepherd and Host

[1] A psalm of David.

I

The LORD is my shepherd;*
there is nothing I lack.[z]

[2] In green pastures you let me graze;
to safe waters you lead me;
[3] you restore my strength.
You guide me along the right path*
for the sake of your name.[a]

[4] Even when I walk through a dark valley,*[b]
I fear no harm for you are at my side;
your rod and staff give me courage.

II

[5] You set a table before me*
as my enemies watch;

---

z Pss 80, 2; 95, 7; 100, 3; Dt 2, 7.—a Prv 4, 11.—b Jb 10, 21-22; Is 50, 10.—c Ps 92, 11.—d Ps 16, 5.—e Ps 27, 4.—f Pss 50, 12; 89, 12; Dt 10, 14; 1 Cor 10, 26.—g Ps 136, 6; Is 42, 5.—h Ps 15, 1.—i Ps 118, 19-20.—j Pss 86, 4; 143, 8.—k Ps 71, 1.

Ps 23: God's loving care for the psalmist is portrayed under the figures of a shepherd for the flock (1-4) and a host's generosity toward a guest (5-6). The imagery of both sections is drawn from traditions of the exodus (Is 40, 11; 49, 10; Jer 31, 10).
23, 1: *My shepherd:* God as good shepherd is common in both the Old Testament and the New Testament (Ez 34, 11-16 and Jn 10, 11-18).
23, 3: *The right path:* connotes "right way" and "way of righteousness."
23, 4: *A dark valley:* a different division of the Hebrew consonants yields the translation "the valley of the shadow of death."
23, 5: *You set a table before me:* this expression occurs in an exodus context in Ps 78, 19. *As my enemies watch:* my enemies see that I am God's friend and guest. *Oil:* a perfumed ointment made from olive oil, used especially at banquets (Ps 104, 15; Mt 26, 7; Lk 7, 37. 46; Jn 12, 2).
23, 6: *Goodness and love:* the blessings of God's covenant with Israel.
Ps 24: The psalm apparently accompanied a ceremony of the entry of God (invisibly enthroned upon the ark), followed by the people, into the temple. The temple commemorated the creation of the world (1-2). The people had to affirm their fidelity before being admitted into the sanctuary (3-6; cf Ps 15). A choir identifies the approaching God and invites the very temple gates to bow down in obeisance (7-10).
24, 4-5: Literally, "the one whose hands are clean." The singular is used for the entire class of worshipers, hence the plural translation.
24, 7. 9: *Lift up your heads, O gates . . . you ancient portals:* the literal meaning is impossible since the portcullis (a gate that moves up and down) was unknown in the ancient world. Extra-biblical parallels suggest a full personification of the circle of gate towers: they are like a council of elders, bowed down and anxious, awaiting the return of the army and the Great Warrior gone to battle.
Ps 25: A lament. Each verse begins with a successive letter of the Hebrew alphabet. Such acrostic psalms are often a series of statements only loosely connected. The psalmist mixes ardent pleas (1-2. 16-22) with expressions of confidence in God who forgives and guides.

You anoint my head with oil;[c]
my cup overflows.[d]
[6] Only goodness and love* will pursue me
all the days of my life;
I will dwell in the house of the LORD[e]
for years to come.

PSALM 24*

The Glory of God in Procession to Zion

[1] A psalm of David.

I

The earth is the LORD's and all it holds,[f]
the world and those who live there.
[2] For God founded it on the seas,
established it over the rivers.[g]

II

[3] Who may go up the mountain of the LORD?[h]
Who can stand in his holy place?
[4] "The clean of hand and pure of heart,*
who are not devoted to idols,
who have not sworn falsely.
[5] They will receive blessings from the LORD,
and justice from their saving God.
[6] Such are the people that love the LORD,
that seek the face of the God of Jacob."
　　　　　　　　　　　　　　　　Selah

III

[7] Lift up your heads, O gates;
rise up, you ancient portals,*
that the king of glory may enter.[i]
[8] Who is this king of glory?
The LORD, a mighty warrior,
the LORD, mighty in battle.
[9] Lift up your heads, O gates;
rise up, you ancient portals,
that the king of glory may enter.
[10] Who is this king of glory?
The LORD of hosts is the king of glory.
　　　　　　　　　　　　　　　　Selah

PSALM 25*

Confident Prayer for Forgiveness and Guidance

[1] Of David.

I

I wait for you, O LORD;
I lift up my soul [2] to my God.[j]
In you I trust; do not let me be disgraced;[k]
do not let my enemies gloat over me.

3 No one is disgraced who waits for
    you,[l]
    but only those who lightly break
    faith.
4 Make known to me your ways, LORD;
    teach me your paths.[m]
5 Guide me in your truth and teach me,
    for you are God my savior.
    For you I wait all the long day,
    because of your goodness, LORD.*
6 Remember your compassion and love,
    O LORD;
    for they are ages old.[n]
7 Remember no more the sins of my
    youth;[o]
    remember me only in light of your
    love.

II
8 Good and upright is the LORD,
    who shows sinners the way,
9 Guides the humble rightly,
    and teaches the humble the way.
10 All the paths of the LORD are faithful
    love
    toward those who honor the covenant
    demands.
11 For the sake of your name, LORD,
    pardon my guilt, though it is great.
12 Who are those who fear the LORD?
    God shows them the way to choose.[p]
13 They live well and prosper,
    and their descendants inherit the
    land.[q]
14 The counsel of the LORD belongs to the
    faithful;
    the covenant instructs them.
15 My eyes are ever upon the LORD,
    who frees my feet from the snare.[r]

III
16 Look upon me, have pity on me,
    for I am alone and afflicted.[s]
17 Relieve the troubles of my heart;
    bring me out of my distress.
18 Put an end to my affliction and suffer-
    ing;
    take away all my sins.
19 See how many are my enemies,
    see how fiercely they hate me.
20 Preserve my life and rescue me;
    do not let me be disgraced, for I trust
    in you.
21 Let honesty and virtue preserve me;
    I wait for you, O LORD.
22 Redeem Israel, God,*
    from all its distress!

PSALM 26*

Prayer of Innocence

1 Of David.

I
Grant me justice, LORD!
    I have walked without blame.[t]
In the LORD I have trusted;
    I have not faltered.
2 Test me, LORD, and try me;
    search my heart and mind.[u]
3 Your love is before my eyes;
    I walk guided by your faithfulness.[v]

II
4 I do not sit with deceivers,
    nor with hypocrites do I mingle.
5 I hate the company of evildoers;
    with the wicked I do not sit.
6 I will wash my hands* in innocence[w]
    and walk round your altar, LORD,
7 Lifting my voice in thanks,
    recounting all your wondrous deeds.
8 LORD, I love the house where you
    dwell,
    the tenting-place of your glory.[x]

III
9 Do not take me away with sinners,
    nor my life with the violent.[y]
10 Their hands carry out their schemes;
    their right hands are full of bribes.
11 But I walk without blame;[z]
    redeem me, be gracious to me![a]
12 My foot stands on level ground;*
    in assemblies I will bless the LORD.[b]

---

l Ps 22, 6; Is 49, 23; Dn 3, 40.—m Pss 27, 11; 86, 11; 119,
12. 35; 143, 8. 10.—n Sir 51, 8.—o Jb 13, 26; Is 64, 8.—p Prv
19, 23.—q Ps 37, 9. 29.—r Pss 123, 1. 2; 141, 8.—s Pss 86, 16;
119, 132.—t Ps 7, 9.—u Pss 17, 3; 139, 23.—v Ps 86, 11.—w
Ps 73, 13.—x Pss 29, 9; 63, 3; Ex 24, 16; 25, 8.—y Ps 28, 3.—z
Ps 101, 6.—a Ps 25, 16.—b Pss 22, 23; 35, 18; 149, 1.

25, 5: *Because of your goodness, LORD:* these words have
been transposed from the end of 7 to preserve the pattern of two
lines per letter of the Hebrew alphabet in the acrostic poem.
    25, 22: A final verse beginning with the Hebrew letter *pe* is
added to the normal 22-letter alphabet. Thus the letters *aleph,
lamed,* and *pe* open the first, middle (v 11), and last lines of the
psalm. Together, they spell *aleph,* the first letter of the alphabet.
    Ps 26: Like a priest washing before approaching the altar (Ex
30, 17-21), the psalmist seeks God's protection upon entering the
temple. 1-3, matched by 11-12, remind God of past integrity
while asking for purification; 4-5, matched by 9-10, pray for inclusion among the just; 6-8, the center of the poem, express the
joy in God at the heart of all ritual.
    26, 6: *I will wash my hands:* the washing of hands was a
liturgical act (Ex 30, 19. 21; 40, 31-32), symbolic of inner as
well as outer cleanness. Cf Is 1, 16.
    26, 12: *On level ground:* in safety, where there is no danger
of tripping and falling. *In assemblies:* at the temple. Having
walked around the altar, the symbol of God's presence, the psalmist blesses God.

PSALM 27*

Trust in God

¹ Of David

A

I

The LORD is my light and my salvation;ᶜ
   whom do I fear?
The LORD is my life's refuge;
   of whom am I afraid?
² When evildoers come at me
   to devour my flesh,*ᵈ
These my enemies and foes
   themselves stumble and fall.
³ Though an army encamp against me,
   my heart does not fear;
Though war be waged against me,
   even then do I trust.

II

⁴ One thing I ask of the LORD;
   this I seek:
To dwell in the LORD's house
   all the days of my life,
To gaze on the LORD's beauty,
   to visit his temple.ᵉ
⁵ For God will hide me in his shelter
   in time of trouble,ᶠ
Will conceal me in the cover of his tent;
   and set me high upon a rock.

---

c Pss 18, 29; 36, 10; 43, 3; Is 10, 17; Mi 7, 8.—d Ps 14, 4.—e
Pss 23, 6; 61, 5.—f Ps 31, 21.—g Ps 24, 6; Hos 5, 15.—h Is 49,
15.—i Pss 25, 4; 86, 11.—j Ps 116, 9; Is 38, 11.—k Ps 18, 2.—l
Pss 30, 4; 88, 5; 143, 7; Prv 1, 12.—m Ps 134, 2.—n Ps 26,
9.—o Ps 12, 2; 55, 22; 62, 5; Prv 26, 24-28.—p 2 Sm 3, 39.

Ps 27: Tradition has handed down the two sections of the
psalm (1-6 and 7-14) as one psalm, though each part could be
understood as complete in itself. Asserting boundless hope that
God will bring rescue (1-3), the psalmist longs for the presence of
God in the temple, protection from all enemies (4-6). In part B
there is a clear shift in tone (7-12); the climax of the poem comes
with "I believe" (13), echoing "I trust" (3).
27, 2: *To devour my flesh:* the psalmist's enemies are rapacious beasts (Pss 7, 3; 17, 12; 22, 14. 17).
27, 8: *Seek God's face* (literally: "to seek his face"): to commune with God in the temple. The idiom is derived from the practice of journeying to sacred places. Cf Hos 5, 15; 2 Sm 21, 1; Ps
24, 6.
27, 13: *In the land of the living:* or "in the land of life," an
epithet of the Jerusalem temple (Pss 52, 7; 116, 9; Is 38, 11),
where the faithful had access to the life-giving presence of God.
Ps 28: A lament asking that the psalmist, who has taken refuge in the temple (2), not be punished with the wicked, who are
headed inevitably toward destruction (1. 3-5). The statement of
praise is exceptionally lengthy and vigorous (6-7). The psalm ends
with a prayer (8-9).
28, 1: *The pit:* a synonym for Sheol, the shadowy place of the
dead.
28, 2: *Your holy place:* the innermost part of the temple, the
holy of holies, containing the ark. Cf 1 Kgs 6, 16. 19-23; 8, 6-8.

⁶ Even now my head is held high
   above my enemies on every side!
I will offer in his tent
   sacrifices with shouts of joy;
   I will sing and chant praise to the
   LORD.

B

I

⁷ Hear my voice, LORD, when I call;
   have mercy on me and answer me.
⁸ "Come," says my heart, "seek God's
   face";*
   your face, LORD, do I seek!ᵍ
⁹ Do not hide your face from me;
   do not repel your servant in anger.
You are my help; do not cast me off;
   do not forsake me, God my savior!
¹⁰ Even if my father and mother forsake
   me,
   the LORD will take me in.ʰ

II

¹¹ LORD, show me your way;
   lead me on a level path
   because of my enemies.ⁱ
¹² Do not abandon me to the will of my
   foes;
   malicious and lying witnesses have
   risen against me.
¹³ But I believe I shall enjoy the LORD's
   goodness
   in the land of the living.*ʲ
¹⁴ Wait for the LORD, take courage;
   be stouthearted, wait for the LORD!

PSALM 28*

Petition and Thanksgiving

¹ Of David.

I

To you, LORD, I call;
   my Rock, do not be deaf to me.ᵏ
If you fail to answer me,
   I will join those who go down to the
   pit.*ˡ
² Hear the sound of my pleading when I
   cry to you,
   lifting my hands toward your holy
   place.*ᵐ
³ Do not drag me off with the wicked,
   with those who do wrong,ⁿ
Who speak peace to their neighbors
   though evil is in their hearts.ᵒ
⁴ Repay them for their deeds,
   for the evil that they do.
For the work of their hands repay them;
   give them what they deserve.ᵖ

Ps

5 They pay no heed to the LORD's works,
    to the deeds of God's hands. *q*
God will tear them down,
    never to be rebuilt.

II

6 Blessed be the LORD,
    who has heard the sound of my plead-
    ing.*

7 The LORD is my strength and my shield,
    in whom my heart trusted and found
    help.
So my heart rejoices;
    with my song I praise my God.

III

8 LORD, you are the strength of your peo-
    ple,
    the saving refuge of your anointed
    king.*

9 Save your people, bless your inheritance;
    feed and sustain them forever!

PSALM 29*

The Lord of Majesty Acclaimed as King of the World

1 A psalm of David.

I

Give to the LORD, you heavenly beings,*
    give to the LORD glory and might;

2 Give to the LORD the glory due God's
    name.
    Bow down before the LORD's holy
    splendor!*

II

3 The voice of the LORD* is over the
    waters;
    the God of glory thunders,
    the LORD, over the mighty waters.

4 The voice of the LORD is power;
    the voice of the LORD is splendor. *s*

5 The voice of the LORD cracks the cedars;
    the LORD splinters the cedars of Leba-
    non,

6 Makes Lebanon leap like a calf,
    and Sirion* like a young bull.

7 The voice of the LORD strikes with fiery
    flame;

8 the voice of the LORD rocks the desert;
    the LORD rocks the desert of Kadesh.*

9 The voice of the LORD twists the oaks
    and strips the forests bare.
    All in his palace say, "Glory!"*

III

10 The LORD sits enthroned above the
    flood!* *t*
    The LORD reigns as king forever!

11 May the LORD give might to his people;*
    may the LORD bless his people with
    peace! *u*

PSALM 30*

Thanksgiving for Deliverance

1 A psalm. A song for the dedication of the
temple.* Of David.

I

2 I praise you, LORD, for you raised me up
    and did not let my enemies rejoice over
    me.

3 O LORD, my God,
    I cried out to you and you healed* me.

4 LORD, you brought me up from Sheol;*
    you kept me from going down to the
    pit. *v*

II

5 Sing praise to the LORD, you faithful;
    give thanks to God's holy name.

---

q Is 5, 12.—r Pss 68, 35; 96, 7-9.—s Pss 46, 7; 77, 18-19;
Jb 37, 4; Is 30, 30.—t Bar 3, 3.—u Ps 68, 36.—v Ps 28, 1; Jon
2, 7.

28, 6: The psalmist shifts to fervent thanksgiving, probably
responding to a priestly or prophetic oracle in 5cd (not usually
transmitted) assuring the worshiper that the prayer has been heard.

28, 8: *Your people . . . your anointed king:* salvation is
more than individual, affecting all the people and their God-given
leader.

Ps 29: The hymn invites the members of the heavenly court to
acknowledge God's supremacy by ascribing glory and might to God
alone (1-2a. 9b). Divine glory and might are dramatically visible
in the storm (3-9a). The storm apparently comes from the Mediterranean onto the coast of Syria-Palestine and then moves inland.
In 10 the divine beings acclaim God's eternal kingship. The psalm
concludes with a prayer that God will impart the power just displayed to the Israelite king and through the king to Israel.

29, 1: *You heavenly beings:* literally, "sons of God," i.e.,
members of the heavenly court who served Israel's God in a variety
of capacities.

29, 3: *The voice of the Lord:* the sevenfold repetition of the
phrase imitates the sound of crashing thunder and may allude to
God's primordial slaying of Leviathan, the seven-headed sea monster of Canaanite mythology.

29, 6: *Sirion:* the Phoenician name for Mount Hermon. Cf Dt
3, 9.

29, 8: *The desert of Kadesh:* probably north of Palestine in
the neighborhood of Lebanon and Hermon.

29, 9b-10: Having witnessed God's supreme power (3-9a), the
gods acknowledge the glory that befits the king of the divine and
human world.

29, 10: *The flood:* God defeated the primordial waters and
made them part of the universe. Cf Pss 89, 10-13 and 93, 3-4.

29, 11: *His people:* God's people, Israel.

Ps 30: An individual thanksgiving in four parts: praise and
thanks for deliverance and restoration (2-4); an invitation to others
to join in (5-6); a flashback to the time before deliverance (7-11);
a return to praise and thanks (12-13). Two sets of images recur:
1) going down, death, silence; 2) coming up, life, praising. God
has delivered the psalmist from one state to the other.

30, 1: *For the dedication of the temple:* a later adaptation
of the psalm to celebrate the purification of the temple in 164
B.C. during the Maccabean Revolt.

30, 3: *Healed:* for God as healer, see also Pss 103, 3; 107,
20; Hos 6, 1; 7, 1; 11, 3; 14, 5.

30, 4: *Sheol . . . pit:* the shadowy underworld residence of
the spirits of the dead, here a metaphor for near death.

6 For divine [...]ts but a moment;
divine fa[...] a lifetime.
[...]omes for the night;
At dusk w[...]re is rejoicing.
but at d[...]

III

7 Complace[...] once said,
[...] be shaken."
"I shal[...]

8 LORD, w[...]u showed me favor
[...]the mighty mountains.
I stoo[...]
But wh[...] hid your face
I was[...]k with terror. *w*

9 To you[...]RD, I cried out;
with[...]Lord I pleaded for mercy:

10 "Wha[...] is there from my lifeblood,
fro[...]y going down to the grave?*
Does[...]t give you thanks
or [...]lare your faithfulness?

11 Hear[...] LORD, have mercy on me;
L[...], be my helper."

IV

12 Yo[...]hanged my mourning into danc-
[...]ng;
[...]u took off my sackcloth
[...]nd clothed me with gladness. *x*

13 W[...]th my whole being I sing
[...]endless praise to you.
O LORD, my God,
forever will I give you thanks.

PSALM 31*

Prayer in Distress and Thanksgiving for Escape

1 For the leader. A psalm of David.

I

2 In you, LORD, I take refuge; *y*
let me never be put to shame.

In your justice deliver me;

3 incline your ear to me;
make haste to rescue me!
Be my rock of refuge,
a stronghold to save me.

4 You are my rock and my fortress; *z*
for your name's sake lead and guide me.

5 Free me from the net they have set for me,
for you are my refuge.

6 Into your hands I commend my spirit;* *a*
you will redeem me, LORD, faithful God.

7 You hate those who serve worthless idols,
but I trust in the LORD.

8 I will rejoice and be glad in your love,
once you have seen my misery,
observed my distress. *b*

9 You will not abandon me into enemy hands,
but will set my feet in a free and open space.

II

10 Be gracious to me, LORD, for I am in distress;
with grief my eyes are wasted,
my soul and body spent.

11 My life is worn out by sorrow,
my years by sighing.
My strength fails in affliction;
my bones are consumed. *c*

12 To all my foes I am a thing of scorn,
to my neighbors, a dreaded sight,
a horror to my friends.
When they see me in the street,
they quickly shy away. *d*

13 I am forgotten, out of mind like the dead;
I am like a shattered dish.*

14 I hear the whispers of the crowd;
terrors are all around* me.
They conspire against me;
they plot to take my life.

15 But I trust in you, LORD;
I say, "You are my God." *e*

16 My times are in your hands;
rescue me from my enemies,
from the hands of my pursuers.

17 Let your face shine on your servant; *f*
save me in your kindness.

18 Do not let me be put to shame,
for I have called to you, LORD.
Put the wicked to shame;
reduce them to silence in Sheol.

19 Strike dumb their lying lips,
proud lips that attack the just
in contempt and scorn. *g*

---

w Ps 104, 29.—x Is 61, 3; Jer 31, 13.—y 2-4: Ps 71, 1-3.—z Ps 18, 2.—a Lk 23, 46; Acts 7, 59.—b Ps 10, 14.—c Pss 32, 3; 38, 10-11.—d Jb 19, 13-19.—e Ps 140, 7; Is 25, 1.—f Ps 67, 1; Nm 6, 24.—g Ps 12, 4.

30, 7: *Complacent:* untroubled existence is often seen as a source of temptation to forget God. Cf Dt 8, 10-18; Hos 13, 6; Prv 30, 9.

30, 10: In the stillness of Sheol no one gives you praise; let me live and be among your worshipers. Cf Pss 6, 6; 88, 11-13; 115, 17; Is 38, 18.

Ps 31: A lament (2-19) with a strong emphasis on trust (4. 6. 15-16), ending with an anticipatory thanksgiving (20-25). As is usual in laments, the affliction is couched in general terms. The psalmist feels overwhelmed by evil people but trusts in the "faithful God" (6).

31, 6: *Into your hands I commend my spirit:* in Lk 23, 46 Jesus breathes his last with this psalm verse. Stephen in Acts 7, 59 alludes to these words as he is attacked by enemies. The verse is used as an antiphon in the Divine Office at Compline, the last prayer of the day.

31, 13: *Like a shattered dish:* a common comparison for something ruined and useless. Cf Is 30, 14; Jer 19, 11; 22, 28.

31, 14: *Terrors are all around:* a cry used in inescapable danger. Cf Jer 6, 25; 20, 10; 46, 5; 49, 29.

Ps

III

20 How great is your goodness, Lord,
   stored up for those who fear you.
   You display it for those who trust you,
   in the sight of all the people.
21 You hide them in the shelter of your
   presence,
   safe from scheming enemies.
   You keep them in your abode,
   safe from plotting tongues.[h]
22 Blessed be the Lord,
   who has shown me wondrous love,
   and been for me a city most secure.
23 Once I said in my anguish,
   "I am shut out from your sight."[i]
   Yet you heard my plea,
   when I cried out to you.
24 Love the Lord, all you faithful.
   The Lord protects the loyal,
   but repays the arrogant in full.
25 Be strong and take heart,
   all you who hope in the Lord.

PSALM 32*

Remission of Sin

1 Of David. A *maskil*.
   I
   Happy the sinner whose fault is removed,
   whose sin is forgiven.[j]
2 Happy those to whom the Lord im-
   putes no guilt,
   in whose spirit is no deceit.
   II
3 As long as I kept silent,* my bones
   wasted away;
   I groaned all the day.[k]
4 For day and night your hand was heavy
   upon me;
   my strength withered as in dry summer heat.   *Selah*
5 Then I declared my sin to you;
   my guilt I did not hide.[l]
   I said, "I confess my faults to the
   Lord,"
   and you took away the guilt of my
   sin.   *Selah*
6 Thus should all your faithful pray
   in time of distress.
   Though flood waters* threaten,
   they will never reach them.[m]
7 You are my shelter; from distress you
   keep me;
   with safety you ring me round. *Selah*

III

8 I will instruct you [in the]
   way you should [go, show you the]
   give you counsel and [keep my eye]
9 Do not be senseless [over you.]
   mules; [like horses or]
   with bit and bridle [their temper is]
   curbed, [
   else they will not com[e near y]ou.

IV

10 Many are the sorrows of t[he wi]cked,
   but love surrounds those[who trust in]
   the Lord.
11 Be glad in the Lord and r[ejoi]ce, you
   just;
   exult, all you upright of he[art.][n]

PSALM 33*

Praise of God's Power
and Providence

I

1 Rejoice, you just, in the Lord;
   praise from the upright is fitting.[o]
2 Give thanks to the Lord on the harp;
   on the ten-stringed lyre offer praise.[p]
3 Sing to God a new song;
   skillfully play with joyful chant.
4 For the Lord's word is true;
   all his works are trustworthy.
5 The Lord loves justice and right
   and fills the earth with goodness.[q]

---

h Ps 27, 5.—i Jon 2, 5.—j Is 1, 18; Ps 65, 3; Rom 4, 7-8.—k
Ps 31, 11.—l Pss 38, 19; 51, 5.—m Ps 18, 5.—n Ps 33, 1.—o
Pss 32, 11; 147, 1.—p Pss 92, 4; 144, 9.—q Ps 119, 64.

Ps 32: An individual thanksgiving and the second of the seven
Penitential Psalms (cf Ps 6). The opening declaration—the forgiven are blessed (1-2)—arises from the psalmist's own experience. At one time the psalmist was stubborn and closed, a victim
of sin's power (3-4), and then became open to the forgiving God
(5-7). Sin here, as often in the Bible, is not only the personal act
of rebellion against God but also the consequences of that act—
frustration and waning of vitality. Having been rescued, the
psalmist can teach others the joys of justice and the folly of sin (8-
11).
32, 3: *I kept silent:* did not confess the sin before God.
32, 6: *Flood waters:* the untamed waters surrounding the
earth, a metaphor for danger.
Ps 33: A hymn in which the just are invited (1-3) to praise
God, who by a mere word (4-5) created the three-tiered universe
of the heavens, the cosmic waters, and the earth (6-9). Human
words, in contrast, effect nothing (10-11). The greatness of
human beings consists in God's choosing them as a special people
and their faithful response (12-22).

II

6 By the LORD's word the heavens were made;
    by the breath of his mouth all their host.*[r]

7 The waters of the sea were gathered as in a bowl;*
    in cellars the deep was confined.[s]

III

8 Let all the earth fear the LORD;
    let all who dwell in the world show reverence.

9 For he spoke, and it came to be,
    commanded, and it stood in place.[t]

10 The LORD foils the plan of nations,
    frustrates the designs of peoples.

11 But the plan of the LORD stands forever,
    wise designs through all generations.[u]

12 Happy the nation whose God is the LORD,
    the people chosen as his very own.[v]

IV

13 From heaven the LORD looks down
    and observes the whole human race,[w]

14 Surveying from the royal throne
    all who dwell on earth.

15 The one who fashioned the hearts of them all
    knows all their works.

V

16 A king is not saved by a mighty army,
    nor a warrior delivered by great strength.

17 Useless is the horse for safety;
    its great strength, no sure escape.

18 But the LORD's eyes are upon the reverent,
    upon those who hope for his gracious help,

19 Delivering them from death,
    keeping them alive in times of famine.

VI

20 Our soul waits for the LORD,
    who is our help and shield.[x]

21 For in God our hearts rejoice;
    in your holy name we trust.

22 May your kindness, LORD, be upon us;
    we have put our hope in you.

PSALM 34*

Thanksgiving to God Who Delivers the Just

1 Of David, when he feigned madness before Abimelech,* who forced him to depart.

I

2 I will bless the LORD at all times;
    praise shall be always in my mouth.[y]

3 My soul will glory in the LORD
    that the poor may hear and be glad.

4 Magnify the LORD with me;
    let us exalt his name together.

II

5 I sought the LORD, who answered me,
    delivered me from all my fears.

6 Look to God that you may be radiant with joy
    and your faces may not blush for shame.

7 In my misfortune I called,
    the LORD heard and saved me from all distress.

8 The angel of the LORD, who encamps with them,
    delivers all who fear God.[z]

9 Learn to savor how good the LORD is;
    happy are those who take refuge in him.[a]

10 Fear the LORD, you holy ones;
    nothing is lacking to those who fear him.[b]

11 The powerful* grow poor and hungry,
    but those who seek the LORD lack no good thing.

Ps

r Gn 2, 1.—s Ps 78, 13; Gn 1, 9-10; Ex 15, 8.—t Ps 148, 5; Gn 1, 3f; Jdt 16, 14.—u Prv 19, 21; Is 40, 6.—v Ps 144, 15; Ex 19, 6; Dt 7, 6.—w Jb 34, 21; Sir 15, 19; Jer 16, 17; 32, 19.—x Ps 115, 9.—y Ps 145, 2.—z Ex 14, 19.—a Ps 2, 12.—b Prv 3, 7.

33, 6: *All their host:* the stars of the sky are commonly viewed as a vast army, e.g., Neh 9, 6; Is 40, 26; 45, 12; Jer 33, 22.

33, 7: *The waters . . . as in a bowl:* ancients sometimes attributed the power keeping the seas from overwhelming land to a primordial victory of the storm-god over personified Sea. God confines the seas as easily as one puts water in a bowl.

Ps 34: A thanksgiving in acrostic form, each line beginning with a successive letter of the Hebrew alphabet. In this psalm one letter is missing and two are in reverse order. The psalmist, fresh from the experience of being rescued (5. 7), can teach the "poor," those who are defenseless, to trust in God alone (4. 12). God will make them powerful (5-11) and give them protection (12-23).

34, 1: *Abimelech:* a scribal error for Achish. In 1 Sm 21, 13-16, David feigned madness before Achish, not Abimelech.

34, 11: *The powerful:* literally, "lions." Fierce animals were sometimes metaphors for influential people.

III

12 Come, children,* listen to me;[c]
   I will teach you the fear of the LORD.
13 Who among you loves life,[d]
   takes delight in prosperous days?
14 Keep your tongue from evil,
   your lips from speaking lies.
15 Turn from evil and do good;[e]
   seek peace and pursue it.
16 The LORD has eyes for the just[f]
   and ears for their cry.
17 The LORD's face is against evildoers
   to wipe out their memory from the
   earth.
18 When the just cry out, the LORD hears
   and rescues them from all distress.
19 The LORD is close to the broken-
   hearted,
   saves those whose spirit is crushed.
20 Many are the troubles of the just,
   but the LORD delivers from them all.
21 God watches over all their bones;
   not a one shall be broken.[g]
22 Evil will slay the wicked;
   those who hate the just are condemned.
23 The LORD redeems loyal servants;
   no one is condemned whose refuge is
   God.

PSALM 35*

Prayer for Help against Unjust Enemies

1 Of David.

I

Oppose, LORD, those who oppose me;*
   war upon those who make war upon
   me.
2 Take up the shield and buckler;
   rise up in my defense.
3 Brandish lance and battle-ax
   against my pursuers.
   Say to my heart,
   "I am your salvation."
4 Let those who seek my life
   be put to shame and disgrace.
   Let those who plot evil against me[h]
   be turned back and confounded.
5 Make them like chaff before the wind,[i]
   with the angel of the LORD driving
   them on.
6 Make their way slippery and dark,
   with the angel of the LORD pursuing
   them.

II

7 Without cause they set their snare for
   me;
   without cause they dug a pit for
   me.
8 Let ruin overtake them unawares;
   let the snare they have set catch
   them;
   let them fall into the pit they have
   dug.[j]
9 Then I will rejoice in the LORD,
   exult in God's salvation.
10 My very bones shall say,
   "O LORD, who is like you,[k]
   Who rescue the afflicted from the powerful,
   the afflicted and needy from the de-
   spoiler?"

III

11 Malicious witnesses come forward,
   accuse me of things I do not know.
12 They repay me evil for good
   and I am all alone.[l]
13 Yet I, when they were ill, put on sackcloth,*
   afflicted myself with fasting,
   sobbed my prayers upon my bosom.
14 I went about in grief as for my brother,
   bent in mourning as for my mother.
15 Yet when I stumbled they gathered
   with glee;
   they gathered against me like strangers.
   They slandered me without ceasing;
16 without respect they mocked me,
   gnashed their teeth against me.

---

c Prv 1, 8; 4, 1.—d 13-17: 1 Pt 3, 10-12.—e Ps 37, 27.—f Ps
33, 18.—g Jn 19, 36.—h Pss 40, 15; 71, 13.—i Pss 1, 4; 83, 14;
Jb 21, 18.—j Pss 7, 16; 9, 16; 57, 7; Prv 26, 27; Eccl 10, 8; Sir
27, 26.—k Ps 86, 8; 89, 7. 9; Ex 15, 11.—l Pss 27, 12; 38, 20-
21; 109, 5; Jer 18, 20.

34, 12: *Children:* the customary term for students in Wisdom
literature.
Ps 35: A lament of a person betrayed by friends. The psalmist
prays that the evildoers be publicly exposed as unjust (1-8), and
gives thanks in anticipation of vindication (9-10). Old friends are
the enemies (11-16). May their punishment come quickly (17-
21)! The last part (22-26) echoes the opening in praying for the
destruction of the psalmist's persecutors. The psalm may appear
vindictive, but one must keep in mind that the psalmist is praying
for *public* redress now of a *public* injustice. There is at this time
no belief in an afterlife in which justice will be redressed.
35, 1-6: The mixture of judicial, martial, and hunting images
shows that the language is figurative. The actual injustice is false
accusation of serious crimes (11. 15. 20-21). The psalmist seeks
lost honor through a trial before God.
35, 13. 15-17: The Hebrew is obscure.

IV

17 Lord, how long will you look on?
Save me from roaring beasts,
my precious life from lions!*m*
18 Then I will thank you in the great assembly;
I will praise you before the mighty
throng.*n*
19 Do not let lying foes smirk at me,
my undeserved enemies wink know-
ingly.*o*
20 They speak no words of peace,
but against the quiet in the land
they fashion deceitful speech.*p*
21 They open wide their mouths against
me.
They say, "Aha! Good!
Our eyes relish the sight!"*q*
22 You see this, LORD; do not be silent;*r*
Lord, do not withdraw from me.
23 Awake, be vigilant in my defense,
in my cause, my God and my
Lord.
24 Defend me because you are just,
LORD;
my God, do not let them gloat over
me.
25 Do not let them say in their hearts,
"Aha! Just what we wanted!"
Do not let them say,
"We have devoured that one!"
26 Put to shame and confound
all who relish my misfortune.
Clothe with shame and disgrace
those who lord it over me.
27 But let those who favor my just cause
shout for joy and be glad.

May they ever say, "Exalted be the
LORD
who delights in the peace of his loyal
servant."
28 Then my tongue shall recount your justice,
declare your praise, all the day long.*s*

PSALM 36*

Human Wickedness and Divine Providence

1 For the leader. Of David, the servant of the
LORD.

I

2 Sin directs the heart of the wicked;
their eyes are closed to the fear of
God.*t*
3 For they live with the delusion:
their guilt will not be known and
hated.*
4 Empty and false are the words of their
mouth;
they have ceased to be wise and do
good.
5 In their beds they hatch plots;
they set out on a wicked way;
they do not reject evil.*u*

II

6 LORD, your love reaches to heaven;
your fidelity, to the clouds.*v*
7 Your justice is like the highest mountains;
your judgments,* like the mighty
deep;
all living creatures you sustain,
LORD.
8 How precious is your love, O God!
We take refuge in the shadow of your
wings.**w*
9 We feast on the rich food of your house;
from your delightful stream*x* you give
us drink.
10 For with you is the fountain of life,*y*
and in your light we see light.*z*
11 Continue your kindness toward your
friends,
your just defense of the honest heart.
12 Do not let the foot of the proud overtake
me,
nor the hand of the wicked disturb
me.
13 There make the evildoers fall;
thrust them down, never to rise.

m Pss 17, 12; 22, 22; 58, 7.—n Pss 22, 23; 26, 12; 35, 18; 40,
10; 149, 1.—o Ps 38, 17.—p Ps 120, 6-7.—q Ps 40, 16; Lam 2,
16.—r Pss 22, 12; 38, 21; 109, 1.—s Ps 71, 15-16.—t Rom 3,
18.—u Mi 2, 1.—v Pss 57, 11; 71, 19.—w Ps 17, 8.—x Gn 2, 8.
10.—y Is 55, 1; Jn 4, 14.—z Ps 80, 4. 8. 20.

Ps 36: A psalm with elements of wisdom (2-5), the hymn (6-
10), and the lament (11-13). The rule of sin over the wicked (2-5)
is contrasted with the rule of divine love and mercy over God's
friends (6-10). The psalm ends with a prayer that God's guidance
never cease (11-13).

36, 3: *Hated:* punished by God.

36, 6-7: *Love . . . judgments:* God actively controls the entire
world.

36, 8: *The shadow of your wings:* metaphor for divine protection. It probably refers to the winged cherubim in the holy of
holies in the temple. Cf 1 Kgs 6, 23-28. 32; 2 Chr 3, 10-13; Ez 1,
4-9.

Ps

PSALM 37*

The Fate of Sinners and the Reward of the Just

[1] Of David.

Aleph

Do not be provoked by evildoers;
    do not envy those who do wrong.[a]
[2] Like grass they wither quickly;
    like green plants they wilt away.[b]

Beth

[3] Trust in the LORD and do good
    that you may dwell in the land* and
    live secure.[c]
[4] Find your delight in the LORD
    who will give you your heart's de-
    sire.[d]

Gimel

[5] Commit your way to the LORD;
    trust that God will act[e]
[6] And make your integrity shine like the
    dawn,
    your vindication like noonday.[f]

Daleth

[7] Be still before the LORD;
    wait for God.
Do not be provoked by the prosperous,
    nor by malicious schemers.

He

[8] Give up your anger, abandon your
    wrath;
    do not be provoked; it brings only
    harm.
[9] Those who do evil will be cut off,
    but those who wait for the LORD will
    possess the land.[g]

Waw

[10] Wait a little, and the wicked will be no
    more;
    look for them and they will not be
    there.
[11] But the poor will possess the land,[h]
    will delight in great prosperity.

Zayin

[12] The wicked plot against the just
    and grind their teeth at them;
[13] But the LORD laughs at them,[i]
    knowing their day is coming.

Heth

[14] The wicked draw their swords;
    they string their bows
To fell the poor and oppressed,
    to slaughter those whose way is hon-
    est.[j]

[15] Their swords will pierce their own
    hearts;
    their bows will be broken.

Teth

[16] Better the poverty of the just
    than the great wealth of the wicked.[k]
[17] The arms of the wicked will be broken;
    the LORD will sustain the just.

Yodh

[18] The LORD watches over the days of the
    blameless;
    their heritage lasts forever.
[19] They will not be disgraced when times
    are hard;
    in days of famine they will have
    plenty.

Kaph

[20] The wicked perish,
    the enemies of the LORD;
Like the beauty of meadows they vanish;
    like smoke they disappear.[l]

Lamedh

[21] The wicked borrow but do not repay;
    the just are generous in giving.
[22] For those blessed by the Lord will pos-
    sess the land,
    but those accursed will be cut off.

Mem

[23] Those whose steps are guided by the
    LORD,[m]
    whose way God approves,
[24] May stumble, but they will never fall,
    for the LORD holds their hand.

Nun

[25] Neither in my youth, nor now in old age
    have I ever seen the just abandoned[n]
    or their children begging bread.

a Prv 3, 31; 23, 17; 24, 1. 19.—b Pss 90, 5-6; 102, 12; 103, 15-16; Jb 14, 2; Is 40, 7.—c Ps 128, 2.—d Prv 10, 24.—e Ps 55, 23; Prv 3, 5; 16, 3.—f Wis 5, 6; Is 58, 10.—g Ps 25, 13; Prv 2, 21; Is 57, 13.—h Mt 5, 4.—i Pss 2, 4; 59, 9; Wis 4, 18.—j Pss 11, 2; 57, 5; 64, 4.—k Prv 15, 16; 16, 8.—l Wis 5, 14.—m Prv 20, 24.—n Jb 4, 7; Sir 2, 10.

Ps 37: The psalm responds to the problem of evil, which the Old Testament often expresses as a question: why do the wicked prosper and the good suffer? The psalm answers that the situation is only temporary. God will reverse things, rewarding the good and punishing the wicked here on earth. The perspective is concrete and earthbound: people's very actions place them among the ranks of the good or wicked. Each group or "way" has its own inherent dynamism—eventual frustration for the wicked, eventual reward for the just. The psalm is an acrostic, i.e., each section begins with a successive letter of the Hebrew alphabet. Each section has its own imagery and logic.

37, 3. 9. 11. 22. 27. 29. 34: *The land:* the promised land, Israel, which became for later interpreters a type or figure of heaven. Cf Heb 11, 9-10. 13-16. The New Testament Beatitudes (Mt 5, 3-12; Lk 6, 20-26) have been influenced by the psalm, especially their total reversal of the present and their interpretation of the happy future as possession of the land.

26 The just always lend generously,
    and their children become a blessing.

Samekh

27 Turn from evil and do good,
    that you may inhabit the land forever. *o*
28 For the LORD loves justice
    and does not abandon the faithful.

Ayin

When the unjust are destroyed,
    and the children of the wicked cut off,
29 The just will possess the land
    and live in it forever. *p*

Pe

30 The mouths of the just utter wisdom; *q*
    their tongues speak what is right.
31 God's teaching is in their hearts; *r*
    their steps do not falter.

Sadhe

32 The wicked spy on the just
    and seek to kill them.
33 But the LORD does not leave the just in
    their power,
    nor let them be condemned when
    tried.

Qoph

34 Wait eagerly for the LORD,
    and keep to the way; *s*
God will raise you to possess the land;
    you will gloat when the wicked are cut
    off.

Resh

35 I have seen ruthless scoundrels,
    strong as flourishing cedars. *t*
36 When I passed by again, they were gone;
    though I searched, they could not be
    found.

Shin

37 Observe the honest, mark the upright;
    those at peace with God have a fu-
    ture. *u*
38 But all sinners will be destroyed;
    the future of the wicked will be cut off.

Taw

39 The salvation of the just is from the
    LORD,
    their refuge in time of distress. *v*

---

o Ps 34, 14-15; Am 5, 14.—p Ps 25, 13; Prv 2, 21; Is 57, 13.—q
Prv 10, 31.—r Ps 40, 9; Dt 6, 6; Is 51, 7; Jer 31, 33.—s Ps 31,
24.—t Ps 92, 8-9; Is 2, 13; Ez 31, 10-11.—u Prv 23, 18; 24, 14.—
v Ps 9, 10; Is 25, 4.—w Ps 6, 2.—x Jb 6, 4; Lam 3, 12; Pss 31, 11;
64, 7.—y Is 1, 5-6.—z Ps 40, 13; Ezr 9, 6.—a Ps 35, 14.—b Ps
102, 4-6.—c Pss 6, 8; 31, 10.—d Ps 13, 4.—e Ps 32, 5; 51, 5.

Ps 38: In this lament, one of the Penitential Psalms (cf Ps 6),
the psalmist acknowledges the sin that has brought physical and
mental sickness and social ostracism. There is no one to turn to for
help; only God can undo the past and restore the psalmist.

---

40 The LORD helps and rescues them,
    rescues and saves them from the wick-
    ed,
    because in God they take refuge.

PSALM 38*

Prayer of an Afflicted Sinner

1 A psalm of David. For remembrance.

I

2 LORD, punish me no more in your anger;
    in your wrath do not chastise me! *w*
3 Your arrows have sunk deep in me; *x*
    your hand has come down upon me.
4 My flesh is afflicted because of your
    anger;
    my frame aches because of my sin. *y*
5 My iniquities overwhelm me,
    a burden beyond my strength. *z*

II

6 Foul and festering are my sores
    because of my folly.
7 I am stooped and deeply bowed; *a*
    all day I go about mourning.
8 My loins burn with fever;
    my flesh is afflicted.
9 I am numb and utterly crushed;
    I wail with anguish of heart. *b*
10 My Lord, my deepest yearning is before
    you;
    my groaning is not hidden from you.
11 My heart shudders, my strength forsakes
    me;
    the very light of my eyes has failed. *c*
12 Friends and companions shun my pain;
    my neighbors stand far off.
13 Those who seek my life lay snares for me;
    they seek my misfortune, they speak
    of ruin;
    they plot treachery all the day.

III

14 But I am like the deaf, hearing nothing,
    like the dumb, saying nothing,
15 Like someone who does not hear,
    who has no answer ready.
16 LORD, I wait for you;
    O Lord, my God, answer me. *d*
17 For I fear they will gloat,
    exult over me if I stumble.

IV

18 I am very near to falling;
    my pain is with me always.
19 I acknowledge my guilt
    and grieve over my sin. *e*
20 But many are my foes without cause,
    a multitude of enemies without
    reason,

Ps

21 Repaying me evil for good,
   harassing me for pursuing good.*f*
22 Forsake me not, O LORD;
   my God, be not far from me!*g*
23 Come quickly to help me,*h*
   my Lord and my salvation!

PSALM 39*

The Vanity of Life

1 For the leader, for Jeduthun.*i* A psalm of David.

I

2 I said, "I will watch my ways,
   lest I sin with my tongue;
   I will set a curb on my mouth."
3 Dumb and silent before the wicked,
   I refrained from any speech.
   But my sorrow increased;
4   my heart smoldered within me.*j*
   In my thoughts a fire blazed up,
   and I broke into speech:

II

5 LORD, let me know my end, the number
   of my days,
   that I may learn how frail I am.
6 You have given my days a very short
   span;
   my life is as nothing before you.
   All mortals are but a breath.*k* *Selah*
7 Mere phantoms, we go our way;
   mere vapor, our restless pursuits;
   we heap up stores without knowing
   for whom.
8 And now, Lord, what future do I have?
   You are my only hope.
9 From all my sins deliver me;
   let me not be the taunt of fools.

III

10 I was silent and did not open my mouth
   because you were the one who did this.
11 Take your plague away from me;
   I am ravaged by the touch of your
   hand.
12 You rebuke our guilt and chasten us;
   you dissolve all we prize like a cobweb.
   All mortals are but a breath. *Selah*
13 Listen to my prayer, LORD, hear my cry;
   do not be deaf to my weeping!
   I sojourn with you like a passing
   stranger,
   a guest, like all my ancestors.*l*
14 Turn your gaze from me, that I may find
   peace
   before I depart to be no more.

PSALM 40*

Gratitude and Prayer for Help

1 For the leader. A psalm of David.

A

I

2 I waited, waited for the LORD;
   who bent down and heard my cry,*m*
3 Drew me out of the pit of destruction,
   out of the mud of the swamp,*n*
   Set my feet upon rock,
   steadied my steps,
4 And put a new song* in my mouth,*o*
   a hymn to our God.
   Many shall look on in awe
   and they shall trust in the LORD.

II

5 Happy those whose trust is the LORD,
   who turn not to idolatry
   or to those who stray after falsehood.*p*
6 How numerous, O LORD, my God,
   you have made your wondrous deeds!
   And in your plans for us
   there is none to equal you.*q*
   Should I wish to declare or tell them,
   too many are they to recount.*r*

III

7 Sacrifice and offering you do not want;**s*
   but ears open to obedience you gave
   me.
   Holocausts and sin-offerings you do not
   require;
8   so I said, "Here I am;
   your commands for me are written in
   the scroll.

f Ps 109, 5.—*g* Pss 22, 2. 12. 20; 35, 22.—*h* Ps 40, 14.—*i* 1 Chr 16, 41; Pss 62, 1; 77, 1.—*j* Jer 20, 9.—*k* Pss 62, 10; 90, 9-10; 144, 4; Jb 7, 6. 16; 14, 1. 5; Eccl 6, 12; Wis 2, 5.—*l* Ps 119, 19; Gn 23, 4; Heb 11, 13; 1 Pt 2, 11.—*m* Lam 3, 25.—*n* Pss 28, 1; 30, 4; 69, 3. 15-16; 88, 5; Prv 1, 12; Jon 2, 7.—*o* Ps 33, 3.—*p* Ps 1, 1; Prv 16, 20; Jer 17, 7.—*q* Ps 35, 10.—*r* Pss 71, 15; 139, 17-18.—*s* 7-9: Heb 10, 5-7; Ps 51, 18-19; Am 5, 22; Hos 6, 6; Is 1, 11-15.

Ps 39: The lament of a mortally ill person who at first had resolved to remain silently submissive (2-4). But the grief was too much and now the psalmist laments the brevity and vanity of life (5-7), yet remaining hopeful (8-10). The psalmist continues to express both acceptance of the illness and hope for healing in 11-14.

Ps 40: A thanksgiving (2-13) has been combined with a lament (14-18), that appears also in Ps 70. The psalmist describes the rescue in spatial terms—being raised up from the swampy underworld to firm earth where one can praise God (2-4). All who trust God will experience like protection (5-6)! The psalm stipulates the precise mode of thanksgiving: not animal sacrifice but open and enthusiastic proclamation of the salvation just experienced (7-11). A prayer for protection concludes (12-18).

40, 4: *A new song:* a song in response to the new action of God (cf Pss 33, 3; 96, 1; 144, 9; 149, 1; Is 42, 10). Giving thanks is not purely a human response but is itself a divine gift.

40, 7-9: Obedience is better than sacrifice (cf 1 Sm 15, 22; Is 1, 10-20; Hos 6, 6; Am 5, 22-25; Mi 6, 6-8; Acts 7, 42-43 [quoting Am 5, 25-26 LXX]). Heb 10, 5-9 quotes the somewhat different Greek version and interprets it as Christ's self-oblation.

⁹ To do your will is my delight;
  my God, your law is in my heart!"ᵗ
¹⁰ I announced your deed to a great assembly;
  I did not restrain my lips;
  you, LORD, are my witness.ᵘ
¹¹ Your deed I did not hide within my heart;
  your loyal deliverance I have proclaimed.
  I made no secret of your enduring kindness
  to a great assembly.

B

I

¹² LORD, do not withhold your compassion from me;
  may your enduring kindness ever preserve me.ᵛ
¹³ For all about me are evils beyond count;
  my sins so overcome me I cannot see.
  They are more than the hairs of my head;
  my courage fails me.ʷ

II

¹⁴ LORD, graciously rescue me!ˣ
  Come quickly to help me, LORD!
¹⁵ Put to shame and confound
  all who seek to take my life.
  Turn back in disgrace
  those who desire my ruin.ʸ
¹⁶ Let those who say "Aha!"ᶻ
  know dismay and shame.
¹⁷ But may all who seek you
  rejoice and be glad in you.

---

t Ps 37, 31.—u Pss 22, 23; 26, 12; 35, 18; 149, 1.—v Ps 89, 34.—w Ps 38, 5. 11; Ezr 9, 6.—x 14-18: Pss 70, 2-6; 71, 12.—y Ps 35, 4. 26.—z Ps 35, 21. 25.—a Ps 35, 27.—b Tb 4, 7-11.—c Pss 31, 12; 38, 12-13; 88, 8; Jb 19, 13-19; Jer 20, 10.—d Ps 55, 14-15; Jn 13, 18.—e Neh 9, 5.

Ps 41: A thanksgiving for rescue from illness (4. 5. 9). Many people, even friends, have interpreted the illness as a divine punishment for sin and have ostracized the psalmist (5-11). The healing shows the return of God's favor and rebukes the psalmist's detractors (12-13).

41, 2: *Happy those concerned for the lowly and poor:* other psalms use the same formula ("Happy those") for those whom God favors. Cf Ps 32, 1-2; 34, 9; 40, 5; 65, 5. The psalmist's statement about God's love of the poor is based on the experience of being rescued (1-3).

41, 10: *Even the friend . . . has scorned me:* Jn 13, 18 cites this verse to characterize Judas as a false friend. *Scorned me:* an interpretation of the unclear Hebrew, "made great the heel against me."

41, 11: *That I may repay them as they deserve:* the healing itself is an act of judgment through which God decides for the psalmist and against the false friends. The prayer is not necessarily for strength to punish enemies.

41, 14: The doxology, not part of the psalm, marks the end of the first of the five books of the Psalter. Compare Pss 72, 18-20; 89, 53; 106, 48.

May those who long for your help
  always say, "The LORD be glorified."ᵃ
¹⁸ Though I am afflicted and poor,
  the Lord keeps me in mind.
  You are my help and deliverer;
  my God, do not delay!

PSALM 41*

Thanksgiving after Sickness

¹ For the leader. A psalm of David.

I

² Happy those concerned for the lowly and poor;*
  when misfortune strikes, the LORD delivers them.ᵇ
³ The LORD keeps and preserves them,
  makes them happy in the land,
  and does not betray them to their enemies.
⁴ The LORD sustains them on their sickbed,
  allays the malady when they are ill.

II

⁵ Once I prayed, "LORD, have mercy on me;
  heal me, I have sinned against you.
⁶ My enemies say the worst of me:
  'When will that one die and be forgotten?'
⁷ When people come to visit me,
  they speak without sincerity.
  Their hearts store up malice;
  they leave and spread their vicious lies.ᶜ
⁸ My foes all whisper against me;
  they imagine the worst about me:
⁹ I have a deadly disease, they say;
  I will never rise from my sickbed.
¹⁰ Even the friend who had my trust,
  who shared my table, has scorned me.*ᵈ
¹¹ But you, LORD, have mercy and raise me up
  that I may repay them as they deserve."*

III

¹² By this I know you are pleased with me,
  that my enemy no longer jeers at me.
¹³ For my integrity you have supported me
  and let me stand in your presence forever.

* * *

¹⁴ Blessed be the LORD, the God of Israel,*
  from all eternity and forever.
  Amen. Amen.ᵉ

SECOND BOOK — PSALMS 42–72

PSALMS 42—43*

Longing for God's Presence in the Temple

1 For the leader. A *maskil* of the Korahites.*

I

2 As the deer longs for streams of water,[f]
   so my soul longs for you, O God.
3 My being thirsts for God, the living God.
   When can I go and see the face of
   God?*[g]
4 My tears have been my food day and
   night,[h]
   as they ask daily, "Where is your
   God?"[i]
5 Those times I recall
   as I pour out my soul,[j]
   When I went in procession with the
   crowd,
   I went with them to the house of God,
   Amid loud cries of thanksgiving,
   with the multitude keeping festival.[k]
6 Why are you downcast, my soul;
   why do you groan within me?
   Wait for God, whom I shall praise again,
   my savior and my God.

II

7 My soul is downcast within me;
   therefore I will remember you
   From the land of the Jordan* and Hermon,
   from the land of Mount Mizar.[l]
8 Here deep calls to deep* in the roar of
   your torrents.
   All your waves and breakers sweep
   over me.[m]
9 At dawn may the LORD bestow faithful
   love
   that I may sing praise through the
   night,
   praise to the God of my life.
10 I say to God, "My rock,
   why do you forget me?[n]
   Why must I go about mourning
   with the enemy oppressing me?"
11 It shatters my bones, when my adversaries reproach me.
   They say to me daily: "Where is your
   God?"
12 Why are you downcast, my soul,
   why do you groan within me?
   Wait for God, whom I shall praise again,
   my savior and my God.

III

1 Grant me justice, God;
   defend me from a faithless people;
   from the deceitful and unjust rescue
   me.[o]
2 You, God, are my strength.
   Why then do you spurn me?
   Why must I go about mourning,
   with the enemy oppressing me?
3 Send your light and fidelity,*
   that they may be my guide[p]
   And bring me to your holy mountain,
   to the place of your dwelling,[q]
4 That I may come to the altar of God,
   to God, my joy, my delight.
   Then I will praise you with the harp,
   O God, my God.
5 Why are you downcast, my soul?
   Why do you groan within me?
   Wait for God, whom I shall praise again,
   my savior and my God.

PSALM 44*

God's Past Favor and Israel's Present Need

1 For the leader. A *maskil* of the Korahites.

I

2 O God, we have heard with our own ears;
   our ancestors have told us[r]

---

f 2-3: Pss 63, 2; 84, 3; 143, 6; Is 26, 9.—g Ps 27, 4.—h Pss
80, 6; 102, 10.—i Ps 79, 10; Jl 2, 17.—j Lam 3, 20.—k Ps 122,
5.—l Ps 43, 3.—m Pss 18, 5; 32, 6; 69, 2; 88, 8; Jon 2, 4.—n
Pss 18, 2; 31, 3-4.—o Ps 119, 154.—p Pss 18, 29; 27, 1; 36,
10; Mi 7, 8.—q Ps 122, 1.—r Ps 78, 3.

Pss 42–43: Pss 42—43 form a single lament of three sections,
each section ending in an identical refrain (42, 6. 12; 43, 5). The
psalmist is in the extreme north of Israel, far from Jerusalem,
and longs for the divine presence that Israel experienced in the
temple liturgy. Despite sadness, the psalmist hopes once again to
join the worshiping crowds.
42, 1: *The Korahites:* a major guild of temple singers (2 Chr
20, 19) whose name appears in the superscriptions of Pss 42;
44—49; 84—85; 87—88.
42, 3: *See the face of God:* "face" designates a personal
presence (Gn 33, 10; Ex 10, 28-29; 2 Sm 17, 11). The expressions
"see God/God's face" occur elsewhere (Pss 11, 7; 17, 15; 63, 3;
cf Ex 24, 10; 33, 7-11; Jb 33, 26) for the presence of God in the
temple.
42, 7: *From the land of the Jordan:* the sources of the
Jordan are in the foothills of Mount Hermon in present-day southern Lebanon. Mount Mizar is presumed to be a mountain in the
same range.
42, 8: *Here deep calls to deep:* to the psalmist, the waters
arising in the north are overwhelming and far from God's presence,
like the waters of chaos (Pss 18, 5; 69, 2-3. 15; Jon 2, 3-6).
43, 3: *Your light and fidelity:* a pair of divine attributes
personified as guides for the pilgrimage. The psalmist seeks divine
protection for the journey to Jerusalem.
Ps 44: In this lament the community reminds God of past favors
which it has always acknowledged (2-9). But now God has abandoned Israel to defeat and humiliation (10-17), though the people
are not conscious of any sin against the covenant (18-23). They
struggle with being God's special people amid divine silence; yet
they continue to pray (24-27).

The deeds you did in their days,
    with your own hand in days of old:
3 You rooted out nations to plant them,[s]
    crushed peoples to make room for
    them.
4 Not with their own swords did they
    conquer the land,[t]
    nor did their own arms bring victory;
It was your right hand, your own arm,
    the light of your face, for you favored
    them.[u]
5 You are my king and my God,[v]
    who bestows victories on Jacob.
6 Through you we batter our foes;
    through your name, trample our ad-
    versaries.
7 Not in my bow do I trust,
    nor does my sword bring me victory.
8 You have brought us victory over our
    enemies,
    shamed those who hate us.
9 In God we have boasted all the day
    long;
    your name we will praise forever.
Selah

II
10 But now you have rejected and dis-
    graced us;[w]
    you do not march out with our ar-
    mies.[x]
11 You make us retreat* before the foe;
    those who hate us plunder us at will.[y]
12 You hand us over like sheep to be
    slaughtered,
    scatter us among the nations.[z]

13 You sell your people for nothing;
    you make no profit from their sale.[a]
14 You make us the reproach of our neigh-
    bors,[b]
    the mockery and scorn of those
    around us.
15 You make us a byword among the na-
    tions;
    the peoples shake their heads at us.
16 All day long my disgrace is before me;
    shame has covered my face
17 At the sound of those who taunt and re-
    vile,
    at the sight of the spiteful enemy.

III
18 All this has come upon us,
    though we have not forgotten you,
    nor been disloyal to your covenant.
19 Our hearts have not turned back,*
    nor have our steps strayed from your
    path.
20 Yet you have left us crushed,
    desolate in a place of jackals;*[c]
    you have covered us with darkness.
21 If we had forgotten the name of our
    God,
    stretched out our hands to another
    god,
22 Would not God have discovered this,
    God who knows the secrets of the
    heart?
23 For you we are slain all the day long,
    considered only as sheep to be
    slaughtered.[d]

IV
24 Awake! Why do you sleep, O Lord?
    Rise up! Do not reject us forever![e]
25 Why do you hide your face;[f]
    why forget our pain and misery?
26 We are bowed down to the ground;[g]
    our bodies are pressed to the earth.
27 Rise up, help us!
    Redeem us as your love demands.

---

s Pss 78, 55; 80, 9f.—t Dt 8, 17f; Jos 24, 12.—u Pss 4, 7; 31, 17; 67, 2; 80, 4; Nm 6, 25; Dn 9, 17.—v Ps 145, 1.—w 10-27: Ps 89, 39-52.—x Ps 60, 12.—y Lv 26, 17; Dt 28, 25.—z Lv 26, 33; Dt 28, 64.—a Dt 32, 30; Is 52, 3.—b 14-17: Pss 79, 4; 80, 7; 123, 3-4; Jb 12, 4; Dn 9, 16.—c Jer 9, 10.—d Rom 8, 36.—e Pss 10, 1; 74, 1; 77, 8; 79, 5; 83, 2.—f Pss 10, 11; 89, 47; Jb 13, 24.—g Ps 119, 25.

44, 11: *You make us retreat:* the corollary of v 4. Defeat, like victory, is God's doing; neither Israel nor its enemies can claim credit (23).

44, 19: *Our hearts have not turned back:* Israel's defeat was not caused by its lack of fidelity.

44, 20: *A place of jackals:* following Israel's defeat and exile (11-12), the land lies desolate, inhabited only by jackals. Cf Is 13, 22; Jer 9, 10; 10, 22. Others take *tannim* as "sea monster" (cf Ez 29, 3; 32, 2) and render: "you crushed us as you did the sea monster."

Ps 45: A song for the Davidic king's marriage to a foreign princess from Tyre in Phoenicia. The court poet sings (2. 18) of God's choice of the king (3. 8), of his role in establishing divine rule (4-8), and of his splendor as he waits for his bride (9-10). The woman is to forget her own house when she becomes wife to the king (11-13). Her majestic beauty today is a sign of the future prosperity of the royal house (14-18). The psalm was retained in the collection when there was no reigning king, and came to be applied to the king who was to come, the messiah.

PSALM 45*

Song for a Royal Wedding

1 For the leader; according to "Lilies." A *mas-kil* of the Korahites. A love song.

I
2 My heart is stirred by a noble theme,
    as I sing my ode to the king.
    My tongue is the pen of a nimble
    scribe.

Ps

II

3 You are the most handsome of men;
    fair speech has graced your lips,
    for God has blessed you forever.[h]

4 Gird your sword upon your hip, mighty
    warrior!
    In splendor and majesty ride on
    triumphant![i]

5 In the cause of truth and justice
    may your right hand show you won-
    drous deeds.

6 Your arrows are sharp;
    peoples will cower at your feet;
    the king's enemies will lose heart.

7 Your throne, O god,* stands forever;[j]
    your royal scepter is a scepter for jus-
    tice.

8 You love justice and hate wrongdoing;
    therefore God, your God, has
    anointed you
    with the oil of gladness above your
    fellow kings.

9 With myrrh, aloes, and cassia
    your robes are fragrant.
    From ivory-paneled palaces*
    stringed instruments bring you joy.

10 Daughters of kings are your lovely
    wives;
    a princess arrayed in Ophir's gold*
    comes to stand at your right hand.

III

11 Listen, my daughter, and understand;
    pay me careful heed.
    Forget your people and your father's
    house,*

12   that the king might desire your
    beauty.
    He is your lord;

13   honor him, daughter of Tyre.
    Then the richest of the people
    will seek your favor with gifts.[k]

14 All glorious is the king's daughter as she
    enters,[l]
    her raiment threaded with gold;

15 In embroidered apparel she is led to the
    king.
    The maids of her train are presented
    to the king.

16 They are led in with glad and joyous
    acclaim;
    they enter the palace of the king.

IV

17 The throne of your fathers your sons
    will have;
    you shall make them princes through
    all the land.[m]

18 I will make your name renowned
    through all generations;
    thus nations shall praise you forever.[n]

PSALM 46*

God, the Protector of Zion

1 For the leader. A song of the Korahites. According to *alamoth.**

I

2 God is our refuge and our strength,
    an ever-present help in distress.[o]

3 Thus we do not fear, though earth be
    shaken*
    and mountains quake to the depths of
    the sea,

4 Though its waters rage and foam
    and mountains totter at its surging.[p]
    The LORD of hosts is with us;*
    our stronghold is the God of Jacob.
              Selah

II

5 Streams of the river gladden the city of
    God,*
    the holy dwelling of the Most High.[q]

6 God is in its midst; it shall not be
    shaken;
    God will help it at break of day.[r]

---

h Song 5, 10-16.—i Ps 21, 5.—j 7-8: Heb 1, 8-9.—k Ps 72,
10-11; Is 60, 5f.—l 14-16: Ez 16, 10-13.—m Gn 17, 6.—n Is 60,
15.—o Ps 48, 4: Is 33, 2.—p Ps 93, 3-4; Jb 9, 5-6; Is 24, 18-20;
54, 10.—q Pss 48, 2-3; 76, 3.—r Is 7, 14.

45, 7: *O god:* the king, in courtly language, is called "god,"
i.e., more than human, representing God to the people. Heb 1, 8-
9 applies 7-8 to Christ.

45, 9: *Ivory-paneled palaces:* literally, "palaces of ivory."
Ivory paneling and furniture decoration have been found in
Samaria and other ancient Near Eastern cities. Cf Am 3, 15.

45, 10: *Ophir's gold:* uncertain location, possibly a region on
the coast of southern Arabia or eastern Africa, famous for its
gold. Cf 1 Kgs 9, 28; 10, 11; Jb 22, 24.

45, 11: *Forget your people and your father's house:* the
bride should no longer consider herself a daughter of her father's
house, but the wife of the king—the queen.

Ps 46: A song of confidence in God's protection of Zion with
close parallels to Ps 48. The dominant note is sounded by the refrain, *The LORD of hosts is with us* (4. 8. 12). The first strophe
(2-4) sings of the security of God's presence even in utter chaos;
the second (5-8), of divine protection of the city from its enemies;
the third (9-12), of God's imposition of imperial peace.

46, 1: *Alamoth:* the melody of the psalm, now lost.

46, 3-4: Figurative ancient Near Eastern language to describe
social and political upheavals.

46, 4b: The first line of the refrain is similar in structure and
meaning to Isaiah's name for the royal child, Immanuel, *With us
is God* (Is 7, 14; 8, 8. 10).

46, 5: Jerusalem is not situated on a river. This description derives from mythological descriptions of the divine abode and symbolizes the divine presence as the source of all life (cf Is 33, 21;
Ez 47, 1-12; Jl 4, 18; Zec 14, 8; Rv 22, 1-2).

7 Though nations rage and kingdoms totter,
God's voice thunders and the earth trembles.[s]
8 The LORD of hosts is with us;
our stronghold is the God of Jacob.
Selah

III
9 Come and see the works of the LORD,
who has done fearsome deeds on earth;[t]
10 Who stops wars to the ends of the earth,
breaks the bow, splinters the spear,
and burns the shields with fire;[u]
11 Who says:
"Be still and confess that I am God!
I am exalted among the nations,
exalted on the earth."[v]
12 The LORD of hosts is with us;
our stronghold is the God of Jacob.
Selah

---

s Pss 2, 1-5; 48, 5-8; 76, 7-9; Is 17, 12-14.—t Ps 48, 9-10.—u Ps 76, 4.—v Ps 40, 11. —w Ps 89, 16; Zep 3, 14.—x Ps 95, 3; Ex 15, 18; Is 24, 23; 52, 7.—y Ps 2, 8.—z Is 58, 14.—a Pss 24, 8. 10; 68, 18-19; 98, 6.—b 8-9: Pss 72, 11; 93, 1; 96, 10; 97, 1; 99, 1; Jer 10, 7.—c Ps 89, 19; Ex 3, 6; Is 2, 2-4.—d Pss 96, 4; 145, 3.—e Ps 50, 2; Lam 2, 15.—f Is 14, 13.—g Jgs 5, 19.—h Ex 15, 14; Jer 4, 31.

Ps 47: A hymn calling on the nations to acknowledge the universal rule of Israel's God (2-5) who is enthroned as king over Israel and the nations (6-10).

47, 5: *Our heritage . . . the glory:* the land of Israel (cf Is 58, 14), which God has given Israel in an act of sovereignty.

47, 6: *God mounts the throne:* "has gone up to the throne," according to the context (9). Christian liturgical tradition has applied the verse to the ascension of Christ.

Ps 48: A Zion hymn, praising the holy city as the invincible dwelling place of God. Unconquerable, it is an apt symbol of God who has defeated all enemies. After seven epithets describing the city (2-3), the psalm describes the victory by the Divine Warrior over hostile kings (4-8). The second half proclaims the dominion of the God of Zion over all the earth (9-12) and invites pilgrims to announce that God is eternally invincible like Zion itself (13-15).

48, 1: *Korahites:* see note on Ps 42, 1.

48, 3: *The heights of Zaphon:* the mountain abode of the Canaanite storm-god Baal in comparable texts. To speak of Zion as if it were Zaphon was to claim for Israel's God what Canaanites claimed for Baal. Though topographically speaking Zion is only a hill, viewed religiously it towers over other mountains as the home of the supreme God (cf Ps 68, 16-17).

48, 6: *When they looked:* the kings are stunned by the sight of Zion, touched by divine splendor. The language is that of holy war, in which the enemy panics and flees at the sight of divine glory.

48, 8: *The ships of Tarshish:* large ships, named after the distant land or port of Tarshish, probably ancient Tartessus in southern Spain, although other identifications have been proposed. Cf Is 2, 16; 60, 9; Jon 1, 3.

PSALM 47*

The Ruler of All the Nations

1 For the leader. A psalm of the Korahites.

I
2 All you peoples, clap your hands;
shout to God with joyful cries.[w]
3 For the LORD, the Most High, inspires awe,
the great king over all the earth,[x]
4 Who made people subject to us,
brought nations under our feet,[y]
5 Who chose a land for our heritage,
the glory* of Jacob, the beloved.[z]
Selah

II
6 God mounts the throne* amid shouts of joy;
the LORD, amid trumpet blasts.[a]
7 Sing praise to God, sing praise;
sing praise to our king, sing praise.

III
8 God is king over all the earth;[b]
sing hymns of praise.
9 God rules over the nations;
God sits upon his holy throne.
10 The princes of the peoples assemble
with the people of the God of Abraham.
For the rulers of the earth belong to God,
who is enthroned on high.[c]

PSALM 48*

The Splendor of the Invincible City

1 A psalm of the Korahites.* A song.

I
2 Great is the LORD and highly praised
in the city of our God:[d]
The holy mountain, 3 fairest of heights,
the joy of all the earth,[e]
Mount Zion, the heights of Zaphon,*[f]
the city of the great king.

II
4 God is its citadel,
renowned as a stronghold.
5 See! The kings assembled,
together they invaded.
6 When they looked* they were astounded;
terrified, they were put to flight![g]
7 Trembling seized them there,
anguish, like a woman's labor,[h]
8 As when the east wind wrecks
the ships of Tarshish!*

III

9 What we had heard we now see*
 in the city of the LORD of hosts,
In the city of our God,
 founded to last forever. *Selah*
10 O God, within your temple
 we ponder your steadfast love.
11 Like your name, O God,
 your praise reaches the ends of the
 earth.[i]
Your right hand is fully victorious.
12 Mount Zion is glad!
The cities of Judah rejoice
 because of your saving deeds![j]

IV

13 Go about Zion, walk all around it,
 note the number of its towers.
14 Consider the ramparts, examine its
 citadels,
 that you may tell future generations:[k]
15 "Yes, so mighty is God,*
 our God who leads us always!"

PSALM 49*

Confidence in God rather than in Riches

1 For the leader. A psalm of the Korahites.*

2 Hear this, all you peoples!
 Give ear, all who inhabit the world,
3 You of lowly birth or high estate,
 rich and poor alike.
4 My mouth shall speak wisdom,
 my heart shall offer insight.[l]
5 I will turn my attention to a problem,*
 expound my question to the music of
 a lyre.

I

6 Why should I fear in evil days,
 when my wicked pursuers ring me
 round,
7 Those who trust in their wealth
 and boast of their abundant riches?[m]
8 One cannot redeem oneself,*
 pay to God a ransom.[n]
9 Too high the price to redeem a life;
 one would never have enough
10 To stay alive forever
 and never see the pit.
11 Anyone can see that the wisest die,
 the fool and the senseless pass away
 too,[o]
 and must leave their wealth to others.[p]
12 Tombs are their homes forever,
 their dwellings through all generations,
 though they gave their names to their
 lands.

13 For all their riches
 mortals do not abide;
 they perish like the beasts.[q]

II

14 This is the destiny of those who trust in
 folly,
 the end of those so pleased with their
 wealth. *Selah*
15 Like sheep they are herded into Sheol,
 where death will be their shepherd.
Straight to the grave they descend,
 where their form will waste away,
Sheol will be their palace.
16 But God will redeem my life, *Selah*
 will take me* from the power of
 Sheol.[r]
17 Do not fear when others become rich,
 when the wealth of their houses grows
 great.
18 When they die they will take nothing
 with them,
 their wealth will not follow them down.[s]
19 When living, they congratulate themselves and say:
 "All praise you, you do so well."
20 But they will join the company of their
 forebears,
 never again to see the light.[t]
21 For all their riches,
 if mortals do not have wisdom,
 they perish like the beasts.

i Mal 1, 11.—j Ps 97, 8.—k Pss 22, 31-32; 71, 18.—l Ps 78, 2;
Mt 13, 35.—m Jb 31, 24.—n Prv 10, 15; 11, 4; Ez 7, 19; Mt 16,
26.—o Eccl 2, 16.—p Ps 39, 7; Sir 11, 18-19.—q Eccl 3, 18-21.—
r Pss 16, 10; 86, 13; 103, 4; 116, 8.—s Sir 11, 18-19; Eccl 5, 15;
1 Tm 6, 7.—t Jb 10, 21-22.

48, 9: *What we had heard we now see:* the glorious things
that new pilgrims had heard about the holy city—its beauty and
awesomeness—they now see with their own eyes. The seeing here
contrasts with the seeing of the hostile kings in 6.
48, 15: *So mighty is God:* Israel's God is like Zion in being
eternal and invincible. The holy city is therefore a kind of "sacrament" of God.
Ps 49: The psalm affirms confidence in God (cf Pss 23; 27, 1-6;
62) in the face of the apparent good fortune of the unjust rich. Cf
Pss 37; 73. Reliance on wealth is misplaced (8-10) for it is of no
avail in the face of death (18-20). After inviting all to listen to this
axiom of faith (2-5), the psalmist depicts the self-delusion of the
ungodly (6-13), whose destiny is to die like ignorant beasts (13. 18;
cf Prv 7, 21-23). Their wealth should occasion no alarm, for they
will come to nought, whereas God will save the just (14-21).
49, 1: *Korahites:* see note on Ps 42, 1.
49, 5: *Problem:* the psalmist's personal solution to the perennial biblical problem of the prosperity of the wicked. *Question:*
parallel in meaning to *problem;* in Wisdom literature it means the
mysterious way of how the world works.
49, 8: *One cannot redeem oneself:* an axiom. For the practice
of redemption, cf Jb 6, 21-23. A play on the first Hebrew word of v
8 and v 16 relates the two verses.
49, 16: *Will take me:* the same Hebrew verb is used of God
"taking up" a favored servant: Enoch in Gn 5, 24; Elijah in 2 Kgs 2,
11-12; the righteous person in Ps 73, 24. The verse apparently
states the hope that God will rescue the faithful psalmist in the
same manner.

PSALM 50*

The Acceptable Sacrifice

1 A psalm of Asaph.

I
The LORD, the God of gods,
   has spoken and summoned the earth
   from the rising of the sun to its setting.[u]
2 From Zion God shines forth,[v]
   perfect in beauty.
3 Our God comes and will not be silent!
   Devouring fire precedes,
   storming fiercely round about.[w]
4 God summons the heavens above
   and the earth to the judgment of his
   people:
5 "Gather my faithful ones before me,
   those who made a covenant with me
   by sacrifice."
6 The heavens proclaim divine justice,
   for God alone is the judge.[x]   *Selah*

II
7 "Listen, my people, I will speak;
   Israel, I will testify against you;
   God, your God, am I.
8 Not for your sacrifices do I rebuke you,
   nor for your holocausts, set before me
   daily.
9 I need no bullock from your house,
   no goats from your fold.[y]

---

u Dt 10, 17; Jos 22, 22.—v Ps 48, 2.—w Ps 97, 3; Dn 7, 10.—
x Pss 19, 2; 97, 6.—y Ps 69, 32; Am 5, 21-22.—z Pss 24, 1; 89,
12; Dt 10, 14; 1 Cor 10, 26.—a Heb 13, 15.—b Ps 77, 3. —c Ps
91, 16.—d 2 Sm 12.

Ps 50: A covenant lawsuit stating that the sacrifice God really
wants is the sacrifice of praise accompanied by genuine obedience
(cf Mi 6, 1-8). It begins with a theophany and the summoning of
the court (1-6). Then in direct address God explains what is required of the faithful (7-15), rebukes the hypocritical worshiper
(16-21), and concludes with a threat and a promise (22-23; cf Is
1, 19-20).
  Ps 51: A lament, the most famous of the seven Penitential
Psalms, prays for the removal of the personal and social disorders
that sin has brought. The poem has two parts of approximately
equal length: 3-10 and 11-19, and a conclusion in 20-21. The two
parts interlock by repetition of "blot out" in the first verse of
each section (3. 11), of "wash (away)" just after the first verse
of each section (4) and just before the last verse (9) of the first
section, and of "heart," "God," and "spirit" in 12 and 19. The
first part (3-10) asks deliverance from sin, which is not just a past
act but its emotional, physical, and social consequences. The second part (11-19) seeks something more profound than wiping the
slate clean: nearness to God, living by the spirit of God (12-13),
like the relation between God and people described in Jer 31, 33-
34. Nearness to God brings joy and the authority to teach sinners
(15-16). Such proclamation is better than offering sacrifice (17-
19). The last two verses ask for the rebuilding of Jerusalem (20-
21).

10 For every animal of the forest is mine,
   beasts by the thousands on my mountains.
11 I know every bird of the heavens;
   the creatures of the field belong to
   me.
12 Were I hungry, I would not tell you,
   for mine is the world and all that fills
   it.[z]
13 Do I eat the flesh of bulls
   or drink the blood of goats?
14 Offer praise as your sacrifice to God;[a]
   fulfill your vows to the Most High.
15 Then call on me in time of distress;[b]
   I will rescue you, and you shall honor
   me."

III
16 But to the wicked God says:
   "Why do you recite my commandments
   and profess my covenant with your
   lips?
17 You hate discipline;
   you cast my words behind you!
18 When you see thieves, you befriend
   them;
   with adulterers you throw in your lot.
19 You give your mouth free rein for evil;
   you harness your tongue to deceit.
20 You sit maligning your own kin,
   slandering the child of your own
   mother.
21 When you do these things should I be
   silent?
   Or do you think that I am like you?
   I accuse you, I lay the charge before
   you.

IV
22 "Understand this, you who forget God,
   lest I attack you with no one to rescue.
23 Those who offer praise as a sacrifice
   honor me;
   to the obedient I will show the salvation of God."[c]

PSALM 51*

The Miserere: Prayer of Repentance

1 For the leader. A psalm of David, 2 when
Nathan the prophet came to him after his affair
with Bathsheba.[d]

I
3 Have mercy on me, God, in your goodness;
   in your abundant compassion blot
   out my offense.

4 Wash away all my guilt;
  from my sin cleanse me.
5 For I know my offense;
  my sin is always before me.*e*
6 Against you alone have I sinned;
  I have done such evil in your sight
  That you are just in your sentence,
  blameless when you condemn.*f*
7 True, I was born guilty,
  a sinner, even as my mother conceived me.**g*
8 Still, you insist on sincerity of heart;
  in my inmost being teach me wisdom.
9 Cleanse me with hyssop,* that I may be pure;
  wash me, make me whiter than snow.*h*
10 Let me hear sounds of joy and gladness;
   let the bones you have crushed rejoice.

II

11 Turn away your face from my sins;
   blot out all my guilt.
12 A clean heart create for me, God;
   renew in me a steadfast spirit.*i*
13 Do not drive me from your presence,
   nor take from me your holy spirit.*j*
14 Restore my joy in your salvation;
   sustain in me a willing spirit.
15 I will teach the wicked your ways,
   that sinners may return to you.
16 Rescue me from death, God, my saving God,
   that my tongue may praise your healing power.*k*
17 Lord, open my lips;
   my mouth will proclaim your praise.
18 For you do not desire sacrifice;*
   a burnt offering you would not accept.*l*
19 My sacrifice, God, is a broken spirit;
   God, do not spurn a broken, humbled heart.

III

20 Make Zion prosper in your good pleasure;*
   rebuild the walls of Jerusalem.*m*
21 Then you will be pleased with proper sacrifice,
   burnt offerings and holocausts;
   then bullocks will be offered on your altar.

PSALM 52*

The Deceitful Tongue

1 For the leader. A *maskil* of David, 2 when Doeg the Edomite went and told Saul, "David went to the house of Ahimelech."*n*

I

3 Why do you glory in evil,
  you scandalous liar?
  All day long 4 you plot destruction;
  your tongue is like a sharpened razor,
  you skillful deceiver.*o*
5 You love evil rather than good,
  lies rather than honest speech.*p*
                                     Selah
6 You love any word that destroys,
  you deceitful tongue.*q*

II

7 Now God will strike you down,
  leave you crushed forever,
  Pluck you from your tent,
  uproot you from the land of the living.*r*
                                     Selah
8 The righteous will look on with awe;
  they will jeer and say:*s*
9 "That one did not take God as a refuge,
  but trusted in great wealth,
  relied on devious plots."*t*

---

e Pss 32, 5; 38, 19; Is 59, 12.—f Rom 3, 4.—g Jb 14, 4.—h Jb 9, 30; Is 1, 18; Ez 36, 25.—i Ez 11, 19.—j Wis 1, 5; 9, 17; Is 63, 11; Hg 2, 5; Rom 8, 9.—k Ps 30, 10.—l Pss 40, 7; 50, 8; Am 5, 21-22; Hos 6, 6; Is 1, 11-15; Heb 10, 5-7.—m Jer 31, 4; Ez 36, 33.—n 1 Sm 21, 8; 22, 6ff.—o Pss 12, 3; 59, 8; 120, 2-3; Sir 51, 3.—p Jer 4, 22; Jn 3, 19-20.—q Jer 9, 4.—r Pss 27, 13; 28, 5; 56, 14; Jb 18, 14; Prv 2, 22; Is 38, 11.—s Pss 44, 14; 64, 9.—t Jb 31, 24; Prv 11, 28.

51, 7: *A sinner, even as my mother conceived me:* literally, "In iniquity was I conceived," an instance of hyperbole: at no time was the psalmist ever without sin. Cf Ps 88, 16, "I am mortally afflicted since youth," i.e., I have always been afflicted. The verse does not imply that the sexual act of conception is sinful.

51, 9: *Hyssop:* a small bush whose many woody twigs make a natural sprinkler. It was prescribed in the Mosaic law as an instrument for sprinkling sacrificial blood or lustral water for cleansing. Cf Ex 12, 22; Lv 14, 4; Nm 19, 18.

51, 18: *For you do not desire sacrifice:* the mere offering of the ritual sacrifice apart from good dispositions is not acceptable to God. Cf Ps 50.

51, 20-21: Most scholars think that these verses were added to the psalm some time after the destruction of the temple in 587 B.C. The verses assume that the rebuilt temple will be an ideal site for national reconciliation.

Ps 52: A condemnation of the powerful and arrogant (3-6), who bring down upon themselves God's judgment (7). The just, those who trust in God alone, are gladdened and strengthened by the downfall of their traditional enemies (8-11).

III

¹⁰ But I, like an olive tree* in the house of
God,ᵘ
trust in God's faithful love forever.
¹¹ I will praise you always
for what you have done.
I will proclaim before the faithfulᵛ
that your name is good.

PSALM 53*

A Lament over Widespread Corruption

¹ For the leader; according to *Mahalath*. A
maskil of David.

I

² Fools say in their hearts,ʷ
"There is no God."ˣ
Their deeds are loathsome and corrupt;
not one does what is right.
³ God looks down from heaven
upon the human race,ʸ
To see if even one is wise,ᶻ
if even one seeks God.
⁴ All have gone astray;
all alike are perverse.
Not one does what is right, not even
one.ᵃ

II

⁵ Will these evildoers never learn?
They devour my people as they devour bread;ᵇ
they do not call upon God.ᶜ

---

u Pss 1, 3; 92, 12-14; Jer 11, 16; 17, 8.—v Pss 22, 23; 26,
12; 35, 18; 149, 1.—w 2-6a: Ps 14, 1-5a.—x Pss 10, 4; 36, 2;
Is 32, 6; Jer 5, 12.—y Pss 11, 4; 102, 20.—z 2b-3: Rom 3, 11-
12.—a Ps 12, 2.—b Ps 27, 2; Is 9, 11.—c Ps 79, 6.—d Ps 85,
2.—e 1 Sm 23, 19; 26, 1.—f Ps 86, 14.—g Ps 118, 7.—h Ps
143, 12.—i Pss 59, 11; 91, 8; 92, 12.—j 2-3: Pss 5, 2-3; 55, 2-
3; 86, 6; 130, 1-2; Lam 3, 56; Jon 2, 3.

52, 10: *Like a green olive tree:* the righteous will flourish in
the house of God like a well-watered olive tree. Cf Pss 92, 14;
128, 3.
Ps 53: A lament of an individual, duplicated in Ps 14, except
that "God" is used for "the LORD," and v 6 is different. See under
Ps 14.
Ps 54: A lament in which the person under attack calls directly
upon God for help (3-5). Refusing to despair, the psalmist hopes
in God, who is active in history and just (6-7). The psalm ends
with a serene promise to return thanks (8-9).
54, 3: *By your name:* one is present in one's name, hence
God as revealed to humans.
Ps 55: The psalmist, betrayed by intimate friends (14-15, 21-
22), prays that God punish those oath breakers and thus be acknowledged as the protector of the wronged. The sufferings of
the psalmist include both ostracism (4) and mental turmoil (5-6),
culminating in the wish to flee society (7-9). The wish for a sudden death for one's enemies (16) occurs elsewhere in the psalms;
an example of such a death is the earth opening under the wicked
Dathan and Abiram (Nm 16, 31-32). The psalmist, confident of
vindication, exhorts others to a like trust in the God of justice (23-
24). The psalm is not so much for personal vengeance as for a
public vindication of God's righteousness now. There was no belief in an afterlife where such vindication could take place.

⁶ They have good reason to fear,
though now they do not fear.
For God will certainly scatter
the bones of the godless.
They will surely be put to shame,
for God has rejected them.

III

⁷ Oh, that from Zion might come
the deliverance of Israel,
That Jacob may rejoice and Israel be
gladᵈ
when God restores the people!

PSALM 54*

Confident Prayer in Great Peril

¹ For the leader. On stringed instruments. A
maskil of David, ² when the Ziphites came and
said to Saul, "David is hiding among us."ᵉ

I

³ O God, by your name* save me.
By your strength defend my cause.
⁴ O God, hear my prayer.
Listen to the words of my mouth.
⁵ The arrogant have risen against me;
the ruthless seek my life;
they do not keep God before them.ᶠ
Selah

II

⁶ God is present as my helper;ᵍ
the Lord sustains my life.
⁷ Turn back the evil upon my foes;
in your faithfulness, destroy them.ʰ
⁸ Then I will offer you generous sacrifice
and praise your gracious name,
LORD,
⁹ Because it has rescued me from every
trouble,
and my eyes look down on my foes.ⁱ

PSALM 55*

A Lament over Betrayal

¹ For the leader. On stringed instruments. A
maskil of David.

I

² Listen, God, to my prayer;ʲ
do not hide from my pleading;
³ hear me and give answer.
I rock with grief; I groan
⁴ at the uproar of the enemy,
the clamor of the wicked.
They heap trouble upon me,
savagely accuse me.
⁵ My heart pounds within me;
death's terrors fall upon me.

6 Fear and trembling overwhelm me;
   shuddering sweeps over me.
7 I say, "If only I had wings like a dove
   that I might fly away and find rest.*k*
8 Far away I would flee;
   I would stay in the desert.*l*   *Selah*
9 I would soon find a shelter
   from the raging wind and storm."

II

10 Lord, check and confuse their scheming.
   I see violence and strife in the city
11   making rounds on its walls day and night.
   Within are mischief and evil;
12   treachery is there as well;
   oppression and fraud never leave its streets.*m*
13 If an enemy had reviled me,
   that I could bear.
   If my foe had viewed me with contempt,
   from that I could hide.
14 But it was you, my other self,
   my comrade and friend,*n*
15 You, whose company I enjoyed,
   at whose side I walked
   in procession in the house of God.

III

16 Let death take them by surprise;
   let them go down alive to Sheol,*o*
   for evil is in their homes and hearts.
17 But I will call upon God,
   and the LORD will save me.
18 At dusk, dawn, and noon
   I will grieve and complain,
   and my prayer will be heard.*p*
19 God will give me freedom and peace
   from those who war against me,
   though there are many who oppose me.
20 God, who sits enthroned forever,*q*
   will hear me and humble them.
   For they will not mend their ways;
   they have no fear of God.
21 They strike out at friends
   and go back on their promises.
22 Softer than butter is their speech,
   but war is in their hearts.
   Smoother than oil are their words,
   but they are unsheathed swords.*r*
23 Cast your care upon the LORD,
   who will give you support.
   God will never allow
   the righteous one to stumble.*s*
24 But you, God, will bring them down
   to the pit of destruction.*t*

These bloodthirsty liars
   will not live half their days,
   but I put my trust in you.*u*

PSALM 56*

Trust in God

1 For the director. According to *Yonath elem rehoqim.** A *miktam* of David, when the Philistines seized him at Gath.*v*

I

2 Have mercy on me, God,
   for I am treated harshly;
   attackers press me all the day.
3 My foes treat me harshly all the day;
   yes, many are my attackers.
   O Most High, 4when I am afraid,
   in you I place my trust.
5 God, I praise your promise;
   in you I trust, I do not fear.*w*
   What can mere flesh do to me?*x*

II

6 All the day they foil my plans;
   their every thought is of evil against me.
7 They hide together in ambush;
   they watch my every step;
   they lie in wait for my life.*y*
8 They are evil; watch them, God!
   Cast down the nations in your anger!
9 My wanderings you have noted;
   are my tears not stored in your vial,*
   recorded in your book?*z*
10 My foes turn back when I call on you.
   This I know: God is on my side.
11 God, I praise your promise;
12   in you I trust, I do not fear.
   What can mere mortals do to me?

---

k Ps 11, 1.—l Jer 9, 1; Rv 12, 6.—m Jer 5, 1; 6, 6; Ez 22, 2; Hb 1, 3; Zep 3, 1.—n Ps 41, 10; Jer 9, 3; Mt 26, 21-24 par.—o Ps 49, 15; Nm 16, 33; Prv 1, 2; Is 5, 14.—p Dn 6, 11.—q Pss 29, 10; 93, 2; Bar 3, 3.—r Pss 12, 3; 28, 3; 57, 5; 62, 5; 64, 4; Prv 26, 24-28; Jer 9, 7.—s Ps 37, 5; Prv 3, 5; 16, 3; 1 Pt 5, 7.—t Ps 28, 1; 30, 4; 40, 3; 88, 5; 143, 7; Prv 1, 12; Jon 2, 7.—u Pss 25, 2; 56, 4; 130, 5.—v 1 Sm 21, 10.—w Ps 130, 5.—x Ps 118, 6; Heb 13, 6.—y Ps 140, 5-6.—z Ps 10, 14; 2 Kgs 20, 5; Is 25, 8; Rv 7, 17.

Ps 56: Beset physically (2-3) and psychologically (6-7), the psalmist maintains a firm confidence in God (5. 9-10). Nothing will prevent the psalmist from keeping the vow to give thanks for God's gift of life (13-14). A refrain (5. 11-12) divides the psalm in two equal parts.
   56, 1: *Yonath elem rehoqim:* Hebrew words probably designating the melody to which the psalm was to be sung.
   56, 9: *Are my tears not stored in your vial:* a unique saying in the Old Testament. The context suggests that the tears are saved because they are precious; God puts a high value on each of the psalmist's troubles.

III

13 I have made vows to you, God;
   with offerings I will fulfill them,*a*
14 Once you have snatched me from death,
   kept my feet from stumbling,
   That I may walk before God
   in the light of the living.

PSALM 57*

Confident Prayer for Deliverance

1 For the director. Do not destroy.* A *miktam*
of David, when he fled from Saul into a cave.*b*
I
2 Have mercy on me, God,
   have mercy on me.
   In you I seek shelter.
   In the shadow of your wings* I seek
      shelter
   till harm pass by.*c*
3 I call to God Most High,
   to God who provides for me.
4 May God send help from heaven to save
      me,
   shame those who trample upon me.
   May God send fidelity and love.
                              Selah
5 I must lie down in the midst of lions
   hungry for human prey.*d*
   Their teeth are spears and arrows;
   their tongue, a sharpened sword.*e*

---

a Nm 30, 3.—b 1 Sm 22, 1.—c Pss 17, 8; 36, 8.—d Pss 17, 11-
12; 22, 22; 58, 7.—e Pss 11, 2; 64, 4.—f Ps 72, 19; Nm 14, 21.—
g Pss 7, 15; 140, 5-6.—h Ps 108, 2.—i Jb 38, 12.—j Pss 9, 12; 18,
50.—k Pss 36, 6; 71, 19.—l Ps 82, 2; Dt 16, 19.—m Pss 64, 4;
140, 3; Rom 3, 13.—n Ps 3, 7.—o Wis 16, 29.—p Ps 37, 2.

Ps 57: Each of the two equal strophes contains a prayer for rescue from enemies, accompanied by joyful trust in God (2-5, 7-11).
The refrain prays that God be manifested as saving (6, 12). Ps 108
is nearly identical to part of this psalm (57, 8-12 = 108, 2-6).

57, 1: *Do not destroy:* probably the title of the melody to which
the psalm was to be sung.

57, 2: *The shadow of your wings:* probably refers to the
wings of the cherubim (powerful winged animals) whose wings
spread over the ark in the inner chamber of the temple (1 Kgs 6, 23-
28).

57, 9: *I will wake the dawn:* by a bold figure the psalmist
imagines the sound of music and singing will waken a new day.

Ps 58: A lament expressing trust in God's power to dethrone all
powers obstructing divine rule of the world. First condemned are
"the gods," the powers that were popularly imagined to control
human destinies (2-3), then "the wicked," the human instruments
of these forces (4-6). The psalmist prays God to prevent them from
harming the just (7-10). The manifestation of justice will gladden
the just; they will see that their God is with them (11-12). The
psalm is less concerned with personal vengeance than with public
vindication of God's justice now.

58, 1: *Do not destroy:* probably the title of the melody to which
the psalm was to be sung.

58, 2: *Gods:* the Bible sometimes understands pagan gods to be
lesser divine beings who are assigned by Israel's God to rule the foreign nations. Here they are accused of injustice, permitting the
human judges under their patronage to abuse the righteous. Cf Ps
82.

58, 5-6: The image is that of a poisonous snake that is controlled
by the voice or piping of its trainer.

---

6 Show yourself over the heavens, God;
   may your glory appear above all the
      earth.*f*
II
7 They have set a trap for my feet;
   my soul is bowed down;
   They have dug a pit before me.
   May they fall into it themselves!*g*
                              Selah
8 My heart is steadfast, God,
   my heart is steadfast.
   I will sing and chant praise.*h*
9 Awake, my soul;
   awake, lyre and harp!
   I will wake the dawn.**i*
10 I will praise you among the peoples,
      Lord;
   I will chant your praise among the na-
      tions.*j*
11 For your love towers to the heavens;
   your faithfulness, to the skies.*k*
12 Show yourself over the heavens, God;
   may your glory appear above all the
      earth.

PSALM 58*

The Dethroning of Unjust Rulers

1 For the leader. Do not destroy.* A *miktam* of
David.
I
2 Do you indeed pronounce justice, O
      gods;*
   do you judge mortals fairly?*l*
3 No, you freely engage in crime;
   your hands dispense violence to the
      earth.
II
4 The wicked have been corrupt since
      birth;
   liars from the womb, they have gone
      astray.
5 Their poison is like the poison of a
      snake,*
   like that of a serpent stopping its
      ears,*m*
6 So as not to hear the voice of the
      charmer
   who casts such cunning spells.
III
7 O God, smash the teeth in their mouths;
   break the jaw-teeth of these lions,
      Lord!*n*
8 Make them vanish like water flowing
      away;*o*
   trodden down, let them wither like
      grass.*p*

Ps

9 Let them dissolve like a snail that oozes
away,*
    like an untimely birth that never sees
the sun. *q*
10 Suddenly, like brambles or thistles,
    have the whirlwind snatch them
away. *r*
11 Then the just shall rejoice to see the vengeance
    and bathe their feet in the blood of
the wicked. *s*
12 Then it will be said:
    "Truly there is a reward for the just;
    there is a God who is judge on earth!"

PSALM 59*

Complaint against Bloodthirsty Enemies

1 For the director. Do not destroy.* A *miktam*
of David, when Saul sent people to watch his
house and kill him. *t*

I

2 Rescue me from my enemies, my God;
    lift me out of reach of my foes.
3 Deliver me from evildoers;
    from the bloodthirsty save me.
4 They have set an ambush for my life;
    the powerful conspire against me.
For no offense or misdeed of mine,
LORD,
5 for no fault they hurry to take up arms.
Come near and see my plight!
6   You, LORD of hosts, are the God of
Israel!
Awake! Punish all the nations.
Have no mercy on these worthless
traitors. *Selah*
7 Each evening they return,
    growling like dogs, prowling the city. *u*
8 Their mouths pour out insult;
    sharp words are on their lips.
    They say: "Who is there to hear?"*
9 You, LORD, laugh at them;
    you deride all the nations. *v*
10 My strength, for you I watch;
    you, God, are my fortress, 11 my lov-
ing God.

II

May God go before me,
    and show me my fallen foes.
12 Slay them, God,
    lest they deceive my people.
Shake them by your power;
    Lord, our shield, bring them down.
13 For the sinful words of their mouths and
lips
    let them be caught in their pride.

For the lies they have told under oath *w*
14   destroy them in anger,
    destroy till they are no more.
Then people will know God rules over
Jacob,
    yes, even to the ends of the earth. *x*
            Selah
15 Each evening they return,
    growling like dogs, prowling the city.
16 They roam about as scavengers;
    if they are not filled, they howl.

III

17 But I shall sing of your strength,
    extol your love at dawn,
For you are my fortress,
    my refuge in time of trouble.
18 My strength, your praise I will sing;
    you, God, are my fortress, my loving
God.

PSALM 60*

Lament after Defeat in Battle

1 For the leader; according to "The Lily
of. . . ." A *miktam* of David (for teaching), 2
when he fought against Aram-Naharaim and
Aram-Zobah; and Joab, coming back, killed
twelve thousand Edomites in the Valley of Salt. *y*

I

3 O God, you rejected us, broke our defenses;
    you were angry but now revive us.
4 You rocked the earth, split it open; *z*
    repair the cracks for it totters.
5 You made your people go through
hardship,
    made us stagger from the wine you
gave us. *a*

---

q Jb 3, 16.—r Jb 21, 18; Hos 13, 3; Na 1, 10.—s Ps 68, 24;
Is 63, 1-6.—t 1 Sm 19, 11.—u Ps 55, 11.—v Pss 2, 4; 37, 13;
Wis 4, 18.—w Prv 12, 13; 18, 7.—x Ps 83, 18-19; Ez 5, 13.—y
2 Sm 8, 2. 3. 13; 1 Chr 18, 2. 3. 12.—z Ps 75, 4; Is 24, 19.—a
Ps 75, 9; Is 51, 17. 21-22; Jer 25, 15.

58, 9: *A snail that oozes away:* empty shells suggested to
ancients that snails melted away as they left a slimy trail.
    Ps 59: A lament in two parts (2-9, 11b-17), each ending in a
refrain (10, 18). Both parts alternate prayer for vindication (2-3,
5b-6; 11b-14) with vivid depictions of the psalmist's enemies (4-
5a. 7-8. 15-16). The near curse in 12-13 is not a crude desire
for revenge but a wish that God's just rule over human affairs be
recognized now.
    59, 1: *Do not destroy:* probably the title of the melody to
which the psalm was to be sung.
    59, 8: *Who is there to hear?:* a sample of the enemies'
godless reflection. The answer is that God hears their blasphemies.
    Ps 60: The community complains that God has let the enemy
win the battle (3-5) and asks for an assurance of victory (6-7).
In the oracle God affirms ownership of the land; the invasion of
other nations is not permanent and will be reversed ultimately
(8-10). With renewed confidence, the community resolves to fight
again (11). The opening lament is picked up again (12-14), but
this time with new awareness of God's power and human limitation.

⁶ Raise up a flag for those who revere
you,
a refuge for them out of bowshot.
Selah
⁷ Help with your right hand and answer
us*
that your loved ones may escape.

II

⁸ In the sanctuary God promised:
"I will exult, will apportion
Shechem;
the valley of Succoth I will measure
out.*
⁹ Gilead is mine, mine is Manasseh;
Ephraim is the helmet for my head,
Judah, my own scepter.*
¹⁰ Moab is my washbowl;*
upon Edom I cast my sandal.ᵇ
I will triumph over Philistia."

III

¹¹ Who will bring me to the fortified
city?*
Who will lead me into Edom?
¹² Was it not you who rejected us, God?
Do you no longer march with our armies?ᶜ
¹³ Give us aid against the foe;
worthless is human help.
¹⁴ We will triumph with the help of God,
who will trample down our foes.

---

b Ru 4, 7-8.—c Ps 44, 10.—d Ps 46, 2.—e Pss 17, 8; 36, 8;
57, 2.—f Pss 21, 5.—g Pss 72, 5; 89, 5. 30. 37.—h Pss 85, 11;
89, 15. 25; Prv 20, 28.—i 2-3. 6-7: Pss 18, 3; 31, 3-4; 42, 10;
118, 8; 146, 3.—j Pss 12, 3; 28, 3; 55, 22; Prv 26, 24-25.—k
Ps 3, 3; Is 26, 4; 60, 19.

60, 7-14: These verses occur again as the second half of Ps
108.
60, 8: *I will apportion . . . measure out:* God lays claim to
these places. *The valley of Succoth:* probably the lower stretch
of the Jabbok valley.
60, 9: *Judah, my own scepter:* an allusion to the Testament
of Jacob, Gn 49, 10.
60, 10: *Moab is my washbowl:* Moab borders the Dead Sea,
hence a metaphor for the country. *Upon Edom I cast my sandal:* an ancient legal gesture of taking possession of land.
60, 11: *The fortified city:* perhaps Bozrah, the fortified capital of Edom. Cf Is 34, 6; 63, 1; Am 1, 12.
Ps 61: A lament of the king who feels himself at the brink of
death (3) and cries out for the strong and saving presence of God
(3b-5). The king cites the prayer being made for him (7-8), and
promises to give thanks to God.
61, 3: *Brink of Sheol:* literally, "edge of the earth," "earth"
being taken in its occasional meaning "the underworld." Cf Jon
2, 3.
61, 6: *In prayer:* added for sense. Vv 7-8 express *the plea* of
v 6.
61, 9: *Then:* Hebrew "just as," i.e., in accord with the vows
referred to in v 6.
Ps 62: A song of trust displaying serenity from experiencing
God's power (the refrains of 2-3 and 6-7) and anger toward unjust enemies (4-5). From the experience of being rescued, the
psalmist can teach others to trust in God (10-13).
62, 1: *'Al Jeduthun:* apparently the Hebrew name for the
melody.

PSALM 61*

Prayer of the King in Time of Danger

¹ For the leader; with stringed instruments. Of
David.

I

² Hear my cry, O God,
listen to my prayer!
³ From the brink of Sheol* I call;
my heart grows faint.
Raise me up, set me on a rock,
⁴ for you are my refuge,
a tower of strength against the foe.ᵈ
⁵ Then I will ever dwell in your tent,
take refuge in the shelter of your
wings.ᵉ *Selah*

II

⁶ O God, when you accept my vows
and hear the plea of those
who revere your name in prayer:*
⁷ "Add to the days of the king's life;
may his years be many generations;ᶠ
⁸ May he reign before God forever;ᵍ
may your love and fidelity preserve
him"—ʰ
⁹ Then* I will sing your name forever,
fulfill my vows day after day.

PSALM 62*

Trust in God Alone

¹ For the leader; *'al Jeduthun.* A psalm of
David.

I

² My soul rests in God alone,ⁱ
from whom comes my salvation.
³ God alone is my rock and my salvation,
my secure height; I shall never fall.
⁴ How long will you set upon people,
all of you beating them down,
As though they were a sagging fence
or a battered wall?
⁵ Even from my place on high
they plot to dislodge me.
They delight in lies;
they bless with their mouths,
but inwardly they curse.ʲ *Selah*

II

⁶ My soul, be at rest in God alone,
from whom comes my hope.
⁷ God alone is my rock and my salvation,
my secure height; I shall not fall.
⁸ My safety and glory are with God,ᵏ
my strong rock and refuge.
⁹ Trust God at all times, my people!
Pour out your hearts to God our refuge! *Selah*

Ps

III

10 Mortals are a mere breath,
　　the powerful but an illusion;[l]
　On a balance they rise;*
　　together they are lighter than air.
11 Do not trust in extortion;
　　in plunder put no empty hope.
　Though wealth increase,
　　do not set your heart upon it.[m]
12 One thing God has said;
　　two things* I have heard:[n]
　Power belongs to God;
13　　so too, Lord, does kindness,
　And you render to each of us
　　according to our deeds.[o]

PSALM 63*

Ardent Longing for God

1 A psalm of David, when he was in the wilderness of Judah.[p]

I

2 O God, you are my God—
　　for you I long!
　For you my body yearns;
　　for you my soul thirsts,
　Like a land parched, lifeless,
　　and without water.[q]
3 So I look to you in the sanctuary
　　to see your power and glory.
4 For your love is better than life;*
　　my lips offer you worship!

II

5 I will bless you as long as I live;
　　I will lift up my hands, calling on your name.
6 My soul shall savor the rich banquet of praise,
　　with joyous lips my mouth shall honor you!
7 When I think of you upon my bed,
　　through the night watches I will recall
8 That you indeed are my help,
　　and in the shadow of your wings I shout for joy.[r]
9 My soul clings fast to you;
　　your right hand upholds me.

III

10 But those who seek my life will come to ruin;
　　they shall go down to the depths of the earth!
11 They shall be handed over to the sword
　　and become the prey of jackals!
12 But the king shall rejoice in God;
　　all who swear by the Lord* shall exult,
　　for the mouths of liars will be shut![s]

PSALM 64*

Treacherous Conspirators Punished by God

1 For the leader. A psalm of David.

I

2 O God, hear my anguished voice;
　　from the foes I dread protect my life.
3 Hide me from the malicious crowd,
　　the mob of evildoers.
4 They sharpen their tongues like swords,
　　ready their bows for arrows of poison words.[t]
5 They shoot at the innocent from ambush,
　　shoot without risk, catch them unawares.*
6 They resolve on their wicked plan;
　　they conspire to set snares;
　　they say: "Who will see us?"
7 They devise wicked schemes,
　　conceal the schemes they devise;
　　the designs of their hearts are hidden.[u]

II

8 But God will shoot arrows at them
　　and strike them unawares.[v]
9 They will be brought down by their own tongues;
　　all who see them will shake their heads.[w]

---

l Pss 39, 6-7; 144, 4; Jb 7, 16; Wis 2, 5.—m Jb 31, 25; Eccl 5, 9; Jer 17, 11; Mt 6, 19-21. 24.—n Jb 40, 5.—o Pss 28, 4; 31, 24; 2 Sm 3, 39; Jb 34, 11; Jer 17, 10; Mt 16, 27; Rom 2, 6; 2 Tm 4, 14.—p 1 Sm 24.—q Pss 42, 2; 143, 6; Is 26, 9.—r Pss 17, 8; 36, 8.—s Ps 107, 42.—t Pss 11, 2; 37, 14; 55, 22; 57, 5.—u Ps 140, 3; Prv 6, 14.—v Pss 7, 13-14; 38, 3; Dt 32, 42.—w Pss 5, 11; 44, 14; 52, 6.

62, 10: *On a balance they rise:* precious objects were weighed by balancing two pans suspended from a beam. The lighter pan rises.

62, 12: *One thing . . . two things:* parallelism of numbers for the sake of variation, a common device in Semitic poetry. One should not literally add up the numbers. Cf Am 1, 3; Prv 6, 16-19; 30, 15. 18. 21.

Ps 63: A psalm expressing the intimate relationship between God and the worshiper. Separated from God (2), the psalmist longs for the divine life given in the temple (3-6), which is based on a close relationship with God (7-9). May all my enemies be destroyed and God's true worshipers continue in giving praise (10-12)!

63, 4: *For your love is better than life:* only here in the Old Testament is anything prized above life—in this case God's love.

63, 12: *All who swear by the Lord:* to swear by a particular god meant that one was a worshiper of that god (Is 45, 23; 48, 1; Zep 1, 5).

Ps 64: A lament of a person overwhelmed by the malice of the wicked who are depicted in the psalms as the enemies of the righteous (2-7). When people see God bringing upon the wicked the evil they intended against others, they will know who is the true ruler of the world (8-10). The final verse is a vow of praise (11).

64, 5: *Catch them unawares:* literally, "suddenly," i.e., "unexpectedly."

¹⁰ Then all will fear and proclaim God's
    deed,
    pondering what has been done.
¹¹ The just will rejoice and take refuge in
    the LORD;
    all the upright will glory in their
    God.ˣ

PSALM 65*

Thanksgiving for God's Blessings

¹ For the leader. A psalm of David. A song.
I
² To you we owe our hymn of praise,
    O God on Zion;
    To you our vows* must be fulfilled,
³   you who hear our prayers.
    To you all flesh must come*ʸ
⁴   with its burden of wicked deeds.
    We are overcome by our sins;
    only you can pardon them.ᶻ
⁵ Happy the chosen ones you bring
    to dwell in your courts.
    May we be filled with the good things of
        your house,
    the blessings of your holy temple!

---

x Pss 36, 8; 57, 2.—y Is 66, 23. —z Pss 32, 1-2; 78, 38; Is 1,
18.—a Is 66, 19.—b Pss 89, 10; 107, 29; Jb 38, 11; Mt 8, 26.—
c Is 17, 12.—d Lv 26, 4; Is 30, 23. 25; Jl 2, 22-23.—e Is 44,
23.—f Ps 65, 14; Is 44, 23.—g 3-4: Ps 18, 45; Mi 7, 17.—h Pss
74, 15; 114, 3; Ex 14, 21f; Jos 3, 1ff; Is 44, 27; 50, 2.

Ps 65: The community, aware of its unworthiness (3-4), gives thanks for divine bounty (5), a bounty resulting from God's creation victory (6-9). At God's touch the earth comes alive with vegetation and flocks (10-14).
65, 2: *Vows:* the Israelites were accustomed to promising sacrifices in the temple if their prayers were heard.
65, 3: *To you all flesh must come:* all must have recourse to God's mercy.
65, 6: *Awesome deeds:* the acts of creating—installing mountains, taming seas, restraining nations (7-8)—that are visible worldwide (6. 9).
65, 10-14: Apparently a description of the agricultural year, beginning with the first fall rains that soften the hard sun-baked soil (10-11).
65, 10: *God's stream:* the fertile waters of the earth derive from God's fertile waters in the heavenly world.
65, 12: *Paths:* probably the tracks of God's storm chariot dropping rain upon earth.
Ps 66: In the first part (1-12), the community praises God for powerful acts for Israel, both in the past (the exodus from Egypt and the entry into the land [6]) and in the present (deliverance from a recent but unspecified calamity [8-12]). In the second part (13-20), an individual from the rescued community fulfills a vow to offer a sacrifice of thanksgiving. As often in thanksgivings, the rescued person steps forward to teach the community what God has done (16-20).
66, 5-6: Cf the events described in Ex 14, 1—15, 21; Jos 3, 11—4, 24, and Ps 114.

II
⁶ You answer us with awesome deeds* of
    justice,
    O God our savior,
    The hope of all the ends of the earth
    and of far distant islands.ᵃ
⁷ You are robed in power,
    you set up the mountains by your
        might.
⁸ You still the roaring of the seas,ᵇ
    the roaring of their waves,
    the tumult of the peoples.ᶜ
⁹ Distant peoples stand in awe of your
        marvels;
    east and west you make resound with
        joy.
¹⁰ You visit the earth and water it,*
    make it abundantly fertile.ᵈ
    God's stream* is filled with water;
    with it you supply the world with
        grain.
    Thus do you prepare the earth:
¹¹   you drench plowed furrows,
    and level their ridges.
    With showers you keep the ground soft,
    blessing its young sprouts.
¹² You adorn the year with your bounty;
    your paths* drip with fruitful rain.
¹³ The untilled meadows also drip;
    the hills are robed with joy.
¹⁴ The pastures are clothed with flocks,
    the valleys blanketed with grain;
    they cheer and sing for joy.ᵉ

PSALM 66*

Praise of God, Israel's Deliverer

¹ For the leader. A song; a psalm.
I
    Shout joyfully to God, all you on earth;
²   sing of his glorious name;
    give him glorious praise.ᶠ
³ Say to God: "How awesome your deeds!
    Before your great strength your
        enemies cringe.
⁴ All on earth fall in worship before you;ᵍ
    they sing of you, sing of your name!"
                                    Selah
II
⁵ Come and see the works of God,*
    awesome in the deeds done for us.
⁶ He changed the sea to dry land;
    through the river they passed on foot.ʰ
    Therefore let us rejoice in him,
⁷   who rules by might forever,
    Whose eyes are fixed upon the nations.
    Let no rebel rise to challenge! *Selah*

8 Bless our God, you peoples;
  loudly sound his praise,
9 Who has kept us alive
  and not allowed our feet to slip.[i]
10 You tested us, O God,
  tried us as silver tried by fire.[j]
11 You led us into a snare;
  you bound us at the waist as captives.
12 You let captors set foot on our neck;*
  we went through fire and water;
  then you led us out to freedom.[k]

III
13 I will bring holocausts* to your house;
  to you I will fulfill my vows,
14 The vows my lips pronounced
  and my mouth spoke in distress.
15 Holocausts of fatlings I will offer you
  and burnt offerings of rams;
  I will sacrifice oxen and goats. *Selah*
16 Come and hear, all you who fear God,
  while I recount what has been done
  for me.
17 I called to the Lord with my mouth;
  praise was upon my tongue.
18 Had I cherished evil in my heart,
  the Lord would not have heard.
19 But God did hear
  and listened to my voice in prayer.
20 Blessed be God, who did not refuse me
  the kindness I sought in prayer.

PSALM 67*

Harvest Thanks and Petition

1 For the leader; with stringed instruments. A
psalm; a song.

I
2 May God be gracious to us* and bless
  us;
  may God's face shine upon us.[l] *Selah*
3 So shall your rule be known upon the
  earth,
  your saving power among all the nations.[m]
4 May the peoples praise you, God;
  may all the peoples praise you!

II
5 May the nations be glad and shout for
  joy;
  for you govern the peoples justly,
  you guide the nations upon the
  earth.[n]   *Selah*
6 May the peoples praise you, God;
  may all the peoples praise you!

III
7 The earth has yielded its harvest;
  God, our God, blesses us.[o]

8 May God bless us still,
  that the ends of the earth may revere
  our God.

PSALM 68*

The Exodus and Conquest, Pledge of Future Help

1 For the leader. A psalm of David; a song.

I
2 God will arise for battle;*
  the enemy will be scattered;
  those who hate God will flee.[p]
3 The wind will disperse them like
  smoke;
  as wax is melted by fire,
  so the wicked will perish before
  God.[q]
4 Then the just will be glad;
  they will rejoice before God;
  they will celebrate with great joy.

---

i Pss 91, 12; 121, 3; 1 Sm 2, 9; Prv 3, 23.—j Is 48, 10.—k Is
43, 2.—l Pss 4, 7; 31, 17; 44, 4; 80, 4; Dn 9, 17.—m Jer 33,
9.—n Ps 98, 9.—o Ps 85, 13; Lv 26, 4; Ez 34, 27; Hos 2, 23-
24.—p Nm 10, 35.—q Ps 97, 5; Jdt 16, 1; Wis 5, 14; Mi 1, 4.

66, 12: *You let captors set foot on our neck:* literally, "you
let men mount our head." Conquerors placed their feet on the
neck of their enemies as a sign of complete defeat. Cf Jos 10, 24.
A ceremonial footstool of the Egyptian king Tutankhamen portrays bound and prostrate bodies of enemies ready for the king's
feet on their heads, and one of Tutankhamen's ceremonial
chariots depicts the king as a sphinx standing with paw atop the
neck of an enemy.
66, 13: *Holocausts:* wholly burnt offerings. Cf Lv 1, 3-13; 6,
1-4; 22, 17-20.
Ps 67: A petition for a bountiful harvest (7), made in the
awareness that Israel's prosperity will persuade the nations to
worship its God.
67, 2: *May God be gracious to us:* the people's petition
echoes the blessing pronounced upon them by the priests. Cf Nm
6, 22-27.
Ps 68: The psalm is extremely difficult because the Hebrew
text is badly preserved and the ceremony that it describes is uncertain. The translation assumes the psalm accompanied the early
autumn Feast of Tabernacles (Sukkoth), which included a procession of the tribes (25-28). Israel was being oppressed by a foreign
power, perhaps Egypt (31-32)—unless Egypt stands for any oppressor. The psalm may have been composed from segments of
ancient poems, which would explain why the transitions are implied rather than explicitly stated. At any rate, v 2 is based on Nm
10, 35-36, and vv 8-9 are derived from Jgs 5, 4-5.
  The argument develops in nine stanzas (each of three to five
poetic lines): 1) confidence that God will destroy Israel's enemies
(2-4); 2) call to praise God as savior (5-7); 3) God's initial rescue
of Israel from Egypt (8), the Sinai encounter (9), and the settlement in Canaan (10-11); 4) the defeat of the Canaanite kings
(12-15); 5) the taking of Jerusalem, where Israel's God will rule
the world (16-19); 6) praise for God's past help and for the future
interventions that will be modeled on the ancient exodus-conquest
(20-24); 7) procession at the Feast of Tabernacles (25-28); 8)
prayer that the defeated enemies bring tribute to the temple (29-
32); 9) invitation for all kingdoms to praise Israel's God (33-36).
68, 2: The opening line alluding to Nm 10, 35 makes clear that
God's assistance in the period of the exodus and conquest is the
model and assurance of all future divine help.

II

5 Sing to God, praise the divine name;
    exalt the rider of the clouds.*
    Rejoice before this God
        whose name is the LORD.[r]
6 Father of the fatherless, defender of
        widows—[s]
    this is the God whose abode is holy,
7 Who gives a home to the forsaken,
    who leads prisoners out to prosperity,
    while rebels live in the desert.*

III

8 God, when you went forth before your
        people,[t]
    when you marched through the des-
        ert,   *Selah*
9 The earth quaked, the heavens shook,
    before God, the One of Sinai,
    before God, the God of Israel.
10 You claimed a land as your own, O God;
11   your people settled there.
    There you poured abundant rains, God,
    graciously given to the poor in their
        need.

IV

12a The Lord announced the news of vic-
        tory:*
13a   "The kings and their armies are in
        desperate flight.[u]

---

r Pss 18, 10; 104, 3; Dt 33, 26; Is 19, 1.—s 6-7: Pss 103, 6;
146, 7. 9; Ex 22, 20-22; Bar 6, 37.—t 8-9: Pss 44, 10; 114, 4.
7; Jgs 5, 4-5; Heb 12, 26.—u Jgs 5, 19. 22.—v Jgs 5, 16.—w
Ps 132, 13-14; Ez 43, 7.—x Ps 47, 8; Eph 4, 8-10.—y Pss 34,
2; 145, 2; Is 46, 3-4; 63, 9.—z Dt 32, 42.—a Pss 58, 11; 1 Kgs
21, 19; 22, 38; Is 63, 1-6.—b Pss 81, 2-3; 87, 7; 149, 3; 150,
3-5; 2 Sm 6, 5.

68, 5: *Exalt the rider of the clouds:* God's intervention is
in the imagery of Canaanite myth in which the storm-god mounted
the storm clouds to ride to battle. Such theophanies occur throughout the psalm: 2-3. 8-10. 12-15. 18-19. 22-24. 29-32. 34-35.
See Dt 33, 26; Ps 18, 8-16; Is 19, 1.
68, 7: *While rebels live in the desert:* rebels must live in
the arid desert, whereas God's people will live in the well-watered
land (vv 8-11).
68, 12-15: The Hebrew text upon which the translation is
based has apparently suffered dislocation and has been substantially rearranged for sense. The version of the defeat of the kings
differs from that in the Book of Joshua, where the people play a
significant role. Here God alone is responsible for the victory
(though the actual battle is not described); Israel only gathers the
spoils. God alone is the source of Israel's success; human effort
is not important.
68, 15: *Zalmon:* generally taken as the name of a mountain
where snow is visible in winter, perhaps to be located in the Golan
Heights or in the mountains of Bashan or Hauran east of the Sea
of Galilee.
68, 17: *The mountain:* Mount Zion, the site of the temple.
68, 23: *Even from Bashan . . . from the depths of the sea:*
the heights and the depths, the farthest places where enemies
might flee.
68, 25-28: *Your procession:* the procession renews God's
original taking up of residence on Zion, described in 16-19.

12b All you people so numerous,
14a   will you stay by the sheepfolds?[v]
13b Every household will share the booty,
14b   perhaps a dove sheathed with silver,
14c   its wings covered with yellow gold."
15 When the Almighty routed the kings
        there,
    the spoils were scattered like snow on
        Zalmon.*

V

16 You high mountains of Bashan,
    you rugged mountains of Bashan,
17 You rugged mountains, why look with
        envy
    at the mountain* where God has cho-
        sen to dwell,
    where the LORD resides forever?[w]
18 God's chariots were myriad, thousands
        upon thousands;
    from Sinai the Lord entered the holy
        place.
19 You went up to its lofty height;
    you took captives, received slaves as
        tribute.[x]
    No rebels can live in the presence of
        God.

VI

20 Blessed be the Lord day by day,
    God, our salvation, who carries us.[y]
                                    Selah
21 Our God is a God who saves;
    escape from death is in the LORD
        God's hands.
22 God will crush the skulls of the enemy,
    the hairy heads of those who walk in
        sin.[z]
23 The Lord has said:
    "Even from Bashan I will fetch them,
    fetch them even from the depths of
        the sea.*
24 You will wash your feet in your enemy's
        blood;
    the tongues of your dogs will lap it
        up."[a]

VII

25 Your procession* comes into view, O
        God,
    your procession into the holy place,
        my God and king.
26 The singers go first, the harpists follow;
    in their midst girls sound the tim-
        brels.[b]
27 In your choirs, bless God;
    bless the LORD, you from Israel's as-
        semblies.

Ps

28 In the lead is Benjamin, few in number;
  there the princes of Judah, a large
    throng,
  the princes of Zebulun, the princes of
    Naphtali, too.^c → too.*c*

VIII
29 Summon again, O God, your power,
  the divine power you once showed for
    us.
30 Show it from your temple on behalf of
    Jerusalem,
  that kings may bring you tribute.
31 Roar at the wild beast of the reeds,*
  the herd of mighty bulls, the lords of
    nations;
  scatter the nations that delight in war.
32 Exact rich tribute from lower Egypt,*^d
  from upper Egypt, gold and silver;
  make Ethiopia extend its hands to
    God.^e

IX
33 You kingdoms of the earth, sing to God;^f
  chant the praises of the Lord, *Selah*
34 Who rides the heights of the ancient
    heavens,
  whose voice is thunder, mighty thun-
    der.
35 Confess the power of God,
  whose majesty protects Israel,
  whose power is in the sky.
36 Awesome is God in his holy place,
  the God of Israel,
  who gives power and strength to his
    people.^g
  Blessed be God!

PSALM 69*

A Cry of Anguish in Great Distress

1 For the leader; according to "Lilies."* Of
David.
I
2 Save me, God,
  for the waters* have reached my
    neck.^h
3 I have sunk into the mire of the deep,
  where there is no foothold.
  I have gone down to the watery depths;
  the flood overwhelms me.ⁱ
4 I am weary with crying out;
  my throat is parched.
  My eyes have failed,
  looking for my God.^j
5 More numerous than the hairs of my
    head
  are those who hate me without cause.^k

Too many for my strength
  are my treacherous enemies.
Must I now restore
  what I did not steal?*
II
6 God, you know my folly;
  my faults are not hidden from you.
7 Let those who wait for you, LORD of
    hosts,
  not be shamed through me.
  Let those who seek you, God of Israel,^l
  not be disgraced through me.
8 For your sake I bear insult,
  shame covers my face.^m
9 I have become an outcast to my kin,
  a stranger to my mother's children.ⁿ
10 Because zeal for your house consumes
    me,*
  I am scorned by those who scorn
    you.*^o
11 I have wept and fasted,^p
  but this led only to scorn.
12 I clothed myself in sackcloth;
  I became a byword for them.
13 They who sit at the gate gossip about me;
  drunkards make me the butt of their
    songs.

III
14 But I pray to you, LORD,
  for the time of your favor.

c Is 8, 23.—d Ez 29, 2ff.—e Is 18, 7; 45, 14.—f Ps 138, 4.—g
Pss 28, 8; 29, 11.—h Pss 18, 5; 93, 3-4; Jb 22, 11.—i Pss 40,
2; 124, 4-5.—j Pss 25, 15; 119, 82; 123, 2; 141, 8; Is 38, 14.—k
Ps 40, 13; Lam 3, 52; Jn 15, 25.—l Ps 40, 17.—m Jer 15, 15.—n
Jb 19, 13-15.—o Ps 119, 139; Jn 2, 17; Rom 15, 3.—p 11-13:
Ps 109, 24-25; Jb 30, 9; Lam 3, 14.

68, 31: *The wild beast of the reeds:* probably the Nile
crocodile, a symbol for Egypt; see 32 and Ez 29, 2-5.
68, 31-32: *Lower Egypt* is the delta area north of Cairo.
Upper Egypt is the Nile Valley from Cairo to Aswan. *Ethiopia*
is still further south.
Ps 69: A lament complaining of suffering in language both
metaphorical (2-3 and 15-16, the waters of chaos) and literal (4.
5. 9. 11-13, exhaustion, alienation from family and community,
false accusation). In the second part the psalmist prays with special
emphasis that the enemies be punished for all to see (23-29).
Despite the pain, the psalmist does not lose hope that all be set
right, and promises public praise (30-37). The psalm, which depicts
the suffering of the innocent just person vividly, is cited often by
the New Testament especially in the passion accounts, e.g., v 5
in Jn 15, 25; v 22 in Mk 15, 23. 36 and parallels and in Jn 19,
29. The psalm prays not so much for personal vengeance as for
public vindication of God's justice. There was, at this time, no
belief in an afterlife where such vindication could take place.
Redress had to take place now, in the sight of all.
69, 1: *"Lilies":* apparently the name of the melody.
69, 2: *Waters:* the waters of chaos from which God created
the world are a common metaphor for extreme distress. Cf Pss
18, 5; 42, 8; 88, 8; Jon 2, 3-6.
69, 5: *What I did not steal:* the psalmist, falsely accused of
theft, is being forced to make restitution.
69, 10: *Zeal for your house consumes me:* the psalmist's
commitment to God's cause brings only opposition. Cf Jn 2, 17. *I
am scorned by those who scorn you:* Rom 15, 3 uses the verse
as an example of Jesus' unselfishness.

God, in your great kindness answer me
   with your constant help. *q*
15 Rescue me from the mire; *r*
   do not let me sink.
   Rescue me from my enemies
   and from the watery depths.
16 Do not let the floodwaters overwhelm
   me,
   nor the deep swallow me,
   nor the mouth of the pit close over me.
17 Answer me, LORD, in your generous
   love;
   in your great mercy turn to me.
18 Do not hide your face from your servant;
   in my distress hasten to answer me! *s*
19 Come and ransom my life;
   because of my enemies redeem me.
20 You know my reproach, my shame, my
   disgrace;
   before you stand all my foes.
21 Insult has broken my heart, and I am
   weak;
   I looked for compassion, but there was
   none,
   for comforters, but found none. *t*
22 Instead they put gall in my food;
   for my thirst they gave me vinegar. *u*

IV
23 Make their own table a snare for them,
   a trap for their friends. *v*
24 Make their eyes so dim they cannot see;
   keep their backs ever feeble.
25 Pour out your wrath upon them;
   let the fury of your anger overtake
   them.
26 Make their camp desolate,
   with none to dwell in their tents. *w*
27 For they pursued the one you struck,
   added to the pain of the one you
   wounded.

28 Add that to their crimes;
   let them not attain to your reward.
29 Strike them from the book of the living;
   do not count them among the just! *x*

V
30 But I am afflicted and in pain;
   let your saving help protect me, God,
31 That I may praise God's name in song*
   and glorify it with thanksgiving.
32 My song will please the LORD more than
   oxen,
   more than bullocks with horns and
   hooves: *y*
33 "See, you lowly ones, and be glad;
   you who seek God, take heart! *z*
34 For the LORD hears the poor,
   does not spurn those in bondage.
35 Let the heavens and the earth sing
   praise,
   the seas and whatever moves in them!"

VI
36 God will rescue Zion,
   rebuild the cities of Judah. *a*
   God's servants shall dwell in the land
   and possess it;
37 it shall be the heritage of their descendants;
   those who love God's name shall dwell
   there. *b*

PSALM 70*

Prayer for Divine Help

1 For the leader; of David. For remembrance.
2 Graciously rescue me, God! *c*
   Come quickly to help me, LORD! *d*
3 Confound and put to shame
   those who seek my life. *e*
   Turn back in disgrace
   those who desire my ruin.
4 Let those who say "Aha!" *f*
   turn back in their shame.
5 But may all who seek you
   rejoice and be glad in you.
   May those who long for your help
   always say, "God be glorified!" *g*
6 Here I am, afflicted and poor.
   God, come quickly!
   You are my help and deliverer.
   LORD, do not delay!

PSALM 71*

Prayer in Time of Old Age

I
1 In you, LORD, I take refuge; *h*
   let me never be put to shame. *i*
2 In your justice rescue and deliver me;
   listen to me and save me!

q Is 49, 8.—r 15-16: Pss 28, 1; 30, 4; 32, 6; 40, 3; 88, 5; Prv
1, 12.—s Pss 102, 3; 143, 7.—t Lam 1, 2.—u Lam 3, 15; Mt
27, 34. 48; Mk 15, 23.—v Rom 11, 9-10.—w Acts 1, 20.—x Ps
139, 16; Ex 32, 32; Is 4, 3; Dn 12, 1; Mal 3, 16; Rv 3, 5.—y
Pss 40, 7; 50, 8-9. 14; 51, 18; Is 1, 11-15; Hos 6, 6; Am 5,
21-22; Heb 10, 5-8.—z Pss 22, 27; 35, 27; 70, 5.—a Is 44, 26;
Ez 36, 10.—b Ps 102, 29; Is 65, 9.—c 2-6: Ps 40, 14-18.—d
Ps 71, 12.—e Ps 35, 4. 26.—f Ps 35, 21. 25.—g Ps 35, 27.—h
1-3: Ps 31, 2-4.—i Ps 25, 2.

69, 31: *That I may praise God's name in song:* the actual
song is cited in 33-35, the word "praise" in 35 referring back to
"praise" in 31.
Ps 70: A lament of a poor and afflicted person (6) who has no
resource except God, and who cries out to be saved from the
enemy. The psalm is almost identical to Ps 40, 14-18.
Ps 71: A lament of an old person (9. 18) whose afflictions are
interpreted by enemies as a divine judgment (11). The first part
of the psalm pleads for help (1-4) on the basis of a hope learned
from a lifetime's experience of God; the second part describes
the menace (9-13) yet remains buoyant (14-16); the third develops
the theme of hope and praise.

Ps

3 Be my rock and refuge,
  my secure stronghold;
  for you are my rock and fortress.*j*
4 My God, rescue me from the power of
  the wicked,
  from the clutches of the violent.*k*
5 You are my hope, Lord;
  my trust, GOD, from my youth.
6 On you I depend since birth;
  from my mother's womb you are my
  strength;*l*
  my hope in you never wavers.
7 I have become a portent to many,*
  but you are my strong refuge!
8 My mouth shall be filled with your
  praise,
  shall sing your glory every day.

II
9 Do not cast me aside in my old age;
  as my strength fails, do not forsake
  me.
10 For my enemies speak against me;
  they watch and plot against me.*m*
11 They say, "God has abandoned that one.
  Pursue, seize the wretch!
  No one will come to the rescue!"
12 God, do not stand far from me;
  my God, hasten to help me.*n*
13 Bring to a shameful end
  those who attack me;
  Cover with contempt and scorn
  those who seek my ruin.*o*
14 I will always hope in you
  and add to all your praise.
15 My mouth shall proclaim your just
  deeds,
  day after day your acts of deliverance,
  though I cannot number them all.*p*
16 I will speak of the mighty works of the
  Lord;
  O GOD, I will tell of your singular
  justice.

III
17 God, you have taught me from my
  youth;
  to this day I proclaim your wondrous
  deeds.
18 Now that I am old and gray,*q*
  do not forsake me, God,
  That I may proclaim your might
  to all generations yet to come,*r*
  Your power 19 and justice, God,
  to the highest heaven.
  You have done great things;*s*
  O God, who is your equal?*t*
20 You have sent me many bitter afflictions,
  but once more revive me.

From the watery depths of the earth
  once more raise me up.
21 Restore my honor;
  turn and comfort me,
22 That I may praise you with the lyre
  for your faithfulness, my God,
  And sing to you with the harp,
  O Holy One of Israel!
23 My lips will shout for joy as I sing your
  praise;
  my soul, too, which you have redeemed.
24 Yes, my tongue shall recount
  your justice day by day.
  For those who sought my ruin
  will have been shamed and disgraced.

PSALM 72*

A Prayer for the King

1 Of Solomon.
I
O God, give your judgment to the king;
  your justice to the son of kings;* *u*
2 That he may govern your people with
  justice,
  your oppressed with right judgment,*v*
3 That the mountains may yield their
  bounty for the people,
  and the hills great abundance,*w*
4 That he may defend the oppressed
  among the people,
  save the poor and crush the oppressor.

II
5 May he live as long as the sun endures,
  like the moon, through all generations.*x*
6 May he be like rain coming down upon
  the fields,
  like showers watering the earth,*y*
7 That abundance may flourish in his
  days,
  great bounty, till the moon be no
  more.

---

j Ps 18, 3.—k Ps 140, 2.—l Ps 22, 11.—m Pss 3, 2; 22, 8.—n Ps 22, 20.—o Pss 35, 4; 40, 15; 70, 3.—p Ps 35, 28.—q Is 46, 3-4.—r Pss 22, 31-32; 48, 14-15; 145, 4.—s Ps 72, 18.—t Ps 86, 8.—u Ps 99, 4; Jer 23, 5.—v Prv 31, 8-9.—w Is 52, 7; 55, 12.—x Ps 89, 37-38; Jer 31, 35.—y Dt 32, 2; Is 45, 8; Hos 6, 3.

71, 7: *A portent to many:* the afflictions of the sufferer are taken as a manifestation of God's anger. Cf Dt 28, 46; Ps 31, 12.

Ps 72: A royal psalm in which the Israelite king, as the representative of God, is the instrument of divine justice (1-4. 12-14) and blessing (5-7. 15-17) for the whole world. The king is human, giving only what he has received from God. Hence intercession must be made for him. The extravagant language is typical of oriental royal courts.

72, 1: *The king . . . the son of kings:* the crown prince is the king's son; the prayer envisages the dynasty.

III
8 May he rule from sea to sea,
  from the river to the ends of the
  earth.*z
9 May his foes kneel before him,
  his enemies lick the dust.ᵃ
10 May the kings of Tarshish and the islands* bring tribute,
   the kings of Arabia and Seba offer
   gifts.ᵇ
11 May all kings bow before him,
   all nations serve him.ᶜ
12 For he rescues the poor when they cry
   out,
   the oppressed who have no one to
   help.
13 He shows pity to the needy and the poorᵈ
   and saves the lives of the poor.
14 From extortion and violence he frees
   them,
   for precious is their blood* in his
   sight.
IV
15 Long may he live, receiving gold from
   Arabia,
   prayed for without cease, blessed day
   by day.

---

z Dt 11, 24; Zec 9, 10.—a Is 49, 23; Mi 7, 17.—b Ps 68, 30;
Is 60, 5-6; 1 Kgs 10, 1ff.—c Pss 47, 8.—d Prv 31, 9.—e Is 27,
6; Hos 14, 6-8; Am 9, 13.—f Ps 21, 7.—g Gn 12, 3; Zec 8, 13.—h
Pss 41, 14; 89, 53; 106, 48; 136, 4.—i Ps 57, 5; Nm 14, 21.—j
Ps 37, 1; Jb 21, 13.—k Jb 15, 27.—l Ps 17, 10.—m Ps 10, 11;
Jb 22, 13.

72, 8: *From sea to sea . . . the ends of the earth:* the
boundaries of the civilized world known at the time: from the
Mediterranean Sea (the western sea) to the Persian Gulf (the
eastern sea), and from the Euphrates (the river) to the islands
and lands of southwestern Europe, "the ends of the earth." The
words may also have a mythic nuance—the earth surrounded by
cosmic waters, hence everywhere.
72, 10: *Tarshish and the islands:* the far west (Ps 48, 6);
Arabia and Seba: the far south (1 Kgs 10, 1).
72, 14: *Their blood:* cf Ps 116, 15.
72, 16: The translation of the difficult Hebrew is tentative.
72, 17: *May the tribes of the earth give blessing with his
name:* an echo of the promise to the ancestors (Gn 12, 3; 26, 4;
28, 14), suggesting that the monarchy in Israel fulfilled the promise
to Abraham, Isaac, and Jacob.
72, 18-19: A doxology marking the end of Book II of the
Psalter.
Ps 73: The opening verse of this probing poem (cf Pss 37, 49)
is actually the psalmist's hard-won conclusion from personal experience: God is just and good! The psalmist describes near loss
of faith (2-12), occasioned by observing the wicked who blasphemed
God with seeming impunity (4-12). Feeling abandoned despite
personal righteousness, the psalmist could not bear the injustice
until an experience of God's nearness in the temple made clear
how deluded the wicked were. Their sudden destruction shows
their impermanence (13-20). The just can thus be confident, for,
as the psalmist now knows, their security is from God (1. 23-28).
73, 9: *They set their mouths against the heavens:* in an
image probably derived from mythic stories of half-divine giants,
the monstrous speech of the wicked is likened to enormous jaws
gaping wide, devouring everything in sight.
73, 10: The Hebrew is obscure.

---

16 May wheat abound in the land,
   flourish even on the mountain
   heights.
   May his fruit increase like Lebanon's,
   his wheat like the grasses of the
   land.*e
17 May his name be blessed forever;
   as long as the sun, may his name endure.*f
   May the tribes of the earth give blessings with his name;
   may all the nations regard him as fa-
   vored.ᵍ
              * * *
18 Blessed be the LORD, the God of Israel,*
   who alone does wonderful deeds.ʰ
19 Blessed be his glorious name forever;
   may all the earth be filled with the
   LORD's glory.ⁱ
   Amen and amen.
20 The end of the psalms of David, son of
   Jesse.

THIRD BOOK — PSALMS 73–89

PSALM 73*
The Trial of the Just

1 A psalm of Asaph.
  How good God is to the upright,
  the Lord, to those who are clean of
  heart!

I
2 But, as for me, I lost my balance;
  my feet all but slipped,
3 Because I was envious of the arrogant
  when I saw the prosperity of the
  wicked.ʲ
4 For they suffer no pain;
  their bodies are healthy and sleek.
5 They are free of the burdens of life;
  they are not afflicted like others.
6 Thus pride adorns them as a necklace;
  violence clothes them as a robe.
7 Out of their stupidity comes sin;
  evil thoughts flood their hearts.ᵏ
8 They scoff and spout their malice;
  from on high they utter threats.ˡ
9 They set their mouths against the
  heavens,*
  their tongues roam the earth.
10 So my people turn to them
   and drink deeply of their words.*
11 They say, "Does God really know?"
   "Does the Most High have any
   knowledge?"ᵐ

Ps

12 Such, then, are the wicked,
    always carefree, increasing their
    wealth.

II

13 Is it in vain that I have kept my heart
    clean,
    washed my hands in innocence?[n]
14 For I am afflicted day after day,
    chastised every morning.
15 Had I thought, "I will speak as they do,"
    I would have betrayed your people.
16 Though I tried to understand all this,
    it was too difficult for me,
17 Till I entered the sanctuary of God
    and came to understand their end.*

III

18 You set them, indeed, on a slippery road;
    you hurl them down to ruin.
19 How suddenly they are devastated;
    undone by disasters forever!
20 They are like a dream after waking,
    Lord,
    dismissed like shadows when you
    arise.[o]

IV

21 Since my heart was embittered
    and my soul deeply wounded,
22 I was stupid and could not understand;
    I was like a brute beast in your pres-
    ence.
23 Yet I am always with you;
    you take hold of my right hand.[p]
24 With your counsel you guide me,
    and at the end receive me with honor.*
25 Whom else have I in the heavens?
    None beside you delights me on earth.
26 Though my flesh and my heart fail,
    God is the rock of my heart, my por-
    tion forever.
27 But those who are far from you perish;
    you destroy those unfaithful to you.
28 As for me, to be near God is my good,
    to make the Lord GOD my refuge.
I shall declare all your works
    in the gates of daughter Zion.

PSALM 74*

Prayer at the Destruction of the Temple

1 A *maskil* of Asaph.

I

Why, God, have you cast us off for-
    ever?*[q]
Why does your anger burn against the
    sheep of your pasture?[r]

2 Remember your flock that you gathered
    of old,
    the tribe you redeemed as your very
    own.
    Remember Mount Zion where you
    dwell.[s]
3 Turn your steps toward the utter ruins,
    toward the sanctuary devastated by
    the enemy.
4 Your foes roared triumphantly in your
    shrine;
    they set up their own tokens of vic-
    tory.
5 They hacked away like foresters gather-
    ing boughs,
    swinging their axes in a thicket of
    trees.
6 They smashed all your engraved work,
    pounded it with hammer and pick.
7 They set your sanctuary on fire;
    the abode of your name they razed
    and profaned.[t]
8 They said in their hearts, "Destroy
    them all!
    Burn all the shrines of God in the
    land!"
9 Now we see no signs,*
    we have no prophets,[u]
    no one who knows how long.

---

n Ps 26, 6; Mal 3, 14.—o Jb 20, 8— p Ps 121, 5.—q Pss 10,
1; 44, 24; 77, 8.—r Ps 80, 5.—s Pss 68, 17; 132, 13; Ex 15,
17; Jer 10, 16; 51, 19.—t Is 64, 10; Ps 79, 1.—u Lam 2, 9.

73, 17: *And came to understand their end:* the psalmist
receives a double revelation in the temple: 1) the end of the
wicked comes unexpectedly (18-20); 2) God is with me.
73, 24: *And at the end receive me with honor:* a perhaps
deliberately enigmatic verse. It is understood by some commentators as reception into heavenly glory, hence the traditional
translation, "receive me into glory." The Hebrew verb can indeed refer to mysterious divine elevation of a righteous person
into God's domain: Enoch in Gn 5, 24; Elijah in 2 Kgs 2, 11-12;
the righteous psalmist in Ps 49, 16. Personal resurrection in the
Old Testament, however, is clearly attested only in the second
century B.C. The verse is perhaps best left unspecified as a reference to God's nearness and protection.
Ps 74: A communal lament sung when the enemy invaded the
temple; it would be especially appropriate at the destruction of
Jerusalem in 587 B.C. Israel's God is urged to look upon the
ruined sanctuary and remember the congregation who worshiped
there (1-11). People and sanctuary are bound together; an attack
on Zion is an attack on Israel. In the second half of the poem, the
community brings before God the story of their origins—their
creation (12-17)—in order to move God to reenact that deed of
creation now. Will God allow a lesser power to destroy the divine
project (18-23)?
74, 1: *Forever:* the word implies that the disaster is already
of long duration. Cf 74, 9 and note.
74, 9: *Now we see no signs:* ancients often asked prophets
to say for how long a divine punishment was to last. Cf 2 Sm 24,
13. Here no prophet has arisen to indicate the duration.

10 How long, O God, shall the enemy
jeer?[v]
Shall the foe revile your name forever?

11 Why draw back your right hand,
why keep it idle beneath your cloak?

II

12 Yet you, God, are my king from of
old,*
winning victories throughout the
earth.

13 You stirred up the sea in your might;[w]
you smashed the heads of the dragons on the waters.[x]

14 You crushed the heads of Leviathan,[y]
tossed him for food to the sharks.

15 You opened up springs and torrents,
brought dry land out of the primeval
waters.

16 Yours the day and yours the night;
you set the moon and sun in place.

17 You fixed all the limits of the earth;
summer and winter you made.[z]

18 Remember how the enemy has jeered,
O LORD,
how a foolish people has reviled your
name.

19 Do not surrender to beasts those who
praise you;
do not forget forever the life of your
afflicted.

20 Look to your covenant,
for the land is filled with gloom;
the pastures, with violence.

---

v Ps 89, 47.—w Ps 89, 10.—x Is 51, 9-10.—y Jb 3, 8; 40,
25; Is 27, 1.—z 16-17: Gn 1.—a Pss 46, 3; 60, 4; 93, 1; 96,
10; 104, 5; 1 Sm 2, 8; Is 24, 19.—b 1 Sm 2, 3; Zec 2, 1-4.—c
Jb 15, 25.—d Mt 24, 23-27.—e Jb 5, 11; 1 Sm 2, 7.—f Ps 60,
5; Jb 21, 20; Is 51, 17. 21-22; Jer 25, 15ff; Hb 2, 16.—g Ps
92, 11.

74, 12-17: Comparable Canaanite literature describes the
storm-god's victory over all-encompassing Sea and its allies
(dragons and Leviathan) and the subsequent peaceful arrangement of the universe, sometimes through the placement of
paired cosmic elements (day and night, sun and moon). Cf Ps
89, 12-13. The psalm apparently equates the enemies attacking
the temple with the destructive cosmic forces already tamed by
God. Why then are those forces now raging untamed against
your own people?

Ps 75: The psalmist gives thanks and rejoices (2. 10) for the
direct intervention of God, which is promised in two oracles (3-
4. 11). Expecting that divine intervention, the psalmist warns
evildoers to repent (5-9).

75, 2: *You said:* supplied for clarity here and in v 11. The
translation assumes in both places that the psalmist is citing an
oracle of God.

75, 5: *Do not raise your horns!:* the horn is the symbol of
strength; to raise one's horn is to exalt one's own power as v
6 explains.

75, 9: *A cup:* "the cup of God's wrath" is the punishment inflicted on the wicked. Cf Is 51, 17; Jer 25, 15-29; 49, 12; Ez
23, 31-33. *Spiced:* literally, "a mixed drink"; spices or drugs
were added to wine. Cf Prv 9, 2. 5.

---

21 Let not the oppressed turn back in
shame;
may the poor and needy praise your
name.

22 Arise, God, defend your cause;
remember the constant jeers of the
fools.

23 Do not ignore the clamor of your foes,
the unceasing uproar of your
enemies.

PSALM 75*

God the Judge of the World

1 For the leader. Do not destroy! A psalm of
Asaph; a song.

I

2 We thank you, God, we give thanks;
we call upon your name,
declare your wonderful deeds.
You said:*

3 "I will choose the time;
I will judge fairly.

4 The earth and all its inhabitants will
quake,
but I have firmly set its pillars."[a]
Selah

II

5 So I say to the boastful: "Do not
boast!"[b]
to the wicked: "Do not raise your
horns!*

6 Do not raise your horns against heaven!
Do not speak arrogantly against the
Rock!"[c]

7 For judgment comes not from east or
from west,
not from the desert or from the
mountains,[d]

8 But from God who decides,
who brings some low and raises
others high.[e]

9 Yes, a cup* is in the LORD's hand,
foaming wine, fully spiced.
When God pours it out,
they will drain it even to the dregs;
all the wicked of the earth must
drink.[f]

10 But I will rejoice forever;
I will sing praise to the God of Jacob,

11 Who has said:
"I will break off all the horns of the
wicked,
but the horns of the just shall be
lifted up."[g]

PSALM 76*

God Defends Zion

¹ For the leader; a psalm with stringed instruments. A song of Asaph.

I

² Renowned in Judah is God,[h]
  whose name is great in Israel.
³ On Salem* is God's tent, a shelter on Zion.
⁴ There the flashing arrows were shattered,
  shield, sword, and weapons of war.[i]
  Selah

II

⁵ Terrible and awesome are you,
  stronger than the ancient mountains.*
⁶ Despoiled are the bold warriors;
  they sleep their final sleep;
  the hands of all the mighty have failed.[j]
⁷ At your roar, O God of Jacob,
  chariots and steeds lay still.
⁸ So terrible and awesome are you;
  who can stand before you and your great anger?[k]
⁹ From the heavens you pronounced sentence;
  the earth was terrified and reduced to silence,
¹⁰ When you arose, O God, for judgment
  to deliver the afflicted of the land.
  Selah
¹¹ Even wrathful Edom praises you;
  the remnant of Hamath* keeps your feast.

III

¹² Make and keep vows to the LORD your God.[l]
  May all present bring gifts to this awesome God,
¹³ Who checks the pride of princes,
  inspires awe among the kings of earth.

PSALM 77*

Confidence in God during National Distress

¹ For the leader; 'al Jeduthun. A psalm of Asaph.

I

² I cry aloud to God,
  cry to God to hear me.
³ On the day of my distress I seek the Lord;

by night my hands are raised unceasingly;[m]
  I refuse to be consoled.
⁴ When I think of God, I groan;
  as I ponder, my spirit grows faint.[n]
  Selah
⁵ My eyes cannot close in sleep;
  I am troubled and cannot speak.
⁶ I consider the days of old;
  the years long past ⁷ I remember.[o]
  In the night I meditate in my heart;
  I ponder and my spirit broods:
⁸ "Will the Lord reject us forever,[p]
  never again show favor?
⁹ Has God's love ceased forever?
  Has the promise failed for all ages?
¹⁰ Has God forgotten mercy,
  in anger withheld compassion?"
  Selah
¹¹ I conclude:* "My sorrow is this,
  the right hand of the Most High has left us."[q]

II

¹² I will remember* the deeds of the LORD;
  yes, your wonders of old I will remember.[r]
¹³ I will recite all your works;
  your exploits I will tell.
¹⁴ Your way, O God, is holy;
  what god is as great as our God?[s]
¹⁵ You alone are the God who did wonders;
  among the peoples you revealed your might.[t]

h Hb 3, 2.—i Pss 46, 10; 122, 6-9.—j 2 Kgs 19, 35; Jer 51, 39; Na 3, 18.—k Dt 7, 21; 1 Sm 6, 20; Na 1, 6; Mal 3, 2.—l Nm 30, 3.—m Pss 50, 15; 88, 2.—n Jon 2, 8.—o Ps 143, 5; Dt 32, 7.—p 8-10: Pss 13, 2; 44, 24; 74, 1; 80, 5; 89, 47; Lam 3, 31.—q Ex 15, 6. 12; Pss 17, 7; 18, 36.—r Ps 143, 5.—s Ps 18, 31; Ex 15, 11.—t Ps 86, 10; 89, 6.

Ps 76: A song glorifying Zion, the mountain of Jerusalem where God destroyed Israel's enemies. Zion is thus the appropriate site to celebrate the victory (3-4), a victory described in parallel scenes (5-7. 8-11). Israel is invited to worship its powerful patron deity (12-13).

76, 3: *Salem:* an ancient name for Jerusalem, used here perhaps on account of its allusion to the Hebrew word for peace, *shalom.* Cf Gn 14, 18; Heb 7, 1-3.

76, 5: *Ancient mountains:* conjectural translation of a difficult Hebrew phrase on the basis of Gn 49, 26. The mountains are part of the structure of the universe (Ps 89, 12-13).

76, 11: *Edom . . . Hamath:* conjectural translation. Israel's neighbors to the southeast and north.

Ps 77: A community lament in which the speaker ("I") describes the anguish of Israel at God's silence when its very existence is at stake (2-11). In response the speaker recites the story of how God brought the people into existence (12-21). The question is thus posed to God: will you allow the people you created to be destroyed?

77, 11: *I conclude:* literally, "I said." The psalmist, after pondering the present distress and God's promises to Israel, has decided that God has forgotten the people.

77, 12: *I will remember:* the verb sometimes means to make present the great deeds of Israel's past by reciting them. Cf Pss 78, 42; 105, 5; 106, 7.

16 With your arm you redeemed your peo-
        ple,
    the descendants of Jacob and Joseph. *u*
                                    Selah
17 The waters saw you, God;
    the waters saw you and lashed about,
    trembled even to their depths. *v*
18 The clouds poured down their rains;
    the thunderheads rumbled;
    your arrows flashed back and forth. *w*
19 The thunder of your chariot wheels re-
        sounded;
    your lightning lit up the world;
    the earth trembled and quaked. *x*
20 Through the sea was your path;
    your way, through the mighty waters,
    though your footsteps were unseen. *y*
21 You led your people like a flock
    under the care of Moses and Aaron. *z*

PSALM 78*

A New Beginning in Zion and David

1 A *maskil* of Asaph.

I

Attend, my people, to my teaching;
    listen to the words of my mouth.
2 I will open my mouth in story,*
    drawing lessons from of old. *a*

---

u Gn 46, 26-27; Neh 1, 10.—v Pss 18, 16; 114, 3; Na 1, 4.—w
Pss 18, 14-15; 29; 144, 6; Jb 37, 3-4; Wis 5, 21; Hb 3, 10-11;
Zec 9, 14.—x Pss 18, 8; 97, 4; 99, 1; Ex 19, 16; Jgs 5, 4-5.—y
Neh 9, 11; Wis 14, 3; Is 51, 10; Hb 3, 15.—z Ps 78, 52; Is 63,
11-14; Hos 12, 14; Mi 6, 4.—a Ps 49, 5; Mt 13, 35.—b Ps 44,
2.—c Ex 10, 2; Dt 4, 9; Jb 8, 8.—d Ps 147, 19; Dt 33, 4.—e Ps
22, 31-32; Dt 4, 9; 6, 7.—f Dt 31, 27; 32, 5.—g Ps 95, 10.—h
Ps 106, 7.—i 13-14: Ex 14—15; Ps 136, 13.—j Ex 14, 22; 15,
8.—k Ps 105, 39; Ex 13, 21; Wis 18, 3.—l Pss 105, 41; 114,
8; Ex 17, 1-7; Nm 20, 2-13; Dt 8, 15; Wis 11, 4; Is 48, 21.—m
Dt 9, 7; Ez 20, 13.—n Ps 106, 14; Ex 16, 2-36.—o Ps 23, 5.

Ps 78: A recital of history to show that past generations did
not respond to God's gracious deeds and were punished by God
making the gift into a punishment. Will Israel now fail to appreciate
God's new act—the choosing of Zion and of David? The tripartite
introduction invites Israel to learn the lessons hidden in its traditions (1-4. 5-7. 8-11); each section ends with the mention of God's
acts. There are two distinct narratives of approximately equal
length: the wilderness events (12-39) and the movement from
Egypt to Canaan (40-72). The structure of both is parallel: gracious
act (12-16. 40-55), rebellion (17-20. 56-58), divine punishment
(21-31. 59-64), God's readiness to forgive and begin anew (32-39.
65-72). The psalm may reflect the reunification program of either
King Hezekiah (late eighth century) or King Josiah (late seventh
century) in that the Northern Kingdom (Ephraim, Joseph) is especially invited to accept Zion and the Davidic king.
78, 2: *Story:* Hebrew *mashal* literally means "comparison"
and can signify a story with a hidden meaning. Mt 13, 35 cites
the verse to explain Jesus' use of parables.
78, 9: *Ephraimite archers:* Ephraim was the most important
tribe of the Northern Kingdom. Its military defeat (here unspecified) demonstrates its infidelity to God, who otherwise would
have protected it.
78, 12. 43: *Zoan:* a city on the arm of the Nile, a former
capital of Egypt.

---

3 We have heard them, we know them;
    our ancestors have recited them to us. *b*
4 We do not keep them from our children;
    we recite them to the next generation,
    The praiseworthy and mighty deeds of
        the LORD,
    the wonders that he performed. *c*
5 God set up a decree in Jacob,
    established a law in Israel: *d*
    What he commanded our ancestors,
    they were to teach their children;
6 That the next generation might come to
        know,
    children yet to be born. *e*
    In turn they were to recite them to their
        children,
7   that they too might put their trust in
        God,
    And not forget the works of God,
    keeping his commandments.
8 They were not to be like their ancestors,
    a rebellious and defiant generation, *f*
    A generation whose heart was not con-
        stant, *g*
    whose spirit was not faithful to God,
9 Like the ranks of Ephraimite archers,*
    who retreated on the day of battle.
10 They did not keep God's covenant;
    they refused to walk by his law.
11 They forgot his works,
    the wondrous deeds he had shown
        them.

II

A

12 In the sight of their ancestors God did
        wonders,
    in the land of Egypt, the plain of
        Zoan.* *h*
13 He split the sea and led them across, *i*
    piling up the waters rigid as walls. *j*
14 God led them with a cloud by day,
    all night with the light of fire. *k*
15 He split rock in the desert,
    gave water to drink, abounding as the
        deep. *l*
16 He made streams flow from crags,
    drew out rivers of water.

B

17 But they went on sinning against him,
    rebelling against the Most High in the
        desert. *m*
18 They tested God in their hearts,
    demanding the food they craved. *n*
19 They spoke against God, and said,
    "Can God spread a table in the des-
        ert?*o*

20 True, when he struck the rock,
    water gushed forth,
    the wadis flooded.
    But can he also provide bread,
    give meat to his people?"

C

21 The LORD heard and grew angry;[p]
    fire blazed up against Jacob;
    anger flared up against Israel.
22 For they did not believe in God,
    did not trust in his saving power.
23 So he commanded the skies above;*
    the doors of heaven he opened.
24 God rained manna upon them for
    food;
    bread from heaven he gave them.[q]
25 All ate a meal fit for heroes;
    food he sent in abundance.
26 He stirred up the east wind in the
    heavens;
    by his power God brought on the
    south wind.
27 He rained meat upon them like dust,
    winged fowl like the sands of the sea,
28 Brought them down in the midst of the
    camp,
    round about their tents.
29 They ate and were well filled;
    he gave them what they had craved.
30 But while they still wanted more,
    and the food was still in their mouths,
31 God's anger attacked them,
    killed their best warriors,
    laid low the youth of Israel.[r]
32 In spite of all this they went on sinning,
    they did not believe in his wonders.

D

33 God ended their days abruptly,
    their years in sudden death.
34 When he slew them, they began to seek
    him;
    they again inquired of their God.[s]
35 They remembered* that God was their
    rock,
    God Most High, their redeemer.
36 But they deceived him with their
    mouths,
    lied to him with their tongues.
37 Their hearts were not constant toward
    him;
    they were not faithful to his covenant.[t]
38 But God is merciful and forgave their
    sin;*
    he did not utterly destroy them.

Time and again he turned back his
    anger,
    unwilling to unleash all his rage.[u]
39 He was mindful that they were flesh,
    a breath that passes and does not re-
    turn.

III

A

40 How often they rebelled against God in
    the desert,
    grieved him in the wasteland.
41 Again and again they tested God,
    provoked the Holy One of Israel.
42 They did not remember his power,
    the day he redeemed them from the
    foe,[v]
43 When he displayed his wonders in
    Egypt,*
    his marvels in the plain of Zoan.[w]
44 God changed their rivers to blood;
    their streams they could not drink.
45 He sent insects that devoured them,[x]
    frogs that destroyed them.
46 He gave their harvest to the caterpillar,
    the fruits of their labor to the locust.
47 He killed their vines with hail,[y]
    their sycamores with frost.
48 He exposed their flocks to deadly hail,
    their cattle to lightning.[z]
49 He unleashed against them his fiery
    breath,
    roar, fury, and distress,
    storming messengers of death.
50 He cleared a path for his anger;
    he did not spare them from death;
    he delivered their beasts to the plague.
51 He struck all the firstborn of Egypt,[a]
    love's first child in the tents of Ham.
52 God led forth his people like sheep;
    he guided them through the desert like
    a flock.[b]

---

p 21f: Nm 11; Dt 32, 22.—q Ps 105, 40; Ex 16, 4. 14; Dt 8,
3; Wis 16, 20; Jn 6, 31.—r Nm 14, 29.—s Dt 32, 15. 18; Is 26,
16.—t Ps 95, 10; Is 29, 13.—u Ps 85, 4; Ex 32, 14; Is 48, 9;
Ez 20, 22.—v Ps 106, 21.—w 43f: Pss 105, 27-36; 135, 9; Ex
7, 14—11, 10; 12, 29-36; Wis 16—18.—x Ex 8, 17.—y Wis 16,
16.—z Ex 9, 3.—a Pss 105, 36; 136, 10; Ex 12, 29.—b Ps 77, 21.

78, 23-31: On the manna and the quail, see Ex 16 and Nm
11. Unlike Ex 16, here both manna and quail are instruments of
punishment, showing that a divine gift can become deadly because
of Israel's apostasy.
    78, 35: *Remembered:* invoked God publicly in worship. Their
words were insincere (36).
    78, 38: God is always ready to forgive and begin anew, as in
choosing Zion and David (65-72).
    78, 43-55: Ex 7—12 records ten plagues. Here there are six
divine attacks upon Egypt; the seventh climactic act is God's bringing Israel to the holy land.

53 He led them on secure and unafraid,
but the sea enveloped their enemies. *c*
54 He brought them to his holy land,
the mountain his right hand had won. *d*
55 God drove out the nations before them,
apportioned them a heritage by lot,
settled the tribes of Israel in their
tents.

B

56 But they tested, rebelled against God
Most High,
his decrees they did not observe.
57 They turned back, deceitful like their
ancestors;
they proved false like a bow with no
tension.
58 They enraged him with their high places;
with their idols they goaded him. *e*

C

59 God heard and grew angry;
he rejected Israel completely.
60 He forsook the shrine at Shiloh,*f
the tent where he dwelt with humans.
61 He gave up his might into captivity,
his glorious ark into the hands of the
foe. *g*
62 God abandoned his people to the sword;
he was enraged against his heritage.
63 Fire consumed their young men;
their young women heard no wedding
songs. *h*
64 Their priests fell by the sword;
their widows made no lamentation.

D

65 Then the Lord awoke as from sleep,
like a warrior from the effects of wine.

---

c Ex 14, 26-28.—d Ex 15, 17.—e Dt 32, 16. 21.—f Jos 18, 1; 1 Sm 1, 3; Jer 7, 12; 26, 6.—g 1 Sm 4, 11. 22.—h Dt 32, 25; Jer 7, 34.—i Pss 48, 2; 50, 2; Lam 2, 15.—j Ps 89, 21; Ez 34, 23; 37, 24; 2 Chr 6, 6.—k 1 Sm 16, 11-13; 2 Sm 7, 8.—l 2 Kgs 25, 9-10; Lam 1, 10.—m Jer 7, 33.—n 1 Mc 7, 17; Jer 14, 16.—o Pss 44, 14; 80, 7; 123, 3-4; Jb 12, 4; Dn 9, 16; Zep 2, 8.—p Pss 13, 2; 44, 24; 89, 47; Dt 4, 24.—q Ps 14, 4; Jer 10, 25.—r Ps 142, 7.

78, 60: *Shiloh:* an important shrine in the north prior to Jerusalem. Despite its holy status, it was destroyed (60-64; cf Jer 7, 12. 14).

78, 68. 70: God's ultimate offer of mercy to the sinful helpless people is Zion and the Davidic king.

Ps 79: A communal lament complaining that the nations have defiled the temple and murdered the holy people, leaving their corpses unburied (1-4). The occasion is probably the destruction of Jerusalem by the Babylonian army in 587 B.C. The people ask how long the withdrawal of divine favor will last (5), pray for action when (6-7), and admit that their own sins have brought about the catastrophe (8-9). They seek to persuade God to act for reasons of honor: the nations who do not call upon the Name are running amok (6); the divine honor is compromised (1. 10. 12); God's own servants suffer (2-4. 11).

66 He put his enemies to flight;
everlasting shame he dealt them.
67 He rejected the tent of Joseph,
chose not the tribe of Ephraim.
68 God chose the tribe of Judah,*
Mount Zion which he favored. *i*
69 He built his shrine like the heavens,
like the earth which he founded forever.
70 He chose David his servant,
took him from the sheepfold. *j*
71 From tending sheep God brought him,
to shepherd Jacob, his people,
Israel, his heritage. *k*
72 He shepherded them with a pure heart;
with skilled hands he guided them.

PSALM 79*

A Prayer for Jerusalem

1 A psalm of Asaph.

I

O God, the nations have invaded your
heritage;
they have defiled your holy temple,
have laid Jerusalem in ruins. *l*
2 They have left the corpses of your servants
as food for the birds of the heavens,
the flesh of your faithful for the
beasts of the earth. *m*
3 They have spilled their blood like water
all around Jerusalem,
and no one is left to bury them. *n*
4 We have become the reproach of our
neighbors,
the scorn and derision of those
around us. *o*

II

5 How long, LORD? Will you be angry
forever?
Will your rage keep burning like
fire?*p*
6 Pour out your wrath on nations that reject you,
on kingdoms that do not call on your
name,*q*
7 For they have devoured Jacob,
laid waste his home.
8 Do not hold past iniquities against us;
may your compassion come quickly,
for we have been brought very low. *r*

III

9 Help us, God our savior,
　for the glory of your name.
Deliver us, pardon our sins
　for your name's sake.[s]
10 Why should the nations say,
　"Where is their God?"[t]
Before our eyes make clear to the nations
　that you avenge the blood of your servants.[u]

IV

11 Let the groans of prisoners come before you;
　by your great power free those doomed to death.[v]
12 Lord, inflict on our neighbors sevenfold
　the disgrace they inflicted on you.[w]
13 Then we, your people, the sheep of your pasture,
　will give thanks to you forever;
　through all ages we will declare your praise.

PSALM 80*

Prayer To Restore God's Vineyard

1 For the leader; according to "Lilies." *Eduth.** A psalm of Asaph.

I

2 Shepherd of Israel, listen,
　guide of the flock of Joseph!
From your throne upon the cherubim
　reveal yourself[x]
3　to Ephraim, Benjamin, and Manasseh.
Stir up your power, come to save us.
4 O LORD of hosts, restore us.
Let your face shine upon us,
　that we may be saved.[y]

II

5 LORD of hosts,
　how long will you burn with anger
　while your people pray?[z]
6 You have fed them the bread of tears,
　made them drink tears in abundance.[a]
7 You have left us to be fought over by our neighbors;
　our enemies deride us.[b]

8 O LORD of hosts, restore us;
　let your face shine upon us,
　that we may be saved.

III

9 You brought a vine* out of Egypt;
　you drove away the nations and planted it.
10 You cleared the ground;
　it took root and filled the land.
11 The mountains were covered by its shadow,
　the cedars of God by its branches. '
12 It sent out boughs as far as the sea,*
　shoots as far as the river.
13 Why have you broken down the walls,
　so that all who pass by pluck its fruit?[c]
14 The boar from the forest strips the vine;
　the beast of the field feeds upon it.[d]
15 Turn again, LORD of hosts;
　look down from heaven and see;
Attend to this vine,
16　the shoot your right hand has planted.
17 Those who would burn or cut it down—
　may they perish at your rebuke.
18 May your help be with the man at your right hand,
　with the one* whom you once made strong.
19 Then we will not withdraw from you;
　revive us, and we will call on your name.
20 LORD of hosts, restore us;
　let your face shine upon us,
　that we may be saved.

s Ez 20, 44; 36, 22.—t Pss 42, 4; 115, 2; Jl 2, 17.—u Jl 4,
21.—v Ps 102, 21.—w Ps 89, 51-52.—x Pss 23, 1-3; 95, 7; 100,
3; Gn 48, 15; Ex 25, 22; 1 Sm 4, 4; 2 Sm 6, 2; Mi 7, 14.—y 4.
8. 20: Pss 4, 7; 31, 17; 67, 2; 85, 5; Nm 6, 25; Dn 9, 17.—z Pss
13, 2; 44, 24; 74, 1; 79, 5; 89, 47; Dt 4, 24.—a Pss 42, 4; 102,
10.—b Pss 44, 14; 79, 4; 123, 3-4; Jb 12, 4; Dn 9, 16; Zep 2,
8.—c Ps 89, 41.—d Hos 2, 14.

Ps 80: A community lament in time of military defeat. Using the familiar image of Israel as a vineyard, the people complain that God has broken down the wall protecting the once splendid vine brought from Egypt (9-14). They pray that God will again turn to them and use the Davidic king to lead them to victory (15-20).

80, 1: *Lilies . . . . Eduth:* the first term is probably the title of the melody to which the psalm was to be sung; the second is unexplained.

80, 9: *A vine:* a frequent metaphor for Israel. Cf Is 5, 1-7; 27, 2-5; Jer 2, 21; Hos 10, 1; Mt 21, 33.

80, 12: *The sea:* the Mediterranean. *The river:* the Euphrates. Cf Gn 15, 18; 1 Kgs 5, 1. The terms may also have a mythic nuance—the seas that surround the earth; sea and river are sometimes paralleled in poetry.

80, 18: *The man at your right hand . . . the one:* the Davidic king who will lead the army in battle.

PSALM 81*

An Admonition to Fidelity

1 For the leader; "upon the *gittith.*"* Of Asaph.

I

2 Sing joyfully to God our strength;[e]
    shout in triumph to the God of Jacob!
3 Take up a melody, sound the timbrel,
    the sweet-sounding harp and lyre.
4 Blow the trumpet at the new moon,
    at the full moon,* on our solemn
    feast.[f]
5 For this is a law in Israel,
    an edict of the God of Jacob,[g]
6 Who made it a decree for Joseph
    when he came out of the land of
    Egypt.

II

I hear a new oracle:*
7   "I relieved their shoulders of the bur-
    den;*
    their hands put down the basket.[h]

---

e Pss 43, 4; 68, 26; 149, 3; 150, 3-4; Jdt 16, 1.—f Lv 23, 24;
Nm 29, 1.—g Ex 23, 14ff.—h Ex 1, 14; 6, 6.—i Ps 95, 8; Ex 2,
23ff; 17, 7; 19, 16; Nm 20, 13; 27, 14.—j Ex 15, 26; Is 55, 2-
3.—k 10-11: Ex 20, 2-6; Dt 5, 6-10.—l Jer 3, 17; 7, 24.—m Is
48, 18.—n Lv 26, 7-8.—o Ps 147, 14; Dt 32, 13-14.—p Is 3, 13-
14.—q Ps 58, 2.—r Dt 1, 17.

Ps 81: At a pilgrimage feast, probably harvest in the fall, the
people assemble in the temple in accord with the Sinai ordinances
(2-6a). They hear a divine word (mediated by a temple speaker)
telling how God rescued them from slavery in Egypt (7-9), gave
them the fundamental commandment of fidelity (9-11), which
would bring punishment if they refused to obey (12-13). But if Israel repents, God will be with them once again, bestowing protection and fertility (14-17).
    81, 1: *Upon the gittith:* probably the title of the melody to
which the psalm was to be sung or a musical instrument.
    81, 4: *New moon . . . full moon:* the pilgrimage feast of har-
vest began with a great assembly (Lv 23, 24; Nm 29, 1), used the
new moon as a sign (Nm 29, 6), and included trumpets (Lv 23,
24).
    81, 6: *I hear a new oracle:* literally, "a tongue I do not know
I hear." A temple official speaks the word of God (6b-17), which
is authoritative and unlike merely human words (cf Nm 24, 4. 16).
    81, 7: *I relieved their shoulders of the burden:* literally,
"his [Israel's] shoulder," hence the plural translation. A reference
to the liberation of Israel from slavery in Egypt. *The basket:* for
carrying clay to make bricks. Cf Ex 1, 14.
    81, 8: *Meribah:* place of rebellion in the wilderness; cf Ex 17,
7; Nm 20, 13.
    81, 10: *There must be no foreign god among you:* as in Pss
50 and 95, Israel is challenged to obey the first commandment of
fidelity to God after the proclamation of the exodus.
    Ps 82: As in Ps 58, the pagan gods are seen as subordinate di-
vine beings to whom Israel's God had delegated oversight of the
foreign countries in the beginning (Dt 32, 8-9 LXX). Now God
arises in the heavenly assembly (1) to rebuke the unjust "gods" (2-
4), who are stripped of divine status and reduced in rank to mortals
(5-7). They are accused of misruling the earth by not upholding the
poor. A short prayer for universal justice concludes the psalm (8).
    82, 5: The gods are blind and unable to declare what is right.
Their misrule shakes earth's foundations (cf Pss 11, 3; 75, 4),
which God made firm in creation (Ps 96, 10).

---

8 In distress you called and I rescued you;
    unseen, I spoke to you in thunder;
    At the waters of Meribah* I tested you
    and said:[i]
                    Selah
9   'Listen, my people, I give you warn-
    ing!
    If only you will obey me, Israel![j]
10 There must be no foreign god among
    you;*[k]
    you must not worship an alien god.
11 I, the LORD, am your God,
    who brought you up from the land of
    Egypt.
    Open wide your mouth that I may fill
    it.'
12 But my people did not listen to my
    words;
    Israel did not obey me.
13 So I gave them over to hardness of
    heart;
    they followed their own designs.[l]
14 But even now if my people would listen,
    if Israel would walk in my paths,[m]
15 In a moment I would subdue their foes,
    against their enemies unleash my
    hand.[n]
16 Those who hate the LORD would trem-
    ble,
    their doom sealed forever.
17 But Israel I would feed with the finest
    wheat,
    satisfy them with honey from the
    rock."[o]

PSALM 82*

The Downfall of Unjust Gods

1 A psalm of Asaph.

I

God rises in the divine council,
    gives judgment in the midst of the
    gods.[p]
2 "How long will you judge unjustly
    and favor the cause of the wicked?[q]
                    Selah
3 Defend the lowly and fatherless;
    render justice to the afflicted and
    needy.
4 Rescue the lowly and poor;
    deliver them from the hand of the
    wicked."[r]

II

5 The gods neither know nor understand,
    wandering about in darkness,
    and all the world's foundations
    shake.*

6 I declare: "Gods though you be,*
　　offspring of the Most High all of you,
7 Yet like any mortal you shall die;
　　like any prince you shall fall."
8 Arise, O God, judge the earth,*
　　for yours are all the nations.

PSALM 83*

Prayer against a Hostile Alliance

1 A song; a psalm of Asaph.

I

2 God, do not be silent;
　　God, be not still and unmoved![s]
3 See how your enemies rage;
　　your foes proudly raise their heads.
4 They conspire against your people,
　　plot against those you protect.[t]
5 They say, "Come, let us wipe out their
　　nation;
　　let Israel's name be mentioned no
　　more!"
6 They scheme with one mind,
　　in league against you:[u]
7 The tents of Ishmael and Edom,*
　　the people of Moab and Hagar,[v]
8 Gebal, Ammon, and Amalek,[w]
　　Philistia and the inhabitants of
　　Tyre.[x]
9 Assyria, too, in league with them
　　gives aid to the descendants of Lot.
　　　　　　　　　　　　　　Selah

II

10 Deal with them as with Midian;*
　　as with Sisera and Jabin at the torrent
　　Kishon,[y]
11 Those destroyed at Endor,
　　who became dung for the ground.[z]
12 Make their nobles like Oreb and Zeeb,
　　all their princes like Zebah and Zal-
　　munna,
13 Who made a plan together,
　　"Let us seize the pastures of God."
14 My God, turn them into withered grass,
　　into chaff flying before the wind.[a]
15 As a fire raging through a forest,
　　a flame setting mountains ablaze,[b]
16 Pursue them with your tempest;
　　terrify them with your storm.[c]
17 Cover their faces with shame,
　　till they pay you homage, LORD.
18 Let them be dismayed and shamed for-
　　ever;
　　let them perish in disgrace.

19 Show them you alone are the LORD,
　　the Most High over all the earth.[d]

PSALM 84*

Prayer of a Pilgrim to Jerusalem

1 For the leader; "upon the *gittith*." A psalm of
the Korahites.

I

2 How lovely your dwelling,
　　O LORD of hosts![e]
3 My soul yearns and pines
　　for the courts of the LORD.[f]
　　My heart and flesh cry out
　　for the living God.
4 As the sparrow finds a home*
　　and the swallow a nest to settle her
　　young,
　　My home is by your altars,
　　LORD of hosts, my king and my
　　God![g]
5 Happy are those who dwell in your
　　house!
　　They never cease to praise you.
　　　　　　　　　　　　　　Selah

II

6 Happy are those who find refuge in
　　you,
　　whose hearts are set on pilgrim roads.

---

s Pss 10, 1; 44, 24; 109, 1.—t Jer 11, 9.—u Ps 2, 2.—v Nm
20, 23; 1 Chr 5, 10. 19.—w Ex 17, 8.—x Jos 13, 2.—y Ex 2, 15;
Is 9, 3; 10, 26.—z Jer 8, 2.—a Pss 1, 4; 35, 5; 58, 10; Is 5, 24;
10, 17; 13; 29, 5; Ez 21, 3.—b Ps 50, 3.—c Jb 27, 21; Jer
25, 32.—d Ps 97, 9; Dt 4, 39; Dn 3, 45.—e Pss 43, 3-4; 122,
1.—f Pss 42, 2-3; 63, 2-3; 143, 6; Is 26, 9.—g Ps 5, 3.

82, 6: *I declare: "Gods though you be"*: in Jn 10, 34 Jesus
uses the verse to prove that those to whom the word of God is addressed can fittingly be called "gods."

82, 8: *Judge the earth:* according to Dt 32, 8-9 LXX, Israel's
God had originally assigned jurisdiction over the foreign nations
to the subordinate deities, keeping Israel as a personal possession. Now God will directly take over the rulership of the whole
world.

Ps 83: The community lament complains to God of the nations'
attempts to wipe out the name of Israel (2-9). The psalmist sees
all Israel's enemies throughout its history united in a conspiracy
(3-9). May God destroy the current crop of enemies as the
enemies of old were destroyed (10-13), and may they be pursued
until they acknowledge the name of Israel's God (14-19).

83, 7-9: Apart from the Assyrians, all the nations listed here
were neighbors of Israel. *The people of . . . Hagar:* a tribe of
the desert regions east of *Ammon* and *Moab* (1 Chr 5, 10. 19-
22). *Gebal* is the Phoenician city of Byblos or perhaps a mountain
region south of the Dead Sea. *The descendants of Lot* are
Moab and Edom (Gn 19, 36-38 and Dt 2, 9). These nations were
never united against Israel in the same period; the psalm has
lumped them all together.

83, 10-13: For the historical events, see Jgs 4—8.

Ps 84: Israelites celebrated three pilgrimage feasts in Jerusalem annually. The psalm expresses the sentiments of the pilgrims
eager to enjoy the divine presence.

84, 4: The desire of a restless bird for a secure home is an
image of the desire of a pilgrim for the secure house of God. Cf
Ps 42, 2-3, where the image for the desire of the pilgrim is the
thirst of the deer for water.

7 As they pass through the Baca valley,*
    they find spring water to drink.
Also from pools the Lord provides
    water
    for those who lose their way.
8 They pass through outer and inner wall
    and see the God of gods on Zion.

III
9 LORD of hosts, hear my prayer;
    listen, God of Jacob.   *Selah*
10 O God, look kindly on our shield;
    look upon the face of your anoint-
    ed.*h

IV
11 Better one day in your courts
    than a thousand elsewhere.
Better the threshold of the house of my
    God
    than a home in the tents of the wick-
    ed.
12 For a sun and shield is the LORD God,
    bestowing all grace and glory.
The LORD withholds no good thing
    from those who walk without re-
    proach.
13 O LORD of hosts,
    happy are those who trust in you!

PSALM 85*

Prayer for Divine Favor

1 For the leader. A psalm of the Korahites.

I
2 You once favored, LORD, your land,
    restored the good fortune of Jacob.*i*

---

h Ps 89, 19.—i Pss 14, 7; 126, 4.—j Ps 78, 38; Ex 32, 14; Is
48, 9.—k Ps 80, 4.—l Pss 79, 5; 89, 47.—m Pss 89, 15; 97, 2.—
n Is 45, 8.—o Ps 67, 7; Lv 26, 4; Ez 34, 27; Hos 2, 23-24; Zec
8, 12.—p Pss 25, 1; 143, 8.—q Jl 2, 13.—r Pss 5, 2; 130, 1-2.

84, 7: *Baca valley:* Hebrew obscure; probably a valley on the
way to Jerusalem.
84, 10: *Our shield . . . your anointed:* the king had a role
in the liturgical celebration. For the king as shield, cf Ps 89, 19.
Ps 85: A national lament reminding God of past favors and forgiveness (2-4) and begging for forgiveness and grace now (5-8).
A speaker represents the people who wait humbly with open
hearts (9-10): God will be active on their behalf (11-14). The
situation suggests the conditions of Judea during the early postexilic period, the fifth century B.C.; the thoughts are similar to
those of postexilic prophets (Hg 1, 5-11; 2, 6-9).
85, 9: The prophet listens to God's revelation. Cf Hb 2, 1.
85, 11-14: Divine activity is personified as pairs of virtues.
Ps 86: An individual lament. The psalmist, "poor and oppressed" (1), "devoted" (2), "your servant" (2. 4. 16), "rescued
from the depths of Sheol" (13), attacked by the ruthless (14), desires only God's protection (1-7. 11-17).

3 You forgave the guilt of your people,
    pardoned all their sins.   *Selah*
4 You withdrew all your wrath,
    turned back your burning anger.*j*

II
5 Restore us once more, God our sav-
       ior;
    abandon your wrath against us.*k*
6 Will you be angry with us forever,
    drag out your anger for all genera-
    tions?*l*
7 Please give us life again,
    that your people may rejoice in
    you.
8 Show us, LORD, your love;
    grant us your salvation.

III
9 I will listen for the word of God;*
    surely the LORD will proclaim peace
To his people, to the faithful,
    to those who trust in him.
10 Near indeed is salvation for the loyal;
    prosperity will fill our land.
11 Love and truth will meet;*
    justice and peace will kiss.*m*
12 Truth will spring from the earth;
    justice will look down from heaven.*n*
13 The LORD will surely grant abundance;
    our land will yield its increase.*o*
14 Prosperity will march before the Lord,
    and good fortune will follow behind.

PSALM 86*

Prayer in Time of Distress

1 A prayer of David.

I
Hear me, LORD, and answer me,
    for I am poor and oppressed.
2 Preserve my life, for I am loyal;
    save your servant who trusts in
    you.
3 You are my God; pity me, Lord;
    to you I call all the day.
4 Gladden the soul of your servant;
    to you, Lord, I lift up my soul.*p*
5 Lord, you are kind and forgiving,
    most loving to all who call on you.*q*
6 LORD, hear my prayer;
    listen to my cry for help.*r*
7 In this time of trouble I call,
    for you will answer me.

Ps

II

8 None among the gods can equal you, O
Lord;
nor can their deeds compare to
yours.[s]
9 All the nations you have made shall
come
to bow before you, Lord,
and give honor to your name.[t]
10 For you are great and do wondrous
deeds;
and you alone are God.

III

11 Teach me, LORD, your way
that I may walk in your truth,[u]
single-hearted and revering your
name.
12 I will praise you with all my heart,
glorify your name forever, Lord my
God.
13 Your love for me is great;
you have rescued me from the depths
of Sheol.[v]
14 O God, the arrogant have risen against
me;
a ruthless band has sought my life;
to you they pay no heed.
15 But you, Lord, are a merciful and gracious God,
slow to anger, most loving and true.[w]
16 Turn to me, have pity on me;
give your strength to your servant;
save this child of your handmaid.[x]
17 Give me a sign of your favor:
make my enemies see, to their confusion,
that you, LORD, help and comfort
me.

PSALM 87*

Zion the True Birthplace of Diaspora Pilgrims

1 A psalm of the Korahites. A song.

I

The LORD loves the city[y]
founded on holy mountains,
2 Loves the gates* of Zion
more than any dwelling in Jacob.
3 Glorious things are said of you,
O city of God!   *Selah*

II

4 From Babylon and Egypt I count
those who acknowledge the LORD.
Philistia, Ethiopia, Tyre,
of them it can be said:
"This one was born there."

5 But of Zion it must be said:*
"They all were born here."[z]
The Most High confirms this;[a]
6 the LORD notes in the register of the
peoples:
"This one was born here."[b]   *Selah*
7 So all sing in their festive dance:
"Within you is my true home."[c]

PSALM 88*

A Despairing Lament

1 A song; a psalm of the Korahites. For the
leader; according to *Mahalath*. For singing; a
maskil of Heman the Ezrahite.

I

2 LORD, my God, I call out by day;
at night I cry aloud in your presence.[d]
3 Let my prayer come before you;
incline your ear to my cry.[e]
4 For my soul is filled with troubles;[f]
my life draws near to Sheol.*
5 I am reckoned with those who go down
to the pit;
I am weak, without strength.
6 My couch is among the dead,
with the slain who lie in the grave.
You remember them no more;
they are cut off from your care.
7 You plunged me into the bottom of the
pit,
into the darkness of the abyss.
8 Your wrath lies heavy upon me;
all your waves crash over me.[g]   *Selah*

---

s Pss 35, 10; 89, 9; Ex 15, 11; Dt 3, 24; Jer 10, 6.—t Ps 22,
28; Zec 14, 16; Rv 15, 4.—u Pss 25, 4; 26, 3; 27, 11; 119, 12.
35; 143, 8. 10.—v Pss 30, 4; 40, 3; Jon 2, 7.—w Pss 103, 8;
130, 7; 145, 8; Ex 34, 6.—x Pss 25, 16; 116, 16; Wis 9, 5.—y
1-2: Pss 76, 2-3; 78, 68-69.—z Gal 4, 26.—a Ps 48, 9.—b Is 4,
3.—c Pss 68, 26; 149, 3.—d Ps 77, 3.—e Ps 119, 170.—f 4-7:
Pss 28, 1; 30, 4; 40, 3; 86, 13; 143, 7; Nm 16, 33; Jb 17, 1; Jon
2, 7.—g Pss 18, 5; 32, 6; 42, 8; 69, 2; Jon 2, 4.

Ps 87: A song of Zion, like Psalms 46, 48, 76, and 132. After
the exile of the sixth century B.C., diaspora Jews from all over
the world (4) made the long pilgrimage to Jerusalem, the city of
God (1-3). Such Jews may have hailed from distant lands, but the
psalm sees them as children of Zion (5-7). The original occasion
may have been Pentecost, which always attracted a large number
of diaspora Jews.
87, 2: *The gates:* the city itself, a common Hebrew idiom.
87, 5-6: The bond between the exile and the holy city was so
strong as to override the exile's citizenship of lesser cities.
Ps 88: A lament in which the psalmist prays for rescue from
the alienation of approaching death. Each of the three stanzas begins with a call to God (2. 10b. 14) and complains of the death
that separates one from God. The tone is persistently grim.
88, 4-8: In imagination the psalmist already experiences the
alienation of Sheol.

9 Because of you my friends shun me;
   you make me loathsome to them;[h]
   Caged in, I cannot escape;
10   my eyes grow dim from trouble.

II

All day I call on you, LORD;
   I stretch out my hands to you.
11 Do you work wonders for the dead?*
   Do the shades arise and praise you?[i]
                                    Selah
12 Is your love proclaimed in the grave,
   your fidelity in the tomb?
13 Are your marvels declared in the dark-
     ness,
   your righteous deeds in the land of
     oblivion?

III

14 But I cry out to you, LORD;
   in the morning my prayer comes be-
     fore you.
15 Why do you reject me, LORD?
   Why hide your face from me?
16 I am mortally afflicted since youth;
   lifeless, I suffer your terrible blows.
17 Your wrath has swept over me;
   your terrors have reduced me to si-
     lence.[j]

---

h Pss 38, 12; 79, 4; 80, 7; 123, 3-4; 142, 8; Jb 12, 4; 19, 13;
Lam 3, 7; Dn 9, 16.—i Pss 6, 6; 30, 10; 115, 17; Is 38, 18.—j
Jb 6, 4; 20, 25.—k Jb 19, 13.—l Is 63, 7.—m Pss 61, 7-8; 132,
11; 2 Sm 7, 8-16.—n Pss 29, 1; 82, 1; Jb 1, 6; 5, 1.—o 7-9: Pss
35, 10; 86, 8; 113, 5; Ex 15, 11; Jer 10, 6.—p 10-11: Pss 65,
8; 74, 13-15; 107, 29; Jb 7, 12; Is 51, 9-10.—q Pss 24, 1-2; 50,
12; Dt 10, 14; 1 Cor 10, 26.

88, 11-13: The psalmist seeks to persuade God to act out of
concern for divine honor: the shades give you no worship, so keep
me alive to offer you praise.
Ps 89: The community laments the defeat of the Davidic king,
to whom God promised kingship as enduring as the heavens (2-5).
The psalm narrates how God became king of the divine beings (6-
9) and how the Davidic king became king of earthly kings (20-
38). Since the defeat of the king calls into question God's promise, the community ardently prays God to be faithful to the original promise to David (39-52).
89, 3-5: David's dynasty is to be as long-lasting as the heavens,
a statement reinforced by using the same verbs (establish, stand)
both of the divine love and loyalty and of the Davidic dynasty and
throne. Cf 29-30.
89, 7: *The gods:* literally, "the sons of gods," "the holy ones"
and "courtiers" of 6 and 8. These heavenly spirits are members
of God's court.
89, 11: *Rahab:* a mythological sea monster whose name is
used in the Bible mainly as a personification of primeval chaos. Cf
Jb 9, 13; 26, 12; Ps 74, 13-14; Is 51, 9.
89, 13: *Zaphon and Amanus:* two sacred mountains in
northern Syria. *Tabor:* a high hill in the valley of Jezreel in
northern Israel. *Hermon:* a mountain in Lebanon, forming the
southern spur of the Anti-Lebanon range.

18 All the day they surge round like a
     flood;
   from every side they close in on
     me.
19 Because of you companions shun me;[k]
   my only friend is darkness.

PSALM 89*

A Lament over God's Promise to David

1 A *maskil* of Ethan the Ezrahite.

I

2 The promises of the LORD I will sing
     forever,[l]
   proclaim your loyalty through all
     ages.
3 For you said, "My love is established
     forever;*
   my loyalty will stand as long as the
     heavens.
4 I have made a covenant with my chosen
     one;
   I have sworn to David my servant:
5 I will make your dynasty stand forever
   and establish your throne through all
     ages."[m]   *Selah*

II

6 The heavens praise your marvels,
     LORD,
   your loyalty in the assembly of the
     holy ones.[n]
7 Who in the skies ranks with the LORD?
   Who is like the LORD among the
     gods?*[o]
8 A God dreaded in the council of the
     holy ones,
   greater and more awesome than all
     who sit there!
9 LORD, God of hosts, who is like you?
   Mighty LORD, your loyalty is always
     present.
10 You rule the raging sea;[p]
   you still its swelling waves.
11 You crushed Rahab* with a mortal
     blow;
   your strong arm scattered your foes.
12 Yours are the heavens, yours the earth;
   you founded the world and every-
     thing in it.[q]
13 Zaphon and Amanus* you created;
   Tabor and Hermon rejoice in your
     name.

14 Mighty your arm, strong your hand,
  your right hand is ever exalted.
15 Justice and judgment are the foundation of your throne;
  love and loyalty march before you.[r]
16 Happy the people who know you,
  LORD,
  who walk in the radiance of your
  face.
17 In your name they sing joyfully all the
  day;
  at your victory they raise the festal
  shout.[s]
18 You are their majestic strength;
  by your favor our horn* is exalted.[t]
19 Truly the LORD is our shield,
  the Holy One of Israel, our king![u]

III

20 Once you spoke in vision;[v]
  to your faithful ones you said:
  "I have set a leader over the warriors;
  I have raised up a hero from the
  army.
21 I have chosen David, my servant;
  with my holy oil I have anointed
  him.
22 My hand will be with him;[w]
  my arm will make him strong.
23 No enemy shall outwit him,
  nor shall the wicked defeat him.
24 I will crush his foes before him,
  strike down those who hate him.
25 My loyalty and love will be with him;
  through my name his horn will be
  exalted.
26 I will set his hand upon the sea,
  his right hand upon the rivers.*
27 He shall cry to me, 'You are my father,[x]
  my God, the Rock that brings me victory!'
28 I myself make him firstborn,
  Most High* over the kings of the
  earth.
29 Forever I will maintain my love for
  him;[y]
  my covenant with him stands firm.
30 I will establish his dynasty forever,
  his throne as the days of the heavens.
31 If his descendants forsake my law,[z]
  do not follow my decrees,
32 If they fail to observe my statutes,
  do not keep my commandments,
33 I will punish their crime with a rod
  and their guilt with lashes.

34 But I will not take my love from
  him,
  nor will I betray my bond of loyalty.[a]
35 I will not violate my covenant;
  the promise of my lips I will not
  alter.[b]
36 By my holiness I swore once for
  all:[c]
  I will never be false to David.
37 His dynasty will continue forever,[d]
  his throne, like the sun before
  me.
38 Like the moon it will stand eternal,
  forever firm like the sky!"*   *Selah*

IV

39 But now you have rejected and
  spurned,[e]
  been enraged at your anointed.
40 You renounced the covenant with your
  servant,
  defiled his crown in the dust.
41 You broke down all his defenses,[f]
  left his strongholds in ruins.
42 All who pass through seize plunder;
  his neighbors deride him.
43 You have exalted the right hand of his
  foes,
  have gladdened all his enemies.[g]
44 You turned back his sharp sword,
  did not support him in battle.
45 You brought to an end his splendor,
  hurled his throne to the ground.

---

r Pss 85, 11-12; 97, 2.—s Ps 47, 2; Zep 3, 14.—t Pss 112, 9;
148, 14.—u Pss 47, 9; 96, 10; 97, 1; 99, 1; Is 6, 3.—v 20-21:
Pss 78, 70; 132, 11-12; 2 Sm 7, 4. 8-16; 1 Chr 17, 3. 7-14; Is
42, 1; Acts 13, 22.—w 22-25: 1 Sm 2, 9-10.—x 27-28: Pss 2, 7;
110, 2-3; 2 Sm 7, 9. 14; Col 1, 15. 18; Rv 1, 5.—y 29-30: Pss
18, 51; 61, 8; 144, 10; 2 Sm 7, 11; Is 55, 3.—z 31-33: Lv 26,
14-33.—a Ps 40, 12; Sir 47, 22.—b Jer 33, 20-21.—c Am 4,
2.—d 37-38: Pss 61, 8; 72, 5; Sir 43, 6.—e 39-47: Ps 44, 10-
25.—f 41-42: Ps 80, 13-14.—g Lam 1, 5.

89, 18, 25: *Horn:* a concrete noun for an abstract quality;
horn is a symbol of strength.
89, 26: *The sea . . . the rivers:* geographically the limits of
the Davidic Empire (the Mediterranean and the Euphrates);
mythologically, the traditional forces of chaos. See note on v 11.
89, 28: *Most High:* a divine title, which is here extended to
David as God's own king. Cf Ps 2, 7-9; Is 9, 5. As God rules over
the members of the heavenly council (6-9), so David, God's surrogate, rules over earthly kings.
89, 37-38: *Like the sun before me . . . like the sky:* as enduring as the heavenly lights. Cf 2-5 and Ps 72, 5. 17.

⁴⁶ You cut short the days of his youth,
   covered him with shame.   *Selah*
⁴⁷ How long, LORD?
   Will you stay hidden forever?
   Must your wrath smolder like
   fire?*ʰ*
⁴⁸ Remember how brief is my life,
   how frail the race you created!*ⁱ*
⁴⁹ What mortal can live and not see
   death?
   Who can escape the power of Sheol?*ʲ*
                  Selah
⁵⁰ Where are your promises of old,
   Lord,
   the loyalty sworn to David?
⁵¹ Remember, Lord, the insults to your
   servants,
   how I bear all the slanders of the nations.*ᵏ*
⁵² Your enemies, LORD, insult your
   anointed;
   they insult my every endeavor.

            * * *

⁵³ Blessed be the LORD forever! Amen and
   amen!**ˡ*

---

h Pss 13, 2; 44, 25; 74, 10; 79, 5; Dt 4, 24.—i Pss 39, 5-6; 62, 10; 90, 9-10; 144, 4; Jb 7, 6. 16; 14, 1. 5; Eccl 6, 12; Wis 2, 5.—j Ps 90, 3.—k Ps 79, 12.—l Pss 41, 14; 72, 18; 106, 48.—m Pss 48, 15; 55, 20; 93, 2; 102, 13; Hb 1, 12.—n 2 Pt 3, 8.—o Pss 103, 14; 104, 29; 146, 4; Gn 3, 19; 1 Mc 2, 63; Jb 34, 14-15; Eccl 3, 20; 12, 7; Sir 40, 11.—p Ps 89, 48.—q Pss 37, 2; 102, 11; 103, 15-16; Jb 14, 1-2; Is 40, 6-8.—r Ps 109, 14-15; Hos 7, 2.—s 9-10: Pss 39, 5-7; 62, 10; 102, 24-25; 144, 4; Gn 6, 3; Jb 7, 6. 16; 14, 5; Prv 10, 27; Eccl 6, 12; Wis 2, 5; Sir 18, 8; Is 65, 20.—t Ps 17, 15.—u Nm 14, 34; Jer 31, 13.—v Ps 33, 22.

89, 53: The doxology at the end of the third book of the Psalms; it is not part of Ps 89.
   Ps 90: A communal lament that describes only in general terms the cause of the community's distress. After confidently invoking God (1), the psalm turns to a complaint contrasting God's eternity with the brevity of human life (2-6) and sees in human suffering the punishment for sin (7-12). The psalm concludes with a plea for God's intervention (13-17).
   90, 3: *Return:* one word of God is enough to return mortals to the dust from which they were created. Humans were created from earth in Gn 2, 7; 3, 19.
   90, 4: The translation reverses the order of the difficult Hebrew verses 3 and 4 to get the probable original order. *A watch in the night:* the night was divided into three sentry periods or watches. Cf Jgs 7, 19.
   90, 5: *You have brought them to their end:* an interpretation of the unclear Hebrew.
   90, 6: *It is dry and withered:* the transitory nature of the grass under the scorching sun was proverbial. Cf Ps 129, 6; Is 40, 6-8.

FOURTH BOOK — PSALMS 90–106

PSALM 90*

God's Eternity and Human Frailty

¹ A prayer of Moses, the man of God.

I

Lord, you have been our refuge
   through all generations.
² Before the mountains were born,
   the earth and the world brought forth,
   from eternity to eternity you are
   God.*ᵐ*
⁴ A thousand years in your eyes*
   are merely a yesterday.*ⁿ*
³ But humans you return to dust,
   saying, "Return,* you mortals!"*ᵒ*
⁴ᶜ Before a watch passes in the night,
⁵ you have brought them to their end;*ᵖ*
They disappear like sleep at dawn;
   they are like grass that dies.
⁶ It sprouts green in the morning;
   by evening it is dry and withered.*�q*

II

⁷ Truly we are consumed by your anger,
   filled with terror by your wrath.
⁸ You have kept our faults before you,
   our hidden sins exposed to your sight.*ʳ*
⁹ Our life ebbs away under your wrath;*ˢ*
   our years end like a sigh.
¹⁰ Seventy is the sum of our years,
   or eighty, if we are strong;
Most of them are sorrow and toil;
   they pass quickly, we are all but gone.
¹¹ Who comprehends your terrible anger?
   Your wrath matches the fear it inspires.
¹² Teach us to count our days aright,
   that we may gain wisdom of heart.
¹³ Relent, O LORD! How long?
   Have pity on your servants!
¹⁴ Fill us at daybreak with your love,*ᵗ*
   that all our days we may sing for joy.
¹⁵ Make us glad as many days as you humbled us,
   for as many years as we have seen
   trouble.*ᵘ*
¹⁶ Show your deeds to your servants,
   your glory to their children.
¹⁷ May the favor of the Lord our God be
   ours.*ᵛ*
Prosper the work of our hands!
Prosper the work of our hands!

Ps

PSALM 91*

Security Under God's Protection

I

1 You who dwell in the shelter of the
 Most High,*
   who abide in the shadow of the Almighty,
2 Say to the LORD, "My refuge and fortress,
   my God in whom I trust."*w*
3 God will rescue you from the fowler's
 snare,
   from the destroying plague,
4 Will shelter you with pinions,
   spread wings that you may take refuge;*x*
   God's faithfulness is a protecting
 shield.
5 You shall not fear the terror of the night
   nor the arrow that flies by day,*y*
6 Nor the pestilence that roams in darkness,
   nor the plague that ravages at noon.*z*
7 Though a thousand fall at your side,
   ten thousand at your right hand,
   near you it shall not come.
8 You need simply watch;
   the punishment of the wicked you
 will see.*a*
9 You have the LORD for your refuge;
   you have made the Most High your
 stronghold.
10 No evil shall befall you,
   no affliction come near your tent.*b*
11 For God commands the angels**c*
   to guard you in all your ways.*d*
12 With their hands they shall support
 you,
   lest you strike your foot against a
 stone.*e*
13 You shall tread upon the asp and the
 viper,
   trample the lion and the dragon.*f*

II

14 Whoever clings to me I will deliver;
   whoever knows my name I will set on
 high.*g*
15 All who call upon me I will answer;*h*
   I will be with them in distress;*i*
   I will deliver them and give them
 honor.
16 With length of days I will satisfy them
   and show them my saving power.*j*

PSALM 92*

A Hymn of Thanksgiving for God's Fidelity

1 A psalm. A sabbath song.

I

2 It is good to give thanks to the LORD,
   to sing praise to your name, Most
 High,*k*
3 To proclaim your love in the morning,
   your faithfulness in the night,
4 With the ten-stringed harp,
   with melody upon the lyre.*l*
5 For you make me jubilant, LORD, by
 your deeds;
   at the works of your hands I shout for
 joy.

II

6 How great are your works, LORD!*m*
   How profound your purpose!
7 A senseless person cannot know this;
   a fool cannot comprehend.
8 Though the wicked flourish like grass
   and all sinners thrive,*n*
   They are destined for eternal destruction;
9   for you, LORD, are forever on high.
10 Indeed your enemies, LORD,
   indeed your enemies shall perish;
   all sinners shall be scattered.*o*

III

11 You have given me the strength of a
 wild bull;*p*
   you have poured rich oil upon me.*q*

---

w Pss 18, 3; 31, 3-4; 42, 10; 142, 6; 2 Sm 22, 3.—x Pss 17,
8; 36, 8; 57, 2; 63, 8; Dt 32, 11; Ru 2, 12; Mt 23, 37.—y Prv
3, 25; Song 3, 8.—z Dt 32, 24.—a Ps 92, 12.—b Prv 12, 21; Dt
7, 15.—c 11-12: Mt 4, 6; Lk 4, 10f.—d Heb 1, 14.—e Ps 121,
3; Prv 3, 23.—f Is 11, 8; Lk 10, 19.—g Pss 9, 11; 119, 132.—h
Jer 33, 3; Zec 13, 9.—i Is 43, 2.—j Prv 3, 2.—k Pss 33, 1; 147,
1.—l Pss 33, 2; 144, 9.—m 6-7: Pss 131, 1; 139, 6. 17; Wis 13,
1; 17, 1.—n Ps 37, 35.—o Pss 68, 1-2; 125, 5.—p Ps 75, 10; Dt
33, 17.—q Ps 23, 5.

Ps 91: A prayer of someone who has taken refuge in the security of the temple (1-2). The psalmist is confident that God's presence will protect the people in every dangerous situation (3-13).
The final verses are an oracle of salvation promising salvation to
those who trust in God (14-16).
  91, 1: *The shelter of the Most High:* basically "hiding
place" but in the psalms a designation for the protected temple
precincts. Cf Pss 27, 5; 31, 21; 61, 5. *The shadow of the Almighty:* literally, "the shadow of the wings of the Almighty." Cf
Pss 17, 8; 36, 8; 57, 2; 63, 8. V 4 makes clear that the shadow
is an image of the safety afforded by the outstretched wings of the
cherubim in the holy of holies.
  91, 11-12: The words are cited in Mt 4, 6; Lk 4, 10-11, as
part of Satan's challenge to Jesus in the desert.
  Ps 92: A hymn of praise and thanks for God's faithful deeds (2-
5). The wicked, deluded by their prosperity (6-9), are punished
(10), whereas the psalmist has already experienced God's protection (11-16).

¹² My eyes look with glee on my wicked
enemies;
  my ears delight in the fall of my foes.ʳ
¹³ The just shall flourish like the palm
tree,
  shall grow like a cedar of Lebanon.ˢ
¹⁴ Planted* in the house of the LORD,
  they shall flourish in the courts of our
  God.
¹⁵ They shall bear fruit even in old age,
  always vigorous and sturdy,
¹⁶ As they proclaim: "The LORD is just;
  our rock, in whom there is no
  wrong."ᵗ

PSALM 93*

God Is a Mighty King

¹ The LORD is king,* robed with
majesty;
  the LORD is robed, girded with
  might.ᵘ
  The world will surely stand in place,
  never to be moved.ᵛ
² Your throne stands firm from of old;
  you are from everlasting, LORD.ʷ
³ The flood* has raised up, LORD;
  the flood has raised up its roar;
  the flood has raised its pounding
  waves.

---

r Ps 91, 8.—s Pss 1, 3; 52, 10; Jer 17, 8.—t Dt 32, 4.—u Pss
47, 8; 96, 10; 97, 1; 99, 1.—v Pss 75, 2-3; 104, 5.—w Pss 55,
20; 90, 2; 102, 13; Hb 1, 12.—x Na 1, 2.—y Jer 51, 56; Lam 3,
64.—z Pss 13, 2; 75, 5; Jer 12, 1.—a Ps 73; Mal 2, 17; 3, 14.—
b Ex 22, 21-22; Dt 24, 17-22.—c Pss 10, 11; 64, 6; 73, 11; Jb
22, 13-14; Ez 9, 9.—d Prv 1, 22; 8, 5.—e Ex 4, 11; Prv 20,
12.—f Ps 33, 15; 1 Cor 3, 20.—g Ps 119, 71; Jb 5, 17.—h 1 Sm
12, 12; Sir 47, 22.

92, 14: *Planted:* the just are likened to trees growing in the
sacred precincts of the temple, which is often seen as the source
of life and fertility because of God's presence. Cf Ps 36, 9. 10; Ez
47, 1-12.
Ps 93: A hymn celebrating the kingship of God, who created
the world (1-2) by defeating the sea (3-4). In the ancient myth
that is alluded to here, Sea completely covered the land, making
it impossible for the human community to live. Sea, or Flood,
roars in anger against God, who is personified in the storm. God's
utterances or decrees are given authority by the victory over Sea
(5).
93, 1: *The LORD is king:* literally, "the LORD reigns." This
psalm, and Pss 47 and 96—99, are sometimes called enthronement psalms. They may have been used in a special liturgy during
which God's ascent to the throne was ritually reenacted. They
have also been interpreted eschatologically, pointing to the coming of God as king at the end-time.
93, 3: *The flood:* the primordial sea was tamed by God in the
act of creation. It is a figure of chaos and rebellion. Cf Ps 46, 4.
Ps 94: A lament of an individual who is threatened by wicked
people. The danger affects the whole community. Calling upon
God as judge (1-2), the psalm complains about oppression of the
holy community by people within (3-7). Bold declarations of faith
follow: denunciation of evildoers (8-11) and assurance to the just
(12-15). The psalm continues with further lament (16-19) and
ends with strong confidence in God's response (20-23).

---

⁴ More powerful than the roar of many
waters,
  more powerful than the breakers of
  the sea,
  powerful in the heavens is the LORD.
⁵ Your decrees are firmly established;
  holiness belongs to your house,
  LORD,
  for all the length of days.

PSALM 94*

A Prayer for Deliverance from the Wicked

I
¹ LORD, avenging God,
  avenging God, shine forth!ˣ
² Rise up, judge of the earth;
  give the proud what they deserve.ʸ

II
³ How long, LORD, shall the wicked,
  how long shall the wicked glory?ᶻ
⁴ How long will they mouth haughty
speeches,
  go on boasting, all these evildoers?ᵃ
⁵ They crush your people, LORD,
  torment your very own.
⁶ They kill the widow and alien;
  the fatherless they murder.ᵇ
⁷ They say, "The LORD does not see;
  the God of Jacob takes no notice."ᶜ

III
⁸ Understand, you stupid people!
  You fools, when will you be wise?ᵈ
⁹ Does the one who shaped the ear not
hear?
  The one who formed the eye not
  see?ᵉ
¹⁰ Does the one who guides nations not rebuke?
  The one who teaches humans not
  have knowledge?
¹¹ The LORD does know human plans;
  they are only puffs of air.ᶠ

IV
¹² Happy those whom you guide, LORD,ᵍ
  whom you teach by your instruction.
¹³ You give them rest from evil days,
  while a pit is being dug for the wicked.
¹⁴ You, LORD, will not forsake your people,
  nor abandon your very own.ʰ
¹⁵ Judgment shall again be just,
  and all the upright of heart will follow
  it.

Ps

V

16 Who will rise up for me against the wicked?
   Who will stand up for me against evildoers?
17 If the LORD were not my help,
   I would long have been silent in the grave.[i]
18 When I say, "My foot is slipping,"
   your love, LORD, holds me up.[j]
19 When cares increase within me,
   your comfort gives me joy.

VI

20 Can unjust judges be your allies,
   those who create burdens in the name of law,
21 Those who conspire against the just
   and condemn the innocent to death?
22 No, the LORD is my secure height,
   my God, the rock where I find refuge,
23 Who will turn back their evil upon them[k]
   and destroy them for their wickedness.
   Surely the LORD our God will destroy them![l]

PSALM 95*

A Call to Praise and Obedience

I

1 Come, let us sing joyfully to the LORD;
   cry out to the rock of our salvation.[m]
2 Let us greet him with a song of praise,
   joyfully sing out our psalms.
3 For the LORD is the great God,
   the great king over all gods,[n]
4 Whose hand holds the depths of the earth;
   who owns the tops of the mountains.
5 The sea and dry land belong to God,
   who made them, formed them by hand.[o]

II

6 Enter, let us bow down in worship;
   let us kneel before the LORD who made us.
7 For this is our God,
   whose people we are,
   God's well-tended flock.[p]

III

   Oh, that today you would hear his voice:[q]
8 Do not harden your hearts as at Meribah,*
   as on the day of Massah in the desert.

9 There your ancestors tested me;
   they tried me though they had seen my works.[r]
10 Forty years I loathed that generation;
   I said: "This people's heart goes astray,
   they do not know my ways."[s]
11 Therefore I swore in my anger:
   "They shall never enter my rest."*

PSALM 96*

God of the Universe

I

1 Sing to the LORD a new song;[t]
   sing to the LORD, all the earth.
2 Sing to the LORD, bless his name;
   announce his salvation day after day.
3 Tell God's glory among the nations;
   among all peoples, God's marvelous deeds.[u]

II

4 For great is the LORD and highly to be praised,
   to be feared above all gods.*[v]
5 For the gods of the nations all do nothing,
   but the LORD made the heavens.[w]
6 Splendor and power go before him;
   power and grandeur are in his holy place.

III

7 Give to the LORD, you families of nations,
   give to the LORD glory and might;
8   give to the LORD the glory due his name![x]

---

i Ps 115, 17.—j Ps 145, 14.—k Pss 7, 16; 9, 16; 35, 8; 57, 7; Prv 26, 27; Eccl 10, 8; Sir 27, 26.—l Ps 107, 42.—m Dt 32, 15.—n Pss 47, 2; 135, 5.—o Ps 24, 1-2.—p Pss 23, 1-3; 100, 3; Mi 7, 14.—q 7c-11: Pss 81, 8; 106, 32; Heb 3, 7-11. 15; 4, 3. 5. 7.—r Nm 14, 22; 20, 2-13; Dt 6, 16; 33, 8.—s Ps 78, 8; Nm 14, 34; Dt 32, 5.—t Ps 98, 1; Is 42, 10.—u Pss 98, 4; 105, 1.—v Pss 48, 2; 95, 3; 145, 3.—w Ps 97, 7; Is 40, 17; 1 Cor 8, 4.—x Ps 29, 2.

Ps 95: Twice the psalm calls the people to praise and worship God (1-2. 6), the king of all creatures (3-5) and shepherd of the flock (7ab). The last strophe warns the people to be more faithful than were their ancestors in the journey to the promised land (7c-11). This invitation to praise God regularly opens the Church's official prayer, the Liturgy of the Hours.

95, 8: *Meribah:* literally, "contention"; the place where the Israelites quarreled with God. *Massah:* "testing," the place where they put God to the trial. Cf Ex 17, 7; Nm 20, 13.

95, 11: *My rest:* the promised land as in Dt 12, 9. Heb 4 applies the verse to the eternal rest of heaven.

Ps 96: A hymn inviting all humanity to praise the glories of Israel's God (1-3), who is the sole God (4-6). To the just ruler of all belongs worship (7-10); even inanimate creation is to offer praise (11-13). This psalm has numerous verbal and thematic contacts with Is 40—55, as does Ps 98. Another version of the psalm is 1 Chr 16, 23-33.

96, 4: For references to other gods, see comments on Pss 58 and 82.

9 Bring gifts and enter his courts;
 bow down to the LORD, splendid in
 holiness.

10 Tremble before God, all the earth;
 say among the nations: The LORD is
 king.*y*
 The world will surely stand fast, never
 to be moved.
 God rules the peoples with fairness.

IV
11 Let the heavens be glad and the earth
 rejoice;
 let the sea and what fills it resound;*z*
12 let the plains be joyful and all that is
 in them.
 Then let all the trees of the forest rejoice
13 before the LORD who comes,
 who comes to govern the earth,*a*
 To govern the world with justice
 and the peoples with faithfulness.

PSALM 97*

The Divine Ruler of All

I
1 The LORD is king; let the earth rejoice;
 let the many islands be glad.*b*
2 Cloud and darkness surround the Lord;
 justice and right are the foundation of
 his throne.*c*
3 Fire goes before him;
 everywhere it consumes the foes.
4 Lightning illumines the world;
 the earth sees and trembles.*d*
5 The mountains melt like wax before the
 LORD,
 before the Lord of all the earth.*e*
6 The heavens proclaim God's justice;
 all peoples see his glory.*f*

---

y Pss 75, 4; 93, 1.—z Ps 98, 7.—a Ps 98, 9.—b Pss 75, 4; 93,
1; 96, 10.—c Pss 85, 11; 89, 15; Ex 19, 6; Dt 4, 11; 5, 22; 1 Kgs
8, 12.—d Pss 18, 8; 50, 3; 77, 18; 99, 1; Jgs 5, 4-5.—e Jdt 16,
15; Mi 1, 4.—f Ps 50, 6.—g Ps 96, 5.—h Ps 48, 12.—i Ps 83,
19.—j Ps 121, 7.—k Ps 112, 4.—l Ps 30, 5.—m Ps 96, 1; Is 42,
10.—n Is 59, 16; 63, 5.—o Ps 47, 6-7.—p Ps 96, 11.—q Is 44,
23; 55, 12.—r Ps 96, 13.—s Ps 67, 5.

Ps 97: The hymn begins with God appearing in a storm, a
traditional picture of some ancient Near Eastern gods (1-6); cf
Ps 18, 8-16; Mi 1, 3-4; Hb 3, 3-15. Israel rejoices in the overthrowing of idol worshipers and their gods (7-9) and the rewarding
of the faithful righteous (10-12).

97, 7: *All gods:* divine beings thoroughly subordinate to Israel's
God. The Greek translates "angels," an interpretation adopted by
Heb 1, 6.

Ps 98: A hymn, similar to Ps 96, extolling God for Israel's
victory (1-3). All nations (4-6) and even inanimate nature (7-8)
are summoned to welcome God's coming to rule over the world (9).

98, 1: *Marvelous deeds . . . victory:* the conquest of all
threats to the peaceful existence of Israel, depicted in the psalms
variously as a cosmic force such as sea, or nations bent on Israel's
destruction, or evildoers seemingly triumphant. *Whose right
hand and holy arm:* God is pictured as a powerful warrior.

II
7 All who serve idols are put to shame,
 who glory in worthless things;
 all gods* bow down before you.*g*
8 Zion hears and is glad,
 and the cities of Judah rejoice
 because of your judgments, O LORD.*h*
9 You, LORD, are the Most High over all
 the earth,*i*
 exalted far above all gods.
10 The LORD loves those who hate evil,
 protects the lives of the faithful,*j*
 rescues them from the hand of the
 wicked.
11 Light dawns for the just;
 gladness, for the honest of heart.*k*
12 Rejoice in the LORD, you just,
 and praise his holy name.*l*

PSALM 98*

The Coming of God

1 A psalm.

I
 Sing a new song to the LORD,
 who has done marvelous deeds,*m*
 Whose right hand and holy arm
 have won the victory.**n*
2 The LORD has made his victory known;
 has revealed his triumph for the nations to see,
3 Has remembered faithful love
 toward the house of Israel.
 All the ends of the earth have seen
 the victory of our God.

II
4 Shout with joy to the LORD, all the earth;
 break into song; sing praise.
5 Sing praise to the LORD with the harp,
 with the harp and melodious song.
6 With trumpets and the sound of the horn
 shout with joy to the King, the LORD.*o*

III
7 Let the sea and what fills it resound,*p*
 the world and those who dwell there.
8 Let the rivers clap their hands,
 the mountains shout with them for
 joy,*q*
9 Before the LORD who comes,
 who comes to govern the earth,*r*
 To govern the world with justice
 and the peoples with fairness.*s*

Ps

PSALM 99*

The Holy King

I

¹ The LORD is king, the peoples tremble;
God is enthroned on the cherubim,*
the earth quakes.[t]
² The LORD is great on Zion,
exalted above all the peoples.
³ Let them praise your great and awesome
name:
holy is God![u]

II

⁴ O mighty king, lover of justice,
you alone have established fairness;
you have created just rule in Jacob.[v]
⁵ Exalt the LORD, our God;
bow down before his footstool;*[w]
holy is God!

III

⁶ Moses and Aaron were among his
priests,
Samuel among those who called on
God's name;
they called on the LORD, who answered them.[x]
⁷ From the pillar of cloud God spoke to
them;
they kept the decrees, the law they
received.[y]
⁸ O LORD, our God, you answered them;
you were a forgiving God,
though you punished their offenses.[z]
⁹ Exalt the LORD, our God;
bow down before his holy mountain;
holy is the LORD, our God.

PSALM 100*

Processional Hymn

¹ A psalm of thanksgiving.

Shout joyfully to the LORD, all you
lands;
² worship the LORD with cries of gladness;
come before him with joyful song.
³ Know that the LORD is God,*
our maker to whom we belong,
whose people we are, God's well-
tended flock.[a]
⁴ Enter the temple gates with praise,
its courts with thanksgiving.
Give thanks to God, bless his name;[b]
⁵ good indeed is the LORD,
Whose love endures forever,
whose faithfulness lasts through every
age.

PSALM 101*

Norm of Life for Rulers

¹ A psalm of David.

I

I sing of love and justice;
to you, LORD, I sing praise.
² I follow the way of integrity;[c]
when will you come to me?
I act with integrity of heart
within my royal court.*[d]
³ I do not allow into my presence
anyone who speaks perversely.
Whoever acts shamefully I hate;
no such person can be my friend.[e]
⁴ I shun the devious of heart;
the wicked I do not tolerate.
⁵ Whoever slanders another in secret
I reduce to silence.[f]
Haughty eyes and arrogant hearts[g]
I cannot endure.

II

⁶ I look to the faithful of the land;*
they alone can be my companions.
Those who follow the way of integrity,[h]
they alone can enter my service.
⁷ No one who practices deceit
can hold a post in my court.
No one who speaks falsely
can be among my advisors.[i]

---

t Pss 18, 8-11; 80, 2; 93, 1; Ex 25, 22; 1 Sm 4, 4; 2 Sm 6,
2.—u Is 6, 3.—v Pss 72, 1; 99, 4; Jer 23, 5.—w Ps 132, 7.—x
Jer 15, 1.—y Ex 33, 9; Nm 12, 5.—z Ex 32, 11; Nm 20, 12.—a
Pss 23, 1; 95, 7; Mi 7, 14; Is 64, 7.—b 4-5: Pss 106, 1; 107,
1; 118, 1; 136, 1; 138, 8; Jer 33, 11.—c Ps 26, 11.—d 1 Kgs
9, 4; Is 33, 15.—e Prv 11, 20.—f Prv 17, 20; 30, 10.—g Prv
21, 4.—h Ps 26, 11; Prv 20, 7.—i Ps 5, 5; Prv 25, 5.

Ps 99: A hymn to God as the king whose grandeur is most
clearly seen on Mount Zion (2) and in the laws given to Israel
(4). Israel is special because of God's word of justice, which was
mediated by the revered speakers, Moses, Aaron, and Samuel
(6-8). The poem is structured by the threefold statement that God
is holy (3. 5. 9) and by the twice-repeated command to praise (5.
9).

99, 1: *Enthroned on the cherubim:* cherubim were composite
beings with animal and human features, common in ancient Near
Eastern art. Two cherubim were placed on the ark (or box) of
the covenant in the holy of holies. Upon them God was believed
to dwell invisibly. Cf Ex 25, 20-22; 1 Sm 4, 4; 2 Sm 6, 2; Ps 80, 2.

99, 5: *Footstool:* a reference to the ark. Cf 1 Chr 28, 2; Ps
132, 7.

Ps 100: A hymn inviting the people to enter the temple courts
with thank offerings for the God who created them.

100, 3: Although the people call on all the nations of the world
to join in their hymn, they are conscious of being the chosen people
of God.

Ps 101: The king, grateful at being God's chosen (1), promises
to be a ruler after God's own heart (2-3), allowing into the royal
service only the God-fearing (3-8).

101, 2: *Within my royal court:* the king promises to make
his own household a model for Israel, banning all officials who
abuse their power.

101, 6: *I look to the faithful of the land:* the king seeks
companions only among those faithful to God.

8 Each morning* I clear the wicked from
   the land,
   and rid the LORD's city of all evildoers.

PSALM 102*

Prayer in Time of Distress

¹The prayer of one afflicted and wasting away
whose anguish is poured out before the LORD.

I

2 LORD, hear my prayer;
   let my cry come to you.
3 Do not hide your face from me
   now that I am in distress.ʲ
   Turn your ear to me;
   when I call, answer me quickly.
4 For my days vanish like smoke;ᵏ
   my bones burn away as in a furnace.
5 I am withered, dried up like grass,
   too wasted to eat my food.
6 From my loud groaning
   I become just skin and bones.
7 I am like a desert owl,
   like an owl among the ruins.
8 I lie awake and moan,
   like a lone sparrow on the roof.
9 All day long my enemies taunt me;
   in their rage, they make my name a
   curse.*
10 I eat ashes like bread,
    mingle my drink with tears.ˡ
11 Because of your furious wrath,
    you lifted me up just to cast me
    down.

---

j Pss 69, 18; 143, 7.—k 4-6: Ps 38, 7-9.—l Pss 42, 4; 80, 6.—
m Pss 109, 23; 144, 4; Jb 8, 9; 14, 2; Eccl 6, 12; Wis 2, 5.—n
Ps 90, 5-6.—o Pss 55, 20; 90, 2; 93, 2; 102, 13; 135, 13; 145,
13; Lam 5, 19; Hb 1, 12.—p Is 59, 19; 66, 18.—q Ps 22, 31-
32.—r Pss 11, 4; 14, 2.—s Ps 79, 11.—t Is 60, 3-4; Zec 2, 15;
8, 22.—u Pss 39, 5; 90, 10; Jb 14, 5.—v 26-28: Heb 1, 10-12.—
w Ps 69, 36-37.

101, 8: *Each morning:* the normal time for the administration of justice (2 Sm 15, 2; Jer 21, 12) and for the arrival of divine aid (Pss 59, 17; 143, 8; Is 33, 2). *I clear the wicked from
the land:* the king, as God's servant, is responsible for seeing
that divine justice is carried out.
Ps 102: A lament, one of the Penitential Psalms. The psalmist, experiencing psychic and bodily disintegration (4-12), cries
out to God (1-3). In the temple precincts where God has promised
to be present, the psalmist recalls God's venerable promises to
save the poor (13-23). The final part (24-29) restates the original complaint and prayer, and emphasizes God's eternity.
102, 9: *They make my name a curse:* enemies use the
psalmist's name in phrases such as, "May you be as wretched as
this person!"
102, 20-23: Both 20-21 and 22-23 depend on 19.
102, 25: *In the midst of my days:* when the normal span of
life is but half completed. Cf Is 38, 10; Jer 17, 11.

---

12 My days are like a lengthening
   shadow;ᵐ
   I wither like the grass.ⁿ

II

13 But you, LORD, are enthroned forever;
   your renown is for all generations.ᵒ
14 You will again show mercy to Zion;
   now is the time for pity;
   the appointed time has come.
15 Its stones are dear to your servants;
   its dust moves them to pity.
16 The nations shall revere your name,
   LORD,
   all the kings of the earth, your glory,ᵖ
17 Once the LORD has rebuilt Zion
   and appeared in glory,
18 Heeding the plea of the lowly,
   not scorning their prayer.
19 Let this be written for the next generation,
   for a people not yet born,
   that they may praise the LORD:�q
20 "The LORD looked down from the holy
   heights,*
   viewed the earth from heaven,ʳ
21 To attend to the groaning of the prisoners,
   to release those doomed to die."ˢ
22 Then the LORD's name will be declared
   on Zion,
   the praise of God in Jerusalem,
23 When all peoples and kingdoms gather
   to worship the LORD.ᵗ

III

24 God has shattered my strength in mid-
   course,
   has cut short my days.
25 I plead, O my God,
   do not take me in the midst of my
   days.*ᵘ
   Your years last through all generations.
26 Of old you laid the earth's foundations;ᵛ
   the heavens are the work of your
   hands.
27 They perish, but you remain;
   they all wear out like a garment;
   Like clothing you change them and
   they are changed,
28   but you are the same, your years have
   no end.
29 May the children of your servants live
   on;
   may their descendants live in your
   presence.ʷ

Ps

PSALM 103*

Praise of Divine Goodness

¹ Of David.

I

Bless the LORD, my soul;
  all my being, bless his holy name!
² Bless the LORD, my soul;
  do not forget all the gifts of God,
³ Who pardons all your sins,
  heals all your ills,
⁴ Delivers your life from the pit,ˣ
  surrounds you with love and compassion,
⁵ Fills your days with good things;
  your youth is renewed like the eagle's.*

II

⁶ The LORD does righteous deeds,
  brings justice to all the oppressed.ʸ
⁷ His ways were revealed to Moses,
  mighty deeds to the people of Israel.
⁸ Merciful and gracious is the LORD,
  slow to anger, abounding in kindness.ᶻ
⁹ God does not always rebuke,
  nurses no lasting anger,
¹⁰ Has not dealt with us as our sins merit,
  nor requited us as our deeds deserve.

III

¹¹ As the heavens tower over the earth,
  so God's love towers over the faithful.ᵃ
¹² As far as the east is from the west,
  so far have our sins been removed from us.
¹³ As a father has compassion on his children,
  so the LORD has compassion on the faithful.
¹⁴ For he knows how we are formed,
  remembers that we are dust.ᵇ
¹⁵ Our days are like the grass;
  like flowers of the field we blossom.ᶜ
¹⁶ The wind sweeps over us and we are gone;
  our place knows us no more.
¹⁷ But the LORD's kindness is forever,
  toward the faithful from age to age.
  He favors the children's children
¹⁸ of those who keep his covenant,
  who take care to fulfill its precepts.

IV

¹⁹ The LORD's throne is established in heaven;
  God's royal power rules over all.
²⁰ Bless the LORD, all you angels,ᵈ
  mighty in strength and attentive,
  obedient to every command.
²¹ Bless the LORD, all you hosts,
  ministers who do God's will.
²² Bless the LORD, all creatures,
  everywhere in God's domain.
  Bless the LORD, my soul!

PSALM 104*

Praise of God the Creator

I

¹ Bless the LORD, my soul!
  LORD, my God, you are great indeed!
  You are clothed with majesty and glory,
² robed in light as with a cloak.
  You spread out the heavens like a tent;ᵉ
³ you raised your palace upon the waters.*
  You make the clouds your chariot;
  you travel on the wings of the wind.
⁴ You make the winds your messengers;
  flaming fire, your ministers.ᶠ

---

x Pss 28, 1; 30, 4; 40, 3; 69, 16; 88, 5; 143, 7; Prv 1, 12; Jon 2, 7.—y Ps 146, 6-7.—z Ps 86, 15; 145, 8; Ex 34, 6-7; Nm 14, 18; Jer 3, 12; Jl 2, 13; Jon 4, 2.—a Is 55, 9.—b Ps 90, 3.—c Pss 37, 2; 90, 5-6; Is 40, 7.—d Ps 148, 2; Dn 3, 58.—e Prv 8, 27-28; Jb 9, 8; Is 40, 22; Gn 1, 6-7; Am 9, 6.—f Heb 1, 7.

Ps 103: The speaker in this hymn begins by praising God for personal benefits (1-5), then moves on to God's mercy toward all the people (6-18). Even sin cannot destroy that mercy (11-13), for the eternal God is well aware of the people's human fragility (14-18). The psalmist invites the heavenly beings to join in praise (19-22).

103, 5: *Your youth is renewed like the eagle's:* because of the eagle's long life it was a symbol of perennial youth and vigor. Cf Is 40, 31.

Ps 104: A hymn praising God who easily and skillfully made rampaging waters and primordial night into a world vibrant with life. The psalmist describes God's splendor in the heavens (1-4), how the chaotic waters were tamed to fertilize and feed the world (5-18), and how primordial night was made into a gentle time of refreshment (19-23). The picture is like Gn 1, 1-2: a dark and watery chaos is made dry and lighted so that creatures might live. The psalmist reacts to the beauty of creation with awe (24-34). May sin not deface God's work (35)!

104, 3: *Your palace upon the waters:* God's heavenly dwelling above the upper waters of the sky. Cf Gn 1, 6-7; Ps 29, 10.

II

5 You fixed the earth on its foundation,*
   never to be moved.
6 The ocean covered it like a garment;
   above the mountains stood the
   waters.
7 At your roar they took flight;
   at the sound of your thunder they
   fled.*g*
8 They rushed up the mountains, down
   the valleys
   to the place you had fixed for them.
9 You set a limit they cannot pass;
   never again will they cover the
   earth.*h*

III

10 You made springs flow into channels
   that wind among the mountains.
11 They give drink to every beast of the
   field;*i*
   here wild asses quench their thirst.
12 Beside them the birds of heaven nest;
   among the branches they sing.
13 You water the mountains from your
   palace;
   by your labor the earth abounds.
14 You raise grass for the cattle
   and plants for our beasts of burden.
   You bring bread from the earth,
15   and wine to gladden our hearts,
   Oil to make our faces gleam,
   food to build our strength.
16 The trees of the LORD drink their
   fill,*
   the cedars of Lebanon, which you
   planted.
17 There the birds build their nests;
   junipers are the home of the stork.*j*

18 The high mountains are for wild goats;
   the rocky cliffs, a refuge for badgers.

IV

19 You made the moon to mark the seasons,*k*
   the sun that knows the hour of its setting.
20 You bring darkness and night falls,
   then all the beasts of the forest roam
   abroad.
21 Young lions roar for prey;
   they seek their food from God.*l*
22 When the sun rises, they steal away
   and rest in their dens.
23 People go forth to their work,
   to their labor till evening falls.

V

24 How varied are your works, LORD!
   In wisdom you have wrought them
   all;
   the earth is full of your creatures.*m*
25 Look at the sea, great and wide!
   It teems with countless beings,
   living things both large and small.*n*
26 Here ships ply their course;
   here Leviathan,* your creature,
   plays.*o*

VI

27 All of these look to you
   to give them food in due time.*p*
28 When you give to them, they gather;
   when you open your hand, they are
   well filled.
29 When you hide your face, they are
   lost.*
   When you take away their breath,
   they perish
   and return to the dust from which
   they came.*q*
30 When you send forth your breath, they
   are created,
   and you renew the face of the earth.

VII

31 May the glory of the LORD endure forever;
   may the LORD be glad in these
   works!
32 If God glares at the earth, it trembles;
   if God touches the mountains, they
   smoke!*r*

---

g Ps 29, 3.—h Jer 5, 22; Gn 9, 11-15.—i 11-14: Ps 147, 8-
9.—j Ez 31, 6.—k Sir 43, 6.—l Jb 38, 39.—m Ps 92, 6; Sir 39,
16.—n Sir 43, 26.—o Jb 3, 8; 40, 25.—p Pss 136, 25; 145, 15-
16.—q Jb 34, 14-15; Eccl 3, 20; Ps 90, 3.—r Ps 144, 5.

104, 5-9: God places the gigantic disk of the earth securely on
its foundation and then, as a warrior, chases away the enveloping
waters and confines them under, above, and around the earth.
104, 16-18: Even the exotic flora and fauna of the high mountains of the Lebanon range receive adequate water.
104, 26: *Leviathan:* a sea monster symbolizing primeval
chaos. Cf Ps 74, 14; Is 27, 1; Jb 40, 25. God does not destroy
chaos but makes it part of the created order.
104, 29-30: On one level, the spirit (or wind) of God is the fall
and winter rains that provide food for all creatures. On another,
it is the breath (or spirit) of God that makes beings live.

33 I will sing to the LORD all my life;
    I will sing praise to my God while I
    live.[s]
34 May my theme be pleasing to God;
    I will rejoice in the LORD.
35 May sinners vanish from the earth,
    and the wicked be no more.
    Bless the LORD, my soul! Hallelu-
    jah!*

PSALM 105*

God's Fidelity to the Promise

I
1 Give thanks to the LORD, invoke his
    name;[t]
    make known among the peoples his
    deeds![u]
2 Sing praise, play music;
    proclaim all his wondrous deeds!
3 Glory in his holy name;
    rejoice, O hearts that seek the LORD!
4 Rely on the mighty LORD;
    constantly seek his face.[v]
5 Recall the wondrous deeds he has
    done,
    his signs and his words of judgment,
6 You descendants of Abraham his ser-
    vant,
    offspring of Jacob, the chosen one!

II
7 The LORD is our God
    who rules the whole earth.
8 He remembers forever his covenant,
    the pact imposed for a thousand gen-
    erations,
9 Which was made with Abraham,
    confirmed by oath to Isaac,[w]
10 And ratified as binding for Jacob,
    an everlasting covenant for Israel:
11 "To you I give the land of Canaan,
    your own allotted heritage."[x]

III
12 When they were few in number,[y]
    a handful, and strangers there,
13 Wandering from nation to nation,
    from one kingdom to another,
14 He let no one oppress them;
    for their sake he rebuked kings:*
15 "Do not touch my anointed,
    to my prophets* do no harm."

IV
16 Then he called down a famine on the
    land,
    destroyed the grain that sustained
    them.[z]
17 He had sent a man ahead of them,
    Joseph, sold as a slave.[a]
18 They shackled his feet with chains;
    collared his neck in iron,[b]
19 Till his prediction came to pass,
    and the word of the LORD proved
    him true.[c]
20 The king sent and released him;
    the ruler of peoples set him free.[d]
21 He made him lord over his palace,
    ruler over all his possessions,[e]
22 To instruct his princes by his word,
    to teach his elders wisdom.

V
23 Then Israel entered Egypt;[f]
    Jacob lived in the land of Ham.*
24 God greatly increased his people,
    made them too many for their
    foes.[g]
25 He turned their hearts to hate his peo-
    ple,
    to treat his servants unfairly.[h]
26 He sent his servant Moses,
    Aaron whom he had chosen.[i]
27 They worked his signs in Egypt*[j]
    and wonders in the land of Ham.

s Ps 146, 2.—t 1-15: 1 Chr 16, 8-22.—u Pss 18, 50; 96, 3;
145, 5; Is 12, 4-5.—v Pss 24, 6; 27, 8.—w Gn 15, 1ff; 26, 3.—x
Gn 12, 7; 15, 18.—y 12-13: Dt 4, 27; 26, 5.—z Gn 41, 54. 57.—
a Gn 37, 28. 36; 45, 5.—b Gn 39, 20.—c Gn 40—41.—d Gn 41,
14.—e Gn 41, 41-44.—f Gn 46, 1—47, 12; Acts 7, 15.—g Ex 1,
7; Acts 7, 17.—h Ex 1, 8-14.—i Ex 3, 10; 4, 27.—j 27-36: Ps
78, 43-51; Ex 7—12.

104, 35: *Hallelujah:* a frequent word in the last third of the
Psalter. The word combines the plural imperative of praise *(halle-
lelu)* with an abbreviated form of the divine name Yah(weh).
    Ps 105: A hymn to God who promised the land of Canaan to
the holy people. Cf Pss 78; 106; 136. Israel is invited to praise
and seek the presence of God (1-6), who is faithful to the promise
of land to the ancestors (7-11). In every phase of the national
story—the ancestors in the land of Canaan (12-15), Joseph in
Egypt (16-22), Israel in Egypt (23-38), Israel in the desert on
the way to Canaan (39-45)—God remained faithful, reiterating
the promise of the land to successive servants.
    105, 14: *Kings:* Pharaoh and Abimelech of Gerar. Cf Gn 12,
17; 20, 6-7.
    105, 15: *My anointed . . . my prophets:* the patriarchs
Abraham, Isaac, and Jacob, who were "anointed" in the sense of
being consecrated and recipients of God's revelation.
    105, 23. 27: *The land of Ham:* a synonym for Egypt. Cf Gn
10, 6.
    105, 27-38: This psalm and Ps 78, 43-51 have an account of
the plagues differing in number or in order from Ex 7, 14—12,
30. Several versions of the exodus story were current.

²⁸ He sent darkness and it grew dark,
  but they rebelled against his word.
²⁹ He turned their waters into blood
  and killed all their fish.
³⁰ Their land swarmed with frogs,
  even the chambers of their kings.
³¹ He spoke and there came swarms of flies,
  gnats through all their country.
³² For rain he gave them hail,
  flashes of lightning throughout their land.
³³ He struck down their vines and fig trees,
  shattered the trees of their country.
³⁴ He spoke and the locusts came,
  grasshoppers without number.^k
³⁵ They devoured every plant in the land;
  they ravaged the crops of their fields.
³⁶ He struck down every firstborn in the land,
  the first fruits of all their vigor.
³⁷ He brought his people out,
  laden with silver and gold;^l
  no stragglers among the tribes.
³⁸ Egypt rejoiced when they left,
  for panic had seized them.

VI

³⁹ He spread a cloud as a cover,
  and made a fire to light up the night.^m
⁴⁰ They asked and he brought them quail;
  with bread from heaven he filled them.ⁿ

---

k Jl 1, 4.—l Ex 12, 33-36.—m Ps 78, 14; Ex 13, 21-22; Wis 18, 3.—n Ps 78, 24-28; Ex 16, 13-15; Nm 11, 31ff; Wis 16, 20.—o Ps 78, 15-16; Ex 17, 1-7; Nm 20, 11.—p Dt 4, 37-40.—q Dt 6, 20-25; 7, 8-11.—r Pss 100, 5; 107, 1; 1 Chr 16, 34; Jer 33, 11; Dn 3, 89.—s Is 56, 1-2.—t Ps 25, 7; Neh 5, 19.—u 6-7: Ps 78, 11-17; Ex 14, 11; Lv 26, 40; 1 Kgs 8, 47; Bar 2, 12; Dn 9, 5.—v Ez 36, 20-22.—w Ex 14, 21-31; Is 50, 2; 63, 11-14; Na 1, 4.

Ps 106: Israel is invited to praise the God whose mercy has always tempered judgment of Israel (1-3). The speaker, on behalf of all, seeks solidarity with the people, who can always count on God's fidelity despite their sin (4-5). Confident of God's mercy, the speaker invites national repentance (6) by reciting from Israel's history eight instances of sin, judgment, and forgiveness. The sins are the rebellion at the Red Sea (6-12; see Ex 14—15), the craving for meat in the desert (13-15; see Nm 11), the challenge to Moses' authority (16-18; see Nm 16), the golden calf episode (19-23; see Ex 32—34), the refusal to take Canaan by the southern route (24-27; see Nm 13—14 and Dt 1—2), the rebellion at Baal-Peor (28-31; see Nm 25, 1-10), the anger of Moses (32-33; see Nm 20, 1-13), and mingling with the nations (34-47). The last, as suggested by its length and generalized language, may be the sin that invites the repentance of the present generation. The text gives the site of each sin: Egypt (7), the desert (14), the camp (16), Horeb (19), in their tents (25), Baal-Peor (28), the waters of Meribah (32), Canaan (38).

⁴¹ He split the rock and water gushed forth;
  it flowed through the desert like a river.^o
⁴² For he remembered his sacred word
  to Abraham his servant.
⁴³ He brought his people out with joy,
  his chosen ones with shouts of triumph.
⁴⁴ He gave them the lands of the nations,
  the wealth of the peoples to own,^p
⁴⁵ That they might keep his laws
  and observe his teachings.^q
Hallelujah!

PSALM 106*

Israel's Confession of Sin

¹ Hallelujah!

A

Give thanks to the LORD, who is good,
  whose love endures forever.^r
² Who can tell the mighty deeds of the LORD,
  proclaim in full God's praise?
³ Happy those who do what is right,
  whose deeds are always just.^s
⁴ Remember me, LORD, as you favor your people;
  come to me with your saving help,^t
⁵ That I may see the prosperity of your chosen,
  rejoice in the joy of your people,
  and glory with your heritage.

B

⁶ We have sinned like our ancestors;^u
  we have done wrong and are guilty.

I

⁷ Our ancestors in Egypt
  did not attend to your wonders.
They did not remember your great love;
  they defied the Most High at the Red Sea.
⁸ Yet he saved them for his name's sake
  to make his power known.^v
⁹ He roared at the Red Sea and it dried up.
  He led them through the deep as through a desert.^w
¹⁰ He rescued them from hostile hands,
  freed them from the power of the enemy.

Ps

11 The waters covered their oppressors;
　　not one of them survived.
12 Then they believed his words
　　and sang songs of praise.ˣ

II

13 But they soon forgot all he had done;
　　they had no patience for his plan.
14 In the desert they gave way to their cravings,
　　tempted God in the wasteland.ʸ
15 So he gave them what they asked
　　and sent among them a wasting disease.ᶻ

III

16 In the camp they challenged Mosesᵃ
　　and Aaron, the holy one of the LORD.
17 The earth opened and swallowed Dathan,
　　it closed on the followers of Abiram.
18 Against that company the fire blazed;
　　flames consumed the wicked.

IV

19 At Horeb they fashioned a calf,ᵇ
　　worshiped a metal statue.
20 They exchanged their glorious God
　　for the image of a grass-eating bull.
21 They forgot the God who saved them,
　　who did great deeds in Egypt,ᶜ
22 Amazing deeds in the land of Ham,
　　fearsome deeds at the Red Sea.
23 He would have decreed their destruction,
　　had not Moses, the chosen leader,
　　Withstood him in the breach*
　　to turn back his destroying anger.ᵈ

V

24 Next they despised the beautiful land;ᵉ
　　they did not believe the promise.
25 In their tents they complained;
　　they did not obey the LORD.
26 So with raised hand he swore
　　to destroy them in the desert,
27 To scatter their descendants among the nations,
　　disperse them in foreign lands.

VI

28 They joined in the rites of Baal of Peor,ᶠ
　　ate food sacrificed to dead gods.
29 They provoked him by their actions,
　　and a plague broke out among them.
30 Then Phinehas rose to intervene,
　　and the plague was brought to a halt.
31 This was counted for him as a righteous deed
　　for all generations to come.

VII

32 At the waters of Meribah they angered God,ᵍ
　　and Moses suffered because of them.*
33 They so embittered his spirit
　　that rash words crossed his lips.

VIII

34 They did not destroy the peoples
　　as the LORD had commanded them,ʰ
35 But mingled with the nations
　　and imitated their ways.ⁱ
36 They worshiped their idols
　　and were ensnared by them.ʲ
37 They sacrificed to the gods*
　　their own sons and daughters,
38 Shedding innocent blood,
　　the blood of their own sons and daughters,
　　Whom they sacrificed to the idols of Canaan,
　　desecrating the land with bloodshed.
39 They defiled themselves by their actions,
　　became adulterers by their conduct.
40 So the LORD grew angry with his people,
　　abhorred his own heritage.
41 He handed them over to the nations,
　　and their adversaries ruled them.ᵏ
42 Their enemies oppressed them,
　　kept them under subjection.
43 Many times did he rescue them,
　　but they kept rebelling and scheming
　　and were brought low by their own guilt.ˡ
44 Still God had regard for their affliction
　　when he heard their wailing.
45 For their sake he remembered his covenant
　　and relented in his abundant love,ᵐ
46 Winning for them compassion
　　from all who held them captive.

---

x Ex 15, 1-21.—y Ps 78, 18; Ex 15, 24; 16, 3; Nm 11, 1-6.—z Ps 78, 26-31; Nm 11, 33.—a 16-18: Nm 16; Dt 11, 6; Is 26, 11.—b 19-20: Ex 32; Dt 9, 8-21; Jer 2, 11; Acts 7, 41; Rom 1, 23.—c Ps 78, 42-58; Dt 32, 18; Jer 2, 32.—d Ex 32, 11; Dt 9, 25; Ez 22, 30.—e 24-27: Lv 26, 33; Nm 14; Dt 1, 25-36; Ez 20, 15. 23.—f 28-31: Nm 25; Dt 26, 14; Sir 45, 23-24.—g 32-33: Ps 95, 8-9; Ex 17, 1-7; Nm 20, 2-13; Dt 6, 16; 33, 8.—h Dt 7, 1; Jgs 2, 1-5.—i Lv 18, 3; Jgs 1, 27-35; 3, 5.—j 36-38: Lv 18, 21; Nm 35, 33; Dt 32, 17; Jgs 2, 11-13. 17. 19; 2 Kgs 16, 3; Bar 4, 7; 1 Cor 10, 20.—k Jgs 2, 14-23.—l Is 63, 7-9.—m Lv 26, 42.

106, 23: *Withstood him in the breach:* the image is that of Moses standing in a narrow break made in the wall to keep anyone from entering.

106, 32: *Moses suffered because of them:* Moses was not allowed to enter the promised land because of his rash words (Nm 20, 12). According to Dt 1, 37, Moses was not allowed to cross because of the people's sin, not his own.

106, 37: *The gods:* Hebrew *shedim,* customarily translated "demons," occurs in parallelism with "gods" in an important inscription from Transjordan and hence is translated "gods."

C

47 Save us, LORD, our God;
gather us from among the nations
That we may give thanks to your holy
name
and glory in praising you.[n]

* * *

48 Blessed be the LORD, the God of Israel,[*]
from everlasting to everlasting!
Let all the people say, Amen![o]
Hallelujah!

FIFTH BOOK — PSALMS 107–150

PSALM 107[*]

God the Savior of Those in Distress

1 "Give thanks to the LORD who is good,
whose love endures forever!"[p]
2 Let that be the prayer of the LORD's redeemed,
those redeemed from the hand of the
foe,[q]
3 Those gathered from foreign lands,
from east and west, from north and
south.[r]

I

4 Some had lost their way in a barren desert;
found no path toward a city to live in.
5 They were hungry and thirsty;
their life was ebbing away.[s]
6 In their distress they cried to the LORD,
who rescued them in their peril,

---

n 1 Chr 16, 35.—o Pss 41, 14; 72, 18; 89, 53; 1 Chr 16, 36;
Neh 9, 5.—p Pss 100, 4-5; 106, 1; Jer 33, 11.—q Is 63, 12.—r
Is 43, 5-6; 49, 12; Zec 8, 7.—s Dt 8, 15; 32, 10; Is 49, 10.—t
Is 35, 8; 40, 3; 43, 19.—u Dt 6, 10.—v Lk 1, 53.—w Is 42, 7.
22; Jb 36, 8-9; Prv 1, 25.—x Ps 106, 43.—y Is 42, 7; 49, 9; 51,
14.—z Jb 6, 6-7; 33, 20.—a Ps 147, 15; Wis 16, 12; Is 55, 11;
Mt 8, 8.—b Sir 43, 25.—c Jon 1, 4.

106, 48: A doxology ending Book IV of the Psalter. It is not
part of the psalm.
Ps 107: A hymn inviting those who have been rescued by God
to give praise (1-3). Four archetypal divine rescues are described,
each ending in thanksgiving: from the sterile desert (4-9), from
imprisonment in gloom (10-16), from mortal illness (17-22), and
from the angry sea (23-32). The number four connotes totality,
all the possible varieties of rescue. The same saving activity of
God is shown in Israel's history (33-41); whenever the people
were endangered God rescued them. The last verses invite people
to ponder the persistent saving acts of God (42-43).

7 Guided them by a direct path[t]
so they reached a city to live in.[u]
8 Let them thank the LORD for such
kindness,
such wondrous deeds for mere mortals.
9 For he satisfied the thirsty,
filled the hungry with good things.[v]

II

10 Some lived in darkness and gloom,
in prison, bound with chains,
11 Because they rebelled against God's
word,
scorned the counsel of the Most
High,[w]
12 Who humbled their hearts through
hardship;
they stumbled with no one to help.[x]
13 In their distress they cried to the LORD,
who saved them in their peril,
14 Led them forth from darkness and
gloom
and broke their chains asunder.[y]
15 Let them thank the LORD for such
kindness,
such wondrous deeds for mere mortals.
16 For he broke down the gates of bronze
and snapped the bars of iron.

III

17 Some fell sick from their wicked ways,
afflicted because of their sins.
18 They loathed all manner of food;[z]
they were at the gates of death.
19 In their distress they cried to the LORD,
who saved them in their peril,
20 Sent forth the word to heal them,[a]
snatched them from the grave.
21 Let them thank the LORD for such
kindness,
such wondrous deeds for mere mortals.
22 Let them offer a sacrifice in thanks,
declare his works with shouts of
joy.

IV

23 Some went off to sea in ships,
plied their trade on the deep waters.[b]
24 They saw the works of the LORD,
the wonders of God in the deep.
25 He spoke and roused a storm wind;
it tossed the waves on high.[c]

26 They rose up to the heavens, sank to
the depths;
their hearts trembled at the danger.
27 They reeled, staggered like drunkards;
their skill was of no avail.[d]
28 In their distress they cried to the LORD,
who brought them out of their peril,
29 Hushed the storm to a murmur;
the waves of the sea were stilled.[e]
30 They rejoiced that the sea grew calm,
that God brought them to the harbor
they longed for.
31 Let them thank the LORD for such
kindness,
such wondrous deeds for mere mortals.
32 Let them praise him in the assembly of
the people,
give thanks in the council of the
elders.

V

33 God changed rivers into desert,*
springs of water into thirsty ground,[f]
34 Fruitful land into a salty waste,
because of the wickedness of its people.[g]
35 He changed the desert into pools of
water,
arid land into springs of water,[h]
36 And settled the hungry there;
they built a city to live in.[i]
37 They sowed fields and planted vineyards,
brought in an abundant harvest.[j]
38 God blessed them, they became very
many,
and their livestock did not decrease.[k]
40 But he poured out contempt on princes,
made them wander the trackless
wastes,[l]
39 Where they were diminished and
brought low
through misery and cruel oppression,
41 While the poor were released from their
affliction;
their families increased like their
flocks.[m]
42 The upright saw this and rejoiced;[n]
all wickedness shut its mouth.
43 Whoever is wise will take note of these
things,[o]
will ponder the merciful deeds of the
LORD.

PSALM 108*

Prayer for Victory

1 A song; a psalm of David.

I

2 My heart is steadfast, God;[p]
my heart is steadfast.
I will sing and chant praise.
3 Awake, my soul; awake, lyre and
harp!
I will wake the dawn.[q]
4 I will praise you among the peoples,
LORD;
I will chant your praise among the
nations.[r]
5 For your love towers to the heavens;
your faithfulness, to the skies.[s]
6 Appear on high over the heavens,
God;
may your glory appear above all the
earth.
7 Help with your right hand and answer
us
that your loved ones may escape.

II

8 God promised in the sanctuary:[t]
"I will exult, I will apportion
Shechem;
the valley of Succoth I will measure
out.
9 Gilead is mine, mine is Manasseh;
Ephraim is the helmet for my head,
Judah, my own scepter.
10 Moab is my washbowl;
upon Edom I cast my sandal;[u]
I will triumph over Philistia."

---

d Is 29, 9.—e Pss 65, 8; 89, 10; Mt 8, 26 par.—f Is 35, 7; 42,
15; 50, 2.—g Gn 19, 23-28; Dt 29, 22; Sir 39, 23.—h Ps 114,
8; Is 41, 8.—i Ez 36, 35.—j Is 65, 21; Jer 31, 5.—k Dt 7, 13-
14.—l Jb 12, 23-25.—m Ps 113, 7.—n Pss 58, 11; 63, 12.—o
Hos 14, 10.—p 2-6: Ps 57, 8-12.—q Jb 38, 12.—r Pss 9, 12; 18,
50; 148, 13.—s Pss 36, 6; 71, 19.—t 8-14: Ps 60, 8-14.—u Ru
4, 7-8.

107, 33-41: God destroyed Sodom and Gomorrah in Gn 18—
19, which the psalm sees as the destruction of the wicked inhabitants of Canaan to prepare the way for Israel (33-34). God then
led Israel through the desert to give them a fertile land (35-38)
and protected them from every danger (39-41).

Ps 108: A prayer compiled from two other psalms: 2-6 are virtually the same as Ps 57, 8-12; 7-14 are the same as Ps 60, 7-14.
An old promise of salvation (8-10) is combined with a confident
assurance (1-6. 14) and petition (7. 12-13).

III

11 Who will bring me to the fortified city?
   Who will lead me into Edom?
12 Was it not you who rejected us, God?
   Do you no longer march with our armies?[v]
13 Give us aid against the foe;
   worthless is human help.
14 We will triumph with the help of God,
   who will trample down our foes.

PSALM 109*

Prayer of a Person Falsely Accused

1 For the leader. A psalm of David.

I

O God, whom I praise, do not be silent,[w]
2   for wicked and treacherous mouths
      attack me.
They speak against me with lying
      tongues;
3 with hateful words they surround
   me,
   attacking me without cause.
4 In return for my love they slander me,
   even though I prayed for them.
5 They repay me evil for good,
   hatred for my love.[x]

II

My enemies say of me:
6 "Find a lying witness,
   an accuser* to stand by his right
   hand,

---

v Ps 44, 10.—w Pss 35, 22; 83, 1.—x Pss 35, 12; 38, 21; Prv
17, 13; Jer 18, 20.—y Acts 1, 20.—z Ex 22, 23; Jer 18, 21.—a
Ps 21, 11; Prv 10, 7.—b Ex 20, 5.—c Ps 90, 8.—d Ps 34, 16.—e
24-25: Ps 69, 11-13.

Ps 109: A lament notable for the length and vehemence of its
prayer against evildoers (6-20); the cry to God (1) and the complaint (22-25) are brief in comparison. The psalmist is apparently
the victim of a slander campaign, potentially devastating in a society where reputation and honor are paramount. In the emotional perspective of the psalm, there are only two types of people: the wicked and their poor victims. The psalmist is a poor victim (22. 31) and by that fact a friend of God and enemy of the
wicked. The psalmist seeks vindication not on the basis of personal virtue but because of God's promise to protect the poor.
109, 6: *An accuser:* Hebrew *satan,* a word occurring in Jb
1—2 and Zec 3, 1-2. In the latter passage Satan stands at the
right hand of the high priest to bring false accusations against him
before God. Here the accuser is human.
109, 20: *May the LORD bring all this:* the psalmist prays
that God ratify the curses of 6-19 and bring them upon the wicked.

---

7 That he may be judged and found
   guilty,
   that his plea may be in vain.
8 May his days be few;
   may another take his office.[y]
9 May his children be fatherless,
   his wife, a widow.[z]
10 May his children be vagrant beggars,
   driven from their hovels.
11 May the usurer snare all he owns,
   strangers plunder all he earns.
12 May no one treat him kindly
   or pity his fatherless children.
13 May his posterity be destroyed,[a]
   his name cease in the next generation.
14 May the LORD remember his fathers'
   guilt;
   his mother's sin not be canceled.[b]
15 May their guilt be always before the
   LORD,[c]
   till their memory is banished from
   the earth,[d]
16 For he did not remember to show kindness,
   but hounded the wretched poor
   and brought death to the broken-
   hearted.
17 He loved cursing; may it come upon
   him;
   he hated blessing; may none come to
   him.
18 May cursing clothe him like a robe;
   may it enter his belly like water,
   seep into his bones like oil.
19 May it be near as the clothes he wears,
   as the belt always around him."

Ps

III

20 May the LORD bring all this* upon my
   accusers,
   upon those who speak evil against
   me.
21 But you, LORD, my God,
   deal kindly with me for your name's
   sake;
   in your great mercy rescue me.
22 For I am sorely in need;
   my heart is pierced within me.
23 Like a lengthening shadow I near my
   end,
   all but swept away like the locust.
24 My knees totter from fasting;[e]
   my flesh has wasted away.
25 I have become a mockery to them;
   when they see me, they shake their
   heads.

26 Help me, LORD, my God;
    save me in your kindness.
27 Make them know this is your hand,
    that you, LORD, have acted.
28 Though they curse, may you bless;
    shame my foes, that your servant may
    rejoice.
29 Clothe my accusers with disgrace;
    make them wear shame like a mantle.
30 I will give fervent thanks to the LORD;
    before all I will praise my God.*f*
31 For God stands at the right hand of the
    poor
    to defend them against unjust accus-
    ers.

PSALM 110*

God Appoints the King both King and Priest

1 A psalm of David.

The LORD says to you, my lord:*
  "Take your throne at my right hand,
  while I make your enemies your footstool."*g*
2 The scepter of your sovereign might
  the LORD will extend from Zion.
  The LORD says: "Rule over your
  enemies!
3 Yours is princely power from the day
  of your birth.
  In holy splendor before the daystar,*
  like the dew I begot you."*h*
4 The LORD has sworn and will not
  waver:
  "Like Melchizedek* you are a priest
  forever."*i*

Ps 110: A royal psalm in which a court singer recites three oracles in which God assures the king that his enemies are conquered (1-2), makes the king "son" in traditional adoption language (3), gives priestly status to the king and promises to be with him in future military ventures (4-7).
110, 1: *The LORD says to you, my lord:* literally, "The LORD says to my lord," a polite form of address of an inferior to a superior. Cf 1 Sm 25, 25; 2 Sm 1, 10. The court singer refers to the king. Jesus in the synoptic gospels (Mt 22, 41-46 and parallels) takes the psalmist to be David and hence "my lord" refers to the messiah, who must be someone greater than David. *Your footstool:* in ancient times victorious kings put their feet on the prostrate bodies of their enemies.
110, 3: *Before the daystar:* possibly an expression for before the world began (Prv 8, 22). *Like the dew I begot you:* an adoption formula as in Pss 2, 7; 89, 27-28.
110, 4: *Like Melchizedek:* Melchizedek was the ancient king of Salem (Jerusalem) who blessed Abraham (Gn 14, 18-20); like other kings of the time he performed priestly functions. Heb 7 sees in Melchizedek a type of Christ.

5 At your right hand is the Lord,
  who crushes kings on the day of
  wrath,*j*
6 Who, robed in splendor, judges nations,
  crushes heads across the wide earth,
7 Who drinks from the brook by the
  wayside*
  and thus holds high the head.*k*

PSALM 111*

Praise of God for Goodness to Israel

1 Hallelujah.

I will praise the LORD with all my
  heart*l*
  in the assembled congregation of the
  upright.*
2 Great are the works of the LORD,
  to be treasured for all their delights.
3 Majestic and glorious is your* work,
  your wise design endures forever.
4 You won renown for your wondrous
  deeds;
  gracious and merciful is the LORD.*m*
5 You gave food to those who fear you,*
  mindful of your covenant forever.
6 You showed powerful deeds to your
  people,
  giving them the lands* of the nations.

---

f Ps 111, 1.— g Mt 22, 44; Acts 2, 34-35; 1 Cor 15, 25; Heb 1, 13; 8, 1; 10, 12-13; 1 Pt 3, 22.—h Pss 2, 7; 89, 27; Is 49, 1.—i Pss 89, 35; 132, 11; Gn 14, 18; Heb 5, 6; 7, 21.—j Ps 2, 9; Rv 2, 27; 12, 5; 19, 15.—k Ps 3, 4.—l Ps 138, 1.—m Ps 103, 8; 112. 4.

110, 7: *Who drinks from the brook by the wayside:* the meaning is uncertain. Some see an allusion to a rite of royal consecration at the Gihon spring (cf 1 Kgs 1, 33. 38). Others find here an image of the divine warrior (or king) pursuing enemies so relentlessly that he does not stop long enough to eat and drink.
Ps 111: A temple singer (1) tells how God is revealed in Israel's history (2-10). The deeds reveal God's very self, powerful, merciful, faithful. The poem is an acrostic, each verse beginning with a successive letter of the Hebrew alphabet.
111, 1: *In the assembled congregation of the upright:* in the temple. Cf Ps 149, 1.
111, 3: *Your:* the psalm refers to God in the third person throughout; the shift to the second person is for the sake of inclusive language.
111, 5: *Food to those who fear you:* probably a reference to the manna in the desert, which elsewhere is seen as a type of the Eucharist. Cf Jn 6, 31-33. 49-51.
111, 6: *Lands:* literally, "inheritance, heritage."

7 The works of your hands are right and
  true,
    reliable all your decrees,
8 Established forever and ever,
    to be observed with loyalty and care.
9 You sent deliverance to your people,
    ratified your covenant forever;
    holy and awesome is your name.
10 The fear of the LORD* is the beginning
  of wisdom;[n]
    prudent are all who live by it.
    Your praise endures forever.

PSALM 112*

The Blessings of the Just

1 Hallelujah!

Happy are those* who fear the LORD,
    who greatly delight in God's com-
    mands.[o]
2 Their descendants shall be mighty in
  the land,
    a generation upright and blessed.
3 Wealth and riches shall be in their
  homes;
    their prosperity* shall endure forever.
4 They shine through the darkness, a light
  for the upright;[p]
    they are gracious, merciful, and just.

---

n Prv 1, 7; 9, 10; Sir 1, 16.—o Pss 1, 1-2; 119, 1-2; 128, 1.—p
Pss 37, 6; 97, 11; Prv 13, 9; Is 58, 10.—q Prv 10, 7; Wis 8, 13.—r
Prv 22, 9; 2 Cor 9, 9.—s Ps 135, 1.—t Ps 148, 13.—u Ps 89, 7-
9.—v Ps 107, 41; 1 Sm 2, 7-8.—w 1 Sm 2, 5; Is 54, 1.—x Ex 19, 6.

111, 10: *The fear of the LORD:* reverence for God, the Hebrew
term for religion.
Ps 112: An acrostic poem detailing the blessings received by
those who remain close to God by obedience to the commandments.
Among their blessings are children (2), wealth that enables them to
be magnanimous (3. 5. 9), and virtue by which they encourage
others (4). The just person is an affront to the wicked, whose hopes
remain unfulfilled (10). The logic resembles Pss 1 and 111.
112, 1: *Happy are those:* literally, "Happy the person." "Person" is used typically, hence the plural translation.
112, 3: *Prosperity:* literally, "justice." In the Second Temple
Period the word acquired the nuance of liberality and almsgiving.
Cf Sir 3, 30; 7, 10; Mt 6, 1-4.
112, 9: *Their horn:* the symbol for vitality and honor.
Ps 113: A hymn exhorting the congregation to praise God's
name, i.e., the way in which God is present in the world; the name is
mentioned three times in 1-3. The divine name is especially honored in the temple (1) but its recognition is not limited by time (2)
and space (3), for God is everywhere active (4-5) especially in rescuing the lowly faithful (7-9).
Ps 114: A hymn celebrating Israel's escape from Egypt, journey
through the wilderness, and entry into the promised land, and the
miracles of nature that bore witness to God's presence in their
midst. In the perspective of the psalm, the people proceed directly
from Egypt into the promised land (1-2). Sea and Jordan, which
stood like soldiers barring the people from their land, flee before
the mighty God as the earth recoils from the battle (3-4). The poet
taunts the natural elements as one taunts defeated enemies (5-6).

5 All goes well for those gracious in lending,
    who conduct their affairs with jus-
    tice.
6 They shall never be shaken;
    the just shall be remembered for-
    ever.[q]
7 They shall not fear an ill report;
    their hearts are steadfast, trusting the
    LORD.
8 Their hearts are tranquil, without fear,
    till at last they look down on their
    foes.
9 Lavishly they give to the poor;
    their prosperity shall endure forever;[r]
    their horn* shall be exalted in honor.
10 The wicked shall be angry to see this;
    they will gnash their teeth and waste
    away;
    the desires of the wicked come to
    nothing.

PSALM 113*

Praise of God's Care of the Poor

1 Hallelujah!

I

Praise, you servants of the LORD,
    praise the name of the LORD.[s]
2 Blessed be the name of the LORD
    both now and forever.
3 From the rising of the sun to its setting
    let the name of the LORD be praised.

II

4 High above all nations is the LORD;
    above the heavens God's glory.[t]
5 Who is like the LORD,
    our God enthroned on high,
6   looking down on heaven and earth?[u]
7 The LORD raises the needy from the
  dust,
    lifts the poor from the ash heap,[v]
8 Seats them with princes,
    the princes of the people,
9 Gives the childless wife a home,
    the joyful mother of children.[w]
Hallelujah!

PSALM 114*

The Lord's Wonders at the Exodus

1 When Israel came forth from Egypt,
    the house of Jacob from an alien peo-
    ple,
2 Judah became God's holy place,
    Israel, God's domain.[x]

Ps

3 The sea beheld and fled;*
   the Jordan turned back.^y
4 The mountains skipped like rams;
   the hills, like lambs of the flock.^z
5 Why was it, sea, that you fled?
   Jordan, that you turned back?
6 You mountains, that you skipped like
   rams?
   You hills, like lambs of the flock?
7 Tremble, earth, before the Lord,^a
   before the God of Jacob,
8 Who turned rock into pools of water,*
   stone into flowing springs.^b

PSALM 115*

The Greatness of the True God

I

1 Not to us, Lord, not to us
   but to your name give glory
   because of your faithfulness and
    love.^c
2 Why should the nations say,
   "Where is their God?"*^d
3 Our God is in heaven;
   whatever God wills is done.^e

II

4 Their idols are silver and gold,^f
   the work of human hands.^g
5 They have mouths but do not speak,
   eyes but do not see.
6 They have ears but do not hear,
   noses but do not smell.
7 They have hands but do not feel,
   feet but do not walk,
   and no sound rises from their throats.
8 Their makers shall be like them,
   all who trust in them.

III

9 The house of Israel trusts in the Lord,^h
   who is their help and shield.ⁱ
10 The house of Aaron trusts in the Lord,
   who is their help and shield.
11 Those who fear the Lord* trust in the
   Lord,
   who is their help and shield.
12 The Lord remembers us and will bless
   us,
   will bless the house of Israel,
   will bless the house of Aaron,
13 Will bless those who fear the Lord,
   small and great alike.

14 May the Lord increase your number,
   you and your descendants.
15 May you be blessed by the Lord,
   who made heaven and earth.
16 The heavens* belong to the Lord,
   but the earth is given to us.^j
17 The dead do not praise the Lord,*
   all those gone down into silence.^k
18 It is we who bless the Lord,
   both now and forever.
Hallelujah!

PSALM 116*

Thanksgiving to God Who Saves from Death

I

1 I love the Lord, who listened
   to my voice in supplication,
2 Who turned an ear to me
   on the day I called.

---

y Ex 14, 21f; Jos 3, 14ff; Pss 66, 6; 74, 15.—z Ps 29, 6; Wis 19, 9.—a Ps 68, 9.—b Ex 17, 6; Nm 20, 11.—c Ez 36, 22-23.—d Ps 79, 10.—e Ps 135, 6.—f 4-10: Ps 135, 15-19; Wis 15, 15-16; Is 44, 9f; Jer 10, 1-5.—g Is 40, 19.—h Ps 118, 2-4.—i Ps 33, 20.—j Gn 1, 28.—k Pss 6, 6; 88, 11ff; Sir 17, 22f; Is 38, 18.

114, 3-4: Pairs of cosmic elements such as sea and rivers, mountains and hills, are sometimes mentioned in creation accounts. Personified here as warriors, the pairs tremble in fear before the Divine Warrior. The quaking also recalls the divine appearance in the storm at Sinai (Ex 19, 16-19) and elsewhere (Jgs 5, 4-5; Ps 18, 8-16).

114, 8: The miracles of giving drink to the people in the arid desert. Cf Ex 17, 1-7; Is 41, 17-18.

Ps 115: A response to the enemy taunt, "Where is your God?" This hymn to the glory of Israel's God (1-3) ridicules the lifeless idols of the nations (4-8), expresses in a litany the trust of the various classes of the people in God (9-11), invokes God's blessing on them as they invoke the divine name (12-15), and concludes as it began with praise of God. Ps 135, 15-18 similarly mocks the Gentile gods and has a similar litany and hymn (Ps 135, 19-21).

115, 2: *Where is their God?:* implies that God cannot help them.

115, 9-11: *The house of Israel . . . the house of Aaron . . . those who fear the Lord:* the laity of Israelite birth, the priests, and the converts to Judaism. Cf Pss 118, 2-4; 135, 19-21. In the New Testament likewise "those who fear the Lord" means converts to Judaism (cf Acts 10, 2. 22. 35; 13, 16. 26).

115, 16: *The heavens:* literally, "the heaven of heavens" or "the highest heavens," i.e., above the firmament. See note on Ps 148, 4.

115, 17: See note on Ps 6, 6.

Ps 116: A thanksgiving in which the psalmist responds to divine rescue from mortal danger (3-4) and from near despair (10-11) with vows and temple sacrifices (13-14. 17-19). The Greek and Latin versions divide the psalm into two parts: 1-9 and 10-19, corresponding to its two major divisions.

3 I was caught by the cords of death;*[l]
the snares of Sheol had seized me;
I felt agony and dread.
4 Then I called on the name of the LORD,
"O LORD, save my life!"

II

5 Gracious is the LORD and just;
yes, our God is merciful.[m]
6 The LORD protects the simple;
I was helpless, but God saved me.
7 Return, my soul, to your rest;
the LORD has been good to you.[n]
8 For my soul has been freed from death,
my eyes from tears, my feet from
stumbling.[o]
9 I shall walk before the LORD
in the land of the living.*[p]

III

10 I kept faith, even when I said,*
"I am greatly afflicted!"[q]

---

l Ps 18, 5; Jon 2, 3.—m Ex 34, 6.—n Ps 13, 6.—o Ps 56, 14;
Is 25, 8; Rv 21, 4.—p Pss 27, 13; 56, 14; Is 38, 11.—q 2 Cor 4,
13.—r Ps 12, 2.—s Ps 72, 14; Is 43, 4.—t Pss 86, 16; 143, 12;
Wis 9, 5.—u Lv 7, 12ff.—v Jon 2, 10.—w Rom 15, 11.—x Pss
100, 5; 136, 1f.—y Ps 115, 9-11.—z Ps 27, 1; Heb 13, 6.

116, 3: *The cords of death:* death is personified here; it attempts to capture the psalmist with snares and nets. Cf Ps 18, 6.
116, 9: *The land of the living:* the phrase elsewhere is an epithet of the Jerusalem temple (cf Pss 27, 13; 52, 7; Is 38, 11). Hence the psalmist probably refers to being present to God in the temple.
116, 10: *I kept faith, even when I said:* even in the days of despair, the psalmist did not lose all hope.
116, 13: *The cup of salvation:* probably the libation of wine poured out in gratitude for rescue. Cf Ex 25, 29; Nm 15, 5. 7. 10.
116, 15: *Too costly in the eyes of the LORD:* the meaning is that the death of God's faithful is grievous to God, not that God is pleased with the death. Cf Ps 72, 14. In Wis 3, 5-6 God accepts the death of the righteous as a sacrificial burnt offering.
Ps 117: This shortest of hymns calls on the nations to acknowledge God's supremacy. The supremacy of Israel's God has been demonstrated to them by the people's secure existence, which is owed entirely to God's gracious fidelity.
Ps 118: A thanksgiving liturgy accompanying a victory procession of the king and the people into the temple precincts. After an invocation in the form of a litany (1-4), the psalmist (very likely speaking in the name of the community) describes how the people confidently implored God's help (5-9) when hostile peoples threatened its life (10-14); vividly God's rescue is recounted (15-18). Then follows a dialogue at the temple gates between the priests and the psalmist as the latter enters to offer the thanksgiving sacrifice (19-25). Finally, the priests impart their blessing (26-27), and the psalmist sings in gratitude (28-29).

11 I said in my alarm,
"No one can be trusted!"[r]
12 How can I repay the LORD
for all the good done for me?
13 I will raise the cup of salvation*
and call on the name of the LORD.
14 I will pay my vows to the LORD
in the presence of all his people.
15 Too costly in the eyes of the LORD*
is the death of his faithful.[s]
16 LORD, I am your servant,
your servant, the child of your maidservant;[t]
you have loosed my bonds.
17 I will offer a sacrifice of thanksgiving
and call on the name of the LORD.[u]
18 I will pay my vows to the LORD[v]
in the presence of all his people,
19 In the courts of the house of the LORD,
in your midst, O Jerusalem.
Hallelujah!

PSALM 117*

The Nations Called To Praise

1 Praise the LORD, all you nations!
Give glory, all you peoples![w]
2 The LORD's love for us is strong;
the LORD is faithful forever.
Hallelujah!

PSALM 118*

Hymn of Thanksgiving

I

1 Give thanks to the LORD, who is good,[x]
whose love endures forever.
2 Let the house of Israel say:
God's love endures forever.
3 Let the house of Aaron say,
God's love endures forever.
4 Let those who fear the LORD say,[y]
God's love endures forever.

II

5 In danger I called on the LORD;
the LORD answered me and set me
free.
6 The LORD is with me; I am not afraid;
what can mortals do against me?[z]

7 The LORD is with me as my helper;
  I shall look in triumph on my foes.
8 Better to take refuge in the LORD[a]
  than to put one's trust in mortals.
9 Better to take refuge in the LORD
  than to put one's trust in princes.

III

10 All the nations surrounded me;
   in the LORD's name I crushed them.
11 They surrounded me on every side;
   in the LORD's name I crushed them.
12 They surrounded me like bees;[b]
   they blazed like fire among thorns;
   in the LORD's name I crushed them.
13 I was hard pressed and falling,
   but the LORD came to my help.[c]
14 The LORD, my strength and might,
   came to me as savior.[d]

IV

15 The joyful shout of deliverance
   is heard in the tents of the victors:
   "The LORD's right hand strikes with
      power;
16   the LORD's right hand is raised;
   the LORD's right hand strikes with
      power."
17 I shall not die but live
   and declare the deeds of the LORD.
18 The LORD chastised me harshly,
   but did not hand me over to death.

V

19 Open the gates of victory;
   I will enter and thank the LORD.[e]
20 This is the LORD's own gate,
   where the victors enter.*
21 I thank you for you answered me;
   you have been my savior.
22 The stone the builders rejected*
   has become the cornerstone.[f]
23 By the LORD has this been done;
   it is wonderful in our eyes.
24 This is the day the LORD has made;
   let us rejoice in it and be glad.
25 LORD, grant salvation!*
   LORD, grant good fortune!

VI

26 Blessed is he
   who comes in the name of the LORD.[g]
   We bless you from the LORD's house.
27   The LORD is God and has given us
   light.

Join in procession with leafy branches
up to the horns of the altar.

VII

28 You are my God, I give you thanks;
   my God, I offer you praise.
29 Give thanks to the LORD, who is good,
   whose love endures forever.

PSALM 119*

A Prayer to God, the Lawgiver

Aleph

1 Happy those whose way is blameless,
  who walk by the teaching of the
  LORD.[h]
2 Happy those who observe God's decrees,
  who seek the Lord with all their
  heart.[i]

---

a 8f: Ps 146, 3.—b Dt 1, 44.—c Ps 129, 1-2.—d Ex 15, 2; Is
12, 2.—e Is 26, 2.—f Mt 21, 42; Lk 20, 17; Acts 4, 11; Rom 9,
33; 1 Pt 2, 7.—g Mt 21, 9; 23, 39.—h Pss 1, 1-2; 15, 2; 112,
1.—i Dt 4, 29.

118, 20: *Where the victors enter:* their victory has demonstrated that God favors them; they are "just" in the biblical sense.
118, 22: *The stone the builders rejected:* a proverb: what
is insignificant to human beings has become great through divine
election. The "stone" may originally have meant the foundation
stone or capstone of the temple. The New Testament interpreted
the verse as referring to the death and resurrection of Christ (Mt
21, 42; Acts 4, 11; cf Is 28, 16 and Rom 9, 33; 1 Pt 2, 7).
118, 25: *Grant salvation:* the Hebrew for this cry has come
into English as "Hosanna." This cry and the words in 26 were
used in the gospels to welcome Jesus entering the temple on
Palm Sunday (Mk 11, 9-10).
Ps 119: This psalm, the longest by far in the psalter, praises
God for giving such splendid laws and instruction for people to
live by. The author glorifies and thanks God for the Torah, prays
for protection from sinners enraged by others' fidelity to the law,
laments the cost of obedience, delights in the law's consolations,
begs for wisdom to understand the precepts, and asks for the rewards of keeping them. Several expected elements do not appear
in the psalm: Mount Sinai with its story of God's revelation and
gift to Israel of instruction and commandments, the temple and
other institutions related to revelation and laws (frequent in other
psalms). The psalm is fascinated with God's word directing and
guiding human life.
The poem is an acrostic; its twenty-two stanzas (of eight verses
each) are in the order of the Hebrew alphabet. Each of the eight
verses within a stanza begins with the same letter. Each verse
contains one word for "instruction." The translation here given
attempts to translate each Hebrew word for "instruction" with
the same English word. There are, however, nine words for "instruction," not eight, so the principle of a different word for "instruction" in each verse cannot be maintained with perfect consistency. The nine words for "instruction" in the translation are:
law, edict, command, precept, word, utterance, way, decree, and
teaching.

3 They do no wrong;
     they walk in God's ways.
4 You have given them the command
     to keep your precepts with care.
5 May my ways be firm
     in the observance of your laws!
6 Then I will not be ashamed
     to ponder all your commands.
7 I will praise you with sincere heart
     as I study your just edicts.
8 I will keep your laws;
     do not leave me all alone.

Beth

9 How can the young walk without fault?
     Only by keeping your words.
10 With all my heart I seek you;
     do not let me stray from your commands.
11 In my heart I treasure your promise,
     that I may not sin against you.
12 Blessed are you, O LORD;
     teach me your laws.[j]
13 With my lips I recite
     all the edicts you have spoken.
14 I find joy in the way of your decrees
     more than in all riches.
15 I will ponder your precepts
     and consider your paths.
16 In your laws I take delight;
     I will never forget your word.

Gimel

17 Be kind to your servant that I may live,
     that I may keep your word.
18 Open my eyes to see clearly
     the wonders of your teachings.
19 I am a sojourner in the land;*[k]
     do not hide your commands from me.

20 At all times my soul is stirred
     with longing for your edicts.
21 With a curse you rebuke the proud
     who stray from your commands.
22 Free me from disgrace and contempt,
     for I observe your decrees.
23 Though princes meet and talk against me,
     your servant studies your laws.
24 Your decrees are my delight;
     they are my counselors.

Daleth

25 I lie prostrate in the dust;[l]
     give me life in accord with your word.
26 I disclosed my ways and you answered me;
     teach me your laws.
27 Make me understand the way of your precepts;
     I will ponder your wondrous deeds.
28 I weep in bitter pain;
     in accord with your word strengthen me.
29 Lead me from the way of deceit;
     favor me with your teaching.
30 The way of loyalty I have chosen;
     I have set your edicts before me.
31 I cling to your decrees, LORD;
     do not let me come to shame.
32 I will run the way of your commands,
     for you open my docile heart.*

He

33 LORD, teach me the way of your laws;
     I shall observe them with care.[m]
34 Give me insight to observe your teaching,
     to keep it with all my heart.
35 Lead me in the path of your commands,[n]
     for that is my delight.
36 Direct my heart toward your decrees
     and away from unjust gain.
37 Avert my eyes from what is worthless;
     by your way give me life.
38 For your servant fulfill your promise
     made to those who fear you.
39 Turn away from me the taunts I dread,
     for your edicts bring good.
40 See how I long for your precepts;
     in your justice give me life.

Ps

---

j Pss 25, 4; 27, 11; 86, 11; 143, 8. 10.—k Ps 39, 13.—l Ps 44, 26.—m Ps 19, 12.—n Pss 25, 4; 27, 11; 86, 11; 143, 8. 10.

119, 19: *A sojourner in the land:* like someone without the legal protection of a native inhabitant, the psalmist has a special need for the guidance of God's teaching.
119, 32: *For you open my docile heart:* literally, "you make broad my heart."

Waw

⁴¹ Let your love come to me, LORD,
   salvation in accord with your promise.
⁴² Let me answer my taunters with a
   word,
   for I trust in your word.
⁴³ Do not take the word of truth from my
   mouth,
   for in your edicts is my hope.
⁴⁴ I will keep your teachings always,
   for all time and forever.
⁴⁵ I will walk freely in an open space
   because I cherish your precepts.
⁴⁶ I will speak openly of your decrees
   without fear even before kings.
⁴⁷ I delight in your commands,
   which I dearly love.
⁴⁸ I lift up my hands to your commands;*
   I study your laws, which I love.

Zayin

⁴⁹ Remember your word to your servant
   by which you give me hope.
⁵⁰ This is my comfort in affliction,
   your promise that gives me life.
⁵¹ Though the arrogant utterly scorn me,
   I do not turn from your teaching.
⁵² When I recite your edicts of old
   I am comforted, LORD.
⁵³ Rage seizes me because of the wicked;
   they forsake your teaching.
⁵⁴ Your laws become my songs
   wherever I make my home.
⁵⁵ Even at night I remember your name
   in observance of your teaching,
   LORD.
⁵⁶ This is my good fortune,
   for I have observed your precepts.

Heth

⁵⁷ My portion is the LORD;
   I promise to keep your words.
⁵⁸ I entreat you with all my heart:
   have mercy on me in accord with
   your promise.
⁵⁹ I have examined my ways
   and turned my steps to your decrees.
⁶⁰ I am prompt, I do not hesitate
   in keeping your commands.

⁶¹ Though the snares of the wicked surround me,
   your teaching I do not forget.
⁶² At midnight I rise to praise you
   because your edicts are just.
⁶³ I am the friend of all who fear you,
   of all who keep your precepts.
⁶⁴ The earth, LORD, is filled with your
   love;ᵒ
   teach me your laws.

Teth

⁶⁵ You have treated your servant well,
   according to your word, O LORD.
⁶⁶ Teach me wisdom and knowledge,
   for in your commands I trust.
⁶⁷ Before I was afflicted I went astray,
   but now I hold to your promise.
⁶⁸ You are good and do what is good;
   teach me your laws.
⁶⁹ The arrogant smear me with lies,
   but I observe your precepts with all
   my heart.
⁷⁰ Their hearts are gross and fat;ᵖ
   as for me, your teaching is my delight.
⁷¹ It was good for me to be afflicted,
   in order to learn your laws.
⁷² Teaching from your lips is more precious to me
   than heaps of silver and gold.

Yodh

⁷³ Your hands made me and fashioned me;
   give me insight to learn your commands.
⁷⁴ Those who fear you rejoice to see me,
   because I hope in your word.
⁷⁵ I know, LORD, that your edicts are just;
   though you afflict me, you are faithful.
⁷⁶ May your love comfort me
   in accord with your promise to your
   servant.
⁷⁷ Show me compassion that I may live,
   for your teaching is my delight.
⁷⁸ Shame the proud for oppressing me unjustly,
   that I may study your precepts.

---

o Ps 33, 5.—p Pss 17, 10; 73, 7; Jb 15, 27.

119, 48: *I lift up my hands to your commands:* to lift up
the hands was an ancient gesture of reverence to God. Here the
picture is applied to God's law.

79 Let those who fear you turn to me,
   those who acknowledge your decrees.
80 May I be wholehearted toward your
   laws,
   that I may not be put to shame.

Kaph

81 My soul longs for your salvation;
   I put my hope in your word.^q
82 My eyes long to see your promise.^r
   When will you comfort me?
83 I am like a wineskin shriveled by
   smoke,^s
   but I have not forgotten your laws.
84 How long can your servant survive?
   When will your edict doom my foes?
85 The arrogant have dug pits for me;
   defying your teaching.
86 All your commands are steadfast.
   Help me! I am pursued without
   cause.
87 They have almost ended my life on
   earth,
   but I do not forsake your precepts.
88 In your kindness give me life,
   to keep the decrees you have spoken.

Lamedh

89 Your word, LORD, stands forever;^t
   it is firm as the heavens.*
90 Through all generations your truth endures;
   fixed to stand firm like the earth.
91 By your edicts they stand firm to this
   day,
   for all things are your servants.
92 Had your teaching not been my delight,
   I would have perished in my affliction.
93 I will never forget your precepts;
   through them you give me life.
94 I am yours; save me,
   for I cherish your precepts.

95 The wicked hope to destroy me,
   but I pay heed to your decrees.
96 I have seen the limits of all perfection,
   but your command is without
   bounds.

Mem

97 How I love your teaching, Lord!
   I study it all day long.
98 Your command makes me wiser than
   my foes,
   for it is always with me.
99 I have more understanding than all my
   teachers,
   because I ponder your decrees.
100 I have more insight than my elders,
   because I observe your precepts.^u
101 I keep my steps from every evil path,
   that I may obey your word.
102 From your edicts I do not turn,
   for you have taught them to me.
103 How sweet to my tongue is your promise,
   sweeter than honey to my mouth!^v
104 Through your precepts I gain insight;
   therefore I hate all false ways.

Nun

105 Your word is a lamp for my feet,
   a light for my path.^w
106 I make a solemn vow
   to keep your just edicts.
107 I am very much afflicted, LORD;
   give me life in accord with your
   word.
108 Accept my freely offered praise;^x
   LORD, teach me your decrees.
109 My life is always at risk,
   but I do not forget your teaching.
110 The wicked have set snares for me,
   but from your precepts I do not
   stray.
111 Your decrees are my heritage forever;
   they are the joy of my heart.
112 My heart is set on fulfilling your laws;
   they are my reward forever.

Samekh

113 I hate every hypocrite;
   your teaching I love.

---

q Ps 130, 6.—r Pss 25, 15; 123, 1-2; 141, 8.—s Jb 30, 30.—t
Is 40, 8.—u Jb 32, 6; Wis 4, 8-9.—v Ps 19, 11.—w Ps 18, 29;
Prv 6, 23.—x Ps 50, 14. 23; Heb 13, 15.

119, 89-91: God's word creates the world, which manifests
that word by its permanence and reliability.

Ps

114 You are my refuge and shield;
  in your word I hope.
115 Depart from me, you wicked,[y]
  that I may observe the commands of
  my God.
116 Sustain me by your promise that I may
  live;
  do not disappoint me in my hope.
117 Strengthen me that I may be safe,
  ever to contemplate your laws.
118 You reject all who stray from your
  laws,
  for vain is their deceit.
119 Like dross you regard all the wicked
  on earth;
  therefore I love your decrees.
120 My flesh shudders with dread of you;
  I hold your edicts in awe.

Ayin

121 I have fulfilled your just edict;
  do not abandon me to my oppressors.
122 Guarantee your servant's welfare;
  do not let the arrogant oppress me.
123 My eyes long to see your salvation
  and the justice of your promise.
124 Act with kindness toward your servant;
  teach me your laws.
125 I am your servant; give me discernment
  that I may know your decrees.
126 It is time for the LORD to act;
  they have disobeyed your teaching.
127 Truly I love your commands
  more than the finest gold.
128 Thus I follow all your precepts;
  every wrong way I hate.

Pe

129 Wonderful are your decrees;
  therefore I observe them.
130 The revelation of your words sheds
  light,
  gives understanding to the simple.
131 I sigh with open mouth,
  yearning for your commands.
132 Turn to me and be gracious,[z]
  your edict for lovers of your name.
133 Steady my feet in accord with your
  promise;
  do not let iniquity lead me.

134 Free me from human oppression,
  that I may keep your precepts.
135 Let your face shine upon your servant;
  teach me your laws.
136 My eyes shed streams of tears
  because your teaching is not followed.

Sadhe

137 You are righteous, LORD,
  and just are your edicts.[a]
138 You have issued your decrees in justice
  and in surpassing faithfulness.
139 I am consumed with rage,
  because my foes forget your words.
140 Your servant loves your promise;
  it has been proved by fire.
141 Though belittled and despised,
  I do not forget your precepts.
142 Your justice is forever right,
  your teaching forever true.
143 Though distress and anguish come
  upon me,
  your commands are my delight.
144 Your decrees are forever just;
  give me discernment that I may live.

Qoph

145 I call with all my heart, O LORD;
  answer me that I may observe your
  laws.
146 I call to you to save me
  that I may keep your decrees.
147 I rise before dawn and cry out;
  I put my hope in your words.
148 My eyes greet the night watches
  as I meditate on your promise.[b]
149 Hear my voice in your love, O LORD;
  by your edict give me life.
150 Malicious persecutors draw near me;
  they are far from your teaching.
151 You are near, O LORD;
  reliable are all your commands.
152 Long have I known from your decrees
  that you have established them forever.

---

y Pss 6, 9; 139, 19; Jb 21, 14.—z Pss 25, 16; 86, 16.—a Tb
3, 2.—b Pss 63, 7; 77, 7.

Resh

153 Look at my affliction and rescue me,
for I have not forgotten your teaching.
154 Take up my cause and redeem me;*c*
for the sake of your promise give me
life.
155 Salvation is far from sinners
because they do not cherish your
laws.
156 Your compassion is great, O LORD;
in accord with your edicts give me
life.
157 Though my persecutors and foes are
many,
I do not turn from your decrees.
158 I view the faithless with loathing,*d*
because they do not heed your
promise.
159 See how I love your precepts, LORD;
in your kindness give me life.
160 Your every word is enduring;
all your just edicts are forever.

Shin

161 Princes persecute me without reason,
but my heart reveres only your
word.

---

c Ps 43, 1.—d Ps 139, 22.—e Ps 72, 7.—f Ps 88, 3.—g Is 53,
6; Jer 50, 6; Lk 15, 1-7.—h Jon 2, 3.—i Ps 12, 3-5; Sir 51, 3.—j
Pss 11, 6; 140, 11; Prv 16, 27.

Ps 120: A thanksgiving, reporting divine rescue (1) yet with
fervent prayer for further protection against lying attackers (2-
4). The psalmist is acutely conscious of living away from God's
own land where divine peace prevails (5-7).
120, 1: *Song of ascents:* Pss 120—134 all begin with this
superscription. Most probably these fifteen psalms once formed a
collection of psalms sung when pilgrims went to Jerusalem, since
one "ascended" to Jerusalem (1 Kgs 12, 28; Pss 24, 3; 122, 4;
Lk 2, 42) or to the house of God or to an altar (1 Kgs 12, 33; 2
Kgs 23, 2; Ps 24, 3). Less probable is the explanation that these
psalms were sung when the exiles when they "ascended" to Jerusalem from Babylonia (cf Ezr 7, 9). The idea, found in the Mishnah,
that the fifteen steps on which the Levites sang corresponded to
these fifteen psalms *(Middot* 2, 5) must underlie the Vulgate
translation *canticum graduum,* "song of the steps" or "gradual
song."
120, 3: *More besides:* a common curse formula in Hebrew
was "May the Lord do such and such evils to you [the evils being
specified], and add still more to them." Cf 1 Sm 3, 17; 14, 44;
25, 22. Here the psalmist is at a loss for a suitable malediction.
120, 4: *Coals of brushwood:* coals made from the stalk of
the broom plant burn with intense heat. The psalmist thinks of
lighted coals cast at his enemies.

162 I rejoice at your promise,
as one who has found rich spoil.
163 Falsehood I hate and abhor;
your teaching I love.
164 Seven times a day I praise you
because your edicts are just.
165 Lovers of your teaching have much
peace;*e*
for them there is no stumbling
block.
166 I look for your salvation, LORD,
and I fulfill your commands.
167 I observe your decrees;
I love them very much.
168 I observe your precepts and decrees;
all my ways are before you.

Taw

169 Let my cry come before you, LORD;*f*
in keeping with your word give me
discernment.
170 Let my prayer come before you;
rescue me according to your promise.
171 May my lips pour forth your praise,
because you teach me your laws.
172 May my tongue sing of your promise,
for all your commands are just.
173 Keep your hand ready to help me,
for I have chosen your precepts.
174 I long for your salvation, LORD;
your teaching is my delight.
175 Let me live to praise you;
may your edicts give me help.
176 I have wandered like a lost sheep;
seek out your servant,
for I do not forget your commands.*g*

PSALM 120*

Prayer of a Returned Exile

1 A song of ascents.*

I

The LORD answered me
when I called in my distress:*h*
2 LORD, deliver me from lying lips,
from treacherous tongues.*i*

II

3 What will the Lord inflict on you,
O treacherous tongue,
and what more besides?*
4 A warrior's sharpened arrows
and fiery coals of brushwood!**j*

III

5 Alas, I was an alien in Meshech,*
   I lived near the tents of Kedar!
6 Too long did I live
   among those who hated peace.
7 When I spoke of peace,
   they were for war.[k]

PSALM 121*

The Lord My Guardian

1 A song of ascents.

I

I raise my eyes toward the mountains.*
   From where will my help come?[l]
2 My help comes from the LORD,
   the maker of heaven and earth.[m]

II

3 God will not allow your foot to slip;[n]
   your guardian does not sleep.
4 Truly, the guardian of Israel
   never slumbers nor sleeps.
5 The LORD is your guardian;
   the LORD is your shade*
   at your right hand.[o]
6 By day the sun cannot harm you,
   nor the moon by night.[p]
7 The LORD will guard you from all evil,
   will always guard your life.[q]
8 The LORD will guard your coming and
   going
   both now and forever.[r]

PSALM 122*

A Pilgrim's Prayer for Jerusalem

1 A song of ascents. Of David.

I

I rejoiced when they said to me,
   "Let us go to the house of the
   LORD."[s]
2 And now our feet are standing
   within your gates, Jerusalem.
3 Jerusalem, built as a city,
   walled round about.*[t]
4 Here the tribes have come,
   the tribes of the LORD,
   As it was decreed for Israel,
   to give thanks to the name of the
   LORD.[u]
5 Here are the thrones of justice,
   the thrones of the house of David.

II

6 For the peace of Jerusalem pray:
   "May those who love you prosper!

7 May peace be within your ramparts,
   prosperity within your towers."[v]
8 For family and friends I say,
   "May peace be yours."
9 For the house of the LORD, our God, I
   pray,
   "May blessings be yours."

PSALM 123*

Reliance on the Lord

1 A song of ascents.

To you I raise my eyes,
   to you enthroned in heaven.[w]
2 Yes, like the eyes of a servant
   on the hand of his master,
   Like the eyes of a maid
   on the hand of her mistress,
   So our eyes are on the LORD our God,
   till we are shown favor.
3 Show us favor, LORD, show us favor,
   for we have our fill of contempt.[x]
4 We have our fill of insult from the insolent,
   of disdain from the arrogant.

---

k Pss 35, 20; 140, 3-4.—l Jer 3, 23.—m Pss 124, 8; 146, 6.—
n Pss 66, 9; 91, 12; 1 Sm 2, 9; Prv 3, 23.—o Pss 16, 8; 73,
23.—p Wis 18, 3; Is 25, 4; 49, 10.—q Ps 97, 10.—r Dt 28, 6.—s
Pss 43, 3-4; 84, 2-5.—t Ps 48, 13-14.—u Dt 16, 16.—v Ps 128,
5.—w Pss 25, 15; 119, 82; 141, 8.—x Ps 44, 13-14; Jb 12, 4.

120, 5: *Meshech* was in the far north (Gn 10, 2) and *Kedar*
was a tribe of the north Arabian desert (Gn 25, 13). The psalmist
may be thinking generally of all aliens living among inhospitable
peoples.

Ps 121: A blessing given to someone embarking on a dangerous journey, whether a soldier going on a campaign or a pilgrim
returning home from the temple. People look anxiously at the
wooded hills. Will God protect them on their journey (1)? The
speaker declares that God is not confined to a place or a time (2),
that every step is guarded (3-4); night and day (5-6) God watches
over their every movement (7-8).

121, 1: *The mountains:* possibly Mount Zion, the site of the
temple and hence of safety, but more probably mountains as a
place of dangers, causing anxiety to the psalmist.

121, 5-6: The image of shade, a symbol of protection, is apt:
God as shade protects from the harmful effects that ancients believed were caused by the sun and moon.

Ps 122: A song of Zion, sung by pilgrims obeying the law to
visit Jerusalem three times on a journey. The singer anticipates
joining the procession into the city (1-3). Jerusalem is a place of
encounter, where the people praise God (4) and hear the divine
justice mediated by the king (5). The very buildings bespeak
God's power (cf Ps 48, 13-15). May the grace of this place transform the people's lives (6-9)!

122, 3: *Walled round about:* literally, "which is joined to
it," probably referring both to the density of the buildings and to
the dense population.

Ps 123: A lament that begins as a prayer of an individual (1),
who expresses by a touching comparison exemplary confidence in
God (2). The psalm ends in prayer that God relieve the people's
humiliation at the hands of the arrogant (3-4).

PSALM 124*

God, the Rescuer of the People

¹ A song of ascents. Of David.

I

Had not the LORD been with us,
let Israel say,*ʸ*
² Had not the LORD been with us,
when people rose against us,
³ They would have swallowed us alive,*ᶻ*
for their fury blazed against us.
⁴ The waters would have engulfed us,
the torrent overwhelmed us;*ᵃ*
⁵   seething waters would have drowned
us.

II

⁶ Blessed be the LORD, who did not leave
us
to be torn by their fangs.
⁷ We escaped with our lives
like a bird from the fowler's snare;
the snare was broken and we escaped.
⁸ Our help is the name* of the LORD,
the maker of heaven and earth.*ᵇ*

---

y Ps 129, 1.—z Prv 1, 12.—a Pss 18, 5; 69, 2.—b Pss 121, 2;
146, 6.—c Prv 10, 25.—d Dt 32, 11.—e Ps 18, 25ff.—f Prv 3,
32.—g Ps 128, 6.—h Ps 14, 7.—i Jb 8, 21.—j Bar 4, 23; Is 65,
19.

Ps 124: A thanksgiving which teaches that Israel's very existence is owed to God who rescues them. In the first part Israel's
enemies are compared to the mythic sea dragon (2b-3a; cf Jer
51, 34) and Flood (3b-5; cf Is 51, 9-10). The psalm heightens the
malice of human enemies by linking them to the primordial
enemies of God's creation. Israel is a bird freed from the trap-
per's snare (6-8)—freed originally from Pharaoh and now from
the current danger.
    124, 8: *Our help is the name:* for the idiom, see Ex 18, 4.
    Ps 125: In response to exilic anxieties about the ancient
promises of restoration, the psalm expresses confidence that God
will surround the people as the mountains surround Zion (1-2).
The just will not be contaminated by the wicked (3). May God
judge between the two groups (4-5).
    125, 3: *The land given to the just:* literally, "the lot of the
just." The promised land was divided among the tribes of Israel
by lot (Nm 26, 55; Jos 18). *The just* are the members of the people who are obedient to God. If the domination of the wicked
were to continue in the land, even the just would be infected by
their evil attitudes.
    Ps 126: A lament probably sung shortly after Israel's return
from exile. The people rejoice that they are in Zion (1-3) but
mere presence in the holy city is not enough; they must pray for
the prosperity and the fertility of the land (4). The last verses are
probably an oracle of promise: the painful work of sowing will be
crowned with life (5-6).
    126, 4: *Like the dry stream beds of the Negeb:* the psalm-
ist prays for rain in such abundance that the dry riverbeds will
run.

PSALM 125*

Israel's Protector

¹ A song of ascents.

I

Like Mount Zion are they
who trust in the LORD,
unshakable, forever enduring.*ᶜ*
² As mountains surround Jerusalem,
the LORD surrounds his people
both now and forever.*ᵈ*

II

³ The scepter of the wicked will not prevail
in the land given to the just,*
Lest the just themselves
turn their hands to evil.

III

⁴ Do good, LORD, to the good,
to those who are upright of heart.*ᵉ*
⁵ But those who turn aside to crooked
ways
may the LORD send down with the
wicked.*ᶠ*
Peace upon Israel!*ᵍ*

PSALM 126*

The Reversal of Zion's Fortunes

¹ A song of ascents.

I

When the LORD restored the fortunes
of Zion,*ʰ*
then we thought we were dreaming.
² Our mouths were filled with laughter;
our tongues sang for joy.*ⁱ*
Then it was said among the nations,
"The LORD has done great things for
them."
³ The LORD has done great things for us;
oh, how happy we were!
⁴ Restore again our fortunes, LORD,
like the dry stream beds of the
Negeb.*

II

⁵ Those who sow in tears
will reap with cries of joy.*ʲ*
⁶ Those who go forth weeping,
carrying sacks of seed,
Will return with cries of joy,
carrying their bundled sheaves.

Ps

PSALM 127*

The Need of God's Blessing

¹ A song of ascents. Of Solomon.

I

Unless the LORD build the house,
  they labor in vain who build.
Unless the LORD guard the city,
  in vain does the guard keep watch.
² It is vain for you to rise early
  and put off your rest at night,
To eat bread earned by hard toil—
  all this God gives to his beloved in
  sleep.*ᵏ*

II

³ Children too are a gift from the LORD,
  the fruit of the womb, a reward.*ˡ*
⁴ Like arrows in the hand of a warrior
  are the children born in one's youth.
⁵ Blessed are they whose quivers are
  full.
  They will never be shamed
  contending with foes at the gate.*

PSALM 128*

The Happy Home of the Just

¹ A song of ascents.

I

Happy are all who fear the LORD,*
  who walk in the ways of God.*ᵐ*
² What your hands provide you will enjoy;
  you will be happy and prosper:*ⁿ*
³ Like a fruitful vine
  your wife within your home,
Like olive plants
  your children around your table.*ᵒ*
⁴ Just so will they be blessed
  who fear the LORD.

II

⁵ May the LORD bless you from Zion,
  all the days of your life*ᵖ*
That you may share Jerusalem's joy
⁶ and live to see your children's children.*�q*
  Peace upon Israel!*ʳ*

PSALM 129*

Against Israel's Enemies

¹ A song of ascents.

I

Much have they oppressed me from my
  youth,
  now let Israel say.*ˢ*
² Much have they oppressed me from my
  youth,*ᵗ*
  yet they have not prevailed.

³ Upon my back the plowers plowed,
  as they traced their long furrows.*ᵘ*
⁴ But the just LORD cut me free
  from the ropes of the yoke of the
  wicked.*

II

⁵ May they be scattered in disgrace,
  all who hate Zion.
⁶ May they be like grass on the rooftops*
  withered in early growth,*ᵛ*
⁷ Never to fill the reaper's hands,
  nor the arms of the binders of
  sheaves,
⁸ With none passing by to call out:
  "The blessing of the LORD be upon
  you!*
  We bless you in the name of the
  LORD!"*ʷ*

PSALM 130*

Prayer for Pardon and Mercy

¹ A song of ascents.

I

Out of the depths* I call to you, LORD;
²   Lord, hear my cry!

---

k Eccl 2, 24.—l Pss 115, 14; 128, 3; Dt 28, 11; Prv 17, 6.—m
Ps 112, 1.—n Ps 112, 3.—o Jb 29, 5; Ps 144, 12.—p Pss 20, 3;
134, 3.—q Jb 42, 16; Prv 17, 6.—r Ps 125, 5.—s Ps 124, 1.—t
Ps 118, 13.—u Is 51, 23.—v Is 37, 27.—w Ps 118, 26.

Ps 127: The psalm puts together two proverbs (1-2 and 3-5) on God establishing "houses" or families. The prosperity of human groups is not the work of humans but the gift of God.

127, 5: *At the gate:* the reference is not to enemies besieging the walls of a city but to adversaries in litigation. Lawcourts functioned in the open area near the main city gate. The more adult sons a man had, the more forceful he would appear in disputes. Cf Prv 31, 23.

Ps 128: A statement that the ever-reliable God will bless the reverent (1). God's blessing is concrete: satisfaction and prosperity, a fertile spouse and abundant children (2-4). The perspective is that of the adult male, ordinarily the ruler and representative of the household to the community. The last verses extend the blessing to all the people for generations to come (5-6).

128, 1: *All who fear the LORD:* literally, singular: "the one fearing," is used in a typical sense and so is translated by the plural.

Ps 129: A psalm giving thanks for God's many rescues of Israel over the long course of their history (1-4); the people pray that their oppressors never know the joy of harvest (5-8).

129, 4: *The ropes of the yoke of the wicked:* usually understood as the rope for yoking animals to the plow. If it is severed, the plowing (cf 3) comes to a halt.

129, 6: *Like grass on the rooftops:* after the spring rains, grass would sprout from the coat of mud with which the flat roofs of simple houses were covered, but when the dry summer began there was no moisture in the thin roof-covering to sustain the grass.

129, 8: *The blessing of the LORD be upon you:* harvesters greeted one another with such blessings. Cf Ru 2, 4.

Ps 130: This lament, a Penitential Psalm, is the *De profundis* used in liturgical prayers for the faithful departed. In deep sorrow the psalmist cries to God (1-2), asking for mercy (3-4). The psalmist's trust (5-6) becomes a model for the people (7-8).

130, 1: *The depths:* Sheol here is a metaphor of total misery. Deep anguish makes the psalmist feel "like those descending to the pit" (Ps 143, 7).

May your ears be attentive
  to my cry for mercy. [x]
3 If you, LORD, mark our sins,
  Lord, who can stand?[y]
4 But with you is forgiveness
  and so you are revered.*

II

5 I wait with longing for the LORD,
  my soul waits for his word. [z]
6 My soul looks for the Lord
  more than sentinels for daybreak. [a]
  More than sentinels for daybreak,
7   let Israel look for the LORD,
  For with the LORD is kindness,
    with him is full redemption,[b]
8 And God will redeem Israel
  from all their sins. [c]

PSALM 131*

Humble Trust in God

1 A song of ascents. Of David.

LORD, my heart is not proud;
  nor are my eyes haughty.
I do not busy myself with great matters,
  with things too sublime for me. [d]
2 Rather, I have stilled my soul,
  hushed it like a weaned child.

---

x Pss 5, 2-3; 55, 2-3; 86, 6; Lam 3, 55-56; Jon 2, 3.—y Na 1, 6.—z Ps 119, 81.—a Is 21, 11; 26, 9.—b Pss 86, 15; 100, 5; 103, 8.—c Ps 25, 22; Mt 1, 21.—d Ps 139, 6.—e Is 66, 12-13.— f 2 Sm 7; 1 Chr 28, 2.—g Ps 99, 5.—h 8-10: Pss 2, 2; 89, 21; 95, 11; Nm 10, 35; 2 Chr 6, 41-42; Sir 24, 7.—i Ps 110, 4; 2 Sm 7, 12.—j 11-14: Ps 68, 17; 1 Kgs 8, 13; Sir 24, 7.—k 2 Chr 6, 41; Is 61, 10.—l Is 11, 1; Jer 33, 15; Ez 29, 21; Zec 3, 8; Lk 1, 69.

130, 4: *And so you are revered:* the experience of God's mercy leads one to a greater sense of God.

Ps 131: A song of trust, in which the psalmist gives up self-sufficiency (1), like a babe enjoying the comfort of its mother's lap (2), thus providing a model for Israel's faith (3).

132: A song for a liturgical ceremony in which the ark, the throne of Israel's God, was carried in procession to the temple. The singer asks that David's care for the proper housing of the ark be regarded with favor (1-5), and tells how it was brought to Jerusalem (6-10). There follows God's promise of favor to the Davidic dynasty (11-12) and to Zion (13-17). The transfer of the ark to the tent in Jerusalem is described in 2 Sm 6.

132, 1: *All his anxious care:* to build the temple. Cf 2 Sm 7, 1-17 and 1 Kgs 8, 17.

132, 2. 5: *Mighty One of Jacob:* one of the titles of Israel's God. Cf Gn 49, 24; Is 49, 26; 60, 16.

132, 6: *Ephrathah:* the homeland of David. Cf Ru 4, 11. *The fields of Jaar:* poetic for Kiriath-jearim, a town west of Jerusalem, where the ark remained for several generations. Cf 1 Sm 7, 1-2 ; 2 Sm 6, 2; 1 Chr 13, 5-6.

132, 17: *A horn sprout for David's line:* the image of the horn, a symbol of strength, is combined with that of a "sprout," a term used for the Davidic descendant (cf Jer 23, 5; 33, 15; Zec 3, 8; 6, 12). Early Christians referred the latter designation to Christ as son of David (Lk 1, 69).

Like a weaned child on its mother's lap,
  so is my soul within me. [e]
3 Israel, hope in the LORD,
  now and forever.

PSALM 132*

The Covenant between David and God

1 A song of ascents.

I

LORD, remember David
  and all his anxious care;*
2 How he swore an oath to the LORD,
  vowed to the Mighty One of Jacob:*
3 "I will not enter the house where I live,[f]
  nor lie on the couch where I sleep;
4 I will give my eyes no sleep,
  my eyelids no rest,
5 Till I find a home for the LORD,
  a dwelling for the Mighty One of Jacob."

6 "We have heard of it in Ephrathah;*
  we have found it in the fields of Jaar.
7 Let us enter God's dwelling;
  let us worship at God's footstool."[g]

8 "Arise, LORD, come to your resting place,[h]
  you and your majestic ark.
9 Your priests will be clothed with justice;
  your faithful will shout for joy."
10 For the sake of David your servant,
  do not reject your anointed.

II

11 The LORD swore an oath to David,
  a pledge never to be broken:[i]
  "Your own offspring[j] I will set upon your throne.
12 If your sons observe my covenant,
  the laws I shall teach them,
  Their sons, in turn,
    shall sit forever on your throne."
13 Yes, the LORD has chosen Zion,
  desired it for a dwelling:
14 "This is my resting place forever;
  here I will dwell, for I desire it.
15 I will bless Zion with meat;
  its poor I will fill with bread.
16 I will clothe its priests with blessing;
  its faithful shall shout for joy. [k]
17 There I will make a horn sprout for David's line;*[l]
  I will set a lamp for my anointed.
18 His foes I will clothe with shame,
  but on him my crown shall gleam."

Ps

PSALM 133*

A Vision of a Blessed Community

1 A song of ascents. Of David.

How good it is, how pleasant,
  where the people* dwell as one!
2 Like precious ointment* on the head,[m]
  running down upon the beard,
Upon the beard of Aaron,
  upon the collar of his robe.
3 Like dew* of Hermon coming down
  upon the mountains of Zion.[n]
There the LORD has lavished blessings,
  life for evermore![o]

PSALM 134*

Exhortation to the Night Watch
To Bless God

1 A song of ascents.

Come, bless the LORD,
  all you servants of the LORD*
Who stand in the house of the LORD
  through the long hours of night.[p]
2 Lift up your hands toward the sanctuary,[q]
  and bless the LORD.
3 May the LORD who made heaven and
  earth[r]
  bless you from Zion.

PSALM 135*

Praise of God, the Ruler and
Benefactor of Israel

1 Hallelujah!

I

Praise the name of the LORD!
  Praise, you servants of the LORD,[s]
2 Who stand in the house of the LORD,
  in the courts of the house of our
  God![t]
3 Praise the LORD; the LORD is good!
  Sing to God's name; it is gracious!
4 For the LORD has chosen Jacob,
  Israel as a treasured possession.*[u]

II

5 I know that the LORD is great,
  our Lord is greater than all gods.[v]

6 Whatever the LORD wishes
  he does in heaven and on earth,
  in the seas and in all the deeps.[w]
7 He raises storm clouds from the end of
  the earth,
  makes lightning and rain,
  brings forth wind from the storehouse.[x]

III

8 He struck down Egypt's firstborn,[y]
  human and beast alike,
9 And sent signs and portents against
  you, Egypt,
  against Pharaoh and all his servants.
10 The Lord struck down many nations,[z]
  slew mighty kings—
11 Sihon, king of the Amorites,
  Og, king of Bashan,
  all the kings of Canaan—
12 And made their land a heritage,
  a heritage for Israel his people.
13 O LORD, your name is forever,
  your renown, from age to age![a]
14 For the LORD defends his people,
  shows mercy to his servants.[b]

---

m Ex 30, 25. 30.—n Hos 14, 6.—o Dt 28, 8; 30, 20.—p Ps
135, 1-2; 1 Chr 9, 33.—q Pss 28, 2; 141, 2.—r Pss 20, 3; 128,
5; Nm 6, 24.—s Ps 113, 1.—t Ps 134, 1.—u Pss 33, 12; 144,
15; Ex 19, 6; Dt 7, 6.—v Ps 95, 3; Ex 18, 11.—w Ps 115, 3.—x
Ps 148, 8; Jer 10, 13; 51, 16; Jb 37, 9.—y 8-9: Pss 78, 51; 105,
27. 36; 136, 10; Ex 12, 29.—z 10-12: Nm 21, 21-35; Dt 2, 24—
3, 17; Ps 136, 17-22.—a Ps 102, 13; Ex 3, 15.—b Dt 32, 36.

Ps 133: A benediction over a peaceful community, most probably the people Israel, but appropriate too for Israelite families
(1). The history of Israel, whether of its ancestors in the book of
Genesis or of later periods, was a history of distinct groups
struggling to live in unity. Here that unity is declared blessed, like
the holy oils upon the priest Aaron or the dew of the rainless summer that waters the crops (2-3).
133, 1: *The people:* literally, "brothers," i.e., male and
female members of a kin group or people—most probably, the
people Israel.
133, 2: *Ointment:* oil was used at the consecration of the high
priest (Ex 30, 22-33).
133, 3: *Dew:* dew was an important source of moisture in the
dry climate (Gn 27, 28; Hos 14, 6). *Hermon:* the majestic snow-
capped mountain visible in the north of Palestine.
Ps 134: A brief liturgy exhorting the temple singers to acknowledge the great deeds of God at a night service (cf Is 30,
29). Mount Zion is the place from which blessings affect the lives
of humans, for there Israel's God dwells.
134, 1: *Servants of the LORD:* priests and Levites. Cf Dt 10,
8; Pss 113, 1; 135, 1; Dn 3, 84-85.
Ps 135: The hymn begins and ends with an invitation to praise
God (1-3, 19-20) for the great act of choosing Israel (4). The
story of Israel's emergence as a people is told in 5-14; God
created and redeemed the people, easily conquering all opposition. God's defeat of hostile powers means that the powers themselves and their images are useless (15-18). The last three verses
appear also in Ps 115, 4-8.
135, 4: Though all nations are God's, Israel has a special
status as God's "treasured" people: Ex 19, 5; Dt 7, 6; 14, 2; 26,
18; Mal 3, 17.

IV

15 The idols of the nations are silver and
    gold,*c*
    the work of human hands.
16 They have mouths but speak not;
    they have eyes but see not;
17 They have ears but hear not;
    no breath is in their mouths.
18 Their makers shall be like them,
    all who trust in them.

V

19 House of Israel, bless the LORD!*d*
    House of Aaron, bless the LORD!
20 House of Levi, bless the LORD!
    You who fear the LORD, bless the
    LORD!
21 Blessed from Zion be the LORD,
    who dwells in Jerusalem!
    Hallelujah!

PSALM 136*

Hymn of Thanksgiving for God's Everlasting Love

I

1 Praise the LORD, who is so good;*e*
    God's love endures forever;
2 Praise the God of gods;
    God's love endures forever;
3 Praise the Lord of lords;
    God's love endures forever;

II

4 Who alone has done great wonders,*f*
    God's love endures forever;

---

c 15-18: Ps 115, 4-6. 8.—d 19-20: Ps 118, 2-4.—e Pss 100,
5; 118, 1.—f Ps 72, 18.—g Gn 1, 9-19.—h Ps 24, 2.—i Jer 31,
35.—j Ex 12, 29. 51; 14, 22. 27; 15, 22; Pss 78, 51-52; 135,
8.—k Dt 4, 34.—l Ex 14, 21f.—m Dt 8, 2. 15.—n 17-22: Ps 135,
10-12.

Ps 136: The hymn praises Israel's God ("the God of gods," 2),
who has created the world in which Israel lives. The refrain occurring after every line suggests that a speaker and chorus sang
the psalm in antiphonal fashion. A single act of God is described
in 4-25: God arranges the heavens and the earth as the environment for human community, and then creates the community by
freeing them and giving them land. In the final section (23-25)
God, who created the people and gave them land, continues to
protect and nurture them.
136, 22: *A heritage for Israel:* the land was given to Israel
by God to be handed on to future generations.

5 Who skillfully made the heavens,*g*
    God's love endures forever;
6 Who spread the earth upon the waters,*h*
    God's love endures forever;
7 Who made the great lights,
    God's love endures forever;
8 The sun to rule the day,
    God's love endures forever;
9 The moon and stars to rule the night,*i*
    God's love endures forever;

III

10 Who struck down the firstborn of
    Egypt,*j*
    God's love endures forever;
11 And led Israel from their midst,
    God's love endures forever;
12 With mighty hand and outstretched
    arm,*k*
    God's love endures forever;
13 Who split in two the Red Sea,
    God's love endures forever;
14 And led Israel through,
    God's love endures forever;
15 But swept Pharaoh and his army into
    the Red Sea,*l*
    God's love endures forever;
16 Who led the people through the des-
    ert,*m*
    God's love endures forever;

IV

17 Who struck down great kings,*n*
    God's love endures forever;
18 Slew powerful kings,
    God's love endures forever;
19 Sihon, king of the Amorites,
    God's love endures forever;
20 Og, king of Bashan,
    God's love endures forever;
21 And made their lands a heritage,
    God's love endures forever;
22 A heritage for Israel,* God's servant,
    God's love endures forever.

V

23 The LORD remembered us in our mis-
    ery,
    God's love endures forever;
24 Freed us from our foes,
    God's love endures forever;
25 And gives food to all flesh,
    God's love endures forever.

VI

26 Praise the God of heaven,
    God's love endures forever.

Ps

PSALM 137*

Sorrow and Hope in Exile

I

1 By the rivers of Babylon
   we sat mourning and weeping
   when we remembered Zion.*o*
2 On the poplars* of that land
   we hung up our harps.*p*
3 There our captors asked us
   for the words of a song;
   Our tormentors, for a joyful song:
   "Sing for us a song of Zion!"
4 But how could we sing a song of the
   LORD
   in a foreign land?

II

5 If I forget you, Jerusalem,
   may my right hand wither.*q*
6 May my tongue stick to my palate
   if I do not remember you,
   If I do not exalt Jerusalem
   beyond all my delights.

III

7 Remember, LORD, against Edom
   that day at Jerusalem.
   They said: "Level it, level it
   down to its foundations!"*r*
8 Fair Babylon, you destroyer,
   happy those who pay you back
   the evil you have done us!*s*
9 Happy those who seize your children
   and smash them against a rock.**t*

PSALM 138*

Hymn of a Grateful Heart

1 Of David.

I

I thank you, LORD, with all my heart;*u*
   before the gods* to you I sing.
2 I bow low toward your holy temple;
   I praise your name for your fidelity
   and love.
For you have exalted over all
   your name and your promise.
3 When I cried out, you answered;
   you strengthened my spirit.

II

4 All the kings of earth will praise you,
   LORD,
   when they hear the words of your
   mouth.

5 They will sing of the ways of the LORD:
   "How great is the glory of the
   LORD!"
6 The LORD is on high, but cares for the
   lowly*v*
   and knows the proud from afar.
7 Though I walk in the midst of dangers,
   you guard my life when my enemies
   rage.
You stretch out your hand;
   your right hand saves me.
8 The LORD is with me to the end.
   LORD, your love endures forever.
   Never forsake the work of your
   hands!

PSALM 139*

The All-knowing and Ever-present God

1 For the leader. A psalm of David.

I

LORD, you have probed me, you know
   me:
2   you know when I sit and stand;**w*
   you understand my thoughts from
   afar.
3 My travels and my rest you mark;
   with all my ways you are familiar.

---

o Ez 3, 15; Lam 3, 48.—p Is 24, 8; Lam 5, 14.—q Jer 51,
50.—r Jer 49, 7; Lam 4, 21-22; Ez 25, 12-14.—s Is 47, 1-3; Jer
50—51.—t Hos 14, 1.—u Ps 9, 1.—v Lk 1, 51-52.—w 2 Kgs 19,
27; Jb 12, 13.

Ps 137: A temple singer refuses to sing the people's sacred
songs in an alien land despite demands from Babylonian captors
(1-4). The singer swears an oath by what is most dear to a musi-
cian—hands and tongue—to exalt Jerusalem always (5-6). The
psalm ends with a prayer that the old enemies of Jerusalem,
Edom and Babylon, be destroyed (7-9).
137, 2: *Poplars:* sometimes incorrectly translated "willow."
The Euphrates poplar is a high tree common on riverbanks in the
Orient.
137, 9: *Happy those who seize your children and smash
them against a rock:* the infants represent the future generations, and so must be destroyed if the enemy is truly to be eradi-
cated.
Ps 138: A thanksgiving to God, who came to the rescue of the
psalmist. Divine rescue was not the result of the psalmist's virtues
but of God's loving fidelity (1-3). The act is not a private transaction but a public act that stirs the surrounding nations to praise
God's greatness and care for the people (4-6). The psalmist, having experienced salvation, trusts that God will always be there in
moments of danger (7-8).
138, 1: *Before the gods:* i.e., heavenly beings, who were
completely subordinate to Israel's God. The earthly temple represents the heavenly palace of God.
Ps 139: A hymnic meditation on God's omnipresence and omniscience. The psalmist is keenly aware of God's all-knowing gaze
(1-6), of God's presence in every part of the universe (7-12), and
of God's control over the psalmist's very self (13-16). Summing
up 1-16, 17-18 express wonder. There is only one place hostile to
God's rule—wicked people. The psalmist prays to be removed
from their company (19-24).
139, 2: *When I sit and stand:* in all my physical movement.

⁴ Even before a word is on my tongue,
  Lord, you know it all.
⁵ Behind and before you encircle me
  and rest your hand upon me.
⁶ Such knowledge is beyond me,
  far too lofty for me to reach.ˣ

II

⁷ Where can I hide from your spirit?
  From your presence, where can I
  flee?
⁸ If I ascend to the heavens, you are
  there;
  if I lie down in Sheol, you are there
  too.ʸ
⁹ If I fly with the wings of dawn*
  and alight beyond the sea,
¹⁰ Even there your hand will guide me,
  your right hand hold me fast.
¹¹ If I say, "Surely darkness shall hide me,
  and night shall be my light"—*
¹² Darkness is not dark for you,
  and night shines as the day.
  Darkness and light are but one.ᶻ

III

¹³ You formed my inmost being;
  you knit me in my mother's womb.ᵃ
¹⁴ I praise you, so wonderfully you made
  me;
  wonderful are your works!
  My very self you knew;
¹⁵   my bones were not hidden from you,
  When I was being made in secret,
  fashioned as in the depths of the
  earth.*

---

x Ps 131, 1.—y Jb 23, 8-9; Jer 23, 23-24.—z Jb 12, 22.—a
Wis 7, 1; Eccl 11, 5; Jb 1, 21.—b Mal 3, 16.—c Jb 11, 7.—d Jb
21, 14.—e Ps 119, 158.—f Pss 17, 3; 26, 2.—g Ps 71, 4.—h Ps
64, 4; Rom 3, 13.—i Jer 18, 22; Pss 56, 7; 57, 7.

139, 9: *Fly with the wings of dawn:* go to the extremities
of the east. *Beyond the sea:* uttermost bounds of the west; the
sea is the Mediterranean.
139, 11: *Night shall be my light:* night to me is what day is
to others.
139, 15: *The depths of the earth:* figurative language for
the womb, stressing the hidden and mysterious operations that
occur there.
139, 24: *My way . . . the ancient paths:* the manner of living of our ancestors, who were faithful to God's will. Cf Jer 6, 16.
Ps 140: A lament seeking rescue from violent and treacherous
foes (2-6). The psalmist remains trusting (7-8), vigorously praying that the plans of the wicked recoil upon themselves (9-12). A
serene statement of praise ends the psalm (13-14). The psalmist
is content to be known as one of "the needy," "the poor," "the
just," "the upright" (13-14), a class of people expecting divine
protection.
140, 4: Similar metaphors for a wicked tongue are used in Pss
52, 4; 55, 22; 58, 5.
140, 6: *Have set a trap . . . have spread a net:* the same
figure, of hunters setting traps, occurs in Pss 9, 16; 31, 5; 35, 7;
64, 6. Cf Mt 22, 15; Lk 11, 54.

---

¹⁶ Your eyes foresaw my actions;
  in your book all are written down;ᵇ
  my days were shaped, before one
  came to be.

IV

¹⁷ How precious to me are your designs, O
  God;
  how vast the sum of them!
¹⁸ Were I to count, they would outnumber
  the sands;
  to finish, I would need eternity.ᶜ
¹⁹ If only you would destroy the wicked,
  O God,
  and the bloodthirsty would depart
  from me!ᵈ
²⁰ Deceitfully they invoke your name;
  your foes swear faithless oaths.
²¹ Do I not hate, Lord, those who hate
  you?
  Those who rise against you, do I not
  loathe?ᵉ
²² With fierce hatred I hate them,
  enemies I count as my own.

V

²³ Probe me, God, know my heart;
  try me, know my concerns.ᶠ
²⁴ See if my way is crooked,
  then lead me in the ancient paths.*

PSALM 140*

Prayer for Deliverance from the Wicked

¹ For the leader. A psalm of David.

I

² Deliver me, Lord, from the wicked;
  preserve me from the violent,ᵍ
³ From those who plan evil in their
  hearts,
  who stir up conflicts every day,
⁴ Who sharpen their tongues like serpents,*
  venom of asps upon their lips.ʰ *Selah*

II

⁵ Keep me, Lord, from the clutches of
  the wicked;
  preserve me from the violent,
  who plot to trip me up.ⁱ
⁶ The arrogant have set a trap for me;
  villains have spread a net,*
  laid snares for me by the wayside.
          Selah

Ps

7 I say to the LORD: You are my God;[j]
listen, LORD, to the words of my
prayer.
8 My revered LORD, my strong helper,
my helmet on the day of battle,
9 LORD, do not grant the desires of the
wicked;
do not let their plots succeed. *Selah*
10 Around me they raise their proud
heads;
may the mischief they threaten overwhelm them.
11 May God rain burning coals upon
them,[k]
cast them into the grave never more
to rise.

III
12 Slanderers will not survive on earth;
evil will quickly entrap the violent.
13 For I know the LORD will secure
justice for the needy, their rights for
the poor.
14 Then the just will give thanks to your
name;
the upright will dwell in your presence.[l]

PSALM 141*

Prayer for Deliverance from the Wicked

1 A psalm of David.

LORD, I call to you;
come quickly to help me;
listen to my plea when I call.
2 Let my prayer be incense* before you;
my uplifted hands an evening sacrifice.[m]
3 Set a guard, LORD, before my mouth,
a gatekeeper at my lips.[n]
4 Do not let my heart incline to evil
or yield to any sin.
I will never feast upon
the fine food of evildoers.
5 Let the just strike me; that is kindness;*
let them rebuke me; that is oil for my
head.[o]
All this I shall not refuse,
but will pray despite these trials.
6 When their leaders are cast over the
cliff,
all will learn that my prayers were
heard.

7 As when a farmer plows a field into
broken clods,
so their bones will be strewn at the
mouth of Sheol.
8 My eyes are upon you, O GOD, my
Lord;[p]
in you I take refuge; do not strip me
of life.
9 Guard me from the trap they have set
for me,
from the snares of evildoers.[q]
10 Into their own nets let all the wicked
fall,
while I make good my own escape.

PSALM 142*

A Prayer in Time of Trouble

1 A *maskil* of David, when he was in the cave.*
A prayer.

2 With full voice I cry to the LORD;
with full voice I beseech the LORD.
3 Before God I pour out my complaint,
lay bare my distress.
4 My spirit is faint within me,[r]
but you know my path.[s]
Along the way I walk
they have hidden a trap for me.[t]
5 I look to my right hand,[u]
but no friend is there.

---

j Ps 31, 15.—k Pss 11, 6; 120, 4; Gn 19, 24.—l Pss 11, 7; 16,
11; 17, 15.—m Ps 134, 2; Ex 30, 8.—n Sir 22, 27.—o Prv 9, 8;
25, 12.—p Pss 25, 15; 123, 1-2.—q Ps 142, 4.—r Ps 143, 4.—s
Ps 139, 24.—t Ps 141, 9.—u Pss 16, 8; 73, 23; 121, 5.

Ps 141: A lament of an individual (1-2) who is keenly aware
that only the righteous can worship God properly and who therefore prays to be protected from the doomed wicked (3-10).
141, 2: *Incense:* literally, "smoke," i.e., the fragrant fumes
arising from the altar at the burning of sacrificial animals or of
aromatic spices; also used in Rv 5, 8 as a symbol of prayer. *My
uplifted hands:* the gesture of supplication. Cf Pss 28, 2; 63, 5;
88, 10; 119, 48; 134, 2; 143, 6.
141, 5-7: The Hebrew text is obscure.
Ps 142: In this lament imploring God for help (2-4b), the
psalmist tells how enemies have set a trap (4c-5), and prays for
rescue (6-8). The speaker feels utterly alone (5), exhausted (7),
and may even be imprisoned (8a). Prison is possibly a metaphor
for general distress. The last two verses are the vow of praise,
made after receiving an assurance of divine help (8cd).
142, 1: *In the cave:* cf 1 Sm 22, 1; 24, 1-3; Ps 57, 1.

There is no escape for me;
    no one cares for me.
6 I cry out to you, LORD,
    I say, You are my refuge,[v]
    my portion in the land of the living.[w]
7 Listen to my cry for help,
    for I am brought very low.[x]
Rescue me from my pursuers,
    for they are too strong for me.
8 Lead me out of my prison,
    that I may give thanks to your name.
Then the just shall gather around me*
    because you have been good to me.

PSALM 143*

A Prayer in Distress

1 A psalm of David.

LORD, hear my prayer;
    in your faithfulness listen to my
    pleading;
    answer me in your justice.
2 Do not enter into judgment with your
    servant;
    before you no living being can be
    just.[y]

---

v Ps 91, 2. 9.—w Pss 16, 5; 27, 13; 116, 9; Is 38, 11.—x Ps
79, 8.—y Eccl 7, 20; Jb 4, 17; Rom 3, 20.—z Ps 7, 6.—a Lam
3, 6.—b Ps 142, 4; Jb 17, 1.—c Ps 77, 6. 12.—d Pss 42, 2; 63,
2.—e Pss 28, 1; 30, 4; 88, 5; Prv 1, 12.—f Pss 25, 4; 27, 11; 86,
11; 119, 12. 35.—g Ps 116, 16.—h Jb 7, 17.—i Pss 62, 10; 90,
9-10; Jb 7, 16; Eccl 6, 12; Wis 2, 5.

142, 8: *Then the just shall gather around me:* in the temple, when the psalmist offers a thanksgiving sacrifice.
    Ps 143: One of the Church's seven Penitential Psalms, this la-
ment is a prayer to be freed from death-dealing enemies. The
psalmist addresses God, aware that there is no equality between
God and humans; salvation is a gift (1-2). Victimized by evil people (3-4), the psalmist recites ("remembers") God's past actions
on behalf of the innocent (5-6). The psalm continues with fervent
prayer (7- 9) and a strong desire for guidance and protection (10-
12).
    143, 3: *They have crushed:* literally, "he crushed"; the sin-
gular is used typically, hence the plural translation.
    Ps 144: The psalm may reflect a ceremony in which the king,
as leader of the army, asked God's help (1-8). In 9 the poem
shifts abruptly from pleading to thanksgiving, and (except for 11)
shifts again to prayer for the people. The first section (1-2) is a
prayer of thanks for victory; the second (3-7a), a humble acknowledgment of human nothingness and a supplication that God
show forth saving power; the third (9-11), a promise of future
thanksgiving; the fourth (12-15), a wish for prosperity and peace.
A prayer for deliverance from treacherous foes serves as a refrain
after the second and third sections (7b-8, 11). Except for its final
section, the psalm is made up almost entirely of verses from other
psalms.
    144, 1-2: Composed of phrases from Ps 18, 3. 35. 47-48.
    144, 3: Similar to Ps 8, 5.
    144, 4: Composed of phrases from Pss 39, 6; 102, 12.

3 The enemy has pursued me;
    they have crushed* my life to the
    ground.[z]
They have left me in darkness
    like those long dead.[a]
4 My spirit is faint within me;
    my heart is dismayed.[b]
5 I remember the days of old;
    I ponder all your deeds;
    the works of your hands I recall.[c]
6 I stretch out my hands to you;
    I thirst for you like a parched land.[d]
                        Selah
7 Hasten to answer me, LORD;
    for my spirit fails me.
Do not hide your face from me,
    lest I become like those descending to
    the pit.[e]
8 At dawn let me hear of your kindness,
    for in you I trust.
Show me the path I should walk,
    for to you I entrust my life.[f]
9 Rescue me, LORD, from my foes,
    for in you I hope.
10 Teach me to do your will,
    for you are my God.
May your kind spirit guide me
    on ground that is level.
11 For your name's sake, LORD, give me
    life;
    in your justice lead me out of distress.
12 In your kindness put an end to my foes;
    destroy all who attack me,
    for I am your servant.[g]

PSALM 144*

A Prayer for Victory and Prosperity

1 Of David.

I

Blessed be the LORD, my rock,*
    who trains my hands for battle,
    my fingers for war;
2 My safeguard and my fortress,
    my stronghold, my deliverer,
My shield, in whom I trust,
    who subdues peoples under me.

II

3 LORD, what are mortals that you notice
    them;*
    human beings, that you take thought
    of them?[h]
4 They are but a breath;*
    their days are like a passing shadow.[i]

Ps

5 LORD, incline your heavens and come;*
   touch the mountains and make them
   smoke.*j*

6 Flash forth lightning and scatter my
   foes;
   shoot your arrows and rout them.

7 Reach out your hand from on high;
   deliver me from the many waters;
   rescue me from the hands of foreign
   foes.

8 Their mouths speak untruth;
   their right hands are raised in lying
   oaths.*

9 O God, a new song I will sing to you;
   on a ten-stringed lyre I will play for
   you.*k*

10 You give victory to kings;
   you delivered David your servant.*l*
   From the menacing sword 11 deliver me;
   rescue me from the hands of foreign
   foes.
   Their mouths speak untruth;
   their right hands are raised in lying
   oaths.

III

12 May our sons be like plants*m*
   well nurtured from their youth,
   Our daughters, like carved columns,
   shapely as those of the temple.

13 May our barns be full
   with every kind of store.
   May our sheep increase by thousands,
   by tens of thousands in our fields;
   may our oxen be well fattened.

14 May there be no breach in the walls,
   no exile, no outcry in our streets.*n*

15 Happy the people so blessed;
   happy the people whose God is the
   LORD.*o*

PSALM 145*

The Greatness and Goodness of God

1 Praise. Of David.

I will extol you, my God and king;
   I will bless your name forever.

2 Every day I will bless you;
   I will praise your name forever.*p*

3 Great is the LORD and worthy of high
   praise;*q*
   God's grandeur is beyond understanding.

4 One generation praises your deeds to
   the next
   and proclaims your mighty works.*r*

5 They speak of the splendor of your
   majestic glory,
   tell of your wonderful deeds.*s*

6 They speak of your fearsome power
   and attest to your great deeds.*t*

7 They publish the renown of your
   abounding goodness
   and joyfully sing of your justice.

8 The LORD is gracious and merciful,
   slow to anger and abounding in love.*u*

9 The LORD is good to all,
   compassionate to every creature.*v*

10 All your works give you thanks, O
   LORD,
   and your faithful bless you.*w*

11 They speak of the glory of your reign
   and tell of your great works,

12 Making known to all your power,
   the glorious splendor of your rule.

13 Your reign is a reign for all ages,
   your dominion for all generations.*x*
   The LORD is trustworthy in every
   word,
   and faithful in every work.

14 The LORD supports all who are falling
   and raises up all who are bowed
   down.*y*

15 The eyes of all look hopefully to you;
   you give them their food in due season.*z*

16 You open wide your hand
   and satisfy the desire of every living
   thing.

---

j Is 63, 19.—k Ps 33, 2-3.—l Ps 18, 51.—m Ps 128, 3.—n Is 65, 19.—o Ps 33, 12.—p Ps 34, 2.—q Pss 48, 2; 95, 3; 96, 4; Jb 36, 26.—r Pss 22, 31-32; 48, 14-15; 71, 18; 78, 4; Ex 10, 2; Dt 4, 9.—s Pss 96, 3; 105, 2.—t Ps 66, 3.—u Pss 86, 5. 15; 103, 8; Ex 34, 6; Sir 2, 11.—v Ps 103, 13; Wis 11, 24.—w Dn 3, 57.—x Pss 10, 16; 102, 13; 146, 10; Lam 5, 19; Dn 3, 100; Rv 11, 15.—y Pss 94, 18; 146, 8.—z Pss 136, 25; 104, 27-28; Mt 6, 25-26.

144, 5-7: Adapted in large part from Pss 18, 10. 15. 17; 104, 32.
144, 8b. 11b: *Their right hands are raised in lying oaths:* the psalmist's enemies give false testimony.
Ps 145: A hymn in acrostic form; every verse begins with a successive letter of the Hebrew alphabet. Acrostic poems usually do not develop ideas but consist rather of loosely connected statements. The singer invites all to praise God (1-3. 21). The "works of God" make God present and invite human praise (4-7); they climax in a confession (8-9). God's mighty acts show forth divine kingship (10-20), a major theme in the literature of early Judaism and in Christianity.

¹⁷ You, LORD, are just in all your ways,
  faithful in all your works.^{*a*}
¹⁸ You, LORD, are near to all who call
  upon you,
  to all who call upon you in truth.^{*b*}
¹⁹ You satisfy the desire of those who fear
  you;
  you hear their cry and save them.^{*c*}
²⁰ You, LORD, watch over all who love
  you,
  but all the wicked you destroy.^{*d*}
²¹ My mouth will speak your praises,
  LORD;
  all flesh will bless your holy name forever.^{*e*}

PSALM 146*

Trust in God the Creator
and Redeemer

¹ Hallelujah!

Praise the LORD, my soul;
² I shall praise the LORD all my life,
  sing praise to my God while I live.^{*f*}

I

³ Put no trust in princes,
  in mere mortals powerless to save.^{*g*}
⁴ When they breathe their last, they re-
  turn to the earth;
  that day all their planning comes to
  nothing.^{*h*}

---

a Dt 32, 4.—b Dt 4, 7; Is 55, 6; 58, 9.—c Ps 34, 18.—d Jgs
5, 31.—e Sir 40, 35.—f Pss 103, 1; 104, 33.—g Ps 118, 8-9.—h
Pss 90, 3; 104, 29; 1 Mc 2, 63; Jb 34, 14-15; Eccl 3, 20; 12, 7;
Sir 40, 11; Is 2, 22.—i Ex 20, 11; Pss 121, 2; 124, 8; Acts 14,
15; Rv 14, 7.—j Ps 103, 6.—k Ps 68, 7; Is 49, 9; 61, 1.—l Ps
145, 14.—m Ps 68, 6; Dt 10, 18.—n Ps 145, 13; Lam 5, 19.—o
Pss 33, 1; 92, 2.—p Is 11, 12; 56, 8; Jer 31, 10.—q Jb 5, 18;
Is 30, 26; 61, 1; Jer 33, 6.—r Is 40, 26.—s Jdt 16, 13; Jer 51,
15.—t Ps 146, 9; 1 Sm 2, 7-8.—u Ps 71, 22.—v Ps 104, 13f; Jb
5, 10; Jer 14, 22; Jl 2, 23.—w Jb 38, 41; Mt 6, 26.—x Pss 20,
8; 33, 16-18.

Ps 146: A hymn of someone who has learned there is no other
source of strength except the merciful God. Only God, not mortal
humans (3-4), can help vulnerable and oppressed people (5-9).
The first of the five hymns that conclude the Psalter.
  Ps 147: The hymn is divided into three sections by the calls to
praise in 1, 7, and 12. The first section praises the powerful
creator who restores exiled Judah (1-6); the second section, the
creator who provides food to animals and humans; the third and
climactic section exhorts the holy city to recognize it has been re-
created and made the place of disclosure for God's word, a word
as life-giving as water.
  147, 8-9: God clothes the fields and feeds the birds. Cf Mt 6,
26. 30.
  147, 10-11: Acknowledging one's dependence upon God
rather than claiming self-sufficiency pleases God. Cf Pss 20, 8;
33, 16-19.

II
⁵ Happy those whose help is Jacob's God,
  whose hope is in the LORD, their
  God,
⁶ The maker of heaven and earth,
  the seas and all that is in them,^{*i*}
Who keeps faith forever,
⁷ secures justice for the oppressed,^{*j*}
  gives food to the hungry.
The LORD sets prisoners free;^{*k*}
⁸ the LORD gives sight to the blind.
The LORD raises up those who are
  bowed down;^{*l*}
  the LORD loves the righteous.
⁹ The LORD protects the stranger,
  sustains the orphan and the widow,^{*m*}
  but thwarts the way of the wicked.
¹⁰ The LORD shall reign forever,
  your God, Zion, through all generations!^{*n*}
Hallelujah!

PSALM 147*

God's Word Restores Jerusalem

¹ Hallelujah!

I

How good to celebrate our God in song;
  how sweet to give fitting praise.^{*o*}
² The LORD rebuilds Jerusalem,
  gathers the dispersed of Israel,^{*p*}
³ Heals the brokenhearted,
  binds up their wounds,^{*q*}
⁴ Numbers all the stars,
  calls each of them by name.^{*r*}
⁵ Great is our Lord, vast in power,
  with wisdom beyond measure.^{*s*}
⁶ The LORD sustains the poor,
  but casts the wicked to the ground.^{*t*}

II

⁷ Sing to the LORD with thanksgiving;
  with the lyre celebrate our God,^{*u*}
⁸ Who covers the heavens with clouds,*
  provides rain for the earth,
  makes grass sprout on the mountains,^{*v*}
⁹ Who gives animals their food
  and ravens what they cry for.^{*w*}
¹⁰ God takes no delight in the strength of
  horses,*
  no pleasure in the runner's stride.^{*x*}
¹¹ Rather the LORD takes pleasure in the
  devout,
  those who await his faithful care.

Ps

III

¹² Glorify the LORD, Jerusalem;
   Zion, offer praise to your God,
¹³ Who has strengthened the bars of your
   gates,
   blessed your children within you,*y*
¹⁴ Brought peace to your borders,
   and filled you with finest wheat. *z*
¹⁵ The LORD sends a command to earth;*
   his word runs swiftly!*a*
¹⁶ Thus snow is spread like wool,
   frost is scattered like ash,*b*
¹⁷ Hail is dispersed like crumbs;
   before such cold the waters freeze.
¹⁸ Again he sends his word and they melt;
   the wind is unleashed and the waters
   flow.
¹⁹ The LORD also proclaims his word to
   Jacob,
   decrees and laws to Israel. *c*
²⁰ God has not done this for other nations;
   of such laws they know nothing.
   Hallelujah!

PSALM 148*

All Creation Summoned To Praise

¹ Hallelujah!
I
Praise the LORD from the heavens;
   give praise in the heights.
² Praise him, all you angels;
   give praise, all you hosts. *d*
³ Praise him, sun and moon;
   give praise, all shining stars.
⁴ Praise him, highest heavens,*
   you waters above the heavens.
⁵ Let them all praise the LORD's name;
   for the LORD commanded and they
   were created,*e*
⁶ Assigned them duties forever,
   gave them tasks that will never
   change.
II
⁷ Praise the LORD from the earth,
   you sea monsters and all deep waters;*f*
⁸ You lightning and hail, snow and clouds,
   storm winds that fulfill his command;
⁹ You mountains and all hills,
   fruit trees and all cedars;*g*
¹⁰ You animals wild and tame,
   you creatures that crawl and fly;*h*
¹¹ You kings of the earth and all peoples,
   princes and all who govern on earth;
¹² Young men and women too,
   old and young alike.

¹³ Let them all praise the LORD's name,
   for his name alone is exalted,
   majestic above earth and heaven.*i*
¹⁴ The LORD has lifted high the horn of
   his people;*
   to the glory of all the faithful,
   of Israel, the people near to their God.
   Hallelujah!

PSALM 149*

Praise God with Song and Sword

¹ Hallelujah!

Sing to the LORD a new song,
   a hymn in the assembly of the faithful.*j*
² Let Israel be glad in their maker,
   the people of Zion rejoice in their
   king.
³ Let them praise his name in festive
   dance,
   make music with tambourine and
   lyre.**k*
⁴ For the LORD takes delight in his people,
   honors the poor with victory.
⁵ Let the faithful rejoice in their glory,
   cry out for joy at their banquet,*
⁶ With the praise of God in their mouths,
   and a two-edged sword in their hands,*l*
⁷ To bring retribution on the nations,
   punishment on the peoples,*m*

---

y Ps 48, 14.—z Ps 81, 17.—a Ps 33, 9.—b Jb 6, 16; 37, 10;
38, 22.—c Ps 78, 5; Bar 3, 37; Dt 4, 7-8.—d Dn 3, 58-63; Ps
103, 20f.—e Ps 33, 9; Gn 1, 3f; Jdt 16, 14.—f Gn 1, 21; Ps 135,
6.—g Is 44, 23.—h Gn 1, 21. 24f; Ps 30, 5; Dt 4, 7.—i Ps 30,
5; Dt 4, 7.—j Pss 22, 23; 26, 12; 35, 18; 40, 10; Jdt 16, 1.—k
Pss 68, 26; 81, 2-3; 87, 7; 150, 3-4.—l Neh 4, 10-12; 2 Mc 15,
27.—m Wis 3, 8.

147, 15-19: God speaks through the thunder of nature and the
word of revealed law. Cf Is 55, 10-11. The weather phenomena
are well known in Jerusalem: a blizzard of snow and hail followed
by a thunderstorm that melts the ice.

Ps 148: A hymn inviting the beings of heaven (1-6) and of
earth (7-14) to praise God. The hymn does not distinguish between
inanimate and animate (and rational) nature.

148, 4: *Highest heavens:* literally, "the heavens of the heavens," i.e., the space above the firmament, where the "upper waters" are stored. Cf Gn 1, 6-7; Dt 10, 14; 1 Kgs 8, 27; Ps 104, 3. 13.

148, 14: *The LORD has lifted high the horn of his people:*
horn = strength, the concrete noun for the abstract. Of all peoples
God has chosen Israel to return praise and thanks in a special way.

Ps 149: A hymn inviting the people of Israel to celebrate their
God in song and festive dance (1-3. 5) because God has chosen
them and given them victory (4). The exodus and conquest are
the defining acts of Israel; the people must be ready to do again
those acts in the future at the divine command (6-9).

149, 3: *Make music with tambourine and lyre:* the verse
recalls the great exodus hymn of Ex 15, 20.

149, 5: *At their banquet:* literally, "upon their couches." The
people reclined to banquet.

8 To bind their kings with chains,
   shackle their nobles with irons,
9 To execute the judgments decreed for
   them—
   such is the glory* of all God's faithful.
   Hallelujah!

n Dn 3, 53.—o Dt 3, 24.—p 3ff: Pss 81, 3-4; 149, 3; 2 Sm 6,
5; 1 Chr 13, 8; 16, 5. 42; 2 Chr 5, 12-13; 7, 6.—q Ps 68, 26;
Ex 15, 20.—r Rv 5, 13.

149, 9: *The glory:* what brings honor to the people is their
readiness to carry out the divine will, here conceived as punishing
injustice done by the nations.
Ps 150: The psalm is a closing doxology both for the fifth book
of the Psalms (107—149) and for the Psalter as a whole. Temple
musicians and dancers are called to lead all beings on earth and
in heaven in praise of God. The psalm proclaims to whom praise
shall be given, and where (1); what praise shall be given, and why
(2); how praise shall be given (3-5), and by whom (6).
150, 1: *His holy sanctuary:* God's temple on earth. *The
mighty dome of heaven:* literally, "[God's] strong vault";
heaven is here imagined as a giant plate separating the inhabited
world from the waters of the heavens.

PSALM 150*

Final Doxology

1 Hallelujah!

Praise God in his holy sanctuary;*[n]
   give praise in the mighty dome of
   heaven.
2 Give praise for his mighty deeds,[o]
   praise him for his great majesty.
3 Give praise with blasts upon the horn,[p]
   praise him with harp and lyre.
4 Give praise with tambourines and dance,
   praise him with flutes and strings.[q]
5 Give praise with crashing cymbals,
   praise him with sounding cymbals.
6 Let everything that has breath
   give praise to the LORD![r]
Hallelujah!

THE BOOK OF PROVERBS

The first word of this book, MISHLE, *has provided the title by which it is generally designated in Jewish and Christian circles. The name "Proverbs," while not an exact equivalent of* MISHLE, *describes the main contents satisfactorily, even though it is hardly an adequate designation for such parts as 1, 1—9, 18 or 31, 10-31. Among some early Christian writers the book was also known by the name of "Wisdom," and in the Roman Missal it was for many centuries referred to as a "Book of Wisdom."*

The Book of Proverbs is an anthology of didactic poetry forming part of the sapiential literature of the Old Testament. Its primary purpose, indicated in the first sentence (1, 2f), is to teach wisdom. It is thus directed particularly to the young and inexperienced (1, 4); but also to those who desire advanced training in wisdom (1, 5f). The wisdom which the book teaches covers a wide field of human and divine activity, ranging from matters purely secular to most lofty moral and religious truths, such as God's omniscience (5, 21; 15, 3-11), power (19, 21; 21, 30), providence (20, 1-24), goodness (15, 29), and the joy and strength resulting from abandonment to him (3, 5; 16, 20; 18, 10). The teaching of the entire book is placed on a firm religious foundation by the principle that "the fear of the Lord is the beginning of knowledge" (1, 7; cf 9, 10).

Prv

To Solomon are explicitly ascribed parts II and V of the book; he is the patron of Hebrew wisdom. Of Agur (part VI) and Lemuel (part VIII), nothing further is known. Parts III and IV are attributed to "the wise." The remaining parts are anonymous.

The manner of compilation is conjectural. Parts II and V. may have circulated first as independent collections, compiled before the fall of Jerusalem, as the references to Solomon (10, 1) and Hezekiah (25, 1) suggest. Parts III, IV and VII would seem to belong together as a third collection of a similar kind. The author of the first nine chapters, a religious sage familiar with the earlier sacred books, was the editor of the whole as we have it, probably in the early part of the fifth century B.C.

Christ and the Apostles often expressly quoted the Proverbs (Jn 7, 38; Rom 12, 20; Jas 4, 6) or repeated their teaching; compare Lk 10, 14, and Prv 25, 7; 1 Pt 4, 8; Jas 5, 20 and Prv 10, 12. The book has an important place in the Latin and Greek liturgies.

On the basis of titles, subject matter, and poetic structure the Book of Proverbs may be divided as follows: I. Introduction: The Value of Wisdom (1, 1—9, 18). II. First Collection of the Proverbs of Solomon (10, 1—22, 16). III. Sayings of the Wise (22, 17—24, 22). IV. Other Sayings of the Wise (24, 23-34). V. Second Collection of the Proverbs of Solomon (25, 1—29, 27). VI. The Words of Agur (30, 1-6). VII. Numerical Proverbs (30, 7-33). VIII. The Words of Lemuel (31, 1-9). IX. The Ideal Wife (31, 10-31).

I: INTRODUCTION: THE VALUE OF WISDOM

CHAPTER 1*

Purpose of the Proverbs of Solomon*

1 The proverbs of Solomon,[a] the son of David,
   king of Israel:
2 That men may appreciate wisdom and discipline,*
   may understand words of intelligence;
3 May receive training in wise conduct,
   in what is right, just and honest;
4 That resourcefulness may be imparted to the simple,*
   to the young man knowledge and discretion.
5 A wise man by hearing them will advance in learning,
   an intelligent man will gain sound guidance,
6 That he may comprehend proverb and parable,
   the words of the wise and their riddles.

7 The fear of the LORD* is the beginning of knowledge;[b]
   wisdom and instruction fools despise.

The Path of the Wicked:
Greed and Violence*

8 Hear, my son, your father's instruction,
   and reject not your mother's teaching;
9 A graceful diadem will they be for your head;
   a torque for your neck.
10 My son, should sinners entice you,
   11 and say,
   "Come along with us!
   Let us lie in wait for the honest man,
   let us, unprovoked, set a trap for the innocent;
12 Let us swallow them up, as the nether world does, alive,
   in the prime of life, like those who go down to the pit!
13 All kinds of precious wealth shall we gain,
   we shall fill our houses with booty;
14 Cast in your lot with us,
   we shall all have one purse!"—

15 My son, walk not in the way with them,
   hold back your foot from their path!
16 [For their feet run to evil,
   they hasten to shed blood.[c]]
17 It is in vain that a net is spread*
   before the eyes of any bird—
18 These men lie in wait for their own blood,
   they set a trap for their own lives.
19 This is the fate of everyone greedy of loot:
   unlawful gain takes away the life of him who acquires it.

Wisdom in Person Gives Warning*

20 Wisdom cries aloud in the street,
   in the open squares she raises her voice;[d]
21 Down the crowded ways she calls out,
   at the city gates she utters her words:
22 "How long, you simple ones, will you love inanity,
23 how long will you turn away at my reproof?
   Lo! I will pour out to you my spirit,
   I will acquaint you with my words.

24 "Because I called and you refused,
   I extended my hand and no one took notice;[e]
25 Because you disdained all my counsel,
   and my reproof you ignored—
26 I, in turn, will laugh at your doom;
   I will mock when terror overtakes you;

a Prv 10, 1; 25, 1; 1 Kgs 4, 32.—b Prv 9, 10; Jb 28, 28; Ps 111, 10; Sir 1, 16.—c Is 59, 7.—d Prv 8, 1-3; 9, 3.—e Is 65, 2. 12; 66, 4; Jer 7, 13.

1, 1-6: This prologue explains the purpose of the book: to educate the inexperienced in knowledge and right conduct, and to increase the learning of the wise man by proverbs, parables and riddles.

1, 2: *Discipline:* education or formation which dispels ignorance and corrects vice.

1, 4: *Simple:* immature and inexperienced, hence easily influenced for good or evil.

1, 7: *Fear of the Lord:* reverential fear and respect for God on account of his sovereignty, goodness and justice toward men. This is the foundation of religion.

1, 8-19: A warning against association with the greedy and the violent who seek to destroy the honest man and to steal his possessions (11-14). The trap which the wicked set for the innocent (11), in the end (19) takes away the life of the wicked themselves.

1, 17: Instructed by the wise man, the youth (of v 4) will recognize the invitation of the wicked (11-14) as a *net* spread before him, and he will thus, like the *bird,* be protected against falling into it.

1, 20-23: Wisdom is here personified: with divine authority she sets forth and proclaims the moral order, instructing and threatening (24-33) the multitudes in the streets and places of assembly.

²⁷ When terror comes upon you like a
storm,
    and your doom approaches like a
whirlwind;
    when distress and anguish befall you.
²⁸ "Then they call me, but I answer not;
    they seek me, but find me not;*
²⁹ Because they hated knowledge,
    and chose not the fear of the LORD;
³⁰ They ignored my counsel,
    they spurned all my reproof;
    And in their arrogance they preferred
arrogance,
    and like fools they hated knowledge:
³¹ "Now they must eat the fruit of their
own way,
    and with their own devices be glut-
ted.*
³² For the self-will of the simple kills
them,
    the smugness of fools destroys them.
³³ But he who obeys me dwells in security,
    in peace, without fear of harm."^f

CHAPTER 2*
The Blessings of Wisdom*

¹ My son, if you receive my words
    and treasure my commands,
² Turning your ear to wisdom,*
    inclining your heart to understand-
ing;
³ Yes, if you call to intelligence,
    and to understanding raise your
voice;
⁴ If you seek her like silver,

---

f Prv 8, 33f.—g Jb 32, 8; Wis 7, 25; Sir 1, 1; Jas 1, 5.—h Prv
5, 3. 20; 6, 24; 7, 5; 22, 14.—i Prv 5, 5f; 7, 27.—j 21f: Prv 10,
7. 30; Jb 18, 17; Pss 21, 9-13; 37, 22. 28.

1, 28: Overtaken by doom, the foolish seek wisdom, but in vain
because they do so too late. Cf Jn 7, 34; 8, 21.
1, 31: Sinners are punished by the bad fruits which their sins
produce. Cf Wis 11, 16.
2—7: These chapters form an ordered discourse in seven "columns" of twenty-two verses each. Chapter 2 introduces the four
topics about which the sage instructs his pupil: the service of God
(3, 1-12. 25-34), the search for wisdom (3, 13-24. 35; 4, 1-9),
the avoidance of evil companions among men (4, 10-27; 5, 21-
23), and among women (5, 1-20; 6, 20—7, 27). The last topic is
treated at a length equal to the first three because the discourse
is meant especially for youths (cf Prv 1, 4).
2, 1-22: The search for wisdom (1-4) leads to the protection
of God (5-8) and of wisdom herself (9ff; cf Prv 1, 20-33) and to
deliverance from evil men (12-15) and evil women (16-19), and
so to lasting happiness (20ff).
2, 2f: *Wisdom, understanding, intelligence:* various names
or aspects of the same gift.
3, 1-12: Many are the rewards for fidelity and trust in God,
and for diffidence of self (1-8). Cf Dt 30, 20; Is 38, 19. The offering of material things for divine worship is blessed by an increase of such goods (9f). Even correction and chastisement are
a mark of God's love and favor (11f).

---

    and like hidden treasures search her
out:
⁵ Then will you understand the fear of
the LORD;
    the knowledge of God you will find;
⁶ For the LORD gives wisdom,
    from his mouth come knowledge and
understanding;^g
⁷ He has counsel in store for the upright,
    he is the shield of those who walk
honestly,
⁸ Guarding the paths of justice,
    protecting the way of his pious ones.
⁹ Then you will understand rectitude and
justice,
    honesty, every good path;
¹⁰ For wisdom will enter your heart,
    knowledge will please your soul,
¹¹ Discretion will watch over you,
    understanding will guard you;
¹² Saving you from the way of evil men,
    from men of perverse speech,
¹³ Who leave the straight paths
    to walk in ways of darkness,
¹⁴ Who delight in doing evil,
    rejoice in perversity;
¹⁵ Whose ways are crooked,
    and devious their paths;
¹⁶ Saving you from the wife of another,
    from the adulteress with her smooth
words,^h
¹⁷ Who forsakes the companion of her
youth
    and forgets the pact with her God;
¹⁸ For her path sinks down to death,
    and her footsteps lead to the shades;ⁱ
¹⁹ None who enter thereon come back
again,
    or gain the paths of life.
²⁰ Thus you may walk in the way of good
men,
    and keep to the paths of the just.
²¹ For the upright will dwell in the land,^j
    the honest will remain in it;
²² But the wicked will be cut off from the
land,
    the faithless will be rooted out of it.

CHAPTER 3*
Attitude toward the Lord*

¹ My son, forget not my teaching,
    keep in mind my commands;

Prv

2 For many days, and years of life,[k]
  and peace, will they bring you.

3 Let not kindness and fidelity leave you;
  bind them around your neck;
4 Then will you win favor and good esteem
  before God and man.

5 Trust in the LORD with all your heart,
  on your own intelligence rely not;
6 In all your ways be mindful of him,
  and he will make straight your paths.

7 Be not wise in your own eyes,[l]
  fear the LORD and turn away from evil;
8 This will mean health for your flesh
  and vigor for your bones.

9 Honor the LORD with your wealth,
  with first fruits of all your produce;[m]
10 Then will your barns be filled with grain,
  with new wine your vats will overflow.

11 The discipline of the LORD, my son,
  disdain not;[n]
  spurn not his reproof;
12 For whom the LORD loves he reproves,
  and he chastises the son he favors.[o]

The Value of Wisdom*

13 Happy the man who finds wisdom,
  the man who gains understanding![p]
14 For her profit is better than profit in silver,
  and better than gold is her revenue;
15 She is more precious than corals,*
  and none of your choice possessions
  can compare with her.[q]

16 Long life is in her right hand,
  in her left are riches and honor;
17 Her ways are pleasant ways,
  and all her paths are peace;
18 She is a tree of life* to those who grasp her,[r]
  and he is happy who holds her fast.

19 The LORD by wisdom founded the earth,
  established the heavens by understanding;
20 By his knowledge the depths break open,
  and the clouds drop down dew.*
21 My son, let not these slip out of your sight;

keep advice and counsel in view;
22 So will they be life to your soul,
  and an adornment for your neck.
23 Then you may securely go your way;
  your foot will never stumble;
24 When you lie down, you need not be afraid,
  when you rest, your sleep will be sweet.
35 Honor is the possession of wise men,
  but fools inherit shame.

Attitude toward Fellow Men*

25 Be not afraid of sudden terror,
  of the ruin of the wicked* when it comes;
26 For the LORD will be your confidence,
  and will keep your foot from the snare.
27 Refuse no one the good on which he has a claim
  when it is in your power to do it for him.
28 Say not to your neighbor, "Go, and come again,
  tomorrow I will give," when you can give at once.
29 Plot no evil against your neighbor,
  against him who lives at peace with you.
30 Quarrel not with a man without cause,
  with one who has done you no harm.
31 Envy not the lawless man
  and choose none of his ways:[s]
32 To the LORD the perverse man is an abomination,
  but with the upright is his friendship.

---

k Prv 4, 10; 9, 11; 10, 27.—l Rom 11, 25; 12, 16.—m Ex 34, 26; Lv 27, 30; Dt 26, 2; Sir 7, 31; 35, 7.—n Heb 12, 5f.—o Jdt 8, 27; Rv 3, 19.—p Prv 8, 34f.—q Prv 8, 11. 19; Wis 7, 8-11.—r Prv 4, 13; 8, 35; 11, 30; Gn 2, 9; 3, 22.—s Prv 23, 17; 24, 1. 19; Ps 37, 1.

3, 13-24: Wisdom, or understanding, is more valuable than silver and gold. Its fruit is long life, riches, honor and happiness (13-18). Even the creation of the universe and its adornment (Gn 1) were not done without wisdom (19f). It is the life of the soul and gives security in work and in repose (21-24).

3, 15: *Corals:* some precious stone may be intended.

3, 18: *A tree of life:* cf Prv 11, 30; 13, 12; Gn 2, 9.

3, 20: For the Hebrews, *the depths* enclosed the great subterranean ocean; the rain and dew descended from the celestial ocean above the firmament; cf Gn 1, 6-10; Jb 26, 8. 12; Pss 18, 16; 24, 2.

3, 25-34: Serving God with confidence in him (25f) requires serving one's neighbor through kindness (27f), peace with the good (29ff), no envy of the wicked (31), because the Lord's friendship and kindness are with the just; his curse is with the wicked.

3, 25: *The ruin of the wicked:* i.e., the ruin that comes upon the wicked.

33 The curse of the LORD is on the house
 of the wicked,
  but the dwelling of the just.he blesses;
34 When he is dealing with the arrogant,
 he is stern,[t]
  but to the humble he shows kindness.

CHAPTER 4

Wisdom: the Supreme Guide of Men*

1 Hear, O children, a father's instruction,
  be attentive, that you may gain
  understanding!
2 Yes, excellent advice I give you;
  my teaching do not forsake.
3 When I was my father's child,
  frail, yet the darling of my mother,
4 He taught me, and said to me:
  "Let your heart hold fast my words:[u]
  keep my commands, that you may
  live!
5 "Get wisdom, get understanding!
  Do not forget or turn aside from the
  words I utter.
6 Forsake her not, and she will preserve
  you;
  love her, and she will safeguard you;
7 The beginning of wisdom is: get wisdom;
  at the cost of all you have, get understanding.
8 Extol her, and she will exalt you;
  she will bring you honors if you embrace her;
9 She will put on your head a graceful
  diadem;
  a glorious crown will she bestow on
  you."

---

t Prv 1, 26.—u 1 Kgs 2, 2ff.—v Prv 3, 2.—w Prv 8, 35.

4, 1-9: The sage speaks as a father admonishing his children to
secure wisdom at any cost.
4, 10-27: The way of wisdom leads directly to life (10-13); it
is a light that grows brighter (18). The wise man is bound to shun
(14-17) the dark and violent path of the wicked (19). Singleness
of purpose and right conduct proceed from the heart of a wise
man as from the source of life (23-26); they save him from destruction on evil paths (4, 27; 5, 21ff).
4, 18: *Till perfect day:* literally, "till the day is established";
this may refer to full daylight or to noonday.
5, 1-20: Understanding and discretion guard a man against the
wiles of an adulteress, which lead astray and beget bitterness,
bloodshed and death (1-6). They destroy honor, waste the years
of life, despoil hard-earned wealth, consume the flesh, and bring
remorse in the end (7-14). Conjugal fidelity and love for one wife
only bring happiness and security (15-20). Cf Prv 6, 20—7, 27.

The Good and the Evil Way*

10 Hear, my son, and receive my words,
  and the years of your life shall be
  many.[v]
11 On the way of wisdom I direct you,
  I lead you on straightforward paths.
12 When you walk, your step will not be
  impeded,
  and should you run, you will not
  stumble.
13 Hold fast to instruction, never let her
  go;
  keep her, for she is your life.
14 The path of the wicked enter not,
  walk not on the way of evil men;
15 Shun it, cross it not,
  turn aside from it, and pass on.
16 For they cannot rest unless they have
  done evil;
  to have made no one stumble steals
  away their sleep.
17 For they eat the bread of wickedness
  and drink the wine of violence.
19 The way of the wicked is like darkness;
  they know not on what they stumble.
18 But the path of the just is like shining
  light,
  that grows in brilliance till perfect
  day.*

20 My son, to my words be attentive,
  to my sayings incline your ear;
21 Let them not slip out of your sight,
  keep them within your heart;
22 For they are life to those who find
  them,[w]
  to man's whole being they are health.

23 With closest custody, guard your heart,
  for in it are the sources of life.
24 Put away from you dishonest talk,
  deceitful speech put far from you.
25 Let your eyes look straight ahead
  and your glance be directly forward.
26 Survey the path for your feet,
  and let all your ways be sure.
27 Turn neither to right nor to left,
  keep your foot far from evil.

CHAPTER 5

Warning against Adultery*

1 My son, to my wisdom be attentive,
  to my knowledge incline your ear,

2 That discretion may watch over you,
and understanding may guard you.
3 The lips of an adulteress drip with honey,
and her mouth is smoother than oil;[x]
4 But in the end she is as bitter as wormwood,
as sharp as a two-edged sword.
5 Her feet go down to death,
to the nether world her steps attain;[y]
6 Lest you see before you the road to life,
her paths will ramble, you know not where.

7 So now, O children, listen to me,
go not astray from the words of my mouth.
8 Keep your way far from her,[z]
approach not the door of her house,
9 Lest you give your honor* to others,[a]
and your years to a merciless one;
10 Lest strangers have their fill of your wealth,
your hard-won earnings go to an alien's house;
11 And you groan in the end,
when your flesh and your body are consumed;
12 And you say, "Oh, why did I hate instruction,
and my heart spurn reproof!
13 Why did I not listen to the voice of my teachers,
nor to my instructors incline my ear!
14 I have all but come to utter ruin,
condemned by the public assembly!"

15 Drink water from your own cistern,
running water from your own well.
16 How may your water sources be dispersed abroad,
streams of water in the streets?
17 Let your fountain be yours alone,
not one shared with strangers;
18 And have joy of the wife of your youth,
19 your lovely hind, your graceful doe.*
Her love will invigorate you always,
through her love you will flourish continually,
22 When you lie down she will watch over you,
and when you wake, she will share your concerns;

wherever you turn, she will guide you.*
20 Why then, my son, should you go astray for another's wife
and accept the embraces of an adulteress?
21 For each man's ways are plain to the LORD's sight;*
all their paths he surveys;[b]
22 By his own iniquities the wicked man will be caught,
in the meshes of his own sin he will be held fast;
23 He will die from lack of discipline,
through the greatness of his folly he will be lost.

CHAPTER 6

Miscellaneous Proverbs*

1 My son, if you have become surety to your neighbor,[c]
given your hand in pledge* to another,
2 You have been snared by the utterance of your lips,
caught by the words of your mouth;
3 So do this, my son, to free yourself,
since you have fallen into your neighbor's power:
Go, hurry, stir up your neighbor!
4 Give no sleep to your eyes,
nor slumber to your eyelids;
5 Free yourself as a gazelle from the snare,
or as a bird from the hand of the fowler.

6 Go to the ant,[d] O sluggard,
study her ways and learn wisdom;
7 For though she has no chief,
no commander or ruler,

---

x Prv 7, 5.—y Prv 2, 18; 7, 27.—z Prv 7, 25.—a 9f: Sir 9, 6.—
b Jb 14, 16; 31, 4; 34, 21.—c 1f: Prv 11, 15; 22, 26; Sir 8, 13;
29, 19.—d Prv 30, 25.

5, 9: *Honor:* the words "life" and "wealth" have also been read in this place. *A merciless one:* the offended husband; cf Prv 6, 34f.

5, 19: *Lovely hind . . . graceful doe:* oriental symbols of feminine beauty and charm; cf Song 2, 7. 9. 17.

5, 22: This is transposed from chapter 6, 22.

5, 21-23: These verses are best read after Prv 4, 27.

6, 1-19: These verses interrupt the discourse of chapters 2—7, which should be read apart from them; they contain four shorter proverbs akin to those in chapter 30.

6, 1: *Given your hand in pledge:* literally, "struck your hands"; this was probably the legal method for closing a contract.

8 She procures her food in the summer,
   stores up her provisions in the harvest.   .
9 How long, O sluggard, will you rest?
   when will you rise from your sleep?
10 A little sleep, a little slumber,
   a little folding of the arms to rest—*
11 Then will poverty come upon you like a
   highwayman,
   and want like an armed man.

12 A scoundrel, a villain, is he
   who deals in crooked talk.
13 He winks his eyes,
   shuffles his feet,
   makes signs with his fingers;
14 He has perversity in his heart,
   is always plotting evil,
   sows discord.
15 Therefore suddenly ruin comes upon
   him;
   in an instant he is crushed beyond
   cure.

16 There are six things the LORD hates,
   yes, seven are an abomination to
   him;*
17 Haughty eyes, a lying tongue,
   and hands that shed innocent blood;
18 A heart that plots wicked schemes,
   feet that run swiftly to evil,
19 The false witness who utters lies,
   and he who sows discord among
   brothers.

Warning against Adultery*

20 Observe, my son, your father's bidding,
   and reject not your mother's teaching;
21 Keep them fastened over your heart always,
   put them around your neck;
23 For the bidding is a lamp, and the
   teaching a light,

and a way to life are the reproofs of
   discipline;
24 To keep you from your neighbor's wife,
   from the smooth tongue of the adulteress. *e*

25 Lust not in your heart after her beauty,
   let her not captivate you with her
   glance!*f*
26 For the price of a loose woman
   may be scarcely a loaf of bread,
   But if she is married,
   she is a trap for your precious life.*
27 Can a man take fire to his bosom,
   and his garments not be burned?
28 Or can a man walk on live coals,
   and his feet not be scorched?
29 So with him who goes in to his neighbor's wife—
   none who touches her shall go unpunished. *g*

30 Men despise not the thief if he steals
   to satisfy his appetite when he is hungry;
31 Yet if he be caught he must pay back
   sevenfold;
   all the wealth of his house he may
   yield up.
32 But he who commits adultery is a fool;
   he who would destroy himself does it.
33 A degrading beating will he get,
   and his disgrace will not be wiped
   away;
34 For vindictive is the husband's wrath, **Prv**
   he will have no pity on the day of
   vengeance;
35 He will not consider any restitution,
   nor be satisfied with the greatest
   gifts.

CHAPTER 7

1 My son, keep my words,
   and treasure my commands.
2 Keep my commands and live,
   my teaching as the apple of your eye;
3 Bind them on your fingers,
   write them on the tablet of your
   heart. *h*
4 Say to Wisdom, "You are my sister!"
   call Understanding, "Friend!"
5 That they may keep you from another's
   wife,

---

e Prv 2, 16; 7, 5.—f Ex 20, 17; Dt 5, 21; Sir 9, 8; 25, 20; Mt
5, 28.—g Sir 9, 9.—h Dt 6, 8.

6, 10: This verse may be regarded as the sluggard's reply or as
a continuation of the remonstrance.
6, 16-19: The seven vices symbolized for the most part by
bodily organs are pride, lying, murder, intrigue, readiness to do
evil, false witness, and the stirring up of discord.
6, 20—7, 27: Parental training and the love of wisdom are an
invaluable and constant help for the young (6, 20-23; 7, 1-4).
They are the best defense against adultery (6, 24; 7, 5. 24f),
which involves the guilty in many dangers and punishments (6,
26-35; 7, 6-27). Cf Prv 5, 1-20.
6, 26: Some interpret the verse in a progressive sense, i.e., to
satisfy the increasing demands of a courtesan a man is reduced to
poverty; if the woman is married, even his very life is endangered.

from the adulteress with her smooth
words.ⁱ

6 For at the window of my house,
through my lattice I looked out—

7 And I saw among the simple ones,
I observed among the young men,
a youth with no sense,

8 Going along the street near the corner,
then walking in the direction of her
house—

9 In the twilight, at dusk of day,
at the time of the dark of night.

10 And lo! the woman comes to meet him,
robed like a harlot, with secret designs—

11 She is fickle and unruly,
in her home her feet cannot rest;

12 Now she is in the streets, now in the
open squares,
and at every corner she lurks in ambush—

13 When she seizes him, she kisses him,
and with an impudent look says to
him:

14 "I owed peace offerings,
and today I have fulfilled my vows;*

15 So I came out to meet you,
to look for you, and I have found
you!

16 With coverlets I have spread my couch,
with brocaded cloths of Egyptian
linen;

17 I have sprinkled my bed with myrrh,
with aloes, and with cinnamon.

18 "Come, let us drink our fill of love,
until morning, let us feast on love!

19 For my husband is not at home,
he has gone on a long journey;

20 A bag of money he took with him,
not till the full moon will he return
home."

21 She wins him over by her repeated urging,
with her smooth lips she leads him astray;^j

22 He follows her stupidly,
like an ox that is led to slaughter;
Like a stag that minces toward the net,

23   till an arrow pierces its liver;
Like a bird that rushes into a snare,
unaware that its life is at stake.

24 So now, O children, listen to me,
be attentive to the words of my
mouth!

25 Let not your heart turn to her ways,
go not astray in her paths;

26 For many are those she has struck down
dead,
numerous, those she has slain.

27 Her house is made up of ways to the
nether world,
leading down into the chambers of
death.^k

CHAPTER 8

The Discourse of Wisdom*

1 Does not Wisdom call,
and Understanding raise her voice?^l

2 On the top of the heights along the
road,
at the crossroads she takes her stand;

3 By the gates at the approaches of the
city,
in the entryways she cries aloud:

4 "To you, O men, I call;
my appeal is to the children of men.

5 You simple ones, gain resource,
you fools,* gain sense.

6 "Give heed! for noble things I speak;
honesty opens my lips.

7 Yes, the truth my mouth recounts,*
but wickedness my lips abhor.

8 Sincere are all the words of my mouth,
no one of them is wily or crooked;

9 All of them are plain to the man of intelligence,
and right to those who attain knowledge.

10 Receive my instruction in preference to
silver,
and knowledge rather than choice
gold.

---

i Prv 2, 16; 6, 24.—j Prv 5, 3; 6, 24.—k Prv 2, 18f; 5, 5.—l
Prv 1, 20f; 9, 3.

7, 14: *"Peace offerings . . . vows":* a portion of the sacrifice
reverted to the donor and had to be eaten on the same day at a
family festival (Lv 7, 11-15). In this figure, the adulteress offers
to share with the foolish young man the deadly feast of her sensuality.

8, 1-36: Wisdom is here personified as in Prv 1, 20-33, to confirm the words of the teacher of wisdom. She exalts her grandeur
and origin, and invites all (1-11) to be attentive to her salutary influence in human society (12-21), for she was privileged to be
present at the creation of the world (22-31). Finally, she promises life and the favor of God to those who find her, death to those
who despise her.

8, 5: *Simple ones . . . fools:* see note on Prv 1, 4.

8, 7f: The truth and sincerity of wisdom are absolute because
they are divine. They can neither deceive nor tolerate deception.
An intelligent man understands and accepts them.

11 [For Wisdom is better than corals,
   and no choice possession can compare with her.*m*]

12 "I, Wisdom, dwell with experience,
   and judicious knowledge I attain,
13 [The fear of the LORD is to hate evil;]
   Pride, arrogance, the evil way,
   and the perverse mouth I hate.*n*
14 Mine are counsel and advice;
   mine is strength; I am understanding.*
15 By me kings reign,
   and lawgivers establish justice;
16 By me princes govern,
   and nobles; all the rulers of earth.

17 "Those who love me I also love,
   and those who seek me find me.
18 With me are riches and honor,*o*
   enduring wealth and prosperity.
19 My fruit is better than gold, yes, than
   pure gold,
   and my revenue than choice silver.*p*
20 On the way of duty I walk,
   along the paths of justice,
21 Granting wealth to those who love me,
   and filling their treasuries.

22 "The LORD begot me, the firstborn of
   his ways,*
   the forerunner of his prodigies of
   long ago;*q*

23 From of old I was poured forth,*
   at the first, before the earth.*r*
24 When there were no depths I was
   brought forth,*
   when there were no fountains or
   springs of water;
25 Before the mountains were settled into
   place,
   before the hills, I was brought forth;
26 While as yet the earth and the fields
   were not made,
   nor the first clods of the world.

27 "When he established the heavens I was
   there,*s*
   when he marked out the vault over
   the face of the deep;
28 When he made firm the skies above,
   when he fixed fast the foundations of
   the earth;
29 When he set for the sea its limit,
   so that the waters should not transgress his command;
30 Then was I beside him as his
   craftsman,*
   and I was his delight day by day,*t*
   Playing before him all the while,
31   playing on the surface of his earth;
   and I found delight in the sons of
   men.

32 "So now, O children, listen to me;
33   instruction and wisdom do not reject!
   Happy the man who obeys me,
   and happy those who keep my ways,
34 Happy the man watching daily at my
   gates,
   waiting at my doorposts;
35 For he who finds me finds life,*u*
   and wins favor from the LORD;
36 But he who misses me harms himself;
   all who hate me love death."

---

m Prv 3, 15; Wis 7, 8.—n Prv 6, 16f; 16, 5.—o Prv 3, 16.—p
Prv 3, 14.—q Wis 9, 9; Sir 1, 1; 24, 9.—r Sir 1, 4.—s Prv 3, 19;
Sir 24, 4f.—t Wis 9, 9.—u Prv 3, 13-18; 4, 22.—v Prv 8, 1f.

8, 14: What is here predicated of wisdom is elsewhere attributed to God (Jb 12, 13-16).

8, 22-31: Wisdom is of divine origin. It is here represented as
a being which existed before all things (22-26) and concurred
with God when he planned and executed the creation of the universe, adorned it with beauty and variety, and established its wonderful order (27-30). Here that plurality of divine Persons is
foreshadowed which was afterward to be fully revealed when
Wisdom in the Person of Jesus Christ became incarnate.

8, 23: *Poured forth:* the exact meaning of the Hebrew is uncertain; the expression must imply the equivalent of "born." The
Hebrews likened the movement of air and of spirit to that of liquids.

8, 24-26: The formless mass from which God created the
heavens and the earth; cf Gn 1, 1f; 2, 4ff.

8, 30: *His craftsman:* furnishing God with the plan, as it
were, for the creation of all things; cf Jb 38, 1f; Wis 7, 22—8,
1. *I was his delight:* the ever-present object of God's complacency.

9, 1-6. 13-18: Wisdom and folly are represented as matrons,
each inviting people to her banquet. Wisdom offers the food and
drink of divine doctrine and virtue which give life (1-6). Unstable
and senseless folly furnishes the stolen bread and water of deceit
and vice which bring death to her guests.

9, 3: *She calls:* i.e., indirectly, through her maidens; but the
text could also mean that wisdom herself publicly proclaims her
invitation.

CHAPTER 9

The Two Banquets*

1 Wisdom has built her house,
   she has set up her seven columns;
2 She has dressed her meat, mixed her
   wine,
   yes, she has spread her table.
3 She has sent out her maidens; she calls*
   from the heights out over the city:*v*
4 "Let whoever is simple turn in here;
   to him who lacks understanding, I
   say,

⁵ Come, eat of my food,
  and drink of the wine I have mixed!
⁶ Forsake foolishness that you may live;
  advance in the way of understanding.
¹¹ For by me your days will be multiplied
  and the years of your life increased."ʷ

⁷ He who corrects an arrogant man earns
  insult;
  and he who reproves a wicked man
  incurs opprobrium.
⁸ Reprove not an arrogant man, lest he
  hate you;
  reprove a wise man, and he will love
  you.ˣ
⁹ Instruct a wise man, and he becomes
  still wiser;
  teach a just man, and he advances in
  learning.

¹⁰ The beginning of wisdom is the fear of
  the LORD,
  and knowledge of the Holy One is
  understanding.ʸ

¹² If you are wise, it is to your own advantage;
  and if you are arrogant, you alone
  shall bear it.

¹³ The woman Folly is fickle,ᶻ
  she is inane, and knows nothing.
¹⁴ She sits at the door of her house
  upon a seat on the city heights,
¹⁵ Calling to passers-by
  as they go on their straight way:
¹⁶ "Let whoever is simple turn in here,
  or who lacks understanding; for to
  him I say,
¹⁷ Stolen water is sweet,
  and bread gotten secretly is pleasing!"*
¹⁸ Little he knows that the shades are
  there,
  that in the depths of the nether world
  are her guests!*

II: FIRST COLLECTION OF THE PROVERBS
OF SOLOMON*

CHAPTER 10

¹ The Proverbs of Solomon:

A wise son makes his father glad,
  but a foolish son is a grief to his
  mother.ᵃ

² Ill-gotten treasures profit nothing,
  but virtue saves from death.ᵇ

³ The LORD permits not the just to
  hunger,
  but the craving of the wicked he
  thwarts.

⁴ The slack hand impoverishes,
  but the hand of the diligent enriches.ᶜ

⁵ A son who fills the granaries in summer
  is a credit;
  a son who slumbers during harvest, a
  disgrace.

⁶ Blessings are for the head of the just,
  but a rod for the back of the fool.

⁷ The memory of the just will be blessed,
  but the name of the wicked will rot.

⁸ A wise man heeds commands,
  but a prating fool will be overthrown.

⁹ He who walks honestly walks securely,
  but he whose ways are crooked will
  fare badly.

¹⁰ He who winks at a fault causes trouble,
  but he who frankly reproves promotes peace.

¹¹ A fountain of life is the mouth of the
  just,
  but the mouth of the wicked conceals
  violence.

¹² Hatred stirs up disputes,
  ᵈbut love covers all offenses.*

¹³ On the lips of the intelligent is found
  wisdom,
  [but the mouth of the wicked conceals violence].

¹⁴ Wise men store up knowledge,
  but the mouth of a fool is imminent
  ruin.

---

w Prv 3, 2. 16; 4, 10; 10, 27.—x Sir 10, 27.—y Prv 1, 7; Jb
28, 28; Ps 111, 10; Sir 1, 16.— z 13-18: Prv 7, 7-27.—a Prv 1,
1; 15, 20; 17, 25; 19, 13; 25, 1; 29, 15.—b Prv 11, 4. 6.—c Prv
6, 11; 12, 24; 13, 4; 20, 13; 28, 19.—d 1 Cor 13, 4-7; 1 Pt 4, 8.

9, 17: The secrecy implies wrongdoing.
9, 18: The banquet chamber of folly is a tomb from which no
one who enters it is released.
10, 1—22, 16: The varied contents of this first collection of
Solomon's proverbs apply mostly to individual life. Each of its
three hundred and seventy-five proverbs is meant to be distinct
from the others, developing one idea through contrasting parallelism in chapters 10—15, and a climactic treatment in 16—22.
10, 12: *Love covers all offenses:* a favorite maxim of the
Apostles; cf 1 Cor 13, 7; Jas 5, 20; 1 Pt 4, 8; also Prv 17, 9.

15 The rich man's wealth is his strong city;
the ruination of the lowly is their poverty.*

16 The just man's recompense leads to life,
the gains of the wicked, to sin.*e*

17 A path to life is his who heeds admonition,
but he who disregards reproof goes astray.*f*

18 It is the lips of the liar that conceal hostility;
but he who spreads accusations is a fool.

19 Where words are many, sin is not wanting;
but he who restrains his lips does well.*g*

20 Like choice silver is the just man's tongue;
the heart of the wicked is of little worth.

21 The just man's lips nourish many,
but fools die for want of sense.

22 It is the LORD's blessing that brings wealth,*h*
and no effort can substitute for it.*

23 Crime is the entertainment of the fool;
so is wisdom for the man of sense.

24 What the wicked man fears will befall him,
but the desire of the just will be granted.

25 When the tempest passes, the wicked man is no more;
but the just man is established forever.

26 As vinegar to the teeth, and smoke to the eyes,
is the sluggard to those who use him as a messenger.

27 The fear of the LORD prolongs life,
but the years of the wicked are brief.*i*

28 The hope of the just brings them joy,
but the expectation of the wicked comes to nought.

29 The LORD is a stronghold to him who walks honestly,
but to evildoers, their downfall.

30 The just man will never be disturbed,
but the wicked will not abide in the land.

31 The mouth of the just yields wisdom,
but the perverse tongue will be cut off.

32 The lips of the just know how to please,
but the mouth of the wicked, how to pervert.

CHAPTER 11

1 False scales are an abomination to the LORD,
but a full weight is his delight.*j*

2 When pride comes, disgrace comes;
but with the humble is wisdom.

3 The honesty of the upright guides them;
the faithless are ruined by their duplicity.

4 Wealth is useless on the day of wrath,*k*
but virtue saves from death.*

5 The honest man's virtue makes his way straight,
but by his wickedness the wicked man falls.*l*

6 The virtue of the upright saves them,
but the faithless are caught in their own intrigue.

7 When a wicked man dies his hope perishes,*m*
and what is expected from strength comes to nought.

8 The just man escapes trouble,
and the wicked man falls into it in his stead.

9 With his mouth the impious man would ruin his neighbor,*n*
but through their knowledge the just make their escape.

---

e Prv 11, 18f.—f Prv 15, 10.—g Prv 17, 27; Sir 20, 17; Jas 1,
19.—h Sir 11, 22.—i Prv 3, 2; 4, 10; 9, 11; 14, 27.—j Prv 16,
11; 20, 10; Lv 19, 35f.—k Prv 10, 2.—l Prv 28, 18.—m Prv 10,
28; Wis 3, 18.—n Prv 29, 5.

10, 15: The inspired author reflects upon the reality of the power of money and the defeat of poverty, without approving these things.

10, 22: The blessing of God rather than our own industry crowns our efforts with success; cf Ps 127, 1f; Mt 6, 25-34.

11, 4: *Wealth . . . death:* not what a man is worth but what he is, counts before God.

Prv

10 When the just prosper, the city rejoices;*o*
   and when the wicked perish, there is jubilation.

11 Through the blessing of the righteous the city is exalted,
   but through the mouth of the wicked it is overthrown.

12 He who reviles his neighbor has no sense,
   but the intelligent man keeps silent.

13 A newsmonger reveals secrets,*p*
   but a trustworthy man keeps a confidence.

14 For lack of guidance a people falls;
   security lies in many counselors.*q*

15 He is in a bad way who becomes surety for another,*r*
   but he who hates giving pledges is safe.

16 A gracious woman wins esteem,
   but she who hates virtue is covered with shame.
   [The slothful become impoverished,
   but the diligent gain wealth.]

17 A kindly man benefits himself,
   but a merciless man harms himself.

18 The wicked man makes empty profits,
   but he who sows virtue has a sure reward.*s*

19 Virtue directs toward life,
   but he who pursues evil does so to his death.

20 The depraved in heart are an abomination to the LORD,
   but those who walk blamelessly are his delight.

21 Truly the evil man shall not go unpunished,
   but those who are just shall escape.

22 Like a golden ring in a swine's snout
   is a beautiful woman with a rebellious disposition.

23 The desire of the just ends only in good;
   the expectation of the wicked is wrath.

24 One man is lavish yet grows still richer;
   another is too sparing, yet is the poorer.

25 He who confers benefits will be amply enriched,
   and he who refreshes others will himself be refreshed.

26 Him who monopolizes grain, the people curse—
   but blessings upon the head of him who distributes it!

27 He who seeks the good commands favor,
   but he who pursues evil will have evil befall him.

28 He who trusts in his riches will fall,
   but like green leaves the just flourish.*t*

29 He who upsets his household has empty air for a heritage;
   and the fool will become slave to the wise man.

30 The fruit of virtue is a tree of life,
   but violence takes lives away.

31 If the just man is punished on earth,
   how much more the wicked and the sinner!*u*

CHAPTER 12

1 He who loves correction loves knowledge,
   but he who hates reproof is stupid.*v*

2 The good man wins favor from the LORD,
   but the schemer is condemned by him.

3 No man is built up by wickedness,
   but the root of the just will never be disturbed.

4 A worthy wife is the crown of her husband,*w*
   but a disgraceful one is like rot in his bones.

5 The plans of the just are legitimate;
   the designs of the wicked are deceitful.

6 The words of the wicked are a deadly ambush,
   but the speech of the upright saves them.

7 The wicked are overthrown and are no more,

o Prv 28, 12; 29, 2.—p Prv 20, 19.—q Prv 15, 22; 20, 18; 24, 6.—r Prv 6, 1f.—s Prv 1C, 16.—t Ps 52, 9f.—u 1 Pt 4, 18.—v Prv 15, 5. 10; 29, 1; Sir 19, 5; 21, 6.—w Sir 26, 1. 16.

but the house of the just stands firm.

8 According to his good sense a man is
praised,
but one with a warped mind is despised.

9 Better a lowly man who supports himself
than one of assumed importance who
lacks bread.*

10 The just man takes care of his beast,
but the heart of the wicked is merciless.

11 He who tills his own land has food in
plenty,
but he who follows idle pursuits is a
fool.*

12 The stronghold of evil men will be demolished,
but the root of the just is enduring.

13 In the sin of his lips the evil man is ensnared,
but the just comes free of trouble.

14 From the fruit of his words a man has
his fill of good things,*
and the work of his hands comes back
to reward him.*

15 The way of the fool seems right in his
own eyes,
but he who listens to advice is wise.

16 The fool immediately shows his anger,
but the shrewd man passes over an
insult.

17 He tells the truth who states what he is
sure of,
but a lying witness speaks deceitfully.*

18 The prating of some men is like sword
thrusts,
but the tongue of the wise is healing.

19 Truthful lips endure forever,
the lying tongue, for only a moment.

20 Deceit is in the hands of those who plot
evil,
but those who counsel peace have
joy.

21 No harm befalls the just,
but the wicked are overwhelmed with
misfortune.

22 Lying lips are an abomination to the
Lord,*
but those who are truthful are his delight.

23 A shrewd man conceals his knowledge,
but the hearts of fools gush forth
folly.

24 The diligent hand will govern,
but the slothful will be enslaved.*

25 Anxiety in a man's heart depresses it,
but a kindly word makes it glad.*

26 The just man surpasses his neighbor,
but the way of the wicked leads them
astray.

27 The slothful man catches not his prey,
but the wealth of the diligent man is
great.

28 In the path of justice there is life,
but the abominable way leads to
death.

CHAPTER 13

1 A wise son loves correction,
but the senseless one heeds no rebuke.

2 From the fruit of his words a man eats
good things,*
but the treacherous one craves violence.

3 He who guards his mouth protects his
life;
to open wide one's lips brings downfall.*

4 The soul of the sluggard craves in vain,
but the diligent soul is amply
satisfied.

5 Anything deceitful the just man hates,
but the wicked brings shame and disgrace.

6 Virtue guards one who walks honestly,
but the downfall of the wicked is
sin.*

7 One man pretends to be rich, yet has
nothing;
another pretends to be poor, yet has
great wealth.

8 A man's riches serve as ransom for his
life,
but the poor man heeds no rebuke.

---

x Sir 10, 26.—y Prv 28, 19; Sir 20, 27.—z Prv 13, 2; 18,
20.—a Prv 14, 5.—b Prv 6, 17.—c Prv 10, 4; 13, 4.—d Prv 15,
13; 17, 22.—e Prv 12, 14; 18, 20.—f Prv 18, 7; 21, 23.—g Prv
11, 3. 5f.

12, 14: Cf Mt 7, 17; Gal 6, 8.

9 The light of the just shines gaily,
but the lamp* of the wicked goes
out. *h*

10 The stupid man sows discord by his insolence,
but with those who take counsel is
wisdom.

11 Wealth quickly gotten dwindles away,
but amassed little by little, it grows. *i*

12 Hope deferred makes the heart sick,
but a wish fulfilled is a tree of life.

13 He who despises the word* must pay
for it,
but he who reveres the commandment will be rewarded.

14 The teaching of the wise is a fountain of
life,
that a man may avoid the snares of
death.

15 Good sense brings favor,
but the way of the faithless is their
ruin.

16 The shrewd man does everything with
prudence,
but the fool peddles folly.

17 A wicked messenger brings on disaster,
but a trustworthy envoy is a healing
remedy.

18 Poverty and shame befall the man who
disregards correction,
but he who heeds reproof is honored.

19 Lust indulged starves the soul,
but fools hate to turn from evil.

20 Walk with wise men and you will become wise,
but the companion of fools will fare
badly. *j*

21 Misfortune pursues sinners,
but the just shall be recompensed
with good.

22 The good man leaves an inheritance to
his children's children,
but the wealth of the sinner is stored
up for the just.

23 A lawsuit devours the tillage of the
poor,
but some men perish for lack of a law
court.

24 He who spares his rod hates his son,

but he who loves him takes care to
chastise him. *k*

25 When the just man eats, his hunger is
appeased;
but the belly of the wicked suffers
want.

CHAPTER 14

1 Wisdom builds her house,
but Folly tears hers down with her
own hands.

2 He who walks uprightly fears the
LORD,
but he who is devious in his ways
spurns him.

3 In the mouth of the fool is a rod for his
back,
but the lips of the wise preserve
them.

4 Where there are no oxen, the crib remains empty;
but large crops come through the
strength of the bull.

5 A truthful witness does not lie,
but a false witness utters lies. *l*

6 The senseless man seeks in vain for wisdom,
but knowledge is easy to the man of
intelligence.

7 To avoid the foolish man, take steps!
But knowing lips one meets with by
surprise.

8 The shrewd man's wisdom gives him
knowledge of his way,
but the folly of fools is their deception.

9 Guilt lodges in the tents of the arrogant,
but favor in the house of the just.

10 The heart knows its own bitterness,
and in its joy no one else shares.

11 The house of the wicked will be destroyed,
but the tent of the upright will
flourish. *m*

12 Sometimes a way seems right to a man,
but the end of it leads to death! *n*

---

h Prv 24, 20.—i Prv 28, 20. 22.—j Sir 6, 34; 8. 17.—k Prv
19, 18; 22, 15; 23, 13f; 29, 15; Sir 30, 1. 8-13.—l Prv 12, 17.—
m Prv 3, 33; 12, 7; 15, 25.—n Prv 16, 25.

13, 9: *Light . . . lamp:* symbols of life and prosperity; cf Prv
4, 18f.
13, 13: *Word:* advice, or God's law.

13 Even in laughter the heart may be sad,
and the end of joy may be sorrow.

14 The scoundrel suffers the consequences
of his ways,
and the good man reaps the fruit of
his paths.

15 The simpleton believes everything,
but the shrewd man measures his
steps.

16 The wise man is cautious and shuns
evil;
the fool is reckless and sure of himself.

17 The quick-tempered man makes a fool
of himself,
but the prudent man is at peace.

18 The adornment of simpletons is folly,
but shrewd men gain the crown of
knowledge.

19 Evil men must bow down before the
good,
and the wicked, at the gates of the
just.

20 Even by his neighbor the poor man is
hated,
but the friends of the rich are many.[o]

21 He sins who despises the hungry;
but happy is he who is kind to the
poor!

22 Do not those who plot evil go astray?
But those intent on good gain kindness and constancy.

23 In all labor there is profit,
but mere talk tends only to penury.

24 The crown of the wise is resourcefulness;
the diadem of fools is folly.

25 The truthful witness saves lives,
but he who utters lies is a betrayer.

26 In the fear of the LORD is a strong defense;
even for one's children he will be a
refuge.

27 The fear of the LORD is a fountain of
life,
that a man may avoid the snares of
death.

28 In many subjects lies the glory of the
king;
but if his people are few, it is the
prince's ruin.

29 The patient man shows much good
sense,
but the quick-tempered man displays
folly at its height.[p]

30 A tranquil mind gives life to the body,
but jealousy rots the bones.

31 He who oppresses the poor blasphemes
his Maker,
but he who is kind to the needy
glorifies him.[q]

32 The wicked man is overthrown by his
wickedness,
but the just man finds a refuge in his
honesty.

33 In the heart of the intelligent wisdom
abides,
but in the bosom of fools it is unknown.

34 Virtue exalts a nation,
but sin is a people's disgrace.

35 The king favors the intelligent servant,
but the worthless one incurs his
wrath.

CHAPTER 15

1 A mild answer calms wrath,[r]
but a harsh word stirs up anger.

2 The tongue of the wise pours out
knowledge,
but the mouth of fools spurts forth
folly.

3 The eyes of the LORD are in every
place,
keeping watch on the evil and the
good.

4 A soothing tongue is a tree of life,
but a perverse one crushes the spirit.

5 The fool spurns his father's admonition,
but prudent is he who heeds reproof.[s]

6 In the house of the just there are ample
resources,
but the earnings of the wicked are in
turmoil.

7 The lips of the wise disseminate knowledge,
but the heart of fools is perverted.

---

o Prv 19, 4. 7; Sir 6, 8, 12.—p Prv 16, 32; 19, 11; Jas 1, 19.—q Prv 17, 5.—r Prv 25, 15; Sir 6, 5.—s Prv 12, 1; 13, 18.

8 The sacrifice of the wicked is an abomination to the LORD,[t]
but the prayer of the upright is his delight.

9 The way of the wicked is an abomination to the LORD,
but he loves the man who pursues virtue.[u]

10 Severe punishment is in store for the man who goes astray;
he who hates reproof will die.

11 The nether world and the abyss* lie open before the LORD;
how much more the hearts of men!

12 The senseless man loves not to be reproved;
to wise men he will not go.

13 A glad heart lights up the face,
but by mental anguish the spirit is broken.[v]

14 The mind of the intelligent man seeks knowledge,
but the mouth of fools feeds on folly.

15 Every day is miserable for the depressed,
but a lighthearted man has a continual feast.

16 Better a little with fear of the LORD*
than a great fortune with anxiety.

17 Better a dish of herbs where love is
than a fatted ox and hatred with it.

18 An ill-tempered man stirs up strife,[w]
but a patient man allays discord.

19 The way of the sluggard is hemmed in as with thorns,
but the path of the diligent is a highway.

20 A wise son makes his father glad,
but a fool of a man despises his mother.[x]

21 Folly is joy to the senseless man,
but the man of understanding goes the straight way.

22 Plans fail when there is no counsel,
but they succeed when counselors are many.[y]

23 There is joy for a man in his utterance,
a word in season, how good it is![z]

24 The path of life leads the prudent man upward,
that he may avoid the nether world below.

25 The LORD overturns the house of the proud,
but he preserves intact the widow's landmark.

26 The wicked man's schemes are an abomination to the LORD,[a]
but the pure speak what is pleasing to him.

27 He who is greedy of gain brings ruin on his own house,
but he who hates bribes will live.

28 The just man weighs well his utterance,
but the mouth of the wicked pours out evil.

29 The LORD is far from the wicked,
but the prayer of the just he hears.

30 A cheerful glance brings joy to the heart;
good news invigorates the bones.

31 He who listens to salutary reproof[b]
will abide among the wise.

32 He who rejects admonition despises his own soul,
but he who heeds reproof gains understanding.

33 The fear of the LORD is training for wisdom,
and humility goes before honors.[c]

CHAPTER 16

1 Man may make plans in his heart,
but what the tongue utters is from the LORD.*

2 All the ways of a man may be pure in his own eyes,
but it is the LORD who proves the spirit.[d]

3 Entrust your works to the LORD,
and your plans will succeed.

---

t Prv 21, 27; Eccl 4, 17; Sir 34, 18ff; Is 1, 11-15.—u Prv 11, 20; 21, 21.—v Prv 12, 25; 17, 22; Sir 30, 22.—w Prv 26, 21; 29, 22; Sir 28, 11.—x Prv 10, 1; 29, 3.—y Prv 11, 14.—z Prv 25, 11; Sir 20, 6.—a Prv 6, 18.—b Prv 25, 12.—c Prv 1, 7; Sir 1, 24.—d Prv 21, 2.

15, 11: *Nether world . . . abyss:* the abode of the dead, signifying the profound obscurity which is open nevertheless to the sight and power of God.

15, 16f: Not the amount of temporal goods but the virtue of their possessor makes them a source of happiness.

16, 1: Words, like actions, often produce results different from those which were planned.

4 The LORD has made everything for his
own ends,
even the wicked for the evil day.*

5 Every proud man is an abomination to
the LORD;*
I assure you that he will not go unpunished.

6 By kindness and piety guilt is expiated,
and by the fear of the LORD man
avoids evil.

7 When the LORD is pleased with a man's
ways,
he makes even his enemies be at
peace with him.

8 Better a little with virtue,
than a large income with injustice.

9 In his mind a man plans his course,
but the LORD directs his steps.*

10 The king's lips are an oracle;
no judgment he pronounces is false.*

11 Balance and scales belong to the LORD;
all the weights used with them are his
concern.*

12 Kings have a horror of wrongdoing,
for by righteousness the throne endures.*

13 The king takes delight in honest lips,
and the man who speaks what is right
he loves.*

14 The king's wrath is like messengers of
death,*
but a wise man can pacify it.

15 In the light of the king's countenance is
life,
and his favor is like a rain cloud in
spring.

16 How much better to acquire wisdom
than gold!
To acquire understanding is more desirable than silver.*

17 The path of the upright avoids misfortune;

he who pays attention to his way
safeguards his life.

18 Pride goes before disaster,
and a haughty spirit before a fall.

19 It is better to be humble with the meek
than to share plunder with the
proud.*

20 He who plans a thing will be successful;
happy is he who trusts in the LORD!

21 The wise man is esteemed for his discernment,
yet pleasing speech increases his persuasiveness.

22 Good sense is a fountain of life to its
possessor,
but folly brings chastisement on
fools.

23 The mind of the wise man makes him
eloquent,
and augments the persuasiveness of
his lips.

24 Pleasing words are a honeycomb,
sweet to the taste and healthful to the
body.

25 Sometimes a way seems right to a man,
but the end of it leads to death!*

26 The laborer's appetite labors for him,
for his mouth urges him on.*

27 A scoundrel is a furnace of evil,
and on his lips there is a scorching fire.

Prv

28 An intriguer sows discord,
and a talebearer separates bosom
friends.*

29 A lawless man allures his neighbor,
and leads him into a way that is not
good.

30 He who winks his eye is plotting trickery;
he who compresses his lips has mischief ready.

31 Gray hair is a crown of glory;*
it is gained by virtuous living.

32 A patient man is better than a warrior,
and he who rules his temper, than he
who takes a city.*

33 When the lot is cast into the lap,
its decision depends entirely on the
LORD.*

---

e Prv 6, 16f; 8, 13.—f Prv 19, 21; 20, 24.—g Prv 11, 1.—h
Prv 25, 5.—i Prv 14, 35; 22, 11.—j Prv 19, 12; 20, 2.—k Prv 8,
10f. 19.—l Prv 11, 2.—m Prv 14, 12.—n Prv 10, 4.—o Prv 6,
14. 19; 17, 9; 26, 22; Sir 28, 15.—p Prv 20, 29.—q Prv 14, 29.

16, 4: Even the wicked, in their punishment, cannot escape
glorifying God's justice.
16, 10: Decisions of supreme judicial authority were presumed
disinterested and correct.
16, 33: The favorable or unfavorable result of chance depends
on God. Deciding strifes and doubts by lot was practiced by the
ancient Hebrews; cf Ex 28, 15-30; Lv 16, 8; Jos 7, 14; 1 Sm 10,
20f.

CHAPTER 17

1 Better a dry crust with peace
    than a house full of feasting with
    strife.

2 An intelligent servant will rule over a
    worthless son,
    and will share the inheritance with
    the brothers.*

3 The crucible for silver, and the furnace
    for gold,
    but the tester of hearts is the LORD.

4 The evil man gives heed to wicked lips,
    and listens to falsehood from a mis-
    chievous tongue.*

5 He who mocks the poor blasphemes his
    Maker;[r]
    he who is glad at calamity will not go
    unpunished.

6 Grandchildren are the crown of old
    men,
    and the glory of children is their
    parentage.

7 Fine words are out of place in a fool;
    how much more, lying words in a
    noble!

8 A man who has a bribe to offer rates it
    a magic stone;
    at every turn it brings him success.

9 He who covers up a misdeed fosters
    friendship,
    but he who gossips about it separates
    friends.

10 A single reprimand does more for a man
    of intelligence
    than a hundred lashes for a fool.

11 On rebellion alone is the wicked man
    bent,
    but a merciless messenger will be sent
    against him.

12 Face a bear robbed of her cubs,
    but never a fool in his folly!

13 If a man returns evil for good,
    from his house evil will not depart.[s]

14 The start of strife is like the opening of
    a dam;
    therefore, check a quarrel before it
    begins!

15 He who condones the wicked,[t] he who
    condemns the just,

are both an abomination to the
LORD.

16 Of what use in the fool's hand are the
    means
    to buy wisdom, since he has no mind
    for it?

17 He who is a friend is always a friend,
    and a brother is born for the time of
    stress.[u]

18 Senseless is the man who gives his hand
    in pledge,
    who becomes surety for his neigh-
    bor.[v]

19 He who loves strife loves guilt;[w]
    he who builds his gate high* courts
    disaster.

20 He who is perverse in heart finds no
    good,
    and a double-tongued man falls into
    trouble.

21 To be a fool's parent is grief for a man;
    the father of a numskull has no joy.

22 A joyful heart is the health of the body,
    but a depressed spirit dries up the
    bones.[x]

23 The wicked man accepts a concealed
    bribe
    to pervert the course of justice.

24 The man of intelligence fixes his gaze
    on wisdom,[y]
    but the eyes of a fool are on the ends
    of the earth.

25 A foolish son is vexation to his father,
    and bitter sorrow to her who bore
    him.[z]

26 It is wrong to fine an innocent man,
    but beyond reason to scourge
    princes.

27 He who spares his words is truly wise,
    and he who is chary of speech is a
    man of intelligence.[a]

28 Even a fool, if he keeps silent, is consid-
    ered wise;
    if he closes his lips, intelligent.

r Prv 14, 31.—s Mt 5, 39; Rom 12, 17; 1 Thes 5, 15; 1 Pt 3,
9.—t Prv 24, 24; Is 5, 23.—u Prv 18, 24.—v Prv 6, 1f; 11, 15.—
w Prv 15, 18.—x Prv 12, 25; 15, 13.—y Eccl 8, 1.—z Prv 10, 1;
29, 15.—a Prv 10, 19; Sir 1, 21; Jas 1, 19.

17, 2: Intelligence and ability are esteemed more highly than
nobility of blood.
17, 4: To justify his own evil ways, a wicked man judges evil
of others. Cf Mt 7, 1-5.
17, 19: *Builds . . . high:* a symbol of arrogance.

CHAPTER 18

1 In estrangement one seeks pretexts:
with all persistence he picks a quarrel.

2 The fool takes no delight in understanding,
but rather in displaying what he thinks.

3 With wickedness comes contempt,
and with disgrace comes scorn.

4 The words from a man's mouth are deep waters,
but the source of wisdom is a flowing brook. *b*

5 It is not good to be partial to the guilty,
and so to reject a rightful claim. *c*

6 The fool's lips lead him into strife,
and his mouth provokes a beating.

7 The fool's mouth is his ruin;
his lips are a snare to his life. *d*

8 The words of a talebearer are like dainty morsels
that sink into one's inmost being. *e*

9 The man who is slack in his work
is own brother to the man who is destructive.

10 The name of the LORD is a strong tower;*
the just man runs to it and is safe.

11 The rich man's wealth is his strong city; *f*
he fancies it a high wall.

12 Before his downfall a man's heart is haughty, *g*
but humility goes before honors.*

13 He who answers before he hears *h*—
his is the folly and the shame.*

14 A man's spirit sustains him in infirmity—
but a broken spirit who can bear?

15 The mind of the intelligent gains knowledge,
and the ear of the wise seeks knowledge.

16 A man's gift clears the way for him,
and gains him access to great men. *i*

17 The man who pleads his case first seems to be in the right;
then his opponent comes and puts him to the test.

18 The lot puts an end to disputes,
and is decisive in a controversy between the mighty.*

19 A brother is a better defense than a strong city,
and a friend is like the bars of a castle.

20 From the fruit of his mouth a man has his fill;*
with the yield of his lips he sates himself. *j*

21 Death and life are in the power of the tongue; *k*
those who make it a friend shall eat its fruit.

22 He who finds a wife finds happiness;
it is a favor he receives from the LORD. *l*

23 The poor man implores,
but the rich man answers harshly.

24 Some friends bring ruin on us,
but a true friend is more loyal than a brother. *m*

CHAPTER 19

1 Better a poor man who walks in his integrity
than he who is crooked in his ways and rich. *n*

2 Without knowledge even zeal is not good;
and he who acts hastily, blunders.

3 A man's own folly upsets his way,
but his heart is resentful against the LORD.

4 Wealth adds many friends,
but the friend of the poor man deserts him. *o*

5 The false witness will not go unpunished,

---

b Prv 20, 5; Jn 7, 38.—c Prv 24, 23; 28, 21.—d Prv 10, 14; 12, 13; 13, 3; Eccl 10, 12.—e Prv 26, 22.—f Prv 10, 15.—g Prv 11, 2; 16, 18; Sir 10, 15.—h Sir 11, 8.—i Prv 21, 14.—j Prv 12, 14; 13, 2.—k Sir 37, 18.—l Prv 12, 4; 19, 14; Sir 7, 26.—m Prv 17, 17.—n Prv 28, 6.—o Prv 14, 20; Sir 13, 20ff.

18, 10f: Religion is a strong support and sure refuge in the struggle of life. The rich foolishly rely on their wealth for such support.
18, 12: Compare the Savior's words: "Whoever exalts himself shall be humbled, but whoever humbles himself shall be exalted" (Mt 23, 12).
18, 13: To speak without first listening is characteristic of a fool; cf Prv 10, 14; Sir 11, 8.
18, 18: See note on Prv 16, 33.
18, 20f: Everyone must accept the consequences, of benefit or harm to himself, which his words produce.

and he who utters lies will not escape.*p*

6 Many curry favor with a noble;·
all are friends of the man who has
something to give.

7 All the poor man's brothers hate him;
how much more do his friends shun
him!

8 He who gains intelligence is his own
best friend;
he who keeps understanding will be
successful.

9 The false witness will not go unpunished,
and he who utters lies will perish.

10 Luxury is not befitting a fool;
much less should a slave rule over
princes.

11 It is good sense in a man to be slow to
anger,
and it is his glory to overlook an offense.

12 The king's wrath is like the roaring of a
lion,
but his favor, like dew on the grass.*q*

13 The foolish son is ruin to his father,*r*
and the nagging of a wife is a persistent leak.

14 Home and possessions are an inheritance from parents,
but a prudent wife is from the
LORD.*s*

15 Laziness plunges a man into deep sleep,
and the sluggard must go hungry.*t*

16 He who keeps the precept keeps his life,
but the despiser of the word will
die.*u*

17 He who has compassion on the poor
lends to the LORD,*v*
and he will repay him for his good
deed.*

18 Chastise your son, for in this there is
hope;
but do not desire his death.*w*

19 The man of violent temper pays the
penalty;
even if you rescue him, you will have
it to do again.

20 Listen to counsel and receive instruction,

that you may eventually become
wise.

21 Many are the plans in a man's heart,
but it is the decision of the LORD that
endures.*x*

22 From a man's greed comes his shame;
rather be a poor man than a liar.

23 The fear of the LORD is an aid to life;
one eats and sleeps without being visited by misfortune.

24 The sluggard loses his hand in the dish;
he will not even lift it to his mouth.*y*

25 If you beat an arrogant man, the simple
learn a lesson;
if you rebuke an intelligent man, he
gains knowledge.*z*

26 He who mistreats his father, or drives
away his mother,
is a worthless and disgraceful son.*a*

27 If a son ceases to hear instruction,
he wanders from words of knowledge.

28 An unprincipled witness perverts justice,
and the mouth of the wicked pours
out iniquity.

29 Rods are prepared for the arrogant,
and blows for the backs of fools.*b*

CHAPTER 20

1 Wine is arrogant, strong drink is riotous;
none who goes astray for it is wise.*c*

2 The dread of the king is as when a lion
roars;*d*
he who incurs his anger forfeits his
life.

3 It is honorable for a man to shun strife,
while every fool starts a quarrel.

4 In seedtime the sluggard plows not;
when he looks for the harvest, it is
not there.

5 The intention in the human heart is like
water far below the surface,

p Dt 19, 16-20; Dn 13, 61.—q Prv 20, 2.—r Prv 10, 1; 17,
25.—s Prv 18, 22.—t Prv 6, 9ff.—u Prv 13, 13; 16, 17.—v Prv
14, 21; 22, 9; 28, 27.—w Prv 13, 24; 23, 13f.—x Prv 16, 9.—y
Prv 26, 15.—z Prv 17, 10; 21, 11.—a Sir 3, 16.—b Prv 26, 3.—
c Prv 23, 29-35.— d Prv 19, 12.

19, 17: Cf Mt 25, 34-40.

but the man of intelligence draws it forth.*e*

6 Many are declared to be men of virtue:
but who can find one worthy of trust?

7 When a man walks in integrity and justice,
happy are his children after him!

8 A king seated on the throne of judgment
dispels all evil with his glance.

9 Who can say, "I have made my heart clean,*f*
I am cleansed of my sin"?*

10 Varying weights, varying measures,
are both an abomination to the LORD.*g*

11 Even by his manners the child betrays
whether his conduct is innocent and right.

12 The ear that hears, and the eye that sees—
the LORD has made them both.

13 Love not sleep, lest you be reduced to poverty;
eyes wide open mean abundant food.

14 "Bad, bad!" says the buyer;
but once he has gone his way, he boasts.*

15 Like gold or a wealth of corals,
wise lips are a precious ornament.

16 Take his garment who becomes surety for another,*h*
and for strangers yield it up!*

17 The bread of deceit is sweet to a man,

but afterward his mouth will be filled with gravel.

18 Plans made after advice succeed;
so with wise guidance wage your war.

19 A newsmonger reveals secrets;
so have nothing to do with a babbler!

20 If one curses his father or mother,
his lamp will go out* at the coming of darkness.*i*

21 Possessions gained hastily at the outset
will in the end not be blessed.

22 Say not, "I will repay evil!"
Trust in the LORD and he will help you.*j*

23 Varying weights are an abomination to the LORD,
and false scales are not good.*k*

24 Man's steps are from the LORD;*l*
how, then, can a man understand his way?*

25 Rashly to pledge a sacred gift is a trap for a man,
or to regret a vow once made.*

26 A wise king winnows the wicked,
and threshes them under the cartwheel.

27 A lamp from the LORD is the breath of man;
it searches through all his inmost being.

28 Kindness and piety safeguard the king,
and he upholds his throne by justice.*m*

29 The glory of young men is their strength,
and the dignity of old men is gray hair.*n*

30 Evil is cleansed away by bloody lashes,
and a scourging to the inmost being.

CHAPTER 21

1 Like a stream is the king's heart in the hand of the Lord;
wherever it pleases him, he directs it.

2 All the ways of a man may be right in his own eyes,
but it is the LORD who proves hearts.*o*

---

e Prv 18, 4.—f 1 Kgs 8, 46; 2 Chr 6, 36; Eccl 7, 20; 1 Jn 1, 8.—g Prv 11, 1; 20, 23.—h Prv 27, 13.—i Prv 30, 11. 17; Ex 21, 17; Lv 20, 9; Mt 15, 4.—j Prv 24, 29; Sir 28, 1; Mt 5, 39; Rom 12, 17. 19; 1 Thes 5, 15; 1 Pt 3, 9.—k Prv 11, 1; 20, 10.—l Prv 16, 9.—m Prv 16, 12.—n Prv 16, 31.—o Prv 16, 2.

20, 9: Man can be free of sin only by the power of God. Cf 1 Kgs 8, 46ff; Jb 4, 17; 14, 4; Pss 51, 2ff; 130, 3f; Rom 3, 23f; 1 Jn 1, 8.

20, 14: What one wishes to buy is valued cheaply in order that it may be obtained at a low price; once purchased, it is deemed more valuable.

20, 16: Caution is again advised in the matter of becoming surety; cf Prv 6, 1ff.

20, 20: *His lamp will go out:* misfortune, even death, awaits him; cf Prv 13, 9; Ex 21, 17.

20, 24: Man is dependent upon God and cannot fully foresee his own course.

20, 25: This verse cautions against making vows without proper reflection; cf Dt 23, 22ff; Eccl 5, 4f.

3 To do what is right and just^p
is more acceptable to the LORD than
sacrifice.*

4 Haughty eyes and a proud heart—
the tillage of the wicked is sin.

5 The plans of the diligent are sure of
profit,
but all rash haste leads certainly to
poverty.

6 He who makes a fortune by a lying
tongue
is chasing a bubble over deadly
snares.

7 The oppression of the wicked will
sweep them away,
because they refuse to do what is
right.

8 The way of the culprit is crooked,
but the conduct of the innocent is
right.

9 It is better to dwell in a corner of the
housetop
than in a roomy house with a quarrelsome woman.^q

10 The soul of the wicked man desires evil;
his neighbor finds no pity in his eyes.

11 When the arrogant man is punished,
the simple are the wiser;
when the wise man is instructed, he
gains knowledge.^r

12 The just man appraises the house of the
wicked:
there is one who brings down the
wicked to ruin.

13 He who shuts his ear to the cry of the
poor
will himself also call and not be
heard.

14 A secret gift allays anger,
and a concealed present, violent
wrath.

15 To practice justice is a joy for the just,
but terror for evildoers.^s

16 The man who strays from the way of
good sense
will abide in the assembly of the
shades.*

17 He who loves pleasure will suffer want;
he who loves wine and perfume will
not be rich.

18 The wicked man serves as ransom for
the just,*
and the faithless man for the righteous.^t

19 It is better to dwell in a wilderness
than with a quarrelsome and vexa-
tious wife.

20 Precious treasure remains in the house
of the wise,
but the fool consumes it.

21 He who pursues justice and kindness
will find life and honor.

22 The wise man storms a city of the
mighty,
and overthrows the stronghold in
which it trusts.

23 He who guards his mouth and his
tongue
keeps himself from trouble.^u

24 Arrogant is the name for the man of
overbearing pride
who acts with scornful effrontery.

25 The sluggard's propensity slays him,
for his hands refuse to work.

26 Some are consumed with avarice all the
day,
but the just man gives unsparingly.

27 The sacrifice of the wicked is an abomination,
the more so when they offer it with a
bad intention.^v

28 The false witness will perish,^w
but he who listens will finally have
his say.

29 The wicked man is brazen-faced,
but the upright man pays heed to his
ways.

30 There is no wisdom, no understanding,
no counsel, against the LORD.

p 1 Sm 15, 22; Hos 6, 6.—q Prv 21, 19; 25, 24; 27, 15; Sir
25, 23.—r Prv 29, 25.—s Prv 10, 29.—t Prv 11, 8.—u Prv 13,
3.—v Prv 15, 8; Sir 34, 18ff.—w Prv 19, 5. 9.

21, 3: External rites or sacrifices do not please God unless accompanied by internal worship and right moral conduct; cf Prv
15, 8; 21, 27; Is 1, 11-15; Am 5, 22; Mal 1, 12.
21, 16: *Assembly of the shades:* cf note on Jb 26, 5.
21, 18: *Wicked . . . ransom for the just:* exemplified in the
history of God's chosen people whom he ransomed from Egypt at
the cost of the life of Pharaoh and his army (Ex 14, 23-31), and
from Babylon by giving to Cyrus, the Persian conqueror, Egypt,
Ethiopia and Seba, the richest lands of the world (Is 43, 1ff).

31 The horse is equipped for the day of
 battle,
  but victory is the LORD's.

CHAPTER 22

1 A good name is more desirable than
 great riches,
  and high esteem, than gold and
  silver.ˣ
2 Rich and poor have a common bond:
  the LORD is the maker of them all.ʸ
3 The shrewd man perceives evil and
 hides,
  while simpletons continue on and
  suffer the penalty.ᶻ
4 The reward of humility and fear of the
 LORD
  is riches, honor and life.
5 Thorns and snares are on the path of
 the crooked;
  he who would safeguard his life will
  shun them.
6 Train a boy in the way he should go;
  even when he is old, he will not
  swerve from it.
7 The rich rule over the poor,
  and the borrower is the slave of the
  lender.
8 He who sows iniquity reaps calamity,ᵃ
  and the rod destroys his labors.
9 The kindly man will be blessed,
  for he gives of his sustenance to the
  poor.

---

x Eccl 7, 1.—y Prv 29, 13.—z Prv 27, 12.—a Jb 4, 8; Sir 7, 3;
Hos 8, 7.—b Mt 5, 8.—c Prv 26, 13.—d Prv 23, 27.—e Prv 5,
1.—f Prv 23, 11.

22, 13: To avoid the effort required for doing good *the sluggard* exaggerates the difficulties that must be overcome.
22, 16: Money gained by exploiting the poor is in turn lost to
those who are more wealthy.
22, 17—24, 22: This collection of proverbs, introduced as
sayings of the wise, is given in the more intimate and personal
form of an address to a pupil called the *son* and is arranged in
strophes instead of couplets.
22, 17—23, 35: The maxims warn against: oppression of the
poor and defenseless (22, 22f), anger (24f), giving surety for
debts (26f), bad manners at a king's table (23, 1f), anxiety for
riches (4f), a grudging host (6ff), intemperance in food and drink
(19ff. 29-35), and adultery (26ff). They exhort to: careful workmanship (22, 29), respect for the rights of orphans (23, 10f), correction of the young (13f), filial piety (15f. 22-25), and fear of
the Lord (17f).
22, 19f: *Amen-em-Ope:* an Egyptian scribe to whom is attributed a collection of maxims in *Thirty* chapters (v 20) composed for the instruction of his children and addressed to a young
man who wishes to enter upon a career. The inspired editor of
Proverbs does not translate these, but uses their materials in constructing a similar collection of proverbs.

10 Expel the arrogant man and discord
 goes out;
  strife and insult cease.
11 The LORD loves the pure of heart;ᵇ
  the man of winning speech has the
  king for his friend.
12 The eyes of the LORD safeguard knowledge,
  but he defeats the projects of the
  faithless.
13 The sluggard says, "A lion is outside;ᶜ
  in the streets I might be slain."*
14 The mouth of the adulteress is a deep
 pit;ᵈ
  he with whom the LORD is angry will
  fall into it.
15 Folly is close to the heart of a child,
  but the rod of discipline will drive it
  far from him.
16 He who oppresses the poor to enrich
 himself
  will yield up his gains to the rich as
  sheer loss.*

III: SAYINGS OF THE WISE*

17 The sayings of the wise:*

Incline your ear, and hear my words,ᵉ
  and apply your heart to my doctrine;
18 For it will be well if you keep them in
 your bosom,
  if they all are ready on your lips.
19 That your trust may be in the LORD,
  I make known to you the words of
  Amen-em-Ope.*
20 Have I not written for you the
 "Thirty,"
  with counsels and knowledge,
21 To teach you truly
  how to give a dependable report to
  one who sends you?
22 Injure not the poor because they are
 poor,
  nor crush the needy at the gate;
23 For the LORD will defend their cause,ᶠ
  and will plunder the lives of those
  who plunder them.
24 Be not friendly with a hotheaded man,
  nor the companion of a wrathful
  man,
25 Lest you learn his ways,
  and get yourself into a snare.

26 Be not one of those who give their hand
in pledge,
of those who become surety for
debts;*g*

27 For if you have not the means to pay,
your bed will be taken from under
you.

28 Remove not the ancient landmark
which your fathers set up. *h*

29 You see a man skilled at his work?
He will stand in the presence of
kings;
he will not stand in the presence of
obscure men.

CHAPTER 23

1 When you sit down to dine with a ruler,
keep in mind who is before you;
2 And put a knife to your throat*
if you have a ravenous appetite.
3 Do not desire his delicacies;
they are deceitful food.

4 Toil not to gain wealth,
cease to be concerned about it;
5 While your glance flits to it, it is gone!
for assuredly it grows wings,
like the eagle that flies toward heaven.

6 Do not take food with a grudging man,
and do not desire his dainties;
7 For in his greed he is like a storm.
"Eat and drink," he says to you,
though his heart is not with you;
8 The little you have eaten you will vomit
up,
and you will have wasted your agreeable words.

9 Speak not for the fool's hearing;
he will despise the wisdom of your
words. *i*

10 Remove not the ancient landmark,*j*
nor invade the fields of orphans;
11 For their redeemer is strong;
he will defend their cause against
you. *k*

12 Apply your heart to instruction,
and your ears to words of knowledge.

13 Withhold not chastisement from a boy;
if you beat him with the rod, he will
not die. *l*
14 Beat him with the rod,*m*
and you will save him from the nether
world.

15 My son, if your heart be wise,
my own heart also will rejoice;
16 And my inmost being will exult,
when your lips speak what is right.

17 Let not your heart emulate sinners,*n*
but be zealous for the fear of the
LORD always;
18 For you will surely have a future,
and your hope will not be cut off. *o*

19 Hear, my son, and be wise,
and guide your heart in the right way.
20 Consort not with winebibbers,
nor with those who eat meat to excess;
21 For the drunkard and the glutton come
to poverty,
and torpor clothes a man in rags.

22 Listen to your father who begot you,
and despise not your mother when
she is old.
23 Get the truth, and sell it not—
wisdom, instruction and understanding.
24 The father of a just man will exult with
glee;
he who begets a wise son will have joy
in him.*p*
25 Let your father and mother have joy;
let her who bore you exult.

26 My son, give me your heart,
and let your eyes keep to my ways.
27 For the harlot is a deep ditch,
and the adulteress a narrow pit;
28 Yes, she lies in wait like a robber,*q*
and increases the faithless among
men.

29 Who scream? Who shriek?*
Who have strife? Who have anxiety?

---

g Prv 6, 1f; 11, 15; 17, 18.—h Prv 23, 10; Dt 19, 14; 27,
17.—i Prv 9, 7.—j Prv 22, 28.—k Prv 22, 23.—l Prv 13, 24; 19,
18; Sir 30, 1.—m Prv 29, 15. 17.—n Prv 3, 31; 24, 1. 19.—o
Prv 24, 14.—p Prv 10, 1.—q Prv 7, 10-27.

23, 2: *Put a knife to your throat:* a proverbial metaphor for
self-restraint.
23, 29-35: A vivid description of the evil effects, physical and
psychological, of drunkenness.

Who have wounds for nothing?
Who have black eyes?
30 Those who linger long over wine,
those who engage in trials of blended
wine.[r]
31 Look not on the wine when it is red,
when it sparkles in the glass.
It goes down smoothly;
32 but in the end it bites like a serpent,
or like a poisonous adder.
33 Your eyes behold strange sights,
and your heart utters disordered
thoughts;
34 You are like one now lying in the
depths of the sea,
now sprawled at the top of the mast.
35 "They struck me, but it pained me not;
they beat me, but I felt it not;
When shall I awake
to seek wine once again?"*

CHAPTER 24

1 Be not emulous of evil men,*
and desire not to be with them;[s]
2 For their hearts plot violence,
and their lips speak of foul play.

3 By wisdom is a house built,
by understanding is it made firm;
4 And by knowledge are its rooms filled
with every precious and pleasing possession.

5 A wise man is more powerful than a
strong man,
and a man of knowledge than a man
of might;[t]

6 For it is by wise guidance that you wage
your war,
and the victory is due to a wealth of
counselors.[u]

7 For a fool, to be silent is wisdom;[v]
not to open his mouth at the gate.*

8 He who plots evil doing—
men call him an intruder.
9 Beyond intrigue and folly and sin,
it is arrogance that men find abominable.

10 If you remain indifferent* in time of adversity,
your strength will depart from you.
11 Rescue those who are being dragged to
death,*
and from those tottering to execution
withdraw not.
12 If you say, "I know not this man!"
does not he who tests hearts perceive
it?
He who guards your life knows it,
and he will repay each one according
to his deeds.[w]

13 If you eat honey, my son, because it is
good,
if virgin honey is sweet to your taste;
14 Such, you must know, is wisdom to
your soul.
If you find it, you will have a future,
and your hope will not be cut off.[x]

15 Lie not in wait against the home of the
just man,
ravage not his dwelling place;
16 For the just man* falls seven times and
rises again,
but the wicked stumble to ruin.

17 Rejoice not when your enemy falls,
and when he stumbles, let not your
heart exult,
18 Lest the LORD see it, be displeased with
you,
and withdraw his wrath from your
enemy.

19 Be not provoked with evildoers,
nor envious of the wicked;
20 For the evil man has no future,
the lamp of the wicked will be put
out.[y]

21 My son, fear the LORD and the king;*
have nothing to do with those who
rebel against them;

---

r Prv 20, 1; Sir 19, 2; Hos 4, 11.—s Prv 3, 31; 23, 17.—t Prv
21, 22.—u Prv 20, 18.— v Sir 6, 21.—w Ps 62, 13; Sir 16, 12;
Mt 16, 27; Rom 2, 6.—x Prv 23, 18.—y Prv 13, 9.

23, 35: Wine makes the drunkard insensible to bodily and
moral harm. His one desire is to indulge again.
  24, 1-22: These verses continue an exhortation to wisdom (vv
3-7. 13f), and against: violence (1f), pride and intrigue (8f), cal-
lousness (10-12), injustice (15f), joy in the failure of others (17f)
or scandal at their success (19f), and rebellion against authority
(21f).
  24, 7: *At the gate:* of the city, where justice was administered
and public affairs discussed; see note on Ru 4, 1. Cf also Pss 69,
13; 127, 5; Prv 22, 22; 31, 23. 31.
  24, 10: *Indifferent:* to those who suffer unjustly.
  24, 11: *Rescue . . . death:* most probably refers to the legal
rescue of those unjustly condemned to death.
  24, 16: *The just man* overcomes every misfortune which oppresses him. *Seven times:* i.e., an indefinite number; cf Mt 18,
21f; Lk 17, 4.
  24, 21f: One owes obedience to God and to supreme civil authority (Mt 22, 21; Rom 13, 1ff; 1 Pt 2, 13f). The punishments
for failure in either duty transcend the limits of private justice.

22 For suddenly arises the destruction they
send,
and the ruin from either one, who can
measure?

IV: OTHER SAYINGS OF THE WISE*

23 These also are sayings of the wise:

To show partiality in judgment is not
good.[z]
24 He who says to the wicked man,
"You are just"—
men will curse him, people will denounce him;
25 But those who convict the evildoer will
fare well,
and on them will come the blessing of
prosperity.

26 He gives a kiss on the lips*
who makes an honest reply.

27 Complete your outdoor tasks,
and arrange your work in the field;
afterward you can establish your
house.*

28 Be not a witness against your neighbor
without just cause,[a]
thus committing folly with your lips.

29 Say not, "As he did to me, so will I do
to him;[b]
I will repay the man according to his
deeds."*

30 I passed by the field of the sluggard,
by the vineyard of the man without
sense;
31 And behold! it was all overgrown with
thistles;
its surface was covered with nettles,
and its stone wall broken down.
32 And as I gazed at it, I reflected;
I saw and learned the lesson:
33 A little sleep, a little slumber,[c]
a little folding of the arms to rest—
34 Then will poverty come upon you like a
highwayman,
and want like an armed man.

V: SECOND COLLECTION OF THE PROVERBS OF SOLOMON

CHAPTER 25

1 These also are proverbs of Solomon.[d]
The men of Hezekiah,* king of Judah,
transmitted them.

2 God has glory in what he conceals,
kings have glory in what they fathom.

3 As the heavens in height, and the earth
in depth,
the heart of kings is unfathomable.

4 Remove the dross from silver,
and it comes forth perfectly purified;
5 Remove the wicked from the presence
of the king,
and his throne is made firm through
righteousness.

6 Claim no honor in the king's presence,*
nor occupy the place of great men;
7 For it is better that you be told, "Come
up closer!"
than that you be humbled before the
prince.[e]

8 What your eyes have seen
bring not forth hastily against an opponent;
For what will you do later on
when your neighbor puts you to
shame?
9 Discuss your case with your neighbor,
but another man's secret do not disclose;
10 Lest, hearing it, he reproach you,
and your ill repute cease not.

11 Like golden apples in silver settings
are words spoken at the proper time.

12 Like a golden earring, or a necklace of
fine gold,
is a wise reprover to an obedient ear.

---

z Prv 18, 5; 28, 21; Lv 19, 15; Dt 1, 17; 16, 19.—a Prv 19,
5; 25, 18.—b Prv 20, 22.—c 33f: Prv 6, 10f.—d Prv 1, 1.—e Lk
14, 8ff.

24, 23-34: This collection of sayings continues in the same
vein as the preceding: it instructs in fairness (23-26) and preparation for the future (27), and warns against vengeance (28f) and
slothfulness (30-34).
24, 26: *He gives a kiss on the lips:* shows himself a true
friend.
24, 27: This verse is commonly interpreted as advocating careful and practical preparation for marriage.
24, 29: This verse indicates great progress from the principle
of the law of Talion (see note on Ex 21, 23ff) toward the teaching found in Rom 12, 17ff. Cf also Prv 25, 21ff.
25, 1: *The men of Hezekiah:* literary men at the royal court
of Hezekiah who are represented as transcribing the proverbs
from other collections. Hezekiah was a reformer of national religious life (2 Chr 29, 25-30).
25, 6f: Compare the lesson on humility which was taught by
Christ (Lk 14, 7-11).

13 Like the coolness of snow in the heat of
the harvest
is a faithful messenger for the one
who sends him.
[He refreshes the soul of his master.]

14 Like clouds and wind when no rain follows
is the man who boastfully promises
what he never gives.

15 By patience is a ruler persuaded,*f*
and a soft tongue will break a bone.

16 If you find honey, eat only what you
need,
lest you become glutted with it and
vomit it up.

17 Let your foot be seldom in your neighbor's house,
lest he have more than enough of
you, and hate you.

18 Like a club, or a sword, or a sharp
arrow,
is the man who bears false witness
against his neighbor.

19 Like an infected tooth or an unsteady
foot
is [dependence on] a faithless man in
time of trouble.

20 Like a moth in clothing, or a maggot in
wood,
sorrow gnaws at the human heart.*g*

21 If your enemy be hungry, give him food
to eat,*
if he be thirsty, give him to drink;*h*
22 For live coals you will heap on his head,
and the LORD will vindicate you.

23 The north wind brings rain,
and a backbiting tongue an angry
countenance.

24 It is better to dwell in a corner of the
housetop
than in a roomy house with a quarrelsome woman.*i*

25 Like cool water to one faint from thirst
is good news from a far country.

26 Like a troubled fountain or a polluted
spring
is a just man who gives way before
the wicked.

27 To eat too much honey is not good;
nor to seek honor after honor.*

28 Like an open city with no defenses
is the man with no check on his feelings.

CHAPTER 26*

1 Like snow in summer, or rain in harvest,
honor for a fool is out of place.

2 Like the sparrow in its flitting, like the
swallow in its flight,
a curse uncalled-for arrives nowhere.

3 The whip for the horse, the bridle for
the ass,
and the rod for the back of fools.*j*

4 Answer not the fool according to his
folly,*
lest you too become like him.

5 Answer the fool according to his folly, **Prv**
lest he become wise in his own eyes.

6 He cuts off his feet, he drinks down violence,
who sends messages by a fool.

7 A proverb in the mouth of a fool*
hangs limp, like crippled legs.

8 Like one who entangles the stone in the
sling
is he who gives honor to a fool.

9 Like a thorn stick brandished by the
hand of a drunkard
is a proverb in the mouth of fools.

10 Like an archer wounding all who pass
by
is he who hires a drunken fool.

11 As the dog returns to his vomit,
so the fool repeats his folly.*k*

---

f Prv 15, 1. 4.—g Sir 30, 24.—h Rom 12, 20.—i Prv 21, 9.—j
Prv 19, 29; Sir 33, 25.—k 2 Pt 2, 2.

25, 21f: Charity is invaluable in resolving enmities and restoring peace. *Live coals:* i.e., either remorse and embarrassment
for the harm done, or increased punishment for refusing reconciliation. Cf Mt 5, 44; Rom 12, 20.
25, 27: *Nor . . . honor after honor:* the text is uncertain.
26, 1-28: Concrete images describe the vices of fools (1-12),
of sluggards (13-16), of meddlers (17-19), of talebearers (20ff),
and of flatterers (23-28).
26, 4f: There is no contradiction between these two proverbs.
In any answer the wise man gives he must protect his own interest
against the fool.
26, 7ff: The fool abuses whatever knowledge he possesses.

12 You see a man wise in his own eyes?
   There is more hope for a fool than for
   him.

13 The sluggard says, "There is a lion in
   the street,
   a lion in the middle of the square!"*l*

14 The door turns on its hinges,
   the sluggard, on his bed!

15 The sluggard loses his hand in the dish;
   he is too weary to lift it to his
   mouth.*m*

16 The sluggard imagines himself wiser
   than seven men who answer with
   good sense.

17 Like the man who seizes a passing dog
   by the ears
   is he who meddles in a quarrel not his
   own.

18 Like a crazed archer
   scattering firebrands and deadly arrows

19 Is the man who deceives his neighbor,
   and then says, "I was only joking."

20 For lack of wood, the fire dies out;
   and when there is no talebearer, strife
   subsides.

21 What a bellows is to live coals, what
   wood is to fire,
   such is a contentious man in enkin-
   dling strife.*n*

22 The words of a talebearer are like dainty
   morsels
   that sink into one's inmost being.*o*

23 Like a glazed finish on earthenware
   are smooth lips with a wicked heart.

24 With his lips an enemy pretends,
   but in his inmost being he maintains
   deceit;

25 When he speaks graciously, trust him
   not,*p*
   for seven abominations* are in his
   heart.

26 A man may conceal hatred under dis-
   simulation,
   but his malice will be revealed in the
   assembly.

27 He who digs a pit falls into it;
   and a stone comes back upon him
   who rolls it.*q*

28 The lying tongue is its owner's enemy,
   and the flattering mouth works ruin.

CHAPTER 27

1 Boast not of tomorrow,
   for you know not what any day may
   bring forth.

2 Let another praise you—not your own
   mouth;
   someone else—not your own lips.

3 Stone is heavy, and sand a burden,
   but a fool's provocation is heavier
   than both.*r*

4 Anger is relentless, and wrath overwhelming—
   but before jealousy who can stand?

5 Better is an open rebuke
   than a love that remains hidden.

6 Wounds from a friend may be accepted
   as well meant,
   but the greetings of an enemy one
   prays against.

7 One who is full, tramples on virgin
   honey;
   but to the man who is hungry, any
   bitter thing is sweet.

8 Like a bird that is far from its nest
   is a man who is far from his home.

9 Perfume and incense gladden the heart,
   but by grief the soul is torn asunder.

10 Your own friend and your father's
   friend forsake not;
   but if ruin befalls you, enter not a
   kinsman's house.
   Better is a neighbor near at hand than a
   brother far away.

11 If you are wise, my son, you will gladden my heart,
   and I will be able to rebut him who
   taunts me.

12 The shrewd man perceives evil and
   hides;
   simpletons continue on and suffer the
   penalty.*s*

13 Take his garment who becomes surety
   for another,*t*

l Prv 22, 13.—m Prv 19, 24.—n Prv 15, 18; 29, 22.—o Prv
18, 8.—p Sir 12, 10; 27, 23.—q Eccl 10, 8; Sir 27, 25f.—r Sir
22, 14f.—s Prv 22, 3.—t Prv 20, 16.

26, 25: *Seven abominations:* many evil intentions.

and for the sake of a stranger, yield it
up!*

14 When one greets his neighbor with a
loud voice in the early morning,
a curse can be laid to his charge.*

15 For a persistent leak on a rainy day
the match is a quarrelsome woman.ᵘ

16 He who keeps her stores up a
stormwind;
he cannot tell north from south.

17 As iron sharpens iron,
so man sharpens his fellow man.

18 He who tends a fig tree eats its fruit,
and he who is attentive to his master
will be enriched.

19 As one face differs from another,
so does one human heart from another.

20 The nether world and the abyss are
never satisfied;ᵛ
so too the eyes of men.

21 As the crucible tests silver and the furnace gold,
so a man is tested by the praise he receives.

22 Though you should pound the fool to
bits
with the pestle, amid the grits in a
mortar,
his folly would not go out of him.

23 Take good care of your flocks,*
give careful attention to your herds;

24 For wealth lasts not forever,
nor even a crown from age to age.

25 When the grass is taken away and the
aftergrowth appears,
and the mountain greens are gathered
in,

26 The lambs will provide you with clothing,

---

u Prv 21, 9; 25, 24.—v Prv 30, 16; Eccl 4, 8.—w Prv 19, 1.—x
Prv 21, 27.

27, 13: See note on Prv 20, 16.
27, 14: The *loud voice* suggests hypocrisy in the greeting.
27, 23-27: The land of Palestine was very suitable for flocks
and herds, which formed the principal source of wealth for their
owners.
28, 2: The meaning of this poorly preserved verse seems to be
that frequent changes of rulers often result from moral corruption
and political disorder.
28, 4: *The law:* religious and moral teaching.
28, 8: *Interest and overcharge* were strictly forbidden in
the old law among Israelites because it was presumed that the
borrower was in distress; cf Ex 22, 25; Lv 25, 35ff; Dt 23, 19;
Ps 15, 5; Ez 18, 8. Civil and divine law will take the offender's
wealth from him.
28, 9: Prayers offered in bad faith are displeasing to God.

and the goats will bring the price of a
field,

27 And there will be ample goat's milk to
supply you,
to supply your household,
and maintenance for your maidens.

CHAPTER 28

1 The wicked man flees although no one
pursues him;
but the just man, like a lion, feels
sure of himself.

2 If a land is rebellious, its princes will be
many;
but with a prudent man it knows security.*

3 A rich man who oppresses the poor
is like a devastating rain that leaves
no food.

4 Those who abandon the law* praise the
wicked man,
but those who keep the law war
against him.

5 Evil men understand nothing of justice,
but those who seek the LORD understand all.

6 Better a poor man who walks in his integrity
than he who is crooked in his ways
and rich.ʷ

7 He who keeps the law is a wise son,
but the gluttons' companion disgraces his father.

8 He who increases his wealth by interest
and overcharge*
gathers it for him who is kind to the
poor.

9 When one turns away his ear from hearing the law,ˣ
even his prayer is an abomination.*

10 He who seduces the upright into an evil
way
will himself fall into his own pit.
[And blameless men will gain prosperity.]

11 The rich man is wise in his own eyes,
but a poor man who is intelligent sees
through him.

12 When the just are triumphant, there is
great jubilation;

but when the wicked gain pre-eminence, people hide.

13 He who conceals his sins prospers not,
but he who confesses and forsakes
them obtains mercy.

14 Happy the man who is always on his
guard;
but he who hardens his heart will fall
into evil.

15 Like a roaring lion or a ravenous bear
is a wicked ruler over a poor people.

16 The less prudent the prince, the more
his deeds oppress.
He who hates ill-gotten gain prolongs
his days.

17 Though a man burdened with human
blood
were to flee to the grave, none should
support him.

18 He who walks uprightly is safe,
but he whose ways are crooked falls
into the pit.

19 He who cultivates his land will have
plenty of food,
but from idle pursuits a man has his
fill of poverty.^{y}

20 The trustworthy man will be richly
blessed;
he who is in haste to grow rich will
not go unpunished.^{z}

21 To show partiality is never good:^{a}
for even a morsel of bread a man may
do wrong.

22 The avaricious man is perturbed about
his wealth,
and he knows not when want will
come upon him.

23 He who rebukes a man gets more
thanks in the end
than one with a flattering tongue.

24 He who defrauds father or mother and
calls it no sin,^{b}
is a partner of the brigand.

25 The greedy man stirs up disputes,
but he who trusts in the LORD will
prosper.

26 He who trusts in himself is a fool,
but he who walks in wisdom is safe.

27 He who gives to the poor suffers no
want,^{c}

but he who ignores them gets many a
curse.

28 When the wicked gain pre-eminence,
other men hide;
but at their fall the just flourish.

CHAPTER 29

1 The man who remains stiff-necked and
hates rebuke
will be crushed suddenly beyond
cure.

2 When the just prevail, the people rejoice;
but when the wicked rule, the people
groan.^{d}

3 He who loves wisdom makes his father
glad,
but he who consorts with harlots
squanders his wealth.^{e}

4 By justice a king gives stability to the
land;
but he who imposes heavy taxes ruins
it.

5 The man who flatters his neighbor
is spreading a net under his feet.

6 The wicked man steps into a snare,
but the just man runs on joyfully.

7 The just man has a care for the rights of
the poor;
the wicked man has no such concern.

8 Arrogant men set the city ablaze,
but wise men calm the fury.^{f}

9 If a wise man disputes with a fool,
he may rage or laugh but can have no
peace.

10 Bloodthirsty men hate the honest man,
but the upright show concern for his
life.

11 The fool gives vent to all his anger;
but by biding his time, the wise man
calms it.^{g}

12 If a ruler listens to lying words,
his servants all become wicked.

13 The poor and the oppressor* have a
common bond:^{h}

---

y Prv 12, 11.—z Prv 13, 11.—a Prv 24, 23.—b Mk 7, 11ff.—c
Prv 19, 17; Sir 4, 3-8.—d Prv 11, 10.—e Prv 5, 10; 10, 1.—f
Prv 11, 11.—g Prv 12, 16; 25, 28; Sir 21, 26.—h Prv 22, 2.

29, 13: God gives life to all classes of people; cf Prv 22, 2.

the Lord gives light to the eyes of both.

14 If a king is zealous for the rights of the poor,
his throne stands firm forever.

15 The rod of correction gives wisdom,
but a boy left to his whims disgraces his mother.[i]

16 When the wicked prevail, crime increases;
but their downfall the just will behold.

17 Correct your son, and he will bring you comfort,
and give delight to your soul.

18 Without prophecy the people become demoralized;
but happy is he who keeps the law.

19 By words no servant can be trained;[j]
for he understands what is said, but obeys not.

20 Do you see a man hasty in his words?[k]
More can be hoped for from a fool!

21 If a man pampers his servant from childhood,
he will turn out to be stubborn.

22 An ill-tempered man stirs up disputes,
and a hotheaded man is the cause of many sins.[l]

23 Man's pride causes his humiliation,
but he who is humble of spirit obtains honor.[m]

24 The accomplice of a thief is his own enemy:*
he hears himself put under a curse, yet discloses nothing.

25 The fear of man brings a snare,
but he who trusts in the LORD is safe.

26 Many curry favor with the ruler,
but the rights of each are from the LORD.

27 The evildoer is an abomination to the just,
and he who walks uprightly is an abomination to the wicked.

VI: THE WORDS OF AGUR
CHAPTER 30

1 The words of Agur,* son of Jakeh the Massaite:

The pronouncement of mortal man: "I am not God;*
I am not God, that I should prevail.

2 Why, I am the most stupid of men,
and have not even human intelligence;

3 Neither have I learned wisdom,
nor have I the knowledge of the Holy One.

4 Who has gone up to heaven and come down again—
who has cupped the wind in his hands?
Who has bound up the waters in a cloak—
who has marked out all the ends of the earth?
What is his name, what is his son's name,
if you know it?"

5 Every word of God is tested;[n]
he is a shield to those who take refuge in him.

6 Add nothing to his words,[o]
lest he reprove you, and you be exposed as a deceiver.

VII: NUMERICAL PROVERBS

7 Two things I ask of you,
deny them not to me before I die:

8 Put falsehood and lying far from me,
give me neither poverty nor riches;
[provide me only with the food I need;]

9 Lest, being full, I deny you,
saying, "Who is the Lord?"
Or, being in want, I steal,
and profane the name of my God.

10 Slander not a servant to his master,
lest he curse you, and you have to pay the penalty.

11 There is a group of people that curses its father,*
and blesses not its mother.[p]

---

i Prv 13, 24; 22, 15; 23, 13f; Sir 22, 6; 30, 1.—j Sir 33, 25f.—k Eccl 5, 1.—l Prv 15, 18; 26, 21.—m Prv 11, 2; 16, 18; 18, 12; Jb 22, 29.—n Ps 12, 7.—o Dt 4, 2.—p Prv 20, 20.

29, 24: *Is his own enemy:* because he not only incurs guilt as an accomplice but, by his silence, brings down on himself the curse invoked on the unknown guilty partner.

30, 1: *Agur:* an unknown person. *Massaite:* from Massa in northern Arabia, elsewhere referred to as an encampment of the Ishmaelites (Gn 25, 14). But the word may not be intended as a place name; it might signify "an oracle," "a prophecy."

30, 1ff: Agur wishes to stress man's insignificance when he is compared to God; cf Job 38—39.

30, 11-14: Perverted people are here classified as unfilial (11), self-righteous (12), proud (13) and rapacious (14).

Prv

¹² There is a group that is pure in its own
    eyes,
    yet is not purged of its filth.
¹³ There is a group—how haughty their
    eyes!
    how overbearing their glance!
¹⁴ There is a group whose incisors are
    swords,
    whose teeth are knives,
    Devouring the needy from the earth,
    and the poor from among men.

¹⁵ The two daughters of the leech are,
    "Give, Give."*
    Three things are never satisfied,
    four never say, "Enough!"
¹⁶ The nether world, and the barren
    womb;^{q}
    the earth, that is never saturated with
    water,
    and fire, that never says, "Enough!"

¹⁷ The eye that mocks a father,
    or scorns an aged mother,
    Will be plucked out by the ravens in the
    valley;
    the young eagles will devour it.

¹⁸ Three things are too wonderful for me,*
    yes, four I cannot understand:
¹⁹ The way of an eagle in the air,
    the way of a serpent upon a rock,
    The way of a ship on the high seas,
    and the way of a man with a maiden.

²⁰ Such is the way of an adulterous
    woman:
    she eats, wipes her mouth,
    and says, "I have done no wrong."*

²¹ Under three things the earth trembles,
    yes, under four it cannot bear up:
²² Under a slave when he becomes king,
    and a fool when he is glutted with
    food;^{r}
²³ Under an odious woman when she is
    wed,
    and a maidservant when she displaces
    her mistress.

²⁴ Four things are among the smallest on
    the earth,
    and yet are exceedingly wise:
²⁵ Ants—a species not strong,
    yet they store up their food in the
    summer;
²⁶ Rock-badgers*—a species not mighty,
    yet they make their home in the
    crags;

²⁷ Locusts—they have no king,
    yet they migrate all in array;
²⁸ Lizards—you can catch them with your
    hands,
    yet they find their way into kings'
    palaces.

²⁹ Three things are stately in their stride,
    yes, four are stately in their carriage:
³⁰ The lion, mightiest of beasts,
    who retreats before nothing;
³¹ The strutting cock, and the he-goat,
    and the king at the head of his peo-
    ple.

³² If you have foolishly been proud*
    or presumptuous—put your hand on
    your mouth;
³³ For the stirring of milk brings forth
    curds,
    and the stirring of anger brings forth
    blood.

VIII: THE WORDS OF LEMUEL

CHAPTER 31

¹ The words of Lemuel, king of Massa.
The advice which his mother gave him:

² What, my son, my first-born!
    what, O son of my womb;
    what, O son of my vows!
³ Give not your vigor to women,
    nor your strength to those who ruin
    kings.^{s}
⁴ It is not for kings, O Lemuel,
    not for kings to drink wine;
    strong drink is not for princes!^{t}
⁵ Lest in drinking they forget what the
    law decrees,
    and violate the rights of all who are in
    need.

---

q Prv 27, 20.—r Prv 19, 10; Eccl 10, 6f.—s Prv 5, 9.—t Prv
20, 1.

30, 15f: *The two daughters . . . "Give, Give":* the text is
obscure but the sense seems to be that *the leech* is insatiable in
its desire for *blood,* just as are *the nether world* for victims, *the
barren womb* for offspring, *the* parched *earth* for *water,* and
fire for fuel (16).
30, 18f: The soaring flight of the eagle, the mysterious movement upon a rock of the serpent which has no feet, the path of the
ship through the trackless deep, and the marvelous procreation of
human life, excite great wonderment.
30, 20: This verse portrays the indifference of an adulterous
woman who thinks there is no trace of her wicked act.
30, 26: *Rock-badgers:* cf note on Ps 104, 18.
30, 32f: The anger aroused by overweening pride threatens an
awesome punishment.

6 Give strong drink to one who is perishing,
and wine to the sorely depressed;
7 When they drink, they will forget their
misery,
and think no more of their burdens.
8 Open your mouth in behalf of the
dumb,
and for the rights of the destitute;
9 Open your mouth, decree what is just,
defend the needy and the poor!

IX: THE IDEAL WIFE

10 When one finds a worthy wife,[u]
her value is far beyond pearls.
11 Her husband, entrusting his heart to
her,
has an unfailing prize.
12 She brings him good, and not evil,*
all the days of her life.
13 She obtains wool and flax
and makes cloth with skillful hands.
14 Like merchant* ships,
she secures her provisions from afar.
15 She rises while it is still night,
and distributes food to her household.

16 She picks out a field to purchase;
out of her earnings she plants a vineyard.
17 She is girt about with strength,
and sturdy are her arms.
18 She enjoys the success of her dealings;
at night her lamp is undimmed.*
19 She puts her hands to the distaff,
and her fingers ply the spindle.
20 She reaches out her hands to the poor,
and extends her arms to the needy.
21 She fears not the snow for her household;
all her charges are doubly clothed.
22 She makes her own coverlets;
fine linen and purple are her clothing.
23 Her husband is prominent at the city
gates
as he sits with the elders of the land.
24 She makes garments and sells them,
and stocks the merchants with belts.
25 She is clothed with strength and dignity,
and she laughs at the days to come.*
26 She opens her mouth in wisdom,
and on her tongue is kindly counsel.
27 She watches the conduct of her household,
and eats not her food in idleness.
28 Her children rise up and praise her;
her husband, too, extols her:
29 "Many are the women of proven worth,
but you have excelled them all."
30 Charm is deceptive and beauty fleeting;
the woman who fears the LORD is to
be praised.*
31 Give her a reward of her labors,
and let her works praise her at the
city gates.

---

u 10-31: Sir 26, 1ff. 13-18.

31, 12: *Good and not evil:* i.e., prosperity, not adversity.
31, 14: *Merchant:* literally, "Canaanite" (cf v 24), probably because the merchant class had been composed chiefly of Canaanites.
31, 18: *Her lamp is undimmed:* indicates abundance of productive work and its accompanying prosperity; cf Prv 20, 20; Jb 18, 6.
31, 25: *Laughs at the days to come:* anticipates the future with gladness free from anxiety.
31, 30: The true charm of the ideal wife is her religious spirit, for she *fears the Lord;* cf note on Prv 1, 7.

Eccl

THE BOOK OF ECCLESIASTES

The title Ecclesiastes *given to this book is the Greek translation of the Hebrew name* Qoheleth *meaning, perhaps, "one who convokes an assembly." The book, however, does not consist of public addresses, but is a treatise, more or less logically developed, on the vanity of all things. Reflections in prose and aphorisms in verse are intermingled in Ecclesiastes, which contains, besides, an introduction and an epilogue.*

The book is concerned with the purpose and value of human life. While admitting the existence of a divine plan, it considers such a plan to be hidden from man, who seeks happiness without ever finding it here below (3, 11; 8, 7. 17). Ecclesiastes applies his "Vanity of vanities" to everything "under the sun," even to that wisdom which seeks to find at last a semblance of good in the things of the world. Merit does not yield happiness for it is often tried by suffering. Riches and pleasures do not avail. Existence is monotonous, enjoyment fleeting and vain; darkness quickly follows. Life, then, is an enigma beyond human ability to solve.

While Ecclesiastes concedes that there is an advantage for man in the enjoyment of certain legitimate pleasures lest he lapse into pessimism and despair, he nevertheless considers this indulgence also vanity unless man returns due thanks to the Creator who has given him all. Under this aspect, earthly wisdom would rise to the higher level of true spiritual wisdom. This true wisdom is not found "under the sun" but is perceived only by the light of faith, inasmuch as it rests with God, who is the final Judge of the good and the bad, and whose reign endures forever. The Epilogue gives the clue to this thought (12, 13f).

The moral teaching of the book is imperfect, like the Old Testament itself (Heb 7, 19), yet it marks an advance in the development of the doctrine of divine retribution. While rejecting the older solution of earthly rewards and punishments, Ecclesiastes looks forward to a more lasting one. The clear answer to the problem was to come with the light of Christ's teaching concerning future life.

The author of the book was a teacher of popular wisdom (12, 9). Qoheleth was obviously only his literary name. Because he is called "David's son, king in Jerusalem," it was commonly thought that he was King Solomon. Such personation, however, was but a literary device to lend greater dignity and authority to the book—a circumstance which does not in any way impugn its inspired character. The Epilogue seems to have been written by an editor, probably a disciple of Qoheleth. The entire work differs considerably in language and style from earlier books of the Old Testament. It reflects a late period of Hebrew, and was probably written about three centuries before Christ.

CHAPTER 1

1 The words of David's son, Qoheleth,*
king in Jerusalem:*a*

Vanity of Toil without Profit

2 Vanity of vanities,* says Qoheleth,
    vanity of vanities! All things are vanity!*b*
3 What profit has man from all the labor *c*
    which he toils at under the sun?*
4 One generation passes and another
        comes,
    but the world forever stays.
5 The sun rises and the sun goes down;
    then it presses on to the place where
        it rises.
6 Blowing now toward the south, then toward the north,
    the wind turns again and again, resuming its rounds.
7 All rivers go to the sea,
    yet never does the sea become full.
    To the place where they go,
    the rivers keep on going.
8 All speech is labored;
    there is nothing man can say.*
    The eye is not satisfied with seeing
    nor is the ear filled with hearing.*d*

9 What has been, that will be; what has been done, that will be done. Nothing is new under the sun.*e* 10 Even the thing of which we say, "See, this is new!" has already existed in the ages that preceded us.*f*

11 There is no remembrance of the men of old;*g* nor of those to come will there be any remembrance among those who come after them.*

I: QOHELETH'S INVESTIGATION OF LIFE

Twofold Introduction. 12 I, Qoheleth, was king over Israel in Jerusalem, 13 and I applied my mind to search and investigate in wisdom all things that are done under the sun.*h*

A thankless task God has appointed
    for men to be busied about.

14 I have seen all things that are done under the sun,*i* and behold, all is vanity and a chase after wind.*

15 What is crooked cannot be made
        straight,
    and what is missing cannot be supplied.

---

a Eccl 7, 27; 12, 8f.—b Eccl 12, 8.—c Eccl 2, 11. 22; 3, 9; 5, 15.—d Eccl 8, 17.—e Eccl 3, 15; 6, 10.—f Eccl 3, 15.—g Eccl 2, 16.—h Eccl 8, 9.—i Eccl 2, 11. 17.

1, 1: *Qoheleth:* see Introduction.
1, 2: *Vanity of vanities:* a Hebrew superlative expressing the supreme degree of futility and emptiness.
1, 3: *Under the sun:* used throughout this book to signify "on the earth."
1, 8: *All speech . . . man can say:* or "All things are wearisome beyond man's power to tell."
1, 11: Men remember nothing long; God, however, never forgets.
1, 14: *Chase after wind:* futility, like an attempt to corral the winds. Cf Hos 12, 2. The ancient versions understood "affliction of spirit." These words are used to conclude sections of the discourse, as far as Eccl 6, 9.

¹⁶ *j* Though I said to myself, "Behold, I have become great and stored up wisdom beyond all who were before me. in Jerusalem, and my mind has broad experience of wisdom and knowledge"; ¹⁷ yet when I applied my mind to know wisdom and knowledge, madness and folly, I learned that this also is a chase after wind. *k*

¹⁸ For in much wisdom there is much sorrow,
   and he who stores up knowledge stores up grief.

CHAPTER 2

Study of Pleasure-seeking. ¹ I said to myself,* "Come, now, let me try you with pleasure and the enjoyment of good things."*l* But behold, this too was vanity. ² Of laughter I said: "Mad!" and of mirth: "What good does this do?" ³ I thought of beguiling my senses with wine, though my mind was concerned with wisdom,* and of taking up folly, until I should understand what is best for men to do under the heavens during the limited days of their life.

⁴ I undertook great works; I built myself houses and planted vineyards; ⁵ I made gardens and parks, and set out in them fruit trees of all sorts. ⁶ And I constructed for myself reservoirs to water a flourishing woodland. ⁷ I acquired male and female slaves, and slaves were born in my house. I also had growing herds of cattle and flocks of sheep, more than all who had been before me in Jerusalem. ⁸ I amassed for myself silver and gold, and the wealth of kings and provinces. I got for myself male and female singers and all human luxuries. ⁹ I became great, and I stored up more than all others before me in Jerusalem; my wisdom, too, stayed with me. ¹⁰ *m* Nothing that my eyes desired did I deny them, nor did I deprive myself of any joy, but my heart rejoiced in the fruit of all my toil. This was my share for all my toil. ¹¹ *n* But when I turned to all the works that my hands had wrought, and to the toil at which I had taken such pains, behold! all was vanity and a chase after wind, with nothing gained under the sun. ¹² For what will the man do who is to come after the king? What men have already done!

Study of Wisdom and Folly. I went on to the consideration of wisdom, madness and folly. ¹³ And I saw that wisdom has the advantage over folly as much as light has the advantage over darkness.

¹⁴ The wise man has eyes in his head,
   but the fool walks in darkness. *o*

Yet I knew that one lot befalls both of them. ¹⁵ So I said to myself, if the fool's lot is to befall me also, why then should I be wise? Where is the profit for me? And I concluded in my heart that this too is vanity. ¹⁶ *p* Neither of the wise man nor of the fool will there be an abiding remembrance, for in days to come both will have been forgotten. How is it that the wise man dies as well as the fool! ¹⁷ Therefore I loathed life, since for me the work that is done under the sun is evil; for all is vanity and a chase after wind.

Study of the Fruits of Toil

To Others the Profits. ¹⁸ And I detested all the fruits of my labor under the sun, because I must leave them to a man who is to come after me. ¹⁹ And who knows whether he will be a wise man or a fool? Yet he will have control over all the fruits of my labor under the sun. This also is vanity. ²⁰ So my feelings turned to despair of all the fruits of my labor under the sun. ²¹ For here is a man who has labored with wisdom and knowledge and skill, and to another, who has not labored over it, he must leave his property. This also is vanity and a great misfortune. ²² *q* For what profit comes to a man from all the toil and anxiety of heart with which he has labored under the sun? ²³ All his days sorrow and grief are his occupation; even at night his mind is not at rest. This also is vanity.

²⁴ *r* There is nothing better for man than to eat and drink and provide himself with good things by his labors. Even this, I realized, is from the hand of God.* ²⁵ For who can eat or drink apart from him? ²⁶ *s* For to whatever man he sees fit he gives wisdom and knowledge and joy; but to the sinner he gives the task of gathering possessions to be given to whatever man God sees fit. This also is vanity and a chase after wind.

Eccl

j Eccl 2, 9.—k Eccl 2, 3; 7, 25.—l Wis 2, 6.—m Eccl 3, 22; 5, 18.—n Eccl 1, 17; Sir 44, 9.—o 14f: Eccl 6, 8; 9, 2f.—p Eccl 1, 11; Wis 2, 4.—q Eccl 1, 3.—r Eccl 3, 12f. 22; 5, 17f; 8, 15.—s Prv 13, 22.

2, 1-11: The author here assumes the role of Solomon.
2, 3: *Though my mind . . . wisdom:* while indulging in pleasure the author hopes to discover wherein man's true happiness consists.
2, 24: Unrestrained indulgence is not advocated here, but legitimate pleasure and the cheerfulness it begets.

CHAPTER 3

Man Cannot Hit on the Right Time To Act

1 There is an appointed time for every-
    thing,
    and a time for every affair under the
    heavens.
2 A time to be born, and a time to die;
    a time to plant, and a time to uproot
    the plant.
3 A time to kill, and a time to heal;
    a time to tear down, and a time to
    build.
4 A time to weep, and a time to laugh;
    a time to mourn, and a time to dance.
5 A time to scatter stones, and a time to
    gather them;
    a time to embrace, and a time to be
    far from embraces.
6 A time to seek, and a time to lose;
    a time to keep, and a time to cast
    away.
7 A time to rend, and a time to sew;
    a time to be silent, and a time to speak.
8 A time to love, and a time to hate;
    a time of war, and a time of peace.

9 *t* What advantage has the worker from
his toil? 10 I have considered the task which
God has appointed for men to be busied
about. 11 *u* He has made everything appropriate to its time, and has put the timeless
into their hearts, without men's ever dis-
covering, from beginning to end, the work
which God has done. 12 I recognized that
there is nothing better than to be glad and
to do well during life. 13 *v* For every man,
moreover, to eat and drink and enjoy the
fruit of all his labor is a gift of God. 14 I
recognized that whatever God does will endure forever; there is no adding to it, or
taking from it. Thus has God done that he
may be revered. 15 *w* What now is has already been; what is to be, already is; and
God restores* what would otherwise be dis-
placed.

The Problem of Retribution. 16 *x* And still
under the sun in the judgment place I saw
wickedness, and in the seat of justice, iniquity. 17 *y* And I said to myself, both the
just and the wicked God will judge, since
there is a time for every affair and on every
work a judgment. 18 I said to myself: As
for the children of men, it is God's way of
testing them and of showing that they are
in themselves like beasts. 19 For the lot of
man and of beast is one lot; the one dies
as well as the other. Both have the same

life-breath, and man has no advantage over
the beast; but all is vanity. 20 *z* Both go to
the same place; both were made from the
dust, and to the dust they both return. 21
a Who knows if the life-breath of the children of men goes upward and the life-
breath of beasts goes earthward? 22 *b* And
I saw that there is nothing better for a man
than to rejoice in his work; for this is his
lot. Who will let him see what is to come
after him?

CHAPTER 4

Vanity of Toil. 1 Again I considered all the
oppressions that take place under the sun:
the tears of the victims with none to comfort them! From the hand of their oppressors comes violence, and there is none to
comfort them!*c* 2 And those now dead, I
declared more fortunate in death than are
the living to be still alive. *d* 3 And better off
than both is the yet unborn, who has not
seen the wicked work that is done under
the sun. 4 Then I saw that all toil and skillful work is the rivalry of one man for another. This also is vanity and a chase after
wind.

5 "The fool folds his arms
    and consumes his own flesh"*—
6 Better is one handful with tranquility
    than two with toil and a chase after
    wind!

Companions and Successors. 7 Again I
found this vanity under the sun: 8 a solitary
man with no companion; with neither son
nor brother. Yet there is no end to all his
toil, and riches do not satisfy his greed.
"For whom do I toil and deprive myself of
good things?" This also is vanity and a
worthless task. 9 Two are better than one:
they get a good wage for their labor. 10 If
the one falls, the other will lift up his companion. Woe to the solitary man! For if he
should fall, he has no one to lift him up.
11 So also, if two sleep together, they keep
each other warm. How can one alone keep
warm? 12 Where a lone man may be overcome, two together can resist. A three-ply
cord is not easily broken.

---

t Eccl 1, 3.—u Eccl 8, 17; 11, 5; Gn 1, 31.—v Eccl 2, 24.—w
Eccl 1, 9.—x Eccl 4, 1.—y Eccl 12, 14.—z Eccl 12, 7; Gn 2, 7;
3, 19; Ps 103, 14; Wis 2, 3; Sir 10, 9; 17, 1; 40, 11.—a Wis 2,
2.—b Eccl 8, 7; 10, 14.—c Eccl 5, 7.—d Eccl 7, 2.

3, 15: *God restores:* the meaning is probably that God allows
no part of his creation to drop out of existence.

4, 5: *Consumes his own flesh:* refuses to work for the necessities of life and consequently suffers hunger and impairs his
bodily health.

¹³ Better is a poor but wise youth than an old but foolish king who no longer knows caution; ¹⁴ for from a prison house* one comes forth in his royalty he was poor at birth. ¹⁵ Then I saw all those who are to live and move about under the sun with the heir apparent who will succeed to his place.* ¹⁶ There is no end to all these people, to all over whom he takes precedence; yet the later generations will not applaud him. This also is vanity and a chase after wind.

Vanity of Many Words. ¹⁷ *e* Guard your step when you go to the house of God. Let your approach be obedience, rather than the fools' offering of sacrifice;* for they know not how to keep from doing evil.

CHAPTER 5

¹ Be not hasty in your utterance and let not your heart be quick to make a promise in God's presence. God is in heaven and you are on earth; therefore let your words be few.

² For nightmares* come with many cares, and a fool's utterance with many words.

³ *f* When you make a vow to God, delay not its fulfillment. For God has no pleasure in fools; fulfill what you have vowed. ⁴ You had better not make a vow than make it and not fulfill it. ⁵ Let not your utterances make you guilty, and say not before his representative, "It was a mistake," lest God be angered by such words and destroy the works of your hands. ⁶ *g* Rather, fear God!

Gain and Loss of Goods. ⁷ *h* If you see oppression of the poor, and violation of rights and justice in the realm, do not be ~~shocked by~~ the fact, for the high official

has another higher than he watching him and above these are others higher still—. ⁸ Yet an advantage for a country in every respect is a king for the arable land.*

⁹ *i* The covetous man is never satisfied with money, and the lover of wealth reaps no fruit from it; so this too is vanity. ¹⁰ Where there are great riches, there are also many to devour them. Of what use are they to the owner except to feast his eyes upon? ¹¹ Sleep is sweet to the laboring man, whether he eats little or much, but the rich man's abundance allows him no sleep.

¹² *j* This is a grievous evil which I have seen under the sun: riches kept by their owner to his hurt. ¹³ Should the riches be lost through some misfortune, he may have a son when he is without means. ¹⁴ *k* As he came forth from his mother's womb, so again shall he depart, naked as he came, having nothing from his labor that he can carry in his hand. ¹⁵ This too is a grievous evil, that he goes just as he came. What then does it profit him to toil for wind? ¹⁶ All the days of his life are passed in gloom and sorrow, under great vexation, sickness and wrath.

¹⁷ *l* Here is what I recognize as good: it is well for a man to eat and drink and enjoy all the fruits of his labor under the sun during the limited days of the life which God gives him; for this is his lot. ¹⁸ Any man to whom God gives riches and property, and grants power to partake of them, so that he receives his lot and finds joy in the fruits of his toil, has a gift from God. ¹⁹ For he will hardly dwell on the shortness of his life, because God lets him busy himself with the joy of his heart.* | Eccl

CHAPTER 6

Limited Worth of Enjoyment. ¹ There is another evil which I have seen under the sun, and it weighs heavily upon man: ² *m* there is the man to whom God gives riches and property and honor, so that he lacks none of all the things he craves; yet God does not grant him power to partake of them, but a stranger devours them. This is vanity and a dire plague. ³ Should a man have a hundred children and live many years, no matter to what great age, still if he has not the full benefit of his goods, or if he is deprived of burial, of this man I proclaim that the child born dead is more fortunate than he.* ⁴ Though it came

e 1 Sm 15, 22: Ho~ ~ ~ ~ Nm ~, 5; Dt 23, 23; Ps 50, 14.—g Eccl 12, 13; Dt 10, 12.—h Eccl 3, 16; 4, 1.—i Prv 28, 22.—j Jb 20, 20.—k Jb 1, 21; 1 Tm 6, 7.—l 17f: Eccl 2, 24.—m Eccl 2, 18f.

4, 14: *Prison house:* probably his mother's womb, from which the king issues without possessions. Cf Eccl 5, 14.

4, 15: The king is no sooner dead than the people transfer their allegiance to his successor.

4, 17: *The fools'* . . . *sacrifice:* unacceptable to God because of their disobedience; cf 1 Sm 15, 22; Hos 6, 6.

5, 2: *Nightmares:* literally, "dreams."

5, 8: The wording of this verse has perhaps never been adequately explained.

5, 19: The meaning is that the joys of life, though temporary, keep a man from dwelling on the ills which afflict humanity.

6, 3: A large family, a long life, an honorable burial, all were highly esteemed by the Hebrews, and it was considered a great misfortune to be deprived of them.

in vain and goes into darkness and its name is enveloped in darkness; [5]though it has not seen or known the sun, yet the dead child is at rest rather than such a man. [6]Should he live twice a thousand years and not enjoy his goods, do not both go to the same place?*

[7]All man's toil is for his mouth,* yet his desire is not fulfilled. [8]For what advantage has the wise man over the fool, or what advantage has the poor man in knowing how to conduct himself in life? [9]"What the eyes see is better than what the desires wander after."* This also is vanity and a chase after wind.

II: QOHELETH'S CONCLUSIONS

[10]Whatever is, was long ago given its name, and the nature of man is known, and that he cannot contend in judgment with one who is stronger than he.* [11]For though there are many sayings that multiply vanity, what profit is there for a man? [12] *n* For who knows what is good for a man in life, the limited days of his vain life (which God has made like a shadow)? Because—who is there to tell a man what will come after him under the sun?

A. Man Cannot Find Out What Is Good for Him To Do

CHAPTER 7

Critique of Sages on the Day of Adversity

[1] A good name is better than good ointment,*
   and the day of death than the day of birth. *o*

[2] It is better to go to the house of mourning than to the house of feasting,
   For that is the end of every man,
   and the living should take it to heart. *p*

[3] Sorrow is better than laughter,
   because when the face is sad the heart grows wiser.

[4] The heart of the wise is in the house of mourning,
   but the heart of fools is in the house of mirth.

[5] It is better to hearken to the wise man's rebuke
   than to hearken to the song of fools;

[6] For as the crackling of thorns under a pot,
   so is the fool's laughter.
   This also is vanity,

[7] For oppression can make a fool of a wise man,

and a bribe corrupts the heart.

[8] Better is the end of speech than its beginning;
   better is the patient spirit than the lofty spirit.

[9] Do not in spirit become quickly discontented,
   for discontent lodges in the bosom of a fool.

[10]Do not say: How is it that former times were better than these? For it is not in wisdom that you ask about this.

[11] Wisdom and an inheritance are good,
   and an advantage to those that see the sun.

[12]For the protection of wisdom is as the protection of money; and the advantage of knowledge is that wisdom preserves the life of its owner.

[13]Consider the work of God. Who can make straight what he has made crooked? [14]On a good day enjoy good things, and on an evil day consider: Both the one and the other God has made, so that man cannot find fault with him in anything.

Critique of Sages on Justice and Wickedness. [15]I have seen all manner of things in my vain days: a just man perishing in his justice, and a wicked one surviving in his wickedness. [16] *q* "Be not just to excess, and be not overwise, lest you be ruined.* [17]Be not wicked to excess, and be not foolish. Why should you die before your time?"* [18]It is good to hold to this rule, and not to let that one* go; but he who fears God will win through at all events.

[19]Wisdom is a better defense for the wise man than would be ten princes in the city, [20] *r* yet there is no man on earth

n Jb 8, 9; 14, 2; Ps 102, 12.—o Eccl 4, 2; Prv 22, 1; Sir 41, 13.—p Eccl 4, 2.—q 16f: Eccl 8, 12ff.—r Jb 25, 4; Prv 20, 9; 1 Kgs 8, 46; Rom 3, 23; Jas 3, 2; 1 Jn 1, 8.

6, 6: *Same place:* the grave.

6, 7: *Mouth:* appetite, and therefore, body.

6, 9: *Better . . . wander after:* the good that is present to us is better than that which is absent and, perhaps, unattainable.

6, 10: The one who is stronger than man is God.

7, 1: *Ointment:* applied to the child at birth; *a good name* remains even after death.

7, 16: St. Jerome explains the warning against excessive justice in reference to the self-righteous man who is so stern that he is never willing to forgive sin in others; cf vv 20ff.

7, 17: Untimely death was traditionally recognized as a divine punishment of the wicked; cf 1 Sm 2, 31-34; Jer 17, 11; Ps 55, 24; Prv 10, 27. This warning against presumptuous wickedness is not an endorsement of any lesser degree of misconduct.

7, 18: *This rule . . . that one:* the sayings cited in vv 16f. Others refer *this* and *that* to riches and wisdom (cf 7, 12), justice and wisdom, or justice and wickedness. This last supposition makes the author's thought hard to follow.

so just as to do good and never sin.* [21] [s] Do not give heed to every word that is spoken lest you hear your servant speaking ill of you, [22] for you know in your heart that you have many times spoken ill of others. [23] All these things I probed in wisdom. I said, "I will acquire wisdom"; but it was beyond me. [24] What exists is far-reaching; it is deep, very deep: who can find it out? [25] [t] I turned my thoughts toward knowledge; I sought and pursued wisdom and reason, and I recognized that wickedness is foolish and folly is madness.

Critique of Sages on Women. [26] [u] More bitter than death I find the woman who is a hunter's trap, whose heart is a snare and whose hands are prison bonds. He who is pleasing to God will escape her, but the sinner will be entrapped by her. [27] Behold, this have I found, says Qoheleth, adding one thing to another that I might discover the answer [28] which my soul still seeks and has not found: One man out of a thousand have I come upon, but a woman among them all I have not found.* [29] Behold, only this have I found out: God made mankind straight, but men have had recourse to many calculations.*

CHAPTER 8

Critique of Sages on the Wise Man and the King

[1] Who is like the wise man,
    and who knows the explanation of things?
A man's wisdom illumines his face,
    but an impudent look is resented.

[2] Observe the precept of the king, and in view of your oath to God, [3] be not hasty to withdraw from the king; do not join in with a base plot, for he does whatever he pleases, [4] because his word is sovereign, and who can say to him, "What are you doing?" [5] "He who keeps the commandment experiences no evil, and the wise man's heart knows times and judgments; [6] for there is a time and a judgment for everything."— Yet it is a great affliction for man [7] [v] that he is ignorant of what is to come; for who will make known to him how it will be? [8] There is no man who is master of the breath of life so as to retain it, and none has mastery of the day of death. There is no exemption from the struggle, nor are the wicked saved by their wickedness. [9] [w] All these things I considered and I applied my mind to every work that is done under the sun, while one man tyrannizes over another to his hurt.

The Problem of Retribution. [10] Meanwhile I saw wicked men approach and enter; and as they left the sacred place, they were praised in the city for what they had done. This also is vanity.* [11] Because the sentence against evildoers is not promptly executed, therefore the hearts of men are filled with the desire to commit evil— [12] because the sinner does evil a hundred times and survives. Though indeed I know that it shall be well with those who fear God, for their reverence toward him; [13] and that it shall not be well with the wicked man, and he shall not prolong his shadowy* days, for his lack of reverence toward God.

[14] This is a vanity which occurs on earth: there are just men treated as though they had done evil and wicked men treated as though they had done justly. This, too, I say is vanity. [15] [x] Therefore I commend mirth, because there is nothing good for man under the sun except eating and drinking and mirth: for this is the accompaniment of his toil during the limited days of the life which God gives him under the sun.* [16] [y] When I applied my heart to know wisdom and to observe what is done on earth, [17] [z] I recognized that man is unable to find out all God's work that is done under the sun, even though neither by day nor by night do his eyes find rest in sleep. However much man toils in searching, he does not find it out; and even if the wise man says that he knows, he is unable to find it out.

B. Man Does Not Know What Is To Come

CHAPTER 9

[1] All this I have kept in mind and recognized:* the just, the wise, and their deeds

---

s 21f: 1 Kgs 8, 46.—t Eccl 1, 17.—u Prv 5, 4.—v Eccl 3, 22; 10, 14.—w Eccl 1, 13f.—x Eccl 2, 24; 9, 7.—y Eccl 1, 13; 3, 10.—z Eccl 3, 11.

7, 20: This is to be understood in the sense of Rom 5, 12. See note there.

7, 28: The author found sincerity rare among men, but among women still more rare.

7, 29: *Calculations:* the many vain attempts and schemes of men to attain happiness by their own efforts.

8, 10: The text is obscure. The Latin has "wicked men buried, who, while still alive, were in the holy place, and were praised in the city as if their works were just."

8, 13: *Shadowy:* perhaps an addition here; cf Eccl 6, 12.

8, 15: See notes on Eccl 2, 24; 5, 19.

9, 1-10: These statements are based on a very imperfect concept of life beyond the grave. With Christian revelation about the future life came the only satisfactory solution of the problem which so perplexed the author.

are in the hand of God. Love from hatred*
man cannot tell; both appear equally vain,
[2] *a* in that there is the same lot for all, for
the just and the wicked, for the good and
the bad, for the clean and the unclean, for
him who offers sacrifice and him who does
not. As it is for the good man, so it is for
the sinner; as it is for him who swears
rashly, so it is for him who fears an oath.
[3] Among all the things that happen under
the sun, this is the worst, that things turn
out the same for all. Hence the minds of
men are filled with evil, and madness is in
their hearts during life; and afterward they
go to the dead.

[4] Indeed, for any among the living there
is hope; a live dog is better off than a dead
lion. [5] *b* For the living know that they are
to die, but the dead no longer know anything. There is no further recompense for
them, because all memory of them is lost.
[6] For them, love and hatred and rivalry
have long since perished. They will never
again have part in anything that is done
under the sun.

[7] *c* Go, eat your bread with joy and
drink your wine with a merry heart, because it is now that God favors your works.
[8] At all times let your garments be white,
and spare not the perfume for your head.
[9] Enjoy life with the wife whom you love,
all the days of the fleeting life that is
granted you under the sun. This is your lot
in life, for the toil of your labors under the
sun. [10] Anything you can turn your hand
to, do with what power you have; for there
will be no work, nor reason, nor knowledge, nor wisdom in the nether world
where you are going.

The Evil Time Not Known. [11] Again I saw
under the sun that the race is not won by
the swift, nor the battle by the valiant, nor
a livelihood by the wise, nor riches by the
shrewd, nor favor by the experts; for a
time of calamity comes to all alike. [12] Man
no more knows his own time* than fish
taken in the fatal net, or birds trapped in
the snare; like these the children of men
are caught when the evil time falls suddenly upon them.

The Uncertain Future and the Sages.
[13] On the other hand I saw this wise deed
under the sun, which I thought sublime.
[14] Against a small city with few men in it
advanced a mighty king, who surrounded
it and threw up great siegeworks about it.
[15] But in the city lived a man who, though

poor, was wise, and he delivered it
through his wisdom. Yet no one remembered this poor man. [16] *d* Though I had
said, "Wisdom is better than force," yet
the wisdom of the poor man is despised
and his words go unheeded.

[17] "The quiet words of the wise are better
     heeded
     than the shout of a ruler of fools"—!

[18] "A fly that dies can spoil the perfumer's
     ointment,
     and a single slip can ruin much that is
     good."

CHAPTER 10

[1] More weighty than wisdom or wealth is
     a little folly!
[2] The wise man's understanding turns
     him to his right;
     the fool's understanding turns him to
     his left.*

[3] When the fool walks through the
streets, in his lack of understanding he
calls everything foolish.

[4] Should the anger of the ruler burst
upon you, forsake not your place; for
mildness abates great offenses.

[5] I have seen under the sun another evil,
like a mistake that proceeds from the
ruler: [6] a fool put in lofty position while the
rich sit in lowly places. [7] I have seen slaves
on horseback, while princes walked on the
ground like slaves.

[8] He who digs a pit may fall into it, *e*
     and he who breaks through a wall
     may be bitten by a serpent.
[9] He who moves stones may be hurt by
     them,
     and he who chops wood is in danger
     from it.

[10] If the iron becomes dull, though at
first he made easy progress, he must increase his efforts; but the craftsman has
the advantage of his skill.

[11] If the serpent bites because it has not
     been charmed,
     then there is no advantage for the
     charmer.

---

a Eccl 2, 14.—b Eccl 1, 11.—c Eccl 2, 1. 24; 8, 15; 11, 9.—d
Prv 24, 5.—e 8f: Prv 26, 27; Sir 27, 29.

9, 1: *Love from hatred:* divine favor or disfavor.
9, 12: *His own time:* the time of death or sudden disaster.
10, 2: It is doubtful whether the author is endorsing either direction; cf Prv 4, 25ff.

¹² Words from the wise man's mouth win
favor,
but the fool's lips consume him.*f*
¹³ The beginning of his words is folly,
and the end of his talk is utter madness;
¹⁴   yet the fool multiplies words.
Man knows not what is to come,
for who can tell him what is to come
after him?*g*
¹⁵ When will the fool be weary of his
labor,
he who knows not the way to the
city?*

Man Does Not Know What Evil Will Come

¹⁶ Woe to you, O land, whose king was a
servant,
and whose princes dine in the morning!
¹⁷ Blessed are you, O land, whose king is
of noble birth,
and whose princes dine at the right
time
(for vigor and not in drinking bouts).
¹⁸ When hands are lazy, the rafters sag;
when hands are slack, the house leaks.
¹⁹ Bread and oil call forth merriment
and wine makes the living glad,
but money answers for everything.
²⁰ Even in your thoughts do not make
light of the king,
nor in the privacy of your bedroom
revile the rich,
Because the birds of the air may carry
your voice,
a winged creature may tell what you
say.

CHAPTER 11

¹ Cast your bread upon the waters;*
after a long time you may find it again.
² Make seven or eight portions;*
you know not what misfortune may
come upon the earth.

---

f Sir 21, 19.—g Eccl 5, 2; 8, 7.—h Eccl 8, 17.

10, 15: *He who . . . city:* perhaps a proverbial expression for
supreme stupidity.
11, 1: This may refer to a spirit of adventure in business or to
generosity in almsgiving. *Waters:* of the ocean, which sometimes
carry lost treasures to the shore.
11, 2: This verse refers either to almsgiving or to the wisdom
of not putting all one's cargo into a single vessel.
11, 10: *Dawn . . . fleeting:* literally, "youth and the dawn [of
life] are vanity."
12, 2: *The sun . . . return:* the cloudy and rainy Palestinian
winter, a natural symbol of old age.

Man Does Not Know What Good Will Come

³ When the clouds are full,
they pour out rain upon the earth.
Whether a tree falls to the south or to
the north,
wherever it falls, there shall it lie.
⁴ One who pays heed to the wind will not
sow,
and one who watches the clouds will
never reap.
⁵ Just as you know not how the breath of
life
fashions the human frame in the
mother's womb,
So you know not the work of God
which he is accomplishing in the universe.*h*
⁶ In the morning sow your seed,
and at evening let not your hand be
idle:
For you know not which of the two will
be successful,
or whether both alike will turn out
well.

Poem on Youth and Old Age. ⁷Light is
sweet! and it is pleasant for the eyes to see
the sun. ⁸However many years a man may
live, let him, as he enjoys them all, remember that the days of darkness will be
many. All that is to come is vanity.

⁹ Rejoice, O young man, while you are
young,
and let your heart be glad in the days
of your youth.
Follow the ways of your heart,
the vision of your eyes;
Yet understand that as regards all this
God will bring you to judgment.
¹⁰ Ward off grief from your heart
and put away trouble from your presence,
though the dawn of youth is fleeting.*

CHAPTER 12

¹ Remember your Creator in the days of
your youth,
before the evil days come
And the years approach of which you
will say,
I have no pleasure in them;
² Before the sun* is darkened,
and the light, and the moon, and the
stars,

while the clouds return* after the rain;

3 When the guardians* of the house tremble,
and the strong men are bent,
And the grinders are idle because they are few,
and they who look through the windows grow blind;

4 When the doors* to the street are shut,
and the sound of the mill is low;
When one waits for the chirp of a bird,
but all the daughters of song are suppressed;

5 And one fears heights,
and perils in the street;
When the almond tree blooms,*
and the locust grows sluggish
and the caper berry is without effect,
Because man goes to his lasting home,
and mourners go about the streets;

6 Before the silver cord is snapped
and the golden bowl* is broken,
And the pitcher is shattered at the spring,
and the broken pulley falls into the well,

7 And the dust returns to the earth as it once was,
and the life breath returns to God who gave it. *i*

8 Vanity of vanities, says Qoheleth,
all things are vanity! *j*

Epilogue. 9 Besides being wise, Qoheleth taught the people knowledge, and weighed, scrutinized and arranged many proverbs. 10 Qoheleth sought to find pleasing sayings, and to write down true sayings with precision. 11 The sayings of the wise are like goads; like fixed spikes are the topics given by one collector.* 12 *k* As to more than these, my son, beware. Of the making of many books there is no end, and in much study there is weariness for the flesh.

13 *l* The last word, when all is heard: Fear God and keep his commandments, for this is man's all;* 14 *m* because God will bring to judgment every work, with all its hidden qualities, whether good or bad.

i Eccl 3, 20f; Jb 34, 15.—j Eccl 1, 2.—k Eccl 1, 18.—l Eccl 5, 6.—m Eccl 11, 9.

12, 3: *Guardians:* the arms; *strong men:* the legs; *grinders:* the teeth; *they who . . . windows:* the eyes.
12, 4: *Doors:* the tightly compressed lips; *sound of the mill:* perhaps the sound of mastication; *daughters of song:* the voice.
12, 5: *The almond tree blooms:* resembling the white hair of age. *The locust . . . sluggish:* an image of the stiffness in movement of the aged. *The caper berry:* a stimulant for appetite.
12, 6: *The golden bowl* suspended by *the silver cord* was a symbol of life; the snapping of the cord and the breaking of the bowl, a symbol of death. *The pitcher . . . the broken pulley:* another pair of metaphors for life and its ending.
12, 11: *Goads . . . one collector:* the *sayings* were stimulants to thought and also *spikes* or centers around which to group correlated pronouncements *of the wise.*
12, 13: *Man's all:* St. Jerome explains: "Unto this is every man born, that, knowing his Maker, he may revere him in fear, honor, and the observance of his commandments."

THE SONG OF SONGS

The Song of Songs, meaning the greatest of songs (1, 1), contains in exquisite poetic form the sublime portrayal and praise of the mutual love of the Lord and his people. The Lord is the Lover and his people are the beloved. Describing this relationship in terms of human love, the author simply follows Israel's tradition. Isaiah (5, 1-7; 54, 4-8), Jeremiah (2, 2f. 32), and Ezekiel (16; 23) all characterize the covenant between the Lord and Israel as a marriage. Hosea the prophet sees the idolatry of Israel in the adultery of Gomer (1—3). He also represents the Lord speaking to Israel's heart (2, 16) and changing her into a new spiritual people, purified by the Babylonian captivity and betrothed anew to her divine Lover "in justice and uprightness, in love and mercy" (2, 21).

The author of the Song, using the same literary figure, paints a beautiful picture of the ideal Israel, the chosen people of the Old and New Testaments, whom the Lord led by degrees to an exalted spiritual union with himself in the bond of perfect love. When the Song is thus interpreted there is no reason for surprise at the tone of the poem, which employs in its descriptions the courtship and marriage customs of the author's time. Moreover, the poem is not an allegory in which each remark, e.g., in the dialogue of the lovers, has a higher meaning. It is a parable in which the true meaning of mutual love comes from the poem as a whole.

While the Song is thus commonly understood by most Catholic scholars, it is also possible to see in it an inspired portrayal of ideal human love. Here we would have from God a description of the sacredness and the depth of married union.

Although the poem is attributed to Solomon in the traditional title (1, 1), the language and style of the work, among other considerations, point to a time after the end of the Babylonian Exile (538 B.C.) as that in which an unknown poet composed this masterpiece. The structure of the Song is difficult to analyze; here it is regarded as a lyric dialogue, with dramatic movement and interest.

The use of marriage as symbol, characteristic of the Song, is found extensively also in the New Testament (Mt 9, 15; 25, 1-13; Jn 3, 29; 2 Cor 11, 2; Eph 5, 23-32; Rv 19, 7ff; 21, 9ff). In Christian tradition, the Song has been interpreted in terms of the union between Christ and the Church and, particularly by St. Bernard, of the union between Christ and the individual soul. Throughout the liturgy, especially in the Little Office, there is a consistent application of the Song of Songs to the Blessed Virgin Mary.

THE SONG OF SONGS BY SOLOMON*

CHAPTER 1

Love's Desires

2 B Let him kiss me with kisses of his mouth!*

More delightful is your love than wine!*[a]

3   Your name spoken is a spreading perfume—

---

a 2f: Song 4, 10.—b Song 4, 10.

1, 1: This title is actually the first verse of chapter 1.

1, 2ff: The marginal letters indicate the speaker of the verses: B—Bride; D—Daughters of Jerusalem; G—Bridegroom. In vv 2-7 the bride and the daughters address the bridegroom who appears here as a king, but more often in the poem as a shepherd. King and shepherd are familiar figures of the Lord in the Sacred Scriptures. Cf Ps 23, 1; Is 40, 11; Jn 10, 1-16.

1, 5: *Daughters of Jerusalem:* the chorus whom the bride addresses and who ask her questions (Song 5, 9; 6, 1), thus developing action within the poem. *Kedar:* a Syrian desert region whose name suggests blackness; tents were often made of black goat hair. *Curtains:* tent coverings of *Salma,* a region close to Kedar.

1, 6: *Swarthy:* tanned by the sun from working in her brothers' vineyards. *My own vineyard:* the bride herself; cf Is 5, 1-7, where Israel is designated as the vineyard and the Lord is the Lover.

1, 7: Here and elsewhere in the Song (3, 1; 5, 8; 6, 1), the bride expresses her desire to be in the company of her lover. These verses point to a certain tension in the poem. Only at the end (Song 8, 5ff) does mutual possession of the lovers become final.

that is why the maidens love you.

4   Draw me!—

D   We will follow you eagerly!

B   Bring me, O king, to your chambers.

D With you we rejoice and exult,
    we extol your love; it is beyond wine:[b]
how rightly you are loved!

Love's Boast

5 B I am as dark—but lovely,
    O daughters of Jerusalem*—
As the tents of Kedar,
    as the curtains of Salma.

6   Do not stare at me because I am swarthy,*
    because the sun has burned me.
My brothers have been angry with me;
    they charged me with the care of the vineyards:
    my own vineyard I have not cared for.

Love's Inquiry

7 B Tell me, you whom my heart loves,*
    where you pasture your flock,

Sng

where you give them rest at midday,
Lest I be found wandering
   after the flocks of your companions.

8 G If you do not know,
   O most beautiful among women,
Follow the tracks of the flock
   and pasture the young ones
   near the shepherds' camps.

Love's Vision

9 G To the steeds of Pharaoh's chariots*
   would I liken you, my beloved:
10 Your cheeks lovely in pendants,
   your neck in jewels.
11 We will make pendants of gold for
   you,
   and silver ornaments.

Love's Union

12 B For the king's banquet
   my nard* gives forth its fragrance.
13 My lover is for me a sachet of myrrh*
   to rest in my bosom.
14 My lover is for me a cluster of henna*
   from the vineyards of Engedi.

15 G Ah, you are beautiful, my beloved,c
   ah, you are beautiful; your eyes are
   doves!*

16 B Ah, you are beautiful, my lover—
   yes, you are lovely.
Our couch, too, is verdant;*
17   the beams of our house are cedars,
   our rafters, cypresses.

CHAPTER 2

1 I am a flower of Sharon,*
   a lily of the valley.

2 G As a lily among thorns,
   so is my beloved among women.

3 B As an apple tree among the trees of the
   woods,
   so is my lover among men.
I delight to rest in his shadow,
   and his fruit is sweet to my mouth.
4 He brings me into the banquet hall*
   and his emblem over me is love.d
5 Strengthen me with raisin cakes,
   refresh me with apples,
   for I am faint with love.e
6 His left hand is under my head

and his right arm embraces me.f
7 I adjure you, daughters of Jerusalem,g
   by the gazelles and hinds* of the
   field,
Do not arouse, do not stir up love
   before its own time.

A Tryst in the Spring

8 B Hark! my lover—here he comes*
   springing across the mountains,
   leaping across the hills.
9 My lover is like a gazelle
   or a young stag.
Here he stands behind our wall,
   gazing through the windows,
   peering through the lattices.
10 My lover speaks; he says to me,
   "Arise, my beloved, my beautiful
   one,
   and come!

11 "For see, the winter is past,
   the rains are over and gone.
12 The flowers appear on the earth,
   the time of pruning the vines has
   come,
   and the song of the dove is heard in
   our land.
13 The fig tree puts forth its figs,
   and the vines, in bloom, give forth
   fragrance.
Arise, my beloved, my beautiful one,
   and come!
14 "O my dove in the clefts of the rock,*
   in the secret recesses of the cliff,

---

c Song 4, 1. 7.—d Song 1, 4.—e Song 5, 8.—f Song 8, 3.—g
Song 3, 5; 8, 4.

1, 9ff: The bridegroom compares the girl's beauty to the rich adornment of the royal chariot of Pharaoh.

1, 12: *Nard:* a precious perfume, a figure of the bride; cf Song 4, 14.

1, 13: *Myrrh:* produced from aromatic resin of balsam or roses.

1, 14: *Henna:* a plant which bears white scented flowers.

1, 15: *Doves:* suggesting innocence and charm.

1, 16f: Though the meeting place of the lovers is but a shepherd's hut of green branches, it becomes a palace with beams of cedar and rafters of cypress when adorned with their love.

2, 1: *Flower of Sharon:* probably the narcissus, which grows in the fertile Plain of Sharon lying between Mount Carmel and Jaffa on the Mediterranean coast.

2, 4ff: *The banquet hall,* the sweet things of the table, the embrace of the bride and bridegroom, express the delicacy of their affection and the intimacy of their love.

2, 7: *By the gazelles and hinds:* the swiftness of these animals and the luster and soft expression of their eyes are suggestive of love; cf Prv 5, 19.

2, 8ff: In this sudden change of scene, the bride pictures her lover hastening toward her dwelling until his voice is heard bidding her come to him.

2, 14: The bride is addressed as though she were a dove in a mountain fastness out of sight and reach.

Let me see you,
let me hear your voice,
For your voice is sweet,
and you are lovely."

15 B Catch us the foxes, the little foxes*
that damage the vineyards; for our
vineyards are in bloom!

16 My lover belongs to me and I to him;
he browses among the lilies. *h*

17 Until the day breathes cool* and the
shadows lengthen,
roam, my lover,
Like a gazelle or a young stag
upon the mountains of Bether. *i*

CHAPTER 3

Loss and Discovery

1 B On my bed at night I sought him*
whom my heart loves—
I sought him but I did not find him. *j*

2 I will rise then and go about the city;
in the streets and crossings I will
seek
Him whom my heart loves.
I sought him but I did not find him.

3 The watchmen came upon me,
as they made their rounds of the
city;
Have you seen him whom my heart
loves?

4 I had hardly left them
when I found him whom my heart
loves.
I took hold of him and would not let
him go
till I should bring him to the home
of my mother, *k*
to the room of my parent.

5 I adjure you, daughters of Jerusalem,

by the gazelles and hinds of the
field,
Do not arouse, do not stir up love
before its own time. *l*

Regal State of the Bridegroom

6 D What is this coming up from the desert,*
like a column of smoke
Laden with myrrh, with frankincense,
and with the perfume of every exotic
dust? *m*

7 Ah, it is the litter of Solomon;
sixty valiant men surround it,
of the valiant men of Israel:

8 All of them expert with the sword,
skilled in battle,
Each with his sword at his side
against danger in the watches of the
night.

9 King Solomon made himself a carriage
of wood from Lebanon.

10 He made its columns of silver,
its roof of gold,
Its seat of purple cloth,
its framework inlaid with ivory.

11 Daughters of Jerusalem, come forth
and look upon King Solomon
In the crown with which his mother
has crowned him
on the day of his marriage,
on the day of the joy of his heart.

CHAPTER 4

The Charms of the Beloved

1 G Ah, you are beautiful, my beloved, *n*
ah, you are beautiful!
Your eyes are doves *o*
behind your veil.
Your hair is like a flock of goats
streaming down the mountains of
Gilead.

2 Your teeth* are like a flock of ewes to
be shorn,
which come up from the washing,
All of them big with twins,
none of them thin and barren.

3 Your lips are like a scarlet strand;
your mouth is lovely.
Your cheek is like a half-pomegranate*
behind your veil.

4 Your neck is like David's tower *p*
girt with battlements;

Sng

---

h Song 6, 3; 7, 10.—i Song 4, 6; 8, 14.—j 1ff: Song 5, 2ff.—k
Song 8, 2.—l Song 2, 7; 8, 4.—m Song 6, 10; 8, 5.—n Song 1,
15.—o 1ff: Song 6, 5ff.—p Song 7, 5.

2, 15: A snatch of song in answer to the request of v 14; cf
Song 8, 13f. *Foxes:* all who threaten to disturb the security of
love symbolized by the vineyard; cf v 16.

2, 17: *Breathes cool:* in the evening when the sun is going
down. Cf Gn 3, 8. *Bether:* a very obscure word; some interpret it
in the sense of ruggedness; others, of spices; still others, of sacrifice (Gn 15, 10).

3, 1ff: See the parallel in Song 5, 2-8.

3, 6ff: The lover is portrayed as King Solomon, escorted by
sixty armed men, coming in royal procession to meet his bride.

4, 2: *Teeth:* praised for whiteness and regularity.

4, 3: *Pomegranate:* a fruit somewhat like an orange, with a
firm skin and deep red color. The girl's cheek is compared, in
roundness and tint, to a half-pomegranate.

A thousand bucklers hang upon it,
all the shields of valiant men.*

5 Your breasts are like twin fawns,*q*
the young of a gazelle
that browse among the lilies.

6 Until the day breathes cool and the
shadows lengthen,*r*
I will go to the mountain of myrrh,
to the hill of incense.*

7 You are all-beautiful, my beloved,
and there is no blemish in you.*

8 Come from Lebanon, my bride,
come from Lebanon, come!
Descend from the top of Amana,
from the top of Senir and Hermon,*
From the haunts of lions,
from the leopards' mountains.

9 You have ravished my heart, my sister,* my bride;*s*
you have ravished my heart with one
glance of your eyes,
with one bead of your necklace.

10 How beautiful is your love, my sister,
my bride,*t*
how much more delightful is your
love than wine,
and the fragrance of your ointments
than all spices!

11 Your lips drip honey,* my bride,
sweetmeats and milk are under your
tongue;
And the fragrance of your garments
is the fragrance of Lebanon.

The Lover and His Garden

12 G You are an enclosed garden, my sister,
my bride,*u*
an enclosed garden, a fountain
sealed.*

13 You are a park that puts forth pomegranates,
with all choice fruits;

14 Nard and saffron, calamus and cinnamon,
with all kinds of incense;
Myrrh and aloes,
with all the finest spices.*

15 You are a garden fountain, a well of
water
flowing fresh from Lebanon.

16 Arise, north wind! Come, south wind!
blow upon my garden*
that its perfumes may spread abroad.

B Let my lover come to his garden
and eat its choice fruits.

CHAPTER 5

1 G I have come to my garden, my sister,
my bride;*v*
I gather my myrrh and my spices,
I eat my honey and my sweetmeats,
I drink my wine and my milk.

D Eat, friends; drink!* Drink freely of
love!

A Fruitless Search

2 B I was sleeping, but my heart kept
vigil;*
I heard my lover knocking:
"Open to me, my sister, my beloved,
my dove, my perfect one!*w*
For my head is wet with dew,
my locks with the moisture of the
night."

3 I have taken off my robe,*
am I then to put it on?
I have bathed my feet,
am I then to soil them?

4 My lover put his hand through the
opening;
my heart trembled within me,
and I grew faint when he spoke.

5 I rose to open to my lover,
with my hands dripping myrrh:
With my fingers dripping choice
myrrh
upon the fittings of the lock.

---

q Song 7, 4.—r Song 2, 17.—s Song 6, 5.—t Song 1, 2f.—u
Song 6, 2. 11.—v Song 6, 2.—w 2ff: Song 3, 1f.

4, 4: The ornaments about her neck are compared to the
trophies on the city walls. Cf 1 Kgs 10, 10; 14, 26ff; Ez 27, 10.
  4, 6: *Mountain of myrrh . . . hill of incense:* spoken figuratively of the bride; cf Song 8, 14.
  4, 7: Cf St. Paul's description of the church in Eph 5, 27. This
verse is also applied to Our Lady, especially in the liturgy of the
feast of the Immaculate Conception.
  4, 8: *Amana . . . Senir and Hermon:* these rugged heights
symbolize obstacles that would separate the lovers; cf Song 2, 14.
  4, 9: *Sister:* a term of endearment; it forms part of the conventional language of love used in this canticle.
  4, 11: *Honey:* sweet words. Cf Prv 5, 3.
  4, 12: *Enclosed garden . . . fountain sealed:* reserved for
the bridegroom alone. The bride's fidelity is implied. Cf Prv 5,
15-19.
  4, 14: These plants are all known for their sweet scent.
  4, 16: The last two lines of the verse are spoken by the girl, inviting her lover to herself, the *garden.*
  5, 1: *Eat, friends; drink!:* the lovers are encouraged to enjoy
the delights of their love, symbol of Christ's union with the
church.
  5, 2-8: A trial similar to that in Song 3, 1ff.
  5, 3f: The bride's hesitation is due, not to levity, but to strong
emotion.

6 I opened to my lover—
but my lover had departed, gone.*x*
I sought him but I did not find him;
I called to him but he did not answer
me.*

7 The watchmen came upon me*y*
as they made their rounds of the
city;
They struck me, and wounded me,
and took my mantle from me,
the guardians of the walls.*

8 I adjure you, daughters of Jerusalem,*z*
if you find my lover—
What shall you tell him?—
that I am faint with love.

The Charms of the Lost Lover

9D How does your lover differ from any
other,
O most beautiful among women?
How does your lover differ from any
other,
that you adjure us so?

10B My lover is radiant and ruddy;*
he stands out among thousands.

11 His head is pure gold;
his locks are palm fronds,
black as the raven.

12 His eyes are like doves
beside running waters,
His teeth would seem bathed in milk,
and are set like jewels.

13 His cheeks are like beds of spice
with ripening aromatic herbs.
His lips are red blossoms;
they drip choice myrrh.

14 His arms are rods of gold
adorned with chrysolites.

His body is a work of ivory
covered with sapphires.

15 His legs are columns of marble
resting on golden bases.
His stature is like the trees on Lebanon,
imposing as the cedars.

16 His mouth is sweetness itself;
he is all delight.
Such is my lover, and such my friend,
O daughters of Jerusalem.

CHAPTER 6

Discovery

1D Where has your lover gone,
O most beautiful among women?
Where has your lover gone
that we may seek him with you?*

2B My lover has come down to his garden,*
to the beds of spice,
To browse in the garden*a*
and to gather lilies.

3 My lover belongs to me and I to him;
he browses among the lilies.*b*

The Charms of the Beloved

4G You are as beautiful as Tirzah, my beloved,*
as lovely as Jerusalem,
as awe-inspiring as bannered troops.

5 Turn your eyes from me,*c*
for they torment me.
Your hair is like a flock of goats
streaming down from Gilead.

6 Your teeth are like a flock of ewes*d*
which come up from the washing,
All of them big with twins,
none of them thin and barren.

7 Your cheek is like a half-pomegranate
behind your veil.

8 There are sixty queens, eighty concubines,
and maidens without number—

9 One alone is my dove, my perfect one,
her mother's chosen,
the dear one of her parent.
The daughters saw her and declared
her fortunate,
the queens and concubines, and they
sang her praises;

---

x Song 3, 1.—y Song 3, 3.—z Song 2, 5.—a Song 4, 12; 5, 1.—
b Song 2, 16; 7, 11.—c Song 4, 9.—d 6f: Song 4, 1ff.

5, 6: The disappearance of the lover seems to be a deliberate
trial and test inflicted on the girl.
5, 7: *The watchmen* do not know the reason for the girl's appearance in the city streets; cf Song 3, 2ff.
5, 10f: In answer to the question of v 9, the girl sings her
lover's praises (vv 10-16). *Gold:* indicates how precious the lover
is. *Palm fronds:* his thick, luxuriant growth of hair.
6, 1: The daughters of Jerusalem are won by this description
of the lover and offer their aid in seeking him.
6, 2f: Determined to share her lover with no one, the girl refuses the aid offered by the daughters in seeking him. She implies
that she had never really lost him, for he *has come down to his
garden.*
6, 4-9: The lover again celebrates her beauty. *Tirzah:* probably meaning "pleasant"; it was the early capital of the northern
kingdom of Israel (1 Kgs 16).

Sng

10 D Who is this that comes forth like the
dawn,*e*
as beautiful as the moon, as resplendent as the sun,
as awe-inspiring as bannered troops?

Love's Meeting

11 B I came down to the nut garden*f*
to look at the fresh growth of the
valley,
To see if the vines were in bloom,
if the pomegranates had blossomed.
12 Before I knew it, my heart had made
me
the blessed one of my kinswomen.*

CHAPTER 7

The Beauty of the Bride

1 D Turn, turn, O Shulammite,*
turn, turn, that we may look at you!

B Why would you look at the Shulammite
as at the dance of the two companies?

2 D How beautiful are your feet in sandals,*
O prince's daughter!
Your rounded thighs are like jewels,
the handiwork of an artist.
3 Your navel is a round bowl
that should never lack for mixed
wine.
Your body is a heap of wheat
encircled with lilies.
4 Your breasts are like twin fawns,
the young of a gazelle.*g*
5 Your neck is like a tower of ivory.*h*
Your eyes are like the pools in
Heshbon
by the gate of Bath-rabbim.
Your nose is like the tower on Lebanon
that looks toward Damascus.*
6 Your head rises like Carmel;
your hair is like draperies of purple;
a king is held captive in its tresses.

Love's Desires

7 G How beautiful you are, how pleasing,
my love, my delight!
8 Your very figure is like a palm tree,*
your breasts are like clusters.
9 I said: I will climb the palm tree,

I will take hold of its branches.
Now let your breasts be like clusters of
the vine
and the fragrance of your breath like
apples,
10 And your mouth like an excellent
wine—

Love's Union

B that flows smoothly for my lover,
spreading over the lips and the
teeth.*
11 I belong to my lover*
and for me he yearns.*i*
12 Come, my lover, let us go forth to the
fields
and spend the night among the villages.
13 Let us go early to the vineyards, and
see
if the vines are in bloom,
If the buds have opened,
if the pomegranates have blossomed;*j*
There will I give you my love.
14 The mandrakes* give forth fragrance,
and at our doors are all choice fruits;

---

e Song 3, 6; 8, 5.—f Song 4, 12ff; 7, 13.—g Song 4, 5.—h
Song 4, 4.—i Song 2, 16; 6, 3.—j Song 6, 11.

6, 12: The text is obscure in Hebrew and in the ancient versions. The Vulgate reads: "I did not know; my soul disturbed me
because of the chariots of Aminadab."

7, 1: *Shulammite:* so called either because the girl is considered to be from Shulam in the plain of Esdraelon (cf 1 Kgs 1, 3)
or because the name may mean "the peaceful one," and thus recall the name of Solomon. *As at the dance of the two companies:* the meaning is uncertain. The question in this verse
could be construed as a refusal to dance; more probably, however, the girl accedes, as the following verses suggest.

7, 2-6: A flattering description of the girl's charms.
Rounded . . . jewels: the meaning of these Hebrew words is not
certain. *Wine* and *wheat* are symbolic of fertility; they are here
associated with parts of the body which have a close relation to
fruitfulness.

7, 5: The comparison emphasizes the stateliness and whiteness
of the neck, and the limpidity of the eyes. *Bath-rabbim:* a proper
name which occurs only here; there was a city of Rabbah northeast of *Heshbon* in Transjordan. Cf Jer 49, 3.

7, 8f: *Palm tree:* a figure of stateliness. The bridegroom is
eager to enjoy the possession of his bride.

7, 10: The bride delicately turns his compliment into an expression of the love and tenderness she feels for him.

7, 11-14: The girl's answer assures him of her affection and
invites him to return with her to the rural delights which are associated with their love and which recall the meeting described in
Song 6, 11f.

7, 14: *Mandrakes:* herbs believed to have power to arouse
love and promote fertility; cf Gn 30, 14ff.

Both fresh and mellowed fruits, my
lover,
I have kept in store for you.

CHAPTER 8

1 Oh, that you were my brother,
nursed at my mother's breasts!
If I met you out of doors, I would kiss
you
and none would taunt me.
2 I would lead you, bring you in
to the home of my mother.[k]
There you would teach me to give you
spiced wine to drink, and pomegranate juice.
3 His left hand is under my head
and his right arm embraces me.[l]

4 I adjure you, daughters of Jerusalem,
by the gazelles and hinds of the
field,
Do not arouse, do not stir up love,
before its own time.[m]

Homecoming

5D Who is this coming up from the desert,[n]
leaning upon her lover?*

G Under the apple tree I awakened you;
it was there that your mother conceived you,

it was there that your parent conceived.

True Love

6B Set me as a seal* on your heart,
as a seal on your arm;
For stern as death is love,
relentless as the nether world is devotion;
its flames are a blazing fire.
7 Deep waters cannot quench love,
nor floods sweep it away.
Were one to offer all he owns to purchase love,
he would be roundly mocked.

Chastity and Its Welcome

8 "Our sister is little*
and she has no breasts as yet.
What shall we do for our sister
when her courtship begins?
9 If she is a wall,
we will build upon it a silver
parapet;
If she is a door,
we will reinforce it with a cedar
plank."
10 I am a wall,
and my breasts are like towers.
So now in his eyes I have become
one to be welcomed.

The Bride and Her Dowry

11B Solomon had a vineyard at Baal-
hamon;*
he gave over the vineyard to caretakers.
For its fruit one would have to pay
a thousand silver pieces.
12 My vineyard is at my own disposal;
the thousand pieces are for you, O
Solomon,
and two hundred for the caretakers
of its fruit.

Life Together

13G O garden-dweller,*
my friends are listening for your
voice,
let me hear it!

14B Be swift, my lover,
like a gazelle or a young stag
on the mountains of spices![o]

---

k Song 3, 4.—l Song 2, 6.—m Song 2, 7; 3, 5.—n Song 3, 6;
6, 10.—o Song 2, 9. 17; 4, 6.

8, 5: The lovers are pictured walking homeward, enjoying the
fulfillment of the desire which the girl expressed in vv 1f. The
groom speaks of their first meeting.
8, 6f: *Seal:* this could be worn bound to the arm, as here, or
suspended at the neck, or as a ring (Jer 22, 24). It was used for
identification and signatures. *Stern . . . relentless:* in human experience, death and the nether world are inevitable, unrelenting;
in the end they always triumph. Love, which is just as certain of
its victory, matches its strength against the natural enemies of
life; waters cannot extinguish it nor floods carry it away. It is
more priceless than all riches.
8, 8ff: The bride affirms her chastity. In 8, 9 she quotes the
course of action which her elder brothers had decided on. While
she is yet immature, they will shelter her in view of eventual marriage. If she is virtuous, she will be honored; if she is unchaste,
she will be kept under strict vigilance. In reply to this she proclaims her virtue and boasts of having found welcome from her
lover.
8, 11f: These enigmatic verses have been variously interpreted. In v 11 the girl alludes to a vineyard of great value which is
compared to her own self in v 12. Her enormous dowry, *a
thousand silver pieces,* is in keeping with her intrinsic worth.
She has been the generous lover, giving herself and a dowry to
her lover, referred to as *Solomon,* and also smaller gifts to her
brothers, *the caretakers* (cf vv 8ff).
8, 13f: As in Song 2, 14f, her lover asks for a word or a song
and she replies in words similar to those found in Song 2, 17.

Sng

THE BOOK OF WISDOM

The Book of Wisdom was written about a hundred years before the coming of Christ. Its author, whose name is not known to us, was a member of the Jewish community at Alexandria, in Egypt. He wrote in Greek, in a style patterned on that of Hebrew verse. At times he speaks in the person of Solomon, placing his teachings on the lips of the wise king of Hebrew tradition in order to emphasize their value. His profound knowledge of the earlier Old Testament writings is reflected in almost every line of the book, and marks him, like Ben Sira, as an outstanding representative of religious devotion and learning among the sages of postexilic Judaism.

The primary purpose of the sacred author was the edification of his co-religionists in a time when they had experienced suffering and oppression, in part at least at the hands of apostate fellow Jews. To convey his message he made use of the most popular religious themes of his time, namely the splendor and worth of divine wisdom (6, 22—11, 1), the glorious events of the Exodus (11, 2-16; 12, 23-27; 15, 18—19, 22), God's mercy (11, 17—12, 22), the folly of idolatry (13, 1—15, 17), and the manner in which God's justice is vindicated in rewarding or punishing the individual soul (1, 1—6, 21). The first ten chapters especially form a preparation for the fuller teachings of Christ and his church. Many passages from this section of the book, notably 3, 1-8, are used by the church in her liturgy.

The principal divisions of the Book of Wisdom are: I. The Reward of Justice (1, 1—6, 21). II. Praise of Wisdom by Solomon (6, 22—11, 1). III. Special Providence of God during the Exodus (11, 2-16; 12, 23-27; 15, 18—19, 22) with digressions on God's mercy (11, 17—12, 22) and on the folly and shame of idolatry (13, 1—15, 17).

I: THE REWARD OF JUSTICE

CHAPTER 1

Exhortation to Justice, the Key to Life

1 Love justice,* you who judge the earth;*a*
  think of the LORD in goodness,
  and seek him in integrity of heart;*b*
2 Because he is found by those who test him not,
  and he manifests himself to those who do not disbelieve him.*c*
3 For perverse counsels separate a man from God,
  and his power, put to the proof, rebukes the foolhardy;*d*
4 Because into a soul that plots evil wisdom enters not,
  nor dwells she in a body under debt of sin.*e*
5 For the holy spirit of discipline* flees deceit
  and withdraws from senseless counsels;
  and when injustice occurs it is rebuked.*f*
6 For wisdom is a kindly spirit,
  yet she acquits not the blasphemer of his guilty lips;
  Because God is the witness of his inmost self*g*
  and the sure observer of his heart
  and the listener to his tongue.*h*
7 For the spirit of the LORD fills the world,*i*
  is all-embracing, and knows what man says.*
8 Therefore no one who utters wicked things can go unnoticed,
  nor will chastising condemnation pass him by.*j*
9 For the devices of the wicked man shall be scrutinized,
  and the sound of his words shall reach the LORD,
  for the chastisement of his transgressions;
10 Because a jealous ear hearkens to everything,*k*
  and discordant grumblings are no secret.
11 Therefore guard against profitless grumbling,
  and from calumny* withhold your tongues;
  For a stealthy utterance does not go unpunished,
  and a lying mouth slays the soul.

a 1 Chr 29, 17; Ps 2, 10; Is 26, 9.—b 1f: Sir 1, 25.—c 1 Chr 28, 9.—d Is 59, 2.—e Sir 15, 7f; Rom 7, 14.—f Is 63, 10.—g Jer 17, 10.—h 6f: Jer 23, 24f.—i Wis 12, 1.—j Prv 19, 5.—k 10f: Nm 14, 27f.

1, 1: *Justice:* not merely the cardinal virtue of that name (cf Wis 8, 7), but the universal moral quality which is the application of Wisdom to moral conduct.
1, 5: *Discipline:* here and elsewhere, another name for Wisdom; *injustice:* the opposite of the virtue in Wis 1, 1.
1, 7: This verse is applied to the Holy Spirit in the liturgy at Pentecost.
1, 11: *Calumny:* speech against God and his providence is meant.

12 Court not death by your erring way of
life,
   nor draw to yourselves destruction by
   the works of your hands.
13 Because God did not make death,[l]
   nor does he rejoice in the destruction
   of the living.
14 For he fashioned all things that they
   might have being;
   and the creatures of the world are
   wholesome,
And there is not a destructive drug
   among them
   nor any domain of the nether world
   on earth,
15 For justice is undying.[m]

The Wicked Reject Immortality
and Justice Alike

16 It was the wicked who with hands and
   words invited death,
   considered it a friend, and pined for it,
   and made a covenant with it,
Because they deserve to be in its possession,[n]

CHAPTER 2

1   they who said among themselves,
   thinking not aright:
"Brief and troublous is our lifetime;[o]
   neither is there any remedy for man's
   dying,
   nor is anyone known to have come
   back from the nether world.
2 For haphazard were we born,
   and hereafter we shall be as though
   we had not been;
Because the breath in our nostrils is a
   smoke
   and reason is a spark at the beating of
   our hearts,
3 And when this is quenched, our body
   will be ashes
   and our spirit will be poured abroad
   like unresisting air.[p]
4 Even our name will be forgotten in time,
   and no one will recall our deeds.

So our life will pass away like the traces
   of a cloud,
   and will be dispersed like a mist
   pursued by the sun's rays
   and overpowered by its heat.
5 For our lifetime is the passing of a
   shadow;
   and our dying cannot be deferred
   because it is fixed with a seal; and no
   one returns.[q]
6 Come, therefore, let us enjoy the good
   things that are real,
   and use the freshness of creation
   avidly.[r]
7 Let us have our fill of costly wine and
   perfumes,
   and let no springtime blossom pass us
   by;
8   let us crown ourselves with rosebuds
   ere they wither.
9 Let no meadow be free from our wantonness;*
   everywhere let us leave tokens of our
   rejoicing,
   for this our portion is, and this our
   lot.[s]
10 Let us oppress the needy just man;
   let us neither spare the widow
   nor revere the old man for his hair
   grown white with time.[t]
11 But let our strength be our norm of justice;
   for weakness proves itself useless.
12 * Let us beset the just one, because he
   is obnoxious to us;
   he sets himself against our doings,
Reproaches us for transgressions of the
   law*
   and charges us with violations of our
   training.[u]
13 He professes to have knowledge of God
   and styles himself a child of the
   LORD.[v]
14 To us he is the censure of our thoughts;
   merely to see him is a hardship for
   us,[w]
15 Because his life is not like other men's,
   and different are his ways.
16 He judges us debased;
   he holds aloof from our paths as from
   things impure.
He calls blest the destiny of the just
   and boasts that God is his Father.[x]
17 Let us see whether his words be true;
   let us find out what will happen to
   him.[y]
18 For if the just one be the son of God, he
   will defend him

Wis

---

l 13f: Ez 18, 32; 33, 11; 2 Pt 3, 9.—m Is 51, 6ff.—n Is 28,
15.—o Jb 14, 1; 7, 9.—p Jb 7, 9; Jas 4, 14.—q Ps 144, 4.—r Is
22, 13; 1 Cor 15, 32.—s Jer 13, 25.—t Ex 22, 22ff; Lv 19, 32.—u
Hos 8, 1.—v Mt 27, 43; Jn 8, 55; 10, 36-39.—w Mt 9, 4.—x Jer
6, 30.—y Gn 37, 20.

2, 9: *Let no meadow . . . wantonness:* the extant Greek
Mss have "Let none of us be without part in our wanton doings."
Most Latin Mss have both forms of this line.

2, 12-20: Often applied to the Passion of our Lord; many have
understood these verses as a direct prophecy. Cf Mt 27, 41-44.

2, 12: *Law:* the law of Moses; *training* has the same meaning.

and deliver him from the hand of his foes.[z]

19 With revilement and torture let us put him to the test
that we may have proof of his gentleness
and try his patience.

20 Let us condemn him to a shameful death;
for according to his own words, God will take care of him."[a]

21 These were their thoughts, but they erred;
for their wickedness blinded them,[b]

22 And they knew not the hidden counsels of God;
neither did they count on a recompense of holiness
nor discern the innocent souls' reward.[c]

23 For God formed man to be imperishable;
the image of his own nature he made him.[d]

24 But by the envy of the devil, death entered the world,
and they who are in his possession experience it.[e]

CHAPTER 3

The Hidden Counsels of God

A. On Suffering

1 But the souls of the just are in the hand of God,[f]
and no torment shall touch them.*

2 They seemed, in the view of the foolish, to be dead;
and their passing away was thought an affliction

3 and their going forth from us, utter destruction.
But they are in peace.[g]

4 For if before men, indeed, they be punished,
yet is their hope full of immortality;

5 Chastised a little, they shall be greatly blessed,
because God tried them
and found them worthy of himself.[h]

6 As gold in the furnace, he proved them,
and as sacrificial offerings* he took them to himself.[i]

7 In the time of their visitation* they shall shine,
and shall dart about as sparks through stubble;[j]

8 They shall judge nations and rule over peoples,
and the LORD shall be their King forever.[k]

9 Those who trust in him shall understand truth,
and the faithful shall abide with him in love:
Because grace and mercy are with his holy ones,[l]
and his care is with his elect.

10 But the wicked shall receive a punishment to match their thoughts,*
since they neglected justice and forsook the LORD.

11 For he who despises wisdom and instruction is doomed.[m]
Vain is their hope, fruitless are their labors,
and worthless are their works.[n]

12 Their wives are foolish and their children wicked;
accursed is their brood.[o]

B. On Childlessness

13 Yes, blessed is she who, childless and undefiled,
knew not transgression of the marriage bed;
she shall bear fruit at the visitation of souls.*

14 So also the eunuch whose hand wrought no misdeed,
who held no wicked thoughts against the LORD—
For he shall be given fidelity's choice reward*
and a more gratifying heritage in the LORD's temple.[p]

15 For the fruit of noble struggles is a glorious one;

---

z Ps 22, 9; Is 42, 1; Mt 27, 43; Jn 5, 18.—a Jas 5, 6.—b Rom 1, 21.—c Ps 18, 24f; Prv 11, 18; Mt 11, 25.—d Gn 1, 26f; Is 54, 16 LXX.—e Gn 3, 1-24; Rom 5, 12.—f Jb 12, 10; 5, 19.—g Is 57, 2.—h Tb 12, 13; 2 Cor 4, 17; 1 Pt 1, 6f.—i Ps 51, 19; Prv 17, 3; Sir 2, 5; Is 48, 10.—j Dn 12, 3; Ob 18; Mal 3, 3; Mt 13, 43.—k Wis 8, 14; Prv 8, 16; Dn 7, 22; 1 Cor 6, 2; Rv 20, 4.—l Wis 4, 15; Jb 10, 12; Jn 15, 10.—m Prv 1, 7.—n 11f: Sir 41, 8.—o Dt 28, 18ff.—p Is 56, 2-5.

3, 1-8: Verses frequently applied to the martyrs.
3, 6: *Offerings:* the image is that of the holocaust, in which the victim is completely consumed by fire.
3, 7: *Visitation:* God's loving judgment of those who have been faithful to him; the same word is used in Wis 14, 11 for the punishment of the wicked at God's final judgment. Cf also Wis 3, 13.
3, 10: *To match their thoughts:* a fate as empty as that which they describe; cf Wis 2, 1-5.
3, 13: *Visitation of souls:* that is, the last judgment. Cf Wis 3, 7-9.
3, 14: *Fidelity's choice reward:* cf Is 56, 1-8. *More gratifying:* better than sons and daughters; cf Is 56, 5.

and unfailing is the root of understanding.*q*

16 But the children of adulterers will remain without issue,
and the progeny of an unlawful bed will disappear.*r*

17 For should they attain long life, they will be held in no esteem,
and dishonored will their old age be at last;

18 While should they die abruptly, they have no hope
nor comfort in the day of scrutiny;

19 for dire is the end of the wicked generation.*s*

CHAPTER 4

1 Better is childlessness with virtue;
for immortal is its memory:*
because both by God is it acknowledged, and by men.*t*

2 When it is present men imitate it,
and they long for it when it is gone;
And forever it marches crowned in triumph,
victorious in unsullied deeds of valor.

3 But the numerous progeny of the wicked shall be of no avail;
their spurious offshoots shall not strike deep root
nor take firm hold.*u*

4 For even though their branches flourish for a time,
they are unsteady and shall be rocked by the wind
and, by the violence of the winds, uprooted;*v*

5 Their twigs shall be broken off untimely,
and their fruit be useless, unripe for eating,
and fit for nothing.

6 For children born of lawless unions
give evidence of the wickedness of their parents, when they are examined.

C. On Early Death

7 But the just man, though he die early, shall be at rest.*w*

8 For the age that is honorable comes not with the passing of time,*x*
nor can it be measured in terms of years.

9 Rather, understanding is the hoary crown for men,
and an unsullied life, the attainment of old age.

10 He who pleased God was loved;*y*
he who lived among sinners was transported—*

11 Snatched away, lest wickedness pervert his mind
or deceit beguile his soul;*z*

12 For the witchery of paltry things obscures what is right
and the whirl of desire transforms the innocent mind.*a*

13 Having become perfect in a short while,
he reached the fullness of a long career;

14 for his soul was pleasing to the LORD,
therefore he sped him out of the midst of wickedness.*b*
But the people saw and did not understand,
nor did they take this into account.*

16 Yes, the just man dead condemns the sinful who live,
and youth swiftly completed
condemns the many years of the wicked man grown old.*c*

17 For they see the death of the wise man
and do not understand what the LORD intended for him,
or why he made him secure.

18 They see, and hold him in contempt;
but the LORD laughs them to scorn.*d*

19 And they shall afterward become dishonored corpses.*e*
and an unceasing mockery among the dead.
For he shall strike them down speechless and prostrate*f*
and rock them to their foundations;
They shall be utterly laid waste
and shall be in grief
and their memory shall perish.

The Final Judgment of the Wicked

20 Fearful shall they come, at the counting up* of their sins,
and their lawless deeds shall convict them to their face.

---

q Sir 1, 18.—r 2 Sm 12, 14.—s Ps 34, 22.—t Sir 16, 1ff; Prv 3, 3f.—u Sir 23, 25.—v Sir 40, 15; Is 40, 24.—w Wis 3, 3.—x 8f: Jb 12, 12; 32, 9; Sir 25, 4ff.—y Gn 5, 24; Sir 44, 16; Heb 11, 5.—z Is 57, 1f.—a Wis 2, 21; Dn 13, 9.—b Gn 19, 22. 29; 2 Pt 2, 7.—c Mt 12, 41f.—d Ps 37, 13.—e Neh 1, 10 LXX; Ps 18, 8; Is 14, 19; Jer 23, 39f.—f 2 Mc 3, 29.

4, 1: The Latin form of this line, "Oh, how fair is the chaste generation in its glory!" is a later adaptation, which is applied in the liturgy to the splendor of virginity.

4, 10f: There are allusions here to Enoch (Gn 5, 21-24), who was young by patriarchal standards, and to Lot (Gn 19, 10f; 2 Pt 2, 7f). Cf also Is 57, 1f.

4, 15: The verse here omitted repeats the last two lines of Wis 3, 9.

4, 20: *Counting up:* the last judgment.

Wis

CHAPTER 5

1 Then shall the just one with great assurance confront[g]
  his oppressors who set at nought his labors.[h]

2 Seeing this, they shall be shaken with dreadful fear,
  and amazed at the unlooked-for salvation.

3 They shall say among themselves, rueful and groaning through anguish of spirit:
  "This is he whom once we held as a laughingstock
  and as a type for mockery, 4fools that we were!

His life we accounted madness,
  and his death dishonored.

5 See how he is accounted among the sons of God;
  how his lot is with the saints![i]

6 We, then, have strayed from the way of truth,[j]
  and the light of justice did not shine for us,
  and the sun did not rise for us.[k]

7 We had our fill of the ways of mischief and of ruin;
  we journeyed through impassable deserts,
  but the way of the LORD we knew not.

8 What did our pride avail us?
  What have wealth and its boastfulness afforded us?[l]

9 All of them passed like a shadow
  and like a fleeting rumor;[m]

10 Like a ship traversing the heaving water,
  of which, when it has passed, no trace can be found,
  no path of its keel in the waves.

11 Or like a bird flying through the air;
  no evidence of its course is to be found—
  But the fluid air, lashed by the beat of pinions,
  and cleft by the rushing force
  Of speeding wings, is traversed:
  and afterward no mark of passage can be found in it.

12 Or as, when an arrow has been shot at a mark,
  the parted air straightway flows together again
  so that none discerns the way it went through—

13 Even so we, once born, abruptly came to nought
  and held no sign of virtue to display,
  but were consumed in our wickedness."[n]

14 Yes, the hope of the wicked is like thistledown borne on the wind,
  and like fine, tempest-driven foam;
  Like smoke scattered by the wind,
  and like the passing memory of the nomad camping for a single day.[o]

15 But the just live forever,
  and in the LORD is their recompense,
  and the thought of them is with the Most High.[p]

16 Therefore shall they receive the splendid crown,
  the beauteous diadem, from the hand of the LORD—
  For he shall shelter them with his right hand,
  and protect them with his arm.[q]

17 He shall take his zeal for armor[r]
  and he shall arm creation to requite the enemy;

18 He shall don justice for a breastplate
  and shall wear sure judgment for a helmet;

19 He shall take invincible rectitude as a shield[s]

20 and whet his sudden anger for a sword,
  And the universe shall war with him against the foolhardy.

21 Well-aimed shafts of lightnings shall go forth
  and from the clouds as from a well-drawn bow shall leap to the mark;[t]

22 and as from his sling, wrathful hailstones shall be hurled.
  The water of the sea shall be enraged against them
  and the streams shall abruptly overflow;[u]

23 A mighty wind shall confront them
  and a tempest winnow them out;
  Thus lawlessness shall lay the whole earth waste
  and evildoing overturn the thrones of potentates.[v]

---

g 1f: 2 Thes 1, 6f.—h Col 2, 15.—i Acts 26, 18; Col 1, 12.—j Prv 4, 18f; Jn 12, 35.—k 6f: Is 59, 6-14.—l Ps 49, 7; Prv 10, 2.—m 9ff: 1 Chr 29, 15; Ps 144, 4; Jb 9, 25f LXX.—n Ez 33, 10.—o Jb 21, 18; Ps 1, 4; 37, 20; Is 17, 13.—p Is 62, 11; Ez 18, 9.—q Ex 33, 22; Is 62, 3; 2 Tm 4, 8; 1 Pt 5, 4.—r 17f: Is 59, 16.—s 19f: Dt 32, 40ff.—t Hb 3, 9ff.—u Dt 11, 4.—v Wis 11, 20; Sir 10, 13f.

CHAPTER 6

Exhortation To Seek Wisdom

1 Hear, therefore, kings, and understand;[w]
   learn, you magistrates of the earth's
   expanse!
2 Hearken, you who are in power over the
   multitude
   and lord it over throngs of peoples!
3 Because authority was given you by the
   LORD
   and sovereignty by the Most High,
   who shall probe your works and
   scrutinize your counsels![x]
4 Because, though you were ministers of his
   kingdom, you judged not rightly,
   and did not keep the law,*
   nor walk according to the will of God,
5 Terribly and swiftly shall he come
   against you,
   because judgment is stern for the
   exalted—
6 For the lowly may be pardoned out of
   mercy[y]
   but the mighty shall be mightily put
   to the test.
7 For the Lord of all shows no partiality,
   nor does he fear greatness,[z]
   Because he himself made the great as
   well as the small,
   and he provides for all alike;
8 but for those in power a rigorous
   scrutiny impends.
9 To you, therefore, O princes, are my
   words addressed[a]
   that you may learn wisdom and that
   you may not sin.
10 For those who keep the holy precepts
   hallowed shall be found holy,
   and those learned in them will have
   ready a response.*
11 Desire therefore my words;
   long for them and you shall be instructed.
12 Resplendent and unfading is Wisdom,

and she is readily perceived by those
   who love her,
   and found by those who seek her.[b]
13 She hastens to make herself known in
   anticipation of men's desire;[c]
14 he who watches for her at dawn shall
   not be disappointed,
   for he shall find her sitting by his gate.
15 For taking thought of her is the perfection of prudence,
   and he who for her sake keeps vigil
   shall quickly be free from care;
16 Because she makes her own rounds,
   seeking those worthy of her,
   and graciously appears to them in the
   ways,
   and meets them with all solicitude.[d]
17 For the first step toward discipline is a
   very earnest desire for her;[e]
   then, care for discipline is love of her;
18 love means the keeping of her laws;
   To observe her laws is the basis for incorruptibility;
19 and incorruptibility makes one close
   to God;
20 thus the desire for Wisdom leads up
   to a kingdom.
21 If, then, you find pleasure in throne and
   scepter, you princes of the peoples,
   honor Wisdom, that you may reign as
   kings forever.

II: PRAISE OF WISDOM BY SOLOMON

Introduction

22 Now what Wisdom is, and how she
   came to be, I shall relate;
   and I shall hide no secrets from you,
   But from the very beginning I shall
   search out
   and bring to light knowledge of her,
   nor shall I diverge from the truth.[f]
23 Neither shall I admit consuming
   jealousy to my company,
   because that can have no fellowship
   with Wisdom.[g]
24 A great number of wise men is the
   safety of the world,
   and a prudent king, the stability of
   his people;[h]
25 so take instruction from my words, to
   your profit.

CHAPTER 7

Solomon Is Like All Other Men

1 I too am a mortal man, the same as all
   the rest,[i]
   and a descendant of the first man
   formed of earth.*

---

w 1f: Wis 1, 1; Sir 33, 19; Mi 3, 1. 9.—x 2 Chr 36, 23; Prv 8,
15f; Jn 19, 11; Rom 13, 1ff.—y 6ff: Lk 12, 48.—z Dt 1, 17; Prv
22, 2.—a 9ff: Dt 4, 10; Ps 2, 11; Sir 32, 14; 1 Jn 3, 7.—b Wis
7, 10; Prv 8, 17; Jer 29, 13.—c 13ff: Prv 8, 3. 17. 34.—d Prv
8, 20f; Sir 15, 1ff.—e 17-21: Ps 2, 10ff; Prv 4, 4-9; 7, 1-4; 8,
15f; Dn 7, 27; Jn 14, 15. 21; 1 Jn 5, 3.—f Tb 12, 7. 11; Mt 13,
11; Jn 15, 15.—g Wis 7, 13; Jas 3, 14f.—h Prv 24, 6; 29, 4; Sir
10, 1ff.—i 1f: Wis 10, 1; Gn 2, 7; Jb 10, 9-12; 33, 6; 1 Cor 15,
47ff.

6, 4: *Law:* that of Moses; cf v 10; Wis 2, 12.
6, 10: *Response:* a suitable plea before the great Judge. Cf
Prv 22, 21; Jb 31, 14; Hb 2, 1; Sir 8, 9.
7, 1: *First man formed of earth:* Adam. The author omits
throughout the book the proper names of the characters in sacred
history of whom he speaks; see especially chapter 10.

And in my mother's womb I was molded
   into flesh

2 in a ten-months' period*—body and
   blood,
   from the seed of man, and the pleasure
   that accompanies marriage.

3 And I too, when born, inhaled the common air,
   and fell upon the kindred earth;
   wailing, I uttered that first sound common to all.

4 In swaddling clothes and with constant
   care I was nurtured.

5 For no king has any different origin or
   birth,

6 but one is the entry into life for all;
   and in one same way they leave it.^j

Solomon Prayed and Wisdom and Riches Came to Him

7 Therefore I prayed, and prudence was
   given me;
   I pleaded, and the spirit of Wisdom
   came to me.^k

8 I preferred her to scepter and throne,^l
   And deemed riches nothing in comparison with her,

9 nor did I liken any priceless gem to her;
   Because all gold, in view of her, is a little
   sand,
   and before her, silver is to be accounted mire.

10 Beyond health and comeliness I loved her,
   And I chose to have her rather than the
   light,
   because the splendor of her never
   yields to sleep.^m

11 Yet all good things together came to me
   in her company,^n
   and countless riches at her hands;

12 And I rejoiced in them all, because Wisdom is their leader,
   though I had not known that she is the
   mother of these.^o

Solomon Prays for Help To Speak of Wisdom

13 Simply I learned about her, and ungrudgingly do I share—
   her riches I do not hide away;^p

14 For to men she is an unfailing treasure;
   those who gain this treasure win the
   friendship of God,
   to whom the gifts they have from discipline* commend them.

15 Now God grant I speak suitably
   and value these endowments at their
   worth:

For he is the guide of Wisdom
   and the director of the wise.

16 For both we and our words are in his hand,
   as well as all prudence and knowledge
   of crafts.^q

17 For he gave me sound knowledge of
   existing things,
   that I might know the organization of
   the universe and the force of its elements,

18 The beginning and the end and the midpoint of times,
   the changes in the sun's course and the
   variations of the seasons.

19 Cycles of years, positions of the stars,

20 natures of animals, tempers of beasts,
   Powers of the winds and thoughts of men,
   uses of plants and virtues of roots—

21 Such things as are hidden I learned, and
   such as are plain;

22 for Wisdom, the artificer of all, taught
   me.^r

Nature and Incomparable Dignity of Wisdom

For in her is a spirit
   intelligent, holy, unique,
Manifold, subtle, agile,
   clear, unstained, certain,
Not baneful, loving the good, keen,^s
   unhampered, beneficent, ^23 kindly,
Firm, secure, tranquil,
   all-powerful, all-seeing,
And pervading all spirits,
   though they be intelligent, pure and
   very subtle.

24 For Wisdom is mobile beyond all motion,
   and she penetrates and pervades all
   things by reason of her purity.^t

25 For she is an aura of the might of God
   and a pure effusion of the glory of the
   Almighty;
   therefore nought that is sullied enters
   into her.

26 For she is the refulgence of eternal light,
   the spotless mirror of the power of God,
   the image of his goodness.^u

27 And she, who is one, can do all things,
   and renews everything while herself
   perduring;

---

j Jb 1, 21; 1 Tm 6, 7f.—k 1 Kgs 3, 5-15; Prv 2, 3-11.—l 8f: Wis
8, 1; 1 Kgs 10, 21; Prv 3, 14ff; 8, 10. 18f; Jb 28, 15-19.—m Prv 6,
23.—n Prv 8, 21.—o Prv 8, 14f.—p Wis 6, 23.—q Wis 3, 1.—r Wis
14, 2; Prv 8, 30.—s 22f: Heb 4, 12f; Jas 3, 17.—t Wis 8, 1.—u 2
Cor 4, 4; Col 1, 15; Heb 1, 3.

7, 2: *In a ten-months' period:* thus the ancients were accustomed to reckon the period of pregnancy.
7, 14: *Discipline:* cf note on Wis 1, 5.

And passing into holy souls from age to age,
  she produces friends of God and prophets.[v]
28 For there is nought God loves, be it not one who dwells with Wisdom.
29 For she is fairer than the sun[w]
  and surpasses every constellation of the stars.
  Compared to light she takes precedence;
30 for that, indeed, night supplants,
  but wickedness prevails not over Wisdom.

CHAPTER 8

1 Indeed, she reaches from end to end* mightily
  and governs all things well.[x]

Solomon Sought Wisdom, the Source of Blessings

2 Her I loved and sought after from my youth;
  I sought to take her for my bride
  and was enamored of her beauty.[y]
3 She adds to nobility the splendor of companionship with God;
  even the LORD of all loved her.
4 For she is instructress in the understanding of God,
  the selector of his works.[z]
5 And if riches be a desirable possession in life,
  what is more rich than Wisdom, who produces all things?[a]
6 And if prudence renders service,[b]
  who in the world is a better craftsman than she?
7 Or if one loves justice,
  the fruits of her works are virtues;
  For she teaches moderation and prudence,
  justice and fortitude,*
  and nothing in life is more useful for men than these.
8 Or again, if one yearns for copious learning,

she knows the things of old, and infers those yet to come.
  She understands the turns of phrases and the solutions of riddles;
  signs and wonders she knows in advance
  and the outcome of times and ages.[c]

Solomon Sought Wisdom as His Counselor and Comfort

9 So I determined to take her to live with me,
  knowing that she would be my counselor while all was well,
  and my comfort in care and grief.
10 For her sake I should have glory among the masses,[d]
  and esteem from the elders, though I be but a youth.
11 I should become keen in judgment,
  and should be a marvel before rulers.
12 They would abide my silence and attend my utterance;
  and as I spoke on further,
  they would place their hands upon their mouths.*
13 For her sake I should have immortality
  and leave to those after me an everlasting memory.[e]
14 I should govern peoples, and nations would be my subjects—[f]
15 terrible princes, hearing of me, would be afraid;
  in the assembly I should appear noble, and in war courageous.
16 Within my dwelling, I should take my repose beside her;
  For association with her involves no bitterness
  and living with her no grief,
  but rather joy and gladness.[g]

Solomon Realizes That Wisdom Is a Gift of God

17 Thinking thus within myself,
  and reflecting in my heart
  That there is immortality in kinship with Wisdom,[h]
18 and good pleasure in her friendship,
  and unfailing riches in the works of her hands,
  And that in frequenting her society there is prudence,
  and fair renown in sharing her discourses,
  I went about seeking to take her for my own.
19 Now, I was a well-favored child,*

v Ex 33, 11; Jb 42, 2; Ps 104, 29; Jl 3, 1.—w 29f: Song 6, 3. 9.—x Wis 7, 24; 15, 1.—y 1 Kgs 3, 7ff; Ps 45, 12; Prv 5, 18; 8, 17.—z Prv 8, 27-31.—a Prv 8, 18f.—b 6f: Prv 8, 14f.—c Prv 1, 6; Sir 39, 1ff; 42, 19f; Dn 2, 21.—d 10ff: 1 Kgs 3, 28; Jb 29, 8ff. 21f.—e Sir 15, 6; 41, 12f; Is 56, 5.—f Wis 3, 8; Ps 18, 48; 47, 4.—g Prv 29, 6; Sir 15, 6; Bar 3, 38.—h Prv 3, 18.

8, 1: *End to end:* from one end of the heavens to the other.
8, 7: *Moderation . . . fortitude:* what are now known as the cardinal virtues.
8, 12: *Hands upon their mouths:* an oft-mentioned sign of respect among the ancients for unanswerable wisdom; cf Jb 40, 4.
8, 19f: Here the sacred writer mentions first bodily, then spiritual, excellence. To make it plain that the latter is the governing factor in the harmonious development of the human person, he then reverses the order.

Wis

and I came by a noble nature;
20 or rather, being noble, I attained an unsullied body.
21 And knowing that I could not otherwise possess her* except God gave it—
and this, too, was prudence, to know whose is the gift—
I went to the LORD and besought him,[i]
and said with all my heart:

CHAPTER 9
Solomon's Prayer

1 God of my fathers, LORD of mercy,[j]
you who have made all things by your word[k]
2 And in your wisdom have established man
to rule the creatures produced by you,[l]
3 To govern the world in holiness and justice,
and to render judgment in integrity of heart:[m]
4 Give me Wisdom, the attendant at your throne,
and reject me not from among your children;[n]
5 For I am your servant, the son of your handmaid,
a man weak and short-lived
and lacking in comprehension of judgment and of laws.[o]
6 Indeed, though one be perfect among the sons of men,
if Wisdom, who comes from you, be not with him,
he shall be held in no esteem.[p]
7 You have chosen me king over your people
and magistrate for your sons and daughters.[q]
8 You have bid me build a temple on your holy mountain
and an altar in the city that is your dwelling place,
a copy of the holy tabernacle which you had established from of old.[r]
9 Now with you is Wisdom, who knows your works
and was present when you made the world;
Who understands what is pleasing in your eyes
and what is conformable with your commands.[s]
10 Send her forth from your holy heavens
and from your glorious throne dispatch her

That she may be with me and work with me,
that I may know what is your pleasure.[t]
11 For she knows and understands all things,
and will guide me discreetly in my affairs
and safeguard me by her glory;[u]
12 Thus my deeds will be acceptable,
and I shall judge your people justly
and be worthy of my father's throne.[v]
13 For what man knows God's counsel,
or who can conceive what the LORD intends?[w]
14 For the deliberations of mortals are timid,
and unsure are our plans.
15 For the corruptible body burdens the soul
and the earthen shelter weighs down the mind that has many concerns.[x]
16 And scarce do we guess the things on earth,
and what is within our grasp we find with difficulty;
but when things are in heaven, who can search them out?[y]
17 Or who ever knew your counsel, except you had given Wisdom
and sent your holy spirit from on high?[z]
18 And thus were the paths of those on earth made straight,
and men learned what was your pleasure,
and were saved by Wisdom.[a]

CHAPTER 10*
Wisdom Preserves Her Followers

1 She preserved the first-formed father* of the world[b]
when he alone had been created;[c]

---

i 1 Kgs 3, 9; 4, 29; Prv 2, 6; Jas 1, 5.—j Ps 86, 15.—k 1f: Gn 1; Ps 33, 6; Prv 3, 19; Jer 10, 12; Jn 1, 3. 10.—l Ps 8, 7ff; Sir 17, 2ff.—m 1 Kgs 3, 6; 9, 4f; Ps 9, 8f.—n 2 Chr 1, 10.—o 1 Kgs 3, 7; Ps 116, 16.—p Wis 3, 17; 1 Kgs 11, 4; 1 Cor 3, 18ff.—q 1 Chr 28, 5.—r Ex 25, 8f; 2 Sm 7, 13; 1 Chr 28, 5; 2 Chr 6, 1f; 7, 7; Tb 1, 4; Pss 15, 1; 48, 2f.—s Dt 6, 17f; Prv 8, 22-31; Jn 1, 1ff. 10.—t Wis 18, 15; Mt 5, 34; Jn 3, 17; 20, 21.—u Wis 8, 8.—v 1 Kgs 3, 6-9.—w Is 40, 13; Bar 3, 31.—x Jb 4, 19.—y Sir 1, 3; Jn 3, 12.—z Jn 14, 26.—a Wis 10, 9; Prv 28, 26.—b 1-16: Heb 11, 17-27.—c Wis 7, 1.

8, 21: *Possess her:* in the Latin, "be continent." Though this verse has often been cited in connection with the virtue of chastity, the original must certainly mean "be possessed of Wisdom."
10, 1-21: This chapter prepares for the following section (11, 2—19, 22) on the history of Israel in the Exodus, by reviewing the dealings of Wisdom with the patriarchs. It has a parallel in Sir 44—50; cf also Wis 18, 9.
10, 1f: Adam.

And she raised him up from his fall,

2 and gave him power to rule all things.^d

3 But when the unjust man* withdrew from her in his anger,

he perished through his fratricidal wrath.^e

4 When on his account the earth was flooded, Wisdom again saved it, piloting the just man* on frailest wood.^f

5 She, when the nations were sunk in universal wickedness, knew the just man,* kept him blameless before God,

and preserved him resolute against pity for his child.^g

6 She delivered the just man* from among the wicked who were being destroyed,^h

when he fled as fire descended upon Pentapolis—

7 Where as a testimony to its wickedness, there yet remain a smoking desert,

Plants bearing fruit that never ripens, and the tomb of a disbelieving soul,* a standing pillar of salt.ⁱ

8 For those who forsook Wisdom first were bereft of knowledge of the right,

And then they left mankind a memorial of their folly—

so that they could not even be hidden in their fall.

9 But Wisdom delivered from tribulations those who served her.^j

10 She, when the just man fled from his brother's anger,^k

guided him in direct ways,*

Showed him the kingdom of God and gave him knowledge of holy things;

She prospered him in his labors and made abundant the fruit of his works,

11 Stood by him against the greed of his defrauders,

and enriched him;^l

12 She preserved him from foes, and secured him against ambush,

And she gave him the prize for his stern struggle

that he might know that devotion to God* is mightier than all else.^m

13 She did not abandon the just man* when he was sold,ⁿ

but delivered him from sin.^o

14 She went down with him into the dungeon,

and did not desert him in his bonds,

Until she brought him the scepter of royalty

and authority over his oppressors,

Showed those who had defamed him false,

and gave him eternal glory.

15 The holy people and blameless race—it was she

who delivered them from the nation that oppressed them.^p

16 She entered the soul of the Lord's servant,*

and withstood fearsome kings with signs and portents;^q

17 she gave the holy ones the recompense of their labors,^r

Conducted them by a wondrous road, and became a shelter for them by day and a starry flame by night.

18 She took them across the Red Sea and brought them through the deep waters—

19 But their enemies she overwhelmed, and cast them up* from the bottom of the depths.

20 Therefore the just despoiled the wicked;

and they sang, O Lord, your holy name

and praised in unison your conquering hand^s—

21 Because Wisdom opened the mouths of the dumb,

and gave ready speech to infants.^t

---

d Gn 1, 28.—e Gn 4, 1-16.—f Wis 14, 5f; Gn 6, 5-9.—g Gn 22, 7-10.—h Gn 18, 22-33; 19, 15-25; 2 Pt 2, 6f.—i Gn 19, 26; Lk 17, 32.—j Wis 16, 8.—k Gn 27, 43ff; 28, 12-15.—l Gn 30, 29f; 31, 5-12.—m Gn 32, 24-29; 1 Tm 4, 8.—n 13f: Gn 37—45.—o Gn 39, 7-10.—p Ex 3, 9; 14, 30; 19, 6.—q Wis 1, 4; 7, 27; Ex 4, 10; Ps 76, 13.—r 17ff; Wis 14, 3; 19, 7; Ex 13, 21f; 14—15; Pss 77, 20f; 78, 13. 53; Is 4, 5f.—s Ex 12, 35f; 15, 1-21.—t Ex 4, 10-15; Ps 8, 3; Mt 11, 25.—u Dt 2, 7; Hos 12, 14.

10, 3: Cain.

10, 4: Noah.

10, 5: Abraham.

10, 6: Lot. *Pentapolis:* the five cities, including Sodom; cf Gn 14, 2.

10, 7: *Disbelieving soul:* Lot's wife; cf Gn 19, 26.

10, 10ff: Jacob.

10, 12: *Devotion to God:* in the Greek this signifies "piety" or "religion," and is the equivalent of the Hebrew "fear of the Lord"; cf Prv 1, 7.

10, 13f: Joseph.

10, 16: Moses.

10, 19: *Cast them up:* their bodies, on the shore.

CHAPTER 11

1 She made their affairs prosper through the holy prophet.^u

III: SPECIAL PROVIDENCE OF GOD DURING THE EXODUS

Introduction

7 They journeyed through the uninhabited desert,*
and in solitudes they pitched their tents;[v]

3 they withstood enemies and took vengeance on their foes.[w]

4 When they thirsted, they called upon you,
and water was given them from the sheer rock,
assuagement for their thirst from the hard stone.

5 For by the things through which their foes were punished
they in their need were benefited.[x]

First Example: Water Punishes the Egyptians and Benefits the Israelites

6 Instead of a spring, when the perennial river*
was troubled with impure blood[y]

7 as a rebuke to the decree for the slaying of infants,
You gave them abundant water in an unhoped-for way,

8 once you had shown by the thirst they then had
how you punished their adversaries.

9 For when they had been tried, though only mildly chastised,[z]
they recognized how the wicked, condemned in anger, were being tormented.

11 Both those afar off and those close by were afflicted:[a]

10 the latter you tested, admonishing them as a father;
the former as a stern king you probed and condemned.

12 For a twofold grief took hold of them[b]
and a groaning at the remembrance of the ones who had departed.

13 For when they heard that the cause of their own torments
was a benefit to these others, they recognized the LORD.

14 Him who of old had been cast out in exposure they indeed mockingly rejected;
but in the end of events, they marveled at him,
since their thirst proved unlike that of the just.[c]

Second Example: Animals Punish the Egyptians and Benefit the Israelites

15 And in return for their senseless, wicked thoughts,
which misled them into worshiping dumb* serpents and worthless insects,
You sent upon them swarms of dumb creatures for vengeance;[d]

16 that they might recognize that a man is punished by the very things through which he sins.[e]

Digression on God's Mercy

17 For not without means was your almighty hand,[f]
that had fashioned the universe from formless matter,
to send upon them a drove of bears or fierce lions,

18 Or new-created, wrathful, unknown beasts
to breathe forth fiery breath,
Or pour out roaring smoke,
or flash terrible sparks from their eyes.

19 Not only could these attack and completely destroy them;
even their frightful appearance itself could slay.

20 Even without these, they could have been killed at a single blast,
pursued by retribution
and winnowed out by your mighty spirit;
But you have disposed all things by measure and number and weight.[g]

21 For with you great strength abides always;
who can resist the might of your arm?[h]

22 Indeed, before you the whole universe is as a grain from a balance,*

v 2ff: Ex 17, 2-6; Nm 20, 1-13; Pss 63, 2; 107, 4-7; Jer 2, 6.—w Ex 17, 8-16; Nm 21, 1ff. 21-35; 31, 1-12; Ps 118, 10ff.—x Wis 16, 1f.—y 6ff: Wis 18, 5; Ex 1, 22; 7, 17-24.—z 9ff: Wis 3, 5; 16, 3f; Dt 8, 2-5; Ps 6, 2; Prv 3, 12; 2 Mc 6, 12-16.—a Ps 6, 2.—b 12f: Wis 16, 8; Ex 14, 4. 18.—c Ex 2, 3.—d Wis 12, 23f; 15, 18—16, 1; Ex 7, 26ff.—e Wis 12, 23. 27; Ex 10, 16; Prv 1, 31f; 26, 27.—f 17ff: Wis 12, 8f; 16, 1. 5; Gn 1, 1f; Dt 32, 24; 2 Kgs 17, 25f; Hos 13, 4-8.—g Jb 4, 9.—h Wis 12, 12; 2 Chr 20, 6.

11, 2ff: Few verses in these later chapters can be fully understood without consulting the passages in the Mosaic books which are indicated in the cross references. The theme of this part of the book is expressed in Wis 11, 5, and is illustrated in the following chapters by five examples drawn from Exodus events.

11, 6ff: *The perennial river:* the Nile; the contrast is between the first plague of Egypt (Ex 7, 17-24) and the water drawn from the rock in Horeb (Ex 17, 5-7; Nm 20, 8-11).

11, 15: *Dumb:* that is, irrational.

11, 22: *Grain from a balance:* a tiny particle used for weighing on sensitive scales.

or a drop of morning dew come down
upon the earth.[i]
23 But you have mercy on all, because you
can do all things;
and you overlook the sins of men that
they may repent.[j]
24 For you love all things that are
and loathe nothing that you have
made;
for what you hated, you would not
have fashioned.[k]
25 And how could a thing remain, unless
you willed it;
or be preserved, had it not been
called forth by you?[l]
26 But you spare all things, because they
are yours, O LORD and lover of
souls,[m]

CHAPTER 12

1 for your imperishable spirit is in all
things![n]
2 Therefore you rebuke offenders little by
little,
warn them, and remind them of the
sins they are committing,
that they may abandon their wickedness and believe in you, O LORD!
3 For, truly, the ancient inhabitants of
your holy land,[o]
4 whom you hated for deeds most
odious—
Works of witchcraft and impious sacrifices;
5 a cannibal feast of human flesh
and of blood, from the midst
of . . .*—
These merciless murderers of children,
6 and parents who took with their own
hands defenseless lives,[p]
You willed to destroy by the hands of
our fathers,
7 that the land that is dearest of all to
you

might receive a worthy colony of
God's children.[q]
8 But even these, as they were men, you
spared,
and sent wasps as forerunners of your
army
that they might exterminate them by
degrees.[r]
9 Not that you were without power to
have the wicked vanquished in battle by the just,
or wiped out at once by terrible
beasts or by one decisive word;[s]
10 But condemning them bit by bit, you
gave them space for repentance.
You were not unaware that their race
was wicked
and their malice ingrained,[t]
And that their dispositions would never
change;
11 for they were a race accursed from
the beginning.
Neither out of fear for anyone
did you grant amnesty for their sins.[u]
12 For who can say to you, "What have
you done?"
or who can oppose your decree?
Or when peoples perish, who can challenge you, their maker;
or who can come into your presence
as vindicator of unjust men?[v]
13 For neither is there any god besides you
who have the care of all,
that you need show you have not unjustly condemned;[w]
14 Nor can any king or prince confront
you on behalf of those you have
punished.[x]
15 But as you are just, you govern all
things justly;
you regard it as unworthy of your
power
to punish one who has incurred no
blame.[y]
16 For your might is the source of justice;
your mastery over all things makes
you lenient to all.[z]
17 For you show your might when the perfection of your power is disbelieved;*
and in those who know you, you rebuke temerity.[a]
18 But though you are master of might,
you judge with clemency,
and with much lenience you govern
us;
for power, whenever you will, attends you.

i Hos 13, 3.—j Wis 12, 10; Dt 9, 27; Acts 17, 30; Rom 2, 4;
11, 32; 2 Pt 3, 9.—k Ps 145, 9.—l Is 41, 4.—m Wis 12, 16; Is
63, 9.—n Wis 1, 7.—o 3ff: Wis 14, 23; Dt 18, 9-12; Pss 5, 6;
106, 28. 34-39; Jer 19, 4f; Ez 16, 3. 20f. 36.—p Nm 33, 52.—q
Dt 11, 12.—r Ex 23, 28ff; Dt 7, 17-24.—s Wis 11, 18; 18, 15;
Nm 16, 21.—t Wis 11, 23; Ps 55, 20; Sir 16, 9.—u Gn 9, 25.—v
2 Sm 16, 10; Eccl 8, 4; Sir 46, 19; Is 45, 9; Dn 4, 32; Rom 9,
19ff.—w Wis 6, 7; Dt 3, 24; 32, 39; Is 44, 6. 8.—x Jer 49, 19;
50, 44.—y Gn 18, 23ff; Dt 32, 4.—z Wis 2, 11; 11, 26; Ps 103,
19.—a Wis 15, 2f; Ex 9, 16.

12, 5: *And of blood, from the midst of . . . :* this line is
obscure in the current Greek text and in all extant translations.
Either one or two words would complete it. The horrible crimes
here spoken of (cf Wis 14, 23) were not unheard of in the ancient
pagan world.
12, 17: The brunt of God's anger and vindictive justice is borne
by those who know him and yet defy his authority and might. Cf
Wis 1, 2; 15, 2, but also Wis 12, 27; 18, 13.

Wis

¹⁹ And you taught your people, by these
 deeds,^b
 that those who are just must be kind;
And you gave your sons good ground
 for hope
 that you would permit repentance for
 their sins.

²⁰ For these were enemies of your ser-
 vants, doomed to death;
 yet, while you punished them with
 such solicitude and pleading,
 granting time and opportunity to
 abandon wickedness,

²¹ With what exactitude you judged your
 sons,
 to whose fathers you gave the sworn
 covenants of goodly promises!^c

²² Us, therefore, you chastise, and our
 enemies with a thousand blows you
 punish,
 that we may think earnestly of your
 goodness when we judge,
 and, when being judged, may look
 for mercy.

Second Example Resumed

²³ Hence those unjust also, who lived a life
 of folly,
 you tormented through their own
 abominations.^d

²⁴ For they went far astray in the paths of
 error,
 taking for gods the worthless and disgusting among beasts,
 deceived like senseless infants.^e

²⁵ Therefore as though upon unreasoning
 children,
 you sent your judgment on them as a
 mockery;^f

²⁶ But they who took no heed of punish-
 ment which was but child's play
 were to experience a condemnation
 worthy of God.

²⁷ For in the things through which they
 suffered distress,
 since they were tortured by the very
 things they deemed gods,
 They saw and recognized the true God
 whom before they had refused to
 know;
 with this, their final condemnation
 came upon them.^g

CHAPTER 13

Digression on False Worship

A. NATURE WORSHIP

¹ For all men were by nature foolish who
 were in ignorance of God,

and who from the good things seen
 did not succeed in knowing him
 who is,*
 and from studying the works did not
 discern the artisan;^h

² But either fire, or wind, or the swift air,
 or the circuit of the stars, or the
 mighty water,
 or the luminaries of heaven,* the governors of the world, they considered gods.ⁱ

³ Now if out of joy in their beauty they
 thought them gods,
 let them know how far more excellent
 is the LORD than these;
 for the original source of beauty
 fashioned them.^j

⁴ Or if they were struck by their might
 and energy,
 let them from these things realize
 how much more powerful is he
 who made them.^k

⁵ For from the greatness and the beauty
 of created things
 their original author, by analogy, is
 seen.

⁶ But yet, for these the blame is less;*
For they indeed have gone astray per-
 haps,
 though they seek God and wish to
 find him.

⁷ For they search busily among his
 works,
 but are distracted by what they see,
 because the things seen are fair.

⁸ But again, not even these are pardon-
 able.

⁹ For if they so far succeeded in knowl-
 edge
 that they could speculate about the
 world,
 how did they not more quickly find
 its LORD?

B. IDOLATRY

¹⁰ But doomed are they, and in dead
 things are their hopes,

---

b 19f: Wis 11, 23; Sir 17, 24.—c Wis 18, 22; Gn 50 24; Dt 7,
6-14; Ps 105, 8ff.—d Wis 11, 16; 16, 1.—e Dt 11, 28; Jer 5, 28;
Rom 1, 23.—f Jer 4, 22.—g Wis 16, 16; Ex 14, 4. 28.—h Acts
14, 17; Eph 4, 17ff.—i Gn 1, 14-19; Dt 4, 19; Jb 31, 26ff.—j Ps
8, 4.—k Jer 10, 2; Bar 6, 39.

13, 1: *Him who is:* the Hebrew sacred name of God; cf Ex 3,
14.
 13, 2: *Luminaries of heaven:* the Latin interprets, "sun and
moon"; *governors:* cf Gn 1, 16.
 13, 6: *The blame is less:* the greater blame is incurred by
those mentioned in Wis 13, 10 and 15, 14ff.

who termed gods things made by human hands:
Gold and silver, the product of art, and likenesses of beasts,
or useless stone, the work of an ancient hand.*l*

The Carpenter and Wooden Idols

11 A carpenter may saw out a suitable tree*m*
and skillfully scrape off all its bark,
And deftly plying his art,
produce something fit for daily use,*n*
12 and use up the refuse from his handiwork in preparing his food, and have his fill;
13 Then the good-for-nothing refuse from these remnants,
crooked wood grown full of knots,
he takes and carves to occupy his spare time.*o*
This wood he models with listless skill,
and patterns it on the image of a man
14 or makes it resemble some worthless beast.
When he has daubed it with red and crimsoned its surface with red stain,
and daubed over every blemish in it,*p*
15 He makes a fitting shrine for it
and puts it on the wall, fastening it with a nail.*q*
16 Thus lest it fall down he provides for it,
knowing that it cannot help itself;
for, truly, it is an image and needs help.*r*
17 But when he prays about his goods or marriage or children,*s*
he is not ashamed to address the thing without a soul.
And for vigor he invokes the powerless;
18 and for life he entreats the dead;
And for aid he beseeches the wholly incompetent,
and about travel, something that cannot even walk.
19 And for profit in business and success with his hands

he asks facility of a thing with hands completely inert.

CHAPTER 14

1 Again, one preparing for a voyage and about to traverse the wild waves
cries out to wood more unsound than the boat that bears him.*t*
2 For the urge for profits devised this latter,
and Wisdom the artificer produced it.
3 But your providence, O Father! guides it,
for you have furnished even in the sea a road,
and through the waves a steady path,*u*
4 Showing that you can save from any danger,
so that even one without skill may embark.*v*
5 But you will that the products of your Wisdom be not idle;
therefore men trust their lives even to frailest wood,
and have been safe crossing the surge on a raft.*w*
6 For of old, when the proud giants were being destroyed,
the hope of the universe, who took refuge on a raft,*
left to the world a future for his race,
under the guidance of your hand.*x*
7 For blest is the wood through which justice comes about;*
8 but the handmade idol is accursed, and its maker as well:
he for having produced it, and it, because though corruptible, it was termed a god.*y*
9 Equally odious to God are the evildoer and his evil deed;
10 and the thing made shall be punished with its contriver.
11 Therefore upon the idols of the nations shall a visitation come,
since they have become abominable amid God's works,
Snares for the souls of men
and a trap for the feet of the senseless.*z*

The Origin and Evils of Idolatry

12 For the source of wantonness is the devising of idols;

l Wis 3, 11; 15, 5. 17; Dt 4, 25-28; 7, 25; 27, 15; Ps 115, 4; Hos 14, 4; Acts 17, 29.—m 11-19: Is 44, 9-20.—n Wis 15, 7; Bar 6, 58.—o Dt 4, 16.—p Jer 10, 9.—q Is 40, 20; 41, 7; 44, 13.—r 1 Sm 5, 3ff; Bar 6, 57.—s 17ff: Wis 15, 15.—t Is 46, 7.— u Ps 107, 23-30; Is 43, 16.—v Wis 16, 8.—w Wis 10, 4.—x Gn 6, 4; 17, 1ff. 21f.—y Rom 1, 23.—z Wis 3, 7; Ex 23, 33; Nm 33, 4; Jos 23, 13; Ps 115, 4; Jer 6, 15; 10, 15; 46, 25; Hos 9, 15.

14, 6: Noah.
14, 7: Often applied to the cross of our Lord.

and their invention was a corruption of life. [a]

13 For in the beginning they were not, nor shall they continue forever; [b]

14 for by the vanity of men they came into the world, and therefore a sudden end is devised for them.

15 For a father, afflicted with untimely mourning, made an image of the child so quickly taken from him, And now honored as a god what was formerly a dead man and handed down to his subjects mysteries and sacrifices.

16 Then, in time, the impious practice gained strength and was observed as law, and graven things were worshiped by princely decrees. [c]

17 Men who lived so far away that they could not honor him in his presence copied the appearance of the distant king And made a public image of him they wished to honor, out of zeal to flatter him when absent, as though present.

18 And to promote this observance among those to whom it was strange, the artisan's ambition provided a stimulus.

19 For he, mayhap in his determination to please the ruler, labored over the likeness to the best of his skill; [d]

20 And the masses, drawn by the charm of the workmanship, soon thought he should be worshiped who shortly before was honored as a man. [e]

21 And this became a snare for mankind, that men enslaved to either grief or tyranny conferred the incommunicable Name on sticks and stones.

22 Then it was not enough for them to err in their knowledge of God; [f] but even though they live in a great war of ignorance, they call such evils peace. [g]

23 For while they celebrate either child-slaying sacrifices or clandestine mysteries, or frenzied carousals in unheard-of rites, [h]

24 They no longer safeguard either lives or pure wedlock; but each either waylays and kills his neighbor, or aggrieves him by adultery.

25 And all is confusion—blood and murder, theft and guile, [i] corruption, faithlessness, turmoil, perjury,

26 Disturbance of good men, neglect of gratitude, besmirching of souls, unnatural lust, disorder in marriage, adultery and shamelessness.

27 For the worship of infamous idols is the reason and source and extremity of all evil. [j]

28 For they either go mad with enjoyment, or prophesy lies, or live lawlessly or lightly forswear themselves. [k]

29 For as their trust is in soulless idols, they expect no harm when they have sworn falsely.

30 But on both counts shall justice overtake them: because they thought ill of God and devoted themselves to idols, [l] and because they deliberately swore false oaths, despising piety.*

31 For not the might of those that are sworn by but the retribution of sinners ever follows upon the transgression of the wicked.*

CHAPTER 15

1 But you, our God, are good and true, slow to anger, and governing all with mercy. [m]

2 For even if we sin, we are yours, and know your might; but we will not sin, knowing that we belong to you. [n]

3 For to know you well is complete justice, and to know your might is the root of immortality. [o]

---

a Rom 1, 23ff.—b Is 2, 18.—c Dn 3, 4ff; 1 Mc 1, 47-50.—d Is 44, 12f LXX.—e Wis 15, 4.—f 22-31: Jer 2, 20; 3, 1-25; Hos 4, 1f. 9-19; Rom 1, 26-31; Gal 5, 19ff; 1 Tm 1, 9f.—g Jer 6, 14; Ez 13, 10.—h Wis 12, 4f; 14, 15; Is 57, 5.—i 25f: Jer 7, 8f; 22, 17.—j Ex 23, 13.—k Jer 5, 31; 29, 26.—l Wis 1, 1. 8; 11, 20; Jer 5, 2. 7.—m Ex 34, 6f; Pss 86, 5. 15; 145, 8. 9. 14.—n Jb 10, 14f LXX.—o Wis 3, 15; Jn 17, 3.

14, 30: *Piety:* the sanctity of oaths.
14, 31: Perjury is a form of deceit which calls for punishment even though it be practiced in the name of a lifeless idol.

⁴ For neither did the evil creation of
men's fancy deceive us,
nor the fruitless labor of painters,ᵖ
A form smeared with varied colors,
⁵   the sight of which arouses yearning in
the senseless man,
till he longs for the inanimate form of
a dead image.
⁶ Lovers of evil things, and worthy of
such hopes
are they who make them and long for
them and worship them.�q

The Potter's Clay Idols

⁷ For truly the potter, laboriously working the soft earth,
molds for our service each several
article:
Both the vessels that serve for clean
purposes
and their opposites, all alike;
As to what shall be the use of each vessel of either class
the worker in clay is the judge.ʳ
⁸ And with misspent toil he molds a
meaningless god from the selfsame
clay;
though he himself shortly before was
made from the earth
And after a little, is to go whence he was
taken,
when the life that was lent him is demanded back.ˢ
⁹ But his concern is not that he is to die
nor that his span of life is brief;
Rather, he vies with goldsmiths and silversmiths
and emulates molders of bronze,
and takes pride in modeling counter-
feits.ᵗ
¹⁰ Ashes his heart is! more worthless than
earth is his hope,ᵘ
and more ignoble than clay his life;
¹¹ Because he knew not the one who
fashioned him,
and breathed into him a quickening
soul,

and infused a vital spirit.ᵛ
¹² Instead, he esteemed our life a play-
thing,
and our span of life a holiday for
gain;
"For one must," says he, "make profit
every way, be it even out of evil."ʷ
¹³ For this man more than any knows that
he is sinning,
when out of earthen stuff he creates
fragile vessels and idols alike.
¹⁴ But all quite senseless, and worse than
childish in mind,
are the enemies of your people who
enslaved them.ˣ
¹⁵ For they esteemed all the idols of the
nations, gods,
which have no use of the eyes for
vision,
nor nostrils to snuff the air,
Nor ears to hear
nor fingers on their hands for feeling;
even their feet are useless to walk
with.ʸ
¹⁶ For a man made them;ᶻ
one whose spirit has been lent him
fashioned them.
For no man succeeds in fashioning a
god like himself;
¹⁷   being mortal, he makes a dead thing
with his lawless hands.
For he is better than the things he worships;
he at least lives, but never they.

Second Example Resumed

¹⁸ And besides, they worship* the most
loathsome beasts—ᵃ
for compared as to folly, these are
worse than the rest,*
¹⁹ Nor for their looks are they good or desirable beasts,
but they have escaped both the approval of God and his blessing.ᵇ

CHAPTER 16

¹ Therefore they* were fittingly punished
by similar creatures,
and were tormented by a swarm of in-
sects.ᶜ
² Instead of this punishment, you benefited your people
with a novel dish, the delight they
craved,
by providing quail for their food;ᵈ
³ That those others, when they desired
food,

p Wis 13, 14.—q Ps 115, 8.—r Wis 13, 11; Jer 18, 3f; Rom 9,
21; 2 Tm 2, 20f.—s Gn 3, 19; Eccl 12, 7.—t Bar 6, 46.—u Jb 13,
12 LXX.—v Gn 2, 7; Zec 12, 1.—w Jas 4, 13f.—x Ex 1, 13.—y
Wis 14, 11; Dt 4, 28; Pss 115, 4-7; 135, 15ff.—z 16f: Wis 13,
10.—a Wis 11, 15; 12, 24.—b Gn 1, 25; 3, 14.—c Wis 11, 15f;
12, 23. 27; Ex 7, 27; 8, 12. 17.—d Wis 11, 13; 19, 11f; Ex 16,
13; Nm 11, 31f; Ps 105, 40.

15, 18ff: The author here returns to the main theme of chapters
11—19, which was interrupted by the digression 13, 1—15, 17.

15, 18: *For . . . rest:* this may mean that the creatures worshiped by the Egyptians (e.g., crocodiles, serpents, scarabs, etc.)
were more patently lacking in intelligence than the general run of
beasts; cf Wis 11, 15; 12, 24.

16, 1: *They:* the Egyptian idolaters.

since the creatures sent to plague
them were so loathsome,
should be turned from even the craving of necessities,
While these, after a brief period of pri-
vation,
partook of a novel dish. *e*

4 For upon those oppressors, inexorable
want had to come;
but these needed only be shown how
their enemies were being tormented. *f*

5 For when the dire venom of beasts came
upon them *g*
and they were dying from the bite of
crooked serpents,
your anger endured not to the end.

6 But as a warning, for a short time they
were terrorized,
though they had a sign* of salvation,
to remind them of the precept of
your law.

7 For he who turned toward it was saved,
not by what he saw,
but by you, the savior of all.

8 And by this also you convinced our foes
that you are he who delivers from all
evil. *h*

9 For the bites of locusts and of flies slew
them,
and no remedy was found to save
their lives
because they deserved to be punished
by such means; *i*

10 But not even the fangs of poisonous reptiles overcame your sons,
for your mercy brought the antidote
to heal them. *j*

11 For as a reminder of your injunctions,
they were stung,
and swiftly they were saved,
Lest they should fall into deep forget-
fulness
and become unresponsive to your
beneficence. *k*

12 For indeed, neither herb nor application cured them,
but your all-healing word, O LORD! *l*

13 For you have dominion over life and
death; *m*
you lead down to the gates of the
nether world, and lead back.

14 Man, however, slays in his malice,
but when the spirit has come away, it
does not return,
nor can he bring back the soul once it
is confined.*

15 But your hand none can escape.

Third Example: A Rain of Manna for Israel instead of the Plague of Storms

16 For the wicked who refused to know
you
were punished by the might of your
arm,
Pursued by unwonted rains and hail-
storms and unremitting down-
pours,
and consumed by fire. *n*

17 For against all expectation, in water
which quenches anything,
the fire grew more active;
For the universe fights on behalf of the
just. *o*

18 For now the flame was tempered *p*
so that the beasts might not be burnt
up that were sent upon the wicked,
but that these might see and know
they were struck by the judgment
of God;

19 And again, even in the water, fire
blazed beyond its strength
so as to consume the produce of the
wicked land.

20 Instead of this, you nourished your people with food of angels
and furnished them bread from heav-
en, ready to hand, untoiled-for,
endowed with all delights and con-
forming to every taste. *q*

21 For this substance of yours revealed
your sweetness toward your children,
and serving the desire of him who received it,
was blended to whatever flavor each
one wished. *r*

22 Yet snow and ice* withstood fire and
were not melted,
that they might know that their
enemies' fruits
Were consumed by a fire that blazed in
the hail
and flashed lightning in the rain. *s*

---

e Wis 11, 15; Ex 8, 10; 16, 3.—f Wis 11, 8f.—g 5f: Nm 21, 4-
9; Dt 32, 24; Jer 8, 7 LXX.—h Gn 48, 16; 2 Mc 1, 24f.—i Ex 8,
16-28; 10, 4-19; Pss 78, 45f; 105, 31. 34; Rv 9, 1-11.—j Dt 32,
33.—k Ps 78, 11.—l Ex 15, 26.—m 13ff: Dt 32, 39; 1 Sm 2, 6;
Tb 13, 2; Ps 78, 34. 39; Eccl 8, 8; Dn 5, 19; 2 Mc 6, 26; 7, 23.—
n Wis 11, 21; 12, 27; Ex 5, 2; 9, 29-34.—o Wis 10, 20; 19, 20;
Ex 9, 23-28; 2 Mc 8, 36; 14, 34.—p 18f: Wis 19, 20f.—q Ex 16,
4; Nm 11, 8; Ps 78, 24f; Jn 6, 31.—r Ps 34, 9.—s Ex 9, 25-31;
10, 12; Ps 148, 8.

16, 6: *Sign:* the brazen serpent; cf Nm 21, 9.
16, 14: *Confined:* in the nether world, in limbo.
16, 22: *Snow and ice:* the manna; cf Wis 16, 27; 19, 21.

23 But this fire, again, that the just might
be nourished,
forgot even its proper strength;[t]
24 For your creation, serving you, its
maker,
grows tense for punishment against
the wicked,
but is relaxed in benefit for those who
trust in you.[u]
25 Therefore at that very time, transformed in all sorts of ways,
it was serving your all-nourishing
bounty
according to what they needed and
desired;
26 That your sons whom you loved might
learn, O LORD,
that it is not the various kinds of
fruits that nourish man,
but it is your word that preserves
those who believe you![v]
27 For what was not destroyed by fire,
when merely warmed by a momentary sunbeam, melted;[w]
28 So that men might know that one must
give you thanks before the sunrise,
and turn to you at daybreak.[x]
29 For the hope of the ingrate melts like a
wintry frost
and runs off like useless water.[y]

CHAPTER 17

Fourth Example: Darkness Afflicts the Egyptians, While the Israelites Have Light

1 For great are your judgments, and
hardly to be described;
therefore the unruly souls were
wrong.[z]
2 For when the lawless thought to enslave
the holy nation,
shackled with darkness, fettered by
the long night,
they lay confined beneath their own
roof as exiles from the eternal providence.[a]
3 For they who supposed their secret sins
were hid[b]

under the dark veil of oblivion
Were scattered in fearful trembling,
terrified by apparitions.
4 For not even their inner chambers kept
them fearless,
for crashing sounds on all sides terrified them,
and mute phantoms with somber
looks appeared.
5 No force, even of fire, was able to give
light,
nor did the flaming brilliance of the
stars
succeed in lighting up that gloomy
night.[c]
6 But only intermittent, fearful fires*
flashed through upon them;
And in their terror they thought beholding these was worse
than the times when that sight was no
longer to be seen.[d]
7 And mockeries of the magic art were in
readiness,
and a jeering reproof of their vaunted
shrewdness.[e]
8 For they who undertook to banish fears
and terrors from the sick soul
themselves sickened with a ridiculous
fear.
9 For even though no monstrous thing
frightened them,
they shook at the passing of insects
and the hissing of reptiles,[f]
10 And perished trembling,
reluctant to face even the air that they
could nowhere escape.
11 For wickedness, of its nature cowardly,
testifies in its own condemnation,
and because of a distressed conscience, always magnifies misfortunes.[g]
12 For fear is nought but the surrender of
the helps that come from reason;
13 and the more one's expectation is of
itself uncertain,
the more one makes of not knowing
the cause that brings on torment.
14 So they, during that night, powerless
though it was,
that had come upon them from the
recesses of a powerless* nether
world,
while all sleeping the same sleep,
15 Were partly smitten by fearsome
apparitions
and partly stricken by their souls'
surrender,

Wis

---

t Wis 19, 21.—u Wis 5, 17. 20; 19, 6; Sir 39, 25ff.—v Dt 8, 3;
Mt 4, 4.—w Ex 16, 21.—x Pss 57, 9f; 92, 3.—y Wis 5, 14; 2 Sm
14, 14.—z Ex 6, 6 LXX.—a Wis 18, 4; Ex 1, 13f; 19, 6; 10,
21ff.—b 3f: Wis 1, 7f; 10, 8; 18, 17.—c Wis 10, 17; Jer 23, 24
LXX.—d Ex 9, 23f.—e Wis 12, 25f; Ex 7, 11f. 22; 8, 3; 9, 11; 10,
2.—f Wis 16, 1; Jer 26, 22 LXX.—g Wis 4, 6; 10, 7; Rom 2, 15.

17, 6: *Fires:* that is, lightnings.
17, 14: *Powerless:* the nether world, the home of darkness,
has no power against God, nor even against such men as do not
submit to it of themselves; cf Wis 1, 14ff.

for fear came upon them, sudden and unexpected.[h]

16 Thus, then, whoever was there fell into that unbarred prison and was kept confined.[i]

17 For whether one was a farmer, or a shepherd,
or a worker at tasks in the wasteland,
Taken unawares, he served out the inescapable sentence;

18 for all were bound by the one bond of darkness.[j]
And were it only the whistling wind,
or the melodious song of birds in the spreading branches,
Or the steady sound of rushing water,

19 or the rude crash of overthrown rocks,
Or the unseen gallop of bounding animals
or the roaring cry of the fiercest beasts,
Or an echo resounding from the hollow of the hills,
these sounds, inspiring terror, paralyzed them.

20 For the whole world shone with brilliant light[k]
and continued its works without interruption;

21 Over them alone was spread oppressive night,
an image of the darkness that next should come upon them;
yet they were to themselves more burdensome than the darkness.

CHAPTER 18

1 But your holy ones had very great light;
And those others, who heard their voices but did not see their forms,
since now they themselves had suffered, called them blest;

2 And because they who formerly had been wronged did not harm them, they thanked them,
and pleaded with them, for the sake of the difference between them.*

3 Instead of this, you furnished the flaming pillar
which was a guide on the unknown way,
and the mild sun for an honorable migration.[l]

4 For those deserved to be deprived of light and imprisoned by darkness,
who had kept your sons confined

through whom the imperishable light of the law was to be given to the world.[m]

Fifth Example: Death of the Egyptian First-born; the Israelites Are Spared

5 When they determined to put to death the infants of the holy ones,
and when a single boy* had been cast forth but saved,
As a reproof you carried off their multitude of sons
and made them perish all at once in the mighty water.[n]

6 That night was known beforehand to our fathers,
that, with sure knowledge of the oaths in which they put their faith, they might have courage.[o]

7 Your people awaited
the salvation of the just and the destruction of their foes.[p]

8 For when you punished our adversaries,
in this you glorified us whom you had summoned.[q]

9 For in secret the holy children of the good were offering sacrifice
and putting into effect with one accord the divine institution,
That your holy ones should share alike the same good things and dangers,[r]
having previously sung the praises of the fathers.*

10 But the discordant cry of their enemies responded,
and the piteous wail of mourning for children was borne to them.[s]

11 And the slave was smitten with the same retribution as his master;
even the plebeian suffered the same as the king.[t]

12 And all alike by a single death had countless dead;
For the living were not even sufficient for the burial,

---

h Ex 11, 9f.—i Wis 18, 4; Ex 10, 23.—j 18f: Lv 26, 36.—k 20f: Ex 10, 23; Is 9, 1; 60, 1ff; 2 Pt 2, 17.—l Ex 13, 21.—m Wis 17, 2; Ps 119, 105; Is 2, 3. 5.—n Wis 11, 7. 14; Ex 1, 16. 22; 2, 3. 6-10; 15, 10; Neh 9, 11.—o Wis 12, 21; Ex 6, 8; 13, 5.—p Ex 14, 13.—q Wis 19, 22; Ex 3, 18; Is 43, 3f.—r Ex 12, 21-28; Sir 44—50.—s Ex 12, 30; Jer 9, 17. 19.—t Ex 11, 5; 12, 29.

18, 2: *The difference between them:* God's distinctive manner of treating the Israelites and the Egyptians according to their respective merits.
18, 5: *Single boy:* Moses.
18, 9: *Praises of the fathers:* cf Sir 44—50; Wis 10.

since at a single instant their nobler offspring were destroyed. [u]

13 For though they disbelieved at every turn on account of sorceries,
at the destruction of the first-born they acknowledged that the people* was God's son. [v]

14 For when peaceful stillness compassed everything
and the night in its swift course was half spent,

15 Your all-powerful word from heaven's royal throne
bounded, a fierce warrior, into the doomed land, [w]

16   bearing the sharp sword of your inexorable decree.
And as he alighted, he filled every place with death;
he still reached to heaven, while he stood upon the earth. [x]

17 Then, forthwith, visions in horrible dreams perturbed them [y]
and unexpected fears assailed them;

18 And cast half-dead, one here, another there,
each was revealing the reason for his dying.

19 For the dreams that disturbed them had proclaimed this beforehand,
lest they perish unaware of why they suffered ill.

20 But the trial of death touched at one time even the just,
and in the desert a plague struck the multitude;
Yet not for long did the anger last. [z]

21 For the blameless man* hastened to be their champion,
bearing the weapon of his special office,
prayer and the propitiation of incense;

He withstood the wrath and put a stop to the calamity,
showing that he was your servant. [a]

22 And he overcame the bitterness
not by bodily strength, not by force of arms;
But by word he overcame the smiter,*
recalling the sworn covenants with their fathers. [b]

23 For when corpses had already fallen one on another in heaps,
he stood in the midst and checked the anger,
and cut off the way to the living. [c]

24 For on his full-length robe was the whole world,
and the glories of the fathers were carved in four rows upon the stones,
and your grandeur* was on the crown upon his head. [d]

25 To these names the destroyer yielded, and these he feared;
for the mere trial of anger was enough. [e]

CHAPTER 19

1 But the wicked, merciless wrath assailed until the end.
For he* knew beforehand what they were yet to do: [f]

2 That though they themselves had agreed to the departure
and had anxiously sent them* on their way,
they would regret it and pursue them. [g]

3 For while they* were still engaged in funeral rites
and were mourning at the burials of the dead,
They adopted another senseless plan;
and those whom they had sent away with entreaty,
they pursued as fugitives. [h]

4 For a compulsion suited to this ending drew them on,
and made them forgetful of what had befallen them,
That they might fill out the torments of their punishment,

5   and your people might experience a glorious* journey
while those others met an extraordinary death.

---

u Nm 33, 4.—v Wis 17, 7; Ex 4, 22f; 12, 12. 29; 13, 2. 13. 15.—w Wis 9, 10; Ex 15, 3.—x 1 Chr 21, 16; Heb 4, 12; Rv 1, 16.—y 17ff: Wis 17, 3f.—z Wis 16, 5; Nm 17, 9-15.—a Nm 16, 7.—b Wis 12, 21; Ex 32, 12f; Ps 20, 8.—c Nm 14, 29f.—d Ex 28, 15-21. 31-38; Sir 45, 8-12; 50, 11.—e 1 Chr 21, 15.—f Ex 14, 4.—g Ex 12, 33; 14, 5. 8.—h Wis 18, 10. 12; Ex 12, 30ff.

18, 13: *People:* the Hebrews.
18, 21: *Blameless man:* Aaron acting according to his office of high priest and intercessor.
18, 22: *Smiter:* the destroying angel; cf v 25.
18, 24: *Glories . . . grandeur:* the name of God and the names of the tribes were inscribed on the high priest's apparel.
19, 1: *He:* i.e., God.
19, 2: *Them:* the Hebrews.
19, 3: *They:* the Egyptians.
19, 5: *Glorious:* more precisely, "wondrous," but the word reflects *glorified* in Wis 18, 8 and 19, 22.

Wis

6 For all creation, in its several kinds, was
   being made over anew,
   serving its natural laws,
   that your children might be pre
   served unharmed.[i]
7 The cloud overshadowed their camp;
   and out of what had before been
   water, dry land was seen emerging:
   Out of the Red Sea an unimpeded road,
   and a grassy plain out of the mighty
   flood.[j]
8 Over this crossed the whole nation sheltered by your hand,
   after they beheld stupendous wonders.
9 For they ranged about like horses,
   and bounded about like lambs,
   praising you, O LORD! their deliverer.[k]
10 For they were still mindful of what had
   happened in their sojourn:
   how instead of the young of animals
   the land brought forth gnats,
   and instead of fishes the river
   swarmed with countless frogs.[l]
11 And later they saw also a new kind of
   bird[m]
   when, prompted by desire, they
   asked for pleasant foods;
12 For to appease them quail came to them
   from the sea.
13 And the punishments came upon the
   sinners
   only after forewarnings from the violence of the thunderbolts.
   For they justly suffered for their own
   misdeeds,
   since indeed they treated their guests
   with the more grievous* hatred.[n]
14 For those others did not receive unfamiliar visitors,[o]
   but these were enslaving beneficent
   guests.
15 And not that only; but what punishment was to be theirs*
   since they received strangers unwillingly!

16 Yet these, after welcoming them with
   festivities,
   oppressed with awful toils
   those who now shared with them the
   same rights.[p]
17 And they were struck with blindness,
   as those others had been at the portals
   of the just—
   When, surrounded by yawning darkness,
   each sought the entrance of his own
   gate.[q]
18 For the elements, in variable harmony
   among themselves,
   like strings of the harp, produce new
   melody,
   while the flow of music steadily persists.
   And this can be perceived exactly from
   a review of what took place.
19 For land creatures were changed into
   water creatures,
   and those that swam went over on to
   the land.
20 Fire in water maintained its own
   strength,[r]
   and water forgot its quenching nature;
21 Flames, by contrast, neither consumed
   the flesh
   of the perishable animals that went
   about in them,
   nor melted the icelike, quick-melting
   kind of ambrosial food.
22 For every way, O LORD! you magnified
   and glorified your people;
   unfailing, you stood by them in every
   time and circumstance.[s]

i Wis 5, 17; 16, 24.—j Ex 14, 21-29.—k Wis 10, 20; 16, 8; Ex
15, 1-18; Ps 114, 4-6.—l Ex 7, 27ff; 8, 12-15; Ps 105, 30f.—m
11f: Wis 16, 2; Ps 78, 18.—n 2 Mc 7, 18. 32.—o 14f: Gn 15, 13;
Ex 2, 22.—p Gn 45, 17-20; 47, 4ff; Ex 1, 11.—q Wis 17, 2; Gn
19, 11.—r 20f: Wis 16, 17ff. 22f. 27.—s Wis 18, 8; Lv 26, 44;
Ps 126, 3.

19, 13: *More grievous:* than that of the people of Sodom; cf
Gn 19.
19, 15: *Theirs:* the people of Sodom.

THE BOOK OF SIRACH
(ECCLESIASTICUS)

The Book of Sirach derives its 'name from the author, Jesus, son of Eleazar, son of Sirach *(50, 27). Its earliest title seems to have been "Wisdom of the Son of Sirach." The designation "Liber Ecclesiasticus," meaning "Church Book," appended to some Greek and Latin manuscripts was due to the extensive use which the church made of this book in presenting moral teaching to catechumens and to the faithful.*

The author, a sage who lived in Jerusalem, was thoroughly imbued with love for the law, the priesthood, the temple, and divine worship. As a wise and experienced observer of life he addressed himself to his contemporaries with the motive of helping them to maintain religious faith and integrity through study of the holy books, and through tradition.

The book contains numerous maxims formulated with care, grouped by affinity, and dealing with a variety of subjects such as the individual, the family, and the community in their relations with one another and with God. It treats of friendship, education, poverty and wealth, the law, religious worship, and many other matters which reflect the religious and social customs of the time.

Written in Hebrew between 200 and 175 B.C., the text was translated into Greek sometime after 132 B.C. by the author's grandson, who also wrote a Foreword which contains information about the book, the author, and the translator himself. Until the close of the nineteenth century Sirach was known only in translations, of which this Greek rendering was the most important. From it the Latin version was made. Between 1896 and 1900, again in 1931, and several times since 1956, manuscripts were discovered containing in all about two thirds of the Hebrew text, which agrees substantially with the Greek. One such text, from Masada, is pre-Christian in date.

Though not included in the Hebrew Bible after the first century A.D., nor accepted by Protestants, the Book of Sirach has always been recognized by the Catholic Church as divinely inspired and canonical. The Foreword, though not inspired, is placed in the Bible because of its antiquity and importance.

The contents of Sirach are of a discursive nature not easily divided into separate parts. Chapters 1—43 deal largely with moral instruction; chapters 44, 1—50, 24 contain a eulogy of the heroes of Israel and some of the patriarchs. There are two appendices in which the author expresses his gratitude to God, and appeals to the unlearned to acquire true wisdom.

The church uses the Book of Sirach extensively in her liturgy.

FOREWORD

Many important truths have been handed down to us through the law, the prophets, and the later authors; and for these the instruction and wisdom of Israel merit praise. Now, those who are familiar with these truths must not only understand them themselves but, as lovers of wisdom, be able, in speech and in writing, to help others less familiar. Such a one was my grandfather, Jesus, who, having devoted himself for a long time to the diligent study of the law, the prophets, and the rest of the books[1] of our ancestors, and having developed a thorough familiarity with them, was moved to write something himself in the nature of instruction and wisdom, in order that those who love wisdom might, by acquainting themselves with what he too had written, make even greater progress in living in conformity with the divine law.

You therefore are now invited to read in it a spirit of attentive good will, with indulgence for any apparent failure on our part, despite earnest efforts, in the interpretation of particular passages. For words spoken originally in Hebrew are not as effective when they are translated into another language. That is true not only of this book but of the law itself, the prophets and the rest of the books, which differ no little when they are read in the original.

I arrived in Egypt in the thirty-eighth year of the reign of King Euergetes,[2] and while there, I found a reproduction of our valuable teaching.[3] I therefore considered myself in duty bound to devote some diligence and industry to the translation of this book. Many sleepless hours of close application have I devoted in the interval to finishing the book for publication, for the benefit of those living abroad who wish to acquire wisdom and are disposed to live their lives according to the standards of the law.

---

[1] *The law, the prophets and the rest of the books:* the Sacred Scriptures of the Old Testament written before the time of Sirach, according to the threefold division of the present Hebrew Bible.

[2] *Thirty-eighth . . . Euergetes:* 132 B.C. The reference is to Ptolemy VII, Physkon Euergetes II (170-163; 145-117 B.C.).

[3] *Reproduction . . . teaching:* may refer to the Septuagint (Greek) translation of Hebrew wisdom writings predating Sirach.

THE WISDOM OF SIRACH

CHAPTER 1

Praise of Wisdom*

1 All wisdom* comes from the LORD
and with him it remains forever.*a*

2 The sand of the seashore, the drops of
rain,
the days of eternity: who can number
these?

3 Heaven's height, earth's breadth,
the depths of the abyss: who can explore these?

4 Before all things else wisdom was
created;
and prudent understanding, from
eternity.

5 To whom has wisdom's root been revealed?
Who knows her subtleties?*b*

6 There is but one, wise and truly awe-inspiring,
seated upon his throne:

7 It is the LORD; he created her,
has seen her and taken note of her.*c*

8 He has poured her forth upon all his
works,
upon every living thing according to
his bounty;
he has lavished her upon his friends.

9 * Fear of the LORD* is glory and splendor,
gladness and a festive crown.

10 Fear of the LORD warms the heart,
giving gladness and joy and length of
days.

11 He who fears the LORD will have a
happy end;
even on the day of his death he will
be blessed.

12 The beginning of wisdom is fear of the
LORD,
which is formed with the faithful in
the womb.*d*

13 With devoted men was she created from
of old,
and with their children her beneficence abides.

14 Fullness of wisdom is fear of the LORD;
she inebriates men with her fruits.*e*

15 Her entire house she fills with choice
foods,
her granaries with her harvest.

16 Wisdom's garland is fear of the LORD,
with blossoms of peace and perfect
health.*f*

17 Knowledge and full understanding she
showers down;
she heightens the glory of those who
possess her.

18 The root of wisdom is fear of the LORD;
her branches are length of days.

19 One cannot justify unjust anger;*
anger plunges a man to his downfall.

20 A patient man need stand firm but for a
time,
and then contentment comes back to
him.

21 For a while he holds back his words,
then the lips of many herald his wisdom.

22 Among wisdom's treasures is the para-
gon of prudence;
but fear of the LORD is an abomination to the sinner.

23 If you desire wisdom, keep the commandments,
and the LORD will bestow her upon
you;

24 For fear of the LORD is wisdom and culture;
loyal humility is his delight.

25 Be not faithless to the fear of the
LORD,*
nor approach it with duplicity of
heart.

26 Play not the hypocrite before men;
over your lips keep watch.

27 Exalt not yourself lest you fall
and bring upon you dishonor;

28 For then the LORD will reveal your
secrets
and publicly cast you down,

29 Because you approached the fear of the
LORD
with your heart full of guile.

a 1 Kgs 3, 9.—b Bar 3, 15.—c Jb 28, 27.—d Jb 28, 28; Ps
111, 10; Prv 1, 7; 9, 10.—e Eccl 12, 13.—f Sir 21, 11.

1, 1-8: The Lord is the source and preserver of wisdom (1); he
created her from eternity, *before all things else* (4-7); all his
works reflect wisdom (2f. 8).

1, 1: *Wisdom:* here the author speaks of true wisdom, namely
God's external revelation of himself. Throughout the book he describes in great detail just what wisdom is; sometimes it is divine;
sometimes it is a synonym for God's law; sometimes it is human.
But the author makes clear that even human wisdom, properly
understood, comes from God.

1, 9-18: Here are described the spiritual and temporal blessings that come during the lifetime of him who fears the Lord, i.e.,
practices true religion.

1, 9: *Fear of the Lord:* see note on Ps 111, 10.

1, 19-22: The disciple of wisdom shuns *unjust* anger which
brings *downfall.* By patience and self-control he preserves calm,
recovers *contentment,* and receives public praise. The sinner, on
the contrary, despises the restraints which religion imposes.

1, 25-29: Infidelity to religion, or the use of it for any but the
single purpose of serving God, is hypocrisy and self-exaltation, deserving of public disgrace.

CHAPTER 2

Duties toward God

¹ My son, when you come to serve the
LORD,*
prepare yourself for trials.ᵍ
² Be sincere of heart and steadfast,
undisturbed in time of adversity.
³ Cling to him, forsake him not;
thus will your future be great.
⁴ Accept whatever befalls you,
in crushing misfortune be patient;
⁵ For in fire gold is tested,
and worthy men in the crucible of
humiliation.ʰ
⁶ Trust God and he will help you;
make straight your ways and hope in
him.
⁷ You who fear the LORD, wait for his
mercy,
turn not away lest you fall.
⁸ You who fear the LORD, trust him,
and your reward will not be lost.
⁹ You who fear the LORD, hope for good
things,
for lasting joy and mercy.
¹⁰ Study the generations long past and
understand;
has anyone hoped in the LORD and
been disappointed?
Has anyone persevered in his fear and
been forsaken?
has anyone called upon him and been
rebuffed?ⁱ
¹¹ Compassionate and merciful is the
LORD;
he forgives sins, he saves in time of
trouble.
¹² Woe to craven hearts and drooping
hands,*

to the sinner who treads a double
path!
¹³ Woe to the faint of heart who trust not,
who therefore will have no shelter!
¹⁴ Woe to you who have lost hope!
what will you do at the visitation of
the LORD?
¹⁵ Those who fear the LORD disobey not
his words;
those who love him keep his ways.ʲ
¹⁶ Those who fear the LORD seek to please
him,
those who love him are filled with his
law.
¹⁷ Those who fear the LORD prepare their
hearts
and humble themselves before him.
¹⁸ Let us fall into the hands of the LORD
and not into the hands of men,
For equal to his majesty
is the mercy that he shows.ᵏ

CHAPTER 3

Duties toward Parents*

¹ Children, pay heed to a father's right;
do so that you may live
² For the LORD sets a father in honor
over his children;
a mother's authority he confirms over
her sons.
³ He who honors his father atones for sins;
⁴ he stores up riches who reveres his
mother.
⁵ He who honors his father is gladdened
by children,
and when he prays he is heard.
⁶ He who reveres his father will live a
long life;
he obeys the LORD who brings comfort to his mother.
⁷ He who fears the LORD honors his
father,
and serves his parents as rulers.
⁸ In word and deed honor your father
that his blessing may come upon
you;ˡ
⁹ For a father's blessing gives a family
firm roots,
but a mother's curse uproots the
growing plant.ᵐ
¹⁰ Glory not in your father's shame,
for his shame is no glory to you!
¹¹ His father's honor is a man's glory;
disgrace for her children, a mother's
shame.
¹² My son, take care of your father when
he is old;
grieve him not as long as he lives.ⁿ

Sir

---

g 2 Tm 3, 12.—h Prv 17, 3; Wis 3, 6; 1 Pt 1, 7.—i Pss 31, 2; 145, 18f.—j Jn 14, 23.—k Sir 18, 3.—l Ex 20, 12; Dt 5, 16; Mt 15, 4; Mk 7, 10; Eph 6, 2.—m Gn 27, 29; 49, 2-27.—n Prv 23, 22.

2, 1-11: Serving God is not without its trials (1); moreover, it must be done with sincerity, steadfastness and fidelity (2f). Misfortune and humiliation merely purify man and prove his worth (4f). Patience and unwavering trust in God are always rewarded with the benefits of God's mercy and of *lasting joy* (6-11).

2, 12-18: A warning to those who compromise their religion in time of affliction; they fail in courage and trust and therefore have no security (12ff). But those who fear the Lord through obedience, reverence, love and humility find his *mercy equal to his majesty* (15-18).

3, 1-16: Besides the virtues that must characterize our conduct toward God, special duties toward our neighbor are enjoined, such as honor and respect toward parents, with corresponding blessings (1-9). Even to old and infirm parents this respect is due (10-13); through it, the sins of children are pardoned (14f). Failure to render respect is blasphemy and merits a curse from God (16). Cf Ex 20, 12; Eph 6, 2f.

¹³ Even if his mind fail, be considerate
with him;
 revile him not in the fullness of your
 strength.
¹⁴ For kindness to a father will not be forgotten,
 it will serve as a sin offering—it will
 take lasting root.
¹⁵ In time of tribulation it will be recalled
 to your advantage,
 like warmth upon frost it will melt
 away your sins.
¹⁶ A blasphemer is he who despises his
 father;
 accursed of his Creator, he who an-
 gers his mother.ᵒ

Humility*

¹⁷ My son, conduct your affairs with
 humility,
 and you will be loved more than a
 giver of gifts.
¹⁸ Humble yourself the more, the greater
 you are,
 and you will find favor with God.ᵖ
¹⁹ For great is the power of God;
 by the humble he is glorified.*
²⁰ What is too sublime for you, seek not,
 into things beyond your strength
 search not.�q
²¹ What is committed to you, attend to;
 for what is hidden is not your concern.
²² With what is too much for you meddle
 not,
 when shown things beyond human
 understanding.
²³ Their own opinion has misled many,
 and false reasoning unbalanced their
 judgment.
²⁴ Where the pupil of the eye is missing,
 there is no light,
 and where there is no knowledge,
 there is no wisdom.
²⁵ A stubborn man will fare badly in the
 end,
 and he who loves danger will perish
 in it.
²⁶ A stubborn man will be burdened with
 sorrow;
 a sinner will heap sin upon sin.
²⁷ For the affliction of the proud man
 there is no cure;
 he is the offshoot of an evil plant.ʳ
²⁸ The mind of a sage appreciates proverbs,
 and an attentive ear is the wise man's
 joy.

Alms for the Poor*

²⁹ Water quenches a flaming fire,
 and alms atone for sins.ˢ
³⁰ He who does a kindness is remembered
 afterward;
 when he falls, he finds a support.

CHAPTER 4

¹ My son, rob not the poor man of his
 livelihood:
 force not the eyes of the needy* to
 turn away.ᵗ
² A hungry man grieve not,
 a needy man anger not;
³ Do not exasperate the downtrodden;
 delay not to give to the needy.
⁴ A beggar in distress do not reject;
 avert not your face from the poor.
⁵ From the needy turn not your eyes,
 give no man reason to curse you;
⁶ For if in the bitterness of his soul he
 curse you,
 his Creator will hear his prayer.
⁷ Endear yourself to the assembly;
 before a ruler bow your head.
⁸ Give a hearing to the poor man,
 and return his greeting with courtesy;
⁹ Deliver the oppressed from the hand of
 the oppressor;
 let not justice be repugnant to you.
¹⁰ To the fatherless be as a father,
 and help their mother as a husband
 would;
 Thus will you be like a son to the Most
 High,
 and he will be more tender to you
 than a mother.

The Rewards of Wisdom*

¹¹ Wisdom instructs her children
 and admonishes those who seek her.

o Prv 19, 26; 30, 11. 14. 17.—p Mt 23, 12.—q Ps 131, 1.—r
Dt 32, 32; Wis 12, 10.—s Dn 4, 27.—t Tb 4, 7-11.

3, 17-27: Humility gives a true estimate of self (17ff). Through
it a man performs duty, avoids what is beyond his understanding and
strength (20ff). Pride, however, begets false greatness, misjudgment,
stubbornness, sorrow, affliction and perdition (23-27).

3, 19: An alternate or additional line would read: "For though
many have been great in the course of time, it is to the humble he
reveals his secrets." Cf Mt 11, 25f; 1 Cor 1, 26-29.

3, 29—4, 10: Mercy and kindness toward those in misfortune
atone for sin and endear a man to God and to his fellow men.

4, 1: *Eyes of the needy:* when they look for help; cf Sir 18, 17.

4, 11-19: The Hebrew text presents wisdom speaking in the
first person, as in ch 24. The precious fruits of wisdom: life, favor,
glory, blessings, God's love, are intended to arouse desire for her
(11-14). Her disciples are like priests (14) and judges (15), even
partners who possess her for themselves and their descendants
(16). They enjoy happiness and penetrate her profound secrets
after surviving her tests (17f). Those who fail her are abandoned
to destruction (19).

¹² He who loves her loves life;
    those who seek her out win her favor.
¹³ He who holds her fast inherits glory;
    wherever he dwells, the LORD bestows blessings.
¹⁴ Those who serve her serve the Holy One;
    those who love her the LORD loves.ᵘ
¹⁵ He who obeys her judges nations;
    he who hearkens to her dwells in her inmost chambers.
¹⁶ If one trusts her, he will possess her;
    his descendants too will inherit her.
¹⁷ She walks with him as a stranger,
    and at first she puts him to the test;
    Fear and dread she brings upon him
    and tries him with her discipline;
    With her precepts she puts him to the proof,
    until his heart is fully with her.
¹⁸ Then she comes back to bring him happiness
    and reveal her secrets to him.
¹⁹ But if he fails her, she will abandon him
    and deliver him into the hands of despoilers.

Sincerity and Justice*

²⁰ Use your time well; guard yourself from evil,
    and bring upon yourself no shame.
²¹ There is a sense of shame laden with guilt,
    and a shame that merits honor and respect.
²² Show no favoritism to your own discredit;
    let no one intimidate you to your own downfall.
²³ Refrain not from speaking at the proper time,
    and hide not away your wisdom;
²⁴ For it is through speech that wisdom becomes known,

and knowledge through the tongue's rejoinder.
²⁵ Never gainsay the truth,
    and struggle not against the rushing stream.
²⁶ Be not ashamed to acknowledge your guilt,
    but of your ignorance rather be ashamed.
²⁷ Do not abase yourself before an impious man,
    nor refuse to do so before rulers.
²⁸ Even to the death fight for truth,
    and the LORD your God will battle for you.
²⁹ Be not surly in your speech,
    nor lazy and slack in your deeds.
³⁰ Be not a lion at home,
    nor sly and suspicious at work.
³¹ Let not your hand be open to receive
    and clenched when it is time to give.

CHAPTER 5

Against Presumption*

¹ Rely not on your wealth;
    say not: "I have the power."ᵛ
² Rely not on your strength
    in following the desires of your heart.
³ Say not: "Who can prevail against me?"
    for the LORD will exact the punishment.
⁴ Say not: "I have sinned, yet what has befallen me?"
    for the LORD bides his time.
⁵ Of forgiveness be not overconfident,
    adding sin upon sin.
⁶ Say not: "Great is his mercy;
    my many sins he will forgive."
⁷ For mercy and anger alike are with him;
    upon the wicked alights his wrath.
⁸ Delay not your conversion to the LORD,
    put it not off from day to day;
⁹ For suddenly his wrath flames forth;
    at the time of vengeance, you will be destroyed.
¹⁰ Rely not upon deceitful wealth,
    for it will be no help on the day of wrath.ʷ

Sincerity in Speech

¹¹ Winnow not in every wind,
    and start not off in every direction.*
¹² Be consistent in your thoughts;
    steadfast be your words.*
¹³ Be swift to hear,
    but slow to answer.ˣ
¹⁴ If you have the knowledge, answer your neighbor;

Sir

---

u Wis 7, 28.—v Lk 12, 19.—w Prv 10, 2; 11, 4. 28.—x Prv 29, 20; Jas 1, 19.

4, 20-31: Besides the interior trials of discipline and precept, the disciple of wisdom is warned against external dangers to his sincerity and justice, namely evil, human respect (20f), compromise of liberty in speech and action (22-25), false shame, and ignorance (26). He must fight for the truth (28), and avoid cynicism and laziness (29), and inconsistency in his conduct (30).

5, 1-10: The vices of the rich are pride and independence (1f), presumption (3), false security (4-7), and impenitence (8), which cannot escape the divine wrath (9f). Cf Prv 18, 23; 19, 1; 28, 6.

5, 11: A proverbial expression condemning inconstancy and advocating sincerity and honesty.

5, 12—6, 1: Proper use of the tongue requires constancy in speech (5, 12), prudence (13f), reserve (15), charity (6, 1), as well as the avoidance of detraction, *calumny* (16) and double talk, which bring shame and disgrace (5, 17; 6, 1).

if not, put your hand over your mouth.
15 Honor and dishonor through talking!
    A man's tongue can be his downfall.
16 Be not called a detractor;
    use not your tongue for calumny;
17 For shame has been created for the thief,
    and the reproach of his neighbor for the double-tongued.

CHAPTER 6

1 Say nothing harmful, small or great;
    be not a foe instead of a friend;
    A bad name and disgrace will you acquire:
    "That for the evil man with double tongue!"*
2 Fall not into the grip of desire,[y]
    lest, like fire, it consume your strength;
3 Your leaves it will eat, your fruits destroy,
    and you will be left a dry tree,
4 For contumacious desire destroys its owner
    and makes him the sport of his enemies.

True Friendship*

5 A kind mouth multiplies friends,
    and gracious lips prompt friendly greetings.
6 Let your acquaintances be many,
    but one in a thousand your confidant.
7 When you gain a friend, first test him,[z]
    and be not too ready to trust him.
8 For one sort of friend is a friend when it suits him,
    but he will not be with you in time of distress.
9 Another is a friend who becomes an enemy,
    and tells of the quarrel to your shame.
10 Another is a friend, a boon companion,
    who will not be with you when sorrow comes.
11 When things go well, he is your other self,
    and lords it over your servants;
12 But if you are brought low, he turns against you
    and avoids meeting you.
13 Keep away from your enemies;
    be on your guard with your friends.
14 A faithful friend is a sturdy shelter;

he who finds one finds a treasure.
15 A faithful friend is beyond price,
    no sum can balance his worth.
16 A faithful friend is a life-saving remedy,
    such as he who fears God finds;
17 For he who fears God behaves accordingly,
    and his friend will be like himself.

Blessings of Wisdom*

18 My son, from your youth embrace discipline;
    thus will you find wisdom with graying hair.
19 As though plowing and sowing, draw close to her;
    then await her bountiful crops.
20 For in cultivating her you will labor but little,
    and soon you will eat of her fruits.
21 How irksome she is to the unruly!
    The fool cannot abide her.
22 She will be like a burdensome stone to test him,
    and he will not delay in casting her aside.
23 For discipline* is like her name,
    she is not accessible to many.
24 Listen, my son, and heed my advice;
    refuse not my counsel.
25 Put your feet into her fetters,
    and your neck under her yoke.
26 Stoop your shoulders and carry her
    and be not irked at her bonds.
27 With all your soul draw close to her;
    with all your strength keep her ways.
28 Search her out, discover her; seek her and you will find her.
    Then when you have her, do not let her go;
29 Thus will you afterward find rest in her,
    and she will become your joy.
30 Her fetters will be your throne of majesty;
    her bonds, your purple cord.

y 2-3: Sir 9, 8; 23, 17; Jb 31, 12; Is 56, 3.—z 7ff: Sir 12, 8f; 37, 1-5; Prv 19, 4.

6, 1: *"That . . . double tongue!":* people will say this against the man whose deceitful tongue has brought him to disgrace.

6, 5-17: True friends are discerned not by prosperity (11) but through the trials of adversity: distress, quarrels (9), sorrow (10) and misfortune (12). Such friends are rare and their value is beyond estimation, a gift from God (14-17).

6, 18-37: The various figures in each of the three strophes urge the search for wisdom through patience (19-23), docility (32-37), and perseverance in trials (25ff), promising rich rewards (28-31). Cf 4, 11-19.

6, 23: *Discipline (musar,* in the sense of wisdom) is a perfect homonym for *musar,* "removed, withdrawn"; thus the path of *discipline* is inaccessible to many.

³¹ You will wear her as your robe of glory,^a
   bear her as your splendid crown.*
³² My son, if you wish, you can be taught;
   if you apply yourself, you will be
   shrewd.
³³ If you are willing to listen, you will
   learn;
   if you give heed, you will be wise.
³⁴ Frequent the company of the elders;
   whoever is wise, stay close to him.
³⁵ Be eager to hear every godly discourse;
   let no wise saying escape you.^b
³⁶ If you see a man of prudence, seek him
   out;
   let your feet wear away his doorstep!
³⁷ Reflect on the precepts of the LORD,
   let his commandments be your constant meditation;
   Then he will enlighten your mind,
   and the wisdom you desire he will
   grant.^c

CHAPTER 7
Conduct in Public Life*

¹ Do no evil, and evil will not overtake
   you;
²   avoid wickedness, and it will turn
   aside from you.
³ Sow not in the furrows of injustice,
   lest you harvest it sevenfold.^d
⁴ Seek not from the LORD authority,
   nor from the king a place of honor.
⁵ Parade not your justice before the LORD,
   and before the king flaunt not your
   wisdom.^e

⁶ Seek not to become a judge
   if you have not strength to root out
   crime,
   Or you will show favor to the ruler
   and mar your integrity.
⁷ Be guilty of no evil before the city's
   populace,
   nor disgrace yourself before the assembly.
⁸ Do not plot to repeat a sin;
   not even for one will you go unpunished.
⁹ Say not: "He will appreciate my many
   gifts;
   the Most High will accept my offerings."^f
¹⁰ Be not impatient in prayers,
   and neglect not the giving of alms.
¹¹ Laugh not at an embittered man;
   be mindful of him who exalts and
   humbles.*
¹² Plot no mischief against your brother,
   nor against your friend and compan-
   ion.
¹³ Delight not in telling lie after lie,
   for it never results in good.
¹⁴ Thrust not yourself into the delibera-
   tions of princes,^g
   and repeat not the words of your
   prayer.*
¹⁵ Hate not laborious tasks,
   nor farming, which was ordained by
   the Most High.^h
¹⁶ Do not esteem yourself better than your
   fellows;
   remember, his wrath will not delay.
¹⁷ More and more, humble your pride;
   what awaits man is worms.ⁱ

Duties of Family Life,
Religion and Charity*

¹⁸ Barter not a friend for money,
   nor a dear brother for the gold of
   Ophir.*
¹⁹ Dismiss not a sensible wife;
   a gracious wife is more precious than
   corals.
²⁰ Mistreat not a servant who faithfully
   serves,
   nor a laborer who devotes himself to
   his task.^j
²¹ Let a wise servant be dear to you as
   your own self;
   refuse him not his freedom.*
²² If you have livestock, look after them;
   if they are dependable, keep them.
²³ If you have sons, chastise them;
   bend their necks* from childhood.^k

---

a Is 62, 3.—b Sir 8, 9.—c Ps 1, 2.—d Prv 22, 8.—e Jb 9, 2;
Ps 143, 2; Prv 25, 6; 1 Cor 4, 4.—f Sir 34, 18; 35, 12.—g Sir
32, 7ff; Mt 6, 7.—h Gn 2, 15; 3, 17.—i Is 66, 24.—j Lv 19, 13;
Dt 24, 14f; Jas 5, 4.—k Sir 30, 8-13; Prv 13, 24.

6, 31: Some forms of the text speak also of the "yoke" of wisdom under the imagery of golden ornaments.

7, 1-17: In the conduct of social relations wisdom forbids *evil*
and *injustice* (1ff), pride (5. 15ff), ambition and human respect
(4. 6), public disorder (7), presumption and impatience toward
God (9f), ridicule (11), *mischief* and deceit toward one's neighbor (8, 12f).

7, 11: *Him who exalts and humbles:* God; cf 1 Sm 2, 7; Ps
75, 8; Lk 1, 52.

7, 14: *Repeat not . . . prayer:* brevity of speech in dealings
with superiors and more especially with God is a sign of reverence
and respect; cf Eccl 5, 1; Mt 6, 7.

7, 18-36: The duties of respect and appreciation, justice and
kindness should characterize relations toward members of the
household (18-28), and also toward God and his priests (29ff),
the poor and afflicted, the living and the dead (32-36).

7, 18: *Ophir* was the port, at present unidentified, to which
the ships of Solomon sailed and from which they brought back
gold and silver; cf note on Ps 45, 10.

7, 21: After six years of service a Hebrew slave was entitled
to freedom; cf Ex 21, 2; Dt 15, 12-15.

7, 23: *Bend their necks:* keep them from rebellious pride; so
with the Greek. Cf Sir 30, 12. The present Hebrew text, which is
probably not original here, reads: "Choose wives for them while
they are young."

24 If you have daughters, keep them chaste,
   and be not indulgent to them.*l*
25 Giving your daughter in marriage ends
   a great task;
   but give her to a worthy man.*m*
26 If you have a wife, let her not seem
   odious to you;
   but where there is ill-feeling, trust
   her not,
27 With your whole heart honor your
   father;
   your mother's birthpangs forget not.*n*
28 Remember, of these parents you were
   born;
   what can you give them for all they
   gave you?
29 With all your soul, fear God,
   revere his priests.
30 With all your strength, love your Creator,
   forsake not his ministers.
31 Honor God and respect the priest;
   give him his portion as you have been
   commanded:*o*
   First fruits and contributions,
   due sacrifices and holy offerings.*
32 To the poor man also extend your hand,
   that your blessing may be complete;
33 Be generous to all the living,
   and withhold not your kindness from
   the dead.*
34 Avoid not those who weep,
   but mourn with those who mourn;*p*
35 Neglect not to visit the sick—
   for these things you will be loved.*q*
36 In whatever you do, remember your last
   days,
   and you will never sin.

CHAPTER 8

Prudence in Dealing with Other Men*

1 Contend not with an influential man,
   lest you fall into his power.
2 Quarrel not with a rich man,
   lest he pay out the price of your
   downfall;
   For gold has dazzled many,
   and perverts the character of princes.*r*
3 Dispute not with a man of railing
   speech,
   heap no wood upon his fire.*s*
4 Be not too familiar with an unruly man,
   lest he speak ill of your forebears.
5 Shame not a repentant sinner;*t*
   remember, we all are guilty.*
6 Insult no man when he is old,

for some of us, too, will grow old.
7 Rejoice not when a man dies;
   remember, we are all to die.
8 Spurn not the discourse of the wise,*u*
   but acquaint yourself with their proverbs;
   From them you will acquire the training
   to serve in the presence of princes.
9 Reject not the tradition of old men
   which they have learned from their
   fathers;
   From it you will obtain the knowledge
   how to answer in time of need.
10 Kindle not the coals of a sinner,
   lest you be consumed in his flaming
   fire.
11 Let not the impious man intimidate
   you;
   it will set him in ambush against you.*
12 Lend not to one more powerful than
   yourself;
   and whatever you lend, count it as
   lost.*v*
13 Go not surety beyond your means;
   think any pledge a debt you must pay.
14 Contend not at law with a judge,
   for he will settle it according to his
   whim.
15 Travel not with a ruthless man,
   lest he weigh you down with calamity;
   For he will go his own way straight,
   and through his folly you will perish
   with him.
16 Provoke no quarrel with a quick-tempered man
   nor ride with him through the desert;
   For bloodshed is nothing to him;
   when there is no one to help you, he
   will destroy you.

---

l Sir 42, 9ff.—m 1 Cor 7, 36ff.—n Ex 20, 12.—o Lv 7, 31; Nm
18, 18.—p Rom 12, 15.—q Mt 25, 36.—r Sir 31, 6; Dt 16, 19.—
s Prv 26, 20.—t 1 Kgs 8, 46; 1 Jn 1, 8.—u 8f: Sir 6, 35.—v Sir
29, 4-7; Prv 17, 18.

7, 31: *First fruits . . . holy offerings:* cf Ex 29, 27; Lv 7,
31-34; Nm 18, 8-20; Dt 18, 1-5.
7, 33: This seems to refer to the observances ordained toward
the dead, that is, proper mourning and burial. Cf 2 Sm 21, 12ff;
Tb 1, 20; 12, 12. When this verse is read in the light of later
teaching, prayers for the souls of the deceased would also be recommended. Cf 2 Mc 12, 43ff.
8, 1-19: A prudent man will be circumspect, avoiding conflict
with the powerful, the rich and insolent, the impious, the irasci-
ble, and with judges (1ff. 10ff. 14. 16). He will seek friendship
not with the undisciplined (4. 12f) and the ruthless (15), nor with
fools and strangers (17ff), but with the wise and the ancients of
the people (8f).
8, 5: *We all are guilty:* cf 1 Kgs 8, 46; 2 Chr 6, 36; Eccl 7,
20; Rom 3, 9f; 1 Jn 1, 8.
8, 11: To give in to the wicked in one instance becomes an occasion of sin for the future.

17 Take no counsel with a fool,
    for he can keep nothing to himself.
18 Before a stranger do nothing that
    should be kept secret,
    for you know not what it will engen-
    der.[w]
19 Open your heart to no man,
    and banish not your happiness.

CHAPTER 9

Advice concerning Women*

1 Be not jealous of the wife of your
    bosom,
    lest you teach her to do evil against
    you.*
2 Give no woman power over you
    to trample upon your dignity.[x]
3 Be not intimate with a strange woman,
    lest you fall into her snares.
4 With a singing girl be not familiar,
    lest you be caught in her wiles.
5 Entertain no thoughts against a virgin,
    lest you be enmeshed in damages for
    her.*
6 Give not yourself to harlots,
    lest you surrender your inheritance.[y]
7 Gaze not about the lanes of the city
    and wander not through its squares.
8 Avert your eyes from a comely woman;
    gaze not upon the beauty of another's
    wife—
    Through woman's beauty many perish,
    for lust for it burns like fire.[z]
9 With a married woman dine not,
    recline not at table to drink by her
    side,
    Lest your heart be drawn to her
    and you go down in blood to the
    grave.

Choice of Friends*

10 Discard not an old friend,

for the new one cannot equal him.
    A new friend is like new wine
    which you drink with pleasure only
    when it has aged.
11 Envy not a sinner's fame,
    for you know not what disaster awaits
    him.
12 Rejoice not at a proud man's success;
    remember he will not reach death un-
    punished.
13 Keep far from the man who has power
    to kill,
    and you will not be filled with the
    dread of death.
    But if you approach him, offend him
    not,
    lest he take away your life;
    Know that you are stepping among
    snares
    and walking over a net.
14 As best you can, take your neighbors'
    measure,
    and associate with the wise.
15 With the learned be intimate;
    let all your conversation be about the
    law of the LORD.
16 Have just men for your table compan-
    ions;
    in the fear of God be your glory.

Concerning Rulers*

17 Skilled artisans are esteemed for their
    deftness;
    but the ruler of his people is the
    skilled sage.
18 Feared in the city is the man of railing
    speech,
    and he who talks rashly is hated.

CHAPTER 10

1 A wise magistrate lends stability to his
    people,
    and the government of a prudent man
    is well ordered.[a]
2 As the people's judge, so are his minis-
    ters;[b]
    as the head of a city, its inhabitants.
3 A wanton king destroys his people,
    but a city grows through the wisdom
    of its princes.[c]
4 Sovereignty over the earth is in the
    hand of God,
    who raises up on it the man of the
    ·hour;
5 Sovereignty over every man is in the
    hand of God,
    who imparts his majesty to the ruler.

---

w Prv 25, 9f.—x Sir 25, 21.—y Prv 5, 3-11; 6, 24; 29, 3.—z Sir
25, 20; 41, 21.—a Wis 6, 24.—b 2f: Prv 29, 12.—c Prv 29, 4. 8.

9, 1-9: Prudence and reserve in dealing with women are the
best defense of morality. To preserve the liberty and dignity of his
person and the integrity of his possessions, a man must avoid
jealousy toward his own wife and familiarity toward all other
women. Cf Sir 25, 12—26, 18.

9, 1: Unjust suspicions often engender hatred between husband
and wife and may prompt a wife to commit those faults of which
heretofore she had been innocent.

9, 5: Cf Ex 22, 15f: Dt 22, 28f; Jb 31, 1.

9, 10-16: In social relations, adherence to *the law of the Lord*
should serve as a guide (15). Associate with true friends (10), with
the just and the learned (14ff); avoid the company of the mighty and
of sinners doomed to punishment (11ff). Cf Sir 8, 1-19.

9, 17—10, 5: Public office as conducted justly or unjustly
benefits or destroys the people, according to the axiom, "as the
prince, so the people." Cf Is 24, 2. God, however, has sovereignty
over both.

The Sin of Pride*

⁶ No matter the wrong, do no violence to
your neighbor,
and do not walk the path of arrogance. *d*

⁷ Odious to the LORD and to men is arrogance,
and the sin of oppression they both
hate.

⁸ Dominion is transferred from one people to another
because of the violence of the arrogant.

⁹ Why are dust and ashes proud?*
even during life man's body decays;

¹⁰ A slight illness—the doctor jests,
a king today—tomorrow he is dead.

¹¹ When a man dies, he inherits corruption;
worms and gnats and maggots. *e*

¹² The beginning of pride is man's stubbornness
in withdrawing his heart from his
Maker;

¹³ For pride is the reservoir of sin,
a source which runs over with vice;
Because of it God sends unheard-of
afflictions
and brings men to utter ruin. *f*

¹⁴ The thrones of the arrogant God overturns
and establishes the lowly in their
stead.

¹⁵ The roots of the proud God plucks up,
to plant the humble in their place:

¹⁶ He breaks down their stem to the level
of the ground,
then digs their roots from the earth.

¹⁷ The traces of the proud God sweeps
away
and effaces the memory of them from
the earth.

¹⁸ Insolence is not allotted to a man,
nor stubborn anger to one born of
woman.

True Glory*

¹⁹ Whose offspring can be in honor?
Those of men.
Which offspring are in honor? Those
who fear God.
Whose offspring can be in disgrace?
Those of men.
Which offspring are in disgrace?
Those who transgress the com-
mandments.

²⁰ Among brethren their leader is in honor;

he who fears God is in honor among
his people.

²¹ Be it tenant or wayfarer, alien or
pauper,
his glory is the fear of the LORD.

²² It is not just to despise a man who is
wise but poor,
nor proper to honor any sinner. *g*

²³ The prince, the ruler, the judge are in
honor;
but none is greater than he who fears
God.

²⁴ When free men serve a prudent slave,
the wise man does not complain. *h*

²⁵ Flaunt not your wisdom in managing
your affairs,
and boast not in your time of need.

²⁶ Better the worker who has plenty of
everything
than the boaster who is without
bread. *i*

²⁷ My son, with humility have self-esteem;
prize yourself as you deserve.

²⁸ Who will acquit him who condemns
himself?
who will honor him who discredits
himself?

²⁹ The poor man is honored for his wisdom
as the rich man is honored for his
wealth;

³⁰ Honored in poverty, how much more so
in wealth!
Dishonored in wealth, in poverty
how much the more!

CHAPTER 11

¹ The poor man's wisdom lifts his head
high
and sets him among princes.

² Praise not a man for his looks;
despise not a man for his appearance.

³ Least is the bee among winged things,
but she reaps the choicest of all harvests.

d Lv 19, 18.—e Jb 17, 14.—f Prv 18, 12.—g Jas 2, 1-4.—h
Prv 17, 2.—i Prv 12, 9.

10, 6-18: Glory displayed through arrogance and pride is false
and displeasing to God and men, because founded on *dust and
ashes* (6-11). It is the denial of the glory due to God, and therefore the source of all sin (12f). Even the memory of the proud is
destroyed and God transfers their power to the lowly (14-18).

10, 9f: The text is uncertain. Its general implication is that
man deteriorates physically even while alive: a slight illness today
may be followed by death tomorrow. The uncertainty of life
leaves no room for pride.

10, 19—11, 6: Regardless of social barriers, genuine honor
among men comes from fear of the Lord and a true estimate of
self. The Lord exalts the lowly and oppressed; transgressors of
the *commandments* merit dishonor and disgrace.

⁴ Mock not the worn cloak
and jibe at no man's bitter day:
For strange are the works of the LORD,
hidden from men his deeds.
⁵ The oppressed often rise to a throne,
and some that none would consider
wear a crown.*
⁶ The exalted often fall into utter disgrace;
the honored are given into enemy
hands.

Moderation*

⁷ Before investigating, find no fault;
examine first, then criticize.
⁸ Before hearing, answer not,
and interrupt no one in the middle of
his speech.ʲ
⁹ Dispute not about what is not your concern;
in the strife of the arrogant take no
part.
¹⁰ My son, why increase your cares,
since he who is avid for wealth will
not be blameless?
Even if you run after it, you will never
overtake it;
however you seek it, you will not find
it.
¹¹ One may toil and struggle and drive,
and fall short all the more.ᵏ
¹² Another goes his way a weakling and a
failure,
with little strength and great misery—
Yet the eyes of the LORD look favorably
upon him;
he raises him free of the vile dust,
¹³ Lifts up his head and exalts him
to the amazement of the many.
¹⁴ Good and evil, life and death,ˡ
poverty and riches, are from the
LORD.*
¹⁵ Wisdom and understanding and knowledge of affairs,*

love and virtuous paths are from the
LORD.
¹⁶ Error and darkness were formed with
sinners from their birth,
and evil grows old with evildoers.
¹⁷ The LORD's gift remains with the just;
his favor brings continued success.
¹⁸ A man may become rich through a
miser's life,
and this is his allotted reward:
¹⁹ When he says: "I have found rest,ᵐ
now I will feast on my possessions,"
He does not know how long it will be
till he dies and leaves it them to
others.*
²⁰ My son, hold fast to your duty, busy
yourself with it,
grow old while doing your task.
²¹ Admire not how sinners live,
but trust in the LORD and wait for his
light;
For it is easy with the LORD
suddenly, in an instant, to make a
poor man rich.
²² God's blessing is the lot of the just man,
and in due time his hopes bear fruit.
²³ Say not: "What do I need?
What further pleasure can be mine?"
²⁴ Say not: "I am independent.
What harm can come to me now?"
²⁵ The day of prosperity makes one forget
adversity;
the day of adversity makes one forget
prosperity.ⁿ
²⁶ For it is easy with the LORD on the day
of death*
to repay man according to his deeds.
²⁷ A moment's affliction brings forgetful-
ness of past delights;
when a man dies, his life is revealed.
²⁸ Call no man happy before his death,
for by how he ends, a man is known. **Sir**

Care in Choosing Friends

²⁹ Bring not every man into your house,
for many are the snares of the crafty
one;
³⁰ Though he seem like a bird confined in
a cage,
yet like a spy he will pick out the
weak spots.
³¹ The talebearer turns good into evil;
with a spark he sets many coals afire.
³² The evil man lies in wait for blood,
and plots against your choicest possessions.

ʲ Prv 18, 13.—ᵏ Ps 127, 2; Eccl 4, 8.—ˡ Jb 1, 21; 2, 10.—ᵐ
Eccl 4, 8; 6, 2; Lk 12, 19.—ⁿ Sir 18, 25.

11, 5: Cf 1 Sm 2, 8; Ps 105, 17-22; Lk 1, 52.
11, 7-25: Discretion regulates a man's conduct toward others
and their affairs (7ff); as regards his own interests, a man should
avoid solicitude for the passing external benefits of life and property (10-14. 18f. 21. 23ff), and cultivate the lasting inward gifts
of wisdom and virtue (15. 17. 20. 22).
11, 14: Divine Providence ultimately governs the lives of men.
Evil: misfortune and calamity sent by God either in punishment or
as an incentive to repentance or to greater virtue.
11, 15f: Some ancient witnesses omit these two verses.
11, 19: Cf the parable of the rich man, Lk 12, 16-21.
11, 26ff: Sirach, writing before Christian revelation, did not
go beyond the hour of death to find full divine retribution.

³³ Avoid a wicked man, for he breeds only evil,
  lest you incur a lasting stain.
³⁴ Lodge a stranger with you, and he will subvert your course,
  and make a stranger of you to your own household.

CHAPTER 12

¹ If you do good, know for whom you are doing it,*
  and your kindness will have its effect.
² Do good to the just man and reward will be yours,
  if not from him, from the LORD.
³ No good comes to him who gives comfort to the wicked,*
  nor is it an act of mercy that he does.
⁴ Give to the good man, refuse the sinner;ᵒ
  refresh the downtrodden, give nothing to the proud man.
⁵ No arms for combat should you give him,
  lest he use them against yourself;
⁶ With twofold evil you will meet
  for every good deed you do for him.
⁷ The Most High himself hates sinners,
  and upon the wicked he takes vengeance.

⁸ In our prosperity we cannot know our friends;*
  in adversity an enemy will not remain concealed.ᵖ
⁹ When a man is successful even his enemy is friendly;
  in adversity even his friend disappears.�q
¹⁰ Never trust your enemy,
  for his wickedness is like corrosion in bronze.
¹¹ Even though he acts humbly and peaceably toward you,
  take care to be on your guard against him.
  Rub him as one polishes a brazen mirror,*
  and you will find that there is still corrosion.
¹² Let him not stand near you,
  lest he oust you and take your place.
  Let him not sit at your right hand,
  lest he then demand your seat,
  And in the end you appreciate my advice,

when you groan with regret, as I warned you.
¹³ Who pities a snake charmer when he is bitten,
  or anyone who goes near a wild beast?
¹⁴ So is it with the companion of the proud man,
  who is involved in his sins:
¹⁵ While you stand firm, he makes no bold move;
  but if you slip, he cannot hold back.
¹⁶ With his lips an enemy speaks sweetly,
  but in his heart he schemes to plunge you into the abyss.
  Though your enemy has tears in his eyes,
  if given the chance, he will never have enough of your blood.
¹⁷ If evil comes upon you, you will find him at hand;
  feigning to help, he will trip you up,
¹⁸ Then he will nod his head and clap his hands
  and hiss repeatedly, and show his true face.

CHAPTER 13

Caution Regarding Associates*

¹ He who touches pitch blackens his hand;
  he who associates with an impious man learns his ways.
² Bear no burden too heavy for you;
  go with no one greater or wealthier than yourself.
  How can the earthen pot go with the metal cauldron?
  When they knock together, the pot will be smashed:
³ The rich man does wrong and boasts of it,
  the poor man is wronged and begs forgiveness.

---

o 4f: Gal 6, 10.—p Prv 17, 17.—q Prv 19, 4-7.

12, 1-7: The limitations to the practice of charity here reflected were removed by Christ, who requires that good be done even to enemies and to those who hate, persecute and calumniate us (Mt 5, 43-48).
12, 3ff: The author advises against generosity to those who would abuse it.
12, 8-18: Through adversity friends are distinguished from enemies; to trust the latter or permit them intimacy is to invite disaster. Cf note on Sir 6, 5-17.
12, 11: *Brazen mirror:* see note on Ex 38, 8.
13, 1—14, 2: By means of various figures Sirach indicates the practical impossibility of genuine and sincere companionship between the poor and the proud rich. He lays down the principle of associating with equals (13, 15).

4 As long as the rich man can use you he
    will enslave you,
    but when you are exhausted, he will
        abandon you.
5 As long as you have anything he will
    speak fair words to you,
    and with smiles he will win your con-
        fidence;
6 When he needs something from you he
    will cajole you,
    then without regret he will im-
        poverish you.
7 While it serves his purpose he will be-
    guile you,
    then twice or three times he will ter-
        rify you;
    When later he sees you he will pass you
        by,
    and shake his head over you.
8 Guard against being presumptuous;
    be not as those who lack sense.
9 When invited by a man of influence,
    keep your distance;
    then he will urge you all the more.
10 Be not bold with him lest you be re-
    buffed,
    but keep not too far away lest you be
        forgotten.
11 Engage not freely in discussion with
    him,
    trust not his many words;
    For by prolonged talk he will test you,
    and though smiling he will probe
        you.
12 Mercilessly he will make of you a
    laughingstock,
    and will not refrain from injury or
        chains.
13 Be on your guard and take care
    never to accompany men of violence.
14 Every living thing loves its own kind,
    every man a man like himself.
15 Every being is drawn to its own kind;
    with his own kind every man as-
        sociates.
16 Is a wolf ever allied with a lamb?
    So it is with the sinner and the just.[r]
17 Can there be peace between the hyena
    and the dog?

Or between the rich and the poor can
    there be peace?*
18 Lion's prey are the wild asses of the
    desert;
    so too the poor are feeding grounds
        for the rich.
19 A proud man abhors lowliness;
    so does the rich man abhor the poor.
20 When a rich man stumbles he is sup-
    ported by a friend;
    when a poor man trips he is pushed
        down by a friend.
21 Many are the supporters for a rich man
    when he speaks;
    though what he says is odious, it wins
        approval.
    When a poor man speaks they make
        sport of him;
    he speaks wisely and no attention is
        paid him.
22 A rich man speaks and all are silent,
    his wisdom they extol to the clouds.
    A poor man speaks and they say: "Who
        is that?"
    If he slips they cast him down.
23 Wealth is good when there is no sin;
    but poverty is evil by the standards of
        the proud.
24 The heart of a man changes his counte-
    nance,
    either for good or for evil.[s]
25 The sign of a good heart is a cheerful
    countenance;
    withdrawn and perplexed is the
        laborious schemer.

CHAPTER 14

1 Happy the man whose mouth brings
    him no grief,
    who is not stung by remorse for sin.[t]
2 Happy the man whose conscience does
    not reproach him,
    who has not lost hope.

The Use of Wealth

3 Wealth ill becomes the mean man;*
    and to the miser, of what use is gold?
4 What he denies himself he collects for
    others,
    and in his possessions a stranger will
        revel.[u]
5 To whom will he be generous who is
    stingy with himself
    and does not enjoy what is his own?
6 None is more stingy than he who is
    stingy with himself;
    he punishes his own miserliness.

Sir

r 2 Cor 6, 14ff.—s Prv 15, 13.—t Sir 19, 15; 25, 8; Jas 3, 2.—
u Eccl 6, 2.

13, 17: The hostility between the dogs which guard the flocks
at night and the rapacious hyenas is proverbial in Palestine.
14, 3-16: The miser does no good even to himself (3-10);
wealth should be wisely used during life, for it must be left behind
at death (11-16). In the light of the gospel, generosity has a
higher motivation and promise of reward than the Old Testament
writer could propose. Cf Mt 6, 19ff; Lk 12, 32ff.

7 If ever he is generous, it is by mistake;
  and in the end he displays his greed.

8 In the miser's opinion his share is too
  small;

9 he refuses his neighbor and brings
  ruin on himself.

10 The miser's eye is rapacious for bread,
   but on his own table he sets it stale.

11 My son, use freely whatever you have
   and enjoy it as best you can;[v]

12 Remember that death does not tarry,
   nor have you been told the grave's appointed time.

13 Before you die, be good to your friend,
   and give him a share in what you possess.[w]

14 Deprive not yourself of present good
   things,
   let no choice portion escape you.

15 Will you not leave your riches to others,
   and your earnings to be divided by
   lot?

16 Give, take, and treat yourself well,
   for in the nether world there are no
   joys to seek.

17 All flesh grows old, like a garment;
   the age-old law is: All must die.[x]

18 As with the leaves that grow on a vigorous tree:
   one falls off and another sprouts—
   So with the generations of flesh and
   blood:
   one dies and another is born.[y]

19 All man's works will perish in decay,
   and his handiwork will follow after
   him.

The Search for Wisdom and Its Blessings*

20 Happy the man who meditates on wisdom,
   and reflects on knowledge;[z]

21 Who ponders her ways in his heart,
   and understands her paths;

22 Who pursues her like a scout,
   and lies in wait at her entry way;

23 Who peeps through her windows,
   and listens at her doors;

24 Who encamps near her house,
   and fastens his tent pegs next to her
   walls;

25 Who pitches his tent beside her,
   and lives as her welcome neighbor;

26 Who builds his nest in her leafage,
   and lodges in her branches;

27 Who takes shelter with her from the
   heat,
   and dwells in her home.

CHAPTER 15

1 He who fears the LORD will do this;
  he who is practiced in the law will
  come to wisdom.

2 Motherlike she will meet him,
  like a young bride she will embrace
  him,

3 Nourish him with the bread of understanding,
  and give him the water of learning to
  drink.[a]

4 He will lean upon her and not fall,
  he will trust in her and not be put to
  shame.

5 She will exalt him above his fellows;
  in the assembly she will make him
  eloquent.

6 Joy and gladness he will find,
  an everlasting name inherit.[b]

7 Worthless men will not attain to her,
  haughty men will not behold her.

8 Far from the impious is she,
  not to be spoken of by liars.

9 Unseemly is praise on a sinner's lips,
  for it is not accorded to him by God.

10 But praise is offered by the wise man's
   tongue;
   its rightful steward will proclaim it.

Man's Free Will

11 Say not: "It was God's doing that I fell
   away";
   for what he hates he does not do.

12 Say not: "It was he who set me astray";
   for he has no need of wicked man.[c]

13 Abominable wickedness the LORD
   hates,
   he does not let it befall those who fear
   him.

14 When God, in the beginning, created
   man,
   he made him subject to his own free
   choice.[d]

15 If you choose you can keep the commandments;
   it is loyalty to do his will.

16 There are set before you fire and water;
   to whichever you choose, stretch
   forth your hand.

---

v Prv 3, 9.—w Sir 4, 1; Tb 4, 7.—x Ps 103, 14ff; Is 40, 6; Jas
1, 10; 1 Pt 1, 24.—y Eccl 1. 4.—z Ps 1, 2.—a Jn 4, 10; 6,
31ff.—b Sir 6, 29-32.—c Jas 1, 13.—d Gn 1, 17.

14, 20—15, 20: From his social teaching the sage now turns
to consider individual responsibility. Happiness is to be found in
the pursuit and possession of wisdom (14, 20—15, 5). Joy and
honor are given, not to the sinner (7ff), but to him who fears God
and observes his law (1-6. 10). The sinner is fully responsible for
his conduct because God, who sees all things (18f), is not the
author of wickedness (11ff. 20): he gives to every man the liberty
to choose between good and evil (14-17).

17 Before man are life and death,
    whichever he chooses shall be given
    him.*e*
18 Immense is the wisdom of the LORD;
    he is mighty in power, and all-seeing.
19 The eyes of God see all he has made;
    he understands man's every deed.*f*
20 No man does he command to sin,
    to none does he give strength for lies.

CHAPTER 16

God's Punishment of Sinners*

1 Desire not a brood of worthless chil-
    dren,
    nor rejoice in wicked offspring.
2 Many though they be, exult not in them
    if they have not the fear of the LORD.
3 Count not on their length of life,*g*
    have no hope in their future.
    For one can be better than a thousand;
    rather die childless than have godless
    children!
4 Through one wise man can a city be
    peopled;
    through a clan of rebels it becomes
    desolate.
5 Many such things has my eye seen,
    even more than these has my ear
    heard.
6 Against a sinful band fire is enkindled,*h*
    upon a godless people wrath flames
    out.*
7 He forgave not the leaders of old*
    who rebelled long ago in their might;*i*
8 He spared not the neighbors of Lot *j*
    whom he detested for their pride;*
9 Nor did he spare the doomed people*

e Dt 30, 15.—f Pss 33, 18; 34, 16; Heb 4, 13.—g 3f: Wis 4,
1f.—h Sir 21, 9.—i Gn 6, 4; Wis 14, 6; Bar 3, 26ff.—j Gn 19,
24ff.—k Nm 14, 29.—l Sir 23, 18.—m Gn 1, 4ff.

16, 1-21: Sinful offspring are a great misfortune (1-4), for
history and experience show how God punishes sin (5-10). He
judges everyone according to his deeds (11ff); no one is hidden
from him or escapes retribution at his hand (15-21).
    16, 6: For Korah and his *band* (6a), see Nm 16, 35; Ps 106,
18; for the disgruntled Israelites (6b), Ps 78, 21f.
    16, 7: *The leaders of old:* the "mighty men of old" who were
destroyed by the flood: Gn 6, 4; Wis 14, 6; Bar 3, 26ff.
    16, 8: The people of Sodom and Gomorrah: Gn 19, 24f; Ez
16, 49f.
    16, 9: The Canaanites: Ex 23, 23f. 27-31; 33, 2; Dt 7, 1; Wis
12, 3.
    16, 10: The Israelites who murmured against Moses: Nm 11,
20; 14, 12. 22ff.
    16, 22—17, 18: In harmony with Gn 1—2, the author de-
scribes God's wisdom in creating the universe and all things in it
(22-28), endowing man with a moral nature, with wisdom and
knowledge and freedom of will according to his own image (17,
1. 6), so that man may govern the earth (3f), praise God's name
(8), obey his law (9-12), and render to him an account of his
deeds (18). Cf Pss 19; 104.

    who were uprooted because of their
    sin;
10 Nor the six hundred thousand foot sol-
    diers*k*
    who perished for the impiety of their
    hearts.*
11 And had there been but one stiffnecked
    man,
    it were a wonder had he gone un-
    punished.
    For mercy and anger alike are with him
    who remits and forgives, though on
    the wicked alights his wrath.
12 Great as his mercy is his punishment;
    he judges men, each according to his
    deeds.
13 A criminal does not escape with his
    plunder;
    a just man's hope God does not leave
    unfulfilled.
14 Whoever does good has his reward,
    which each receives according to his
    deeds.
15 Say not: "I am hidden from God;
    in heaven who remembers me?
    Among so many people I cannot be
    known;
    what am I in the world of spirits?
16 Behold, the heavens, the heaven of
    heavens,
    the earth and the abyss tremble at his
    visitation;
17 The roots of the mountains, the earth's
    foundations,
    at his mere glance, quiver and quake.
18 Of me, therefore, he will take no
    thought;
    with my ways who will concern him-
    self?
19 If I sin, no eye will see me;
    if all in secret I am disloyal, who is to
    know?*l*
20 Who tells him of just deeds
    and what could I expect for doing my
    duty?"
21 Such are the thoughts of senseless men,
    which only the foolish knave will
    think.

Divine Wisdom Seen in Creation*

22 Hearken to me, my son, take my ad-
    vice,
    apply your mind to my words,
23 While I propose measured wisdom,
    and impart accurate knowledge.
24 When at the first God created his works
    and, as he made them, assigned their
    tasks,*m*

Sir

²⁵ He ordered for all time what they were
to do
and their domains from generation to
generation.
They were not to hunger, nor grow
weary,
nor ever cease from their tasks.
²⁶ Not one should ever crowd its neighbor,
nor should they ever disobey his word.
²⁷ Then the LORD looked upon the earth,
and filled it with his blessings.ⁿ
²⁸ Its surface he covered with all manner
of life
which must return into it again.

CHAPTER 17

¹ The LORD from the earth created man,
and in his own image he made him.^o
² Limited days of life he gives him^p
and makes him return to earth again.
³ He endows man with a strength of his
own,
and with power over all things else on
earth.
⁴ He puts the fear of him in all flesh,
and gives him rule over beasts and
birds.
⁵ He forms men's tongues and eyes and
ears,
and imparts to them an understanding heart.
⁶ With wisdom and knowledge he fills
them;
good and evil he shows them.
⁷ He looks with favor upon their hearts,
and shows them his glorious works,
⁸ That they may describe the wonders of
his deeds
and praise his holy name.
⁹ He has set before them knowledge,
a law of life as their inheritance;
¹⁰ An everlasting covenant* he has made
with them,
his commandments he has revealed to
them.
¹¹ His majestic glory their eyes beheld,
his glorious voice their ears heard.
¹² He says to them, "Avoid all evil";
each of them he gives precepts about
his fellow men.
¹³ Their ways are ever known to him,
they cannot be hidden from his eyes.
¹⁴ Over every nation he places a ruler,*
but the LORD's own portion is Israel.^q
¹⁵ All their actions are clear as the sun to
him,
his eyes are ever upon their ways.

¹⁶ Their wickedness cannot be hidden
from him;
all of their sins are before the LORD.
¹⁷ A man's goodness God cherishes like a
signet ring,
a man's virtue, like the apple of his
eye.
¹⁸ Later he will rise up and repay them,
and requite each one of them as they
deserve.^r

Appeal for a Return to God*

¹⁹ But to the penitent he provides a way
back,
he encourages those who are losing
hope!
²⁰ Return to the LORD and give up sin,
pray to him and make your offenses
few.
²¹ Turn again to the Most High and away
from sin,
hate intensely what he loathes;
²² Who in the nether world can glorify the
Most High^s
in place of the living who offer their
praise?
²³ No more can the dead give praise than
those who have never lived;
they glorify the LORD who are alive
and well.
²⁴ How great the mercy of the LORD,
his forgiveness of those who return to
him!
²⁵ The like cannot be found in men,
for not immortal is any son of man.
²⁶ Is anything brighter than the sun? Yet it
can be eclipsed.
How obscure* then the thoughts of
flesh and blood!
²⁷ God watches over the hosts of highest
heaven,
while all men are dust and ashes.

n Gn 1, 20ff.—o Gn 2, 7; 3, 19.—p 2ff: Gn 1, 26ff; Ps 8, 4-
8.—q Ex 19, 5; Dt 4, 19f; 32, 8f; Dn 10, 13-21; 12, 1; Rom 13,
1.—r Jb 19, 25; Jl 3, 4.—s 22f: Pss 6, 6; 115, 17; Is 38, 18.

17, 10: *An everlasting covenant . . . his commandments:*
the various covenants which God entered into with mankind, e.g., Gn
2, 15ff; 17, 1-22, especially on Mount Sinai where the people saw
God's glory and heard his voice (Ex 19, 16—24, 18).
17, 14: *Ruler:* this may refer to civil authority or to angels
placed over nations as guardians; see note on Dt 32, 8, and the
cross references above.
17, 19-27: Exhorting the sinner to return to God (19ff. 24ff),
the author implies that the Lord will postpone death for a repentant sinner so that he may fulfill his destiny of praising God on
earth (22f). In the light of Christian teaching, the gift of final
penitence extends this divine purpose into life everlasting. See
note on Ps 6, 6; cf also Ez 18, 23; 33, 11-16.
17, 26: *Obscure:* literally, evil; compare Gn 6, 5. Though
moral fault is not excluded, the thought here is the inability to
understand the merciful designs of God. Cf Wis 9, 14-18.

CHAPTER 18

The Divine Power and Mercy*

1 The Eternal is the judge of all things
without exception;
the LORD alone is just.

2 Whom has he made equal to describing
his works,
and who can probe his mighty deeds?

3 Who can measure his majestic power,
or exhaust the tale of his mercies?

4 One cannot lessen, nor increase,
nor penetrate the wonders of the
LORD.

5 When a man ends he is only beginning,
and when he stops he is still bewildered.

6 What is man, of what worth is he?
the good, the evil in him, what are
these?

7 The sum of a man's days is great
if it reaches a hundred years: *t*

8 Like a drop of sea water, like a grain of
sand,
so are these few years among the days
of eternity.

9 That is why the LORD is patient with
men
and showers upon them his mercy.

10 He sees and understands that their
death is grievous,
and so he forgives them all the more.

11 Man may be merciful to his fellow man,
but the LORD's mercy reaches all
flesh,

12 Reproving, admonishing, teaching,
as a shepherd guides his flock; *u*

13 Merciful to those who accept his guidance,
who are diligent in his precepts.

---

t Ps 90, 10.—u Jn 10, 11.—v Sir 20, 13.—w Nm 30, 3; Dt 23,
22; Ps 50, 14; Prv 20, 25; Eccl 5, 4.—x Sir 7, 16.—y Sir 11, 25.

18, 1-13: Not only are God's justice and power beyond man's
understanding (1-5), his mercy also is boundless and surpasses all
human compassion (6-13).
18, 14-27: The practice of charity is an art which avoids every
offense to the recipient (14-18). Prudence directs the changing
circumstances of daily life toward the attainment of its reward *at
the time of visitation*, i.e., the day of reckoning (19-27).
18, 19: *Merit . . . ransom:* almsgiving is often portrayed in
the Bible as a means of approach to the forgiving mercy of God.
Cf Sir 3, 29f; 29, 11f; Tb 12, 12f; Dn 4, 24; Lk 16, 9; Acts 10,
31.
18, 22f: The usual object of a vow in Old Testament times was
the offering of a bloody sacrifice.
18, 28f: A general statement on the teaching of wisdom, serving either as a conclusion to the preceding section or as an introduction to the following one. The neighbors of the wise man are
regarded as the field into which he channels the waters of wisdom
to encourage growth. Cf Sir 24, 28-31.

The Necessity of Prudence

14 My son, to your charity add no reproach,*
nor spoil any gift by harsh words.

15 Like dew that abates a burning wind,
so does a word improve a gift.

16 Sometimes the word means more than
the gift;
both are offered by a kindly man.

17 Only a fool upbraids before giving;
a grudging gift wears out the expectant eyes. *v*

18 Be informed before speaking;
before sickness prepare the cure.

19 Before you are judged, seek merit for
yourself,
and at the time of visitation you will
have a ransom.*

20 Before you have fallen, humble yourself;
when you have sinned, show repentance.

21 Delay not to forsake sins,
neglect it not till you are in distress.

22 Let nothing prevent the prompt payment of your vows;*
wait not to fulfill them when you are
dying. *w*

23 Before making a vow have the means to
fulfill it;
be not one who tries the LORD.

24 Think of wrath and the day of death,
the time of vengeance when he will
hide his face. *x*

25 Remember the time of hunger in the
time of plenty,
poverty and want in the day of
wealth. *y*

26 Between morning and evening the
weather changes;
before the LORD all things are fleeting.

27 A wise man is circumspect in all things;
when sin is rife he keeps himself from
wrongdoing.

28 Any learned man should make wisdom
known,*
and he who attains to her should declare her praise;

29 Those trained in her words must show
their wisdom,
dispensing sound proverbs like life-
giving waters.

Sir

Self-Control*

30 Go not after your lusts,^z
but keep your desires in check.
31 If you satisfy your lustful appetites
they will make you the sport of your
enemies.
32 Have no joy in the pleasures of a moment
which bring on poverty redoubled;
33 Become not a glutton and a winebibber
with nothing in your purse.

CHAPTER 19

1 He who does so grows no richer;
he who wastes the little he has will be
stripped bare.
2 Wine and women make the mind giddy,
and the companion of harlots becomes reckless.^a
4 He who lightly trusts in them has no
sense,
and he who strays after them sins
against his own life.
3 Rottenness and worms will possess him,
for contumacious desire destroys its
owner.

The Proper Use of Speech*

5 He who gloats over evil will meet with
evil,
and he who repeats an evil report has
no sense.
6 Never repeat gossip,
and you will not be reviled.^b
7 Tell nothing to friend or foe;
if you have a fault, reveal it not,^c
8 For he who hears it will hold it against
you,
and in time become your enemy.
9 Let anything you hear die within you;
be assured it will not make you burst.
10 When a fool hears something, he is in
labor,
like a woman giving birth to a child.
11 Like an arrow lodged in a man's thigh
is gossip in the breast of a fool.
12 Admonish your friend—he may not
have done it;
and if he did, that he may not do it
again.^d
13 Admonish your neighbor—he may not
have said it;
and if he did, that he may not say it
again.
14 Admonish your friend—often it may be
slander;

every story you must not believe.
15 Then, too, a man can slip and not mean
it;
who has not sinned with his tongue?^e
16 Admonish your neighbor before you
break with him;
thus will you fulfill the law of the
Most High.^f

How To Recognize True Wisdom*

17 All wisdom is fear of the LORD;
perfect wisdom is the fulfillment of
the law.^g
18 The knowledge of wickedness is not
wisdom,
nor is there prudence in the counsel
of sinners.
19 There is a shrewdness that is detestable,
while the simple man may be free
from sin.
20 There are those with little understanding who fear God,
and those of great intelligence who
violate the law.
21 There is a shrewdness keen but dishonest,
which by duplicity wins a judgment.
22 There is the wicked man who is bowed
in grief,
but is full of guile within;
23 He bows his head and feigns not to
hear,
but when not observed, he will take
advantage of you:
24 Even though his lack of strength keeps
him from sinning,
when he finds the opportunity, he
will do harm.
25 One can tell a man by his appearance;
a wise man is known as such when
first met.
26 A man's attire, his hearty laughter and
his gait,
proclaim him for what he is.

---

z Rom 6, 12; 13, 14.—a Prv 20, 1; 23, 20ff.—b Prv 25, 10.—c
Sir 8, 18f.—d Lv 19, 17; Mt 18, 15; Lk 17, 3.—e Sir 14, 1; Jas
3, 2.—f Lv 19, 17.—g Sir 1, 1. 12. 14; Jb 28, 28; Ps 111, 10;
Prv 1, 7; 9, 10.

18, 30—19, 4: Inordinate gratification of the senses makes a
man unreasonable, the slave of passion, *the sport of his
enemies.* In the end it destroys him physically and spiritually.
19, 5-16: An excellent commentary on the eighth commandment of the Decalogue, forbidding intemperance in speech
through calumny, rash judgment, and detraction (5f), and incul-
cating discreet silence in defense of self and of neighbor (7-11).
Justice requires that an accused neighbor be given a hearing, and
charity urges fraternal correction; both together fulfill *the law of
the Most High* (12-16); cf Mt 7, 1f; 18, 15f.
19, 17-26: True and false wisdom as here described are synonymous with virtue and vice, with *the fulfillment of the law*
and the violation of it.

CHAPTER 20

Conduct of the Wise and the Foolish

1 An admonition can be inopportune,*
  and a man may be wise to hold his peace.
2 It is much better to admonish than to lose one's temper,
  for one who admits his fault will be kept from disgrace.
3 Like a eunuch lusting for intimacy with a maiden
  is he who does right under compulsion.*
4 One man is silent and is thought wise,
  another is talkative and is disliked.
5 One man is silent because he has nothing to say;
  another is silent, biding his time.ʰ
6 A wise man is silent till the right time comes,
  but a boasting fool ignores the proper time.
7 He who talks too much is detested;
  he who pretends to authority is hated.

8 Some misfortunes bring success;*
  some things gained are a man's loss.
9 Some gifts do one no good,
  and some must be paid back double.*
10 Humiliation can follow fame,
  while from obscurity a man can lift up his head.
11 A man may buy much for little,
  but pay for it seven times over.
12 A wise man makes himself popular by a few words,

but fools pour forth their blandishments in vain.
13 A gift from a rogue will do you no good,
  for in his eyes his one gift is equal to seven.
14 He gives little and criticizes often,
  and like a crier he shouts aloud.
He lends today, he asks it back tomorrow;
  hateful indeed is such a man.
15 A fool has no friends,
  nor thanks for his generosity;
16 Those who eat his bread have an evil tongue.
How many times they laugh him to scorn!

17 A fall to the ground is less sudden than a slip of the tongue;*
  that is why the downfall of the wicked comes so quickly.
18 Insipid food is the untimely tale;
  the unruly are always ready to offer it.
19 A proverb when spoken by a fool is unwelcome,
  for he does not utter it at the proper time.
20 A man through want may be unable to sin,
  yet in this tranquility he cannot rest.
21 One may lose his life through shame,
  and perish through a fool's intimidation.
22 A man makes a promise to a friend out of shame,
  and has him for his enemy needlessly.
23 A lie is a foul blot in a man,
  yet it is constantly on the lips of the unruly.
24 Better a thief than an inveterate liar,
  yet both will suffer disgrace;
25 A liar's way leads to dishonor,
  his shame remains ever with him.
26 A wise man advances himself by his words,*
  a prudent man pleases the great.
27 He who works his land has abundant crops,
  he who pleases the great is pardoned his faults.
28 Favors and gifts blind the eyes;
  like a muzzle over the mouth they silence reproof.ⁱ
29 Hidden wisdom and unseen treasure—
  of what value is either?

---

h Sir 20, 1; Prv 10, 19; 17, 28.—i Ex 23, 8; Dt 16, 19.

20, 1-7: Wisdom indicates the proper times for speech and silence, that is, the occasions when the most benefit can be gained from them.
20, 3: The sense is that violence or force against a person can prevent an external act of sin or compel a good deed without eliminating the internal sin or desire of wrongdoing. Cf Sir 20, 20.
20, 8-16: In a series of paradoxes the author indicates how much true and lasting values differ from apparent ones.
20, 9: *And some . . . double:* or perhaps, "but some are doubly precious."
20, 17-25: The ill-timed speech of *the wicked, the unruly* and *a fool* is repulsive (17ff); human respect exposes one to intimidation, rash promises and enmity (21ff); lies bring dishonor and lasting disgrace (23ff).
20, 26-30: Unlike the fool who invites disaster through misuse of his tongue, the sage through prudent speech gains in honor and esteem among the great (26f). He must beware, however, of accepting bribes, lest he share in evil through silence when he should reprove (28ff).

Sir

30 Better the man who hides his folly
   than the one who hides his wisdom.

CHAPTER 21

Sin Must Be Avoided*

1 My son, if you have sinned, do so no
   more,
   and for your past sins pray to be forgiven.
2 Flee from sin as from a serpent
   that will bite you if you go near it;
   Its teeth are lion's teeth,
   destroying the souls of men.
3 Every offense is a two-edged sword;
   when it cuts, there can be no healing.
4 Violence and arrogance wipe out
   wealth;
   so too a proud man's home is destroyed.
5 Prayer from a poor man's lips is heard
   at once,
   and justice is quickly granted him.
6 He who hates correction walks the sinner's path,
   but he who fears the LORD repents in
   his heart.
7 Widely known is the boastful speaker,
   but the wise man knows his own
   faults.
8 He who builds his house with another's
   money
   is collecting stones for his funeral
   mound.
9 A band of criminals is like a bundle of
   tow;
   they will end in a flaming fire.*j*
10 The path of sinners is smooth stones
   that end in the depths of the nether
   world.*

The Wise and the Foolish Differ*

11 He who keeps the law controls his impulses;
   he who is perfect in fear of the LORD
   has wisdom.
12 He can never be taught who is not
   shrewd,
   but one form of shrewdness is
   thoroughly bitter.
13 A wise man's knowledge wells up in a
   flood,
   and his counsel, like a living spring;*k*
14 A fool's mind is like a broken jar—
   no knowledge at all can it hold.
15 When an intelligent man hears words of
   wisdom,

he approves them and adds to them;
The wanton hears them with scorn
   and casts them behind his back.
16 A fool's chatter is like a load on a journey,
   but there is charm to be found upon
   the lips of the wise.
17 The views of a prudent man are sought
   in an assembly,
   and his words are considered with
   care.
18 Like a house in ruins is wisdom to a
   fool;
   the stupid man knows it only as inscrutable words.
19 Like fetters on the legs is learning to a
   fool,
   like a manacle on his right hand.
20 A fool raises his voice in laughter,
   but a prudent man at the most smiles
   gently.*l*
21 Like a chain of gold is learning to a wise
   man,
   like a bracelet on his right arm.

22 The fool steps boldly into a house,
   while the well-bred man remains outside;*m*
23 A boor peeps through the doorway of a
   house,
   but a cultured man keeps his glance
   cast down.
24 It is rude for one to listen at a door;
   a cultured man would be overwhelmed by the disgrace of it.
25 The lips of the impious talk of what is
   not their concern,
   but the words of the prudent are carefully weighed.
26 Fools' thoughts are in their mouths,
   wise men's words are in their hearts.

---

j Ps 21, 9.—k Prv 13, 14; 16, 22.—l Eccl 7, 6.—m Prv 25, 17.

21, 1-10: Under various figures the consequences of sin are
described as destructive of wealth, and even of bodily life, and deserving of death and a place in the depths of the nether world
(2ff. 6a. 8ff). Through prayer, forgiveness can be sought (1), and
through fear of the Lord, repentance is achieved (1. 5. 6b).
21, 10: *The path of sinners . . . nether world:* eternal retribution is not yet proposed in this reference. It became clearly
revealed through the teaching of Christ; cf Mt 7, 13f; 25, 41-46;
Lk 16, 19-31.
21, 11-28: The mind of the wise man is a fountain of knowledge (13. 15); his will is trained to keep the law (11); his words
are gracious, valued, carefully weighed, sincere (16f. 25f); his
conduct is respectful, cultured and restrained (20. 22ff). The
fool's mind is devoid of knowledge and impenetrable to it (12. 14.
18f); his will rejects it (15); his talk is burdensome (16), his
laughter unrestrained (20), his conversation shallow and meddlesome (25f); his conduct is bold and rude (22ff); his abuse of
others redounds on himself (27f).

27 When a godless man curses his adver-
     sary,*
   he really curses himself.
28 A slanderer besmirches himself,
   and is hated by his neighbors.

CHAPTER 22

On Laziness and Foolishness

1 The sluggard is like a stone in the mud;*
   everyone hisses at his disgrace.
2 The sluggard is like a lump of dung;
   whoever touches him wipes his hands.
3 An unruly child is a disgrace to its
     father;
   if it be a daughter, she brings him to
     poverty.[n]
4 A thoughtful daughter becomes a trea-
     sure to her husband,
   a shameless one is her father's grief.
5 A hussy shames her father and her hus-
     band;
   by both she is despised.
6 Like a song in time of mourning is in-
     opportune talk,*
   but lashes and discipline are at all
     times wisdom.
7 Teaching a fool is like gluing a broken
     pot,[o]
   or like disturbing a man in the depths
     of sleep;
8 He talks with a slumberer who talks
     with a fool,
   for when it is over, he will say,
     "What was that?"
9 Weep over the dead man, for his light
     has gone out;

weep over the fool, for sense has left
   him.
10 Weep but a little over the dead man, for
     he is at rest;
   but worse than death is the life of a
     fool.
11 Seven days of mourning for the dead,
   but for the wicked fool a whole
     lifetime.[p]
12 Speak but seldom with the stupid man,
   be not the companion of a brute;
13 Beware of him lest you have trouble
   and be spattered when he shakes
     himself;
   Turn away from him and you will find
     rest
   and not be wearied by his lack of
     sense.
14 What is heavier than lead,
   and what is its name but "Fool"?
15 Sand and salt and an iron mass
   are easier to bear than a stupid man.[q]
16 Masonry bonded with wooden beams*
   is not loosened by an earthquake;
   Neither is a resolve constructed with
     careful deliberation
   shaken in a moment of fear.
17 A resolve that is backed by prudent
     understanding
   is like the polished surface of a
     smooth wall.
18 Small stones lying on an open height
   will not remain when the wind blows;
   Neither can a timid resolve based on
     foolish plans
   withstand fear of any kind.

The Preservation of Friendship*

19 One who jabs the eye brings tears:
   he who pierces the heart bares its
     feelings.
20 He who throws stones at birds drives
   them away,
   and he who insults a friend breaks up
     the friendship.
21 Should you draw a sword against a
     friend,
   despair not, it can be undone.
22 Should you speak sharply to a friend,
   fear not, you can be reconciled.
   But a contemptuous insult, a confi-
     dence broken,
   or a treacherous attack will drive
     away any friend.
23 Make fast friends with a man while he is
     poor;

---

n Prv 17, 21; 19, 13.—o 7-11: Prv 23, 9.—p Gn 50, 10.—q
Prv 27, 3.

21, 27: *Adversary:* this can be understood in the sense that,
if a man curses one who led him into sin, he implicitly curses himself for having yielded to the sin; or in the sense that the enemy
is the man's own sinful nature; or even in the sense that the
enemy is the devil, since the Hebrew word used here is *satan.* Cf
1 Chr 21, 1; Zec 3, 2; 2 Pt 2, 12f; Jude 9.
22, 1-15: To Sirach, a lazy person and an unruly child are a
cause of shame and disgrace; everyone wishes to be rid of them
(1-5). A wicked fool is as senseless as a man asleep or dead, but
the grief he causes others lasts a lifetime (7-11). He is like a
brute, troublesome and intolerable (12-15).
22, 6: *Like a song . . . is . . . talk:* some understand *talk* in
the sense of a rebuke unheeded by the unruly as a joyful song is
out of place among mourners. Corporal punishment, however, is
always effective.
22, 16ff: A prudent mind firmly resolved is undisturbed by violent and conflicting thoughts, whereas a foolish person is tossed
about by the winds of fear, like small stones whipped about by
high winds.
22, 19-26: As disputes and violence weaken friendship, and
disloyalty and abuse of confidence destroy it utterly (19-22. 24.
26), so kindness to a poor man in time of poverty and adversity
builds up friendship and merits a share in his prosperity and inheritance (23. 25).

thus will you enjoy his prosperity
with him.
In time of trouble remain true to him,
so as to share in his inheritance when
it comes.
24 Before flames burst forth an oven
smokes;
so does abuse come before bloodshed.
25 From a friend in need of support
no one need hide in shame;
26 But from him who brings harm to his
friend
all will stand aloof who hear of it.

Prayer*

27 Who will set a guard over my mouth,
and upon my lips an effective seal,
That I may not fail through them,
that my tongue may not destroy me?[r]

CHAPTER 23

1 LORD, Father and Master of my life,*
permit me not to fall by them!
2 Who will apply the lash to my thoughts,
to my mind the rod of discipline,
That my failings may not be spared,
nor the sins of my heart overlooked;
3 Lest my failings increase,
and my sins be multiplied;
Lest I succumb to my foes,
and my enemy rejoice over me?
4 LORD, Father and God of my life,
abandon me not into their control!
5 A brazen look allow me not;
ward off passion from my heart,
6 Let not the lustful cravings of the flesh
master me,
surrender me not to shameless desires.

The Proper Use of the Tongue*

7 Give heed, my children, to the instruction that I pronounce,
for he who keeps it will not be enslaved.
8 Through his lips is the sinner ensnared;
the railer and the arrogant man fall
thereby.
9 Let not your mouth form the habit of
swearing,
or becoming too familiar with the
Holy Name.[s]
10 Just as a slave that is constantly under
scrutiny*
will not be without welts,
So one who swears continually by the
Holy Name

will not remain free from sin.
11 A man who often swears heaps up obligations;
the scourge will never be far from his
house.
If he swears in error, he incurs guilt;
if he neglects his obligation, his sin is
doubly great.[t]
If he swears without reason he cannot
be found just,
and all his house will suffer affliction.
12 There are words which merit death;
may they never be heard among
Jacob's heirs.
For all such words are foreign to the devout,
who do not wallow in sin.
13 Let not your mouth become used to
coarse talk,
for in it lies sinful matter.
14 Keep your father and mother in mind
when you sit among the mighty,
Lest in their presence you commit a
blunder
and disgrace your upbringing,
By wishing you had never been born
or cursing the day of your birth.[u]
15 A man who has the habit of abusive language
will never mature in character as long
as he lives

Sins of the Flesh*

16 Two types of men multiply sins,
a third* draws down wrath;

---

r Ps 141, 3.—s Ex 20, 7; Lv 19, 12; Dt 5, 11; Mt 5, 33ff.—t
Lv 5, 4ff.—u Sir 7, 27; Ex 20, 12; Dt 5, 16.

22, 27—23, 6: The sage implores the divine assistance to
preserve him through stern discipline from sins of the tongue (22,
27; 23, 1); ignorance of mind and weakness of will (2f) and inclinations of the senses and the flesh, lest he fall into the hands of
his enemies, or become a prey of shameful desires (3-6).
23, 1: *Lord, Father and Master of my life:* these words express the tender personal relationship between the author's soul
and God, the need of his assistance, and the truth of his providence.
23, 7-15: A warning against sins of the tongue through misuse
of the Holy Name, thoughtless swearing which involves obligation
and incurs guilt (7-11), blasphemy (12), talk that is coarse and
blundersome (13f), and the incorrigible habit of *abusive language* (15).
23, 10: *As a slave . . . under scrutiny,* so is he who calls on
God to witness the truth of what he says.
23, 16-27: From sins of the tongue the author proceeds to
treat of sins of the flesh and their dire consequences. The passion
of lust tyrannizes over its victims and, like fire, consumes and utterly destroys them (16f. 22-26). The false security of the adulterer serves but to aggravate his inevitable fate (18-21). Only the
fear of the Lord and observance of his commandments can assure
moral safety (27).
23, 16: *Two types . . . a third:* three kinds of sins of impurity, with increasing degrees of gravity: solitary sins (16), fornication (17) and adultery (18-21).

For burning passion is a blazing fire,
  not to be quenched till it burns itself
  out:
A man given to sins of the flesh,
  who never stops until the fire breaks
  forth;
17 The rake to whom all bread is sweet
  and who is never through till he dies;*v*
18 And the man who dishonors his marriage bed
  and says to himself, "Who can see
  me?
Darkness surrounds me, walls hide me;
  no one sees me; why should I fear to
  sin?"*w*
Of the Most High he is not mindful,
19   fearing only the eyes of men;
He does not understand that the eyes of
  the LORD,
  ten thousand times brighter than the
  sun,
Observe every step a man takes
  and peer into hidden corners.
20 He who knows all things before they
  exist
  still knows them all after they are
  made.
21 Such a man will be punished in the
  streets of the city;*x*
  when he least expects it, he will be
  apprehended.*

22 So also with the woman who is unfaithful to her husband
  and offers as heir her son by a
  stranger.
23 First, she has disobeyed the law of the
  Most High;
  secondly, she has wronged her husband;
Thirdly, in her wanton adultery

---

v Prv 9, 17.—w Is 29, 15.—x 21f: Lv 20, 10; Dt 22, 21.—y Sir
1, 10-18. 24; Prv 3, 1f.—z 3ff: Sir 1, 1; Prv 2, 6; 8, 22-36; Wis
7, 24f.

23, 21: Cf Lv 20, 10; Dt 22, 22.
23, 23: The detailed evil of adultery includes disobedience to
God's law (Ex 20, 14), injustice to a partner in marriage, and disgraceful offspring.
23, 24f: The judgment of *the assembly* determined the il-
legitimacy of children born of adultery or incest and excluded
them from the "community of the Lord" (Dt 23, 3). Cf Wis 3, 16-
19; 4, 3-6.
24, 1-27: In this chapter Wisdom speaks in the first person,
describing her origin, her dwelling place in Israel, and the reward
she gives her followers. As in Prv 8, Wisdom is described as a
being who comes from God and is distinct from him. While we do
not say with certainty that this description applies to a personal
being, it does foreshadow the beautiful doctrine of the Word of
God later developed in St. John's Gospel (Jn 1, 1-14). In the
liturgy this chapter is applied to the Blessed Virgin because of her
constant and intimate association with Christ, the Incarnate Wisdom.

she has borne children by another
  man.*
24 Such a woman will be dragged before
  the assembly,*
  and her punishment will extend to
  her children;
25 Her children will not take root;
  her branches will not bring forth
  fruit.
26 She will leave an accursed memory;
  her disgrace will never be blotted out.
27 Thus all who dwell on the earth shall
  know,
  and all who inhabit the world shall
  understand,
That nothing is better than the fear of
  the LORD,
  nothing more salutary than to obey
  his commandments.*y*

CHAPTER 24

Praise of Wisdom

1 Wisdom sings her own praises,*
  before her own people she proclaims
  her glory;
2 In the assembly of the Most High she
  opens her mouth,
  in the presence of his hosts she declares her worth:
3 "From the mouth of the Most High I
  came forth,*z*
  and mistlike covered the earth.
4 In the highest heavens did I dwell,
  my throne on a pillar of cloud.
5 The vault of heaven I compassed alone,
  through the deep abyss I wandered.
6 Over waves of the sea, over all the land,
  over every people and nation I held
  sway.
7 Among all these I sought a resting
  place;
  in whose inheritance should I abide?
8 "Then the Creator of all gave me his
  command,
  and he who formed me chose the spot
  for my tent,
Saying, 'In Jacob make your dwelling,
  in Israel your inheritance.'
9 Before all ages, in the beginning, he
  created me,
  and through all ages I shall not cease
  to be.
10 In the holy tent I ministered before
  him,
  and in Zion I fixed my abode.

Sir

11 Thus in the chosen city he has given me rest,
in Jerusalem is my domain.
12 I have struck root among the glorious people,
in the portion of the LORD, his heritage.

13 "Like a cedar on Lebanon I am raised aloft,
like a cypress on Mount Hermon,
14 Like a palm tree in Engedi,
like a rosebush in Jericho,
Like a fair olive tree in the field,
like a plane tree growing beside the water.
15 Like cinnamon, or fragrant balm, or precious myrrh,
I give forth perfume;*a*
Like galbanum and onycha and sweet spices,
like the odor of incense in the holy place.*
16 I spread out my branches like a terebinth,
my branches so bright and so graceful.
17 I bud forth delights like the vine,
my blossoms become fruit fair and rich.
18 Come to me, all you that yearn for me,
and be filled with my fruits;*
19 You will remember me as sweeter than honey,
better to have than the honeycomb.
20 He who eats of me will hunger still,*
he who drinks of me will thirst for more;*b*
21 He who obeys me will not be put to shame,
he who serves me will never fail."

22 All this is true of the book of the Most High's covenant,*c*
the law which Moses commanded us as an inheritance for the community of Jacob.*
23 It overflows, like the Pishon, with wisdom—*d*
like the Tigris in the days of the new fruits.
24 It runs over, like the Euphrates, with understanding,
like the Jordan at harvest time.
25 It sparkles like the Nile with knowledge,
like the Gihon* at vintage time.

26 The first man never finished comprehending wisdom,
nor will the last succeed in fathoming her.
27 For deeper than the sea are her thoughts;
her counsels, than the great abyss.
28 Now I, like a rivulet from her stream,*
channeling the waters into a garden,
29 Said to myself, "I will water my plants,
my flower bed I will drench";
And suddenly this rivulet of mine became a river,
then this stream of mine, a sea.
30 Thus do I send my teachings forth shining like the dawn,
to become known afar off.
31 Thus do I pour out instruction like prophecy
and bestow it on generations to come.

CHAPTER 25

Those Who Are Worthy of Praise*

1 With three things I am delighted,
for they are pleasing to the LORD and to men:
Harmony among brethren, friendship among neighbors,
and the mutual love of husband and wife.
2 Three kinds of men I hate;
their manner of life I loathe indeed:
A proud pauper, a rich dissembler,
and an old man lecherous in his dotage.

---

a Ex 30, 22-25.—b Is 55, 1; Jn 6, 35.—c Ex 24, 7.—d 23ff: Gn 2, 11-14.

24, 15: These substances were associated with worship, being mentioned in Ex 30, 22f. 34 as the ingredients of the anointing oil and the sacred incense. Israel was a priestly nation.
24, 18: Compare the words of the Savior in Mt 11, 28ff.
24, 20: So pleasing is wisdom to man that, far from being satiated, he will always desire more.
24, 22: Here the author begins to speak once more, Wisdom having ended her discourse in the preceding verse. Wisdom and the law of Moses are now identified.
24, 25: *Gihon:* understood by some to have been a name for the Nile; cf Gn 2, 13.
24, 28-31: Spoken by the author. He had at first drawn a small portion of the water of wisdom for his own private benefit, but finding it so useful, he soon began to let others share in this boon by teaching them the lessons of wisdom.
25, 1-11: While praising brotherly love, love of neighbor, and conjugal love, the sage condemns their opposites in the arrogant pauper who despises his brother, the fraudulent rich man who cheats his neighbor, and the lecherous old man unfaithful to his wife (1f). This last, sensual from his youth, lacks the mature blessings of judgment and wisdom in old age (3-6), and the joy of a peaceful household, where honesty and dignity, friendship, wisdom and fear of God prevail (7-11).

3 What you have not saved in your youth,
how will you acquire in your old age?
4 How becoming to the gray-haired is
judgment,
and a knowledge of counsel to those
on in years!
5 How becoming to the aged is wisdom,
understanding and prudence to the
venerable!
6 The crown of old men is wide experience;
their glory, the fear of the LORD.

7 There are nine who come to my mind as
blessed,
a tenth whom my tongue proclaims:
The man who finds joy in his children,
and he who lives to see his enemies'
downfall.
8 Happy is he who dwells with a sensible
wife,
and he who plows not like a donkey
yoked with an ox.*
Happy is he who sins not with his
tongue,
and he who serves not his inferior.
9 Happy is he who finds a friend
and he who speaks to attentive ears.
10 He who finds wisdom is great indeed,
but not greater than he who fears the
LORD.
11 Fear of the LORD surpasses all else,
its possessor is beyond compare.

Wicked and Virtuous Women*

12 Worst of all wounds is that of the heart,
worst of all evils is that of a woman.
13 Worst of all sufferings is that from one's
foes,

---

e Sir 25, 8; Prv 18, 22; 31, 10ff.—f Sir 36, 24.

25, 8: *Like a donkey yoked with an ox:* incompatibility between husband and wife.

25, 12-25: Wickedness in a woman is most grievous, painful
and bitter to her husband. Through it she becomes vengeful,
dangerous and intolerable, jealous, talkative, intemperate and unchaste. Even her very appearance is changed (12-17). The worst
of all evils, a source of grief, a snare and a disgrace to her husband, she depresses his mind, saddens and breaks his heart, destroys his strength (18-22). She must not be indulged but made
obedient or punished (24f).

25, 23: According to the account in Gn 3, to which Ben Sirach
refers, sin, the cause of death, originated in woman: Eve, the first
human being to sin, induced Adam to follow her example. But it
is through Adam, as head of the race, that original sin and its
punishment of spiritual death are presented by St. Paul (Rom 5)
as having entered the world, to become the occasion for the redemptive work of Christ our Lord.

26, 1-4. 13-18: *A good wife* is as a gift from God, bringing
joy and peace, happiness and contentment to her husband (1-4)
through *her thoughtfulness,* reserve, modesty and chastity,
beauty, grace and virtue (13-18).

26, 2: *Worthy:* gifted spiritually, mentally and physically. Cf
Prv 31, 10.

---

worst of all vengeance is that of one's
enemies:
14 No poison worse than that of a serpent,
no venom greater than that of a
woman.
15 With a dragon or a lion I would rather
dwell
than live with an evil woman.
16 Wickedness changes a woman's looks,
and makes her sullen as a female
bear.
17 When her husband sits among his
neighbors,
a bitter sigh escapes him unawares.
18 There is scarce any evil like that in a
woman;
may she fall to the lot of the sinner!
19 Like a sandy hill to aged feet
is a railing wife to a quiet man.
20 Stumble not through woman's beauty,
nor be greedy for her wealth;
21 The man is a slave, in disgrace and
shame,
when a wife supports her husband.
22 Depressed mind, saddened face,
broken heart—this from an evil wife.
Feeble hands and quaking knees—
from a wife who brings no happiness
to her husband.
23 In woman was sin's beginning,
and because of her we all die.*
24 Allow water no outlet,
and be not indulgent to an erring
wife.
25 If she walks not by your side,
cut her away from you.

CHAPTER 26

1 Happy the husband of a good wife,*
twice-lengthened are his days;e
2 A worthy* wife brings joy to her husband,
peaceful and full is his life.
3 A good wife is a generous gift
bestowed upon him who fears the
LORD;f
4 Be he rich or poor, his heart is content,
and a smile is ever on his face.

5 There are three things at which my
heart quakes,
a fourth before which I quail:
Though false charges in public, trial before all the people,
and lying testimony are harder to
bear than death,

⁶ A jealous wife is heartache and mourning*
and a scourging tongue like the other
three.
⁷ A bad wife is a chafing yoke;
he who marries her seizes a scorpion.
⁸ A drunken wife arouses great anger,
for she does not hide her shame.
⁹ By her eyelids and her haughty stare
an unchaste wife can be recognized.

¹⁰ Keep a strict watch over an unruly wife,
lest, finding an opportunity, she
make use of it;ᵍ
¹¹ Follow close if her eyes are bold,
and be not surprised if she betrays
you:
¹² As a thirsty traveler with eager mouth
drinks from any water that he finds,
So she settles down before every tent-
peg
and opens her quiver for every arrow.

¹³ A gracious wife delights her husband,
her thoughtfulness puts flesh on his
bones;
¹⁴ A gift from the LORD is her governed
speech,
and her firm virtue is of surpassing
worth.
¹⁵ Choicest of blessings is a modest wife,
priceless her chaste person.
¹⁶ Like the sun rising in the LORD's
heavens,
the beauty of a virtuous wife is the
radiance of her home.
¹⁷ Like the light which shines above the
holy lampstand,*
are her beauty of face and graceful
figure.
¹⁸ Golden columns on silver bases
are her shapely limbs and steady
feet.*

Dangers to Integrity and Friendship

¹⁹ These two bring grief to my heart,
and the third arouses my horror:
A wealthy man reduced to want;
illustrious men held in contempt;
And the man who passes from justice to
sin,
for whom the LORD makes ready the
sword.ʰ
²⁰ A merchant can hardly remain upright,*
nor a shopkeeper free from sin;

CHAPTER 27

¹ For the sake of profit many sin,
and the struggle for wealth blinds the
eyes.ⁱ
² Like a peg driven between fitted stones,
between buying and selling sin is
wedged in.
³ Unless you earnestly hold fast to the
fear of the LORD,
suddenly your house will be thrown
down.

⁴ When a sieve is shaken, the husks appear;
so do a man's faults when he speaks.
⁵ As the test of what the potter molds is
in the furnace,
so in his conversation is the test of a
man.ʲ
⁶ The fruit of a tree shows the care it has
had;
so too does a man's speech disclose
the bent of his mind.ᵏ
⁷ Praise no man before he speaks,
for it is then that men are tested.
⁸ If you strive after justice you will attain
it,
and put it on like a splendid robe.
⁹ Birds nest with their own kind,
and fidelity comes to those who live
by it.

---

g Sir 42, 11.—h Ez 18, 24ff.—i Sir 7, 18; 31, 6; Prv 30, 8f.—j
1 Pt 1, 7.—k Mt 7, 20.

26, 6-12: A repetition of the thought expressed in Sir 25, 12-
25.
26, 17f: The *holy lampstand* and the *golden columns* stood
in the holy place of the ancient Tabernacle (Ex 25, 31-40; 26,
32).
26, 18: Among the additions found here in some manuscripts
are the following lines:
"My son, take care in the prime of life
not to surrender your strength to strangers;
Single out from the land a goodly field
and there with confidence sow the seed of your increase;
So shall you have your offspring around you,
and in confidence shall they grow up.

"Though a woman for hire be thought of as a trifle,
a married woman is a deadly snare for those who embrace
her. [Cf Prv 6, 26.]

"A wife's complaint should be made in meekness,
and show itself in a slight flush;
But a loud-mouthed, scolding wife
is a trumpet signaling for battle:
Any human being who answers that challenge
will spend his life amid the turbulence of war."

26, 20—27, 15: From proper conduct in family life, the
author proceeds to social morality, warning especially against injustice in commerce (26, 20—27, 3), and perversity of speech in
business (4-7). The pursuit of *justice* in these matters is all the
more meritorious as it is difficult (8ff). The discourses of the devout are marked with wisdom, but the conversations of the wicked, with offense, swearing, *cursing*, quarrels and even
bloodshed (11-15).

10 As a lion crouches in wait for prey,
   so do sins for evildoers.
11 Ever wise are the discourses of the devout,
   but the godless man, like the moon,
   is inconstant.
12 Limit the time you spend among fools,
   but frequent the company of
   thoughtful men.
13 The conversation of the wicked is offensive,
   their laughter is wanton guilt.
14 Their oath-filled talk makes the hair
   stand on end,
   their brawls make one stop one's ears.
15 Wrangling among the haughty ends in
   bloodshed,
   their cursing is painful to hear.*l*

16 He who betrays a secret cannot be
   trusted,*
   he will never find an intimate friend.*m*
17 Cherish your friend, keep faith with
   him;
   but if you betray his confidence, follow him not;
18 For as an enemy might kill a man,
   you have killed your neighbor's
   friendship.
19 Like a bird released from the hand,
   you have let your friend go and cannot recapture him;
20 Follow him not, for he is far away,
   he has fled like a gazelle from the
   trap.
21 A wound can be bound up, and an insult forgiven,
   but he who betrays secrets does hopeless damage.*n*

Malice, Anger and Vengeance

22 He who has shifty eyes plots mischief
   and no one can ward him off;
23 In your presence he uses honeyed talk,
   and admires your every word,
   But later he changes his tone
   and twists your words to your ruin.*o*
24 There is nothing that I hate so much,
   and the LORD hates him as well.*p*
25 As a stone falls back on him who throws
   it up,*q*
   so a blow struck in treachery injures
   more than one.
26 As he who digs a pit falls into it,
   and he who lays a snare is caught in
   it,
27 Whoever does harm will be involved in
   it,
   without knowing how it came upon
   him.

28 Mockery and abuse will be the lot of the
   proud,
   and vengeance lies in wait for them
   like a lion.
29 The trap seizes those who rejoice in pitfalls,
   and pain will consume them before
   they die;
30 Wrath and anger are hateful things,
   yet the sinner hugs them tight.

CHAPTER 28

1 The vengeful will suffer the LORD's
   vengeance,
   for he remembers their sins in detail.*r*
2 Forgive your neighbor's injustice;
   then when you pray, your own sins
   will be forgiven.*s*

3 Should a man nourish anger against his
   fellows
   and expect healing from the LORD?*t*
4 Should a man refuse mercy to his fellows,
   yet seek pardon for his own sins?
5 If he who is but flesh cherishes wrath,
   who will forgive his sins?
6 Remember your last days, set enmity
   aside;
   remember death and decay, and cease
   from sin!*u*
7 Think of the commandments, hate not
   your neighbor;
   of the Most High's covenant, and
   overlook faults.

8 Avoid strife and your sins will be fewer,
   for a quarrelsome man kindles disputes,
9 Commits the sin of disrupting friendship

---

l Sir 23, 9-15.—m Prv 11, 13; 20, 19.—n Sir 22, 20.—o Prv
26, 24ff.—p Prv 6, 13. 16.—q 25f: Ps 7, 16f; Prv 26, 27; Eccl
10, 8.—r Dt 32, 35; Rom 12, 19.—s Mt 6, 14.—t Mt 18, 23ff.—
u Sir 7, 36; 38, 20.

27, 16—28, 11: Betrayal of *confidence* through indiscretion
destroys *friendship* and does irreparable harm (16-21); cf Sir
22, 22. False friendship based on hypocrisy and deceit is hateful
to God and man (22ff); it soon becomes a victim of its own
treachery (25ff). The same fate awaits the malicious and *vengeful* (27, 28—28, 1). They can obtain mercy and forgiveness only
by first forgiving their neighbor, being mindful of death and of the
commandments of the Most High (28, 2-7). And they must avoid
quarrels and *strife* (8-11).

and sows discord among those at peace.[v]

10 The more wood, the greater the fire,[w]
the more underlying it, the fiercer the fight;
The greater a man's strength, the sterner his anger,
the greater his power, the greater his wrath.

11 Pitch and resin make fires flare up,
and insistent quarrels provoke bloodshed.

The Evil Tongue*

12 If you blow upon a spark, it quickens into flame,
if you spit on it, it dies out;
yet both you do with your mouth!

13 Cursed be gossips, and the double-tongued,
for they destroy the peace of many.[x]

14 A meddlesome tongue subverts many,
and makes them refugees among the peoples;
It destroys walled cities,
and overthrows powerful dynasties.

15 A meddlesome tongue can drive virtuous women from their homes
and rob them of the fruit of their toil;

16 Whoever heeds it has no rest,
nor can he dwell in peace.

17 A blow from a whip raises a welt,
but a blow from the tongue smashes bones;

18 Many have fallen by the edge of the sword,
but not as many as by the tongue.[y]

19 Happy he who is sheltered from it,
and has not endured its wrath;
Who has not borne its yoke
nor been fettered with its chains;

20 For its yoke is a yoke of iron
and its chains are chains of bronze!

21 Dire is the death it inflicts,
besides which even the nether world is a gain;

22 It will not take hold among the just
nor scorch them in its flame,

23 But those who forsake the LORD will fall victims to it,
as it burns among them unquenchably!
It will hurl itself against them like a lion;
like a panther, it will tear them to pieces.

24 As you hedge round your vineyard with thorns,
set barred doors over your mouth;[z]

25 As you seal up your silver and gold,
so balance and weigh your words.

26 Take care not to slip by your tongue
and fall victim to your foe waiting in ambush.

CHAPTER 29

Loans, Alms and Surety*

1 He does a kindness who lends to his neighbor,
and he fulfills the precepts who holds out a helping hand.[a]

2 Lend to your neighbor in his hour of need,
and pay back your neighbor when a loan falls due;[b]

3 Keep your promise, be honest with him,
and you will always come by what you need.

4 Many a man who asks for a loan
adds to the burdens of those who help him;

5 When he borrows, he kisses the lender's hand
and speaks with respect of his creditor's wealth;
But when payment is due he disappoints him
and says he is helpless to meet the claim.

6 If the lender is able to recover barely half,
he considers this an achievement;
If not, he is cheated of his wealth
and acquires an enemy at no extra charge;
With curses and insults the borrower pays him back,
with abuse instead of honor.

---

v Prv 15, 18.—w 10ff: Prv 26, 20f.—x Sir 5, 16f.—y Jas 3, 5ff.—z Sir 22, 27; Ps 141, 3.—a Dt 15, 8; Ps 112, 5; Prv 19, 17.—b Ex 22, 24ff; Lv 25, 36; Mt 5, 42.

28, 12-26: Further treatment of sins of the tongue and their havoc; cf Sir 5, 12—6, 1; 19, 5-16; 20, 17-25; 23, 7-15. *Gossips* and the *double-tongued* destroy domestic peace (12-16). The *whip, the sword, chains, even the nether world,* are not so cruel as the suffering inflicted by an evil tongue (17-21). Not *the just* but *those who forsake the Lord* are *victims* of their evil tongues (22f). Therefore, guard your mouth and tongue as you would guard treasure against an enemy (24ff).

29, 1-20: Some practical maxims concerning the use of wealth. Give *to a poor man* (8f), lend to a needy neighbor, but repay *when a loan falls due* lest the lender's burden be increased (1-5) and his kindness abused (6f); through charity build up defense against evil (10-13). *Go surety for your neighbor according to your means, but take care* (20) not to fall, for the shameless play false and bring their protectors and themselves to misfortune and ruin (14-19).

7 Many refuse to lend, not out of mean-
ness,
but from fear of being cheated.

8 To a poor man, however, be generous;
keep him not waiting for your alms;
9 Because of the precept, help the needy,
and in their want, do not send them
away empty-handed. *c*

10 Spend your money for your brother and
friend,
and hide it not under a stone to
perish;
11 Dispose of your treasure as the Most
High commands,
for that will profit you more than the
gold. *d*
12 Store up almsgiving in your treasure
house,
and it will save you from every evil;
13 Better than a stout shield and a sturdy
spear
it will fight for you against the foe.

14 A good man goes surety for his neighbor,
and only the shameless would play
him false; *e*
15 Forget not the kindness of your backer,
for he offers his very life for you.
16 The wicked turn a pledge on their behalf into misfortune,
and the ingrate abandons his protector;
17 Going surety has ruined many prosperous men
and tossed them about like waves of
the sea, *f*
18 Has exiled men of prominence
and sent them wandering through
foreign lands.
19 The sinner through surety comes to
grief,
and he who undertakes too much falls
into lawsuits.

20 Go surety for your neighbor according
to your means,
but take care lest you fall thereby.

Frugality and Its Rewards*

21 Life's prime needs are water, bread,
and clothing,
a house, too, for decent privacy. *g*
22 Better a poor man's fare under the
shadow of one's own roof
than sumptuous banquets among
strangers. *h*
23 Be it little or much, be content with
what you have,
and pay no heed to him who would
disparage your home;
24 A miserable life it is to go from house to
house,
for as a guest you dare not open your
mouth.
25 The visitor has no thanks for filling the
cups;
besides, you will hear these bitter
words:
26 "Come here, stranger, set the table,
give me to eat the food you have!
27 Away, stranger, for one more worthy;
for my brother's visit I need the
room!"
28 Painful things to a sensitive man
are abuse at home and insults from
his creditors.

CHAPTER 30

The Training of Children*

1 He who loves his son chastises him
often,
that he may be his joy when he grows
up. *i*
2 He who disciplines his son will benefit
from him,
and boast of him among his intimates.
3 He who educates his son makes his
enemy jealous,
and shows his delight in him among
his friends.
4 At the father's death, he will seem not
dead,
since he leaves after him one like
himself,
5 Whom he looks upon through life with
joy,
and even in death, without regret:
6 The avenger he leaves against his foes,
and the one to repay his friends with
kindness.

Sir

---

c Sir 4, 1ff; Lv 19, 9f; 23, 22; Dt 15, 8.—d Sir 17, 17; Tb 4,
7ff.—e Sir 8, 13.—f Prv 6, 1f; 11, 15.—g Sir 39, 26.—h Sir 40,
29.—i Prv 13, 24; 23, 13; 29, 15; Heb 12, 7.

29, 21-28: The man who provides his own basic *needs* of
food, clothing and dwelling, and is content with what he has, preserves his freedom and self-respect (21ff). But if he lives as a
guest, even among the rich, he exposes himself to insult and
abuse (24-28).
30, 1-13: Sound discipline and careful education of children
correct frivolity and stubbornness, prevent remorse and humiliation, and bring to parents lasting joy and delight, prestige among
friends, jealousy of enemies, perpetuation and vindication of
themselves through their offspring (1-6). Lack of discipline and
overindulgence of children bring *sorrow* and disappointment,
terror and *grief* (7-13).

7 He who spoils his son will have wounds
to bandage,
and will quake inwardly at every outcry.
8 A colt untamed turns out stubborn;
a son left to himself grows up unruly.
9 Pamper your child and he will be a terror for you,
indulge him and he will bring you
grief.
10 Share not in his frivolity lest you share
in his sorrow,
when finally your teeth are clenched
in remorse.
11 Give him not his own way in his youth,
and close not your eyes to his follies.
12 Bend him to the yoke when he is young,
thrash his sides while he is still small,
Lest he become stubborn, disobey you,
and leave you disconsolate.*j*
13 Discipline your son, make heavy his
yoke,
lest his folly humiliate you.

Health of Soul and Body*

14 Better a poor man strong and robust,
than a rich man with wasted frame.
15 More precious than gold is health and
well-being,
contentment of spirit than coral.
16 No treasure greater than a healthy
body;
no happiness, than a joyful heart!
17 Preferable is death to a bitter life,*k*
unending sleep to constant illness.*
18 Dainties set before one who cannot eat
are like the offerings placed before a
tomb.*l*
19 What good is an offering to an idol
that can neither taste nor smell?
20 So it is with the afflicted man
who groans at the good things his
eyes behold!

21 Do not give in to sadness,
torment not yourself with brooding;*m*
22 Gladness of heart is the very life of man,
cheerfulness prolongs his days.
23 Distract yourself, renew your courage,
drive resentment far away from you;
For worry has brought death to many,
nor is there aught to be gained from
resentment.*n*
24 Envy and anger shorten one's life,
worry brings on premature old age.

25 One who is cheerful and gay while at
table
benefits from his food.*o*

CHAPTER 31

The Proper Attitude toward Riches*

1 Keeping watch over riches wastes the
flesh,
and the care of wealth drives away
rest.
2 Concern for one's livelihood banishes
slumber;
more than a serious illness it disturbs
repose.*
3 The rich man labors to pile up wealth,
and his only rest is wanton pleasure;
4 The poor man toils for a meager subsistence,
and if ever he rests, he finds himself
in want.
5 The lover of gold will not be free from
sin,
for he who pursues wealth is led
astray by it.
6 Many have been ensnared by gold,
though destruction lay before their
eyes;*p*
7 It is a stumbling block to those who are
avid for it,
a snare for every fool.

8 Happy the rich man found without
fault,*
who turns not aside after gain!*q*
9 Who is he, that we may praise him?
he, of all his kindred, has done wonders,
10 For he has been tested by gold and
come off safe,

---

j Sir 7, 23.—k Sir 41, 2.—l Tb 4, 17.—m Sir 38, 20; Prv 12,
25; 15, 13; 17, 22.—n Sir 38, 18f.—o Prv 15, 15.—p Sir 8, 2.—
q Sir 5, 1. 10.

30, 14-25: Health of mind and body and joy of heart are
judged more precious than wealth (14ff); bitterness, *constant
illness* and affliction more difficult to bear than *death* (17-20).
Sadness, resentment, anxiety, *envy and anger shorten* . . .
life; they should be dispelled by *cheerfulness* and *gladness of
heart,* which help to prolong one's days (21-25).
30, 17: *Preferable is death . . . constant illness:* the true
value of human suffering was revealed through the passion and
death of Christ. It serves as reparation for sin, and when united
with Christ's suffering, as merit for eternal life.
31, 1-11: Solicitude for acquiring wealth and anxiety over
preserving it disturb *repose* and easily lead to sin and ruin (1-7).
Cf Mt 6, 25-34. A *rich man* who has not sinned or been seduced
by wealth is worthy of praise (8-11).
31, 2: The Hebrew adds a verse that seems out of place here:
"A faithful comrade drives away reproach, and the friend who
keeps secrets is as dear as life."
31; 8ff: The church in her liturgy applies this passage to holy
confessors of the Faith.

and this remains his glory;
He could have sinned but did not,
   could have done evil but would not,
11 So that his possessions are secure,
   and the assembly recounts his
   praises.*r*

Table Etiquette*

12 If you are dining with a great man,
   bring not a greedy gullet to his table,
Nor cry out, "How much food there is
   here!"
13   Remember that gluttony is evil.
No creature is greedier than the eye:
   therefore it weeps for any cause.*s*
15 Recognize that your neighbor feels as
   you do,
   and keep in mind your own dislikes:
14 Toward what he eyes, do not put out a
   hand;
   nor reach when he does for the same
   dish.
16 Behave at table like a favored guest,
   and be not greedy, lest you be despised.
17 Be the first to stop, as befits good manners;
   gorge not yourself, lest you give offense.*t*
18 If there are many with you at table,
   be not the first to reach out your
   hand.
19 Does not a little suffice for a well-bred
   man?
   When he lies down, it is without discomfort.*u*
20 Distress and anguish and loss of sleep,
   and restless tossing for the glutton!
Moderate eating ensures sound slumber
   and a clear mind next day on rising.
21 If perforce you have eaten too much,
   once you have emptied your
   stomach,* you will have relief.
22 Listen to me, my son, and scorn me not;
   later you will find my advice good.
In whatever you do, be moderate,
   and no sickness will befall you.

23 On a man generous with food, blessings
   are invoked;
   and this testimony to his goodness is
   lasting;*v*
24 He who is miserly with food is denounced in public,
   and this testimony to his stinginess is
   lasting.
25 Let not wine-drinking be the proof of
   your strength,
   for wine has been the ruin of many.
26 As the furnace probes the work of the
   smith,
   so does wine the hearts of the insolent.
27 Wine is very life to man
   if taken in moderation.
Does he really live who lacks the wine
   which was created for his joy?*w*
28 Joy of heart, good cheer and merriment
   are wine drunk freely at the proper
   time.
29 Headache, bitterness and disgrace
   is wine drunk amid anger and strife.
30 More and more wine is a snare for the
   fool;
   it lessens his strength and multiplies
   his wounds.
31 Rebuke not your neighbor when wine is
   served,
   nor put him to shame while he is
   merry;
Use no harsh words with him
   and distress him not in the presence
   of others.

CHAPTER 32

1 If you are chosen to preside at dinner,
   be not puffed up,
   but with the guests be as one of themselves;
Take care of them first before you sit
   down;
2   when you have fulfilled your duty,
   then take your place,
To share in their joy
   and win praise for your hospitality.
3 Being older, you may talk; that is only
   your right,
   but temper your wisdom, not to disturb the singing.
4 When wine is present, do not pour out
   discourse,
   and flaunt not your wisdom at the
   wrong time.
5 Like a seal of carnelian in a setting of
   gold

Sir

---

r Prv 29, 14.—s Sir 37, 28ff; Prv 23, 1f.—t Sir 37, 29.—u
Eccl 5, 11.—v Prv 22, 9.—w Ps 104, 15; 1 Tm 5, 23.

31, 12—32, 13: A man observing etiquette at table avoids
greed and selfishness (31, 12f), is considerate of a neighbor's
likes and dislikes and *generous* toward him (14f. 23f), observes
proper manners (16ff), is *moderate* in *eating* and drinking (19-
22. 25-30). A good host makes himself one with his guests, is
solicitous for them (32, 1f), provides conversation and diversion
(3-6), is modest in speech (7f. 10), is respectful of elders (9), polite in comportment and grateful to God for his *favors* (11ff).

31, 21: *Emptied your stomach:* the practice of induced vom-
iting, well-known among pagan Romans, and less well-known
among the Jews, seems to be referred to here.

is a concert when wine is served.

6 Like a gold mounting with an emerald
seal
is string music with delicious wine.

7 Young man, speak only when necessary,[x]
when they have asked you more than
once;

8 Be brief, but say much in those few
words,
be like the wise man, taciturn.

9 When among your elders be not forward,
and with officials be not too insistent.

10 Like the lightning that flashes before a
storm
is the esteem that shines on modesty.

11 When it is time to leave, tarry not;
be off for home! There take your
ease,

12 And there enjoy doing as you wish,
but without sin or words of pride.

13 Above all, give praise to your Creator,
who showers his favors upon you.

The Providence of God

14 He who would find God must accept
discipline;*
he who seeks him obtains his request.[y]

15 He who studies the law masters it,
but the hypocrite finds it a trap.[z]

16 His judgment is sound who fears the
LORD;
out of obscurity he draws forth a clear
plan.[a]

17 The sinner turns aside reproof
and distorts the law to suit his purpose.[b]

18 The thoughtful man will not neglect direction;
the proud and insolent man is de-
terred by nothing.

19 Do nothing without counsel,
and then you need have no regrets.[c]

20 Go not on a way that is set with snares,
and let not the same thing trip you
twice.

21 Be not too sure even of smooth roads,
22 be careful on all your paths.

23 Whatever you do, be on your guard,
for in this way you will keep the commandments.

24 He who keeps the law preserves himself;

and he who trusts in the LORD shall
not be put to shame.

CHAPTER 33

1 No evil can harm the man who fears the
LORD;
through trials, again and again he is
safe.[d]

2 He who hates the law is without wisdom,
and is tossed about like a boat in a
storm.

3 The prudent man trusts in the word of
the LORD,
and the law is dependable for him as
a divine oracle.*

4 Prepare your words and you will be listened to;
draw upon your training, and then
give your answer.

5 Like the wheel of a cart is the mind of a
fool;*
his thoughts revolve in circles.

6 A fickle friend is like the stallion
that neighs, no matter who the rider.

7 Why is one day more important than
another,
when it is the sun that lights up every
day?

8 It is due to the LORD's wisdom that
they differ;
it is through him the seasons and
feasts come and go.[e]

9 Some he dignifies and sanctifies,
and others he lists as ordinary days.[f]

10 So too, all men are of clay,
for from earth man was formed;[g]

11 Yet with his great knowledge the LORD
makes men unlike;
in different paths he has them walk.

12 Some he blesses and makes great,
some he sanctifies and draws to himself.

x 7ff: Sir 7, 14.—y Sir 4, 13.—z Sir 2, 16.—a Ps 37, 6.—b Sir
21, 6; Prv 12, 1.—c Sir 37, 16; Tb 4, 18.—d Ps 91, 10.—e Gn
1, 14.—f Ex 20, 11.—g Gn 2, 7.

32, 14—33, 4: God is shown to reveal himself through the discipline of his law, a clear and safe plan of life for the pious Jew of
old. *Direction* and *counsel* are aids in following it (14ff. 18-24;
33, 1. 3f). Sinners and hypocrites, hating *the law* or distorting it,
fail in wisdom and are devoid of security (32, 15. 17f; 33, 2).
33, 3: *Oracle:* as the answer given through the Urim and
Thummim to the high priest is true, so the law proves itself true
to him who obeys it. Cf Ex 28, 30; Nm 27, 21.
33, 5-15: Contrasts observable in the physical universe as well
as in the moral order serve the purposes of divine wisdom (5-9).
All creatures are *like clay . . . in the hands of their
Creator*—the fool and the wise man, the sinner, and the just (10-
15). This does not imply that man is created to be a sinner: God
is not the author of wickedness. Cf Jas 1, 13f.

Others he curses and brings low,
and expels them from their place.
13 Like clay in the hands of a potter,
to be molded according to his pleasure,
So are men in the hands of their
Creator,
to be assigned by him their function.*h*
14 As evil contrasts with good, and death
with life,
so are sinners in contrast with the
just;*i*
15 See now all the works of the Most High:
they come in pairs, the one the opposite of the other.

16 Now I am the last to keep vigil,*
like a gleaner after the vintage;
17 Since by the LORD's blessing I have
made progress
till like a vintager I have filled my
winepress,
18 I would inform you that not for myself
only have I toiled,
but for every seeker after wisdom.

Property and Servants*

19 Listen to me, O leaders of the multitude;
O rulers of the assembly, give ear!*j*
20 Let neither son nor wife, neither
brother nor friend,
have power over you as long as you
live.
21 While breath of life is still in you,
let no man have dominion over you.
Give not to another your wealth,
lest then you have to plead with him;
22 Far better that your children plead with
you
than that you should look to their
generosity.
23 Keep control over all your affairs;

let no one tarnish your glory.
24 When your few days reach their limit,
at the time of death distribute your
inheritance.

25 Fodder and whip and loads for an ass;
the yoke and harness and the rod of
his master.
27 Food, correction and work for a slave;
and for a wicked slave, punishment
in the stocks.
26 Make a slave work and he will look for
his rest;
let his hands be idle and he will seek
to be free.*k*
28 Force him to work that he be not idle,
for idleness is an apt teacher of mischief.
29 Put him to work, for that is what befits
him;
if he becomes unruly, load him with
chains.
30 But never lord it over any human being,
and do nothing unjust.
31 If you have but one slave, treat him like
yourself,
for you have acquired him with your
life's blood;*l*
32 If you have but one slave, deal with him
as a brother,
for you need him as you need your
life:
33 If you mistreat him and he runs away,
in what direction will you look for
him?

CHAPTER 34

Trust in the Lord and Not in Dreams*

1 Empty and false are the hopes of the
senseless,
and fools are borne aloft by dreams.
2 Like a man who catches at shadows or
chases the wind,
is the one who believes in dreams.
3 What is seen in dreams is to reality
what the reflection of a face is to the
face itself.
4 Can the unclean produce the clean?
can the liar ever speak the truth?*m*
5 Divination, omens and dreams all are
unreal;
what you already expect, the mind
depicts.
6 Unless it be a vision specially sent by
the Most High,
fix not your heart on it;
7 For dreams have led many astray,

---

h Wis 15, 7; Jer 18, 1-6; Rom 9, 20f.—i Sir 42, 25.—j Wis 6,
1f.—k Prv 29, 19.—l Sir 7, 21.—m Jb 14, 4.

33, 16ff: Here the author refers to himself as the most recent
of the writers who have endeavored to present true wisdom to
their readers.
33, 19-33: Public officials should reject every influence that
would restrict their freedom in the management of their affairs.
They must make their own household subservient to them rather
than be subservient to it (19-24). Slaves are to be given *food* and
work and *correction* but never to be treated unjustly (25-29).
Great care should be taken of good slaves (30-33).
34, 1-17: Confidence placed in *dreams*, divinations and
omens is false because these are devoid of reality (1-8). True
confidence is founded on *knowledge* and *experience* (9-12),
and above all on the fear of the Lord, with its accompanying
blessings of divine assistance and protection (13-17).

and those who believed in them have perished.

8 The law is fulfilled without fail,
and perfect wisdom is found in the mouth of the faithful man.

9 A man with training gains wide knowledge;
a man of experience speaks sense.

10 One never put to the proof knows little,
whereas with travel a man adds to his resourcefulness.

11 I have seen much in my travels,
learned more than ever I could say.

12 Often I was in danger of death,
but by these attainments I was saved.

13 Lively is the courage of those who fear the LORD,
for they put their hope in their savior;

14 He who fears the LORD is never alarmed,
never afraid; for the LORD is his hope.[n]

15 Happy the soul that fears the LORD!
In whom does he trust, and who is his support?

16 The eyes of the LORD are upon those who love him;
he is their mighty shield and strong support,
A shelter from the heat, a shade from the noonday sun,
a guard against stumbling, a help against falling.[o]

17 He buoys up the spirits, brings a sparkle to the eyes,
gives health and life and blessing.

True Worship of God*

18 Tainted his gifts who offers in sacrifice ill-gotten goods!
Mock presents from the lawless win not God's favor.[p]

19 The Most High approves not the gifts of the godless,
nor for their many sacrifices does he forgive their sins.

20 Like the man who slays a son in his father's presence
is he who offers sacrifice from the possessions of the poor.

21 The bread of charity is life itself for the needy;[q]
he who withholds it is a man of blood.

22 He slays his neighbor who deprives him of his living;

he sheds blood who denies the laborer his wages.

23 If one man builds up and another tears down,
what do they gain but trouble?

24 If one man prays and another curses,
whose voice will the LORD hear?

25 If a man again touches a corpse after he has bathed,
what did he gain by the purification?[r]

26 So with a man who fasts for his sins,
but then goes and commits them again:
Who will hear his prayer,
and what has he gained by his mortification?

CHAPTER 35*

1 To keep the law is a great oblation,[s]
and he who observes the commandments sacrifices a peace offering.

2 In works of charity one offers fine flour,*
and when he gives alms he presents his sacrifice of praise.

3 To refrain from evil pleases the LORD,
and to avoid injustice is an atonement.

4 Appear not before the LORD empty-handed,
for all that you offer is in fulfillment of the precepts.[t]

5 The just man's offering enriches the altar
and rises as a sweet odor before the Most High.

6 The just man's sacrifice is most pleasing,
nor will it ever be forgotten.

7 In generous spirit pay homage to the LORD,
be not sparing of freewill gifts.[u]

n Pss 23, 4; 112, 7f; Prv 3, 23ff; 28, 1.—o Pss 33, 18; 34, 16.—p Sir 35, 11; Prv 21, 27.—q 21f: Lv 19, 13; Dt 24, 14f; Tb 4, 14.—r Nm 19, 11f; Prv 26, 11; 2 Pt 2, 22.—s 1ff: 1 Sm 15, 22; Ps 51, 18f; Is 1, 11-18; Hos 6, 6; Am 5, 21-24.—t Ex 23, 15; 34, 20; Dt 16, 16.—u Sir 7, 31.

34, 18-26: To be acts of true religion, sacrifice and penance must be accompanied by the proper moral dispositions. To offer to God goods taken from the poor (18-22), or to practice penance without interior reform, is a mockery, worthless in the sight of God (23-26). Cf Mt 15, 4-7; Mk 7, 9-13.

35, 1-24: Keeping *the commandments* of the law and avoiding *injustice* constitute sacrifice pleasing and acceptable to God (1ff). Offerings also should be made to him, cheerfully and generously; these he *repays . . . sevenfold* (4-10). Extortion from widows and orphans is injustice, which God quickly repays (11-18). Punishing the *proud* and the *merciless* and coming to the aid of the distressed, he *requites* all *according to* their *deeds* (19-24).

35, 2: *Fine flour,* together with oil and frankincense, was a prescribed offering to God; cf Lv 2, 1ff.

⁸ With each contribution show a cheerful
   countenance,
   and pay your tithes in a spirit of joy. *v*
⁹ Give to the Most High as he has given
   to you,
   generously, according to your means.

¹⁰ For the LORD is one who always repays,
   and he will give back to you sevenfold. *w*
¹¹ But offer no bribes, these he does not
   accept!
   Trust not in sacrifice of the fruits of
   extortion, *x*
¹² For he is a God of justice,
   who knows no favorites. *y*
¹³ Though not unduly partial toward the
   weak,
   yet he hears the cry of the oppressed. *
¹⁴ He is not deaf to the wail of the orphan, *z*
   nor to the widow when she pours out
   her complaint;

¹⁵ Do not the tears that stream down her
   cheek
   cry out against him that causes them
   to fall?
¹⁶ He who serves God willingly is heard;
   his petition reaches the heavens.
¹⁷ The prayer of the lowly pierces the
   clouds;
   it does not rest till it reaches its goal,
¹⁸ Nor will it withdraw till the Most High
   responds,
   judges justly and affirms the right.

¹⁹ God indeed will not delay,
   and like a warrior, will not be still*a*
²⁰ Till he breaks the back of the merciless
   and wreaks vengeance upon the
   proud;
²¹ Till he destroys the haughty root and
   branch,
   and smashes the scepter of the wicked;

²² Till he requites mankind according to
   its deeds,
   and repays men according to their
   thoughts;
²³ Till he defends the cause of his people,
   and gladdens them by his mercy.
²⁴ Welcome is his mercy in time of distress
   as rain clouds in time of drought.

CHAPTER 36

A Prayer for God's People*

¹ Come to our aid, O God of the universe,
   and put all the nations in dread of
   you!
² Raise your hand against the heathen,
   that they may realize your power.
³ As you have used us to show them your
   holiness,
   so now use them to show us your
   glory.
⁴ Thus they will know, as we know,
   that there is no God but you.

⁵ Give new signs and work new wonders;
   show forth the splendor of your right
   hand and arm;
⁶ Rouse your anger, pour out wrath,
   humble the enemy, scatter the foe. *b*
⁷ Hasten the day, bring on the time;
⁹   crush the heads of the hostile rulers.
⁸ Let raging fire consume the fugitive,
   and your people's oppressors meet
   destruction.

¹⁰ Gather all the tribes of Jacob,
   that they may inherit the land as of
   old.
¹¹ Show mercy to the people called by
   your name;
   Israel, whom you named your first-
   born. *c*
¹² Take pity on your holy city,
   Jerusalem, your dwelling place. *d*
¹³ Fill Zion with your majesty,
   your temple with your glory.

¹⁴ Give evidence of your deeds of old;
   fulfill the prophecies spoken in your
   name,
¹⁵ Reward those who have hoped in you,
   and let your prophets be proved true.
¹⁶ Hear the prayer of your servants,
   for you are ever gracious to your people;
¹⁷ Thus it will be known to the very ends
   of the earth
   that you are the eternal God.

Sir

---

v 2 Cor 9, 7.—w Prv 19, 17.—x Sir 34, 18f; Prv 21, 27.—y Dt
10, 17; 2 Chr 19, 7; Jb 34, 19; Wis 6, 7; Acts 10, 34; Rom 2, 11;
Gal 2, 6; 1 Pt 1, 17.—z 14f: Ex 22, 22.—a Is 42, 13ff: 2 Pt 3,
9.—b Ps 79, 6.—c Ex 4, 22.—d 2 Chr 6, 41; Ps 132, 8. 14; Is
2, 1ff; Mi 4, 1ff.

35, 13: Cf Lv 19, 15.
36, 1-17: Making an act of faith and hope in the supreme Lord
of the universe, the author begs God to continue manifesting his
holiness and *mercy* through *Israel*, his people (1ff. 10-13), and
his *power* and justice through the punishment of the nations (2.
5-9), that all the earth may acknowledge him *the eternal God*
(4. 14-17).

Choice of Associates*

¹⁸ The throat can swallow any food,
   yet some foods are more agreeable
   than others;
¹⁹ As the palate tests meat by its savor,
   so does a keen mind insincere words.
²⁰ A deceitful character causes grief,
   but an experienced man can turn the
   tables on him.
²¹ Though any man may be accepted as a
   husband,
   yet one girl will be more suitable than
   another:
²² A woman's beauty makes her husband's
   face light up,
   for it surpasses all else that charms
   the eye;ᵉ
²³ And if, besides, her speech is kindly,
   his lot is beyond that of mortal men.
²⁴ A wife is her husband's richest treasure,
   a helpmate, a steadying column.ᶠ
²⁵ A vineyard with no hedge will be overrun;
   a man with no wife becomes a homeless wanderer.
²⁶ Who will trust an armed band
   that shifts from city to city?
²⁷ Or a man who has no nest,
   but lodges where night overtakes
   him?ᵍ

CHAPTER 37

¹ Every friend declares his friendship,
   but there are friends who are friends
   in name only. ʰ
² Is it not a sorrow unto death
   when your bosom companion becomes your enemy?
³ "Alas, my companion! Why were you
   created
   to blanket the earth with deceit?"
⁴ A false friend will share your joys,
   but in time of trouble he stands afar
   off.
⁵ A true friend will fight with you against
   the foe,
   against your enemies he will be your
   shield-bearer.
⁶ Forget not your comrade during the
   battle,
   and neglect him not when you distribute your spoils.
⁷ Every counselor points out a way,
   but some counsel ways of their own;
⁸ Be on the alert when one proffers advice,

find out first of all what he wants.
   For he may be thinking of himself
   alone;
   why should the profit fall to him?
⁹ He may tell you how good your way will
   be,
   and then stand by to watch your misfortune.
¹⁰ Seek no advice from one who regards
   you with hostility;
   from those who envy you, keep your
   intentions hidden.
¹¹ Speak not to a woman about her rival,
   nor to a coward about war,
   to a merchant about business,
   to a buyer about value,
   to a miser about generosity,
   to a cruel man about mercy,
   to a lazy man about work,
   to a seasonal laborer about the harvest,
   to an idle slave about a great task:
   pay no attention to any advice they
   give.
¹² Instead, associate with a religious man,
   who you are sure keeps the commandments;
   Who is like-minded with yourself
   and will feel for you if you fall.
¹³ Then, too, heed your own heart's counsel;
   for what have you that you can depend on more?
¹⁴ A man's conscience can tell him his
   situation
   better than seven watchmen in a lofty
   tower.
¹⁵ Most important of all, pray to God
   to set your feet in the path of truth.

Wisdom and Temperance

¹⁶ A word is the source of every deed;*
   a thought, of every act.ⁱ

---

e Sir 26, 13ff.—f Gn 2, 18; Prv 18, 22.—g Prv 27, 8.—h Sir
6, 7ff.—i Sir 32, 19.

36, 18—37, 15: In the choice of wife, friend or associate, experience is a discerner of character (18-21). *Beauty* and *kindly
speech* make a woman desirable as wife (22f). The good wife becomes *her husband's richest treasure*, his *helpmate* in establishing his household (24-27). *A true friend* fights for his comrade and shares his spoils with him (37, 5f); a false one deceives
and abandons him in time of need (1-4). A true counselor and associate should be sought among those who keep the commandments, not among those who break them and seek their own advantage (7-12). In all things *pray to God* for light and follow
conscience (13ff).
37, 16-25: Thoughts determine action. Wisdom is the source
of *good* and *life;* folly, of *evil* and *death* (16ff). If the fruits of
a man's wisdom benefit himself, he may be praised in his own
lifetime; if they benefit his people, his praise endures after him,
in their lives (19-25).

17 The root of all conduct is the mind;
  four branches it shoots forth:
18 Good and evil, death and life,
  their absolute mistress is the tongue.*j*
19 A man may be wise and benefit many,
  yet be of no use to himself.
20 Though a man may be wise, if his
    words are rejected
  he will be deprived of all enjoyment.
21 When a man is wise to his own advan-
    tage,
  the fruits of his knowledge are seen in
    his own person;
22 When a man is wise to his people's ad-
    vantage,
  the fruits of his knowledge are en-
    during:*k*
23 Limited are the days of one man's life,
  but the life of Israel is days without
    number.
24 One wise for himself has full enjoy-
    ment,
  and all who see him praise him;
25 One wise for his people wins a heritage
    of glory,
  and his name endures forever.*l*

26 My son, while you are well, govern your
    appetite*
  so that you allow it not what is bad
    for you;
27 For not every food is good for everyone,
  nor is everything suited to every
    taste.*m*
28 Be not drawn after every enjoyment,*n*
  neither become a glutton for choice
    foods,
29 For sickness comes with overeating,
  and gluttony brings on biliousness.
30 Through lack of self-control many have
    died,

j Prv 18, 21.—k Sir 15, 1ff.—l Sir 39, 9; 44, 13f.—m 1 Cor 6,
12; 10, 23.—n 28f: Sir 31, 13. 16ff.—o Ex 15, 25.—p Is 38,
2f.—q Lv 2, 1ff.—r Sir 22, 9f.

37, 26-30: Temperance and self-control should govern a
man's appetite for food, which is intended not to destroy but to
preserve life.
38, 1-15: The profession of medicine comes from *God,* who
makes the earth yield healing herbs and gives the physician
knowledge of their virtue (1-8). In illness the sick man should
cleanse his soul from sin and petition God for help through an offering of sacrifice; the physician, too, does well to invoke God
that he may understand the illness and apply the proper remedy
(9-14). The sinner, in contrast, defies both his Maker and the
doctor (15).
38, 16-23: A period of mourning for the deceased and care for
their burial is becoming (16ff). But grief should not be excessive,
for it neither helps the dead, who cannot return, nor fails to harm
the living. The mourner's own end will quickly follow, and the
time to prepare for it is now (19-23).

but the abstemious man prolongs his
life.

CHAPTER 38

Sickness and Death

1 Hold the physician in honor, for he is
    essential to you,*
  and God it was who established his
    profession.
2 From God the doctor has his wisdom,
  and the king provides for his suste-
    nance.
3 His knowledge makes the doctor distin-
    guished,
  and gives him access to those in au-
    thority.
4 God makes the earth yield healing herbs
  which the prudent man should not
    neglect;
5 Was not the water sweetened by a twig
  that men might learn his power?*o*
6 He endows men with the knowledge
  to glory in his mighty works,
7 Through which the doctor eases pain
  and the druggist prepares his
    medicines;
8 Thus God's creative work continues
    without cease
  in its efficacy on the surface of the
    earth.

9 My son, when you are ill, delay not,
  but pray to God, who will heal you:*p*
10 Flee wickedness; let your hands be just,
  cleanse your heart of every sin;
11 Offer your sweet-smelling oblation and
    petition,
  a rich offering according to your
    means.*q*
12 Then give the doctor his place
  lest he leave; for you need him too.
13 There are times that give him an advan-
    tage,
14   and he too beseeches God
  That his diagnosis may be correct
  and his treatment bring about a cure.
15 He who is a sinner toward his Maker
  will be defiant toward the doctor.

16 My son, shed tears for one who is dead*
  with wailing and bitter lament;
  As is only proper, prepare the body,
  absent not yourself from his burial:*r*
17 Weeping bitterly, mourning fully,

Sir

pay your tribute of sorrow, as he deserves,

18 One or two days, to prevent gossip;
then compose yourself after your
grief,

19 For grief can bring on an extremity
and heartache destroy one's health. *s*

20 Turn not your thoughts to him again;
cease to recall him; think rather of
the end. *t*

21 Recall him not, for there is no hope of
his return;
it will not help him, but will do you
harm. *u*

22 Remember that his fate will also be
yours;
for him it was yesterday, for you
today. *v*

23 With the departed dead, let memory
fade;
rally your courage, once the soul has
left.

Vocations of the Craftsman and the Scribe*

24 The scribe's profession increases his
wisdom;
whoever is free from toil can become
a wise man.

25 How can he become learned who guides
the plow,
who thrills in wielding the goad like a
lance,
Who guides the ox and urges on the
bullock,
and whose every concern is for cattle?

26 His care is for plowing furrows,
and he keeps a watch on the beasts in
the stalls.

27 So with every engraver and designer
who, laboring night and day,
Fashions carved seals,
and whose concern is to vary the pattern.
His care is to produce a vivid impression,
and he keeps watch till he finishes his
design.

28 So with the smith standing near his
anvil,
forging crude iron.
The heat from the fire sears his flesh,
yet he toils away in the furnace heat.
The clang of the hammer deafens his
ears,
his eyes are fixed on the tool he is
shaping.

His care is to finish his work,
and he keeps watch till he perfects it
in detail.

29 So with the potter sitting at his labor,
revolving the wheel with his feet.
He is always concerned for his products,
and turns them out in quantity.

30 With his hands he molds the clay,
and with his feet softens it.
His care is for proper coloring,
and he keeps watch on the fire of his
kiln.

31 All these men are skilled with their
hands,
each one an expert at his own task;

32 Without them no city could be lived in,
and wherever they stay, they need
not hunger.

33 They do not occupy the judge's bench,
nor are they prominent in the assembly;
They set forth no decisions or judgments,
nor are they found among the rulers;

34 Yet they maintain God's ancient handiwork,
and their concern is for exercise of
their skill.

CHAPTER 39

1 How different the man who devotes
himself
to the study of the law of the Most
High!
He explores the wisdom of the men of
old
and occupies himself with the
prophecies;

2 He treasures the discourses of famous
men,
and goes to the heart of involved sayings;

3 He studies obscure parables,
and is busied with the hidden meanings of the sages.

---

s Prv 12, 25; 15, 13; 17, 22.—t Sir 7, 36; 18, 24; 30, 21.—u
2 Sm 12, 23; Wis 2, 1.—v Jas 4, 13ff.

38, 24—39, 11: More excellent than the useful service of
craftsmen—farmer, engraver, smith, potter (25-34)—is the profession of the scribe (24), who studies and meditates on *the law
of the Most High*, seeks him in prayer of thanksgiving, petition
and repentance for sin (39, 1. 6f), *explores the wisdom* of the
past and present, travels abroad to observe the conduct of many
peoples, and attends rulers and great men. Through the spirit of
understanding granted by God, he will show forth his wisdom to
the glory of God's law, gaining renown for generations to come
(2-5. 8-11).

⁴ He is in attendance on the great,
and has entrance to the ruler.
⁵ He travels among the peoples of foreign
lands
to learn what is good and evil among
men.
⁶ His care is to seek the LORD, his
Maker,
to petition the Most High,
To open his lips in prayer,
to ask pardon for his sins.
Then, if it pleases the LORD Almighty,
he will be filled with the spirit of
understanding;
He will pour forth his words of wisdom
and in prayer give thanks to the
LORD,
⁷ Who will direct his knowledge and his
counsel,
as he meditates upon his mysteries.
⁸ He will show the wisdom of what he has
learned
and glory in the law of the LORD's
covenant.
⁹ Many will praise his understanding;
his fame can never be effaced;
Unfading will be his memory,
through all generations his name will
live;ʷ
¹⁰ Peoples will speak of his wisdom,
and in assembly sing his praises.
¹¹ While he lives he is one out of a
thousand,
and when he dies his renown will not
cease.

Praise of God the Creator*

¹² Once more I will set forth my theme
to shine like the moon in its fullness!
¹³ Listen, my faithful children: open up
your petals,
like roses planted near running waters;
¹⁴ Send up the sweet odor of incense,
break forth in blossoms like the lily.
Send up the sweet odor of your hymn of
praise;

---

w Sir 37, 25; 44, 14.—x Gn 1, 31; Eccl 3, 11.—y Gn 1, 6-10;
Ex 14, 21f; Jos 3, 16.—z Sir 15, 19; 42, 20.—a Jos 1, 2-6.—b
Sir 29, 21.

39, 12-35: The sage invites his disciples to join him in joyfully
proclaiming his favorite theme: *The works of God are all of
them good; in its own time every need is supplied* (12-16.
32-35). He describes God's omniscience, supreme power and wisdom, whereby all created things, good in themselves, are ever
present to him, obey him, and fulfill their intended purpose (17-
21), bringing blessing to the virtuous, but evil and punishment to
the wicked who misuse them (22-31). Cf similar hymns of praise,
Sir 36, 1-17; 42, 15—43, 35.

bless the LORD for all he has done!
¹⁵ Proclaim the greatness of his name,
loudly sing his praises,
With music on the harp and all stringed
instruments;
sing out with joy as you proclaim:

¹⁶ The works of God are all of them good;
in its own time every need is sup-
plied.ˣ
¹⁷ At his word the waters become still as in
a flask;
he had but to speak and the reservoirs
were made.ʸ
¹⁸ He has but to command and his will is
done;
nothing can limit his achievement.
¹⁹ The works of all mankind are present to
him;
not a thing escapes his eye.ᶻ
²⁰ His gaze spans all the ages;
to him there is nothing unexpected.
²¹ No cause then to say: "What is the purpose of this?"
Everything is chosen to satisfy a
need.
²² His blessing overflows like the Nile;
like the Euphrates it enriches the surface of the earth.
²³ Again, his wrath expels the nations
and turns fertile land into a salt
marsh.ᵃ
²⁴ For the virtuous his paths are level,
to the haughty they are steep;
²⁵ Good things for the good he provided
from the beginning,
but for the wicked good things and
bad.
²⁶ Chief of all needs for human life
are water and fire, iron and salt,
The heart of the wheat, milk and
honey,
the blood of the grape, and oil, and
cloth;ᵇ
²⁷ For the good all these are good,
but for the wicked they turn out evil.
²⁸ There are storm winds created to
punish,
which in their fury can dislodge
mountains;
When destruction must be, they hurl all
their force
and appease the anger of their
Maker.
²⁹ In his treasury also, kept for the proper
time,

Sir

are fire and hail, famine, disease,

30 Ravenous beasts, scorpions, vipers,
and the avenging sword to extermi
nate the wicked;

31 In doing his bidding they rejoice,
in their assignments they disobey not
his command.

32 So from the first I took my stand,
and wrote down as my theme:

33 The works of God are all of them good;
every need when it comes he fills. *c*

34 No cause then to say: "This is not as
good as that";
for each shows its worth at the proper
time.

35 So now with full joy of heart proclaim
and bless the name of the Holy One.

CHAPTER 40

Joys and Miseries of Life

1 A great anxiety has God allotted,*
and a heavy yoke, to the sons of
men; *d*
From the day one leaves his mother's
womb
to the day he returns to the mother of
all the living,*

2 His thoughts, the fear in his heart,
and his troubled forebodings till the
day he dies—

3 Whether he sits on a lofty throne
or grovels in dust and ashes,

4 Whether he bears a splendid crown
or is wrapped in the coarsest of
cloaks—

5 Are of wrath and envy, trouble and
dread,
terror of death, fury and strife.
Even when he lies on his bed to rest,
his cares at night disturb his sleep.

6 So short is his rest it seems like none,
till in his dreams he struggles as he
did by day,
Terrified by what his mind's eye sees,
like a fugitive being pursued;

7 As he reaches safety, he wakes up
astonished that there was nothing to
fear.

8 So it is with all flesh, with man and with
beast,
but for sinners seven times more.

9 Plague and bloodshed, wrath and the
sword,
plunder and ruin, famine and death: *e*

10 For the wicked, these were created evil,

and it is they who bring on destruction.

11 All that is of earth returns to earth,
and what is from above returns
above.*

12 All that comes from bribes or injustice
will be wiped out,
but loyalty remains for ages.

13 Wealth out of wickedness is like a wadi
in spate:
like a mighty stream with lightning
and thunder,

14 Which, in its rising, rolls along the
stones,
but suddenly, once and for all, comes
to an end. *f*

15 The offshoot of violence will not
flourish,
for the root of the godless is on sheer
rock;

16 Or they are like reeds on the riverbank,
withered before all other plants.

17 But goodness will never be cut off,
and justice endures forever.
Wealth or wages can make life sweet,*
but better than either is finding a
treasure.

18 A child or a city will preserve one's
name,
but better than either, attaining wisdom. *g*

19 Sheepfolds and orchards bring flourishing health;
but better than either, a devoted
wife;

20 Wine and music delight the soul,
but better than either, conjugal
love. *h*

---

c Sir 39, 16; Gn 1, 31; Eccl 3, 11.—d Gn 3, 17; Jb 7, 1; 14,
1; Eccl 2, 23.—e Sir 39, 28ff.—f Sir 23, 25; Wis 4, 3ff.—g Prv
19, 14.—h Ps 104, 15.

40, 1-16: The former idyllic description of the universe is contrasted with the picture of the evils afflicting humanity. Every
man, high or low, is burdened from birth to death with fears, anxieties and troubles, by day and often by night, the time appointed
for rest (1-7). For sinners, the suffering is much greater (8ff).
What they gained by violence and injustice is quickly destroyed;
but *justice endures forever* (14ff).
40, 1: *Mother of all the living:* the earth from which man
was taken. Cf Gn 2, 7; 3, 19f; Jb 1, 21; Ps 139, 15.
40, 11: *All that is of earth . . . returns above:* a reference
to bodily mortality and to the divine origin of life from the Spirit
of God. Cf Sir 41, 10; Gn 2, 7; 3, 19; Jb 34, 14f; Pss 104, 29f;
146, 4; Eccl 12, 7. The Greek and the Latin render the second
half of the verse: "all waters shall return to the sea."
40, 17-27: Of the many treasures making life sweet, such as
health, children, friends, *music, vigor,* the best are called true
conjugal love, wisdom, and above all, *fear of God;* cf Sir 25,
6-11.

21 The flute and the harp offer sweet
melody,
but better than either, a voice that is
true.
22 Charm and beauty delight the eye,
but better than either, the flowers of
the field.[i]
23 A friend, a neighbor, are timely guides,
but better than either, a prudent
wife.
24 A brother, a helper, for times of stress;
but better than either, charity that
rescues.
25 Gold and silver make one's way secure,
but better than either, sound judgment.
26 Wealth and vigor build up confidence,
but better than either, fear of God.
Fear of the LORD leaves nothing wanting;
he who has it need seek no other support;
27 The fear of God is a paradise of blessings;
its canopy, all that is glorious.[j]

28 My son, live not the life of a beggar,*
better to die than to beg;
29 When one has to look to another's table,
his life is not really a life.
His neighbor's delicacies bring revul-
sion of spirit
to one who understands inward feelings:[k]
30 In the mouth of the shameless man begging is sweet,
but within him it burns like fire.

CHAPTER 41

1 O death! how bitter the thought of you*
for the man at peace amid his possessions,

i Mt 6, 28f.—j Is 4, 5.—k Sir 29, 24.—l Sir 30, 17.—m Sir 38,
20ff.—n 5ff: Sir 3, 9ff; Wis 3, 16-19.—o Sir 40, 11; Wis 4,
19.—p Prv 10, 7.—q Prv 22, 1; Eccl 7, 1.

40, 28ff: Among the Jews, beggary was considered degrading
to human dignity; it was agreeable only to the shameless, who had
lost their sense of honor. Cf Sir 29, 22f.
41, 1-13: Whether *death* seems *bitter* to one who enjoys
peace, success and pleasure, or welcome to one who is weak and
in despair, it comes to all and must be accepted as the will of God
(1-4). As the human body passes away (11), so do those who have
sinned through the body and their offspring alike, who, needy and
accursed, pass on with their parents as if they had never been (5-
10). Only the good name of the virtuous endures (11ff).
41, 13: After this verse many texts repeat Sir 20, 29f.
41, 14—42, 8: The author illustrates the subject of true and
false shame with numerous and detailed examples of sin (14-24)
and virtue (42, 1-8), following the norm of the commandments.

For the man unruffled and always successful,
who still can enjoy life's pleasures.
2 O death! how welcome your sentence
to the weak man of failing strength,
Tottering and always rebuffed,
with no more sight, with vanished
hope.[l]
3 Fear not death's decree for you;
remember, it embraces those before
you, and those after.[m]
4 Thus God has ordained for all flesh;
why then should you reject the will of
the Most High?
Whether one has lived a thousand
years, a hundred, or ten,
in the nether world he has no claim
on life.

5 A reprobate line are the children of sinners,[n]
and witless offspring are in the homes
of the wicked.
6 Their dominion is lost to sinners' children,
and reproach abides with their descendants.
7 Children curse their wicked father,
for they suffer disgrace through him.
8 Woe to you, O sinful men,
who forsake the law of the Most
High.
9 If you have children, calamity will seize
them;
you will beget them only for groaning.
When you stumble, there is lasting joy;
at death, you become a curse.
10 Whatever is of nought returns to
nought,
so too the godless from void to void.[o]
11 Man's body is a fleeting thing,
but a virtuous name will never be annihilated.[p]
12 Have a care for your name, for it will
stand by you
better than precious treasures in the
thousands;[q]
13 The boon of life is for limited days,
but a good name, for days without
number.*

True and False Shame*

14 My children, heed my instruction about
shame;
judge of disgrace only according to
my rules,
For it is not always well to be ashamed,

nor is it always the proper thing to blush:

15 Before father and mother be ashamed of immorality,
before master and mistress, of falsehood;
16 Before prince and ruler, of flattery;
before the public assembly, of crime;
17 Before friend and companion, of disloyalty,
and of breaking an oath or agreement.
18 Be ashamed of theft from the people where you settle,
and of stretching out your elbow when you dine;
19 Of refusing to give when asked,
of defrauding another of his appointed share,
20 Of failing to return a greeting,
and of rebuffing a friend;
21 Of gazing at a married woman,
and of entertaining thoughts about another's wife;*r*
Of trifling with a servant girl you have,
and of violating her couch;
22 Of using harsh words with friends,
and of following up your gifts with insults;*s*
23 Of repeating what you hear,
and of betraying secrets—*t*
24 These are the things you should rightly avoid as shameful
if you would be looked upon by everyone with favor.

CHAPTER 42

1 But of these things be not ashamed,
lest you sin through human respect:*u*
2 Of the law of the Most High and his precepts,
or of the sentence to be passed upon the sinful;
3 Of sharing the expenses of a business or a journey,
or of dividing an inheritance or property;
4 Of accuracy of scales and balances,
or of tested measures and weights;*v*
5 Of acquiring much or little,
or of bargaining in dealing with a merchant;
Of constant training of children,
or of beating the sides of a disloyal servant;*w*
6 Of a seal to keep an erring wife at home,
or of a lock placed where there are many hands;

7 Of numbering every deposit,
or of recording all that is given or received;
8 Of chastisement of the silly and the foolish,
or of the aged and infirm answering for wanton conduct.
Thus you will be truly cautious
and recognized by all men as discreet.

A Father's Care for His Daughter*

9 A daughter is a treasure that keeps her father wakeful,
and worry over her drives away rest:*x*
Lest she pass her prime unmarried,
or when she is married, lest she be disliked;
10 While unmarried, lest she be seduced,
or, as a wife, lest she prove unfaithful;
Lest she conceive in her father's home,
or be sterile in that of her husband.
11 Keep a close watch on your daughter,
lest she make you the sport of your enemies,
A byword in the city, a reproach among the people,
an object of derision in public gatherings.
See that there is no lattice in her room,
no place that overlooks the approaches to the house.*y*
12 Let her not parade her charms before men,*z*
or spend her time with married women;
13 For just as moths come from garments,
so harm to women comes from women:
14 Better a man's harshness than a woman's indulgence,
and a frightened daughter than any disgrace.

The Works of God in Nature*

15 Now will I recall God's works;
what I have seen, I will describe.

r Sir 9, 8; Mt 5, 28.—s Sir 18, 14; 20, 13.—t Sir 27, 16.—u Prv 24, 23; Jas 2, 1.— v Prv 11, 1.—w Sir 30, 1-13; 33, 25-33.—x Sir 7, 24f.—y Sir 26, 10.—z 12: Sir 9, 1-9.

42, 9-14: The author considers a daughter to be a source of anxiety to her father, lest she fail to marry, or *be seduced,* or lest, marrying, she be *disliked, prove unfaithful,* or find herself *sterile* (9f). He is advised to *keep a close watch* on her at home, and on her companionship while abroad, lest he suffer on her account among the people (11-14).

42, 15—43, 35: These verses comprise a new section. In them the author contemplates God's power, beauty and goodness as manifested in the mighty work of creating and preserving the universe (42, 15ff. 23. 25; 43, 1-27), his omniscience (42, 18ff), his perfect wisdom (21f), his eternity (24). The conclusion is a fervent hymn of praise (43, 28-35). Cf Sir 16, 22—18, 13.

At God's word were his works brought
  into being;
they do his will as he has ordained for
  them.*a*
16 As the rising sun is clear to all,
  so the glory of the LORD fills all his
  works;
17 Yet even God's holy ones must fail
  in recounting the wonders of the
  LORD,
Though God has given these, his hosts,
  the strength
  to stand firm before his glory.
18 He plumbs the depths and penetrates
  the heart;
  their innermost being he understands.
The Most High possesses all knowledge,
  and sees from of old the things that
  are to come:
19 He makes known the past and the future,
  and reveals the deepest secrets.
20 No understanding does he lack;
  no single thing escapes him.*b*
21 Perennial is his almighty wisdom;
  he is from all eternity one and the
  same,
22 With nothing added, nothing taken
  away;
  no need of a counselor for him!*c*
23 How beautiful are all his works!
  even to the spark and fleeting vision!
24 The universe lives and abides forever;
  to meet each need, each creature is
  preserved.
25 All of them differ, one from another,
  yet none of them has he made in vain,
For each in turn, as it comes, is good;
  can one ever see enough of their
  splendor?*d*

CHAPTER 43

1 The clear vault of the sky shines forth*e*
  like heaven itself, a vision of glory.
2 The orb of the sun, resplendent at its
  rising:
  what a wonderful work of the Most
  High!
3 At noon it seethes the surface of the
  earth,
  and who can bear its fiery heat?
4 Like a blazing furnace of solid metal,
  it sets the mountains aflame with its
  rays;

By its fiery darts the land is consumed;
  the eyes are dazzled by its light.
5 Great indeed is the LORD who made it,
  at whose orders it urges on its steeds.
6 The moon, too, that marks the changing times,
  governing the seasons, their lasting
  sign,*f*
7 By which we know the feast days and
  fixed dates,
  this light-giver which wanes in its
  course:
8 As its name says, each month it renews
  itself;
  how wondrous in this change!
9 The beauty, the glory, of the heavens
  are the stars
  that adorn with their sparkling the
  heights of God,*g*
10 At whose command they keep their
  place
  and never relax in their vigils.
A weapon against the flood waters
  stored on high,
  lighting up the firmament by its brilliance,
11 Behold the rainbow! Then bless its
  Maker,
  for majestic indeed is its splendor;*h*
12 It spans the heavens with its glory,
  this bow bent by the mighty hand of
  God.
13 His rebuke marks out the path for the
  lightning,
  and speeds the arrows of his judgment to their goal.
14 At it the storehouse is opened,
  and like vultures the clouds hurry
  forth.
15 In his majesty he gives the storm its
  power
  and breaks off the hailstones.
16 The thunder of his voice makes the
  earth writhe;
  before his might the mountains
  quake.
17 A word from him drives on the south
  wind,
  the angry north wind, the hurricane
  and the storm.
18 He sprinkles the snow like fluttering
  birds;
  it comes to settle like swarms of locusts.
19 Its shining whiteness blinds the eyes,
  the mind is baffled by its steady fall.
20 He scatters frost like so much salt;

a Ps 77, 12f.—b Sir 39, 19; Wis 1, 6-10.—c Is 40, 13; Rom
11, 34.—d Sir 33, 15.—e 1ff: Ps 19, 2f.—f Lv 23, 5; Nm 28, 11-
14; Ps 81, 4.—g Ps 8, 4.—h Gn 9, 13.

it shines like blossoms on the thorn-bush.

21 Cold northern blasts he sends
that turn the ponds to lumps of ice.
He freezes over every body of water,
and clothes each pool with a coat of mail.

22 When the mountain growth is scorched with heat,
and the flowering plains as though by flames,

23 The dripping clouds restore them all,
and the scattered dew enriches the parched land.

24 His is the plan that calms the deep,
and plants the islands in the sea.

25 Those who go down to the sea tell part of its story,
and when we hear them we are thunderstruck;[i]

26 In it are his creatures, stupendous, amazing,
all kinds of life, and the monsters of the deep.

27 For him each messenger succeeds,
and at his bidding accomplishes his will.[j]

28 More than this we need not add;
let the last word be, he is all in all!*

29 Let us praise him the more, since we cannot fathom him,
for greater is he than all his works;

30 Awful indeed is the LORD's majesty,
and wonderful is his power.

31 Lift up your voices to glorify the LORD,
though he is still beyond your power to praise;

32 Extol him with renewed strength,
and weary not, though you cannot reach the end:

33 For who can see him and describe him?
or who can praise him as he is?[k]

34 Beyond these, many things lie hid;
only a few of his works have we seen.

35 It is the LORD who has made all things,
and to those who fear him he gives wisdom.[l]

CHAPTER 44

Praise of Israel's Great Ancestors

1 Now will I praise those godly men,*
our ancestors, each in his own time:*

2 The abounding glory of the Most High's portion,
his own part, since the days of old.
Subduers of the land in kingly fashion,
men of renown for their might,[ll]

3 Or counselors in their prudence,

or seers of all things in prophecy;[m]

4 Resolute princes of the folk,
and governors with their staves;
Authors skilled in composition,
and forgers of epigrams with their spikes;

5 Composers of melodious psalms,
or discoursers on lyric themes;

6 Stalwart men, solidly established
and at peace in their own estates—

7 All these were glorious in their time,
each illustrious in his day.

8 Some of them have left behind a name
and men recount their praiseworthy deeds;

9 But of others there is no memory,
for when they ceased, they ceased.
And they are as though they had not lived,
they and their children after them.

10 Yet these also were godly men
whose virtues have not been forgotten;

11 Their wealth remains in their families,
their heritage with their descendants;

12 Through God's covenant with them their family endures,
their posterity for their sake.

13 And for all time their progeny will endure,
their glory will never be blotted out;

14 Their bodies are peacefully laid away,
but their name lives on and on.[n]

15 At gatherings their wisdom is retold,
and the assembly proclaims their praise.

The Early Patriarchs

16 [ENOCH* walked with the LORD and was taken up,[o]

i Ps 104, 25-30.—j Ps 33, 6.—k Ps 106, 2.—l Jb 28, 28.—ll Dt 32, 8f.—m Sir 39, 1.—n Wis 3, 3.—o Sir 49, 14; Gn 5, 18-24; Heb 11, 5.

43, 28: *All in all:* the perfections reflected in creation are found in a transcendent way in God, who alone is their source.

44, 1—50, 24: As in the previous section God's wisdom shone forth in the works of nature, so in these chapters it is also revealed through the history of God's people as seen in the lives of their patriarchs, prophets, priests and rulers. The example of these great men, whose virtues are here recalled, constitutes a high point of the author's teaching and illustrates his belief in the canonical Scriptures.

44, 1-15: The reader is here introduced to those men of Israel, later mentioned by name, who through various achievements and beneficial social activities have acquired great renown (1-8. 14f); and also to those who, though forgotten, endure through the fruit of their *virtues* and through their families because of *God's covenant with them* (9-13).

44, 16: *Enoch:* because of his friendship with God and also by reason of his unusual disappearance from the earth, this prophet's renown was great among the chosen people, particularly in the two centuries just before the coming of Christ; cf Gn 5, 21-24; Heb 11, 5. The present verse is an expansion of the original text; cf Sir 49, 14.

that succeeding generations might
learn by his example.]

17 NOAH, found just and perfect,
renewed the race in the time of devastation.*p*

Because of his worth there were survivors,
and with a sign to him the deluge
ended;

18 A lasting agreement was made with
him,
that never should all flesh be destroyed.

19 ABRAHAM, father of many peoples,
kept his glory without stain:*q*

20 He observed the precepts of the Most
High,
and entered into an agreement with
him;
In his own flesh he incised the ordinance,*
and when tested he was found loyal.*r*

21 For this reason, God promised him with
an oath
that in his descendants the nations
would be blessed,
That he would make him numerous as
the grains of dust,
and exalt his posterity like the stars;
That he would give them an inheritance
from sea to sea,

and from the River* to the ends of
the earth.

22 And for ISAAC he renewed the same
promise
because of Abraham, his father.

The covenant with all his forebears was
confirmed,
and the blessing rested upon the head
of JACOB.*s*

23 God acknowledged him as the first-born,
and gave him his inheritance.

He fixed the boundaries for his tribes,
and their division into twelve.

CHAPTER 45

Praise of Moses, Aaron and Phinehas

1 From him was to spring the man*
who won the favor of all:*t*

Dear to God and men,
MOSES, whose memory is held in
benediction.

2 God's honor*u* devolved upon him,*
and the LORD strengthened him with
fearful powers;*v*

3 God wrought swift miracles at his words
and sustained him in the king's presence.

He gave him the commandments for his
people,
and revealed to him his glory.*w*

4 For his trustworthiness and meekness
God selected him from all mankind;*x*

5 He permitted him to hear his voice,
and led him into the cloud,

Where, face to face,* he gave him the
commandments,
the law of life and understanding,

That he might teach his precepts to
Jacob,
his judgments and decrees to Israel.

6 He raised up also, like Moses in holiness,*
his brother AARON, of the tribe of
Levi.*y*

7 He made him perpetual in his office
when he bestowed on him the priesthood* of his people;

He established him in honor
and crowned him with lofty majesty;

8 He clothed him with splendid apparel,
and adorned him with the glorious
vestments:

Breeches and tunic and robe
with pomegranates around the hem,

9 And a rustle of bells round about,
through whose pleasing sound at each
step

---

p Gn 6, 8—9, 29; Heb 11, 7.—q Gn 12, 1—25, 10; Gal 3, 6;
Heb 11, 8-19.—r Gn 17, 10; 22, 1.—s Gn 26, 3. 5. 24; 27, 28f;
28, 14.—t Ex 2, 2; 11, 3; 33, 11; Nm 12, 7.—u Ex 7, 1—13,
22.—v 2-5: Ex 7—Dt 34.—w Ex 4, 17; 7, 1.—x Nm 12, 3. 7.—y
6ff: Ex 28f; Wis 18, 24.

44, 20: *In his own flesh . . . ordinance:* the covenant of circumcision; cf Gn 17, 10-14. *And when tested . . . loyal:* Abraham's willingness to sacrifice his son Isaac at the Lord's command; cf Gn 22, 9-12.

44, 21: *The River:* the Euphrates; cf Gn 2, 14.

45, 1-5: *Moses manifested God's power through miracles (1ff),*
God's authority through the promulgation of the commandments and
the law (5), and God's mercy through the intimacy granted him by
the Lord for his own faithfulness and meekness (4f). The very personification of the old covenant, Moses was also a type of Christ, the
Prophet and Legislator of the new; cf Dt 18, 15.

45, 2: *God's honor devolved upon him:* Moses was actually
God's substitute in dealing with Pharaoh, hence God entrusted his
own honor to Moses.

45, 5: *Face to face:* on God's intimacy with Moses, see Ex
33, 11; Nm 12, 8. St. Paul alluded to this in 1 Cor 13, 12.

45, 6-21: The author here expresses his reverence and esteem
for the priesthood of the old covenant. He recalls God's choice of
Aaron and his sons for this sublime office (6f), and describes in detail
the beauty of the high priest's vestments (8-13). He relates the ordination of Aaron at the hands of Moses, his brother (15), and describes
the priestly functions, of offering sacrifice to God (16), and of blessing
(15), teaching, governing and judging the people (17); the *inheritance* of the high priest (20ff); the punishment of those *families* who
were *jealous* of Aaron (18f); and the confirmation of the covenant of
the priesthood with Aaron's descendants through *Phinehas* (23ff).

45, 7: The *priesthood* of Aaron was superseded by the priesthood of Christ; cf Heb 7, 18-28.

He would be heard within the
sanctuary,
and the children of his race would be
remembered;

10 The sacred vestments of gold, of violet,
and of crimson, wrought with embroidery;
The breastpiece for decision, the ephod
and cincture

11 with scarlet yarn, the work of the
weaver;
Precious stones with seal engravings
in golden settings, the work of the
jeweler,
To commemorate in incised letters
each of the tribes of Israel;

12 On his turban the diadem of gold,
its plate wrought with the insignia of
holiness,
Majestic, glorious, renowned for splendor,
a delight to the eyes, beauty supreme.

13 Before him, no one was adorned with
these,
nor may they ever be worn by any
Except his sons and them alone,
generation after generation, for all
time.

14 His cereal offering is wholly burnt
with the established sacrifice twice
each day;

15 For Moses ordained him
and anointed him with the holy oil,
In a lasting covenant with him
and with his family, as permanent as
the heavens,
That he should serve God in his priesthood
and bless his people in his name.

16 He chose him from all mankind
to offer holocausts and choice offerings,
To burn sacrifices of sweet odor for a
memorial,
and to atone for the people of Israel.

17 He gave to him his laws,
and authority to prescribe and to
judge:
To teach the precepts to his people,
and the ritual to the descendants of
Israel.

18 Men of other families were inflamed
against him,

were jealous of him in the desert,
The followers of Dathan and Abiram,
and the band of Korah in their defiance. z

19 But the LORD saw this and became
angry,
he destroyed them in his burning
wrath.
He brought down upon them a miracle,
and consumed them with his flaming
fire.

20 Then he increased the glory of Aaron a
and bestowed upon him his inheritance:
The sacred offerings he allotted to him,
with the showbread as his portion,

21 The oblations of the LORD are his food,
a gift to him and his descendants.

22 But he holds no land among the people
nor shares with them their heritage;
For the LORD himself is his portion,
his inheritance in the midst of Israel.

23 PHINEHAS too, the son of Eleazar,
was the courageous third of his line
When, zealous for the God of all,
he met the crisis of his people b
And, at the prompting of his noble
heart,
atoned for the children of Israel.

24 Therefore on him again God conferred
the right,
in a covenant of friendship, to provide for the sanctuary,
So that he and his descendants
should possess the high priesthood
forever.

25 For even his covenant with David,
the son of Jesse of the tribe of Judah,
Was an individual heritage through one
son alone;
but the heritage of Aaron is for all his
descendants. c

26 And now bless the LORD
who has crowned you with glory!
May he grant you wisdom of heart
to govern his people in justice,
Lest their welfare should ever be forgotten,
or your authority, throughout all
time.

---

z Nm 16, 1ff.—a 20f: Nm 18, 11-21; Dt 10, 9.—b Nm 25, 7-
13; Ps 106, 30f; 1 Mc 2, 26. 54.—c 2 Sm 7, 12-16.

CHAPTER 46

Joshua, Caleb and the Judges

1 Valiant leader was JOSHUA, son of
Nun,*
assistant to Moses in the prophetic office,
Formed to be, as his name implies,
the great savior of God's chosen
ones,
To punish the enemy
and to win the inheritance for Israel.*d*

2 What glory was his when he raised his
arm,
to brandish his javelin against the
city!*e*

3 And who could withstand him
when he fought the battles of the
LORD?*

4 Did he not by his power stop the sun,
so that one day became two?*f*

5 He called upon the Most High God
when his enemies beset him on all
sides,
And God Most High gave answer to
him
in hailstones of tremendous power,

6 Which he rained down upon the hostile
army
till on the slope he destroyed the foe;
That all the doomed nations might
know
that the LORD was watching over his
people's battles.
And because he was a devoted follower
of God

7 and in Moses' lifetime showed himself loyal,

He and CALEB,* son of Jephunneh,
when they opposed the rebel assembly,
Averted God's anger from the people
and suppressed the wicked complaint—*g*

8 Because of this, they were the only two
spared
from the six hundred thousand infantry,
To lead the people into their inheritance,
the land flowing with milk and
honey.*h*

9 And the strength he gave to Caleb
remained with him even in his old
age
Till he won his way onto the summits of
the land;
his family too received an inheritance,*i*

10 That all the people of Jacob might know
how good it is to be a devoted follower of the LORD.

11 The JUDGES,* too, each one of them,
whose hearts were not deceived,
Who did not abandon God:
may their memory be ever blessed,*j*

12 Their bones return to life from their
resting place,
and their names receive fresh luster
in their children!

13 Beloved of his people, dear to his
Maker,
dedicated from his mother's womb,
Consecrated to the LORD as a prophet,
was SAMUEL, the judge and priest.
At God's word he established the kingdom
and anointed princes to rule the people.*k*

14 By the law of the LORD he judged the
nation,
when he visited the encampments of
Jacob.

15 As a trustworthy prophet he was sought
out
and his words proved him true as a
seer.

16 He, too, called upon God,
and offered him a suckling lamb;*l*

17 Then the LORD thundered forth from
heaven,
and the tremendous roar of his voice
was heard.*m*

---

d Ex 17, 9; Nm 27, 18; Dt 34, 9; Jos 1, 1-4.—e Jos 8, 18.—f
Jos 10, 13.—g Nm 13, 30; 14, 6.—h Nm 14, 22-38.—i Jos 14,
6; 15, 13.—j Jgs 1, 1—16, 31.—k 1 Sm 1, 10ff; 8, 4ff; 10, 1;
16, 13.—l 1 Sm 7, 9.—m Sir 12, 18.

46, 1-6: *Joshua:* whose name means "the LORD is savior"
(1), was the instrument through which God delivered his people in
miraculous ways (2-6) by destroying their enemies, whose land he
gave to the Israelites as an *inheritance* (1).

46, 3: *The battles of the Lord:* cf Jos 6—10.

46, 7-10: *Caleb,* who with Joshua advised Moses and the people in the desert to conquer Canaan, despite the counsel of their
companion scouts and the rebellion of the people, merited to lead
the Israelites of the succeeding generation into the Promised
Land. Caleb in his old age received as his inheritance a portion of
land which he himself had previously conquered; cf Jos 15, 13f.

46, 11-20: Of the *Judges* praised and blessed for their fidelity
to God in opposing idolatry, *Samuel,* a man of spotless integrity,
was the greatest (11f. 19). He was judge of the entire nation, and
was also a prophet and priest who through his sacrificial offering
obtained victory over the Philistines. He anointed the kingdom,
anointed kings (13-18), and even after his death foretold the
king's fate and *put an end to wickedness* (20).

Sir

18 He brought low the rulers of the enemy
   and destroyed all the lords of the
   Philistines.
19 When Samuel approached the end of
   his life,
   he testified before the LORD and his
   anointed prince,
   "No bribe or secret gift have I taken
   from any man!"
   and no one dared gainsay him.[n]
20 Even when he lay buried, his guidance
   was sought;
   he made known to the king his fate,
   And from the grave he raised his voice
   as a prophet, to put an end to wickedness.[o]

CHAPTER 47

Nathan, David and Solomon

1 After him came NATHAN*
  who served in the presence of
  David.[p]
2 Like the choice fat of the sacred offerings,
  so was DAVID in Israel.[q]
3 He made sport of lions as though they
  were kids,
  and of bears, like lambs of the flock.[r]
4 As a youth he slew the giant
  and wiped out the people's disgrace,
  When his hand let fly the slingstone
  that crushed the pride of Goliath.[s]
5 Since he called upon the Most High
  God,
  who gave strength to his right arm
  To defeat the skilled warrior
  and raise up the might of his people,
6 Therefore the women sang his praises
  and ascribed to him tens of thousands.
  When he assumed the royal crown, he
  battled[t]
7 and subdued the enemy on every
  side.
  He destroyed the hostile Philistines
  and shattered their power till our own
  day.[u]
8 With his every deed he offered thanks
  to God Most High, in words of
  praise.
  With his whole being he loved his
  Maker
  and daily had his praises sung;
9 He added beauty to the feasts
  and solemnized the seasons of each
  year

With string music before the altar,
  providing sweet melody for the
  psalms[v]
10 So that when the Holy Name was
   praised,
   before daybreak the sanctuary would
   resound.
11 The LORD forgave him his sins
   and exalted his strength forever;
   He conferred on him the rights of royalty
   and established his throne in Israel.[w]
12 Because of his merits he had as his successor*
   a wise son, who lived in security:[x]
13 SOLOMON reigned during an era of
   peace,
   for God made tranquil all his borders.
   He built a house to the name of God,
   and established a lasting sanctuary.[y]
14 How wise you were when you were
   young,
   overflowing with instruction, like the
   Nile in flood![z]
15 Your understanding covered the whole
   earth,
   and, like a sea, filled it with knowledge.
16 Your fame reached distant coasts,
   and their peoples came to hear you;
17 With song and story and riddle,
   and with your answers, you astounded the nations.
18 You were called by that glorious name
   which was conferred upon Israel.*
   Gold you gathered like so much iron,

n 1 Sm 12, 3.—o 1 Sm 28, 14.—p 2 Sm 7, 2.—q 1 Sm 16,
11.—r 1 Sm 17, 35.—s 1 Sm 17, 49.—t 1 Sm 18, 7.—u 2 Sm 5,
6-25.—v 1 Chr 16, 4ff; 23, 2ff; 25, 1-7.—w 2 Sm 12, 13; 7, 12-
16.—x 1 Kgs 2, 12.—y 1 Kgs 5, 1. 5.— z 14-18: 1 Kgs 5, 9-14;
10, 14-28.

47, 1-11: *David,* a youthful and fearless warrior, the favorite
of all Israel, by defeating *Goliath,* the boastful Philistine giant,
removed *the people's disgrace* and greatly strengthened their
power (1-7). *With his whole being he loved* and praised God,
and his devotion to divine worship led him to develop liturgical
cult. David fell into sin, but repenting, received pardon from God
and the promise of an everlasting kingdom (8-11).
47, 12-24: *Solomon,* son and successor of David, inherited
peace through his father's conquests. He built the magnificent
temple of Jerusalem (12f) and received from God the favor of unparalleled wisdom, through which he obtained great fame (14-
17). Luxury and sensuality, however, brought disgrace upon him,
and because of his oppressive burdens, he disposed the kingdom
for division after his death (19-21. 23f). Nevertheless God did not
withdraw his promise of establishing his throne in the descendants
of David (22).
47, 18: Cf 2 Sm 12, 25, where Solomon is called Jedidiah,
"beloved of the Lord." The same term is used of Israel in Jer 11,
15.

you heaped up silver as though it
were lead;
19 But you abandoned yourself to women
and gave them dominion over your
body.*ᵃ*
20 You brought dishonor upon your reputation,
shame upon your marriage,
Wrath upon your descendants,
and groaning upon your domain;
21 Thus two governments came into
being,
when in Ephraim kingship was
usurped.*ᵇ*
22 But God does not withdraw his mercy,
nor permit even one of his promises
to fail.
He does not uproot the posterity of his
chosen one,
nor destroy the offspring of his
friend.
So he gave to Jacob a remnant,
to David a root from his own family.*ᶜ*
23 Solomon finally slept with his fathers,
and left behind him one of his sons,
Expansive* in folly, limited in sense,
REHOBOAM, who by his policy made
the people rebel;
Until one arose who should not be remembered,
the sinner who led Israel into sin,*ᵈ*
Who brought ruin to Ephraim
24   and caused them to be exiled from
their land.

Elijah and Elisha

Their sinfulness grew more and more,
25   and they lent themselves to every
evil,*

---

a 1 Kgs 11, 1ff.—b 1 Kgs 12, 1ff.—c 2 Sm 7, 15; Ps 89,
34ff.—d 1 Kgs 11, 43; 12, 13. 21; 13, 34; 2 Kgs 17, 6ff.—e 1
Kgs 17, 1.—f 1 Kgs 17, 1; 2 Kgs 1, 9-14.—g 1 Kgs 17, 22.—h 1
Kgs 21, 19; 2 Kgs 1, 17.—i 1 Kgs 19, 8ff.—j 1 Kgs 19, 15ff.—k
2 Kgs 2, 11.—l Mal 3, 23f; Mt 17, 10.—m 2 Kgs 2, 9; 3, 13.—n
13f: 2 Kgs 13, 21.

47, 23: *Expansive:* the name *Rehoboam* means "the people
is expansive," that is, widespread. *The sinner:* Jeroboam; cf 1
Kgs 12, 2. 20. 26-32.
47, 25—48, 11: The prophetic ministry of *Elijah* amid widespread idolatry is here described as a judgment by fire (47, 25f).
Through his preaching, miracles and vengeance against God's
enemies within and without Israel, the prophet succeeded for a
time in destroying idols and in restoring faith and the worship of
the true God (48, 2-8). His miraculous departure from this life
gave rise to the belief that he did not die but would return before
the end of the world to *put an end to wrath* and restore the
tribes of Israel (9ff). Cf Mt 17, 9-13.
48, 12-16: *Elisha* fearlessly continued the work of his predecessor by numerous miracles (12ff), but the obstinacy of the
people eventually brought on the destruction of the kingdom of Israel and the dispersion of its subjects. *Judah,* however, survived
under the rule of Davidic kings, both good and bad (15f).

CHAPTER 48

1 Till like a fire there appeared the
prophet
whose words were as a flaming furnace.*ᵉ*
2 Their staff of bread he shattered,
in his zeal he reduced them to straits;
3 By God's word he shut up the heavens
and three times brought down fire.*ᶠ*
4 How awesome are you, ELIJAH!
Whose glory is equal to yours?
5 You brought a dead man back to life
from the nether world, by the will of
the LORD.*ᵍ*
6 You sent kings down to destruction,
and nobles, from their beds of sickness.*ʰ*
7 You heard threats at Sinai,
at Horeb avenging judgments.*ⁱ*
8 You anointed kings who should inflict
vengeance,
and a prophet as your successor.*ʲ*
9 You were taken aloft in a whirlwind,
in a chariot with fiery horses.*ᵏ*
10 You are destined, it is written, in time
to come
to put an end to wrath before the day
of the LORD,
To turn back the hearts of fathers toward their sons,
and to re-establish the tribes of
Jacob.*ˡ*
11 Blessed is he who shall have seen you
before he dies,
12 O Elijah, enveloped in the whirlwind!*ᵐ*

Then ELISHA, filled with a twofold portion of his spirit,*
wrought many marvels by his mere
word.
During his lifetime he feared no one,
nor was any man able to intimidate
his will.
13 Nothing was beyond his power;*ⁿ*
beneath him flesh was brought back
into life.
14 In life he performed wonders,
and after death, marvelous deeds.
15 Despite all this the people did not repent,
nor did they give up their sins,
Until they were rooted out of their land
and scattered all over the earth.
But Judah remained, a tiny people,

Sir

with its rulers from the house of David.[o]

16 Some of these did what was right,
but others were extremely sinful.

Hezekiah and Isaiah*

17 HEZEKIAH fortified his city
and had water brought into it;[p]
With iron tools he cut through the rock
and he built reservoirs for water.

18 During his reign Sennacherib led an invasion,
and sent his adjutant;
He shook his fist at Zion
and blasphemed God in his pride.[q]

19 The people's hearts melted within them,
and they were in anguish like that of childbirth.

20 But they called upon the Most High God
and lifted up their hands to him;
He heard the prayer they uttered,
and saved them through ISAIAH.[r]

21 God struck the camp of the Assyrians
and routed them with with a plague.[s]

22 For Hezekiah did what was right
and held fast to the paths of David,
As ordered by the illustrious prophet
Isaiah, who saw the truth in visions.

23 In his lifetime he turned back the sun
and prolonged the life of the king.[t]

24 By his powerful spirit he looked into the future[u]
and consoled the mourners of Zion;

25 He foretold what should be till the end of time,
hidden things yet to be fulfilled.

CHAPTER 49

Josiah and the Prophets*

1 The name JOSIAH is like blended incense,
made lasting by a skilled perfumer.[v]
Precious is his memory, like honey to the taste,
like music at a banquet.

2 For he grieved over our betrayals
and destroyed the abominable idols.

3 He turned to God with his whole heart,
and, though times were evil, he practiced virtue.

4 Except for David, Hezekiah and Josiah,
they all were wicked;
They abandoned the law of the Most High,

these kings of Judah, right to the very end.

5 So he gave over their power to others,
their glory to a foolish foreign nation

6 Who burned the holy city
and left its streets desolate,
As JEREMIAH had foretold;[w] 7 for they
had treated him badly
who even in the womb had been made a prophet,
To root out, pull down, and destroy,
and then to build and to plant.[x]

8 EZEKIEL beheld the vision
and described the different creatures
of the chariot;[y]

9 He also referred to JOB,
who always persevered in the right path.[z]

10 Then, too, the TWELVE PROPHETS—
may their bones return to life from
their resting place!—
Gave new strength to Jacob
and saved him by their faith and hope.

The Heroes after the Exile

11 How can we fittingly praise ZERUBBABEL,*
who was like a signet ring on God's
right hand,[a]

12 And Jeshua, Jozadak's son?
In their time they built the house of God;
They erected the holy temple,
destined for everlasting glory.

13 Extolled be the memory of NEHEMIAH!
He rebuilt our ruined walls,
Restored our shattered defenses,
and set up gates and bars.[b]

---

o 2 Kgs 15, 29; 18, 11.—p 2 Kgs 20, 20; 2 Chr 32, 3ff. 30.—q
2 Kgs 18, 13ff; Is 36, 1ff.—r 2 Kgs 19, 20.—s 2 Kgs 19, 35; Is
37, 36.—t 2 Kgs 20, 11; Is 38, 8.—u 24f: 2 Kgs 20, 17; Is 40,
1ff; 42, 9; 46, 10; 48, 6; 61, 2.—v 2 Kgs 22, 1; 2 Chr 34, 1.—w
2 Kgs 25, 9; 2 Chr 36, 19.—x Jer 1, 5. 10.—y Ez 1, 4ff.—z Ez
14, 14. 20.—a 11f: Ezr 3, 2; Hg 1, 12; Zec 3, 1.—b Neh 1, 1;
3, 1.

48, 17-25: The fidelity, trust and courage of King *Hezekiah*
(17. 22), the zeal of the prophet *Isaiah*, and the prayer of the
people (20) availed with God. The Assyrian oppressors were
routed (18f. 21), the king's life was prolonged, and consolations
were granted the people through Isaiah's prophecies concerning
the future (23ff), especially the coming of the Messiah and the
establishment of his kingdom; cf Is 7, 14; 9, 6f; 40—65.

49, 1-10: The author's praise of King *Josiah* (1-3), of the
prophets *Jeremiah* and *Ezekiel* and likewise the minor prophets
(7-10) derives from their spirit of fidelity to the Lord and his law
amid the infidelity of kings and people (4ff. 10).

49, 11ff: *Zerubbabel* and *Jeshua*, in rebuilding the temple,
and *Nehemiah*, the governor, in repairing the walls of the Holy
City, also restored what these constructions signify, namely, religious worship and civil authority as prescribed in the law.

The Earliest Patriarchs

14 Few on earth have been made the equal
   of ENOCH,*
   for he was taken up bodily.^{c}
15 Was ever a man born like JOSEPH?
   Even his dead body was provided for.^{d}
16 Glorious, too, were SHEM and SETH and
   ENOS;
   but beyond that of any living being
   was the splendor of ADAM.^{e}

CHAPTER 50

Simon, Son of Jochanan

1 The greatest among his brethren, the
   glory of his people,
   was SIMON the priest, son of Jochanan,*
   In whose time the house of God was
   renovated,
   in whose days the temple was reinforced.
2 In his time also the wall was built
   with powerful turrets for the temple
   precincts;
3 In his time the reservoir was dug,
   the pool with a vastness like the sea's.
4 He protected his people against
   brigands,
   and strengthened his city against the
   enemy.
5 How splendid he was as he appeared
   from the tent,
   as he came from within the veil!
6 Like a star shining among the clouds,
   like the full moon at the holyday season;
7 Like the sun shining upon the temple,
   like the rainbow appearing in the
   cloudy sky;

8 Like the blossoms on the branches in
   springtime,
   like a lily on the banks of a stream;
   Like the trees of Lebanon in summer,
9   like the fire of incense at the sacrifice;
   Like a vessel of beaten gold,
   studded with precious stones;
10 Like a luxuriant olive tree thick with
   fruit,
   like a cypress standing against the
   clouds;
11 Vested in his magnificent robes,
   and wearing his garments of splendor,^{f}
   As he ascended the glorious altar
   and lent majesty to the court of the
   sanctuary.

12 When he received the sundered victims
   from the priests
   while he stood before the sacrificial
   wood,
   His brethren ringed him about like a
   garland,
   like a stand of cedars on Lebanon;
13 All the sons of Aaron in their dignity
   clustered around him like poplars,
   With the offerings to the LORD in their
   hands,
   in the presence of the whole assembly
   of Israel.
14 Once he had completed the services at
   the altar
   with the arranging of the sacrifices
   for the Most High,
15 And had stretched forth his hand for
   the cup,^{g}
   to offer blood of the grape,
   And poured it out at the foot of the
   altar,
   a sweet-smelling odor to the Most
   High God,
16 The sons of Aaron would sound a blast,
   the priests, on their trumpets of
   beaten metal;
   A blast to resound mightily
   as a reminder before the Most High.^{h}
17 Then all the people with one accord
   would quickly fall prostrate to the
   ground
   In adoration before the Most High,
   before the Holy One of Israel.
18 Then hymns would re-echo,
   and over the throng sweet strains of
   praise resound.
19 All the people of the land would shout
   for joy,

---

c Sir 44, 16; Gn 5, 18-24.—d Gn 37—50; Ex 13, 19; Jos 24,
32.—e Gn 1, 27; 4, 25f.—f Sir 45, 8-12; Ex 28, 2-5; 39, 1-21.—
g 15f: Nm 15, 5; 28, 7.—h Nm 10, 10.

49, 14ff: The patriarchs here mentioned were glorious because of their spirit of religion, i.e., their profound reverence for
God and obedience to him. *The splendor of Adam,* moreover,
was due to his direct origin from God.

50, 1-21: The *son of Jochanan* here mentioned was Simon II,
in whose time as high priest (219-196 B.C.) great works were accomplished for the benefit of public worship and welfare (1-4). The
author, a contemporary of this high priest, describes in great detail
and by numerous comparisons the impression of awful majesty received, the lofty joy aroused, at the sight of the high priest fully
vested entering the sanctuary, ascending the altar (6-11), and, in
the presence of the whole assembly of Israel, encircled by assistant
priests bearing offerings, sacrificing the burnt offering on the Day of
Atonement, while the trumpets blast and the people bow down in
adoration of *the Most High* (12-17). The hymnody, the joyful
shouts of the multitude, and finally the high priest's blessing, in
which he pronounces—once only in the year, on this occasion—the
holy name of Yahweh, climax the description of this most solemn
Jewish liturgical function (18-21).

praying to the Merciful One,
As the high priest completed the services at the altar
by presenting to God the sacrifice due;
20 Then coming down he would raise his hands
over all the congregation of Israel.[i]
The blessing of the LORD would be upon his lips,
the name of the LORD would be his glory.
21 Then again the people would lie prostrate
to receive from him the blessing of the Most High.

22 And now, bless the God of all,*
who has done wondrous things on earth;
Who fosters men's growth from their mother's womb,
and fashions them according to his will!
23 May he grant you joy of heart
and may peace abide among you;
24 May his goodness toward us endure in Israel
as long as the heavens are above.

Epilogue and Canticles

25 My whole being loathes two nations,*
the third is not even a people:*
26 Those who live in Seir* and Philistia,
and the degenerate folk who dwell in Shechem.[j]
27 Wise instruction, appropriate proverbs,*
I have written in this book,
I, Jesus, son of Eleazar, son of Sirach,
as they gushed forth from my heart's understanding.
28 Happy the man who meditates upon these things,
wise the man who takes them to heart!
29 If he puts them into practice, he can cope with anything,
for the fear of the LORD is his lamp.

CHAPTER 51

1 I gave you thanks, O God of my father;*
I praise you, O God my savior!
I will make known your name, refuge of my life;[k]
2 you have been my helper against my adversaries.
You have saved me from death,

and kept back my body from the pit,
From the clutches of the nether world
you have snatched my feet;[l]
3 you have delivered me, in your great mercy,
From the scourge of a slanderous tongue,
and from lips that went over to falsehood;
From the snare of those who watched for my downfall,
and from the power of those who sought my life;[m]
From many a danger you have saved me,
4 from flames that hemmed me in on every side;[n]
From the midst of unremitting fire,
5 from the deep belly of the nether world;
From deceiving lips and painters of lies,
6 from the arrows of dishonest tongues.
I was at the point of death,
my soul was nearing the depths of the nether world;[o]
7 I turned every way, but there was no one to help me,
I looked for one to sustain me, but could find no one.[p]
8 But then I remembered the mercies of the LORD,
his kindness through ages past;
For he saves those who take refuge in him,
and rescues them from every evil.
9 So I raised my voice from the very earth,
from the gates of the nether world, my cry.

---

i Nm 6, 23-26.—j 2 Kgs 17, 24; Jn 4, 9.—k Ps 138, 1.—l Ps 91, 3.—m Pss 40, 5; 91, 3.—n Ps 66, 12.—o Pss 88, 4; 94, 17.—p Pss 22, 12; 142, 5.

50, 22ff: Praise and thanksgiving are given to God for his wondrous works, and a blessing is invoked on man that he may enjoy peace and gladness of heart and the abiding goodness of the Most High.
50, 25f: The author's abhorrence of the pagan Edomites (Idumeans), Philistines and Samaritans can be understood in the light of Old Testament thinking, which does not always distinguish between hatred of evildoers and hatred of the evil they do.
50, 25: *Not even a people:* the Samaritans.
50, 26: *Seir:* Mount Seir in the territory of the Edomites. *Shechem:* a city in Samaria.
50, 27ff: These verses contain the subscription of the author, *Jesus, son of Eleazar, son of Sirach,* to his long and beautiful treatise on wisdom as applying to all of human life, integrating it under the direction of *the fear of the Lord.*
51, 1-12: A canticle of praise and thanks to God for delivering the author from slander, dangers, destruction, death, the nether world, and evil of every kind.

¹⁰ I called out: O LORD, you are my
    father,
  you are my champion and my savior;
  Do not abandon me in time of trouble,
    in the midst of storms and dangers. *q*
¹¹ I will ever praise your name
    and be constant in my prayers to you.
  Thereupon the LORD heard my voice,
    he listened to my appeal;
¹² He saved me from evil of every kind
    and preserved me in time of trouble.
  For this reason I thank him and I praise
    him;
    I bless the name of the LORD.*
¹³ * When I was young and innocent,
    I sought wisdom. *r*
¹⁴ She came to me in her beauty,
    and until the end I will cultivate her.
¹⁵ As the blossoms yielded to ripening
    grapes,
    the heart's joy,

---

q Ps 89, 27.—r Sir 34, 11.—s Prv 4, 6.—t Prv 8, 5.—u Sir 6,
20.—v Sir 6, 25.—w Sir 2, 8; Jb 34, 11; Jn 9, 4.

51, 12: After this verse the Hebrew text gives the litany of
praise contained below. It is similar to Ps 136. Though not found
in any versions, and therefore of doubtful authenticity, the litany
seems from internal evidence to go back to the time of Sirach:

> Give thanks to the Lord, for he is good, for his mercy endures
> forever;
> Give thanks to the God of glory, for his mercy endures forever;
> Give thanks to the guardian of Israel, for his mercy endures for-
> ever;
> Give thanks to the creator of the universe, for his mercy en-
> dures forever;
> Give thanks to the redeemer of Israel, for his mercy endures
> forever;
> Give thanks to him who gathers the dispersed of Israel, for his
> mercy endures forever;
> Give thanks to him who builds his city and his sanctuary, for his
> mercy endures forever;
> Give thanks to him who makes a horn to sprout forth, for the
> house of David, for his mercy endures forever;
> Give thanks to him who has chosen for his priests the sons of
> Zadok, for his mercy endures forever;
> Give thanks to the shield of Abraham, for his mercy endures
> forever;
> Give thanks to the rock of Isaac, for his mercy endures forever;
> Give thanks to the mighty one of Jacob, for his mercy endures
> forever;
> Give thanks to him who has chosen Zion, for his mercy endures
> forever;
> Give thanks to the king over kings of kings, for his mercy en-
> dures forever;
> He has lifted up the horn of his people, be this his praise from
> all his faithful ones,
> From the children of Israel, the people close to him. Alleluia!
> (Cf Ps 148, 14.)

51, 13-30: An alphabetic canticle describing: a) the approach
to wisdom through prayer, persistent study and instruction (13-
17), purification from sin, enlightenment and ardent desire; b)
the possession of wisdom (18-22). The author concludes with an
urgent invitation to receive *instruction in wisdom* from
him, and to live by it, because wisdom gives herself *to those who
seek her* (23-26); and for their labor, God will reward them in
the end (27-30). Cf Mt 11, 28; Eccl 12, 14.

In the Greek of 13f there is an expansion introducing Solomon as
the speaker. This deviates from the original author's intent. It reads,
"Publicly, in my prayer, facing the temple, I asked for her."

  My feet kept to the level path
    because from earliest youth I was
    familiar with her.
¹⁶ In the short time I paid heed,
    I met with great instruction.
¹⁷ Since in this way I have profited,
    I will give my teacher grateful praise.
¹⁸ I became resolutely devoted to her—
    the good I persistently strove for.
¹⁹ I burned with desire for her,
    never turning back.
  I became preoccupied with her,
    never weary of extolling her.
  My hand opened her gate
    and I came to know her secrets.
²⁰ For her I purified my hands;
    in cleanness I attained to her.
  At first acquaintance with her, I gained
    understanding
    such that I will never forsake her. *s*
²¹ My whole being was stirred as I learned
    about her;
    therefore I have made her my prize
    possession.
²² The LORD has granted me my lips as a
    reward,
    and my tongue will declare his
    praises.
²³ Come aside to me, you untutored,
    and take up lodging in the house of
    instruction; *t*
²⁴ How long will you be deprived of wis-
    dom's food,
    how long will you endure such bitter
    thirst?
²⁵ I open my mouth and speak of her:
    gain, at no cost, wisdom for your-
    selves. *u*
²⁶ Submit your neck to her yoke,
    that your mind may accept her teach-
    ing.
  For she is close to those who seek her,
    and the one who is in earnest finds
    her. *v*
²⁷ See for yourselves! I have labored only a
    little,
    but have found much.
²⁸ Acquire but a little instruction;
    you will win silver and gold through
    her.
²⁹ Let your spirits rejoice in the mercy of
    God,
    and be not ashamed to give him
    praise.
³⁰ Work at your tasks in due season,
    and in his own time God will give you
    your reward. *w*

THE PROPHETIC BOOKS

The prophetic books bear the names of the four major and twelve minor prophets, besides Lamentations and Baruch. The terms "major" and "minor" refer merely to the length of the respective compositions and not to any distinction in the prophetic office. Jonah is a story of the mission of the prophet rather than a collection of prophecies. Lamentations and Daniel are listed among the hagiographa in the Hebrew Bible, not among the prophetic books. The former contains a series of elegies on the fate of Jerusalem; the latter is apocalyptic in character. Daniel, who lived far removed from Palestine, was not called by God to preach; yet the book is counted as prophecy. Baruch, though excluded from the Hebrew canon, is found in the Septuagint version, and the church has always acknowledged it to be sacred and inspired.

The prophetic books, together with the oral preaching of the prophets, were the result of the institution of prophetism, in which a succession of Israelites chosen by God and appointed by him to be prophets received communications from him and transmitted them to the people in his name (Dt 18, 15-20). The prophets were spokesmen of God, intermediaries between him and his people. The communications they received from God came through visions, dreams, and ecstasies and were transmitted to the people through sermons, writings, and symbolic actions.

The office of prophet was due to a direct call from God. It was not the result of heredity, just as it was not a permanent gift but a transient one, subject entirely to the divine will. The prophets preserved and developed revealed religion (1 Sm 12, 6-25), denounced idolatry (1 Kgs 14, 1-13), defended the moral law (2 Sm 12, 1-15), gave counsel in political matters (Is 31, 1ff), and often also in matters of private life (1 Sm 9, 6-9). At times miracles confirmed their preaching, and their predictions of the future intensified the expectation of the Messiah and of his kingdom.

The prophetic literature in this volume contains the substance of the prophets' authentic preaching, resumes, and genuine samples of such preaching. Some parts were recorded by the prophets themselves, some by persons other than the prophets who uttered them.

The prophecies express judgments of the people's moral conduct, on the basis of the Mosaic alliance between God and Israel. They teach sublime truths and lofty morals. They contain exhortations, threats, announcements of punishment, promises of deliverance, made with solemn authority and in highly imaginative language. In the affairs of men, their prime concern is the interests of God, especially in what pertains to the chosen people through whom the Messiah is to come; hence their denunciations of idolatry and of that externalism in worship which excludes the interior spirit of religion. They are concerned also with the universal nature of the moral law, with personal responsibility, with the person and office of the Messiah, and with the conduct of foreign nations.

In content, the literary genre of prophecy uses warning and threat besides exhortation and promise to declare in God's name events of the near and distant future (Is 8—9). In form, the divine source of prophetic declaration appears in: "The word (or oracle) of the Lord," or "Thus says the Lord," followed by the announcement of a coming event and its moral cause (Hos 4, 7-10). Divine exhortation and promise are introduced by such forms as: "Hear this word, O men of Israel, that the Lord pronounces over you" (Am 3, 1). Kindly and persuasive tones pervade the promises of reward and even the threats of punishment (Am 5, 14-15).

Disregard for exact chronological perspective in the prophecies is an additional characteristic. Predictions of the immediate and distant future are often interrelated, not on the basis of years separating the events but on the analogy of the pattern joining present with very distant, though similar, conditions and circumstances. This is prophetic compenetration, idealization in which persons and things of the more immediate present, in the prophet's day, fade into a wider and more perfect order of persons and things of the future; the former are figures and types of the latter. Thus, some details of what the Psalmist said of the kingdom of David and Solomon (Ps 72) went beyond what was fulfilled in these men, as St. Thomas points out, and found their realization only in the kingdom of Christ. St. Jerome before him, and still earlier the apostles themselves—Peter (Acts 2, 14-36) and Paul (Gal 4, 21-31)—taught us that through anticipation in types we discover in Sacred Scripture the truth of things to come.

Thus the universal blessing for mankind, often promised by God through the mouths of his prophets in figures and types, was in time to become personalized and to confer its full benefit on us through the Word made flesh, who became for us the New Covenant through his life, death, and resurrection, as the prophets had foretold.

THE BOOK OF ISAIAH

The greatest of the prophets appeared at a critical moment of Israel's history. The second half of the eighth century B.C. witnessed the collapse of the northern kingdom under the hammerlike blows of Assyria (722), while Jerusalem itself saw the army of Sennacherib drawn up before its walls (701). In the year that Uzziah, king of Judah, died (742), Isaiah received his call to the prophetic office in the Temple of Jerusalem. Close attention should be given to chapter 6, where this divine summons to be the ambassador of the Most High is circumstantially described.

The vision of the Lord enthroned in glory stamps an indelible character on Isaiah's ministry and provides the key to the understanding of his message. The majesty, holiness and glory of the Lord took possession of his spirit and, conversely, he gained a new awareness of human pettiness and sinfulness. The enormous abyss between God's sovereign holiness and man's sin overwhelmed the prophet. Only the purifying coal of the seraphim could cleanse his lips and prepare him for acceptance of the call: "Here I am, send me!"

The ministry of Isaiah may be divided into three periods, covering the reigns of Jotham (742-735), Ahaz (735-715), and Hezekiah (715-687). To the first period belong, for the most part, the early oracles (1—5) which exposed the moral breakdown of Judah and its capital, Jerusalem. With the accession of Ahaz, the prophet became adviser to the king, whose throne was threatened by the Syro-Ephraimite coalition. Rejecting the plea of Isaiah for faith and courage, the weak Ahaz turned to Assyria for help. From this period came the majority of messianic oracles found in the section of Immanuel prophecies (6—12).

Hezekiah succeeded his father and undertook a religious reform which Isaiah undoubtedly supported. But the old intrigues began again, and the king was soon won over to the pro-Egyptian party. Isaiah denounced this "covenant with death" and again summoned Judah to faith in Yahweh as her only hope. But it was too late; the revolt had already begun. Assyria acted quickly and her army, after ravaging Judah, laid siege to Jerusalem (701). "I shut up Hezekiah like a bird in his cage," boasts the famous inscription of Sennacherib. But Yahweh delivered the city, as Isaiah had promised: God is the Lord of history, and Assyria but an instrument in his hands.

Little is known about the last days of this great religious leader, whose oracles, of singular poetic beauty and power, constantly reminded his wayward people of their destiny and the fidelity of Yahweh to his promises.

The complete Book of Isaiah is an anthology of poems composed chiefly by the great prophet, but also by disciples, some of whom came many years after Isaiah. In 1—39 most of the oracles come from Isaiah and faithfully reflect the situation in eighth-century Judah. To disciples deeply influenced by the prophet belong sections such as the Apocalypse of Isaiah (24—27), the oracles against Babylon (13—14), and probably the poems of 34—35.

Chapters 40—55, sometimes called the Deutero-Isaiah, are generally attributed to an anonymous poet who prophesied toward the end of the Babylonian exile. From this section come the great messianic oracles known as the songs of the Servant, whose mysterious destiny of suffering and glorification is fulfilled in the passion and glorification of Christ. Chapters 56—66 contain oracles from a later period and were composed by disciples who inherited the spirit and continued the work of the great prophet.

The principal divisions of the Book of Isaiah are the following: A. The Book of Judgment: *I. Indictment of Israel and Judah (1, 1—5, 30). II. Immanuel Prophecies (6, 1—12, 6). III. Oracles against the Pagan Nations (13, 1—23, 18). IV. Apocalypse of Isaiah (24, 1—27, 13). V. The Lord Alone, Israel's and Judah's Salvation (28, 1—33, 24). VI. The Lord, Zion's Avenger (34, 1—35, 10). VII. Historical Appendix (36, 1—39, 8).* B. The Book of Consolation: *I. The Lord's Glory in Israel's Liberation (40, 1—48, 21). II. Expiation of Sin, Spiritual Liberation of Israel (49, 1—55, 13). III. Return of the First Captives (56, 1—66, 24).*

A. THE BOOK OF JUDGMENT

I: INDICTMENT OF ISRAEL AND JUDAH

CHAPTER 1

Israel's Sinfulness. ¹The vision* which Isaiah, son of Amoz, had concerning Judah and Jerusalem in the days of Uzziah, Jotham, Ahaz and Hezekiah, kings of Judah.

² Hear, O heavens, and listen, O earth,
    for the LORD speaks:
  Sons have I raised and reared,
    but they have disowned me!ᵃ
³ An ox knows its owner,
    and an ass, its master's manger;
  But Israel* does not know,
    my people has not understood.
⁴ Ah! sinful nation, people laden with
    wickedness,
  evil race, corrupt children!
  They have forsaken the LORD,
    spurned the Holy One of Israel,*
    apostatized.ᵇ
⁵ Where would you yet be struck,*
    you that rebel again and again?
  The whole head is sick,
    the whole heart faint.
⁶ From the sole of the foot to the head
    there is no sound spot:
  Wound and welt and gaping gash,
    not drained, or bandaged,
    or eased with salve.
⁷ Your country is waste,
    your cities burnt with fire;

---

a Dt 32, 1. 5f.—b Is 5, 24; Dt 32, 15.—c Rom 9, 29.—d Ps 50,
8-13; Sir 34, 19; Mi 6, 7.—e Prv 15, 8; Jer 6, 20.—f Prv 1, 28;
Sir 34, 21-25.—g Ex 23, 6; Dt 24, 17; Sir 4, 9f; Jer 22, 3; Ez 22,
7; Zec 7, 9f.—h Ps 51, 9.

1, 1: The title of the book: an editorial addition. *Isaiah:* meaning "the salvation of the Lord," or "The Lord is salvation." *Amoz:* not the minor prophet. *Judah:* the southern kingdom of the tribes of Judah and Benjamin. *Uzziah:* also called Azariah; cf 2 Kgs 15, 1; 2 Chr 26, 1.
1, 3: *Israel:* not the northern kingdom, as in Is 9, 11, exclusively, which Isaiah usually calls "Ephraim" from the tribe bordering on the southern kingdom, but the entire chosen people; cf Is 8, 14.
1, 4: *Holy One of Israel:* a title used frequently by Isaiah, rarely by other writers.
1, 5-8: Sufferings inflicted upon God's people for their sins.
1, 8: *Daughter Zion:* Jerusalem. *Hut . . . shed:* for the shelter of watchmen and laborers.
1, 9: *Lord of hosts:* God, who is the Creator and Ruler of the heavenly armies of the angels, stars, etc. *Remnant:* St. Paul uses this text in Rom 9, 29, where he speaks of God's saving mercy toward the Jews and Gentiles. *Sodom . . . Gomorrah:* cf Gn 19.
1, 11: *The number of your sacrifices:* however numerous, they are not acceptable without the right dispositions on the part of the worshipers.
1, 13: *Octaves with wickedness:* the solemnity of the feasts marred by evil deeds.
1, 15: *Spread out your hands:* in prayer.

Your land before your eyes
    strangers devour
  [a waste, like Sodom overthrown]—
⁸ And daughter Zion* is left
    like a hut in a vineyard,
  Like a shed in a melon patch,
    like a city blockaded.

⁹ Unless the LORD of hosts*
    had left us a scanty remnant,
  We had become as Sodom,
    we should be like Gomorrah.ᶜ
¹⁰ Hear the word of the LORD,
    princes of Sodom!
  Listen to the instruction of our God,
    people of Gomorrah!
¹¹ What care I for the number of your sac-
    rifices?*
    says the LORD.
  I have had enough of whole-burnt rams
    and fat of fatlings;
  In the blood of calves, lambs and goats
    I find no pleasure.ᵈ

¹² When you come in to visit me,
    who asks these things of you?
¹³ Trample my courts no more!
  Bring no more worthless offerings;
    your incense is loathsome to me.
  New moon and sabbath, calling of as-
    semblies,
  octaves with wickedness:* these I
    cannot bear.ᵉ
¹⁴ Your new moons and festivals I detest;
    they weigh me down, I tire of the
    load.
¹⁵ When you spread out your hands,*
    I close my eyes to you;
  Though you pray the more,
    I will not listen.
  Your hands are full of blood!ᶠ
¹⁶   Wash yourselves clean!
  Put away your misdeeds from before my
    eyes;
    cease doing evil; ¹⁷learn to do good.
  Make justice your aim: redress the
    wronged,
    hear the orphan's plea, defend the
    widow.ᵍ

¹⁸ Come now, let us set things right,
    says the LORD:
  Though your sins be like scarlet,
    they may become white as snow;
  Though they be crimson red,
    they may become white as wool.ʰ
¹⁹ If you are willing, and obey,

Is

you shall eat the good things of the
land;

[20] But if you refuse and resist,
the sword shall consume you:
for the mouth of the LORD has spoken!

[21] How has she turned adulteress,
the faithful city, so upright!*
Justice used to lodge within her,
but now, murderers.[i]

[22] Your silver is turned to dross,
your wine is mixed with water.

[23] Your princes are rebels
and comrades of thieves;
Each one of them loves a bribe
and looks for gifts.
The fatherless they defend not,
and the widow's plea does not reach
them.[j]

[24] Now, therefore, says the Lord,
the LORD of hosts, the Mighty One of
Israel:
Ah! I will take vengeance on my foes
and fully repay my enemies![k]

[25] I will turn my hand against you,
and refine your dross in the furnace,
removing all your alloy.

[26] I will restore your judges as at first,
and your counselors as in the beginning;
After that you shall be called
city of justice, faithful city.[l]

[27] Zion shall be redeemed by judgment,
and her repentant ones by justice.*

[28] Rebels and sinners alike shall be
crushed,
those who desert the LORD shall be
consumed.

[29] You shall be ashamed of the terebinths
which you prized,
and blush for the groves which you
chose.*

[30] You shall become like a tree with falling
leaves,
like a garden that has no water.

[31] The strong man shall turn to tow,
and his work shall become a spark;
Both shall burn together,
and there shall be none to quench the
flames.

CHAPTER 2

Zion, the Messianic Capital. [1] This is what
Isaiah, son of Amoz, saw concerning
Judah and Jerusalem.*

[2] In days to come,*
The mountain of the LORD's house[m]
shall be established as the highest
mountain
and raised above the hills.
All nations shall stream toward it;[n]

[3] many peoples shall come and say:
"Come, let us climb the LORD's mountain,
to the house of the God of Jacob,
That he may instruct us in his ways,
and we may walk in his paths."[o]
For from Zion shall go forth instruction,
and the word of the LORD from Jerusalem.*

[4] He shall judge between the nations,
and impose terms on many peoples.
They shall beat their swords into plowshares
and their spears into pruning hooks;
One nation shall not raise the sword
against another,
nor shall they train for war again.[p]

[5] O house of Jacob, come,
let us walk in the light of the LORD!

The Lord's Judgment against Idols

[6] You have abandoned your people,
the house of Jacob,
Because they are filled with fortune-
tellers
and soothsayers,* like the Philistines;
they covenant with strangers.[q]

[7] Their land is full of silver and gold,

---

i Jer 3, 8; Hos 2, 7.—j Ex 23, 8; Dt 16, 19.—k Dt 32, 41.—l
Jer 33, 7ff; Zec 8, 3.—m 2ff: Mi 4, 1ff.—n Is 56, 7.—o Zec 8,
20-23.—p Is 9, 7; 11, 4; Ps 72, 3f; Zec 9, 10.—q Is 8, 19; 19, 3.

1, 21: A picture of Jerusalem, once so faithful to God. Apostasy from the covenant is often likened by the prophets to unfaithfulness to the marriage vow.

1, 27: This verse is the key to the whole Book of Isaiah. Zion's
defiant persistence in sin has demanded a divine *judgment,* by
which her survivors will be cleansed and will return to God in *justice;* cf Is 40, 2.

1, 29: *Terebinths which you prized . . . groves which you
chose:* as popular shrines for idolatrous worship.

2, 1: An editorial addition introducing chapters 2-5.

2, 2-4: The messianic destiny which ensures Judah's later restoration. In the messianic kingdom the prophets generally see *the
Lord's house* as the seat of authority and the source of clear and
certain doctrine; also, its rule willingly accepted by all peoples,
maintained by spiritual sanctions, and tending to universal peace.
This passage is found substantially unchanged in Mi 4, 1-3; it
probably, although not certainly, has Isaiah as its author.

2, 3: *Zion . . . Jerusalem:* types of the earthly center of the
messianic kingdom.

2, 6: *Fortunetellers and soothsayers:* divination was
strictly forbidden; cf Dt 18, 9-14.

and there is no end to their treasures;
Their land is full of horses,
and there is no end to their chariots.
8 Their land is full of idols;
they worship the works of their
hands,
that which their fingers have made.*r*

9 But man is abased,
each one brought low.
[Do not pardon them!]
10 Get behind the rocks,
hide in the dust,
From the terror of the LORD
and the splendor of his majesty!*s*
11 The haughty eyes of man will be lowered,
the arrogance of men will be abased,
and the LORD alone will be exalted,
on that day.*
12 For the LORD of hosts will have his
day
against all that is proud and arrogant,
all that is high, and it will be brought
low;
13 Yes, against all the cedars of Lebanon*
and all the oaks of Bashan,
14 Against all the lofty mountains
and all the high hills,
15 Against every lofty tower
and every fortified wall,
16 Against all the ships of Tarshish*
and all stately vessels.
17 Human pride will be abased,
the arrogance of men brought low,
And the LORD alone will be exalted, on
that day

18   The idols will perish forever.

19 Men will go into caves in the rocks
and into holes in the earth,
From the terror of the LORD

---

r Is 31, 1ff.—s 2 Thes 1, 9.—t Lv 26, 26; Ez 4, 16.

2, 11: *That day:* the day of the Lord, a day of retribution,
often referred to, especially by the minor prophets, and described
in terms of natural phenomena: earthquake, fire, storm.
2, 13: *Lebanon:* Mount Lebanon in Syria, famed for its
cedars. *Bashan:* the wooded uplands east of the Jordan River.
2, 16: *Tarshish:* cf note on Ps 48, 8.
3, 1-12: Anarchy will reign in Jerusalem and Judah. In the
prevailing desperation, even the most unworthy and the least
qualified will be sought as rulers.

and the splendor of his majesty,
when he arises to overawe the earth.

20 On that day men will throw to the
moles and the bats the idols of silver and
gold which they made for worship.

21 They go into caverns in the rocks
and into crevices in the cliffs,
From the terror of the LORD
and the splendor of his majesty,
when he arises to overawe the earth.

22 As for you, let man alone,
in whose nostrils is but a breath;
for what he is worth?

CHAPTER 3

Judgment of Judah and Jerusalem

1 The Lord, the LORD of hosts,*
shall take away from Jerusalem and
from Judah
support and prop [all supplies of
bread and water]:*t*

2 Hero and warrior,
judge and prophet, fortuneteller and
elder,
3 The captain of fifty and the nobleman,
counselor, skilled magician, and expert charmer.

4 I will make striplings their princes;
the fickle shall govern them,
5 And the people shall oppress one another,
yes, every man his neighbor.
The child shall be bold toward the
elder,
and the base toward the honorable.
6 When a man seizes his brother
in his father's house, saying,
"You have clothes! Be our ruler,
and take in hand this ruin!"—
7   Then shall he answer in that day:
"I will not undertake to cure this,
when in my own house there is no
bread or clothing!
You shall not make me ruler of the
people."

8 Jerusalem is crumbling, Judah is falling;
for their speech and their deeds are
before the LORD,

Is

a provocation in the sight of his majesty.

9 Their very look bears witness against them;
their sin like Sodom they vaunt,
They hide it not. Woe to them!
they deal out evil to themselves.

10 Happy the just, for it will be well with them,
the fruit of their works they will eat.

11 Woe to the wicked man! All goes ill,
with the work of his hands he will be repaid.

12 My people—a babe in arms will be their tyrant,
and women will rule them!
O my people, your leaders mislead,
they destroy the paths you should follow.

13 The LORD rises to accuse,
standing to try his people.

14 The Lord enters into judgment
with his people's elders and princes:
It is you who have devoured the vineyard;
the loot wrested from the poor is in your houses.

15 What do you mean by crushing my people,
and grinding down the poor when they look to you?
says the Lord, the GOD of hosts.ᵘ

16 The LORD said:ᵛ
Because the daughters of Zion are haughty,
and walk with necks outstretched
Ogling and mincing as they go,
their anklets tinkling with every step,

17 The Lord shall cover the scalps of Zion's daughters with scabs,
and the LORD shall bare their heads.*

18 On that day the LORD will do away with the finery of the anklets, sunbursts, and crescents; 19 the pendants, bracelets, and veils; 20 the headdresses, bangles, cinctures, perfume boxes, and amulets; 21 the signet rings, and the nose rings;* 22 the court dresses, wraps, cloaks, and purses; 23 the mirrors, linen tunics, turbans, and shawls.

24 Instead of perfume there will be stench,
instead of the girdle, a rope,

And for the coiffure, baldness;
for the rich gown, a sackcloth skirt.
Then, instead of beauty:

25 Your men will fall by the sword,
and your champions, in war;

26 Her gates will lament and mourn,
as the city sits desolate on the ground.

CHAPTER 4

1 Seven women will take hold of one man*
on that day, saying:
"We will eat our own food
and wear our own clothing;
Only let your name be given us,
put an end to our disgrace!"

The Messianic Branch

2   On that day,
The branch of the LORD* will be luster and glory,
and the fruit of the earth will be honor and splendor
for the survivors of Israel.ʷ

3 He who remains in Zion
and he that is left in Jerusalem
Will be called holy:
every one marked down for life* in Jerusalem.ˣ

4 When the Lord washes away
the filth of the daughters of Zion,
And purges Jerusalem's blood from her midst
with a blast of searing judgment,

5 Then will the LORD create,
over the whole site of Mount Zion
and over her place of assembly,
A smoking cloud by day
and a light of flaming fire by night.ʸ

6 For over all, his glory will be shelter and protection:

---

u Lv 25, 42. 55.—v 16ff: Is 32, 11f.—w Is 11, 1; Jer 23, 5; 33, 15.—x Is 6, 13; 10, 20; Ob 17.—y Ex 13, 21.

3, 17: *Bare their heads:* a mark of social disgrace; cf Nm 5, 18.

3, 21: *Nose rings:* of gold, a feminine ornament in the East; cf note on Gn 24, 22.

4, 1: *Seven women . . . one man:* the disproportion of the sexes due to war leaves the female population almost without male partners. The women are eager to marry, not for support, but to avoid the disgrace of being childless.

4, 2: *Branch of the Lord:* divine blessings in general, which later culminated in the Messiah; cf Jer 23, 5; Zec 3, 8; 6, 12.

4, 3: *Marked down for life:* in God's list of his elect; cf Ex 32, 32.

shade from the parching heat of day,
refuge and cover from storm and
rain.

CHAPTER 5

The Vineyard Song

1 Let me now sing of my friend,
my friend's song concerning his vineyard.
My friend had a vineyard*
on a fertile hillside;
2 He spaded it, cleared it of stones,
and planted the choicest vines;
Within it he built a watchtower,
and hewed out a wine press.
Then he looked for the crop of grapes,
but what it yielded was wild grapes.

3 Now, inhabitants of Jerusalem and men
of Judah,
judge between me and my vineyard:
4 What more was there to do for my vineyard
that I had not done?
Why, when I looked for the crop of
grapes,
did it bring forth wild grapes?
5 Now, I will let you know
what I mean to do to my vineyard:
Take away its hedge, give it to grazing,
break through its wall, let it be trampled!
6 Yes, I will make it a ruin:
it shall not be pruned or hoed,
but overgrown with thorns and
briers;
I will command the clouds
not to send rain upon it.
7 The vineyard of the LORD of hosts is
the house of Israel,
and the men of Judah are his
cherished plant;
He looked for judgment, but see,
bloodshed!
for justice, but hark, the outcry!*

---

z Mi 2, 2.—a Is 6, 12.—b Am 6, 5f.—c Hb 2, 5.

5, 1: *My friend had a vineyard:* the Lord and his chosen
people.
5, 7: *Judgment . . . bloodshed . . . justice . . . outcry:* in
Hebrew, these adversative terms constitute a play on words.
5, 8-10: Land-grabbers who unjustly acquire property will be
impoverished instead of enriched.
5, 10: *Ten acres:* a field requiring ten days of plowing by a
yoke of oxen. *Liquid measure:* in Hebrew, a "bath," i.e., about
ten gallons. *Homer:* a dry measure of about ten bushels. *Ephah:*
a dry measure of about one bushel.
5, 14: *Nether world:* cf note on Ps 6, 6.

Doom of the Unjust

8 Woe to you who join house to house,*
who connect field with field,
Till no room remains, and you are left
to dwell
alone in the midst of the land!²
9 In my hearing the LORD of hosts has
sworn:
Many houses shall be in ruins,
large ones and fine, with no one to
live in them.ᵃ
10 Ten acres* of vineyard
shall yield but one liquid measure,
And a homer of seed
shall yield but an ephah.
17 Lambs shall graze there at pasture,
and kids shall eat in the ruins of the
rich.

11 Woe to those who demand strong
drink
as soon as they rise in the morning,
And linger into the night
while wine inflames them!
12 With harp and lyre, timbrel and flute,
they feast on wine;
But what the LORD does, they regard
not,
the work of his hands they see not.ᵇ
13 Therefore my people go into exile,
because they do not understand;
Their nobles die of hunger,
and their masses are parched with
thirst.
14 Therefore the nether world* enlarges its
throat
and opens its maw without limit;
Down go their nobility and their masses,
their throngs and their revelry.ᶜ
15 Men shall be abased, each one brought
low,
and the eyes of the haughty lowered,
16 But the LORD of hosts shall be exalted
by his judgment,
and God the Holy shall be shown
holy by his justice.

18 Woe to those who tug at guilt with
cords of perversity,
and at sin as if with cart ropes!
19 To those who say, "Let him make
haste
and speed his work, that we may see
it;

Is

On with the plan of the Holy One of
Israel!
> let it come to pass, that we may know
> it!"[d]

20 Woe to those who call evil good, and
good evil,
> who change darkness into light, and
> light into darkness,
> who change bitter into sweet, and
> sweet into bitter!

21 Woe to those who are wise in their own
sight,
> and prudent in their own esteem![e]

22 Woe to the champions at drinking
wine,
> the valiant at mixing strong drink![f]

23 To those who acquit the guilty for
bribes,
> and deprive the just man of his
> rights![g]

24 Therefore, as the tongue of fire licks up
stubble,
> as dry grass shrivels in the flame,
> Even so their root shall become rotten
> and their blossom scatter like dust;
> For they have spurned the law of the
> LORD of hosts,
> and scorned the word of the Holy
> One of Israel.

25 Therefore the wrath of the LORD blazes
against his people,
> he raises his hand to strike them;
> When the mountains quake,
> their corpses shall be like refuse in
> the streets.
> For all this, his wrath is not turned
> back,
> and his hand is still outstretched.

Invasion*

26 He will give a signal to a far-off nation,
> and whistle to them from the ends of
> the earth;
> speedily and promptly will they
> come.

27 None of them will stumble with weariness,
> none will slumber and none will
> sleep.
> None will have his waist belt loose,
> nor the thong of his sandal broken.

28 Their arrows are sharp,
> and all their bows are bent.

The hoofs of their horses seem like flint,
> and their chariot wheels like the hur-
> ricane.

29 Their roar is that of the lion,
> like the lion's whelps they roar;
> They growl and seize the prey,
> they carry it off and none will rescue
> it.

30 [They will roar over it, on that day,
> with a roaring like that of the sea.][h]

II: IMMANUEL PROPHECIES

CHAPTER 6

Call of Isaiah. [1] In the year King Uzziah
died,* I saw the Lord seated on a high and
lofty throne,[i] with the train of his garment
filling the temple.* [2] Seraphim were stationed above; each of them had six wings:
with two they veiled their faces, with two
they veiled their feet, and with two they
hovered aloft.[j]

[3] "Holy, holy, holy is the LORD of
hosts!" they cried one to the other. "All
the earth is filled with his glory!" [4] [k] At
the sound of that cry, the frame of the
door shook and the house was filled with
smoke.*

[5] Then I said, "Woe is me, I am
doomed!* For I am a man of unclean lips,
living among a people of unclean lips; yet
my eyes have seen the King, the LORD of
hosts!"[l] [6] Then one of the seraphim flew to
me, holding an ember which he had taken
with tongs from the altar.

[7] He touched my mouth with it. "See,"
he said, "now that this has touched your

---

d Jer 5, 12: 2 Pt 3, 4.—e Prv 3, 7; Rom 12, 16.—f Sir 31, 3.—
g Ex 23, 8; Prv 17, 15.—h Is 8, 22.—i Jn 12, 41.—j Rv 4, 8.—k
1 Kgs 8, 10f; Rv 15, 8.—l Gn 32, 3; Ex 20, 19; 33, 20; Jgs 6, 22;
13, 22.

5, 26-30: A description of the invading Assyrian army, God's
instrument for punishing his people.

6, 1: *In the year King Uzziah died:* 742 B.C.

6, 1ff: *Temple:* the holy place, just in front of the holy of
holies. *Seraphim:* literally "the burning ones," are celestial beings who surround the throne of God. Each has six wings. Reverence for the divine majesty causes them to veil their faces with
two wings; modesty, to veil their extremities in similar fashion;
alacrity in God's service, to extend two wings in preparation for
flight. *Holy, holy, holy:* God's perfect interior holiness whose
exterior manifestation is *his glory.* These words are found in the
Roman liturgy just before the Canon of the Mass.

6, 4: *Smoke:* reminiscent of the clouds which surrounded God
at Mount Sinai; cf Ex 19, 16-19; Dt 4, 11f.

6, 5: *Doomed:* it was popularly believed that to see God would
lead to one's death; cf Gn 32, 31; Ex 33, 20; Jgs 13, 22.

lips,* your wickedness is removed, your sin purged."*m*

⁸ Then I heard the voice of the Lord saying, "Whom shall I send? Who will go for us?" "Here I am," I said; "send me!" ⁹ And he replied: Go and say to this people:*

Listen carefully, but you shall not understand!
Look intently, but you shall know nothing!*n*
10 You are to make the heart of this people sluggish,
    to dull their ears and close their eyes;
Else their eyes will see, their ears hear,
    their heart understand,
    and they will turn and be healed.*o*

11 "How long, O Lord?" I asked. And he replied:

Until the cities are desolate,
    without inhabitants,
Houses, without a man,
    and the earth is a desolate waste.
12 Until the LORD removes men far away,
    and the land is abandoned more and more.*
13 If there be still a tenth part in it,
    then this in turn shall be laid waste;
As with a terebinth or an oak

---

m Jer 1, 9; Dn 10, 16.—n Mt 13, 14f; Mk 4, 12; Lk 8, 10; Acts 28, 26f.—o Jer 5, 21; Jn 12, 40.—p Is 10, 22.—q 2 Kgs 16, 5; 2 Chr 28, 5-15.—r Is 36, 2; 2 Chr 32, 3.—s Is 8, 6ff.

6, 7: *Touched your lips:* Isaiah is thus symbolically purified to be worthy of his vocation as God's prophet. In the Roman liturgy, the celebrant at Mass makes reference to this incident just before he reads the gospel.
6, 9f: The truth that the nation will remain impenitent is vividly foretold, as if its obstinacy would be caused, instead of merely occasioned, by the prophet's warning. Cf Mt 13, 13ff; Mk 4, 12; Lk 8, 10.
6, 12: Several limited deportations in the time of Isaiah would later culminate in the Babylonian Exile.
7, 1: *Days of Ahaz:* who ruled from 735 to 715 B.C. This attack against Jerusalem by the kings of *Aram* (Syria) and Israel was occasioned by Ahaz' refusal to enter with them into an anti-Assyrian alliance; cf 2 Kgs 16.
7, 3: *Shear-jashub:* this name means "a remnant will return."
7, 6: *Son of Tabeel:* an adherent of Jerusalem's enemies. His appointment would interrupt the lawful succession from David.
7, 9: *Within sixty years and five:* if the text is correct, its reference is unknown.
7, 11: *Deep . . . sky:* an extraordinary or miraculous sign that would prove God's firm will to save the royal house of David from its oppressors.
7, 12: *Tempt the Lord:* Ahaz expresses in this hypocritical way his preference for depending upon the might of Assyria rather than upon God.

whose trunk remains when its leaves have fallen.
[Holy offspring is the trunk.]*p*

CHAPTER 7

Birth of Immanuel. ¹ In the days of Ahaz,* king of Judah, son of Jotham, son of Uzziah, Rezin, king of Aram, and Pekah, king of Israel, son of Remaliah, went up to attack Jerusalem,*q* but they were not able to conquer it. ² When word came to the house of David that Aram was encamped in Ephraim, the heart of the king and the heart of the people trembled, as the trees of the forest tremble in the wind.

³ *r* Then the LORD said to Isaiah: Go out to meet Ahaz, you and your son Shear-jashub,* at the end of the conduit of the upper pool, on the highway of the fuller's field, ⁴ and say to him: Take care you remain tranquil and do not fear; let not your courage fail before these two stumps of smoldering brands [the blazing anger of Rezin and the Arameans, and of the son of Remaliah], ⁵ because of the mischief that Aram [Ephraim and the son of Remaliah] plots against you, saying, ⁶ "Let us go up and tear Judah asunder, make it our own by force, and appoint the son of Tabeel* king there."

7 Thus says the LORD:
    This shall not stand, it shall not be!
8 Damascus is the capital of Aram,
    and Rezin the head of Damascus;
Samaria is the capital of Ephraim,
    and Remaliah's son the head of Samaria.
9 But within sixty years and five,*
    Ephraim shall be crushed, no longer a nation.
Unless your faith is firm
    you shall not be firm!*s*

10 Again the LORD spoke to Ahaz: 11 Ask for a sign from the LORD, your God; let it be deep as the nether world, or high as the sky!* 12 But Ahaz answered, "I will not ask! I will not tempt the LORD!"* 13 Then he said: Listen, O house of David! Is is not enough for you to weary men, must you also weary my God? 14 Therefore the

Is

Lord himself will give you this sign:* the virgin shall be with child, and bear a son, and shall name him Immanuel. ¹⁵He shall be living on curds and honey* by the time he learns to reject the bad and choose the good. ¹⁶For before the child learns to reject the bad and choose the good, the land of those two kings whom you dread shall be deserted.

¹⁷The LORD shall bring upon you and your people and your father's house days worse than any since Ephraim seceded from Judah. [This means the king of Assyria.] ¹⁸On that day

The LORD shall whistle
    for the fly that is in the farthest
      streams of Egypt,
    and for the bee in the land of Assyria.
¹⁹ All of them shall come and settle
    in the steep ravines and in the rocky
      clefts,
    on all thornbushes and in all pas-
      tures.

²⁰On that day the LORD shall shave with the razor hired from across the River [with the king of Assyria] the head, and the hair between the legs. It shall also shave off the beard.* ²¹On that day a man shall keep a heifer or a couple of sheep, ²²and from their abundant yield of milk he shall live on curds; curds and honey shall be the food of all who remain in the land. ²³On that day every place where there used to be a thousand vines, worth a thousand pieces of silver, shall be turned to briers and thorns. ²⁴Men shall go there with bow and arrows; for all the country shall be briers and thorns. ²⁵For fear of briers and thorns you shall not go upon any mountainside which used to be hoed with the mattock; they shall be grazing land for cattle and shall be trampled upon by sheep.

CHAPTER 8

The Son of Isaiah. ¹The LORD said to me: Take a large cylinder-seal, and inscribe on it in ordinary letters:* "Belonging to Maher-shalal-hash-baz." ²And I took reliable witnesses,* Uriah the priest, and Zechariah, son of Jeberechiah. ³Then I went to the prophetess* and she conceived and bore a son. The LORD said to me: Name him Maher-shalal-hash-baz, ⁴for

before the child knows how to call his father or mother by name, the wealth of Damascus and the spoil of Samaria shall be carried off by the king of Assyria.

⁵Again the LORD spoke to me:

⁶ Because this people* has rejected
    the waters of Shiloah that flow
      gently,ᵗ
And melts with fear before the loftiness
    of Rezin and Remaliah's son,
⁷ Therefore the LORD raises against them
    the waters of the River, great and
      mighty
    [the king of Assyria and all his
      power].
It shall rise above all its channels,
    and overflow all its banks;
⁸ It shall pass into Judah, and flood it all
      throughout:
    up to the neck it shall reach;
It shall spread its wings
    the full width of your land, Im-
      manuel!

⁹ Know, O peoples, and be appalled!
    Give ear, all you distant lands!

---

t Jn 9, 7. 11.

7, 14: The *sign* proposed by Isaiah was concerned with the preservation of Judah in the midst of distress (cf Is 7, 15. 17), but more especially with the fulfillment of God's earlier promise to David (2 Sm 7, 12-16) in the coming of *Immanuel* (meaning, "With us is God") as the ideal king (cf Is 9, 5-6; 11, 1-5). The church has always followed St. Matthew in seeing the transcendent fulfillment of this verse in Christ and his Virgin Mother. The prophet need not have known the full force latent in his own words; and some Catholic writers have sought a preliminary and partial fulfillment in the conception and birth of the future King Hezekiah, whose mother, at the time Isaiah spoke, would have been a young, unmarried woman (Hebrew, *almah*). The Holy Spirit was preparing, however, for another Nativity which alone could fulfill the divinely given terms of Immanuel's mission, and in which the perpetual virginity of the Mother of God was to fulfill also the words of this prophecy in the integral sense intended by the divine Wisdom.
7, 15: *Curds and honey:* the restricted diet of those who remain after devastation has changed the once fertile fields of Judah into grazing land; cf Is 7, 21-25.
7, 20: God will use the Assyrians *from across the River* (the Euphrates) as his instrument *(razor)* to inflict disgrace and suffering upon his people.
8, 1: *Ordinary letters:* easily read by all. *Maher-shalal-hash-baz:* a symbolic name to be given to another son of Isaiah (v 3); it means "quick spoils; speedy plunder," and describes what the Assyrians will do.
8, 2: *Reliable witnesses:* who would testify that Isaiah had indeed prophesied the future destruction. *Uriah the priest:* cf 2 Kgs 16, 10.
8, 3: *The prophetess:* wife of Isaiah.
8, 6ff: *This people:* Judah. *Waters of Shiloah:* the stream that flows into the pool of Shiloah in Jerusalem, its slow current symbolizing the silent, divine protection which Judah has rejected. God will therefore summon the mighty Assyrian army, symbolized by *the River* (Euphrates), to devastate Judah, which, however, will not be entirely destroyed, because it is the land of *Immanuel.*

Arm, but be crushed! Arm, but be crushed!

10 Form a plan,* and it shall be thwarted;
make a resolve, and it shall not be carried out,
for "With us is God!"

Disciples of Isaiah. 11 For thus said the LORD to me, taking hold of me and warning me not to walk in the way of this people:*u*

12 Call not alliance what this people calls alliance,
and fear not, nor stand in awe of what they fear.

13 But with the LORD of hosts make your alliance—
for him be your fear and your awe.

14 Yet he shall be a snare, an obstacle and a stumbling stone
to both the houses of Israel,
A trap and a snare
to those who dwell in Jerusalem;*u*

15 And many among them shall stumble and fall,
broken, snared, and captured.

16 The record is to be folded and the sealed instruction kept among my disciples.* 17 For I will trust in the LORD, who is hiding his face from the house of Jacob; yes, I will wait for him. 18 Look at me and the children whom the Lord has given me: we are signs* and portents

in Israel from the LORD of hosts who dwells on Mount Zion. 19 *v* And when they say to you, "Inquire of mediums and fortunetellers (who chirp and mutter!*); should not a people inquire of their gods, apply to the dead on behalf of the living?"—20 then this document will furnish its instruction. That kind of thing they will surely say.*

The Prince of Peace. 23 First he degraded the land of Zebulun and the land of Naphtali;* but in the end he has glorified the seaward road, the land west of the Jordan, the District of the Gentiles.

Anguish has taken wing, dispelled is darkness:
for there is no gloom where but now there was distress.

CHAPTER 9

1 The people who walked in darkness*w*
have seen a great light;
Upon those who dwelt in the land of gloom
a light has shone.

2 You have brought them abundant joy and great rejoicing,
As they rejoice before you as at the harvest,
as men make merry when dividing spoils.

3 For the yoke that burdened them,
the pole on their shoulder,
And the rod of their taskmaster
you have smashed, as on the day of Midian.

4 For every boot that tramped in battle,
every cloak rolled in blood,
will be burned as fuel for flames.*x*

5 For a child* is born to us, a son is given us;
upon his shoulder dominion rests.
They name him Wonder-Counselor, God-Hero,
Father-Forever, Prince of Peace.*xx*

6 His dominion is vast
and forever peaceful,
From David's throne, and over his kingdom,
which he confirms and sustains
By judgment and justice,
both now and forever.

tt Ez 3, 14.—u Rom 9, 33; 1 Pt 2, 8.—v Lv 19, 31; Dt 18, 10ff.—w 1f: Mt 4, 15f.—x Sir 39, 9.—xx Ps 72, 7; Lk 2, 11. 14.

8, 10: The *plan* of Israel's enemies will be *thwarted* because, as the name "Immanuel" signifies, *With us is God.*
8, 16: *Kept among my disciples:* for preservation and transmission.
8, 18: *Signs:* Isaiah and his sons had symbolic names.
8, 19: *Chirp and mutter:* a mocking reference to the sounds uttered by necromancers, as if the dead were speaking; all such practices were forbidden.
8, 21f: These verses have been transposed and placed within Is 14, 25, which affords the context in which they can be understood.
8, 23: *Zebulun . . . Naphtali:* northern Palestine, which was first to be attacked by the Assyrians; God, however, redeems it, as he redeems all his people. *Seaward road:* from Damascus, across southern Galilee to the Mediterranean Sea. *District of the Gentiles:* northern Galilee, inhabited by pagans; cf Jos 20, 7; Is 9, 1. Mt 4, 15f refers to this, since Jesus began his public mission in Galilee.
9, 5: *A child:* the Immanuel of Is 7, 14 and 8, 8; cf Is 11, 1. 2. 9. In Christian tradition and liturgy, this passage is used to refer to Christ. *Upon his shoulder dominion rests:* authority. *Wonder-Counselor:* remarkable for his wisdom and prudence. *God-Hero:* a warrior and a defender of his people, like God himself. *Father-Forever:* ever devoted to his people. *Prince of Peace:* his reign will be characterized by peace.

Is

The zeal of the Lord of hosts will do this!*y*

Fall of the Northern Kingdom

7 The Lord has sent word against Jacob,
    it falls upon Israel;
8 And all the people know it,
    Ephraim and those who dwell in Samaria,
    those who say in arrogance and pride of heart,
9 "Bricks have fallen,
    but we will build with cut stone;
Sycamores are felled,
    but we will replace them with cedars."
10 But the Lord raises up their foes against them
    and stirs up their enemies to action:
11 Aram* on the east and the Philistines on the west
    devour Israel with open mouth.
For all this, his wrath is not turned back,
    and his hand is still outstretched!

12 The people do not turn to him who struck them,
    nor seek the Lord of hosts.
13 So the Lord severs from Israel head and tail,
    palm branch and reed in one day.
14 [The elder and the noble are the head,
    the prophet who teaches falsehood is the tail.]
15 The leaders of this people mislead them
    and those to be led are engulfed.*z*
16 For this reason the Lord does not spare their young men,
    and their orphans and widows he does not pity;
They are wholly profaned and sinful,
    and every mouth gives vent to folly.
For all this, his wrath is not turned back,
    his hand is still outstretched!

17 For wickedness burns like fire,
    devouring brier and thorn;
It kindles the forest thickets,
    which go up in columns of smoke.
18 At the wrath of the Lord of hosts the land quakes,
    and the people are like fuel for fire;
No man spares his brother,
    each devours the flesh of his neighbor.

19 Though they hack on the right, they are hungry;
    though they eat on the left, they are not filled.
20 Manasseh devours Ephraim,* and Ephraim Manasseh;
    together they turn on Judah.
For all this, his wrath is not turned back,
    his hand is still outstretched!

CHAPTER 10

Social Injustice

1 Woe to those who enact unjust statutes
    and who write oppressive decrees,*a*
2 Depriving the needy of judgment
    and robbing my people's poor of their rights,
Making widows their plunder,
    and orphans their prey!*b*
3 What will you do on the day of punishment,
    when ruin comes from afar?
To whom will you flee for help?
    Where will you leave your wealth,
4 Lest it sink beneath the captive
    or fall beneath the slain?
For all this, his wrath is not turned back,
    his hand is still outstretched!

Assyria the Unconscious Instrument of God

5 Woe to Assyria! My rod in anger,
    my staff in wrath.
6 Against an impious nation* I send him,
    and against a people under my wrath I order him
To seize plunder, carry off loot,
    and tread them down like the mud of the streets.
7 But this is not what he intends,
    nor does he have this in mind;
Rather, it is in his heart to destroy,

---

y Jer 23, 5; Lk 1, 32f.—z Is 28, 7; Jer 2, 8; 5, 31; 20, 6; 23, 13f; 29, 30ff; Ez 13, 1-7; 22, 28; Mi 3, 11.—a Jer 8, 8.—b Is 1, 23.

9, 11: *Aram:* the Syrian kingdom, with its capital at Damascus.

9, 20: *Manasseh . . . Ephraim:* two of the leading tribes of the northern kingdom.

10, 6f: *Impious nation:* Israel. It was God's intention to use Assyria merely to punish, not to destroy, his people.

to make an end of nations not a few.
8 "Are not my commanders all kings?" he
    says,
9   "Is not Calno like Carchemish,*c*
    Or Hamath like Arpad,
    or Samaria like Damascus?*
10 Just as my hand reached out to idola-
    trous kingdoms
    that had more images than Jerusalem
    and Samaria,
11 Just as I treated Samaria and her idols,
    shall I not do to Jerusalem and her
    graven images?"*d*

12 [But when the LORD has brought to
an end all his work on Mount Zion and in
Jerusalem,

I will punish the utterance
    of the king of Assyria's proud heart,
13   and the boastfulness of his haughty
    eyes. For he says:]

"By my own power I have done it,
    and by my wisdom, for I am shrewd.
I have moved the boundaries of peo-
    ples,
    their treasures I have pillaged,
    and, like a giant, I have put down the
    enthroned.
14 My hand has seized like a nest
    the riches of nations;
As one takes eggs left alone,
    so I took in all the earth;
No one fluttered a wing,
    or opened a mouth, or chirped!"

15 Will the axe boast against him who
    hews with it?
    Will the saw exalt itself above him
    who wields it?
As if a rod could sway him who lifts it,
    or a staff him who is not wood!
16 Therefore the Lord, the LORD of hosts,
    will send among his fat ones* lean-
    ness,

And instead of his glory there will be
    kindling
    like the kindling of fire.
17 The Light of Israel will become a fire,
    Israel's Holy One a flame,
That burns and consumes his briers
    and his thorns in a single day.
18 His splendid forests and orchards
    will be consumed, soul and body;
19 And the remnant of the trees in his
    forest
    will be so few,
Like poles set up for signals,
    that any boy can record them.
20   On that day
The remnant of Israel,
    the survivors of the house of Jacob,
    will no more lean upon him who
    struck them;
But they will lean upon the LORD,
    the Holy One of Israel, in truth.
21 A remnant will return,* the remnant of
    Jacob,
    to the mighty God.
22 For though your people, O Israel,
    were like the sand of the sea,
Only a remnant of them will return;
    their destruction is decreed
    as overwhelming justice demands.*e*

23 Yes, the destruction he has decreed,
the Lord, the GOD of hosts, will carry out
within the whole land. 24 Therefore thus
says the Lord, the GOD of hosts: O my
people, who dwell in Zion, do not fear the
Assyrian, though he strikes you with a
rod, and raises his staff against you. 25 For
only a brief moment more, and my anger
shall be over; but them I will destroy in
wrath. 26 Then the LORD of hosts will raise
against them a scourge such as struck Midian at the rock of Oreb; and he will raise
his staff over the sea as he did against
Egypt.*f* 27 On that day,*

His burden shall be taken from your
    shoulder,
    and his yoke shattered from your
    neck.

Sennacherib's Invasion

He has come up from the direction of
    Rimmon,
28   he has reached Aiath, passed through
    Migron,
    at Michmash his supplies are stored.

---

c Is 36, 19; Am 6, 2.—d Is 36, 20.—e Rom 9, 27f.—f Jgs 7,
25.

10, 9: *Calno . . . Damascus:* cities captured by the Assyrians.
    10, 16: *His fat ones:* the strong men of the king of Assyria.
    10, 21: *A remnant will return:* in Hebrew, *shear-jashub,*
an allusion to the name of Isaiah's son, Shear-jashub; cf Is 7, 3.
    10, 27-32: A poetic description of the progress of the Assyrian
army, advancing from the north through Judah to the gates of
Jerusalem.

29 They cross the ravine:
"We will spend the night at Geba."
Ramah is in terror,
Gibeah of Saul has fled.

30 Cry and shriek, O daughter of Gallim!
Hearken, Laishah! Answer her,
Anathoth!

31 Madmenah is in flight,
the inhabitants of Gebim seek refuge.

32 Even today he will halt at Nob,*
he will shake his fist at the mount of
daughter Zion,
the hill of Jerusalem!

33 Behold, the Lord, the LORD of hosts,
lops off the boughs with terrible violence;
The tall of stature are felled,
and the lofty ones brought low;

34 The forest thickets are felled with the
axe,
and Lebanon in its splendor falls.

CHAPTER 11

The Rule of Immanuel

1 But a shoot shall sprout from the stump
of Jesse,*
and from his roots a bud shall blos-
som.g

2 The spirit of the Lord shall rest upon
him:h
a spirit of wisdom and of understanding,
A spirit of counsel and of strength,
a spirit of knowledge and of fear of
the Lord,*

3 and his delight shall be the fear of the
LORD.
Not by appearance shall he judge,
nor by hearsay shall he decide,

4 But he shall judge the poor with justice,
and decide aright for the land's
afflicted.i
He shall strike the ruthless with the rod
of his mouth,
and with the breath of his lips he
shall slay the wicked.

5 Justice shall be the band around his
waist,
and faithfulness a belt upon his hips.

6 Then the wolf shall be a guest of the
lamb,*

and the leopard shall lie down with
the kid;
The calf and the young lion shall
browse together,
with a little child to guide them.j

7 The cow and the bear shall be neighbors,
together their young shall rest;
the lion shall eat hay like the ox.

8 The baby shall play by the cobra's den,
and the child lay his hand on the
adder's lair.

9 There shall be no harm or ruin on all
my holy mountain;
for the earth shall be filled with
knowledge of the LORD,
as water covers the sea.k

Union of Ephraim and Judah

10   On that day,
The root of Jesse,
set up as a signal for the nations,
The Gentiles shall seek out,
for his dwelling shall be glorious.l

11   On that day,
The Lord shall again take it in handm
to reclaim the remnant of his people
that is left from Assyria and Egypt,
Pathros, Ethiopia, and Elam,
Shinar, Hamath, and the isles of the
sea.*

12 He shall raise a signal to the nations
and gather the outcasts of Israel;
The dispersed of Judah he shall assemble
from the four corners of the earth.

13 The envy of Ephraim shall pass away,
and the rivalry of Judah be removed;
Ephraim shall not be jealous of Judah,

---

g Lk 3, 32.—h Mt 3, 16; Mk 1, 10.—i Pss 72, 2. 4; 98, 9; 2
Thes 2, 8.—j Is 65, 25.—k Hb 2, 14.—l Is 49, 22; Rom 15, 12.—
m Is 27, 13; Mi 7, 12; Zec 10, 10.

10, 32ff: Just when the enemy is about to capture Jerusalem,
God intervenes and destroys the hostile army.
11, 1: *Jesse:* David's father. *Shoot . . . stump:* after the
Babylonian exile only *a stump* of the Davidic dynasty will remain; from it will arise the new *shoot*, the messianic King.
11, 2f: The source of the traditional names of the gifts of the
Holy Spirit. The Septuagint and the Vulgate read "piety" for
fear of the Lord in its first occurrence, thus listing seven gifts.
11, 6-9: This picture of the idyllic harmony of paradise is a
dramatic symbol of the universal peace and justice of messianic
times.
11, 11: *Pathros . . . sea:* where God's people lived in exile.
Pathros: upper Egypt. *Elam:* east of Babylonia. *Shinar:*
Babylonia. *Hamath:* on the Orontes River in Syria. *Isles:* or
coastlands, in the Mediterranean.

and Judah shall not be hostile to Ephraim;[n]

14 But they shall swoop down on the foothills
of the Philistines to the west,
together they shall plunder the Kedemites;*
Edom and Moab shall be their possessions,
and the Ammonites their subjects.

15 The Lord shall dry up the tongue of the
Sea of Egypt,*
and wave his hand over the Euphrates in his fierce anger
And shatter it into seven streamlets,
so that it can be crossed in sandals.[o]

16 There shall be a highway for the remnant of his people
that is left from Assyria,
As there was for Israel
when he came up from the land of
Egypt.

CHAPTER 12

Song of Thanksgiving*

1 On that day, you will say:
I give you thanks, O LORD;
though you have been angry with me,
your anger has abated, and you have
consoled me.

2 God indeed is my savior;
I am confident and unafraid.
My strength and my courage is the
LORD,
and he has been my savior.[p]

3 With joy you will draw water
at the fountain of salvation, 4and say
on that day:

---

n Ez 37, 16-17.—o Ex 14, 29.—p Ex 15, 2; Ps 118. 14.—q Ex
15, 1.—r Is 41, 14. 16; 54, 1; Zep 3, 14; Zec 2, 10.—s Is 5,
26.—t Jer 50, 9.—u Jer 46, 10; Jl 1, 15.—v Ez 7, 17.—w Is 21,
3; Ps 48, 7; Mi 4, 9.

11, 14: *Kedemites:* tribes in the Arabian Desert.
11, 15: *Tongue . . . Egypt:* the body of water between Egypt
and Palestine.
12, 1-6: Israel's thanksgiving to the Lord, expressed in language like that of the Psalms.
13, 2: *To them:* the Medes (v 17) and Persians, who would
destroy Babylon. *Gates of the volunteers:* the mustering places
of Babylon's enemies for war against her.
13, 3: *Dedicated soldiers:* in the sense that they will wage a
"holy war" and carry out God's plan.
13, 6ff: *Day of the Lord:* described often in prophetical writings, it generally signified the coming of the Lord in power and
majesty to destroy his enemies and inaugurate his kingdom. Here
it refers to the overthrow of Babylon. The figures used convey the
idea of horror and destruction. Read vv 6-8 with vv 14-16.

Give thanks to the LORD, acclaim his
name;
among the nations make known his
deeds,
proclaim how exalted is his name.

5 Sing praise to the LORD for his glorious
achievement;
let this be known throughout all the
earth.[q]

6 Shout with exultation, O city of Zion,
for great in your midst
is the Holy One of Israel![r]

III: ORACLES AGAINST THE PAGAN NATIONS

CHAPTER 13

Babylon. [1]An oracle concerning Babylon; a vision of Isaiah, son of Amoz.

2 Upon the bare mountains set up a signal;
cry out to them,*
Wave for them to enter
the gates of the volunteers.[s]

3 I have commanded my dedicated soldiers,*
I have summoned my warriors,
eager and bold to carry out my anger.

4 Listen! the rumble on the mountains:
that of an immense throng!
Listen! the noise of kingdoms,
nations assembled!
The LORD of hosts is mustering
an army for battle.[t]

5 They come from a far-off country,
and from the end of the heavens,
The LORD and the instruments of his
wrath,
to destroy all the land.

6 Howl, for the day of the LORD* is near;
as destruction from the Almighty it
comes.[u]

7 Therefore all hands fall helpless,[v]
the bows of the young men fall from
their hands.
Every man's heart melts 8in terror.
Pangs and sorrows take hold of them,
like a woman in labor they writhe;
They look aghast at each other,
their faces aflame.[w]

9 Lo, the day of the LORD comes,
cruel, with wrath and burning anger;
To lay waste the land
and destroy the sinners within it!

Is

10 The stars and constellations of the
     heavens
       send forth no light;
     The sun is dark when it rises,
       and the light of the moon does not
       shine.[x]
11 Thus I will punish the world for its evil
     and the wicked for their guilt.
     I will put an end to the pride of the ar-
     rogant,
       the insolence of tyrants I will hum-
       ble.[y]
12 I will make mortals more rare than pure
     gold,
       men, than gold of Ophir.*
13 For this I will make the heavens trem-
     ble
       and the earth shall be shaken from its
       place,
     At the wrath of the LORD of hosts
       on the day of his burning anger.

14 Like a hunted gazelle,
       or a flock that no one gathers,
     Every man shall turn to his kindred
       and flee to his own land.[z]
15 Everyone who is caught shall be run
     through;
       to a man, they shall fall by the sword.
16 Their infants shall be dashed to pieces
       in their sight;
     their houses shall be plundered
       and their wives ravished.[a]

17 I am stirring up against them the
     Medes,
       who think nothing of silver
     and take no delight in gold.[b]
18 The fruit of the womb they shall not
     spare,
       nor shall they have eyes of pity for
       children.
19 And Babylon, the jewel of kingdoms,
       the glory and pride of the Chaldeans,
     Shall be overthrown by God
       like Sodom and like Gomorrah.
20 She shall never be inhabited,
       nor dwelt in, from age to age;
     The Arab shall not pitch his tent there,
       nor shepherds couch their flocks.[c]

21 But wildcats shall rest there
       and owls shall fill the houses;
     There ostriches shall dwell,
       and satyrs* shall dance.[d]

22 Desert beasts shall howl in her castles,
       and jackals in her luxurious palaces.
     Her time is near at hand
       and her days shall not be prolonged.

CHAPTER 14

The King of Babylon. [1]When the LORD
has pity on Jacob and again chooses Israel
and settles them on their own soil, the
aliens will join them and be counted with
the house of Jacob.[e] [2]The house of Israel
will take them and bring them along to its
place, and possess them as male and
female slaves on the Lord's soil, making
captives of its captors and ruling over its
oppressors.[f] [3]On the day the LORD relieves you of sorrow and unrest and the
hard service in which you have been enslaved,[g] [4]you will take up this taunt-song*
against the king of Babylon:[h]

How the oppressor has reached his end!
     how the turmoil is stilled!
5 The LORD has broken the rod of the
     wicked,
       the staff of the tyrants
6 That struck the peoples in wrath
     relentless blows;
     That beat down the nations in anger,
       with oppression unchecked.

7 The whole earth rests peacefully,
     song breaks forth;
8 The very cypresses rejoice over you,
     and the cedars of Lebanon:
     "Now that you are laid to rest,
       there will be none to cut us down."[i]

9 The nether world below is all astir
     preparing for your coming;
     It awakens the shades to greet you,
       all the leaders of the earth;
     It has the kings of all nations
       rise from their thrones.
10 All of them speak out
     and say to you,
     "You too have become weak like us,
       you are the same as we.

---

x Is 24, 23.—y Is 2, 17; Jer 50, 32.—z Jer 50, 16.—a Na 3,
10.—b Is 21, 2; Jer 51, 11. 28.—c Is 51, 62.—d Is 34, 13f; 35,
7.—e Is 56, 3; 60, 4; Ps 102, 14; Jer 24, 6; Zec 1, 17.—f Is 66,
20.—g Jer 30, 10.—h Hb 2, 6.—i Ez 31, 16.

13, 12: *Ophir:* cf note to Ps 45, 10.
13, 21: *Satyrs:* in the popular mind, demons of goatlike form
dwelling in ruins, symbols of immorality; cf Lv 17, 7.
14, 4-21: This *taunt-song,* or satire, is one of the finest in
the Bible.

11 Down to the nether world your pomp is
    brought,
    the music of your harps.
The couch beneath you is the maggot,
    your covering, the worm."*j*

12 How have you fallen from the heavens,
    O morning star,* son of the dawn!
How are you cut down to the ground,
    you who mowed down the nations!
13 You said in your heart:*k*
    "I will scale the heavens;
Above the stars of God
    I will set up my throne;
I will take my seat on the Mount of As-
    sembly,
    in the recesses of the North.*
14 I will ascend above the tops of the
    clouds;
    I will be like the Most High!"*l*
15 Yet down to the nether world you go
    to the recesses of the pit!

16 When they see you they will stare,
    pondering over you:
"Is this the man who made the earth
    tremble,
    and kingdoms quake?
17 Who made the world a desert,
    razed its cities,
    and gave his captives no release?
18 All the kings of the nations lie in glory,
    each in his own tomb;
19 But you are cast forth without burial,
    loathsome and corrupt,
Clothed as those slain at sword-point,
    a trampled corpse.
Going down to the pavement of the pit,
20   you will never be one with them in
    the grave."
For you have ruined your land,
    you have slain your people!

Let him not be named forever,
    that scion of an evil race!
21 Make ready to slaughter his sons

---

j Sir 10, 13.—k Jer 51, 53; Am 9, 2.—l Ez 28, 2.—m Jer
51, 62.

14, 12: *Morning star:* the king of Babylon. The Vulgate
has "Lucifer," a name applied by the church Fathers to Satan.
14, 13: *Recesses of the North:* see note on Ps 48, 3.
14, 21f: *He . . . clouds:* the two verses have been transposed from chap. 8.
14, 28: *The year that King Ahaz died:* 715 B.C.
14, 29: *Rod:* an Assyrian oppressor whose identity is uncertain. *Flying saraph:* a poisonous serpent, distinguished by its
speedy movement; cf note on Nm 21, 6.

---

    for the guilt of their fathers;
Lest they rise and possess the earth,
    and fill the breadth of the world with
    tyrants.

22 I will rise up against them, says the
LORD of hosts, and cut off from Babylon
name and remnant, progeny and offspring,
says the LORD.*m* 23 I will make it a haunt
of hoot owls and a marshland; I will sweep
it with the broom of destruction, says the
LORD of hosts.

Assyria

24   The LORD of hosts has sworn:
As I have resolved,
    so shall it be;
As I have proposed,
    so shall it stand:
25 I will break the Assyrian in my land
    and trample him on my mountains;
21 * He shall pass through it hard-pressed
    and hungry,
    and in his hunger he shall become en-
    raged,
    and curse his king and his gods.
He shall look upward,
    but there shall be strict darkness
    without any dawn;
22 He shall gaze at the earth,
    but there shall be distress and dark-
    ness,
    with the light blacked out by its
    clouds.
(25) Then his yoke shall be removed from
    them,
    and his burden from their shoulder.
26 This is the plan proposed for the whole
    earth,
    and this the hand outstretched over
    all nations.
27 The LORD of hosts has planned;
    who can thwart him?
His hand is stretched out;
    who can turn it back?

Philistia. 28 In the year that King Ahaz
died,* there came this oracle:

29 Rejoice not, O Philistia, not a man of
    you,
    that the rod* which smote you is bro-
    ken;
For out of the serpent's root shall come
    an adder,
    its fruit shall be a flying saraph.
30 In my pastures the poor shall eat,

Is

and the needy lie down in safety;
But I will kill your root with famine
　that shall slay even your remnant.
31 Howl, O gate; cry out, O city!
　Philistia, all of you melts away!
For there comes a smoke from the
　north,
　without a straggler in the ranks.
32 What will one answer the messengers of
　the nation?
　"The LORD has established Zion,
　and in her the afflicted of his people
　find refuge."[n]

CHAPTER 15

Moab

1　　　Oracle on Moab:
Laid waste in a night,
　Ar of Moab is destroyed;
Laid waste in a night,
　Kir of Moab is destroyed.[o]
2 Up goes daughter Dibon[p]
　to the high places to weep;
Over Nebo and over Medeba
　Moab wails.
Every head is shaved,
　every beard sheared off.*
3 In the streets they wear sackcloth,
　lamenting and weeping;
On rooftops and in the squares
　everyone wails.
4 Heshbon and Elealeh cry out,
　they are heard as far as Jahaz.
At this the loins of Moab tremble,
　his soul quivers within him;[q]
5 The heart of Moab cries out,
　his fugitives reach Zoar
　[Eglath-shelishiyah].
The ascent of Luhith
　they climb weeping;
On the way to Horonaim
　they utter rending cries.[r]

6 The waters of Nimrim
　have become a waste;
The grass is withered,
　new growth is gone,
　nothing is green.
7 So now whatever they have acquired or
　stored away
　they carry across the Gorge of the
　Poplars,
8 For the cry has gone round
　the land of Moab;
As far as Eglaim the wailing,

and to Beer-elim, the wail.
9 The waters of Dimon were filled with
　blood,*
　but I will bring still more upon
　Dimon:
Lions for those who are fleeing from
　Moab
　and for those who remain in the land!

CHAPTER 16

1 Send them forth, hugging the earth like
　reptiles,
　from Sela across the desert,
　to the mount of daughter Zion.
2 Like flushed birds,
　like startled nestlings,
Are the daughters of Moab
　at the fords of the Arnon.*
3 Offer counsel, take their part:*
　at high noon let your shadow be like
　the night,
To hide the outcasts,
　to conceal the fugitives.
4 Let the outcasts of Moab live with you,
　be their shelter from the destroyer.
When the struggle is ended, the ruin
　complete,
　and they have done with trampling
　the land,
5 A throne shall be set up in mercy,
　and on it shall sit in fidelity
　[in David's tent]
A judge upholding right
　and prompt to do justice.[s]

6 We have heard of the pride of Moab,
　how very proud he is,
With his haughty, arrogant insolence
　that his empty words do not match.[t]

7 Therefore Moab wails for Moab,*
　everywhere they wail;
For the raisin cakes* of Kir-hareseth
　they sigh, stricken with grief.[u]

---

n Pss 87, 5; 102, 17f; Zep 3, 12.—o Is 16, 7.—p Jer 48, 38f.—q Jer 48, 34.—r Is 16, 9; Jer 48, 3.—s Is 32, 1.—t Jer 48, 29.—u Is 15, 3.

15, 2: *Every head . . . sheared off:* traditional signs of grief.
15, 9: There is in the Hebrew a play on words: *Dimon* and *dam,* the latter signifying "blood."
16, 2: *The Arnon:* principal river of Moab.
16, 3-5: Directed to Jerusalem, which should receive the suffering Moabites with mercy, as befits the city of David's family, who were partly descended from Ruth the Moabite.
16, 7-14: Moab had been prosperous; now it has become a desert.
16, 7: *Raisin cakes:* masses of dried compressed grapes used as food (cf 2 Sm 6, 19; 1 Chr 16, 3; Ct 2, 5), and also in pagan cult (Hos 3, 1).

⁸ The terraced slopes of Heshbon languish,
the vines of Sibmah,
Whose clusters overpowered
the lords of nations,
While they reached as far as Jazer
and scattered over the desert,*
And whose branches spread forth
and extended over the sea.
⁹ Therefore I weep with Jazer
for the vines of Sibmah;
I water you with tears,
Heshbon and Elealeh;
For on your summer fruits and harvests
the battle cry has fallen. ᵛ
¹⁰ From the orchards are taken away
joy and gladness,
In the vineyards there is no singing,
no shout of joy;
In the wine presses no one treads
grapes,
the vintage shout is stilled. ʷ

¹¹ Therefore for Moab
my breast moans like a lyre,
and my heart for Kir-hareseth. ˣ
¹² When Moab grows weary on the high
places,ʸ
he shall enter his sanctuary to pray,
but it shall avail him nothing.*

¹³ * This is the word the LORD spoke
against Moab in times past. ¹⁴ But now the
LORD has spoken: In three years, like
those of a hireling, the glory of Moab shall
be degraded despite all its great multitude;
there shall be a remnant, very small and
weak.

---

v Is 15, 5; Jer 48, 32.—w Is 24, 8.—x Is 15, 5; Jer 48, 36.—y
Jer 48, 13.—z Jer 49, 23.—a Is 10, 16.—b Is 24, 13.—c Mi 5,
12.—d Is 27, 10.—e Jer 2, 32; Hos 8, 14.

16, 8: *Desert:* to the east. *Sea:* the Dead Sea.
16, 12: In vain do the Moabites appeal to their god Chemosh.
16, 13f: A prose application of the preceding poetic oracle
against Moab (15, 1—16, 12); cf Jer 4, 8. *Like those of a
hireling:* who fulfills his period of service according to the shortest manner of reckoning; cf Is 21, 16.
17, 1: *Damascus:* capital of Syria, destroyed in 732 B.C.
17, 3: *Ephraim:* Israel, leagued with Syria against Assyria
and Judah; destroyed in 721 B.C. *Aram:* Syria.
17, 5: *Valley of Rephaim:* a fertile plain to the southwest of
Jerusalem; cf Jos 15, 8; 2 Sm 5, 18.
17, 6: Olives not easily picked by hand were knocked from the
tree by means of a long stick; cf Is 24, 13.
17, 8: *Sacred poles:* see note on Ex 34, 13. *Incense stands:*
small altars on which incense was burned in idolatrous worship; cf
Is 27, 9; Lv 26, 30.
17, 10: *Pagan plants:* literally, "plants of delight," understood by some as planted in honor of the god of fertility.

CHAPTER 17

Damascus

¹   Oracle on Damascus:*
Lo, Damascus shall cease to be a city
and become a ruin;ᶻ
² Her cities shall be forever abandoned,
given over to flocks to lie in undisturbed.
³ The fortress shall be lost to Ephraim*
and the kingdom to Damascus;
The remnant of Aram shall have the
same glory
as the Israelites,
says the LORD of hosts.

⁴   On that day
The glory of Jacob shall fade,
and his full body grow thin,ᵃ
⁵ Like the reaper's mere armful of stalks
when he gathers the standing grain;
Or as when one gleans the ears
in the Valley of Rephaim.*
⁶ Only a scattering of grapes shall be left!
As when an olive tree has been
beaten,
Two or three olives remain at the very
top,
four or five on its fruitful branches,*
says the LORD, the God of Israel. ᵇ

⁷ On that day man shall look to his
maker,
his eyes turned toward the Holy One
of Israel. ᶜ
⁸ He shall not look to the altars, his
handiwork,
nor shall he regard what his fingers
have made:
the sacred poles* or the incense
stands.

⁹ On that day his strong cities shall be
like those abandoned by the Hivites
and Amorites
When faced with the children of Israel:
they shall be laid waste. ᵈ
¹⁰ For you have forgotten God, your
savior,
and remembered not the Rock, your
strength.
Therefore, though you plant your
pagan plants*
and set out your foreign vine slips,ᵉ

Is

11 Though you make them grow the day
you plant them
and make your sprouts blossom on
the next morning,
The harvest shall disappear on the day
of the grievous blow,
the incurable blight.

12 Ah! the roaring of many peoples*
that roar like the roar of the seas!
The surging of nations
that surge like the surging of mighty
waves!

13 But God shall rebuke them,
and they shall flee far away;
Windswept, like chaff on the mountains,
like tumbleweed in a storm.

14 In the evening, they spread terror,
before morning, they are gone!
Such is the portion of those who despoil
us,
the lot of those who plunder us.

CHAPTER 18
Ethiopia

1 Ah, land of buzzing insects,*
beyond the rivers of Ethiopia,*

2 Sending ambassadors by sea,
in papyrus boats on the waters!
Go, swift messengers,
to a nation tall and bronzed,
To a people dreaded near and far,
a nation strong and conquering,
whose land is washed by rivers.*f*

3 All you who inhabit the world,
who dwell on earth,
When the signal is raised on the mountain, look!
When the trumpet blows, listen!

4 For thus says the LORD to me:
I will quietly look on from where I
dwell,
Like the glowing heat of sunshine,
like a cloud of dew at harvest time.

5 Before the vintage, when the flowering
is ended,
and the blooms are succeeded by ripening grapes,
Then comes the cutting of branches
with pruning hooks
and the discarding of the lopped-off
shoots.

6 They shall all be left to the mountain
birds of prey,
and to the beasts in the land;

The birds of prey shall summer on them
and on them all the beasts of the
earth shall winter.

7 Then will gifts be brought to the LORD
of hosts from a people tall and bronzed,
from a people dreaded near and far, a nation strong and conquering, whose land is
washed by rivers—to Mount Zion where
dwells the name of the LORD of hosts.*g*

CHAPTER 19
Egypt

1 Oracle on Egypt:
See, the LORD is riding on a swift cloud
on his way to Egypt;
The idols of Egypt tremble before him,
the hearts of the Egyptians melt
within them.

2 I will rouse Egypt against Egypt:
brother will war against brother,
Neighbor against neighbor,
city against city, kingdom against
kingdom.

3 The courage of the Egyptians ebbs away
within them,
and I will bring to nought their counsel;
They shall consult idols and charmers,
ghosts and spirits.*h*

4 I will deliver Egypt
into the power of a cruel master,*
A harsh king who shall rule over them,
says the Lord, the LORD of hosts.*i*

5 The waters shall be drained from the
sea,
the river shall shrivel and dry up;*j*

6 Its streams shall become foul,
and the canals of Egypt shall dwindle
and dry up.
Reeds and rushes shall wither away,

7 and bulrushes on the bank of the
Nile;

---

f Is 18, 7.—g Is 45, 14; Zep 3, 10; Mal 1, 11.—h Is 44, 25.—i
Ez 29, 19; 30, 10.—j Ez 30, 12; 32, 2.

17, 12f: *Many peoples:* the hordes that accompanied the invading Assyrians, whom God repels just as he vanquished the
primeval waters of chaos; see notes on Jb 3, 8; 7, 12; Ps 89, 11.

18, 1: *Land of buzzing insects:* the region of the Upper Nile
where these multiplied with great rapidity.

18, 1f: *Papyrus boats:* light and serviceable vessels made of
bundles of papyrus stalks and sealed with pitch. Egypt, ruled by a
dynasty from *Ethiopia,* had invited Judah to join a coalition
against Assyria, but Isaiah bade the *ambassadors* return to their
own people.

19, 4: *Cruel master:* the king of Assyria.

All the sown land along the Nile
   shall dry up and blow away, and be
   no more.
8 The fishermen shall mourn and lament,
   all who cast hook in the Nile;
   Those who spread their nets in the
   water
   shall pine away.
9 The linen-workers shall be disappointed,
   the combers and weavers shall turn
   pale;[k]
10 The spinners shall be crushed,
   all the hired laborers shall be despon-
   dent.

11 Utter fools are the princes of Zoan!*
   the wisest of Pharaoh's advisers give
   stupid counsel.
   How can you say to Pharaoh,
   "I am a disciple of wise men, of ancient kings"?
12 Where then are your wise men?
   Let them tell you and make known
   What the LORD of hosts had planned
   against Egypt.
13 The princes of Zoan have become fools,
   the princes of Memphis have been
   deceived.
   The chiefs of her tribes
   have led Egypt astray.
14 The LORD has prepared among them
   a spirit of dizziness,
   And they have made Egypt stagger in
   whatever she does,
   as a drunkard staggers in his vomit.
15 Egypt shall have no work to do[l]
   for head or tail, palm branch or
   reed.*

16 On that day the Egyptians shall be like
women, trembling with fear, because of
the LORD of hosts shaking his fist at
them.[m] 17 And the land of Judah shall be a
terror to the Egyptians. Every time they
remember Judah, they shall stand in dread

because of the plan which the LORD of
hosts has in mind for them.[n]
   18 On that day there shall be five cities*
in the land of Egypt speaking the language
of Canaan and swearing by the LORD of
hosts; one shall be called "City of the
Sun."
   19 On that day there shall be an altar to
the LORD in the land of Egypt, and a sacred pillar to the LORD near the boundary.
20 It shall be a sign and a witness to the
LORD of hosts in the land of Egypt, when
they cry out to the LORD against their oppressors, and he sends them a savior to defend and deliver them. 21 The LORD shall
make himself known to Egypt, and the
Egyptians shall know the LORD in that
day; they shall offer sacrifices and oblations, and fulfill the vows they make to the
LORD.[o] 22 Although the LORD shall smite
Egypt severely, he shall heal them; they
shall turn to the LORD and he shall be won
over and heal them.
   23 On that day there shall be a highway
from Egypt to Assyria; the Assyrians shall
enter Egypt, and the Egyptians enter Assyria, and Egypt shall serve Assyria.
   24 On that day Israel shall be a third
party with Egypt and Assyria, a blessing in
the midst of the land,[p] 25 when the LORD
of hosts blesses it: "Blessed be my people
Egypt, and the work of my hands Assyria,
and my inheritance, Israel."

CHAPTER 20

Captivity of Egypt and Ethiopia. 1 In the
year the general sent by Sargon, king of
Assyria, fought against Ashdod and captured it, 2 the LORD gave a warning
through Isaiah,* the son of Amoz: Go and
take off the sackcloth from your waist, and
remove the sandals from your feet. This he
did, walking naked and barefoot. 3 Then
the LORD said: Just as my servant Isaiah
has gone naked and barefoot for three
years as a sign and portent against Egypt
and Ethiopia, 4 so shall the king of Assyria
lead away captives from Egypt, and exiles
from Ethiopia, young and old, naked and
barefoot, with buttocks uncovered [the
shame of Egypt]. 5 They shall be dismayed
and ashamed because of Ethiopia, their
hope, and because of Egypt, their boast.[q]

---

k Ez 27, 7.—l Is 9, 14.—m Na 3, 13.—n Ex 14, 25.—o Zec 14, 16. 18.—p Gn 12, 2.—q Is 30, 3. 5.

19, 11. 13: *Zoan:* later known as Tanis, and *Memphis* (in Hebrew, *Noph*) were the key cities of the Nile Delta.
19, 15: *Head or tail, palm branch or reed:* the leaders or the people; cf Is 9, 13f.
19, 18: *Five cities:* colonies of Jews living together and speaking their languages, Hebrew and Aramaic; cf Jer, chap. 43, *City of the Sun:* the meaning is uncertain, but the reference seems to be to the city known later as Heliopolis.
20, 2-6: The symbolic act of the prophet conveyed the idea that Assyria would lead captive the Egyptians and Ethiopians. The Judeans and their allies would then realize the folly of having trusted in them.

⁶The inhabitants of this coastland shall say on that day, "Look at our hope! We have fled here for help and deliverance from the king of Assyria; where can we flee now?"ʳ

CHAPTER 21

Fall of Babylon

¹   Oracle on the wastelands by the sea:*
Like whirlwinds sweeping in waves
    through the Negeb,
there comes from the desert,
    from the fearful land,
² A cruel sight, revealed to me:
    the traitor betrays,
    the despoiler spoils.
"Go up, Elam; besiege, O Media;*
    I will put an end to all groaning!"ˢ
³ Therefore my loins are filled with an-
    guish,
pangs have seized me like those of a
    woman in labor;
I am too bewildered to hear,
    too dismayed to look.ᵗ
⁴ My mind reels,
    shuddering assails me;
My yearning for twilight
    has turned into dread.

⁵ They set the table,
    spread out the rugs;
    they eat, they drink.*
Rise up, O princes,
    oil the shield!
⁶ For thus says my Lord to me:
    Go, station a watchman,
    let him tell what he sees.
⁷ If he sees a chariot,
    a pair of horses,
Someone riding an ass,
    someone riding a camel,
Then let him pay heed,
    very close heed.
⁸   Then the watchman cried,
"On the watchtower, O my Lord,
    I stand constantly by day;
And I stay at my post
    through all the watches of the night.ᵘ
⁹ Here he comes now:
    a single chariot,
    a pair of horses;
He calls out and says,
    'Fallen, fallen is Babylon,

And all the images of her gods
    are smashed to the ground.' "ᵛ

¹⁰ O my people who have been threshed,
    beaten on my threshing floor!
What I have heard
    from the LORD of hosts,
The God of Israel,
    I have announced to you.ʷ

Edom

¹¹   Oracle on Edom:
They call to me from Seir,*
    "Watchman, how much longer the
    night?
Watchman, how much longer the
    night?"
¹²   The watchman replies,
"Morning has come, and again night.
    If you will ask, ask; come back
    again."

Arabia

¹³   Oracle on Arabia:*
In the thicket in the nomad country
    spend the night,
    O caravans of Dedanites.
¹⁴ Meet the thirsty, bring them water;
    you who dwell in the land of Tema,
    greet the fugitives with bread.
¹⁵ They flee from the sword,
    from the whetted sword;
From the taut bow,
    from the fury of battle.

¹⁶ For thus says the Lord to me: In another year, like those of a hireling,* all the glory of Kedar shall come to an end. ¹⁷ Few of Kedar's stalwart archers shall remain, for the LORD, the God of Israel, has spoken.

---

r Is 31, 3; 36, 6.—s Is 13, 17.—t Ps 38, 8.—u Hb 2, 1.—v Is 46, 1; Jer 50, 2; 51, 8; Rv 14, 8.—w Is 51, 23.

21, 1: *Wastelands by the sea:* Babylonia. *Negeb:* the desert south of Judah.
21, 2: *Elam . . . Media:* nations which, under the leadership of Cyrus, captured Babylon in 538 B.C. *End to all groaning:* those who were captives of Babylon shall be freed.
21, 5: Babylon is destroyed while its leaders are feasting; cf Dn 5. *Oil the shield:* shields were oiled and greased so as to divert blows more easily.
21, 11f: *Seir:* another name for Edom. The Edomites ask the prophet how much longer they must suffer *(the night* of suffering); he answers ambiguously: "Liberation *(morning)* and further suffering *(night),*" but perhaps they will later receive a more encouraging answer *(ask; come back again).*
21, 13f: *Arabia:* that is, *the nomad country. Dedanites:* an Arab tribe associated with Edom and Tema, and living east of the Red Sea; cf Gn 10, 7; 25, 3; Jer 25, 23.
21, 16: *Year . . . of a hireling:* see note on Is 16, 14. *Kedar:* a nomad tribe in Arabia; cf Is 42, 11; 60, 7; Ps 120, 5.

CHAPTER 22

Jerusalem

1   Oracle of the Valley of Vision:*
What is the matter with you now, that
     you have gone up,
all of you, to the housetops,
2 O city full of noise and chaos,
     O wanton town!
Your slain are not slain with the sword,
     nor killed in battle.*
3 All your leaders fled away together,
     fled afar off;
All who were in you were captured to-
     gether,
captured without the use of a bow.*
4 At this I say: Turn away from me,
     let me weep bitterly;
Do not try to comfort me
     for the ruin of the daughter of my
     people.*
5 It is a day of panic, rout and confusion,
     from the Lord, the GOD of hosts, in
     the Valley of Vision.
Walls crash;
     they cry for help to the mountains.*
6 Elam* takes up the quivers,
     Aram mounts the horses,
     and Kir uncovers the shields.
7 Your choice valleys are filled with
     chariots,
     and horses are posted at the gates,
8   and shelter over Judah is removed.

* On that day you looked to the
weapons in the House of the Forest; 9 you
saw that the breaches in the City of David
were many; you collected the water of the
lower pool. 10 You numbered the houses
of Jerusalem, tearing some down to
strengthen the wall; 11 you made a reservoir between the two walls for the water

---

x Is 32, 13.—y 2 Kgs 25, 4.—z Jer 6, 26; 9, 1; 14, 17.—a Is
37, 3.—b Jl 2, 17.—c Is 56, 12; Wis 2, 6; 1 Cor 15, 32.—d 2 Kgs
18, 18. 37.

22, 1-8: *Valley of Vision:* while the people live in revelry and
disorder, the prophet foresees the impending doom of the city.
22, 6: *Elam, Aram, Kir:* all allies of Assyria. *Kir:* perhaps the
same people referred to in Am 1, 5.
22, 8-11: Defense measures, in which the inhabitants of Jerusalem placed their trust instead of relying on God. *House of the
Forest:* an armory built by Solomon; its columns of wood
suggested the trees of a forest; cf 1 Kgs 7, 2; 10, 17.
22, 15: *Shebna:* referred to as the scribe in Is 36, 3.
22, 20: *Eliakim:* also referred to in Is 36, 3; he is described
as loyal to God.
22, 22: *Key:* symbol of authority; cf Mt 16, 19; Rv 3, 7.

---

of the old pool. But you did not look to the
city's Maker, nor did you consider him
who built it long ago.

12 On that day the Lord,
     the GOD of hosts, called on you
To weep and mourn,
     to shave your head and put on sack-
     cloth.*
13 But look! you feast and celebrate,
     you slaughter oxen and butcher
     sheep,
You eat meat and drink wine:
     "Eat and drink, for tomorrow we
     die!"*
14 This reaches the ears of the LORD of
     hosts—
You shall not be pardoned this wick-
     edness till you die,
     says the Lord, the GOD of hosts.

Shebna and Eliakim

15 Thus says the Lord, the GOD of hosts:
     Up, go to that official,
     Shebna,* master of the palace,
16 Who has hewn for himself a sepulcher
     on a height
     and carved his tomb in the rock:
"What are you doing here, and what
     people have you here,
     that here you have hewn for yourself
     a tomb?"
17 The LORD shall hurl you down head-
     long, mortal man!
     He shall grip you firmly
18 And roll you up and toss you like a ball
     into an open land
To perish there, you and the chariots
     you glory in,
     you disgrace to your master's house!
19 I will thrust you from your office
     and pull you down from your station.

20 On that day I will summon my servant
     Eliakim,* son of Hilkiah;*
21 I will clothe him with your robe,
     and gird him with your sash,
     and give over to him your authority.
He shall be a father to the inhabitants of
     Jerusalem,
     and to the house of Judah.
22 I will place the key* of the House of
     David on his shoulder;

Is

when he opens, no one shall shut,
when he shuts, no one shall open.[e]

23 I will fix him like a peg in a sure spot,
to be a place of honor for his family;

24 On him shall hang all the glory of his
family:*
descendants and offspring,
all the little dishes, from bowls to
jugs.

25 On that day, says the LORD of hosts,
the peg fixed in a sure spot shall give way,
break off and fall, and the weight that
hung on it shall be done away with; for the
LORD has spoken.

CHAPTER 23

Tyre and Sidon

1　　Oracle on Tyre:
Wail, O ships of Tarshish,*
for your port is destroyed;
From the land of the Kittim*
the news reaches them.

2 Silence! you who dwell on the coast,
you merchants of Sidon,
Whose messengers crossed the sea

3 over the deep waters.
The grain of Shihor,* the harvest of the
Nile, was her revenue,
and she the merchant among nations.

4 Shame, O Sidon, fortress on the sea,
for the sea has spoken:*
"I have not been in labor, nor given
birth,
nor raised young men,
nor reared virgins."

5 When it is heard in Egypt
they shall be in anguish at the news of
Tyre.

6 Pass over to Tarshish, wailing,
you who dwell on the coast!

7 Is this your wanton city,
whose origin is from of old,
Whose feet have taken her
to dwell in distant lands?

8 Who has planned such a thing
against Tyre, the bestower of crowns,
Whose merchants are princes,
whose traders are the earth's honored
men?

9 The LORD of hosts has planned it,
to disgrace all pride of majesty,

to degrade all the earth's honored
men.[f]

10 Cross to your own land,
O ship of Tarshish;
the harbor is no more.

11 His hand he stretches out over the sea,
he shakes kingdoms;
The LORD has ordered the destruction
of Canaan's strongholds.*

12 You shall exult no more, he says,
you who are now oppressed, virgin
daughter Sidon.
Arise, pass over to the Kittim,
even there you shall find no rest.[g]

13 * [This people is the land of the Chaldeans, not Assyria.]

She whom the impious founded,
setting up towers for her,
Has had her castles destroyed,
and has been turned into a ruin.[h]

14 Lament, O ships of Tarshish,
for your haven is destroyed.

15 On that day, Tyre shall be forgotten
for seventy years. With the days of another
king, at the end of seventy years,* it shall
be for Tyre as in the song about the harlot:[i]

16 Take a harp, go about the city,
O forgotten harlot;
Pluck the strings skillfully, sing many
songs,
that they may remember you.

17 At the end of the seventy years the
LORD shall visit Tyre. She shall return to
her hire and deal with all the world's kingdoms on the face of the earth.[j] 18 But her
merchandise and her hire shall be sacred to
the LORD. It shall not be stored up or laid
away, but from her merchandise those
who dwell before the LORD shall eat their
fill and clothe themselves in choice attire.*

---

e Rv 3, 7.—f Ez 28, 7.—g Ez 28, 21f.—h Ez 26, 7.—i Jer 25,
11.—j Ez 27, 12.

22, 24f: If Eliakim should anger God, he and his family (compared here to dishes, bowls and jugs) will suffer disaster.
23, 1-4. 12ff: These verses refer to Sidon, vv 5-11 to Tyre.
23, 1: *Kittim:* Cyprus.
23, 3: *Shihor:* a synonym for the Nile.
23, 4: *The sea* brings to distant coasts the news that Sidon
must disown her children; her people are dispersed.
23, 11: *Canaan's strongholds:* the fortresses of Phoenicia.
23, 13: The gloss here identifies *she whom the impious
founded* with *the land of the Chaldeans.*
23, 15: *Seventy years:* a conventional period of time indicating simply a long disaster; cf Jer 25, 11 and 29, 10.
23, 18: Describes the conversion of Tyre.

IV: APOCALYPSE OF ISAIAH *

CHAPTER 24

Devastation of the World:
A Remnant Saved

1 Lo, the LORD empties the land and lays it waste;
  he turns it upside down,
  scattering its inhabitants: [k]
2 Layman and priest alike,
  servant and master,
  The maid as her mistress,
  the buyer as the seller,
  The lender as the borrower,
  the creditor as the debtor.
3 The earth is utterly laid waste, utterly stripped,
  for the LORD has decreed this thing.
4 The earth mourns and fades,
  the world languishes and fades;
  both heaven and earth languish.
5 The earth is polluted because of its inhabitants,
  who have transgressed laws, violated statutes,
  broken the ancient covenant.*
6 Therefore a curse devours the earth,
  and its inhabitants pay for their guilt;
  Therefore they who dwell on earth turn pale,
  and few men are left.
7 The wine mourns, the vine languishes,
  all the merry-hearted groan. [l]
8 Stilled are the cheerful timbrels,
  ended the shouts of the jubilant,
  stilled is the cheerful harp. [m]
9 They cannot sing and drink wine;
  strong drink is bitter to those who partake of it.
10 Broken down is the city of chaos,*
  shut against entry, every house. [n]
11 In the streets they cry out for lack of wine;

all joy has disappeared
  and cheer has left the land. [o]
12 In the city nothing remains but ruin;
  its gates are battered and desolate.
13 Thus it is within the land,
  and among the peoples,
  As with an olive tree after it is beaten,
  as with a gleaning when the vintage is done. [p]
14 These* lift up their voice in acclaim;
  from the sea they proclaim the majesty of the LORD:
15 "For this, in the coastlands,
  give glory to the LORD!
  In the coastlands of the sea,
  to the name of the LORD, the God of Israel!" [q]
16 From the end of the earth we hear songs:
  "Splendor to the Just One!"

But I said, "I am wasted, wasted away.
  Woe is me! The traitors betray:
  with treachery have the traitors betrayed!
17 Terror, pit, and trap [r]
  are upon you, inhabitant of the earth;
18 He who flees at the sound of terror
  will fall into the pit;
  He who climbs out of the pit
  will be caught in the trap.
  For the windows on high will be opened
  and the foundations of the earth will shake.
19 The earth will burst asunder,
  the earth will be shaken apart,
  the earth will be convulsed.
20 The earth will reel like a drunkard,
  and it will sway like a hut;
  Its rebellion will weigh it down,
  until it falls, never to rise again." [s]

21 On that day the LORD will punish
  the host of the heavens* in the heavens,
  and the kings of the earth on the earth. [t]
22 They will be gathered together
  like prisoners into a pit;
  They will be shut up in a dungeon,
  and after many days they will be punished.
23 Then the moon will blush [u]
  and the sun grow pale,
  For the LORD of hosts will reign

---

k Is 13, 9; Hos 4, 9.—l Jl 1, 10.—m Jer 7, 34; Hos 2, 13.—n Is 25, 2.—o Jer 48, 33; Lam 5, 14f.—p Is 17, 6; Mi 7, 1.—q Is 42, 10. 12; Zep 2, 11.—r 17f: Jer 48, 43f.—s Is 9, 14.—t Ps 76, 13.—u Is 13, 10; Jl 3, 3f; 4, 15.

24, 1—27, 13: This section, probably composed at a later date, contains oracles on the day of the Lord, combined with hymns of thanksgiving and of supplication.
24, 5: _Ancient covenant:_ God's commandments to all mankind.
24, 10: _City of chaos:_ a symbol of godlessness as opposed to Jerusalem, the city of God.
24, 14: _These:_ the saved.
24, 21: _Host of the heavens:_ the stars, which were regarded by the pagans as gods; cf Dt 4, 19; Jer 8, 2.

Is

on Mount Zion and in Jerusalem,
glorious in the sight of his elders.*

CHAPTER 25

1 O Lord, you are my God,*
I will extol you and praise your name;
For you have fulfilled your wonderful
plans of old,
faithful and true. *v*

2 For you have made the city a heap,
the fortified city a ruin;
The castle of the insolent is a city no
more,
nor ever to be rebuilt. *w*

3 Therefore a strong people will honor
you,
fierce nations will fear you.

4 For you are a refuge to the poor,
a refuge to the needy in distress;
Shelter from the rain,
shade from the heat. *x*
As with the cold rain,

5   as with the desert heat,
even so you quell the uproar of the
wanton.

6 On this mountain* the Lord of hosts
will provide for all peoples
A feast of rich food and choice wines,
juicy, rich food and pure, choice
wines.

7 On this mountain he will destroy
the veil that veils all peoples,
The web that is woven over all nations;*y*

8   he will destroy death forever.
The Lord God will wipe away
the tears from all faces;
The reproach of his people he will remove
from the whole earth; for the Lord
has spoken.

9   On that day it will be said:
"Behold our God, to whom we looked
to save us!
This is the Lord for whom we
looked;
let us rejoice and be glad that he has
saved us!"*z*

10 For the hand of the Lord will rest on
this mountain,
but Moab* will be trodden down
as a straw is trodden down in the
mire. *a*

11 He will stretch forth his hands in Moab
as a swimmer extends his hands to
swim;

He will bring low their pride
as his hands sweep over them. *b*

12 The high-walled fortress he will raze,
and strike it down level with the
earth, with the very dust. *c*

CHAPTER 26

The Divine Vindicator. 1 On that day they
will sing this song in the land of Judah:

"A strong city have we;
he sets up walls and ramparts to protect us.

2 Open up the gates
to let in a nation that is just,
one that keeps faith. *d*

3 A nation of firm purpose you keep in
peace;
in peace, for its trust in you."*e*

4 Trust in the Lord forever!
For the Lord is an eternal Rock.*f*

5 He humbles those in high places,
and the lofty city he brings down;
He tumbles it to the ground,
levels it with the dust.*g*

6 It is trampled underfoot by the needy,
by the footsteps of the poor.

7 The way of the just is smooth;
the path of the just you make level. *h*

8 Yes, for your way and your judgments,
O Lord,
we look to you;
Your name and your title
are the desire of our souls.

9 My soul yearns for you in the night,
yes, my spirit within me keeps vigil
for you;
When your judgment dawns upon the
earth,
the world's inhabitants learn justice. *i*

10 The wicked man, spared, does not learn
justice;
in an upright land he acts perversely,
and sees not the majesty of the
Lord.*j*

v Ex 15, 2.—w Jer 9, 11.—x Is 14, 32; 32, 2; Na 1, 7.—y Is
60, 1. 3; 1 Cor 15, 53ff; Rv 7, 17; 21, 4.—z Is 30, 18f.—a Zep
2, 9f.—b Is 16, 6f. 14.—c Is 26, 5.—d Ps 118, 19f.—e Is 32,
17f; 54, 13.—f Is 30, 29; Ps 62, 8.—g Is 25, 12; 32, 19.—h Ps
23, 3f; Prv 11, 3. 5.—i Ps 94, 15.—j Is 5, 12.

24, 23: *His elders:* the heavenly courtiers surrounding the
throne of God.
25, 1-8: Victory in messianic times.
25, 6: *This mountain:* Zion, symbol of the heavenly Jerusalem.
25, 10: *Moab:* symbol of God's enemies.

11 O LORD, your hand is uplifted,
    but they behold it not;
  Let them be shamed when they see
      your zeal for your people:
    let the fire prepared for your enemies
      consume them.
12 O LORD, you mete out peace to us,
    for it is you who have accomplished
      all we have done. *k*
13 O LORD, our God, other lords than you
      have ruled us;
    it is from you only that we can call
      upon your name.

14 Dead they are, they have no life,
    shades that cannot rise;
  For you have punished and destroyed
      them,
    and wiped out all memory of them.
15 You have increased the nation, O
      LORD,
    increased the nation to your own
      glory,
    and extended far all the borders of
      the land. *l*
16 O LORD, oppressed by your punish-
      ment,
    we cried out in anguish under your
      chastising. *m*
17 As a woman about to give birth
    writhes and cries out in her pains,
    so were we in your presence, O
      LORD. *n*
18 We conceived and writhed in pain,
    giving birth to wind;
  Salvation we have not achieved for the
      earth,
    the inhabitants of the world cannot
      bring it forth.
19 But your dead shall live, their corpses
      shall rise;
    awake and sing, you who lie in the
      dust. *o*
  For your dew is a dew of light,
    and the land of shades gives birth.*

Day of the Lord: Reward and Punishment

20 Go, my people, enter your chambers,
    and close your doors behind you;
  Hide yourselves for a brief moment,
    until the wrath is past.
21 See, the LORD goes forth from his
      place,
    to punish the wickedness of the
      earth's inhabitants;
  The earth will reveal the blood upon
      her,
    and no longer conceal her slain. *p*

CHAPTER 27

1   On that day,
  The LORD will punish with his sword
    that is cruel, great, and strong,
  Leviathan the fleeing serpent,
    Leviathan the coiled serpent;
    and he will slay the dragon* that is in
      the sea. *q*

2   On that day—
  The pleasant vineyard, sing about it! *r*
3   I, the LORD, am its keeper,
    I water it every moment;
  Lest anyone harm it,
    night and day I guard it. *s*
4 I am not angry,
    but if I were to find briers and
      thorns,
  In battle I should march against them;
    I should burn them all. *t*
8 Expunging and expelling, I should
      strive against them,
    carrying them off with my cruel wind
      in time of storm. *u*

6 In days to come Jacob shall take root,
    Israel shall sprout and blossom,
    covering all the world with fruit.
7 Is he to be smitten as his smiter was
      smitten?
    or slain as his slayer was slain?*
5 Or shall he cling to me for refuge?*
    He must make peace with me;
    peace shall he make with me! *v*
9 This, then, shall be the expiation of
      Jacob's guilt,
    this the whole fruit of the removal of
      his sin:
  He shall pulverize all the stones of the
      altars
    like pieces of chalk;

---

k Jer 29, 11.—l Is 54, 2f; Neh 9, 23.—m Hos 6, 1.—n Mi 4,
10.—o Ez 37, 5f; Dn 12, 2; Hos 6, 2.—p Mi 1, 3.—q Jb 40, 25-
32; Ez 32, 2.—r Is 5, 1.—s Is 5, 2ff; Ps 121, 4f.—t Is 10, 17.—u
Jer 18, 17.—v Is 37, 31; Rom 11, 12.

26, 19: This verse refers to the restoration of Israel in messianic times under the figure of the resurrection of the dead; cf
Ez, chap. 37.
27, 1: *Leviathan . . . dragon:* symbols of the forces of evil
which God vanquishes even as he overcame primeval chaos; cf
notes on Jb 3, 8; 7, 12.
27, 7: God's people will not be treated as sternly as were their
enemies.
27, 5. 9: Israel will *make peace with* God and destroy all
signs of idolatrous worship.

Is

no sacred poles or incense altars shall
stand.

¹⁰ For the fortified city* shall be desolate,
an abandoned pasture, a forsaken
wilderness,
where calves shall browse and lie.ʷ
Its boughs shall be destroyed,
¹¹ its branches shall wither and be broken off,
and women shall come to build a fire
with them.
This is not an understanding people;
therefore their maker shall not spare
them,
nor shall he who formed them have
mercy on them.ˣ

¹² On that day,
The LORD shall beat out the grain
between the Euphrates and the Wadi
of Egypt,*
and you shall be gleaned one by one,
O sons of Israel.

¹³ On that day,*
A great trumpet shall blow,
and the lost in the land of Assyria
and the outcasts in the land of Egypt
Shall come and worship the LORD
on the holy mountain, in Jerusalem.ʸ

V: THE LORD ALONE, ISRAEL'S AND JUDAH'S SALVATION

CHAPTER 28

The Fate of Samaria

¹ Woe to the majestic garland
of the drunkard Ephraim,*
To the fading blooms of his glorious
beauty,
on the head of him who is stupefied
with wine.ᶻ
² Behold, the LORD has a strong one and
a mighty,*
who, like a downpour of hail, a destructive storm,
Like a flood of water, great and overflowing,
levels to the ground with violence;ᵃ
³ With feet that will trample
the majestic garland of the drunkard
Ephraim.
⁴ The fading blooms of his glorious
beauty
on the head of the fertile valley

Will be like an early fig before summer:
when a man sees it,
he picks and swallows it at once.

⁵ On that day the LORD of hosts
will be a glorious crown
And a brilliant diadem
to the remnant of his people,
⁶ A spirit of justice
to him who sits in judgment,
And strength to those
who turn back the battle at the gate.

Against Judah

⁷ But these also stagger from wine
and stumble from strong drink:
Priest and prophet stagger from strong
drink,
overpowered by wine;
Led astray by strong drink
staggering in their visions,
tottering when giving judgment.ᵇ
⁸ Yes, all the tables
are covered with filthy vomit,
with no place left clean.
⁹ "To whom would he impart knowledge?*
To whom would he convey the message?
To those just weaned from milk,
those taken from the breast? ¹⁰ For he
says,
'Command on command, command on
command,
rule on rule, rule on rule,
here a little, there a little!' "
¹¹ Yes, with stammering lips and in a
strange language*

---

w Is 6, 11.—x Jer 4, 22.—y Hos 11, 11.—z Hos 7, 5; Am 6,
6.—a Is 30, 30.—b Is 56, 10. 12.

27, 10f: *The fortified city:* symbol of the powers of evil; see
note on Is 24, 10.
27, 12: *The Euphrates and the Wadi of Egypt:* the ideal
borders of Israel; cf Gn 15, 18; 2 Kgs 24, 7.
27, 13: The triumph of God's people is described in eschatological language; they will gather in Jerusalem from *Assyria* and *Egypt.*
28, 1: *Ephraim:* the northern kingdom. Its capital, Samaria,
was built upon a hill, suggestive of a *majestic garland* adorning
the head of the drunken kingdom.
28, 2: *A strong one and a mighty:* Assyria.
28, 9f: The words of those who ridicule Isaiah. The Hebrew of
v 10, by its very sound, conveys the idea of mocking imitation of
what the prophet says, as though he spoke like a stammering
child: SAU LASAU, SAU LASAU, CAU LACAU, CAU LACAU,
ZE'ER SHAM, ZE'ER SHAM. But in v 13 God repeats these
words in deadly earnest, putting them in the mouth of the victorious pagan army.
28, 11: God will answer the mockers and defend Isaiah.
Strange language: spoken by the invading army.

he will speak to this people[c]

12 to whom he said:
This is the resting place,
give rest to the weary;
Here is repose—
but they would not listen.

13 So for them the word of the LORD shall be:
"Command on command, command on command,
Rule on rule, rule on rule,
here a little, there a little!"
So that when they walk, they stumble backward,
broken, ensnared, and captured.

14 Therefore, hear the word of the LORD, you arrogant,
who rule this people in Jerusalem:

15 Because you say, "We have made a covenant with death,
and with the nether world* we have made a pact;
When the overwhelming scourge passes,
it will not reach us;
For we have made lies our refuge,
and in falsehood we have found a hiding place,"—[d]

16 Therefore, thus says the Lord GOD:
See, I am laying a stone in Zion,*
a stone that has been tested,
A precious cornerstone as a sure foundation;

he who puts his faith in it shall not be shaken.[e]

17 I will make of right a measuring line,
of justice a level.—
Hail shall sweep away the refuge of lies,
and waters shall flood the hiding place.

18 Your covenant with death shall be canceled
and your pact with the nether world shall not stand.
When the overwhelming scourge passes,
you shall be trampled down by it.

19 Whenever it passes, it shall take you;
morning after morning it shall pass,
By day and by night;
terror alone shall convey the message.

20 For the bed shall be too short to stretch out in,
and the cover too narrow to wrap in.

21 For the LORD shall rise up as on Mount Perazim,*
bestir himself as in the Valley of Gibeon,
To carry out his work, his singular work,
to perform his deed, his strange deed.[f]

22 Now, be arrogant no more
lest your bonds be tightened,
For I have heard from the Lord, the GOD of hosts,
the destruction decreed for the whole earth.[g]

23 Give ear and hear my voice,*
pay attention and listen to what I say:

24 Is the plowman forever plowing,
always loosening and harrowing his land for planting?

25 When he has leveled the surface,
does he not scatter gith and sow cumin,*
Put in wheat and barley,
with spelt as its border?

26 He has learned this rule,
instructed by his God.

27 Gith is not threshed with a sledge,
nor does a cartwheel roll over cumin.*

---

c Jer 5, 15; 1 Cor 14, 21; Dt 28, 49; Bar 4, 15.—d Wis 1, 16; Jer 5, 12.—e Ps 118, 22; Mt 21, 42; Acts 4, 11; Rom 9, 33; 1 Pt 2, 6.—f Jos 10, 10; 2 Sm 5, 20; 1 Chr 14, 11.—g Is 10, 23.

28, 15. 18: *A covenant with death, and with the nether world:* an alliance with foreign powers, such as Egypt and Babylon, to prevent death and destruction. *Have made lies . . . a hiding place:* this confidence in human aid proves to be false and deceitful, incapable of averting the dreaded disaster. *Overwhelming scourge:* the flood of the Assyrian invasion; cf Is 8, 7f.

28, 16: *A stone in Zion:* the true and *sure foundation* of salvation promised by God to the Davidic dynasty (cf Is 7, 13-16; 9, 1-6), which the Apostles saw fulfilled in Christ the universal Savior; cf 1 Pt 2, 6-8; Rom 9, 33; 10, 9ff. *Cornerstone:* the assurance of salvation rejected by Israel in the prophet's time, is reflected by the psalmist (Ps 118, 22) and fulfilled in the Person of Christ; cf Mt 21, 42; Lk 20, 17; Acts 4, 11; Rom 9, 33; 1 Pt 2, 7.

28, 21: *Mount Perazim . . . Valley of Gibeon:* where David defeated the Philistines; cf 2 Sm 5, 20. 25; 1 Chr 14, 11. 16.

28, 23-29: The practical variation of the farmer's work taught him by God reflects God's dealing with his people, wisely adapted to circumstances; he does not crush their weakness altogether; cf ch 29.

28, 25: *Gith . . . cumin:* herbs used in seasoning food. *Spelt:* a variety of wheat.

But gith is beaten out with a staff,
and cumin crushed for food with a
rod.

28 No, he does nor thresh it unendingly,
nor does he crush it
with his noisy cartwheels and horses.

29 This too comes from the LORD of hosts;
wonderful is his counsel and great his
wisdom.

CHAPTER 29

The Fall of Jerusalem

1 Woe to Ariel, Ariel,*
the city where David encamped!
Add year to year,
let the feasts come round. *h*

2 But I will bring distress upon Ariel,
with mourning and grief.
You shall be to me like Ariel, *i*

3 I will encamp like David against you;
I will encircle you with outposts
and set up siege works against you. *j*

4 Prostrate you shall speak from the
earth,
and from the base dust your words
shall come.
Your voice shall be like a ghost's from
the earth,
and your words like chirping* from
the dust.

5 The horde of your arrogant shall be like
fine dust,
the horde of the tyrants like flying
chaff.
Then suddenly, in an instant, *k*

6 you shall be visited by the LORD of
hosts,
With thunder, earthquake, and great
noise,
whirlwind, storm, and the flame of
consuming fire.

7 Then like a dream,*
a vision in the night,
Shall be the horde of all the nations
who war against Ariel
with all the earthworks of her besiegers.

8 As when a hungry man dreams he is
eating
and awakens with an empty stomach,
Or when a thirsty man dreams he is
drinking

and awakens faint and dry,
So shall the horde of all the nations be,
who make war against Zicn.

Blindness and Perversity

9 Be irresolute, stupefied;*
blind yourselves and stay blind!
Be drunk, but not from wine,
stagger, but not from strong drink! *l*

10 For the LORD has poured out on you
a spirit of deep sleep.
He has shut your eyes [the prophets]
and covered your heads [the seers]. *m*

11 For you the revelation of all this has
become like the words of a sealed scroll.
When it is handed to one who can read,
with the request, "Read this," he replies,
"I cannot; it is sealed." *n* 12 When it is
handed to one who cannot read, with the
request, "Read this," he replies, "I cannot
read."

13 The Lord said:
Since this people draws near with words
only
and honors me with their lips alone,
though their hearts are far from me,
And their reverence for me has become
routine observance of the precepts of
men, *o*

14 Therefore I will again deal with this
people
in surprising and wondrous fashion:
The wisdom of its wise men shall perish
and the understanding of its prudent
men be hid. *p*

15 Woe to those who would hide their
plans
too deep for the LORD!
Who work in the dark, saying,
"Who sees us, or who knows us?" *q*

16 Your perversity is as though the potter
were taken to be the clay:

h 2 Sm 5, 9.—i Is 33, 7.—j 2 Kgs 25, 1; Ez 4, 2.—k Is 17, 13;
Ps 18, 43; Jb 21, 18.—l Is 19, 14; 28, 7f.—m Is 6, 10; Rom 11,
8.—n Dn 12, 4.—o Ez 33, 31; Mt 15, 8f; Mk 7, 6f.—p Jer 49,
7; 1 Cor 1, 19.—q Is 30, 1; Ez 8, 12; Jn 3, 19f.

29, 1f: *Ariel:* variously interpreted to mean "lion of God" or
"hearth (altar) of God," a poetic name for Jerusalem; or perhaps
to be read as Uru-el, "foundation of God," an archaic name for
the Jebusite city of Jerusalem; *like* that *Ariel,* against which
David encamped, it will be besieged by God.
29, 4: *Chirping:* see note on Is 8, 19.
29, 7f: Just when the Assyrians think their capture of Jerusalem to be certain, the Lord will snatch victory from their hands
and save his city.
29, 9-12: Jerusalem in her blindness refuses to believe God's
revelation that she will be saved.

As though what is made should say of
its maker,
"He made me not!"
Or the vessel should say of the potter,
"He does not understand."[r]

Redemption*

17 But a very little while,
and Lebanon shall be changed into an
orchard,
and the orchard be regarded as a forest![s]

18 On that day the deaf shall hear
the words of a book;
And out of gloom and darkness,
the eyes of the blind shall see.[t]

19 The lowly will ever find joy in the
LORD,
and the poor rejoice in the Holy One
of Israel.[u]

20 For the tyrant will be no more
and the arrogant will have gone;
All who are alert to do evil will be cut
off,[v]

21   those whose mere word condemns a
man,
Who ensnare his defender at the gate,
and leave the just man with an empty
claim.[w]

22 Therefore thus says the LORD,
the God of the house of Jacob,
who redeemed Abraham:*
Now Jacob shall have nothing to be
ashamed of,
nor shall his face grow pale.[x]

23 When his children see
the work of my hands in his midst,
They shall keep my name holy;
they shall reverence the Holy One of
Jacob,
and be in awe of the God of Israel.

24 Those who err in spirit shall acquire
understanding,

---

r Is 45, 9; Jer 18, 6; Rom 9, 20.—s Is 32, 15.—t Is 35, 5; 42,
6f.—u Is 61, 1—v Is 28, 22.—w Am 5, 10. 12.—x Is 45, 17.—y
Is 1, 4.—z Is 31, 1; 36, 6.—a Is 20, 5; Jer 2, 36f.—b Is 19,
11.—c Is 36, 6.—d Is 8, 1. 16; Jer 36, 2; Heb 2, 2.—e Is 1, 4;
Jer 7, 28.

29, 17-24: The prophet presents God's plan of redemption in
terms of unheard-of natural phenomena as if such changes in nature took place, e.g., the change of the cedars of Lebanon into an
orchard (v 17).
29, 22: *Who redeemed Abraham:* by freeing him from the
idolatry of his native land.
30, 6: *Flying saraph:* see note on Nm 21, 6.
30, 7: *Rahab:* Egypt, here as elsewhere (cf Ps 87, 4), is compared to the stormy, impetuous sea monster (cf Is 51, 9; Jb 26,
12; Ps 89, 11), which yet, when asked for aid by Judah, becomes
silent, *quelled.*
30, 8: Isaiah will write down his condemnation of the people
so that (vv 12-18) its fulfillment may afterward be admitted.

and those who find fault shall receive
instruction.

CHAPTER 30

Futile Alliance with Egypt

1 Woe to the rebellious children,
says the LORD,
Who carry out plans that are not mine,
who weave webs that are not inspired
by me,
adding sin upon sin.[y]

2 They go down to Egypt,
but my counsel they do not seek.
They find their strength in Pharaoh's
protection
and take refuge in Egypt's shadow;[z]

3 Pharaoh's protection shall be your
shame,
and refuge in Egypt's shadow your
disgrace.[a]

4 When their princes are at Zoan
and their messengers reach Hanes,[b]

5 All shall be ashamed
of a people that gain them nothing,
Neither help nor benefit,
but only shame and reproach.[c]

6   [Oracle on the Beasts of the
Negeb]

Through the distressed and troubled
land
of the lioness and roaring lion,
of the viper and flying saraph,*
They carry their riches on the backs of
asses
and their treasures on the humps of
camels
To a people good for nothing,

7   to Egypt whose help is futile and
vain.
Therefore I call her
"Rahab* quelled."

8 Now come, write it on a tablet they can
keep,
inscribe it in a record;*
That it may be in future days
an eternal witness:[d]

9 This is a rebellious people,
deceitful children,
Children who refuse
to obey the law of the LORD.[e]

10 They say to the seers, "Have no visions";
to the prophets, "Do not descry for
us what is right;

speak flatteries to us, conjure up illusions.*f*

11 Out of the way! Out of our path!
    Let us hear no more
    of the Holy One of Israel."*g*

12 Therefore, thus says the Holy One of
    Israel:
    Because you reject this word,
    And put your trust in what is crooked
        and devious,
        and depend on it,

13 This guilt of yours shall be
    like a descending rift
    Bulging out in a high wall
        whose crash comes suddenly, in an
        instant.*h*

14 It crashes like a potter's jar
    smashed beyond rescue,
    And among its fragments cannot be
        found
    a sherd to scoop fire from the hearth
        or dip water from the cistern.*i*

15 For thus said the Lord GOD,
    the Holy One of Israel:
    By waiting and by calm you shall be
        saved,
        in quiet and in trust your strength
        lies.
    But this you did not wish.*j*

16 "No," you said,
    "Upon horses we will flee."

    —Very well, flee!
    "Upon swift steeds we will ride."
    —Not so swift as your pursuers.*k*

17 A thousand shall tremble at the threat
        of one;
    if five threaten you, you shall flee,
    Until you are left like a flagstaff on the
        mountaintop,
    like a flag on the hill.

18 Yet the LORD is waiting to show you
        favor,
    and he rises to pity you;
    For the LORD is a God of justice:
    blessed are all who wait for him!*l*

19 O people of Zion, who dwell in Jerusa-
        lem,
    no more will you weep;
    He will be gracious to you when you cry
        out,
    as soon as he hears he will answer
        you.*m*

20 The Lord will give you the bread you
        need
    and the water for which you thirst.

No longer will your Teacher* hide him-
        self,
    but with your own eyes you shall see
        your Teacher,

21 While from behind, a voice shall sound
        in your ears:
    "This is the way; walk in it,"
    when you would turn to the right or
        to the left.*n*

22 And you shall consider unclean your
        silver-plated idols
    and your gold-covered images;
    You shall throw them away like filthy
        rags
    to which you say, "Begone!"*o*

Zion's Future Prosperity

23 He will give rain for the seed
    that you sow in the ground,
    And the wheat that the soil produces
    will be rich and abundant.
    On that day your cattle will graze
    in spacious meadows;*p*

24 The oxen and the asses that till the
        ground
    will eat silage tossed to them
    with shovel and pitchfork.

25 Upon every high mountain and lofty
        hill
    there will be streams of running
        water.
    On the day of the great slaughter,
    when the towers fall,*q*

26 The light of the moon will be like that
        of the sun
    and the light of the sun will be seven
        times greater
    [like the light of seven days].
    On the day the LORD binds up the
        wounds of his people,
    he will heal the bruises left by his
        blows.*r*

Divine Judgment on Assyria*

27 See the name of the LORD coming from
        afar
    in burning wrath, with lowering
        clouds!

---

f Jer 5, 31.—g Jb 21, 14f.—h Ez 13, 14.—i Jer 19, 11.—j Is 7, 4; Mi 7, 7.—k Is 31, 3.—l Ps 34, 9; Jer 17, 7.—m Is 58, 9.—n Jer 31, 33f.—o Is 31, 7.—p Lv 26, 3. 5.—q Jl 4, 18.—r Jer 30, 17.

30, 20: *Teacher:* God, who in the past taught in a veiled manner through his prophets, will in future help them to understand
his teaching clearly. This was eminently true when the Son of God
became Man.

30, 27-33: God's punishment of Assyria. *The name of the*
Lord: God himself; cf Ps 20, 2.

His lips are filled with fury,
   his tongue is like a consuming fire;
28 His breath, like a flood in a ravine
   that reaches suddenly to the neck,
Will winnow the nations with a destructive winnowing,
   and with repeated winnowings will he
   battle against them
[and a bridle on the jaws of the peoples to send them astray].

30 The LORD will make his glorious voice
   heard,
   and let it be seen how his arm descends
In raging fury and flame of consuming
   fire,
   in driving storm and hail.
31 When the LORD speaks, Assyria will be
   shattered,
   as he strikes with the rod;
32 While at every sweep of the rod
   which the LORD will bring down on
   him in punishment,
29 You will sing
   as on a night when a feast is observed,
And be merry of heart,
   as one marching along with a flute
Toward the mountain of the LORD,
   toward the Rock of Israel,
   accompanied by the timbrels and
   lyres.
33 For the pyre* has long been ready,
   prepared for the king;
Broad and deep it is piled
   with dry grass and wood in abundance,
And the breath of the LORD, like a
   stream of sulphur,
   will set it afire.

CHAPTER 31

Against the Egyptian Alliance

1 Woe to those who go down to Egypt for
   help,
   who depend upon horses;

s Is 30, 2; 36, 6.—t Ps 146, 3ff.—u Ps 91, 4.—v Jer 3, 12.—w
Is 30, 22.—x Is 37, 36.

30, 29-33: *Pyre:* on which the corpse of the king of Assyria is
burned. This is the occasion of festal rejoicing for the Israelites,
who are now free from his yoke.
31, 9: *Crag:* the king as the rallying point of the princes.

Who put their trust in chariots because
   of their number,
   and in horsemen because of their
   combined power,
But look not to the Holy One of Israel
   nor seek the LORD!s
2 Yet he too is wise and will bring disaster;
   he will not turn from what he has
   threatened to do.
He will rise up against the house of the
   wicked
   and against those who help evildoers.
3 The Egyptians are men, not God,
   their horses are flesh, not spirit;
When the LORD stretches forth his
   hand,
   the helper shall stumble, the one
   helped shall fall,
   and both of them shall perish to-
   gether.t

4   Thus says the LORD to me:
As a lion or a lion cub
   growling over its prey,
With a band of shepherds
   assembled against it,
Is neither frightened by their shouts
   nor disturbed by their noise,
So shall the LORD of hosts come down
   to wage war upon the mountain and
   hill of Zion.
5 Like hovering birds, so the LORD of
   hosts
   shall shield Jerusalem,
To protect and deliver,
   to spare and rescue it.u

6 Return, O children of Israel, to him
whom you have utterly deserted.v 7 On
that day each one of you shall spurn his
sinful idols of silver and gold, which he
made with his hands.w

Downfall of Assyria

8 Assyria shall fall by a sword not wielded
   by man,
   no mortal sword shall devour him;
He shall flee before the sword,
   and his young men shall be impressed
   as laborers.x
9 He shall rush past his crag* in panic,
   and his princes shall flee in terror
   from his standard,
Says the LORD who has a fire in Zion
   and a furnace in Jerusalem.

CHAPTER 32

The Kingdom of Justice

¹ See, a king will reign justly
  and princes will rule rightly.*y*
² Each of them will be a shelter from the
    wind,
  a retreat from the rain.
  They will be like streams of water in a
    dry country,
    like the shade of a great rock in a
      parched land.*z*
³ The eyes of those who see will not be
    closed;
    the ears of those who hear will be at-
      tentive.
⁴ The flighty will become wise and capa-
    ble,
    and the stutterers will speak fluently
      and clearly.
⁵ No more will the fool be called noble,
    nor the trickster be considered hon-
      orable.
⁶ For the fool speaks foolishly,
    planning evil in his heart:
  How to do wickedness,
    to speak perversely against the LORD,
  To let the hungry go empty
    and the thirsty be without drink.*a*
⁷ And the trickster uses wicked trickery,
    planning crimes:
  How to ruin the poor with lies,
    and the needy when they plead their
      case.
⁸ But the noble man plans noble things,
    and by noble things he stands.

The Women of Jerusalem

⁹ O complacent ladies, rise up and hear
    my voice,
    overconfident women, give heed to
      my words.
¹⁰ In a little more than a year
    you overconfident ones will be shak-
      en;
  The vintage will fail,
    there will be no harvest.*b*
¹¹ Tremble, you who are complacent!
    Shudder, you who are overconfident!
  Strip yourselves bare,
    with only a loincloth to cover you.*c*
¹² Beat your breasts
    for the pleasant fields, the fruitful
      vine,

¹³ And the soil of my people,
    overgrown with thorns and briers;
  For all the joyful houses,
    the wanton city.*d*
¹⁴ Yes, the castle* will be forsaken,
    the noisy city deserted;*e*
¹⁹ Down it comes, as trees come down in
    the forest!
  The city will be utterly laid low.
  Hill and tower will become wasteland
    forever
    for wild asses to frolic in, and flocks
      to pasture,
¹⁵ Until the spirit from on high*
    is poured out on us.

  Then will the desert become an orchard
    and the orchard be regarded as a for-
      est.*f*
¹⁶ Right will dwell in the desert
    and justice abide in the orchard.
¹⁷ Justice will bring about peace;
    right will produce calm and security.*g*
¹⁸ My people will live in peaceful country,
    in secure dwellings and quiet resting
      places. *h*
²⁰ Happy are you who sow beside every
    stream,
    and let the ox and the ass go freely!*i*

CHAPTER 33

Overthrow of Assyria

¹ Woe, O destroyer never destroyed,
    O traitor never betrayed!
  When you finish destroying, you will be
    destroyed;
    when wearied with betraying, you
      will be betrayed.

² O LORD, have pity on us, for you we
    wait.
  Be our strength every morning,
    our salvation in time of trouble!*j*
³ At the roaring sound, peoples flee;
    when you rise in your majesty, na-
      tions are scattered.

---

y Is 16, 5; Ps 72, 2ff; Jer 23, 5.—z Is 4, 6; 25, 4.—a Prv 10,
32; Eccl 10, 12f.—b Zep 1, 13.—c Jer 4, 8.—d Is 7, 23; 34,
13.—e Is 27, 10.—f Is 35, 1; 44, 3.—g Is 54, 13f; Ps 72, 7; Jas
3, 18.—h Mi 4, 4.—i Is 30, 23.— j Is 25, 9.

32, 14. 19: *The castle:* the citadel of Jerusalem. *Hill and
tower:* the fortified hill, in Hebrew *Ophel,* with its stronghold
called "the great projecting tower" in Neh 3, 27.
32, 15-18. 20: Extraordinary peace and prosperity will come
to Israel under just rulers.

⁴ Men gather spoil as caterpillars are
    gathered up;
    they rush upon it like the onrush of
    locusts. *k*
⁵ The LORD is exalted, enthroned on
    high;
    he fills Zion with right and justice. *l*
⁶ That which makes her seasons lasting,
    the riches that save her, are wisdom
    and knowledge;
    the fear of the LORD is her treasure. *m*

⁷ See, the men of Ariel cry out in the
    streets,
    the messengers of Shalem* weep bit-
    terly.
⁸ The highways are desolate,
    travelers have quit the paths,
    Covenants are broken, their terms are
    spurned;
    yet no man gives it a thought. *n*
⁹ The country languishes in mourning,
    Lebanon withers with shame;
    Sharon* is like the steppe,
    Bashan and Carmel are stripped
    bare. *o*

¹⁰ Now will I rise up, says the LORD,
    now will I be exalted, now be lifted
    up.
¹¹ You conceive dry grass, bring forth
    stubble;
    my spirit shall consume you like fire.
¹² The peoples shall be as in a limekiln,
    like brushwood cut down for burning
    in the fire. *p*

¹³ Hear, you who are far off, what I have
    done;
    you who are near, acknowledge my
    might.
¹⁴ On Zion sinners are in dread,
    trembling grips the impious:
    "Who of us can live with the consuming
    fire?
    who of us can live with the everlast-
    ing flames?" *q*
¹⁵ He who practices virtue and speaks
    honestly,
    who spurns what is gained by oppres-
    sion,

Brushing his hands free of contact with
    a bribe,
    stopping his ears lest he hear of
    bloodshed,
    closing his eyes lest he look on evil—*r*
¹⁶ He shall dwell on the heights,
    his stronghold shall be the rocky fast-
    ness,
    his food and drink in steady supply.

Restoration of Zion

¹⁷ Your eyes will see a king* in his splen-
    dor,
    they will look upon a vast land.
¹⁸ Your mind will dwell on the terror:
    "Where is he who counted, where is
    he who weighed?
    Where is he who counted the tow-
    ers?"
¹⁹ To the people of alien tongue you will
    look no more,
    the people of obscure speech,
    stammering in a language not under-
    stood.
²⁰ Look to Zion, the city of our festivals;
    let your eyes see Jerusalem
    as a quiet abode, a tent not to be
    struck,
    Whose pegs will never be pulled up,
    nor any of its ropes severed.

²² Indeed the LORD will be there with us,
    majestic;
    yes, the LORD our judge, the LORD
    our lawgiver,
    the LORD our king, he it is who will
    save us.
²¹ In a place of rivers and wide streams
    on which no boat is rowed,
    where no majestic ship* passes,
²³ The rigging hangs slack;
    it cannot hold the mast in place,
    nor keep the sail spread out.
    Then the blind will divide great spoils
    and the lame will carry off the loot.
²⁴ No one who dwells there will say, "I am
    sick";
    the people who live there will be for-
    given their guilt.

VI: THE LORD, ZION'S AVENGER

CHAPTER 34

Judgment upon Edom

¹ Come near, O nations, and hear;
    be attentive, O peoples!

---

k 2 Chr 20, 25.—l Is 1, 26.—m Prv 9, 10.—n Jgs 5, 6.—o Na
1, 4.—p Is 10, 17.—q Na 1, 6.—r Pss 15, 2-6; 24, 4f.

33, 7: *Ariel . . . Shalem:* Jerusalem; cf Is 29, 1; Gn 14, 18.
33, 9: *Sharon:* the fertile plain near the Mediterranean.
33, 17: *King:* the messianic King, or God; cf v 22.
33, 21. 23: *Boat . . . majestic ship:* of a foreign oppressor.

Is

Let the earth and what fills it listen,
  the world and all it produces.[s]
2 The LORD is angry with all the nations
  and is wrathful against all their host;
  he has doomed them and given them
  over to slaughter.
3 Their slain shall be cast out,
  their corpses shall send up a stench;
  The mountains shall run with their
  blood,[t]
4 and all the hills shall rot;
  The heavens shall be rolled up like a
  scroll,
  and all their host shall wither away,
  As the leaf wilts on the vine,
  or as the fig withers on the tree.[u]

5 When my sword has drunk its fill in the
  heavens,
  lo, it shall come down in judgment
  upon Edom, a people I have
  doomed.[v]
6 The LORD has a sword filled with
  blood,[w]
  greasy with fat,
  With the blood of lambs and goats,
  with the fat of rams' kidneys;
  For the LORD has a sacrifice in Bozrah,
  a great slaughter in the land of Edom.
7 Wild oxen shall be struck down with
  fatlings,
  and bullocks with bulls;
  Their land shall be soaked with blood,
  and their earth greasy with fat.
8 For the LORD has a day of vengeance,
  a year of requital by Zion's defender.[x]
9 Edom's streams shall be changed into
  pitch
  and her earth into sulphur,
  and her land shall become burning
  pitch;
10 Night and day it shall not be quenched,
  its smoke shall rise forever.
  From generation to generation she shall
  lie waste,
  never again shall anyone pass through
  her.
11 But the desert owl and hoot owl shall
  possess her,
  the screech owl and raven shall dwell
  in her.
  The LORD will measure her with line
  and plummet
  to be an empty waste
  for satyrs* to dwell in.[y]

12 Her nobles shall be no more,
  nor shall kings be proclaimed there;
  all her princes are gone.[z]
13 Her castles shall be overgrown with
  thorns,
  her fortresses with thistles and briers.
  She shall become an abode for jackals
  and a haunt for ostriches.[a]
14 Wildcats shall meet with desert beasts,
  satyrs shall call to one another;
  There shall the lilith* repose,
  and find for herself a place to rest.
15 There the hoot owl shall nest and lay
  eggs,
  hatch them out and gather them in
  her shadow;
  There shall the kites assemble,
  none shall be missing its mate.

16 Look in the book of the LORD* and
  read:
  No one of these shall be lacking,
  For the mouth of the LORD has ordered
  it,
  and his spirit shall gather them
  there.[b]
17 It is he who casts the lot for them,
  and with his hand he marks off their
  shares of her;
  They shall possess her forever,
  and dwell there from generation to
  generation.

CHAPTER 35

Israel's Deliverance*

1 The desert and the parched land will
  exult;
  the steppe will rejoice and bloom.[c]
2 They will bloom with abundant flowers,
  and rejoice with joyful song.
  The glory of Lebanon will be given to
  them,
  the splendor of Carmel and Sharon;

---

s Dt 32, 1.—t Ez 32, 4. 6.—u Is 13, 10; Ez 32, 7f; 4, 15.—v
Jer 46, 10.—w 6f: Jer 49, 12f.—x Is 13, 9; 63, 4.—y Is 14, 23;
Zep 2, 14.—z Ob 18.—a Is 13, 21; Hos 9, 6.—b Jos 18, 10; Ps
78, 55.—c Is 55, 12f.

34, 11: *Satyrs:* see note on Is 13, 21; cf Is 34, 14.
34, 14: *Lilith:* a female demon thought to roam about the desert.
34, 16: *Book of the Lord:* God's list of all his creatures; cf Ps
69, 29, ''the book of the living''; Ps 139, 16, ''your book.''
35, 1-10: Similar to the description of the return from the
Exile, as found in chaps. 40-55.

They will see the glory of the LORD,
the splendor of our God.[d]
3 Strengthen the hands that are feeble,
make firm the knees that are weak,[e]
4 Say to those whose hearts are frightened:
Be strong, fear not!
Here is your God,
he comes with vindication;
With divine recompense
he comes to save you.[f]
5 Then will the eyes of the blind be
opened,
the ears of the deaf be cleared;[g]
6 Then will the lame leap like a stag,
then the tongue of the dumb will
sing.[h]

Streams will burst forth in the desert,
and rivers in the steppe.
7 The burning sands will become pools,
and the thirsty ground, springs of
water;
The abode where jackals lurk
will be a marsh for the reed and
papyrus.
8 A highway will be there,
called the holy way;
No one unclean may pass over it,
nor fools go astray on it.
9 No lion will be there,
nor beast of prey go up to be met
upon it.
It is for those with a journey to make,
and on it the redeemed will walk.[i]
10 Those whom the LORD has ransomed
will return
and enter Zion singing,
crowned with everlasting joy;
They will meet with joy and gladness,
sorrow and mourning will flee.[j]

---

d Is 60, 13; Ps 96, 12.—e Jb 4, 3f; Heb 12, 12.—f Is 41, 10;
Zec 8, 13.—g Is 29, 18; 32, 3.—h Is 41, 18; 43, 10. 19.—i Is 62,
10; Lv 26, 6.—j Is 51, 11.—k 2 Kgs 18, 13; 2 Chr 32, 1.—l Is
30, 2.—m 2 Kgs 18, 4.—n Is 10, 5f.

36, 1—39, 8: Except for 38, 9-20, this historical appendix
describing the siege, etc., is paralleled in 2 Kgs 18, 13—20, 19,
which, however, has certain details proper to itself. The events
are also recorded in substantially the same way in the cuneiform
inscriptions of Sennacherib.
36, 7: The Assyrians pretend that Hezekiah's removal of the
high places and altars (illegal sanctuaries) was taken by the
Lord as an insult. They declare to Jerusalem's emissaries that the
city therefore no longer has a right to the Lord's protection and
that they are the ones who truly carry out his will (cf v 10).
36, 11: The Jewish emissaries ask that the conversation be
carried on in *Aramaic,* not in *Judean,* for they fear the effect of
the Assyrian claims upon the morale of the people.

VII: HISTORICAL APPENDIX

CHAPTER 36

Invasion of Sennacherib.* [1] In the fourteenth year of King Hezekiah, Sennacherib, king of Assyria, went on an expedition against all the fortified cities of
Judah and captured them.[k] [2] From Lachish the king of Assyria sent his commander with a great army to King
Hezekiah in Jerusalem. When he stopped
at the conduit of the upper pool, on the
highway of the fuller's field, [3] there came
out to him the master of the palace,
Eliakim, son of Hilkiah, and Shebna the
scribe, and the herald Joah, son of Asaph.
[4] The commander said to them, "Tell King
Hezekiah: Thus says the great king, the
king of Assyria, 'On what do you base this
confidence of yours? [5] Do you think mere
words substitute for strategy and might in
war? On whom, then, do you rely, that
you rebel against me? [6] This Egypt, the
staff on which you rely, is in fact a broken
reed which pierces the hand of anyone who
leans on it. That is what Pharaoh, king of
Egypt, is to all who rely on him.[l] [7] But if
you say to me: "We rely on the LORD, our
God," is not he the one whose high places
and altars Hezekiah removed,* commanding Judah and Jerusalem to worship before
this altar?'[m]
[8] "Now, make a wager with my lord the
king of Assyria: 'I will give you two
thousand horses, if you can put riders on
them.' [9] How then can you repulse even
one of the least servants of my lord? And
yet you rely on Egypt for chariots and
horsemen! [10] 'Was it without the LORD's
will that I have come up to destroy this
land? The LORD said to me, "Go up and
destroy that land!" ' "[n]
[11] Then Eliakim and Shebna and Joah
said to the commander, "Please speak to
your servants in Aramaic; we understand
it. Do not speak to us in Judean within
earshot of the people who are on the
wall."*
[12] But the commander replied, "Was it
to you and your master that my lord sent
me to speak these words? Was it not
rather to the men sitting on the wall,
who, with you, will have to eat their own
excrement and drink their own urine?"
[13] Then the commander stepped forward

Is

and cried out in a loud voice in Judean, "Listen to the words of the great king, the king of Assyria. [14]Thus says the king: 'Do not let Hezekiah deceive you, since he cannot deliver you. [15]Let not Hezekiah induce you to rely on the LORD, saying, "The LORD will surely save us; this city will not be handed over to the king of Assyria." ' [16]Do not listen to Hezekiah, for the king of Assyria says: 'Make peace with me and surrender! Then each of you will eat of his own vine and of his own fig tree, and drink the water of his own cistern,[o] [17]until I come to take you to a land like your own, a land of grain and wine, of bread and vineyards. [18]Do not let Hezekiah seduce you by saying, "The LORD will save us." Has any of the gods of the nations ever rescued his land from the hand of the king of Assyria?[p] [19]Where are the gods of Hamath and Arpad? Where are the gods of Sepharvaim? Where are the gods of Samaria? Have they saved Samaria from my hand?[q] [20]Which of all the gods of these lands ever rescued his land from my hand? Will the LORD then save Jerusalem from my hand?' " [21]But they remained silent and did not answer him one word, for the king had ordered them not to answer him.

[22]Then the master of the palace, Eliakim, son of Hilkiah, Shebna the scribe, and the herald Joah, son of Asaph, came to Hezekiah with their garments torn, and reported to him what the commander had said.

CHAPTER 37

[1]When King Hezekiah heard this, he tore his garments, wrapped himself in sackcloth, and went into the temple of the LORD. [2]He sent Eliakim, the master of the palace, and Shebna the scribe, and the elders of the priests, wrapped in sackcloth, to tell the prophet Isaiah, son of Amoz: [3]"Thus says Hezekiah: 'This is a day of distress, of rebuke, and of disgrace. Children are at the point of birth, but there is no strength to bring them forth.* [4]Perhaps the LORD, your God, will hear the words of the commander, whom his master, the king of Assyria, sent to taunt the living God, and will rebuke him for the words which the LORD, your God, has heard. Send up a prayer for the remnant that is here.' "

[5]When the servants of King Hezekiah had come to Isaiah, [6]he said to them: "Tell this to your master: 'Thus says the LORD: Do not be frightened by the words you have heard, with which the servants of the king of Assyria have blasphemed me.[r] [7]I am about to put in him such a spirit that, when he hears a certain report, he will return to his own land, and there I will cause him to fall by the sword.' "

[8]When the commander returned to Lachish and heard that the king of Assyria had left there, he found him besieging Libnah. [9]The king of Assyria heard a report that Tirhakah,* king of Ethiopia, had come out to fight against him. Again he sent envoys to Hezekiah with this message: "Thus shall you say to Hezekiah, king of Judah: [10]'Do not let your God on whom you rely deceive you by saying that Jerusalem will not be handed over to the king of Assyria.[s] [11]You yourself have heard what the kings of Assyria have done to all the countries: They doomed them! Will you, then, be saved? [12]Did the gods of the nations whom my fathers destroyed save them? Gozen, Haran, Rezeph, and the Edenites in Telassar? [13]Where is the king of Hamath, the king of Arpad, or a king of the cities of Sepharvaim, Hena or Ivvah?' "

[14]Hezekiah took the letter from the hand of the messengers and read it; then he went up to the temple of the LORD, and spreading it out before him, [15]he prayed to the LORD: [16]"O LORD of hosts, God of Israel, enthroned upon the cherubim! You alone are God over all the kingdoms of the earth. You have made the heavens and the earth.* [17]Incline your ear, O LORD, and listen! Open your eyes, O LORD, and see! Hear all the words of the letter that Sennacherib sent to taunt the living God. [18]Truly, O LORD, the kings of Assyria have laid waste all the nations and their

---

o 1 Kgs 4, 25; Zec 3, 10.—p Is 37, 11.—q Is 10, 9; 37, 13.—r Is 41, 10-14; 51, 7.—s Is 36, 14.

37, 3: A proverbial expression. In the Bible the pangs of childbirth often typify extreme anguish; cf Is 13, 8; Jer 6, 24; Mi 4, 9f. In this instance there is reference to the desperate situation of Hezekiah from which he was scarcely able to free himself.

37, 9: *Tirhakah:* may have been general of the Egyptian army in 701 B.C.; later he became king, one of the Ethiopian dynasty of Egyptian kings (c. 690-664 B.C.). Many consider that this account in Isaiah combines features of two originally distinct sieges of Jerusalem by Sennacherib.

37, 16: In contrast to the empty boasting of the Assyrians, Hezekiah proclaims the Lord as *God over all the kingdoms of the earth.*

lands, [19] and cast their gods into the fire; they destroyed them because they were not gods but the work of human hands, wood and stone. [t] [20] Therefore, O LORD, our God, save us from his hand, that all the kingdoms of the earth may know that you, O LORD, alone are God."

Punishment of Sennacherib. [21] Then Isaiah, son of Amoz, sent this message to Hezekiah: Thus says the LORD, the God of Israel: In answer to your prayer for help against Sennacherib, king of Assyria, [22] this is the word the LORD has spoken concerning him: [u]

She despises you, laughs you to scorn,
the virgin daughter Zion;
Behind you she wags her head,
daughter Jerusalem.
[23] Whom have you insulted and blasphemed,
against whom have you raised your voice
And lifted up your eyes on high?
Against the Holy One of Israel! [v]
[24] Through your servants you have insulted the Lord:
You said, "With my many chariots
I climbed the mountain heights,
the recesses of Lebanon;
I cut down its lofty cedars,
its choice cypresses;
I reached the remotest heights,
its forest park.
[25] I dug wells and drank water in foreign lands;
I dried up with the soles of my feet
all the rivers of Egypt."

[26] Have you not heard?
Long ago I prepared it,
From days of old I planned it,
now I have brought it to pass:
That you should reduce fortified cities
into heaps of ruins,

[27] While their inhabitants, shorn of power,
are dismayed and ashamed,
Becoming like the plants of the field,
like the green growth,
like the scorched grass on the housetops.
[28] I am aware whether you stand or sit;
I know whether you come or go,
and also your rage against me.
[29] Because of your rage against me
and your fury which has reached my ears,
I will put my hook in your nose
and my bit in your mouth,
and make you return the way you came.

[30] This shall be a sign for you: [*]
this year you shall eat the aftergrowth,
next year, what grows of itself;
But in the third year, sow and reap,
plant vineyards and eat their fruit!
[31] The remaining survivors of the house of Judah
shall again strike root below
and bear fruit above. [w]
[32] For out of Jerusalem shall come a remnant,
and from Mount Zion, survivors.
The zeal of the LORD of hosts shall do this.

[33] Therefore, thus says the LORD concerning the king of Assyria: He shall not reach this city, nor shoot an arrow at it, nor come before it with a shield, nor cast up siegeworks against it. [34] He shall return by the same way he came, without entering the city, says the LORD. [x] [35] I will shield and save this city for my own sake, and for the sake of my servant David. [y]

[36] The angel of the LORD went forth and struck down one hundred and eighty-five thousand in the Assyrian camp. [z] Early the next morning, there they were, all the corpses of the dead. [*] [37] So Sennacherib, the king of Assyria, broke camp and went back home to Nineveh. [a]

[38] When he was worshiping in the temple of his god Nisroch, his sons Adrammelech and Sharezer slew him with the sword and fled into the land of Ararat. [*] His son Esarhaddon reigned in his stead.

---

t Jer 16, 20.—u 2 Kgs 19, 21.—v Is 1, 4.—w Is 27, 6.—x Is 37, 29.—y 1 Kgs 15, 4f.—z Is 10, 12; 17, 14.—a 2 Kgs 19, 35f.

37, 30: *You:* Hezekiah. *A sign:* it is difficult to know the nature of this sign. Either it is merely a proverbial expression to signify that prosperity follows adversity, or it indicates that after two years the normal conditions of life will be resumed.

37, 36: The destruction of Sennacherib's army is also recorded by Herodotus, a Greek historian of the fifth century B.C. It was probably due to the bubonic plague, but the sacred author attributes it to its ultimate cause, God through his angel.

37, 38: The violent death of Sennacherib (681 B.C.) is also mentioned in non-biblical sources. It occurred twenty years after his invasion of Judea.

Is

CHAPTER 38

Sickness and Recovery of Hezekiah. * [1] In those days,* when Hezekiah was mortally ill, the prophet Isaiah, son of Amoz, came and said to him: "Thus says the LORD: Put your house in order, for you are about to die; you shall not recover."[b] [2] Then Hezekiah turned his face to the wall and prayed to the LORD: [3] "O LORD, remember how faithfully and wholeheartedly I conducted myself in your presence, doing what was pleasing to you!" And Hezekiah wept bitterly.[c]

[4] Then the word of the LORD came to Isaiah: [5] "Go, tell Hezekiah:* Thus says the LORD, the God of your father David: I have heard your prayer and seen your tears. I will heal you: in three days you shall go up to the LORD's temple; I will add fifteen years to your life. [6] I will rescue you and this city from the hand of the king of Assyria; I will be a shield to this city."[d]

[21] Isaiah then ordered a poultice of figs to be taken and applied to the boil, that he might recover. [22] Then Hezekiah asked, "What is the sign that I shall go up to the temple of the LORD?"

[7] [Isaiah answered:] "This will be the sign for you from the LORD that he will do what he has promised: [8] See, I will make the shadow cast by the sun on the stairway to the terrace of Ahaz* go back the ten steps it has advanced." So the sun came back the ten steps it had advanced.[e]

Hezekiah's Hymn of Thanksgiving. [9] The song of Hezekiah, king of Judah, after he had been sick and had recovered from his illness:

[10] Once I said,
     "In the noontime of life* I must depart!
     To the gates of the nether world I shall be consigned
     for the rest of my years."[f]
[11] I said, "I shall see the LORD* no more
     in the land of the living.
     No longer shall I behold my fellow men
     among those who dwell in the world."
[12] My dwelling, like a shepherd's tent,
     is struck down and borne away from me;
     You have folded up my life, like a weaver
     who severs the last thread.*

Day and night you give me over to torment;[g]
[13] I cry out until the dawn.
Like a lion he breaks all my bones;
     [day and night you give me over to torment].
[14] Like a swallow I utter shrill cries;
     I moan like a dove.
My eyes grow weak, gazing heavenward:
     O Lord, I am in straits; be my surety!

[15] What am I to say or tell him?*
     He has done it!
I shall go on through all my years
     despite the bitterness of my soul.
[16] Those live whom the LORD protects;
     yours . . . the life of my spirit.*
You have given me health and life;
[17]   thus is my bitterness transformed into peace.
You have preserved my life
     from the pit of destruction,
When you cast behind your back
     all my sins.*
[18] For it is not the nether world that gives you thanks,*

---

b 2 Kgs 20, 1.—c 2 Kgs 18, 5f.—d Is 37, 35.—e 2 Kgs 20, 9. 11.—f Jb 17, 11; Ps 102, 25.—g Jb 7, 6.

38, 1—39, 8: The events of this section—sickness and recovery of Hezekiah, embassy of Merodach-baladan—point forward to Babylon (cc 40-66). They occurred prior to the events of Is 36, 1—37, 38, which point back to Assyria (Is 1, 1—35, 10).

38, 1: *In those days:* a time prior to the siege of Jerusalem in 701 B.C.

38, 5: Since Hezekiah died in 687 B.C. this sickness of his seems to have been in 702 B.C., that is, *fifteen years* before.

38, 8: *Stairway to the terrace of Ahaz:* this interpretation is based on a reading of the Hebrew text revised according to the Dead Sea Scroll of Isaiah; cf 2 Kgs 23, 12. Many translate the phrase as "steps of Ahaz" and understand this as referring to a sundial.

38, 10: *In the noontime of life:* long before the end of a full span of life; cf Pss 55, 24; 102, 25.

38, 11: *See the Lord:* go to the temple and take part in its service.

38, 12: These two metaphors emphasize the suddenness and finality of death.

38, 15: *What am I to say or tell him?:* a rhetorical question, as if the poet were at a loss in giving fitting expression to his gratitude; cf Ps 116, 12. *He has done it:* accomplished the cure. *Despite the bitterness:* even though the one praying was previously so dejected.

38, 16: *Yours . . . the life of my spirit:* the current Hebrew text is corrupt. The revised Latin psalter renders it: "You have revived my soul."

38, 17: *You cast behind your back all my sins:* figurative language to express the divine forgiveness of sins, as if God no longer saw or cared about them. This expression is ordinarily used of men forgetting God; cf 1 Kgs 14, 9; Ez 23, 35; Ps 50, 17.

38, 18f: See note on Ps 6, 6.

nor death that praises you;
Neither do those who go down into the
    pit
await your kindness. [h]
19 The living, the living give you thanks,
    as I do today.
Fathers declare to their sons,
    O God, your faithfulness.
20 The LORD is our savior;
    we shall sing to stringed instruments
In the house of the LORD
    all the days of our life.

CHAPTER 39

Embassy from Merodach-baladan. [1] At
that time when Merodach-baladan,* son of
Baladan, king of Babylon, heard that
Hezekiah had recovered from his sickness,
he sent letters and gifts to him. [i] [2] Hezekiah
was pleased at this, and therefore showed
the messengers his treasury, the silver and
gold, the spices and fine oil, his whole armory, and everything that was in his
storerooms; there was nothing in his house
or in his whole realm that he did not show
them. [j]
[3] Then Isaiah the prophet came to King
Hezekiah and asked him, "What did these
men say to you? Where did they come
from?" Hezekiah answered, "They came
to me from a distant land, from Babylon."
[4] "What did they see in your house?" he
asked. Hezekiah replied, "They saw everything in my house; there is nothing in my
storerooms that I did not show them."
[5] Then Isaiah said to Hezekiah, "Hear
the word of the LORD of hosts: [6] Behold,
the days shall come when all that is in your
house, and everything that your fathers
have stored up until this day, shall be carried off to Babylon;* nothing shall be

left, says the LORD. [k] [7] Some of your own
bodily descendants shall be taken and
made servants in the palace of the king of
Babylon." [l] [8] Hezekiah replied to Isaiah,
"The word of the LORD which you have
spoken is favorable."* For he thought,
"There will be peace and security in my
lifetime." [m]

B. THE BOOK OF CONSOLATION

I: THE LORD'S GLORY IN ISRAEL'S LIBERATION

CHAPTER 40

Promise of Salvation

1 Comfort, give comfort to my people,
    says your God.
2 Speak tenderly to Jerusalem, and pro-
    claim to her
    that her service* is at an end,
    her guilt is expiated;
Indeed, she has received from the hand
    of the LORD
    double for all her sins. [n]
3   A voice cries out:*
In the desert prepare the way of the
    LORD!
Make straight in the wasteland a
    highway for our God! [o]
4 Every valley shall be filled in,
    every mountain and hill shall be
    made low;
The rugged land shall be made a plain,
    the rough country, a broad valley.
5 Then the glory of the LORD shall be re-
    vealed,
    and all mankind shall see it together;
    for the mouth of the LORD has spo-
    ken.

6 A voice says, "Cry out!"
    I answer, "What shall I cry out?"
"All mankind is grass,
    and all their glory like the flower of
    the field. [p]
7 The grass withers, the flower wilts,
    when the breath of the LORD blows
    upon it.
    [So then, the people is the grass.]
8 Though the grass withers and the
    flower wilts,
    the word of our God stands for ever."

9 Go up onto a high mountain,
    Zion, herald of glad tidings;
Cry out at the top of your voice,
    Jerusalem, herald of good news!

---

h Pss 6, 6; 88, 11-13.—i 1-8: 2 Kgs 20, 12.—j 2 Chr 32,
25ff.—k 2 Kgs 24, 13; 25, 13ff.—l 2 Chr 33, 11; Dn 1, 2f.—m
2 Chr 32, 26.—n Is 50, 21.—o Mt 3, 3; Jn 1, 23.—p Jb 8, 12;
14, 2; Ps 37, 2; Sir 14, 18; Jas 1, 10; 1 Pt 1, 24.

39, 1: *Merodach-baladan:* twice king of Babylon, probably
from 721 to 710 B.C., and again for nine months, in 704-703.
This visit of his messengers, certainly before 701, was in reality
a political one. Babylon hoped to lead an anti-Assyrian confederation composed of neighboring states.
39, 6: Because Judah preferred to follow a pro-Babylonian
policy, instead of trusting in God, it would later be exiled to Babylon.
39, 8: *Favorable:* for the Exile would not occur in his
lifetime.
40, 2: *Service:* servitude and exile.
40, 3-5: The figurative language here describes the actual return of the exiles from Babylon to Jerusalem. It is the Lord who
leads them; their road is made easy for them. Mt 3, 3 and parallels see in the verses a prophecy of the Baptizer and Christ.

Fear not to cry out
  and say to the cities of Judah:
    Here is your God!
[10] Here comes with power
    the Lord GOD,
  who rules by his strong arm;
Here is his reward with him,
  his recompense before him.
[11] Like a shepherd he feeds his flock;
  in his arms he gathers the lambs,
Carrying them in his bosom,
  and leading the ewes with care.[q]

Power of the Creator To Save His People

[12] Who has cupped in his hand the waters
    of the sea,
  and marked off the heavens with a
    span?*
Who has held in a measure the dust of
    the earth,
  weighed the mountains in scales
  and the hills in a balance?
[13] Who has directed the spirit of the
    LORD,
  or has instructed him as his coun-
    selor?[r]
[14] Whom did he consult to gain knowl-
    edge?
  Who taught him the path of judg-
    ment,
  or showed him the way of under-
    standing?

[15] Behold, the nations count as a drop of
    the bucket,
  as dust on the scales;
  the coastlands weigh no more than
    powder.
[16] Lebanon would not suffice for fuel,*
  nor its animals be enough for
    holocausts.
[17] Before him all the nations are as
    nought,
  as nothing and void he accounts
    them.

[18] To whom can you liken God?[s]
  With what equal can you confront
    him?
[19] An idol, cast by a craftsman,
  which the smith plates with gold
  and fits with silver chains?[t]
[20] Mulberry wood, the choice portion
  which a skilled craftsman picks out
    for himself,

Choosing timber that will not rot,
  to set up an idol that will not be un-
    steady?[u]

[6] One man helps another,*
  one says to the other, "Keep on!"
[7] The craftsman encourages the gold-
    smith,
  the one who beats with the hammer,
  him who strikes on the anvil;
He says the soldering is good,
  and he fastens it with nails to steady
    it.

[21] Do you not know? Have you not heard?
  Was it not foretold you from the be-
    ginning?
  Have you not understood? Since the
    earth was founded
[22] He sits enthroned above the vault of the
    earth,
  and its inhabitants are like grasshop-
    pers;
He stretches out the heavens like a veil,
  spreads them out like a tent to dwell
    in.[v]
[23] He brings princes to nought
  and makes the rulers of the earth as
    nothing.
[24] Scarcely are they planted or sown,
  scarcely is their stem rooted in the
    earth,
When he breathes upon them and they
    wither,
  and the stormwind carries them away
    like straw.

[25] To whom can you liken me as an equal?
  says the Holy One.
[26] Lift up your eyes on high
  and see who has created* these:
He leads out their army and numbers
    them,
  calling them all by name.
By his great might and the strength of
    his power
  not one of them is missing![w]

---

q Is 49, 9f; 63, 11; Ez 34, 23; 37, 24; Jn 10, 11.—r Wis 9, 13;
Rom 11, 34; 1 Cor 2, 16; Jb 38, 1ff.—s 18f: Acts 17, 29.—t Ps
115, 4-7.—u Is 44, 13.—v Ps 104, 2.—w Ps 147, 4f.

40, 12: *Span:* the distance between the extended little finger
and the thumb. *Measure:* literally, "third"; here a small container.
40, 16: *Lebanon . . . fuel:* the famed cedars would not be
enough to keep the fires of sacrifice burning.
40, 6-7: These two verses have been transposed from chap.
41.
40, 26: *Created:* see note on Gn 1, 1. *By name:* for he is
their Creator.

27 Why, O Jacob, do you say,*
    and declare, O Israel,
    "My way is hidden from the LORD,
        and my right is disregarded by my
        God"?
28 Do you not know
        or have you not heard?
    The LORD is the eternal God,
        creator of the ends of the earth.
    He does not faint nor grow weary,
        and his knowledge is beyond
        scrutiny.
29 He gives strength to the fainting;
        for the weak he makes vigor abound.
30 Though young men faint and grow
        weary,
    and youths stagger and fall,
31 They that hope in the LORD will renew
        their strength,
    they will soar as with eagles' wings;
    They will run and not grow weary,
        walk and not grow faint.

CHAPTER 41

The Liberator of Israel

1 Keep silence before me, O coastlands;*
        you peoples, wait for my words!
    Let them draw near and speak;
        let us come together for judgment.

2 Who has stirred up from the East the
        champion of justice,*
    and summoned him to be his atten-
        dant?
    To him he delivers the nations
        and subdues the kings;
    With his sword he reduces them to
        dust,
    with his bow, to driven straw.
3 He pursues them, passing on without
        loss,
    by a path his feet do not even tread.
4 Who has performed these deeds?
        He who has called forth the genera-
        tions since the beginning.ˣ

---

x Is 44, 7; 46, 10.—y 8f: Is 44, 1f. 21; 45, 4.

40, 27f: God's people, here called *Jacob* and *Israel*, must not give way to discouragement: their *Lord is the eternal God.*
41, 1-4: It is generally agreed that these verses describe the vocation and victory of Cyrus, whom the Lord used as his instrument to redeem Israel.
41, 2: Cyrus is the *champion of justice* and God's *attendant.*
41, 14: *Redeemer:* in Hebrew, *goel,* one who frees another from slavery and avenges his sufferings; cf Lv 25, 48; Dt 19, 6. 12.

I, the LORD, am the first,
        and with the last I will also be.
5 The coastlands see, and fear;
        the ends of the earth tremble:
    these things are near, they come to
        pass.

8 But you, Israel, my servant,ʸ
        Jacob, whom I have chosen,
    offspring of Abraham my friend—
9 You whom I have taken from the ends
        of the earth
    and summoned from its far-off
        places,
    You whom I have called my servant,
        whom I have chosen and will not cast
        off—
10 Fear not, I am with you;
        be not dismayed; I am your God.
    I will strengthen you, and help you,
        and uphold you with my right hand
        of justice.

11 Yes, all shall be put to shame and dis-
        grace
    who vent their anger against you;
    Those shall perish and come to nought
        who offer resistance.
12 You shall seek out, but shall not find,
        those who strive against you;
    They shall be as nothing at all
        who do battle with you.

13 For I am the LORD, your God,
        who grasp your right hand;
    It is I who say to you, "Fear not,
        I will help you."
14 Fear not, O worm Jacob,
        O maggot Israel;
    I will help you, says the LORD;
        your redeemer* is the Holy One of Is-
        rael.
15 I will make of you a threshing sledge,
        sharp, new, and double-edged,
    To thresh the mountains and crush
        them,
    to make the hills like chaff.
16 When you winnow them, the wind shall
        carry them off
    and the storm shall scatter them.
    But you shall rejoice in the LORD,
        and glory in the Holy One of Israel.

17 The afflicted and the needy seek water
        in vain,
    their tongues are parched with thirst.

I, the LORD, will answer them;
    I, the God of Israel, will not forsake them.

18 I will open up rivers on the bare heights,
    and fountains in the broad valleys;
I will turn the desert into a marshland,
    and the dry ground into springs of water.

19 I will plant in the desert the cedar,
    acacia, myrtle, and olive;
I will set in the wasteland the cypress,
    together with the plane tree and the pine,

20 That all may see and know,
    observe and understand,
That the hand of the LORD has done this,
    the Holy One of Israel has created it.

21 Present your case, says the LORD;*
    bring forward your reasons, says the King of Jacob.

22 Let them come near and foretell to us
    what it is that shall happen!
What are the things of long ago?
    Tell us, that we may reflect on them
And know their outcome;
    or declare to us the things to come!

23 Foretell the things that shall come afterward,
    that we may know that you are gods!
Do something, good or evil,
    that will put us in awe and in fear.

24 Why, you are nothing and your work is nought!
    To choose you is an abomination.

25 I have stirred up one from the north,
    and he comes;
    from the east I summon him* by name;
He shall trample the rulers down like red earth,
    as the potter treads the clay.

26 Who announced this from the beginning, that we might know;
    beforehand, that we might say it is true?
Not one of you foretold it, not one spoke;
    no one heard you say,

27 "The first news for Zion: they are coming now,"
    or, "For Jerusalem I will pick out a bearer of the glad tidings."

28 When I look, there is not one,
    no one of them to give counsel,
    to make an answer when I question them.

29 Ah, all of them are nothing,
    their works are nought,
    their idols are empty wind!

CHAPTER 42

The Servant of the Lord

1 Here is my servant* whom I uphold,
    my chosen one with whom I am pleased,
Upon whom I have put my spirit;
    he shall bring forth justice to the nations,[z]

2 Not crying out, not shouting,
    not making his voice heard in the street.

3 A bruised reed he shall not break,
    and a smoldering wick he shall not quench,*

4 Until he establishes justice on the earth;
    the coastlands* will wait for his teaching.

5 Thus says God, the LORD,
    who created the heavens and stretched them out,
    who spreads out the earth with its crops,
Who gives breath to its people
    and spirit to those who walk on it:

6 I, the LORD, have called you for the victory of justice,
    I have grasped you by the hand;
I formed you, and set you
    as a covenant of the people,
    a light for the nations,[a]

7 To open the eyes of the blind,
    to bring out prisoners from confinement,
    and from the dungeon, those who live in darkness.

---

z Is 45, 6; 49, 6.—a Is 45, 13.

41, 21-24: An indictment of idols.
41, 25: *I summon him:* Cyrus.
42, 1-4: *Servant:* there are three other "Servant-of-the-Lord" oracles, Is 49, 1-7; 50, 4-11; 52, 13—53, 12. Many identifications have been proposed, e.g., historical Israel, ideal Israel, an Old Testament historical character before or during the lifetime of the prophet, the prophet himself. The New Testament and Christian tradition, however, have seen a fulfillment of these prophecies in Jesus Christ.
42, 3: A reference to the mercy of Christ.
42, 4: *Coastlands:* the lands of the Mediterranean. In the Old Testament the word often refers to the pagan lands of the west.

⁸ I am the LORD, this is my name;
  my glory I give to no other,
  nor my praise to idols.
⁹ See, the earlier things have come to
    pass,
  new ones I now foretell;
Before they spring into being,
  I announce them to you.

The Salvation of Israel
despite Its Sins

¹⁰ Sing to the LORD a new song,
  his praise from the end of the earth:
Let the sea and what fills it resound,
  the coastlands, and those who dwell
    in them.
¹¹ Let the steppe and its cities cry out,
  the villages where Kedar* dwells;
Let the inhabitants of Sela exult,
  and shout from the top of the moun-
    tains.
¹² Let them give glory to the LORD,
  and utter his praise in the coastlands.

¹³ The LORD goes forth like a hero,
  like a warrior he stirs up his ardor;
He shouts out his battle cry,
  against his enemies he shows his
    might:ᵇ
¹⁴ I have looked away, and kept silence,
  I have said nothing, holding myself
    in;
But now, I cry out as a woman in labor,
  gasping and panting.
¹⁵ I will lay waste mountains and hills,
  all their herbage I will dry up;
I will turn the rivers into marshes,
  and the marshes I will dry up.ᶜ
¹⁶ I will lead the blind on their journey;
  by paths unknown I will guide them.
I will turn darkness into light before
    them,
  and make crooked ways straight.
These things I do for them,
  and I will not forsake them.ᵈ
¹⁷ They shall be turned back in utter
    shame
  who trust in idols;
Who say to molten images,

"You are our gods."
¹⁸ You who are deaf, listen,*
  you who are blind, look and see!
¹⁹ Who is blind but my servant,
  or deaf like the messenger I send?
²⁰ You see many things without taking
    note;
  your ears are open, but without hear-
    ing.
²¹ Though it pleased the LORD in his jus-
    tice
  to make his law great and glorious,
²² This is a people* despoiled and plun-
    dered,
  all of them trapped in holes,
    hidden away in prisons.
They are taken as booty, with no one to
    rescue them;
  as spoil, with no one to demand their
    return.
²³ Who of you gives ear to this?
  Who listens and pays heed for the
    time to come?
²⁴ Who was it that gave Jacob to be plun-
    dered,
  Israel to the despoilers?*
Was it not the LORD, against whom we
    have sinned?
  In his ways they refused to walk,
    his law they disobeyed.
²⁵ So he poured out wrath upon them,
  his anger, and the fury of battle;
It blazed round about them, yet they
    did not realize,
  it burned them, but they took it not
    to heart.

CHAPTER 43

Promises of Redemption and Restoration

¹ But now, thus says the LORD,
  who created you, O Jacob, and
    formed you, O Israel:
Fear not, for I have redeemed you;
  I have called you by name: you are
    mine.
² When you pass through the water, I will
    be with you;
  in the rivers you shall not drown.
When you walk through fire, you shall
    not be burned;
  the flames shall not consume you.
³ For I am the LORD, your God,
  the Holy One of Israel, your savior.
I give Egypt as your ransom,

---

b Ex 14, 3.—c Ex 9, 25; 10, 15; 14, 21; Ps 105, 33ff.—d Ex
13, 21.

42, 11: *Kedar:* cf footnote to Is 21, 16. *Sela:* Petra, the capital of Edom.
42, 18-20: Because of their unbelief, the Lord rebukes his
people, whom he calls his *servant,* his *messenger.*
42, 22: *A people:* Israel in exile.
42, 24: *Despoilers:* the Assyrians and Babylonians.

Ethiopia and Seba* in return for you.

4 Because you are precious in my eyes
and glorious, and because I love you,
I give men in return for you
and peoples in exchange for your
life. [e]

5 Fear not, for I am with you;
from the east I will bring back your
descendants,
from the west I will gather you.

6 I will say to the north: Give them up!
and to the south: Hold not back!
Bring back my sons from afar,
and my daughters from the ends of
the earth: [f]

7 Everyone who is named as mine,
whom I created for my glory,
whom I formed and made.

8 Lead out the people who are blind
though they have eyes,
who are deaf though they have ears.

9 Let all the nations gather together,
let the peoples assemble!
Who among them could have revealed
this,
or foretold to us the earlier things?*
Let them produce witnesses to prove
themselves right,
that one may hear and say, "It is
true!"

10 You are my witnesses, says the LORD,
my servants whom I have chosen
To know and believe in me
and understand that it is I.
Before me no god was formed,
and after me there shall be none.

11 It is I, I the LORD;
there is no savior but me.

12 It is I who foretold, I who saved;
I made it known, not any strange god
among you;
You are my witnesses, says the LORD.
I am God, 13 yes, from eternity I am
He;
There is none who can deliver from my
hand:
who can countermand what I do? [g]

14 Thus says the LORD, your redeemer,*
the Holy One of Israel:
For your sakes I send to Babylon;
I will lower all the bars,
and the Chaldeans shall cry out in
lamentation.

15 I am the LORD, your Holy One,
the creator of Israel, your King.

16 Thus says the LORD,
who opens a way in the sea
and a path in the mighty waters, [h]

17 Who leads out chariots and horsemen,
a powerful army,
Till they lie prostrate together, never to
rise,
snuffed out and quenched like a
wick. [i]

18 Remember not the events of the past,
the things of long ago consider not;*

19 See, I am doing something new!
Now it springs forth, do you not perceive it?
In the desert I make a way,
in the wasteland, rivers.

20 Wild beasts honor me,
jackals and ostriches,
For I put water in the desert
and rivers in the wasteland
for my chosen people to drink,

21 The people whom I formed for myself,
that they might announce my praise.

22 Yet you did not call upon me, O
Jacob,*
for you grew weary of me, O Israel.

23 You did not bring me sheep for your
holocausts,
nor honor me with your sacrifices.
I did not exact from you the service of
offerings,
nor weary you for frankincense. [j]

24 You did not buy me sweet cane* for
money,
nor fill me with the fat of your sacrifices;
Instead, you burdened me with your
sins,
and wearied me with your crimes.

25 It is I, I, who wipe out,
for my own sake, your offenses;
your sins I remember no more.

---

e Dt 4, 37; Hos 11, 1.—f Is 49, 22; Ez 16, 20.—g Is 41, 4.—h
Is 51, 10f; Ex 14, 21.—i Ex 15, 4.—j Jer 6, 20.

43, 3f: *Egypt . . . Ethiopia and Seba:* countries which God
permitted the Persians to conquer in return for having given Israel its freedom.
43, 9: Only God can know and predict future events; cf Is 41,
1-5. 21-29.
43, 14-17: The destruction of Babylon.
43, 18: No need to think solely of the past wonders of the
exodus from Egypt; equally great is the exodus from Babylon.
43, 22-28: The reason for the liberation of the Israelites is not
their fidelity but rather God's mercy.
43, 24: *Sweet cane:* a fragrant substance used in making incense and the sacred anointing oil; cf Ex 30, 23; Jer 6, 20.

26 Would you have me remember, have us
come to trial?
Speak up, prove your innocence!
27 Your first father* sinned;
your spokesmen rebelled against me
28 Till I repudiated the holy gates,
put Jacob under the ban,
and exposed Israel to scorn.

CHAPTER 44

1 Hear then, O Jacob, my servant,
Israel, whom I have chosen.
2 Thus says the LORD who made you,
your help, who formed you from the
womb:
Fear not, O Jacob, my servant,
the darling* whom I have chosen.
3 I will pour out water upon the thirsty
ground,
and streams upon the dry land;
I will pour out my spirit upon your offspring,
and my blessing upon your descendants.
4 They shall spring up amid the verdure
like poplars beside the flowing waters.^k
5 One shall say, "I am the LORD's,"
another shall be named after Jacob,
And this one shall write on his hand,*
"The LORD's,"
and Israel shall be his surname.^l

The True God and False Gods

6 Thus says the LORD, Israel's King
and redeemer, the LORD of hosts:
I am the first and I am the last;
there is no God but me.^m
7 Who is like me? Let him stand up and
speak,
make it evident, and confront me
with it.
Who of old announced future events?

Let them foretell to us the things to
come.
8 Fear not, be not troubled:
did I not announce and foretell it long
ago?
You are my witnesses! Is there a God
or any Rock* besides me?ⁿ

9 * Idol makers all amount to nothing,
and their precious works are of no avail, as
they themselves give witness. To their
shame, they neither see nor know anything; and they are more deaf than men
are.^o 10 Indeed, all the associates of anyone
who forms a god, or casts an idol to no
purpose, will be put to shame; 11 they will
all assemble and stand forth, to be reduced
to fear and shame.

12 The smith fashions an iron image,
works it over the coals, shapes it with hammers, and forges it with his strong arm. He
is hungry and weak, drinks no water and
becomes exhausted.^p
13 The carpenter stretches a line and
marks with a stylus the outline of an idol.
He shapes it with a plane and measures it
off with a compass, making it like a man in
appearance and dignity, to occupy a
shrine. 14 He cuts down cedars, takes a
holm or an oak, and lays hold of other
trees of the forest, which the Lord had
planted and the rain made grow 15 to serve
man for fuel. With a part of their wood he
warms himself, or makes a fire for baking
bread; but with another part he makes a
god which he adores, an idol which he
worships. 16 Half of it he burns in the fire,
and on its embers he roasts his meat; he
eats what he has roasted until he is full,
and then warms himself and says, "Ah! I
am warm, I feel the fire." 17 Of what remains he makes a god, his idol, and prostrate before it in worship, he implores it,
"Rescue me, for you are my god."
18 The idols have neither knowledge nor
reason; their eyes are coated so that they
cannot see, and their hearts so that they
cannot understand. 19 Yet he does not reflect, nor have the intelligence and sense to
say, "Half of the wood I burned in the fire,
and on its embers I baked bread and
roasted meat which I ate. Shall I then
make an abomination out of the rest, or
worship a block of wood?" 20 He is chasing
ashes*—a thing that cannot save itself
when the flame consumes it; yet he does

Is

---

k Is 54, 1ff.—l Is 43, 7; 45, 14.—m Is 41, 44; 43, 15; 45, 21;
48, 3. 12; 51, 15; 54, 5.—n Is 43, 10. 12; Dt 32, 4.—o Is 48, 5.
7.—p Wis 13, 11ff.

43, 27: *First father:* Adam or Jacob, or collectively "early
ancestors." *Spokesmen:* leaders, priests, prophets.
44, 2: *The darling:* see note on Dt 32, 15; cf also Dt 33, 5.
26.
44, 5: *Write on his hand:* an allusion to the Babylonian custom of tattooing the owner's name on the hand of his slave; cf
also Rv 13, 16.
44, 8: *Rock:* place of refuge; said of God in Dt 32, 4. 18; 1 Sm
2, 2; etc.
44, 9-20: Satire on the makers and worshipers of idols.
44, 20: *Chasing ashes:* exerting efforts in vain; cf Hos 12, 2;
Eccl 1, 14; 2, 11. 17.

not say, "Is not this thing in my right hand
a fraud?"

21 Remember this, O Jacob,
    you, O Israel, who are my servant!
I formed you to be a servant to me;
    O Israel, by me you shall never be
        forgotten:
22 I have brushed away your offenses like a
        cloud,
    your sins like a mist;
    return to me, for I have redeemed
    you.

23 Raise a glad cry, you heavens: the LORD
        has done this;
    shout, you depths of the earth.
Break forth, you mountains, into song,
    you forest, with all your trees.
For the LORD has redeemed Jacob,
    and shows his glory through Israel.

Cyrus, Anointed of the Lord, Liberator of Israel

24 Thus says the LORD, your redeemer,
    who formed you from the womb:
I am the LORD, who made all things,
    who alone stretched out the heavens;
    when I spread out the earth, who was
        with me?^{q}
25 It is I who bring to nought the omens of
        liars,
    who make fools of diviners;
I turn wise men back
    and make their knowledge foolish.
26 It is I who confirm the words of my ser-
        vants,
    I carry out the plan announced by my
        messengers;
I say to Jerusalem: Be inhabited;
    to the cities of Judah: Be rebuilt;
    I will raise up their ruins.
27 It is I who said to the deep: Be dry;
    I will dry up your wellsprings.^{r}
28 I say of Cyrus:* My shepherd,
    who fulfills my every wish;
He shall say of Jerusalem, "Let her be
        rebuilt,"
    and of the temple, "Let its founda-
        tions be laid."^{s}

CHAPTER 45

1 Thus says the LORD to his anointed,*
    Cyrus,
    whose right hand I grasp,
Subduing nations before him,
    and making kings run in his service,

Opening doors before him
    and leaving the gates unbarred:
2 I will go before you
    and level the mountains;
Bronze doors* I will shatter,
    and iron bars I will snap.^{t}
3 I will give you treasures out of the dark-
        ness,
    and riches that have been hidden
        away,
That you may know that I am the
    LORD,
    the God of Israel, who calls you by
    your name.

4 For the sake of Jacob, my servant,
    of Israel my chosen one,
I have called you by your name,
    giving you a title, though you knew
    me not.^{u}
5 I am the LORD and there is no other,
    there is no God besides me.
It is I who arm you, though you know
    me not,
6   so that toward the rising and the set-
        ting of the sun
    men may know that there is none be-
        sides me.*
I am the LORD, there is no other;
7   I form the light, and create the dark-
        ness,
I make well-being and create woe;*
    I, the LORD, do all these things.
8 Let justice descend, O heavens, like
        dew from above,
    like gentle rain let the skies drop it
        down.
Let the earth open and salvation bud
    forth;
    let justice also spring up!*
    I, the LORD, have created this.^{v}

---

q Is 40, 22; Jb 9, 8.—r Is 42, 15; 51, 10.—s Jer 3, 15; Ez 34,
23.—t Ps 107, 16.—u Is 40, 26.—v Pss 72, 6; 85, 11.

44, 28: *Cyrus:* king of Persia (559-529 B.C.) and conqueror
of Babylon (538 B.C.), who liberated the Jews, permitting them
to return to their native land and to rebuild Jerusalem and the
Temple.

45, 1: *Anointed:* in Hebrew, *meshiah,* from which the word
"Messiah" is derived; from its Greek translation, *Christos,* we
have the name "Christ." Applied to kings, "anointed" originally
referred only to those of Israel, but it is here given to *Cyrus* because he is the agent of the Lord.

45, 2: *Bronze doors:* of Babylon.

45, 6: The Gentiles will come to know the true God; cf also vv
20-25.

45, 7: *Create woe:* God permits evil for the sake of a greater
good.

45, 8: The Vulgate rendering gives a more precise Messianic
sense to this verse, using "just one" and "savior" in place of *justice* and *salvation.* The Advent liturgy uses the Vulgate form,
Rorate coeli desuper . . . ., to express the world's longing for
the coming of Christ.

9 Woe to him who contends with his
   Maker;[w]
   a potsherd among potsherds of the
   earth!*
   Dare the clay say to its modeler, "What
   are you doing?"
   or, "What you are making has no
   hands"?
10 Woe to him who asks a father, "What
   are you begetting?"
   or a woman, "What are you giving
   birth to?"

11 Thus says the LORD,
   the Holy One of Israel, his maker:
   You question me about my children,
   or prescribe the work of my hands for
   me!
12 It was I who made the earth
   and created mankind upon it;
   It was my hands that stretched out the
   heavens;
   I gave the order to all their host.
13 It was I who stirred up one* for the
   triumph of justice;
   all his ways I make level.
   He shall rebuild my city
   and let my exiles go free
   Without price or ransom,
   says the LORD of hosts.

14   Thus says the LORD:
   The earnings of Egypt, the gain of
   Ethiopia,
   and the Sabeans,* tall of stature,
   Shall come over to you and belong to
   you;
   they shall follow you, coming in
   chains.
   Before you they shall fall prostrate,
   saying in prayer:

---

w Jer 18, 6; Rom 9, 20.—x Is 43, 3.—y Is 55, 8; Prv 25, 2.—z
Rom 14, 11; Phil 2, 10.

45, 9: No one may challenge God's freedom of action,
exemplified here by the selection of Cyrus as his anointed.
45, 13: *One:* Cyrus, called by God for the deliverance and restoration of Israel.
45, 14: *Egypt . . . Ethiopia . . . Sabeans:* the Egyptians and
their allies who, when conquered by Cyrus, are seen as acknowledging the God of Israel to be the one true God; cf Is 43, 3.
45, 15: *God is hidden:* he dwells invisibly in the holy of
holies.
45, 18: *Waste:* an allusion to the beginning of creation, when
the earth was *waste and void* (Gn 1, 2), the same Hebrew
word, *tohu,* being used in both passages. The further reference
here is to Palestine, which God wishes again to be inhabited by
the returning exiles.
45, 20: *Who bear wooden idols:* in their religious processions. The gods of the pagans have feet but cannot walk; cf Ps
115, 7; Bar 6, 25.

"With you only is God, and nowhere
   else;
   the gods are nought.[x]
15 Truly with you God is hidden,*
   the God of Israel, the savior![y]
16 Those are put to shame and disgrace
   who vent their anger against him;
   Those go in disgrace
   who carve images.
17 Israel, you are saved by the LORD,
   saved forever!
   You shall never be put to shame or disgrace
   in future ages."

18   For thus says the LORD,
   The creator of the heavens,
   who is God,
   The designer and maker of the earth
   who established it,
   Not creating it to be a waste,*
   but designing it to be lived in:
   I am the LORD, and there is no other.
19   I have not spoken from hiding
   nor from some dark place of the
   earth,
   And I have not said to the descendants
   of Jacob,
   "Look for me in an empty waste."
   I, the LORD, promise justice,
   I foretell what is right.

20 Come and assemble, gather together,
   you fugitives from among the gentiles!
   They are without knowledge who bear
   wooden idols*
   and pray to gods that cannot save.
21 Come here and declare
   in counsel together:
   Who announced this from the beginning
   and foretold it from of old?
   Was it not I, the LORD,
   besides whom there is no other God?
   There is no just and saving God but
   me.

22 Turn to me and be safe,
   all you ends of the earth,
   for I am God; there is no other!
23 By myself I swear,
   uttering my just decree
   and my unalterable word:
   To me every knee shall bend;
   by me every tongue shall swear,[z]
24 Saying, "Only in the LORD
   are just deeds and power.

Before him in shame shall come
 all who vent their anger against him.
25 In the LORD shall be the vindication
 and the glory
 of all the descendants of Israel."

CHAPTER 46

The Gods of Babylon

1 Bel bows down, Nebo* stoops,
 their idols are upon beasts and cattle;
They must be borne up on shoulders,
 carried as burdens by the weary.

2 They stoop and bow down together;
 unable to save those who bear them,
 they too go into captivity.

3 Hear me, O house of Jacob,
 all who remain of the house of Israel,
My burden since your birth,
 whom I have carried from your in-
 fancy.ᵃ

4 Even to your old age I am the same,
 even when your hair is gray I will
 bear you;
It is I who have done this, I who will
 continue,
 and I who will carry you to safety.

5 Whom would you compare me with, as
 an equal,
 or match me against, as though we
 were alike?

6 There are those who pour out gold from
 a purse
 and weigh out silver on the scales;
Then they hire a goldsmith to make it
 into a god
 before which they fall down in worship.

7 They lift it to their shoulders to carry;
 when they set it in place again, it
 stays,
 and does not move from the spot.
Although they cry out to it, it cannot
 answer;
 it delivers no one from distress.

8 Remember this and be firm,
 bear it well in mind, you rebels;
 remember the former things, those
 long ago:

9 I am God, there is no other;
 I am God, there is none like me.

10 At the beginning I foretell the outcome;
 in advance, things not yet done.

I say that my plan shall stand,
 I accomplish my every purpose.

11 I call from the east a bird of prey,*
 from a distant land, one to carry out
 my plan.
Yes, I have spoken, I will accomplish it;
 I have planned it, and I will do it.

12 Listen to me, you fainthearted,
 you who seem far from the victory of
 justice:

13 I am bringing on my justice, it is not far
 off,
 my salvation shall not tarry;
I will put salvation within Zion,
 and give to Israel my glory.

CHAPTER 47

The Fall of Babylon*

1 Come down, sit in the dust,
 O virgin daughter Babylon;
Sit on the ground, dethroned,
 O daughter of the Chaldeans.
No longer shall you be called
 dainty and delicate.

2 Take the millstone and grind flour,
 remove your veil;
Strip off your train, bare your legs,
 pass through the streams.

3 Your nakedness shall be uncovered
 and your shame be seen;
I will take vengeance,
 I will yield to no entreaty,
 says our redeemer,

4 Whose name is the LORD of hosts,
 the Holy One of Israel.

5 Go into darkness and sit in silence,
 O daughter of the Chaldeans.
No longer shall you be called
 sovereign mistress of kingdoms.

6 Angry at my people,
 I profaned my inheritance,
And I gave them into your hand;
 but you showed them no mercy,
And upon old men
 you laid a very heavy yoke.

7 You said, "I shall remain always,
 a sovereign mistress forever!"

---

a Is 44, 2.

46, 1: *Bel . . . Nebo:* gods of Babylon; their complete helplessness is here contrasted with God's omnipotence.
46, 11: *From the east a bird of prey:* Cyrus; cf Is 41, 2-4.
47, 1-15: A taunt-song, mocking Babylon, once queen of the nations, now made a slave girl.

But you did not lay these things to
   heart,
   you disregarded their outcome.*b*

8 Now hear this, voluptuous one,
   enthroned securely,
Saying to yourself,
   "I, and no one else!
I shall never be a widow,
   or suffer the loss of my children"—*c*

9 Both these things shall come to you
   suddenly, in a single day:
Complete bereavement and widowhood
   shall come upon you
For your many sorceries
   and the great number of your spells;*

10 Because you felt secure in your wickedness,
   and said, "No one sees me."

Your wisdom and your knowledge
   led you astray,
And you said to yourself,
   "I, and no one else!"

11 But upon you shall come evil
   you will not know how to predict;
Disaster shall befall you
   which you cannot allay.
Suddenly there shall come upon you
   ruin which you will not expect.

12 Keep up, now, your spells
   and your many sorceries;
Perhaps you can make them avail,
   perhaps you can strike terror!

13 You wearied yourself with many con-
   sultations,
   at which you toiled from your youth;
Let the astrologers stand forth to save
   you,
   the stargazers who forecast at each
    new moon
   what would happen to you.

14 Lo, they are like stubble,
   fire consumes them;
They cannot save themselves
   from the spreading flames.
This is no warming ember,
   no fire to sit before.

15 Thus do your wizards serve you
   with whom you have toiled from your
    youth;
Each wanders his own way,
   with none to save you.

---

b Is 14, 13f.—c Zep 2, 15; Rv 18, 7.—d Is 42, 9.—e Is 43,
22ff.

47, 9. 13. 15: Babylon was known for its sorcery and astrol-
ogy.

CHAPTER 48

Exhortations to the Exiles

1 Hear this, O house of Jacob
   called by the name Israel,
   sprung from the stock of Judah,
You who swear by the name of the
   Lord
   and invoke the God of Israel
   without sincerity or justice,

2 Though you are named after the holy
   city
   and rely on the God of Israel,
   whose name is the Lord of hosts.

3 Things of the past I foretold long ago,
   they went forth from my mouth, I let
    you hear of them;
   then suddenly I took action and they
    came to be.

4 Because I know that you are stubborn
   and that your neck is an iron sinew
   and your forehead bronze,

5 I foretold them to you of old;
   before they took place I let you hear
    of them,
That you might not say, "My idol did
    them,
   my statue, my molten image com-
    manded them."

6 Now that you have heard, look at all
   this;
   must you not admit it?*d*

From now on I announce new things to
   you,
   hidden events of which you knew
    not.

7 Now, not long ago, they are brought
   into being,
   and beforetime you did not hear of
    them,
   so that you cannot claim to have
    known them;

8 You neither heard nor knew,
   they did not reach your ears be-
    forehand.
Yes, I know you are utterly treacherous,
   a rebel you were called from birth.*e*

9 For the sake of my name I restrain my
   anger,
   for the sake of my renown I hold it
    back from you,
   lest I should destroy you.

10 See, I have refined you like silver,

Is

tested you in the furnace of affliction.*j*

11 For my sake, for my own sake, I do
this;
why should I suffer profanation?
My glory I will not give to another.

12 Listen to me, Jacob,
Israel, whom I named!
I, it is I who am the first,
and also the last am I.*g*

13 Yes, my hand laid the foundations of
the earth;
my right hand spread out the
heavens.
When I call them,
they stand forth at once.*h*

14 All of you assemble and listen:
Who among you foretold these
things?
The LORD's friend* shall do his will
against Babylon and the progeny of
Chaldea.

15 I myself have spoken, I have called him,
I have brought him, and his way succeeds!

16 Come near to me and hear this!
Not from the beginning did I speak it
in secret;
At the time it comes to pass, I am present:
"Now the Lord* GOD has sent me,
and his spirit."

17 Thus says the LORD, your redeemer,
the Holy One of Israel:
I, the LORD, your God,
teach you what is for your good,
and lead you on the way you should
go.

18 If you would hearken to my commandments,
your prosperity would be like a river,
and your vindication like the waves of
the sea;

19 Your descendants would be like the
sand,
and those born of your stock like its
grains,
Their name never cut off
or blotted out from my presence.

20 Go forth from Babylon, flee from
Chaldea!
With shouts of joy proclaim this,
make it known;
Publish it to the ends of the earth, and
say,

"The LORD has redeemed his servant
Jacob.

21 They did not thirst
when he led them through dry lands;
Water from the rock he set flowing for
them;
he cleft the rock, and waters welled
forth."*i*

22 [There is no peace for the wicked,
says the LORD.]

II: EXPIATION OF SIN, SPIRITUAL LIBERATION OF ISRAEL

CHAPTER 49

The Servant of the Lord*

1 Hear me, O coastlands,
listen, O distant peoples.*j*
The LORD called me from birth,
from my mother's womb he gave me
my name.*

2 He made of me a sharp-edged sword
and concealed me in the shadow of
his arm.
He made me a polished arrow,
in his quiver he hid me.*

3 You are my servant, he said to me,
Israel,* through whom I show my
glory.

4 Though I thought I had toiled in vain,
and for nothing, uselessly, spent my
strength,
Yet my reward is with the LORD,
my recompense is with my God.*k*

5 For now the LORD has spoken
who formed me as his servant from
the womb,
That Jacob may be brought back to him

---

f Is 1, 25; Jer 6, 29f; Zec 13, 9; Mal 3, 2.—g Is 41, 4; 44, 6;
48, 12; Rv 1, 8. 17.—h Is 40, 22. 26; 45, 12. 18.—i Ex 17, 6;
Nm 20, 11.—j Is 41, 9; 43, 1; 44, 2. 24; 46, 3.—k Is 40, 27.

48, 14: *The Lord's friend:* Cyrus, who carries out God's
plans.
48, 16: *"Now the Lord . . . spirit":* said by Cyrus; cf v 14.
49, 1-7: The second of the four "Servant-of-the-Lord" oracles.
49, 1: *Gave me my name:* designated me for a special office
(cf Jer 1, 5), or perhaps, made me renowned (cf Ps 45, 18).
49, 2: The servant was made ready and fit for the preaching of
God's word.
49, 3: *Israel:* the Servant is identified with the people of Israel as their ideal representative; however, since vv 5f seem to
distinguish the Servant from Israel, some regard the word *Israel*
here as a gloss.

and Israel gathered to him;
And I am made glorious in the sight of
the LORD,
and my God is now my strength!
6 It is too little, he says, for you to be my
servant,
to raise up the tribes of Jacob,
and restore the survivors of Israel;[l]
I will make you a light to the nations,
that my salvation may reach to the
ends of the earth.*
7 Thus says the LORD,
the redeemer and the Holy One of Israel,
To the one despised, whom the nations
abhor,
the slave of rulers:
When kings see you, they shall stand
up,
and princes shall prostrate themselves
Because of the LORD who is faithful,
the Holy One of Israel who has chosen you.[m]

The Liberation and Restoration of Zion

8   Thus says the LORD:
In a time of favor I answer you,
on the day of salvation I help you,
To restore the land
and allot the desolate heritages,[n]
9 Saying to the prisoners: Come out!
To those in darkness: Show yourselves!
Along the ways they shall find pasture,
on every bare height shall their pastures be.[o]
10 They shall not hunger or thirst,
nor shall the scorching wind or the
sun strike them;
For he who pities them leads them
and guides them beside springs of
water.[p]
11 I will cut a road through all my mountains,
and make my highways level.[q]
12 See, some shall come from afar,

others from the north and the west,
and some from the land of Syene.*
13 Sing out, O heavens, and rejoice, O
earth,
break forth into song, you mountains.
For the LORD comforts his people
and shows mercy to his afflicted.
14 But Zion said, "The LORD has forsaken
me;
my Lord has forgotten me."[r]
15 Can a mother forget her infant,
be without tenderness for the child of
her womb?
Even should she forget,
I will never forget you.[s]
16 See, upon the palms of my hands I have
written your name;*
your walls are ever before me.
17 Your rebuilders make haste,
as those who tore you down and laid
you waste
go forth from you;
18 Look about and see,
they are all gathering and coming to
you.
As I live, says the LORD,
you shall be arrayed with them all as
with adornments,
like a bride you shall fasten them on
you.
19 Though you were waste and desolate,
a land of ruins,
Now you shall be too small for your inhabitants,
while those who swallowed you up
will be far away.
20 The children whom you had lost
shall yet say to you,
"This place is too small for me,
make room for me to live in."
21 You shall ask yourself:
"Who has borne me these?
I was bereft and barren
[exiled and repudiated];
who has reared them?
I was left all alone;
where then do these come from?"[t]

22   Thus says the Lord GOD:
See, I will lift up my hand to the nations,
and raise my signal to the peoples;
They shall bring your sons in their
arms,

---

l Is 42, 1-6; 44, 5; 45, 14; Lk 2, 32; Acts 13, 46f.—m Is 49,
23; 55, 5.—n 2 Cor 6, 2.—o Is 42, 7. 18ff.—p Is 51, 14; Rv 7,
16.—q Is 40, 3f.—r Is 40, 27.—s Is 43, 4; 44, 21; 46, 3f.—t Is
54, 1ff.

49, 6: The Servant's vocation will be not only the restoration
of Israel but the conversion of the world; cf Lk 2, 32.
49, 12: *Syene:* now called Aswan, at the first cataract of the
Nile in southern Egypt.
49, 16: *Upon the palms . . . name:* for continual remembrance; cf Ex 13, 9. 16; Dt 6, 6-9.

Is

and your daughters shall be carried
on their shoulders. [u]

23 Kings shall be your foster fathers,
their princesses your nurses;
Bowing to the ground, they shall worship you
and lick the dust at your feet.
Then you shall know that I am the
LORD,
and those who hope in me shall never
be disappointed.

24   Thus says the LORD:
Can booty be taken from a warrior?
or captives be rescued from a tyrant?

25 Yes, captives can be taken from a warrior,
and booty be rescued from a tyrant;
Those who oppose you I will oppose,
and your sons I will save.

26 I will make your oppressors eat their
own flesh,
and they shall be drunk with their
own blood
as with the juice of the grape.
All mankind shall know
that I, the LORD, am your savior,
your redeemer, the mighty one of
Jacob. [v]

CHAPTER 50

Salvation Only through the Lord's Servant

1   Thus says the LORD:
Where is the bill of divorce
with which I dismissed your
mother?*
Or to which of my creditors
have I sold you?
It was for your sins that you were sold,
for your crimes that your mother was
dismissed. [w]

2 Why was no one there when I came?
Why did no one answer when I
called?*
Is my hand too short to ransom?
Have I not the strength to deliver?
Lo, with my rebuke I dry up the sea,
I turn rivers into a desert;
Their fish rot for lack of water,
and die of thirst. [x]

3 I clothe the heavens in mourning,
and make sackcloth their vesture.

4 The Lord GOD has given me*
a well-trained tongue,
That I might know how to speak to the
weary

a word that will rouse them.
Morning after morning
he opens my ear that I may hear;

5 And I have not rebelled,
have not turned back.*

6 I gave my back to those who beat me,
my cheeks to those who plucked my
beard;*
My face I did not shield
from buffets and spitting. [y]

7 The Lord GOD is my help,
therefore I am not disgraced;
I have set my face like flint,
knowing that I shall not be put to
shame. [z]

8 He is near who upholds my right;
if anyone wishes to oppose me,
let us appear together.
Who disputes my right?
Let him confront me.

9 See, the Lord GOD is my help;
who will prove me wrong?
Lo, they will all wear out like cloth,
the moth will eat them up. [a]

10 Who among you fears the LORD,*
heeds his servant's voice,
And walks in darkness
without any light,
Trusting in the name of the LORD
and relying on his God? [b]

11 All of you kindle flames
and carry about you fiery darts;
Walk by the light of your own fire
and by the flares you have burnt!
This is your fate from my hand:
you shall lie down in a place of pain.

CHAPTER 51

Exhortation To Trust in the Lord

1 Listen to me, you who pursue justice,
who seek the LORD;

---

u Is 5, 26; 13, 2.—w Is 19, 2; Ez 38, 21; Zec 14, 13.—w Dt 24,
1-4; Mt 19, 3; Mk 10, 2ff; Is 54, 6ff.—x Ex 7, 18; Ps 105, 29.—
y 2 Sm 10, 4ff; Mt 26, 67; 27, 30.—z Ez 3, 9.—a Is 51, 6-8; Ps
102, 27.—b Is 43, 1f; 44, 1f.

50, 1: Responding to the people's complaint of utter abandonment by God, the prophet shows that their sins were responsible
for their banishment. Since there was no bill of divorce, the bond
between the Lord and his people still exists and he will ultimately
save them.
50, 2: Israel's faith in God is weak; she does not answer his
call, nor believe in his promises of deliverance.
50, 4-11: The third of the four "Servant-of-the-Lord" oracles;
in vv 4-9 the Servant speaks; in vv 10f God reproves the people
for not following the Servant.
50, 5: The Servant does not refuse the divine vocation.
50, 6: He willingly submits to insults and beatings. *Plucked
my beard:* a grave insult.
50, 10f: Instead of trusting in the Lord and his Servant, the
people rely on their own devices, to their own destruction.

Look to the rock from which you were
hewn,
to the pit* from which you were
quarried;^c

² Look to Abraham, your father,
and to Sarah, who gave you birth;
When he was but one I called him,
I blessed him and made him many.^d

³ Yes, the LORD shall comfort Zion
and have pity on all her ruins;
Her deserts he shall make like Eden,
her wasteland like the garden of the
LORD;
Joy and gladness shall be found in her,
thanksgiving and the sound of song.

⁴ Be attentive to me, my people;*
my folk, give ear to me.
For law shall go forth from my presence,
and my judgment, as the light of the
peoples.^e

⁵ I will make my justice come speedily;
my salvation shall go forth
[and my arm shall judge the nations];
In me shall the coastlands hope,
and my arm they shall await.

⁶ Raise your eyes to the heavens,
and look at the earth below;
Though the heavens grow thin like
smoke,
the earth wears out like a garment
and its inhabitants die like flies,
My salvation shall remain forever
and my justice shall never be dismayed.*

⁷ Hear me, you who know justice,
you people who have my teaching at
heart:
Fear not the reproach of men,
be not dismayed at their revilings.

⁸ They shall be like a garment eaten by
moths,
like wool consumed by grubs;
But my justice shall remain forever

and my salvation, for all generations.^f

⁹ Awake, awake, put on strength,
O arm of the LORD!
Awake as in the days of old,
in ages long ago!
Was it not you who crushed Rahab,*
you who pierced the dragon?^g

¹⁰ Was it not you who dried up the sea,
the waters of the great deep,*
Who made the depths of the sea into a
way
for the redeemed to pass over?

¹¹ Those whom the LORD has ransomed
will return
and enter Zion singing,
crowned with everlasting joy;
They will meet with joy and gladness,
sorrow and mourning will flee.

¹² I, it is I who comfort you.
Can you then fear mortal man,
who is human only, to be looked
upon as grass,

¹³ And forget the LORD, your maker,
who stretched out the heavens
and laid the foundations of the earth?
All the day you are in constant dread
of the fury of the oppressor;
But when he sets himself to destroy,
what is there of the oppressor's
fury?

¹⁴ The oppressed shall soon be released;
they shall not die and go down into
the pit,
nor shall they want for bread.

¹⁵ For I am the LORD, your God,
who stirs up the sea so that its waves
roar;
the LORD of hosts by name.^h

¹⁶ I have put my words into your mouth
and shielded you in the shadow of my
hand,
I, who stretched out the heavens,
who laid the foundations of the earth,
who say to Zion: You are my people.

---

c Rom 9, 30f.—d Ez 33, 24; Gn 12, 2ff; 22, 17.—e Is 2, 3.—f
Is 50, 9.—g Ex 15, 16; Jb 9, 13; 26, 12; Pss 74, 13; 89, 11.—h
Jer 31, 35.

51, 1: *Rock . . . pit:* your glorious ancestry.
51, 4f: The conversion of the Gentiles.
51, 6: God's *salvation* and *justice* are eternal, in contrast to
the impermanence of *the heavens* and *the earth:* cf Mt 24, 35.
51, 9: *Rahab:* see note on Is 30, 7. *The dragon:* see notes on
Is 27, 1; Ps 74, 13.
51, 10: *Great deep:* another reference to the primeval chaos
of Gn 1, 2.

The Cup of the Lord

¹⁷ Awake, awake!
Arise, O Jerusalem,
You who drank at the LORD's hand
the cup of his wrath;

Who drained to the dregs
 the bowl of staggering! [i]
18 She has no one to guide her
 of all the sons she bore;
She has no one to grasp her by the
 hand,
 of all the sons she reared!—
19 Your misfortunes are double;
 who is there to condole with you?
Desolation and destruction, famine and
 sword!
Who is there to comfort you?
20 Your sons lie helpless
 at every street corner
 like antelopes in a net.
They are filled with the wrath of the
 LORD,
 the rebuke of your God.

21 But now, hear this, O afflicted one,
 drunk, but not with wine, [j]
22 Thus says the LORD, your Master,
 your God, who defends his people:
See, I am taking from your hand
 the cup of staggering;
The bowl of my wrath
 you shall no longer drink.
23 I will put it into the hands of your tormentors,
 those who ordered you
 to bow down, that they might walk
 over you,
While you offered your back like the
 ground,
 like the street for them to walk on.

CHAPTER 52

Let Zion Rejoice

1 Awake, awake!
 Put on your strength, O Zion;
Put on your glorious garments,
 O Jerusalem, holy city.
No longer shall the uncircumcised
 or the unclean enter you.
2 Shake off the dust,
 ascend to the throne, Jerusalem;
Loose the bonds from your neck,
 O captive daughter Zion!
3 For thus says the LORD:
You were sold for nothing,
 and without money you shall be redeemed.
4 Thus says the Lord GOD:
To Egypt in the beginning my people
 went down,

to sojourn there;
Assyria, too, oppressed them for
 nought.
5 But now, what am I to do here?
 says the LORD.
My people have been taken away without redress;
 their rulers make a boast of it, says
 the LORD;
 all the day my name is constantly reviled.
6 Therefore on that day my people shall
 know my renown,
 that it is I who have foretold it. Here
 I am!
7 How beautiful upon the mountains*
 are the feet of him who brings glad
 tidings,
Announcing peace, bearing good news,
 announcing salvation, and saying to
 Zion,
 "Your God is King!" [k]

8 Hark! Your watchmen raise a cry,
 together they shout for joy,
For they see directly, before their eyes,
 the LORD restoring Zion. [l]
9 Break out together in song,
 O ruins of Jerusalem!
For the LORD comforts his people,
 he redeems Jerusalem.
10 The LORD has bared his holy arm
 in the sight of all the nations;
All the ends of the earth will behold
 the salvation of our God.

11 Depart, depart, come forth from there,
 touch nothing unclean!
Out from there!* Purify yourselves,
 you who carry the vessels of the
 LORD.
12 Yet not in fearful haste will you come
 out,
 nor leave in headlong flight,
For the LORD comes before you,
 and your rear guard is the God of Israel. [m]

i Jer 25, 15ff; Ez 23, 32ff.—j Is 29, 9.—k Is 40, 9; Rom 10, 15.—l Is 62, 6.—m Ex 12, 11.

52, 7-10: God leads his people back from Babylon to Zion, from whose ruined walls *watchmen . . . shout for joy;* cf Rom 10, 15.
52, 11: *From there:* from Babylon. *Vessels of the Lord:* taken to Babylon by Nebuchadnezzar, now carried back by the exiled priests returning in procession to Zion; cf Ezr 1, 7.

Suffering and Triumph of the Servant of the Lord*

13 See, my servant shall prosper,
  he shall be raised high and greatly
    exalted.
14 Even as many were amazed at him—
  so marred was his look beyond that of
    man,
  and his appearance beyond that of
    mortals—[n]
15 So shall he startle many nations,
  because of him kings shall stand
    speechless;
  For those who have not been told shall
    see,
  those who have not heard shall pon-
    der it.[o]

CHAPTER 53

1 Who would believe what we have
    heard?
  To whom has the arm of the LORD
    been revealed?[p]
2 He grew up like a sapling before him,[q]
  like a shoot from the parched earth;
  There was in him no stately bearing to
    make us look at him,
  nor appearance that would attract us
    to him.*
3 He was spurned* and avoided by men,
  a man of suffering, accustomed to in-
    firmity,
  One of those from whom men hide their
    faces,
  spurned, and we held him in no es-
    teem.[r]

4 Yet it was our infirmities that he bore,*
  our sufferings that he endured,

While we thought of him as stricken,
  as one smitten by God and afflicted.[s]
5 But he was pierced for our offenses,
  crushed for our sins,
  Upon him was the chastisement that
    makes us whole,
  by his stripes we were healed.[t]
6 We had all gone astray like sheep,
  each following his own way;
  But the LORD laid upon him
  the guilt of us all.[u]

7 Though he was harshly treated, he sub-
    mitted
  and opened not his mouth;
  Like a lamb led to the slaughter
  or a sheep before the shearers,
  he was silent and opened not his
    mouth.[v]
8 Oppressed and condemned, he was
    taken away,
  and who would have thought any
    more of his destiny?
  When he was cut off from the land of
    the living,
  and smitten for the sin of his people,
9 A grave was assigned him among the
    wicked
  and a burial place with evildoers,
  Though he had done no wrong
  nor spoken any falsehood.[w]
10 [But the LORD was pleased*
  to crush him in infirmity.]

  If he gives his life as an offering for sin,
  he shall see his descendants in a long
    life,
  and the will of the LORD shall be ac-
    complished through him.
11 Because of his affliction
  he shall see the light in fullness of
    days;
  Through his suffering, my servant shall
    justify many,
  and their guilt he shall bear.
12 Therefore I will give him his portion
    among the great,
  and he shall divide the spoils with the
    mighty,
  Because he surrendered himself to
    death
  and was counted among the wicked;
  And he shall take away the sins of
    many,
  and win pardon for their offenses.[x]

---

n Ps 69, 8.—o Mi 7, 16.—p Is 52, 10; Jn 12, 38; Rom 10,
16.—q Is 11, 1.—r Jb 19, 18; Ps 31, 11ff; Mk 9, 11.—s Jer 10,
19; Mt 8, 17.—t 1 Cor 15, 3; 1 Pt 2, 24.—u Lv 16, 21ff.—v Mt
26, 63; Acts 8, 32.—w 1 Pt 2, 22f; 1 Jn 3, 5.—x Mk 15, 28; Lk
22, 37.

52, 13—53, 12: The last of the four "Servant-of-the-Lord"
oracles. An extraordinary description of the sinless Servant, who
by his voluntary suffering atones for the sins of his people, and
saves them from just punishment at the hands of God. Only in
Jesus Christ is the prophecy perfectly fulfilled.
  53, 2: Only God appreciated his Servant's true greatness.
  53, 3: Because he suffered, he was regarded as a sinner and
therefore as one to be *spurned.*
  53, 4ff: He did indeed suffer but it was for the sins of mankind,
and through his sufferings men are *healed.*
  53, 10ff: Because he fulfilled the divine will by suffering for
the sins of others, the Servant will be rewarded by the Lord. *See
the light:* enjoy happiness. This line may originally have read,
"he shall drink and eat to the full"—at the thanksgiving sacrifice
at which *he shall divide the spoils* (v 12).

CHAPTER 54

The New Zion

¹ Raise a glad cry, you barren one* who
did not bear,
break forth in jubilant song, you who
were not in labor,
For more numerous are the children of
the deserted wife
than the children of her who has a
husband,
says the LORD.*ʸ*
² Enlarge the space for your tent,
spread out your tent cloths unsparingly;
lengthen your ropes and make firm
your stakes.*ᶻ*
³ For you shall spread abroad to the right
and to the left;
your descendants shall dispossess the
nations
and shall people the desolate cities.

⁴ Fear not, you shall not be put to shame;
you need not blush, for you shall not
be disgraced.
The shame of your youth you shall
forget,
the reproach of your widowhood no
longer remember.
⁵ For he who has become your husband is
your Maker;
his name is the LORD of hosts;
Your redeemer* is the Holy One of Israel,
called God of all the earth.

⁶ The LORD calls you back,
like a wife forsaken and grieved in
spirit,
A wife married in youth and then cast
off,
says your God.*ᵃ*
⁷ For a brief moment I abandoned you,
but with great tenderness I will take
you back.
⁸ In an outburst of wrath, for a moment
I hid my face from you;
But with enduring love I take pity on
you,
says the LORD, your redeemer.

⁹ This is for me like the days of Noah,
when I swore that the waters of Noah
should never again deluge the earth;
So I have sworn not to be angry with
you,
or to rebuke you.*ᵇ*

¹⁰ Though the mountains leave their place
and the hills be shaken,
My love shall never leave you
nor my covenant of peace be shaken,
says the LORD, who has mercy on
you.*ᶜ*
¹¹ O afflicted one, storm-battered and un-
consoled,*
I lay your pavements in carnelians,
and your foundations in sapphires;*ᵈ*
¹² I will make your battlements of rubies,
your gates of carbuncles,
and all your walls of precious stones.
¹³ All your sons shall be taught by the
LORD,
and great shall be the peace of your
children.
¹⁴ In justice shall you be established,
far from the fear of oppression,
where destruction cannot come near
you.
¹⁵ Should there be any attack, it shall not
be of my making;
whoever attacks you shall fall before
you.
¹⁶ Lo, I have created the craftsman
who blows on the burning coals
and forges weapons as his work;
It is I also who have created
the destroyer to work havoc.
¹⁷ No weapon fashioned against you shall
prevail;
every tongue you shall prove false
that launches an accusation against
you.
This is the lot of the servants of the
LORD,
their vindication from me, says the
LORD.

CHAPTER 55

An Invitation to Grace

¹ All you who are thirsty,*
come to the water!

---

y Gal 4, 27.—z Is 49, 20.—a Mal 2, 14f.—b Gn 9, 15.—c Pss
76, 5; 46, 3.—d Rv 21, 18-21.

54, 1: Jerusalem, pictured as a wife who had been *barren* and
deserted, now suddenly finds herself with innumerable children
(the returning exiles); cf Gal 4, 27 for the application of this text
to the church, the New Zion.
54, 5: *Redeemer:* cf note on Is 41, 14.
54, 11f: Cf Rv 21. *Afflicted one:* Jerusalem; *carnelians:*
reddish quartz, hard and durable; *carbuncles:* another precious
stone of red color.
55, 1ff: God's salvation is freely extended to his people and to
all nations; through him will the *benefits assured to David* be
renewed; cf Is 12, 3; Jn 7, 37.

You who have no money,
   come, receive grain and eat;
Come, without paying and without cost,
   drink wine and milk!*e*
2 Why spend your money for what is not bread;
   your wages for what fails to satisfy?
Heed me, and you shall eat well,
   you shall delight in rich fare.
3 Come to me heedfully,
   listen, that you may have life.
I will renew with you the everlasting covenant,
   the benefits assured to David.*f*
4 As I made him a witness to the peoples,
   a leader and commander of nations,
5 So shall you summon a nation you knew not,
   and nations that knew you not shall run to you,
Because of the LORD, your God,
   the Holy One of Israel, who has glorified you.*g*

6 Seek the LORD while he may be found,
   call him while he is near.
7 Let the scoundrel forsake his way,
   and the wicked man his thoughts;
Let him turn to the LORD for mercy;
   to our God, who is generous in forgiving.
8 For my thoughts are not your thoughts,
   nor are your ways my ways, says the LORD.
9 As high as the heavens are above the earth,
   so high are my ways above your ways
   and my thoughts above your thoughts.

10 For just as from the heavens
   the rain and snow come down
And do not return there
   till they have watered the earth,

making it fertile and fruitful,
Giving seed to him who sows
   and bread to him who eats,
11 So shall my word be
   that goes forth from my mouth;
It shall not return to me void,
   but shall do my will,
   achieving the end for which I sent it.

12 Yes, in joy you shall depart,
   in peace you shall be brought back;
Mountains and hills shall break out in song before you,
   and all the trees of the countryside shall clap their hands.
13 In place of the thornbush, the cypress shall grow,
   instead of nettles,* the myrtle.
This shall be to the LORD's renown,
   an everlasting imperishable sign.

III: RETURN OF THE FIRST CAPTIVES

CHAPTER 56

The Lord's House Open to All*

1   Thus says the LORD:
Observe what is right, do what is just;
   for my salvation is about to come,
   my justice, about to be revealed.
2 Happy is the man who does this,
   the son of man who holds to it;
Who keeps the sabbath free from profanation,
   and his hand from any evildoing.
3 Let not the foreigner say,
   when he would join himself to the LORD,
   "The LORD will surely exclude me from his people";
Nor let the eunuch say,
   "See, I am a dry tree."*
4   For thus says the LORD:
To the eunuchs who observe my sabbaths
   and choose what pleases me
   and hold fast to my covenant,*h*
5 I will give, in my house
   and within my walls, a monument and a name*
Better than sons and daughters;
   an eternal, imperishable name will I give them.

6 And the foreigners who join themselves to the LORD,
   ministering to him,

---

e Jn 4, 10ff; 6, 35; 7, 37ff; Rv 21, 6; 22, 17.—f 2 Sm 7, 12-16.—g Acts 13, 34.—h Wis 3, 14f.

55, 13: *Thornbush . . . nettles:* suggestive of the desert and therefore symbolic of suffering and hardship; *cypress, myrtle:* suggestive of fertile land and therefore symbolic of joy and strength.

56, 1-8: Participation in the future messianic salvation is offered to all who believe in the Lord and keep his commandments, regardless of origin or social condition.

56, 3: Eunuchs had originally been excluded from the community of the Lord; cf Dt 23, 2; Wis 3, 14. *Dry tree:* unable to produce the fruit of offspring.

56, 5: *A monument and a name:* a memorial inscription to prevent oblivion for the one who had no children; cf 2 Sm 18, 18; Neh 7, 15; 13, 14.

Loving the name of the LORD,
and becoming his servants—
All who keep the sabbath free from profanation
and hold to my covenant,
7 Them I will bring to my holy mountain
and make joyful in my house of prayer;
Their holocausts and sacrifices
will be acceptable on my altar,
For my house shall be called
a house of prayer for all peoples. [i]
8 Thus says the Lord GOD,
who gathers the dispersed of Israel:
Others will I gather to him
besides those already gathered.

Blind Leaders

9 * All you wild beasts* of the field,
come and eat,
all you beasts in the forest! [j]
10 My watchmen are blind,
all of them unaware;
They are all dumb dogs,
they cannot bark;
Dreaming as they lie there,
loving their sleep.
11 They are relentless dogs,
they know not when they have enough.
These are the shepherds
who know no discretion;
Each of them goes his own way,
every one of them to his own gain:
12 "Come, I will fetch some wine;
let us carouse with strong drink,
And tomorrow will be like today,
or even greater." [k]

CHAPTER 57

1 The just man perishes,
but no one takes it to heart;
Devout men are swept away,
with no one giving it a thought.
Though he is taken away from the presence of evil,
the just man 2 enters into peace;
There is rest on his couch
for the sincere, straightforward man.

Faithless People

3 But you, draw near,
you sons of a sorceress,
adulterous, wanton race!
4 Of whom do you make sport,

at whom do you open wide your mouth,
and put out your tongue?
Are you not rebellious children,
a worthless race;
5 You who are in heat among the terebinths,
under every green tree;
You who immolate children in the wadies,
behind the crevices in the cliffs? [l]

6 Among the smooth stones* of the wadi
is your portion,
these are your lot;
To these you poured out libations,
and brought offerings.
Should I decide not to punish these things?
7 Upon a high and lofty mountain
you made your bed,
and there you went up to offer sacrifice. [m]
8 Behind the door and the doorpost
you placed your indecent symbol.
Deserting me, you spread out
your high, wide bed;
And of those whose embraces you love
you carved the symbol and gazed upon it
9 While you approached the king* with scented oil,
and multiplied your perfumes;
While you sent your ambassadors far away,
down even to the nether world.
10 Though worn out by your many misdeeds,
you never said, "It is hopeless";
New strength you found,
and so you did not weaken.

11 Of whom were you afraid? Whom did you fear,

---

i 1 Kgs 8, 29f; Mt 21, 13.—j Ez 34, 5.—k Is 28, 7ff; Wis 2, 7.—l Jer 7, 31; 19, 5; Ez 20, 28. 31.—m Hos 4, 13; Jer 2, 20; Ez 6, 13.

56, 9—57, 13: This section is apparently preexilic, written in the manner of the older prophets who condemned the pagan rites of Baal worship.
56, 9: *Wild beasts:* foreign nations, which are invited to come and ravage Israel.
57, 6: *Smooth stones:* the Hebrew word for this expression has the same consonants as the word for "portion"; instead of making the Lord their portion (cf Ps 16, 5), the people adored slabs of stone which they took from the streambeds in valleys and set up as idols; cf Jer 3, 9. Therefore, it is implied, they will be swept away as by a sudden torrent of waters carrying them down the rocky-bottomed gorge to destruction and death without burial.
57, 9: *The king:* the pagan god Moloch. *Ambassadors:* children sent to him through a sacrificial death.

that you became false
And did not remember me
or give me any thought?
Was I to remain silent and unseeing,
so that you would not have me to fear?
¹² I will expose your justice*
and your works;
¹³ They shall not help you when you cry
out,
nor save you in your distress.

All these* the wind shall carry off,
the breeze shall bear away;
But he who takes refuge in me shall inherit the land,
and possess my holy mountain.

Comfort for the Afflicted

¹⁴ Build up, build up, prepare the way,
remove the stumbling blocks from
my people's path. ⁿ
¹⁵ For thus says he who is high and
exalted,
living eternally, whose name is the
Holy One:
On high I dwell, and in holiness,
and with the crushed and dejected in
spirit,
To revive the spirits of the dejected,
to revive the hearts of the crushed. ᵒ
¹⁶ I will not accuse forever,
nor always be angry;
For their spirits would faint before me,
the souls that I have made.
¹⁷ Because of their wicked avarice I was
angry,
and struck them, hiding myself in
wrath,
as they went their own rebellious
way. ᵖ
¹⁸ I saw their ways,
but I will heal them and lead them;
I will give full comfort
to them and to those who mourn for
them,
¹⁹ I, the Creator, who gave them life.

Peace, peace to the far and the near,
says the LORD; and I will heal them.
²⁰ But the wicked are like the tossing sea
which cannot be calmed,

And its waters cast up mud and filth.
²¹ No peace for the wicked! says my
God. �q

CHAPTER 58

True Fasting

¹ Cry out full-throated and unsparingly,
lift up your voice like a trumpet blast;
Tell my people their wickedness,
and the house of Jacob their sins.*
² They seek me day after day,*
and desire to know my ways,
Like a nation that has done what is just
and not abandoned the law of their
God;
They ask me to declare what is due
them,
pleased to gain access to God.
³ "Why do we fast, and you do not see it?
afflict ourselves, and you take no note
of it?"

Lo, on your fast day you carry out your
own pursuits,
and drive all your laborers.
⁴ Yes, your fast ends in quarreling and
fighting,
striking with wicked claw.
Would that today you might fast
so as to make your voice heard on
high!
⁵ Is this the manner of fasting I wish,
of keeping a day of penance:
That a man bow his head like a reed,
and lie in sackcloth and ashes?
Do you call this a fast,
a day acceptable to the LORD?ʳ
⁶ This, rather, is the fasting that I wish:
releasing those bound unjustly,
untying the thongs of the yoke;
Setting free the oppressed,
breaking every yoke;
⁷ Sharing your bread with the hungry,
sheltering the oppressed and the
homeless;
Clothing the naked when you see them,
and not turning your back on your
own. ˢ

⁸ Then your light shall break forth like
the dawn,
and your wound shall quickly be
healed;
Your vindication shall go before you,
and the glory of the LORD shall be
your rear guard.

---

n Is 40, 3f.—o Is 61, 2f.—p Is 56, 11.—q Is 48, 21.—r Zec 7,
5.—s Ez 18, 7. 16; Mt 25, 35.

57, 12: *Justice:* here used ironically.
57, 13: *All these:* the wicked mentioned in Is 57, 3-10.
58, 1: This command is directed to the prophet.
58, 2-14: Merely external worship does not avail with God; it
must be joined to internal sincerity.

9 Then you shall call, and the LORD will
answer,
   you shall cry for help, and he will
say: Here I am!
If you remove from your midst oppression,
   false accusation and malicious
speech;
10 If you bestow your bread on the hungry
and satisfy the afflicted;
Then light shall rise for you in the darkness,
   and the gloom shall become for you
like midday;
11 Then the LORD will guide you always
   and give you plenty even on the
parched land.
He will renew your strength,
   and you shall be like a watered garden,
   like a spring whose water never fails.*t*
12 The ancient ruins shall be rebuilt for
your sake,
   and the foundations from ages past
you shall raise up;
"Repairer of the breach," they shall call
you,
"Restorer of ruined homesteads."*u*

13 If you hold back your foot on the sabbath
from following your own pursuits on
my holy day;
If you call the sabbath a delight,
and the LORD's holy day honorable;
If you honor it by not following your
ways,
seeking your own interests, or speaking with malice—
14 Then you shall delight in the LORD,
   and I will make you ride on the
heights of the earth;
I will nourish you with the heritage of
Jacob, your father,
   for the mouth of the LORD has
spoken.

CHAPTER 59

Sin and Confession

1 Lo, the hand of the LORD is not too
short to save,
   nor his ear too dull to hear.*v*
2 Rather, it is your crimes
that separate you from your God,

It is your sins that make him hide his
face
   so that he will not hear you.
3 For your hands are stained with blood,
your fingers with guilt;
Your lips speak falsehood,
and your tongue utters deceit.*w*
4 No one brings suit justly,
no one pleads truthfully;
They trust in emptiness* and tell lies;
   they conceive mischief and bring
forth malice.
5 They hatch adders' eggs,*
and weave spiders' webs:
Whoever eats their eggs will die,
   if one of them is pressed, it will hatch
as a viper;*x*
6 Their webs cannot serve as clothing,
   nor can they cover themselves with
their works.
Their works are evil works,
   and deeds of violence come from
their hands.
7 Their feet run to evil,
   and they are quick to shed innocent
blood;
Their thoughts are destructive
thoughts,
   plunder and ruin are on their highways.*y*
8 The way of peace they know not,
   and there is nothing that is right in
their paths;
Their ways they have made crooked,
   whoever treads them knows no
peace.

9 That is why right is far from us*
and justice does not reach us.
We look for light, and lo, darkness;
for brightness, but we walk in gloom!
10 Like blind men we grope along the
wall,
   like people without eyes we feel our
way.
We stumble at midday as at dusk,
in Stygian darkness, like the dead.
11 We all growl like bears,
   like doves we moan without ceasing.

---

t Is 51, 3; Ps 24.—u Is 61, 4.—v Is 50, 2; Nm 11, 23.—w Is
1, 15.—x Jb 20, 12-16.—y Rom 3, 15.

59, 4: *Emptiness:* things having no value.
59, 5f: A proverb signifying evil works—*adders' eggs*—and
useless devices—*spiders' webs;* the former do positive harm to
oneself and others, the latter serve no useful purpose.
59, 9-15: Spoken by the people through the mouth of the
prophet.

We look for right, but it is not there;
for salvation, and it is far from us.[z]

12 For our offenses before you are many,
our sins bear witness against us.
Yes, our offenses are present to us,
and our crimes we know:

13 Transgressing, and denying the LORD,
turning back from following our
God,
Threatening outrage, and apostasy,
uttering words of falsehood the heart
has conceived.

14 Right is repelled,
and justice stands far off;
For truth stumbles in the public square,
uprightness cannot enter.

15 Honesty is lacking,
and the man who turns from evil is
despoiled.

The Redeemer in Zion

The LORD saw this, and was aggrieved
that right did not exist.

16 He saw that there was no one,
and was appalled that there was none
to intervene;
So his own arm brought about the victory,
and his justice lent him its support.

17 He put on justice as his breastplate,
salvation, as the helmet on his head;
He clothed himself with garments of
vengeance,
wrapped himself in a mantle of zeal.[a]

18 He repays his enemies their deserts,
and requites his foes with wrath.

19 Those in the west shall fear the name of
the LORD,
and those in the east, his glory;
For it shall come like a pent-up river
which the breath of the LORD drives
on.

20 He shall come to Zion a redeemer
to those of Jacob who turn from sin,
says the LORD.[b]

21 This is the covenant with them
which I myself have made, says the
LORD:

My spirit which is upon you
and my words that I have put into
your mouth
Shall never leave your mouth,
nor the mouths of your children
Nor the mouths of your children's children
from now on and forever, says the
LORD.

CHAPTER 60

Glory of the New Zion

1 Rise up in splendor! Your light has
come,*
the glory of the Lord shines upon
you.

2 See, darkness covers the earth,
and thick clouds cover the peoples;
But upon you the LORD shines,
and over you appears his glory.

3 Nations shall walk by your light,
and kings by your shining radiance.[c]

4 Raise your eyes and look about;
they all gather and come to you:
Your sons come from afar,
and your daughters in the arms of
their nurses.[d]

5 Then you shall be radiant at what you
see,
your heart shall throb and overflow,
For the riches of the sea shall be
emptied out before you,
the wealth of nations shall be brought
to you.

6 Caravans of camels shall fill you,
dromedaries from Midian and
Ephah;
All from Sheba shall come
bearing gold and frankincense,
and proclaiming the praises of the
LORD.

7 All the flocks of Kedar shall be gathered
for you,
the rams of Nebaioth shall be your
sacrifices;
They will be acceptable offerings on my
altar,
and I will enhance the splendor of my
house.

8 What are these that fly along like
clouds,
like doves* to their cotes?

9 All the vessels of the sea are assembled,

---

z Is 38, 14.—a Wis 5, 17ff; Eph 6, 14; 1 Thes 5, 8.—b Rom
11, 26f.—c Is 42, 6; 45, 14; 49, 6.—d Is 49, 18.

60, 1-6: The Church makes use of these verses for the first
reading of the Mass on the feast of Epiphany, for she sees in them
symbols of her universality.
60, 8f: *Like clouds, like doves:* the white sails of *the ships
of Tarshish;* cf note on Ps 48, 8.

with the ships of Tarshish in the lead,
To bring your children from afar
    with their silver and gold,
In the name of the LORD, your God,
    the Holy One of Israel, who has
    glorified you.

10 Foreigners shall rebuild your walls,
    and their kings shall be your atten-
    dants;
Though I struck you in my wrath,
    yet in my good will I have shown you
    mercy.
11 Your gates shall stand open constantly;
    day and night they shall not be closed
But shall admit to you the wealth of na-
    tions,
    and their kings, in the vanguard.[e]
12 For the people or kingdom shall perish
    that does not serve you;
    those nations shall be utterly de-
    stroyed.
13 The glory of Lebanon* shall come to
    you:
    the cypress, the plane and the pine,
To bring beauty to my sanctuary,
    and glory to the place where I set my
    feet.[f]
14 The children of your oppressors shall
    come,
    bowing low before you;
All those who despised you
    shall fall prostrate at your feet.
They shall call you "City of the LORD,"
    "Zion of the Holy One of Israel."

15 Once you were forsaken,
    hated and unvisited,
Now I will make you the pride of the
    ages,
    a joy to generation after generation.[g]
16 You shall suck the milk of nations,
    and be nursed at royal breasts;
You shall know that I, the LORD, am
    your savior,
    your redeemer, the mighty one of
    Jacob.
17 In place of bronze I will bring gold,
    instead of iron, silver;
In place of wood, bronze,
    instead of stones, iron;
I will appoint peace your governor,
    and justice your ruler.

18 No longer shall violence be heard of in
    your land,

or plunder and ruin within your
    boundaries.
You shall call your walls "Salvation"
    and your gates "Praise."
19 No longer shall the sun
    be your light by day,
Nor the brightness of the moon
    shine upon you at night;
The LORD shall be your light forever,
    your God shall be your glory.[h]
20 No longer shall your sun go down,
    or your moon withdraw,
For the LORD will be your light forever,
    and the days of your mourning shall
    be at an end.
21 Your people shall all be just,
    they shall always possess the land,
They, the bud of my planting,
    my handiwork to show my glory.
22 The smallest shall become a thousand,
    the youngest, a mighty nation;
I, the LORD, will swiftly accomplish
    these things
    when their time comes.[i]

CHAPTER 61

The Mission to the Afflicted

1 The spirit of the Lord GOD is upon
    me,*
    because the LORD has anointed me;
He has sent me to bring glad tidings to
    the lowly,
    to heal the brokenhearted,
To proclaim liberty to the captives
    and release to the prisoners,[j]
2 To announce a year of favor from the
    LORD
    and a day of vindication by our God,
    to comfort all who mourn;[k]
3 To place on those who mourn in Zion
    a diadem instead of ashes,
To give them oil of gladness in place of
    mourning,
    a glorious mantle instead of a listless
    spirit.
They will be called oaks of justice,
    planted by the LORD to show his
    glory.

---

e Rv 21, 25.—f Is 35, 2.—g Ez 16.—h Rv 21, 23; 22, 5.—i Gn
12, 2; 17, 6.—j Is 42, 1; 48, 16; Lk 4, 18f.—k Mt 5, 5.

60, 13: *Glory of Lebanon:* the cedars, together with the
cypress, the plane and the pine, all precious, durable wood.

61, 1f: This was spoken by the prophet in regard to the restoration of Zion, but quoted by Christ as referring to his mission;
cf Lk 4, 18f. *Year of favor . . . day of vindication:* the time of
God's salvation.

The Reward of Israel

4 They shall rebuild the ancient ruins,
 the former wastes they shall raise up
And restore the ruined cities,
 desolate now for generations.[l]
5 Strangers shall stand ready to pasture
 your flocks,
 foreigners shall be your farmers and
 vinedressers.
6 You yourselves shall be named priests
 of the LORD,
 ministers of our God you shall be
 called.
You shall eat the wealth of the nations
 and boast of riches from them.

7 Since their shame was double
 and disgrace and spittle were their
 portion,
They shall have a double inheritance in
 their land,
 everlasting joy shall be theirs.[m]
8 For I, the LORD, love what is right,
 I hate robbery and injustice;
I will give them their recompense faithfully,
 a lasting covenant I will make with
 them.[n]
9 Their descendants shall be renowned
 among the nations,
 and their offspring among the peoples;
All who see them shall acknowledge
 them
 as a race the LORD has blessed.

10 I rejoice heartily in the LORD,
 in my God is the joy of my soul;
For he has clothed me with a robe of
 salvation,
 and wrapped me in a mantle of justice,
Like a bridegroom adorned with a
 diadem,
 like a bride bedecked with her jewels.
11 As the earth brings forth its plants,
 and a garden makes its growth spring
 up,

---

l Is 58, 12.—m Is 40, 2.—n Is 55, 3; 59, 21.—o Rv 2, 17; 3,
12.—p Is 49, 15f; 54, 1ff.—q Is 52, 10.

62, 2: *New name:* figurative expression for a new state of
happiness; cf Rv 2, 17; 3, 12.
62, 6f: *Remind the Lord . . . give no rest to him:* figuratively, as though to make certain that the Lord will remember his
pledge to Jerusalem. Cf Lk 11, 7f.

So will the Lord GOD make justice and
 praise
 spring up before all the nations.

CHAPTER 62

Jerusalem the Lord's Bride

1 For Zion's sake I will not be silent,
 for Jerusalem's sake I will not be
 quiet,
Until her vindication shines forth like
 the dawn
 and her victory like a burning torch.

2 Nations shall behold your vindication,
 and all kings your glory;
You shall be called by a new name*
 pronounced by the mouth of the
 LORD.[o]
3 You shall be a glorious crown in the
 hand of the LORD,
 a royal diadem held by your God.
4 No more shall men call you "Forsak-
 en,"
 or your land "Desolate,"
But you shall be called "My Delight,"
 and your land "Espoused."
For the LORD delights in you,
 and makes your land his spouse.[p]
5 As a young man marries a virgin,
 your Builder shall marry you;
And as a bridegroom rejoices in his
 bride
 so shall your God rejoice in you.

Restoration of Zion

6 Upon your walls, O Jerusalem,
 I have stationed watchmen;
Never, by day or by night,
 shall they be silent.
O you who are to remind the LORD,*
 take no rest
7 And give no rest to him,
 until he re-establishes Jerusalem
And makes of it
 the pride of the earth.

8 The LORD has sworn by his right hand
 and by his mighty arm:
No more will I give your grain
 as food to your enemies;
Nor shall foreigners drink your wine,
 for which you toiled.[q]
9 But you who harvest the grain shall eat
 it,
 and you shall praise the LORD;

Is

You who gather the grapes shall drink
the wine
in the courts of my sanctuary. *r*

10 Pass through, pass through the gates,
prepare the way for the people; *s*
Build up, build up the highway,
clear it of stones,
raise up a standard over the nations.*

11 See, the LORD proclaims
to the ends of the earth:
Say to daughter Zion,
your savior comes!
Here is his reward with him,
his recompense before him. *t*

12 They shall be called the holy people,
the redeemed of the LORD,
And you shall be called "Frequented,"
a city that is not forsaken. *u*

CHAPTER 63

Punishment of Edom*

1 Who is this that comes from Edom,
in crimsoned garments, from Bozrah—
This one arrayed in majesty,
marching in the greatness of his
strength?
"It is I, I who announce vindication,
I who am mighty to save."

2 Why is your apparel red,
and your garments like those of the
wine presser? *v*

3 "The wine press I have trodden alone,
and of my people there was no one
with me.
I trod them in my anger,
and trampled them down in my
wrath;
Their blood spurted on my garments;
all my apparel I stained.

4 For the day of vengeance was in my
heart,
my year for redeeming was at hand. *w*

5 I looked about, but there was no one to
help,
I was appalled that there was no one
to lend support;
So my own arm brought about the victory
and my own wrath lent me its support. *x*

6 I trampled down the peoples in my
anger,
I crushed them in my wrath,

and I let their blood run out upon the
ground."

Prayer for the Return
of God's Favor*

7 The favors of the LORD I will recall,
the glorious deeds of the LORD,
Because of all he has done for us;
for he is good to the house of Israel,
He has favored us according to his
mercy
and his great kindness. *y*

8 He said: They are indeed my people,
children who are not disloyal;
So he became their savior
9   in their every affliction.
It was not a messenger or an angel,
but he himself who saved them.
Because of his love and pity
he redeemed them himself,
Lifting them and carrying them
all the days of old. *z*

10 But they rebelled, and grieved
his holy spirit;
So he turned on them like an enemy,
and fought against them.

11 Then they remembered the days of old
and Moses, his servant;
Where is he who brought up out of the
sea
the shepherd of his flock?
Where is he who put his holy spirit
in their midst;

12 Whose glorious arm
was the guide at Moses' right;
Who divided the waters before them,
winning for himself eternal renown;

13 Who led them without stumbling
through the depths
like horses in the open country,

14 Like cattle going down into the plain,
the spirit of the LORD guiding them?
Thus you led your people,
bringing glory to your name.

---

r Dt 12, 17f; 14, 23.—s Is 58, 14.—t Is 40, 10.—u Is 62, 4.—v
Rv 19, 13.—w Is 34, 8; 61, 2.—x Is 59, 16.—y Is 26, 15.—z Dt
4, 37f.

62, 10: The command is given to the workmen to begin the reconstruction of the city.
63, 1-6: In a dramatic dialogue between God and the prophet,
the Lord is portrayed as the sole avenger of justice against his
enemies.
63, 7—64, 11: A prayer probably composed toward the end
of the exile, in which the prophet, after recalling God's blessings
on Israel in its past history (63, 7-10), especially at the Exodus
(11-14), begs the Lord to come once more to the aid of his people
(63, 15—64, 3), who now humbly confess their sins (4-11).

15 Look down from heaven and regard us
from your holy and glorious palace!
Where is your zealous care and your
might,
your surge of pity and your mercy?[a]
O Lord, hold not back,
16 for you are our father.
Were Abraham not to know us,
nor Israel to acknowledge us,
You, LORD, are our father,
our redeemer you are named forever.
17 Why do you let us wander, O LORD,
from your ways,
and harden our hearts so that we fear
you not?
Return for the sake of your servants,
the tribes of your heritage.
18 Why have the wicked invaded your holy
place,
why have our enemies trampled your
sanctuary?
19 Too long have we been like those you
do not rule,
who do not bear your name.

Oh, that you would rend the heavens
and come down,
with the mountains quaking before
you,

CHAPTER 64

1 As when brushwood is set ablaze,
or fire makes the water boil!
Thus your name would be made known
to your enemies
and the nations would tremble before
you,
2 While you wrought awesome deeds we
could not hope for,
3 such as they had not heard of from of
old.
No ear has ever heard, no eye ever seen,
any God but you
doing such deeds for those who wait
for him.[b]

4 Would that you might meet us doing
right,
that we were mindful of you in our
ways!
Behold, you are angry, and we are sinful;

5 all of us have become like unclean
men,
all our good deeds are like polluted
rags;
We have all withered like leaves,
and our guilt carries us away like the
wind.
6 There is none who calls upon your
name,
who rouses himself to cling to you;
For you have hidden your face from us
and have delivered us up to our guilt.
7 Yet, O LORD, you are our father;
we are the clay and you the potter:
we are all the work of your hands.
8 Be not so very angry, LORD,
keep not our guilt forever in mind;
look upon us, who are all your people.
9 Your holy cities have become a desert,
Zion is a desert, Jerusalem a waste.[c]
10 Our holy and glorious temple
in which our fathers praised you
Has been burned with fire;
all that was dear to us is laid waste.
11 Can you hold back, O LORD, after all
this?
Can you remain silent, and afflict us
so severely?

CHAPTER 65

Necessity of Punishment

1 I was ready to respond to those who
asked me not,
to be found by those who sought me
not.
I said: Here I am! Here I am!
To a nation that did not call upon my
name.[d]

2 I have stretched out my hands all the
day
to a rebellious people,
Who walk in evil paths
and follow their own thoughts,[e]
3 People who provoke me
continually, to my face,
Offering sacrifices in the groves
and burning incense on bricks,
4 Living among the graves
and spending the night in caverns,
Eating swine's flesh,
with carrion broth in their dishes,
5 Crying out, "Hold back,

Is

a Dt 26, 15; Bar 2, 16.—b 1 Cor 2, 9.—c Ps 79, 1.—d Rom 10,
20.—e Rom 10, 21.

do not touch me; I am too sacred for
you!"*

These things enkindle my wrath,
fire that burns all the day.
6 Lo, before me it stands written;
I will not be quiet until I have paid in
full
7 Your crimes and the crimes of your
fathers as well,
says the LORD.
Since they burned incense on the mountains,
and disgraced me on the hills,
I will at once pour out in full measure
their recompense into their laps.

Fate of the Good and the Bad in Israel

8 Thus says the LORD:
When the juice is pressed from grapes,
men say, "Do not discard them,
for there is still good in them";
Thus will I do with my servants:
I will not discard them all;
9 From Jacob I will save offspring,
from Judah, those who are to inherit
my mountains;
My chosen ones shall inherit the land,
my servants shall dwell there.
10 Sharon shall be a pasture for the flocks
and the valley of Achor a resting
place for the cattle
of my people who have sought me.

11 But you who forsake the LORD,
forgetting my holy mountain,
You who spread a table for Fortune
and fill cups of blended wine for Destiny,*
12 You I will destine for the sword;
you shall all go down in slaughter.
Since I called and you did not answer,
I spoke and you did not listen,
But did what was evil in my sight
and preferred things which displease
me,*f*
13 therefore thus says the Lord GOD:
Lo, my servants shall eat,
but you shall go hungry;
My servants shall drink,
but you shall be thirsty;
My servants shall rejoice,
but you shall be put to shame;
14 My servants shall shout
for joy of heart,
But you shall cry out for grief of heart

and howl for anguish of spirit.
15 The Lord GOD shall slay you,
and the name you leave
Shall be used by my chosen ones for
cursing;
but my servants shall be called by another name
16 By which he will be blessed
on whom a blessing is invoked in the
land;
He who takes an oath in the land
shall swear by the God of truth;
For the hardships of the past shall be
forgotten,
and hidden from my eyes.

The World Renewed

17 Lo, I am about to create new heavens
and a new earth;
The things of the past shall not be remembered
or come to mind.*g*
18 Instead, there shall always be rejoicing
and happiness
in what I create;
For I create Jerusalem to be a joy
and its people to be a delight;
19 I will rejoice in Jerusalem
and exult in my people.
No longer shall the sound of weeping be
heard there,
or the sound of crying;
20 No longer shall there be in it
an infant who lives but a few days,
or an old man who does not round
out his full lifetime;
He dies a mere youth who reaches but a
hundred years,
and he who fails of a hundred shall be
thought accursed.

21 They shall live in the houses they build,
and eat the fruit of the vineyards they
plant;
22 They shall not build houses for others
to live in,
or plant for others to eat.
As the years of a tree, so the years of my
people;
and my chosen ones shall long enjoy

---

f Is 66, 4; Prv 1, 24; Jer 7, 13.—g Is 66, 22; Rv 21, 1.

65, 5: *I am too sacred for you:* the uncleanness of pork, obvious to a Semite, is what these people claim has made them sacred! The prophet ridicules them. Some translate: "I will render
you sacred," and understand this as referring to the concept of
sacredness as something contagious.
65, 11f: *Destiny:* the Hebrew also has a play on the words:
Destiny and *destine; meni* and *manithi.*

the produce of their hands.

23 They shall not toil in vain,
nor beget children for sudden destruction;
For a race blessed by the LORD
are they and their offspring.

24 Before they call, I will answer;
while they are yet speaking, I will
hearken to them.

25 The wolf and the lamb shall graze alike,
and the lion shall eat hay like the ox
[but the serpent's food shall be
dust].*h*
None shall hurt or destroy
on all my holy mountain, says the
LORD.*

CHAPTER 66

True and False Worship

1   Thus says the LORD:
The heavens are my throne,
the earth is my footstool.
What kind of house can you build for
me;
what is to be my resting place?*i*

2 My hand made all these things
when all of them came to be, says the
LORD.
This is the one whom I approve:
the lowly and afflicted man who
trembles at my word.

3 Merely slaughtering an ox is like slaying
a man;
sacrificing a lamb, like breaking a
dog's neck;
Bringing a cereal offering, like offering
swine's blood;
burning incense, like paying homage
to an idol.
Since these have chosen their own ways
and taken pleasure in their own
abominations,*j*

4 I in turn will choose ruthless treatment
for them*
and bring upon them what they fear.
Because, when I called, no one answered,
when I spoke, no one listened;

Because they did what was evil in my
sight,
and chose what gave me displeasure,*k*

5 Hear the word of the LORD,
you who tremble at his word:
Your brethren who, because of my
name,
hate and reject you, say,
"Let the LORD show his glory
that we may see your joy";
but they shall be put to shame.

6 A sound of roaring from the city,
a sound from the temple,
The sound of the LORD
repaying his enemies their deserts!*l*

Mother Zion

7 Before she comes to labor,*
she gives birth;*m*
Before the pains come upon her,
she safely delivers a male child.

8 Who ever heard of such a thing,
or saw the like?
Can a country be brought forth in one
day,
or a nation be born in a single moment?
Yet Zion is scarcely in labor
when she gives birth to her children.

9 Shall I bring a mother to the point of
birth,
and yet not let her child be born? says
the LORD;
Or shall I who allow her to conceive,
yet close her womb? says your God.

10 Rejoice with Jerusalem and be glad because of her,
all you who love her;
Exult, exult with her,
all you who were mourning over her!

11 Oh, that you may suck fully
of the milk of her comfort,
That you may nurse with delight
at her abundant breasts!

12   For thus says the LORD:
Lo, I will spread prosperity over her
like a river,
and the wealth of the nations like an
overflowing torrent.
As nurslings, you shall be carried in her
arms,
and fondled in her lap;

13 As a mother comforts her son,

Is

---

h Is 11, 6-9.—i 2 Sm 7, 4ff; 1 Kgs 8, 27; Acts 7, 49; 17, 24.—j
Lv 11, 7.—k Is 65, 12; Prv 1, 24; Jer 7, 13.—l Jl 4, 16; Am 1,
2.—m 7-9: Is 49, 18-21; 54, 1.

65, 25: See note on Is 11, 6-9.
66, 4f: Worship which is merely external is as evil as though
it were idolatry.
66, 7-9: The absence of labor in Zion's childbearing is a symbol of the joyful begetting of the new people of God.

so will I comfort you;
in Jerusalem you shall find your comfort.

14 When you see this, your heart shall rejoice,
and your bodies flourish like the grass;
The LORD's power shall be known to his servants,
but to his enemies, his wrath.

15 Lo, the LORD shall come in fire,
his chariots like the whirlwind,
To wreak his wrath with burning heat
and his punishment with fiery flames.

16 For the LORD shall judge all mankind
by fire and sword,
and many shall be slain by the LORD.

17 They who sanctify and purify themselves to go to the groves, as followers of one who stands within, they who eat swine's flesh, loathsome things and mice, shall all perish with their deeds and their thoughts, says the LORD.[n]

Gathering of the Nations. 18 I come to gather nations of every language; they shall come and see my glory.* 19 I will set a sign among them; from them I will send fugitives to the nations: to Tarshish, Put and Lud, Mosoch, Tubal and Javan, to the distant coastlands that have never heard of my fame, or seen my glory; and they shall proclaim my glory among the nations.

20 They shall bring all your brethren from all the nations as an offering to the LORD, on horses and in chariots, in carts, upon mules and dromedaries, to Jerusalem, my holy mountain, says the LORD, just as the Israelites bring their offering to the house of the LORD in clean vessels. 21 Some of these I will take as priests and Levites, says the LORD.

Lasting Reward and Punishment

22 As the new heavens and the new earth which I will make
Shall endure before me, says the LORD,
so shall your race and your name endure.[o]

23 From one new moon to another,
and from one sabbath to another,
All mankind shall come to worship before me, says the LORD.

24 They shall go out and see the corpses[p]
of the men who rebelled against me;
Their worm shall not die,
nor their fire be extinguished;
and they shall be abhorrent to all mankind.*

n Lv 11, 29.—o Is 65, 17; Rv 21, 1.—p Mk 9, 45.

66, 18-21: God summons the neighboring nations to Zion and from among them will send some to far distant lands to proclaim his glory. *All your brethren:* Jews in exile.
66, 24: God's enemies lie dead outside the walls of the New Jerusalem; just as in the past, corpses, filth and refuse lay in the Valley of Hinnom outside the city, where huge fires were constantly burning; cf Jos 15, 8; 2 Chr 28, 3; Mk 9, 45-48.

THE BOOK OF JEREMIAH

The Book of Jeremiah combines history, biography, and prophecy. It portrays a nation in crisis and introduces the reader to an extraordinary leader upon whom the Lord placed the heavy burden of the prophetic office. Jeremiah was born about 650 B.C. of a priestly family from the little village of Anathoth, near Jerusalem. While still very young he was called to his task in the thirteenth year of King Josiah (628), whose reform, begun with enthusiasm and hope, ended with his death on the battlefield of Megiddo (609) as he attempted to stop the northward march of the Egyptian Pharaoh Neco.

The prophet heartily supported the reform of the pious King Josiah, which began in 629 B.C. Nineveh, the capital of Assyria, fell in 612, preparing the way for the new colossus, Babylon, which was soon to put an end to Judean independence.

After the death of Josiah the old idolatry returned. Jeremiah opposed it with all his strength. Arrest, imprisonment, and public disgrace were his lot. Jeremiah saw in the nation's impenitence the sealing of its doom. Nebuchadnezzar captured Jerusalem and carried King Jehoiachin into exile (22, 24).

During the years 598-587, Jeremiah attempted to counsel Zedekiah in the face of bitter opposition. The false prophet Hananiah proclaimed that the yoke of Babylon was broken and a strong pro-Egyptian party in Jerusalem induced Zedekiah to revolt. Nebuchadnezzar took swift and terrible vengeance; Jerusalem was destroyed in 587 and its leading citizens sent into exile. About this time Jeremiah uttered the great oracle of the "New Covenant" (31, 31-34) sometimes called "The Gospel before the Gospel." This passage contains his most sublime teaching and is a landmark in Old Testament theology.

The prophet remained amidst the ruins of Jerusalem, but was later forced into Egyptian exile by a band of conspirators. There, according to an old tradition, he was murdered by his own countrymen. The influence of Jeremiah was greater after his death than before. The exiled community read and meditated the lessons of the prophet, and his influence can be seen in Ezekiel, certain of the psalms, and the second part of Isaiah. Shortly after the exile, the Book of Jeremiah as we have it today was published in a final edition. It is divided as follows: I. Oracles in the Days of Josiah (1, 1—6, 30). II. Oracles Mostly in the Days of Jehoiakim (7, 1—20, 18). III. Oracles in the Last Years of Jerusalem (21, 1—33, 26). IV. Fall of Jerusalem (34, 1—45, 5). V. Oracles against the Nations (46, 1—51, 64). VI. Historical Appendix (52, 1-34).

I: ORACLES IN THE DAYS OF JOSIAH

CHAPTER 1

¹ The words of Jeremiah, son of Hilkiah, of a priestly family in Anathoth,* in the land of Benjamin. ² The word of the LORD first came to him in the days of Josiah, son of Amon, king of Judah, in the thirteenth year of his reign,ᵃ ³ and continued through the reign of Jehoiakim, son of Josiah, king of Judah, and until the downfall* and exile of Jerusalem in the fifth month of the eleventh year of Zedekiah, son of Josiah, king of Judah.ᵇ

Call of Jeremiah

⁴ The word of the LORD came to me thus:

a Jer 25, 3.—b Jer 25, 1.—c Jer 49, 1; Gal 1, 15f.—d Is 6, 7.—e Ez 11, 3. 7; 24, 3.

1, 1: *Anathoth:* a village about three miles northeast of Jerusalem, where Solomon exiled Abiathar (1 Kgs 2, 26f); it is probable that Jeremiah belonged to the *priestly family* of Abiathar.

1, 3: *Until the downfall:* these words were originally prefixed as a title to a collection of Jeremiah's prophecies which lacked chapters 40-44. The new title in Jer 40, 1 and the oracles that follow clearly show that Jeremiah continued to prophesy after the destruction of Jerusalem in 587 B.C.

1, 5: Jeremiah was destined to the office of prophet before his birth; cf Is 49, 1. 5; Lk 1, 15; Gal 1, 15f. *I knew you:* I loved you and chose you. *I dedicated you:* I set you apart to be a prophet. Some Fathers and later theologians understand this to mean that Jeremiah was freed from original sin before his birth. The context does not justify this conclusion. *The nations:* the pagan neighbors of Judah, besides the great world powers—Assyria, Babylonia, Egypt—intimately associated with Judah's destiny.

1, 6: *I am too young:* Jeremiah's youth (he was less than thirty years old) must not be an obstacle to the responsibilities of the prophetic office; God will supply for his human defects (cf vv 7f).

1, 11: *The watching-tree:* the almond tree, which is the first to blossom in the springtime as though it had not slept. The Hebrew name contains a play on words with "I am watching."

1, 13: *Boiling cauldron . . . the north:* symbol of an invasion from the north; cf vv 14f.

⁵ Before I formed you in the womb I
knew you.*
before you were born I dedicated
you,
a prophet to the nations I appointed
you.ᶜ

⁶ "Ah, Lord GOD!" I said,
"I know not how to speak; I am too
young."*

⁷ But the LORD answered me,

Say not, "I am too young."
To whomever I send you, you shall
go;
whatever I command you, you shall
speak.

⁸ Have no fear before them,
because I am with you to deliver you,
says the LORD.

⁹ Then the LORD extended his hand and touched my mouth, saying,

See, I place my words in your mouth!ᵈ
¹⁰   This day I set you
over nations and over kingdoms,
To root up and to tear down,
to destroy and to demolish,
to build and to plant.

¹¹ The word of the LORD came to me with the question: What do you see, Jeremiah? "I see a branch of the watching-tree,"* I replied. ¹² Then the LORD said to me: Well have you seen, for I am watching to fulfill my word. ¹³ ᵉ A second time the word of the LORD came to me with the question: What do you see? "I see a boiling cauldron," I replied, "that appears from the north."*

¹⁴ And from the north, said the LORD to

Jer

me, evil will boil over upon all who dwell in the land.*f*

15 Lo, I am summoning
   all the kingdoms of the north, says the LORD;
   Each king shall come and set up his throne
   at the gateways of Jerusalem,
   Opposite her walls all around
   and opposite all the cities of Judah.*g*
16 I will pronounce my sentence against them
   for all their wickedness in forsaking me,
   And in burning incense to strange gods
   and adoring their own handiwork.*h*

17 But do you gird your loins;
   stand up and tell them
   all that I command you.
   Be not crushed on their account,
   as though I would leave you crushed before them;
18 For it is I this day
   who have made you a fortified city,
   A pillar of iron, a wall of brass,
   against the whole land:
   Against Judah's kings and princes,
   against its priests and people.*i*
19 They will fight against you, but not prevail over you,
   for I am with you to deliver you, says the LORD.

CHAPTER 2

Infidelity of Israel. * ¹This word of the LORD came to me: ²Go, cry out this message for Jerusalem to hear!

   I remember the devotion* of your youth,
   how you loved me as a bride,
   Following me in the desert,
   in a land unsown.*j*
3 Sacred to the LORD was Israel,
   the first fruits* of his harvest;
   Should anyone presume to partake of them,
   evil would befall him, says the LORD.*k*

4 Listen to the word of the LORD, O house of Jacob!
   All you clans of the house of Israel,
5   thus says the LORD:
   What fault did your fathers find in me
   that they withdrew from me,

   Went after empty idols,
   and became empty themselves?*l*
6 They did not ask, "Where is the LORD
   who brought us up from the land of Egypt,
   Who led us through the desert,
   through a land of wastes and gullies,
   Through a land of drought and darkness,
   through a land which no one crosses,
   where no man dwells?"*m*

7 When I brought you into the garden land
   to eat its goodly fruits,
   You entered and defiled my land,
   you made my heritage loathsome.*n*
8 The priests asked not,
   "Where is the LORD?"
   Those who dealt with the law* knew me not:
   the shepherds rebelled against me.
   The prophets prophesied by Baal,
   and went after useless idols.*o*
9 Therefore will I yet accuse you, says the LORD,
   and even your children's children I will accuse.*p*
10 Pass over to the coast of the Kittim* and see,
   send to Kedar and carefully inquire:
   Where has the like of this been done?
11 Does any other nation change its gods?—
   yet they are not gods at all!
   But my people have changed their glory for useless things.*q*
12 Be amazed at this, O heavens,
   and shudder with sheer horror, says the LORD.
13 Two evils have my people done:

---

f Jer 4, 6; 6, 1.—g Jer 6, 22.—h Is 2, 8.—i Jer 6, 27; 15, 20; Ez 3, 8.—j Dt 2, 7; 32, 9-12; Mi 6, 4.—k Jer 12, 14; Ex 4, 22; Dt 7, 6; 14, 2.—l Is 5, 4; Mi 6, 3.—m Ex 20, 2f; Dt 8, 14; Is 63, 11ff.—n Lv 18, 24f; Dt 8, 7-10; 32, 13f.—o Jer 8, 8ff; 23, 1. 13.—p Ex 20, 5.—q Jer 16, 20; Ps 106, 20.

2, 1—3, 5: These verses probably contain the earliest of Jeremiah's preachings. The covenant relationship, symbolized by the figure of a marriage, was frequently broken by Israel, seen here as an unfaithful wife unworthy of reconciliation with God (Jer 3, 1-5).
2, 2: *Devotion:* Israel's gratitude, fidelity, and love for God.
2, 3: *First fruits:* an offering to God which became his exclusive property, and could therefore not be put to profane use; cf Lv 22, 1.
2, 8: *Those who dealt with the law:* the priests. *The shepherds:* the kings and nobles.
2, 10: *Kittim:* a Phoenician colony in Cyprus. *Kedar:* a nomad tribe of the Syrian desert. These two names represent West and East.

they have forsaken me, the source of
   living waters;
They have dug themselves cisterns,
   broken cisterns, that hold no water.[r]

14 Is Israel a slave, a bondman by birth?*
   Why then has he become booty?
15 Against him lions roar
   full-throated cries.
They have made his land a waste;
   his cities are charred ruins, without
   inhabitant.[s]
16 Yes, the people of Memphis* and
   Tahpanhes
shave the crown of your head.
17 Has not the forsaking of the LORD,
   your God,
done this to you?[t]
18 And now, why go to Egypt,*
   to drink the waters of the Nile?
Why go to Assyria,
   to drink the waters of the Euphrates?
19 Your own wickedness chastises you,
   your own infidelities punish you.
Know then, and see, how evil and bitter
   is your forsaking the LORD, your
   God,
And showing no fear of me,
   says the Lord, the GOD of hosts.[u]

20 Long ago you broke your yoke,[v]
   you tore off your bonds.
"I will not serve," you said.
On every high hill, under every green
   tree,
   you gave yourself to harlotry.*
21 I had planted you, a choice vine
   of fully tested stock;
How could you turn out obnoxious to
   me,
   a spurious vine?[w]

---

r Jer 17, 13; Ps 36, 9; Is 1, 4.—s Jer 9, 11.—t Jer 4, 18; 30,
15.—u Prv 5, 22; Hos 5, 5.—v Jer 3, 6. 13; Jgs 10, 6.—w Ex 15,
17; Ps 80, 9; Is 5, 4.—x Jb 9, 30.—y Jer 18, 12.— z Jer 48, 27;
Rom 6, 21.—a Jer 11, 13; Dt 32, 38; Jgs 10, 14.—b Jer 5, 3;
Neh 9, 26.

2, 14: *Bondman by birth:* a perpetual slave, different from
the debt-slave, who was to be freed after six years; cf Ex 21, 2.
2, 16: *Memphis:* the capital of Lower Egypt. *Tahpanhes:* a
frontier city of Egypt, east of the Delta. *Shave the crown of
your head:* the spoliation of Judah at the hands of the Egyptians.
2, 18: *Egypt* and *Assyria* were the protecting foreign powers
favored by rival parties within Judah. The desire for such foreign
alliances is a further desertion of the Lord, *the source of living
waters* (v 13), in favor of the above-named powers, symbolized
by *the Nile* and *the Euphrates* rivers.
2, 20: *Harlotry:* idolatry (because Israel is the bride of God).
2, 23: *The Valley:* of Ben-hinnom, south of Jerusalem, site of
the infamous sanctuary of Topheth where children were sacrificed to Molech; cf Jer 7, 31.

22 Though you scour it with soap,
   and use much lye,
The stain of your guilt is still before
   me,
   says the Lord GOD.[x]
23 How can you say, "I am not defiled,
   I have not gone after the Baals"?
Consider your conduct in the Valley,*
   recall what you have done:
A frenzied she-camel, coursing near and
   far,
24   breaking away toward the desert,
Snuffing the wind in her ardor—
   who can restrain her lust?
No beasts need tire themselves seeking
   her;
   in her month they will meet her.

25 Stop wearing out your shoes
   and parching your throat!
But you say, "No use! no!
   I love these strangers,
   and after them I must go."[y]
26 As the thief is shamed when caught,
   so shall the house of Israel be
   shamed:
They, their kings and their princes,
   their priests and their prophets;[z]
27 They who say to a piece of wood, "You
   are my father,"
and to a stone, "You gave me birth."
They turn to me their backs, not their
   faces;
   yet, in their time of trouble they cry
   out,
   "Rise up and save us!"
28 Where are the gods you made for yourselves?
   Let them rise up!
Will they save you in your time of
   trouble?
For as numerous as your cities
   are your gods, O Judah!
And as many as the streets of Jerusalem
are the altars you have set up for
   Baal.[a]

29 How dare you still plead with me?
   You have all rebelled against me, says
   the LORD.
30 In vain I struck your children;
   the correction they did not take.
Your sword devoured your prophets
   like a ravening lion.[b]
31 You, of this generation,
   take note of the word of the Lord:
Have I been a desert to Israel,

a land of darkness?
Why do my people say, "We have
moved on,
we will come to you no more"?
³² Does a virgin forget her jewelry,
a bride her sash?
Yet my people have forgotten me
days without number.*c*

³³ How well you pick your way
when seeking love!
You who, in your wickedness,
have gone by ways unclean!
³⁴ You, on whose clothing there is
the life-blood of the innocent,
whom you found committing no
burglary;
³⁵ Yet withal you say, "I am innocent;
at least, his anger is turned away from
me."
Behold, I will judge you
on that word of yours, "I have not
sinned."
³⁶ How very base you have become
in changing your course!
By Egypt will you be shamed,
as you were shamed by Assyria.*d*
³⁷ From there also shall you go away
with hands upon your head;
For the LORD has rejected those in
whom you trust,
with them you will have no success.*e*

CHAPTER 3

¹ If a man sends away his wife*f*
and, after leaving him,
she marries another man,
Does the first husband come back to
her?
Would not the land be wholly defiled?
But you have sinned with many lovers,
and yet you would return to me! says
the LORD.*

² Lift your eyes to the heights, and see,
where have men not lain with you?
By the waysides you waited for them
like an Arab* in the desert.
You defiled the land
by your wicked harlotry.*g*
³ Therefore the showers were withheld,
the spring rain failed.
But because you have a harlot's brow,
you refused to blush.*h*
⁴ Even now do you not call me, "My
father,

you who are the bridegroom of my
youth"?
⁵ "Will he keep his wrath forever,
will he hold his grudge to the end?"
This is what you say; yet you do
all the evil you can.

Judah and Israel. ⁶ The LORD said to me
in the days of King Josiah: See now what
rebellious Israel has done! She has gone up
every high mountain, and under every
green tree she has played the harlot.*i* ⁷ And
I thought, after she has done all this she
will return to me. But she did not return.
Then, even though her traitor sister Judah
saw ⁸ that for all the adulteries rebellious
Israel had committed, I put her away and
gave her a bill of divorce, nevertheless her
traitor sister Judah was not frightened; she
too went off and played the harlot.*j* ⁹ Eager
to sin, she polluted the land, committing
adultery with stone and wood.*k* ¹⁰ With all
this, the traitor sister Judah did not return
to me wholeheartedly, but insincerely,
says the LORD.

Restoration of Israel. ¹¹ Then the LORD
said to me: Rebel Israel is inwardly more
just than traitorous Judah.*l* ¹² Go, proclaim
these words toward the north, and say:

Return, rebel Israel, says the LORD,
I will not remain angry with you;
For I am merciful, says the LORD,
I will not continue my wrath forever.*m*
¹³ Only know your guilt:
how you rebelled against the LORD,
your God,
How you ran hither and yon to strangers
[under every green tree]
and would not listen to my voice, says
the LORD.*n*
¹⁴ Return, rebellious children, says the
LORD,*

---

c Jer 13, 25; Dt 32, 18.—d 2 Chr 28, 16-21.—e 2 Sm 13,
19.—f Dt 24, 1-4.—g Ex 16, 24f.—h Jer 6, 15; 8, 12.—i Jer 2,
20; Dt 12, 2.—j 2 Kgs 17, 6. 18-23; Ez 23, 11.—k Jer 2, 27.—l
Ez 16, 51; 23, 11.—m Dt 4, 29ff.—n Jer 2, 20. 25; Lv 26, 40.—

3, 1: Such remarriage of divorced spouses was forbidden by Dt
24, 1-4. Under this figure the prophet sees the presumption of
Judah, the unfaithful spouse, who thinks she can return to the
Lord after uniting herself to other gods.
3, 2: *An Arab:* a marauding nomad who lay in wait for caravans.
3, 14-18: A remnant of Israel (14) will reunite with Judah
(18). The elementary cult of the Lord represented by *the ark of
the covenant* will now be replaced by a more deeply spiritual
and universal alliance, symbolized by his throne in the ideal Jerusalem around which *all nations will be gathered together*
(17).

for I am your Master;
I will take you, one from a city, two
  from a clan,
and bring you to Zion. [o]

15 I will appoint over you shepherds after
  my own heart,
who will shepherd you wisely and
  prudently. [p]

16 When you multiply and become fruitful
  in the land,
says the LORD,
They will in those days no longer say,
"The ark of the covenant of the
  LORD!"
They will no longer think of it, or remember it,
or miss it, or make another.

17 At that time they will call Jerusalem
the LORD's throne; there all nations will be
gathered together to honor the name of the
LORD at Jerusalem, and they will walk no
longer in their hardhearted wickedness. [q]
18 In those days the house of Judah will
join the house of Israel; together they will
come from the land of the north to the
land which I gave to your fathers as a
heritage. [r]

Conditions for Forgiveness

19 I had thought:
How I should like to treat you as
  sons,
And give you a pleasant land,
a heritage most beautiful among the
  nations!
You would call me, "My Father," I
  thought,
and never cease following me. [s]

20 But like a woman faithless to her lover,
even so have you been faithless to me,
O house of Israel, says the LORD. [t]

21 A cry is heard on the heights!

---

o Jer 23, 3; Is 10, 21f.—p Ez 34, 23; Jn 21, 15.—q Is 2, 2.—r
Jer 30, 3; 31, 8.—s Jer 31, 9. 20; Is 63, 16.—t Jer 5, 11.—u
Hos 3, 5.—v Jer 14, 8.—w Jer 16, 11f; 22, 21.—x Jer 25, 5.—y
Jer 12, 16; Dt 10, 20; Is 65, 16.—z Hos 10, 12; Mt 13, 7. 22.—a
Jer 9, 24.

3, 24: *Shame-god:* literally, shame, a term commonly substituted for Baal, the Canaanite god with many local shrines.

4, 2: *As the Lord lives:* this oath, made sincerely, implies Israel's return to God and loyal adherence to him. Thus the ancient
promises are fulfilled; cf Gn 12, 3; 18, 18; 22, 18; 26, 4; Ps 72,
17.

4, 4: The mere external rite of circumcision avails nothing unless accompanied by the removal of blindness and obstinacy of
heart; cf Rom 2, 25. 29; 1 Cor 7, 19; Gal 5, 6; 6, 13. 15.

the plaintive weeping of Israel's children,
Because they have perverted their ways
and forgotten the LORD, their God.

22 Return, rebellious children,
and I will cure you of your rebelling.
"Here we are, we now come to you
because you are the LORD, our God. [u]

23 Deceptive indeed are the hills,
the thronging mountains;
In the LORD, our God, alone
is the salvation of Israel. [v]

24 The shame-god* has devoured
our fathers' toil from our youth,
Their sheep and their cattle,
their sons and their daughters.

25 Let us lie down in our shame,
let our disgrace cover us,
for we have sinned against the LORD,
  our God,
From our youth to this day, we and our
  fathers also;
we listened not to the voice of the
LORD, our God." [w]

CHAPTER 4

1 If you wish to return, O Israel, says the
  LORD,
return to me.
If you put your detestable things out of
  my sight,
and do not stray, [x]

2 Then you can swear, "As the LORD
  lives,"*
in truth, in judgment, and in justice;
Then shall the nations use his name in
  blessing,
and glory in him. [y]

3 For to the men of Judah and of Jerusalem, thus says the LORD:

Till your untilled ground,
sow not among thorns. [z]

4 For the sake of the LORD, be circumcised,*
remove the foreskins of your hearts,
O men of Judah and citizens of Jerusalem;
Lest my anger break out like fire,
and burn till none can quench it,
because of your evil deeds. [a]

The Invasion from the North

5 Proclaim it in Judah,
make it heard in Jerusalem;

Blow the trumpet through the land,
  summon the recruits!
Say, "Fall in, let us march
  to the fortified cities."
6 Bear the standard to Zion,
  seek refuge without delay!
Evil I bring from the north,
  and great destruction.
7 Up comes the lion from his lair,
  the destroyer of nations has set out,
  has left his place,
To turn your land into desolation,
  till your cities lie waste and empty. *b*
8 So gird yourselves with sackcloth,
  mourn and wail:
"The blazing wrath of the LORD
  is not turned away from us." *c*

9   In that day, says the LORD,
The king will lose heart, and the
  princes;
  the priests will be amazed,
  and the prophets stunned.
10 "Alas! Lord GOD," they will say,
  "you only deceived us*
When you said: Peace shall be yours;
  for the sword touches our very
  soul." *d*
11 At that time it will be said
  of this people and of Jerusalem,
"From the glaring heights through the
  desert
  a wind comes toward the daughter of
  my people."
  Not to winnow, not to cleanse,
12   does this wind from the heights come
  at my bidding;
And I myself now pronounce
  sentence upon them. *e*

13 See! like storm clouds he advances,
  like a hurricane his chariots;
Swifter than eagles are his steeds:
  "Woe to us! we are ruined."
14 Cleanse your heart of evil, O Jerusalem,
  that you may be saved.
How long must your pernicious
  thoughts
  lodge within you?
15 Listen! They proclaim it from Dan,
  from Mount Ephraim they announce
  destruction:
16 "Make this known to the nations,
  announce it to Jerusalem:
The besiegers are coming from the distant land,

  shouting their war cry against the
  cities of Judah." *f*
17 Like watchmen of the fields they surround her,
  for she has rebelled against me, says
  the LORD. *g*
18 Your conduct, your misdeeds, have
  done this to you;
how bitter is this disaster of yours,
how it reaches to your very heart! *h*

19 My breast! my breast! how I suffer!*
  The walls of my heart!
My heart beats wildly,
  I cannot be still;
For I have heard the sound of the trumpet,
  the alarm of war.
20 Ruin after ruin is reported;
  the whole earth is laid waste.
In an instant my tents are ravaged;
  in a flash, my shelters. *i*
21 How long must I see that signal,
  hear that trumpet sound!

22 Fools my people are,
  they know me not;
Senseless children they are,
  having no understanding;
They are wise in evil,
  but know not how to do good. *j*
23 I looked at the earth, and it was waste
  and void;
  at the heavens, and their light had
  gone out! *k*
24 I looked at the mountains, and they
  were trembling,
  and all the hills were crumbling!
25 I looked and behold, there was no man;
  even the birds of the air had flown
  away!
26 I looked and behold, the garden land
  was a desert,
  with all its cities destroyed
  before the LORD, before his blazing
  wrath. *l*

27   For thus says the LORD:
Waste shall the whole land be;
  I will [not] wholly destroy it. *m*
28 Because of this the earth shall mourn,
  the heavens above shall darken;

---

b Jer 2, 15; 5, 6.—c Jer 6, 26; Is 5, 25.—d Jer 6, 14.—e Jer
1, 16.—f Jer 5, 15.—g Jer 6, 3.—h Jer 2, 17. 19.—i Jer 10,
20.—j Dt 32, 5f. 28.—k Is 24, 1. 3.—l Lv 26, 31.—m Jer 5, 18.

4, 10; *You only deceived us:* the false prophets blame their
deception on God; cf Jer 14, 13-16.
4, 19ff: Probably the prophet's own anguish at the coming destruction of Judah.

I have spoken, I will not repent,
  I have resolved, I will not turn back.[n]
29 At the shout of horseman and bowman
    each city takes to flight;
  They shrink into the thickets,
    they scale the rocks:
  All the cities are abandoned,
    and no one dwells in them.
30 You now who are doomed, what do you
    mean
  by putting on purple,
    bedecking yourself with gold,
  Shading your eyes with cosmetics,
    beautifying yourself in vain?
  Your lovers spurn you,
    they seek your life.
31 Yes, I hear the moaning, as of a woman
    in travail,
  like the anguish of a mother with her
    first child—
  The cry of daughter Zion gasping,
    as she stretches forth her hands:
  "Ah, woe is me! I sink exhausted
    before the slayers!"[o]

CHAPTER 5

Universal Corruption

1 Roam the streets of Jerusalem,
    look about and observe,
  Search through her public places,
    to find even one
  Who lives uprightly
    and seeks to be faithful,
    and I will pardon her!
2 Though they say, "As the LORD lives,"
    they swear falsely.
3   O LORD, do your eyes not look for
    honesty?
  You struck them, but they did not
    cringe;
    you laid them low, but they refused
    correction;
  They set their faces harder than stone,
    and refused to return to you.[p]
4 It is only the lowly, I thought,
    who are foolish;
  For they know not the way of the
    LORD,
    their duty to their God.[q]
5 I will go to the great ones
    and speak with them;

For they know the way of the LORD,
    their duty to their God.
But, one and all, they had broken the
    yoke,[r]
  torn off the harness.[r]
6 Therefore lions from the forest slay
    them,
  wolves of the desert ravage them,
  Leopards keep watch round their cities:
    all who come out are torn to pieces
  For their many crimes
    and their numerous rebellions.

7 Why should I pardon you these things?
  Your sons have forsaken me,
    they swear by gods that are not.
  I fed them, but they committed adul-
    tery;
    to the harlot's house they throng.
8 Lustful stallions they are,
    each neighs after another's wife.[s]
9 Shall I not punish them for these
    things?
  says the LORD;
  On a nation such as this shall I not take
    vengeance?
10 Climb to her terraces, and ravage them,
    destroy them [not] wholly.
  Tear away her tendrils,
    they do not belong to the LORD.[t]
11 For they have openly rebelled against
    me,
  both the house of Israel and the house
    of Judah,
    says the LORD.[u]
12 They denied the LORD,*
    saying, "Not he—
  No evil shall befall us,
    neither sword nor famine shall we
    see.[v]
13 The prophets have become wind,
    and the word is not in them.
  May their threats be carried out
    against themselves!"

14 Now, for this that you have said,
    says the LORD, the God of hosts—
  Behold, I make my words
    in your mouth, a fire,
  And this people is the wood
    that it shall devour!—
15 Beware, I will bring against you
    a nation from afar,
  O house of Israel, says the LORD;
  A long-lived nation, an ancient nation,

Jer

---

n Is 24, 4.—o Jer 6, 24.—p Jer 2, 30.—q Jer 8, 7.—r Jer 6,
13.—s Jer 13, 27.—t Jer 2, 21.—u Jer 3, 20.—v Jer 14, 13; Is
28, 15.

5, 12: *They denied the Lord:* the people act as though God
does not exist and will not interfere.

a people whose language you know
not,
whose speech you cannot understand.[w]

16 Their quivers are like open graves;
all of them are warriors.

17 They will devour your harvest and your
bread,
devour your sons and your daughters,
Devour your sheep and cattle,
devour your vines and fig trees;
They will beat flat with the sword
the fortified city in which you trust.[x]

18 Yet even in those days, says the LORD, I
will not wholly destroy you.[y] 19 And when
they ask, "Why has the LORD done all
these things to us?" say to them, "As you
have forsaken me to serve strange gods in
your own land, so shall you serve strangers
in a land not your own."

20 Announce this to the house of Jacob,
proclaim it in Judah:

21 Pay attention to this,
foolish and senseless people
Who have eyes and see not,
who have ears and hear not.[z]

22 Should you not fear me, says the LORD,
should you not tremble before me?
I made the sandy shore the sea's limit,
which by eternal decree it may not
overstep.
Toss though it may, it is to no avail;
though its billows roar, they cannot
pass.[a]

23 But this people's heart is stubborn and
rebellious;
they turn and go away,

24 And say not in their hearts,
"Let us fear the LORD, our God,
Who gives us rain
early and late,* in its time;
Who watches for us
over the appointed weeks of harvest."[b]

25 Your crimes have prevented these
things,
your sins have turned back these
blessings from you.[c]

26 For there are among my people criminals;
like fowlers they set traps,
but it is men they catch.[d]

27 Their houses are as full of treachery
as a bird-cage is of birds;

Therefore they grow powerful and rich,
28 fat and sleek.
They go their wicked way;
justice they do not defend
By advancing the claim of the fatherless
or judging the cause of the poor.[e]

29 Shall I not punish these things? says the
LORD;
on a nation such as this shall I not
take vengeance?

30 A shocking, horrible thing
has happened in the land:

31 The prophets prophesy falsely,
and the priests teach as they wish;
Yet my people will have it so;
what will you do when the end
comes?[f]

CHAPTER 6

The Enemy at the Gates

1 Flee, sons of Benjamin,
out of Jerusalem!
Blow the trumpet in Tekoa,
raise a signal over Beth-haccherem;
For evil threatens from the north,
and mighty destruction.[g]

2 O lovely and delicate
daughter Zion, you are ruined!

3 Against her, shepherds come with their
flocks;*
all around, they pitch their tents,
each one grazes his portion.[h]

4 "Prepare for war against her,
Up! let us rush upon her at midday!
Alas! the day is waning,
evening shadows lengthen;

5 Up! let us rush upon her by night,
destroy her palaces!"[i]

6   For thus says the LORD of
hosts:
Hew down her trees,
throw up a siege mound against Jerusalem.
Woe to the city marked for punishment;
nought but oppression within her![j]

---

w Dt 28, 49.—x Dt 28, 31.—y Jer 4, 27.—z Is 6, 9.—a Jb 38,
10f.—b Gn 8, 22; Dt 11, 14.—c Jer 2, 17. 19.—d Prv 1, 11.—e
Jer 12, 1; Is 1, 23.—f Jer 14, 14; Mi 2, 11.—g Jer 1, 14f.—h
Jer 4, 17.—i 2 Chr 36, 19.—j Jer 32, 24; Zep 3, 1-4.

5, 24: *Rain early and late:* autumn and spring rains respectively. *Appointed weeks of harvest:* the seven weeks between
the Passover (Dt 16, 9f) and Pentecost, during which it ordinarily
did not rain.
6, 3: *Shepherds . . . with their flocks:* foreign invaders with
their armies.

7 As the well gushes out its waters,
so she gushes out her wickedness.
Violence and destruction resound in
her;
ever before me are wounds and
blows. *k*
8 Be warned, O Jerusalem,
lest I be estranged from you;
Lest I turn you into a desert,
a land where no man dwells.
9 Thus says the LORD of hosts:
Glean, glean like a vine
the remnant of Israel;
Pass your hand, like a vintager,
repeatedly over the tendrils.
10 To whom shall I speak?
whom shall I warn, and be heard?
See! their ears are uncircumcised,
they cannot give heed;
See, the word of the LORD has become
for them
an object of scorn, which they will
not have. *l*
11 Therefore my wrath brims up within
me,
I am weary of holding it in;
I will pour it out upon the child in the
street,
upon the young men gathered together.
Yes, all will be taken, husband and
wife,
graybeard with ancient. *m*
12 Their houses will fall to strangers,
their fields and their wives as well;
For I will stretch forth my hand
against those who dwell in this land,
says the LORD. *n*
13 Small and great alike, all are greedy for
gain;
prophet and priest, all practice
fraud. *o*
14 They would repair, as though it were
nought,*
the injury to my people:
"Peace, peace!" they say,
though there is no peace. *p*

15 They are odious; they have done abominable things,
yet they are not at all ashamed,
they know not how to blush.
Hence they shall be among those who
fall;
in their time of punishment they shall
go down,
says the LORD. *q*
16 Thus says the LORD:
Stand beside the earliest roads,
ask the pathways of old*
Which is the way to good, and walk it;
thus you will find rest for your souls.
But they said, "We will not walk
it." *r*
17 When I raised up watchmen* for them:
"Hearken to the sound of the trumpet!"
they said, "We will not hearken."
18 Therefore hear, O nations,
and know, O earth,
what I will do with them:
19 See, I bring evil upon this people,
the fruit of their own schemes,
Because they heeded not my words,
because they despised my law. *s*
20 Of what use to me incense that comes
from Sheba,
or sweet cane from far-off lands?
Your holocausts find no favor with me,
your sacrifices please me not. *t*
21 Therefore, thus says the LORD:
See, I will place before this people
obstacles to bring them down;
Fathers and sons alike,
neighbors and friends shall perish. *u*
22 Thus says the LORD:
See, a people comes from the land of
the north,
a great nation, roused from the ends
of the earth. *v*
23 Bow and javelin they wield;
cruel and pitiless are they.
They sound like the roaring sea
as they ride forth on steeds,
Each in his place, for battle
against you, daughter Zion.
24 We hear the report of them;
helpless fall our hands,
Anguish takes hold of us,
throes like a mother's in child-birth. *w*
25 Go not forth into the field,

k Is 57, 20.—l Jer 7, 26; 20, 8.—m Ez 9, 6.—n Jer 8, 10; Dt
28, 30ff.—o Jer 8, 10; 23, 11.—p Jer 8, 11.—q Jer 3, 3; 8,
12.—r Jer 7, 23f; 18, 15.—s Prv 1, 31.—t Is 1, 11; 43, 24.—u
Is 8, 14f.—v Jer 1, 15; 5, 15.—w Jer 4, 31.

6, 14: *As though it were nought:* the false assurance of well-
being given by priest and prophet cannot reduce the harm which universal materialism and corruption have done to the people.
6, 16: *Earliest roads . . . pathways of old:* history and the
lessons to be learned from it.
6, 17: *Watchmen:* the prophets who, like Jeremiah, had upheld God's moral law.

Jer

step not into the street,
Beware of the enemy's sword;
terror on every side!

26 O daughter of my people, gird on sackcloth,
roll in the ashes.
Mourn as for an only child
with bitter wailing,
For sudden upon us
comes the destroyer.[x]

27 A tester among my people I have appointed you,
to search and test their way.[y]

28 Arch-rebels are they all,
dealers in slander,
all of them corrupt.

29 The bellows roars,
the lead is consumed by the fire;
In vain has the smelter refined,
the wicked are not drawn off.

30 "Silver rejected" they shall be called,
for the LORD has rejected them.

II: ORACLES MOSTLY IN THE DAYS OF JEHOIAKIM

CHAPTER 7

The Temple Sermon.* [1] The following
message came to Jeremiah from the LORD:
[2] Stand at the gate of the house of the
LORD, and there proclaim this message:
Hear the word of the LORD, all you of
Judah who enter these gates to worship the
LORD! [3] Thus says the LORD of hosts, the
God of Israel: Reform your ways and your
deeds, so that I may remain with you in
this place.[z] [4] Put not your trust in the deceitful words: "This is the temple of the
LORD! The temple of the LORD! The temple of the LORD!"[a] [5] Only if you
thoroughly reform your ways and your
deeds; if each of you deals justly with his
neighbor; [6] if you no longer oppress the
resident alien,* the orphan, and the
widow; if you no longer shed innocent
blood in this place, or follow strange gods
to your own harm,[b] [7] will I remain with
you in this place, in the land which I gave
your fathers long ago and forever.[c]

[8] But here you are, putting your trust in
deceitful words to your own loss! [9] Are you
to steal and murder, commit adultery and
perjury, burn incense to Baal, go after
strange gods that you know not,[d] [10] and yet
come to stand before me in this house
which bears my name, and say: "We are
safe; we can commit all these abomina-

tions again"?[e] [11] Has this house which
bears my name become in your eyes a den
of thieves? I too see what is being done,
says the LORD.[f] [12] You may go to Shiloh,*
which I made the dwelling place of my
name in the beginning. See what I did to it
because of the wickedness of my people Israel.[g] [13] And now, because you have committed all these misdeeds, says the LORD,
because you did not listen, though I spoke
to you untiringly; because you did not answer, though I called you, [14] I will do to
this house named after me, in which you
trust, and to this place which I gave to you
and your fathers, just as I did to Shiloh.[h]
[15] I will cast you away from me, as I cast
away all your brethren, all the offspring of
Ephraim.[i]

Abuses in Worship. [16] You, now, do not
intercede for this people; raise not in their
behalf a pleading prayer![j] Do not urge me,
for I will not listen to you. [17] Do you not
see what they are doing in the cities of
Judah, in the streets of Jerusalem? [18] The
children gather wood, their fathers light
the fire, and the women knead dough to
make cakes for the queen of heaven,*
while libations are poured out to strange
gods in order to hurt me.[k] [19] Is it I whom
they hurt, says the LORD; is it not rather
themselves, to their own confusion?[l] [20] See
now, says the Lord GOD, my anger and my
wrath will pour out upon this place, upon
man and beast, upon the trees of the field
and the fruits of the earth; it will burn
without being quenched.[m]

[21] Thus says the LORD of hosts, the God
of Israel: Heap your holocausts upon your
sacrifices; eat up the flesh! [22] In speaking
to your fathers on the day I brought them
out of the land of Egypt, I gave

---

x Jer 25, 34; Am 8, 10.—y Jer 1, 18.—z Jer 18, 11; 26, 13.—
a Mi 3, 11.—b Ex 22, 21-24.—c Dt 4, 40.—d Jer 44, 17.—e Jer
32, 34.—f Mt 21, 13.—g Jos 18, 1.—h Jer 26, 9.—i 1 Kgs 9, 7;
2 Kgs 17, 23.—j Jer 11, 14; 14, 11.—k Jer 44, 17. 19.—l Jb 35,
6.—m Jer 36, 29; 2 Kgs 22, 17.

7, 1-15: *The temple of the Lord* will not serve as a place of
refuge for the Jews against their enemies if they fail to reform
their evil ways.

7, 6: *The resident alien:* specially protected by law; cf Ex
20, 10; Nm 9, 14; 15, 14; Dt 5, 14; 28, 43.

7, 12: *Shiloh:* original place of worship from the time of
Joshua to that of Samuel. The sanctuary was later rejected by
God and destroyed by the Philistines; cf 1 Sm 1, 9; 4, 3f; Ps 78,
60. 68f.

7, 18: *Queen of heaven:* the Assyro-Babylonian Ishtar, goddess of fertility, whose worship was introduced under King Manasseh and was revived after Josiah's death. *Cakes* shaped like
stars (Ishtar was identified with the planet Venus) were offered
in her honor.

them no command* concerning holocaust or sacrifice. [23] This rather is what I commanded them: Listen to my voice; then I will be your God and you shall be my people. Walk in all the ways that I command you, so that you may prosper.[n]
[24] But they obeyed not, nor did they pay heed. They walked in the hardness of their evil hearts and turned their backs, not their faces, to me.[o] [25] From the day that your fathers left the land of Egypt even to this day, I have sent you untiringly all my servants the prophets.[p] [26] Yet they have not obeyed me nor paid heed; they have stiffened their necks and done worse than their fathers.[q] [27] When you speak all these words to them, they will not listen to you either; when you call to them, they will not answer you. [28] Say to them: This is the nation which does not listen to the voice of the LORD, its God, or take correction. Faithfulness has disappeared; the word itself is banished from their speech.

[29] Cut off your dedicated hair* and throw
　it away!
on the heights intone an elegy;[r]
For the LORD has rejected and cast off
　the generation that draws down his
　wrath.

[30] The people of Judah have done what is evil in my eyes, says the LORD. They have defiled the house which bears my name by setting up in it their abominable idols.[s] [31] In the Valley of Ben-hinnom they have built the high place of Topheth to immolate in fire their sons and their daughters, such a thing as I never commanded or had in mind. [32] Therefore, beware! days will come, says LORD, when Topheth and the Valley of Ben-hinnom will no longer be called such, but rather

the Valley of Slaughter. For lack of space, Topheth will be a burial place.[t] [33] The corpses of this people will be food for the birds of the sky and for the beasts of the field, which no one will drive away.[u] [34] In the cities of Judah and in the streets of Jerusalem I will silence the cry of joy, the cry of gladness, the voice of the bridegroom and the voice of the bride; for the land will be turned to rubble.[v]

CHAPTER 8

[1] At that time, says the LORD, the bones of the kings and princes of Judah, the bones of the priests and the prophets, and the bones of the citizens of Jerusalem will be emptied out of their graves[w] [2] and spread out before the sun and the moon and the whole army of heaven,* which they loved and served, which they followed, consulted, and worshiped. They will not be gathered up for burial, but will lie like dung upon the ground.[x] [3] Death will be preferred to life by all the survivors of this wicked race who remain in any of the places to which I banish them, says the LORD of hosts.

Israel's Conduct Incomprehensible

[4]　　Tell them: Thus says the LORD:
When someone falls, does he not rise
　　again?
if he goes astray, does he not turn
　　back?
[5] Why do these people rebel
　with obstinate resistance?
Why do they cling to deceptive idols,
　refuse to turn back?[y]
[6] I listen closely:
　they speak what is not true;
No one repents of his wickedness,
　saying "What have I done!"
Everyone keeps on running his course,
　like a steed dashing into battle.[z]
[7] Even the stork in the air
　knows its seasons;
Turtledove, swallow and thrush
　observe their time of return,
But my people do not know
　the ordinance of the LORD.[a]

[8] How can you say, "We are wise,[b]
　we have the law of the LORD"?
Why, that has been changed into false-
　hood
　by the lying pen of the scribes!*

n Jer 11, 4; Lv 26, 3. 12.—o Jer 17, 23.—p 2 Chr 36, 15f; Bar 1, 19.—q Jer 19, 15; 2 Chr 30, 8.—r Jer 9, 17-21.—s Jer 32, 34.—t Jer 19, 6; 32, 35.—u Jer 16, 4; 34, 20.—v Jer 16, 9.—w Bar 2, 24.—x Dt 4, 19.—y Jer 5, 3; 7, 24. 26.—z Jb 34, 31f.—a Is 1, 3.—b Mal 2, 8; Rom 2, 17-23.

7, 22: *I gave them no command:* right conduct rather than mere external cult was God's will concerning his people (v 23).

7, 29: *Dedicated hair:* the unshorn hair of the nazirite, regarded as sacred because of a vow, temporary or permanent, to abstain from cutting or shaving the hair, from contact with a corpse, and from all products of the vine; cf Nm 6, 4-8. The cutting of this hair was a sign of extreme mourning.

8, 2: *Army of heaven:* the stars, worshiped by the pagan nations and even by the inhabitants of Jerusalem during the reigns of Manasseh and Amon.

8, 8f: *Lying pen of the scribes:* because the interpretations and ordinances of the scribes ran counter to the *word of the Lord.*

Jer

⁹ The wise are confounded,
    dismayed and ensnared;
Since they have rejected the word of the
    LORD,
    of what avail is their wisdom?*c*

Shameless in Their Crimes

¹⁰ Therefore, I will give their wives to
    strangers,
    their fields to spoilers.
Small and great alike, all are greedy for
    gain,
    prophet and priest, all practice
    fraud.*d*
¹¹ They would repair, as though it were
    nought,
    the injury to the daughter of my peo-
    ple:*
"Peace, peace!" they say,
    though there is no peace.*e*
¹² They are odious; they have done abom-
    inable things,
    yet they are not at all ashamed,
    they know not how to blush.
Hence they shall be among those who
    fall;
    in their time of punishment they shall
    go down,
    says the LORD.*f*

Threats of Punishment

¹³ I will gather them all in, says the LORD:
    no grapes on the vine,
No figs on the fig trees,
    foliage withered!
¹⁴ Why do we remain here?
    Let us form ranks and enter the
    walled cities,
    to perish there;
For the LORD has wrought our destruc-
    tion,
    he has given us poison to drink,
    because we have sinned against the
    LORD.*g*
¹⁵ We wait for peace to no avail;
    for a time of healing, but terror
    comes instead.*h*
¹⁶ From Dan is heard
    the snorting of his steeds;
The neighing of his stallions
    shakes the whole land.
They come devouring the land and all it
    contains,
    the city and those who dwell in it.
¹⁷ Yes, I will send against you
    poisonous snakes,

Against which no charm will work
    when they bite you, says the LORD.*i*

The Prophet's Grief over the People's Suffering

¹⁸ My grief is incurable,
    my heart within me is faint.
¹⁹ Listen! the cry of the daughter of my
    people,
    far and wide in the land!
Is the LORD no longer in Zion,
    is her King no longer in her midst?
[Why do they provoke me with their
    idols,
    with their foreign nonentities?]*j*
²⁰ "The harvest has passed, the summer is
    at an end,
    and yet we are not safe!"
²¹ I am broken by the ruin of the daughter
    of my people.
    I am disconsolate; horror has seized
    me.*k*
²² Is there no balm in Gilead,*
    no physician there?
Why grows not new flesh
    over the wound of the daughter of my
    people?*l*
²³ Oh, that my head were a spring of
    water,
    my eyes a fountain of tears,
That I might weep day and night
    over the slain of the daughter of my
    people!

CHAPTER 9

The Corruption of the People

¹ Would that I had in the desert
    a travelers' lodge!
That I might leave my people
    and depart from them.
They are all adulterers,
    a faithless band.
² They ready their tongues like a drawn
    bow;
    with lying, and not with truth,
    they hold forth in the land.
They go from evil to evil,
    but me they know not, says the
    LORD.

---

c 1 Cor 3, 20.—d Jer 6, 13; Dt 28, 30.—e Jer 6, 14.—f Jer 6, 15.—g Jer 9, 14; 23, 15.—h Jer 14, 19.—i Dt 32, 24.—j Dt 32, 21; Mi 4, 9.—k Jer 14, 17.—l Jer 46, 11.

8, 11: *Daughter of my people:* the people itself personified as a woman.
8, 22: *Gilead:* noted for its healing balm but unable to heal the moral wound of the people.

³ Be on your guard, everyone against his
neighbor;
　put no trust in any brother.
Every brother apes Jacob, the supplanter,*
　every friend is guilty of slander.
⁴ Each one deceives the other,
　no one speaks the truth.
They have accustomed their tongues to
lying,
　and are perverse, and cannot re-
pent.ᵐ
⁵ Violence upon violence,
　deceit upon deceit:
They refuse to recognize me,
　says the LORD.

⁶　　Therefore, thus says the LORD
　　of hosts:
I will smelt them and test them;
　how else should I deal with their
wickedness?
⁷ A murderous arrow is his tongue,
　his mouth utters deceit;
He speaks cordially with his friends,
　but in his heart he lays an ambush!ⁿ
⁸ For these things, says the LORD,
　shall I not punish them?
On a nation such as this
　shall I not take vengeance?ᵒ

Dirge over the Ravaged Land

⁹ Over the mountains, break out in cries
of lamentation,
　over the pasture lands, intone a dirge:
They are scorched, and no man crosses
them,
　unheard is the bleat of the flock;
Birds of the air as well as beasts,
　all have fled, and are gone.ᵖ
¹⁰ I will turn Jerusalem into a heap of
ruins,
　a haunt of jackals;
The cities of Judah I will make into a
waste,
　where no one dwells.�q

¹¹ Who is so wise that he can understand this? Let him to whom the mouth of
the LORD has spoken make it known:

---

m Jer 12, 6.—n Pss 28, 3; 62, 4.—o Jer 5, 9. 29.—p Jer 4, 25;
12, 4.—q Is 13, 22.—r Ps 107, 43; Hos 14, 10.—s Jer 7, 24; 19,
4f.—t Jer 23, 15.—u Lv 26, 33; Dt 28, 36. 64.—v Jer 14, 17.—
w Jer 14, 16.—x Prv 21, 30.

9, 3: *Jacob, the supplanter:* in Hebrew, a play on words.
Jacob, as his name indicates ("he supplants"), deprived his
brother Esau of his birthright; cf Gn 25, 26. 33.

Why is the land ravaged,
　scorched like a wasteland un-
traversed?ʳ

¹²The LORD answered: Because they
have abandoned my law, which I set before them, and have not followed it or listened to my voice, ¹³but followed rather
the hardness of their hearts and the Baals,
as their fathers had taught them;ˢ ¹⁴therefore, thus says the LORD of hosts, the God
of Israel: See now, I will give them wormwood to eat and poison to drink.ᵗ ¹⁵I will
scatter them among nations whom neither
they nor their fathers have known; I will
send the sword to pursue them until I have
completely destroyed them.ᵘ

¹⁶　　Thus says the LORD of hosts:
Attention! tell the wailing women to
come,
　summon the best of them;
¹⁷ Let them come quickly
　and intone a dirge for us,
That our eyes may be wet with weeping,
　our cheeks run with tears.ᵛ
¹⁸ The dirge is heard from Zion:
　Ruined we are, and greatly ashamed;
We must leave the land,
　give up our homes!
¹⁹ Hear, you women, the word of the
LORD,
　let your ears receive his message.
Teach your daughters this dirge,
　and each other this lament.
²⁰ Death has come up through our windows,
　has entered our palaces;
It cuts down the children in the street,
　young people in the squares.ʷ
²¹ The corpses of the slain
　lie like dung on a field,
Like sheaves behind the harvester,
　with no one to gather them.

True Glory

²²　　Thus says the LORD:
Let not the wise man glory in his wisdom,
　nor the strong man glory in his
strength,
　nor the rich man glory in his riches;ˣ
²³ But rather, let him who glories, glory in
this,
　that in his prudence he knows me,

Jer

Knows that I, the LORD, bring about
kindness,
justice and uprightness on the earth;
For with such am I pleased, says the
LORD.

Circumcision Worthless. ²⁴ See, days are
coming, says the LORD, when I will de-
mand an account of all those circumcised
in their flesh:^y ²⁵ Egypt and Judah, Edom
and the Ammonites, Moab and the desert
dwellers who shave their temples.* For all
these nations, like the whole house of Israel, are uncircumcised in heart.

CHAPTER 10

The Folly of Idolatry. ¹ Hear the word
which the LORD speaks to you, O house of
Israel. ² Thus says the LORD:

Learn not the customs of the nations,
and have no fear of the signs of the
heavens,*
though the nations fear them.^z
³ For the cult idols of the nations are
nothing,
wood cut from the forest,
Wrought by craftsmen with the adze,^a
⁴ adorned with silver and gold.
With nails and hammers they are fastened,
that they may not totter.^b
⁵ Like a scarecrow in a cucumber field
are they,
they cannot speak;
They must be carried about,
for they cannot walk.
Fear them not, they can do no harm,
neither is it in their power to do
good.^c
⁶ No one is like you, O LORD,
great are you,
great and mighty is your name.^d
⁷ Who would not fear you,
King of the nations,
for it is your due!
Among all the wisest of the nations,
and in all their domain,
there is none like you.^e

⁸ One and all they are dumb and sense-
less,
these idols they teach about are
wooden:
⁹ Silver strips brought from Tarshish,
and gold from Ophir,

The work of the craftsman
and the handiwork of the smelter,
Clothed with violet and purple—
all of them the work of artisans.

¹¹ Thus shall you say of them: Let the
gods that did not make heaven and earth
perish from the earth, and from beneath
these heavens!^f

¹⁰ The LORD is true God,
he is the living God, the eternal King,
Before whose anger the earth quakes,
whose wrath the nations cannot endure:^g
¹² He who made the earth by his power,
established the world by his wisdom,
and stretched out the heavens by his
skill.^h
¹³ When he thunders, the waters in the
heavens roar,
and he brings up clouds from the end
of the earth;
He makes the lightning flash in the
rain,
and releases stormwinds from their
chambers.
¹⁴ Every man is stupid, ignorant;
every artisan is put to shame by his
idol:
He has molded a fraud,
without breath of life.ⁱ
¹⁵ Nothingness are they, a ridiculous
work;
they will perish in their time of
punishment.
¹⁶ Not like these is the portion of Jacob:
he is the creator of all things;
Israel is his very own tribe,
LORD of hosts is his name.^j

Abandonment of Judah

¹⁷ Lift your bundle and leave the land,
O city living in a state of siege!
¹⁸ For thus says the LORD:
Behold, this time
I will sling away the inhabitants of
the land;
I will hem them in,

y Jer 4, 4.—z Bar 6, 6.—a Wis 13, 11; Is 44, 9.—b Is 40, 19;
41, 7.—c Ps 115, 4-8; Bar 6, 15.—d Ps 86, 8ff.—e Jer 5, 22; Ps
47, 2. 8.—f Ps 96, 5.—g Ps 10, 16.—h Ps 104, 5.—i Rom 1,
22f.—j Jer 31, 35.

9, 25: *Desert dwellers . . . temples:* Arab tribesmen who
cut off their hair and shaved their temples in honor of the pagan
god of Dushara. This was forbidden the Israelites (Lv 19, 27).
10, 2: *Signs of the heavens:* phenomena in the sky
superstitiously regarded by the pagans as dire omens.

that they may be taken.
19 Woe is me! I am undone,
  my wound is incurable;
Yet I had thought:
  if I make light of my wound, I can
    bear it.
20 My tent is ruined,
  all its cords are severed.
My sons have left me, they are no more:
  no one to pitch my tent,
  no one to raise its curtains. *k*
21 Yes, the shepherds were stupid as cat-
    tle,
  the LORD they sought not;
Therefore they had no success,
  and all their flocks were scattered. *l*
22 Listen! a noise! it comes closer,
  a great uproar from the northern
    land:
To turn the cities of Judah
  into a desert haunt of jackals.

Prayer of Jeremiah

23 You know, O LORD,
  that man is not master of his way;
Man's course is not within his choice,
  nor is it for him to direct his step.
24 Punish us, O LORD, but with equity,
  not in anger, lest you have us dwindle
    away.
25 Pour out your wrath on the nations that
    know you not,
  on the tribes that call not upon your
    name;
For they have devoured Jacob utterly,
  and laid waste his dwelling. *m*

CHAPTER 11

Plea for Fidelity to the Covenant. ¹The following message came to Jeremiah from the
LORD: ²Speak to the men of Judah and to
the citizens of Jerusalem, ³saying to them:
Thus says the LORD, the God of Israel:
Cursed be the man who does not observe
the terms of this covenant, *n* ⁴which I enjoined upon your fathers the day I brought
them up out of the land of Egypt, that iron
foundry, saying: Listen to my voice and do
all that I command you. Then you shall be
my people, and I will be your God. *o* ⁵Thus
I will fulfill the oath which I swore to your

fathers, to give them a land flowing with
milk and honey: the one you have today.
"Amen, LORD," I answered.
6 Then the LORD said to me: Proclaim
all these words in the cities of Judah and in
the streets of Jerusalem: Hear the words of
this covenant and obey them. ⁷Urgently
and constantly I warned your fathers to
obey my voice, from the day I brought
them up out of the land of Egypt even to
this day. ⁸But they did not listen or give
ear. Each one followed the hardness of his
evil heart, till I brought upon them all the
threats of this covenant which they had
failed to observe as I commanded them. *p*
9 A conspiracy has been found, the
LORD said to me, among the men of Judah
and the citizens of Jerusalem. ¹⁰They have
returned to the crimes of their forefathers
who refused to obey my words. They also
have followed and served strange gods; the
covenant which I had made with their
fathers, the house of Israel and the house
of Judah have broken. *q* ¹¹Therefore, thus
says the LORD: See, I bring upon them
misfortune which they cannot escape.
Though they cry out to me, I will not listen to them. *r* ¹²Then the cities of Judah
and the citizens of Jerusalem will go and
cry out to the gods to which they have
been offering incense. But these gods will
give them no help whatever when misfortune strikes. *s*

13 For as numerous as your cities
    are your gods, O Judah!
And as many as the streets of Jerusalem
    are the altars for offering sacrifice to
      Baal. *t*

14 Do not intercede on behalf of this people, nor utter a plea for them. I will not listen when they call to me at the time of
their misfortune. *u*

Sacrifices of No Avail

15 What right has my beloved in my
      house,
    while she prepares her plots?
Can vows and sacred meat turn away
    your misfortune from you?
Will you still be jubilant
16   when you hear the great invasion?
A spreading olive tree, goodly to be-
      hold,

Jer

k Jer 4, 20.—l Jer 23, 1; Ez 34, 5f.—m Ps 79, 6f.—n Dt 27,
26.—o Dt 4, 20; 1 Kgs 8, 51.—p 2 Kgs 17, 14.—q Dt 31, 16; Ez
20, 21-30.—r Jer 14, 12; Mi 3, 4.—s Dt 32, 37f.—t Jer 2, 28;
Hos 10, 1.—u Jer 7, 16; 14, 11.

the LORD has named you;
Now he sets fire to it,
its branches burn.

17 The LORD of hosts who planted you
has decreed misfortune for you because of
the evil done by the house of Israel and by
the house of Judah, who provoked me by
sacrificing to Baal. *v*

The Plot against Jeremiah. 18 I knew it because the LORD informed me; at that time
you, O LORD, showed me their doings.

CHAPTER 12

1 You would be in the right, O LORD,
  if I should dispute with you;
    even so, I must discuss the case with
    you.
  Why does the way of the godless
    prosper,
    why live all the treacherous in con-
    tentment? *w*
2 You planted them; they have taken
  root,
    they keep on growing and bearing
    fruit.
  You are upon their lips,
    but far from their inmost thoughts. *x*
3 You, O Lord, know me, you see me,
    you have found that at heart I am
    with you. *y*
  Pick them out like sheep for the slaughter,
    set them apart for the day of car-
    nage. *

4 How long must the earth mourn,
    the green of the whole countryside
    wither?
  For the wickedness of those who dwell
  in it
    beasts and birds disappear,
    because they say, "God does not see
    our ways."

5 If running against men has wearied you,
    how will you race against horses?
  And if in a land of peace you fall headlong,
    what will you do in the thickets of the
    Jordan?

6 For even your own brothers, the members of your father's house, betray you;
they have recruited a force against you. Do
not believe them, even if they are friendly
to you in their words. *z*

19 * Yet I, like a trusting lamb led to
slaughter, had not realized that they were
hatching plots against me: "Let us destroy
the tree in its vigor; let us cut him off from
the land of the living, so that his name will
be spoken no more." *a*

20 But, you, O LORD of hosts, O just
    Judge,
  searcher of mind and heart,
  Let me witness the vengeance you take
    on them,
      for to you I have entrusted my
      cause! *b*

21 Therefore, thus says the LORD concerning the men of Anathoth who seek
your life, saying, "Do not prophesy in the
name of the LORD; else you shall die by
our hand." *c* 22 Therefore, thus says the
LORD of hosts: I am going to punish them.
The young men shall die by the sword;
their sons and daughters shall die by
famine. *d* 23 None shall be spared among
them, for I will bring misfortune upon the
men of Anathoth, the year of their punishment. *e*

The Lord's Complaint

7 I abandon my house,
    cast off my heritage;
  The beloved of my soul I deliver
    into the hand of her foes. *f*
8 My heritage has turned on me
    like a lion in the jungle;
  Because she has roared against me,
    I treat her as an enemy. *g*
9 My heritage is a prey for hyenas,
    is surrounded by vultures;
  Come, gather together, all you beasts of
    the field,
    come and eat! *h*
10 Many shepherds have ravaged my vine-
    yard,
    have trodden my heritage underfoot;
  The portion that delighted me they
    have turned
    into a desert waste. *i*
11 They have made it a mournful waste,
    desolate it lies before me,

v Is 5, 2.—w Jb 21, 7; Mal 3, 15.—x Is 29, 13.—y Jer 17, 18;
Jb 23, 10.—z Jer 9, 4.—a Jer 18, 18; 20, 10; Wis 2, 20.—b Jer
15, 15.—c Am 7, 13. 16.—d Jer 18, 21f.—e Jer 23, 12.—f Ps
78, 62; Lam 2, 1f.—g Ps 106, 40.—h 2 Kgs 24, 2; Is 56, 9.—i
Jer 6, 3; Is 63, 18.

12, 3: Jeremiah does not seek private vengeance but the
punishment of the wicked by the Lord; cf Jer 20, 12. Nevertheless, the prophet's reaction to persecution shows the difference
between the spirit of the Old Testament and the New.
12, 19-23: These verses have been transposed from ch 11.

Desolate, all the land,
   because no one takes it to heart.
12 Upon every desert height
   brigands have come up.
The LORD has a sword which consumes
   the land, from end to end:
   no peace for all mankind.*j*
13 They have sown wheat and reaped
   thorns,
   they have tired themselves out to no
   purpose;
They recoil before their harvest,
   the flaming anger of the LORD.

Judah's Neighbors. 14 Thus says the
LORD against all my evil neighbors* who
plunder the heritage which I gave my people Israel as their own: See, I will pluck
them up from their land; the house of
Judah I will pluck up in their midst.*k*
15 But after plucking them up, I will pity
them again and bring them back, each to
his heritage, each to his land.*l* 16 And if
they carefully learn my people's custom of
swearing by my name, "As the LORD
lives," they who formerly taught my people to swear by Baal shall be built up in the
midst of my people.*m* 17 But if they do not
obey, I will uproot and destroy that nation
entirely, says the LORD.*n*

CHAPTER 13

Judah's Corruption.* 1 The LORD said to
me: Go buy yourself a linen loincloth;
wear it on your loins, but do not put it in
water. 2 I bought the loincloth, as the
LORD commanded, and put it on. 3 A second time the word of the LORD came to me
thus: 4 Take the loincloth which you
bought and are wearing, and go now to the
Parath; there hide it in a cleft of the rock.
5 Obedient to the LORD's command, I
went to the Parath and buried the
loincloth. 6 After a long interval, he said to
me: Go now to the Parath and fetch the
loincloth which I told you to hide there.
7 Again I went to the Parath, sought out

and took the loincloth from the place
where I had hid it. But it was rotted, good
for nothing! 8 Then the message came to
me from the LORD: 9 Thus says the LORD:
So also I will allow the pride of Judah to
rot, the great pride of Jerusalem.*o* 10 This
wicked people who refuse to obey my
words, who walk in the stubbornness of
their hearts, and follow strange gods to
serve and adore them, shall be like this
loincloth which is good for nothing.*p*
11 For, as close as the loincloth clings to a
man's loins, so had I made the whole
house of Israel and the whole house of
Judah cling to me, says the LORD; to be
my people, my renown, my praise, my
beauty. But they did not listen.*q*

The Broken Wineflask. 12 Now speak to
them this word: Thus says the LORD, the
God of Israel: Every wineflask is meant to
be filled with wine. If they reply, "Do we
not know that every wineflask is meant to
be filled with wine?" 13 say to them: Thus
says the LORD: Beware! I am filling with
drunkenness all the inhabitants of this
land, the kings who succeed to David's
throne, the priests and prophets, and all
the citizens of Jerusalem.*r* 14 I will dash
them against each other, fathers and sons
together, says the LORD; I will show no
compassion, I will not spare or pity, but
will destroy them.*s*

A Last Warning

15 Give ear, listen humbly,
   for the LORD speaks.
16 Give glory to the LORD, your God,
   before it grows dark;
Before your feet stumble
   on darkening mountains;
Before the light you look for turns to
   darkness,
   changes into black clouds.*t*
17 If you do not listen to this in your pride,
   I will weep in secret many tears;
My eyes will run with tears
   for the LORD's flock, led away to
   exile.*u*

Exile

18 Say to the king and to the queen
   mother:
   come down from your throne;
From your heads fall
   your magnificent crowns.*v*
19 The cities of the Negeb are besieged,

Jer

---

j Is 42, 25; 57, 21.—k 2 Kgs 24, 2.—l Am 9, 14.—m Dt 6,
13.—n Is 60, 12.—o Prv 16, 18.—p Jer 2, 20; 7, 24; 16, 11.—q
Ex 19, 5; Dt 26, 18f.—r Jer 25, 15-18; Is 51, 17.—s Jer 19,
10f.—t Prv 4, 18f; Is 5, 30; Am 8, 9.—u Jer 14, 17; Ps 119,
136.—v Jer 22, 26; 2 Kgs 24, 12. 15.

12, 14: *My evil neighbors:* nations surrounding Israel, the
land belonging to the Lord; cf Is 8, 8.
13, 1-11: This is probably a vision of the prophet symbolizing
the religious corruption of Judah at the hands of the Babylonians,
represented here by the river *Parath,* the Euphrates; though a
spring of the same name, northeast of Anathoth, may be directly
meant.

with no one to relieve them;
All Judah is banished
in universal exile.

Jerusalem's Disgrace

20 Lift up your eyes and see
men coming from the north.
Where is the flock entrusted to you,
the sheep that were your glory?*w*
21 What will you say when they place as
rulers over you
those whom you taught to be your
lovers?
Will not pangs seize you
like those of a woman giving birth?*x*
22 If you ask in your heart
why these things befall you:
For your great guilt your skirts are
stripped away
and you are violated.*y*
23 Can the Ethiopian change his skin?
the leopard his spots?
As easily would you be able to do good,
accustomed to evil as you are.*z*
24 I will scatter them like chaff that flies
when the desert wind blows.*a*
25 This is your lot, the portion measured
out to you
from me, says the LORD.
Because you have forgotten me,
and trusted in the lying idol,*b*
26 I now will strip off your skirts from
you,
so that your shame will appear.*c*
27 Your adulteries, your neighings,
your shameless prostitutions:
On the hills in the highlands
I see these horrible crimes of yours.
Woe to you, Jerusalem, how long will it
yet be
before you become clean!*d*

CHAPTER 14

The Great Drought. ¹The word of the
LORD that came to Jeremiah concerning
the drought:*e*

2 Judah mourns,
her gates are lifeless;
Her people sink down in mourning:
from Jerusalem ascends a cry of anguish.*f*
3 The nobles send their servants for
water,
but when they come to the cisterns
They find no water

and return with empty jars.*g*
Ashamed, despairing, they cover their
heads
4 because of the stricken soil;
Because there is no rain in the land
the farmers are ashamed, they cover
their heads.*h*
5 Even the hind in the field deserts her
offspring
because there is no grass.
6 The wild asses stand on the bare
heights,
gasping for breath like jackals;
Their eyes grow dim,
because there is no vegetation to be
seen.
7 Even though our crimes bear witness
against us,
take action, O LORD, for the honor of
your name—
Even though our rebellions are many,
though we have sinned against you.*i*
8 O Hope of Israel, O LORD,
our savior in time of need!
Why should you be a stranger in this
land,
like a traveler who has stopped but
for a night?
9 Why are you like a man dumbfounded,
a champion who cannot save?
You are in our midst, O LORD,
your name we bear:
do not forsake us!*j*

10   Thus says the LORD of this people:
They so love to wander
that they do not spare their feet.
The LORD has no pleasure in them;
now he remembers their guilt,
and will punish their sins.*k*

¹¹Then the LORD said to me: Do not intercede for this people.*l* ¹²If they fast, I
will not listen to their supplication. If they
offer holocausts or cereal offerings, I will
not accept them. Rather, I will destroy
them with the sword, famine, and pestilence.*m*
¹³Ah! Lord GOD, I replied, it is the
prophets who say to them, "You shall not
see the sword; famine shall not befall you.
Indeed, I will give you lasting peace in this
place."*n*

w Jer 6, 22f.—x 2 Kgs 16, 7.—y Is 47, 2f.—z Ps 55, 20.—a
Pss 1, 4; 83, 14.—b Jb 20, 29.—c Ez 16, 32.—d Jer 2, 20.— e
Lv 26, 19f.—f Is 3, 26.—g Am 4, 8.—h Dt 28, 23.—i Dn 9, 4-
14.—j Is 59, 1f; 63, 19.—k Jer 2, 25.—l Jer 11, 14; Ex 32,
10.— m Jer 6, 20; Is 1, 11. 13.—n Jer 4, 10; 5, 12.

¹⁴Lies these prophets utter in my name, the LORD said to me. I did not send them; I gave them no command nor did I speak to them. Lying visions, foolish divination, dreams of their own imagination, they prophesy to you.⁰ ¹⁵Therefore, thus says the LORD: Concerning the prophets who prophesy in my name, though I did not send them; who say, "Sword and famine shall not befall this land": by the sword and famine shall these prophets meet their end.ᵖ ¹⁶The people to whom they prophesy shall be cast out into the streets of Jerusalem by famine and the sword. No one shall bury them, their wives, their sons, or their daughters, for I will pour out upon them their own wickedness.�q ¹⁷Speak to them this word:

Let my eyes stream with tears
　day and night, without rest,
Over the great destruction which over-
　whelms
　　the virgin daughter of my people,
　　over her incurable wound.ʳ
¹⁸ If I walk out into the field,
　look! those slain by the sword;
If I enter the city,
　look! those consumed by hunger.
Even the prophet and the priest
　forage in a land they know not.

¹⁹ Have you cast Judah off completely?
　Is Zion loathsome to you?
Why have you struck us a blow
　that cannot be healed?
We wait for peace, to no avail;
　for a time of healing, but terror
　comes instead.ˢ
²⁰ We recognize, O LORD, our wicked-
　ness,
　the guilt of our fathers;
　that we have sinned against you.ᵗ
²¹ For your name's sake spurn us not,
　disgrace not the throne of your glory;
　remember your covenant with us,
　and break it not.ᵘ
²² Among the nations' idols is there any
　that gives rain?
　Or can the mere heavens send show-
　ers?
Is it not you alone, O LORD,

our God, to whom we look?
You alone have done all these
　things.ᵛ

CHAPTER 15

¹The LORD said to me: Even if Moses and Samuel stood before me, my heart would not turn toward this people. Send them away from me.ʷ ²If they ask you where they should go, tell them, Thus says the LORD: Whoever is marked for death, to death; whoever is marked for the sword, to the sword; whoever is marked for famine, to famine; whoever is marked for captivity, to captivity.ˣ ³Four kinds of scourge I have decreed against them, says the LORD: the sword to slay them; dogs to drag them about; the birds of the sky and the beasts of the earth to devour and destroy them.ʸ ⁴And I will make them an object of horror to all the kingdoms of the earth because of what Manasseh, son of Hezekiah, king of Judah, did in Jerusalem.ᶻ

Scene of Tragedy

⁵ Who will pity you, Jerusalem,
　who will console you?
Who will stop to ask
　about your welfare?ᵃ
⁶ You have disowned me, says the LORD,
　turned your back upon me;
And so I stretched out my hand to de-
　stroy you,
　I was weary of sparing you.ᵇ
⁷ I winnowed them with the fan
　in every city gate.
I destroyed my people through bereave-
　ment;
　they returned not from their evil
　ways.ᶜ
⁸ Their widows were more numerous be-
　fore me
　than the sands of the sea.
I brought against the mother of youths
　the spoiler at midday;
Suddenly I struck her
　with anguish and terror.
⁹ The mother of seven swoons away,
　gasping out her life;
Her sun sets in full day,
　she is disgraced, despairing.
Their survivors I will give to the sword
　before their enemies, says the LORD.ᵈ

---

o Jer 5, 31; 23, 16.—p Jer 5, 12f.—q Jer 7, 33; 19, 7.—r Jer 9, 17.—s Jer 8, 15; 2 Chr 36, 16.—t Ps 106, 6; Dn 9, 5. 8.—u Jer 14, 7; Lv 26, 44; Ps 25, 11.—v Jer 5, 24; Zec 10, 1.—w Ps 99, 6; Ez 14, 14. 16.—x Jer 14, 12; Ez 5, 12.—y Ez 14, 21.—z Jer 24, 9; 2 Kgs 21, 11-16; 23, 26; 24, 3f.—a Is 51, 19.—b Am 7, 8.—c Is 41, 16.—d 1 Sm 2, 5.

Jeremiah's Complaint

10 Woe to me, mother, that you gave me
    birth!
    a man of strife and contention to all
      the land!
I neither borrow nor lend,
    yet all curse me.*e*

11 Tell me, LORD, have I not served you
    for their good?
    Have I not interceded with you
    in the time of misfortune and an-
      guish?*f**

15   You know I have.
Remember me, LORD, visit me,
    and avenge me on my persecutors.
Because of your long-suffering banish
    me not;
    know that for you I have borne in-
      sult.*g*

16 When I found your words, I devoured
    them;
    they became my joy and the happi-
      ness of my heart,
Because I bore your name,
    O LORD, God of hosts.

17 I did not sit celebrating
    in the circle of merrymakers;
Under the weight of your hand I sat
    alone
    because you filled me with indigna-
      tion.*h*

18 Why is my pain continuous,
    my wound incurable, refusing to be
      healed?
You have indeed become for me a
    treacherous brook,*
    whose waters do not abide!*i*

19   Thus the LORD answered me:
If you repent, so that I restore you,
    in my presence you shall stand;
If you bring forth the precious without
    the vile,
    you shall be my mouthpiece.
Then it shall be they who turn to you,
    and you shall not turn to them;

20 And I will make you toward this people
    a solid wall of brass.
Though they fight against you,
    they shall not prevail,
For I am with you,
    to deliver and rescue you, says the
      LORD.*j*

21 I will free you from the hand of the
    wicked,
    and rescue you from the grasp of the
      violent.

CHAPTER 16

Jeremiah's Life a Warning. ¹This message
came to me from the LORD: ²Do not
marry any woman; you shall not have sons
or daughters in this place, ³for thus says
the LORD concerning the sons and
daughters who will be born in this place,
the mothers who will give them birth, the
fathers who will beget them in this land:
⁴Of deadly disease they shall die. Un-
lamented and unburied they will lie like
dung on the ground. Sword and famine
will make an end of them, and their
corpses will become food for the birds of
the sky and the beasts of the field.*k*

⁵Go not into a house of mourning, the
LORD continued: go not there to lament or
offer sympathy. For I have withdrawn my
friendship from this people, says the
LORD, my kindness and my pity.*l* ⁶They
shall die, the great and the lowly, in this
land, and shall go unburied* and un-
lamented.* No one will gash himself or
shave his head for them.*m* ⁷They will not
break bread with the bereaved to console
them in their bereavement; they will not
give them the cup of consolation to drink
over the death of father or mother.*n*

⁸Enter not a house where people are celebrating, to sit with them eating and
drinking. ⁹For thus says the LORD of
hosts, the God of Israel: Before your very
eyes and during your lifetime I will silence
from this place the cry of joy and the cry of
gladness, the voice of the bridegroom and
the voice of the bride.*o*

¹⁰When you proclaim all these words to
this people and they ask you: "Why has
the LORD pronounced all these great evils
against us? What is our crime? What sin
have we committed against the LORD, our
God?"*p*—¹¹ *q* you shall answer them: It is
because your fathers have forsaken me,
says the LORD, and followed strange gods,
which they served and worshiped; but

---

e Jer 20, 14.—f Jer 39, 11-14.—g Jer 11, 20; 12, 3; Ps 69,
8.—h Ps 25, 4.—i Jer 14, 19; 30, 15.—j Jer 1, 18; 6, 27.—k Jer
7, 33; 22, 18.—l Ez 24, 16f.—m Lv 19, 28; Dt 14, 1.—n Ez 24,
17.—o Jer 7, 34; 25, 10.—p Jer 2, 35; 5, 19; 13, 22.—q Jer 22,
9; Dt 29, 25.

15, 12-14: These verses are omitted because v 12 is a dittography of 17, 1. Verses 13-14 are a dittography of 17, 3f.

15, 18: *A treacherous brook:* that dries up when its waters
are needed. The prophet complains that he cannot rely on God
with unfailing assurance of his assistance.

16, 6f: These verses refer to popular mourning practices,
sometimes connected with pagan superstition; cf Dt 14, 1f.

me they have forsaken, and my law they have not observed. ¹²And you have done worse than your fathers. Here you are, every one of you, walking in the hardness of his evil heart instead of listening to me. *ʳ* ¹³I will cast you out of this land into a land that neither you nor your fathers have known; there you can serve strange gods day and night, because I will not grant you my mercy.

Return from Exile. ¹⁴However, days will surely come, says the LORD, when it will no longer be said, "As the LORD lives, who brought the Israelites out of Egypt"; *ˢ* ¹⁵but rather, "As the LORD lives, who brought the Israelites out of the land of the north and out of all the countries to which he had banished them." I will bring them back to the land which I gave their fathers. *ᵗ*

Double Punishment. ¹⁶Look! I will send many fishermen, says the LORD, to catch them. After that, I will send many hunters to hunt them out from every mountain and hill and from the clefts of the rocks. *ᵘ* ¹⁷For my eyes are upon all their ways; they are not hidden from me, nor does their guilt escape my view. *ᵛ* ¹⁸I will at once repay them double for their crime and their sin of profaning my land with their detestable corpses of idols, and filling my heritage with their abominations. *ʷ*

Conversion of the Heathen

¹⁹ O LORD, my strength, my fortress,
  my refuge in the day of distress!
To you will the nations come
  from the ends of the earth, and say,
"Mere frauds are the heritage of our
  fathers,
  empty idols of no use." *ˣ*
²⁰ Can man make for himself gods?
  These are not gods. *ʸ*
²¹ Look, then: I will give them knowledge;
  this time I will leave them in no
  doubt
Of my strength and my power:
  they shall know that my name is
  LORD. *ᶻ*

CHAPTER 17

The Sin of Judah and Its Punishment

¹ The sin of Judah is written
  with an iron stylus,
Engraved with a diamond point
  upon the tablets of their hearts. *ᵃ*

[And the horns of their altars, ²when their sons remember their altars and their sacred poles, beside the green trees, on the high hills, ³the peaks in the highland.]

Your wealth and all your treasures
  I will give as spoil.
In recompense for all your sins
  throughout your borders,
⁴ You will relinquish your hold on your
  heritage
  which I have given you.
I will enslave you to your enemies
  in a land that you know not:
For a fire has been kindled by my wrath
  that will burn forever. *ᵇ*

True Wisdom

⁵   Thus says the LORD:
Cursed is the man who trusts in human
  beings,
  who seeks his strength in flesh,
  whose heart turns away from the
  LORD. *ᶜ*
⁶ He is like a barren bush in the desert
  that enjoys no change of season,
But stands in a lava waste,
  a salt and empty earth.
⁷ Blessed is the man who trusts in the
  LORD,
  whose hope is the LORD. *ᵈ*
⁸ He is like a tree planted beside the waters
  that stretches out its roots to the
  stream:
It fears not the heat when it comes,
  its leaves stay green;
In the year of drought it shows no distress,
  but still bears fruit. *ᵉ*
⁹ More tortuous than all else is the human
  heart,
  beyond remedy; who can understand
  it?
¹⁰ I, the LORD, alone probe the mind
  and test the heart,
To reward everyone according to his
  ways,

---

r Jer 7, 24ff.—s Jer 23, 7f.—t Jer 24, 6.—u 2 Kgs 24, 2; Lam 4, 19.—v Jer 32, 19; Jb 34, 21.—w Is 40, 2.—x Jer 2, 11; Is 2, 2f.—y Jer 2, 11; Gal 4, 8.—z Am 5, 8.—a Jb 19, 24.—b Jer 5, 19; Dt 32, 22.—c Ps 146, 2f.—d Ps 1, 3.—e Is 58, 11.

according to the merit of his deeds.*f*
11 A partridge that mothers a brood not
   her own
   is the man who acquires wealth un-
      justly:
   In midlife it will desert him;
      in the end he is only a fool.*g*

The Source of Life

12 A throne of glory, exalted from the be-
      ginning,
   such is our holy place.*h*
13 O hope of Israel, O LORD!
   all who forsake you shall be in dis-
      grace;
   The rebels in the land shall be put to
      shame;
   they have forsaken the source of liv-
      ing waters
      [the LORD].*i*

Prayer for Vengeance

14 Heal me, LORD, that I may be healed;
   save me, that I may be saved,
   for it is you whom I praise.
15 See how they say to me,
   "Where is the word of the LORD?
   Let it come to pass!"*j*
16 Yet I did not press you to send calam-
      ity;
   the day without remedy I have not
      desired.
   You know what passed my lips;
   it is present before you.
17 Do not be my ruin,
   you, my refuge in the day of misfor-
      tune.*k*
18 Let my persecutors, not me, be con-
      founded;
   let them, not me, be broken.
   Bring upon them the day of misfortune,
   crush them with repeated destruc-
      tion.*l*

Observance of the Sabbath. 19 Thus said
the LORD to me: Go, stand at the Gate of
Benjamin,* where the kings of Judah
enter and leave, and at the other gates of
Jerusalem.*m* 20 There say to them: Hear
the word of the LORD, you kings of
Judah, and all Judah, and all you citizens
of Jerusalem who enter these gates!
21 Thus says the LORD: As you love your
lives, take care not to carry burdens on
the sabbath day, to bring them in through

the gates of Jerusalem.*n* 22 Bring no burden
from your homes on the sabbath. Do no
work whatever, but keep holy the sabbath,
as I commanded your fathers,*o* 23 though
they did not listen or give ear, but stiffened their necks so as not to hear or take
correction.*p* 24 If you obey me wholeheartedly, says the LORD, and carry no burden
through the gates of this city on the sabbath, keeping the sabbath holy and abstaining from all work on it,*q* 25 then,
through the gates of this city, kings who sit
upon the throne of David will continue to
enter, riding in their chariots or upon their
horses, along with their princes, and the
men of Judah, and the citizens of Jerusalem. This city will remain inhabited forever.*r* 26 To it people will come from the
cities of Judah and the neighborhood of
Jerusalem, from the land of Benjamin and
from the foothills, from the hill country
and the Negeb, to bring holocausts and
sacrifices, cereal offerings and incense and
thank offerings to the house of the LORD.*s*
27 But if you do not obey me and keep holy
the sabbath, if you carry burdens and
come through the gates of Jerusalem on
the sabbath, I will set unquenchable fire to
its gates, which will consume the palaces
of Jerusalem.*t*

CHAPTER 18

The Potter's Vessel.* 1 This word came to
Jeremiah from the LORD: 2 Rise up, be off
to the potter's house; there I will give you
my message. 3 I went down to the potter's
house and there he was, working at the
wheel. 4 Whenever the object of clay which
he was making turned out badly in his
hand, he tried again, making of the clay
another object of whatever sort he
pleased.*u* 5 Then the word of the Lord
came to me: 6 Can I not do to you, house of
Israel, as this potter has done? says the
LORD. Indeed, like clay in the hand of the
potter, so are you in my hand, house of
Israel.*v* 7 *w* Sometimes I threaten to up-

f Jer 32, 19; 1 Sm 16, 7; Eccl 12, 14.—g Prv 13, 11; Lk 12,
20.—h Jer 14, 21.—i Jer 2, 13.—j Is 5, 19; 2 Pt 3, 4.—k Jer 16,
19.—l Jer 15, 15; 18, 20-23; Ps 35, 5f.—m Jer 7, 2.—n Neh 13,
15-19.—o Ex 20, 8; 23, 12.—p Jer 5, 3; 7, 24.—q Is 58, 14.—r
Jer 22, 4.—s Jer 32, 44.—t Ez 22, 8.—u Rom 9, 20f.—v Wis 15,
7; Is 45, 9.—w Jer 1, 10.

17, 19: *The Gate of Benjamin:* probably the northern gate of
the temple area and city wall of Jerusalem; cf Jer 20, 2; 37, 12;
38, 7.
18, 1-12: The lesson of the potter is not that God deals arbitrarily with his people, but that he is almighty to destroy or restore, accordingly as they disobey him or fulfill his plans.

uproot and tear down and destroy a nation or a kingdom. [8]But if that nation which I have threatened turns from its evil, I also repent of the evil which I threatened to do.[x] [9]Sometimes, again, I promise to build up and plant a nation or a kingdom. [10]But if that nation does what is evil in my eyes, refusing to obey my voice, I repent of the good with which I promised to bless it.[y]

[11]And now, tell this to the men of Judah and the citizens of Jerusalem: Thus says the LORD: Take care! I am fashioning evil against you and making a plan. Return, each of you, from his evil way; reform your ways and your deeds.[z] [12]But they will say, "No use! We will follow our own devices; each one of us will behave according to the stubbornness of his evil heart!"[a]

Judah's Apostasy Unnatural

[13]   Therefore thus says the LORD:
Ask among the nations—
    who has ever heard the like?
Truly horrible things
    has virgin Israel done![b]
[14] Does the snow of Lebanon*
    desert the rocky heights?
Do the gushing waters dry up
    that flow fresh down the mountains?
[15] Yet my people have forgotten me:
    they burn incense to a thing that does
        not exist.
They stumble out of their ways,
    the paths of old,
To travel on bypaths,
    not the beaten track.[c]
[16] Their land shall be turned into a desert,
    an object of lasting ridicule:
All passers-by will be amazed,
    will shake their heads.[d]
[17] Like the east wind, I will scatter them
    before their enemies;

I will show them my back, not my face,
    in their day of disaster.[e]

Another Prayer for Vengeance.

[18]"Come," they said, "let us contrive a plot against Jeremiah. It will not mean the loss of instruction from the priests, nor of counsel from the wise, nor of messages from the prophets. And so, let us destroy him by his own tongue; let us carefully note his every word."[f]

[19] Heed me, O LORD,
    and listen to what my adversaries
        say.
[20] Must good be repaid with evil
    that they should dig a pit to take my
        life?
Remember that I stood before you
    to speak in their behalf,
    to turn away your wrath from them.[g]
[21] So now, deliver their children to
        famine,[h]
    do away with them by the sword.
Let their wives be made childless and
        widows;
    let their men die of pestilence,
    their young men be slain by the
        sword in battle.*
[22] May cries be heard from their homes,
    when suddenly you send plunderers
        against them.
For they have dug a pit to capture me,
    they have hid snares for my feet;
[23] But you, O LORD, know
    all their plans to slay me.
Forgive not their crime,
    blot not out their sin in your sight!
Let them go down before you,
    proceed against them in the time of
        your anger.[i]

CHAPTER 19

Symbol of the Potter's Flask.

[1]Thus said the LORD: Go, buy a potter's earthen flask. Take along some of the elders of the people and of the priests, [2]and go out toward the Valley of Ben-hinnom, at the entrance of the Potsherd Gate;* there proclaim the words which I will speak to you: [3]Listen to the word of the LORD, kings of Judah and citizens of Jerusalem: Thus says the LORD of hosts, the God of Israel: I am going to bring such evil upon this place that all who hear of it will feel their ears tingle. [4]This is because they have forsaken me and alienated this place

---

x Jer 26, 3; Is 55, 7; Ez 18, 21. 27.—y Nm 14, 22f.—z Jer 7, 3; 25, 5; 35, 15.—a Jer 2, 25; 7, 24.—b Jer 2, 10f; 5, 30.—c Jer 2, 13. 32.—d Jer 19, 8; Lv 26, 32; 1 Kgs 9, 8.—e Prv 1, 24-31.—f Jer 11, 19; Ps 35, 15f.—g Ps 35, 12.—h Ps 109, 9f.—i Neh 4, 5; Pss 35, 4; 37, 32f.

18, 14: *Lebanon:* here apparently including Mount Hermon, whose snow-capped peak can be seen from parts of Palestine all year round. The prophet contrasts the certainties of nature with Israel's unnatural desertion of the Lord for idols (v 15).

18, 21: In the Old Testament a man's family was regarded as part of his personality, to be rewarded or punished along with him; cf Jos 7, 24ff.

19, 2: *Potsherd Gate:* in the south wall of Jerusalem, through which potsherds and other refuse were carried to the Valley of Ben-hinnom.

by burning in it incense to strange gods which neither they nor their fathers knew; and the kings of Judah have filled this place with the blood of the innocent.*j* [5] They have built high places for Baal to immolate their sons in fire as holocausts to Baal: such a thing as I neither commanded nor spoke of, nor did it ever enter my mind.*k* [6] Therefore, days will come, says the LORD, when this place will no longer be called Topheth, or the Valley of Ben-hinnom, but rather, the Valley of Slaughter.*l* [7] In this place I will foil the plan of Judah and Jerusalem; I will make them fall by the sword before their enemies, by the hand of those that seek their lives. Their corpses I will give as food to the birds of the sky and the beasts of the field.*m* [8] I will make this city an object of amazement and derision. Because of all its wounds, every passer-by will be amazed and will catch his breath. [9] I will have them eat the flesh of their sons and daughters; they shall eat one another's flesh during the strict siege by which their enemies and those who seek their lives will confine them.*n*

[10] And you shall break the flask in the sight of the men who went with you, [11] and say to them: Thus says the LORD of hosts: Thus will I smash this people and this city, as one smashes a clay pot so that it cannot be repaired. And Topheth shall be a burial place, for lack of place to bury elsewhere.*o* [12] Thus I will do to this place and to its inhabitants, says the LORD; I will make this city like Topheth.*p* [13] And the houses of Jerusalem and the palaces of the kings of Judah shall be defiled like the place of Topheth, all the houses upon whose roofs they burnt incense to the whole host of heaven and poured out libations to strange gods.*q*

[14] When Jeremiah returned from Topheth, where the LORD had sent him to prophesy, he stood in the court of the house of God and said to all the people:*r* [15] Thus says the LORD of hosts, the God of Israel: I will surely bring upon this city all the evil with which I threatened it, because they have stiffened their necks and have not obeyed my words.*s*

CHAPTER 20

[1] Jeremiah was heard prophesying these things by the priest Pashhur,*t* son of

Immer, chief officer in the house of the LORD.* [2] So he had the prophet scourged and placed in the stocks at the upper Gate of Benjamin in the house of the LORD.*u* [3] The next morning, after Pashhur had released Jeremiah from the stocks, the prophet said to him: *v* Instead of Pashhur, the LORD will name you "Terror on every side."* [4] For thus says the LORD: Indeed, I will deliver you to terror, you and all your friends. Your own eyes shall see them fall by the sword of their enemies. All Judah I will deliver to the king of Babylon,* who shall take them captive to Babylon or slay them with the sword. [5] All the wealth of this city, all it has toiled for and holds dear, all the treasures of the kings of Judah, I will give as plunder into the hands of their foes, who shall seize it and carry it away to Babylon.*w* [6] You, Pashhur, and all the members of your household shall go into exile. To Babylon you shall go, you and all your friends; there you shall die and be buried, because you have prophesied lies to them.*x*

Jeremiah's Interior Crisis

[7] You duped me,* O LORD, and I let myself be duped;
　you were too strong for me, and you triumphed.
All the day I am an object of laughter;
　everyone mocks me.
[8] Whenever I speak, I must cry out,
　violence and outrage is my message;
The word of the LORD has brought me
　derision and reproach all the day.
[9] I say to myself, I will not mention him,
　I will speak in his name no more.
But then it becomes like fire burning in
　my heart,

j Jer 1, 16; 2 Kgs 21, 16; 24, 4.—k Jer 7, 31f; 32, 35.—l Jer 7, 32.—m Jer 7, 33.—n Lv 26, 29.—o Jer 7, 32.—p 2 Kgs 23, 10.—q Jer 32, 29.—r Jer 26, 2.—s Jer 7, 26; Prv 29, 1.—t Jer 21, 1.—u Jer 29, 26.—v Jer 6, 25.—w 2 Kgs 20, 17; 24, 12-16.—x Jer 14, 13f; 28, 15.

20, 1: *Chief officer in the house of the Lord:* head of the temple police; cf Jer 29, 26. By entering the temple court (Jer 19, 14), Jeremiah had put himself under Pashhur's jurisdiction.
20, 3: *Terror on every side:* Pashhur will share the fate of doomed Jerusalem and will experience personally all that the people as a whole have had to endure.
20, 4: *Babylon:* mentioned here for the first time as the land of exile. The prophecy probably dates from after 605 B.C., when Nebuchadnezzar defeated Egypt and made the Chaldean empire dominant in Syria and Palestine.
20, 7: *You duped me:* to be understood in the light of Jeremiah's intimate dealings with God; cf Jer 15, 18.

imprisoned in my bones;
I grow weary holding it in,
I cannot endure it.*y*

10 Yes, I hear the whisperings of many:
"Terror on every side!
Denounce! let us denounce him!"
All those who were my friends
are on the watch for any misstep of
mine.
"Perhaps he will be trapped; then we
can prevail,
and take our vengeance on him."*z*

11 But the LORD is with me, like a mighty
champion:
my persecutors will stumble, they
will not triumph.
In their failure they will be put to utter
shame,
to lasting, unforgettable confusion.*a*

12 O LORD of hosts, you who test the just,
who probe mind and heart,
Let me witness the vengeance you take
on them,
for to you I have entrusted my
cause.*b*

13 Sing to the LORD,
praise the LORD,
For he has rescued the life of the poor
from the power of the wicked!*c*

14 Cursed be the day*
on which I was born!
May the day my mother gave me birth
never be blessed!*d*

15 Cursed be the man who brought the
news
to my father, saying,
"A child, a son, has been born to you!"
filling him with great joy.

16 Let that man be like the cities
which the LORD relentlessly overthrew;
Let him hear war cries in the morning,
battle alarms at noonday,*e*

17 because he did not dispatch me in the
womb!
Then my mother would have been my
grave,
her womb confining me forever.*f*

18 Why did I come forth from the womb,
to see sorrow and pain,
to end my days in shame?*g*

III: ORACLES IN THE LAST YEARS OF JERUSALEM

CHAPTER 21

Fate of Zedekiah and Jerusalem. ¹ The
message which came to Jeremiah from the
LORD when King Zedekiah* sent him
Pashhur, son of Malchiah, and the priest
Zephaniah, son of Maaseiah, with this request: ² Inquire for us of the LORD, because Nebuchadnezzar, king of Babylon,
is attacking us. Perhaps the LORD will deal
with us according to all his wonderful
works, so that he will withdraw from us.
³ But Jeremiah answered them: This is
what you shall report to Zedekiah: ⁴ Thus
says the LORD, the God of Israel: I will
turn back in your hands the weapons with
which you intend to fight the king of
Babylon and the Chaldeans who besiege
you outside the walls. These weapons I
will pile up in the midst of this city,*h* ⁵ and
I myself will fight against you with outstretched hand and mighty arm, in anger,
and wrath, and great rage!*i* ⁶ I will strike
the inhabitants of this city, both man and
beast; they shall die in a great pestilence.*j*
⁷ After that, says the LORD, I will hand
over Zedekiah, king of Judah, and his
ministers and the people in this city who
survive pestilence, sword, and famine, into
the hand of Nebuchadnezzar, king of
Babylon, into the hands of their enemies
and those who seek their lives. He shall
strike them with the edge of the sword,
without quarter, without pity or mercy.*k*
⁸ And to this people you shall say: Thus
says the LORD: See, I am giving you a
choice between life and death.*l* ⁹ Whoever
remains in this city shall die by the sword
or famine or pestilence. But whoever
leaves and surrenders to the besieging
Chaldeans shall live and have his life as
booty. ¹⁰ For I have turned against this
city, for its woe and not for its good, says
the LORD. It shall be given into the power
of the king of Babylon who shall burn it
with fire.*

y Jer 6, 11; Jb 32, 18.—z Jb 19, 19; Ps 31, 13; Lk 20, 20.—a
Jer 1, 8; 15, 20.—b Jer 11, 20.—c Pss 35, 9f; 109, 30f.—d Jer
15, 10; Jb 3, 1-10; 10, 18.—e Gn 19, 25; Is 13, 19.—f Jb 3, 10f;
10, 19.—g Jb 14, 1.—h Jer 37, 8ff.—i Is 63, 10; Lam 2, 4f.—j
Jer 16, 4.—k Jer 24, 8ff; Dt 28, 49f.—l Jer 21, 9; Dt 30, 15. 19.

20, 14-18: Deception, sorrow and terror have brought the
prophet close to the point of despair; nevertheless he has expressed his utmost confidence in the triumph of God's will (vv
11ff); cf Jb 3, 12.

21, 1: *Zedekiah:* brother of Jehoiakim, appointed king by
Nebuchadnezzar after he had carried Jehoiachin away to captivity (2 Kgs 24, 17). *Pashhur:* different from the one in Jer 20, 1ff
but also one of Jeremiah's enemies; cf Jer 38, 1. 4.

21, 10: Jeremiah consistently pointed out the uselessness of
resistance to Babylon, since the Lord had delivered Judah to
Nebuchadnezzar (Jer 27, 6). Because of this the prophet was denounced and imprisoned as a traitor (Jer 37, 13f).

Oracles regarding the Kings

11 To the royal house of Judah:*
Hear the word of the LORD, 12 O house
of David!
Thus says the LORD:
Each morning dispense justice,
rescue the oppressed from the hand
of the oppressor,
Lest my fury break out like fire
which burns without being quenched,
because of the evil of your deeds. *m*
13 Beware! I am against you, Valley-site,
Rock of the Plain,* says the LORD.
You who say, "Who will attack us,
who can penetrate our retreats?"
14 I will punish you, says the LORD,
as your deeds deserve!
I will kindle a fire in its forest*
that shall devour all its surroundings. *n*

CHAPTER 22

1 The LORD told me this: Go down to
the palace of the king of Judah and there
deliver this message: 2 You shall say: Listen to the word of the LORD, king of
Judah, who sit on the throne of David,
you, your ministers, and your people that
enter by these gates! *o* 3 Thus says the
LORD: Do what is right and just. Rescue
the victim from the hand of his oppressor.
Do not wrong or oppress the resident
alien, the orphan, or the widow, and do
not shed innocent blood in this place. *p* 4 If
you carry out these commands, kings who
succeed to the throne of David will continue to enter the gates of this palace, riding in chariots or mounted on horses, with
their ministers, and their people. 5 But if
you do not obey these commands, I swear
by myself, says the LORD: this palace shall
become rubble. 6 For thus says the LORD
concerning the palace of the king of Judah:

Though you be to me like Gilead,
like the peak of Lebanon,*
I will turn you into a waste,
a city uninhabited.
7 Against you I will send destroyers,
each with his axe:
They shall cut down your choice cedars,
and cast them into the fire. *q*

8 Many people will pass by this city and
ask one another: "Why has the LORD done
this to so great a city?" *r* 9 And the answer
will be given: "Because they have deserted

their covenant with the LORD, their God,
by worshiping and serving strange gods." *s*

Jehoahaz

10 Weep not for him who is dead,*
mourn not for him!
Weep rather for him who is going away;
never again will he see
the land of his birth. *t*

11 Thus says the LORD concerning Shallum,* son of Josiah, king of Judah, who
succeeded his father as king. He has left
this place never to return. 12 Rather, he
shall die in the place where they exiled
him; this land he shall not see again.

Jehoiakim

13 Woe to him who builds his house on
wrong,
his terraces on injustice;
Who works his neighbor without pay,*
and gives him no wages. *u*
14 Who says, "I will build myself a
spacious house,
with airy rooms,"
Who cuts out windows for it,
panels it with cedar,
and paints it with vermillion.
15 Must you prove your rank among kings*
by competing with them in cedar?
Did not your father eat and drink?
He did what was right and just,
and it went well with him. *v*

m Jer 4, 4; 22, 3; Zec 7, 9.—n 2 Kgs 25, 9; 2 Chr 36, 19.—o
Jer 17, 20.—p Jer 21, 12; Ex 22, 21-24; Dt 24, 17.—q Jer 21,
14.—r Dt 29, 24ff.—s Jer 19, 4; 40, 2f.—t 2 Chr 35, 23ff.—u Lv
19, 13; Dt 24, 14; Hb 2, 9. 12.—v 2 Kgs 23, 25.

21, 11—23, 8: This section contains an editor's collection of
Jeremiah's oracles against the kings of Judah. They are placed in
the chronological order of the kings, and are prefaced by the oracles against the kings of Judah in general (Jer 21, 11—22, 9).
21, 13: *Valley-site, Rock of the Plain:* Mount Zion, surrounded by valleys, was regarded by the royal house as im-
pregnable. Despite this natural fortification, God shows derisively
that it is no more than a rock rising from the plain, undefendable
against the attack of his fury.
21, 14: *Its forest:* probably the royal palace, built of cedar
wood; cf Jer 22, 14; in 1 Kgs 7, 2 the armory of Solomon's palace
is called "the house of the forest of Lebanon."
22, 6: *Gilead . . . Lebanon:* both were known for their trees;
cf v 7.
22, 10: *Him who is dead:* Josiah. His successor, Jehoahaz,
who is going away, was deported by Pharaoh Neco to Egypt,
where he died (2 Kgs 23, 33f).
22, 11: *Shallum:* Jehoahaz is called this only here. Presumably it was his name at birth, while Jehoahaz was his royal name.
22, 13: *Without pay:* either by forced labor in public works,
or inasmuch as workers were defrauded of their hire. Despite the
impoverishment caused in Judah by the payment of foreign tribute, Jehoiakim embarked on a program of lavish building in Jerusalem (v 14). Social injustice is the cause of much of the prophetic condemnation of the kings (v 17).
22, 15f: Josiah, the reforming king, prospered materially
without oppressing his people; he embodied all the ideals of kingship.

¹⁶ Because he dispensed justice to the
    weak and the poor,
    it went well with him.
Is this not true knowledge of me?
    says the LORD.^w
¹⁷ But your eyes and heart are set on noth-
    ing
    except on your own gain,
On shedding innocent blood,
    on practicing oppression and extor-
    tion.^x

¹⁸ Therefore, thus says the LORD con-
cerning Jehoiakim, son of Josiah, king of
Judah:

They shall not lament him,
    "Alas! my brother"; "Alas! sister."*
They shall not lament him,
    "Alas, Lord! alas, Majesty!"^y
¹⁹ The burial of an ass* shall he be given,
    dragged forth and cast out
    beyond the gates of Jerusalem.^z

Jeconiah

²⁰ Scale Lebanon and cry out,*
    in Bashan lift up your voice;
Cry out from Abarim,
    for all your lovers are crushed.^a
²¹ I spoke to you when you were secure,
    but you answered, "I will not listen."
This has been your way from your
    youth,
    not to listen to my voice.
²² The wind shall shepherd all your
    shepherds,
    your lovers shall go into exile.
Surely then you shall be ashamed and
    confounded

because of all your wickedness.
²³ You who dwell on Lebanon,
    who nest in the cedars,
How you shall groan when pains come
    upon you,
    like the pangs of a woman in travail!

²⁴ As I live, says the LORD, if you, Co-
niah,* son of Jehoiakim, king of Judah,
are a signet ring on my right hand, I will
snatch you from it. ²⁵ I will deliver you
into the hands of those who seek your life;
the hands of those whom you fear; the
hands of Nebuchadnezzar, king of Baby-
lon, and the Chaldeans.^b ²⁶ I will cast you
out, you and the mother who bore you,*
into a different land from the one you were
born in; and there you shall die.^c
²⁷ Neither of them shall come back to the
land for which they yearn.^d

²⁸ Is this man Coniah a vessel despised, to
    be broken up,
    an instrument that no one wants?
Why are he and his descendants cast
    out?
    why thrown into a land they know
    not?
²⁹ O land, land, land,
    hear the word of the LORD—
³⁰   Thus says the LORD:
  ^e Write this man down as one child-
    less,*
    who will never thrive in his lifetime!
No descendant of his shall achieve
    a seat on the throne of David
    as ruler again over Judah.

CHAPTER 23

Messianic Reign.* ¹ ^f Woe to the shepherds who mislead and scatter the flock

---

w Prv 31, 9.—x Ez 22, 13. 27.—y Jer 16, 4ff; 1 Kgs 13, 30.—z
Jer 36, 30.—a Jer 30, 14f; Dt 32, 49.—b Jer 21, 7; 34, 20.—c
2 Kgs 24, 15.—d Jer 44, 14.—e Jer 36, 30; 1 Chr 3, 16f; Mt 1,
12.—f Jer 22, 22.

22, 18: *"Alas! my brother"; "Alas! sister":* customary
cries of mourning.
22, 19: *The burial of an ass:* no burial at all, except to be
cast outside the city as refuse. This prophecy regards the popular
feeling toward Jehoiakim rather than the actual circumstances of
his burial. According to 2 Kgs 24, 5 he was buried with his fathers
in Jerusalem. However, his grave may have been profaned by
Nebuchadnezzar.
22, 20-23: The prophet first apostrophizes Jerusalem, which
is bidden to scale *Lebanon, Bashan,* and *Abarim,* i.e., the highest surrounding mountains to the north, northeast, and southeast,
to gaze on the ruin of its *lovers,* i.e., the false leaders of Judah,
called its *shepherds* (22); cf Jer 2, 8. The year is 597 B.C., after
Nebuchadnezzar's deportation of Jehoiachin. Jerusalem still
stands (23), apparently as secure as the heights of Lebanon, but
destruction is to follow (cf v 6).
22, 24: *Coniah:* a shortened form of Jeconiah, the name
which Jeremiah gives the king called elsewhere in the Bible
Jehoiachin. *A signet ring:* the seal used by important men—in a
sense, their most valuable possession—mounted in a ring worn
constantly on the hand. The Lord says that even were Jehoiachin
such a precious possession, he would reject him. The words in vv

24-30 date from the short three-month reign of Jehoiachin, before he was carried away by Nebuchadnezzar.
22, 26: *You and the mother who bore you:* the queen
mother held a special position in the monarchy of Judah, and in
the Books of Kings she is invariably mentioned by name along
with the king (1 Kgs 15, 2; 2 Kgs 18, 2). Jehoiachin did indeed
die in Babylon.
22, 30: *Childless:* Jehoiachin is so considered because none
of his descendants will be king. From the Book of Ezekiel, who
dates his oracles according to Jehoiachin's fictitious regnal years,
it is evident that the people expected Jehoiachin to return. The
above prophecy of Jeremiah was uttered to dispel this hope (Jer
28, 4). Of the seven sons born to Jehoiachin in exile, none became
king. His grandson Zerubbabel presided for a time over the
Jewish community after the return from exile, but not as king.
23, 1-8: With the false rulers who have governed his people the
Lord contrasts himself, the good shepherd, who will in the times of
restoration appoint worthy rulers (1-4). A messianic King will arise
from the line of David who will rule over Judah and Israel with the
justice of the Lord, fulfilling all the kingly ideals (5f). *"The Lord
our justice"* is probably an ironic wordplay on the name of the
weak King Zedekiah ("The Lord is justice"); the messianic King
will be in reality what Zedekiah's name falsely proclaims him. The
final verses, 7-8, were probably added during the exile.

of my pasture, says the LORD. ²Therefore, thus says the LORD, the God of Israel, against the shepherds who shepherd my people: You have scattered my sheep and driven them away. You have not cared for them, but I will take care to punish your evil deeds.ᵍ ³I myself will gather the remnant of my flock from all the lands to which I have driven them and bring them back to their meadow; there they shall increase and multiply.ʰ ⁴I will appoint shepherds for them who will shepherd them so that they need no longer fear and tremble; and none shall be missing, says the LORD.ⁱ

⁵ Behold, the days are coming, says the
    LORD,
    when I will raise up a righteous shoot
      to David;
  As king he shall reign and govern
      wisely,
    he shall do what is just and right in
      the land.ʲ
⁶ In his days Judah shall be saved,
    Israel shall dwell in security.
  This is the name they give him:
    "The LORD our justice."ᵏ

⁷ ˡ Therefore, the days will come, says the LORD, when they shall no longer say, "As the LORD lives, who brought the Israelites out of the land of Egypt"; ⁸but rather, "As the LORD lives, who brought the descendants of the house of Israel up from the land of the north"—and from all the lands to which I banished them; they shall again live on their own land.

The False Prophets*

⁹   Concerning the prophets:
  My heart within me is broken,
    my bones all tremble;
  I am like a man who is drunk,
    overcome by wine,
  Because of the LORD,
    because of his holy words.
¹⁰ With adulterers the land is filled;
  on their account the land mourns,
    the pasture ranges are seared.ᵐ
  Theirs is an evil course,
    theirs is unjust power.
¹¹ Both prophet and priest are godless!
  In my very house I find their wickedness,
  says the LORD.ⁿ
¹² Hence their way shall become for them
  slippery ground.

In the darkness they shall lose their
    footing,
    and fall headlong;
Evil I will bring upon them:
  the year of their punishment, says the
    LORD.ᵒ
¹³ Among Samaria's prophets
    I saw unseemly deeds:
  They prophesied by Baal
    and led my people Israel astray.ᵖ
¹⁴ But among Jerusalem's prophets
    I saw deeds still more shocking:
  Adultery, living in lies,
    siding with the wicked,
    so that no one turns from evil;
  To me they are all like Sodom,
    its citizens like Gomorrah.�q

¹⁵Therefore, thus says the LORD of hosts against the prophets:

Behold, I will give them wormwood to
    eat,
    and poison to drink;
For from Jerusalem's prophets
  ungodliness has gone forth into the
    whole land.ʳ

¹⁶   Thus says the LORD of hosts:
  Listen not to the words of your prophets,
    who fill you with emptiness;
  Visions of their own fancy they speak,
    not from the mouth of the LORD.ˢ
¹⁷ They say to those who despise the word
    of the LORD,*
  "Peace shall be yours";
  And to everyone who walks in hardness
    of heart,
  "No evil shall overtake you."ᵗ
¹⁸ Now, who has stood in the council of
    the LORD,
    to see him and to hear his word?
    Who has heeded his word, so as to
    announce it?ᵘ

---

g Ez 34, 4ff; Zec 11, 16f.—h Jer 29, 14; 32, 37.—i Jer 3, 15; Ez 34, 11f.—j Jer 33, 14ff; Is 4, 2; 9, 5f; 11, 1-5.—k Dn 9, 24.—l 7f: Jer 16, 14f.—m Jer 4, 22; 5, 7f; 9, 2. 10.—n Jer 6, 13.—o Ps 35, 6.—p 1 Kgs 18, 19.—q Jer 29, 21ff; Is 1, 9f.—r Jer 8, 14; 9, 14.—s Jer 14, 14.—t Jer 5, 12; Ez 13, 10; Mi 3, 11; Zec 10, 2.—u Jb 15, 8; Is 40, 13; 1 Cor 2, 16.

23, 9-40: After the collection of oracles against the kings, the editor of the book placed this collection of oracles against the false prophets. With them are associated the priests, for both have betrayed their trust as instructors in the religion of the Lord; cf Jer 2, 8; 4, 9; 6, 13f.

23, 17-20: Not only are the false prophets personally immoral, but they encourage immorality by prophesying good of those who do evil. The true prophet, on the other hand, sees the inevitable consequences of sin.

¹⁹ See, the storm of the LORD!
His wrath breaks forth
In a whirling storm
that bursts upon the heads of the
wicked.^v

²⁰ The anger of the LORD shall not abate
until he has done and fulfilled
what he has determined in his heart.
When the time comes,
you shall fully understand.

²¹ I did not send these prophets,
yet they ran;
I did not speak to them,
yet they prophesied.^w

²² Had they stood in my council,
and did they but proclaim to my people my words,
They would have brought them back
from evil ways
and from their wicked deeds.

²³ Am I a God near at hand only, says the
LORD,^x
and not a God far off?*

²⁴ Can a man hide in secret
without my seeing him? says the
LORD.
Do I not fill
both heaven and earth? says the
LORD.

²⁵ I have heard the prophets who proph-
esy lies in my name say, "I had a dream! I
had a dream!" ²⁶ How long will this continue? Is my name in the hearts of the
prophets who prophesy lies and their own
deceitful fancies? ²⁷ By their dreams which
they recount to each other, they think to
make my people forget my name, just as
their fathers forgot my name for Baal.^y
²⁸ Let the prophet who has a dream re-

count his dream; let him who has my word
speak my word truthfully!

What has straw to do with the wheat?*
says the LORD.^z

²⁹ Is not my word like fire, says the LORD,
like a hammer shattering rocks?

³⁰ Therefore I am against the prophets,
says the LORD, who steal my words from
each other.^a ³¹ Yes, I am against the
prophets, says the LORD, who borrow
speeches to pronounce oracles. ³² Yes, I
am against the prophets who prophesy
lying dreams, says the LORD, and who
lead my people astray by recounting their
lies and by their empty boasting. From
me they have no mission or command,
and they do this people no good at all,
says the LORD.^b

³³ * And when this people, or a prophet
or a priest asks you, "What is the burden
of the LORD?" you shall answer, "You are
the burden, and I cast you off, says the
LORD." ³⁴ If a prophet or a priest or anyone else mentions "the burden of the
LORD," I will punish that man and his
house. ³⁵ Thus you shall ask, when speaking to one another, "What answer did the
LORD give?" or, "What did the LORD
say?" ³⁶ But the burden of the LORD you
shall mention no more. For each man his
own word becomes the burden so that you
pervert the words of the living God, the
LORD of hosts, our God. ³⁷ Thus shall you
ask the prophet, "What answer did the
LORD give?" or, "What did the LORD
say?" ³⁸ But if you ask about "the burden
of the LORD," then thus says the LORD:
Because you use this phrase, "the burden
of the LORD," though I forbade you to use
it, ³⁹ therefore I will lift you on high and
cast you from my presence, you and the
city which I gave to you and your fathers.
⁴⁰ And I will bring upon you eternal re-
proach, eternal, unforgettable shame.^c

CHAPTER 24

The Two Baskets of Figs.* ¹ The LORD
showed me two baskets of figs placed before the temple of the LORD.^d—This was
after Nebuchadnezzar, king of Babylon,
had exiled from Jerusalem Jeconiah, son of
Jehoiakim, king of Judah, and the princes
of Judah, the artisans and the skilled
workers, and brought them to Babylon.—
² One basket contained excellent figs, the

v Jer 30, 23.—w Jer 29, 9.—x Jer 16, 17; Ps 139, 8.—y Jgs
3, 7; 8, 33.—z Nm 12, 6.—a Dt 18, 20.—b Jer 28, 15ff.—c Jer
20, 11.—d Am 8, 1f.

23, 23: *Near at hand only . . . far off:* God knows not
merely the present but also the future.

23, 28f: *Straw . . . wheat:* such is the contrast between false
and true prophecy. True prophecy is like fire (cf Jer 5, 14; 20, 9),
producing violent results (v 29); Jeremiah's own life is a testimony of that.

23, 33-40: A wordplay on *massa,* which means both oracle
(usually of woe) and burden. In 34ff it appears that the word
massa itself is forbidden the people in the meaning of a divine
oracle. Doubtless this was because of some association unknown
to us. In Hos 2, 18 it is forbidden to call God "Baal" ("master"),
because of the association of this title with the Canaanite god.

24, 1-10: Jeremiah, like Ezekiel, saw that no good could be
expected from the people who had been left in Judah under
Zedekiah or who had fled into Egypt; good was to be hoped for
only from those who would pass through the purifying experience
of the exile to form the new Israel.

Jer

early-ripening kind. But the other basket contained very bad figs, so bad they could not be eaten. ³Then the LORD said to me: What do you see, Jeremiah?*e* "Figs," I replied; "the good ones are very good, but the bad ones very bad, so bad they cannot be eaten." ⁴Thereupon this word of the LORD came to me: ⁵Thus says the LORD, the God of Israel: Like these good figs, even so will I regard with favor Judah's exiles whom I sent away from this place into the land of the Chaldeans.*f* ⁶I will look after them for their good, and bring them back to this land, to build them up, not to tear them down; to plant them, not to pluck them out.*g* ⁷I will give them a heart with which to understand that I am the LORD. They shall be my people and I will be their God, for they shall return to me with their whole heart.*h* ⁸And like the figs that are bad, so bad they cannot be eaten—yes, thus says the LORD—even so will I treat Zedekiah, king of Judah, and his princes, the remnant of Jerusalem remaining in this land and those who have settled in the land of Egypt.*i* ⁹I will make them an object of horror to all the kingdoms of the earth, a reproach and a byword, a taunt and a curse, in all the places to which I will drive them.*j* ¹⁰I will send upon them the sword, famine, and pestilence, until they have disappeared from the land which I gave them and their fathers.*k*

CHAPTER 25

Seventy Years of Exile. * ¹The word that came to Jeremiah concerning all the people of Judah, in the fourth year of Jehoiakim, son of Josiah, king of Judah (the first year of Nebuchadnezzar, king of Babylon).*l* ²This word the prophet Jeremiah spoke to all the people of Judah and all the citizens of Jerusalem: ³Since the thirteenth year of Josiah, son of Amon, king of Judah, to this day—these three and twenty years—the word of the LORD has come to me and I spoke to you untiringly, but you would not listen.*m* ⁴Though you refused to listen or pay heed, the LORD has sent you without fail all his servants the prophets*n* ⁵with this message: Turn back, each of you, from your evil way and from your evil deeds; then you shall remain in the land which the LORD gave you and your fathers, from of old and forever. ⁶Do not

follow strange gods to serve and adore them, lest you provoke me with your handiwork, and I bring evil upon you.*o* ⁷But you would not listen to me, says the LORD, and so you provoked me with your handiwork to your own harm.*p* ⁸Hence, thus says the LORD of hosts: Since you would not listen to my words, ⁹lo! I will send for and fetch all the tribes of the north, says the LORD (and I will send to Nebuchadnezzar, king of Babylon, my servant); I will bring them against this land, against its inhabitants, and against all these neighboring nations. I will doom them, making them an object of horror, of ridicule, of everlasting reproach.*q* ¹⁰Among them I will bring to an end the song of joy and the song of gladness, the voice of the bridegroom and the voice of the bride, the sound of the millstone and the light of the lamp. ¹¹This whole land shall be a ruin and a desert. Seventy years these nations shall be enslaved to the king of Babylon;*r* ¹²but when the seventy years have elapsed, I will punish the king of Babylon and the nation and the land of the Chaldeans for their guilt, says the LORD. Their land I will turn into everlasting desert.*s* ¹³Against that land I will fulfill all the words I have spoken against it [all that is written in this book, which Jeremiah prophesied against all the nations]. ¹⁴They also shall be enslaved to great nations and mighty kings, and thus I will repay them according to their own deeds and according to their own handiwork.*t*

The Cup of Judgment on the Nations. ¹⁵For thus said the LORD, the God of Israel, to me:* Take this cup of foaming wine from my hand, and have all the nations to whom I will send you drink it.*u* ¹⁶They shall drink, and be convulsed,

e Jer 1, 11.—f Jer 29, 11; Lv 26, 44f.—g Jer 12, 15; Am 9, 15.—h Jer 30, 22; 31, 1; 32, 37; Bar 2, 31.—i Jer 29, 18.—j Jer 15, 4; Dt 28, 37.—k Jer 14, 12.—l Jer 36, 1.—m Jer 1, 2.—n 2 Chr 36, 15.—o Jer 7, 6f.—p Jer 7, 17ff.—q Jer 1, 15; 43, 10.—r Lv 26, 32-35.—s Is 13, 20ff.—t Jer 27, 7; 50, 9. 41f; 51, 6. 24.—u Rv 14, 10.

25, 1-14: *The fourth year of Jehoiakim:* 605 B.C. Officially, *the first year of Nebuchadnezzar* began the following year; but as early as his victory over Egypt at Carchemish in 605, Nebuchadnezzar was the dominant power in the Near East, in whom Jeremiah now saw the fulfillment of his prophecy of the enemy to come from the north (cf Jer 1, 13; 6, 22ff). In vv 11f occurs for the first time the prophecy of the seventy years' exile; cf Jer 29, 10. This Jeremiah intends as a round number, to signify that the present generation must die out.

25, 15ff: Jeremiah is a prophet to the nations (cf 1, 5) as well as to his own people. All the nations mentioned here appear again in the more extensive collection of Jeremiah's oracles against the nations in chapters 46-51.

and go mad, because of the sword I will send among them.[v] [17]I took the cup from the hand of the LORD and gave drink to all the nations to which the LORD sent me: [18][Jerusalem, the cities of Judah, her kings and her princes, to make them a ruin and a desert, an object of ridicule and cursing, as they are today;] [19]Pharaoh, king of Egypt, and his servants, his princes, all the people under him, native [20]and foreign; all the kings of the land of Uz;* all the kings of the land of the Philistines: Ashkelon, Gaza, Ekron, and the remnant of Ashdod; [21]Edom, Moab, and the Ammonites; [22]all the kings of Tyre, of Sidon, and of the shores beyond the sea;* [23]Dedan and Tema and Buz,* all the desert dwellers who shave their temples; [24][all the kings of Arabia;] [25]all the kings of Zimri, of Elam, of the Medes; [26]all the kings of the north, near and far, one after the other; all the kingdoms upon the face of the earth [and after them the king of Sheshach* shall drink].

[27]Tell them: Thus says the LORD of hosts, the God of Israel: Drink! become drunk and vomit; fall, never to rise, before the sword that I will send among you![w] [28]If they refuse to take the cup from your hand and drink, say to them: Thus says the LORD of hosts: You must drink![x] [29]For since with this city, which is called by my name, I begin to inflict evil, how can you possibly be spared? You shall not be spared! I will call down the sword upon all who inhabit the earth, says the LORD of hosts.

[30]Prophesy against them all these things and say to them:

The LORD roars from on high,
    from his holy dwelling he raises his voice;
Mightily he roars over the range,

a shout like that of vintagers over the grapes.[y]
[31] To all who inhabit the earth to its very ends
    the uproar spreads;
For the LORD has an indictment against the nations,
    he is to pass judgment upon all mankind:
The godless shall be given to the sword,
    says the LORD.
[32]   Thus says the LORD of hosts:
Lo! calamity stalks
    from nation to nation;
A great storm is unleashed
    from the ends of the earth.

[33] On that day, those whom the LORD has slain will be strewn from one end of the earth to the other. None will mourn them, none will gather them for burial; they shall lie like dung on the field.[z]

[34] Howl, you shepherds, and wail!
    roll in the dust, leaders of the flock!
The time for your slaughter has come;
    like choice rams you shall fall.
[35] There is no flight for the shepherds,
    no escape for the leaders of the flock.[a]
[36] Listen! Wailing from the shepherds,
    howling by the leaders of the flock!
For the LORD lays waste their grazing place,
[37]   desolate lie the peaceful pastures;
[38] The lion leaves his lair,
    and their land is made desolate
By the sweeping sword,
    by the burning wrath of the LORD.[b]

CHAPTER 26

Jeremiah Threatened with Death. [1]In the beginning of the reign* of Jehoiakim, son of Josiah, king of Judah, this message came from the LORD: [2]Thus says the LORD: Stand in the court of the house of the LORD and speak to the people of all the cities of Judah who come to worship in the house of the LORD; whatever I command you, tell them, and omit nothing.[c] [3]Perhaps they will listen and turn back, each from his evil way, so that I may repent of the evil I have planned to inflict upon them for their evil deeds.[d] [4]Say to them: Thus says the LORD: If you disobey me, not living according to the law I placed before you [5]and not listening

v Jer 51, 7.—w Ob 1, 16.—x Jer 49, 12.—y Jer 51, 14.—z Jer 8, 2; 16, 4. 6.—a Jer 32, 4.—b Jer 4, 7.—c Jer 7, 2.—d Jer 18, 3.

25, 20: *Uz:* the homeland of Job, in Edomite or Arabian territory.
25, 22: *The shores beyond the sea:* Phoenician commercial colonies planted throughout the Mediterranean world.
25, 23: *Dedan and Tema and Buz:* North Arabian tribes.
25, 25: *Sheshach:* Babylon. The word is formed from *babel* by substituting letters of the Hebrew alphabet in inverse order.
26, 1: *The beginning of the reign:* a technical expression for the time between a king's accession to the throne and the beginning of his first official (calendar) year as king. Jehoiakim's first regnal year was 608 B.C.

to the words of my servants the prophets, whom I send you constantly though you do not obey them,[e] [6]I will treat this house like Shiloh, and make this the city which all the nations of the earth shall refer to when cursing another.[f]

[7]Now the priests, the prophets, and all the people heard Jeremiah speak these words in the house of the LORD. [8]When Jeremiah finished speaking all that the LORD bade him speak to all the people, the priests and prophets laid hold of him, crying, "You must be put to death! [9]Why do you prophesy in the name of the LORD: 'This house shall be like Shiloh,' and 'This city shall be desolate and deserted'?" And all the people gathered about Jeremiah in the house of the LORD.

[10]When the princes of Judah were informed of these things, they came up from the king's palace to the house of the LORD and held court at the New Gate of the house of the LORD. [11]The priests and prophets said to the princes and to all the people, "This man deserves death; he has prophesied against this city, as you have heard with your own ears."[g] [12]Jeremiah gave this answer to the princes and all the people: "It was the LORD who sent me to prophesy against this house and city all that you have heard. [13]Now, therefore, reform your ways and your deeds; listen to the voice of the LORD your God, so that the LORD will repent of the evil with which he threatens you.[h] [14]As for me, I am in your hands; do with me what you think good and right. [15]But mark well: if you put me to death, it is innocent blood you bring on yourselves, on this city and its citizens. For in truth it was the LORD who sent me to you, to speak all these things for you to hear."

[16]Thereupon the princes and all the people said to the priests and the prophets, "This man does not deserve death; it is in the name of the LORD, our God, that he speaks to us." [17]At this, some of the elders of the land came forward and said to all the people assembled, [18]"Micah of Moresheth* used to prophesy in the days of Hezekiah, king of Judah, and he told all the people of Judah: Thus says the LORD of hosts:

Zion shall become a plowed field,
    Jerusalem a heap of ruins,
    and the temple mount a forest ridge.[i]

[19]Did Hezekiah, king of Judah, and all Judah condemn him to death? Did they not rather fear the LORD and entreat the favor of the LORD, so that he repented of the evil with which he had threatened them? But we are on the point of committing this great evil to our own undoing."[j]

The Fate of Uriah. [20]There was another man who prophesied in the name of the LORD, Uriah, son of Shemaiah, from Kiriath-jearim; he prophesied the same things against this city and land as Jeremiah did. [21]When King Jehoiakim and all his officers and princes were informed of his words, the king sought to kill him. But Uriah heard of it and fled in fear to Egypt. [22]Thereupon King Jehoiakim sent Elnathan, son of Achbor, and others with him into Egypt [23]to bring Uriah back to the king, who had him slain by the sword and his corpse cast into the common grave. [24]But Ahikam, son of Shaphan,* protected Jeremiah, so that he was not handed over to the people to be put to death.

CHAPTER 27

Serve Babylon or Perish.* [1][In the beginning of the reign of Jehoiakim, son of Josiah, king of Judah,]* . . . this message came to Jeremiah from the LORD: [2]Thus said the LORD to me: Make for yourself bands and yoke bars and put them over your shoulders. [3]Send to the kings of Edom, of Moab, of the Ammonites, of Tyre, and of Sidon, through the ambassadors who have come to Jerusalem to Zedekiah, king of Judah, [4]and charge them thus: Tell your masters: Thus says the LORD of hosts, the God of Israel: [5]It

---

e Jer 25, 4.—f Jer 7, 12. 14.—g Jer 38, 4.—h Jer 7, 3.—i Mi 1, 1; 3, 12.—j 2 Chr 32, 26.

26, 18: *Micah of Moresheth:* the prophet Micah, who appears among the canonical minor prophets (cf Mi 1, 1).

26, 24: *Ahikam, son of Shaphan:* one of Josiah's officials (2 Kgs 22, 12) and father of Gedaliah, Jeremiah's friend, who was governor of Judah after Zedekiah's deportation (cf Jer 39, 14; 40, 5ff).

27, 1—29, 32: A special collection of Jeremiah's prophecies dealing with false prophets. From stylistic peculiarities, quite evident in the Hebrew, it is plain that these three chapters once existed independently of the other prophecies of Jeremiah.

27, 1: *[In the beginning of the reign of Jehoiakim . . . Judah]:* this gloss cannot be correct because according to Jer 28, 1 the time is the fourth year of Zedekiah, 594 B.C., the occasion of an embassy of the neighboring states (v 3), doubtless for the purpose of laying plans against Nebuchadnezzar.

was I who made the earth, and man and beast on the face of the earth, by my great power, with my outstretched arm; and I can give them to whomever I think fit.[k] [6]Now I have given all these lands into the hand of Nebuchadnezzar, king of Babylon, my servant; even the beasts of the field I have given him for his use.[l] [7]All nations shall serve him and his son and his grandson, until the time of his land, too, shall come. Then it in turn shall serve great nations and mighty kings.[m] [8]Meanwhile, if any nation or kingdom will not serve Nebuchadnezzar, king of Babylon, or will not bend its neck under the yoke of the king of Babylon, I will punish that nation with sword, famine, and pestilence, says the LORD, until I give them into his hand.[n]

[9]You, however, must not listen to your prophets,* to your diviners and dreamers, to your soothsayers and sorcerers, who say to you, "You need not serve the king of Babylon."[o] [10]For they prophesy lies to you, in order to drive you far from your land, to make me banish you so that you will perish.[p] [11]The people that submits its neck to the yoke of the king of Babylon to serve him I will leave in peace on its own land, says the LORD, to till it and dwell in it.[q]

[12]To Zedekiah, king of Judah, I spoke the same words: Submit your necks to the yoke of the king of Babylon; serve him and his people, so that you may live.[r] [13]Why should you and your people die by sword, famine, and pestilence, with which the LORD has threatened the nation that will not serve the king of Babylon?[s] [14]Do not listen to the words of those prophets who say, "You need not serve the king of Babylon," for they prophesy lies to you.[t] [15]I did not send them, says the LORD, but they prophesy falsely in my name, with the result that I must banish you, and you will perish, you and the prophets who are prophesying to you.[u]

[16] [v] To the priests and to all the people I spoke as follows: Thus says the LORD: Do not listen to the words of your prophets who prophesy to you: "The vessels of the house of the LORD will be brought back from Babylon soon now," for they prophesy lies to you. [17]Do not listen to them! Serve the king of Babylon that you may live; else this city will become a heap of ruins. [18]If they were prophets, if the word of the LORD were with them, they would intercede with the LORD of hosts, that the vessels which remain in the house of the LORD and in the palace of the king of Judah and in Jerusalem might not be taken to Babylon. [19] * For thus says the LORD of hosts concerning the pillars, the bronze sea, the stands, and the rest of the vessels that remain in this city, [20]which Nebuchadnezzar, king of Babylon, did not take when he exiled Jeconiah, son of Jehoiakim, king of Judah, from Jerusalem to Babylon, along with all the nobles of Judah and Jerusalem—[21]yes, thus says the LORD of hosts, the God of Israel, concerning the vessels that remain in the house of the LORD, in the palace of the king of Judah, and in Jerusalem:[vv] [22]To Babylon they shall be brought, and there they shall remain, until the day I look for them, says the LORD; then I will bring them back and restore them to this place.

CHAPTER 28

The Two Yokes. [1]That same year, in [the beginning of] the reign of Zedekiah, king of Judah, in the fifth month of the fourth year, the prophet Hananiah, son of Azzur, from Gibeon, said to me in the house of the LORD in the presence of the priests and all the people: [2]"Thus says the LORD of hosts, the God of Israel: 'I will break the yoke of the king of Babylon. [3]Within two years I will restore to this place all the vessels of the temple of the LORD which Nebuchadnezzar, king of Babylon, took away from this place to Babylon. [4]And I will bring back to this place Jeconiah, son of Jehoiakim, king of Judah, and all the exiles of Judah who went to Babylon,' says the LORD, 'for I will break the yoke of the king of Babylon.' "

[5]The prophet Jeremiah answered the prophet Hananiah in the presence of the priests and all the people assembled in the house of the LORD, [6]and said: Amen! thus

---

k Jer 32, 17.—l Jer 25, 9; 43, 10; Ez 30, 21. 25.—m Jer 25, 11; 2 Chr 36, 20.—n Jer 25, 9; Bar 2, 22.—o Jer 29, 8.—p Jer 14, 13-16.—q Bar 2, 21.—r Jer 38, 17.—s Jer 24, 8ff.—t Jer 14, 14; 23, 21.—u Jer 20, 6.—v Jer 28, 3; 2 Chr 36, 7. 10. 18.—vv 21f: 2 Kgs 25, 13-17; 2 Chr 36, 18. 22.

27, 9: *Your prophets:* seers and diviners served the Gentile kings as the professional prophets served the kings of Judah.

27, 19-22: This prophecy was fulfilled after Zedekiah's disastrous defeat; cf 2 Kgs 25, 13ff.

may the LORD do! May he fulfill the things you have prophesied by bringing the vessels of the house of the LORD and all the exiles back from Babylon to this place! [7]But now, listen to what I am about to state in your hearing and the hearing of all the people. [8]From of old, the prophets who were before you and me prophesied war, woe, and pestilence against many lands and mighty kingdoms. [9]But the prophet who prophesies peace is recognized as truly sent by the LORD only when his prophetic prediction is fulfilled.[w]

[10]Thereupon the prophet Hananiah took the yoke from the neck of the prophet Jeremiah, broke it, [11]and said in the presence of all the people: "Thus says the LORD: 'Even so, within two years I will break the yoke of Nebuchadnezzar, king of Babylon, from off the neck of all the nations.'" At that, the prophet Jeremiah went away.

[12]Some time after the prophet Hananiah had broken the yoke from off the neck of the prophet Jeremiah, the word of the LORD came to Jeremiah: [13]Go tell Hananiah this: Thus says the LORD: By breaking a wooden yoke, you forge an iron yoke! [14]For thus says the LORD of hosts, the God of Israel: A yoke of iron I will place on the necks of all these nations serving Nebuchadnezzar, king of Babylon, and they shall serve him; even the beasts of the field I give him.[x]

[15]To the prophet Hananiah the prophet Jeremiah said: Hear this, Hananiah! The LORD has not sent you, and you have raised false confidence in this people. [16]For this, says the LORD, I will dispatch you from the face of the earth; this very year you shall die, because you have preached rebellion against the LORD.[y] [17]That same year, in the seventh month, Hananiah the prophet died.

CHAPTER 29

Letter to the Exiles in Babylon. [1]This is the contents of the letter which the prophet Jeremiah sent from Jerusalem to the remaining elders among the exiles, to the priests, the prophets, and all the people who were exiled by Nebuchadnezzar from Jerusalem to Babylon. [2]This was after King Jeconiah and the queen mother, the courtiers, the princes of Judah and

Jerusalem, the artisans and the skilled workmen had left Jerusalem.[z] [3]Delivered in Babylon by Elasah,* son of Shaphan, and by Gemariah, son of Hilkiah, whom Zedekiah, king of Judah, sent to the king of Babylon, the letter read:

[4]Thus says the LORD of hosts, the God of Israel, to all the exiles whom I exiled from Jerusalem to Babylon: [5]Build houses to dwell in; plant gardens, and eat their fruits. [6]Take wives and beget sons and daughters; find wives for your sons and give your daughters husbands, so that they may bear sons and daughters. There you must increase in number, not decrease. [7]Promote the welfare of the city to which I have exiled you; pray for it to the LORD, for upon its welfare depends your own.[a]

[10]Thus says the LORD: Only after seventy years have elapsed for Babylon will I visit you and fulfill for you my promise to bring you back to this place.[b] [11]For I know well the plans I have in mind for you, says the LORD, plans for your welfare, not for woe! plans to give you a future full of hope. [12]When you call me, when you go to pray to me, I will listen to you.[c] [13]When you look for me, you will find me. Yes, when you seek me with all your heart, [14]you will find me with you, says the LORD, and I will change your lot; I will gather you together from all the nations and all the places to which I have banished you, says the LORD, and bring you back to the place from which I have exiled you.[d]

[16]Thus says the LORD concerning the king who sits on David's throne, and all the people who remain in this city, your brethren who did not go with you into exile; [17]thus says the LORD of hosts: I am sending against them sword, famine and pestilence. I will make them like rotten figs, too bad to be eaten. [18]I will pursue them with sword, famine, and pestilence, and make them an object of horror to all the kingdoms of the earth, of malediction, astonishment, ridicule, and reproach to all

---

w Dt 18, 22.—x Jer 27, 6f; Dt 28, 48.—y Dt 13, 6.—z 2 Kgs 24, 15.—a 1 Tm 2, 1f.—b Jer 25, 11; 2 Chr 36, 21f; Ezr 1, 1; Dn 9, 2; Zec 1, 12; 7, 5.—c Jer 33, 3.—d Jer 23, 3. 8.

29, 3: *Elasah:* possibly the brother of Ahikam (cf Jer 26, 24). *Gemariah:* perhaps the son of the high priest Hilkiah; cf 2 Kgs 22, 4. Zedekiah had dispatched these men to Nebuchadnezzar for some other purpose, possibly the payment of tribute, but Jeremiah took advantage of their mission to send his letter by them.

the nations among which I will banish them.[e] [19] For they did not listen ·to my words, says the LORD, though I kept sending them my servants the prophets, only to have them go unheeded, says the LORD.[f]

[20] You, now, listen to the word of the LORD, all you exiles whom I sent away from Jerusalem to Babylon. [15] As for your saying, "The LORD has raised up for us prophets here in Babylon"—[8] thus says the LORD of hosts, the God of Israel: Do not let yourselves be deceived by the prophets and diviners who are among you; do not listen to those among you who dream dreams.[g] [9] For they prophesy lies to you in my name; I did not send them, says the LORD.[h] [21] This is what the LORD of hosts, the God of Israel, has to say about those who prophesy lies to you in my name, Ahab, son of Kolaiah, and Zedekiah, son of Maaseiah: I am handing them over to Nebuchadnezzar, king of Babylon, who will slay them before your eyes.[i] [22] All the exiles of Judah in Babylon will pattern a curse after them: "May the LORD make you like Zedekiah and Ahab, whom the king of Babylon roasted in the flames." [23] For they are criminals in Israel, committing adultery with their neighbors' wives, and alleging in my name things I did not command. I know, I am witness, says the LORD.[j]

The False Prophet Shemaiah. [24] Say this to Shemaiah, the Nehelamite: [25] Thus says the LORD of hosts, the God of Israel: Because you sent letters on your own authority to all the people of Jerusalem, to all the priests and to Zephaniah, the priest, son of Maaseiah, with this message: [26] * "The LORD has appointed you priest in place of the priest Jehoiada, so that there may be police officers in the house of the LORD, to take action against all madmen and those who pose as prophets, by putting them into the stocks or the pillory. [27] Why, then, do you not rebuke Jeremiah of Anathoth who poses as a prophet among you? [28] For he sent us in Babylon this message: It will be a long time; build houses to live in; plant gardens and eat their fruits. . . ."

[29] When the priest Zephaniah read this letter to the prophet, [30] the word of the LORD came to Jeremiah: [31] Send the message to all the exiles: Thus says the LORD concerning Shemaiah, the Nehelamite: Because Shemaiah prophesies to you without a mission from me, and raises false confidence, [32] says the LORD, I will therefore punish Shemaiah, the Nehelamite, and his offspring. None of them shall survive among this people to see the good I will do to this people, says the LORD, because he preached rebellion against the LORD.

CHAPTER 30

The Restoration. * [1] The following message came to Jeremiah from the LORD: [2] Thus says the LORD, the God of Israel: Write all the words I have spoken to you in a book.[k] [3] For behold, the days will come, says the LORD, when I will change the lot of my people (of Israel and Judah, says the LORD), and bring them back to the land which I gave to their fathers; they shall have it as their possession.[l]

[4] These are the words which the LORD spoke to Israel and to Judah: [5] thus says the LORD:

A cry of dismay we hear;
    fear reigns, not peace.
[6] Inquire, and see:
    since when do men bear children?
Why, then, do I see all these men,
    with their hands on their loins
    like women in childbirth?
Why have all their faces turned
    deathly pale?[m]
[7] How mighty is that day—
    none like it!
A time of distress for Jacob,
    though he shall be saved from it.[n]

---

e Jer 15, 4; 24, 9; 34, 17f.—f Jer 25, 4.—g Jer 27, 9. 14.—h Jer 5, 31.—i Jer 14, 14.—j Jer 23, 14.—k Jer 36, 2; Hb 2, 2; Rv 1, 11.—l Jer 29, 14; 31, 8. 10. 23; 32, 37. 44; Ez 39, 25; Am 9, 14.—m Jer 6, 24; 50, 43.—n Am 5, 18; Zep 1, 14f.

29, 26-29: The words of Jeremiah to the false prophet Shemaiah are not fully preserved in the current Hebrew text, as is seen in the incomplete sentence of this translation (vv 25-28). In his letter to Zephaniah Shemaiah reminds him of his authority, as Pashhur's successor, to imprison Jeremiah. Zephaniah, however, merely reads the letter to Jeremiah but does not imprison him.

30, 1—31, 40: These two chapters do not belong chronologically to those that precede and follow. They contain mainly oracles of salvation which Jeremiah originally uttered on behalf of the conquered remnants of the northern kingdom; then, after Judah began to share Samaria's fate, the oracles were extended to include Judah. Their composition is to be placed early in Jeremiah's ministry, probably after the fall of Nineveh (612 B.C.), when Josiah assumed power over the North; cf 2 Kgs 23, 15ff.

Jer

⁸On that day, says the LORD of hosts, "I will break his yoke from off your necks and snap your bonds." Strangers shall no longer enslave them;ᵒ ⁹instead, they shall serve the LORD, their God, and David, their king,* whom I will raise up for them.ᵖ

¹⁰ But you, my servant Jacob, fear not,
  says the LORD,
  be not dismayed, O Israel!
Behold, I will deliver you from the far-off land,
  your descendants, from their land of exile;
Jacob shall again find rest,
  shall be tranquil and undisturbed,�q
¹¹ for I am with you, says the LORD, to deliver you.
I will make an end of all the nations
  among which I have scattered you;
  but of you I will not make an end.
I will chastise you as you deserve,
  I will not let you go unpunished.ʳ

¹² For thus says the LORD:
Incurable is your wound,
  grievous your bruise;ˢ
¹³ There is none to plead your cause,
  no remedy for your running sore,
  no healing for you.
¹⁴ All your lovers have forgotten you,
  they do not seek you.
I struck you as an enemy would strike,
  punished you cruelly;ᵗ
¹⁵ Why cry out over your wound?
  your pain is without relief.
Because of your great guilt,
  your numerous sins,
  I have done this to you.ᵘ

¹⁶ Yet all who devour you shall be devoured,
  all your enemies shall go into exile.
All who plunder you shall be plundered,
  all who pillage you I will hand over to pillage.ᵛ
¹⁷ For I will restore you to health;
  of your wounds I will heal you, says the LORD.
"The outcast" they have called you,
  "with no avenger."ʷ

¹⁸ Thus says the LORD:
See! I will restore the tents of Jacob,
  his dwellings I will pity;
City shall be rebuilt upon hill,
  and palace restored as it was.ˣ

¹⁹ From them will resound songs of praise,
  the laughter of happy men.
I will make them not few, but many;
  they will not be tiny, for I will glorify them.ʸ
²⁰ His sons shall be as of old,
  his assembly before me shall stand firm;
  I will punish all his oppressors.ᶻ
²¹ His leader* shall be one of his own,
  and his rulers shall come from his kin.
When I summon him, he shall approach me;
  how else should one take the deadly risk
  of approaching me? says the LORD.
²² You shall be my people,
  and I will be your God.ᵃ

²³ See, the storm of the LORD!
  His wrath breaks forth
In a whirling storm
  that bursts upon the heads of the wicked.ᵇ
²⁴ The anger of the LORD will not abate
  until he has done and fulfilled
  what he has determined in his heart.
When the time comes,
  you will fully understand.ᶜ

CHAPTER 31

Good News of the Return

¹ At that time, says the LORD,
  I will be the God of all the tribes of Israel,
  and they shall be my people.ᵈ
² Thus says the LORD:
The people that escaped the sword*
  have found favor in the desert.

---

o Is 14, 5f; Ez 34, 27.—p Ez 34, 23; 37, 24; Hos 3, 5; Lk 1, 69.—q Jer 46, 27; Is 43, 5.—r Jer 46, 28; Ez 11, 16f; Am 9, 8f.—s Jer 10, 19; 14, 17; 15, 18.—t Jer 22, 22; Lam 1, 19.—u Jer 15, 18.—v Jer 2, 3.—w Jer 33, 6.—x Jer 33, 7, 11; Ezr 6, 3-15; Ez 36, 10.—y Is 35, 10; 51, 11.—z Is 49, 26.—a Jer 24, 7; 31, 1. 33; 32, 38; Lv 26, 12; Ez 11, 20; 36, 28.—b Jer 23, 19.—c Jer 23, 20.—d Jer 30, 22.

30, 9: *David, their king:* the messianic King of the Davidic line, often called David by the prophets; cf Ez 34, 23f; 37, 24f; Hos 3, 5.

30, 21: *His leader:* probably not the messianic King, but simply any one of the rulers of the restored Israel, who will no longer be foreigners, and with whom the Lord will be on terms of intimacy, as with the whole people. *The deadly risk of approaching me:* to approach God unsummoned brings death; cf Lv 16, 1f.

31, 2: *The people that escaped the sword:* the exiles who were not killed but deported; they *have found favor in the desert,* across which they were driven into captivity. The prophet alludes to the first desert wandering of Israel (Ex 16ff), in which the people found the Lord. *His rest:* the land of promise. The perfect fulfillment of this promised rest is found only in the New Testament (Heb, chapters 3 and 4).

As Israel comes forward to be given his
rest,
3 the LORD appears to him from afar:
With age-old love I have loved you;
so I have kept my mercy toward
you.*e*
4 Again I will restore you, and you shall
be rebuilt,
O virgin Israel;
Carrying your festive tambourines,
you shall go forth dancing with the
merrymakers.
5 Again you shall plant vineyards
on the mountains of Samaria;
those who plant them shall enjoy the
fruits.*f*
6 Yes, a day will come when the watchmen
will call out on Mount Ephraim:
"Rise up, let us go to Zion,
to the LORD, our God."*g*

The Road of Return

7 For thus says the LORD:
Shout with joy for Jacob,
exult at the head of the nations;
proclaim your praise and say:
The LORD has delivered his people,
the remnant of Israel.*h*
8 Behold, I will bring them back
from the land of the north;
I will gather them from the ends of the
world,
with the blind and the lame in their
midst,
The mothers and those with child;
they shall return as an immense
throng.*i*
9 They departed in tears,
but I will console them and guide
them;
I will lead them to brooks of water,
on a level road, so that none shall
stumble.
For I am a father to Israel,
Ephraim is my first-born.*j*
10 Hear the word of the LORD, O nations,
proclaim it on distant coasts, and say:

He who scattered Israel, now gathers
them together,
he guards them as a shepherd his
flock.
11 The LORD shall ransom Jacob,
he shall redeem him from the hand of
his conqueror.*k*
12 Shouting, they shall mount the heights
of Zion,
they shall come streaming to the
LORD's blessings:
The grain, the wine, and the oil,
the sheep and the oxen;
They themselves shall be like watered
gardens,
never again shall they languish.*l*
13 Then the virgins shall make merry and
dance,
and young men and old as well.
I will turn their mourning into joy,
I will console and gladden them after
their sorrows.
14 I will lavish choice portions upon the
priests,
and my people shall be filled with my
blessings,
says the LORD.

End of Rachel's Mourning

15 Thus says the LORD:
In Ramah* is heard the sound of moaning,
of bitter weeping!
Rachel mourns her children,
she refuses to be consoled
because her children are no more.*m*
16 Thus says the LORD:
Cease your cries of mourning,
wipe the tears from your eyes.
The sorrow you have shown shall have
its reward,
says the LORD,
they shall return from the enemy's
land.
17 There is hope for your future, says the
LORD;
your sons shall return to their own
borders.*n*
18 I hear, I hear Ephraim pleading:
You chastised me, and I am chastened;
I was an untamed calf.
If you allow me, I will return,
for you are the LORD, my God.*o*
19 I turn in repentance;
I have come to myself, I strike my
breast;

e Dt 7, 8; 10, 15; Is 43, 4; 63, 9; Hos 11, 1. 4.—f Is 65, 21;
Am 9, 14.—g Is 2, 3; 27, 13; Mi 4, 2.—h Is 12, 6.—i Jer 3, 18;
23, 3. 8; Is 35, 5f.—j Ex 4, 22.—k Is 44, 23; 48, 20.—l Is 58,
11.—m Mt 2, 18.—n Jer 29, 10-14.—o Lv 26, 40ff.

31, 15: *Ramah:* a village about five miles north of Jerusalem,
where Rachel was buried (1 Sm 10, 2). *Rachel:* said to mourn
for her children since she was the ancestress of Ephraim, the
chief of the northern tribes. Mt 2, 18 applies this verse to the
slaughter of the innocents by Herod.

I blush with shame,
    I bear the disgrace of my youth.*p*
20 Is Ephraim not my favored son,
    the child in whom I delight?
Often as I threaten him,
    I still remember him with favor;
My heart stirs for him,
    I must show him mercy, says the
    LORD.*q*

Summons To Return Home

21 Set up road markers,
    put up guideposts;
Turn your attention to the highway,
    the road by which you went.
Turn back, O virgin Israel,
    turn back to these your cities.
22 How long will you continue to stray,
    rebellious daughter?
The LORD has created a new thing upon
    the earth:
    the woman must encompass the
    man* with devotion.

23 Thus says the LORD of hosts, the God
of Israel: When I change their lot in the
land of Judah and her cities, they shall
again repeat this greeting: "May the LORD
bless you, holy mountain, abode of justice!" *r* 24 Judah and all her cities, the farmers and those who lead the flock, shall
dwell there together. 25 For I will refresh
the weary soul; every soul that languishes I
will replenish. 26 Upon this I awoke and
opened my eyes; but my sleep was sweet to
me.*
27 The days are coming, says the LORD,
when I will seed the house of Israel and the
house of Judah with the seed of man and
the seed of beast. 28 As I once watched over
them to uproot and pull down, to destroy,
to ruin, and to harm, so I will watch over
them to build and to plant, says the
LORD.*s* 29 In those days they shall no
longer say,

"The fathers ate unripe grapes,*t*
    and the children's teeth are set on
    edge,"*

30 but through his own fault only shall anyone die: the teeth of him who eats the unripe grapes shall be set on edge.
The New Covenant.* 31 The days are coming, says the LORD, when I will make a
new covenant with the house of Israel and
the house of Judah.*u* 32 It will not be like
the covenant I made with their fathers the
day I took them by the hand to lead them
forth from the land of Egypt; for they
broke my covenant and I had to show myself their master, says the LORD.*v* 33 But
this is the covenant which I will make with
the house of Israel after those days, says
the LORD. I will place my law within
them, and write it upon their hearts; I will
be their God, and they shall be my people.*w* 34 No longer will they have need to
teach their friends and kinsmen how to
know the LORD. All, from least to greatest, shall know me, says the LORD, for I
will forgive their evildoing and remember
their sin no more.*x*

Certainty of God's Promise

35   Thus says the LORD,
He who gives the sun to light the day,
    moon and stars to light the night;
Who stirs up the sea till its waves roar,
    whose name is LORD of hosts:*y*
36 If ever these natural laws give way
    in spite of me, says the LORD,
Then shall the race of Israel cease
    as a nation before me forever. *z*

---

p Dt 30, 1ff.—q Hos 11, 8.—r Jer 30, 3; Ps 122, 8.—s Jer 1,
10; 18, 7.—t Dt 24, 16; Ez 18, 2.—u Jer 32, 40; Heb 9, 15.—v
Ex 24, 7f; Dt 5, 2.—w Jer 32, 40; Ez 37, 26; Heb 10, 16.—x Is
54, 13.—y Gn 1, 14-18.—z Jer 33, 20f.

31, 22: *The woman must encompass the man:* the words
"with devotion," not in the Hebrew, are added for the sense. No
fully satisfactory explanation has been given this text. Among the
more probable are these: (a) Formerly the man (the Lord) en-
compassed the woman (Israel) with mercy and devotion; now in
the spiritual religion of Israel which will follow on the restoration, this order will be reversed. (b) So secure will Israel be
after the restoration that women will no longer need the natural
protection of their husbands, but even weak women can protect
men. (c) St. Jerome in his commentary on this verse understood
it of Mary's virginal conception of Christ. "The Lord has created
a new thing on earth; without seed of man, without carnal union
and conception, 'a woman will encompass a man' within her
womb—One who, though He will later appear to advance in wisdom and age through the stages of infancy and childhood, yet,
while confined for the usual number of months in his mother's
womb, will already be perfect man."
31, 26: *I awoke . . . sweet to me:* probably said by the
prophet himself.
31, 29: *"The fathers . . . on edge":* a proverb used in Israel,
expressing the idea that children suffer for the sins of their parents (cf Ez 18, 2). The Israel of the restoration will be characterized instead by personal responsibility and retribution for one's
acts (v 30; cf vv 31-34).
31, 31-34: The *new covenant* to be made with Israel is a
common theme of the prophets, beginning with Hosea. According
to Jeremiah, the qualities of the new covenant that make it different from the old are: (a) It will not be broken, but will last forever; (b) Its law will be written in the heart, not merely on tablets
of stone; (c) The knowledge of God will be so generally shown
forth in the life of the people that it will no longer be necessary
to put it into words of instruction. In the fullest sense, this
prophecy was fulfilled only through the work of Jesus Christ; cf
Lk 22, 20; 1 Cor 11, 25.

³⁷   Thus says the LORD:
If the heavens on high can be measured,
   or the foundations below the earth be
   sounded,
Then will I cast off the whole race of Israel
   because of all they have done, says
   the LORD.

Rebuilding of Jerusalem. ³⁸ The days are coming, says the LORD, when the city shall be rebuilt as the LORD's,^a from the Tower of Hananel to the Corner Gate.* ³⁹ The measuring line shall be stretched from there straight to the hill Gareb and then turn to Goah. ⁴⁰ The whole valley of corpses and ashes,* all the slopes toward the Kidron Valley, as far as the corner of the Horse Gate at the east, shall be holy to the LORD. Never again shall the city be rooted up or thrown down.

CHAPTER 32

Pledge of Restoration.* ¹ This message came to Jeremiah from the LORD in the tenth year of Zedekiah,* king of Judah, the eighteenth year of Nebuchadnezzar. ² At that time the army of the king of Babylon was besieging Jerusalem, and the prophet Jeremiah was imprisoned in the quarters of the guard, at the king's

---

a Neh 12, 38; Zec 14, 10f.—b Jer 33, 1; 37, 20; 38, 6; 39, 14.—c Jer 26, 9; 34, 2; 37, 6-10.—d Jer 34, 3; 38, 18. 23; 39, 4-7.—e Jer 39, 7; 52, 11.—f l v 25, 24-34; Ru 4, 4.—g Jer 36, 4.—h 2 Kgs 19, 15; Jb 42, 2.

31, 38: *From the Tower of Hananel to the Corner Gate:* from the northeast to the northwest.

31, 40: *Valley of corpses and ashes:* the Valley of Ben-hinnom, which joins the Kidron at the southeast of ancient Jerusalem. *The Horse Gate:* in the eastern city wall, at the southeast corner of the temple area.

32, 1-44: This chapter recounts a prophecy "in action." At the Lord's command, Jeremiah fulfills his family duty to purchase the land of his cousin, carrying out all the legal forms, including records, to testify that Judah will be restored and that the life of the past will be resumed.

32, 1: *The tenth year of Zedekiah:* 588 B.C. *The eighteenth year of Nebuchadnezzar:* dating his reign from his victory at Carchemish; see note on Jer 25, 1-14.

32, 6-9: Jeremiah's imprisonment by the weak-willed Zedekiah was a technical custody that did not deprive him of all freedom of action. The siege maintained by the Chaldeans (v 2) was only now beginning (v 24), and could be bypassed by individual persons going to and fro between Jerusalem and nearby Anathoth.

32, 7: *The first right of purchase:* the obligation of the closest relative to redeem the property of one in economic distress, so that the ancestral land might remain within the family (Lv 25, 25-28); see note on Ru 2, 20.

32, 11: *The sealed copy . . . and the open one:* the legal deed of sale was written on a scroll, which was then rolled up and sealed; about it was rolled another scroll, left unsealed, containing a copy or a summary of the first.

32, 14: *In an earthen jar:* the first of the Dead Sea Scrolls were found in such a jar.

---

palace.^b ³ Zedekiah, king of Judah, had imprisoned him there, remonstrating: "How dare you prophesy: Thus says the LORD: I am handing over this city to the king of Babylon, who will capture it.^c ⁴ Neither shall Zedekiah, king of Judah, escape the hands of the Chaldeans; rather shall he be handed over to the king of Babylon. They shall meet and speak face to face,^d ⁵ and Zedekiah shall be taken to Babylon. There he shall remain, until I attend to him, says the LORD; in fighting the Chaldeans, you cannot win!"^e

⁶ * This message came to me from the LORD, said Jeremiah: ⁷ Hanamel, son of your uncle Shallum, will come to you with the offer:^f "Buy for yourself my field in Anathoth, since you, as nearest relative, have the first right of purchase."* ⁸ Then, as the LORD foretold, Hanamel, my uncle's son, came to me to the quarters of the guard and said, "Please buy my field in Anathoth, in the district of Benjamin; as nearest relative, you have the first claim to possess it; make it yours." I knew this was what the LORD meant, ⁹ so I bought the field in Anathoth from my cousin Hanamel, paying him the money, seventeen silver shekels.

¹⁰ When I had written and sealed the deed, called witnesses, and weighed out the silver on the scales, ¹¹ I accepted the deed of purchase, both the sealed copy, containing title and conditions, and the open one.* ¹² This deed of purchase I gave to Baruch, son of Neriah, son of Mahseiah, in the presence of my cousin Hanamel and of the witnesses who had signed the deed, and before all the men of Judah who happened to be in the quarters of the guard.^g

¹³ In their presence I gave Baruch this charge: ¹⁴ Thus says the LORD of hosts, the God of Israel: Take these deeds, both the sealed and the open deed of purchase, and put them in an earthen jar,* so that they can be kept there a long time. ¹⁵ For thus says the LORD of hosts, the God of Israel: Houses and fields and vineyards shall again be bought in this land.

¹⁶ After giving the deed of purchase to Baruch, son of Neriah, I prayed thus to the LORD: ¹⁷ Ah, Lord GOD, you have made heaven and earth by your great might, with your outstretched arm; nothing is impossible to you.^h ¹⁸ You continue your kindness through a thousand generations; and you repay the fathers' guilt,

even into the lap of their sons who follow them. O God, great and mighty, whose name is LORD of hosts,[i] [19]great in counsel, mighty in deed, whose eyes are open to all the ways of men, giving to each according to his ways, according to the fruit of his deeds:[j] [20]you have wrought signs and wonders in the land of Egypt and to this day, both in Israel and among all other men, until now you have gained renown.[k] [21]With strong hand and outstretched arm you brought your people Israel out of the land of Egypt amid signs and wonders and great terror. [22]This land you gave them, as you had promised their fathers under oath, a land flowing with milk and honey.[l] [23]They entered and took possession of it, but they did not listen to your voice; by your law they did not live, and what you commanded they failed to do. Hence you let all these evils befall them.[m] [24]See, the siegeworks have arrived at this city to breach it; the city will be handed over to the Chaldeans who are attacking it, amid sword, famine, and pestilence. What you threatened has happened, you see it yourself;[n] [25]and yet you tell me, O Lord GOD: Buy the field with money, call in witnesses. But the city has already been handed over to the Chaldeans!

[26]Then this word of the LORD came to Jeremiah: [27]I am the LORD, the God of all mankind! Is anything impossible to me? [28]This now is what the LORD says: I will hand over this city to the Chaldeans, for Nebuchadnezzar, king of Babylon, to take. [29]The Chaldeans who are attacking it shall enter this city and set fire to it, burning it and its houses, on the roofs of which incense was burned to Baal and libations were poured out to strange gods as a provocation to me.[o] [30]The Israelites and the Judeans from their youth have done only what is evil in my eyes; the Israelites did nothing but provoke me with the works of their hands, says the LORD.[p] [31]From the day it was built to this day, this city has excited my anger and wrath, [32]so that I must put it out of my sight for all the wickedness the Israelites and Judeans, with their kings and their princes, their priests and their prophets, the men of Judah and the citizens of Jerusalem, have done to provoke me.[q] [33]They turned their backs to me, not their faces; though I kept teaching them, they would not listen to my correction.[r] [34]They defiled the house named after me by the horrid idols they set up in it.[s] [35]They built high places to Baal in the Valley of Ben-hinnom, and immolated their sons and daughters to Molech,* bringing sin upon Judah; this I never commanded them, nor did it even enter my mind that they should practice such abominations.[t]

[36]Now, therefore, thus says the LORD, the God of Israel, concerning this city, which as you say is handed over to the king of Babylon amid sword, famine, and pestilence: [37]Behold, I will gather them together from all the lands to which in anger, wrath, and great rage I banish them; I will bring them back to this place and settle them here in safety.[u] [38]They shall be my people, and I will be their God.[v] [39]One heart and one way I will give them, that they may fear me always, to their own good and that of their children after them. [40]I will make with them an eternal covenant, never to cease doing good to them; into their hearts I will put the fear of me, that they may never depart from me.[w] [41]I will take delight in doing good to them: I will replant them firmly in this land, with all my heart and soul.[x]

[42]For thus says the LORD: Just as I brought upon this people all this great evil, so I will bring upon them all the good I promise them.[y] [43]Fields shall again be bought in this land, which you call a desert, without man or beast, handed over to the Chaldeans.[z] [44]Fields shall be bought with money, deeds written and sealed, and witnesses shall be used in the land of Benjamin, in the suburbs of Jerusalem, in the cities of Judah and of the hill country, in the cities of the foothills and of the Negeb, when I change their lot, says the LORD.[a]

CHAPTER 33

Restoration of Jerusalem. [1]The word of the LORD came to Jeremiah a second time

---

i Ex 20, 5f; Dt 5, 9.—j Jb 34, 21; Ps 33, 13ff.—k Ex 6, 6; Dt 4, 34; Ps 135, 9.—l Jer 11, 5; Gn 15, 18; 17, 8; 26, 3.—m Jer 7, 24ff; Dn 9, 10-14.—n Jer 21, 5; 33, 4.—o Jer 21, 10; 37, 8ff.—p Jer 3, 25; 44, 8.—q Jer 2, 26; Is 3, 8.—r Jer 7, 24.—s Jer 7, 30; 2 Kgs 21, 4f.—t Jer 7, 31; 19, 5; Ps 106, 37f.—u Jer 23, 3; 29, 14; Is 11, 12; Ez 11, 17.—v Jer 24, 7; 31, 33.—w Jer 31, 31ff.—x Dt 30, 9.—y Jer 33, 10-14; Zec 8, 13.—z Jer 33, 10.—a Jer 17, 26; 33, 7.

32, 35: *Molech:* the god to whom human sacrifice was offered in the Valley of Ben-hinnom. Here, as in Jer 19, 5, he is given the name *Baal;* see note on Lv 18, 21.

while he was still imprisoned in the quarters of the guard: ²Thus says the LORD who made the earth and gave it form and firmness, whose name is LORD: ³Call to me, and I will answer you; I will tell to you things great beyond reach of your knowledge.[b] ⁴Thus says the LORD, the God of Israel, concerning the houses of this city and the palaces of Judah's kings, which are being destroyed in the face of siegeworks and the sword:[c] ⁵men come to battle the Chaldeans, and these houses will be filled with the corpses of those whom I slay in my anger and wrath, when I hide my face from this city for all their wickedness.[d]

⁶Behold, I will treat and assuage the city's wounds; I will heal them, and reveal to them an abundance of lasting peace.[e] ⁷I will change the lot of Judah and the lot of Israel, and rebuild them as of old.[f] ⁸I will cleanse them of all the guilt they incurred by sinning against me; all their offenses by which they sinned and rebelled against me, I will forgive.[g] ⁹Then Jerusalem shall be my joy, my praise, my glory, before all the nations of the earth, as they hear of all the good I will do among them. They shall be in fear and trembling over all the peaceful benefits I will give her.

¹⁰Thus says the LORD: In this place of which you say, "How desolate it is, without man, without beast!" and in the cities of Judah, in the streets of Jerusalem that are now deserted, without man, without citizen, without beast, there shall yet be heard[h] ¹¹the cry of joy, the cry of gladness, the voice of the bridegroom, the voice of the bride, the sound of those who bring thank offerings to the house of the LORD, singing, "Give thanks to the LORD

of hosts, for the LORD is good; his mercy endures forever." For I will restore this country as of old, says the LORD.[i]

¹²Thus says the LORD of hosts: In this place, now desolate, without man or beast, and in all its cities there shall again be sheepfolds for the shepherds to couch their flocks. ¹³In the cities of the hill country, of the foothills, and of the Negeb, in the land of Benjamin and the suburbs of Jerusalem, and in the cities of Judah, flocks will again pass under the hands of the one who counts them, says the LORD.

¹⁴ * The days are coming, says the LORD, when I will fulfill the promise I made to the house of Israel and Judah. ¹⁵In those days, in that time, I will raise up for David a just shoot; he shall do what is right and just in the land.[j] ¹⁶In those days Judah shall be safe and Jerusalem shall dwell secure; this is what they shall call her: "The LORD our justice." ¹⁷For thus says the LORD: Never shall David lack a successor on the throne of the house of Israel,[k] ¹⁸nor shall priests of Levi ever be lacking, to offer holocausts before me, to burn cereal offerings, and to sacrifice victims.[l]

This word of the LORD also came to Jeremiah: ¹⁹Thus says the LORD: ²⁰If you can break my covenant with day,[m] and my covenant with night, so that day and night no longer alternate in sequence, ²¹then can my covenant with my servant David also be broken, so that he will not have a son to be king upon his throne, and my covenant with the priests of Levi who minister to me. ²²Like the host of heaven which cannot be numbered, and the sands of the sea which cannot be counted, I will multiply the descendants of my servant David and the Levites who minister to me.

²³This word of the LORD came to Jeremiah: ²⁴Have you not noticed what these people are saying: "The LORD has rejected the two tribes which he had chosen"? They spurn my people as if it were no longer a nation in their eyes.[n] ²⁵ [o] Thus says the LORD: When I have no covenant with day and night, and have given no laws to heaven and earth, ²⁶then too will I reject the descendants of Jacob and of my servant David, so as not to take from his descendants rulers for the race of Abraham, Isaac, and Jacob. For I will change their lot and show them mercy.

---

b Is 48, 6.—c Jer 32, 24.—d Jer 21, 4ff.—e Is 57, 18.—f Jer 30, 3; 32, 44.—g Ez 36, 25.—h Jer 32, 43.—i 1 Chr 16, 34; Ezr 3, 11; Ps 136, 1.—j Jer 23, 5; Ps 72, 1-4. 12ff; Is 11, 1.—k 2 Sm 7, 16; 1 Kgs 2, 4; Ps 89, 4f. 29. 36f.—l Ez 44, 15f.—m 20f: Jer 31, 36f; Ps 89, 37f.—n Rom 11, 1f.—o 25f: Jer 31, 36f; 32, 44.

33, 14-26: This is the longest continuous passage in the Book of Jeremiah that is lacking in the Greek. It appears to be the post-exilic composition of an inspired writer who used parts of the prophecies of Jeremiah—often, however, in a sense different from the prophet's. The prediction of an eternal Davidic dynasty (14-17) to fulfill the prophecy of Nathan (2 Sm 7, 11-16), and of a perpetual priesthood and sacrifice (18), was not to be realized in the restoration of the Jewish nation. It finds its fulfillment only in Jesus of Nazareth, who combined with his messianic Davidic kingship an eternal priesthood; cf Heb 6, 20; 7, 24f.

IV: FALL OF JERUSALEM

CHAPTER 34

Fate of Zedekiah. ¹This word came to Jeremiah from the LORD while Nebuchadnezzar, king of Babylon, and his armies and the earth's kingdoms subject to him, as well as the other peoples, were all attacking Jerusalem and all her cities:ᵖ ²Thus says the LORD, the God of Israel: Go to Zedekiah, king of Judah, and tell him: Thus says the LORD: I am handing this city over to the king of Babylon; he will destroy it with fire. q ³Neither shall you escape his hand; rather you will be captured and fall into his hands. You shall see the king of Babylon and speak to him face to face. Then you shall be taken to Babylon.ʳ

⁴But if you obey the word of the LORD, Zedekiah, king of Judah, then, says the LORD to you, you shall not die by the sword. ⁵You shall die in peace, and they will lament you as their lord, and burn spices for your burial as they did for your fathers, the kings who preceded you from the first; it is I who make this promise, says the LORD.

⁶The prophet Jeremiah told all these things to Zedekiah, king of Judah, in Jerusalem, ⁷while the armies of the king of Babylon were attacking Jerusalem and the remaining cities of Judah, Lachish, and Azekah,* since these alone were left of the fortified cities of Judah.

The Pact Broken.* ⁸This is the word that came to Jeremiah from the LORD after King Zedekiah had made an agreement with all the people in Jerusalem to issue an edict of emancipation. ⁹Everyone was to free his Hebrew slaves, male and female, so that no one should hold a man of Judah, his brother, in slavery.ˢ ¹⁰All the princes and the others who entered the agreement consented to set free their male and female servants, so that they should be slaves no longer. But though they agreed and freed them, ¹¹afterward they took back their male and female slaves whom they had set free and again forced them into service.

¹²Then this word of the LORD came to Jeremiah: ¹³Thus says the LORD, the God of Israel: The day I brought your fathers out of the land of Egypt, out of the place where they were slaves, I made this covenant with them: ¹⁴Every seventh year each of you shall set free his Hebrew brother who has sold himself to you; six years he shall serve you, but then you shall let him go free. Your fathers, however, did not heed me or obey me. ¹⁵Today you indeed repented and did what is right in my eyes by proclaiming the emancipation of your brethren and making an agreement before me in the house that is named after me. ¹⁶But then you changed your mind and profaned my name by taking back your male and female slaves to whom you had given their freedom; you forced them once more into slavery.ᵗ ¹⁷Therefore, thus says the LORD: You did not obey me by proclaiming your neighbors and kinsmen free. I now proclaim you free, says the LORD, for the sword, famine, and pestilence. I will make you an object of horror to all the kingdoms of the earth. ¹⁸ * The men who violated my covenant and did not observe the terms of the agreement which they made before me, I will make like the calf which they cut in two, between whose two parts they passed. ¹⁹The princes of Judah and of Jerusalem, the courtiers, the priests, and the common people, who passed between the parts of the calf, ²⁰I will hand over, all of them, to their enemies, to those who seek their lives: their corpses shall be food for the birds of the air and the beasts of the field.ᵘ

²¹Zedekiah, too, king of Judah, and his princes, I will hand over to their enemies, to those who seek their lives, to the

---

p Jer 52, 4; 2 Kgs 25, 1.—q Jer 21, 10; 32, 3. 28.—r Jer 32, 4; 52, 11.—s Ex 21, 2ff; Lv 25, 39. 46; Dt 15, 12-15.—t Lv 19, 12.—u Jer 7, 33; 16, 4; 19, 7.

34, 7: *Lachish and Azekah:* fortress towns to the southwest of Jerusalem which Nebuchadnezzar besieged to prevent help coming to Jerusalem from Egypt. Between 1935 and 1938, archaeologists found at Lachish several letters written on pottery fragments which date from 598 or 588 B.C., and which mention both Lachish and Azekah.

34, 8-22: While the Chaldean siege of Jerusalem was in progress, the citizens of Jerusalem made a covenant at Zedekiah's instigation to free their brother Judeans who were in slavery. Doubtless this was both to provide additional free defenders for the city and to offer reparation for past violations of the law, according to which Hebrew slaves were to serve no longer than six years (Dt 15, 12-15). But when the siege was temporarily lifted, probably because of the help promised by Pharaoh Hophra (cf Jer 37, 5), the inhabitants of Jerusalem broke the covenant and once more pressed their brethren into slavery (v 11).

34, 18f: As the Bible (Gn 15, 10-17) and also contemporary inscriptions make clear, agreements were sometimes ratified by walking between the divided pieces of animals while the contracting parties invoked on themselves a fate similar to that of the slaughtered beast if they should fail to keep their word. *The agreement:* that mentioned in vv 10. 15.

soldiers of the king of Babylon who have at present withdrawn from you.*v* *22* I will give the command, says the LORD, and bring them back to this city. They shall attack and capture it, and destroy it with fire; the cities of Judah I will turn into a desert where no man dwells.*w*

CHAPTER 35

The Faithful Rechabites. *1* This word came to Jeremiah from the LORD in the days of Jehoiakim, son of Josiah, king of Judah: *2* Approach the Rechabites* and speak to them; bring them into the house of the LORD, to one of the rooms, and give them wine to drink. *3* So I went and brought Jaazaniah, son of Jeremiah, son of Habazziniah, his brothers and all his sons, the whole company of the Rechabites, *4* into the house of the LORD, to the room of the sons of Hanan,* son of Igdaliah, the man of God, next to the princes' room, above the room of Maaseiah, son of Shallum, keeper of the doorway. *5* I set before these Rechabite men bowls full of wine and offered them cups to drink the wine.

6 "We do not drink wine," they said to me: "Jonadab,* Rechab's son, our father, forbade us in these words: 'Neither you nor your children shall ever drink wine. *7* Build no house and sow no seed; neither plant nor own a vineyard. You shall dwell in tents all your life, so that you may live long on the earth where you are wayfarers.' *8* Now we have heeded Jonadab, Rechab's son, our father, in all his prohibitions. All our lives we have not drunk wine, neither we, nor our wives, nor our sons, nor our daughters. *9* We build no houses to live in; we own no vineyards or fields or crops, *10* and we live in tents; we obediently do everything our father

Jonadab commanded us. *11* But when Nebuchadnezzar, king of Babylon, invaded this land, we decided to come into Jerusalem to escape the army of the Chaldeans and the army of Aram;* that is why we are now living in Jerusalem."

12 Then this word of the LORD came to Jeremiah: *13* Thus says the LORD of hosts, the God of Israel: Go, say to the men of Judah and to the citizens of Jerusalem: Will you not take correction and obey my words? says the LORD.*x* *14* The advice of Jonadab, Rechab's son, by which he forbade his children to drink wine, has been followed: to this day they have not drunk it; they obeyed their father's command. Me, however, you have not obeyed, although I spoke to you untiringly and insistently.*y* *15* I kept sending you all my servants the prophets, telling you to turn back, all of you, from your evil way; to reform your conduct, and not follow strange gods or serve them, if you would remain on the land which I gave you and your fathers; but you did not heed me or obey me.*z* *16* Yes, the children of Jonadab, Rechab's son, observed the command which their father laid on them; but this people does not obey me! *17* Now, therefore, says the LORD God of hosts, the God of Israel: I will bring upon Judah and all the citizens of Jerusalem every evil that I threatened; because when I spoke they did not obey, when I called they did not answer.*a*

18 But to the company of the Rechabites Jeremiah said: Thus says the LORD of hosts, the God of Israel: Since you have obeyed the command of Jonadab, your father, kept all his commands and done everything he commanded you, *19* thus therefore says the LORD of hosts, the God of Israel: Never shall there fail to be a descendant of Jonadab, Rechab's son, standing in my service.

CHAPTER 36

Baruch Writes the Prophecies of Jeremiah. *1* In the fourth year of Jehoiakim, son of Josiah, king of Judah, this word came to Jeremiah from the LORD: *2* Take a scroll and write on it all the words I have spoken to you against Israel, Judah, and all the nations, from the day I first spoke to you, in the days of Josiah, until today. *3* Perhaps, when the house of Judah hears all the evil I have in mind

---

v Jer 37, 5. 11.—w Jer 37, 8; 52, 7-13; 2 Chr 36, 17. 19.—x Jer 32, 33.—y Jer 7, 13; 25, 3; 2 Chr 36, 15f.—z Jer 25, 4f. 7.—a Jer 11, 8f.

35, 2: *The Rechabites:* reactionaries who believed that the Lord could not be well served except by maintaining the original nomadic conditions of Israel's life. Without sharing their convictions, the prophet holds up their fidelity to their ideals as an example to put to shame his faithless countrymen. *In the days of Jehoiakim:* probably in 599 or 598 B.C.

35, 4: *The sons of Hanan:* probably the disciples of this *man of God* or prophet. *Maaseiah:* possibly the father of the priest Zephaniah (Jer 29, 25; 37, 3). *Keeper of the doorway:* a priestly function of responsibility; cf Jer 52, 24.

35, 6: *Jonadab:* a contemporary of King Jehu; cf 2 Kgs 10, 15ff.

35, 11: *The army of Aram:* Nebuchadnezzar enlisted the help of Judah's foreign neighbors in his assault on Jerusalem.

to do to them, they will turn back each from his evil way, so that I may forgive their wickedness and their sin.[b] 4 So Jeremiah called Baruch, son of Neriah, who wrote down on a scroll, as Jeremiah dictated, all the words which the LORD had spoken to him.

9 In the ninth month, in the fifth year of Jehoiakim, son of Josiah, king of Judah, a fast to placate the LORD was proclaimed for all the people of Jerusalem and all who came from Judah's cities to Jerusalem. 5 Then Jeremiah charged Baruch: I cannot go to the house of the LORD; I am prevented* from doing so. 6 Do you go on the fast day and read publicly in the LORD's house the LORD's words from the scroll you wrote at my dictation; read them also to all the men of Judah who come up from their cities. 7 Perhaps they will lay their supplication before the LORD and will all turn back from their evil way; for great is the fury of anger with which the LORD has threatened this people.[c]

8 Baruch, son of Neriah, did everything the prophet Jeremiah commanded; from the book-scroll he read the LORD's words in the LORD's house. 10 It was in the room of Gemariah,* son of the scribe Shaphan, in the upper court of the LORD's house, at the entrance of the New Temple-Gate, that Baruch publicly read the words of Jeremiah from his book.

11 Now Micaiah, son of Gemariah, son of Shaphan, heard all the words of the LORD read from the book. 12 So he went down to the king's palace, into the scribe's chamber,* where the princes were just then in session: Elishama, the scribe, Delaiah, son of Shemaiah, Elnathan, son of Achbor, Gemariah, son of Shaphan, Zedekiah, son of Hananiah, and the other princes. 13 To them Micaiah reported all that he had heard Baruch read publicly from his book. 14 Thereupon the princes sent Jehudi, son of Nethaniah, son of Shelemiah, son of Cushi, to Baruch with the order: "Come, and bring with you the scroll you read publicly to the people." Scroll in hand, Baruch, son of Neriah, went to them. 15 "Sit down," they said to him, "and read it to us." Baruch read it to them, 16 and when they heard all its words, they were frightened and said to one another,

"We must certainly tell the king all these things." 17 Then they asked Baruch: "Tell us, please, how you came to write down all these words." 18 "Jeremiah dictated all these words to me," Baruch answered them, "and I wrote them down with ink in the book." 19 At this the princes said to Baruch, "Go into hiding, you and Jeremiah; let no one know where you are."

20 Leaving the scroll in safekeeping in the room of Elishama the scribe, they entered the room where the king was. When they told him everything that had happened, 21 he sent Jehudi to fetch the scroll. Jehudi brought it from the room of Elishama the scribe, and read it to the king and to all the princes who were in attendance on the king. 22 Now the king was sitting in his winter house, since it was the ninth month, and fire was burning in a brazier before him. 23 Each time Jehudi finished reading three or four columns, the king would cut off the piece with a scribe's knife* and cast it into the fire in the brazier, until the entire roll was consumed in the fire. 24 Hearing all these words did not frighten the king and his ministers or cause them to rend their garments. 25 And though Elnathan, Delaiah, and Gemariah urged the king not to burn the scroll, he would not listen to them, 26 but commanded Jerahmeel, a royal prince, and Seraiah, son of Azriel, and Shelemiah, son of Abdeel, to arrest Baruch, the secretary, and the prophet Jeremiah. But the LORD kept them concealed.

27 This word of the LORD came to Jeremiah, after the king burned the scroll with the text Jeremiah had dictated to Baruch: 28 Take another scroll, and write on it everything that the first scroll contained, which Jehoiakim, king of Judah, burned up. 29 And against Jehoiakim, king of Judah, say this: Thus says the

---

b Jer 26, 3; Is 55, 6f.—c 2 Kgs 22, 13.

36, 5: *I am prevented:* probably because of his temple sermon (Jer 7, 1-15), or because of temporary ritual uncleanness.
36, 10: *Gemariah:* member of a family friendly to Jeremiah, which had rights to a room in the fortress of the temple gateway overlooking the court of the temple; from a window in this room Baruch read Jeremiah's prophetic sermon to the people.
36, 12: *The scribe's chamber:* the office of the royal secretary.
36, 23: *A scribe's knife:* used to sharpen the reeds which were employed as pens.

LORD: You burned that scroll, saying, "Why did you write on it: Babylon's king shall surely come and lay waste this land and empty it of man and beast?" [30] The LORD now says of Jehoiakim, king of Judah:[d] No descendant of his shall succeed to David's throne; his corpse shall be cast out, exposed to the heat of day, to the cold of night.* [31] I will punish him and his descendants and his ministers for their wickedness; against them and the citizens of Jerusalem and the men of Judah I will fulfill all the threats of evil which went unheeded.

[32] Jeremiah took another scroll, and gave it to his secretary, Baruch, son of Neriah; he wrote on it at Jeremiah's dictation all the words contained in the book which Jehoiakim, king of Judah, had burned in the fire, and many others of the same kind in addition.

CHAPTER 37

Jeremiah in the Dungeon. [1] Coniah, son of Jehoiakim, was succeeded by King Zedekiah, son of Josiah; he was made king over the land of Judah by Nebuchadnezzar, king of Babylon.[e] [2] Neither he, nor his ministers, nor the people of the land would listen to the words of the LORD spoken by Jeremiah the prophet. [3] Yet King Zedekiah sent Jehucal, son of Shelemiah, and Zephaniah, son of Maaseiah the priest, to the prophet Jeremiah with this request: "Pray to the LORD, our God, for us."[f] [4] At this time Jeremiah had not yet been put into prison;* he still came and went freely among the people. [5] Also, Pharaoh's army* had set out from Egypt, and when the Chaldeans who were besieging Jerusalem heard this report they marched away from the city.[g]

[6] This word of the LORD then came to the prophet Jeremiah: [7] Thus says the LORD, the God of Israel: Give this answer to the king of Judah who sent you to me to consult me: Pharaoh's army which has set out to help you will return to its own land, Egypt.[h] [8] The Chaldeans shall return to the fight against this city; they shall capture it and destroy it with fire.[i]

[9] Thus says the LORD: Do not deceive yourselves with the thought that the Chaldeans will leave you for good, because they shall not leave! [10] Even if you were to defeat the whole Chaldean army now attacking you, and only the wounded remained, each in his tent, these would rise up and destroy the city with fire.[j]

[11] When the Chaldean army lifted the siege of Jerusalem at the threat of the army of Pharaoh,[k] [12] Jeremiah set out from Jerusalem for the district of Benjamin, to take part with his family in the division of an inheritance. [13] But when he reached the Gate of Benjamin, he met the captain of the guard, a man named Irijah, son of Shelemiah, son of Hananiah; he seized the prophet Jeremiah, saying, "You are deserting to the Chaldeans!" [14] "That is a lie!" Jeremiah answered, "I am not deserting to the Chaldeans." Without listening, Irijah kept Jeremiah in custody and brought him to the princes.

[15] The princes were enraged, and had Jeremiah beaten and thrown into prison in the house of Jonathan the scribe, which they were using as a jail.[l] [16] And so Jeremiah entered the vaulted dungeon, where he remained a long time.

[17] Once King Zedekiah had him brought to his palace and he asked him secretly whether there was any message from the LORD. Yes! Jeremiah answered: you shall be handed over to the king of Babylon.[m] [18] Jeremiah then asked King Zedekiah: In what have I wronged you, or your ministers, or this people, that you should put me in prison?[n] [19] And where are your own prophets now, [20] who prophesied to you that the king of Babylon would not attack you or this land? Hear now, my lord king, and grant my petition: do not send me back into the house of Jonathan the scribe, or I shall die there.

[21] King Zedekiah ordered that Jeremiah be confined in the quarters of the guard, and given a loaf of bread each day from the bakers' shop until all the bread in the city was eaten up. Thus Jere-

d Jer 22, 19.—e Jer 52, 1; 2 Kgs 24, 17; 2 Chr 36, 10.—f Jer 21, 1.—g Ez 17, 15; 29, 6f.—h Ez 17, 17.—i Jer 34, 22.—j Jer 21, 4.—k Zec 14, 10.—l Jer 38, 6-13.—m Jer 21, 7; 32, 3; 34, 21.—n Jer 26, 19.

36, 30: Jehoiakim's son Jehoiachin was named king, but reigned only three months; he was known better for his thirty-seven-year exile in Babylon. *His corpse shall be cast out:* see note on Jer 22, 19.

37, 4: *Put into prison:* as described in Jer 32, 1ff. Chronologically, the present episode follows Jer 34, 1-7.

37, 5: *Pharaoh's army:* the force sent by Pharaoh Hophra which caused the Chaldeans momentarily to lift the siege of Jerusalem (cf Jer 34, 21).

Jer

miah remained in the quarters of the guard.*o*

CHAPTER 38

Jeremiah in the Miry Cistern. [1] Shephatiah, son of Mattan, Gedaliah, son of Pashhur, Jucal, son of Shelemiah, and Passhur, son of Malchiah, heard Jeremiah speaking these words to all the people:* [2] Thus says the LORD: He who remains in this city shall die by sword, or famine, or pestilence; but he who goes out to the Chaldeans shall live; his life shall be spared him as booty, and he shall live.*p* [3] Thus says the LORD: This city shall certainly be handed over to the army of the king of Babylon; he shall capture it.

[4] "This man ought to be put to death," the princes said to the king; "he demoralizes the soldiers* who are left in this city, and all the people, by speaking such things to them; he is not interested in the welfare of our people, but in their ruin."*q* [5] King Zedekiah answered: "He is in your power"; for the king could do nothing with them. [6] And so they took Jeremiah and threw him into the cistern of Prince Malchiah, which was in the quarters of the guard, letting him down with ropes. There was no water in the cistern, only mud, and Jeremiah sank into the mud.*r*

[7] Now Ebed-melech, a Cushite,* a courtier in the king's palace, heard that they had put Jeremiah into the cistern. The king happened just then to be at the Gate of Benjamin, [8] and Ebed-melech went there from the palace and said to him, [9] "My lord king, these men have been at fault in all they have done to the prophet Jeremiah, casting him into the cistern. He will die of famine on the spot, for there is no more food in the city."*s* [10] Then the king ordered Ebed-melech the Cushite to take three men along with him, and draw the prophet Jeremiah out of the cistern before he should die. [11] Ebed-melech took the men along with him, and went first to the linen closet in the palace, from which he took some old, tattered rags; these he sent down to Jeremiah in the cistern, with ropes. [12] Then he said to Jeremiah, "Put the old, tattered rags between your armpits and the ropes." Jeremiah did so, [13] and they drew him up with the ropes out of the cistern. But Jeremiah remained in the quarters of the guard.

[14] Once King Zedekiah summoned the prophet Jeremiah to come to him at the third entrance to the house of the LORD. "I have a question to ask you," the king said to Jeremiah; "hide nothing from me."*t* Jeremiah answered Zedekiah: [15] If I tell you anything, you will have me killed, will you not? If I counsel you, you will not listen to me!*u* [16] But King Zedekiah swore to Jeremiah secretly: "As the LORD lives who gave us the breath of life, I will not kill you; nor will I hand you over to these men who seek your life."

[17] Thereupon Jeremiah said to Zedekiah: Thus says the LORD God of hosts, the God of Israel: If you surrender to the princes of Babylon's king, you shall save your life; this city shall not be destroyed with fire, and you and your family shall live.*v* [18] But if you do not surrender to the princes of Babylon's king, this city shall fall into the hands of the Chaldeans, who shall destroy it with fire, and you shall not escape their hands.*w*

[19] King Zedekiah, however, said to Jeremiah, "I am afraid of the men of Judah who have deserted to the Chaldeans; I may be handed over to them, and they will mistreat me."*x* [20] You will not be handed over, Jeremiah answered. Please obey the voice of the LORD and do as I tell you; then it shall go well with you, and your life will be spared.*y* [21] But if you refuse to surrender, this is what the LORD shows me: [22] All the women left in the house of Judah's king shall be brought out to the princes of Babylon's king, and they shall taunt you thus:

"They betrayed you, outdid you,
    your good friends!
Now that your feet are stuck in the
    mud,
    they slink away."*z*

---

o Jer 32, 2; 38, 28.—p Jer 21, 9f; 39, 18; 45, 5.—q Jer 26, 11.—r Jer 37, 14f.—s Jer 52, 6.—t Jer 37, 16.—u Lk 22, 67f.— v Jer 27, 12f; 2 Kgs 24, 12.—w Jer 32, 4.—x 1 Sm 31, 4.—y 2 Chr 20, 20.—z Jb 6, 15; 19, 13f. 19.

38, 1: Jeremiah enjoyed sufficient liberty *in the quarters of the guard* (Jer 37, 21) to speak to the people; cf Jer 32, 6-9. *Gedaliah, son of Pashhur:* the latter is possibly the Pashhur of Jer 20, 1. *Pashhur, son of Malchiah:* mentioned in Jer 21, 1.

38, 4: *He demoralizes the soldiers:* literally, "he weakens their hands." One of the Lachish ostraca (see note on Jer 34, 7) uses the same expression of the princes in Jerusalem.

38, 7: *A Cushite:* an Ethiopian. Ebed-melech evidently held a position of some authority at court.

23 All your wives and sons shall be led forth to the Chaldeans, and you shall not escape their hands; you shall be handed over to the king of Babylon, and this city shall be destroyed with fire.*a*
24 Then Zedekiah said to Jeremiah, "Let no one know about this conversation, or you shall die. 25 If the princes hear I spoke to you, if they come and ask you, 'Tell us what you said to the king; do not hide it from us, or we will kill you,' or, 'What did the king say to you?' 26 give them this answer: 'I petitioned the king not to send me back to Jonathan's house to die there.' "
27 When all the princes came to Jeremiah, they questioned him, and he answered them in the very words the king had commanded. They said no more to him, for nothing had been heard of the earlier conversation. 28 Thus Jeremiah stayed in the quarters of the guard till the day Jerusalem was taken.*b*

CHAPTER 39

Jeremiah and Gedaliah. When Jerusalem was taken. . . . 1 In the tenth month of the ninth year* of Zedekiah,*c* king of Judah, Nebuchadnezzar, king of Babylon, and all his army marched against Jerusalem and besieged it. 2 On the ninth day of the fourth month, in the eleventh year* of Zedekiah, a breach was made in the city's defenses. 3 All the princes of the king of Babylon came and occupied the middle gate: Nergal-sharezer, of Simmagir, the chief officer, Nebushazban, the high dignitary, and all the other princes of the king of Babylon. . . . 4 When Zedekiah, king of Judah, saw them, he and all his warriors fled by night, leaving the city on the Royal Garden Road* through the gate

---

a Jer 41, 10.—b Jer 39, 14.—c 1f: Jer 52, 4-16; 2 Kgs 25, 1-12; Ez 24, 1.—d Jer 52, 7.—e Jer 32, 4f; 38, 18.—f Jer 34, 21.—g Jer 32, 4f; Ez 12, 13.—h Jer 21, 10; 34, 2; 52, 13.—i 2 Kgs 25, 11.—j 2 Kgs 25, 12. 22.—k Jer 40, 4.—l Jer 26, 24; 38, 28.—m Jer 21, 10; Dn 9, 12.—n Jer 45, 5; Pss 25, 3; 36, 40.

39, 1: *The tenth month of the ninth year:* the month Tebet (mid-December to mid-January) of the year 589/8 B.C.
39, 2: *The ninth day of the fourth month, in the eleventh year:* in July of 587 B.C.
39, 4: *The Royal Garden Road:* along the southeast side of the city; the royal garden was in the Kidron Valley. *The gate between the two walls:* the southernmost city gate, at the end of the Tyropoean Valley. *The Arabah:* the Jordan Valley. Zedekiah was attempting to escape across the Jordan when he was captured near Jericho.
39, 5: *Riblah:* Nebuchadnezzar's headquarters in Syria, which had also been used by Pharaoh Neco (2 Kgs 23, 33).

---

between the two walls. He went in the direction of the Arabah,*d* 5 but the Chaldean army pursued them, and overtook and captured Zedekiah in the desert near Jericho. He was brought to Riblah,* in the land of Hamath, where Nebuchadnezzar, king of Babylon, pronounced sentence upon him.*e* 6 As Zedekiah looked on, his sons were slain at Riblah by order of the king of Babylon, who slew also all the nobles of Judah.*f* 7 He then blinded Zedekiah and bound him in chains to bring him to Babylon.*g*
8 The Chaldeans set fire to the king's palace and the houses of the people, and demolished the walls of Jerusalem.*h* 9 Nebuzaradan, chief of the bodyguard, deported to Babylon the rest of the people left in the city, those who had deserted to him, and the rest of the workmen.*i* 10 But some of the poor who had no property were left in the land of Judah by Nebuzaradan, chief of the bodyguard, and were given at the same time vineyards and farms.*j*
11 Concerning Jeremiah, Nebuchadnezzar, king of Babylon, gave the following orders through Nebuzaradan, chief of the bodyguard: 12 "Take him and look after him; let no harm befall him, but treat him as he himself requests."*k* 13 Thereupon Nebuzaradan, chief of the bodyguard, and Nebushazban, the high dignitary, and Nergal-sharezer, the chief officer, and all the nobles of the king of Babylon, 14 had Jeremiah taken out of the quarters of the guard, and entrusted to Gedaliah, son of Ahikam, son of Shaphan, to be brought home. And so he remained among the people.*l*

A Word of Comfort for Ebed-melech. 15 While Jeremiah was still imprisoned in the quarters of the guard, the word of the Lord came to him: 16 Go, tell this to Ebed-melech the Cushite: Thus says the Lord of hosts, the God of Israel: Behold, I am now fulfilling the words I spoke against this city, for evil and not for good; and this before your very eyes.*m* 17 But on that day I will rescue you, says the Lord; you shall not be handed over to the men of whom you are afraid. 18 I will make certain that you escape and do not fall by the sword. Your life shall be spared as booty, because you trusted in me, says the Lord.*n*

CHAPTER 40

Jeremiah Still in Judah. [1]This word* came to Jeremiah from the LORD, after Nebuzaradan, captain of the bodyguard, had released him in Ramah, where he had found him a prisoner in chains, among the captives of Jerusalem and Judah who were being exiled to Babylon.[o] [2]When the captain of the bodyguard took charge of Jeremiah, he said to him, "The LORD, your God, foretold the ruin of this place. [3]Now he has brought about in deed what he threatened; because you sinned against the LORD and did not obey his voice, this fate has befallen you. [4]And now, I am freeing you today from the fetters that bind your hands; if it seems good to you to come with me to Babylon, you may come: I will look after you well. But if it does not please you to come to Babylon, you need not come. See, the whole land is before you; go wherever you think good and proper";[p] [5]and then, before he left—"or go to Gedaliah, son of Ahikam, son of Shaphan, whom the king of Babylon has appointed ruler over the cities of Judah; stay with him among the people, or go wherever you please." The captain of the bodyguard gave him food and gifts and let him go.[q] [6]Jeremiah went to Gedaliah, son of Ahikam, in Mizpah,* and stayed with him among the people left in the land.[r]

[7]When the army leaders who were still in the field with all their men heard that the king of Babylon had given Gedaliah, son of Ahikam, charge of the land, of men, women, and children, and of those poor who had not been led captive to Babylon, [8]they came with their men to Gedaliah in Mizpah: Ishmael, son of Nethaniah; Johanan, son of Kareah; Seraiah, son of Tanhumeth; the sons of Ephai of Netophah; and Jezaniah* of Beth-maacah. [9]Gedaliah, son of Ahikam, son of Shaphan, adjured them and their men not to be afraid to serve the Chaldeans: to stay in the land and submit to the king of Babylon, for their own welfare,[s] [10]saying that he himself would remain in Mizpah, as their intermediary with the Chaldeans who should come to them. They were to collect the wine, the fruit, and the oil, to store them in jars, and to settle in the cities they occupied.

[11]When the people of Judah in Moab, those among the Ammonites, those in Edom, and those in all other lands heard that the king of Babylon had left a remnant in Judah, and had appointed over them Gedaliah, son of Ahikam, son of Shaphan, [12]they all returned to the land of Judah from the places to which they had scattered. They went to Gedaliah at Mizpah and had a rich harvest of wine and fruit.

Assassination of Gedaliah. [13]Now Johanan, son of Kareah, and all the leaders of the armies in the field came to Gedaliah in Mizpah [14]and asked him whether he did not know that Baalis, the king of the Ammonites,* had sent Ishmael, son of Nethaniah, to assassinate him.[t] [15]But Gedaliah, son of Ahikam, would not believe them. Then Johanan, son of Kareah, said secretly to Gedaliah in Mizpah: "Let me go and kill Ishmael, son of Nethaniah; no one will know it. Why should he be allowed to kill you? All the Jews who have now rallied to you will be dispersed and the remnant of Judah will perish." [16]Nevertheless, Gedaliah, son of Ahikam, answered Johanan, son of Kareah, "You shall do nothing of the kind; you have lied about Ishmael."

CHAPTER 41

[1]In the seventh month Ishmael, son of Nethaniah, son of Elishama, of royal descent, one of the king's nobles, came with ten men to Gedaliah, son of Ahikam, at Mizpah.[u] And while they were together at table in Mizpah, [2]Ishmael, son of Nethaniah, and the ten who were with him, rose up and attacked with swords Gedaliah, son of Ahikam, son of Shaphan, whom the king of Babylon had made ruler over the land; and they killed

---

o Jer 39, 14.—p Jer 39, 12.—q Jer 39, 14; 2 Kgs 25, 22.—r Jer 39, 14.—s Jer 27, 12f; 2 Kgs 25, 24.—t Jer 41, 1ff. 10.—u Jer 40, 14ff; 2 Kgs 25, 25.

40, 1: *This word:* actually, no further word of the Lord is recorded until Jer 42, 7ff. This is a title affixed to the following chapters after they were attached to an earlier form of the book ending with chapter 39.

40, 6: *Mizpah:* some five miles northwest of Jerusalem, where Israel chose its first king (1 Sm 10, 17-24). Presumably Jerusalem had been damaged too much by the Chaldean conquest to remain a seat of government.

40, 8: *Jezaniah:* the seal ring of a high official of this name was discovered in 1932 at the site usually identified with Mizpah, Tell en-Nasbe.

40, 14: *The Ammonites:* they resented the survival of their ancient enemy, Judah. *Ishmael:* their willing tool, who doubtless aspired to rule over Judah himself, as he was of the house of David; cf Jer 41, 1.

him. ³Ishmael also slew all the men of Judah of military age who were with Gedaliah and the Chaldean soldiers who were there.

⁴The second day after the murder of Gedaliah, before anyone knew of it, ⁵eighty men with beards shaved off, clothes in rags, and with gashes on their bodies came from Shechem, Shiloh, and Samaria, bringing food offerings and incense for the house of the LORD. ⁶Ishmael, son of Nethaniah, went out from Mizpah to meet them, weeping as he went. ⁷"Come to Gedaliah, son of Ahikam," he said as he met them. When they were once inside the city, Ishmael, son of Nethaniah, and his men slew them and threw them into the cistern. ⁸But there were ten among them who pleaded with Ishmael: "Do not kill us; we have stores buried in the field: wheat and barley, oil and honey." And so he spared them and did not kill them, as he had killed their companions. ⁹The cistern into which Ishmael threw all the corpses of the men he had killed was the large one made by King Asa to defend himself against Baasha, king of Israel; this cistern Ishmael, son of Nethaniah, filled with the slain.ᵛ

¹⁰Ishmael, son of Nethaniah, led away the remnant of the people left in Mizpah and the princesses,* whom Nebuzaradan, captain of the bodyguard, had confided to Gedaliah, son of Ahikam. With these captives, Ishmael, son of Nethaniah, set out to make his way to the Ammonites.

Flight to Egypt. ¹¹But when Johanan, son of Kareah, and the other army leaders with him heard of the crimes Ishmael, son of Nethaniah, had committed, ¹²they took all their men and set out to attack Ishmael, son of Nethaniah. They overtook him at the Great Waters in Gibeon.* ¹³At the sight of Johanan, son of Kareah, and the other army leaders, the people who were Ishmael's captives rejoiced. ¹⁴All of those whom Ishmael had brought away from Mizpah went over to Johanan, son of Kareah. ¹⁵But Ishmael, son of Nethaniah, escaped from Johanan and fled to the Ammonites with eight men. ¹⁶Then Johanan, son of Kareah, and all his army leaders took charge of the remnant of the people, both the soldiers and the women and children with their guardians, whom Ishmael, son of Nethaniah, had brought away from Mizpah after he killed Gedaliah, son of Ahikam. From Gibeon, ¹⁷they retreated to the lodging place of Chimham near Bethlehem, where they stopped, intending to flee into Egypt. ¹⁸They were afraid of the Chaldeans, because Ishmael, son of Nethaniah, had slain Gedaliah, son of Ahikam, whom the king of Babylon had made ruler in the land of Judah.

CHAPTER 42

¹Then all the army leaders, Johanan, son of Kareah, Azariah, son of Hoshaiah, and all the people, high and low, approached the prophet Jeremiah ²and said, "Grant our petition; pray for us to the LORD, your God, for all this remnant. We are now few who once were many, as you well see. ³Let the LORD, your God, show us what way we should take and what we should do." ⁴Very well! the prophet Jeremiah answered them: I will pray to the LORD, your God, as you desire; whatever the LORD answers you, I will tell you; I will withhold nothing from you.ʷ ⁵And they said to Jeremiah, "May the LORD be our witness: we will truly and faithfully follow all the instructions the LORD, your God, will send us.ˣ ⁶Whether it is pleasant or difficult, we will obey the command of the LORD, our God, to whom we are sending you, so that it will go well with us for obeying the command of the LORD, our God."ʸ

⁷Ten days passed before the word of the LORD came to Jeremiah. ⁸Then he called Johanan, son of Kareah, his army leaders, and all the people, high and low, ⁹and said to them: Thus says the LORD, the God of Israel, to whom you sent me to offer your prayer: ¹⁰If you remain quietly in this land I will build you up, and not tear you down; I will plant you, not uproot you; for I regret the evil I have done you.ᶻ ¹¹Do not fear the king of Babylon, before whom you are now afraid; do not fear him, says the LORD, for I am with you to save you,

---

v 1 Kgs 15, 16; 2 Chr 16, 6.—w 1 Sm 3, 18.—x Jgs 11, 10.— y Jer 7, 23; Dt 5, 33; 6, 3.—z Jer 31, 28; 32, 41.

41, 10: *The princesses:* of the royal house of Judah. They had not been deported to Babylon with the men of this house.

41, 12: *Gibeon:* today called El-Jib; it is northwest of Jerusalem. The most recent excavations have revealed the extensive dimensions of the city spring and well, called here *the Great Waters;* cf 2 Sm 2, 12ff.

to rescue you from his power.[a] [12]I will grant you mercy, so that he will be sorry for you and let you return to your land.[b] [13]But if you disobey the voice of the LORD, your God, and decide not to remain in this land, [14]saying, "No, we will go to Egypt, where we will see no more of war, hear the trumpet alarm no longer, nor hunger for bread; there we will live";[c] [15]then listen to the word of the LORD, remnant of Judah: Thus says the LORD of hosts, the God of Israel: If you are determined to go to Egypt, when you arrive there to stay, [16]the sword you fear shall reach you in the land of Egypt; the hunger you dread shall cling to you no less in Egypt, and there you shall die.[d] [17]All those men who determine to go to Egypt to stay, shall die by the sword, famine, and pestilence; not one shall survive or escape the evil that I will bring upon them.[e] [18]For thus says the LORD of hosts, the God of Israel: Just as my furious anger was poured out upon the citizens of Jerusalem, so shall my anger be poured out on you when you reach Egypt. You shall become an example of malediction and horror, a curse and a reproach, and you shall never see this place again.[f]

[19]It is the LORD who has spoken to you, remnant of Judah; do not go to Egypt! You can never say that I did not warn you this day. [20]At the cost of your lives you have deceived me, sending me to the LORD, your God, saying, "Pray for us to the LORD, our God; make known to us all that the LORD, our God, shall say, and we will do it." [21]Today I proclaim his message, but you obey the voice of the LORD, your God, in nothing that he has commissioned me to make known to you.[g] [22]Have no doubt of this, you shall die by the sword, famine, and pestilence in the place where you wish to go and settle.[h]

CHAPTER 43

[1]When Jeremiah finished speaking to the people all these words of the LORD, their God, with which the LORD had sent him to them, [2]Azariah, son of Hoshaiah, Johanan, son of Kareah, and all the insolent men shouted to Jeremiah: "You lie; it was not the LORD, our God, who sent you to tell us not to go to Egypt to settle. [3]It is Baruch, son of Neriah, who stirs you up against us, to hand us over to the

Chaldeans to be killed or exiled to Babylon."[i]

[4]Johanan, son of Kareah, and the rest of the leaders and the people did not obey the LORD's command to stay in the land of Judah.[j] [5]Instead, Johanan, son of Kareah, and all the army leaders took along the whole remnant of Judah that had been dispersed among the nations and had returned thence to dwell again in the land of Judah: [6]men, women, and children, the princesses and everyone whom Nebuzaradan, captain of the bodyguard, had entrusted to Gedaliah, son of Ahikam, son of Shaphan; also Jeremiah, the prophet, and Baruch, son of Neriah.[k] [7]Against the LORD's command they went to Egypt, and arrived at Tahpanhes. . . .[l]

Jeremiah in Egypt. [8]This word of the LORD came to Jeremiah in Tahpanhes: [9]Take with you large stones and sink them in mortar in the brickyard at the entrance to the royal building* in Tahpanhes, while the men of Judah look on, [10]and then say to them: Thus says the LORD of hosts, the God of Israel: I will send for my servant Nebuchadnezzar, king of Babylon, and bring him here. He will set his throne upon these stones which I, Jeremiah, have sunk, and stretch his canopy over them.[m] [11]He shall come and strike the land of Egypt: with death, whoever is marked for death; with exile, everyone destined for exile; with the sword, all who are intended for the sword.[n] [12]He shall set fire to the temples of Egypt's gods, and burn the gods or carry them off. As a shepherd delouses his cloak, he shall delouse the land of Egypt and depart victorious.[o] [13]He shall smash the obelisks of the temple of the sun in the land of Egypt and destroy with fire the temples of the Egyptian gods.

CHAPTER 44

[1]This word came to Jeremiah for all the people of Judah who were living in Egypt, at Migdol, Tahpanhes, and Memphis, and in Upper Egypt: [2] * Thus says the LORD

a Jer 30, 10f.—b Ps 106, 45f; Prv 16, 7.—c Dt 28, 68.—d Jer 44, 13f. 27.—e Jer 29, 17f; 44, 14. 28.—f Jer 44, 12.—g Zec 7, 11f.—h Jer 44, 12; Hos 9, 6.—i Jer 38, 4.—j Jer 41, 16.—k Jer 41, 10.—l Jer 42, 13f; 44, 1.—m Jer 27, 6; Ex 29, 19.—n Jer 46, 13; Ez 30, 10.—o Jer 46, 25; Ez 30, 13f.

43, 9: *The royal building:* residence of the Egyptian governor.

44, 2-30: Chronologically, this is the last of Jeremiah's prophecies to his countrymen. The narrative leaves him an old man nearing seventy, rejected by his people. According to tradition, he was murdered in Egypt by fellow Judeans.

of hosts, the God of Israel: You have seen all the evil I brought on Jerusalem and the other cities of Judah. Today they are ruins and uninhabited,*p* ³because of the evil they did to provoke me, going after strange gods, serving them and sacrificing to them, gods which neither they, nor you, nor your fathers knew.*q* ⁴Though I kept sending to you all my servants the prophets, with the plea not to commit this horrible deed which I hate, ⁵they would not listen or accept the warning to turn away from the evil of sacrificing to strange gods.*r* ⁶Therefore the fury of my anger poured forth in flame over the cities of Judah and the streets of Jerusalem, so that they became the ruinous waste they are today.

⁷Now thus says the LORD God of hosts, the God of Israel: Why do you inflict so great an evil upon yourselves? Will you root out from Judah man and wife, child and nursling, and not leave yourselves even a remnant? ⁸Will you go on provoking me by the works of your hands, by sacrificing to strange gods here in the land of Egypt where you have come to live? Will you be rooted out and become a curse and a disgrace among all the nations of the earth?*s* ⁹Have you forgotten the evil deeds which your fathers, and the kings of Judah and their wives, and you yourselves and your wives have done in the land of Judah and the streets of Jerusalem?*t* ¹⁰To this day they have not been crushed; they do not fear or follow the law and the statutes which I set before you and your fathers.*u*

¹¹Hence, thus says the LORD of hosts, the God of Israel: I have determined evil against you; and I will uproot all Judah. ¹²I will take away the remnant of Judah who insisted on coming to dwell in Egypt, so that they shall be wholly destroyed. In the land of Egypt they shall fall by the sword or be consumed by hunger. High and low, they shall die by the sword, or by hunger, and become an example of malediction, a horror, a curse and a reproach.*v* ¹³Thus will I punish those who live in Egypt, just as I punished Jeru-

salem with sword, hunger, and pestilence. None of the remnant of Judah that have come to settle in the land of Egypt shall escape or survive.*w* ¹⁴None shall return to the land of Judah, though they yearn to return and live there. Only scattered refugees shall return.

¹⁵From all the men who knew that their wives were burning incense to strange gods, from all the women who were present in the immense crowd, and from all the people who lived in Lower and Upper Egypt, Jeremiah received this answer: ¹⁶"We will not listen to what you say in the name of the LORD.*x* ¹⁷Rather will we continue doing what we had proposed; we will burn incense to the queen of heaven and pour out libations to her, as we and our fathers, our kings and princes have done in the cities of Judah and the streets of Jerusalem. Then we had enough food to eat and we were well off; we suffered no misfortune.*y* ¹⁸But since we stopped burning incense to the queen of heaven and pouring out libations to her, we are in need of everything and are being destroyed by the sword and by hunger. ¹⁹And when we burned incense to the queen of heaven and poured out libations to her, was it without our husbands' consent that we baked for her cakes in her image and poured out libations to her?"*z*

²⁰To all the people, men and women, who gave him this answer, Jeremiah said: ²¹Was it not this that the LORD remembered and brought to mind, that you burned incense in the cities of Judah and the streets of Jerusalem: you, your fathers, your kings and princes, and the people generally?*a* ²²The LORD could no longer bear your evil deeds, the horrible things which you were doing; and so your land became a waste, a desert, a thing accursed and without inhabitants, as it is today.*b* ²³Because you burned incense and sinned against the LORD, not obeying the voice of the LORD, not living by his law, his statutes, and his decrees, this evil has befallen you at the present day.*c*

²⁴Jeremiah said further to all the people, including the women: Hear the word of the LORD, all you Judeans in the land of Egypt: ²⁵Thus says the LORD of hosts, the God of Israel: You and your wives have stated your intentions, and kept them in fact: "We will continue to fulfill the vows

Jer

p Jer 34, 22; Lv 26, 32f.—q Jer 11, 17; Dt 32, 17.—r Jer 7, 24. 26; 19, 4.—s Jer 25, 6f.—t 1 Kgs 11, 1. 8; Ezr 9, 7. 14.—u Jer 7, 24.—v Jer 42, 15. 18. 22.—w Jer 43, 11.—x Jer 6, 16f.—y Jer 5, 3; 7, 18.—z Jer 7, 18.—a Jer 11, 13.—b Jer 15, 6.—c 2 Kgs 17, 15; Dn 9, 11f.

we have made to burn incense to the queen of heaven and to pour out libations to her." Very well! keep your vows, carry out your resolutions! [26] But listen then to the word of the LORD, all you people of Judah who live in Egypt; I swear by my own great name, says the LORD, in the whole land of Egypt no man of Judah shall henceforth pronounce my name, saying, "As the Lord GOD lives." [27] I am watching over them to do evil, not good. All the men of Judah in Egypt shall perish by the sword or famine until they are utterly destroyed. [d] [28] Those who escape the sword to return from the land of Egypt to the land of Judah shall be few in number. The whole remnant of Judah who came to settle in Egypt shall know whose word stands, mine or theirs. [e]

[29] That you may know how surely my threats of punishment for you shall be fulfilled, this shall be a sign to you, says the LORD, that I will punish you in this place. [30] Thus says the LORD: See! I will hand over Pharaoh Hophra,* king of Egypt, to his enemies, to those who seek his life, just as I handed over Zedekiah, king of Judah, to his enemy and mortal foe, Nebuchadnezzar, king of Babylon. [f]

CHAPTER 45

A Message to Baruch.* [1] This is the message that the prophet Jeremiah gave to Baruch, son of Neriah, when he wrote in a book the prophecies that Jeremiah dictated in the fourth year of Jehoiakim, son of Josiah, king of Judah: [g] [2] Thus says the LORD, God of Israel, to you, Baruch, [3] because you said, "Alas! the LORD adds grief to my pain; [h] I am weary from groaning, and can find no rest": [4] say this to him, says the LORD: What I have built, I am tearing down; what I have planted, I am uprooting: even the whole land. [i] [5] And do you seek great things for yourself? Seek them not! I am bringing evil on all mankind, says the LORD, but your life I will leave you as booty, wherever you may go. [j]

V: ORACLES AGAINST THE NATIONS*

CHAPTER 46

[1] This is the word of the LORD that came to the prophet Jeremiah against the nations.

Against Egypt. [2] Concerning Egypt. Against the army of Pharaoh Neco, king of Egypt, which was defeated at Carchemish on the Euphrates* by Nebuchadnezzar, king of Babylon, in the fourth year of Jehoiakim, son of Josiah, king of Judah:

[3] Prepare shield and buckler!
    march to battle!
[4] Harness the horses,
    mount, charioteers!
Fall in with your helmets;
    polish your spears, put on your
        breastplates.
[5] What do I see?
    With broken ranks
They fall back;
    their heroes are routed,
They flee headlong
    without making a stand.
Terror on every side,
    says the LORD! [k]
[6] The swift cannot flee,
    nor the hero escape:
There in the north, on the Euphrates'
        bank,
    they stumble and fall.

[7] Who is this that surges forward like the
        Nile,
    like rivers of billowing waters?
[8] Egypt surges like the Nile,
    like rivers of billowing waters.
"I will surge forward," he says, "and
        cover the earth,
    destroying the city and its people. [l]
[9] Forward, horses!
    drive madly, chariots!

d Ez 7, 3-7.—e Dt 28, 62; Is 10, 22.—f Jer 39, 5ff; 46, 25f; Ez 29, 3f; 30, 21.—g Jer 36, 4. 18. 32.—h Lam 1, 3; 5, 5.—i Jer 18, 7; Is 5, 5f.—j Jer 25, 26-29.—k Jer 6, 25; 49, 29.—l Ez 29, 3; 32, 2.

44, 30: *Hophra:* killed by his own people. The ruler of Egypt at the time of its conquest by Nebuchadnezzar was Hophra's successor Amasis, who was also slain by his enemies.

45, 1-5: At the conclusion of his narrative, Baruch appends a prophecy given him personally by Jeremiah when he first wrote down Jeremiah's words (cf chap. 36). The future revealed by the prophet had depressed Baruch; this prophecy was to assure him of his personal safety, while repeating the Lord's determination to destroy Judah.

46—51: In these chapters most of Jeremiah's oracles against the foreign nations have been gathered together and placed at the end of his book; in the Greek text they appear with the other oracles against the nations, in chap. 25. In general, they are in chronological order: 46, 1—49, 33, from the fourth year of Jehoiakim; 49, 34-39, at the beginning of Zedekiah's reign; 50, 1—51, 64, from the fourth year of Zedekiah.

46, 2: *Carchemish on the Euphrates:* the western terminus of the Mesopotamian trade route, where Nebuchadnezzar defeated Neco in 605 B.C., thus gaining undisputed control of Syria and Palestine.

Set out, warriors,
Cush and Put, bearing your shields,
Men of Lud, stretching your bows!"
[10] But this is the day of the Lord GOD of
hosts,
a day of vengeance, vengeance on his
foes!
The sword devours, is sated, drunk
with their blood:
for the Lord GOD of hosts holds a
slaughter feast
in the northland, on the Euphrates. [m]
[11] Go up to Gilead, and take balm,
O virgin daughter Egypt!
No use to multiply remedies;
for you there is no cure. [n]
[12] The nations hear of your shame,
your cries fill the earth.
Warrior trips over warrior,
both fall together. [o]

[13] [p] The message which the LORD gave
to the prophet Jeremiah concerning the
advance of Nebuchadnezzar, king of Babylon, to attack the land of Egypt:*
[14] Announce it in Egypt, publish it in
Migdol,
proclaim it in Memphis and Tahpanhes!
Say: Take your stand, prepare yourselves,
the sword has already devoured your
neighbors. [q]
[15] Why has Apis* fled,
your mighty one failed to stand?
The LORD thrust him down;
[16]   he stumbled repeatedly, and fell.
They said one to another,
"Up! let us return to our own people,
To the land of our birth,
away from the destroying sword." [r]
[17] Call Pharaoh, king of Egypt, by the
name
"The noise that let its time go by."*

[18] As I live, says the King
whose name is LORD of hosts,
Like Tabor among the mountains he
shall come,
like Carmel* above the sea.
[19] Pack your baggage for exile,
capital city of daughter Egypt;
Memphis shall become a desert,
an empty ruin.
[20] Egypt is a pretty heifer,
from the north a horsefly lights upon
her.
[21] The mercenaries in her ranks
are like fatted calves;
They too turn and flee together,
stand not their ground,
When the day of their ruin comes upon
them,
the time of their punishment.
[22] She sounds like a retreating reptile!
Yes, they come in force;
like woodchoppers, they attack her
with axes.
[23] They cut down her forest, says the
LORD,
impenetrable though it be;
More numerous than locusts,
they cannot be counted.
[24] Disgraced is daughter Egypt,
handed over to the people of the
north.

[25] The LORD of hosts, the God of Israel,
has said: See! I will punish Amon* of
Thebes, and Egypt, her gods and her
kings, Pharaoh, and those who trust in
him. [s] [26] I will hand them over to those who
seek their lives, to Nebuchadnezzar, king
of Babylon, and his ministers. But later on
Egypt shall be inhabited again, as in times
past, says the LORD. [t]

[27] But you, my servant Jacob, fear not;
be not dismayed, O Israel.
Behold, I will deliver you from the far-
off land,
your descendants, from their land of
exile.
Jacob shall again find rest,
shall be tranquil and undisturbed. [u]
[28] You, my servant Jacob, never fear, says
the LORD,
for I am with you;
I will make an end of all the nations
to which I have driven you,
But of you I will not make an end:
I will chastise you as you deserve,
I will not let you go unpunished. [v]

m Dt 32, 42; Is 13, 9; Ez 39, 17-20.—n Jer 8, 22; 51, 8; Ez
30, 21f.—o Ez 32, 9-12.—p Jer 43, 10f; 44, 30; Is 19, 1.—q Jer
44, 1.—r Lv 26, 37.—s Ez 30, 15f.—t Jer 44, 30; Ez 30, 4; 32,
11f.—u Jer 30, 10; 43, 5.—v Jer 30, 11.

46, 13: In 601 B.C. Nebuchadnezzar advanced against Egypt
and even entered the country, but finally had to withdraw to
Syria.
46, 15: *Apis:* the chief god of Memphis, venerated in the form
of a black bull.
46, 17: *"The noise . . . go by":* in Hebrew there is wordplay
here on the name Hophra, who still made a pretense of power
though his career was at an end.
46, 18: *Tabor . . . Carmel:* outstanding mountains of Palestine, symbols of strength, to which Nebuchadnezzar is compared.
46, 25: *Amon:* the sun-god worshiped at Thebes, in Upper
Egypt.

Jer

CHAPTER 47

Against the Philistines. ¹This is the word that came from the LORD to the prophet Jeremiah concerning the Philistines, before Pharaoh attacked Gaza:ʷ ²Thus says the LORD:

* Behold: waters are rising from the north,
    a torrent in flood;
It shall flood the land and all that is in it,
    the cities and their people.
All the people of the land
    set up a wailing cry.
³ They hear the stamping hooves of his steeds,
    the rattling chariots, the rumbling wheels.
Father turn not to save their children;
    their hands fall helpless
⁴ Because of the day which has come
    to ruin all the Philistines,
And cut off from Tyre and Sidon*
    the last of their allies.
Yes, the LORD is destroying the Philistines,
    the remnant from the coasts of Caphtor.ˣ
⁵ Gaza is shaved bald,ʸ
    Ashkelon is reduced to silence;
Ashdod, the remnant of their strength,
    how long will you gash yourself?*
⁶ Alas, sword of the LORD!
    how long till you find rest?
Return into your scabbard;
    stop, be still!*
⁷ How can it find rest
    when the LORD has commanded it?
Against Ashkelon and the seashore
    he has appointed it.ᶻ

CHAPTER 48

Against Moab.* ¹Concerning Moab, thus says the LORD of hosts, the God of Israel:

Woe to Nebo, it is laid waste;
    Kiriathaim is disgraced and captured,
Disgraced and overthrown is the stronghold:
² Moab's glory is no more.
Evil they plan against Heshbon:
    "Come, let us put an end to her as a people."
You, too, Madmen, shall be reduced to silence;
    behind you stalks the sword.

³ Listen! a cry from Horonaimᵃ
    of ruin and great destruction!
⁴ Moab is crushed,
    their outcry is heard in Zoar.
⁵ The ascent of Luhith
    they climb weeping;
On the descent to Horonaim
    the cry of destruction is heard.
⁶ "Flee, save your lives,
    to survive like the wild ass in the desert!"
⁷ Because you trusted in your works and your treasures,
    you also shall be captured.
Chemosh* shall go into exile,
    his priests and princes with him.ᵇ
⁸ The destroyer comes upon every city,
    not a city escapes;
Ruined is the valley,
    wasted the plain, as the LORD has said.
⁹ Set up a memorial for Moab,
    for it is an utter wasteland;
Its cities are turned into ruins
    where no one dwells.
¹⁰ [Cursed be he who does the LORD's work remissly,
    cursed he who holds back his sword from blood.]
¹¹ Moab has been tranquil from his youth,
    has rested upon his lees;
He was not poured from one flask to another,
    he went not into exile.
Thus he kept his taste,
    and his scent was not lost.ᶜ

¹²Hence, the days shall come, says the LORD, when I will send him coopers to turn him over; they shall empty his flasks and break his jars. ¹³Chemosh shall dis-

---

w Ez 25, 15f; Zep 2, 4.—x Jer 25, 22; Ez 25, 16f; Am 1, 8; 9, 7.—y Am 1, 7.—z Zep 2, 5f.—a 3ff: Is 15, 5.—b Nm 21, 29.— c Zep 1, 12.

47, 2-7: This prophecy was fulfilled in 605/4 B.C.
47, 4: *Tyre and Sidon:* Phoenician cities associated commercially with the Philistines, and enemies of Nebuchadnezzar; cf Jer 27, 1-4. Nebuchadnezzar carried out a thirteen-year siege of Tyre which was only partially successful. *Caphtor:* probably the island of Crete, the traditional place of origin of the Philistines; cf Am 9, 7.
47, 5: Of the ancient Philistine cities, neither Gath nor Ekron (Jer 25, 20) is mentioned in this period of waning independence of the seacoast.
47, 6: Words of the Philistines.
48, 1-47: Moab was one of the Israelites' bitterest enemies. According to Flavius Josephus, Moab and Ammon were conquered by Nebuchadnezzar in his twenty-third year, 582 B.C., five years after the destruction of Jerusalem.
48, 7: *Chemosh:* chief god of the Moabites.

appoint Moab, as Israel was disappointed by Bethel in which they trusted. *d*

14 How can you say, "We are heroes,
   men valiant in war"?
15 The ravager of Moab and his cities advances,
   the flower of his youth goes down to be slaughtered,
   says the King, the LORD of hosts by name.
16 Near at hand is Moab's ruin,
   his disaster hastens apace.
17 Mourn for him, all you his neighbors,
   all you who knew him well!
   Say: How the strong staff is broken,
   the glorious rod!
18 Come down from glory, sit on the ground,
   you that dwell in Dibon;
   Moab's ravager has come up against you,
   he has ruined your strongholds. *e*
19 Stand by the wayside, watch closely,
   you that dwell in Aroer;
   Ask the man who flees, the woman who tries to escape:
   say to them, "What has happened?" *f*
20 Moab is disgraced, yes, destroyed,
   howl and cry out;
   Publish it at the Arnon,
   Moab is ruined! *g*

21 For judgment has come on the land of the plateau: on Holon, Jahzah, and Mephaath, *h* 22 on Dibon, Nebo, and Beth-diblathaim, 23 on Kiriathaim, Beth-gamul, and Beth-meon, 24 on Kerioth and on Bozrah: on all the cities of Moab, far and near.

25 Moab's strength is broken,
   his might is shattered, says the LORD.

26 Because he boasted against the LORD, make Moab drunk so that he retches and vomits, and he too becomes a laughingstock. 27 Is Israel a laughingstock to you? Was she caught among thieves, that you shake your head whenever you speak of her? *i*

28 Leave the cities, dwell in the crags,
   you that dwell in Moab.
   Be like a dove that nests
   out of reach on the edge of a chasm.

29 We have heard of the pride of Moab, *j*
   pride beyond bounds:
   His loftiness, his pride, his scorn,
   his insolence of heart.
30 I know, says the LORD, his arrogance;
   liar in boast, liar in deed.
31 And so I wail over Moab,
   over all Moab I cry,
   over the men of Kir-heres I moan. *k*
32 More than for Jazer I weep over you,
   vineyard of Sibmah.
   Your tendrils trailed down to the sea,
   as far as Jazer they stretched.
   Upon your harvest, upon your vintage,
   the ravager has fallen. *l*
33 Joy and jubilation are at an end
   in the fruit gardens of the land of Moab.
   I drain the wine from the wine vats,
   the treader treads no more,
   the vintage shout is stilled.

34 The cry of Heshbon and Elealeh is heard as far as Jahaz; they call from Zoar to Horonaim, and to Eglath-shelishiyah, for even the waters of Nimrim turn into a desert. *m* 35 I will leave no one in Moab, says the LORD, to offer a holocaust on the high place, or to burn incense to his gods. 36 Hence the wail of flutes for Moab is in my heart; for the men of Kir-heres the wail of flutes is in my heart: the wealth they acquired has perished. *n* 37 Every head has been made bald, every beard shaved; every hand is gashed, and the loins of all are clothed in sackcloth. *o* 38 On every roof of Moab and in all his squares there is mourning; I have shattered Moab like a pot that no one wants, says the LORD. 39 How terror seizes Moab, and wailing! How he turns his back in shame! Moab has become a laughingstock and a horror to all his neighbors! 40 For thus says the LORD:

Behold, like an eagle he soars,
   spreads his wings over Moab. *p*
41 Cities are taken,
   strongholds seized:
   On that day the hearts of Moab's heroes
   are like the heart of a woman in travail. *q*
42 Moab shall be destroyed, no more a people,
   because he boasted against the LORD. *r*

Jer

d Is 16, 12.—e Nm 21, 30.—f Dt 2, 3b.—g Is 16, 7.—h Is 15, 4.—i Zep 2, 8ff.—j 29f: Is 16, 6.—k Is 16, 7.—l Is 16, 8f.—m Is 15, 4f.—n Is 16, 11.—o Jer 47, 5; Is 15, 2f; Ez 7, 18.—p Jer 49, 22.—q Jer 6, 24; 30, 6.—r Zep 2, 9f.

43 Terror, pit, and trap be upon you,
  people of Moab, says the LORD. *s*
44 He who flees from the terror
  falls into the pit;
He who climbs from the pit
  is caught in the trap;
For I will bring these things upon Moab
  in the year of their punishment, says
  the LORD.
45 In Heshbon's shadow stop short
  the exhausted refugees;
For fire breaks forth from Heshbon,
  and a blaze from the house of Sihon:
It consumes the brow of Moab,
  the skull of the noisemakers. *t*

46 Woe to you, O Moab,
  you are ruined, O people of Chemosh!
Your sons are taken into exile,
  your daughters into captivity.
47 But I will change the lot of Moab
  in the days to come, says the LORD. *u*

Thus far the judgment on Moab.

CHAPTER 49

Against the Ammonites. 1 Concerning the
Ammonites, thus says the LORD:

Has Israel no sons?
  has he no heir?
When then has Milcom* disinherited
  Gad,
  why have his people settled in Gad's
  cities?
2 But the days are coming, says the
  LORD,
  when against Rabbah of the Ammonites*
I will sound the battle alarm;
She shall become a mound of ruins,
  and her daughter cities shall be destroyed by fire.
Israel shall inherit those who disinherited her,
  says the LORD. *v*
3 Howl, Heshbon, for the ravager approaches,
  shriek, daughters of Rabbah!
Put on sackcloth and mourn,
  run to and fro, gashing yourselves;
For Milcom goes into exile
  along with his priests and captains. *w*

4 Why do you glory in your strength,
  your ebbing strength, rebellious
  daughter?

You who trust in your treasures, saying,
  "Who can come against me?"
5 I am bringing terror upon you,
  says the Lord GOD of hosts,
  from all round about you;
You shall be scattered, each man in
  headlong flight,
  with no one to rally the fugitives. *x*
6 But afterward I will change the lot
  of the Ammonites, says the LORD.

Against Edom.* 7 Concerning Edom, thus
says the LORD of hosts:

Is there no more wisdom in Teman,*
  has counsel perished from the prudent,
  has their wisdom become corrupt?
8 Flee, retreat, hide in deep holes,
  you who live in Dedan:
For I will bring destruction upon Esau*
  when I come to punish him. *y*
9 If vintagers came upon you,
  they would leave no gleanings;
If thieves by night,
  they would destroy as they pleased. *z*
10 So I myself will strip Esau;
  I will uncover his retreats so that he
  cannot hide.
He is ruined: sons, and brothers,
  and neighbors, so that he is no
  more. *a*
11 Leave your orphans behind, I will keep
  them alive;
  your widows, let them trust in me. *b*

12 For thus says the LORD: Even those
not sentenced to drink the cup must drink
it! Shall you then go unpunished? You
shall not go unpunished; you shall surely
drink it. *c* 13 By my own self I have sworn,
says the LORD: Bozrah* shall become an
object of horror and a disgrace, a desola-

---

s Is 24, 17f.—t Nm 21, 28f.—u Jer 49, 39.—v Am 1, 14.—w
Is 15, 2ff.—x Jer 48, 47.—y Ez 25, 13.—z Ob 5.—a Mal 1, 3.—b
Dt 10, 18; Ps 68, 6.—c Jer 25, 15. 28; Lam 4, 21f.

49, 1: *Milcom:* chief god of the Ammonites. The Transjordan
tribe of Gad bordered on Ammon, and after the collapse of the
northern kingdom the Ammonites occupied its territory.
   49, 2: *Rabbah of the Ammonites:* or Rabbath-Ammon, capital of the Ammonite kingdom. The modern Amman is the capital
of the kingdom of Jordan.
   49, 7-22: *Edom:* this implacable enemy from ancient times
profited from Judah's downfall; cf Ob 11f.
   49, 7: *Teman:* a district of Edom, used here for the whole
country; it was famous for its wise men; cf Jb 2, 11.
   49, 8: *Esau:* Jacob's brother, the traditional ancestor of the
Edomites; cf Gn 36.
   49, 13: *Bozrah:* capital of Edom, southeast of the Dead Sea.

tion and a curse; she and all her cities shall become ruins forever.[d]

[14] I have heard a report from the LORD,
    a herald has been sent among the nations:
Gather together, move against her,
    rise up for battle.
[15] Small will I make you among the nations,
    despised among men![e]
[16] The terror you spread beguiled you,
    and your presumption of heart;
You that live in rocky crags,
    that hold the heights of the hill:
Though you build your nest high as the eagle,
    from there I will drag you down, says the LORD.[f]

[17] Edom shall become an object of horror. Every passer-by shall be appalled and catch his breath at all her wounds. [18] As when Sodom, Gomorrah, and their neighbors were overthrown, says the LORD, not a man shall dwell there: no one shall visit there.[g]

[19] As when a lion comes up from the thicket of Jordan
    to the permanent feeding grounds,
So I, in an instant, will drive men off;
    and whom I choose I will establish there!
For who is like me? who can call me to account?
    What shepherd can stand against me?[h]
[20] Therefore, hear the counsel of the LORD,
    which he has taken against Edom;
Hear the plans he has made
    against those that live in Teman:
They shall be dragged away, even the smallest sheep,
    their own pasture shall be aghast because of them.
[21] At the noise of their fall the earth quakes,
    to the Red Sea the outcry is heard!

[22] See! like an eagle he soars aloft,
    and spreads his wings over Bozrah;
On that day the hearts of Edom's heroes shall be
    like the heart of a woman in travail.[i]

Against Damascus. Concerning Damascus:

[23] Hamath and Arpad* are covered with shame,
    they have heard bad news;
Worried, they toss like the sea
    which cannot rest.[j]
[24] Damascus is weakened, she turns to flee,
    panic has seized her.
Distress and pangs take hold of her,
    like those of a woman in travail.
[25] How can the city of glory be forsaken,
    the town of delight!
[26] But now her young men shall fall in her streets,
    and all her warriors shall be stilled.
On that day, says the LORD of hosts,
[27] I will set fire to the wall of Damascus,
    and it shall devour the palaces of Ben-hadad.*

Against Arabia. [28] Of Kedar and the kingdoms of Hazor, defeated by Nebuchadnezzar, king of Babylon, thus says the LORD:

Rise up, attack Kedar,
    ravage the Easterners.[k]
[29] Their tents and herds shall be taken away,
    their tent curtains and all their goods;
Their camels they shall carry off for themselves,
    and shout from upon them, "Terror on every side!"[l]
[30] Flee! leave your homes, hide in deep holes,
    you that live in Hazor, says the LORD;
For counsel has been taken against you,
    a plan has been formed against you
    [Nebuchadnezzar, king of Babylon].
[31] Rise up! set out against a nation that is at peace,
    that lives secure, says the LORD,
That has no gates or bars,
    and dwells alone.
[32] Their camels shall be your booty,
    their many herds your spoil;

Jer

---

d Is 34, 6; Ez 35, 3-9; Ob 16.—e Ob 2.—f Jer 48, 29f.—g Jer 50, 40; Dt 29, 23.—h Jer 12, 5; 25, 9; 50, 44f.—i Jer 4, 13.—j Is 36, 19; 37, 13.—k Is 21, 16.—l Jer 4, 20.

49, 23: *Hamath and Arpad:* independent Aramean states to the north of Damascus; the invasion is conceived as coming from the north. The situation is of the eighth century B.C. Cf Is 10, 9ff.

49, 27: *The palaces of Ben-hadad:* the royal palaces in Damascus where at least three kings bore this name; cf 1 Kgs 15, 18; 20.

I will scatter to the winds those who
  shave their temples,
  from all sides I will bring ruin upon
    them,
  says the LORD.*m*
33 Hazor shall become a haunt of jackals,
  a desert forever,
  Where no man lives,
  no human being stays.

Against Elam. 34 The following word of
the LORD against Elam* came to the
prophet Jeremiah at the beginning of the
reign of Zedekiah, king of Judah: 35 Thus
says the LORD of hosts:

Behold, I will break the bow of Elam,
  the mainstay of their might.
36 I will bring upon Elam the four winds
  from the four ends of the heavens:
  I will scatter them to all these winds, till
    there is no nation
  to which the outcasts of Elam shall
    not come.
37 I will break Elam before their foes,
  before those who seek their life;
  I will bring evil upon them,
  my burning wrath, says the LORD.
  I will send the sword to pursue them
  until I have completely made an end
    of them;
38 My throne I will set up in Elam
  and destroy from there king and
    princes,
  says the LORD.
39 But in the days to come I will change
  the lot of Elam, says the LORD.

CHAPTER 50

The First Prophecy against Babylon. 1 The
word which the LORD spoke against Babylon,* against the land of the Chaldeans,
through the prophet Jeremiah:*n*

2 Announce and publish it among the na-
    tions;
  publish it, hide it not, but say:
  Babylon is taken, Bel* confounded,
    Merodach shattered;
  her images are put to shame, her idols
    shattered.
3 A people from the north advances
    against her
  to turn her land into a desert,
  So that no one shall live there,
  because man and beast have fled
    away.*o*
4 In those days, at that time, says the
    LORD,

the men of Israel and of Judah shall
    come,
  Weeping as they come, to seek the
    LORD, their God;*p*
5 to their goal in Zion they shall ask
    the way.
  "Come, let us join ourselves to the
    LORD
  with covenant everlasting, never to
    be forgotten."*q*
6 Lost sheep were my people,
  their shepherds misled them,
  straggling on the mountains;
  From mountain to hill they wandered,
  losing the way to their fold.*r*
7 Whoever came upon them devoured
    them,
  and their enemies said, "We incur no
    guilt,
  Because they sinned against the LORD,
  the hope of their fathers, their abode
    of justice."*s*
8 Flee from Babylon, leave the land of the
    Chaldeans,
  be like the rams at the head of the
    flock.*t*
9 See, I am stirring up against Babylon
  a band of great nations from the
    north;
  from there they advance, and she
    shall be taken.
  Their arrows are arrows of the skilled
    warrior;
  none shall return without effect.*u*
10 Chaldea shall be their plunder,
  and all her plunderers shall be en-
    riched,
  says the LORD.
11 Yes, rejoice and exult,
  you that plunder my portion;
  Frisk like calves on the green,
    snort like stallions!
12 Your mother shall be sorely put to
    shame,

---

m Jer 9, 25.—n Jer 51, 1; Is 13, 1-14; 21, 1-10.—o Jer 51,
48; Is 13, 17.—p Jer 3, 18; Ps 126, 6.—q Jer 31, 31; 32, 40.—r
Is 53, 6; 1 Pt 2, 25.—s Jer 31, 23.—t Jer 51, 6. 45; Is 48, 20.—
u Jer 51, 27.

49, 34: *Elam:* the ancient kingdom to the east of Babylonia.
50, 1—51, 58: A collection of miscellaneous prophecies
against Babylon which now stands as the introduction to the story
in Jer 51, 59-64. The Greek text of Jer 50, 1 omits *through the
prophet Jeremiah*, and it is in fact likely that these oracles are
not Jeremiah's, but were composed by other inspired writers
after the fall of Jerusalem, who may have used some of
Jeremiah's texts. Babylon fell to the Persians in 538 B.C.
50, 2: *Bel:* originally the name of the god of Nippur in
Mesopotamia, then identified with *Merodach* (Marduk), chief
god of Babylon.

she that bore you shall be abashed;
See, the last of the nations,
a desert, dry and waste. *v*

13 Because of the LORD's wrath she shall
be empty,
and become a total desert;
Everyone who passes by Babylon will
be appalled
and catch his breath, at all her
wounds. *w*

14 Take your posts encircling Babylon,
you who bend the bow;
Shoot at her, spare not your arrows, *x*

15 raise the war cry against her on all
sides.
She surrenders, her bastions fall,
her walls are torn down:*
Vengeance of the LORD is this! Take revenge on her,
as she has done, do to her;
for she sinned against the LORD. *y*

16 Cut off from Babylon the sower
and him who wields the sickle in harvest time!
Before the destroying sword,
each of them turns to his own people,
everyone flees to his own land. *z*

17 A stray sheep was Israel
that lions pursued;
Formerly the king of Assyria devoured
her,
now Nebuchadnezzar of Babylon
gnaws her bones. *a*

18 Therefore, thus says the LORD of
hosts, the God of Israel:

I will punish the king of Babylon and
his land,
as once I punished the king of Assyria; *b*

19 But I will bring back Israel to her fold,
to feed on Carmel and Bashan,
And on Mount Ephraim and Gilead,
till she has her fill. *c*

20 In those days, at that time, says the
LORD:

They shall seek Israel's guilt, but it
shall be no more,
and Judah's sins, but these shall no
longer be found;
for I will forgive the remnant I preserve. *d*

21 Attack the land of Merathaim,*
and those who live in Pekod;
Slaughter and doom them, says the
LORD,
do all I have commanded you.

22 Battle alarm in the land,
dire destruction!

23 How has the hammer of the whole earth
been broken and shattered!
What an object of horror
Babylon has become among the nations. *e*

24 You ensnared yourself, and were
caught,
O Babylon, before you knew it!
You were discovered and seized,
because you challenged the LORD. *f*

25 The LORD opens his armory
and brings forth the weapons of his
wrath;
For the Lord GOD of hosts has work to
do
in the land of the Chaldeans. *g*

26 Come upon her from every side,
open her granaries,
Pile up her goods in heaps and doom it,
leave not a remnant.

27 Slay all her oxen,
let them go down to the slaughter;
Woe to them! their day has come,
the time of their punishment.

28 Listen! the fugitives, the escaped
from the land of Babylon:
They announce in Zion
the vengeance of the LORD, our
God. *h*

29 Call up against Babylon archers,
all who bend the bow;
Encamp around her,
let no one escape.
Repay her for her deeds;
as she has done, do to her,
For she insulted the LORD,
the Holy One of Israel. *i*

30 Therefore her young men shall fall in
her streets,

---

v Jer 51, 43; Is 13, 20ff.—w Jer 25, 12.—x Jer 51, 11; Is 21,
2.—y Jer 51, 11. 44. 58; Ps 137, 8.—z Is 13, 14.—a 2 Kgs 17,
24; 18, 14.—b Is 10, 12; 14, 24f.—c Jer 23, 3; Ez 34, 13f.—d
Jer 31, 34; Is 43, 25; Mi 7, 19.—e Jer 51, 20; Is 14, 6.—f Jer
51, 57.—g Jer 51, 11f; Is 13, 5.—h Jer 51, 10f.—i Jer 51, 56.

50, 15: *Her walls are torn down:* the prophet is not predicting the details of Babylon's downfall, but describing such a downfall in conventional language. Actually, Babylon was surrendered
peaceably, without destruction.

50, 21: *Merathaim,* "twice bitter," and *Pekod,* "punishment," are here symbolic terms for Babylonia, though probably
they suggest also the names of regions in that country.

all her warriors shall perish on that
   day,
says the LORD.*j*

31 I am against you, man of insolence,
   says the Lord GOD of hosts;
For your day has come,
   the time for me to punish you.
32 Insolence stumbles and falls;
   there is no one to raise him up.
I will kindle in his cities a fire
   that shall devour everything around
   him.
33   Thus says the LORD of hosts:
Oppressed are the men of Israel,
   and with them the men of Judah;
All their captors hold them fast
   and refuse to let them go.
34 Strong is their avenger,
   whose name is LORD of hosts;
He will defend their cause with success,
   and give rest to the earth,
   but unrest to those who live in Babylon.*k*

35 A sword upon the Chaldeans, says the
   LORD,
   upon Babylon's people, her princes
   and wise men!
36 A sword upon the soothsayers,
   that they may become fools!
A sword upon her warriors,
   that they may tremble;
37 A sword upon her motley throng,
   that they may become women!
A sword upon her treasures,
   that they may be plundered;*l*
38 A sword upon her waters,
   that they may dry up!
For it is a land of idols,
   and they shall be made frantic by
   fearful things.*m*
39 Hence, wildcats and desert beasts shall
   dwell there,
   and ostriches shall occupy it;
Never again shall it be peopled, or lived
   in,
   from age to age.*n*
40 As when God overturned Sodom
   and Gomorrah, with their neighbors,
   says the LORD,
Not a man shall dwell there,
   no human being shall tarry there.*o*

41 See! a people comes from the north,
   a great nation, and mighty kings
   roused from the ends of the earth.*p*

42 Bow and javelin they wield,
   cruel and pitiless are they;
They sound like the roaring sea,
   as they ride forth on steeds,
Each in his place for battle
   against you, daughter Babylon.
43 The king of Babylon hears news of
   them,
   and helpless fall his hands;
Anguish seizes him,
   throes like a mother's in childbirth.*q*
44 As when a lion comes up from the Jordan's thicket
   to the permanent feeding grounds,
So I, in one instant, will drive them off,
   and whom I choose I will establish
   there;
For who is like me? who calls me to account?
   what shepherd can stand against me?*r*
45 Therefore hear the counsel of the LORD
   which he has taken against Babylon;
Hear the plans he has made
   against the land of the Chaldeans:
They shall be dragged away, even the
   smallest sheep;
   their own pasture shall be aghast because of them.*s*
46 At the cry "Babylon is captured!" the
   earth quakes;
   the outcry is heard among the nations.*t*

CHAPTER 51

The Second Prophecy against Babylon

1   Thus says the LORD:
See! I rouse against Babylon,
   and against those who live in
   Chaldea,
   a destroying wind.
2 Against Babylon I will send winnowers
   to winnow her and lay waste her land;
They shall besiege her from all sides
   on the day of affliction.*u*
3 Let the bowman draw his bow,
   and flaunt his coat of mail;
Spare not her young men,
   doom her entire army.*v*
4 The slain shall fall in the land of
   Chaldea,
   the transfixed, in her streets;*w*

---

j Jer 49, 26; 51, 4.—k Jer 51, 36.—l Jer 51, 30; Na 3, 13.—m
Jer 51, 32. 36.—n Jer 51, 37; Is 13, 21f.—o Jer 51, 43.—p Jer
51, 27f.—q Is 13, 7.—r Jer 49, 19.—s Jer 51, 12. 29.—t Jer 51,
29.—u Jer 15, 7; Is 41, 16.—v Jer 50, 14. 29.—w Jer 50, 30.

5 For Israel and Judah are not widowed
   of their God, the LORD of hosts,
And the Chaldean land is full of guilt
   to be punished by the Holy One of Israel.

6 Flee out of Babylon;
   let each one save his life,
   perish not for her guilt;
This is a time of vengeance for the
   LORD,
   he pays her her due.*x*

7 Babylon was a golden cup in the hand
   of the LORD
   which made the whole earth drunk;
The nations drank its wine,
   with this they have become mad.*y*

8 Babylon suddenly falls and is crushed:
   howl over her!
Bring balm for her wounds,
   in case she can be healed.*z*

9 "We have tried to heal Babylon,
   but she cannot be healed.
   Leave her, let us go, each to his own
   land."
Her judgment reaches heaven,
   it touches the clouds.*a*

10 The LORD has brought to light our just
   cause;
   come, let us tell in Zion
   what the LORD, our God, has done.*b*

11 Sharpen the arrows,
   fill the quivers;
The LORD has stirred up the spirit of
   Media's kings;*
   Babylon he is resolved to destroy.
Yes, it is the vengeance of the LORD,
   vengeance for his temple.*c*

12 Against the walls of Babylon raise a signal,
   make strong the watch;
Post sentries,
   arrange ambushes!
For the LORD has planned and he will
   carry out
   his threat against the inhabitants of
   Babylon.

13 You who dwell by mighty waters,
   rich in treasure,

Your end has come,
   the term at which you shall be cut
   off!*d*

14 The LORD of hosts has sworn by himself:
   I will fill you with men as numerous
   as locusts, *
   who shall raise over you the vintage
   shout!

15 He has sworn who made the earth by
   his power,
   and established the world by his wisdom,
   and stretched out the heavens by his
   skill.*e*

16 When he thunders, the waters in the
   heavens roar,
   and he brings up clouds from the end
   of the earth;
He makes the lightning flash in the
   rain,
   and releases stormwinds from their
   chambers.

17 Every man is stupid, ignorant;
   every artisan is put to shame by his
   idol:
He molded a fraud,
   without breath of life.

18 Nothingness are they, a ridiculous
   work,
   that will perish in their time of
   punishment.

19 Not like these is the portion of Jacob,
   he is the creator of all things;
Israel is his very own tribe,
   LORD of hosts is his name.

20 You are my hammer,
   my weapon for war;
With you I shatter nations,
   with you I destroy kingdoms.

21 With you I shatter horse and rider,
   with you I shatter chariot and driver.*f*

22 With you I shatter man and wife,
   with you I shatter old and young,
   with you I shatter youth and
   maiden.*g*

23 With you I shatter the shepherd and his
   flock,
   with you I shatter the farmer and his
   team,
   with you I shatter satraps and prefects.

24 Thus will I repay Babylon,
   and all who live in Chaldea
All the evil they did to Zion,

---

x Jer 50, 8. 15. 29; Is 48, 20.—y Rv 14, 8; 17, 4.—z Rv 18,
9-18.—a Is 13, 14; Rv 18, 5.—b Jer 50, 28.—c 2 Kgs 17, 6; Is
13, 17.—d Na 2, 1.—e Jer 10, 12.—f Dn 7, 7. 19. 23.—g Is 13,
16. 18.

51, 11: *Media's kings:* the Medes dwelt with the Persians in
the land now known as Iran. At the time these words were written the Medes were the dominant people of the two, but within a
short time the Persians had gained the ascendancy.

Jer

as you shall see with your own eyes,
says the LORD.[h]

25 Beware! I am against you,
destroying mountain,
destroyer of the entire earth, says the
LORD;
I will stretch forth my hand against you,
roll you down over the cliffs,
and make you a burnt mountain:[i]

26 They will not take from you a cornerstone,
or a foundation stone;
Ruins forever shall you be,
says the LORD.[j]

27 Raise a signal on the earth,
blow the trumpet among the nations;
Dedicate peoples to war against her,
summon against her the kingdoms,
Ararat, Minni, and Ashkenaz;*
Appoint recruiting officers against her,
send up horses like bristling locusts.[k]

28 Dedicate peoples to war against her:
the king of Media,
Its governors and all its prefects,
every land in his domain.

29 The earth quakes and writhes,
the LORD's plan against Babylon is
carried out,
Turning the land of Babylon
into a desert where no one lives.

30 Babylon's warriors have ceased to fight,
they remain in their strongholds;
Dried up is their strength,
they have become women.
Burned are their homes,
and broken their bars.

31 One runner meets another,
herald meets herald,
Telling the king of Babylon
that all his city is taken.[l]

32 The fords have been seized,
and the fortresses set on fire,
while warriors are in panic.

33 For thus says the LORD of hosts, the
God of Israel:

Daughter Babylon is like a threshing
floor
at the time it is trodden;
Yet a little while,
and the harvest time will come for
her.[m]

34 He has consumed me,* routed me,
[Nebuchadnezzar, king of Babylon,]
he has left me as an empty vessel;

He has swallowed me like a dragon:
filled his belly with my delights, and
cast me out.

35 My torn flesh be upon Babylon,
says the city on Zion;
My blood upon the people of Chaldea,
says Jerusalem.

36 But now, thus says the LORD:
Surely I will defend your cause,
I will avenge you;
I will dry up her sea,
and drain her fountain.

37 Babylon shall become a heap of ruins,
a haunt of jackals;
A place of horror and ridicule,
where no one lives.[n]

38 They all roar like lions,
growl like lion cubs.[o]

39 When they are parched, I will set a
drink before them
to make them drunk, that they may
be overcome
with perpetual sleep, never to awak-
en, says the LORD.

40 I will bring them down like lambs to the
slaughter,
like rams and goats.

41 How has she been seized, made captive,
the glory of the whole world!
What a horror has Babylon become
among nations:[p]

42 against Babylon the sea rises,
she is overwhelmed by the roaring
waves!

43 Her cities have become a desert,
parched and arid land
Where no man lives,
and no one passes through.

44 I will punish Bel in Babylon,
and make him disgorge what he swallowed;
peoples shall stream to him no more.
The wall of Babylon falls!

45 Leave her, my people, let each one
save himself
from the burning wrath of the LORD.

46 Be not discouraged for fear of rumors
spread in the land; this year the rumor
comes, then violence in the land, tyrant

---

h Jer 25, 14; 50, 29; Ps 137, 8.—i Rv 8, 7; 18, 8f.—j Jer 25,
12; Ps 118, 22.—k Na 3, 17.—l 2 Chr 30, 6; Jb 1, 14-18.—m Rv
14, 15.—n Is 25, 2.—o Na 2, 11f.—p Is 13, 19.

51, 27: *Ararat, Minni, and Ashkenaz:* regions or people in
what is now Armenia, subject at this time to Media.
51, 34: *Me, my:* refers to Jerusalem.

against tyrant.[q] [47]But behold, the days are coming when I will punish the idols of Babylon; her whole land shall be put to shame, and all her slain shall lie fallen within her. [48]Then heaven, and earth, and everything in them shall shout over Babylon with joy, when the destroyers come against her from the north, says the LORD.[r] [49]Babylon, too, must fall, O slain of Israel, as at the hands of Babylon have fallen the slain of all the earth.

[50] You who have escaped the sword,
    go on, stand not still;
Remember the LORD from afar,
    let Jerusalem come to your minds.
[51] We are ashamed because we have heard taunts,
    confusion covers our faces; strangers have entered
    the holy places of the house of the LORD.[s]
[52] But behold, the days are coming, says the LORD,
    when I will punish her idols,
    and in her whole land the wounded will groan.
[53] Though Babylon scale the heavens,
    and make her strong heights inaccessible,
    destroyers from me shall reach her, says the LORD.[t]
[54] Hear! loud cries from Babylon,
    dire destruction from the land of the Chaldeans;
[55] For the LORD lays Babylon waste,
    stills her loud cry,
Though her waves were roaring like mighty waters,
    and their clamor was heard afar.
[56] For the destroyer comes upon her, [Babylon,]

her heroes are captured, their bows broken;
The LORD is a God who requites,
    he will surely repay.[u]

[57]I will make her princes and her wise men drunk, her governors, her prefects, and her warriors, so that they sleep an eternal sleep, never to awaken, says the King, whose name is the LORD of hosts. [58]Thus says the LORD of hosts:

The walls of spacious Babylon shall be leveled utterly;
    her lofty gates shall be destroyed by fire.
The toil of the nations is for nothing;
    for the flames the peoples weary themselves.[v]

The Prophecy Sent to Babylon. [59]This was the errand given by the prophet Jeremiah to Seraiah,* son of Neriah, son of Mahseiah, when he went to Babylon for the king in the fourth year of the reign of Zedekiah; Seraiah was chief quartermaster. [60]Jeremiah had written all the misfortune that was to befall Babylon in a single book:* all these words that were written against Babylon. [61]And Jeremiah said to Seraiah: When you reach Babylon, see that you read aloud all these words,[w] [62]and then say: O LORD, you yourself threatened to destroy this place, so that neither man nor beast should dwell in it, since it would remain an everlasting desert. [63]When you have finished reading this book, tie a stone to it and throw it in the Euphrates,[x] [64]and say: Thus shall Babylon sink. Never shall she rise, because of the evil I am bringing upon her. [To "weary themselves" are the words of Jeremiah.]*

VI: HISTORICAL APPENDIX*

CHAPTER 52

Capture of Jerusalem. [1]Zedekiah was twenty-one years old when he became king, and he reigned eleven years in Jerusalem.[y] His mother's name was Hamutal, daughter of Jeremiah of Libnah. [2]He did what was evil in the eyes of the LORD, just as Jehoiakim had done. [3]Indeed, what was done in Jerusalem and in Judah so angered the LORD that he cast them out from his presence.
Zedekiah rebelled against the king of Babylon. [4] [z] In the tenth month of the

q Mt 24, 6f.—r Rv 18, 20.—s Pss 44, 16f; 78, 1-4.—t Is 14, 13.—u Na 1, 2.—v Hb 2, 13.—w Jer 50, 1-51.—x Rv 18, 21.—y 1-27: 2 Kgs 24, 18—25, 21.—z 4-16: Jer 39, 1-10.

51, 59: *Seraiah:* the brother of Baruch; cf Jer 32, 12. *The king:* Zedekiah. Perhaps Seraiah went to Babylon to explain away the presence of foreign ambassadors in Jerusalem that same year; cf Jer 27, 3.
51, 60: Jeremiah prophesied against Babylon, even as he foretold Judah's release from Babylon's power (Jer 3, 14-18; 32, 15; 33, 6-9. 12f); but his *book* against Babylon was thrown in the Euphrates (v 63). The preceding oracles were composed by later writers; see note on Jer 50, 1—51, 58.
51, 64: *To "weary themselves" are the words of Jeremiah:* an editorial remark concerning the end of v 58.
52, 1-34: This supplement to the Book of Jeremiah was taken by the final editor from 2 Kgs 24, 18—25, 30 and placed here in order to show the fulfillment of Jeremiah's prophecies. In part this repeats the history given in Jer 39—41; the history of Gedaliah in 2 Kgs 25, 22-26, however, has not been reproduced here.

ninth year of his reign, on the tenth day of the month,* Nebuchadnezzar, king of Babylon, and his whole army advanced against Jerusalem, encamped around it, and built siege walls on every side. ⁵The siege of the city continued until the eleventh year of King Zedekiah.

⁶On the ninth day of the fourth month, when famine had gripped the city and the people had no more bread, ⁷the city walls were breached. Then all the soldiers took to flight and left the city by night through the gate between the two walls which was near the king's garden. With the Chaldeans surrounding the city, they went in the direction of the Arabah. ⁸But the Chaldean army pursued the king and overtook Zedekiah in the desert near Jericho, while his whole army fled from him.

⁹The king, therefore, was arrested and brought to Riblah, in the land of Hamath, to the king of Babylon, who pronounced sentence on him. ¹⁰As Zedekiah looked on, the king of Babylon slew his sons as well as all the princes of Judah at Riblah. ¹¹Then he blinded Zedekiah, bound him with fetters, and had him brought to Babylon and kept in prison until the day of his death.

Destruction of Jerusalem. ¹²On the tenth day of the fifth month (this was in the nineteenth year* of Nebuchadnezzar, king of Babylon), Nebuzaradan, captain of the bodyguard, came to Jerusalem as the representative of the king of Babylon. ¹³He burned the house of the LORD, the palace of the king, and all the houses of Jerusalem; every large building he destroyed with fire. ¹⁴And the Chaldean troops who were with the captain of the guard tore down all the walls that surrounded Jerusalem.

¹⁵Then Nebuzaradan, captain of the guard, led into exile the rest of the people left in the city, and those who had deserted to the king of Babylon, and the rest of the artisans. ¹⁶But some of the country's poor, Nebuzaradan, captain of the guard, left behind as vinedressers and farmers.

¹⁷The bronze pillars that belonged to the house of the LORD, and the wheeled carts and the bronze sea in the house of the LORD, the Chaldeans broke into pieces; they carried away all the bronze to Babylon. ¹⁸They took also the pots, the shovels, the snuffers, the bowls, the pans, and all the bronze vessels used for service. ¹⁹The basins also, the fire holders, the bowls, the pots, the lampstands, the pans, the sacrificial bowls which were of gold or silver, these too the captain of the guard carried off, ²⁰as well as the two pillars, the one sea, and the twelve oxen of bronze under the sea, and the wheeled carts which King Solomon had made for the house of the LORD. The bronze of all these furnishings could not be weighed.

²¹Each of the pillars was eighteen cubits high and twelve cubits in diameter; each was four fingers thick, and hollow inside. ²²A bronze capital five cubits high surmounted the one pillar, and a network with pomegranates encircled the capital, all of brass; and so for the other pillar. The pomegranates . . . ²³there were ninety-six pomegranates. There were a hundred pomegranates, all around the network.

²⁴The captain of the guard also took Seraiah, the high priest, Zephaniah, the second priest, and the three keepers of the entry. ²⁵And from the city he took one courtier, a commander of soldiers, and seven men in the personal service of the king who were present in the city, and the scribe of the army commander who mustered the people of the land, and sixty of the common people who were in the city. ²⁶The captain of the guard, Nebuzaradan, arrested these and brought them to the king of Babylon at Riblah, ²⁷who had them struck down and put to death in Riblah, in the land of Hamath.

Thus was Judah exiled from her land. ²⁸ * This is the number of the people whom Nebuchadnezzar led away captive: in his seventh year, three thousand and twenty-three people of Judah; ²⁹in the eighteenth year of Nebuchadnezzar, eight hundred and thirty-two persons from Jerusalem; ³⁰in the twenty-third year of Nebuchadnezzar, Nebuzaradan, captain of

---

52, 4: *In the tenth month of the ninth year of his reign, on the tenth day of the month:* January 15, 588 B.C. Cf Jer 39, 1.

52, 12: *On the tenth day of the fifth month . . . nineteenth year:* the tenth of Ab—July/August in 587 B.C.

52, 28-30: These verses are missing in the Greek text and have not been taken from 2 Kgs 25, but from some other source using a different system of chronology. Besides the deportations of 598 and 587 B.C., mention is made here of a final one that took place in the year 582/1, possibly as a sequel to the murder of Gedaliah; cf Jer 41, 2.

the guard, exiled seven hundred and forty-five people of Judah: four thousand six hundred persons in all.

Favor Shown to Jehoiachin.* [31] *a* In the thirty-seventh year of the exile of Jehoiachin, king of Judah, on the twenty-

---

a 31-34: 2 Kgs 25, 27-30.

52, 31-34: In the year 561/0 B.C., Jehoiachin was released from prison by Nebuchadnezzar's successor Awel-Marduk (Evil-merodach), who reigned only two years. Babylonian records confirm the fact that Jehoiachin and his family were supported at public expense.

52, 32: *The other kings:* who had also been brought as captives to Babylon.

fifth day of the twelfth month, Evil-merodach, king of Babylon, in the inaugural year of his reign, took up the case of Jehoiachin, king of Judah, and released him from prison. [32] He spoke kindly to him and gave him a throne higher than that of the other kings* who were with him in Babylon. [33] Jehoiachin took off his prison garb and ate at the king's table as long as he lived. [34] The allowance given him by the king of Babylon was a perpetual allowance, in fixed daily amounts, all the days of his life until the day of his death.

THE BOOK OF LAMENTATIONS

The sixth century B.C. was an age of crisis, a turning point in the history of Israel. With the destruction of the temple and the interruption of its ritual, the exile of the leaders and loss of national sovereignty, an era came to an end. Not long after the fall of Jerusalem (587) an eyewitness of the national humiliation composed these five laments. They combine confession of sin, grief over the suffering and humiliation of Zion, submission to merited chastisement, and strong faith in the constancy of Yahweh's love and power to restore. The union of poignant grief and unquenchable hope reflects the constant prophetic vision of the weakness of man and the strength of God's love; it also shows how Israel's faith in Yahweh could survive the shattering experience of national ruin.

As a literary work, the Book of Lamentations is carefully constructed according to a familiar structural device. The first four poems are acrostics in which the separate stanzas begin with successive letters of the Hebrew alphabet from the first to the last. Far from destroying the spontaneous pathos of the songs, this literary feature permits a symbolic and disciplined expression of the profound grief, the sinful responsibility, and the enduring hope of the suffering community. The figure of Israel as the bride of Yahweh, familiar from the prophets, appears here again; but now Zion is a desolate widow, the Judaea Capta of Titus' memorial coins, sustained only by the faith that God's chastisement will eventually give place to his infinite compassion.

CHAPTER 1

Jerusalem Abandoned and Disgraced*

[1] How lonely she is now,
    the once crowded city!
Widowed is she
    who was mistress over nations;
The princess among the provinces
    has been made a toiling slave.

[2] Bitterly she weeps at night,
    tears upon her cheeks,
With not one to console her
    of all her dear ones;
Her friends have all betrayed her
    and become her enemies. *a*

---

a Jer 30, 14; Ez 16, 37.—b Dt 28, 65; Jer 45, 3.—c Jer 14, 2.

1, 1-22: In this poem the poet first describes Jerusalem's miserable state after the destruction wrought by the Chaldeans (vv 1-11a); in v 11b the city itself takes up the lament.

[3] Judah has fled into exile
    from oppression and cruel slavery;
Yet where she lives among the nations
    she finds no place to rest:
All her persecutors come upon her
    where she is narrowly confined. *b*

[4] The roads to Zion mourn
    for lack of pilgrims going to her feasts;
All her gateways are deserted,
    her priests groan,
Her virgins sigh;
    she is in bitter grief. *c*

[5] Her foes are uppermost,
    her enemies are at ease;
The LORD has punished her
    for her many sins.
Her little ones have gone away,
    captive before the foe.

Lam

6 Gone from daughter Zion
  is all her glory:
Her princes, like rams
  that find no pasture,
Have gone off without strength
  before their captors.

7 Jerusalem is mindful of the days
  of her wretched homelessness,
When her people fell into enemy hands,
  and she had no one to help her;
When her foes gloated over her,
  laughed at her ruin.

8 Through the sin of which she is guilty,
  Jerusalem is defiled;
All who esteemed her think her vile
  now that they see her nakedness;
She herself groans
  and turns away.[d]

9 Her filth is on her skirt;
  she gave no thought how she would
  end.
Astounding is her downfall,
  with no one to console her.
Look, O LORD, upon her misery,
  for the enemy has triumphed!

10 The foe stretched out his hand
  to all her treasures;
She has seen those nations
  enter her sanctuary
Whom you forbade to come
  into your assembly.[e]

11 All her people groan,
  searching for bread;
They give their treasures for food,
  to retain the breath of life.
"Look, O LORD, and see
  how worthless I have become!"[f]

12 "Come, all you who pass by the way,
  look and see
Whether there is any suffering like my
    suffering,
  which has been dealt me
When the LORD afflicted me
  on the day of his blazing wrath.

13 "From on high he sent fire
  down into my very frame;
He spread a net for my feet,
  and overthrew me.
He left me desolate,
  in pain all the day.[g]

14 "He has kept watch over my sins;
  by his hand they have been plaited;
They have settled about my neck,*
  he has brought my strength to its
  knees;

The Lord has delivered me into their
  grip,
  I am unable to rise.

15 "All the mighty ones in my midst
  the Lord has cast away;
He summoned an army against me
  to crush my young men;
The LORD has trodden in the wine press
  virgin daughter Judah.[h]

16 "At this I weep,
  my eyes run with tears:
Far from me are all who could console
  me,
  any who might revive me;
My sons were reduced to silence
  when the enemy prevailed."[i]

17 Zion stretched out her hands,
  but there was no one to console her;
The LORD gave orders against Jacob
  for his neighbors to be his foes;
Jerusalem has become in their midst
  a thing unclean.[j]

18 "The LORD is just;
  I had defied his command.
Listen, all you peoples,
  and behold my suffering:
My maidens and my youths
  have gone into captivity.[k]

19 "I cried out to my lovers,*
  but they failed me.
My priests and my elders
  perished in the city;
Where they sought food for themselves,
  they found it not.[l]

20 "Look, O LORD, upon my distress:
  all within me is in ferment,
My heart recoils within me
  from my monstrous rebellion.
In the streets the sword bereaves,
  at home death stalks.[m]

21 "Give heed to my groaning;
  there is no one to console me.
All my enemies rejoice at my misfor-
    tune:
  it is you who have wrought it.
Bring on the day you have proclaimed,
  that they may be even as I.

---

d Is 47, 2; Jer 13, 22. 26.—e Jer 51, 51.—f Jer 52, 6.—g Ez
12, 13.—h Jer 8, 16.—i Jer 13, 17; 14, 17.—j Ps 74, 7.—k Dt
28, 41.—l Jer 30, 14.—m Lam 2, 11.

1, 14: *They have been plaited . . . my neck:* the sins of the
people have been bound together and laid as a yoke on their back;
cf Mt 23, 4.
    1, 19: *My lovers:* Zion's foreign allies, who failed to help her,
as the prophets had warned.

22 "Let all their evil come before you;*
   deal with them
As you have dealt with me
   for all my sins;
My groans are many,
   and I am sick at heart."[n]

CHAPTER 2

The Lord's Wrath against Zion*

1 How the Lord in his wrath
   has detested daughter Zion!
He has cast down from heaven to earth
   the glory of Israel,*
Unmindful of his footstool
   on the day of his wrath.

2 The Lord has consumed without pity
   all the dwellings of Jacob;
He has torn down in his anger
   the fortresses of daughter Judah;
He has brought to the ground in dishonor
   her king and her princes.

3 He broke off, in fiery wrath,
   the horn* that was Israel's whole
   strength;
He withheld the support of his right
   hand
   when the enemy approached;
He blazed up in Jacob like a flaming fire
   devouring all about it.[o]

4 Like an enemy he made taut his bow;
   with his arrows in his right hand
He took his stand as a foe, and slew
   all on whom the eye doted;
Over the tent of daughter Zion
   he poured out his wrath like fire.[p]

5 The Lord has become an enemy,
   he has consumed Israel:
Consumed all her castles
   and destroyed her fortresses;
For daughter Judah he has multiplied
   moaning and groaning.

6 He has demolished his shelter like a garden booth,
   he has destroyed his dwelling;
In Zion the LORD has made
   feast and sabbath to be forgotten;
He has scorned in fierce wrath
   both king and priest.[q]

7 The Lord has disowned his altar,
   rejected his sanctuary;
The walls of her towers
   he has handed over to the enemy,
Who shout in the house of the LORD
   as on a feast day.[r]

8 The LORD marked for destruction
   the wall of daughter Zion:
He stretched out the measuring line;*
   his hand brought ruin, yet he did not
   relent—
He brought grief on wall and rampart
   till both succumbed.[s]

9 Sunk into the ground are her gates;
   he has removed and broken her bars.
Her king and her princes are among the
   pagans;
   priestly instruction is wanting,
And her prophets have not received
   any vision from the LORD.[t]

10 On the ground in silence sit
   the old men of daughter Zion;
They strew dust* on their heads
   and gird themselves with sackcloth;
The maidens of Jerusalem
   bow their heads to the ground.[u]

11 Worn out from weeping are my eyes,
   within me all is in ferment;
My gall is poured out on the ground*
   because of the downfall of the daughter of my people,
As child and infant faint away
   in the open spaces of the town.[v]

12 They ask their mothers,
   "Where is the cereal?"—in vain,
As they faint away like the wounded
   in the streets of the city,
And breathe their last
   in their mothers' arms.[w]

13 To what can I liken or compare you,
   O daughter Jerusalem?
What example can I show you for your
   comfort,
   virgin daughter Zion?
For great as the sea is your downfall;
   who can heal you?[x]

14 Your prophets had for you

---

n Lam 3, 64.—o Lam 1, 12.—p Jer 30, 14.—q Lam 1, 4; Is 1,
13; 5, 5.—r Ez 24, 21.—s Jer 52, 13.—t Dt 28, 36.—u Is 3,
26.—v Lam 3, 48.—w Lam 1, 11.—x Lam 1, 12.

1, 22: Zion fully acknowledges her guilt and the justness of divine punishment; nevertheless, she pleads that her enemies also
be punished for their guilt.
2, 1: *The glory of Israel:* the temple. *His footstool:* the ark
of the covenant (1 Chr 28, 2; Pss 99, 5; 132, 7); or again, the
temple (Ez 43, 7).
2, 3: *Horn:* symbol of power and strength; cf Lam 2, 17; 1 Sm
2, 10; Lk 1, 69; etc.
2, 8: *The measuring line:* used not only in building, but in
deciding what must be destroyed; cf Is 34, 11; 2 Kgs 21, 13.
2, 10: *They strew dust:* as a sign of penance; cf Jb 2, 12.
2, 11: *My gall is poured out on the ground:* I am afflicted
with bitter sorrow; cf Jb 16, 13.

Lam

false and specious visions;
They did not lay bare your guilt,
  to avert your fate;
They beheld for you in vision
  false and misleading portents.*y*

15 All who pass by
  clap their hands at you;
They hiss and wag their heads
  over daughter Jerusalem:
"Is this the all-beautiful city,
  the joy of the whole earth?"*z*

16 All your enemies
  open their mouths against you;
They hiss and gnash their teeth.
  They say, "We have devoured her.
This at last is the day we hoped for;
  we have lived to see it!"*a*

17 The LORD has done as he decreed:
  he has fulfilled the threat
He set forth from days of old;
  he has destroyed and had no pity,
Letting the enemy gloat over you
  and exalting the horn of your foes.*b*

18 Cry out to the Lord;
  moan, O daughter Zion!
Let your tears flow like a torrent
  day and night;
Let there be no respite for you,
  no repose for your eyes.

19 Rise up, shrill in the night,
  at the beginning of every watch;
Pour out your heart like water
  in the presence of the Lord;
Lift up your hands to him
  for the lives of your little ones
[Who faint from hunger
  at the corner of every street].

20 "Look, O LORD, and consider:
  whom have you ever treated thus?
Must women eat their offspring,*
  their well-formed children?
Are priest and prophet to be slain
  in the sanctuary of the LORD?*c*

21 "Dead in the dust of the streets
  lie young and old;
My maidens and young men
  have fallen by the sword;
You have slain on the day of your
    wrath,
  slaughtered without pity.*d*

22 "You summoned as for a feast day
  terrors against me from all sides;
There was not, on the day of your wrath,
  either fugitive or survivor;

Those whom I bore and reared
  my enemy has utterly destroyed."*e*

CHAPTER 3

Sufferings of the Prophet and His People

1 I am a man who knows affliction*
    from the rod of his anger,*f*
2 One whom he has led and forced to
      walk
    in darkness, not in the light;
3 Against me alone he brings back his
      hand
    again and again all the day.

4 He has worn away my flesh and my skin,
    he has broken my bones;*g*
5 He has beset me round about
    with poverty and weariness;
6 He has left me to dwell in the dark
    like those long dead.*h*

7 He has hemmed me in with no escape
    and weighed me down with chains;
8 Even when I cry out for help,
    he stops my prayer;*i*
9 He has blocked my ways with fitted
      stones,
    and turned my paths aside.

10 A lurking bear he has been to me,
    a lion in ambush!*j*
11 He deranged my ways, set me astray,
    left me desolate.*k*
12 He bent his bow, and set me up
    as the target for his arrow.*l*
13 He pierces my sides
    with shafts from his quiver.*m*
14 I have become a laughingstock for all
      nations,
    their taunt all the day long;*n*
15 He has sated me with bitter food,
    made me drink my fill of worm-
      wood.*o*
16 He has broken my teeth with gravel,
    pressed my face in the dust;
17 My soul is deprived of peace,
    I have forgotten what happiness is;
18 I tell myself my future is lost,
    all that I hoped for from the LORD.

---

y Is 58, 1; Jer 2, 8; 23, 16.—z Jer 18, 16.—a Lam 3, 46.—b
Dt 28, 15.—c Lam 4, 10.—d Lam 3, 43; 2 Chr 36, 17; Jer 6,
11.—e Jer 42, 17.—f Jer 20, 18.—g Jb 30, 30; Is 38, 13.—h Ps
143, 3.—i Ps 22, 2.—j Jb 10, 16; Hos 13, 8.—k Lam 1, 13.—l
Lam 2, 4; Jb 16, 12.—m Jb 6, 4; Ps 38, 3.—n Jb 30, 9; Ps 69,
13.—o Jer 9, 14; 23, 15.

2, 20: *Must women eat their offspring:* extreme famine in
a besieged city sometimes led to this form of cannibalism; cf Lam
4, 10; 2 Kgs 6, 28f; Bar 2, 3; Ez 5, 10.
3, 1-21: The author identifies Zion's sufferings with his own.

19 The thought of my homeless poverty
   is wormwood and gall;
20 Remembering it over and over
   leaves my soul downcast within me.
21 But I will call this to mind,
   as my reason to have hope:

22 The favors of the LORD are not
   exhausted,
   his mercies are not spent;*p*
23 They are renewed each morning,
   so great is his faithfulness.
24 My portion is the LORD, says my soul;
   therefore will I hope in him.*q*

25 Good is the LORD to one who waits for
   him,
   to the soul that seeks him;*r*
26 It is good to hope in silence
   for the saving help of the LORD.
27 It is good for a man to bear
   the yoke* from his youth.

28 Let him sit alone and in silence,
   when it is laid upon him.
29 Let him put his mouth to the dust;*
   there may yet be hope.*s*
30 Let him offer his cheek to be struck,
   let him be filled with disgrace.*t*

31 For the Lord's rejection
   does not last forever;*u*
32 Though he punishes, he takes pity,
   in the abundance of his mercies;*v*
33 He has no joy in afflicting
   or grieving the sons of men.*w*

34 When anyone tramples underfoot
   all the prisoners in the land,
35 When he distorts men's rights
   in the very sight of the Most High,
36 When he presses a crooked claim,
   the Lord does not look on unconcerned.

37 Who commands, so that it comes to
   pass,
   except the Lord ordains it;
38 Except it proceeds from the mouth of
   the Most High,
   whether the thing be good or bad!*x*
39 Why should any living man complain,
   any mortal, in the face of his sins?*y*

40 Let us search and examine our ways
   that we may return to the LORD!*z*
41 Let us reach out our hearts
   toward God in heaven!
42 We have sinned and rebelled;
   you have not forgiven us.

43 You veiled yourself in wrath and pursued us,
   you slew us and took no pity;*a*
44 You wrapped yourself in a cloud
   which prayer could not pierce.
45 You have made us offscourings and refuse
   among the nations.*b*

46 All our enemies
   have opened their mouths against us;
47 Terror and the pit have been our lot,
   desolation and destruction;*c*
48 My eyes run with streams of water
   over the downfall of the daughter of
   my people.*d*

49 My eyes flow without ceasing,
   there is no respite,
50 Till the LORD from heaven
   looks down and sees.
51 My eyes torment my soul
   at the sight of all the daughters of my
   city.

52 Those who were my enemies without
   cause
   hunted me down like a bird;
53 They struck me down alive in the pit,
   and sealed me in with a stone.*e*
54 The waters flowed over my head,
   and I said, "I am lost!"

55 I called upon your name, O LORD,*f*
   from the bottom of the pit;
56 You heard me call, "Let not your ear
   be deaf to my cry for help!"
57 You came to my aid when I called to
   you;
   you said, "Have no fear!"

58 You defended me in mortal danger,
   you redeemed my life.
59 You see, O LORD, how I am wronged;
   do me justice!*g*
60 You see all their vindictiveness,
   all their plots against me.

61 You hear their insults, O LORD,
   [all their plots against me],
62 The whispered murmurings of my foes,
   against me all the day;
63 Whether they sit or stand,
   see, I am their taunt song.

p Neh 9, 31.—q Pss 16, 5; 73, 26.—r Ps 130, 6; Is 30, 18.—s
Jb 42, 6.—t Is 50, 6; Mt 5, 39.—u Ps 103, 9.—v Is 54, 8f.—w
Heb 12, 10f.—x Is 45, 7.—y Prv 19, 3.—z Jl 2, 12f.—a Lam 2,
21.—b 1 Cor 4, 13.—c Is 24, 17; Jer 48, 43.—d Ps 119, 136.—e
Jer 37, 16; 38, 6-9.—f 55f: Ps 130, 1f.—g Ps 35, 23.

3, 27: *To bear the yoke:* to do God's will; cf Jer 2, 20.
3, 29: *Let him put his mouth to the dust:* in humble submission; cf Ps 72, 9.

Lam

64 Requite them as they deserve, O LORD,
   according to their deeds;
65 Give them hardness of heart,
   as your curse upon them; *h*
66 Pursue them in wrath and destroy them
   from under your heavens!

CHAPTER 4

Miseries of the Besieged City

1 How tarnished is the gold,
   how changed the noble metal;
   How the sacred stones lie strewn
   at every street corner!

2 Zion's precious sons,
   fine gold their counterpart,
   Now worth no more than earthen jars
   made by the hands of a potter! *i*

3 Even the jackals bare their breasts
   and suckle their young;
   The daughter of my people has become
   as cruel
   as the ostrich* in the desert. *j*

4 The tongue of the suckling cleaves
   to the roof of its mouth in thirst;
   The babes cry for food,
   but there is no one to give it to them.

5 Those accustomed to dainty food
   perish in the streets;
   Those brought up in purple
   now cling to the ash heaps. *k*

6 The punishment of the daughter of my
   people
   is greater than the penalty of Sodom,
   Which was overthrown in an instant
   without the turning of a hand. *l*

7 Brighter than snow were her princes,
   whiter than milk,
   More ruddy than coral,
   more precious than sapphire.

8 Now their appearance is blacker than
   soot,
   they are unrecognized on the streets;
   Their skin shrinks on their bones,
   as dry as wood. *m*

9 Better for those who perish by the
   sword
   than for those who die of hunger,
   Who waste away, as though pierced
   through,
   lacking the fruits of the field!

10 The hands of compassionate women
   boiled their own children,
   To serve them as mourners' food
   in the downfall of the daughter of my
   people. *n*

11 The LORD has spent his anger,
   poured out his blazing wrath;
   He has kindled a fire in Zion
   that has consumed her foundations. *o*

12 The kings of the earth did not believe,
   nor any of the world's inhabitants,
   That enemy or foe could enter
   the gates of Jerusalem.

13 Because of the sins of her prophets*
   and the crimes of her priests,
   Who shed in her midst
   the blood of the just!—*p*

14 They staggered blindly in the streets,
   soiled with blood,
   So that people could not touch
   even their garments: *q*

15 "Away, you unclean!" they cried to
   them,
   "Away, away, do not draw near!"
   If they left and wandered among the nations,
   nowhere could they remain.

16 The LORD himself has dispersed them,
   he regards them no more;
   He does not receive the priests with
   favor,
   nor show kindness to the elders.

17 Our eyes ever wasted away,
   looking in vain for aid;
   From our watchtower we watched
   for a nation* that could not save us.

18 Men dogged our steps
   so that we could not walk in our
   streets;
   Our end drew near, and came;
   our time had expired.

19 Our pursuers were swifter
   than eagles in the air,
   They harassed us on the mountains
   and waylaid us in the desert. *r*

---

h Jer 11, 20; 2 Tm 4, 14.—i Jer 19, 11.—j Jb 39, 16.—k Dt
28, 56.—l Gn 19, 23-29; 2 Pt 2, 6; Jude 1, 7.—m Lam 3, 4.—n
Lam 2, 20; Dt 28, 56f; 2 Kgs 6, 29.—o Jer 7, 20; Ez 5, 13.—p
Jer 6, 13.—q Is 59, 10.—r Jer 4, 13; Hb 1, 8.

4, 3: *Cruel as the ostrich:* see note on Jb 39, 14ff. Jerusalem, in her distress, has abandoned her children.
4, 13ff: The priests and the false prophets lulled the people
into an illusory security (Jer 2, 8; 5, 31; 6, 13; etc.), condoning
and entering into their crimes so that they themselves became unclean.
4, 17: *A nation:* Egypt, which failed to give effective aid
against Babylon.

20 The anointed one of the LORD, our
   breath of life,*
   was caught in their snares,
   He in whose shadow we thought
   we could live on among the nations. *s*

21 Though you rejoice and are glad, O
   daughter Edom,
   you who dwell in the land of Uz,*
   To you also shall the cup be passed;
   you shall become drunk and naked. *t*

22 Your chastisement is completed, O
   daughter Zion,
   he will not prolong your exile;
   But your wickedness, O daughter
   Edom, he will punish,
   he will lay bare your sins. *u*

CHAPTER 5

The Prophet's Lament and Supplication

1 Remember, O LORD, what has befallen
   us,
   look, and see our disgrace:

2 Our inherited lands have been turned
   over to strangers,
   our homes to foreigners. *v*

3 We have become orphans, fatherless;
   widowed are our mothers.

4 The water we drink we must buy,
   for our own wood we must pay.

---

s Lam 2, 9; Ez 19, 4. 8.—t Lam 1, 21; Jer 25, 15.—u Is 40,
2.—v Ps 79, 1.—w Jer 6, 25.—x Lam 4, 8.—y Zec 14, 2.—z Lam
4, 16.—a Jer 16, 9; 25, 10; Am 8, 10.—b Pss 9, 8; 45, 7; 102,
13. 27.—c Pss 13, 1; 42, 10.—d Ps 80, 19f.—e Jer 14, 19.

4, 20: *Our breath of life:* the king. This is a royal epithet borrowed from Egyptian usage, while *the anointed one of the
Lord* is Israelite. After the disaster of 598 B.C. (2 Kgs 24, 1-17),
Jerusalem could have hoped to live in peace amidst her neighbors; but they (vv 21f) as well as Babylon turned against her to
ensure her total devastation in 587 B.C.
4, 21: *Uz:* see note on Jer 25, 20.
5, 6: In its state of abjection, Judah was forced to depend on
its traditional enemies to the west and the east for subsistence.
Mesopotamia is here called by the name it had long borne, *Assyria,* though in these times the power of the Assyrians had been
superseded by that of the Chaldeans.
5, 7: *Our fathers:* collective responsibility, for good and for
evil, was recognized in the Old Testament; cf Jer 31, 29. But the
present generation is also personally guilty of sin (v 16).
5, 8: Administrations imposed by foreign powers were notori-
ously corrupt and inept. The Hebrew word for "slave" is the same
as that used for an official (servant of the ruler); the author
doubtless intends the double meaning here.
5, 14: *The gate:* the place of assembly, where city decisions
were made and judgment given by the elders and other notables;
see note on Ru 4, 1.

5 On our necks is the yoke of those who
   drive us;
   we are worn out, but allowed no rest.

6 To Egypt we submitted,
   and to Assyria, to fill our need of
   bread.*

7 Our fathers,* who sinned, are no more;
   but we bear their guilt.

8 Slaves rule over us;
   there is no one to rescue us from their
   hands.*

9 At the peril of our lives we bring in our
   sustenance,
   in the face of the desert heat; *w*

10 Our skin is shriveled up, as though by a
   furnace,
   with the searing blasts of famine. *x*

11 The wives in Zion were ravished by the
   enemy,
   the maidens in the cities of Judah; *y*

12 Princes were gibbeted by them,
   elders shown no respect. *z*

13 The youths carry the millstones,
   boys stagger under their loads of
   wood;

14 The old men have abandoned the gate,*
   the young men their music.

15 The joy of our hearts has ceased,
   our dance has turned into mourning; *a*

16 The garlands have fallen from our
   heads:
   woe to us, for we have sinned!

17 Over this our hearts are sick,
   at this our eyes grow dim:

18 That Mount Zion should be desolate,
   with jackals roaming there!

19 You, O LORD, are enthroned forever;
   your throne stands from age to age. *b*

20 Why, then, should you forget us,
   abandon us so long a time? *c*

21 Lead us back to you, O LORD, that we
   may be restored:
   give us anew such days as we had of
   old. *d*

22 For now you have indeed rejected us,
   and in full measure turned your
   wrath against us. *e*

Lam

THE BOOK OF BARUCH

The opening verses of this book ascribe it, or at least its first part, to Baruch, the well-known secretary of the prophet Jeremiah. It contains five very different compositions, the first and the last in prose, the others in poetic form. The prose sections were certainly composed in Hebrew, though the earliest known form of the book is in Greek.

An observance of the feast of Booths with a public prayer of penitence and petition (1, 15—3, 8), such as is supposed by the introduction (1, 1-14), would not have been possible during the lifetime of Baruch after the fall of Jerusalem; this indeed is suggested in the prayer itself (2, 26). The prayer is therefore to be understood as the pious reflection of a later Jewish writer upon the circumstances of the exiles in Babylon as he knew them from the Book of Jeremiah. He expresses in their name sentiments called for by the prophet, and ascribes the wording of these sentiments to the person most intimately acquainted with Jeremiah's teaching, namely, Baruch. The purpose of this literary device is to portray for his own and later generations the spirit of repentance which prompted God to bring the Exile to an end.

The lesson thus gained is followed by a hymn in praise of Wisdom (3, 9—4, 4), exalting the law of Moses as the unique gift of God to Israel, the observance of which is the way to life and peace. The ideal city of Jerusalem is then represented (4, 5-29) as the solicitous mother of all exiles, who is assured in the name of God that all her children will be restored to her (4, 30—5, 9).

The final chapter is really a separate work, with a title of its own (6, 1). It is patterned after the earlier letter of Jeremiah (Jer 29), in the spirit of the warnings against idolatry contained in Jer 10 and Is 44. Its earnestness is impressive, but in restating previous inspired teachings at a later day, it does so with no special literary grace.

Thus the principal divisions of the book are seen to be: I. Prayer of the Exiles (1, 1—3, 8). II. Praise of Wisdom in the Law of Moses (3, 9—4, 4). III. Jerusalem Bewails and Consoles Her Captive Children (4, 5-29). IV. Jerusalem Consoled: The Captivity about To End (4, 30—5, 9). V. The Letter of Jeremiah against Idolatry (6, 1-72).

I: PRAYER OF THE EXILES

CHAPTER 1

Meeting in Babylon. ¹Now these are the words of the scroll which Baruch, son of Neriah, son of Mahseiah, son of Zedekiah, son of Hasadiah, son of Hilkiah, wrote in Babylon,*a* ²in the fifth year [on the seventh day of the month,* at the time when the Chaldeans took Jerusalem and burnt it with fire].*b* ³ *c* And Baruch read the words of this scroll for Jeconiah, son of Jehoiakim, king of Judah, to hear it, as well as all the people who came to the reading:*d* ⁴the nobles, the kings' sons, the elders, and the whole people, small and great alike—all who lived in Babylon by the river Sud.*

⁵They wept and fasted and prayed before the LORD, ⁶and collected such funds as each could furnish.*e* ⁷These they sent to Jerusalem, to Jehoiakim, son of Hilkiah, son of Shallum, the priest, and to the priests and the whole people who were with him in Jerusalem. ⁸[This was when

he* received the vessels of the house of the LORD that had been removed from the temple, to restore them to the land of Judah, on the tenth of Sivan. These silver vessels Zedekiah, son of Josiah, king of Judah, had made ⁹after Nebuchadnezzar, king of Babylon, carried off Jeconiah, and the princes, and the skilled workers, and the nobles, and the people of the land

---

a Jer 32, 12; 36, 4; 45, 1-5.—b 2 Kgs 25, 8ff.—c 2 Kgs 24, 8-17; Jer 22, 24-30; 51, 59-64.—d 3-4: 2 Kgs 23, 1-2.—e Dt 16, 17.

1, 2: *In the fifth year on the seventh day of the month:* Jerusalem fell on the seventh day of the fifth month; cf 2 Kgs 25, 8; Jer 52, 12. Either the text read originally "the fifth month," or it refers to the observance of an anniversary of the fall of Jerusalem in 587 B.C.

1, 4: *The river Sud:* one of the Babylonian canals, not otherwise identified. In ancient non-biblical Hebrew fragments discovered in 1952, there is reference to a river "Sur" in a similar context.

1, 8f: *He:* possibly Baruch; less likely *Jehoiakim . . . the priest* (v 7), a member of the high-priestly family not mentioned elsewhere. The *silver vessels* here described are distinct from the vessels referred to in 2 Kgs 25, 14 and Ezr 1, 7ff. The author of this note may have thought of the *fifth year* (v 1) of Zedekiah, in view of Jer 28, 1; 29, 1ff. A "fifth year," again with no month mentioned, is given in Ez 1, 2 for the inaugural vision of Ezekiel's prophetic career.

964

from Jerusalem, as captives, and brought them to Babylon.]

¹⁰Their message was: "We send you funds, with which you are to procure holocausts, sin offerings, and frankincense, and to prepare cereal offerings; offer these on the altar of the LORD our God, *f* ¹¹and pray for the life of Nebuchadnezzar, king of Babylon, and that of Belshazzar, his son,* that their lifetimes may equal the duration of the heavens above the earth;*g* ¹²and that the LORD may give us strength, and light to our eyes, that we may live under the protective shadow of Nebuchadnezzar, king of Babylon, and that of Belshazzar, his son, and serve them long, finding favor in their sight.

Confession of Guilt. ¹³"Pray for us also to the LORD, our God; for we have sinned against the LORD, our God, and the wrath and anger of the LORD have not yet been withdrawn from us at the present day. ¹⁴And read out publicly this scroll which we send you, in the house of the LORD, on the feast day and during the days of assembly:*h*

¹⁵"Justice is with the LORD, our God; and we today are flushed with shame, we men of Judah and citizens of Jerusalem,*i* ¹⁶that we, with our kings and rulers and priests and prophets, and with our fathers, ¹⁷have sinned in the LORD's sight ¹⁸and disobeyed him. We have neither heeded the voice of the LORD, our God, nor followed the precepts which the LORD set before us. ¹⁹From the time the LORD led our fathers out of the land of Egypt until the present day, we have been disobedient to the LORD, our God, and only too ready to disregard his voice. ²⁰And the evils and the curse which the LORD enjoined upon Moses, his servant, at the time he led our fathers forth from the land of Egypt to give us the land flowing with milk and honey, cling to us even today.*j* ²¹For we did not heed the voice of the LORD, our God, in all

the words of the prophets whom he sent us, ²²but each of us went off after the devices of our own wicked hearts, served other gods, and did evil in the sight of the LORD, our God.

CHAPTER 2

¹"And the LORD fulfilled the warning he had uttered against us: against our judges, who governed Israel, against our kings and princes, and against the men of Israel and Judah. ²He brought down upon us evils so great that there has not been done anywhere under heaven what has been done in Jerusalem, as was written in the law of Moses:*k* ³that one after another of us should eat* the flesh of his son or of his daughter. ⁴He has made us subject to all the kingdoms round about us, a reproach and a horror among all the nations round about to which the LORD has scattered us.*l* ⁵We are brought low, not raised up, because we sinned against the LORD, our God, not heeding his voice.

⁶"Justice is with the LORD, our God; and we, like our fathers, are flushed with shame even today.*m* ⁷All the evils of which the LORD had warned us have come upon us; ⁸and we did not plead before the LORD, or turn, each from the figments of his evil heart. ⁹And the LORD kept watch over the evils, and brought them home to us; for the LORD is just in all the works he commanded us to do,*n* ¹⁰but we did not heed his voice, or follow the precepts of the LORD which he set before us.

Prayer for Deliverance. ¹¹"And now, LORD, God of Israel, you who led your people out of the land of Egypt with your mighty hand, with signs and wonders and great might, and with your upraised arm, so that you have made for yourself a name till the present day:*o* ¹²we have sinned, been impious, and violated, O LORD, our God, all your statutes.*p* ¹³Let your anger be withdrawn from us, for we are left few in number among the nations to which you scattered us. ¹⁴Hear, O LORD, our prayer of supplication, and deliver us for your own sake: grant us favor in the presence of our captors, ¹⁵that the whole earth may know that you are the LORD, our God, and that Israel and his descendants bear your name.*q* ¹⁶O LORD, look down from your holy dwelling and take thought of us; turn, O LORD, your ear to hear us.*r* ¹⁷Look

---

f Jer 17, 26.—g Dt 11, 21; Jer 29, 7; Dn 5, 1-2; 1 Tm 2, 1f.—h Ex 23, 14ff; Lv 23, 35f; Hos 9, 5; Sir 50, 6.—i Bar 2, 6; 3, 8; Neh 9, 6-37; Ezr 9, 6-15; Dn 9, 4-19.—j Lv 26, 14-39; Dt 28, 15-68.—k 2f: 2 Kgs 6, 28f; Jer 19, 9; Lam 2, 20; 4, 10; Ez 5, 10.—l Jer 29, 18.—m Bar 1, 15.—n Jer 1, 12; 31, 28; 44, 27.—o Dt 6, 21-22.—p Ps 106, 6.—q Sir 36, 11; Jer 14, 9.—r Dt 26, 15.

1, 11: *Nebuchadnezzar . . . Belshazzar, his son:* as in Dn 5, 1f. Later Jewish tradition seems to have simplified the history of the past by making the last Chaldean ruler of Babylon the son of the conqueror of Jerusalem.

2, 3: *One after another of us should eat:* see note on Lam 2, 20.

directly at us, and behold: it is not the dead in the nether world, whose spirits have been taken from within them, who will give glory and vindication to the LORD.[s] [18] He whose soul is deeply grieved, who walks bowed and feeble, with failing eyes and famished soul, will declare your glory and justice, LORD![t]

[19] "Not on the just deeds of our fathers and our kings do we base our plea for mercy in your sight, O LORD, our God. [20] You have brought your wrath and anger down upon us, as you had warned us through your servants the prophets: [21] 'Thus says the LORD: Bend your shoulders to the service of the king of Babylon, that you may continue in the land I gave your fathers:[u] [22] for if you do not hear the LORD's voice so as to serve the king of Babylon,

[23] I will make to cease from the cities of Judah
and from the streets of Jerusalem
The sounds of joy and the sounds of gladness,
the voice of the bridegroom
and the voice of the bride;
And all the land shall be deserted,
without inhabitants.'[v]

[24] But we did not heed your voice, or serve the king of Babylon, and you fulfilled the threats you had made through your servants the prophets, to have the bones of our kings and the bones of our fathers brought out from their burial places.[w] [25] And indeed, they lie exposed* to the heat of day and the frost of night. They died in dire anguish, by hunger and the sword and plague.[x] [26] And you reduced the house which bears your name* to what it is today, for the wickedness of the kingdom of Israel and the kingdom of Judah.[y]

God's Promises Recalled. [27] "But with us, O LORD, our God, you have dealt in all your clemency and in all your great mercy. [28] This was your warning through your servant Moses, the day you ordered him to write down your law in the presence of the Israelites: [29] If you do not heed my voice, surely this great and numerous throng will dwindle away among the nations to which I will scatter them. [30] For I know they will not heed me, because they are a stiff-necked people. But in the land of their captivity they shall have a change of heart;[z] [31] they shall know that I, the LORD, am their God. I will give them hearts, and

heedful ears;[a] [32] and they shall praise me in the land of their captivity, and shall invoke my name.[b] [33] Then they shall turn back from their stiff-necked stubbornness, and from their evil deeds, because they shall remember the fate of their fathers who sinned against the LORD.[c] [34] And I will bring them back to the land which with my oath I promised to their fathers, to Abraham, Isaac and Jacob; and they shall rule it. I will make them increase; they shall not then diminish. [35] And I will establish for them, as an eternal covenant, that I will be their God, and they shall be my people; and I will not again remove my people Israel from the land I gave them.[d]

CHAPTER 3

[1] "LORD Almighty, God of Israel, afflicted souls and dismayed spirits call to you. [2] Hear, O LORD, for you are a God of mercy; and have mercy on us, who have sinned against you: [3] for you are enthroned forever, while we are perishing forever.[e] [4] LORD Almighty, God of Israel, hear the prayer of Israel's few, the sons of those who sinned against you; they did not heed the voice of the LORD, their God, and the evils cling to us. [5] Remember at this time not the misdeeds of our fathers, but your own hand and name: [6] for you are the LORD our God; and you, O LORD, we will praise! [7] For this, you put into our hearts the fear of you: that we may call upon your name, and praise you in our captivity, when we have removed from our hearts all the wickedness of our fathers who sinned against you.[f] [8] Behold us today in our captivity, where you scattered us, a reproach, a curse, and a requital for all the misdeeds of our fathers, who withdrew from the LORD, our God."

II: PRAISE OF WISDOM IN THE LAW OF MOSES

[9] Hear, O Israel, the commandments of life:
listen, and know prudence![g]

---

s Ps 6, 6; Is 38, 18.—t Zep 2, 3.—u Jer 27, 12.—v Jer 7, 34.—w Jer 8, 1f.—x Jer 7, 34; 14, 12; 31, 30.—y Jer 7, 10-15.—z Dt 30, 1f; 31, 27.—a Jer 24, 7; Ez 36, 26; Ps 40, 7.—b Tb 13, 7.—c 33ff: Dt 30, 1-10.—d Jer 31; Lam 4, 22.—e Pss 29, 10; 102, 12f.—f Jer 31, 33.—g Prv 4, 20ff.

2, 25: *They lie exposed:* probably an allusion to Jer 36, 30; see note on Jer 22, 19.

2, 26: *The house which bears your name:* the temple of Jerusalem. *What it is today:* during the exile it lay in ruins.

10 How is it, Israel,
   that you are in the land of your foes,
   grown old in a foreign land,
   Defiled with the dead,
11   accounted with those destined for the
     nether world?*h*
12 You have forsaken the fountain of wisdom!*i*
13   Had you walked in the way of God,
     you would have dwelt in enduring
     peace.*j*
14 Learn where prudence is,
   where strength, where understanding;
   That you may know also
   where are length of days, and life,
   where light of the eyes, and peace.*k*

15 Who has found the place of wisdom,*l*
   who has entered into her treasures?
16 Where are the rulers of the nations,
   they who lorded it over the wild
   beasts of the earth,*m*
17   and made sport of the birds of the
     heavens:
   They who heaped up the silver
   and the gold in which men trust;
   of whose possessions there was no
   end?
18 They schemed anxiously for money,
   but there is no trace of their work:
19 They have vanished down into the
   nether world,
   and others have risen up in their
   stead.

20 Later generations have seen the light,
   have dwelt in the land,
   But the way to understanding they have
   not known,
21   they have not perceived her paths, or
     reached her;
   their offspring were far from the way
   to her.
22 She has not been heard of in Canaan,*
   nor seen in Teman.*n*

23 The sons of Hagar who seek knowledge
   on earth,
   the merchants of Midian and Teman,
   the phrasemakers seeking knowledge,
   These have not known the way to wisdom,
   nor have they her paths in mind.

24 O Israel, how vast is the house of God,*
   how broad the scope of his dominion:
25 Vast and endless,
   high and immeasurable!
26 In it were born the giants,
   renowned at the first,
   stalwarts, skilled in war.*o*
27 Not these did God choose,
   nor did he give them the way of
   understanding;*p*
28 They perished for lack of prudence,
   perished through their folly.*q*
29 Who has gone up to the heavens and
   taken her,
   or brought her down from the
   clouds?*r*
30 Who has crossed the sea and found her,
   bearing her away rather than choice
   gold?
31 None knows the way to her,
   nor has any understood her paths.

32 Yet he who knows all things knows her;
   he has probed her by his knowledge—
   He who established the earth for all
   time,
   and filled it with four-footed beasts;
33 He who dismisses the light, and it departs,
   calls it, and it obeys him trembling;
34 Before whom the stars at their posts
   shine and rejoice;
35 When he calls them, they answer,
   "Here we are!"
   shining with joy for their Maker.*s*
36 Such is our God;
   no other is to be compared to him:
37 He has traced out all the way of understanding,
   and has given her to Jacob, his servant,
   to Israel, his beloved son.*t*

38 Since then she has appeared on earth,
   and moved among men.*u*

---

h Ps 88, 5.—i Jer 2, 13; Jn 4, 10. 14.—j Is 48, 18.—k Prv 3,
2; 8, 14.—l 15ff: Jb 28, 1-28.—m Jer 27, 6.—n Jer 49, 7; Ez
28, 4-5; Zec 9, 2; Jb 2, 11.—o Gn 6, 4; Wis 14, 6.—p 1 Sm 16,
7-10.—q Sir 10, 8.—r Dt 30, 12f; Sir 24, 4; Rom 10, 6f.—s Jb
38, 7; Ps 147, 4; Is 40, 26.—t Ps 147, 19; Sir 24, 8-12.—u Wis
9, 18; Jn 1, 14.

3, 22f: Despite the renown for wisdom of the peoples of *Canaan* or Phoenicia (Ez 28, 3f), of *Teman* (Jer 49, 7), of *the sons of Hagar* or the Arabians, they did not possess true wisdom, which is found only in the law of God.

3, 24: *The house of God:* here, the created universe.

CHAPTER 4

¹ She is the book of the precepts of God,
   the law that endures forever;
   All who cling to her will live,
      but those will die who forsake her.ᵛ
² Turn, O Jacob, and receive her:
      walk by her light toward splendor.ʷ
³ Give not your glory to another,
      your privileges to an alien race.
⁴ Blessed are we, O Israel;
      for what pleases God is known to us!ˣ

III: JERUSALEM BEWAILS AND CONSOLES HER CAPTIVE CHILDREN

⁵ Fear not, my people!
      Remember, Israel,
⁶ You were sold to the nations
      not for your destruction;
   It was because you angered God
      that you were handed over to your
      foes.ʸ
⁷ For you provoked your Makerᶻ
      with sacrifices to demons, to no-gods;
⁸ You forsook the Eternal God who
      nourished you,
   and you grieved Jerusalem who fos-
      tered you.
⁹ She indeed saw coming upon you
      the anger of God; and she said:

   "Hear, you neighbors of Zion!
      God has brought great mourning
      upon me,
¹⁰ For I have seen the captivity
      that the Eternal God has brought
      upon my sons and daughters.
¹¹ With joy I fostered them;
      but with mourning and lament I let
      them go.
¹² Let no one gloat over me, a widow,
      bereft of many:
   For the sins of my children I am left
      desolate,
      because they turned from the law of
      God,ᵃ
¹³ and did not acknowledge his statutes;
   In the ways of God's commandments
      they did not walk,
      nor did they tread the disciplined
      paths of his justice.
¹⁴ "Let Zion's neighbors come,
      to take note of the captivity of my
      sons and daughters,
      brought upon them by the Eternal
      God.

¹⁵ He has brought against them a nation
      from afar,
      a nation ruthless and of alien speech,
   That has neither reverence for age
      nor tenderness for childhood;ᵇ
¹⁶ They have led away this widow's
      cherished sons,
      have left me solitary, without
      daughters.
¹⁷ What can I do to help you?
¹⁸ He who has brought this evil upon
      you
      must himself deliver you from your
      enemies' hands.ᶜ
¹⁹ Farewell, my children, farewell:
      I am left desolate.
²⁰ I have taken off the garment of peace,
      have put on sackcloth for my prayer
      of supplication,
      and while I live I will cry out to the
      Eternal God.ᵈ

²¹ "Fear not, my children; call upon God,
      who will deliver you from oppression
      at enemy hands.ᵉ
²² I have trusted in the Eternal God for
      your welfare,
      and joy has come to me from the
      Holy One
   Because of the mercy that will swiftly
      reach you
      from your eternal savior.
²³ With mourning and lament I sent you
      forth,
      but God will give you back to me
      with enduring gladness and joy.ᶠ
²⁴ As Zion's neighbors lately saw you
      taken captive,
      so shall they soon see God's salvation
      come to you,
      with great glory and the splendor of
      the Eternal God.ᵍ

²⁵ "My children, bear patiently the angerʰ
      that has come from God upon you;
   Your enemies have persecuted you,
      and you will soon see their destruc-
      tion
      and trample upon their necks.*

v Dt 4, 6-8; Prv 8, 35f; Sir 24, 22.—w Prv 4, 13. 19.—x Dt 4,
32-37; 33, 29.—y Jgs 2, 14; Is 50, 1; 52, 3.—z 7-8: Dt 32, 13-
18; 1 Cor 10, 20.—a Lam 1, 1. 2. 7.—b Dt 28, 49f; Jer 5, 15;
6, 22f.—c Jer 32, 42.—d Jdt 9, 1; Est 4, 16.—e Jer 51, 5.—f Jer
31, 12f.—g Is 60, 1ff.—h Is 51, 23.

4, 25: *Trample upon their necks:* love of enemies was not
an Old Testament ideal. The Babylonians are considered here,
however, to be God's enemies as well as Israel's.

²⁶ My pampered children have trodden
rough roads,
carried off by their enemies like
sheep in a raid. *i*

²⁷ Fear not, my children; call out to God!
He who brought this upon you will
remember you.*j*

²⁸ As your hearts have been disposed to
stray from God,
turn now ten times the more to seek
him;

²⁹ For he who has brought disaster upon
you
will, in saving you, bring you back
enduring joy."*k*

IV: JERUSALEM CONSOLED: THE CAPTIVITY ABOUT TO END

³⁰ Fear not, Jerusalem!
He who gave you your name is your
encouragement.*l*

³¹ Fearful are those who harmed you,
who rejoiced at your downfall;

³² Fearful are the cities where your children were enslaved,
fearful the city that took your sons.*m*

³³ As that city rejoiced at your collapse,*n*
and made merry at your downfall,
so shall she grieve over her own desolation.

³⁴ I will take from her the joyous throngs,
and her exultation shall be turned to
mourning:

³⁵ For fire shall come upon her*o*
from the Eternal God, for a long
time,
and demons shall dwell in her from
that time on.*

³⁶ Look to the east, Jerusalem!
behold the joy that comes to you from
God.*p*

³⁷ Here come your sons whom you once
let go,
gathered in from the east and from
the west
By the word of the Holy One,
rejoicing in the glory of God.

CHAPTER 5

¹ Jerusalem, take off your robe of mourning and misery;
put on the splendor of glory from
God forever:*q*

² Wrapped in the cloak of justice from
God,
bear on your head the mitre
that displays the glory of the eternal
name.*r*

³ For God will show all the earth your
splendor:

⁴ you will be named by God forever
the peace of justice, the glory of
God's worship.*s*

⁵ Up, Jerusalem! stand upon the heights;
look to the east and see your children
Gathered from the east and the west
at the word of the Holy One,
rejoicing that they are remembered
by God.

⁶ Led away on foot by their enemies they
left you:
but God will bring them back to you
borne aloft in glory as on royal
thrones.*t*

⁷ For God has commanded
that every lofty mountain be made
low,
And that the age-old depths and gorges
be filled to level ground,
that Israel may advance secure in the
glory of God.*u*

⁸ The forests and every fragrant kind of
tree
have overshadowed Israel at God's
command;*v*

⁹ For God is leading Israel in joy
by the light of his glory,
with his mercy and justice for company.

V: THE LETTER OF JEREMIAH AGAINST IDOLATRY

CHAPTER 6

¹A copy of the letter which Jeremiah
sent to those who were being led captive to
Babylon by the king of the Babylonians, to
convey to them what God had commanded
him:*w*

For the sins you committed before God,
you are being led captive to Babylon by
Nebuchadnezzar, king of the Babylo-

---

i Lam 2, 22.—j Is 40, 1.—k Is 35, 10.—l Ps 46, 5; Is 60, 14.—
m Jer 51, 43.—n 33f: Is 13, 20ff; 47, 1-11; Jer 50, 13.—o Is 34,
9-14.—p Is 60, 4f.—q Is 52, 1.—r Ex 39, 30; Wis 18, 24; Is 61,
10; 62, 3.—s Is 1, 26; 32, 17; Jer 33, 16.—t Is 49, 22.—u Is 40,
3f.—v Is 41, 19.—w Jer 29, 1.

4, 35: Deserts and desolate places were looked upon as the
special habitations of *demons;* Tb 8, 3; Lk 11, 24.

nians. ² When you reach Babylon you will be there many years, a period seven generations* long; after which I will bring you back from there in peace. ³ And now in Babylon you will see borne upon men's shoulders gods of silver and gold and wood, which cast fear upon the pagans.ˣ ⁴ Take care that you yourselves do not imitate their alien example and stand in fear of them, ⁵ when you see the crowd before them and behind worshiping them. Rather, say in your hearts, "You, O Lᴏʀᴅ, are to be worshiped!"; ⁶ for my angel is with you, and he is the custodian of your lives.ʸ

⁷ Their tongues are smoothed by woodworkers; they are covered with gold and silver—but they are a fraud, and cannot speak.ᶻ ⁸ People bring gold, as to a maiden in love with ornament, ⁹ and furnish crowns for the heads of their gods. Then sometimes the priests take the silver and gold from their gods and spend it on themselves, ¹⁰ or give part of it to the harlots on the terrace.* They trick them out in garments like men, these gods of silver and gold and wood; ¹¹ but though they are wrapped in purple clothing, they are not safe from corrosion or insects. ¹² They wipe their faces clean of the house dust which is thick upon them. ¹³ Each has a scepter, like the human ruler of a district; but none does away with those that offend against it. ¹⁴ Each has in its right hand an axe or dagger, but it cannot save itself from war or pillage. Thus it is known they are not gods; do not fear them.

¹⁵ As useless as one's broken tools ¹⁶ are their gods, set up in their houses; their eyes are full of dust from the feet of those who enter. ¹⁷ Their courtyards are walled in like those of a man brought to execution for a crime against the king; the priests reinforce their houses with gates and bars and bolts, lest they be carried off by robbers. ¹⁸ They light more lamps for them than for themselves, yet not one of these can they see. ¹⁹ They are like any beam in the house; it is said their hearts are eaten away. Though the insects out of the ground consume them and their garments, they do not feel it. ²⁰ Their faces are blackened by the smoke of the house. ²¹ Bats and swallows alight on their bodies and on their heads; and cats as well as birds.

²² Know, therefore, that they are not gods, and do not fear them.

²³ Despite the gold that covers them for adornment, unless someone wipes away the corrosion, they do not shine; nor did they feel anything when they were molded. ²⁴ They are bought at any price, and there is no spirit in them. ²⁵ Having no feet, they are carried on men's shoulders, displaying their shame to all; and those who worship them are put to confusionᵃ ²⁶ because, if they fall to the ground, the worshipers must raise them up. They neither move of themselves if one sets them upright, nor come upright if they fall; but one puts gifts beside them as beside the dead. ²⁷ * Their priests resell their sacrifices for their own advantage. Even their wives cure parts of the meat, but do not share it with the poor and the weak;ᵇ ²⁸ the menstruous and women in childbed handle their sacrifices. Knowing from this that they are not gods, do not fear them.

²⁹ How can they be called gods? For women bring the offerings to these gods of silver and gold and wood; ³⁰ and in their temples the priests squat with torn tunic and with shaven hair and beard, and with their heads uncovered.ᶜ ³¹ They shout and wail before their gods as others do at a funeral banquet. ³² The priests take some of their clothing and put it on their wives and children. ³³ * Whether they are treated well or ill by anyone, they cannot requite it; they can neither set up a king nor remove him.ᵈ ³⁴ Similarly, they cannot give anyone riches or coppers; if one fails to fulfill a vow to them, they cannot exact it of him. ³⁵ They neither save a man from death, nor deliver the weak from the strong.ᵉ ³⁶ To no blind man do they restore his sight, nor do they save any man in an emergency. ³⁷ They neither pity the widow nor benefit the orphan. ³⁸ These gilded

---

x Is 46, 7; Jer 10, 1-16.—y Ex 23, 20.—z Ps 135, 16.—a Wis 13, 16.—b Lv 12, 4; 15, 19f; Dt 14, 28f.—c Lv 10, 6; 21, 5. 10.—d Dn 2, 21.—e Pss 68, 6; 146, 7ff.

6, 2: *Seven generations:* possibly an indication of the date of this composition by an author writing for his contemporaries for whom the conditions of the exile were still realities. He has multiplied the *seventy years* of Jer 29, 10 by three or four.

6, 10: *Harlots on the terrace:* cult prostitutes, common in the idolatrous religions of the Gentiles.

6, 27-31: From the point of view of Jewish ritual law, the practices named here were grotesque and depraved; cf Lv 12, 2ff; 15, 19-23.

6, 33-39: All that the gods cannot do, the true God does; cf 1 Sm 2, 7; Dt 23, 22; Pss 68, 6; 146, 7-9; Is 35, 4f.

and silvered wooden statues are like stones from the mountains; and their worshipers will be put to shame. ³⁹How then can it be thought or claimed that they are gods?

⁴⁰Even the Chaldeans themselves have no respect for them; for when they see a deaf mute, incapable of speech, they bring forward Bel* and ask the god to make noise, as though the man could understand; ⁴¹and they are themselves unable to reflect and abandon these gods, for they have no sense. ⁴² * And their women, girt with cords, sit by the roads, burning chaff for incense;*f* ⁴³and whenever one of them is drawn aside by some passerby who lies with her, she mocks her neighbor who has not been dignified as she has, and has not had her cord broken. ⁴⁴All that takes place around these gods is a fraud: how then can it be thought or claimed that they are gods?

⁴⁵They are produced by woodworkers and goldsmiths, and they are nothing else than what these craftsmen wish them to be. ⁴⁶Even those who produce them are not long-lived; ⁴⁷how then can what they have produced be gods? They have left frauds and opprobrium to their successors. ⁴⁸For when war or disaster comes upon them, the priests deliberate among themselves where they can hide with them. ⁴⁹How then can one not know that these are no-gods, which do not save themselves either from war or from disaster? ⁵⁰They are wooden, gilded and silvered; they will later be known for frauds. To all peoples and kings it will be clear that they are not gods, but human handiwork; and that God's work is not in them.

⁵¹Who does not know that they are not gods? ⁵²They set no king over the land, nor do they give men rain. ⁵³They neither vindicate their own rights, nor do they recover what is unjustly taken, for they are unable; ⁵⁴they are like crows between heaven and earth. For when fire breaks out in the temple of these wooden or gilded or silvered gods, though the priests

flee and are safe, they themselves are burnt up in the fire like beams. ⁵⁵They cannot resist a king, or enemy forces. ⁵⁶How then can it be admitted or thought that they are gods?

They are safe from neither thieves nor bandits, these wooden and silvered and gilded gods; ⁵⁷those who seize them strip off the gold and the silver, and go away with the clothing that was on them, and they cannot help themselves. ⁵⁸How much better to be a king displaying his valor, or a handy tool in a house, the joy of its owner, than these false gods; or the door of a house, that keeps safe those who are within, rather than these false gods; or a wooden post in a palace, rather than these false gods!*g* ⁵⁹The sun and moon and stars are bright, and obedient in the service for which they are sent. ⁶⁰Likewise the lightning, when it flashes, is a goodly sight; and the same wind blows over all the land. ⁶¹The clouds, too, when commanded by God to proceed across the whole world, fulfill the order; ⁶²and fire, sent from on high to burn up the mountains and the forests, does what has been commanded. But these false gods are not their equal, whether in beauty or in power; ⁶³so that it is unthinkable, and cannot be claimed, that they are gods. They can neither execute judgment, nor benefit man. ⁶⁴Know, therefore, that they are not gods, and do not fear them.

⁶⁵Kings they neither curse nor bless. ⁶⁶They show the nations no signs in the heavens, nor are they brilliant like the sun, nor shining like the moon. ⁶⁷The beasts which can help themselves by fleeing to shelter are better than they are. ⁶⁸Thus in no way is it clear to us that they are gods; so do not fear them. ⁶⁹For like a scarecrow in a cucumber patch, that is no protection, are their wooden, gilded, silvered gods. ⁷⁰Just like a thornbush in a garden on which perches every kind of bird, or like a corpse hurled into darkness, are their silvered and gilded wooden gods. ⁷¹From the rotting of the purple and the linen upon them, it can be known that they are not gods; they themselves will in the end be consumed, and be a disgrace in the land. ⁷²The better for the just man who has no idols: he shall be far from disgrace!

---

f 42-43: Jer 3, 2.—g Wis 13, 10-15; 15, 7ff.

6, 40: *Bel:* cf note on Jer 50, 2.

6, 42f: This seems to refer to the obligation of Babylonian women to serve once in their lives as cult prostitutes. The unbroken cord was a sign that this duty had not yet been fulfilled. *Chaff:* burnt as an aphrodisiac or for use in erotic rites.

Bar

THE BOOK OF EZEKIEL

Ezekiel's complex character makes him one of the most interesting figures in Israelite prophecy. In many ways he resembles the more primitive type of prophet represented by Elijah and Elisha; yet he clearly depends on all his predecessors in prophecy, and his teaching is a development of theirs. His unique contribution to the history of prophetism lies in his manifest interest in the temple and the liturgy, an interest paralleled in no other prophet—not even Jeremiah who, like Ezekiel, was also a priest. Particularly because of this interest, Ezekiel's influence on postexilic religion was enormous, and not without reason has he been called "the father of Judaism." This has resulted in his prophecies reaching us with the evident marks of editing and addition by the postexilic circles that shared his intense interest. However, we may be sure that in this book we have throughout what is in substance the prophet's own work.

Ezekiel became a prophet in Babylon—the first prophet to receive the call to prophesy outside the Holy Land. As one of the exiles deported by Nebuchadnezzar in 597, his first task was to prepare his fellow countrymen in Babylon for the final destruction of Jerusalem, which they believed to be inviolable. Accordingly, the first part of his book consists of reproaches for Israel's past and present sins and the confident prediction of yet a further devastation of the land of promise and a more general exile. In 587, when Nebuchadnezzar destroyed Jerusalem, Ezekiel was vindicated before his unbelieving compatriots.

After this time, Ezekiel's message changes. From now on his prophecy is characterized by the promise of salvation in a new covenant, and he is anxious to lay down the conditions necessary to obtain it. Even as Jeremiah had believed, Ezekiel thought that the exiles were the hope of Israel's restoration, once God's allotted time for the exile had been accomplished. His final eight chapters are an utopian vision of the Israel of the future, rid of its past evils and re-established firmly under the rule of the Lord. The famous vision of the dry bones in chapter 37 expresses his firm belief in a forthcoming restoration, Israel rising to new life from the graveyard of Babylon. But Ezekiel's new covenant, like Jeremiah's, was to see its true fulfillment only in the New Testament.

Perhaps no other prophet has stressed the absolute majesty of God as Ezekiel does. This appears not only in the tremendous vision by the river Chebar with which his prophecy opens, but throughout the book. Ultimately, says Ezekiel, whatever God does to or for man is motivated by zeal for his own holy name. The new heart and the new spirit which must exist under the new covenant cannot be the work of man; they too must be the work of God. By such teachings he helped prepare for the New Testament doctrine of salvation through grace.

The Book of Ezekiel is divided as follows: I. Call of the Prophet (1, 1—3, 27). II. Before the Siege of Jerusalem (4, 1—24, 27). III. Prophecies against Foreign Nations (25, 1—32, 32). IV. Salvation for Israel (33, 1—39, 29). V. The New Israel (40, 1—48, 35).

I: CALL OF THE PROPHET

CHAPTER 1

The Vision: God on the Cherubim. ¹ In the thirtieth year,* on the fifth day of the fourth month, while I was among the exiles by the river Chebar, the heavens opened, and I saw divine visions.*ᵃ*—² On the fifth day of the month, the fifth year,* that is, of King Jehoiachin's exile, ³ the word of the LORD came to the priest Ezekiel, the son of Buzi, in the land of the Chaldeans by the river Chebar.—There the hand of the LORD came upon me.

⁴ As I looked, a stormwind came from the North,* a huge cloud with flashing fire [enveloped in brightness], from the midst of which [the midst of the fire] something gleamed like electrum. ⁵ Within it were fig-

---

a Ez 3, 23; 10, 20; 43, 3.

1, 1: *The thirtieth year,* which corresponds to the fifth year of exile (v 2), has never been satisfactorily explained; possibly it refers to the prophet's age. *The river Chebar:* probably a canal near Nippur, southeast of Babylon, one of the sites on which the Jewish exiles were settled.

1, 2: *The fifth day of the* fourth *month, the fifth year:* July 31, 593 B.C.; cf v 1.

1, 4: *The North:* the abode of God; see notes on Jb 37, 22; Ps 48, 3. *Electrum:* an alloy of gold and silver, used here for some undetermined bright metal.

ures resembling four living creatures*
that looked like this: their form was human,
6 but each had four faces and four wings,
7 and their legs went straight down; the soles
of their feet were round. They sparkled
with a gleam like burnished bronze.
10 * Their faces were like this: *b* each of
the four had the face of a man, but on the
right side was the face of a lion, and on the
left side the face of an ox, and finally each
had the face of an eagle. 9 Their faces [and
their wings] looked out on all their four
sides; they did not turn when they moved,
but each went straight forward. 12 [Each
went straight forward; wherever the spirit
wished to go, there they went; they did not
turn when they moved.]
8 Human hands were under their wings,
and the wings of one touched those of another. 11 Each had two wings spread out
above so that they touched one another's,
while the other two wings of each covered
his body. 13 In among the living creatures
something like burning coals of fire could
be seen; they seemed like torches, moving
to and fro among the living creatures. The
fire gleamed, and from it came forth flashes
of lightning.
15 As I looked at the living creatures, I
saw wheels on the ground, one beside each
of the four living creatures. 16 The wheels
had the sparkling appearance of chrysolite,
and all four of them looked the same: they
were constructed as though one wheel were
within another. 17 They could move in any
of the four directions they faced, without
veering as they moved. 18 *c* The four of
them had rims, and I saw that their rims
were full of eyes all around. 19 When the
living creatures moved, the wheels moved
with them; and when the living creatures
were raised from the ground, the wheels

also were raised. 20 Wherever the spirit
wished to go, there the wheels went, and
they were raised together with the living
creatures; for the spirit of the living creatures was in the wheels.
22 * Over the heads of the living creatures, something like a firmament could be
seen, seeming like glittering crystal,
stretched straight out above their heads.
23 Beneath the firmament their wings were
stretched out, one toward the other. [Each
of them had two covering his body.] 24 Then
I heard the sound of their wings, like the
roaring of mighty waters, like the voice of
the Almighty. When they moved, the
sound of the tumult was like the din of an
army. [And when they stood still, they lowered their wings.]
26 Above the firmament over their heads
something like a throne could be seen, looking like sapphire. Upon it was seated, up
above, one who had the appearance of a
man.* 27 Upward from what resembled his
waist I saw what gleamed like electrum;
downward from what resembled his waist
I saw what looked like fire; he was surrounded with splendor. 28 Like the bow
which appears in the clouds on a rainy day
was the splendor that surrounded him.
Such was the vision of the likeness of the
glory of the LORD.

CHAPTER 2

Eating of the Scroll. When I had seen it,
I fell upon my face and heard a voice that
said to me: 1 Son of man,* stand up! I wish
to speak with you. 2 As he spoke to me,
spirit* entered into me and set me on my
feet, and I heard the one who was speaking
3 say to me: Son of man, I am sending you
to the Israelites, rebels who have rebelled
against me; they and their fathers have revolted against me to this very day. 4 Hard
of face and obstinate of heart are they to
whom I am sending you. But you shall say
to them: Thus says the LORD God! 5 And
whether they heed or resist—for they are
a rebellious house—they shall know that a
prophet has been among them. 6 But as for
you, son of man, fear neither them nor their
words when they contradict you and reject
you, and when you sit on scorpions.*
Neither fear their words nor be dismayed
at their looks, for they are a rebellious
house. 7 [But speak my words to them,
whether they heed or resist, for they are

---

b Rv 4, 6f.—c Ez 10, 12; Rv 4, 6. 8.

1, 5: *Four living creatures:* identified as cherubim in Ez 10, 20f.
1, 10-22: Note the changed order of the verses and the omission of the textually uncertain verses 14 and 21. Such changes also occur elsewhere in this book.
1, 22f. 26: This symbolic description of God's throne is similar to that in Ex 24, 9f.
1, 26: *One who had the appearance of a man:* God appearing in human form (v 28); cf Ex 33, 18-23.
2, 1: *Son of man:* a formal way of saying simply "man"; God's habitual way of addressing the prophet throughout this book. Probably the title is used to emphasize the separation of the divine and the human.
2, 2: *Spirit:* vital power, coming from God, which enables the prophet to hear the word of God; cf Ez 8, 3; 9, 24; 11, 1.
2, 6: *When you sit on scorpions:* the prophet must be prepared for the bitterest opposition.

rebellious.] [8] As for you, son of man, obey me when I speak to you: be not rebellious like this house of rebellion, but open your mouth and eat what I shall give you.

[9] [d] It was then I saw a hand stretched out to me, in which was a written scroll [10] which he unrolled before me. It was covered with writing front and back, and written on it was: Lamentation and wailing and woe!

CHAPTER 3

[1] He said to me: Son of man, eat what is before you; eat this scroll, then go, speak to the house of Israel. [2] So I opened my mouth and he gave me the scroll to eat. [3] [e] Son of man, he then said to me, feed your belly and fill your stomach with this scroll I am giving you. I ate it, and it was as sweet as honey* in my mouth. He said: [4] Son of man, go now to the house of Israel, and speak my words to them.

[5] Not to a people with difficult speech and barbarous language am I sending you, [6] nor to the many peoples [with difficult speech and barbarous language] whose words you cannot understand. If I were to send you to these, they would listen to you; [7] but the house of Israel will refuse to listen to you, since they will not listen to me. For the whole house of Israel is stubborn of brow and obstinate in heart. [8] But I will make your face as hard as theirs, and your brow as stubborn as theirs, [9] like diamond, harder than flint. Fear them not, nor be dismayed at their looks, for they are a rebellious house.

[10] Son of man, he said to me, take into your heart all my words that I speak to you; hear them well. [11] Now go to the exiles, to your countrymen, and say to them: Thus says the Lord God!—whether they heed or resist!

[12] Then spirit lifted me up, and I heard behind me the noise of a loud rumbling as the glory of the Lord* rose from its place: [13] the noise made by the wings of the living creatures striking one another, and by the wheels alongside them, a loud rumbling. [14] The spirit which had lifted me up seized me, and I went off spiritually stirred, while the hand of the Lord rested heavily upon me. [15] Thus I came to the exiles who lived at Tel-abib* by the river Chebar, and for seven days I sat among them distraught.

The Prophet as Watchman.* [17] Thus the word of the Lord came to me: Son of man, I have appointed you a watchman for the house of Israel. [f] When you hear a word from my mouth, you shall warn them for me.

[18] If I say to the wicked man, You shall surely die; and you do not warn him or speak out to dissuade him from his wicked conduct so that he may live: that wicked man shall die for his sin, but I will hold you responsible for his death. [19] If, on the other hand, you have warned the wicked man, yet he has not turned away from his evil nor from his wicked conduct, then he shall die for his sin, but you shall save your life.

[20] If a virtuous man turns away from virtue and does wrong when I place a stumbling block before him, he shall die. He shall die for his sin, and his virtuous deeds shall not be remembered; but I will hold you responsible for his death if you did not warn him. [21] When, on the other hand, you have warned a virtuous man not to sin, and he has in fact not sinned, he shall surely live because of the warning, and you shall save your own life.

Ezekiel's Dumbness.* [22] The hand of the Lord came upon me, and he said to me: Get up and go out into the plain, where I will speak with you. [23] [g] So I got up and went out into the plain, and I saw that the glory of the Lord was in that place, like the glory I had seen by the river Chebar. I fell prone, [24] but then spirit entered into me and set me on my feet, and he spoke with me.

He said to me: Go shut yourself up in your house. [25] [As for you, son of man, they will put cords upon you and bind you with them, so that you cannot go out among them.] [26] I will make your tongue stick to your palate so that you will be dumb* and unable to rebuke them for

d Rv 5, 1.—e Rv 10, 9f.—f Ez 33, 7.—g Ez 1, 3; 10, 15. 20. 22; 43, 3.

3, 3: *As sweet as honey:* though the prophet must foretell terrible things, the word of God is sweet to him who receives it.

3, 12: *The glory of the Lord:* the divine presence, manifested here in visible form.

3, 15: *Tel-abib:* one of the sites where the exiles were settled, probably near Nippur.

3, 17-21: This passage refers to one of the prophet's most characteristic qualities. It was placed here by an editor, though it properly belongs to a later stage in Ezekiel's ministry; cf chapter 33.

3, 22-27: This passage also belongs to a later period, with Ez 24, 25ff and 33, 21f, during the time of the final siege of Jerusalem, when Ezekiel's prophecies consisted mainly of symbolic actions rather than words.

3, 26: *Dumb:* unwilling to speak to the people in exile while Jerusalem was being besieged; cf Ez 24, 27.

being a rebellious house. ²⁷ Only when I speak with you and open your mouth, shall you say to them: Thus says the LORD God! Let him heed who will, and let him resist who will, for they are a rebellious house.

II: BEFORE THE SIEGE OF JERUSALEM

CHAPTER 4

Acts Symbolic of Siege and Exile. ¹⁶ At the end of seven days . . . :* ¹ As for you, son of man, take a clay tablet; lay it in front of you, and draw on it a city [Jerusalem]. ² Raise a siege against it: build a tower, lay out a ramp, pitch camps, and set up battering rams all around. ³ Then take an iron griddle and set it up as an iron wall between you and the city. Fix your gaze on it: it shall be in the state of siege, and you shall besiege it. This shall be a sign for the house of Israel. ⁴ Then you shall lie on your left side, while I place the sins of the house of Israel upon you. As many days as you lie thus, you shall bear their sins. ⁵ For the years of their sins I allot you the same number of days, three hundred and ninety, during which you will bear the sins of the house of Israel. ⁶ When you finish this, you are to lie down again, but on your right side, and bear the sins of the house of Judah forty days;* one day for each year I have allotted you. ⁷ Fixing your gaze on the siege of Jerusalem, with bared arm* you shall prophesy against it. ⁸ See, I will bind you with cords so that you cannot turn from one side to the other until you have completed the days of your siege.

⁹ * Again, take wheat and barley, and beans and lentils, and millet and spelt; put them in a single vessel and make bread out of them. Eat it for as many days as you lie upon your side, three hundred and ninety. ¹⁰ The food you eat shall be twenty shekels a day by weight; each day the same. ¹¹ And the water you drink shall be the sixth of a hin by measure; each day the same. ¹⁶ *h* Then he said to me: Son of man, I am breaking the staff of bread* in Jerusalem. They shall eat bread which they have weighed out anxiously, and they shall drink water which they have measured out fearfully, ¹⁷ so that, owing to the scarcity of bread and water, everyone shall be filled with terror and waste away because of his sins.

¹² For your food you must bake barley loaves over human excrement in their sight, said the LORD. ¹³ Thus the Israelites shall eat their food unclean among the nations where I scatter them.*i* ¹⁴ "Oh no, LORD God!" I protested. "Never have I been made unclean, and from my youth till now, never have I eaten carrion flesh or that torn by wild beasts: never has any unclean meat entered my mouth." ¹⁵ Very well, he replied, I allow you cow's dung in place of human excrement; bake your bread on that.

CHAPTER 5

¹ As for you, son of man, take a sharp sword and use it like a barber's razor, passing it over your head and beard. Then take a set of scales and divide the hair you have cut. ² Burn a third in the fire, within the city,* when the days of your siege are completed; place another third around the city and strike it with the sword; the final third strew in the wind, and pursue it with the sword. ³ [But of the last take a small number and tie them in the hem of your garment. ⁴ Then take some of these and throw them in the midst of the fire and burn them.]

Say to the whole house of Israel: ⁵ Thus says the LORD GOD: This is Jerusalem! In the midst of the nations I placed her, surrounded by foreign countries. ⁶ But she rebelled against my ordinances more wickedly than the nations, and against my statutes more than the foreign countries surrounding her; she has spurned my ordinances and has not lived by my statutes. ⁷ Therefore thus says the Lord GOD: Because you have been more rebellious than the nations surrounding you, not living by my statutes nor fulfilling my ordinances, but acting according to the ordinances of the surrounding nations; ⁸ therefore thus

---

h Ez 5, 16; 14, 13.—i Hos 9, 4.

3, 16: *At the end of seven days . . . :* the incomplete sentence probably contained some such words as "the word of the Lord came to me." For *seven days,* see v 15. (This verse has been transposed from ch 3.)

4, 5f: *Three hundred and ninety* days . . . *forty days:* symbolically representing the respective lengths of the periods of exile of northern Israelites and Judahites. Northern Israel had already fallen to Assyria in 722 B.C. The letters in the Hebrew phrase for *the days of your siege* (v 8), each of which has its own numerical value, add up to three hundred and ninety. Forty years represent one generation.

4, 7: *Bared arm:* a symbol of unrestrained power.

4, 9-17: This action represents the scarcity of food during the siege of Jerusalem, and the consequent need to eat whatever is at hand. *Twenty shekels:* about nine ounces. *The sixth of a hin:* about one quart.

4, 16: *Breaking the staff of bread:* reducing the supply of bread which sustains the life of man as the walking staff sustains the traveler on his journey; cf Ez 5, 16; 14, 13; Lv 26, 26; Ps 105, 16; Is 3, 1.

5, 2: *The city:* the one drawn on the tablet.

says the Lord GOD: See, I am coming at you!* I will inflict punishments in your midst while the nations look on. ⁹Because of all your abominations I will do with you what I have never done before, the like of which I will never do again. ¹⁰This means that fathers within you shall eat sons, and sons shall eat fathers.* I will inflict punishments upon you and scatter all that remain of your people in every direction.

¹¹Therefore, as I live, says the Lord GOD, because you have defiled my sanctuary with all your detestable abominations, I swear to cut you down. I will not look upon you with pity nor have mercy. ¹²A third of your people shall die of pestilence and perish of hunger within you; another third shall fall by the sword all around you; and a third I will scatter in every direction, and I will pursue them with the sword. ¹⁶ *j* When I loose against you the cruel, destructive arrows of hunger, I will break your staff of bread; ¹⁷I will send famine against you, and wild beasts that shall rob you of your children. Pestilence and bloodshed shall stalk through you, and I will bring the sword upon you. I, the LORD, have spoken!

¹³Thus shall my anger spend itself, and I will wreak my fury upon them till I am appeased; they shall know that I, the LORD, have spoken in my jealousy when I spend my fury upon them. ¹⁴I will make you a waste and a reproach among the nations that surround you, which every passer-by may see. ¹⁵When I execute judgment upon you in anger and fury and with furious chastisements, you shall be a reproach and an object of scorn, a terrible warning to the nations that surround you. I, the LORD, have spoken!

CHAPTER 6

Against the Mountains of Israel. ¹Thus the word of the LORD came to me: ²Son of man, turn toward the mountains of Israel, and prophesy against them: ³Mountains of Israel, hear the word of the Lord GOD. Thus says the Lord GOD [to the mountains and hills, the ravines and valleys]:*ᵏ* See, I am bringing a sword against you, and I will destroy your high places.* ⁴Your altars shall be laid waste, your incense stands shall be broken, and I will cast down your slain ones before your idols; ⁵I will scatter their bones all around your altars.* ⁶In all your dwelling places cities shall be made deso-

late and high places laid waste, so that your altars will be made desolate and laid waste, your idols broken and removed, and your incense stands smashed to bits. ⁷[The slain shall fall in your midst, and you shall know that I am the LORD. ⁸I have warned you.]

When some of your people have escaped to other nations from the sword, and have been scattered over the foreign lands, ⁹then those who have escaped will remember me among the nations to which they have been exiled, after I have broken their adulterous hearts that turned away from me [and their eyes which lusted after idols]. They shall loathe themselves because of their evil deeds, all their abominations. ¹⁰Then they shall know that it was not in vain that I, the LORD, threatened to inflict this calamity upon them.

¹¹Thus says the Lord GOD: Clap your hands, stamp your feet,* and cry "Alas!" because of all the abominations of the house of Israel, for which they shall fall by the sword, by famine, and by pestilence. ¹²He that is far off shall die of pestilence, he that is near shall fall by the sword, and he that is besieged shall perish by famine; so will I spend my fury upon them. ¹³Then shall they know that I am the LORD, when their slain shall lie amid their idols, all about their altars, on every high hill and mountaintop, beneath every green tree and leafy oak,* wherever they offered appeasing odors to any of their gods. ¹⁴I will stretch out my hand against them, and wherever they live I will make the land a desolate waste, from the desert to Riblah;* thus shall they know that I am the LORD.

CHAPTER 7

The End Has Come. ¹Thus the word of the LORD came to me: ²Son of man, now

---

j Ez 4, 16; 14, 13.—k Ez 36, 1.

5, 8: *I am coming at you:* an expression borrowed from the language of warfare in which enemies attacked one another with the sword. *You* in vv 8-17 is Jerusalem.

5, 10: *Fathers . . . shall eat sons, and sons . . . fathers:* see note on Lam 2, 20.

6, 3: *High places:* the sanctuaries on the mountaintops where illegal worship, whether of the Lord or of Canaanite deities, was performed.

6, 5: *Scatter their bones . . . altars:* dead men's bones defiled a place; cf 2 Kgs 23, 14.

6, 11: *Clap your hands, stamp your feet:* here evidently signs of mourning; in Ez 25, 6, signs of joy.

6, 13: *Every green tree and leafy oak:* sacred groves had a long history in Palestine as places of worship; cf Dt 12, 2; note on Gn 12, 6.

6, 14: *From the desert to Riblah:* the whole land, from the far south to the far north.

say: Thus says the Lord GOD to the land of Israel: An end! The end has come upon the four corners of the land! ³Now the end is upon you; I will unleash my anger against you and judge you according to your conduct and lay upon you the consequences of all your abominations. ⁴I will not look upon you with pity nor have mercy; I will bring your conduct down upon you, and the consequences of your abominations shall be in your midst; then shall you know that I am the LORD.

⁵Thus says the Lord GOD: Disaster upon disaster! See it coming! ⁶An end is coming, the end is coming upon you! See it coming! ⁷The climax has come for you who dwell in the land! The time has come, near is the day: a time of consternation, not of rejoicing. ⁸Soon now I will pour out my fury upon you and spend my anger upon you; I will judge you according to your conduct and lay upon you the consequences of all your abominations. ⁹I will not look upon you with pity nor have mercy; I will deal with you according to your conduct, and the consequences of your abominations shall be in your midst; then shall you know that it is I, the LORD, who strike.

¹⁰See, the day of the LORD! See, the end is coming! Lawlessness is in full bloom, insolence flourishes, ¹¹violence has risen to support wickedness. It shall not be long in coming, nor shall it delay. ¹² * The time has come, the day dawns. Let not the buyer rejoice nor the seller mourn, for wrath shall be upon all the throng. ¹³The seller shall not regain what he sold as long as he lives, for wrath shall be upon all the throng. Because of his sins, no one shall preserve his life. ¹⁴They shall sound the trumpet and make everything ready, yet no one shall go to war, for my wrath is upon all the throng.

---

l Is 15, 2; Jer 48, 37.—m Prv 11, 4; Sir 5, 10; Zep 1, 18.—n Dn 14, 6.

7, 12f: Mundane affairs will cease to have any meaning in view of the disaster that is to come.
7, 18: *Baldness:* shaving the head was a sign of mourning.
7, 22: *My treasure:* the temple of Jerusalem.
8, 3: *The statue of jealousy which stirs up jealousy:* the statue which provokes the Lord's jealousy for his honor. This was probably the statue of the goddess Asherah erected by the wicked King Manasseh (cf 2 Kgs 21, 7; 2 Chr 33, 7. 15). Though it had been removed by King Josiah (2 Kgs 23, 6), it had no doubt been set up again in the repaganizing of Jerusalem that followed on Josiah's death.
8, 5: *He:* an angel accompanies Ezekiel in these visions and represents the voice of the Lord; cf Ez 40, 3f.

¹⁵The sword is outside; pestilence and hunger are within. He that is in the country shall die by the sword; pestilence and famine shall devour those in the city. ¹⁶Even those who escape and flee to the mountains like the doves of the valleys— I will put them all to death, each one for his own sins. ¹⁷All their hands shall be limp, and all their knees shall run with water. ¹⁸ *l* They shall put on sackcloth, and horror shall cover them; shame shall be on all their faces and baldness* on all their heads. ¹⁹They shall fling their silver into the streets, and their gold shall be considered refuse.*m* Their silver and gold cannot save them on the day of the LORD's wrath. They shall not be allowed to satisfy their craving or fill their bellies, for this has been the occasion of their sin. ²⁰In the beauty of their ornaments they put their pride: they made of them their abominable images [their idols]. For this reason I make them refuse. ²¹I will hand them over as booty to foreigners, to be spoiled and defiled by the wicked of the earth. ²²I will turn away my face from them, and my treasure* shall be profaned: robbers shall enter and profane it.

²³They shall wreak slaughter, for the land is filled with bloodshed and the city full of violence. ²⁴I will bring in the worst of the nations, who shall take possession of their houses. I will put an end to their proud strength, and their sanctuaries shall be profaned. ²⁵When anguish comes they shall seek peace, but there will be none. ²⁶There shall be disaster after disaster, rumor after rumor. Prophetic vision shall fade; instruction shall be lacking to the priest, and counsel to the elders, ²⁷while the prince shall be enveloped in terror, and the hands of the common people shall tremble. I will deal with them according to their conduct, and according to their judgments I will judge them; thus they shall know that I am the LORD.

CHAPTER 8

Vision of Abominations in the Temple. ³Spirit lifted me up in the air and brought me in divine visions to Jerusalem,*n* to the entrance of the north gate, where stood the statue of jealousy which stirs up jealousy.* ⁵He* said to me: Son of man, look toward the north! I looked toward the north and saw northward of the gate the altar of the statue of jealousy. ⁶Son of man, he asked me, do you see what they are doing? Do you see the great abominations that the house of Israel is practicing here, so that I must depart from my sanctuary? But you shall see still greater abominations!

⁷Then he brought me to the entrance of the court, where I saw there was a hole in the wall. ⁸Son of man, he ordered, dig through the wall. I dug through the wall and saw a door. ⁹Enter, he said to me, and see the abominable evils which they are doing here. ¹⁰I entered and saw that all around upon the wall were pictured the figures of all kinds of creeping things and loathsome beasts* [all the idols of the house of Israel]. ¹¹Before these stood seventy of the elders of the house of Israel, among whom stood Jaazaniah, son of Shaphan, each of them with his censer in his hand, and the fragrance of the incense was rising upward. ¹²Then he said to me: Do you see, son of man, what each of these elders of the house of Israel is doing in his idol room? They think: "The LORD cannot see us; the LORD has forsaken the land." ¹³He continued: You shall see still greater abominations that they are practicing.

¹⁴Then he brought me to the entrance of the north gate of the temple, and I saw sitting there the women who were weeping for Tammuz.* ¹⁵Then he said to me: Do you see this, son of man? You shall see other abominations, greater than these! ¹⁶Then he brought me into the inner court of the LORD's house, and there at the door of the LORD's temple, between the vestibule and the altar, were about twenty-five men with their backs to the LORD's temple and their faces toward the east; they were bowing down to the sun.* ¹⁷Do you see, son of man? he asked me. Is it such a trivial matter for the house of Judah to do the abominable things they have done here—for they have filled the land with violence, and again and again they have provoked me—that now they must also put the branch to my nose?* ¹⁸Therefore I in turn will act furiously: I will not look upon them with pity nor will I show mercy.

CHAPTER 9

Slaughter of the Idolaters. ¹Then he cried loud for me to hear: Come, you scourges of the city! ²With that I saw six men coming from the direction of the upper gate which faces the north, each with a destroying weapon in his hand. In their midst was a man dressed in linen, with a writer's case at his waist. They entered and stood beside the bronze altar. ³Then he called to the man dressed in linen with the writer's case at his waist, ⁴ ᵒ saying to him: * Pass through the city [through Jerusalem] and mark an X on the foreheads of those who moan and groan over all the abominations that are practiced within it. ⁵To the others I heard him say: Pass through the city after him and strike! Do not look on them with pity nor show any mercy! ⁶Old men, youths and maidens, women and children—wipe them out! But do not touch any marked with the X; begin at my sanctuary. So they began with the men [the elders] who were in front of the temple. ⁷Defile the temple, he said to them, and fill the courts with the slain; then go out and strike in the city.

⁸As they began to strike, I was left alone. I fell prone, crying out, "Alas, Lord GOD! Will you destroy all that is left of Israel when you pour out your fury on Jerusalem?" ⁹He answered me: The sins of the house of Israel are great beyond measure; the land is filled with bloodshed, the city with lawlessness. They think that the LORD has forsaken the land, that he does not see them. ¹⁰I, however, will not look upon them with pity, nor show any mercy. I will bring down their conduct upon their heads.

¹¹Then I saw the man dressed in linen with the writing case at his waist make his report: "I have done as you ordered."

---

o Ex 12, 7; Rv 7, 3.

8, 10: *Creeping things and loathsome beasts:* probably Egyptian deities, which were represented in animal form. During the last days of Jerusalem King Zedekiah was allied with Egypt, trusting in it for protection against the Chaldeans.

8, 14: *Weeping for Tammuz:* the withering of trees and plants in autumn was thought to be due to the descent of *Tammuz,* the Babylonian god of fertility, to the nether world of the dead; this descent was bewailed by the women.

8, 16: *Bowing down to the sun:* sun worship had been made an important part of Judahite idolatry by the impious kings; cf 2 Kgs 23, 11.

8, 17: *Put the branch to my nose:* the meaning is uncertain. Perhaps it refers to an Egyptian practice imported into Judah; the Egyptian sun god Re is pictured with a vine branch at his nose, signifying the transfer of creative power (divine breath) to living things. Such rites were abominable to the Lord.

9, 4: Ezekiel is pre-eminently the prophet of personal retribution; the innocent inhabitants of Jerusalem are to be spared when the idolatrous are punished. *An X:* literally, the Hebrew letter taw, which had the form of a cross.

²⁴ * Spirit lifted me up and brought me back to the exiles in Chaldea [in a vision, by God's spirit]. Then the vision I had seen left me, ²⁵ and I told the exiles everything the LORD had shown me.

CHAPTER 10

God's Glory Leaves Jerusalem. ¹ * On the fifth day of the sixth month, in the sixth year,* as I was sitting in my house, and the elders of Judah sat before me, the hand of the Lord GOD fell upon me there. ² I looked up and saw a form that looked like a man. Downward from what seemed to be his waist, there was fire; from his waist upward there seemed to be a brightness like the sheen of electrum. He stretched out what appeared to be a hand and seized me by the hair of my head. . . .*

⁴ I saw there the glory of the God of Israel, like the vision I had seen in the plain. The cherubim were stationed to the right of the temple; ²⁰ these were the living creatures I had seen beneath the God of Israel by the river Chebar,^p whom I now recognized to be cherubim. ²¹ Each had four faces and four wings; something like human hands were under their wings. ²² Their faces looked just like those I had seen by the river Chebar; each one went straight forward. ¹⁴ ^q Each had four faces: the first face was that of an ox, the second that of a man, the third that of a lion, and the fourth that of an eagle. ¹⁵ Such were the living creatures I had seen by the river Chebar.

⁹ ^r I also saw four wheels beside them, one wheel beside each cherub; the wheels appeared to have the luster of chrysolite stone. ¹⁰ All four of them seemed to be made the same, as though there were a wheel within a wheel. ¹¹ When they moved, they went in any one of their four directions without veering as they moved; for in whichever direction they were faced, they went straight towards it without veering as they moved. ¹² ^s The rims of the four wheels were full of eyes all around. ¹³ I heard the wheels given the name "wheelwork." ¹⁶ ^t When the cherubim moved, the wheels went beside them; when the cherubim lifted their wings to rise from the earth, even then the wheels did not leave their sides. ¹⁷ When they stood still, the wheels stood still; when they rose, the wheels rose with them; for the living creatures' spirit was in them.

¹ I looked and saw in the firmament above the cherubim what appeared to be sapphire stone; something like a throne could be seen upon it. ² He said to the man dressed in linen: Go within the wheelwork under the cherubim; fill both your hands with burning coals* from among the cherubim, then scatter them over the city. As I looked on, he entered.

The glory of the God of Israel had gone up from the cherubim, upon which it had been, to the threshold of the temple. ³ As the man entered, the cloud filled the inner court, ⁴ and the glory of the LORD rose from over the cherubim to the threshold of the temple; the temple was filled with the cloud, and all the court was bright with the glory of the LORD. ⁵ The noise of the wings of the cherubim could be heard as far as the outer court; it was like the voice of God the Almighty when he speaks.

⁶ When he had commanded the man dressed in linen to take fire from within the wheelwork, among the cherubim, the man entered and stood by one of the wheels. ⁷ Thereupon its cherub stretched out his hand toward the fire that was among the cherubim. He took up some of it and put it in the hands of the one dressed in linen, who took it and came out. ⁸ [Something like human hands could be seen under the wings of the cherubim.]

¹⁸ Then the glory of the LORD left the threshold of the temple and rested upon the cherubim. ¹⁹ These lifted their wings, and I saw them rise from the earth, the wheels rising along with them. They stood at the entrance of the eastern gate of the LORD's house, and the glory of the God of

---

p Ez 1, 1. 3.—q Ez 1, 10.—r Ez 1, 15f.—s Ez 1, 18.—t Ez 1, 19.

9, 24f: These verses have been transposed from ch 11.

10, 1: In chapters 8, 1—11, 25 of the current Hebrew text, several visions involving the temple of Jerusalem were combined to form a single continuous vision. The redistribution of verses in this translation is an attempt to separate the original visions (10, 1. 2. 4. have been transposed from ch 8).

10, 1: *The fifth day of the sixth month, in the sixth year:* September 17, 592 B.C.

10, 2: The dots indicate the omission of some words describing the prophet's being transported in his visions to the court of the temple.

10, 2: The *burning coals* within the wheelwork under God's throne, a sign of the divine presence (cf Ez 28, 14; Ps 18, 13), symbolize the judgment to be visited on the city.

Ez

Israel was up above them. ²² * Then the cherubim lifted their wings, and the wheels went along with them, while up above them was the glory of the God of Israel. ²³ And the glory of the LORD rose from the city and took a stand on the mountain which is to the east of the city.

CHAPTER 11

Judgment of the Princes. ¹ Spirit lifted me up and brought me to the east gate of the temple. At the entrance of the gate I saw twenty-five men, among whom were Jaazaniah, son of Azzur, and Pelatiah, son of Benaiah, princes of the people. ² The LORD said to me: Son of man, these are the men who are planning evil and giving wicked counsel in this city. ³ "Shall we not," they say, "be building houses soon? The city is the kettle, and we are the meat."* ⁴ Therefore prophesy against them, son of man, prophesy! ⁵ Then the spirit of the LORD fell upon me, and he told me to say: Thus says the LORD: This is the way you talk, house of Israel, and what you are plotting I well know. ⁶ You have slain many in this city and have filled its streets with your slain. ⁷ Therefore thus says the Lord GOD: Your slain whom you have placed within it, they are the meat, and the city is the kettle; but you I will take out of it. ⁸ You fear the sword, but the sword I will bring upon you, says the Lord GOD. ⁹ I will bring you out of the city, and hand you over to foreigners, and inflict punishments upon you. ¹⁰ By the sword you shall fall; at the boundaries of Israel I will judge you; thus you shall know that I am the LORD. ¹¹ The city shall not be a kettle for you, nor shall you be the meat within it. At the boundaries of Israel I will judge you, ¹² and you shall know that I am the LORD, by whose statutes you have not lived, and whose ordinances you have not kept; rather, you have acted according to the ordinances of the nations around you.

¹³ While I was prophesying, Pelatiah, the son of Benaiah, died. I fell prone and cried out in a loud voice: "Alas, Lord GOD! will you utterly wipe out what remains of Israel?"

Restoration of the Exiles. ¹⁴ Thus the word of the LORD came to me: ¹⁵ * Son of man, it is about your kinsmen, your fellow exiles, and the whole house of Israel that the inhabitants of Jerusalem say, "They are far away from the LORD; to us the land of Israel has been given as our possession." ¹⁶ Therefore say. Thus says the Lord GOD: Though I have removed them far among the nations and scattered them over foreign countries—and was for a while their only sanctuary in the countries to which they had gone—¹⁷ I will gather you from the nations and assemble you from the countries over which you have been scattered, and I will restore to you the land of Israel. ¹⁸ They shall return to it and remove from it all its detestable abominations. ¹⁹ ^u I will give them a new heart and put a new spirit within them; I will remove the stony heart from their bodies, and replace it with a natural heart, ²⁰ so that they will live according to my statutes, and observe and carry out my ordinances; thus they shall be my people and I will be their God. ²¹ But as for those whose hearts are devoted to their detestable abominations, I will bring down their conduct upon their heads, says the Lord GOD.

CHAPTER 12

Acts Symbolic of the Exile. ¹ Thus the word of the LORD came to me: ² Son of man, you live in the midst of a rebellious house; they have eyes to see but do not see, and ears to hear but do not hear, for they are a rebellious house. ³ Now, son of man, during the day while they are looking on, prepare your baggage as though for exile, and again while they are looking on, migrate from where you live to another place; perhaps they will see that they are a rebellious house. ⁴ You shall bring out your baggage like an exile in the daytime while they are looking on; in the evening, again while they are looking on, you shall go out like one of those driven into exile; ⁵ while they look on, dig a hole in the wall* and pass through it; ⁶ while they look on, shoulder the burden and set out in the darkness; cover your face that you may not

---

u Ez 36, 26; Jer 31, 33.

10, 22f: These verses have been transposed from ch 11.

11, 3: These words reflect the false confidence of the inhabitants of Jerusalem in the face of the Chaldean invasion. Jerusalem, they think, is like an iron kettle protecting the meat within it from harm; but cf Ez 24, 3-6.

11, 15-21: Like Jeremiah (cf chapter 29), Ezekiel knows that no reform is to be expected from the men of Judah who remained in Palestine; but the exiles will be the ones to form the new Israel. The new, spiritual covenant will replace the former covenant; cf Jer 24, 7.

12, 5: *Dig a hole in the wall:* the exiles are to leave Jerusalem through the broken walls of the ruined city.

see the land, for I have made you a sign for the house of Israel.

⁷I did as I was told. During the day I brought out my baggage as though it were that of an exile, and at evening I dug a hole through the wall with my hand and, while they looked on, set out in the darkness, shouldering my burden.

⁸Then, in the morning, the word of the LORD came to me: ⁹Son of man, did not the house of Israel, that rebellious house, ask you what you were doing? ¹⁰Tell them: Thus says the Lord GOD: This oracle concerns Jerusalem and the whole house of Israel within it. ¹¹I am a sign for you: as I have done, so shall it be done to them; as captives they shall go into exile. ¹²The prince who is among them shall shoulder his burden and set out in darkness, going through a hole that he has dug in the wall, and covering his face lest he be seen by anyone. ¹³ ᵛ But I will spread my net over him, and he shall be taken in my snare. I will bring him to Babylon, into the land of the Chaldeans—but he shall not see it*—and there he shall die. ¹⁴All his retinue, his aides, and his troops I will scatter in every direction, and pursue them with the sword. ¹⁵Then shall they know that I am the LORD, when I disperse them among the nations and scatter them over foreign lands. ¹⁶Yet I will leave a few of them to escape the sword, famine and pestilence, so that they may tell of all their abominations among the nations to which they will come; thus they shall know that I am the LORD.

¹⁷Thus the word of the LORD came to me: ¹⁸Son of man, eat your bread trembling, and drink your water shaking with anxiety. ¹⁹Then say to the people of the land: Thus says the Lord GOD of the inhabitants of Jerusalem [to the land of Israel]: They shall eat their bread in anxiety and drink their water in horror, that their land may be emptied of the violence of all its inhabitants that now fills it. ²⁰Inhabited

---

v Ez 17, 20; 32, 3.

12, 13: *But he shall not see it:* Zedekiah was blinded by Nebuchadnezzar before being deported to Babylonia; cf 2 Kgs 25, 7.

12, 22. 27: These words were used against Ezekiel because of the apparent failure of his prophecies; cf Jer 20, 7ff.

13, 3-23: These verses have been transposed according to the following order: 7-8. 10-16. 3-4. 6. 9. 17. 22-23. 18-21.

13, 10: To the confidence which the people had in their defenses against the Chaldeans, the false prophets contributed the illusion of security by predictions of peace, like men who whitewash a wall rather than allow its defects to be seen.

---

cities shall be in ruins, and the land shall be a waste; thus you shall know that I am the LORD.

Prophecy Ridiculed. ²¹Thus the word of the LORD came to me: ²²Son of man, what is this proverb that you have in the land of Israel: "The days drag on, and no vision ever comes to anything"?* ²³Say to them therefore: Thus says the Lord GOD: I will put an end to this proverb; they shall never quote it again in Israel. Rather, say to them: The days are at hand, and also the fulfillment of every vision. ²⁵Whatever I speak is final, and it shall be done without further delay. In your days, rebellious house, whatever I speak I will bring about, says the Lord GOD.

²⁴There shall no longer be any false visions or deceitful divinations within the house of Israel, because it is I, the LORD, who will speak.

²⁶Thus the word of the LORD came to me: ²⁷Son of man, listen to the house of Israel saying, "The vision he sees is a long way off; he prophesies of the distant future!" ²⁸Say to them therefore: Thus says the Lord GOD: None of my words shall be delayed any longer; whatever I speak is final, and it shall be done, says the Lord GOD.

CHAPTER 13

Against the Prophets of Peace. ¹Thus the word of the LORD came to me: ²Son of man, prophesy against the prophets of Israel, prophesy! Say to those who prophesy their own thought: Hear the word of the LORD:* ⁵You did not step into the breach, nor did you build a wall about the house of Israel that would stand firm against attack on the day of the LORD. ⁷Was not the vision you saw false, and your divination lying? ⁸Therefore thus says the Lord GOD: Because you have spoken falsehood and have seen lying visions, therefore see! I am coming at you, says the Lord GOD.

¹⁰For the very reason that they led my people astray, saying, "Peace!" when there was no peace, and that, as one built a wall, they would cover it with whitewash,* ¹¹say then to the whitewashers: I will bring down a flooding rain; hailstones shall fall, and a stormwind shall break out. ¹²And when the wall has fallen, will you not be asked: Where is the whitewash you spread on? ¹³Therefore thus says the Lord GOD: In my fury I will let loose stormwinds; be-

Ez

cause of my anger there shall be a flooding rain, and hailstones shall fall with destructive wrath. ¹⁴I will tear down the wall that you have whitewashed and level it to the ground, laying bare its foundations. When it falls, you shall be crushed beneath it; thus you shall know that I am the LORD. ¹⁵When I have spent my fury on the wall and its whitewashers, I tell you there shall be no wall, nor shall there be whitewashers—¹⁶those prophets of Israel who prophesied to Jerusalem and saw for it visions of peace when there was no peace, says the Lord GOD.

Against False Prophets in Chaldea. ³ *w* Thus says the Lord GOD: Woe to those prophets who are fools, who follow their own spirit and have seen no vision. ⁴Like foxes among ruins are your prophets, O Israel! ⁶Their visions are false and their divination lying. They say, "Thus says the LORD!" though the LORD did not send them; then they wait for him to fulfill their word! ⁹But I will stretch out my hand against the prophets who have false visions and who foretell lies. They shall not belong to the community of my people, nor be recorded in the register of the house of Israel, nor enter the land of Israel; thus you shall know that I am the LORD.

Against False Prophetesses. ¹⁷Now, son of man, turn toward the daughters of your people who prophesy their own thoughts; against these, prophesy: Thus says the Lord GOD: ²²Because you have disheartened the upright man with lies when I did not wish him grieved, and have encouraged the wicked man not to turn from his evil conduct and save his life; ²³therefore you shall no longer see false visions and practice divination, but I will rescue my people from your power. Thus you shall know that I am the LORD.

Against Sorceresses. ¹⁸Woe to those who sew bands for everyone's wrists and make veils* for every size of head so as to entrap their owners. Do you think to entrap the lives of my people, yet keep yourselves alive? ¹⁹You dishonor me before my people with handfuls of barley and crumbs of bread,* killing those who should not die and keeping alive those who should not live, lying to my people who willingly hear lies. ²⁰Therefore thus says the Lord GOD: See! I am coming at those bands of yours in which you entrap men's lives: I will tear them from their arms and set free those

you have caught. ²¹I will tear off your veils and rescue my people from your power, so that they shall no longer be prey to your hands. Thus you shall know that I am the LORD.

CHAPTER 14

Prophecy Useless for Idolaters. ¹When certain elders of Israel came and sat down before me, ²the word of the LORD came to me: ³Son of man, these men have the memory of their idols fresh in their hearts, and they keep the occasion of their sin before them. Why should I allow myself to be consulted by them? ⁴Therefore speak with them, and say to them: Thus says the Lord GOD: If anyone of the house of Israel, holding the memory of his idols in his heart and keeping the occasion of his sin before him, has recourse to a prophet, I, the LORD, will be his answer in person because of his many idols. ⁵Thus would I bring back to their senses the house of Israel, who have become estranged from me through all their idols.

⁶Therefore say to the house of Israel: Thus says the Lord GOD: Return and be converted from your idols; turn yourselves away from all your abominations. ⁷For if anyone of the house of Israel or any alien resident in Israel is estranged from me, and holds the memory of his idols in his heart and keeps the occasion of his sin before him, yet asks a prophet to consult me for him, I, the LORD, will be his answer in person. ⁸I will turn against that man, and make of him an example and a byword. I will cut him off from the midst of my people. Thus you shall know that I am the LORD.

⁹ ˣ As for the prophet, if he is beguiled into speaking a word, I, the LORD, shall have beguiled that prophet;* I will stretch out my hand against him and root him out of my people Israel. ¹⁰Each shall receive punishment for his sin, the inquirer and the prophet shall be punished alike, ¹¹so that the house of Israel may no longer stray from me and may no longer be defiled by all their sins. Thus they shall be my

---

w Ex 14, 9; 34, 2; Jer 23, 1.—x 1 Kgs 22, 23.

13, 18: *Sew bands . . . make veils:* magical practices believed to give to the sorceresses power over those on whom they placed these objects.

13, 19: *Handfuls of barley and crumbs of bread:* used in divination and forecasting the future.

14, 9: *I, the Lord, shall have beguiled that prophet:* the ancient Israelites attributed to God every action, good or evil; cf 1 Sm 18, 10; 2 Sm 24, 1ff. We would say, rather, that God permitted this deceit.

people, and I will be their God, says the Lord GOD.

Personal Responsibility. * [12] Thus the word of the LORD came to me: [13] *y* Son of man, when a land sins against me by breaking faith, I stretch out my hand against it and break its staff of bread, I let famine loose upon it and cut off from it both man and beast; [14] and even if these three men were in it, Noah, Daniel, and Job,* they could save only themselves by their virtue, says the Lord GOD. [15] If I were to cause wild beasts to prowl the land, depopulating it so that it became a waste, traversed by none because of the wild beasts, [16] and these three men were in it, as I live, says the Lord GOD, I swear they could save neither sons nor daughters; they alone would be saved, and the land would be a waste. [17] Or if I brought the sword upon this country, commanding the sword to pass through the land cutting off from it man and beast, [18] and these three men were in it, as I live, says the Lord GOD, they would be unable to save either sons or daughters; they alone would be saved. [19] Or if I were to send pestilence into this land, pouring out upon it my bloodthirsty fury, cutting off from it man and beast, [20] even if Noah, Daniel, and Job were in it, as I live, says the Lord GOD, I swear that they could save neither son nor daughter; they would save only themselves by their virtue.

[21] Thus says the Lord GOD: Even though I send Jerusalem my four cruel punishments, the sword, famine, wild beasts, and pestilence, to cut off from it man and beast, [22] still some survivors shall be left in it who will bring out sons and daughters; when they come out to you, you shall see their conduct and their actions and be consoled regarding the evil I have brought on Jerusalem [all that I have brought upon it]. [23] They shall console you when you see their conduct and actions,

for you shall then know that it was not without reason that I did to it what I did, says the Lord GOD.

CHAPTER 15

Parable of the Vine. [1] Thus the word of the LORD came to me: [2] Son of man, what makes the wood of the vine better than any other wood? That branch among the trees of the forest! [3] Can you use its wood to make anything worthwhile? Can you make even a peg from it, to hang on it any kind of vessel? [4] If you throw it on the fire as fuel and the fire devours both ends and even the middle is scorched, is it still good for anything? [5] Why, even when it was whole it was good for nothing; how much less, when the fire has devoured and scorched it, can it be used for anything! [6] Therefore, thus says the Lord GOD: Like the wood of the vine among the trees of the forest, which I have destined as fuel for the fire, do I make the inhabitants of Jerusalem. [7] I will set my face against them; they have escaped from the fire, but the fire shall devour them. Thus you shall know that I am the LORD, when I turn my face against them. [8] I will make the land a waste, because they have broken faith, says the Lord GOD.

CHAPTER 16

The Faithless Spouse [1] Thus the word of the LORD came to me: [2] Son of man, make known to Jerusalem her abominations. [3] Thus says the Lord GOD to Jerusalem: By origin and birth you are of the land of Canaan; your father was an Amorite and your mother a Hittite.* [4] As for your birth, the day you were born your navel cord was not cut; you were neither washed with water nor anointed, nor were you rubbed with salt, nor swathed in swaddling clothes. [5] No one looked on you with pity or compassion to do any of these things for you. Rather, you were thrown out on the ground as something loathsome, the day you were born.

[6] Then I passed by and saw you weltering in your blood. I said to you: Live in your blood [7] and grow like a plant in the field. You grew and developed, you came to the age of puberty; your breasts were formed, your hair had grown, but you were still stark naked. [8] Again I passed by and saw you that you were now old enough for love. So I spread the corner of my

---

y Ez 4, 16.

14, 12-23: The doctrine of personal responsibility before God was not new (cf Ez 3, 16-21; 18; 33, 1-20); but it had not been emphasized by the prophets before the Exile, who mostly predicted national retribution and called for national repentance.

14, 14: *Noah, Daniel, and Job:* proverbially virtuous men. The Daniel named here may be the traditional just judge of the ancient past, celebrated in Canaanite literature, who is possibly reflected in Dn 13, but is not the hero of Dn 1—12.

16, 3f: *By origin and birth . . . Canaan . . . Amorite . . . Hittite:* the inhabitants of Jerusalem and Judah absorbed not only pre-Israelite racial strains, but also many elements of the country's pagan cult and customs.

Ez

cloak over you to cover your nakedness;* I swore an oath to you and entered into a covenant with you; you became mine, says the Lord GOD. [9] Then I bathed you with water, washed away your blood, and anointed you with oil. [10] I clothed you with an embroidered gown, put sandals of fine leather on your feet; I gave you a fine linen sash and silk robes to wear. [11] I adorned you with jewelry: I put bracelets on your arms, a necklace about your neck, [12] a ring in your nose, pendants in your ears, and a glorious diadem upon your head. [13] Thus you were adorned with gold and silver; your garments were of fine linen, silk, and embroidered cloth. Fine flour, honey, and oil were your food. You were exceedingly beautiful, with the dignity of a queen. [14] You were renowned among the nations for your beauty, perfect as it was, because of my splendor which I had bestowed on you, says the Lord GOD.

[15] But you were captivated by your own beauty, you used your renown to make yourself a harlot, and you lavished your harlotry on every passer-by, whose own you became. [16] * You took some of your gowns and made for yourself gaudy high places, where you played the harlot. . . . [17] You took the splendid gold and silver ornaments that I had given you and made for yourself male images, with which also you played the harlot. [18] You took your embroidered gowns to cover them; my oil and my incense you set before them; [19] the food that I had given you, the fine flour, the oil, and the honey with which I fed you, you set before them as an appeasing odor, says the Lord GOD. [20] *z* The sons and daughters you had borne me you took and offered as sacrifices* to be devoured by them! Was it not enough that you had become a harlot? [21] *a* You slaughtered and immolated my children to them, making them pass through fire. [22] And through all your abominations and harlotries you remembered nothing of when you were a girl, stark naked and weltering in your blood.

[23] Then after all your evildoing—woe, woe to you! says the Lord GOD—[24] you raised for yourself a platform and a dais* in every public place. [25] *b* At every street corner you built a dais for yourself to use your beauty obscenely, spreading your legs for every passer-by, playing the harlot countless times. [26] You played the harlot with the Egyptians, your lustful neighbors, so many times that I was provoked to anger. [27] Therefore I stretched out my hand against you, I diminished your allowance and delivered you over to the will of your enemies, the Philistines, who revolted at your lewd conduct. [28] You also played the harlot with the Assyrians, because you were not satisfied; and after playing the harlot with them, you were still not satisfied. [29] Again and again you played the harlot, now going to Chaldea, the land of the traders; but despite this, you were still not satisfied.

[30] How wild your lust! says the Lord GOD, that you did all these things, acting like a shameless prostitute, [31] building your platform at every street corner and erecting your dais in every public place! Yet you were unlike a prostitute, since you disdained payment. [32] The adulterous wife receives, instead of her husband, payment. [33] All harlots receive gifts. But you rather bestowed your gifts on all your lovers, bribing them to come to you from all sides for your harlotry. [34] Thus in your harlotry you were different from all other women. No one sought you out for prostitution. Since you gave payment instead of receiving it, how different you were!

[35] Therefore, harlot, hear the word of the LORD! [36] Thus says the Lord GOD: Because you poured out your lust and revealed your nakedness in your harlotry with your lovers and abominable idols, and because you sacrificed the life-blood of your children to them, [37] *c* I will now gather together all your lovers whom you tried to please, whether you loved them or loved them not; I will gather them against you from all sides and expose you naked for them to see. [38] I will inflict on you the sentence of adulteresses and murderesses; I will wreak fury and jealousy upon you.

---

z Ex 20, 26. 31; 23, 37ff; Lv 18, 21; 20, 2; Dt 12, 31; 18, 10; 2 Kgs 21, 6; 23, 10; 24, 4; Jer 7, 31; 19, 5; 32, 34; Mi 6, 7.—a 2 Kgs 16, 3; 17, 17; 21, 6; 23, 10.—b Ez 23, 8; Is 57, 7; Jer 2, 20; 3, 2; 5, 7; 13, 27; Hos 2, 4; 4, 13.—c Ez 23, 10.

16, 8: *I spread the corner of my cloak over you to cover your nakedness:* and also to signify the intention of marriage; cf Ru 3, 9.

16, 16: Fine robes were used to cover a couch for harlotry; cf Prv 7, 16f. In the allegory of this chapter the viewpoint often shifts from the figure (harlotry) to the reality (idolatry).

16, 20f: Human sacrifice was introduced under Judah's impious kings; cf 2 Kgs 16, 3; 17, 17; Jer 7, 31.

16, 24: *A platform and a dais:* associated with ritual prostitution, which the Israelites borrowed from Canaanite practice.

39 I will hand you over to them to tear down your platform and demolish your dais; they shall strip you of your garments and take away your splendid ornaments, leaving you stark naked. **40** They shall lead an assembly against you to stone you and hack you with their swords. **41** *d* They shall burn your apartments with fire and inflict punishments on you while many women look on. Thus I will put an end to your harlotry, and you shall never again give payment. **42** When I have wreaked my fury upon you I will cease to be jealous of you, I will be quiet and no longer vexed. **43** Because you did not remember what happened when you were a girl, but enraged me with all these things, therefore in return I am bringing down your conduct upon your head, says the Lord GOD. For did you not add lewdness to the rest of your abominable deeds?

44 See, everyone who is fond of proverbs will say of you, 'Like mother, like daughter.' **45** Yes, you are the true daughter of the mother* who spurned her husband and children, and you are a true sister to those who spurned their husbands and children—your mother was a Hittite and your father an Amorite. **46** Your elder sister was Samaria* with her daughters, living to the north of you; and your younger sister, living to the south of you, was Sodom with her daughters. **47** Yet not only in their ways did you walk, and act as abominably as they did; in a very short time you became more corrupt in all your ways than they. **48** As I live, says the Lord GOD, I swear that your sister Sodom, with her daughters, has not done as you and your daughters have done! **49** *e* And look at the guilt of your sister Sodom: she and her daughters were proud, sated with food, complacent in their prosperity, and they gave no help to the poor and needy. **50** Rather, they became haughty and committed abominable crimes in my presence; then, as you have seen, I removed them. **51** Samaria did not commit half your sins! You have done more abominable things than they, and have even made your sisters

appear just, with all the abominable deeds you have done. **52** You, then, bear your shame; you are an argument in favor of your sisters! In view of your sinful deeds, more abominable than theirs, they appear just in comparision with you. Blush for shame, and bear the shame of having made your sisters appear just.

53 I will restore their fortunes, the fortune of Sodom and her daughters and of Samaria and her daughters [and I will restore your fortune along with them], **54** that you may bear your shame and be disgraced for all the comfort you brought them. **55** Yes, your sisters, Sodom and her daughters, Samaria and her daughters, shall return to their former state [you and your daughters shall return to your former state]. **56** Was not your sister Sodom kept in bad repute by you while you felt proud of yourself, **57** before your wickedness became evident? Now you are like her, reproached by the Edomites and all your neighbors, despised on all sides by the Philistines. **58** The penalty of your lewdness and your abominations—you must bear it all, says the LORD.

59 For thus speaks the Lord GOD: I will deal with you according to what you have done, you who despised your oath, breaking a covenant. **60** Yet I will remember the covenant I made with you when you were a girl, and I will set up an everlasting covenant with you. **61** Then you shall remember your conduct and be ashamed when I take your sisters, those older and younger than you, and give them to you as daughters, even though I am not bound by my covenant with you. **62** For I will re-establish my covenant with you, that you may know that I am the LORD, **63** that you may remember and be covered with confusion, and that you may be utterly silenced for shame when I pardon you for all you have done, says the Lord GOD.

CHAPTER 17

The Eagles and the Vine. **1** Thus the word of the LORD came to me: **2** Son of man, propose a riddle, and speak this proverb to the house of Israel: **3** Thus speaks the Lord GOD:

The great eagle, with great wings, with
    long pinions,
  with thick plumage, many-hued,
    came to Lebanon.

---

d 2 Kgs 25, 9.—e Gn 19, 24.

16, 45: *True daughter of the mother:* Jerusalem has followed in the footsteps of its heathen forebears; cf v 3.

16, 46: *Your elder sister was Samaria:* Samaria can be called an elder sister in view of the relatively greater importance of the northern kingdom, Israel, during most of Old Testament history. Also, the relatively insignificant Sodom of ancient history can be called *your younger sister.*

Ez

He took the crest of the cedar,
4   tearing off its topmost branch,
And brought it to a land of tradesmen,
     set it in a city of merchants.
5 Then he took some seed of the land,
     and planted it in a seedbed;
A shoot by plentiful waters,
     like a willow he placed it,
6 To sprout and grow up a vine,
     dense and low-lying,
Its branches turned toward him,
     its roots lying under him.
Thus it became a vine, produced
     branches
     and put forth shoots.
7 But there was another great eagle,
     great of wing, rich in plumage;
To him this vine bent its roots,
     sent out its branches,
That he might water it more freely
     than the bed where it was planted.
8 In a fertile field by plentiful waters it
     was planted,
     to grow branches, bear fruit,
     and become a majestic vine.

9 Say: Thus says the Lord GOD: Can it prosper? Will he not rather tear it out by the roots and strip off its fruit, so that all its green growth will wither when he pulls it up by the roots? [No need of a mighty arm or many people to do this.] 10 True, it is planted, but will it prosper? Will it not rather wither, when touched by the east wind, in the bed where it grew? 11 * Thus the word of the LORD came to me: 12 Son of man, say now to the rebellious house: Do you not understand what this means? It is this: The king of Babylon came to Jerusalem and took away its king and princes with him to Babylon. 13 Then he selected a man of the royal line with whom he made a covenant, binding him under oath, while removing the nobles of the land, 14 so that the kingdom would remain a modest one, without aspirations, and would keep his covenant and obey him. 15 But this man rebelled against him, sending envoys to Egypt to obtain horses and a great army. Can he prosper? Can he who does such things escape? Can he break a covenant and still go free? 16 As I live, says the Lord GOD, in the home of the king who set him up to rule, whose oath he spurned, whose covenant with him he broke, there in Babylon I swear he shall die! 17 When ramps are cast up and siege towers are built for the destruction of many lives, he shall not be saved in the conflict by Pharaoh with a great army and numerous troops. 18 He spurned his oath, breaking his covenant. Though he gave his hand in pledge, he did all these things. He shall not escape!

19 Therefore say: Thus says the Lord GOD: As I live, my oath which he spurned, my covenant which he broke, I swear to bring down upon his head. 20 f I will spread my net over him, and he shall be taken in my snare. I will bring him to Babylon and enter into judgment with him there over his breaking faith with me. 21 All the crack troops among his forces shall fall by the sword, and the survivors shall be scattered in every direction. Thus you shall know that I, the LORD, have spoken.

22 Therefore say: Thus says the Lord GOD:

I, too, will take from the crest of the
     cedar,
     from its topmost branches tear off a
        tender shoot,
And plant it on a high and lofty moun-
     tain;
23   on the mountain heights of Israel I
     will plant it.*
It shall put forth branches and bear
     fruit,
     and become a majestic cedar.
Birds of every kind shall dwell beneath
     it,
     every winged thing in the shade of its
        boughs.
24 And all the trees of the field shall know
     that I, the LORD,
Bring low the high tree,
     lift high the lowly tree,
Wither up the green tree,
     and make the withered tree bloom.

As I, the LORD, have spoken, so will I do.

CHAPTER 18

Personal Responsibility. 1 Thus the word of the LORD came to me: Son of man,

---

f Ez 12, 13; 32, 3.

17, 11-21: These verses explain the foregoing allegory. In 597 B.C. Nebuchadnezzar removed King Jehoiachin and took him into exile; in his place he set Zedekiah, Jehoiachin's uncle, on the throne and received from him the oath of loyalty. But Zedekiah was beguiled into rebellion by Pharaoh Hophra of Egypt, and thereby merited punishment; cf 2 Kgs 24, 10—25, 7.

17, 22f: *I, too, will take from the crest of the cedar . . . plant it:* the Lord will restore Israel under a messianic King from the same Davidic dynasty.

²what is the meaning of this proverb that you recite in the land of Israel:

"Fathers have eaten green grapes,ᵍ
     thus their children's teeth are on edge"?*

³As I live, says the Lord GOD: I swear that there shall no longer be anyone among you who will repeat this proverb in Israel. ⁴For all lives are mine; the life of the father is like the life of the son, both are mine; only the one who sins shall die.

⁵If a man is virtuous—if he does what is right and just, ⁶if he does not eat on the mountains,* nor raise his eyes to the idols of the house of Israel; if he does not defile his neighbor's wife, nor have relations with a woman in her menstrual period; ⁷ʰ if he oppresses no one, gives back the pledge received for a debt, commits no robbery; if he gives food to the hungry and clothes the naked; ⁸if he does not lend at interest nor exact usury; if he holds off from evildoing, judges fairly between a man and his opponent; ⁹if he lives by my statutes and is careful to observe my ordinances, that man is virtuous—he shall surely live, says the Lord GOD.

¹⁰But if he begets a son who is a thief, a murderer, or who does any of these things ¹¹(though the father does none of them), a son who eats on the mountains, defiles the wife of his neighbor, ¹²oppresses the poor and needy, commits robbery, does not give back a pledge, raises his eyes to idols, does abominable things, ¹³lends at interest and exacts usury—this son certainly shall not live. Because he practiced all these abominations, he shall surely die; his death shall be his own fault.

¹⁴On the other hand, if a man begets a son who, seeing all the sins his father commits, yet fears and does not imitate him; ¹⁵a son who does not eat on the mountains, or raise his eyes to the idols of the house of Israel, or defile his neighbor's wife; ¹⁶who does not oppress anyone, or exact a pledge, or commit robbery; who gives his food to the hungry and clothes the naked; ¹⁷who holds off from evildoing,

accepts no interest or usury, but keeps my ordinances and lives by my statutes—this one shall not die for the sins of his father, but shall surely live. ¹⁸Only the father, since he violated rights, and robbed, and did what was not good among his people, shall in truth die for his sins. ¹⁹You ask: "Why is not the son charged with the guilt of his father?" Because the son has done what is right and just, and has been careful to observe all my statutes, he shall surely live. ²⁰ ⁱ Only the one who sins shall die. The son shall not be charged with the guilt of his father, nor shall the father be charged with the guilt of his son. The virtuous man's virtue shall be his own, as the wicked man's wickedness shall be his.

²¹But if the wicked man turns away from all the sins he committed, if he keeps all my statutes and does what is right and just, he shall surely live, he shall not die. ²²None of the crimes he committed shall be remembered against him; he shall live because of the virtue he has practiced. ²³ ʲ Do I indeed derive any pleasure from the death of the wicked? says the Lord GOD. Do I not rather rejoice when he turns from his evil way that he may live?

²⁴And if the virtuous man turns from the path of virtue to do evil, the same kind of abominable things that the wicked man does, can he do this and still live? None of his virtuous deeds shall be remembered, because he has broken faith and committed sin; because of this, he shall die. ²⁵ ᵏ You say, "The LORD's way is not fair!" Hear now, house of Israel: Is it my way that is unfair, or rather, are not your ways unfair? ²⁶When a virtuous man turns away from virtue to commit iniquity, and dies, it is because of the iniquity he committed that he must die. ²⁷But if a wicked man, turning from the wickedness he has committed, does what is right and just, he shall preserve his life; ²⁸since he has turned away from all the sins which he committed, he shall surely live, he shall not die. ²⁹And yet the house of Israel says, "The LORD's way is not fair!" Is it my way that is not fair, house of Israel, or rather, is it not that your ways are not fair?

³⁰ ˡ Therefore I will judge you, house of Israel, each one according to his ways, says the Lord GOD. Turn and be converted from all your crimes, that they may be no cause of guilt for you. ³¹Cast away from

---

g Jer 13, 29.—h Is 58, 7; Mt 25, 35.—i Dt 24, 16; 2 Kgs 14, 6; 2 Chr 25, 4.—j Ez 33, 11; 2 Pt 3, 9.—k Ez 33, 20.—l Mt 3, 2; Lk 3, 3.

18, 2: *Fathers . . . on edge:* a proverb by which the people claimed that they were being punished for their ancestors' sins rather than for their own; cf Jer 31, 29.

18, 6: *Eat on the mountains:* partake of ritual meals at the heathen high places.

you all the crimes you have committed, and make for yourselves a new heart and a new spirit. Why should you die, O house of Israel? [32] *m* For I have no pleasure in the death of anyone who dies, says the Lord GOD. Return and live!

CHAPTER 19

[1] As for you, son of man, raise a lamentation over the prince of Israel:

Allegory of the Lions*

[2] What a lioness was your mother,
  a lion of lions!
Among young lions she couched
  to rear her whelps.
[3] One whelp she raised up,
  a young lion he became;
He learned to seize prey,
  men he devoured.
[4] Then nations raised cries against him,
  in their pit he was caught;
They took him away with hooks
  to the land of Egypt.
[5] Then she saw that in vain she had waited,
  her hope was destroyed.
She took another of her whelps,
  him she made a young lion.
[6] He prowled among the lions,
  a young lion he became;
He learned to seize prey,
  men he devoured;
[7] He ravaged their strongholds,
  their cities he wasted.
The land and all in it were appalled
  at the noise of his roar.
[8] Nations laid out against him
  snares all about him;
They spread their net to take him,
  in their pit he was caught.
[9] They put him in a cage and took him away
  to the king of Babylon,
So that his voice would not be heard
  on the mountains of Israel.

Allegory of the Vine Branch

[10] Your mother was like a vine*
  planted by the water;
Fruitful and branchy was she
  because of the abundant water.
[11] One strong branch she put out
  as a royal scepter.
Stately was her height
  amid the dense foliage;

Notably tall was she
  with her many clusters.
[12] But she was torn up in fury
  and flung to the ground;
The east wind withered her up,
  her fruit was torn off;
Then her strong branch withered up;
  fire devoured it. *n*
[13] So now she is planted in the desert,
  in a land dry and parched,
[14] For fire came out of the branch
  and devoured her shoots;
She is now without a strong branch,
  a ruler's scepter.

This is a lamentation and serves as a lamentation.

CHAPTER 20

Israel's History of Infidelity. [1] In the seventh year, on the tenth day of the fifth month,* some of the elders of Israel came to consult the LORD and sat down before me. [2] Then the word of the LORD came to me: [3] Son of man, speak with the elders of Israel and say to them: Thus says the Lord GOD: Have you come to consult me? As I live! I swear I will not allow myself to be consulted by you, says the Lord GOD.

[4] Will you judge them? Will you judge, son of man? Make known to them the abominations of their ancestors [5] in these words: Thus speaks the Lord GOD: The day I chose Israel, I swore to the descendants of the house of Jacob; in the land of Egypt I revealed myself to them and swore: I am the LORD, your God. [6] That day I swore to bring them out of the land of Egypt to the land I had scouted for them, a land flowing with milk and honey, a jewel among all lands. [7] Then I said to them: Throw away, each of you, the detestable things that have held your eyes; do not defile yourselves with the idols of Egypt: I am the LORD, your God.

[8] But they rebelled against me and refused to listen to me; none of them threw away the detestable things that had held their eyes, they did not abandon the idols

---

m Ez 18, 23; 33, 11; 2 Pt 3, 9.—n Hos 13, 15.

19, 2-9: The meaning of this allegory is uncertain. Probably the two *young lions* are Jehoahaz and Zedekiah, sons of the same mother, who were deported to Egypt and Babylonia respectively. Cf 2 Kgs 23, 31-34; 24, 18ff.
19, 10-14: *A vine:* Judah. *One strong branch:* the Davidic king.
20, 1: *The seventh year, on the tenth day of the fifth month:* August 14, 591 B.C.

of Egypt. Then I thought of pouring out my fury on them and spending my anger on them there in the land of Egypt; ⁹but I acted for my name's sake, that it should not be profaned in the sight of the nations among whom they were, in whose presence I had made myself known to them, revealing that I would bring them out of the land of Egypt. ¹⁰Therefore I led them out of the land of Egypt and brought them into the desert. ¹¹ ₒ Then I gave them my statutes and made known to them my ordinances, which everyone must keep, to have life through them. ¹² ₚ I also gave them my sabbaths to be a sign between me and them, to show that it was I, the LORD, who made them holy.

¹³But the house of Israel rebelled against me in the desert. They did not observe my statutes, and they despised my ordinances that bring life to those who keep them. My sabbaths, too, they desecrated grievously. Then I thought of pouring out my fury on them in the desert to put an end to them, ¹⁴but I acted for my name's sake, that it should not be profaned in the sight of the nations in whose presence I had brought them out. ¹⁵Nevertheless I swore to them in the desert not to bring them to the land I had given them, a land flowing with milk and honey, a jewel among all lands. ¹⁶So much were their hearts devoted to their idols, they had not lived by my statutes, but despised my ordinances and desecrated my sabbaths. ¹⁷But I looked on them with pity, not wanting to destroy them, so I did not put an end to them in the desert.

¹⁸Then I said to their children in the desert: Do not observe the statutes of your parents or keep their ordinances; do not defile yourselves with their idols. ¹⁹I am the LORD, your God: observe my statutes and be careful to keep my ordinances; ²⁰keep holy my sabbaths, as a sign between me and you to show that I am the LORD, your God. ²¹But their children rebelled against me: they did not observe my statutes or keep my ordinances that

bring life to those who observe them, and my sabbaths they desecrated. Then I thought of pouring out my fury on them, of spending my anger on them in the desert; ²²but I stayed my hand, acting for my name's sake, lest it be profaned in the sight of the nations in whose presence I brought them out. ²³Nevertheless I swore to them in the desert that I would disperse them among the nations and scatter them over foreign lands; ²⁴for they did not keep my ordinances, but despised my statutes and desecrated my sabbaths, with eyes only for the idols of their fathers. ²⁵Therefore I gave them statutes that were not good,* and ordinances through which they could not live. ²⁶I let them become defiled by their gifts, by their immolation of every first-born, so as to make them an object of horror.

²⁷Therefore speak to the house of Israel, son of man, and tell them: Thus says the Lord GOD: In this way also your fathers blasphemed me, breaking faith with me: ²⁸when I had brought them to the land I had sworn to give them, and they saw all its high hills and leafy trees, there they offered their sacrifices [there they brought their offensive offerings], there they sent up appeasing odors, and there they poured out their libations. ²⁹I asked them: To what sort of high place do you betake yourselves?—and so they call it a high place even to the present day. ³⁰Therefore say to the house of Israel: Thus says the Lord GOD: Will you defile yourselves like your fathers? Will you lust after their detestable idols? ³¹By offering your gifts, by making your children pass through the fire, you defile yourselves with all your idols even to this day. Shall I let myself be consulted by you, house of Israel? As I live! says the Lord GOD: I swear I will not let myself be consulted by you.

³²What you are thinking of shall never happen: "We shall be like the nations, like the peoples of foreign lands, serving wood and stone." ³³As I live, says the Lord GOD, with a mighty hand and outstretched arm, with poured-out wrath, I swear I will be king over you! ³⁴With a mighty hand and outstretched arm, with poured-out wrath, I will bring you out from the nations and gather you from the countries over which you are scattered; ³⁵ * then

---

ₒ Lv 18, 5; Rom 10, 5.—ₚ Ex 20, 8; 31, 13; Dt 5, 12.

20, 25f: *I gave them statutes that were not good:* the Lord permitted them to adopt pagan practices, including the abominable sacrifice of their newborn infants, which could only merit their destruction. See note on Ez 14, 9.
20, 35-38: Exile in the pagan lands will serve the same purpose as the desert journey after the Exodus from Egypt: the rebellious will be eliminated, and only a remnant will survive.

Ez

I will lead you to the desert of the peoples, where I will enter into judgment with you face to face. ³⁶Just as I entered into judgment with your fathers in the desert of the land of Egypt, so will I enter into judgment with you, says the Lord GOD. ³⁷I will count you with the staff and bring back but a small number. ³⁸I will separate from you those who have rebelled and transgressed against me; from the land where they sojourned as aliens I will bring them out, but they shall not return to the land of Israel. Thus you shall know that I am the LORD.

³⁹As for you, house of Israel, thus says the Lord GOD: Come, each one of you, destroy your idols! Then listen to me, and never again profane my holy name with your gifts and your idols. ⁴⁰For on my holy mountain, on the mountain height of Israel, says the Lord GOD, there the whole house of Israel without exception shall worship me; there I will accept them, and there I will claim your tributes and the first fruits of your offerings, and all that you dedicate. ⁴¹As a pleasing odor I will accept you, when I have brought you from among the nations and gathered you out of the countries over which you were scattered; and by means of you I will manifest my holiness in the sight of the nations. ⁴²Thus you shall know that I am the LORD, when I bring you back to the land of Israel, the land which I swore to give to your fathers. ⁴³There you shall recall your conduct and all the deeds by which you defiled yourselves; and you shall loathe yourselves because of the evil things you did. ⁴⁴And you shall know that I am the LORD when I deal with you thus, for my name's sake, and not according to your evil conduct and corrupt actions, O house of Israel, says the Lord GOD.

CHAPTER 21

The Sword of the Lord. ¹Thus the word of the LORD came to me: ² * Son of man, look southward, preach toward the south, and prophesy against the forest of the southern land. ³Hear the word of the LORD! you shall say to the southern forest. Thus says the Lord GOD: See! I am kindling a fire in you that shall devour all trees, the green as well as the dry. The blazing flame shall not be quenched, but from south to north every face shall be scorched by it. ⁴Everyone shall see that I, the LORD, have kindled it, and it shall not be quenched.

⁵But I said, "Alas! Lord GOD, they say to me, 'Is not this the one who is forever spinning parables?' " ⁶Then the word of the LORD came to me: ⁷Son of man, look toward Jerusalem, preach against their sanctuary, and prophesy against the land of Israel, ⁸saying to the land of Israel: Thus says the LORD: See! I am coming at you; I will draw my sword from its sheath and cut off from you the virtuous and the wicked.* ⁹Thus my sword shall leave its sheath against everyone from south to north, ¹⁰and everyone shall know that I, the LORD, have drawn my sword from its sheath, and it shall not be sheathed again.

Act Symbolic of the City's Fall. ¹¹As for you, son of man, groan! with shattered strength groan bitterly while they look on. ¹²And when they ask you, "Why are you groaning?", you shall say: Because of a report;* when it comes every heart shall fail, every hand shall fall helpless, every spirit shall be daunted, and every knee shall run with water. See, it is coming, it is here! says the Lord GOD.

Song of the Sword. ¹³Thus the word of the LORD came to me: ¹⁴Son of man, prophesy! say: Thus says the LORD:

A sword, a sword has been sharpened,
     a sword, a sword has been burnished:
¹⁵ To work slaughter has it been sharpened,
     to flash lightning has it been burnished.
Why should I now withdraw it?
     You have spurned the rod and every judgment!
¹⁶ I have given it over to the burnisher
     that he might hold it in his hand,
A sword sharpened and burnished
     to be put in the hand of a slayer.
¹⁷ Cry out and wail, son of man,
     for it is destined for my people;
It is for all the princes of Israel,
     victims of the sword with my people.

21, 2ff: The southern kingdom, Judah, is likened to a forest about to be burned; cf Jer 21, 14.

21, 8: *Cut off from you the virtuous and the wicked:* a more complete devastation of Jerusalem than that described in Ez 9, 6.

21, 12: *A report:* the news of the fall of Jerusalem; cf Ez 33, 21f.

Therefore, slap your thigh,* ¹⁸for the sword has been tested; and why should it not be so? says the Lord GOD, since you have spurned the rod.

¹⁹ As for you, son of man, prophesy,
    brushing one hand against the other:
While the sword is doubled and tripled,
    this sword of slaughter,
This great sword of slaughter
    which threatens all around,
²⁰ That every heart may tremble;
    for many will be the fallen.
At all their gates
    I have appointed the sword for
    slaughter,
Fashioned to flash lightning,
    burnished for slaughter.
²¹ Cleave to the right! destroy!
    to the left! wherever your edge is
    turned.

²² Then I, too, shall brush one hand against the other* and wreak my fury. I, the LORD, have spoken.

Nebuchadnezzar at the Crossroads.
²³ Thus the word of the LORD came to me: ²⁴ Son of man, make for yourself two roads over which the sword of the king of Babylon can come. Both roads shall lead out from the same land. Then put a signpost at the head of each road, ²⁵ so that the sword can come to Rabbah of the Ammonites or to Judah's capital, Jerusalem. ²⁶ For at the fork where the two roads divide stands the king of Babylon, divining;* he has shaken the arrows, inquired of the teraphim, inspected the liver. ²⁷ In his right hand is the divining arrow marked "Jerusalem,"* bidding him to give the order for slaying, to raise his voice in the battle cry, to post

---

21, 17: *Slap your thigh:* a gesture signifying grief and dread.
21, 22: *Brush one hand against the other:* a gesture signifying the rejection of responsibility; cf Ez 22, 13; Nm 24, 10.
21, 26: Three forms of divination are mentioned: *arrow* divination, consisting in the use of differently marked arrows extracted or shaken from a case at random; the consultation of the *teraphim* or household idols; and *liver* divination, scrutiny of the configurations of the livers of newly slaughtered animals, a common form of divination in Mesopotamia.
21, 27f: An *arrow marked "Jerusalem"* is picked out, which *marks* the guilt of the city's inhabitants for having broken their oath of allegiance to Nebuchadnezzar.
21, 33-37: In the preceding section Nebuchadnezzar is represented as deciding whether to attack Jerusalem or Rabbath-Ammon. As it happened, Jerusalem was chosen for attack; later, however, the Chaldeans also invaded Ammon. The present oracle against Ammon is inserted here, rather than in chapters 25-32, in order to complement the oracle against Jerusalem.

---

battering-rams at the gates, to cast up a ramp, to build a siege tower. ²⁸ In their eyes this is but a lying oracle; yet they are bound by the oaths they have sworn, and the arrow taken in hand marks their guilt.
²⁹ Therefore thus says the Lord GOD: Because you have drawn attention to your guilt, with your crimes laid bare and your sinfulness in all your wicked deeds revealed (because attention has been drawn to you), you shall be taken in hand. ³⁰ And as for you, depraved and wicked prince of Israel, whose day is coming when your life of crime will be ended, ³¹ thus says the Lord GOD: Off with the turban and away with the crown! Nothing shall be as it was! Up with the low and down with the high! ³² Twisted, twisted, twisted will I leave it; it shall not be the same until he comes who has the claim against the city; and to him I will hand it over.

Against the Ammonites.* ³³ As for you, son of man, prophesy: Thus says the Lord GOD against the Ammonites and their insults: A sword, a sword is drawn for slaughter, burnished to consume and to flash lightning, ³⁴ because you planned with false visions and lying divinations to lay it on the necks of depraved and wicked men whose day has come when their crimes are at an end. ³⁵ Return it to its sheath! In the place where you were created, in the land of your origin, I will judge you. ³⁶ I will pour out my indignation upon you, breathing my fiery wrath upon you; I will hand you over to ravaging men, artisans of destruction. ³⁷ You shall be fuel for the fire, your blood shall flow throughout the land. You shall not be remembered, for I, the LORD, have spoken.

CHAPTER 22

Crimes of Jerusalem. ¹ Thus the word of the LORD came to me: ² You, son of man, would you judge, would you judge the bloody city? Then make known all her abominations, ³ and say: Thus says the Lord GOD: Woe to the city which sheds blood within herself so that her time has come, and which has made idols for her own defilement. ⁴ By the blood which you shed you have been made guilty, and with the idols you made you have become defiled; you have brought on your day, so that the end of your years has come. Therefore I make you an object of scorn

Ez

to the nations and a laughingstock to all foreign lands. ⁵Those near you and those far off shall deride you because of your foul reputation and your great perversity. ⁶See! the princes of Israel, family by family, are in you only for bloodshed. ⁷Within you, father and mother are despised; in your midst, they extort from the resident alien; within you, they oppress orphans and widows. ⁸What is holy to me you have spurned, and my sabbaths you have desecrated. ⁹There are those in you who slander to cause bloodshed; within you are those who feast on the mountains; in your midst are those who do lewd things. ¹⁰In you are those who uncover the nakedness of their fathers, and in you those who coerce women in their menstrual period. ¹¹ � There are those in you who do abominable things with the wives of their neighbors, men who defile their daughters-in-law by incest, men who coerce their sisters, the daughters of their own fathers. ¹²There are those in you who take bribes to shed blood. You exact interest and usury; you despoil your neighbors violently; and me you have forgotten, says the Lord GOD.

¹³See, I am brushing one hand against the other because of the unjust profits you have made and because of the bloodshed in your midst. ¹⁴Can your heart remain firm, will your hands be strong, in the days when I deal with you? I, the LORD, have spoken, and I will act. ¹⁵I will disperse you among the nations and scatter you over foreign lands, so that I may purge your uncleanness. ¹⁶In you I will allow myself to be profaned in the eyes of the nations; thus you shall know that I am the LORD.

¹⁷Thus the word of the LORD came to me: ¹⁸Son of man, the house of Israel has become dross for me. All of them are bronze and tin, iron and lead [in the midst of a furnace]: dross from silver have they become. ¹⁹Therefore thus says the Lord GOD: Because all of you have become dross, therefore I must gather you together within Jerusalem. ²⁰Just as silver, bronze, iron, lead, and tin are gathered into a furnace and smelted in the roaring flames, so I will gather you together in my furious wrath, put you in, and smelt you. ²¹When I have assembled you, I will blast you with the fire of my anger and smelt you with it. ²²You shall be smelted by it just as silver

is smelted in a furnace. Thus you shall know that I, the Lord, have poured out my fury on you.

²³Thus the word of the LORD came to me: ²⁴Son of man, say to her: You are a land unrained on [that is, not rained on] at the time of my fury. ²⁵Her princes are like roaring lions that tear prey; they devour people, seizing their wealth and precious things, and make widows of many within her. ²⁶Her priests violate my law and profane what is holy to me; they do not distinguish between the sacred and the profane, nor teach the difference between the unclean and the clean; they pay no attention to my sabbaths, so that I have been profaned in their midst. ²⁷ ʳ Her nobles within her are like wolves that tear prey, shedding blood and destroying lives to get unjust gain. ²⁸Her prophets cover them with whitewash, pretending to visions that are false and performing lying divinations, saying, "Thus says the Lord GOD," although the LORD has not spoken. ²⁹The people of the land practice extortion and commit robbery; they afflict the poor and the needy, and oppress the resident alien without justice. ³⁰Thus I have searched among them for someone who could build a wall or stand in the breach before me to keep me from destroying the land; but I found no one. ³¹Therefore I have poured out my fury upon them; with my fiery wrath I have consumed them; I have brought down their conduct upon their heads, says the Lord GOD.

CHAPTER 23

The Two Sisters. ¹Thus the word of the LORD came to me: ²Son of man, there were two women, daughters of the same mother, ³who even as young girls played the harlot in Egypt. There the Egyptians caressed their bosoms and fondled their virginal breasts. ⁴Oholah was the name of the elder, and the name of her sister was Oholibah.* They became mine and bore sons and daughters. [As for their names: Samaria is Oholah, and Jerusalem is Oholibah.] ⁵Oholah became a harlot faith-

q Jer 5, 7f.—r Mi 3, 11; Zep 3, 3.

23, 4: *Oholah . . . Oholibah:* symbolic names. The first, standing for Samaria, may be read to mean "her own tent"; the latter, standing for Jerusalem, means "my tent is in her." The references seem to be to the schismatic temple and cult of the Lord in Samaria, as opposed to their authentic counterpart in Jerusalem.

less to me; she lusted after her lovers, the Assyrians, warriors [6] dressed in purple, governors and officers, all of them attractive young men, knights mounted on horses. [7] Thus she gave herself as a harlot to them, to all the elite of the Assyrians, and she defiled herself with all those for whom she lusted [with all their idols]. [8] She did not give up the harlotry which she had begun in Egypt, when they had lain with her as a young girl, fondling her virginal breasts and pouring out their impurities on her. [9] Therefore I handed her over to her lovers, the Assyrians for whom she had lusted. [10] [s] They exposed her nakedness, her sons and daughters they took away, and herself they slew with the sword. Thus she became a byword for women, for they punished her grievously.

[11] Though her sister Oholibah saw all this, her lust was more depraved than her sister's, and she outdid her in harlotry. [12] She too lusted after the Assyrians, governors and officers, warriors impeccably clothed, knights mounted on horses, all of them attractive young men. [13] I saw that she had defiled herself. Both had gone down the same path, [14] yet she went further in her harlotry. When she saw men drawn on the wall, the images of Chaldeans drawn with vermillion, [15] with sashes girded about their waists, flowing turbans on their heads, all looking like chariot warriors, the portraits of Babylonians, natives of Chaldea, [16] she lusted for them; no sooner had she set eyes on them than she sent messengers to them in Chaldea. [17] Then the Babylonians came to her, to the love couch, and defiled her with their intercourse. As soon as she was defiled by them, she became disgusted with them. [18] Her harlotry was discovered and her shame was revealed, and I became disgusted with her as I had become disgusted with her sister. [19] But she played the harlot all the more, recalling the days of her girlhood, when she had been a harlot in the land of Egypt. [20] She lusted for the lechers of Egypt, whose members are like that of an ass, and whose heat is like those of stallions. [21] You yearned for the lewdness of your girlhood, when the Egyptians fondled

s Ez 16, 37.

23, 23: *Pekod, Shoa and Koa:* peoples living about the Tigris, part of "greater Babylonia."

your breasts, caressing your bosom. [22] Therefore, Oholibah, thus says the Lord GOD: I will now stir up your lovers against you, those with whom you are disgusted, and I will bring them against you from every side: [23] the men of Babylon and all of Chaldea, Pekod, Shoa and Koa,* along with all those of Assyria, attractive young men, all of them governors and officers, charioteers and warriors, all of them horsemen. [24] They shall come against you from the north with chariots and wagons and many peoples. Shields, bucklers, and helmets they shall array against you everywhere. [25] I will leave it to them to judge, and they will judge you by their own ordinances. I will let loose my jealousy against you, so that they shall deal with you in fury, cutting off your nose and ears; and what is left of you shall fall by the sword. They shall take away your sons and daughters, and what is left of you shall be devoured by fire. [26] They shall strip off your clothes and seize your splendid ornaments. [27] I will put an end to your lewdness and to the harlotry you began in Egypt; you shall no longer look toward it, nor shall you remember Egypt again.

[28] For thus says the Lord GOD: I am now handing you over to those whom you hate, to those who fill you with disgust. [29] They shall deal with you in hatred, seizing all that you have worked for and leaving you stark naked, so that your indecent nakedness is exposed. Your lewdness and harlotry [30] have brought these things upon you, because you played the harlot with the nations by defiling yourself with their idols.

[31] Because you followed in the path of your sister, I will hand you her cup. [32] Thus says the Lord GOD:

The cup of your sister you shall drink,
    so wide and deep, which holds so
      much,
[33] Filled with destruction and grief,
    a cup of dismay, the cup of your sister.

[34] You shall drain it dry, and gnaw at the very sherds of the cup, and you shall tear out your breasts; for I have spoken, says the Lord GOD. [35] Therefore thus says the Lord GOD: Because you have forgotten me and cast me behind your back, it is for you to bear the penalty of your lewdness and harlotry.

36 Then the LORD said to me: Son of man, would you judge Oholah and Oholibah? Then make known to them their abominations. 37 For they committed adultery, and blood is on their hands. They committed adultery with their idols; to feed them they immolated the children they had borne me. 38 [This, too, they did to me: they defiled my sanctuary and desecrated my sabbaths. 39 On the very day they slew their children for their idols, they entered my sanctuary to desecrate it. Thus they acted within my house.] 40 Moreover, they sent for men who had to come from afar,* to whom messengers were sent. And so they came—and for them you bathed yourself, painted your eyes, and put on ornaments. 41 You sat on a couch prepared for them, with a table spread before it, on which you had set my incense and oil. 42 Then was heard the shout of a carefree mob in the city, and these were men brought in from the desert, who put bracelets on the women's arms and splendid diadems on their heads. 43 So I said: "Oh, this woman jaded with adulteries! Now they will commit whoredom with her, and as for her. . . ." 44 And indeed they did come to her as men come to a harlot. Thus they came to Oholah and Oholibah, the lewd women. 45 But just men shall punish them with the sentence meted out to adulteresses and murderesses, for they have committed adultery, and blood is on their hands.

46 Thus says the Lord GOD: Summon an assembly against them, and deliver them over to terror and plunder. 47 The assembly shall stone them and hack them to pieces with their swords. They shall slay their sons and daughters, and burn their houses with fire. 48 Thus I will put an end to lewdness in the land, and all the women will be warned not to imitate your lewdness. 49 They shall inflict on you the penalty of your lewdness, and you shall pay for your sins of idolatry. Thus you shall know that I am the LORD.

CHAPTER 24

Allegory of the Pot. 1 On the tenth day of the tenth month, in the ninth year,* the word of the LORD came to me: 2 Son of man, write down this date today, for this very day the king of Babylon has invested Jerusalem. 3 Propose this parable to the rebellious house: Thus says the Lord GOD:

* Set up the pot, set it up,
  then pour in some water.
4 Put in it pieces of meat,
  all good pieces: thigh and shoulder;
  Fill it with the choicest joints
5 taken from the pick of the flock.
Then pile the wood beneath it;
  bring to a boil these pieces
  and the joints that are in it.
6 Take out its pieces, one by one,
  without casting lots for it.

Therefore, thus says the Lord GOD: Woe to the bloody city,[t] a pot containing rust, whose rust has not been removed. 7 For the blood she shed is in her midst: she poured it on the bare rock; she did not pour it out on the earth, to be covered with dust.* 8 To work up my wrath, to excite my vengeance, she put her blood on the bare rock, not to be covered; 9 Therefore, thus says the Lord GOD:

I, too, will heap up a great bonfire,
10 piling on wood and kindling the fire,
Till the meat has been cooked,
  till the broth has boiled.

11 Then I will set the pot empty on the coals till its metal glows red hot, till the impurities in it melt, and its rust disappears. 12 Yet not even with fire will its great rust be removed. 13 Because you have sullied yourself with lewdness when I would have purified you, and you refused to be purified of your uncleanness, therefore you shall not be purified until I wreak my fury on you. 14 I, the LORD, have spoken; it is coming, for I will bring it about without fail. I will not have pity nor repent. By your conduct and your deeds you shall be judged, says the Lord GOD.

Symbol of the Destruction of the Temple. 15 Thus the word of the LORD came to me:

---

t Na 3, 1; Hb 2, 12.

23, 40: *Men who had to come from afar:* ambassadors from Assyria and Babylon. Alliances with these countries aided in the corruption of both Israel and Judah.

24, 1: *The tenth day of the tenth month, in the ninth year:* January 15, 588 B.C. The same date is given in Jer 52, 4.

24, 3ff: This present comparison of the inhabitants of Jerusalem to meat boiled in a pot symbolizes their punishment rather than their supposed protection as in Ez 11, 3.

24, 7: *Blood . . . to be covered with dust:* since blood was sacred to God, it had to be covered with earth (Lv 17, 13); the blood of a murdered man that was left uncovered cried to heaven for vengeance; cf Jb 16, 18; Gn 4, 10.

¹⁶Son of man, by a sudden blow I am taking away from you the delight of your eyes, but do not mourn or weep or shed any tears. ¹⁷Groan in silence, make no lament for the dead, bind on your turban, put your sandals on your feet, do not cover your beard, and do not eat the customary bread.* ¹⁸That evening my wife died, and the next morning I did as I had been commanded. ¹⁹Then the people asked me, "Will you not tell us what all these things that you are doing mean for us?" I therefore spoke to the people that morning, ²⁰saying to them: Thus the word of the LORD came to me: ²¹Say to the house of Israel: Thus says the Lord GOD: I will now desecrate my sanctuary, the stronghold of your pride, the delight of your eyes, the desire of your soul. The sons and daughters you left behind shall fall by the sword. ²⁴Ezekiel shall be a sign for you: all that he did you shall do when it happens. Thus you shall know that I am the LORD. ²² *You shall do as I have done, not covering your beards nor eating the customary bread. ²³Your turbans shall remain on your heads, your sandals on your feet. You shall not mourn or weep, but you shall rot away because of your sins and groan one to another.

End of Ezekiel's Dumbness. ²⁵ᵗᵗ As for you, son of man, truly, on the day I take away from them their bulwark, their glorious joy, the delight of their eyes, the desire of their soul, and the pride of their hearts, their sons and daughters, ²⁶that day the fugitive will come to you, that you may hear it for yourself; ²⁷that day your mouth shall be opened and you shall be dumb no longer. Thus you shall be a sign to them, and they shall know that I am the LORD.

III: PROPHECIES AGAINST FOREIGN NATIONS

CHAPTER 25

Against Ammon. ¹Thus the word of the LORD came to me: ²Son of man, turn toward the Ammonites and prophesy against them. ³ᵘ Say to the Ammonites: Hear the word of the LORD! Thus says the Lord GOD: Because you cried out your joy over the desecration of my sanctuary, the devastation of the land of Israel, and the exile of the house of Judah, ⁴therefore I will deliver you into the possession of the Easterners.* They shall set up their encampments among you and pitch their tents; they shall eat your fruits and drink your milk. ⁵I will make Rabbah a pasture for camels, and the villages of the Ammonites a resting place for flocks. Thus you shall know that I am the LORD.

⁶For thus says the Lord GOD: Because you clapped your hands and stamped your feet, rejoicing most maliciously in your heart over the land of Israel, ⁷therefore I will stretch out my hand against you. I will make you plunder for the nations, I will cut you off from the peoples, and remove you from the lands. I will destroy you, and thus you shall know that I am the LORD.

Against Moab. ⁸ᵛ Thus says the Lord God: Because Moab said, "See! the house of Judah is like all other nations," ⁹therefore I will clear the shoulder of Moab* totally of its cities, the jewels of the land: Beth-jesimoth, Baal-meon, and Kiriathaim. ¹⁰I will hand her over, along with the Ammonites, into the possession of the Easterners, that she may not be remembered among the peoples. ¹¹Thus I will execute judgment upon Moab, that they may know that I am the LORD.

Against Edom. ¹² ʷ Thus says the Lord GOD: Because Edom has taken vengeance on the house of Judah and has made itself grievously guilty by taking vengeance on them, ¹³therefore thus says the Lord GOD: I will stretch out my hand against Edom and cut off from it man and beast. I will make it a waste from Teman to Dedan; they shall fall by the sword. ¹⁴My vengeance upon Edom I will entrust to my people Israel, who will deal with Edom in accordance with my anger and my fury; thus they shall know my vengeance, says the Lord GOD.

Against the Philistines. ¹⁵Thus says the Lord GOD: Because the Philistines have acted revengefully, and have taken vengeance with destructive malice in their hearts, with an undying enmity, ¹⁶therefore thus says the Lord GOD: See! I am

Ez

---

tt 25ff: Ez 3, 22-27.—u Jer 40, 14; 41, 10; 49, 2; Am 1, 13ff; Zep 2, 8ff.—v Sir 50, 26; Is 15, 1-9; 16, 1-14; Jer 48, 1-47; Am 2, 1ff; Zep 2, 8f.—w 12ff: Ez 35, 1ff; Is 34, 5; Jer 49, 7-22; Jl 4, 19; Am 1, 11f; Ob 1-21.

24, 17: *The customary bread:* eaten as a mourning observance; cf Jer 16, 7. The other gestures here forbidden were also popular mourning customs.

24, 22f: The fall of the city will be so sudden and final that the exiles will have no time to go into mourning.

25, 4: *The Easterners:* nomadic tribes to the east of Ammon and Moab.

25, 9: *The shoulder of Moab:* the edge of the Moabite plateau.

stretching out my hand against the Philistines; I will cut off the Cherethites* and wipe out the remnant on the seacoast. [17] I will execute great acts of vengeance on them, punishing them furiously. Thus they shall know that I am the LORD, when I wreak my vengeance on them.

CHAPTER 26

Against the City of Tyre. [1] On the first day of the . . . month in the eleventh year, the word of the LORD came to me: [2] Son of man, because of what Tyre said of Jerusalem:

"Aha! it is broken, the gateway to the peoples;
   now that it is ruined, its wealth reverts to me!"
[3]   therefore thus says the Lord GOD:
See! I am coming at you, Tyre;
   I will churn up against you many nations,
   even as the sea churns up its waves;[x]
[4] They shall destroy the walls of Tyre
   and raze her towers.
I will scrape the ground from her
   and leave her a bare rock;*
[5] She shall be a drying place for nets
   in the midst of the sea.

I have spoken, says the Lord GOD: and she shall be booty for the nations. [6] And her daughters* on the mainland shall be slaughtered by the sword; thus they shall know that I am the LORD.

[7] For thus says the Lord GOD: I am now bringing up against Tyre from the north Nebuchadnezzar the king of Babylon, the king of kings, with horses and chariots, with cavalry and a great and mighty army.

[8] Your daughters on the mainland
   he shall slay with the sword;
He shall place a siege tower against you,
   cast up a ramp about you,
   and raise his shields against you.
[9] He shall pound your walls with battering-rams
   and break down your towers with his weapons.
[10] The surge of his horses shall cover you with dust,
   amid the noise of steeds, of wheels and of chariots.

Your walls shall shake as he enters your gates,
   even as one enters a city that is breached.
[11] With the hoofs of his horses
   he shall trample all your streets;
Your people he shall slay by the sword;
   your mighty pillars he shall pull to the ground.
[12] Your wealth shall be plundered,
   your merchandise pillaged;
Your walls shall be torn down,
   your precious houses demolished;
Your stones, your timber, and your clay
   shall be cast into the sea.
[13] I will put an end to the noise of your songs,
   and the sound of your lyres shall be heard no more.
[14] I will make you a bare rock;
   a drying place for nets shall you be.

Never shall you be rebuilt, for I have spoken, says the Lord GOD.

[15] Thus says the Lord GOD to Tyre: At the noise of your fall, at the groaning of the wounded, when the sword slays in your midst, shall not the isles quake? [16] All the princes of the sea* shall step down from their thrones, lay aside their robes, and strip off their embroidered garments. They shall be clothed in mourning and, sitting on the ground, they shall tremble at every moment and be horrified at you. [17] Then they shall utter a lament over you:

How have you perished, gone from the seas,
   city most prized!
Once she was mighty on the sea,
   she and her dwellers,
Who spread terror into all
   that dwelt by the sea.
[18] On this, the day of your fall,
   the islands quake!

The isles in the sea are terrified at your passing.

---

x Is 26, 1-21; 47, 4; Jl 4, 4f; Zec 9, 2ff.

25, 16: *Cherethites:* a people forming part of the Philistine nation; cf Zep 2, 5.
26, 4f: *A bare rock:* the Tyre of Ezekiel's time was situated on a rocky island just off the Phoenician coast; it was not until the time of Alexander the Great that it was connected by a causeway to the mainland.
26, 6: *Her daughters:* tributary towns and villages on the mainland.
26, 16: *The princes of the sea:* the rulers of the islands and coastal cities leagued commercially with Tyre.

[19] For thus says the Lord GOD: When I make you a city desolate like cities that are no longer inhabited, when I churn up the abyss against you, and its mighty waters cover you, [20] then I will thrust you down with those who descend into the pit,* those of the bygone age; and I will make you dwell in the nether lands, in the everlasting ruins, with those who go down to the pit, so that you may never return to take your place in the land of the living. [21] I will make you a devastation, and you shall be no more; you shall be sought, but never again found, says the Lord GOD.

CHAPTER 27

The Ship Tyre. [1] Thus the word of the LORD came to me: [2] As for you, son of man, utter a lament over Tyre, [3] and say to Tyre that is situated at the approaches of the sea, that brought the trade of the peoples to many a coastland: Thus says the Lord GOD:

Tyre, you said, "I am a ship,
    perfect in beauty."
[4] In the midst of the sea your builders
        placed you,
    perfected your beauty.
[5] With cypress from Senir* they built for
        you
    all of your decks;
Cedar from Lebanon they took
    to make you a mast;
[6] From the highest oaks of Bashan*
    they made your oars;
Your bridge they made of cypress wood
    from the coasts of Kittim.
[7] Fine embroidered linen from Egypt
    became your sail [to serve you as a
        banner].
Purple and scarlet from the coasts of
        Elishah*
    covered your cabin.
[8] Citizens of Sidon and Arvad
    served as your oarsmen;
Skilled men of Zemer were in you
    to be your mariners;

[9] The elders and experts of Gebal* were
        in you
    to caulk your seams.

Every ship and sailor on the sea came to you to carry trade. [10] Persia and Lud and Put were in your army as warriors; shield and helmet they hung upon you, increasing your splendor. [11] The men of Arvad were all about your walls, and the Gamadites were in your towers; they hung their bucklers all around on your walls, and made perfect your beauty. [12] Tarshish traded with you, so great was your wealth, exchanging silver, iron, tin, and lead for your wares. [13] Javan, Tubal, and Meshech were also traders with you, exchanging slaves and articles of bronze for your goods. [14] From Beth-togarmah horses, steeds, and mules were exchanged for your wares. [15] The Rhodanites trafficked with you; many coastlands traded with you; ivory tusks and ebony wood they gave you for payment. [16] Edom traded with you, so many were your products, exchanging garnets, purple, embroidered cloth, fine linen, coral, and rubies for your wares. [17] Judah and the land of Israel trafficked with you, exchanging Minnith wheat, figs, honey, oil, and balm for your goods. [18] Damascus traded with you, so great was your wealth, exchanging Helbon wine and Zahar wool. [19] Javan exchanged wrought iron, cassia, and aromatic cane from Uzal for your wares. [20] Dedan traded with you for riding gear. [21] The trade of Arabia and of all the sheikhs of Kedar belonged to you; they dealt in lambs, rams, and goats. [22] The merchants of Sheba and Raamah also traded with you, exchanging for your wares the very choicest spices, all kinds of precious stones, and gold. [23] Haran, Canneh, and Eden, the merchants of Sheba, Asshur, and Chilmad [24] traded with you, marketing with you rich garments, violet mantles, embroidered cloth, varicolored carpets, and firmly woven cords. [25] Ships of Tarshish journeyed for you in your merchandising.

You were full and heavily laden
    in the heart of the sea.
[26] Through the deep waters your oarsmen
        brought you home,
But the east wind smashed you
    in the heart of the sea.
[27] Your wealth, your goods, your wares,
    your sailors, and your crew,

[the caulkers of your seams, those who

26, 20: *Those who descend into the pit:* the dead, pictured as dwelling in a place or cave of darkness.

27, 5: *Senir:* another name for Mount Hermon; cf Dt 3, 9.

27, 6: *Bashan:* northern Transjordan, which, like Lebanon, was noted for its great forests. *Kittim:* probably Cyprus.

27, 7: *Elishah:* probably another term for Cyprus.

27, 8f: *Sidon . . . Arvad . . . Zemer . . . Gebal:* Phoenician cities in Tyre's orbit of influence; the last-named is the classical Byblos.

Ez

traded for your goods, all your warriors
who were in you, and all the great crowd
within you]

Sank into the heart of the sea
on the day of your shipwreck.

28 Hearing the shouts of your mariners,
the shores begin to quake.

29 Down from their ships
come all who ply the oar;
The sailors, all the mariners of the sea,
stand on the shore,

30 Making their voice heard on your behalf,
shouting bitter cries,
Strewing dust on their heads,
rolling in the ashes.

31 For you they shave their heads
and put on sackcloth,
For you they weep in anguish,
with bitter lament.

32 In their mourning they utter a lament
over you;
thus they wail over you:
Who was ever destroyed like Tyre
in the midst of the sea?

33 With your goods which you drew from
the seas
you filled many peoples;
With your great wealth and merchandise
you enriched the kings of the earth.

34 Now you are wrecked in the sea,
in the watery depths;
Your wares and all your crew
have gone down with you.

35 All who dwell on the coastlands
are aghast over you,
Their kings are terrified,
their faces convulsed.

36 The traders among the peoples
now hiss at you;
You have become a horror,
and you shall be no more.

CHAPTER 28

The Prince of Tyre. 1 Thus the word of
the LORD came to me: 2 Son of man, say to
the prince of Tyre: Thus says the Lord
GOD:

Because you are haughty of heart,
you say, "A god am I!
I occupy a godly throne
in the heart of the sea!"—
And yet you are a man, and not a god,
however you may think yourself like
a god.

3 Oh yes, you are wiser than Daniel,*
there is no secret that is beyond you.

4 By your wisdom and your intelligence
you have made riches for yourself;
You have put gold and silver
into your treasuries.

5 By your great wisdom applied to your
trading
you have heaped up your riches;
your heart has grown haughty from
your riches—

6   therefore thus says the Lord GOD:
Because you have thought yourself
to have the mind of a god,

7 Therefore I will bring against you
foreigners, the most barbarous of nations.
They shall draw their swords
against your beauteous wisdom,
they shall run them through your
splendid apparel.

8 They shall thrust you down to the pit,
there to die
a bloodied corpse, in the heart of the
sea.

9 Will you then say, "I am a god!"
when you face your murderers?
No, you are a man, not a god,
handed over to those who will slay
you.

10 You shall die the death of the uncircumcised
at the hands of foreigners,
for I have spoken,
says the Lord GOD.

11 Thus the word of the LORD came to
me: 12 Son of man, utter a lament over the
king of Tyre, saying to him: Thus says the
Lord GOD:

* You were stamped with the seal of
perfection,
of complete wisdom and perfect
beauty.

13 In Eden, the garden of God, you were,
and every precious stone was your
covering

[carnelian, topaz, and beryl, chrysolite,
onyx, and jasper, sapphire, garnet, and
emerald];

Of gold your pendants and jewels
were made, on the day you were
created.

28, 3: *Wiser than Daniel:* see note on Ez 14, 14.
28, 12-19: This picture of Tyre and its fall recalls images of
the earthly paradise portraying the creation of man in perfection
and his fall (Gn, chapters 2-3).

14 With the Cherub I placed you;
  you were on the holy mountain of
    God,*
  walking among the fiery stones.
15 Blameless you were in your conduct
    from the day you were created,
  Until evil was found in you,
16   the result of your far-flung trade;
  violence was your business, and you
    sinned.
  Then I banned you from the mountain
    of God;
  the Cherub drove you from among
    the fiery stones.
17 You became haughty of heart because
    of your beauty;
  for the sake of splendor you debased
    your wisdom.
  I cast you to the earth, so great was your
    guilt;
  I made you a spectacle in the sight of
    kings.
18 Because of your guilt, your sinful trade,
  I have profaned your sanctuaries,
  And I have brought out fire from your
    midst
  which will devour you.
  I have reduced you to dust on the earth
    in the sight of all who should see you.
19 Among the peoples, all who knew you
    stand aghast at you;
  You have become a horror,
    you shall be no more.

Against Sidon. 20 *y* Thus the word of the
LORD came to me: Son of man, look toward Sidon, 21 *z* and prophesy against it:
22 Thus says the Lord GOD: *a* See! I am
coming at you, Sidon; I will be glorified in
your midst. Then they shall know that I
am the LORD, when I inflict punishments
upon it and use it to manifest my holiness.

23 Into it I will send pestilence,
  and blood shall flow in its streets.
  Within it shall fall those slain
    by the sword that comes against it
    from every side.

Thus they shall know that I am the LORD.
24 Sidon shall no longer be a tearing thorn
for the house of Israel, a brier that
scratches them more than all the others
about them who despise them; thus they
shall know that I am the LORD.
25 Thus says the Lord GOD: When I
gather the house of Israel from the peoples
among whom they are scattered, then I
will manifest my holiness through them in
the sight of the nations. Then they shall
live on their land which I gave to my servant Jacob; 26 they shall live on it in security, building houses and planting vineyards. They shall dwell secure while I inflict punishments on all their neighbors
who despised them; thus they shall know
that I, the LORD, am their God.

CHAPTER 29

Egypt the Crocodile. 1 On the twelfth day
of the tenth month in the tenth year,* the
word of the LORD came to me: 2 Son of
man, set your face against Pharaoh, king
of Egypt, and prophesy against him and
against all Egypt.* 3 Say this to him: Thus
says the Lord GOD:

  See! I am coming at you, Pharaoh,
    king of Egypt,
  Great crouching monster
    amidst your Niles:*
  Who say, "The Niles are mine;
    it is I who made them!"

4 I will put hooks in your jaws and make
the fish of your Niles stick to your scales,
then draw you up from the midst of your
Niles along with all the fish of your Niles
sticking to your scales.

5 I will cast you into the desert,
    you and all the fish of your Niles;
  You shall fall upon the open field,
    you shall not be taken up or buried;
  To the beasts of the earth and the birds
      of the air
    I give you as food,
6 That all who dwell in Egypt may know
    that I am the LORD.
  Because you have been a reed staff
    for the house of Israel: *b*
7 When they held you in hand, you splin-
      tered,
    throwing every shoulder out of joint;
  When they leaned on you, you broke,

---

y Is 23, 1-18.—z Jer 47, 4.—a Jl 4, 4; Zec 9, 2ff.—b Is 36, 6.

28, 14: *The holy mountain of God:* the residence of God
was sometimes designated as a mountain; cf Is 14, 13. *The fiery
stones:* associated with the divine presence; cf Ez 1, 13; Ps 18,
13.
29, 1: *The twelfth day of the tenth month in the tenth
year:* January 7, 587 B.C. The siege of Jerusalem had begun a
year earlier; cf Ez 24, 1.
29, 2: Egypt was allied with Judah against the Chaldeans.
29, 3: *Niles:* the many rivulets of the Nile as it branches out
into the Delta.

Ez

bringing each one of them down headlong;

⁸ therefore thus says the Lord GOD: See! I will bring the sword against you, and cut off from you both man and beast. ⁹ The land of Egypt shall become a desolate waste; thus they shall know that I am the LORD.

Because you said, "The Niles are mine; it is I who made them," ¹⁰ therefore see! I am coming at you and against your Niles; I will make the land of Egypt a waste and a desolation from Migdol to Syene,* and even to the frontier of Ethiopia. ¹¹ No foot of man or beast shall pass through it; they shall not pass through it, and it will be uninhabited for forty years. ¹² I will make the land of Egypt the most desolate of lands, and its cities shall be the most deserted of cities for forty years; and I will scatter the Egyptians among the nations and strew them over foreign lands. ¹³ Yet thus says the Lord GOD: At the end of forty years I will gather the Egyptians from the peoples among whom they are scattered, ¹⁴ and I will restore Egypt's fortune, bringing them back to the land of Pathros, the land of their origin,* where it will be the lowliest ¹⁵ of kingdoms, never more to set itself above the nations. I will make them few, that they may not dominate the nations. ¹⁶ No longer shall they be for the house of Israel to trust in, but the living reminder of its guilt for having turned to follow after them. Thus they shall know that I am the LORD.

The Wages of Nebuchadnezzar. ¹⁷ On the first day of the first month in the twenty-seventh year,* the word of the LORD came to me: ¹⁸ Son of man, Nebuchadnezzar, the king of Babylon, has led his army in an exhausting campaign against Tyre.* Their heads became bald and their shoulders were galled; but neither he nor his army received any wages from Tyre for the campaign he led against it. ¹⁹ Therefore thus says the Lord GOD: ᶜ I am now giving the land of Egypt to Nebuchadnezzar, king of Babylon. He shall carry off its riches, plundering and pillaging it for the wages of his soldiers, who did it for me; ²⁰ as payment for his toil I have given him the land of Egypt, says the Lord GOD.

²¹ On that day I will make a horn sprout for the house of Israel, and I will cause you to speak out in their midst; thus they shall know that I am the LORD.

CHAPTER 30

The Day of the Lord against Egypt. ¹ Thus the word of the LORD came to me: ² Son of man, speak this prophecy: Thus says the Lord GOD: Cry, Oh, the day! ³ for near is the day, near is the day of the Lord; a day of clouds, doomsday for the nations shall it be. ⁴ Then a sword shall come upon Egypt, and anguish shall be in Ethiopia, when the slain fall in Egypt, when her riches are seized and her foundations are overthrown. ⁵ Ethiopia, Put, Lud, all Arabia, Libya, and people of the allied territory shall fall by the sword with them. ⁶ Those who support Egypt shall fall, and down shall come her proud strength; from Migdol to Syene they shall fall there by the sword, says the Lord GOD. ⁷ She shall be the most devastated of lands, and her cities shall be the most desolate of all. ⁸ Then they shall know that I am the LORD, when I set fire to Egypt and when all who help her are broken. ⁹ On that day messengers shall hasten forth at my command to terrify unsuspecting Ethiopia; they shall be in anguish on the day of Egypt, which is surely coming.

¹⁰ Thus says the Lord GOD: I will put an end to the throngs of Egypt by the hand of Nebuchadnezzar, king of Babylon. ¹¹ He and his people with him, the most ruthless of nations, shall be brought in to devastate the land. They shall draw their swords against Egypt, and fill the land with the slain. ¹² I will turn the Niles into dry land and sell the land over to the power of the wicked. The land and everything in it I will hand over to foreigners to devastate. I, the LORD, have spoken.

¹³ ᵈ Thus says the Lord GOD: I will put an end to the great ones of Memphis and

---

c Jer 46, 2.—d Zec 13, 2.

29, 10: *From Migdol to Syene:* from the northern to the southern extremity of Egypt. *Syene* is the modern Assuan.

29, 14: *Pathros, the land of their origin:* upper Egypt, that is, southern Egypt, where the Egyptians were thought to have originated; Is 11, 11; Jer 44, 1. 15.

29, 17: *The first day of the first month in the twenty-seventh year:* April 26, 571 B.C. This is the latest date attached to any prophecy in Ezekiel.

29, 18f: The fulfillment of Ezekiel's prophecy against Tyre (chapters 26-28) was a thirteen-year siege of the city by Nebuchadnezzar (587-574 B.C.). Tyre seems to have been taken, but its resources were exhausted and the booty was small. Therefore Ezekiel now prophesies that Nebuchadnezzar will collect his wages as God's instrument in the punishment of Tyre, by plundering Egypt.

the princes of the land of Egypt, that they may be no more. I will cast fear into the land of Egypt, and devastate Pathros. [14] I will set fire to Zoan, and inflict punishments on Thebes. [15] I will pour out my wrath on Pelusium, Egypt's stronghold, and cut down the crowds in Memphis. [16] I will set fire to Egypt; Syene shall writhe in anguish; Thebes shall be breached and its walls shall be demolished. [17] The young men of On and of Pibeseth shall fall by the sword, and the cities themselves shall go into captivity. [18] In Tehaphnehes the day shall be darkened when I break the scepter of Egypt. Her haughty pride shall cease from her, clouds shall cover her, and her daughters shall go into captivity. [19] Thus will I inflict punishments on Egypt, that they may know that I am the LORD.

Pharaoh's Broken Arm. [20] On the seventh day of the first month in the eleventh year,* the word of the LORD came to me: [21] * Son of man, I have broken the arm of Pharaoh, the king of Egypt, and see, it has not been bound up with bandages and healing remedies that it may be strong enough to hold the sword. [22] Therefore thus says the Lord GOD: See! I am coming at Pharaoh, the king of Egypt. I will break his strong arm, so that the sword drops from his hand. [23] I will scatter the Egyptians among the nations and strew them over foreign lands. [24] But I will strengthen the arms of the king of Babylon, and put my sword in his hand, which he will bring against Egypt so as to plunder and pillage it. [25] [I will make the arms of the king of Babylon strong, but the arms of Pharaoh shall drop.] Then they shall know that I am the LORD, when I put my sword in the hand of the king of Babylon for him to wield against the land of Egypt. [26] [I will scatter the Egyptians among the nations and strew them over foreign lands.] Thus they shall know that I am the LORD.

30, 20: *The seventh day of the first month in the eleventh year:* April 29, 587 B.C.

30, 21-26: This oracle was uttered during the siege of Jerusalem, which had now lasted more than a year (Ez 24, 1). Pharaoh Hophra went to the aid of Jerusalem, causing the Chaldeans to lift the siege temporarily; cf Jer 34, 21; 37, 6f. In the prophet's eyes, this was interfering with the divine punishment of Judah that was to be inflicted by the Chaldeans. The Egyptians were routed by the Chaldeans, and were able to offer no more help to Jerusalem; cf chapter 31.

31, 1: *The first day of the third month in the eleventh year:* June 21, 587 B.C.

CHAPTER 31

Allegory of the Cypress. [1] On the first day of the third month in the eleventh year,* the word of the LORD came to me: [2] Son of man, say to Pharaoh, the king of Egypt, and to his hordes: What are you like in your greatness?

[3] Behold, a cypress [cedar] in Lebanon,
  beautiful of branch, lofty of stature,
  amid the very clouds lifted its crest.

[4] Waters made it grow, the abyss made it flourish,
  sending its rivers round where it was planted,
  turning its streams to all the trees of the field.

[5] Thus it grew taller than every other tree of the field,
  and longer of branch because of the abundant water.

[6] In its boughs nested all the birds of the air,
  under its branches all beasts of the field gave birth,
  in its shade dwelt numerous peoples of every race.

[7] It became beautiful and stately in its spread of foliage,
  for its roots were turned toward abundant water.

[8] The cedars in the garden of God were not its equal,
  nor could the fir trees match its boughs,
  Neither were the plane trees like it for branches;
  no tree in the garden of God matched its beauty.

[9] I made it beautiful, with much foliage,
  the envy of all Eden's trees in the garden of God.

[10] Therefore thus says the Lord GOD: Because it became lofty in stature, raising its crest among the clouds, and because it became proud in heart at its height, [11] I have handed it over to the mightiest of the nations, which has dealt with it in keeping with its wickedness. I humilated it. [12] Foreigners, the most ruthless of the nations, cut it down and left it on the mountains. Its foliage was brought low in all the valleys, its branches lay broken in all the ravines of the land, and all the peoples of the land withdrew from its shade, abandoning it.

Ez

¹³ On its fallen trunk rested all the birds of
the air,
    and by its branches were all the
    beasts of the field.

¹⁴Thus no tree may grow lofty in stature
or raise its crest among the clouds; no tree
fed by water may stand by itself in its loftiness.

    For all of them are destined for death,
      for the land below,
    For the company of mortals,
      those who go down into the pit.

¹⁵Thus says the Lord GOD: On the day
he went down to the nether world I made
the abyss close up over him; I stopped its
streams so that the deep waters were held
back. I cast gloom over Lebanon because
of him, so that all the trees in the land
drooped on his account. ¹⁶At the crash of
his fall I made the nations rock, when I
cast him down to the nether world with
those who go down into the pit. In the
land below, all Eden's trees were consoled,
Lebanon's choice and best, all that were
fed by water. ¹⁷They too have come down
with him to the nether world, to those
slain by the sword; those who dwelt in his
shade are dispersed among the nations.
¹⁸Which was your equal in glory or size
among the trees of Eden? Yet you have
been brought down with the trees of Eden
to the land below. You shall lie with the
uncircumcised, with those slain by the
sword. Such are Pharaoh and all his
hordes, says the Lord GOD.

CHAPTER 32

Dirge over Pharaoh. ¹On the first day of
the twelfth month in the twelfth year,* the
word of the LORD came to me: ²Son of
man, utter a lament over Pharaoh, the
king of Egypt, saying to him: Lion of the
nations, you are destroyed.

    You were like a monster in the sea,
      spouting in your streams,
    Stirring the water with your feet
      and churning its streams.

³Thus says the Lord GOD:

    I will spread my net over you
      [with a host of many nations],
      and draw you up in my seine.ᵉ
⁴ I will leave you on the land;
      on the open field I will cast you.
    I will have all the birds of the air alight
      on you,

    and all the beasts of the earth eat
      their fill of you.
⁵ I will leave your flesh on the mountains,
      and fill the valleys with your carcass.
⁶ I will water the land with what flows
      from you,
    and the river beds shall be filled with
      your blood.
⁷ When I snuff you out I will cover the
      heavens,
    and all their stars I will darken;
    The sun I will cover with clouds,
      and the moon shall not give its light.ᶠ
⁸ All the shining lights in the heavens
    I will darken on your account,
    And I will spread darkness over your
      land,
      says the Lord GOD.

⁹I will grieve the hearts of many peoples
when I lead you captive among the nations, to lands which you do not know.
¹⁰Many peoples shall be appalled at you,
and their kings shall shudder over you in
horror when they see me brandish my
sword, and on the day of your downfall
every one of them shall continuously tremble for his own life. ¹¹For thus says the
Lord GOD: The sword of the king of Babylon shall come upon you.

¹² I will cut down your horde with the
      blades of warriors,
    all of them the most ruthless of the
      nations;
    They shall lay waste the glory of Egypt,
      and all her hordes shall be destroyed.
¹³ I will have all of her animals perish
      beside her abundant waters;
    The foot of man shall stir them no
      longer,
    nor shall the hoof of beast disturb
      them.
¹⁴ Then will I make their waters clear,
      and their streams flow like oil,
      says the Lord GOD.

¹⁵When I turn Egypt into a waste, the
land shall be devastated of all that is in it;
when I strike all who live there, they shall
know that I am the LORD. ¹⁶This is a
dirge, and it shall be sung: the daughters
of the nations shall chant it; over Egypt
and all its hordes shall they chant it, says
the Lord GOD.

Dirge over Egypt. ¹⁷On the fifteenth day
of the first month in the twelfth year,

---

e Ez 12, 13; 17, 20.—f Is 13, 10; Jl 2, 10; 4, 15; Mt 24, 29.

32, 1: *The first day of the twelfth month in the twelfth
year:* March 3, 585 B.C.

the word of the LORD came to me: [18]Son of man, lament over the throngs of Egypt, for the mighty nations have thrust them down to the bottom of the earth, with those who go down into the pit. [20]In the midst of those slain by the sword shall they fall, and place shall be made with them for all their hordes. Then from the midst of the nether world, the mighty warriors shall speak to Egypt: [19]"Whom do you excel in beauty? [21]Come down, you and your allies, lie with the uncircumcised, with those slain by the sword."

[22]There is Assyria with all her company, all of them slain, [23]whose graves have been made in the recesses of the pit; her company is around Egypt's grave, all of them slain, fallen by the sword, who spread terror in the land of the living. [24]There is Elam with all her throng about Egypt's grave, all of them slain, fallen by the sword: they have gone down uncircumcised to the bottom of the earth, who spread their terror in the land of the living, and they bear their disgrace with those who go down into the pit; [25]in the midst of the slain they are placed. [26]There are Meshech and Tubal and all their throng about her grave, all of them uncircumcised, slain by the sword, for they spread their terror in the land of the living.

[27]They do not lie with the mighty men fallen of old,* who went down to the nether world with their weapons of war, whose swords were placed under their heads and whose shields were laid over their bones, though the mighty men caused terror in the land of the living. [28]But in the midst of the uncircumcised shall you lie, with those slain by the sword. [29]There are Edom, her kings, and all her princes, who despite their might have been placed with those slain by the sword; with the uncircumcised they lie, and with those who go down into the pit. [30]There are all the princes of the north and all the Sidonians, who have gone down with the slain, because of the terror their might inspired; they lie uncircumcised with those slain by the sword and bear their disgrace with those who go down to the pit. [31]When Pharaoh sees these, he shall be comforted for all his hordes slain by the

sword—Pharaoh and all his army, says the Lord GOD. [32]Since he spread his terror in the land of the living, therefore is he laid to rest among the uncircumcised, with those slain by the sword—Pharaoh and all his hordes, says the Lord GOD.

IV: SALVATION FOR ISRAEL

CHAPTER 33

The Prophet a Watchman. [1]Thus the word of the LORD came to me: [2]Son of man, speak thus to your countrymen: When I bring the sword against a country, and the people of this country select one of their number to be their watchman, [3]and the watchman, seeing the sword coming against the country, blows the trumpet to warn the people, [4]anyone hearing but not heeding the warning of the trumpet and therefore slain by the sword that comes against him, shall be responsible for his own death. [5]He heard the trumpet blast yet refused to take warning; he is responsible for his own death, for had he taken warning he would have escaped with his life. [6]But if the watchman sees the sword coming and fails to blow the warning trumpet, so that the sword comes and takes anyone, I will hold the watchman responsible for that person's death, even though that person is taken because of his own sin.

[7] [g] You, son of man, I have appointed watchman for the house of Israel; when you hear me say anything, you shall warn them for me. [8]If I tell the wicked man that he shall surely die, and you do not speak out to dissuade the wicked man from his way, he [the wicked man] shall die for his guilt, but I will hold you responsible for his death. [9]But if you warn the wicked man, trying to turn him from his way, and he refuses to turn from his way, he shall die for his guilt, but you shall save yourself.

Individual Retribution. [10]As for you, son of man, speak to the house of Israel: You people say, "Our crimes and our sins weigh us down; we are rotting away because of them. How can we survive?" [11] [h] Answer them: As I live, says the LORD, I swear I take no pleasure in the death of the wicked man, but rather in the wicked man's conversion, that he may live. Turn, turn from your evil ways! Why should you die, O house of Israel?

---

g Ez 3, 17.—h Ez 18, 23-32.

32, 27: *The mighty men fallen of old:* the semilegendary heroes of the prehistoric past, who were thought to have once dominated the world; cf Is 14, 9.

¹²As for you, son of man, tell your countrymen: The virtue which a man has practiccd will not save him on the day that he sins; neither will the wickedness that a man has done bring about his downfall on the day that he turns from his wickedness [nor can the virtuous man, when he sins, remain alive]. ¹³Though I say to the virtuous man that he shall surely live, if he then presumes on his virtue and does wrong, none of his virtuous deeds shall be remembered; because of the wrong he has done, he shall die. ¹⁴And though I say to the wicked man that he shall surely die, if he turns away from his sin and does what is right and just, ¹⁵giving back pledges, restoring stolen goods, living by the statutes that bring life, and doing no wrong, he shall surely live, he shall not die. ¹⁶None of the sins he committed shall be held against him; he has done what is right and just, he shall surely live.

¹⁷Yet your countrymen say, "The way of the LORD is not fair!"; but it is their way that is not fair. ¹⁸When a virtuous man turns away from what is right and does wrong, he shall die for it. ¹⁹But when a wicked man turns away from wickedness and does what is right and just, because of this he shall live. ²⁰ ⁱ And still you say, "The way of the LORD is not fair!"? I will judge every one of you according to his ways, O house of Israel.

The Fugitive from Jerusalem.* ²¹On the fifth day of the tenth month, in the twelfth year of our exile, the fugitive came to me from Jerusalem and said, "The city is taken!" ²²The hand of the LORD had come upon me the evening before the fugitive arrived, and he opened my mouth when the fugitive reached me in the morning. My mouth was opened, and I was dumb no longer.

The Survivors in Judah.* ²³Thus the word of the Lord came to me: ²⁴Son of man, they who live in the ruins on the land of Israel reason thus: "Abraham, though but a single individual, received possession of the land; we, therefore, being many, have as permanent possession the land that has been given to us." ²⁵Give them this answer: Thus says the Lord GOD: You eat on the mountains, you raise your eyes to your idols, you shed blood—yet you would keep possession of the land? ²⁶You rely on your sword, you do abominable things, each one of you defiles his neighbor's

wife—yet you would keep possession of the land? ²⁷Tell them this: Thus says the Lord GOD: As I live, those who are in the ruins shall fall by the sword; those who are in the open field I have given to the wild beasts for food; and those who are in fastnesses and in caves shall die by the plague. ²⁸I will make the land a desolate waste, so that its proud strength will come to an end, and the mountains of Israel shall be so desolate that no one will cross them. ²⁹Thus they shall know that I am the LORD, when I make the land a desolate waste because of all the abominable things they have done.

The Prophet's False Popularity. ³⁰As for you, son of man, your countrymen are talking about you along the walls and in the doorways of houses. They say to one another, "Come and hear the latest word that comes from the LORD."* ³¹My people come to you as people always do; they sit down before you and hear your words, but they will not obey them, for lies are on their lips and their desires are fixed on dishonest gain. ³²For them you are only a ballad singer, with a pleasant voice and a clever touch. They listen to your words, but they will not obey them. ³³But when it comes—and it is surely coming!—they shall know that there was a prophet among them.

CHAPTER 34

Parable of the Shepherds. ¹Thus the word of the LORD came to me: ²Son of man, prophesy against the shepherds of Israel,* in these words prophesy to them [to the shepherds]: Thus says the Lord GOD: Woe to the shepherds of Israel who have been pasturing themselves!ʲ Should not shepherds, rather, pasture sheep? ³You have fed off their milk, worn their

---

i Ez 18, 25.—j Ez 13, 3; Jer 23, 1.

33, 21f: January 8, 585 B.C. According to Jeremiah (39, 2), Jerusalem was taken in July, 587. Some MSS read "eleventh" for *twelfth* year (January, 586); even so, there was ample time between the fall of Jerusalem and the arrival of the fugitive from that city to journey to Babylon. However, this is the fugitive sent to fulfill the promise of Ez 24, 25. 27, the eyewitness who would release Ezekiel from his dumbness; cf Ez 2, 26f.

33, 23-29: News brought by the fugitive furnished the occasion of this prophecy. Like Jeremiah, Ezekiel rejects the idea that the survivors in Judah have any claim to the land. The new Israel is to be formed from the exiles.

33, 30: The fulfillment of Ezekiel's prophecies about Jerusalem was responsible for this temporary enthusiasm among the unstable people.

34, 2: *The shepherds of Israel:* the leaders of the people.

wool, and slaughtered the fatlings, but the sheep you have not pastured. ⁴You did not strengthen the weak nor heal the sick nor bind up the injured. You did not bring back the strayed nor seek the lost, but you lorded it over them harshly and brutally. ⁵So they were scattered for lack of a shepherd, and became food for all the wild beasts. My sheep were scattered ⁶and wandered over all the mountains and high hills; my sheep were scattered over the whole earth, with no one to look after them or to search for them.

⁷ Therefore, shepherds, hear the word of the LORD: ⁸As I live, says the Lord GOD, because my sheep have been given over to pillage, and because my sheep have become food for every wild beast, for lack of a shepherd; because my shepherds did not look after my sheep, but pastured themselves and did not pasture my sheep; ⁹because of this, shepherds, hear the word of the LORD: ¹⁰Thus says the Lord GOD: I swear I am coming against these shepherds. I will claim my sheep from them and put a stop to their shepherding my sheep so that they may no longer pasture themselves. I will save my sheep, that they may no longer be food for their mouths.

¹¹For thus says the Lord GOD: I myself will look after and tend my sheep. ¹²As a shepherd tends his flock when he finds himself among his scattered sheep, so will I tend my sheep. I will rescue them from every place where they were scattered when it was cloudy and dark. ¹³I will lead them out from among the peoples and gather them from the foreign lands; I will bring them back to their own country and pasture them upon the mountains of Israel [in the land's ravines and all its inhabited places]. ¹⁴In good pastures will I pasture them, and on the mountain heights of Israel shall be their grazing ground. There they shall lie down on good grazing ground, and in rich pastures shall they be pastured on the mountains of Israel. ¹⁵I myself will pasture my sheep; I myself will give them rest, says the Lord GOD. ¹⁶The lost I will seek out, the strayed I

will bring back, the injured I will bind up, the sick I will heal [but the sleek and the strong I will destroy], shepherding them rightly.

Separation of the Sheep. ¹⁷As for you, my sheep, says the Lord GOD, I will judge between one sheep and another, between rams and goats. ¹⁸Was it not enough for you to graze on the best pasture, that you had to trample the rest of your pastures with your feet? Was it not enough for you to drink the clearest water, that you had to foul the remainder with your feet? ¹⁹Thus my sheep had to graze on what your feet had trampled and drink what your feet had fouled. ²⁰Therefore thus says the Lord GOD: Now will I judge between the fat and the lean sheep. ²¹Because you push with side and shoulder, and butt all the weak sheep with your horns until you have driven them out, ²²I will save my sheep so that they may no longer be despoiled, and I will judge between one sheep and another. ²³ ᵏ I will appoint one shepherd over them to pasture them, my servant David;* he shall pasture them and be their shepherd. ²⁴I, the Lord, will be their God, and my servant David shall be prince among them. I, the LORD, have spoken.

²⁵I will make a covenant of peace with them, and rid the country of ravenous beasts, that they may dwell securely in the desert and sleep in the forests. ²⁶I will place them about my hill, sending rain in due season, rains that shall be a blessing to them. ²⁷The trees of the field shall bear their fruits, and the land its crops, and they shall dwell securely on their own soil. Thus they shall know that I am the LORD when I break the bonds of their yoke and free them from the power of those who enslaved them. ²⁸They shall no longer be despoiled by the nations or devoured by beasts of the earth, but shall dwell secure, with no one to frighten them. ²⁹I will prepare for them peaceful fields for planting; they shall no longer be carried off by famine in the land, or bear the reproaches of the nations. ³⁰Thus they shall know that I, the LORD, am their God, and they are my people, the house of Israel, says the Lord GOD. ³¹[You, my sheep, you are the sheep of my pasture, and I am your God, says the Lord GOD.]

---

k Is 40, 21; Hos 3, 5; Jn 10, 11. 14.

34, 23: *One shepherd . . . my servant David:* a messianic Davidic King who will rule over the restored Israel (vv 25-31) in the name of the Lord.

Ez

CHAPTER 35

Against Edom.* [1]Thus the word of the LORD came to me:[l] [2]Son of man, set your face against Mount Seir, and prophesy against it. [3]Say to it: Thus says the Lord GOD: See! I am coming at you, Mount Seir. I will stretch out my hand against you and make you a desolate waste. [4]Your cities I will turn into ruins, and you shall be a waste; thus you shall know that I am the LORD.

[5]Because you never let die your hatred for the Israelites, whom you delivered over to the power of the sword at the time of their trouble, when their crimes came to an end, [6]therefore, as I live, says the Lord GOD, you have been guilty of blood, and blood, I swear, shall pursue you. [7]I will make Mount Seir a desolate waste, and cut off from it any traveler. [8]With the slain I will fill your hills, your valleys, and all your ravines [in them the slain shall fall by the sword]: [9]desolate will I make you forever, and leave your cities without inhabitants; thus you shall know that I am the LORD.

[10]Because you said: The two nations and the two lands* have become mine; we shall possess them—although the LORD was there—[11]therefore, as I live, says the Lord GOD, I will deal with you according to your anger and your envy which you have exercised [in your hatred] against them. I will make myself known among you when I judge you, [12]and you shall know that I am the LORD.

I have heard all the contemptuous things you have uttered against the mountains of Israel: "They are desolate, they have been given us to devour." [13]I have heard the insolent and wild words you have spoken against me. [14]Thus says the Lord GOD: Just as you rejoiced over my land because it was desolate, so will I do to you. [15]In keeping with your glee over the devastation of the inheritance of the house of Israel, so will I treat you. A waste shall you be, Mount Seir, you and the whole of Edom. Thus they shall know that I am the LORD.

CHAPTER 36

Regeneration of the Land. [1]As for you, son of man, prophesy to the mountains of Israel: Mountains of Israel,[m] hear the word of the LORD! [2]Thus says the Lord GOD: Because the enemy has said of you, Ha! the everlasting heights have become our possession" [3][therefore prophesy in these words: Thus says the Lord GOD:]; because you have been ridiculed and despised on all sides for having become a possession for the rest of the nations, and have become a byword and a popular jeer; [4]therefore, mountains of Israel, hear the word of the LORD: [Thus says the Lord GOD to the mountains and hills, the ravines and valleys, the desolate ruins and abandoned cities, which have been given over to the pillage and mockery of the remaining nations round about; [5]therefore thus says the Lord GOD:] Truly, with burning jealousy I speak against the rest of the nations [and against all of Edom] who with wholehearted joy and utter contempt have considered my land their possession to be delivered over to plunder. [6][Therefore, prophesy concerning the land of Israel, and say to the mountains and hills, the ravines and valleys: Thus says the Lord GOD:] With jealous fury I speak, because you have borne the reproach of the nations. [7]Therefore do I solemnly swear that your neighboring nations shall bear their own reproach.

[8]As for you, mountains of Israel, you shall grow branches and bear fruit for my people Israel, for they shall soon return. [9]See, I come to you, it is to you that I turn; you will be tilled and sown, [10]and I will settle crowds of men upon you, the whole house of Israel; cities shall be repeopled, and ruins rebuilt. [11]I will settle crowds of men and beasts upon you, to multiply and be fruitful. I will repeople you as in the past, and be more generous to you than in the beginning; thus you shall know that I am the LORD.

[12][My people Israel are the ones whom I will have walk upon you; they shall take possession of you, and you shall be their heritage. Never again shall you rob them of their children.]

[13]Thus says the Lord GOD: Because they have said of you, "You are a land that devours men,* and you rob your peo-

---

l 1ff: Ez 25, 12ff.—m Ez 6, 3.

35, 1-15: After the fall of Jerusalem, Edom assisted the Chaldeans in devastating the land and subduing the population, and ended by occupying part of Judah's former territory. For this reason these oracles against Edom are found in the context of the city's fall.

35, 10: *The two nations and the two lands:* the superseded kingdoms of Israel and Judah and their territories.

36, 13: *A land that devours men:* destroys its own population, as could be seen in its disastrous political history.

ple of their children"; [14] therefore, never again shall you devour men or rob your people of their children, says the Lord GOD. [15] No more will I permit you to hear the reproach of nations, or bear insults from peoples, or rob your people of their children, says the Lord GOD.

Regeneration of the People. [16] Thus the word of the LORD came to me: [17] Son of man, when the house of Israel lived in their land, they defiled it by their conduct and deeds. In my sight their conduct was like the defilement of a menstruous woman. [18] Therefore I poured out my fury upon them [because of the blood which they poured out on the ground, and because they defiled it with idols]. [19] I scattered them among the nations, dispersing them over foreign lands; according to their conduct and deeds I judged them. [20] *n* But when they came among the nations [wherever they came], they served to profane my holy name, because it was said of them: "These are the people of the LORD, yet they had to leave their land." [21] So I have relented because of my holy name which the house of Israel profaned among the nations where they came. [22] Therefore say to the house of Israel: Thus says the Lord GOD: Not for your sakes do I act, house of Israel, but for the sake of my holy name, which you profaned among the nations to which you came. [23] I will prove the holiness of my great name, profaned among the nations, in whose midst you have profaned it. Thus the nations shall know that I am the LORD, says the Lord GOD, when in their sight I prove my holiness through you. [24] For I will take you away from among the nations, gather you from all the foreign lands, and bring you back to your own land. [25] *o* I will sprinkle clean water upon you to cleanse you from all your impurities, and from all your idols I will cleanse you. [26] *p* I will give you a new heart and place a new spirit within you, taking from your bodies your stony hearts and giving you natural hearts. [27] *q* I will put my spirit within you and make you live by my statutes, careful to observe my decrees. [28] You shall live in the land I gave

n Is 52, 5; Rom 2, 24.—o Ps 51, 4; Zec 13, 1; Hb 10, 22; Jn 3, 5.—p Jer 31, 33.—q Ez 37, 14; 39, 29; Is 42, 1; 44, 3; 59, 21; Hg 2, 5; Jl 3, 1f.

37, 1-14: This vision is a prediction of the restoration of Israel under the figure of a resurrection from the dead; it is not concerned with the doctrine of resurrection itself.

your fathers; you shall be my people, and I will be your God. [29] I will save you from all your impurities; I will order the grain to be abundant, and I will not send famine against you. [30] I will increase the fruit on your trees and the crops in your fields; thus you shall no longer bear among the nations the reproach of famine. [31] Then you shall remember your evil conduct, and that your deeds were not good; you shall loathe yourselves for your sins and your abominations. [32] Not for your sakes do I act, says the Lord GOD—let this be known to you! Be ashamed and abashed because of your conduct, O house of Israel.

[33] Thus says the Lord GOD: When I purify you from all your crimes, I will repeople the cities, and the ruins shall be rebuilt; [34] the desolate land shall be tilled, which was formerly a wasteland exposed to the gaze of every passer-by. [35] "This desolate land has been made into a garden of Eden," they shall say. "The cities that were in ruins, laid waste, and destroyed are now repeopled and fortified." [36] Thus the neighboring nations that remain shall know that I, the LORD, have rebuilt what was destroyed and replanted what was desolate. I, the LORD, have promised, and I will do it.

[37] Thus says the Lord GOD: This also I will be persuaded to do for the house of Israel: to multiply them like sheep. [38] As with sacrificial sheep, the sheep of Jerusalem on its feast days, the cities which were in ruins shall be filled with flocks of men; thus they shall know that I am the LORD.

CHAPTER 37

Vision of the Dry Bones. * [1] The hand of the LORD came upon me, and he led me out in the spirit of the LORD and set me in the center of the plain, which was now filled with bones. [2] He made me walk among them in every direction so that I saw how many they were on the surface of the plain. How dry they were! [3] He asked me: Son of man, can these bones come to life? "Lord GOD," I answered, "you alone know that." [4] Then he said to me: Prophesy over these bones, and say to them: Dry bones, hear the word of the LORD! [5] Thus says the Lord GOD to these bones: See! I will bring spirit into you, that you may come to life. [6] I will put sinews upon

Ez

you, make flesh grow over you, cover you with skin, and put spirit in you so that you may come to life and know that I am the LORD. [7] I prophesied as I had been told, and even as I was prophesying I heard a noise; it was a rattling as the bones came together, bone joining bone. [8] I saw the sinews and the flesh come upon them, and the skin cover them, but there was no spirit in them. [9] Then he said to me: Prophesy to the spirit, prophesy, son of man, and say to the spirit: Thus says the Lord GOD: From the four winds come, O spirit, and breathe into these slain that they may come to life. [10] I prophesied as he told me, and the spirit came into them; they came alive and stood upright, a vast army. [11] Then he said to me: Son of man, these bones are the whole house of Israel. They have been saying, "Our bones are dried up, our hope is lost, and we are cut off." [12] Therefore, prophesy and say to them: Thus says the Lord GOD: O my people, I will open your graves and have you rise from them, and bring you back to the land of Israel. [13] Then you shall know that I am the LORD, when I open your graves and have you rise from them, O my people! [14] I will put my spirit in you that you may live, and I will settle you upon your land; thus you shall know that I am the LORD. I have promised, and I will do it, says the LORD.

The Two Sticks. [15] * Thus the word of the LORD came to me: [16] Now, son of man, take a single stick, and write on it: Judah and those Israelites who are associated with him. Then take another stick and write on it: Joseph [the stick of Ephraim] and all the house of Israel associated with him. [17] Then join the two sticks together, so that they form one stick in your hand. [18] When your countrymen ask you, "Will you not tell us what you mean by all this?", [19] answer them: Thus says the Lord GOD: [I will take the stick of Joseph, which is in the hand of Ephraim, and of the tribes of Israel associated with him, and I will join to it the stick of Judah, making them a single stick; they shall be one in my hand. [20] The sticks on which you write you shall hold up before them to see. [21] Tell them: Thus speaks the Lord GOD:] I will take the Israelites from among the nations to which they have come, and gather them from all sides to bring them back to their land. [22] I will make them

one nation upon the land, in the mountains of Israel, and there shall be one prince for them all. Never again shall they be two nations, and never again shall they be divided into two kingdoms.

[23] No longer shall they defile themselves with their idols, their abominations, and all their transgressions. I will deliver them from all their sins of apostasy, and cleanse them so that they may be my people and I may be their God. [24] r My servant David shall be prince over them, and there shall be one shepherd for them all; they shall live by my statutes and carefully observe my decrees. [25] They shall live on the land which I gave to my servant Jacob, the land where their fathers lived; they shall live on it forever, they, and their children, and their children's children, with my servant David their prince forever. [26] s I will make with them a covenant of peace; it shall be an everlasting covenant with them, and I will multiply them, and put my sanctuary among them forever. [27] My dwelling shall be with them; I will be their God, and they shall be my people. [28] Thus the nations shall know that it is I, the LORD, who make Israel holy, when my sanctuary shall be set up among them forever.

CHAPTER 38

First Prophecy against Gog. [1] Thus the word of the LORD came to me:* [2] Son of man, turn toward Gog* [the land of Magog], t the chief prince of Meshech and Tubal, and prophesy against him: [3] Thus says the Lord GOD: See! I am coming at you, Gog, chief prince of Meshech and Tubal. [4] I will lead you forth with all your army, horses and riders all handsomely outfitted, a great horde with bucklers

---

r Ez 34, 23; Jer 23, 5; 33, 15.—s Ps 110, 4.—t Rv 20, 7f.

37, 15-22: The symbolic action of joining two sticks into one signifies the future union of Israel and Judah under one messianic King.

38, 1—39, 20: These three oracles against Gog may refer either to a specific foreign invasion in the future, or to the apocalyptic struggle between good and evil at the end of time. By some they are ascribed to a later author than Ezekiel, who lived after the exile and the return to Palestine.

38, 2: *Gog:* the name is almost certainly a symbolic one taken from that of Gyges, king of Lydia, whether or not the prophet has a specific person in mind. The gloss *Magog* may be an Akkadian expression, *mat-Gog,* "the land of Gog." *Meshech* and *Tubal,* as well as *Gomer* and *Beth-togarmah* (v 6), were countries around the Black Sea, the northernmost countries known to the Hebrews: *the north* (cf also v 15) was the traditional direction from which invasion was expected; cf Jer 1, 13ff.

and shields, all of them carrying swords: [5]Persia, Cush, and Put with them [all with shields and helmets], [6]Gomer with all its troops, Beth-togarmah from the recesses of the north with all its troops, many peoples with you. [7]Prepare yourself, be ready, you and all your horde assembled about you, and be at my disposal. [8]After many days you will be mustered [in the last years you will come] against a nation which has survived the sword, which has been assembled from many peoples [on the mountains of Israel which were long a ruin], which has been brought forth from among the peoples and all of whom now dwell in security. [9]You shall come up like a sudden storm, advancing like a cloud to cover the earth, you and all your troops and the many peoples with you.

[10]Thus says the Lord GOD: At that time thoughts shall arise in your mind, and you shall devise an evil scheme: [11]"I will go up against a land of open villages and attack the peaceful people who are living in security, all of them living without walls, having neither bars nor gates, [12]to plunder and pillage, turning my hand against the ruins that were repeopled and against a people gathered from the nations, a people concerned with cattle and goods, who dwell at the navel of the earth."* [13]Sheba and Dedan, the merchants of Tarshish and all her young lions shall ask you: "Is it for plunder that you have come? Is it for pillage that you have summoned your horde, to carry off silver and gold, to take away cattle and goods, to seize much plunder?"

[17]Thus says the Lord GOD: It is of you that I spoke in ancient times through my servants, the prophets of Israel, who prophesied in those days that I would bring you against them. [18]But on that day, the day when Gog invades the land of Israel, says the Lord GOD, my fury shall be aroused. In my anger [19]and in my jealousy, in my fiery wrath, I swear: On that day there shall be a great shaking upon the land of Israel. [20]Before me shall tremble the fish of the sea and the birds of the air, the beasts of the field and all the reptiles that crawl upon the ground, and all men who are on the land. Mountains

---

38, 12: *Who dwell at the navel of the earth:* the people of Israel (cf v 18; also Ez 5, 5). Many ancient peoples spoke of their own homelands as "the navel," that is, the center of the earth.

shall be overturned, and cliffs shall tumble, and every wall shall fall to the ground. [21]Against him I will summon every terror, says the Lord GOD, every man's sword against his brother. I will hold judgment with him in pestilence and bloodshed; [22]flooding rain and hailstones, fire and brimstone, I will rain upon him, upon his troops, and upon the many peoples with him. [23]I will prove my greatness and holiness and make myself known in the sight of many nations; thus they shall know that I am the LORD.

Second Prophecy against Gog. [14]Therefore prophesy, son of man, and say to Gog: Thus says the Lord GOD: When my people Israel are dwelling in security, will you not bestir yourself [15]and come from your home in the recesses of the north, you and many peoples with you, all mounted on horses, a great horde and a mighty army? [16]You shall come up against my people Israel like a cloud covering the land. In the last days I will bring you against my land, that the nations may know of me, when in their sight I prove my holiness through you, O Gog.

CHAPTER 39

Third Prophecy against Gog. [1]Now, son of man, prophesy against Gog in these words: Thus says the Lord GOD: See! I am coming at you, Gog, chief prince of Meshech and Tubal. [2]I will turn you about, I will urge you on, and I will make you come up from the recesses of the north; I will lead you against the mountains of Israel. [3]Then I will strike the bow from your left hand, and make the arrows drop from your right. [4]Upon the mountains of Israel you shall fall, you and all your troops and the peoples who are with you. To birds of prey of every kind and to the wild beasts I am giving you to be eaten. [5]On the open field you shall fall, for I have decreed it, says the Lord God.

[6]I will send fire upon Magog and upon those who live securely in the coastlands; thus they shall know that I am the LORD. [7]I will make my holy name known among my people Israel; I will no longer allow my holy name to be profaned. Thus the nations shall know that I am the LORD, the Holy One in Israel. [8]Yes, it is coming and shall be fulfilled, says the Lord GOD. This is the day I have decreed.

Ez

⁹Then shall those who live in the cities of Israel go out and burn weapons: [shields and bucklers,] bows and arrows, clubs and lances; for seven years they shall make fires with them. ¹⁰They shall not have to bring in wood from the fields or cut it down in the forests, for they shall make fires with the weapons. Thus they shall plunder those who plundered them and pillage those who pillaged them, says the Lord GOD.

¹¹On that day I will give Gog for his tomb a well-known place in Israel, the Valley of Abarim* east of the sea [it is blocked to travelers]. Gog shall be buried there with all his horde, and it shall be named "Valley of Hamon-gog." ¹²To purify the land, the house of Israel shall need seven months to bury them. ¹³All the people of the land shall bury them and gain renown for it, when I reveal my glory, says the Lord GOD. ¹⁴Men shall be permanently employed to pass through the land burying those who lie unburied, so as to purify the land. For seven months they shall keep searching. ¹⁵When they pass through, should they see a human bone, let them put up a marker beside it, until others have buried it in the Valley of Hamon-gog. ¹⁶[Also the name of the city shall be Hamonah.] Thus the land shall be purified.

¹⁷As for you, son of man, says the Lord GOD, say to birds of every kind and to all the wild beasts: Come together, from all sides gather for the slaughter I am about to provide for you, a great slaughter on the mountains of Israel: you shall have flesh to eat and blood to drink. ¹⁸You shall eat the flesh of warriors and drink the blood of the princes of the land [rams, lambs, and goats, bullocks, fatlings of Bashan, all of them]. ¹⁹From the slaughter which I will provide for you, you shall eat fat until you are filled and drink blood until you are drunk. ²⁰You shall be filled at my table with horses and riders, with warriors and soldiers of every kind, says the Lord GOD.

Israel's Return. ²¹Thus I will display my glory among the nations, and all the nations shall see the judgment I have executed and the hand I have laid upon them. ²²From that day forward the house of Israel shall know that I am the LORD, their God. ²³The nations shall know that because of its sins the house of Israel went into exile; for they transgressed against me, and I hid my face from them and handed them over to their foes, so that all of them fell by the sword. ²⁴According to their uncleanness and their transgressions I dealt with them, hiding my face from them.

²⁵Therefore, thus says the Lord GOD: Now I will restore the fortunes of Jacob and have pity on the whole house of Israel, and I will be jealous for my holy name. ²⁶They shall forget their disgrace and all the times they broke faith with me, when they live in security on their land with no one to frighten them. ²⁷When I bring them back from among the peoples, I will gather them from the lands of their enemies, and will prove my holiness through them in the sight of many nations. ²⁸ ᵘ Thus they shall know that I, the LORD, am their God, since I who exiled them among the nations, will gather them back on their land, not leaving any of them behind. ²⁹No longer will I hide my face from them, for I have poured out my spirit upon the house of Israel, says the Lord GOD.

V: THE NEW ISRAEL*
The New Temple
CHAPTER 40

The Man with a Measure. ¹On the tenth day of the month beginning the twenty-fifth year of our exile, fourteen years after the city was taken, that very day the hand of the LORD came upon me and brought me ²in divine visions to the land of Israel, where he set me down on a very high mountain. On it there seemed to be a city being built before me. ³When he had brought me there, all at once I saw a man whose appearance was that of bronze; he was standing in the gate, holding a linen cord and a measuring rod. ⁴The man said to me, "Son of man, look carefully and listen intently, and pay strict attention to all that I will show you, for you have been

---

u Ez 36, 23.

39, 11: *The Valley of Abarim:* in the Abarim mountains east of the Jordan. *Hamom-gog:* means "the horde of Gog."

40, 1—48, 35: This lengthy vision of the new Israel is dated (Ez 40, 1) April 28, 573 B.C. It is largely concerned with the new temple and the prescriptions to govern it, but other details of the restored commonwealth are included, forming a kind of program for the future. The literary form of the vision has been aptly termed "utopian": it is plain that the prophet did not expect a literal fulfillment of much of what he described. The passage doubtless underwent successive additions, both from the prophet and from later inspired writers.

brought here so that I might show it to you. Tell the house of Israel all that you see." [5] [Then I saw an outer wall that completely surrounded the temple. The man was holding a measuring rod six cubits long, each cubit being a cubit and a handbreadth;* he measured the width and the height of the structure, each of which was found to be one rod.]

The East Gate.* [6] Then he went to the gate which faced the east, climbed its steps, and measured the gate's threshold, which was found to be a rod wide. [7] The cells were a rod long and a rod wide, and the pilasters between the cells measured five cubits. The threshold of the gate adjoining the vestibule of the gate toward the inside measured one rod. [8] He measured the vestibule of the gate, [9] which was eight cubits, and its pilasters, which were two cubits. The vestibule of the gate was toward the inside. [10] The cells of the east gate were three on either side, of equal size, and the pilasters on either side were also of equal size. [11] He measured the gate's entrance, which was ten cubits wide, while the width of the gate's passage itself was thirteen cubits. [12] The border before each of the cells on both sides was one cubit; the cells themselves were six cubits on either side, from opening to opening. [13] He measured the gate from the back wall of one cell to the back wall of the cell on the opposite side: the width was twenty-five cubits. [14] He measured the vestibule, which was twenty-five cubits. The pilasters adjoining the court on either side were six cubits. [15] The length of the gate from the front entrance to the front of the vestibule on the inside was fifty cubits. [16] Within the gateway on both sides there were splayed windows let into the cells [and into their pilasters]; likewise, within

the vestibule on both sides there were windows. The pilasters were decorated with palms.

The Outer Court. [17] Then he brought me to the outer court,* where there were chambers and a pavement. The pavement was laid all around the court, and the chambers, which were on the pavement, were thirty in number. [18] The pavement lay alongside the gates, as wide as the gates were long; this was the lower pavement. [19] He measured the width of the court from the front of the lower gate to the front of the inner gate; it was one hundred cubits between them.

The North Gate. Then he proceeded north, [20] where, on the outer court, there was a gate facing north, whose length and width he measured. [21] Its cells, three on either side, its pilasters, and its vestibule had the same measurements as those of the first gate; it was fifty cubits long and twenty-five cubits wide. [22] Its windows, the windows of its vestibule, and its palm decorations were of the same proportions as those of the gate facing the east. Seven steps led up to it, and its vestibule was toward the inside. [23] The inner court had a gate opposite the north gate, just as at the east gate; he measured one hundred cubits from one gate to the other.

The South Gate. [24] Then he led me south, to where there was a southern gate, whose cells, pilasters, and vestibule he measured; they were the same size as the others. [25] The gate and its vestibule had windows on both sides, like the other windows. It was fifty cubits long and twenty-five cubits wide. [26] It was ascended by seven steps; its vestibule was toward the inside; and it was decorated with palms here and there on its pilasters. [27] The inner court also had a southern gate; from gate to gate he measured one hundred cubits.

Gates of the Inner Court.* [28] Then he brought me to the inner court by the south gate, where he measured the south gate. Its dimensions were the same as the others; [29] its cells, its pilasters, and its vestibule were the same size as the others. The gate and its vestibule had windows on both sides; and it was fifty cubits long and twenty-five cubits wide. [31] But its vestibule was toward the outer court; palms were on its pilasters, and it had a stairway of eight steps. [32] Then he brought me to the gate facing the east, where he measured the

---

40, 5: *A cubit and a handbreadth:* the ordinary cubit consisted of six handbreadths; the great cubit, of seven. In measuring the temple, a rod six great cubits long was used. The ordinary cubit was about one and a half feet, or, more exactly, 17.5 inches; the large cubit, 20.4 inches.

40, 6-16: The east gate, leading into the outer court of the temple, is described more fully than the north and south gates, which, however, were of the same dimensions. On the west side of the outer court there was a large building instead of a gate (Ez 41, 12).

40, 17: *The outer court:* the court outside the temple area proper, which had its own inner court (vv 28-37).

40, 28-37: The gates leading into the inner court of the temple area correspond to the gates leading into the outer court, with the exception that their vestibules are on the outer rather than the inner side. (Verse 30, a dittography of v 29, is omitted.)

Ez

gate, whose dimensions were found to be the same. ³³Its cells, its pilasters, and its vestibule were the same size as the others; the gate and its vestibule had windows on both sides; it was fifty cubits long and twenty-five cubits wide. ³⁴But its vestibule was toward the outer court; palms were on its pilasters here and there, and it had a stairway of eight steps. ³⁵Then he brought me to the north gate, where he measured the dimensions ³⁶of its cells, its pilasters, and its vestibule, and found them the same. The gate and its vestibule had windows on both sides; it was fifty cubits long and twenty-five cubits wide. ³⁷Its vestibule was toward the outer court; palms were on its pilasters here and there, and it had a stairway of eight steps.

Side Rooms. ³⁸There was a chamber opening off the vestibule of the gate, where the holocausts were rinsed. ³⁹In the vestibule of the gate there were two tables on either side, on which were slaughtered the sin offerings and guilt offerings. ⁴⁰Along the wall of the vestibule, but outside, near the entrance of the north gate, were two tables, and on the other side of the vestibule of the gate there were two tables. ⁴¹There were four tables on either side of the gate [eight tables], on which the sacrifices were slaughtered. ⁴²There were four tables for holocausts, made of cut stone, one and a half cubits long, one and a half cubits wide, and one cubit high. ⁴³The ledges, a handbreadth wide, were set on the inside all around, and on them were laid the instruments with which the holocausts were slaughtered. On the tables themselves the flesh was laid. ⁴⁴He then led me to the inner court where there were two chambers, one beside the north gate, facing south, and the other beside the south gate, facing north. ⁴⁵He said to me, "This chamber which faces south is for the priests who have charge of the temple, ⁴⁶and the chamber which faces north is for the priests who have charge of the altar. These are the Zadokites,* the only Levites who may come near to minister to the LORD." ⁴⁷Then he measured the court, which was a hundred cubits long and a hundred cubits wide, a perfect square. The altar stood in front of the temple.

The Temple Building.* ⁴⁸Then he brought me into the vestibule of the temple and measured the pilasters on each side, which

were five cubits. The width of the doorway was fourteen cubits, and the side walls on either side of the door measured three cubits. ⁴⁹The vestibule was twenty cubits wide and twelve cubits deep; ten steps led up to it, and there were columns by the pilasters, one on either side.

CHAPTER 41

¹Then he brought me to the nave and measured the pilasters, which were six cubits thick on either side. ²The width of the entrance was ten cubits, and the walls at either side of it measured five cubits each. He measured the length of the nave, which was found to be forty cubits, while its width was twenty.

³Then he went in beyond and measured the pilasters flanking that entrance, which were two cubits; the width of the entrance was six cubits, and the walls at either side of it extended seven cubits each. ⁴He measured the space beyond the nave, twenty cubits long and twenty cubits wide, and said to me, "This is the holy of holies."*

⁵Then he measured the wall of the temple, which was six cubits thick; the side chambers, which extended all the way around the temple, had a width of four cubits. ⁶There were thirty side chambers built one above the other in three stories, and there were offsets in the outside wall of the temple that enclosed the side chambers; these served as supports, so that there were no supports in the temple wall proper. ⁷There was a broad circular passageway that led upward to the side chambers, for the temple was enclosed all the way around and all the way upward; therefore the temple had a broad way running upward so that one could pass from the lowest to the middle and the highest story. ⁸About the temple was a raised pavement completely enclosing it—the foundations of the side chambers—a full rod of six cubits in extent. ⁹The width of the outside wall which enclosed the side chambers

---

40, 46: *The Zadokites:* descendants of the priestly line of Zadok; cf 2 Sm 15, 24-29; 1 Kgs 1, 32ff; 2, 35.

40, 48—41, 15: The description of Ezekiel's visionary temple closely follows the description of the temple of Solomon (1 Kgs 6).

40, 49—41, 4: *Vestibule . . . nave . . . holy of holies:* the three divisions of the temple building in progressing order of sanctity. The last is called "the inner sanctuary" in 1 Kgs 6.

was five cubits. Between the side chambers of the temple [10] and the chambers of the court was an open space twenty cubits wide going all around the temple. [11] The side chambers had entrances to the open space, one entrance on the north and another on the south. The width of the wall surrounding the open space was five cubits. [12] The building* fronting the free area on the west side was seventy cubits front to back; the wall of the building was five cubits thick all around, and it measured ninety cubits from side to side. [13] He measured the temple, which was one hundred cubits long. The free area, together with the building and its walls, was a hundred cubits in length. [14] The façade of the temple, along with the free area, on the east side, was one hundred cubits wide. [15] He measured the building which lay the length of the free area and behind it, and together with its walls on both sides it was one hundred cubits.

Interior of the Temple. The inner nave and the outer vestibule [16] were paneled with precious wood all around, covered from the ground to the windows. There were splayed windows with trellises about them [facing the threshold]. [17] As high as the lintel of the door, even into the interior part of the temple as well as outside, on every wall on every side in both the inner and outer rooms were carved [18] the figures of cherubim and palmtrees: a palmtree between every two cherubim. Each cherub had two faces: [19] a man's face looking at a palmtree on one side, and a lion's face looking at a palmtree on the other; thus they were figured on every side throughout the whole temple. [20] From the ground to the lintel of the door the cherubim and palmtrees were carved on the walls. [21] The way into the nave was a square doorframe. In front of the holy place was something that looked like [22] a wooden altar,* three cubits in height, two cubits long, and two cubits wide. It had corners, and its base and sides were of wood. He said to me, "This is the table which is before the LORD." [23] The nave had a double door, and also the holy place had [24] a double

door. Each door had two movable leaves; two leaves were on one doorjamb and two on the other. [25] Carved upon them [on the doors of the nave] were cherubim and palmtrees, like those carved on the walls. Before the vestibule outside was a wooden lattice. [26] There were splayed windows [and palmtrees] on both side walls of the vestibule, and the side chambers of the temple. . . .

CHAPTER 42

Other Structures. [1] Then he led me north to the outer court, bringing me to some chambers on the north that lay across the free area and which were also across from the building. [2] Their length was a hundred cubits on the north side, and they were fifty cubits wide. [3] Across the twenty cubits of the inner court and the pavement of the outer court, there were three parallel rows of them on different levels. [4] In front of the chambers, to the inside, was a walk ten cubits broad and a wall of one cubit; but the entrances of the chambers were on the north. [5] The outermost chambers were the lowest, for the system of levels set them at a level lower than the closest chambers and those in between;* [6] for they were in three rows and had no foundations to conform with the foundations of the courts, therefore they were on a lower terrace of the ground than the closest and the middle chambers. [7] On the far side there was a wall running parallel to the chambers along the outer court; its length before these chambers was fifty cubits, [8] for the length of the chambers belonging to the outer court was fifty cubits, but along its entire length the wall measured one hundred cubits. [9] Below these chambers there was the way in from the east, so that one could enter from the outer court [10] where the wall of the court began.

To the south along the side of the free area and the building there were also chambers, [11] before which was a passage. These looked like the chambers to the north, just as long and just as wide, with the same exits and plan and entrances. [12] Below the chambers to the south there was an entrance at the beginning of the way which led to the back wall, by which one could enter from the east. [13] He said to me, "The north and south chambers which border on the free area are the sanctuary chambers; here the priests who draw near to the LORD shall eat the most

---

41, 12: *The building:* the function of this structure lying behind the temple is never specified.

41, 22: *A wooden altar:* the altar of incense, standing in the nave at the entrance to the holy of holies.

42, 5f: The three rows of identical chambers, since they rested on different ground levels, necessarily had roofs on correspondingly different levels.

Ez

sacred meals, and here they shall keep the most sacred offerings: cereal offerings, sin offerings, and guilt offerings; for it is a holy place.* [14] When the priests have once entered, they shall not leave the holy place for the outer court until they have left here the clothing in which they ministered, for it is holy. They shall put on other garments, and then approach the place destined for the people."

Measuring the Outer Court. [15] When he had finished measuring the inner temple area, he brought me out by way of the gate which faces east and measured all the limits of the court. [16] He measured the east side: five hundred cubits by his measuring rod. Then he turned [17] and measured the north side: five hundred cubits by the measuring rod. He turned [18] to the south and measured five hundred cubits by the measuring rod. [19] Then he turned to the west and measured five hundred cubits by the measuring rod. [20] Thus he measured it in the four directions, five hundred cubits long and five hundred cubits wide. It was surrounded by a wall, to separate the sacred from the profane.

Restoration of the Temple

CHAPTER 43

The Return of the Lord. [1] Then he led me to the gate which faces the east, [2] and there I saw the glory of the God of Israel coming from the east. I heard a sound like the roaring of many waters, and the earth shone with his glory. [3] *v* The vision was like that which I had seen when he came to destroy the city, and like that which I had seen by the river Chebar. I fell prone [4] as the glory of the LORD entered the temple by way of the gate which faces the east, [5] but spirit lifted me up and brought me to the inner court. And I saw that the temple was filled with the glory of the LORD. [6] Then I heard someone speaking to me from the temple, while the man stood beside me. [7] The voice said to me: Son of man, this is where my throne shall be, this is where I will set the soles of my feet; here I will dwell among the Israelites forever. Never again shall they and their kings profane my holy name with their harlotries and with the corpses of their kings [their high places]. [8] When they placed their threshold against my threshold* and their doorpost next to mine, so that only a

wall was between us, they profaned my holy name by their abominable deeds; therefore I consumed them in my wrath. [9] From now on they shall put far from me their harlotry and the corpses of their kings, and I will dwell in their midst forever.

The Law of the Temple. [10] As for you, son of man, describe the temple to the house of Israel [that they may be ashamed of their sins], both its measurements and its design; [11] [and if they are ashamed of all that they have done,] make known to them the form and design of the temple, its exits and entrances, all its statutes and laws; write these down for them to see, that they may carefully observe all its laws and statutes. [12] This is the law of the temple: its whole surrounding area on the mountain top shall be most sacred.

The Altar. [13] These were the measurements of the altar* in cubits of one cubit plus a handbreadth. Its base was one cubit high and one cubit deep, with a rim around its edge of one span. The height of the altar itself was as follows: [14] from its base at the bottom up to the lower ledge it was two cubits high, and this ledge was one cubit deep; from the lower to the upper ledge it was four cubits high, and this ledge also was one cubit deep; [15] the hearth of the altar was four cubits high, and extending from the top of the hearth were the four horns of the altar. [16] The hearth was a square: twelve cubits long and twelve cubits wide. [17] The upper ledge was also a square: fourteen cubits long and fourteen cubits wide. The lower ledge, likewise a square, was sixteen cubits long and sixteen cubits wide, with a half-cubit rim surrounding it. And there was a base of one cubit all around. The steps of the altar face the east.

[18] Then he said to me: Son of man, thus says the Lord GOD: These are the statutes for the altar when it is set up for the offering of holocausts upon it and for the

---

v Ez 1, 1.

42, 13: The function of these chambers is explained again in Ez 46, 19f.

43, 8: *They placed their threshold against my threshold:* the preexilic temple and the royal palace belonged to the same complex of buildings, and this physical proximity was reflected in the use made of the temple by kings like Ahaz and Manasseh, who treated it as their private chapel for pagan rites. In the new Israel the temple is free, even physically, from civil jurisdiction; cf Ez 45, 7f.

43, 13: *The altar:* of holocausts, standing in the inner court of the temple area; cf Ez 40, 47.

sprinkling of blood against it. ¹⁹Give a young bull as a sin offering to the priests, the Levites who are of the line of Zadok, who draw near me to minister to me, says the Lord GOD. ²⁰Take some of its blood and put it on the four horns of the altar, and on the four corners of the ledge, and on the rim all around. Thus you shall purify it and make atonement for it. ²¹Then take the bull of the sin offering, which is to be burnt in a designated part of the temple, outside the sanctuary. ²²On the second day present an umblemished he-goat as a sin offering, to purify the altar as was done with the bull. ²³When you have finished the purification, bring an unblemished young bull and an unblemished ram from the flock, ²⁴and present them before the LORD; the priests shall strew salt on them and offer them to the LORD as holocausts. ²⁵Daily for seven days you shall offer a he-goat as a sin offering, and a young bull and a ram from the flock, all unblemished, shall be offered ²⁶for seven days. Thus atonement shall be made for the altar, and it shall be purified and dedicated. ²⁷And when these days are over, from the eighth day on, the priests shall offer your holocausts and peace offerings on the altar. Then I will accept you, says the Lord GOD.

CHAPTER 44

The Closed Gate. ¹Then he brought me back to the outer gate of the sanctuary, facing the east; but it was closed. ²He said to me: This gate is to remain closed; it is not to be opened for anyone to enter by it; since the LORD, the God of Israel, has entered by it, it shall remain closed. ³Only the prince may sit down in it to eat his meal in the presence of the LORD. He must enter by way of the vestibule of the gate, and leave by the same way.*

44, 3: The prince stands at the eastern gate of the inner court while his sacrifice is offered up (Ez 46, 2); he then goes to the vestibule of the outer court, there to partake of his sacrificial meal. The closed outer gate on the eastern side signifies that the Lord has entered the temple permanently, not to depart again.

44, 7ff: In the preexilic temple various menial services had been performed by foreigners; cf Jos 9, 22-27. In the new temple the Levites will perform these services (vv 10-14).

44, 10-14: Levites other than the Zadokite priesthood of Jerusalem had performed priestly functions at the various sanctuaries and high places in Israel and Judah, where the worship of the Lord had often been corrupted with pagan elements. The demotion of the Levites to menial service in the temple was enforced in the actual restoration after the exile, and explains why relatively few Levites were willing to return; cf Ezr 8, 15ff.

The New Law

Admission to the Temple. ⁴Then he brought me by way of the north gate to the façade of the temple, and when I looked I saw the glory of the LORD filling the LORD's temple, and I fell prone. ⁵Then he said to me: Son of man, pay strict attention, look carefully, and listen intently to all that I will tell you about the statutes and laws of the LORD's temple; be attentive in regard to those who are to be admitted to the temple and all those who are to be excluded from the sanctuary. ⁶Say to that rebellious house, the house of Israel: Thus says the Lord GOD: Enough of all these abominations of yours, O house of Israel! ⁷You have admitted foreigners, uncircumcised both in heart and flesh, to my sanctuary to profane it when you offered me food, fat, and blood;* thus you have broken my covenant by all your abominations. ⁸Instead of caring for the service of my temple, you have appointed such as these to serve me in my sanctuary in your stead. ⁹Thus says the Lord GOD: No foreigners, uncircumcised in heart and in flesh, shall ever enter my sanctuary; none of the foreigners who live among the Israelites.

Levites.* ¹⁰But as for the Levites who departed from me when Israel strayed from me to pursue their idols, they shall bear the consequences of their sin. ¹¹They shall serve in my sanctuary as gatekeepers and temple servants; they shall slaughter the holocausts and the sacrifices for the people, and they shall stand before the people to minister for them. ¹²Because they used to minister for them before their idols, and became an occasion of sin to the house of Israel, therefore I have sworn an oath against them, says the Lord GOD: they shall bear the consequences of their sin. ¹³They shall no longer draw near me to serve as my priests, nor shall they touch any of my sacred things, or the most sacred things. Thus they shall bear their disgrace because of all their abominable deeds. ¹⁴But I will set them to the service of the temple, for all its work and for everything that is to be done in it.

Priests. ¹⁵As for the levitical priests, however, the Zadokites who cared for my sanctuary when the Israelites strayed from me, they shall draw near me to minister to me, and they shall stand before me to offer me fat and blood, says the Lord GOD. [16] It is they who shall enter my sanctuary, they who shall approach my table to minister to me, and they who shall carry out my service. [17] Whenever they enter the gates of the inner court, they shall wear linen garments; they shall not put on anything woolen when they minister at the gates of the inner court or within the temple. [18] *w* They shall have linen turbans on their heads and linen drawers on their loins; they shall not gird themselves with anything that causes sweat. [19] *x* When they are to go out to the people in the outer court, they shall take off the garments in which they ministered and leave them in the chambers of the sanctuary, putting on other garments; thus they will not transmit holiness to the people* with their garments.

[20] *y* They shall not shave their heads nor let their hair hang loose, but they shall keep their hair carefully trimmed. [21] *z* No priest shall drink wine when he is to enter the inner court. [22] *a* They shall not take for their wives either widows or divorced women, but only virgins of the race of Israel; however, they may marry women who are the widows of priests. [23] *b* They shall teach my people to distinguish between the sacred and the profane, and make known to them the difference between the clean and the unclean. [24] In capital cases they shall stand as judges, judging them according to my decrees. They shall observe my laws and statutes on all my festivals, and keep my sabbaths holy.

[25] *c* They shall not make themselves unclean by coming near any dead person, unless it be their father, mother, son, daughter, brother, or maiden sister; for these they may make themselves unclean. [26] After a priest has been cleansed, he must wait an additional seven days, [27] and on the day he enters the inner court to minister in the sanctuary, he shall present his sin offering, says the Lord GOD. [28] *d* They shall have no inheritance, for I am their inheritance; you shall give them no property in Israel, for I am their property. [29] *e* They shall eat the cereal offering, the sin offering, and the guilt offering; whatever is under the ban* in Israel shall be theirs. [30] *f* All the choicest first fruits of every kind, and all the best of your offerings of every kind, shall belong to the priests;

likewise the best of your dough you shall give to the priests to bring a blessing down upon your house. [31] *g* The priests shall not eat anything, whether flesh or fowl, that has died of itself or has been killed by wild beasts.

CHAPTER 45

The Sacred Tract. [1] When you apportion the land into inheritances, you shall set apart a sacred tract of land for the LORD, twenty-five thousand cubits long and twenty thousand wide; its whole area shall be sacred. [2] Of this land a square plot, five hundred by five hundred cubits, surrounded by a free space of fifty cubits, shall be assigned to the sanctuary. [3] Also from this sector measure off a strip, twenty-five thousand cubits long and ten thousand wide, within which shall be the sanctuary, the holy of holies. [4] This shall be the sacred part of the land belonging to the priests, the ministers of the sanctuary, who draw near to minister to the LORD; it shall be a place for their homes and pasture land for their cattle. [5] Also there shall be a strip twenty-five thousand cubits long and ten thousand wide as property for the Levites, the ministers of the temple, that they may have cities to live in. [6] As property of the City you shall designate a strip five thousand cubits wide and twenty-five thousand long, parallel to the sacred tract; this shall belong to the whole house of Israel. [7] The prince shall have a section bordering on both sides of the combined sacred tract and City property, extending westward on the western side and eastward on the eastern side, corresponding in length to one of the tribal portions from the western boundary to the eastern boundary [8] of the land. This shall be his property in Israel, so that the princes of Israel will no longer oppress my people, but will leave the land to the house of Israel according to their tribes.

---

w Ex 28, 40. 42; 29, 9; 38, 28; Lv 6, 3.—x Ez 42, 13. 14.—y Lv 21, 5.—z Lv 10, 9.—a Lv 21, 7. 14.—b Dt 17, 9; 19, 17.—c Lv 21, 1ff. 11.—d Nm 18, 20; Dt 18, 1.—e Lv 2, 3. 10; 6, 9. 22; 7, 9; 10, 12; Nm 18, 9; 18, 14.—f Ex 34, 26; Dt 18, 4.—g Lv 22, 8.

44, 19: *Thus they will not transmit holiness to the people:* holiness was thought of as something physical, as though it were communicable, and therefore not to be brought in contact with unconsecrated persons.

44, 29: *Under the ban:* dedicated to the Lord, withdrawn from profane use.

Weights and Measures.* [9]Thus says the Lord GOD: Enough, you princes of Israel! Put away violence and oppression, and do what is right and just! Stop evicting my people! says the Lord GOD. [10] [h] You shall have honest scales, an honest ephah, and an honest liquid measure. [11]The ephah and the liquid measure shall be of the same size: the liquid measure equal to a tenth of a homer, and the ephah equal to a tenth of a homer; by the homer they shall be determined. [12] [i] The shekel shall be twenty gerahs. Twenty shekels, twenty-five shekels, plus fifteen shekels shall be your mina.

Offerings. [13]These are the offerings you shall make: one sixth of an ephah from each homer of wheat, and one sixth of an ephah from each homer of barley. [14]The regulation for oil: for every measure of oil, a tenth of a measure, computed by the kor* of ten liquid measures [or a homer, for ten liquid measures make a homer]. [15]One sheep from the flock for every two hundred from the pasturage of Israel, for sacrifice—holocausts and peace offerings and atonement sacrifices, says the Lord GOD. [16]All the people of the land shall be bound to this offering [for the prince in Israel]. [17]It shall be the duty of the prince to provide the holocausts, cereal offerings, and libations on the feasts, new moons, and sabbaths, on all the festivals of the house of Israel. He shall offer the sin offerings, cereal offerings, holocausts, and peace offerings, to make atonement on behalf of the house of Israel.

The Passover. [18]Thus says the Lord GOD: On the first day of the first month you shall use an unblemished young bull as a sacrifice to purify the sanctuary. [19]Then the priest shall take some of the blood from the sin offering and put it on the doorposts of the temple, on the four corners of the ledge of the altar, and on the doorposts of the gates of the inner court. [20]You shall repeat this on the first day of the seventh month for those who have sinned through inadvertence or ignorance; thus you shall make atonement for the temple. [21] [j] On the fourteenth day of the first month you shall observe the feast of the Passover; for seven days unleavened bread is to be eaten. [22]On that day the prince shall offer on his own behalf, and on behalf of all the people of the land, a bull as a sin offering. [23]On each of the seven days of the feast he shall offer as a holocaust to the LORD seven bulls and seven rams without blemish, and as a sin offering he shall offer one male goat each day. [24]As a cereal offering he shall offer one ephah for each bull and one ephah for each ram; and he shall offer one hin* of oil for each ephah.

The Feast of Booths. [25]On the fifteenth day of the seventh month, the feast day, and for seven days, he shall perform the same rites, making the same sin offerings, the same holocausts, the same cereal offerings and offerings of oil.

CHAPTER 46

Sabbaths. [1]Thus says the Lord GOD: The gate toward the east of the inner court shall remain closed throughout the six working days, but on the sabbath and on the day of the new moon it shall be open. [2]The prince shall enter from outside by way of the vestibule of the gate and remain standing at the doorpost of the gate; then while the priests offer his holocausts and peace offerings, he shall worship at the threshold of the gate and then leave; the gate shall not be closed until evening. [3]The people of the land shall worship before the LORD at the door of this gate on the sabbaths and new moons. [4] [k] The holocausts which the prince presents to the LORD on the sabbath shall consist of six unblemished lambs and an unblemished ram, [5]together with a cereal offering of one ephah for the ram, whatever he pleases for the lambs, and a hin of oil for each ephah. [6] [l] On the day of the new moon he shall provide an unblemished young bull, also six lambs and a ram without blemish, [7]with a cereal offering of one ephah for the bull and one for the ram, for the lambs as much as he has at hand, and for each ephah a hin of oil.

h Lv 19, 15; Dt 25, 13-16; Hos 12, 8; Am 8, 5; Mi 6, 10f.—i
Ex 30, 13; Lv 27, 25; Nm 3, 47; 18, 16.—j Ex 12, 6; Lv 23, 5;
Nm 28, 16.—k Nm 28, 9f.—l Nm 28, 11-15.

45, 9-12: Besides the land monopoly fostered by royal greed and collusion with the wealthy (Mi 2, 2; Is 3, 12-15; 5, 8-10), one grave social evil of preexilic Israel was dishonesty in business; cf Hos 12, 8; Am 8, 5. *Ephah:* a dry measure; *liquid measure:* in Hebrew, a "bath," standardized according to the homer (a dry measure of about 10 bushels, or 80 gallons). In v 12 reference is made to the change in value of the *mina:* before the exile it was valued at 50 shekels, but afterward, in imitation of Babylonian practice, the 60-shekel mina was adopted. The shekel was a unit of weight slightly less than half an ounce. As a monetary unit, the value obviously differed greatly, depending on whether it wa_ a gold or a silver shekel.

45, 14: *Kor:* both a liquid and a dry measure, corresponding to the homer.

45, 24: *Hin:* a sixth part of the liquid measure called a bath.

Ez

Ritual Laws. [8] The prince shall always enter and depart by the vestibule of the gate. [9] *m* When the people of the land enter the presence of the LORD to worship on the festivals, if they enter by the north gate they shall leave by the south gate, and if they enter by the south gate they shall leave by the north gate; no one shall return by the gate through which he has entered, but he shall leave by the opposite gate. [10] The prince shall be in their midst when they enter, and he shall also leave with them. [11] On the feasts and festivals the cereal offering shall be an ephah for a bull, an ephah for a ram, but for the lambs as much as one pleases, and a hin of oil with each ephah. [12] When the prince makes a freewill offering to the LORD, whether holocausts or peace offerings, the eastern gate shall be opened for him, and he shall offer his holocausts or his peace offerings as on the sabbath; then he shall leave, and the gate shall be closed after his departure. [13] *n* He shall offer as a daily holocaust to the LORD an unblemished yearling lamb; this he shall offer every morning. [14] With it every morning he shall provide as a cereal offering one sixth of an ephah, with a third of a hin of oil to moisten the fine flour. This cereal offering to the LORD is mandatory with the established holocaust. [15] *o* The lamb, the cereal offering, and the oil are to be offered every morning as an established holocaust.

The Prince and the Land. [16] Thus says the Lord GOD: If the prince makes a gift of part of his inheritance to any of his sons, it shall belong to his sons; that property is theirs by inheritance. [17] But if he makes a gift of part of his inheritance to one of his servants, it shall belong to the latter only until the year of release,* when it shall revert to the prince. Only the inheritance given to his sons is permanent. [18] The prince shall not seize any part of the inheritance of the people by evicting them from their property. He shall provide an inheritance for his sons from his own property, so that none of my people will be driven from their property.

The Temple Kitchens. [19] Then he brought me by the entrance which is on the side of the gate to the chambers [of the sanctuary, reserved to the priests] which face the north. There, at their west end, I saw a place, [20] concerning which he said to me, "Here the priests cook the guilt offerings and the sin offerings, and bake the cereal offerings, so that they do not have to take them into the outer court at the risk of transmitting holiness to the people." [21] Then he led me into the outer court and had me pass around the four corners of the court, and I saw that in each corner there was another court: [22] in the four corners of the court, minor courts, forty cubits long and thirty wide, all four of them the same size. [23] A wall of stones surrounded each of the four, and hearths were built beneath the stones all the way around. [24] He said to me, "These are the kitchens where temple ministers cook the sacrifices of the people."

CHAPTER 47

The Wonderful Stream. * [1] Then he brought me back to the entrance of the temple, and I saw water flowing out from beneath the threshold of the temple toward the east, for the façade of the temple was toward the east; the water flowed down from the southern side of the temple, south of the altar. *p* [2] He led me outside by the north gate, and around to the outer gate facing the east, where I saw water trickling from the southern side. [3] Then when he had walked off to the east with a measuring cord in his hand, he measured off a thousand cubits and had me wade through the water, which was ankle-deep. [4] He measured off another thousand and once more had me wade through the water, which was now knee-deep. Again he measured off a thousand and had me wade; the water was up to my waist. [5] Once more he measured off a thousand, but there was now a river through which I could not wade; for the water had risen so high it had become a river that could not be crossed except by swimming. [6] He asked me, "Have you seen this, son of man?" Then he brought me to the bank of the river, where he had me sit. [7] Along the bank of the river I saw very many trees on both sides. [8] He said to me, "This water

m Ex 23, 17; 34, 23; Dt 16, 16.—n Ex 29, 38-42; Nm 28, 3-8.—o Ex 29, 42.—p Sir 24, 28f; Jl 4, 18; Zec 13, 1; Rv 22, 1f.

46, 17: *The year of release:* the jubilee year; cf Lv 25, 23-55.
47, 1-12: The wonderful and superabundant stream flowing from the temple, restoring to fertility traditionally arid ground, is symbolic of the return of the conditions of primeval paradise; cf Gn 2, 10-14. Water signifies great blessings, just as dryness signifies a curse; cf Ez 26, 5. 14.

flows into the eastern district down upon the Arabah, and empties into the sea, the salt waters, which it makes fresh. ⁹Wherever the river flows, every sort of living creature that can multiply shall live, and there shall be abundant fish, for wherever this water comes the sea shall be made fresh. ¹⁰Fishermen shall be standing along it from En-gedi to En-eglaim,* spreading their nets there. Its kinds of fish shall be like those of the Great Sea, very numerous. ¹¹Only its marshes and swamps shall not be made fresh; they shall be left for salt. ¹²Along both banks of the river, fruit trees of every kind shall grow; their leaves shall not fade, nor their fruit fail. Every month they shall bear fresh fruit, for they shall be watered by the flow from the sanctuary. Their fruit shall serve for food, and their leaves for medicine.

The New Israel

Boundaries of the Land.* ¹³Thus says the Lord GOD: These are the boundaries within which you shall apportion the land among the twelve tribes of Israel [Joseph having two portions]. ¹⁴All of you shall have a like portion in this land which I swore to give to your fathers, that it might fall to you as your inheritance. ¹⁵ �q This is the boundary of the land on the north side: from the Great Sea in the direction of Hethlon, past Labo of Hamath, to Zedad, ¹⁶Berothah, and Sibraim, along the frontiers of Hamath and Damascus, to Hazar-enon which is on the border of the Hauran. ¹⁷Thus the border shall extend from the sea to Hazar-enon, with the frontier of Hamath and Damacus to the north. This is the northern boundary. ¹⁸The eastern boundary: between the Hauran—toward Damascus—and Gilead on the one side, and the land of Israel on the other side, the Jordan shall form the boundary down to the eastern sea as far as Tamar. This is the eastern boundary. ¹⁹The south-

ern boundary: from Tamar to the waters of Meribath-kadesh, thence to the Wadi of Egypt, and on to the Great Sea. This is the southern boundary. ²⁰The western boundary: the Great Sea forms the boundary up to a point parallel to Labo of Hamath. This is the western boundary.

The Northern Portions. ²¹You shall distribute this land among yourselves according to the tribes of Israel. ²² ʳ You shall allot it as inheritances for yourselves and for the aliens resident in your midst who have bred children among you. The latter shall be to you like native Israelites; along with you they shall receive inheritances among the tribes of Israel. ²³In whatever tribe the alien may be resident, there you shall assign him his inheritance, says the Lord God.

CHAPTER 48

¹This is the list* of the tribes.ˢ Dan: at the northern extremity, adjoining Hamath, all along from the approaches to Hethlon through Labo of Hamath to Hazar-enon, on the northerly border with Damascus, with his possession reaching from the eastern to the western boundary. ²Asher: on the frontier of Dan, from the eastern to the western boundary. ³Naphtali: on the frontier of Asher, from the eastern to the western boundary. ⁴Manasseh: on the frontier of Naphtali, from the eastern to the western boundary. ⁵Ephraim: on the frontier of Manasseh, from the eastern to the western boundary. ⁶Reuben: on the frontier of Ephraim, from the eastern to the western boundary. ⁷Judah: on the frontier of Reuben, from the eastern to the western boundary.

The Sacred Tract. ⁸On the frontier of Judah, from the eastern to the western boundary there shall be the tract which you shall set apart, twenty-five thousand cubits from north to south, and as wide as one of the tribal portions from the eastern to the western boundary. In the center of the tract shall be the sanctuary. ⁹The tract that you set aside for the LORD shall be twenty-five thousand cubits across by twenty thousand north and south. ¹⁰In this sacred tract the priests shall have twenty-five thousand cubits on the north, ten thousand on the west, ten thousand on the east, and twenty-five thousand on the south; and the sanctuary of the LORD shall be in its center. ¹¹The consecrated priests,

---

q Nm 34, 7ff.—r Ex 12, 48; Lv 19, 34; 24, 22; Nm 9, 14; Jos 8, 33.—s Ez 47, 15ff.

47, 10: *From En-gedi to En-eglaim:* the former was about halfway down the western shore of the Dead Sea, the latter may have been at its northern extremity.

47, 13-20: These boundaries of the restored Israel correspond to those of the Davidic kingdom at its fullest extent, the so-called "ideal boundaries" of the promised land; cf Nm 34, 3-12.

48, 1-29: This distribution of the land among the tribes does not correspond to the geographical realities of Palestine. It is a description of the ideal order, like that in Ez 47, 1-12.

Ez

the Zadokites, who fulfilled my service and did not stray along with the Israelites as the Levites did, [12] shall have within this tract of land their own most sacred domain, next to the territory of the Levites. [13] The Levites shall have a territory corresponding to that of the priests, twenty-five thousand cubits by ten thousand. The whole tract shall be twenty-five thousand cubits across and twenty thousand north and south. [14] They may not sell or exchange or alienate this, the best part of the land, for it is sacred to the LORD. [15] The remaining five thousand cubits along the twenty-five-thousand-cubit line are profane land, assigned to the City for dwellings and pasture; the City shall be at their center. [16] These are the dimensions of the City: the north side, forty-five hundred cubits; the south side, forty-five hundred cubits; the east side, forty-five hundred cubits; and the west side, forty-five hundred cubits. [17] The pasture lands of the City shall extend north two hundred and fifty cubits, south two hundred and fifty cubits, east two hundred and fifty cubits, and west two hundred and fifty cubits. [18] There shall remain an area along the sacred tract, ten thousand cubits to the east and ten thousand to the west, whose produce shall provide food for the workers of the City. [19] The workers in the City shall be taken from all the tribes of Israel. [20] The entire tract shall be twenty-five thousand by twenty-five thousand cubits; as a perfect square you shall set apart the sacred tract together with the City property. [21] The remainder shall belong to the prince: the land on both sides of the sacred tract and the City property, extending along the twenty-five-thousand-cubit line eastward to the eastern boundary, and westward along the twenty-five-thousand-cubit line to the western boundary, a territory parallel with the tribal portions for the prince. The sacred tract and the sanctuary of the temple shall be in the middle. [22] Thus, except for the property of the Levites and the City property, which lie in the midst of the prince's property, the territory between the portions of Judah and of Benjamin shall belong to the prince.

The Southern Portions. [23] These are the remaining tribes. Benjamin: from the eastern to the western boundary. [24] Simeon: on the frontier of Benjamin, from the eastern to the western boundary. [25] Issachar: on the frontier of Simeon, from the eastern to the western boundary. [26] Zebulun: on the frontier of Issachar, from the eastern to the western boundary. [27] Gad: on the frontier of Zebulun, from the eastern to the western boundary. [28] Along the frontier of Gad shall be the southern boundary, which shall extend from Tamar to the waters of Meribath-kadesh, and from there to the Wadi of Egypt, and on to the Great Sea. [29] Such is the land which you shall apportion as inheritances among the tribes of Israel, and these are their portions, says the Lord GOD.

The Gates of the City. [30] These are the exits of the City, the gates of which are named after the tribes of Israel. On the north side, measuring forty-five hundred cubits, [31] there shall be three gates: the gate of Reuben, the gate of Judah, and the gate of Levi. [32] On the east side, measuring forty-five hundred cubits, there shall be three gates: the gate of Joseph, the gate of Benjamin, and the gate of Dan. [33] On the south side, measuring forty-five hundred cubits, there shall be three gates: the gate of Simeon, the gate of Issachar, and the gate of Zebulun. [34] On the west side, measuring forty-five hundred cubits, there shall be three gates: the gate of Gad, the gate of Asher, and the gate of Naphtali. [35] The perimeter of the City is eighteen thousand cubits. The name of the City shall henceforth be "The LORD is here."

THE BOOK OF DANIEL

This Book takes its name, not from the author, who is actually unknown, but from its hero, a young Jew taken early to Babylon, where he lived at least until 538 B.C. Strictly speaking, the book does not belong to the prophetic writings but rather to a distinctive type of literature known as "apocalyptic," of which it is an early specimen. Apocalyptic writing enjoyed its greatest popularity from 200 B.C. to 100 A.D., a time of distress and persecution for Jews, and later, for Christians. Though subsequent in time to the prophetic, apocalyptic literature has its roots in the teaching of the prophets, who often pointed ahead to the day of the Lord, the consummation of history. For both prophet and apocalyptist Yahweh was the Lord of history, and he would ultimately vindicate his people.

This work was composed during the bitter persecution carried on by Antiochus IV Epiphanes (167-164) and was written to strengthen and comfort the Jewish people in their ordeal.

The Book contains stories originating in and transmitted by popular traditions which tell of the trials and triumphs of the wise Daniel and his three companions. The moral is that men of faith can resist temptation and conquer adversity. The characters are not purely legendary but rest on older historical tradition. What is more important than the question of historicity, and closer to the intention of the author, is the fact that a persecuted Jew of the second century B.C. would quickly see the application of these stories to his own plight.

There follows a series of visions promising deliverance and glory to the Jews in the days to come. The great nations of the ancient world have risen in vain against Yahweh; his kingdom shall overthrow existing powers and last forever. Under this apocalyptic imagery are contained some of the best elements of prophetic teaching: the insistence on right conduct, the divine control over events, the certainty that the kingdom of God will ultimately triumph. The arrival of the kingdom is a central theme of the synoptic gospels, and Jesus, in calling himself the "Son of Man," reminds us that he fulfills the destiny of this mysterious figure in the seventh chapter of Daniel.

The added episodes of Susanna, Bel, and the Dragon, found only in the Greek version, are edifying short stories with a didactic purpose.

These three sections constitute the divisions of the Book of Daniel: I. Daniel and the Kings of Babylon (1, 1—6, 29). II. Daniel's Visions (7, 1—12, 13). III. Appendix (13, 1—14, 42).

I: DANIEL AND THE KINGS OF BABYLON

CHAPTER 1

The Food Test. [1] In the third year of the reign of Jehoiakim, king of Judah, King Nebuchadnezzar of Babylon came and laid siege to Jerusalem.[a] [2][b] The Lord handed over to him Jehoiakim, king of Judah, and some of the vessels of the temple of God, which he carried off to the land of Shinar,* and placed in the temple treasury of his god.

[3] The king told Ashpenaz, his chief chamberlain, to bring in some of the Israelites of royal blood and of the nobility, [4] young men without any defect, handsome, intelligent and wise, quick to learn, and prudent in judgment, such as could take their place in the king's palace; they were to be taught the language and literature of the Chaldeans; [5] after three years' training they were to enter the king's service. The king allotted them a daily portion of food and wine from the royal table. [6] Among these were men of Judah: Daniel, Hananiah, Mishael, and Azariah. [7] The chief chamberlain changed their names: Daniel to Belteshazzar, Hananiah to Shadrach, Mishael to Meshach, and Azariah to Abednego.*

[8] But Daniel was resolved not to defile himself with the king's food or wine; so he begged the chief chamberlain to spare him this defilement.* [9] Though God had given

---

a 2 Kgs 24, 1; 2 Chr 36, 6; Jer 25, 1.—b Dn 5, 2; Gn 10, 10; 2 Kgs 24, 2; 2 Chr 36, 7.

1, 2: Shinar: ancient name for Babylonia, a deliberate archaism in this text; cf Gn 10, 10; 11, 2.
1, 7: The young men are given Babylonian names as a sign of their adoption by the king.
1, 8: *This defilement:* the bread, meat, and wine of the Gentiles, which were unclean (Hos 9, 3; Tb 1, 12; Jdt 10, 5; 12, 1f) because they might have been offered to idols or prepared over firewood taken from a sacred grove. Only raw vegetables and water were safe from this danger (v 12).

Daniel the favor and sympathy of the chief chamberlain, [10] he nevertheless said to Daniel, "I am afraid of my lord the king; it is he who allotted your food and drink. If he sees that you look wretched by comparison with the other young men of your age, you will endanger my life with the king." [11] Then Daniel said to the steward whom the chief chamberlain had put in charge of Daniel, Hananiah, Mishael, and Azariah, [12] "Please test your servants for ten days. Give us vegetables to eat and water to drink. [13] Then see how we look in comparison with the other young men who eat from the royal table, and treat your servants according to what you see." [14] He acceded to this request, and tested them for ten days; [15] after ten days they looked healthier and better fed than any of the young men who ate from the royal table. [16] So the steward continued to take away the food and wine they were to receive, and gave them vegetables.

[17] To these four young men God gave knowledge and proficiency in all literature and science, and to Daniel the understanding of all visions and dreams. [18] At the end of the time the king had specified for their preparation, the chief chamberlain brought them before Nebuchadnezzar. [19] When the king had spoken with all of them, none was found equal to Daniel, Hananiah, Mishael, and Azariah; and so they entered the king's service. [20] In any question of wisdom or prudence which the king put to them, he found them ten times better than all the magicians and enchanters in his kingdom. [21] c Daniel remained there until the first year of King Cyrus.*

CHAPTER 2

The King's Dream.* [1] In the second year of his reign, King Nebuchadnezzar had a dream which left his spirit no rest and robbed him of his sleep. [2] So he ordered that the magicians, enchanters, sorcerers, and Chaldeans* be summoned to interpret the dream for him. When they came and presented themselves to the king, [3] he said to them, "I had a dream which will allow my spirit no rest until I know what it means." [4] The Chaldeans answered the king [Aramaic]:* "O king, live forever! Tell your servants the dream and we will give its meaning." [5] The king answered the Chaldeans, "This is what I have decided:

unless you tell me the dream and its meaning, you shall be cut to pieces and your houses destroyed. [6] But if you tell me the dream and its meaning, you shall receive from me gifts and presents and great honors. Now tell me the dream and its meaning."

[7] Again they answered, "Let the king tell his servants the dream and we will give its meaning." [8] But the king replied: "I know for certain that you are bargaining for time, since you know what I have decided. [9] If you do not tell me the dream, there can be but one decree for you. You have framed a false and deceitful interpretation to present me with till the crisis is past. Tell me the dream, therefore, that I may be sure that you can also give its correct interpretation."

[10] The Chaldeans answered the king: "There is not a man on earth who can do what you ask, O king; never has any king, however great and mighty, asked such a thing of any magician, enchanter, or Chaldean. [11] What you demand, O king, is too difficult; there is no one who can tell it to the king except the gods who do not dwell among men." [12] At this the king became violently angry and ordered all the wise men of Babylon to be put to death. [13] When the decree was issued that the wise men should be slain, Daniel and his companions were also sought out.

[14] Then Daniel prudently took counsel with Arioch, the captain of the king's guard, who had set out to kill the wise men of Babylon: [15] "O officer of the king," he asked, "what is the reason for this harsh order from the king?" When Arioch told him, [16] Daniel went and·asked for time from the king, that he might give him the interpretation.

[17] Daniel went home and informed his companions Hananiah, Mishael, and Azariah, [18] that they might implore the mercy of the God of heaven in regard to

---

c Dn 6, 28.

1, 21: *The first year of King Cyrus:* the year of this Persian king's conquest of Babylon, 539/8 B.C.

2, 1-49: The chronology of v 1 is in conflict with that of Dn 1, 5. 18, and in v 25 Daniel appears to be introduced to the king for the first time. It seems that the story of this chapter was originally entirely independent of chapter 1, and later retouched slightly to fit its present setting.

2, 2: *Chaldeans:* here probably astrologers, who were so associated with the Chaldeans in the Hebrew mind that in the later language they are sometimes simply called by the name of that people.

2, 4: *Aramaic:* from Dn 2, 4 to 7, 28 the text of Daniel is in Aramaic, not Hebrew, as indicated by this gloss.

this mystery, so that Daniel and his companions might not perish with the rest of the wise men of Babylon. ¹⁹During the night the mystery was revealed to Daniel in a vision, and he blessed the God of heaven:

²⁰ "Blessed be the name of God forever and ever,
   for wisdom and power are his.
²¹ He causes the changes of the times and seasons,
   makes kings and unmakes them.
   He gives wisdom to the wise
   and knowledge to those who understand.
²² He reveals deep and hidden things
   and knows what is in the darkness,
   for the light dwells with him. *d*
²³ To you, O God of my fathers,
   I give thanks and praise,
   because you have given me wisdom and power.
   Now you have shown me what we asked of you,
   you have made known to us the king's dream."

²⁴ So Daniel went to Arioch, whom the king had appointed to destroy the wise men of Babylon, and said to him, "Do not put the wise men of Babylon to death. Bring me before the king, and I will tell him the interpretation of the dream." Arioch quickly brought Daniel to the king and said, ²⁵ "I have found a man among the Judean captives who can give the interpretation to the king." ²⁶The king asked Daniel, whose name was Belteshazzar, "Can you tell me the dream that I had, and its meaning?" ²⁷In the king's presence Daniel made this reply:

"The mystery about which the king has inquired, the wise men, enchanters, magicians, and astrologers could not explain to the king. ²⁸But there is a God in heaven who reveals mysteries, and he has shown King Nebuchadnezzar what is to happen in days to come; this was the dream you saw as you lay in bed. ²⁹To you in your bed there came thoughts about what should happen in the future, and he who reveals mysteries showed you what is to be. ³⁰To me also this mystery has been revealed; not that I am wiser than any other living person, but in order that its meaning may be made known to the king, that you may understand the thoughts in your own mind.

³¹ "In your vision, O king, you saw a statue, very large and exceedingly bright, terrifying in appearance as it stood before you. ³²The head of the statue was pure gold, its chest and arms were silver, its belly and thighs bronze, ³³the legs iron, its feet partly iron and partly tile.* ³⁴While you looked at the statue, a stone which was hewn from a mountain without a hand being put to it, struck its iron and tile feet, breaking them in pieces. ³⁵The iron, tile, bronze, silver, and gold all crumbled at once, fine as the chaff on the threshing floor in summer, and the wind blew them away without leaving a trace. But the stone that struck the statue became a great mountain and filled the whole earth.

³⁶ * "This was the dream; the interpretation we shall also give in the king's presence. ³⁷You, O king, are the king of kings; to you the God of heaven has given dominion and strength, power and glory; ³⁸men, wild beasts, and birds of the air, wherever they may dwell, he has handed over to you, making you ruler over them all; you are the head of gold. ³⁹Another kingdom shall take your place, inferior to yours, then a third kingdom, of bronze, which shall rule over the whole earth. ⁴⁰There shall be a fourth kingdom, strong as iron; it shall break in pieces and subdue all these others, just as iron breaks in pieces and crushes everything else. ⁴¹The feet and toes you saw, partly of potter's tile and partly of iron, mean that it shall be a divided kingdom, but yet have some of the hardness of iron. As you saw the iron mixed with clay tile, ⁴²and the toes partly iron and partly tile, the kingdom shall be partly strong and partly fragile. ⁴³The iron mixed with clay tile means that they shall seal their alliances by intermarriage, but they shall not stay united, any more than iron mixes with clay. ⁴⁴ *e* In the lifetime of

---

d Jn 1, 9; 8, 12; 1 Cor 4, 5; 1 Jn 1, 6.—e Mt 21, 44; Lk 20, 18.

2, 33: *Partly tile:* terra cotta tile was much in use among the Babylonians for decoration and for actual construction.

2, 36-45: The four successive kingdoms in this apocalyptic perspective are the Babylonian (gold), the Median (silver), the Persian (bronze), and the Hellenistic (iron). The last, after Alexander's death, was divided among his generals (vv 41f). The two resulting kingdoms, which most affected the Jews, were the dynasty of the Ptolemies in Egypt and that of the Seleucids in Syria, who tried in vain, by war and through intermarriage, to restore the unity of Alexander's empire (v 43). The stone hewn from the mountain is the messianic kingdom awaited by the Jews (vv 44f). Our Lord made this image personal to himself; cf Lk 20, 17f.

Dn

those kings the God of heaven will set up a kingdom that shall never be destroyed or delivered up to another people; rather, it shall break in pieces all these kingdoms and put an end to them, and it shall stand forever. 45 That is the meaning of the stone you saw hewn from the mountain without a hand being put to it, which broke in pieces the tile, iron, bronze, silver, and gold. The great God has revealed to the king what shall be in the future; this is exactly what you dreamed, and its meaning is sure."

46 Then King Nebuchadnezzar fell down and worshiped Daniel and ordered sacrifice and incense offered to him. 47 To Daniel the king said, "Truly your God is the God of gods and Lord of kings and a revealer of mysteries; that is why you were able to reveal this mystery." 48 He advanced Daniel to a high post, gave him many generous presents, made him ruler of the whole province of Babylon and chief prefect over all the wise men of Babylon. 49 At Daniel's request the king made Shadrach, Meshach, and Abednego administrators of the province of Babylon, while Daniel himself remained at the king's court.

CHAPTER 3

The Fiery Furnace. 1 King Nebuchadnezzar had a golden statue made, sixty cubits high and six cubits wide, which he set up in the plain of Dura* in the province of Babylon. 2 He then ordered the satraps,* prefects, and governors, the counselors, treasurers, judges, magistrates and all the officials of the provinces to be summoned to the dedication of the statue which he had set up. 3 The satraps, prefects, and governors, the counselors, treasurers, judges, and magistrates and all the officials of the provinces, all these came together for the dedication and stood before the statue which King Nebuchadnezzar had set up. 4 A herald cried out: "Nations and peoples of every language, when you hear the sound of the trumpet, flute, lyre, harp, psaltery,* bagpipe, and all the other musical instruments, 5 you are ordered to fall down and worship the golden statue which King Nebuchadnezzar has set up. 6 Whoever does not fall down and worship shall be instantly cast into a white-hot furnace."* 7 Therefore, as soon as they heard the sound of the trumpet, flute, lyre,

harp, psaltery, bagpipe, and all the other musical instruments, the nations and peoples of every language all fell down and worshiped the golden statue which King Nebuchadnezzar had set up.

8 At that point, some of the Chaldeans came and accused the Jews 9 to King Nebuchadnezzar: "O king, live forever! 10 O king, you issued a decree that everyone who heard the sound of the trumpet, flute, lyre, harp, psaltery, bagpipe, and all the other musical instruments should fall down and worship the golden statue; 11 whoever did not was to be cast into a white-hot furnace. 12 There are certain Jews whom you have made administrators of the province of Babylon: Shadrach, Meshach, Abednego; these men, O king, have paid no attention to you; they will not serve your god or worship the golden statue which you set up."

13 Nebuchadnezzar flew into a rage and sent for Shadrach, Meshach, and Abednego, who were promptly brought before the king. 14 King Nebuchadnezzar questioned them: "Is it true, Shadrach, Meshach, and Abednego, that you will not serve my god, or worship the golden statue that I set up? 15 Be ready now to fall down and worship the statue I had made, whenever you hear the sound of the trumpet, flute, lyre, harp, psaltery, bagpipe, and all the other musical instruments; otherwise, you shall be instantly cast into the white-hot furnace; and who is the God that can deliver you out of my hands?" 16 Shadrach, Meshach, and Abednego answered King Nebuchadnezzar, "There is no need for us to defend ourselves before you in this matter. 17 If our God, whom we serve, can save us* from the white-hot furnace and from your hands, O king, may he save us! 18 But even if he will not, know, O king, that we will not serve your god or worship the golden statue which you set up."

19 Nebuchadnezzar's face became livid with utter rage against Shadrach, Meshach,

---

3, 1: *Dura:* several places in Babylonia bore this name. Probably the present reference is to one a few miles south of Babylon. Colossi of the type mentioned here were not uncommon in antiquity; a cubit was seventeen and a half inches.

3, 2: *Satraps:* the Persian major governors.

3, 4: *Psaltery:* a harplike instrument.

3, 6: Death by fire was not unknown as a punishment in Babylonia; cf Jer 29, 22.

3, 17: *If our God . . . can save us:* the youths do not question the efficacy of the divine power, but whether it will be exercised (v 18).

and Abednego. He ordered the furnace to be heated seven times more than usual [20] and had some of the strongest men in his army bind Shadrach, Meshach, and Abednego and cast them into the white-hot furnace. [21] They were bound and cast into the white-hot furnace with their coats, hats, shoes and other garments, [22] for the king's order was urgent. So huge a fire was kindled in the furnace that the flames devoured the men who threw Shadrach, Meshach, and Abednego into it. [23] But these three fell, bound, into the midst of the white-hot furnace.

[24] * They walked about in the flames, singing to God and blessing the Lord. [25] In the fire Azariah stood up and prayed aloud:

[26] "Blessed are you, and praiseworthy,
   O Lord, the God of our fathers,
   and glorious forever is your name.
[27] For you are just in all you have done;
   all your deeds are faultless, all your
      ways right,
   and all your judgments proper.
[28] You have executed proper judgments
   in all that you have brought upon us
   and upon Jerusalem, the holy city of
      our fathers.
   By a proper judgment you have done all
      this
   because of our sins;
[29] For we have sinned and transgressed
      by departing from you,
   and we have done every kind of evil.
[30] Your commandments we have not
      heeded or observed,
   nor have we done as you ordered us
      for our good.
[31] Therefore all you have brought upon
      us,
   all you have done to us,
   you have done by a proper judgment.
[32] You have handed us over to our
      enemies,
   lawless and hateful rebels;
   to an unjust king, the worst in all the
      world.
[33] Now we cannot open our mouths;
   we, your servants, who revere you,
   have become a shame and a reproach.
[34] For your name's sake, do not deliver us
      up forever,

or make void your covenant.
[35] Do not take away your mercy from us,
   for the sake of Abraham, your be-
      loved,
   Isaac your servant, and Israel your
      holy one,
[36] To whom you promised to multiply
      their offspring
   like the stars of heaven,
   or the sand on the shore of the sea.
[37] For we are reduced, O Lord, beyond
      any other nation,
   brought low everywhere in the world
      this day
   because of our sins.
[38] We have in our day no prince, prophet,
      or leader,
   no holocaust, sacrifice, oblation, or
      incense,
   no place to offer first fruits, to find
      favor with you.
[39] But with contrite heart and humble
      spirit
   let us be received;
[40] As though it were holocausts of rams
      and bullocks,
   or thousands of fat lambs,
   So let our sacrifice be in your presence
      today
   as we follow you unreservedly;
   for those who trust in you cannot be
      put to shame.
[41] And now we follow you with our whole
      heart,
   we fear you and we pray to you.
[42] Do not let us be put to shame,
   but deal with us in your kindness and
      great mercy.
[43] Deliver us by your wonders,
   and bring glory to your name, O
      Lord:
[44] Let all those be routed
   who inflict evils on your servants;
   Let them be shamed and powerless,
   and their strength broken;
[45] Let them know that you alone are the
      Lord God,
   glorious over the whole world."

[46] Now the king's men who had thrown them in continued to stoke the furnace with brimstone, pitch, tow, and faggots. [47] The flames rose forty-nine cubits above the furnace, [48] and spread out, burning the Chaldeans nearby. [49] But the angel of the Lord went down into the furnace with Azariah and his companions, drove the

---

3, 24-90: These verses are inspired additions to the Aramaic text of Daniel, translated from the Greek form of the book. They were originally composed in Hebrew or Aramaic, which has not been preserved. The church has always regarded them as part of the canonical Scriptures.

fiery flames out of the furnace, ⁵⁰and
made the inside of the furnace as though a
dew-laden breeze were blowing through it.
The fire in no way touched them or caused
them pain or harm. ⁵¹Then these three in
the furnace with one voice sang, glorifying
and blessing God:

⁵² "Blessed are you, O Lord, the God of
our fathers,
praiseworthy and exalted above all
forever;
And blessed is your holy and glorious
name,
praiseworthy and exalted above all
for all ages.
⁵³ Blessed are you in the temple of your
holy glory,
praiseworthy and glorious above all
forever.
⁵⁴ Blessed are you on the throne of your
kingdom,
praiseworthy and exalted above all
forever.
⁵⁵ Blessed are you who look into the depths
from your throne upon the cherubim,
praiseworthy and exalted above all
forever.
⁵⁶ Blessed are you in the firmament of
heaven,
praiseworthy and glorious forever.
⁵⁷ Bless the Lord, all you works of the
Lord,
praise and exalt him above all forever.
⁵⁸ Angels of the Lord, bless the Lord,
praise and exalt him above all for-
ever.
⁵⁹ You heavens, bless the Lord,
praise and exalt him above all forever.^f
⁶⁰ All you waters above the heavens, bless
the Lord,
praise and exalt him above all forever.
⁶¹ All you hosts of the Lord, bless the
Lord;
praise and exalt him above all forever.
⁶² Sun and moon, bless the Lord;
praise and exalt him above all forever.
⁶³ Stars of heaven, bless the Lord;
praise and exalt him above all forever.
⁶⁴ Every shower and dew, bless the Lord;
praise and exalt him above all for-
ever.

⁶⁵ All you winds, bless the Lord;
praise and exalt him above all forever.
⁶⁶ Fire and heat, bless the Lord;
praise and exalt him above all forever.
⁶⁷ [Cold and chill, bless the Lord;
praise and exalt him above all forever.
⁶⁸ Dew and rain, bless the Lord;
praise and exalt him above all forever.]
⁶⁹ Frost and chill, bless the Lord;
praise and exalt him above all forever.
⁷⁰ Ice and snow, bless the Lord;
praise and exalt him above all forever.
⁷¹ Nights and days, bless the Lord;
praise and exalt him above all forever.
⁷² Light and darkness, bless the Lord;
praise and exalt him above all for-
ever.
⁷³ Lightnings and clouds, bless the Lord;
praise and exalt him above all for-
ever.
⁷⁴ Let the earth bless the Lord,
praise and exalt him above all forever.
⁷⁵ Mountains and hills, bless the Lord;
praise and exalt him above all for-
ever.
⁷⁶ Everything growing from the earth,
bless the Lord;
praise and exalt him above all forever.
⁷⁷ You springs, bless the Lord;
praise and exalt him above all forever.
⁷⁸ Seas and rivers, bless the Lord;
praise and exalt him above all forever.
⁷⁹ You dolphins and all water creatures,
bless the Lord;
praise and exalt him above all forever.
⁸⁰ All you birds of the air, bless the Lord;
praise and exalt him above all for-
ever.
⁸¹ All you beasts, wild and tame, bless the
Lord;
praise and exalt him above all forever.
⁸² You sons of men, bless the Lord;

f 59f: Ps 148, 4.

praise and exalt him above all forever.
83 O Israel, bless the Lord;
praise and exalt him above all forever.
84 Priests of the Lord, bless the Lord;
praise and exalt him above all forever.
85 Servants of the Lord, bless the Lord;
praise and exalt him above all forever.
86 Spirits and souls of the just, bless the
Lord;
praise and exalt him above all forever.
87 Holy men of humble heart, bless the
Lord;
praise and exalt him above all forever.
88 Hananiah Azariah, Mishael, bless the
Lord;
praise and exalt him above all forever.
For he has delivered us from the nether
world,
and saved us from the power of
death;
He has freed us from the raging flame
and delivered us from the fire.
89 Give thanks to the Lord, for he is good,
for his mercy endures forever.
90 Bless the God of gods, all you who fear
the Lord;
praise him and give him thanks,
because his mercy endures forever."

Hearing them sing, and astonished at seeing them alive, 91 King Nebuchadnezzar rose in haste and asked his nobles, "Did we not cast three men bound into the fire?" "Assuredly, O king," they answered. 92 "But," he replied, "I see four men unfettered and unhurt, walking in the fire, and the fourth looks like a son of God."* 93 Then Nebuchadnezzar came to

g Dn 4, 31; 7, 14.—h Gn 41, 38.

3, 92: *A son of God:* an angel; cf Jb 1, 6.
3, 98—4, 34: This section has the form of a letter written by Nebuchadnezzar to his subjects.
3, 99: *The most high God:* the Jews, especially in the diaspora, used this title to distinguish their God from those of the pagans. On the lips of a polytheist (so also in v 93) it was merely the title of another god. It was an ancient divine name used in Canaan; cf Gn 14, 18.
4, 5: *After the name of my god:* Belteshazzar, the Babylonian name given to Daniel at the king's orders (Dn 1, 7), is Balatsu-ussur, "protect his life." In the king's intention, this would be an abbreviation for *Bel-balatsu-ussur.* It would thus include an appeal to the god Bel, originally the name of the city god of Nippur, and later identified with Marduk, the chief god of Babylon. Daniel's use of the name would refer the prayer rather to the true God.

the opening of the white-hot furnace and called to Shadrach, Meshach, and Abednego: "Servants of the most high God, come out." Thereupon Shadrach, Meshach, and Abednego came out of the fire. 94 When the satraps, prefects, governors, and nobles of the king came together, they saw that the fire had had no power over the bodies of these men; not a hair of their heads had been singed, nor were their garments altered; there was not even a smell of fire about them. 95 Nebuchadnezzar exclaimed, "Blessed be the God of Shadrach, Meshach, and Abednego, who sent his angel to deliver the servants that trusted in him; they disobeyed the royal command and yielded their bodies rather than serve or worship any god except their own God. 96 Therefore I decree for nations and peoples of every language that whoever blasphemes the God of Shadrach, Meshach, and Abednego shall be cut to pieces and his house destroyed. For there is no other God who can rescue like this." 97 Then the king promoted Shadrach, Meshach, and Abednego in the province of Babylon.

Vision of the Great Tree.* 98 King Nebuchadnezzar to the nations and peoples of every language, wherever they dwell on earth: abundant peace! 99 It has seemed good to me to publish the signs and wonders which the most high God* has accomplished in my regard.

100 How great are his signs, how mighty
his wonders;
his kingdom is an everlasting kingdom,
and his dominion endures through all
generations. g

CHAPTER 4

1 I, Nebuchadnezzar, was at home in my palace, content and prosperous. 2 I had a terrifying dream as I lay in bed, and the images and the visions of my mind frightened me. 3 So I issued a decree that all the wise men of Babylon should be brought before me to give the interpretation of the dream. 4 When the magicians, enchanters, Chaldeans, and astrologers had come in, I related the dream before them; but none of them could tell me its meaning. 5 h Finally there came before me Daniel, whose name is Belteshazzar after the name of my god,* and in whom is the spirit of the holy

God. I repeated the dream to him: ⁶"Belteshazzar, chief of the magicians, I know that the spirit of the holy God is in you and no mystery is too difficult for you; tell me the meaning of the visions that I saw in my dream.

⁷"These were the visions I saw while in bed: I saw a tree of great height at the center of the world. ⁸It was large and strong, with its top touching the heavens, and it could be seen to the ends of the earth. ⁹Its leaves were beautiful and its fruit abundant, providing food for all. Under it the wild beasts found shade, in its branches the birds of the air nested; all men ate of it. ¹⁰In the vision I saw while in bed, a holy sentinel* came down from heaven, ¹¹and cried out:

* " 'Cut down the tree and lop off its branches,
     strip off its leaves and scatter its fruit;
     let the beasts flee its shade, and the
       birds its branches.
¹² But leave in the earth its stump and roots,
     fettered with iron and bronze, in the
       grass of the field.
     Let him be bathed with the dew of
       heaven;
     his lot be to eat, among beasts, the
       grass of the earth.
¹³ Let his mind be changed from the
       human;
     let him be given the sense of a beast,
       till seven years pass over him.
¹⁴ By decree of the sentinels is this decided,
     by order of the holy ones, this sentence;
     That all who live may know
       that the Most High rules over the
       kingdom of men:
     He can give it to whom he will,
       or set over it the lowliest of men.'ⁱ

¹⁵"This is the dream that I, King Nebuchadnezzar, had. Now, Belteshazzar, tell me its meaning. Although none of the wise men in my kingdom can tell me the meaning, you can, because the spirit of the holy God is in you."

¹⁶Then Daniel, whose name was Belteshazzar, was appalled for a while, terrified by his thoughts. "Belteshazzar," the king said to him, "let not the dream or its meaning terrify you." ¹⁷"My lord," Belteshazzar replied, "this dream should be for your enemies, and its meaning for your foes.* The large, strong tree that you saw, with its top touching the heavens, that could be seen by the whole earth, ¹⁸which had beautiful foliage and abundant fruit, providing food for all, under which the wild beasts lived, and in whose branches the birds of the air dwelt—¹⁹you are that tree, O king, large and strong! Your majesty has become so great as to touch the heavens, and your rule extends over the whole earth. ²⁰As for the king's vision of a holy sentinel that came down from heaven and proclaimed: 'Cut down the tree and destroy it, but leave in the earth its stump and roots, fettered with iron and bronze in the grass of the field; let him be bathed with the dew of heaven; and let his lot be among wild beasts till seven years pass over him'—²¹this is its meaning, O king: this is the sentence which the Most High has passed upon my lord king: ²² ʲ You shall be cast out from among men and dwell with wild beasts; you shall be given grass to eat like an ox and be bathed with the dew of heaven;* seven years shall pass over you, until you know that the Most High rules over the kingdom of men and gives it to whom he will. ²³The command that the stump and roots of the tree are to be left means that your kingdom shall be preserved for you, once you have learned it is heaven that rules. ²⁴ ᵏ Therefore, O king, take my advice; atone for your sins by good deeds, and for your misdeeds by kindness to the poor; then your prosperity will be long."*

²⁵All this happened to King Nebuchadnezzar. ²⁶Twelve months later, as he was walking on the roof of the royal palace in Babylon, ²⁷the king said, "Babylon the great! Was it not I, with my great strength, who built it as a royal residence for my splendor and majesty?"* ²⁸While these words were still on the king's lips, a voice spoke from heaven, "It has been decreed for you, King Nebuchadnezzar, that your

i 1 Sm 2, 8; 16, 11; Is 62, 6.—j Dn 5, 21.—k Sir 3, 30; 4, 8.

4, 10: *A holy sentinel:* an angel. This term is found in the Bible only in this chapter of Daniel, but it is common in later Jewish literature.
4, 11ff: As the tree is Nebuchadnezzar (v 19), the description passes from metaphor to the reality.
4, 17: *"This dream . . . for your foes":* Daniel speaks as a courtier.
4, 22: The description is of a form of insanity called lycanthropy, in which the patient acts like a wolf.
4, 24: A classic Scriptural text for the efficacy of good works.
4, 27: The words attributed to the king are similar to the boastings in the royal inscriptions by which the Mesopotamian kings testified to their mighty works.

kingdom is taken from you! [29] You shall be cast out from among men, and shall dwell with wild beasts; you shall be given grass to eat like an ox, and seven years shall pass over you, until you learn that the Most High rules over the kingdom of men and gives it to whom he will." [30] * At once this was fulfilled. Nebuchadnezzar was cast out from among men, he ate grass like an ox, and his body was bathed with the dew of heaven, until his hair grew like the feathers of an eagle, and his nails like the claws of a bird.

[31] *l* When this period was over, I, Nebuchadnezzar, raised my eyes to heaven; my reason was restored to me, and I blessed the Most High, I praised and glorified him who lives forever:

His dominion is an everlasting dominion,
    and his kingdom endures through all generations.
[32] All who live on the earth are counted as nothing;
    he does as he pleases with the powers of heaven
    as well as with those who live on the earth.
There is no one who can stay his hand or say to him, "What have you done?"

[33] At the same time my reason returned to me, and for the glory of my kingdom, my majesty and my splendor returned to me. My nobles and lords sought me out; I was restored to my kingdom, and became much greater than before. [34] Therefore, I, Nebuchadnezzar, now praise and exalt and glorify the King of heaven, because all his works are right and his ways just; and those who walk in pride he is able to humble.

---

l Dn 3, 100; 7, 14.

4, 30ff: There is no certainty of any such thing happening to Nebuchadnezzar as is described here. Some scholars think that the Nebuchadnezzar of this chapter is actually Nabonidus, the father of Belshazzar, who was mysteriously absent from Babylon for a number of years. The Biblical author's chief interest was not in the historicity of this popular tale, but in the object lesson it contained for the proud "divine" kings of the Seleucid dynasty.
5, 1: *King Belshazzar:* Belshazzar was actually the crown prince, but he had been given royal authority in Babylon by his father Nabonidus.
5, 2: *Nebuchadnezzar, his father:* several kings of Babylon intervened between Nebuchadnezzar and Belshazzar. Either the term *father* is used here in the broad sense of "remote predecessor," or the name *Nebuchadnezzar* is used for "Nabonidus."

CHAPTER 5

The Writing on the Wall. [1] King Belshazzar* gave a great banquet for a thousand of his lords, with whom he drank. [2] Under the influence of the wine, he ordered the gold and silver vessels which Nebuchadnezzar, his father,* had taken from the temple in Jerusalem, to be brought in so that the king, his lords, his wives and his entertainers might drink from them. [3] When the gold and silver vessels taken from the house of God in Jerusalem had been brought in, and while the king, his lords, his wives and his entertainers were drinking [4] wine from them, they praised their gods of gold and silver, bronze and iron, wood and stone.

[5] Suddenly, opposite the lampstand, the fingers of a human hand appeared, writing on the plaster of the wall in the king's palace. When the king saw the wrist and hand that wrote, [6] his face blanched; his thoughts terrified him, his hip joints shook, and his knees knocked. [7] The king shouted for the enchanters, Chaldeans, and astrologers to be brought in. "Whoever reads this writing and tells me what it means," he said to the wise men of Babylon, "shall be clothed in purple, wear a golden collar about his neck, and be third in the government of the kingdom." [8] But though all the king's wise men came in, none of them could either read the writing or tell the king what it meant. [9] Then King Belshazzar was greatly terrified; his face went ashen, and his lords were thrown into confusion.

[10] When the queen heard of the discussion between the king and his lords, she entered the banquet hall and said, "O king, live forever! Be not troubled in mind, nor look so pale! [11] There is a man in your kingdom in whom is the spirit of the holy God; during the lifetime of your father he was seen to have brilliant knowledge and god-like wisdom. In fact, King Nebuchadnezzar, your father, made him chief of the magicians, enchanters, Chaldeans, and astrologers, [12] because of the extraordinary mind possessed by this Daniel, whom the king named Belteshazzar. He knew and understood how to interpret dreams, explain enigmas, and solve difficulties. Now therefore, summon Daniel to tell you what this means."

13 Then Daniel was brought into the presence of the king. The king asked him, "Are you the Daniel, the Jewish exile, whom my father, the king, brought from Judah? 14 I have heard that the spirit of God is in you, that you possess brilliant knowledge and extraordinary wisdom. 15 Now, the wise men and enchanters were brought in to me to read this writing and tell me its meaning, but they could not say what the words meant. 16 But I have heard that you can interpret dreams and solve difficulties; if you are able to read the writing and tell me what it means, you shall be clothed in purple, wear a gold collar about your neck, and be third in the government of the kingdom."

17 Daniel answered the king: "You may keep your gifts, or give your presents to someone else; but the writing I will read for you, O king, and tell you what it means. 18 The Most High God gave your father Nebuchadnezzar a great kingdom and glorious majesty. 19 Because he made him so great, the nations and peoples of every language dreaded and feared him. Whomever he wished, he killed or let live; whomever he wished, he exalted or humbled. 20 But when his heart became proud and his spirit hardened by insolence, he was put down from his royal throne and deprived of his glory; 21 *m* he was cast out from among men and was made insensate as a beast; he lived with wild asses, and ate grass like an ox; his body was bathed with the dew of heaven, until he learned that the Most High God rules over the kingdom of men and appoints over it whom he will. 22 You, his son, Belshazzar, have not humbled your heart, though you knew all this; 23 you have rebelled against the Lord of heaven. You had the vessels of his temple brought before you, so that you and your nobles, your wives and your entertainers, might drink wine from them; and you praised the gods of silver and gold, bronze and iron, wood and stone, that neither see nor hear nor have intelligence. But the God in whose hand is your life breath and the whole course of your life, you did not glorify. 24 By him were the wrist and hand sent, and the writing set down.

25 "This is the writing that was inscribed: MENE, TEKEL, and PERES.* These words mean: 26 * MENE, God has numbered your kingdom and put an

end to it; 27 TEKEL, you have been weighed on the scales and found wanting; 28 PERES, your kingdom has been divided and given to the Medes and Persians."

29 Then by order of Belshazzar they clothed Daniel in purple, with a gold collar about his neck, and proclaimed him third in the government of the kingdom. 30 The same night Belshazzar, the Chaldean king, was slain:

CHAPTER 6

1 And Darius the Mede* succeeded to the kingdom at the age of sixty-two.

In the Lions' Den. 2 Darius decided to appoint over his entire kingdom one hundred and twenty satraps, to safeguard his interests; 3 these were accountable to three supervisors, one of whom was Daniel. 4 Daniel outshone all the supervisors and satraps because an extraordinary spirit was in him, and the king thought of giving him authority over the entire kingdom. 5 Therefore the supervisors and satraps tried to find grounds for accusation against Daniel as regards the administration. But they could accuse him of no wrongdoing; because he was trustworthy, no fault of neglect or misconduct was to be found in him. 6 Then these men said to themselves, "We shall find no grounds for accusation against this Daniel unless by way of the law of his God." 7 So these supervisors and satraps went thronging to the king and said to him, "King Darius, live forever! 8 *n* All the supervisors of the kingdom, the prefects, satraps, nobles, and governors are agreed that the following prohibition ought to be put in force by royal decree: no one is to address any petition to god or

m Dn 4, 22.—n Est 1, 19.

5, 25: *Mene, Tekel, and Peres:* these seem to be the Aramaic names of weights and monetary values: the mina, the shekel (the sixtieth part of a mina), and the parsu (a half-mina).

5, 26ff: Daniel interprets these three terms by a play on the words: *Mene,* connected with the verb meaning to number; *Tekel,* with the verb meaning to weigh; *Peres,* with the verb meaning to divide. There is also a play on the last term with the word for Persians.

6, 1: *Darius the Mede:* unknown in profane history. The Median kingdom had already been conquered by Cyrus the Persian, and it was Cyrus who captured Babylon. Evidently the author of Daniel has deliberately adopted an apocalyptic view of history, derived from prophecy (cf Is 13, 17ff; Jer 51, 11. 28ff), according to which the Medes formed the second of four world kingdoms preceding the messianic times; see note on Dn 2, 36-45. The character of Darius the Mede has probably been modeled on that of the Persian King Darius the Great (522-486 B.C.), the second successor of Cyrus.

man for thirty days, except to you, O king; otherwise he shall be cast into a den of lions. ⁹Now, O king, issue the prohibition over your signature, immutable and irrevocable* under Mede and Persian law." ¹⁰So King Darius signed the prohibition and made it law.

¹¹Even after Daniel heard that this law had been signed, he continued his custom of going home to kneel in prayer and give thanks to his God in the upper chamber three times a day, with the windows open toward Jerusalem. ¹²So these men rushed in and found Daniel praying and pleading before his God. ¹³Then they went to remind the king about the prohibition: "Did you not decree, O king, that no one is to address a petition to god or man for thirty days, except to you, O king; otherwise he shall be cast into a den of lions?" The king answered them, "The decree is absolute, irrevocable under the Mede and Persian law." ¹⁴To this they replied, "Daniel, the Jewish exile, has paid no attention to you, O king, or to the decree you issued; three times a day he offers his prayer." ¹⁵The king was deeply grieved at this news and he made up his mind to save Daniel; he worked till sunset to rescue him. ¹⁶But these men insisted. "Keep in mind, O king," they said, "that under the Mede and Persian law every royal prohibition or decree is irrevocable." ¹⁷So the king ordered Daniel to be brought and cast into the lions' den.* To Daniel he said, "May your God, whom you serve so constantly, save you." ¹⁸To forestall any tampering, the king sealed with his own ring and the rings of the lords the stone that had been brought to block the opening of the den.

¹⁹Then the king returned to his palace for the night; he refused to eat and he dismissed the entertainers. Since sleep was impossible for him, ²⁰the king rose very early the next morning and hastened to the lions' den. ²¹As he drew near, he cried out to Daniel sorrowfully, "O Daniel, servant of the living God, has the God whom you serve so constantly been able to save you from the lions?" ²² *o* Daniel answered the king: "O king, live forever! ²³My God has sent his angel and closed the lions' mouths so that they have not hurt me. For I have been found innocent before him; neither to you have I done any harm, O king!" ²⁴This gave the king great joy. At his order Daniel was removed from the den, unhurt because he trusted in his God. ²⁵The king then ordered the men who had accused Daniel, along with their children and their wives, to be cast into the lions' den. Before they reached the bottom of the den, the lions overpowered them and crushed all their bones.

²⁶Then King Darius wrote to the nations and peoples of every language, wherever they dwell on the earth: "All peace to you! ²⁷I decree that throughout my royal domain the God of Daniel is to be reverenced and feared:

"For he is the living God, enduring forever;
    his kingdom shall not be destroyed,
    and his dominion shall be without end.
²⁸ He is a deliverer and savior,
    working signs and wonders in heaven and on earth,
    and he delivered Daniel from the lions' power." *p*

²⁹So Daniel fared well during the reign of Darius and the reign of Cyrus the Persian.

II: DANIEL'S VISIONS

CHAPTER 7

Vision of the Four Beasts.* ¹In the first year of King Belshazzar of Babylon, Daniel had a dream as he lay in bed, and was terrified by the visions of his mind. Then he wrote down the dream; the account began: ²In the vision I saw during the night, suddenly the four winds of heaven stirred up the great sea.* ³from which emerged four immense beasts, each

---

o 1 Mc 2, 60.—p Dn 1, 21.

6, 9: *Immutable and irrevocable:* the passages in Est 1, 19 and 8, 8 also refer to the immutability of Medo-Persian laws. The historian Diodorus Siculus indicates that such a concept existed in the time of Darius III (335-331 B.C.), the last of the Persian kings. Cf vv 13. 16.

6, 17: *The lions' den:* a pit too deep to be easily scaled; its opening was blocked with a stone (v 18).

7, 1-27: The significance of this vision is the same as that of Nebuchadnezzar's dream in chapter 2; see note on Dn 2, 36-45. To the four succeeding world kingdoms, Babylonian, Median, Persian, and Greek, is opposed the messianic kingdom of the people of God. The imagery of this chapter has been used extensively in the Revelation of St. John, where it is applied to the Roman empire, the persecutor of the church.

7, 2: *The great sea:* the primordial ocean beneath the earth, according to primitive cosmology (Gn 7, 11; 49, 25). This was thought to contain various monsters (Is 27, 1; Jb 7, 12), and in particular mythological monsters symbolizing the chaos which God had vanquished in ancient times (Jb 9, 13; 26, 13; etc.).

Dn

different from the others. [4] The first was like a lion, but with eagle's wings.* While I watched, the wings were plucked; it was raised from the ground to stand on two feet like a man, and given a human mind. [5] The second was like a bear;* it was raised up on one side, and among the teeth in its mouth were three tusks. It was given the order, "Up, devour much flesh." [6] After this I looked and saw another beast, like a leopard;* on its back were four wings like those of a bird, and it had four heads. To this beast dominion was given. [7] After this, in the visions of the night I saw the fourth beast,* different from all the others, terrifying, horrible, and of extraordinary strength; it had great iron teeth with which it devoured and crushed, and what was left it trampled with its feet. [8] I was considering the ten horns it had, when suddenly another, a little horn, sprang out of their midst, and three of the previous horns were torn away to make room for it. This horn had eyes like a man, and a mouth that spoke arrogantly. [9] * As I watched,

Thrones were set up
  and the Ancient One took his throne.
His clothing was snow bright,
  and the hair on his head as white as
    wool;
His throne was flames of fire,
  with wheels of burning fire.
[10] A surging stream of fire
  flowed out from where he sat;
Thousands upon thousands were ministering to him,
  and myriads upon myriads attended
    him. [q]

The court was convened, and the books were opened. [11] I watched, then, from the first of the arrogant words which the horn spoke, until the beast was slain and its body thrown into the fire to be burnt up. [12] The other beasts, which also lost their dominion, were granted a prolongation of life for a time and a season. [13] As the visions during the night continued, I saw

One like a son of man* coming,
  on the clouds of heaven;
When he reached the Ancient One
  and was presented before him,
[14] He received dominion, glory, and kingship;
nations and peoples of every language
  serve him.

His dominion is an everlasting dominion
  that shall not be taken away,
  his kingship shall not be destroyed. [r]

[15] I, Daniel, found my spirit anguished within its sheath of flesh, and I was terrified by the visions of my mind. [16] I approached one of those present and asked him what all this meant in truth; in answer, he made known to me the meaning of the things: [17] "These four great beasts stand for four kingdoms which shall arise on the earth. [18] But the holy ones of the Most High shall receive the kingship, to possess it forever and ever."

[19] But I wished to make certain about the fourth beast, so very terrible and different from the others, devouring and crushing with its iron teeth and bronze claws, and trampling with its feet what was left; [20] about the ten horns on its head, and the other one that sprang up, before which three horns fell; about the horn with the eyes and the mouth that spoke arrogantly, which appeared greater than its fellows. [21] For, as I watched, that horn made war against the holy ones and was victorious [22] until the Ancient One arrived; judgment was pronounced in favor of the holy ones of the Most High, and the time came

---

q Rv 5, 11.—r Dn 3, 100; 4, 31; Mi 4, 7; Lk 1, 32.

7, 4: The representation of the Babylonian empire as a winged lion, a common motif in Babylonian art, symbolizes the bestial power hostile to God. The two wings that *were plucked* represent Nebuchadnezzar and Belshazzar. *On two feet like a man . . . a human mind:* contrasts with what is said in Dn 4, 13. 30.
7, 5: *A bear:* represents the Median empire, its *three tusks* symbolizing its destructive nature; hence, the command: *"Up, devour much flesh."*
7, 6: *A leopard:* used to symbolize the swiftness with which Cyrus the Persian established his kingdom. *Four heads:* corresponding to the four Persian kings of Dn 11, 2.
7, 7f: Alexander's empire was *different from all the others* in that it was Western rather than Oriental in inspiration. The *ten horns* represent the kings of the Seleucid dynasty, the only part of the Hellenistic empire that concerned the author. The *little horn* is Antiochus IV Epiphanes (175-163 B.C.), the worst of the Seleucid kings, who usurped the throne.
7, 9f: A vision of the heavenly throne of God *(the Ancient One),* who sits in judgment (symbolized by *fire*) over the nations. Some of the details of the vision, depicting the divine majesty and omnipotence, are to be found in Ez 1.
7, 13f: *One like a son of man:* in contrast to the worldly kingdoms opposed to God, which appear as beasts, the glorified people of God that will form his kingdom on earth is represented in human form (v 18). Just as our Lord applied the figure of the stone hewn from the mountain to himself (Dn 2, 36-45), he also made the title, "Son of Man," his most characteristic way of referring to himself, as the One in whom and through whom the salvation of God's people came to be realized.

when the holy ones possessed the kingdom. ²³ He answered me thus:

"The fourth beast shall be a fourth
    kingdom on earth,
    different from all the others;
It shall devour the whole earth,
    beat it down, and crush it.
²⁴ The ten horns shall be ten kings
    rising out of that kingdom;
    another shall rise up after them,
Different from those before him,
    who shall lay low three kings.
²⁵ He shall speak against the Most High
    and oppress the holy ones of the Most
    High,
    thinking to change the feast days and
    the law.*
They shall be handed over to him
    for a year, two years, and a half-year.
²⁶ But when the court is convened,
    and his power is taken away
    by final and absolute destruction,
²⁷ Then the kingship and dominion and
    majesty
    of all the kingdoms under the
    heavens
    shall be given to the holy people of
    the Most High,
Whose kingdom shall be everlasting:
    all dominions shall serve and obey
    him."

²⁸ The report concluded: I, Daniel, was greatly terrified by my thoughts, and my

---

7, 25: The reference is to the persecutions of Antiochus IV and his attempt to force the Jews to give up their customs and to adopt Hellenistic ways (1 Mc 1, 33f). *A year, two years, and a half-year:* an indefinite, evil period of time. As seven is the Jewish "perfect" number, half of it signifies great imperfection. Actually, this corresponds fairly accurately to the duration of Antiochus' persecution.

7, 28: This verse ends the Aramaic part of the Book of Daniel.

8, 1-27: This vision repeats the major part of the preceding one, though in a more explicit fashion. As explained in vv 20ff, *the two-horned ram* represents the combined kingdom of the Medes and Persians, destroyed by Alexander's Hellenistic empire originating in the west. Once again the author is interested only in the Seleucid dynasty, which emerged from the dissolution of Alexander's empire after his death in 323 B.C.

8, 2: *The fortress of Susa:* the royal palace of the Persian kings in the ancient territory of Elam, east of Babylonia. *The river Ulai:* a canal along the northern side of Susa.

8, 9: *The little horn,* as in chapter 7, is Antiochus IV. *The glorious country:* Palestine.

8, 10ff: *The host of heaven:* ordinarily meaning the stars, here refers to the people of God; cf Dn 12, 3. *The prince of the host:* God himself, with whose holy religion Antiochus interfered (1 Mc 1, 45).

8, 13: *The desolating sin:* the Hebrew contains a wordplay *(shomem)* on the name Baal Shamem ("lord of the heavens," the Greek Zeus Olympios), referring to the statue with which Antiochus profaned the temple of Jerusalem (2 Mc 6, 2).

---

face blanched, but I kept the matter to myself.*

CHAPTER 8

Vision of the Ram and He-goat.* ¹ After this first vision, I, Daniel, had another, in the third year of the reign of King Belshazzar. ² In my vision I saw myself in the fortress of Susa* in the province of Elam; I was beside the river Ulai. ³ I looked up and saw standing by the river a ram with two great horns, the one larger and newer than the other. ⁴ I saw the ram butting toward the west, north, and south. No beast could withstand it or be rescued from its power; it did what it pleased and became very powerful.

⁵ As I was reflecting, a he-goat with a prominent horn on its forehead suddenly came from the west across the whole earth without touching the ground. ⁶ It approached the two-horned ram I had seen standing by the river, and rushed toward it with savage force. ⁷ I saw it attack the ram with furious blows when they met, and break both its horns. It threw the ram, which had not the force to withstand it, to the ground, and trampled upon it; and no one could rescue it from its power.

⁸ The he-goat became very powerful, but at the height of its power the great horn was shattered, and in its place came up four others, facing the four winds of heaven. ⁹ Out of one of them came a little horn* which kept growing toward the south, the east, and the glorious country. ¹⁰ Its power extended to the host of heaven,* so that it cast down to earth some of the host and some of the stars and trampled on them. ¹¹ It boasted even against the prince of the host, from whom it removed the daily sacrifice, and whose sanctuary it cast down, ¹² as well as the host, while sin replaced the daily sacrifice. It cast truth to the ground, and was succeeding in its undertaking.

¹³ I heard a holy one speaking, and another said to whichever one it was that spoke, "How long shall the events of this vision last concerning the daily sacrifice, the desolating sin* which is placed there, the sanctuary, and the trampled host?" ¹⁴ He answered him, "For two thousand three hundred evenings and mornings; then the sanctuary shall be purified."

¹⁵ While I, Daniel, sought the meaning of the vision I had seen, a manlike figure

stood before me, [16] and on the Ulai I heard a human voice that cried out, "Gabriel,* explain the vision to this man." [17] When he came near where I was standing, I fell prostrate in terror. But he said to me, "Understand, son of man, that the vision refers to the end time."* [18] As he spoke to me, I fell forward in a faint; he touched me and made me stand up. [19] "I will show you," he said, "what is to happen later in the period of wrath; for at the appointed time, there will be an end. [20] "The two-horned ram you saw represents the kings of the Medes and Persians. [21] The he-goat is the king of the Greeks, and the great horn on its forehead is the first king. [22] The four that rose in its place when it was broken are four kingdoms that will issue from his nation, but without his strength.

[23] "After their reign,
    when sinners have reached their
      measure,
There shall arise a king, impudent
    and skilled in intrigue.
[24] He shall be strong and powerful,
    bring about fearful ruin,
    and succeed in his undertaking.
He shall destroy powerful peoples;
[25]   his cunning shall be against the holy
      ones,
    his treacherous conduct shall suc-
      ceed.
He shall be proud of heart
    and destroy many by stealth.
But when he rises against the prince of
    princes,
    he shall be broken without a hand
      being raised.
[26] The vision of the evenings and the
    mornings
    is true, as spoken;
Do you, however, keep this vision un-
    disclosed,
because the days are to be many."

[27] I, Daniel, was weak and ill for some days; then I arose and took care of the king's affairs. But I was appalled at the vision, which I could not understand.

CHAPTER 9

Gabriel and the Seventy Weeks. [1] It was the first year that Darius,* son of Ahasuerus, of the race of the Medes, reigned over the kingdom of the Chaldeans;

[2] *s* in the first year of his reign I, Daniel, tried to understand in the Scriptures the counting of the years of which the LORD spoke to the prophet Jeremiah: that for the ruins of Jerusalem seventy years* must be fulfilled.

[3] I turned to the Lord God, pleading in earnest prayer, with fasting, sackcloth, and ashes. [4] *t* I prayed to the LORD, my God, and confessed, "Ah, Lord, great and awesome God, you who keep your merciful covenant toward those who love you and observe your commandments! [5] *u* We have sinned, been wicked and done evil; we have rebelled and departed from your commandments and your laws. [6] We have not obeyed your servants the prophets, who spoke in your name to our kings, our princes, our fathers, and all the people of the land. [7] Justice, O Lord, is on your side; we are shamefaced even to this day: the men of Judah, the residents of Jerusalem, and all Israel, near and far, in all the countries to which you have scattered them because of their treachery toward you. [8] O LORD, we are shamefaced, like our kings, our princes, and our fathers, for having sinned against you. [9] But yours, O Lord, our God, are compassion and forgiveness! Yet we rebelled against you [10] and paid no heed to your command, O LORD, our God, to live by the law you gave us through your servants the prophets. [11] *v* Because all Israel transgressed your law and went astray, not heeding your voice, the sworn malediction, recorded in the law of Moses, the servant of God, was poured out over us for our sins. [12] You carried out the threats you spoke against us and against those who governed us, by bringing upon us in Jerusalem the greatest calamity that has ever occurred under heaven. [13] As it is

---

s 2f: Jer 25, 11; 29, 10.—t Neh 1, 5.—u Bar 1, 17.—v Dt 27, 15.

8, 16: The angel Gabriel is mentioned here for the first time in the Bible. There is wordplay in the preceding verse on *geber—manlike figure.*

8, 17: *The end time:* the day of the Lord, when God sits in judgment on his enemies (v 19).

9, 1: *Darius:* see the note on Dn 6, 1.

9, 2: *Seventy years:* the prophet Jeremiah (25, 11; 29, 10) prophesied a Babylonian captivity of seventy years, a round number signifying the complete passing away of the existing generation. Jeremiah's prophecy was fulfilled in the capture of Babylon by Cyrus and the subsequent return of the Jews to Palestine. However, the author of Daniel, living during the persecution of Antiochus, sees the conditions of the exile still existing; therefore in his meditation he extends Jeremiah's number to seventy weeks of years (v 24), i.e., seven times seventy years, to characterize the Jewish victory over the Seleucids as the ultimate fulfillment of the prophecy.

written* in the law of Moses, this calamity came full upon us. As we did not appease the LORD, our God, by turning back from our wickedness and recognizing his constancy, ¹⁴ so the LORD kept watch over the calamity and brought it upon us. You, O LORD, our God, are just in all that you have done, for we did not listen to your voice.

¹⁵ *w* "Now, O Lord, our God, who led your people out of the land of Egypt with a strong hand, and made a name for yourself even to this day, we have sinned, we are guilty. ¹⁶ O Lord, in keeping with all your just deeds, let your anger and your wrath be turned away from your city Jerusalem, your holy mountain. On account of our sins and the crimes of our fathers, Jerusalem and your people have become the reproach of all our neighbors. ¹⁷ Hear, therefore, O God, the prayer and petition of your servant; and for your own sake, O Lord, let your face shine upon your desolate sanctuary. ¹⁸ *x* Give ear, O my God, and listen; open your eyes and see our ruins and the city which bears your name. When we present our petition before you, we rely not on our just deeds, but on your great mercy. ¹⁹ O Lord, hear! O Lord, pardon! O Lord, be attentive and act without delay, for your own sake, O my God, because this city and your people bear your name!"

²⁰ I was still occupied with my prayer, confessing my sin and the sin of my people Israel, presenting my petition to the LORD, my God, on behalf of his holy mountain— ²¹ *y* I was still occupied with this prayer, when Gabriel, the one whom I had seen before in vision, came to me in rapid flight at the time of the evening sacrifice.* ²² He instructed me in these words: "Daniel, I have now come to give you understanding. ²³ When you began your petition, an answer was given which I have come to announce, because you are beloved. Therefore, mark the answer and understand the vision.

²⁴ "Seventy weeks* are decreed
for your people and for your holy city:
Then transgression will stop and sin
will end,
guilt will be expiated,
Everlasting justice will be introduced,
vision and prophecy ratified,
and a most holy will be anointed.
²⁵   Know and understand this:
From the utterance of the word
that Jerusalem was to be rebuilt*
Until one who is anointed and a leader,
there shall be seven weeks.
During sixty-two weeks
it shall be rebuilt,
With streets and trenches,
in time of affliction.
²⁶ After the sixty-two weeks
an anointed* shall be cut down
when he does not possess the city;
And the people of a leader who will
come
shall destroy the sanctuary.
Then the end shall come like a torrent;
until the end there shall be war,
the desolation that is decreed.
²⁷ For one week* he shall make
a firm compact with the many;
Half the week
he shall abolish sacrifice and oblation;

---

w Bar 2, 11; Ex 14, 22.—*x* Jer 25, 29.—*y* Dn 8, 16.

9, 13: *As it is written:* the first time that this formula of Scriptural citation is used in the Bible. The reference (v 11) is to the sanctions of Lv 26, 14ff; Dt 28, 15ff.

9, 21: *At the time of the evening sacrifice:* between three and four in the afternoon.

9, 24: *Seventy weeks:* i.e., of years. Just as Jeremiah's seventy years was an approximation (see note on v 2), the four hundred and ninety years here is not to be taken literally. Similarly, the distribution of the "weeks" in the following verses indicates only relative proportions of the total figure. *A most holy:* an expression used almost always of an object, the altar or the temple, but once (1 Chr 23, 13) of Aaron the high priest. The author sees the definitive establishment of the kingdom of God, realized in the reconsecration of the temple after Antiochus' desecration, or personified in the holy community (like the Son of Man of chapter 7). The Fathers of the church almost unanimously understood the reference to be to Christ, the final realization of the prophecy.

9, 25: *From the utterance . . . to be rebuilt:* from the time of Jeremiah's prophecy. *One . . . anointed and a leader:*

either Cyrus, who was called the anointed of the Lord to end the exile (Is 45, 1), or the high priest Joshua, who presided over the rebuilding of the altar of sacrifice after the exile (Ezr 3, 2). *Seven weeks:* forty-nine years, an approximation of the time of the exile. *During sixty-two weeks . . . rebuilt:* a period of 434 years, roughly approximating the interval between the rebuilding of Jerusalem after the exile and the beginning of the Seleucid persecution.

9, 26: *An anointed:* doubtless the high priest Onias III, murdered in 171 B.C., from which the author dates the beginning of the persecution. Onias was in exile when he was killed. *A leader:* Antiochus IV.

9, 27: *One week:* the final phase of the period in view, the time of Antiochus' persecution; *he* is Antiochus himself. *The many:* the faithless Jews who allied themselves with the heathen; cf 1 Mc 1, 11ff. *Half the week:* three and a half years; see note on Dn 7, 25. The temple was desecrated by Antiochus from 167 to 165 B.C. *The temple wing:* probably the main portal. *The horrible abomination:* see note on Dn 8, 13. Perhaps an inscription was placed on the portal of the temple dedicating it to the Olympian Zeus. Our Lord referred to this passage in his own prediction of the destruction of Jerusalem (Mt 24, 15).

Dn

On the temple wing shall be the horrible abomination
until the ruin that is decreed
is poured out upon the horror."z

CHAPTER 10

Vision of the Hellenistic Wars.* [1] In the third year of Cyrus, king of Persia, a revelation was given to Daniel, who had been named Belteshazzar. The revelation was certain: a great war; he understood it from the vision. [2] In those days, I, Daniel, mourned* three full weeks. [3] I ate no savory food, I took no meat or wine, and I did not anoint myself at all until the end of the three weeks.

[4] On the twenty-fourth day of the first month* I was on the bank of the great river, the Tigris. [5] As I looked up, I saw a man* dressed in linen with a belt of fine gold around his waist. [6] His body was like chrysolite, his face shone like lightning, his eyes were like fiery torches, his arms and feet looked like burnished bronze, and his voice sounded like the roar of a multitude. [7] I alone, Daniel, saw the vision; but great fear seized the men who were with me; they fled and hid themselves, although they did not see the vision. [8] So I was left alone, seeing this great vision. No strength remained in me; I turned the color of death and was powerless. [9] When I heard the sound of his voice, I fell face forward in a faint.

[10] But then a hand touched me, raising me to my hands and knees. [11] "Daniel, beloved," he said to me, "understand the words which I am speaking to you; stand up, for my mission now is to you." When he said this to me, I stood up trembling. [12] "Fear not, Daniel," he continued; "from the first day you made up your mind to acquire understanding and humble yourself before God, your prayer was heard. Because of it I started out, [13] but the prince of the kingdom of Persia* stood in my way for twenty-one days, until finally Michael, one of the chief princes, came to help me. I left him there with the prince of the kings of Persia, [14] and came to make you understand what shall happen to your people in the days to come; for there is yet a vision concerning those days."

[15] While he was speaking thus to me, I fell forward and kept silent. [16] Then something like a man's hand touched my lips;

I opened my mouth and said to the one facing me, "My lord, I was seized with pangs at the vision and I was powerless. [17] How can my lord's servant speak with you, my lord? For now no strength or even breath is left in me." [18] The one who looked like a man touched me again and strengthened me, saying, [19] "Fear not, beloved, you are safe; take courage and be strong." [20] When he spoke to me, I grew strong and said, "Speak, my lord, for you have strengthened me." "Do you know," he asked, "why I have come to you? Soon I must fight the prince of Persia again. When I leave, the prince of Greece will come; [21] a but I shall tell you what is written in the truthful book. No one supports me against all these except Michael, your prince, [1] standing* as a reinforcement and a bulwark for me. [2] Now I shall tell you the truth.

CHAPTER 11

"Three kings of Persia* are yet to come; and a fourth shall acquire the greatest riches of all. Strengthened by his riches, he shall rouse all the kingdom of Greece. [3] But a powerful king shall appear and rule with great might, doing as he pleases. [4] No sooner shall he appear than his kingdom shall be broken and divided in the four directions under heaven; but not among his descendants or in keeping with his mighty rule, for his kingdom shall be torn to pieces and belong to others than they.

---

z Mt 24, 15; 2 Mc 6, 2.—a Rv 12, 7.

10, 1—12, 13: This final vision repeats some of the material contained in the others. It is concerned with history of the worldly kingdoms from the time of Cyrus to the defeat of the tyrant Antiochus.

10, 2: *Mourned:* perhaps the author intends to recall the interruption in the rebuilding of the temple, which occurred during this time (Ezr 4, 1-4).

10, 4: *The first month:* the month Nisan (mid-March to mid-April).

10, 5f: The heavenly person of the vision is probably the angel Gabriel, as in Dn 9, 21. *Chrysolite:* or topaz, a yellowish precious stone.

10, 13: *The prince of the kingdom of Persia:* the guardian angel of Persia. The later Judaism ascribed protecting angels to various groups of human society, often as little more than personifications. *Michael:* the angel who is the protector of God's people (v 21).

10, 1f: *Standing . . . truth:* these are the first two verses of ch 11.

11, 2-4: The *three kings of Persia* who follow Cyrus are uncertain, since there were more than three Persian kings between Cyrus and the dissolution of the kingdom. The *fourth* is doubtless Xerxes I (486-465 B.C.), the great campaigner against Greece. The *powerful king* is Alexander the Great, who ended the Persian empire by his victory at Issus in 333 B.C.

⁵ * "The king of the south shall grow strong, but one of his princes shall grow stronger still and govern a domain greater than his. ⁶After some years they shall become allies: the daughter of the king of the south shall come to the king of the north in the interest of peace. But her bid for power shall fail: and her line shall not be recognized, and she shall be given up, together with those who brought her, her son and her husband. But later ⁷a descendant of her line shall succeed to his rank, and shall come against the rampart and enter the stronghold of the king of the north, and conquer them. ⁸Even their gods, with their molten images and their precious vessels of silver and gold, he shall carry away as booty into Egypt. For years he shall have nothing to do with the king of the north. ⁹Then the latter shall invade the land of the king of the south, and return to his own country.

¹⁰"But his sons shall prepare and assemble a great armed host, which shall advance like a flood, then withdraw. When it returns and surges around the stronghold, ¹¹the king of the south, provoked, shall go out to fight against the king of the north, whose great host shall make a stand but shall be given into his hand ¹²and be carried off. In the pride of his heart, he shall lay low tens of thousands, but he shall not triumph. ¹³For the king of the north shall raise another army, greater than before; after some years he shall attack with this large army and great resources. ¹⁴ ᵇ In those times many shall resist the king of the south, and outlaws of your people shall rise up in fulfillment of vision, but they shall fail. ¹⁵When the king of the north comes, he shall set up siegeworks and take the fortified city by storm. The power of the south shall not withstand him, and not even his picked troops shall have the strength to resist. ¹⁶He shall attack him

and do as he pleases, with no one to withstand him. He shall stop in the glorious land, dealing destruction. ¹⁷He shall set himself to penetrate the entire strength of his kingdom. He shall conclude an agreement with him and give him a daughter in marriage in order to destroy the kingdom, but this shall not succeed in his favor. ¹⁸He shall turn to the coastland and take many, but a leader shall put an end to his shameful conduct, so that he cannot renew it against him. ¹⁹He shall turn to the strongholds of his own land, but shall stumble and fall, to be found no more. ²⁰In his stead one shall arise who will send a tax collector through the glorious kingdom, but he shall soon be destroyed, though not in conflict or in battle.

²¹"There shall rise in his place a despicable person, to whom the royal insignia shall not be given. By stealth and fraud he shall seize the kingdom. ²²Armed might shall be completely overwhelmed by him and crushed, and even the prince of the covenant. ²³After allying with him, he shall treacherously rise to power with a small party. ²⁴By stealth he shall enter prosperous provinces and do that which his fathers or grandfathers never did; he shall distribute spoil, booty, and riches among them and devise plots against their strongholds; but only for a time. ²⁵He shall call on his strength and cleverness to meet the king of the south with a great army; the king of the south shall prepare for battle with a very large and strong army, but he shall not succeed because of the plots devised against him. ²⁶Even his table companions shall seek to destroy him, his army shall be overwhelmed, and many shall fall slain. ²⁷The two kings, resolved on evil, shall sit at table together and exchange lies, but they shall have no success, because the appointed end is not yet.

²⁸"He shall turn back toward his land with great riches, his mind set against the holy covenant; he shall arrange matters and return to his land. ²⁹At the time appointed he shall come again to the south, but this time it shall not be as before. ³⁰When ships of the Kittim* confront him, he shall lose heart and retreat. Then he shall direct his rage and energy against the holy covenant; those who forsake it he shall once more single out. ³¹Armed forces shall move at his command and defile

---

b Is 19, 1.

11, 5-45: These verses describe the dynastic histories of the Ptolemies in Egypt *(the king of the south)* and the Seleucids in Syria *(the king of the north)*, the two divisions of the Hellenistic empire that were of interest to the author (v 6). In vv 10-20 is described the struggle between the two kingdoms for the control of Palestine, in which the Seleucids were eventually victorious. The reference in v 20 is to Seleucus IV, who sent Heliodorus to plunder the temple treasure in Jerusalem (2 Mc 3). Finally, vv 21-45 describe the career of Antiochus IV and his persecution, in details that have been seen above.

11, 30: *Kittim:* originally this word meant Cypriots or other island dwellers. Here it means the Romans, who forced Antiochus to withdraw from Egypt during his second campaign there.

Dn

the sanctuary stronghold, abolishing the daily sacrifice and setting up the horrible abomination. [32] By his deceit he shall make some who were disloyal to the covenant apostatize; but those who remain loyal to their God shall take strong action. [33] The nation's wise men shall instruct the many; though for a time they will become victims of the sword, of flames, exile, and plunder. [34] When they fall, few people shall help them, but many shall join them out of treachery. [35] Of the wise men, some shall fall, so that the rest may be tested, refined, and purified, until the end time which is still appointed to come.

[36] * "The king shall do as he pleases, exalting himself and making himself greater than any god; he shall utter dreadful blasphemies against the God of gods. He shall prosper only till divine wrath is ready, for what is determined must take place. [37] He shall have no regard for the gods of his ancestors or for the one in whom women delight; for no god shall he have regard, because he shall make himself greater than all. [38] Instead, he shall give glory to the god of strongholds; a god unknown to his fathers he shall glorify with gold, silver, precious stones, and other treasures. [39] To defend the strongholds he shall station a people of a foreign god. Whoever acknowledges him he shall provide with abundant honor; he shall make them rule over the many and distribute the land as a reward.

[40] "At the appointed time the king of the south shall come to grips with him, but the king of the north shall overwhelm him with chariots and horsemen and a great fleet, passing through the countries like a flood. [41] He shall enter the glorious land and many shall fall, except Edom, Moab, and the chief part of Ammon, which shall escape from his power. [42] He shall extend his power over the countries, and not even the land of Egypt shall escape. [43] He shall control the riches of gold and silver and all the treasures of Egypt; Libya and Ethiopia shall be in his train. [44] When news from the east and the north terrifies him, he shall set out with great fury to slay and to doom many. [45] He shall pitch the tents of his royal pavilion between the sea and the glorious holy mountain, but he shall come to his end with none to help him.

CHAPTER 12

[1] "At that time there shall arise
    Michael, the great prince,
    guardian of your people; [c]
It shall be a time unsurpassed in distress
    since nations began until that time.
At that time your people shall escape,
    everyone who is found written in the
    book. *
[2] Many of those who sleep
    in the dust of the earth shall awake; *
Some shall live forever,
    others shall be an everlasting horror
    and disgrace. [d]
[3] But the wise shall shine brightly
    like the splendor of the firmament,
And those who lead the many to justice
    shall be like the stars forever. [e]

[4] "As for you, Daniel, keep secret the message and seal the book until the end time; many shall fall away and evil shall increase."

[5] I, Daniel, looked and saw two others, one standing on either bank of the river. [6] One of them said to the man clothed in linen, who was upstream, "How long shall it be to the end of these appalling things?" [7] [f] The man clothed in linen, who was upstream, lifted his right and left hands to heaven; and I heard him swear by him who lives forever that it should be for a year, two years, a half-year; * and that, when the power of the destroyer of the holy people was brought to an end, all these things should end. [8] I heard, but I did not understand; so I asked, "My lord, what follows this?" [9] "Go, Daniel," he said, "because the words are to be kept secret and sealed until the end time. [10] Many shall be refined, purified, and tested, but the wicked shall prove wicked; none of them shall have understanding, but the wise shall have it. [11] From the time that the daily sacrifice is abolished and the horrible

---

c Rv 12, 7.—d Mt 25, 46; Jn 5, 29.—e Wis 3, 7.—f Rv 10, 5f.

11, 36-39: Instead of venerating Apollo, one of *the gods of his ancestors,* Antiochus venerated, and even identified himself with, Zeus Olympios, whom the Romans equated with the god of their fortress in Rome, Jupiter Capitolinus, *the god of strongholds.*

12, 1: *Written in the book:* the book of God's predestination.
12, 2: The first Israelites who have fallen (Dn 11, 33ff) *shall awake,* that is, rise to *live forever.* A resurrection of the wicked as in later, Christian teaching (Jn 5, 28f) is implied here if the *others* are included in the *many;* but cf Is 66, 24.
12, 7: *A year, two years, a half-year:* see note on Dn 7, 25. The author's perspective is the end of Antiochus, and beyond, the final consummation of all things.

abomination is set up, there shall be one thousand two hundred and ninety days. ¹²Blessed is the man who has patience and perseveres until the one thousand three hundred and thirty-five days. ¹³Go, take your rest, you shall rise for your reward at the end of days."

III: APPENDIX*
CHAPTER 13

Susanna's Virtue. ¹In Babylon there lived a man named Joakim, ²who married a very beautiful and God-fearing woman, Susanna, the daughter of Hilkiah; ³her pious parents had trained their daughter according to the law of Moses. ⁴Joakim was very rich; he had a garden near his house, and the Jews had recourse to him often because he was the most respected of them all.

⁵That year, two elders of the people were appointed judges, of whom the Lord said, "Wickedness has come out of Babylon: from the elders who were to govern the people as judges." ⁶These men, to whom all brought their cases, frequented the house of Joakim. ⁷When the people left at noon, Susanna used to enter her husband's garden for a walk. ⁸When the old men saw her enter every day for her walk, they began to lust for her. ⁹They suppressed their consciences; they would not allow their eyes to look to heaven, and did not keep in mind just judgments. ¹⁰Though both were enamored of her, they did not tell each other their trouble, ¹¹for they were ashamed to reveal their lustful desire to have her. ¹²Day by day they watched eagerly for her. ¹³One day they said to each other, "Let us be off for home, it is time for lunch." So they went out and parted; ¹⁴but both turned back, and when they met again, they asked each other the reason. They admitted their lust, and then they agreed to look for an occasion when they could meet her alone.

¹⁵One day, while they were waiting for the right moment, she entered the garden as usual, with two maids only. She decided to bathe, for the weather was warm. ¹⁶Nobody else was there except the two elders, who had hidden themselves and were watching her. ¹⁷"Bring me oil and soap," she said to the maids, "and shut the garden doors while I bathe." ¹⁸They did as she said; they shut the garden doors and left by the side gate to fetch what she had ordered, unaware that the elders were hidden inside.

¹⁹As soon as the maids had left, the two old men got up and hurried to her. ²⁰"Look," they said, "the garden doors are shut, and no one can see us; give in to our desire, and lie with us. ²¹If you refuse, we will testify against you that you dismissed your maids because a young man was here with you."

²²"I am completely trapped," Susanna groaned. "If I yield, it will be my death; if I refuse, I cannot escape your power. ²³Yet it is better for me to fall into your power without guilt than to sin before the Lord." ²⁴Then Susanna shrieked, and the old men also shouted at her, ²⁵as one of them ran to open the garden doors. ²⁶When the people in the house heard the cries from the garden, they rushed in by the side gate to see what had happened to her. ²⁷At the accusations by the old men, the servants felt very much ashamed, for never had any such thing been said about Susanna.

²⁸When the people came to her husband Joakim the next day, the two wicked elders also came, fully determined to put Susanna to death. Before all the people they ordered: ²⁹"Send for Susanna, the daughter of Hilkiah, the wife of Joakim." When she was sent for, ³⁰she came with her parents, children and all her relatives. ³¹Susanna, very delicate and beautiful, ³²was veiled; but those wicked men ordered her to uncover her face so as to sate themselves with her beauty. ³³All her relatives and the onlookers were weeping.

³⁴In the midst of the people the two elders rose up and laid their hands on her head. ³⁵Through her tears she looked up to heaven, for she trusted in the Lord wholeheartedly. ³⁶The elders made this accusation: "As we were walking in the garden alone, this woman entered with two girls and shut the doors of the garden, dismissing the girls. ³⁷A young man, who was hidden there, came and lay with her. ³⁸When we, in a corner of the garden, saw this crime, we ran toward them. ³⁹We saw them lying together, but the man we

Dn

13, 1—14, 42: The short stories in these two chapters may have originally been about some other Daniel or Daniels than the hero of the main part of the book. They exist now only in Greek, but probably were first composed in Hebrew or Aramaic. They are excluded from the Jewish canon of Scripture, but the church has always included them among the inspired writings.

could not hold, because he was stronger than we; he opened the doors and ran off. 40 Then we seized this one and asked who the young man was, 41 but she refused to tell us. We testify to this." The assembly believed them, since they were elders and judges of the people, and they condemned her to death.

42 But Susanna cried aloud: "O eternal God, you know what is hidden and are aware of all things before they come to be: 43 you know that they have testified falsely against me. Here I am about to die, though I have done none of the things with which these wicked men have charged me."

44 The Lord heard her prayer. 45 As she was being led to execution, God stirred up the holy spirit of a young boy named Daniel, 46 and he cried aloud: "I will have no part in the death of this woman." 47 All the people turned and asked him, "What is this you are saying?" 48 He stood in their midst and continued, "Are you such fools, O Israelites! To condemn a woman of Israel without examination and without clear evidence? 49 Return to court, for they have testified falsely against her."

50 Then all the people returned in haste. To Daniel the elders said, "Come, sit with us and inform us, since God has given you the prestige of old age." 51 But he replied, "Separate these two far from one another that I may examine them."

52 After they were separated one from the other, he called one of them and said: "How you have grown evil with age! Now have your past sins come to term: 53 g passing unjust sentences, condemning the innocent, and freeing the guilty, although the Lord says, 'The innocent and the just you shall not put to death.' 54 Now, then, if you were a witness, tell me under what tree you saw them together." 55 "Under a mastic tree,"* he answered. "Your fine lie has cost you your head," said Daniel; "for the angel of God shall receive the sentence from him and split you in two." 56 Putting him to one side, he ordered the other one to be brought. "Offspring of Canaan, not of Judah," Daniel said to him, "beauty has seduced you, lust has subverted your conscience. 57 This is how you acted with the daughters of Israel, and in their fear they yielded to you; but a daughter of Judah did not tolerate your wickedness.* 58 Now then, tell me under what tree you surprised them together." 59 "Under an oak,"

he said. "Your fine lie has cost you also your head," said Daniel; "for the angel of God waits with a sword to cut you in two so as to make an end of you both."

60 The whole assembly cried aloud, blessing God who saves those that hope in him. 61 h They rose up against the two elders, for by their own words Daniel had convicted them of perjury. According to the law of Moses, they inflicted on them the penalty they had plotted to impose on their neighbor: 62 they put them to death. Thus was innocent blood spared that day.

63 Hilkiah and his wife praised God for their daughter Susanna, as did Joakim her husband and all her relatives, because she was found innocent of any shameful deed. 64 And from that day onward Daniel was greatly esteemed by the people.

CHAPTER 14

Bel and the Dragon. 1 After King Astyages* was laid with his fathers, Cyrus the Persian succeeded to his kingdom. 2 Daniel was the king's favorite and was held in higher esteem than any of the friends of the king.* 3 The Babylonians had an idol called Bel,* and every day they provided for it six barrels of fine flour, forty sheep, and six measures of wine. 4 The king worshiped it and went every day to adore it; but Daniel adored only his God. 5 When the king asked him, "Why do you not adore Bel?" Daniel replied, "Because I worship not idols made with hands, but only the living God who made heaven and earth and has dominion over all mankind." 6 Then the king continued, "You do not think Bel is a living god? Do you not see how much he eats and drinks every day?"

---

g Ex 23, 7.—h 61f: Dt 19, 18. 19.

13, 55-59: The contrast between the *mastic tree*, which is small, and the majestic *oak* emphasizes the contradiction between the statements of the two elders. In the Greek text there is a play on words between the names of these two trees and the mortal punishment decreed by Daniel for the elders.

13, 57: Besides the evident moral intent of this story, it appears to have served the purpose of contrasting the northern and the southern kingdom, Israel and Judah, in favor of the latter.

14, 1: *King Astyages:* the last of the Median kings, defeated by Cyrus in 550 B.C. This story preserves the fiction of a successive Median and Persian rule of Babylon.

14, 2: This verse in the Septuagint Greek text reads: "There was once a priest, Daniel by name, the son of Abal, a favorite of the king of Babylon." This may represent an earlier form of the story, before it was attached to the Book of Daniel.

14, 3: *Bel:* see the note on Dn 4, 5.

⁷ Daniel began to laugh. "Do not be deceived, O king," he said; "it is only clay inside and bronze outside; it has never taken any food or drink." ⁸ Enraged, the king called his priests and said to them, "Unless you tell me who it is that consumes these provisions, you shall die. ⁹ But if you can show that Bel consumes them, Daniel shall die for blaspheming Bel." Daniel said to the king, "Let it be as you say!" ¹⁰ There were seventy priests of Bel, besides their wives and children.

When the king went with Daniel into the temple of Bel, ¹¹ the priests of Bel said, "See, we are going to leave. Do you, O king, set out the food and prepare the wine; then shut the door and seal it with your ring. ¹² If you do not find that Bel has eaten it all when you return in the morning, we are to die; otherwise Daniel shall die for his lies against us." ¹³ They were not perturbed, because under the table they had made a secret entrance through which they always came in to consume the food. ¹⁴ After they departed the king set the food before Bel, while Daniel ordered his servants to bring some ashes, which they scattered through the whole temple; the king alone was present. Then they went outside, sealed the closed door with the king's ring, and departed. ¹⁵ The priests entered that night as usual, with their wives and children, and they ate and drank everything.

¹⁶ Early the next morning, the king came with Daniel. ¹⁷ "Are the seals unbroken, Daniel?" he asked. And Daniel answered, "They are unbroken, O king." ¹⁸ As soon as he had opened the door, the king looked at the table and cried aloud, "Great you are, O Bel; there is no trickery in you." ¹⁹ But Daniel laughed and kept the king from entering. "Look at the floor," he said; "whose footprints are these?" ²⁰ "I see the footprints of men, women, and children!" said the king. ²¹ The angry king arrested the priests, their wives, and their children. They showed him the secret door by which they used to enter to consume what was on the table. ²² He put them to death, and handed Bel over to Daniel, who destroyed it and its temple.

²³ There was a great dragon which the Babylonians worshiped. ²⁴ "Look!" said the king to Daniel, "you cannot deny that this is a living god, so adore it." ²⁵ But Daniel answered, "I adore the Lord, my God, for he is the living God. ²⁶ Give me permission, O king, and I will kill this dragon without sword or club." "I give you permission," the king said. ²⁷ Then Daniel took some pitch, fat, and hair; these he boiled together and made into cakes. He put them into the mouth of the dragon, and when the dragon ate them, he burst asunder. "This," he said, "is what you worshiped."

²⁸ When the Babylonians heard this, they were angry and turned against the king. "The king has become a Jew," they said; "he has destroyed Bel, killed the dragon, and put the priests to death." ²⁹ They went to the king and demanded: "Hand Daniel over to us, or we will kill you and your family." ³⁰ When he saw himself threatened with violence, the king was forced to hand Daniel over to them. ³¹ They threw Daniel into a lions' den, where he remained six days. ³² In the den were seven lions, and two carcasses and two sheep had been given to them daily. But now they were given nothing, so that they would devour Daniel.

³³ In Judea there was a prophet, Habakkuk; he mixed some bread in a bowl with the stew he had boiled, and was going to bring it to the reapers in the field, ³⁴ when an angel of the Lord told him, "Take the lunch you have to Daniel in the lions' den at Babylon." ³⁵ But Habakkuk answered, "Babylon, sir, I have never seen, and I do not know the den!" ³⁶ ⁱ The angel of the Lord seized him by the crown of his head and carried him by the hair; with the speed of the wind, he set him down in Babylon above the den. ³⁷ "Daniel, Daniel," cried Habakkuk, "take the lunch God has sent you." ³⁸ "You have remembered me, O God," said Daniel; "you have not forsaken those who love you." ³⁹ While Daniel began to eat, the angel of the Lord at once brought Habakkuk back to his own place.

⁴⁰ On the seventh day the king came to mourn for Daniel. As he came to the den and looked in, there was Daniel, sitting there! ⁴¹ The king cried aloud, "You are great, O Lord, the God of Daniel, and there is no other besides you!" ⁴² Daniel he took out, but those who had tried to destroy him he threw into the den, and they were devoured in a moment before his eyes.

ⁱ Ez 8, 3.

THE BOOK OF HOSEA

Hosea belonged to the northern kingdom and began his prophetic career in the last years of Jeroboam II (786-746 B.C.). Some believe that he was a priest, others that he was a cult prophet; the prophecy, our only source of information concerning his life, gives us no certain answer in the matter. The collected oracles reveal a very sensitive, emotional man who could pass quickly from violent anger to the deepest tenderness. The prophecy pivots around his own unfortunate marriage to Gomer, a personal tragedy which profoundly influenced his teaching. In fact, his own prophetic vocation and message were immeasurably deepened by the painful experience he underwent in his married life.

Gomer, the adulteress, symbolized faithless Israel. And just as Hosea could not give up his wife forever even when she played the harlot, so Yahweh could not renounce Israel, who had been betrothed to him. God would chastise, but it would be the chastisement of the jealous lover, longing to bring back the beloved to the fresh and pure joy of their first love.

Israel's infidelity took the form of idolatry and ruthless oppression of the poor. No amount of mechanically offered sacrifices could atone for her serious sins. Chastisement alone remained; God would have to strip her of the rich ornaments bestowed by her false lovers and thus bring her back to the true lover. A humiliated Israel would again seek Yahweh. The eleventh chapter of Hosea is one of the summits of Old Testament theology; God's love for his people has never been expressed more tenderly. Hosea began the tradition of describing the relation between Yahweh and Israel in terms of marriage. This symbolism appears later on in the Old Testament; and, in the New, both St. John and St. Paul express in the same imagery the union between Christ and his church.

The Book of Hosea is divided as follows: I. The Prophet's Marriage and Its Lesson (1, 1—3, 5). II. Israel's Guilt and Punishment (4, 1—14, 10).

I: THE PROPHET'S MARRIAGE AND ITS LESSON*

CHAPTER 1

Marriage with an Unfaithful Wife. ¹The word of the LORD that came to Hosea, the son of Beeri, in the days of Uzziah, Jotham, Ahaz, Hezekiah, kings of Judah, and in the days of Jeroboam, son of Joash, king of Israel. ²In the beginning of the LORD's speaking to Hosea, the LORD said to Hosea:

Go, take a harlot wife* and harlot's children,
for the land gives itself to harlotry,
turning away from the LORD.

³So he went and took Gomer, the daughter of Diblaim; and she conceived and bore him a son. ⁴Then the LORD said to him:

Give him the name Jezreel,*
for in a little while
I will punish the house of Jehu
for the bloodshed at Jezreel

And bring to an end the kingdom
of the house of Israel;
⁵ On that day I will break the bow of Israel
in the valley of Jezreel.

⁶When she conceived again and bore a daughter, the LORD said to him:

Give her the name Lo-ruhama;*
I no longer feel pity for the house of Israel:
rather, I abhor them utterly.

1—3: This section is ordinarily thought to be biographical, the prophet's personal tragedy figuring as the relation of God to his people Israel. Hosea's marriage to a harlot wife represents Israel's infidelity to her Lord; hence the symbolic names of the children (Hos 1, 4-9). In Hos 2, 4-25 the Lord protests this infidelity and decrees its consequences, but promises restoration in return for amendment; his punishments are medicinal. In chapter 3 Hosea once more takes back his wife, but only conditionally, signifying God's long-suffering love for Israel and hope for her return.
1, 2: *A harlot wife:* this does not necessarily mean that Gomer was a harlot when Hosea married her; the verse describes the event in its final consequences.
1, 4: *Jezreel:* the strategic valley in northern Israel where Jehu brought the dynasty of Omri to an end through bloodshed (2 Kgs 9—10). Jeroboam II was the last king but one of the house of Jehu; the prophecy in this verse was fulfilled by the murder of his son, who reigned only six months (2 Kgs 15, 8-10).
1, 6: *Lo-ruhama:* "she is not pitied." The "pity" that is here withheld from Israel is God's gratuitous love which inspires his beneficent acts.

7 Yet for the house of Judah I feel pity;
  I will save them by the LORD, their
    God;
But I will not save them by war,
  by sword or bow, by horses or horse-
    men.*

8 After she weaned Lo-ruhama, she conceived and bore a son. 9 Then the LORD
said:

Give him the name of Lo-ammi,*
  for you are not my people,
  and I will not be your God.

CHAPTER 2

Israel's Punishment and Restoration

4 Protest against your mother, protest!*
  for she is not my wife,
  and I am not her husband.
Let her remove her harlotry from be-
    fore her,
  her adultery from between her
    breasts,
5 Or I will strip her naked,*
  leaving her as on the day of her birth;
I will make her like the desert,
  reduce her to an arid land,
  and slay her with thirst.
6 I will have no pity on her children,
  for they are the children of harlotry.

1, 7: The terrible punishments announced by the prophets were
so fully realized that later generations made a point of recalling
the same prophets' messages of consolation also, even though it
meant taking these from another context. Thus, an editor placed
the words of Hos 2, 1ff after the repudiation of Israel in Hos 1,
9; here the more natural order has been restored. The present
verse is another example of the same thing. In addition, it may be
the work of a later hand, dating from a time when the prophecies
of Hosea were circulated in the south, after the dissolution of the
northern kingdom that he had prophesied. The second part of the
verse emphasizes the power of the Lord, who needs no human
agents to fulfill his will. It may refer to the deliverance of Jerusalem from the siege of Sennacherib (2 Kgs 19, 35ff).
  1, 9: *Lo-ammi:* "not my people."
  2, 4: The Lord speaks of Israel, still using the example of
Hosea's wife.
  2, 5: *I will strip her naked:* contemporary documents indicate that this was a conventional punishment for adultery.
  2, 7: *My lovers:* the local fertility deities to whom, rather
than to the Lord (v 10), the unfaithful Israelites attributed the
produce of the land.
  2, 15: *The days of the Baals:* ritual observances held in various local shrines in honor of Baal.
  2, 8f: The crop failures, blight, etc., sent by the Lord (vv 11-
14) have as their purpose to make Israel see the folly of her ways.
  2, 16f: Israel's journey in the desert represents for Hosea the
time of Israel's fidelity, before it was corrupted by the ways of
Canaan; cf Jer 2, 2-7; Am 5, 25. Thus, he pictures a restoration
in terms of a new entry into the promised land.

7 Yes, their mother has played the harlot;
  she that conceived them has acted
    shamefully.
"I will go after my lovers,"* she said,
  "who give me my bread and my
    water,
  my wool and my flax, my oil and my
    drink."

10 Since she has not known
    that it was I who gave her
    the grain, the wine, and the oil,
  And her abundance of silver,
    and of gold, which they used for
      Baal,
11 Therefore I will take back my grain in
    its time,
    and my wine in its season;
  I will snatch away my wool and my flax,
    with which she covers her nakedness.
12 So now I will lay bare her shame
    before the eyes of her lovers,
    and no one can deliver her out of my
      hand.
13 I will bring an end to all her joy,
    her feasts, her new moons, her sab-
      baths,
    and all her solemnities.
14 I will lay waste her vines and fig trees,
    of which she said, "These are the hire
    my lovers have given me";
  I will turn them into rank growth
    and wild beasts shall devour them.
15 I will punish her for the days of the
    Baals,*
    for whom she burnt incense
  While she decked herself out with her
    rings and her jewels,
    and, in going after her lovers,
    forgot me, says the LORD.

8 Therefore, I will hedge in her way with
    thorns*
    and erect a wall against her,
    so that she cannot find her paths.
9 If she runs after her lovers, she shall not
    overtake them;
    if she looks for them she shall not
    find them.
  Then she shall say,
    "I will go back to my first husband,
    for it was better with me then than
      now."

16 So I will allure her;*
    I will lead her into the desert
    and speak to her heart.

Hos

¹⁷ From there I will give her the vineyards
    she had,
    and the valley of Achor as a door of
      hope.
She shall respond there as in the days of
    her youth,
    when she came up from the land of
      Egypt.
¹⁸   On that day, says the LORD,
She shall call me "My husband,"
    and never again "My baal."*
¹⁹ Then will I remove from her mouth the
    names of the Baals,
    so that they shall no longer be in-
      voked.
²⁰ I will make a covenant for them on that
    day,
    with the beasts of the field,
With the birds of the air,
    and with the things that crawl on the
      ground.
Bow and sword and war
    I will destroy from the land,
    and I will let them take their rest in
      security.
²¹ I will espouse you to me forever:*
    I will espouse you in right and in jus-
      tice,
    in love and in mercy;
²² I will espouse you in fidelity,
    and you shall know the LORD.

²³ On that day I will respond, says the
    LORD;
    I will respond to the heavens,
    and they shall respond to the earth;
²⁴ The earth shall respond to the grain,
    and wine, and oil,
    and these shall respond to Jezreel.
²⁵ I will sow him for myself in the land,
    and I will have pity on Lo-ruhama.
I will say to Lo-ammi, "You are my
    people,"
    and he shall say, "My God!"ᵃ

CHAPTER 3

Triumph of Love

¹ * Again the LORD said to me:

Give your love to a woman
    beloved of a paramour, an adulteress;
Even as the LORD loves the people of Is-
    rael,
    though they turn to other gods
    and are fond of raisin cakes.*

² So I bought her for fifteen pieces of
silver and a homer* and a lethech of barley. ³ Then I said to her:

"Many days you shall wait for me;
    you shall not play the harlot
Or belong to any man;
    I in turn will wait for you."
⁴ For the people of Israel shall remain
    many days
    without king or prince,
Without sacrifice or sacred pillar,*
    without ephod or household idols.
⁵ Then the people of Israel shall turn
    back
    and seek the LORD, their God,
    and David, their king;*
They shall come trembling to the LORD
    and to his bounty, in the last days. ᵇ
¹ * The number of the Israelites
    shall be like the sand of the sea,
    which can be neither measured nor
    counted.

---

a Rom 9, 25; 1 Pt 2, 10.—b Ez 34, 23.

2, 18: *My baal:* the word means "lord, master." It was commonly used by women of their husbands, but it is to be shunned as
a title for the Lord because of its association with the pagan god
Baal. Probably it had been so used by many Israelites, who saw
little if any difference between the worship of the Lord and the
worship of Baal.
2, 21f: The Lord will once more espouse Israel; the qualities
ascribed to the renewed people are the bridal gift (cf Gn 24, 53)
with which he will endow it. *In right and in justice:* two terms
dear to Hosea, used by him especially to condemn the popular social injustice and corruption of the legal processes. Here they
mean right conduct in general. *Love:* one of the most characteristic words of Hosea's prophecy. It means a dutiful love, based on
a social relation; here it refers to the covenant between God and
his people. It is a love fulfilled by the performance of mutual obligations. *Mercy:* from the same root as the word translated *pity*
in Hos 1, 6; cf v 25. *And you shall know the Lord:* another
characteristic expression of Hosea; cf Hos 4, 1; 5, 4; 6, 3. 6. It
means not an abstract but a practical knowledge, i.e., acknowledgment of his will, obedience to his law.
3, 1-5: Hosea is instructed to take Gomer back, redeeming her
from her paramours. On condition of her amendment, she will be
restored to her former position as wife. This in turn signifies
God's enduring love for his people. He will put the people through
a period of trial—the dissolution of the kingdom—in order that
they may return to him wholeheartedly.
3, 1: *Raisin cakes:* offerings to the fertility goddess Ashera,
the female counterpart of Baal; cf Jer 7, 18; 44, 19.
3, 2: *Homer:* about ten bushels. *Lethech:* a half-homer.
3, 4: *Sacred pillar:* the stone massebah, originally perhaps a
phallic symbol, representing Baal. These were also used, with another signification, in Israelite worship; see notes on Gn 28, 18;
Ex 34, 13. *Ephod:* an instrument used in consulting the deity; cf
1 Sm 23, 6-12; 30, 7; see notes on Ex 28, 6. 15-30. *Household
idols:* images regarded as the tutelary deities of the household; cf
Gn 31, 19; Jgs 17, 5; 18, 14. 17f.
3, 5: *David, their king:* the messianic King of the Davidic line
who will restore the kingdom of God's people; cf Jer 23, 5; Ez
34, 23f. *The last days:* the messianic age.
3, 1-3: These verses *(The number . . . Ruhama)* (transposed
from ch 2) continue the conditional promise of restoration made
in Hos 3, 1-5, reversing the dire predictions of chapter 1; the
symbolic names now become names of honor: *Jezreel,* "God
sows"; *Ammi,* "my people"; *Ruhama,* "she is pitied."

Whereas they were called
"Lo-ammi,"
They shall be called,
"Children of the living God."ᶜ

2 Then the people of Judah and of Israel
shall be gathered together;
They shall appoint for themselves one
head
and come up from other lands,
for great shall be the day of Jezreel.

3 Say to your brothers, "Ammi,"
and to your sisters, "Ruhama."

II: ISRAEL'S GUILT AND PUNISHMENT

CHAPTER 4

Crimes of Israel

1 Hear the word of the LORD, O people of
Israel,
for the LORD has a grievance
against the inhabitants of the land:
There is no fidelity, no mercy,
no knowledge of God in the land.

2 False swearing, lying, murder, stealing
and adultery!
in their lawlessness, bloodshed follows bloodshed. ᵈ

3 Therefore the land mourns,
and everything that dwells in it languishes:
The beasts of the field,
the birds of the air,
and even the fish of the sea perish.

Guilt of the Priests

4 But let no one protest, let no one complain;
with you is my grievance, O priests!*

5 You shall stumble in the day,
and the prophets shall stumble with
you at night;

---

c Rom 9, 26.—d Ex 20, 13-17.—e Is 24, 2.

4, 4ff: Hosea is particularly severe with the *priests* in the
northern kingdom, who had led the way in the general apostasy
from God's law. The *prophets* here associated with the priests (v
5) were doubtless cult prophets, who were often unworthy of
their pretended calling; cf Jer 2, 8; 4, 9f; 6, 13f; 23, 9-40.
4, 12: *Wood . . . wand:* an idol used in divination.
4, 14: *With prostitutes you offer sacrifice:* the ritual prostitution practiced at the Canaanite shrines was introduced even
into sanctuaries dedicated to the Lord. In comparison, the adultery that had become common in Israel was a far less reprehensible crime.
4, 15: *Gilgal:* not the Gilgal of the south (Jos 4, 19f), but a
sanctuary north of Bethel where there was an association of cult
prophets (2 Kgs 2, 1ff; 4, 38). *Beth-aven:* literally, "house of iniquity," Hosea's nickname for Bethel, or a scribal substitute for
Bethel, "house of god," in this context. Bethel was one of the
royal shrines of Israel, where there was a schismatic public worship of the Lord; cf 1 Kgs 12, 26-30.

I will destroy your mother.

6 My people perish for want of knowl-
edge!
Since you have rejected knowledge,
I will reject you from my priesthood;
Since you have ignored the law of your
God,
I will also ignore your sons.

7 One and all they sin against me,
exchanging their glory for shame.

8 They feed on the sin of my people,
and are greedy for their guilt.

9 The priests shall fare no better than the
people:
I will punish them for their ways,
and repay them for their deeds. ᵉ

10 They shall eat but not be satisfied,
they shall play the harlot but not increase,
Because they have abandoned the LORD

11 to practice harlotry.

Old wine and new
deprive my people of understanding.

12 They consult their piece of wood,
and their wand* makes pronouncements for them,
For the spirit of harlotry has led them
astray;
they commit harlotry, forsaking their
God.

13 On the mountaintops they offer sacrifice
and on the hills they burn incense,
Beneath oak and poplar and terebinth,
because of their pleasant shade.
That is why your daughters play the
harlot,
and your daughters-in-law are adulteresses.

14 Am I then to punish your daughters for
their harlotry,
your daughters-in-law for their adultery?
You yourselves consort with harlots,
and with prostitutes you offer sacrifice!*
So must a people without understanding come to ruin.

15 Though you play the harlot, O Israel,
let not Judah become guilty!
Come not to Gilgal,*
nor up to Beth-aven,
to swear, "As the Lord lives!"

16 For Israel is as stubborn as a heifer;

Hos

will the LORD now give them broad
  pastures
  as though they were lambs?
[17] Ephraim* is an associate of idols,
  let him alone!
[18] When their carousing is over,
  they give themselves to harlotry;
  in their arrogance they love shame.
[19] The wind has bound them up in its pinions;*
  they shall have only shame from their
  altars.

CHAPTER 5

Guilt of the Leaders

[1] Hear this, O priests,
  Pay attention, O house of Israel,
  O household of the king, give ear!
  It is you who are called to judgment.*f*
  For you have become a snare at Mizpah,*
  and a net spread upon Tabor.
[2] In their perversity they have sunk into
  wickedness,
  and I am rejected by them all.

[3] I know Ephraim,
  and Israel is not hidden from me;
  Now Ephraim has played the harlot,
  Israel is defiled.
[4] Their deeds do not allow them
  to return to their God;
  For the spirit of harlotry is in them,
  and they do not recognize the LORD.

[5] The arrogance of Israel bears witness
  against him;
  Ephraim stumbles in his guilt,
  and Judah stumbles with them.
[6] With their flocks and their herds they
  shall go
  to seek the LORD, but they shall not
  find him:
  he has withdrawn himself from them.
[7] They have been untrue to the LORD,
  for they have begotten illegitimate
  children;
  Now shall the new moon devour them
  together with their fields.

Political Upheavals*

[8] Blow the horn in Gibeah,
  the trumpet in Ramah!
  Sound the alarm in Beth-aven:
  "Look behind you, O Benjamin!"*

[9] Ephraim shall become a waste
  on the day of chastisement:
  Against the tribes of Israel
  I announce what is sure to be.
[10] The princes of Judah have become
  like those that move a boundary line;*
  Upon them I will pour out
  my wrath like water.*g*

[11] Is Ephraim maltreated, his rights
  violated?
  No, he has willingly gone after filth!*
[12] I am like a moth for Ephraim,
  like maggots* for the house of Judah.
[13] When Ephraim saw his infirmity,
  and Judah his sore,
  Ephraim went to Assyria,
  and Judah sent to the great king.*
  But he cannot heal you
  nor take away your sore.
[14] For I am like a lion to Ephraim,
  like a young lion to the house of
  Judah;
  It is I who rend the prey and depart,
  I carry it away and no one can save it
  from me.

Insincere Conversion

[15] I will go back to my place
  until they pay for their guilt
  and seek my presence.*

---

f Mi 3, 1.—g Dt 19, 14; 27, 17.

4, 17: *Ephraim:* the heartland of the northern kingdom. During the latter part of Hosea's prophetic career, Ephraim was all that remained of Israel after the Assyrians had overrun Transjordan and Galilee.
4, 19: The Israelites shall be carried from their country as by a whirlwind. To this their idolatry has brought them.
5, 1: *Mizpah:* probably the Mizpah in Transjordan is meant; cf Jos 11, 8. *Tabor:* the mountain that dominates the valley of Jezreel.
5, 8-14: This passage refers to the Syro-Ephraimite war of 735-734 B.C., when a coalition of Arameans and Israelites attempted to dethrone the king of Judah. Judah repulsed the attempt with the aid of Assyria, and the latter devastated both Aram and Israel; cf 2 Kgs 16, 5-9. Hosea condemns both Israel and Judah for the war.
5, 8: A vision of invasion, from *Gibeah* and *Ramah* in northern Judah, into Israel.
5, 10: *Like those that move a boundary line:* comparison of the invaders to a classic case of social injustice; cf Dt 19, 14; 27, 17; Prv 23, 10f.
5, 11: *Gone after filth:* by allying himself with Aram.
5, 12: *Moth . . . maggots:* internal corruption will work the Lord's punishment on both Israel and Judah.
5, 13: *Ephraim went . . . the great king:* in 738 B.C. the Israelite king Manahem had to pay tribute to the Assyrian king Tiglath-pileser III, whose vassal he became (2 Kgs 15, 19f). Under the threat of the Syro-Ephraimite invasion King Ahaz of Judah also submitted himself and his country to Tiglath-pileser (2 Kgs 16, 7-9). "The great king" was the title used by the Assyrian kings.
5, 15: The Lord withdraws himself from Israel, hoping for its repentance.

CHAPTER 6

* In their affliction, they shall look for
me:
1   "Come, let us return to the LORD,
For it is he who has rent, but he will
heal us;
he has struck us, but he will bind our
wounds.
2 He will revive us after two days;*
on the third day he will raise us up,
to live in his presence. *h*
3 Let us know, let us strive to know the
LORD;
as certain as the dawn is his coming,
and his judgment shines forth like the
light of day!
He will come to us like the rain,
like spring rain that waters the earth."

4 What can I do with you, Ephraim?
What can I do with you, Judah?
Your piety* is like a morning cloud,
like the dew that early passes away.
5 For this reason I smote them through
the prophets,
I slew them by the words of my
mouth;
6 For it is love that I desire, not sacrifice,
and knowledge of God rather than
holocausts. *i*
7 But they, in their land, violated the
covenant;
there they were untrue to me.

8 Gilead is a city of evildoers,
tracked with blood.
9 As brigands ambush a man,
a band of priests slay on the way to
Shechem,

---

h 1 Cor 15, 4.—i 1 Sm 15, 22; Eccl 4, 17; Mt 9, 13; 12, 7.

6, 1: *In . . . me:* this is the last line of ch 5.
6, 2: *After two days; on the third day:* after a short lapse
of time.
6, 4: *Piety:* the word is translated "love" in Hos 2, 21 and in
v 6 below.
6, 11: *Harvest:* when the land will reap the consequences of
its sins.
7, 3-7: This passage refers to the dynastic upheavals of Israel's
declining days. Between the death of Jeroboam II and the fall of
Samaria to the Assyrians, a matter of some twenty-five years, there
were four separate dynasties on the throne and as many murdered
kings. The prophet compares the Israelite nobles who were inflamed
with passion to an overheated oven that consumes what it is supposed to bake; thus the land consumes its kings. *Regale:* with wine
(v 3). Like fire smoldering through the night and blazing up in the
morning, the sleeping anger of plotters soon breaks out in open
rebellion; the succession of night and morning suggests the short
reigns of the various kings of this troubled period.
7, 8: *A hearth cake unturned:* burnt on one side, half baked
on the other, and therefore useless. Israel's decline in power is
ascribed to its disastrous meddling in the power politics of the
neighboring nations.

---

committing monstrous crime.
10 In the house of Israel I have seen a horrible thing:
there harlotry is found in Ephraim,
Israel is defiled.
11 For you also, O Judah,
a harvest* has been appointed.

CHAPTER 7

1 When I would bring about the restoration of my people,
when I would heal Israel,
The guilt of Ephraim stands out,
the wickedness of Samaria;
They practice falsehood,
thieves break in, bandits plunder
abroad.
2 Yet they do not remind themselves
that I remember all their wickedness.
Even now their crimes surround them,
present to my sight.

Failure of the Monarchy*

3 In their wickedness they regale the king,
the princes too, with their deceits.
4 They are all kindled to wrath
like a blazing oven,
Whose fire the baker desists from stirring
once the dough is kneaded until it has
risen.
5 On the day of our king,
the princes are overcome with the
heat of wine.
He extends his hand among dis-
semblers;
6   the plotters approach with hearts like
ovens.
All the night their anger sleeps;
in the morning it flares like a blazing
fire.
7 They are all heated like ovens,
and consume their rulers.
All their kings have fallen;
none of them calls upon me.

Foreign Alliances

8 Ephraim mingles with the nations,
Ephraim is a hearth cake unturned.*
9 Strangers have sapped his strength,
but he takes no notice of it;
Of gray hairs, too, there is a sprinkling,
but he takes no notice of it.
10 The arrogance of Israel bears witness
against him;

Hos

yet they do not return to the LORD,
their God,
nor seek him, for all that.

11 Ephraim is like a dove,
silly and senseless;
They call upon Egypt,
they go to Assyria.

12 Even as they go I will spread my net
around them,
like birds in the air I will bring them
down.
In an instant I will send them captive
from their land.

Perversity of Israel

13 Woe to them, they have strayed from
me!
Ruin to them, they have sinned
against me!
Though I wished to redeem them,
they spoke lies against me.

14 They have not cried to me from their
hearts
when they wailed upon their beds;
For wheat and wine they lacerated
themselves,*
while they rebelled against me.

15 Though I trained and strengthened
their arms,
yet they devised evil against me.

16 They have again become useless,
like a treacherous bow.
Their princes shall fall by the sword
because of the insolence of their
tongues;
thus they shall be mocked in the land
of Egypt.

CHAPTER 8

1 A trumpet to your lips,
you who watch over the house of the
LORD!
Since they have violated my covenant,
and sinned against my law,

2 While to me they cry out,
"O God of Israel, we know you!"

3 The men of Israel have thrown away
what is good;
the enemy shall pursue them.

4 * They made kings, but not by my authority;
they established princes, but without
my approval.
With their silver and gold they made
idols for themselves, to their own destruction.

5 Cast away your calf, O Samaria!
my wrath is kindled against them;
How long will they be unable to attain
innocence in Israel?

6 The work of an artisan,
no god at all,
Destined for the flames—
such is the calf of Samaria!

7 When they sow the wind,
they shall reap the whirlwind;
The stalk of grain that forms no ear
can yield no flour;
Even if it could,
strangers would swallow it.

8 Israel is swallowed up;
he is now among the nations
a thing of no value.

9 They went up to Assyria—
a wild ass off on its own—
Ephraim bargained for lovers.

10 Even though they bargain with the nations,
I will now gather an army;
King and princes shall shortly
succumb under the burden.

11 When Ephraim made many altars to expiate sin,
his altars became occasions of sin.*

12 Though I write for him my many ordinances,
they are considered as a stranger's.

13 Though they offer sacrifice,
immolate flesh and eat it,
the LORD is not pleased with them.
He shall still remember their guilt
and punish their sins;
they shall return to Egypt.

14 Israel has forgotten his maker
and built palaces.
Judah, too, has fortified many cities;
but I will send fire upon his cities,
to devour their castles.*j*

---

j Am 2, 5.

7, 14: *They lacerated themselves:* a common oriental practice in prayers of earnest impetration (1 Kgs 18, 28); the practice
was forbidden in Israelite religion (Lv 19, 28; Dt 14, 1).

8, 4-6: Israel's monarchy and separate sanctuary are here associated, as in 1 Kgs 12, 20-33; both were the result of rebellion
against the divinely approved Davidic dynasty and the Jerusalem
temple with the ark of the covenant. The calf image set up by
Jeroboam I in the royal shrines prevented Israel from attaining
innocence (vv 5f).

8, 11: The very multiplicity of sanctuaries throughout the land
was a danger to the purity of worship. The local shrines were
speedily assimilated to the cult places used by the Canaanites, and
the Lord was identified with the god Baal worshiped there. Thus
the Deuteronomic writers, influenced by prophetic ideas, ended
by restricting sacrificial worship to the one temple in Jerusalem.

CHAPTER 9

Exile without Worship

*R*joice not, O Israel,
    exult not like the nations!
*F*or you have been unfaithful to your
        God,
    loving a harlot's hire
    upon every threshing floor.*
Threshing floor and wine press shall not
        nourish them,
    the new wine shall fail them.
3 They shall not dwell in the LORD's
        land;
    Ephraim shall return to Egypt,
    and in Assyria they shall eat unclean
        food.
4 They shall not pour libations of wine to
        the LORD,
    or proffer their sacrifices before him.
    Theirs will be like mourners' bread,*
        that makes unclean all who eat of it;
    Such food as they have shall be for
        themselves;
    it cannot enter the house of the
        LORD.
5 What will you do on the festival day,
    the day of the LORD's feast?*
6 When they go from the ruins,
    Egypt shall gather them in, Memphis
        shall bury them.
    Weeds shall overgrow their silver trea-
        sures,
    and thorns invade their tents.

The Prophet Ridiculed

7 They have come, the days of punish-
        ment!
    they have come, the days of recom-
        pense!

Let Israel know it!
    "The prophet is a fool,
    the man of the spirit is mad!"
Because your iniquity is great,
    great, too, is your hostility.
8 A prophet is Ephraim's watchman with
        God,
    yet a fowler's snare is on all his ways,
    hostility in the house of his God.
9 They have sunk to the depths of corrup-
        tion,
    as in the days of Gibeah;*
He shall remember their iniquity
    and punish their sins.

Crime of Baal-peor

10 Like grapes in the desert,
    I found Israel;
Like the first fruits of the fig tree in its
        prime,
    I considered your fathers.
When they came to Baal-peor*
    and consecrated themselves to the
        Shame,
    they became as abhorrent as the thing
        they loved.
11 The glory of Ephraim flies away like a
        bird:
    no birth, no carrying in the womb, no
        conception.
Were they to bear children,
    I would slay the darlings of their
        womb.
12 Even though they bring up their chil-
        dren,
    I will make them childless, till not
        one is left.
Woe to them
    when I turn away from them!

13 Ephraim, as I saw, was like Tyre,
    planted in a beauteous spot;
But Ephraim shall bring out
    his children to the slayer.
14 Give them, O LORD!
    give them what?
Give them an unfruitful womb,*
    and dry breasts!

Crime of Gilgal

15 All their wickedness is in Gilgal;*
    yes, there they incurred my hatred
Because of their wicked deeds
    I will drive them out of my house.
I will love them no longer;
    all their princes are rebels.*k*

---

k 1 Sm 8, 5.

9, 1f: *Upon every threshing floor:* an allusion to harvest festivals in honor of Baal, to whom the Israelites had attributed the
fertility of the land; cf Hos 2, 7.
9, 4: *Mourners' bread:* bread eaten at funeral rites; cf Dt
26, 13f. Contact with a corpse made a person ritually unclean, together with everything he touched. Such bread could not be offered to the Lord.
9, 5: *The Lord's feast:* doubtless the autumn feast of Booths,
the most important of the Israelite public celebrations; cf Lv 23,
34.
9, 9: *The days of Gibeah:* a reference to the outrage committed at Gibeah in the days of the Judges (Jgs 19, 22-30).
9, 10: At *Baal-peor* (Nm 25, 1-5) the Israelites consecrated
themselves to Baal, here called *the Shame.*
9, 14: *An unfruitful womb:* this appears to be a reversal of
the ancient blessing of Joseph contained in Gn 49, 25f, in which
the increase, hence fruitfulness, promised to the patriarch is even
signified by the name of his son Ephraim, on whose descendants
the prophet now invokes the curse of extinction.
9, 15: *Gilgal:* see note on Hos 4, 15.

Hos

16 Ephraim is stricken,
      their root is dried up;
      they shall bear no fruit.

17 My God will disown them
      because they have not listened to
         him;
      they shall be wanderers among the
         nations.

CHAPTER 10

Punishment of Idolatry

1 Israel is a luxuriant vine
      whose fruit matches its growth.
   The more abundant his fruit,
      the more altars he built;
   The more productive his land,
      the more sacred pillars* he set up.
2 Their heart is false,
      now they pay for their guilt;
   God shall break down their altars
      and destroy their sacred pillars.
3 If they would say,
      "We have no king"—
   Since they do not fear the LORD,
      what can the king do for them?
4 Nothing but make promises,
      swear false oaths, and make alliances,
   While justice grows wild
      like wormwood* in a plowed field!

5 The inhabitants of Samaria fear
      for the calf of Beth-aven;*
   The people mourn for it
      and its priests wail over it,
      because the glory has departed from
         it.
6 It too shall be carried to Assyria,
      as an offering to the great king.
   Ephraim shall be taken into captivity,
      Israel be shamed by his schemes.

7 The king of Samaria shall disappear,
      like foam upon the waters.
8 The high places of Aven shall be de-
         stroyed,
      the sin of Israel;
      thorns and thistles shall overgrow
         their altars.
   Then they shall cry out to the moun-
      tains, "Cover us!"
   and to the hills, "Fall upon us!"*l*

9 Since the days of Gibeah
      you have sinned, O Israel.
   There they took their stand;
      war was not to reach them
         Gibeah.*m*
10 Against the wanton people I came
      and I chastised them;*n*
   I gathered troops against them
      when I chastised them for their t
         crimes.*

Time To Seek the Lord

11 Ephraim was a trained heifer,
      willing to thresh;
   I myself laid a yoke
      upon her fair neck;
   Ephraim was to be harnessed, Judah
      was to plow,
   Jacob was to break his furrows:

12 "Sow for yourselves justice,
      reap the fruit of piety;
   Break up for yourselves a new field,
      for it is time to seek the LORD,
      till he come and rain down justice
         upon you."*o*
13 But you have cultivated wickedness,
      reaped perversity,
      and eaten the fruit of falsehood.

   Because you have trusted in your
         chariots,
      and in your many warriors,
14 Turmoil shall break out among your
         tribes
      and all your fortresses shall be rav-
         aged
   As Salman ravaged Beth-arbel* in time
         of war,
      smashing mothers and their chil-
         dren.*p*

---

l Is 2, 19; Lk 23, 30; Rv 6, 16.—m Jgs 20, 1.—n Jer 4, 3.—o
Is 45, 8.—p Jgs 8, 10ff.

10, 1: *Sacred pillars:* see note on Hos 3, 4.
10, 4: *Justice . . . like wormwood:* the administration of justice, which should have been the mainstay of the people, has in
corrupt hands become another instrument of oppression; cf Am 6,
13.
10, 5: *The calf of Beth-aven:* see notes on Hos 4, 15; 8, 4ff.
10, 10: *Their two crimes:* possibly the outrage described in
Jgs 19 is conceived as a double crime, of adultery and murder. Or
the prophet regards the proclamation of the monarchy (cf 1 Sm
10, 23f) as a crime.
10, 14: *As Salman ravaged Beth-arbel:* allusion to an invasion not otherwise mentioned in the Bible. Salman may have been
the Moabite king of this name mentioned in an inscription of Tiglath-pileser III. There were several Beth-arbels in Palestine; this
one was probably in Transjordan.

15 So shall it be done to you, Bethel,
   because of your utter wickedness:
At dawn the king of Israel
   shall perish utterly.

CHAPTER 11

When Israel Was a Child

1 When Israel was a child I loved him,
   out of Egypt* I called my son.*q*
2 The more I called them,
   the farther they went from me,
Sacrificing to the Baals
   and burning incense to idols.
3 Yet it was I who taught Ephraim to
     walk,
   who took them in my arms;
4 I drew them with human cords,
   with bands of love;*
I fostered them like one
   who raises an infant to his cheeks;
Yet, though I stooped to feed my child,
   they did not know that I was their
     healer.

5 He shall return to the land of Egypt,
   and Assyria shall be his king;
6 The sword shall begin with his cities
   and end by consuming his solitudes.
Because they refused to repent,
   their own counsels shall devour
     them.
7 His people are in suspense about re-
     turning to him;
   and God, though in unison they cry
     out to him,
   shall not raise them up.

End of the Exile

8 How could I give you up, O Ephraim,
   or deliver you up, O Israel?
How could I treat you as Admah,
   or make you like Zeboiim?*

---

q Mt 2, 15.—r Gn 19, 24f.—s Gn 25, 26; 32, 25.

11, 1: *Out of Egypt:* Hosea, like most of the prophets, dates
the real beginning of Israel from the time of Moses and the
Exodus. Mt 2, 15 applies this text to the return of the Christ Child
from Egypt.
11, 4: *I drew them . . . with bands of love:* not forcing them
like draft animals, but drawing them with kindness and affection.
11, 8: *Admah . . . Zeboiim:* cities destroyed with Sodom and
Gomorrah (Dt 29, 22).
12, 2: *He comes . . . Egypt:* allusion to the commercial and
military pacts with the great powers, consistently condemned by
the prophets as derogatory of the Lord's claim on his people.
12, 3-7: Contemporary Israel and the Israel represented by its
ancestor Jacob (Israel) are here alternated, a splendid example
of the Hebrew concept of "corporate personality" or easy transition from the individual to the community of which he is part.
Hosea recalls the history of Jacob as it now appears in Genesis,
but with some differences of detail and order.

My heart is overwhelmed,
   my pity is stirred.*r*
9 I will not give vent to my blazing anger,
   I will not destroy Ephraim again;
For I am God and not man,
   the Holy One present among you;
   I will not let the flames consume you.

10 They shall follow the LORD,
   who roars like a lion;
When he roars,
   his sons shall come frightened from
     the west,
11 Out of Egypt they shall come trem-
     bling, like sparrows,
   from the land of Assyria, like doves;
And I will resettle them in their homes,
   says the LORD.

CHAPTER 12

Infidelity of Israel

1 Ephraim has surrounded me with lies,
   the house of Israel, with deceit;
Judah is still rebellious against God,
   against the Holy One, who is faithful.
2 Ephraim chases the wind,
   ever pursuing the gale.
His lies and falsehoods are many:
   he comes to terms with Assyria,
   and carries oil to Egypt.*

3 * The LORD has a grievance against Is-
     rael:
   he shall punish Jacob for his conduct,
   for his deeds he shall repay him.
4 In the womb he supplanted his brother,
   and as a man he contended with
     God;*s*
5 He contended with the angel and
     triumphed,
   entreating him with tears.
At Bethel he met God
   and there he spoke with him:
6 The LORD, the God of hosts,
   the LORD is his name!
7 You shall return by the help of your
     God,
   if you remain loyal and do right
   and always hope in your God.

8 A merchant who holds a false balance,
   who loves to defraud!
9 Though Ephraim says,
   "How rich I have become;
   I have made a fortune!"

Hos

All his gain shall not suffice him
  for the guilt of his sin.
¹⁰ I am the LORD, your God,
  since the land of Egypt;
  I will again have you live in tents,
  as in that appointed time.
¹¹ I granted many visions
  and spoke to the prophets,
  through whom I set forth examples.
¹² In Gilead is falsehood, they have come
  to nought,
  in Gilgal they sacrifice to bullocks;
  Their altars are like heaps of stones
  in the furrows of the field.

¹³ When Jacob fled to the land of Aram,
  he served for a wife;
  for a wife Israel tended sheep.ᵗ
¹⁴ By a prophet* the LORD brought Israel
  out of Egypt,
  and by a prophet they were pro-
  tected.ᵘ
¹⁵ Ephraim has exasperated his lord;
  therefore he shall cast his bloodguilt
  upon him
  and repay him for his outrage.

CHAPTER 13

¹ Ephraim's word caused fear,
  for he was exalted in Israel;
  but he sinned through Baal and died.

Punishment for Ingratitude

² Now they continue to sin,
  making for themselves molten images,
  Silver idols according to their fancy,
  all of them the work of artisans.
  "To these," they say, "offer sacrifice."
  Men kiss calves!
³ Therefore, they shall be like a morning
  cloud
  or like the dew that early passes
  away,
  Like chaff storm-driven from the
  threshing floor
  or like smoke out of the window.

⁴ I am the LORD, your God,
  since the land of Egypt;
  You know no God besides me,
  and there is no savior but me.ᵛ
⁵ I fed you in the desert,
  in the torrid land.
⁶ They ate their fill;
  when filled, they became proud of
  heart
  and forgot me.

⁷ Therefore, I will be like a lion to them,
  like a panther by the road I will keep
  watch.
⁸ I will attack them like a bear robbed of
  its young,
  and tear their hearts from their
  breasts;
  I will devour them on the spot like a
  lion,
  as though a wild beast were to rend
  them.

⁹ Your destruction, O Israel!
  who is there to help you?
¹⁰ Where now is your king,
  that he may rescue you in all your
  cities?
  And your rulers, of whom you said,
  "Give me a king and princes"?ʷ
¹¹ I give you a king in my anger,
  and I take him away in my wrath.*
¹² The guilt of Israel is wrapped up,
  his sin is stored away.
¹³ The birth pangs shall come for him,
  but he shall be an unwise child;
  For when it is time he shall not present
  himself
  where children break forth.*
¹⁴ Shall I deliver them from the power of
  the nether world?*
  shall I redeem them from death?ˣ
  Where are your plagues, O death!
  where is your sting, O nether world!
  My eyes are closed to compassion.

¹⁵ Though he be fruitful among his fellows,
  an east wind shall come, a wind from
  the LORD,
  rising from the desert,
  That shall dry up his spring,
  and leave his fountain dry.
  It shall loot his land
  of every precious thing.ʸ

---

t Gn 28, 5; 29, 20.—u Ex 14, 21f.—v Is 43, 11.—w 1 Sm 8,
5.—x 1 Cor 15, 54.—y Ex 19, 12.

12, 14: *A prophet:* Moses.
13, 11: *I give you a king . . . in my wrath:* the Lord
punishes the people of the northern kingdom by giving them incompetent kings who are soon deposed.
13, 13: Israel's sin is such as to warrant its destruction (v 12),
because it refuses to do penance. It will therefore perish as surely
as the unborn child which dies in its mother's body because it does
not properly employ the only way to safety.
13, 14: *Shall . . . nether world:* a vigorous affirmation of
the Lord's determination to destroy Israel. St. Paul cites these
words in a different sense (1 Cor 15, 54f), that of the ultimate
victory of life over death in the resurrection of the body on the
last day, wrought through the merits of Christ's passion and resurrection.

CHAPTER 14

¹ Samaria shall expiate her guilt,
for she has rebelled against her God.
They shall fall by the sword,
their little ones shall be dashed to
pieces,
their expectant mothers shall be
ripped open.

Sincere Conversion

² Return, O Israel, to the LORD, your
God;
you have collapsed through your
guilt.
³ Take with you words,
and return to the LORD;
Say to him, "Forgive all iniquity,
and receive what is good, that we may
render
as offerings the bullocks from our
stalls.
⁴ Assyria will not save us,
nor shall we have horses to mount;
We shall say no more, 'Our god,'
to the work of our hands;
for in you the orphan finds compassion."
⁵ I will heal their defection,

14, 10: A later addition in the style of the wisdom literature.

I will love them freely;
for my wrath is turned away from
them.
⁶ I will be like the dew for Israel:
he shall blossom like the lily;
He shall strike root like the Lebanon
cedar,
⁷ and put forth his shoots.
His splendor shall be like the olive tree
and his fragrance like the Lebanon
cedar.
⁸ Again they shall dwell in his shade
and raise grain;
They shall blossom like the vine,
and his fame shall be like the wine of
Lebanon.

⁹ Ephraim! What more has he to do with
idols?
I have humbled him, but I will
prosper him.
"I am like a verdant cypress tree"—
Because of me you bear fruit!

*   *   *

¹⁰ Let him who is wise understand these
things;
let him who is prudent know them.
Straight are the paths of the LORD,
in them the just walk,
but sinners stumble in them.*

THE BOOK OF JOEL

This prophecy is rich in apocalyptic imagery and strongly eschatological in tone. It was composed about 400 B.C. Its prevailing theme is the day of the Lord.

A terrible invasion of locusts ravaged Judah. So frightful was the scourge that the prophet visualized it as a symbol of the coming day of the Lord. In the face of this threatening catastrophe, the prophet summoned the people to repent, to turn to the Lord with fasting and weeping. They were ordered to convoke a solemn assembly in which the priests would pray for deliverance. The Lord answered their prayer and promised to drive away the locusts and bless the land with peace and prosperity. To these material blessings would be added an outpouring of the spirit on all flesh. St. Peter, in his first discourse before the people at Pentecost (Acts 2, 16-21), sees in the coming of the Holy Spirit the fulfillment of this promise (1, 1—3, 5).

The concluding poem pictures the nations gathered in the Valley of Jehoshaphat, where the Lord is about to pass judgment. Israel's enemies are summoned to hear the solemn indictment; their evil deeds are at last requited. The tumultuous throng assembled in the valley of decision is made up of the enemies of God and they face inevitable destruction. The oracle changes abruptly from the terrifying image of judgment to a vision of Israel restored and forever secure from her enemies. God is both the vindicator of his people and the source of their blessing (4, 1-21).

CHAPTER 1

The Land Invaded. ¹The word of the LORD which came to Joel, the son of Pethuel.

² Hear this, you elders!
Pay attention, all you who dwell in the land!
Has the like of this happened in your days,
or in the days of your fathers?
³ Tell it to your children,
and your children to their children,
and their children to the next generation.
⁴ What the cutter left,
the locust swarm has eaten;
What the locust swarm left,
the grasshopper has eaten;
And what the grasshopper left,
the devourer* has eaten.

⁵ Wake up, you drunkards, and weep;
wail, all you drinkers of wine,
Because the juice of the grape
will be withheld from your mouths.
⁶ For a people* has invaded my land,
mighty and without number;
His teeth are the teeth of a lion,
and his molars those of a lioness.
⁷ He has laid waste my vine,
and blighted my fig tree;
He has stripped it, sheared off its bark;
its branches are made white.

⁸ Lament like a virgin girt with sackcloth
for the spouse of her youth.
⁹ Abolished are offering and libation
from the house of the LORD;
In mourning are the priests,
the ministers of the LORD.
¹⁰ The field is ravaged,
the earth mourns,
Because the grain is ravaged,
the must has failed,
the oil languishes.

¹¹ Be appalled, you husbandmen!
wail, you vinedressers!
Over the wheat and the barley,
because the harvest of the field has perished.
¹² The vine has dried up,
the fig tree is withered;
The pomegranate, the date palm also,
and the apple,
all the trees of the field are dried up;
Yes, joy has withered away
from among mankind.

¹³ Gird yourselves and weep, O priests!
wail, O ministers of the altar!
Come, spend the night in sackcloth,
O ministers of my God!
The house of your God is deprived
of offering and libation.
¹⁴ Proclaim a fast,
call an assembly;
Gather the elders,
all who dwell in the land,
Into the house of the LORD, your God,
and cry to the LORD!ᵃ

¹⁵ Alas, the day!
for near is the day of the LORD,
and it comes as ruin from the Almighty.
¹⁶ From before our very eyes
has not the food been cut off;
And from the house of our God,
joy and gladness?
¹⁷ The seed lies shriveled under its clods;
the stores are destroyed,
The barns are broken down,
for the grain has failed.
¹⁸ How the beasts groan!
The herds of cattle are bewildered!
Because they have no pasturage,
even the flocks of sheep have perished.

¹⁹ To you, O LORD, I cry!
for fire has devoured the pastures of the plain,
and flame has enkindled all the trees of the field.
²⁰ Even the beasts of the field
cry out to you;
For the streams of water are dried up,
and fire has devoured the pastures of the plain.

CHAPTER 2

The Day of the Lord

¹ Blow the trumpet in Zion,
sound the alarm on my holy mountain!
Let all who dwell in the land tremble,
for the day of the LORD is coming;

---

a Jl 2, 15.

1, 4: *Cutter . . . locust . . . grasshopper . . . devourer:* these names refer to various species of locusts; they can only be approximate.
1, 6: *A people:* the locusts compared to an invading army.

2 Yes, it is near, a day of darkness and of
gloom,
a day of clouds and somberness!
Like dawn spreading over the mountains,
a people numerous and mighty!
Their like has not been from of old,
nor will it be after them,
even to the years of distant generations.

3 Before them a fire devours,
and after them a flame enkindles;
Like the garden of Eden is the land before them,
and after them a desert waste;
from them there is no escape.

4 Their appearance is that of horses;
like steeds they run.

5 As with the rumble of chariots
they leap on the mountaintops;
As with the crackling of a fiery flame
devouring stubble;
Like a mighty people
arrayed for battle.

6 Before them peoples are in torment,
every face blanches.

7 Like warriors they run,
like soldiers they scale the wall;
They advance, each in his own lane,
without swerving from their paths.

8 No one crowds another,
each advances in his own track;
Though they fall into the ditches,
they are not checked.

9 They assault the city,
they run upon the wall,
they climb into the houses;
In at the windows
they come like thieves.

10 Before them the earth trembles,
the heavens shake;
The sun and the moon are darkened,
and the stars withhold their brightness.[b]

11 The LORD raises his voice
at the head of his army;
For immense indeed is his camp,

yes, mighty, and it does his bidding.
For great is the day of the LORD,
and exceedingly terrible; who can
bear it?[c]

12 Yet even now, says the LORD,
return to me with your whole heart,
with fasting, and weeping, and
mourning;

13 Rend your hearts, not your garments,
and return to the LORD, your God.
For gracious and merciful is he,
slow to anger, rich in kindness,
and relenting in punishment.[d]

14 Perhaps he will again relent
and leave behind him a blessing,
Offerings and libations
for the LORD, your God.[e]

15 Blow the trumpet in Zion!
proclaim a fast,
call an assembly;[f]

16 Gather the people,
notify the congregation;
Assemble the elders,
gather the children
and the infants at the breast;
Let the bridegroom quit his room,
and the bride her chamber.

17 Between the porch and the altar*
let the priests, the ministers of the
LORD, weep,
And say, "Spare, O LORD, your people,
and make not your heritage a reproach,
with the nations ruling over them!
Why should they say among the peoples,
'Where is their God?' "

Blessings for God's People. 18 Then the
LORD was stirred to concern for his land
and took pity on his people. 19 The LORD
answered and said to his people:

See, I will send you
grain, and wine, and oil,
and you shall be filled with them;
No more will I make you
a reproach among the nations.

20 No, the northerner* I will remove far
from you,
and drive him out into a land arid and
waste,
With his van toward the eastern sea,
and his rear toward the western sea;
And his foulness shall go up,
and his stench shall go up.

---

b Jl 4, 15; Is 13, 10; Ez 32, 7f; Mt 24, 29; Mk 13, 24; Lk 21,
25f.—c Jer 30, 7; Am 5, 18; Zep 1, 15.—d Ps 86, 5; Jon 4, 2.—e
Jon 3, 9.—f Jl 1, 14.

2, 17: The priests stood in the open space between the outdoor
altar of holocausts and the temple building, facing the latter in
order thereby to look toward God present in the holy of holies.

2, 20: *The northerner:* the locusts, that are compared to an
invading army, which in Palestine came from the north; cf Jer 1,
14f; 4, 6; Ez 26, 7; 38, 6. 15.

JI

21 Fear not, O land!
exult and rejoice!
for thc LORD has done great things.
22 Fear not, beasts of the field!
for the pastures of the plain are
green;
The tree bears its fruit,
the fig tree and the vine give their
yield.

23 And do you, O children of Zion, exult
and rejoice in the LORD, your God!
He has given you the teacher of justice:*
he has made the rain come down for
you,
the early and the late rain as before.*g*
24 The threshing floors shall be full of
grain
and the vats shall overflow with wine
and oil.

25 And I will repay you for the years
which the locust has eaten,
The grasshopper, the devourer, and the
cutter,
my great army which I sent among
you.
26 You shall eat and be filled,
and shall praise the name of the
LORD, your God,
Because he has dealt wondrously with
you;
my people shall nevermore be put to
shame.
27 And you shall know that I am in the
midst of Israel;
I am the LORD, your God, and there
is no other;
my people shall nevermore be put to
shame.

CHAPTER 3

1 Then afterward I will pour out*h*
my spirit* upon all mankind.
Your sons and daughters shall prophesy,
your old men shall dream dreams,
your young men shall see visions;
2 Even upon the servants and the handmaids,
in those days, I will pour out my
spirit.

3 And I will work wonders in the heavens
and on the earth,
blood, fire, and columns of smoke;

4 The sun will be turned to darkness,
and the moon to blood,
At the coming of the day of the LORD,
the great and terrible day. *i*
5 Then everyone shall be rescued
who calls on the name of the LORD;
For on Mount Zion there shall be a
remnant,
as the LORD has said,
And in Jerusalem survivors
whom the LORD shall call.*j*

CHAPTER 4

Judgment upon the Nations

1 Yes, in those days, and at that time,
when I would restore the fortunes
of Judah and Jerusalem,
2 I will assemble all the nations
and bring them down to the Valley of
Jehoshaphat,*
And I will enter into judgment with
them there
on behalf of my people and my inheritance, Israel;
Because they have scattered them
among the nations,
and divided my land.
3 Over my people they have cast lots;
they gave a boy for a harlot,
and sold a girl for the wine they
drank.

4 Moreover, what are you to me, Tyre
and Sidon, and all the regions of Philistia?
Would you take vengeance upon me by
some action? But if you do take action
against me, swiftly, speedily, I will return
your deed upon your own head. 5 You took
my silver and my gold, and brought my
precious treasures into your temples! 6 You
sold the people of Judah and Jerusalem to
the Greeks, removing them far from their

---

g Hos 10, 12.—h 1-5: Is 44, 3; Acts 2, 17-21.—i Jl 2, 10.—j
Rom 10, 13.

2, 23: *The teacher of justice:* the rain sent by God to show
his fidelity to his promises, and to teach his people to be faithful
to his commandments; cf Dt 11, 14. There is also a play on words
here between the Hebrew word *moreh* (teacher) and the Hebrew word *yoreh* (the early rain). The expression likewise has a
messianic connotation; cf Is 30, 20. The founder of the Essene
sect of Qumran (second century B.C.) was known as "The
Teacher of Justice."

3, 1f: *I will pour out my spirit:* in the Old Testament the
spirit is the gift of God bestowed on those acting as his agents.
The promise of the spirit is quoted by St. Peter in Acts 2, 17-21
as fulfilled in an eminent way by the gift of the Holy Spirit, the
Third Person of the Blessed Trinity, bestowed on the Apostles.

4, 2: *Valley of Jehoshaphat:* a symbolic name of the place of
final judgment (v 14). The name Jehoshaphat signifies "Yahweh
judges." This place has been popularly identified with the Kidron
Valley.

own country! [7]See, I rouse them from the place into which you have sold them, and I will return your deed upon your own head. [8]I will sell your sons and your daughters to the people of Judah, who shall sell them to the Sabeans,* a nation far off. Indeed, the LORD has spoken.

[9] Declare this among the nations:
    proclaim a war,
    rouse the warriors to arms!
    Let all the soldiers
    report and march!
[10] Beat your plowshares into swords,
    and your pruning hooks into spears;
    let the weak man say, "I am a war-
    rior!"*

[11] Hasten and come, all you neighboring
    peoples,
    assemble there!
    [Bring down, O Lord, your warriors!*]
[12] Let the nations bestir themselves and
    come up
    to the Valley of Jehoshaphat;
    For there will I sit in judgment
    upon all the neighboring nations.

[13] Apply the sickle,[k]
    for the harvest is ripe;

Come and tread,
    for the wine press is full;
The vats overflow,
    for great is their malice.*
[14] Crowd upon crowd
    in the valley of decision;
For near is the day of the LORD
    in the valley of decision.
[15] Sun and moon are darkened,
    and the stars withhold their bright-
    ness.[l]
[16] The LORD roars from Zion,
    and from Jerusalem raises his voice;
The heavens and the earth quake,
    but the LORD is a refuge to his peo-
    ple,
    a stronghold to the men of Israel.[m]

Salvation for God's Elect

[17] Then shall you know that I, the LORD,
    am your God,
    dwelling on Zion, my holy mountain;
Jerusalem shall be holy,
    and strangers shall pass through her
    no more.
[18] And then, on that day,[n]
    the mountains shall drip new wine,
    and the hills shall flow with milk;
And the channels of Judah
    shall flow with water:
A fountain shall issue from the house of
    the LORD,
    to water the Valley of Shittim.*
[19] Egypt shall be a waste,
    and Edom a desert waste,
Because of violence done to the people
    of Judah,
    because they shed innocent blood in
    their land.
[20] But Judah shall abide forever,
    and Jerusalem for all generations.
[21] I will avenge their blood,
    and not leave it unpunished.
    The LORD dwells in Zion.

k Rv 14, 15.—l Jl 2, 10; 3, 4.—m Jer 25, 30; Am 1, 2.—n Am 9, 13; Ez 47, 1-12; Zec 14, 8.

4, 8: *Sabeans:* a south Arabian people known for their commerce.
4, 10: This imagery is used in the reverse sense in Is 2, 4; Mi 4, 3. Here the warlike weapons are made in response to God's summons to armies which he selected to expel forever the unlawful invaders from the land of his chosen people.
4, 11: *Warriors:* the angels; cf Zec 14, 5.
4, 13: Because of their numerous crimes, the nations are ripe for punishment. The use of warlike weapons against them is likened to the onslaught on the fields and vines at harvest time.
4, 18: *The Valley of Shittim,* or "the ravine of the acacia trees": perhaps a part of the Kidron Valley southeast of Jerusalem; the prophetic picture of a stream of water flowing from a fountain in the temple of Jerusalem is to be found in Ez 47, 1. The Shittim east of the Jordan (see note on Nm 25, 1) is hardly referred to here.

THE BOOK OF AMOS

Amos was a shepherd of Tekoa in Judah, who exercised his ministry during the prosperous reign of Jeroboam II (786-746 B.C.). He prophesied in Israel at the great cult center of Bethel, from which he was finally expelled by the priest in charge of this royal sanctuary. The poetry of Amos, who denounces the hollow prosperity of the northern kingdom, is filled with imagery and language taken from his own pastoral background. The book is an anthology of his oracles and was compiled either by the prophet or by some of his disciples.

The prophecy begins with a sweeping indictment of Damascus, Philistia, Tyre, and Edom; but the forthright herdsman saves his climactic denunciation for Israel, whose injustice and idolatry are sins against the light granted to her. Israel could indeed expect the day of Yahweh, but it would be a day of darkness and not light. When Amos prophesied the overthrow of the sanctuary, the fall of the royal house, and the captivity of the people, it was more than Israelite officialdom could bear. The priest of Bethel drove Amos from the shrine—but not before hearing a terrible sentence pronounced upon himself.

Amos is a prophet of divine judgment, and the sovereignty of Yahweh in nature and history dominates his thought. But he was no innovator; his conservatism was in keeping with the whole prophetic tradition calling the people back to the high moral and religious demands of Yahweh's revelation. In common with the other prophets, Amos knew that divine punishment is never completely destructive; it is part of the hidden plan of God to bring salvation to men. The perversity of the human will may retard, but it cannot totally frustrate, this design of a loving God. The last oracle opens up a perspective of restoration under a Davidic king.

The Book of Amos may be divided as follows: I. Judgment of the Nations (1, 1—2, 16). II. Words and Woes for Israel (3, 1—6, 14). III. Symbolic Visions: Threats and Promises (7, 1—9, 8b); Epilogue: Messianic Perspective (9, 8c-15).

I: JUDGMENT OF THE NATIONS

CHAPTER 1

¹ The words of Amos, a shepherd from Tekoa,ᵃ which he received in vision concerning Israel, in the days of Uzziah, king of Judah, and in the days of Jeroboam, son of Joash, king of Israel, two years before the earthquake:*

² The LORD will roar from Zion,
    and from Jerusalem raise his voice:
The pastures of the shepherds will languish,
    and the summit of Carmel wither.ᵇ

Aram

³   Thus says the LORD:
For three crimes of Damascus, and for four,*
    I will not revoke my word;
Because they threshed Gilead
    with sledges of iron,
⁴ I will send fire* upon the house of Hazael,
    to devour the castles of Ben-hadad.
⁵ I will break the bar of Damascus;*
    I will root out those who live in the Valley of Aven,
And the sceptered ruler of Beth-eden;
    the people of Aram shall be exiled to Kir,
    says the LORD.

Philistia

⁶   Thus says the LORD:
For three crimes of Gaza, and for four,
    I will not revoke my word;
Because they took captive whole groups
    to hand over to Edom,
⁷ I will send fire upon the wall of Gaza,
    to devour her castles;
⁸ I will root out those who live in Ashdod,
    and the sceptered ruler of Ashkelon;
I will turn my hand against Ekron,
    and the last of the Philistines shall perish,
    says the Lord God.

---

a Zec 14, 5.—b Jer 25, 30; Jl 3, 16.

1, 1: *The earthquake:* which according to Hebrew tradition marked the crime of Uzziah when he attempted to offer incense in the temple (2 Chr 26, 16-21). Zechariah mentions it several centuries later (Zec 14, 5).

1, 3: *For three crimes . . . four:* crime after crime, an indefinite number; cf Am 1, 6. The series of judgments on the foreign nations shows that the Lord demands the observance of the moral order everywhere; Israel and Judah, despite their privileged position, are no exception. *I will not revoke my word:* God will not withdraw his threat of punishment against each of these nations. *They threshed Gilead:* the people of Aram under King Hazael had devastated Gilead; cf 2 Kgs 10, 32f.

1, 4: *Fire:* devastation caused by the Assyrians (Am 1, 7. 10. 12. 14; 2, 2. 5); cf 1 Sm 15, 18. *Hazael* and *Ben-hadad;* kings of the Arameans whose capital was *Damascus* (v 5); they fought against Israel (2 Kgs 13, 3), and had long occupied the region of Gilead (v 3) in Transjordan.

1, 5: *Bar of Damascus:* the beam securing the main gate of the city against invaders, symbol of its defenses. *Valley of Aven* ("vale of wickedness") and *Beth-eden* ("house of pleasure"): Aramean territory from southwest to northeast.

Tyre

9 Thus says the LORD:
For three crimes of Tyre, and for four,
  I will not revoke my word;
Because they delivered whole groups
    captive to Edom,
  and did not remember the pact of
    brotherhood,*
10 I will send fire upon the wall of Tyre,
  to devour her castles.

Edom

11 Thus says the LORD:
For three crimes of Edom, and for four,
  I will not revoke my word;
Because he pursued his brother* with
    the sword,
  choking up all pity;
Because he persisted in his anger
  and kept his wrath to the end,
12 I will send fire upon Teman,
  and it will devour the castles of Boz-
    rah.*

Ammon

13 Thus says the LORD:
For three crimes of the Ammonites, and
    for four,
  I will not revoke my word;
Because they ripped open expectant
    mothers in Gilead,
  while extending their territory,
14 I will kindle a fire upon the wall of Rabbah,*

1, 9: *Pact of brotherhood:* Hiram of Tyre had made a pact with Solomon and called him brother (1 Kgs 5, 12; 9, 13).

1, 11: *Pursued his brother:* the Edomites were descended from Esau, the brother of Jacob (Gn 25—27); nevertheless they constantly nourished enmity against Jacob's descendants, the Israelites.

1, 12: *Teman and Bozrah:* two of the chief cities of Edom; cf Jer 49, 20.

1, 14: *Rabbah:* now called Amman, the modern capital of the Hashemite Kingdom of Jordan.

2, 1: Here the prophet stresses the gravity of Moab's violation of the Semitic custom of providing honorable burial for the dead.

2, 4: *The lies:* false gods, who exist only in the minds of their worshipers. The crimes of Judah are infidelity and idolatry, in contrast to the sins for which the surrounding nations are judged.

2, 6-13: The detailed crimes of Israel are placed in strong contrast with the benefits with which the Lord favored his people.

2, 6: *A pair of sandals:* indicating how cheaply the rich regarded the poor.

2, 8: *Upon garments . . . any altar:* usurers kept the garments taken as pledges from the poor; but instead of restoring them to their owners before nightfall (Ex 22, 25; Dt 24, 12), they used them in idolatrous worship. *Wine . . . their god:* under the guise of a religious ceremony they drink the wine obtained through unjust fines.

---

and it will devour her castles
Amid clamor on the day of battle
  and stormwind in a time of tempest.
15 Their king shall go into captivity,
  he and his princes with him, says the
    LORD.

CHAPTER 2

Moab

1 Thus says the LORD:
For three crimes of Moab, and for four,
  I will not revoke my word;
Because he burned to ashes
  the bones of Edom's king,*
2 I will send fire upon Moab,
  to devour the castles of Kerioth;
Moab shall meet death amid uproar
  and shouts and trumpet blasts.
3 I will root out the judge from her midst,
  and her princes I will slay with him,
    says the LORD.

Judah

4 Thus says the LORD:
For three crimes of Judah, and for four,
  I will not revoke my word;
Because they spurned the law of the
    LORD,
  and did not keep his statutes;
Because the lies* which their fathers
    followed
  have led them astray,
5 I will send fire upon Judah,
  to devour the castles of Jerusalem.

Israel

6 Thus says the LORD:
For three crimes of Israel, and for
    four,*
  I will not revoke my word;
Because they sell the just man for silver,
  and the poor man for a pair of san-
    dals.*
7 They trample the heads of the weak
  into the dust of the earth,
  and force the lowly out of the way.
Son and father go to the same prosti-
    tute,
  profaning my holy name.
8 Upon garments taken in pledge
  they recline beside any altar;*

Am

And the wine of those who have been
fined
they drink in the house of their god.

9 Yet it was I who destroyed the Amorites
before them,
who were as tall as the cedars,
and as strong as the oak trees.
I destroyed their fruit above,
and their roots beneath.[c]

10 It was I who brought you up from the
land of Egypt,
and who led you through the desert
for forty years,
to occupy the land of the Amorites:[d]

11 I who raised up prophets among your
sons,
and nazirites* among your young
men.
Is this not so, O men of Israel?
says the LORD.

12 But you gave the nazirites wine to
drink,
and commanded the prophets not to
prophesy.

13 Beware, I will crush you into the
ground
as a wagon crushes when laden with
sheaves.

14 Flight shall perish from the swift,
and the strong man shall not retain
his strength;
The warrior shall not save his life,

15 nor the bowman stand his ground;
The swift of foot shall not escape,
nor the horseman save his life.

16 And the most stouthearted of warriors
shall flee naked on that day, says the
LORD.

II: WORDS AND WOES FOR ISRAEL

CHAPTER 3

First Word. [1] Hear this word, O men of
Israel, that the LORD pronounces over
you, over the whole family that I brought
up from the land of Egypt:

2 You alone have I favored,
more than all the families of the
earth;
Therefore I will punish you
for all your crimes.*

3 Do two walk together
unless they have agreed?

4 Does a lion roar in the forest
when it has no prey?

Does a young lion cry out from its den
unless it has seized something?

5 Is a bird brought to earth by a snare
when there is no lure for it?
Does a snare spring up from the ground
without catching anything?

6 If the trumpet sounds in a city,
will the people not be frightened?
If evil befalls a city,
has not the LORD caused it?*

7 Indeed, the Lord GOD does nothing
without revealing his plan
to his servants, the prophets.

8 The lion roars—
who will not be afraid!
The Lord GOD speaks—
who will not prophesy!

9 Proclaim this in the castles of Ashdod,
in the castles of the land of Egypt:
"Gather about the mountain of
Samaria,
and see the great disorders within
her,
the oppression in her midst."*

10 For they know not how to do what is
right,
says the LORD,
Storing up in their castles
what they have extorted and robbed.

11   Therefore, thus says the Lord GOD:
An enemy shall surround the land,
and strip you of your strength,
and pillage your castles.

12   Thus says the LORD:
As the shepherd snatches from the
mouth of the lion
a pair of legs or the tip of an ear of his
sheep,
So the Israelites who dwell in Samaria
shall escape
with the corner of a couch or a piece
of a cot.

13 Hear and bear witness against the
house of Jacob, says the Lord GOD, the
God of hosts:

---

c Nm 21, 24; Dt 2, 24.—d Ex 14, 21; Dt 8, 2. 14.

2, 11: *Nazirites:* see note on Nm 6, 1ff.
3, 2: God's choice of Israel brought its own responsibility.
3, 6: The sufferings which sinful man experiences through the
permissive will of God are presented here, as elsewhere in the
Old Testament, simply as caused by the Lord.
3, 9: Israel's southern neighbors, beyond Judah, are invited by
the prophetic orator to witness the moral disorders of God's people.

14 On the day when I punish Israel for his
crimes,
I will visit also the altars of Bethel:
The horns of the altar shall be broken
off
and fall to the ground.
15 Then will I strike the winter house
and the summer house;
The ivory apartments* shall be ruined,
and their many rooms shall be no
more,
says the LORD.

CHAPTER 4

Second Word

1 Hear this word, women of the mountain
of Samaria,
you cows of Bashan,*
You who oppress the weak
and abuse the needy;
Who say to your lords,
"Bring drink for us!"
2 The Lord GOD has sworn by his holiness:
Truly the days are coming upon you
When they shall drag you away with
hooks,
the last of you with fishhooks;
3 You shall go out through the breached
walls
each by the most direct way,
And you shall be cast into the mire,
says the LORD.

4 Come to Bethel and sin,
to Gilgal, and sin the more;*
Each morning bring your sacrifices,
every third day, your tithes;
5 Burn leavened food as a thanksgiving
sacrifice,
proclaim publicly your freewill offerings,
For so you love to do, O men of Israel,
says the Lord GOD.

e Hg 2, 17.—f Gn 19, 24.

3, 15: *Ivory apartments:* rooms containing furniture inlaid
in ivory, similar to the pieces discovered in the excavations at
Samaria.
4, 1: *Bashan:* the region east of the Sea of Galilee, famous
for its rich pasture and fattened herds, to which Amos likens the
indolent women of Samaria.
4, 4f: This invitation to the sanctuaries of the northern kingdom is ironical. Pilgrimages to the shrines of *Bethel* and *Gilgal*
were the more displeasing to God because they were contrary to
his will and ineffective toward improvement of morals.
4, 10: *Pestilence like that of Egypt:* plagues were well
known in Egypt; cf Dt 7, 15; 28, 27. 60. *Stench of your camps:*
caused by the unburied bodies.

6 Though I have made your teeth
clean of food in all your cities,
and have made bread scarce in all
your dwellings,
Yet you returned not to me,
says the LORD.
7 Though I also withheld the rain from
you
when the harvest was still three
months away;
I sent rain upon one city
but not upon another;
One field was watered by rain,
but another without rain dried up;
8 Though two or three cities staggered to
one city
for water that did not quench their
thirst;
Yet you returned not to me,
says the LORD.
9 I struck you with blight and searing
wind;
your many gardens and vineyards,
your fig trees and olive trees the locust devoured;
Yet you returned not to me,
says the LORD.*e*
10 I sent upon you a pestilence like that of
Egypt,*
and with the sword I slew your young
men;
Your horses I let be captured,
to your nostrils I brought the stench
of your camps;
Yet you returned not to me,
says the LORD.
11 I brought upon you such upheaval
as when God overthrew Sodom and
Gomorrah:
you were like a brand plucked from
the fire;
Yet you returned not to me,
says the LORD.*f*
12 So now I will deal with you in my own
way, O Israel!
and since I will deal thus with you,
prepare to meet your God, O Israel:
13 Him who formed the mountains, and
created the wind,
and declares to man his thoughts;
Who made the dawn and the darkness,
and strides upon the heights of the
earth:
The LORD, the God of hosts by
name.

Am

CHAPTER 5

Third Word

[1] Hear this word which I utter over you,
    a lament, O house of Israel:
[2] She is fallen, to rise no more,
    the virgin Israel;
    She lies abandoned upon her land,
    with no one to raise her up.

[3]   For thus says the Lord GOD:
    The city that marched out with a
      thousand
    shall be left with a hundred,
    Another that marched out with a hun-
      dred
    shall be left with ten,
    of the house of Israel.

[4] For thus says the LORD
    to the house of Israel:
    Seek me, that you may live,
[5]   but do not seek Bethel;
    Do not come to Gilgal,
    and do not cross to Beer-sheba.
    For Gilgal shall be led into exile,
    and Bethel shall become nought.
[6] Seek the LORD, that you may live,
    lest he come upon the house of
      Joseph* like a fire
    That shall consume, with none to
      quench it
    for the house of Israel:
[8] He who made the Pleiades and Orion,
    who turns darkness into dawn,
    and darkens day into night;
    Who summons the waters of the sea,
    and pours them out upon the surface
    of the earth;[g]
[9] Who flashes destruction upon the strong,
    and brings ruin upon the fortress;
    whose name is LORD.

First Woe

[7] Woe to those who turn judgment to
    wormwood
    and cast justice to the ground!
[10] They hate him who reproves at the gate*
    and abhor him who speaks the truth.
[11] Therefore, because you have trampled
    upon the weak
    and exacted of them levies of grain,
    Though you have built houses of hewn
      stone,
    you shall not live in them!
    Though you have planted choice vine-
      yards,
    you shall not drink their wine![h]

[12] Yes, I know how many are your crimes,
    how grievous your sins:
    Oppressing the just, accepting bribes,
    repelling the needy at the gate!
[13] Therefore the prudent man is silent at
    this time,
    for it is an evil time.

[14] Seek good and not evil,
    that you may live;
    Then truly will the LORD, the God of
      hosts,
    be with you as you claim!
[15] Hate evil and love good,
    and let justice prevail at the gate;
    Then it may be that the LORD, the God
    of hosts,
    will have pity on the remnant of
    Joseph.[i]

[16] Therefore, thus says the LORD,
    the God of hosts, the Lord:
    In every square there shall be lamenta-
      tion,
    and in every street they shall cry,
    Alas! Alas!
    They shall summon the farmers to wail
    and professional mourners to lament,
[17] And in every vineyard there shall be
    lamentation
    when I pass through your midst, says
    the LORD.

Second Woe

[18] Woe to those who yearn for the day of
    the LORD!*
    What will this day of the LORD mean
    for you?
    Darkness and not light![j]
[19] As if a man were to flee from a lion,
    and a bear should meet him;
    Or as if on entering his house
    he were to rest his hand against the
    wall,
    and a snake should bite him.

---

g Am 9, 6.—h Zep 1, 13.—i Ps 97, 10; Rom 12, 9.—j Jer 30,
7; Jl 2, 11; Zep 1, 15.

5, 6: *House of Joseph:* the kingdom of Israel or northern
kingdom, the chief tribes of which were descended from Ephraim
and Manasseh, the sons of Joseph; cf Am 5. 15; 6, 6.
5, 10: *At the gate:* see note on Ps 127, 5.
5, 18: *Day of the Lord:* a technical expression which in earliest times referred to God's special intervention in human affairs.
Through it his power and justice triumphed in his people. The
present passage is the first instance in which it means a day of
punishment of sinners. During the exile it assumed the meaning of
a time when God would avenge Israel against her oppressors and
bring about her restoration (Jer 50, 27; Ez 30, 3ff). Still later it
came to mean the day of final judgment of the world when the
good will be rewarded and the wicked punished (Mal 3, 19ff; Jl
2, 1ff; Zep 1, 14ff).

20 Will not the day of the LORD be darkness and not light,
   gloom without any brightness?

21 * I hate, I spurn your feasts,
   I take no pleasure in your solemnities;[k]

22 Your cereal offerings I will not accept,
   nor consider your stall-fed peace offerings.

23 Away with your noisy songs!
   I will not listen to the melodies of your harps.
   But if you would offer me holocausts,

24   then let justice surge like water,
   and goodness like an unfailing stream.

25 Did you bring me sacrifices and offerings[l]
   for forty years in the desert, O house of Israel?*

26 You will carry away Sakkuth, your king,
   and Kaiwan, your star god,*
   the images that you have made for yourselves;

27 For I will exile you beyond Damascus,
   say I, the LORD, the God of hosts by name.

CHAPTER 6

Third Woe

1 * Woe to the complacent in Zion,
   to the overconfident on the mount of Samaria,*

---

k Is 1, 11; Jer 6, 20; Mal 1, 12.—l Acts 7, 42.—m Lk 6, 24.—n Jer 51, 14.

5, 21-27: The Lord condemns, not ritual worship in itself, but the cult whose exterior rites and solemnity have no relation to interior morality and justice. The Israelites falsely worshiped him as neighboring nations adored Baal or Chamos, deities which were thought to protect their respective peoples against their enemies in return for ritual observances, without any relation to right conduct.

5, 25: The meaning is not certain; according to some, the idea is that during the forty years' wandering in the desert the simple, rudimentary worship of God was accompanied by the practice of justice, in contrast to the elaborate ritual unaccompanied by works of justice in the prophet's time.

5, 26: *Sakkuth . . . star god:* although the text is uncertain, it seems quite probable that reference is made to the Assyrian deities, Sakkuth, god of war and light, and Kaiwan, the planet Saturn. The people will go into exile, from which these gods have been unable to save them.

6, 1-7: The luxury of the people in Samaria will be punished by exile. They failed to learn the lesson from *Calneh, Hamath* and *Gath* at the approach of the powerful and warlike Assyrians.

6, 1: *The complacent in Zion . . . the overconfident . . . of Samaria:* the proud and self-interested rulers of Judah and Israel.

6, 12: *Can horses . . . oxen?:* one cannot change the course of nature, as the Israelites attempted to do by their sins of injustice.

Leaders of a nation favored from the first,
   to whom the people of Israel have recourse![m]

2 Pass over to Calneh and see,
   go from there to Hamath the great,
   and down to Gath of the Philistines!
Are you better than these kingdoms,
   or is your territory wider than theirs?

3 You would put off the evil day,
   yet you hasten the reign of violence!

4 Lying upon beds of ivory,
   stretched comfortably on their couches,
They eat lambs taken from the flock,
   and calves from the stall!

5 Improvising to the music of the harp,
   like David, they devise their own accompaniment.

6 They drink wine from bowls
   and anoint themselves with the best oils;
   yet they are not made ill by the collapse of Joseph!

7 Therefore, now they shall be the first to go into exile,
   and their wanton revelry shall be done away with.

8 The Lord GOD has sworn by his very self,
   say I, the LORD, the God of hosts:
I abhor the pride of Jacob,
   I hate his castles,
   and I give over the city with everything in it;[n]

9 Should there remain ten men
   in a single house, these shall die.

10 Only a few shall be left
   to carry the dead out of the houses;
If one says to a man inside a house,
   "Is anyone with you?" and he answers, "No one,"
Then he shall say, "Silence!"
   for no one must mention the name of the LORD.

11 Indeed, the LORD has given the command
   to shatter the great house to bits,
   and reduce the small house to rubble.

12 Can horses run across a cliff?
   or can one plow the sea with oxen?*
Yet you have turned judgment into gall,
   and the fruit of justice into wormwood.

Am

13 You rejoice in Lodebar,
    and say, "Have we not, by our own
      strength,
    seized for ourselves Karnaim?"*
14 Beware, I am raising up against you, O
    house of Israel,
    say I, the LORD, the God of hosts,
A nation* that shall oppress you
    from Labo of Hamath even to the
    Wadi Arabah.

III: SYMBOLIC VISIONS: THREATS AND PROMISES

CHAPTER 7

Vision of Locusts. ¹This is what the Lord
GOD showed me: He was forming a locust
swarm when the late growth began to
come up (the late growth after the king's
mowing*). ²While they were eating all the
grass in the land, I said:

Forgive, O Lord GOD!
How can Jacob stand?
He is so small!

³And the LORD repented of this: "It
shall not be," said the Lord GOD.
Vision of Fire. ⁴Then the Lord GOD
showed me this: he called for a judgment
by fire.* It had devoured the great abyss,
and was consuming the land, ⁵when I said:

Cease, O Lord GOD!
How can Jacob stand?
He is so small!

⁶The LORD repented of this. "This also
shall not be," said the Lord GOD.
Vision of the Plummet. ⁷Then the Lord
GOD showed me this: he was standing by a
wall, plummet in hand.* ⁸The LORD
asked me, "What do you see, Amos?" And
when I answered, "A plummet," the LORD
said:

See, I will lay the plummet
    in the midst of my people Israel;
    I will forgive them no longer.
⁹ The high places of Isaac shall be laid
    waste,
    and the sanctuaries of Israel made de-
      solate;
    I will attack the house of Jeroboam
      with the sword.
Amos and Amaziah. ¹⁰Amaziah, the
priest of Bethel, sent word to Jeroboam,

king of Israel: "Amos has conspired
against you here within Israel; the country
cannot endure all his words. ¹¹For this is
what Amos says:

Jeroboam shall die by the sword,
    and Israel shall surely be exiled from
      its land."

¹²To Amos, Amaziah said: "Off with
you, visionary, flee to the land of Judah!
There earn your bread by prophesying,
¹³but never again prophesy in Bethel; for
it is the king's sanctuary and a royal temple." ¹⁴Amos answered Amaziah, "I was
no prophet, nor have I belonged to a company of prophets; I was a shepherd and a
dresser of sycamores.* ¹⁵The LORD took
me from following the flock, and said to
me, Go, prophesy to my people Israel.
¹⁶Now hear the word of the LORD!"

You say: prophesy not against Israel,
    preach not against the house of Isaac.
17   Now thus says the LORD:
Your wife shall be made a harlot in the
    city,
    and your sons and daughters shall fall
      by the sword;
Your land shall be divided by measur-
    ing line,
    and you yourself shall die in an un-
      clean land;
Israel shall be exiled far from its land.

CHAPTER 8

Vision of the Fruit Basket. ¹This is what
the Lord GOD showed me: a basket of ripe
fruit. ²"What do you see, Amos?" he
asked. I answered, "A basket of ripe
fruit." Then the LORD said to me:

The time is ripe to have done with my
    people Israel;
    I will forgive them no longer.

6, 13: *Lodebar . . . Karnaim:* in Transjordan; they had been
captured by the Israelites. Perhaps it is in irony that reference is
made to these two cities, for the root of the first suggests "nothing" and that of the second, "horns" or "strength."
6, 14: *A nation:* Assyria.
7, 1: *The king's mowing:* the first mowing, a portion of
which was payable to the king as a tax.
7, 4: *Fire:* understood by many as a burning drought.
7, 7: *Plummet in hand:* signifying that God is about to withdraw his mercy from his people and that the nation is to be measured for destruction.
7, 14f: Amos denies that he belonged to the class of professional prophets; his vocation is due to the personal intervention of
the Lord.

3 The temple songs shall become wailings
   on that day,
   says the Lord GOD.
Many shall be the corpses,
   strewn everywhere.—Silence!

Against Greed

4 Hear this, you who trample upon the
   needy
   and destroy the poor of the land!
5 "When will the new moon be over,"
   you ask,
   "that we may sell our grain,
   and the sabbath, that we may display
   the wheat?
We will diminish the ephah,*
   add to the shekel,
   and fix our scales for cheating!
6 We will buy the lowly man for silver,
   and the poor man for a pair of sandals;
   even the refuse of the wheat we will
   sell!"

7 The LORD has sworn by the pride of
   Jacob:*
   Never will I forget a thing they have
   done!
8 Shall not the land tremble because of
   this,
   and all who dwell in it mourn,
   While it rises up and tosses like the
   Nile,
   and settles back like the river of
   Egypt?*
9 On that day, says the Lord GOD,
   I will make the sun set at midday
   and cover the earth with darkness in
   broad daylight.
10 I will turn your feasts into mourning
   and all your songs into lamentations.
I will cover the loins of all with sackcloth

---

o Tb 2, 6; 1 Mc 1, 41.—p Ps 139, 8.

8, 5: *Ephah:* a standard of measure; a little more than a
bushel.
8, 7: *The pride of Jacob:* the sinful pride detested by God
(Am 6, 8), in contrast to God himself, who is the true Pride of
Jacob.
8, 8: The figure is based on the annual flooding of the river
Nile.
8, 14: *Dan and Beer-sheba,* the extreme northern and
southern limits of the country, where idolatrous worship was offered.
9, 1-8: There will be no escape from God's punishment, symbolized here by the destruction of a building, probably the schismatic temple at Bethel.
9, 3: *Serpent:* the sea monster of familiar legend, subdued by
God at the time of creation and lurking still in the ocean depths;
cf Ps 89, 10f.

---

and make every head bald.
I will make them mourn as for an only
   son,
   and bring their day to a bitter end.*o*

11 Yes, days are coming, says the Lord
   GOD,
   when I will send famine upon the
   land:
Not a famine of bread, or thirst for
   water,
   but for hearing the word of the
   LORD.
12 Then shall they wander from sea to sea
   and rove from the north to the east
In search of the word of the LORD,
   but they shall not find it.

13 On that day, fair virgins and young men
   shall faint from thirst;
14 Those who swear by the shameful idol
   of Samaria,
   "By the life of your god, O Dan!"
   "By the life of your love, O Beer-
   sheba!"
   those shall fall, never to rise again.*

CHAPTER 9

Vision of the Altar.* [1]I saw the Lord
standing beside the altar, and he said:

Strike the bases, so that the doorjambs
   totter
   till you break them off on the heads
   of them all!
Those who are left I will slay with the
   sword;
   not one shall flee,
   no survivor shall escape.
2 Though they break through to the
   nether world,
   even from there my hand shall bring
   them out;
Though they climb to the heavens,
   I will bring them down;*p*
3 Though they hide on the summit of
   Carmel,
   there too I will hunt them out and
   take them away;
Though they hide from my gaze
   in the bottom of the sea,
   I will command the serpent* there to
   bite them;
4 Though they are led into captivity by
   their enemies,
   there will I command the sword to
   slay them.

Am

I will fix my gaze upon them
  for evil, and not for good,[q]
5 I, the Lord GOD of hosts.
I melt the earth with my touch,
  so that all who dwell on it mourn,
While it all rises up like the Nile,
  and settles back like the river of
  Egypt;
6 I have built heaven, my upper chamber,
  and established my vault over the
  earth;
I summon the waters of the sea
  and pour them out upon the surface
  of the earth,
  I, the LORD by name.[r]
7 Are you not like the Ethiopians to me,
  O men of Israel, says the LORD?
Did I not bring the Israelites from the
  land of Egypt
  as I brought the Philistines from
  Caphtor
  and the Arameans* from Kir?[s]
8 The eyes of the Lord GOD are on this
  sinful kingdom:
  I destroy it from off the face of the
  earth.

EPILOGUE: MESSIANIC PERSPECTIVE

But I will not destroy the house of
  Jacob completely,
  says the LORD.
9 For see, I have given the command
  to sift the house of Israel among all
  the nations,
As one sifts with a sieve,
  letting no pebble fall to the ground.
10 By the sword shall all sinners among my
  people die,
  those who say, "Evil will not reach or
  overtake us."

11 * On that day I will raise up
  the fallen hut of David;
I will wall up its breaches,
  raise up its ruins,
  and rebuild it as in the days of old,[t]
12 That they may conquer what is left of
  Edom
  and all the nations that shall bear my
  name,
  say I, the LORD, who will do this.
13 Yes, days are coming,
  says the LORD,
When the plowman shall overtake the
  reaper,
  and the vintager, him who sows the
  seed;
The juice of grapes shall drip down the
  mountains,
  and all the hills shall run with it.[u]
14 I will bring about the restoration of my
  people Israel;
  they shall rebuild and inhabit their
  ruined cities,
Plant vineyards and drink the wine,
  set out gardens and eat the fruits.
15 I will plant them upon their own
  ground;
  never again shall they be plucked
From the land I have given them,
  say I, the LORD, your God.

---

q Jer 44, 11.—r Am 5, 8.—s Dt 2, 23; Jer 47, 4.—t Acts 15,
16.—u Jl 3, 18.

9, 7: *The Ethiopians . . . the Philistines . . . the Arameans:* by nature Israel is not different from any other nation. It was not because of any merit on Israel's part that God delivered them from Egypt. *Caphtor:* the island of Crete.
9, 11f: In Acts 15, 15ff St. James interprets this passage in a messianic sense. *Fallen hut:* the kingdom. *The nations that shall bear my name:* the Gentile peoples who shall be converted to the Lord, that is, conquered by him, and therefore shall bear his name.

THE BOOK OF OBADIAH

The twenty-one verses of this book contain the shortest and sternest prophecy in the Old Testament. Nothing is known of the author, although his oracle against Edom, a long-standing enemy of Israel, indicates a date of composition sometime in the fifth century B.C. During this period the Edomites had been forced to abandon their ancient home near the Gulf of Aqaba and had settled in southern Judah, where they appear among the adversaries of the Jews returning from exile.

The prophecy is a bitter cry for vengeance against Edom for its heinous crimes. The mountain of Esau will be occupied and ravaged by the enemy but Zion shall remain inviolate. Judah and Israel shall again form one nation; and that triumphant refrain of Israelite eschatology will be heard once more: "The Kingdom is the Lord's!" Many of the verses in this prophecy can be paralleled in Jer 49, 7-22, but it is difficult to determine the precise relationship between these similar passages.

Title and Theme

1 The vision of Obadiah.

[Thus says the Lord GOD:]

Of Edom we have heard a message from the LORD,
and a herald has been sent among the nations:
"Up! let us go to war against him!"[a]

Edom Shall Perish

2 See, I make you small among the nations;[b]
you are held in dire contempt.
3 The pride of your heart has deceived you:
you who dwell in the clefts of the rock,
whose abode is in the heights,
Who say in your heart,
"Who will bring me down to earth?"
4 Though you go as high as the eagle,
and your nest be set among the stars,
From there will I bring you down,
says the LORD.
5 If thieves came to you, if robbers by night,[c]
how could you be thus destroyed:
would they not steal merely till they had enough?
If vintagers came to you,
would they not leave some gleanings?*
6 How they search Esau,
seek out his hiding places!

7 To the border they drive you—
all your allies;
They deceive you, they overpower you—
those at peace with you;
Those who eat your bread
lay snares beneath you:
There is no understanding in him!*
8 Shall I not, says the LORD, on that day
make the wise men* disappear from Edom,
and understanding from the mount of Esau?[d]
9 Your warriors, O Teman,* shall be crushed,
till all on Mount Esau are destroyed.

The Cause

10 Because of violence to your brother Jacob,*
disgrace shall cover you
and you shall be destroyed forever.[e]
11 On the day when you stood by,
on the day when aliens carried off his possessions,
And strangers entered his gates
and cast lots over Jerusalem,
you too were one of them.*

12 Gaze not upon the day of your brother,
the day of his disaster;
Exult not over the children of Judah
on the day of their ruin;
Speak not haughtily
on the day of distress!
13 Enter not the gate of my people
on the day of their calamity;
Gaze not, you at least, upon his misfortune
on the day of his calamity;
Lay not hands upon his possessions
on the day of his calamity!
14 Stand not at the crossroads
to slay his refugees;
Betray not his fugitives
on the day of distress!

Judgment upon the Nations

15 For near is the day of the LORD[f]
for all the nations!
As you have done, so shall it be done to you,

---

a Jer 49, 14.—b 2ff: Jer 49, 15f.—c Jer 49, 9.—d Is 29, 14; 1 Cor 1, 19.—e Gn 27, 41f.—f 15f: Ps 137, 7ff.

5: Something of value may escape the robber, and the vintager always leaves something for the gleaners, but God's devastation of Edom will be complete.
7: *There is no understanding in him:* Edom's faithless allies assure one another that he does not have sense enough to be able to defend himself.
8: *The wise men:* Edom was proverbial for its wise men; cf Jer 49, 7.
9: *Teman:* one of the names used for the land southeast of Palestine, here synonymous with Edom. *Esau:* here used as the name of the land.
10: *Your brother Jacob:* Esau, also called Edom, and Jacob, the father of Judah, were the sons of Isaac (Gn 25, 24ff).
11: After the devastation of Judah, Edom occupied the southern part of its territory. Edomites also joined the invading Chaldean forces (13) and assisted them in capturing the people of Judah (14).

your deed shall come back upon your
own head;
16 As you have drunk* upon my holy
mountain,
so shall all the nations drink continually.
Yes, they shall drink and swallow,
and shall become as though they had
not been.

Judah Shall Be Restored

17 But on Mount Zion there shall be a portion saved;*
the mountain shall be holy,
And the house of Jacob shall take possession
of those that dispossessed them.
18 The house of Jacob shall be a fire,
and the house of Joseph a flame;
The house of Esau shall be stubble,
and they shall set them ablaze and devour them;
Then none shall survive of the house of
Esau,
for the LORD has spoken.
19 They shall occupy the Negeb, the
mount of Esau,

and the foothills of the Philistines;
And they shall occupy the lands of
Ephraim
and the lands of Samaria,
and Benjamin shall occupy Gilead.
20 The captives of this host of the children
of Israel
shall occupy the Canaanite land as far
as Zarephath,*
And the captives of Jerusalem who are
in Sepharad
shall occupy the cities of the Negeb.
21 And saviors* shall ascend Mount Zion
to rule the mount of Esau,
and the kingship shall be the LORD's.

16: *As you have drunk:* the Lord addresses the people of
Judah. As the people of Jerusalem have drunk the cup of retribution, so shall the nations, and especially Edom (18), suffer punishment. This metaphorical use of drinking the cup of God's wrath is
common in the Bible; cf Jb 21, 20; Is 19, 14; Jer 25, 15f.
17ff: The Israelites shall be restored and shall occupy the lands
of those who oppressed them. The survivors of Judah shall be rejoined by the returned exiles from northern Israel.
20: *Zarephath:* a town in Phoenicia, north of Tyre; cf 1 Kgs
17, 10. Ezekiel's ideal boundaries of the new Israel (Ez 47, 13ff)
extend farther north. *Sepharad:* probably Sardis in western Asia
Minor. The later rabbis thought it to be Spain.
21: *Saviors:* the victorious Israelites who will rule over their
enemies after the fashion of the ancient Judges; cf Jgs 3, 9. 15.
31; 10, 1.

THE BOOK OF JONAH

*Written in the postexilic era, probably in the fifth century B.C., this book is a didactic
story with an important theological message. It concerns a disobedient prophet who attempted to run away from his divine commission, was cast overboard and swallowed by a great
fish, rescued in a marvelous manner, and sent on his way to Nineveh, the traditional enemy
of Israel. To the surprise of Jonah, the wicked city listened to his message of doom and repented immediately. All, from king to lowliest subject, humbled themselves in sackcloth and
ashes. Seeing their repentance, God did not carry out the punishment he had planned for
them. Whereupon Jonah complained to God about the unexpected success of his mission; he
was bitter because Yahweh, instead of destroying, had led the people to repentance and then
spared them.*

*From this partly humorous story, a very sublime lesson may be drawn. Jonah stands for
a narrow and vindictive mentality, all too common among the Jews of that period. Because
they were the chosen people, a good many of them cultivated an intolerant nationalism which
limited the mercy of God to their nation. It was abhorrent to their way of thinking that nations as wicked as Assyria should escape his wrath.*

*The prophecy, which is both instructive and entertaining, strikes directly at this view-
point. It is a parable of mercy, showing that God's threatened punishments are but the expression of a merciful will which moves all men to repent and seek forgiveness. The universality of the story contrasts sharply with the particularistic spirit of many in the postexilic
community. The book has also prepared the way for the gospel with its message of redemption for all, both Jew and Gentile.*

CHAPTER 1

The First Mission. ¹This is the word of the LORD that came to Jonah,^{*a*} son of Amittai:* ²"Set out for the great city of Nineveh, and preach against it; their wickedness has come up before me."^{*b*} ³But Jonah made ready to flee to Tarshish* away from the LORD. He went down to Joppa, found a ship going to Tarshish, paid the fare, and went aboard to journey with them to Tarshish, away from the LORD.

⁴The LORD, however, hurled a violent wind upon the sea, and in the furious tempest that arose the ship was on the point of breaking up. ⁵Then the mariners became frightened and each one cried to his god. To lighten the ship for themselves, they threw its cargo into the sea. Meanwhile, Jonah had gone down into the hold of the ship, and lay there fast asleep. ⁶The captain came to him and said, "What are you doing asleep? Rise up, call upon your God! Perhaps God will be mindful of us so that we may not perish."

⁷Then they said to one another, "Come, let us cast lots to find out on whose account we have met with this misfortune." So they cast lots, and thus singled out Jonah. ⁸"Tell us," they said, "what is your business? Where do you come from? What is your country, and to what people do you belong?" ⁹"I am a Hebrew," Jonah answered them; "I worship the LORD, the God of heaven, who made the sea and the dry land."

¹⁰Now the men were seized with great fear and said to him, "How could you do such a thing!"—They knew that he was fleeing from the LORD, because he had told them.—¹¹"What shall we do with you," they asked, "that the sea may quiet down for us?" For the sea was growing more and more turbulent. ¹²Jonah said to them, "Pick me up and throw me into the sea, that it may quiet down for you; since I know it is because of me that this violent storm has come upon you."

¹³Still the men rowed hard to regain the land, but they could not, for the sea grew ever more turbulent. ¹⁴Then they cried to the LORD: "We beseech you, O LORD, let us not perish for taking this man's life; do not charge us with shedding innocent blood, for you, LORD, have done as you saw fit."* ¹⁵Then they took Jonah and threw him into the sea, and the sea's raging abated. ¹⁶Struck with great fear of the LORD, the men offered sacrifice and made vows to him.

CHAPTER 2

¹But the LORD sent a large fish, that swallowed Jonah; and he remained in the belly of the fish three days and three nights.^{*c*} ²From the belly of the fish Jonah said this prayer to the LORD, his God:

Psalm of Thanksgiving

³ Out of my distress I called to the LORD,
 and he answered me;
From the midst of the nether world I
  cried for help,
 and you heard my voice.^{*d*}
⁴ For you cast me into the deep, into the
  heart of the sea,
 and the flood enveloped me;
All your breakers and your billows
 passed over me.^{*e*}
⁵ Then I said, "I am banished from your
  sight!
 yet would I again look upon your
  holy temple."^{*f*}
⁶ The waters swirled about me, threatening my life;
 the abyss enveloped me;
 seaweed clung about my head.^{*g*}
⁷ Down I went to the roots of the mountains;
 the bars of the nether world
 were closing behind me forever,
But you brought up my life from the
  pit,
 O LORD, my God.^{*h*}

⁸ When my soul fainted within me,
 I remembered the LORD;
My prayer reached you
 in your holy temple.^{*i*}

---

a 2 Kgs 14, 25.—b Jon 3, 3; 4, 11.—c Mt 12, 40; 16, 4; Lk 11, 30; 1 Cor 15, 4.—d Pss 18, 7; 120, 1.—e Ps 42, 8.—f Ps 31, 23; Is 38, 11.—g Pss 18, 5; 69, 2.—h Pss 16, 10; 30, 4.—i Pss 5, 8; 18, 7; 88, 3.

1, 1: *Jonah, son of Amittai:* a prophet of this name lived at the time of Jeroboam II (786-746 B.C.).

1, 3: *Tarshish:* identified by many with Tartessus, an ancient Phoenician colony in southwest Spain; precise identification with any particular Phoenician center in the western Mediterranean is uncertain. To the Hebrews it stood for the far west.

1, 14: Since it has pleased the Lord to punish Jonah, the mariners ask that in ridding themselves of him they be not charged with the crime of murder.

9 Those who worship vain idols
    forsake their source of mercy.*j*
10 But I, with resounding praise,
    will sacrifice to you;
What I have vowed I will pay:
    deliverance is from the LORD.*k*

11 Then the LORD commanded the fish to spew Jonah upon the shore.

CHAPTER 3

Conversion of Nineveh. 1 The word of the LORD came to Jonah a second time: 2 "Set out for the great city of Nineveh, and announce to it the message that I will tell you." 3 So Jonah made ready and went to Nineveh, according to the LORD's bidding. Now Nineveh was an enormously large city; it took three days to go through it. 4 Jonah began his journey through the city, and had gone but a single day's walk announcing, "Forty days more and Nineveh shall be destroyed,"* 5 when the people of Nineveh believed God; they proclaimed a fast and all of them, great and small, put on sackcloth.*l*

6 When the news reached the king of Nineveh, he rose from his throne, laid aside his robe, covered himself with sackcloth, and sat in the ashes. 7 Then he had this proclaimed throughout Nineveh, by decree of the king and his nobles: "Neither man nor beast, neither cattle nor sheep, shall taste anything; they shall not eat, nor shall they drink water. 8 Man and beast shall be covered with sackcloth* and call loudly to God; every man shall turn from his evil way and from the violence he has in hand. 9 Who knows, God may relent and forgive, and withhold his blazing wrath, so that we shall not perish."*m* 10 When God saw by their actions how they turned from their evil way, he repented of the evil that he had threatened to do to them; he did not carry it out.

CHAPTER 4

Jonah's Anger: God's Reproof. 1 But this was greatly displeasing to Jonah, and he became angry.* 2 "I beseech you, LORD," he prayed, "is not this what I said while I

was still in my own country? This is why I fled at first to Tarshish. I knew that you are a gracious and merciful God, slow to anger, rich in clemency, loathe to punish.*n* 3 And now, LORD, please take my life from me; for it is better for me to die than to live."*o* 4 But the LORD asked, "Have you reason to be angry?"

5 Jonah then left the city for a place to the east of it, where he built himself a hut and waited under it in the shade, to see what would happen to the city. 6 And when the LORD God provided a gourd plant,* that grew up over Jonah's head, giving shade that relieved him of any discomfort, Jonah was very happy over the plant. 7 But the next morning at dawn God sent a worm which attacked the plant, so that it withered. 8 And when the sun arose, God sent a burning east wind; and the sun beat upon Jonah's head till he became faint. Then he asked for death, saying, "I would be better off dead than alive."

9 But God said to Jonah, "Have you reason to be angry over the plant?" "I have reason to be angry," Jonah answered, "angry enough to die." 10 Then the LORD said, "You are concerned over the plant which cost you no labor and which you did not raise; it came up in one night and in one night it perished.* 11 And should I not be concerned over Nineveh, the great city, in which there are more than a hundred and twenty thousand persons who cannot distinguish their right hand from their left, not to mention the many cattle?"

---

j Ps 31, 7.—k Ps 50, 14.—l Mt 12, 41; Lk 11, 32.—m Jl 2, 14.—n Ps 86, 5; Jl 2, 13.—o 1 Kgs 19, 4.

3, 4: *Shall be destroyed:* the Hebrew expression reminds the reader of the "overthrowing" of the wicked cities, Sodom and Gomorrah, by a special act of God.

3, 8: *Beast . . . sackcloth:* the animals carried the signs of this repentance, as on occasions of joy they bore garlands.

4, 1: *He became angry:* because of his narrowly nationalistic vindictiveness, Jonah did not wish the Lord to forgive the Ninevites.

4, 6: *Gourd plant:* the Hebrew word, *kikayon,* means here a wide-leafed plant of the cucumber or castor-bean variety.

4, 10f: Jonah is selfish in bemoaning his personal loss of a shady gourd plant without any concern over the threat of loss of life to the Ninevites through the destruction of their city. If God in his kindness provided the plant for his prophet without the latter's effort or merit, how much more is he disposed to show love and mercy toward all men, Jew and Gentile, when they repent of their sins and implore his pardon! God's providence is also shown here to extend even to animals.

THE BOOK OF MICAH

Micah was a contemporary of Isaiah. Of his personal life and call we know nothing except that he came from the obscure village of Moresheth in the foothills. His were the broad vistas of the Judean lowland and the distant sea on the western horizon. With burning eloquence he attacked the rich exploiters of the poor, fraudulent merchants, venal judges, corrupt priests and prophets. To the man of the countryside the vices of the nation seemed centered in its capitals, for both Samaria and Jerusalem are singled out for judgment. An interesting notice in Jer 26, 17f informs us that the reform of Hezekiah was influenced by the preaching of Micah.

The prophecy may be divided into three parts: I. The impending judgment of the Lord, followed by an exposition of its causes, Israel's sins. Censure of Judah's leaders for betrayal of their responsibility (1, 1—3, 12). II. The glory of the restored Zion. A prince of David's house will rule over a reunited Israel. (St. Matthew's Nativity narrative points to Christ's birth in Bethlehem as the fulfillment of this prophecy.) A remnant shall survive the chastisement of Judah and her adversaries shall be destroyed (4, 1—5, 14). III. The case against Israel, in which the Lord is portrayed as the plaintiff who has maintained fidelity to the covenant. The somber picture closes with a prayer for national restoration and a beautiful expression of trust in God's pardoning mercy (6, 1—7, 20).

It should be noted that each of these three divisions begins with reproach and the threat of punishment, and ends on a note of hope and promise.

I: PUNISHMENT OF ISRAEL'S SINS

CHAPTER 1

Divine Judgment. ¹The word of the LORD which came to Micah of Moresheth in the days of Jotham, Ahaz, and Hezekiah, kings of Judah: that is, the vision he received concerning Samaria and Jerusalem.

² Hear, O peoples, all of you,
give heed, O earth, and all that fills you![a]
Let the Lord GOD be witness against you,
the Lord from his holy temple!*
³ For see, the LORD comes forth from his place,[b]
he descends and treads upon the heights of the earth.
⁴ The mountains melt under him
and the valleys split open,
Like wax before the fire,
like water poured down a slope.

---

a Dt 32, 1; Is 1, 2.—b 3f: Is 26, 21; Na 1, 5; Hb 3, 10.—c Hos 9, 1.—d Jb 30, 29.

1, 2: *His holy temple:* God's heavenly temple; the prophet pictures a theophany (3f).
1, 7: The comparison of the unfaithful people with a prostitute, first found in Hosea, is frequent with the prophets; probably ritual prostitution is meant; cf Am 2, 7f; Hos 4, 14.

---

⁵ For the crime of Jacob all this comes to pass,
and for the sins of the house of Israel.
What is the crime of Jacob?
Is it not Samaria?
And what is the sin of the house of Judah?
Is it not Jerusalem?
⁶ I will make Samaria a stone heap in the field,
a place to plant for vineyards;
I will throw down into the valley her stones,
and lay bare her foundations.
⁷ All her idols shall be broken to pieces,[c]
all her wages shall be burned in the fire,
and all her statues I will destroy.
As the wages of a harlot they were gathered,
and to the wages of a harlot shall they return.*

⁸ For this reason I lament and wail,
I go barefoot and naked;
I utter lamentation like the jackals,
and mourning like the ostriches.[d]
⁹ There is no remedy for the blow she has been struck;
rather, it has come even to Judah,
It reaches to the gate of my people,
even to Jerusalem.

1071

¹⁰ Publish it not in Gath,*
   weep not at all;
In Beth-leaphrah
   roll in the dust.^e
¹¹ Pass by,
   you who dwell in Shaphir!
The inhabitants of Zaanan
   come not forth from their city.
The lamentation of Beth-ezel
   finds in you its grounds.
¹² How can the inhabitants of Maroth
   hope for good?
For evil has come down from the LORD
   to the gate of Jerusalem.
¹³ Harness steeds to the chariots,
   O inhabitants of Lachish;
Lachish, the beginning of sin
   for daughter Zion,
Because there were in you
   the crimes of Israel.
¹⁴ Therefore you shall give parting gifts
   to Moresheth-gath;
Beth-achzib is a deception
   to the kings of Israel.
¹⁵ Yet must I bring to you the conqueror,
   O inhabitants of Mareshah;
Even to Adullam shall go
   the glory of Israel.

¹⁶ Make yourself bald, pluck out your
   hair,
   for the children whom you cherish;
Let your baldness be as the eagle's,
   because they are exiled from you.*

CHAPTER 2

Social Evils

¹ Woe to those who plan iniquity,
   and work out evil on their couches;
In the morning light they accomplish it
   when it lies within their power.
² They covet fields, and seize them;
   houses, and they take them;
They cheat an owner of his house,
   a man of his inheritance.*
³   Therefore thus says the LORD:
Behold, I am planning against this race
   an evil
     from which you shall not withdraw
     your necks;
Nor shall you walk with head high,
   for it will be a time of evil.

⁴ On that day a satire shall be sung over
   you,
   and there shall be a plaintive chant:

"Our ruin is complete,
   our fields are portioned out among
   our captors,
The fields of my people are measured
   out,
   and no one can get them back!"
⁵ Thus you shall have no one
   to mark out boundaries by lot*
   in the assembly of the LORD.

⁶ "Preach not," they preach,
   "let them not preach of these
   things!"*
The shame will not withdraw.
⁷ How can it be said, O house of Jacob,
   "Is the LORD short of patience,
   or are such his deeds?"
Do not my words promise good
   to him who walks uprightly?

⁸ But of late my people has risen up as an
   enemy:
   you have stripped off the mantle covering the tunic
Of those who go their way in confidence,
   as though it were spoils of war.
⁹ The women of my people you drive out
   from their pleasant houses;
From their children you take away
   forever the honor I gave them.*
¹⁰ "Up! Be off,
   this is no place to rest";
For any trifle you exact
   a crippling pledge.*
¹¹ If one, acting on impulse, should make
   the futile claim:

---

e 2 Sm 1, 20.

1, 10-15: The Judean cities here named were in the vicinity of Moresheth, the region with which Micah was most familiar. They were to experience divine chastisement. In the Hebrew, wordplays on the names of these cities abound. The text is partly obscure.

1, 16: Shaving the head was a sign of mourning; cf Is 3, 24; Am 8, 10.

2, 2: Land monopoly, also denounced by Isaiah, was a chronic vice in Judah. To protect the poor against it, a man's *inheritance*, his ancestral property, was supposed to be inviolate; cf 1 Kgs 21, 1-4; but the wealthy in their greed were enslaving men for their debts and depriving them of their land.

2, 5: *To mark out boundaries by lot:* an allusion to the initial distribution of the land of Palestine among the Israelites; cf Jos 13—21. The appropriate punishment of those greedy for land will be the loss of their land to their enemies (v 4), a loss that will be irrevocable.

2, 6f: The words in quotation marks are the protestations of the people against the prophet's predictions of doom.

2, 9: *The honor I gave them:* their dignity as free Israelites.

2, 10: *A crippling pledge:* Israelite law forbade exacting pledges for loans that would work hardship on the borrower (Ex 22, 25f; Dt 24, 6. 10-13. 17); but the law was habitually violated.

"I pour you wine and strong drink as
my prophecy,"
then he would be the prophet of this
people.
12 I will gather you, O Jacob, each and
every one,*
I will assemble all the remnant of
Israel;
I will group them like a flock in the
fold,
like a herd in the midst of its corral;
they shall not be thrown into panic by
men.
13 With a leader to break the path
they shall burst open the gate and go
out through it;
Their king shall go through before
them,
and the LORD at their head.

CHAPTER 3

Downfall of Present Leaders

1   And I said:
Hear, you leaders of Jacob,
rulers of the house of Israel!
Is it not your duty to know what is
right,
2   you who hate what is good, and love
evil?
You who tear their skin from them,
and their flesh from their bones!*f*
3 They eat the flesh of my people,
and flay their skin from them,
and break their bones.
They chop them in pieces like flesh in a
kettle,
and like meat in a caldron.
4 When they cry to the LORD,
he shall not answer them;
Rather shall he hide his face from them
at that time,
because of the evil they have done.

5 Thus says the LORD regarding the
prophets*
who lead my people astray;

---

f Am 2, 7.—g Ez 13, 10.—h Jer 15, 9; Am 8, 9; Zec 13, 3.—i
Ez 22, 27; Zep 3, 3.—j Jer 26, 18.—k 1ff: Is 2, 2ff.

2, 12f: This messianic passage concerning the restoration after
the Babylonian exile seems out of place here and is probably a
later addition.
3, 5-8: Almost all the prophetic books contain oracles against
the false prophets. Here Micah accuses them of prophesying for
venal motives and determining the prophecy by the price that is
paid them; he contrasts his own disinterested preaching of the
word of God.
4, 1ff: See note on Is 2, 2ff.

Who, when their teeth have something
to bite,
announce peace,
But when one fails to put something in
their mouth,
proclaim war against him.*g*
6 Therefore you shall have night, not vision,
darkness, not divination;
The sun shall go down upon the prophets,
and the day shall be dark for them.*h*
7 Then shall the seers be put to shame,
and the diviners confounded;
They shall cover their lips, all of them,
because there is no answer from God.
8 But as for me, I am filled with power,
with the spirit of the LORD,
with authority and with might;
To declare to Jacob his crimes
and to Israel his sins.

9 Hear this, you leaders of the house of
Jacob,
you rulers of the house of Israel!
You who abhor what is just,
and pervert all that is right;
10 Who build up Zion with bloodshed,
and Jerusalem with wickedness!
11 Her leaders render judgment for a
bribe,
her priests give decisions for a salary,
her prophets divine for money,
While they rely on the LORD, saying,
"Is not the LORD in the midst of us?
No evil can come upon us!"*i*

12 Therefore, because of you,
Zion shall be plowed like a field,
and Jerusalem reduced to a rubble,
And the mount of the temple
to a forest ridge.*j*

II: THE NEW ISRAEL

CHAPTER 4

The People To Be Restored

1 In days to come*
the mount of the LORD's house
Shall be established higher than the
mountains;
it shall rise high above the hills,
And peoples shall stream to it:*k*
2   Many nations shall come, and say,
"Come, let us climb the mount of the
LORD,

to the house of the God of Jacob,
That he may instruct us in his ways,
  that we may walk in his paths."
For from Zion shall go forth instruction,
  and the word of the LORD from Jerusalem.
3 He shall judge between many peoples
  and impose terms on strong and distant nations;
They shall beat their swords into plowshares,
  and their spears into pruning hooks;
One nation shall not raise the sword
  against another,
  nor shall they train for war again.
4 Every man shall sit under his own vine
  or under his own fig tree, undisturbed;
  for the mouth of the LORD of hosts
  has spoken.[l]
5 For all the peoples walk
  each in the name of its god,
But we will walk in the name of the
  LORD,
  our God, forever and ever.

6 On that day, says the LORD,
  I will gather the lame,
And I will assemble the outcasts,
  and those whom I have afflicted.
7 I will make of the lame a remnant,
  and of those driven far off a strong
  nation;
And the LORD shall be king over them
  on Mount Zion,
  from now on forever.[m]
8 And you, O Magdal-eder,*
  hillock of daughter Zion!
Unto you shall it come:
  the former dominion shall be restored,
  the kingdom of daughter Jerusalem.

9 Now why do you cry out so?
  Are you without a king?
Or has your counselor perished,
  That you are seized with pains
  like a woman in travail?
10 Writhe in pain, grow faint,
  O daughter Zion,
  like a woman in travail;
For now shall you go forth from the
  city
  and dwell in the fields;
To Babylon shall you go,
  there shall you be rescued.

There shall the LORD redeem you
  from the hand of your enemies.*
11 How many nations are gathered against
  you!
They say, "Let her be profaned,
  let our eyes see Zion's downfall!"
12 But they know not the thoughts of the
  LORD,
  nor understand his counsel,
When he has gathered them
  like sheaves on the threshing floor.
13 Arise and thresh, O daughter Zion;
  your horn I will make iron
And your hoofs bronze,
  that you may crush many peoples;
You shall devote their spoils to the
  LORD,
  and their riches to the Lord of the
  whole earth.[n]

Restoration through the Messiah

14 Now fence yourself in, Bat-gader!*
"They have laid siege against us!"
With the rod they strike on the cheek
  the ruler of Israel.

CHAPTER 5

1 But you, Bethlehem-Ephrathah,[o]
  too small to be among the clans of
  Judah,
From you shall come forth for me
  one who is to be ruler in Israel;
Whose origin is from of old,
  from ancient times.*
2 (Therefore the Lord will give them up,
  until the time
  when she who is to give birth* has
  borne,
And the rest of his brethren shall return
  to the children of Israel.)[p]

---

l Hos 14, 8; Am 9, 14.—m Is 6, 13; Dn 7, 14: Zep 3, 19; Lk
1, 32.—n Is 41, 15; Hos 10, 11.—o Ru 1, 2; 1 Sm 17, 12; Mt 2,
6; Jn 7, 42.—p 2f: Is 7, 14; 11, 1f.

4, 8: *Magdal-eder:* "tower of the flock," an ancient place
name (cf Gn 35, 21), here used symbolically of Jerusalem.
  4, 10: *For now . . . your enemies:* probably a later addition
to the text, when the prediction of exile had been fulfilled in the
Babylonian captivity. The prophet sees the exile as the means
whereby God will purify and restore his people.
  4, 14: *Bat-gader:* "fenced-in maiden," another symbolic
name for Jerusalem, then under siege from the Assyrians.
  5, 1: In contrast to Bat-gader (Mi 4, 14), where the *ruler of
Israel,* the reigning king, is in peril of his life from the Assyrians,
is the tiny city and clan of Bethlehem-Ephrathah, from which
comes the ancient Davidic dynasty *(whose origin is from of old,
from ancient times)* with its messianic King, *one who is to be
ruler in Israel.*
  5, 2: *She who is to give birth:* the mother of the Messiah; cf
Is 7, 14.

³ He shall stand firm and shepherd his
flock
by the strength of the LORD,
in the majestic name of the LORD, his
God;
And they shall remain, for now his
greatness
shall reach to the ends of the earth;
⁴ he shall be peace.

If Assyria invades our country*
and treads upon our land,
We shall raise against it seven shepherds,
eight men of royal rank;
⁵ And they shall tend the land of Assyria
with the sword,
and the land of Nimrod* with the
drawn sword;
And we shall be delivered from Assyria,
if it invades our land
and treads upon our borders.

⁶ The remnant of Jacob shall be
in the midst of many peoples,
Like dew coming from the LORD,
like raindrops on the grass,
Which wait for no man,
nor tarry for the sons of men.
⁷ And the remnant of Jacob shall be
among the nations,
in the midst of many peoples,
Like a lion among beasts of the forest,
like a young lion among flocks of
sheep;
When it passes through, it tramples
and tears, and there is none to deliver.

---

q Hos 3, 4; 10, 1f.—r Is 6, 2; Ob 1.—s Jer 2, 5.—t Ex 15, 20.

5, 4f: This passage, expressing confidence in Judah's ability to
deliver itself from Assyria, is in contrast with the preceding messianic oracle, which ascribes deliverance to the Lord and his
agent. Some believe that here the prophet is quoting the words of
the defiant men of Judah. The *shepherds* and *men of royal
rank* are one and the same: warriors capable of routing Assyria.
The same kind of numerical progression is used by Amos (1, 3),
and elsewhere in the Bible.
5, 5: *Nimrod:* the legendary ancestor of the Mesopotamians;
cf Gn 10, 10ff.
5, 9-13: Part of the messianic restoration will consist in the
removal of everything that has drawn Israel away from the Lord;
this includes not only the objects of false worship, but also the ar-
maments in which the idolaters had trusted.
5, 12f: *Sacred pillars . . . sacred poles:* see note on Ex 34,
13.
6, 5: *From Shittim to Gilgal:* from the east to the west side
of the Jordan; the events described in Jos 3—5 are meant. The
text is defective; however, it is evident that this verse continues
the remembrance of God's deeds of mercy to Israel, beginning
with the Exodus (v 4) and extending to the conquest, deeds which
have provoked so little response from his people.

⁸ Your hand shall be lifted above your
foes,
and all your enemies shall be destroyed.
⁹ On that day, says the LORD,*
I will destroy the horses from your midst
and ruin your chariots;
¹⁰ I will demolish the cities of your land
and tear down all your fortresses.
¹¹ I will abolish the means of divination
from your use,
and there shall no longer be soothsayers among you.
¹² I will abolish your carved images
and the sacred pillars from your
midst;
And you shall no longer adore
the works of your hands.�q
¹³ I will tear out the sacred poles* from
your midst,
and destroy your cities.
¹⁴ I will wreak vengeance in anger and
wrath
upon the nations that have not hearkened.

III: ADMONITION

CHAPTER 6

Accusation and Answer

¹ Hear, then, what the LORD says:
Arise, present your plea before the
mountains,
and let the hills hear your voice!ʳ
² Hear, O mountains, the plea of the
LORD,
pay attention, O foundations of the
earth!
For the LORD has a plea against his people,
and he enters into trial with Israel.

³ O my people, what have I done to you,
or how have I wearied you? Answer
me!ˢ
⁴ For I brought you up from the land of
Egypt,
from the place of slavery I released
you;
And I sent before you Moses,
Aaron, and Miriam.ᵗ
⁵ My people, remember what Moab's
King Balak planned,
and how Balaam, the son of Beor, answered him
. . . from Shittim to Gilgal,*

that you may know the just deeds of
the LORD. *u*

6 With what shall I come before the
LORD,*
and bow before God most high?
Shall I come before him with
holocausts,
with calves a year old?*v*
7 Will the LORD be pleased with
thousands of rams,
with myriad streams of oil?
Shall I give my first-born* for my
crime,
the fruit of my body for the sin of my
soul?
8 You have been told, O man, what is
good,
and what the LORD requires of you:
Only to do the right and to love goodness,
and to walk humbly with your God. *w*

9 Hark! the LORD cries to the city.*
[It is wisdom to fear your name!]
Hear, O tribe and city council,
12 You whose rich men are full of violence,
whose inhabitants speak falsehood
with deceitful tongues in their heads!
10 Am I to bear any longer criminal hoard-
ing
and the meager ephah that is accursed?
11 Shall I acquit criminal balances,
bags of false weights?

13 Rather I will begin to strike you
with devastation because of your sins.
15 You shall sow, yet not reap,
tread out the olive, yet pour no oil,
and the grapes, yet drink no wine. *x*
14 You shall eat, without being satisfied,
food that will leave you empty;
What you acquire, you cannot save;
what you do save, I will deliver up to
the sword.*y*
16 You have kept the decrees of Omri,
and all the works of the house of
Ahab,
and you have walked in their counsels;
Therefore I will deliver you up to ruin,
and your citizens to derision;

and you shall bear the reproach of the
nations.*

CHAPTER 7

Condemnation and Prayer

1 Alas! I am as when the fruit is gathered,
as when the vines have been gleaned;
There is no cluster to eat,
no early fig that I crave.
2 The faithful are gone from the earth,
among men the upright are no more!
They all lie in wait to shed blood,
each one ensnares the other. *z*
3 Their hands succeed at evil;
the prince makes demands,
The judge is had for a price,
the great man speaks as he pleases,*a*
4 The best of them is like a brier,
the most upright like a thorn hedge.
The day announced by your watchmen!
your punishment has come;
now is the time of your confusion.
5 Put no trust in a friend,*
have no confidence in a companion;
Against her who lies in your bosom
guard the portals of your mouth. *b*
6 For the son dishonors his father,
the daughter rises up against her
mother,
The daughter-in-law against her
mother-in-law,
and a man's enemies are those of his
household. *c*
7 But as for me, I will look to the LORD,
I will put my trust in God my savior;
my God will hear me!*d*

---

u Nm 22, 23.—v 6f: Hos 6, 6; 8, 13; Am 5, 21.—w Dt 26, 16;
Zec 7, 9; Mt 23, 23.—x Dt 28, 38; Am 5, 11; Hg 1, 6.—y Hos 4,
10.—z Is 1, 21; Hos 4, 2.—a Is 1, 23.—b Jer 9, 3.—c Mt 10,
35f.—d Is 8, 17.

6, 6ff: The people ask how they shall worship the Lord, pro-
posing the various forms of sacrifice. The prophet replies that
sacrifice avails nothing without the true spirit of religion. This is
one of the best expressions of the prophetic teaching on religion,
the preparation for such New Testament passages as Jas 1, 27.
6, 7: *Shall I give my first-born:* through Canaanite influence
the abominable practice of human sacrifice had been introduced
under impious kings (cf 2 Kgs 16, 3; 21, 6).
6, 9: *The city:* Jerusalem as the embodiment of the crimes of
the entire land.
6, 16: Judah has followed the example of the northern kingdom epitomized in the semipaganism of Omri and his son Ahab (1
Kgs 16, 25-34), copying both the corrupted worship and the social injustice of their reigns.
7, 5f: Corresponding to the widespread civil corruption and
apostasy from religion is the breakdown of normal human and
family relations.

8 Rejoice not over me, O my enemy!*
   though I have fallen, I will arise;
   though I sit in darkness, the LORD is
      my light.
9 The wrath of the LORD I will endure
   because I have sinned against him,
   Until he takes up my cause,
   and establishes my right.
   He will bring me forth to the light;
   I will see his justice.
10 When my enemy sees this,
   shame shall cover her:
   She who said to me,
   "Where is the LORD, thy God?"
   My eyes shall see her downfall;
   now shall she be trampled underfoot,
   like the mire in the streets.

11 It is the day for building your walls;*
   on that day the boundary shall be
      taken away.
12 It is the day; and they shall come to you
   from Assyria and from Egypt,
   From Tyre even to the River,
   from sea to sea, and from mountain
      to mountain;*e*
13 And the land shall be a waste
   because of its citizens,
   as a result of their deeds.

---

e Zec 14, 16.—f Jer 10, 6; Acts 10, 43.—g Ps 105, 6; Is 41,
8; 63, 16.

7, 8ff: The unnamed enemy of Judah mentioned in these verses
may be Assyria or one of the neighboring countries, such as
Edom, which stood by to profit at Judah's downfall.
7, 11ff: This prophecy of restoration and repopulation of the
promised land by the Jews now in exile appears to be from the
period after the destruction of Jerusalem by the Chaldeans (587
B.C.).
7, 14-17: This prayer appears to be from the time after the return from exile (537 B.C.), when the people, few in number, possessed only a fragment of their former land, and were surrounded
by hostile nations.

14 Shepherd your people with your staff,*
   the flock of your inheritance,
   That dwells apart in a woodland,
   in the midst of Carmel.
   Let them feed in Bashan and Gilead,
   as in the days of old;
15 As in the days when you came from the
      land of Egypt,
   show us wonderful signs.

16 The nations shall behold and be put to
      shame,
   in spite of all their strength;
   They shall put their hands over their
      mouths;
   their ears shall become deaf.
17 They shall lick the dust like the serpent,
   like reptiles on the ground;
   They shall come quaking from their
      fastnesses,
   trembling in fear of you [the LORD,
      our God].

18 Who is there like you, the God who re-
      moves guilt
   and pardons sin for the remnant of
      his inheritance;
   Who does not persist in anger forever,
   but delights rather in clemency,*f*
19 And will again have compassion on us,
   treading underfoot our guilt?
   You will cast into the depths of the sea
   all our sins;
20 You will show faithfulness to Jacob,
   and grace to Abraham,
   As you have sworn to our fathers
   from days of old.*g*

THE BOOK OF NAHUM

   *Shortly before the fall of Nineveh in 612 B.C., Nahum uttered his prophecy against the
hated city. To understand the prophet's exultant outburst of joy over the impending destruction it is necessary to recall the savage cruelty of Assyria, which had made it the scourge of
the ancient Near East for almost three centuries. The royal inscriptions of Assyria afford the
best commentary on the burning denunciation of "the bloody city." In the wake of their conquests, mounds of heads, impaled bodies, enslaved citizens, and avaricious looters testified
to the ruthlessness of the Assyrians. Little wonder that Judah joined in the general outburst
of joy over the destruction of Nineveh!*

   *But Nahum is not a prophet of unrestrained revenge. God's moral government of the
world is asserted. Yahweh is the avenger but he is also merciful, a citadel in the day of*

distress. Nineveh's doom was a judgment on the wicked city. Before many years passed, Jerusalem too was to learn the meaning of such a judgment.

The book is divided as follows: The Lord's Coming in Judgment (1, 2—2, 1. 3). The Fall of Nineveh (2, 2—3, 19).

CHAPTER 1

¹ Oracle about Nineveh. The book of the vision of Nahum of Elkosh.

The Lord's Coming in Judgment

² * A jealous and avenging God* is the LORD,
     an avenger is the LORD, and angry;
The LORD brings vengeance on his adversaries,
     and lays up wrath for his enemies;
³ The LORD is slow to anger, yet great in power,
     and the LORD never leaves the guilty unpunished.
In hurricane and tempest is his path,
     and clouds are the dust at his feet;*ᵃ*
⁴ He rebukes the sea and leaves it dry,
     and all the rivers he dries up.*ᵇ*
Withered are Bashan and Carmel,
     and the bloom of Lebanon fades;*
⁵ The mountains quake before him,
     and the hills dissolve;
The earth is laid waste before him,
     the world and all who dwell in it.
⁶ Before his wrath, who can stand firm,*ᶜ*
     and who can face his blazing anger?
His fury is poured out like fire,
     and the rocks are rent asunder before him.*
⁷ The LORD is good,
     a refuge on the day of distress;
He takes care of those who have recourse to him,
⁸   when the flood rages;
He makes an end of his opponents,
     and his enemies he pursues with darkness.

⁹ What are you imputing to the LORD?*
     It is he who will make an end!
The enemy shall not rise a second time;
¹⁰ As when a tangle of thornbushes is set aflame,
     like dry stubble, they shall be utterly consumed.
¹² For, says the LORD,
     be they* ever so many and so vigorous,

still they shall be mown down and disappear.
Though I have humbled you,
     I will humble you no more.
¹³ Now will I break his yoke from off you,
     and burst asunder your bonds.*ᵈ*
¹¹ From you he came
     who devised evil against the LORD,
     the scoundrel planner.*

¹⁴ The LORD has commanded regarding you:*
     no descendant shall come to bear your name;
From your temple I will abolish
     the carved and the molten image;
     I will make your grave a mockery.

CHAPTER 2

¹ See, upon the mountains there advances
     the bearer of good news, announcing peace!
Celebrate your feasts, O Judah,
     fulfill your vows!
For nevermore shall you be invaded
     by the scoundrel; he is completely destroyed.*ᵉ*
³ The LORD will restore the vine of Jacob,
     the pride of Israel,
Though ravagers have ravaged them
     and ruined the tendrils.

---

a Ex 19, 16ff.—b Is 33, 9; Hb 3, 6ff.—c Zep 1, 15; 2, 3.—d Is 9, 4; 10, 27.—e Is 52, 7; Rom 10, 15.

1, 2-8: A poem written in the style of the alphabetic psalms; cf Pss 9A; 25; 111; 119. Here, however, most of the verses beginning with the letters of the second half of the alphabet are not preserved.
1, 2: *A jealous . . . God:* see note on Ex 20, 5.
1, 4: *Bashan, Carmel* and *Lebanon* were famous for their forests.
1, 6f: The coming of God in judgment has two aspects: to those who oppose him it will be unbearable; to *those who have recourse to him* it will bring strength and consolation.
1, 9: *What are you imputing to the Lord?:* the people of Judah are asked what they think God has in mind.
1, 12f: *They:* the enemies of Judah. *You:* Judah. *His yoke:* the dominion of the Assyrian king over Judah.
1, 11: *From you . . . the scoundrel planner:* addressed to Nineveh, the capital city of Sennacherib, king of Assyria, who besieged Jerusalem c. 700 B.C.
1, 14: *You:* the king of Assyria.

The Fall of Nineveh

2 The hammer comes up against you;*
　　guard the rampart,
Keep watch on the road, gird your
　　loins,
　　marshal all your strength!
4 The shields of his warriors are crim-
　　soned,
　　the soldiers colored in scarlet;
Fiery steel are the chariots
　　on the day of his mustering.
The horses are frenzied;
5　　the chariots dash madly through the
　　streets
And wheel in the squares,
　　looking like firebrands,
　　flashing like lightning bolts.
6 His picked troops are called,
　　ranks break at their charge;
To the wall they rush,
　　the mantelet* is set up.
7 The river gates are opened,
　　the palace shudders,
8 Its mistress is led forth captive,
　　and her handmaids,* under guard,
Moaning like doves,
　　beating their breasts.
9 Nineveh is like a pool
　　whose waters escape;
"Stop! Stop!"
　　but none turns back.
10 "Plunder the silver, plunder the gold!"
　　There is no end to the treasure,
　　to their wealth in precious things of
　　every kind!

11 Emptiness, desolation, waste;
　　melting hearts and trembling knees,
Writhing in every frame,
　　every face blanched!*f*
12 Where is the lions' cave,
　　the young lions' den,
Where the lion* went in and out,
　　and the cub, with no one to disturb
　　them?

---

f Jl 2, 6.—g Hb 2, 12.—h Mi 1, 7; Rv 17, 1f.—i Is 47, 3; Jer
13, 26; Hos 2, 12.—j Jer 46, 25.

2, 2: *The hammer comes up against you:* the enemy is
about to crush Nineveh.
2, 6: *Mantelet:* a movable shelter protecting the besiegers.
2, 8: *Mistress . . . and her handmaids:* either the queen of
Nineveh with the ladies of her court, or the statue of Ishtar,
Nineveh's chief goddess, with her temple prostitutes.
2, 12: *The lion:* the king of Assyria.
3, 5f: The punishment of adulteresses.
3, 8: *No-amon:* No was the Egyptian name of the capital of
Upper Egypt, called Thebes by the Greeks; its tutelary deity was
Amon. This great city was destroyed by the Assyrians in 663 B.C.

13 The lion snatched enough for his cubs,
　　and strangled for his lionesses;
He filled his dens with prey,
　　and his caves with plunder.
14 I come against you,
　　says the LORD of hosts,
I will consume in smoke your chariots,
　　and the sword shall devour your
　　young lions;
Your preying on the land I will bring to
　　an end,
　　the cry of your lionesses shall be
　　heard no more.

CHAPTER 3

Ruin Imminent and Inevitable

1 Woe to the bloody city, all lies,
　　full of plunder, whose looting never
　　stops!*g*
2 The crack of the whip, the rumbling
　　sounds of wheels;
　　horses a-gallop, chariots bounding,
3 Calvary charging,
The flame of the sword, the flash of the
　　spear,
　　the many slain, the heaping corpses,
　　the endless bodies to stumble upon!
4 For the many debaucheries of the har-
　　lot,
　　fair and charming, a mistress of
　　witchcraft,
Who enslaved nations with her harlot-
　　ries,
　　and peoples by her witchcraft:*h*
5 I am come against you,*i*
　　and I will strip your skirt from you;
I will show your nakedness to the na-
　　tions,
　　to the kingdoms your shame!*
6 I will cast filth upon you,
　　disgrace you and put you to shame;
7 Till everyone who sees you runs from
　　you, saying,
　　"Nineveh is destroyed; who can pity
　　her?
　　Where can one find any to console
　　her?"

8 Are you better than No-amon*
　　that was set among the streams,
Surrounded by waters,
　　with the flood for her rampart
　　and water her wall?*j*
9 Ethiopia was her strength, and Egypt,
　　and others without end;

Put and the Libyans were her auxiliaries.

10 Yet even she went captive into exile,
even her little ones were dashed to
pieces
at the corner of every street;
For her nobles they cast lots,
and all her great men were put into
chains.

11 You, too, shall drink of this till you
faint away;
you, too, shall seek a refuge from the
foe. *k*

12 All your fortresses are but fig trees,
bearing early figs
That fall, when shaken,
into the hungry mouth.

13 See, the troops are women in your
midst;
to your foes the gates of your land are
open wide,
fire has consumed their bars. *l*

14 Draw water for the siege,*
strengthen your fortresses;
Go down into the mud and tread the
clay,
take hold of the brick mold!

15 There the fire shall consume you,
the sword shall cut you down.

Multiply like the grasshoppers,
multiply like the locusts!

16 Make your couriers more numerous
than the stars,

17 your garrisons as many as grasshoppers,
And your scribes as locust swarms
gathered on the rubble fences on a
cold day!
Yet when the sun warms them,
the grasshoppers will spread their
wings and fly,
and vanish, no one knows where.

18 Alas! how your shepherds slumber, O
king of Assyria,
your nobles have gone to rest.
Your people are scattered upon the
mountains,
with none to gather them.

19 There is no healing for your hurt,
your wound is mortal.
All who hear this news of you
clap their hands over you;
For who has not been overwhelmed,
steadily, by your malice?

k Mi 2, 11.—l Jer 51, 30.

3, 14: An ironic exhortation to prepare the city for a futile defense. *Go down . . . brick mold:* make bricks for the city walls.

THE BOOK OF HABAKKUK

*This prophecy dates from the years 605-597 B.C., or between the great Babylonian vic-
tory at Carchemish and Nebuchadnezzar's invasion of Judah which culminated in the capture of Jerusalem. The situation of Judah was desperate at this time, with political intrigue
and idolatry widespread in the small kingdom. The first two chapters consist of a dialogue
between the prophet and the Lord. For what may be the first time in Israelite literature, a
man questions the ways of God, as Habakkuk calls him to account for his government of the
world. To this question God replies that he has prepared a chastising rod, Babylon, which
will be the avenging instrument in his hand. There is added the divine assurance that the just
Israelite will not perish in the calamities about to be visited on the nation.*

*The third chapter is a magnificent religious lyric, filled with reminiscences of Israel's
past and rich in literary borrowings from the poetry of ancient Canaan, though still expressing authentic Israelite faith. God appears in all his majestic splendor and executes vengeance on Judah's enemies. The prophecy ends with a joyous profession of confidence in the
Lord, the Savior.*

CHAPTER 1

¹ The oracle which Habakkuk the prophet received in vision.

The Prophet's Complaint and Its Answer

² How long, O LORD? I cry for help*
　but you do not listen!
I cry out to you, "Violence!"
　but you do not intervene.
³ Why do you let me see ruin;
　why must I look at misery?
Destruction and violence are before me;
　there is strife, and clamorous discord.
⁴ This is why the law is benumbed,
　and judgment is never rendered:
Because the wicked circumvent the just;
　this is why judgment comes forth perverted.

⁵ Look over the nations and see,*
　and be utterly amazed!
For a work is being done in your days
　that you would not have believed,
　were it told.ᵃ

---

a Acts 13, 41.

1, 2-4: Traditionally, these verses have been taken as the prophet's complaint against the internal evils of Judah; the language used is that employed by Amos, Isaiah, and Jeremiah to condemn the social abuses of their day. In vv 5ff the Lord answers this complaint by indicating the Chaldean empire as his instrument for punishing his people for these sins.
1, 5: *Look over the nations and see:* after Nebuchadnezzar's defeat of Egypt in 605 B.C., there could be little doubt that it was the Chaldean ambition to dominate the entire Near East.
1, 8: *Wolves at evening:* the wolf is apparently thought of as more rabid and vicious in the evening when setting out for prey (Jer 5, 6; Zep 3, 3).
1, 11: *Veers like the wind:* the conquests of the ancient Near East were mainly raiding expeditions to collect tribute. As far as administration of conquered territories was concerned, both the Assyrians and Chaldeans were usually content to install friendly rulers and then depart. *This culprit:* though the Chaldeans were used by God as the agents of his punishment, this did not diminish their own guilt as ruthless marauders.
1, 12—2, 1: It is generally thought that this complaint is directed against the Chaldeans and their terrible destruction. But it may well be a continuation of Hb 1, 2-4, against the wicked Judahites who have merited God's punishment.
1, 12: *O Rock:* an ancient title celebrating the Lord's power; cf Ps 18, 32.
1, 15: The *he* of this and the following verses, to whom is attributed such extensive evil and the destruction of many peoples, may be the wicked of Judah embodied in King Jehoiakim, ally of the powerful Pharaoh Neco of Egypt; the devastation wrought by Jehoiakim and Neco together is condemned.
1, 16: *He sacrifices to his net:* in v 15 the wicked ruler in question is represented as catching men in a net. This verse alludes to some rite involving the sacrificial veneration of the weapons of war.

⁶ For see, I am raising up Chaldea,
　that bitter and unruly people,
That marches the breadth of the land
　to take dwellings not his own.
⁷ Terrible and dreadful is he,
　from himself derive his law and his majesty.
⁸ Swifter than leopards are his horses,
　and keener than wolves at evening.*
His horses prance,
　his horsemen come from afar:
They fly like the eagle hastening to devour;
⁹ 　each comes for the rapine,
Their combined onset is that of a stormwind
　that heaps up captives like sand.
¹⁰ He scoffs at kings,
　and princes are his laughingstock;
He laughs at any fortress,
　heaps up a ramp, and conquers it.
¹¹ Then he veers like the wind* and is gone—
　this culprit who makes his own strength his god!

¹² Are you not from eternity, O LORD,*
　my holy God, immortal?
O LORD, you have marked him for judgment,
　O Rock,* you have readied him for punishment!
¹³ Too pure are your eyes to look upon evil,
　and the sight of misery you cannot endure.
Why, then, do you gaze on the faithless in silence
　while the wicked man devours
　one more just than himself?
¹⁴ You have made man like the fish of the sea,
　like creeping things without a ruler.
¹⁵ He* brings them all up with his hook,
　he hauls them away with his net,
He gathers them in his seine;
　and so he rejoices and exults.
¹⁶ Therefore he sacrifices to his net,*
　and burns incense to his seine;
For thanks to them his portion is generous,
　and his repast sumptuous.
¹⁷ Shall he, then, keep on brandishing his sword
　to slay peoples without mercy?

Hb

CHAPTER 2

1 I will stand at my guard post,
  and station myself upon the rampart,
And keep watch to see what he will say
    to me,
  and what answer he will give to my
    complaint. *b*

2 Then the LORD answered me and said:
  Write down the vision
Clearly upon the tablets,
  so that one can read it readily.
3 For the vision still has its time,
  presses on to fulfillment, and will not
    disappoint;
If it delays, wait for it,
  it will surely come, it will not be late.
4 The rash man has no integrity;*c*
  but the just man, because of his faith,
    shall live.*
Wealth, too, is treacherous:
  the proud, unstable man—
5 He who opens wide his throat like the
    nether world,
  and is insatiable as death,
Who gathers to himself all the nations,
  and rallies to himself all the peo-
    ples—
6 Shall not all these take up a taunt
    against him,
  satire and epigrams about him, to
    say:

Woe to him who stores up what is not
    his:
  how long can it last!
  he loads himself down with debts.
7 Shall not your creditors rise suddenly?
  Shall not they who make you tremble
    awake?
  You shall become their spoil!
8 Because you despoiled many peoples
  all the rest of the nations shall despoil
    you;
Because of men's blood shed,
  and violence done to the land,
  to the city and to all who dwell in it.

9 Woe to him who pursues evil gain for
    his household,
  setting his nest on high
  to escape the reach of misfortune!
10 You have devised shame for your
    household,
  cutting off many peoples, forfeiting
    your own life:

11 For the stone in the wall shall cry out,*
  and the beam in the woodwork shall
    answer it!
12 Woe to him who builds a city by
    bloodshed,
  and establishes a town by wicked-
    ness!*d*
13 Is not this from the LORD of hosts:
  peoples toil for the flames,*
  and nations grow weary for nought!*e*
14 But the earth shall be filled
  with the knowledge of the LORD's
    glory
  as water covers the sea.*f*

15 Woe to you who give your neighbors
  a flood of your wrath to drink,
  and make them drunk, till their
    nakedness is seen!
16 You are filled with shame instead of
    glory;
  drink, you too, and stagger!
On you shall revert the cup from the
    LORD's right hand,
  and utter shame on your glory.
17 For the violence done to Lebanon* shall
    cover you,
  and the destruction of the beasts shall
    terrify you;
Because of men's blood shed,
  and violence done to the land,
  to the city and to all who dwell in it.

19 Woe to him who says to wood,
    "Awake!"
  to dumb stone, "Arise!"
  Can such a thing give oracles?
See, it is overlaid with gold and silver,
  but there is no life breath in it.

---

b Ps 85, 9.—c Rom 1, 17; Gal 3, 11; Heb 10, 38.—d Ez 24, 9; Na 3, 1.—e Jer 51, 58.—f Is 11, 9.

2, 4: *The just man, because of his faith, shall live:* the faith which here enables the virtuous man to survive the impending doom is both a confident belief in God's justice, and patience in awaiting its execution. St. Paul quotes these words (Rom 1, 17; Gal 3, 11; Heb 10, 38) to confirm his teaching that man receives justification and supernatural life through faith in Christ.
2, 11f: The palaces, built at the expense of gross injustice (vv 6-10), call down vengeance on their builders. This is typical prophetic language for the condemnation of social crimes within Israel and Judah.
2, 13: *Peoples toil for the flames:* they build only to have fire consume their work, when they build contrary to God's will.
2, 17: *The violence done to Lebanon:* the spoliation of the cedar forests of Lebanon, used in lavish building projects by the great conquerors; cf Is 14, 8; 37, 24. *The destruction of the beasts:* the killing off of the wild animals through excessive hunting by the same conquerors; cf Bar 3, 16.

¹⁸ Of what avail is the carved image,*
  that its maker should carve it?
Or the molten image and lying oracle,
  that its very maker should trust in it,
  and make dumb idols?
²⁰ But the LORD is in his holy temple;
  silence before him, all the earth!ᵍ

CHAPTER 3

Canticle

¹ Prayer of Habakkuk, the prophet. To a plaintive tune.*

² O LORD, I have heard your renown,
  and feared, O LORD, your work.
In the course of the years revive it,*
  in the course of the years make it
  known;
  in your wrath remember compassion!

³ * God comes from Teman,*
  the Holy One from Mount Paran.
Covered are the heavens with his glory,
  and with his praise the earth is filled.
⁴ His splendor spreads like the light;
  rays shine forth from beside him,
  where his power is concealed.
⁵ Before him goes pestilence,
  and the plague follows in his steps.
⁶ He pauses to survey the earth;
  his look makes the nations tremble.
The eternal mountains are shattered,
  the age-old hills bow low
  along his ancient ways.

⁷ I see the tents of Cushan collapse;
  trembling are the pavilions of the
  land of Midian.
⁸ Is your anger against the streams, O
  LORD?

Is your wrath against the streams,
  your rage against the sea,
That you drive the steeds
  of your victorious chariot?
⁹ Bared and ready is your bow,
  filled with arrows is your quiver.
Into streams you split the earth;
¹⁰ at sight of you the mountains tremble.
A torrent of rain descends;
  the ocean gives forth its roar.
The sun forgets to rise,
¹¹ the moon remains in its shelter,
At the light of your flying arrows,
  at the gleam of your flashing spear.ʰ

¹² In wrath you bestride the earth,
  in fury you trample the nations.
¹³ You come forth to save your people,
  to save your anointed one.*
You crush the heads of the wicked,
  you lay bare their bases at the neck.ⁱ
¹⁴ You pierce with your shafts the heads of
  their princes
  whose boast would be of devouring
  the wretched in their lair.
¹⁵ You tread the sea with your steeds
  amid the churning of the deep
  waters.

¹⁶ I hear, and my body trembles;
  at the sound, my lips quiver.
Decay invades my bones,
  my legs tremble beneath me.
I await the day of distress
  that will come upon the people who
  attack us.

¹⁷ For though the fig tree blossom not
  nor fruit be on the vines,
Though the yield of the olive fail
  and the terraces produce no nourishment,
Though the flocks disappear from the
  fold
  and there be no herd in the stalls,
¹⁸ Yet will I rejoice in the LORDʲ
  and exult in my saving God.
¹⁹ GOD, my Lord, is my strength;
  he makes my feet swift as those of
  hinds
  and enables me to go upon the
  heights.

For the leader; with stringed instruments.

---

g Ps 11, 4.—h Jos 10, 12.—i Is 51, 9ff.—j 18f: Ps 18, 32f; Mi
7, 7.

2, 18-20: Idolatrous worship is here shown to be folly by contrasting man-made idols with the majesty of the one true God.
3, 1: A later liturgical rubric. So also the end of v 19.
3, 2: *In the course of the years revive it:* renew today your wondrous deeds of the past.
3, 3-15: Cf the theophanies in Dt 33, 2f; Jgs 5, 4f; Pss 18, 8-16; 68, 8f; 77, 17-21; 97, 1-5; Na 1, 3-6, etc. Conventional language is employed to describe the appearance of the Lord, as in Ex 19, 16-19.
3, 3: *Teman:* a region in Edom. *Mount Paran:* in the territory of Edom, or the northern part of the Sinaitic peninsula. The Lord is represented as coming from Sinai, where he had appeared to Moses and given Israel the covenant and the law.
3, 13: *Your anointed one:* the theocratic king, the head of God's people.

THE BOOK OF ZEPHANIAH

The title of the prophecy informs us that the ministry of Zephaniah took place during the reign of Josiah (640-609 B.C.). The protest against the worship of false gods, and the condemnation of the pro-Assyrian court ministers who served as regents during Josiah's minority, allow us to place the work in the first decade of the reign. Accordingly, the prophecy of Zephaniah comes rightly before that of Jeremiah, who was probably influenced by it in both language and ideas.

The age of Zephaniah was a time of religious degradation, when the old idolatries reappeared and men worshiped sun, moon, and stars. Rites completely alien to the pure monotheism taught by Moses flourished in Jerusalem. To the corrupt city Zephaniah announced the impending judgment, the day of the Lord. The prophecy may be divided into three sections, corresponding to the three chapters of the book:

The Day of the Lord: A day of doom. The last few verses of this oracle give the classic description of the Day of the Lord as an overwhelming disaster. The Christian hymn Dies Irae *is based on this passage (1, 2-18).*

The Day of the Lord: A day of judgment of the nations, traditional enemies of God's people (2, 1-15).

Reproach and Promise for Jerusalem: Despite Judah's infidelities, the Lord in his mercy will spare a holy remnant, which will finally enjoy peace. The prophecy closes with a hymn of joy sung by the remnant restored to Zion (3, 1-20).

CHAPTER 1

¹ The word of the LORD which came to Zephaniah, the son of Cushi, the son of Gedaliah, the son of Amariah, the son of Hezekiah, in the days of Josiah, the son of Amon, king of Judah.

The Day of the Lord:
A Day of Doom

² I will completely sweep away all things
   from the face of the earth, says the LORD.
³ I will sweep away man and beast,
   I will sweep away the birds of the sky,
   and the fishes of the sea.
I will overthrow the wicked;
   I will destroy mankind
   from the face of the earth, says the LORD. [a]
⁴ I will stretch out my hand against Judah,
   and against all the inhabitants of Jerusalem;
I will destroy from this place the last vestige of Baal,
   the very names of his priests,
⁵ And those who adore the host of heaven* on the roofs,
with those who adore the LORD
   but swear by Milcom; [b]
⁶ And those who have fallen away from the LORD,
   and those who do not seek the LORD.

⁷ Silence in the presence of the Lord GOD!
   for near is the day of the LORD,
Yes, the LORD has prepared a slaughter feast,
   he has consecrated his guests.*
⁸   On the day of the LORD's slaughter feast
I will punish the princes, and the king's sons,
   and all that dress in foreign apparel.
⁹ I will punish, on that day,
   all who leap over the threshold,*
Who fill the house of their master
   with violence and deceit.
¹⁰   On that day, says the LORD,

---

a Hos 4, 3.—b Jer 8, 2; 19, 13.

1, 5: *The host of heaven:* the stars, the worship of which was introduced into Judah by the Assyrians. *Milcom:* the god of the Ammonites; cf 1 Kgs 11, 5. 7. 33; 2 Kgs 23, 13.
1, 7: *He has consecrated his guests:* God has prepared those whom he has invited to share as soldiers in the booty, as beast and bird scavengers of carrion, on the day of slaughter. Cf Jer 46, 10; Ez 39, 17.
1, 9: *Leap over the threshold:* the reference is to a superstitious custom of the pagans, witnessed to at least in regard to the worship of Dagon (1 Sm 5, 5).

A cry will be heard from the Fish Gate,
a wail from the New Quarter,
loud crashing from the hills.
11 Wail, O inhabitants of the Mortar!*
for all the merchants will be destroyed,
all who weigh out silver, done away
with.
12 At that time I will explore Jerusalem
with lamps;
I will punish the men who thicken on
their lees,*
Who say in their hearts,
"Neither good nor evil can the LORD
do."
13 Their wealth shall be given to pillage
and their houses to devastation;
They will build houses, but shall not
dwell in them,
plant vineyards, but not drink their
wine. *c*
14 Near is the great day of the LORD,
near and very swiftly coming;
Hark, the day of the LORD!
bitter, then, the warrior's cry.
15 A day of wrath is that day, *d*
a day of anguish and distress,
A day of destruction and desolation,
a day of darkness and gloom,
A day of thick black clouds,
16   a day of trumpet blasts and battle
alarm
Against fortified cities,
against battlements on high. *e*
17 I will hem men in
till they walk like the blind,
because they have sinned against the
LORD;
And their blood shall be poured out like
dust,
and their brains like dung.
18 Neither their silver nor their gold
shall be able to save them
on the day of the LORD's wrath,
When in the fire of his jealousy

all the earth shall be consumed.
For he shall make an end, yes, a sudden
end,
of all who live on the earth. *f*

CHAPTER 2

The Day of the Lord: A Day
of Judgment

1 Gather, gather yourselves together,
O nation without shame!*
2 Before you are driven away,
like chaff that passes on;
Before there comes upon you
the blazing anger of the LORD;
Before there comes upon you
the day of the LORD's anger.
3 Seek the LORD, all you humble of the
earth,
who have observed his law;
Seek justice, seek humility;
perhaps you may be sheltered
on the day of the LORD's anger.
4 For Gaza shall be forsaken,
and Ashkelon shall be a waste,
Ashdod they shall drive out at midday,
and Ekron* shall be uprooted. *g*
5 Woe to you who dwell by the seacoast,
to the Cretan folk!*
The word of the LORD is against you,
I will humble you, land of the Philistines,
and leave you to perish without an inhabitant!
6 The coastland of the Cretans shall become
fields for shepherds, and folds for
flocks.
7 The coast shall belong
to the remnant of the house of Judah;
by the sea they shall pasture.
In the houses of Ashkelon at evening
they shall couch their flocks,
For the LORD their God shall visit
them,
and bring about their restoration.
8 I have heard the revilings uttered by
Moab,
and the insults of the Ammonites,
When they reviled my people
and made boasts against their territory.
9 Therefore, as I live, says the LORD of
hosts,
the God of Israel,

---

c Am 5, 11.—d Jer 30, 7; Jl 2, 11; Am 5, 18.—e Am 2, 2.—f
Zep 3, 8; Ez 7, 19.—g Am 1, 6ff; Zec 9, 5.

1, 10f: *The New Quarter . . . the Mortar:* sections of Jerusalem (cf 2 Kgs 22, 14).

1, 12: *The men who thicken on their lees:* those who are
overconfident because, like bottles of wine in which the sediment
has settled to the bottom, they have remained at peace and undisturbed for a long time.

2, 1: *Nation without shame:* Judah.

2, 4: *Gaza . . . Ashkelon . . . Ashdod . . . Ekron:* four of the
five cities of the Philistine confederation. The fifth city, Gath, is
not mentioned, perhaps because it was already destroyed.

2, 5: *Cretan folk:* the Philistines, who came from Crete; see
note on Dt 2, 23.

Moab shall become like Sodom,
the land of Ammon like Gomorrah:
A field of nettles and a salt pit
and a waste forever.
The remnant of my people shall plunder them,
the survivors of my nation dispossess
them.

10 Such shall be the requital of their pride,
because they reviled and boasted
against
the people of the LORD of hosts.

11 The LORD shall inspire them with fear
when he makes all the gods of earth
to waste away;
Then, each from its own place,
all the coastlands of the nations shall
adore him.

12 You too, O Cushites,*
shall be slain by the sword of the
LORD.

13 He will stretch out his hand against the
north,
to destroy Assyria;
He will make Nineveh a waste,
dry as the desert.

14 In her midst shall settle in droves
all the wild life of the hollows;
The screech owl and the desert owl
shall roost in her columns;
Their call shall resound from the window,
the raven's croak from the doorway. *h*

15 Is this the exultant city*
that dwelt secure;
That told herself,
"There is no other than I!"
How has she become a waste,
a lair for wild beasts?
Whoever passes by her
hisses, and shakes his fist!

CHAPTER 3

Reproach and Promise for Jerusalem

1 Woe to the city, rebellious and polluted,
to the tyrannical city!

2 She hears no voice,
accepts no correction;
In the LORD she has not trusted,
to her God she has not drawn near. *i*

3 Her princes in her midst
are roaring lions;
Her judges are wolves of the night

that have had no bones to gnaw by
morning. *j*

4 Her prophets are insolent,
treacherous men;
Her priests profane what is holy,
and do violence to the law. *k*

5 The LORD within her is just,
who does no wrong;
Morning after morning he renders judgment
unfailingly, at dawn.

6 I have destroyed nations,
their battlements are laid waste;
I have made their streets deserted,
with no one passing through;
Their cities are devastated,
with no man dwelling in them. *l*

7 I said, "Surely now you will fear me,
you will accept correction";
She should not fail to see
all I have visited upon her.
Yet all the more eagerly have they done
all their corrupt deeds.

8 Therefore, wait for me, says the LORD,
against the day when I arise as accuser;
For it is my decision to gather together
the nations,
to assemble the kingdoms,
In order to pour out upon them my
wrath,
all my blazing anger;
For in the fire of my jealousy
shall all the earth be consumed. *m*

9 For then I will change and purify
the lips of the peoples,
That they all may call upon the name of
the LORD,
to serve him with one accord;

10 From beyond the rivers of Ethiopia
and as far as the recesses of the
North,
they shall bring me offerings.

11   On that day
You need not be ashamed
of all your deeds,
your rebellious actions against me;
For then will I remove from your midst
the proud braggarts,

---

h Is 34, 11.—i Jer 2, 30; 7, 28.—j Ez 22, 27; Mi 3, 11.—k Jer
23, 32.—l Jer 2, 15.—m Zep 1, 18.

2, 12: *Cushites:* the Egyptians, at this time under a Cushite or
Ethiopian dynasty.
2, 15: *The exultant city:* Nineveh.

And you shall no longer exalt yourself
on my holy mountain.

12 But I will leave as a remnant in your
midst
a people humble and lowly,
Who shall take refuge in the name of
the Lord:ⁿ
13   the remnant of Israel.
They shall do no wrong
and speak no lies;
Nor shall there be found in their mouths
a deceitful tongue;
They shall pasture and couch their
flocks
with none to disturb them.^o
14 Shout for joy, O daughter Zion!
sing joyfully, O Israel!
Be glad and exult with all your heart,
O daughter Jerusalem!^p
15 The LORD has removed the judgment
against you,
he has turned away your enemies;
The King of Israel, the LORD, is in your
midst,
you have no further misfortune to
fear.

n Hos 14, 4.—o Mi 4, 4.—p Zec 9, 9.—q Mt 14, 27.—r Mi 4, 6.

16 On that day, it shall be said to Jerusalem:
Fear not, O Zion, be not discouraged!^q
17 The LORD, your God, is in your midst,
a mighty savior;
He will rejoice over you with gladness,
and renew you in his love,
He will sing joyfully because of you,
18   as one sings at festivals.

I will remove disaster from among you,
so that none may recount your disgrace.
19 Yes, at that time I will deal
with all who oppress you:
I will save the lame,
and assemble the outcasts;
I will give them praise and renown
in all the earth, when I bring about
their restoration.^r
20 At that time I will bring you home,
and at that time I will gather you;
For I will give you renown and praise,
among all the peoples of the earth,
When I bring about your restoration
before your very eyes, says the LORD.

Hg

THE BOOK OF HAGGAI

*Postexilic prophecy begins with Haggai, who received the word of the Lord in the sec-
ond year of Darius (520 B.C.). The Jews who returned from the Exile in Babylonia had encountered formidable obstacles in their efforts to re-establish Jewish life in Judah. The
Samaritans had succeeded in blocking the rebuilding of the temple; but after Darius acceded
to the throne (522), permission was given to resume the work. At this critical moment, when
defeatism and a certain lethargy had overtaken his repatriated countrymen, Haggai came
forward with his exhortations to them to complete the great task. The first oracle, an appeal
to the Jews, is contained in chapter 1. To this appeal Haggai added a short oracle of encouragement (2, 1-9) for the sake of those who gloomily contrasted the former magnificence of
Solomon's temple with the second temple: the Lord would be present in this new abode, and
its glory, enhanced by the offerings of the Gentiles, would surpass the ancient splendor.*

The prophecy may be divided into five oracles:

*The call to rebuild the temple. The economic distress so apparent in Judah is due to the
Jews' neglect of the Lord while they provide for their own needs (1, 1-15).*

The future glory of the new temple, surpassing that of the old (2, 1-9).

*Unworthiness of a people, who may be the Samaritans, to offer sacrifice at the newly
restored altar. This oracle is cast in the literary form of a torah, an instruction given the people by a priest (2, 10-14).*

A promise of immediate blessings, which follows upon the undertaking (chapter 1) to rebuild the temple (2, 15-19).

A pledge to Zerubbabel, descendant of David, repository of the Messianic hopes (2, 20-23).

CHAPTER 1

Exhortation To Rebuild the Temple of the Lord. ¹On the first day of the sixth month in the second year* of King Darius, the word of the LORD came through the prophet Haggai to the governor of Judah, Zerubbabel, son of Shealtiel, and to the high priest Joshua, son of Jehozadak:ᵃ ²Thus says the LORD of hosts: This people says: "Not now has the time come to rebuild the house of the LORD." ³(Then this word of the LORD came through Haggai, the prophet:) ⁴Is it time for you to dwell in your own paneled houses,ᵇ while this house lies in ruins?*

⁵ Now thus says the LORD of hosts:
    Consider your ways!
⁶ You have sown much, but have brought
    in little;
    you have eaten, but have not been
        satisfied;
    You have drunk, but have not been
        exhilarated;
    have clothed yourselves, but not been
        warmed;
    And he who earned wages
        earned them for a bag with holes in
        it.ᶜ

⁷   Thus says the LORD of hosts:
    Consider your ways!
⁸   Go up into the hill country;
        bring timber, and build the house
    That I may take pleasure in it
        and receive my glory, says the LORD.
⁹ You expected much, but it came to lit-
        tle;
        and what you brought home, I blew
        away.
    For what cause? says the LORD of hosts.
    Because my house lies in ruins,
        while each of you hurries to his own
        house.ᵈ
¹⁰ Therefore the heavens withheld from
        you their dew,
        and the earth her crops.ᵉ
¹¹ And I called for a drought
        upon the land and upon the moun-
        tains;

    Upon the grain, and upon the wine, and
        upon the oil,
        and upon all that the ground brings
        forth;
    Upon men and upon beasts,
        and upon all that is produced by hand.

¹² Then Zerubbabel, son of Shealtiel, and the high priest Joshua, son of Jehozadak, and all the remnant of the people* listened to the voice of the LORD, their God, and to the words of the prophet Haggai, because the LORD, their God, had sent him, and the people feared because of the LORD. ¹³And the LORD's messenger, Haggai, proclaimed to the people as the message of the LORD: I am with you, says the LORD.

¹⁴Then the LORD stirred up the spirit of the governor of Judah, Zerubbabel, son of Shealtiel, and the spirit of the high priest Joshua, son of Jehozadak, and the spirit of all the remnant of the people, so that they came and set to work on the house of the LORD of hosts, their God, ¹⁵on the twenty-fourth day of the sixth month.

CHAPTER 2

Future Glory of the New Temple. In the second year of King Darius, ¹on the twenty-first day of the seventh month, the word of the LORD came through the prophet Haggai: ²Tell this to the governor of Judah, Zerubbabel, son of Shealtiel, and to the high priest Joshua, son of Jehozadak, and to the remnant of the people:

³ Who is left among you
        that saw this house in its former
        glory?
    And how do you see it now?
        Does it not seem like nothing in your
        eyes?

---

a Ezr 4, 24; 5, 1; 6, 14.—b 2 Sm 7, 2.—c Dt 28, 38ff; Mi 6, 15.—d 2 Kgs 25, 9.—e Gn 27, 28; Am 4, 6-9.

1, 1: *The sixth month in the second year:* August/September in 520 B.C.
1, 4: *The luxury of the homes of the wealthy with their paneled houses* contrasts sadly with the ruined state of the Lord's *house.*
1, 12: *The remnant of the people:* a technical term in Haggai and Zechariah for the returned exiles.

⁴ But now take courage, Zerubbabel, says
   the LORD,
   and take courage, Joshua, high
     priest, son of Jehozadak,
And take courage, all you people of the
   land,
   says the LORD, and work!
For I am with you, says the LORD of
   hosts.*f*
⁵ This is the pact that I made with you
   when you came out of Egypt,
And my spirit continues in your midst;
   do not fear!*g*

⁶   For thus says the LORD of
   hosts:*
One moment yet, a little while,
   and I will shake the heavens and the
     earth,
   the sea and the dry land.*h*
⁷ I will shake all the nations,
   and the treasures of all the nations
     will come in,
And I will fill this house with glory,
   says the LORD of hosts.*i*
⁸ Mine is the silver and mine the gold,
   says the LORD of hosts.
⁹ Greater will be the future glory of this
   house
   than the former, says the LORD of
     hosts;
And in this place I will give peace,
   says the LORD of hosts!*j*

Offerings of the Unclean Rejected. ¹⁰On
the twenty-fourth day of the ninth month,
in the second year of King Darius, the
word of the LORD came to the prophet
Haggai: ¹¹Thus says the LORD of hosts:
Ask the priests for a decision:*k* ¹²If a man
carries sanctified flesh in the fold of his
garment and the fold touches bread, or

pottage, or wine, or oil, or any other food,
do they become sanctified? "No," the
priests answered.* ¹³Then Haggai said: If
a person unclean from contact with a
corpse touches any of these, do they become unclean? The priests answered,
"They become unclean."*l* ¹⁴Then Haggai
continued:

So is this people, and so is this nation
   in my sight, says the LORD:
And so are all the works of their hands;
   and what they offer there is unclean.

Promise of Immediate Blessings. * ¹⁵But
now, consider from this day forward. Before there was a stone laid upon a stone in
the temple of the LORD, ¹⁶how did you
fare?

When one went to a heap of grain for
   twenty measures,
   it would yield but ten;
When another went to the vat to draw
   fifty measures,
   there would be but twenty.*m*
¹⁷ I struck you in all the works of your
   hands
   with blight, searing wind, and hail,
   yet you did not return to me, says the
     LORD.

¹⁸[Consider from this day forward: from
the twenty-fourth day of the ninth
month.* From the day on which the temple of the LORD was founded, consider!]

¹⁹ Indeed, the seed has not sprouted,
   nor have the vine, the fig, the pome-
     granate
   and the olive tree yet borne.
From this day, I will bless!

Pledge to Zerubbabel. ²⁰The message of
the LORD came a second time to Haggai on
the twenty-fourth day of the month:*
²¹Tell this to Zerubbabel, the governor of
Judah:

I will shake the heavens and the earth;
²² I will overthrow the thrones of kingdoms,
   destroy the power of the kingdoms of
     the nations.
I will overthrow the chariots and their
   riders,
   and the riders with their horses
   shall go down by one another's
     sword.*n*

---

f Zec 8, 9.—g Ex 29, 45; Lv 26, 45.—h Heb 12, 26.—i Gn 49,
10; Is 60, 5. 9. 11; Mal 3, 1; Rv 21, 26.—j Is 2, 2ff; Zec 6, 13.—
k Dt 17, 8-13; Zec 7, 3.—l Nm 19, 11; 13, 22.—m Is 5, 10.—n
Ez 38, 21; Dn 2, 44; Zec 14, 13; Lk 1, 52.

2, 6-9: From the later period of Ezekiel's preaching onward,
the temple became, as here, one of the dominant messianic
themes. *Greater will be the future glory of this house than
the former:* because Christ will enter it.
   2, 12ff: According to the ritual concepts of the Jews, uncleanness was more contagious than sacredness. Inasmuch as the people were unclean, their offerings became unclean (Nm 19, 22).
   2, 15-19: This prophecy is intimately linked with chapter 1,
and should be read with it.
   2, 18: *The ninth month:* the ordinal *ninth* has been copied
incorrectly from Hg 2, 10. This note properly concerns the *twenty-
fourth day of the sixth month, on which the temple of the
Lord was founded* (Hg 1, 15).
   2, 20: *The month:* probably again the sixth month, as in Hg 1,
15 and 2, 18; see note on the latter.

23   On that day, says the LORD of hosts,[o]

I will take you, Zerubbabel,
     son of Shealtiel, my servant, says the LORD,
And I will set you as a signet ring;

for I have chosen you, says the LORD of hosts.*

---

o Song 8, 6; Sir 49, 11; Is 42, 1; 44, 1f.

2, 23: This promise to Zerubbabel, reversing the punishment of his grandfather (Jer 22, 24), is a continuation of the messianic hope; cf Zec 6, 11f.

THE BOOK OF ZECHARIAH

Zechariah's initial prophecy is dated to 520 B.C., the same year as that in which Haggai received the prophetic call. The first eight chapters of the Book of Zechariah contain oracles which certainly belong to him while the last six (sometimes called "Deutero-Zechariah") represent the work of one or more unknown authors. In the prophecies proper to Zechariah eight symbolic visions are recorded, all meant to promote the work of rebuilding the temple and to encourage the returned exiles, especially their leaders, Joshua and Zerubbabel. In the final chapter of this first division Zechariah portrays the messianic future under the figure of a prosperous land to which the nations come in pilgrimage, eager to follow the God of Israel.

The second part of Zechariah is divided into two sections, each with its own introductory title. The first (9—11) consists of oracles whose historical background, date and authorship are extremely difficult to determine. With 9, 9 begins the messianic vision of the coming of the Prince of Peace. The verses describing the triumphant appearance of the humble king are taken up by the four Evangelists to describe the entry of Christ into Jerusalem on Palm Sunday. Chapter 12 is introduced by an oracle proclaiming the victory of God's people over the heathen. The prophecy closes by describing, in apocalyptic imagery, the final assault of the enemy on Jerusalem, after which the messianic age begins.

CHAPTER 1

Necessity of Conversion. [1] In the second year of Darius, in the eighth month,* the word of the LORD came to the prophet Zechariah, son of Berechiah, son of Iddo:[a] [2] The LORD was indeed angry with your fathers. . . . [3] and say to them: Thus says the LORD of hosts: Return to me, says the LORD of hosts, and I will return to you, says the LORD of hosts. [4] Be not like your fathers whom the former prophets warned: Thus says the LORD of hosts: Turn from your evil ways and from your wicked deeds. But they would not listen or pay attention to me, says the LORD.[b] [5] Your fathers, where are they? And the prophets, can they live forever? [6] But my words and my decrees, which I entrusted to my servants the prophets, did not these overtake your fathers? Then they repented and admitted: "The LORD of hosts has treated us according to our ways and deeds, just as he had determined he would."[c]

The Four Horsemen. [7] In the second year of Darius, on the twenty-fourth day of Shebat, the eleventh month,* the word of the LORD came to the prophet Zechariah, son of Berechiah, son of Iddo, in the following way: [8] I had a vision during the night. There appeared the driver of a red horse,* standing among myrtle trees in a shady place, and behind him were red, sorrel, and white horses.[d] [9] Then I asked, "What are these, my lord?"; and the angel who spoke with me answered me, "I will show you what these are." [10] The man who was standing among the myrtle trees spoke up and said, "These are they whom the LORD has sent to patrol the earth."[e] [11] And they answered the angel of the LORD who was standing among the myrtle trees and said, "We have patrolled the earth; see, the whole earth is tranquil and at rest!"

---

a Ezr 4, 24; 5, 1; 6, 14.—b Jer 25, 5; 35, 15; Mal 3, 7.—c Lam 2, 17; Lv 26, 14ff; Dt 28, 15.—d Rv 6, 4.—e Zec 6, 7.

1, 1: *The second year . . . eighth month:* October/November, 520 B.C.

1, 7: *The second year . . . eleventh month:* January/February, 519 B.C.

1, 8-11: *The driver of a red horse:* apparently distinct from *the man,* or *angel of the Lord . . . standing among the myrtle trees,* who spoke with the prophet. The four horsemen are sent by God to the four corners of the earth (Zec 2, 10), to see if the whole earth is at peace.

¹² ᶠ Then the angel of the Lord spoke out and said, "O LORD of hosts, how long will you be without mercy for Jerusalem and the cities of Judah that have felt your anger these seventy years?"* ¹³ To the angel who spoke with me, the LORD replied with comforting words.ᵍ

¹⁴ And the angel who spoke with me said to me, Proclaim: Thus says the LORD of hosts: I am deeply moved for the sake of Jerusalem and Zion,ʰ ¹⁵ and I am exceedingly angry with the complacent nations;* whereas I was but a little angry, they added to the harm.ⁱ ¹⁶ Therefore, says the LORD: I will turn to Jerusalem in mercy; my house shall be built in it, says the LORD of hosts, and a measuring line* shall be stretched over Jerusalem.ʲ ¹⁷ Proclaim further: Thus says the LORD of hosts: My cities shall again overflow with prosperity; the LORD will again comfort Zion, and again choose Jerusalem.ᵏ

CHAPTER 2

Four Horns and Four Blacksmiths. ¹ I raised my eyes and looked: there were four horns.* ² Then I asked the angel who spoke with me what these were. He answered me, "These are the horns that scattered Judah and Israel and Jerusalem."

³ Then the LORD showed me four blacksmiths. And I asked, "What are these coming to do?" ⁴ And he said, "Here are the horns that scattered Judah, so that no man raised his head anymore; but these have come to terrify them: to cast down the horns of the nations that raised their horns to scatter the land of Judah."

---

f Zec 7, 5; Jer 25, 11; Dn 9, 2.—g Jer 29, 10.—h Zec 8, 2; Jl 2, 18.—i Is 47, 6; Ob 10-14.—j Zec 8, 3; Ezr 6, 14.—k Is 51, 3.—l Rv 11, 1.—m Dt 28, 64.—n Ez 36, 11.—o Dt 32, 10; Ps 17, 8.—p Ez 37, 26.—q Hg 1, 1; 1 Chr 21, 1.—r Rom 8, 33; Jude 9.—s Lk 15, 22.

1, 12: *These seventy years:* see note on Jer 25, 1-14.

1, 15: *The complacent nations:* the neighbors of Judah, especially Edom, which enjoyed their present prosperity and security at Judah's expense.

1, 16: *Measuring line:* not for devastation, as in Is 34, 11, but for reconstruction.

2, 1-4: *Four horns:* symbolic of the hostile forces which, from the four corners of the earth, invaded and devastated *the land of Judah. Four blacksmiths:* the powers used by God to destroy these enemies of his people.

2, 8: *That young man:* the angel or *man with a measuring line* of v 5.

2, 10: *The land of the north:* Babylonia (v 11).

3, 3: *Filthy garments:* symbolic of mourning for the dead, or of national catastrophe, and implying acknowledgment of guilt (v 5).

The New Jerusalem. ⁵ Again I raised my eyes and looked: there was a man with a measuring line in his hand.ˡ ⁶ "Where are you going?" I asked. "To measure Jerusalem," he answered; "to see how great is its width and how great its length."ᵐ

⁷ Then the angel who spoke with me advanced, and another angel came out to meet him ⁸ and said to him, "Run, tell this to that young man:* People will live in Jerusalem as though in open country, because of the multitude of men and beasts in her midst.ⁿ ⁹ But I will be for her an encircling wall of fire, says the LORD, and I will be the glory in her midst."

¹⁰ Up, up! Flee from the land of the north,* says the LORD; for I scatter you to the four winds of heaven, says the LORD. ¹¹ Up, escape to Zion! you who dwell in daughter Babylon. ¹² For thus said the LORD of hosts (after he had already sent me) concerning the nations that have plundered you: Whoever touches you touches the apple of my eye.ᵒ ¹³ See, I wave my hand over them; they become plunder for their slaves. Thus you shall know that the LORD of hosts has sent me.

¹⁴ Sing and rejoice, O daughter Zion! See, I am coming to dwell among you, says the LORD.ᵖ ¹⁵ Many nations shall join themselves to the LORD on that day, and they shall be his people, and he will dwell among you, and you shall know that the LORD of hosts has sent me to you. ¹⁶ The LORD will possess Judah as his portion in the holy land, and he will again choose Jerusalem. ¹⁷ Silence, all mankind, in the presence of the LORD! for he stirs forth from his holy dwelling.

CHAPTER 3

Joshua the High Priest. ¹ Then he showed me Joshua the high priest standing before the angel of the LORD, while Satan stood at his right hand to accuse him.�q ² And the angel of the LORD said to Satan, "May the LORD rebuke you, Satan; may the LORD who has chosen Jerusalem rebuke you! Is not this man a brand snatched from the fire?"ʳ

³ Now Joshua was standing before the angel, clad in filthy garments.* ⁴ He spoke and said to those who were standing before him, "Take off his filthy garments, and clothe him in festal garments."ˢ ⁵ He also said, "Put a clean miter on his head."

Zec

And they put a clean miter on his head and clothed him with the garments. Then the angel of the LORD, standing, said, "See, I have taken away your guilt."

6 The angel of the LORD then gave Joshua this assurance: 7 "Thus says the LORD of hosts: If you walk in my ways and heed my charge, you shall judge my house and keep my courts, and I will give you access among these standing here. 8 Listen, O Joshua, high priest! You and your associates who sit before you are men of good omen.* Yes, I will bring my servant the Shoot. *t* 9 Look at the stone that I have placed before Joshua, one stone with seven facets.* I will engrave its inscription, says the LORD of hosts, and I will take away the guilt of the land in one day. *u* 10 On that day, says the LORD of hosts, you will invite one another under your vines and fig trees." *v*

CHAPTER 4

4 Then I said to the angel who spoke with me, "What are these things, my lord?" 5 And the angel who spoke with me replied, "Do you not know what these things are?" "No, my lord," I answered. 6 Then he said to me, "This is the LORD's message to Zerubbabel: Not by an army, nor by might, but by my spirit, says the LORD of hosts. 7 What are you, O great mountain?* Before Zerubbabel you are but a plain. He shall bring out the capstone amid exclamations of 'Hail, Hail' to it." *w*

8 This word of the LORD then came to me: 9 The hands of Zerubbabel have laid the foundations of this house, *x* and his hands shall finish it; then you shall know that the LORD of hosts has sent me to you. 10 *y* For even they who were scornful on that day of small beginnings shall rejoice to see the select stone in the hands of Zerubbabel. These seven facets are the eyes of the LORD that range over the whole earth.

The Lampstand. 1 Then the angel who spoke with me returned and awakened me, like a man awakened from his sleep. 2 "What do you see?" he asked me. "I see a lampstand all of gold, with a bowl at the top," I replied; "on it are seven lamps with their tubes, *z* 3 and beside it are two olive trees, one on the right and the other on the left." *a* 11 I then asked him, "What are these two olive trees at each side of the

lampstand?" 12 And again I asked, "What are the two olive tufts which freely pour out fresh oil through the two golden channels?" 13 "Do you not know what these are?" he said to me. "No, my lord," I answered him. 14 He said, "These are the two anointed* who stand by the LORD of the whole earth."

CHAPTER 5

The Flying Scroll. * 1 Then I raised my eyes again and saw a scroll flying. *b* 2 "What do you see?" he asked me. I answered, "I see a scroll flying; it is twenty cubits long and ten cubits wide." 3 Then he said to me: "This is the curse which is to go forth over the whole earth; in accordance with it shall every thief be swept away, and in accordance with it shall every perjurer be expelled from here. 4 I will send it forth, says the LORD of hosts, and it shall come into the house of the thief, or into the house of him who perjures himself with my name; it shall lodge within his house, consuming it, timber and stones." *c*

The Flying Bushel. * 5 Then the angel who spoke with me came forward and said to me, "Raise your eyes and see what this is

---

t Is 4, 2; 11, 1; Jer 23, 5; 33, 15.—u Zec 4, 10.—v 1 Kgs 4, 25.—w Ezr 3, 11f; Ps 118, 22.—x Ezr 6, 14ff.—y Zec 3, 9.—z Rv 1, 12.—a Rv 11, 4.—b Ez 2, 9.—c Lv 19, 12.

3, 8: *Men of good omen:* the restoration of the priesthood is a sign of the coming of the messianic times. *My servant the Shoot:* identified, in the earliest form of Zec 6, 11f as the prophet composed it, with Zerubbabel, direct descendant of King David and rebuilder of the temple; and, as such, a type of the Messiah; cf Jer 23, 5.

3, 9: *One stone with seven facets:* apparently the same as the *select stone* of Zec 4, 10, which seems to be a precious gem. The *seven facets* are explained in Zec 4, 10 as signifying the Lord's vigilance over the world. *I will engrave its inscription:* the same Hebrew verb for *engrave* is used in Ex 28, 9. 11 in regard to the inscriptions on the twelve precious stones of the priestly breastpiece.

4, 7: *Great mountain:* figure of the obstacles confronting Zerubbabel in building the temple. *A plain:* figure of the ease with which he will overcome these obstacles.

4, 1ff. 11-14: *The two anointed:* literally, "the two sons of oil," Joshua, the anointed high priest, and Zerubbabel, the anointed prince. Just as the two olive trees in this imagery supply the sacred seven-branched lampstand (Ex 25, 31-40) with oil (v 12), so these two men, in ministering to the community, *stand by* (serve) *the Lord.*

5, 1-4: The enormous scroll, thirty feet by fifteen (the dimensions in length and breadth of the portico of Solomon's temple, 1 Kgs 6, 3), contains a list of maledictions on sinners, similar to that in Dt 27, 15-26. The *thief* and the *perjurer* represent all sinners, who are expelled from the holy community.

5, 5-11: The *woman* sealed in the *bushel container* is a figure of the general corruption of the people of Judah. She is removed from the Holy Land and transported to *Shinar,* that is, Babylonia, where a dwelling is being prepared for her; this is a symbol of the reign of *Wickedness* in pagan lands, contrasted with the reign of holiness in the Lord's dwelling on Mount Zion.

that comes forth." 6"What is it?" I asked. And he answered, "This is a bushel container coming. This is their guilt in all the land." 7Then a leaden cover was lifted, and there was a woman sitting inside the bushel. 8"This is Wickedness," he said; and he thrust her inside the bushel, pushing the leaden cover into the opening. 9Then I raised my eyes and saw two women coming forth with a wind ruffling their wings, for they had wings like the wings of a stork. As they lifted up the bushel into the air, 10I said to the angel who spoke with me, "Where are they taking the bushel?" 11He replied, "To build a temple for it in the land of Shinar; when the temple is ready, they will deposit it there in its place."*d*

CHAPTER 6

Four Chariots.* 1Again I raised my eyes and saw four chariots coming out from between two mountains; and the mountains were of bronze. 2The first chariot had red horses, the second chariot black horses,*e* 3the third chariot white horses, and the fourth chariot spotted horses—all of them strong horses. 4I asked the angel who spoke with me, "What are these, my lord?" 5The angel said to me in reply, "These are the four winds of the heavens, which are coming forth after being reviewed by the LORD of all the earth."*f* 6The chariot with the black horses was turning toward the land of the north, the red and the white horses went after them, and the spotted ones went toward the land of the south. 7As these strong horses emerged, eager to set about patrolling the earth, he said, "Go, patrol the earth!" Then, as they patrolled the earth, 8he called out to me and said, "See, they that

go forth to the land of the north will make my spirit rest in the land of the north."

The Coronation. 9This word of the LORD then came to me: 10Take from the returned captives Heldai, Tobijah, Jedaiah; and go the same day to the house of Josiah, son of Zephaniah (these had come from Babylon). 11Silver and gold you shall take, and make a crown; place it on the head of [Joshua, son of Jehozadak, the high priest] Zerubbabel.* 12And say to him: Thus says the LORD of hosts: Here is a man whose name is Shoot, and where he is he shall sprout, and he shall build the temple of the LORD.*g* 13Yes, he shall build the temple of the LORD, and taking up the royal insignia, he shall sit as ruler upon his throne. The priest shall be at his right hand, and between the two of them there shall be friendly understanding.*h* 14The crown itself shall be a memorial offering in the temple of the LORD in favor of Heldai, Tobijah, Jedaiah, and the son of Zephaniah. 15And they who are from afar shall come and build the temple of the LORD,*i* and you shall know that the LORD of hosts has sent me to you. And if you heed carefully the voice of the LORD your God. . . .

CHAPTER 7

True Fasting. 1In the fourth year of Darius the king [the word of the LORD came to Zechariah], on the fourth day of Chislev, the ninth month,* 2Bethel-sarezer sent Regemmelech and his men to implore favor of the LORD 3and to ask the priests of the house of the LORD of hosts, and the prophets, "Must I mourn and abstain in the fifth month as I have been doing these many years?"*j* 4Thereupon this word of the LORD of hosts came to me: 5Say to all the people of the land and to the priests: When you fasted and mourned in the fifth and in the seventh month these seventy years, was it really for me that you fasted?*k* 6And when you were eating and drinking, was it not for yourselves that you ate, and for yourselves that you drank? 7Were not these the words which the LORD spoke through the former prophets, when Jerusalem and the surrounding cities were inhabited and at peace, when the Negeb and the foothills were inhabited?*l* 8[This word of the LORD came to Zechariah: 9Thus says the LORD of hosts:] Render true judgment, and show kindness and compassion toward each other.*m* 10Do not oppress the

---

d Gn 11, 2ff.—e Zec 1, 8; Rv 6, 4.—f Ps 104, 4.—g Zec 3, 8; Eph 2, 20; Heb 3, 3.—h Ps 110, 4; Heb 3, 1.—i Eph 2, 19f.—j Zec 8, 19.—k Is 58, 5; Rom 14, 6.—l Jer 17, 26.—m Is 58, 6.

6, 1-8: The *four chariots* represent the angelic hosts sent by the Lord to the four ends of the earth. The chariot with the *black horses* brings the *spirit,* i.e., anger of the Lord against the land of the north, Babylonia.

6, 11: *Make a crown; place it on the head of [Joshua, son of Jehozadak, the priest] Zerubbabel:* according to the current Hebrew text, Joshua the high priest is to be crowned. However, since the crown is a sign of royalty, the original text must have had the name of Zerubbabel here, not that of Joshua. In Zec 3, 8 Joshua is a different man from the one called the *Shoot,* and in v 12 it is upon the *Shoot* that the crown is to be placed.

7, 1: *The fourth year of Darius . . . the fourth day of Chislev, the ninth month:* November, 518 B.C.

widow or the orphan, the alien or the poor; do not plot evil against one another in your hearts.[n] [11]But they refused to listen; they stubbornly turned their backs and stopped their ears so as not to hear.[o] [12]And they made their hearts diamond-hard so as not to hear the teaching and the message that the LORD of hosts had sent by his spirit through the former prophets.[p] [13]Then the LORD of hosts in his great anger said that, as they had not listened when he called, so he would not listen when they called,[q] [14]but would scatter them with a whirlwind among all the nations that they did not know. Thus the land was left desolate after them with no one traveling to and fro; they made the pleasant land into a desert.[r]

CHAPTER 8

In the Days of the Messiah. [1]This word of the LORD of hosts came: Thus says the LORD of hosts:

[2] I am intensely jealous for Zion,
    stirred to jealous wrath for her.[s]
[3]   Thus says the LORD:
I will return to Zion,
    and I will dwell within Jerusalem;
Jerusalem shall be called the faithful city,
    and the mountain of the LORD of hosts,
    the holy mountain.[t]

[4]Thus says the LORD of hosts: Old men and old women, each with staff in hand because of old age, shall again sit in the streets of Jerusalem. [5]The city shall be filled with boys and girls playing in her streets. [6]Thus says the LORD of hosts: Even if this should seem impossible in the eyes of the remnant of this people, shall it in those days be impossible in my eyes also, says the LORD of hosts? [7]Thus says the LORD of hosts: Lo, I will rescue my people from the land of the rising sun, and from the land of the setting sun.[u] [8]I will bring them back to dwell within Jerusalem. They shall be my people, and I will be their God, with faithfulness and justice.[v]

[9]Thus says the LORD of hosts: Let your hands be strong, you who in these days hear these words spoken by the prophets on the day when the foundation of the house of the LORD of hosts was laid for the building of the temple.[w] [10]For before those days there were no wages for men, or hire for beasts; those who came and went had no security from the enemy, for I set every man against his neighbor. [11]But now I will not deal with the remnant of this people as in former days, says the LORD of hosts, [12]for it is the seedtime of peace: the vine shall yield its fruit, the land shall bear its crops, and the heavens shall give their dew; all these things I will have the remnant of the people possess. [13]Just as you were a curse among the nations, O house of Judah and house of Israel, so will I save you that you may be a blessing; do not fear, but let your hands be strong.[x]

[14]Thus says the LORD of hosts: As I determined to harm you when your fathers provoked me to wrath, says the LORD of hosts, and I did not relent,[y] [15]so again in these days I have determined to favor Jerusalem and the house of Judah; do not fear! [16]These then are the things you should do: Speak the truth to one another; let there be honesty and peace in the judgments at your gates,[z] [17]and let none of you plot evil against another in his heart, nor love a false oath. For all these things I hate, says the LORD.[a]

[18]This word of the LORD of hosts came to me: [19]Thus says the LORD of hosts: The fast days of the fourth, the fifth, the seventh, and the tenth months shall become occasions of joy and gladness, cheerful festivals for the house of Judah; only love faithfulness and peace.* [20]Thus says the LORD of hosts: There shall yet come peoples, the inhabitants of many cities; [21]and the inhabitants of one city shall approach those of another, and say, "Come! let us go to implore the favor of the LORD"; and, "I too will go to seek the LORD."[b] [22]Many peoples and strong nations shall come to seek the LORD of hosts in Jerusalem and to implore the favor of the LORD.[c] [23]Thus says the LORD of hosts: In those days ten men of every na-

---

n Ex 22, 21-24; Dt 24, 17; Is 1, 17; Jer 5, 28.—o Neh 9, 29; Hos 4, 16.—p Ez 11, 19; 36, 26; Neh 9, 29.—q Is 1, 15; Mi 3, 4.—r Dt 4, 27.—s Na 1, 2.—t Is 2, 2; Jer 31, 23.—u Is 11, 11; Jer 30, 18.—v Jer 4, 2.—w Ezr 5, 11; Hg 2, 18.—x Is 19, 24; Jer 42, 18; Hg 2, 19; Zep 3, 20.—y Jer 31, 28.—z Zec 7, 9.—a Zec 7, 10.—b Is 2, 3.—c Is 60, 3.

8, 19: The fast day of *the fourth* month recalled the fall of Jerusalem in June, 587 B.C. (2 Kgs 25, 3f); that of *the fifth* month, the burning of the temple by Nebuzaradan in July of the same year (2 Kgs 25, 8f); that of *the seventh* month, the murder of Gedaliah in September of the same year (Jer 41, 1f); that of *the tenth* month, the beginning of the final siege of Jerusalem in January, 588 B.C. (2 Kgs 25, 1).

tionality, speaking different tongues, shall take hold, yes, take hold of every Jew by the edge of his garment and say, "Let us go with you, for we have heard that God is with you."[d]

CHAPTER 9

Invasion by the Lord *

1   An oracle:
The word of the LORD is upon the land of Hadrach,
    and Damascus is its resting place,
For the cities of Aram are the LORD's,
    as are all the tribes of Israel,
2 Hamath also, on its border,
    Tyre, too, and Sidon, however wise they be.[e]
3 Tyre built herself a stronghold,
    and heaped up silver like dust,
    and gold like the mire of the streets.
4 Lo, the LORD will strip her of her possessions,
    and smite her power on the sea,
    and she shall be devoured by fire.[f]
5 Ashkelon shall see it and be afraid;
    Gaza also: she shall be in great anguish;
    Ekron, too, for her hope shall come to nought.
The king shall disappear from Gaza,
    and Ashkelon shall not be inhabited,
6   and the baseborn* shall occupy Ashdod.
I will destroy the pride of the Philistine[g]

---

d Is 66, 23.—e Jer 49, 23.—f Is 23, 1-18; Ez 26, 1—28, 26.—g Am 1, 8.—h Is 62, 11; Jer 23, 5; Mt 21, 5; Jn 12, 15.—i Hos 1, 7.—j Is 42, 7; Ez 24, 8.—k Is 61, 7.

9, 1-8: Divine judgment is about to fall on the surrounding hostile peoples: *Aram* (Syria), including the cities of *Hadrach* and *Damascus;* Phoenicia, with its cities of *Tyre* and *Sidon;* Philistia, with its cities of *Ashkelon, Gaza, Ekron,* and *Ashdod.*
9, 6: *The baseborn:* people of mixed ancestry.
9, 7: *Remnant:* see note on Hg 1, 12. *The Jebusites:* the pre-Israelite inhabitants of Jerusalem, conquered by David and incorporated into Israel.
9, 8: *My house:* the Holy Land: cf Hos 8, 1; 9, 15; Jer 12, 7.
9, 9: The Messiah will come, not as a conquering warrior, but in lowliness and peace. Not like the last kings of Judah, who rode in chariots and on horses (Jer 17, 25; 22, 4), but like the princes of old (Gn 49, 11; Jgs 5, 10; 10, 4), the Messiah will ride on an ass. The Evangelists see a literal fulfillment of this prophecy in the Savior's triumphant entry into Jerusalem (Mt 21, 4f; Jn 12, 14f).
9, 10: *The River:* the Euphrates; see note on Ps 72, 8.
9, 11: *The blood of your covenant with me:* the covenant between the Lord and Israel sealed with sacrificial blood (Ex 24, 8).
9, 12: *The waiting prisoners:* the exiles awaiting the return to their country, where they will receive a double compensation for the double punishment they had suffered; cf Is 40, 2; 61, 7.

---

7   and take from his mouth his bloody meat,
    and his abominations from between his teeth:
He also shall become a remnant* for our God,
    and shall be like a family in Judah,
    and Ekron shall be like the Jebusites.
8 I will encamp by my house* as a guard
    that none may pass to and fro;
No oppressor shall pass over them again,
    for now I have regard for their affliction.

Restoration under the Messiah

9 Rejoice heartily, O daughter Zion,[h]
    shout for joy, O daughter Jerusalem!
See, your king shall come to you;
    a just savior is he,
Meek, and riding on an ass,
    on a colt, the foal of an ass.*
10 He shall banish the chariot from Ephraim,
    and the horse from Jerusalem;
The warrior's bow shall be banished,
    and he shall proclaim peace to the nations.
His dominion shall be from sea to sea,
    and from the River* to the ends of the earth.[i]
11 As for you, for the blood of your covenant with me,*
    I will bring forth your prisoners from the dungeon.[j]
12 In the return to the fortress
    of the waiting prisoners,*
This very day, I will return you double for your exile.[k]
13 For I will bend Judah as my bow,
    I will arm myself with Ephraim;
I will arouse your sons, O Zion,
    [against your sons, O Yavan,]
    and I will use you as a warrior's sword.
14 The LORD shall appear over them,
    and his arrow shall shoot forth as lightning;
The LORD God shall sound the trumpet,
    and come in a storm from the south.
15 The LORD of hosts shall be a shield over them,
    they shall overcome slingstones
    and trample them underfoot;
They shall drink blood like wine,

Zec

till they are filled with it like libation
bowls,
like the corners of the altar.
16 And the LORD, their God, shall save
them on that day,
his people, like a flock.
For they are the jewels in a crown
raised aloft over his land.[l]
17 For what wealth is theirs, and what
beauty!
grain that makes the youths flourish,
and new wine, the maidens!

CHAPTER 10

The New Order of Things

1 Ask of the LORD rain in the spring season!
It is the LORD who makes the storm
clouds,
And sends men the pouring rain;
for everyone, grassy fields.[m]
2 For the teraphim* speak nonsense,
the diviners have false visions:
Deceitful dreams they tell,
empty comfort they offer.
This is why they wander like sheep,
wretched: they have no shepherd.[n]
3 My wrath is kindled against the
shepherds,
and I will punish the leaders;
For the LORD of hosts will visit his
flock,
the house of Judah,
and make them his stately war horse.
4 From him shall come leader and chief,
from him warrior's bow and every
officer.
5 They shall all be warriors,
trampling the mire of the streets in
battle;
They shall wage war because the LORD
is with them,
and shall put the horsemen to rout.
6 I will strengthen the house of Judah,
the house of Joseph I will save;
I will bring them back, because I have
mercy on them,
they shall be as though I had never
cast them off,
for I am the LORD, their God, and I
will hear them.
7 Then Ephraim shall be valiant men,
and their hearts shall be cheered as by
wine.
Their children shall see it and be glad,
their hearts shall rejoice in the LORD.

8 I will whistle for them to come together,
and when I redeem them
they will be as numerous as before.[o]
9 I sowed them among the nations,
yet in distant lands they remember
me;
they shall rear their children and return.
10 I will bring them back from the land of
Egypt,
and gather them from Assyria.
I will bring them into Gilead and into
Lebanon,
but these shall not suffice them;[p]
11 I will cross over to Egypt
and smite the waves of the sea
and all the depths of the Nile shall be
dried up.
The pride of Assyria shall be cast down,
and the scepter of Egypt taken away.[q]
12 I will strengthen them in the LORD,
and they shall walk in his name, says
the LORD.[r]

CHAPTER 11

1 Open your doors, O Lebanon,
that the fire may devour your cedars!
2 Wail, you cypress trees,
for the cedars are fallen,
the mighty have been despoiled.
Wail, you oaks of Bashan,
for the impenetrable forest is cut
down!
3 Hark! the wailing of the shepherds,
their glory has been ruined.
Hark! the roaring of the young lions,
the jungle of the Jordan is laid waste.

Allegory of the Shepherds.* 4Thus said
the LORD, my God: Shepherd the flock

---

l Is 62, 3.—m Dt 11, 14; Jer 14, 22.— n Jer 10, 8; Ez 34, 5.—
o Ez 36, 37.—p Is 11, 11; 49, 20; Hos 11, 11.—q Is 11, 15; Ez
30, 13.—r Mi 4, 5.

10, 2: *Teraphim:* household idols, used for divination; cf Gn
31, 19. 34f; Jgs 17, 5; 18, 17f. 20; Ez 21, 26; Hos 3, 4.
11, 4-17: In this allegory the prophet becomes the good
shepherd of God's flock, which is being slaughtered; he is the defender of the people exploited by bad rulers. *The three
shepherds,* rulers in general, are to destroy one another in a
short time *(a single month).* The service of the good shepherd is
contemptuously valued at *thirty pieces of silver,* the legal
indemnity (Ex 21, 32) for a gored slave. The prophet is thus a
type of Christ whose mission of salvation to his people was appraised by the Sanhedrists, the false shepherds, at the same base
price (Mt 26, 14ff). In the case of the prophet as well as of Christ
(Mt 27, 5), the money is thrown into the temple treasury, i.e.,
paid to God, showing thereby how shamefully his divine love and
care are requited.

to be slaughtered. ⁵For they who buy them slay them with impunity; while those who sell them say, "Blessed be the LORD, I have become rich!" Even their own shepherds do not feel for them.ˢ ⁶(Nor shall I spare the inhabitants of the earth any more, says the LORD. Yes, I will deliver each of them into the power of his neighbor, or into the power of his king; they shall crush the earth, and I will not deliver it out of their power.)

⁷So I became the shepherd of the flock to be slaughtered for the sheep merchants. I took two staffs, one of which I called "Favor," and the other, "Bonds," and I fed the flock.ᵗ ⁸In a single month I did away with the three shepherds. I wearied of them, and they behaved badly toward me. ⁹"I will not feed you," I said. "What is to die, let it die; what is to perish, let it perish, and let those that are left devour one another's flesh."ᵘ

¹⁰Then I took my staff "Favor" and snapped it asunder, breaking off the covenant which I had made with all peoples; ¹¹that day it was broken off. The sheep merchants who were watching me understood that this was the word of the LORD. ¹²I said to them, "If it seems good to you, give me my wages; but if not, let it go." And they counted out my wages, thirty pieces of silver.ᵛ ¹³But the LORD said to me, "Throw it in the treasury, the handsome price at which they valued me." So I took the thirty pieces of silver and threw them into the treasury in the house of the LORD.ʷ

¹⁴Then I snapped asunder my other staff, "Bonds," breaking off the brotherhood between Judah and Israel. ¹⁵The LORD said to me: This time take the gear of a foolish shepherd. ¹⁶For I will raise up a shepherd in the land who will take no note of those that perish, nor seek the strays, nor heal the injured, nor feed what

---

s Jer 50, 7.—t Hos 5, 6.—u Jer 15, 2.—v Ex 21, 32; Mt 26, 15.—w Mt 27, 9f.—x Ez 34, 2ff.—y Jn 10, 12.—z Is 42, 5.—a Is 51, 17; Jer 51, 7.—b Mt 21, 44.—c Ob 18.—d Ex 32, 34.—e Jer 6, 26; Jn 19, 34; Rv 1, 7.

12, 1-9: Under the image of the deliverance of Judah and Jerusalem from invading enemies, the prophet foretells the ultimate victory of God's people in the messianic age.

12, 10: The divine blessings *(a spirit of grace and petition)* will be poured out on God's people through the intervention of an unnamed sufferer *(him whom they have thrust through),* similar to the Servant of the Lord in Is 52, 13—53, 12. In Jn 19, 37 the Evangelist sees in this passage a prophecy fulfilled in the piercing of Christ's side.

survives—he will eat the flesh of the fat ones and tear off their hoofs!ˣ

¹⁷ Woe to my foolish shepherd
  who forsakes the flock!
May the sword fall upon his arm
  and upon his right eye;
Let his arm wither away entirely,
  and his right eye be blind forever!ʸ

CHAPTER 12

Jerusalem God's Instrument.* ¹An oracle: the word of the LORD concerning Israel. Thus says the LORD, who spreads out the heavens, lays the foundations of the earth, and forms the spirit of man within him:ᶻ ²See, I will make Jerusalem a bowl to stupefy all peoples round about. [Judah will be besieged, even Jerusalem.]ᵃ ³On that day I will make Jerusalem a weighty stone for all peoples. All who attempt to lift it shall injure themselves badly, and all the nations of the earth shall be gathered against her.ᵇ ⁴On that day, says the LORD, I will strike every horse with fright, and its rider with madness. I will strike blind all the horses of the peoples, but upon the house of Judah I will open my eyes, ⁵and the princes of Judah shall say to themselves, "The inhabitants of Jerusalem have their strength in the LORD of hosts, their God." ⁶On that day I will make the princes of Judah like a brazier of fire in the woodland, and like a burning torch among sheaves, and they shall devour right and left all the surrounding peoples; but Jerusalem shall still abide on its own site.ᶜ ⁷The LORD shall save the tents of Judah first, that the glory of the house of David and the glory of the inhabitants of Jerusalem may not be exalted over Judah. ⁸On that day, the LORD will shield the inhabitants of Jerusalem, and the weakling among them shall be like David on that day, and the house of David godlike, like an angel of the LORD before them.ᵈ ⁹On that day I will seek the destruction of all nations that come against Jerusalem.

Messianic Jerusalem. ¹⁰I will pour out on the house of David and on the inhabitants of Jerusalem a spirit of grace and petition;ᵉ and they shall look on him whom they have thrust through, and they shall mourn for him as one mourns for an only son, and they shall grieve over him as one grieves over a firstborn.*

11 * On that day the mourning in Jerusalem shall be as great as the mourning of Hadadrimmon in the plain of Megiddo.*f* 12 And the land shall mourn, each family apart: the family of the house of David, and their wives; the family of the house of Nathan, and their wives; 13 the family of the house of Levi, and their wives; the family of Shemei, and their wives; 14 and all the rest of the families, each family apart, and the wives apart.

CHAPTER 13

The End of Falsehood. 1 On that day there shall be open to the house of David and to the inhabitants of Jerusalem, a fountain to purify from sin* and uncleanness.*g* 2 On that day, says the LORD of hosts, I will destroy the names of the idols from the land, so that they shall be mentioned no more; I will also take away the prophets and the spirit of uncleanness from the land.*h* 3 If a man still prophesies, his parents, father and mother, shall say to him, "You shall not live, because you have spoken a lie in the name of the LORD." When he prophesies, his parents, father and mother, shall thrust him through.*i*

4 On that day, every prophet shall be ashamed to prophesy his vision, neither shall he assume the hairy mantle* to mislead, 5 but he shall say, "I am no prophet, I am a tiller of the soil, for I have owned land since my youth."*j* 6 And if anyone asks him, "What are these wounds on your chest?"* he shall answer, "With these I was wounded in the house of my dear ones."

The Song of the Sword

7 Awake, O sword, against my shepherd,
　　against the man who is my associate,
　　says the LORD of hosts.
Strike the shepherd
　　that the sheep may be dispersed,*
　　and I will turn my hand against the
　　little ones.*k*
8 In all the land, says the LORD,
　　two thirds of them shall be cut off
　　and perish,
　　and one third shall be left.
9 I will bring the one third through fire,
　　and I will refine them as silver is re-
　　fined,
　　and I will test them as gold is tested.*l*

They shall call upon my name,
　　and I will hear them.
I will say, "They are my people,"
　　and they shall say, "The LORD is my
　　God."

CHAPTER 14

The Fight for Jerusalem.* 1 Lo, a day shall come for the LORD when the spoils shall be divided in your midst. 2 And I will gather all the nations against Jerusalem for battle: the city shall be taken, houses plundered, women ravished; half of the city shall go into exile, but the rest of the people shall not be removed from the city. 3 Then the LORD shall go forth and fight against those nations, fighting as on a day of battle. 4 That day his feet shall rest upon the Mount of Olives, which is opposite Jerusalem to the east. The Mount of Olives shall be cleft in two from east to west by a very deep valley, and half of the mountain shall move to the north and half of it to the south. 5 And the valley of the LORD's mountain shall be filled up when the valley of those two mountains reaches its edge; it shall be filled up as it was filled up by the earthquake in the days of King Uzziah of Judah. Then the LORD, my

---

f 2 Chr 35, 22-25.—g Heb 9, 14; 1 Pt 1, 18f; Rv 1, 5.—h Mi 5, 12; 2 Pt 2, 1.—i Dt 18, 20; Mi 3, 5ff.—j Am 7, 14.—k Mt 26, 31.—l Jer 30, 22; Ps 66, 10.

12, 11: The mourning for the pierced victim in Jerusalem is compared to a lamentation *in the plain of Megiddo* apparently over a certain personage called *Hadadrimmon.* The reference is no longer clear. Both *Hadad* and *Rimmon* were names of the Semitic storm god, often identified with the god Baal. Some see here a reference to the annual mourning by the pagans over the death of the fertility god. According to others, *Hadadrimmon* is the name of a place near Megiddo, and the reference would then be to the mourning over the death of King Josiah, who was killed in battle there; cf 2 Chr 35, 22-25.

13, 1: *A fountain to purify from sin:* in contrast to the lustral water used in ritual purification; cf Nm 19, 9. 13. 20; 31, 23. The Lord himself is the *fountain* of living water (Jer 2, 13); cf Is 12, 2ff.

13, 4: *Hairy mantle:* worn by prophets as a mark of their calling; cf 2 Kgs 1, 8; Mt 3, 4.

13, 6: *Wounds on your chest:* literally, "wounds between your hands." The false prophets, like the prophet of Baal (1 Kgs 18, 28), apparently inflicted wounds on themselves; to defend himself against the accusation of being a false prophet, a man will deny having inflicted wounds on himself and say instead that he received them at home, "*in the house of my dear ones.*" In the liturgy this text is applied to Christ in an accommodated sense.

13, 7: When the shepherd is killed, the sheep are scattered. In Mt 26, 31 the Evangelist quotes from this verse, in somewhat different form, the words, *I will smite the shepherd, and the sheep of the flock will be scattered,* as said by Christ shortly before his arrest in the Garden of Olives and the flight of the Apostles.

14, 1-21: An apocalyptic description of the day of the Lord, in which Jerusalem, the figure of God's elect, after much suffering (siege: vv 1ff; riot: v 13; plague: vv 12, 15), is rescued by the Lord (vv 4f) and given great blessings (vv 6-11. 14. 16-21).

God, shall come, and all his holy ones with him.

⁶On that day there shall no longer be cold or frost. ⁷There shall be one continuous day, known to the LORD, not day and night, for in the evening time there shall be light.*m*

⁸On that day, living waters shall flow from Jerusalem, half to the eastern sea, and half to the western sea, and it shall be so in summer and in winter.*n* ⁹The LORD shall become king over the whole earth; on that day the LORD shall be the only one, and his name the only one.*o*

¹⁰And from Geba to Rimmon in the Negeb, all the land shall turn into a plain; but Jerusalem shall remain exalted in its place. From the Gate of Benjamin to the place of the First Gate, to the Corner Gate; and from the Tower of Hananel to the king's wine presses,*p* ¹¹they shall occupy her. Never again shall she be doomed; Jerusalem shall abide in security.*q*

¹²And this shall be the plague with which the LORD shall strike all the nations that have fought against Jerusalem: their flesh shall rot while they stand upon their feet, and their eyes shall rot in their sockets, and their tongues shall rot in their mouths.

¹³On that day there shall be among them a great tumult from the LORD: every man shall seize the hand of his neighbor,

m Rv 21, 23.—n Zec 13, 1; Ez 47, 1-8; Jl 3, 18.—o Dt 6, 4; Eph 4, 5f; Rv 11, 15.—p Zec 12, 6; Neh 3, 6; 12, 38.—q Jer 31, 40; Rv 22, 3.—r Lv 23, 34. 43; Neh 8, 14; Is 60, 6. 9.—s Mt 21, 12; Jn 2, 13-16.

and the hand of each shall be raised against that of his neighbor. ¹⁴Judah also shall fight against Jerusalem. The riches of all the surrounding nations shall be gathered together, gold, silver, and garments, in great abundance.

¹⁵Similar to this plague shall be the plague upon the horses, mules, camels, asses, and upon all the beasts that are in those camps.

¹⁶All who are left of all the nations that came against Jerusalem shall come up year after year to worship the King, the LORD of hosts, and to celebrate the feast of Booths.*r* ¹⁷If any of the families of the earth does not come up to Jerusalem to worship the King, the LORD of hosts, no rain shall fall upon them. ¹⁸And if the family of Egypt does not come up, or enter, upon them shall fall the plague which the LORD will inflict upon all the nations that do not come up to celebrate the feast of Booths. ¹⁹This shall be the punishment of Egypt, and the punishment of all the nations that do not come up to celebrate the feast of Booths.

²⁰On that day there shall be upon the bells of the horses, "Holy to the LORD." The pots in the house of the LORD shall be as the libation bowls before the altar. ²¹And every pot in Jerusalem and in Judah shall be holy to the LORD of hosts; and all who come to sacrifice shall take them and cook in them. On that day there shall no longer be any merchant in the house of the LORD of hosts.*s*

THE BOOK OF MALACHI

This work was composed by an anonymous writer shortly before Nehemiah's arrival in Jerusalem (455 B.C.). Because of the sharp reproaches he was leveling against the priests and rulers of the people, the author probably wished to conceal his identity. To do this he made a proper name out of the Hebrew expression for "My Messenger" (Malachi), which occurs in 1, 1 and 3, 1. The historical value of the prophecy is considerable in that it gives us a picture of life in the Jewish community returned from Babylon, between the period of Haggai and the reform measures of Ezra and Nehemiah. It is likely that the author's trenchant criticism of abuses and religious indifference in the community prepared the way for these necessary reforms.

The chosen people had made a sorry return for divine love. The priests, who should have been leaders, had dishonored God by their blemished sacrifices. In his first chapter, the writer foresees the time when all nations will offer a pure oblation (1, 11)—a prophecy whose fulfillment the church sees in the Sacrifice of the Mass. The author then turns from priests to people, denouncing their marriages with pagans and their callous repudiation of Israelite wives. Imbued with the rationalist and critical spirit of the times, many had wearied God with the question, "Where is the God of justice?" To this question the prophet replies that the day of the Lord is coming. But first the forerunner must come, who will prepare the soil for repentance and true worship. The gospel writers point to John the Baptizer as the forerunner ushering in the messianic age, the true day of the Lord. When the ground is prepared God will appear, measuring out rewards and punishments and purifying the nation in the furnace of judgment. He will create a new order in which the ultimate triumph of good is inevitable.

CHAPTER 1

[1] An oracle. The word of the LORD to Israel through Malachi.

Israel Preferred to Edom

[2] I have loved you, says the LORD;
    but you say, "How have you loved us?"[a]
[3] Was not Esau Jacob's brother? says the LORD:*
    yet I loved Jacob, but hated Esau;
I made his mountains a waste,
    his heritage a desert for jackals.[b]
[4] If Edom says, "We have been crushed but we will rebuild the ruins,"
Thus says the LORD of hosts:
    They indeed may build, but I will tear down,
And they shall be called the land of guilt,[c]
    the people with whom the LORD is angry forever.
[5] Your own eyes shall see it, and you will say,
    "Great is the LORD, even beyond the land of Israel."[d]

Sins of the Priests and Levites

[6] A son honors his father,
    and a servant fears his master;
If then I am a father,
    where is the honor due to me?
And if I am a master,
    where is the reverence due to me?—
So says the LORD of hosts to you, O priests,
    who despise his name.
But you ask, "How have we despised your name?"
[7]   By offering polluted food on my altar!
Then you ask, "How have we polluted it?"
    By saying the table of the LORD may be slighted!
[8] When you offer a blind animal for sacrifice,[e]

is this not evil?
When you offer the lame or the sick,
    is it not evil?
Present it to your governor; see if he will accept it,
    or welcome you, says the LORD of hosts.*
[9] So now if you implore God for mercy on us,
    when you have done the like
Will he welcome any of you?
    says the LORD of hosts.
[10] Oh, that one among you would shut the temple gates*
    to keep you from kindling fire on my altar in vain!
I have no pleasure in you, says the LORD of hosts;
    neither will I accept any sacrifice from your hands,
[11] For from the rising of the sun, even to its setting,
    my name is great among the nations;
And everywhere they bring sacrifice to my name,
    and a pure offering;
For great is my name among the nations,
    says the LORD of hosts.[f]
[12] But you behave profanely toward me by thinking

---

a Dt 7, 6ff; Ez 16; Am 1, 11.—b Gn 25, 23; Rom 9, 13.—c Is 34, 5f; 63, 1-6; Jer 49, 7-22; Ob 21.—d Is 60.—e Lv 22, 19-25; Dt 15, 21.—f Ps 113, 3; Is 59, 19.

1, 3ff: The thought passes from the person *Esau* to his descendants, *Edom*, and from the person *Jacob* to his descendants, *Israel. Loved:* preferred; *hated:* rejected; cf Gn 25, 21ff. St. Paul uses this passage as an example of God's freedom of choice in calling the Gentiles to the faith (Rom 9, 13).
1, 8: The offering in sacrifice of a *lame, sick* or *blind* animal was forbidden in the law (Lv 22, 17-25; Dt 17, 1).
1, 10f: The imperfect sacrifices offered without sincerity by the people of Judah are displeasing to the Lord. He will rather be pleased with the offerings of the Gentile nations throughout the world *(from the rising of the sun, even to its setting),* which anticipate the *pure offering* to be sacrificed in messianic times, the universal Sacrifice of the Mass, as we are told by the Council of Trent.

the LORD's table and its offering may
be polluted,
and its food slighted.

¹³ You also say, "What a burden!"
and you scorn it, says the LORD of
hosts;
You bring in what you seize, or the
lame, or the sick;
yes, you bring it as a sacrifice.
Shall I accept it from your hands?
says the LORD.

¹⁴ Cursed is the deceiver, who has in his
flock a male,
but under his vow sacrifices to the
LORD a gelding;
For a great King am I, says the LORD of
hosts,
and my name will be feared among
the nations.

CHAPTER 2

¹ And now, O priests, this commandment
is for you:
If you do not listen,

² And if you do not lay it to heart,
to give glory to my name, says the
LORD of hosts,
I will send a curse upon you
and of your blessing I will make a
curse.
Yes, I have already cursed it,
because you do not lay it to heart.ᵍ

³ Lo, I will deprive you of the shoulder*
and I will strew dung in your faces,
The dung of your feasts,
and you will be carried off with it.

⁴ Then you will know that I sent you this
commandment
because I have a covenant with Levi,
says the LORD of hosts.ʰ

⁵ My covenant with him was one of life
and peace;
fear I put in him, and he feared me,
and stood in awe of my name.ⁱ

⁶ True doctrine was in his mouth,

---

g Lv 26, 14-45; Dt 28, 15-68.—h Nm 25, 12f.—i Nm 25, 12; Ez
37, 26ff.—j Dt 33, 8-11.—k Lv 10, 10f; Dt 17, 9f; Jer 18, 18; Hg
2, 12.—l Mt 23, 9; Jb 31, 15; Eph 4, 6.—m Ezr 9, 2; Neh 13, 25.

2, 3: *I will deprive you of the shoulder:* this part of a sacrificial animal, allotted by the law (Dt 18, 3) to the priests, will be
withheld from them.
2, 10-16: Intermarriage of Israelites with foreigners was forbidden according to Dt 7, 1-4. After the exile this law was strictly
enforced (Ezr 9—10). Foreign marriages are here portrayed as a
violation of the covenant (v 10), which made the sacrifices offered
by the offenders unacceptable to God (v 13). They were all the
more reprehensible when accompanied by the divorce of Israelite
wives (vv 14ff). This gradual return to the primitive ideal of the
indissolubility of marriage was fully realized in New Testament
times through the teaching of Christ; cf Mt 19, 3-12.

---

and no dishonesty was found upon his
lips;
He walked with me in integrity and uprightness,
and turned many away from evil.ʲ

⁷ For the lips of the priest are to keep
knowledge,
and instruction is to be sought from
his mouth,
because he is the messenger of the
LORD of hosts.ᵏ

⁸ But you have turned aside from the
way,
and have caused many to falter by
your instruction;
You have made void the covenant of
Levi,
says the LORD of hosts.

⁹ I, therefore, have made you contemptible
and base before all the people,
Since you do not keep my ways,
but show partiality in your decisions.

Sins of the People

¹⁰ Have we not all the one Father?*
Has not the one God created us?
Why then do we break faith with each
other,
violating the covenant of our fathers?ˡ

¹¹ Judah has broken faith; an abominable
thing
has been done in Israel and in Jerusalem.
Judah has profaned the temple which
the LORD loves,
and has married an idolatrous
woman.ᵐ

¹² May the LORD cut off from the man
who does this
both witness and advocate out of the
tents of Jacob,
and anyone to offer sacrifice to the
LORD of hosts!

¹³ This also you do: the altar of the LORD
you cover
with tears, weeping and groaning,
Because he no longer regards your sacrifice
nor accepts it favorably from your
hand;

¹⁴ And you say, "Why is it?"—
Because the LORD is witness
between you and the wife of your
youth,

With whom you have broken faith
  though she is your companion, your
  betrothed wife.[n]
15 Did he not make one being, with flesh
  and spirit:
  and what does that one require but
  godly offspring?
  You must then safeguard life that is
  your own,
  and not break faith with the wife of
  your youth.[o]
16 For I hate divorce,
  says the LORD, the God of Israel,
  And covering one's garment with injustice,
  says the LORD of hosts;
  You must then safeguard life that is
  your own,
  and not break faith.

17 You have wearied the LORD with your
  words,
  yet you say, "How have we wearied
  him?"
  By your saying, "Every evildoer
  is good in the sight of the LORD,
  And he is pleased with him";
  or else, "Where is the just God?"

CHAPTER 3

The Messenger of the Covenant

1 Lo, I am sending my messenger
  to prepare the way before me;*
  And suddenly there will come to the
  temple
  the LORD whom you seek,
  And the messenger of the covenant
  whom you desire.
  Yes, he is coming, says the LORD of
  hosts.[p]
2 But who will endure the day of his coming?
  And who can stand when he appears?
  For he is like the refiner's fire,
  or like the fuller's lye.
3 He will sit refining and purifying
  [silver],
  and he will purify the sons of Levi,
  Refining them like gold or like silver
  that they may offer due sacrifice to
  the LORD.[q]
4 Then the sacrifice of Judah and Jerusalem
  will please the LORD,
  as in the days of old, as in years gone
  by.

5 I will draw near to you for judgment,
  and I will be swift to bear witness
  Against the sorcerers, adulterers, and
  perjurers,
  those who defraud the hired man of
  his wages,
  Against those who defraud widows and
  orphans;
  those who turn aside the stranger,
  and those who do not fear me, says
  the LORD of hosts.

6 Surely I, the LORD, do not change,*
  nor do you cease to be sons of Jacob.
7 Since the days of your fathers you have
  turned aside
  from my statutes, and have not kept
  them.
  Return to me, and I will return to you,
  says the LORD of hosts.
  Yet you say, "How must we return?"[r]
8   Dare a man rob God? Yet you are
  robbing me!
  And you say, "How do we rob you?"
  In tithes and in offerings![s]
9 You are indeed accursed,
  for you, the whole nation, rob me.
10 Bring the whole tithe
  into the storehouse,*
  That there may be food in my house,
  and try me in this, says the LORD of
  hosts:
  Shall I not open for you the floodgates
  of heaven,
  to pour down blessing upon you
  without measure?[t]
11 For your sake I will forbid the locust
  to destroy your crops;
  And the vine in the field will not be barren,
  says the LORD of hosts.

12 Then all nations will call you blessed,
  for you will be a delightful land,
  says the LORD of hosts.
13 You have defied me in word, says the
  LORD,

---

n Gn 31, 49f; Prv 5, 18ff.—o Gn 2, 7. 22ff.—p Is 40, 3; Mt 11,
10; Mk 1, 2; Lk 1, 17; 7, 27.—q Is 1, 25; Zec 13, 9.—r Zec 1,
3f; Acts 7, 51.—s Neh 13, 10-14.—t 2 Chr 31, 10f; Neh 10, 38;
13, 12; Prv 3, 9f.

3, 1: *My messenger . . . before me:* in v 23 this messenger
is called Elijah. In Mt 11, 10 these words are quoted by Christ as
referring to John the Baptizer, who prepared the way for the
coming of the Savior; cf Mt 3, 1ff. 11f; 17, 11ff; Mk 1, 2-8; Lk
3, 2-18; Jn 1, 31-34.
3, 6f: God is faithful to his promises. He will not abandon the
Israelites, who are still his people.
3, 10: *Storehouse:* the temple treasury.

yet you ask, "What have we spoken
against you?"

14 You have said, "It is vain to serve
God,
and what do we profit by keeping his
command,
And going about in penitential dress
in awe of the LORD of hosts?[u]

15 Rather must we call the proud blessed;
for indeed evildoers prosper,
and even tempt God with impunity."

16 Then they who fear the LORD spoke
with one another,
and the LORD listened attentively;
And a record book* was written before
him
of those who fear the LORD and trust
in his name.[v]

17 And they shall be mine, says the LORD
of hosts,
my own special possession, on the
day I take action.
And I will have compassion on them,
as a man has compassion on his son
who serves him.[w]

18 Then you will again see the distinction
between the just and the wicked;
Between him who serves God,
and him who does not serve him.

---

u Jb 21, 14f; 22, 17; Ps 73, 11f.—v Rv 20, 12.—w Ex 19, 5;
Dt 7, 6; Pss 103, 13; 135, 4.—x Is 13, 9; 34, 8; Jl 3, 3; Zep 1,
18; 2 Pt 3, 7.—y Lk 1, 78f.—z Ex 20; Lv 26; Dt 4, 1. 5f.—a Mt
11, 14; 17, 10; Mk 9, 10ff; Lk 1, 17.

3, 16: *Record book:* see note on Ex 32, 32.

3, 23: *Elijah:* described in 2 Kgs 2, 11 as taken heavenward
in a fiery chariot. Here his return to earth seems to be foretold.
Jewish tradition has interpreted this literally; Christ declared it to
be fulfilled in the coming cf John the Baptizer (Mt 17, 10-13).

3, 24: The words in fine print, a repetition of v 23a-d, have
been added by the scribes so that the collection of the twelve
minor prophets will not end with the threat of doom.

19 For lo, the day is coming, blazing like
an oven,
when all the proud and all evildoers
will be stubble,
And the day that is coming will set
them on fire,
leaving them neither root nor branch,
says the LORD of hosts.[x]

20 But for you who fear my name, there
will arise
the sun of justice with its healing
rays;
And you will gambol like calves out of
the stall

21 and tread down the wicked;[y]
They will become ashes under the soles
of your feet,
on the day I take action, says the
LORD of hosts.

22 Remember the law of Moses my servant,
which I enjoined upon him on
Horeb,
The statutes and ordinances
for all Israel.[z]

23 Lo, I will send you
Elijah,* the prophet,
Before the day of the LORD comes,
the great and terrible day,

24 To turn the hearts of the fathers to their
children,
and the hearts of the children to their
fathers,[a]
Lest I come and strike
the land with doom.

Lo, I will send you
Elijah, the prophet,
Before the day of the LORD comes,
the great and terrible day.*

THE
NEW TESTAMENT

PREFACE TO THE NEW AMERICAN BIBLE
FIRST EDITION OF THE NEW TESTAMENT

The New Testament translation has been approached with essentially the same fidelity to the thought and individual style of the biblical writers as was applied in the Old Testament. In some cases, however, the problem of marked literary peculiarities had to be met. What by any Western standard are the limited vocabularies and stylistic infelicities of the evangelists cannot be retained in the exact form in which they appear in the originals without displeasing the modern ear. A compromise is here attempted whereby some measure of the poverty of the evangelists' expression is kept and placed at the service of their message in its richness. Similarly, the syntactical shortcomings of Paul, his frequent lapses into anacoluthon, and the like, are rendered as they occur in his epistles rather than "smoothed out." Only thus, the translators suppose, will contemporary readers have some adequate idea of the kind of writing they have before them. When the prose of the original flows more smoothly, as in Luke, Acts, and Hebrews, it is reflected in the translation.

The Gospel according to John comprises a special case. Absolute fidelity to his technique of reiterated phrasing would result in an assault on the English ear, yet the softening of the vocal effect by substitution of other words and phrases would destroy the effectiveness of his poetry. Again, resort is had to compromise. This is not an easy matter when the very repetitiousness which the author deliberately employed is at the same time regarded by those who read and speak English to be a serious stylistic defect. Only those familiar with the Greek originals can know what a relentless tattoo Johannine poetry can produce. A similar observation could be made regarding other New Testament books as well. Matthew and Mark are given to identical phrasing twice and three times in the same sentence. As for the rhetorical overgrowth and mixed figures of speech in the letters of Peter, James, and Jude, the translator must resist a powerful compulsion to tidy them up if only to render these letters intelligibly.

Without seeking refuge in complaints against the inspired authors, however, the translators of *The New American Bible* here state that what they have attempted is a translation rather than a paraphrase. To be sure, all translation can be called paraphrase by definition. Any striving for complete fidelity will shortly end in infidelity. Nonetheless, it must be pointed out that the temptation to improve overladen sentences by the consolidation or elimination of multiplied adjectives, or the simplification of clumsy hendiadys, has been resisted here. For the most part, rhetorically ineffective words and phrases are retained in this translation in some form, even when it is clear that a Western contemporary writer would never have employed them.

The spelling of proper names in *The New American Bible* follows the customary forms found in most English Bibles since the Authorized Version.

Despite the arbitrary character of the divisions into numbered verses (a scheme which in its present form is only four centuries old), the translators have made a constant effort to keep within an English verse the whole verbal content of the Greek verse. At times the effort has not seemed worth the result since it often does violence to the original author's flow of expression, which preceded it by so many centuries. If this translation had been prepared for purposes of public reading only, the editors would have forgone the effort at an early stage. But since they never departed from the threefold objective of preparing a translation suitable for liturgical use, private reading, and the purposes of students, the last-named consideration prevailed. Those familiar with Greek should be able to discover how the translators of the New Testament have rendered any given original verse of scripture, if their exegetical or theological tasks require them to know this. At the same time, the fact should be set down here that the editors did not commit themselves in the synoptic gospels to rendering repeated words or phrases identically.

This leads to a final consideration: the Greek text used for the New Testament. Here, punctuation and verse division are at least as important as variant readings. In general, Nestle-Aland's *Novum Testamentum Graece* (25th edition, 1963) was followed. Additional help was derived from *The Greek New Testament* (Aland, Black, Metzger, Wikgren), produced for the use of translators by the United Bible Societies in 1966. However, the editors did not confine themselves strictly to these texts; at times, they inclined toward readings otherwise attested. The omission of alternative translations does not mean that the translators think them without merit, but only that in every case they had to make a choice.

Poorly attested readings do not occur in this translation. Doubtful readings of some merit appear within brackets; public readers may include such words or phrases, or omit them entirely without any damage to sense. Parentheses are used, as ordinarily in English, as a punctuation device. Material they enclose is in no sense textually doubtful. It is simply thought to be parenthetical in the intention of the biblical author, even though there is no such punctuation mark in Greek. The difficulty in dealing with quotation marks is well known. Since they do not appear in any form in the original text, wherever they occur here they constitute an editorial decision.

PREFACE TO THE REVISED EDITION

The New Testament of *The New American Bible,* a fresh translation from the Greek text, was first published in complete form in 1970, together with the Old Testament translation that had been completed the previous year. Portions of the New Testament had appeared earlier, in somewhat different form, in the provisional Mass lectionary of 1964 and in the *Lectionary for Mass* of 1970.

Since 1970 many different printings of the New Testament have been issued by a number of publishers, both separately and in complete bibles, and the text has become widely known both in the United States and in other English-speaking countries. Most American Catholics have been influenced by it because of its widespread use in the liturgy, and it has received a generally favorable reception from many other Christians as well. It has taken its place among the standard contemporary translations of the New Testament, respected for its fidelity to the original and its attempt to render this into current American English.

Although the scriptures themselves are timeless, translations and explanations of them quickly become dated in an era marked by rapid cultural change to a degree never previously experienced. The explosion of biblical studies that has taken place in our century and the changing nature of our language itself require periodic adjustment both in translations and in the accompanying explanatory materials. The experience of actual use of the New Testament of *The New American Bible,* especially in oral proclamation, has provided a basis for further improvement. Accordingly, it was decided in 1978 to proceed with a thorough revision of the New Testament to reflect advances in scholarship and to satisfy needs identified through pastoral experience.

For this purpose a steering committee was formed to plan, organize, and direct the work of revision, to engage collaborators, and to serve as an editorial board to coordinate the work of the various revisers and to determine the final form of the text and the explanatory materials. Guidelines were drawn up and collaborators selected in 1978 and early 1979, and November of 1980 was established as the deadline for manuscripts. From December 1980 through September 1986 the editorial board met a total of fifty times and carefully reviewed and revised all the material in order to ensure accuracy and consistency of approach. The editors also worked together with the bishops' ad hoc committee that was appointed by the National Conference of Catholic Bishops in 1982 to oversee the revision.

The threefold purpose of the translation that was expressed in the preface to the first edition has been maintained in the revision: to provide a version suitable for liturgical proclamation, for private reading, and for purposes of study. Special attention has been given to the first of these purposes, since oral proclamation demands special qualities in a translation, and experience had provided insights and suggestions that could lead to improvement in this area. Efforts have also been made, however, to facilitate devotional reading by providing suitable notes and introductory materials, and to assist the student by achieving greater accuracy and consistency in the translation and supplying more abundant information in the introductions and notes.

The primary aim of the revision is to produce a version as accurate and faithful to the meaning of the Greek original as is possible for a translation. The editors have consequently moved in the direction of a formal-equivalence approach to translation, matching the vocabulary, structure, and even word order of the original as closely as possible in the receptor language. Some other contemporary biblical versions have adopted, in varying degrees, a dynamic-equivalence approach, which attempts to respect the individuality of each language by expressing the meaning of the original in a linguistic structure suited to English, even though this may be very different from the corresponding Greek structure. While this approach often results in fresh and brilliant renderings, it has the disadvantages of more or less radically abandoning traditional biblical and liturgical terminology and phraseology, of expanding the text to include what more properly belongs in notes, commentaries, or preaching, and of tending toward paraphrase. A more formal approach seems better suited to the specific purposes intended for this translation.

At the same time, the editors have wished to produce a version in English that reflects contemporary American usage and is readily understandable to ordinary educated people, but one that will be recognized as dignified speech, on the level of formal rather than colloquial usage. These aims are not in fact contradictory, for there are different levels of language in current use: the language of formal situations is not that of colloquial conversation, though people understand both and may pass from one to the other without adverting to the transition. The liturgy is a formal situation that requires a level of discourse more dignified, formal, and hieratic than the world of business, sport, or informal communication. People readily understand this more formal level even though they may not often use it; our passive vocabulary is much larger than our active vocabulary. Hence this revision, while avoiding archaisms, does not shrink from traditional biblical terms that are easily understood even though not in common use in everyday speech. The level of language consciously aimed at is one appropriate for liturgical proclamation; this may also permit the translation to serve the purposes of devotional reading and serious study.

A particular effort has been made to insure consistency of vocabulary. Always to translate a given Greek word by the same English equivalent would lead to ludicrous results and to infidelity to the meaning of the text. But in passages where a particular Greek term retains the same meaning, it has been rendered in the same way insofar as this has been feasible; this is particularly significant in the case of terms that have a specific theological meaning. The synoptic gospels have been carefully translated so as to reveal both the similarities and the differences of the Greek.

An especially sensitive problem today is the question of discrimination in language. In recent years there has been much discussion about allegations of anti-Jewish expressions in the New Testament and of language that discriminates against various minorities. Above all, however, the question of discrimination against women affects the largest number of people and arouses the greatest degree of interest and concern. At present there is little agreement about these problems or about the best way to deal with them. In all these areas the present translation attempts to display a sensitivity appropriate to the present state of the questions under discussion, which are not yet resolved and in regard to which it is impossible to please everyone, since intelligent and sincere participants in the debate hold mutually contradictory views.

The primary concern in this revision is fidelity to what the text says. When the meaning of the Greek is inclusive of both sexes, the translation seeks to reproduce such inclusivity insofar as this is possible in normal English usage, without resort to inelegant circumlocutions or neologisms that would offend against the dignity of the language. Although the generic sense of *man* is traditional in English, many today reject it; its use has therefore generally been avoided, though it is retained in cases where no fully satisfactory equivalent could be found. English does not possess a gender-inclusive third personal pronoun in the singular, and this translation continues to use the masculine resumptive pronoun after *everyone* or *anyone*, in the traditional way, where this cannot be avoided without infidelity to the meaning.

The translation of the Greek word *adelphos,* particularly in the plural form *adelphoi*, poses an especially delicate problem. While the term literally means *brothers* or other male blood relatives, even in profane Greek the plural can designate two persons, one of either sex, who were born of the same parents. It was adopted by the early Christians to designate, in a figurative sense, the members of the Christian community, who were conscious of a new familial relationship to one another by reason of their adoption as children of God. They are consequently addressed as *adelphoi*. This has traditionally been rendered into English by *brothers* or, more archaically, *brethren*. There has never been any doubt that this designation includes *all* the members of the Christian community, both male and female. Given the absence in English of a corresponding term that explicitly includes both sexes, this translation retains the usage of *brothers,* with the inclusive meaning that has been traditionally attached to it in this biblical context.

Since the New Testament is the product of a particular time and culture, the views expressed in it and the language in which they are expressed reflect a particular cultural conditioning, which sometimes makes them quite different from contemporary ideas and concerns. Discriminatory language should be eliminated insofar as possible whenever it is unfaithful to the meaning of the New Testament, but the text should not be altered in order to adjust it to contemporary concerns. This translation does not introduce any changes, expansions, additions to, or subtractions from the text of scripture. It further retains the traditional biblical ways of speaking about God and about Christ, including the use of masculine nouns and pronouns.

The Greek text followed in this translation is that of the third edition of *The Greek New Testament,* edited by Kurt Aland, Matthew Black, Carlo Martini, Bruce Metzger, and Allen Wikgren, and published by the United Bible Societies in 1975. The same text, with a different critical apparatus and variations in punctuation and typography, was published as the twenty-sixth edition of the Nestle-Aland *Novum Testamentum Graece* in 1979 by the Deutsche Bibelstiftung, Stuttgart. This edition has also been consulted. When variant readings occur, the translation, with few exceptions, follows the reading that was placed in the text of these Greek editions, though the occurrence of the principal variants is pointed out in the notes.

The editors of the Greek text placed square brackets around words or portions of words of which the authenticity is questionable because the evidence of textual witnesses is inconclusive. The same has been done in the translation insofar as it is possible to reproduce this convention in English. It should be possible to read the text either with or without the disputed words, but in English it is not always feasible to provide this alternative, and in some passages the bracketed words must be included to make sense. As in the first edition, parentheses do not indicate textual uncertainty, but are simply a punctuation device to indicate a passage that in the editors' judgment appears parenthetical to the thought of the author.

Citations from the Old Testament are placed within quotation marks; longer citations are set off as block quotations in a separate indented paragraph. The sources of such citations, as well as those of many more or less subtle allusions to the Old Testament, are identified in the biblical cross-reference section at the bottom of each page. Insofar as possible, the translation of such Old Testament citations agrees with that of *The New American Bible* Old Testament whenever the underlying Greek agrees with the Hebrew (or, in some cases, the Aramaic or Greek) text from which the Old Testament translation was made. But citations in the New Testament frequently follow the Septuagint or some other version, or were made from memory; hence, in many cases the translation in the New Testament passage will not agree with what appears in the Old Testament. Some of these cases are explained in the notes.

It is a further aim of the revised edition to supply explanatory materials more abundantly than in the first edition. In most cases the introductions and notes have been entirely rewritten and expanded, and the cross-references checked and revised. It is intended that these materials should reflect the present state of sound biblical scholarship and should be presented in such a form that they can be assimilated by the ordinary intelligent reader without specialized biblical training. While they have been written with the ordinary educated Christian in mind, not all technical vocabulary can be entirely dispensed with in approaching the Bible, any more than in any other field. It is the hope of the editors that these materials, even if they sometimes demand an effort, will help the reader to a fuller and more intelligent understanding of the New Testament and a fruitful appropriation of its meaning for personal spiritual growth.

The New American Bible is a Roman Catholic translation. This revision, however, like the first edition, has been accomplished with the collaboration of scholars from other Christian churches, both among the revisers and on the editorial board, in response to the encouragement of Vatican Council II *(Dei Verbum,* 22). The editorial board expresses gratitude to all who have collaborated in the revision: to all the revisers, consultants, and bishops who contributed to it, to reviewers of the first edition, and to those who voluntarily submitted suggestions. May this translation fulfill its threefold purpose, "so that the word of the Lord may speed forward and be glorified" (2 Thes 3, 1).

The Feast of St. Jerome
September 30, 1986

THE REVISED NEW TESTAMENT

BOOKS OF THE NEW TESTAMENT

Page

The Gospel according to Matthew 6
The Gospel according to Mark 67
The Gospel according to Luke 95
The Gospel according to John 142
The Acts of the Apostles 179
The Letter to the Romans 221
The First Letter to the Corinthians 242
The Second Letter to the Corinthians 265
The Letter to the Galatians 283
The Letter to the Ephesians 292
The Letter to the Philippians 300
The Letter to the Colossians 307
The First Letter to the Thessalonians 313
The Second Letter to the Thessalonians 317
The First Letter to Timothy 321
The Second Letter to Timothy 328
The Letter to Titus 332
The Letter to Philemon 335
The Letter to the Hebrews 337
The Letter to James 356
The First Letter of Peter 362
The Second Letter of Peter 368
The First Letter of John 373
The Second Letter of John 379
The Third Letter of John 380
The Letter of Jude 382
The Book of Revelation 385

THE GOSPELS

The collection of writings that constitutes the New Testament begins with four gospels. Next comes the Acts of the Apostles, followed by twenty-one letters that are attributed to Paul, James, Peter, John, and Jude. Finally, at the end of the early church's scriptures stands the Revelation to John. Virtually all Christians agree that these twenty-seven books constitute the "canon," a term that means "rule" and designates the list of writings that are regarded as authoritative for Christian faith and life.

It is the purpose of this Introduction to describe those features that are common to the four gospels. A similar treatment of the letters of the New Testament is provided in the two Introductions that appear before the Letter to the Romans and before the Letter of James, respectively. The Acts of the Apostles, a work that is both historical and theological, and Revelation, an apocalyptic work, have no counterparts in the New Testament; the special Introductions prefixed to these books treat of the literary characteristics proper to each of them.

While the New Testament contains four writings called "gospels," there is in reality only one gospel running through all of the Christian scriptures, the gospel of and about Jesus Christ. Our English word "gospel" translates the Greek term *euangelion,* meaning "good news." This noun was used in the plural by the Greek translators of the Old Testament to render the Hebrew term for "good news" (2 Sm 4, 10; possibly also 18, 22.25). But it is the corresponding verb *euangelizomai,* "to proclaim good news," that was especially significant in preparing for the New Testament idea of "gospel," since this term is used by Deutero-Isaiah for announcing the great victory of God that was to establish his universal kingship and inaugurate the new age (Is 40, 9; 52, 7; 61, 1).

Paul used the word *euangelion* to designate the message that he and the other apostles proclaimed, the "gospel of God" (Rom 1, 1; 15, 16; 2 Cor 11, 7; 1 Thes 2, 2.8.9). He often referred to it simply as "the gospel" (Rom 1, 16; 10, 16; 11, 28; etc) or, because of its content and origin, as "the gospel of Christ" (Rom 15, 19; 1 Cor 9, 12; 1 Thes 3, 2; etc). Because of its personal meaning for him and his own particular manner of telling the story about Jesus Christ and of explaining the significance of his cross and resurrection, Paul also referred to this message as "my gospel" (Rom 2, 16; cf Gal 1, 11; 2, 2) or "our gospel" (2 Cor 4, 3; 1 Thes 1, 5; 2 Thes 2, 14).

It was Mark, as far as we know, who first applied the term "gospel" to a book telling the story of Jesus; see Mk 1, 1 and the note there. This form of presenting Jesus' life, works, teachings, passion, and resurrection was developed further by the other evangelists; see the Introduction to each gospel. The first three of the canonical gospels, Matthew, Mark, and Luke, are so similar at many points when viewed together, particularly when arranged in parallel columns or lines, that they are called "synoptic" gospels, from the Greek word for such a general view. The fourth gospel, John, often differs significantly from the synoptics in outline and approach. This work never uses the word "gospel" or its corresponding verb; nevertheless, its message concerns the same Jesus, and the reader is urged to believe in him as the Messiah, "that through this belief you may have life in his name" (20, 31).

From the second century onward, the practice arose of designating each of these four books as a "gospel," understood as a title, and of adding a phrase with a name that identified the traditional author, e.g., "The Gospel according to Matthew." The arrangement of the canon that was adopted, with the four gospels grouped together at the beginning followed by Acts, provides a massive focus upon Jesus and allows Acts to serve as a framework for the letters of the New Testament. This order, however, conceals the fact that Luke's two volumes, a gospel and Acts, were intended by their author to go together. It further obscures the point that Paul's letters were written before any of our gospels, though the sayings and deeds of Jesus stand behind all the New Testament writings.

THE GOSPEL ACCORDING TO MATTHEW

INTRODUCTION

The position of the Gospel according to Matthew as the first of the four gospels in the New Testament reflects both the view that it was the first to be written, a view that goes back to the late second century A.D., and the esteem in which it was held by the church; no other was so frequently quoted in the noncanonical literature of earliest Christianity. Although the majority of scholars now reject the opinion about the time of its composition, the high estimation of this work remains. The reason for that becomes clear upon study of the way in which Matthew presents his story of Jesus, the demands of Christian discipleship, and the breaking-in of the new and final age through the ministry but particularly through the death and resurrection of Jesus.

The gospel begins with a narrative prologue (1, 1—2, 23), the first part of which is a genealogy of Jesus starting with Abraham, the father of Israel (1, 1-17). Yet at the beginning of that genealogy Jesus is designated as "the son of David, the son of Abraham" (1, 1). The kingly ancestor who lived about a thousand years after Abraham is named first, for this is the genealogy of Jesus Christ, the Messiah, the royal anointed one (1, 16). In the first of the episodes of the infancy narrative that follow the genealogy, the mystery of Jesus' person is declared. He is conceived of a virgin by the power of the Spirit of God (1, 18-25). The first of the gospel's fulfillment citations, whose purpose it is to show that he was the one to whom the prophecies of Israel were pointing, occurs here (1, 23): he shall be named Emmanuel, for in him God is with us.

The announcement of the birth of this newborn king of the Jews greatly troubles not only King Herod but all Jerusalem (2, 1-3), yet the Gentile magi are overjoyed to find him and offer him their homage and their gifts (2, 10-11). Thus his ultimate rejection by the mass of his own people and his acceptance by the Gentile nations is foreshadowed. He must be taken to Egypt to escape the murderous plan of Herod. By his sojourn there and his subsequent return after the king's death he relives the Exodus experience of Israel. The words of the Lord spoken through the prophet Hosea, "Out of Egypt I called my son," are fulfilled in him (2, 15); if Israel was God's son, Jesus is so in a way far surpassing the dignity of that nation, as his marvelous birth and the unfolding of his story show (see 3, 17; 4, 1-11; 11, 27; 14, 33; 16, 16; 27, 54). Back in the land of Israel, he must be taken to Nazareth in Galilee because of the danger to his life in Judea, where Herod's son Archelaus is now ruling (2, 22-23). The sufferings of Jesus in the infancy narrative anticipate those of his passion, and if his life is spared in spite of the dangers, it is because his destiny is finally to give it on the cross as "a ransom for many" (20, 28). Thus the word of the angel will be fulfilled, ". . . he will save his people from their sins" (1, 21; cf 26, 28).

In 4, 12 Matthew begins his account of the ministry of Jesus, introducing it by the preparatory preaching of John the Baptist (3, 1-12), the baptism of Jesus that culminates in God's proclaiming him his "beloved Son" (3, 13-17), and the temptation in which he proves his true sonship by his victory over the devil's attempt to deflect him from the way of obedience to the Father (4, 1-11). The central message of Jesus' preaching is the coming of the kingdom of heaven and the need for repentance, a complete change of heart and conduct, on the part of those who are to receive this great gift of God (4, 17). Galilee is the setting for most of his ministry; he leaves there for Judea only in 19, 1, and his ministry in Jerusalem, the goal of his journey, is limited to a few days (21, 1—25, 46).

In this extensive material there are five great discourses of Jesus, each concluding with the formula "When Jesus finished these words" or one closely similar (7, 28; 11, 1; 13, 53; 19, 1; 26, 1). These are an important structure of the gospel. In every case the discourse is preceded by a narrative section, each narrative and discourse together constitut-

ing a "book" of the gospel. The discourses are, respectively, the "Sermon on the Mount" (5, 3—7, 27), the missionary discourse (10, 5-42), the parable discourse (13, 3-52), the "church order" discourse (18, 3-35), and the eschatological discourse (24, 4—25, 46). In large measure the material of these discourses came to Matthew from his tradition, but his work in modifying and adding to what he had received is abundantly evident. No other evangelist gives the teaching of Jesus with such elegance and order as he.

    In the "Sermon on the Mount" the theme of righteousness is prominent, and even at this early stage of the ministry the note of opposition is struck between Jesus and the Pharisees, who are designated as "the hypocrites" (6, 2.5.16). The righteousness of his disciples must surpass that of the scribes and Pharisees; otherwise, in spite of their alleged following of Jesus, they will not enter into the kingdom of heaven (5, 20). Righteousness means doing the will of the heavenly Father (7, 21), and his will is proclaimed in a manner that is startling to all who have identified it with the law of Moses. The antitheses of the Sermon (5, 21-48) both accept (5, 21-30.43-48) and reject (5, 31-42) elements of that law, and in the former case the understanding of the law's demands is deepened and extended. The antitheses are the best commentary on the meaning of Jesus' claim that he has come not to abolish but to fulfill the law (5, 17). What is meant by fulfillment of the law is not the demand to keep it exactly as it stood before the coming of Jesus, but rather his bringing the law to be a lasting expression of the will of God, and in that fulfillment there is much that will pass away. Should this appear contradictory to his saying that "until heaven and earth pass away" not even the smallest part of the law will pass (5, 18), that time of fulfillment is not the dissolution of the universe but the coming of the new age, which will occur with Jesus' death and resurrection. While righteousness in the new age will continue to mean conduct that is in accordance with the law, it will be conduct in accordance with the law as expounded and interpreted by Jesus (cf 28, 20, ". . . all that I have commanded you").

    Though Jesus speaks harshly about the Pharisees in the Sermon, his judgment is not solely a condemnation of them. The Pharisees are portrayed as a negative example for his disciples, and his condemnation of those who claim to belong to him while disobeying his word is no less severe (7, 21-23.26-27).

    In 4, 23 a summary statement of Jesus' activity speaks not only of his teaching and proclaiming the gospel but of his "curing every disease and illness among the people"; this is repeated almost verbatim in 9, 35. The narrative section that follows the Sermon on the Mount (8, 1—9, 38) is composed principally of accounts of those merciful deeds of Jesus, but it is far from being simply a collection of stories about miraculous cures. The nature of the community that Jesus will establish is shown; it will always be under the protection of him whose power can deal with all dangers (8, 23-27), but it is only for those who are prepared to follow him at whatever cost (8, 16-22), not only believing Israelites but Gentiles who have come to faith in him (8, 10-12). The disciples begin to have some insight, however imperfect, into the mystery of Jesus' person. They wonder about him whom "the winds and the sea obey" (8, 27), and they witness his bold declaration of the forgiveness of the paralytic's sins (9, 2). That episode of the narrative moves on two levels. When the crowd sees the cure that testifies to the authority of Jesus, the Son of Man, to forgive sins (9, 6), they glorify God "who had given such authority to human beings" (9, 8). The forgiveness of sins is now not the prerogative of Jesus alone but of "human beings," that is, of the disciples who constitute the community of Jesus, the church. The ecclesial character of this narrative section could hardly be more plainly indicated.

    The end of the section prepares for the discourse on the church's mission (10, 5-42). Jesus is moved to pity at the sight of the crowds who are like sheep without a shepherd

(9, 36), and he sends out the twelve disciples to make the proclamation with which his own ministry began, "The kingdom of heaven is at hand" (10, 7, cf 4, 17), and to drive out demons and cure the sick as he has done (10, 1). Their mission is limited to Israel (10, 5-6) as Jesus' own was (15, 24), yet in v 16 that perspective broadens and the discourse begins to speak of the mission that the disciples will have after the resurrection and of the severe persecution that will attend it (10, 18). Again, the discourse moves on two levels: that of the time of Jesus and that of the time of the church.

The narrative section of the third book (11, 2—12, 50) deals with the growing opposition to Jesus. Hostility toward him has already been manifested (8, 10; 9, 3.10-13.34), but here it becomes more intense. The rejection of Jesus comes, as before, from Pharisees, who take "counsel against him to put him to death" (12, 14) and repeat their earlier accusation that he drives out demons because he is in league with demonic power (12, 22-24). But they are not alone in their rejection. Jesus complains of the lack of faith of "this generation" of Israelites (11, 16-19) and reproaches the towns "where most of his mighty deeds had been done" for not heeding his call to repentance (11, 20-24). This dark picture is relieved by Jesus' praise of the Father who has enabled "the childlike" to accept him (11, 25-27), but on the whole the story is one of opposition to his word and blindness to the meaning of his deeds. The whole section ends with his declaring that not even the most intimate blood relationship with him counts for anything; his only true relatives are those who do the will of his heavenly Father (12, 48-50).

The narrative of rejection leads up to the parable discourse (13, 3-52). The reason given for Jesus' speaking to the crowds in parables is that they have hardened themselves against his clear teaching, unlike the disciples to whom knowledge of "the mysteries of the kingdom has been granted" (13, 10-16). In 13, 36 he dismisses the crowds and continues the discourse to his disciples alone, who claim, at the end, to have understood all that he has said (13, 51). But, lest the impression be given that the church of Jesus is made up only of true disciples, the explanation of the parable of the weeds among the wheat (13, 37-43), as well as the parable of the net thrown into the sea "which collects fish of every kind" (13, 47-49), shows that it is composed of both the righteous and the wicked, and that separation between the two will be made only at the time of the final judgment.

In the narrative that constitutes the first part of the fourth book of the gospel (13, 54—17, 27), Jesus is shown preparing for the establishment of his church with its teaching authority that will supplant the blind guidance of the Pharisees (15, 13-14), whose teaching, curiously said to be that of the Sadducees also, is repudiated by Jesus as the norm for his disciples (16,6.11-12). The church of Jesus will be built on Peter (16, 18), who will be given authority to bind and loose on earth, an authority whose exercise will be confirmed in heaven (16, 19). The metaphor of binding and loosing has a variety of meanings, among them that of giving authoritative teaching. This promise is made to Peter directly after he has confessed Jesus to be the Messiah, the Son of the living God (16, 16), a confession that he has made as the result of revelation given to him by the heavenly Father (16, 17); Matthew's ecclesiology is based on his high christology.

Directly after that confession Jesus begins to instruct his disciples about how he must go the way of suffering and death (16, 21). Peter, who has been praised for his confession, protests against this and receives from Jesus the sharpest of rebukes for attempting to deflect Jesus from his God-appointed destiny. The future rock upon whom the church will be built is still a man of "little faith" (see 14, 31). Both he and the other disciples must know not only that Jesus will have to suffer and die but that they too will have to follow him on the way of the cross if they are truly to be his disciples (16, 24-25).

The discourse following this narrative (18, 1-35) is often called the "church order" discourse, although that title is perhaps misleading since the emphasis is not on the structure of the church but on the care that the disciples must have for one another in respect to guarding each other's faith in Jesus (18, 6-7), to seeking out those who have wandered from the fold (18, 10-14), and to repeated forgiving of their fellow disciples who have offended them (18, 21-35). But there is also the obligation to correct the sinful fellow Christian and, should one refuse to be corrected, separation from the community is demanded (18, 15-18).

The narrative of the fifth book (19, 1—23, 39) begins with the departure of Jesus and his disciples from Galilee for Jerusalem. In the course of their journey Jesus for the third time predicts the passion that awaits him at Jerusalem and also his resurrection (20, 17-19). At his entrance into the city he is hailed as the Son of David by the crowds accompanying him (21, 9). He cleanses the temple (21, 12-17), and in the few days of his Jerusalem ministry he engages in a series of controversies with the Jewish religious leaders (21, 23-27; 22, 15-22.23-33.34-40.41-46), meanwhile speaking parables against them (21, 28-32.33-46), against all those Israelites who have rejected God's invitation to the messianic banquet (22, 1-10), and against all, Jew and Gentile, who have accepted but have shown themselves unworthy of it (22, 11-14). Once again, the perspective of the evangelist includes not only the time of Jesus' ministry but that of the preaching of the gospel after his resurrection. The narrative culminates in Jesus' denunciation of the scribes and Pharisees, reflecting not only his own opposition to them but that of Matthew's church (23, 1-36), and in Jesus' lament over Jerusalem (23, 37-39).

In the discourse of the fifth book (24, 1—25, 46), the last of the great structural discourses of the gospel, Jesus predicts the destruction of the temple and his own final coming. The time of the latter is unknown (24, 36.44), and the disciples are exhorted in various parables to live in readiness for it, a readiness that entails faithful attention to the duties of the interim period (24, 45—25, 30). The coming of Jesus will bring with it the great judgment by which the everlasting destiny of all will be determined (25, 31-46).

The story of Jesus' passion and resurrection (26, 1—28, 20), the climax of the gospel, throws light on all that has preceded. In Mt "righteousness" means both the faithful response to the will of God demanded of all to whom that will is announced and also the saving activity of God for his people (see 3, 15; 5, 6; 6, 33). The passion supremely exemplifies both meanings of that central Matthean word. In Jesus' absolute faithfulness to the Father's will that he drink the cup of suffering (26, 39), the incomparable model for Christian obedience is given; in his death "for the forgiveness of sins" (26, 28), the saving power of God is manifested as never before.

Matthew's portrayal of Jesus in his passion combines both the majestic serenity of the obedient Son who goes his destined way in fulfillment of the scriptures (26, 52-54), confident of his ultimate vindication by God, and the depths of fear and abandonment that he feels in face of death (26, 38-39; 27, 46). These two aspects are expressed by an Old Testament theme that occurs often in the narrative, i.e., the portrait of the suffering Righteous One who complains to God in his misery, but is certain of eventual deliverance from his terrible ordeal.

The passion-resurrection of God's Son means nothing less than the turn of the ages, a new stage of history, the coming of the Son of Man in his kingdom (28, 18; cf 16, 28). That is the sense of the apocalyptic signs that accompany Jesus' death (27, 51-53) and resurrection (28, 2). Although the old age continues, as it will until the manifestation of Jesus' triumph at his parousia, the final age has now begun. This is known only to those who have seen the Risen One and to those, both Jews and Gentiles, who have believed in *their announcement of Jesus' triumph and have themselves become his disciples (cf 28, 19). To them he is constantly, though invisibly, present (28, 20), verifying the name Emmanuel, "God is with us" (cf 1, 23).*

The questions of authorship, sources, and the time of composition of this gospel have received many answers, none of which can claim more than a greater or lesser degree of probability. The one now favored by the majority of scholars is the following.

The ancient tradition that the author was the disciple and apostle of Jesus named Matthew (see 10, 3) is untenable because the gospel is based, in large part, on the Gospel according to Mark (almost all the verses of that gospel have been utilized in this), and it is hardly likely that a companion of Jesus would have followed so extensively an account that came from one who admittedly never had such an association rather than rely on his own memories. The attribution of the gospel to the disciple Matthew may have been due to his having been responsible for some of the traditions found in it, but that is far from certain.

The unknown author, whom we shall continue to call Matthew for the sake of convenience, drew not only upon the Gospel according to Mark but upon a large body of material (principally, sayings of Jesus) not found in Mk that corresponds, sometimes exactly, to material found also in the Gospel according to Luke. This material, called "Q" (probably from the first letter of the German word Quelle, meaning "source"), represents traditions, written and oral, used by both Matthew and Luke. Mark and Q are sources common to the two other synoptic gospels; hence the name the "Two-Source Theory" given to this explanation of the relation among the synoptics.

In addition to what Matthew drew from Mk and Q, his gospel contains material that is found only there. This is often designated "M," written or oral tradition that was available to the author. Since Mk was written shortly before or shortly after A.D. 70 (see Introduction to Mk), Mt was composed certainly after that date, which marks the fall of Jerusalem to the Romans at the time of the First Jewish Revolt (A.D. 66-70), and probably at least a decade later since Matthew's use of Mk presupposes a wide diffusion of that gospel. The post-A.D. 70 date is confirmed within the text by 22, 7, which refers to the destruction of Jerusalem.

As for the place where the gospel was composed, a plausible suggestion is that it was Antioch, the capital of the Roman province of Syria. That large and important city had a mixed population of Greek-speaking Gentiles and Jews. The tensions between Jewish and Gentile Christians there in the time of Paul (see Gal 2, 1-14) in respect to Christian obligation to observe Mosaic law are partially similar to tensions that can be seen between the two groups in Matthew's gospel. The church of Matthew, originally strongly Jewish Christian, had become one in which Gentile Christians were predominant. His gospel answers the question how obedience to the will of God is to be expressed by those who live after the "turn of the ages," the death and resurrection of Jesus.

The principal divisions of the Gospel according to Matthew are the following:

I.   The Infancy Narrative (1, 1—2, 23)
II.   The Proclamation of the Kingdom (3, 1—7, 29)
III. Ministry and Mission in Galilee (8, 1—11, 1)
IV.   Opposition from Israel (11, 2—13, 53)
V.   Jesus, the Kingdom, and the Church (13, 54—18, 35)
VI.   Ministry in Judea and Jerusalem (19, 1—25, 46)
VII. The Passion and Resurrection (26, 1—28, 20)

I. THE INFANCY NARRATIVE*

CHAPTER 1

The Genealogy of Jesus. 1 *a* The book of the genealogy of Jesus Christ, the son of David, the son of Abraham.*

2 *b* Abraham became the father of Isaac, Isaac the father of Jacob, Jacob the father of Judah and his brothers. *c* 3 Judah became the father of Perez and Zerah, whose mother was Tamar. *d* Perez became the father of Hezron, Hezron the father of Ram, 4 *e* Ram the father of Amminadab. Amminadab became the father of Nahshon, Nahshon the father of Salmon, 5 *f* Salmon the father of Boaz, whose mother was Rahab. Boaz became the father of Obed, whose mother was Ruth. Obed became the father of Jesse, 6 *g* Jesse the father of David the king.

David became the father of Solomon, whose mother had been the wife of Uriah. 7 *h* Solomon became the father of Rehoboam, Rehoboam the father of Abijah, Abijah the father of Asaph.* 8 Asaph became the father of Jehoshaphat, Jehoshaphat the father of Joram, Joram the father of Uzziah. 9 Uzziah became the father of

Jotham, Jotham the father of Ahaz, Ahaz the father of Hezekiah. 10 Hezekiah became the father of Manasseh, Manasseh the father of Amos,* Amos the father of Josiah. 11 Josiah became the father of Jechoniah and his brothers at the time of the Babylonian exile.

12 *i* After the Babylonian exile, Jechoniah became the father of Shealtiel, Shealtiel the father of Zerubbabel, 13 Zerubbabel the father of Abiud. Abiud became the father of Eliakim, Eliakim the father of Azor, 14 Azor the father of Zadok. Zadok became the father of Achim, Achim the father of Eliud, 15 Eliud the father of Eleazar. Eleazar became the father of Matthan, Matthan the father of Jacob, 16 Jacob the father of Joseph, the husband of Mary. Of her was born Jesus who is called the Messiah.

17 Thus the total number of generations from Abraham to David is fourteen generations; from David to the Babylonian exile, fourteen generations; from the Babylonian exile to the Messiah, fourteen generations.*

The Birth of Jesus.* 18 Now this is how the birth of Jesus Christ came about.

a Gn 5, 1 / 1 Chr 17, 11 / Gn 22, 18.—b 2-17: Lk 3, 23-38.—c Gn 21, 3; 25, 26; 29, 35; 1 Chr 2, 1.—d Gn 38, 29-30; Ru 4, 18; 1 Chr 2, 4-9.—e Ru 4, 19-20; 1 Chr 2, 10-11.—f Ru 4, 21-22; 1 Chr 2, 11-12.—g 2 Sm 12, 24; 1 Chr 2, 15; 3, 5.—h 7-11: 2 Kgs 25, 1-21; 1 Chr 3, 10-15.— i 12-16: 1 Chr 3, 16-19.

1, 1—2, 23: The infancy narrative forms the prologue of the gospel. Consisting of a genealogy and five stories, it presents the coming of Jesus as the climax of Israel's history, and the events of his conception, birth, and early childhood as the fulfillment of Old Testament prophecy. The genealogy is probably traditional material that Matthew edited. In its first two sections (Mt 1, 2-11) it was drawn from Ru 4, 18-22 and 1 Chr 1—3. Except for Jechoniah, Shealtiel, and Zerubbabel, none of the names in the third section (Mt 1, 12-16) is found in any Old Testament genealogy. While the genealogy shows the continuity of God's providential plan from Abraham on, discontinuity is also present. The women Tamar (Mt 1, 3), Rahab and Ruth (Mt 1, 5), and the wife of Uriah, Bathsheba (Mt 1, 6), bore their sons through unions that were in varying degrees strange and unexpected. These "irregularities" culminate in the supreme "irregularity" of the Messiah's birth of a virgin mother; the age of fulfillment is inaugurated by a creative act of God.

Drawing upon both biblical tradition and Jewish stories, Matthew portrays Jesus as reliving the Exodus experience of Israel and the persecutions of Moses. His rejection by his own people and his passion are foreshadowed by the troubled reaction of "all Jerusalem" to the question of the magi who are seeking the "newborn king of the Jews" (Mt 2, 2-3), and by Herod's attempt to have him killed. The magi who do him homage prefigure the Gentiles who will accept the preaching of the gospel. The infancy narrative proclaims who Jesus is, the savior of his people from their sins (Mt 1, 21), Emmanuel in whom "God is with us" (Mt 1, 23), and the Son of God (Mt 2, 15).

1, 1: *The Son of David, the son of Abraham:* two links of the genealogical chain are singled out. Although the later, David is placed first in order to emphasize that Jesus is the royal Mes-

siah. The mention of Abraham may be due not only to his being the father of the nation Israel but to Matthew's interest in the universal scope of Jesus' mission; cf Gn 22, 18, ". . . . in your descendants all the nations of the earth shall find blessing."

1, 7: The successor of Abijah was not Asaph but Asa (see 1 Chr 3, 10). Some textual witnesses read the latter name; however, *Asaph* is better attested. Matthew may have deliberately introduced the psalmist Asaph into the genealogy (and in v 10 the prophet Amos) in order to show that Jesus is the fulfillment not only of the promises made to David (see 2 Sm 7) but of all the Old Testament.

1, 10: *Amos:* some textual witnesses read *Amon,* who was the actual successor of Manasseh (see 1 Chr 3, 14).

1, 17: Matthew is concerned with fourteen generations, probably because fourteen is the numerical value of the Hebrew letters forming the name of David. In the second section of the genealogy (6b-11), three kings of Judah, Ahaziah, Joash, and Amaziah, have been omitted (see 1 Chr 3, 11-12), so that there are fourteen generations in that section. Yet the third (12-16) apparently has only thirteen. Since Matthew here emphasizes that each section has fourteen, it is unlikely that the thirteen of the last was due to his oversight. Some scholars suggest that *Jesus who is called the Messiah* (16b) doubles the final member of the chain: *Jesus,* born within the family of David, opens up the new age as *Messiah,* so that in fact there are fourteen generations in the third section. This is perhaps too subtle, and the hypothesis of a slip not on the part of Matthew but of a later scribe seems likely. On *Messiah,* see the note on Lk 2, 11.

1, 18-25: This first story of the infancy narrative spells out what is summarily indicated in v 16. The virginal conception of Jesus is the work of the Spirit of God. Joseph's decision to divorce Mary is overcome by the heavenly command that he take her into his home and accept the child as his own. The natural genealogical line is broken but the promises to David are fulfilled; through Joseph's adoption the child belongs to the family of David. Matthew sees the virginal conception as the fulfillment of Is 7, 14.

Mt

When his mother Mary was betrothed to Joseph,* but before they lived together, she was found with child through the holy Spirit. [19] Joseph her husband, since he was a righteous man,* yet unwilling to expose her to shame, decided to divorce her quietly. [20] *j* Such was his intention when, behold, the angel of the Lord* appeared to him in a dream and said, "Joseph, son of David, do not be afraid to take Mary your wife into your home. For it is through the holy Spirit that this child has been conceived in her. [21] She will bear a son and you are to name him Jesus,* because he will save his people from their sins." [22] All this took place to fulfill what the Lord had said through the prophet:

[23] *k* "Behold, the virgin shall be with child
    and bear a son,
and they shall name him Emmanuel,"

which means "God is with us."* [24] When Joseph awoke, he did as the angel of the Lord had commanded him and took his wife into his home. [25] He had no relations with her until she bore a son,* and he named him Jesus.*l*

CHAPTER 2

The Visit of the Magi. *[1] When Jesus was born in Bethlehem of Judea, in the days of King Herod,* behold, magi from the east arrived in Jerusalem, [2] saying, "Where is the newborn king of the Jews? We saw his star* at its rising and have come to do him homage."*m* [3] When King Herod heard this,

he was greatly troubled, and all Jerusalem with him. [4] Assembling all the chief priests and the scribes of the people, he inquired of them where the Messiah was to be born.* [5] *n* They said to him, "In Bethlehem of Judea, for thus it has been written through the prophet:

[6] 'And you, Bethlehem, land of Judah,
    are by no means least among the rulers of Judah;
since from you shall come a ruler,
    who is to shepherd my people Israel.' "

[7] Then Herod called the magi secretly and ascertained from them the time of the star's appearance. [8] He sent them to Bethlehem and said, "Go and search diligently for the child. When you have found him, bring me word, that I too may go and do him homage." [9] After their audience with the king they set out. And behold, the star that they had seen at its rising preceded them, until it came and stopped over the place where the child was. [10] They were overjoyed at seeing the star, [11] *o* and on entering the house they saw the child with Mary his mother. They prostrated themselves and did him homage. Then they opened their treasures and offered him gifts of gold, frankincense, and myrrh.* [12] And having been warned in a dream not to return to Herod, they departed for their country by another way.

Jesus, in whom God is with his people. The name Emmanuel is alluded to at the end of the gospel where the risen Jesus assures his disciples of his continued presence, ". . . I am with you always, until the end of the age" (Mt 28, 20).

1, 25: *Until she bore a son:* the evangelist is concerned to emphasize that Joseph was not responsible for the conception of Jesus. The Greek word translated "until" does not imply normal marital conduct after Jesus' birth, nor does it exclude it.

2, 1-12: The future rejection of Jesus by Israel and his acceptance by the Gentiles are retrojected into this scene of the narrative.

2, 1: *In the days of King Herod:* Herod reigned from 37 to 4 B.C. *Magi:* originally a designation of the Persian priestly caste, the word became used of those who were regarded as having more than human knowledge. Matthew's magi are astrologers.

2, 2: *We saw his star:* it was a common ancient belief that a new star appeared at the time of a ruler's birth. Matthew also draws upon the Old Testament story of Balaam, who had prophesied that "A star shall advance from Jacob" (Nm 24, 17), though there the star means not an astral phenomenon but the king himself.

2, 4: Herod's consultation with the chief priests and scribes has some similarity to a Jewish legend about the child Moses in which the "sacred scribes" warn Pharaoh about the imminent birth of one who will deliver Israel from Egypt and the king makes plans to destroy him.

2, 11: Cf Ps 72, 10.15; Is 60, 6. These Old Testament texts led to the interpretation of the magi as kings.

---

j Mt 2, 13.19; Lk 1, 35.—k Is 7, 14 LXX.—l Lk 2, 7.—m Nm 24, 17.—n 5-6: Mi 5, 1; 2 Sm 5, 2.—o Ps 72, 10-11.15; Is 60, 6.

1, 18: *Betrothed to Joseph:* betrothal was the first part of the marriage, constituting a man and woman as husband and wife. Subsequent infidelity was considered adultery. The betrothal was followed some months later by the husband's taking his wife into his home, at which time normal married life began.

1, 19: *A righteous man:* as a devout observer of the Mosaic law, Joseph wished to break his union with someone whom he suspected of gross violation of the law. It is commonly said that the law required him to do so, but the texts usually given in support of that view, e.g., Dt 22, 20-21, do not clearly pertain to Joseph's situation. *Unwilling to expose her to shame:* the penalty for proved adultery was death by stoning; cf Dt 22, 21-23.

1, 20: *The angel of the Lord:* in the Old Testament a common designation of God in communication with a human being. *In a dream:* see Mt 2, 13.19.22. These dreams may be meant to recall the dreams of Joseph, son of Jacob the patriarch (Gn 37, 5-11.19). A closer parallel is the dream of Amram, father of Moses, related by Josephus (*Antiquities* 2, 9, 3 §§212, 215-16).

1, 21: *Jesus:* in first-century Judaism the Hebrew name Joshua (Greek *Iēsous*) meaning "Yahweh helps" was interpreted as "Yahweh saves."

1, 23: *God is with us:* God's promise of deliverance to Judah in Isaiah's time is seen by Matthew as fulfilled in the birth of

PALESTINE
IN THE TIME OF CHRIST

0 10 20
MILES

Sidon
DAMASCUS
Zarephath
R. Leontes
MT. LEBANON
MT. HERMON
Tyre
Caesarea
Philippi
Iturea
Trachonitis
Paneas
Batanea
UPPER
GALILEE
Chorazin
Bethsaida
Gaulanitis
Auranitis
Capernaum
SEA OF GALILEE
Magdala
Gamala
Cana
Tiberias
Nazareth
MT. TABOR
Gadara
LOWER
Gadarenes
DECAPOLIS
Dor
Plain of Esdraelon
GALILEE
Jezreel
Caesarea
SAMARIA
River Jordan
Gerasa
Samaria
Sychar
MT. EBAL
Jacobs Well
MT. GERIZIM
Joppa
Plain of Sharon
Arimathea
PEREA
Lydda
Ephraim
Philadelphia
BEYOND THE JORDAN
Jericho
MT. OF OLIVES
Azotus
JERUSALEM
Bethany
Ashkelon
Bethlehem
JUDAH
Macherus
R. Arnon
Gaza
Hebron
Wilderness of Judah
Engedi
DEAD SEA
Masada
Beer-sheba

MEDITERRANEAN SEA

PHOENICIA

GALILEE

Mt

PALESTINE IN THE TIME OF CHRIST (37 B.C.—36 A.D.) — **(a)** Herod the Great becomes king under the Romans in 37 (and is kept by Caesar Augustus in 29). Herod's reign is one of continual fear of plots and he does not hesitate to execute his own relatives and children, while erecting magnificent edifices. **(b)** Jesus is born sometime before Herod's death (7-6 B.C.?). **(c)** In 4 B.C. Herod's kingdom is divided among his sons. Archelaus becomes ethnarch of Judea but is deposed in 6 A.D. and **Judea** and **Samaria** become part of the Roman province of Syria. Antipas becomes tetrarch of **Galilee** and **Perea** until 39 A.D. Philip becomes tetrarch of **Trachonitis** until his death in 34 A.D. **(d)** In 7 A.D. Annas is made high priest. **(e)** In 15 A.D. Tiberius Caesar becomes Roman Emperor. **(f)** In 26 A.D. Joseph Caiaphas is made high priest. **(g)** In 26 A.D. Pontius Pilate is sent as governor of Judea and outrages the Jews by letting the Romans bring ensigns into the temple.

JERUSALEM
IN THE
NEW TESTAMENT PERIOD

THE TEMPLE OF
JERUSALEM
AS REBUILT BY
HEROD

JERUSALEM IN THE NEW TESTAMENT PERIOD — (a) This period in the history of Jerusalem rivals the Solomonic period in the external glories added to it by Herod the Great. There is the great fortress **Antonia** of the temple enclosure, three great towers, Phasael, Hippicus, and Mariamne, as well as the magnificent **palace**—all at the north-corner. The most splendid addition is the rebuilt **temple** (started in 19 B.C. and finally completed in 62 A.D.). **(b)** It is to this city that Jesus is brought as an infant (Lk 2, 22-38) and as a youth (Lk 2, 41-52). It is here that during his public ministry Jesus cleanses the **temple** (Jn 2, 13-25), heals a man at the pool of **Bethesda** (Jn 5, 1-47), attends the feast of Tabernacles (Jn 7, 2; 10. 21), and the Dedication (Jn 10, 22-39). **(c)** Jesus spends the final week of his life in and around the city (Mt 27; Jn 12, 12—19, 42). **(d)** After his resurrection Jesus appears to various people (Lk 24) and his disciples (Jn 20, 26-29; Lk 24, 49) in Jerusalem and ascends from the **Mount of Olives** nearby (Lk 24, 50-53).

The Flight to Egypt. [13]* When they had departed, behold, the angel of the Lord appeared to Joseph in a dream and said, "Rise, take the child and his mother, flee to Egypt,* and stay there until I tell you. Herod is going to search for the child to destroy him." [14] Joseph rose and took the child and his mother by night and departed for Egypt. [15] He stayed there until the death of Herod, that what the Lord had said through the prophet[p] might be fulfilled, "Out of Egypt I called my son."*

The Massacre of the Infants. [16] When Herod realized that he had been deceived by the magi, he became furious. He ordered the massacre of all the boys in Bethlehem and its vicinity two years old and under, in accordance with the time he had ascertained from the magi. [17] Then was fulfilled what had been said through Jeremiah the prophet:

[18] [q] "A voice was heard in Ramah,
    sobbing and loud lamentation;
Rachel weeping for her children,
    and she would not be consoled,
    since they were no more."*

The Return from Egypt. [19] When Herod had died, behold, the angel of the Lord appeared in a dream to Joseph in Egypt [20] and said,[r] "Rise, take the child and his mother and go to the land of Israel, for those who sought the child's life are dead."* [21] He rose, took the child and his mother, and went to the land of Israel. [22] But when he heard that Archelaus was ruling over Judea in place of his father Herod,* he was afraid to go back there. And because he had been warned in a dream, he departed for the region of Galilee. [23] [s] He went and dwelt in a town called Nazareth, so that what had been spoken through the prophets might be fulfilled, "He shall be called a Nazorean."*

II. THE PROCLAMATION OF THE KINGDOM

CHAPTER 3

The Preaching of John the Baptist.[*][t] [1] In those days John the Baptist appeared, preaching in the desert of Judea* [2] [and] saying, "Repent,* for the kingdom of heaven is at hand!"[u] [3] It was of him that the prophet Isaiah[v] had spoken when he said:

"A voice of one crying out in the desert,
    'Prepare the way of the Lord,
    make straight his paths.' " *

---

p Hos 11, 1.—q Jer 31, 15.—r Ex 4, 19.—s Mt 13, 54; Mk 1, 9; Lk 2, 39; 4, 34; Jn 19, 19.—t 1-12: Mk 1, 2-8; Lk 3, 2-17.—u Mt 4, 17; 10, 7.—v Is 40, 3.

2, 13-23: Biblical and nonbiblical traditions about Moses are here applied to the child Jesus, though the dominant Old Testament type is not Moses but Israel (see v 15).

2, 13: *Flee to Egypt:* Egypt was a traditional place of refuge for those fleeing from danger in Palestine (see 1 Kgs 11, 40; Jer 26, 21), but the main reason why the child is to be taken to Egypt is that he may relive the Exodus experience of Israel.

2, 15: The fulfillment citation is taken from Hos 11, 1. Israel, God's son, was called out of Egypt at the time of the Exodus; Jesus, the Son of God, will similarly be called out of that land in a new exodus. The father-son relationship between God and the nation is set in a higher key. Here the son is not a group adopted as "son of God," but the child who, as conceived by the holy Spirit, stands in unique relation to God. He is son of David and of Abraham, of Mary and of Joseph, but, above all, of God.

2, 18: Jer 31, 15 portrays Rachel, wife of the patriarch Jacob, weeping for her children taken into exile at the time of the Assyrian invasion of the northern kingdom (722-21 B.C.). Bethlehem was traditionally identified with Ephrath, the place near which Rachel was buried (see Gn 35, 19; 48, 7), and the mourning of Rachel is here applied to her lost children of a later age. *Ramah:* about six miles north of Jerusalem. The lamentation of Rachel is so great as to be heard at a far distance.

2, 20: *For those who sought the child's life are dead:* Moses, who had fled from Egypt because the Pharaoh sought to kill him (see Ex 2, 15), was told to return there, "for all the men who sought your life are dead" (Ex 4, 19).

2, 22: With the agreement of the emperor Augustus, Archelaus received half of his father's kingdom, including Judea, after Herod's death. He had the title "ethnarch" (i.e., "ruler of a nation") and reigned from 4 B.C. to A.D. 6.

2, 23: *Nazareth . . . he shall be called a Nazorean:* the tradition of Jesus' residence in Nazareth was firmly established, and Matthew sees it as being in accordance with the foreannounced plan of God. The town of Nazareth is not mentioned in the Old Testament, and no such prophecy can be found there. The vague expression "through the prophets" may be due to Matthew's seeing a connection between Nazareth and certain texts in which there are words with a remote similarity to the name of that town. Some such Old Testament texts are Is 11, 1 where the Davidic king of the future is called "a bud" *(neṣer)* that shall blossom from the roots of Jesse, and Jgs 13, 5.7 where Samson, the future deliverer of Israel from the Philistines, is called one who shall be consecrated (a *nāzîr*) to God.

3, 1-12: Here Matthew takes up the order of Jesus' ministry found in the gospel of Mark, beginning with the preparatory preaching of John the Baptist.

3, 1: Unlike Luke, Matthew says nothing of the Baptist's origins and does not make him a relative of Jesus. *The desert of Judea:* the barren region west of the Dead Sea extending up the Jordan valley.

3, 2: *Repent:* the Baptist calls for a change of heart and conduct, a turning of one's life from rebellion to obedience toward God. *The kingdom of heaven is at hand:* "heaven" (literally, "the heavens") is a substitute for the name "God" that was avoided by devout Jews of the time out of reverence. The expression "the kingdom of heaven" occurs only in the gospel of Matthew. It means the effective rule of God over his people. In its fullness it includes not only human obedience to God's word, but the triumph of God over physical evils, supremely over death. In the expectation found in Jewish apocalyptic, the kingdom was to be ushered in by a judgment in which sinners would be condemned and perish, an expectation shared by the Baptist. This was modified in Christian understanding where the kingdom was seen as being established in stages, culminating with the parousia of Jesus.

3, 3: See the note on Jn 1, 23.

4 *w* John wore clothing made of camel's hair and had a leather belt around his waist. His food was locusts and wild honey.* 5 At that time Jerusalem, all Judea, and the whole region around the Jordan were going out to him 6 and were being baptized by him in the Jordan River as they acknowledged their sins.*

7 When he saw many of the Pharisees and Sadducees* coming to his baptism, he said to them, "You brood of vipers! Who warned you to flee from the coming wrath? *x* 8 Produce good fruit as evidence of your repentance. 9 And do not presume to say to yourselves, 'We have Abraham as our father.' For I tell you, God can raise up children to Abraham from these stones. *y* 10 Even now the ax lies at the root of the trees. Therefore every tree that does not bear good fruit will be cut down and thrown into the fire. 11 *z* I am baptizing you with water, for repentance, but the one who is coming after me is mightier than I. I am not worthy to carry his sandals. He will baptize you with the holy Spirit and fire.* 12 *a* His winnowing fan is in his hand. He will clear his threshing floor and gather his wheat into his barn, but the chaff he will burn with unquenchable fire."*

The Baptism of Jesus.* 13 *b* Then Jesus came from Galilee to John at the Jordan to be baptized by him. 14 *John tried to prevent him, saying, "I need to be baptized by you, and yet you are coming to me?" 15 Jesus said to him in reply, "Allow it now, for thus it is fitting for us to fulfill all righteousness." Then he allowed him. 16 *c* After Jesus was baptized, he came up from the water and behold, the heavens were opened [for him], and he saw the Spirit of God descending like a dove [and] coming upon him.* 17 And a voice came from the heavens, saying, "This is my beloved Son,* with whom I am well pleased." *d*

CHAPTER 4

The Temptation of Jesus.* 1 *e* Then Jesus was led by the Spirit into the desert to be tempted by the devil. 2 *f* He fasted for forty days and forty nights,* and afterwards he

---

w Mt 11, 7-8; 2 Kgs 1, 8; Zec 13, 4.—x Mt 12, 34; 23, 33; Is 59, 5.—y Jn 8, 33.39; Rom 9, 7-8; Gal 4, 21-31.—z Jn 1, 26-27.33; Acts 1, 5.—a Mt 13, 30; Is 41, 16; Jer 15, 7.—b 13-17: Mk 1, 9-11; Lk 3, 21-22; Jn 1, 31-34.—c Is 42, 1.—d Mt 12, 18; 17, 5; Gn 22, 2; Ps 2, 7; Is 42, 1.—e 1-11: Mk 1, 12-13; Lk 4, 1-13.—f Ex 24, 18; Dt 8, 2.

3, 4: The clothing of John recalls the austere dress of the prophet Elijah (2 Kgs 1, 8). The expectation of the return of Elijah from heaven to prepare Israel for the final manifestation of God's kingdom was widespread, and according to Matthew this expectation was fulfilled in the Baptist's ministry (Mt 11, 14; 17, 11-13).

3, 6: Ritual washing was practiced by various groups in Palestine between 150 B.C. and A.D. 250. John's baptism may have been related to the purificatory washings of the Essenes at Qumran.

3, 7: *Pharisees and Sadducees:* the former were marked by devotion to the law, written and oral, and the scribes, experts in the law, belonged predominantly to this group. The Sadducees were the priestly aristocratic party, centered in Jerusalem. They accepted as scripture only the first five books of the Old Testament, followed only the letter of the law, rejected the oral legal traditions, and were opposed to teachings not found in the Pentateuch, such as the resurrection of the dead. Matthew links both of these groups together as enemies (Mt 16, 1.6.11.12; cf Mk 8, 11-13.15). The threatening words that follow are addressed to them rather than to "the crowds" as in Lk 3, 7. *The coming wrath:* the judgment that will bring about the destruction of unrepentant sinners.

3, 11: *Baptize you with the holy Spirit and fire:* the water baptism of John will be followed by an "immersion" of the repentant in the cleansing power of the Spirit of God, and of the unrepentant in the destroying power of God's judgment. However, some see *the holy Spirit* and *fire* as synonymous, and the effect of this "baptism" as either purification or destruction. See the note on Lk 3, 16.

3, 12: The discrimination between the good and the bad is compared to the procedure by which a farmer separates wheat

and chaff. The *winnowing fan* was a forklike shovel with which the threshed wheat was thrown into the air. The kernels fell to the ground; the light chaff, blown off by the wind, was gathered and burned up.

3, 13-17: The baptism of Jesus is the occasion on which he is equipped for his ministry by the holy Spirit and proclaimed to be the Son of God.

3, 14-15: This dialogue, peculiar to Matthew, reveals John's awareness of Jesus' superiority to him as the mightier one who is coming and who will baptize with the holy Spirit (11). His reluctance to admit Jesus among the sinners whom he is baptizing with water is overcome by Jesus' response. *To fulfill all righteousness:* in this gospel to *fulfill* usually refers to fulfillment of prophecy, and *righteousness* to moral conduct in conformity with God's will. Here, however, as in Mt 5, 6 and Mt 6, 33, *righteousness* seems to mean the saving activity of God. *To fulfill all righteousness* is to submit to the plan of God for the salvation of the human race. This involves Jesus' identification with sinners; hence the propriety of his accepting John's baptism.

3, 16: *The Spirit . . . coming upon him:* cf Is 42, 1.

3, 17: *This is my beloved Son:* the Marcan address to Jesus (Mk 1, 11) is changed into a proclamation. The Father's voice speaks in terms that reflect Is 42, 1, Ps 2, 7, and Gn 22, 2.

4, 1-11: Jesus, proclaimed Son of God at his baptism, is subjected to a triple temptation. Obedience to the Father is a characteristic of true sonship, and Jesus is tempted by the devil to rebel against God, overtly in the third case, more subtly in the first two. Each refusal of Jesus is expressed in language taken from the Book of Deuteronomy (Dt 8, 3; 6, 13.16). The testings of Jesus resemble those of Israel during the wandering in the desert and later in Canaan, and the victory of Jesus, the true Israel and the true Son, contrasts with the failure of the ancient and disobedient "son," the old Israel. In the temptation account Matthew is almost identical with Luke; both seem to have drawn upon the same source.

4, 2: *Forty days and forty nights:* the same time as that during which Moses remained on Sinai (Ex 24, 18). The time reference, however, seems primarily intended to recall the forty years during which Israel was tempted in the desert (Dt 8, 2).

was hungry. ³The tempter approached and said to him, "If you are the Son of God, command that these stones become loaves of bread." ⁴He said in reply, "It is written:ᵍ

'One does not live by bread alone,
but by every word that comes forth
from the mouth of God.' "*

⁵ * Then the devil took him to the holy city, and made him stand on the parapet of the temple, ⁶and said to him, "If you are the Son of God, throw yourself down. For it is written:

'He will command his angels concerning you,'
and 'with their hands they will support you,
lest you dash your foot against a stone.' "ʰ

⁷Jesus answered him, "Again it is written, 'You shall not put the Lord, your God, to the test.' "ⁱ ⁸Then the devil took him up to a very high mountain, and showed him all the kingdoms of the world in their magnificence, ⁹and he said to him, "All these I shall give to you, if you will prostrate yourself and worship me."* ¹⁰At this, Jesus said to him, "Get away, Satan! It is written:

'The Lord, your God, shall you worship
and him alone shall you serve.' "ʲ

¹¹Then the devil left him and, behold, angels came and ministered to him.

The Beginning of the Galilean Ministry.* ¹²ᵏWhen he heard that John had been arrested, he withdrew to Galilee. ¹³He left Nazareth and went to live in Capernaum by the sea, in the region of Zebulun and Naphtali,ˡ ¹⁴that what had been said through Isaiah the prophet might be fulfilled:

¹⁵ "Land of Zebulun and land of Naphtali,ᵐ
the way to the sea, beyond the Jordan,
Galilee of the Gentiles,
¹⁶ the people who sit in darkness
have seen a great light,
on those dwelling in a land overshadowed by death
light has arisen."ⁿ

¹⁷From that time on, Jesus began to preach and say,ᵒ "Repent, for the kingdom of heaven is at hand."*

The Call of the First Disciples.* ¹⁸ᵖAs he was walking by the Sea of Galilee, he saw two brothers, Simon who is called Peter, and his brother Andrew, casting a net into the sea; they were fishermen. ¹⁹He said to them, "Come after me, and I will make you fishers of men." ²⁰At once they left their nets and followed him.* ²¹He walked along from there and saw two other brothers, James, the son of Zebedee, and his brother John. They were in a boat, with their father Zebedee, mending their nets. He called them, ²²and immediately they left their boat and their father and followed him.

Ministering to a Great Multitude.* ²³He went around all of Galilee, teaching in their synagogues,* proclaiming the gospel of the kingdom, and curing every disease and ill-

Mt

---

g Dt 8, 3.—h Ps 91, 11-12.—i Dt 6, 16.—j Mt 16, 23; Dt 6, 13.—k 12-13: Mk 1, 14-15; Lk 4, 14.31.—l Jn 2, 12.—m 15-16: Is 8, 23 LXX; 9, 1.—n Lk 1, 79.—o Mt 3, 2.—p 18-22: Mk 1, 16-20; Lk 5, 1-11.

4, 4: Cf Dt 8, 3. Jesus refuses to use his power for his own benefit and accepts whatever God wills.

4, 5-7: The devil supports his proposal by an appeal to the scriptures, Ps 91, 11a.12. Unlike Israel (Dt 6, 16), Jesus refuses to "test" God by demanding from him an extraordinary show of power.

4, 9: The worship of Satan to which Jesus is tempted is probably intended to recall Israel's worship of false gods. His refusal is expressed in the words of Dt 6, 13.

4, 12-17: Isaiah's prophecy of the light rising upon Zebulun and Naphtali (Is 8, 23—9, 1) is fulfilled in Jesus' residence at Capernaum. The territory of these two tribes was the first to be devastated (733-32 B.C.) at the time of the Assyrian invasion. In order to accommodate Jesus' move to Capernaum to the prophecy, Matthew speaks of that town as being "in the region of Zebulun and Naphtali" (13), whereas it was only in the territory of the latter, and he understands the sea of the prophecy, the Mediterranean, as the sea of Galilee.

4, 17: At the beginning of his preaching Jesus takes up the words of John the Baptist (Mt 3, 2) although with a different meaning; in his ministry the kingdom of heaven has already begun to be present (Mt 12, 28).

4, 18-22: The call of the first disciples promises them a share in Jesus' work and entails abandonment of family and former way of life. Three of the four, Simon, James, and John, are distinguished among the disciples by a closer relation with Jesus (Mt 17, 1; 26, 37).

4, 20: Here and in v 22, as in Mark (Mk 1, 16-20) and unlike the Lucan account (Lk 5, 1-11), the disciples' response is motivated only by Jesus' invitation, an element that emphasizes his mysterious power.

4, 23-25: This summary of Jesus' ministry concludes the narrative part of the first book of Matthew's gospel (chs 3-4). The activities of his ministry are teaching, proclaiming the gospel, and healing; cf Mt 9, 35.

4, 23: *Their synagogues:* Matthew usually designates the Jewish synagogues as *their synagogue(s)* (Mt 9, 35; 10, 17; 12, 9; 13, 54) or, in address to Jews, *your synagogues* (Mt 23, 34), an indication that he wrote after the break between church and synagogue.

ness among the people.*q* *24*His fame spread to all of Syria,* and they brought to him all who were sick with various diseases and racked with pain, those who were possessed, lunatics, and paralytics, and he cured them. *25*And great crowds from Galilee, the Decapolis,* Jerusalem, and Judea, and from beyond the Jordan followed him.*r*

CHAPTER 5

The Sermon on the Mount. *1* *When he saw the crowds,* he went up the mountain, and after he had sat down, his disciples came to him.*2*He began to teach them, saying:

The Beatitudes*
3 "Blessed are the poor in spirit,*
for theirs is the kingdom of heaven.*s*
4 Blessed are they who mourn,*t*
for they will be comforted.*
5 Blessed are the meek,*u*
for they will inherit the land.*
6 Blessed are they who hunger and thirst
for righteousness,*
for they will be satisfied.
7 Blessed are the merciful,
for they will be shown mercy.*v*

8 Blessed are the clean of heart,*w*
for they will see God.*
9 Blessed are the peacemakers,
for they will be called children of God.
10 Blessed are they who are persecuted for the sake of righteousness,*
for theirs is the kingdom of heaven.*x*
*11*Blessed are you when they insult you and persecute you and utter every kind of evil against you [falsely] because of me.*y* *12*Rejoice and be glad, for your reward will be great in heaven.*z* Thus they persecuted the prophets who were before you.*

The Similes of Salt and Light.* *13* *a*"You are the salt of the earth. But if salt loses its taste, with what can it be seasoned? It is no longer good for anything but to be thrown out and trampled underfoot.* *14*You are the light of the world. A city set on a mountain cannot be hidden.*b* *15*Nor do they light a lamp and then put it under a bushel basket; it is set on a lampstand, where it gives light to all in the house.*c* *16*Just so, your light must shine before others, that they may see your good deeds and glorify your heavenly Father.*d*

---

q Mt 9, 35; Mk 1, 39; Lk 4, 15.44.—r Mk 3, 7-8; Lk 6, 17-19.—s 3-12: Lk 6, 20-23.—t Is 61, 2-3; Rv 21, 4.—u Gn 13, 15; Ps 37, 11.—v Mt 18, 33; Jas 2, 13.—w Pss 24, 4-5; 73, 1.—x 1 Pt 2, 20; 3, 14; 4, 14.—y Mt 10, 22; Acts 5, 41.—z 2 Chr 36, 16; Heb 11, 32-38; Jas 5, 10.—a Mk 9, 50; Lk 14, 34-35.—b Jn 8, 12.—c Mk 4, 21; Lk 8, 16; 11, 33.—d Jn 3, 21.

4, 24: *Syria:* the Roman province to which Palestine belonged.

4, 25: *The Decapolis:* a federation of Greek cities in Palestine, originally ten in number, all but one east of the Jordan.

5, 1—7, 29: The first of the five discourses that are a central part of the structure of this gospel. It is the discourse section of the first book and contains sayings of Jesus derived from Q and from M. The Lucan parallel is in that gospel's "Sermon on the Plain" (Lk 6, 20-49), although some of the sayings in Matthew's "Sermon on the Mount" have their parallels in other parts of Luke. The careful topical arrangement of the sermon is probably not due only to Matthew's editing; he seems to have had a structured discourse of Jesus as one of his sources. The form of that source may have been as follows: four beatitudes (Mt 5, 3-4.6.11-12), a section on the new righteousness with illustrations (Mt 5, 17.20-24.27-28.33-48), a section on good works (Mt 6, 1-6.16-18), and three warnings (Mt 7, 1-2.15-21.24-27).

5, 1-2: Unlike Luke's sermon, this is addressed not only to the disciples but to the crowds (see Mt 7, 28).

5, 3-12: The form *Blessed are (is)* occurs frequently in the Old Testament in the Wisdom literature and in the psalms. Although modified by Matthew, the first, second, fourth, and ninth beatitudes have Lucan parallels (Mt 5, 3 // Lk 6, 20; Mt 5, 4 // Lk 6, 21b; Mt 5, 6 // Lk 6, 21a; Mt 5, 11-12 // Lk 5, 22-23). The others were added by the evangelist and are probably his own composition. A few manuscripts, Western and Alexandrian, and many versions and patristic quotations give the second and third beatitudes in inverted order.

5, 3: *The poor in spirit:* in the Old Testament, the *poor* ('*ānāwîm*) are those who are without material possessions and whose confidence is in God (see Is 61, 1; Zep 2, 3; in the NAB the word is translated *lowly* and *humble,* respectively, in those texts). Matthew added *in spirit* in order either to indicate that only the devout poor were meant or to extend the beatitude to all, of whatever social rank, who recognized their complete dependence on God. The same phrase *poor in spirit* is found in the Qumran literature (1QM 14, 7).

5, 4: Cf Is 61, 2, "(The Lord has sent me) . . . to comfort all who mourn." *They will be comforted:* here the passive is a "theological passive" equivalent to the active "God will comfort them"; so also in vv 6 and 7.

5, 5: Cf Ps 37, 11, ". . . the meek shall possess the land." In the psalm "the land" means the land of Palestine; here it means the kingdom.

5, 6: *For righteousness:* a Matthean addition. For the meaning of *righteousness* here, see the note on Mt 3, 14-15.

5, 8: Cf Ps 24, 4. Only one "whose heart is clean" can take part in the temple worship. To be with God in the temple is described in Ps 42, 3 as "beholding his face," but here the promise to *the clean of heart* is that they will *see God* not in the temple but in the coming kingdom.

5, 10: *Righteousness* here, as usually in Matthew, means conduct in conformity with God's will.

5, 12: *The prophets who were before you:* the disciples of Jesus stand in the line of the persecuted prophets of Israel. Some would see the expression as indicating also that Matthew considered all Christian disciples as prophets.

5, 13-16: By their deeds the disciples are to influence the world for good. They can no more escape notice than *a city set on a mountain.* If they fail in good works, they are as useless as flavorless salt or as a lamp whose light is concealed.

5, 13: The unusual supposition of salt losing its flavor has led some to suppose that the saying refers to the salt of the Dead Sea that, because chemically impure, could lose its taste.

Teaching about the Law.* [17]"Do not think that I have come to abolish the law or the prophets. I have come not to abolish but to fulfill. [18]Amen, I say to you, until heaven and earth pass away, not the smallest letter or the smallest part of a letter will pass from the law, until all things have taken place.[e] [19]Therefore, whoever breaks one of the least of these commandments and teaches others to do so will be called least in the kingdom of heaven. But whoever obeys and teaches these commandments will be called greatest in the kingdom of heaven.* [20]I tell you, unless your righteousness surpasses that of the scribes and Pharisees, you will not enter into the kingdom of heaven.

Teaching about Anger. [21] *"You have heard that it was said to your ancestors,[f] 'You shall not kill; and whoever kills will be liable to judgment.'* [22]But I say to you, whoever is angry* with his brother will be liable to judgment,[g] and whoever says to his brother, 'Raqa,' will be answerable to the Sanhedrin, and whoever says, 'You fool,' will be liable to fiery Gehenna.* [23]Therefore, if you bring your gift to the altar, and there recall that your brother has anything against you,[h] [24]leave your gift there at the altar, go first and be reconciled

with your brother, and then come and offer your gift. [25]Settle with your opponent quickly while on the way to court with him.[i] Otherwise your opponent will hand you over to the judge, and the judge will hand you over to the guard, and you will be thrown into prison. [26]Amen, I say to you, you will not be released until you have paid the last penny.

Teaching about Adultery. [27]"You have heard that it was said,[j] 'You shall not commit adultery.'* [28]But I say to you, everyone who looks at a woman with lust has already committed adultery with her in his heart. [29] * If your right eye causes you to sin, tear it out and throw it away.[k] It is better for you to lose one of your members than to have your whole body thrown into Gehenna. [30]And if your right hand causes you to sin, cut it off and throw it away. It is better for you to lose one of your members than to have your whole body go into Gehenna.

Teaching about Divorce. [31]"It was also said, 'Whoever divorces his wife must give her a bill of divorce.'[l] [32]But I say to you, whoever divorces his wife (unless the marriage is unlawful) causes her to commit

Mt

---

e Lk 16, 17.—f Ex 20, 13; Dt 5, 17.—g Jas 1, 19-20.—h Mk 11, 25.—i 25-26: Mt 18, 34-35; Lk 12, 58-59.—j Ex 20, 14; Dt 5, 18.—k 29-30: Mt 18, 8-9; Mk 9, 43-47.—l Mt 19, 3-9; Dt 24, 1.

5, 17-20: This statement of Jesus' position concerning the Mosaic law is composed of traditional material from Matthew's sermon documentation (see the note on Mt 5, 1—7, 29), other Q material (cf Mt 18 and Lk 16, 17), and the evangelist's own editorial touches. *To fulfill* the law appears at first to mean a literal enforcement of the law in the least detail: *until heaven and earth pass away* nothing of the law will pass (18). Yet the "passing away" of heaven and earth is not necessarily the end of the world understood, as in much apocalyptic literature, as the dissolution of the existing universe. The "turning of the ages" comes with the apocalyptic event of Jesus' death and resurrection, and those to whom this gospel is addressed are living in the new and final age, prophesied by Isaiah as the time of "new heavens and a new earth" (Is 65, 17; 66, 22). Meanwhile, during Jesus' ministry when the kingdom is already breaking in, his mission remains within the framework of the law, though with significant anticipation of the age to come, as the following antitheses (vv 21-48) show.

5, 19: Probably *these commandments* means those of the Mosaic law. But this is an interim ethic "until heaven and earth pass away."

5, 21-48: Six examples of the conduct demanded of the Christian disciple. Each deals with a commandment of the law, introduced by *You have heard that it was said to your ancestors* or an equivalent formula, followed by Jesus' teaching in respect to that commandment, *But I say to you;* thus their designation as

"antitheses." Three of them accept the Mosaic law but extend or deepen it (21-22; 27-28; 43-44); three reject it as a standard of conduct for the disciples (31-32; 33-37; 38-39).

5, 21: Cf Ex 20, 13; Dt 5, 17. The second part of the verse is not an exact quotation from the Old Testament, but cf Ex 21, 12.

5, 22: Anger is the motive behind murder, as the insulting epithets are steps that may lead to it. They, as well as the deed, are all forbidden. *Raqa:* an Aramaic word *rēqā'* or *rēqâ* probably meaning "imbecile," "blockhead," a term of abuse. The ascending order of punishment, *judgment* (by a local council?), trial before *the Sanhedrin,* condemnation to *Gehenna,* points to a higher degree of seriousness in each of the offenses. *Sanhedrin:* the highest judicial body of Judaism. *Gehenna:* in Hebrew *gêhinnōm,* "Valley of Hinnom," or *gê ben-hinnōm,* "Valley of the son of Hinnom," southwest of Jerusalem, the center of an idolatrous cult during the monarchy in which children were offered in sacrifice (see 2 Kgs 23, 10; Jer 7, 31). In Jos 18, 16 (Septuagint, Codex Vaticanus) the Hebrew is transliterated into Greek as *gaienna,* which appears in the New Testament as *geenna.* The concept of punishment of sinners by fire either after death or after the final judgment is found in Jewish apocalyptic literature (e.g., Enoch 90, 26) but the name *geenna* is first given to the place of punishment in the New Testament.

5, 22-26: Reconciliation with an offended brother is urged in the admonition of vv 23-24 and the parable of vv 25-26 (// Lk 12, 58-59). The severity of the judge in the parable is a warning of the fate of unrepentant sinners in the coming judgment by God.

5, 27: See Ex 20, 14; Dt 5, 18.

5, 29-30: No sacrifice is too great to avoid total destruction in Gehenna.

adultery, and whoever marries a divorced woman commits adultery.*m

Teaching about Oaths. 33 n "Again you have heard that it was said to your ancestors, 'Do not take a false oath, but make good to the Lord all that you vow.'* 34 o But I say to you, do not swear at all;* not by heaven, for it is God's throne; 35 nor by the earth, for it is his footstool; nor by Jerusalem, for it is the city of the great King. 36 Do not swear by your head, for you cannot make a single hair white or black. 37 Let your 'Yes' mean 'Yes,' and your 'No' mean 'No.' Anything more is from the evil one.*

Teaching about Retaliation.* 38 "You have heard that it was said,p 'An eye for an eye and a tooth for a tooth.' 39 q But I say to you, offer no resistance to one who is evil. When someone strikes you on [your] right cheek, turn the other one to him as well. 40 If anyone wants to go to law with you over your tunic, hand him your cloak as well. 41 Should anyone press you into ser-

vice for one mile,* go with him for two miles r 42 Give to the one who asks of you, and do not turn your back on one who wants to borrow.s

Love of Enemies.* 43 t "You have heard that it was said, 'You shall love your neighbor and hate your enemy.'u 44 But I say to you, love your enemies, and pray for those who persecute you, 45 that you may be children of your heavenly Father, for he makes his sun rise on the bad and the good, and causes rain to fall on the just and the unjust. 46 For if you love those who love you, what recompense will you have? Do not the tax collectors* do the same? 47 And if you greet your brothers only, what is unusual about that? Do not the pagans do the same?* 48 So be perfect,* just as your heavenly Father is perfect.v

CHAPTER 6

Teaching about Almsgiving.* 1 "[But] take care not to perform righteous deeds in order that people may see them;w otherwise, you will have no recompense from

---

m Lk 16, 18; 1 Cor 7, 10-11.—n Lv 19, 12; Nm 30, 3.—o 34-37: Ps 48, 3; Sir 23, 9; Is 66, 1; Jas 5, 12.—p Ex 21, 24; Lv 24, 19-20.—q 39-42: Lk 6, 29-30.—r Lam 3, 30.—s Dt 15, 7-8.—t 43-48: Lk 6, 27.32-36.—u Lv 19, 18.—v Lk 11, 44; 19, 2; Dt 18, 13; Jas 1, 4; 1 Pt 1, 16; 1 Jn 3, 3.—w Mt 23, 5.

5, 31-32: See Dt 24, 1-5. The Old Testament commandment that a bill of divorce be given to the woman assumes the legitimacy of divorce itself. It is this that Jesus denies. *(Unless the marriage is unlawful):* this "exceptive clause," as it is often called, occurs also in Mt 19, 9, where the Greek is slightly different. There are other sayings of Jesus about divorce that prohibit it absolutely (see Mk 10, 11-12; Lk 16, 18; cf 1 Cor 7, 10.11b), and most scholars agree that they represent the stand of Jesus. Matthew's "exceptive clauses" are understood by some as a modification of the absolute prohibition. It seems, however, that the unlawfulness that Matthew gives as a reason why a marriage must be broken refers to a situation peculiar to his community: the violation of Mosaic law forbidding marriage between persons of certain blood and/or legal relationship (Lv 18, 6-18). Marriages of that sort were regarded as incest *(porneia),* but some rabbis allowed Gentile converts to Judaism who had contracted such marriages to remain in them. Matthew's "exceptive clause" is against such permissiveness for Gentile converts to Christianity; cf the similar prohibition of *porneia* in Acts 15, 20.29. In this interpretation, the clause constitutes no exception to the absolute prohibition of divorce when the marriage is lawful.

5, 33: This is not an exact quotation of any Old Testament text, but see Ex 20, 7, Dt 5, 11, and Lv 19, 12. The purpose of an oath was to guarantee truthfulness by one's calling on God as witness.

5, 34-36: The use of these oath formularies that avoid the divine name is in fact equivalent to swearing by it, for all the things sworn by are related to God.

5, 37: *Let your 'Yes' mean 'Yes,' and your 'No' mean 'No':* literally, "let your speech be 'Yes, yes,' 'No, no.' " Some have understood this as a milder form of oath, permitted by Jesus. In view of v 34, "Do not swear at all," that is unlikely. *From the evil one:* i.e., from the devil. Oath-taking presupposes a sinful weakness of the human race, namely, the tendency to lie. Jesus demands of his disciples a truthfulness that makes oaths unnecessary.

5, 38-42: See Lv 24, 20. The Old Testament commandment was meant to moderate vengeance; the punishment should not exceed the injury done. Jesus forbids even this proportionate retaliation. Of the five examples that follow, only the first deals directly with retaliation for evil; the others speak of liberality.

5, 41: Roman garrisons in Palestine had the right to requisition the property and services of the native population.

5, 43-48: See Lv 19, 18. There is no Old Testament commandment demanding hatred of one's enemy, but the "neighbor" of the love commandment was understood as one's fellow countryman. Both in the Old Testament (Ps 139, 19-22) and at Qumran (1QS 9, 21) hatred of evil persons is assumed to be right. Jesus extends the love commandment to the enemy and the persecutor. His disciples, as children of God, must imitate the example of their Father, who grants his gifts of sun and rain to both the good and the bad.

5, 46: *Tax collectors:* Jews who were engaged in the collection of indirect taxes such as tolls and customs. See the note on Mk 2, 14.

5, 47: Jesus' disciples must not be content with merely usual standards of conduct; see v 20 where the verb "surpass" (Greek *perisseuō*) is cognate with the *unusual (perisson)* of this verse.

5, 48: *Perfect:* in the gospels this word occurs only in Matthew, here and in Mt 19, 21. The Lucan parallel (Lk 6, 36) demands that the disciples be *merciful.*

6, 1-18: The sermon continues with a warning against doing good in order to be seen and gives three examples, almsgiving (2-4), prayer (5-15), and fasting (16-18). In each, the conduct of *the hypocrites* (2) is contrasted with that demanded of the disciples. The sayings about *reward* found here and elsewhere (Mt 5, 12.46; 10, 41-42) show that this is a genuine element of Christian moral exhortation. Possibly to underline the difference between the Christian idea of *reward* and that of *the hypocrites,* the evangelist uses two different Greek verbs to express the rewarding of the disciples and that of *the hypocrites;* in the latter case it is the verb *apechō,* a commercial term for giving a receipt for what has been paid in full (2.5.16).

your heavenly Father. ²When you give alms, do not blow a trumpet before you, as the hypocrites* do in the synagogues and in the streets to win the praise of others. Amen, I say to you, they have received their reward.ˣ ³But when you give alms, do not let your left hand know what your right is doing, ⁴so that your almsgiving may be secret. And your Father who sees in secret will repay you.

Teaching about Prayer. ⁵"When you pray, do not be like the hypocrites, who love to stand and pray in the synagogues and on street corners so that others may see them. Amen, I say to you, they have received their reward. ⁶But when you pray, go to your inner room, close the door, and pray to your Father in secret. And your Father who sees in secret will repay you. ⁷ * In praying, do not babble like the pagans, who think that they will be heard because of their many words.* ⁸Do not be like them. Your Father knows what you need before you ask him.

The Lord's Prayer. ⁹ * "This is how you are to pray:ʸ

Our Father in heaven,*
    hallowed be your name,
¹⁰   your kingdom come,*
    your will be done,

on earth as in heaven.ᶻ
¹¹ ᵃ Give us today our daily bread;*
¹²   and forgive us our debts,*
    as we forgive our debtors;ᵇ
¹³   and do not subject us to the final
    test,*
    but deliver us from the evil one.ᶜ
¹⁴ * If you forgive others their transgressions, your heavenly Father will forgive you.ᵈ ¹⁵But if you do not forgive others, neither will your Father forgive your transgressions.ᵉ

Teaching about Fasting. ¹⁶"When you fast,* do not look gloomy like the hypocrites. They neglect their appearance, so that they may appear to others to be fasting. Amen, I say to you, they have received their reward. ¹⁷But when you fast, anoint your head and wash your face, ¹⁸so that you may not appear to be fasting, except to your Father who is hidden. And your Father who sees what is hidden will repay you.

Treasure in Heaven. ¹⁹ * "Do not store up for yourselves treasures on earth, where moth and decay destroy, and thieves break in and steal.ᶠ ²⁰But store up treasures in heaven, where neither moth nor decay de-

Mt

---

x Jn 12, 43.—y 9-13: Lk 11, 2-4.—z Mt 26, 42.—a Prv 30, 8-9.—b Mt 18, 21-22; Sir 28, 2 —c Jn 17, 15; 2 Thes 3, 3.—d Mt 18, 35; Sir 28, 1-5; Mk 11, 25.—e Jas 2, 13.—f Jas 5, 2-3.

6, 2: *The hypocrites:* the scribes and Pharisees, see Mt 23, 13.15.23.25.27.29. The designation reflects an attitude resulting not only from the controversies at the time of Jesus' ministry but from the opposition between Pharisaic Judaism and the church of Matthew.*They have received their reward:* they desire praise and have received what they were looking for.

6, 7-15: Matthew inserts into his basic traditional material an expansion of the material on prayer that includes the model prayer, the "Our Father." That prayer is found in Lk 11, 2-4 in a different context and in a different form.

6, 7: The example of what Christian prayer should be like contrasts it now not with the prayer of the hypocrites but with that of *the pagans.* Their babbling probably means their reciting a long list of divine names, hoping that one of them will force a response from the deity.

6, 9-13: Matthew's form of the "Our Father" follows the liturgical tradition of his church. Luke's less developed form also represents the liturgical tradition known to him, but it is probably closer than Matthew's to the original words of Jesus.

6, 9: *Our Father in heaven:* this invocation is found in many rabbinic prayers of the post-New Testament period. *Hallowed be your name:* though the "hallowing" of the divine name could be understood as reverence done to God by human praise and by obedience to his will, this is more probably a petition that God hallow his own name, i.e., that he manifest his glory by an act of power (cf Ez 36, 23), in this case, by the establishment of his kingdom in its fullness.

6, 10: *Your kingdom come:* this petition sets the tone of the prayer, and inclines the balance toward divine rather than human action in the petitions that immediately precede and follow it. *Your will be done, on earth as in heaven:* a petition that the divine purpose to establish the kingdom, a purpose present now *in heaven,* be executed *on earth.*

6, 11: *Give us today our daily bread:* the rare Greek word *epiousios,* here *daily,* occurs in the New Testament only here and in Lk 11, 3. A single occurrence of the word outside of these texts and of literature dependent on them has been claimed, but the claim is highly doubtful. The word may mean *daily* or "future" (other meanings have also been proposed). The latter would conform better to the eschatological tone of the whole prayer. So understood, the petition would be for a speedy coming of the kingdom (*today*), which is often portrayed in both the Old Testament and the New under the image of a feast (Is 25, 6; Mt 8, 11; 22, 1-10; Lk 13, 29; 14, 15-24).

6, 12: *Forgive us our debts:* the word *debts* is used metaphorically of sins, "debts" owed to God (see Lk 11, 4). The request is probably for forgiveness at the final judgment.

6, 13: Jewish apocalyptic writings speak of a period of severe trial before the end of the age, sometimes called the "messianic woes." This petition asks that the disciples be spared that *final test.*

6, 14-15: These verses reflect a set pattern called "Principles of Holy Law." Human action now will be met by a corresponding action of God at the final judgment.

6, 16: The only fast prescribed in the Mosaic law was that of the Day of Atonement (Lv 16, 31), but the practice of regular fasting was common in later Judaism; cf *Didache* 9, 1.

6, 19-34: The remaining material of this chapter is taken almost entirely from Q. It deals principally with worldly possessions, and the controlling thought is summed up in v 24: the disciple can serve only one master and must choose between God and wealth *(mammon).* See further the note on Lk 16, 9.

stroys, nor thieves break in and steal.
21 For where your treasure is, there also
will your heart be. *g*

The Light of the Body.* 22 "The lamp of
the body is the eye. If your eye is sound,
your whole body will be filled with light;
23 but if your eye is bad, your whole body
will be in darkness. And if the light in you
is darkness, how great will the darkness
be. *h*

God and Money. 24 "No one can serve two
masters. *i* He will either hate one and love
the other, or be devoted to one and despise
the other. You cannot serve God and mammon.*

Dependence on God.* 25 *j* "Therefore I
tell you, do not worry about your life, what
you will eat [or drink], or about your body,
what you will wear. Is not life more than
food and the body more than clothing?
26 Look at the birds in the sky; they do not
sow or reap, they gather nothing into
barns, yet your heavenly Father feeds
them. Are not you more important than
they? *k* 27 Can any of you by worrying add a
single moment to your life-span?* 28 Why
are you anxious about clothes? Learn from
the way the wild flowers grow. They do
not work or spin. 29 But I tell you that not
even Solomon in all his splendor was
clothed like one of them. 30 If God so
clothes the grass of the field, which grows
today and is thrown into the oven tomorrow, will he not much more provide for
you, O you of little faith?* 31 So do not
worry and say, 'What are we to eat?' or
'What are we to drink?' or 'What are we to
wear?' 32 All these things the pagans seek.
Your heavenly Father knows that you need
them all. 33 But seek first the kingdom [of
God] and his righteousness,* and all these
things will be given you besides. 34 Do not
worry about tomorrow; tomorrow will take
care of itself. Sufficient for a day is its own
evil.

CHAPTER 7

Judging Others. 1 * *l* "Stop judging,* that
you may not be judged. *m* 2 For as you
judge, so will you be judged, and the measure with which you measure will be measured out to you. *n* 3 Why do you notice the
splinter in your brother's eye, but do not
perceive the wooden beam in your own
eye? 4 How can you say to your brother,
'Let me remove that splinter from your
eye,' while the wooden beam is in your
eye? 5 You hypocrite,* remove the wooden
beam from your eye first; then you will see
clearly to remove the splinter from your
brother's eye.

Pearls before Swine. 6 "Do not give what
is holy to dogs,* or throw your pearls before swine, lest they trample them underfoot, and turn and tear you to pieces. *o*

The Answer to Prayers. 7 *p* "Ask and it
will be given to you; seek and you will
find; knock and the door will be opened to
you. *q* 8 For everyone who asks, receives;
and the one who seeks, finds; and to the
one who knocks, the door will be opened. *r*
9 Which one of you would hand his son a
stone when he asks for a loaf of bread,*

---

g 20-21: Lk 12, 33-34.—h 22-23: Lk 11, 34-36.—i Lk 16,
13.—j 25-33: Lk 12, 22-31.—k Pss 145, 15-16; 147, 9.—l 1-5:
Lk 6, 37-38.41-42.—m Rom 2, 1-2; 1 Cor 4, 5.—n Wis 12, 22;
Mk 4, 24.—o Prv 23, 9.—p 7-11: Mk 11, 24; Lk 11, 9-13.—q
Mt 18, 19.—r Lk 18, 1-8; Jn 14, 13.

6, 22-23: In this context the parable probably points to the
need for the disciple to be enlightened by Jesus' teaching on the
transitory nature of earthly riches.

6, 24: *Mammon:* an Aramaic word meaning wealth or property.

6, 25-34: Jesus does not deny the reality of human needs (32),
but forbids making them the object of anxious care and, in effect,
becoming their slave.

6, 27: *Life-span:* the Greek word can also mean "stature." If
it is taken in that sense, the word here translated *moment* (literally, "cubit") must be translated literally as a unit not of time but
of spatial measure. The cubit is about eighteen inches.

6, 30: *Of little faith:* except for the parallel in Lk 12, 28, the
word translated *of little faith* is found in the New Testament only
in Matthew. It is used by him of those who are disciples of Jesus
but whose faith in him is not as deep as it should be (see Mt 8, 26;
14, 31; 16, 8 and the cognate noun in Mt 17, 20).

6, 33: *Righteousness:* see the note on Mt 3, 14-15.

7, 1-12: In v 1 Matthew returns to the basic traditional material of the sermon (Lk 6, 37-38.41-42). The governing thought is
the correspondence between conduct toward one's fellows and
God's conduct toward the one so acting.

7, 1: This is not a prohibition against recognizing the faults of
others, which would be hardly compatible with vv 5 and 6, but
against passing judgment in a spirit of arrogance, forgetful of
one's own faults.

7, 5: *Hypocrite:* the designation previously given to the
scribes and Pharisees is here given to the Christian disciple who
is concerned with the faults of another and ignores his own more
serious offenses.

7, 6: *Dogs* and *swine* were Jewish terms of contempt for Gentiles. This saying may originally have derived from a Jewish
Christian community opposed to preaching the gospel *(what is
holy, pearls)* to Gentiles. In the light of Mt 28,19 that can hardly
be Matthew's meaning. He may have taken the saying as applying
to a Christian dealing with an obstinately impenitent fellow Christian (Mt 18, 17).

7, 9-10: There is a resemblance between a stone and a round
loaf of bread and between a serpent and the scaleless fish called
barbut.

[10] or a snake when he asks for a fish? [11] If you then, who are wicked, know how to give good gifts to your children, how much more will your heavenly Father give good things to those who ask him.[s]

The Golden Rule. [12] "Do to others whatever you would have them do to you.[t] This is the law and the prophets.*

The Narrow Gate. [13] * "Enter through the narrow gate;* for the gate is wide and the road broad that leads to destruction, and those who enter through it are many.[u] [14] How narrow the gate and constricted the road that leads to life. And those who find it are few.

False Prophets. * [15] "Beware of false prophets, who come to you in sheep's clothing, but underneath are ravenous wolves.[v] [16] [w] By their fruits you will know them. Do people pick grapes from thornbushes, or figs from thistles? [17] Just so, every good tree bears good fruit, and a rotten tree bears bad fruit. [18] A good tree cannot bear bad fruit, nor can a rotten tree bear good fruit. [19] Every tree that does not bear good fruit will be cut down and thrown into the fire. [20] So by their fruits you will know them.[x]

The True Disciple. * [21] "Not everyone who says to me, 'Lord, Lord,' will enter the kingdom of heaven, but only the one who does the will of my Father in heaven.[y]

[22] Many will say to me on that day,[z] 'Lord, Lord, did we not prophesy in your name? Did we not drive out demons in your name? Did we not do mighty deeds in your name?'[a] [23] Then I will declare to them solemnly, 'I never knew you.* Depart from me, you evildoers.'[b]

The Two Foundations. [24] * "Everyone who listens to these words of mine and acts on them will be like a wise man who built his house on rock.[c] [25] The rain fell, the floods came, and the winds blew and buffeted the house.[d] But it did not collapse; it had been set solidly on rock. [26] And everyone who listens to these words of mine but does not act on them will be like a fool who built his house on sand. [27] The rain fell, the floods came, and the winds blew and buffeted the house. And it collapsed and was completely ruined."

[28] * When Jesus finished these words, the crowds were astonished at his teaching, [29] [e] for he taught them as one having authority, and not as their scribes.*

III. MINISTRY AND MISSION IN GALILEE*

CHAPTER 8

The Cleansing of a Leper. [1] [f] When Jesus came down from the mountain, great

Mt

---

s 1 Jn 5, 14-15.—t Lk 6, 31.—u Lk 13, 24.—v 2 Pt 2, 1.—w 16-17: Mt 12, 33; Lk 6, 43-44.—x Mt 3, 10.—y Is 29, 13; Lk 6, 46.—z 22-23: Lk 13, 26-27.—a Mt 25, 11-12.—b Pss 5, 5; 6, 9.—c 24-27: Lk 6, 47-49.—d 25-26: Prv 10, 25.—e Mk 1, 22; Lk 4, 32.—f 1-4: Mk 1, 40-44; Lk 5, 12-14.

7, 12: See Lk 6, 31. This saying, known since the eighteenth century as the "Golden Rule," is found in both positive and negative form in pagan and Jewish sources, both earlier and later than the gospel. *This is the law and the prophets* is an addition probably due to the evangelist.

7, 13-28: The final section of the discourse is composed of a series of antitheses, contrasting two kinds of life within the Christian community, that of those who obey the words of Jesus and that of those who do not. Most of the sayings are from Q and are found also in Luke.

7, 13-14: The metaphor of the "two ways" was common in pagan philosophy and in the Old Testament. In Christian literature it is found also in the *Didache* (1-6) and the *Epistle of Barnabas* (18-20).

7, 15-20: Christian disciples who claimed to speak in the name of God were called *prophets* (15) in Mt 10, 41 and in Mt 23, 34. They were presumably an important group within the church of Matthew. As in the case of the Old Testament prophets, there were both true and false ones, and for Matthew the difference could be recognized by the quality of their deeds, the *fruits* (16). The mention of *fruits* leads to the comparison with trees, some producing good fruit, others bad.

7, 21-23: The attack on the false prophets is continued, but is broadened to include those disciples who perform works of healing and exorcism in the name of Jesus (*Lord*) but live evil

lives. Entrance into the kingdom is only for those who do the will of the Father. On the day of judgment *(on that day)* the morally corrupt prophets and miracle workers will be rejected by Jesus.

7, 23: *I never knew you:* cf Mt 10, 33. *Depart from me, you evildoers:* cf Ps 6, 9.

7, 24-27: The conclusion of the discourse (cf Lk 6, 47-49). Here the relation is not between saying and doing as in vv 15-23 but between hearing and doing, and the words of Jesus are applied to every Christian *(everyone who listens)*.

7, 28-29: *When Jesus finished these words:* this or a similar formula is used by Matthew to conclude each of the five great discourses of Jesus (cf Mt 11, 1; 13, 53; 19, 1; 26, 1).

7, 29: *Not as their scribes:* scribal instruction was a faithful handing down of the traditions of earlier teachers; Jesus' teaching is based on his own authority. *Their scribes:* for the implications of *their*, see the note on Mt 4, 23.

8, 1—9, 38: This narrative section of the second book of the gospel is composed of nine miracle stories, most of which are found in Mark, although Matthew does not follow the Marcan order and abbreviates the stories radically. The stories are arranged in three groups of three, each group followed by a section composed principally of sayings of Jesus about discipleship. Verse 9, 35 is an almost verbatim repetition of Mt 4, 23. Each speaks of Jesus' teaching, preaching, and healing. The teaching and preaching form the content of chs 5-7; the healing, that of chs 8-9. Some scholars speak of a portrayal of Jesus as "Messiah of the Word" in 5-7 and "Messiah of the Deed" in 8-9. That is accurate so far as it goes, but there is also a strong emphasis on discipleship in 8-9; these chapters have not only christological but ecclesiological import.

crowds followed him. [2] And then a leper* approached, did him homage, and said, "Lord, if you wish, you can make me clean." [3] He stretched out his hand, touched him, and said, "I will do it. Be made clean." His leprosy was cleansed immediately. [4] Then Jesus said to him, "See that you tell no one, but go show yourself to the priest, and offer the gift that Moses prescribed;[g] that will be proof for them."*

The Healing of a Centurion's Servant.*

[5] [h] When he entered Capernaum, a centurion* approached him and appealed to him, [6] saying, "Lord, my servant is lying at home paralyzed, suffering dreadfully." [7] He said to him, "I will come and cure him." [8] The centurion said in reply,* "Lord, I am not worthy to have you enter under my roof; only say the word and my servant will be healed. [9] For I too am a person subject to authority, with soldiers subject to me. And I say to one, 'Go,' and he goes; and to another, 'Come here,' and he comes; and to my slave, 'Do this,' and he does it." [10] When Jesus heard this, he was amazed and said to those following him, "Amen, I say to you, in no one in Israel* have I found such faith. [11] [t] I say to you,* many will come from the east and the west, and will recline with Abraham, Isaac, and Jacob at the banquet in the kingdom of heaven, [12] but the children of the kingdom will be driven out into the outer darkness, where there will be wailing and grinding of teeth." [13] And Jesus said to the centurion, "You may go; as you have believed, let it be done for you." And at that very hour [his] servant was healed.

The Cure of Peter's Mother-in-Law.* [14] [j]

Jesus entered the house of Peter, and saw his mother-in-law lying in bed with a fever. [15] He touched her hand, the fever left her, and she rose and waited on him.[k]

Other Healings. [16] When it was evening,

they brought him many who were possessed by demons, and he drove out the spirits by a word* and cured all the sick, [17] to fulfill what had been said by Isaiah the prophet:[l]

> "He took away our infirmities
> and bore our diseases."*

The Would-be Followers of Jesus.*

[18] [m] When Jesus saw a crowd around him, he gave orders to cross to the other side.* [19] [n] A scribe approached and said to him, "Teacher,* I will follow you wherever you go." [20] Jesus answered him, "Foxes have dens and birds of the sky have nests, but the Son of Man* has nowhere to rest his head." [21] Another of [his] disciples said to him, "Lord, let me go first and bury my

---

g Lv 14, 2-32; Lk 17, 14.—h 5-13: Lk 7, 1-10; Jn 4, 46-53.—i 11-12: Mt 13, 42.50; 22, 13; 24, 51; 25, 30; Lk 13, 28-29.—j 14-16: Mk 1, 29-34; Lk 4, 38-41.—k Mt 9, 25.—l Is 53, 4.—m Mk 4, 35.—n 19-22: Lk 9, 57-60.

8, 2: *A leper:* see the note on Mk 1, 40.

8, 4: Cf Lv 14, 2-9. *That will be proof for them:* the Greek can also mean "that will be proof against them." It is not clear whether *them* refers to the priests or the people.

8, 5-13: This story comes from Q (see Lk 7, 1-10) and is also reflected in Jn 4, 46-54. The similarity between the Q story and the Johannine is due to a common oral tradition, not to a common literary source. As in the later story of the daughter of the Canaanite woman (Mt 15, 21-28) Jesus here breaks with his usual procedure of ministering only to Israelites and anticipates the mission to the Gentiles.

8, 5: *A centurion:* a military officer commanding a hundred men. He was probably in the service of Herod Antipas, tetrarch of Galilee; see the note on Mt 14, 1.

8, 8-9: Acquainted by his position with the force of a command, the centurion expresses faith in the power of Jesus' mere word.

8, 10: *In no one in Israel:* there is good textual attestation (e.g., Codex Sinaiticus) for a reading identical with that of Lk 7, 9, "not even in Israel." But that seems to be due to a harmonization of Matthew with Luke.

8, 11-12: Matthew inserts into the story a Q saying (see Lk 13, 28-29) about the entrance of Gentiles into the kingdom and the exclusion of those Israelites who, though descended from the patriarchs and members of the chosen nation *(the children of the kingdom),* refused to believe in Jesus. *There will be wail-*

ing and grinding of teeth: the first occurrence of a phrase used frequently in this gospel to describe final condemnation (Mt 13, 42.50; 22, 13; 24, 51; 25, 30). It is found elsewhere in the New Testament only in Lk 13, 28.

8, 14-15: Cf Mk 1, 29-31. Unlike Mark, Matthew has no implied request by others for the woman's cure. Jesus acts on his own initiative, and the cured woman rises and waits not on "them" (Mk 1, 31) but on *him.*

8, 16: *By a word:* a Matthean addition to Mk 1, 34; cf Mt 8, 8.

8, 17: This fulfillment citation from Is 53, 4 follows the MT, not the LXX. The prophet speaks of the Servant of the Lord who suffers vicariously for the sins ("infirmities") of others; Matthew takes the *infirmities* as physical afflictions.

8, 18-22: This passage between the first and second series of miracles about following Jesus is taken from Q (see Lk 9, 57-62). The third of the three sayings found in the source is absent from Matthew.

8, 18: *The other side:* i.e., of the Sea of Galilee.

8, 19: *Teacher:* for Matthew, this designation of Jesus is true, for he has Jesus using it of himself (Mt 10, 24.25; 23, 8; 26, 18), yet when it is used of him by others they are either his opponents (Mt 9, 11; 12, 38; 17, 24; 22, 16.24.36) or, as here and in Mt 19, 16, well-disposed persons who cannot see more deeply. Thus it reveals an inadequate recognition of who Jesus is.

8, 20: *Son of Man:* see the note on Mk 8, 31. This is the first occurrence in Mt of a term that appears in the New Testament only in sayings of Jesus, except for Acts 7, 56 and possibly Mt 9, 6 (// Mk 2, 10; Lk 5, 24). In Mt it refers to Jesus in his ministry (seven times, as here), in his passion and resurrection (nine times, e.g., Mt 17, 22), and in his glorious coming at the end of the age (thirteen times, e.g., Mt 24, 30).

father." ²²But Jesus answered him, "Follow me, and let the dead bury their dead."*

The Calming of the Storm at Sea. ²³ *o* He
got into a boat and his disciples followed him.* ²⁴Suddenly a violent storm* came up on the sea, so that the boat was being swamped by waves; but he was asleep. ²⁵ *p* They came and woke him, saying, "Lord, save us!* We are perishing!" ²⁶He said to them, "Why are you terrified, O you of little faith?"* Then he got up, rebuked the winds and the sea, and there was great calm. ²⁷The men were amazed and said, "What sort of man is this, whom even the winds and the sea obey?"

The Healing of the Gadarene Demoniacs.
²⁸ *q* When he came to the other side, to the territory of the Gadarenes,* two demoniacs who were coming from the tombs met him. They were so savage that no one could travel by that road. ²⁹They cried out, "What have you to do with us,* Son of God? Have you come here to torment us before the appointed time?" ³⁰Some distance away a herd of many swine were feeding.* ³¹The demons pleaded with him, "If you drive us out, send us into the herd of swine."*r* ³²And he said to them, "Go then!" They came out and entered the swine, and the whole herd rushed down the steep bank into the sea where they

drowned. ³³The swineherds ran away, and when they came to the town they reported everything, including what had happened to the demoniacs. ³⁴Thereupon the whole town came out to meet Jesus, and when they saw him they begged him to leave their district.

CHAPTER 9

The Healing of a Paralytic. ¹ *s* He entered
a boat, made the crossing, and came into his own town.* ²And there people brought to him a paralytic lying on a stretcher. When Jesus saw their faith, he said to the paralytic, "Courage, child, your sins are forgiven."*t* ³At that, some of the scribes* said to themselves, "This man is blaspheming." ⁴Jesus knew what they were thinking, and said, "Why do you harbor evil thoughts? ⁵Which is easier, to say, 'Your sins are forgiven,' or to say, 'Rise and walk'? ⁶ * But that you may know that the Son of Man has authority on earth to forgive sins"—he then said to the paralytic, "Rise, pick up your stretcher, and go home." *u* ⁷He rose and went home. ⁸When the crowds saw this they were struck with awe and glorified God who had given such authority to human beings.*

---

o 23-27: Mk 4, 35-40; Lk 8, 22-25.—p 25-26: Ps 107, 28-29.—q 28-34: Mk 5, 1-17; Lk 8, 26-37.—r Lk 4, 34.41.—s 1-8: Mk 2, 3-12; Lk 5, 18-26.—t Lk 7, 48.—u Jn 5, 27.

8, 22: *Let the dead bury their dead:* the demand of Jesus overrides what both the Jewish and the Hellenistic world regarded as a filial obligation of the highest importance. See the note on Lk 9, 60.

8, 23: *His disciples followed him:* the first miracle in the second group (Mt 8, 23—9, 8) is introduced by a verse that links it with the preceding sayings by the catchword "follow." In Mk the initiative in entering the boat is taken by the disciples (Mk 4, 35-41); here, Jesus enters first and the disciples follow.

8, 24: *Storm:* literally, "earthquake," a word commonly used in apocalyptic literature for the shaking of the old world when God brings in his kingdom. All the synoptics use it in depicting the events preceding the parousia of the Son of Man (Mt 24, 7; Mk 13, 8; Lk 21, 11). Matthew has introduced it here and in his account of the death and resurrection of Jesus (Mt 27, 51-54; 28, 2).

8, 25: The reverent plea of the disciples contrasts sharply with their reproach of Jesus in Mk 4, 38.

8, 26: *You of little faith:* see the note on Mt 6, 30. *Great calm:* Jesus' calming the sea may be meant to recall the Old Testament theme of God's control over the chaotic waters (Pss 65, 8; 89, 10; 93, 3-4; 107, 29).

8, 28: *Gadarenes:* this is the reading of Codex Vaticanus, supported by other important textual witnesses. The original reading of Codex Sinaiticus was Gazarenes, later changed to

Gergesenes, and a few versions have Gerasenes. Each of these readings points to a different territory connected, respectively, with the cities Gadara, Gergesa (modern Jerash). There is the same confusion of readings in the parallel texts, Mk 5, 1 and Lk 8, 26; there the best reading seems to be "Gerasenes," whereas "Gadarenes" is probably the original reading in Mt. The town of Gadara was about five miles southeast of the Sea of Galilee, and Josephus (*Life* 9 §42) refers to it as possessing territory that lay on that sea. *Two demoniacs:* Mark (5, 1-20) has one.

8, 29: *What have you to do with us?:* see the note on Jn 2, 4. *Before the appointed time:* the notion that evil spirits were allowed by God to afflict human beings until the time of the final judgment is found in Enoch 16, 1 and Jubilees 10, 7-10.

8, 30: The tending of pigs, animals considered unclean by Mosaic law (Lv 11, 6-7), indicates that the population was Gentile.

9, 1: *His own town:* Capernaum; see Mt 4, 13.

9, 3: *Scribes:* see the note on Mk 2, 6. Matthew omits the reason given in the Marcan story for the charge of blasphemy: "Who but God alone can forgive sins?" (Mk 2, 7).

9, 6: It is not clear whether "But that you may know . . . to forgive sins" is intended to be a continuation of the words of Jesus or a parenthetical comment of the evangelist to those who would hear or read this gospel. In any case, Matthew here follows the Marcan text.

9, 8: *Who had given such authority to human beings:* a significant difference from Mk 2, 12 ("They . . . glorified God, saying, 'We have never seen anything like this' "). Matthew's extension to *human beings* of the authority to forgive sins points to the belief that such authority was being claimed by Matthew's church.

The Call of Matthew. ⁹*As Jesus passed on from there,ᵛ he saw a man named Matthew* sitting at the customs post. He said to him, "Follow me." And he got up and followed him. ¹⁰While he was at table in his house,* many tax collectors and sinners came and sat with Jesus and his disciples.ʷ ¹¹The Pharisees saw this and said to his disciples, "Why does your teacher* eat with tax collectors and sinners?" ¹²He heard this and said, "Those who are well do not need a physician, but the sick do.* ¹³Go and learn the meaning of the words,ˣ 'I desire mercy, not sacrifice.'* I did not come to call the righteous but sinners."

The Question about Fasting. ¹⁴ʸThen the disciples of John approached him and said, "Why do we and the Pharisees fast [much], but your disciples do not fast?" ¹⁵Jesus answered them, "Can the wedding guests mourn as long as the bridegroom is with them? The days will come when the bridegroom is taken away from them, and then they will fast.* ¹⁶No one patches an old cloak with a piece of unshrunken cloth,* for its fullness pulls away from the cloak and the tear gets worse. ¹⁷People do not put new wine into old wineskins. Otherwise the skins burst, the wine spills out, and the skins are ruined. Rather, they pour new wine into fresh wineskins, and both are preserved."

The Official's Daughter and the Woman with a Hemorrhage. ¹⁸*While he was saying these things to them,ᶻ an official* came forward, knelt down before him, and said, "My daughter has just died. But come, lay your hand on her, and she will live." ¹⁹Jesus rose and followed him, and so did his disciples. ²⁰A woman suffering hemorrhages for twelve years came up behind him and touched the tassel* on his cloak. ²¹She said to herself, "If only I can touch his cloak, I shall be cured."ᵃ ²²Jesus turned around and saw her, and said, "Courage, daughter! Your faith has saved you." And from that hour the woman was cured.

²³When Jesus arrived at the official's house and saw the flute players and the crowd who were making a commotion, ²⁴he said, "Go away! The girl is not dead but sleeping."* And they ridiculed him. ²⁵When the crowd was put out, he came and took her by the hand, and the little girl arose. ²⁶And news of this spread throughout all that land.

The Healing of Two Blind Men.* ²⁷ᵇ And as Jesus passed on from there, two blind men

---

v 9-13: Mk 2, 14-17; Lk 5, 27-32.—w Mt 11, 19; Lk 15, 1-2.—x Mt 12, 7; Hos 6, 6.—y 14-17: Mk 2, 18-22; Lk 5, 33-39.—z 18-26: Mk 5, 22-43; Lk 8, 41-56.—a Mt 14, 36; Nm 15, 37.—b 27-31: Mt 20, 29-34.

9, 9-17: In this section the order is the same as that of Mk 2, 13-22.

9, 9: *A man named Matthew:* Mark names this tax collector Levi (Mk 2, 14). No such name appears in the four lists of the twelve who were the closest companions of Jesus (Mt 10, 2-4; Mk 3, 16-19; Lk 6, 14-16; Acts 1, 13 [eleven, because of the defection of Judas Iscariot]), whereas all four list a Matthew, designated in Mt 10, 3 as "the tax collector." The evangelist may have changed the "Levi" of his source to *Matthew* so that this man, whose call is given special notice, like that of the first four disciples (Mt 4, 18-22), might be included among the twelve. Another reason for the change may be that the disciple Matthew was the source of traditions peculiar to the church for which the evangelist was writing.

9, 10: *His house:* it is not clear whether *his* refers to Jesus or Matthew. *Tax collectors:* see the note on Mt 5, 46. Table association with such persons would cause ritual impurity.

9, 11: *Teacher:* see the note on Mt 8, 19.

9, 12: See the note on Mk 2, 17.

9, 13: *Go and learn . . . not sacrifice:* Matthew adds the prophetic statement of Hos 6, 6 to the Marcan account (see also Mt 12, 7). If mercy is superior to the temple sacrifices, how much more to the laws of ritual impurity.

9, 15: Fasting is a sign of mourning and would be as inappropriate at this time of joy, when Jesus is proclaiming the kingdom, as it would be at a marriage feast. Yet the saying looks forward to the time when Jesus will no longer be with the disciples visibly, the time of Matthew's church. *Then they will fast:* see *Didache* 8, 1.

9, 16-17: Each of these parables speaks of the unsuitability of attempting to combine the old and the new. Jesus' teaching is not a patching up of Judaism, nor can the gospel be contained within the limits of Mosaic law.

9, 18-34: In this third group of miracles, the first (18-26) is clearly dependent on Mark (Mk 5, 21-43). Though it tells of two miracles, the cure of the woman had already been included within the story of the raising of the official's daughter, so that the two were probably regarded as a single unit. The other miracles seem to have been derived from Mark and Q respectively, though there Matthew's own editing is much more evident.

9, 18: *Official:* literally, "ruler." Mark calls him "one of the synagogue officials" (Mk 5, 22). *My daughter has just died:* Matthew heightens the Marcan "my daughter is at the point of death" (Mk 5, 23).

9, 20: *Tassel:* possibly "fringe." The Mosaic law prescribed that tassels be worn on the corners of one's garment as a reminder to keep the commandments (see Nm 15, 37-39; Dt 22, 12).

9, 24: *Sleeping:* sleep is a biblical metaphor for death (see Ps 87, 6 LXX; Dn 12, 2; 1 Thes 5, 10). Jesus' statement is not a denial of the child's real death, but an assurance that she will be roused from her sleep of death.

9, 27-31: This story was probably composed by Matthew out of Mark's story of the healing of a blind man named Bartimaeus (Mk 10, 46-52). Mark places the event late in Jesus' ministry, just before his entrance into Jerusalem, and Matthew has followed his Marcan source at that point in his gospel also (see Mt 20, 29-34). In each of the Matthean stories the single blind man of Mark becomes two. The reason why Matthew would have given a double version of the Marcan story and placed the earlier one here may be that he wished to add a story of Jesus' curing the blind at this point in order to prepare for Jesus' answer to the emissaries of the Baptist (Mt 11, 4-6) in which Jesus, recounting his works, begins with his giving sight to the blind.

followed [him], crying out, "Son of David,* have pity on us!"*c* 28 When he entered the house, the blind men approached him and Jesus said to them, "Do you believe that I can do this?" "Yes, Lord," they said to him. 29 Then he touched their eyes and said, "Let it be done for you according to your faith." 30 And their eyes were opened. Jesus warned them sternly, "See that no one knows about this." 31 But they went out and spread word of him through all that land.

The Healing of a Mute Person.* 32 *d* As they were going out, a demoniac who could not speak was brought to him, 33 and when the demon was driven out the mute person spoke. The crowds were amazed and said, "Nothing like this has ever been seen in Israel."*e* 34 But the Pharisees said,*f* "He drives out demons by the prince of demons."*

The Compassion of Jesus. 35 *g* Jesus went around to all the towns and villages, teaching in their synagogues, proclaiming the gospel of the kingdom, and curing every disease and illness.* 36 *h* At the sight of the crowds, his heart was moved with pity for them because they were troubled and abandoned, like sheep without a shepherd.* 37 *i* Then he said to his disci-

ples, "The harvest is abundant but the laborers are few; 38 so ask the master of the harvest to send out laborers for his harvest."*

CHAPTER 10

The Mission of the Twelve. 1 * Then he summoned his twelve disciples* and gave them authority over unclean spirits to drive them out and to cure every disease and every illness.*j* 2 The names of the twelve apostles* are these: first, Simon called Peter, and his brother Andrew; James, the son of Zebedee, and his brother John; 3 Philip and Bartholomew, Thomas and Matthew the tax collector; James, the son of Alphaeus, and Thaddeus; 4 Simon the Cananean, and Judas Iscariot who betrayed him.

The Commissioning of the Twelve. 5 *k* Jesus sent out these twelve* after instructing them thus, "Do not go into pagan territory or enter a Samaritan town. 6 *l* Go rather to the lost sheep of the house of Israel. 7 As you go, make this proclamation: 'The kingdom of heaven is at hand.'*m* 8 * Cure the sick, raise the dead, cleanse lepers, drive out demons. Without cost you have received; without cost you are to give. 9 *n* Do not take gold or silver or copper for your belts; 10 *o* no sack for the journey, or a

c Mt 15, 22.—d 32-34: Mt 12, 22-24; Lk 11, 14-15.—e Mk 2, 12; 7, 37.—f Mt 10, 25; Mk 3, 22.—g Mt 4, 23; Lk 8, 1.—h Nm 27, 17; 1 Kgs 22, 17; Jer 50, 6; Ez 34, 5; Mk 6, 34.—i 37-38: Lk 10, 2; Jn 4, 35.—j 1-4: Mk 3, 14-19; Lk 6, 13-16; Acts 1, 13.—k 5-15: Mk 6, 7-13; Lk 9, 1-6.—l Mt 15, 24.—m Mt 3, 2; 4, 17.—n 9-10: Mk 6, 8-9; Lk 9, 3; 10, 4.—o Lk 10, 7; 1 Cor 9, 14; 2 Tm 5, 18.

9, 27: *Son of David:* this messianic title is connected once with the healing power of Jesus in Mark (Mk 10, 47-48) and Luke (Lk 18, 38-39) but more frequently in Matthew (see also Mt 12, 23; 15, 22; 20, 30-31).

9, 32-34: The source of this story seems to be Q (see Lk 11, 14-15). As in the preceding healing of the blind, Matthew has two versions of this healing, the later in Mt 12, 22-24 and the earlier here.

9, 34: This spiteful accusation foreshadows the growing opposition to Jesus in chs 11 and 12.

9, 35: See the notes on Mt 4, 23-25 and Mt 8, 1—9, 38.

9, 36: See Mk 6, 34; Nm 27, 17; 1 Kgs 22, 17.

9, 37-38: This Q saying (see Lk 10, 2) is only imperfectly related to this context. It presupposes that only God *(the master of the harvest)* can take the initiative in sending out preachers of the gospel, whereas in Matthew's setting it leads into ch 10, where Jesus does so.

10, 1—11, 1: After an introductory narrative (10, 1-4), the second of the discourses of the gospel. It deals with the mission now to be undertaken by the disciples (5-15), but the perspective broadens and includes the missionary activity of the church between the time of the resurrection and the parousia.

10, 1: *His twelve disciples:* although, unlike Mark (Mk 3, 13-14) and Luke (Lk 6, 12-16), Matthew has no story of Jesus' choosing the Twelve, he assumes that the group is known to the

reader. The earliest New Testament text to speak of it is 1 Cor 15, 5. The number probably is meant to recall the twelve tribes of Israel and implies Jesus' authority to call all Israel into the kingdom. While Luke (Lk 6, 13) and probably Mark (Mk 4, 10.34) distinguish between the Twelve and a larger group also termed disciples, Matthew tends to identify the disciples and the Twelve. *Authority . . . every illness:* activities the same as those of Jesus; see Mt 4, 23; 9, 35; 10, 8. The Twelve also share in his proclamation of the kingdom (Mt 10, 7). But although he teaches (Mt 4, 23; 7, 28; 9, 35), they do not. Their commission to teach comes only after Jesus' resurrection, after they have been fully instructed by him (Mt 28, 20).

10, 2-4: Here, for the only time in Matthew, the Twelve are designated *apostles.* The word "apostle" means "one who is sent," and therefore fits the situation here described. In the Pauline letters, the place where the term occurs most frequently in the New Testament, it means primarily one who has seen the risen Lord and has been commissioned to proclaim the resurrection. With slight variants in Luke and Acts, the names of those who belong to this group are the same in the four lists given in the New Testament (see the note on Mt 9, 9). *Cananean:* this represents an Aramaic word meaning "zealot." The meaning of that designation is unclear (see the note on Lk 6, 15).

10, 5-6: Like Jesus (Mt 15, 24), the Twelve are sent only to Israel. This saying may reflect an original Jewish Christian refusal of the mission to the Gentiles, but for Matthew it expresses rather the limitation that Jesus himself observed during his ministry.

10, 8-11: The Twelve have received their own call and mission through God's gift, and the benefits they confer are likewise to be given freely. They are not to take with them money, provisions, or unnecessary clothing; their lodging and food will be provided by those who receive them.

second tunic, or sandals, or walking stick. The laborer deserves his keep. [11] *p* Whatever town or village you enter, look for a worthy person in it, and stay there until you leave. [12] As you enter a house, wish it peace. [13] If the house is worthy, let your peace come upon it; if not, let your peace return to you.* [14] *q* Whoever will not receive you or listen to your words—go outside that house or town and shake the dust from your feet.* [15] Amen, I say to you, it will be more tolerable for the land of Sodom and Gomorrah on the day of judgment than for that town.*r*

Coming Persecutions. [16] *s* "Behold, I am sending you like sheep in the midst of wolves; so be shrewd as serpents and simple as doves. [17] *But beware of people,*t* for they will hand you over to courts and scourge you in their synagogues,*u* [18] and you will be led before governors and kings for my sake as a witness before them and the pagans. [19] When they hand you over, do not worry about how you are to speak or what you are to say. You will be given at that moment what you are to say.*v* [20] For it will not be you who speak but the Spirit of your Father speaking through you. [21] *w* Brother will hand over brother to death, and the father his child; children will rise up against parents and have them put to death.* [22] You will be hated by all because of my name, but whoever endures to the end* will be saved. [23] When they persecute you in one town, flee to another. Amen, I say to you, you will not finish the towns of Israel before the Son of Man comes.* [24] *x* No disciple is above his teacher, no slave above his master. [25] It is enough for the disciple that he become like his teacher, for the slave that he become like his master. If they have called the master of the house Beelzebul,* how much more those of his household!

Courage under Persecution. [26] *y* "Therefore do not be afraid of them. Nothing is concealed that will not be revealed, nor secret that will not be known.* [27] What I say to you in the darkness, speak in the light; what you hear whispered, proclaim on the housetops. [28] And do not be afraid of those who kill the body but cannot kill the soul; rather, be afraid of the one who can destroy both soul and body in Gehenna.*a* [29] Are not two sparrows sold for a small coin? Yet not one of them falls to the ground without your Father's knowledge. [30] Even all the hairs of your head are counted. [31] So do not be afraid; you are worth more than many sparrows. [32] Everyone who acknowledges me before others I will acknowledge before my heavenly Father.* [33] But whoever denies me before others, I will deny before my heavenly Father.*b*

Jesus: A Cause of Division. [34] *c* "Do not think that I have come to bring peace upon the earth. I have come to bring not peace but the sword. [35] For I have come to set

> a man 'against his father,
>   a daughter against her mother,
>   and a daughter-in-law against her mother-in-law;
> [36] and one's enemies will be those of his household.'

p 11-15: Mk 6, 10-11; Lk 9, 4-5; 10, 5-12.—q Acts 13, 51; 18, 6.—r Mt 11, 24; Gn 19, 1-29; Jude 7.—s Lk 10, 3.—t 17-22: Mk 13, 9-13; Lk 21, 12-19.—u Acts 5, 40.—v Ex 4, 11-12; Jer 1, 6-10; Lk 12, 11-12.—w 21-22: Mt 24, 9.13.—x 24-25: Lk 6, 40; Jn 13, 16; 15, 20.—y 26-33: Lk 12, 2-9.—z Mk 4, 22; Lk 8, 17; 1 Tm 5, 25.—a Jas 4, 12.—b Mk 8, 38; Lk 9, 26; 2 Tm 2, 12; Rv 3, 5.—c 34-35: Lk 12, 51-53.

10, 13: The greeting of peace is conceived of not merely as a salutation but as an effective word. If it finds no worthy recipient, it will return to the speaker.

10, 14: *Shake the dust from your feet:* this gesture indicates a complete disassociation from such unbelievers.

10, 17: The persecutions attendant upon the post-resurrection mission now begin to be spoken of. Here Matthew brings into the discourse sayings found in Mk 13, which deals with events preceding the parousia.

10, 21: See Mi 7, 6, which is cited in vv 35.36.

10, 22: *To the end:* the original meaning was probably "until the parousia." But it is not likely that Matthew expected no missionary disciples to suffer death before then, since he envisages the martyrdom of other Christians (21). For him, *the end* is probably that of the individual's life (see 28).

10, 23: *Before the Son of Man comes:* since the coming of the Son of Man at the end of the age had not taken place when this gospel was written, much less during the mission of the Twelve during Jesus' ministry, Matthew cannot have meant the coming to refer to the parousia. It is difficult to know what he understood it to be: perhaps the "proleptic parousia" of Mt 28, 16-20, or the destruction of the temple in A.D. 70, viewed as a coming of Jesus in judgment on unbelieving Israel.

10, 25: *Beelzebul:* see Mt 9, 34 for the charge linking Jesus with "the prince of demons," who is named *Beelzebul* in Mt 12, 24. The meaning of the name is uncertain; possibly, "lord of the house."

10, 26: The *concealed* and *secret* coming of the kingdom is to be proclaimed by them, and no fear must be allowed to deter them from that proclamation.

10, 32-33: In the Q parallel (Lk 12, 8-9), the Son of Man will acknowledge those who have acknowledged Jesus, and those who deny him will be denied (by the Son of Man) before the angels of God at the judgment. Here Jesus and the Son of Man are identified, and the acknowledgment or denial will be before his heavenly Father.

The Conditions of Discipleship. [37] *d* "Whoever loves father or mother more than me is not worthy of me, and whoever loves son or daughter more than me is not worthy of me; [38] and whoever does not take up his cross* and follow after me is not worthy of me. [39] *e* Whoever finds his life will lose it, and whoever loses his life for my sake will find it.*

Rewards. [40] "Whoever receives you receives me,* and whoever receives me receives the one who sent me. *f* [41] Whoever receives a prophet* because he is a prophet will receive a prophet's reward, and whoever receives a righteous man because he is righteous will receive a righteous man's reward. [42] And whoever gives only a cup of cold water to one of these little ones to drink because he is a disciple—amen, I say to you, he will surely not lose his reward." *g*

CHAPTER 11

[1] When Jesus finished giving these commands to his twelve disciples,* he went away from that place to teach and to preach in their towns.

IV. OPPOSITION FROM ISRAEL

The Messengers from John the Baptist. [2] * *h* When John heard in prison* of the works of the Messiah, he sent his disciples to him [3] with this question, "Are you the one who is to come, or should we look for another?"* [4] Jesus said to them in reply, "Go and tell John what you hear and see: [5] * the blind regain their sight, the lame walk, lepers are cleansed, the deaf hear, the dead are raised, and the poor have the good news proclaimed to them. *i* [6] And blessed is the one who takes no offense at me."

Jesus' Testimony to John.* [7] As they were going off, Jesus began to speak to the crowds about John, "What did you go out to the desert to see? A reed swayed by the wind? *j* [8] Then what did you go out to see? Someone dressed in fine clothing? Those who wear fine clothing are in royal palaces. [9] Then why did you go out? To see a prophet?* Yes, I tell you, and more than a prophet. [10] This is the one about whom it is written:

'Behold, I am sending my messenger ahead of you;

he will prepare your way before you.' *k*

[11] Amen, I say to you, among those born of women there has been none greater than John the Baptist; yet the least in the kingdom of heaven is greater than he.* [12] From the days of John the Baptist until now, the kingdom of heaven suffers violence,* and

Mt

---

d 37-39: Mt 16, 24-25; Lk 14, 26-27.—e Mk 8, 35; Lk 9, 24; Jn 12, 25.—f Lk 10, 16; Jn 12, 44; 13, 20.—g Mt 25, 40; Mk 9, 41.—h 2-11: Lk 7, 18-28.—i Is 26, 19; 29, 18-19; 35, 5-6; 61, 1.—j Mt 3, 3.5.—k Ex 23, 20; Mal 3, 1; Mk 1, 2; Lk 1, 76.

10, 38: The first mention of the cross in Matthew, explicitly that of the disciple, but implicitly that of Jesus *(and follow after me)*. Crucifixion was a form of capital punishment used by the Romans for offenders who were not Roman citizens.

10, 39: One who denies Jesus in order to save one's earthly life will be condemned to everlasting destruction; loss of earthly life for Jesus' sake will be rewarded by everlasting life in the kingdom.

10, 40-42: All who receive the disciples of Jesus receive him, and God who sent him, and will be rewarded accordingly.

10, 41: *A prophet:* one who speaks in the name of God; here, the Christian prophets who proclaim the gospel. *Righteous man:* since righteousness is demanded of all the disciples, it is difficult to take the *righteous man* of this verse and *one of these little ones* (42) as indicating different groups within the followers of Jesus. Probably all three designations are used here of Christian missionaries as such.

11, 1: The closing formula of the discourse refers back to the original addressees, the Twelve.

11, 2—12, 50: The narrative section of the third book deals with the growing opposition to Jesus. It is largely devoted to disputes and attacks relating to faith and discipleship and thus contains much sayings-material, drawn in large part from Q.

11, 2: *In prison:* see Mt 4, 12; 14, 1-12. *The works of the Messiah:* the deeds of chs 8-9.

11, 3: The question probably expresses a doubt of the Baptist that Jesus is *the one who is to come* (cf Mal 3, 1) because his mission has not been one of fiery judgment as John had expected (Mt 3, 2).

11, 5-6: Jesus' response is taken from passages of Isaiah (Is 26, 19; 29, 18-19; 35, 5-6; 61, 1) that picture the time of salvation as marked by deeds such as those that Jesus is doing. The beatitude is a warning to the Baptist not to disbelieve because his expectations have not been met.

11, 7-19: Jesus' rebuke of John is counterbalanced by a reminder of the greatness of the Baptist's function (7-15) that is followed by a complaint about those who have heeded neither John nor Jesus (16-19).

11, 9-10: In common Jewish belief there had been no prophecy in Israel since the last of the Old Testament prophets, Malachi. The coming of a new prophet was eagerly awaited, and Jesus agrees that John was such. Yet he was *more than a prophet*, for he was the precursor of the one who would bring in the new and final age. The Old Testament quotation is a combination of Mal 3, 1 and Ex 23, 20, with the significant change that the *before me* of Malachi becomes *before you*. The messenger now precedes not God, as in the original, but Jesus.

11, 11: John's preeminent greatness lies in his function of announcing the imminence of the kingdom (Mt 3, 1). But to be in the kingdom is so great a privilege that the least who has it is greater than the Baptist.

11, 12: The meaning of this difficult saying is probably that the opponents of Jesus are trying to prevent people from accepting the kingdom and to snatch it away from those who have received it.

the violent are taking it by force.[l] [13] All the prophets and the law* prophesied up to the time of John. [14] And if you are willing to accept it, he is Elijah, the one who is to come.[m] [15] Whoever has ears ought to hear.

[16] [n] "To what shall I compare this generation?* It is like children who sit in marketplaces and call to one another, [17] 'We played the flute for you, but you did not dance, we sang a dirge but you did not mourn.' [18] For John came neither eating nor drinking, and they said, 'He is possessed by a demon.'[o] [19] The Son of Man came eating and drinking and they said, 'Look, he is a glutton and a drunkard, a friend of tax collectors and sinners.' But wisdom is vindicated by her works."[p]

Reproaches to Unrepentant Towns. [20] [q] Then he began to reproach the towns where most of his mighty deeds had been done, since they had not repented. [21] "Woe to you, Chorazin! Woe to you, Bethsaida! For if the mighty deeds done in your midst had been done in Tyre and Sidon,* they would long ago have repented in sackcloth and ashes.[r] [22] But I tell you, it will be more tolerable for Tyre and Sidon on the day of judgment than for you. [23] And as for you, Capernaum:

'Will you be exalted to heaven?[s]

You will go down to the netherworld.'*

For if the mighty deeds done in your midst had been done in Sodom, it would have remained until this day. [24] But I tell you, it will be more tolerable for the land of Sodom on the day of judgment than for you."[t]

The Praise of the Father. [25] [u] At that time Jesus said in reply,* "I give praise to you, Father, Lord of heaven and earth, for although you have hidden these things from the wise and the learned you have revealed them to the childlike. [26] Yes, Father, such has been your gracious will. [27] All things have been handed over to me by my Father. No one knows the Son except the Father, and no one knows the Father except the Son and anyone to whom the Son wishes to reveal him.[v]

The Gentle Mastery of Christ. [28] * "Come to me, all you who labor and are burdened,* and I will give you rest. [29] [w] Take my yoke upon you and learn from me, for I am meek and humble of heart; and you will find rest for yourselves.* [30] For my yoke is easy, and my burden light."

CHAPTER 12

Picking Grain on the Sabbath.[1] *At that time Jesus was going through a field of grain on the sabbath.[x] His disciples were hungry and began to pick the heads of grain and eat them.[y] [2] When the Pharisees saw this, they said to him, "See, your disciples are doing what is unlawful* to do on

---

l Lk 16, 16.—m Mt 17, 10-13; Mal 3, 23; Lk 1, 17.—n 16-19: Lk 7, 31-35.—o Lk 1, 15.—p Mt 9, 10-11.—q 20-24: Lk 10, 12-15.—r Jl 4, 4-7.—s Is 14, 13-15.—t Mt 10, 15.—u 25-27: Lk 10, 21-22.—v Jn 3, 35; 6, 46; 7, 28; 10, 15.—w Sir 51, 26; Jer 6, 16.—x 1-8: Mk 2, 23-28; Lk 6, 1-5.—y Dt 23, 26.

11, 13: *All the prophets and the law:* Matthew inverts the usual order, "law and prophets," and says that both have *prophesied.* This emphasis on the prophetic character of the law points to its fulfillment in the teaching of Jesus and to the transitory nature of some of its commandments (see the note on Mt 5, 17-20).

11, 16-19: See Lk 7, 31-35. The meaning of the parable (16-17) and its explanation (18-19b) is much disputed. A plausible view is that the *children* of the parable are two groups, one of which proposes different entertainments to the other that will not agree with either proposal. The first represents John, Jesus, and their disciples; the second those who reject John for his asceticism and Jesus for his table association with those despised by the religiously observant. Verse 19c *(her works)* forms an inclusion with v 2 ("the works of the Messiah"). The original form of the saying is better preserved in Lk 7, 35, ". . . wisdom is vindicated by all her children." There John and Jesus are the children of Wisdom; here the works of Jesus the Messiah are those of divine Wisdom, of which he is the embodiment. Some important textual witnesses, however, have essentially the same reading as in Luke.

11, 21: Tyre and Sidon were pagan cities denounced for their wickedness in the Old Testament; cf Jl 4, 4-7.

11, 23: Capernaum's pride and punishment are described in language taken from the taunt song against the king of Babylon (Is 14, 13-15).

11, 25-27: This Q saying, identical with Lk 10, 21-22 except for minor variations, introduces a joyous note into this section, so dominated by the theme of unbelief. While *the wise and the learned,* the scribes and Pharisees, have rejected Jesus' preaching and the significance of his mighty deeds, *the childlike* have accepted them. Acceptance depends upon the Father's revelation, but this is granted to those who are open to receive it and refused to the arrogant. Jesus can speak of all mysteries because he is *the Son* and there is perfect reciprocity of knowledge between him and the Father; what has been *handed over* to him is revealed only to those whom he wishes.

11, 28-29: These verses are peculiar to Matthew and are similar to Ben Sirach's invitation to learn wisdom and submit to her yoke (Sir 51, 23.26).

11, 28: *Who labor and are burdened:* burdened by the law as expounded by the scribes and Pharisees (Mt 23, 4).

11, 29: In place of the yoke of the law, complicated by scribal interpretation, Jesus invites the burdened to take the yoke of obedience to his word, under which they *will find rest;* cf Jer 6, 16.

12, 1-14: Matthew here returns to the Marcan order that he left in Mt 9, 18. The two stories depend on Mk 2, 23-28 and Mk 3, 1-6, respectively, and are the only places in either gospel that deal explicitly with Jesus' attitude toward sabbath observance.

12, 1-2: The picking of the heads of grain is here equated with reaping, which was forbidden on the sabbath (Ex 34, 21).

the sabbath." ³He said to them,* "Have you not read what David*z* did when he and his companions were hungry, ⁴how he went into the house of God and ate the bread of offering,*a* which neither he nor his companions but only the priests could lawfully eat? ⁵ * Or have you not read in the law that on the sabbath the priests serving in the temple violate the sabbath and are innocent?*b* ⁶I say to you, something greater than the temple is here. ⁷If you knew what this meant, 'I desire mercy, not sacrifice,'*c* you would not have condemned these innocent men.* ⁸ *d* For the Son of Man is Lord of the sabbath."*

The Man with a Withered Hand. ⁹ *e* Moving on from there, he went into their synagogue. ¹⁰And behold, there was a man there who had a withered hand. They questioned him, "Is it lawful to cure on the sabbath?"* so that they might accuse him. ¹¹He said to them, "Which one of you who has a sheep that falls into a pit on the sabbath will not take hold of it and lift it out?* ¹²How much more valuable is a person than a sheep. So it is lawful to do good on the sabbath." ¹³Then he said to the man, "Stretch out your hand." He stretched it out, and it was restored as sound as the other. ¹⁴But the Pharisees* went out and took counsel against him to put him to death.*f*

z 3-4: 1 Sm 21, 2-7.—a Lv 24, 5-9.—b Lv 24, 8; Nm 28, 9-10.—c Hos 6, 6.—d Jn 5, 16-17.—e 9-15: Mk 3, 1-6; Lk 6, 6-11.—f Jn 5, 18.—g 18-21: Is 42, 1-4.—h 22-24: Mt 9, 32-34; Lk 11, 14-15.—i Mt 9, 27.—j Mt 10, 25; Mk 3, 22.—k 25-29: Mk 3, 23-27; Lk 11, 17-22.

12, 3-4: See 1 Sm 21, 2-7. In the Marcan parallel (Mk 2, 25-26) the high priest is mistakenly called Abiathar, although in 1 Sm this action is attributed to Ahimelech. The Old Testament story is not about a violation of the sabbath rest; its pertinence to this dispute is that a violation of the law was permissible because of David's men being without food.

12, 5-6: This and the following argument (7) are peculiar to Matthew. The temple service seems to be the changing of the showbread on the sabbath (Lv 24, 8) and the doubling on the sabbath of the usual daily holocausts (Nm 28, 9-10). The argument is that the law itself requires work that breaks the sabbath rest, because of the higher duty of temple service. If temple duties outweigh the sabbath law, how much more does the presence of Jesus, with his proclamation of the kingdom *(something greater than the temple)*, justify the conduct of his disciples.

12, 7: See the note on Mt 9, 13.

12, 8: The ultimate justification for the disciples' violation of the sabbath rest is that Jesus, the Son of Man, has supreme authority over the law.

12, 10: Rabbinic tradition later than the gospels allowed relief to be given to a sufferer on the sabbath if life was in danger. This may also have been the view of Jesus' Pharisaic contemporaries. But the case here is not about one in danger of death.

12, 11: Matthew omits the question posed by Jesus in Mk 3, 4 and substitutes one about rescuing a sheep on the sabbath, similar to that in Lk 14, 5.

The Chosen Servant.* ¹⁵When Jesus realized this, he withdrew from that place. Many [people] followed him, and he cured them all,* ¹⁶but he warned them not to make him known. ¹⁷This was to fulfill what had been spoken through Isaiah the prophet:

¹⁸ "Behold, my servant whom I have chosen,*g*
    my beloved in whom I delight;
I shall place my spirit upon him,
    and he will proclaim justice to the Gentiles.
¹⁹ He will not contend* or cry out,
    nor will anyone hear his voice in the streets.
²⁰ A bruised reed he will not break,
    a smoldering wick he will not quench,
until he brings justice to victory.
²¹   And in his name the Gentiles will hope."*

Jesus and Beelzebul.* ²² *h* Then they brought to him a demoniac who was blind and mute. He cured the mute person so that he could speak and see. ²³ *i* All the crowd was astounded, and said, "Could this perhaps be the Son of David?"* ²⁴ *j* But when the Pharisees heard this, they said, "This man drives out demons only by the power of Beelzebul, the prince of demons."* ²⁵ *k* But he knew what they were thinking and said to them,* "Every king-

12, 14: See Mk 3, 6. Here the plan to bring about Jesus' death is attributed to the Pharisees only. This is probably due to the situation of Matthew's church, when the sole opponents were the Pharisees.

12, 15-21: Matthew follows Mk 3, 7-12 but summarizes his source in two verses (15.16) that pick up the withdrawal, the healings, and the command for silence. To this he adds a fulfillment citation from the first Servant Song (Is 42, 1-4) that does not correspond exactly to either the Hebrew or the LXX of that passage. It is the longest Old Testament citation in this gospel, emphasizing the meekness of Jesus, the Servant of the Lord, and foretelling the extension of his mission to the Gentiles.

12, 15: Jesus' knowledge of the Pharisees' plot and his healing *all* are peculiar to Matthew.

12, 19: The servant's not contending is seen as fulfilled in Jesus' withdrawal from the disputes narrated in 1-14.

12, 21: Except for a minor detail, Matthew here follows the LXX, although the meaning of the Hebrew ("the coastlands will wait for his teaching") is similar.

12, 22-32: For the exorcism, see the note on Mt 9, 32-34. The long discussion combines Marcan and Q material (Mk 3, 22-30; Lk 11, 19-20.23; 12, 10). Mark 3, 20-21 is omitted, with a consequent lessening of the sharpness of Mt 12, 48.

12, 23: See the note on Mt 9, 27.

12, 24: See the note on Mt 10, 25.

12, 25-26: Jesus' first response to the Pharisees' charge is that if it were true, Satan would be destroying his own kingdom.

dom divided against itself will be laid waste, and no town or house divided against itself will stand. 26 And if Satan drives out Satan, he is divided against himself; how, then, will his kingdom stand? 27 And if I drive out demons by Beelzebul, by whom do your own people* drive them out? Therefore they will be your judges. 28 *l* But if it is by the Spirit of God that I drive out demons, then the kingdom of God has come upon you.* 29 How can anyone enter a strong man's house and steal his property, unless he first ties up the strong man? Then he can plunder his house.* 30 *m* Whoever is not with me is against me, and whoever does not gather with me scatters.* 31 *n* Therefore, I say to you, every sin and blasphemy will be forgiven people, but blasphemy against the Spirit* will not be forgiven. 32 And whoever speaks a word against the Son of Man will be forgiven; but whoever speaks against the holy Spirit will not be forgiven, either in this age or in the age to come.

A Tree and Its Fruits. 33 *o* "Either declare* the tree good and its fruit is good, or declare the tree rotten and its fruit is rotten, for a tree is known by its fruit. 34 *p* You brood of vipers, how can you say good things when you are evil? For from the

fullness of the heart the mouth speaks.* 35 A good person brings forth good out of a store of goodness, but an evil person brings forth evil out of a store of evil. 36 *q* I tell you, on the day of judgment people will render an account for every careless word they speak.* 37 By your words you will be acquitted, and by your words you will be condemned."

The Demand for a Sign. * 38 Then some of the scribes and Pharisees said to him, "Teacher,* we wish to see a sign from you." *r* 39 He said to them in reply, "An evil and unfaithful* generation seeks a sign, but no sign will be given it except the sign of Jonah the prophet. 40 Just as Jonah was in the belly of the whale three days and three nights,* so will the Son of Man be in the heart of the earth three days and three nights. 41 * At the judgment, the men of Nineveh will arise with this generation and condemn it, because they repented at the preaching of Jonah; and there is something greater than Jonah here. 42 At the judgment the queen of the south will arise with this generation and condemn it, because she came from the ends of the earth to hear the wisdom of Solomon; and there is something greater than Solomon here. *s*

l Lk 11, 20.—m Lk 11, 23.—n 31-32: Mk 3, 28-30; Lk 12, 10.—o 33-35: Lk 6, 43-45.—p Mt 3, 7; 23, 33; 15, 11-12; Lk 3, 7.—q 36-37: Jas 3, 1-2.—r 38-42: Mt 16, 1-4; Jon 2, 1; 3, 1-10; Mk 8, 11-12; Lk 11, 29-32.—s 1 Kgs 10, 1-10.

12, 27: Besides pointing out the absurdity of the charge, Jesus asks how the work of Jewish exorcists *(your own people)* is to be interpreted. Are they, too, to be charged with collusion with Beelzebul? For an example of Jewish exorcism see Josephus, *Antiquities* 8, 2, 5 §§42-49.

12, 28: The Q parallel (Lk 11, 20) speaks of the "finger" rather than of the "spirit" of God. While the difference is probably due to Matthew's editing, he retains *the kingdom of God* rather than changing it to his usual "kingdom of heaven." *Has come upon you:* see Mt 4, 17.

12, 29: A short parable illustrates what Jesus is doing. The *strong man* is Satan, whom Jesus has tied up and whose *house* he is plundering. Jewish expectation was that Satan would be chained up in the last days (Rv 20, 2); Jesus' exorcisms indicate that those days have begun.

12, 30: This saying, already attached to the preceding verses in Q (see Lk 11, 23), warns that there can be no neutrality where Jesus is concerned. Its pertinence in a context where Jesus is addressing not the neutral but the bitterly opposed is not clear. The accusation of scattering, however, does fit the situation. Jesus is the shepherd of God's people (Mt 2, 6), his mission is to the lost sheep of Israel (Mt 15, 24); the Pharisees, who oppose him, are guilty of scattering the sheep.

12, 31: *Blasphemy against the Spirit:* the sin of attributing to Satan (24) what is the work of the Spirit of God (28).

12, 33: *Declare:* literally, "make." The meaning of this verse is obscure. Possibly it is a challenge to the Pharisees to de-

clare either Jesus and his exorcisms good or both of hem bad. A tree is known by its fruit; if the fruit is good, so must the tree be. If the driving out of demons is good, so must its source be.

12, 34: The admission of Jesus' goodness cannot be made by the Pharisees, for they are evil, and the words that proceed from their evil hearts cannot be good.

12, 36-37: If on the day of judgment people will be held accountable for even their *careless* words, the vicious accusations of the Pharisees will surely lead to their condemnation.

12, 38-42: This section is mainly from Q (see Lk 11, 29-32). Mk 8, 11-12, which Matthew has followed in Mt 16, 1-4, has a similar demand for a sign. The scribes and Pharisees refuse to accept the exorcisms of Jesus as authentication of his claims and demand a sign that will end all possibility of doubt. Jesus' response is that no such sign will be given. Because his opponents are evil and see him as an agent of Satan, nothing will convince them.

12, 38: *Teacher:* see the note on Mt 8, 19. In Mt 16, 1 the request is for a sign "from heaven" (Mk 8, 11).

12, 39: *Unfaithful:* literally, "adulterous." The covenant between God and Israel was portrayed as a marriage bond, and unfaithfulness to the covenant as adultery; cf Hos 2, 4-15; Jer 3, 6-10.

12, 40: See Jon 2, 1. While in Q the sign was simply Jonah's preaching to the Ninevites (Lk 11, 30.32), Matthew here adds Jonah's sojourn *in the belly of the whale* for *three days and three nights*, a prefiguration of Jesus' sojourn in the abode of the dead and, implicitly, of his resurrection.

12, 41-42: The Ninevites who *repented* (see Jon 3, 1-10) and *the queen of the south* (i.e., of Sheba; see 1 Kgs 10, 1-13) were pagans who responded to lesser opportunities than have been offered to Israel in the ministry of Jesus, *something greater than Jonah* or *Solomon*. At the final judgment they will condemn the faithless *generation* that has rejected him.

The Return of the Unclean Spirit.* [43] [t]
"When an unclean spirit goes out of a person it roams through arid regions searching for rest but finds none. [44] Then it says, 'I will return to my home from which I came.' But upon returning, it finds it empty, swept clean, and put in order. [45] Then it goes and brings back with itself seven other spirits more evil than itself, and they move in and dwell there; and the last condition of that person is worse than the first. Thus it will be with this evil generation."

The True Family of Jesus.* [46] [u] While he was still speaking to the crowds, his mother and his brothers appeared outside, wishing to speak with him. [[47] Someone told him, "Your mother and your brothers are standing outside, asking to speak with you."]* [48] But he said in reply to the one who told him, "Who is my mother? Who are my brothers?" [49] And stretching out his hand toward his disciples, he said, "Here are my mother and my brothers. [50] For whoever does the will of my heavenly Father is my brother, and sister, and mother."

---

t 43-45: Lk 11, 24-26.—u 46-50: Mk 3, 31-35; Lk 8, 19-21.—v 1-15: Mk 4, 1-12; Lk 8, 4-10.—w Mt 25, 29; Mk 4, 25; Lk 8, 18; 19, 26.

12, 43-45: Another Q passage; cf Mt 11, 24-26. Jesus' ministry has broken Satan's hold over Israel, but the refusal of *this evil generation* to accept him will lead to a worse situation than what preceded his coming.

12, 46-50: See Mk 3, 31-35. Matthew has omitted Mk 3, 20-21, which is taken up in Mk 3, 31 (see the note on Mt 12, 22-32), yet the point of the story is the same in both gospels: natural kinship with Jesus counts for nothing; only one who *does the will of* his *heavenly Father* belongs to his true family.

12, 47: This verse is omitted in some important textual witnesses, including Codex Sinaiticus (original reading) and Codex Vaticanus.

13, 1-53: The discourse in parables is the third great discourse of Jesus in Mt and constitutes the second part of the third book of the gospel. Matthew follows the Marcan outline (Mk 4, 1-35) but has only two of Mark's parables, the five others being from Q and M. In addition to the seven parables, the discourse gives the reason why Jesus uses this type of speech (10-15), declares the blessedness of those who understand his teaching (16-17), explains the parable of the sower (18-23) and of the weeds (36-43), and ends with a concluding statement to the disciples (51-52).

13, 3: *In parables:* the word "parable" (Greek *parabolē*) is used in the LXX to translate the Hebrew *māshāl*, a designation covering a wide variety of literary forms such as axioms, proverbs, similitudes, and allegories. In the New Testament the same breadth of meaning of the word is found, but there it primarily designates stories that are illustrative comparisons between Christian truths and events of everyday life. Sometimes the event has a strange element that is quite different from usual experience (e.g., in v 33, the enormous amount of dough in the parable of the yeast); this is meant to sharpen the curiosity of the hearer. If each detail of such a story is given a figurative meaning, the story is an allegory. Those who maintain a sharp distinction be-

---

CHAPTER 13

The Parable of the Sower. [1] *On that day, Jesus went out of the house and sat down by the sea. [v] [2] Such large crowds gathered around him that he got into a boat and sat down, and the whole crowd stood along the shore. [3] And he spoke to them at length in parables,* saying: "A sower went out to sow.* [4] And as he sowed, some seed fell on the path, and birds came and ate it up. [5] Some fell on rocky ground, where it had little soil. It sprang up at once because the soil was not deep, [6] and when the sun rose it was scorched, and it withered for lack of roots. [7] Some seed fell among thorns, and the thorns grew up and choked it. [8] But some seed fell on rich soil, and produced fruit, a hundred or sixty or thirtyfold. [9] Whoever has ears ought to hear."

The Purpose of Parables. [10] The disciples approached him and said, "Why do you speak to them in parables?" [11] He said to them in reply, "Because knowledge of the mysteries of the kingdom of heaven has been granted to you, but to them it has not been granted.* [12] [w] To anyone who has, more will be given* and he will grow rich; from anyone who has not, even what he

---

tween parable and allegory insist that a parable has only one point of comparison, and that while parables were characteristic of Jesus' teaching, to see allegorical details in them is to introduce meanings that go beyond their original intention and even falsify it. However, to exclude any allegorical elements from a parable is an excessively rigid mode of interpretation, now abandoned by many scholars.

13, 3-8: Since in Palestine sowing often preceded plowing, much of the seed is scattered on ground that is unsuitable. Yet while much is wasted, the seed that falls on good ground bears fruit in extraordinarily large measure. The point of the parable is that, in spite of some failure because of opposition and indifference, the message of Jesus about the coming of the kingdom will have enormous success.

13, 11: Since a parable is figurative speech that demands reflection for understanding, only those who are prepared to explore its meaning can come to know it. To understand is a gift of God, granted to the disciples but not to the crowds. In Semitic fashion, both the disciples' understanding and the crowd's obtuseness are attributed to God. The question of human responsibility for the obtuseness is not dealt with, although it is asserted in v 13. *The mysteries:* as in Lk 8, 10; Mk 4, 11 has "the mystery." The word is used in Dn 2, 18.19.27 and in the Qumran literature (1QpHab 7, 8; 1QS 3, 23; 1QM 3, 9) to designate a divine plan or decree affecting the course of history that can be known only when revealed. *Knowledge of the mysteries of the kingdom of heaven* means recognition that the kingdom has become present in the ministry of Jesus.

13, 12: In the New Testament use of this axiom of practical "wisdom" (see Mt 25, 29; Mk 4, 25; Lk 8, 18; 19, 26), the reference transcends the original level. God gives further understanding to one who accepts the revealed mystery; from the one who does not, he will take it away (note the "theological passive," *more will be given, what he has will be taken away*).

has will be taken away. [13] [x] This is why I speak to them in parables, because 'they look but do not see and hear but do not listen or understand.'* [14] [y] Isaiah's prophecy is fulfilled in them, which says:

'You shall indeed hear but not understand,
you shall indeed look but never see.
[15] Gross is the heart of this people,
they will hardly hear with their ears,
they have closed their eyes,
lest they see with their eyes
and hear with their ears
and understand with their heart and be converted
and I heal them.'

The Privilege of Discipleship.* [16] [z] "But blessed are your eyes, because they see, and your ears, because they hear. [17] Amen, I say to you, many prophets and righteous people longed to see what you see but did not see it, and to hear what you hear but did not hear it.

The Explanation of the Parable of the Sower.* [18] [a] "Hear then the parable of the sower. [19] The seed sown on the path is the one who hears the word of the kingdom without understanding it, and the evil one comes and steals away what was sown in his heart. [20] The seed sown on rocky ground is the one who hears the word and receives it at once with joy. [21] But he has no root and lasts only for a time. When some tribulation or persecution comes because

of the word, he immediately falls away. [22] The seed sown among thorns is the one who hears the word, but then worldly anxiety and the lure of riches choke the word and it bears no fruit. [23] But the seed sown on rich soil is the one who hears the word and understands it, who indeed bears fruit and yields a hundred or sixty or thirtyfold."

The Parable of the Weeds among the Wheat.* [24] He proposed another parable to them. "The kingdom of heaven may be likened to a man who sowed good seed in his field. [25] While everyone was asleep his enemy came and sowed weeds* all through the wheat, and then went off. [26] When the crop grew and bore fruit, the weeds appeared as well. [27] The slaves of the householder came to him and said, 'Master, did you not sow good seed in your field? Where have the weeds come from?' [28] He answered, 'An enemy has done this.' His slaves said to him, 'Do you want us to go and pull them up?' [29] He replied, 'No, if you pull up the weeds you might uproot the wheat along with them. [30] Let them grow together until harvest*; then at harvest time I will say to the harvesters, "First collect the weeds and tie them in bundles for burning; but gather the wheat into my barn." ' " [b]

The Parable of the Mustard Seed.* [31] [c] He proposed another parable to them. "The kingdom of heaven is like a mustard seed that a person took and sowed in a field. [32]

---

x Jn 9, 39.—y 14-15: Is 6, 9-10; Jn 12, 40; Acts 28, 26-27; Rom 11, 8.—z 16-17: Lk 10, 23-24; 1 Pt 1, 10-12.—a 18-23: Mk 4, 13-20; Lk 8, 11-15.—b Mt 3, 12.—c 31-32: Mk 4, 30-32; Lk 13, 18-19.

13, 13: *Because 'they look . . . or understand':* Matthew softens his Marcan source, which states that Jesus speaks in parables so that the crowds may not understand (Mk 4, 12), and makes such speaking a punishment given *because* they have not accepted his previous clear teaching. However, his citation of Is 6, 9-10 in v 14 supports the harsher Marcan view.

13, 16-17: Unlike the unbelieving crowds, the disciples have seen that which the *prophets* and the *righteous* of the Old Testament *longed to see* without having their longing fulfilled.

13, 18-23: See Mk 4, 14-20; Lk 8, 11-15. In this explanation of the parable the emphasis is on the various types of soil on which the seed falls, i.e., on the dispositions with which the preaching of Jesus is received. The second and third types particularly are explained in such a way as to support the view held by many scholars that the explanation derives not from Jesus but from early Christian reflection upon apostasy from the faith that was the consequence of persecution and worldliness respectively. Others, however, hold that the explanation may come basically from Jesus even though it was developed in the light of later Christian experience. The four types of persons envisaged are (1) those

who never accept *the word of the kingdom* (19); (2) those who believe for a while but fall away because of *persecution* (20-21); (3) those who believe, but in whom *the word* is choked by *worldly anxiety* and the seduction of *riches* (22); (4) those who respond to *the word* and produce *fruit* abundantly (23).

13, 24-30: This parable is peculiar to Matthew. The comparison in v 24 does not mean that *the kingdom of heaven may be likened* simply to the person in question but to the situation narrated in the whole story. The refusal of *the householder* to allow his *slaves* to separate *the wheat* from *the weeds* while they are still growing is a warning to the disciples not to attempt to anticipate the final judgment of God by a definitive exclusion of sinners from the kingdom. In its present stage it is composed of the good and the bad. The judgment of God alone will eliminate the sinful. Until then there must be patience and the preaching of repentance.

13, 25: *Weeds:* darnel, a poisonous weed that in its first stage of growth resembles wheat.

13, 30: *Harvest:* a common biblical metaphor for the time of God's judgment; cf Jer 51, 33; Jl 4, 13; Hos 6, 11.

13, 31-33: See Mk 4, 30-32; Lk 13, 18-21. The parables of the mustard seed and the yeast illustrate the same point: the amazing contrast between the small beginnings of the kingdom and its marvelous expansion.

32 *d* It is the smallest of all the seeds, yet when full-grown it is the largest of plants. It becomes a large bush, and the 'birds of the sky come and dwell in its branches.' "*

The Parable of the Yeast. 33 He spoke to them another parable. "The kingdom of heaven is like yeast* that a woman took and mixed with three measures of wheat flour until the whole batch was leavened." *e*

The Use of Parables. 34 *f* All these things Jesus spoke to the crowds in parables. He spoke to them only in parables,* 35 to fulfill what had been said through the prophet:*

"I will open my mouth in parables,
    I will announce what has lain hidden
        from the foundation [of the
        world]." *g*

The Explanation of the Parable of the Weeds. 36 Then, dismissing the crowds,* he went into the house. His disciples approached him and said, "Explain to us the parable of the weeds in the field." 37 *He said in reply, "He who sows good seed is the Son of Man, 38 the field is the world,* the good seed the children of the kingdom. The weeds are the children of the evil one, 39 and the enemy who sows them is the devil. The harvest is the end of the age,* and the harvesters are angels. 40 Just as weeds are collected and burned [up] with fire, so will it be at the end of the age.

41 The Son of Man will send his angels, and they will collect out of his kingdom* all who cause others to sin and all evildoers. 42 *h* They will throw them into the fiery furnace, where there will be wailing and grinding of teeth. 43 *i* Then the righteous will shine like the sun in the kingdom of their Father. Whoever has ears ought to hear.*

More Parables.* 44 *j* "The kingdom of heaven is like a treasure buried in a field,* which a person finds and hides again, and out of joy goes and sells all that he has and buys that field. 45 Again, the kingdom of heaven is like a merchant searching for fine pearls. 46 When he finds a pearl of great price, he goes and sells all that he has and buys it. 47 Again, the kingdom of heaven is like a net thrown into the sea, which collects fish of every kind. 48 When it is full they haul it ashore and sit down to put what is good into buckets. What is bad they throw away. 49 Thus it will be at the end of the age. The angels will go out and separate the wicked from the righteous 50 and throw them into the fiery furnace, where there will be wailing and grinding of teeth.

Treasures New and Old. 51 "Do you understand* all these things?" They an-

Mt

---

d Ez 17, 23; 31, 6; Dn 4, 7-9.17-19.—e Lk 13, 20-21.—f 34-35: Mk 4, 33-34.—g Ps 78, 2.—h Mt 8, 12; Rv 21, 8.—i Dn 12, 3.—j 44-45: Prv 2, 4; 4, 7.

13, 32: See Dn 4, 7-9.17-19, where the birds nesting in the tree represent the people of Nebuchadnezzar's kingdom. See also Ez 17, 23 and 31, 6.

13, 33: Except in this Q parable and in Mt 16, 12, *yeast* (or "leaven") is, in New Testament usage, a symbol of corruption (see Mt 16, 6.11-12; Mk 8, 15; Lk 12, 1; 1 Cor 5, 6-8; Gal 5, 9). *Three measures:* an enormous amount, enough to feed a hundred people. The exaggeration of this element of the parable points to the greatness of the kingdom's effect.

13, 34: *Only in parables:* see vv 10-15.

13, 35: *The prophet:* some textual witnesses read "Isaiah the prophet." The quotation is actually from Ps 78, 2; the first line corresponds to the LXX text of the psalm. The psalm's title ascribes it to Asaph, the founder of one of the guilds of temple musicians. He is called "the prophet" (NAB "the seer") in 2 Chr 29, 30, but it is doubtful that Matthew adverted to that; for him, any Old Testament text that could be seen as fulfilled in Jesus was prophetic.

13, 36: *Dismissing the crowds:* the return of Jesus to the house marks a break with the crowds, who represent unbelieving Israel. From now on his attention is directed more and more to his disciples and to their instruction. The rest of the discourse is addressed to them alone.

13, 37-43: In the explanation of the parable of the weeds emphasis lies on the fearful end of the wicked, whereas the parable itself concentrates on patience with them until judgment time.

13, 38: *The field is the world:* this presupposes the resurrection of Jesus and the granting to him of "all power in heaven and on earth" (Mt 28, 18).

13, 39: *The end of the age:* this phrase is found only in Mt (13, 40.49; 24, 3; 28, 20).

13, 41: *His kingdom:* the *kingdom* of *the Son of Man* is distinguished from that of the Father (43); see 1 Cor 15, 24-25. The church is the place where Jesus' kingdom is manifested, but his royal authority embraces the entire world; see the note on Mt 13, 38.

13, 43: See Dn 12, 3.

13, 44-50: The first two of the last three parables of the discourse have the same point. The *person* who *finds* a buried *treasure* and the *merchant* who finds a *pearl of great price* sell *all* that they have to acquire these finds; similarly, the one who understands the supreme value of the kingdom gives up whatever he must to obtain it. The *joy* with which this is done is made explicit in the first parable, but it may be presumed in the second also. The concluding parable of the fishnet resembles the explanation of the parable of the weeds with its stress upon the final exclusion of evil persons from the kingdom.

13, 44: In the unsettled conditions of Palestine in Jesus' time, it was not unusual to guard valuables by burying them in the ground.

13, 51: Matthew typically speaks of the understanding of the disciples.

swered, "Yes." [52] And he replied, "Then every scribe who has been instructed in the kingdom of heaven is like the head of a household who brings from his storeroom both the new and the old."* [53] When Jesus finished these parables, he went away from there.

V. JESUS, THE KINGDOM, AND THE CHURCH

The Rejection at Nazareth. [54] * He came to his native place and taught the people in their synagogue.[k] They were astonished* and said, "Where did this man get such wisdom and mighty deeds?[l] [55] Is he not the carpenter's son? Is not his mother named Mary and his brothers James, Joseph, Simon, and Judas?[m] [56] Are not his sisters all with us? Where did this man get all this?" [57] And they took offense at him. But Jesus said to them, "A prophet is not without honor except in his native place and in his own house."[n] [58] And he did not work many mighty deeds there because of their lack of faith.

CHAPTER 14

Herod's Opinion of Jesus. [1] * [o] At that time Herod the tetrarch* [p] heard of the reputation of Jesus[q] [2] and said to his servants, "This man is John the Baptist. He

has been raised from the dead; that is why mighty powers are at work in him."

The Death of John the Baptist. [3] [r] Now Herod had arrested John, bound [him], and put him in prison on account of Herodias,* the wife of his brother Philip, [4] for John had said to him, "It is not lawful for you to have her."[s] [5] Although* he wanted to kill him, he feared the people, for they regarded him as a prophet.[t] [6] But at a birthday celebration for Herod, the daughter of Herodias performed a dance before the guests and delighted Herod [7] so much that he swore to give her whatever she might ask for. [8] Prompted by her mother, she said, "Give me here on a platter the head of John the Baptist." [9] The king was distressed, but because of his oaths and the guests who were present, he ordered that it be given, [10] and he had John beheaded in the prison. [11] His head was brought in on a platter and given to the girl, who took it to her mother. [12] His disciples came and took away the corpse and buried him; and they went and told Jesus.

The Return of the Twelve and the Feeding of the Five Thousand. * [13] [u] When Jesus heard of it, he withdrew in a boat to a deserted place by himself. The crowds heard of this and followed him on foot from their

---

k 54-58: Mk 6, 1-6; Lk 4, 16-30.—l Mt 2, 23; Jn 1, 46; 7, 15.—m Mt 12, 46; 27, 56; Jn 6, 42.—n Jn 4, 44.—o 1-12: Mk 6, 14-29.—p Lk 3, 1.—q 1-2: Lk 9, 7-9.—r 3-4: Lk 3, 19-20.—s Lv 18, 16; 20, 21.—t Mt 21, 26.—u 13-21: Mt 15, 32-38; Mk 6, 32-44; Lk 9, 10-17; Jn 6, 1-13.

13, 52: Since Matthew tends to identify the disciples and the Twelve (see the note on Mt 10, 1), this saying about the Christian *scribe* cannot be taken as applicable to all who accept the message of Jesus. While the Twelve are in many ways representative of all who believe in him, they are also distinguished from them in certain respects. The church of Matthew has leaders among whom are a group designated as "scribes" (Mt 23, 34). Like the scribes of Israel, they are teachers. It is the Twelve and these their later counterparts to whom this verse applies. The *scribe . . . instructed in the kingdom of heaven* knows both the teaching of Jesus (*the new*) and the law and prophets (*the old*) and provides in his own teaching *both the new and the old* as interpreted and fulfilled by *the new*. On the translation *head of a household* (for the same Greek word translated *householder* in v 27), see the note on Mt 24, 45-51.

13, 54—17, 27: This section is the narrative part of the fourth book of the gospel.

13, 54-58: After the Sermon on the Mount the crowds are in admiring astonishment at Jesus' teaching (Mt 7, 28); here the astonishment is of those who take *offense at him.* Familiarity with his background and family leads them to regard him as pretentious. Matthew modifies his Marcan source (Mk 6, 1-6). Jesus is not the carpenter but *the carpenter's son* (55), "and among his own kin" is omitted (57), *he did not work many mighty deeds*

in face of such unbelief (58) rather than the Marcan ". . . he was not able to perform any mighty deed there" (Mk 6, 5), and there is no mention of his townspeople's lack of faith.

14, 1-12: The murder of the Baptist by Herod Antipas prefigures the death of Jesus (see Mt 17, 12). The Marcan source (Mk 6, 14-29) is much reduced and in some points changed. In Mk Herod reveres John as a holy man and the desire to kill him is attributed to Herodias (Mk 6, 19.20), whereas here that desire is Herod's from the beginning (5).

14, 1: *Herod the tetrarch:* Herod Antipas, son of Herod the Great. When the latter died, his territory was divided among three of his surviving sons, Archelaus who received half of it (Mt 2, 23), Herod Antipas who became ruler of Galilee and Perea, and Philip who became ruler of northern Transjordan. Since he received a quarter of his father's domain, Antipas is accurately designated *tetrarch* ("ruler of a fourth [part]"), although in v 9 Matthew repeats the "king" of his Marcan source (Mk 6, 26).

14, 3: Herodias was not the wife of Herod's half-brother Philip but of another half-brother, Herod Boethus. The union was prohibited by Lv 18, 16; 20, 21. According to Josephus (*Antiquities* 18, 5, 2 §§116-19), Herod imprisoned then executed John because he feared that the Baptist's influence over the people might enable him to lead a rebellion.

14, 13-21: The feeding of the five thousand is the only miracle of Jesus that is recounted in all four gospels. The principal reason for that may be that it was seen as anticipating the Eucharist and the final banquet in the kingdom (Mt 8, 11; 26, 29), but it looks not only forward but backward, to the feeding of Israel with manna in the desert at the time of the Exodus (Ex 16), a miracle that in some contemporary Jewish expectation would be repeated in the messianic age (2 Baruch 29, 8). It may also be meant to recall Elisha's feeding a hundred men with small provisions (2 Kgs 4, 42-44).

towns. [14]When he disembarked and saw the vast crowd, his heart was moved with pity for them, and he cured their sick. [15]When it was evening, the disciples approached him and said, "This is a deserted place and it is already late; dismiss the crowds so that they can go to the villages and buy food for themselves." [16][Jesus] said to them, "There is no need for them to go away; give them some food yourselves." [17]But they said to him, "Five loaves and two fish are all we have here." [18]Then he said, "Bring them here to me," [19]and he ordered the crowds to sit down on the grass. Taking* the five loaves and the two fish, and looking up to heaven, he said the blessing, broke the loaves, and gave them to the disciples, who in turn gave them to the crowds. [20]They all ate and were satisfied, and they picked up the fragments left over*—twelve wicker baskets full. [21]Those who ate were about five thousand men, not counting women and children.

The Walking on the Water.* [22] *v* Then he made the disciples get into the boat and precede him to the other side, while he dismissed the crowds. [23]After doing so, he went up on the mountain by himself to pray. When it was evening he was there alone. *w* [24]Meanwhile the boat, already a few miles offshore, was being tossed about by the waves, for the wind was against it. [25]During the fourth watch of the night,* he came toward them, walking on the sea. [26]When the disciples saw him walking on the sea they were terrified. "It is a ghost," they said, and they cried out in fear. [27]At once [Jesus] spoke to them, "Take courage, it is I;* do not be afraid." [28]Peter said to him in reply, "Lord, if it is you, command me to come to you on the water." [29]He said, "Come." Peter got out of the boat and began to walk on the water toward Jesus. [30] *x* But when he saw how [strong] the wind was he became frightened; and, beginning to sink, he cried out, "Lord, save me!" [31]Immediately Jesus stretched out his hand and caught him, and said to him, "O you of little faith,* why did you doubt?" [32]After they got into the boat, the wind died down. [33]*y* Those who were in the boat did him homage, saying, "Truly, you are the Son of God."*

The Healings at Gennesaret. [34] *z* After making the crossing, they came to land at Gennesaret. [35]When the men of that place recognized him, they sent word to all the surrounding country. People brought to him all those who were sick [36]and begged him that they might touch only the tassel on his cloak, and as many as touched it were healed. *a*

CHAPTER 15

The Tradition of the Elders.* [1] *b* Then Pharisees and scribes came to Jesus from Jerusalem and said, [2]"Why do your disciples break the tradition of the elders?* They do not wash [their] hands when they

---

v 22-33: Mk 6, 45-52; Jn 6, 16-21.—w Mk 1, 35; Lk 5, 16; 6, 12.—x 30-31: Mt 8, 25-26.—y Mt 16, 16.—z 34-36: Mk 6, 53-56.—a Mt 9, 20-22.—b 1-20: Mk 7, 1-23.

14, 19: The *taking*, saying the blessing, breaking, and giving to the disciples correspond to the actions of Jesus over the bread at the Last Supper (Mt 26, 26). Since they were usual at any Jewish meal, that correspondence does not necessarily indicate a eucharistic reference here. Matthew's silence about Jesus' dividing the fish among the people (Mk 6, 41) is perhaps more significant in that regard.

14, 20: *The fragments left over:* as in Elisha's miracle, food was *left over* after all had been fed. The word *fragments* (Greek *klasmata*) is used, in the singular, of the broken bread of the Eucharist in *Didache* 9, 3-4.

14, 22-33: The disciples, laboring against the turbulent sea, are saved by Jesus. For his power over the waters, see the note on Mt 8, 26. Here that power is expressed also by his *walking on the sea* (25; cf Ps 77, 20; Jb 9, 8). Matthew has inserted into the Marcan story (Mk 6, 45-52) material that belongs to his special traditions on Peter (28-31).

14, 25: *The fourth watch of the night:* between 3 a.m. and 6 a.m. The Romans divided the twelve hours between 6 p.m. and 6 a.m. into four equal parts called "watches."

14, 27: *It is I:* see the note on Mk 6, 50.

14, 31: *You of little faith:* see the note on Mt 6, 30. *Why did you doubt?:* the verb is peculiar to Matthew and occurs elsewhere only in Mt 28, 17.

14, 33: This confession is in striking contrast to the Marcan parallel (Mk 6, 51) where the disciples are "completely astounded."

15, 1-20: This dispute begins with the question of the Pharisees and scribes why Jesus' disciples are breaking *the tradition of the elders* about washing one's hands before eating (2). Jesus' counterquestion accuses his opponents of breaking *the commandment of God for the sake of* their tradition (3) and illustrates this by their interpretation of the commandment of the Decalogue concerning parents (4-6). Denouncing them as hypocrites, he applies to them a derogatory prophecy of Isaiah (7-8). Then with a wider audience (*the crowd*, 10) he goes beyond the violation of tradition with which the dispute has started. The parable (11) is an attack on the Mosaic law concerning clean and unclean foods, similar to those antitheses that abrogate the law (Mt 5, 31-32.33-34.38-39). After a warning to his disciples not to follow the moral guidance of the Pharisees (13-14), he explains the *parable* (15) to them, saying that defilement comes not from what *enters the mouth* (17) but from the evil thoughts and deeds that rise from within, *from the heart* (18-20). The last verse returns to the starting point of the dispute (eating *with unwashed hands*). Because of Matthew's omission of Mk 7, 19b, some scholars think that Matthew has weakened the Marcan repudiation of the Mosaic food laws. But that half verse is ambiguous in the Greek, which may be the reason for its omission here.

15, 2: *The tradition of the elders:* see the note on Mk 7, 5. The purpose of the handwashing was to remove defilement caused by contact with what was ritually unclean.

eat a meal."[c] [3] He said to them in reply, "And why do you break the commandment of God* for the sake of your tradition? [4] For God said, 'Honor your father and your mother,' and 'Whoever curses father or mother shall die.'[d] [5] But you say, 'Whoever says to father or mother, "Any support you might have had from me is dedicated to God,"* [6] need not honor his father.' You have nullified the word of God for the sake of your tradition. [7] Hypocrites, well did Isaiah prophesy about you when he said:

[8]   'This people honors me with their lips,*
    but their hearts are far from me;[e]
[9]   in vain do they worship me,
    teaching as doctrines human precepts.' "[f]

[10] He summoned the crowd and said to them, "Hear and understand.[g] [11] It is not what enters one's mouth that defiles that person; but what comes out of the mouth is what defiles one." [12] Then his disciples approached and said to him, "Do you know that the Pharisees took offense when they heard what you said?" [13] He said in reply,* "Every plant that my heavenly Father has not planted will be uprooted. [14] Let them alone; they are blind guides [of the blind]. If a blind person leads a blind person, both will fall into a pit."[h] [15] Then Peter* said to him in reply, "Explain [this] parable to us." [16] He said to them, "Are even you still without understanding? [17] Do you not realize that everything that enters the mouth passes into the stomach and is expelled into the latrine? [18] But the things that come out of the mouth come from the heart, and they defile.[i] [19] For from the heart come evil thoughts, murder, adultery, unchastity, theft, false witness, blasphemy.* [20] These are what defile a person, but to eat with unwashed hands does not defile."

The Canaanite Woman's Faith.* [21][j] Then Jesus went from that place and withdrew to the region of Tyre and Sidon. [22] And behold, a Canaanite woman of that district came and called out, "Have pity on me, Lord, Son of David! My daughter is tormented by a demon." [23] But he did not say a word in answer to her. His disciples came and asked him, "Send her away, for she keeps calling out after us." [24] He said in reply, "I was sent only to the lost sheep of the house of Israel."* [25] But the woman

came and did him homage, saying, "Lord, help me."[k] [26] He said in reply, "It is not right to take the food of the children* and throw it to the dogs." [27] She said, "Please, Lord, for even the dogs eat the scraps that fall from the table of their masters." [28] Then Jesus said to her in reply, "O woman, great is your faith!* Let it be done for you as you wish." And her daughter was healed from that hour.[l]

The Healing of Many People. [29] Moving on from there Jesus walked by the Sea of Galilee, went up on the mountain, and sat down there. [30] Great crowds came to him, having with them the lame, the blind, the deformed, the mute, and many others. They placed them at his feet, and he cured them.[m] [31] The crowds were amazed when they saw the mute speaking, the deformed made whole, the lame walking, and the blind able to see, and they glorified the God of Israel.

The Feeding of the Four Thousand.* [32][n] Jesus summoned his disciples and said, "My heart is moved with pity for the

---

c Lk 11, 38.—d Ex 20, 12; 21, 17; Lv 20, 9; Dt 5, 16; Prv 20, 20.—e Is 29, 13 LXX.—f Col 2, 23.—g Mk 7, 14.—h Mt 23, 16.19.24; Lk 6, 39; Jn 9, 40.—i Mt 12, 34.—j 21-28: Mk 7, 24-30.—k Mt 10, 6.—l Mt 8, 10.—m Is 35, 5-6.—n 32-39: Mk 8, 1-10.

15, 3-4: For the commandment see Ex 20, 12 (// Dt 5, 16); 21, 17. The honoring of one's parents had to do with supporting them in their needs.

15, 5: See the note on Mk 7, 11.

15, 8: The text of Is 29, 13 is quoted approximately according to the Septuagint.

15, 13-14: Jesus leads his disciples away from the teaching authority of the Pharisees.

15, 15: Matthew specifies *Peter* as the questioner, unlike Mk 7, 17. Given his tendency to present the disciples as more understanding than in his Marcan source, it is noteworthy that here he retains the Marcan rebuke, although in a slightly milder form. This may be due to his wish to correct the Jewish Christians within his church who still held to the food laws and thus separated themselves from Gentile Christians who did not observe them.

15, 19: The Marcan list of thirteen things that defile (Mk 7, 21-22) is here reduced to seven that partially cover the content of the Decalogue.

15, 21-28: See the note on Mt 8, 5-13.

15, 24: See the note on Mt 10, 5-6.

15, 26: *The children:* the people of Israel. *Dogs:* see the note on Mt 7, 6.

15, 28: As in the case of the cure of the centurion's servant (Mt 8, 10), Matthew ascribes Jesus' granting the request to the woman's *great faith,* a point not made equally explicit in the Marcan parallel (Mk 7, 24-30).

15, 32-39: Most probably this story is a doublet of that of the feeding of the five thousand (Mt 14, 13-21). It differs from it notably only in that Jesus takes the initiative, not the disciples (32), and in the numbers: the crowd has been with Jesus *three days* (32), *seven loaves* are multiplied (36), *seven baskets* of *fragments* remain after the feeding (37), and *four thousand* men are fed (38).

crowd, for they have been with me now for three days and have nothing to eat. I do not want to send them away hungry, for fear they may collapse on the way." ³³The disciples said to him, "Where could we ever get enough bread in this deserted place to satisfy such a crowd?" ³⁴Jesus said to them, "How many loaves do you have?" "Seven," they replied, "and a few fish." ³⁵He ordered the crowd to sit down on the ground. ³⁶Then he took the seven loaves and the fish, gave thanks,* broke the loaves, and gave them to the disciples, who in turn gave them to the crowds. ³⁷They all ate and were satisfied. They picked up the fragments left over—seven baskets full.⁰ ³⁸Those who ate were four thousand men, not counting women and children. ³⁹And when he had dismissed the crowds, he got into the boat and came to the district of Magadan.

CHAPTER 16

The Demand for a Sign. ¹ ᵖThe Pharisees and Sadducees came and, to test him, asked him to show them a sign from heaven.* ²He said to them in reply, "[In the evening you say, 'Tomorrow will be fair, for the sky is red'; ³ �q and, in the

morning, 'Today will be stormy, for the sky is red and threatening.' You know how to judge the appearance of the sky, but you cannot judge the signs of the times.]* ⁴An evil and unfaithful generation seeks a sign, but no sign will be given it except the sign of Jonah."* Then he left them and went away.ʳ

The Leaven of the Pharisees and Sadducees.* ⁵ˢIn coming to the other side of the sea, the disciples had forgotten to bring bread. ⁶ᵗJesus said to them, "Look out, and beware of the leaven* of the Pharisees and Sadducees." ⁷ * They concluded among themselves, saying, "It is because we have brought no bread." ⁸When Jesus became aware of this he said, "You of little faith, why do you conclude among yourselves that it is because you have no bread? ⁹Do you not yet understand, and do you not remember the five loaves for the five thousand, and how many wicker baskets you took up?ᵘ ¹⁰Or the seven loaves for the four thousand, and how many baskets you took up?ᵛ ¹¹How do you not comprehend that I was not speaking to you about bread? Beware of the leaven of the Pharisees and Sadducees." ¹²Then they understood* that he was not telling them to beware of the leaven of bread, but of the teaching of the Pharisees and Sadducees.

Peter's Confession about Jesus.* ¹³ʷWhen Jesus went into the region of Caesarea Philippi* he asked his disciples,

Mt

---

o Mt 16, 10.—p 1-10: Mk 8, 11-21.—q Lk 12, 54-56.—r Mt 12, 39; Jon 2, 1.—s 5-12: Mk 8, 14-21.—t Lk 12, 1.—u Mt 14, 17-21; Jn 6, 9.—v Mt 15, 34-38.—w 13-16: Mk 8, 27-29; Lk 9, 18-20.

15, 36: *Gave thanks:* see Mt 14, 19, "said the blessing." There is no difference in meaning. The thanksgiving was a blessing of God for his benefits.

16, 1: *A sign from heaven:* see the note on Mt 12, 38-42.

16, 2-3: The answer of Jesus in these verses is omitted in many important textual witnesses, and it is very uncertain that it is an original part of this gospel. It resembles Lk 12, 54-56 and may have been inserted from there. It rebukes the Pharisees and Sadducees who are able to read indications of coming weather but not the indications of the coming kingdom in the signs that Jesus does offer, his mighty deeds and teaching.

16, 4: See the notes on Mt 12, 39.40.

16, 5-12: Jesus' warning his disciples against *the teaching of the Pharisees and Sadducees* comes immediately before his promise to confer on Peter the authority to bind and to loose on earth (19), an authority that will be confirmed in heaven. Such authority most probably has to do, at least in part, with teaching. The rejection of the teaching authority of the Pharisees (see also Mt 12, 12-14) prepares for a new one derived from Jesus.

16, 6: *Leaven:* see the note on Mt 13, 33. *Sadducees:* Matthew's Marcan source speaks rather of "the leaven of Herod" (Mk 8, 15).

16, 7-11: The disciples, men *of little faith,* misunderstand Jesus' metaphorical use of *leaven,* forgetting that, as the feeding of the crowds shows, he is not at a loss to provide them with bread.

16, 12: After his rebuke, the disciples understand that by *leaven* he meant the corrupting influence of *the teaching of the Pharisees and Sadducees.* The evangelist probably understands this *teaching* as common to both groups. Since at the time of Jesus' ministry the two differed widely on points of teaching, e.g., the resurrection of the dead, and at the time of the evangelist the Sadducee party was no longer a force in Judaism, the supposed common *teaching* fits neither period. The disciples' eventual understanding of Jesus' warning contrasts with their continuing obtuseness in the Marcan parallel (Mk 8, 14-21).

16, 13-20: The Marcan confession of Jesus as Messiah, made by Peter as spokesman for the other disciples (Mk 8, 27-29; cf also Lk 9, 18-20), is modified significantly here. The confession is of Jesus both as *Messiah* and as *Son of the living God* (16). Jesus' response, drawn principally from material peculiar to Matthew, attributes the confession to a divine revelation granted to Peter alone (17) and makes him the *rock* on which Jesus *will build* his *church* (18) and the disciple whose authority in the church *on earth* will be confirmed *in heaven,* i.e., by God (19).

16, 13: *Caesarea Philippi:* situated about twenty miles north of the Sea of Galilee in the territory ruled by Philip, a son of Herod the Great, tetrarch from 4 B.C. until his death in A.D. 34 (see the note on Mt 14, 1). He rebuilt the town of Paneas, naming it *Caesarea* in honor of the emperor, and *Philippi* ("of Philip") to distinguish it from the seaport in Samaria that was also called Caesarea. *Who do people say that the Son of Man is?:* although the question differs from the Marcan parallel (Mk 8, 27: "Who . . . that I am?"), the meaning is the same, for Jesus here refers to himself as *the Son of Man* (cf 15).

"Who do people say that the Son of Man is?" [14] They replied, "Some say John the Baptist,* others Elijah, still others Jeremiah or one of the prophets." [x] [15] He said to them, "But who do you say that I am?" [16] [y] Simon Peter said in reply, "You are the Messiah, the Son of the living God."* [17] Jesus said to him in reply, "Blessed are you, Simon son of Jonah. For flesh and blood* has not revealed this to you, but my heavenly Father. [18] And so I say to you, you are Peter, and upon this rock I will build my church,* and the gates of the netherworld shall not prevail against it. [z] [19] I will give you the keys to the kingdom of heaven.* Whatever you bind on earth shall be bound in heaven; and whatever you loose on earth shall be loosed in heaven." [a] [20] [b] Then he strictly ordered his disciples to tell no one that he was the Messiah.*

The First Prediction of the Passion.* [21] [c] From that time on, Jesus began to show his disciples that he* must go to Jerusalem and suffer greatly from the elders, the chief priests, and the scribes, and be killed and on the third day be raised. [d] [22] * Then Peter took him aside and began to rebuke him, "God forbid, Lord! No such thing shall ever happen to you." [23] He turned and said to Peter, "Get behind me, Satan! You are an obstacle to me. You are thinking not as God does, but as human beings do." [e]

---

x Mt 14, 2.—y Jn 6, 69.—z Jn 1, 42.—a Is 22, 22; Rv 3, 7.—b Mk 8, 30; Lk 9, 21.—c 21-28: Mk 8, 31—9, 1; Lk 9, 22-27.—d Mt 17, 22-23; 20, 17-19.—e Mt 4, 10.

16, 14: *John the Baptist:* see Mt 14, 2. *Elijah:* cf Mal 3, 23-24; Sir 48, 10; and see the note on Mt 3, 4. *Jeremiah:* an addition of Matthew to the Marcan source.

16, 16: *The Son of the living God:* see Mt 2, 15; 3, 17. The addition of this exalted title to the Marcan confession eliminates whatever ambiguity was attached to the title Messiah. This, among other things, supports the view proposed by many scholars that Matthew has here combined his source's confession with a post-resurrectional confession of faith in Jesus as *Son of the living God* that belonged to the appearance of the risen Jesus to Peter; cf 1 Cor 15, 5; Lk 24, 34.

16, 17: *Flesh and blood:* a Semitic expression for human beings, especially in their weakness. *Has not revealed this . . . but my heavenly Father:* that Peter's faith is spoken of as coming not through human means but through a revelation from God is similar to Paul's description of his recognition of who Jesus was; see Gal 1, 15-16, ". . . when he [God] . . . was pleased to reveal his Son to me. . . ."

16, 18: *You are Peter, and upon this rock I will build my church:* the Aramaic word *kēpā'* meaning *rock* and transliterated into Greek as *Kēphas* is the name by which Peter is called in the Pauline letters (1 Cor 1, 12; 3, 22; 9, 5; 15, 4; Gal 1, 18; 2, 9.11.14) except in Gal 2, 7-8 ("Peter"). It is translated as *Petros* ("Peter") in Jn 1, 42. The presumed original Aramaic of Jesus' statement would have been, in English, "You are the Rock *(Kēpā')* and upon this rock *(kēpā')* I will build my church." The Greek text probably means the same, for the difference in gender between the masculine noun *petros,* the disciple's new name, and the feminine noun *petra* (rock) may be due simply to the unsuitability of using a feminine noun as the proper name of a male. Although the two words were generally used with slightly different nuances, they were also used interchangeably with the same meaning, "rock." *Church:* this word (Greek *ekklēsia)* occurs in the gospels only here and in Mt 18, 17 (twice). There are several possibilities for an Aramaic original. Jesus' *church* means the community that he *will* gather and that, like a building, will have Peter as its solid foundation. That function of Peter consists in his being witness to Jesus as *the Messiah, the Son of the living God. The gates of the netherworld shall not prevail against it:* the netherworld (Greek *Hadēs,* the abode of the dead) is conceived of as a walled city whose *gates* will not close in upon the church of Jesus, i.e., it will not be overcome by the power of death.

16, 19: *The keys to the kingdom of heaven:* the image of *the keys* is probably drawn from Is 22, 15-25, where Eliakim, who succeeds Shebnah as master of the palace, is given "the key

of the house of David," which he authoritatively "opens" and "shuts" (Is 22, 22). *Whatever you bind . . . loosed in heaven:* there are many instances in rabbinic literature of the binding-loosing imagery. Of the several meanings given there to the metaphor, two are of special importance here: the giving of authoritative teaching, and the lifting or imposing of the ban of excommunication. It is disputed whether the image of *the keys* and that of binding and loosing are different metaphors meaning the same thing. In any case, the promise of the keys is given to Peter alone. In Mt 18, 18 all the disciples are given the power of binding and loosing, but the context of that verse suggests that there the power of excommunication alone is intended. That *the keys* are those to *the kingdom of heaven* and that Peter's exercise of authority in the church *on earth* will be confirmed *in heaven* show an intimate connection between, but not an identification of, the church and *the kingdom of heaven.*

16, 20: Cf Mk 8, 30. Matthew makes explicit that the prohibition has to do with speaking of Jesus as *the Messiah;* see the note on Mk 8, 27-30.

16, 21-23: This first prediction of the passion follows Mk 8, 31-33 in the main and serves as a corrective to an understanding of Jesus' messiahship as solely one of glory and triumph. By his addition of *from that time on* (21) Matthew has emphasized that Jesus' revelation of his coming suffering and death marks a new phase of the gospel. Neither this nor the two later passion predictions (Mt 17, 22-23; 20, 17-19) can be taken as sayings that, as they stand, go back to Jesus himself. However, it is probable that he foresaw that his mission would entail suffering and perhaps death, but was confident that he would ultimately be vindicated by God (see Mt 26, 29).

16, 21: *He:* the Marcan parallel (Mk 8, 31) has "the Son of Man." Since Matthew has already designated Jesus by that title (13), its omission here is not significant. The Matthean prediction is equally about the sufferings of the Son of Man. *Must:* this necessity is part of the tradition of all the synoptics; cf Mk 8, 31; Lk 9, 21. *The elders, the chief priests, and the scribes:* see the note on Mk 8, 31. *On the third day:* so also Lk 9, 22, against the Marcan "after three days" (Mk 8, 31). Matthew's formulation is, in the Greek, almost identical with the pre-Pauline fragment of the kerygma in 1 Cor 15, 4, and also with Hos 6, 2, which many take to be the Old Testament background to the confession that Jesus was raised *on the third day.* Josephus uses "after three days" and "on the third day" interchangeably (*Antiquities* 7, 11, 6 §§280-81; 8, 8, 1-2 §§214, 218) and there is probably no difference in meaning between the two phrases.

16, 22-23: Peter's refusal to accept Jesus' predicted suffering and death is seen as a satanic attempt to deflect Jesus from his God-appointed course, and the disciple is addressed in terms that recall Jesus' dismissal of the devil in the temptation account (Mt 4, 10: "Get away, Satan!"). Peter's satanic purpose is emphasized by Matthew's addition to the Marcan source of the words *You are an obstacle to me.*

The Conditions of Discipleship.* 24 Then Jesus said to his disciples, "Whoever wishes to come after me must deny himself,* take up his cross, and follow me./ 25 For whoever wishes to save his life will lose it,g but whoever loses his life for my sake will find it.* 26 What profit would there be for one to gain the whole world and forfeit his life? Or what can one give in exchange for his life? 27 h For the Son of Man will come with his angels in his Father's glory, and then he will repay everyone according to his conduct.* 28 Amen, I say to you, there are some standing here who will not taste death until they see the Son of Man coming in his kingdom."*

CHAPTER 17

The Transfiguration of Jesus.* 1 i After six days Jesus took Peter, James, and John his brother, and led them up a high mountain by themselves.* 2 And he was transfigured before them; his face shone like the sun* and his clothes became white as light./ 3 And behold, Moses and Elijah appeared to them, conversing with him.* 4 Then Peter said to Jesus in reply, "Lord, it is good that we are here. If you wish, I will make three tents* here, one for you, one for Moses, and one for Elijah." 5 k While he was still speaking, behold, a bright cloud cast a shadow over them,* then from the cloud came a voice that said, "This is my beloved Son, with whom I am well pleased; listen to him." 6 *When the disciples heard this, they fell prostrate and were very much afraid. 7 But Jesus came and touched them, saying, "Rise, and do not be afraid." 8 And when the disciples raised their eyes, they saw no one else but Jesus alone.

The Coming of Elijah.* 9 l As they were coming down from the mountain, Jesus charged them, "Do not tell the vision* to anyone until the Son of Man has been raised from the dead." 10 m Then the disciples asked him, "Why do the scribes say that Elijah must come first?"* 11 He said in reply,* "Elijah will indeed come and re-

Mt

---

f Lk 14, 27.—g Lk 17, 33; Jn 12, 25.—h Mt 25, 31-33; Jb 34, 11; Ps 62, 13; Jer 17, 10; 2 Thes 1, 7-8.—i 1-8: Mk 9, 2-8; Lk 9, 28-36.—j Mt 28, 3; Dn 7, 9; 10, 6; Rv 4, 4; 7, 9; 19, 14.—k Mt 3, 17; Dt 18, 15; 2 Pt 1, 17.—l 9-13: Mk 9, 9-13.—m Mal 3, 23-24.

16, 24-28: A readiness to follow Jesus even to giving up one's life for him is the condition for true discipleship; this will be repaid by him at the final judgment.

16, 24: *Deny himself:* to deny someone is to disown him (see Mt 10, 33; 26, 34-35) and to deny oneself is to disown oneself as the center of one's existence.

16, 25: See the notes on Mt 10, 38.39.

16, 27: The parousia and final judgment are described in Mt 25, 31 in terms almost identical with these.

16, 28: *Coming in his kingdom:* since the *kingdom* of the *Son of Man* has been described as "the world" and Jesus' sovereignty precedes his final coming in glory (Mt 13, 38.41), the *coming* in this verse is not the parousia as in the preceding but the manifestation of Jesus' rule after his resurrection; see the notes on Mt 13, 38.41.

17, 1-8: The account of the transfiguration confirms that Jesus is the *Son* of God (5) and points to fulfillment of the prediction that he will come *in his Father's glory* at the end of the age (Mt 16, 27). It has been explained by some as a resurrection appearance retrojected into the time of Jesus' ministry, but that is not probable since the account lacks many of the usual elements of the resurrection-appearance narratives. It draws upon motifs from the Old Testament and noncanonical Jewish apocalyptic literature that express the presence of the heavenly and the divine, e.g., brilliant light, white garments, and the overshadowing cloud.

17, 1: These three disciples are also taken apart from the others by Jesus in Gethsemane (Mt 26, 37). *A high mountain:* this has been identified with Tabor or Hermon, but probably no specific mountain was intended by the evangelist or by his Marcan source (Mk 9, 2). Its meaning is theological rather than geographical, possibly recalling the revelation to Moses on Mount Sinai (Ex 24, 12-18) and to Elijah at the same place (1 Kgs 19, 8-18; Horeb= Sinai).

17, 2: *His face shone like the sun:* this is a Matthean addition; cf Dn 10, 6. *His clothes became white as light:* cf Dn 7, 9, where the clothing of God appears "snow bright." For the *white* garments of other heavenly beings, see Rv 4, 4; 7, 9; 19, 14.

17, 3: See the note on Mk 9, 5.

17, 4: *Three tents:* the booths in which the Israelites lived during the feast of Tabernacles (cf Jn 7, 2) were meant to recall their ancestors' dwelling in booths during the journey from Egypt to the promised land (Lv 23, 39-42). The same Greek word, *skēnē*, here translated *tents*, is used in the LXX for the booths of that feast, and some scholars have suggested that there is an allusion here to that liturgical custom.

17, 5: *Cloud cast a shadow over them:* see the note on Mk 9, 7. *This is my beloved Son . . . listen to him:* cf Mt 3, 17. The voice repeats the baptismal proclamation about Jesus, with the addition of the command *listen to him.* The latter is a reference to Dt 18, 15 in which the Israelites are commanded to *listen* to the prophet like Moses whom God will raise up for them. The command to *listen* to Jesus is general, but in this context it probably applies particularly to the preceding predictions of his passion and resurrection (Mt 16, 21) and of his coming (Mt 16, 27.28).

17, 6-7: A Matthean addition; cf Dn 10, 9-10.18-19.

17, 9-13: In response to the disciples' question about the expected return of Elijah, Jesus interprets the mission of the Baptist as the fulfillment of that expectation. But that was not suspected by those who opposed and finally killed him, and Jesus predicts a similar fate for himself.

17, 9: *The vision:* Matthew alone uses this word to describe the transfiguration. *Until the Son of Man has been raised from the dead:* only in the light of Jesus' resurrection can the meaning of his life and mission be truly understood; until then no testimony to *the vision* will lead people to faith.

17, 10: See the notes on Mt 3, 4; 16, 14.

17, 11-12: The preceding question and this answer may reflect later controversy with Jews who objected to the Christian claims for Jesus that Elijah had not yet come.

store all things;[n] [12]but I tell you that Elijah has already come,[o] and they did not recognize him but did to him whatever they pleased. So also will the Son of Man suffer at their hands." [13]Then the disciples understood that he was speaking to them of John the Baptist.*

The Healing of a Boy with a Demon.* [14] [p] When they came to the crowd a man approached, knelt down before him, [15]and said, "Lord, have pity on my son, for he is a lunatic* and suffers severely; often he falls into fire, and often into water. [16]I brought him to your disciples, but they could not cure him." [17]Jesus said in reply, "O faithless and perverse* generation, how long will I be with you? How long will I endure you? Bring him here to me."[q] [18]Jesus rebuked him and the demon came out of him,* and from that hour the boy was cured. [19]Then the disciples approached Jesus in private and said, "Why could we not drive it out?" [20]*He said to them, "Because of your little faith. Amen, I say to you, if you have faith the size of a mustard seed, you will say to this moun-tain, 'Move from here to there,' and it will move. Nothing will be impossible for you." [r] [21]*

The Second Prediction of the Passion.* [22] [s] As they were gathering in Galilee, Jesus said to them, "The Son of Man is to be handed over to men, [23]and they will kill him, and he will be raised on the third day." And they were overwhelmed with grief.

Payment of the Temple Tax.* [24]When they came to Capernaum, the collectors of the temple tax* approached Peter and said, "Doesn't your teacher pay the temple tax?"[t] [25]"Yes," he said. When he came into the house, before he had time to speak, Jesus asked him, "What is your opinion, Simon? From whom do the kings of the earth take tolls or census tax? From their subjects or from foreigners?"* [26]When he said, "From foreigners," Jesus said to him, "Then the subjects are exempt.* [27]But that we may not offend

---

n Lk 1, 17.—o 12-13: Mt 11, 14.—p 14-21: Mk 9, 14-29; Lk 9, 37-43.—q Dt 32, 5 LXX.—r Mt 21, 21; Lk 17, 6; 1 Cor 13, 2.—s 22-23: Mt 16, 21; 20, 18-19.—t Ex 30, 11-16; Neh 10, 33.

17, 13: See Mt 11, 14.

17, 14-20: Matthew has greatly shortened the Marcan story (Mk 9, 14-29). Leaving aside several details of the boy's illness, he concentrates on the need for faith, not so much on the part of the boy's father (as does Mark, for Matthew omits Mk 9, 22b-24) but on that of his own disciples whose inability to drive out the demon is ascribed to their *little faith* (20).

17, 15: *A lunatic:* this description of the boy is peculiar to Matthew. The word occurs in the New Testament only here and in Mt 4, 24 and means one affected or struck by the moon. The symptoms of the boy's illness point to epilepsy, and attacks of this were thought to be caused by phases of the moon.

17, 17: *Faithless and perverse:* so Matthew and Luke (Lk 9, 41) against Mark's *faithless* (Mk 9, 19). The Greek word here translated *perverse* is the same as that in Dt 32, 5 LXX, where Moses speaks to his people. There is a problem in knowing to whom the reproach is addressed. Since the Matthean Jesus normally chides his disciples for their *little faith* (as in 20), it would appear that the charge of lack of faith could not be made against them and that the reproach is addressed to unbelievers among the Jews. However in v 20b (*if you have faith the size of a mustard seed*), which is certainly addressed to the disciples, they appear to have not even the smallest faith; if they had, they would have been able to cure the boy. In the light of v 20b the reproach of v 17 could have applied to the disciples. There seems to be an inconsistency between the charge of *little faith* in v 20a and that of not even a little in v 20b.

17, 18: *The demon came out of him:* not until this verse does Matthew indicate that the boy's illness is a case of demoniacal possession.

17, 20: The entire verse is an addition of Matthew who (according to the better attested text) omits the reason given for the

disciples' inability in Mk 9, 29. *Little faith:* see the note on Mt 6, 30. *Faith the size of a mustard seed . . . and it will move:* a combination of a Q saying (cf Lk 17, 6) with a Marcan saying (cf Mk 11, 23).

17, 21: Some manuscripts add, "But this kind does not come out except by prayer and fasting"; this is a variant of the better reading of Mk 9, 29.

17, 22-23: The second passion prediction (cf Mt 16, 21-23) is the least detailed of the three and may be the earliest. In the Marcan parallel the disciples do not understand (Mk 9, 32); here they understand and are *overwhelmed with grief* at the prospect of Jesus' death (23).

17, 24-27: Like Mt 14, 28-31 and Mt 16, 16b-19, this episode comes from Matthew's special material on Peter. Although the question of *the collectors* concerns Jesus' payment of *the temple tax*, it is put to *Peter*. It is he who receives instruction from Jesus about freedom from the obligation of payment and yet why it should be made. The means of doing so is provided miraculously. The pericope deals with a problem of Matthew's church, whether its members should pay the temple tax, and the answer is given through a word of Jesus conveyed to Peter. Some scholars see here an example of the teaching authority of Peter exercised in the name of Jesus (see Mt 16, 19). The specific problem was a Jewish Christian one and may have arisen when the Matthean church was composed largely of that group.

17, 24: *The temple tax:* before the destruction of the Jerusalem temple in A.D. 70 every male Jew above nineteen years of age was obliged to make an annual contribution to its upkeep (cf Ex 30, 11-16; Neh 10, 33). After the destruction the Romans imposed upon Jews the obligation of paying that tax for the temple of Jupiter Capitolinus. There is disagreement about which period the story deals with.

17, 25: *From their subjects or from foreigners?:* the Greek word here translated *subjects* literally means "sons."

17, 26: *Then the subjects are exempt:* just as *subjects* are not bound by laws applying to *foreigners*, neither are Jesus and his disciples, who belong to the kingdom of heaven, bound by the duty of paying the temple tax imposed on those who are not of the kingdom. If the Greek is translated "sons," the freedom of Jesus, the Son of God, and of his disciples, children ("sons") of the kingdom (cf Mt 13, 38), is even more clear.

them,* go to the sea, drop in a hook, and take the first fish that comes up. Open its mouth and you will find a coin worth twice the temple tax. Give that to them for me and for you."

CHAPTER 18*

The Greatest in the Kingdom. [1] [u] At that time the disciples* approached Jesus and said, "Who is the greatest in the kingdom of heaven?" [2] He called a child over, placed it in their midst, [3] and said, "Amen, I say to you, unless you turn and become like children,* you will not enter the kingdom of heaven. [v] [4] Whoever humbles himself like this child is the greatest in the kingdom of heaven. [w] [5] And whoever receives one child such as this in my name receives me.*

Temptations to Sin. [6] [x] "Whoever causes one of these little ones* who believe in me

to sin, it would be better for him to have a great millstone hung around his neck and to be drowned in the depths of the sea. [7] Woe to the world because of things that cause sin! Such things must come, but woe to the one through whom they come!* [8] [y] If your hand or foot causes you to sin,* cut it off and throw it away. It is better for you to enter into life maimed or crippled than with two hands or two feet to be thrown into eternal fire. [9] And if your eye causes you to sin, tear it out and throw it away. It is better for you to enter into life with one eye than with two eyes to be thrown into fiery Gehenna.

The Parable of the Lost Sheep. [10] [z] "See that you do not despise one of these little ones, for I say to you that their angels in heaven always look upon the face of my heavenly Father.* [11] [a] [12] What is your opinion? If a man has a hundred sheep and

---

u 1-5: Mk 9, 36-37; Lk 9, 46-48.—v Mt 19, 14; Mk 10, 15; Lk 18, 17.—w Mt 23, 12.—x 6-7: Mk 9, 42; Lk 17, 1-2.—y 8-9: Mt 5, 29-30; Mk 9, 43-47.—z 10-14: Ez 34, 1-3.16; Lk 15, 3-7.—a Lk 19, 10.

17, 27: *That we may not offend them:* though they are *exempt* (26), Jesus and his disciples are to avoid giving offense; therefore the tax is to be paid. *A coin worth twice the temple tax:* literally, "a stater," a Greek coin worth two double drachmas. Two double drachmas were equal to the Jewish shekel and the tax was a half-shekel. *For me and for you:* not only Jesus but Peter pays the tax, and this example serves as a standard for the conduct of all the disciples.

18, 1-35: This discourse of the fourth book of the gospel is often called the "church order" discourse, but it lacks most of the considerations usually connected with church order, such as various offices in the church and the duties of each, and deals principally with the relations that must obtain among the members of the church. Beginning with the warning that greatness in *the kingdom of heaven* is measured not by rank or power but by childlikeness (1-5), it deals with the care that the disciples must take not to cause the *little ones to sin* or to neglect them if they stray from the community (6-14), the correction of members who sin (15-18), the efficacy of the prayer of the disciples because of the presence of Jesus (19-20), and the forgiveness that must be repeatedly extended to sinful members who repent (21-35).

18, 1: The initiative is taken not by Jesus as in the Marcan parallel (Mk 9, 33-34) but by the disciples. *Kingdom of heaven:* this may mean *the kingdom* in its fullness, i.e., after the parousia and the final judgment. But what follows about causes of sin, church discipline, and forgiveness, all dealing with the present age, suggests that the question has to do with rank also in the church, where *the kingdom* is manifested here and now, although only partially and by anticipation; see the notes on Mt 3, 2; 4, 17.

18, 3: *Become like children:* the child is held up as a model for the disciples not because of any supposed innocence of children but because of their complete dependence on, and trust in, their parents. So must the disciples be, in respect to God.

18, 5: Cf Mt 10, 40.

18, 6: *One of these little ones:* the thought passes from the child of vv 2-4 to the disciples, *little ones* because of their becoming *like children*. It is difficult to know whether this is a designation of all who are disciples or of those who are insignificant in contrast to others, e.g., the leaders of the community. Since

apart from this chapter the designation *little ones* occurs in Mt only in 10, 42 where it means disciples as such, that is its more likely meaning here. *Who believe in me:* since discipleship is impossible without at least some degree of faith, this further specification seems superfluous. However, it serves to indicate that the warning against causing a *little one* to sin is principally directed against whatever would lead such a one to a weakening or loss of faith. The Greek verb *skandalizein,* here translated *causes . . . to sin,* means literally "causes to stumble"; what the stumbling is depends on the context. It is used of falling away from faith in Mt 13, 21. According to the better reading of Mk 9, 42, in *me* is a Matthean addition to the Marcan source. *It would be better . . . depths of the sea:* cf Mk 9, 42.

18, 7: This is a Q saying; cf Lk 17, 1. The inevitability of *things that cause sin* (literally, "scandals") does not take away the responsibility of *the one through whom they come.*

18, 8-9: These verses are a doublet of Mt 5, 29-30. In that context they have to do with causes of sexual sin. As in the Marcan source from which they have been drawn (Mk 9, 42-48), they differ from the first warning about scandal, which deals with causing another person to sin, for they concern what *causes* oneself to sin and they do not seem to be related to another's loss of faith, as the first warning is. It is difficult to know how Matthew understood the logical connection between these verses and vv 6-7.

18, 10-14: The first and last verses are peculiar to Mt. The parable itself comes from Q; see Lk 15, 3-7. In Lk it serves as justification for Jesus' table-companionship with sinners; here, it is an exhortation for the disciples to seek out fellow disciples who have gone *astray.* Not only must no one cause a little disciple to sin, but those who have strayed must be sought out and, if possible, brought back to the community. The joy of the shepherd on finding the sheep, though not absent in Mt (13), is more emphasized in Lk. By his addition of vv 10 and 14, Matthew has drawn out explicitly the application of the parable to the care of the *little ones.*

18, 10: *Their angels in heaven . . . my heavenly Father:* for the Jewish belief in angels as guardians of nations and individuals, see Dn 10, 13.20-21; Tb 5, 4-7; 1QH 5, 20-22; as intercessors who present the prayers of human beings to God, see Tb 13, 12.15. The high worth of the *little ones* is indicated by their being represented before God by these heavenly beings.

18, 11: Some manuscripts add, "For the Son of Man has come to save what was lost"; cf Mt 9, 13. This is practically identical with Lk 19, 10 and is probably a copyist's addition from that source.

one of them goes astray, will he not leave the ninety-nine in the hills and go in search of the stray? [13] And if he finds it, amen, I say to you, he rejoices more over it than over the ninety-nine that did not stray. [14] In just the same way, it is not the will of your heavenly Father that one of these little ones be lost.

A Brother Who Sins.* [15] "If your brother* sins [against you], go and tell him his fault between you and him alone. If he listens to you, you have won over your brother. [b] [16] If he does not listen, take one or two others along with you, [c] so that 'every fact may be established on the testimony of two or three witnesses.' * [17] If he refuses to listen to them, tell the church.* If he refuses to listen even to the church, then treat him as you would a Gentile or a tax collector. [d] [18] [e] Amen, I say to you, whatever you bind on earth shall be bound in heaven, and whatever you loose on earth shall be loosed in heaven.* [19] *Again, [amen,] I say to you, if two of you agree on earth about

anything for which they are to pray, it shall be granted to them by my heavenly Father. [j] [20] [g] For where two or three are gathered together in my name, there am I in the midst of them." *

The Parable of the Unforgiving Servant.* [21] [h] Then Peter approaching asked him, "Lord, if my brother sins against me, how often must I forgive him? As many as seven times?" [22] Jesus answered, "I say to you, not seven times but seventy-seven times.* [23] That is why the kingdom of heaven may be likened to a king who decided to settle accounts with his servants. [i] [24] When he began the accounting, a debtor was brought before him who owed him a huge amount.* [25] Since he had no way of paying it back, his master ordered him to be sold, along with his wife, his children, and all his property, in payment of the debt. [26] At that, the servant fell down, did him homage, and said, 'Be patient with me, and I will pay you back in full.' * [27] Moved with compassion the master of that servant let him go and forgave him the

---

b Lv 19, 17; Sir 19, 13; Gal 6, 1.—c Dt 19, 15; Jn 8, 17; 1 Tm 5, 19.—d 1 Cor 5, 1-13.—e Mt 16, 19; Jn 20, 23.—f Mt 7, 7-8; Jn 15, 7.—g 1 Cor 5, 4.—h 21-22: Mt 6, 12; Lk 17, 4.—i Mt 25, 19.

18, 15-20: Passing from the duty of Christian disciples toward those who have strayed from their number, the discourse now turns to how they are to deal with one who sins and yet remains within the community. First there is to be private correction (15); if this is unsuccessful, further correction before *two or three witnesses* (16); if this fails, the matter is to be brought before the assembled community (*the church*), and if the sinner refuses to attend to the correction of *the church*, he is to be expelled (17). The church's judgment will be ratified *in heaven*, i.e., by God (18). This three-step process of correction corresponds, though not exactly, to the procedure of the Qumran community; see 1QS 5, 25—6, 1; 6, 24—7, 25; CD 9, 2-8. The section ends with a saying about the favorable response of God to prayer, even to that of a very small number, for Jesus is in the midst of any gathering of his disciples, however small (19-20). Whether this prayer has anything to do with the preceding judgment is uncertain. *Won over:* literally, "gained."

18, 15: *Your brother:* a fellow disciple; see Mt 23, 8. The bracketed words, *against you,* are widely attested but they are not in the important codices Sinaiticus and Vaticanus or in some other textual witnesses. Their omission broadens the type of sin in question. *Won over:* literally, "gained."

18, 16: Cf Dt 19, 15.

18, 17: *The church:* the second of the only two instances of this word in the gospels; see the note on Mt 16, 18. Here it refers not to the entire *church* of Jesus, as in Mt 16, 18, but to the local congregation. *Treat him . . . a Gentile or a tax collector:* just as the observant Jew avoided the company of Gentiles and tax collectors, so must the congregation of Christian disciples separate itself from the arrogantly sinful member who refuses to repent even when convicted of his sin by the whole *church*. Such a one is to be set outside the fellowship of the community. The harsh language about *Gentile* and *tax collector* probably reflects a stage of the Matthean *church* when it was principally composed of Jewish Christians. That time had long since passed, but the principle of exclusion for such a sinner remained. Paul makes a similar demand for excommunication in 1 Cor 5, 1-13.

18, 18: Except for the plural of the verbs *bind* and *loose*, this verse is practically identical with Mt 16, 19b, and many scholars understand it as granting to all the disciples what was previously given to Peter alone. For a different view, based on the different contexts of the two verses, see the note on Mt 16, 19.

18, 19-20: Some take these verses as applying to prayer on the occasion of the church's gathering to deal with the sinner of v 17. Unless an *a fortiori* argument is supposed, this seems unlikely. God's answer to the prayer of *two or three* envisages a different situation from one that involves the entire congregation. In addition, the object of this prayer is expressed in most general terms as *anything for which they are to pray.*

18, 20: *For where two or three . . . midst of them:* the presence of Jesus guarantees the efficacy of the prayer. This saying is similar to one attributed to a rabbi executed in A.D. 135 at the time of the second Jewish revolt: ". . . When two sit and there are between them the words of the Torah, the divine presence (Shekinah) rests upon them" (*Pirqê 'Abôt* 3, 3).

18, 21-35: The final section of the discourse deals with the forgiveness that the disciples are to give to their fellow disciples who sin against them. To the question of Peter how often forgiveness is to be granted (21), Jesus answers that it is to be given without limit (22) and illustrates this with the parable of the unmerciful servant (23-34), warning that his *heavenly Father* will give those who do not forgive the same treatment as that given to the unmerciful servant (35). Verses 21-22 correspond to Lk 17, 4; the parable and the final warning are peculiar to Mt. That the parable did not originally belong to this context is suggested by the fact that it really does not deal with repeated forgiveness, which is the point of Peter's question and Jesus' reply.

18, 22: *Seventy-seven times:* the Greek corresponds exactly to the LXX of Gn 4, 24. There is probably an allusion, by contrast, to the limitless vengeance of Lamech in the Gn text. In any case, what is demanded of the disciples is limitless forgiveness.

18, 24: *A huge amount:* literally, "ten thousand talents." The talent was a unit of coinage of high but varying value depending on its metal (gold, silver, copper) and its place of origin. It is mentioned in the New Testament only here and in Mt 25, 14-30.

18, 26: *Pay you back in full:* an empty promise, given the size of the debt.

loan. ²⁸When that servant had left, he found one of his fellow servants who owed him a much smaller amount.* He seized him and started to choke him, demanding, 'Pay back what you owe.' ²⁹Falling to his knees, his fellow servant begged him, 'Be patient with me, and I will pay you back.' ³⁰But he refused. Instead, he had him put in prison until he paid back the debt. ³¹Now when his fellow servants saw what had happened, they were deeply disturbed, and went to their master and reported the whole affair. ³²His master summoned him and said to him, 'You wicked servant! I forgave you your entire debt because you begged me to. ³³Should you not have had pity on your fellow servant, as I had pity on you?'ʲ ³⁴Then in anger his master handed him over to the torturers until he should pay back the whole debt.* ³⁵ᵏ So will my heavenly Father do to you, unless each of you forgives his brother from his heart.''*

j Sir 28, 4.—k Mt 6, 15; Jas 2, 13.—l 3-9: Mk 10, 2-12.—m Gn 1, 27.—n Gn 2, 24; 1 Cor 6, 16; Eph 5, 31.—o Dt 24, 1-4.—p Mt 5, 32; Lk 16, 18; 1 Cor 7, 10-11.

18, 28: *A much smaller amount:* literally, "a hundred denarii." A denarius was the normal daily wage of a laborer. The difference between the two debts is enormous and brings out the absurdity of the conduct of the Christian who has received the great forgiveness of God and yet refuses to forgive the relatively minor offenses done to him.

18, 34: Since the debt is so great as to be unpayable, the punishment will be endless.

18, 35: The Father's forgiveness, already given, will be withdrawn at the final judgment for those who have not imitated his forgiveness by their own.

19, 1—23, 39: The narrative section of the fifth book of the gospel. The first part (Mt 19, 1—20, 34) has for its setting the journey of Jesus from Galilee to Jerusalem; the second (Mt 21, 1—23, 39) deals with Jesus' ministry in Jerusalem up to the final great discourse of the gospel (chs 24-25). Matthew follows the Marcan sequence of events, though adding material both special to this gospel and drawn from Q. The second part ends with the denunciation of the scribes and Pharisees (Mt 23, 1-36) followed by Jesus' lament over Jerusalem (37-39). This long and important speech raises a problem for the view that Mt is structured around five other discourses of Jesus (see Introduction) and that this one has no such function in the gospel. However, it is to be noted that this speech lacks the customary concluding formula that follows the five discourses (see the note on Mt 7, 28), and that those discourses are all addressed either exclusively (chs 10, 18, 24-25) or primarily (chs 5-7, 13) to the disciples, whereas this is addressed primarily to the scribes and Pharisees (13-36). Consequently, it seems plausible to maintain that the evangelist did not intend to give it the structural importance of the five other discourses, and that, in spite of its being composed of sayings-material, it belongs to the narrative section of this book. In that regard, it is similar to the sayings-material of Mt 11, 7-30. Some have proposed that Matthew wished to regard it as part of the final discourse of chs 24-25, but the intervening material (Mt 24, 1-4) and the change in matter and style of those chapters do not support that view.

19, 1-12: In giving Jesus' teaching on divorce (3-9), Matthew here follows his Marcan source (Mk 10, 2-12) as he does Q in Mt 5, 31-32 (cf Lk 16, 18). Verses 10-12 are peculiar to Mt.

VI. MINISTRY IN JUDEA AND JERUSALEM

CHAPTER 19

Marriage and Divorce. ¹ *When Jesus* finished these words,* he left Galilee and went to the district of Judea across the Jordan. ²Great crowds followed him, and he cured them there. ³ ˡ Some Pharisees approached him, and tested him,* saying, "Is it lawful for a man to divorce his wife for any cause whatever?" ⁴* He said in reply, "Have you not read 'that from the beginning the Creator 'made them male and female'ᵐ ⁵and said, 'For this reason a man shall leave his father and mother and be joined to his wife, and the two shall become one flesh'?ⁿ ⁶So they are no longer two, but one flesh. Therefore, what God has joined together, no human being must separate." ⁷They said to him, "Then why did Mosesᵒ command that the man give the woman a bill of divorce and dismiss [her]?"* ⁸He said to them, "Because of the hardness of your hearts Moses allowed you to divorce your wives, but from the beginning it was not so. ⁹ ᵖ I say to you,* whoever divorces his wife (unless the marriage

19, 1: *When Jesus finished these words:* see the note on Mt 7, 28-29. *The district of Judea across the Jordan:* an inexact designation of the territory. Judea did not extend *across the Jordan;* the territory east of the river was Perea. The route to Jerusalem by way of Perea avoided passage through Samaria.

19, 3: *Tested him:* the verb is used of attempts of Jesus' opponents to embarrass him by challenging him to do something they think impossible (Mt 16, 1; Mk 8, 11; Lk 11, 16) or by having him say something that they can use against him (Mt 22, 18.35; Mk 10, 2; 12, 15). *For any cause whatever:* this is peculiar to Mt and has been interpreted by some as meaning that Jesus was being asked to take sides in the dispute between the schools of Hillel and Shammai on the reasons for divorce, the latter holding a stricter position than the former. It is unlikely, however, that to ask Jesus' opinion about the differing views of two Jewish schools, both highly respected, could be described as "testing" him, for the reason indicated above.

19, 4-6: Matthew recasts his Marcan source, omitting Jesus' question about Moses' command (Mk 10, 3) and having him recall at once two Genesis texts that show the will and purpose of *the Creator* in making human beings *male and female* (Gn 1, 27), namely, that *a man* may *be joined to his wife* in marriage in the intimacy of *one flesh* (Gn 2, 24). *What God has* thus *joined* must not be separated by any *human being.* (The NAB translation of the Hebrew *bāsār* of Gn 2, 24 as "body" rather than "flesh" obscures the reference of Mt to that text.)

19, 7: See Dt 24, 1-4.

19, 9: Moses' concession to human sinfulness (*the hardness of your hearts,* 8) is repudiated by Jesus, and the original will of the Creator is reaffirmed against that concession. (*Unless the marriage is unlawful*): see the note on Mt 5, 31-32. There is some evidence suggesting that Jesus' absolute prohibition of divorce was paralleled in the Qumran community (see 11QTemple 57, 17-19; CD 4, 12b—5, 14). Matthew removes Mark's setting of this verse as spoken to the disciples alone "in the house" (Mk 10, 10) and also his extension of the divorce prohibition to the case of a woman's divorcing her husband (Mt 10, 12), probably because in Palestine, unlike the places where Roman and Greek law prevailed, the woman was not allowed to initiate the divorce.

is unlawful) and marries another commits adultery." [10] [His] disciples said to him, "If that is the case of a man with his wife, it is better not to marry." [11] He answered, "Not all can accept [this] word,* but only those to whom that is granted. [12] Some are incapable of marriage because they were born so; some, because they were made so by others; some, because they have renounced marriage* for the sake of the kingdom of heaven. Whoever can accept this ought to accept it."

Blessing of the Children.* [13] Then children were brought to him that he might lay his hands on them and pray.[q] The disciples rebuked them, [14] but Jesus said, "Let the children come to me, and do not prevent them; for the kingdom of heaven belongs to such as these." [r] [15] After he placed his hands on them, he went away.

The Rich Young Man.* [16] [s] Now someone approached him and said, "Teacher, what good must I do to gain eternal life?"* [17] He answered him, "Why do you ask me about the good? There is only One who is good.* If you wish to enter into life, keep the commandments." [18] * He asked him, "Which ones?" And Jesus replied, " 'You shall not kill;[t] you shall not commit adultery; you shall not steal; you shall not bear false witness; [19] honor your father and your mother'; and 'you shall love your neighbor as yourself.' " [20] The young man* said to him, "All of these I have observed. What do I still lack?" [21] Jesus said to him, "If you wish to be perfect,* go, sell what you have and give to [the] poor, and you will have treasure in heaven. Then come, follow me." [u] [22] When the young man heard this statement, he went away sad, for he had many possessions. [23] * Then Jesus said to his disciples, "Amen, I say to you, it will be hard for one who is rich to enter the kingdom of heaven. [24] Again I say to you, it is easier for a camel to pass through the eye of a needle than for one who is rich to enter the kingdom of God." [v] [25] * When the disciples heard this, they were greatly astonished and said, "Who then can be saved?" [26] Jesus looked at them and said, "For human beings this is impossible, but for God all things are possible." [w] [27] Then Peter said to him in reply, "We have given up everything and followed you. What will

---

q 13-15: Mk 10, 13-16; Lk 18, 15-17.—r Mt 18, 3; Acts 8, 36.—s 16-30: Mk 10, 17-31; Lk 18, 18-30.—t 18-19: Ex 20, 12-16; Dt 5, 16-20 / Lv 19, 18; Rom 13, 9.—u Mt 5, 48; 6, 20.— v Mt 7, 14.—w Gn 18, 14; Jb 42, 2; Lk 1, 37.

19, 11: *[This] word:* probably the disciples' *it is better not to marry* (10). Jesus agrees but says that celibacy is not for all but only for those *to whom that is granted* by God.

19, 12: *Incapable of marriage:* literally, "eunuchs." Three classes are mentioned, eunuchs from birth, eunuchs by castration, and those who have voluntarily *renounced marriage* (literally, "have made themselves eunuchs") *for the sake of the kingdom,* i.e., to devote themselves entirely to its service. Some scholars take the last class to be those who have been divorced by their spouses and have refused to enter another marriage. But it is more likely that it is rather those who have chosen never to marry, since that suits better the optional nature of the decision: *whoever can . . . ought to accept it.*

19, 13-15: This account is understood by some as intended to justify the practice of infant baptism. That interpretation is based principally on the command not to *prevent* the children from coming, since that word sometimes has a baptismal connotation in the New Testament; see Acts 8, 36.

19, 16-30: Cf Mk 10, 17-31. This story does not set up a "two-tier" morality, that of those who seek (only) *eternal life* (16) and that of those who *wish to be perfect* (21). It speaks rather of the obstacle that riches constitute for the following of Jesus and of the impossibility, humanly speaking, for one who has *many possessions* (22) *to enter the kingdom* (24). Actual renunciation of riches is not demanded of all; Matthew counts the rich Joseph of Arimathea as a disciple of Jesus (Mt 27, 57). But only the poor in spirit (Mt 5, 3) can *enter the kingdom* and, as here, such poverty may entail the sacrifice of one's *possessions.* The Twelve, who *have given up everything* (27) to follow Jesus, will have as their reward a share in Jesus' (the Son of

Man's) *judging the twelve tribes of Israel* (28), and all who have similarly sacrificed family or property for his sake *will inherit eternal life* (29).

19, 16: *Gain eternal life:* this is equivalent to "entering into life" (17) and "being saved" (25); the *life* is that of the new age after the final judgment (see Mt 25, 46). It probably is also equivalent here to "entering the kingdom of heaven" (23) or "the kingdom of God" (24), but see the notes on Mt 3, 2; 4, 17; 18, 1 for the wider reference of *the kingdom* in Mt.

19, 17: By Matthew's reformulation of the Marcan question and reply (Mk 10, 17-18) Jesus' repudiation of the term "good" for himself has been softened. Yet the Marcan assertion that "no one is good but God alone" stands, with only unimportant verbal modification.

19, 18-19: The first five commandments cited are from the Decalogue (see Ex 20, 12-16; Dt 5, 16-20). Matthew omits Mark's "you shall not defraud" (Mt 10, 19; see Dt 24, 14) and adds Lv 19, 18. This combination of commandments of the Decalogue with Lv 19, 18 is partially the same as Paul's enumeration of the demands of Christian morality in Rom 13, 9.

19, 20: *Young man:* in Mt alone of the synoptics the questioner is said to be a *young man;* thus the Marcan "from my youth" (Mk 10, 20) is omitted.

19, 21: *If you wish to be perfect: to be perfect* is demanded of all Christians; see Mt 5, 48. In the case of this man, it involves selling his possessions and giving to the poor; only so can he *follow* Jesus.

19, 23-24: Riches are an obstacle to entering *the kingdom* that cannot be overcome by human power. The comparison with the impossibility of a camel's passing *through the eye of a needle* should not be mitigated by such suppositions as that *the eye of a needle* means a low or narrow gate. *The kingdom of God:* as in Mt 12, 28; 21, 31.43, instead of Mt's usual *kingdom of heaven.*

19, 25-26: See the note on Mk 10, 23-27.

there be for us?"[x] [28] [y] Jesus said to them, "Amen, I say to you that you who have followed me, in the new age, when the Son of Man is seated on his throne of glory, will yourselves sit on twelve thrones, judging the twelve tribes of Israel.* [29] And everyone who has given up houses or brothers or sisters or father or mother or children or lands for the sake of my name will receive a hundred times more, and will inherit eternal life. [30] [z] But many who are first will be last, and the last will be first.*

CHAPTER 20

The Workers in the Vineyard.* [1]"The kingdom of heaven is like a landowner who went out at dawn to hire laborers for his vineyard. [2] After agreeing with them for the usual daily wage, he sent them into his vineyard. [3] Going out about nine o'clock, he saw others standing idle in the marketplace, [4] and he said to them, 'You too go into my vineyard, and I will give you what is just.'* [5] So they went off. [And] he went out again around noon, and around three o'clock, and did likewise. [6] Going out about five o'clock, he found others standing around, and said to them, 'Why do you stand here idle all day?' [7] They answered, 'Because no one has hired us.' He said to them, 'You too go into my vineyard.' [8] When it was evening the owner of the vineyard said to his foreman, 'Summon the laborers and give them their pay,[a] beginning with the last and ending with the first.'* [9] When those who had started about five o'clock came, each received the usual daily wage. [10] So when the first came, they thought that they would receive more, but each of them also got the usual wage. [11] And on receiving it they grumbled against the landowner, [12] saying, 'These last ones worked only one hour, and you have made them equal to us, who bore the day's burden and the heat.' [13] He said to one of them in reply, 'My friend, I am not cheating you.* Did you not agree with me for the usual daily wage? [14] * Take what is yours and go. What if I wish to give this last one the same as you? [15] [Or] am I not free to do as I wish with my own money? Are you envious because I am generous?' [16] Thus, the last will be first, and the first will be last."*

The Third Prediction of the Passion.* [17] As Jesus was going up to Jerusalem,[b] he took the twelve [disciples] aside by themselves, and said to them on the way, [18]"Behold, we are going up to Jerusalem, and the Son of Man will be handed over to the chief priests and the scribes, and they will condemn him to death, [19] and hand him over to the Gentiles to be mocked and scourged and crucified, and he will be raised on the third day."

---

x Mt 4, 20.22.—y Mt 25, 31; Dn 7, 9.22; Lk 22, 30; Rv 3, 21; 20, 4.—z Mt 20, 16.—a Lv 19, 13; Dt 24, 15.—b 17-19: Mt 16, 21; 17, 22-23; Mk 10, 32-34; Lk 18, 31-33.

19, 28: This saying, directed to the Twelve, is from Q; see Lk 22, 29-30. *The new age:* the Greek word here translated "new age" occurs in the New Testament only here and in Ti 3, 5. Literally, it means "rebirth" or "regeneration," and is used in Ti of spiritual rebirth through baptism. Here it means the "rebirth" effected by the coming of the kingdom. Since that coming has various stages (see the notes on Mt 3, 2; 4, 17), *the new age* could be taken as referring to the time after the resurrection when the Twelve will govern the true Israel, i.e., the church of Jesus. (For "judge" in the sense of "govern," cf Jgs 12, 8.9.11; 15, 20; 16, 31; Ps 2, 10.) But since it is connected here with the time when *the Son of Man* will be *seated on his throne of glory,* language that Matthew uses in Mt 25, 31 for the time of final judgment, it is more likely that what the Twelve are promised is that they will be joined with Jesus then in judging the people of Israel.

19, 30: Different interpretations have been given to this saying, which comes from Mk 10, 31. In view of Matthew's associating it with the following parable (Mt 20, 1-15) and substantially repeating it (in reverse order) at the end of that parable (Mt 20, 16), it may be that his meaning is that all who respond to the call of Jesus, at whatever time (*first* or *last*), will be the same in respect to inheriting the benefits of the kingdom, which is the gift of God.

20, 1-16: This parable is peculiar to Mt. It is difficult to know whether the evangelist composed it or received it as part of his traditional material and, if the latter is the case, what its original reference was. In its present context its close association with Mt 19, 30 suggests that its teaching is the equality of all the disciples in the reward of inheriting eternal life.

20, 4: *What is just:* although the wage is not stipulated as in the case of those first hired, it will be fair.

20, 8: *Beginning with the last . . . the first:* this element of the parable has no other purpose than to show how *the first* knew what *the last* were given (12).

20, 13: *I am not cheating you:* literally, "I am not treating you unjustly."

20, 14-15: The owner's conduct involves no violation of justice (4.13), and that all the workers receive the same wage is due only to his generosity to the latest arrivals; the resentment of the first comes from envy.

20, 16: See the note on Mt 19, 30.

20, 17-19: Cf Mk 10, 32-34. This is the third and the most detailed of the passion predictions (Mt 16, 21-23; 17, 22-23). It speaks of Jesus' being *handed over to the Gentiles* (Mt 27, 2), his being *mocked* (Mt 27, 27-30), *scourged* (Mt 27, 26), and *crucified* (Mt 27, 31.35). In all but the last of these points Matthew agrees with his Marcan source, but whereas Mk speaks of Jesus' being killed (Mk 10, 34), Mt has the specific *to be . . . crucified.*

The Request of James and John.* ²⁰ *c* Then the mother* of the sons of Zebedee approached him with her sons and did him homage, wishing to ask him for something. ²¹ He said to her, "What do you wish?" She answered him, "Command that these two sons of mine sit, one at your right and the other at your left, in your kingdom." ²² Jesus said in reply, "You do not know what you are asking.* Can you drink the cup that I am going to drink?" They said to him, "We can." ²³ He replied, "My cup you will indeed drink, but to sit at my right and at my left [, this] is not mine to give but is for those for whom it has been prepared by my Father." ²⁴ When the ten heard this, they became indignant at the two brothers.*d* ²⁵ But Jesus summoned them and said, "You know that the rulers of the Gentiles lord it over them, and the great ones make their authority over them felt. ²⁶ But it shall not be so among you. Rather, whoever wishes to be great among you shall be your servant; ²⁷ whoever wishes to be first among you shall be your slave.*e* ²⁸ Just so, the Son of Man did not come to be served but to serve and to give his life as a ransom* for many."*f*

The Healing of Two Blind Men.* ²⁹ As they left Jericho,*g* a great crowd followed him. ³⁰ Two blind men were sitting by the roadside, and when they heard that Jesus was passing by, they cried out, "[Lord,]* Son of David, have pity on us!" *h* ³¹ The crowd warned them to be silent, but they called out all the more, "Lord, Son of David, have pity on us!" ³² Jesus stopped and called them and said, "What do you want me to do for you?" ³³ They answered him, "Lord, let our eyes be opened." ³⁴ Moved with pity, Jesus touched their eyes. Immediately they received their sight, and followed him.

CHAPTER 21

The Entry into Jerusalem.* ¹ *i* When they drew near Jerusalem and came to Bethphage* on the Mount of Olives, Jesus sent two disciples, ² saying to them, "Go into the village opposite you, and immediately you will find an ass tethered, and a colt with her.* Untie them and bring them here to me. ³ And if anyone should say anything to you, reply, 'The master has need of them.' Then he will send them at

---

c 20-28: Mk 10, 35-45.—d 24-27: Lk 22, 25-27.—e Mk 9, 35.—f Mt 26, 28; Is 53, 12; Rom 5, 6; 1 Tm 2, 6.—g 29-34: Mk 10, 46-52; Lk 18, 35-43.—h Mt 9, 27.—i 1-11: Mk 11, 1-11; Lk 19, 28-38; Jn 12, 12-15.

20, 20-28: Cf Mk 10, 35-45. The request of the sons of Zebedee, made through their mother, for the highest places of honor in the *kingdom*, and the indignation of *the* other *ten* disciples at this request, show that neither *the two brothers* nor the others have understood that what makes for greatness in the kingdom is not lordly power but humble service. Jesus gives the example, and his ministry of service will reach its highest point when he gives his life for the deliverance of the human race from sin.

20, 20-21: The reason for Matthew's making the *mother* the petitioner (cf Mk 10, 35) is not clear. Possibly he intends an allusion to Bathsheba's seeking the kingdom for Solomon; see 1 Kgs 1, 11-21. *Your kingdom:* see the note on Mt 16, 28.

20, 22: *You do not know what you are asking:* the Greek verbs are plural and, with the rest of the verse, indicate that the answer is addressed not to the woman but to her sons. *Drink the cup:* see the note on Mk 10, 38-40. Matthew omits the Marcan "or be baptized with the baptism with which I am baptized" (Mk 10, 38).

20, 28: *Ransom:* this noun, which occurs in the New Testament only here and in the Marcan parallel (Mt 10, 45), does not necessarily express the idea of liberation by payment of some price. The cognate verb is used frequently in the LXX of God's liberating Israel from Egypt or from Babylonia after the Exile; see Ex 6, 6; 15, 13; Ps 77 (76 LXX), 16; Is 43, 1; 44, 22. The liberation brought by Jesus' death will be *for many;* cf Is 53, 12. *Many* does not mean that some are excluded, but is a Semitism designating the collectivity who benefit from the service of the one, and is equivalent to "all." While there are few verbal contacts between this saying and the fourth Servant Song (Is 52, 13—53, 12), the ideas of that passage are reflected here.

20, 29-34: The cure of the blind men is probably symbolic of what will happen to the disciples, now blind to the meaning of Jesus' passion and to the necessity of their sharing his suffering.

As the men are given sight, so, after the resurrection, will the disciples come to see that to which they are now blind. Matthew has abbreviated his Marcan source (Mk 10, 46-52) and has made Mk's one man two. Such doubling is characteristic of this gospel; see Mt 8, 28-34 (// Mk 5, 1-20) and the note on Mt 9, 27-31.

20, 30: *[Lord]:* some important textual witnesses omit this, but that may be because copyists assimilated this verse to Mt 9, 27. *Son of David:* see the note on Mt 9, 27.

21, 1-11: Jesus' coming to Jerusalem is in accordance with the divine will that he must go there (cf Mt 16, 21) to suffer, die, and be raised. He prepares for his entry into the city in such a way as to make it a fulfillment of the prophecy of Zec 9, 9 (2) that emphasizes the humility of the *king who comes* (5). That prophecy, absent from the Marcan parallel account (Mk 11, 1-11) although found also in the Johannine account of the entry (Jn 12, 15), is the center of the Matthean story. During the procession from Bethphage to Jerusalem, Jesus is acclaimed as the Davidic messianic king by the crowds who accompany him (9). On his arrival *the whole city was shaken,* and to the inquiry of the amazed populace about Jesus' identity the crowds with him reply that he is *the prophet, from Nazareth in Galilee* (10.11).

21, 1: *Bethphage:* a village that can no longer be certainly identified. Mk mentions it before Bethany (Mk 11, 1), which suggests that it lay to the east of the latter. *The Mount of Olives:* the hill east of Jerusalem that is spoken of in Zec 14, 4 as the place where the Lord will come to rescue Jerusalem from the enemy nations.

21, 2: *An ass tethered, and a colt with her:* instead of the one animal of Mk 11, 2, Mt has two, as demanded by his understanding of Zec 9, 9.

once." [4] This happened so that what had been spoken through the prophet* might be fulfilled:

[5] "Say to daughter Zion,
　'Behold, your king comes to you,
　　meek and riding on an ass,
　　and on a colt, the foal of a beast of
　　　burden.' "[j]

[6] The disciples went and did as Jesus had ordered them. [7] They brought the ass and the colt and laid their cloaks over them, and he sat upon them.* [8] [k] The very large crowd spread their cloaks on the road, while others cut branches from the trees and strewed them on the road.* [9] The crowds preceding him and those following kept crying out and saying:

"Hosanna* to the Son of David;
　blessed is he who comes in the name
　　of the Lord;
　hosanna in the highest." [l]

[10] And when he entered Jerusalem the whole city was shaken* and asked, "Who is this?" [11] And the crowds replied, "This is Jesus the prophet,* from Nazareth in Galilee."

The Cleansing of the Temple. * [12] [m] Jesus entered the temple area and drove out all those engaged in selling and buying there. [n] He overturned the tables of the money changers and the seats of those who were selling doves.* [13] And he said to them, "It is written: [o]

'My house shall be a house of prayer,'*
　but you are making it a den of
　　thieves."

[14] The blind and the lame* approached him in the temple area, and he cured them. [p] [15] When the chief priests and the scribes saw the wondrous things* he was doing, and the children crying out in the temple area, "Hosanna to the Son of David," they were indignant [16] and said to him, "Do you hear what they are saying?" Jesus said to them, "Yes; and have you never read the text, [q] 'Out of the mouths of infants and nurslings you have brought forth praise'?"* [17] And leaving them, he went out of the city to Bethany, and there he spent the night.

Mt

---

j Is 62, 11; Zec 9, 9.—k 2 Kgs 9, 13.—l Ps 118, 25-26.—m 12-17: Mk 11, 15-19; Lk 19, 45-48; Jn 2, 14-22.—n Lv 5, 7.—o Is 56, 7; Jer 7, 11.—p 2 Sm 5, 8 LXX.—q Ps 8, 2 LXX; Wis 10, 21.

21, 4-5: *The prophet:* this fulfillment citation is actually composed of two distinct Old Testament texts, Is 62, 11 (*Say to daughter Zion*) and Zec 9, 9. The *ass* and the *colt* are the same animal in the prophecy, mentioned twice in different ways, the common Hebrew literary device of poetic parallelism. That Matthew takes them as two is one of the reasons why some scholars think that he was a Gentile rather than a Jewish Christian who would presumably not make that mistake (see Introduction).

21, 7: *Upon them:* upon the two animals; an awkward picture resulting from Matthew's misunderstanding of the prophecy.

21, 8: *Spread . . . on the road:* cf 2 Kgs 9, 13. There is a similarity between the cutting and strewing of the *branches* and the festivities of Tabernacles (Lv 23, 39-40); see also 2 Mc 10, 5-8 where the celebration of the rededication of the temple is compared to that of Tabernacles.

21, 9: *Hosanna:* the Hebrew means "(O LORD) grant salvation"; see Ps 118, 25, but that invocation had become an acclamation of jubilation and welcome. *Blessed is he . . . in the name of the Lord:* see Ps 118, 26 and the note on Jn 12, 13. *In the highest:* probably only an intensification of the acclamation, although *Hosanna in the highest* could be taken as a prayer, "May God save (him)."

21, 10: *Was shaken:* in the gospels this verb is peculiar to Mt where it is used also of the earthquake at the time of the crucifixion (Mt 27, 51) and of the terror of the guards of Jesus' tomb at the appearance of the angel (Mt 28, 4). For Matthew's use of the cognate noun, see the note on Mt 8, 24.

21, 11: *The prophet:* see Mt 16, 14 ("one of the prophets") and Mt 21, 46.

21, 12-17: Matthew changes the order of Mk (11, 11.12.15) and places the cleansing of the temple on the same day as the entry into Jerusalem, immediately after it. The activities going on in *the temple area* were not secular but connected with the temple worship. Thus Jesus' attack on those so engaged and his charge that they were *making* God's *house of prayer a den of thieves* (12-13) constituted a claim to authority over the religious practices of Israel and were a challenge to the priestly authorities. Verses 14-17 are peculiar to Mt. Jesus' healings and his countenancing the children's cries of praise rouse the indignation of *the chief priests and the scribes* (15). These two groups appear in the infancy narrative (Mt 2, 4) and have been mentioned in the first and third passion predictions (Mt 16, 21; 20, 18). Now, as the passion approaches, they come on the scene again, exhibiting their hostility to Jesus.

21, 12: These activities were carried on in the court of the Gentiles, the outermost court of *the temple area.* Animals for sacrifice were sold; the *doves* were for those who could not afford a more expensive offering; see Lv 5, 7. *Tables of the money changers:* only the coinage of Tyre could be used for the purchases; other money had to be exchanged for that.

21, 13: *'My house . . . prayer':* cf Is 56, 7. Matthew omits the final words of the quotation, "for all peoples" ("all nations"), possibly because for him the worship of the God of Israel by all nations belongs to the time after the resurrection; see Mt 28, 19. *A den of thieves:* the phrase is taken from Jer 7, 11.

21, 14: *The blind and the lame:* according to 2 Sm 5, 8 (LXX) *the blind and the lame* were forbidden to enter "the house of the Lord," the temple. These are the last of Jesus' healings in Mt.

21, 15: *The wondrous things:* the healings.

21, 16: *'Out of the mouths . . . praise':* cf Ps 8, 3 (LXX).

The Cursing of the Fig Tree.* [18] r When he was going back to the city in the morning, he was hungry. [19] Seeing a fig tree by the road, he went over to it, but found nothing on it except leaves. And he said to it, "May no fruit ever come from you again." And immediately the fig tree withered. s [20] When the disciples saw this, they were amazed and said, "How was it that the fig tree withered immediately?" [21] t Jesus said to them in reply, "Amen, I say to you, if you have faith and do not waver, not only will you do what has been done to the fig tree, but even if you say to this mountain, 'Be lifted up and thrown into the sea,' it will be done.* [22] Whatever you ask for in prayer with faith, you will receive." u

The Authority of Jesus Questioned.* [23] v When he had come into the temple area, the chief priests and the elders of the people approached him as he was teaching and said, "By what authority are you doing these things?* And who gave you this authority?" w [24] Jesus said to them in reply, "I shall ask you one question,* and if you answer it for me, then I shall tell you by what authority I do these things. [25] Where was John's baptism from? Was it of heavenly or of human origin?" They discussed this among themselves and said, "If we say 'Of heavenly origin,' he will say to us, 'Then why did you not believe him?' [26] x But if we say, 'Of human origin,' we fear the crowd, for they all regard John as a prophet."* [27] So they said to Jesus in reply, "We do not know." He himself said to them, "Neither shall I tell you by what authority I do these things.*

The Parable of the Two Sons.* [28] "What is your opinion? A man had two sons. He came to the first and said, 'Son, go out and work in the vineyard today.' [29] He said in reply, 'I will not,' but afterwards he changed his mind and went. [30] The man came to the other son and gave the same order. He said in reply, 'Yes, sir,' but did not go. [31] Which of the two did his father's will?" They answered, "The first." Jesus said to them, "Amen, I say to you, tax collectors and prostitutes are entering the kingdom of God before you.* [32] When John came to you in the way of righteousness, you did not believe him; but tax collectors and prostitutes did. y Yet even when you saw that, you did not later change your minds and believe him.*

---

r 18-22: Mk 11, 12-14.20-24.—s Jer 8, 13; Lk 13, 6-9.—t Mt 17, 20; Lk 17, 6.—u Mt 7, 7; 1 Jn 3, 22.—v 23-27: Mk 11, 27-33; Lk 20, 1-8.—w Jn 2, 18.—x Mt 14, 5.—y Lk 7, 29-30.

21, 18-22: In Mk the effect of Jesus' cursing the fig tree is not immediate; see Mk 11, 14.20. By making it so, Matthew has heightened the miracle. Jesus' act seems arbitrary and ill-tempered, but it is a prophetic action similar to those of Old Testament prophets that vividly symbolize some part of their preaching; see, e.g., Ez 12, 1-20. It is a sign of the judgment that is to come upon the Israel that with all its apparent piety lacks the fruit of good deeds (Mt 3, 10) and will soon bear the punishment of its fruitlessness (43). Some scholars propose that this story is the development in tradition of a parable of Jesus about the destiny of a fruitless tree, such as Lk 13, 6-9. Jesus' answer to the question of the amazed disciples (20) makes the miracle an example of the power of prayer made with unwavering *faith* (21-22).

21, 21: See Mt 17, 20.

21, 23-27: Cf Mk 11, 27-33. This is the first of five controversies between Jesus and the religious authorities of Judaism in Mt 21, 23—22, 46, presented in the form of questions and answers.

21, 23: *These things:* probably his entry into the city, his cleansing of the temple, and his healings there.

21, 24: To reply by counterquestion was common in rabbinical debate.

21, 26: *We fear . . . as a prophet:* cf Mt 14, 5.

21, 27: Since through embarrassment on the one hand and fear on the other the religious authorities claim ignorance of the origin of John's baptism, they show themselves incapable of speaking with authority; hence Jesus refuses to discuss with them the grounds of his authority.

21, 28-32: The series of controversies is interrupted by three parables on the judgment of Israel (Mt 21, 28—22, 14) of which this, peculiar to Mt, is the first. The second (Mt 21, 33-46) comes from Mk (12, 1-12), and the third (Mt 22, 1-14) from Q; see Lk 14, 15-24. This interruption of the controversies is similar to that in Mk, although Mk has only one parable between the first and second controversy. As regards Mt's first parable, vv 28-30 if taken by themselves could point simply to the difference between saying and doing, a theme of much importance in this gospel (cf Mt 7, 21; 12, 50); that may have been the parable's original reference. However, it is given a more specific application by the addition of vv 31-32. The two sons represent, respectively, the religious leaders and the religious outcasts who followed John's call to repentance. By the answer they give to Jesus' question (31) the leaders condemn themselves. There is much confusion in the textual tradition of the parable. Of the three different forms of the text given by important textual witnesses, one has the leaders answer that the son who agreed to go but did not was the one who did the father's will. Although some scholars accept that as the original reading, their arguments in favor of it seem unconvincing. The choice probably lies only between a reading that puts the son who agrees and then disobeys before the son who at first refuses and then obeys, and the reading followed in the present translation. The witnesses to the latter reading are slightly better than those that support the other.

21, 31: *Entering . . . before you:* this probably means "they enter; you do not."

21, 32: Cf Lk 7, 29-30. Although the thought is similar to that of the Lucan text, the formulation is so different that it is improbable that the saying comes from Q. *Came to you . . . way of righteousness:* several meanings are possible: that John himself was righteous, that he taught righteousness to others, or that he had an important place in God's plan of salvation. For the last, see the note on Mt 3, 14-15.

The Parable of the Tenants.* ³³"Hear another parable.ᶻ There was a landowner who planted a vineyard,ᵃ put a hedge around it, dug a wine press in it, and built a tower.* Then he leased it to tenants and went on a journey. ³⁴When vintage time drew near, he sent his servants* to the tenants to obtain his produce. ³⁵But the tenants seized the servants and one they beat, another they killed, and a third they stoned. ³⁶Again he sent other servants, more numerous than the first ones, but they treated them in the same way. ³⁷Finally, he sent his son to them, thinking, 'They will respect my son.' ³⁸But when the tenants saw the son, they said to one another, 'This is the heir. Come, let us kill him and acquire his inheritance.'* ³⁹ᵇ They seized him, threw him out of the vineyard, and killed him.* ⁴⁰What will the owner of the vineyard do to those tenants when he comes?" ⁴¹They answered* him, "He will put those wretched men to a wretched death and lease his vineyard to other tenants who will give him the produce at the proper times." ⁴²Jesus said to them, "Did you never read in the scriptures:ᶜ

'The stone that the builders rejected
    has become the cornerstone;
by the Lord has this been done,
    and it is wonderful in our eyes'?*
⁴³Therefore, I say to you, the kingdom of God will be taken away from you and given to a people that will produce its fruit.* [⁴⁴The one who falls on this stone will be dashed to pieces; and it will crush anyone on whom it falls.]"* ⁴⁵When the chief priests and the Pharisees* heard his parables, they knew that he was speaking about them. ⁴⁶And although they were attempting to arrest him, they feared the crowds, for they regarded him as a prophet.

CHAPTER 22

The Parable of the Wedding Feast.* ¹ ᵈ Jesus again in reply spoke to them in parables, saying, ²"The kingdom of heaven may be likened to a king who gave a wedding feast* for his son. ³He dispatched his servants to summon the invited guests to the feast, but they refused to come. ⁴A second time he sent other servants,* saying,

---

z 33-46: Mk 12, 1-12; Lk 20, 9-19.—a Is 5, 1-2.7.—b Heb 13, 12.—c Ps 118, 22-23; Is 28, 16; Acts 4, 11; 1 Pt 2, 7.—d 1-14: Lk 14, 15-24.

21, 33-46: Cf Mk 12, 1-12. In this parable there is a close correspondence between most of the details of the story and the situation that it illustrates, the dealings of God with his people. Because of that heavy allegorizing, some scholars think that it does not in any way go back to Jesus, but represents the theology of the later church. That judgment applies to the Marcan parallel as well, although the allegorizing has gone farther in Mt. There are others who believe that while many of the allegorical elements are due to church sources, they have been added to a basic parable spoken by Jesus. This view is now supported by the Gospel of Thomas, #65, where a less allegorized and probably more primitive form of the parable is found.

21, 33: *Planted a vineyard . . . a tower:* cf Is 5, 1-2. The *vineyard* is defined in Is 5, 7 as "the house of Israel."

21, 34-35: *His servants:* Mt has two sendings of *servants* as against Mk's three sendings of a single servant (Mk 11, 2-5a) followed by a statement about the sending of "many others" (Mk 11, 2.5b). That these *servants* stand for the prophets sent by God to Israel is clearly implied but not made explicit here, but see Mt 23, 37. *His produce:* cf Mk 12, 2, "some of the produce." The *produce* is the good works demanded by God, and his claim to them is total.

21, 38: *Acquire his inheritance:* if a Jewish proselyte died without heir, the tenants of his land would have final claim on it.

21, 39: *Threw him out . . . and killed him:* the change in the Marcan order where the son is killed and his corpse then thrown out (Mk 12, 8) was probably made because of the tradition that Jesus died outside the city of Jerusalem; see Jn 19, 17; Heb 13, 12.

21, 41: *They answered:* in Mk 12, 9 the question is answered by Jesus himself; here the leaders answer and so condemn themselves; cf v 31. Matthew adds that the new *tenants* to whom the vineyard will be transferred *will give* the owner *the produce at the proper times.*

21, 42: Cf Ps 118, 22-23. The psalm was used in the early church as a prophecy of Jesus' resurrection; see Acts 4, 11; 1 Pt 2, 7. If, as some think, the original parable ended at v 39, it was thought necessary to complete it by a reference to Jesus' vindication by God.

21, 43: Peculiar to Mt. *Kingdom of God:* see the note on Mt 19, 23-24. Its presence here instead of Mt's usual "kingdom of heaven" may indicate that the saying came from Matthew's own traditional material. *A people that will produce its fruit:* believing Israelites and Gentiles, the church of Jesus.

21, 44: The majority of textual witnesses omit this verse. It is probably an early addition to Mt from Lk 20, 18 with which it is practically identical.

21, 45: *The Pharisees:* Matthew inserts into the group of Jewish leaders (23) those who represented the Judaism of his own time.

22, 1-14: This parable is from Q; see Lk 14, 15-24. It has been given many allegorical traits by Matthew, e.g., the burning of the *city* of the guests who refused the invitation (7), which corresponds to the destruction of Jerusalem by the Romans in A.D. 70. It has similarities with the preceding parable of the tenants: the sending of two groups of *servants* (3.4), the murder of the *servants* (6), the punishment of the *murderers* (7), and the entrance of a new group into a privileged situation of which the others had proved themselves unworthy (8-10). The parable ends with a section that is peculiar to Mt (11-14), which some take as a distinct parable. Mt presents the *kingdom* in its double aspect, already present and something that can be entered here and now (1-10), and something that will be possessed only by those present members who can stand the scrutiny of the final judgment (11-14). The parable is not only a statement of God's judgment on Israel but a warning to Matthew's church.

22, 2: *Wedding feast:* the Old Testament's portrayal of final salvation under the image of a banquet (Is 25, 6) is taken up also in Mt 8, 11; cf Lk 13, 15.

22, 3-4: *Servants . . . other servants:* probably Christian missionaries in both instances; cf Mt 23, 34.

'Tell those invited: "Behold, I have prepared my banquet, my calves and fattened cattle are killed, and everything is ready; come to the feast." ' 5 Some ignored the invitation and went away, one to his farm, another to his business. 6 The rest laid hold of his servants, mistreated them, and killed them.e 7 The king was enraged and sent his troops, destroyed those murderers, and burned their city.* 8 Then he said to his servants, 'The feast is ready, but those who were invited were not worthy to come. 9 Go out, therefore, into the main roads and invite to the feast whomever you find.' 10 The servants went out into the streets and gathered all they found, bad and good alike,* and the hall was filled with guests. 11 But when the king came in to meet the guests he saw a man there not dressed in a wedding garment.* 12 He said to him, 'My friend, how is it that you came in here without a wedding garment?' But he was reduced to silence. 13 Then the king said to his attendants, 'Bind his hands and feet, and cast him into the darkness outside,f where there will be wailing and grinding of teeth.'* 14 Many are invited, but few are chosen."

Paying Taxes to the Emperor.* 15 Then the Pharisees* went off and plotted how they might entrap him in speech.g 16 They sent their disciples to him, with the Herodians,* saying, "Teacher, we know that you are a truthful man and that you teach the way of God in accordance with the truth. And you are not concerned with anyone's opinion, for you do not regard a person's status. 17 Tell us, then, what is your opinion: Is it lawful* to pay the census tax to Caesar or not?" 18 Knowing their malice, Jesus said, "Why are you testing me, you hypocrites? 19 Show me the coin that pays the census tax." Then they handed him the Roman coin.* 20 He said to them, "Whose image is this and whose inscription?" 21 They replied, "Caesar's."* At that he said to them, "Then repay to Caesar what belongs to Caesar and to God what belongs to God."h 22 When they heard this they were amazed, and leaving him they went away.

The Question about the Resurrection.* 23 i On that day Sadducees approached him, saying that there is no resurrection.* They put this question to him, 24 j saying, "Teacher, Moses said, 'If a man dies* without children, his brother shall marry

---

e Mt 21, 35.—f Mt 8, 12; 25, 30.—g 15-22: Mk 12, 13-17; Lk 20, 20-26.—h Rom 13, 7.—i 23-33: Mk 12, 18-27; Lk 20, 27-40.—j Gn 38, 8; Dt 25, 5-6.

22, 7: See the note on vv 1-14.

22, 10: *Bad and good alike:* cf Mt 13, 47.

22, 11: *A wedding garment:* the repentance, change of heart and mind, that is the condition for entrance into the kingdom (Mt 3, 2; 4, 17) must be continued in a life of good deeds (Mt 7, 21-23).

22, 13: *Wailing and grinding of teeth:* the Christian who lacks the wedding garment of good deeds will suffer the same fate as those Jews who have rejected Jesus; see the note on Mt 8, 11-12.

22, 15-22: The series of controversies between Jesus and the representatives of Judaism (see the note on Mt 21, 23-27) is resumed. As in the first (Mt 21, 23-27), here and in the following disputes Matthew follows his Marcan source with few modifications.

22, 15: *The Pharisees:* while Matthew retains the Marcan union of Pharisees and Herodians in this account, he clearly emphasizes the Pharisees' part. They alone are mentioned here, and the Herodians are joined with them only in a prepositional phrase of v 16. *Entrap him in speech:* the question that they will pose is intended to force Jesus to take either a position contrary to that held by the majority of the people or one that will bring him into conflict with the Roman authorities.

22, 16: *Herodians:* see the note on Mk 3, 6. They would favor payment of the tax; the Pharisees did not.

22, 17: *Is it lawful:* the law to which they refer is the law of God.

22, 19: *They handed him the Roman coin:* their readiness in producing the money implies their use of it and their acceptance of the financial advantages of the Roman administration in Palestine.

22, 21: *Caesar's:* the emperor Tiberius (A.D. 14-37). *Repay to Caesar what belongs to Caesar:* those who willingly use the coin that is Caesar's should *repay* him in kind. The answer avoids taking sides in the question of the lawfulness of the tax. *To God what belongs to God:* Jesus raises the debate to a new level. Those who have hypocritically asked about tax in respect to its relation to the law of God should be concerned rather with repaying God with the good deeds that are his due; cf Mt 21, 41.43.

22, 23-33: Here Jesus' opponents are the *Sadducees,* members of the powerful priestly party of his time; see the note on Mt 3, 7. Denying the resurrection of the dead, a teaching of relatively late origin in Judaism (cf Dn 12, 2), they appeal to a law of the Pentateuch (Dt 25, 5-10) and present a case based on it that would make resurrection from the dead ridiculous (24-28). Jesus chides them for knowing neither *the scriptures* nor *the power of God* (29). His argument in respect to God's *power* contradicts the notion, held even by many proponents as well as by opponents of the teaching, that the life of those raised from the dead would be essentially a continuation of the type of life they had had before death (30). His argument based on the scriptures (31-32) is of a sort that was accepted as valid among Jews of the time.

22, 23: *Saying that there is no resurrection:* in the Marcan parallel (Mk 12, 18) the Sadducees are correctly defined as those "who say there is no resurrection"; see also Lk 20, 27. Matthew's rewording of Mk can mean that these particular Sadducees deny the resurrection, which would imply that he was not aware that the denial was characteristic of the party. For some scholars this is an indication of his being a Gentile Christian; see the note on Mt 21, 4-5.

22, 24: *'If a man dies . . . his brother':* this is known as the "law of the levirate," from the Latin *levir,* "brother-in-law." Its purpose was to continue the family line of the deceased *brother* (Dt 25, 6).

his wife and raise up descendants for his brother.' [25] Now there were seven brothers among us. The first married and died and, having no descendants, left his wife to his brother. [26] The same happened with the second and the third, through all seven. [27] Finally the woman died. [28] Now at the resurrection, of the seven, whose wife will she be? For they all had been married to her." [29] Jesus said to them in reply, "You are misled because you do not know the scriptures or the power of God.* [30] At the resurrection they neither marry nor are given in marriage but are like the angels in heaven. [31] And concerning the resurrection of the dead, have you not read what was said to you* by God, [32] 'I am the God of Abraham, the God of Isaac, and the God of Jacob'?[k] He is not the God of the dead but of the living." [33] When the crowds heard this, they were astonished at his teaching.

The Greatest Commandment.* [34] [l] When the Pharisees heard that he had silenced the Sadducees, they gathered together, [35] and one of them [a scholar of the law]* tested him by asking, [36] "Teacher, which commandment in the law is the greatest?"* [37] He said to him,* "You shall love the Lord, your God, with all your heart, with all your soul, and with all your mind.[m] [38] This is the greatest and the first commandment. [39] The second is like it:* You shall love your neighbor as yourself.[n] [40] The whole law and the prophets depend on these two commandments."* [o]

The Question about David's Son.* [41] [p] While the Pharisees were gathered together, Jesus questioned them,* [42] saying, "What is your opinion about the Messiah? Whose son is he?" They replied, "David's."* [43] He said to them, "How, then, does David, inspired by the Spirit, call him 'lord,' saying:

[44] 'The Lord said to my lord,
"Sit at my right hand
    until I place your enemies under your feet"'? [q]

[45] If David calls him 'lord,' how can he be his son?"* [46] No one was able to answer him a word, nor from that day on did anyone dare to ask him any more questions.[r]

---

k Ex 3, 6.—l 34-40: Mk 12, 28-34; Lk 10, 25-28.—m Dt 6, 5.—n Lv 19, 18; Jas 2, 8.—o Rom 13, 8-10; Gal 5, 14.—p 41-46: Mk 12, 35-37; Lk 20, 41-44.—q Ps 110, 1; Acts 2, 35; Heb 1, 13.—r Lk 20, 40.

22, 29: The sexual relationships of this world will be transcended; the risen body will be the work of the creative *power of God.*

22, 31-32: Cf Ex 3, 6. In the Pentateuch, which the Sadducees accepted as normative for Jewish belief and practice, God speaks even now (*to you*) of himself as the God of the patriarchs who died centuries ago. He identifies himself in relation to them, and because of their relation to him, the living God, they too are alive. This might appear no argument for the resurrection, but simply for life after death as conceived in Wis 3, 1-3. But the general thought of early first-century Judaism was not influenced by that conception; for it human immortality was connected with the existence of the body.

22, 34-40: The Marcan parallel (Mk 12, 28-34) is an exchange between Jesus and a scribe who is impressed by the way in which Jesus has conducted himself in the previous controversy (Mk 12, 28), who compliments him for the answer he gives him (Mk 12, 32), and who is said by Jesus to be "not far from the kingdom of God" (Mk 12, 34). Matthew has sharpened that scene. The questioner, as the representative of other Pharisees, tests Jesus by his question (34-35), and both his reaction to Jesus' reply and Jesus' commendation of him are lacking.

22, 35: [*A scholar of the law*]: meaning "scribe." Although this reading is supported by the vast majority of textual witnesses, it is the only time that the Greek word so translated occurs in Mt. It is relatively frequent in Lk, and there is reason to think that it may have been added here by a copyist since it occurs in the Lucan parallel (Lk 10, 25-28). *Tested:* see the note on Mt 19, 3.

22, 36: For the devout Jew all the commandments were to be kept with equal care, but there is evidence of preoccupation in Jewish sources with the question put to Jesus.

22, 37-38: Cf Dt 6, 5. Matthew omits the first part of Mk's fuller quotation (Mk 12, 29; Dt 6, 4-5), probably because he considered its monotheistic emphasis needless for his church. The love of God must engage the total person (*heart, soul, mind*).

22, 39: Jesus goes beyond the extent of the question put to him and joins to *the greatest and the first commandment* a second, that of *love of neighbor,* Lv 19, 18; see the note on Mt 19, 18-19. This combination of the two commandments may already have been made in Judaism.

22, 40: The double commandment is the source from which *the whole law and the prophets* are derived.

22, 41-46: Having answered the questions of his opponents in the preceding three controversies, Jesus now puts a question to them about the sonship of the Messiah. Their easy response (43a) is countered by his quoting a verse of Ps 110 that raises a problem for their response (43b-45). They are unable to solve it and *from that day on* their questioning of him is ended.

22, 41: *The Pharisees . . . questioned them:* Mk is not specific about who are questioned (Mk 12, 35).

22, 42-44: *David's:* this view of the Pharisees was based on such Old Testament texts as Is 11, 1-9; Jer 23, 5; and Ez 34, 23; see also the extrabiblical Psalms of Solomon 17, 21. *How, then . . . saying:* Jesus cites Ps 110, 1, accepting the Davidic authorship of the psalm, a common view of his time. The psalm was probably composed for the enthronement of a Davidic king of Judah. Matthew assumes that the Pharisees interpret it as referring to the Messiah, although there is no clear evidence that it was so interpreted in the Judaism of Jesus' time. It was widely used in the early church as referring to the exaltation of the risen Jesus. *My lord:* understood as the Messiah.

22, 45: Since Matthew presents Jesus both as Messiah (Mt 16, 16) and as Son of David (Mt 1, 1; see also the note on Mt 9, 27), the question is not meant to imply Jesus' denial of Davidic sonship. It probably means that although he is the Son of David, he is someone greater, Son of Man and Son of God, and recognized as greater by David who calls him my *'lord.'*

CHAPTER 23*

Denunciation of the Scribes and Pharisees. [1] s Then Jesus spoke to the crowds and to his disciples, [2] saying, "The scribes and the Pharisees have taken their seat on the chair of Moses.* [3] Therefore, do and observe all things whatsoever they tell you, but do not follow their example. For they preach but they do not practice. [4] t They tie up heavy burdens* [hard to carry] and lay them on people's shoulders, but they will not lift a finger to move them. [5] u All their works are performed to be seen. They widen their phylacteries and lengthen their tassels.* [6] v They love places of honor at banquets,* seats of honor in synagogues, [7] greetings in marketplaces, and the salutation 'Rabbi.' [8] *As for you, do not be called 'Rabbi.' You have but one teacher, and you are all brothers. [9] Call no one on earth your father; you have but one Father in heaven. [10] Do not be called 'Mas-

---

s 1-39: Mk 12, 38-39; Lk 11, 37-52; 13, 34-35.—t Lk 11, 46.—u Mt 6, 1-6; Ex 13, 9.16; Nm 15, 38-39; Dt 6, 8; 11, 18.—v 6-7: Mk 12, 38-39; Lk 11, 43; 20, 46.—w Mt 20, 26.—x Lk 14, 11; 18, 14.—y Lk 11, 52.

ter'; you have but one master, the Messiah. [11] The greatest among you must be your servant. w [12] Whoever exalts himself will be humbled; but whoever humbles himself will be exalted. x

[13] *"Woe to you, scribes and Pharisees, you hypocrites. You lock the kingdom of heaven* before human beings. You do not enter yourselves, nor do you allow entrance to those trying to enter. y [14] *

[15] "Woe to you, scribes and Pharisees, you hypocrites. You traverse sea and land to make one convert, and when that happens you make him a child of Gehenna twice as much as yourselves.*

23, 1-39: The final section of the narrative part of the fifth book of the gospel is a denunciation by Jesus of the scribes and the Pharisees (see the note on Mt 3, 7). It depends in part on Mk and Q (cf Mk 12, 38-39; Lk 11, 37-52; 13, 34-35), but in the main it is peculiar to Mt. (For the reasons against considering this extensive body of sayings-material either as one of the structural discourses of this gospel or as part of the one that follows in chs 24-25, see the note on Mt 19, 1—23, 39.) While the tradition of a deep opposition between Jesus and the Pharisees is well founded, this speech reflects an opposition that goes beyond that of Jesus' ministry and must be seen as expressing the bitter conflict between Pharisaic Judaism and the church of Matthew at the time when the gospel was composed. The complaint often made that the speech ignores the positive qualities of Pharisaism and of its better representatives is true, but the complaint overlooks the circumstances that gave rise to the invective. Nor is the speech purely anti-Pharisaic. The evangelist discerns in his church many of the same faults that he finds in its opponents and warns his fellow Christians to look to their own conduct and attitudes.

23, 2-3: *Have taken their seat . . . Moses:* it is uncertain whether this is simply a metaphor for Mosaic teaching authority or refers to an actual *chair* on which the teacher sat. It has been proved that there was a seat so designated in synagogues of a later period than that of this gospel. *Do and observe . . . they tell you:* since the Matthean Jesus abrogates Mosaic law (Mt 5, 31-42), warns his disciples against the teaching of the Pharisees (Mt 14, 1-12), and, in this speech, denounces the Pharisees as blind guides in respect to their teaching on oaths (16-22), this commandment to *observe all things whatsoever they* (the scribes and Pharisees) *tell you* cannot be taken as the evangelist's understanding of the proper standard of conduct for his church. The saying may reflect a period when the Matthean community was largely Jewish Christian and was still seeking to avoid a complete break with the synagogue. Matthew has incorporated this traditional material into the speech in accordance with his view of the course of salvation history, in which he portrays the time of Jesus' ministry as marked by the fidelity to the law, although with significant pointers to the new situation that would exist after his death and resurrection (see the note on Mt 5, 17-20). The crowds and the disciples (1) are exhorted not to *follow* the *example* of the Jewish leaders, whose deeds do not conform to their teaching (3).

23, 4: *Tie up heavy burdens:* see the note on Mt 11, 28.

23, 5: To the charge of preaching but not practicing (3), Jesus adds that of acting in order to earn praise. The disciples have already been warned against this same fault (see the note on Mt 6, 1-18). *Phylacteries:* the Mosaic law required that during prayer small boxes containing parchments on which verses of scripture were written be worn on the left forearm and the forehead (see Ex 13, 9.16; Dt 6, 8; 11, 18). *Tassels:* see the note on Mt 9, 20. The widening of *phylacteries* and the lengthening of *tassels* were for the purpose of making these evidences of piety more noticeable.

23, 6-7: Cf Mk 12, 38-39. *'Rabbi':* literally, "my great one," a title of respect for teachers and leaders.

23, 8-12: These verses, warning against the use of various titles, are addressed to the disciples alone. While only the title *'Rabbi'* has been said to be used in addressing the scribes and Pharisees (7), the implication is that *Father* and *'Master'* also were. The prohibition of these titles to the disciples suggests that their use was present in Matthew's church. The Matthean Jesus forbids not only the titles but the spirit of superiority and pride that is shown by their acceptance. *Whoever exalts . . . will be exalted:* cf Lk 14, 11.

23, 13-36: This series of seven "woes," directed against the *scribes and Pharisees* and addressed to them, is the heart of the speech. The phrase *woe* to occurs often in the prophetic and apocalyptic literature, expressing horror of a sin and punishment for those who commit it. *Hypocrites:* see the note on Mt 6, 2. The hypocrisy of the *scribes and Pharisees* consists in the difference between their speech and action (3) and in demonstrations of piety that have no other purpose than to enhance their reputation as religious persons (5).

23, 13: *You lock the kingdom of heaven:* cf Mt 16, 19 where Jesus tells Peter that he will give him the keys to *the kingdom of heaven.* The purpose of the authority expressed by that metaphor is to give entrance into the kingdom (the kingdom is closed only to those who reject the authority); here the charge is made that the authority of the *scribes and Pharisees* is exercised in such a way as to be an obstacle to entrance. Cf Lk 11, 52 where the accusation against the "scholars of the law" (Mt's scribes) is that they "have taken away the key of knowledge."

23, 14: Some manuscripts add a verse here or after v 12, "Woe to you, scribes and Pharisees, you hypocrites. You devour the houses of widows and, as a pretext, recite lengthy prayers. Because of this, you will receive a very severe condemnation." Cf Mk 12, 40; Lk 20, 47. This "woe" is almost identical with Mk 12, 40 and seems to be an interpolation derived from that text.

23, 15: In the first century A.D. until the First Jewish Revolt against Rome (A.D. 66-70), many Pharisees conducted a vigorous missionary campaign among Gentiles. *Convert:* literally, "proselyte," a Gentile who accepted Judaism fully by submitting to circumcision and all other requirements of Mosaic law. *Child of Gehenna:* worthy of everlasting punishment; for *Gehenna,* see the note on Mt 5, 22. *Twice as much as yourselves:* possibly this refers simply to the zeal of the *convert,* surpassing that of the one who converted him.

16 * "Woe to you, blind guides, who say, 'If one swears by the temple, it means nothing, but if one swears by the gold of the temple, one is obligated.'ᶻ ¹⁷Blind fools, which is greater, the gold, or the temple that made the gold sacred? ¹⁸And you say, 'If one swears by the altar, it means nothing, but if one swears by the gift on the altar, one is obligated.' ¹⁹You blind ones, which is greater, the gift, or the altar that makes the gift sacred? ²⁰ ᵃ One who swears by the altar swears by it and all that is upon it; ²¹one who swears by the temple swears by it and by him who dwells in it; ²²one who swears by heaven swears by the throne of God and by him who is seated on it.

²³"Woe to you, scribes and Pharisees, you hypocrites. You pay tithes* of mint and dill and cummin, and have neglected the weightier things of the law: judgment and mercy and fidelity. [But] these you should have done, without neglecting the others.ᵇ ²⁴Blind guides, who strain out the gnatᶜ and swallow the camel!*

²⁵ * "Woe to you, scribes and Pharisees, you hypocrites.ᵈ You cleanse the outside of cup and dish, but inside they are full of plunder and self-indulgence. ²⁶Blind Pharisee, cleanse first the inside of the cup, so that the outside also may be clean.

²⁷ * "Woe to you, scribes and Pharisees, you hypocrites. You are like whitewashed tombs, which appear beautiful on the outside, but inside are full of dead men's bones and every kind of filth. ²⁸Even so, on the outside you appear righteous, but inside you are filled with hypocrisy and evildoing.ᵉ

²⁹ * "Woe to you, scribes and Pharisees,* you hypocrites. You build the tombs of the prophets and adorn the memorials of the righteous, ³⁰and you say, 'If we had lived in the days of our ancestors, we would not have joined them in shedding the prophets' blood.'ᶠ ³¹Thus you bear witness against yourselves that you are the children of those who murdered the prophets;ᵍ ³²now fill up what your ancestors measured out! ³³You serpents, you brood of vipers, how can you flee from the judgment of Gehenna?ʰ ³⁴ * Therefore, behold, I send to you prophets and wise men and scribes;ⁱ some of them you will kill and crucify, some of them you will scourge

---

ances while inner purity is ignored. The *scribes and Pharisees* are compared to cups carefully washed on the outside but filthy within. *Self-indulgence:* the Greek word here translated means lack of self-control, whether in drinking or in sexual conduct.

23, 27-28: The sixth *woe*, like the preceding one, deals with concern for externals and neglect of what is *inside*. Since contact with dead bodies, even when one was unaware of it, caused ritual impurity (Nm 19, 11-22), tombs were whitewashed so that no one would contract such impurity inadvertently.

23, 29-36: The final *woe* is the most serious indictment of all. It portrays the *scribes and Pharisees* as standing in the same line as their *ancestors* who murdered *the prophets* and *the righteous.*

23, 29-32: In spite of honoring the slain dead by building their *tombs* and adorning their *memorials,* and claiming that they would not have joined in their ancestors' crimes if they *had lived* in their *days,* the *scribes and Pharisees* are true *children* of their ancestors and are defiantly ordered by Jesus to *fill up* what those *ancestors measured out.* This order reflects the Jewish notion that there was an allotted measure of suffering that had to be completed before God's final judgment would take place.

23, 34-36: There are important differences between the Matthean and the Lucan form of this Q material; cf Lk 11, 49-51. In Lk the one who sends the emissaries is the "wisdom of God." If, as many scholars think, that is the original wording of Q, Matthew, by making Jesus the sender, has presented him as the personified divine wisdom. In Lk, wisdom's emissaries are the Old Testament "prophets" and the Christian "apostles." Mt's *prophets and wise men and scribes* are probably Christian disciples alone; cf Lk 11, 41 and see the note on Mt 13, 52. *You will kill:* see Mt 24, 9. *Scourge in your synagogues . . . town to town:* see Mt 10, 17.23 and the note on Mt 10, 17. *All the righteous blood shed upon the earth:* the slaying of the disciples is in continuity with all the shedding of *righteous blood* beginning with that of *Abel.* The persecution of Jesus' disciples by *this generation* involves the persecutors in the guilt of their murderous ancestors. *The blood of Zechariah:* see the note on Lk 11, 51. By identifying him as *the son of Barachiah* Matthew understands him to be Zechariah the Old Testament minor prophet; see Zec 1, 1.

---

z Mt 15, 14.—a 20-22: Mt 5, 34-35.—b Lv 27, 30; Dt 14, 22; Lk 11, 42.—c Lv 11, 41-45.—d 25-26: Mk 7, 4; Lk 11, 39.—e Lk 16, 15; 18, 9.—f Lk 11, 47.—g Acts 7, 52.—h Mt 3, 7; 12, 34.—i 34-36: Mt 5, 12; Gn 4, 8; 2 Chr 24, 20-22; Zec 1, 1; Lk 11, 49-51; Rv 18, 24.

23, 16-22: An attack on the casuistry that declared some oaths binding (*one is obligated*) and others not (*it means nothing*) and held the binding oath to be the one made by something of lesser value (*the gold; the gift on the altar*). Such teaching, which inverts the order of values, reveals the teachers to be *blind guides;* cf Mt 15, 14. Since the Matthean Jesus forbids all oaths to his disciples (Mt 5, 33-37), this *woe* does not set up a standard for Christian moral conduct, but ridicules the Pharisees on their own terms.

23, 23: The Mosaic law ordered tithing of the produce of the land (Lv 27, 30; Dt 14, 22-23), and the scribal tradition is said here to have extended this law to even the smallest herbs. The practice is criticized not in itself but because it shows the Pharisees' preoccupation with matters of less importance while they neglect *the weightier things of the law.*

23, 24: Cf Lv 11, 41-45 that forbids the eating of any "swarming creature." The Pharisees' scrupulosity about minor matters and neglect of greater ones (23) is further brought out by this contrast between straining liquids that might contain a tiny "swarming creature" and yet swallowing *the camel.* The latter was one of the unclean animals forbidden by the law (Lv 11, 4), but it is hardly possible that the scribes and Pharisees are being denounced as guilty of so gross a violation of the food laws. To *swallow the camel* is only a hyperbolic way of speaking of their neglect of what is important.

23, 25-26: The ritual washing of utensils for dining (cf Mk 7, 4) is turned into a metaphor illustrating a concern for appear-

Mt

in your synagogues and pursue from town to town, ³⁵so that there may come upon you all the righteous blood shed upon earth, from the blood of Abel to the blood of Zechariah, the son of Barachiah, whom you murdered between the sanctuary and the altar. ³⁶Amen, I say to you, all these things will come upon this generation.

The Lament over Jerusalem.* ³⁷ *j* "Jerusalem, Jerusalem, you who kill the prophets and stone those sent to you, how many times I yearned to gather your children together, as a hen gathers her young under her wings, but you were unwilling! *k* ³⁸Behold, your house will be abandoned, desolate.*l* ³⁹I tell you, you will not see me again until you say, 'Blessed is he who comes in the name of the Lord.' "*m*

j 37-39: Lk 13, 34-35; 19, 41-44.—k Mt 21, 35.—l Jer 12, 7.—m Ps 118, 26.—n 1-44: Mk 13, 1-37; Lk 21, 5-36.—o Dn 2, 28 LXX.—p Is 19, 2.—q Mt 10, 17.

23, 37-39: Cf Lk 13, 34-35. The denunciation of Pharisaic Judaism ends with this lament over *Jerusalem*, which has repeatedly rejected and murdered those whom God has *sent to her*. *How many times:* this may refer to various visits of Jesus to the city, an aspect of his ministry found in Jn but otherwise not in the synoptics. *As a hen . . . under her wings:* for imagery similar to this, see Pss 17, 8; 91, 4. *Your house . . . desolate:* probably an allusion to the destruction of the temple in A.D. 70. *You will not see me . . . in the name of the Lord:* Israel will not see Jesus again until he comes in glory for the final judgment. The acclamation has been interpreted in contrasting ways, as an indication that Israel will at last accept Jesus at that time, and as its troubled recognition of him as its dreaded judge who will pronounce its condemnation; in support of the latter view see Mt 24, 30.

24, 1—25, 46: The discourse of the fifth book, the last of the five around which the gospel is structured. It is called the "eschatological" discourse since it deals with the coming of the new age (the *eschaton*) in its fullness, with events that will precede it, and with how the disciples are to conduct themselves while awaiting an event that is as certain as its exact time is unknown to all but the Father (Mt 24, 36). The discourse may be divided into two parts, Mt 24, 1-44 and Mt 24, 45—25, 46. In the first, Matthew follows his Marcan source (Mk 13, 1-37) closely. The second is drawn from Q and from the evangelist's own traditional material. Both parts show Matthew's editing of his sources by deletions, additions, and modifications. The vigilant waiting that is emphasized in the second part does not mean a cessation of ordinary activity and concentration only on what is to come, but a faithful accomplishment of duties at hand, with awareness that the end, for which the disciples must always be ready, will entail the great judgment by which the everlasting destiny of all will be determined.

24, 2: As in Mk, Jesus predicts the destruction of the temple. By omitting the Marcan story of the widow's contribution (Mk 12, 41-44) that immediately precedes the prediction in that gospel, Matthew has established a close connection between it and Mt 23, 38, ". . . your house will be abandoned desolate."

24, 3: *The Mount of Olives:* see the note on Mt 21, 1. *The disciples:* cf Mk 13, 3-4 where only Peter, James, John, and Andrew put the question that is answered by the discourse. In both gospels, however, the question is put *privately:* the ensuing discourse is only for those who are *disciples* of Jesus. *When will this happen . . . end of the age?:* Matthew distinguishes carefully between the destruction of the temple *(this)* and the *coming* of Jesus that will bring *the end of the age.* In Mk the two events are more closely connected, a fact that may be explained by

---

CHAPTER 24

The Destruction of the Temple Foretold. ¹ * *n* Jesus left the temple area and was going away, when his disciples approached him to point out the temple buildings. ²* He said to them in reply, "You see all these things, do you not? Amen, I say to you, there will not be left here a stone upon another stone that will not be thrown down."

The Beginning of Calamities. ³As he was sitting on the Mount of Olives,* the disciples approached him privately and said, "Tell us, when will this happen, and what sign will there be of your coming, and of the end of the age?" ⁴ * Jesus said to them in reply, "See that no one deceives you. ⁵For many will come in my name, saying, 'I am the Messiah,' and they will deceive many. ⁶You will hear of wars* and reports of wars; see that you are not alarmed, for these things must happen, but it will not yet be the end.*o* ⁷Nation will rise against nation, and kingdom against kingdom; there will be famines and earthquakes from place to place.*p* ⁸All these are the beginning of the labor pains.* ⁹Then they will hand you over to persecution, and they will kill you.*q* You will be hated by all nations*

Mark's believing that the one would immediately succeed the other. *Coming:* this translates the Greek word *parousia,* which is used in the gospels only here and in vv 27, 37, and 39. It designated the official visit of a ruler to a city or the manifestation of a saving deity, and it was used by Christians to refer to the final coming of Jesus in glory, a term first found in the New Testament with that meaning in 1 Thes 2, 19. *The end of the age:* see the note on Mt 13, 39.

24, 4-14: This section of the discourse deals with calamities in the world (6-7) and in the church (9-12). The former *must happen* before *the end* comes (6), but they are only *the beginning of the labor pains* (8). (It may be noted that the Greek word translated *the end* in v 6 and in vv 13-14 is not the same as the phrase "the end of the age" in v 3, although the meaning is the same.) The latter are sufferings of the church, from within and without, that will last until the *gospel is preached . . . to all nations. Then the end will come* and those who have endured the sufferings with fidelity *will be saved* (13-14).

24, 6-7: The disturbances mentioned here are a commonplace of apocalyptic language, as is the assurance that they *must happen* (see Dn 2, 28 LXX), for that is the plan of God. *Kingdom against kingdom:* see Is 19, 2.

24, 8: *The labor pains:* the tribulations leading up to the end of the age are compared to the pains of a woman about to give birth. There is much attestation for rabbinic use of the phrase "the woes (or birth pains) of the Messiah" after the New Testament period, but in at least one instance it is attributed to a rabbi who lived in the late first century A.D. In this Jewish usage it meant the distress of the time preceding the coming of the Messiah; here, the *labor pains* precede the coming of the Son of Man in glory.

24, 9-12: Matthew has used Mk 13, 9-12 in his missionary discourse (Mt 10, 17-21) and omits it here. Besides the sufferings, including death, and the hatred of *all nations* that the disciples will have to endure, there will be worse affliction within the church itself. This is described in vv 10-12, which are peculiar to because of my name. [10] And then many will be led into sin; they will betray and hate one another. [11] Many false prophets will arise and deceive many; [12] and because of the increase of evildoing, the love of many will grow cold. [13] But the one who perseveres to the end will be saved.[r] [14] And this gospel of the kingdom will be preached throughout the world as a witness to all nations,* and then the end will come.[s]

The Great Tribulation.* [15] "When you see the desolating abomination* spoken of through Daniel the prophet standing in the holy place (let the reader understand),[t] [16] then those in Judea must flee* to the mountains, [17] * a person on the housetop must not go down to get things out of his house,[u] [18] a person in the field must not return to get his cloak. [19] Woe to pregnant women and nursing mothers in those days. [20] Pray that your flight not be in winter or on the sabbath,* [21] for at that time there will be great tribulation,[v] such as has not been since the beginning of the world until now, nor ever will be.* [22] And if those days had not been shortened, no one would be saved; but for the sake of the elect they will be shortened. [23] If anyone says to you then, 'Look, here is the Messiah!' or, 'There he is!' do not believe it.[w] [24] False messiahs and false prophets will arise, and they will perform signs and wonders so great as to deceive, if that were possible, even the elect. [25] Behold, I have told it to you beforehand. [26] So if they say to you, 'He is in the desert,' do not go out there; if they say, 'He is in the inner rooms,' do not believe it.* [27] For just as lightning comes from the east and is seen as far as the west, so will the coming of the Son of Man be.[x] [28] Wherever the corpse is, there the vultures will gather.

The Coming of the Son of Man. [29] "Immediately after the tribulation of those days,

    the sun will be darkened,
       and the moon will not give its light,
    and the stars will fall from the sky,
       and the powers of the heavens will be shaken.* [y]

---

r Mt 10, 22.—s Mt 28, 19; Rom 10, 18.—t Dn 9, 27; 11, 31; 12, 11; Mk 13, 14.—u Lk 17, 31.—v Dn 12, 1.—w Lk 17, 23.— x 27-28: Lk 17, 24.37.—y Is 13, 10.13; Ez 32, 7; Am 8, 9.

Mt. *Will be led into sin:* literally, "will be scandalized," probably meaning that they will become apostates; see Mt 13, 21 where "fall away" translates the same Greek word as here. *Betray:* in the Greek this is the same word as the *hand over* of v 9. The handing over to persecution and hatred from outside will have their counterpart within the church. *False prophets:* these are Christians; see the note on Mt 7, 15-20. *Evildoing:* see Mt 7, 23. Because of the apocalyptic nature of much of this discourse, the literal meaning of this description of the church should not be pressed too hard. However, there is reason to think that Mt's addition of these verses reflects in some measure the condition of his community.

24, 14: Except for the last part *(and then the end will come),* this verse substantially repeats Mk 13, 10. The Matthean addition raises a problem since what follows in vv 15-23 refers to the horrors of the First Jewish Revolt including the destruction of the temple, and Matthew, writing after that time, knew that the parousia of Jesus was still in the future. A solution may be that the evangelist saw the events of those verses as foreshadowing the cosmic disturbances that he associates with the parousia (29) so that the period in which the former took place could be understood as belonging to *the end.*

24, 15-28: Cf Mk 13, 14-23; Lk 17, 23-24.37. A further stage in the tribulations that will precede the coming of the Son of Man, and an answer to the question of v 3a, "when will this (the destruction of the temple) happen?"

24, 15: *The desolating abomination:* in 167 B.C. the Syrian king Antiochus IV Epiphanes desecrated the temple by setting up in it a statue of Zeus Olympios (see 1 Mc 1, 54). That event is referred to in Dn 12, 11 LXX as the "desolating abomination" (NAB "horrible abomination") and the same Greek term is used here; cf also Dn 9, 27; 11, 31. Although the desecration had taken place before Dn was written, it is presented there as a future event, and Matthew sees that "prophecy" fulfilled in the desecration of the temple by the Romans. *In the holy place:* the temple; more precise than Mk's *where he should not* (Mk 13,

14). *Let the reader understand:* this parenthetical remark, taken from Mk 13, 14, invites *the reader* to realize the meaning of Dn's "prophecy."

24, 16: The tradition that the Christians of Jerusalem fled from that city to Pella, a city of Transjordan, at the time of the First Jewish Revolt is found in Eusebius *(Ecclesiastical History,* 3, 5, 3), who attributes the flight to "a certain oracle given by revelation before the war." The tradition is not improbable but the Matthean command, derived from its Marcan source, is vague in respect to the place of flight (*to the mountains*), although some scholars see it as applicable to the flight to Pella.

24, 17-19: Haste is essential, and the journey will be particularly difficult for women who are burdened with unborn or infant children.

24, 20: *On the sabbath:* this addition to *in winter* (cf Mk 13, 18) has been understood as an indication that Mt was addressed to a church still observing the Mosaic law of sabbath rest and the scribal limitations upon the length of journeys that might lawfully be made on that day. That interpretation conflicts with Mt's view on sabbath observance (cf Mt 12, 1-14). The meaning of the addition may be that those undertaking on the sabbath a journey such as the one here ordered would be offending the sensibilities of law-observant Jews and would incur their hostility.

24, 21: For the unparalleled distress of that time, see Dn 12, 1.

24, 26-28: Claims that the Messiah is to be found in some distant or secret place must be ignored. *The coming of the Son of Man* will be as clear as *lightning* is to all and as *the corpse* of an animal is to *vultures;* cf Lk 17, 24.37. Here there is clear identification of *the Son of Man* and the Messiah; cf v 23.

24, 29: The answer to the question of v 3b, "What will be the sign of your coming?" *Immediately after . . . those days:* the shortening of time between the preceding *tribulation* and the parousia has been explained as Matthew's use of a supposed device of Old Testament prophecy whereby certainty that a predicted event will occur is expressed by depicting it as imminent. While it is questionable that that is an acceptable understanding of the Old Testament predictions, it may be applicable here, for Matthew knew that the parousia had not come *immediately after* the fall of Jerusalem, and it is unlikely that he is attributing a mistaken calculation of time to Jesus. *The sun . . . be shaken:* cf Is 13, 10.13.

Mt

30 And then the sign of the Son of Man* will appear in heaven, and all the tribes of the earth will mourn, and they will see the Son of Man coming upon the clouds of heaven with power and great glory.ᶻ 31 And he will send out his angels* with a trumpet blast, and they will gather his elect from the four winds, from one end of the heavens to the other.ᵃ

The Lesson of the Fig Tree.* 32 "Learn a lesson from the fig tree. When its branch becomes tender and sprouts leaves, you know that summer is near. 33 In the same way, when you see all these things, know that he is near, at the gates. 34 Amen, I say to you, this generation* will not pass away until all these things have taken place. 35 Heaven and earth will pass away, but my words will not pass away.ᵇ

The Unknown Day and Hour.* 36 "But of that day and hour no one knows, neither the angels of heaven, nor the Son,* but the Father alone.ᶜ 37 * For as it was in the days of Noah, so it will be at the coming of the Son of Man.ᵈ 38 In [those] days before the flood, they were eating and drinking, marrying and giving in marriage, up to the day that Noah entered the ark. 39 They did not know until the flood came and carried them all away. So will it be [also] at the coming of the Son of Man. 40 * Two men will be out in the field; one will be taken,

and one will be left.ᵉ 41 Two women will be grinding at the mill; one will be taken, and one will be left. 42 * Therefore, stay awake! ᶠ For you do not know on which day your Lord will come. 43 Be sure of this: if the master of the house had known the hour of night when the thief was coming, he would have stayed awake and not let his house be broken into.ᵍ 44 So too, you also must be prepared, for at an hour you do not expect, the Son of Man will come.

The Faithful or the Unfaithful Servant.* 45 ʰ "Who, then, is the faithful and prudent servant, whom the master has put in charge of his household to distribute to them their food at the proper time?* 46 Blessed is that servant whom his master on his arrival finds doing so. 47 Amen, I say to you, he will put him in charge of all his property. 48 But if that wicked servant says to himself, 'My master is long delayed,'* 49 and begins to beat his fellow servants, and eat and drink with drunkards, 50 the servant's master will come on an unexpected day and at an unknown hour 51 and will punish him severely* and assign him a place with the hypocrites, where there will be wailing and grinding of teeth.ⁱ

24, 36: Many textual witnesses omit *nor the Son*, which follows Mk 13, 32. Since its omission can be explained by reluctance to attribute this ignorance to *the Son*, the reading that includes it is probably original.

24, 37-39: Cf Lk 17, 26-27. *In the days of Noah:* the Old Testament account of the flood lays no emphasis upon what is central for Matthew, i.e., the unexpected coming of the flood upon those who were unprepared for it.

24, 40-41: Cf Lk 17, 34-35. *Taken . . . left:* the former probably means *taken* into the kingdom; the latter, *left* for destruction. People in the same situation will be dealt with in opposite ways. In this context, the discrimination between them will be based on their readiness for the coming of the Son of Man.

24, 42-44: Cf Lk 12, 39-40. The theme of vigilance and readiness is continued with the bold comparison of the Son of Man to a thief who comes to break into a house.

24, 45-51: The second part of the discourse (see the note on Mt 24, 1 —25, 46) begins with this parable of *the faithful* or unfaithful *servant;* cf Lk 12, 41-46. It is addressed to the leaders of Matthew's church; *the servant has* been *put in charge* of his master's *household* (45) even though that *household* is composed of those who are his *fellow servants* (49).

24, 45: *To distribute . . . proper time:* readiness for the master's return means a vigilance that is accompanied by faithful performance of the duty assigned.

24, 48: *My master . . . delayed:* the note of delay is found also in the other parables of this section; cf Mt 25, 5.19.

24, 51: *Punish him severely:* the Greek verb, found in the New Testament only here and in the Lucan parallel (Lk 12, 46), means, literally, "cut in two." *With the hypocrites:* see the note on Mt 6, 2. Matthew classes the unfaithful Christian leader with the unbelieving leaders of Judaism. *Wailing and grinding of teeth:* see the note on Mt 8, 11-12.

---

z Dn 7, 13; Zec 12, 12-14; Rv 1, 7.—a Is 27, 13; 1 Cor 15, 52; 1 Thes 4, 16.—b Is 40, 8.—c Acts 1, 7.—d 37-39: Gn 6, 5—7. 23; Lk 17, 26-27; 2 Pt 3, 6.—e 40-41: Lk 17, 34-35.—f 42-44: Mt 25, 13; Lk 12, 39-40.—g 1 Thes 5, 2.—h 45-51: Lk 12, 41-46.—i Mt 13, 42; 25, 30.

24, 30: *The sign of the Son of Man:* perhaps this means *the sign* that is the glorious appearance *of the Son of Man;* cf Mt 12, 39-40 where "the sign of Jonah" is Jonah's being in the "belly of the whale." *Tribes of the earth will mourn:* peculiar to Mt; cf Zec 12, 12-14. *Coming upon the clouds . . . glory:* cf Dn 7, 13, although there the "one like a son of man" comes to God to receive kingship; here *the Son of Man* comes from heaven for judgment.

24, 31: *Send out his angels:* cf Mt 13, 41 where they are sent out to collect the wicked for punishment. *Trumpet blast:* cf Is 27, 13; 1 Thes 4, 16.

24, 32-35: Cf Mk 13, 28-31.

24, 34: The difficulty raised by this verse cannot be satisfactorily removed by the supposition that *this generation* means the Jewish people throughout the course of their history, much less the entire human race. Perhaps for Matthew it means the *generation* to which he and his community belonged.

24, 36-44: The statement of v 34 is now counterbalanced by one that declares that the exact time of the parousia is known only to *the Father* (36), and the disciples are warned to be always ready for it. This section is drawn from Mk and Q (cf Lk 17, 26-27.34-35; 12, 39-40).

CHAPTER 25

The Parable of the Ten Virgins.* ¹"Then* the kingdom of heaven will be like ten virgins who took their lamps and went out to meet the bridegroom. ²Five of them were foolish and five were wise.* ³The foolish ones, when taking their lamps, brought no oil with them, ⁴but the wise brought flasks of oil with their lamps. ⁵Since the bridegroom was long delayed, they all became drowsy and fell asleep. ⁶At midnight, there was a cry, 'Behold, the bridegroom! Come out to meet him!' ⁷Then all those virgins got up and trimmed their lamps. ⁸The foolish ones said to the wise, 'Give us some of your oil, for our lamps are going out.' ⁹But the wise ones replied, 'No, for there may not be enough for us and you. Go instead to the merchants and buy some for yourselves.' ¹⁰While they went off to buy it, the bridegroom came and those who were ready went into the wedding feast with him. Then the door was locked. ¹¹ * Afterwards the other virgins came and said, 'Lord, Lord, open the door for us!'ʲ ¹²But he said in reply, 'Amen, I say to you, I do not know you.' ¹³Therefore, stay awake,* for you know neither the day nor the hour.ᵏ

The Parable of the Talents.* ¹⁴ ˡ "It will be as when a man who was going on a journey* called in his servants and entrusted his possessions to them. ¹⁵To one he gave five talents;* to another, two; to a third, one—to each according to his ability. Then he went away. Immediately ¹⁶the one who received five talents went and traded with them, and made another five. ¹⁷Likewise, the one who received two made another two. ¹⁸But the man who received one went off and dug a hole in the ground and buried his master's money.* ¹⁹After a long time the master of those servants came back and settled accounts with them. ²⁰The one who had received five talents came forward bringing the additional five.* He said, 'Master, you gave me five talents. See, I have made five more.' ²¹His master said to him, 'Well done, my good and faithful servant. Since you were faithful in small matters, I will give you great responsibilities. Come, share your master's joy.'ᵐ ²²[Then] the one who had received two talents also came forward and said, 'Master, you gave me two talents. See, I have made two more.' ²³His master said to him, 'Well done, my good and faithful servant. Since you were faithful in small matters, I will give you great responsibilities. Come, share your master's joy.' ²⁴Then the one who had received the one talent came forward and said, 'Master, I knew you were a demanding person, harvesting where you did not plant and gathering where you did not scatter; ²⁵so out of fear I went off and buried your talent in the ground. Here it is back.' ²⁶His master said to him in reply, 'You wicked, lazy servant!* So you knew that I harvest where I did not plant and gather where I did not scatter? ²⁷Should you not then have put my money in the bank so that I could have got it back with interest on my return? ²⁸Now then! Take the talent from him and give it to the one with ten. ²⁹ ⁿ For to everyone who has, more will be given and he will grow rich; but from the one who has not, even what he has will be taken away.* ³⁰And throw this useless servant into the darkness outside, where there will be wailing and grinding of teeth.'*

---

j 11-12: Mt 7, 21.23; Lk 13, 25.27.—k Mt 24, 42; Mk 13, 33.—l 14-30: Lk 19, 12-27.—m Lk 16, 10.—n Mt 13, 12; Mk 4, 25; Lk 8, 18; 19, 26.

25, 1-13: Peculiar to Mt.

25, 1: *Then:* at the time of the parousia. *Kingdom . . . will be like:* see the note on Mt 13, 24-30.

25, 2-4: *Foolish . . . wise:* cf the contrasted "wise man" and "fool" of Mt 7, 24.26, where the two are distinguished by good deeds and lack of them, and such deeds may be signified by the *oil* of this parable.

25, 11-12: *Lord, Lord:* cf Mt 7, 21. *I do not know you:* cf Mt 7, 23, where the Greek verb is different but synonymous.

25, 13: *Stay awake:* some scholars see this command as an addition to the original parable of Matthew's traditional material, since in v 5 all the virgins, wise and foolish, fall asleep. The wise virgins are adequately equipped for their task, and *stay awake* may mean no more than to be prepared; cf Mt 24, 42.44.

25, 14-30: Cf Lk 19, 12-27.

25, 14: *It will be as when . . . journey:* literally, "For just as a man who was going on a journey." Although the comparison is not completed, the sense is clear; the kingdom of heaven is like the situation here described. Faithful use of one's gifts will lead to participation in the fullness of the kingdom, lazy inactivity to exclusion from it.

25, 15: *Talents:* see the note on Mt 18, 24.

25, 18: *Buried his master's money:* see the note on Mt 13, 44.

25, 20-23: Although the first two servants have received and doubled large sums, their faithful trading is regarded by the master as fidelity *in small matters* only, compared with the *great responsibilities* now to be given to them. The latter are unspecified. *Share your master's joy:* probably the joy of the banquet of the kingdom; cf Mt 8, 11.

25, 26-30: *Wicked, lazy servant:* this man's inactivity is not negligible but seriously culpable. As punishment, he loses the gift he had received, that is now given to the first servant, whose possessions are already great.

25, 29: See the note on Mt 13, 12 where there is a similar application of this maxim.

25, 30: See the note on Mt 8, 11-12.

The Judgment of the Nations.* [31]"When the Son of Man comes in his glory, and all the angels with him,[o] he will sit upon his glorious throne,* [32] and all the nations* will be assembled before him. And he will separate them one from another, as a shepherd separates the sheep from the goats.[p] [33] He will place the sheep on his right and the goats on his left. [34] Then the king will say to those on his right, 'Come, you who are blessed by my Father. Inherit the kingdom prepared for you from the foundation of the world. [35] [q] For I was hungry and you gave me food, I was thirsty and you gave me drink, a stranger and you welcomed me, [36] naked and you clothed me, ill and you cared for me, in prison and you visited me.' [37] Then the righteous* will answer him and say, 'Lord, when did we see you hungry and feed you, or thirsty and give you drink? [38] When did we see you a stranger and welcome you, or naked and clothe you? [39] When did we see you ill or in prison, and visit you?' [40] [r] And the king will say to them in reply, 'Amen, I say to you, whatever you did for one of these least brothers of mine, you did for me.' [41] [s] Then he will say to those on his left, 'Depart from me, you accursed, into the eternal fire prepared for the devil and his angels.* [42] For I was hungry and you gave me no food,[t] I was thirsty and you gave me

no drink, [43] a stranger and you gave me no welcome, naked and you gave me no clothing, ill and in prison, and you did not care for me.' [44] *Then they will answer and say, 'Lord, when did we see you hungry or thirsty or a stranger or naked or ill or in prison, and not minister to your needs?' [45] He will answer them, 'Amen, I say to you, what you did not do for one of these least ones, you did not do for me.' [46] And these will go off to eternal punishment, but the righteous to eternal life."[u]

VII. THE PASSION AND RESURRECTION

CHAPTER 26

The Conspiracy against Jesus. [1] * When Jesus finished all these words,* he said to his disciples, [2] [v] "You know that in two days' time it will be Passover, and the Son of Man will be handed over to be crucified." [3] Then the chief priests and the elders of the people assembled in the palace of the high priest, who was called Caiaphas,* [4] and they consulted together to arrest Jesus by treachery and put him to death.[w] [5] But they said, "Not during the festival,* that there may not be a riot among the people."

---

o Mt 16, 27; Dt 33, 2 LXX.—p Ez 34, 17.—q 35-36: Is 58, 7; Ez 18, 7.—r Mt 10, 40.42.—s Mt 7, 23; Lk 13, 27.—t 42-43: Jb 22, 7; Jas 2, 15-16.—u Dn 12, 2.—v 2-5: Mk 14, 1-2; Lk 22, 1-2.—w Jn 11, 47-53.

25, 31-46: The conclusion of the discourse, which is peculiar to Mt, portrays the final judgment that will accompany the parousia. Although often called a "parable," it is not really such, for the only parabolic elements are the depiction of *the Son of Man* as *a shepherd* and of *the righteous* and the wicked as *sheep* and *goats* respectively (32-33). The criterion of judgment will be the deeds of mercy that have been done for the *least* of *Jesus' brothers* (40). A difficult and important question is the identification of these *least brothers.* Are they all people who have suffered hunger, thirst, etc. (35.36) or a particular group of such sufferers? Scholars are divided in their response and arguments can be made for either side. But leaving aside the problem of what the traditional material that Matthew edited may have meant, it seems that a stronger case can be made for the view that in the evangelist's sense the sufferers are Christians, probably Christian missionaries whose sufferings were brought upon them by their preaching of the gospel. The criterion of judgment for *all the nations* is their treatment of those who have borne to the world the message of Jesus, and this means ultimately their acceptance or rejection of Jesus himself; cf Mt 10, 40, "Whoever receives you, receives me."

25, 31: See the note on Mt 16, 27.

25, 32: *All the nations:* before the end the gospel will have been preached throughout the world (Mt 24, 14); thus the Gentiles will be judged on their response to it. But the phrase *all the nations* includes the Jews also, for at the judgment "the Son of Man . . . will repay everyone according to his conduct" (Mt 16, 27).

25, 37-40: *The righteous* will be astonished that in caring for the needs of the sufferers they were ministering to the *Lord* himself. *One of these least brothers of mine:* cf Mt 10, 42.

25, 41: *Fire prepared . . . his angels:* cf 1 Enoch 10, 13 where it is said of the evil angels and Semyaza, their leader, "In those days they will lead them into the bottom of the fire—and in torment—in the place (where) they will be locked up forever."

25, 44-45: The *accursed* (41) will be likewise astonished that their neglect of the sufferers was neglect of the *Lord* and will receive from him a similar answer.

26, 1—28, 20: The five books with alternating narrative and discourse (Mt 3, 1—25, 46) that give this gospel its distinctive structure lead up to the climactic events that are the center of Christian belief and the origin of the Christian church, the passion and resurrection of Jesus. In his passion narrative (chs 26-27) Matthew follows his Marcan source closely but with omissions (e.g., Mk 14, 51-52) and additions (e.g., Mt 27, 3-10.19). Some of the additions indicate that he utilized traditions that he had received from elsewhere; others are due to his own theological insight (e.g., Mt 26, 28, ". . . for the forgiveness of sins"; Mt 27, 52). In his editing Matthew also altered Mk in some minor details. But there is no need to suppose that he knew any passion narrative other than Mark's.

26, 1-2: *When Jesus finished all these words:* see the note on Mt 7, 28-29. *"You know . . . crucified":* Matthew turns Mk's statement of the time (Mk 14, 1) into Jesus' final prediction of his passion. *Passover:* see the note on Mk 14, 1.

26, 3: *Caiaphas* was high priest from A.D. 18 to 36.

26, 5: *Not during the festival:* the plan to delay Jesus' arrest and execution until after *the festival* was not carried out, for according to the synoptics he was arrested on the night of Nisan 14 and put to death the following day. No reason is given why the plan was changed.

The Anointing at Bethany.* [6] [x] Now when Jesus was in Bethany in the house of Simon the leper, [7] a woman came up to him with an alabaster jar of costly perfumed oil, and poured it on his head while he was reclining at table. [8] When the disciples saw this, they were indignant and said, "Why this waste? [9] It could have been sold for much, and the money given to the poor." [10] Since Jesus knew this, he said to them, "Why do you make trouble for the woman? She has done a good thing for me. [11] The poor you will always have with you; but you will not always have me.[y] [12] In pouring this perfumed oil upon my body, she did it to prepare me for burial.* [13] Amen, I say to you, wherever this gospel is proclaimed in the whole world, what she has done will be spoken of, in memory of her."

The Betrayal by Judas. [14] [z] Then one of the Twelve, who was called Judas Iscariot,* went to the chief priests [15] [a] and said, "What are you willing to give me if I hand him over to you?"* They paid him thirty pieces of silver, [16] and from that time on he looked for an opportunity to hand him over.

Preparations for the Passover. [17] [b] On the first day of the Feast of Unleavened Bread,* the disciples approached Jesus and said, "Where do you want us to prepare for you to eat the Passover?"[c] [18] * He said, "Go into the city to a certain man and tell him, 'The teacher says, "My appointed time draws near; in your house I shall celebrate the Passover with my disciples." ' " [19] The disciples then did as Jesus had ordered, and prepared the Passover.

The Betrayer. [20] When it was evening, he reclined at table with the Twelve. [21] And while they were eating, he said, "Amen, I say to you, one of you will betray me."* [22] Deeply distressed at this, they began to say to him one after another, "Surely it is not I, Lord?" [23] He said in reply, "He who has dipped his hand into the dish with me is the one who will betray me. [24] The Son of Man indeed goes, as it is written of him,[d] but woe to that man by whom the Son of Man is betrayed. It would be better for that man if he had never been born."* [25] Then Judas, his betrayer, said in reply, "Surely it is not I, Rabbi?" He answered, "You have said so."*

The Lord's Supper. [26] * [e] While they were eating,[f] Jesus took bread, said the blessing, broke it, and giving it to his disciples said, "Take and eat; this is my body."* [27] Then he took a cup, gave thanks,* and

Mt

---

x 6-13: Mk 14, 3-9; Jn 12, 1-8.—y Dt 15, 11.—z 14-16: Mk 14, 10-11; Lk 22, 3-6.—a Zec 11, 12.—b 17-25: Mk 14, 12-21; Lk 22, 7-23.—c Ex 12, 14-20.—d Is 53, 8-10—e 26-30: Mk 14, 22-26; Lk 22, 14-23; 1 Cor 11, 23-25.—f 26-27: 1 Cor 10, 16.

26, 6-13: See the notes on Mk 14, 3-9 and Jn 12, 1-8.

26, 12: *To prepare me for burial:* cf Mk 14, 8. In accordance with the interpretation of this act as Jesus' *burial* anointing, Matthew, more consistent than Mark, changes the purpose of the visit of the women to Jesus' tomb; they do not go to anoint him (Mk 16, 1) but "to see the tomb" (Mt 28, 1).

26, 14: *Iscariot:* see the note on Lk 6, 16.

26, 15: The motive of avarice is introduced by Judas's question about the price for betrayal, which is absent in the Marcan source (Mk 14, 10-11). *Hand him over:* the same Greek verb is used to express the saving purpose of God by which Jesus is handed over to death (cf Mt 17, 22; 20, 18; 26, 2) and the human malice that hands him over. *Thirty pieces of silver:* the price of the betrayal is found only in Mt. It is derived from Zec 11, 12 where it is the wages paid to the rejected shepherd, a cheap price (Zec 11, 13). That amount is also the compensation paid to one whose slave has been gored by an ox (Ex 21, 32).

26, 17: *The first day of the Feast of Unleavened Bread:* see the note on Mk 14, 1. Matthew omits Mk's "when they sacrificed the Passover lamb."

26, 18: By omitting much of Mk 14, 13-15, adding *My appointed time draws near,* and turning the question into a statement, *in your house I shall celebrate the Passover,* Matthew has given this passage a solemnity and majesty greater than that of his source.

26, 21: Given Matthew's interest in the fulfillment of the Old Testament, it is curious that he omits the Marcan designation of Jesus' betrayer as "one who is eating with me" (Mk 14, 18), since that is probably an allusion to Ps 41, 10. However, the shocking fact that the betrayer is one who shares table fellowship with Jesus is emphasized in v 23.

26, 24: *It would be better . . . born:* the enormity of the deed is such that it would be better not to exist than to do it.

26, 25: Peculiar to Mt. *You have said so:* cf Mt 26, 64; 27, 11. This is a half-affirmative. Emphasis is laid on the pronoun and the answer implies that the statement would not have been made if the question had not been asked.

26, 26-29: See the note on Mk 14, 22-24. The Marcan-Matthean is one of the two major New Testament traditions of the words of Jesus when instituting the Eucharist. The other (and earlier) is the Pauline-Lucan (1 Cor 11, 23-25; Lk 22, 19-20). Each shows the influence of Christian liturgical usage, but the Marcan-Matthean is more developed in that regard than the Pauline-Lucan. The words over the bread and cup succeed each other without the intervening meal mentioned in 1 Cor 11, 25; Lk 22, 20; and there is parallelism between the consecratory words *(this is my body . . . this is my blood).* Matthew follows Mk closely but with some changes.

26, 26: See the note on Mt 14, 19. *Said the blessing:* a prayer blessing God. *Take and eat:* literally, *Take, eat. Eat* is an addition to Mk's "take it" (literally, "take"; Mk 14, 22). *This is my body:* the bread is identified with Jesus himself.

26, 27-28: *Gave thanks:* see the note on Mt 15, 36. *Gave it to them . . . all of you:* cf Mk 14, 23-24. In the Marcan sequence the disciples drink and then Jesus says the interpretative words. Matthew has changed this into a command to *drink* followed by those words. *My blood:* see Lv 17, 11 for the concept that the *blood* is "the seat of life" and that when placed on the altar it "makes atonement." *Which will be shed:* the present participle, "being shed" or "going to be shed," is future in relation to the Last Supper. *On behalf of:* Greek *peri;* see the note on Mk 14, 24. *Many:* see the note on Mt 20, 28. *For the forgiveness of sins:* a Matthean addition. The same phrase occurs in Mk 1, 4 in connection with John's baptism but Matthew avoids it there (Mt 3, 11). He places it here probably because he wishes to emphasize that it is the sacrificial death of Jesus that brings *forgiveness of sins.*

gave it to them, saying, "Drink from it, all of you, 28 for this is my blood of the covenant, which will be shed on behalf of many for the forgiveness of sins.g 29 I tell you, from now on I shall not drink this fruit of the vine until the day when I drink it with you new in the kingdom of my Father."* 30 Then, after singing a hymn, they went out to the Mount of Olives.*

Peter's Denial Foretold. 31 h Then Jesus said to them, "This night all of you will have your faith in me shaken,* for it is written:

'I will strike the shepherd,
    and the sheep of the flock will be dispersed';i

32 but after I have been raised up, I shall go before you to Galilee." 33 Peter said to him in reply, "Though all may have their faith in you shaken, mine will never be." 34 j Jesus said to him, "Amen, I say to you, this very night before the cock crows,* you will deny me three times."k 35 Peter said to him, "Even though I should have to die with you, I will not deny you." And all the disciples spoke likewise.

The Agony in the Garden. 36 * l Then Jesus came with them to a place called Gethsemane,* and he said to his disciples,m "Sit here while I go over there and pray." 37 n He took along Peter and the two sons of Zebedee,* and began to feel sorrow and distress. 38 Then he said to them, "My soul is sorrowful even to death.* Remain here and keep watch with me."o 39 He advanced a little and fell prostrate in prayer, saying, "My Father,* if it is possible, let this cup pass from me; yet, not as I will, but as you will."p 40 When he returned to his disciples he found them asleep. He said to Peter, "So you could not keep watch with me for one hour? 41 Watch and pray that you may not undergo the test.* The spirit is willing, but the flesh is weak." 42 Withdrawing a second time, he prayed again, "My Father,q if it is not possible that this cup pass without my drinking it, your will be done!"* 43 Then he returned once more and found them asleep, for they could not keep their eyes open. 44 He left them and withdrew again and prayed a third time, saying the same thing again. 45 Then he returned to his disciples and said to them, "Are you still sleeping and taking your rest? Behold, the hour is at hand when the Son of Man is to be handed over to sinners.r 46 Get up, let us go. Look, my betrayer is at hand."

The Betrayal and Arrest of Jesus. 47 s While he was still speaking, Judas, one of the Twelve, arrived, accompanied by a large crowd, with swords and clubs, who

---

g Ex 24, 8; Is 53, 12.—h 31-35: Mk 14, 7-31.—i Zec 13, 7; Jn 16, 32.—j 34-35: Lk 22, 33-34; Jn 13, 37-38.—k Mt 26, 69-75.—l 36-46: Mk 14, 32-42; Lk 22, 39-46.—m Jn 18, 1.—n 37-39: Heb 5, 7.—o Ps 42, 6.12; Jon 4, 9.—p Jn 4, 34; 6, 38; Phil 2, 8.—q Mt 6, 10; Heb 10, 9.—r Jn 12, 23; 13, 1; 17, 1.—s 47-56: Mk 14, 43-50; Lk 22, 47-53; Jn 18, 3-11.

26, 29: Although his death will interrupt the table fellowship he has had with the disciples, Jesus confidently predicts his vindication by God and a new table fellowship with them at the banquet of the kingdom.

26, 30: See the note on Mk 14, 26.

26, 31: *Will have . . . shaken:* literally, "will be scandalized in me"; see the note on Mt 24, 9-12. *I will strike . . . dispersed:* cf Zec 13, 7.

26, 34: *Before the cock crows:* see the note on Mt 14, 25. The third watch of the night was called "cockcrow." *Deny me:* see the note on Mt 16, 24.

26, 36-56: Cf Mk 14, 32-52. The account of Jesus in Gethsemane is divided between that of his agony (36-46) and that of his betrayal and arrest (47-56). Jesus' *sorrow and distress* (37) in face of death is unrelieved by the presence of his three disciples who, though urged to *watch with* him (38.41), fall asleep (40.43). He prays that *if . . . possible* his death may be avoided (39) but that his Father's will be done (39.42.44). Knowing then that his death must take place, he announces to his companions that *the hour* for his being *handed over* has come (45). Judas arrives with an armed band provided by the Sanhedrin and greets Jesus with a kiss, the prearranged sign for his identification (47-49). After his arrest, he rebukes a disciple who has attacked *the*

high priest's servant with a *sword* (51-54), and chides those who have come out to seize him with *swords and clubs* as if he were *a robber* (55-56). In both rebukes Jesus declares that the treatment he is now receiving is the fulfillment of the scriptures (55.56). The subsequent flight of *all the disciples* is itself the fulfillment of his own prediction (cf 31). In this episode, Matthew follows Mk with a few alterations.

26, 36: *Gethsemane:* the Hebrew name means "oil press" and designates an olive orchard on the western slope of the Mount of Olives; see the note on Mt 21, 1. The name appears only in Mt and Mk. The place is called a "garden" in Jn 18, 1.

26, 37: *Peter and the two sons of Zebedee:* cf Mt 17, 1.

26, 38: Cf Ps 42, 6.12. In the Septuagint (Ps 41, 5.12) the same Greek word for *sorrowful* is used as here. *To death:* i.e., "enough to die"; cf Jon 4, 9.

26, 39: *My Father:* see the note on Mk 14, 36. Matthew omits the Aramaic *'abbā'* and adds the qualifier *my. This cup:* see the note on Mk 10, 38-40.

26, 41: *Undergo the test:* see the note on Mt 6, 13. In that verse "the final test" translates the same Greek word as is here translated *the test,* and these are the only instances of the use of that word in Mt. It is possible that the passion of Jesus is seen here as an anticipation of the great tribulation that will precede the parousia (see the notes on Mt 24, 8; 24, 21) to which Mt 6, 13 refers, and that just as Jesus prays to be delivered from death (39), so he exhorts the disciples to pray that they will not have to *undergo* the great *test* that his passion would be for them. Some scholars, however, understand *not undergo* (literally, "not enter") *the test* as meaning not that the disciples may be spared *the test* but that they may not yield to the temptation of falling away from Jesus because of his passion even though they will have to endure it.

26, 42: *Your will be done:* cf Mt 6, 10.

had come from the chief priests and the elders of the people. [48] His betrayer had arranged a sign with them, saying, "The man I shall kiss is the one; arrest him." [49] Immediately he went over to Jesus and said, "Hail, Rabbi!"* and he kissed him. [50] Jesus answered him, "Friend, do what you have come for." Then stepping forward they laid hands on Jesus and arrested him. [51] And behold, one of those who accompanied Jesus put his hand to his sword, drew it, and struck the high priest's servant, cutting off his ear. [52] Then Jesus said to him, "Put your sword back into its sheath, for all who take the sword will perish by the sword. [53] Do you think that I cannot call upon my Father and he will not provide me at this moment with more than twelve legions of angels? [54] But then how would the scriptures be fulfilled which say that it must come to pass in this way?" [55] At that hour Jesus said to the crowds, "Have you come out as against a robber, with swords and clubs to seize me? Day after day I sat teaching in the temple area, yet you did not arrest me.* [56] But all this has come to pass that the writings of the prophets may be fulfilled." Then all the disciples left him and fled.[t]

Jesus before the Sanhedrin.* [57] [u] Those who had arrested Jesus led him away to

Caiaphas* the high priest, where the scribes and the elders were assembled. [58] Peter was following him at a distance as far as the high priest's courtyard, and going inside he sat down with the servants to see the outcome. [59] The chief priests and the entire Sanhedrin* kept trying to obtain false testimony against Jesus in order to put him to death, [60] [v] but they found none, though many false witnesses came forward. Finally two* came forward [61] who stated, "This man said, 'I can destroy the temple of God and within three days rebuild it.'" [62] The high priest rose and addressed him, "Have you no answer? What are these men testifying against you?" [63] But Jesus was silent.* Then the high priest said to him, "I order you to tell us under oath before the living God whether you are the Messiah, the Son of God."[w] [64] Jesus said to him in reply, "You have said so.* But I tell you:

> From now on you will see 'the Son of Man
> seated at the right hand of the Power'
> and 'coming on the clouds of heaven.'"[x]

[65] Then the high priest tore his robes and said, "He has blasphemed!* What further

t Mt 26, 31.—u 57-68: Mk 14, 53-65; Lk 22, 54-55.63-71; Jn 18, 12-14.19-24.—v 60-61: Dt 19, 15; Jn 2, 19; Acts 6, 14.—w Is 53, 7.—x Ps 110, 1; Dn 7, 13.

26, 49: *Rabbi:* see the note on Mt 23, 6-7. Jesus is so addressed twice in Mt (cf 25), both times by Judas. For the significance of the closely related address "teacher" in Mt, see the note on Mt 8, 19.

26, 55: *Day after day . . . arrest me:* cf Mk 14, 49. This suggests that Jesus had taught for a relatively long period in Jerusalem, whereas Mt 21, 1-11 puts his coming to the city for the first time only a few days before.

26, 57-68: Following Mk 14, 53-65, Matthew presents the nighttime appearance of Jesus before *the Sanhedrin* as a real trial. After *many false witnesses* bring charges against him that do not suffice for the death sentence (60), *two came forward* who charge him with claiming to be able to *destroy the temple . . . and within three days* to *rebuild it* (60-61). Jesus makes no answer even when challenged to do so by *the high priest,* who then orders him to declare *under oath . . . whether* he is *the Messiah, the Son of God* (62-63). Matthew changes Mk's clear affirmative response (Mk 14, 62) to the same one as that given to Judas (cf 25), but follows Mk almost verbatim in Jesus' predicting that his judges will see him *(the Son of Man) seated at the right hand of God and coming on the clouds of heaven* (64). *The high priest* then charges him with blasphemy (65), a charge with which the other members of *the Sanhedrin* agree by declaring that *he deserves to die* (66). They then attack him (67) and mockingly demand that he *prophesy* (68). This account contains elements that are contrary to the judicial procedures prescribed in the Mishnah, the Jewish code of law that dates in written form from ca. A.D. 200, e.g., trial on a feast day, a night session of the court, pronouncement of a verdict of condemnation at the same session at which testimony was re-

ceived. Consequently, some scholars regard the account entirely as a creation of the early Christians without historical value. However, it is disputable whether the norms found in the Mishnah were in force at the time of Jesus. More to the point is the question whether the Matthean-Marcan night trial derives from a combination of two separate incidents, a nighttime preliminary investigation (cf Jn 18, 13.19-24) and a formal trial on the following morning (cf Lk 22, 66-71).

26, 57: *Caiaphas:* see the note on Mt 26, 3.

26, 59: *Sanhedrin:* see the note on Lk 22, 66.

26, 60-61: *Two:* cf Dt 19, 15. *I can destroy . . . rebuild it:* there are significant differences from the Marcan parallel (Mk 14, 58). Matthew omits "made with hands" and "not made with hands" and changes Mk's "will destroy" and "will build another" to *can destroy* and (can) *rebuild.* The charge is probably based on Jesus' prediction of the temple's destruction; see the notes on Mt 23, 37-39; 24, 2; and Jn 2, 19. A similar prediction by Jeremiah was considered as deserving death; cf Jer 7, 1-15; 26, 1-8.

26, 63: *Silent:* possibly an allusion to Is 53, 7. *I order you . . . living God:* peculiar to Mt; cf Mk 14, 61.

26, 64: *You have said so:* see the note on Mt 26, 25. *From now on . . . heaven:* the Son of Man who is to be crucified (cf Mt 20, 19) will be seen in glorious majesty (cf Ps 110, 1) and *coming on the clouds of heaven* (cf Dn 7, 13). *The Power:* see the note on Mk 14, 61-62.

26, 65: *Blasphemed:* the punishment for *blasphemy* was death by stoning (see Lv 24, 10-16). According to the Mishnah, to be guilty of *blasphemy* one had to pronounce "the Name itself," i.e. Yahweh; cf *Sanhedrin* 7, 4.5. Those who judge the gospel accounts of Jesus' trial by the later Mishnah standards point out that Jesus uses the surrogate "the Power," and hence no Jewish court would have regarded him as guilty of *blasphemy;* others hold that the Mishnah's narrow understanding of *blasphemy* was a later development.

need have we of witnesses? You have now heard the blasphemy; [66]what is your opinion?" They said in reply, "He deserves to die!" [67]*Then they spat in his face and struck him, while some slapped him,[y] [68]saying, "Prophesy for us, Messiah: who is it that struck you?"

Peter's Denial of Jesus. [69][z] Now Peter

was sitting outside in the courtyard. One of the maids came over to him and said, "You too were with Jesus the Galilean." [70]But he denied it in front of everyone,* saying, "I do not know what you are talking about!" [71]As he went out to the gate, another girl saw him and said to those who were there, "This man was with Jesus the Nazorean." [72]Again he denied it with an oath, "I do not know the man!" [73]A little later the bystanders came over and said to Peter, "Surely you too are one of them; even your speech gives you away."* [74]At that he began to curse and to swear, "I do not know the man." And immediately a cock crowed. [75]Then Peter remembered the word that Jesus had spoken: "Before the cock crows you will deny me three times." He went out and began to weep bitterly.[a]

CHAPTER 27

Jesus before Pilate. [1]* When it was

morning,[b] all the chief priests and the elders of the people took counsel* against Jesus to put him to death. [2]They bound

him, led him away, and handed him over to Pilate, the governor.

The Death of Judas. [3] [c] Then Judas, his betrayer, seeing that Jesus had been condemned, deeply regretted what he had done. He returned the thirty pieces of silver* to the chief priests and elders,[d] [4]saying, "I have sinned in betraying innocent blood." They said, "What is that to us? Look to it yourself." [5]Flinging the money into the temple, he departed and went off and hanged himself.* [6]The chief priests gathered up the money, but said, "It is not lawful to deposit this in the temple treasury, for it is the price of blood." [7]After consultation, they used it to buy the potter's field as a burial place for foreigners. [8]That is why that field even today is called the Field of Blood. [9]Then was fulfilled what had been said through Jeremiah the prophet,* "And they took the thirty pieces of silver, the value of a man with a price on his head, a price set by some of the Israelites, [10]and they paid it out for the potter's field just as the Lord had commanded me."[e]

Jesus Questioned by Pilate. [11] [f] Now Jesus stood before the governor, and he questioned him, "Are you the king of the Jews?"* Jesus said, "You say so." [12]And when he was accused by the chief priests

---

y Wis 2, 19; Is 50, 6.—z 69-75: Mk 14, 66-72; Lk 22, 56-62; Jn 18, 17-18.25-27.—a Mt 26, 34.—b 1-2: Mk 15, 1; Lk 23, 1; Jn 18, 28.—c 3-10: Acts 1, 18-19.—d Mt 26, 15.—e Zec 11, 12-13.—f 11-14: Mk 15, 2-5; Lk 23, 2-3; Jn 18, 29-38.

26, 67-68: The physical abuse, apparently done to Jesus by the members of the Sanhedrin themselves, recalls the sufferings of the Isaian Servant of the Lord; cf Is 50, 6. The mocking challenge to *prophesy* is probably motivated by Jesus' prediction of his future glory (64).

26, 70: *Denied it in front of everyone:* see Mt 10, 33. Peter's repentance (75) saves him from the fearful destiny of which Jesus speaks there.

26, 73: *Your speech . . . away:* Matthew explicates Mk's "you too are a Galilean" (Mk 14, 70).

27, 1-31: Cf Mk 15, 1-20. Matthew's account of the Roman trial before *Pilate* is introduced by a consultation of the Sanhedrin after which Jesus is *handed over to . . . the governor* (1-2). Matthew follows his Marcan source closely but adds some material that is peculiar to him, the death of *Judas* (3-10), possibly the name *Jesus* as the name of *Barabbas* also (16-17), the intervention of Pilate's *wife* (19), Pilate's washing *his hands* in token of his disclaiming responsibility for Jesus' death (24), and the assuming of that responsibility by *the whole people* (25).

27, 1-2: There is scholarly disagreement about the meaning of the Sanhedrin's taking *counsel* (*symboulion elabon*; cf Mt 12, 14; 22, 15; 27, 7; 28, 12); see the note on Mk 15, 1. Some understand it as a discussion about the strategy for putting their death sentence against *Jesus* into effect since they lacked the right to do so themselves. Others see it as the occasion for their passing

that sentence, holding that Matthew, unlike Mark (Mk 14, 64), does not consider that it had been passed in the night session (Mt 26, 66). Even in the latter interpretation, his handing *him over to Pilate* is best explained on the hypothesis that they did not have competence to put their sentence into effect, as is stated in Jn 18, 31.

27, 3: *The thirty pieces of silver:* see Mt 26, 15.

27, 5-8: For another tradition about the death of Judas, cf Acts 1, 18-19. The two traditions agree only in the purchase of a *field* with *the money* paid to Judas for his betrayal of Jesus and the name given to the *field, the Field of Blood.* In Acts Judas himself buys the field and its name comes from his own blood shed in his fatal accident on it. *The potter's field:* this designation of the field is based on the fulfillment citation in v 10.

27, 9-10: Cf Mt 26, 15. Matthew's attributing this text to Jeremiah is puzzling, for there is no such text in that book, and *the thirty pieces of silver* thrown by Judas "into the temple" (5) recall rather Zec 11, 12-13. It is usually said that the attribution of the text to Jeremiah is due to Matthew's combining the Zechariah text with texts from Jeremiah that speak of a *potter* (Jer 18, 2-3), the buying of a *field* (Jer 32, 6-9), or the breaking of a potter's flask at Topheth in the valley of Ben-Hinnom with the prediction that it will become a burial place (Jer 19, 1-13).

27, 11: *King of the Jews:* this title is used of Jesus only by pagans. The Matthean instances are, besides this verse, Mt 2, 2; 27, 29.37. Matthew equates it with "Messiah"; cf Mt 2, 2.4 and Mt 27, 17.22 where he has changed "the king of the Jews" of his Marcan source (Mk 15, 9.12) to "(Jesus) called Messiah." The normal political connotation of both titles would be of concern to the Roman *governor. You say so:* see the note on Mt 26, 25. An unqualified affirmative response is not made because Jesus' kingship is not what Pilate would understand it to be.

and elders,* he made no answer.[g] [13]Then Pilate said to him, "Do you not hear how many things they are testifying against you?" [14]But he did not answer him one word, so that the governor was greatly amazed.

The Sentence of Death.* [15] [h] Now on the occasion of the feast the governor was accustomed to release to the crowd one prisoner whom they wished. [16]And at that time they had a notorious prisoner called [Jesus] Barabbas.* [17]So when they had assembled, Pilate said to them, "Which one do you want me to release to you, [Jesus] Barabbas, or Jesus called Messiah?" [18]For he knew that it was out of envy that they had handed him over.* [19]While he was still seated on the bench, his wife sent him a message, "Have nothing to do with that righteous man. I suffered much in a dream today because of him."* [20]The chief priests and the elders persuaded the crowds to ask for Barabbas but to destroy Jesus.[i] [21]The governor said to them in reply, "Which of the two do you want me to release to you?" They answered, "Barabbas!" [22]Pilate said to them, "Then what shall I do with Jesus called Messiah?"

They all said, "Let him be crucified!"* [23]But he said, "Why? What evil has he done?" They only shouted the louder, "Let him be crucified!" [24]* When Pilate saw that he was not succeeding at all, but that a riot was breaking out instead, he took water and washed his hands in the sight of the crowd, saying, "I am innocent of this man's blood. Look to it yourselves."[j] [25]And the whole people said in reply, "His blood be upon us and upon our children." [26]Then he released Barabbas to them, but after he had Jesus scourged,* he handed him over to be crucified.

Mockery by the Soldiers. [27][k] Then the soldiers of the governor took Jesus inside the praetorium* and gathered the whole cohort around him. [28]They stripped off his clothes and threw a scarlet military cloak* about him. [29]Weaving a crown out of thorns,* they placed it on his head, and a reed in his right hand. And kneeling before him, they mocked him, saying, "Hail, King of the Jews!"[l] [30]They spat upon him* and took the reed and kept striking him on the head.[m] [31]And when they had mocked him, they stripped him of the cloak, dressed him in his own clothes, and led him off to crucify him.

g Is 53, 7.—h 15-26: Mk 15, 6-15; Lk 23, 17-25; Jn 18, 39—19, 16.—i Acts 3, 14.—j Dt 21, 1-8.—k 27-31: Mk 15, 16-20; Jn 19, 2-3.—l Mt 27, 11.—m Is 50, 6.

27, 12-14: Cf Mt 26, 62-63. As in the trial before the Sanhedrin, Jesus' silence may be meant to recall Is 53, 7. *Greatly amazed:* possibly an allusion to Is 52, 14-15.

27, 15-26: The choice that Pilate offers *the crowd* between *Barabbas* and *Jesus* is said to be in accordance with a custom of releasing at the Passover feast *one prisoner* chosen by *the crowd* (15). This custom is mentioned also in Mk 15, 6 and Jn 18, 39 but not in Lk; see the note on Lk 23, 17. Outside of the gospels there is no direct attestation of it, and scholars are divided in their judgment of the historical reliability of the claim that there was such a practice.

27, 16-17: *[Jesus] Barabbas:* it is possible that the double name is the original reading; *Jesus* was a common Jewish name; see the note on Mt 1, 21. This reading is found in only a few textual witnesses, although its absence in the majority can be explained as an omission of *Jesus* made for reverential reasons. That name is bracketed because of its uncertain textual attestation. The Aramaic name *Barabbas* means "son of the father"; the irony of the choice offered between him and Jesus, the true son of the Father, would be evident to those addressees of Mt who knew that.

27, 18: Cf Mk 14, 10. This is an example of the tendency, found in varying degree in all the gospels, to present Pilate in a relatively favorable light and emphasize the hostility of the Jewish authorities and eventually of the people.

27, 19: Jesus' innocence is declared by a Gentile woman. *In a dream:* in Mt's infancy narrative, dreams are the means of divine communication; cf Mt 1, 20; 2, 12.13.19.22.

27, 22: *Let him be crucified:* incited by the chief priests and elders (20), the crowds demand that Jesus be executed by crucifixion, a peculiarly horrible form of Roman capital punishment. The Marcan parallel, "Crucify him" (Mk 15, 3), addressed

to Pilate, is changed by Matthew to the passive, probably to emphasize the responsibility of the crowds.

27, 24-25: Peculiar to Mt. *Took water . . . blood:* cf Dt 21, 1-8, the handwashing prescribed in the case of a murder when the killer is unknown. The elders of the city nearest to where the corpse is found must wash their hands, declaring, "Our hands did not shed this blood." *Look to it yourselves:* cf v 4. *The whole people:* Matthew sees in those who speak these words *the* entire *people:* (Greek *laos*) of Israel. *His blood . . . and upon our children:* cf Jer 26, 15. The responsibility for Jesus' death is accepted by the nation that was God's special possession (Ex 19, 5), his own *people* (Hos 2, 25), and they thereby lose that high privilege; see Mt 21, 43 and the note on that verse. The controversy between Matthew's church and Pharisaic Judaism about which was the true people of God is reflected here. As the Second Vatican Council has pointed out, guilt for Jesus' death is not attributable to all the Jews of his time or to any Jews of later times.

27, 26: *He had Jesus scourged:* the usual preliminary to crucifixion.

27, 27: *The praetorium:* the residence of the Roman *governor.* His usual place of residence was at Caesarea Maritima on the Mediterranean coast, but he went to Jerusalem during the great feasts, when the influx of pilgrims posed the danger of a nationalistic riot. It is disputed whether *the praetorium* in Jerusalem was the old palace of Herod in the west of the city or the fortress of Antonia northwest of the temple area. *The whole cohort:* normally six hundred soldiers.

27, 28: *Scarlet military cloak:* so Mt as against the royal purple of Mk 15, 17 and Jn 19, 2.

27, 29: *Crown out of thorns:* probably of long *thorns* that stood upright so that it resembled the "radiant" *crown,* a diadem with spikes worn by Hellenistic kings. The soldiers' purpose was mockery, not torture. *A reed:* peculiar to Mt; a mock scepter.

27, 30: *Spat upon him:* cf Mt 26, 67 where there also is a possible allusion to Is 50, 6.

Mt

The Way of the Cross.* [32] As they were going out, they met a Cyrenian named Simon; this man they pressed into service to carry his cross. [n]

The Crucifixion. [33] [o] And when they came to a place called Golgotha (which means Place of the Skull), [34] [p] they gave Jesus wine to drink mixed with gall.* But when he had tasted it, he refused to drink. [35] After they had crucified him, they divided his garments* by casting lots;[q] [36] then they sat down and kept watch over him there. [37] And they placed over his head the written charge* against him: This is Jesus, the King of the Jews. [38] Two revolutionaries* were crucified with him, one on his right and the other on his left. [39] [r] Those passing by reviled him, shaking their heads* [40] and saying, "You who would destroy the temple and rebuild it in three days, save yourself, if you are the Son of God, [and] come down from the cross!"[s] [41] Likewise the chief priests with the scribes and elders mocked him and said,

[42] "He saved others; he cannot save himself. So he is the king of Israel!* Let him come down from the cross now, and we will believe in him. [43] *He trusted in God; let him deliver him now if he wants him. For he said, 'I am the Son of God.' "[t] [44] The revolutionaries who were crucified with him also kept abusing him in the same way.

The Death of Jesus. [45] [u] From noon onward,[v] darkness came over the whole land until three in the afternoon.* [46] And about three o'clock Jesus cried out in a loud voice, *"Eli, Eli, lema sabachthani?"** which means, "My God, my God, why have you forsaken me?"[w] [47] Some of the bystanders who heard it said, "This one is calling for Elijah."* [48] Immediately one of them ran to get a sponge; he soaked it in wine, and putting it on a reed, gave it to him to drink.[x] [49] But the rest said, "Wait, let us see if Elijah comes to save him." [50] But Jesus cried out again in a loud voice, and gave up his spirit.* [51] [y] And behold, the veil of the sanctuary was torn in two from top to bottom.* The earth quaked, rocks

---

n Mk 15, 21; Lk 23, 26.—o 33-44: Mk 15, 22-32; Lk 23, 32-38; Jn 19, 17-19.23-24.—p Ps 69, 21.—q Ps 22, 19.—r Ps 22, 8.—s Mt 4, 3.6; 26, 61.—t Ps 22, 9; Wis 2, 12-20.—u 45-46: Mk 15, 33-41; Lk 23, 44-49; Jn 19, 28-30.—v Am 8, 9.—w Ps 22, 2.—x Ps 69, 21.—y Ex 26, 31-36; Ps 68, 9; 77, 19.

27, 32: See note on Mk 15, 21. *Cyrenian named Simon:* Cyrenaica was a Roman province on the north coast of Africa and Cyrene was its capital city. The city had a large population of Greek-speaking Jews. *Simon* may have been living in Palestine or have come there for the Passover as a pilgrim. *Pressed into service:* see the note on Mt 5, 41.

27, 34: *Wine . . . mixed with gall:* cf Mk 15, 23 where the drink is "wine drugged with myrrh," a narcotic. Mt's text is probably an inexact allusion to Ps 69, 22. That psalm belongs to the class called the individual lament, in which a persecuted just man prays for deliverance in the midst of great suffering and also expresses confidence that his prayer will be heard. That theme of the suffering Just One is frequently applied to the sufferings of Jesus in the passion narratives.

27, 35: The clothing of an executed criminal went to his executioner(s), but the description of that procedure in the case of Jesus, found in all the gospels, is plainly inspired by Ps 22, 19. However, that psalm verse is quoted only in Jn 19, 24.

27, 37: The offense of a person condemned to death by crucifixion was written on a tablet that was displayed on his cross. The *charge* against *Jesus* was that he had claimed to be the *King of the Jews* (cf Mt 27, 11), i.e., the Messiah (cf Mt 27, 17.22).

27, 38: *Revolutionaries:* see the note on Jn 18, 40 where the same Greek word as that found here is used for Barabbas.

27, 39-40: *Reviled him . . . heads:* cf Ps 22, 8. *You who would destroy . . . three days:* cf Mt 26, 61. *If you are the Son of God:* the same words as those of the devil in the temptation of Jesus; cf Mt 4, 3.6.

27, 42: *King of Israel:* in their mocking of Jesus the members of the Sanhedrin call themselves and their people not "the Jews" but *Israel.*

27, 43: Peculiar to Mt. *He trusted in God . . . wants him:* cf Ps 22, 9. *He said . . . of God:* probably an allusion to Wis 2, 12-20 where the theme of the suffering Just One appears.

27, 45: Cf Amos 8, 9 where on the day of the Lord "the sun will set at midday."

27, 46: *Eli, Eli, lema sabachthani?:* Jesus cries out in the words of Ps 22, 2a, a psalm of lament that is the Old Testament passage most frequently drawn upon in this narrative. In Mk the verse is cited entirely in Aramaic, which Matthew partially retains but changes the invocation of God to the Hebrew *Eli,* possibly because that is more easily related to the statement of the following verse about Jesus' calling for Elijah.

27, 47: *Elijah:* see the note on Mt 3, 4. This prophet, taken up into heaven (2 Kgs 2, 11), was believed to come to the help of those in distress, but the evidences of that belief are all later than the gospels.

27, 50: *Gave up his spirit:* cf the Marcan parallel (Mk 15, 37), "breathed his last." Matthew's alteration expresses both Jesus' control over his destiny and his obedient giving up of his life to God.

27, 51-53: *Veil of the sanctuary . . . bottom:* cf Mk 15, 38; Lk 23, 45. Lk puts this event immediately before the death of Jesus. There were two veils in the Mosaic tabernacle on the model of which the temple was constructed, the outer one before the entrance of the Holy Place and the inner one before the Holy of Holies (see Ex 26, 31-36). Only the high priest could pass through the latter and that only on the Day of Atonement (see Lv 16, 1-18). Probably the *torn veil* of the gospels is the inner one. The meaning of the scene may be that now, because of Jesus' death, all people have access to the presence of God, or that the temple, its holiest part standing exposed, is now profaned and will soon be destroyed. *The earth quaked . . . appeared to many:* peculiar to Mt. The earthquake, the splitting of the *rocks,* and especially the resurrection of the dead *saints* indicate the coming of the final age. In the Old Testament the coming of God is frequently portrayed with the imagery of an earthquake (see Pss 68, 9; 77, 19), and Jesus speaks of the earthquakes that will accompany the "labor pains" that signify the beginning of the dissolution of the old world (Mt 24, 7-8). For the expectation of the resurrection of the dead at the coming of the new and final age, see Dn 12, 1-3. Matthew knows that the end of the old age has not yet come (Mt 28, 20), but the new age has broken in with the death (and resurrection; cf the earthquake in Mt 28, 2) of Jesus; see the note on Mt 16, 28. *After his resurrection:* this qualification seems to be due to Matthew's wish to assert the primacy of Jesus' *resurrection* even though he has placed the resurrection of the dead *saints* immediately after Jesus' death.

were split, [52] tombs were opened, and the bodies of many saints who had fallen asleep were raised. [z] [53] And coming forth from their tombs after his resurrection, they entered the holy city and appeared to many. [54] *The centurion and the men with him who were keeping watch over Jesus feared greatly when they saw the earthquake and all that was happening, and they said, "Truly, this was the Son of God!" [55] There were many women there, looking on from a distance,* who had followed Jesus from Galilee, ministering to him. [56] Among them were Mary Magdalene and Mary the mother of James and Joseph, and the mother of the sons of Zebedee. [a]

The Burial of Jesus. * [57] [b] When it was evening, there came a rich man from Arimathea named Joseph, who was himself a disciple of Jesus. [c] [58] He went to Pilate and asked for the body of Jesus; then Pilate ordered it to be handed over. [59] Taking the body, Joseph wrapped it [in] clean linen [60] and laid it in his new tomb that he had hewn in the rock. Then he rolled a huge stone across the entrance to the tomb and departed. [61] But Mary Magdalene and the other Mary remained sitting there, facing the tomb.

z Dn 12, 1-3.—a Mt 13, 55.—b 57-61: Mk 15, 42-47; Lk 23, 50-56; Jn 19, 38-42.—c Is 53, 9.—d Mt 12, 40; 16, 21; 17, 23; 20, 19.—e 1-10: Mk 16, 1-8; Lk 24, 1-12; Jn 20, 1-10.

27, 54: Cf Mk 15, 39. The Christian confession of faith is made by Gentiles, not only *the centurion,* as in Mk, but the other soldiers *who were keeping watch over Jesus* (cf 36).

27, 55-56: *Looking on from a distance:* cf Ps 38, 12. *Mary Magdalene . . . Joseph:* these two women are mentioned again in v 61 and Mt 28, 1 and are important as witnesses of the reality of the empty tomb. A *James* and *Joseph* are referred to in Mt 13, 55 as brothers of Jesus.

27, 57-61: Cf Mk 15, 42-47. Matthew drops Mk's designation of *Joseph* of Arimathea as "a distinguished member of the council" (the Sanhedrin), and makes him *a rich man* and *a disciple of Jesus.* The former may be an allusion to Is 53, 9 (the Hebrew reading of that text is disputed and the one followed in the NAB OT has nothing about the rich, but they are mentioned in the LXX version). That the tomb was the *new tomb* of a *rich man* and that it was seen by the women are indications of an apologetic intent of Matthew; there could be no question about the identity of Jesus' burial place. *The other Mary:* the mother of James and Joseph (56).

27, 62-66: Peculiar to Mt. The story prepares for Mt 28, 11-15 and the Jewish charge that the tomb was empty because the *disciples* had stolen the body of Jesus (Mt 28, 13.15).

27, 62: *The next day . . . preparation:* the sabbath. According to the synoptic chronology, in that year *the day of preparation* (for the sabbath) was the Passover; cf Mk 15, 42. *The Pharisees:* the principal opponents of Jesus during his ministry and, in Matthew's time, of the Christian church, join with *the chief priests* to guarantee against a possible attempt of Jesus' *disciples* to steal his body.

27, 64: *This last imposture . . . the first:* the claim that Jesus *has been raised from the dead* is clearly the *last imposture; the first* may be either his claim that he would be *raised up* (63) or his claim that he was the one with whose ministry the kingdom of God had come (see Mt 12, 28).

The Guard at the Tomb. * [62] The next day, the one following the day of preparation,* the chief priests and the Pharisees gathered before Pilate [63] and said, "Sir, we remember that this imposter while still alive said, 'After three days I will be raised up.' [d] [64] Give orders, then, that the grave be secured until the third day, lest his disciples come and steal him and say to the people, 'He has been raised from the dead.' This last imposture would be worse than the first." * [65] Pilate said to them, "The guard is yours;* go secure it as best you can." [66] So they went and secured the tomb by fixing a seal to the stone and setting the guard.

CHAPTER 28*

The Resurrection of Jesus. [1] After the sabbath, [e] as the first day of the week was dawning,* Mary Magdalene and the other Mary came to see the tomb. [2] * And behold, there was a great earthquake; for an

27, 65: *The guard is yours:* literally, "have a guard" or "you have a guard." Either the imperative or the indicative could mean that Pilate granted the petitioners some Roman soldiers as guards, which is the sense of the present translation. However, if the verb is taken as an indicative it could also mean that Pilate told them to use their own Jewish guards.

28, 1-20: Except for vv 1-8, based on Mk 16, 1-8, the material of this final chapter is peculiar to Mt. Even where he follows Mk, Matthew has altered his source so greatly that a very different impression is given from that of the Marcan account. The two points that are common to the resurrection testimony of all the gospels are that the tomb of Jesus had been found empty and that the risen Jesus had appeared to certain persons, or, in the original form of Mk, that such an appearance was promised as soon to take place (see Mk 16, 7). On this central and all-important basis, Matthew has constructed an account that interprets the resurrection as the turning of the ages (2-4), shows the Jewish opposition to Jesus as continuing *to the present* in the claim that the resurrection is a deception perpetrated by the *disciples* who stole his body from the tomb (11-15), and marks a new stage in the mission of *the disciples* once limited to Israel (10, 5-6); now they are to *make disciples of all nations.* In this work they will be strengthened by the presence of the exalted Son of Man, who will be with them *until* the kingdom comes in fullness at *the end of the age* (16-20).

28, 1: *After the sabbath . . . dawning:* since the sabbath ended at sunset, this could mean in the early evening, for *dawning* can refer to the appearance of the evening star; cf Lk 23, 54. However, it is probable that Matthew means the morning dawn of the day after the sabbath, as in the similar though slightly different text of Mk, "when the sun had risen" (Mk 16, 2). *Mary Magdalene and the other Mary:* see the notes on Mt 27, 55-56; 57-61. *To see the tomb:* cf Mk 16, 1-2 where the purpose of the women's visit is to anoint Jesus' body.

28, 2-4: Peculiar to Mt. *A great earthquake:* see the note on Mt 27, 51-53. *Descended from heaven:* this trait is peculiar to Mt, although his interpretation of the "young man" of his Marcan source (Mk 16, 5) as an *angel* is probably true to Mk's intention; cf Lk 24, 23 where the "two men" of Mt 24, 4 are said to be "angels." *Rolled back the stone . . . upon it:* not to allow the risen Jesus to leave the tomb but to make evident that the tomb is empty (see 6). Unlike the apocryphal Gospel of Peter (9, 35—11, 44), the New Testament does not describe the resurrection of Jesus, nor is there anyone who sees it. *His appearance was like lightning . . . snow:* see the note on Mt 17, 2.

Mt

angel of the Lord descended from heaven, approached, rolled back the stone, and sat upon it.*f* ³His appearance was like lightning and his clothing was white as snow.*g* ⁴The guards were shaken with fear of him and became like dead men. ⁵Then the angel said to the women in reply, "Do not be afraid! I know that you are seeking Jesus the crucified. ⁶ * He is not here, for he has been raised just as he said. Come and see the place where he lay. ⁷Then go quickly and tell his disciples, 'He has been raised from the dead, and he is going before you to Galilee; there you will see him.' Behold, I have told you."*h* ⁸Then they went away quickly from the tomb, fearful yet overjoyed, and ran to announce* this to his disciples. ⁹ * And behold, Jesus met them on their way and greeted them.*i* They approached, embraced his feet, and did him homage. ¹⁰Then Jesus said to them, "Do not be afraid. Go tell my brothers to go to Galilee, and there they will see me."

The Report of the Guard. * ¹¹While they were going, some of the guard went into the city and told the chief priests all that had happened. ¹²They assembled with the elders and took counsel; then they gave a large sum of money to the soldiers, ¹³telling them, "You are to say, 'His disciples came by night and stole him while we were asleep.' ¹⁴And if this gets to the ears of the governor, we will satisfy [him] and keep you out of trouble." ¹⁵The soldiers took the money and did as they were instructed. And this story has circulated among the Jews to the present [day].

The Commissioning of the Disciples. * ¹⁶ *j* The eleven* disciples went to Galilee, to the mountain to which Jesus had ordered them. ¹⁷When they saw him, they worshiped, but they doubted.* ¹⁸Then Jesus approached and said to them, "All power in heaven and on earth*k* has been given to me.* ¹⁹Go, therefore,* and make disciples of all nations, baptizing them in the name of the Father, and of the Son, and of the holy Spirit,*l* ²⁰teaching them to observe all that I have commanded you.* And behold, I am with you always, until the end of the age."*m*

---

f Mt 25, 51.—g Mt 17, 2.—h Mt 26, 32.—i 9-10: Jn 20, 17.— j 16-20: Mk 16, 14-16; Lk 24, 36-49; Jn 20, 19-23.—k Dn 7, 14 LXX.—l Acts 1, 8.—m Mt 1, 23; 13, 39; 24, 3.

28, 6-7: Cf Mk 16, 6-7. *Just as he said:* a Matthean addition referring to Jesus' predictions of his resurrection, e.g., Mt 16, 21; 17, 23; 20, 19. *Tell his disciples:* like the angel of the Lord of the infancy narrative, the angel interprets a fact and gives a commandment about what is to be done; cf Mt 1, 20-21. Matthew omits Mk's "and Peter" (Mk 16, 7); considering his interest in Peter, this omission is curious. Perhaps the reason is that the Marcan text may allude to a first appearance of Jesus to Peter alone (cf 1 Cor 15, 5; Lk 24, 34) which Matthew has already incorporated into his account of Peter's confession at Caesarea Philippi; see the note on Mt 16, 16. *He is going . . . Galilee:* like Mk 16, 7, a reference to Jesus' prediction at the Last Supper (Mt 26, 32; Mk 14, 28). Matthew changes Mk's "as he told you" to a declaration of the angel.

28, 8: Contrast Mk 16, 8 where the women in their fear "said nothing to anyone."

28, 9-10: Although these verses are peculiar to Mt, there are similarities between them and Jn's account of the appearance of Jesus to Mary Magdalene (Jn 20, 17). In both there is a touching of Jesus' body, and a command of Jesus to bear a message to his disciples, designated as his *brothers.* Matthew may have drawn upon a tradition that appears in a different form in Jn. Jesus' words to the women are mainly a repetition of those of the angel (5a; 7b).

28, 11-15: This account indicates that the dispute between Christians and Jews about the empty tomb was not whether the tomb was empty but why.

28, 16-20: This climactic scene has been called a "proleptic parousia," for it gives a foretaste of the final glorious coming of the Son of Man (Mt 26, 64). Then his triumph will be manifest to all; now it is revealed only to *the disciples,* who are commissioned to announce it to *all nations* and bring them to belief in Jesus and obedience to his commandments.

28, 16: *The eleven:* the number recalls the tragic defection of Judas Iscariot. *To the mountain .. . ordered them:* since the message to *the disciples* was simply that they were to go to Galilee (10), some think that *the mountain* comes from a tradition of the message known to Matthew and alluded to here. For the significance of *the mountain,* see the note on Mt 17, 1.

28, 17: *But they doubted:* the Greek can also be translated, "but some doubted." The verb occurs elsewhere in the New Testament only in Mt 14, 31 where it is associated with Peter's being of "little faith." For the meaning of that designation, see the note on Mt 6, 30.

28, 18: *All power . . . me:* the Greek word here translated *power* is the same as that found in the LXX translation of Dn 7, 13-14 where one "like a son of man" is given *power* and an everlasting kingdom by God. The risen Jesus here claims universal power, i.e., *in heaven and on earth.*

28, 19: *Therefore:* since universal power belongs to the risen Jesus (18), he gives the eleven a mission that is universal. They are to *make disciples of all nations.* While *all nations* is understood by some scholars as referring only to *all* Gentiles, it is probable that it included the Jews as well. *Baptizing them:* baptism is the means of entrance into the community of the risen One, the Church. *In the name of the Father . . . holy Spirit:* this is perhaps the clearest expression in the New Testament of trinitarian belief. It may have been the baptismal formula of Matthew's church, but primarily it designates the effect of baptism, the union of the one baptized with the Father, Son, and holy Spirit.

28, 20: *All that I have commanded you:* the moral teaching found in this gospel, preeminently that of the Sermon on the Mount (chs 5-7). The commandments of Jesus are the standard of Christian conduct, not the Mosaic law as such, even though some of the Mosaic commandments have now been invested with the authority of Jesus. *Behold, I am with you always:* the promise of Jesus' real though invisible presence echoes the name Emmanuel given to him in the infancy narrative; see the note on Mt 1, 23. *End of the age:* see the notes on Mt 13, 39 and Mt 24, 3.

THE GOSPEL ACCORDING TO MARK

INTRODUCTION

This shortest of all New Testament gospels is likely the first to have been written, yet it often tells of Jesus' ministry in more detail than either Matthew or Luke (for example, the miracle stories at 5, 1-20 or 9, 14-29). It recounts what Jesus did in a vivid style, where one incident follows directly upon another. In this almost breathless narrative, Mark stresses Jesus' message about the kingdom of God now breaking into human life as good news (1, 14-15) and Jesus himself as the gospel of God (1, 1; 8, 35; 10, 29). Jesus is the Son whom God has sent to rescue humanity by serving and by sacrificing his life (10, 45).

The opening verse about good news in Mark (1, 1) serves as a title for the entire book. The action begins with the appearance of John the Baptist, a messenger of God attested by scripture. But John points to a mightier one, Jesus, at whose baptism God speaks from heaven, declaring Jesus his Son. The Spirit descends upon Jesus, who eventually, it is promised, will baptize "with the holy Spirit." This presentation of who Jesus really is (1, 1-13) is rounded out with a brief reference to the temptation of Jesus and how Satan's attack fails. Jesus as Son of God will be victorious, a point to be remembered as one reads of Jesus' death and the enigmatic ending to Mark's Gospel.

The key verses at 1, 14-15, which are programmatic, summarize what Jesus proclaims as gospel: fulfillment, the nearness of the kingdom, and therefore the need for repentance and for faith. After the call of the first four disciples, all fishermen (1, 16-20), we see Jesus engaged in teaching (1, 21.22.27), preaching (1, 38.39), and healing (1, 29-31.34.40-45), and exorcising demons (1,22-27.34.39). The content of Jesus' teaching is only rarely stated, and then chiefly in parables (ch 4) about the kingdom. His cures, especially on the sabbath (3, 1-5); his claim, like God, to forgive sins (2, 3-12); his table fellowship with tax collectors and sinners (2, 14-17); and the statement that his followers need not now fast but should rejoice while Jesus is present (2, 18-22), all stir up opposition that will lead to Jesus' death (3, 6).

In Mark, Jesus is portrayed as immensely popular with the people in Galilee during his ministry (2, 2; 3, 7; 4, 1). He appoints twelve disciples to help preach and drive out demons, just as he does (3, 13-19). He continues to work many miracles; the blocks 4, 35—6, 44 and 6, 45—7, 10 are cycles of stories about healings, miracles at the Sea of Galilee, and marvelous feedings of the crowds. Jesus' teaching in ch 7 exalts the word of God over "the tradition of the elders" and sees defilement as a matter of the heart, not of unclean foods. Yet opposition mounts. Scribes charge that Jesus is possessed by Beelzebul (3, 22). His relatives think him "out of his mind" (3, 21). Jesus' kinship is with those who do the will of God, in a new eschatological family, not even with mother, brothers, or sisters by blood ties (3, 31-35; cf 6, 1-6). But all too often his own disciples do not understand Jesus (4, 13.40; 6, 52; 8, 17-21). The fate of John the Baptist (6, 17-29) hints ominously at Jesus' own passion (9, 13; cf 8, 31).

A breakthrough seemingly comes with Peter's confession that Jesus is the Christ (Messiah; 8, 27-30). But Jesus himself emphasizes his passion (8, 31; 9, 31; 10, 33-34), not glory in the kingdom (10, 35-45). Momentarily he is glimpsed in his true identity when he is transfigured before three of the disciples (9, 2-8), but by and large Jesus is depicted in Mark as moving obediently along the way to his cross in Jerusalem. Occasionally there are miracles (9, 17-27; 10, 46-52; 11, 12-14.20-21, the only such account in Jerusalem), sometimes teachings (10, 2-11.23-31), but the greatest concern is with discipleship (8,

34—9, 1; 9, 33-50). For the disciples do not grasp the mystery being revealed (9, 32; 10, 32.38). One of them will betray him, Judas (14, 10-11.43-45); one will deny him, Peter (14, 27.31.54.66-72); all eleven men will desert Jesus (14, 27.50).

The passion account, with its condemnation of Jesus by the Sanhedrin (14, 53.55-65; 15, 1a) and sentencing by Pilate (15, 1b-15), is prefaced with the entry into Jerusalem (11, 1-11), ministry and controversies there (11, 15—12, 44), Jesus' Last Supper with the disciples (14, 1-26), and his arrest at Gethsemane (14, 32-52). A chapter of apocalyptic tone about the destruction of the temple (13, 1-2.14-23) and the coming of the Son of Man (13, 24-27), a discourse filled with promises (13, 11.31) and admonitions to be watchful (13, 2.23.37), is significant for Mark's Gospel, for it helps one see that God, in Jesus, will be victorious after the cross and at the end of history.

The Gospel of Mark ends in the most ancient manuscripts with an abrupt scene at Jesus' tomb, which the women find empty (16, 1-8). His own prophecy of 14, 28 is reiterated, that Jesus goes before the disciples into Galilee; "there you will see him." These words may imply resurrection appearances there, or Jesus' parousia there, or the start of Christian mission, or a return to the roots depicted in 1, 9.14-15 in Galilee. Other hands have attached additional endings after 16, 8; see the note on 16, 9-20.

The framework of Mark's Gospel is partly geographical: Galilee (1, 14—9, 49), through the area "across the Jordan" (10, 1) and through Jericho (10, 46-52), to Jerusalem (11, 1—16, 8). Only rarely does Jesus go into Gentile territory (5, 1-20; 7, 24-37), but those who acknowledge him there and the centurion who confesses Jesus at the cross (15, 39) presage the gospel's expansion into the world beyond Palestine.

Mark's Gospel is even more oriented to christology. Jesus is the Son of God (1, 11; 9, 7; 15, 39; cf 1, 1; 14, 61). He is the Messiah, the anointed king of Davidic descent (12, 35; 15, 32), the Greek for which, Christos, has, by the time Mark wrote, become in effect a proper name (1, 1; 9, 41). Jesus is also seen as Son of Man, a term used in Mark not simply as a substitute for "I" or for humanity in general (cf 2, 10.27-28; 14, 21) or with reference to a mighty figure who is to come (13, 26; 14, 62), but also in connection with Jesus' predestined, necessary path of suffering and vindication (8, 31; 10, 45).

The unfolding of Mark's story about Jesus is sometimes viewed by interpreters as centered around the term "mystery." The word is employed just once, at 4, 11, in the singular, and its content there is the kingdom, the open secret that God's reign is now breaking into human life with its reversal of human values. There is a related sense in which Jesus' real identity remained a secret during his lifetime, according to Mark, although demons and demoniacs knew it (1, 24; 3, 11; 5, 7); Jesus warned against telling of his mighty deeds and revealing his identity (1, 44; 3, 12; 5, 43; 7, 36; 8, 26.30), an injunction sometimes broken (1, 45; cf 5, 19-20). Further, Jesus teaches by parables, according to Mark, in such a way that those "outside" the kingdom do not understand, but only those to whom the mystery has been granted by God.

Mark thus shares with Paul, as well as with other parts of the New Testament, an emphasis on election (13, 20.22) and upon the gospel as Christ and his cross (cf 1 Cor 1, 23). Yet in Mark the person of Jesus is also depicted with an unaffected naturalness. He reacts to events with authentic human emotion: pity (1, 44), anger (3, 5), triumph (4, 40), sympathy (5, 36; 6, 34), surprise (6, 9), admiration (7, 29; 10, 21), sadness (14, 33-34), and indignation (14, 48-49).

Although the book is anonymous, apart from the ancient heading "According to Mark" in manuscripts, it has traditionally been assigned to John Mark, in whose mother's house (at Jerusalem) Christians assembled (Acts 12, 12). This Mark was a cousin of Barnabas (Col 4, 10) and accompanied Barnabas and Paul on a missionary journey (Acts 12, 25; 13, 3; 15, 36-39). He appears in Pauline letters (Phlm 24; 2 Tm 4, 11) and with Peter

(1 Pt 5, 13). Papias (ca. A.D. 135) described Mark as Peter's "interpreter," a view found in other patristic writers. Petrine influence should not, however, be exaggerated. The evangelist has put together various oral and possibly written sources—miracle stories, parables, sayings, stories of controversies, and the passion—so as to speak of the crucified Messiah for Mark's own day.

Traditionally, the gospel is said to have been written shortly before A.D. 70 in Rome, at a time of impending persecution and when destruction loomed over Jerusalem. Its audience seems to have been Gentile, unfamiliar with Jewish customs (hence 7, 3-4.11). The book aimed to equip such Christians to stand faithful in the face of persecution (13, 9-13), while going on with the proclamation of the gospel begun in Galilee (13, 10; 14, 9). Modern research often proposes as the author an unknown Hellenistic Jewish Christian, possibly in Syria, and perhaps shortly after the year 70.

The principal divisions of the Gospel according to Mark are the following:

I. The Preparation for the Public Ministry of Jesus (1, 1-13)
II. The Mystery of Jesus (1, 14—8, 26)
III. The Mystery Begins to Be Revealed (8, 27—9, 32)
IV. The Full Revelation of the Mystery (9, 33—16, 8)
    The Longer Ending (16, 9-20)
    The Shorter Ending
    The Freer Logion (in the note on 16, 9-20)

I. THE PREPARATION FOR THE PUBLIC MINISTRY OF JESUS*

CHAPTER 1

[1] The beginning of the gospel of Jesus Christ [the Son of God].*

The Preaching of John the Baptist. [2] [a] As it is written in Isaiah the prophet:*

"Behold, I am sending my messenger ahead of you;
he will prepare your way.[b]
[3] A voice of one crying out in the desert:
'Prepare the way of the Lord,
make straight his paths.' "[c]

[4] John [the] Baptist appeared in the desert proclaiming a baptism of repentance for the forgiveness of sins. [5] People of the whole Judean countryside and all the inhabitants of Jerusalem were going out to him and were being baptized by him in the Jordan River as they acknowledged their sins. [6] John was clothed in camel's hair, with a leather belt around his waist.* He fed on locusts and wild honey. [7] And this is what he proclaimed: "One mightier than I is coming after me. I am not worthy to stoop and loosen the thongs of his sandals. [8] [d] I have baptized you with water; he will baptize you with the holy Spirit."*

The Baptism of Jesus. [9] [e] It happened in those days that Jesus came from Nazareth of Galilee and was baptized in the Jordan by John. [10] On coming up out of the water

a 2-8: Mt 3,1-11; Lk 3, 2-16.—b Mal 3, 1.—c Is 40, 3; Jn 1, 23.—d Jn 1, 27; Acts 1, 5; 11, 16.—e 9-11: Mt 3, 13-17; Lk 3, 21-23; Jn 1, 32-33.

1, 1-13: The prologue of the Gospel according to Mark begins with the title (1) followed by three events preparatory to Jesus' preaching: (1) the appearance in the Judean wilderness of John, baptizer, preacher of repentance, and precursor of Jesus (2-8); (2) the baptism of Jesus, at which a voice from heaven acknowledges Jesus to be God's Son, and the holy Spirit descends on him (9-11); (3) the temptation of Jesus by Satan (12-13).

1, 1: *The gospel of Jesus Christ [the Son of God]:* the "good news" of salvation in and through Jesus, crucified and risen, acknowledged by the Christian community as Messiah (Mk 8, 29; 14, 61-62) and Son of God (Mk 1, 11; 9, 7; 15, 39), although some important manuscripts here omit *the Son of God.*

1, 2-3: Although Mark attributes the prophecy to Isaiah, the text is a combination of Mal 3, 1; Is 40, 3; and Ex 23, 20; cf Mt 11, 10; Lk 7, 27. John's ministry is seen as God's prelude to the saving mission of his Son. *The way of the Lord:* this prophecy of Deutero-Isaiah concerning the end of the Babylonian exile is here applied to the coming of Jesus; John the Baptist is to prepare the way for him.

1, 6: *Clothed in camel's hair . . . waist:* the Baptist's garb recalls that of Elijah in 2 Kgs 1, 8. Jesus speaks of the Baptist as Elijah who has already come (Mk 9, 11-13; Mt 17, 10-12; cf Mal 3, 23-24; Lk 1, 17).

1, 8-9: Through the life-giving baptism with the holy Spirit (8), Jesus will create a new people of God. But first he identifies himself with the people of Israel in submitting to John's baptism of repentance and in bearing on their behalf the burden of God's decisive judgment (9; cf 4). As in the desert of Sinai, so here in the wilderness of Judea, Israel's sonship with God is to be renewed.

he saw the heavens being torn open and the Spirit, like a dove, descending upon him.* [11] And a voice came from the heavens, "You are my beloved Son; with you I am well pleased."[f]

The Temptation of Jesus.* [12] At once the Spirit drove him out into the desert,[g] [13] and he remained in the desert for forty days, tempted by Satan. He was among wild beasts, and the angels ministered to him.

II. THE MYSTERY OF JESUS

The Beginning of the Galilean Ministry. [14] After John had been arrested,* Jesus came to Galilee proclaiming the gospel of God:[h] [15] "This is the time of fulfillment. The kingdom of God is at hand. Repent, and believe in the gospel."[i]

The Call of the First Disciples.* [16] As he passed by the Sea of Galilee,[j] he saw Simon and his brother Andrew casting their nets into the sea; they were fishermen. [17] Jesus said to them, "Come after me, and I will make you fishers of men." [18] Then they left their nets and followed him. [19] He walked along a little farther and saw James, the son of Zebedee, and his brother John. They too were in a boat mènding their nets. [20] Then he called them. So they left their father Zebedee in the boat along with the hired men and followed him.

The Cure of a Demoniac. [21] * Then they came to Capernaum, and on the sabbath he entered the synagogue and taught.[k] [22] The people were astonished at his teaching, for he taught them as one having authority and not as the scribes.[l] [23] In their synagogue was a man with an unclean spirit;* [24] he cried out, "What have you to do with us,* Jesus of Nazareth? Have you come to destroy us? I know who you are—the Holy One of God!"* [25] Jesus rebuked him and said, "Quiet! Come out of him!" [26] The unclean spirit convulsed him and with a loud cry came out of him. [27] All were amazed and asked one another, "What is this? A new teaching with authority. He commands even the unclean spirits and they obey him." [28] His fame spread everywhere throughout the whole region of Galilee.

The Cure of Simon's Mother-in-Law. [29] [m] On leaving the synagogue he entered the house of Simon and Andrew with James and John. [30] Simon's mother-in-law lay sick with a fever. They immediately told him about her. [31] He approached, grasped her hand, and helped her up. Then the fever left her and she waited on them.

Other Healings. [32] When it was evening, after sunset, they brought to him all who were ill or possessed by demons. [33] The whole town was gathered at the door. [34] He cured many who were sick with various diseases, and he drove out many demons, not permitting them to speak because they knew him.

---

f Ps 2, 7.—g 12-13: Mt 4, 1-11; Lk 4, 1-13.—h 14-15: Mt 4, 12-17; Lk 4, 14-15.—i Mt 3, 2.—j 16-20: Mt 4, 18-22; Lk 5, 2-11.—k 21-28: Lk 4, 31-37.—l Mt 7, 28-29.—m 29-34: Mt 8, 14-16; Lk 4, 38-41.

1, 10-11: *He saw the heavens . . . and the Spirit . . . upon him:* indicating divine intervention in fulfillment of promise. Here the descent of the Spirit on Jesus is meant, anointing him for his ministry; cf Is 11, 2; 42, 1; 61, 1; 63, 9. *A voice . . . with you I am well pleased:* God's acknowledgment of Jesus as his unique Son, the object of his love. His approval of Jesus is the assurance that Jesus will fulfill his messianic mission of salvation.

1, 12-13: The same Spirit who descended on Jesus in his baptism now drives him into the desert for forty days. The result is radical confrontation and temptation by Satan who attempts to frustrate the work of God. The presence of wild beasts may indicate the horror and danger of the desert regarded as the abode of demons or may reflect the paradise motif of harmony among all creatures; cf Is 11, 6-9. The presence of ministering angels to sustain Jesus recalls the angel who guided the Israelites in the desert in the first Exodus (Ex 14, 19; 23, 20) and the angel who supplied nourishment to Elijah in the wilderness (1 Kgs 19, 5-7). The combined forces of good and evil were present to Jesus in the desert. His sustained obedience brings forth the new Israel of God there where Israel's rebellion had brought death and alienation.

1, 14-15: *After John had been arrested:* in the plan of God, Jesus was not to proclaim the good news of salvation prior to the termination of the Baptist's active mission. *Galilee:* in the Mar-

can account, scene of the major part of Jesus' public ministry before his arrest and condemnation. *The gospel of God:* not only the good news from God but about God at work in Jesus Christ. *This is the time of fulfillment:* i.e., of God's promises. *The kingdom of God . . . repent:* see the note on Mt 3, 2.

1, 16-20: These verses narrate the call of the first disciples. See the notes on Mt 4, 18-22 and Mt 4, 20.

1, 21-45: The account of a single day's ministry of Jesus on a sabbath in and outside the synagogue of Capernaum (21-31) combines teaching and miracles of exorcism and healing. Mention is not made of the content of the teaching but of the effect of astonishment and alarm on the people. Jesus' teaching with authority, making an absolute claim on the hearer, was in the best tradition of the ancient prophets, not of the scribes. The narrative continues with events that evening (32-34; see the notes on Mt 8, 14-17) and the next day (35-39). The cleansing in vv 40-45 stands as an isolated story.

1, 23: *An unclean spirit:* so called because of the spirit's resistance to the holiness of God. The spirit knows and fears the power of Jesus to destroy his influence; cf Mk 1, 32.34; 3, 11; 6, 13.

1, 24: *What have you to do with us?:* see the note on Jn 2, 4.

1, 24-25: *The Holy One of God:* not a confession but an attempt to ward off Jesus' power, reflecting the notion that use of the precise name of an opposing spirit would guarantee mastery over him. Jesus silenced the cry of the unclean spirit and drove him out of the man.

Jesus Leaves Capernaum. [35] [n] Rising very early before dawn, he left and went off to a deserted place, where he prayed. [36] Simon and those who were with him pursued him [37] and on finding him said, "Everyone is looking for you." [38] He told them, "Let us go on to the nearby villages that I may preach there also. For this purpose have I come." [39] So he went into their synagogues, preaching and driving out demons throughout the whole of Galilee.

The Cleansing of a Leper. [40] [o] A leper* came to him [and kneeling down] begged him and said, "If you wish, you can make me clean." [41] Moved with pity, he stretched out his hand, touched him, and said to him, "I do will it. Be made clean." [p] [42] The leprosy left him immediately, and he was made clean. [q] [43] Then, warning him sternly, he dismissed him at once. [44] Then he said to him, "See that you tell no one anything, but go, show yourself to the priest and offer for your cleansing what Moses prescribed; that will be proof for them." [r] [45] The man went away and began to publicize the whole matter. He spread the report abroad so that it was impossible for Jesus to enter a town openly. He remained outside in deserted places, and people kept coming to him from everywhere.

CHAPTER 2

The Healing of a Paralytic. [1] * When Jesus returned to Capernaum [s] after some days, it became known that he was at home.* [2] Many gathered together so that there was no longer room for them, not even around the door, and he preached the word to them. [3] They came bringing to him a paralytic carried by four men. [4] Unable to get near Jesus because of the crowd, they opened up the roof above him. After they had broken through, they let down the mat on which the paralytic was lying. [5] When Jesus saw their faith, he said to the paralytic, "Child, your sins are forgiven."* [6] Now some of the scribes* were sitting there asking themselves, [7] "Why does this man speak that way? He is blaspheming.* Who but God alone can forgive sins?" [t] [8] Jesus immediately knew in his mind what they were thinking to themselves, so he said, "Why are you thinking such things in your hearts? [9] Which is easier, to say to the paralytic, 'Your sins are forgiven,' or to say, 'Rise, pick up your mat and walk'? [10] But that you may know that the Son of Man has authority to forgive sins on earth"*— [11] he said to the paralytic, "I say to you, rise, pick up your mat, and go home." [12] He rose, picked up his mat at once, and went away in the sight of everyone. They were all astounded and glorified God, saying, "We have never seen anything like this."

The Call of Levi. [13] [u] Once again he went out along the sea. All the crowd came to him and he taught them.* [14] [v] As he passed by,* he saw Levi, son of Alphaeus, sitting at the customs post. He said to him, "Follow me." And he got up and followed him. [15] While he was at table in his house,*

Mk

---

n 35-39: Lk 4, 42-44.—o 40-44: Mt 8, 2-4; Lk 5, 12-14.—p Mk 5, 30.—q Lk 17, 14.—r Lv 14, 2-32.—s 1-12: Mt 9, 2-8; Lk 5, 18-26.—t Is 43, 25.—u Mk 4, 1.—v 14-17: Mt 9, 9-13; Lk 5, 27-32.

1, 40: *A leper:* for the various forms of skin disease, see Lv 13, 1-50 and the note on Lv 13, 2-4. There are only two instances in the Old Testament in which God is shown to have cured a leper (Nm 12, 10-15 and 2 Kgs 5, 1-14). The law of Moses provided for the ritual purification of a leper. In curing the leper, Jesus assumes that the priests will reinstate the cured man into the religious community. See also the note on Lk 5, 14.

2, 1—3, 6: This section relates a series of conflicts between Jesus and the scribes and Pharisees in which the growing opposition of the latter leads to their plot to put Jesus to death (Mk 3, 6).

2, 1-2: *He was at home:* to the crowds that gathered in and outside the house Jesus *preached the word,* i.e., the gospel concerning the nearness of the kingdom and the necessity of repentance and faith (Mk 1, 14).

2, 5: It was the faith of the paralytic and those who carried him that moved Jesus to heal the sick man. Accounts of other miracles of Jesus reveal more and more his emphasis on faith as the requisite for exercising his healing powers (Mk 5, 34; 9, 23-24; 10, 52).

2, 6: *Scribes:* trained in oral interpretation of the written law; in Mark's gospel, adversaries of Jesus, with one exception (Mk 12, 28.34).

2, 7: *He is blaspheming:* an accusation made here and repeated during the trial of Jesus (Mk 14, 60-64).

2, 10: *But that you may know that the Son of Man . . . on earth:* although vv 8-9 are addressed to the scribes, the sudden interruption of thought and structure in v 10 seems not addressed to them nor to the paralytic. Moreover, the early public use of the designation "Son of Man" to unbelieving scribes is most unlikely. The most probable explanation is that Mark's insertion of v 10 is a commentary addressed to Christians for whom he recalls this miracle and who already accept in faith that Jesus is Messiah and Son of God.

2, 13: *He taught them:* see the note on Mk 1, 21-45.

2, 14: *As he passed by:* see the note on Mk 1, 16-20. *Levi, son of Alphaeus:* see the note on Mt 9, 9. *Customs post:* such tax collectors paid a fixed sum for the right to collect customs duties within their districts. Since whatever they could collect above this amount constituted their profit, the abuse of extortion was widespread among them. Hence, Jewish customs officials were regarded as sinners (16), outcasts of society, and disgraced along with their families. *He got up and followed him:* i.e., became a disciple of Jesus.

2, 15: *In his house:* cf v 1; Mt 9, 10. Lk 5, 29 clearly calls it Levi's house.

many tax collectors and sinners sat with Jesus and his disciples; for there were many who followed him. 16 * Some scribes who were Pharisees saw that he was eating with sinners and tax collectors and said to his disciples, "Why does he eat with tax collectors and sinners?" 17 Jesus heard this and said to them [that], "Those who are well do not need a physician,* but the sick do. I did not come to call the righteous but sinners."

The Question about Fasting. * 18 The disciples of John and of the Pharisees were accustomed to fast. *w* People came to him and objected, "Why do the disciples of John and the disciples of the Pharisees fast, but your disciples do not fast?" 19 Jesus answered them, "Can the wedding guests fast* while the bridegroom is with them? As long as they have the bridegroom with them they cannot fast. 20 But the days will come when the bridegroom is taken away from them, and then they will fast on that day. 21 No one sews a piece of unshrunken cloth on an old cloak. If he does, its fullness pulls away, the new from the old, and the tear gets worse. 22 Likewise, no one pours new wine into old wineskins. Otherwise, the wine will burst the skins, and both the wine and the skins are ruined. Rather, new wine is poured into fresh wineskins."

The Disciples and the Sabbath. * 23 As he was passing through a field of grain on the sabbath, his disciples began to make a path while picking the heads of grain. *x* 24 At this the Pharisees said to him, "Look, why are they doing what is unlawful on the sabbath?" *y* 25 He said to them, "Have you never read what David did* when he was in need and he and his companions were hungry? 26 How he went into the house of God when Abiathar was high priest and ate the bread of offering that only the priests could lawfully eat, and shared it with his companions?" *z* 27 Then he said to them, "The sabbath was made for man,* not man for the sabbath. *a* 28 That is why the Son of Man is lord even of the sabbath." *

CHAPTER 3

A Man with a Withered Hand. 1 *Again he entered the synagogue. *b* There was a man there who had a withered hand. 2 They watched him closely to see if he would cure him on the sabbath so that they might accuse him. 3 He said to the man with the withered hand, "Come up here before us." 4 Then he said to them, "Is it lawful to do good on the sabbath rather than to do evil, to save life rather than to destroy it?" But they remained silent. 5 Looking around at them with anger and grieved at their hardness of heart, he said to the man, "Stretch out your hand." He stretched it out and his hand was restored. *c* 6 The Pharisees went out and immediately took counsel with the Herodians against him to put him to death. *

---

w 18-22: Mt 9, 14-17; Lk 5, 33-39.—x 23-28: Mt 12, 1-8; Lk 6, 1-5.—y Dt 23, 25.—z 1 Sm 21, 2-7 / Lv 24, 5-9.—a 2 Mc 5, 19.—b 1-6: Mt 12, 9-14; Lk 6, 6-11.—c Lk 14, 4.

2, 16-17: This and the following conflict stories reflect a similar pattern: a statement of fact, a question of protest, and a reply by Jesus.

2, 17: *Do not need a physician:* this maxim of Jesus with its implied irony was uttered to silence his adversaries who objected that he ate with *tax collectors and sinners* (16). Because the scribes and Pharisees were self-righteous, they were not capable of responding to Jesus' call to repentance and faith in the gospel.

2, 18-22: This conflict over the question of fasting has the same pattern as vv 16-17; see the notes on Mt 9, 15 and Mt 9, 16-17.

2, 19: *Can the wedding guests fast?:* the bridal metaphor expresses a new relationship of love between God and his people in the person and mission of Jesus to his disciples. It is the inauguration of the new and joyful messianic time of fulfillment and the passing of the old. Any attempt at assimilating the Pharisaic practice of fasting, or of extending the preparatory discipline of John's disciples beyond the arrival of the bridegroom, would be as futile as sewing *a piece of unshrunken cloth on an old cloak* or pouring *new wine into old wineskins* with the resulting destruction of both cloth and wine (21-22). Fasting is rendered superfluous during the earthly ministry of Jesus; cf v 20.

2, 23-28: This conflict regarding the sabbath follows the same pattern as in vv 18-22.

2, 25-26: *Have you never read what David did?:* Jesus defends the action of his disciples on the basis of 1 Sm 21, 2-7 in which an exception is made to the regulation of Lv 24, 9 because of the extreme hunger of David and his men. According to 1 Sm, the priest who gave the bread to David was Ahimelech, father of Abiathar.

2, 27: *The sabbath was made for man:* a reaffirmation of the divine intent of the sabbath to benefit Israel as contrasted with the restrictive Pharisaic tradition added to the law.

2, 28: *The Son of Man is lord even of the sabbath:* Mark's comment on the theological meaning of the incident is to benefit his Christian readers; see the note on Mk 2, 10.

3, 1-5: Here Jesus is again depicted in conflict with his adversaries over the question of sabbath-day observance. His opponents were already ill disposed toward him because they regarded Jesus as a violator of the sabbath. Jesus' question *Is it lawful to do good on the sabbath rather than to do evil?* places the matter in the broader theological context outside the casuistry of the scribes. The answer is obvious. Jesus heals the man with the withered hand in the sight of all and reduces his opponents to silence; cf Jn 5, 17-18.

3, 6: In reporting the plot of the Pharisees and Herodians to put Jesus to death after this series of conflicts in Galilee, Mark uses a pattern that recurs in his account of later controversies in Jerusalem (Mk 11, 17-18; 12, 13-17). The help of the Herodians, supporters of Herod Antipas, tetrarch of Galilee and Perea, is needed to take action against Jesus. Both series of conflicts point to their gravity and to the impending passion of Jesus.

The Mercy of Jesus. [7] * Jesus withdrew toward the sea with his disciples.[d] A large number of people [followed] from Galilee and from Judea. [8] Hearing what he was doing, a large number of people came to him also from Jerusalem, from Idumea, from beyond the Jordan, and from the neighborhood of Tyre and Sidon. [9] He told his disciples to have a boat ready for him because of the crowd, so that they would not crush him. [10] He had cured many and, as a result, those who had diseases were pressing upon him to touch him.[e] [11] * And whenever unclean spirits saw him they would fall down before him and shout, "You are the Son of God."[f] [12] He warned them sternly not to make him known.

The Mission of the Twelve. [13] [g] He went up the mountain* and summoned those whom he wanted and they came to him. [14] [h] He appointed twelve [whom he also named apostles] that they might be with him* and he might send them forth to preach [15] and to have authority to drive out demons: [16] [he appointed the twelve:] Simon, whom he named Peter;* [17] James, son of Zebedee, and John the brother of James, whom he named Boanerges, that is, sons of thunder;[i] [18] Andrew, Philip, Bartholomew, Matthew, Thomas, James the son of Alphaeus; Thaddeus, Simon the Cananean, [19] and Judas Iscariot who betrayed him.

Blasphemy of the Scribes. [20] * He came home.* Again [the] crowd gathered, making it impossible for them even to eat.[j] [21] When his relatives heard of this they set out to seize him, for they said, "He is out of his mind."[k] [22] The scribes who had come from Jerusalem said, "He is possessed by Beelzebul,"* and "By the prince of demons he drives out demons."[l]

Jesus and Beelzebul. [23] Summoning them, he began to speak to them in parables, "How can Satan drive out Satan? [24] If a kingdom is divided against itself, that kingdom cannot stand. [25] And if a house is divided against itself, that house will not be able to stand. [26] And if Satan has risen up against himself and is divided, he cannot stand; that is the end of him. [27] But no one can enter a strong man's house to plunder his property unless he first ties up the strong man. Then he can plunder his house. [28] Amen, I say to you, all sins and all blasphemies that people utter will be forgiven them.[m] [29] But whoever blasphemes against the holy Spirit* will never have forgiveness, but is guilty of an everlasting sin." [30] For they had said, "He has an unclean spirit."

Jesus and His Family. [31] [n] His mother and his brothers arrived. Standing outside they sent word to him and called him. [32] A crowd seated around him told him, "Your mother and your brothers* [and your sisters] are outside asking for you." [33] But he said to them in reply, "Who are my mother and [my] brothers?" [34] And looking around at those seated in the circle he said, "Here are my mother and my brothers. [35] [For] whoever does the will of God is my brother and sister and mother."

Mk

---

d 7-12: Mt 4, 23-25; 12, 15; Lk 6, 17-19.—e Mk 5, 30.—f Mk 1, 34; Lk 4, 41.—g 13-19: Mk 10, 1-4; Lk 6, 12-16.—h Mk 6, 7.—i Mt 16, 18; Jn 1, 42.—j Mk 2, 2.—k Jn 10, 20.—l 22-30: Mt 12, 24-32; Lk 11, 15-22; 12, 10.—m Lk 12, 10.—n 31-35: Mt 12, 46-50; Lk 8, 19-21.

3, 7-19: This overview of the Galilean ministry manifests the power of Jesus to draw people to himself through his teaching and deeds of power. The crowds of Jews from many regions surround Jesus (7-12). This phenomenon prepares the way for creating a new people of Israel. The choice and mission of the Twelve is the prelude (13-19).

3, 11-12: See the note on Mk 1, 24-25.

3, 13: *He went up the mountain:* here and elsewhere the mountain is associated with solemn moments and acts in the mission and self-revelation of Jesus (Mk 6, 46; 9, 2-8; 13, 3). Jesus acts with authority as he *summoned those whom he wanted and they came to him.*

3, 14-15: *He appointed twelve [whom he also named apostles] that they might be with him:* literally "he made," i.e., instituted them as apostles to extend his messianic mission through them (Mk 6, 7-13). See the notes on Mt 10, 1 and Mt 10, 2-4.

3, 16: *Simon, whom he named Peter:* Mark indicates that Simon's name was changed on this occasion. Peter is first in all lists of the apostles (Mt 10, 2; Lk 6, 14; Acts 1, 13; cf 1 Cor 15, 5-8).

3, 20-35: Within the narrative of the coming of Jesus' relatives (20-21) is inserted the account of the unbelieving scribes from Jerusalem who attributed Jesus' power over demons to Beelzebul (22-30); see the note on Mk 5, 21-43. There were those even among the relatives of Jesus who disbelieved and regarded Jesus as *out of his mind* (21). Against this background, Jesus is informed of the arrival of his mother and brothers [and sisters] (32). He responds by showing that not family ties but doing God's will (35) is decisive in the kingdom; cf the note on Mt 12, 46-50.

3, 20: *He came home:* cf Mk 2, 1-2 and see the note on Mk 2, 15.

3, 22: *By Beelzebul:* see the note on Mt 10, 25. Two accusations are leveled against Jesus: (1) that *he is possessed* by an unclean spirit, and (2) *by the prince of demons he drives out demons.* Jesus answers the second charge by a parable (24-27) and responds to the first charge in vv 28-29.

3, 29: *Whoever blasphemes against the holy Spirit:* this sin is called *an everlasting sin* because it attributes to Satan, who is the power of evil, what is actually the work of the holy Spirit, namely, victory over the demons.

3, 32: *Your brothers:* see the note on Mk 6, 3.

CHAPTER 4

The Parable of the Sower. [1] * On another occasion [o] he began to teach by the sea.* A very large crowd gathered around him so that he got into a boat on the sea and sat down. And the whole crowd was beside the sea on land.[p] [2] And he taught them at length in parables, and in the course of his instruction he said to them, [3] * "Hear this! A sower went out to sow. [4] And as he sowed, some seed fell on the path, and the birds came and ate it up. [5] Other seed fell on rocky ground where it had little soil. It sprang up at once because the soil was not deep. [6] And when the sun rose, it was scorched and it withered for lack of roots. [7] Some seed fell among thorns, and the thorns grew up and choked it and it produced no grain. [8] And some seed fell on rich soil and produced fruit. It came up and grew and yielded thirty, sixty, and a hundredfold." [9] He added, "Whoever has ears to hear ought to hear."

The Purpose of the Parables. [10] And when he was alone, those present along with the Twelve questioned him about the parables. [11] * He answered them, "The mystery of the kingdom of God has been granted to you. But to those outside everything comes in parables, [12] so that

'they may look and see but not perceive,
    and hear and listen but not understand,
in order that they may not be converted
    and be forgiven.' " [q]

[13] * Jesus said to them, "Do you not understand this parable? [r] Then how will you understand any of the parables? [14] The sower sows the word. [15] These are the ones on the path where the word is sown. As soon as they hear, Satan comes at once and takes away the word sown in them. [16] And these are the ones sown on rocky ground who, when they hear the word, receive it at once with joy. [17] But they have no root; they last only for a time. Then when tribulation or persecution comes because of the word, they quickly fall away. [18] Those sown among thorns are another sort. They are the people who hear the word, [19] but worldly anxiety, the lure of riches, and the craving for other things intrude and choke the word, and it bears no fruit. [20] But those sown on rich soil are the ones who hear the

word and accept it and bear fruit thirty and sixty and a hundredfold."

Parable of the Lamp. [21] [s] He said to them, "Is a lamp brought in to be placed under a bushel basket or under a bed, and not to be placed on a lampstand? [t] [22] For there is nothing hidden except to be made visible; nothing is secret except to come to light. [u] [23] Anyone who has ears to hear ought to hear." [24] He also told them, "Take care what you hear. The measure with which you measure will be measured out to you, and still more will be given to you. [v] [25] To the one who has, more will be given; from the one who has not, even what he has will be taken away." [w]

Seed Grows of Itself. * [26] He said, "This is how it is with the kingdom of God; it is as if a man were to scatter seed [x] on the land [27] and would sleep and rise night and day and the seed would sprout and grow, he knows not how. [28] Of its own accord the land yields fruit, first the blade, then the ear, then the full grain in the ear. [29] And

---

o 1-12: Mt 13, 1-13; Lk 8, 4-10.—p Mk 2, 13; Lk 5, 1.—q Is 6, 9; Jn 12, 40; Acts 28, 26; Rom 11, 8.—r 13-20: Mt 13, 18-23; Lk 8, 11-15.—s 21-25: Lk 8, 16-18.—t Mt 5, 15; Lk 11, 33.—u Mt 10, 26; Lk 12, 2.—v Mt 7, 2; Lk 6, 38.—w Mt 13, 12; Lk 19, 26.—x 26-29: Jas 5, 7.

4, 1-34: *In parables* (2): see the note on Mt 13, 3. The use of parables is typical of Jesus' enigmatic method of teaching the crowds (2-9.12) as compared with the interpretation of the parables he gives to his disciples (10-25.33-34), to each group according to its capacity to understand (9-11). The key feature of the parable at hand is the sowing of the seed (3), representing the breakthrough of the kingdom of God into the world. The various types of soil refer to the diversity of response accorded the word of God (4-7). The climax of the parable is the harvest of thirty, sixty, and a hundredfold, indicating the consummation of the kingdom (8). Thus both the present and the future action of God, from the initiation to the fulfillment of the kingdom, is presented through this and other parables (26-29.30-32).

4, 1: *By the sea:* the shore of the Sea of Galilee or a boat near the shore (Mk 2, 13; 3, 7-8) is the place where Mark depicts Jesus teaching the crowds. By contrast the mountain is the scene of Jesus at prayer (Mk 6, 46) or in the process of forming his disciples (Mk 3, 13; 9, 2).

4, 3-8: See the note on Mt 13, 3-8.

4, 11-12: These verses are to be viewed against their background in Mk 3, 6.22 concerning the unbelief and opposition Jesus encountered in his ministry. It is against this background that the distinction in Jesus' method becomes clear of presenting the kingdom to the disbelieving crowd in one manner and to the disciples in another. To the former it is presented in parables and the truth remains hidden; for the latter the parable is interpreted and the mystery is partially revealed because of their faith; see the notes on Mt 13, 11 and Mt 13, 13.

4, 13-20: See the note on Mt 13, 18-23.

4, 26-29: Only Mark records the parable of the seed's growth. Sower and harvester are the same. The emphasis is on the power of the seed to grow of itself without human intervention (27). Mysteriously it produces *blade* and *ear* and *full grain* (28). Thus the kingdom of God initiated by Jesus in proclaiming the word develops quietly yet powerfully until it is fully established by him at the final judgment (29); cf Rv 14, 15.

when the grain is ripe, he wields the sickle at once, for the harvest has come."

The Mustard Seed. 30 *y* He said, "To what shall we compare the kingdom of God, or what parable can we use for it? 31 It is like a mustard seed that, when it is sown in the ground, is the smallest of all the seeds on the earth. 32 But once it is sown, it springs up and becomes the largest of plants and puts forth large branches, so that the birds of the sky can dwell in its shade." * 33 With many such parables *z* he spoke the word to them as they were able to understand it. 34 Without parables he did not speak to them, but to his own disciples he explained everything in private.

The Calming of a Storm at Sea. 35 * On that day, as evening drew on, he said to them, "Let us cross to the other side." *a* 36 Leaving the crowd, they took him with them in the boat just as he was. And other boats were with him. 37 A violent squall came up and waves were breaking over the boat, so that it was already filling up. 38 Jesus was in the stern, asleep on a cushion. They woke him and said to him, "Teacher, do you not care that we are perishing?" 39 He woke up, rebuked the wind, and said to the sea, "Quiet! Be still!" * The wind ceased and there was great calm. 40 Then he asked them, "Why

---

y 30-32: Mt 13, 31-32; Lk 13, 18-19.—z 33-34: Mt 13, 34.—a 35-40: Mt 8, 18.23-37; Lk 8, 22-25.—b Mk 1, 27.—c 1-20: Mt 8, 28-34; Lk 8, 26-39.—d Mt 12, 45; Lk 8, 2; 11, 26.

4, 32: The universality of the kingdom of God is indicated here; cf Ez 17, 23; 31, 6; Dn 4, 17-19.

4, 35—5, 43: After the chapter on parables, Mark narrates four miracle stories: Mk 4, 35-41; 5, 1-20; and two joined together in Mk 5, 21-43. See also the notes on Mt 8, 23-34 and Mt 9, 8-26.

4, 39: *Quiet! Be still!:* as in the case of silencing a demon (Mk 1, 25), Jesus rebukes the wind and subdues the turbulence of the sea by a mere word; see the note on Mt 8, 26.

4, 41: Jesus is here depicted as exercising power over wind and sea. In the Christian community this event was seen as a sign of Jesus' saving presence amid persecutions that threatened its existence.

5, 1: *The territory of the Gerasenes:* the reference is to pagan territory; cf Is 65, 1. Another reading is "Gadarenes"; see the note on Mt 8, 28.

5, 2-6: The man was an outcast from society, dominated by unclean spirits (8.13), living among the tombs. The prostration before Jesus (6) indicates Jesus' power over evil spirits.

5, 7: *What have you to do with me?:* cf Mk 1, 24 and see the note on Jn 2, 4.

5, 9: *Legion is my name:* the demons were numerous and the condition of the possessed man was extremely serious; cf Mt 12, 45.

5, 11: *Herd of swine:* see the note on Mt 8, 30.

---

are you terrified? Do you not yet have faith?" 41 *b* They were filled with great awe and said to one another, "Who then is this whom even wind and sea obey?" *

CHAPTER 5

The Healing of the Gerasene Demoniac. 1 *c* They came to the other side of the sea, to the territory of the Gerasenes.* 2 When he got out of the boat, at once a man* from the tombs who had an unclean spirit met him. 3 The man had been dwelling among the tombs, and no one could restrain him any longer, even with a chain. 4 In fact, he had frequently been bound with shackles and chains, but the chains had been pulled apart by him and the shackles smashed, and no one was strong enough to subdue him. 5 Night and day among the tombs and on the hillsides he was always crying out and bruising himself with stones. 6 Catching sight of Jesus from a distance, he ran up and prostrated himself before him, 7 crying out in a loud voice, "What have you to do with me,* Jesus, Son of the Most High God? I adjure you by God, do not torment me!" 8 (He had been saying to him, "Unclean spirit, come out of the man!") 9 He asked him, "What is your name?" He replied, "Legion is my name.* There are many of us." *d* 10 And he pleaded earnestly with him not to drive them away from that territory.

11 Now a large herd of swine* was feeding there on the hillside. 12 And they pleaded with him, "Send us into the swine. Let us enter them." 13 And he let them, and the unclean spirits came out and entered the swine. The herd of about two thousand rushed down a steep bank into the sea, where they were drowned. 14 The swineherds ran away and reported the incident in the town and throughout the countryside. And people came out to see what had happened. 15 As they approached Jesus, they caught sight of the man who had been possessed by Legion, sitting there clothed and in his right mind. And they were seized with fear. 16 Those who witnessed the incident explained to them what had happened to the possessed man and to the swine. 17 Then they began to beg him to leave their district. 18 As he was getting into the boat, the man who had been possessed pleaded to remain with him.

Mk

[19] But he would not permit him but told him instead, "Go home* to your family and announce to them all that the Lord in his pity has done for you." [20] Then the man went off and began to proclaim in the Decapolis what Jesus had done for him; and all were amazed.

Jairus's Daughter and the Woman with a Hemorrhage.* [21] When Jesus had crossed again [in the boat] to the other side, a large crowd gathered around him, and he stayed close to the sea.[e] [22] One of the synagogue officials, named Jairus, came forward.[f] Seeing him he fell at his feet [23] and pleaded earnestly with him, saying, "My daughter is at the point of death. Please, come lay your hands on her* that she may get well and live." [24] He went off with him, and a large crowd followed him and pressed upon him.

[25] There was a woman afflicted with hemorrhages for twelve years. [26] She had suffered greatly at the hands of many doctors and had spent all that she had. Yet she was not helped but only grew worse. [27] She had heard about Jesus and came up behind him in the crowd and touched his cloak. [28] She said, "If I but touch his clothes, I shall be cured."* [29] Immediately her flow of blood dried up. She felt in her body that she was healed of her affliction. [30] Jesus, aware at once that power had gone out from him, turned around in the crowd and asked, "Who has touched my clothes?" [31] But his disciples said to him, "You see how the crowd is pressing upon you, and yet you ask, 'Who touched me?' " [32] And he looked around to see who had done it. [33] The woman, realizing what had happened to her, approached in fear and trembling. She fell down before Jesus and told him the whole truth. [34] He said to her, "Daughter, your faith has saved you. Go in peace and be cured of your affliction."[g]

[35] While he was still speaking, people from the synagogue official's house arrived and said, "Your daughter has died; why trouble the teacher any longer?"* [36] Disregarding the message that was reported, Jesus said to the synagogue official, "Do not be afraid; just have faith." [37] He did not allow anyone to accompany him inside except Peter, James, and John, the brother of James. [38] When they arrived at the house of the synagogue official, he caught sight of a commotion, people weeping and wailing loudly. [39][h] So he went in and said to them, "Why this commotion and weeping? The child is not dead but asleep."* [40] And they ridiculed him. Then he put them all out. He took along the child's father and mother and those who were with him and entered the room where the child was. [41] He took the child by the hand and said to her, "*Talitha koum,*" which means, "Little girl, I say to you, arise!"* [42] The girl, a child of twelve, arose immediately and walked around. [At that] they were utterly astounded. [43] He gave strict orders that no one should know this and said that she should be given something to eat.

CHAPTER 6

The Rejection at Nazareth. [1][i] He departed from there and came to his native place,* accompanied by his disciples. [2] * When the sabbath came he began to teach in the synagogue, and many who heard him were astonished. They said, "Where did this man get all this? What kind of wisdom has been given him? What mighty

---

e Mk 2, 13.—f 22-43: Mt 9, 18-26; Lk 8, 41-56.—g Lk 7, 30.—h 39-40: Acts 9, 40.—i 1-6: Mt 13, 54-58; Lk 4, 16-30.

5, 19: *Go home:* Jesus did not accept the man's request *to remain with him* as a disciple (18), yet invited him to announce to his own people what the Lord had done for him, i.e., proclaim the gospel message to his pagan family; cf Mk 1, 14.39; 3, 14; 13, 10.

5, 21-43: The story of the raising to life of Jairus's daughter is divided into two parts: vv 21-24 and 35-43. Between these two separated parts the account of the cure of the hemorrhage victim (25-34) is interposed. This technique of intercalating or sandwiching one story within another occurs several times in Mk: 3, 19b-21 (22-30) 31-35; 6, 6b-13 (14-29) 30; 11, 12-14 (15-19) 20-25; 14, 53 (54) 55-65 (66-73).

5, 23: *Lay your hands on her:* this act for the purpose of healing is frequent in Mk (6, 5; 7, 32-35; 8, 23-25; 16, 18) and is also found in Mt 9, 18; Lk 4, 40; 13, 13; Acts 9, 17; 28, 8.

5, 28: Both in the case of Jairus and his daughter (23) and in the case of the hemorrhage victim, the inner conviction that physical contact (30) accompanied by faith in Jesus' saving power could effect a cure was rewarded.

5, 35: The faith of Jairus was put to a twofold test: (1) that his daughter might be cured and, now that she had died, (2) that she might be restored to life. His faith contrasts with the lack of faith of the crowd.

5, 39: *Not dead but asleep:* the New Testament often refers to death as sleep (Mt 27, 52; Jn 11, 11; 1 Cor 15, 6; 1 Thes 4, 13-15); see the note on Mt 9, 24.

5, 41: *Arise:* the Greek verb *egeirein* is the verb generally used to express resurrection from death (Mk 6, 14.16; Mt 11, 5; Lk 7, 14) and Jesus' own resurrection (Mk 16, 6; Mt 28, 6; Lk 24, 6).

6, 1: *His native place:* the Greek word *patris* here refers to Nazareth (cf Mk 1, 9; Lk 4, 16.23-24), though it can also mean native land.

6, 2-6: See the note on Mt 13, 54-58.

deeds are wrought by his hands! [3] [j] Is he not the carpenter,* the son of Mary, and the brother of James and Joses and Judas and Simon? And are not his sisters here with us?" And they took offense at him. [4] [k] Jesus said to them, "A prophet is not without honor except in his native place and among his own kin and in his own house."* [5] So he was not able to perform any mighty deed there,* apart from curing a few sick people by laying his hands on them. [6] He was amazed at their lack of faith.

The Mission of the Twelve. He went around to the villages in the vicinity teaching. [7] [l] He summoned the Twelve* and began to send them out two by two and gave them authority over unclean spirits. [8] * He instructed them to take nothing for the journey but a walking stick—no food, no sack, no money in their belts. [9] They were, however, to wear sandals but not a second tunic. [10] He said to them, "Wherever you enter a house, stay there until you leave from there.* [11] Whatever place does not welcome you or listen to you, leave there and shake the dust off your feet in

testimony against them." [12] So they w off and preached repentance. [13] They dr out many demons, and they anointed v oil many who were sick[m] and cu them.*

Herod's Opinion of Jesus.* [14] K Herod* heard about it, for his fame become widespread, and people were ing,[n] "John the Baptist has been rai from the dead; that is why mighty pow are at work in him."[o] [15] Others were s ing, "He is Elijah"; still others, "He prophet like any of the prophets."[p] [16] when Herod learned of it, he said, "I John whom I beheaded. He has b raised up."

The Death of John the Baptist.* [17] He was the one who had John arrested bound in prison on account of Herod the wife of his brother Philip, whom had married.[q] [18] John had said to Her "It is not lawful for you to have y brother's wife."[r] [19] Herodias* harbore grudge against him and wanted to kill h but was unable to do so. [20] Herod fea John, knowing him to be a righteous holy man, and kept him in custody. WI he heard him speak he was very mu perplexed, yet he liked to listen to hi [21] She had an opportunity one day wh Herod, on his birthday, gave a banquet his courtiers, his military officers, and t

---

j Mk 15, 40; Mt 12, 46; Jn 6, 42.—k Jn 4, 44.—l 7-11: Mt 10, 1.9-14; Lk 9, 15; 10, 4-11.—m Jas 5, 14.—n 14-16: Lk 9, 7-8.—o 14-29: Mt 14, 1-12.—p Mt 16, 14.—q Lk 3, 19-20.—r Lv 18, 16.

6, 3: *Is he not the carpenter?:* no other gospel calls Jesus a carpenter. Some witnesses have "the carpenter's son," as in Mt 13, 55. *Son of Mary:* contrary to Jewish custom, which calls a man the son of his father, this expression may reflect Mark's own faith that God is the Father of Jesus (Mk 1, 1.11; 8, 38; 13, 32; 14, 36). *The brother of James . . . Simon:* in Semitic usage, the terms 'brother,' 'sister' are applied not only to children of the same parents, but to nephews, nieces, cousins, half-brothers, and half-sisters; cf Gn 14, 16; 29, 15; Lv 10, 4. While one cannot suppose that the meaning of a Greek word should be sought in the first place from Semitic usage, the Septuagint often translates the Hebrew *'āḥ* by the Greek word *adelphos,* "brother," as in the cited passages, a fact that may argue for a similar breadth of meaning in some New Testament passages. For instance, there is no doubt that in v 17, "brother" is used of Philip, who was actually the half-brother of Herod Antipas. On the other hand, Mark may have understood the terms literally; see also Mk 3, 31-32; Mt 12, 46; 13, 55-56; Lk 8, 19; Jn 7, 3.5. The question of meaning here would not have arisen but for the faith of the church in Mary's perpetual virginity.

6, 4: *A prophet is not without honor except . . . in his own house:* a saying that finds parallels in other literatures, especially Jewish and Greek, but without reference to a prophet. Comparing himself to previous Hebrew prophets whom the people rejected, Jesus intimates his own eventual rejection by the nation especially in view of the dishonor his own relatives had shown him (Mk 3, 21) and now his townspeople as well.

6, 5: *He was not able to perform any mighty deed there:* according to Mark, Jesus' power could not take effect because of a person's lack of faith.

6, 7-13: The preparation for the mission of the Twelve is seen in the call (1) of the first disciples to be fishers of men (Mk 1, 16-20), (2) then of the Twelve set apart to be with Jesus and to receive authority to preach and expel demons (Mk 3, 13-19). Now

they are given the specific mission to exercise that authorit word and power as representatives of Jesus during the tim their formation.

6, 8-9: In Mk the use of a *walking stick* (8) and *sandals* is permitted, but not in Mt 10, 10 nor in Lk 10, 4. Mark does mention any prohibition to visit pagan territory and to en Samaritan towns. These differences indicate a certain adapta to conditions in and outside of Palestine and suggest in Mark's count a later activity in the church. For the rest, Jesus required his apostles a total dependence on God for food and shelter; cf 6, 35-44; 8, 1-9.

6, 10-11: Remaining in the same house as a guest (10) rath than moving to another offering greater comfort avoided any i pression of seeking advantage for oneself and prevented dishon to one's host. Shaking the dust off one's feet served as testimo against those who rejected the call to repentance.

6, 13: *Anointed with oil . . . cured them:* a common medi inal remedy, but seen here as a vehicle of divine power f healing.

6, 14-16: The various opinions about Jesus anticipate th theme of his identity that reaches its climax in Mk 8, 27-30.

6, 14: *King Herod:* see the note on Mt 14, 1.

6, 17-29: Similarities are to be noted between Mark's accoun of the imprisonment and death of John the Baptist in thi pericope, and that of the passion of Jesus (Mk 15, 1-47). Hero and Pilate, each in turn, acknowledges the holiness of life of on over whom he unjustly exercises the power of condemnation an death (Mk 6, 26-27; 15, 9-10.14-15). The hatred of Herodias to ward John parallels that of the Jewish leaders toward Jesus. Afte the deaths of John and of Jesus, well-disposed persons request the bodies of the victims of Herod and of Pilate in turn to give them respectful burial (Mk 6, 29; 15, 45-46).

6, 19: *Herodias:* see the note on Mt 14, 3.

leading men of Galilee. [22] Herodias's own daughter came in and performed a dance that delighted Herod and his guests. The king said to the girl, "Ask of me whatever you wish and I will grant it to you." [23] He even swore [many things] to her, "I will grant you whatever you ask of me, even to half of my kingdom." [s] [24] She went out and said to her mother, "What shall I ask for?" She replied, "The head of John the Baptist." [25] The girl hurried back to the king's presence and made her request, "I want you to give me at once on a platter the head of John the Baptist." [26] The king was deeply distressed, but because of his oaths and the guests he did not wish to break his word to her. [27] [t] So he promptly dispatched an executioner with orders to bring back his head. He went off and beheaded him in the prison. [28] He brought in the head on a platter and gave it to the girl. The girl in turn gave it to her mother. [29] When his disciples heard about it, they came and took his body and laid it in a tomb.

The Return of the Twelve. [30] The apostles[*] gathered together with Jesus and reported all they had done and taught. [u] [31] [*] He said to them, "Come away by yourselves to a deserted place and rest a while." People were coming and going in great numbers, and they had no opportunity even to eat. [v] [32] So they went off in the boat by themselves to a deserted place. [w] [33] People saw them leaving and many came to know about it. They hastened there on foot from all the towns and arrived at the place before them.

The Feeding of the Five Thousand. [34] When he disembarked and saw the vast crowd, his heart was moved with pity for them, for they were like sheep without a shepherd; and he began to teach them many things. [35] [*] By now it was already late and his disciples approached him and said, "This is a deserted place and it is already very late. [36] Dismiss them so that they can go to the surrounding farms and villages and buy themselves something to eat." [37] He said to them in reply, "Give them some food yourselves." But they said to him, "Are we to buy two hundred days' wages worth of food and give it to them to eat?" [38] He asked them, "How many loaves do you have? Go and see." And when they had found out they said, "Five loaves and two fish." [39] So he gave orders to have them sit down in groups on the green

grass. [40] The people took their places in rows by hundreds and by fifties.[*] [41] Then, taking the five loaves and the two fish and looking up to heaven, he said the blessing, broke the loaves, and gave them to [his] disciples to set before the people; he also divided the two fish among them all.[*] [42] They all ate and were satisfied. [43] And they picked up twelve wicker baskets full of fragments and what was left of the fish. [44] Those who ate [of the loaves] were five thousand men.

The Walking on the Water.[*] [45] Then he made his disciples get into the boat[x] and precede him to the other side toward Bethsaida,[*] while he dismissed the crowd. [46] And when he had taken leave of them, he went off to the mountain to pray.[*] [47] When it was evening, the boat was far out on the sea and he was alone on shore. [48] Then he saw that they were tossed about while rowing, for the wind was against them. About the fourth watch of the night, he came toward them walking on the sea.[*] He meant to pass by them. [49] But when they saw him walking on the sea, they thought it was a

---

s Est 5, 3.—t 27-28: Lk 9, 9.—u Lk 9, 10.—v Mk 3, 20; Mt 14, 13; Lk 9, 10.—w 32-44: Mt 14, 13-21; Lk 9, 10-17; Jn 6, 1-13—x 45-51: Mt 14, 22-32; Jn 6, 15-21.

6, 30: *Apostles:* here, and in some manuscripts at 3, 14, Mark calls apostles (i.e., those sent forth) the Twelve whom Jesus sends as his emissaries, empowering them to preach, to expel demons, and to cure the sick (13). Only after Pentecost is the title used in the technical sense.

6, 31-34: The withdrawal of Jesus with his disciples to a desert place to rest attracts a great number of people to follow them. Toward this people of the new exodus Jesus is moved with pity; he satisfies their spiritual hunger by teaching them many things, thus gradually showing himself the faithful shepherd of a new Israel; cf Nm 27, 17; Ez 34, 15.

6, 35-44: See the note on Mt 14, 13-21. Compare this section with Mk 8, 1-9. The various accounts of the multiplication of loaves and fishes, two each in Mark and in Matthew and one each in Luke and in John, indicate the wide interest of the early church in their eucharistic gatherings; see, e.g., Mk 6, 41; 8, 6; 14, 22; and recall also the sign of bread in Ex 16; Dt 8, 3-16; Pss 78, 24-25; 105, 40; Wis 16, 20-21.

6, 40: *The people . . . in rows by hundreds and by fifties:* reminiscent of the groupings of Israelites encamped in the desert (Ex 18, 21-25) and of the wilderness tradition of the prophets depicting the transformation of the wasteland into pastures where the true shepherd feeds his flock (Ez 34, 25-26) and makes his people beneficiaries of messianic grace.

6, 41: On the language of this verse as eucharistic (cf Mk 14, 22), see the notes on Mt 14, 19.20. Jesus observed the Jewish table ritual of blessing God before partaking of food.

6, 45-52: See the note on Mt 14, 22-33.

6, 45: *To the other side toward Bethsaida:* a village at the northeastern shore of the Sea of Galilee.

6, 46: *He went off to the mountain to pray:* see Mk 1, 35-38. In Jn 6, 15 Jesus withdrew to evade any involvement in the false messianic hopes of the multitude.

6, 48: *Walking on the sea:* see the notes on Mt 14, 22-33 and on Jn 6, 19.

ghost and cried out. ⁵⁰They had all seen him and were terrified. But at once he spoke with them, "Take courage, it is I, do not be afraid!"* ⁵¹He got into the boat with them and the wind died down. They were [completely] astounded. ⁵²They had not understood the incident of the loaves.* On the contrary, their hearts were hardened.ʸ

The Healings at Gennesaret. ⁵³ ᶻ After making the crossing, they came to land at Gennesaret and tied up there. ⁵⁴As they were leaving the boat, people immediately recognized him. ⁵⁵They scurried about the surrounding country and began to bring in the sick on mats to wherever they heard he was. ⁵⁶Whatever villages or towns or countryside he entered, they laid the sick in the marketplaces and begged him that they might touch only the tassel on his cloak; and as many as touched it were healed.ᵃ

---

y Mk 4, 13.—z 53-56: Mt 14, 34-36.—a Mk 5, 27-28; Acts 5, 15.—b 1-23: Mt 15, 1-20.—c Is 29, 13.—d Ex 21, 17; Lv 20, 9; Dt 5, 16; Eph 6, 2.—e 14-23: Mt 15, 10-20.—f Mk 4, 10.13.—g Acts 10, 15.

6, 50: *It is I. do not be afraid!:* literally, "I am." This may reflect the divine revelatory formula of Ex 3, 14; Is 41, 4.10.14; 43, 1-3.10.13. Mark implies the hidden identity of Jesus as Son of God.

6, 52: *They had not understood . . . the loaves:* the revelatory character of this sign and that of the walking on the sea completely escaped the disciples. *Their hearts were hardened:* in Mk 3, 5-6 hardness of heart was attributed to those who did not accept Jesus and plotted his death. Here the same disposition prevents the disciples from comprehending Jesus' self-revelation through signs; cf Mk 8, 17.

7, 1-23: See the note on Mt 15, 1-20. Against the Pharisees' narrow, legalistic, and external practices of piety in matters of purification (2-5), external worship (6-7), and observance of commandments, Jesus sets in opposition the true moral intent of the divine law (8-13). But he goes beyond contrasting the law and Pharisaic interpretation of it. The parable of vv 14-15 in effect sets aside the law itself in respect to clean and unclean food. He thereby opens the way for unity between Jew and Gentile in the kingdom of God, intimated by Jesus' departure for pagan territory beyond Galilee. For similar contrast see Mk 2, 1—3, 6; 3, 20-35; 6, 1-6.

7, 3: *Carefully washing their hands:* refers to ritual purification.

7, 5: *Tradition of the elders:* the body of detailed, unwritten, human laws regarded by the scribes and Pharisees to have the same binding force as that of the Mosaic law; cf Gal 1, 14.

7, 11: *Qorban:* a formula for a gift to God, dedicating the offering to the temple, so that the giver might continue to use it for himself but not give it to others, even needy parents.

7, 16: Verse 16, "Anyone who has ears to hear ought to hear," is omitted because it is lacking in some of the best Greek manuscripts and was probably transferred here by scribes from Mk 4, (9).23.

7, 17: *Away from the crowd . . . the parable:* in this context of privacy the term *parable* refers to something hidden, about to be revealed to the disciples; cf Mk 4, 10-11.34. Jesus sets the Mosaic food laws in the context of the kingdom of God where they are abrogated, and he declares moral defilement the only cause of uncleanness.

7, 19: *(Thus he declared all foods clean):* if this bold declaration goes back to Jesus, its force was not realized among Jewish Christians in the early church; cf Acts 10, 1—11, 18.

CHAPTER 7

The Tradition of the Elders.* ¹Now when the Pharisees with some scribes who had come from Jerusalem gathered around him,ᵇ ²they observed that some of his disciples ate their meals with unclean, that is, unwashed, hands. ³(For the Pharisees and, in fact, all Jews, do not eat without carefully washing their hands,* keeping the tradition of the elders. ⁴And on coming from the marketplace they do not eat without purifying themselves. And there are many other things that they have traditionally observed, the purification of cups and jugs and kettles [and beds].) ⁵So the Pharisees and scribes questioned him, "Why do your disciples not follow the tradition of the elders* but instead eat a meal with unclean hands?" ⁶He responded, "Well did Isaiah prophesy about you hypocrites, as it is written:ᶜ

'This people honors me with their lips,
  but their hearts are far from me;
⁷ In vain do they worship me,
  teaching as doctrines human precepts.'

⁸You disregard God's commandment but cling to human tradition." ⁹He went on to say, "How well you have set aside the commandment of God in order to uphold your tradition! ¹⁰For Moses said, 'Honor your father and your mother,' and 'Whoever curses father or mother shall die.'ᵈ ¹¹Yet you say, 'If a person says to father or mother, "Any support you might have had from me is *qorban*"'* (meaning, dedicated to God), ¹²you allow him to do nothing more for his father or mother. ¹³You nullify the word of God in favor of your tradition that you have handed on. And you do many such things." ¹⁴ ᵉ He summoned the crowd again and said to them, "Hear me, all of you, and understand. ¹⁵Nothing that enters one from outside can defile that person; but the things that come out from within are what defile." [16]*

¹⁷ ᶠ When he got home away from the crowd his disciples questioned him about the parable.* ¹⁸He said to them, "Are even you likewise without understanding? Do you not realize that everything that goes into a person from outside cannot defile, ¹⁹ ᵍ since it enters not the heart but the stomach and passes out into the latrine?" (Thus he declared all foods clean.)* ²⁰"But what comes out of a person, that is what

defiles. [21] [h] From within people, from their hearts, come evil thoughts, unchastity, theft, murder, [22] adultery, greed, malice, deceit, licentiousness, envy, blasphemy, arrogance, folly. [23] All these evils come from within and they defile."

The Syrophoenician Woman's Faith. [24] [i] From that place he went off to the district of Tyre.* He entered a house and wanted no one to know about it, but he could not escape notice. [25] Soon a woman whose daughter had an unclean spirit heard about him. She came and fell at his feet. [26] The woman was a Greek, a Syrophoenician by birth, and she begged him to drive the demon out of her daughter.[j] [27] He said to her, "Let the children be fed first.* For it is not right to take the food of the children and throw it to the dogs." [28] She replied and said to him, "Lord, even the dogs under the table eat the children's scraps." [29] Then he said to her, "For saying this, you may go. The demon has gone out of your daughter." [30] When the woman went home, she found the child lying in bed and the demon gone.

The Healing of a Deaf Man. [31] [k] Again he left the district of Tyre and went by way of Sidon to the Sea of Galilee, into the district of the Decapolis. [32] And people brought to him a deaf man who had a speech impediment and begged him to lay his hand on him. [33] He took him off by himself away from the crowd. He put his finger into the man's ears and, spitting, touched his tongue; [34] then he looked up to heaven and groaned, and said to him, "*Ephphatha!*" (that is, "Be opened!") [35] And [immediately] the man's ears were opened, his speech impediment was removed, and he spoke plainly. [36] He ordered them not to tell anyone. But the more he ordered them not to, the more they proclaimed it.* [37] They were exceedingly astonished and they said, "He has done all things well. He makes the deaf hear and [the] mute speak." [l]

CHAPTER 8

The Feeding of the Four Thousand. * [1] In those days when there again was a great crowd without anything to eat, [m] he summoned the disciples and said, [2] "My heart is moved with pity for the crowd, because they have been with me now for three days and have nothing to eat. [3] If I send them

away hungry to their homes, they will collapse on the way, and some of them have come a great distance." [4] His disciples answered him, "Where can anyone get enough bread to satisfy them here in this deserted place?" [5] Still he asked them, "How many loaves do you have?" "Seven," they replied. [6] He ordered the crowd to sit down on the ground. Then, taking the seven loaves he gave thanks, broke them, and gave them to his disciples to distribute, and they distributed them to the crowd.* [7] They also had a few fish. He said the blessing over them and ordered them distributed also. [8] They ate and were satisfied. They picked up the fragments left over—seven baskets. [9] There were about four thousand people.

He dismissed them [10] and got into the boat with his disciples and came to the region of Dalmanutha.

The Demand for a Sign. [11] * The Pharisees came forward and began to argue with him,[n] seeking from him a sign from heaven to test him.[o] [12] He sighed from the depth of his spirit and said, "Why does this generation seek a sign? Amen, I say to you, no sign will be given to this generation."

---

h Jer 17, 9.—i 24-30: Mt 15, 21-28.—j Mt 8, 29.—k 31-37: Mt 15, 29-31.—l Mt 15, 31.—m 1-10: Mk 6, 34-44; Mt 15, 32-39.—n 11-13: Mt 12, 38-39; 16, 1-4.—o Lk 11, 16.

7, 24-37: The withdrawal of Jesus to the district of Tyre may have been for a respite (24), but he soon moved onward to Sidon and, by way of the Sea of Galilee, to the Decapolis. These districts provided a Gentile setting for the extension of his ministry of healing because the people there acknowledged his power (29.37). The actions attributed to Jesus (33-35) were also used by healers of the time.

7, 27-28: The figure of a household in which children at table are fed first and then their leftover food is given to the dogs under the table is used effectively to acknowledge the prior claim of the Jews to the ministry of Jesus; however, Jesus accedes to the Gentile woman's plea for the cure of her afflicted daughter because of her faith.

7, 36: *The more they proclaimed it:* the same verb *proclaim* attributed here to the crowd in relation to the miracles of Jesus is elsewhere used in Mark for the preaching of the gospel on the part of Jesus, of his disciples, and of the Christian community (Mk 1, 14; 13, 10; 14, 9). Implied in the action of the crowd is a recognition of the salvific mission of Jesus; see the note on Mt 11, 5-6.

8, 1-10: The two accounts of the multiplication of loaves and fishes (Mk 8, 1-10 and Mk 6, 31-44) have eucharistic significance. Their similarity of structure and themes but dissimilarity of detail are considered by many to refer to a single event that, however, developed in two distinct traditions, one Jewish Christian and the other Gentile Christian, since Jesus in Mark's presentation (Mk 7, 24-37) has extended his saving mission to the Gentiles.

8, 6: See the note on Mk 6, 41.

8, 11-12: The objection of the Pharisees that Jesus' miracles are unsatisfactory for proving the arrival of God's kingdom is comparable to the request of the crowd for a sign in Jn 6, 30-31. Jesus' response shows that a sign originating in human demand will not be provided; cf Nm 14, 11.22.

¹³Then he left them, got into the boat again, and went off to the other shore.

The Leaven of the Pharisees. ¹⁴ ᵖ They had forgotten to bring bread, and they had only one loaf with them in the boat. ¹⁵He enjoined them, "Watch out, guard against the leaven of the Pharisees and the leaven of Herod."* ¹⁶They concluded among themselves that it was because they had no bread. ¹⁷When he became aware of this he said to them, "Why do you conclude that it is because you have no bread? Do you not yet understand or comprehend? Are your hearts hardened? �q ¹⁸Do you have eyes and not see, ears and not hear? And do you not remember,ʳ ¹⁹when I broke the five loaves for the five thousand, how many wicker baskets full of fragments you picked up?" They answered him, "Twelve." ²⁰"When I broke the seven loaves for the four thousand, how many full baskets of fragments did you pick up?" They answered [him], "Seven." ²¹He said to them, "Do you still not understand?"

The Blind Man of Bethsaida. * ²²When they arrived at Bethsaida, they brought to him a blind man and begged him to touch him. ²³He took the blind man by the hand and led him outside the village. Putting spittle on his eyes he laid his hands on him and asked, "Do you see anything?" ˢ ²⁴Looking up he replied, "I see people looking like trees and walking." ²⁵Then he laid hands on his eyes a second time and he saw clearly; his sight was restored and he could see everything distinctly. ²⁶Then he sent him home and said, "Do not even go into the village."

III. THE MYSTERY BEGINS TO BE REVEALED

Peter's Confession about Jesus. * ²⁷Now Jesus and his disciples set out for the villages of Caesarea Philippi. ᵗ Along the way he asked his disciples, "Who do people say that I am?" ²⁸They said in reply, "John the Baptist, others Elijah, still others one of the prophets." ²⁹And he asked them, "But who do you say that I am?" Peter said to him in reply, "You are the Messiah." ³⁰Then he warned them not to tell anyone about him.

The First Prediction of the Passion. ³¹ ᵘ He began to teach them that the Son of Man* must suffer greatly and be rejected by the elders, the chief priests, and the scribes, and be killed, and rise after three days. ³²He spoke this openly. Then Peter took him aside and began to rebuke him. ³³At this he turned around and, looking at his disciples, rebuked Peter and said, "Get behind me, Satan. You are thinking not as God does, but as human beings do."

The Conditions of Discipleship. ³⁴He summoned the crowd with his disciples and said* to them, "Whoever wishes to come after me must deny himself, take up his

---

p 14-21: Mt 16, 5-12; Lk 12, 1.—q Mk 4, 13.—r Jer 5, 21; Ez 12, 2.—s Mk 7, 33; Jn 9, 6.—t 27-30: Mt 16, 13-20; Lk 9, 18-21.—u 31-38: Mt 16, 21-27; Lk 9, 22-26.

8, 15: *The leaven of the Pharisees . . . of Herod:* the corruptive action of leaven (1 Cor 5, 6-8; Gal 5, 9) was an apt symbol of the evil dispositions both of the Pharisees (Mk 8, 11-13; 7, 5-13) and of Herod (Mk 6, 14-29) toward Jesus. The disciples of Jesus are warned against sharing such rebellious attitudes toward Jesus; cf vv 17, 21.

8, 22-26: Jesus' actions and the gradual cure of the blind man probably have the same purpose as in the case of the deaf man (Mk 7, 31-37). Some commentators regard the cure as an intended symbol of the gradual enlightenment of the disciples concerning Jesus' messiahship.

8, 27-30: This episode is the turning point in Mark's account of Jesus in his public ministry. Popular opinions concur in regarding him as a prophet. The disciples by contrast believe him to be the Messiah. Jesus acknowledges this identification but prohibits them from making his messianic office known to avoid confusing it with ambiguous contemporary views on the nature of that office. See further the notes on Mt 16, 13-20.

8, 31: *Son of Man:* an enigmatic title. It is used in Dn 7, 13-14 as a symbol of "the saints of the Most High," the faithful Is-

raelites who receive the everlasting kingdom from the Ancient One (God). They are represented by a human figure that contrasts with the various beasts who represent the previous kingdoms of the earth. In the Jewish apocryphal books of 1 Enoch and 4 Ezra the "Son of Man" is not, as in Dn, a group, but a unique figure of extraordinary spiritual endowments, who will be revealed as the one through whom the everlasting kingdom decreed by God will be established. It is possible though doubtful that this individualization of the Son of Man figure had been made in Jesus' time, and therefore his use of the title in that sense is questionable. Of itself, this expression means simply a human being, or, indefinitely, someone, and there are evidences of this use in pre-Christian times. Its use in the New Testament is probably due to Jesus' speaking of himself in that way, "a human being," and the later church's taking this in the sense of the Jewish apocrypha and applying it to him with that meaning. *Rejected by the elders, the chief priests, and the scribes:* the supreme council called the Sanhedrin was made up of seventy-one members of these three groups and presided over by the high priest. It exercised authority over the Jews in religious matters. See the note on Mt 8, 20.

8, 34-35: This utterance of Jesus challenges all believers to authentic discipleship and total commitment to himself through self-renunciation and acceptance of the cross of suffering, even to the sacrifice of life itself. *Whoever wishes to save his life will lose it . . . will save it:* an expression of the ambivalence of life and its contrasting destiny. Life seen as mere self-centered earthly existence and lived in denial of Christ ends in destruction, but when lived in loyalty to Christ, despite earthly death, it arrives at fullness of life.

Mk

cross, and follow me.[v] [35] For whoever wishes to save his life will lose it, but whoever loses his life for my sake and that of the gospel* will save it.[w] [36] What profit is there for one to gain the whole world and forfeit his life? [37] What could one give in exchange for his life? [38] Whoever is ashamed of me and of my words in this faithless and sinful generation, the Son of Man will be ashamed of when he comes in his Father's glory with the holy angels."[x]

CHAPTER 9

[1] [y] He also said to them, "Amen, I say to you, there are some standing here who will not taste death until they see that the kingdom of God has come in power."*

The Transfiguration of Jesus.* [2] After six days Jesus took Peter, James, and John and led them up a high mountain apart by themselves.[z] And he was transfigured before them, [3] and his clothes became dazzling white, such as no fuller on earth could bleach them. [4] Then Elijah appeared to them along with Moses, and they were conversing with Jesus. [5] Then Peter said to Jesus in reply, "Rabbi, it is good that we are here! Let us make three tents: one for you, one for Moses, and one for Elijah."* [6] He hardly knew what to say, they were so terrified. [7] Then a cloud came, casting a shadow over them;* then from the cloud came a voice, "This is my beloved Son. Listen to him." [8] Suddenly, looking around, they no longer saw anyone but Jesus alone with them.

The Coming of Elijah.* [9] As they were coming down from the mountain, he charged them not to relate what they had seen to anyone, except when the Son of Man had risen from the dead.[a] [10] So they kept the matter to themselves, questioning what rising from the dead meant. [11] [b] Then they asked him, "Why do the scribes say that Elijah must come first?" [12] He told them, "Elijah will indeed come first and restore all things, yet how is it written regarding the Son of Man that he must suffer greatly and be treated with contempt? [13] But I tell you that Elijah has come and they did to him whatever they pleased, as it is written of him."[c]

The Healing of a Boy with a Demon.* [14] When they came to the disciples,[d] they saw a large crowd around them and scribes arguing with them. [15] Immediately on see-ing him, the whole crowd was utterly amazed. They ran up to him and greeted him. [16] He asked them, "What are you arguing about with them?" [17] Someone from the crowd answered him, "Teacher, I have brought to you my son possessed by a mute spirit. [18] Wherever it seizes him, it throws him down; he foams at the mouth, grinds his teeth, and becomes rigid. I asked your disciples to drive it out, but they were unable to do so." [19] He said to them in reply, "O faithless generation, how long will I be with you? How long will I endure you? Bring him to me." [20] They brought the boy to him. And when he saw him, the spirit immediately threw the boy into convulsions. As he fell to the ground, he began to roll around and foam at the mouth. [21] Then he questioned his father, "How long has this been happening to him?" He replied, "Since childhood. [22] It has often thrown

---

v Mt 10, 38-39; 16, 24-27; Lk 14, 26-27.—w Jn 12, 25.—x Mt 10, 33; Lk 12, 8.—y Mt 16, 28; Lk 9, 27.—z 2-13: Mt 17, 1-13; Lk 9, 28-36.—a Mk 8, 31.—b 11-12: Is 53, 3; Mal 3, 23.—c 1 Kgs 19, 2-10.—d 14-29: Mt 17, 14-21; Lk 9, 37-43.

8, 35: *For my sake and that of the gospel:* Mark here, as at Mk 10, 29, equates Jesus with the gospel.

9, 1: *There are some standing . . . come in power:* understood by some to refer to the establishment by God's power of his kingdom on earth in and through the church; more likely, as understood by others, a reference to the imminent parousia.

9, 2-8: Mk and Mt 17, 1 place the transfiguration of Jesus six days after the first prediction of his passion and death and his instruction to the disciples on the doctrine of the cross; Lk 9, 28 has "about eight days." Thus the transfiguration counterbalances the prediction of the passion by affording certain of the disciples insight into the divine glory that Jesus possessed. His glory will overcome his death and that of his disciples; cf 2 Cor 3, 18; 2 Pt 1, 16-19. The heavenly voice (7) prepares the disciples to understand that in the divine plan Jesus must die ignominiously before his messianic glory is made manifest; cf Lk 24, 25-27. See further the note on Mt 17, 1-8.

9, 5: Moses and Elijah represent respectively law and prophecy in the Old Testament and are linked to Mt. Sinai; cf Ex 19, 16—20, 17; 1 Kgs 19, 2.8-14. They now appear with Jesus as witnesses to the fulfillment of the law and the prophets taking place in the person of Jesus as he appears in glory.

9, 7: *A cloud came, casting a shadow over them:* even the disciples enter into the mystery of his glorification. In the Old Testament the cloud covered the meeting tent, indicating the Lord's presence in the midst of his people (Ex 40, 34-35) and came to rest upon the temple in Jerusalem at the time of its dedication (1 Kgs 8, 10).

9, 9-13: At the transfiguration of Jesus his disciples had seen Elijah. They were perplexed because, according to the rabbinical interpretation of Mal 3, 23-24, Elijah was to come first. Jesus' response shows that Elijah has come, in the person of John the Baptist, to prepare for the day of the Lord. Jesus *must suffer greatly and be treated with contempt* (12) like the Baptist (13); cf Mk 6, 17-29.

9, 14-29: The disciples' failure to effect a cure seems to reflect unfavorably on Jesus (14-18.22). In response Jesus exposes their lack of trust in God (19) and scores their lack of prayer (29), i.e., of conscious reliance on God's power when acting in Jesus' name. For Mt, see the note on Mt 17, 14-20. Luke 9, 37-43 centers attention on Jesus' sovereign power.

him into fire and into water to kill him. But if you can do anything, have compassion on us and help us." ²³ Jesus said to him, " 'If you can!' Everything is possible to one who has faith." ²⁴ Then the boy's father cried out, "I do believe, help my unbelief!" ²⁵ Jesus, on seeing a crowd rapidly gathering, rebuked the unclean spirit and said to it, "Mute and deaf spirit, I command you: come out of him and never enter him again!" ²⁶ Shouting and throwing the boy into convulsions, it came out. He became like a corpse, which caused many to say, "He is dead!" ²⁷ But Jesus took him by the hand, raised him, and he stood up. ²⁸ When he entered the house, his disciples asked him in private, "Why could we not drive it out?" ²⁹ He said to them, "This kind can only come out through prayer."*

The Second Prediction of the Passion. ³⁰ ᵉ They left from there and began a journey through Galilee, but he did not wish anyone to know about it.ᶠ ³¹ He was teaching his disciples and telling them, "The Son of Man is to be handed over to men and they will kill him, and three days after his death he will rise." ³² But they did not understand the saying, and they were afraid to question him.

IV. THE FULL REVELATION OF THE MYSTERY

The Greatest in the Kingdom.* ³³ They came to Capernaum and, once inside the house, he began to ask them, "What were you arguing about on the way?"ᵍ ³⁴ But they remained silent. They had been discussing among themselves on the way who was the greatest. ³⁵ Then he sat down, called the Twelve, and said to them, "If anyone wishes to be first, he shall be last of all and the servant of all."ʰ ³⁶ Taking a child he placed it in their midst, and putting his arms around it he said to them, ³⁷ "Whoever receives one child such as this in my name, receives me; and whoever receives me, receives not me but the One who sent me."ⁱ

Another Exorcist.* ³⁸ John said to him,ʲ "Teacher, we saw someone driving out demons in your name, and we tried to prevent him because he does not follow us." ³⁹ Jesus replied, "Do not prevent him. There is no one who performs a mighty deed in my name who can at the same time speak ill of me. ⁴⁰ For whoever is not against us is for us.ᵏ ⁴¹ Anyone who gives you a cup of water to drink because you belong to Christ, amen, I say to you, will surely not lose his reward.ˡ

Temptations to Sin. ⁴² ᵐ "Whoever causes one of these little ones who believe [in me] to sin, it would be better for him if a great millstone were put around his neck and he were thrown into the sea. ⁴³ If your hand causes you to sin, cut it off. It is better for you to enter into life maimed than with two hands to go into Gehenna,* into the unquenchable fire. [⁴⁴]* ⁴⁵ And if your foot causes you to sin, cut if off. It is better for you to enter into life crippled than with two feet to be thrown into Gehenna. [⁴⁶]* ⁴⁷ And if your eye causes you to sin, pluck it out. Better for you to enter into the kingdom of God with one eye than with two eyes to be thrown into Gehenna, ⁴⁸ where 'their worm does not die, and the fire is not quenched.'ⁿ

The Simile of Salt. ⁴⁹ "Everyone will be salted with fire.* ⁵⁰ Salt is good, but if salt becomes insipid, with what will you restore its flavor? Keep salt in yourselves and you will have peace with one another."ᵒ

---

e Jn 7, 1.—f 30-32: Mk 8, 31; Mt 17, 22-23; Lk 9, 43-45.—g 33-37: Mt 18, 1-5; Lk 9, 46-48.—h Mt 20, 27.—i Mt 10, 40; 18, 5; Jn 13, 20.—j 38-41: Nm 11, 28; Lk 9, 49-50; 1 Cor 12, 3.—k Mt 12, 30.—l Mt 10, 42; 1 Cor 3, 23.—m 42-47: Mt 5, 29-30; 18, 6-9; Lk 17, 1-2.—n Is 66, 24.—o Lv 2, 13; Mt 5, 13; Lk 14, 34-35; Col 4, 6.

9, 29: *This kind can only come out through prayer:* a variant reading adds "and through fasting."

9, 33-37: Mark probably intends this incident and the sayings that follow as commentary on the disciples' lack of understanding (32). Their role in Jesus' work is one of service, especially to the poor and lowly. Children were the symbol Jesus used for the *anawim,* the poor in spirit, the lowly in the Christian community.

9, 38-41: Jesus warns against jealousy and intolerance toward others, such as exorcists who do *not follow us.* The saying in v 40 is a broad principle of the divine tolerance. Even the smallest courtesies shown to those who teach in Jesus' name do not go unrewarded.

9, 43.45.47: *Gehenna:* see the note on Mt 5, 22.

9, 44.46: These verses, lacking in some important early manuscripts, are here omitted as scribal additions. They simply repeat v 48, itself a modified citation of Is 66, 24.

9, 49: *Everyone will be salted with fire:* so the better manuscripts. Some add "every sacrifice will be salted with salt." The purifying and preservative use of salt in food (Lv 2, 13) and the refinement effected through fire refer here to comparable effects in the spiritual life of the disciples of Jesus.

CHAPTER 10

Marriage and Divorce. ¹ He set out from there and went into the district of Judea [and] across the Jordan. Again crowds gathered around him and, as was his custom, he again taught them. [2] * The Pharisees approached and asked, "Is it lawful for a husband to divorce his wife?" They were testing him.[p] [3] He said to them in reply, "What did Moses command you?" [4] They replied, "Moses permitted him to write a bill of divorce and dismiss her." [q] [5] But Jesus told them, "Because of the hardness of your hearts he wrote you this commandment. [6] But from the beginning of creation, 'God made them male and female.[r] [7] For this reason a man shall leave his father and mother [and be joined to his wife],[s] [8] and the two shall become one flesh.' So they are no longer two but one flesh. [9] Therefore what God has joined together, no human being must separate." [10] In the house the disciples again questioned him about this. [11] [t] He said to them, "Whoever divorces his wife and marries another commits adultery against her; [12] and if she divorces her husband and marries another, she commits adultery."

Blessing of the Children. [13] [u] And people were bringing children to him that he might touch them, but the disciples rebuked them.[v] [14] When Jesus saw this he became indignant and said to them, "Let the children come to me; do not prevent them, for the kingdom of God belongs to such as these. [15] Amen, I say to you, whoever does not accept the kingdom of God like a child* will not enter it." [w] [16] Then he embraced them and blessed them, placing his hands on them.

The Rich Man. [17] [x] As he was setting out on a journey, a man ran up, knelt down before him, and asked him, "Good teacher, what must I do to inherit eternal life?" [18] Jesus answered him,"Why do you call me good?* No one is good but God alone. [19] You know the commandments: 'You shall not kill; you shall not commit adultery; you shall not steal; you shall not bear false witness; you shall not defraud; honor your father and your mother.' " [y] [20] He replied and said to him, "Teacher, all of these I have observed from my youth." [21] Jesus, looking at him, loved him and said to him, "You are lacking in one thing. Go, sell what you have, and give to [the] poor and you will have treasure in heaven; then come, follow me." [22] At that statement his face fell, and he went away sad, for he had many possessions.

[23] * Jesus looked around and said to his disciples, "How hard it is for those who

have wealth to enter the kingdom of God!" [z] [24] The disciples were amazed at his words. So Jesus again said to them in reply, "Children, how hard it is to enter the kingdom of God! [25] It is easier for a camel to pass through [the] eye of [a] needle than for one who is rich to enter the kingdom of God." [26] They were exceedingly astonished and said among themselves, "Then who can be saved?" [27] Jesus looked at them and said, "For human beings it is impossible, but not for God. All things are possible for God." [28] Peter began to say to him, "We have given up everything and followed you." [29] Jesus said, "Amen, I say to you, there is no one who has given up house or brothers or sisters or mother or father or children or lands for my sake and for the sake of the gospel [30] who will not receive a hundred times more now in this present age: houses and brothers and sisters and mothers and children and lands, with persecutions, and eternal life in the age to come. [31] But many that are first will be last, and [the] last will be first." [a]

The Third Prediction of the Passion. [32] [b] They were on the way, going up to Jerusalem, and Jesus went ahead of them. They were amazed, and those who followed were afraid. Taking the Twelve aside again, he began to tell them what was

---

p 2-12: Mt 19, 3-9.—q Dt 24, 1-4.—r Gn 1, 27.—s 7-8: Gn 2, 24; 1 Cor 6, 16; Eph 5, 31.—t 11-12: Mt 5, 32; Lk 16, 18; 1 Cor 7, 10-11.—u 13-16: Mt 19, 13-15; Lk 18, 15-17.—v Lk 9, 47.—w Mt 18, 3.—x 17-31: Mt 19, 16-30; Lk 18, 18-30.—y Ex 20, 12-16; Dt 5, 16-21.—z Prv 11, 28.—a Mt 19, 30; Lk 13, 30.—b 32-34: Mk 8, 31; Mt 20, 17-19; Lk 18, 31-33.

10, 2-9: In the dialogue between Jesus and the Pharisees on the subject of divorce, Jesus declares that the law of Moses permitted divorce (Dt 24, 1) only *because of the hardness of your hearts* (4-5). In citing Gn 1, 27 and Gn 2, 24, Jesus proclaims permanence to be the divine intent from the beginning concerning human marriage (6-8). He reaffirms this with the declaration that *what God has joined together, no human being must separate* (9). See further the notes on Mt 5, 31-32 and Mt 19, 3-9.

10, 15: *Whoever does not accept the kingdom of God like a child:* i.e., in total dependence upon and obedience to the gospel; cf Mt 18, 3-4.

10, 18: *Why do you call me good?:* Jesus repudiates the term "good" for himself and directs it to God, the source of all goodness who alone can grant the gift of eternal life; cf Mt 19, 16-17.

10, 23-27: In the Old Testament wealth and material goods are considered a sign of God's favor (Jb 1, 10; Ps 128, 1-2; Is 3, 10). The words of Jesus in 23-25 provoke astonishment among the disciples because of their apparent contradiction of the Old Testament concept (24.26). Since wealth, power, and merit generate false security, Jesus rejects them utterly as a claim to enter the kingdom. Achievement of salvation is beyond human capability and depends solely on the goodness of God who offers it as a gift (27).

going to happen to him. [33]"Behold, we are going up to Jerusalem, and the Son of Man will be handed over to the chief priests and the scribes, and they will condemn him to death and hand him over to the Gentiles [34]who will mock him, spit upon him, scourge him, and put him to death, but after three days he will rise."

Ambition of James and John. [35] [c] Then James and John, the sons of Zebedee, came to him and said to him, "Teacher, we want you to do for us whatever we ask of you." [36]He replied, "What do you wish [me] to do for you?" [37]They answered him, "Grant that in your glory we may sit one at your right and the other at your left." [38] [d] Jesus said to them, "You do not know what you are asking. Can you drink the cup that I drink or be baptized with the baptism with which I am baptized?"* [39]They said to him, "We can." Jesus said to them, "The cup that I drink, you will drink, and with the baptism with which I am baptized, you will be baptized; [40]but to sit at my right or at my left is not mine to give but is for those for whom it has been prepared." [41]When the ten heard this, they became indignant at James and John. [42] * Jesus summoned them and said to them,[e] "You know that those who are recognized as rulers over the Gentiles lord it over them, and their great ones make their authority over them felt. [43]But it shall not be so among you. Rather, whoever wishes to be great among you will be your servant;

---

c 35-45: Mt 20, 20-28.—d Lk 12, 50.—e 42-45: Lk 22, 25-27.—f 46-52: Mt 20, 29-34; Lk 18, 35-43.—g 1-10: Mt 21, 1-9; Lk 19, 29-38; Jn 12, 12-15.—h 9-10: 2 Sm 7, 16; Ps 118, 26.

10, 38-40: *Can you drink the cup . . . I am baptized?*: the metaphor of drinking the cup is used in the Old Testament to refer to acceptance of the destiny assigned by God; see the note on Ps 11, 6. In Jesus' case, this involves divine judgment on sin that Jesus the innocent one is to expiate on behalf of the guilty (Mk 14, 24; Is 53, 5). His baptism is to be his crucifixion and death for the salvation of the human race; cf Lk 12, 50. The request of James and John for a share in the glory (35-37) must of necessity involve a share in Jesus' sufferings, the endurance of tribulation and suffering for the gospel (39). The authority of assigning places of honor in the kingdom is reserved to God (40).

10, 42-45: Whatever authority is to be exercised by the disciples must, like that of Jesus, be rendered as service to others (45) rather than for personal aggrandizement (42-44). The service of Jesus is his passion and death for the human race (45); cf Mk 14, 24; Is 53, 11-12; Mt 26, 28; Lk 22, 19-20.

10, 46-52: See the notes on Mk 9, 27-31 and Mt 20, 29-34.

11, 1-11: In Mark's account Jesus takes the initiative in ordering the preparation for his entry into Jerusalem (1-6) even as he later orders the preparation of his last Passover supper (Mk 14, 12-16). In vv 9-10 the greeting Jesus receives stops short of proclaiming him Messiah. He is greeted rather as the prophet of the coming messianic kingdom. Contrast Mt 21, 9.

[44]whoever wishes to be first among you will be the slave of all. [45]For the Son of Man did not come to be served but to serve and to give his life as a ransom for many."

The Blind Bartimaeus. * [46]They came to Jericho.[f] And as he was leaving Jericho with his disciples and a sizable crowd, Bartimaeus, a blind man, the son of Timaeus, sat by the roadside begging. [47]On hearing that it was Jesus of Nazareth, he began to cry out and say, "Jesus, son of David, have pity on me." [48]And many rebuked him, telling him to be silent. But he kept calling out all the more, "Son of David, have pity on me." [49]Jesus stopped and said, "Call him." So they called the blind man, saying to him, "Take courage; get up, he is calling you." [50]He threw aside his cloak, sprang up, and came to Jesus. [51]Jesus said to him in reply, "What do you want me to do for you?" The blind man replied to him, "Master, I want to see." [52]Jesus told him, "Go your way; your faith has saved you." Immediately he received his sight and followed him on the way.

Mk

CHAPTER 11

The Entry into Jerusalem. * [1]When they drew near to Jerusalem,[g] to Bethphage and Bethany at the Mount of Olives, he sent two of his disciples [2]and said to them, "Go into the village opposite you, and immediately on entering it, you will find a colt tethered on which no one has ever sat. Untie it and bring it here. [3]If anyone should say to you, 'Why are you doing this?' reply, 'The Master has need of it and will send it back here at once.' " [4]So they went off and found a colt tethered at a gate outside on the street, and they untied it. [5]Some of the bystanders said to them, "What are you doing, untying the colt?" [6]They answered them just as Jesus had told them to, and they permitted them to do it. [7]So they brought the colt to Jesus and put their cloaks over it. And he sat on it. [8]Many people spread their cloaks on the road, and others spread leafy branches that they had cut from the fields. [9]Those preceding him as well as those following kept crying out:[h]

"Hosanna!
Blessed is he who comes in the name
of the Lord!

10   Blessed is the kingdom of our father
        David that is to come!
     Hosanna in the highest!"

11 He entered Jerusalem and went into the temple area. He looked around at everything and, since it was already late, went out to Bethany with the Twelve. *i*

Jesus Curses a Fig Tree. * 12 The next day as they were leaving Bethany he was hungry. *j* 13 Seeing from a distance a fig tree in leaf, he went over to see if he could find anything on it. When he reached it he found nothing but leaves; it was not the time for figs. 14 And he said to it in reply, "May no one ever eat of your fruit again!" And his disciples heard it.

Cleansing of the Temple. * 15 They came to Jerusalem, *k* and on entering the temple area he began to drive out those selling and buying there. He overturned the tables of the money changers and the seats of those who were selling doves. 16 He did not permit anyone to carry anything through the temple area. 17 Then he taught them saying, "Is it not written:

    'My house shall be called a house of
       prayer for all peoples'?
       But you have made it a den of
        thieves." *l*

18 The chief priests and the scribes came to hear of it and were seeking a way to put him to death, yet they feared him because the whole crowd was astonished at his teaching. 19 When evening came, they went out of the city. *m*

The Withered Fig Tree. 20 *n* Early in the morning, as they were walking along, they saw the fig tree withered to its roots. 21 Peter remembered and said to him, "Rabbi, look! The fig tree that you cursed has withered." 22 Jesus said to them in reply, "Have faith in God. 23 Amen, I say to you, whoever says to this mountain, 'Be lifted up and thrown into the sea,' and does not doubt in his heart but believes that what he says will happen, it shall be done for him. *o* 24 Therefore I tell you, all that you ask for in prayer, believe that you will receive it and it shall be yours. *p* 25 When you stand to pray, forgive anyone against whom you have a grievance, so that your heavenly Father may in turn forgive you your transgressions. *q* [26]"*

The Authority of Jesus Questioned. *
27 They returned once more to Jerusalem. *r*

As he was walking in the temple area, the chief priests, the scribes, and the elders approached him 28 and said to him, "By what authority are you doing these things? Or who gave you this authority to do them?" 29 Jesus said to them, "I shall ask you one question. Answer me, and I will tell you by what authority I do these things. 30 Was John's baptism of heavenly or of human origin? Answer me." 31 They discussed this among themselves and said, "If we say, 'Of heavenly origin,' he will say, '[Then] why did you not believe him?' 32 But shall we say, 'Of human origin'?"—they feared the crowd, for they all thought John really was a prophet. 33 So they said to Jesus in reply, "We do not know." Then Jesus said to them, "Neither shall I tell you by what authority I do these things."

CHAPTER 12

Parable of the Tenants. * 1 He began to speak to them in parables. *s* "A man planted a vineyard, put a hedge around it, dug a wine press, and built a tower. Then he leased it to tenant farmers and left on a journey. *t* 2 At the proper time he sent a servant to the tenants to obtain from them some of the produce of the vineyard. 3 But they seized him, beat him, and sent him away empty-handed. 4 Again he sent them another servant. And that one they beat over the head and treated shamefully. 5 He

i Mt 21, 10.17.—j 12-14: Mt 21, 18-20; Lk 13, 6-9.—k 15-18: Mt 21, 12-13; Lk 19, 45-46; Jn 2, 14-16.—l Is 56, 7; Jer 7, 11.—m Lk 21, 37.—n 20-24: Mt 21, 20-22.—o Mt 17, 20-21; Lk 17, 6.—p Mt 7, 7; Jn 11, 22; 14, 13.—q Mt 6, 14; 18, 35.—r 27-33: Mt 21, 23-27; Lk 20, 1-8.—s 1-12: Mt 21, 33-46; Lk 20, 9-19.—t Is 5, 1-7; Jer 2, 21.

11, 12-14: Jesus' search for fruit on the fig tree recalls the prophets' earlier use of this image to designate Israel; cf Jer 8, 13; 29, 17; Jl 1, 7; Hos 9, 10.16. Cursing the fig tree is a parable in action representing Jesus' judgment (20) on barren Israel and the fate of Jerusalem for failing to receive his teaching; cf Is 34, 4; Hos 2, 14; Lk 13, 6-9.

11, 15-19: See the note on Mt 21, 12-17.

11, 26: This verse, which reads, "But if you do not forgive, neither will your heavenly Father forgive your transgressions," is omitted in the best manuscripts. It was probably added by copyists under the influence of Mt 6, 15.

11, 27-33: The mounting hostility toward Jesus came from the chief priests, the scribes, and the elders (27); the Herodians and the Pharisees (Mk 12, 13); and the Sadducees (Mk 12, 18). By their rejection of God's messengers, John the Baptist and Jesus, they incurred the divine judgment implied in vv 27-33 and confirmed in the parable of the vineyard tenants (Mk 12, 1-12).

12, 1-12: The vineyard denotes Israel (Is 5, 1-7). The tenant farmers are the religious leaders of Israel. God is the owner of the vineyard. His servants are his messengers, the prophets. The beloved son is Jesus (Mk 1, 11; 9, 7; Mt 3, 17; 17, 5; Lk 3, 22; 9, 35). The punishment of the tenants refers to the religious leaders, and the transfer of the vineyard to others refers to the people of the new Israel.

sent yet another whom they killed. So, too, many others; some they beat, others they killed. [6] He had one other to send, a beloved son. He sent him to them last of all, thinking, 'They will respect my son.' [7] But those tenants said to one another, 'This is the heir. Come, let us kill him, and the inheritance will be ours.' [8] So they seized him and killed him, and threw him out of the vineyard. [9] What [then] will the owner of the vineyard do? He will come, put the tenants to death, and give the vineyard to others. [10] Have you not read this scripture passage: [u]

'The stone that the builders rejected
    has become the cornerstone;
[11] by the Lord has this been done,
    and it is wonderful in our eyes'?"

[12] They were seeking to arrest him, but they feared the crowd, for they realized that he had addressed the parable to them. So they left him and went away.

Paying Taxes to the Emperor. [13] * They sent some Pharisees[v] and Herodians to him to ensnare him[w] in his speech.* [14] They came and said to him, "Teacher, we know that you are a truthful man and that you are not concerned with anyone's opinion. You do not regard a person's status but teach the way of God in accordance with the truth. Is it lawful to pay the census tax to Caesar or not? Should we pay or should we not pay?" [15] Knowing their hypocrisy he said to them, "Why are you testing me? Bring me a denarius to look at." [16] They brought one to him and he said to them, "Whose image and inscription is this?" They replied to him, "Caesar's." [17] So Jesus said to them, "Repay to Caesar what belongs to Caesar and to God what belongs to God." They were utterly amazed at him.[x]

---

u 10-11: Ps 118, 22-23; Is 28, 16.—v 13-27: Mt 22, 15-33; Lk 20, 20-39.—w Mk 3, 6.—x Rom 13, 7.—y Dt 25, 5.—z Ex 3, 6.—a 28-34: Mt 22, 34-40; Lk 10, 25-28.—b Dt 6, 4-5.—c Lv 19, 18; Rom 13, 9; Gal 5, 14; Jas 2, 8.—d Dt 6, 4; Ps 40, 7-9.—e Mt 22, 46; Lk 20, 40.—f 35-37: Mt 22, 41-45; Lk 20, 41-44.

12, 13-34: In the ensuing conflicts (cf also Mk 2, 1—3, 6) Jesus vanquishes his adversaries by his responses to their questions and reduces them to silence (34).

12, 13-17: See the note on Mt 22, 15-22.

12, 18-27: See the note on Mt 22, 23-33.

12, 28-34: See the note on Mt 22, 34-40.

12, 35-37: Jesus questions the claim of the scribes about the Davidic descent of the Messiah, not to deny it (Mt 1, 1; Acts 2, 20.34; Rom 1, 3; 2 Tm 2, 8) but to imply that he is more than this. His superiority derives from his transcendent origin, to which David himself attested when he spoke of the Messiah with the name "Lord" (Ps 110, 1). See also the note on Mt 22, 41-46.

The Question about the Resurrection.* [18] Some Sadducees, who say there is no resurrection, came to him and put this question to him, [19] saying, "Teacher, Moses wrote for us, 'If someone's brother dies, leaving a wife but no child, his brother must take the wife and raise up descendants for his brother.'[y] [20] Now there were seven brothers. The first married a woman and died, leaving no descendants. [21] So the second married her and died, leaving no descendants, and the third likewise. [22] And the seven left no descendants. Last of all the woman also died. [23] At the resurrection [when they arise] whose wife will she be? For all seven had been married to her." [24] Jesus said to them, "Are you not misled because you do not know the scriptures or the power of God? [25] When they rise from the dead, they neither marry nor are given in marriage, but they are like the angels in heaven. [26] As for the dead being raised, have you not read in the Book of Moses, in the passage about the bush, how God told him, 'I am the God of Abraham, [the] God of Isaac, and [the] God of Jacob'?[z] [27] He is not God of the dead but of the living. You are greatly misled."

The Greatest Commandment.* [28] One of the scribes,[a] when he came forward and heard them disputing and saw how well he had answered them, asked him, "Which is the first of all the commandments?" [29] Jesus replied, "The first is this: 'Hear, O Israel! The Lord our God is Lord alone! [30] You shall love the Lord your God with all your heart, with all your soul, with all your mind, and with all your strength.'[b] [31] The second is this: 'You shall love your neighbor as yourself.' There is no other commandment greater than these."[c] [32] The scribe said to him, "Well said, teacher. You are right in saying, 'He is One and there is no other than he.' [33] And 'to love him with all your heart, with all your understanding, with all your strength, and to love your neighbor as yourself' is worth more than all burnt offerings and sacrifices."[d] [34] And when Jesus saw that [he] answered with understanding, he said to him, "You are not far from the kingdom of God." And no one dared to ask him any more questions.[e]

The Question about David's Son.* [35] As Jesus was teaching in the temple area he said.[f] "How do the scribes claim that the

Messiah is the son of David? [36]David himself, inspired by the holy Spirit, said:

'The Lord said to my lord,
"Sit at my right hand
     until I place your enemies under your
     feet." ' [g]

[37]David himself calls him 'lord'; so how is he his son?" [The] great crowd heard this with delight.

Denunciation of the Scribes.* [38]In the course of his teaching he said,[h] "Beware of the scribes, who like to go around in long robes and accept greetings in the marketplaces, [39]seats of honor in synagogues, and places of honor at banquets. [40]They devour the houses of widows and, as a pretext, recite lengthy prayers. They will receive a very severe condemnation."

The Poor Widow's Contribution.* [41]He sat down opposite the treasury and observed how the crowd put money into the treasury.[i] Many rich people put in large sums. [42]A poor widow also came and put in two small coins worth a few cents. [43]Calling his disciples to himself, he said to them, "Amen, I say to you, this poor widow put in more than all the other contributors to the treasury. [44]For they have all contributed from their surplus wealth, but she, from her poverty, has contributed all she had, her whole livelihood."

CHAPTER 13

The Destruction of the Temple Foretold.* [1]As he was making his way out of the temple area one of his disciples said to him, "Look, teacher, what stones and what buildings!"[j] [2]Jesus said to him, "Do you see these great buildings? There will not be one stone left upon another that will not be thrown down."

The Signs of the End. [3] * As he was sitting on the Mount of Olives opposite the temple area, Peter, James, John, and Andrew asked him privately,[k] [4]"Tell us, when will this happen, and what sign will there be when all these things are about to come to an end?" [5]Jesus began to say to them, "See that no one deceives you.[l] [6]Many will come in my name saying, 'I am he,' and they will deceive many. [7]When you hear of wars and reports of wars do not be alarmed; such things must happen, but it will not yet be the end. [8]Nation will rise against nation and kingdom against kingdom. There will be earthquakes from place to place and there will be famines. These are the beginnings of the labor pains.

The Coming Persecution. [9][m] "Watch out for yourselves. They will hand you over to the courts. You will be beaten in synagogues. You will be arraigned before governors and kings because of me, as a witness before them. [10]But the gospel must first be preached to all nations.* [11]When they lead you away and hand you over, do not worry beforehand about what you are to say.[n] But say whatever will be given to you at that hour. For it will not be you who are speaking but the holy Spirit. [12]Brother will hand over brother to death, and the father his child; children will rise up against parents and have them put to death. [13]You will be hated by all because of my name. But the one who perseveres to the end will be saved.

The Great Tribulation. [14] [o] "When you see the desolating abomination standing* where he should not (let the reader understand), then those in Judea must flee to the mountains,[p] [15][and] a person on a housetop must not go down or enter to get anything out of his house,[q] [16]and a person in

---

g Ps 110, 1.—h 38-40: Mt 23, 1-7; Lk 11, 43; 20, 45-47.—i 41-44: Lk 21, 1-4.—j 1-2: Mt 24, 1-2; Lk 21, 5-6.—k 3-8: Mt 24, 3-8; Lk 21, 7-11.—l Eph 5, 6; 2 Thes 2, 3.—m 9-13: Mt 24, 9-14; Lk 21, 12-19.—n 11-12: Mt 10, 19-22; Lk 12, 11-12.—o 14-23: Mt 24, 15-22; Lk 21, 20-24.—p Dn 9, 27; Mt 24, 15.—q Lk 17, 31.

12, 38-40: See the notes on Mk 7, 1-23 and Mt 23, 1-39.

12, 41-44: See the note on Lk 21, 1-4.

13, 1-2: The reconstructed temple with its precincts, begun under Herod the Great ca. 20 B.C., was completed only some seven years before it was destroyed by fire in A.D. 70 at the hands of the Romans; cf Jer 26, 18; Mt 24, 1-2. For the dating of the reconstruction of the temple, see further the note on Jn 2, 20.

13, 3-37: Jesus' prediction of the destruction of the temple (2) provoked questions that the four named disciples put to him in private regarding the time and the sign when all *these things are about to come to an end* (3-4). The response to their questions was Jesus' eschatological discourse prior to his imminent death. It contained instruction and consolation exhorting the disciples and the church to faith and obedience through the trials that would confront them (5-13). The sign is the presence of *the desolating abomination* (14; see Dn 9, 27), i.e., of the Roman power profaning the temple. Flight from Jerusalem is urged rather than defense of the city through misguided messianic hope (14-23). Intervention will occur only after destruction (24-27), which will happen before the end of the first Christian generation (28-31). No one but the Father knows the precise time, or that of the parousia (32); hence the necessity of constant vigilance (33-37). Luke sets the parousia at a later date, after "the time of the Gentiles" (Lk 21, 24). See also the notes on Mt 24, 1—25, 46.

13, 10: *The gospel . . . to all nations:* the period of the Christian mission.

13, 14: The participle *standing* is masculine, in contrast to the neuter at Mt 24, 15.

a field must not return to get his cloak. [17]Woe to pregnant women and nursing mothers in those days. [18]Pray that this does not happen in winter. [19]For those times will have tribulation such as has not been since the beginning of God's creation until now, nor ever will be.[r] [20]If the Lord had not shortened those days, no one would be saved; but for the sake of the elect whom he chose, he did shorten the days. [21]If anyone says to you then, 'Look, here is the Messiah! Look, there he is!' do not believe it. [22]False messiahs and false prophets will arise and will perform signs and wonders in order to mislead, if that were possible, the elect. [23]Be watchful! I have told it all to you beforehand.

The Coming of the Son of Man. [24] [s]"But in those days after that tribulation

> the sun will be darkened,
>   and the moon will not give its light,[t]
> [25] and the stars will be falling from the sky,
>   and the powers in the heavens will be shaken.

[26] [u] And then they will see 'the Son of Man coming in the clouds' with great power and

---

r Dn 12, 1.—s 24-27: Mt 24, 29-31; Lk 21, 25-27.—t Is 13, 10; Ez 32, 7; Jl 2, 10.—u Mk 14, 62; Dn 7, 13-14.—v 28-32: Mt 24, 32-36; Lk 21, 29-33.—w 33-37: Mt 24, 42; 25, 13-15.—x Mt 25, 14-30; Lk 19, 12-27.—y 1-2: Mt 26, 2-5; Lk 22, 1-2; Jn 11, 45-53.—z 3-9: Mt 26, 6-13; Jn 12, 1-8.

13, 26: *Son of Man . . . with great power and glory:* Jesus cites this text from Dn 7, 13 in his response to the high priest, *Are you the Messiah?* (Mk 14, 61). In Ex 34, 5; Lv 16, 2; and Nm 11, 25 the clouds indicate the presence of the divinity. Thus in his role of Son of Man, Jesus is a heavenly being who will come in power and glory.

14, 1—16, 8: In the movement of Mark's gospel the cross is depicted as Jesus' way to glory in accordance with the divine will. Thus the passion narrative is seen as the climax of Jesus' ministry.

14, 1: *The Passover and the Feast of Unleavened Bread:* the connection between the two festivals is reflected in Ex 12, 3-20; 34, 18; Lv 23, 4-8; Nm 9, 2-14; 28, 16-17; Dt 16, 1-8. The Passover commemorated the redemption from slavery and the departure after the Passover lamb was sacrificed in the temple in the afternoon of the fourteenth day of the month of Nisan. With the Passover supper on the same evening was associated the eating of unleavened bread. The latter was continued through Nisan 21, a reminder of the affliction of the Israelites and of the haste surrounding their departure. Praise and thanks to God for his goodness in the past were combined at this dual festival with the hope of future salvation. *The chief priests . . . to death:* the intent to put Jesus to death was plotted for a long time but delayed for fear of the crowd (Mk 3, 6; 11, 18; 12, 12).

14, 3-9: At Bethany on the Mount of Olives, a few miles from Jerusalem, *in the house of Simon the leper,* Jesus defends a woman's loving action of anointing his head with perfumed oil in view of his impending death and burial as a criminal, in which case his body would not be anointed. See further the note on Jn 12, 7. He assures the woman of the remembrance of her deed in the worldwide preaching of the good news.

glory,* [27]and then he will send out the angels and gather [his] elect from the four winds, from the end of the earth to the end of the sky.

The Lesson of the Fig Tree. [28] [v] "Learn a lesson from the fig tree. When its branch becomes tender and sprouts leaves, you know that summer is near. [29]In the same way, when you see these things happening, know that he is near, at the gates. [30]Amen, I say to you, this generation will not pass away until all these things have taken place. [31]Heaven and earth will pass away, but my words will not pass away.

Need for Watchfulness. [32]"But of that day or hour, no one knows, neither the angels in heaven, nor the Son, but only the Father. [33] [w] Be watchful! Be alert! You do not know when the time will come. [34]It is like a man traveling abroad. He leaves home and places his servants in charge, each with his work, and orders the gatekeeper to be on the watch.[x] [35]Watch, therefore; you do not know when the lord of the house is coming, whether in the evening, or at midnight, or at cockcrow, or in the morning. [36]May he not come suddenly and find you sleeping. [37]What I say to you, I say to all: 'Watch!' "

CHAPTER 14

The Conspiracy against Jesus. [1] * The Passover and the Feast of Unleavened Bread* were to take place in two days' time.[y] So the chief priests and the scribes were seeking a way to arrest him by treachery and put him to death. [2]They said, "Not during the festival, for fear that there may be a riot among the people."

The Anointing at Bethany. * [3]When he was in Bethany reclining at table in the house of Simon the leper,[z] a woman came with an alabaster jar of perfumed oil, costly genuine spikenard. She broke the alabaster jar and poured it on his head. [4]There were some who were indignant. "Why has there been this waste of perfumed oil? [5]It could have been sold for more than three hundred days' wages and the money given to the poor." They were infuriated with her. [6]Jesus said, "Let her alone. Why do you make trouble for her? She has done a good thing for me. [7]The poor you will always have with you, and whenever you wish you can do good to them, but you will not always have me. [8]She has done what

Mk

she could. She has anticipated anointing my body for burial. [9] Amen, I say to you, wherever the gospel is proclaimed to the whole world, what she has done will be told in memory of her."

The Betrayal by Judas. [10] *a* Then Judas Iscariot, one of the Twelve, went off to the chief priests to hand him over to them. [11] When they heard him they were pleased and promised to pay him money. Then he looked for an opportunity to hand him over.

Preparations for the Passover. [12] *b* On the first day of the Feast of Unleavened Bread, when they sacrificed the Passover lamb,* his disciples said to him, "Where do you want us to go and prepare for you to eat the Passover?" [13] He sent two of his disciples and said to them, "Go into the city and a man will meet you, carrying a jar of water.* Follow him. [14] Wherever he enters, say to the master of the house, 'The Teacher says, "Where is my guest room where I may eat the Passover with my disciples?" ' [15] Then he will show you a large upper room furnished and ready. Make the preparations for us there." [16] The disciples then went off, entered the city, and found it just as he had told them; and they prepared the Passover.

The Betrayer. [17] *c* When it was evening, he came with the Twelve. [18] And as they reclined at table and were eating, Jesus said, "Amen, I say to you, one of you will betray me, one who is eating with me."* [19] They began to be distressed and to say to him, one by one, "Surely it is not I?" [20] He said to them, "One of the Twelve, the one who dips with me into the dish. [21] For the

Son of Man indeed goes, as it is written of him,* but woe to that man by whom the Son of Man is betrayed. It would be better for that man if he had never been born."

The Lord's Supper. [22] *While they were eating,*d* he took bread, said the blessing, broke it, and gave it to them, and said, "Take it; this is my body." [23] Then he took a cup, gave thanks, and gave it to them, and they all drank from it. [24] He said to them, "This is my blood of the covenant, which will be shed* for many. [25] Amen, I say to you, I shall not drink again the fruit of the vine until the day when I drink it new in the kingdom of God." [26] Then, after singing a hymn,* they went out to the Mount of Olives.*e*

Peter's Denial Foretold.* [27] Then Jesus said to them, "All of you will have your faith shaken, for it is written:

'I will strike the shepherd,
   and the sheep will be dispersed.'*f*

[28] But after I have been raised up, I shall go before you to Galilee." [29] Peter said to him, "Even though all should have their faith shaken, mine will not be." [30] Then Jesus said to him, "Amen, I say to you, this very night before the cock crows twice you will deny me three times." [31] But he vehemently replied, "Even though I should have to die with you, I will not deny you." And they all spoke similarly.

The Agony in the Garden. [32] *Then they came to a place named Gethsemane,*g* and he said to his disciples, "Sit here while I

14, 22-24: The actions and words of Jesus express within the framework of the Passover meal and the transition to a new covenant the sacrifice of himself through the offering of his body and blood in anticipation of his passion and death. His *blood of the covenant* both alludes to the ancient rite of Ex 24, 4-8 and indicates the new community that the sacrifice of Jesus will bring into being (Mt 26, 26-28; Lk 22, 19-20; 1 Cor 11, 23-25).

14, 24: *Which will be shed:* see the note on Mt 26, 27-28. *For many:* the Greek preposition *hyper* is a different one from that at Mt 26, 28 but the same as that found at Lk 22, 19.20 and 1 Cor 11, 24. The sense of both words is vicarious, and it is difficult in Hellenistic Greek to distinguish between them. For *many* in the sense of "all," see the note on Mt 20, 28.

14, 26: *After singing a hymn:* Pss 114-118, thanksgiving songs concluding the Passover meal.

14, 27-31: Jesus predicted that the Twelve would waver in their faith, even abandon him, despite their protestations to the contrary. Yet he reassured them that after his resurrection he would regather them in Galilee (Mk 16, 7; cf Mt 26, 32; 28, 7.10.16; Jn 21), where he first summoned them to be his followers as he began to preach the good news (Mk 1, 14-20).

14, 32-34: The disciples who had witnessed the raising to life of the daughter of Jairus (Mk 5, 37) and the transfiguration of their Master (Mk 9, 2) were now invited to witness his degradation and agony and to watch and pray with him.

---

a 10-11: Mt 26, 14-16; Lk 22, 3-6.—b 12-16: Mt 26, 17-19; Lk 22, 7-13.—c 17-21: Mt 26, 20-24; Lk 22, 21-23; Jn 13, 21-26.—d 22-25: Mt 26, 26-30; Lk 22, 19-20; 1 Cor 11, 23-25.—e 26-31: Mt 26, 30-35; Lk 22, 34.39; Jn 13, 36-38.—f Zec 13, 7; Jn 16, 32.—g 32-42: Mt 26, 36-46; Lk 22, 40-46.

14, 12: *The first day of the Feast of Unleavened Bread . . . the Passover lamb:* a less precise designation of the day for sacrificing the Passover lamb as evidenced by some rabbinical literature. For a more exact designation, see the note on Mk 14, 1. It was actually Nisan 14.

14, 13: *A man . . . carrying a jar of water:* perhaps a prearranged signal, for only women ordinarily carried water in jars. The Greek word used here, however, implies simply a person and not necessarily a male.

14, 18: *One of you will betray me, one who is eating with me:* contrasts the intimacy of table fellowship at the Passover meal with the treachery of the traitor; cf Ps 41, 10.

14, 21: *The Son of Man indeed goes, as it is written of him:* a reference to Ps 41, 10 cited by Jesus concerning Judas at the Last Supper; cf Jn 13, 18-19.

pray." [h] [33] He took with him Peter, James, and John, and began to be troubled and distressed. [34] Then he said to them, "My soul is sorrowful even to death. Remain here and keep watch." [35] He advanced a little and fell to the ground and prayed that if it were possible the hour might pass by him; [36] he said, "Abba, Father,* all things are possible to you. Take this cup away from me, but not what I will but what you will." [37] When he returned he found them asleep. He said to Peter, "Simon, are you asleep? Could you not keep watch for one hour? [38] Watch and pray that you may not undergo the test. [i] The spirit is willing but the flesh is weak."* [39] Withdrawing again, he prayed, saying the same thing. [40] Then he returned once more and found them asleep, for they could not keep their eyes open and did not know what to answer him. [41] He returned a third time and said to them, "Are you still sleeping and taking your rest? It is enough. The hour has come. Behold, the Son of Man is to be handed over to sinners. [42] Get up, let us go. See, my betrayer is at hand."

The Betrayal and Arrest of Jesus.
[43] [j] Then, while he was still speaking, Judas, one of the Twelve, arrived, accompanied by a crowd with swords and clubs

---

h Jn 18, 1.—i Rom 7, 5.—j 43-50: Mt 26, 47-56; Lk 22, 47-53; Jn 18, 3-11.—k 53-65: Mt 26, 57-68; Lk 22, 54-55.63-65.67-71; Jn 18, 12-13.—l Mk 15, 29; 2 Cor 5, 1.—m Mk 13, 26; Ps 110, 1; Dn 7, 13; Mt 24, 30.

14, 36: *Abba, Father:* an Aramaic term, here also translated by Mark, Jesus' special way of addressing God with filial intimacy. The word *'abbā'* seems not to have been used in earlier or contemporaneous Jewish sources to address God without some qualifier. Cf Rom 8, 15; Gal 4, 6 for other occurrences of the Aramaic word in the Greek New Testament. *Not what I will but what you will:* note the complete obedient surrender of the human will of Jesus to the divine will of the Father; cf Jn 4, 34; 8, 29; Rom 5, 19; Phil 2, 8; Heb 5, 8.

14, 38: *The spirit is willing but the flesh is weak:* the spirit is drawn to what is good yet found in conflict with the flesh, inclined to sin; cf Ps 51, 7.12. Everyone is faced with this struggle, the full force of which Jesus accepted on our behalf and, through his bitter passion and death, achieved the victory.

14, 53: *They led Jesus away . . . came together:* Mark presents a formal assembly of the whole Sanhedrin (chief priests, elders, and scribes) at night, leading to the condemnation of Jesus (64), in contrast to Lk 22, 66.71, where Jesus is condemned in a daytime meeting of the council; see also Jn 18, 13.19-24.

14, 57-58: See the notes on Mt 26, 60-61 and Jn 2, 19.

14, 61-62: *The Blessed One:* a surrogate for the divine name, which Jews did not pronounce. *I am:* indicates Jesus' acknowledgment that he is the Messiah and Son of God; cf Mk 1, 1. Contrast Mt 26, 64 and Lk 22, 67-70, in which Jesus leaves his interrogators to answer their own question. *You will see the Son of Man . . . with the clouds of heaven:* an allusion to Dn 7, 13 and Ps 110, 1, portending the enthronement of Jesus as judge in the transcendent glory of God's kingdom. *The Power:* another surrogate for the name of God.

---

who had come from the chief priests, the scribes, and the elders. [44] His betrayer had arranged a signal with them, saying, "The man I shall kiss is the one; arrest him and lead him away securely." [45] He came and immediately went over to him and said, "Rabbi." And he kissed him. [46] At this they laid hands on him and arrested him. [47] One of the bystanders drew his sword, struck the high priest's servant, and cut off his ear. [48] Jesus said to them in reply, "Have you come out as against a robber, with swords and clubs, to seize me? [49] Day after day I was with you teaching in the temple area, yet you did not arrest me; but that the scriptures may be fulfilled." [50] And they all left him and fled. [51] Now a young man followed him wearing nothing but a linen cloth about his body. They seized him, [52] but he left the cloth behind and ran off naked.

Jesus before the Sanhedrin. [53] [k] They led Jesus away to the high priest, and all the chief priests and the elders and the scribes came together.* [54] Peter followed him at a distance into the high priest's courtyard and was seated with the guards, warming himself at the fire. [55] The chief priests and the entire Sanhedrin kept trying to obtain testimony against Jesus in order to put him to death, but they found none. [56] Many gave false witness against him, but their testimony did not agree. [57] * Some took the stand and testified falsely against him, alleging, [58] "We heard him say, 'I will destroy this temple made with hands and within three days I will build another not made with hands.' " [l] [59] Even so their testimony did not agree. [60] The high priest rose before the assembly and questioned Jesus, saying, "Have you no answer? What are these men testifying against you?" [61] But he was silent and answered nothing. Again the high priest asked him and said to him, "Are you the Messiah, the son of the Blessed One?"* [62] Then Jesus answered, "I am;

and 'you will see the Son of Man
　　seated at the right hand of the Power
　　　and coming with the clouds of
　　　heaven.' " [m]

[63] At that the high priest tore his garments and said, "What further need have we of witnesses? [64] You have heard the blasphemy. What do you think?" They all condemned him as deserving to die. [65] Some

began to spit on him. They blindfolded him and struck him and said to him, "Prophesy!" And the guards greeted him with blows.[n]

Peter's Denial of Jesus. 66 [o] While Peter was below in the courtyard, one of the high priest's maids came along. 67 Seeing Peter warming himself, she looked intently at him and said, "You too were with the Nazarene, Jesus." 68 But he denied it saying, "I neither know nor understand what you are talking about." So he went out into the outer court. [Then the cock crowed.]* 69 The maid saw him and began again to say to the bystanders, "This man is one of them." 70 Once again he denied it. A little later the bystanders said to Peter once more, "Surely you are one of them; for you too are a Galilean." 71 He began to curse and to swear, "I do not know this man about whom you are talking." 72 And immediately a cock crowed a second time. Then Peter remembered the word that Jesus had said to him, "Before the cock crows twice you will deny me three times." He broke down and wept.[p]

CHAPTER 15

Jesus before Pilate. 1 [q] As soon as morning came,[r] the chief priests with the elders and the scribes, that is, the whole Sanhedrin, held a council.* They bound Jesus, led him away, and handed him over to Pilate. 2 Pilate questioned him, "Are you the king of the Jews?"* He said to him in reply, "You say so." 3 The chief priests accused him of many things. 4 Again Pilate questioned him, "Have you no answer? See how many things they accuse you of." 5 Jesus gave him no further answer, so that Pilate was amazed.

The Sentence of Death. * 6 Now on the occasion of the feast he used to release to them one prisoner whom they requested.[s] 7 A man called Barabbas* was then in prison along with the rebels who had committed murder in a rebellion. 8 The crowd came forward and began to ask him to do for them as he was accustomed. 9 Pilate answered, "Do you want me to release to you the king of the Jews?" 10 For he knew that it was out of envy that the chief priests had handed him over. 11 But the chief priests stirred up the crowd to have him release Barabbas for them instead. 12 Pilate again said to them in reply, "Then what [do you want] me to do with [the man you call] the king of the Jews?" 13 They shouted again, "Crucify him."* 14 Pilate said to them, "Why? What evil has he done?" They only shouted the louder, "Crucify him." 15 So Pilate, wishing to satisfy the crowd, released Barabbas to them and, after he had Jesus scourged, handed him over to be crucified.*

Mockery by the Soldiers. 16 [t] The soldiers led him away inside the palace, that is, the praetorium,* and assembled the whole cohort. 17 They clothed him in purple and, weaving a crown of thorns, placed it on him. 18 They began to salute him with, "Hail, King of the Jews!" 19 and kept striking his head with a reed and spitting upon him. They knelt before him in homage. 20 And when they had mocked him, they stripped him of the purple cloak, dressed him in his own clothes, and led him out to crucify him.

The Way of the Cross. 21 They pressed into service a passer-by, Simon, a Cyrenian,* who was coming in from the country, the father of Alexander and Rufus, to carry his cross.[u]

The Crucifixion. 22 [v] They brought him to the place of Golgotha (which is translated

---

n Lk 22, 63-65.—o 66-72: Mt 26, 69-75; Lk 22, 56-62; Jn 18, 16-18.25-27.—p Jn 13, 38.—q 1-5: Mt 27, 1-2.11-14; Lk 23, 1-3.—r Jn 18, 28.—s 6-15: Mt 27, 15-26; Lk 23, 17-25; Jn 18, 39-40.—t 16-20: Mt 27, 27-31; Jn 19, 2-3.—u Mt 27, 32; Lk 23, 26.—v 22-38: Mt 27, 33-51; Lk 23, 32-46; Jn 19, 17-30.

14, 68: *[Then the cock crowed]:* found in most manuscripts, perhaps in view of vv 30 and 72, but omitted in others.

15, 1: *Held a council:* the verb here, *poieō,* can mean either "convene a council" or "take counsel." This reading is preferred to a variant "reached a decision" (cf Mk 3, 6), which Mk 14, 64 describes as having happened at the night trial; see the note on Mt 27, 1-2. *Handed him over to Pilate:* lacking authority to execute their sentence of condemnation (Mk 14, 64), the Sanhedrin had recourse to Pilate to have Jesus tried and put to death (15); cf Jn 18, 31.

15, 2: *The king of the Jews:* in the accounts of the evangelists a certain irony surrounds the use of this title as an accusation against Jesus (see the note on Mk 15, 26). While Pilate uses this term (2.9.12), he is aware of the evil motivation of the chief priests who handed Jesus over for trial and condemnation (10; Lk 23, 14-16.20; Mt 27, 18.24; Jn 18, 38; 19, 4.6.12).

15, 6-15: See the note on Mt 27, 15-26.

15, 7: *Barabbas:* see the note on Mt 27, 16-17.

15, 13: *Crucify him:* see the note on Mt 27, 22.

15, 15: See the note on Mt 27, 26.

15, 16: *Praetorium:* see the note on Mt 27, 27.

15, 21: *They pressed into service . . . Simon, a Cyrenian:* a condemned person was constrained to bear his own instrument of torture, at least the crossbeam. The precise naming of Simon and his sons is probably due to their being known among early Christian believers to whom Mark addressed his gospel. See also the notes on Mt 27, 32 and Lk 23, 26-32.

Place of the Skull). [23] They gave him wine drugged with myrrh, but he did not take it. [24] *w* Then they crucified him and divided his garments by casting lots for them to see what each should take.* [25] It was nine o'clock in the morning* when they crucified him. [26] The inscription of the charge against him read, "The King of the Jews."* [27] With him they crucified two revolutionaries, one on his right and one on his left. *x* [28]* [29] Those passing by reviled him, shaking their heads and saying,*y* "Aha! You who would destroy the temple and rebuild it in three days,* [30] save yourself by coming down from the cross." [31] Likewise the chief priests, with the scribes, mocked him among themselves and said, "He saved others; he cannot save himself. [32] Let the Messiah, the King of Israel, come down now from the cross that we may see and believe." Those who were crucified with him also kept abusing him. *z*

w Ps 22, 18.—x Lk 23, 33.—y Jn 2, 19.—z Lk 23, 39.—a Ps 22, 2.—b 39-41: Mt 27, 54-56; Lk 23, 47-49.—c Mk 6, 3; Lk 8, 2-3.—d 42-47: Mt 27, 57-61; Lk 23, 50-56; Jn 19, 38-42.—e 1-8: Mt 28, 1-8; Lk 24, 1-10; Jn 20, 1-10.—f 1-2: Mt 28, 1; Lk 23, 56.

15, 24: See the notes on Mt 27, 35 and Jn 19, 23-25a.

15, 25: *It was nine o'clock in the morning:* literally, "the third hour," thus between 9 a.m. and 12 noon. Cf vv 33.34.42 for Mark's chronological sequence, which may reflect liturgical or catechetical considerations rather than the precise historical sequence of events; contrast the different chronologies in the other gospels, especially Jn 19, 14.

15, 26: *The inscription . . . the King of the Jews:* the political reason for the death penalty falsely charged by the enemies of Jesus. See further the notes on Mt 27, 37 and Jn 19, 19.

15, 28: This verse, "And the scripture was fulfilled that says, 'And he was counted among the wicked,' " is omitted in the earliest and best manuscripts. It contains a citation from Is 53, 12, and was probably introduced from Lk 22, 37.

15, 29: See the note on Mt 27, 39-40.

15, 34: An Aramaic rendering of Ps 22, 2. See also the note on Mt 27, 46.

15, 35: *Elijah:* a verbal link with *Eloi* (34). See the note on Mk 9, 9-13; cf Mal 3, 23-24. See also the note on Mt 27, 47.

15, 38: See the note on Mt 27, 51-53.

15, 39: The closing portion of Mark's gospel returns to the theme of its beginning in the Gentile centurion's climactic declaration of belief that Jesus *was the Son of God*. It indicates the fulfillment of the good news announced in the prologue (Mk 1, 1) and may be regarded as the firstfruit of the passion and death of Jesus.

15, 40-41: See the note on Mt 27, 55-56.

15, 43: *Joseph of Arimathea:* see the note on Mt 27, 57-61.

16, 1-8: The purpose of this narrative is to show that the tomb is empty and that Jesus *has been raised* (6) and *is going before you to Galilee* (7) in fulfillment of Mk 14, 28. The women find the tomb empty, and an angel stationed there announces to them what has happened. They are told to proclaim the news to Peter and the disciples in order to prepare them for a reunion with him. Mark's composition of the gospel ends at v 8 with the women telling no one, because they were afraid. This abrupt termination causes some to believe that the original ending of this gospel may have been lost. See the following note.

The Death of Jesus. [33] At noon darkness came over the whole land until three in the afternoon. [34] And at three o'clock Jesus cried out in a loud voice, "*Eloi, Eloi, lema sabachthani?*"* which is translated, "My God, my God, why have you forsaken me?" *a* [35] Some of the bystanders who heard it said, "Look, he is calling Elijah."* [36] One of them ran, soaked a sponge with wine, put it on a reed, and gave it to him to drink, saying, "Wait, let us see if Elijah comes to take him down." [37] Jesus gave a loud cry and breathed his last. [38] The veil of the sanctuary was torn in two from top to bottom.* [39] *b* When the centurion who stood facing him saw how he breathed his last he said, "Truly this man was the Son of God!"* [40] There were also women looking on from a distance. *c* Among them were Mary Magdalene, Mary the mother of the younger James and of Joses, and Salome.* [41] These women had followed him when he was in Galilee and ministered to him. There were also many other women who had come up with him to Jerusalem.

The Burial of Jesus. [42] *d* When it was already evening, since it was the day of preparation, the day before the sabbath, [43] Joseph of Arimathea,* a distinguished member of the council, who was himself awaiting the kingdom of God, came and courageously went to Pilate and asked for the body of Jesus. [44] Pilate was amazed that he was already dead. He summoned the centurion and asked him if Jesus had already died. [45] And when he learned of it from the centurion, he gave the body to Joseph. [46] Having bought a linen cloth, he took him down, wrapped him in the linen cloth and laid him in a tomb that had been hewn out of the rock. Then he rolled a stone against the entrance to the tomb. [47] Mary Magdalene and Mary the mother of Joses watched where he was laid.

CHAPTER 16

The Resurrection of Jesus. * [1] When the sabbath was over, *e* Mary Magdalene, Mary, the mother of James, and Salome bought spices so that they might go and anoint him. *f* [2] Very early when the sun had risen, on the first day of the week, they came to the tomb. [3] They were saying to one another, "Who will roll back the stone for us from the entrance to the tomb?" [4] When they looked up, they saw that the

Mk

stone had been rolled back; it was very large. ⁵On entering the tomb they saw a young man sitting on the right side, clothed in a white robe, and they were utterly amazed.ᵍ ⁶He said to them, "Do not be amazed! You seek Jesus of Nazareth, the crucified. He has been raised; he is not here. Behold, the place where they laid him. ⁷But go and tell his disciples and Peter, 'He is going before you to Galilee; there you will see him, as he told you.' "ʰ ⁸Then they went out and fled from the tomb, seized with trembling and bewilderment. They said nothing to anyone, for they were afraid.

THE LONGER ENDING*

The Appearance to Mary Magdalene. [⁹ⁱWhen he had risen, early on the first day of the week, he appeared first to Mary Magdalene, out of whom he had driven seven demons. ¹⁰ʲShe went and told his companions who were mourning and weeping. ¹¹When they heard that he was alive and had been seen by her, they did not believe.

The Appearance to Two Disciples. ¹²ᵏ After this he appeared in another form to two of them walking along on their way to the country. ¹³They returned and told the others; but they did not believe them either.

---

g Jn 20, 12.—h Mk 14, 28.—i 9-20: Mt 28, 1-10; Jn 20, 11-18.—j 10-11: Lk 24, 10-11; Jn 20, 18.—k 12-14: Lk 24, 13-35.—l Lk 24, 36-49; 1 Cor 15, 5.—m 15-16: Mk 13, 10; Mt 28, 18-20; Lk 24, 47; Jn 20, 21.—n Mt 10, 1; Lk 10, 19; Acts 28, 3-6.—o Lk 24, 50-53.—p 1 Tm 3, 16.

16, 9-20: This passage, termed the Longer Ending to the Marcan gospel by comparison with a much briefer conclusion found in some less important manuscripts, has traditionally been accepted as a canonical part of the gospel and was defined as such by the Council of Trent. Early citations of it by the Fathers indicate that it was composed by the second century, although vocabulary and style indicate that it was written by someone other than Mark. It is a general resume of the material concerning the appearances of the risen Jesus, reflecting, in particular, traditions found in Luke (24) and John (20).

The Shorter Ending: Found after v 8 before the Longer Ending in four seventh-to-ninth-century Greek manuscripts as well as in

The Commissioning of the Eleven. ¹⁴ˡ[But] later, as the eleven were at table, he appeared to them and rebuked them for their unbelief and hardness of heart because they had not believed those who saw him after he had been raised. ¹⁵ᵐHe said to them, "Go into the whole world and proclaim the gospel to every creature. ¹⁶Whoever believes and is baptized will be saved; whoever does not believe will be condemned. ¹⁷These signs will accompany those who believe: in my name they will drive out demons, they will speak new languages. ¹⁸They will pick up serpents [with their hands], and if they drink any deadly thing, it will not harm them. They will lay hands on the sick, and they will recover."ⁿ

The Ascension of Jesus. ¹⁹So then the Lord Jesus, after he spoke to them, was taken up into heaven and took his seat at the right hand of God.ᵒ ²⁰But they went forth and preached everywhere, while the Lord worked with them and confirmed the word through accompanying signs.]ᵖ

THE SHORTER ENDING*

[And they reported all the instructions briefly to Peter's companions. Afterwards Jesus himself, through them, sent forth from east to west the sacred and imperishable proclamation of eternal salvation. Amen.]

---

one Old Latin version, where it appears alone without the Longer Ending.

The Freer Logion: Found after v 14 in a fourth-fifth century manuscript preserved in the Freer Gallery of Art, Washington, DC, this ending was known to Jerome in the fourth century. It reads: "And they excused themselves, saying, 'This age of lawlessness and unbelief is under Satan, who does not allow the truth and power of God to prevail over the unclean things dominated by the spirits [or, does not allow the unclean things dominated by the spirits to grasp the truth and power of God]. Therefore reveal your righteousness now.' They spoke to Christ. And Christ responded to them, 'The limit of the years of Satan's power is completed, but other terrible things draw near. And for those who sinned I was handed over to death, that they might return to the truth and no longer sin, in order that they might inherit the spiritual and incorruptible heavenly glory of righteousness. But . . . .' "

THE GOSPEL ACCORDING TO LUKE

INTRODUCTION

The Gospel according to Luke is the first part of a two-volume work that continues the biblical history of God's dealings with humanity found in the Old Testament, showing how God's promises to Israel have been fulfilled in Jesus and how the salvation promised to Israel and accomplished by Jesus has been extended to the Gentiles. The stated purpose of the two volumes is to provide Theophilus and others like him with certainty—assurance— about earlier instruction they have received (1, 4). To accomplish his purpose, Luke shows that the preaching and teaching of the representatives of the early church are grounded in the preaching and teaching of Jesus, who during his historical ministry (Acts 1, 21-22) prepared his specially chosen followers and commissioned them to be witnesses to his resurrection and to all else that he did (Acts 10, 37-42). This continuity between the historical ministry of Jesus and the ministry of the apostles is Luke's way of guaranteeing the fidelity of the church's teaching to the teaching of Jesus.

Luke's story of Jesus and the church is dominated by a historical perspective. This history is first of all salvation history. God's divine plan for human salvation was accomplished during the period of Jesus, who through the events of his life (22, 22) fulfilled the Old Testament prophecies (4, 21; 18, 31; 22, 37; 24, 26-27.44), and this salvation is now extended to all humanity in the period of the church (Acts 4, 12). This salvation history, moreover, is a part of human history. Luke relates the story of Jesus and the church to events in contemporary Palestinian (1, 5; 3, 1-2; Acts 4, 6) and Roman (2, 1-2; 3, 1; Acts 11, 28; 18, 2.12) history, for, as Paul says in Acts 26, 26, "this was not done in a corner." Finally, Luke relates the story of Jesus and the church to contemporaneous church history. Luke is concerned with presenting Christianity as a legitimate form of worship in the Roman world, a religion that is capable of meeting the spiritual needs of a world empire like that of Rome. To this end, Luke depicts the Roman governor Pilate declaring Jesus innocent of any wrongdoing three times (Acts 23, 29; 25, 25; 26, 31-32). At the same time Luke argues in Acts that Christianity is the logical development and proper fulfillment of Judaism and is therefore deserving of the same toleration and freedom traditionally accorded Judaism by Rome (Acts 13, 16-41; 23, 6-9; 24, 10-21; 26, 2-23).

The prominence given to the period of the church in the story has important consequences for Luke's interpretation of the teachings of Jesus. By presenting the time of the church as a distinct phase of salvation history, Luke accordingly shifts the early Christian emphasis away from the expectation of an imminent parousia to the day-to-day concerns of the Christian community in the world. He does this in the gospel by regularly emphasizing the words "each day" (9, 23; cf Mk 8, 34; 11, 3; 16, 19; 19, 47) in the sayings of Jesus. Although Luke still believes the parousia to be a reality that will come unexpectedly (12, 38.45-46), he is more concerned with presenting the words and deeds of Jesus as guides for the conduct of Christian disciples in the interim period between the ascension and the parousia and with presenting Jesus himself as the model of Christian life and piety.

Throughout the gospel, Luke calls upon the Christian disciple to identify with the master Jesus, who is caring and tender toward the poor and lowly, the outcast, the sinner, and the afflicted, toward all those who recognize their dependence on God (4, 18; 6, 20-23; 7, 36-50; 14, 12-14; 15, 1-32; 16, 19-31; 18, 9-14; 19, 1-10; 21, 1-4), but who is severe toward the proud and self-righteous, and particularly toward those who place their material wealth before the service of God and his people (6, 24-26; 12, 13-21; 16, 13-15.19-31; 18, 9-14.15-25; cf 1, 50-53). No gospel writer is more concerned than Luke with the mercy and compassion of Jesus (7, 41-43; 10, 29-37; 13, 6-9; 15, 11-32). No *gospel writer is more concerned with the role of the Spirit in the life of Jesus and the Christian disciple (1, 35.41; 2, 25-27; 4, 1.14.18; 10, 21; 11, 13; 24, 49), with the importance of prayer (3, 21; 5, 16; 6, 12; 9, 28; 11, 1-13; 18, 1-8), or with Jesus' concern for women (7, 11-17.36-50; 8, 2-3; 10, 38-42). While Jesus calls all humanity to repent (5, 32; 10, 13; 11, 32; 13, 1-5; 15, 7-10; 16, 30; 17, 3-4; 24, 47), he is particularly demanding of those who would be his disciples. Of them he demands absolute and total detachment from family and material possessions (9, 57-62; 12, 32-34; 14, 25-35). To all who respond in faith and repentance to the word Jesus preaches, he brings salvation (2, 30-32; 3, 6; 7, 50; 8, 48.50; 17, 19; 19, 9) and peace (2, 14; 7, 50; 8, 48; 19, 38.42) and life (10, 25-28; 18, 26-30).*

Early Christian tradition, from the late second century on, identifies the author of this gospel and of the Acts of the Apostles as Luke, a Syrian from Antioch, who is mentioned in the New Testament in Col 4, 14, Phlm 24, and 2 Tm 4, 11. The prologue of the gospel makes it clear that Luke is not part of the first generation of Christian disciples but is himself dependent upon the traditions he received from those who were eyewitnesses and ministers of the word (1, 2). His two-volume work marks him as someone who was highly literate both in the Old Testament traditions according to the Greek versions and in Hellenistic Greek writings.

Among the likely sources for the composition of this gospel (1, 3) were the Gospel of Mark, a written collection of sayings of Jesus known also to the author of the Gospel of Matthew (Q; see Introduction to Matthew), and other special traditions that were used by Luke alone among the gospel writers. Some hold that Luke used Mark only as a complementary source for rounding out the material he took from other traditions. Because of its dependence on the Gospel of Mark and because details in Luke's Gospel (13, 35a; 19, 43-44; 21, 20; 23, 28-31) imply that the author was acquainted with the destruction of the city of Jerusalem by the Romans in A.D. 70, the Gospel of Luke is dated by most scholars after that date; many propose A.D. 80-90 as the time of composition.

Luke's consistent substitution of Greek names for the Aramaic or Hebrew names occurring in his sources (e.g., 23, 33 // Mk 15, 22; 18, 41 // Mk 10, 51), his omission from the gospel of specifically Jewish Christian concerns found in his sources (e.g., Mk 7, 1-23), his interest in Gentile Christians (2, 30-32; 3, 6.38; 4, 16-30; 13, 28-30; 14, 15-24; 17, 11-19; 24, 47-48), and his incomplete knowledge of Palestinian geography, customs, and practices are among the characteristics of this gospel that suggest that Luke was a non-Palestinian writing to a non-Palestinian audience that was largely made up of Gentile Christians.

The principal divisions of the Gospel according to Luke are the following:

 I. *The Prologue (1, 1-4)*
 II. *The Infancy Narrative (1, 5—2, 52)*
 III. *The Preparation for the Public Ministry (3, 1—4, 13)*
 IV. *The Ministry in Galilee (4, 14—9, 50)*
 V. *The Journey to Jerusalem: Luke's Travel Narrative (9, 51—19, 27)*
 VI. *The Teaching Ministry in Jerusalem (19, 28—21, 38)*
 VII. *The Passion Narrative (22, 1—23, 56)*
 VIII. *The Resurrection Narrative (24, 1-53)*

I. THE PROLOGUE*

CHAPTER 1

¹Since many have undertaken to compile a narrative of the events that have been fulfilled among us,*a* ²just as those who were eyewitnesses from the beginning and ministers of the word have handed them down to us,*b* ³I too have decided, after investigating everything accurately anew, to write it down in an orderly sequence for you, most excellent Theophilus, ⁴so that you may realize the certainty of the teachings you have received.

II. THE INFANCY NARRATIVE*

Announcement of the Birth of John.
⁵In the days of Herod, King of Judea,* there was a priest named Zechariah of the priestly division of Abijah; his wife was from the daughters of Aaron, and her name was Elizabeth.*c* ⁶Both were righteous in the eyes of God, observing all the commandments and ordinances of the Lord blamelessly. ⁷But they had no child,* because Elizabeth was barren and both were advanced in years.*d* ⁸Once when he was serving as priest in his division's turn

before God, ⁹according to the practice of the priestly service, he was chosen by lot to enter the sanctuary of the Lord to burn incense.*e* ¹⁰Then, when the whole assembly of the people was praying outside at the hour of the incense offering, ¹¹the angel of the Lord appeared to him, standing at the right of the altar of incense. ¹²Zechariah was troubled by what he saw, and fear came upon him. ¹³But the angel said to him, "Do not be afraid,* Zechariah, because your prayer has been heard. Your wife Elizabeth will bear you a son, and you shall name him John.*f* ¹⁴And you will have joy and gladness, and many will rejoice at his birth, ¹⁵for he will be great in the sight of [the] Lord. He will drink neither wine nor strong drink.* He will be filled with the holy Spirit even from his mother's womb,*g* ¹⁶and he will turn many of the children of Israel to the Lord their God. ¹⁷He will go before him in the spirit and power of Elijah* to turn the hearts of fathers toward children and the disobedient to the understanding of the righteous, to prepare a people fit for the

a 1-4: Acts 1, 1; 1 Cor 15, 3.—b Lk 24, 48; Jn 15, 27; Acts 1, 21-22.—c 1 Chr 24, 10.—d Gn 18, 11; Jgs 13, 2-5; 1 Sm 1, 5-6.—e Ex 30, 7.—f Lk 1, 57.60.63; Mt 1, 20-21.—g Lk 7, 33; Nm 6, 1-21; Jgs 13, 4; 1 Sm 1, 11 LXX.

1, 1-4: The Gospel according to Luke is the only one of the synoptic gospels to begin with a literary prologue. Making use of a formal, literary construction and vocabulary, the author writes the prologue in imitation of Hellenistic Greek writers and, in so doing, relates his story about Jesus to contemporaneous Greek and Roman literature. Luke is not only interested in the words and deeds of Jesus, but also in the larger context of the birth, ministry, death, and resurrection of Jesus as the fulfillment of the promises of God in the Old Testament. As a second- or third-generation Christian, Luke acknowledges his debt to earlier *eyewitnesses* and *ministers of the word*, but claims that his contribution to this developing tradition is a complete and accurate account, told in an orderly manner, and intended to provide *Theophilus* ("friend of God," literally) and other readers with certainty about earlier teachings they have received.

1, 5—2, 52: Like the Gospel according to Matthew, this gospel opens with an infancy narrative, a collection of stories about the birth and childhood of Jesus. The narrative uses early Christian traditions about the birth of Jesus, traditions about the birth and circumcision of John the Baptist, and canticles such as the Magnificat (Lk 1, 46-55) and Benedictus (Lk 1, 67-79), composed of phrases drawn from the Greek Old Testament. It is largely, however, the composition of Luke who writes in imitation of Old Testament birth stories, combining historical and legendary details, literary ornamentation and interpretation of scripture, to answer in advance the question, "Who is Jesus Christ?" The focus of the narrative, therefore, is primarily christological. In this section Luke announces many of the themes that will become prominent in the rest of the gospel: the centrality of Jerusalem and the temple, the journey motif, the universality of salvation, joy and peace, concern for the lowly, the importance of women, the presentation of Jesus as savior, Spirit-guided revelation and prophecy, and the fulfillment of Old Testament promises. The account presents parallel scenes (diptychs) of angelic announcements of the birth of John the Baptist and of Jesus, and of

the birth, circumcision, and presentation of John and Jesus. In this parallelism, the ascendency of Jesus over John is stressed: John is prophet of the Most High (Lk 1, 76); Jesus is Son of the Most High (Lk 1, 32). John is great in the sight of the Lord (Lk 1, 15); Jesus will be Great (a LXX attribute, used absolutely, of God) (Lk 1, 32). John will go before the Lord (Lk 1, 16-17); Jesus will be Lord (Lk 1, 43; 2, 11).

1, 5: *In the days of Herod, King of Judea:* Luke relates the story of salvation to events in contemporary world history. Here and in Lk 3, 1-2, he connects his narrative with events in Palestinian history; in Lk 2, 1-2 and Lk 3, 1, he casts the Jesus story in the light of events of Roman history. Herod the Great, the son of the Idumean Antipater, was declared "King of Judea" by the Roman Senate in 40 B.C., but became the undisputed ruler of Palestine only in 37 B.C. He continued as king until his death in 4 B.C. *Priestly division of Abijah:* a reference to the eighth of the twenty-four divisions of priests who, for a week at a time, twice a year, served in the Jerusalem temple.

1, 7: *They had no child:* though childlessness was looked upon in contemporary Judaism as a curse or punishment for sin, it is intended here to present Elizabeth in a situation similar to that of some of the great mothers of important Old Testament figures: Sarah (Gn 15, 3; 16, 1); Rebekah (Gn 25, 21); Rachel (Gn 29, 31; 30, 1); the mother of Samson and wife of Manoah (Jgs 13, 2-3); Hannah (1 Sm 1, 2).

1, 13: *Do not be afraid:* a stereotyped Old Testament phrase spoken to reassure the recipient of a heavenly vision (Gn 15, 1; Jos 1, 9; Dn 10, 12.19 and elsewhere in Lk 1, 30; 2, 10). *You shall name him John:* the name means "Yahweh has shown favor," an indication of John's role in salvation history.

1, 15: *He will drink neither wine nor strong drink:* like Samson (Jgs 13, 4-5) and Samuel (1 Sm 1, 11 LXX and 4QSamᵃ), John is to be consecrated by Nazirite vow and set apart for the Lord's service.

1, 17: *He will go before him in the spirit and power of Elijah:* John is to be the messenger sent before Yahweh, as described in Mal 3, 1-2. He is cast, moreover, in the role of the Old Testament fiery reformer, the prophet Elijah, who according to Mal 3, 23 (4, 5) is sent before "the great and terrible day of the Lord comes."

Lord."[h] [18]Then Zechariah said to the angel, "How shall I know this? For I am an old man, and my wife is advanced in years." [19]And the angel said to him in reply, "I am Gabriel,* who stand before God. I was sent to speak to you and to announce to you this good news.[i] [20]But now you will be speechless and unable to talk* until the day these things take place, because you did not believe my words, which will be fulfilled at their proper time."[j]

[21]Meanwhile the people were waiting for Zechariah and were amazed that he stayed so long in the sanctuary. [22]But when he came out, he was unable to speak to them, and they realized that he had seen a vision in the sanctuary. He was gesturing to them but remained mute. [23]Then, when his days of ministry were completed, he went home. [24]After this time his wife Elizabeth conceived, and she went into seclusion for five months, saying, [25]"So has the Lord done for me at a time when he has seen fit to take away my disgrace before others."[k]

Announcement of the Birth of Jesus.*
[26]In the sixth month, the angel Gabriel was sent from God to a town of Galilee called Nazareth, [27]to a virgin betrothed to a man named Joseph, of the house of David, and the virgin's name was Mary.[l] [28]And coming to her, he said, "Hail, favored one! The Lord is with you."[m] [29]But she was greatly troubled at what was said and pondered what sort of greeting this might be. [30]Then the angel said to her, "Do not be afraid, Mary, for you have found favor with God. [31][n]Behold, you will conceive in your womb and bear a son, and you shall name him Jesus. [32][o] He will be great and will be called Son of the Most High,* and the Lord God will give him the throne of David his father, [33]and he will rule over the house of Jacob forever, and of his kingdom there will be no end."[p] [34]But Mary said to the angel, "How can this be, since I have no relations with a man?"* [35]And the angel said to her in reply, "The holy Spirit will come upon you, and the power of the Most High will overshadow you. Therefore the child to be born will be called holy, the Son of God.[q] [36]And behold, Elizabeth, your relative, has also conceived* a son in her old age, and this is the sixth month for her who was called barren; [37]for nothing will be impossible for God."[r] [38]Mary said, "Behold, I am the handmaid of the Lord. May it be done to me accord-

ing to your word." Then the angel departed from her.

Mary Visits Elizabeth.
[39]During those days Mary set out and traveled to the hill country in haste to a town of Judah, [40]where she entered the house of Zechariah and greeted Elizabeth. [41]When Elizabeth heard Mary's greeting, the infant leaped in her womb, and Elizabeth, filled with the holy Spirit,[s] [42]cried out in a loud voice and said, "Most blessed are you among women, and blessed is the fruit of your womb.[t] [43]And how does this happen to me, that the mother of my Lord* should come to me? [44]For at the moment the sound of your greeting reached my ears, the infant in my womb leaped for joy.[45]Blessed are you who believed* that

h Sir 48, 10; Mal 3, 1; 3, 23-24; Mt 11, 14; 17, 11-13.—i Dn 8, 16; 9, 21.—j Lk 1, 45.—k Gn 30, 23.—l Lk 2, 5; Mt 1, 16.18.—m Jgs 6, 12; Ru 2, 4; Jdt 13, 18.—n Gn 16, 11; Jgs 13, 3; Is 7, 14; Mt 1, 21-23.—o 32-33: 2 Sm 7, 12.13.16; Is 9, 7.—p Dn 2, 44; 7, 14; Mi 4, 7; Mt 28, 18.—q Mt 1, 20.—r Gn 18, 14; Jer 32, 27; Mt 19, 26.—s Lk 1, 15; Gn 25, 22 LXX.—t Lk 11, 27-28; Jgs 5, 24; Jdt 13, 18 / Dt 28, 4.

1, 19: *I am Gabriel:* "the angel of the Lord" is identified as Gabriel, the angel who in Dn 9, 20-25 announces the seventy weeks of years and the coming of an anointed one, a prince. By alluding to Old Testament themes in vv 17 and 19, such as the coming of the day of the Lord and the dawning of the messianic era, Luke is presenting his interpretation of the significance of the births of John and Jesus.

1, 20: *You will be speechless and unable to talk:* Zechariah's becoming mute is the sign given in response to his question in v 18. When Mary asks a similar question in Lk 1, 34, unlike Zechariah who was punished for his doubt, she, in spite of her doubt, is praised and reassured (35-37).

1, 26-38: The announcement to Mary of the birth of Jesus is parallel to the announcement to Zechariah of the birth of John. In both the angel Gabriel appears to the parent who is troubled by the vision (11-12.26-29) and then told by the angel not to fear (13.30). After the announcement is made (14-17.31-33) the parent objects (18.34) and a sign is given to confirm the announcement (20.36). The particular focus of the announcement of the birth of Jesus is on his identity as Son of David (32-33) and Son of God (32.35).

1, 32: *Son of the Most High:* cf Lk 1, 76 where John is described as "prophet of the Most High." "Most High" is a title for God commonly used by Luke (Lk 1, 35.76; 6, 35; 8, 28; Acts 7, 48; 16, 17).

1, 34: Mary's questioning response is a denial of sexual relations and is used by Luke to lead to the angel's declaration about the Spirit's role in the conception of this child (35). According to Luke, the virginal conception of Jesus takes place through the holy Spirit, the power of God, and therefore Jesus has a unique relationship to Yahweh: he is Son of God.

1, 36-37: The sign given to Mary in confirmation of the angel's announcement to her is the pregnancy of her aged relative Elizabeth. If a woman past the childbearing age could become pregnant, why, the angel implies, should there be doubt about Mary's pregnancy, for *nothing will be impossible for God.*

1, 43: Even before his birth, Jesus is identified in Lk as the *Lord.*

1, 45: *Blessed are you who believed:* Luke portrays Mary as a believer whose faith stands in contrast to the disbelief of Zechariah (Lk 1, 20). Mary's role as believer in the infancy narrative should be seen in connection with the explicit mention of her presence among "those who believed" after the resurrection at the beginning of the Acts of the Apostles (Acts 1, 14).

what was spoken to you by the Lord would be fulfilled."*u*

The Canticle of Mary. [46] *v* And Mary said:*

"My soul proclaims the greatness of the Lord;*w*

[47] my spirit rejoices in God my savior.*x*

[48] For he has looked upon his handmaid's lowliness;
behold, from now on will all ages call me blessed.*y*

[49] The Mighty One has done great things for me,
and holy is his name.*z*

[50] His mercy is from age to age
to those who fear him.*a*

[51] He has shown might with his arm,
dispersed the arrogant of mind and heart.*b*

[52] He has thrown down the rulers from their thrones
but lifted up the lowly.*c*

[53] The hungry he has filled with good things;
the rich he has sent away empty.*d*

[54] He has helped Israel his servant,
remembering his mercy,*e*

[55] according to his promise to our fathers,
to Abraham and to his descendants forever."*f*

[56] Mary remained with her about three months and then returned to her home.

The Birth of John. * [57] When the time arrived for Elizabeth to have her child she gave birth to a son. [58] Her neighbors and relatives heard that the Lord had shown his great mercy toward her, and they rejoiced with her.*g* [59] When they came on the eighth day to circumcise*h* the child, they were going to call him Zechariah after his father,* [60] but his mother said in reply, "No. He will be called John."*i* [61] But they answered her, "There is no one among your relatives who has this name." [62] So they made signs, asking his father what he wished him to be called. [63] He asked for a tablet and wrote, "John is his name," and all were amazed. [64] Immediately his mouth was opened, his tongue freed, and he spoke blessing God.*j* [65] Then fear came upon all their neighbors, and all these matters were discussed throughout the hill country of Judea. [66] All who heard these things took them to heart, saying, "What, then, will this child be?" For surely the hand of the Lord was with him.

The Canticle of Zechariah. [67] Then Zechariah his father, filled with the holy Spirit, prophesied, saying:

[68] "Blessed be the Lord, the God of Israel,*
for he has visited and brought redemption to his people.*k*

[69] He has raised up a horn for our salvation*
within the house of David his servant,*l*

u Lk 1, 20.—v 46-55: 1 Sm 2, 1-10.—w Ps 35, 9; Is 61, 10; Hb 3, 18.—x Ti 3, 4; Jude 25.—y Lk 11, 27; 1 Sm 1, 11; 2 Sm 16, 12; 2 Kgs 14, 26; Ps 113, 7.—z Dt 10, 21; Pss 71, 19; 111, 9; 126, 2-3.—a Pss 89, 2; 103, 13.17.—b Pss 89, 10; 118, 15; Jer 32, 17 (39, 17 LXX).—c 1 Sm 2, 7; 2 Sm 22, 28; Jb 5, 11; 12, 19; Ps 147, 6; Sir 10, 14; Jas 4, 6; 1 Pt 5, 5.—d 1 Sm 2, 5; Ps 107, 9.—e Ps 98, 3; Is 41, 8-9.—f Gn 13, 15; 17, 7; 18, 18; 22, 17-18; Mi 7, 20.—g Lk 1, 14.—h Lk 2, 21; Gn 17, 10.12; Lv 12, 3.—i Lk 1, 13.—j Lk 1, 20.—k Lk 7, 16; Pss 41, 13; 72, 18; 106, 48; 111, 9.—l Ps 18, 3.

1, 46-55: Although Mary is praised for being the mother of the Lord and because of her belief, she reacts as the servant in a psalm of praise, the Magnificat. Because there is no specific connection of the canticle to the context of Mary's pregnancy and her visit to Elizabeth, the Magnificat (with the possible exception of v 48) may have been a Jewish Christian hymn that Luke found appropriate at this point in his story. Even if not composed by Luke, it fits in well with themes found elsewhere in Lk: joy and exultation in the Lord; the lowly being singled out for God's favor; the reversal of human fortunes; the fulfillment of Old Testament promises. The loose connection between the hymn and the context is further seen in the fact that a few Old Latin manuscripts identify the speaker of the hymn as Elizabeth, even though the overwhelming textual evidence makes Mary the speaker.

1, 57-66: The birth and circumcision of John above all emphasize John's incorporation into the people of Israel by the sign of the covenant (Gn 17, 1-12). The narrative of John's circumcision also prepares the way for the subsequent description of the circumcision of Jesus in Lk 2, 21. At the beginning of his two-volume work Luke shows those who play crucial roles in the inauguration of Christianity to be wholly a part of the people of Israel. At the end of the Acts of the Apostles (21, 20; 22, 3; 23, 6-9; 24, 14-16; 26, 2-8.22-23) he will argue that Christianity is the direct descendant of Pharisaic Judaism.

1, 59: The practice of Palestinian Judaism at this time was to name the child at birth; moreover, though naming a male child after the father is not completely unknown, the usual practice was to name the child after the grandfather (see 61). The naming of the child John and Zechariah's recovery from his loss of speech should be understood as fulfilling the angel's announcement to Zechariah in Lk 1, 13 and 20.

1, 68-79: Like the canticle of Mary (46-55) the canticle of Zechariah is only loosely connected with its context. Apart from vv 76-77, the hymn in speaking of *a horn for our salvation* (69) and *the daybreak from on high* (78) applies more closely to Jesus and his work than to John. Again like Mary's canticle, it is largely composed of phrases taken from the Greek Old Testament and may have been a Jewish Christian hymn of praise that Luke adapted to fit the present context by inserting vv 76-77 to give Zechariah's reply to the question asked in v 66.

1, 69: *A horn for our salvation:* the horn is a common Old Testament figure for strength (Pss 18, 3; 75, 5-6; 89, 18; 112, 9; 148, 14). This description is applied to God in Ps 18, 3 and is here transferred to Jesus. The connection of the phrase with *the house of David* gives the title messianic overtones and may indicate an allusion to a phrase in Hannah's song of praise (1 Sm 2, 10), "the horn of his anointed."

70 even as he promised through the mouth
of his holy prophets from of old:
71   salvation from our enemies and from
the hand of all who hate us,*m*
72 to show mercy to our fathers*n*
and to be mindful of his holy
covenant*o*
73 and of the oath he swore to Abraham
our father,*p*
and to grant us that, 74 rescued from
the hand of enemies,
without fear we might worship him 75 in
holiness and righteousness
before him all our days.*q*
76 And you, child, will be called prophet
of the Most High,
for you will go before the Lord* to
prepare his ways,*r*
77 to give his people knowledge of salvation
through the forgiveness of their sins,
78 because of the tender mercy of our
God*s*
by which the daybreak from on high*
will visit us*t*
79 to shine on those who sit in darkness
and death's shadow,
to guide our feet into the path of
peace."

80 The child grew and became strong in
spirit, and he was in the desert until the
day of his manifestation to Israel.*u*

CHAPTER 2

The Birth of Jesus. 1 * In those days a decree went out from Caesar Augustus* that
the whole world should be enrolled. 2 This
was the first enrollment, when Quirinius
was governor of Syria. 3 So all went to be
enrolled, each to his own town. 4 And
Joseph too went up from Galilee from the
town of Nazareth to Judea, to the city of
David that is called Bethlehem, because he
was of the house and family of David,*v* 5 to
be enrolled with Mary, his betrothed, who
was with child.*w* 6 While they were there,
the time came for her to have her child,
7 and she gave birth to her firstborn son.*
She wrapped him in swaddling clothes and
laid him in a manger, because there was no
room for them in the inn.*x*

8 * Now there were shepherds in that region living in the fields and keeping the
night watch over their flock. 9 The angel of
the Lord appeared to them and the glory of
the Lord shone around them, and they
were struck with great fear.*y* 10 The angel
said to them, "Do not be afraid; for behold, I proclaim to you good news of great

---

m Ps 106, 10.—n Ps 106, 45-46.—o 72-73: Gn 17, 7; Lv 26,
42; Ps 105, 8-9; Mi 7, 20.—p 73-74: Gn 22, 16-17.—q Ti 2,
12.—r Is 40, 3; Mal 3, 1; Mt 3, 3; 11, 10.—s Mal 3, 20.—t 78-
79: Is 60, 1-2.—u Lk 2, 40; Mt 3, 1.—v Mi 5, 2; Mt 2, 6.—w Lk
1, 27; Mt 1, 18.—x Mt 1, 25.—y Lk 1, 11.26.

1, 76: *You will go before the Lord:* here *the Lord* is most
likely a reference to Jesus (contrast 15-17 where Yahweh is
meant) and John is presented as the precursor of Jesus.

1, 78: *The daybreak from on high:* three times in the LXX
(Jer 23, 5; Zec 3, 8; 6, 12), the Greek word used here for *day-
break* translates the Hebrew word for "scion, branch," an Old
Testament messianic title.

2, 1-2: Although universal registrations of Roman citizens are
attested in 28 B.C., 8 B.C., and A.D. 14 and enrollments in individual provinces of those who are not Roman citizens are also attested, such a universal census of the Roman world under Caesar
Augustus is unknown outside the New Testament. Moreover,
there are notorious historical problems connected with Luke's
dating of the census *when Quirinius was governor of Syria*, and
the various attempts to resolve the difficulties have proved unsuccessful. P. Sulpicius Quirinius became legate of the province of
Syria in A.D. 6-7 when Judea was annexed to the province of
Syria. At that time, a provincial census of Judea was taken up. If
Quirinius had been legate of Syria previously, it would have to
have been before 10 B.C. because the various legates of Syria
from 10 B.C. to 4 B.C. (the death of Herod) are known, and such
a dating for an earlier census under Quirinius would create additional problems for dating the beginning of Jesus' ministry (Lk 3,
1.23). A previous legateship after 4 B.C. (and before A.D. 6)
would not fit with the dating of Jesus' birth in the days of Herod

(Lk 1, 5; Mt 2, 1). Luke may simply be combining Jesus' birth in
Bethlehem with his vague recollection of a census under Quirinius
(see also Acts 5, 37) to underline the significance of this birth for
the whole Roman world: through this child born in Bethlehem
peace and salvation come to the empire.

2, 1: *Caesar Augustus:* the reign of the Roman emperor
Caesar Augustus is usually dated from 27 B.C. to his death in A.D.
14. According to Greek inscriptions, Augustus was regarded in
the Roman Empire as "savior" and "god," and he was credited
with establishing a time of peace, the *pax Augusta*, throughout
the Roman world during his long reign. It is not by chance that
Luke relates the birth of Jesus to the time of Caesar Augustus:
the real savior (11) and peace-bearer (14; see also Lk 19, 38) is
the child born in Bethlehem. The great emperor is simply God's
agent (like the Persian king Cyrus in Is 44, 28—45, 1) who provides the occasion for God's purposes to be accomplished. *The
whole world:* that is, the whole Roman world: Rome, Italy, and
the Roman provinces.

2, 7: *Firstborn son:* the description of Jesus as *firstborn son*
does not necessarily mean that Mary had other sons. It is a legal
description indicating that Jesus possessed the rights and privileges of the firstborn son (Gn 27; Ex 13, 2; Nm 3, 12-13; 18, 15-
16; Dt 21, 15-17). See the notes on Mt 1, 25 and Mk 6, 3.
Wrapped him in swaddling clothes: there may be an allusion
here to the birth of another descendant of David, his son Solomon,
who though a great king was wrapped in swaddling clothes like
any other infant (Wis 7, 4-6). *Laid him in a manger:* a feeding
trough for animals. A possible allusion to Is 1, 3 LXX.

2, 8-20: The announcement of Jesus' birth to the shepherds is in
keeping with Luke's theme that the lowly are singled out as the
recipients of God's favors and blessings (see also Lk 1, 48.52).

joy that will be for all the people. [11] [z] For today in the city of David a savior has been born for you who is Messiah and Lord.* [12] And this will be a sign for you: you will find an infant wrapped in swaddling clothes and lying in a manger." [13] And suddenly there was a multitude of the heavenly host with the angel, praising God and saying:

[14] "Glory to God in the highest[a]
      and on earth peace to those on whom
      his favor rests."*

The Visit of the Shepherds. [15] When the angels went away from them to heaven, the shepherds said to one another, "Let us go, then, to Bethlehem to see this thing that has taken place, which the Lord has made known to us." [16] So they went in haste and found Mary and Joseph, and the infant lying in the manger. [17] When they saw this, they made known the message that had been told them about this child. [18] All who heard it were amazed by what had been told them by the shepherds. [19] And Mary kept all these things, reflecting on them in her heart. [20] Then the shepherds returned, glorifying and praising God for all they had heard and seen, just as it had been told to them.

The Circumcision and Naming of Jesus. [21] When eight days were completed for his

circumcision,* he was named Jesus, the name given him by the angel before he was conceived in the womb.[b]

The Presentation in the Temple. [22] * When the days were completed for their purification* according to the law of Moses, they took him up to Jerusalem to present him to the Lord,[c] [23] just as it is written in the law of the Lord, "Every male that opens the womb shall be consecrated to the Lord,"[d] [24] and to offer the sacrifice of "a pair of turtledoves or two young pigeons," in accordance with the dictate in the law of the Lord.

[25] Now there was a man in Jerusalem whose name was Simeon. This man was righteous and devout, awaiting the consolation of Israel,* and the holy Spirit was upon him. [26] It had been revealed to him by the holy Spirit that he should not see death before he had seen the Messiah of the Lord. [27] He came in the Spirit into the temple; and when the parents brought in the child Jesus to perform the custom of the law in regard to him, [28] he took him into his arms and blessed God, saying:

[29] "Now, Master, you may let your ser-
      vant go
      in peace, according to your word,
[30] for my eyes have seen your salvation,[e]

---

z Mt 1, 21; 16, 16; Jn 4, 42; Acts 2, 36; 5, 31; Phil 2, 11.—a Lk 19, 38.—b Lk 1, 31; Gn 17, 12; Mt 1, 21.—c 22-24: Lv 12, 2-8.—d Ex 13, 2.12.—e 30-31: Lk 3, 6; Is 40, 5 LXX; 52, 10.

2, 11: The basic message of the infancy narrative is contained in the angel's announcement: this child is *savior, Messiah,* and *Lord.* Luke is the only synoptic gospel writer to use the title *savior* for Jesus (Lk 2, 11; Acts 5, 31; 13, 23; see also Lk 1, 69; 19, 9; Acts 4, 12). As savior, Jesus is looked upon by Luke as the one who rescues humanity from sin and delivers humanity from the condition of alienation from God. The title *christos,* "Christ," is the Greek equivalent of the Hebrew *māšîaḥ,* "Messiah," "anointed one." Among certain groups in first-century Palestinian Judaism, the title was applied to an expected royal leader from the line of David who would restore the kingdom to Israel (see Acts 1, 6). The political overtones of the title are played down in Lk and instead the Messiah of the Lord (26) or the Lord's anointed is the one who now brings salvation to all humanity, Jew and Gentile (29-32). *Lord* is the most frequently used title for Jesus in Lk and Acts. In the New Testament it is also applied to Yahweh, as it is in the Old Testament. When used of Jesus it points to his transcendence and dominion over humanity.

2, 14: *On earth peace to those on whom his favor rests:* the peace that results from the Christ event is for those whom God has favored with his grace. This reading is found in the oldest representatives of the Western and Alexandrian text traditions and is the preferred one; the Byzantine text tradition, on the other hand, reads: "on earth peace, good will toward men." The peace of which Luke's gospel speaks (Lk 2, 14; 7, 50; 8, 48; 10, 5-6; 19, 38.42; 24, 36) is more than the absence of war of the *pax Augusta;* it also includes the security and well-being characteristic of peace in the Old Testament.

2, 21: Just as John before him had been incorporated into the people of Israel through his circumcision, so too this child (see the note on Lk 1, 57-66).

2, 22-40: The presentation of Jesus in the temple depicts the parents of Jesus as devout Jews, faithful observers of the law of the Lord (23.24.39), i.e., the law of Moses. In this respect, they are described in a fashion similar to the parents of John (Lk 1, 6) and Simeon (25) and Anna (36-37).

2, 22: *Their purification:* syntactically, *their* must refer to Mary and Joseph, even though the Mosaic law never mentions the purification of the husband. Recognizing the problem, some Western scribes have altered the text to read "his purification," understanding the presentation of Jesus in the temple as a form of purification; the Vulgate version has a Latin form that could be either "his" or "her." According to the Mosaic law (Lv 12, 2-8), the woman who gives birth to a boy is unable for forty days to touch anything sacred or to enter the temple area by reason of her legal impurity. At the end of this period she is required to offer a year-old lamb as a burnt offering and a turtledove or young pigeon as an expiation of sin. The woman who could not afford a lamb offered instead two turtledoves or two young pigeons, as Mary does here. *They took him up to Jerusalem to present him to the Lord:* as the firstborn son (Lk 2, 7) Jesus was consecrated to the Lord as the law required (Ex 13, 2.12), but there was no requirement that this be done at the temple. The concept of a presentation at the temple is probably derived from 1 Sm 1, 24-28, where Hannah offers the child Samuel for sanctuary services. The law further stipulated (Nm 3, 47-48) that the firstborn should be redeemed by the parents through their payment of five shekels to a member of a priestly family. About this legal requirement Luke is silent.

2, 25: *Awaiting the consolation of Israel:* Simeon here and later Anna who speak about the child to all who were awaiting the redemption of Jerusalem represent the hopes and expectations of faithful and devout Jews who at this time were looking forward to the restoration of God's rule in Israel. The birth of Jesus brings these hopes to fulfillment.

31   which you prepared in sight of all the
     peoples,
32   a light for revelation to the Gentiles,
     and glory for your people Israel."*f*

33 The child's father and mother were
amazed at what was said about him; 34 and
Simeon blessed them and said to Mary his
mother, "Behold, this child is destined for
the fall and rise of many in Israel, and to be
a sign that will be contradicted*g* 35 (and you
yourself a sword will pierce)* so that the
thoughts of many hearts may be revealed."
36 There was also a prophetess, Anna, the
daughter of Phanuel, of the tribe of Asher.
She was advanced in years, having lived
seven years with her husband after her
marriage, 37 and then as a widow until she
was eighty-four. She never left the temple,
but worshiped night and day with fasting
and prayer. 38 And coming forward at that
very time, she gave thanks to God and
spoke about the child to all who were
awaiting the redemption of Jerusalem.*h*

The Return to Nazareth. 39 When they had
fulfilled all the prescriptions of the law of
the Lord, they returned to Galilee, to their
own town of Nazareth.*i* 40 The child grew
and became strong, filled with wisdom;
and the favor of God was upon him.*j*

The Boy Jesus in the Temple.* 41 Each
year his parents went to Jerusalem for the
feast of Passover,*k* 42 and when he was
twelve years old, they went up according to
festival custom. 43 After they had com-

pleted its days, as they were returning, the
boy Jesus remained behind in Jerusalem,
but his parents did not know it. 44 Thinking that he was in the caravan, they journeyed for a day and looked for him among
their relatives and acquaintances, 45 but not
finding him, they returned to Jerusalem to
look for him. 46 After three days they found
him in the temple, sitting in the midst of
the teachers, listening to them and asking
them questions, 47 and all who heard him
were astounded at his understanding and
his answers. 48 When his parents saw him,
they were astonished, and his mother said
to him, "Son, why have you done this to
us? Your father and I have been looking
for you with great anxiety." 49 And he said
to them, "Why were you looking for me?
Did you not know that I must be in my
Father's house?"* 50 But they did not
understand what he said to them. 51 He
went down with them and came to
Nazareth, and was obedient to them; and
his mother kept all these things in her
heart.*l* 52 And Jesus advanced [in] wisdom
and age and favor before God and man.*m*

III. THE PREPARATION FOR THE PUBLIC MINISTRY

CHAPTER 3
The Preaching of John the Baptist.* 1 In
the fifteenth year of the reign of Tiberius
Caesar,* when Pontius Pilate was governor

---

f Is 42, 6; 46, 13; 49, 6; Acts 13, 47; 26, 23.—g Lk 12, 51; Is
8, 14; Jn 9, 39; Rom 9, 33; 1 Cor 1, 23; 1 Pt 2, 7-8.—h Is 52,
9.—i Mt 2, 23.—j Lk 1, 80; 2, 52.—k Ex 12, 24-27; 23, 15; Dt
16, 1-8.—l Lk 2, 19.—m Lk 1, 80; 2, 40; 1 Sm 2, 26.

2, 35: *(And you yourself a sword will pierce):* Mary herself
will not be untouched by the various reactions to the role of Jesus
(34). Her blessedness as mother of Jesus will be challenged by
her son who describes true blessedness as "hearing the word of
God and observing it" (Lk 11, 27-28 and Lk 8, 20-21).

2, 41-52: This story's concern with an incident from Jesus'
youth is unique in the canonical gospel tradition. It presents Jesus
in the role of the faithful Jewish boy, raised in the traditions of Israel, and fulfilling all that the law requires. With this episode,
the infancy narrative ends just as it began, in the setting of the
Jerusalem temple.

2, 49: *I must be in my Father's house:* this phrase can also
be translated, "I must be about my Father's work." In either
translation, Jesus refers to God as his Father. His divine sonship,
and his obedience to his heavenly Father's will, take precedence
over his ties to his family.

3, 1-20: Although Luke is indebted in this section to his
sources, the Gospel of Mark and a collection of sayings of John
the Baptist, he has clearly marked this introduction to the ministry of Jesus with his own individual style. Just as the gospel began
with a long periodic sentence (Lk 1, 1-4), so too this section (1-
2). He casts the call of John the Baptist in the form of an Old Testament prophetic call (2) and extends the quotation from Isaiah
found in Mk 1, 3 (Is 40, 3) by the addition of Is 40, 4-5 in vv 5-6.

In doing so, he presents his theme of the universality of salvation,
which he has announced earlier in the words of Simeon (Lk 2, 30-
32). Moreover, in describing the expectation of the people (15),
Luke is characterizing the time of John's preaching in the same
way as he had earlier described the situation of other devout Israelites in the infancy narrative (Lk 2, 25-26.37-38). In vv 7-18
Luke presents the preaching of John the Baptist who urges the
crowds to reform in view of *the coming wrath* (7.9: eschatological preaching), and who offers the crowds certain standards for
reforming social conduct (10-14: ethical preaching), and who announces to the crowds the coming of *one mightier than* he (15-
18: messianic preaching).

3, 1: *Tiberius Caesar:* Tiberius succeeded Augustus as emperor in A.D. 14 and reigned until A.D. 37. The fifteenth year of
his reign, depending on the method of calculating his first regnal
year, would have fallen between A.D. 27 and 29. *Pontius Pilate:*
prefect of Judea from A.D. 26 to 36. The Jewish historian
Josephus describes him as a greedy and ruthless prefect who had
little regard for the local Jewish population and their religious
practices (see Lk 13, 1). *Herod:* i.e., Herod Antipas, the son of
Herod the Great. He ruled over Galilee and Perea from 4 B.C. to
A.D. 39. His official title *tetrarch* means literally, "ruler of a
quarter," but came to designate any subordinate prince. *Philip:*
also a son of Herod the Great, tetrarch of the territory to the
north and east of the Sea of Galilee from 4 B.C. to A.D. 34. Only
two small areas of this territory are mentioned by Luke.
Lysanias: nothing is known about this Lysanias who is said here
to have been tetrarch of Abilene, a territory northwest of Damascus.

of Judea,[n] and Herod was tetrarch of Galilee, and his brother Philip tetrarch of the region of Ituraea and Trachonitis, and Lysanias was tetrarch of Abilene, [2] during the high priesthood of Annas and Caiaphas,* the word of God came to John[o] the son of Zechariah in the desert. [3] * He went throughout [the] whole region of the Jordan, proclaiming a baptism of repentance for the forgiveness of sins,[p] [4] as it is written in the book of the words of the prophet Isaiah:[q]

"A voice of one crying out in the desert:
'Prepare the way of the Lord,[r]
    make straight his paths.*
[5] Every valley shall be filled
    and every mountain and hill shall be made low.
The winding roads shall be made straight,
    and the rough ways made smooth,
[6] and all flesh shall see the salvation of God.' "[s]

[7] He said to the crowds who came out to be baptized by him, "You brood of vipers! Who warned you to flee from the coming wrath?[t] [8] Produce good fruits as evidence of your repentance; and do not begin to say to yourselves, 'We have Abraham as our father,' for I tell you, God can raise up children to Abraham from these stones.[u] [9] Even now the ax lies at the root of the trees. Therefore every tree that does not produce good fruit will be cut down and thrown into the fire."[v]

[10] And the crowds asked him, "What then should we do?" [11] He said to them in reply, "Whoever has two cloaks should share with the person who has none. And whoever has food should do likewise." [12] Even tax collectors came to be baptized and they said to him, "Teacher, what should we do?"[w] [13] He answered them, "Stop collecting more than what is prescribed." [14] Soldiers also asked him, "And what is it that we should do?" He told them, "Do not practice extortion, do not falsely accuse anyone, and be satisfied with your wages."

[15] x Now the people were filled with expectation, and all were asking in their hearts whether John might be the Messiah. [16] John answered them all, saying,[y] "I am baptizing you with water, but one mightier than I is coming. I am not worthy to loosen the thongs of his sandals. He will baptize you with the holy Spirit and fire.* [17] His winnowing fan* is in his hand to clear his threshing floor and to gather the wheat into his barn, but the chaff he will burn with unquenchable fire."[z] [18] Exhorting them in many other ways, he preached good news to the people. [19] * Now Herod the tetrarch,[a] who had been censured by him because of Herodias, his brother's wife, and because of all the evil deeds Herod had committed, [20] added still another to these by [also] putting John in prison.

---

n 1-20: Mt 3, 1-12; Mk 1, 1-8; Jn 1, 19-28.—o Lk 1, 80.—p Acts 13, 24; 19, 4.—q 4-6: Is 40, 3-5.—r Jn 1, 23.—s Lk 2, 30-31.—t Mt 12, 34.—u Jn 8, 39.—v Mt 7, 19; Jn 15, 6.—w Lk 7, 29.—x 15-16: Acts 13, 25.—y Lk 7, 19-20; Jn 1, 27; Acts 1, 5; 11, 16.—z Mt 3, 12.—a 19-20: Mt 14, 3-4; Mk 6, 17-18.

3, 2: *During the high priesthood of Annas and Caiaphas:* after situating the call of John the Baptist in terms of the civil rulers of the period, Luke now mentions the religious leadership of Palestine (see the note on Lk 1, 5). Annas had been high priest A.D. 6-15. After being deposed by the Romans in A.D. 15 he was succeeded by various members of his family and eventually by his son-in-law, Caiaphas, who was high priest A.D. 18-36. Luke refers to Annas as high priest at this time (but see Jn 18, 13.19), possibly because of the continuing influence of Annas or because the title continued to be used for the ex-high priest. *The word of God came to John:* Luke is alone among the New Testament writers in associating the preaching of John with a call from God. Luke is thereby identifying John with the prophets whose ministries began with similar calls. In Lk 7, 26 John will be described as "more than a prophet"; he is also the precursor of Jesus (Lk 7, 27), a transitional figure inaugurating the period of the fulfillment of prophecy and promise.

3, 3: See the note on Mt 3, 2.

3, 4: The Essenes from Qumran used the same passage to explain why their community was in the desert studying and observing the law and the prophets (1QS 8, 12-15).

3, 16: *He will baptize you with the holy Spirit and fire:* in contrast to John's baptism with water, Jesus is said to baptize with the holy Spirit and with fire. From the point of view of the early Christian community, the Spirit and fire must have been understood in the light of the fire symbolism of the pouring out of the Spirit at Pentecost (Acts 2, 1-4); but as part of John's preaching, the Spirit and fire should be related to their purifying and refining characteristics (Ez 36, 25-27; Mal 3, 2-3). See the note on Mt 3, 11.

3, 17: *Winnowing fan:* see the note on Mt 3, 12.

3, 19-20: Luke separates the ministry of John the Baptist from that of Jesus by reporting the imprisonment of John before the baptism of Jesus (21-22). Luke uses this literary device to serve his understanding of the periods of salvation history. With John the Baptist, the time of promise, the period of Israel, comes to an end; with the baptism of Jesus and the descent of the Spirit upon him, the time of fulfillment, the period of Jesus, begins. In his second volume, the Acts of the Apostles, Luke will introduce the third epoch in salvation history, the period of the church.

The Baptism of Jesus.* [21] [b] After all the people had been baptized and Jesus also had been baptized and was praying,* heaven was opened [22] [c] and the holy Spirit descended upon him in bodily form like a dove. And a voice came from heaven, "You are my beloved Son; with you I am well pleased."*

The Genealogy of Jesus.* [23] [d] When Jesus began his ministry he was about thirty years of age. He was the son, as was thought, of Joseph, the son of Heli,[e] [24] the son of Matthat, the son of Levi, the son of Melchi, the son of Jannai, the son of Joseph, [25] the son of Mattathias, the son of Amos, the son of Nahum, the son of Esli, the son of Naggai, [26] the son of Maath, the son of Mattathias, the son of Semein, the son of Josech, the son of Joda, [27] the son of Joanan, the son of Rhesa, the son of Zerubbabel, the son of Shealtiel, the son of Neri,[f] [28] the son of Melchi, the son of Addi, the son of Cosam, the son of Elmadam, the son of Er, [29] the son of Joshua, the son of Eliezer, the son of Jorim, the son of Matthat, the son of Levi, [30] the son of Simeon, the son of Judah, the son of Joseph, the son of Jonam, the son of Eliakim, [31] [g] the son of Melea, the son of Menna, the son of Mattatha, the son of Nathan, the son of David,* [32] the son of Jesse,[h] the son of Obed, the son of Boaz, the son of Sala, the son of Nahshon, [33] the son of Amminadab, the son of Admin, the son of Arni, the son of Hezron, the son of Perez,[i]

the son of Judah,[j] [34] the son of Jacob, the son of Isaac, the son of Abraham,[k] the son of Terah, the son of Nahor, [35] the son of Serug, the son of Reu, the son of Peleg, the son of Eber, the son of Shelah, [36] the son of Cainan, the son of Arphaxad, the son of Shem,[l] the son of Noah, the son of Lamech, [37] the son of Methuselah, the son of Enoch, the son of Jared, the son of Mahalaleel, the son of Cainan, [38] the son of Enos, the son of Seth, the son of Adam,[m] the son of God.

CHAPTER 4

The Temptation of Jesus.* [1] [n] Filled with the holy Spirit,* Jesus returned from the Jordan and was led by the Spirit into the desert [2] for forty days,* to be tempted by the devil. He ate nothing during those days, and when they were over he was hungry.[o] [3] The devil said to him, "If you are the Son of God, command this stone to become bread." [4] Jesus answered him, "It is written, 'One does not live by bread alone.' "[p] [5] Then he took him up and showed him all the kingdoms of the world in a single instant. [6] The devil said to him, "I shall give to you all this power and their glory; for it has been handed over to me, and I may give it to whomever I wish.[q] [7] All this will be yours, if you worship me." [8] Jesus said to him in reply, "It is written:

'You shall worship the Lord, your God,
　　and him alone shall you serve.' "[r]

[9] Then he led him to Jerusalem,* made him stand on the parapet of the temple, and

---

b 21-22: Mt 3, 13-17; Mk 1, 9-11.—c Lk 9, 35; Ps 2, 7; Is 42, 1; Mt 12, 18; 17, 5; Mk 9, 7; Jn 1, 32; 2 Pt 1, 17.—d 23-38: Mt 1, 1-17.—e Lk 4, 22; Jn 6, 42.—f 1 Chr 3, 17; Ez 3, 2.—g 2 Sm 5, 14.—h 31-32: 1 Sm 16, 1.18.—i 31-33: Ru 4, 17-22; 1 Chr 2, 1-15.—j Gn 29, 35; 38, 29.—k Gn 21, 3; 25, 26; 1 Chr 1, 34; 28, 34.—l 34-36: Gn 11, 10-26; 1 Chr 1, 24-27.—m 36-38: Gn 4, 25—5, 32; 1 Chr 1, 1-4.—n 1-13: Mt 4, 1-11; Mk 1, 12-13.—o Heb 4, 15.—p Dt 8, 3.—q Jer 27, 5; Mt 28, 18.—r Dt 6, 13.

3, 21-22: This episode in Luke focuses on the heavenly message identifying Jesus as *Son* and, through the allusion to Is 42, 1, as Servant of Yahweh. The relationship of Jesus to the Father has already been announced in the infancy narrative (Lk 1, 32.35; 2, 49); it occurs here at the beginning of Jesus' Galilean ministry and will reappear in Lk 9, 35 before another major section of Luke's gospel, the travel narrative (Lk 9, 51—19, 27). Elsewhere in Luke's writings (Lk 4, 18; Acts 10, 38), this incident will be interpreted as a type of anointing of Jesus.

3, 21: *Was praying:* Luke regularly presents Jesus at prayer at important points in his ministry: here at his baptism; at the choice of the Twelve (Lk 6, 12); before Peter's confession (Lk 9, 18); at the transfiguration (Lk 9, 28); when he teaches his disciples to pray (Lk 11, 1); at the Last Supper (Lk 22, 32); on the Mount of Olives (Lk 22, 41); on the cross (Lk 23, 46).

3, 22: *You are my beloved Son; with you I am well pleased:* this is the best attested reading in the Greek manuscripts. The Western reading, "You are my Son, this day I have begotten you," is derived from Ps 2, 7.

3, 23-38: Whereas Mt 1, 2 begins the genealogy of Jesus with Abraham to emphasize Jesus' bonds with the people of Israel, Luke's universalism leads him to trace the descent of Jesus beyond Israel to Adam and beyond that to God (38) to stress again Jesus' divine sonship.

3, 31: *The son of Nathan, the son of David:* in keeping with Jesus' prophetic role in Lk and Acts (e.g., Lk 7, 16.39; 9, 8; 13, 33; 24, 19; Acts 3, 22-23; 7, 37) Luke traces Jesus' Davidic ancestry through the prophet Nathan (see 2 Sm 7, 2) rather than through King Solomon, as Mt 1, 6-7.

4, 1-13: See the note on Mt 4, 1-11.

4, 1: *Filled with the holy Spirit:* as a result of the descent of the Spirit upon him at his baptism (Lk 3, 21-22), Jesus is now equipped to overcome the devil. Just as the Spirit is prominent at this early stage of Jesus' ministry (1.14.18), so too it will be at the beginning of the period of the church in Acts (Acts 1, 4; 2, 4.17).

4, 2: *For forty days:* the mention of forty days recalls the forty years of the wilderness wanderings of the Israelites during the Exodus (Dt 8, 2).

4, 9: *To Jerusalem:* the Lucan order of the temptations concludes on the parapet of the temple in Jerusalem, the city of destiny in Luke-Acts. It is in Jerusalem that Jesus will ultimately face his destiny (Lk 9, 51; 13, 33).

said to him, "If you are the Son of God, throw yourself down from here, [10]for it is written:

> 'He will command his angels concerning you,
> to guard you,'[s]

[11]and:

> 'With their hands they will support you,
> lest you dash your foot against a stone.' "[t]

[12]Jesus said to him in reply, "It also says, 'You shall not put the Lord, your God, to the test.' "[u] [13]When the devil had finished every temptation,[v] he departed from him for a time.*

IV. THE MINISTRY IN GALILEE

The Beginning of the Galilean Ministry. [14] [w] Jesus returned to Galilee in the power of the Spirit, and news of him spread* throughout the whole region.[x] [15]He taught in their synagogues and was praised by all.

The Rejection at Nazareth.* [y] [16]He came to Nazareth, where he had grown up, and went according to his custom* into the synagogue on the sabbath day. He stood up to read [17]and was handed a scroll of the prophet Isaiah. He unrolled the scroll and found the passage where it was written:

[18] "The Spirit of the Lord is upon me,*
> because he has anointed me
> to bring glad tidings to the poor.[z]

He has sent me to proclaim liberty to captives
and recovery of sight to the blind,
> to let the oppressed go free,
[19] and to proclaim a year acceptable to the Lord."

[20]Rolling up the scroll, he handed it back to the attendant and sat down, and the eyes of all in the synagogue looked intently at him. [21]He said to them, "Today this scripture passage is fulfilled in your hearing."* [22]And all spoke highly of him and were amazed at the gracious words that came from his mouth. They also asked, "Isn't this the son of Joseph?"[a] [23]He said to them, "Surely you will quote me this proverb, 'Physician, cure yourself,' and say, 'Do here in your native place the things that we heard were done in Capernaum.' " * [24]And he said, "Amen, I say to you, no prophet is accepted in his own native place. [25] * Indeed, I tell you, there were many widows in Israel in the days of Elijah when the sky was closed for three and a half years and a severe famine spread over the entire land.[b] [26]It was to none of these that Elijah was sent, but only to a widow in Zarephath[c] in the land of Sidon.* [27]Again, there were many lepers in Israel during the time of Elisha the prophet; yet not one of them was cleansed, but only Naaman the Syrian."[d] [28]When the people in the synagogue heard this, they were all filled with fury. [29]They rose up, drove him out of the town, and led him to the brow of the hill on which their town

---

s Ps 91, 11.—t Ps 91, 12.—u Dt 6, 16; 1 Cor 10, 9.—v Lk 22, 3; Jn 13, 2.27; Heb 4, 15 .—w 14-15: Mt 4, 12-17; Mk 1, 14-15.—x Lk 5, 15; Mt 3, 16.—y 16-30: Mt 13, 53-58; Mk 6, 1-6.—z 18-19: Is 61, 1-2; 58, 6.—a Lk 3, 23; Jn 6, 42.—b 1 Kgs 17, 1-7; 18, 1; Jas 5, 17.—c 1 Kgs 17, 9.—d 2 Kgs 5, 1-14.

4, 13: *For a time:* the devil's opportune time will occur before the passion and death of Jesus (Lk 22, 3.31-32.53).

4, 14: *News of him spread:* a Lucan theme; see Lk 4, 37; 5, 15; 7, 17.

4, 16-30: Luke has transposed to the beginning of Jesus' ministry an incident from his Marcan source, which situated it near the end of the Galilean ministry (Mk 6, 1-6a). In doing so, Luke turns the initial admiration (22) and subsequent rejection of Jesus (28-29) into a foreshadowing of the whole future ministry of Jesus. Moreover, the rejection of Jesus in his own hometown hints at the greater rejection of him by Israel (Acts 13, 46).

4, 16: *According to his custom:* Jesus' practice of regularly attending synagogue is carried on by the early Christians' practice of meeting in the temple (Acts 2, 46; 3, 1; 5, 12).

4, 18: *The Spirit of the Lord is upon me, because he has anointed me:* see the note on Lk 3, 21-22. As this incident develops, Jesus is portrayed as a prophet whose ministry is compared to that of the prophets Elijah and Elisha. Prophetic anointings are known in first-century Palestinian Judaism from the Qumran literature that speaks of prophets as God's anointed ones. *To bring glad tidings to the poor:* more than any other gospel writer Luke is concerned with Jesus' attitude toward the economically and socially poor (see Lk 6, 20.24; 12, 16-21; 14, 12-14;

16, 19-26; 19, 8). At times, the poor in Luke's gospel are associated with the downtrodden, the oppressed and afflicted, the forgotten and the neglected (Lk 4, 18; 6, 20-22; 7, 22; 14, 12-14), and it is they who accept Jesus' message of salvation.

4, 21: *Today this scripture passage is fulfilled in your hearing:* this sermon inaugurates the time of fulfillment of Old Testament prophecy. Luke presents the ministry of Jesus as fulfilling Old Testament hopes and expectations (Lk 7, 22); for Luke, even Jesus' suffering, death, and resurrection are done in fulfillment of the scriptures (Lk 24, 25-27.44-46; Acts 3, 18).

4, 23: *The things that we heard were done in Capernaum:* Luke's source for this incident reveals an awareness of an earlier ministry of Jesus in Capernaum that Luke has not yet made use of because of his transposition of this Nazareth episode to the beginning of Jesus' Galilean ministry. It is possible that by use of the future tense *you will quote me . . . .,* Jesus is being portrayed as a prophet.

4, 25-26: The references to Elijah and Elisha serve several purposes in this episode: they emphasize Luke's portrait of Jesus as a prophet like Elijah and Elisha; they help to explain why the initial admiration of the people turns to rejection; and they provide the scriptural justification for the future Christian mission to the Gentiles.

4, 26: *A widow in Zarephath in the land of Sidon:* like Naaman the Syrian in v 27, a non-Israelite becomes the object of the prophet's ministry.

had been built, to hurl him down head-long. 30 But he passed through the midst of them and went away.

The Cure of a Demoniac. 31 * Jesus then went down to Capernaum,*e* a town of Galilee.*f* He taught them on the sabbath, 32 and they were astonished at his teaching because he spoke with authority.*g* 33 In the synagogue there was a man with the spirit of an unclean demon,*h* and he cried out in a loud voice, 34 "Ha! What have you to do with us, Jesus of Nazareth? Have you come to destroy us?* I know who you are—the Holy One of God!"*i* 35 Jesus rebuked him and said, "Be quiet! Come out of him!" Then the demon threw the man down in front of them and came out of him without doing him any harm. 36 They were all amazed and said to one another, "What is there about his word? For with authority and power he commands the unclean spirits, and they come out." 37 And news of him spread everywhere in the surrounding region.

The Cure of Simon's Mother-in-Law. 38 *j* After he left the synagogue, he entered the house of Simon.* Simon's mother-in-law was afflicted with a severe fever, and they interceded with him about her. 39 He stood over her, rebuked the fever, and it left her. She got up immediately and waited on them.

Other Healings. *k* 40 At sunset, all who had people sick with various diseases brought them to him. He laid his hands on each of

them and cured them. 41 And demons also came out from many, shouting, "You are the Son of God."*l* But he rebuked them and did not allow them to speak because they knew that he was the Messiah.*

Jesus Leaves Capernaum. *m* 42 At daybreak, Jesus left and went to a deserted place. The crowds went looking for him, and when they came to him, they tried to prevent him from leaving them.* 43 But he said to them, "To the other towns also I must proclaim the good news of the kingdom of God, because for this purpose I have been sent."*n* 44 And he was preaching in the synagogues of Judea.*

CHAPTER 5

The Call of Simon the Fisherman. *o* 1 *p* While the crowd was pressing in on Jesus and listening to the word of God, he was standing by the Lake of Gennesaret. 2 He saw two boats there alongside the lake; the fishermen had disembarked and were washing their nets. 3 Getting into one of the boats, the one belonging to Simon, he asked him to put out a short distance from the shore. Then he sat down and taught the crowds from the boat. 4 *q* After he had finished speaking, he said to Simon, "Put out into deep water and lower your nets for a catch." 5 Simon said in reply, "Master,

---

4, 42: *They tried to prevent him from leaving them:* the reaction of these strangers in Capernaum is presented in contrast to the reactions of those in his hometown who rejected him (28-30).

4, 44: *In the synagogues of Judea:* instead of *Judea,* which is the best reading of the manuscript tradition, the Byzantine text tradition and other manuscripts read "Galilee," a reading that harmonizes Lk with Mt 4, 23 and Mk 1, 39. Up to this point Luke has spoken only of a ministry of Jesus in Galilee. Luke may be using *Judea* to refer to the land of Israel, the territory of the Jews, and not to a specific portion of it.

5, 1-11: This incident has been transposed from his source, Mk 1, 16-20, which places it immediately after Jesus makes his appearance in Galilee. By this transposition Luke uses this example of Simon's acceptance of Jesus to counter the earlier rejection of him by his hometown people, and since several incidents dealing with Jesus' power and authority have already been narrated, Luke creates a plausible context for the acceptance of Jesus by Simon and his partners. Many commentators have noted the similarity between the wondrous catch of fish reported here (4-9) and the post-resurrectional appearance of Jesus in Jn 21, 1-11. There are traces in Luke's story that the post-resurrectional context is the original one: in v 8 Simon addresses Jesus as *Lord* (a post-resurrectional title for Jesus—see Lk 24, 34; Acts 2, 36—that has been read back into the historical ministry of Jesus) and recognizes himself as a sinner (an appropriate recognition for one who has denied knowing Jesus—Lk 22, 54-62). As used by Luke, the incident looks forward to Peter's leadership in Luke-Acts (Lk 6, 14; 9, 20; 22, 31-32; 24, 34; Acts 1, 15; 2, 14-40; 10, 11-18; 15, 7-12) and symbolizes the future success of Peter as fisherman (Acts 2, 41).

---

e 31-37: Mk 1, 21-28.—f Mt 4, 13; Jn 2, 12.—g Mt 7, 28-29.—h 33-34: Lk 8, 28; Mt 8, 29; Mk 1, 23-24; 5, 7.—i Lk 4, 41; Jn 6, 69.—j 38-39: Mt 8, 14-15; Mk 1, 29-31.—k 40-41: Mt 8, 16; Mk 1, 32-34.—l Lk 4, 34; Mt 8, 29; Mk 3, 11-12.—m 42-44: Mk 1, 35-39.—n Lk 8, 1; Mk 1, 14-15.—o 1-11: Mt 4, 18-22; Mk 1, 16-20.—p 1-3: Mt 13, 1-2; Mk 2, 13; 3, 9-10; 4, 1-2.—q 4-9: Jn 21, 1-11.

4, 31-44: The next several incidents in Jesus' ministry take place in Capernaum and are based on Luke's source, Mk 1, 21-39. To the previous portrait of Jesus as prophet (16-30) they now add a presentation of him as teacher (31-32), exorcist (32-37.41), healer (38-40), and proclaimer of God's kingdom (43).

4, 34: *What have you to do with us?:* see the note on Jn 2, 4. *Have you come to destroy us?:* the question reflects the current belief that before the day of the Lord control over humanity would be wrested from the evil spirits, evil destroyed, and God's authority over humanity reestablished. The synoptic gospel tradition presents Jesus carrying out this task.

4, 38: *The house of Simon:* because of Luke's arrangement of material, the reader has not yet been introduced to Simon (cf Mk 1, 16-18.29-31). Situated as it is before the call of Simon (Lk 5, 1-11), it helps the reader to understand Simon's eagerness to do what Jesus says (Lk 5, 5) and to follow him (Lk 5, 11).

4, 41: *They knew that he was the Messiah:* that is, the Christ (see the note on Lk 2, 11).

we have worked hard all night and have caught nothing, but at your command I will lower the nets." [6] When they had done this, they caught a great number of fish and their nets were tearing. [7] They signaled to their partners in the other boat to come to help them. They came and filled both boats so that they were in danger of sinking. [8] When Simon Peter saw this, he fell at the knees of Jesus and said, "Depart from me, Lord, for I am a sinful man." [9] For astonishment at the catch of fish they had made seized him and all those with him, [10] and likewise James and John, the sons of Zebedee, who were partners of Simon. Jesus said to Simon, "Do not be afraid; from now on you will be catching men."[r] [11] When they brought their boats to the shore, they left everything* and followed him.[s]

The Cleansing of a Leper.[t] [12] Now there was a man full of leprosy* in one of the towns where he was; and when he saw Jesus, he fell prostrate, pleaded with him, and said, "Lord, if you wish, you can make me clean." [13] Jesus stretched out his hand,

---

r Jer 16, 16.—s Mt 19, 27.—t 12-16: Mt 8, 2-4; Mk 1, 40-45.—u Lk 8, 56; Lv 14, 2-32; Mk 7, 36.—v Mk 1, 35.—w 17-26: Mt 9, 1-8; Mk 2, 1-12.—x Lk 7, 49; Is 43, 25.—y Lk 6, 8; 9, 47.—z 24-25: Jn 5, 8-9.27.—a 27-32: Mt 9, 9-13; Mk 2, 13-17.—b 29-30: Lk 15, 1-2.

5, 11: *They left everything:* in Mk 1, 16-20 and Mt 4, 18-22 the fishermen who follow Jesus leave their nets and their father; in Luke, they leave *everything* (see also Lk 5, 28; 12, 33; 14, 33; 18, 22), an indication of Luke's theme of complete detachment from material possessions.

5, 12: *Full of leprosy:* see the note on Mk 1, 40.

5, 14: *Show yourself to the priest ... what Moses prescribed:* this is a reference to Lv 14, 2-9 that gives detailed instructions for the purification of one who had been a victim of leprosy and thereby excluded from contact with others (see Lv 13, 45-46.49; Nm 5, 2-3). *That will be proof for them:* see the note on Mt 8, 4.

5, 17—6, 11: From his Marcan source, Luke now introduces a series of controversies with Pharisees: controversy over Jesus' power to forgive sins (17-26); controversy over his eating and drinking with tax collectors and sinners (27-32); controversy over not fasting (33-36); and finally two episodes narrating controversies over observance of the sabbath (1-11).

5, 17: *Pharisees:* see the note on Mt 3, 7.

5, 19: *Through the tiles:* Luke has adapted the story found in Mk to his non-Palestinian audience by changing "opened up the roof" (Mk 2, 4, a reference to Palestinian straw and clay roofs) to *through the tiles,* a detail that reflects the Hellenistic Greco-Roman house with tiled roof.

5, 20: *As for you, your sins are forgiven:* literally, "O man, your sins are forgiven you." The connection between the forgiveness of sins and the cure of the paralytic reflects the belief of first-century Palestine (based on the Old Testament: Ex 20, 5; Dt 5, 9) that sickness and infirmity are the result of sin, one's own or that of one's ancestors (see also Lk 13, 2; Jn 5, 14; 9, 2).

5, 21: *The scribes:* see the note on Mk 2, 6.

5, 24: See the notes on Mt 9, 6 and Mk 2, 10.

5, 28: *Leaving everything behind:* see the note on Lk 5, 11.

---

touched him, and said, "I do will it. Be made clean." And the leprosy left him immediately. [14] Then he ordered him not to tell anyone, but "Go, show yourself to the priest and offer for your cleansing what Moses prescribed;* that will be proof for them."[u] [15] The report about him spread all the more, and great crowds assembled to listen to him and to be cured of their ailments, [16] but he would withdraw to deserted places to pray.[v]

The Healing of a Paralytic.[w] [17] * One day as Jesus was teaching, Pharisees* and teachers of the law were sitting there who had come from every village of Galilee and Judea and Jerusalem; and the power of the Lord was with him for healing. [18] And some men brought on a stretcher a man who was paralyzed; they were trying to bring him in and set [him] in his presence. [19] But not finding a way to bring him in because of the crowd, they went up on the roof and lowered him on the stretcher through the tiles* into the middle in front of Jesus. [20] When he saw their faith, he said, "As for you, your sins are forgiven."* [21] Then the scribes* and Pharisees began to ask themselves, "Who is this who speaks blasphemies? Who but God alone can forgive sins?"[x] [22] Jesus knew their thoughts and said to them in reply, "What are you thinking in your hearts?[y] [23] Which is easier, to say, 'Your sins are forgiven,' or to say, 'Rise and walk'? [24] [z] But that you may know that the Son of Man has authority on earth to forgive sins"—he said to the man who was paralyzed, "I say to you, rise, pick up your stretcher, and go home."* [25] He stood up immediately before them, picked up what he had been lying on, and went home, glorifying God. [26] Then astonishment seized them all and they glorified God, and, struck with awe, they said, "We have seen incredible things today."

The Call of Levi. [a] [27] After this he went out and saw a tax collector named Levi sitting at the customs post. He said to him, "Follow me." [28] And leaving everything behind,* he got up and followed him. [29] [b] Then Levi gave a great banquet for him in his house, and a large crowd of tax collectors and others were at table with them. [30] The Pharisees and their scribes complained to his disciples, saying, "Why do you eat and drink with tax collectors and sinners?" [31] Jesus said to them in reply,

"Those who are healthy do not need a physician, but the sick do. ³²I have not come to call the righteous to repentance but sinners."

The Question about Fasting.ᶜ ³³And they said to him, "The disciples of John fast often and offer prayers, and the disciples of the Pharisees do the same; but yours eat and drink." ³⁴ * Jesus answered them, "Can you make the wedding guests* fast while the bridegroom is with them? ³⁵But the days will come, and when the bridegroom is taken away from them, then they will fast in those days." ³⁶*And he also told them a parable. "No one tears a piece from a new cloak to patch an old one. Otherwise, he will tear the new and the piece from it will not match the old cloak. ³⁷Likewise, no one pours new wine into old wineskins. Otherwise, the new wine will burst the skins, and it will be spilled, and the skins will be ruined. ³⁸Rather, new wine must be poured into fresh wineskins. ³⁹[And] no one who has been drinking old wine desires new, for he says, 'The old is good.' "*

CHAPTER 6

Debates about the Sabbath.* ¹ ᵈ While he was going through a field of grain on a sabbath, his disciples were picking the heads of grain, rubbing them in their hands, and eating them.ᵉ ²Some Pharisees said, "Why are you doing what is unlawful on the sabbath?" ³ ᶠ Jesus said to them in reply,

"Have you not read what David did when he and those [who were] with him were hungry? ⁴[How] he went into the house of God, took the bread of offering,* which only the priests could lawfully eat, ate of it, and shared it with his companions."ᵍ ⁵Then he said to them, "The Son of Man is lord of the sabbath."

⁶ ʰ On another sabbath he went into the synagogue and taught, and there was a man there whose right hand was withered. ⁷The scribes and the Pharisees watched him closely to see if he would cure on the sabbath so that they might discover a reason to accuse him.ⁱ ⁸But he realized their intentions and said to the man with the withered hand, "Come up and stand before us." And he rose and stood there.ʲ ⁹Then Jesus said to them, "I ask you, is it lawful to do good on the sabbath rather than to do evil, to save life rather than to destroy it?" ¹⁰Looking around at them all, he then said to him, "Stretch out your hand." He did so and his hand was restored. ¹¹But they became enraged and discussed together what they might do to Jesus.

The Mission of the Twelve.* ¹² ᵏ In those days he departed to the mountain to pray, and he spent the night in prayer* to God. ¹³When day came, he called his disciples to himself, and from them he chose Twelve,* whom he also named apostles: ¹⁴ ˡ Simon, whom he named Peter,* and his brother Andrew, James, John, Philip, Barthol-

---

ᶜ 33-39: Mt 9, 14-17; Mk 2, 18-22.—ᵈ 1-5: Mt 12, 1-8; Mk 2, 23-28.—ᵉ Dt 23, 26.—ᶠ 3-4: 1 Sm 21, 1-6.—ᵍ Lv 24, 5-9.—ʰ 6-11: Mt 12, 9-14; Mk 3, 1-6.—ⁱ Lk 14, 1.—ʲ Lk 5, 22; 9, 47.—ᵏ 12-16: Mt 10, 1-4; Mk 3, 13-19.—ˡ 14-16: Acts 1, 13.

5, 34-35: See the notes on Mt 9, 15 and Mk 2, 19.

5, 34: *Wedding guests:* literally, "sons of the bridal chamber."

5, 36-39: See the notes on Mt 9, 16-17 and Mk 2, 19.

5, 39: *The old is good:* this saying is meant to be ironic and offers an explanation for the rejection by some of the new wine that Jesus offers: satisfaction with old forms will prevent one from sampling the new.

6, 1-11: The two episodes recounted here deal with gathering grain and healing, both of which were forbidden on the sabbath. In his defense of his disciples' conduct and his own charitable deed, Jesus argues that satisfying human needs such as hunger and performing works of mercy take precedence even over the sacred sabbath rest. See also the notes on Mt 12, 1-14 and Mk 2, 25-26.

6, 4: *The bread of offering:* see the note on Mt 12, 5-6.

6, 12-16: See the notes on Mt 10, 1—11, 1 and Mk 3, 14-15.

6, 12: *Spent the night in prayer:* see the note on Lk 3, 21.

6, 13: *He chose Twelve:* the identification of this group as the *Twelve* is a part of early Christian tradition (see 1 Cor 15, 5), and in Mt and Lk, the Twelve are associated with the twelve tribes of Israel (Lk 22, 29-30; Mt 19, 28). After the fall of Judas from his position among the Twelve, the need is felt on the part of the early community to reconstitute this group before the Christian ministry begins at Pentecost (Acts 1, 15-26). From Luke's perspective, they are an important group who because of their association with Jesus from the time of his baptism to his ascension (Acts 1, 21-22) provide the continuity between the historical Jesus and the church of Luke's day and who as the original eyewitnesses guarantee the fidelity of the church's beliefs and practices to the teachings of Jesus (Lk 1, 1-4). *Whom he also named apostles:* only Luke among the gospel writers attributes to Jesus the bestowal of the name *apostles* upon the Twelve. See the note on Mt 10, 2-4. "Apostle" becomes a technical term in early Christianity for a missionary sent out to preach the word of God. Although Luke seems to want to restrict the title to the Twelve (only in Acts 4, 4.14 are Paul and Barnabas termed apostles), other places in the New Testament show an awareness that the term was more widely applied (1 Cor 15, 5-7; Gal 1, 19; 1 Cor 1, 1; 9, 1; Rom 16, 7).

6, 14: *Simon, whom he named Peter:* see the note on Mk 3, 16.

omew, ¹⁵ Matthew, Thomas, James the son of Alphaeus, Simon who was called a Zealot,* ¹⁶ and Judas the son of James, and Judas Iscariot,* who became a traitor.

Ministering to a Great Multitude. ^{m 17} And he came down with them and stood on a stretch of level ground. A great crowd of his disciples and a large number of the people from all Judea and Jerusalem and the coastal region of Tyre and Sidon* ¹⁸ came to hear him and to be healed of their diseases; and even those who were tormented by unclean spirits were cured. ¹⁹ Everyone in the crowd sought to touch him because power came forth from him and healed them all.

Sermon on the Plain. ⁿ ²⁰ * And raising his eyes toward his disciples he said:

"Blessed are you who are poor,*
  for the kingdom of God is yours.
²¹ Blessed are you who are now hungry,
  for you will be satisfied.
Blessed are you who are now weeping,
  for you will laugh.^o
²² Blessed are you when people hate you,
  and when they exclude and insult you,
  and denounce your name as evil
  on account of the Son of Man.^p

²³ Rejoice and leap for joy on that day! Behold, your reward will be great in heaven. For their ancestors treated the prophets in the same way.^q

²⁴ But woe to you who are rich,
  for you have received your consolation.^r
²⁵ But woe to you who are filled now,
  for you will be hungry.

Woe to you who laugh now,
  for you will grieve and weep.^s
²⁶ Woe to you when all speak well of you,
  for their ancestors treated the false
  prophets in this way.^t

Love of Enemies.* ^{27 u} "But to you who hear I say, love your enemies, do good to those who hate you,^v ²⁸ bless those who curse you, pray for those who mistreat you.^w ²⁹ To the person who strikes you on one cheek, offer the other one as well, and from the person who takes your cloak, do not withhold even your tunic. ³⁰ Give to everyone who asks of you, and from the one who takes what is yours do not demand it back. ³¹ Do to others as you would have them do to you.^x ³² For if you love those who love you, what credit is that to you? Even sinners love those who love them. ³³ And if you do good to those who do good to you, what credit is that to you? Even sinners do the same. ³⁴ If you lend money to those from whom you expect repayment, what credit [is] that to you? Even sinners lend to sinners, and get back the same amount.^y ³⁵ But rather, love your enemies and do good to them, and lend expecting nothing back; then your reward will be great and you will be children of the Most High, for he himself is kind to the ungrateful and the wicked.^z ³⁶ Be merciful, just as [also] your Father is merciful.

Lk

(46-49). Almost all the words of Jesus reported by Lk are found in Mt's version, but because Mt includes sayings that were related to specifically Jewish Christian problems (e.g., Mt 5, 17-20; 6, 1-8.16-18) that Luke did not find appropriate for his predominantly Gentile Christian audience, the "Sermon on the Mount" is considerably longer. Lk's sermon may be outlined as follows: an introduction consisting of blessings and woes (20-26); the love of one's enemies (27-36); the demands of loving one's neighbor (37-42); good deeds as proof of one's goodness (43-45); a parable illustrating the result of listening to and acting on the words of Jesus (46-49). At the core of the sermon is Jesus' teaching on the love of one's enemies (27-36) that has as its source of motivation God's graciousness and compassion for all humanity (35-36) and Jesus' teaching on the love of one's neighbor (37-42) that is characterized by forgiveness and generosity.

6, 20-26: The introductory portion of the sermon consists of blessings and woes that address the real economic and social conditions of humanity (the poor—the rich; the hungry—the satisfied; those grieving—those laughing; the outcast—the socially acceptable). By contrast, Matthew emphasizes the religious and spiritual values of disciples in the kingdom inaugurated by Jesus ("poor in spirit," Mt 5, 5; "hunger and thirst for righteousness," Mt 5, 6). In the sermon, *blessed* extols the fortunate condition of persons who are favored with the blessings of God; the woes, addressed as they are to the disciples of Jesus, threaten God's profound displeasure on those so blinded by their present fortunate situation that they do not recognize and appreciate the real values of God's kingdom. In all the blessings and woes, the present condition of the persons addressed will be reversed in the future.

6, 27-36: See the notes on Mt 5, 43-48 and Mt 5, 48.

m 17-19: Mt 4, 23-25; Mk 3, 7-10.—n 20-26: Mt 5, 1-12.—o Ps 126, 5-6; Is 61, 3; Jer 31, 25; Rv 7, 16-17.—p Jn 15, 19; 16, 2; 1 Pt 4, 14.—q Lk 11, 47-48; 23, 30-31.—r Jas 5, 1.—s Is 65, 13-14.—t Jas 4, 4.—u 27-36: Mt 5, 38-48.—v Prv 25, 21; Rom 12, 20-21.—w Rom 12, 14; 1 Pt 3, 9.—x Mt 7, 12.—y Dt 15, 7-8.—z Lv 25, 35-36.

6, 15: *Simon who was called a Zealot:* the Zealots were the instigators of the First Revolt of Palestinian Jews against Rome in A.D. 66-70. Because the existence of the Zealots as a distinct group during the lifetime of Jesus is the subject of debate, the meaning of the identification of Simon as a Zealot is unclear.

6, 16: *Judas Iscariot:* the name *Iscariot* may mean "man from Kerioth."

6, 17: *The coastal region of Tyre and Sidon:* not only Jews from Judea and Jerusalem, but even Gentiles from outside Palestine come to hear Jesus (see Lk 2, 31-32; 3, 6; 4, 24-27).

6, 20-49: Luke's "Sermon on the Plain" is the counterpart to Mt's "Sermon on the Mount" (Mt 5, 1—7, 27). It is addressed to the disciples of Jesus, and, like the sermon in Mt, it begins with beatitudes (20-22) and ends with the parable of the two houses

Judging Others.* [37] [a] "Stop judging and you will not be judged. Stop condemning and you will not be condemned. Forgive and you will be forgiven. [b] [38] Give and gifts will be given to you; a good measure, packed together, shaken down, and overflowing, will be poured into your lap. For the measure with which you measure will in return be measured out to you." [c] [39] And he told them a parable, "Can a blind person guide a blind person? Will not both fall into a pit? [d] [40] No disciple is superior to the teacher; but when fully trained, every disciple will be like his teacher. [e] [41] Why do you notice the splinter in your brother's eye, but do not perceive the wooden beam in your own? [42] How can you say to your brother, 'Brother, let me remove that splinter in your eye,' when you do not even notice the wooden beam in your own eye? You hypocrite! Remove the wooden beam from your eye first; then you will see clearly to remove the splinter in your brother's eye.

A Tree Known by Its Fruit. [f] [43] * "A good tree does not bear rotten fruit, nor does a rotten tree bear good fruit. [44] For every tree is known by its own fruit. For people do not pick figs from thornbushes, nor do they gather grapes from brambles. [45] A good person out of the store of goodness in his heart produces good, but an evil person out of a store of evil produces evil; for from the fullness of the heart the mouth speaks.

The Two Foundations. [46] [g] "Why do you call me, 'Lord, Lord,' but not do what I command? [47] * I will show you what someone is like who comes to me, listens to my words, and acts on them. [h] [48] That one is like a person building a house, who dug deeply and laid the foundation on rock; when the flood came, the river burst against that house but could not shake it because it had been well built. [49] But the one who listens and does not act is like a person who built a house on the ground without a foundation. When the river burst against it, it collapsed at once and was completely destroyed."

CHAPTER 7

The Healing of a Centurion's Slave. [i] [1] * When he had finished all his words to the people, he entered Capernaum.* [2] A centurion* there had a slave who was ill and about to die, and he was valuable to him.

[3] When he heard about Jesus, he sent elders of the Jews to him, asking him to come and save the life of his slave. [4] They approached Jesus and strongly urged him to come, saying, "He deserves to have you do this for him, [5] for he loves our nation and he built the synagogue for us." [6] And Jesus went with them, but when he was only a short distance from the house, the centurion sent friends to tell him, "Lord, do not trouble yourself, for I am not worthy to have you enter under my roof.* [7] Therefore, I did not consider myself worthy to come to you; but say the word and let my servant be healed. [8] For I too am a person subject to authority, with soldiers subject to me. And I say to one, 'Go,' and he goes; and to another, 'Come here,' and he comes; and to my slave, 'Do this,' and he does it." [9] When Jesus heard this he was amazed at him and, turning, said to the crowd following him, "I tell you, not even in Israel have I found such faith." [10] When the messengers returned to the house, they found the slave in good health.

Raising of the Widow's Son.* [11] [j] Soon afterward he journeyed to a city called Nain,

---

a 37-42: Mt 7, 1-5.—b Mt 6, 14; Jas 2, 13.—c Mk 4, 24.—d Mt 15, 14; 23, 16-17.24.—e Mt 10, 24-25; Jn 13, 16; 15, 20.—f 43-45: Mt 7, 16-20; 12, 33.35.—g Mt 7, 21; Rom 2, 13; Jas 1, 22.—h 47-49: Mt 7, 24-27.—i 1-10: Mt 8, 5-13; Jn 4, 43-54.—j 11-17: Lk 4, 25-26; 1 Kgs 17, 17-24.

6, 37-42: See the notes on Mt 7, 1-12; 7, 1; 7, 5.

6, 43-46: See the notes on Mt 7, 15-20 and Mt 12, 33.

6, 47-49: See the note on Mt 7, 24-27.

7, 1—8, 3: The episodes in this section present a series of reactions to the Galilean ministry of Jesus and reflect some of Luke's particular interests: the faith of a Gentile (1-10); the prophet Jesus' concern for a widowed mother (11-17); the ministry of Jesus directed to the afflicted and unfortunate of Is 61, 1 (18-23); the relation between John and Jesus and their role in God's plan for salvation (24-35); a forgiven sinner's manifestation of love (36-50); the association of women with the ministry of Jesus (Lk 8, 1-3).

7, 1-10: This story about the faith of the centurion, a Gentile who cherishes the Jewish nation (5), prepares for the story in Acts of the conversion by Peter of the Roman centurion Cornelius who is similarly described as one who is generous to the Jewish nation (Acts 10, 2). See also Acts 10, 34-35 in the speech of Peter: "God shows no partiality . . . the person who fears him and acts righteously is acceptable to him." See also the notes on Mt 8, 5-13 and Jn 4, 43-54.

7, 2: *A centurion:* see the note on Mt 8, 5.

7, 6: *I am not worthy to have you enter under my roof:* to enter the house of a Gentile was considered unclean for a Jew; cf Acts 10, 28.

7, 11-17: In the previous incident Jesus' power was displayed for a Gentile whose servant was dying; in this episode it is displayed toward a widowed mother whose only son has already died. Jesus' power over death prepares for his reply to John's disciples in v 22: "the dead are raised." This resuscitation in alluding to the prophet Elijah's resurrection of the only son of a widow of Zarephath (1 Kgs 17, 8-24) leads to the reaction of the crowd: "A great prophet has arisen in our midst" (16).

and his disciples and a large crowd accompanied him. [12] As he drew near to the gate of the city, a man who had died was being carried out, the only son of his mother, and she was a widow. A large crowd from the city was with her.[k] [13] When the Lord saw her, he was moved with pity for her and said to her, "Do not weep." [14] He stepped forward and touched the coffin; at this the bearers halted, and he said, "Young man, I tell you, arise!" [15] The dead man sat up and began to speak, and Jesus gave him to his mother.[l] [16] Fear seized them all, and they glorified God, exclaiming, "A great prophet has arisen in our midst," and "God has visited his people."[m] [17] This report about him spread through the whole of Judea and in all the surrounding region.

The Messengers from John the Baptist.[*] [18] [n] The disciples of John told him about all these things. John summoned two of his disciples [19] and sent them to the Lord to ask, "Are you the one who is to come, or should we look for another?"[o] [20] When the men came to him, they said, "John the Baptist has sent us to you to ask, 'Are you the one who is to come, or should we look for another?' " [21] At that time he cured many of their diseases, sufferings, and evil

---

k Lk 8, 42; 1 Kgs 17, 17.—l 1 Kgs 17, 23; 2 Kgs 4, 36.—m Lk 1, 68; 19, 44.—n 18-23: Mt 11, 2-6.—o Mal 3, 1; Rv 1, 4.8; 4, 8.—p Lk 4, 18; Is 35, 5-6; 61, 1.—q 24-30: Mt 11, 7-15.—r Lk 1, 76.—s Mal 3, 1 / Is 40, 3.—t 29-30: Lk 3, 7.12; Mt 21, 32.— u 31-35: Mt 11, 16-19.—v Lk 15, 2.—w Lk 11, 37; 14, 1.

7, 18-23: In answer to John's question, *Are you the one who is to come?*—a probable reference to the return of the fiery prophet of reform, Elijah, "before the day of the Lord comes, the great and terrible day" (Mal 3, 23)—Jesus responds that his role is rather to bring the blessings spoken of in Is 61, 1 to the oppressed and neglected of society (22; cf Lk 4, 18).

7, 23: *Blessed is the one who takes no offense at me:* this beatitude is pronounced on the person who recognizes Jesus' true identity in spite of previous expectations of what "the one who is to come" would be like.

7, 24-30: In his testimony to John, Jesus reveals his understanding of the relationship between them: John is the precursor of Jesus (27); John is the messenger spoken of in Mal 3, 1 who in Mal 3, 23 is identified as Elijah. Taken with the previous episode, it can be seen that Jesus identifies John as precisely the person John envisioned Jesus to be: the Elijah who prepares the way for the coming of the day of the Lord.

7, 31-35: See the note on Mt 11, 16-19.

7, 36-50: In this story of the pardoning of the sinful woman Luke presents two different reactions to the ministry of Jesus. A Pharisee, suspecting Jesus to be a prophet, invites Jesus to a festive banquet in his house, but the Pharisee's self-righteousness leads to little forgiveness by God and consequently little love shown toward Jesus. The sinful woman, on the other hand, manifests a faith in God (50) that has led her to seek forgiveness for her sins, and because so much was forgiven, she now overwhelms Jesus with her display of love; cf the similar contrast in attitudes in Lk 18, 9-14. The whole episode is a powerful lesson on the relation between forgiveness and love.

---

spirits; he also granted sight to many who were blind. [22] And he said to them in reply, "Go and tell John what you have seen and heard: the blind regain their sight, the lame walk, lepers are cleansed, the deaf hear, the dead are raised, the poor have the good news proclaimed to them.[p] [23] And blessed is the one who takes no offense at me."[*]

Jesus' Testimony to John. [24] [*] When the messengers of John had left, Jesus began to speak to the crowds about John.[q] "What did you go out to the desert to see—a reed swayed by the wind? [25] Then what did you go out to see? Someone dressed in fine garments? Those who dress luxuriously and live sumptuously are found in royal palaces. [26] Then what did you go out to see? A prophet? Yes, I tell you, and more than a prophet.[r] [27] This is the one about whom scripture says:

'Behold, I am sending my messenger
     ahead of you,
  he will prepare your way before
     you.'[s]

[28] I tell you, among those born of women, no one is greater than John; yet the least in the kingdom of God is greater than he." [29] [t] (All the people who listened, including the tax collectors, and who were baptized with the baptism of John, acknowledged the righteousness of God; [30] but the Pharisees and scholars of the law, who were not baptized by him, rejected the plan of God for themselves.)

[31] [*] "Then to what shall I compare the people of this generation? What are they like?[u] [32] They are like children who sit in the marketplace and call to one another,

'We played the flute for you, but you
     did not dance.
  We sang a dirge, but you did not
     weep.'

[33] For John the Baptist came neither eating food nor drinking wine, and you said, 'He is possessed by a demon.' [34] The Son of Man came eating and drinking and you said, 'Look, he is a glutton and a drunkard, a friend of tax collectors and sinners.'[v] [35] But wisdom is vindicated by all her children."

The Pardon of the Sinful Woman.[*] [36] [w] A Pharisee invited him to dine with him, and

Lk

he entered the Pharisee's house and reclined at table.*[37] Now there was a sinful woman in the city who learned that he was at table in the house of the Pharisee.[x] Bringing an alabaster flask of ointment,[y] [38] she stood behind him at his feet weeping and began to bathe his feet with her tears. Then she wiped them with her hair, kissed them, and anointed them with the ointment. [39] When the Pharisee who had invited him saw this he said to himself, "If this man were a prophet, he would know who and what sort of woman this is who is touching him, that she is a sinner." [40] Jesus said to him in reply, "Simon, I have something to say to you." "Tell me, teacher," he said. [41] "Two people were in debt to a certain creditor; one owed five hundred days' wages* and the other owed fifty. [42] Since they were unable to repay the debt, he forgave it for both. Which of them will love him more?" [43] Simon said in reply, "The one, I suppose, whose larger debt was forgiven." He said to him, "You have judged rightly." [44] Then he turned to the woman and said to Simon, "Do you see this woman? When I entered your house, you did not give me water for my feet, but she has bathed them with her tears and wiped them with her hair. [45] You did not give me a kiss, but she has not ceased kissing my feet since the time I entered. [46] You did not anoint my head with oil, but she anointed my feet with ointment. [47] So I tell you, her many sins have been forgiven; hence, she has shown great love.* But the one to whom little is forgiven, loves little." [48] He said to her, "Your sins are forgiven."[z] [49] The others at table said to themselves, "Who is this who even forgives sins?"[a] [50] But he said to the woman, "Your faith has saved you; go in peace."

CHAPTER 8

Galilean Women Follow Jesus.* [1] Afterward he journeyed from one town and village to another, preaching and proclaiming the good news of the kingdom of God.[b] Accompanying him were the Twelve [2] [c] and some women who had been cured of evil spirits and infirmities, Mary, called Magdalene, from whom seven demons had gone out, [3] Joanna, the wife of Herod's steward Chuza, Susanna, and many others who provided for them out of their resources.

The Parable of the Sower.[d] [4] * When a large crowd gathered, with people from one town after another journeying to him, he spoke in a parable.* [5] "A sower went out to sow his seed. And as he sowed, some seed fell on the path and was trampled, and the birds of the sky ate it up. [6] Some seed fell on rocky ground, and when it grew, it withered for lack of moisture. [7] Some seed fell among thorns, and the thorns grew with it and choked it. [8] And some seed fell on good soil, and when it grew, it produced fruit a hundredfold." After saying this, he called out, "Whoever has ears to hear ought to hear."[e]

The Purpose of the Parables.[f] [9] Then his disciples asked him what the meaning of this parable might be. [10] He answered, "Knowledge of the mysteries of the kingdom of God has been granted to you; but to the rest, they are made known through parables so that 'they may look but not see, and hear but not understand.'[g]

The Parable of the Sower Explained.* [11] [h] "This is the meaning of the parable. The

---

x Mt 26, 7; Mk 14, 3.—y 37-38: Jn 12, 3.—z Lk 5, 20; Mt 9, 20; Mk 2, 5.—a Lk 5, 21.—b Lk 4, 43.—c 2-3: Lk 23, 49; 24, 10; Mt 27, 55-56; Mk 15, 40-41; Jn 19, 5.—d 4-8: Mt 13, 1-9; Mk 4, 1-9.—e Lk 14, 35; Mt 11, 15; 13, 43; Mk 4, 23.—f 9-10: Mt 13, 10-13; Mk 4, 10-12.—g Is 6, 9.—h 11-15: Mt 13, 18-23; Mk 4, 13-20.

7, 36: *Reclined at table:* the normal posture of guests at a banquet. Other oriental banquet customs alluded to in this story include the reception by the host with a kiss (45), washing the feet of the guests (44), and the anointing of the guests' heads (46).

7, 41: *Days' wages:* one denarius is the normal daily wage of a laborer.

7, 47: *Her many sins have been forgiven; hence, she has shown great love:* literally, "her many sins have been forgiven, seeing that she has loved much." That the woman's sins have been forgiven is attested by the great love she shows toward Jesus. Her love is the consequence of her forgiveness. This is also the meaning demanded by the parable in vv 41-43.

8, 1-3: Luke presents Jesus as an itinerant preacher traveling in the company of the Twelve and of the Galilean women who are sustaining them out of their means. These Galilean women will later accompany Jesus on his journey to Jerusalem and become witnesses to his death (Lk 23, 49) and resurrection (Lk 24, 9-11, where Mary Magdalene and Joanna are specifically mentioned; cf also Acts 1, 14). The association of women with the ministry of Jesus is most unusual in the light of the attitude of first-century Palestinian Judaism toward women. The more common attitude is expressed in Jn 4, 27, and early rabbinic documents caution against speaking with women in public.

8, 4-21: The focus in this section is on how one should hear the word of God and act on it. It includes the parable of the sower and its explanation (4-15), a collection of sayings on how one should act on the word that is heard (16-18), and the identification of the mother and brothers of Jesus as the ones who hear the word and act on it (19-21). See also the notes on Mt 13, 1-53 and Mk 4, 1-34.

8, 4-8: See the note on Mt 13, 3-8.

8, 11-15: On the interpretation of the parable of the sower, see the note on Mt 13, 18-23.

seed is the word of God.[i] [12]Those on the path are the ones who have heard, but the devil comes and takes away the word from their hearts that they may not believe and be saved. [13]Those on rocky ground are the ones who, when they hear, receive the word with joy, but they have no root; they believe only for a time and fall away in time of trial. [14]As for the seed that fell among thorns, they are the ones who have heard, but as they go along, they are choked by the anxieties and riches and pleasures of life, and they fail to produce mature fruit. [15]But as for the seed that fell on rich soil, they are the ones who, when they have heard the word, embrace it with a generous and good heart, and bear fruit through perseverance.

The Parable of the Lamp.* [16] [j] "No one who lights a lamp conceals it with a vessel or sets it under a bed; rather, he places it on a lampstand so that those who enter may see the light.[k] [17]For there is nothing hidden that will not become visible, and nothing secret that will not be known and come to light.[l] [18]Take care, then, how you hear. To anyone who has, more will be given, and from the one who has not, even what he seems to have will be taken away."[m]

Jesus and His Family.*[n] [19]Then his mother and his brothers* came to him but were unable to join him because of the crowd. [20] [o] He was told, "Your mother and your brothers are standing outside and they wish to see you." [21]He said to them in reply, "My mother and my brothers are those who hear the word of God and act on it."*

The Calming of a Storm at Sea.[p] [22] * One day he got into a boat with his disciples and said to them, "Let us cross to the other side of the lake." So they set sail, [23]and while they were sailing he fell asleep. A squall blew over the lake, and they were taking in water and were in danger. [24]They came and woke him saying, "Master, master, we are perishing!" He awakened, rebuked the wind and the waves, and they subsided and there was a calm. [25]Then he asked them, "Where is your faith?" But they were filled with awe and amazed and said to one another, "Who then is this, who commands even the winds and the sea, and they obey him?"

The Healing of the Gerasene Demoniac.[q] [26]Then they sailed to the territory of the Gerasenes,* which is opposite Galilee. [27]When he came ashore a man from the town who was possessed by demons met him. For a long time he had not worn clothes; he did not live in a house, but lived among the tombs. [28] [r] When he saw Jesus, he cried out and fell down before him; in a loud voice he shouted, "What have you to do with me, Jesus, son of the Most High God? I beg you, do not torment me!" [29]For he had ordered the unclean spirit to come out of the man. (It had taken hold of him many times, and he used to be bound with chains and shackles as a restraint, but he would break his bonds and be driven by the demon into deserted places.) [30]Then Jesus asked him, "What is your name?"* He replied, "Legion," because many demons had entered him. [31]And they pleaded with him not to order them to depart to the abyss.*

[32]A herd of many swine was feeding there on the hillside, and they pleaded with

---

i 1 Pt 1, 23.—j 16-18: Mk 4, 21-25.—k Lk 11, 33; Mt 5, 15.—l Lk 12, 2; Mt 10, 26.—m Lk 19, 26; Mt 13, 12; 25, 29.— n 19-21: Mt 12, 46-50; Mk 3, 31-35.—o 20-21: Lk 11, 27-28.— p 22-25: Mt 8, 18.23-27; Mk 4, 35-41.—q 26-39: Mt 8, 28-34; Mk 5, 1-20.—r 28-29: Lk 4, 33-35; Mt 8, 29; Mk 1, 23-24.

8, 16-18: These sayings continue the theme of responding to the word of God. Those who hear the word must become a light to others (16); even the mysteries of the kingdom that have been made known to the disciples (9-10) must come to light (17); a generous and persevering response to the word of God leads to a still more perfect response to the word.

8, 19: *His brothers:* see the note on Mk 6, 3.

8, 21: The family of Jesus is not constituted by physical relationship with him but by obedience to the word of God. In this, Luke agrees with the Marcan parallel (Mk 3, 31-35), although by omitting Mk 3, 33 and especially Mk 3, 20-21 Luke has softened the Marcan picture of Jesus' natural family. Probably he did this because Mary has already been presented in Lk 1, 38 as the obedient handmaid of the Lord who fulfills the requirement for belonging to the eschatological family of Jesus; cf also Lk 11, 27-28.

8, 22-56: This section records four miracles of Jesus that manifest his power and authority: (1) the calming of a storm on the lake (22-25); (2) the exorcism of a demoniac (26-39); (3) the cure of a hemorrhaging woman (40-48); (4) the raising of Jairus's daughter to life (49-56). They parallel the same sequence of stories at Mk 4, 35—5, 43.

8, 26: *Gerasenes:* other manuscripts read Gadarenes or Gergesenes. See also the note on Mt 8, 28. *Opposite Galilee:* probably Gentile territory (note the presence in the area of pigs—unclean animals to Jews) and an indication that the person who receives salvation (36) is a Gentile.

8, 30: *What is your name?:* the question reflects the popular belief that knowledge of the spirit's name brought control over the spirit. *Legion:* to Jesus' question the demon replies with a Latin word transliterated into Greek. The Roman legion at this period consisted of 5,000 to 6,000 foot soldiers; hence the name implies a very large number of demons.

8, 31: *Abyss:* the place of the dead (Rom 10, 7) or the prison of Satan (Rv 20, 3) or the subterranean "watery deep" that symbolizes the chaos before the order imposed by creation (Gn 1, 2).

him to allow them to enter those swine; and he let them. ³³ The demons came out of the man and entered the swine, and the herd rushed down the steep bank into the lake and was drowned. ³⁴ When the swineherds saw what had happened, they ran away and reported the incident in the town and throughout the countryside. ³⁵ People came out to see what had happened and, when they approached Jesus, they discovered the man from whom the demons had come out sitting at his feet.* He was clothed and in his right mind, and they were seized with fear. ³⁶ Those who witnessed it told them how the possessed man had been saved. ³⁷ The entire population of the region of the Gerasenes asked Jesus to leave them because they were seized with great fear. So he got into a boat and returned. ³⁸ The man from whom the demons had come out begged to remain with him, but he sent him away, saying, ³⁹ "Return home and recount what God has done for you." The man went off and proclaimed throughout the whole town what Jesus had done for him.

Jairus's Daughter and the Woman with a Hemorrhage.* ⁴⁰ ˢ When Jesus returned, the crowd welcomed him, for they were all waiting for him. ⁴¹ And a man named Jairus, an official of the synagogue, came forward. He fell at the feet of Jesus and begged him to come to his house, ⁴² because he had an only daughter,* about twelve years old, and she was dying. As he went, the crowds almost crushed him. ⁴³ And a woman afflicted with hemorrhages for twelve years,* who [had spent her whole livelihood on doctors and] was unable to be cured by anyone, ⁴⁴ came up behind him and touched the tassel on his cloak. Immediately her bleeding stopped. ⁴⁵ Jesus then asked, "Who touched me?" While all were denying it, Peter said, "Master, the crowds are pushing and pressing in upon you." ⁴⁶ But Jesus said, "Someone has touched me; for I know that power has gone out from me." ᵗ ⁴⁷ When the woman realized that she had not escaped notice, she came forward trembling. Falling down before him, she explained in the presence of all the people why she had touched him and how she had been healed immediately. ⁴⁸ He said to her, "Daughter, your faith has saved you; go in peace." ᵘ

⁴⁹ While he was still speaking, someone from the synagogue official's house arrived and said, "Your daughter is dead; do not trouble the teacher any longer." ⁵⁰ On hearing this, Jesus answered him, "Do not be afraid; just have faith and she will be saved." ⁵¹ When he arrived at the house he allowed no one to enter with him except Peter and John and James, and the child's father and mother. ⁵² ᵛ All were weeping and mourning for her, when he said, "Do not weep any longer, for she is not dead, but sleeping."* ⁵³ And they ridiculed him, because they knew that she was dead. ⁵⁴ But he took her by the hand and called to her, "Child, arise!" ⁵⁵ Her breath returned and she immediately arose. He then directed that she should be given something to eat. ⁵⁶ Her parents were astounded, and he instructed them to tell no one what had happened.

CHAPTER 9

The Mission of the Twelve.* ¹ ʷ He summoned the Twelve and gave them power and authority over all demons and to cure diseases, ² and he sent them to proclaim the kingdom of God and to heal [the sick]. ³ He said to them, "Take nothing for the journey,* neither walking stick, nor sack, nor food, nor money, and let no one take a second tunic. ⁴ Whatever house you enter,

---

s 40-56: Mt 9, 18-26; Mk 5, 21-43.—t Lk 6, 19.—u Lk 7, 50; 17, 19; 18, 42.—v Lk 7, 13.—w 1-6: Mt 10, 1.5-15; Mk 6, 7-13.

8, 35: *Sitting at his feet:* the former demoniac takes the position of a disciple before the master (Lk 10, 39; Acts 22, 3).

8, 40-56: Two interwoven miracle stories, one a healing and the other a resuscitation, present Jesus as master over sickness and death. In the Lucan account, faith in Jesus is responsible for the cure (48) and for the raising to life (50).

8, 42: *An only daughter:* cf the son of the widow of Nain whom Luke describes as an "only" son (Lk 7, 12; see also Lk 9, 38).

8, 43: *Afflicted with hemorrhages for twelve years:* according to the Mosaic law (Lv 15, 25-30) this condition would render the woman unclean and unfit for contact with other people.

8, 52: *Sleeping:* her death is a temporary condition; cf Jn 11, 11-14.

9, 1-6: Armed with the power and authority that Jesus himself has been displaying in the previous episodes, the Twelve are now sent out to continue the work that Jesus has been performing throughout his Galilean ministry: (1) proclaiming the kingdom (Lk 4, 43; 8, 1); (2) exorcising demons (Lk 4, 33-37.41; 8, 26-39) and (3) healing the sick (Lk 4, 38-40; 5, 12-16.17-26; 6, 6-10; 7, 1-10.17.22; 8, 40-56).

9, 3: *Take nothing for the journey:* the absolute detachment required of the disciple (Lk 14, 33) leads to complete reliance on God (Lk 12, 22-31).

stay there and leave from there.ˣ ⁵And as for those who do not welcome you, when you leave that town, shake the dust from your feet* in testimony against them."ʸ ⁶Then they set out and went from village to village proclaiming the good news and curing diseases everywhere.

Herod's Opinion of Jesus.ᶻ ⁷ * Herod the tetrarch* heard about all that was happening, and he was greatly perplexed because some were saying, "John has been raised from the dead";ᵃ ⁸ others were saying, "Elijah has appeared"; still others, "One of the ancient prophets has arisen." ⁹ ᵇ But Herod said, "John I beheaded. Who then is this about whom I hear such things?" And he kept trying to see him.*

The Return of the Twelve and the Feeding of the Five Thousand.ᶜ ¹⁰When the apostles returned, they explained to him what they had done. He took them and withdrew in private to a town called Bethsaida. ¹¹The crowds, meanwhile, learned of this and followed him. He received them and spoke to them about the kingdom of God, and he healed those who needed to be cured. ¹²As the day was drawing to a close, the Twelve approached him and said, "Dismiss the crowd so that they can go to the surrounding villages and farms and find lodging and provisions; for we are in a deserted place here." ¹³ ᵈ He said to them, "Give them some food yourselves." They replied, "Five loaves and two fish are all we have, unless we ourselves go and buy food for all these people." ¹⁴Now the men there numbered about five thousand. Then he said to his disciples, "Have them sit down in groups of [about] fifty." ¹⁵They did so and

made them all sit down. ¹⁶Then taking* the five loaves and the two fish, and looking up to heaven, he said the blessing over them, broke them, and gave them to the disciples to set before the crowd.ᵉ ¹⁷They all ate and were satisfied. And when the leftover fragments were picked up, they filled twelve wicker baskets.

Peter's Confession about Jesus.*¹⁸ ᶠ Once when Jesus was praying in solitude,* and the disciples were with him, he asked them, "Who do the crowds say that I am?" ¹⁹They said in reply, "John the Baptist; others, Elijah; still others, 'One of the ancient prophets has arisen.' "ᵍ ²⁰Then he said to them, "But who do you say that I am?" Peter said in reply, "The Messiah of God."* ²¹He rebuked them and directed them not to tell this to anyone.

The First Prediction of the Passion. ²²He said, "The Son of Man must suffer greatly and be rejected by the elders, the chief priests, and the scribes, and be killed and on the third day be raised."ʰ

The Conditions of Discipleship. ⁱ ²³Then he said to all, "If anyone wishes to come after me, he must deny himself and take up his cross daily* and follow me.ʲ ²⁴For whoever wishes to save his life will lose it, but whoever loses his life for my sake will save it.ᵏ ²⁵What profit is there for one to gain the whole world yet lose or forfeit himself? ²⁶Whoever is ashamed of me and of my words, the Son of Man will be ashamed of when he comes in his glory and in the glory of the Father and of the holy angels.ˡ ²⁷Truly I say to you, there are

---

x Lk 10, 5-7.—y Lk 10, 10-11; Acts 13, 51.—z 7-9: Mt 14, 1-12; Mk 6, 14-29.—a 7-8: Lk 9, 19; Mt 16, 14; Mk 8, 28.—b Lk 23, 8.—c 10-17: Mt 14, 13-21; Mk 6, 30-44; Jn 6, 1-14.—d 13-17: 2 Kgs 4, 42-44.—e Lk 22, 19; 24, 30-31; Acts 2, 42; 20, 11; 27, 35.—f 18-21: Mt 16, 13-20; Mk 8, 27-30.—g Lk 9, 7-8.—h Lk 24, 7.26; Mt 16, 21; 20, 18-19; Mk 8, 31; 10, 33-34.—i 23-27: Mt 16, 24-28; Mk 8, 34—9, 1.—j Lk 14, 27; Mt 10, 38.—k Lk 17, 33; Mt 10, 39; Jn 12, 25.—l Lk 12, 9; Mt 10, 33; 2 Tm 2, 12.

9, 5: *Shake the dust from your feet:* see the note on Mt 10, 14.

9, 7-56: This section in which Luke gathers together incidents that focus on the identity of Jesus is introduced by a question that Herod is made to ask in this gospel: "Who then is this about whom I hear such things?" (9). In subsequent episodes, Luke reveals to the reader various answers to Herod's question: Jesus is one in whom God's power is present and who provides for the needs of God's people (10-17); Peter declares Jesus to be "the Messiah of God" (18-21); Jesus says he is the suffering Son of Man (22.43-45); Jesus is the Master to be followed, even to death (23-27); Jesus is God's Son, his Chosen One (28-36).

9, 7: *Herod the tetrarch:* see the note on Lk 3, 1.

9, 9: *And he kept trying to see him:* this indication of Herod's interest in Jesus prepares for Lk 13, 31-33 and for Lk 23, 8-12 where Herod's curiosity about Jesus' power to perform miracles remains unsatisfied.

9, 16: *Then taking . . . .:* the actions of Jesus recall the institution of the Eucharist in Lk 22, 19; see also the note on Mt 14, 19.

9, 18-22: This incident is based on Mk 8, 27-33, but Luke has eliminated Peter's refusal to accept Jesus as suffering Son of Man (Mk 8, 32) and the rebuke of Peter by Jesus (Mk 8, 33). Elsewhere in the gospel, Luke softens the harsh portrait of Peter and the other apostles found in his Marcan source (cf Lk 22, 39-46, which similarly lacks a rebuke of Peter that occurs in the source, Mk 8, 37-38).

9, 18: *When Jesus was praying in solitude:* see the note on Lk 3, 21.

9, 20: *The Messiah of God:* on the meaning of this title in first-century Palestinian Judaism, see the notes on Lk 2, 11 and on Mt 16, 13-20 and Mk 8, 27-30.

9, 23: *Daily:* this is a Lucan addition to a saying of Jesus, removing the saying from a context that envisioned the imminent suffering and death of the disciple of Jesus (as does the saying in Mk 8, 34-35) to one that focuses on the demands of daily Christian existence.

some standing here who will not taste death until they see the kingdom of God."

The Transfiguration of Jesus.* [28] [m] About eight days after he said this, he took Peter, John, and James and went up the mountain to pray.* [29] While he was praying his face changed in appearance and his clothing became dazzling white. [30] And behold, two men were conversing with him, Moses and Elijah,* [31] [n] who appeared in glory and spoke of his exodus that he was going to accomplish in Jerusalem.* [32] Peter and his companions had been overcome by sleep, but becoming fully awake, they saw his glory* and the two men standing with him. [o] [33] As they were about to part from him, Peter said to Jesus, "Master, it is good that we are here; let us make three tents,* one for you, one for Moses, and one for Elijah." But he did not know what he was saying. [34] While he was still speaking, a cloud came and cast a shadow over them,* and they became frightened when they entered the cloud. [35] [p] Then from the cloud came a voice that said, "This is my chosen Son; listen to him."* [36] After the voice had spoken, Jesus was found alone. They fell silent and did not at that time* tell anyone what they had seen.

The Healing of a Boy with a Demon.* [37] [q] On the next day, when they came down from the mountain, a large crowd met him. [38] There was a man in the crowd who cried out, "Teacher, I beg you, look at my son; he is my only child. [39] For a spirit seizes him and he suddenly screams and it con-

vulses him until he foams at the mouth; it releases him only with difficulty, wearing him out. [40] I begged your disciples to cast it out but they could not." [41] Jesus said in reply, "O faithless and perverse generation, how long will I be with you and endure you? Bring your son here." [42] As he was coming forward, the demon threw him to the ground in a convulsion; but Jesus rebuked the unclean spirit, healed the boy, and returned him to his father. [43] And all were astonished by the majesty of God.

The Second Prediction of the Passion. [r] While they were all amazed at his every deed, he said to his disciples, [44] "Pay attention to what I am telling you. The Son of Man is to be handed over to men." [45] But they did not understand this saying; its meaning was hidden from them so that they should not understand it, and they were afraid to ask him about this saying.

The Greatest in the Kingdom. [s] [46] * An argument arose among the disciples about which of them was the greatest. [t] [47] Jesus realized the intention of their hearts and took a child and placed it by his side [48] and said to them, "Whoever receives this child in my name receives me, and whoever receives me receives the one who sent me. For the one who is least among all of you is the one who is the greatest." [u]

Another Exorcist. [v] [49] Then John said in reply, "Master, we saw someone casting out demons in your name and we tried to prevent him because he does not follow in our company." [50] Jesus said to him, "Do not prevent him, for whoever is not against you is for you."

---

m 28-36: Mt 17, 1-8; Mk 9, 2-8.—n Lk 9, 22; 13, 33.—o Jn 1, 14; 2 Pt 1, 16.—p Lk 3, 22; Dt 18, 15; Ps 2, 7; Is 42, 1; Mt 3, 17; 12, 18; Mk 1, 11; 2 Pt 1, 17-18.—q 37-43: Mt 17, 14-18; Mk 9, 14-27.—r 43-45: Lk 18, 32-34; Mt 17, 22-23; Mk 9, 30-32.—s 46-48: Mt 18, 1-5; Mk 9, 33-37.—t Lk 22, 24.—u Lk 10, 16; Mt 10, 40; Jn 13, 20.—v 49-50: Mk 9, 38-40.

9, 28-36: Situated shortly after the first announcement of the passion, death, and resurrection, this scene of Jesus' transfiguration provides the heavenly confirmation to Jesus' declaration that his suffering will end in glory (32); see also the notes on Mt 17, 1-8 and Mk 9, 2-8.

9, 28: *Up the mountain to pray:* the "mountain" is the regular place of prayer in Lk (see Lk 6, 12; 22, 39-41).

9, 30: *Moses and Elijah:* the two figures represent the Old Testament law and the prophets. At the end of this episode, the heavenly voice will identify Jesus as the one to be listened to now (35). See also the note on Mk 9, 5.

9, 31: *His exodus that he was going to accomplish in Jerusalem:* Luke identifies the subject of the conversation as the *exodus* of Jesus, a reference to the death, resurrection, and ascension of Jesus that will take place in Jerusalem, the city of destiny (see Lk 9, 51). The mention of *exodus,* however, also calls to mind the Israelite Exodus from Egypt to the promised land.

9, 32: *They saw his glory:* the *glory* that is proper to God is here attributed to Jesus (see Lk 24, 26).

9, 33: *Let us make three tents:* in a possible allusion to the feast of Tabernacles, Peter may be likening his joy on the occasion of the transfiguration to the joyful celebration of this harvest festival.

9, 34: *Over them:* it is not clear whether *them* refers to Jesus, Moses, and Elijah, or to the disciples. For the cloud casting its shadow, see the note on Mk 9, 7.

9, 35: Like the heavenly voice that identified Jesus at his baptism prior to his undertaking the Galilean ministry (Lk 3, 22), so too here before the journey to the city of destiny is begun (51) the heavenly voice again identifies Jesus as Son. *Listen to him:* the two representatives of Israel of old depart (33) and Jesus is left alone (36) as the teacher whose words must be heeded (see also Acts 3, 22).

9, 36: *At that time:* i.e., before the resurrection.

9, 37-43a: See the note on Mk 9, 14-29.

9, 46-50: These two incidents focus on attitudes that are opposed to Christian discipleship: rivalry and intolerance of outsiders.

V. THE JOURNEY TO JERUSALEM: LUKE'S TRAVEL NARRATIVE*

Departure for Jerusalem; Samaritan Inhospitality. [51] * When the days for his being taken up* were fulfilled, he resolutely determined to journey to Jerusalem,[w] [52] and he sent messengers ahead of him.[x] On the way they entered a Samaritan* village to prepare for his reception there, [53] but they would not welcome him because the destination of his journey was Jerusalem. [54] When the disciples James and John saw this they asked, "Lord, do you want us to call down fire from heaven to consume them?"[y] [55] Jesus turned and rebuked them, [56] and they journeyed to another village.

The Would-be Followers of Jesus.* [57] [z] As they were proceeding on their journey someone said to him, "I will follow you wherever you go." [58] Jesus answered him, "Foxes have dens and birds of the sky have nests, but the Son of Man has nowhere to rest his head." [59] And to another he said, "Follow me." But he replied, "[Lord,] let me go first and bury my father." [60] But he answered him, "Let the dead bury their dead.* But you, go and proclaim the kingdom of God." [61] [a] And another said, "I will follow you, Lord, but first let me say farewell to my family at home." [62] [To him] Jesus said, "No one who sets a hand to the plow and looks to what was left behind is fit for the kingdom of God."

CHAPTER 10

The Mission of the Seventy-two.* [1] After this the Lord appointed seventy[-two]* others whom he sent ahead of him in pairs to every town and place he intended to visit.[b] [2] He said to them, "The harvest is abundant but the laborers are few; so ask the master of the harvest to send out laborers for his harvest.[c] [3] Go on your way; behold, I am sending you like lambs among wolves.[d] [4] Carry no money bag,[e] no sack, no sandals;[f] and greet no one along the way.* [5] Into whatever house you enter, first say, 'Peace to this household.'* [6] If a peaceful person* lives there, your peace will rest on him; but if not, it will return to you. [7] Stay in the same house and eat and drink what is offered to you, for the la-

---

w Lk 9, 53; 13, 22.33; 17, 11; 18, 31; 19, 28; 24, 51; Acts 1, 2.9-11.22.—x Mal 3, 1.—y 2 Kgs 1, 10.12.—z 57-60: Mt 8, 19-22.—a 61-62: 1 Kgs 19, 20.—b Mk 6, 7.—c Mt 9, 37-38; Jn 4, 35.—d Mt 10, 16.—e Lk 9, 3; 2 Kgs 4, 29.—f 4-11: Mt 10, 7-14.

9, 51—18, 14: The Galilean ministry of Jesus finishes with the previous episode and a new section of Luke's gospel begins, the journey to Jerusalem. This journey is based on Mk 10, 1-52, but Luke uses his Marcan source only in Lk 18, 15—19, 27. Before that point he has inserted into his gospel a distinctive collection of sayings of Jesus and stories about him that he has drawn from Q, a collection of sayings of Jesus used also by Matthew, and from his own special traditions. All of the material collected in this section is loosely organized within the framework of a journey of Jesus to Jerusalem, the city of destiny, where his exodus (suffering, death, resurrection, ascension) is to take place (Lk 9, 31), where salvation is accomplished, and from where the proclamation of God's saving word is to go forth (Lk 24, 47; Acts 1, 8). Much of the material in the Lucan travel narrative is teaching for the disciples. During the course of this journey Jesus is preparing his chosen Galilean witnesses for the role they will play after his exodus (Lk 9, 31): they are to be his witnesses to the people (Acts 10, 39; 13, 31) and thereby provide certainty to the readers of Luke's gospel that the teachings they have received are rooted in the teachings of Jesus (Lk 1, 1-4).

9, 51-55: Just as the Galilean ministry began with a rejection of Jesus in his hometown, so too the travel narrative begins with the rejection of him by Samaritans. In this episode Jesus disassociates himself from the attitude expressed by his disciples that those who reject him are to be punished severely. The story alludes to 2 Kgs 1,10.12, where the prophet Elijah takes the course of action Jesus rejects, and Jesus thereby rejects the identification of himself with Elijah.

9, 51: *Days for his being taken up:* like the reference to his exodus in v 31, this is probably a reference to all the events (suffering, death, resurrection, ascension) of his last days in Jerusalem. *He resolutely determined:* literally, "he set his face."

9, 52: *Samaritan:* Samaria was the territory between Judea and Galilee west of the Jordan river. For ethnic and religious reasons, the Samaritans and the Jews were bitterly opposed to one another (see Jn 4, 9).

9, 57-62: In these sayings Jesus speaks of the severity and the unconditional nature of Christian discipleship. Even family ties and filial obligations, such as burying one's parents, cannot distract one no matter how briefly from proclaiming the kingdom of God. The first two sayings are paralleled in Mt 8, 19-22; see also the notes there.

9, 60: *Let the dead bury their dead:* i.e., let the spiritually dead (those who do not follow) bury their physically dead. See also the note on Mt 8, 22.

10, 1-12: Only the Gospel of Luke contains two episodes in which Jesus sends out his followers on a mission: the first (Lk 9,1-6) is based on the mission in Mk 6, 6b-13 and recounts the sending out of the Twelve; here in vv 1-12 a similar report based on Q becomes the sending out of seventy-two in this gospel. The episode continues the theme of Jesus preparing witnesses to himself and his ministry. These witnesses include not only the Twelve but also the seventy-two who may represent the Christian mission in Luke's own day. Note that the instructions given to the Twelve and to the seventy-two are similar and that what is said to the seventy-two in v 4 is directed to the Twelve in Lk 22, 35.

10, 1: *Seventy[-two]:* important representatives of the Alexandrian and Caesarean text types read "seventy," while other important Alexandrian texts and Western readings have "seventy-two."

10, 4: *Carry no money bag . . . greet no one along the way:* because of the urgency of the mission and the singlemindedness required of missionaries, attachment to material possessions should be avoided and even customary greetings should not distract from the fulfillment of the task.

10, 5: *First say, 'Peace to this household':* see the notes on Lk 2, 14 and Mt 10, 13.

10, 6: *A peaceful person:* literally, "a son of peace."

borer deserves his payment. Do not move about from one house to another.[g] [8]Whatever town you enter and they welcome you, eat what is set before you,[h] [9]cure the sick in it and say to them, 'The kingdom of God is at hand for you.'[i] [10]Whatever town you enter and they do not receive you, go out into the streets and say,[j] [11]'The dust of your town that clings to our feet, even that we shake off against you.' Yet know this: the kingdom of God is at hand.[k] [12]I tell you, it will be more tolerable for Sodom on that day than for that town.[l]

Reproaches to Unrepentant Towns.* [13] [m] "Woe to you, Chorazin! Woe to you, Bethsaida![n] For if the mighty deeds done in your midst had been done in Tyre and Sidon, they would long ago have repented, sitting in sackcloth and ashes. [14]But it will be more tolerable for Tyre and Sidon at the judgment than for you. [15] [o] And as for you, Capernaum, 'Will you be exalted to heaven? You will go down to the netherworld.'* [16]Whoever listens to you listens to me. Whoever rejects you rejects me. And whoever rejects me rejects the one who sent me."[p]

Return of the Seventy-two. [17]The seventy[-two] returned rejoicing, and said, "Lord, even the demons are subject to us because of your name." [18]Jesus said, "I have observed Satan fall like lightning* from the sky.[q] [19]Behold, I have given you the power 'to tread upon serpents' and scorpions and upon the full force of the enemy and nothing will harm you.[r] [20]Nevertheless, do not rejoice because the spirits are subject to you, but rejoice because your names are written in heaven."[s]

Praise of the Father.[t] [21]At that very moment he rejoiced [in] the holy Spirit and said, "I give you praise, Father, Lord of heaven and earth, for although you have hidden these things from the wise and the learned you have revealed them to the childlike.* Yes, Father, such has been your gracious will.[u] [22]All things have been handed over to me by my Father. No one knows who the Son is except the Father, and who the Father is except the Son and anyone to whom the Son wishes to reveal him."[v]

The Privileges of Discipleship.[w] [23]Turning to the disciples in private he said, "Blessed are the eyes that see what you see. [24]For I say to you, many prophets and kings desired to see what you see, but did not see it, and to hear what you hear, but did not hear it."

The Greatest Commandment.[x] [25] * There was a scholar of the law* who stood up to test him and said, "Teacher, what must I do to inherit eternal life?"[y] [26]Jesus said to him, "What is written in the law? How do you read it?" [27]He said in reply, "You shall love the Lord, your God, with all your heart, with all your being, with all your strength, and with all your mind, and your neighbor as yourself."[z] [28]He replied to him, "You have answered correctly; do this and you will live."[a]

The Parable of the Good Samaritan. [29]But because he wished to justify himself, he said to Jesus, "And who is my neighbor?" [30]Jesus replied, "A man fell victim to robbers as he went down from Jerusalem to Jericho. They stripped and beat him and went off leaving him half-dead. [31] * A priest happened to be going down that

g Lk 9, 4; Mt 10, 10; 1 Cor 9, 6-14; 1 Tm 5, 18.—h 1 Cor 10, 27.—i Mt 3, 2; 4, 17; Mk 1, 15.—j 10-11: Lk 9, 5.—k Acts 13, 51; 18, 6.—l Mt 10, 15; 11, 24.—m 13-15: Mt 11, 20-24.—n 13-14: Is 23; Ez 26—28; Jl 3, 4-8; Am 1, 1-10; Zec 9, 2-4.—o Is 14, 13-15.—p Mt 10, 40; Jn 5, 23; 13, 20; 15, 23.—q Is 14, 12; Jn 12, 31; Rv 12, 7-12.—r Ps 19, 13; Mk 16, 18.—s Ex 32, 32; Dn 12, 1; Mt 7, 22; Phil 4, 3; Heb 12, 23; Rv 3, 5; 21, 27.—t 21-22: Mt 11, 25-27.—u 1 Cor 1, 26-28.—v Jn 3, 35; 10, 15.—w 23-24: Mt 13, 16-17.—x 25-28: Mt 22, 34-40; Mk 12, 28-34.—y Lk 18, 18; Mt 19, 16; Mk 10, 17.—z Lv 19, 18; Dt 6, 5; 10, 12; Jos 22, 5; Mt 19, 19; 22, 37-39; Rom 13, 9; Gal 5, 14; Jas 2, 8.—a Lv 18, 5; Prv 19, 16; Rom 10, 5; Gal 3, 12.

10, 13-16: The call to repentance that is a part of the proclamation of the kingdom brings with it a severe judgment for those who hear it and reject it.

10, 15: *The netherworld:* the underworld, the place of the dead (Acts 2, 27.31), here contrasted with heaven; see also the note on Mt 11, 23.

10, 18: *I have observed Satan fall like lightning:* the effect of the mission of the seventy-two is characterized by the Lucan Jesus as a symbolic fall of Satan. As the kingdom of God is gradually being established, evil in all its forms is being defeated; the dominion of Satan over humanity is at an end.

10, 21: *Revealed them to the childlike:* a restatement of the theme announced in Lk 8, 10: the mysteries of the kingdom are revealed to the disciples. See also the note on Mt 11, 25-27.

10, 25-37: In response to a question from a Jewish legal expert about inheriting eternal life, Jesus illustrates the superiority of love over legalism through the story of the good Samaritan. The law of love proclaimed in the "Sermon on the Plain" (Lk 6, 27-36) is exemplified by one whom the legal expert would have considered ritually impure (see Jn 4, 9). Moreover, the identity of the "neighbor" requested by the legal expert (29) turns out to be a Samaritan, the enemy of the Jew (see the note on Lk 9, 52).

10, 25: *Scholar of the law:* an expert in the Mosaic law, and probably a member of the group elsewhere identified as the scribes (Lk 5, 21).

10, 31-32: *Priest . . . Levite:* those religious representatives of Judaism who would have been expected to be models of "neighbor" to the victim pass him by.

road, but when he saw him, he passed by on the opposite side. [32] Likewise a Levite came to the place, and when he saw him, he passed by on the opposite side. [33] But a Samaritan traveler who came upon him was moved with compassion at the sight. [34] He approached the victim, poured oil and wine over his wounds and bandaged them. Then he lifted him up on his own animal, took him to an inn and cared for him. [35] The next day he took out two silver coins and gave them to the innkeeper with the instruction, 'Take care of him. If you spend more than what I have given you, I shall repay you on my way back.' [36] Which of these three, in your opinion, was neighbor to the robbers' victim?" [37] He answered, "The one who treated him with mercy." Jesus said to him, "Go and do likewise."

Martha and Mary. * [38] *b* As they continued their journey he entered a village where a woman whose name was Martha welcomed him. [39] She had a sister named Mary [who] sat beside the Lord at his feet* listening to

---

b 38-39: Jn 11, 1; 12, 2-3.—c 1-4: Mt 6, 9-15.—d 5-8: Lk 18, 1-5.—e 9-13: Mt 7, 7-11.—f Mt 21, 22; Mk 11, 24; Jn 14, 13; 15, 7; 1 Jn 5, 14-15.

10, 38-42: The story of Martha and Mary further illustrates the importance of hearing the words of the teacher and the concern with women in Lk.

10, 39: *Sat beside the Lord at his feet:* it is remarkable for first-century Palestinian Judaism that a woman would assume the posture of a disciple at the master's feet (see also Lk 8, 35; Acts 22, 3), and it reveals a characteristic attitude of Jesus toward women in this gospel (see Lk 8, 2-3).

10, 42: *There is need of only one thing:* some ancient versions read, "there is need of few things"; another important, although probably inferior, reading found in some manuscripts is, "there is need of few things, or of one."

11, 1-13: Luke presents three episodes concerned with prayer. The first (1-4) recounts Jesus teaching his disciples the Christian communal prayer, the "Our Father"; the second (5-8), the importance of persistence in prayer; the third (9-13), the effectiveness of prayer.

11, 1-4: The Matthean form of the "Our Father" occurs in the "Sermon on the Mount" (Mt 6, 9-15); the shorter Lucan version is presented while Jesus is at prayer (see the note on Lk 3, 21) and his disciples ask him to teach them to pray just as John taught his disciples to pray. In answer to their question, Jesus presents them with an example of a Christian communal prayer that stresses the fatherhood of God and acknowledges him as the one to whom the Christian disciple owes daily sustenance (3), forgiveness (4), and deliverance from the final trial (4). See also the notes on Mt 6, 9-13.

11, 2: *Your kingdom come:* in place of this petition, some early church Fathers record: "May your holy Spirit come upon us and cleanse us," a petition that may reflect the use of the "Our Father" in a baptismal liturgy.

11, 3-4: *Daily bread:* see the note on Mt 6, 11. *The final test:* see the note on Mt 6, 13.

11, 13: *The holy Spirit:* this is a Lucan editorial alteration of a traditional saying of Jesus (see Mt 7, 11). Luke presents the gift of the holy Spirit as the response of the Father to the prayer of the Christian disciple.

---

him speak. [40] Martha, burdened with much serving, came to him and said, "Lord, do you not care that my sister has left me by myself to do the serving? Tell her to help me." [41] The Lord said to her in reply, "Martha, Martha, you are anxious and worried about many things. [42] There is need of only one thing.* Mary has chosen the better part and it will not be taken from her."

CHAPTER 11

The Lord's Prayer. *c* [1] * He was praying in a certain place, and when he had finished, one of his disciples said to him, "Lord, teach us to pray just as John taught his disciples."* [2] He said to them, "When you pray, say:

> Father, hallowed be your name,
> your kingdom come.*
> [3] Give us each day our daily bread*
> [4] and forgive us our sins
> for we ourselves forgive everyone in debt to us,
> and do not subject us to the final test."

Further Teachings on Prayer. *d* [5] And he said to them, "Suppose one of you has a friend to whom he goes at midnight and says, 'Friend, lend me three loaves of bread, [6] for a friend of mine has arrived at my house from a journey and I have nothing to offer him,' [7] and he says in reply from within, 'Do not bother me; the door has already been locked and my children and I are already in bed. I cannot get up to give you anything.' [8] I tell you, if he does not get up to give him the loaves because of their friendship, he will get up to give him whatever he needs because of his persistence.

The Answer to Prayer. *e* [9] "And I tell you, ask and you will receive; seek and you will find; knock and the door will be opened to you.* [10] For everyone who asks, receives; and the one who seeks, finds; and to the one who knocks, the door will be opened. [11] What father among you would hand his son a snake when he asks for a fish? [12] Or hand him a scorpion when he asks for an egg? [13] If you then, who are wicked, know how to give good gifts to your children, how much more will the Father in heaven give the holy Spirit* to those who ask him?"

Lk

Jesus and Beelzebul. [g] 14 He was driving out a demon [that was] mute, and when the demon had gone out, the mute person spoke and the crowds were amazed. 15 Some of them said, "By the power of Beelzebul, the prince of demons, he drives out demons." [h] 16 Others, to test him, asked him for a sign from heaven. [i] 17 But he knew their thoughts and said to them, "Every kingdom divided against itself will be laid waste and house will fall against house. 18 And if Satan is divided against himself, how will his kingdom stand? For you say that it is by Beelzebul that I drive out demons. 19 If I, then, drive out demons by Beelzebul, by whom do your own people* drive them out? Therefore they will be your judges. 20 But if it is by the finger of God that [I] drive out demons, then the kingdom of God has come upon you. [j] 21 When a strong man fully armed guards his palace, his possessions are safe. 22 But when one stronger* than he attacks and overcomes him, he takes away the armor on which he relied and distributes the spoils. 23 Whoever is not with me is against me, and whoever does not gather with me scatters. [k]

The Return of the Unclean Spirit. [l] 24 "When an unclean spirit goes out of someone, it roams through arid places searching for rest but, finding none, it says, 'I shall return to my home from which I came.' 25 But upon returning, it finds it swept clean and put in order. 26 Then it goes and brings back seven other spirits more wicked than itself who move in and dwell there, and the last condition of that person is worse than the first." [m]

True Blessedness. * 27 While he was speaking, a woman from the crowd called out and said to him, "Blessed is the womb that carried you and the breasts at which you nursed." [n] 28 He replied, "Rather, blessed are those who hear the word of God and observe it."

The Demand for a Sign. * 29 While still more people gathered in the crowd, he said to them, [o] "This generation is an evil generation; it seeks a sign, but no sign will be given it, except the sign of Jonah. [p] 30 Just as Jonah became a sign to the Ninevites, so will the Son of Man be to this generation. 31 At the judgment the queen of the south will rise with the men of this generation and she will condemn them, because she came from the ends of the earth to hear the wisdom of Solomon, and there is something greater than Solomon here. [q] 32 At the judgment the men of Nineveh will arise with this generation and condemn it, because at the preaching of Jonah they repented, and there is something greater than Jonah here. [r]

The Simile of Light. 33 "No one who lights a lamp hides it away or places it [under a bushel basket], but on a lampstand so that those who enter might see the light. [s] 34 The lamp of the body is your eye. [t] When your eye is sound, then your whole body is filled with light, but when it is bad, then your body is in darkness. 35 Take care, then, that the light in you not become darkness. 36 If your whole body is full of light, and no part of it is in darkness, then it will be as full of light as a lamp illuminating you with its brightness."

Denunciation of the Pharisees and Scholars of the Law. * 37 [u] After he had spoken, a Pharisee invited him to dine at his home. He entered and reclined at table to eat. [v] 38 The Pharisee was amazed to see that he did not observe the prescribed washing before the meal. [w] 39 The Lord said to him, "Oh you Pharisees! [x] Although you cleanse the outside of the cup and the dish, inside you are filled with plunder and evil. 40 You fools! Did not the maker of the outside also

g 14-23: Mt 12, 22-30; Mk 3, 20-27.—h Mt 9, 34.—i Mt 12, 38; 16, 1; Mk 8, 11; 1 Cor 1, 22.—j Ex 8, 19.—k Lk 9, 50; Mk 9, 40.—l 24-26: Mt 12, 43-45.—m Jn 5, 14.—n Lk 1, 28.42.48.—o 29-32: Mt 12, 38-42; Mk 8, 12.—p Mt 16, 1.4; Jn 6, 30; 1 Cor 1, 22.—q 1 Kgs 10, 1-10; 2 Chr 9, 1-12.—r Jon 3, 8.10.—s Lk 8, 16; Mt 5, 15; Mk 4, 21.—t 34-36: Mt 6, 22-23.— u 37-54: Lk 20, 45-47; Mt 23, 1-36; Mk 12, 38-40.—v Lk 7, 36; 14, 1.—w Mt 15, 2; Mk 7, 2-5.—x Mt 23, 25-26.

11, 19: *Your own people:* the Greek reads "your sons." Other Jewish exorcists (see Acts 19, 13-20), who recognize that the power of God is active in the exorcism, would themselves convict the accusers of Jesus. See also the note on Mt 12, 27.

11, 22: *One stronger:* i.e., Jesus. Cf Lk 3, 16 where John the Baptist identifies Jesus as "more powerful than I."

11, 27-28: The beatitude in v 28 should not be interpreted as a rebuke of the mother of Jesus; see the note on Lk 8, 21. Rather, it emphasizes (like Lk 2, 35) that attentiveness to God's word is more important than biological relationship to Jesus.

11, 29-32: The "sign of Jonah" in Lk is the preaching of the need for repentance by a prophet who comes from afar. Cf Mt 12, 38-42 (and see the notes there) where the "sign of Jonah" is interpreted by Jesus as his death and resurrection.

11, 37-54: This denunciation of the Pharisees (39-44) and the scholars of the law (45-52) is set by Luke in the context of Jesus' dining at the home of a Pharisee. Controversies with or reprimands of Pharisees are regularly set by Luke within the context of Jesus' eating with Pharisees (see Lk 5, 29-39; 7, 36-50; 14, 1-24). A different compilation of similar sayings is found in Mt 23 (see also the notes there).

make the inside? [41] But as to what is within, give alms, and behold, everything will be clean for you. [42] Woe to you Pharisees! You pay tithes of mint and of rue and of every garden herb, but you pay no attention to judgment and to love for God. These you should have done, without overlooking the others.[y] [43] Woe to you Pharisees! You love the seat of honor in synagogues and greetings in marketplaces.[z] [44] Woe to you! You are like unseen graves* over which people unknowingly walk."[a]

[45] Then one of the scholars of the law* said to him in reply, "Teacher, by saying this you are insulting us too."[b] [46] And he said, "Woe also to you scholars of the law! You impose on people burdens hard to carry, but you yourselves do not lift one finger to touch them. [47] [c] Woe to you! You build the memorials of the prophets whom your ancestors killed. [48] Consequently, you bear witness and give consent to the deeds of your ancestors, for they killed them and you do the building. [49] [d] Therefore, the wisdom of God said, 'I will send to them prophets and apostles;* some of them they

---

y Lv 27, 30; Mt 23, 23.—z Lk 20, 46; Mt 23, 6; Mk 12, 38-39.—a Mt 23, 27.—b Mt 23, 4.—c 47-48: Mt 23, 29-32.—d 49-51: Mt 23, 34-36.—e Gn 4, 8; 2 Chr 24, 20-22.—f Mt 23, 13.—g Lk 6, 11; Mt 22, 15-22.—h Lk 20, 20.—i Mt 16, 6; Mk 8, 15.—j 2-9: Mt 10, 26-33.—k Lk 8, 17; Mk 4, 22.—l Lk 12, 24; 21, 18; Acts 27, 34.—m Lk 9, 26; Mk 8, 38; 2 Tm 2, 12.—n Mt 12, 31-32; Mk 3, 28-29.—o 11-12: Lk 21, 12-15; Mt 10, 17-20; Mk 13, 11.

11, 44: *Unseen graves:* contact with the dead or with human bones or graves (see Nm 19, 16) brought ritual impurity. Jesus presents the Pharisees as those who insidiously lead others astray through their seeming attention to the law.

11, 45: *Scholars of the law:* see the note on Lk 10, 25.

11, 49: *I will send to them prophets and apostles:* Jesus connects the mission of the church (apostles) with the mission of the Old Testament prophets who often suffered the rebuke of their contemporaries.

11, 51: *From the blood of Abel to the blood of Zechariah:* the murder of Abel is the first murder recounted in the Old Testament (Gn 4, 8). The Zechariah mentioned here may be the Zechariah whose murder is recounted in 2 Chr 24, 20-22, the last murder presented in the Hebrew canon of the Old Testament.

12, 1: See the notes on Mk 8, 15 and Mt 16, 5-12.

12, 2-9: Luke presents a collection of sayings of Jesus exhorting his followers to acknowledge him and his mission fearlessly and assuring them of God's protection even in times of persecution. They are paralleled in Mt 10, 26-33.

12, 5: *Gehenna:* see the note on Mt 5, 22.

12, 6: *Two small coins:* the Roman copper coin, the assarion (Latin *as*), was worth about one-sixteenth of a denarius (see the note on Lk 7, 41).

12, 10-12: The sayings about the holy Spirit are set in the context of fearlessness in the face of persecution (2-9; cf Mt 12, 31-32). The holy Spirit will be presented in Luke's second volume, the Acts of the Apostles, as the power responsible for the guidance of the Christian mission and the source of courage in the face of persecution.

---

will kill and persecute' [50] in order that this generation might be charged with the blood of all the prophets shed since the foundation of the world, [51] from the blood of Abel to the blood of Zechariah* who died between the altar and the temple building. Yes, I tell you, this generation will be charged with their blood! [e] [52] Woe to you, scholars of the law! You have taken away the key of knowledge. You yourselves did not enter and you stopped those trying to enter."[f] [53] When he left, the scribes and Pharisees began to act with hostility toward him and to interrogate him about many things,[g] [54] for they were plotting to catch him at something he might say.[h]

CHAPTER 12

The Leaven of the Pharisees.* [1] Meanwhile, so many people were crowding together that they were trampling one another underfoot.[i] He began to speak, first to his disciples, "Beware of the leaven—that is, the hypocrisy—of the Pharisees.

Courage under Persecution.* [2] [j] "There is nothing concealed that will not be revealed, nor secret that will not be known.[k] [3] Therefore whatever you have said in the darkness will be heard in the light, and what you have whispered behind closed doors will be proclaimed on the housetops. [4] I tell you, my friends, do not be afraid of those who kill the body but after that can do no more. [5] I shall show you whom to fear. Be afraid of the one who after killing has the power to cast into Gehenna;* yes, I tell you, be afraid of that one. [6] Are not five sparrows sold for two small coins?* Yet not one of them has escaped the notice of God. [7] Even the hairs of your head have all been counted. Do not be afraid. You are worth more than many sparrows.[l] [8] I tell you, everyone who acknowledges me before others the Son of Man will acknowledge before the angels of God. [9] But whoever denies me before others will be denied before the angels of God.[m]

Sayings about the holy Spirit.* [10] "Everyone who speaks a word against the Son of Man will be forgiven, but the one who blasphemes against the holy Spirit will not be forgiven.[n] [11] When they take you before synagogues and before rulers and authorities,[o] do not worry about how or what your defense will be or about what you are

Lk

to say. [12] For the holy Spirit will teach you at that moment what you should say."

Saying against Greed. [13] * Someone in the crowd said to him, "Teacher, tell my brother to share the inheritance with me." [14] He replied to him, "Friend, who appointed me as your judge and arbitrator?" [p] [15] Then he said to the crowd, "Take care to guard against all greed, for though one may be rich, one's life does not consist of possessions." [q]

Parable of the Rich Fool. [16] Then he told them a parable. "There was a rich man whose land produced a bountiful harvest. [17] He asked himself, 'What shall I do, for I do not have space to store my harvest?' [18] And he said, 'This is what I shall do: I shall tear down my barns and build larger ones. There I shall store all my grain and other goods [19] [r] and I shall say to myself, "Now as for you, you have so many good things stored up for many years, rest, eat, drink, be merry!" ' [s] [20] But God said to him, 'You fool, this night your life will be demanded of you; and the things you have prepared, to whom will they belong?' [21] Thus will it be for the one who stores up treasure for himself but is not rich in what matters to God."*

Dependence on God. [22] [t] He said to [his] disciples, "Therefore I tell you, do not worry about your life and what you will eat, or about your body and what you will wear. [23] For life is more than food and the body more than clothing. [24] Notice the ravens: they do not sow or reap; they have neither storehouse nor barn, yet God feeds them. How much more important are you than birds! [u] [25] Can any of you by worrying add a moment to your life-span? [26] If even the smallest things are beyond your control, why are you anxious about the rest? [27] Notice how the flowers grow. They do not toil or spin. But I tell you, not even Solomon in all his splendor was dressed like one of them. [v] [28] If God so clothes the grass in the field that grows today and is thrown into the oven tomorrow, will he not much more provide for you, O you of little faith? [29] As for you, do not seek what you are to eat and what you are to drink, and do not worry anymore. [30] All the nations of the world seek for these things, and your Father knows that you need them. [31] Instead, seek his kingdom, and these other things will be given you besides. [32] Do not be afraid any longer, little flock, for your

Father is pleased to give you the kingdom. [w] [33] Sell your belongings and give alms. Provide money bags for yourselves that do not wear out, an inexhaustible treasure in heaven that no thief can reach nor moth destroy. [x] [34] For where your treasure is, there also will your heart be.

Vigilant and Faithful Servants. * [35] [y] "Gird your loins and light your lamps [36] and be like servants who await their master's return from a wedding, ready to open immediately when he comes and knocks. [z] [37] Blessed are those servants whom the master finds vigilant on his arrival. Amen, I say to you, he will gird himself, have them recline at table, and proceed to wait on them. [38] And should he come in the second or third watch and find them prepared in this way, blessed are those servants. [39] [a] Be sure of this: if the master of the house had known the hour when the thief was coming, he would not have let his house be broken into. [40] You also must be prepared, for at an hour you do not expect, the Son of Man will come."

[41] Then Peter said, "Lord, is this parable meant for us or for everyone?" [42] And the Lord replied, "Who, then, is the faithful and prudent steward whom the master will put in charge of his servants to distribute [the] food allowance at the proper time? [43] Blessed is that servant whom his master on arrival finds doing so. [44] Truly, I say to you, he will put him in charge of all his property. [45] But if that servant says to himself, 'My master is delayed in coming,'* and begins to beat the menservants and the maidservants, to eat and drink and get

p Ex 2, 14; Acts 7, 27.—q 1 Tm 6, 9-10.—r 19-21: Mt 6, 19-21; 1 Tm 6, 17.—s 19-20: Sir 11, 19.—t 22-32: Mt 6, 25-34.—u Lk 12, 7.—v 1 Kgs 10, 4-7; 2 Chr 9, 3-6.—w Lk 22, 29; Rv 1, 6.—x Lk 18, 22; Mt 6, 20-21; Mk 10, 21.—y 35-46: Mt 24, 45-51.—z Mt 25, 1-13; Mk 13, 35-37.—a 39-40: Mt 24, 43-44; 1 Thes 5, 2.

12, 13-34: Luke has joined together sayings contrasting those whose focus and trust in life is on material possessions, symbolized here by the rich fool of the parable (16-21), with those who recognize their complete dependence on God (21), those whose radical detachment from material possessions symbolizes their heavenly treasure (33-34).

12, 21: *Rich in what matters to God:* literally, "rich for God."

12, 35-48: This collection of sayings relates to Luke's understanding of the end time and the return of Jesus. Luke emphasizes for his readers the importance of being faithful to the instructions of Jesus in the period before the parousia.

12, 45: *My master is delayed in coming:* this statement indicates that early Christian expectations for the imminent return of Jesus had undergone some modification. Luke cautions his readers against counting on such a delay and acting irresponsibly. Cf the similar warning in Mt 24, 48.

drunk, ⁴⁶then that servant's master will come on an unexpected day and at an unknown hour and will punish him severely and assign him a place with the unfaithful. ⁴⁷That servant who knew his master's will but did not make preparations nor act in accord with his will shall be beaten severely;ᵇ ⁴⁸and the servant who was ignorant of his master's will but acted in a way deserving of a severe beating shall be beaten only lightly. Much will be required of the person entrusted with much, and still more will be demanded of the person entrusted with more.

Jesus: A Cause of Division.* ⁴⁹"I have come to set the earth on fire, and how I wish it were already blazing! ⁵⁰There is a baptism* with which I must be baptized, and how great is my anguish until it is accomplished!ᶜ ⁵¹Do you think that I have come to establish peace on the earth?ᵈ No, I tell you, but rather division.ᵉ ⁵²From now on a household of five will be divided, three against two and two against three; ⁵³a father will be divided against his son and a son against his father, a mother against her daughter and a daughter against her

mother, a mother-in-law against her daughter-in-law and a daughter-in-law against her mother-in-law."ᶠ

Signs of the Times. ᵍ ⁵⁴He also said to the crowds, "When you see [a] cloud rising in the west you say immediately that it is going to rain—and so it does; ⁵⁵and when you notice that the wind is blowing from the south you say that it is going to be hot—and so it is. ⁵⁶You hypocrites! You know how to interpret the appearance of the earth and the sky; why do you not know how to interpret the present time?

Settlement with an Opponent. ʰ ⁵⁷"Why do you not judge for yourselves what is right? ⁵⁸If you are to go with your opponent before a magistrate, make an effort to settle the matter on the way; otherwise your opponent will turn you over to the judge, and the judge hand you over to the constable, and the constable throw you into prison. ⁵⁹I say to you, you will not be released until you have paid the last penny."*

CHAPTER 13

A Call to Repentance.* ¹At that time some people who were present there told him about the Galileans whose blood Pilate* had mingled with the blood of their sacrifices. ²He said to them in reply, "Do you think that because these Galileans suffered in this way they were greater sinners than all other Galileans?ⁱ ³By no means! But I tell you, if you do not repent,ʲ you will all perish as they did! ⁴Or those eighteen people who were killed when the tower at Siloam fell on them*—do you think they were more guilty than everyone else who lived in Jerusalem? ⁵By no means! But I tell you, if you do not repent, you will all perish as they did!"

The Parable of the Barren Fig Tree.* ⁶ᵏ And he told them this parable: "There once was a person who had a fig tree planted in his orchard, and when he came in search of fruit on it but found none, ⁷he said to the gardener, 'For three years now I have come in search of fruit on this fig tree but have found none. [So] cut it down. Why should it exhaust the soil?' ⁸He said to him in reply, 'Sir, leave it for this year also, and I shall cultivate the ground around it and fertilize it; ⁹it may bear fruit in the future. If not you can cut it down.' "

b Jas 4, 17.—c Mk 10, 38-39.—d 51-53: Mt 10, 34-35.—e Lk 2, 14.—f Mi 7, 6.—g 54-56: Mt 16, 2-3.—h 57-59: Mt 5, 25-26.—i Jn 9, 2.—j 3-5: Jn 8, 24.—k 6-9: Jer 8, 13; Hb 3, 17; Mt 21, 19; Mk 11, 13.

12, 49-53: Jesus' proclamation of the kingdom is a refining and purifying fire. His message that meets with acceptance or rejection will be a source of conflict and dissension even within families.

12, 50: *Baptism:* i.e., his death.

12, 59: *The last penny:* Greek, *lepton,* a very small amount. Mt 5, 26 has for "the last penny" the Greek word *kodrantēs* (Latin *quadrans,* "farthing").

13, 1-5: The death of the Galileans at the hands of Pilate (1) and the accidental death of those on whom the tower fell (4) are presented by the Lucan Jesus as timely reminders of the need for all to repent, for the victims of these tragedies should not be considered outstanding sinners who were singled out for punishment.

13, 1: The slaughter of the Galileans by Pilate is unknown outside Lk; but from what is known about Pilate from the Jewish historian Josephus, such a slaughter would be in keeping with the character of Pilate. Josephus reports that Pilate had disrupted a religious gathering of the Samaritans on Mt. Gerizim with a slaughter of the participants (*Antiquities* 18, 4, 1 §§86-87), and that on another occasion Pilate had killed many Jews who had opposed him when he appropriated money from the temple treasury to build an aqueduct in Jerusalem (*Jewish War* 2, 9, 4 §§175-77; *Antiquities* 18, 3, 2 §§60-62).

13, 4: Like the incident mentioned in v 1, nothing of this accident in Jerusalem is known outside Lk and the New Testament.

13, 6-9: Following on the call to repentance in vv 1-5, the parable of the barren fig tree presents a story about the continuing patience of God with those who have not yet given evidence of their repentance (see Lk 3, 8). The parable may also be alluding to the delay of the end time, when punishment will be meted out, and the importance of preparing for the end of the age because the delay will not be permanent (8-9).

Cure of a Crippled Woman on the Sabbath.* [10] He was teaching in a synagogue on the sabbath. [11] And a woman was there who for eighteen years had been crippled by a spirit; she was bent over, completely incapable of standing erect. [12] When Jesus saw her, he called to her and said, "Woman, you are set free of your infirmity." [13] He laid his hands on her, and she at once stood up straight and glorified God. [14] *l* But the leader of the synagogue, indignant that Jesus had cured on the sabbath, said to the crowd in reply, "There are six days when work should be done. Come on those days to be cured, not on the sabbath day." [15] * The Lord said to him in reply, "Hypocrites! Does not each one of you on the sabbath untie his ox or his ass from the manger and lead it out for watering?*m* [16] This daughter of Abraham, whom Satan has bound* for eighteen years now, ought she not to have been set free on the sabbath day from this bondage?"*n* [17] When he said this, all his adversaries were humiliated; and the whole crowd rejoiced at all the splendid deeds done by him.

The Parable of the Mustard Seed.*o* [18] * Then he said, "What is the kingdom of God like? To what can I compare it? [19] It is like a mustard seed that a person took and planted in the garden. When it was fully grown, it became a large bush and 'the birds of the sky dwelt in its branches.'"*p*

The Parable of the Yeast.*q* [20] Again he said, "To what shall I compare the kingdom of God? [21] It is like yeast that a woman took and mixed [in] with three measures of wheat flour until the whole batch of dough was leavened."

The Narrow Door; Salvation and Rejection.* [22] He passed through towns and villages, teaching as he went and making his way to Jerusalem. [23] Someone asked him, "Lord, will only a few people be saved?" He answered them, [24] *r* "Strive to enter through the narrow gate, for many, I tell you, will attempt to enter but will not be strong enough.*s* [25] After the master of the house has arisen and locked the door, then will you stand outside knocking and saying, 'Lord, open the door for us.' He will say to you in reply, 'I do not know where you are from.'*t* [26] And you will say, 'We ate and drank in your company and you taught in our streets.' [27] *u* Then he will say to you, 'I do not know where [you] are

from. Depart from me, all you evildoers!' [28] *v* And there will be wailing and grinding of teeth when you see Abraham, Isaac, and Jacob and all the prophets in the kingdom of God and you yourselves cast out. [29] And people will come from the east and the west and from the north and the south and will recline at table in the kingdom of God.*w* [30] For behold, some are last who will be first, and some are first who will be last."*x*

Herod's Desire to Kill Jesus. [31] At that time some Pharisees came to him and said, "Go away, leave this area because Herod wants to kill you." [32] He replied, "Go and tell that fox, 'Behold, I cast out demons and I perform healings today and tomorrow, and on the third day I accomplish my purpose.* [33] Yet I must continue on my way today,*y* tomorrow, and the following day, for it is impossible that a prophet should die outside of Jerusalem.'*

---

l Lk 6, 7; 14, 3; Ex 20, 8-11; Dt 5, 12-15; Mt 12, 10; Mk 3, 2-4; Jn 5, 16; 7, 23; 9, 14.16.—m Lk 14, 5; Dt 22, 4; Mt 12, 11.—n Lk 19, 9.—o 18-19: Mt 13, 31-32; Mk 4, 30-32.—p Ez 17, 23-24; 31, 6.—q 20-21: Mt 13, 33.—r 24-30: Mt 7, 13-14.21-23.—s Mk 10, 25.—t Mt 25, 10-12.—u Ps 6, 9; Mt 7, 23; 25, 41.—v 28-29: Mt 8, 11-12.—w Ps 107, 2-3.—x Mt 19, 20; 20, 16; Mk 10, 31.—y Lk 2, 38; Jn 6, 30; 8, 20.

13, 10-17: The cure of the crippled woman on the sabbath and the controversy that results furnishes a parallel to an incident that will be reported by Lk in 14, 1-6, the cure of the man with dropsy on the sabbath. A characteristic of Lk's style is the juxtaposition of an incident that reveals Jesus' concern for a man with an incident that reveals his concern for a woman; cf, e.g., Lk 7, 11-17 and Lk 8, 49-56.

13, 15-16: If the law as interpreted by Jewish tradition allowed for the untying of bound animals on the sabbath, how much more should this woman who has been bound by Satan's power be freed on the sabbath from her affliction.

13, 16: *Whom Satan has bound:* affliction and infirmity are taken as evidence of Satan's hold on humanity. The healing ministry of Jesus reveals the gradual wresting from Satan of control over humanity and the establishment of God's kingdom.

13, 18-21: Two parables are used to illustrate the future proportions of the kingdom of God that will result from its deceptively small beginning in the preaching and healing ministry of Jesus. They are paralleled in Mt 13, 31-33 and Mk 4, 30-32.

13, 22-30: These sayings of Jesus follow in Lk upon the parables of the kingdom (18-21) and stress that great effort is required for entrance into the kingdom (24) and that there is an urgency to accept the present opportunity to enter because the narrow door will not remain open indefinitely (25). Lying behind the sayings is the rejection of Jesus and his message by his Jewish contemporaries (26) whose places at table in the kingdom will be taken by Gentiles from the four corners of the world (29). Those called last (the Gentiles) will precede those to whom the invitation to enter was first extended (the Jews). See also Lk 14, 15-24.

13, 32: Nothing, not even Herod's desire to kill Jesus, stands in the way of Jesus' role in fulfilling God's will and in establishing the kingdom through his exorcisms and healings.

13, 33: *It is impossible that a prophet should die outside of Jerusalem:* Jerusalem is the city of destiny and the goal of the journey of the prophet Jesus. Only when he reaches the holy city will his work be accomplished.

The Lament over Jerusalem.^z [34] "Jerusalem, Jerusalem, you who kill the prophets and stone those sent to you, how many times I yearned to gather your children together as a hen gathers her brood under her wings, but you were unwilling! [35] Behold, your house will be abandoned. [But] I tell you, you will not see me until [the time comes when] you say, 'Blessed is he who comes in the name of the Lord.' "^a

CHAPTER 14

Healing of the Man with Dropsy on the Sabbath.* [1] ^b On a sabbath he went to dine at the home of one of the leading Pharisees, and the people there were observing him carefully.^c [2] In front of him there was a man suffering from dropsy.* [3] Jesus spoke to the scholars of the law and Pharisees in reply, asking, "Is it lawful to cure on the sabbath or not?"^d [4] But they kept silent; so he took the man and, after he had healed him, dismissed him. [5] Then he said to them, "Who among you, if your son or ox* falls into a cistern, would not immediately pull him out on the sabbath day?"^e [6] But they were unable to answer his question.^f

Conduct of Invited Guests and Hosts.* [7] ^g He told a parable to those who had been invited, noticing how they were choosing the places of honor at the table. [8] ^h "When you are invited by someone to a wedding banquet, do not recline at table in the place of honor. A more distinguished guest than you may have been invited by him, [9] and the host who invited both of you may approach you and say, 'Give your place to this man,' and then you would proceed with embarrassment to take the lowest place. [10] Rather, when you are invited, go and take the lowest place so that when the host comes to you he may say, 'My friend, move up to a higher position.' Then you will enjoy the esteem of your companions at the table. [11] For everyone who exalts himself will be humbled, but the one who humbles himself will be exalted."ⁱ [12] Then he said to the host who invited him, "When you hold a lunch or a dinner, do not invite your friends or your brothers or your relatives or your wealthy neighbors, in case they may invite you back and you have repayment.^j [13] Rather, when you hold a banquet, invite the poor, the crippled, the lame, the blind; [14] blessed indeed will you be because of their inability to repay you. For you will be repaid at the resurrection of the righteous."^k

The Parable of the Great Feast.* [15] One of his fellow guests on hearing this said to him, "Blessed is the one who will dine in the kingdom of God." [16] ^l He replied to him, "A man gave a great dinner to which he invited many. [17] When the time for the dinner came, he dispatched his servant to say to those invited, 'Come, everything is now ready.' [18] But one by one, they all began to excuse themselves. The first said to him, 'I have purchased a field and must go to examine it; I ask you, consider me excused.' [19] And another said, 'I have purchased five yoke of oxen and am on my way to evaluate them; I ask you, consider me excused.' [20] And another said, 'I have just married a woman, and therefore I cannot come.' [21] The servant went and reported this to his master. Then the master of the house in a rage commanded his servant, 'Go out quickly into the streets and alleys of the town and bring in here the poor and the crippled, the blind and the lame.' [22] The servant reported, 'Sir, your orders have been carried out and still there is room.' [23] The master then ordered the servant, 'Go out to the highways and hedgerows and make people come in that my home may be filled. [24] For, I tell you, none of those men who were invited will taste my dinner.' "

---

z 34-35: Lk 19, 41-44; Mt 23, 37-39.—a Lk 19, 38; 1 Kgs 9, 7-8; Ps 118, 26; Jer 7, 4-7.13-15; 12, 7; 22, 5.—b 1-6: Lk 6, 6-11; 13, 10-17.—c Lk 11, 37.—d Lk 6, 9; Mk 3, 4.—e Lk 13, 15; Dt 22, 4; Mt 12, 11.—f Mt 22, 46.—g Lk 11, 43; Mt 23, 6; Mk 12, 38-39.—h 8-10: Prv 25, 6-7.—i Lk 18, 14.—j Lk 6, 32-35.—k Jn 5, 29.—l 16-24: Mt 22, 2-10.

14, 1-6: See the note on Lk 13, 10-17.

14, 2: *Dropsy:* an abnormal swelling of the body because of the retention and accumulation of fluid.

14, 5: *Your son or ox:* this is the reading of many of the oldest and most important New Testament manuscripts. Because of the strange collocation of *son* and *ox*, some copyists have altered it to "your ass or ox," on the model of the saying in Lk 13, 15.

14, 7-14: The banquet scene found only in Luke provides the opportunity for these teachings of Jesus on humility and presents a setting to display Luke's interest in Jesus' attitude toward the rich and the poor (see the notes on Lk 4, 18; 6, 20-26; 12, 13-34).

14, 15-24: The parable of the great dinner is a further illustration of the rejection by Israel, God's chosen people, of Jesus' invitation to share in the banquet in the kingdom and the extension of the invitation to other Jews whose identification as the poor, crippled, blind, and lame (21) classifies them among those who recognize their need for salvation, and to Gentiles (23). A similar parable is found in Mt 22, 1-10.

Sayings on Discipleship.* [25] Great crowds were traveling with him, and he turned and addressed them, [26] [m] "If anyone comes to me without hating his father* and mother, wife and children, brothers and sisters, and even his own life, he cannot be my disciple. [n] [27] Whoever does not carry his own cross and come after me cannot be my disciple. [o] [28] Which of you wishing to construct a tower does not first sit down and calculate the cost to see if there is enough for its completion? [29] Otherwise, after laying the foundation and finding himself unable to finish the work the onlookers should laugh at him [30] and say, 'This one began to build but did not have the resources to finish.' [31] Or what king marching into battle would not first sit down and decide whether with ten thousand troops he can successfully oppose another king advancing upon him with twenty thousand troops? [32] But if not, while he is still far away, he will send a delegation to ask for peace terms. [33] In the same way, everyone of you who does not renounce all his possessions cannot be my disciple. [p]

The Simile of Salt.* [34] "Salt is good, but if salt itself loses its taste, with what can its flavor be restored? [q] [35] It is fit neither for the soil nor for the manure pile; it is thrown out. Whoever has ears to hear ought to hear." [r]

CHAPTER 15

The Parable of the Lost Sheep. [s] [1] * The tax collectors and sinners were all drawing near to listen to him, [2] but the Pharisees and scribes began to complain, saying, "This man welcomes sinners and eats with them." [t] [3] So to them he addressed this parable. [4] [u] "What man among you having a hundred sheep and losing one of them would not leave the ninety-nine in the desert and go after the lost one [v] until he finds it? [w] [5] And when he does find it, he sets it on his shoulders with great joy [6] and, upon his arrival home, he calls together his friends and neighbors and says to them, 'Rejoice with me because I have found my lost sheep.' [7] I tell you, in just the same way there will be more joy in heaven over one sinner who repents than over ninety-nine righteous people who have no need of repentance. [x]

The Parable of the Lost Coin. [8] "Or what woman having ten coins* and losing one would not light a lamp and sweep the house, searching carefully until she finds it? [9] And when she does find it, she calls together her friends and neighbors and says to them, 'Rejoice with me because I have found the coin that I lost.' [10] In just the same way, I tell you, there will be rejoicing among the angels of God over one sinner who repents."

The Parable of the Lost Son. [11] Then he said, "A man had two sons, [12] and the younger son said to his father, 'Father, give me the share of your estate that should come to me.' So the father divided the property between them. [13] After a few days, the younger son collected all his belongings and set off to a distant country where he squandered his inheritance on a life of dissipation. [y] [14] When he had freely spent everything, a severe famine struck that country, and he found himself in dire need. [15] So he hired himself out to one of the local citizens who sent him to his farm to tend the swine. [16] And he longed to eat his fill of the pods on which the swine fed, but nobody gave him any. [17] Coming to his senses he thought, 'How many of my father's hired workers have more than enough food to eat, but here am I, dying from hunger. [18] I shall get up and go to my father and I shall say to him, "Father, I

m 26-27: Mt 10, 37-38.—n Lk 9, 57-62; 18, 29; Jn 12, 25.—o Lk 9, 23; Mt 16, 24; Mk 8, 34.—p Lk 5, 11.—q Mt 5, 13; Mk 9, 50.—r Lk 8, 8; Mt 11, 15; 13, 9; Mk 4, 9.23.—s 1-7: Mt 9, 10-13.—t Lk 5, 30; 19, 7.—u 4-7: Mt 18, 12-14.—v 4-6: Lk 19, 10.—w Ez 34, 11-12.16.—x Ez 18, 23.—y Prv 29, 3.

14, 25-33: This collection of sayings, most of which are peculiar to Lk, focuses on the total dedication necessary for the disciple of Jesus. No attachment to family (26) or possessions (33) can stand in the way of the total commitment demanded of the disciple. Also, acceptance of the call to be a disciple demands readiness to accept persecution and suffering (27) and a realistic assessment of the hardships and costs (28-32).

14, 26: *Hating his father . . . :* cf the similar saying in Mt 10, 37. The disciple's family must take second place to the absolute dedication involved in following Jesus (see also Lk 9, 59-62).

14, 34-35: The simile of salt follows the sayings of Jesus that demanded of the disciple total dedication and detachment from family and possessions and illustrates the condition of one who does not display this total commitment. The halfhearted disciple is like salt that cannot serve its intended purpose. See the simile of salt in Mt 5, 13 and the note there.

15, 1-32: To the parable of the lost sheep (1-7) that Luke shares with Matthew (Mt 18, 12-14), Luke adds two parables (the lost coin, 8-10; the prodigal son, 11-32) from his own special tradition to illustrate Jesus' particular concern for the lost and God's love for the repentant sinner.

15, 8: *Ten coins:* literally, "ten drachmas." A drachma was a Greek silver coin.

have sinned against heaven and against you. [19] I no longer deserve to be called your son; treat me as you would treat one of your hired workers." ' [20] So he got up and went back to his father. While he was still a long way off, his father caught sight of him, and was filled with compassion. He ran to his son, embraced him and kissed him. [21] His son said to him, 'Father, I have sinned against heaven and against you; I no longer deserve to be called your son.' [22] But his father ordered his servants, 'Quickly bring the finest robe and put it on him; put a ring on his finger and sandals on his feet. [23] Take the fattened calf and slaughter it. Then let us celebrate with a feast, [24] because this son of mine was dead, and has come to life again; he was lost, and has been found.' Then the celebration began. [25] Now the older son had been out in the field and, on his way back, as he neared the house, he heard the sound of music and dancing. [26] He called one of the servants and asked what this might mean. [27] The servant said to him, 'Your brother has returned and your father has slaughtered the fattened calf because he has him back safe and sound.' [28] He became angry, and when he refused to enter the house, his father

came out and pleaded with him. [29] He said to his father in reply, 'Look, all these years I served you and not once did I disobey your orders; yet you never gave me even a young goat to feast on with my friends. [30] But when your son returns who swallowed up your property with prostitutes, for him you slaughter the fattened calf.' [31] He said to him, 'My son, you are here with me always; everything I have is yours. [32] But now we must celebrate and rejoice, because your brother was dead and has come to life again; he was lost and has been found.' "

CHAPTER 16

The Parable of the Dishonest Steward.[*] [1] Then he also said to his disciples, "A rich man had a steward who was reported to him for squandering his property. [2] He summoned him and said, 'What is this I hear about you? Prepare a full account of your stewardship, because you can no longer be my steward.' [3] The steward said to himself, 'What shall I do, now that my master is taking the position of steward away from me? I am not strong enough to dig and I am ashamed to beg. [4] I know what I shall do so that, when I am removed from the stewardship, they may welcome me into their homes.' [5] He called in his master's debtors one by one. To the first he said, 'How much do you owe my master?' [6] He replied, 'One hundred measures[*] of olive oil.' He said to him, 'Here is your promissory note. Sit down and quickly write one for fifty.' [7] Then to another he said, 'And you, how much do you owe?' He replied, 'One hundred kors[*] of wheat.' He said to him, 'Here is your promissory note; write one for eighty.' [8] And the master commended that dishonest steward for acting prudently.

Application of the Parable.[*] "For the children of this world are more prudent in dealing with their own generation than are the children of light.[*] [z] [9] I tell you, make friends for yourselves with dishonest wealth,[*] so that when it fails, you will be welcomed into eternal dwellings.[a] [10] [*] The person who is trustworthy in very small matters is also trustworthy in great ones; and the person who is dishonest in very small matters is also dishonest in great ones.[b] [11] If, therefore, you are not trustworthy with dishonest wealth, who

z Eph 5, 8; 1 Thes 5, 5.—a Lk 12, 33.—b Lk 19, 17; Mt 25, 20-23.

16, 1-8a: The parable of the dishonest steward has to be understood in the light of the Palestinian custom of agents acting on behalf of their masters and the usurious practices common to such agents. The dishonesty of the steward consisted in the squandering of his master's property (1) and not in any subsequent graft. The master commends the dishonest steward who has forgone his own usurious commission on the business transaction by having the debtors write new notes that reflected only the real amount owed the master (i.e., minus the steward's profit). The dishonest steward acts in this way in order to ingratiate himself with the debtors because he knows he is being dismissed from his position (3). The parable, then, teaches the prudent use of one's material goods in light of an imminent crisis.

16, 6: *One hundred measures:* literally, "one hundred *baths.*" A *bath* is a Hebrew unit of liquid measurement equivalent to eight or nine gallons.

16, 7: *One hundred kors:* a *kor* is a Hebrew unit of dry measure for grain or wheat equivalent to ten or twelve bushels.

16, 8b-13: Several originally independent sayings of Jesus are gathered here by Luke to form the concluding application of the parable of the dishonest steward.

16, 8b-9: The first conclusion recommends the prudent use of one's wealth (in the light of the coming of the end of the age) after the manner of the children of this world, represented in the parable by the dishonest steward.

16, 9: *Dishonest wealth:* literally, "mammon of iniquity." Mammon is the Greek transliteration of a Hebrew or Aramaic word that is usually explained as meaning "that in which one trusts." The characterization of this wealth as *dishonest* expresses a tendency of wealth to lead one to dishonesty. *Eternal dwellings:* or, "eternal tents," i.e., heaven.

16, 10-12: The second conclusion recommends constant fidelity to those in positions of responsibility.

Lk

will trust you with true wealth? [12] If you are not trustworthy with what belongs to another, who will give you what is yours? [13] No servant can serve two masters.* He will either hate one and love the other, or be devoted to one and despise the other. You cannot serve God and mammon." [c]

A Saying against the Pharisees. [14] * The Pharisees, who loved money,* heard all these things and sneered at him. [15] And he said to them, "You justify yourselves in the sight of others, but God knows your hearts; for what is of human esteem is an abomination in the sight of God. [d]

Sayings about the Law. [16] "The law and the prophets lasted until John;* but from then on the kingdom of God is proclaimed, and everyone who enters does so with violence. [e] [17] It is easier for heaven and earth to pass away than for the smallest part of a letter of the law to become invalid. [f]

Sayings about Divorce. [18] "Everyone who divorces his wife and marries another commits adultery, and the one who marries a woman divorced from her husband commits adultery. [g]

The Parable of the Rich Man and Lazarus.* [19] "There was a rich man* who dressed in purple garments and fine linen and dined sumptuously each day. [20] And lying at his door was a poor man named Lazarus, covered with sores, [h] [21] who would gladly have eaten his fill of the scraps that fell from the rich man's table. Dogs even used to come and lick his sores. [22] When the poor man died, he was carried away by angels to the bosom of Abraham. The rich man also died and was buried, [23] and from the netherworld,* where he was in torment, he raised his eyes and saw Abraham far off and Lazarus at his side. [24] And he cried out, 'Father Abraham, have pity on me. Send Lazarus to dip the tip of his finger in water and cool my tongue, for I am suffering torment in these flames.' [25] Abraham replied, 'My child, remember that you received what was good during your lifetime while Lazarus likewise received what was bad; but now he is comforted here, whereas you are tormented. [i] [26] Moreover, between us and you a great chasm is established to prevent anyone from crossing who might wish to go from our side to yours or from your side to ours.' [27] He said, 'Then I beg you, father, send him to my father's house, [28] for I have

five brothers, so that he may warn them, lest they too come to this place of torment.' [29] But Abraham replied, 'They have Moses and the prophets. Let them listen to them.' [30] * He said, 'Oh no, father Abraham, but if someone from the dead goes to them, they will repent.' [31] Then Abraham said, 'If they will not listen to Moses and the prophets, neither will they be persuaded if someone should rise from the dead.' " [j]

CHAPTER 17

Temptations to Sin. [1] [k] He said to his disciples, "Things that cause sin will inevitably occur, but woe to the person through whom they occur. [2] It would be better for him if a millstone were put around his neck and he be thrown into the sea than for him to cause one of these little ones to sin. [3] Be on your guard!* If your brother sins, rebuke him; and if he repents, forgive him. [l] [4] And if he wrongs you seven times in one day and returns to you seven times saying, 'I am sorry,' you should forgive him." [m]

---

c Mt 6, 24.—d Lk 18, 9-14.—e Mt 11, 12-13.—f Mt 5, 18.—g Mt 5, 32; 19, 9; Mk 10, 11-12; 1 Cor 7, 10-11.—h Mt 15, 27; Mk 7, 28.—i Lk 6, 24-25.—j Jn 5, 46-47; 11, 44-48.—k 1-2: Mt 18, 6-7.—l Mt 18, 15.—m Mt 6, 14; 18, 21-22.35; Mk 11, 25.

16, 13: The third conclusion is a general statement about the incompatibility of serving God and being a slave to riches. To be dependent upon wealth is opposed to the teachings of Jesus who counseled complete dependence on the Father as one of the characteristics of the Christian disciple (Lk 12, 22-39). *God and mammon:* see the note on Lk 16, 9. Mammon is used here as if it were itself a god.

16, 14-18: The two parables about the use of riches in ch 16 are separated by several isolated sayings of Jesus on the hypocrisy of the Pharisees (14-15), on the law (16-17), and on divorce (18).

16, 14-15: The Pharisees are here presented as examples of those who are slaves to wealth (see Lk 16, 13) and, consequently, they are unable to serve God.

16, 16: John the Baptist is presented in Luke's gospel as a transitional figure between the period of Israel, the time of promise, and the period of Jesus, the time of fulfillment. With John, the fulfillment of the Old Testament promises has begun.

16, 19-31: The parable of the rich man and Lazarus again illustrates Luke's concern with Jesus' attitude toward the rich and the poor. The reversal of the fates of the rich man and Lazarus (22-23) illustrates the teachings of Jesus in Luke's "Sermon on the Plain" (Lk 6, 20-21.24-25).

16, 19: The oldest Greek manuscript of Lk dating from ca. A.D. 175-225 records the name of the rich man as an abbreviated form of "Nineveh," but there is very little textual support in other manuscripts for this reading. "Dives" of popular tradition is the Latin Vulgate's translation for "rich man."

16, 23: *The netherworld:* see the note on Lk 10, 15.

16, 30-31: A foreshadowing in Luke's gospel of the rejection of the call to repentance even after Jesus' resurrection.

17, 3a: *Be on your guard:* the translation takes v 3a as the conclusion to the saying on scandal in vv 1-2. It is not impossible that it should be taken as the beginning of the saying on forgiveness in vv 3b-4.

Saying of Faith. [5] And the apostles said to the Lord, "Increase our faith." [6] The Lord replied, "If you have faith the size of a mustard seed, you would say to [this] mulberry tree, 'Be uprooted and planted in the sea,' and it would obey you. [n]

Attitude of a Servant. * [7] "Who among you would say to your servant who has just come in from plowing or tending sheep in the field, 'Come here immediately and take your place at table'? [8] Would he not rather say to him, 'Prepare something for me to eat. Put on your apron and wait on me while I eat and drink. You may eat and drink when I am finished'? [9] Is he grateful to that servant because he did what was commanded? [10] So should it be with you. When you have done all you have been commanded, say, 'We are unprofitable servants; we have done what we were obliged to do.' "

The Cleansing of Ten Lepers. * [11] As he continued his journey to Jerusalem, [o] he traveled through Samaria and Galilee. * [12] As he was entering a village, ten lepers

---

n Mt 17, 20; 21, 21; Mk 11, 23.—o Lk 9, 51-53; 13, 22.33; 18, 31; 19, 28; Jn 4, 4.—p Lk 18, 38; Mt 9, 27; 15, 22.—q Lk 5, 14; Lv 14, 2-32; Mt 8, 4; Mk 1, 44.—r Lk 7, 50; 18, 42.—s Jn 3, 3.—t Lk 17, 23; Mt 24, 23; Mk 13, 21.—u Lk 17, 21; Mt 24, 23.26; Mk 13, 21.—v Mt 24, 27.—w Lk 9, 22; 18, 32-33; Mt 16, 21; 17, 22-23; 20, 18-19; Mk 8, 31; 9, 31; 10, 33-34.—x 26-27: Gn 6—8; Mt 24, 37-39.—y 28-29: Gn 18, 20-21; 19, 1-29.—z Mt 24, 17-18; Mk 13, 15-16.—a 31-32: Gn 19, 17.26.—b Lk 9, 24; Mt 10, 39; 16, 25; Mk 8, 35; Jn 12, 25.

17, 7-10: These sayings of Jesus, peculiar to Luke, which continue his response to the apostles' request to increase their faith (5-6), remind them that Christian disciples can make no claim on God's graciousness; in fulfilling the exacting demands of discipleship, they are only doing their duty.

17, 11-19: This incident recounting the thankfulness of the cleansed Samaritan leper is narrated only in Luke's gospel and provides an instance of Jesus holding up a non-Jew (18) as an example to his Jewish contemporaries (cf Lk 10, 33 where a similar purpose is achieved in the story of the good Samaritan). Moreover, it is the faith in Jesus manifested by the foreigner that has brought him salvation (19; cf the similar relationship between faith and salvation in Lk 7, 50; 8, 48.50).

17, 11: *Through Samaria and Galilee:* or, "between Samaria and Galilee."

17, 14: See the note on Lk 5, 14.

17, 20-37: To the question of the Pharisees about the time of the coming of God's kingdom, Jesus replies that the kingdom is *among you* (20-21). The emphasis has thus been shifted from an imminent observable coming of the kingdom to something that is already present in Jesus' preaching and healing ministry. Luke has also appended further traditional sayings of Jesus about the unpredictable suddenness of the day of the Son of Man, and assures his readers that in spite of the delay of that day (Lk 12, 45), it will bring judgment unexpectedly on those who do not continue to be vigilant.

17, 21: *Among you:* the Greek preposition translated as *among* can also be translated as "within." In the light of other statements in Luke's gospel about the presence of the kingdom (see Lk 10, 9.11; 11, 20) "among" is to be preferred.

---

met [him]. They stood at a distance from him [13] and raised their voice, saying, "Jesus, Master! Have pity on us!" [p] [14] And when he saw them, he said, "Go show yourselves to the priests." * As they were going they were cleansed. [q] [15] And one of them, realizing he had been healed, returned, glorifying God in a loud voice; [16] and he fell at the feet of Jesus and thanked him. He was a Samaritan. [17] Jesus said in reply, "Ten were cleansed, were they not? Where are the other nine? [18] Has none but this foreigner returned to give thanks to God?" [19] Then he said to him, "Stand up and go; your faith has saved you." [r]

The Coming of the Kingdom of God. [20] * Asked by the Pharisees when the kingdom of God would come, he said in reply, "The coming of the kingdom of God cannot be observed, [s] [21] and no one will announce, 'Look, here it is,' or, 'There it is.' [t] For behold, the kingdom of God is among you." *

The Day of the Son of Man. [22] Then he said to his disciples, "The days will come when you will long to see one of the days of the Son of Man, but you will not see it. [23] There will be those who will say to you, 'Look, there he is,' [or] 'Look, here he is.' Do not go off, do not run in pursuit. [u] [24] For just as lightning flashes and lights up the sky from one side to the other, so will the Son of Man be [in his day]. [v] [25] But first he must suffer greatly and be rejected by this generation. [w] [26] As it was in the days of Noah, [x] so it will be in the days of the Son of Man; [27] they were eating and drinking, marrying and giving in marriage up to the day that Noah entered the ark, and the flood came and destroyed them all. [28] [y] Similarly, as it was in the days of Lot: they were eating, drinking, buying, selling, planting, building; [29] on the day when Lot left Sodom, fire and brimstone rained from the sky to destroy them all. [30] So it will be on the day the Son of Man is revealed. [31] [z] On that day, a person who is on the housetop and whose belongings are in the house must not go down to get them, and likewise a person in the field must not return to what was left behind. [a] [32] Remember the wife of Lot. [33] Whoever seeks to preserve his life will lose it, but whoever loses it will save it. [b] [34] I tell you, on that night there will be two people in one bed;

Lk

one will be taken, the other left. [35] *c* And there will be two women grinding meal together; one will be taken, the other left." [36]* [37] They said to him in reply, "Where, Lord?" He said to them, "Where the body is, there also the vultures will gather." *d*

CHAPTER 18

The Parable of the Persistent Widow. [1] * Then he told them a parable about the necessity for them to pray always without becoming weary. *e* He said, [2] "There was a judge in a certain town who neither feared God nor respected any human being. [3] And a widow in that town used to come to him and say, 'Render a just decision for me against my adversary.' [4] For a long time the judge was unwilling, but eventually he thought, 'While it is true that I neither fear God nor respect any human being, [5] *f* because this widow keeps bothering me I shall deliver a just decision for her lest she finally come and strike me.' "* [6] The Lord said, "Pay attention to what the dishonest judge says. [7] Will not God then secure the rights of his chosen ones who call out to him day and night? Will he be slow to answer them? [8] I tell you, he will see to it that justice is done for them speedily. But when the Son of Man comes, will he find faith on earth?"

The Parable of the Pharisee and the Tax Collector. [9] He then addressed this parable to those who were convinced of their own righteousness and despised everyone else. *g* [10] "Two people went up to the temple area to pray; one was a Pharisee and the other was a tax collector. [11] The Pharisee took up his position and spoke this prayer to himself, 'O God, I thank you that I am not like the rest of humanity—greedy, dishonest, adulterous—or even like this tax collector. [12] I fast twice a week, and I pay tithes on my whole income.' *h* [13] But the tax collector stood off at a distance and would not even raise his eyes to heaven but beat his breast and prayed, 'O God, be merciful to me a sinner.' *i* [14] I tell you, the latter went home justified, not the former; for everyone who exalts himself will be humbled, and the one who humbles himself will be exalted." *j*

Saying on Children and the Kingdom. [15] * People were bringing even infants to him that he might touch them,* and when the disciples saw this, they rebuked them. *k*

[16] Jesus, however, called the children to himself and said, "Let the children come to me and do not prevent them; for the kingdom of God belongs to such as these. [17] Amen, I say to you, whoever does not accept the kingdom of God like a child will not enter it." *l*

The Rich Official. [18] *m* An official asked him this question, "Good teacher, what must I do to inherit eternal life?" *n* [19] Jesus answered him, "Why do you call me good? No one is good but God alone. [20] You know the commandments, 'You shall not commit adultery; you shall not kill; you shall not steal; you shall not bear false witness; honor your father and your mother.' " *o* [21] And he replied, "All of these I have observed from my youth." [22] *p* When Jesus heard this he said to him, "There is still one thing left for you: sell all that you have and distribute it to the poor, and you will have a treasure in heaven. Then come, follow me."* [23] But when he heard this he became quite sad, for he was very rich.

---

c Mt 24, 40-41.—d Jb 39, 30; Mt 24, 28.—e Rom 12, 12; Col 4, 2; 1 Thes 5, 17.—f Lk 11, 8.—g Lk 16, 5; Mt 23, 25-28.—h Mt 23, 23.—i Ps 51, 3.—j Lk 14, 11; Mt 23, 12.—k 15-17: Mt 19, 13-15; Mk 10, 13-16.—l Mt 18, 3.—m 18-30: Mt 19, 16-30; Mk 10, 17-31.—n Lk 10, 25.—o Ex 20, 12-16; Dt 5, 16-20.—p Lk 12, 33; Sir 29, 11; Mt 6, 20.

17, 36: The inclusion of v 36, "There will be two men in the field; one will be taken, the other left behind," in some Western manuscripts appears to be a scribal assimilation to Mt 24, 40.

18, 1-14: The particularly Lucan material in the travel narrative concludes with two parables on prayer. The first (1-8) teaches the disciples the need of persistent prayer so that they not fall victims to apostasy (8). The second (9-14) condemns the self-righteous, critical attitude of the Pharisee and teaches that the fundamental attitude of the Christian disciple must be the recognition of sinfulness and complete dependence on God's graciousness. The second parable recalls the story of the pardoning of the sinful woman (Lk 7, 36-50) where a similar contrast is presented between the critical attitude of the Pharisee Simon and the love shown by the pardoned sinner.

18, 5: *Strike me:* the Greek verb translated as *strike* means "to strike under the eye" and suggests the extreme situation to which the persistence of the widow might lead. It may, however, be used here in the much weaker sense of "to wear one out."

18, 15—19, 27: Luke here includes much of the material about the journey to Jerusalem found in his Marcan source (Mk 10, 1-52) and adds to it the story of Zacchaeus (Lk 19, 1-10) from his own particular tradition and the parable of the gold coins (minas) (Lk 19, 11-27) from Q, the source common to Lk and Mt.

18, 15-17: The sayings on children furnish a contrast to the attitude of the Pharisee in the preceding episode (9-14) and that of the wealthy official in the following one (18-23) who think that they can lay claim to God's favor by their own merit. The attitude of the disciple should be marked by the receptivity and trustful dependence characteristic of the child.

18, 22: Detachment from material possessions results in the total dependence on God demanded of one who would inherit eternal life. *Sell all that you have:* the original saying (cf Mk 10, 21) has characteristically been made more demanding by Luke's addition of "all."

On Riches and Renunciation. [24] Jesus looked at him [now sad] and said, "How hard it is for those who have wealth to enter the kingdom of God! [25] For it is easier for a camel to pass through the eye of a needle than for a rich person to enter the kingdom of God." [26] Those who heard this said, "Then who can be saved?" [27] And he said, "What is impossible for human beings is possible for God."[q] [28] Then Peter said, "We have given up our possessions and followed you." [29] [r] He said to them, "Amen, I say to you, there is no one who has given up house or wife or brothers or parents or children for the sake of the kingdom of God [30] who will not receive [back] an overabundant return in this present age and eternal life in the age to come."

The Third Prediction of the Passion.[s] [31] * Then he took the Twelve aside and said to them, "Behold, we are going up to Jerusalem and everything written by the prophets about the Son of Man will be fulfilled.* [32] [t] He will be handed over to the

Gentiles and he will be mocked and insulted and spat upon; [33] and after they have scourged him they will kill him, but on the third day he will rise." [34] But they understood nothing of this; the word remained hidden from them and they failed to comprehend what he said.[u]

The Healing of the Blind Beggar.[v] [35] Now as he approached Jericho a blind man was sitting by the roadside begging, [36] and hearing a crowd going by, he inquired what was happening. [37] They told him, "Jesus of Nazareth is passing by." [38] [w] He shouted, "Jesus, Son of David,* have pity on me!" [39] The people walking in front rebuked him, telling him to be silent, but he kept calling out all the more, "Son of David, have pity on me!" [40] Then Jesus stopped and ordered that he be brought to him; and when he came near, Jesus asked him, [41] "What do you want me to do for you?" He replied, "Lord, please let me see."[x] [42] Jesus told him, "Have sight; your faith has saved you."[y] [43] He immediately received his sight and followed him, giving glory to God. When they saw this, all the people gave praise to God.

---

q Mk 14, 36.—r 29-30: Lk 14, 26.—s 31-34: Lk 24, 25-27.44; Mt 20, 17-19; Mk 10, 32-34; Acts 3, 18.—t 32-33: Lk 9, 22.44.—u Mk 9, 32.—v 35-43: Mt 20, 29-34; Mk 10, 46-52.—w 38-39: Lk 17, 13; Mt 9, 27; 15, 22.—x Mk 10, 36.—y Lk 7, 50; 17, 19.—z Lk 5, 30; 15, 2.—a Ex 21, 37; Nm 5, 6-7; 2 Sm 12, 6.—b Lk 13, 16; Mt 21, 31.—c Lk 15, 4-10; Ez 34, 16.

18, 31-33: The details included in this third announcement of Jesus' suffering and death suggest that the literary formulation of the announcement has been directed by the knowledge of the historical passion and death of Jesus.

18, 31: *Everything written by the prophets . . . will be fulfilled:* this is a Lucan addition to the words of Jesus found in the Marcan source (Mk 10, 32-34). Luke understands the events of Jesus' last days in Jerusalem to be the fulfillment of Old Testament prophecy, but, as is usually the case in Luke-Acts, the author does not specify which Old Testament prophets he has in mind; cf Lk 24, 25.27.44; Acts 3, 8; 13, 27; 26, 22-23.

18, 38: *Son of David:* the blind beggar identifies Jesus with a title that is related to Jesus' role as Messiah (see the note on Lk 2, 11). Through this Son of David, salvation comes to the blind man. Note the connection between salvation and house of David mentioned earlier in Zechariah's canticle (Lk 1, 69). See also the note on Mt 9, 27.

19, 1-10: The story of the tax collector Zacchaeus is unique to this gospel. While a rich man (2), Zacchaeus provides a contrast to the rich man of Lk 18, 18-23 who cannot detach himself from his material possessions to become a follower of Jesus. Zacchaeus, according to Luke, exemplifies the proper attitude toward wealth: he promises to give half of his possessions to the poor (8) and consequently is the recipient of salvation (9-10).

19, 9: *A descendant of Abraham:* literally, "a son of Abraham." The tax collector Zacchaeus, whose repentance is attested by his determination to amend his former ways, shows himself to be a true descendant of Abraham, the true heir to the promises of God in the Old Testament. Underlying Luke's depiction of Zacchaeus as a descendant of Abraham, the father of the Jews (Lk 1, 73; 16, 22-31), is his recognition of the central place occupied by Israel in the plan of salvation.

19, 10: This verse sums up for Luke his depiction of the role of Jesus as savior in this gospel.

CHAPTER 19

Zacchaeus the Tax Collector. * [1] He came to Jericho and intended to pass through the town. [2] Now a man there named Zacchaeus, who was a chief tax collector and also a wealthy man, [3] was seeking to see who Jesus was; but he could not see him because of the crowd, for he was short in stature. [4] So he ran ahead and climbed a sycamore tree in order to see Jesus, who was about to pass that way. [5] When he reached the place, Jesus looked up and said to him, "Zacchaeus, come down quickly, for today I must stay at your house." [6] And he came down quickly and received him with joy. [7] When they all saw this, they began to grumble, saying, "He has gone to stay at the house of a sinner."[z] [8] But Zacchaeus stood there and said to the Lord, "Behold, half of my possessions, Lord, I shall give to the poor, and if I have extorted anything from anyone I shall repay it four times over."[a] [9] And Jesus said to him, "Today salvation[b] has come to this house because this man too is a descendant of Abraham.* [10] [c] For the Son of Man has come to seek and to save what was lost." *

The Parable of the Ten Gold Coins.* 11 *d* While they were listening to him speak, he proceeded to tell a parable because he was near Jerusalem and they thought that the kingdom of God would appear there immediately. 12 So he said, "A nobleman went off to a distant country to obtain the kingship for himself and then to return.*e* 13 He called ten of his servants and gave them ten gold coins* and told them, 'Engage in trade with these until I return.' 14 His fellow citizens, however, despised him and sent a delegation after him to announce, 'We do not want this man to be our king.' 15 But when he returned after obtaining the kingship, he had the servants called, to whom he had given the money, to learn what they had gained by trading. 16 The first came forward and said, 'Sir, your gold coin has earned ten additional ones.' 17 He replied, 'Well done, good servant! You have been faithful in this very small matter; take charge of ten cities.'*f* 18 Then the second came and reported, 'Your gold coin, sir, has earned five more.' 19 And to this servant too he said, 'You, take charge of five cities.' 20 Then the other servant came and said, 'Sir, here is your gold coin; I kept it stored away in a handkerchief, 21 for I was afraid of you, because you are a demanding person; you take up what you did not lay down and you harvest what you did not plant.' 22 He said to him, 'With your own words I shall condemn you, you wicked servant. You knew I was a demanding person, taking up what I did not lay down and harvesting what I did not plant; 23 why did you not put my money in a bank? Then on my return I would have collected it with interest.' 24 And to those standing by he said, 'Take

the gold coin from him and give it to the servant who has ten.' 25 But they said to him, 'Sir, he has ten gold coins.' 26 'I tell you, to everyone who has, more will be given, but from the one who has not, even what he has will be taken away.*g* 27 Now as for those enemies of mine who did not want me as their king, bring them here and slay them before me.' "

VI. THE TEACHING MINISTRY IN JERUSALEM*

The Entry into Jerusalem.* *h* 28 After he had said this, he proceeded on his journey up to Jerusalem. 29 As he drew near to Bethphage and Bethany at the place called the Mount of Olives, he sent two of his disciples.*i* 30 He said, "Go into the village opposite you, and as you enter it you will find a colt tethered on which no one has ever sat. Untie it and bring it here.*j* 31 And if anyone should ask you, 'Why are you untying it?' you will answer, 'The Master has need of it.' " 32 So those who had been sent went off and found everything just as he had told them.*k* 33 And as they were untying the colt, its owners said to them, "Why are you untying this colt?" 34 They answered, "The Master has need of it." 35 *l* So they brought it to Jesus, threw their cloaks over the colt, and helped Jesus to mount. 36 As he rode along, the people were spreading their cloaks on the road; 37 and now as he was approaching the slope of the Mount of Olives, the whole multitude of his disciples began to praise God aloud with joy for all the mighty deeds they had seen. 38 They proclaimed:

---

d 11-27: Mt 25, 14-30.—e Mk 13, 34.—f Lk 16, 10.—g Lk 8, 18; Mt 13, 12; Mk 4, 25.—h 28-40: Mt 21, 1-11; Mk 11, 1-11; Jn 12, 12-19.—i Zec 14, 4.—j Nm 19, 2; Dt 21, 3, 1 Sm 6, 7; Zec 9, 9.—k Lk 22, 13.—l 35-36: 2 Kgs 9, 13.

however, it furnishes a correction to the expectation of the imminent end of the age and of the establishment of the kingdom in Jerusalem (11). Jesus is not on his way to Jerusalem to receive the kingly power; for that, he must go away and only after returning from the distant country (a reference to the parousia) will reward and judgment take place.

19, 13: *Ten gold coins:* literally, "ten minas." A mina was a monetary unit that in ancient Greece was the equivalent of one hundred drachmas.

19, 28—21, 38: With the royal entry of Jesus into Jerusalem, a new section of Luke's gospel begins, the ministry of Jesus in Jerusalem before his death and resurrection. Luke suggests that this was a lengthy ministry in Jerusalem (Lk 19, 47; 20, 1; 21, 37-38; 22, 53) and it is characterized by Jesus' daily teaching in the temple (Lk 21, 37-38). For the story of the entry of Jesus into Jerusalem, see also Mt 21, 1-11; Mk 11, 1-10; Jn 12, 12-19 and the notes there.

19, 11-27: In this parable Luke has combined two originally distinct parables: (1) a parable about the conduct of faithful and productive servants (13.15b-26) and (2) a parable about a rejected king (12.14-15a.27). The story about the conduct of servants occurs in another form in Mt 25, 14-20. The story about the rejected king may have originated with a contemporary historical event. After the death of Herod the Great, his son Archelaus traveled to Rome to receive the title of king. A delegation of Jews appeared in Rome before Caesar Augustus to oppose the request of Archelaus. Although not given the title of king, Archelaus was made ruler over Judea and Samaria. As the story is used by Luke,

"Blessed is the king who comes
in the name of the Lord.*
Peace in heaven
and glory in the highest."*m*

[39] Some of the Pharisees in the crowd said to him, "Teacher, rebuke your disciples." * [40] He said in reply, "I tell you, if they keep silent, the stones will cry out!"

The Lament for Jerusalem.* [41] *n* As he drew near, he saw the city and wept over it,*o* [42] saying, "If this day you only knew what makes for peace—but now it is hidden from your eyes.*p* [43] * For the days are coming upon you when your enemies will raise a palisade against you; they will encircle you and hem you in on all sides.*q* [44] They will smash you to the ground and your children within you, and they will not leave one stone upon another within you because you did not recognize the time of your visitation." *r*

The Cleansing of the Temple. [45] *s* Then Jesus entered the temple area* and proceeded to drive out those who were selling things,*t* [46] saying to them, "It is written, 'My house shall be a house of prayer, but you have made it a den of thieves.' "*u* [47] And every day he was teaching in the temple area.*v* The chief priests, the scribes, and the leaders of the people, meanwhile, were seeking to put him to death,*w* [48] but they could find no way to accomplish their purpose because all the people were hanging on his words.

CHAPTER 20*

The Authority of Jesus Questioned. *x* [1] One day as he was teaching the people in the temple area and proclaiming the good news, the chief priests and scribes, together with the elders, approached him [2] and said to him, "Tell us, by what authority are you doing these things? Or who is the one who gave you this authority?"*y* [3] He said to them in reply, "I shall ask you a question. Tell me, [4] was John's baptism of heavenly or of human origin?"*z* [5] They discussed this among themselves, and said, "If we say, 'Of heavenly origin,' he will say, 'Why did you not believe him?'*a* [6] But if we say, 'Of human origin,' then all the people will stone us, for they are convinced that John was a prophet." [7] So they answered that they did not know from where it came. [8] Then Jesus said to them, "Neither shall I tell you by what authority I do these things."

The Parable of the Tenant Farmers.* [9] *b* Then he proceeded to tell the people this parable. "[A] man planted a vineyard, leased it to tenant farmers, and then went on a journey for a long time.*c* [10] At harvest time he sent a servant*d* to the tenant farmers to receive some of the produce of the vineyard. But they beat the servant and sent him away empty-handed. [11] So he proceeded to send another servant, but him also they beat and insulted and sent away empty-handed. [12] Then he proceeded to send a third, but this one too they wounded and threw out. [13] The owner of the vineyard said, 'What shall I do? I shall

m Lk 2, 14; Ps 118, 26.—n 41-44: Lk 13, 34-35.—o 2 Kgs 8, 11-12; Jer 14, 17; 15, 5.—p Lk 8, 10; Is 6, 9-10; Mt 13, 14; Mk 4, 12; Acts 28, 26-27; Rom 11, 8.10.—q Is 29, 3.—r Lk 1, 68; 21, 6; Ps 137, 9; Mt 24, 2; Mk 13, 2.—s 45-46: Mt 21, 12-13; Mk 11, 15-17; Jn 2, 13-17.—t Mal 3, 1 / Hos 9, 15.—u Is 56, 7; Jer 7, 11.—v 47-48: Lk 20, 19; 22, 2; Mt 21, 46; Mk 11, 18; 12, 12; 14, 1-2; Jn 5, 18; 7, 30.—w Lk 21, 37; 22, 53; Jn 18, 20.—x 1-8: Mt 21, 23-27; Mk 11, 27-33.—y Acts 4, 7.—z Lk 3, 3.16.—a Mt 21, 32.—b 9-19: Mt 21, 33-46; Mk 12, 1-12.—c Is 5, 1-7.—d 10-12: 2 Chr 36, 15-16.

19, 38: *Blessed is the king who comes in the name of the Lord:* only in Lk is Jesus explicitly given the title *king* when he enters Jerusalem in triumph. Luke has inserted this title into the words of Ps 118, 26 that heralded the arrival of the pilgrims coming to the holy city and to the temple. Jesus is thereby acclaimed as *king* (see Lk 1, 32) and as the one *who comes* (see Mal 3, 1; Lk 7, 19). *Peace in heaven . . . :* the acclamation of the disciples of Jesus in Lk echoes the announcement of the angels at the birth of Jesus (Lk 2, 14). The peace Jesus brings is associated with the salvation to be accomplished here in Jerusalem.

19, 39: *Rebuke your disciples:* this command, found only in Lk, was given so that the Roman authorities would not interpret the acclamation of Jesus as king as an uprising against them; cf Lk 23, 2-3.

19, 41-44: The lament for Jerusalem is found only in Lk. By not accepting Jesus (the one who mediates peace), Jerusalem will not find peace but will become the victim of devastation.

19, 43-44: Luke may be describing the actual disaster that befell Jerusalem in A.D. 70 when it was destroyed by the Romans during the First Revolt.

19, 45-46: Immediately upon entering the holy city, Jesus in a display of his authority enters the temple (see Mal 3, 1-3) and lays claim to it after cleansing it that it might become a proper place for his teaching ministry in Jerusalem (Lk 19, 47; 20, 1; 21, 37; 22, 53). See Mt 21, 12-17; Mk 11, 15-19; Jn 2, 13-17 and the notes there.

20, 1-47: The Jerusalem religious leaders or their representatives, in an attempt to incriminate Jesus with the Romans and to discredit him with the people, pose a number of questions to him (about his authority, 2; about payment of taxes, 22; about the resurrection, 28-33).

20, 9-19: This parable about an absentee landlord and a tenant farmers' revolt reflects the social and economic conditions of rural Palestine in the first century. The synoptic gospel writers use the parable to describe how the rejection of the landlord's son becomes the occasion for the vineyard to be taken away from those to whom it was entrusted (the religious leadership of Judaism that rejects the teaching and preaching of Jesus; 19).

send my beloved son; maybe they will respect him.'[e] [14] But when the tenant farmers saw him they said to one another, 'This is the heir. Let us kill him that the inheritance may become ours.' [15] So they threw him out of the vineyard and killed him.* What will the owner of the vineyard do to them? [16] He will come and put those tenant farmers to death and turn over the vineyard to others." When the people heard this, they exclaimed, "Let it not be so!" [17] But he looked at them and asked, "What then does this scripture passage mean:

'The stone which the builders rejected has become the cornerstone'?[f]

[18] Everyone who falls on that stone will be dashed to pieces; and it will crush anyone on whom it falls." [19] The scribes and chief priests sought to lay their hands on him at that very hour, but they feared the people, for they knew that he had addressed this parable to them.[g]

Paying Taxes to the Emperor.[h] [20] They watched him closely and sent agents pretending to be righteous who were to trap him in speech,[i] in order to hand him over to the authority and power of the governor.* [21] They posed this question to him, "Teacher, we know that what you say and teach is correct, and you show no partiality, but teach the way of God in accordance with the truth.[j] [22] Is it lawful for us to pay tribute to Caesar or not?"* [23] Recognizing their craftiness he said to them, [24] "Show me a denarius;* whose image and name does it bear?" They replied, "Caesar's." [25] So he said to them, "Then repay to Caesar what belongs to Caesar and to God what belongs to God."[k] [26] They were unable to trap him by something he might say before the people, and so amazed were they at his reply that they fell silent.

The Question about the Resurrection.[l] [27] Some Sadducees,* those who deny that there is a resurrection, came forward and put this question to him,[m] [28] * saying, "Teacher, Moses wrote for us, 'If someone's brother dies leaving a wife but no child, his brother must take the wife and raise up descendants for his brother.'[n] [29] Now there were seven brothers; the first married a woman but died childless. [30] Then the second [31] and the third married her, and likewise all the seven died childless. [32] Finally the woman also died. [33] Now at the resurrection whose wife will

that woman be? For all seven had been married to her." [34] Jesus said to them, "The children of this age marry and remarry; [35] but those who are deemed worthy to attain to the coming age and to the resurrection of the dead neither marry nor are given in marriage. [36] They can no longer die, for they are like angels; and they are the children of God because they are the ones who will rise.* [37] That the dead will rise even Moses made known in the passage about the bush, when he called 'Lord' the God of Abraham, the God of Isaac, and the God of Jacob;[o] [38] and he is not God of the dead, but of the living, for to him all are alive."[p] [39] Some of the scribes said in reply, "Teacher, you have answered well." [40] And they no longer dared to ask him anything.[q]

The Question about David's Son.* [41] [r] Then he said to them, "How do they claim that the Messiah is the Son of David? [42] For David himself in the Book of Psalms says:[s]

---

e Lk 3, 22.—f Ps 118, 22; Is 28, 16.—g Lk 19, 47-48; 22, 2; Mt 21, 46; Mk 11, 18; 12, 12; 14, 1-2; Jn 5, 18; 7, 30.—h 20-26: Mt 22, 15-22; Mk 12, 13-17.—i Lk 11, 54.—j Jn 3, 2.—k Rom 13, 6-7.—l 27-40: Mt 22, 23-33; Mk 12, 18-27.—m Acts 23, 8.—n Gn 38, 8; Dt 25, 5.—o Ex 3, 2.6.15-16.—p Rom 14, 8-9.—q Mt 22, 46; Mk 12, 34.—r 41-44: Mt 22, 41-45; Mk 12, 35-37.—s 42-43: Ps 110, 1.

20, 15: *They threw him out of the vineyard and killed him:* cf Mk 12, 8. Luke has altered his Marcan source and reports that the murder of the son takes place outside the vineyard to reflect the tradition of Jesus' death outside the walls of the city of Jerusalem (see Heb 13, 12).

20, 20: *The governor:* i.e., Pontius Pilate, the Roman administrator responsible for the collection of taxes and maintenance of order in Palestine.

20, 22: Through their question the agents of the Jerusalem religious leadership hope to force Jesus to take sides on one of the sensitive political issues of first-century Palestine. The issue of nonpayment of taxes to Rome becomes one of the focal points of the First Jewish Revolt (A.D. 66-70) that resulted in the Roman destruction of Jerusalem and the temple. See also the note on Mt 22, 15-22.

20, 24: *Denarius:* a Roman silver coin (see the note on Lk 7, 41).

20, 27: *Sadducees:* see the note on Mt 3, 7.

20, 28-33: The Sadducees' question, based on the law of levirate marriage recorded in Dt 25, 5-10, ridicules the idea of the resurrection. Jesus rejects their naive understanding of the resurrection (35-36) and then argues on behalf of the resurrection of the dead on the basis of the written law (37-38) that the Sadducees accept. See also the notes on Mt 22, 23-33.

20, 36: *Because they are the ones who will rise:* literally, "being sons of the resurrection."

20, 41-44: After successfully answering the three questions of his opponents, Jesus now asks them a question. Their inability to respond implies that they have forfeited their position and authority as the religious leaders of the people because they do not understand the scriptures. This series of controversies between the religious leadership of Jerusalem and Jesus reveals Jesus as the authoritative teacher whose words are to be listened to (see Lk 9, 35). See also the notes on Mt 22, 41-46.

'The Lord said to my lord,
"Sit at my right hand

43   till I make your enemies your footstool." '

44 Now if David calls him 'lord,' how can he be his son?"

Denunciation of the Scribes. [t]

45 Then, within the hearing of all the people, he said to [his] disciples, 46 "Be on guard against the scribes, who like to go around in long robes and love greetings in marketplaces, seats of honor in synagogues, and places of honor at banquets. [u] 47 They devour the houses of widows and, as a pretext, recite lengthy prayers. They will receive a very severe condemnation."

CHAPTER 21

The Poor Widow's Contribution.*

1 [v] When he looked up he saw some wealthy people putting their offerings into the treasury 2 and he noticed a poor widow putting in two small coins. 3 He said, "I tell you truly, this poor widow put in more than all the rest; 4 for those others have all made offerings from their surplus wealth, but she, from her poverty, has offered her whole livelihood."

The Destruction of the Temple Foretold. [w]

5 *While some people were speaking about how the temple was adorned with costly stones and votive offerings, he said, 6 "All that you see here—the days will come when there will not be left a stone upon another stone that will not be thrown down." [x]

The Signs of the End.

7 [y] Then they asked him, "Teacher, when will this happen? And what sign will there be when all these things are about to happen?" 8 He answered, "See that you not be deceived, for many will come in my name, saying, 'I am he,' and 'The time has come.' * Do not follow them! [z] 9 When you hear of wars and insurrections, do not be terrified; for such things must happen first, but it will not immediately be the end." 10 Then he said to them, "Nation will rise against nation, and kingdom against kingdom. [a] 11 There will be powerful earthquakes, famines, and plagues from place to place; and awesome sights and mighty signs will come from the sky.

The Coming Persecution.

12 [b] "Before all this happens,* however, they will seize and persecute you, they will hand you over to the synagogues and to prisons, and they will have you led before kings and governors because of my name. [c] 13 It will lead to your giving testimony. 14 Remember, you are not to prepare your defense beforehand, 15 [d] for I myself shall give you a wisdom in speaking * that all your adversaries will be powerless to resist or refute. 16 [e] You will even be handed over by parents, brothers, relatives, and friends, and they will put some of you to death. [f] 17 You will be hated by all because of my name, 18 but not a hair on your head will be destroyed. [g] 19 By your perseverance you will secure your lives. [h]

The Great Tribulation.*

20 [i] "When you see Jerusalem surrounded by armies, know

Lk

---

t 45-47: Lk 11, 37-54; Mt 23, 1-36; Mk 12, 38-40.—u Lk 14, 7-11.—v 1-4: Mk 12, 41-44.—w 5-6: Mt 24, 1-2; Mk 13, 1-2.— x Lk 19, 44.—y 7-19: Mt 24, 3-14; Mk 13, 3-13.—z Lk 17, 23; Mk 13, 5.6.21; 1 Jn 2, 18.—a 2 Chr 15, 6; Is 19, 2.—b 12-15: Lk 12, 11-12; Mt 10, 17-20; Mk 13, 9-11.—c Jn 16, 2; Acts 25, 24.—d Acts 6, 10.—e 16-18: Mt 10, 21-22.—f Lk 12, 52-53.— g Lk 12, 7; 1 Sm 14, 45; Mt 10, 30; Acts 27, 34.—h Lk 8, 15.—i 20-24: Mt 24, 15-21; Mk 13, 14-19.

21, 1-4: The widow is another example of the poor ones in this gospel whose detachment from material possessions and dependence on God leads to their blessedness (Lk 6, 20). Her simple offering provides a striking contrast to the pride and pretentiousness of the scribes denounced in the preceding section (Lk 20, 45-47). The story is taken from Mk 12, 41-44.

21, 5-36: Jesus' eschatological discourse in Lk is inspired by Mk 13, but Luke has made some significant alterations to the words of Jesus found there. Luke maintains, though in a modified form, the belief in the early expectation of the end of the age (see 27.28.31.32.36), but, by focusing attention throughout the gospel on the importance of the day-to-day following of Jesus and by reinterpreting the meaning of some of the signs of the end from

Mk 13, he has come to terms with what seemed to the early Christian community to be a delay of the parousia. Mark, for example, described the desecration of the Jerusalem temple by the Romans (Mk 13, 14) as the apocalyptic symbol (see Dn 9, 27; 12, 11) accompanying the end of the age and the coming of the Son of Man. Luke (Lk 21, 20-24), however, removes the apocalyptic setting and separates the historical destruction of Jerusalem from the signs of the coming of the Son of Man by a period that he refers to as "the times of the Gentiles" (Lk 21, 24). See also the notes on Mt 24, 1-36 and Mk 13, 1-37.

21, 8: *The time has come:* in Lk, the proclamation of the imminent end of the age has itself become a false teaching.

21, 12: *Before all this happens . . . :* to Luke and his community, some of the signs of the end just described (10-11) still lie in the future. Now in dealing with the persecution of the disciples (12-19) and the destruction of Jerusalem (20-24) Luke is pointing to eschatological signs that have already been fulfilled.

21, 15: *A wisdom in speaking:* literally, "a mouth and wisdom."

21, 20-24: The actual destruction of Jerusalem by Rome in A.D. 70 upon which Luke and his community look back provides the assurance that, just as Jesus' prediction of Jerusalem's destruction was fulfilled, so too will be his announcement of their final redemption (27-28).

that its desolation is at hand.[j] [21]Then those in Judea must flee to the mountains. Let those within the city escape from it, and let those in the countryside not enter the city,[k] [22]for these days are the time of punishment when all the scriptures are fulfilled. [23]Woe to pregnant women and nursing mothers in those days, for a terrible calamity will come upon the earth and a wrathful judgment upon this people.[l] [24]They will fall by the edge of the sword and be taken as captives to all the Gentiles; and Jerusalem will be trampled underfoot by the Gentiles until the times of the Gentiles* are fulfilled.[m]

The Coming of the Son of Man.[n] [25]"There will be signs in the sun, the moon, and the stars, and on earth nations will be in dismay, perplexed by the roaring of the sea and the waves.[o] [26]People will die of fright in anticipation of what is coming upon the world, for the powers of the heavens* will be shaken.[p] [27]And then they will see the Son of Man coming in a cloud with power and great glory.[q] [28]But when these signs begin to happen, stand erect and raise your heads because your redemption is at hand."[r]

The Lesson of the Fig Tree.[s] [29]He taught them a lesson. "Consider the fig tree and all the other trees. [30]When their buds burst open, you see for yourselves and know that summer is now near; [31]in the same way, when you see these things happening, know that the kingdom of God is near. [32]Amen, I say to you, this generation will not pass away until all these things have taken place.[t] [33]Heaven and earth will pass away, but my words will not pass away.[u]

Exhortation to be Vigilant. [34]"Beware that your hearts do not become drowsy from carousing and drunkenness and the anxieties of daily life, and that day catch you by surprise[v] [35]like a trap. For that day will assault everyone who lives on the face of the earth. [36]Be vigilant at all times and pray that you have the strength to escape the tribulations that are imminent and to stand before the Son of Man."[w]

Ministry in Jerusalem.[37]During the day, Jesus was teaching in the temple area, but at night he would leave and stay at the place called the Mount of Olives.[x] [38]And all the people would get up early each morning to listen to him in the temple area.

VII. THE PASSION NARRATIVE*

CHAPTER 22

The Conspiracy against Jesus. [1] [y] Now the feast of Unleavened Bread, called the Passover,* was drawing near, [2] [z] and the chief priests and the scribes were seeking a way to put him to death, for they were afraid of the people. [3] [a] Then Satan entered into Judas,* the one surnamed Iscariot, who was counted among the Twelve,[b] [4]and he went to the chief priests and temple guards to discuss a plan for handing him over to them. [5]They were pleased and agreed to pay him money. [6]He accepted their offer and sought a favorable opportunity to hand him over to them in the absence of a crowd.

Preparations for the Passover.[c] [7]When the day of the Feast of Unleavened Bread arrived, the day for sacrificing the Passover lamb,[d] [8]he sent out Peter and John, instructing them, "Go and make preparations for us to eat the Passover." [9]They asked him, "Where do you want us to

---

j 20-22: Lk 19, 41-44.—k Lk 17, 31.—l 1 Cor 7, 26.—m Tb 14, 5; Ps 79, 1; Is 63, 18; Jer 21, 7; Rom 11, 25; Rv 11, 2.—n 25-28: Mt 24, 29-31; Mk 13, 24-27.—o Wis 5, 22; Is 13, 10; Ez 32, 7; Jl 2, 10; 3, 3-4; 4, 15; Rv 6, 12-14.—p Hg 2, 6.21.—q Dn 7, 13-14; Mt 26, 64; Rv 1, 7.—r Lk 2, 38.—s 29-33: Mt 24, 32-35; Mk 13, 28-31.—t Lk 9, 27; Mt 16, 28.—u Lk 16, 17.—v Lk 12, 45-46; Mt 24, 48-50; 1 Thes 5, 3.6-7.—w Mk 13, 33.—x Lk 19, 47; 22, 39.—y 1-2: Mt 26, 1-5; Mk 14, 1-2; Jn 11, 47-53.— z Lk 19, 47-48; 20, 19; Mt 21, 46; Mk 12, 12; Jn 5, 18; 7, 30.— a 3-6: Mt 26, 14-16; Mk 14, 10-11; Jn 13, 2.27.—b Acts 1, 17.—c 7-13: Mt 26, 17-19; Mk 14, 12-16.—d Ex 12, 6.14-20.

21, 24: *The times of the Gentiles:* a period of indeterminate length separating the destruction of Jerusalem from the cosmic signs accompanying the coming of the Son of Man.

21, 26: *The powers of the heavens:* the heavenly bodies mentioned in v 25 and thought of as cosmic armies.

22, 1—23, 56a: The passion narrative. Luke is still dependent upon Mk for the composition of the passion narrative but has incorporated much of his own special tradition into the narrative. Among the distinctive sections in Lk are: (1) the tradition of the institution of the Eucharist (Lk 22, 15-20); (2) Jesus' farewell discourse (Lk 22, 21-38); (3) the mistreatment and interrogation of Jesus (Lk 22, 63-71); (4) Jesus before Herod and his second appearance before Pilate (Lk 23, 6-16); (5) words addressed to the women followers on the way to the crucifixion (Lk 23, 27-32); (6) words to the penitent thief (Lk 23, 39-41); (7) the death of Jesus (Lk 23, 46.47b-49). Luke stresses the innocence of Jesus (Lk 23, 4.14-15.22) who is the victim of the powers of evil (Lk 22, 3.31.53) and who goes to his death in fulfillment of his Father's will (Lk 22, 42.46). Throughout the narrative Luke emphasizes the mercy, compassion, and healing power of Jesus (Lk 22, 51; 23, 43) who does not go to death lonely and deserted, but is accompanied by others who follow him on the way of the cross (Lk 23, 26-31.49).

22, 1: *Feast of Unleavened Bread, called the Passover:* see the note on Mk 14, 1.

22, 3: *Satan entered into Judas:* see the note on Lk 4, 13.

make the preparations?" [10] And he answered them, "When you go into the city, a man will meet you carrying a jar of water.* Follow him into the house that he enters [11] and say to the master of the house, 'The teacher says to you, "Where is the guest room where I may eat the Passover with my disciples?" ' [12] He will show you a large upper room that is furnished. Make the preparations there." [13] Then they went off and found everything exactly as he had told them, and there they prepared the Passover.[e]

The Last Supper.[f] [14] When the hour came, he took his place at table with the apostles. [15] He said to them, "I have eagerly desired to eat this Passover* with you before I suffer, [16] for, I tell you, I shall not eat it [again] until there is fulfillment in the kingdom of God."[g] [17] Then he took a cup,* gave thanks, and said, "Take this and share it among yourselves; [18] for I tell you [that] from this time on I shall not drink of the fruit of the vine until the kingdom of God comes." [19] [h] Then he took the bread, said the blessing, broke it, and gave it to them, saying, "This is my body, which will be given for you; do this in memory of me."* [20] And likewise the cup after they had eaten, saying, "This cup is the new covenant in my blood, which will be shed for you.[i]

The Betrayal Foretold.[j] [21] "And yet behold, the hand of the one who is to betray me is with me on the table; [22] for the Son of Man indeed goes as it has been determined; but woe to that man by whom he is betrayed." [23] And they began to debate

among themselves who among them would do such a deed.

The Role of the Disciples. [24] * Then an argument broke out among them[k] about which of them should be regarded as the greatest. [25] [l] He said to them, "The kings of the Gentiles lord it over them and those in authority over them are addressed as 'Benefactors';* [26] but among you it shall not be so. Rather, let the greatest among you be as the youngest, and the leader as the servant.[m] [27] For who is greater: the one seated at table or the one who serves? Is it not the one seated at table? I am among you as the one who serves. [28] It is you who have stood by me in my trials; [29] and I confer a kingdom on you, just as my Father has conferred one on me,[n] [30] that you may eat and drink at my table in my kingdom; and you will sit on thrones judging the twelve tribes of Israel.[o]

Peter's Denial Foretold.[p] [31] "Simon, Simon, behold Satan has demanded to sift all of you* like wheat,[q] [32] but I have prayed* that your own faith may not fail; and once you have turned back, you must strengthen your brothers." [33] He said to him, "Lord, I am prepared to go to prison and to die with you."[r] [34] But he replied, "I tell you, Peter, before the cock crows this day, you will deny three times that you know me."[s]

Instructions for the Time of Crisis. [35] [t] He said to them, "When I sent you forth without a money bag or a sack or sandals, were you in need of anything?" "No, nothing," they replied. [36] [u] He said to them,* "But now one who has a money bag should take

---

e Lk 19, 32.—f 14-20: Mt 26, 20.26-30; Mk 14, 17.22-26; 1 Cor 11, 23-25.—g Lk 13, 29.—h Lk 24, 30; Acts 27, 35.—i Ex 24, 8; Jer 31, 31; 32, 40; Zec 9, 11.—j 21-23: Ps 41, 10; Mt 26, 21-25; Mk 14, 18-21; Jn 13, 21-30.—k Lk 9, 46; Mt 18, 1; Mk 9, 34.—l 25-27: Mt 20, 25-27; Mk 10, 42-44; Jn 13, 3-16.—m Mt 23, 11; Mk 9, 35.—n Lk 12, 32.—o Mt 19, 28.—p 31-34: Mt 26, 33-35; Mk 14, 29-31; Jn 13, 37-38.—q Jb 1, 6-12; Am 9, 9.—r Lk 22, 54.—s Lk 22, 54-62.—t Lk 9, 3; 10, 4; Mt 10, 9-10; Mk 6, 7-9.—u Lk 22, 49.

22, 10: *A man will meet you carrying a jar of water:* see the note on Mk 14, 13.

22, 15: *This Passover:* Luke clearly identifies this last supper of Jesus with the apostles as a Passover meal that commemorated the deliverance of the Israelites from slavery in Egypt. Jesus reinterprets the significance of the Passover by setting it in the context of the kingdom of God (16). The "deliverance" associated with the Passover finds its new meaning in the blood that will be shed (20).

22, 17: Because of a textual problem in vv 19 and 20, some commentators interpret this cup as the eucharistic cup.

22, 19c-20: *Which will be given . . . do this in memory of me:* these words are omitted in some important Western text manuscripts and a few Syriac manuscripts. Other ancient text

types, including the oldest papyrus manuscript of Lk dating from the late second or early third century, contain the longer reading presented here. The Lucan account of the words of institution of the Eucharist bears a close resemblance to the words of institution in the Pauline tradition (see 1 Cor 11, 23-26). See also the notes on Mt 26, 26-29; 26, 27-28; and Mk 14, 22-24.

22, 24-38: The Gospel of Luke presents a brief farewell discourse of Jesus; compare the lengthy farewell discourses and prayer in Jn, chs 13-17.

22, 25: *'Benefactors':* this word occurs as a title of rulers in the Hellenistic world.

22, 31: *All of you:* literally, "you." The translation reflects the meaning of the Greek text that uses a second person plural pronoun here.

22, 31-32: Jesus' prayer for Simon's faith and the commission to strengthen his brothers anticipates the post-resurrection prominence of Peter in the first half of Acts, where he appears as the spokesman for the Christian community and the one who begins the mission to the Gentiles (Acts 10—11).

22, 36: In contrast to the ministry of the Twelve and of the seventy-two during the period of Jesus (Lk 9, 3; 10, 4), in the future period of the church the missionaries must be prepared for the opposition they will face in a world hostile to their preaching.

Lk

it, and likewise a sack, and one who does not have a sword should sell his cloak and buy one. 37 For I tell you that this scripture must be fulfilled in me, namely, 'He was counted among the wicked'; and indeed what is written about me is coming to fulfillment."*v* 38 Then they said,"Lord, look, there are two swords here." But he replied, "It is enough!"*

The Agony in the Garden. *w* 39 Then going out he went, as was his custom, to the Mount of Olives, and the disciples followed him. 40 When he arrived at the place he said to them, "Pray that you may not undergo the test."*x* 41 After withdrawing about a stone's throw from them and kneeling, he prayed,*y* 42 saying, "Father, if you are willing, take this cup away from me; still, not my will but yours be done."*z* *[43 And to strengthen him an angel from heaven appeared to him. 44 He was in such agony and he prayed so fervently that his sweat became like drops of blood falling on the ground.] 45 When he rose from prayer and returned to his disciples, he found them sleeping from grief. 46 He said to them, "Why are you sleeping? Get up and pray that you may not undergo the test."*a*

The Betrayal and Arrest of Jesus.b 47 While he was still speaking, a crowd approached and in front was one of the Twelve, a man named Judas. He went up to Jesus to kiss him. 48 Jesus said to him, "Judas, are you betraying the Son of Man with a kiss?" 49 His disciples realized what was about to happen, and they asked, "Lord, shall we strike with a sword?"*c* 50 And one of them struck the high priest's servant and cut off his right ear. *d* 51 But Jesus said in reply, "Stop, no more of this!" Then he touched the servant's ear and healed him.* 52 And Jesus said to the chief priests and temple guards and elders who had come for him, "Have you come out as against a robber, with swords and clubs?*e* 53 Day after day I was with you in the temple area, and you did not seize me; but this is your hour, the time for the power of darkness."*f*

Peter's Denial of Jesus. 54 *g* After arresting him they led him away and took him into the house of the high priest; Peter was following at a distance.*h* 55 They lit a fire in the middle of the courtyard and sat around it, and Peter sat down with them. 56 When a maid saw him seated in the light, she looked intently at him and said, "This man

too was with him." 57 But he denied it saying, "Woman, I do not know him." 58 A short while later someone else saw him and said, "You too are one of them"; but Peter answered, "My friend, I am not." 59 About an hour later, still another insisted, "Assuredly, this man too was with him, for he also is a Galilean." 60 But Peter said, "My friend, I do not know what you are talking about." Just as he was saying this, the cock crowed, 61 and the Lord turned and looked at Peter;* and Peter remembered the word of the Lord, how he had said to him, "Before the cock crows today, you will deny me three times."*i* 62 He went out and began to weep bitterly. 63 *j* The men who held Jesus in custody were ridiculing and beating him. 64 They blindfolded him and questioned him, saying, "Prophesy! Who is it that struck you?" 65 And they reviled him in saying many other things against him.

Jesus before the Sanhedrin.* 66 *k* When day came the council of elders of the people met, both chief priests and scribes,*l* and they brought him before their Sanhedrin.* 67 They said, "If you are the Messiah, tell us," but he replied to them, "If I tell you, you will not believe,*m* 68 and if I question, you will not respond. 69 But from this time on the Son of Man will be

v Is 53, 12.—w 39-46: Mt 26, 30.36-46; Mk 14, 26.32-42; Jn 18, 1-2.—x Lk 22, 46.—y Heb 5, 7-8.—z Mt 6, 10.—a Lk 22, 40.—b 47-53: Mt 26, 47-56; Mk 14, 43-50; Jn 18, 3-4.—c Lk 22, 36.—d Jn 18, 26.—e Lk 22, 37.—f Lk 19, 47; 21, 37; Jn 7, 30; 8, 20; Col 1, 13.—g 54-62: Mt 26, 57-58.69-75; Mk 14, 53-54.66-72; Jn 18, 12-18.25-27.—h Lk 22, 33.—i Lk 22, 34.—j 63-65: Mt 26, 67-68; Mk 14, 65.—k 66-71: Mt 26, 59-66; Mk 14, 55-64.—l Mt 27, 1; Mk 15, 1.—m Jn 3, 12; 8, 45; 10, 24.

22, 38: *It is enough!:* the farewell discourse ends abruptly with these words of Jesus spoken to the disciples when they take literally what was intended as figurative language about being prepared to face the world's hostility.

22, 43-44: These verses, though very ancient, were probably not part of the original text of Lk. They are absent from the oldest papyrus manuscripts of Lk and from manuscripts of wide geographical distribution.

22,51: *And healed him:* only Luke recounts this healing of the injured servant.

22, 61: Only Luke recounts that *the Lord turned and looked at Peter.* This look of Jesus leads to Peter's weeping bitterly over his denial (62).

22, 66-71: Luke recounts one daytime trial of Jesus (66-71) and hints at some type of preliminary nighttime investigation (54-65). Mark (and Matthew who follows Mk) has transferred incidents of this day into the nighttime interrogation with the result that there appear to be two Sanhedrin trials of Jesus in Mk (and Mt); see the note on Mk 14, 53.

22, 66: *Sanhedrin:* the word is a Hebraized form of a Greek word meaning a "council," and refers to the elders, chief priests, and scribes who met under the high priest's leadership to decide religious and legal questions that did not pertain to Rome's interests. Jewish sources are not clear on the competence of the Sanhedrin to sentence and to execute during this period.

seated at the right hand of the power of God."[n] [70]They all asked, "Are you then the Son of God?" He replied to them, "You say that I am." [71]Then they said, "What further need have we for testimony? We have heard it from his own mouth."

CHAPTER 23

Jesus before Pilate.[o] [1] * Then the whole assembly of them arose and brought him before Pilate. [2]They brought charges against him, saying, "We found this man misleading our people; he opposes the payment of taxes to Caesar and maintains that he is the Messiah, a king."[p] [3]Pilate asked him, "Are you the king of the Jews?" He said to him in reply, "You say so."[q] [4]Pilate then addressed the chief priests and the crowds, "I find this man not guilty." [5]But they were adamant and said, "He is inciting the people with his teaching throughout all Judea, from Galilee where he began even to here."[r]

Jesus before Herod. [6] * On hearing this Pilate asked if the man was a Galilean; [7]and upon learning that he was under Herod's jurisdiction, he sent him to Herod who was in Jerusalem at that time.[s] [8]Herod was very glad to see Jesus; he had

n Ps 110, 1; Dn 7, 13-14; Acts 7, 56.—o 1-5: Mt 27, 1-2.11-14; Mk 15, 1-5; Jn 18, 28-38.—p Lk 20, 22-25; Acts 17, 7; 24, 5.—q Lk 22, 70; 1 Tm 6, 13.—r Lk 23, 14.22.41; Mt 27, 24; Jn 19, 4.6; Acts 13, 28.—s Lk 3, 1; 9, 7.—t Lk 9, 9; Acts 4, 27-28.—u Mk 15, 5.—v Mt 27, 12; Mk 15, 3.—w Mt 27, 28-30; Mk 15, 17-19; Jn 19, 2-3.—x Lk 23, 4.22.41.—y Lk 23, 22; Jn 19, 12-14.—z 18-25: Mt 27, 20-26; Mk 15, 6-7.11-15; Jn 18, 38b-40; 19, 14-16; Acts 3, 13-14.—a 26-32: Mt 27, 32.38; Mk 15, 21.27; Jn 19, 17.—b 28-31: Lk 19, 41-44; 21, 23-24.

23, 1-5.13-25: Twice Jesus is brought before Pilate in Luke's account, and each time Pilate explicitly declares Jesus innocent of any wrongdoing (4.14.22). This stress on the innocence of Jesus before the Roman authorities is also characteristic of John's gospel (Jn 18, 38; 19, 4.6). Luke presents the Jerusalem Jewish leaders as the ones who force the hand of the Roman authorities (1-2.5.10.13.18.21.23-25).

23, 6-12: The appearance of Jesus before Herod is found only in this gospel. Herod has been an important figure in Lk (Lk 9, 7-9; 13, 31-33) and has been presented as someone who has been curious about Jesus for a long time. His curiosity goes unrewarded. It is faith in Jesus, not curiosity, that is rewarded (Lk 7, 50; 8, 48.50; 17, 19).

23, 17: This verse, "He was obliged to release one prisoner for them at the festival," is not part of the original text of Lk. It is an explanatory gloss from Mk 15, 6 (also Mt 27, 15) and is not found in many early and important Greek manuscripts. On its historical background, see the notes on Mt 27, 15-26.

23, 26-32: An important Lucan theme throughout the gospel has been the need for the Christian disciple to follow in the footsteps of Jesus. Here this theme comes to the fore with the story of Simon of Cyrene who takes up the cross and follows Jesus (see Lk 9, 23; 14, 27) and with the large crowd who likewise follow Jesus on the way of the cross. See also the note on Mk 15, 21.

been wanting to see him for a long time, for he had heard about him and had been hoping to see him perform some sign.[t] [9]He questioned him at length, but he gave him no answer.[u] [10]The chief priests and scribes, meanwhile, stood by accusing him harshly.[v] [11][Even] Herod and his soldiers treated him contemptuously and mocked him, and after clothing him in resplendent garb, he sent him back to Pilate.[w] [12]Herod and Pilate became friends that very day, even though they had been enemies formerly. [13]Pilate then summoned the chief priests, the rulers, and the people [14]and said to them, "You brought this man to me and accused him of inciting the people to revolt. I have conducted my investigation in your presence and have not found this man guilty of the charges you have brought against him,[x] [15]nor did Herod, for he sent him back to us. So no capital crime has been committed by him.[16] [y] Therefore I shall have him flogged and then release him." [17]*

The Sentence of Death. [z] [18]But all together they shouted out, "Away with this man! Release Barabbas to us." [19](Now Barabbas had been imprisoned for a rebellion that had taken place in the city and for murder.) [20]Again Pilate addressed them, still wishing to release Jesus, [21]but they continued their shouting, "Crucify him! Crucify him!" [22]Pilate addressed them a third time, "What evil has this man done? I found him guilty of no capital crime. Therefore I shall have him flogged and then release him." [23]With loud shouts, however, they persisted in calling for his crucifixion, and their voices prevailed. [24]The verdict of Pilate was that their demand should be granted. [25]So he released the man who had been imprisoned for rebellion and murder, for whom they asked, and he handed Jesus over to them to deal with as they wished.

The Way of the Cross.[*] [26] [a] As they led him away they took hold of a certain Simon, a Cyrenian, who was coming in from the country; and after laying the cross on him, they made him carry it behind Jesus. [27]A large crowd of people followed Jesus, including many women who mourned and lamented him. [28] [b] Jesus turned to them and said, "Daughters of Jerusalem, do not weep for me; weep instead for yourselves and for your children, [29]for indeed, the days are coming when people will say, 'Blessed are the barren, the wombs that never bore and the breasts that never nursed.' [30] At that time people will say to the mountains, 'Fall upon us!' and to the hills, 'Cover us!'[c] [31] for if these things are done when the wood is green what will happen when it is dry?" [32] Now two others, both criminals, were led away with him to be executed.

The Crucifixion.[d] [33] When they came to the place called the Skull, they crucified him and the criminals there, one on his right, the other on his left.[e] [34] [Then Jesus said, "Father, forgive them, they know not what they do."]* They divided his garments by casting lots.[f] [35] The people stood by and watched; the rulers, meanwhile, sneered at him and said,[g] "He saved others, let him save himself if he is the chosen one, the Messiah of God."[h] [36] Even the soldiers jeered at him. As they approached to offer him wine[i] [37] they called out, "If you are King of the Jews, save yourself." [38] Above him there was an inscription that read, "This is the King of the Jews."

[39] * Now one of the criminals hanging there reviled Jesus, saying, "Are you not the Messiah? Save yourself and us." [40] The other, however, rebuking him, said in reply, "Have you no fear of God, for you are subject to the same condemnation? [41] And indeed, we have been condemned justly, for the sentence we received corresponds to our crimes, but this man has done nothing criminal."[j] [42] Then he said, "Jesus, remember me when you come into your kingdom."[k] [43] He replied to him, "Amen, I say to you, today you will be with me in Paradise."[l]

The Death of Jesus.[m] [44] It was now about noon[n] and darkness came over the whole land until three in the afternoon* [45] because of an eclipse of the sun. Then the veil of the temple was torn down the middle.[o] [46] Jesus cried out in a loud voice, "Father, into your hands I commend my spirit"; and when he had said this he breathed his last.[p] [47] The centurion who witnessed what had happened glorified God and said, "This man was innocent* beyond doubt." [48] When all the people who had gathered for this spectacle saw what had happened, they returned home beating their breasts;[q] [49] but all his acquaintances stood at a distance, including the women who had followed him from Galilee and saw these events.[r]

The Burial of Jesus.[s] [50] Now there was a virtuous and righteous man named Joseph who, though he was a member of the council, [51] had not consented to their plan of action. He came from the Jewish town of Arimathea and was awaiting the kingdom of God.[t] [52] He went to Pilate and asked for the body of Jesus. [53] After he had taken the body down, he wrapped it in a linen cloth and laid him in a rock-hewn tomb in which no one had yet been buried.[u] [54] It was the day of preparation, and the sabbath was about to begin. [55] The women who had come from Galilee with him followed behind, and when they had seen the tomb and the way in which his body was laid in it,[v] [56] they returned and prepared spices and perfumed oils. Then they rested on the sabbath according to the commandment.[w]

VIII. THE RESURRECTION NARRATIVE*

CHAPTER 24

The Resurrection of Jesus. [1] [x] But at daybreak on the first day of the week they took the spices they had prepared and went to

c Hos 10, 8; Rv 6, 16.—d 33-43: Mt 27, 33-44; Mk 15, 22-32; Jn 19, 17-24.—e Lk 22, 37; Is 53, 12.—f Nm 15, 27-31; Ps 22, 19; Mt 5, 44; Acts 7, 60.—g 35-36: Ps 22, 8-9.—h Lk 4, 23.—i Ps 69, 22; Mt 27, 48; Mk 15, 36.—j Lk 23, 4.14.22.—k Lk 9, 27; 23, 2.3.38.—l 2 Cor 12, 3; Rv 2, 7.—m 44-49: Mt 27, 45-56; Mk 15, 33-41; Jn 19, 25-30.—n 44-45: Am 8, 9.—o Ex 26, 31-33; 36, 35.—p Ps 31, 6; Acts 7, 59.—q Lk 18, 13; Zec 12, 10.—r Lk 8, 1-3; 23, 55-56; 24, 10; Ps 38, 12.—s 50-56: Mt 27, 57-61; Mk 15, 42-47; Jn 19, 38-42; Acts 13, 29.—t Lk 2, 25.38.—u Lk 19, 30; Acts 13, 29.—v Lk 8, 2; 23, 49; 24, 10.—w Ex 12, 16; 20, 10; Dt 5, 14.—x 1-8: Mt 28, 1-8; Mk 16, 1-8; Jn 20, 1-17.

23, 34a: *[Then Jesus said, "Father, forgive them, they know not what they do."]:* this portion of v 34 does not occur in the oldest papyrus manuscript of Lk and in other early Greek manuscripts and ancient versions of wide geographical distribution.

23, 39-43: This episode is recounted only in this gospel. The penitent sinner receives salvation through the crucified Jesus. Jesus' words to the penitent thief reveal Luke's understanding that the destiny of the Christian is "to be with Jesus."

23, 44: *Noon . . . three in the afternoon:* literally, the sixth and ninth hours. See the note on Mk 15, 25.

23, 47: *This man was innocent:* or, "This man was righteous."

24, 1-53: The resurrection narrative in Lk consists of five sections: (1) the women at the empty tomb (Lk 23, 56b—24, 12); (2) the appearance to the two disciples on the way to Emmaus (Lk 24, 13-35); (3) the appearance to the disciples in Jerusalem (Lk 24, 36-43); (4) Jesus' final instructions (Lk 24, 44-49); (5) the ascension (Lk 24, 50-53). In Lk, all the resurrection appearances take place in and around Jerusalem; moreover, they are all recounted as having taken place on Easter Sunday. A consistent theme throughout the narrative is that the suffering, death, and resurrection of Jesus were accomplished in fulfillment of Old Testament promises and of Jewish hopes (19a.21.26-27.44.46). In his second volume, Acts, Luke will argue that Christianity is the fulfillment of the hopes of Pharisaic Judaism and its logical development (see Acts 24, 10-21).

the tomb. ²They found the stone rolled away from the tomb; ³but when they entered, they did not find the body of the Lord Jesus. ⁴While they were puzzling over this, behold, two men in dazzling garments appeared to them.*y* ⁵They were terrified and bowed their faces to the ground. They said to them, "Why do you seek the living one among the dead?*z* ⁶He is not here, but he has been raised.* Remember what he said to you while he was still in Galilee, ⁷that the Son of Man must be handed over to sinners and be crucified, and rise on the third day."*a* ⁸And they remembered his words.*b* ⁹ *c* Then they returned from the tomb and announced all these things to the eleven and to all the others.* ¹⁰The women were Mary Magdalene, Joanna, and Mary the mother of James; the others who accompanied them also told this to the apostles,*d* ¹¹but their story seemed like nonsense and they did not believe them. ¹² *e* But Peter got up and ran to the tomb, bent down, and saw the burial cloths alone; then he went home amazed at what had happened.*

---

y 2 Mc 3, 26; Acts 1, 10.—z Acts 2, 9.—a Lk 9, 22.44; 17, 25; 18, 32-33; Mt 16, 21; 17, 22-23; Mk 9, 31; Acts 17, 3.—b Jn 2, 22.—c 9-11: Mk 16, 10-11; Jn 20, 18.—d Lk 8, 2-3; Mk 16, 9.—e Jn 20, 3-7.—f Mk 16, 12-13.—g Jn 20, 14; 21, 4.—h Mt 2, 23; 21, 11; Acts 2, 22.—i Lk 1, 54.68; 2, 38.—j 22-23: Lk 24, 1-11; Mt 28, 1-8; Mk 16, 1-8.—k Jn 20, 3-10.—l 25-26: Lk 9, 22; 18, 31; 24, 44; Acts 3, 24; 17, 3.—m Lk 24, 44; Dt 18, 25; Ps 22, 1-18; Is 53; 1 Pt 1, 10-11.

24, 6a: *He is not here, but he has been raised:* this part of the verse is omitted in important representatives of the Western text tradition, but its presence in other text types and the slight difference in wording from Mt 28, 6 and Mk 16, 6 argue for its retention.

24, 9: The women in this gospel do not flee from the tomb and tell no one, as in Mk 16, 8, but return and tell the disciples about their experience. The initial reaction to the testimony of the women is disbelief (11).

24, 12: This verse is missing from the Western textual tradition but is found in the best and oldest manuscripts of other text types.

24, 13-35: This episode focuses on the interpretation of scripture by the risen Jesus and the recognition of him in the breaking of the bread. The references to the quotations of scripture and explanation of it (25-27), the kerygmatic proclamation (34), and the liturgical gesture (30) suggest that the episode is primarily catechetical and liturgical rather than apologetic.

24, 13: *Seven miles:* literally, "sixty stades." A stade was 607 feet. Some manuscripts read "160 stades" or more than eighteen miles. The exact location of Emmaus is disputed.

24, 16: A consistent feature of the resurrection stories is that the risen Jesus was different and initially unrecognizable (Lk 24, 37; Mk 16, 12; Jn 20, 14; 21, 4).

24, 26: *That the Messiah should suffer . . . :* Luke is the only New Testament writer to state explicit!y of a suffering Messiah (26.46; Acts 3, 18; 17, 3; 26, 23). The idea of a suffering Messiah is not found in the Old Testament or in other Jewish literature prior to the New Testament period, although the idea is hinted at in Mk 8, 31-33. See the notes on Mt 26, 63 and Mt 26, 67-68.

The Appearance on the Road to Emmaus.* ¹³Now that very day two of them were going to a village seven miles* from Jerusalem called Emmaus,*f* ¹⁴and they were conversing about all the things that had occurred. ¹⁵And it happened that while they were conversing and debating, Jesus himself drew near and walked with them, ¹⁶ *g* but their eyes were prevented from recognizing him.* ¹⁷He asked them, "What are you discussing as you walk along?" They stopped, looking downcast. ¹⁸One of them, named Cleopas, said to him in reply, "Are you the only visitor to Jerusalem who does not know of the things that have taken place there in these days?" ¹⁹And he replied to them, "What sort of things?" They said to him, "The things that happened to Jesus the Nazarene, who was a prophet mighty in deed and word before God and all the people,*h* ²⁰how our chief priests and rulers both handed him over to a sentence of death and crucified him. ²¹ *i* But we were hoping that he would be the one to redeem Israel; and besides all this, it is now the third day since this took place. ²² *j* Some women from our group, however, have astounded us: they were at the tomb early in the morning ²³and did not find his body; they came back and reported that they had indeed seen a vision of angels who announced that he was alive. ²⁴ *k* Then some of those with us went to the tomb and found things just as the women had described, but him they did not see." ²⁵ *l* And he said to them, "Oh, how foolish you are! How slow of heart to believe all that the prophets spoke! ²⁶Was it not necessary that the Messiah should suffer* these things and enter into his glory?" ²⁷Then beginning with Moses and all the prophets, he interpreted to them what referred to him in all the scriptures.*m* ²⁸As they approached the village to which they were going, he gave the impression that he was going on farther. ²⁹But they urged him, "Stay with us, for it is nearly evening and the day is almost over." So he went in to stay with them. ³⁰And it happened that, while he was with them at table, he took bread, said the blessing, broke it, and gave it to them. ³¹With that their eyes were opened and they recognized him, but he vanished from their sight. ³²Then they said to each other, "Were not our hearts burning [within us] while he spoke to us on the way and opened the scriptures to us?"

Lk

33 So they set out at once and returned to Jerusalem where they found gathered together the eleven and those with them 34 who were saying, "The Lord has truly been raised and has appeared to Simon!" n 35 Then the two recounted what had taken place on the way and how he was made known to them in the breaking of the bread.

The Appearance to the Disciples in Jerusalem. 36 * While they were still speaking about this,o he stood in their midst and said to them, "Peace be with you."p 37 But they were startled and terrified and thought that they were seeing a ghost.q 38 Then he said to them, "Why are you troubled? And why do questions arise in your hearts? 39 *Look at my hands and my feet, that it is I myself. Touch me and see, because a ghost does not have flesh and bones as you can see I have." 40 r And as he said this, he showed them his hands and his feet. 41 While they were still incredulous for joy and were amazed, he asked them, "Have you anything here to eat?" 42 They gave him a piece of baked fish;s 43 he took it and ate it in front of them.

44 He said to them, "These are my words that I spoke to you while I was still with you, that everything written about me in the law of Moses and in the prophets and psalms must be fulfilled."t 45 Then he opened their minds to understand the scriptures.u 46 And he said to them,v "Thus it is written that the Messiah would suffer and rise from the dead on the third day* 47 and that repentance, for the forgiveness of sins, would be preached in his name to all the nations, beginning from Jerusalem.w 48 You are witnesses of these things.x 49 And [behold] I am sending the promise of my Father* upon you; but stay in the city until you are clothed with power from on high."y

The Ascension.* 50 z Then he led them [out] as far as Bethany, raised his hands, and blessed them. 51 As he blessed them he parted from them and was taken up to heaven. 52 They did him homage and then returned to Jerusalem with great joy,a 53 and they were continually in the temple praising God.*

---

n 1 Cor 15, 4-5.—o 36-53: Mk 16, 14-19; Jn 20, 19-20.—p 1 Cor 15, 5.—q Mt 14, 26.—r 40-41: Jn 21, 5.9-10.13.—s Acts 10, 41.—t Lk 18, 31; 24, 27; Mt 16, 21; Jn 5, 39.46.—u Jn 20, 9.—v Lk 9, 22; Is 53; Hos 6, 2.—w Mt 3, 2; 28, 19-20; Mk 16, 15-16; Acts 10, 41.—x Acts 1, 8.—y Jn 14, 26; Acts 1, 4; 2, 3-4.—z 50-51: Mk 16, 19; Acts 1, 9-11.—a Acts 1, 12.

24, 36-43.44-49: The Gospel of Luke, like each of the other gospels (Mt 28, 16-20; Mk 16, 14-15; Jn 20, 19-23), focuses on an important appearance of Jesus to the Twelve in which they are commissioned for their future ministry. As in vv 6 and 12, so in vv 36 and 40 there are omissions in the Western text.

24, 39-42: The apologetic purpose of this story is evident in the concern with the physical details and the report that Jesus ate food.

24, 46: See the note on Lk 24, 26.

24, 49: *The promise of my Father:* i.e., the gift of the holy Spirit.

24, 50-53: Luke brings his story about the time of Jesus to a close with the report of the ascension. He will also begin the story of the time of the church with a recounting of the ascension. In the gospel, Luke recounts the ascension of Jesus on Easter Sunday night, thereby closely associating it with the resurrection. In Acts (1, 3.9-11; 13, 31) he historicizes the ascension by speaking of a forty-day period between the resurrection and the ascension. The Western text omits some phrases in vv 51 and 52, perhaps to avoid any chronological conflict with Acts 1 about the time of the ascension.

24, 53: The Gospel of Luke ends as it began (Lk 1, 9), in the Jerusalem temple.

THE GOSPEL ACCORDING TO JOHN

INTRODUCTION

    The Gospel according to John is quite different in character from the three synoptic gospels. It is highly literary and symbolic. It does not follow the same order or reproduce the same stories as the synoptic gospels. To a much greater degree, it is the product of a developed theological reflection and grows out of a different circle and tradition. It was probably written in the 90s of the first century.

    The Gospel of John begins with a magnificent prologue, which states many of the major themes and motifs of the gospel, much as an overture does for a musical work. The prologue proclaims Jesus as the preexistent and incarnate Word of God who has revealed the Father to us. The rest of the first chapter forms the introduction to the gospel proper and consists of the Baptist's testimony about Jesus (there is no baptism of Jesus in this gospel—John simply points him out as the Lamb of God), followed by stories of the call of the first disciples, in which various titles predicated of Jesus in the early church are presented.

The gospel narrative contains a series of "signs"—the gospel's word for the wondrous deeds of Jesus. The author is primarily interested in the significance of these deeds, and so interprets them for the reader by various reflections, narratives, and discourses. The first sign is the transformation of water into wine at Cana (2, 1-11); this represents the replacement of the Jewish ceremonial washings and symbolizes the entire creative and transforming work of Jesus. The second sign, the cure of the royal official's son (4, 46-54) simply by the word of Jesus at a distance, signifies the power of Jesus' life-giving word. The same theme is further developed by other signs, probably for a total of seven. The third sign, the cure of the paralytic at the pool with five porticoes in ch 5, continues the theme of water offering newness of life. In the preceding chapter, to the woman at the well in Samaria Jesus had offered living water springing up to eternal life, a symbol of the revelation that Jesus brings; here Jesus' life-giving word replaces the water of the pool that failed to bring life. Chapter 6 contains two signs, the multiplication of loaves and the walking on the waters of the Sea of Galilee. These signs are connected much as the manna and the crossing of the Red Sea are in the Passover narrative and symbolize a new exodus. The multiplication of the loaves is interpreted for the reader by the discourse that follows, where the bread of life is used first as a figure for the revelation of God in Jesus and then for the Eucharist. After a series of dialogues reflecting Jesus' debates with the Jewish authorities at the Feast of Tabernacles in chs 7 and 8, the sixth sign is presented in ch 9, the sign of the young man born blind. This is a narrative illustration of the theme of conflict in the preceding two chapters; it proclaims the triumph of light over darkness, as Jesus is presented as the Light of the world. This is interpreted by a narrative of controversy between the Pharisees and the young man who had been given his sight by Jesus, ending with a discussion of spiritual blindness and spelling out the symbolic meaning of the cure. And finally, the seventh sign, the raising of Lazarus in ch 11, is the climax of signs. Lazarus is presented as a token of the real life that Jesus, the Resurrection and the Life, who will now ironically be put to death because of his gift of life to Lazarus, will give to all who believe in him once he has been raised from the dead.

After the account of the seven signs, the "hour" of Jesus arrives, and the author passes from sign to reality, as he moves into the discourses in the upper room that interpret the meaning of the passion, death, and resurrection narratives that follow. The whole gospel of John is a progressive revelation of the glory of God's only Son, who comes to reveal the Father and then returns in glory to the Father. The author's purpose is clearly expressed in what must have been the original ending of the gospel at the end of ch 20: "Now Jesus did many other signs in the presence of [his] disciples that are not written in this book. But these are written that you may [come to] believe that Jesus is the Messiah, the Son of God, and that through this belief you may have life in his name."

Critical analysis makes it difficult to accept the idea that the gospel as it now stands was written by one person. Chapter 21 seems to have been added after the gospel was completed; it exhibits a Greek style somewhat different from that of the rest of the work. The prologue (1, 1-18) apparently contains an independent hymn, subsequently adapted to serve as a preface to the gospel. Within the gospel itself there are also some inconsistencies, e.g., there are two endings of Jesus' discourse in the upper room (14, 31; 18, 1). To solve these problems, scholars have proposed various rearrangements that would produce a smoother order. However, most have come to the conclusion that the inconsistencies were probably produced by subsequent editing in which homogeneous materials were added to a shorter original.

Other difficulties for any theory of eyewitness authorship of the gospel in its present form are presented by its highly developed theology and by certain elements of its literary style. For instance, some of the wondrous deeds of Jesus have been worked into highly effective dramatic scenes (ch 9); there has been a careful attempt to have these followed by discourses that explain them (chs 5 and 6); and the sayings of Jesus have been woven into long discourses of a quasi-poetic form resembling the speeches of personified Wisdom in the Old Testament.

The gospel contains many details about Jesus not found in the synoptic gospels, e.g., that Jesus engaged in a baptizing ministry (3, 22) before he changed to one of preaching and signs; that Jesus' public ministry lasted for several years (see the note on 2, 13); that he traveled to Jerusalem for various festivals and met serious opposition long before his death (2, 14-25; chs 5 and 7-8); and that he was put to death on the day before Passover (18, 28). These events are not always in chronological order because of the development and editing that took place. However, the accuracy of much of the detail of the fourth gospel constitutes a strong argument that the Johannine tradition rests upon the testimony of an eyewitness. Although tradition identified this person as John, the son of Zebedee, most modern scholars find that the evidence does not support this.

The fourth gospel is not simply history; the narrative has been organized and adapted to serve the evangelist's theological purposes as well. Among them are the opposition to the synagogue of the day and to John the Baptist's followers, who tried to exalt their master at Jesus' expense, the desire to show that Jesus was the Messiah, and the desire to convince Christians that their religious belief and practice must be rooted in Jesus. Such theological purposes have impelled the evangelist to emphasize motifs that were not so clear in the synoptic account of Jesus' ministry, e.g., the explicit emphasis on his divinity.

The polemic between synagogue and church produced bitter and harsh invective, especially regarding the hostility toward Jesus of the authorities—Pharisees and Sadducees—who are combined and referred to frequently as "the Jews" (see the note on 1, 19). These opponents are even described in 8, 44 as springing from their father the devil, whose conduct they imitate in opposing God by rejecting Jesus, whom God has sent. On the other hand, the author of this gospel seems to take pains to show that women are not inferior to men in the Christian community: the woman at the well in Samaria (ch 4) is presented as a prototype of a missionary (4, 4-42), and the first witness of the resurrection is a woman (20, 11-18).

The final editing of the gospel and arrangement in its present form probably dates from between A.D. 90 and 100. Traditionally, Ephesus has been favored as the place of composition, though many support a location in Syria, perhaps the city of Antioch, while some have suggested other places, including Alexandria.

The principal divisions of the Gospel according to John are the following:

I. *Prologue (1, 1-18)*
II. *The Book of Signs (1, 19—12, 50)*
III. *The Book of Glory (13, 1—20, 31)*
IV. *Epilogue: The Resurrection Appearance in Galilee (21, 1-25)*

I. PROLOGUE*

CHAPTER 1

1 In the beginning* was the Word,
    and the Word was with God,
    and the Word was God. *a*
2 He was in the beginning with God.
3 All things came to be through him,
    and without him nothing came to
    be. *b*
    What came to be* 4through him was
        life,
    and this life was the light of the
        human race; *c*
5 the light shines in the darkness, *d*
    and the darkness has not overcome
        it.*

6A man named John was sent* from God. *e*
7He came for testimony,* to testify to the
light, so that all might believe through
him. *f* 8He was not the light, but came to
testify to the light. *g* 9The true light, which
enlightens everyone, was coming into the
world. *h*

10 He was in the world,
    and the world came to be through
        him,
    but the world did not know him.
11 He came to what was his own,
    but his own people* did not accept
        him.
12 *i* But to those who did accept him he
gave power to become children of God, to
those who believe in his name, 13 *j* who
were born not by natural generation nor by
human choice nor by a man's decision but
of God.*
14 And the Word became flesh*
    and made his dwelling among us,
    and we saw his glory,
    the glory as of the Father's only Son,
    full of grace and truth. *k*
15John testified to him and cried out, saying, "This was he of whom I said, *l* 'The
one who is coming after me ranks ahead of
me because he existed before me.' " *
16From his fullness we have all received,
grace in place of grace,* 17because while
the law was given through Moses, grace
and truth came through Jesus Christ. *m* 18No

---

a Jn 10, 30; Gn 1, 1-5; Jb 28, 12-27; Prv 8, 22-25; Wis 9, 1-2; 1 Jn 1, 1-2; Col 1, 1.15; Rv 3, 14; 19, 13.—b Ps 33, 9; Wis 9, 1; Sir 42, 15; 1 Cor 8, 6; Col 1, 16; Heb 1, 2; Rv 3, 14.—c Jn 5, 26; 8, 12; 1 Jn 1, 2.—d Jn 3, 19; 8, 12; 9, 5; 12, 35.46; Wis 7, 29-30; 1 Thes 5, 4; 1 Jn 2, 8.—e Mt 3, 1; Mk 1, 4; Lk 3, 2-3.—f Jn 1, 19-34; 5, 33.—g Jn 5, 35.—h Jn 3, 19; 8, 12; 9, 39; 12, 46.—i Jn 3, 11-12; 5, 43-44; 12, 46-50; Gal 3, 26; 4, 6-7; Eph 1, 5; 1 Jn 3, 2.—j Jn 3, 5-6.—k Ex 16, 10; 24, 17; 25, 8-9; 33, 22; 34, 6; Sir 24, 4.8; Is 60, 1; Ez 43, 7; Jl 4, 17; Hb 2, 14; 1 Jn 1, 2; 4, 2; 2 Jn 7.—l Jn 1, 30; 3, 27-30.—m Jn 7, 19; Ex 31, 18; 34, 28.

1, 1-18: The prologue states the main themes of the gospel: life, light, truth, the world, testimony, and the preexistence of Jesus Christ, the incarnate *Logos,* who reveals God the Father. In origin, it was probably an early Christian hymn. Its closest parallel is in other christological hymns, Col 1, 15-20 and Phil 2, 6-11. Its core (1-5.10-11.14) is poetic in structure, with short phrases linked by "staircase parallelism," in which the last word of one phrase becomes the first word of the next. Prose inserts (at least 6-8 and 15) deal with John the Baptist.

1, 1: *In the beginning:* also the first words of the Old Testament (Gn 1, 1). *Was:* this verb is used three times with different meanings in this verse: existence, relationship, and predication. *The Word* (Greek *logos):* this term combines God's dynamic, creative word (Genesis), personified preexistent Wisdom as the instrument of God's creative activity (Proverbs), and the ultimate intelligibility of reality (Hellenistic philosophy). *With God:* the Greek preposition here connotes communication with another. *Was God:* lack of a definite article with "God" in Greek signifies predication rather than identification.

1, 3: *What came to be:* while the oldest manuscripts have no punctuation here, the corrector of Bodmer Papyrus P75, some manuscripts, and the Ante-Nicene Fathers take this phrase with what follows, as staircase parallelism. Connection with v 3 reflects fourth-century anti-Arianism.

1, 5: The ethical dualism of light and darkness is paralleled in intertestamental literature and in the Dead Sea Scrolls. *Overcome:* "comprehend" is another possible translation, but cf Jn 12, 35; Wis 7, 29-30.

1, 6: John was *sent* just as Jesus was "sent" (Jn 4, 34) in divine mission. Other references to John the Baptist in this gospel emphasize the differences between them and John's subordinate role.

1, 7: *Testimony:* the testimony theme of Jn is introduced, which portrays Jesus as if on trial throughout his ministry. All testify to Jesus: John the Baptist, the Samaritan woman, scripture, his works, the crowds, the Spirit, and his disciples.

1, 11: *What was his own . . . his own people:* first a neuter, literally, "his own property/possession" (probably = Israel), then a masculine, "his own people" (the Israelites).

1, 13: Believers in Jesus become children of God not through any of the three natural causes mentioned but through God who is the immediate cause of the new spiritual life. *Were born:* the Greek verb can mean "begotten" (by a male) or "born" (from a female or or of parents). The variant "he who was begotten," asserting Jesus' virginal conception, is weakly attested in Old Latin and Syriac versions.

1, 14: *Flesh:* the whole person, used probably against docetistic tendencies (cf 1 Jn 4, 2; 2 Jn 7). *Made his dwelling:* literally, "pitched his tent/tabernacle." Cf the tabernacle or tent of meeting that was the place of God's presence among his people (Ex 25, 8-9). The incarnate Word was the new mode of God's presence among his people. The Greek verb has the same consonants as the Aramaic word for God's presence (Shekinah). *Glory:* God's visible manifestation of majesty in power, which once filled the tabernacle (Ex 40, 34) and the temple (1 Kgs 8, 10-11.27), is now centered in Jesus. *Only Son:* Greek, *monogenēs,* but see the note on Jn 1, 18. *Grace and truth:* these words may represent two Old Testament terms describing Yahweh in covenant relationship with Israel (cf Ex 34, 6), thus God's "love" and "fidelity." The Word shares Yahweh's covenant qualities.

1, 15: This verse, interrupting vv 14 and 16, seems drawn from v 30.

1, 16: *Grace in place of grace:* replacement of the Old Covenant with the New (cf 17). Other possible translations are "grace upon grace" (accumulation) and "grace for grace" (correspondence).

Jn

one has ever seen God. The only Son, God,* who is at the Father's side, has revealed him.[n]

II. THE BOOK OF SIGNS

John the Baptist's Testimony to Himself.
[19]*And this is the testimony of John. When the Jews* from Jerusalem sent priests and Levites [to him] to ask him, "Who are you?" [20]he admitted and did not deny it, but admitted,[o] "I am not the Messiah."* [21]So they asked him, "What are you then? Are you Elijah?"* And he said, "I am not." "Are you the Prophet?" He answered, "No."[p] [22]So they said to him, "Who are you, so we can give an answer to those who sent us? What do you have to say for yourself?" [23]He said:

"I am 'the voice of one crying out in the desert,[q]

"Make straight the way of the Lord," '*

as Isaiah the prophet said." [24]Some Pharisees* were also sent. [25]They asked him, "Why then do you baptize if you are not the Messiah or Elijah or the Prophet?"[r] [26]John answered them, "I baptize with water; * but there is one among you whom you do not recognize,[s] [27]the one who is coming after me, whose sandal strap I am not worthy to untie." [28]This happened in Bethany across the Jordan,* where John was baptizing.

John the Baptist's Testimony to Jesus.
[29]The next day he saw Jesus coming toward him and said, "Behold, the Lamb of God,* who takes away the sin of the world.[t] [30]He is the one of whom I said,[u] 'A man is coming after me who ranks ahead of me because he existed before me.'* [31]I did not know him,* but the reason why I came baptizing with water was that he might be made known to Israel."[v] [32]John testified further, saying, "I saw the Spirit come down like a dove* from the sky and remain upon him. [33]I did not know him,[v] but the one who sent me to baptize with water told me, 'On whomever you see the Spirit come down and remain, he is the one who will baptize with the holy Spirit.'[w] [34] [x] Now I have seen and testified that he is the Son of God."*

The First Disciples.[y]
[35]The next day John was there again with two of his disciples,

n Jn 5, 37; 6, 46; Ex 33, 20; Jgs 13, 21-22; 1 Tm 6, 16; 1 Jn 4, 12.—o Jn 3, 28; Lk 3, 15; Acts 13, 25.—p Dt 18, 15.18; 2 Kgs 2, 11; Sir 48, 10; Mal 3, 1.23; Mt 11, 14; 17, 11-13; Mk 9, 13; Acts 3, 22.—q Is 40, 3; Mt 3, 3; Mk 1, 2; Lk 3, 4.—r Ez 36, 25; Zec 13, 1; Mt 16, 14.—s Mt 3, 11; Mk 1, 7-8; Lk 3, 16; Acts 13, 25.—t Jn 1, 36; Ex 12; Is 53, 7; Rv 5—7; 17, 14.—u Jn 1, 15; Mt 3, 11; Mk 1, 7; Lk 3, 16.—v Song 5, 2; Is 11, 2; Hos 11, 11; Mt 3, 16; Mk 1, 10; Lk 3, 21-22.—w Is 42, 1; Mt 3, 11; Mk 1, 8; Lk 3, 16.—x Is 42, 1; Mt 3, 17; Mk 1, 11; Lk 9, 35.—y 35-51: Mt 4, 18-22; Mk 1, 16-20; Lk 5, 1-11.

1, 18: *The only Son, God:* while the vast majority of later textual witnesses have another reading, "the Son, the only one" or "the only Son," the translation above follows the best and earliest manuscripts, *monogenēs theos*, but takes the first term to mean not just "Only One" but to include a filial relationship with the Father, as at Lk 9, 38 ("only child") or Heb 11, 17 ("only son") and as translated at Jn 1, 14. The Logos is thus "only Son" and God but not Father/God.

1, 19-51: The testimony of John the Baptist about the Messiah and Jesus' self-revelation to the first disciples. This section constitutes the introduction to the gospel proper and is connected with the prose inserts in the prologue. It develops the major theme of testimony in four scenes: John's negative testimony about himself; his positive testimony about Jesus; the revelation of Jesus to Andrew and Peter; the revelation of Jesus to Philip and Nathanael.

1, 19: *The Jews:* throughout most of the gospel, the "Jews" does not refer to the Jewish people as such but to the hostile authorities, both Pharisees and Sadducees, particularly in Jerusalem, who refuse to believe in Jesus. The usage reflects the atmosphere, at the end of the first century, of polemics between church and synagogue, or possibly it refers to Jews as representative of a hostile world (10-11).

1, 20: *Messiah:* the anointed agent of Yahweh, usually considered to be of Davidic descent. See further the note on Jn 1, 41.

1, 21: *Elijah:* the Baptist did not claim to Le Elijah returned to earth (cf Mal 3, 23; Mt 11, 14). *The Prophet:* probably the prophet like Moses (Dt 18, 15; cf Acts 3, 22).

1, 23: This is a repunctuation and reinterpretation (as in the synoptic versions and Septuagint) of the Hebrew text of Is 40, 3, which reads, "A voice cries out: In the desert prepare the way of the LORD."

1, 24: *Some Pharisees:* other translations, such as "Now they had been sent from the Pharisees," misunderstand the grammatical construction. This is a different group from that in v 19; the priests and Levites would have been Sadducees, not Pharisees.

1, 26: *I baptize with water:* the synoptics add "but he will baptize you with the holy Spirit" (Mk 1, 8) or ". . . holy Spirit and fire" (Mt 3, 11; Lk 3, 16). John's emphasis is on purification and preparation for a better baptism.

1, 28: *Bethany across the Jordan:* site unknown. Another reading is "Bethabara."

1, 29: *The Lamb of God:* the background for this title may be the victorious apocalyptic lamb who would destroy evil in the world (Rv 5—7; 17, 14); the paschal lamb, whose blood saved Israel (Ex 12); and/or the suffering servant led like a lamb to the slaughter as a sin-offering (Is 53, 7.10).

1, 30: *He existed before me:* possibly as Elijah (to come, 27); for the evangelist and his audience, Jesus' preexistence would be implied (see the note on Jn 1, 1).

1, 31: *I did not know him:* this gospel shows no knowledge of the tradition (Lk 1) about the kinship of Jesus and John the Baptist. *The reason why I came baptizing with water:* in this gospel, John's baptism is not connected with forgiveness of sins; its purpose is revelatory, that Jesus may be made known to Israel.

1, 32: *Like a dove:* a symbol of the new creation (Gn 8, 8) or the community of Israel (Hos 11, 11). *Remain:* the first use of a favorite verb in Jn, emphasizing the permanency of the relationship between Father and Son (as here) and between the Son and the Christian. Jesus is the permanent bearer of the Spirit.

1, 34: *The Son of God:* this reading is supported by good Greek manuscripts, including the Chester Beatty and Bodmer Papyri and the Vatican Codex, but is suspect because it harmonizes this passage with the synoptic version: "This is my beloved Son" (Mt 3, 17; Mk 1, 11; Lk 3, 22). The poorly attested alternate reading, "God's chosen One," is probably a reference to the Servant of Yahweh (Is 42, 1).

³⁶and as he watched Jesus walk by, he said, "Behold, the Lamb of God."* ³⁷The two disciples* heard what he said and followed Jesus. ³⁸Jesus turned and saw them following him and said to them, "What are you looking for?" They said to him, "Rabbi" (which translated means Teacher), "where are you staying?" ³⁹He said to them, "Come, and you will see." So they went and saw where he was staying, and they stayed with him that day. It was about four in the afternoon.* ⁴⁰Andrew, the brother of Simon Peter, was one of the two who heard John and followed Jesus. ⁴¹He first found his own brother Simon and told him, "We have found the Messiah"* (which is translated Anointed). ᶻ ⁴²Then he brought him to Jesus. Jesus looked at him and said, "You are Simon the son of John;* you will be called Cephas" (which is translated Peter).ᵃ

⁴³The next day he* decided to go to Galilee, and he found Philip. And Jesus said to him, "Follow me." ⁴⁴Now Philip was from Bethsaida, the town of Andrew and Peter. ⁴⁵Philip found Nathanael and told him, "We have found the one about whom Moses wrote in the law, and also the prophets, Jesus, son of Joseph, from Nazareth."ᵇ ⁴⁶But Nathanael said to him, "Can anything good come from Naza-

reth?" Philip said to him, "Come and see." ⁴⁷Jesus saw Nathanael coming toward him and said of him, "Here is a true Israelite.* There is no duplicity in him." ⁴⁸ ᶜ Nathanael said to him, "How do you know me?" Jesus answered and said to him, "Before Philip called you, I saw you under the fig tree."* ⁴⁹Nathanael answered him, "Rabbi, you are the Son of God;* you are the King of Israel."ᵈ ⁵⁰Jesus answered and said to him, "Do you believe because I told you that I saw you under the fig tree?* You will see greater things than this." ⁵¹And he said to him, "Amen, amen,* I say to you, you will see the sky opened and the angels of God ascending and descending on the Son of Man."ᵉ

CHAPTER 2

The Wedding at Cana. ¹ * On the third day there was a wedding* in Cana* in Galilee, and the mother of Jesus was there.ᶠ ²Jesus and his disciples were also invited to the wedding. ³When the wine ran short, the mother of Jesus said to him, "They have no wine." ⁴ * [And] Jesus said to her, "Woman, how does your concern affect me? My hour has not yet come."ᵍ ⁵His mother said to the servers, "Do what-

z Jn 4, 25.—a Mt 16, 18; Mk 3, 16.—b Jn 21, 2.—c Mi 4, 4; Zec 3, 10.—d Jn 12, 13; Ex 4, 22; Dt 14, 1; 2 Sm 7, 14; Jb 1, 6; 2, 1; 38, 7; Pss 2, 7; 29, 1; 89, 27; Wis 2, 18; Sir 4, 10; Dn 3, 25; Hos 11, 1; Mt 14, 33; 16, 16; Mk 13, 32.—e Gn 28, 10-17; Dn 7, 13.—f Jn 4, 46; Jgs 14, 12; Tb 11, 8.—g Jn 7, 30; 8, 20; 12, 23; 13, 1; Jgs 11, 12; 1 Kgs 17, 18; 2 Kgs 3, 13; 2 Chr 35, 21; Hos 14, 9; Mk 1, 24; 5, 7; 7, 30; 8, 20; 12, 23; 13, 1.

1, 36: John the Baptist's testimony makes his disciples' following of Jesus plausible.

1, 37: *The two disciples:* Andrew (40) and, traditionally, John, son of Zebedee (see the note on Jn 13, 23).

1, 39: *Four in the afternoon:* literally, the tenth hour, from sunrise, in the Roman calculation of time. Some suggest that the next day, beginning at sunset, was the sabbath; they would have stayed with Jesus to avoid travel on it.

1, 41: *Messiah:* the Hebrew word *māšiaḥ*, "anointed one" (see the note on Lk 2, 11), appears in Greek as the transliterated *messias* only here and in Jn 4, 25. Elsewhere the Greek translation *christos* is used.

1, 42: *Simon, the son of John:* in Mt 16, 17, Simon is called *Bariōna,* "son of Jonah," a different tradition for the name of Simon's father. *Cephas:* in Aramaic = the Rock; cf Mt 16, 18. Neither the Greek equivalent *Petros* nor, with one isolated exception, *Cephas* is attested as a personal name before Christian times.

1, 43: *He:* grammatically, could be Peter, but logically is probably Jesus.

1, 47: *A true Israelite. There is no duplicity in him:* Jacob was the first to bear the name "Israel" (Gn 32, 29), but Jacob was a man of duplicity (Gn 27, 35-36).

1, 48: *Under the fig tree:* a symbol of messianic peace (cf Mi 4, 4; Zec 3, 10).

1, 49: *Son of God:* this title is used in the Old Testament, among other ways, as a title of adoption for the Davidic king (2 Sm 7, 14; Pss 2, 7; 89, 27), and thus here, with *King of Israel,* in a messianic sense. For the evangelist, Son of God also points to Jesus' divinity (cf Jn 20, 28).

1, 50: Possibly a statement: "You [singular] believe because I saw you under the fig tree."

1, 51: The double "Amen" is characteristic of John. *You* is plural in Greek. The allusion is to Jacob's ladder (Gn 28, 12).

2, 1—6, 71: Signs revealing Jesus as the Messiah to all Israel. "Sign" (*sēmeion*) is John's symbolic term for Jesus' wondrous deeds (see Introduction). The Old Testament background lies in the Exodus story (cf Dt 11, 3; 29, 2). John is interested primarily in what the *sēmeia* signify: God's intervention in human history in a new way through Jesus.

2, 1-11: The first sign. This story of replacement of Jewish ceremonial washings (6) presents the initial revelation about Jesus at the outset of his ministry. He manifests his glory; the disciples believe. There is no synoptic parallel.

2, 1: *Cana:* unknown from the Old Testament. *The mother of Jesus:* she is never named in John.

2, 4: This verse may seek to show that Jesus did not work miracles to help his family and friends, as in the apocryphal gospels. *Woman:* a normal, polite form of address, but unattested in reference to one's mother. Cf also Jn 19, 26. *How does your concern affect me?:* literally, "What is this to me and to you?"—a Hebrew expression of either hostility (Jgs 11, 12; 2 Chr 35, 21; 1 Kgs 17, 18) or denial of common interest (Hos 14, 9; 2 Kgs 3, 13). Cf Mk 1, 24; 5, 7, used by demons to Jesus. *My hour has not yet come:* the translation as a question ("Has not my hour now come?"), while preferable grammatically and supported by Greek Fathers, seems unlikely from a comparison with Jn 7, 6.30. The "hour" is that of Jesus' passion, death, resurrection, and ascension (Jn 13, 1).

Jn

ever he tells you."[h] [6]Now there were six stone water jars there for Jewish ceremonial washings,[i] each holding twenty to thirty gallons.* [7]Jesus told them, "Fill the jars with water." So they filled them to the brim. [8]Then he told them, "Draw some out now and take it to the headwaiter." * So they took it. [9]And when the headwaiter tasted the water that had become wine, without knowing where it came from (although the servers who had drawn the water knew), the headwaiter called the bridegroom [10]and said to him, "Everyone serves good wine first, and then when people have drunk freely, an inferior one; but you have kept the good wine until now." [11]Jesus did this as the beginning of his signs* in Cana in Galilee and so revealed his glory, and his disciples began to believe in him.[j]

[12] * After this, he and his mother, [his] brothers, and his disciples went down to Capernaum and stayed there only a few days.*

Cleansing of the Temple. [13] * Since the Passover* of the Jews was near,[k] Jesus went up to Jerusalem. [14] * He found in the temple area those who sold oxen, sheep, and doves,* as well as the money-changers seated there.[l] [15]He made a whip out of cords and drove them all out of the temple area, with the sheep and oxen, and spilled the coins of the money-changers and over-

turned their tables, [16]and to those who sold doves he said, "Take these out of here, and stop making my Father's house a marketplace."[m] [17]His disciples recalled the words of scripture,[n] "Zeal for your house will consume me." * [18]At this the Jews answered and said to him, "What sign can you show us for doing this?"[o] [19]Jesus answered and said to them,[p] "Destroy this temple and in three days I will raise it up." * [20]The Jews said, "This temple has been under construction for forty-six years,* and you will raise it up in three days?" [21]But he was speaking about the temple of his body. [22]Therefore, when he was raised from the dead, his disciples remembered that he had said this, and they came to believe the scripture and the word Jesus had spoken.[q]

[23]While he was in Jerusalem for the feast of Passover, many began to believe in his name when they saw the signs he was doing.[r] [24]But Jesus would not trust himself to them because he knew them all, [25]and did not need anyone to testify about human nature. He himself understood it well.[s]

CHAPTER 3

Nicodemus. * [1] [t] Now there was a Pharisee named Nicodemus, a ruler of the Jews.* [2]He came to Jesus at night and said

---

h Gn 41, 55.—i Jn 3, 25; Lv 11, 33; Am 9, 13-14; Mt 15, 2; 23, 25-26; Mk 7, 2-4; Lk 11, 38.—j Jn 4, 54.—k 13-22: Mt 21, 12-13; Mk 11, 15-17; Lk 19, 45-46.—l Ex 30, 11-16; Lv 5, 7.—m Zec 14, 21.—n Ps 69, 9.—o Jn 6, 30.—p Mt 24, 2; 26, 61; 27, 40; Mk 13, 2; 14, 58; 15, 29; Lk 21, 6; Acts 6, 14.—q Jn 5, 39; 12, 16; 14, 26; 20, 9; Mt 12, 6; Lk 24, 6-8; Rv 21, 22.—r Jn 4, 45.—s 1 Kgs 8, 39; Pss 33, 15; 94, 11; Sir 42, 18; Jer 17, 10; 20, 12.—t Jn 7, 50-51; 19, 39.

2, 6: *Twenty to thirty gallons:* literally, "two or three measures"; the Attic liquid measure contained 39.39 liters. The vast quantity recalls prophecies of abundance in the last days; cf Am 9, 13-14; Hos 14, 7; Jer 31, 12.

2, 8: *Headwaiter:* used of the official who managed a banquet, but there is no evidence of such a functionary in Palestine. Perhaps here a friend of the family acted as master of ceremonies; cf Sir 32, 1.

2, 11: *The beginning of his signs:* the first of seven (see Introduction).

2, 12—3, 21: The next three episodes take place in Jerusalem. Only the first is paralleled in the synoptic gospels.

2, 12: This transitional verse may be a harmonization with the synoptic tradition in Lk 4, 31 and Mt 4, 13. There are many textual variants. John depicts no extended ministry in Capernaum as do the synoptics.

2, 13-22: This episode indicates the post-resurrectional replacement of the temple by the person of Jesus.

2, 13: *Passover:* this is the first Passover mentioned in John; a second is mentioned in Jn 6, 4, a third in Jn 13, 1. Taken literally, they point to a ministry of at least two years.

2, 14-22: The other gospels place the cleansing of the temple in the last days of Jesus' life (Mt, on the day Jesus entered

Jerusalem; Mk, on the next day). The order of events in the gospel narratives is often determined by theological motives rather than by chronological data.

2, 14: *Oxen, sheep, and doves:* intended for sacrifice. The doves were the offerings of the poor (Lv 5, 7). *Money-changers:* for a temple tax paid by every male Jew more than nineteen years of age, with a half-shekel coin (Ex 30, 11-16), in Tyrian currency. See the note on Mt 17, 24.

2, 17: Ps 69, 10, changed to future tense to apply to Jesus.

2, 19: This saying about the destruction of the temple occurs in various forms (Mt 24, 2; 27, 40; Mk 13, 2; 15, 29; Lk 21, 6; cf Acts 6, 14). Mt 26, 61 has: "I *can* destroy the temple of God . . ."; see the note there. In Mk 14, 58, there is a metaphorical contrast with a new temple: "I will destroy this temple *made with hands* and within three days I will build another *not made with hands.*" Here it is symbolic of Jesus' resurrection and the resulting community (see Jn 2, 21 and Rv 21, 2). *In three days:* an Old Testament expression for a short, indefinite period of time; cf Hos 6, 2.

2, 20: *Forty-six years:* based on references in Josephus (*Jewish Wars* 1, 21, 1 #401; *Antiquities* 15, 11, 1 §380), possibly the spring of A.D. 28. Cf the note on Lk 3, 1.

3, 1-21: Jesus instructs Nicodemus on the necessity of a new birth from above. This scene in Jerusalem at Passover exemplifies the faith engendered by signs (Jn 2, 23). It continues the self-manifestation of Jesus in Jerusalem begun in ch 2. This is the first of the Johannine discourses, shifting from dialogue to monologue (11-15) to reflection of the evangelist (16-21). The shift from singular through v 10 to plural in v 11 may reflect the early church's controversy with the Jews.

3, 1: *A ruler of the Jews:* most likely a member of the Jewish council, the Sanhedrin; see the note on Mk 8, 31.

to him, "Rabbi, we know that you are a teacher who has come from God, for no one can do these signs that you are doing unless God is with him." [u] 3 Jesus answered and said to him, "Amen, amen, I say to you, no one can see the kingdom of God without being born* from above." 4 Nicodemus said to him, "How can a person once grown old be born again? Surely he cannot reenter his mother's womb and be born again, can he?" [v] 5 Jesus answered, "Amen, amen, I say to you, no one can enter the kingdom of God without being born of water and Spirit. [w] 6 What is born of flesh is flesh and what is born of spirit is spirit. [x] 7 Do not be amazed that I told you, 'You must be born from above.' 8 The wind* blows where it wills, and you can hear the sound it makes, but you do not know where it comes from or where it goes; so it is with everyone who is born of the Spirit." [y] 9 Nicodemus answered and said to him, "How can this happen?" 10 Jesus answered and said to him, "You are the teacher of Israel and you do not understand this? 11 Amen, amen, I say to you, we speak of what we know and we testify to what we have seen, but you people do not accept our testimony. [z] 12 If I tell you about earthly things and you do not believe, how will you believe if I tell you about heavenly things? [a] 13 No one has gone up to heaven except the one who has come down from heaven, the Son of Man. [b] 14 And just as Moses lifted up* the serpent in the desert, so must the Son of Man be lifted up, [c] 15 so that everyone who believes in him may have eternal life." *

16 For God so loved the world that he gave* his only Son, so that everyone who believes in him might not perish but might have eternal life. [d] 17 For God did not send his Son into the world to condemn* the world, but that the world might be saved through him. [e] 18 Whoever believes in him will not be condemned, but whoever does not believe has already been condemned, because he has not believed in the name of the only Son of God. [f] 19 And this is the verdict, [g] that the light came into the world, but people preferred darkness to light, because their works were evil. * 20 For everyone who does wicked things hates the light and does not come toward the light, so that his works might not be exposed. [h] 21 But whoever lives the truth comes to the light, so that his works may be clearly seen as done in God. [i]

Final Witness of the Baptist. 22 * After this, Jesus and his disciples went into the region of Judea, where he spent some time with them baptizing. [j] 23 John was also baptizing in Aenon near Salim,* because there was an abundance of water there, and people came to be baptized, 24 [k] for John had not yet been imprisoned.* 25 Now a dispute arose between the disciples of John and a Jew* about ceremonial washings. 26 So they came to John and said to him, "Rabbi, the one who was with you across the Jordan, to whom you testified, here he is baptizing and everyone is coming to him." [l] 27 John answered and said, "No one can receive anything except what has been given him from heaven. [m] 28 You yourselves can testify that I said [that] I am not the

---

u Jn 9, 4.16.33; 10, 21; 11, 10; 13, 30; Mt 22, 16; Mk 12, 14; Lk 20, 21.—v Jn 1, 13.—w Jn 1, 32; 7, 39; 19, 30.34-35; Is 32, 15; 44, 3; Ez 36, 25-27; Jl 3, 1-2.—x Jn 6, 63; 1 Cor 15, 44-50.—y Eccl 11, 4-5; Acts 2, 2-4.—z Jn 3, 32.34; 8, 14; Mt 11, 27.—a Jn 6, 62-65; Wis 9, 16-17; 1 Cor, 15, 40; 2 Cor 5, 1; Phil 2, 10; 3, 19-20.—b Jn 1, 18; 6, 62; Dn 7, 13; Rom 10, 6; Eph 4, 9.—c Jn 8, 28; 12, 32.34; Nm 21, 4-9; Wis 16, 5-7.—d 1 Jn 4, 9.—e Jn 5, 22.30; 8, 15-18; 12, 47.—f Jn 5, 24; Mk 16, 16.—g Jn 1, 5.9-11; 8, 12; 9, 5.—h Jb 24, 13-17.—i Gn 47, 29 LXX; Jos 2, 14 LXX; 2 Sm 2, 6 LXX; 15, 20 LXX; Tb 4, 6 LXX; 13, 6; Is 26, 10 LXX; Mt 5, 14-16.—j 22-23: Jn 4, 1-2.—k Mt 4, 12; 14, 3; Mk 1, 14; 6, 17; Lk 3, 20.—l Jn 1, 26.32-34.36.—m Jn 19, 11; 1 Cor 4, 7; 2 Cor 3, 5; Heb 5, 4.

3, 3: *Born:* see the note on Jn 1, 13. *From above:* the Greek adverb *anóthen* means both "from above" and "again." Jesus means "from above" (see Jn 3, 31), but Nicodemus misunderstands it as "again." This misunderstanding serves as a springboard for further instruction.

3, 8: *Wind:* the Greek word *pneuma* (as well as the Hebrew *rûaḥ*) means both "wind" and "spirit." In the play on the double meaning, "wind" is primary.

3, 14: *Lifted up:* in Nm 21, 9, Moses simply "mounted" a serpent upon a pole. John here substitutes a verb implying glorification. Jesus, exalted to glory at his cross and resurrection, represents healing for all.

3, 15: *Eternal life:* used here for the first time in John, this term stresses quality of life rather than duration.

3, 16: *Gave:* as a gift in the incarnation, and also "over to death" in the crucifixion; cf Rom 8, 32.

3, 17-19: *Condemn:* the Greek root means both judgment and condemnation. Jesus' purpose is to save, but his coming provokes judgment; some condemn themselves by turning from the light.

3, 19: Judgment is not only future but is partially realized here and now.

3, 22-26: Jesus' ministry in Judea is only loosely connected with Jn 2, 13—3, 21; cf Jn 1, 19-36. Perhaps John the Baptist's further testimony was transposed here to give meaning to "water" in v 5. Jesus is depicted as baptizing (22); contrast Jn 4, 2.

3, 23: *Aenon near Salim:* site uncertain, either in the upper Jordan valley or in Samaria.

3, 24: A remark probably intended to avoid objections based on a chronology like that of the synoptics (Mt 4, 12; Mk 1, 14).

3, 25: *A Jew:* some think Jesus is meant. Many manuscripts read "Jews."

Messiah, but that I was sent before him.[n] [29]The one who has the bride is the bridegroom; the best man,* who stands and listens for him, rejoices greatly at the bridegroom's voice. So this joy of mine has been made complete.[o] [30]He must increase; I must decrease."[p]

The One from Heaven.* [31]The one who comes from above is above all. The one who is of the earth is earthly and speaks of earthly things. But the one who comes from heaven [is above all].[q] [32]He testifies to what he has seen and heard, but no one accepts his testimony.[r] [33]Whoever does accept his testimony certifies that God is trustworthy.[s] [34]For the one whom God sent speaks the words of God. He does not ration his gift* of the Spirit. [35]The Father loves the Son and has given everything over to him.[t] [36]Whoever believes in the Son has eternal life, but whoever disobeys the Son will not see life, but the wrath of God remains upon him.[u]

CHAPTER 4

[1] * Now when Jesus learned that the Pharisees had heard that Jesus was making and baptizing more disciples than John [2](although Jesus himself was not baptizing, just his disciples),* [3]he left Judea and returned to Galilee.

The Samaritan Woman. [4]He had to* pass through Samaria. [5]So he came to a town of Samaria called Sychar,* near the plot of land that Jacob had given to his son Joseph.[v] [6]Jacob's well was there. Jesus, tired from his journey, sat down there at the well. It was about noon.

[7]A woman of Samaria came to draw water. Jesus said to her, "Give me a drink." [8]His disciples had gone into the town to buy food. [9]The Samaritan woman said to him, "How can you, a Jew, ask me, a Samaritan woman, for a drink?"[w] (For Jews use nothing in common with Samaritans.)* [10]Jesus answered and said to her,[x] "If you knew the gift of God and who is saying to you, 'Give me a drink,' you would have asked him and he would have given you living water."* [11][The woman] said to him, "Sir,* you do not even have a bucket and the cistern is deep; where then can you get this living water? [12]Are you greater than our father Jacob, who gave us this cistern and drank from it himself with his children and his flocks?"[y] [13]Jesus answered and said to her, "Everyone who drinks this water will be thirsty again; [14]but whoever drinks the water I shall give will never thirst; the water I shall give will become in him a spring of water welling up to eternal life."[z] [15]The woman said to him, "Sir, give me this water, so that I may not be thirsty or have to keep coming here to draw water."

[16]Jesus said to her, "Go call your husband and come back." [17]The woman answered and said to him, "I do not have a husband." Jesus answered her, "You are right in saying, 'I do not have a husband.' [18]For you have had five husbands, and the one you have now is not your husband. What you have said is true."[a] [19]The woman said to him, "Sir, I can see that you are a prophet.[b] [20]Our ancestors worshiped on this mountain;* but you people say that

---

n Jn 1, 20-23; Lk 3, 15.—o Jn 15, 11; 17, 13; Mt 9, 15.—p 2 Sm 3, 1.—q Jn 8, 23.—r Jn 3, 11.—s 33-34: Jn 8, 26; 12, 44-50; 1 Jn 5, 10.—t Jn 13, 3; Mt 11, 27; 28, 18; Lk 10, 22.—u Jn 3, 16; 1 Jn 5, 13.—v Gn 33, 18-19; 48, 22; Jos 24, 32.—w Sir 50, 25-26; Mt 10, 5.—x Sir 24, 20-21; Is 55, 1; Jer 2, 13.—y Jn 8, 53; Mt 12, 41.—z Jn 6, 35.58; 7, 37-39; Is 44, 3; 49, 10; Jl 4, 18; Rv 7, 16; 21, 6.—a 2 Kgs 17, 24-34.—b Jn 9, 17; Hos 1, 3.

3, 29: *The best man:* literally, "the friend of the groom," the *shoshben* of Jewish tradition, who arranged the wedding. Competition between him and the groom would be unthinkable.

3, 31-36: It is uncertain whether these are words by the Baptist, Jesus, or the evangelist. They are reflections on the two preceding scenes.

3, 34: *His gift:* of God or to Jesus, perhaps both. This verse echoes vv 5 and 8.

4, 1-42: Jesus in Samaria. The self-revelation of Jesus continues with his second discourse, on his mission to "half-Jews." It continues the theme of replacement, here with regard to cult (21). Water (7-15) serves as a symbol (as at Cana and in the Nicodemus episode).

4, 2: An editorial refinement of Jn 3, 22, perhaps directed against followers of John the Baptist who claimed that Jesus imitated him.

4, 4: *He had to:* a theological necessity; geographically, Jews often bypassed Samaria by taking a route across the Jordan.

4, 5: *Sychar:* Jerome identifies this with Shechem, a reading found in Syriac manuscripts.

4, 9: Samaritan women were regarded by Jews as ritually impure, and therefore Jews were forbidden to drink from any vessel they had handled.

4, 10: *Living water:* the water of life, i.e., the revelation that Jesus brings; the woman thinks of "flowing water," so much more desirable than stagnant cistern water. On John's device of such misunderstanding, cf the note on Jn 3, 3.

4, 11: *Sir:* the Greek *kyrios* means "master" or "lord," as a respectful mode of address for a human being or a deity; cf Jn 4, 19. It is also the word used in the Septuagint for the Hebrew *'ădônai*, substituted for the tetragrammaton YHWH.

4, 20: *This mountain:* Gerizim, on which a temple was erected in the fourth century B.C. by Samaritans to rival Mt. Zion in Jerusalem; cf Dt 27, 4 (Mt. Ebal = the Jews' term for Gerizim) the place to worship is in Jerusalem." [c] [21] Jesus said to her, "Believe me, woman, the hour is coming when you will worship the Father neither on this mountain nor in Jerusalem. [22] You people worship what you do not understand; we worship what we understand, because salvation is from the Jews. [d] [23] But the hour is coming, and is now here, when true worshipers will worship the Father in Spirit and truth;* and indeed the Father seeks such people to worship him. [24] God is Spirit, and those who worship him must worship in Spirit and truth." [e] [25] The woman said to him, "I know that the Messiah is coming,[f] the one called the Anointed; when he comes, he will tell us everything."* [26] Jesus said to her, "I am he,* the one who is speaking with you." [g]

[27] At that moment his disciples returned, and were amazed that he was talking with a woman,* but still no one said, "What are you looking for?" or "Why are you talking with her?" [28] The woman left her water jar and went into the town and said to the people, [29] "Come see a man who told me everything I have done. Could he possibly be the Messiah?" [30] They went out of the town and came to him. [31] Meanwhile, the disciples urged him, "Rabbi, eat." [32] But he said to them, "I have food to eat of which you do not know." [33] So the disciples said to one another, "Could someone have brought him something to eat?" [34] Jesus said to them, "My food is to do the will of the one who sent me and to finish his work. [h] [35] Do you not say, 'In four months* the harvest will be here'? I tell you, look up and see the fields ripe for the harvest. [i] [36] The reaper is already* receiving his payment and gathering crops for eternal life,

so that the sower and reaper can rejoice together.[j] [37] For here the saying is verified that 'One sows and another reaps.' [k] [38] I sent you to reap what you have not worked for; others have done the work, and you are sharing the fruits of their work."

[39] Many of the Samaritans of that town began to believe in him because of the word of the woman* who testified, "He told me everything I have done." [40] When the Samaritans came to him, they invited him to stay with them; and he stayed there two days. [41] Many more began to believe in him because of his word, [42] and they said to the woman, "We no longer believe because of your word; for we have heard for ourselves, and we know that this is truly the savior of the world." [l]

Return to Galilee. [43] * After the two days, he left there for Galilee. [44] [m] For Jesus himself testified that a prophet has no honor in his native place.* [45] When he came into Galilee, the Galileans welcomed him, since they had seen all he had done in Jerusalem at the feast; for they themselves had gone to the feast.

Second Sign at Cana.* [46] [n] Then he returned to Cana in Galilee, where he had made the water wine. Now there was a royal official whose son was ill in Capernaum. [47] When he heard that Jesus had arrived in Galilee from Judea, he went to him and asked him to come down and heal his son, who was near death. [48] Jesus said to him, "Unless you people see signs and wonders, you will not believe." [o] [49] The royal official said to him, "Sir, come down before my child dies." [50] Jesus said to him, "You may go; your son will live." The man believed what Jesus said to him and left. [p] [51] While he was on his way back, his slaves

c Dt 11, 29; 27, 4; Jos 8, 33; Ps 122, 1-5.—d 2 Kgs 17, 27; Ps 76, 2-3.—e 2 Cor 3, 17.—f Jn 1, 41.—g Jn 9, 37.—h Jn 5, 30.36; 6, 38; 9, 4; 17, 4.—i Mt 9, 37-38; Lk 10, 2; Rv 14, 15.—j Ps 126, 5-6; Am 9, 13-14.—k Dt 20, 6; 28, 30; Jb 31, 8; Mi 6, 15.—l 1 Jn 4, 14.—m Mt 13, 57; Mk 6, 4; Lk 4, 24.—n 46-54: Jn 2, 1-11; Mt 8, 5-13; 15, 21-28; Mk 7, 24-30; Lk 7, 1-10.—o Jn 2, 18.23; Wis 8, 8; Mt 12, 38; 1 Cor 1, 22.—p 1 Kgs 17, 23.

4, 23: *In Spirit and truth:* not a reference to an interior worship within one's own spirit. The Spirit is the spirit given by God that reveals truth and enables one to worship God appropriately (Jn 14, 16-17). Cf "born of water and Spirit" (Jn 3, 5).

4, 25: The expectations of the Samaritans are expressed here in Jewish terminology. They did not expect a messianic king of the house of David but a prophet like Moses (Dt 18, 15).

4, 26: *I am he:* it could also be translated "I am," an Old Testament self-designation of Yahweh (Is 43, 3, etc.); cf Jn 6, 20; 8, 24.28.58; 13, 19; 18, 5.6.8. See the note on Mk 6, 50.

4, 27: *Talking with a woman:* a religious and social restriction that Jesus is pictured treating as unimportant.

4, 35: *'In four months . . .':* probably a proverb; cf Mt 9, 37-38.

4, 36: *Already:* this word may go with the preceding verse rather than with 36.

4, 39: The woman is presented as a missionary, described in virtually the same words as the disciples are in Jesus' prayer (Jn 17, 20).

4, 43-54: Jesus' arrival in Cana in Galilee; the second sign. This section introduces another theme, that of the life-giving word of Jesus. It is explicitly linked to the first sign (Jn 2, 11). The royal official believes (50). The natural life given his son is a sign of eternal life.

4, 44: Probably a reminiscence of tradition as in Mk 6, 4. Cf Gospel of Thomas # 31: "No prophet is acceptable in his village, no physician heals those who know him."

4, 46-54: The story of the cure of the royal official's son may be a third version of the cure of the centurion's son (Mt 8, 5-13) or servant (Lk 7, 1-10). Cf also Mt 15, 21-28 // Mk 7, 24-30.

met him and told him that his boy would live. [52] He asked them when he began to recover. They told him, "The fever left him yesterday, about one in the afternoon." [53] The father realized that just at that time Jesus had said to him, "Your son will live," and he and his whole household came to believe. [54] [Now] this was the second sign Jesus did when he came to Galilee from Judea. [q]

CHAPTER 5*

Cure on a Sabbath. [1] After this, there was a feast* of the Jews, and Jesus went up to Jerusalem. [r] [2] Now there is in Jerusalem at the Sheep [Gate]* a pool called in Hebrew Bethesda, with five porticoes. [s] [3] In these lay a large number of ill, blind, lame, and crippled.* [4] * [5] One man was there who had been ill for thirty-eight years. [6] When Jesus saw him lying there and knew that he had been ill for a long time, he said to him, "Do you want to be well?" [7] The sick man answered him, "Sir, I have no one to put me into the pool when the water is stirred up; while I am on my way, someone else gets down there before me." [8] Jesus said to him, "Rise, take up your mat, and walk." [t] [9] Immediately the man became well, took up his mat, and walked. [u]

Now that day was a sabbath. [10] So the Jews said to the man who was cured, "It is the sabbath, and it is not lawful for you to carry your mat." [v] [11] He answered them, "The man who made me well told me, 'Take up your mat and walk.' " [12] They asked him, "Who is the man who told you, 'Take it up and walk'?" [13] The man who was healed did not know who it was, for Jesus had slipped away, since there was a crowd there. [w] [14] After this Jesus found him in the temple area and said to him, [x] "Look, you are well; do not sin anymore, so that nothing worse may happen to you."* [15] The man went and told the Jews that Jesus was the one who had made him well. [16] Therefore, the Jews began to persecute Jesus because he did this on a sabbath. [y] [17] But Jesus answered them, [z] "My Father is at work until now, so I am at work."* [18] For this reason the Jews tried all the more to kill him, because he not only broke the sabbath but he also called God his own father, making himself equal to God. [a]

The Work of the Son. [19] Jesus answered and said to them, "Amen, amen, I say to you, a son cannot do anything on his own, but only what he sees his father doing; [b] for what he does, his son will do also.* [20] For the Father loves his Son and shows him everything that he himself does, and he will show him greater works than these, so that you may be amazed. [c] [21] For just as the Father raises the dead and gives life,* so also does the Son give life to whomever he

q Jn 2, 11.—r Jn 6, 4.—s Neh 3, 1.32; 12, 39.—t Mt 9, 6; Mk 2, 11; Lk 5, 24; Acts 3, 6.—u Mk 2, 12; Lk 5, 25 / Jn 9, 14.—v Ex 20, 8; Jer 17, 21-27; Mk 3, 2; Lk 13, 10; 14, 1.—w Mt 8, 18; 13, 36; Mk 4, 36; 7, 17.—x Jn 8, 11; 9, 2; Ez 18, 20.—y Jn 7, 23; Mt 12, 8.—z Ex 20, 11.—a Jn 7, 1.25; 8, 37.40; 10, 33.36; 14, 28; Gn 3, 5-6; Wis 2, 16; Mt 26, 4; 2 Thes 2, 4.—b Jn 3, 34; 8, 26; 12, 49; 9, 4; 10, 30.—c Jn 3, 35.

5, 1-47: The self-revelation of Jesus continues in Jerusalem at a feast. The third sign (cf Jn 2, 11; 4, 54) is performed, the cure of a paralytic by Jesus' life-giving word. The water of the pool fails to bring life; Jesus' word does.

5, 1: The reference in vv 45-46 to Moses suggests that the feast was Pentecost. The connection of that feast with the giving of the law to Moses on Sinai, attested in later Judaism, may already have been made in the first century. The feast could also be Passover (cf Jn 6, 4). John stresses that the day was a sabbath (9).

5, 2: There is no noun with *Sheep.* "Gate" is supplied on the grounds that there must have been a gate in the NE wall of the temple area where animals for sacrifice were brought in; cf Neh 3, 1.32; 12, 39. *Hebrew:* more precisely, Aramaic. *Bethesda:* preferred to variants "Be(th)zatha" and "Bethsaida"; *bêt-'eš-datayîn* is given as the name of a double pool northeast of the temple area in the Qumran Copper Roll. *Five porticoes:* a pool excavated in Jerusalem actually has five porticoes.

5, 3: The Caesarean and Western recensions, followed by the Vulgate, add "waiting for the movement of the water." Apparently an intermittent spring in the pool bubbled up occasionally (see 7). This turbulence was believed to cure.

5, 4: Toward the end of the second century in the West and among the fourth-century Greek Fathers, an additional verse was known: "For [from time to time] an angel of the Lord used to come down into the pool; and the water was stirred up, so the first one to get in [after the stirring of the water] was healed of whatever disease afflicted him." The angel was a popular explanation of the turbulence and the healing powers attributed to it. This verse is missing from all early Greek manuscripts and the earliest versions, including the original Vulgate. Its vocabulary is markedly non-Johannine.

5, 14: While the cure of the paralytic in Mk 2, 1-12 is associated with the forgiveness of sins, Jesus never drew a one-to-one connection between sin and suffering (cf Jn 9, 3; Lk 12, 1-5), as did Ez 18, 20.

5, 17: Sabbath observance (10) was based on God's resting on the seventh day (cf Gn 2, 2-3; Ex 20, 11). Philo and some rabbis insisted that God's providence remains active on the sabbath, keeping all things in existence, giving life in birth and taking it away in death. Other rabbis taught that God rested from creating, but not from judging (= ruling, governing). Jesus here claims the same authority to work as the Father, and, in the discourse that follows, the same divine prerogatives: power over life and death (21.24-26) and judgment (22.27).

5, 19: This proverb or parable is taken from apprenticeship in a trade: the activity of a son is modeled on that of his father. Jesus' dependence on the Father is justification for doing what the Father does.

5, 21: *Gives life:* in the Old Testament, a divine prerogative (Dt 32, 39; 1 Sm 2, 6; 2 Kgs 5, 7; Tob 13, 2; Is 26, 19; Dan 12, 2).

wishes.*d* 22 Nor does the Father judge anyone, but he has given all judgment* to his
Son,*e* 23 so that all may honor the Son just
as they honor the Father. Whoever does
not honor the Son does not honor the
Father who sent him. 24 Amen, amen, I say
to you, whoever hears my word and believes in the one who sent me has eternal
life and will not come to condemnation,
but has passed from death to life.*f*
25 Amen, amen, I say to you, the hour is
coming and is now here when the dead will
hear the voice of the Son of God, and those
who hear will live.*g* 26 For just as the
Father has life in himself, so also he gave to
his Son the possession of life in himself.*h*
27 And he gave him power to exercise judgment, because he is the Son of Man.*i* 28 *
Do not be amazed at this, because the hour
is coming in which all who are in the tombs
will hear his voice*j* 29 and will come out,
those who have done good deeds to the resurrection of life, but those who have done
wicked deeds to the resurrection of condemnation.*k*

d Jn 11, 25; Dt 32, 39; 1 Sm 2, 6; 2 Kgs 5, 7; Tb 13, 2; Wis
16, 13; Is 26, 19; Dn 7, 10.13; 12, 2; Rom 4, 17; 2 Cor 1, 9.—e
Acts 10, 42; 17, 31.—f Jn 3, 18; 8, 51; 1 Jn 3, 14.—g Jn 5, 28;
8, 51; 11, 25-26; Eph 2, 1; 5, 14; Rv 3, 1.—h Jn 1, 4; 1 Jn 5,
11.—i Jn 5, 22; Dn 7, 13.22; Mt 25, 31; Lk 21, 36.—j Jn 11,
43.—k Dn 12, 2; Mt 16, 27; 25, 46; Acts 24, 15; 2 Cor 5, 10.—l
Jn 6, 38.—m 31-32: Jn 8, 13-14.18.—n Jn 1, 19-27; Mt 11, 10-
11.—o 1 Jn 5, 9.—p Jn 1, 8; Ps 132, 17; Sir 48, 1.—q Jn 10,
25.—r Jn 8, 18; Dt 4, 12.15; 1 Jn 5, 9.—s 1 Jn 2, 14.—t Jn 12,
16; 19, 28; 20, 9; Lk 24, 27.44; 1 Pt 1, 10.—u 1 Jn 2, 15.—v
Mt 24, 5.24.—w Jn 12, 43.—x Dt 31, 26.—y Jn 5, 39; Dt 18,
15; Lk 16, 31; 24, 44.—z 1-13: Mt 14, 13-21; Mk 6, 32-44; Lk
9, 10-17.

5, 22: *Judgment:* another divine prerogative, often expressed
as acquittal or condemnation (Dt 32, 36; Ps 43, 1).

5, 28-29: While vv 19-27 present realized eschatology, vv 28-
29 are future eschatology; cf Dn 12, 2.

5, 32: *Another:* likely the Father, who in four different ways
gives testimony to Jesus, as indicated in the verse groupings 33-
34, 36, 37-38, 39-40.

5, 35: *Lamp:* cf Ps 132, 17: "I will place a lamp for my
Anointed (= David)," and possibly the description of Elijah in Sir
48, 1. But only *for a while,* indicating the temporary and subordinate nature of John's mission.

5, 39: *You search:* this may be an imperative: "Search the
scriptures, because you think that you have eternal life through
them."

5, 41: *Praise:* the same Greek word means "praise" or
"honor" (from others) and "glory" (from God). There is a play on
this in v 44.

6, 1-15: This story of the multiplication of the loaves is the
fourth sign (cf the note on Jn 5, 1-47). It is the only miracle story
found in all four gospels (occurring twice in Mk and Mt). See the
notes on Mt 14, 13-21 and Mt 15, 32-39. John differs on the roles
of Philip and Andrew, the proximity of Passover (4), and the allusion to Elisha (see 9). The story here symbolizes the food that
is readily available through Jesus. It connotes a new exodus and
has eucharistic overtones.

6, 1: *[Of Tiberias]:* the awkward apposition represents a later
name of the Sea of Galilee. It was probably originally a marginal
gloss.

30 "I cannot do anything on my own; I
judge as I hear, and my judgment is just,
because I do not seek my own will but the
will of the one who sent me.*l*

Witnesses to Jesus. 31 *m* "If I testify on
my own behalf, my testimony cannot be
verified. 32 But there is another* who testifies on my behalf, and I know that the
testimony he gives on my behalf is true.
33 You sent emissaries to John, and he testified to the truth.*n* 34 I do not accept testimony from a human being, but I say this
so that you may be saved.*o* 35 He was a
burning and shining lamp,* and for a while
you were content to rejoice in his light.*p*
36 But I have testimony greater than
John's. The works that the Father gave me
to accomplish, these works that I perform
testify on my behalf that the Father has
sent me.*q* 37 Moreover, the Father who
sent me has testified on my behalf. But you
have never heard his voice nor seen his
form,*r* 38 and you do not have his word remaining in you, because you do not believe
in the one whom he has sent.*s* 39 You
search* the scriptures, because you think
you have eternal life through them; even
they testify on my behalf.*t* 40 But you do
not want to come to me to have life.

Unbelief of Jesus' Hearers. 41 "I do not accept human praise;* 42 moreover, I know
that you do not have the love of God in
you.*u* 43 I came in the name of my Father,
but you do not accept me; yet if another
comes in his own name, you will accept
him.*v* 44 How can you believe, when you
accept praise from one another and do not
seek the praise that comes from the only
God?*w* 45 Do not think that I will accuse
you before the Father: the one who will accuse you is Moses, in whom you have
placed your hope.*x* 46 For if you had believed Moses, you would have believed me,
because he wrote about me.*y* 47 But if you
do not believe his writings, how will you
believe my words?"

CHAPTER 6

Multiplication of the Loaves. * 1 *z* After
this, Jesus went across the Sea of Galilee
[of Tiberias].* 2 A large crowd followed
him, because they saw the signs he was
performing on the sick. 3 Jesus went up on
the mountain, and there he sat down with
his disciples. 4 The Jewish feast of Passover

was near.*ᵃ* ⁵When Jesus raised his eyes and saw that a large crowd was coming to him, he said to Philip,*ᵇ* "Where can we buy enough food for them to eat?"* ⁶He said this to test him, because he himself knew what he was going to do.* ⁷Philip answered him, "Two hundred days' wages* worth of food would not be enough for each of them to have a little [bit]."*ᶜ* ⁸One of his disciples, Andrew, the brother of Simon Peter, said to him, ⁹"There is a boy here who has five barley loaves* and two fish; but what good are these for so many?"*ᵈ* ¹⁰Jesus said, "Have the people recline." Now there was a great deal of grass* in that place. So the men reclined, about five thousand in number.*ᵉ* ¹¹Then Jesus took the loaves, gave thanks, and distributed them to those who were reclining, and also as much of the fish as they wanted.*ᶠ* ¹²When they had had their fill, he said to his disciples, "Gather the fragments left over, so that nothing will be wasted." ¹³So they collected them, and filled twelve wicker baskets* with fragments from the five barley loaves that had been more than they could eat. ¹⁴When the people saw the sign he had done, they said, "This is truly the Prophet,* the one who is to come into the world."*ᵍ* ¹⁵Since Jesus knew that they were going to come and carry him off to make him king, he withdrew again to the mountain alone.*ʰ*

Walking on the Water. *ᵢ When it was evening, his disciples went down to the sea, ¹⁷embarked in a boat, and went across the sea to Capernaum. It had already grown dark, and Jesus had not yet come to them. ¹⁸The sea was stirred up because a strong wind was blowing. ¹⁹When they had rowed about three or four miles, they saw Jesus walking on the sea* and coming near the boat, and they began to be afraid.*ʲ* ²⁰But he said to them, "It is I.* Do not be afraid." ²¹They wanted to take him into the boat, but the boat immediately arrived at the shore to which they were heading.

The Bread of Life Discourse. ²² *The next day, the crowd that remained across the sea saw that there had been only one boat there, and that Jesus had not gone along with his disciples in the boat, but only his disciples had left. ²³Other boats came from Tiberias near the place where they had eaten the bread when the Lord gave thanks.* ²⁴When the crowd saw that neither Jesus nor his disciples were there, they themselves got into boats and came to Capernaum looking for Jesus. ²⁵And when they found him across the sea they said to him, "Rabbi, when did you get here?" ²⁶Jesus answered them and said, "Amen, amen, I say to you, you are looking for me not because you saw signs but because you ate the loaves and were filled. ²⁷Do not work for food that perishes but for the food that endures for eternal life,* which the Son of Man will give you. For on him the Father, God, has set his seal."*ᵏ* ²⁸So they said to him, "What can we do to accomplish the works of God?" ²⁹Jesus answered and said to them, "This is the work of God, that you believe in the one he sent." ³⁰So they said to him, "What sign can you do, that we may see and believe in you? What can you do?*ˡ* ³¹ * Our ancestors ate manna in the desert, as it is written: *ᵐ*

---

a Jn 2, 13; 11, 55.—b Nm 11, 13.—c Mt 20, 2.—d 2 Kgs 4, 42-44.—e Mt 14, 21; Mk 6, 44.—f Jn 21, 13.—g Dt 18, 15.18; Mal 3, 1.23; Acts 3, 22.—h Jn 18, 36.—i 16-21: Mt 14, 22-27; Mk 6, 45-52.—j Jb 9, 8; Pss 29, 3-4; 77, 20; Is 43, 16.—k Jn 6, 50.51.54.58.—l Mt 16, 1-4; Lk 11, 29-30.—m Ex 16, 4-5; Nm 11, 7-9; Ps 78, 24.

6, 5: Jesus takes the initiative (in the synoptics, the disciples do), possibly pictured as (cf Jn 6, 14) the new Moses (cf Nm 11, 13).

6, 6: Probably the evangelist's comment; in this gospel Jesus is never portrayed as ignorant of anything.

6, 7: *Days' wages:* literally, "denarii"; a Roman denarius is a day's wage in Mt 20, 2.

6, 9: *Barley loaves:* the food of the poor. There seems an allusion to the story of Elisha multiplying the barley bread in 2 Kgs 4, 42-44.

6, 10: *Grass:* implies springtime, and therefore Passover. *Five thousand:* so Mk 6, 39.44 and parallels.

6, 13: *Baskets:* the word describes the typically Palestinian wicker basket, as in Mk 6, 43 and parallels.

6, 14: *The Prophet:* probably the prophet like Moses (see the note on Jn 1, 21). *The one who is to come into the world:* probably Elijah; cf Mal 3, 1.23.

6, 16-21: The fifth sign is a nature miracle, portraying Jesus sharing Yahweh's power. Cf the parallel stories following the multiplication of the loaves in Mk 6, 45-52 and Mt 14, 22-33.

6, 19: *Walking on the sea:* although the Greek (cf Jn 6, 16) could mean "on the seashore" or "by the sea" (cf Jn 21, 1), the parallels, especially Mt 14, 25, make clear that Jesus walked upon the water. John may allude to Job 9, 8: God "treads upon the crests of the sea."

6, 20: *It is I:* literally, "I am." See also the notes on Jn 4, 26 and Mk 6, 50.

6, 22-71: Discourse on the bread of life; replacement of the manna. Verses 22-34 serve as an introduction, vv 35-59 constitute the discourse proper, vv 60-71 portray the reaction of the disciples and Peter's confession.

6, 23: Possibly a later interpolation, to explain how the crowd got to Capernaum.

6, 27: *The food that endures for eternal life:* cf Jn 4, 14, on water "springing up to eternal life."

6, 31: *Bread from heaven:* cf Ex 16, 4.15.32-34 and the notes there; Ps 78, 24. The manna, thought to have been hidden by Jeremiah (2 Mc 2, 5-8), was expected to reappear miraculously at Passover, in the last days.

'He gave them bread from heaven to eat.' "

32 So Jesus said to them, "Amen, amen, I say to you, it was not Moses who gave the bread from heaven; my Father gives you the true bread from heaven.ⁿ 33 For the bread of God is that which comes down from heaven and gives life to the world."

34 ᵒ So they said to him, "Sir, give us this bread always." 35 * Jesus said to them, "I am the bread of life; whoever comes to me will never hunger, and whoever believes in me will never thirst.ᵖ 36 But I told you that although you have seen [me], you do not believe.�q 37 Everything that the Father gives me will come to me, and I will not reject anyone who comes to me, 38 because I came down from heaven not to do my own will but the will of the one who sent me.ʳ 39 And this is the will of the one who sent me, that I should not lose anything of what he gave me, but that I should raise it [on] the last day.ˢ 40 For this is the will of my Father, that everyone who sees the Son and believes in him may have eternal life, and I shall raise him [on] the last day." ᵗ

41 The Jews murmured about him because he said, "I am the bread that came down from heaven," 42 and they said, "Is this not Jesus, the son of Joseph? Do we not know his father and mother? Then how can he say, 'I have come down from heaven'?" ᵘ 43 Jesus answered and said to them, "Stop murmuring* among yourselves.ᵛ 44 No one can come to me unless the Father who sent me draw him, and I will raise him on the last day. 45 It is written in the prophets:

'They shall all be taught by God.'

Everyone who listens to my Father and learns from him comes to me.ʷ 46 Not that anyone has seen the Father except the one who is from God; he has seen the Father.ˣ 47 Amen, amen, I say to you, whoever believes has eternal life. 48 I am the bread of life. 49 Your ancestors ate the manna in the desert, but they died;ʸ 50 this is the bread that comes down from heaven so that one may eat it and not die. 51 I am the living bread that came down from heaven; whoever eats this bread will live forever; and the bread that I will give is my flesh for the life of the world." ᶻ

52 The Jews quarreled among themselves, saying, "How can this man give us [his] flesh to eat?" 53 Jesus said to them, "Amen, amen, I say to you, unless you eat the flesh of the Son of Man and drink his blood, you do not have life within you. 54 Whoever eats* my flesh and drinks my blood has eternal life, and I will raise him on the last day. 55 For my flesh is true food, and my blood is true drink. 56 Whoever eats my flesh and drinks my blood remains in me and I in him. 57 Just as the living Father sent me and I have life because of the Father, so also the one who feeds on me will have life because of me.ᵃ 58 This is the bread that came down from heaven. Unlike your ancestors who ate and still died, whoever eats this bread will live forever." 59 These things he said while teaching in the synagogue in Capernaum.

The Words of Eternal Life.* 60 Then many of his disciples who were listening said, "This saying is hard; who can accept it?" 61 Since Jesus knew that his disciples were murmuring about this, he said to them, "Does this shock you? 62 What if you were to see the Son of Man ascending to where he was before?* 63 It is the spirit that gives life, while the flesh* is of no avail. The words I have spoken to you are spirit and life. 64 But there are some of you who do not believe." Jesus knew from the beginning the ones who would not believe and the one who would betray him.ᵇ 65 And he said, "For this reason I have told you that

---

n Mt 6, 11.—o Jn 4, 15.—p Is 55, 1-3; Am 8, 11-13.—q Jn 20, 29.—r Jn 4, 34; Mt 26, 39; Heb 10, 9.—s Jn 10, 28-29; 17, 12; 18, 9.—t 1 Jn 2, 25.—u Mt 13, 54-57; Mk 6, 1-4; Lk 4, 22.—v Ex 16, 2.7.8; Lk 4, 22.—w Is 54, 13; Jer 31, 33-34.—x Jn 1, 18; 7, 29; Ex 33, 20.—y 1 Cor 10, 3.5.—z Mt 26, 26-27; Lk 22, 19.—a Jn 5, 26.—b Jn 13, 11.

6, 35-59: Up to v 50, "bread of life" is a figure for God's revelation in Jesus; in vv 51-58, the eucharistic theme comes to the fore. There may thus be a break between vv 50 and 51.

6, 43: *Murmuring:* the word may reflect the Greek of Ex 16, 2.7.8.

6, 54-58: *Eats:* the verb used in these verses is not the classical Greek verb used of human eating, but that of animal eating: "munch," "gnaw." This may be part of John's emphasis on the reality of the flesh and blood of Jesus (cf Jn 6, 55), but the same verb eventually became the ordinary verb in Greek meaning "eat."

6, 60-71: These verses refer more to themes of vv 35-50 than to those of 51-58 and seem to be addressed to members of the Johannine community who found it difficult to accept the high christology reflected in the bread of life discourse.

6, 62: This unfinished conditional sentence is obscure. Probably there is a reference to vv 49-51. This claim provokes incredulity (60); and so Jesus is pictured as asking what his disciples will say when he goes up to heaven.

6, 63: *Spirit . . . flesh:* probably not a reference to the eucharistic body of Jesus but to the supernatural and the natural, as in Jn 3, 6. *Spirit and life:* all Jesus said about the bread of life is the revelation of the Spirit.

no one can come to me unless it is granted him by my Father."

66 As a result of this, many [of] his disciples returned to their former way of life and no longer accompanied him. 67 Jesus then said to the Twelve, "Do you also want to leave?" 68 Simon Peter answered him, "Master, to whom shall we go? You have the words of eternal life. 69 We have come to believe and are convinced that you are the Holy One of God." c 70 Jesus answered them, "Did I not choose you twelve? Yet is not one of you a devil?" 71 He was referring to Judas, son of Simon the Iscariot; it was he who would betray him, one of the Twelve. d

CHAPTER 7

The Feast of Tabernacles. 1 * After this, Jesus moved about within Galilee; but he did not wish to travel in Judea, because the Jews were trying to kill him. e 2 But the Jewish feast of Tabernacles was near. f 3 So his brothers* said to him, "Leave here and go to Judea, so that your disciples also may see the works you are doing. 4 No one works in secret if he wants to be known publicly. If you do these things, manifest yourself to the world." g 5 For his brothers did not believe in him. 6 So Jesus said to them, "My time* is not yet here, but the time is always right for you. 7 The world cannot hate you, but it hates me, because I testify to it that its works are evil. h 8 You go up to the feast. I am not going up* to this feast, because my time has not yet been fulfilled." 9 After he had said this, he stayed on in Galilee.

10 But when his brothers had gone up to the feast, he himself also went up, not openly but [as it were] in secret. 11 The Jews were looking for him at the feast and saying, "Where is he?" 12 And there was considerable murmuring about him in the crowds. Some said, "He is a good man," [while] others said, "No; on the contrary, he misleads the crowd." 13 Still, no one spoke openly about him because they were afraid of the Jews. i

The First Dialogue. * 14 When the feast was already half over, Jesus went up into the temple area and began to teach. 15 j The Jews were amazed and said, "How does he know scripture without having studied?" * 16 Jesus answered them and said, "My teaching is not my own but is from the one who sent me. 17 Whoever chooses to do his will* shall know whether my teaching is from God or whether I speak on my own. k 18 Whoever speaks on his own seeks his own glory, but whoever seeks the glory of the one who sent him is truthful, and there is no wrong in him. 19 Did not Moses give you the law? Yet none of you keeps the law. Why are you trying to kill me?" l 20 The crowd answered, "You are possessed!* Who is trying to kill you?" m 21 Jesus answered and said to them, "I performed one work* and all of you are amazed n 22 because of it. Moses gave you circumcision—not that it came from Moses but rather from the patriarchs—and you circumcise a man on the sabbath. o 23 If a man can receive circumcision on a sabbath so that the law of Moses may not be broken, are you angry with me because I made a whole person well on a sabbath? p 24 Stop judging by appearances, but judge justly." q

---

c Jn 11, 27; Mt 16, 16; Mk 1, 24; Lk 4, 34.—d Jn 12, 4; 13, 2.27.—e Jn 5, 18; 8, 37.40.—f Ex 23, 16; Lv 23, 34; Nm 29, 12; Dt 16, 13-16; Zec 14, 16-19.—g Jn 14, 22.—h Jn 15, 18.—i Jn 9, 22; 19, 38; 20, 19.—j Lk 2, 47.—k Jn 6, 29.—l Acts 7, 53.—m Jn 8, 48-49; 10, 20.—n Jn 5, 1-9.—o Gn 17, 10; Lv 12, 3.—p Jn 5, 2-9.16; Mt 12, 11-12; Lk 14, 5.—q Jn 8, 15; Lv 19, 15; Is 11, 3-4.

7—8: These chapters contain events about the feast of Tabernacles (Sukkoth, Ingathering: Ex 23, 16; Tents, Booths: Dt 16, 13-16), with its symbols of booths (originally built to shelter harvesters), rain (water from Siloam poured on the temple altar), and lights (illumination of the Court of the Women). They continue the theme of the replacement of feasts (Passover, Jn 2, 13; 6, 4; Hanukkah, Jn 10, 22; Pentecost, Jn 5, 1), here accomplished by Jesus as the Living Water. These chapters comprise seven miscellaneous controversies and dialogues. There is a literary inclusion with Jesus in hiding in Jn 7, 4.10 and 8, 59. There are frequent references to attempts on his life: Jn 7, 1.13.19.25.30.32.44; 8, 37.40.59.

7, 3: *Brothers:* these relatives (cf Jn 2, 12 and see the note on Mk 6, 3) are never portrayed as disciples until after the resurrection (Acts 1, 14). Mt 13, 55 and Mk 6, 3 give the names of four of them. Jesus has already performed works/signs in Judea; cf Jn 2, 23; 3, 2; 4, 45; 5, 8.

7, 6: *Time:* the Greek word means "opportune time," here a synonym for Jesus' "hour" (see the note on Jn 2, 4), his death and resurrection. In the wordplay, any time is suitable for Jesus' brothers, because they are not dependent on God's will.

7, 8: *I am not going up:* an early attested reading "not yet" seems a correction, since Jesus in the story does go up to the feast. "Go up," in a play on words, refers not only to going up to Jerusalem but also to exaltation at the cross, resurrection, and ascension; cf Jn 3, 14; 6, 62; 20, 17.

7, 14-31: Jesus teaches in the temple; debate with the Jews.

7, 15: *Without having studied:* literally, "How does he know letters without having learned?" Children were taught to read and write by means of the scriptures. But here more than Jesus' literacy is being discussed; the people are wondering how he can teach like a rabbi. Rabbis were trained by other rabbis and traditionally quoted their teachers.

7, 17: *To do his will:* presumably a reference back to the "work" of Jn 6, 29: belief in the one whom God has sent.

7, 20: *You are possessed:* literally, "You have a demon." The insane were thought to be possessed by a demoniacal spirit.

7, 21: *One work:* the cure of the paralytic (Jn 5, 1-9) because of the reference to the sabbath (Jn 7, 22; 5, 9-10).

25 So some of the inhabitants of Jerusalem said, "Is he not the one they are trying to kill? 26 And look, he is speaking openly and they say nothing to him. Could the authorities* have realized that he is the Messiah? 27 But we know where he is from. When the Messiah comes, no one will know where he is from." *r* 28 So Jesus cried out in the temple area as he was teaching and said, "You know me and also know where I am from. Yet I did not come on my own, but the one who sent me, whom you do not know, is true. *s* 29 I know him, because I am from him, and he sent me." *t* 30 So they tried to arrest him, but no one laid a hand upon him, because his hour had not yet come. *u* 31 But many of the crowd began to believe in him, and said, "When the Messiah comes, will he perform more signs than this man has done?" *v*

Officers Sent to Arrest Jesus.* 32 The Pharisees heard the crowd murmuring about him to this effect, and the chief priests and the Pharisees sent guards to arrest him. 33 So Jesus said, "I will be with

r Heb 7, 3.—s Jn 8, 19.—t Jn 6, 46; 8, 55.—u Jn 7, 44; 8, 20; Lk 4, 29-30.—v Jn 2, 11; 10, 42; 11, 45.—w Jn 13, 33; 16, 16.—x Jn 8, 21; 12, 36; 13, 33.36; 16, 5; Dt 4, 29; Prv 1, 28; Is 55, 6; Hos 5, 6.—y Rv 21, 6.—z Jn 4, 10.14; 19, 34; Is 12, 3; Ez 47, 1.—a Jn 16, 7.—b Dt 18, 15.18.—c 2 Sm 7, 12-14; Pss 89, 3-4; 132, 11; Mi 5, 1; Mt 2, 5-6.—d Jn 12, 42.—e Jn 3, 1; 19, 39.—f Dt 1, 16-17.

7, 26: *The authorities:* the members of the Sanhedrin (same term as Jn 3, 1).

7, 32-36: Jesus announces his approaching departure (cf also Jn 8, 21; 12, 36; 13, 33) and complete control over his destiny.

7, 35: *Dispersion:* or "diaspora": Jews living outside Palestine. *Greeks:* probably refers to the Gentiles in the Mediterranean area; cf Jn 12, 20.

7, 37-39: Promise of living water through the Spirit.

7, 38: *Living water:* not an exact quotation from any Old Testament passage; in the gospel context the gift of the Spirit is meant; cf Jn 3, 5. *From within him:* either Jesus or the believer; if Jesus, it continues the Jesus-Moses motif (water from the rock, Ex 17, 6; Nm 20, 11) as well as Jesus as the new temple (cf Ez 47, 1). Grammatically, it goes better with the believer.

7, 39: *No Spirit yet:* Codex Vaticanus and early Latin, Syriac, and Coptic versions add "given." In this gospel, the sending of the Spirit cannot take place until Jesus' glorification through his death, resurrection, and ascension; cf Jn 20, 22.

7, 40-53: Discussion of the Davidic lineage of the Messiah.

7, 53—8, 11: The story of the woman caught in adultery is a later insertion here, missing from all early Greek manuscripts. A Western text-type insertion, attested mainly in Old Latin translations, it is found in different places in different manuscripts: here, or after Jn 7, 36, or at the end of this gospel, or after Lk 21, 38, or at the end of that gospel. There are many non-Johannine features in the language, and there are also many doubtful readings within the passage. The style and motifs are similar to those of Luke, and it fits better with the general situation at the end of Lk 21, but it was probably inserted here because of the allusion to Jer 17, 13 (cf the note on Jn 8, 6) and the statement, "I do not judge anyone," in Jn 8, 15. The Catholic Church accepts this passage as canonical scripture.

you only a little while longer, and then I will go to the one who sent me. *w* 34 You will look for me but not find [me], and where I am you cannot come." *x* 35 So the Jews said to one another, "Where is he going that we will not find him? Surely he is not going to the dispersion* among the Greeks to teach the Greeks, is he? 36 What is the meaning of his saying, 'You will look for me and not find [me], and where I am you cannot come'?"

Rivers of Living Water.* 37 On the last and greatest day of the feast, Jesus stood up and exclaimed, "Let anyone who thirsts come to me and drink. *y* 38 Whoever believes in me, as scripture says:

'Rivers of living water* will flow from within him.' " *z*

39 He said this in reference to the Spirit that those who came to believe in him were to receive. There was, of course, no Spirit yet,* because Jesus had not yet been glorified. *a*

Discussion about the Origins of the Messiah.* 40 Some in the crowd who heard these words said, "This is truly the Prophet." *b* 41 Others said, "This is the Messiah." But others said, "The Messiah will not come from Galilee, will he? 42 Does not scripture say that the Messiah will be of David's family and come from Bethlehem, the village where David lived?" *c* 43 So a division occurred in the crowd because of him. 44 Some of them even wanted to arrest him, but no one laid hands on him.

45 So the guards went to the chief priests and Pharisees, who asked them, "Why did you not bring him?" 46 The guards answered, "Never before has anyone spoken like this one." 47 So the Pharisees answered them, "Have you also been deceived? 48 Have any of the authorities or the Pharisees believed in him? *d* 49 But this crowd, which does not know the law, is accursed." 50 Nicodemus, one of their members who had come to him earlier, said to them, *e* 51 "Does our law condemn a person before it first hears him and finds out what he is doing?" *f* 52 They answered and said to him, "You are not from Galilee also, are you? Look and see that no prophet arises from Galilee."

CHAPTER 8

A Woman Caught in Adultery.* [53 Then each went to his own house, 1 while Jesus went to the Mount of Olives.* *g* ²But early in the morning he arrived again in the temple area, and all the people started coming to him, and he sat down and taught them. ³Then the scribes and the Pharisees brought a woman who had been caught in adultery and made her stand in the middle. ⁴They said to him, "Teacher, this woman was caught in the very act of committing adultery. ⁵Now in the law, Moses commanded us to stone such women.* So what do you say?"*h* ⁶They said this to test him, so that they could have some charge to bring against him. Jesus bent down and began to write on the ground with his finger.* ⁷But when they continued asking him, he straightened up and said to them,*i* "Let the one among you who is without sin be the first to throw a stone at her."* ⁸Again he bent down and wrote on the ground. ⁹And in response, they went away one by one, beginning with the elders. So he was left alone with the woman before him. ¹⁰Then Jesus straightened up and said to her, "Woman, where are they? Has no one condemned you?"*j* ¹¹She replied, "No one, sir." Then Jesus said, "Neither do I condemn you. Go, [and] from now on do not sin any more."]*k*

The Light of the World.* ¹²Jesus spoke to them again, saying, "I am the light of the world. Whoever follows me will not walk in darkness, but will have the light of life."*l* ¹³So the Pharisees said to him, "You testify on your own behalf, so your testimony cannot be verified." ¹⁴Jesus answered and said to them, "Even if I do testify on my own behalf, my testimony can be verified,* because I know where I came from and where I am going. But you do not know where I come from or where I am going.*m* ¹⁵You judge by appearances,* but I do not judge anyone.*n* ¹⁶And even if I should judge, my judgment is valid, because I am not alone, but it is I and the Father who sent me.*o* ¹⁷Even in your law* it is written that the testimony of two men can be verified.*p* ¹⁸I testify on my behalf and so does the Father who sent me."*q* ¹⁹So they said to him, "Where is your father?" Jesus answered, "You know neither me nor my Father. If you knew me, you would know my Father also."*r* ²⁰He spoke these words while teaching in the treasury in the temple area. But no one arrested him, because his hour had not yet come.*s*

Jesus, the Father's Ambassador.* ²¹He said to them again, "I am going away and you will look for me, but you will die in your sin.* Where I am going you cannot come."*t* ²²So the Jews said, "He is not going to kill himself, is he, because he said, 'Where I am going you cannot come'?"* ²³He said to them, "You belong to what is below, I belong to what is above. You belong to this world, but I do not belong to this world.*u* ²⁴That is why I told you that you will die in your sins. For if you do not believe that I AM,* you will die in your sins."*v* ²⁵So they said to him, "Who are you?"*w* Jesus said to them, "What I told you from the beginning.* ²⁶I have much to

---

g 1-2: Lk 21, 37-38.—h Lv 20, 10; Dt 22, 22-29.—i Dt 17, 7.—j Ez 33, 11.—k Jn 5, 14.—l Jn 1, 4-5.9; 12, 46; Ex 13, 22; Is 42, 6; Zec 14, 8.—m Jn 5, 31.—n Jn 12, 47; 1 Sm 16, 7.—o Jn 5, 30.—p Dt 17, 6; 19, 15; Nm 35, 30.—q Jn 5, 23.37.—r Jn 7, 28; 14, 7; 15, 21.—s Jn 7, 30.—t Jn 7, 34; 13, 33.—u Jn 3, 31; 17, 14; 18, 36.—v Ex 3, 14; Dt 32, 39; Is 43, 10.—w Jn 10, 24.

8, 1: *Mount of Olives:* not mentioned elsewhere in the gospel tradition outside of passion week.

8, 5: Lv 20, 10 and Dt 22, 22 mention only death, but Dt 22, 23-24 prescribes stoning for a betrothed virgin.

8, 6: Cf Jer 17, 13 (RSV): "Those who turn away from thee shall be written in the earth, for they have forsaken the LORD, the fountain of living water"; cf Jn 7, 38.

8, 7: The first stones were to be thrown by the witnesses (Dt 17, 7).

8, 12-20: Jesus the light of the world. Jesus replaces the four torches of the illumination of the temple as the light of joy.

8, 14: *My testimony can be verified:* this seems to contradict Jn 5, 31, but the emphasis here is on Jesus' origin from the Father and his divine destiny. *Where I am going:* indicates Jesus' passion and glorification.

8, 15: *By appearances:* literally, "according to the flesh." *I do not judge anyone:* superficial contradiction of Jn 5, 22.27.30; here the emphasis is that the judgment is not by material standards.

8, 17: *Your law:* a reflection of later controversy between church and synagogue.

8, 21-30: He whose ambassador I am is with me. Jesus' origin is from God; he can reveal God.

8, 21: *You will die in your sin:* i.e., of disbelief; cf v 24. *Where I am going you cannot come:* except through faith in Jesus' passion-resurrection.

8, 22: The Jews suspect that he is referring to his death. Johannine irony is apparent here; Jesus' death will not be self-inflicted but destined by God.

8, 24.28: *I AM:* an expression that late Jewish tradition understood as Yahweh's own self-designation (Is 43, 10); see the note on Jn 4, 26. Jesus is here placed on a par with Yahweh.

8, 25: *What I told you from the beginning:* this verse seems textually corrupt, with several other possible translations: "(I am) what I say to you"; "Why do I speak to you at all?" The earliest attested reading (Bodmer Papyrus P⁶⁶) has (in a second hand), "I told you at the beginning what I am also telling you (now)." The answer here (cf Prv 8, 22) seems to hinge on a misunderstanding of v 24 "*that* I AM" as "*what* I am."

say about you in condemnation. But the one who sent me is true, and what I heard from him I tell the world." [x] [27] They did not realize that he was speaking to them of the Father. [28] So Jesus said [to them], "When you lift up the Son of Man, then you will realize that I AM, and that I do nothing on my own, but I say only what the Father taught me. [y] [29] The one who sent me is with me. He has not left me alone, because I always do what is pleasing to him." [30] Because he spoke this way, many came to believe in him.

Jesus and Abraham. [*] [31] Jesus then said to those Jews who believed in him, [*] "If you remain in my word, you will truly be my disciples, [32] and you will know the truth, and the truth will set you free." [z] [33] They answered him, "We are descendants of Abraham and have never been enslaved to anyone. [*] How can you say, 'You will become free'?" [a] [34] Jesus answered them, "Amen, amen, I say to you, everyone who commits sin is a slave of sin. [b] [35] A slave does not remain in a household forever, but a son[*] always remains. [c] [36] So if a son frees you, then you will truly be free. [37] I know that you are descendants of Abraham. But you are trying to kill me, because my word has no room among you. [38] I tell

you what I have seen in the Father's presence; then do what you have heard from the Father." [*]

[39] They answered and said to him, "Our father is Abraham." Jesus said to them, [d] "If you were Abraham's children, you would be doing the works of Abraham. [*] [40] But now you are trying to kill me, a man who has told you the truth that I heard from God; Abraham did not do this. [41] You are doing the works of your father!" [So] they said to him, "We are not illegitimate. We have one Father, God." [e] [42] Jesus said to them, "If God were your Father, you would love me, for I came from God and am here; I did not come on my own, but he sent me. [f] [43] Why do you not understand what I am saying? Because you cannot bear to hear my word. [44] You belong to your father the devil and you willingly carry out your father's desires. He was a murderer from the beginning and does not stand in truth, because there is no truth in him. When he tells a lie, he speaks in character, because he is a liar and the father of lies. [g] [45] But because I speak the truth, you do not believe me. [46] Can any of you charge me with sin? If I am telling the truth, why do you not believe me? [h] [47] Whoever belongs to God hears the words of God; for this reason you do not listen, because you do not belong to God." [i]

[48] The Jews answered and said to him, "Are we not right in saying that you are a Samaritan[*] and are possessed?" [49] Jesus answered, "I am not possessed; I honor my Father, but you dishonor me. [50] I do not seek my own glory; there is one who seeks it and he is the one who judges. [j] [51] Amen, amen, I say to you, whoever keeps my word will never see death." [k] [52] [So] the Jews said to him, "Now we are sure that you are possessed. Abraham died, as did the prophets, yet you say, 'Whoever keeps my word will never taste death.' [53] Are you greater than our father Abraham,[*] who died? Or the prophets, who died? Who do you make yourself out to be?" [l] [54] Jesus answered, "If I glorify myself, my glory is worth nothing; but it is my Father who glorifies me, of whom you say, 'He is our God.' [55] You do not know him, but I know him. And if I should say that I do not know him, I would be like you a liar. But I do know him and I keep his word. [m] [56] Abraham your father rejoiced to see my day; he

---

x Jn 12, 44-50.—y Jn 3, 14; 12, 32.34.—z Is 42, 7; Gal 4, 31.—a Mt 3, 9.—b Rom 6, 16-17.—c Gn 21, 10; Gal 4, 30; Heb 3, 5-6.—d Gn 26, 5; Rom 4, 11-17; Jas 2, 21-23.—e Mal 2, 10.—f 1 Jn 5, 1.—g Gn 3, 4; Wis 1, 13; 2, 24; Acts 13, 10; 1 Jn 3, 8-15.—h Heb 4, 15; 1 Pt 2, 22; 1 Jn 3, 5.—i Jn 10, 26; 1 Jn 4, 6.—j Jn 7, 18.—k Jn 5, 24-29; 6, 40.47; 11, 25-26.—l Jn 4, 12.—m Jn 7, 28-29.

8, 31-59: Jesus' origin ("before Abraham") and destiny are developed; the truth will free them from sin (34) and death (51).

8, 31: *Those Jews who believed in him:* a rough editorial suture, since in v 37 they are described as trying to kill Jesus.

8, 33: *Have never been enslaved to anyone:* since, historically, the Jews were enslaved almost continuously, this verse is probably Johannine irony, about slavery to sin.

8, 35: *A slave . . . a son:* an allusion to Ishmael and Isaac (Gn 16 and 21), or to the release of a slave after six years (Ex 21, 2; Dt 15, 12).

8, 38: *The Father:* i.e., God. It is also possible, however, to understand the second part of the verse as a sarcastic reference to descent of the Jews from the devil (44), "You do what you have heard from [your] father."

8, 39: *The works of Abraham:* Abraham believed; cf Rom 4, 11-17; Jas 2, 21-23.

8, 48: *Samaritan:* therefore interested in magical powers; cf Acts 7, 14-24.

8, 53: *Are you greater than our father Abraham?:* cf Jn 4, 12.

saw it* and was glad."[n] [57] So the Jews said to him, "You are not yet fifty years old and you have seen Abraham?"* [58] Jesus said to them,[o] "Amen, amen, I say to you, before Abraham came to be, I AM."* [59] So they picked up stones to throw at him; but Jesus hid and went out of the temple area.[p]

CHAPTER 9

The Man Born Blind. [1]*As he passed by he saw a man blind from birth.[q] [2]His disciples asked him,[r] "Rabbi, who sinned, this man or his parents, that he was born blind?"* [3]Jesus answered, "Neither he nor his parents sinned; it is so that the works of God might be made visible through him.[s] [4]We have to do the works of the one who sent me while it is day. Night is coming when no one can work.[t] [5]While I am in the world, I am the light of the world."[u] [6]When he had said this, he spat on the ground and made clay with the saliva, and smeared the clay on his eyes,[v] [7]and said to him, "Go wash* in the Pool of Siloam" (which means Sent). So he went and washed, and came back able to see.[w]

[8]His neighbors and those who had seen him earlier as a beggar said, "Isn't this the one who used to sit and beg?" [9]Some said, "It is," but others said, "No, he just looks like him." He said, "I am." [10]So they said to him, "[So] how were your eyes opened?" [11]He replied, "The man called Jesus made clay and anointed my eyes and told me, 'Go to Siloam and wash.' So I went there and washed and was able to see." [12]And they said to him, "Where is he?" He said, "I don't know."

[13]They brought the one who was once blind to the Pharisees. [14]Now Jesus had made clay* and opened his eyes on a sabbath.[x] [15]So then the Pharisees also asked him how he was able to see. He said to them, "He put clay on my eyes, and I washed, and now I can see." [16]So some of the Pharisees said, "This man is not from God, because he does not keep the sabbath." [But] others said, "How can a sinful man do such signs?" And there was a division among them.[y] [17]So they said to the blind man again, "What do you have to say about him, since he opened your eyes?" He said, "He is a prophet."[z]

[18]Now the Jews did not believe that he had been blind and gained his sight until they summoned the parents of the one who had gained his sight. [19]They asked them, "Is this your son, who you say was born blind? How does he now see?" [20]His parents answered and said, "We know that this is our son and that he was born blind. [21]We do not know how he sees now, nor do we know who opened his eyes. Ask him, he is of age; he can speak for himself." [22] [a] His parents said this because they were afraid of the Jews, for the Jews had already agreed that if anyone acknowledged him as the Messiah, he would be expelled from the synagogue.* [23]For this reason his parents said, "He is of age; question him." [b]

[24]So a second time they called the man who had been blind and said to him, "Give God the praise!* We know that this man is a sinner."[c] [25]He replied, "If he is a sinner, I do not know. One thing I do know is that I was blind and now I see." [26]So they said

---

n Gn 17, 17; Mt 13, 17; Lk 17, 22.—o Jn 1, 30; 17, 5.—p Jn 10, 31.39; 11, 8; Lk 4, 29-30.—q 1-2: Is 42, 7.—r Ex 20, 5; Ez 18, 20; Lk 13, 2.—s Jn 5, 14; 11, 4.—t Jn 11, 9-10; 12, 35-36.—u Jn 8, 12.—v Jn 5, 11; Mk 7, 33; 8, 23.—w 2 Kgs 5, 10-14.—x Jn 5, 9.—y Jn 3, 2; Mt 12, 10-11; Lk 13, 10-11; 14, 1-4.—z Jn 4, 19.—a Jn 7, 13; 12, 42; 16, 2; 19, 38.—b Jn 12, 42.—c Jos 7, 19; 1 Sm 6, 5 LXX.

8, 56: *He saw it:* this seems a reference to the birth of Isaac (Gn 17, 7; 21, 6), the beginning of the fulfillment of promises about Abraham's seed.

8, 57: The evidence of the third-century Bodmer Papyrus P[75] and the first hand of Codex Sinaiticus indicates that the text originally read: "How can Abraham have seen you?"

8, 58: *Came to be, I AM:* the Greek word used for "came to be" is the one used of all creation in the prologue, while the word used for "am" is the one reserved for the Logos.

9, 1—10, 21: Sabbath healing of the man born blind. This fifth sign is introduced to illustrate the saying, "I am the light of the world" (Jn 8, 12; 9, 5). The narrative of conflict about Jesus contrasts Jesus (light) with the Jews (blindness, 39-41).The theme of water is reintroduced in the reference to the pool of Siloam. Ironically, Jesus is being judged by the Jews, yet the Jews are judged by the Light of the world; cf Jn 3, 19-21.

9, 2: See the note on Jn 5, 14, and Ex 20, 5, that parents' sins were visited upon their children. Jesus denies such a cause and emphasizes the purpose: the infirmity was providential.

9, 7: *Go wash:* perhaps a test of faith; cf 2 Kgs 5, 10-14. The water tunnel Siloam (= Sent) is used as a symbol of Jesus, sent by his Father.

9, 14: In using spittle, kneading clay, and healing, Jesus had broken the sabbath rules laid down by Jewish tradition.

9, 22: This comment of the evangelist (in terms used again in Jn 12, 42 and Jn 16, 2) envisages a situation after Jesus' ministry. Rejection/excommunication from the synagogue of Jews who confessed Jesus as Messiah seems to have begun ca. A.D. 85, when the curse against the *mînîm* or heretics was introduced into the "Eighteen Benedictions."

9, 24: *Give God the praise!:* an Old Testament formula of adjuration to tell the truth; cf Jos 7, 19; 1 Sm 6, 5 LXX. Cf Jn 5, 41.

to him, "What did he do to you? How did he open your eyes?" [27] He answered them, "I told you already and you did not listen. Why do you want to hear it again? Do you want to become his disciples, too?" [28] They ridiculed him and said, "You are that man's disciple; we are disciples of Moses! [29] We know that God spoke to Moses, but we do not know where this one is from."[d] [30] The man answered and said to them, "This is what is so amazing, that you do not know where he is from, yet he opened my eyes. [31] We know that God does not listen to sinners, but if one is devout and does his will, he listens to him.[e] [32] It is unheard of that anyone ever opened the eyes of a person born blind.* [33] If this man were not from God, he would not be able to do anything."[f] [34] They answered and said to him, "You were born totally in sin, and are you trying to teach us?" Then they threw him out.

[35] When Jesus heard that they had thrown him out, he found him and said, "Do you believe in the Son of Man?" [36] He answered and said, "Who is he, sir, that I may believe in him?" [37] Jesus said to him, "You have seen him and the one speaking with you is he."[g] [38] He said, "I do believe, Lord," and he worshiped him. [39] * Then Jesus said, "I came into this world for judgment, so that those who do not see might see, and those who do see might become blind."[h]

[40] Some of the Pharisees who were with him heard this and said to him, "Surely we are not also blind, are we?"[i] [41] Jesus said to them, "If you were blind, you would have no sin; but now you are saying, 'We see,' so your sin remains.[j]

CHAPTER 10

The Good Shepherd. [1] * "Amen, amen, I say to you,[k] whoever does not enter a sheepfold* through the gate but climbs over elsewhere is a thief and a robber. [2] But whoever enters through the gate is the shepherd of the sheep. [3] The gatekeeper opens it for him, and the sheep hear his voice, as he calls his own sheep by name and leads them out. [4] When he has driven out all his own, he walks ahead of them, and the sheep follow him,[l] because they recognize his voice.* [5] But they will not follow a stranger; they will run away from him, because they do not recognize the voice of strangers." [6] Although Jesus used this figure of speech,* they did not realize what he was trying to tell them.

[7] * So Jesus said again, "Amen, amen, I say to you, I am the gate for the sheep. [8] All who came [before me]* are thieves and robbers, but the sheep did not listen to them. [9] I am the gate. Whoever enters through me will be saved, and will come in and go out and find pasture. [10] A thief comes only to steal and slaughter and destroy; I came so that they might have life and have it more abundantly. [11] I am the good shepherd. A good shepherd lays down his life for the sheep.[m] [12] A hired man, who is not a shepherd and whose sheep are not his own, sees a wolf coming and leaves the sheep and runs away, and the wolf catches and scatters them.[n] [13] This is because he works for pay and has no concern for the sheep. [14] I am the good shepherd, and I know mine and mine know me, [15] just as the Father knows me and I know the Father; and I will lay down my life for the sheep.[o] [16] I have other sheep* that do not belong to this fold. These also I must lead, and they will hear my voice, and there will be one flock, one

d Ex 33, 11.—e Jn 10, 21; Pss 34, 16; 66, 18; Prv 15, 29; Is 1, 15.—f Jn 3, 2.—g Jn 4, 26; Dn 7, 13.—h Mt 13, 33-35.—i Mt 15, 14; 23, 26; Rom 2, 19.—j Jn 15, 22.—k 1-5: Gn 48, 15; 49, 24; Pss 23, 1-4; 80, 2; Jer 23, 1-4; Ez 34, 1-31; Mi 7, 14.—l Mi 2, 12-13.—m Ps 23, 1-4; Is 40, 11; 49, 9-10; Heb 13, 20; Rv 7, 17.—n Zec 11, 17.—o Jn 15, 13; 1 Jn 3, 16.

9, 32: *A person born blind:* the only Old Testament cure from blindness is found in Tobit (cf Tb 7, 7; 11, 7-13; 14, 1-2), but Tobit was not born blind.

9, 39-41: These verses spell out the symbolic meaning of the cure; the Pharisees are not the innocent blind, willing to accept the testimony of others.

10, 1-21: The good shepherd discourse continues the theme of attack on the Pharisees that ends ch 9. The figure is allegorical: the hired hands are the Pharisees who excommunicated the cured blind man. It serves as a commentary on ch 9. For the shepherd motif, used of Yahweh in the Old Testament, cf Ex 34; Gn 48, 15; 49, 24; Mi 7, 14; Pss 23, 1-4; 80, 1.

10, 1: *Sheepfold:* a low stone wall open to the sky.

10, 4: *Recognize his voice:* the Pharisees do not recognize Jesus, but the people of God, symbolized by the blind man, do.

10, 6: *Figure of speech:* John uses a different word for illustrative speech than the "parable" of the synoptics, but the idea is similar.

10, 7-10: In vv 7-8, the figure is of a gate for the shepherd to come to the sheep; in vv 9-10, the figure is of a gate for the sheep to *come in and go out.*

10, 8: *[Before me]:* these words are omitted in many good early manuscripts and versions.

10, 16: *Other sheep:* the Gentiles, possibly a reference to "God's dispersed children" of Jn 11, 52 destined to be gathered into one, or "apostolic Christians" at odds with the community of the beloved disciple.

shepherd.*p* 17 This is why the Father loves me, because I lay down my life in order to take it up again.*q* 18 No one takes it from me, but I lay it down on my own. I have power to lay it down, and power to take it up again.* This command I have received from my Father."*r*

19 Again there was a division among the Jews because of these words.*s* 20 Many of them said, "He is possessed and out of his mind; why listen to him?"*t* 21 Others said, "These are not the words of one possessed; surely a demon cannot open the eyes of the blind, can he?"*u*

Feast of the Dedication. 22 The feast of the Dedication* was then taking place in Jerusalem. It was winter.*v* 23 And Jesus walked about in the temple area on the Portico of Solomon.* 24 So the Jews gathered around him and said to him, "How long are you going to keep us in suspense?* If you are the Messiah, tell us plainly."*w* 25 Jesus answered them, "I told you* and you do not believe. The works I do in my Father's name testify to me.*x* 26 But you do not believe, because you are not among my sheep.*y* 27 My sheep hear my voice; I know them, and they follow me. 28 I give them eternal life, and they shall never perish. No one can take them out of my hand.*z* 29 My Father, who has given them to me, is greater than all,* and no one can take them out of the Father's hand.*a* 30 The Father and I are one."**b*

31 The Jews again picked up rocks to stone him.*c* 13 Jesus answered them, "I

have shown you many good works from my Father. For which of these are you trying to stone me?" 33 The Jews answered him, "We are not stoning you for a good work but for blasphemy. You, a man, are making yourself God."*d* 34 Jesus answered them,*e* "Is it not written in your law, 'I said, "You are gods" '?* 35 If it calls them gods to whom the word of God came, and scripture cannot be set aside, 36 can you say that the one whom the Father has consecrated* and sent into the world blasphemes because I said, 'I am the Son of God'?*f* 37 If I do not perform my Father's works, do not believe me; 38 but if I perform them, even if you do not believe me, believe the works, so that you may realize [and understand] that the Father is in me and I am in the Father."*g* 39 [Then] they tried again to arrest him; but he escaped from their power.

40 He went back across the Jordan to the place where John first baptized, and there he remained.*h* 41 Many came to him and said, "John performed no sign,* but everything John said about this man was true." 42 And many there began to believe in him.*i*

CHAPTER 11

The Raising of Lazarus.* 1 Now a man was ill, Lazarus from Bethany,*j* the village of

---

p Jn 11, 52; Is 56, 8; Jer 23, 3; Ez 34, 23; 37, 24; Mi 2, 12.— q Heb 10, 10.—r Jn 19, 11.—s Jn 7, 43; 9, 16.—t Jn 7, 20; 8, 48.—u Jn 3, 2.—v 1 Mc 4, 54.59.—w Lk 22, 67.—x Jn 8, 25 / Jn 5, 36; 10, 38.—y Jn 8, 45.47.—z Dt 32, 39.—a Wis 3, 1; Is 43, 13.—b Jn 1, 1; 12, 45; 14, 9; 17, 21.—c Jn 8, 59.—d Jn 5, 18; 19, 7; Lv 24, 16.—e Ps 82, 6.—f Jn 5, 18.—g Jn 14, 10- 11.20.—h Jn 1, 28.—i Jn 2, 23; 7, 31; 8, 30.—j 1-2: Jn 12, 1-8; Lk 10, 38-42; 16, 19-31.

10, 18: *Power to take it up again:* contrast the role of the Father as the efficient cause of the resurrection in Acts 2, 24; 4, 10; etc.; Rom 1, 4; 4, 24. Yet even here is added: *This command I have received from my Father.*

10, 22: *Feast of the Dedication:* an eight-day festival of lights (Hebrew, Hanukkah) held in December, three months after the feast of Tabernacles (Jn 7, 2), to celebrate the Maccabees' rededication of the altar and reconsecration of the temple in 164 B.C., after their desecration by Antiochus IV Epiphanes (Dn 8, 13; 9, 27; cf 1 Mc 4, 36-59; 2 Mc 1, 18—2, 19; 10, 1-8).

10, 23: *Portico of Solomon:* on the east side of the temple area, offering protection against the cold winds from the desert.

10, 24: *Keep us in suspense:* literally, "How long will you take away our life?" Cf Jn 11, 48-50. *If you are the Messiah, tell us plainly:* cf Lk 22, 67. This is the climax of Jesus' encounters with the Jewish authorities. There has never yet been an open confession before them.

10, 25: *I told you:* probably at Jn 8, 25, which was an evasive answer.

10, 29: The textual evidence for the first clause is very divided; it may also be translated: "As for the Father, what he has given me is greater than all," or "My Father is greater than all, in what he has given me."

10, 30: This is justification for v 29; it asserts unity of power and reveals that the words and deeds of Jesus are the words and deeds of God.

10, 34: This is a reference to the judges of Israel who, since they exercised the divine prerogative to judge (Dt 1, 17), were called "gods"; cf Ex 21, 6, besides Ps 82, 6, from which the quotation comes.

10, 36: *Consecrated:* this may be a reference to the rededicated altar at the Hanukkah feast; see the note on Jn 10, 22.

10, 41: *Performed no sign:* this is to stress the inferior role of John the Baptist. The Transjordan topography recalls the great witness of John the Baptist to Jesus, as opposed to the hostility of the authorities in Jerusalem.

11, 1-44: The raising of Lazarus, the longest continuous narrative in John outside of the Passion account, is the climax of the signs. It leads directly to the decision of the Sanhedrin to kill Jesus. The theme of life predominates. Lazarus is a token of the real life that Jesus dead and raised will give to all who believe in him. Johannine irony is found in the fact that Jesus' gift of life leads to his own death. The story is not found in the synoptics, but cf Mk 5, 21 and parallels; Lk 7, 11-17. There are also parallels between this story and Luke's parable of the rich man and poor Lazarus (Lk 16, 19-31). In both a man named Lazarus dies; in Luke, there is a request that he return to convince his contemporaries of the need for faith and repentance, while in John, Lazarus does return and some believe but others do not.

Mary and her sister Martha. [2] Mary was the one who had anointed the Lord with perfumed oil and dried his feet with her hair; it was her brother Lazarus who was ill. [3] So the sisters sent word to him, saying, "Master, the one you love is ill." [4] When Jesus heard this he said, "This illness is not to end in death,* but is for the glory of God, that the Son of God may be glorified through it."[k] [5] Now Jesus loved Martha and her sister and Lazarus. [6] So when he heard that he was ill, he remained for two days in the place where he was. [7] Then after this he said to his disciples, "Let us go back to Judea." [8] The disciples said to him, "Rabbi, the Jews were just trying to stone you, and you want to go back there?"[l] [9] Jesus answered, "Are there not twelve hours in a day? If one walks during the day,[m] he does not stumble, because he sees the light of this world.[n] [10] But if one walks at night, he stumbles, because the light is not in him."* [11] He said this, and then told them, "Our friend Lazarus is asleep, but I am going to awaken him." [12] So the disciples said to him, "Master, if he is asleep, he will be saved." [13] But Jesus was talking about his death, while they thought that he meant ordinary sleep.[o] [14] So then Jesus said to them clearly, "Lazarus has died. [15] And I am glad for you that I was not there, that you may believe. Let us go to him." [16] So Thomas, called Didymus,* said to his fellow disciples, "Let us also go to die with him."[p]

[17] When Jesus arrived, he found that Lazarus had already been in the tomb for four days. [18] Now Bethany was near Jerusalem, only about two miles* away. [19] And many of the Jews had come to Martha and Mary to comfort them about their brother.[q] [20] When Martha heard that Jesus was coming, she went to meet him; but Mary sat at home. [21] Martha said to Jesus, "Lord, if you had been here, my brother would not have died.[r] [22] [But] even now I know that whatever you ask of God, God will give you." [23] Jesus said to her, "Your brother will rise." [24] Martha said to him, "I know he will rise, in the resurrection on the last day."[s] [25] Jesus told her, "I am the resurrection and the life; whoever believes in me, even if he dies, will live,[t] [26] and everyone who lives and believes in me will never die. Do you believe this?" [27] [u] She said to him, "Yes, Lord. I have come to believe that you are the Messiah, the Son of God, the one who is coming into the world."*

[28] When she had said this, she went and called her sister Mary secretly, saying, "The teacher is here and is asking for you." [29] As soon as she heard this, she rose quickly and went to him. [30] For Jesus had not yet come into the village, but was still where Martha had met him. [31] So when the Jews who were with her in the house comforting her saw Mary get up quickly and go out, they followed her, presuming that she was going to the tomb to weep there. [32] When Mary came to where Jesus was and saw him, she fell at his feet and said to him, "Lord, if you had been here, my brother would not have died." [33] When Jesus saw her weeping and the Jews who had come with her weeping, he became perturbed* and deeply troubled, [34] and said, "Where have you laid him?" They said to him, "Sir, come and see." [35] And Jesus wept.[v] [36] So the Jews said, "See how he loved him." [37] But some of them said, "Could not the one who opened the eyes of the blind man have done something so that this man would not have died?"

[38] So Jesus, perturbed again, came to the tomb. It was a cave, and a stone lay across it. [39] Jesus said, "Take away the stone." Martha, the dead man's sister, said to him, "Lord, by now there will be a stench; he has been dead for four days." [40] Jesus said to her, "Did I not tell you that if you believe you will see the glory of God?" [41] So they took away the stone. And Jesus raised his eyes and said, "Father,* I thank you

k Jn 9, 3.24.—l Jn 8, 59; 10, 31.—m Jn 8, 12; 9, 4.—n 9-10: Jn 12, 35; 1 Jn 2, 10.—o Mt 9, 24.—p Jn 14, 5.22.—q Jn 12, 9.17-18.—r Jn 11, 32.—s Jn 5, 29; 6, 39-40.44.54; 12, 48; Is 2, 2; Mi 4, 1; Acts 23, 8; 24, 15.—t Jn 5, 24; 8, 51; 14, 6; Dn 12, 2.—u Jn 1, 9; 6, 69.—v Lk 19, 41.

11, 4: *Not to end in death:* this is misunderstood by the disciples as referring to physical death, but it is meant as spiritual death.

11, 10: *The light is not in him:* the ancients apparently did not grasp clearly the entry of light *through* the eye; they seem to have thought of it as being *in* the eye; cf Lk 11, 34; Mt 6, 23.

11, 16: *Called Didymus: Didymus* is the Greek word for twin. Thomas is derived from the Aramaic word for twin; in an ancient Syriac version and in the Gospel of Thomas (#80, 11-12) his given name, Judas, is supplied.

11, 18: *About two miles:* literally, "about fifteen stades"; a stade was 607 feet.

11, 27: The titles here are a summary of titles given to Jesus earlier in the gospel.

11, 33: *Became perturbed:* a startling phrase in Greek, literally, "He snorted in spirit," perhaps in anger at the presence of evil (death).

11, 41: *Father:* in Aramaic, *'abbā'.* See the note on Mk 14, 36.

for hearing me. [42] I know that you always hear me; but because of the crowd here I have said this, that they may believe that you sent me."[w] [43] And when he had said this, he cried out in a loud voice,* "Lazarus, come out!" [44] The dead man came out, tied hand and foot with burial bands, and his face was wrapped in a cloth. So Jesus said to them, "Untie him and let him go."

Session of the Sanhedrin. [45] Now many of the Jews who had come to Mary and seen what he had done began to believe in him.[x] [46] But some of them went to the Pharisees and told them what Jesus had done. [47] So the chief priests and the Pharisees convened the Sanhedrin and said, "What are we going to do? This man is performing many signs.[y] [48] If we leave him alone, all will believe in him, and the Romans will come* and take away both our land and our nation." [49] [z] But one of them, Caiaphas, who was high priest that year,* said to them, "You know nothing, [50] nor do you consider that it is better for you that one man should die instead of the people, so that the whole nation may not perish." [51] He did not say this on his own, but since he was high priest for that year, he prophesied that Jesus was going to die for the nation, [52] and not only for the nation, but also to gather into one the dispersed children of God.* [53] So from that day on they planned to kill him.[a]

[54] So Jesus no longer walked about in public among the Jews, but he left for the region near the desert, to a town called Ephraim,* and there he remained with his disciples.

The Last Passover. [55] Now the Passover of the Jews was near, and many went up from the country to Jerusalem before Passover to purify* themselves.[b] [56] They looked for Jesus and said to one another as they were in the temple area, "What do you think? That he will not come to the feast?" [57] For the chief priests and the Pharisees had given orders that if anyone knew where he was, he should inform them, so that they might arrest him.

CHAPTER 12

The Anointing at Bethany.[c] [1] * Six days before Passover Jesus came to Bethany, where Lazarus was, whom Jesus had raised from the dead.[d] [2] They gave a dinner for him there, and Martha served, while Lazarus was one of those reclining at table with him.[e] [3] Mary took a liter of costly perfumed oil made from genuine aromatic nard and anointed the feet of Jesus* and dried them with her hair; the house was filled with the fragrance of the oil.[f] [4] Then Judas the Iscariot, one [of] his disciples, and the one who would betray him, said, [5] "Why was this oil not sold for three hundred days' wages* and given to the poor?" [6] He said this not because he cared about the poor but because he was a thief and held the money bag and used to steal the contributions.[g] [7] So Jesus said, "Leave her alone. Let her keep this for the day of my burial.* [8] You always have the poor with you, but you do not always have me."[h]

[9] [The] large crowd of the Jews found out that he was there and came, not only because of Jesus, but also to see Lazarus, whom he had raised from the dead.[i] [10] And the chief priests plotted to kill Lazarus too, [11] because many of the Jews were turning away and believing in Jesus because of him.[j]

---

w Jn 12, 30.—x Lk 16, 31.—y Jn 12, 19; Mt 26, 3-5; Lk 22, 2; Acts 4, 16.—z 49-50: Jn 18, 13-14.—a Jn 5, 18; 7, 1; Mt 12, 14.—b Jn 2, 13; 5, 1; 6, 4; 18, 28; Ex 19, 10-11.15; Nm 9, 6-14; 19, 12; Dt 16, 6; 2 Chr 30, 1.3.15-18.—c 1-11: Mt 26, 6-13; Mk 14, 3-9.—d 1-2: Jn 11, 1.—e Lk 10, 38-42.—f Jn 11, 2.—g Jn 13, 29.—h Dt 15, 11.—i Jn 11, 19.—j Jn 11, 45.

11, 43: *Cried out in a loud voice:* a dramatization of Jn 5, 28: "the hour is coming when all who are in the tombs will hear his voice."

11, 48: *The Romans will come:* Johannine irony; this is precisely what happened after Jesus' death.

11, 49: *That year:* emphasizes the conjunction of the office and the year. Actually, Caiaphas was high priest A.D. 18-36. The Jews attributed a gift of prophecy, sometimes unconscious, to the high priest.

11, 52: *Dispersed children of God:* perhaps the "other sheep" of Jn 10, 16.

11, 54: *Ephraim* is usually located about twelve miles northeast of Jerusalem, where the mountains descend into the Jordan valley.

11, 55: *Purify:* prescriptions for purity were based on Ex 19, 10-11.15; Nm 9, 6-14; 2 Chr 30, 1-3.15-18.

12, 1-8: This is probably the same scene of anointing found in Mk 14, 3-9 (see the note there) and Mt 26, 6-13. The anointing by a penitent woman in Lk 7, 36-38 is different. Details from these various episodes have become interchanged.

12, 3: *The feet of Jesus:* so Mk 14, 3; but in Mt 26, 6, Mary anoints Jesus' head as a sign of regal, messianic anointing.

12, 5: *Days' wages:* literally, "denarii." A denarius is a day's wage in Mt 20, 2; see the note on Jn 6, 7.

12, 7: Jesus' response reflects the rabbinical discussion of what was the greatest act of mercy, almsgiving or burying the dead. Those who favored proper burial of the dead thought it an essential condition for sharing in the resurrection.

The Entry into Jerusalem.* [12] [k] On the next day, when the great crowd that had come to the feast heard that Jesus was coming to Jerusalem, [13] they took palm branches* and went out to meet him, and cried out:

"Hosanna!
Blessed is he who comes in the name of the Lord,
[even] the king of Israel." [l]

[14] Jesus found an ass and sat upon it, as is written:

[15] "Fear no more, O daughter Zion;*
see, your king comes, seated upon an ass's colt." [m]

[16] His disciples did not understand this at first, but when Jesus had been glorified they remembered that these things were written about him and that they had done this* for him. [n] [17] * So the crowd that was with him when he called Lazarus from the tomb and raised him from death continued to testify. [18] This was [also] why the crowd went to meet him, because they heard that he had done this sign. [19] So the Pharisees said to one another, "You see that you are gaining nothing. Look, the whole world* has gone after him." [o]

The Coming of Jesus' Hour.* [20] Now there were some Greeks* among those who had come up to worship at the feast. [p] [21] They came to Philip, who was from Bethsaida in Galilee, and asked him, "Sir, we would like to see Jesus." [q] [22] Philip went and told Andrew; then Andrew* and Philip went and told Jesus. [r] [23] Jesus answered them, [s] "The hour has come for the Son of Man to be glorified.* [24] Amen, amen, I say to you, unless a grain of wheat falls to the ground and dies, it remains just a grain of wheat; [t] but if it dies, it produces much fruit.* [25] Whoever loves his life* loses it, and whoever hates his life in this world will preserve it for eternal life. [u] [26] Whoever serves me must follow me, and where I am, there also will my servant be. The Father will honor whoever serves me. [v]

[27] "I am troubled* now. Yet what should I say? 'Father, save me from this hour'? But it was for this purpose that I came to this hour. [w] [28] Father, glorify your name." Then a voice came from heaven, "I have glorified it and will glorify it again." [x] [29] The crowd there heard it and said it was thunder; but others said, "An angel has spoken to him." [y] [30] Jesus answered and said, "This voice did not come for my sake but for yours. [z] [31] Now is the time of judgment on this world; now the ruler of this world* will be driven out. [a] [32] And when I am lifted up from the earth, I will draw everyone to myself." [b] [33] He said this indi-

Jn

---

k 12-19: Mt 21, 1-16; Mk 11, 1-10; Lk 19, 28-40.—l Jn 1, 49; Lv 23, 40; 1 Mc 13, 51; 2 Mc 10, 7; Rv 7, 9.—m Is 40, 9; Zec 9, 9.—n Jn 2, 22.—o Jn 11, 47-48.—p Acts 10, 2.—q Jn 1, 44.—r Jn 1, 40.—s Jn 2, 4.—t Is 53, 10-12; 1 Cor 15, 36.—u Mt 10, 39; 16, 25; Mk 8, 35; Lk 9, 24; 17, 33.—v Jn 14, 3; 17, 24; Mt 16, 24; Mk 8, 34; Lk 9, 23.—w Jn 6, 38; 18, 11; Mt 26, 38-39; Mk 14, 34-36; Lk 22, 42; Heb 5, 7-8.—x Jn 2, 11; 17, 5; Dn 4, 31.34.—y Ex 9, 28; 2 Sm 22, 14; Jb 37, 4; Ps 29, 3; Lk 22, 43; Acts 23, 9.—z Jn 11, 42.—a Jn 16, 11; Lk 10, 18; Rv 12, 9.—b Jn 3, 14; 8, 28; Is 52, 13.

12, 12-19: In Jn, the entry into Jerusalem follows the anointing whereas in the synoptics it precedes. In John, the crowd, not the disciples, are responsible for the triumphal procession.

12, 13: *Palm branches:* used to welcome great conquerors; cf 1 Mc 13, 51; 2 Mc 10, 7. They may be related to the *lûlāb,* the twig bundles used at the feast of Tabernacles. *Hosanna:* see Ps 118, 25-26. The Hebrew word means: "(O Lord), grant salvation." *He who comes in the name of the Lord:* referred in Ps 118, 26 to a pilgrim entering the temple gates, but here a title for Jesus (see the notes on Mt 11, 3 and Jn 6, 14; 11, 27). *The king of Israel:* perhaps from Zep 3, 14-15, in connection with the next quotation from Zec 9, 9.

12, 15: *Daughter Zion:* Jerusalem. *Ass's colt:* symbol of peace, as opposed to the war horse.

12,16: *They had done this:* the antecedent of *they* is ambiguous.

12, 17-18: There seem to be two different crowds in these verses. There are some good witnesses to the text that have an-

other reading for v 17: "Then the crowd that was with him began to testify that he had called Lazarus out of the tomb and raised him from the dead."

12, 19: *The whole world:* the sense is that everyone is following Jesus, but John has an ironic play on *world;* he alludes to the universality of salvation (Jn 3, 17; 4, 42).

12, 20-36: This announcement of glorification by death is an illustration of "the whole world" (19) going after him.

12, 20: *Greeks:* not used here in a nationalistic sense. These are probably Gentile proselytes to Judaism; cf Jn 7, 35.

12, 21-22: *Philip . . . Andrew:* the approach is made through disciples who have distinctly Greek names, suggesting that access to Jesus was mediated to the Greek world through his disciples. Philip and Andrew were from Bethsaida (Jn 1, 44); Galileans were mostly bilingual. *See:* here seems to mean "have an interview with."

12, 23: Jesus' response suggests that only after the crucifixion could the gospel encompass both Jew and Gentile.

12, 24: This verse implies that through his death Jesus will be accessible to all. *It remains just a grain of wheat:* this saying is found in the synoptic triple and double traditions (Mk 8, 35 // Mt 16, 25 // Lk 9, 24; Mt 10, 39 // Lk 9, 33). John adds the phrases (25) *in this world* and *for eternal life.*

12, 25: *His life:* the Greek word *psychē* refers to a person's natural life. It does not mean "soul," for Hebrew anthropology did not postulate body/soul dualism in the way that is familiar to us.

12, 27: *I am troubled:* perhaps an allusion to the Gethsemane agony scene of the synoptics.

12, 31: *Ruler of this world:* Satan.

cating the kind of death he would die. ³⁴ So the crowd answered him, "We have heard from the law that the Messiah remains forever.* Then how can you say that the Son of Man must be lifted up? Who is this Son of Man?"ᶜ ³⁵ Jesus said to them, "The light will be among you only a little while. Walk while you have the light, so that darkness may not overcome you. Whoever walks in the dark does not know where he is going.ᵈ ³⁶ While you have the light, believe in the light, so that you may become children of the light."ᵉ

Unbelief and Belief among the Jews.* After he had said this, Jesus left and hid from them. ³⁷ ᶠ Although he had performed so many signs in their presence they did not believe in him, ³⁸ * in order that the word which Isaiah the prophet spoke might be fulfilled:

> "Lord, who has believed our preaching,
>   to whom has the might of the Lord
>   been revealed?"ᵍ

³⁹ For this reason they could not believe, because again Isaiah said:

⁴⁰ "He blinded their eyes
   and hardened their heart,
   so that they might not see with their
      eyes
   and understand with their heart and
      be converted,
   and I would heal them."ʰ

⁴¹ Isaiah said this because he saw his glory* and spoke about him.ⁱ ⁴² Nevertheless, many, even among the authorities, believed in him, but because of the Pharisees they did not acknowledge it openly in order not to be expelled from the synagogue.ʲ ⁴³ For they preferred human praise to the glory of God.ᵏ

Recapitulation. ⁴⁴ Jesus cried out and said, "Whoever believes in me believes not only in me but also in the one who sent me,ˡ ⁴⁵ and whoever sees me sees the one who sent me.ᵐ ⁴⁶ I came into the world as light, so that everyone who believes in me might not remain in darkness.ⁿ ⁴⁷ And if anyone hears my words and does not observe them, I do not condemn him, for I did not come to condemn the world but to save the world.ᵒ ⁴⁸ Whoever rejects me and does not accept my words has something to judge him: the word that I spoke, it will condemn him on the last day,ᵖ ⁴⁹ because I did not speak on my own, but the Father

who sent me commanded me what to say and speak.�q ⁵⁰ And I know that his commandment is eternal life. So what I say, I say as the Father told me."

III. THE BOOK OF GLORY*

CHAPTER 13

The Washing of the Disciples' Feet.* ¹ Before the feast of Passover,* Jesus knew that his hour had come to pass from this world to the Father. He loved his own in the world and he loved them to the end.ʳ ² The devil had already induced* Judas, son of Simon the Iscariot, to hand him over. So, during supper,ˢ ³ fully aware that the Father had put everything into his power and that he had come from God and was returning to God,ᵗ ⁴ he rose from supper and took off his outer garments. He took a towel and tied it around his waist. ⁵ * Then

---

c Pss 89, 5; 110, 4; Is 9, 7; Dn 7, 13-14; Rv 20, 1-6.—d Jn 9, 4; 11, 10; Jb 5, 14.—e Eph 5, 8.—f 37-43: Dt 29, 2-4; Mk 4, 11-12; Rom 9—11.—g Is 53, 1; Rom 10, 16.—h Is 6, 9-10; Mt 13, 13-15; Mk 4, 12.—i Jn 5, 39; Is 6, 1.4.—j Jn 9, 22.—k Jn 5, 44.—l Jn 13, 20; 14, 1.—m Jn 14, 7-9.—n Jn 1, 9; 8, 12.—o Jn 3, 17.—p Lk 10, 16; Heb 4, 12.—q Jn 14, 10.31; Dt 18, 18-19.—r Jn 2, 4; 7, 30; 8, 20; Mt 26, 17.45; Mk 14, 12.41; Lk 22, 7.—s Jn 6, 71; 17, 12; Mt 26, 20-21; Mk 14, 17-18; Lk 22, 3.—t Jn 3, 35.

12, 34: There is no passage in the Old Testament that states precisely that *the Messiah remains forever.* Perhaps the closest is Ps 89, 37.

12, 37-50: These verses, on unbelief of the Jews, provide an epilogue to the Book of Signs.

12, 38-41: John gives a historical explanation of the disbelief of the Jewish people, not a psychological one. The Old Testament had to be fulfilled; the disbelief that met Isaiah's message was a foreshadowing of the disbelief that Jesus encountered. In Jn 12, 42 and also in Jn 3, 20, we see that there is no negation of freedom.

12, 41: *His glory:* Isaiah saw the glory of Yahweh enthroned in the heavenly temple, but in John the antecedent of *his* is Jesus.

13, 1—19, 42: The Book of Glory. There is a major break here; the word "sign" is used again only in Jn 20, 30. In this phase of Jesus' return to the Father, the discourses (chs 13-17) precede the traditional narrative of the passion (chs 18-20) to interpret them for the Christian reader. This is the only extended example of esoteric teaching of disciples in John.

13, 1-20: Washing of the disciples' feet. This episode occurs in John at the place of the narration of the institution of the Eucharist in the synoptics. It may be a dramatization of Lk 22, 27: "I am your servant." It is presented as a "model" ("pattern") of the crucifixion. It symbolizes cleansing from sin by sacrificial death.

13, 1: *Before the feast of Passover:* this would be Thursday evening, before the day of preparation; in the synoptics, the Last Supper is a Passover meal taking place, in John's chronology, on Friday evening. *To the end:* or, "completely."

13, 2: *Induced:* literally, "The devil put into the heart that Judas should hand him over."

13, 5: The act of washing another's feet was one that could not be required of the lowliest Jewish slave. It is an allusion to the humiliating death of the crucifixion.

he poured water into a basin and began to wash the disciples' feet[u] and dry them with the towel around his waist. [6]He came to Simon Peter, who said to him, "Master, are you going to wash my feet?" [7]Jesus answered and said to him, "What I am doing, you do not understand now, but you will understand later." [8]Peter said to him, "You will never wash my feet." Jesus answered him, "Unless I wash you, you will have no inheritance with me."[v] [9]Simon Peter said to him, "Master, then not only my feet, but my hands and head as well." [10]Jesus said to him, "Whoever has bathed* has no need except to have his feet washed, for he is clean all over; so you are clean, but not all."[w] [11]For he knew who would betray him; for this reason, he said, "Not all of you are clean."[x]

[12]So when he had washed their feet [and] put his garments back on and reclined at table again, he said to them, "Do you realize what I have done for you? [13]You call me 'teacher' and 'master,' and rightly so, for indeed I am.[y] [14]If I, therefore, the master and teacher, have washed your feet, you ought to wash one another's feet. [15]I have given you a model to follow, so that as I have done for you, you should

also do.[z] [16]Amen, amen, I say to you, no slave is greater than his master nor any messenger* greater than the one who sent him.[a] [17]If you understand this, blessed are you if you do it. [18]I am not speaking of all of you. I know those whom I have chosen. But so that the scripture might be fulfilled, 'The one who ate my food has raised his heel against me.'[b] [19]From now on I am telling you before it happens, so that when it happens you may believe that I AM. [20]Amen, amen, I say to you, whoever receives the one I send receives me, and whoever receives me receives the one who sent me."[c]

Announcement of Judas' Betrayal.[d] [21]When he had said this, Jesus was deeply troubled and testified, "Amen, amen, I say to you, one of you will betray me." [22]The disciples looked at one another, at a loss as to whom he meant. [23]One of his disciples, the one whom Jesus loved,* was reclining at Jesus' side.[e] [24]So Simon Peter nodded to him to find out whom he meant. [25]He leaned back against Jesus' chest and said to him, "Master, who is it?"[f] [26]Jesus answered, "It is the one to whom I hand the morsel* after I have dipped it." So he dipped the morsel and [took it and] handed it to Judas, son of Simon the Iscariot. [27]After he took the morsel, Satan entered him. So Jesus said to him, "What you are going to do, do quickly."[g] [28][Now] none of those reclining at table realized why he said this to him. [29]Some thought that since Judas kept the money bag, Jesus had told him, "Buy what we need for the feast," or to give something to the poor.[h] [30]So he took the morsel and left at once. And it was night.

The New Commandment. [31] * When he had left, Jesus said,* "Now is the Son of Man glorified, and God is glorified in him. [32][If God is glorified in him,] God will also glorify him in himself, and he will glorify him at once.[i] [33]My children, I will be with you only a little while longer. You will look for me, and as I told the Jews, 'Where I go you cannot come,' so now I say it to you.[j] [34]I give you a new commandment:* love one another. As I have loved you, so you also should love one another.[k] [35]This is how all will know that you are my disciples, if you have love for one another."

Peter's Denial Predicted. [36]Simon Peter said to him, "Master, where .are you

---

u 1 Sm 25, 41.—v 2 Sm 20, 1.—w Jn 15, 3.—x Jn 6, 70.—y Mt 23, 8.10.—z Lk 22, 27; 1 Pt 2, 21.—a Jn 15, 20; Mt 10, 24; Lk 6, 40.—b Ps 41, 10.—c Mt 10, 40; Mk 9, 37; Lk 9, 48.—d 21-30: Mt 26, 21-25; Mk 14, 18-21; Lk 22, 21-23.—e Jn 19, 26; 20, 2; 21, 7.20; Mt 10, 37.—f Jn 21, 20.—g Jn 13, 2; Lk 22, 3.—h Jn 12, 5-6.—i Jn 17, 1-5.—j Jn 7, 33; 8, 21.—k Jn 15, 12-13.17; Lv 19, 18; 1 Thes 4, 9; 1 Jn 2, 7-10; 3, 23; 2 Jn 5.

13, 10: *Bathed:* many have suggested that this passage is a symbolic reference to baptism. The Greek root involved is used in baptismal contexts in 1 Cor 6, 11; Eph 5, 26; Ti 3, 5; Heb 10, 22.

13, 16: *Messenger:* the Greek has *apostolos,* the only occurrence of the term in John. It is not used in the technical sense here.

13, 23: *The one whom Jesus loved:* also mentioned in Jn 19, 26; 20, 2; 21, 7. A disciple, called "another disciple" or "the other disciple," is mentioned in Jn 18, 15 and Jn 20, 2; in the latter reference he is identified with the disciple whom Jesus loved. There is also an unnamed disciple in Jn 1, 35-40; see the note on Jn 1, 37.

13, 26: *Morsel:* probably the bitter herb dipped in salt water.

13, 31—17, 26: Two farewell discourses and a prayer. These seem to be Johannine compositions, including sayings of Jesus at the Last Supper and on other occasions, modeled on similar farewell discourses in Greek literature and the Old Testament (of Moses, Joshua, David).

13, 31-38: Introduction: departure and return. Terms of coming and going predominate. These verses form an introduction to the last discourse of Jesus, which extends through chs 14 to 17. In it John has collected Jesus' words to *his own* (Jn 13, 1). There are indications that several speeches have been fused together, e.g., in Jn 14, 31 and Jn 17, 1.

13, 34: *I give you a new commandment:* this puts Jesus on a par with Yahweh. The commandment itself is not new; cf Lv 19, 18 and the note there.

going?" Jesus answered [him], "Where I am going, you cannot follow me now, though you will follow later."[l] [37] Peter said to him, "Master, why can't I follow you now? I will lay down my life for you." [38] Jesus answered, "Will you lay down your life for me? Amen, amen, I say to you, the cock will not crow before you deny me three times.[m]

CHAPTER 14

Last Supper Discourses. [1] * "Do not let your hearts be troubled. You have faith* in God; have faith also in me. [2] In my Father's house there are many dwelling places. If there were not, would I have told you that I am going to prepare a place for you? [3] And if I go and prepare a place for you, I will come back again* and take you to myself, so that where I am you also may be.[n] [4] Where [I] am going you know the way." * [5] Thomas said to him, "Master, we do not know where you are going; how can we know the way?" [6] Jesus said to him, "I am the way and the truth* and the life. No one comes to the Father except through me.[o] [7] If you know me, then you will also know my Father.* From now on you do know him and have seen him."[p] [8] Philip said to him, "Master, show us the Father,* and that will be enough for us."[q] [9] Jesus said to him, "Have I been with you for so long a time and you still do not know me, Philip? Whoever has seen me has seen the Father.

How can you say, 'Show us the Father'?[r] [10] Do you not believe that I am in the Father and the Father is in me? The words that I speak to you I do not speak on my own. The Father who dwells in me is doing his works.[s] [11] Believe me that I am in the Father and the Father is in me, or else, believe because of the works themselves.[t] [12] Amen, amen, I say to you, whoever believes in me will do the works that I do, and will do greater ones than these, because I am going to the Father.[u] [13] And whatever you ask in my name, I will do, so that the Father may be glorified in the Son.[v] [14] If you ask anything of me in my name, I will do it.

The Advocate. [15] "If you love me, you will keep my commandments.[w] [16] And I will ask the Father, and he will give you another Advocate* to be with you always,[x] [17] the Spirit of truth,* which the world cannot accept, because it neither sees nor knows it. But you know it, because it remains with you, and will be in you.[y] [18] I will not leave you orphans; I will come to you.* [19] In a little while the world will no longer see me, but you will see me, because I live and you will live.[z] [20] On that day you will realize that I am in my Father and you are in me and I in you.[a] [21] Whoever has my commandments and observes them is the one who loves me. And whoever loves me will be loved by my Father, and I will love him and reveal myself to him."[b] [22] Judas, not the Iscariot,* said to him, "Master, [then] what happened that you will reveal yourself to us and not to the world?"[c]

---

l Mk 14, 27; Lk 22, 23.—m Jn 18, 27; Mt 26, 33-35; Mk 14, 29-31; Lk 22, 33-34.—n Jn 12, 26; 17, 24; 1 Jn 2, 28.—o Jn 8, 31-47.—p Jn 8, 19; 12, 45.—q Ex 24, 9-10; 33, 18.—r Jn 1, 18; 10, 30; 12, 45; 2 Cor 4, 4; Col 1, 15; Heb 1, 3.—s Jn 1, 1; 10, 37-38; 12, 49.—t Jn 10, 38.—u Jn 1, 50; 5, 20.—v Jn 15, 7.16; 16, 23-24; Mt 7, 7-11.—w Jn 15, 10; Dt 6, 4-9; Ps 119; Wis 6, 18; 1 Jn 5, 3; 2 Jn 6.—x Jn 15, 26; Lk 24, 49; 1 Jn 2, 1.—y Jn 16, 13; Mt 28, 20; 2 Jn 1-2.—z Jn 16, 16.—a Jn 10, 38; 17, 21; Is 2, 17; 4, 2-3.—b Jn 16, 27; 1 Jn 2, 5; 3, 24.—c Jn 7, 4; Acts 10, 40-41.

14, 1-31: Jesus' departure and return. This section is a dialogue marked off by a literary inclusion in vv 1 and 27: "Do not let your hearts be troubled."

14, 1: *You have faith:* could also be imperative: "Have faith."

14, 3: *Come back again:* a rare Johannine reference to the parousia; cf 1 Jn 2, 28.

14, 4: *The way:* here, of Jesus himself; also a designation of Christianity in Acts 9, 2; 19, 9.23; 22, 4; 24, 14.22.

14, 6: *The truth:* in John, the divinely revealed reality of the Father manifested in the person and works of Jesus. The possession of truth confers knowledge and liberation from sin (Jn 8, 32).

14, 7: An alternative reading, "If you knew me, then you would have known my Father also," would be a rebuke, as in Jn 8, 19.

14, 8: *Show us the Father:* Philip is pictured asking for a theophany like Ex 24, 9-10; 33, 18.

14, 16: *Another Advocate:* Jesus is the first advocate (paraclete); see 1 Jn 2, 1, where Jesus is an advocate in the sense of intercessor in heaven. The Greek term derives from legal terminology for an advocate or defense attorney, and can mean spokesman, mediator, intercessor, comforter, consoler, although no one of these terms encompasses the meaning in John. The Paraclete in John is a teacher, a witness to Jesus, and a prosecutor of the world, who represents the continued presence on earth of the Jesus who has returned to the Father.

14, 17: *The Spirit of truth:* this term is also used at Qumran, where it is a moral force put into a person by God, as opposed to the spirit of perversity. It is more personal in John; it will teach the realities of the new order (26), and testify to the truth (6). While it has been customary to use masculine personal pronouns in English for the Advocate, the Greek word for "spirit" is neuter, and the Greek text and manuscript variants fluctuate between masculine and neuter pronouns.

14, 18: *I will come to you:* indwelling, not parousia.

14, 22: *Judas, not the Iscariot:* probably not the brother of Jesus in Mk 6, 3 // Mt 13, 55 or the apostle named Jude in Lk 6, 16, but Thomas (see the note on Jn 11, 16), although other readings have "Judas the Cananean."

²³Jesus answered and said to him, "Whoever loves me will keep my word, and my Father will love him, and we will come to him and make our dwelling with him. *d* ²⁴Whoever does not love me does not keep my words; yet the word you hear is not mine but that of the Father who sent me.

²⁵"I have told you this while I am with you. ²⁶The Advocate, the holy Spirit that the Father will send in my name—he will teach you everything and remind you of all that [I] told you. *e* ²⁷Peace* I leave with you; my peace I give to you. Not as the world gives do I give it to you. Do not let your hearts be troubled or afraid. *f* ²⁸You heard me tell you, 'I am going away and I will come back to you.' *g* If you loved me, you would rejoice that I am going to the Father; for the Father is greater than I.* ²⁹And now I have told you this before it happens, so that when it happens you may believe. *h* ³⁰I will no longer speak much with you, for the ruler of the world* is coming. He has no power over me, ³¹but the world must know that I love the Father and that I do just as the Father has commanded me. Get up, let us go. *i*

CHAPTER 15

The Vine and the Branches. ¹ * "I am the true vine,* and my Father is the vine grower. *j* ²He takes away every branch in me that does not bear fruit, and everyone that does he prunes* so that it bears more fruit. ³You are already pruned because of the word that I spoke to you. *k* ⁴Remain in me, as I remain in you. Just as a branch cannot bear fruit on its own unless it remains on the vine, so neither can you unless you remain in me. ⁵I am the vine, you are the branches. Whoever remains in me and I in him will bear much fruit, because without me you can do nothing. ⁶ *l* Anyone who does not remain in me will be thrown out like a branch and wither; people will gather them and throw them into a fire and they will be burned.* ⁷If you remain in me and my words remain in you, ask for whatever you want and it will be done for you. *m* ⁸By this is my Father glorified, that you bear much fruit and become my disciples. *n* ⁹As the Father loves me, so I also love you. Remain in my love. *o* ¹⁰If you keep my commandments, you will remain in my love, just as I have kept my Father's commandments and remain in his love. *p*

¹¹"I have told you this so that my joy might be in you and your joy might be complete. *q* ¹²This is my commandment: love one another as I love you. *r* ¹³No one has greater love than this, *s* to lay down one's life for one's friends.* ¹⁴You are my friends if you do what I command you. ¹⁵I no longer call you slaves, because a slave does not know what his master is doing. I have called you friends,* because I have told you everything I have heard from my Father. *t* ¹⁶It was not you who chose me, but I who chose you and appointed you to go and bear fruit that will remain, so that whatever you ask the Father in my name he may give you. *u* ¹⁷This I command you: love one another. *v*

The World's Hatred.* ¹⁸"If the world hates you, realize that it hated me first. *w* ¹⁹If you belonged to the world, the world

Jn

---

d Rv 3, 20.—e Jn 15, 26; 16, 7.13-14; Ps 51, 13; Is 63, 10.—f Jn 16, 33; Eph 2, 14-18.—g Jn 8, 40.—h Jn 13, 19; 16, 4.—i Jn 6, 38.—j Ps 80, 9-17; Is 5, 1-7; Jer 2, 21; Ez 15, 2; 17, 5-10; 19, 10.—k Jn 13, 10.—l Ez 15, 6-7; 19, 10-14.—m Jn 14, 13; Mt 7, 7; Mk 11, 24; 1 Jn 5, 14.—n Mt 5, 16.—o Jn 17, 23.—p Jn 8, 29; 14, 15.—q Jn 16, 22; 17, 13.—r Jn 13, 34.—s Rom 5, 6-8; 1 Jn 3, 16.—t Dt 34, 5; Jos 24, 29; 2 Chr 20, 7; Ps 89, 21; Is 41, 8; Rom 8, 15; Gal 4, 7; Jas 2, 23.—u Jn 14, 13; Dt 7, 6.—v Jn 13, 34; 1 Jn 3, 23; 4, 21.—w Jn 7, 7; 14, 17; Mt 10, 22; 24, 9; Mk 13, 13; Lk 6, 22; 1 Jn 3, 13.

14, 27: *Peace:* the traditional Hebrew salutation *šālôm;* but Jesus' "Shalom" is a gift of salvation, connoting the bounty of messianic blessing.

14, 28: *The Father is greater than I:* because he *sent, gave,* etc., and Jesus is "a man who has told you the truth that I heard from God" (Jn 8, 40).

14, 30: *The ruler of the world:* Satan; cf Jn 12, 31; 16, 11.

15, 1—16, 4: Discourse on the union of Jesus with his disciples. His words become a monologue and go beyond the immediate crisis of the departure of Jesus.

15, 1-17: Like Jn 10, 1-5, this passage resembles a parable. Israel is spoken of as a vineyard at Is 5, 1-7; Mt 21, 33-46 and as a vine at Ps 80, 9-17; Jer 2, 21; Ez 15, 2; 17, 5-10; 19, 10; Hos 10, 1. The identification of the vine as the Son of Man in Ps 80,

16, and Wisdom's description of herself as a vine in Sir 24, 17, are further background for portrayal of Jesus by this figure. There may be secondary eucharistic symbolism here; cf Mk 14, 25, "the fruit of the vine."

15, 2: *Takes away . . . prunes:* in Greek there is a play on two related verbs.

15, 6: Branches were cut off and dried on the wall of the vineyard for later use as fuel.

15, 13: *For one's friends:* or: "those whom one loves." In 9-13a, the words for love are related to the Greek *agapaō.* In 13b-15, the words for love are related to the Greek *phileō.* For John, the two roots seem synonymous and mean "to love"; cf also Jn 21, 15-17. The word *philos* is used here.

15, 15: *Slaves . . . friends:* in the Old Testament, Moses (Dt 34, 5), Joshua (Jos 24, 29), and David (Ps 89, 21) were called "servants" or "slaves of Yahweh"; only Abraham (Is 41, 8; 2 Chr 20, 7; cf Jas 2, 23) was called a "friend of God."

15, 18—16, 4: The hostile reaction of the world. There are synoptic parallels, predicting persecution, especially at Mt 10, 17-25; 24, 9-10.

would love its own; but because you do not belong to the world, and I have chosen you out of the world, the world hates you.[x] [20] Remember the word I spoke to you,* 'No slave is greater than his master.' If they persecuted me, they will also persecute you. If they kept my word, they will also keep yours.[y] [21] And they will do all these things to you on account of my name,* because they do not know the one who sent me.[z] [22] If I had not come and spoken* to them, they would have no sin; but as it is they have no excuse for their sin.[a] [23] Whoever hates me also hates my Father.[b] [24] If I had not done works among them that no one else ever did, they would not have sin; but as it is, they have seen and hated both me and my Father.[c] [25] But in order that the word written in their law* might be fulfilled, 'They hated me without cause.'[d]

[26] "When the Advocate comes whom I will send* you from the Father, the Spirit of truth that proceeds from the Father, he will testify to me.[e] [27] And you also testify, because you have been with me from the beginning.[f]

CHAPTER 16

[1] "I have told you this so that you may not fall away. [2] They will expel you from the synagogues; in fact, the hour* is coming when everyone who kills you will think he is offering worship to God.[g] [3] They will do this because they have not known either the Father or me.[h] [4] I have told you this so that when their hour comes you may remember that I told you.[i]

Jesus' Departure; Coming of the Advocate.* "I did not tell you this from the beginning, because I was with you. [5] But now I am going to the one who sent me, and not one of you asks me,* 'Where are you going?'[j] [6] But because I told you this, grief has filled your hearts. [7] But I tell you the truth, it is better for you that I go. For if I do not go, the Advocate will not come to you.[k] But if I go, I will send him to you. [8] *And when he comes he will convict the world in regard to sin and righteousness and condemnation: [9] sin, because they do not believe in me;[l] [10] righteousness, because I am going to the Father and you will no longer see me; [11] condemnation, because the ruler of this world has been condemned.[m]

[12] "I have much more to tell you, but you cannot bear it now. [13] But when he comes, the Spirit of truth, he will guide you to all truth.[n] He will not speak on his own, but he will speak what he hears, and will declare to you the things that are coming.* [14] He will glorify me, because he will take from what is mine and declare it to you. [15] Everything that the Father has is mine; for this reason I told you that he will take from what is mine and declare it to you.

[16] "A little while and you will no longer see me, and again a little while later and you will see me."[o] [17] So some of his disciples said to one another, "What does this mean that he is saying to us, 'A little while and you will not see me, and again a little while and you will see me,' and 'Because I am going to the Father'?" [18] So they said, "What is this 'little while' [of which he

---

x Jn 17, 14-16; 1 Jn 4, 5.—y Jn 13, 16; Mt 10, 24.—z Jn 8, 19; 16, 3.—a Jn 8, 21.24; 9, 41.—b Jn 5, 23; Lk 10, 16; 1 Jn 2, 23.—c Jn 3, 2; 9, 32; Dt 4, 32-33.—d Ps 35, 19; 69, 4.—e Jn 14, 16.26; Mt 10, 19-20.—f Lk 1, 2; Acts 1, 8.—g Jn 9, 22; 12, 42; Mt 10, 17; Lk 21, 12; Acts 26, 11.—h Jn 15, 21.—i Jn 13, 19; 14, 29.—j Jn 7, 33; 13, 36; 14, 5.—k Jn 7, 39; 14, 16-17.26; 15, 26.—l Jn 8, 21-24; 15, 22.—m Jn 12, 31.—n Jn 14, 17.26; 15, 26; Pss 25, 5; 143, 10; 1 Jn 2, 27; Rv 7, 17.—o Jn 7, 33; 14, 19.

15, 20: *The word I spoke to you:* a reference to Jn 13, 16.

15, 21: *On account of my name:* the idea of persecution for Jesus' name is frequent in the New Testament (Mt 10, 22; 24, 9; Acts 9, 14). For John, association with Jesus' name implies union with Jesus.

15, 22.24: Jesus' words *(spoken)* and deeds *(works)* are the great motives of credibility. *They have seen and hated:* probably means that they have seen his works and still have hated; but the Greek can be read: "have seen both me and my Father and still have hated both me and my Father." *Works . . . that no one else ever did:* so Yahweh in Dt 4, 32-33.

15, 25: *In their law:* law is here used as a larger concept than the Pentateuch, for the reference is to Ps 35, 19 or Ps 69, 5. See the notes on Jn 10, 34; 12, 34. *Their* law reflects the argument of the church with the synagogue.

15, 26: *Whom I will send:* in Jn 14, 16.26, the Paraclete is to be sent by the Father, at the request of Jesus. Here the Spirit comes from both Jesus and the Father in mission; there is no reference here to the eternal procession of the Spirit.

16, 2: *Hour:* of persecution, not Jesus' "hour" (see the note on Jn 2, 4).

16, 4b-33: A duplicate of Jn 14, 1-31 on departure and return.

16, 5: *Not one of you asks me:* the difficulty of reconciling this with Simon Peter's question in Jn 13, 36 and Thomas' words in Jn 14, 5 strengthens the supposition that the last discourse has been made up of several collections of Johannine material.

16, 8-11: These verses illustrate the forensic character of the Paraclete's role: in the forum of the disciples' conscience he prosecutes the world. He leads believers to see (a) that the basic sin was and is refusal to believe in Jesus; (b) that, although Jesus was found guilty and apparently died in disgrace, in reality righteousness has triumphed, for Jesus has returned to his Father; (c) finally, that it is *the ruler of this world* Satan, who has been condemned through Jesus' death (Jn 12, 32).

16, 13: *Declare to you the things that are coming:* not a reference to new predictions about the future, but interpretation of what has already occurred or been said.

speaks]? We do not know what he means."
[19] Jesus knew that they wanted to ask him,
so he said to them, "Are you discussing
with one another what I said, 'A little while
and you will not see me, and again a little
while and you will see me'? [20] Amen,
amen, I say to you, you will weep and
mourn, while the world rejoices; you will
grieve, but your grief will become joy.[p]
[21] When a woman is in labor, she is in anguish because her hour has arrived; but
when she has given birth to a child, she no
longer remembers the pain because of her
joy that a child has been born into the
world.[q] [22] So you also are now in anguish.
But I will see you again, and your hearts
will rejoice, and no one will take your joy
away from you.[r] [23] On that day you will not
question me about anything. Amen, amen,
I say to you, whatever you ask the Father
in my name he will give you.[s] [24] Until now
you have not asked anything in my name;
ask and you will receive, so that your joy
may be complete.

[25] [t] "I have told you this in figures of
speech. The hour is coming when I will no

---

p Ps 126, 6.—q Is 26, 17-18; Jer 31, 13; Mic 4, 9.—r Jn 14,
19; 15, 11; 20, 20.—s Jn 14, 13.—t Mt 13, 34-35.—u Jn 14,
13.—v Jn 1, 1.—w Jn 8, 29; Zec 13, 7; Mt 26, 31; Mk 14, 27.—
x Jn 14, 27.—y Jn 13, 31.—z Jn 3, 35; Mt 28, 18.—a Jn 1, 17;
Wis 14, 7; 15, 3; 1 Jn 5, 20.—b Jn 1, 1.2; 12, 28; Phil 2, 6.9-
11.—c Jn 17, 20.—d Jn 16, 15; 2 Thes 1, 10.12.

16, 25: See the note on Jn 10, 6. Here, possibly a reference to
Jn 15, 1-16 or Jn 16, 21.

16, 30: The reference is seemingly to the fact that Jesus could
anticipate their question in v 19. The disciples naively think they
have the full understanding that is the climax of "the hour" of
Jesus' death, resurrection, and ascension (25), but the only part
of the hour that is at hand for them is their share in the passion
(32).

16, 32: *You will be scattered:* cf Mk 14, 27 and Mt 26, 31,
where both cite Zec 13, 7 about the sheep being dispersed.

17, 1-26: Climax of the last discourse(s). Since the sixteenth
century, this chapter has been called the "high priestly prayer" of
Jesus. He speaks as intercessor, with words addressed directly to
the Father and not to the disciples, who supposedly only overhear.
Yet the prayer is one of petition, for immediate (6-19) and future
(20-21) disciples. Many phrases reminiscent of the Lord's Prayer
occur. Although still in the world (13), Jesus looks on his earthly
ministry as a thing of the past (4.12). Whereas Jesus has up to
this time stated that the disciples should follow him (Jn 13,
33.36), now he wishes them to be with him in union with the
Father (12-14).

17, 1: The action of looking up to heaven and the address
Father are typical of Jesus at prayer; cf Jn 11, 41 and Lk 11, 2.

17, 2: Another possible interpretation is to treat the first line
of the verse as parenthetical and the second as an appositive to
the clause that ends v 1: *so that your son may glorify you
(just as . . . all people), so that he may give eternal life. . . .*

17, 3: This verse was clearly added in the editing of the gospel
as a reflection on the preceding verse; Jesus nowhere else refers
to himself as Jesus Christ.

17, 6: *I revealed your name:* perhaps the name *I AM;* cf Jn
8, 24.28.58; 13, 19.

---

longer speak to you in figures but I will tell
you clearly about the Father.* [26] On that
day you will ask in my name, and I do not
tell you that I will ask the Father for you.[u]
[27] For the Father himself loves you, because you have loved me and have come to
believe that I came from God. [28] I came
from the Father and have come into the
world. Now I am leaving the world and
going back to the Father."[v] [29] His disciples
said, "Now you are talking plainly, and not
in any figure of speech. [30] Now we realize
that you know everything and that you do
not need to have anyone question you. Because of this we believe that you came from
God."* [31] Jesus answered them, "Do you
believe now? [32] Behold, the hour is coming
and has arrived when each of you will be
scattered* to his own home and you will
leave me alone. But I am not alone, because the Father is with me.[w] [33] I have told
you this so that you might have peace in
me. In the world you will have trouble, but
take courage, I have conquered the
world."[x]

CHAPTER 17

The Prayer of Jesus.* [1] When Jesus had
said this, he raised his eyes to heaven* and
said, "Father, the hour has come. Give
glory to your son, so that your son may
glorify you,[y] [2] just as you gave him authority over all people,[z] so that he may give
eternal life to all you gave him.* [3] Now this
is eternal life,[a] that they should know you,
the only true God, and the one whom you
sent, Jesus Christ.* [4] I glorified you on
earth by accomplishing the work that you
gave me to do. [5] Now glorify me, Father,
with you, with the glory that I had with
you before the world began.[b]

[6] "I revealed your name* to those whom
you gave me out of the world. They belonged to you, and you gave them to me,
and they have kept your word. [7] Now they
know that everything you gave me is from
you, [8] because the words you gave to me I
have given to them, and they accepted
them and truly understood that I came
from you, and they have believed that you
sent me. [9] I pray for them. I do not pray for
the world but for the ones you have given
me, because they are yours,[c] [10] and everything of mine is yours and everything of
yours is mine, and I have been glorified in
them.[d] [11] And now I will no longer be in

the world, but they are in the world, while I am coming to you. Holy Father, keep them in your name that you have given me, so that they may be one just as we are. ¹² When I was with them I protected them in your name that you gave me, and I guarded them, and none of them was lost except the son of destruction, in order that the scripture might be fulfilled. *e* ¹³ But now I am coming to you. I speak this in the world so that they may share my joy completely. *f* ¹⁴ I gave them your word, and the world hated them, because they do not belong to the world any more than I belong to the world. *g* ¹⁵ I do not ask that you take them out of the world *h* but that you keep them from the evil one.* ¹⁶ They do not belong to the world any more than I belong to the world. ¹⁷ Consecrate them in the truth. Your word is truth. *i* ¹⁸ As you sent me into the world, so I sent them into the world. *j* ¹⁹ And I consecrate myself for them, so that they also may be consecrated in truth.

²⁰ "I pray not only for them, but also for those who will believe in me through their word, ²¹ so that they may all be one, as you, Father, are in me and I in you, that they also may be in us, that the world may believe that you sent me. *k* ²² And I have given them the glory you gave me, so that they may be one, as we are one, ²³ I in them and you in me, that they may be brought to perfection as one, that the world may know that you sent me, and that you loved them even as you loved me. ²⁴ Father, they are your gift to me. I wish that where I am* they also may be with me, that they may see my glory that you gave me, because you loved me before the foundation of the world. *l* ²⁵ Righteous Father, the world also does not know you, but I know you, and they know that you sent me. *m* ²⁶ I made known to them your name and I will make it known,* that the love with which you loved me may be in them and I in them."

CHAPTER 18

Jesus Arrested. * ¹ When he had said this, Jesus went out* with his disciples across the Kidron valley to where there was a garden, into which he and his disciples entered. *n* ² Judas his betrayer also knew the place, because Jesus had often met there with his disciples. ³ So Judas got a band of soldiers* and guards from the chief priests and the Pharisees and went there with lanterns, torches, and weapons. *o* ⁴ Jesus, knowing everything that was going to happen to him, went out and said to them, "Whom are you looking for?" ⁵ They answered him, "Jesus the Nazorean."* He said to them, "I AM." Judas his betrayer was also with them. ⁶ When he said to them, "I AM," they turned away and fell to the ground. ⁷ So he again asked them, "Whom are you looking for?" They said, "Jesus the Nazorean." ⁸ Jesus answered, "I told you that I AM. So if you are looking for me, let these men go." ⁹ *p* This was to fulfill what he had said, "I have not lost any of those you gave me."* ¹⁰ Then Simon Peter, who had a sword, drew it, struck the high priest's slave, and cut off his right ear. The slave's name was Malchus.* ¹¹ Jesus said to Peter, "Put your sword into its scabbard. Shall I not drink the cup* that the Father gave me?" *q*

¹² *r* So the band of soldiers, the tribune, and the Jewish guards seized Jesus, bound

e Jn 13, 18; 18, 9; Ps 41, 10; Mt 26, 24; Acts 1, 16.—f Jn 15, 11.—g Jn 15, 19.—h Mt 6, 13; 2 Thes 3, 3; 1 Jn 5, 18.—i 1 Pt 1, 22—j Jn 20, 21-22.—k Jn 10, 30; 14, 10-11.20.—l Jn 14, 3; 1 Thes 4, 17.—m Jn 1, 10.—n 2 Sm 15, 23; Mt 26, 30.36; Mk 14, 26.32; Lk 22, 39.—o Mt 26, 47-51; Mk 14, 43-44; Lk 22, 47.—p Jn 6, 39; 10, 28; 17, 12.—q Mt 20, 22; 26, 39; Mk 10, 38; Lk 22, 42.—r 12-14: Mt 26, 57-58; Mk 14, 53-54; Lk 22, 54-55.

17, 15: Note the resemblance to the petition of the Lord's Prayer, "deliver us from the evil one." Both probably refer to the devil rather than to abstract evil.

17, 24: *Where I am:* Jesus prays for the believers ultimately to join him in heaven. Then they will not see his glory as in a mirror but clearly (2 Cor 3, 18; 1 Jn 3, 2).

17, 26: *I will make it known:* through the Advocate.

18, 1-14: John does not mention the agony in the garden and the kiss of Judas, nor does he identify the place as Gethsemane or the Mount of Olives.

18, 1: *Jesus went out:* see Jn 14, 31, where it seems he is leaving the supper room. *Kidron valley:* literally, "the winter-flowing Kidron"; this wadi has water only during the winter rains.

18, 3: *Band of soldiers:* seems to refer to Roman troops, either the full cohort of 600 men (1/10 of a legion), or more likely the maniple of 200 under their tribune (12). In this case, John is hinting at Roman collusion in the action against Jesus before he was brought to Pilate. The lanterns and torches may be symbolic of the hour of darkness.

18, 5: *Nazorean:* the form found in Mt 26, 71 (see the note on Mt 2, 23) is here used, not *Nazarene* of Mark. *I AM:* or "I am he," but probably intended by the evangelist as an expression of divinity (cf their appropriate response in 6); see the note on Jn 8, 24. John sets the confusion of the arresting party against the background of Jesus' divine majesty.

18, 9: The citation may refer to Jn 6, 39; Jn 10, 28; or Jn 17, 12.

18, 10: Only John gives the names of the two antagonists; both John and Luke mention the right ear.

18, 11: The theme of the cup is found in the synoptic account of the agony (Mk 14, 36 and parallels).

him, [13] and brought him to Annas* first. He was the father-in-law of Caiaphas, who was high priest that year.[s] [14] It was Caiaphas who had counseled the Jews that it was better that one man should die rather than the people.[t]

Peter's First Denial.[u] [15] Simon Peter and another disciple* followed Jesus. Now the other disciple was known to the high priest, and he entered the courtyard of the high priest with Jesus. [16] But Peter stood at the gate outside. So the other disciple, the acquaintance of the high priest, went out and spoke to the gatekeeper and brought Peter in. [17] Then the maid who was the gatekeeper said to Peter, "You are not one of this man's disciples, are you?" He said, "I am not." [18] Now the slaves and the guards were standing around a charcoal fire that they had made, because it was cold, and were warming themselves. Peter was also standing there keeping warm.

The Inquiry before Annas.[v] [19] The high priest questioned Jesus about his disciples and about his doctrine. [20] Jesus answered him, "I have spoken publicly to the world.

I have always taught in a synagogue or in the temple area* where all the Jews gather, and in secret I have said nothing.[w] [21] Why ask me? Ask those who heard me what I said to them. They know what I said." [22] When he had said this, one of the temple guards standing there struck Jesus and said, "Is this the way you answer the high priest?"[x] [23] Jesus answered him, "If I have spoken wrongly, testify to the wrong; but if I have spoken rightly, why do you strike me?" [24] Then Annas sent him bound to Caiaphas* the high priest.[y]

Peter Denies Jesus Again.[z] [25] Now Simon Peter was standing there keeping warm. And they said to him, "You are not one of his disciples, are you?" He denied it and said, "I am not." [26] One of the slaves of the high priest, a relative of the one whose ear Peter had cut off, said, "Didn't I see you in the garden with him?" [27] Again Peter denied it. And immediately the cock crowed.*

The Trial before Pilate. [28] [a] Then they brought Jesus from Caiaphas to the praetorium.* It was morning. And they themselves did not enter the praetorium, in order not to be defiled so that they could eat the Passover. [29] So Pilate came out to them and said, "What charge do you bring [against] this man?" [30] They answered and said to him, "If he were not a criminal, we would not have handed him over to you." [31] At this, Pilate said to them, "Take him yourselves, and judge him according to your law." The Jews answered him, "We do not have the right to execute anyone,"* [32] in order that the word of Jesus might be fulfilled that he said indicating the kind of death[b] he would die.* [33] So Pilate went back into the praetorium and summoned Jesus and said to him, "Are you the King of the Jews?" [34] Jesus answered, "Do you say this on your own or have others told you about me?" [35] Pilate answered, "I am not a Jew, am I? Your own nation and the chief priests handed you over to me. What have you done?"[c] [36] Jesus answered, "My kingdom does not belong to this world. If my kingdom did belong to this world, my attendants [would] be fighting to keep me from being handed over to the Jews. But as it is, my kingdom is not here."[d] [37] So Pilate said to him, "Then you are a king?" Jesus answered, "You say I am a king.* For this I was born and for this I came into

s Lk 3, 2.—t Jn 11, 49-50.—u 15-18: Mt 26, 58.69-70; Mk 14, 54.66-68; Lk 22, 54-57.—v 19-24: Mt 26, 59-66; Mk 14, 55-64; Lk 22, 66-71.—w Jn 6, 59; 7, 14.26; Is 48, 16; Mt 26, 55; Mk 4, 23; Lk 19, 47; 22, 53.—x Acts 23, 2.—y Mt 26, 57.— z 25-27: Mt 26, 71-75; Mk 14, 69-72; Lk 22, 58-62.—a 28-38a: Mt 27, 1-2.11-25; Mk 15, 1-5; Lk 23, 1-5.—b Jn 3, 14; 8, 28; 12, 32-33.—c Jn 1, 11.—d Jn 1, 10; 8, 23.

18, 13: *Annas:* only John mentions an inquiry before Annas; cf Jn 18, 16.19-24; see the note on Lk 3, 2. It is unlikely that this nighttime interrogation before Annas is the same as the trial before Caiaphas placed by Matthew and Mark at night and by Luke in the morning.

18, 15-16: *Another disciple . . . the other disciple:* see the note on Jn 13, 23.

18, 20: *I have always taught . . . in the temple area:* cf Mk 14, 49 for a similar statement.

18, 24: *Caiaphas:* see Mt 26, 3.57; Lk 3, 2; and the notes there. John may leave room here for the trial before Caiaphas described in the synoptic gospels.

18, 27: Cockcrow was the third Roman division of the night, lasting from midnight to 3 a.m.

18, 28: *Praetorium:* see the note on Mt 27, 27. *Morning:* literally, "the early hour," or fourth Roman division of the night, 3 to 6 a.m. *The Passover:* the synoptic gospels give the impression that the Thursday night supper was the Passover meal (Mk 14, 12); for John that meal is still to be eaten Friday night.

18, 31: *We do not have the right to execute anyone:* only John gives this reason for their bringing Jesus to Pilate. Jewish sources are not clear on the competence of the Sanhedrin at this period to sentence and to execute for political crimes.

18, 32: The Jewish punishment for blasphemy was stoning (Lv 24, 16). In coming to the Romans to ensure that Jesus would be crucified, the Jewish authorities fulfilled his prophecy that he would be exalted (Jn 3, 14; 12, 32-33). There is some historical evidence, however, for Jews crucifying Jews.

18, 37: *You say I am a king:* see Mt 26, 64 for a similar response to the high priest. It is at best a reluctant affirmative.

the world, to testify to the truth. Everyone who belongs to the truth listens to my voice." [e] [38] Pilate said to him, "What is truth?"

When he had said this, he again went out to the Jews and said to them, "I find no guilt in him. [f] [39] But you have a custom that I release one prisoner to you at Passover.* Do you want me to release to you the King of the Jews?" [40] They cried out again, "Not this one but Barabbas!"* Now Barabbas was a revolutionary.

CHAPTER 19

[1] [g] Then Pilate took Jesus and had him scourged.* [2] And the soldiers wove a crown out of thorns and placed it on his head, and clothed him in a purple cloak, [3] and they came to him and said, "Hail, King of the Jews!" And they struck him repeatedly. [4] Once more Pilate went out and said to them, "Look, I am bringing him out to you, so that you may know that I find no guilt in him." [h] [5] So Jesus came out, wearing the crown of thorns and the purple cloak. And he said to them, "Behold, the man!" [i] [6] When the chief priests and the guards saw him they cried out, "Crucify him, crucify him!" Pilate said to them, "Take him yourselves and crucify him. I find no guilt in him." [j] [7] The Jews answered, [k] "We have a law, and according to that law he ought to die, because he made himself the Son of God."* [8] Now when Pilate heard this statement, he became even

more afraid, [9] and went back into the praetorium and said to Jesus, "Where are you from?" Jesus did not answer him. [l] [10] So Pilate said to him, "Do you not speak to me? Do you not know that I have power to release you and I have power to crucify you?" [11] Jesus answered [him], "You would have no power over me if it had not been given to you from above. For this reason the one who handed me over to you has the greater sin." [m] [12] Consequently, Pilate tried to release him; but the Jews cried out, "If you release him, you are not a Friend of Caesar.* Everyone who makes himself a king opposes Caesar." [n]

[13] When Pilate heard these words he brought Jesus out and seated him* on the judge's bench in the place called Stone Pavement, in Hebrew, Gabbatha. [14] It was preparation day for Passover, and it was about noon.* And he said to the Jews, "Behold, your king!" [15] They cried out, "Take him away, take him away! Crucify him!" Pilate said to them, "Shall I crucify your king?" The chief priests answered, "We have no king but Caesar." [16] Then he handed him over to them to be crucified.*

The Crucifixion of Jesus. So they took Jesus, [17] [o] and carrying the cross himself* he went out to what is called the Place of the Skull, in Hebrew, Golgotha. [18] There they crucified him, and with him two others, one on either side, with Jesus in the middle. [19] Pilate also had an inscription written and put on the cross. It read, "Jesus the Nazorean, the King of the Jews."* [20] Now many

---

e Jn 8, 47; 1 Tm 6, 13.—f 38b-40: Mt 27, 15-26; Mk 15, 6-15; Lk 23, 18-25; Acts 3, 14.—g 1-16: Mt 27, 27-31; Mk 15, 16-20; Lk 23, 13-25.—h Jn 18, 38.—i Is 52, 14.—j Jn 18, 31; 19, 15.—k Jn 10, 33-36; Lv 24, 16.—l Jn 7, 28.—m Jn 3, 27; 10, 18; Rom 13, 1.—n Acts 17, 7.—o 17-22: Mt 27, 32-37; Mk 15, 21-26; Lk 23, 26-35.

18, 39: See the note on Mt 27, 15.

18, 40: *Barabbas:* see the note on Mt 27, 16-17. *Revolutionary:* a guerrilla warrior fighting for nationalistic aims, though the term can also denote a robber. See the note on Mt 27, 38.

19, 1: Luke places the mockery of Jesus at the midpoint in the trial when Jesus was sent to Herod. Mark and Matthew place the scourging and mockery at the end of the trial after the sentence of death. Scourging was an integral part of the crucifixion penalty.

19, 7: *Made himself the Son of God:* this question was not raised in John's account of the Jewish interrogations of Jesus as it was in the synoptic account. Nevertheless, see Jn 5, 18; 8, 53; 10, 36.

19, 12: *Friend of Caesar:* a Roman honorific title bestowed upon high-ranking officials for merit.

19, 13: *Seated him:* others translate "(Pilate) sat down." In John's thought, Jesus is the real judge of the world, and John may here be portraying him seated on the judgment bench. *Stone Pavement:* in Greek *lithostrotos;* under the fortress Antonia, one of the conjectured locations of the praetorium, a massive

stone pavement has been excavated. *Gabbatha* (Aramaic rather than Hebrew) probably means "ridge, elevation."

19, 14: *Noon:* Mk 15, 25 has Jesus crucified "at the third hour," which means either 9 a.m. or the period from 9 to 12. Noon, the time when, according to John, Jesus was sentenced to death, was the hour at which the priests began to slaughter Passover lambs in the temple; see Jn 1, 29.

19, 16: *He handed him over to them to be crucified:* in context this would seem to mean "handed him over to the chief priests." Lk 23, 25 has a similar ambiguity. There is a polemic tendency in the gospels to place the guilt of the crucifixion on the Jewish authorities and to exonerate the Romans from blame. But John later mentions the Roman soldiers (23), and it was to these soldiers that Pilate handed Jesus over.

19, 17: *Carrying the cross himself:* a different picture from that of the synoptics, especially Lk 23, 26, where Simon of Cyrene is made to carry the cross, walking behind Jesus. In John's theology, Jesus remained in complete control and master of his destiny (cf Jn 10, 18). *Place of the Skull:* the Latin word for skull is *Calvaria;* hence "Calvary." *Golgotha* is actually an Aramaic rather than a Hebrew word.

19, 19: The inscription differs with slightly different words in each of the four gospels. John's form is fullest and gives the equivalent of the Latin *INRI = Iesus Nazarenus Rex Iudaeorum.* Only John mentions its polyglot character (20) and Pilate's role in keeping the title unchanged (21-22).

of the Jews read this inscription, because the place where Jesus was crucified was near the city; and it was written in Hebrew, Latin, and Greek. [21] So the chief priests of the Jews said to Pilate, "Do not write 'The King of the Jews,' but that he said, 'I am the King of the Jews.' "[p] [22] Pilate answered, "What I have written, I have written."

[23] * When the soldiers had crucified Jesus,[q] they took his clothes and divided them into four shares, a share for each soldier.[r] They also took his tunic, but the tunic was seamless, woven in one piece from the top down. [24] So they said to one another, "Let's not tear it, but cast lots for it to see whose it will be," in order that the passage of scripture might be fulfilled [that says]:

"They divided my garments among them,
and for my vesture they cast lots."

This is what the soldiers did. [25] [s] Standing by the cross of Jesus were his mother and his mother's sister, Mary the wife of Clopas, and Mary of Magdala.* [26] When Jesus saw his mother* and the disciple there whom he loved, he said to his mother, "Woman, behold, your son."[t] [27] Then he said to the disciple, "Behold, your mother." And from that hour the disciple took her into his home.

[28] [u] After this, aware that everything was now finished, in order that the scripture might be fulfilled,* Jesus said, "I thirst."[v] [29] There was a vessel filled with common wine.* So they put a sponge soaked in wine on a sprig of hyssop and put it up to his mouth. [30] When Jesus had taken the wine, he said, "It is finished."[w] And bowing his head, he handed over the spirit.*

The Blood and Water. [31] Now since it was preparation day, in order that the bodies might not remain on the cross on the sabbath, for the sabbath day of that week was a solemn one, the Jews asked Pilate that their legs be broken and they be taken down.[x] [32] So the soldiers came and broke the legs of the first and then of the other one who was crucified with Jesus. [33] But when they came to Jesus and saw that he was already dead, they did not break his legs, [34] [y] but one soldier thrust his lance into his side, and immediately blood and water flowed out.* [35] An eyewitness has testified, and his testimony is true; he knows* that he is speaking the truth, so that you also may [come to] believe.[z] [36] For this happened so that the scripture passage might be fulfilled:

"Not a bone of it will be broken."[a]

[37] And again another passage says:

"They will look upon him whom they have pierced."[b]

The Burial of Jesus.* [38] [c] After this, Joseph of Arimathea, secretly a disciple of

---

p Jn 18, 33; Lk 19, 14.—q 23-27: Mt 27, 38-44; Mk 15, 27-32; Lk 23, 36-43.—r 23-24: Ps 22, 19; Mt 27, 35; Mk 15, 24; Lk 23, 34.—s Mt 27, 55; Mk 15, 40-41; Lk 8, 2; 23, 49.—t Jn 13, 23.—u 28-30: Mt 27, 45-56; Mk 15, 33-41; Lk 23, 44-49.—v Pss 22, 16; 69, 22.—w Jn 4, 34; 10, 18; 17, 4; Lk 23, 46.—x Ex 12, 16; Dt 21, 23.—y Nm 20, 11; 1 Jn 5, 6.—z Jn 7, 37-39; 21, 24.—a Ex 12, 46; Nm 9, 12; Ps 34, 21.—b Nm 21, 9; Zec 12, 10; Rv 1, 7.—c 38-42: Mt 27, 57-60; Mk 15, 42-46; Lk 34, 50-54.

19, 23-25a: While all four gospels describe the soldiers casting lots to divide Jesus' garments (see the note on Mt 27, 35), only John quotes the underlying passage from Ps 22, 19, and only John sees each line of the poetic parallelism literally carried out in two separate actions (23a; 23b-24).

19, 25: It is not clear whether four women are meant, or three (i.e., Mary the wife of Cl[e]opas [cf Lk 24, 18] is in apposition with his mother's sister) or two (his mother and his mother's sister, i.e., Mary of Cl[e]opas and Mary of Magdala). Only John mentions the mother of Jesus here. The synoptics have a group of women looking on from a distance at the cross (Mk 15, 40).

19, 26-27: This scene has been interpreted literally, of Jesus' concern for his mother; and symbolically, e.g., in the light of the Cana story in ch 2 (the presence of the mother of Jesus, the address woman, and the mention of the hour) and of the upper room in ch 13 (the presence of the beloved disciple; the hour). Now that the hour has come (28), Mary (a symbol of the church?) is given a role as the mother of Christians (personified by the beloved disciple); or, as a representative of those seeking salvation,

she is supported by the disciple who interprets Jesus' revelation; or Jewish and Gentile Christianity (or Israel and the Christian community) are reconciled.

19, 28: The scripture . . . fulfilled: either in the scene of vv 25-27, or in the I thirst of v 28. If the latter, Pss 22, 16 and 69, 22 deserve consideration.

19, 29: Wine: John does not mention the drugged wine, a narcotic that Jesus refused as the crucifixion began (Mk 15, 23), but only this final gesture of kindness at the end (Mk 15, 36). Hyssop, a small plant, is scarcely suitable for carrying a sponge (Mark mentions a reed) and may be a symbolic reference to the hyssop used to daub the blood of the paschal lamb on the doorpost of the Hebrews (Ex 12, 22).

19, 30: Handed over the spirit: there is a double nuance of dying (giving up the last breath or spirit) and that of passing on the holy Spirit; see Jn 7, 39, which connects the giving of the Spirit with Jesus' glorious return to the Father, and Jn 20, 22, where the author portrays the conferral of the Spirit.

19, 34-35: John probably emphasizes these verses to show the reality of Jesus' death, against the Docetist heretics. In the blood and water there may also be a symbolic reference to the Eucharist and baptism.

19, 35: He knows: it is not certain from the Greek that this he is the eyewitness of the first part of the sentence. May [come to] believe: see the note on Jn 20, 31.

19, 38-42: In the first three gospels there is no anointing on Friday. In Mt and Lk, the women come to the tomb on Sunday morning precisely to anoint Jesus.

Jesus for fear of the Jews, asked Pilate if he could remove the body of Jesus. And Pilate permitted it. So he came and took his body. [39] Nicodemus, the one who had first come to him at night, also came bringing a mixture of myrrh and aloes weighing about one hundred pounds.[d] [40] They took the body of Jesus and bound it with burial cloths along with the spices, according to the Jewish burial custom. [41] Now in the place where he had been crucified there was a garden, and in the garden a new tomb, in which no one had yet been buried. [42] So they laid Jesus there because of the Jewish preparation day; for the tomb was close by.

CHAPTER 20*

The Empty Tomb.* [1] On the first day of the week,[e] Mary of Magdala came to the tomb early in the morning, while it was still dark,* and saw the stone removed from the tomb.[f] [2] So she ran* and went to Simon Peter and to the other disciple whom Jesus loved, and told them, "They have taken the Lord from the tomb, and we don't know where they put him." [3] *So Peter and the other disciple went out and came to the tomb. [4] They both ran, but the other disciple ran faster than Peter and arrived at the tomb first; [5] he bent down and saw the burial cloths there, but did not go in. [6] [g] When Simon Peter arrived after him, he went into the tomb and saw the burial cloths* there, [7] and the cloth that had covered his head, not with the burial cloths but rolled up in a separate place.[h] [8] Then the other disciple also went in, the one who had arrived at the tomb first, and he saw and believed. [9] [i] For they did not yet understand the scripture that he had to rise from the dead.* [10] Then the disciples returned home.

The Appearance to Mary of Magdala.* [11] But Mary stayed outside the tomb weeping.[j] And as she wept, she bent over into the tomb [12] and saw two angels in white sitting there, one at the head and one at the feet where the body of Jesus had been. [13] And they said to her, "Woman, why are you weeping?" She said to them, "They have taken my Lord, and I don't know where they laid him." [14] When she had said this, she turned around and saw Jesus there, but did not know it was Jesus.[k] [15] Jesus said to her, "Woman, why are you weeping? Whom are you looking for?"[l] She thought it was the gardener and said to him, "Sir, if you carried him away, tell me where you laid him, and I will take him." [16] Jesus said to her, "Mary!" She turned and said to him in Hebrew, "Rabbouni,"* which means Teacher. [17] Jesus said to her, "Stop holding on to me,* for I have not yet ascended to the Father. But go to my brothers and tell them, 'I am going to my Father and your Father, to my God and your God.' "[m] [18] Mary of Magdala went and announced to the disciples, "I have seen the Lord," and what he told her.

d Jn 3, 1-2; 7, 50; Ps 45, 9.—e 1-10: Mt 28, 1-10; Mk 16, 1-11; Lk 24, 1-12.—f Jn 19, 25.—g Lk 24, 12.—h Jn 11, 44; 19, 40.—i Acts 2, 26-27; 1 Cor 15, 4.—j 11-18: Mk 16, 9-11.—k Jn 21, 4; Mk 16, 12; Lk 24, 16; 1 Cor 15, 43-44.—l 15-17: Mt 28, 9-10.—m Acts 1, 9.

20, 1-31: The risen Jesus reveals his glory and confers the Spirit. This story fulfills the basic need for testimony to the resurrection. What we have here is not a record but a series of single stories.

20, 1-10: The story of the empty tomb is found in both the Matthean and the Lucan traditions; John's version seems to be a fusion of the two.

20, 1: *Still dark:* according to Mark the sun had risen, Matthew describes it as "dawning," and Luke refers to early dawn. Mary sees the stone removed, not the empty tomb.

20, 2: Mary runs away, not directed by an angel/young man as in the synoptic accounts. The plural "we" in the second part of her statement might reflect a tradition of more women going to the tomb.

20, 3-10: The basic narrative is told of Peter alone in Lk 24, 12, a verse missing in important manuscripts and which may be borrowed from tradition similar to John. Cf also Lk 24, 24.

20, 6-8: Some special feature about the state of the burial cloths caused the beloved disciple to believe. Perhaps the details emphasized that the grave had not been robbed.

20, 9: Probably a general reference to the scriptures is intended, as in Lk 24, 26 and 1 Cor 15, 4. Some individual Old Testament passages suggested are Ps 16, 10; Hos 6, 2; Jon 2, 1.2.11.

20, 11-18: This appearance to Mary is found only in Jn, but cf Mt 28, 8-10 and Mk 16, 9-11.

20, 16: *Rabbouni:* Hebrew or Aramaic for "my master."

20, 17: *Stop holding on to me:* see Mt 28, 9, where the women take hold of his feet. *I have not yet ascended:* for John and many of the New Testament writers, the ascension in the theological sense of going to the Father to be glorified took place with the resurrection as one action. This scene in John dramatizes such an understanding, for by Easter night Jesus is glorified and can give the Spirit. Therefore his ascension takes place immediately after he has talked to Mary. In such a view, the ascension after forty days described in Acts 1, 1-11 would be simply a termination of earthly appearances or, perhaps better, an introduction to the conferral of the Spirit upon the early church, modeled on Elisha's being able to have a (double) share in the spirit of Elijah if he saw him being taken up (same verb as ascending) into heaven (2 Kgs 2, 9-12). *To my Father and your Father, to my God and your God:* this echoes Ru 1, 16: "Your people shall be my people, and your God my God." The Father of Jesus will now become the Father of the disciples because, once ascended, Jesus can give them the Spirit that comes from the Father and they can be reborn as God's children (Jn 3, 5). That is why he calls them *my brothers.*

Appearance to the Disciples.* [19] On the evening of that first day of the week,[n] when the doors were locked, where the disciples* were, for fear of the Jews, Jesus came and stood in their midst and said to them, "Peace be with you." [20] When he had said this, he showed them his hands and his side.* The disciples rejoiced when they saw the Lord.[o] [21] [Jesus] said to them again,[p] "Peace be with you. As the Father has sent me, so I send you."* [22] And when he had said this, he breathed on them and said to them,[q] "Receive the holy Spirit.* [23] [r] Whose sins you forgive are forgiven them, and whose sins you retain are retained."*

Thomas. [24] Thomas, called Didymus, one of the Twelve, was not with them when Jesus came. [25] So the other disciples said to him, "We have seen the Lord." But he said to them, "Unless I see the mark of the nails in his hands and put my finger into the nailmarks and put my hand into his side, I will not believe." [s] [26] Now a week later his disciples were again inside and Thomas was with them. Jesus came, although the doors were locked, and stood in their midst and said, "Peace be with you." [t] [27] Then he said to Thomas, "Put your finger here and see my hands, and bring your hand and put it into my side, and do not be unbelieving, but believe." [28] [u] Thomas answered and said to him, "My

Lord and my God!" * [29] Jesus said to him, "Have you come to believe because you have seen me?[v] Blessed are those who have not seen and have believed."*

Conclusion.* [30] Now Jesus did many other signs in the presence of [his] disciples that are not written in this book.[w] [31] But these are written that you may [come to] believe that Jesus is the Messiah, the Son of God, and that through this belief you may have life in his name.[x]

IV. EPILOGUE

THE RESURRECTION APPEARANCE IN GALILEE

CHAPTER 21

The Appearance to the Seven Disciples. [1] * After this, Jesus revealed himself again to his disciples at the Sea of Tiberias. He revealed himself in this way.[y] [2] Together were Simon Peter, Thomas called Didymus, Nathanael from Cana in Galilee, Zebedee's sons,* and two others of his disciples. [3] * Simon Peter said to them, "I am going fishing." They said to him, "We also will come with you." So they went out and got into the boat, but that night they caught nothing.[z] [4] When it was already dawn, Jesus was standing on the shore; but the disciples did not realize that it was Jesus.[a] [5] Jesus said to them, "Children, have you caught anything to eat?" They

n 19 23: Mt 28, 16 20; Mk 16, 14 18; Lk 24, 36 44. —o Jn 14, 27.—p Jn 17, 18; Mt 28, 19; Mk 16, 15; Lk 24, 47-48.—q Gn 2, 7; Ez 37, 9; 1 Cor 15, 45.—r Mt 16, 19; 18, 18.—s 1 Jn 1, 1.—t Jn 21, 14.—u Jn 1, 1.—v Jn 4, 48; Lk 1, 45; 1 Pt 1, 8.—w Jn 21, 25.—x Jn 3, 14.15; 1 Jn 5, 13.—y Mt 26, 32; 28, 7.—z Mt 4, 18; Lk 5, 4-10.—a Jn 20, 14; Mt 28, 17; Lk 24, 16.

20, 19-29: The appearances to the disciples, without or with Thomas (cf Jn 11, 16; 14, 5), have rough parallels in the other gospels only for vv 19-23; cf Lk 24, 36-39; Mk 16, 14-18.

20, 19: *The disciples:* by implication from v 24, this means ten of the Twelve, presumably in Jerusalem. *Peace be with you:* although this could be an ordinary greeting, John intends here to echo Jn 14, 27. The theme of rejoicing in v 20 echoes Jn 16, 22.

20, 20: *Hands and . . . side:* Lk 24, 39-40 mentions "hands and feet," based on Ps 22, 17.

20, 21: By means of this sending, the Eleven were made apostles, that is, "those sent" (cf Jn 17, 18), though John does not use the noun in reference to them (see the note on Jn 13, 16). A solemn mission or "sending" is also the subject of the post-resurrection appearances to the Eleven in Mt 28, 19; Lk 24, 47; Mk 16, 15.

20, 22: This action recalls Gn 2, 7, where God breathed on the first man and gave him life; just as Adam's life came from God, so now the disciples' new spiritual life cumes from Jesus. Cf also the revivification of the dry bones in Ez 37. This is the author's version of Pentecost. Cf also the note on Jn 19, 30.

20, 23: The Council of Trent defined that this power to forgive sins is exercised in the sacrament of penance. See Mt 16, 19 and Mt 18, 18.

20, 28: *My Lord and my God:* this forms a literary inclusion with the first verse of the gospel: "and the Word was God."

20, 29: This verse is a beatitude on future generations; faith, not sight, matters.

20, 30-31: These verses are clearly a conclusion to the gospel and express its purpose. While many manuscripts read *come to believe,* possibly implying a missionary purpose for John's gospel, a small number of quite early ones read "continue to believe," suggesting that the audience consists of Christians whose faith is to be deepened by the book; cf Jn 19, 35.

21, 1-23: There are many non-Johannine peculiarities in this chapter, some suggesting Lucan Greek style; yet this passage is closer to John than Jn 7, 53—8, 11. There are many Johannine features as well. Its closest parallels in the synoptic gospels are found in Lk 5, 1-11 and Mt 14, 28-31. Perhaps the tradition was ultimately derived from John but preserved by some disciple other than the writer of the rest of the gospel. The appearances narrated seem to be independent of those in ch 20. Even if a later addition, the chapter was added before publication of the gospel, for it appears in all manuscripts.

21, 2: *Zebedee's sons:* the only reference to James and John in this gospel (but see the note on Jn 1, 37). Perhaps the phrase was originally a gloss to identify, among the five, the *two others of his disciples.* The anonymity of the latter phrase is more Johannine (Jn 1, 35). The total of seven may suggest the community of the disciples in its fullness.

21, 3-6: This may be a variant of Luke's account of the catch of fish; see the note on Lk 5, 1-11.

answered him, "No."ᵇ ⁶So he said to them, "Cast the net over the right side of the boat and you will find something." So they cast it, and were not able to pull it in because of the number of fish. ⁷So the disciple whom Jesus loved said to Peter, "It is the Lord." When Simon Peter heard that it was the Lord, he tucked in his garment, for he was lightly clad, and jumped into the sea. ⁸The other disciples came in the boat, for they were not far from shore, only about a hundred yards, dragging the net with the fish. ⁹ ᶜ When they climbed out on shore, they saw a charcoal fire with fish on it and bread.* ¹⁰Jesus said to them, "Bring some of the fish you just caught." ¹¹So Simon Peter went over and dragged the net ashore full of one hundred fifty-three* large fish. Even though there were so many, the net was not torn.ᵈ ¹²Jesus said to them, "Come, have breakfast." And none of the disciples dared to ask him,* "Who are you?" because they realized it was the Lord. ¹³Jesus came over and took the bread and gave it to them, and in like manner the fish.ᵉ ¹⁴This was now the third timeᶠ Jesus was revealed to his disciples after being raised from the dead.*

Jesus and Peter.* ¹⁵When they had finished breakfast, Jesus said to Simon Peter,* "Simon, son of John, do you love me more than these?"* He said to him, "Yes, Lord, you know that I love you." He said to him, "Feed my lambs." ¹⁶He then said to him a second time, "Simon, son of John, do you love me?" He said to him, "Yes, Lord, you know that I love you." He said to him, "Tend my sheep." ¹⁷He said to him the third time, "Simon, son of John, do you love me?" Peter was distressed that he had said to him a third time, "Do you love me?" and he said to him, "Lord, you know everything; you know that I love you." [Jesus] said to him, "Feed my sheep.ᵍ ¹⁸Amen, amen, I say to you,ʰ when you were younger, you used to dress yourself and go where you wanted; but when you grow old, you will stretch out your hands, and someone else will dress you and lead you where you do not want to go."* ¹⁹He said this signifying by what kind of death he would glorify God. And when he had said this, he said to him, "Follow me."ⁱ

The Beloved Disciple. ²⁰Peter turned and saw the disciple following whom Jesus loved, the one who had also reclined upon his chest during the supper and had said, "Master, who is the one who will betray you?"ʲ ²¹When Peter saw him, he said to Jesus, "Lord, what about him?" ²²Jesus said to him, "What if I want him to remain until I come?* What concern is it of yours? You follow me."ᵏ ²³So the word spread among the brothers that that disciple would not die. But Jesus had not told him that he would not die, just "What if I want him to remain until I come? [What concern is it of yours?]"*

Conclusion. ²⁴It is this disciple who testifies to these things and has written them,* and we know that his testimony is true.ˡ ²⁵There are also many other things that Jesus did, but if these were to be described individually, I do not think the whole world would contain the books that would be written.ᵐ

. b Lk 24, 41.—c Lk 24, 41-43.—d 2 Chr 2, 16.—e Lk 24, 42.—f Jn 20, 19.26.—g Jn 13, 37-38; 18, 15-18.25-27; Mt 26, 69-75; Mk 14, 66-72; Lk 22, 55-62.—h Acts 21, 11.14; 2 Pt 1, 14.—i Jn 13, 36.—j Jn 13, 25.—k Mt 16, 28.—l Jn 19, 35.—m Jn 20, 30.

21, 9.12-13: It is strange that Jesus already has fish since none have yet been brought ashore. This meal may have had eucharistic significance for early Christians since v 13 recalls Jn 6, 11, which uses the vocabulary of Jesus' action at the Last Supper; but see also the note on Mt 14, 19.

21, 11: The exact number 153 is probably meant to have a symbolic meaning in relation to the apostles' universal mission; Jerome claims that Greek zoologists catalogued 153 species of fish. Or 153 is the sum of the numbers from 1 to 17. Others invoke Ez 47, 10.

21, 12: *None . . . dared to ask him:* is Jesus' appearance strange to them? Cf Lk 24, 16; Mk 16, 12; Jn 20, 14. The disciples do, however, recognize Jesus *before* the breaking of the bread (opposed to Lk 24, 35).

21, 14: This verse connects chs 20 and 21; cf Jn 20, 19.26.

21, 15-23: This section constitutes Peter's rehabilitation and emphasizes his role in the church.

21, 15-17: In these three verses there is a remarkable variety of synonyms: two different Greek verbs for *love* (see the note on Jn 15, 13); two verbs for *feed/tend;* two nouns for *sheep;* two verbs for *know.* But apparently there is no difference of meaning. The threefold confession of Peter is meant to counteract his earlier threefold denial (Jn 18, 17.25.27). The First Vatican Council cited these verses in defining that Jesus after his resurrection gave Peter the jurisdiction of supreme shepherd and ruler over the whole flock.

21, 15: *More than these:* probably "more than these disciples do" rather than "more than you love them" or "more than you love these things [fishing, etc.]."

21, 18: Originally probably a proverb about old age, now used as a figurative reference to the crucifixion of Peter.

21, 22: *Until I come:* a reference to the parousia.

21, 23: This whole scene takes on more significance if the disciple is already dead. The death of the apostolic generation caused problems in the church because of a belief that Jesus was to have returned first. Loss of faith sometimes resulted; cf 2 Pt 3, 4.

21, 24: *Who . . . has written them:* this does not necessarily mean he wrote them with his own hand. The same expression is used in Jn 19, 22 of Pilate, who certainly would not have written the inscription himself. *We know:* i.e., the Christian community; cf Jn 1, 14.16.

THE ACTS OF THE APOSTLES

INTRODUCTION

The Acts of the Apostles, the second volume of Luke's two-volume work, continues Luke's presentation of biblical history, describing how the salvation promised to Israel in the Old Testament and accomplished by Jesus has now under the guidance of the holy Spirit been extended to the Gentiles. This was accomplished through the divinely chosen representatives (10, 41) whom Jesus prepared during his historical ministry (1, 21-22) and commissioned after his resurrection as witnesses to all that he taught (1, 8; 10, 37-43; Lk 24, 48). Luke's preoccupation with the Christian community as the Spirit-guided bearer of the word of salvation rules out of his book detailed histories of the activity of most of the preachers. Only the main lines of the roles of Peter and Paul serve Luke's interest.

Peter was the leading member of the Twelve (1, 13.15), a miracle worker like Jesus in the gospel (3, 1-10; 5, 1-11.15; 9, 32-35.36-42), the object of divine care (5, 17-21; 12, 6-11), and the spokesman for the Christian community (2, 14-36; 3, 12-26; 4, 8-12; 5, 29-32; 10, 34-43; 15, 7-11), who, according to Luke, was largely responsible for the growth of the community in the early days (2, 4; 4, 4). Paul eventually joined the community at Antioch (11, 25-26), which subsequently commissioned him and Barnabas to undertake the spread of the gospel to Asia Minor. This missionary venture generally failed to win the Jews of the diaspora to the gospel but enjoyed success among the Gentiles (13, 14—14, 27).

Paul's refusal to impose the Mosaic law upon his Gentile converts provoked very strong objection among the Jewish Christians of Jerusalem (15, 1), but both Peter and James supported his position (15, 6-21). Paul's second and third missionary journeys (16, 36—21, 16) resulted in the same pattern of failure among the Jews generally but of some success among the Gentiles. Paul, like Peter, is presented as a miracle worker (14, 8-18; 19, 12; 20, 7-12; 28, 7-10) and the object of divine care (16, 25-31).

In Acts, Luke has provided a broad survey of the church's development from the resurrection of Jesus to Paul's first Roman imprisonment, the point at which the book ends. In telling this story, Luke describes the emergence of Christianity from its origins in Judaism to its position as a religion of worldwide status and appeal. Originally a Jewish Christian community in Jerusalem, the church was placed in circumstances impelling it to include within its membership people of other cultures: the Samaritans (8, 4-25), at first an occasional Gentile (8, 26-30; 10, 1-48), and finally the Gentiles on principle (11, 20-21). Fear on the part of the Jewish people that Christianity, particularly as preached to the Gentiles, threatened their own cultural heritage caused them to be suspicious of Paul's gospel (13, 42-45; 15, 1-5; 28, 17-24). The inability of Christian missionaries to allay this apprehension inevitably created a situation in which the gospel was preached more and more to the Gentiles. Toward the end of Paul's career, the Christian communities, with the exception of those in Palestine itself (9, 31), were mainly of Gentile membership. In tracing the emergence of Christianity from Judaism, Luke is insistent upon the prominence of Israel in the divine plan of salvation (see the note on 1, 26; see also 2, 5-6; 3, 13-15; 10, 36; 13, 16-41; 24, 14-15) and that the extension of salvation to the Gentiles has been a part of the divine plan from the beginning (see 15, 13-18; 26, 22-23).

In the development of the church from a Jewish Christian origin in Jerusalem, with its roots in Jewish religious tradition, to a series of Christian communities among the Gentiles of the Roman empire, Luke perceives the action of God in history laying open the heart of all humanity to the divine message of salvation. His approach to the history of the *church is motivated by his theological interests. His history of the apostolic church is the story of a Spirit-guided community and a Spirit-guided spread of the Word of God (1, 8). The travels of Peter and Paul are in reality the travels of the Word of God as it spreads from Jerusalem, the city of destiny for Jesus, to Rome, the capital of the civilized world of Luke's day. Nonetheless, the historical data he utilizes are of value for the understanding of the church's early life and development and as general background to the Pauline epistles. In the interpretation of Acts, care must be exercised to determine Luke's theological aims and interests and to evaluate his historical data without either exaggerating their literal accuracy or underestimating their factual worth.*

Finally, an apologetic concern is evident throughout Acts. By stressing the continuity between Judaism and Christianity (13, 16-41; 23, 6-9; 24, 10-21; 26, 2-23), Luke argues that Christianity is deserving of the same toleration accorded Judaism by Rome. Part of Paul's defense before Roman authorities is to show that Christianity is not a disturber of the peace of the Roman Empire (24, 5.12-13; 25, 7-8). Moreover, when he stands before Roman authorities, he is declared innocent of any crime against the empire (18, 13-15; 23, 29; 25, 25-27; 26, 31-32). Luke tells his story with the hope that Christianity will be treated as fairly.

Concerning the date of Acts, see the Introduction to the Gospel according to Luke.

The principal divisions of the Acts of the Apostles are the following:

  I.   *The Preparation for the Christian Mission (1, 1—2, 13)*
  II. *The Mission in Jerusalem (2, 14—8, 3)*
  III. *The Mission in Judea and Samaria (8, 4—9, 43)*
  IV. *The Inauguration of the Gentile Mission (10, 1—15, 35)*
  V.   *The Mission of Paul to the Ends of the Earth (15, 36—28, 31)*

I. THE PREPARATION FOR THE CHRISTIAN MISSION

CHAPTER 1*

The Promise of the Spirit. [1] In the first book,[a] Theophilus, I dealt with all that Jesus did and taught [2] until the day he was taken up, after giving instructions through the holy Spirit to the apostles whom he had chosen.[b] [3] He presented himself alive to them by many proofs after he had suffered, appearing to them during forty days* and speaking about the kingdom of God.[c] [4] While meeting with them, he enjoined them not to depart from Jerusalem, but to wait for "the promise of the Father* about which you have heard me speak;[d] [5] for John baptized with water, but in a few days you will be baptized with the holy Spirit."[e]

The Ascension of Jesus. [6] When they had gathered together they asked him, "Lord, are you at this time going* to restore the

---

a Lk 1, 1-4.—b Mt 28, 19-20; Lk 24, 44-49; Jn 20, 22; 1 Tm 3, 16.—c Acts 10, 41; 13, 31.—d Jn 14, 16.17.26.—e Acts 11, 16; Mt 3, 11; Mk 1, 8; Lk 3, 16; Jn 1, 26; Eph 1, 13.

1, 1-26: This introductory material (1-2) connects Acts with the Gospel of Luke, shows that the apostles were instructed by the risen Jesus (3-5), points out that the parousia or second coming in glory of Jesus will occur as certainly as his ascension occurred (6-11), and lists the members of the Twelve, stressing their role as a body of divinely mandated witnesses to his life, teaching, and resurrection (12-26).

1, 3: *Appearing to them during forty days:* Luke considered especially sacred the interval in which the appearances and instructions of the risen Jesus occurred and expressed it therefore in terms of the sacred number forty (cf Dt 8, 2). In his gospel, however, Luke connects the ascension of Jesus with the resurrection by describing the ascension on Easter Sunday evening (Lk 24, 50-53). What should probably be understood as one event (resurrection, glorification, ascension, sending of the Spirit—the paschal mystery) has been historicized by Luke when he writes of a visible ascension of Jesus after forty days and the descent of the Spirit at Pentecost. For Luke, the ascension marks the end of the appearances of Jesus except for the extraordinary appearance to Paul. With regard to Luke's understanding of salvation history, the ascension also marks the end of the time of Jesus (Lk 24, 50-53) and signals the beginning of the time of the church.

1, 4: *The promise of the Father:* the holy Spirit, as is clear from the next verse. This gift of the Spirit was first promised in Jesus' final instructions to his chosen witnesses in Luke's gospel (Lk 24, 49) and formed part of the continuing instructions of the risen Jesus on the kingdom of God, of which Luke speaks in v 3.

1, 6: The question of the disciples implies that in believing Jesus to be the Christ (see the note on Lk 2, 11) they had expected him to be a political leader who would restore self-rule to Israel during his historical ministry. When this had not taken place, they ask if it is to take place at this time, the period of the church.

THE JOURNEYS OF
ST. PAUL

—— 1st Journey	······ 3rd Journey
···· 2nd Journey	—— Voyage to Rome

0 50 100 150 200
MILES

THE JOURNEYS OF ST. PAUL (Acts 13—28) — (a) On his first missionary journey (44 45-49 50 A.D.) Paul visits the island of **Cyprus**, then **Pamphylia, Pisidia** and **Lycaonia**, all in Asia Minor, and establishes churches at **Pisidian Antioch, Iconium** and **Derbe** (Acts 13—14). **(b)** After the Apostolic Council of Jerusalem Paul, accompanied by Silas and later also by Timothy and Luke, makes his second missionary journey (50-53 A.D.) first revisiting the churches previously established by him in **Asia Minor** and then the region of **Galatia** (Acts 16, 6). At **Troas** Paul has a vision in which a man from Macedonia invites him to preach the gospel to his countrymen. Paul accordingly sails for **Europe** and preaches the gospel in **Philippi, Thessalonica, Beroea,** and then in **Athens** and **Corinth**. Then he returns to **Antioch** by way of **Ephesus** and **Jerusalem** (Acts 15, 36—18, 22). **(c)** On his third missionary journey (53 54-58 A.D.) Paul visits nearly the same regions as on the second, but makes **Ephesus**, where he remains nearly three years, the center of his missionary activity. He lays plans also for another missionary journey, intending to leave **Jerusalem** for **Rome** and **Spain**. But persecutions by the Jews hinder him from accomplishing his purpose. After two years of imprisonment at **Caesarea** he finally reaches **Rome**, where he is kept another two years in chains (Acts 18, 23—28, 31).

Acts

Map labels:

BRITAIN 10

SPAIN – 3

1 – ROME

4 – SCYTHIA

PATRAS 4
2 – PATMOS
ACHAIA – 4

BITHYNIA – 4 – 7
GALATIA
ASIA MINOR – 2 – CAPPADOCIA – 4
PHRYGIA – 5
EPHESUS – 2
SYRIA – 11
ANTIOCH – 1
PHOENICIA – 11
JERUSALEM – 9
JUDEA – 12

6 – PARTHIA
ARMENIA – 7 – 8
MESOPOTAMIA – 10 6 – 7 – INDIA
PERSIA
6 – 10

ARABIA – 7 – 8 – 11

EGYPT – 10
NORTH AFRICA – 10

6 – 7 – 8 –
ETHIOPIA

**DISPERSION
OF THE TWELVE APOSTLES
AND PROPAGATION OF THE GOSPEL**
According to the sacred text
or multi-century tradition

1 PETER
2 JOHN
3 JAMES THE GREATER
4 ANDREW
5 PHILIP
6 THOMAS
7 BARTHOLOMEW
8 MATTHEW
9 JAMES THE LESS
10 SIMON THE ZEALOT
11 JUDE THADDEUS
12 MATTHIAS

DISPERSION OF THE TWELVE APOSTLES AND PROPAGATION OF THE GOSPEL — (a) The apostles were twelve men chosen by Jesus to enjoy special jurisdiction and to teach; they were called the Twelve most likely after the number of the twelve Patriarchs, the heads of the tribes of Israel. **(b)** Within the circle of Jesus' disciples, the Twelve were given a privileged position: they alone were present with him at the Last Supper (Mk 14, 17); later they exercised leadership over the primitive community in Jerusalem (Acts 1, 26; 2, 14; 5, 20f), and were responsible for the information about Jesus that developed into the Gospel traditions (Acts 6,

2.4). **(c)** Of the original Twelve, all except Judas were from Galilee (cf. Acts 1, 11; 2, 7), and it is certain that two of them were married, namely, Peter and Philip. **(d)** For a while after the descent of the Holy Spirit upon them, the Twelve (with Matthias replacing Judas) restricted their activities to Palestine, until Divine Providence indicated to them different missionary lands. **(e)** The New Testament is silent about the missionary work of the majority of them, but apocryphal literature has supplied us with many accounts — historical as well as legendary: most of them died through martyrdom for their faith in Jesus.

kingdom to Israel?" [7] He answered them,[f] "It is not for you to know the times or seasons that the Father has established by his own authority.* [8] But you will receive power when the holy Spirit comes upon you,[g] and you will be my witnesses in Jerusalem, throughout Judea and Samaria, and to the ends of the earth."* [9] When he had said this, as they were looking on, he was lifted up, and a cloud took him from their sight.[h] [10] While they were looking intently at the sky as he was going, suddenly two men dressed in white garments stood beside them.[i] [11] They said, "Men of Galilee, why are you standing there looking at the sky? This Jesus who has been taken up from you into heaven will return in the same way as you have seen him going into heaven."[j] [12] [k] Then they returned to Jerusalem from the mount called Olivet, which is near Jerusalem, a sabbath day's journey away.

The First Community in Jerusalem.
[13] When they entered the city they went to the upper room where they were staying,

---

f Mt 24, 36; 1 Thes 5, 1-2.—g Acts 2, 1-13; 10, 39; Is 43, 10; Mt 28, 19; Lk 24, 47-48.—h 2 Kgs 2, 11; Mk 16, 19; Lk 24, 51.—i Jn 20, 17.—j Lk 24, 51; Eph 4, 8-10; 1 Pt 3, 22; Rv 1, 7.—k 12-14: Lk 6, 14-16.—l Lk 23, 49.—m Ps 41, 10; Lk 22, 47.—n Mt 27, 3-10.—o Pss 69, 26; 109, 8; Jn 17, 12.—p Acts 1, 8-9; 10, 39.—q Prv 16, 33.—r Lv 23, 15-21; Dt 16, 9-11.—s 2-3: Jn 3, 8.

1, 7: This verse echoes the tradition that the precise time of the parousia is not revealed to human beings; cf Mk 13, 32; 1 Thes 5, 1-3.

1, 8: Just as Jerusalem was the city of destiny in the Gospel of Luke (the place where salvation was accomplished), so here at the beginning of Acts, Jerusalem occupies a central position. It is the starting point for the mission of the Christian disciples to "the ends of the earth," the place where the apostles were situated and the doctrinal focal point in the early days of the community (Acts 15, 2.6). *The ends of the earth:* for Luke, this means Rome.

1, 18: Luke records a popular tradition about the death of Judas that differs from the one in Mt 27, 5, according to which Judas hanged himself. Here, although the text is not certain, Judas is depicted as purchasing a piece of property with the betrayal money and being killed on it in a fall.

1, 26: The need to replace Judas was probably dictated by the symbolism of the number twelve, recalling the twelve tribes of Israel. This symbolism also indicates that for Luke (see Lk 22, 30) the Christian church is a reconstituted Israel.

2, 1-41: Luke's pentecostal narrative consists of an introduction (1-13), a speech ascribed to Peter declaring the resurrection of Jesus and its messianic significance (14-36), and a favorable response from the audience (37-41). It is likely that the narrative telescopes events that took place over a period of time and on a less dramatic scale. The Twelve were not originally in a position to proclaim publicly the messianic office of Jesus without incurring immediate reprisal from those religious authorities in Jerusalem who had brought about Jesus' death precisely to stem the rising tide in his favor.

2, 2: *There came from the sky a noise like a strong driving wind:* wind and spirit are associated in Jn 3, 8. The sound of a great rush of wind would herald a new action of God in the history of salvation.

Peter and John and James and Andrew, Philip and Thomas, Bartholomew and Matthew, James son of Alphaeus, Simon the Zealot, and Judas son of James. [14] All these devoted themselves with one accord to prayer, together with some women, and Mary the mother of Jesus, and his brothers.[l]

The Choice of Judas's Successor. [15] During those days Peter stood up in the midst of the brothers (there was a group of about one hundred and twenty persons in the one place). He said, [16] "My brothers, the scripture had to be fulfilled which the holy Spirit spoke beforehand through the mouth of David, concerning Judas, who was the guide for those who arrested Jesus.[m] [17] He was numbered among us and was allotted a share in this ministry. [18] [n] He bought a parcel of land with the wages of his iniquity, and falling headlong, he burst open in the middle, and all his insides spilled out.* [19] This became known to everyone who lived in Jerusalem, so that the parcel of land was called in their language 'Akeldama,' that is, Field of Blood. [20] For it is written in the Book of Psalms:

'Let his encampment become desolate,
    and may no one dwell in it.'

And:

'May another take his office.'[o]

[21] Therefore, it is necessary that one of the men who accompanied us the whole time the Lord Jesus came and went among us, [22] beginning from the baptism of John until the day on which he was taken up from us, become with us a witness to his resurrection."[p] [23] So they proposed two, Joseph called Barsabbas, who was also known as Justus, and Matthias. [24] Then they prayed, "You, Lord, who know the hearts of all, show which one of these two you have chosen [25] to take the place in this apostolic ministry from which Judas turned away to go to his own place." [26] [q] Then they gave lots to them, and the lot fell upon Matthias, and he was counted with the eleven apostles.*

CHAPTER 2

The Coming of the Spirit. [1] * When the time for Pentecost was fulfilled, they were all in one place together.[r] [2] And suddenly there came from the sky a noise like a strong driving wind,* and it filled the entire house in which they were.[s]

3 Then there appeared to them tongues as of fire,* which parted and came to rest on each one of them.[t] 4 And they were all filled with the holy Spirit and began to speak in different tongues,* as the Spirit enabled them to proclaim.[u]

5 Now there were devout Jews from every nation under heaven staying in Jerusalem. 6 At this sound, they gathered in a large crowd, but they were confused because each one heard them speaking in his own language. 7 They were astounded, and in amazement they asked, "Are not all these people who are speaking Galileans?[v] 8 Then how does each of us hear them in his own native language? 9 We are Parthians, Medes, and Elamites, inhabitants of Mesopotamia, Judea and Cappadocia, Pontus and Asia, 10 Phrygia and Pamphylia, Egypt and the districts of Libya near Cyrene, as well as travelers from Rome, 11 both Jews and converts to Judaism, Cretans and Arabs, yet we hear them speaking in our own tongues of the mighty acts of God."[w] 12 They were all astounded and bewildered, and said to one another, "What does this mean?" 13 But others said, scoffing, "They have had too much new wine."[x]

II. THE MISSION IN JERUSALEM

Peter's Speech at Pentecost. 14 * Then Peter stood up with the Eleven, raised his voice, and proclaimed to them, "You who are Jews, indeed all of you staying in Jerusalem. Let this be known to you, and listen to my words. 15 These people are not drunk, as you suppose, for it is only nine o'clock in the morning. 16 No, this is what was spoken through the prophet Joel:

17 'It will come to pass in the last days,'
    God says,
    'that I will pour out a portion of my spirit
    upon all flesh.
Your sons and your daughters shall prophesy,
    your young men shall see visions,
    your old men shall dream dreams.[y]
18 Indeed, upon my servants and my handmaids
    I will pour out a portion of my spirit
    in those days,
    and they shall prophesy.
19 And I will work wonders in the heavens above

and signs on the earth below:
    blood, fire, and a cloud of smoke.
20 The sun shall be turned to darkness,
    and the moon to blood,
    before the coming of the great and splendid day of the Lord,
21 and it shall be that everyone shall be saved who calls on the name of the Lord.'[z]

22 You who are Israelites, hear these words. Jesus the Nazorean was a man commended to you by God with mighty deeds, wonders, and signs, which God worked through him in your midst, as you yourselves know.[a] 23 This man, delivered up by the set plan and foreknowledge of God, you killed, using lawless men to crucify him.[b] 24 But God raised him up, releasing him from the throes of death, because it was impossible for him to be held by it.[c] 25 For David says of him:

'I saw the Lord ever before me,[d]
    with him at my right hand I shall not be disturbed.
26 Therefore my heart has been glad and my tongue has exulted;
    my flesh, too, will dwell in hope,
27 because you will not abandon my soul to the nether world,
    nor will you suffer your holy one to see corruption.[e]
28 You have made known to me the paths of life;
    you will fill me with joy in your presence.'

29 My brothers, one can confidently say to you about the patriarch David that he died and was buried, and his tomb is in our

---

t Lk 3, 16.—u Acts 1, 5; 4, 31; 8, 15.17; 10, 44; 11, 15-16; 15, 8; 19, 6; Ps 104, 30; Jn 20, 33.—v Acts 1, 11.—w Acts 10, 46.—x 1 Cor 14, 23.—y Is 2, 2; 44, 3; Jl 3, 1-5.—z Rom 10, 13.—a Acts 10, 38; Lk 24, 19.—b 1 Thes 2, 15.—c Acts 13, 34.—d 25-28: Ps 16, 8-11.—e Acts 13, 35.

2, 3: *Tongues as of fire:* see Ex 19, 18 where fire symbolizes the presence of God to initiate the covenant on Sinai. Here the holy Spirit acts upon the apostles, preparing them to proclaim the new covenant with its unique gift of the Spirit (38).

2, 4: *To speak in different tongues:* ecstatic prayer in praise of God, interpreted in vv 6 and 11 as speaking in foreign languages, symbolizing the worldwide mission of the church.

2, 14-36: The first of six discourses in Acts (along with Acts 3, 12-26; 4, 8-12; 5, 29-32; 10, 34-43; 13, 16-41) dealing with the resurrection of Jesus and its messianic import. Five of these are attributed to Peter, the final one to Paul. Modern scholars term these discourses in Acts the "kerygma," the Greek word for proclamation (cf 1 Cor 15, 11).

midst to this day. ³⁰ But since he was a prophet and knew that God had sworn an oath to him that he would set one of his descendants upon his throne,*ᶠ* ³¹ he foresaw and spoke of the resurrection of the Messiah, that neither was he abandoned to the netherworld nor did his flesh see corruption.*ᵍ* ³² God raised this Jesus; of this we are all witnesses. ³³ Exalted at the right hand of God,* he received the promise of the holy Spirit from the Father and poured it forth, as you [both] see and hear.*ʰ* ³⁴ For David did not go up into heaven, but he himself said:

'The Lord said to my Lord,*ⁱ*

"Sit at my right hand

³⁵   until I make your enemies your footstool." '

³⁶ Therefore let the whole house of Israel know for certain that God has made him both Lord and Messiah, this Jesus whom you crucified."*ʲ*

³⁷ Now when they heard this, they were cut to the heart, and they asked Peter and the other apostles, "What are we to do, my brothers?"*ᵏ* ³⁸ Peter [said] to them, "Repent and be baptized,* every one of you, in the name of Jesus Christ for the forgiveness of your sins; and you will receive the gift of the holy Spirit.*ˡ* ³⁹ For the promise is made to you and to your children and to all those far off, whomever the Lord our God will call."*ᵐ* ⁴⁰ He testified with many other arguments, and was exhorting them, "Save yourselves from this corrupt generation."*ⁿ* ⁴¹ Those who accepted his message

were baptized, and about three thousand persons were added that day.*ᵒ*

Communal Life.* ⁴² *ᵖ* They devoted themselves to the teaching of the apostles and to the communal life, to the breaking of the bread and to the prayers.*�q* ⁴³ Awe came upon everyone, and many wonders and signs were done through the apostles.*ʳ* ⁴⁴ All who believed were together and had all things in common;*ˢ* ⁴⁵ they would sell their property and possessions and divide them among all according to each one's need. ⁴⁶ Every day they devoted themselves to meeting together in the temple area and to breaking bread in their homes. They ate their meals with exultation and sincerity of heart, ⁴⁷ praising God and enjoying favor with all the people. And every day the Lord added to their number those who were being saved.

CHAPTER 3

Cure of a Crippled Beggar. ¹ * Now Peter and John were going up to the temple area for the three o'clock hour of prayer.* ² *ᵗ* And a man crippled from birth was carried and placed at the gate of the temple called "the Beautiful Gate" every day to beg for alms from the people who entered the temple. ³ When he saw Peter and John about to go into the temple, he asked for alms. ⁴ But Peter looked intently at him, as did John, and said, "Look at us." ⁵ He paid attention to them, expecting to receive something from them. ⁶ * Peter said, "I have neither silver nor gold, but what I do have I give

---

f 2 Sm 7, 12; Ps 132, 11.—g Acts 13, 35; Ps 16, 10.—h Acts 1, 4-5.—i 34-35: Ps 110, 1.—j Acts 9, 22; Rom 10, 9; Phil 2, 11.—k Lk 3, 10.—l Acts 3, 19; 16, 31; Lk 3, 3.—m Is 57, 19; Jl 3, 5; Eph 2, 17.—n Dt 32, 5; Ps 78, 8; Lk 9, 41; Phil 2, 15.—o Acts 2, 47; 4, 4; 5, 14; 6, 7; 11, 21.24; 21, 20.—p 42-47: Acts 4, 32-35.—q Acts 1, 14; 6, 4.—r Acts 5, 12-16.—s Acts 4, 32.34-35.—t 2-8: Acts 14, 8-10.

2, 33: *At the right hand of God:* or "by the right hand of God."

2, 38: *Repent and be baptized:* repentance is a positive concept, a change of mind and heart toward God reflected in the actual goodness of one's life. It is in accord with the apostolic teaching derived from Jesus (42) and ultimately recorded in the four gospels. Luke presents baptism in Acts as the expected response to the apostolic preaching about Jesus and associates it with the conferring of the Spirit (Acts 1, 5; 10, 44-48; 11, 16).

2, 42-47: The first of three summary passages (along with Acts 4, 32-37 and 5, 12-16) that outline, somewhat idyllically, the chief characteristics of the Jerusalem community: adherence to the teachings of the Twelve and the centering of its religious life in the eucharistic liturgy (42); a system of distribution of goods that led wealthier Christians to sell their possessions when the needs of the community's poor required it (44 and the note on Acts 4, 32-37); and continued attendance at the temple, since in this initial stage there was little or no thought of any dividing line between Christianity and Judaism (46).

3, 1—4, 31: This section presents a series of related events: the dramatic cure of a lame beggar (Acts 3, 1-10) produces a large audience for the kerygmatic discourse of Peter (Acts 3, 11-26). The Sadducees, taking exception to the doctrine of resurrection, have Peter, John, and apparently the beggar as well, arrested (Acts 4, 1-4) and brought to trial before the Sanhedrin. The issue concerns the authority by which Peter and John publicly teach religious doctrine in the temple (Acts 4, 5-7). Peter replies with a brief summary of the kerygma, implying that his authority is prophetic (Acts 4, 8-12). The court warns the apostles to abandon their practice of invoking prophetic authority in the name of Jesus (Acts 4, 13-18). When Peter and John reply that the prophetic role cannot be abandoned to satisfy human objections, the court nevertheless releases them, afraid to do otherwise since the beggar, lame from birth and over forty years old, is a well-known figure in Jerusalem and the facts of his cure are common property (Acts 4, 19-22). The narrative concludes with a prayer of the Christian community imploring divine aid against threats of persecution (Acts 4, 23-31).

3, 1: *For the three o'clock hour of prayer:* literally, "at the ninth hour of prayer." With the day beginning at 6 a.m., the ninth hour would be 3 p.m.

3, 6-10: The miracle has a dramatic cast; it symbolizes the saving power of Christ and leads the beggar to enter the temple, where he hears Peter's proclamation of salvation through Jesus.

you: in the name of Jesus Christ the Nazorean, [rise and] walk." [u] [7] Then Peter took him by the right hand and raised him up, and immediately his feet and ankles grew strong. [8] He leaped up, stood, and walked around, and went into the temple with them, walking and jumping and praising God. [v] [9] When all the people saw him walking and praising God, [10] they recognized him as the one who used to sit begging at the Beautiful Gate of the temple, and they were filled with amazement and astonishment at what had happened to him.

Peter's Speech. [11] As he clung to Peter and John, all the people hurried in amazement toward them in the portico called "Solomon's Portico." [w] [12] When Peter saw this, he addressed the people, "You Israelites, why are you amazed at this, and why do you look so intently at us as if we had made him walk by our own power or piety? [x] [13] The God of Abraham, [the God] of Isaac, and [the God] of Jacob, the God of our ancestors, has glorified* his servant Jesus whom you handed over and denied in Pilate's presence, when he had decided to release him. [y] [14] You denied the Holy and Righteous One* and asked that a murderer be released to you. [z] [15] The author of life* you put to death, but God raised him from the dead; of this we are witnesses. [a] [16] And by faith in his name, this man, whom you see and know, his name has made strong, and the faith that comes

through it has given him this perfect health, in the presence of all of you. [17] Now I know, brothers, that you acted out of ignorance,* just as your leaders did; [b] [18] but God has thus brought to fulfillment what he had announced beforehand through the mouth of all the prophets,* that his Messiah would suffer. [c] [19] Repent, therefore, and be converted, that your sins may be wiped away, [d] [20] and that the Lord may grant you times of refreshment and send you the Messiah already appointed for you, Jesus,* [21] whom heaven must receive until the times of universal restoration* of which God spoke through the mouth of his holy prophets from of old. [22] For Moses said:*

'A prophet like me will the Lord, your
　　God, raise up for you
　　from among your own kinsmen;
to him you shall listen in all that he may
　　say to you. [e]
[23] Everyone who does not listen to that
　　prophet
　　will be cut off from the people.' [f]

[24] Moreover, all the prophets who spoke, from Samuel and those afterwards, also announced these days. [25] You are the children of the prophets and of the covenant that God made with your ancestors when he said to Abraham, 'In your offspring all the families of the earth shall be blessed.' [g] [26] For you first, God raised up his servant and sent him to bless you by turning each of you from your evil ways." [h]

---

u Acts 4, 10.—v Is 35, 6; Lk 7, 22.—w Acts 5, 12; Jn 10, 23.—x Acts 14, 15.—y Ex 3, 6.15; Is 52, 13; Lk 23, 14-25.—z Mt 27, 20-21; Mk 15, 11; Lk 23, 18; Jn 18, 40.—a Acts 4, 10; 5, 31 / Acts 1, 8; 2, 32.—b Acts 13, 27; Lk 23, 34; 1 Cor 2, 8; 1 Tm 1, 13.—c Lk 18, 31.—d Acts 2, 38.—e Acts 7, 37; Dt 18, 15.18.—f Lv 23, 29; Dt 18, 19.—g Gn 12, 3; 18, 18; 22, 18; Sir 44, 19-21; Gal 3, 8-9.—h Acts 13, 46; Rom 1, 16.

3, 13: *Has glorified:* through the resurrection and ascension of Jesus, God reversed the judgment against him on the occasion of his trial. *Servant:* the Greek word can also be rendered as "son" or even "child" here and also in Acts 3, 26; Acts 4, 25 (applied to David); Acts 4, 27; and Acts 4, 30. Scholars are of the opinion, however, that the original concept reflected in the words identified Jesus with the suffering Servant of the Lord of Is 52, 13—53, 12.

3, 14: *The Holy and Righteous One:* so designating Jesus emphasizes his special relationship to the Father (see Lk 1, 35; 4, 34) and emphasizes his sinlessness and religious dignity that are placed in sharp contrast with the guilt of those who rejected him in favor of Barabbas.

3, 15: *The author of life:* other possible translations of the Greek title are "leader of life" or "pioneer of life." The title clearly points to Jesus as the source and originator of salvation.

3, 17: *Ignorance:* a Lucan motif, explaining away the actions not only of the people but also of their leaders in crucifying Jesus. On this basis the presbyters in Acts could continue to appeal to the Jews in Jerusalem to believe in Jesus, while affirming their involvement in his death because they were unaware of his messianic dignity. See also Acts 13, 27 and Lk 23, 34.

3, 18: *Through the mouth of all the prophets:* Christian prophetic insight into the Old Testament saw the crucifixion and death of Jesus as the main import of messianic prophecy. The Jews themselves did not anticipate a suffering Messiah; they usually understood the Servant Song in Is 52, 13—53, 12 to signify their own suffering as a people. In his typical fashion (cf Lk 18, 31; 24, 25.27.44), Luke does not specify the particular Old Testament prophecies that were fulfilled by Jesus. See also the note on Lk 24, 26.

3, 20: *The Lord . . . and send you the Messiah already appointed for you, Jesus:* an allusion to the parousia or second coming of Christ, judged to be imminent in the apostolic age. This reference to its nearness is the only explicit one in Acts. Some scholars believe that this verse preserves a very early christology, in which the title "Messiah" (Greek "Christ") is applied to him as of his parousia, his second coming (contrast Acts 2, 36). This view of a future messiahship of Jesus is not found elsewhere in the New Testament.

3, 21: *The times of universal restoration:* like "the times of refreshment" (20), an apocalyptic designation of the messianic age, fitting in with the christology of v 20 that associates the messiahship of Jesus with his future coming.

3, 22: A loose citation of Dt 18, 15, which teaches that the Israelites are to learn the will of Yahweh from no one but their prophets. At the time of Jesus, some Jews expected a unique prophet to come in fulfillment of this text. Early Christianity applied this tradition and text to Jesus and used them especially in defense of the divergence of Christian teaching from traditional Judaism.

CHAPTER 4

¹While they were still speaking to the people, the priests, the captain of the temple guard, and the Sadducees* confronted them, ²disturbed that they were teaching the people and proclaiming in Jesus the resurrection of the dead.ⁱ ³They laid hands on them and put them in custody until the next day, since it was already evening. ⁴But many of those who heard the word came to believe and [the] number of men grew to [about] five thousand.

Before the Sanhedrin. ⁵On the next day, their leaders, elders, and scribes were assembled in Jerusalem, ⁶with Annas the high priest, Caiaphas, John, Alexander, and all who were of the high-priestly class. ⁷They brought them into their presence and questioned them, "By what power or by what name have you done this?" ⁸Then Peter, filled with the holy Spirit, answered them, "Leaders of the people and elders:ʲ ⁹If we are being examined today about a good deed done to a cripple, namely, by what means he was saved, ¹⁰then all of you and all the people of Israel should know that it was in the name of Jesus Christ the Nazorean whom you crucified, whom God raised from the dead; in his name this man stands before you healed. ¹¹ᵏ He is 'the stone rejected by you, the builders, which has become the cornerstone.'* ¹² ˡ There is no salvation through anyone else, nor is there any other name under heaven given to the human race by which we are to be saved."*

¹³Observing the boldness of Peter and John and perceiving them to be uneducated, ordinary men, they were amazed, and they recognized them as the companions of Jesus. ¹⁴Then when they saw the man who had been cured standing there with them, they could say nothing in reply. ¹⁵So they ordered them to leave the Sanhedrin, and conferred with one another, saying, ¹⁶"What are we to do with these men? Everyone living in Jerusalem knows that a remarkable sign was done through them, and we cannot deny it. ¹⁷But so that it may not be spread any further among the people, let us give them a stern warning never again to speak to anyone in this name."ᵐ

¹⁸So they called them back and ordered them not to speak or teach at all in the name of Jesus. ¹⁹Peter and John, however, said to them in reply, "Whether it is right in the sight of God for us to obey you rather than God, you be the judges.ⁿ ²⁰It is impossible for us not to speak about what we have seen and heard." ²¹After threatening them further, they released them, finding no way to punish them, on account of the people who were all praising God for what had happened. ²²For the man on whom this sign of healing had been done was over forty years old.

Prayer of the Community. ²³After their release they went back to their own people and reported what the chief priests and elders had told them. ²⁴And when they heard it, they raised their voices to God with one accord and said, "Sovereign Lord, maker of heaven and earth and the sea and all that is in them, ²⁵you said by the holy Spirit through the mouth of our father David, your servant:

'Why did the Gentiles rageᵒ
    and the peoples entertain folly?
²⁶ The kings of the earth took their stand
    and the princes gathered together
        against the Lord and against his
        anointed.'

²⁷Indeed they gathered in this city against your holy servant Jesus whom you anointed, Herod* and Pontius Pilate, together with the Gentiles and the peoples of Israel,ᵖ ²⁸to do what your hand and [your] will had long ago planned to take place. ²⁹And now, Lord, take note of their threats, and enable your servants to speak your word with all boldness, ³⁰as you stretch forth [your] hand to heal, and signs

Acts

---

i Acts 23, 6-8; 24, 21.—j Mt 10, 20.—k Ps 118, 22; Is 28, 16; Mt 21, 42; Mk 12, 10; Lk 20, 17; Rom 9, 33; 1 Pt 2, 7.—l Mt 1, 21; 1 Cor 3, 11.—m Acts 5, 28.—n Acts 5, 29-32.—o 25-26: Ps 2, 1-2.—p Lk 23, 12-13.

4, 1: *The priests, the captain of the temple guard, and the Sadducees:* the priests performed the temple liturgy; the temple guard was composed of Levites, whose captain ranked next after the high priest. The Sadducees, a party within Judaism at this time, rejected those doctrines, including bodily resurrection, which they believed alien to the ancient Mosaic religion. The Sadducees were drawn from priestly families and from the lay aristocracy.

4, 11: Early Christianity applied this citation from Ps 118, 22 to Jesus; cf Mk 12, 10; 1 Pt 2, 7.

4, 12: In the Roman world of Luke's day, salvation was often attributed to the emperor who was hailed as "savior" and "god." Luke, in the words of Peter, denies that deliverance comes through anyone other than Jesus.

4, 27: *Herod:* Herod Antipas, ruler of Galilee and Perea from 4 B.C. to A.D. 39, who executed John the Baptist and before whom Jesus was arraigned; cf Lk 23, 6-12.

and wonders are done through the name of your holy servant Jesus." [31] As they prayed, the place where they were gathered shook,* and they were all filled with the holy Spirit and continued to speak the word of God with boldness. [q]

Life in the Christian Community.*

[32] The community of believers was of one heart and mind, and no one claimed that any of his possessions was his own, but they had everything in common. [33] With great power the apostles bore witness to the resurrection of the Lord Jesus, and great favor was accorded them all. [34] [r] There was no needy person among them, for those who owned property or houses would sell them, bring the proceeds of the sale, [35] and put them at the feet of the apostles, and they were distributed to each according to need.

[36] [s] Thus Joseph, also named by the apostles Barnabas (which is translated "son of encouragement"), a Levite, a Cypriot by birth, [37] sold a piece of property that he owned, then brought the money and put it at the feet of the apostles.

CHAPTER 5

Ananias and Sapphira. *

[1] A man named Ananias, however, with his wife Sapphira, sold a piece of property. [2] He retained for himself, with his wife's knowledge, some of the purchase price, took the remainder, and put it at the feet of the apostles. [3] But Peter said, "Ananias, why has Satan filled your heart so that you lied to the holy Spirit and retained part of the price of the land? [t] [4] While it remained unsold, did it not remain yours? And when it was sold, was it not still under your control? Why did you contrive this deed? You have lied not to human beings, but to God." [5] When Ananias heard these words, he fell down and breathed his last, and great fear came upon all who heard of it. [6] The young men came and wrapped him up, then carried him out and buried him.

[7] After an interval of about three hours, his wife came in, unaware of what had happened. [8] Peter said to her, "Tell me, did you sell the land for this amount?" She answered, "Yes, for that amount." [9] Then

Peter said to her, "Why did you agree to test the Spirit of the Lord? Listen, the footsteps of those who have buried your husband are at the door, and they will carry you out." [10] At once, she fell down at his feet and breathed her last. When the young men entered they found her dead, so they carried her out and buried her beside her husband. [11] And great fear came upon the whole church and upon all who heard of these things. [u]

Signs and Wonders of the Apostles.*

[12] Many signs and wonders were done among the people at the hands of the apostles. They were all together in Solomon's portico. [v] [13] None of the others dared to join them, but the people esteemed them. [14] Yet more than ever, believers in the Lord, great numbers of men and women, were added to them. [15] Thus they even carried the sick out into the streets and laid them on cots and mats so that when Peter came by, at least his shadow might fall on one or another of them. [w] [16] A large number of people from the towns in the vicinity of Jerusalem also gathered, bringing the sick and those disturbed by unclean spirits, and they were all cured.

---

q Acts 2, 4.—r 34-35: Acts 2, 44-45.—s 36-37: Acts 9, 27; 11, 22.30; 12, 25; 13, 15; 1 Cor 9, 6; Gal 2, 1.9.13; Col 4, 10.— t Lk 22, 3; Jn 13, 2.—u Acts 2, 43; 5, 5; 19, 17.—v Acts 2, 43; 6, 8; 14, 3; 15, 12.—w Acts 19, 11-12; Mk 6, 56.

4, 31: *The place . . . shook:* the earthquake is used as a sign of the divine presence in Ex 19, 18; Is 6, 4. Here the shaking of the building symbolizes God's favorable response to the prayer. Luke may have had as an additional reason for using the symbol in this sense the fact that it was familiar in the Hellenistic world. Ovid and Virgil also employ it.

4, 32-37: This is the second summary characterizing the Jerusalem community (see the note on Acts 2, 42-47). It emphasizes the system of the distribution of goods and introduces Barnabas, who appears later in Acts as the friend and companion of Paul, and who, as noted here (37), endeared himself to the community by a donation of money through the sale of property. This sharing of material possessions continues a practice that Luke describes during the historical ministry of Jesus (Lk 8, 3) and is in accord with the sayings of Jesus in Luke's gospel (Lk 12, 33; 16, 9.11.13).

5, 1-11: The sin of Ananias and Sapphira did not consist in the withholding of part of the money but in their deception of the community. Their deaths are ascribed to a lie to the holy Spirit (3.9), i.e., they accepted the honor accorded them by the community for their generosity, but in reality they were not deserving of it.

5, 12-16: This, the third summary portraying the Jerusalem community, underscores the Twelve as its bulwark, especially because of their charismatic power to heal the sick; cf Acts 2, 42-47; 4, 32-37.

Trial before the Sanhedrin.* ¹⁷Then the high priest rose up and all his companions, that is, the party of the Sadducees, and, filled with jealousy,^x ¹⁸laid hands upon the apostles and put them in the public jail. ¹⁹But during the night, the angel of the Lord opened the doors of the prison, led them out, and said,^y ²⁰"Go and take your place in the temple area, and tell the people everything about this life." ²¹When they heard this, they went to the temple early in the morning and taught. When the high priest and his companions arrived, they convened the Sanhedrin, the full senate of the Israelites, and sent to the jail to have them brought in. ²²But the court officers who went did not find them in the prison, so they came back and reported, ²³"We found the jail securely locked and the guards stationed outside the doors, but when we opened them, we found no one inside." ²⁴When they heard this report, the captain of the temple guard and the chief priests were at a loss about them, as to what this would come to. ²⁵Then someone came in and reported to them, "The men whom you put in prison are in the temple area and are teaching the people." ²⁶Then the captain and the court officers went and brought them in, but without force, because they were afraid of being stoned by the people.^z

²⁷When they had brought them in and made them stand before the Sanhedrin, the high priest questioned them, ²⁸"We gave you strict orders [did we not?] to stop teaching in that name. Yet you have filled Jerusalem with your teaching and want to bring this man's blood upon us."^a ²⁹But Peter and the apostles said in reply, "We must obey God rather than men.^b ³⁰The God of our ancestors raised Jesus,^c though you had him killed by hanging him on a tree.* ³¹God exalted him at his right hand * as leader and savior to grant Israel repentance and forgiveness of sins.^d ³²We are witnesses of these things, as is the holy Spirit that God has given to those who obey him."^e

³³When they heard this, they became infuriated and wanted to put them to death. ³⁴But a Pharisee in the Sanhedrin named Gamaliel,* a teacher of the law, respected by all the people, stood up, ordered the men to be put outside for a short time,^f ³⁵and said to them, "Fellow Israelites, be careful what you are about to do to these men. ³⁶ * Some time ago, Theudas appeared, claiming to be someone important, and about four hundred men joined him, but he was killed, and all those who were loyal to him were disbanded and came to nothing. ³⁷After him came Judas the Galilean at the time of the census. He also drew people after him, but he too perished and all who were loyal to him were scattered. ³⁸So now I tell you, have nothing to do with these men, and let them go. For if this endeavor or this activity is of human origin, it will destroy itself. ³⁹But if it comes from God, you will not be able to destroy them; you may even find yourselves fighting against God." They were persuaded by him. ⁴⁰After recalling the apostles, they had them flogged, ordered them to stop speaking in the name of Jesus, and dismissed them.^g ⁴¹So they left the presence of the Sanhedrin, rejoicing that they had been found worthy to suffer dishonor for the sake of the name.^h ⁴²And all day long, both at the temple and in their homes, they did not stop teaching and proclaiming the Messiah, Jesus.ⁱ

Acts

---

x Acts 4, 1-3.6.—y Acts 12, 7-10; 16, 25-26.—z Lk 20, 19.—a Mt 27, 25.—b Acts 4, 19.—c Acts 2, 23-24.—d Acts 2, 38.—e Lk 24, 48; Jn 15, 26.—f Acts 22, 3.—g Mt 10, 17; Acts 4, 17-18.—h Mt 5, 10-11; 1 Pt 4, 13.—i Acts 2, 46; 5, 20-21.25; 8, 35; 17, 3; 18, 5.28; 19, 4-5.

5, 17-42: A second action against the community is taken by the Sanhedrin in the arrest and trial of the Twelve; cf Acts 4, 1-3. The motive is the jealousy of the religious authorities over the popularity of the apostles (17) who are now charged with the defiance of the Sanhedrin's previous order to them to abandon their prophetic role (28; cf Acts 4, 18). In this crisis the apostles are favored by a miraculous release from prison (18-24). (For similar incidents involving Peter and Paul, see Acts 12, 6-11; 16, 25-29.) The real significance of such an event, however, would be manifest only to people of faith, not to unbelievers; since the Sanhedrin already judged the Twelve to be inauthentic prophets, it could disregard reports of their miracles. When the Twelve immediately resumed public teaching, the Sanhedrin determined to invoke upon them the penalty of death (33) prescribed in Dt 13, 6-10. Gamaliel's advice against this course finally prevailed, but it did not save the Twelve from the punishment of scourging (40) in a last endeavor to shake their conviction of their prophetic mission.

5, 30: *Hanging him on a tree:* that is, crucifying him (cf also Gal 3, 13).

5, 31: *At his right hand:* see the note on Acts 2, 33.

5, 34: *Gamaliel:* in Acts 22, 3, Paul identifies himself as a disciple of this Rabbi Gamaliel I who flourished in Jerusalem between A.D. 25 and 50.

5, 36-37: Gamaliel offers examples of unsuccessful contemporary movements to argue that if God is not the origin of this movement preached by the apostles it will perish by itself. The movement initiated by Theudas actually occurred when C. Cuspius Fadus was governor, A.D. 44-46. Luke's placing of Judas the Galilean after Theudas and at the time of the census (see the note on Lk 2, 1-2) is an indication of the vagueness of his knowledge of these events.

CHAPTER 6

The Need for Assistants. [1] At that time, as the number of disciples continued to grow, the Hellenists complained against the Hebrews* because their widows were being neglected in the daily distribution.[j] [2] * So the Twelve called together the community of the disciples and said, "It is not right for us to neglect the word of God to serve at table.* [3] Brothers, select from among you seven reputable men, filled with the Spirit and wisdom, whom we shall appoint to this task, [4] whereas we shall devote ourselves to prayer and to the ministry of the word." [5] The proposal was acceptable to the whole community, so they chose Stephen, a man filled with faith and the holy Spirit, also Philip, Prochorus, Nicanor, Timon, Parmenas, and Nicholas of Antioch, a convert to Judaism. [6] [k] They presented these men to the apostles who prayed and laid hands on them.* [7] The word of God continued to spread, and the number of the disciples in Jerusalem increased greatly; even a large group of priests were becoming obedient to the faith.[l]

Accusation against Stephen. [8] * Now Stephen, filled with grace and power, was working great wonders and signs among the people. [9] Certain members of the so-called Synagogue of Freedmen, Cyrenians, and Alexandrians, and people from Cilicia and Asia, came forward and debated with Stephen, [10] but they could not withstand the wisdom and the spirit with which he spoke.[m] [11] Then they instigated some men to say, "We have heard him speaking blasphemous words against Moses and God."[n] [12] They stirred up the people, the elders, and the scribes, accosted him, seized him, and brought him before the Sanhedrin. [13] They presented false witnesses* who testified, "This man never stops saying things against [this] holy place and the law. [14] For we have heard him claim that this Jesus the Nazorean will destroy this place and change the customs that Moses handed down to us."[o] [15] All those who sat in the Sanhedrin looked intently at him and saw that his face was like the face of an angel.

CHAPTER 7

Stephen's Discourses. [1] Then the high priest asked, "Is this so?" [2] [p] And he replied,* "My brothers and fathers, listen. The God of glory appeared to our father Abraham while he was in Mesopotamia,* before he had settled in Haran, [3] and said to him, 'Go forth from your land and

---

j Acts 2, 45; 4, 34-35.—k Acts 1, 24; 13, 3; 14, 23.—l Acts 9, 31; 12, 24; 16, 5; 19, 20; 28, 30-31.—m Lk 21, 15.—n Mt 26, 59-61; Mk 14, 55-58; Acts 21, 21.—o Mt 26, 59-61; 27, 40; Jn 2, 19.—p Gn 11, 31; 12, 1; Ps 29, 3.

6, 1-7: *The Hellenists . . . the Hebrews:* the Hellenists were not necessarily Jews from the diaspora, but were more probably Palestinian Jews who spoke only Greek. The Hebrews were Palestinian Jews who spoke Hebrew or Aramaic and who may also have spoken Greek. Both groups belong to the Jerusalem Jewish Christian community. The conflict between them leads to a restructuring of the community that will better serve the community's needs. The real purpose of the whole episode, however, is to introduce Stephen as a prominent figure in the community whose long speech and martyrdom will be recounted in ch 7.

6, 2-4: The essential function of the Twelve is the "service of the word," including development of the kerygma by formulation of the teachings of Jesus.

6, 2: *To serve at table:* some commentators think that it is not the serving of food that is described here but rather the keeping of the accounts that recorded the distribution of food to the needy members of the community. In any case, after Stephen and the others are chosen, they are never presented carrying out the task for which they were appointed (2-3). Rather, two of their number, Stephen and Philip, are presented as preachers of the Christian message. They, the Hellenist counterpart of the Twelve, are active in the ministry of the word.

6, 6: *They . . . laid hands on them:* the customary Jewish way of designating persons for a task and invoking upon them the divine blessing and power to perform it.

6, 8—8, 1: The summary (Acts 6, 7) on the progress of the Jerusalem community, illustrated by the conversion of the priests, is followed by a lengthy narrative regarding Stephen. Stephen's

defense is not a response to the charges made against him but takes the form of a discourse that reviews the fortunes of God's word to Israel and leads to a prophetic declaration: a plea for the hearing of that word as announced by Christ and now possessed by the Christian community.

The charges that Stephen depreciated the importance of the temple and the Mosaic law and elevated Jesus to a stature above Moses (Acts 6, 13-14) were in fact true. Before the Sanhedrin, no defense against them was possible. With Stephen, who thus perceived the fuller implications of the teachings of Jesus, the differences between Judaism and Christianity began to appear. Luke's account of Stephen's martyrdom and its aftermath shows how the major impetus behind the Christian movement passed from Jerusalem, where the temple and law prevailed, to Antioch in Syria, where these influences were less pressing.

6, 13: *False witnesses:* here, and in his account of Stephen's execution (Acts 7, 54-60), Luke parallels the martyrdom of Stephen with the death of Jesus.

7, 2-53: Stephen's speech represents Luke's description of Christianity's break from its Jewish matrix. Two motifs become prominent in the speech: (1) Israel's reaction to God's chosen leaders in the past reveals that the people have consistently rejected them; and (2) Israel has misunderstood God's choice of the Jerusalem temple as the place where he is to be worshiped.

7, 2: *God . . . appeared to our father Abraham . . . in Mesopotamia:* the first of a number of minor discrepancies between the data of the Old Testament and the data of Stephen's discourse. According to Gn 12, 1, God first spoke to Abraham in Haran. The main discrepancies are these: in v 16 it is said that Jacob was buried in Shechem, whereas Gn 50, 13 says he was buried at Hebron; in the same verse it is said that the tomb was purchased by Abraham, but in Gn 33, 19 and Jos 24, 32 the purchase is attributed to Jacob himself.

[from] your kinsfolk to the land that I will show you.' *q* 4 So he went forth from the land of the Chaldeans and settled in Haran. And from there, after his father died, he made him migrate to this land where you now dwell. *r* 5 Yet he gave him no inheritance in it, not even a foot's length, but he did promise to give it to him and his descendants as a possession, even though he was childless. *s* 6 And God spoke thus, *t* 'His descendants shall be aliens in a land not their own, where they shall be enslaved and oppressed for four hundred years; 7 but I will bring judgment on the nation they serve,' God said, 'and after that they will come out and worship me in this place.' *u* 8 Then he gave him the covenant of circumcision, and so he became the father of Isaac, and circumcised him on the eighth day, as Isaac did Jacob, and Jacob the twelve patriarchs. *v*

9 "And the patriarchs, jealous of Joseph, sold him into slavery in Egypt; but God was with him *w* 10 and rescued him from all his afflictions. He granted him favor and wisdom before Pharaoh, the king of Egypt, who put him in charge of Egypt and [of] his entire household. *x* 11 Then a famine and great affliction struck all Egypt and Canaan, and our ancestors could find no food; *y* 12 but when Jacob heard that there was grain in Egypt, he sent our ancestors there a first time. *z* 13 The second time, Joseph made himself known to his brothers, and Joseph's family became known to Pharaoh. *a* 14 Then Joseph sent for his father Jacob, inviting him and his whole clan, seventy-five persons; *b* 15 and Jacob went down to Egypt. And he and our ancestors died *c* 16 and were brought back to Shechem and placed in the tomb that Abraham had purchased for a sum of money from the sons of Hamor at Shechem. *d*

17 "When the time drew near for the fulfillment of the promise that God pledged to Abraham, the people had increased and become very numerous in Egypt, *e* 18 until another king who knew nothing of Joseph came to power [in Egypt]. *f* 19 He dealt shrewdly with our people and oppressed [our] ancestors by forcing them to expose their infants, that they might not survive. 20 At this time Moses was born, and he was extremely beautiful. For three months he was nursed in his father's house; *g* 21 but when he was exposed, Pharaoh's daughter adopted him and brought him up as her own son. *h* 22 Moses was educated [in] all the wisdom of the Egyptians and was powerful in his words and deeds.

23 *i* "When he was forty years old, he decided to visit his kinsfolk, the Israelites. 24 When he saw one of them treated unjustly, he defended and avenged the oppressed man by striking down the Egyptian. 25 He assumed [his] kinsfolk would understand that God was offering them deliverance through him, but they did not understand. 26 *j* The next day he appeared to them as they were fighting and tried to reconcile them peacefully, saying, 'Men, you are brothers. Why are you harming one another?' 27 Then the one who was harming his neighbor pushed him aside, saying, 'Who appointed you ruler and judge over us? 28 Are you thinking of killing me as you killed the Egyptian yesterday?' 29 Moses fled when he heard this and settled as an alien in the land of Midian, where he became the father of two sons. *k*

30 *l* "Forty years later, an angel appeared to him in the desert near Mount Sinai in the flame of a burning bush. 31 When Moses saw it, he was amazed at the sight, and as he drew near to look at it, the voice of the Lord came, 32 'I am the God of your fathers, the God of Abraham, of Isaac, and of Jacob.' Then Moses, trembling, did not dare to look at it. 33 But the Lord said to him, 'Remove the sandals from your feet, for the place where you stand is holy ground. 34 I have witnessed the affliction of my people in Egypt and have heard their groaning, and I have come down to rescue them. Come now, I will send you to Egypt.' 35 This Moses, whom they had rejected with the words, 'Who appointed you ruler and judge?' God sent as [both] ruler and deliverer, through the angel who appeared to him in the bush. *m* 36 This man led them out, performing wonders and signs in the land of Egypt, at the Red Sea, and in the desert for forty years. *n* 37 It was this Moses who said to the Israel-

q Gn 12, 1.—r Gn 12, 5; 15, 7.—s Gn 12, 7; 13, 15; 15, 2; 16, 1; Dt 2, 5.—t 6-7: Gn 15, 13-14.—u Ex 3, 12.—v Gn 17, 10-14; 21, 2-4.—w Gn 37, 11.28; 39, 2.3.21.23.—x Gn 41, 37-43; Ps 105, 21; Wis 10, 13-14.—y Gn 41, 54-57; 42, 5.—z Gn 42, 1-2.—a Gn 45, 3-4.16.—b Gn 45, 9-11.18-19; 46, 27; Ex 1, 5 LXX; Dt 10, 22.—c Gn 46, 5-6; 49, 33.—d Gn 23, 3-20; 33, 19; 49, 29-30; 50, 13; Jos 24, 32.—e Ex 1, 7.—f Ex 1, 8.—g Ex 2, 2; Heb 11, 23.—h Ex 2, 3-10.—i 23-24: Ex 2, 11-12.—j 26-28: Ex 2, 13-14.—k Ex 2, 15.21-22; 18, 3-4.—l 30-34: Ex 3, 2-3.—m Ex 2, 14.—n Ex 7, 3.10; 14, 21; Nm 14, 33.

Acts

ites, 'God will raise up for you, from among your own kinsfolk, a prophet like me.'[o] [38]It was he who, in the assembly in the desert, was with the angel who spoke to him on Mount Sinai and with our ancestors, and he received living utterances to hand on to us.[p]

[39]"Our ancestors were unwilling to obey him; instead, they pushed him aside and in their hearts turned back to Egypt,[q] [40]saying to Aaron, 'Make us gods who will be our leaders. As for that Moses who led us out of the land of Egypt, we do not know what has happened to him.'[r] [41]So they made a calf in those days, offered sacrifice to the idol, and reveled in the works of their hands.[s] [42]Then God turned and handed them over to worship the host of heaven, as it is written in the book of the prophets:[t]

'Did you bring me sacrifices and offerings
for forty years in the desert, O house of Israel?[u]

[43] No, you took up the tent of Moloch
and the star of [your] god Rephan,
the images that you made to worship.
So I shall take you into exile beyond Babylon.'

[44]Our ancestors had the tent of testimony in the desert just as the One who spoke to Moses directed him to make it according to the pattern he had seen.[v] [45]Our ancestors who inherited it brought it with Joshua when they dispossessed the nations that God drove out from before our ancestors, up to the time of David,[w] [46]who found favor in the sight of God and asked that he might find a dwelling place for the house of Jacob.[x] [47]But Solomon built a house for him.[y] [48]Yet the Most High does not dwell in houses made by human hands. As the prophet says:[z]

[49] 'The heavens are my throne,
the earth is my footstool.
What kind of house can you build for me?
says the Lord,
or what is to be my resting place?[a]

[50] Did not my hand make all these things?'

Conclusion. [51]"You stiff-necked people, uncircumcised in heart and ears, you always oppose the holy Spirit; you are just like your ancestors. [52]Which of the proph-

ets did your ancestors not persecute? They put to death those who foretold the coming of the righteous one, whose betrayers and murderers you have now become.[b] [53]You received the law as transmitted by angels, but you did not observe it."[c]

Stephen's Martyrdom. [54]When they heard this, they were infuriated, and they ground their teeth at him. [55] [d] But he, filled with the holy Spirit, looked up intently to heaven and saw the glory of God and Jesus standing at the right hand of God,* [56]and he said, "Behold, I see the heavens opened and the Son of Man standing at the right hand of God." [57]But they cried out in a loud voice, covered their ears,* and rushed upon him together. [58]They threw him out of the city, and began to stone him. The witnesses laid down their cloaks at the feet of a young man named Saul.[e] [59]As they were stoning Stephen,[f] he called out, "Lord Jesus, receive my spirit."* [60]Then he fell to his knees and cried out in a loud voice, "Lord, do not hold this sin against them"; and when he said this, he fell asleep.[g]

CHAPTER 8

[1]Now Saul was consenting to his execution.[h]

Persecution of the Church. On that day, there broke out a severe persecution* of the church in Jerusalem, and all were scattered throughout the countryside of Judea and Samaria, except the apostles.* [2]De-

o Dt 18, 15; Acts 3, 22.—p Ex 19, 3; 20, 1-17; Dt 5, 4-22; 6, 4-25.—q Nm 14, 3.—r Ex 32, 1.23.—s Ex 32, 4-6.—t 42-43: Am 5, 25-27.—u Jer 7, 18; 8, 2; 19, 13.—v Ex 25, 9.40.—w Jos 3, 14-17; 18, 1; 2 Sm 7, 5-7.—x 2 Sm 7, 1-2; 1 Kgs 8, 17; Ps 132, 1-5.—y 1 Kgs 6, 1; 1 Chr 17, 12.—z Acts 17, 24.—a Is 66, 1-2.—b 2 Chr 36, 16; Mt 23, 31.34.—c Gal 3, 19; Heb 2, 2.—d 55-56: Mt 26, 64; Mk 14, 62; Lk 22, 69; Acts 2, 34.—e Acts 22, 20.—f Ps 31, 6; Lk 23, 46.—g Mt 27, 46.50; Mk 15, 34; Lk 23, 46.—h Acts 22, 20.

7, 55: *He . . . saw . . . Jesus standing at the right hand of God:* Stephen affirms to the Sanhedrin that the prophecy Jesus made before them has been fulfilled (Mk 14, 62).

7, 57: *Covered their ears:* Stephen's declaration, like that of Jesus, is a scandal to the court, which regards it as blasphemy.

7, 59: Compare Lk 23, [34].46.

8, 1-40: Some idea of the severity of the persecution that now breaks out against the Jerusalem community can be gathered from Acts 22, 4 and Acts 26, 9-11. Luke, however, concentrates on the fortunes of the word of God among people, indicating how the dispersal of the Jewish community resulted in the conversion of the Samaritans (4-17.25). His narrative is further expanded to include the account of Philip's acceptance of an Ethiopian (26-39).

8, 1: *All were scattered . . . except the apostles:* this observation leads some modern scholars to conclude that the persecution was limited to the Hellenist Christians and that the Hebrew Christians were not molested, perhaps because their attitude to-vout men buried Stephen and made a loud lament over him. ³Saul, meanwhile, was trying to destroy the church;* entering house after house and dragging out men and women, he handed them over for imprisonment.ⁱ

III. THE MISSION IN JUDEA AND SAMARIA

Philip in Samaria. ⁴Now those who had been scattered went about preaching the word.ʲ ⁵Thus Philip went down to [the] city of Samaria and proclaimed the Messiah to them.ᵏ ⁶With one accord, the crowds paid attention to what was said by Philip when they heard it and saw the signs he was doing. ⁷For unclean spirits, crying out in a loud voice, came out of many possessed people, and many paralyzed and crippled people were cured.ˡ ⁸There was great joy in that city.

Simon the Magician. ⁹A man named Simon used to practice magic* in the city and astounded the people of Samaria, claiming to be someone great. ¹⁰All of them, from the least to the greatest, paid attention to him, saying, "This man is the 'Power of God' that is called 'Great.' " ¹¹They paid attention to him because he had astounded them by his magic for a long time, ¹²but once they began to believe Philip as he preached the good news about the kingdom of God and the name of Jesus Christ, men and women alike were baptized.ᵐ ¹³Even Simon himself believed and, after being baptized, became devoted to Philip; and when he saw the signs and

mighty deeds that were occurring, he was astounded.

¹⁴Now when the apostles in Jerusalem heard that Samaria had accepted the word of God, they sent them Peter and John, ¹⁵who went down and prayed for them, that they might receive the holy Spirit, ¹⁶for it had not yet fallen upon any of them; they had only been baptized in the name of the Lord Jesus.* ¹⁷Then they laid hands on them and they received the holy Spirit.ⁿ

¹⁸ * When Simon saw that the Spirit was conferred by the laying on of the apostles' hands, he offered them money ¹⁹and said, "Give me this power too, so that anyone upon whom I lay my hands may receive the holy Spirit." ²⁰But Peter said to him, "May your money perish with you, because you thought that you could buy the gift of God with money. ²¹You have no share or lot in this matter, for your heart is not upright before God. ²²Repent of this wickedness of yours and pray to the Lord that, if possible, your intention may be forgiven. ²³For I see that you are filled with bitter gall and are in the bonds of iniquity." ²⁴Simon said in reply, "Pray for me to the Lord, that nothing of what you have said may come upon me." ²⁵So when they had testified and proclaimed the word of the Lord, they returned to Jerusalem and preached the good news to many Samaritan villages.

Philip and the Ethiopian.* ²⁶Then the angel of the Lord spoke to Philip, "Get up and head south on the road that goes down from Jerusalem to Gaza, the desert route."

---

i Acts 9, 1.13; 22, 4; 26, 9-11; 1 Cor 5, 9; Gal 1, 13.—j Acts 11, 19.—k Acts 6, 5; 21, 8-9.—l Mk 16, 17.—m Acts 1, 3; 19, 8; 28, 23.31.—n Acts 2, 4; 4, 31; 10, 44-47; 15, 8-9; 19, 2.6.

ward the law and temple was still more in line with that of their fellow Jews (see the charge leveled against the Hellenist Stephen in Acts 6, 13-14). Whatever the facts, it appears that the Twelve took no public stand regarding Stephen's position, choosing, instead, to await the development of events.

8, 3: *Saul . . . was trying to destroy the church:* like Stephen, Saul was able to perceive that the Christian movement contained the seeds of doctrinal divergence from Judaism. A pupil of Gamaliel, according to Acts 22, 3, and totally dedicated to the law as the way of salvation (Gal 1, 13-14), Saul accepted the task of crushing the Christian movement, at least insofar as it detracted from the importance of the temple and the law. His vehement opposition to Christianity reveals how difficult it was for a Jew of his time to accept a messianism that differed so greatly from the general expectation.

8, 9-13.18-24: Sorcerers were well known in the ancient world. Probably the incident involving Simon and his altercation with Peter is introduced to show that the miraculous charisms possessed by members of the Christian community (6-7) were not to be confused with the magic of sorcerers.

8, 16: Here and in Acts 10, 44-48 and Acts 19, 1-6, Luke distinguishes between baptism in the name of the Lord Jesus and the reception of the Spirit. In each case, the Spirit is conferred through members of the Twelve (Peter and John) or their representative (Paul). This may be Luke's way of describing the role of the church in the bestowal of the Spirit. Elsewhere in Acts, baptism and the Spirit are more closely related (Acts 1, 5; 11, 16).

8, 18-20: Simon attempts to buy the gift of God (20) with money. Peter's cursing of Simon's attempt so to use his money expresses a typically Lucan attitude toward material wealth (cf Lk 6, 24; 12, 16-21; 16, 13).

8, 26-40: In the account of the conversion of the Ethiopian eunuch, Luke adduces additional evidence to show that the spread of Christianity outside the confines of Judaism itself was in accord with the plan of God. He does not make clear whether the Ethiopian was originally a convert to Judaism or, as is more probable, a "God-fearer" (Acts 10, 1), i.e., one who accepted Jewish monotheism and ethic and attended the synagogue but did not consider himself bound by other regulations such as circumcision and observance of the dietary laws. The story of his conversion to Christianity is given a strong supernatural cast by the introduction of an angel (26), instruction from the holy Spirit (29), and the strange removal of Philip from the scene (39).

27 So he got up and set out. Now there was an Ethiopian eunuch, a court official of the Candace,* that is, the queen of the Ethiopians, in charge of her entire treasury, who had come to Jerusalem to worship,ᵒ 28 and was returning home. Seated in his chariot, he was reading the prophet Isaiah. 29 The Spirit said to Philip, "Go and join up with that chariot." 30 * Philip ran up and heard him reading Isaiah the prophet and said, "Do you understand what you are reading?" 31 He replied, "How can I, unless someone instructs me?" So he invited Philip to get in and sit with him.ᵖ 32 This was the scripture passage he was reading:�q

"Like a sheep he was led to the slaughter,
    and as a lamb before its shearer is silent,
        so he opened not his mouth.
33 In [his] humiliation justice was denied him.
    Who will tell of his posterity?
        For his life is taken from the earth."

34 Then the eunuch said to Philip in reply, "I beg you, about whom is the prophet saying this? About himself, or about someone else?" 35 Then Philip opened his mouth and, beginning with this scripture passage, he proclaimed Jesus to him. 36 r As they traveled along the road they came to some water, and the eunuch said, "Look, there is water. What is to prevent my being baptized?" [37] * 38 Then he ordered the chariot to stop, and Philip and the eunuch both went down into the water, and he baptized him. 39 When they came out of the water, the Spirit of the Lord snatched Philip away, and the eunuch saw him no more, but continued on his way rejoicing.ˢ 40 Philip came to Azotus, and went about proclaiming the good news to all the towns until he reached Caesarea.ᵗ

CHAPTER 9

Saul's Conversion. 1 * Now Saul, still breathing murderous threats against the disciples of the Lord,ᵘ went to the high priestᵛ 2 and asked him for letters to the synagogues in Damascus, that, if he should find any men or women who belonged to the Way,* he might bring them back to Jerusalem in chains. 3 On his journey, as he was nearing Damascus, a light from the sky suddenly flashed around him.ʷ 4 He

fell to the ground and heard a voice saying to him, "Saul, Saul, why are you persecuting me?"ˣ 5 He said, "Who are you, sir?" The reply came, "I am Jesus, whom you are persecuting.ʸ 6 Now get up and go into the city and you will be told what you must do."ᶻ 7 The men who were traveling with him stood speechless, for they heard the voice but could see no one.ᵃ 8 Saul got up from the ground, but when he opened his eyes he could see nothing;* so they led him by the hand and brought him to Damascus.ᵇ 9 For three days he was unable to see, and he neither ate nor drank.

Saul's Baptism. 10 c There was a disciple in Damascus named Ananias, and the Lord said to him in a vision, "Ananias." He answered, "Here I am, Lord." 11 The Lord said to him, "Get up and go to the street called Straight and ask at the house of Judas for a man from Tarsus named Saul. He is there praying,ᵈ 12 and [in a vision] he has seen a man named Ananias

o Is 56, 3-5.—p Jn 16, 13.—q 32-33: Is 53, 7-8 LXX.—r Acts 10, 47.—s 1 Kgs 18, 12.—t Acts 21, 8.—u Acts 8, 3; 9, 13; 22, 4; 1 Cor 15, 9; Gal 1, 13-14.—v 1-2: Acts 9, 14; 26, 10.—w 1 Cor 9, 1; 15, 8; Gal 1, 16.—x Acts 22, 6; 26, 14.—y Acts 22, 8; 26, 15; Mt 25, 40.—z Acts 22, 10; 26, 16.—a Acts 22, 9; 26, 13-14.—b Acts 22, 11.—c 10-19: Acts 22, 12-16.—d Acts 21, 39.

8, 27: *The Candace:* Candace is not a proper name here but the title of a Nubian queen.

8, 30-34: Philip is brought alongside the carriage at the very moment when the Ethiopian is pondering the meaning of Is 53, 7-8, a passage that Christianity, from its earliest origins, has applied to Jesus; cf the note on Acts 3, 13.

8, 37: The oldest and best manuscripts of Acts omit this verse, which is a Western text reading: "And Philip said, 'If you believe with all your heart, you may.' And he said in reply, 'I believe that Jesus Christ is the Son of God.' "

9, 1-19: This is the first of three accounts of Paul's conversion (with Acts 22, 3-16 and Acts 26, 2-18) with some differences of detail owing to Luke's use of different sources. Paul's experience was not visionary but was precipitated by the appearance of Jesus, as he insists in 1 Cor 15, 8. The words of Jesus, "Saul, Saul, why are you persecuting me?" related by Luke with no variation in all three accounts, exerted a profound and lasting influence on the thought of Paul. Under the influence of this experience he gradually developed his understanding of justification by faith (see the letters to the Galatians and Romans) and of the identification of the Christian community with Jesus Christ (see 1 Cor 12, 27). That Luke would narrate this conversion three times is testimony to the importance he attaches to it. This first account occurs when the word is first spread to the Gentiles. At this point, the conversion of the hero of the Gentile mission is recounted. The emphasis in the account is on Paul as a divinely chosen instrument (15).

9, 2: *The Way:* a name used by the early Christian community for itself (Acts 18, 26; 19, 9.23; 22, 4; 24, 14.22). The Essene community at Qumran used the same designation to describe its mode of life.

9, 8: *He could see nothing:* a temporary blindness (18) symbolizing the religious blindness of Saul as persecutor (cf Acts 26, 18).

come in and lay [his] hands on him, that he may regain his sight." [13] But Ananias replied, "Lord, I have heard from many sources about this man, what evil things he has done to your holy ones* in Jerusalem. [e] [14] And here he has authority from the chief priests to imprison all who call upon your name." [f] [15] But the Lord said to him, "Go, for this man is a chosen instrument of mine to carry my name before Gentiles, kings, and Israelites, [g] [16] and I will show him what he will have to suffer for my name." [17] So Ananias went and entered the house; laying his hands on him, he said, "Saul, my brother, the Lord has sent me, Jesus who appeared to you on the way by which you came, that you may regain your sight and be filled with the holy Spirit." [18] Immediately things like scales fell from his eyes and he regained his sight. He got up and was baptized, [19] and when he had eaten, he recovered his strength.

Saul Preaches in Damascus.* He stayed some days with the disciples in Damascus, [20] and he began at once to proclaim Jesus in the synagogues, that he is the Son of God.* [21] All who heard him were astounded and said, "Is not this the man who in Jerusalem ravaged those who call upon this name, and came here expressly to take them back in chains to the chief priests?" [22] But Saul grew all the stronger and confounded [the] Jews who lived in Damascus, proving that this is the Messiah.

e Acts 8, 3; 9, 1.—f Acts 9, 1-2; 26, 10; 1 Cor 1, 2; 2 Tm 2, 22.—g Acts 22, 15; 26, 1; 27, 24.—h 24-25: 2 Cor 11, 32-33.—i 26-27: Gal 1, 18.—j Acts 11, 25.

9, 13: *Your holy ones:* literally, "your saints."

9, 19-30: This is a brief resume of Paul's initial experience as an apostolic preacher. At first he found himself in the position of being regarded as an apostate by the Jews and suspect by the Christian community of Jerusalem. His acceptance by the latter was finally brought about through his friendship with Barnabas (27).

9, 20: *Son of God:* the title "Son of God" occurs in Acts only here, but cf the citation of Ps 2, 7 in Paul's speech at Antioch in Pisidia (Acts 13, 33).

9, 26: This visit of Paul to Jerusalem is mentioned by Paul in Gal 1, 18.

9, 29: *Hellenists:* see the note on Acts 6, 1-7.

9, 31-43: In the context of the period of peace enjoyed by the community through the cessation of Paul's activities against it, Luke introduces two traditions concerning the miraculous power exercised by Peter as he was making a tour of places where the Christian message had already been preached. The towns of Lydda, Sharon, and Joppa were populated by both Jews and Gentiles and their Christian communities may well have been mixed.

9, 36: *Tabitha (Dorcas),* respectively the Aramaic and Greek words for "gazelle," exemplifies the right attitude toward material possessions expressed by Jesus in the Lucan Gospel (Lk 6, 30; 11, 41; 12, 33; 18, 22; 19, 8).

Saul Visits Jerusalem. [23] After a long time had passed, the Jews conspired to kill him, [24] [h] but their plot became known to Saul. Now they were keeping watch on the gates day and night so as to kill him, [25] but his disciples took him one night and let him down through an opening in the wall, lowering him in a basket.

[26] [i] When he arrived in Jerusalem* he tried to join the disciples, but they were all afraid of him, not believing that he was a disciple. [27] Then Barnabas took charge of him and brought him to the apostles, and he reported to them how on the way he had seen the Lord and that he had spoken to him, and how in Damascus he had spoken out boldly in the name of Jesus. [28] He moved about freely with them in Jerusalem, and spoke out boldly in the name of the Lord. [29] He also spoke and debated with the Hellenists,* but they tried to kill him. [30] And when the brothers learned of this, they took him down to Caesarea and sent him on his way to Tarsus. [j]

The Church at Peace. [31] * The church throughout all Judea, Galilee, and Samaria was at peace. It was being built up and walked in the fear of the Lord, and with the consolation of the holy Spirit it grew in numbers.

Peter Heals Aeneas at Lydda. [32] As Peter was passing through every region, he went down to the holy ones living in Lydda. [33] There he found a man named Aeneas, who had been confined to bed for eight years, for he was paralyzed. [34] Peter said to him, "Aeneas, Jesus Christ heals you. Get up and make your bed." He got up at once. [35] And all the inhabitants of Lydda and Sharon saw him, and they turned to the Lord.

Peter Restores Tabitha to Life. [36] Now in Joppa there was a disciple named Tabitha (which translated means Dorcas).* She was completely occupied with good deeds and almsgiving. [37] Now during those days she fell sick and died, so after washing her, they laid [her] out in a room upstairs. [38] Since Lydda was near Joppa, the disciples, hearing that Peter was there, sent two men to him with the request, "Please come to us without delay." [39] So Peter got up and went with them. When he arrived, they took him to the room upstairs where all the widows came to him weeping and showing

Acts

him the tunics and cloaks that Dorcas had made while she was with them. [40] Peter sent them all out and knelt down and prayed. Then he turned to her body and said, "Tabitha, rise up." She opened her eyes, saw Peter, and sat up.[k] [41] He gave her his hand and raised her up, and when he had called the holy ones and the widows, he presented her alive. [42] This became known all over Joppa, and many came to believe in the Lord. [43] [l] And he stayed a long time in Joppa with Simon, a tanner.*

IV. THE INAUGURATION OF THE GENTILE MISSION

CHAPTER 10

The Vision of Cornelius.[m] [1] * Now in Caesarea there was a man named Cornelius, a centurion of the Cohort called the Italica,* [2] devout and God-fearing along with his whole household, who used to give alms generously* to the Jewish people and pray to God constantly. [3] One afternoon about three o'clock,* he saw plainly in a vision an angel of God come in to him and say to him, "Cornelius." [4] He looked intently at him and, seized with fear, said, "What is it, sir?" He said to him, "Your prayers and almsgiving have ascended as a memorial offering before God. [5] Now send some men to Joppa and summon one Simon who is called Peter. [6] He is staying with another Simon, a tanner, who has a house by the sea."[n] [7] When the angel who spoke to him had left, he called two of his servants and a devout soldier* from his staff, [8] explained everything to them, and sent them to Joppa.

The Vision of Peter. [9] * The next day, while they were on their way and nearing the city, Peter went up to the roof terrace to pray at about noontime.* [10] He was hungry and wished to eat, and while they were making preparations he fell into a trance. [11] [o] He saw heaven opened and something resembling a large sheet coming down, lowered to the ground by its four corners. [12] In it were all the earth's four-legged animals and reptiles and the birds of the sky. [13] A voice said to him, "Get up, Peter. Slaughter and eat." [14] But Peter said, "Certainly not, sir. For never have I eaten anything profane and unclean."[p] [15] The voice spoke to him again, a second time, "What God has made clean, you are not to call profane."[q] [16] This happened three times, and then the object was taken up into the sky.

[17] * While Peter was in doubt about the meaning of the vision he had seen, the men sent by Cornelius asked for Simon's house and arrived at the entrance. [18] They called out inquiring whether Simon, who is called Peter, was staying there. [19] As Peter was pondering the vision, the Spirit said [to him], "There are three men here looking for you.[r] [20] So get up, go downstairs, and accompany them without hesitation, because I have sent them." [21] Then Peter went down to the men and said, "I am the one you are looking for. What is the reason for your being here?" [22] They answered, "Cornelius, a centurion, an upright and God-fearing man, respected by the whole Jewish nation, was directed by a holy angel to summon you to his house and to hear what you have to say."[s] [23] So he invited them in and showed them hospitality.

The next day he got up and went with them, and some of the brothers from Joppa

---

k Mk 5, 40-41.—l Acts 10, 6.—m 1-8: Acts 10, 30-33.—n Acts 9, 43.—o 11-20: Acts 11, 5-12.—p Lv 11, 1-47; Ez 4, 14.—q Mk 7, 15-19; Gal 2, 12.—r Acts 13, 2.—s Lk 7, 4-5.

9, 43: The fact that Peter lodged with a tanner would have been significant to both the Gentile and the Jewish Christians, for Judaism considered the tanning occupation unclean.

10, 1-48: The narrative centers on the conversion of Cornelius, a Gentile and a "God-fearer" (see the note on Acts 8, 26-40). Luke considers the event of great importance, as is evident from his long treatment of it. The incident is again related in Acts 11, 1-18 where Peter is forced to justify his actions before the Jerusalem community and alluded to in Acts 15, 7-11 where at the Jerusalem "Council" Peter supports Paul's missionary activity among the Gentiles. The narrative divides itself into a series of distinct episodes, concluding with Peter's presentation of the Christian kerygma (34-43) and a pentecostal experience undergone by Cornelius's household preceding their reception of baptism (44-48).

10, 1: *The Cohort called the Italica:* this battalion was an auxiliary unit of archers formed originally in Italy but transferred to Syria shortly before A.D. 69.

10, 2: *Used to give alms generously:* like Tabitha (Acts 9, 36), Cornelius exemplifies the proper attitude toward wealth (see the note on Acts 9, 36).

10, 3: *About three o'clock:* literally, "about the ninth hour." See the note on Acts 3, 1.

10, 7: *A devout soldier:* by using this adjective, Luke probably intends to classify him as a "God-fearer" (see the note on Acts 8, 26-40).

10, 9-16: The vision is intended to prepare Peter to share the food of Cornelius's household without qualms of conscience (48). The necessity of such instructions to Peter reveals that at first not even the apostles fully grasped the implications of Jesus' teaching on the law. In Acts, the initial insight belongs to Stephen.

10, 9: *At about noontime:* literally, "about the sixth hour."

10, 17-23: The arrival of the Gentile emissaries with their account of the angelic apparition illuminates Peter's vision: he is to be prepared to admit Gentiles, who were considered unclean like the animals of his vision, into the Christian community.

went with him. [24] * On the following day he entered Caesarea. Cornelius was expecting them and had called together his relatives and close friends. [25] *t* When Peter entered, Cornelius met him and, falling at his feet, paid him homage. [26] Peter, however, raised him up, saying, "Get up. I myself am also a human being." [27] While he conversed with him, he went in and found many people gathered together [28] *u* and said to them, "You know that it is unlawful for a Jewish man to associate with, or visit, a Gentile, but God has shown me that I should not call any person profane or unclean.* [29] And that is why I came without objection when sent for. May I ask, then, why you summoned me?"

[30] Cornelius replied, "Four days ago* at this hour, three o'clock in the afternoon, I was at prayer in my house when suddenly a man in dazzling robes stood before me and said, [31] 'Cornelius, your prayer has been heard and your almsgiving remembered before God. [32] Send therefore to Joppa and summon Simon, who is called Peter. He is a guest in the house of Simon, a tanner, by the sea.' [33] So I sent for you immediately, and you were kind enough to come. Now therefore we are all here in the presence of God to listen to all that you have been commanded by the Lord."

Peter's Speech.* [34] Then Peter proceeded to speak and said,* "In truth, I see that God shows no partiality. *v* [35] Rather, in every nation whoever fears him and acts uprightly is acceptable to him. [36] * You

know the word [that] he sent to the Israelites* as he proclaimed peace through Jesus Christ, who is Lord of all,*w* [37] what has happened all over Judea, beginning in Galilee after the baptism that John preached,*x* [38] how God anointed Jesus of Nazareth* with the holy Spirit and power. He went about doing good and healing all those oppressed by the devil, for God was with him.*y* [39] We are witnesses* of all that he did both in the country of the Jews and [in] Jerusalem. They put him to death by hanging him on a tree. [40] This man God raised [on] the third day and granted that he be visible, [41] not to all the people, but to us, the witnesses chosen by God in advance, who ate and drank with him after he rose from the dead.*z* [42] He commissioned us*a* to preach to the people and testify that he is the one appointed by God as judge of the living and the dead.* [43] To him all the prophets bear witness, that everyone who believes in him will receive forgiveness of sins through his name."

The Baptism of Cornelius. [44] *b* While Peter was still speaking these things, the holy Spirit fell upon all who were listening to the word.* [45] The circumcised believers who had accompanied Peter were astounded that the gift of the holy Spirit should have been poured out on the Gentiles also, [46] for they could hear them speaking in tongues and glorifying God. Then Peter responded, [47] "Can anyone

---

t 25-26: Acts 14, 13-15; Rv 19, 10.—u Gal 2, 11-16.—v Dt 17, 2; 2 Chr 19, 7; Jb 34, 19; Wis 6, 7; Rom 2, 11; Gal 2, 6; Eph 6, 9; 1 Pt 1, 17.—w Is 52, 7; Na 2, 1.—x Mt 4, 12; Mk 1, 14; Lk 4, 14.—y Is 61, 1; Lk 4, 18.—z Lk 24, 41-43.—a Acts 1, 8; 3, 15; 17, 31; Lk 24, 48; Rom 14, 9; 2 Tm 4, 1.—b Acts 11, 15; 15, 8.

10, 24-27: So impressed is Cornelius with the apparition that he invites close personal friends to join him in his meeting with Peter. But his understanding of the person he is about to meet is not devoid of superstition, suggested by his falling down before him. For a similar experience of Paul and Barnabas, see Acts 14, 11-18.

10, 28: Peter now fully understands the meaning of his vision; see the note on Acts 10, 17-23.

10, 30: *Four days ago:* literally, "from the fourth day up to this hour."

10, 34-43: Peter's speech to the household of Cornelius typifies early Christian preaching to Gentiles.

10, 34-35: The revelation of God's choice of Israel to be the people of God did not mean he withheld the divine favor from other people.

10, 36-43: These words are more directed to Luke's Christian readers than to the household of Cornelius, as indicated by the opening words, "You know." They trace the continuity between the preaching and teaching of Jesus of Nazareth and the procla-

mation of Jesus by the early community. The emphasis on this divinely ordained continuity (41) is meant to assure Luke's readers of the fidelity of Christian tradition to the words and deeds of Jesus.

10, 36: *To the Israelites:* Luke, in the words of Peter, speaks of the prominent position occupied by Israel in the history of salvation.

10, 38: *Jesus of Nazareth:* God's revelation of his plan for the destiny of humanity through Israel culminated in Jesus of Nazareth. Consequently, the ministry of Jesus is an integral part of God's revelation. This viewpoint explains why the early Christian communities were interested in conserving the historical substance of the ministry of Jesus, a tradition leading to the production of the four gospels.

10, 39: *We are witnesses:* the apostolic testimony was not restricted to the resurrection of Jesus but also included his historical ministry. This witness, however, was theological in character; the Twelve, divinely mandated as prophets, were empowered to interpret his sayings and deeds in the light of his redemptive death and resurrection. The meaning of these words and deeds was to be made clear to the developing Christian community as the bearer of the word of salvation (cf Acts 1, 21-26). *Hanging him on a tree:* see the note on Acts 5, 30.

10, 42: *As judge of the living and the dead:* the apostolic preaching to the Jews appealed to their messianic hope, while the preaching to Gentiles stressed the coming divine judgment; cf 1 Thes 1, 10.

10, 44: Just as the Jewish Christians received the gift of the Spirit, so too do the Gentiles.

withhold the water for baptizing these people, who have received the holy Spirit even as we have?"[c] [48]He ordered them to be baptized in the name of Jesus Christ. [49]Then they invited him to stay for a few days.

CHAPTER 11

The Baptism of the Gentiles Explained.*

[1]Now the apostles and the brothers who were in Judea heard that the Gentiles too had accepted the word of God. [2]So when Peter went up to Jerusalem the circumcised believers confronted him, [3]saying, "You entered* the house of uncircumcised people and ate with them." [4]Peter began and explained it to them step by step, saying, [5] [d] "I was at prayer in the city of Joppa when in a trance I had a vision, something resembling a large sheet coming down, lowered from the sky by its four corners, and it came to me. [6]Looking intently into it, I observed and saw the four-legged animals of the earth, the wild beasts, the reptiles, and the birds of the sky. [7]I also heard a voice say to me, 'Get up, Peter. Slaughter and eat.' [8]But I said, 'Certainly not, sir, because nothing profane or unclean has ever entered my mouth.' [9]But a second time a voice from heaven answered, 'What God has made clean, you are not to call profane.' [10]This happened three times, and then everything was drawn up again into the sky. [11]Just then three men appeared at the house where we were, who had been sent to me from Caesarea. [12]The Spirit told me to accompany them without discriminating. These six brothers* also went with me, and we entered the man's house. [13]He related to us how he had seen [the] angel standing in his house, saying, 'Send someone to Joppa and summon Simon, who is called Peter,[e] [14]who will speak words to you by which you and all your household will be saved.' [15]As I began to speak, the holy Spirit fell upon them as it had upon us at the beginning,[f] [16]and I remembered the word of the Lord, how he had said, 'John baptized with water but you will be baptized with the holy Spirit.'[g] [17]If then God gave them the same gift he gave to us when we came to believe in the Lord Jesus Christ, who was I to be able to hinder God?"[h] [18]When they heard this, they stopped objecting and glorified God, saying, "God has then granted life-giving repentance to the Gentiles too."

The Church at Antioch.* [19]Now those who had been scattered by the persecution that arose because of Stephen went as far as Phoenicia, Cyprus, and Antioch, preaching the word to no one but Jews.[i] [20]There were some Cypriots and Cyrenians among them, however, who came to Antioch and began to speak to the Greeks as well, proclaiming the Lord Jesus. [21]The hand of the Lord was with them and a great number who believed turned to the Lord. [22]The news about them reached the ears of the church in Jerusalem, and they sent Barnabas [to go] to Antioch. [23]When he arrived and saw the grace of God, he rejoiced and encouraged them all to remain faithful to the Lord in firmness of heart, [24]for he was a good man, filled with the holy Spirit and faith. And a large number of people was added to the Lord. [25]Then he went to Tarsus to look for Saul, [26]and when he had found him he brought him to Antioch. For a whole year they met with the church and taught a large number of people, and it was in Antioch that the disciples were first called Christians.*

The Prediction of Agabus.* [27]At that time some prophets came down from Jerusalem

c Acts 8, 36.—d 5-12: Acts 10, 11-20.—e Acts 10, 3-5.22.30-32.—f Acts 10, 44.—g Acts 1, 5; 19, 4; Lk 3, 16.—h Acts 15, 8-9.—i Acts 8, 1-4.

11, 1-18: The Jewish Christians of Jerusalem were scandalized to learn of Peter's sojourn in the house of the Gentile Cornelius. Nonetheless, they had to accept the divine directions given to both Peter and Cornelius. They concluded that the setting aside of the legal barriers between Jew and Gentile was an exceptional ordinance of God to indicate that the apostolic kerygma was also to be directed to the Gentiles. Only in ch 15 at the "Council" in Jerusalem does the evangelization of the Gentiles become the official position of the church leadership in Jerusalem.

11, 3: *You entered . . . :* alternatively, this could be punctuated as a question.

11, 12: *These six brothers:* companions from the Christian community of Joppa (see Acts 10, 23).

11, 19-26: The Jewish Christian antipathy to the mixed community was reflected by the early missionaries generally. The few among them who entertained a different view succeeded in introducing Gentiles into the community at Antioch (in Syria). When the disconcerted Jerusalem community sent Barnabas to investigate, he was so favorably impressed by what he observed that he persuaded his friend Saul to participate in the Antioch mission.

11, 26: *Christians:* "Christians" is first applied to the members of the community at Antioch because the Gentile members of the community enable it to stand out clearly from Judaism.

11, 27-30: It is not clear whether the prophets from Jerusalem came to Antioch to request help in view of the coming famine or whether they received this insight during their visit there. The former supposition seems more likely. Suetonius and Tacitus speak of famines during the reign of Claudius (A.D. 41-54), while the Jewish historian Josephus mentions a famine in Judea in A.D. 46-48. Luke is interested, rather, in showing the charity of the Antiochene community toward the Jewish Christians of Jerusalem despite their differences on mixed communities.

to Antioch, [28] and one of them named Agabus stood up and predicted by the Spirit that there would be a severe famine all over the world, and it happened under Claudius.[j] [29] So the disciples determined that, according to ability,[k] each should send relief to the brothers who lived in Judea. [30] This they did, sending it to the presbyters* in care of Barnabas and Saul.

CHAPTER 12

Herod's Persecution of the Christians.*
[1] About that time King Herod laid hands upon some members of the church to harm them. [2] He had James, the brother of John,* killed by the sword, [3] and when he saw that this was pleasing to the Jews he proceeded to arrest Peter also. (It was [the] feast of Unleavened Bread.) [4] He had him taken into custody and put in prison under the guard of four squads of four soldiers each. He intended to bring him before the people after Passover.* [5] Peter thus was being kept in prison, but prayer by the church was fervently being made to God on his behalf.[l]

[6] On the very night before Herod was to bring him to trial, Peter, secured by double chains, was sleeping between two soldiers, while outside the door guards kept watch on the prison. [7] Suddenly the angel

j Acts 21, 10.—k 29-30: Acts 12, 25.—l Jas 5, 16.—m Acts 12, 25; 15, 37.—n Acts 5, 22-24.

11, 30: *Presbyters:* this is the same Greek word that elsewhere is translated "elders," primarily in reference to the Jewish community.

12, 1-19: Herod Agrippa ruled Judea A.D. 41-44. While Luke does not assign a motive for his execution of James and his intended execution of Peter, the broad background lies in Herod's support of Pharisaic Judaism. The Jewish Christians had lost the popularity they had had in Jerusalem (Acts 2, 47), perhaps because of suspicions against them traceable to the teaching of Stephen.

12, 2: *James, the brother of John:* this James, the son of Zebedee, was beheaded by Herod Agrippa ca. A.D. 44.

12, 3.4: *Feast of Unleavened Bread . . . Passover:* see the note on Lk 22, 1.

12, 17: *To James:* this James is not the son of Zebedee mentioned in v 2, but is James, the "brother of the Lord" (Gal 1, 19), who in chs 15 and 21 is presented as leader of the Jerusalem Christian community. *He left and went to another place:* the conjecture that Peter left for Rome at this time has nothing to recommend it. His chief responsibility was still the leadership of the Jewish Christian community in Palestine (see Gal 2, 7). The concept of the great missionary effort of the church was yet to come (see Acts 13, 1-3).

12, 20-23: Josephus gives a similar account of Herod's death that occurred in A.D. 44. Early Christian tradition considered the manner of it to be a divine punishment upon his evil life. See 2 Kgs 19, 35 for the figure of the angel of the Lord in such a context.

of the Lord stood by him and a light shone in the cell. He tapped Peter on the side and awakened him, saying, "Get up quickly." The chains fell from his wrists. [8] The angel said to him, "Put on your belt and your sandals." He did so. Then he said to him, "Put on your cloak and follow me." [9] So he followed him out, not realizing that what was happening through the angel was real; he thought he was seeing a vision. [10] They passed the first guard, then the second, and came to the iron gate leading out to the city, which opened for them by itself. They emerged and made their way down an alley, and suddenly the angel left him. [11] Then Peter recovered his senses and said, "Now I know for certain that [the] Lord sent his angel and rescued me from the hand of Herod and from all that the Jewish people had been expecting." [12] When he realized this, he went to the house of Mary, the mother of John who is called Mark, where there were many people gathered in prayer.[m] [13] When he knocked on the gateway door, a maid named Rhoda came to answer it. [14] She was so overjoyed when she recognized Peter's voice that, instead of opening the gate, she ran in and announced that Peter was standing at the gate. [15] They told her, "You are out of your mind," but she insisted that it was so. But they kept saying, "It is his angel." [16] But Peter continued to knock, and when they opened it, they saw him and were astounded. [17] He motioned to them with his hand to be quiet and explained [to them] how the Lord had led him out of the prison, and said, "Report this to James* and the brothers." Then he left and went to another place. [18] At daybreak there was no small commotion among the soldiers over what had become of Peter.[n] [19] Herod, after instituting a search but not finding him, ordered the guards tried and executed. Then he left Judea to spend some time in Caesarea.

Herod's Death. [20] * He had long been very angry with the people of Tyre and Sidon, who now came to him in a body. After winning over Blastus, the king's chamberlain, they sued for peace because their country was supplied with food from the king's territory. [21] On an appointed day, Herod, attired in royal robes, [and] seated on the rostrum, addressed them publicly. [22] The assembled crowd cried out, "This is the voice of a god, not of a man." [23] At once the angel of the Lord struck him down because he did not ascribe the honor to God, and he was eaten by worms and breathed his last. [24] But the word of God continued to spread and grow.[o]

Mission of Barnabas and Saul.

[25] After Barnabas and Saul completed their relief mission, they returned to Jerusalem,* taking with them John, who is called Mark.[p]

CHAPTER 13

[1] * Now there were in the church at Antioch prophets and teachers: Barnabas, Symeon who was called Niger, Lucius of Cyrene, Manaen who was a close friend of Herod the tetrarch, and Saul. [2] While they were worshiping the Lord and fasting, the holy Spirit said, "Set apart for me Barnabas and Saul for the work to which I have called them." [3] Then, completing their fasting and prayer, they laid hands on them and sent them off.

First Mission Begins in Cyprus.

[4] * So they, sent forth by the holy Spirit, went down to Seleucia and from there sailed to Cyprus. [5] When they arrived in Salamis, they proclaimed the word of God in the Jewish synagogues. They had John* also as their assistant. [6] When they had traveled through the whole island as far as Paphos, they met a magician named Bar-Jesus who was a Jewish false prophet.* [7] He was with the proconsul Sergius Paulus, a man of intelligence, who had summoned Barnabas and Saul and wanted to hear the word of God. [8] But Elymas the magician (for that is

what his name means) opposed them in an attempt to turn the proconsul away from the faith. [9] But Saul, also known as Paul,* filled with the holy Spirit, looked intently at him [10] and said, "You son of the devil, you enemy of all that is right, full of every sort of deceit and fraud. Will you not stop twisting the straight paths of [the] Lord? [11] Even now the hand of the Lord is upon you. You will be blind, and unable to see the sun for a time." Immediately a dark mist fell upon him, and he went about seeking people to lead him by the hand. [12] When the proconsul saw what had happened, he came to believe, for he was astonished by the teaching about the Lord.

Paul's Arrival at Antioch in Pisidia.

[13] From Paphos, Paul and his companions set sail and arrived at Perga in Pamphylia. But John left them and returned to Jerusalem.[q] [14] They continued on from Perga and reached Antioch in Pisidia. On the sabbath they entered [into] the synagogue and took their seats. [15] After the reading of the law and the prophets, the synagogue officials sent word to them, "My brothers, if one of you has a word of exhortation for the people, please speak."

Paul's Address in the Synagogue.

[16] * So Paul got up, motioned with his hand, and said, "Fellow Israelites and you others who are God-fearing,* listen. [17] The God of this people Israel chose our ancestors and exalted the people during their sojourn in the land of Egypt.[r] With uplifted arms he led them out of it [18] and for about forty years he put up with* them in the desert.[s] [19] When he had destroyed seven nations in the land of Canaan, he gave them their

---

o Acts 6, 7.—p Acts 11, 29-30.—q Acts 15, 38.—r Ex 6, 1.6; 12, 51.—s Ex 16, 1.35; Nm 14, 34.

12, 25: *They returned to Jerusalem:* many manuscripts read "from Jerusalem," since Acts 11, 30 implies that Paul and Barnabas are already in Jerusalem. This present verse could refer to a return visit or subsequent relief mission.

13, 1-3: The impulse for the first missionary effort in Asia Minor is ascribed to the prophets of the Antiochene community, under the inspiration of the holy Spirit. Just as the Jerusalem community had earlier been the center of missionary activity, so too Antioch becomes the center from which the missionaries Barnabas and Saul are sent out.

13, 4—14, 27: The key event in Luke's account of the first missionary journey is the experience of Paul and Barnabas at Pisidian Antioch (Acts 13, 14-52). The Christian kerygma proclaimed by Paul in the synagogue was favorably received. Some Jews and "God-fearers" (see the note on Acts 8, 26-40) became interested and invited the missionaries to speak again on the following sabbath (Acts 13, 42). By that time, however, the appearance of a large number of Gentiles from the city had so discon-

certed the Jews that they became hostile toward the apostles (Acts 13, 44-50). This hostility of theirs appears in all three accounts of Paul's missionary journeys in Acts, the Jews of Iconium (Acts 14, 1-2) and Beroea (Acts 17, 11) being notable exceptions.

13, 5: *John:* that is, John Mark (see Acts 12, 12.25).

13, 6: *A magician named Bar-Jesus who was a Jewish false prophet:* that is, he posed as a prophet. Again Luke takes the opportunity to dissociate Christianity from the magical acts of the time (7-11); see also Acts 8, 18-24.

13, 9: *Saul, also known as Paul:* there is no reason to believe that his name was changed from Saul to Paul upon his conversion. The use of a double name, one Semitic (Saul), the other Greco-Roman (Paul), is well attested (cf Acts 1, 23, Joseph Justus; Acts 12, 12.25, John Mark).

13, 16-41: This is the first of several speeches of Paul to Jews proclaiming that the Christian church is the logical development of Pharisaic Judaism (see also Acts 24, 10-21; 26, 2-23).

13, 16: *Who are God-fearing:* see the note on Acts 8, 26-40.

13, 18: *Put up with:* some manuscripts read "sustained."

land as an inheritance[t] [20] at the end of about four hundred and fifty years.* After these things he provided judges up to Samuel [the] prophet.[u] [21] Then they asked for a king. God gave them Saul, son of Kish, a man from the tribe of Benjamin, for forty years.[v] [22] Then he removed him and raised up David as their king; of him he testified, 'I have found David, son of Jesse, a man after my own heart; he will carry out my every wish.'[w] [23] From this man's descendants God, according to his promise, has brought to Israel a savior, Jesus.[x] [24] John heralded his coming by proclaiming a baptism of repentance to all the people of Israel;[y] [25] and as John was completing his course, he would say, 'What do you suppose that I am? I am not he. Behold, one is coming after me; I am not worthy to unfasten the sandals of his feet.'[z]

[26] "My brothers, children of the family of Abraham, and those others among you who are God-fearing, to us this word of salvation has been sent. [27] The inhabitants of Jerusalem and their leaders failed to recognize him, and by condemning him they fulfilled the oracles of the prophets that are read sabbath after sabbath. [28] For even

---

t Dt 7, 1; Jos 14, 1-2.—u Jgs 2, 16; 1 Sm 3, 20.—v 1 Sm 8, 5.19; 9, 16; 10, 1.20-21.24; 11, 15.—w 1 Sm 13, 14; 16, 12-13; Ps 89, 20-21.—x Is 11, 1.—y Mt 3, 1-2; Mk 1, 4-5; Lk 3, 2-3.—z Mt 3, 11; Mk 1, 7; Lk 3, 16; Jn 1, 20.27.—a Mt 27, 20.22-23; Mk 15, 13-14; Lk 23, 4.14-15. 21-23; Jn 19, 4-6.15.—b Mt 27, 59-60; Mk 15, 46; Lk 23, 53; Jn 19, 38.41-42.—c Acts 2, 24.32; 3, 15; 4, 10; 17, 31.—d Acts 1, 3.8; 10, 39.41; Mt 28, 8-10.16-20; Mk 16, 9.12-20; Lk 24, 13-53; Jn 20, 11-29; 21, 1-23.—e Ps 2, 7.—f Is 55, 3.—g Ps 16, 10.—h Acts 2, 29; 1 Kgs 2, 10.—i Rom 3, 20.—j Hb 1, 5.—k Acts 3, 26; Rom 1, 16.

13, 20: *At the end of about four hundred and fifty years:* the manuscript tradition makes it uncertain whether the mention of four hundred and fifty years refers to the sojourn in Egypt before the Exodus, the wilderness period and the time of the conquest (see Ex 12, 40-41), as the translation here suggests, or to the time between the conquest and the time of Samuel, the period of the judges, if the text is read, "After these things, for about four hundred and fifty years, he provided judges."

13, 31: The theme of the Galilean witnesses is a major one in the Gospel of Luke and in Acts and is used to signify the continuity between the teachings of Jesus and the teachings of the church and to guarantee the fidelity of the church's teachings to the words of Jesus.

13, 38-39: *Justified:* the verb is the same as that used in Paul's letters to speak of the experience of justification and, as in Paul, is here connected with the term "to have faith" ("every believer"). But this seems the only passage about Paul in Acts where justification is mentioned. In Lucan fashion it is paralleled with "forgiveness of sins" (a theme at Acts 2, 38; 3, 19; 5, 31; 10, 43) based on Jesus' resurrection (37) rather than his cross, and is put negatively (38). Therefore, some would translate, "in regard to everything from which you could not be acquitted . . . every believer is acquitted."

though they found no grounds for a death sentence, they asked Pilate to have him put to death,[a] [29] and when they had accomplished all that was written about him, they took him down from the tree and placed him in a tomb.[b] [30] But God raised him from the dead,[c] [31] and for many days he appeared to those who had come up with him from Galilee to Jerusalem.[d] These are [now] his witnesses before the people.* [32] We ourselves are proclaiming this good news to you that what God promised our ancestors [33] he has brought to fulfillment for us, [their] children, by raising up Jesus, as it is written in the second psalm, 'You are my son; this day I have begotten you.'[e] [34] And that he raised him from the dead never to return to corruption he declared in this way, 'I shall give you the benefits assured to David.'[f] [35] That is why he also says in another psalm, 'You will not suffer your holy one to see corruption.'[g] [36] Now David, after he had served the will of God in his lifetime, fell asleep, was gathered to his ancestors, and did see corruption.[h] [37] But the one whom God raised up did not see corruption. [38] You must know, my brothers, that through him forgiveness of sins is being proclaimed to you, [and] in regard to everything from which you could not be justified* under the law of Moses, [39] in him every believer is justified.[i] [40] Be careful, then, that what was said in the prophets not come about:

[41] 'Look on, you scoffers,
    be amazed and disappear.
For I am doing a work in your days,
    a work that you will never believe
    even if someone tells you.' "[j]

[42] As they were leaving, they invited them to speak on these subjects the following sabbath. [43] After the congregation had dispersed, many Jews and worshipers who were converts to Judaism followed Paul and Barnabas, who spoke to them and urged them to remain faithful to the grace of God.

Address to the Gentiles. [44] On the following sabbath almost the whole city gathered to hear the word of the Lord. [45] When the Jews saw the crowds, they were filled with jealousy and with violent abuse contradicted what Paul said. [46] [k] Both Paul and Barnabas spoke out boldly and said, "It was necessary that the word of God be

Acts

spoken to you first, but since you reject it and condemn yourselves as unworthy of eternal life, we now turn to the Gentiles.* ⁴⁷For so the Lord has commanded us, 'I have made you a light to the Gentiles, that you may be an instrument of salvation to the ends of the earth.' "ⁱ

⁴⁸The Gentiles were delighted when they heard this and glorified the word of the Lord. All who were destined for eternal life came to believe, ⁴⁹and the word of the Lord continued to spread through the whole region. ⁵⁰The Jews, however, incited the women of prominence who were worshipers and the leading men of the city, stirred up a persecution against Paul and Barnabas, and expelled them from their territory. ⁵¹ ᵐ So they shook the dust from their feet in protest against them and went to Iconium.* ⁵²The disciples were filled with joy and the holy Spirit.

CHAPTER 14

Paul and Barnabas at Iconium. ¹In Iconium they entered the Jewish synagogue together and spoke in such a way that a great number of both Jews and Greeks came to believe, ²although the disbelieving Jews stirred up and poisoned the minds of the Gentiles against the brothers. ³So they stayed for a considerable period, speaking out boldly for the Lord, who confirmed the word about his grace by granting signs and wonders to occur through their hands. ⁿ ⁴The people of the city were divided: some were with the Jews; others, with the apostles. ⁵When there was an attempt by both the Gentiles and the Jews, together with their leaders, to attack and stone them, ᵒ ⁶they realized it and fled to the Lycaonian cities of Lystra and Derbe and to the surrounding countryside, ⁷where they continued to proclaim the good news.

Paul and Barnabas at Lystra. ⁸ * At Lystra there was a crippled man, lame from birth, who had never walked. ⁹He listened to Paul speaking, who looked intently at him, saw that he had the faith to be healed, ¹⁰and called out in a loud voice, "Stand up straight on your feet." He jumped up and began to walk about. ¹¹When the crowds saw what Paul had done, they cried out in Lycaonian, "The gods have come down to us in human form." ᵖ ¹²They called Barnabas "Zeus" and Paul "Hermes,"* be-

cause he was the chief speaker. ¹³And the priest of Zeus, whose temple was at the entrance to the city, brought oxen and garlands to the gates, for he together with the people intended to offer sacrifice.

¹⁴The apostles Barnabas and Paul tore their garments* when they heard this and rushed out into the crowd, shouting, ¹⁵ * "Men, why are you doing this? We are of the same nature as you, human beings. We proclaim to you good news that you should turn from these idols to the living God, 'who made heaven and earth and sea and all that is in them.'�q ¹⁶In past generations he allowed all Gentiles to go their own ways;ʳ ¹⁷yet, in bestowing his goodness, he did not leave himself without witness, for he gave you rains from heaven and fruitful seasons, and filled you with nourishment and gladness for your hearts."ˢ ¹⁸Even with these words, they scarcely restrained the crowds from offering sacrifice to them.

¹⁹ ᵗ However, some Jews from Antioch and Iconium arrived and won over the crowds. They stoned Paul and dragged him out of the city, supposing that he was dead. ²⁰But when the disciples gathered around him, he got up and entered the city. On the following day he left with Barnabas for Derbe.

End of the First Mission. ²¹After they had proclaimed the good news to that city and

---

l Is 49, 6.—m Mt 10, 14; Mk 6, 11; Lk 9, 5; 10, 11.—n Mk 16, 17-20.—o 2 Tm 3, 11.—p Acts 28, 6.—q Acts 3, 12; 10, 26; Ex 20, 11; Ps 146, 6.—r Acts 17, 30.—s Wis 13, 1.—t 19-20: 2 Cor 11, 25; 2 Tm 3, 11.

13, 46: The refusal to believe frustrates God's plan for his chosen people; however, no adverse judgment is made here concerning their ultimate destiny. Again, Luke, in the words of Paul, speaks of the priority of Israel in the plan for salvation (see Acts 10, 36).

13, 51: See the note on Lk 9, 5.

14, 8-18: In an effort to convince his hearers that the divine power works through his word, Paul cures the cripple. However, the pagan tradition of the occasional appearance of gods among human beings leads the people astray in interpreting the miracle. The incident reveals the cultural difficulties with which the church had to cope. Note the similarity of the miracle worked here by Paul to the one performed by Peter in Acts 3, 2-10.

14, 12: *Zeus . . . Hermes:* in Greek religion, Zeus was the chief of the Olympian gods, the "father of gods and men"; Hermes was a son of Zeus and was usually identified as the herald and messenger of the gods.

14, 14: *Tore their garments:* a gesture of protest.

14, 15-17: This is the first speech of Paul to Gentiles recorded by Luke in Acts (cf Acts 17, 22-31). Rather than showing how Christianity is the logical outgrowth of Judaism, as he does in speeches before Jews, Luke says that God excuses past Gentile ignorance and then presents a natural theology arguing for the recognition of God's existence and presence through his activity in natural phenomena.

made a considerable number of disciples, they returned to Lystra and to Iconium and to Antioch. [22] They strengthened the spirits of the disciples and exhorted them to persevere in the faith, saying, "It is necessary for us to undergo many hardships to enter the kingdom of God." [u] [23] They appointed presbyters* for them in each church and, with prayer and fasting, commended them to the Lord in whom they had put their faith. [24] Then they traveled through Pisidia and reached Pamphylia. [25] After proclaiming the word at Perga they went down to Attalia. [26] From there they sailed to Antioch, where they had been commended to the grace of God for the work they had now accomplished. [v] [27] And when they arrived, they called the church together and reported what God had done with them and how he had opened the door of faith to the Gentiles. [28] Then they spent no little time with the disciples.

CHAPTER 15

Council of Jerusalem. [1] * Some who had come down from Judea were instructing the brothers, [w] "Unless you are circumcised according to the Mosaic practice, [x] you cannot be saved."* [2] Because there arose no little dissension and debate by Paul and Barnabas with them, it was decided that Paul, Barnabas, and some of the others should go up to Jerusalem to the apostles and presbyters about this question. [3] They were sent on their journey by the church, and passed through Phoenicia and Samaria telling of the conversion of the Gentiles, and brought great joy to all the brothers. [4] When they arrived in Jerusalem, they were welcomed by the church, as well as by the apostles and the presbyters, and they reported what God had done with them. [5] But some from the party of the Pharisees who had become believers stood up and said, "It is necessary to circumcise them and direct them to observe the Mosaic law."

[6] * The apostles and the presbyters met together to see about this matter. [7] * After much debate had taken place, Peter got up and said to them, "My brothers, you are well aware that from early days God made his choice among you that through my mouth the Gentiles would hear the word of the gospel and believe. [y] [8] And God, who knows the heart, bore witness by granting them the holy Spirit just as he did us. [z] [9] He made no distinction between us and them, for by faith he purified their hearts. [a] [10] Why, then, are you now putting God to the test by placing on the shoulders of the disciples a yoke that neither our ancestors nor we have been able to bear? [b] [11] On the contrary, we believe that we are saved through the grace of the Lord Jesus, [c] in the same way as they."* [12] The whole assembly fell silent, and they listened while Paul and Barnabas described the signs and wonders God had worked among the Gentiles through them.

James on Dietary Law. [13] * After they had fallen silent, James responded, "My

Acts

---

u 1 Thes 3, 3.—v Acts 13, 1-3.—w 1-4: Gal 2, 1-9.—x Lv 12, 3; Gal 5, 2.—y Acts 10, 27-43.—z Acts 10, 44-48.—a Acts 10, 34-35.—b Mt 23, 4; Gal 5, 1.—c Gal 2, 16; 3, 11; Eph 2, 5-8.

14, 23: *They appointed presbyters:* the communities are given their own religious leaders by the traveling missionaries. The structure in these churches is patterned on the model of the Jerusalem community (Acts 11, 30; 15, 2.5.22; 21, 18).

15, 1-35: The Jerusalem "Council" marks the official rejection of the rigid view that Gentile converts were obliged to observe the Mosaic law completely. From here to the end of Acts, Paul and the Gentile mission become the focus of Luke's writing.

15, 1-5: When some of the converted Pharisees of Jerusalem discover the results of the first missionary journey of Paul, they urge that the Gentiles be taught to follow the Mosaic law. Recognizing the authority of the Jerusalem church, Paul and Barnabas go there to settle the question of whether Gentiles can embrace a form of Christianity that does not include this obligation.

15, 6-12: The gathering is possibly the same as that recalled by Paul in Gal 2, 1-10. Note that in v 2 it is only the apostles and presbyters, a small group, with whom Paul and Barnabas are to meet. Here Luke gives the meeting a public character because he wishes to emphasize its doctrinal significance (see Acts 15, 22).

15, 7-11: Paul's refusal to impose the Mosaic law on the Gentile Christians is supported by James on the ground that within his own experience God bestowed the holy Spirit upon Cornelius and his household without preconditions concerning the adoption of the Mosaic law (see Acts 10, 44-47).

15, 11: In support of Paul, Peter formulates the fundamental meaning of the gospel: that all are invited to be saved through faith in the power of Christ.

15, 13-35: Some scholars think that this apostolic decree suggested by James, the immediate leader of the Jerusalem community, derives from another historical occasion than the meeting in question. This seems to be the case if the meeting is the same as the one related in Gal 2, 1-10. According to that account, nothing was imposed upon Gentile Christians in respect to Mosaic law; whereas the decree instructs Gentile Christians of mixed communities to abstain from meats sacrificed to idols and from bloodmeats, and to avoid marriage within forbidden degrees of consanguinity and affinity (Lv 18), all of which practices were especially abhorrent to Jews. Luke seems to have telescoped two originally independent incidents here: the first a Jerusalem "Council" that dealt with the question of circumcision, and the second a Jerusalem decree dealing mainly with Gentile observance of dietary laws (see Acts 21, 25 where Paul seems to be learning of the decree for the first time).

brothers, listen to me. [14] Symeon* has described how God first concerned himself with acquiring from among the Gentiles a people for his name. [15] The words of the prophets agree with this, as is written:

[16] 'After this I shall return[d]
    and rebuild the fallen hut of David;
    from its ruins I shall rebuild it
    and raise it up again,
[17] so that the rest of humanity may seek
    out the Lord,
    even all the Gentiles on whom my
    name is invoked.
Thus says the Lord who accomplishes
    these things,
[18]   known from of old.'

[19] [e] It is my judgment, therefore, that we ought to stop troubling the Gentiles who turn to God, [20] but tell them by letter to avoid pollution from idols, unlawful marriage, the meat of strangled animals, and blood.[f] [21] For Moses, for generations now, has had those who proclaim him in every town, as he has been read in the synagogues every sabbath."

Letter of the Apostles. [22] Then the apostles and presbyters, in agreement with the whole church, decided to choose representatives and to send them to Antioch with Paul and Barnabas. The ones chosen were Judas, who was called Barsabbas, and Silas, leaders among the brothers. [23] This is the letter delivered by them: "The apostles and the presbyters, your brothers, to the brothers in Antioch, Syria, and Cilicia of Gentile origin: greetings. [24] Since we have heard that some of our number [who went out] without any mandate from us have upset you with their teachings and disturbed your peace of mind, [25] we have with one accord decided to choose representatives and to send them to you along with our beloved Barnabas and Paul, [26] who have dedicated their lives to the name of our Lord Jesus Christ. [27] So we are sending Judas and Silas who will also convey this same message by word of mouth: [28] [g] 'It is the decision of the holy Spirit and of us not to place on you any burden beyond these necessities, [29] namely, to abstain from meat sacrificed to idols, from blood, from meats of strangled animals, and from unlawful marriage. If you keep free of these, you will be doing what is right. Farewell.' "[h]

Delegates at Antioch. [30] And so they were sent on their journey. Upon their arrival in Antioch they called the assembly together and delivered the letter. [31] When the people read it, they were delighted with the exhortation. [32] Judas and Silas, who were themselves prophets, exhorted and strengthened the brothers with many words. [33] After they had spent some time there, they were sent off with greetings of peace from the brothers to those who had commissioned them. [34] * [35] But Paul and Barnabas remained in Antioch, teaching and proclaiming with many others the word of the Lord.

V. THE MISSION OF PAUL TO THE ENDS OF THE EARTH

Paul and Barnabas Separate. [36] * After some time, Paul said to Barnabas, "Come, let us make a return visit to see how the brothers are getting on in all the cities where we proclaimed the word of the Lord." [37] Barnabas wanted to take with them also John, who was called Mark, [38] but Paul insisted that they should not take with them someone who had deserted them at Pamphylia and who had not continued with them in their work.[i] [39] So sharp was their disagreement that they separated. Barnabas took Mark and sailed to Cyprus. [40] But Paul chose Silas and departed after being commended by the brothers to the grace of the Lord. [41] He traveled through Syria and Cilicia bringing strength to the churches.

---

d 16-17: Am 9, 11-12.—e 19-20: Acts 15, 28-29; 21, 25.—f Gn 9, 4; Lv 3, 17; 17, 10-14.—g 28-29: Acts 15, 19-20.—h Gn 9, 4; Lv 3, 17; 17, 10-14.—i Acts 13, 13.

15, 14: *Symeon:* elsewhere in Acts he is called either Peter or Simon. The presence of the name Symeon here suggests that, in the source Luke is using for this part of the Jerusalem "Council" incident, the name may have originally referred to someone other than Peter (see Acts 13, 1 where the Antiochene Symeon Niger is mentioned). As the text now stands, however, it is undoubtedly a reference to Simon Peter (7).

15, 34: Some manuscripts add, in various wordings, "But Silas decided to remain there."

15, 36—18, 22: This continuous narrative recounts Paul's second missionary journey. On the internal evidence of the Lucan account, it lasted about three years. Paul first visited the communities he had established on his first journey (Acts 16, 1-5), then pushed on into Macedonia, where he established communities at Philippi, Thessalonica, and Beroea (Acts 16, 7—17, 5). To escape the hostility of the Jews of Thessalonica, he left for Greece and while resident in Athens attempted, without success, to establish an effective Christian community there. From Athens he proceeded to Corinth and, after a stay of a year and a half, returned to Antioch by way of Ephesus and Jerusalem (Acts 17, 16—18, 22). Luke does not concern himself with the structure or statistics of the communities but aims to show the general progress of the gospel in the Gentile world as well as its continued failure to take root in the Jewish community.

CHAPTER 16

Paul in Lycaonia: Timothy. ¹He reached [also] Derbe and Lystra where there was a disciple named Timothy, the son of a Jewish woman who was a believer, but his father was a Greek.ʲ ²The brothers in Lystra and Iconium spoke highly of him,ᵏ ³and Paul wanted him to come along with him. On account of the Jews of that region, Paul had him circumcised,* for they all knew that his father was a Greek. ⁴As they traveled from city to city, they handed on to the people for observance the decisions reached by the apostles and presbyters in Jerusalem. ⁵Day after day the churches grew stronger in faith and increased in number.

Through Asia Minor. ⁶They traveled through the Phrygian and Galatian territory because they had been prevented by the holy Spirit from preaching the message in the province of Asia. ⁷When they came to Mysia, they tried to go on into Bithynia, but the Spirit of Jesus* did not allow them, ⁸so they crossed through Mysia and came down to Troas. ⁹During [the] night Paul had a vision. A Macedonian stood before him and implored him with these words, "Come over to Macedonia and help us."

j 1 Tm 1, 2; 2 Tm 1, 5.—k Phil 2, 20.—l 22-23: 2 Cor 11, 25; Phil 1, 30; 1 Thes 2, 2.

16, 3: *Paul had him circumcised:* he did this in order that Timothy might be able to associate with the Jews and so perform a ministry among them. Paul did not object to the Jewish Christians' adherence to the law. But he insisted that the law could not be imposed on the Gentiles. Paul himself lived in accordance with the law, or as exempt from the law, according to particular circumstances (see 1 Cor 9, 19-23).

16, 7: *The Spirit of Jesus:* this is an unusual formulation in Luke's writings. The parallelism with v 6 indicates its meaning, the holy Spirit.

16, 10-17: This is the first of the so-called "we-sections" in Acts, where Luke writes as one of Paul's companions. The other passages are Acts 20, 5-15; 21, 1-18; 27, 1—28, 16. Scholars debate whether Luke may not have used the first person plural simply as a literary device to lend color to the narrative. The realism of the narrative, however, lends weight to the argument that the "we" includes Luke or another companion of Paul whose data Luke used as a source.

16, 11-40: The church at Philippi became a flourishing community to which Paul addressed one of his letters (see Introduction to the Letter to the Philippians).

16, 14: *A worshiper of God:* a "God-fearer." See the note on Acts 8, 26-40.

16, 16: *With an oracular spirit:* literally, "with a Python spirit." The Python was the serpent or dragon that guarded the Delphic oracle. It later came to designate a "spirit that pronounced oracles" and also a ventriloquist who, it was thought, had such a spirit in the belly.

16, 20: *Magistrates:* in Greek, *stratēgoi,* the popular designation of the *duoviri,* the highest officials of the Roman colony of Philippi.

¹⁰When he had seen the vision, we* sought passage to Macedonia at once, concluding that God had called us to proclaim the good news to them.

Into Europe. ¹¹ * We set sail from Troas, making a straight run for Samothrace, and on the next day to Neapolis, ¹²and from there to Philippi, a leading city in that district of Macedonia and a Roman colony. We spent some time in that city.¹³On the sabbath we went outside the city gate along the river where we thought there would be a place of prayer. We sat and spoke with the women who had gathered there. ¹⁴One of them, a woman named Lydia, a dealer in purple cloth, from the city of Thyatira, a worshiper of God,* listened, and the Lord opened her heart to pay attention to what Paul was saying. ¹⁵After she and her household had been baptized, she offered us an invitation, "If you consider me a believer in the Lord, come and stay at my home," and she prevailed on us.

Imprisonment at Philippi. ¹⁶As we were going to the place of prayer, we met a slave girl with an oracular spirit,* who used to bring a large profit to her owners through her fortune-telling. ¹⁷She began to follow Paul and us, shouting, "These people are slaves of the Most High God, who proclaim to you a way of salvation." ¹⁸She did this for many days. Paul became annoyed, turned, and said to the spirit, "I command you in the name of Jesus Christ to come out of her." Then it came out at that moment.

¹⁹When her owners saw that their hope of profit was gone, they seized Paul and Silas and dragged them to the public square before the local authorities. ²⁰They brought them before the magistrates* and said, "These people are Jews and are disturbing our city ²¹and are advocating customs that are not lawful for us Romans to adopt or practice." ²² ˡ The crowd joined in the attack on them, and the magistrates had them stripped and ordered them to be beaten with rods. ²³After inflicting many blows on them, they threw them into prison and instructed the jailer to guard them securely. ²⁴When he received these instructions, he put them in the innermost cell and secured their feet to a stake.

Deliverance from Prison. ²⁵About midnight, while Paul and Silas were praying and singing hymns to God as the prisoners

Acts

listened, [26] there was suddenly such a severe earthquake that the foundations of the jail shook; all the doors flew open, and the chains of all were pulled loose. [27] When the jailer woke up and saw the prison doors wide open, he drew [his] sword and was about to kill himself, thinking that the prisoners had escaped. [28] But Paul shouted out in a loud voice, "Do no harm to yourself; we are all here." [29] He asked for a light and rushed in and, trembling with fear, he fell down before Paul and Silas. [30] Then he brought them out and said, "Sirs, what must I do to be saved?" [31] And they said, "Believe in the Lord Jesus and you and your household will be saved." [32] So they spoke the word of the Lord to him and to everyone in his house. [33] He took them in at that hour of the night and bathed their wounds; then he and all his family were baptized at once. [34] He brought them up into his house and provided a meal and with his household rejoiced at having come to faith in God.

[35] But when it was day, the magistrates sent the lictors* with the order, "Release those men." [36] The jailer reported the[se] words to Paul, "The magistrates have sent orders that you be released. Now, then, come out and go in peace." [37] But Paul said to them, "They have beaten us publicly, even though we are Roman citizens and have not been tried, and have thrown us into prison.[m] And now, are they going to release us secretly? By no means. Let them come themselves and lead us out."* [38] The lictors reported these words to the magistrates, and they became alarmed when they heard that they were Roman citizens.[n] [39] So they came and placated them, and led them out and asked that they leave the city. [40] When they had come out of the prison, they went to Lydia's house where they saw and encouraged the brothers, and then they left.

CHAPTER 17

Paul in Thessalonica. [1] When they took the road through Amphipolis and Apollonia, they reached Thessalonica, where there was a synagogue of the Jews.[o] [2] Following his usual custom, Paul joined them, and for three sabbaths he entered into discussions with them from the scriptures, [3] expounding and demonstrating that the Messiah had to suffer and rise from the

dead, and that "This is the Messiah, Jesus, whom I proclaim to you."[p] [4] Some of them were convinced and joined Paul and Silas; so, too, a great number of Greeks who were worshipers, and not a few of the prominent women. [5] But the Jews became jealous and recruited some worthless men loitering in the public square, formed a mob, and set the city in turmoil. They marched on the house of Jason,[q] intending to bring them before the people's assembly. [6] * When they could not find them, they dragged Jason and some of the brothers before the city magistrates, shouting, "These people who have been creating a disturbance all over the world have now come here, [7] and Jason has welcomed them.[r] They all act in opposition to the decrees of Caesar and claim instead that there is another king, Jesus."* [8] They stirred up the crowd and the city magistrates who, upon hearing these charges, [9] took a surety payment from Jason and the others before releasing them.

Paul in Beroea. [10] The brothers immediately sent Paul and Silas to Beroea during the night. Upon arrival they went to the synagogue of the Jews. [11] These Jews were more fair-minded than those in Thessalonica, for they received the word with all willingness and examined the scriptures daily to determine whether these things were so.[s] [12] Many of them became believers, as did not a few of the influential Greek women and men. [13] But when the Jews of Thessalonica learned that the word of God had now been proclaimed by Paul in Beroea also, they came there too to cause a commotion and stir up the crowds. [14] So the brothers at once sent Paul on his way to the seacoast, while Silas and Timothy remained behind.[t] [15] After Paul's escorts had taken him to Athens, they came away with instructions for Silas and Timothy to join him as soon as possible.

---

m Acts 22, 25.—n Acts 22, 29.—o 1 Thes 2, 1-2.—p Acts 3, 18; Lk 24, 25-26.46.—q Rom 16, 21.—r Lk 23, 2; Jn 19, 12-15.—s Jn 5, 39.—t 1 Thes 3, 1-2.

16, 35: *The lictors:* the equivalent of police officers, among whose duties were the apprehension and punishment of criminals.

16, 37: *Paul's Roman citizenship* granted him special privileges in regard to criminal process. Roman law forbade under severe penalty the beating of Roman citizens (see also Acts 22, 25).

17, 6-7: The accusations against Paul and his companions echo the charges brought against Jesus in Lk 23, 2.

17, 7: *There is another king, Jesus:* a distortion into a political sense of the apostolic proclamation of Jesus and the kingdom of God (see Acts 8, 12).

Paul in Athens.* [16]While Paul was waiting for them in Athens, he grew exasperated at the sight of the city full of idols. [17]So he debated in the synagogue with the Jews and with the worshipers, and daily in the public square with whoever happened to be there. [18]Even some of the Epicurean and Stoic philosophers* engaged him in discussion. Some asked, "What is this scavenger trying to say?" Others said, "He sounds like a promoter of foreign deities," because he was preaching about 'Jesus' and 'Resurrection.' [19]They took him and led him to the Areopagus* and said, "May we learn what this new teaching is that you speak of? [u] [20]For you bring some strange notions to our ears; we should like to know what these things mean." [21]Now all the Athenians as well as the foreigners residing there used their time for nothing else but telling or hearing something new.

Paul's Speech at the Areopagus. [22]Then Paul stood up at the Areopagus and said:*

"You Athenians, I see that in every respect you are very religious. [23]For as I walked around looking carefully at your shrines, I even discovered an altar inscribed, 'To an Unknown God.'* What therefore you unknowingly worship, I proclaim to you. [24]The God who made the world and all that is in it, the Lord of heaven and earth, does not dwell in sanctuaries made by human hands, [v] [25]nor is he served by human hands because he needs anything. Rather it is he who gives to everyone life and breath and everything. [26]He made from one* the whole human race to dwell on the entire surface of the earth, and he fixed the ordered seasons and the boundaries of their regions, [27]so that people might seek God, even perhaps grope for him and find him, though indeed he is not far from any one of us. [w] [28]For 'In him we live and move and have our being,'* as even some of your poets have said, 'For we too are his offspring.' [29]Since therefore we are the offspring of God, we ought not to think that the divinity is like an image fashioned from gold, silver, or stone by human art and imagination. [x] [30]God has overlooked the times of ignorance, but now he demands that all people everywhere repent [31]because he has established a day on which he will 'judge the world with justice' through a man he has appointed, and he has provided confirmation for all by raising him from the dead." [y]

[32]When they heard about resurrection of the dead, some began to scoff, but others said, "We should like to hear you on this some other time." [33]And so Paul left them. [34]But some did join him, and became believers. Among them were Dionysius, a member of the Court of the Areopagus, a woman named Damaris, and others with them.

---

u 1 Cor 1, 22.—v Acts 7, 48-50; Gn 1, 1; 1 Kgs 8, 27; Is 42, 5.—w Jer 23, 23; Wis 13, 6; Rom 1, 19.—x Acts 19, 26; Is 40, 18-20; 44, 10-17; Rom 1, 22-23.—y Acts 10, 42.

17, 16-21: Paul's presence in Athens sets the stage for the great discourse before a Gentile audience in vv 22-31. Although Athens was a politically insignificant city at this period, it still lived on the glories of its past and represented the center of Greek culture. The setting describes the conflict between Christian preaching and Hellenistic philosophy.

17, 18: *Epicurean and Stoic philosophers:* for the followers of Epicurus (342-271 B.C.), the goal of life was happiness attained through sober reasoning and the searching out of motives for all choice and avoidance. The Stoics were followers of Zeno, a younger contemporary of Alexander the Great. Zeno and his followers believed in a type of pantheism that held that the spark of divinity was present in all reality and that, in order to be free, each person must live "according to nature." *This scavenger:* literally, "seed-picker," as of a bird that picks up grain. The word is later used of scrap collectors and of people who take other people's ideas and propagate them as if they were their own. *Promoter of foreign deities:* according to Xenophon, Socrates was accused of promoting new deities. The accusation against Paul echoes the charge against Socrates. *'Jesus' and 'Resurrection':* the Athenians are presented as misunderstanding Paul from the outset; they think he is preaching about Jesus and a goddess named *Anastasis,* i.e., Resurrection.

17, 19: *To the Areopagus:* the "Areopagus" refers either to the Hill of Ares west of the Acropolis or to the Council of Athens, which at one time met on the hill but which at this time assembled in the Royal Colonnade (*Stoa Basileios*).

17, 22-31: In Paul's appearance at the Areopagus he preaches his climactic speech to Gentiles in the cultural center of the ancient world. The speech is more theological than christological. Paul's discourse appeals to the Greek world's belief in divinity as responsible for the origin and existence of the universe. It contests the common belief in a multiplicity of gods supposedly exerting their powers through their images. It acknowledges that the attempt to find God is a constant human endeavor. It declares, further, that God is the judge of the human race, that the time of the judgment has been determined, and that it will be executed through a man whom God raised from the dead. The speech reflects sympathy with pagan religiosity, handles the subject of idol worship gently, and appeals for a new examination of divinity, not from the standpoint of creation but from the standpoint of judgment.

17, 23: *'To an Unknown God':* ancient authors such as Pausanias, Philostratus, and Tertullian speak of Athenian altars with no specific dedication as altars of "unknown gods" or "nameless altars."

17, 26: *From one:* many manuscripts read "from one blood." *Fixed . . . seasons:* or "fixed limits to the epochs."

17, 28: *'In him we live and move and have our being':* some scholars understand this saying to be based on an earlier saying of Epimenides of Knossos (6th century B.C.). *'For we too are his offspring':* here Paul is quoting Aratus of Soli, a third-century B.C. poet from Cilicia.

Acts

CHAPTER 18

Paul in Corinth. [1] After this he left Athens and went to Corinth. [2] There he met a Jew named Aquila,ᶻ a native of Pontus, who had recently come from Italy with his wife Priscilla* because Claudius had ordered all the Jews to leave Rome. He went to visit them [3] and, because he practiced the same trade, stayed with them and worked, for they were tentmakers by trade. [4] Every sabbath, he entered into discussions in the synagogue, attempting to convince both Jews and Greeks.

[5] When Silas and Timothy came down from Macedonia, Paul began to occupy himself totally with preaching the word, testifying to the Jews that the Messiah was Jesus. [6] When they opposed him and reviled him, he shook out his garments* and said to them, "Your blood be on your heads! I am clear of responsibility. From now on I will go to the Gentiles."ᵃ [7] So he left there and went to a house belonging to a man named Titus Justus, a worshiper of God;* his house was next to a synagogue.ᵇ [8] Crispus,* the synagogue official,ᶜ came to believe in the Lord along with his entire household, and many of the Corinthians who heard believed and were baptized. [9] ᵈ One night in a vision the Lord said to Paul, "Do not be afraid. Go on speaking, and do not be silent, [10] for I am with you. No one will attack and harm you, for I have many people in this city." [11] He settled there for a year and a half and taught the word of God among them.

Accusations before Gallio. [12] But when Gallio was proconsul of Achaia,* the Jews rose up together against Paul and brought him to the tribunal, [13] saying, "This man is inducing people to worship God contrary to the law."* [14] When Paul was about to reply, Gallio spoke to the Jews, "If it were a matter of some crime or malicious fraud, I should with reason hear the complaint of you Jews; [15] but since it is a question of arguments over doctrine and titles and your own law, see to it yourselves. I do not wish to be a judge of such matters." [16] And he drove them away from the tribunal. [17] They all seized Sosthenes, the synagogue official, and beat him in full view of the tribunal. But none of this was of concern to Gallio.

Return to Syrian Antioch. [18] Paul remained for quite some time, and after saying farewell to the brothers he sailed for Syria, together with Priscilla and Aquila. At Cenchreae he had his hair cutᵉ because he had taken a vow.* [19] When they reached Ephesus, he left them there, while he entered the synagogue and held discussions with the Jews. [20] Although they asked him to stay for a longer time, he did not consent, [21] but as he said farewell he promised, "I shall come back to you again, God willing." Then he set sail from Ephesus. [22] Upon landing at Caesarea, he went up and greeted the church* and then went down to Antioch. [23] *. After staying there some time, he left and traveled in orderly sequence through the Galatian country and Phrygia, bringing strength to all the disciples.

Apollos. [24] A Jew named Apollos,ᶠ a native of Alexandria, an eloquent speaker, arrived in Ephesus. He was an authority on the scriptures.* [25] He had been instructed in the Way of the Lord and, with ardent spirit, spoke and taught, accurately Jesus, although he knew only the baptism

z Rom 16, 3.—a Acts 13, 51; Mt 10, 14; 27, 24-25; Mk 6, 11; Lk 9, 5; 10, 10-11.—b Acts 13, 46-47; 28, 28.—c 1 Cor 1, 14.—d 9-10: Jer 1, 8.—e Acts 21, 24; Nm 6, 18.—f 1 Cor 1, 12.

18, 2: *Aquila . . . Priscilla:* both may already have been Christians at the time of their arrival in Corinth (see Acts 18, 26). According to 1 Cor 16, 19, their home became a meeting place for Christians. *Claudius:* the Emperor Claudius expelled the Jews from Rome ca. A.D. 40. The Roman historian Suetonius gives as reason for the expulsion disturbances among the Jews "at the instigation of Chrestos," probably meaning disputes about the messiahship of Jesus.

18, 6: *Shook out his garments:* a gesture indicating Paul's repudiation of his mission to the Jews there; cf Acts 28, 17-31.

18, 7: *A worshiper of God:* see the note on Acts 8, 26-40.

18, 8: *Crispus:* in 1 Cor 1, 14, Paul mentions that Crispus was one of the few he himself baptized at Corinth.

18, 12: *When Gallio was proconsul of Achaia:* Gallio's proconsulship in Achaia is dated to A.D. 51-52 from an inscription discovered at Delphi. This has become an important date in establishing a chronology of the life and missionary work of Paul.

18, 13: *Contrary to the law:* Gallio (15) understands this to be a problem of Jewish, not Roman, law.

18, 18: *He had his hair cut because he had taken a vow:* a reference to a Nazirite vow (see Nm 6, 1-21, especially, 6, 18) taken by Paul (see also Acts 21, 23-27).

18, 22: *He went up and greeted the church:* "going up" suggests a visit to the church in Jerusalem.

18, 23—21, 16: Luke's account of Paul's third missionary journey devotes itself mainly to his work at Ephesus (Acts 19, 1—20, 1). There is a certain restiveness on Paul's part and a growing conviction that the Spirit bids him return to Jerusalem and prepare to go to Rome (Acts 19, 21).

18, 24-25: Apollos appears as a preacher who knows the teaching of Jesus in the context of John's baptism of repentance. Aquila and Priscilla instruct him more fully. He is referred to in 1 Cor 1, 12; 3, 5-6.22.

of John. ²⁶ He began to speak boldly in the synagogue; but when Priscilla and Aquila heard him, they took him aside and explained to him the Way [of God]* more accurately. ²⁷ And when he wanted to cross to Achaia, the brothers encouraged him and wrote to the disciples there to welcome him. After his arrival he gave great assistance to those who had come to believe through grace. ²⁸ He vigorously refuted the Jews in public, establishing from the scriptures that the Messiah is Jesus.

CHAPTER 19

Paul in Ephesus. ¹ * While Apollos was in Corinth, Paul traveled through the interior of the country and came [down] to Ephesus where he found some disciples. ² He said to them, "Did you receive the holy Spirit when you became believers?" They answered him, "We have never even heard that there is a holy Spirit." ³ He said, "How were you baptized?" They replied, "With the baptism of John." ⁴ Paul then said, "John baptized with a baptism of repentance, telling the people to believe in the one who was to come after him, that is, in Jesus." ^g ⁵ When they heard this, they were baptized in the name of the Lord Jesus. ⁶ And when Paul laid [his] hands on them, the holy Spirit came upon them, and they spoke in tongues and prophesied. ^h ⁷ Altogether there were about twelve men.

⁸ He entered the synagogue, and for three months debated boldly with persuasive arguments about the kingdom of God. ⁹ But when some in their obstinacy and disbelief disparaged the Way before the assembly, he withdrew and took his disciples with him and began to hold daily discussions in the lecture hall of Tyrannus.

---

g Acts 1, 5; 11, 16; 13, 24-25; Mt 3, 11; Mk 1, 8; Lk 3, 16.—h Acts 8, 15-17; 10, 44.46.—i Acts 5, 15-16; Lk 8, 44-47.—j Acts 23, 11; Rom 1, 13; 15, 22-32.

18, 26: *The Way [of God]:* for the Way, see the note on Acts 9, 2. Other manuscripts here read "the Way of the Lord," "the word of the Lord," or simply "the Way."

19, 1-6: Upon his arrival in Ephesus, Paul discovers other people at the same religious stage as Apollos, though they seem to have considered themselves followers of Christ, not of the Baptist. On the relation between baptism and the reception of the Spirit, see the note on Acts 8, 16.

19, 24: *Miniature silver shrines of Artemis:* the temple of Artemis at Ephesus was one of the seven wonders of the ancient world. Artemis, originally the Olympian virgin hunter, moon goddess, and goddess of wild nature, was worshiped at Ephesus as an Asian mother goddess and goddess of fertility. She was one of the most widely worshiped female deities in the Hellenistic world (see Acts 18, 27).

¹⁰ This continued for two years with the result that all the inhabitants of the province of Asia heard the word of the Lord, Jews and Greeks alike. ¹¹ So extraordinary were the mighty deeds God accomplished at the hands of Paul ¹² that when face cloths or aprons that touched his skin were applied to the sick, their diseases left them and the evil spirits came out of them. ⁱ

The Jewish Exorcists. ¹³ Then some itinerant Jewish exorcists tried to invoke the name of the Lord Jesus over those with evil spirits, saying, "I adjure you by the Jesus whom Paul preaches." ¹⁴ When the seven sons of Sceva, a Jewish high priest, tried to do this, ¹⁵ the evil spirit said to them in reply, "Jesus I recognize, Paul I know, but who are you?" ¹⁶ The person with the evil spirit then sprang at them and subdued them all. He so overpowered them that they fled naked and wounded from that house. ¹⁷ When this became known to all the Jews and Greeks who lived in Ephesus, fear fell upon them all, and the name of the Lord Jesus was held in great esteem. ¹⁸ Many of those who had become believers came forward and openly acknowledged their former practices. ¹⁹ Moreover, a large number of those who had practiced magic collected their books and burned them in public. They calculated their value and found it to be fifty thousand silver pieces. ²⁰ Thus did the word of the Lord continue to spread with influence and power.

Paul's Plans. ²¹ When this was concluded, Paul made up his mind to travel through Macedonia and Achaia, and then to go on to Jerusalem, saying, "After I have been there, I must visit Rome also." ^j ²² Then he sent to Macedonia two of his assistants, Timothy and Erastus, while he himself stayed for a while in the province of Asia.

The Riot of the Silversmiths. ²³ About that time a serious disturbance broke out concerning the Way. ²⁴ There was a silversmith named Demetrius who made miniature silver shrines of Artemis* and provided no little work for the craftsmen. ²⁵ He called a meeting of these and other workers in related crafts and said, "Men, you know well that our prosperity derives from this work. ²⁶ As you can now see and hear, not only in Ephesus but throughout most of the province of Asia this Paul has persuaded and misled a great number of people by saying that gods made by hands are not gods at all. *k* ²⁷The danger grows, not only that our business will be discredited, but also that the temple of the great goddess Artemis will be of no account, and that she whom the whole province of Asia and all the world worship will be stripped of her magnificence."

²⁸When they heard this, they were filled with fury and began to shout, "Great is Artemis of the Ephesians!" ²⁹The city was filled with confusion, and the people rushed with one accord into the theater, seizing Gaius and Aristarchus, the Macedonians, Paul's traveling companions.*l* ³⁰Paul wanted to go before the crowd, but the disciples would not let him, ³¹and even some of the Asiarchs* who were friends of his sent word to him advising him not to venture into the theater. ³²Meanwhile, some were shouting one thing, others something else; the assembly was in chaos, and most of the people had no idea why they had come together. ³³Some of the crowd prompted Alexander, as the Jews pushed him forward, and Alexander signaled with his hand that he wished to explain something to the gathering. ³⁴But when they recognized that he was a Jew, they all shouted in unison, for about two hours, "Great is Artemis of the Ephesians!" ³⁵Finally the town clerk restrained the crowd and said, "You Ephesians, what person is there who does not know that the city of the Ephesians is the guardian of the temple* of the great Artemis and of her image that fell from the sky? ³⁶Since these things are undeniable, you must calm yourselves and not do anything rash. ³⁷The men you brought here are not temple robbers, nor have they insulted our goddess. ³⁸If Demetrius and his fellow craftsmen have a complaint against anyone, courts are in session, and there are proconsuls. Let them bring charges against one another. ³⁹If you have anything

further to investigate, let the matter be settled in the lawful assembly, ⁴⁰for, as it is, we are in danger of being charged with rioting because of today's conduct. There is no cause for it. We shall [not]* be able to give a reason for this demonstration." With these words he dismissed the assembly.

CHAPTER 20

Journey to Macedonia and Greece. ¹When the disturbance was over, Paul had the disciples summoned and, after encouraging them, he bade them farewell and set out on his journey to Macedonia.*m* ²As he traveled throughout those regions, he provided many words of encouragement for them. Then he arrived in Greece, ³where he stayed for three months. But when a plot was made against him by the Jews as he was about to set sail for Syria, he decided to return by way of Macedonia.

Return to Troas. ⁴ *n* Sopater, the son of Pyrrhus, from Beroea, accompanied him, as did Aristarchus and Secundus from Thessalonica, Gaius from Derbe, Timothy, and Tychicus and Trophimus from Asia ⁵who went on ahead and waited for us* at Troas.*o* ⁶We sailed from Philippi after the feast of Unleavened Bread,* and rejoined them five days later in Troas, where we spent a week.

Eutychus Restored to Life. ⁷On the first day of the week* when we gathered to break bread, Paul spoke to them because he was going to leave on the next day, and he kept on speaking until midnight. ⁸There were many lamps in the upstairs room where we were gathered, ⁹and a young man named Eutychus who was sitting on the window sill was sinking into a deep sleep as Paul talked on and on. Once overcome by sleep, he fell down from the third story and when he was picked up, he was dead. ¹⁰ *p* Paul went down,* threw

---

k Acts 17, 29.—l Col 4, 10.—m 1 Cor 16, 1.—n Rom 16, 21.—o Acts 21, 29; 2 Tm 4, 20.—p 1 Kgs 17, 17-24; 2 Kgs 4, 30-37; Mt 9, 24; Mk 5, 39; Lk 8, 52.

19, 31: *Asiarchs:* the precise status and role of the Asiarchs is disputed. They appear to have been people of wealth and influence who promoted the Roman imperial cult and who may also have been political representatives in a league of cities in the Roman province of Asia.

19, 35: *Guardian of the temple:* this title was accorded by Rome to cities that provided a temple for the imperial cult. Inscriptional evidence indicates that Ephesus was acknowledged as the temple keeper of Artemis and of the imperial cult. *That fell from the sky:* many scholars think that this refers to a meteorite that was worshiped as an image of the goddess.

19, 40: Some manuscripts omit the negative in *[not] be able,* making the meaning, "There is no cause for which we shall be able to give a reason for this demonstration."

20, 5: The second "we-section" of Acts begins here. See the note on Acts 16, 10-17.

20, 6: *Feast of Unleavened Bread:* see the note on Lk 22, 1.

20, 7: *The first day of the week:* the day after the sabbath and the first day of the Jewish week, apparently chosen originally by the Jerusalem community for the celebration of the liturgy of the Eucharist in order to relate it to the resurrection of Christ.

20, 10: The action of Paul in throwing himself upon the dead boy recalls that of Elijah in 1 Kgs 17, 21 where the son of the widow of Zarephath is revived and that of Elisha in 2 Kgs 4, 34 where the Shunamite woman's son is restored to life.

himself upon him, and said as he embraced him, "Don't be alarmed; there is life in him." [11] Then he returned upstairs, broke the bread, and ate; after a long conversation that lasted until daybreak, he departed. [12] And they took the boy away alive and were immeasurably comforted.

Journey to Miletus. [13] We went ahead to the ship and set sail for Assos where we were to take Paul on board, as he had arranged, since he was going overland. [14] When he met us in Assos, we took him aboard and went on to Mitylene. [15] We sailed away from there on the next day and reached a point off Chios, and a day later we reached Samos, and on the following day we arrived at Miletus. [16] * Paul had decided to sail past Ephesus in order not to lose time in the province of Asia, for he was hurrying to be in Jerusalem, if at all possible, for the day of Pentecost.

Paul's Farewell Speech at Miletus. [17] From Miletus he had the presbyters of the church at Ephesus summoned. [18] When they came to him, he addressed them, "You know how I lived among you the whole time from the day I first came to the province of Asia. [19] I served the Lord with all humility and with the tears and trials that came to me because of the plots of the Jews, [20] and I did not at all shrink from telling you what was for your benefit, or from teaching you in public or in your homes. [21] I earnestly bore witness for both Jews and Greeks to repentance before God and to faith in our Lord Jesus. [22] But now, compelled by the Spirit, I am going to Jerusalem. What will happen to me there I do not know, [23] except that in one city after another the holy Spirit has been warning me that imprisonment and hardships await me.[q] [24] Yet I consider life of no importance to me, if only I may finish my course and the ministry that I received from the Lord Jesus, to bear witness to the gospel of God's grace.[r]

[25] "But now I know that none of you to whom I preached the kingdom during my travels will ever see my face again. [26] And so I solemnly declare to you this day that I am not responsible for the blood of any of you, [27] for I did not shrink from proclaiming to you the entire plan of God. [28] [s] Keep watch over yourselves and over the whole flock of which the holy Spirit has appointed you overseers,* in which you tend the church of God that he acquired with his own blood. [29] I know that after my departure savage wolves will come among you, and they will not spare the flock.[t] [30] And from your own group, men will come forward perverting the truth to draw the disciples away after them.[u] [31] So be vigilant and remember that for three years, night and day, I unceasingly admonished each of you with tears.[v] [32] And now I commend you to God and to that gracious word of his that can build you up and give you the inheritance among all who are consecrated. [33] I have never wanted anyone's silver or gold or clothing. [34] You know well that these very hands have served my needs and my companions.[w] [35] In every way I have shown you that by hard work of that sort we must help the weak, and keep in mind the words of the Lord Jesus who himself said, 'It is more blessed to give than to receive.' "[x]

[36] When he had finished speaking he knelt down and prayed with them all. [37] They were all weeping loudly as they threw their arms around Paul and kissed him, [38] for they were deeply distressed that he had said that they would never see his face again. Then they escorted him to the ship.

CHAPTER 21

Arrival at Tyre. [1] * When we had taken leave of them we set sail, made a straight run for Cos, and on the next day for Rhodes, and from there to Patara. [2] Finding a ship crossing to Phoenicia, we went on board and put out to sea. [3] We caught sight of Cyprus but passed by it on our left and sailed on toward Syria and put in at Tyre where the ship was to unload cargo.

---

q Acts 9, 16.—r 2 Tm 4, 7.—s Jn 21, 15-17; 1 Pt 5, 2.—t Jn 10, 12.—u Mt 7, 15; 2 Pt 2, 1-3; 1 Jn 2, 18-19.—v 1 Thes 2, 11.—w 1 Cor 4, 12; 1 Thes 2, 9; 2 Thes 3, 8.—x Sir 4, 31.

20, 16-35: Apparently aware of difficulties at Ephesus and neighboring areas, Paul calls the presbyters together at Miletus, about thirty miles from Ephesus. He reminds them of his dedication to the gospel (18-21), speaks of what he is about to suffer for the gospel (22-27), and admonishes them to guard the community against false prophets, sure to arise upon his departure (28-31). He concludes by citing a saying of Jesus (35) not recorded in the gospel tradition. Luke presents this farewell to the Ephesian presbyters as Paul's last will and testament.

20, 28: *Overseers:* see the note on Phil 1, 1. *The church of God:* because the clause "that he acquired with his own blood" following "the church of God" suggests that "his own blood" refers to God's blood, some early copyists changed "the church of God" to "the church of the Lord." Some prefer the translation "acquired with the blood of his own," i.e., Christ.

21, 1-18: The third "we-section" of Acts (see the note on Acts 16, 10-17).

[4] There we sought out the disciples and stayed for a week. They kept telling Paul through the Spirit not to embark for Jerusalem. [5] At the end of our stay we left and resumed our journey. All of them, women and children included, escorted us out of the city, and after kneeling on the beach to pray, [6] we bade farewell to one another. Then we boarded the ship, and they returned home.

Arrival at Ptolemais and Caesarea. [7] We continued the voyage and came from Tyre to Ptolemais, where we greeted the brothers and stayed a day with them. [8] On the next day we resumed the trip and came to Caesarea, where we went to the house of Philip the evangelist, who was one of the Seven,* and stayed with him.[y] [9] He had four virgin daughters gifted with prophecy. [10] We had been there several days when a prophet named Agabus* came down from Judea. [11] [z] He came up to us, took Paul's belt, bound his own feet and hands with it, and said, "Thus says the holy Spirit: This is the way the Jews will bind the owner of this belt in Jerusalem, and they will hand him over to the Gentiles."* [12] When we heard this, we and the local residents begged him not to go up to Jerusalem. [13] Then Paul replied, "What are you doing, weeping and breaking my heart? I am prepared not only to be bound but even to die in Jerusalem for the name of the Lord Jesus." [14] [a] Since he would not be dissuaded we let the matter rest, saying,[b] "The Lord's will be done."*

Paul and James in Jerusalem. [15] After these days we made preparations for our journey, then went up to Jerusalem. [16] Some of the disciples from Caesarea came along to lead us to the house of Mnason, a Cypriot, a disciple of long standing, with whom we were to stay. [17] * When we reached Jerusalem the brothers welcomed us warmly. [18] The next day, Paul accompanied us on a visit to James, and all the presbyters were present. [19] He greeted them, then proceeded to tell them in detail what God had accomplished among the Gentiles through his ministry. [20] They praised God when they heard it but said to him, "Brother, you see how many thousands of believers there are from among the Jews, and they are all zealous observers of the law. [21] They have been informed that you are teaching all the Jews who live among the Gentiles to abandon Moses and that you are telling them not to circumcise their children or to observe their customary practices. [22] What is to be done? They will surely hear that you have arrived. [23] * So do what we tell you. We have four men who have taken a vow.[c] [24] Take these men and purify yourself with them, and pay their expenses* that they may have their heads shaved. In this way everyone will know that there is nothing to the reports they have been given about you but that you yourself live in observance of the law. [25] [d] As for the Gentiles who have come to believe, we sent them our decision that they abstain from meat sacrificed to idols, from blood, from the meat of strangled animals, and from unlawful marriage."* [26] So Paul took the men, and on the next day after purifying himself together with them entered the temple to give notice of the day when the purification would be completed and the offering made for each of them.[e]

Paul's Arrest. [27] When the seven days were nearly completed, the Jews from the province of Asia noticed him in the temple, stirred up the whole crowd, and laid hands

---

y Acts 6, 5; 8, 5-6.—z Acts 11, 28; 20, 23.—a Acts 19, 15-16.—b Mt 6, 10; 26, 39; Mk 14, 36; Lk 22, 42.—c 23-27: Acts 18, 18; Nm 6, 1-21.—d Acts 15, 19-20.28-29.—e 1 Cor 9, 20.

21, 8: *One of the Seven:* see the note on Acts 6, 2-4.

21, 10: *Agabus:* mentioned in Acts 11, 28 as the prophet who predicted the famine that occurred when Claudius was emperor.

21, 11: The symbolic act of Agabus recalls those of Old Testament prophets. Compare Is 20, 2; Ez 4, 1; Jer 13, I.

21, 14: The Christian disciples' attitude reflects that of Jesus (see Lk 22, 42).

21, 17-26: The leaders of the Jewish Christians of Jerusalem inform Paul that the Jews there believe he has encouraged the Jews of the diaspora to abandon the Mosaic law. According to Acts, Paul had no objection to the retention of the law by the Jewish Christians of Jerusalem and left the Jews of the diaspora who accepted Christianity free to follow the same practice.

21, 23-26: The leaders of the community suggest that Paul, on behalf of four members of the Jerusalem community, make the customary payment for the sacrifices offered at the termination of the Nazirite vow (see Nm 6, 1-24) in order to impress favorably the Jewish Christians in Jerusalem with his high regard for the Mosaic law. Since Paul himself had once made this vow (Acts 18, 18), his respect for the law would be on public record.

21, 24: *Pay their expenses:* according to Nm 6, 14-15 the Nazirite had to present a yearling lamb for a holocaust, a yearling ewe lamb for a sin offering, and a ram for a peace offering, along with food and drink offerings, upon completion of the period of the vow.

21, 25: Paul is informed about the apostolic decree, seemingly for the first time (see the note on Acts 15, 13-35). The allusion to the decree was probably introduced here by Luke to remind his readers that the Gentile Christians themselves were asked to respect certain Jewish practices deriving from the law.

on him, [28] *f* shouting, "Fellow Israelites, help us. This is the man who is teaching everyone everywhere against the people and the law and this place, and what is more, he has even brought Greeks into the temple and defiled this sacred place."* [29] For they had previously seen Trophimus the Ephesian in the city with him and supposed that Paul had brought him into the temple. [30] The whole city was in turmoil with people rushing together. They seized Paul and dragged him out of the temple, and immediately the gates were closed. [31] While they were trying to kill him, a report reached the cohort commander* that all Jerusalem was rioting. [32] He immediately took soldiers and centurions and charged down on them. When they saw the commander and the soldiers they stopped beating Paul. [33] The cohort commander came forward, arrested him, and ordered him to be secured with two chains; he tried to find out who he might be and what he had done. [34] Some in the mob shouted one thing, others something else; so, since he was unable to ascertain the truth because of the uproar, he ordered Paul to be brought into the compound. [35] When he reached the steps, he was carried by the soldiers because of the violence of the mob,

[36] *g* for a crowd of people followed and shouted, "Away with him!"*

[37] Just as Paul was about to be taken into the compound, he said to the cohort commander, "May I say something to you?" He replied, "Do you speak Greek? [38] So then you are not the Egyptian* who started a revolt some time ago and led the four thousand assassins into the desert?" *h* [39] Paul answered, "I am a Jew, of Tarsus in Cilicia, a citizen of no mean city; I request you to permit me to speak to the people." [40] When he had given his permission, Paul stood on the steps and motioned with his hand to the people; and when all was quiet he addressed them in Hebrew.*

CHAPTER 22

Paul's Defense before the Jerusalem Jews.* [1] "My brothers and fathers, listen to what I am about to say to you in my defense." [2] When they heard him addressing them in Hebrew they became all the more quiet. And he continued, [3] "I am a Jew, born in Tarsus in Cilicia, but brought up in this city. At the feet of Gamaliel I was educated strictly in our ancestral law and was zealous for God, just as all of you are today. *i* [4] I persecuted this Way to death, binding both men and women and delivering them to prison. *j* [5] Even the high priest and the whole council of elders can testify on my behalf. For from them I even received letters to the brothers and set out for Damascus to bring back to Jerusalem in chains for punishment those there as well.

[6] "On that journey as I drew near to Damascus, about noon a great light from the sky suddenly shone around me. *k* [7] I fell to the ground and heard a voice saying to me, 'Saul, Saul, why are you persecuting me?' *l* [8] I replied, 'Who are you, sir?' And he said to me, 'I am Jesus the Nazorean whom you are persecuting.' *m* [9] My companions saw the light but did not hear the voice of the one who spoke to me. *n* [10] I asked, 'What shall I do, sir?' The Lord answered me, 'Get up and go into Damascus, and there you will be told about everything appointed for you to do.' *o* [11] Since I could see nothing because of the brightness of that light, I was led by hand by my companions and entered Damascus. *p*

[12] *q* "A certain Ananias, a devout observer of the law, and highly spoken of by

---

f Rom 15, 31.—g Acts 22, 22; Lk 23, 18; Jn 19, 15.—h Acts 5, 36-37.—i Acts 5, 34; 26, 4-5; 2 Cor 11, 22; Gal 1, 13-14; Phil 3, 5-6.—j Acts 8, 3; 9, 1-2; 22, 19; 26, 9-11; Phil 3, 6.—k Acts 9, 3; 26, 13; 1 Cor 15, 8.—l Acts 9, 4; 26, 14.—m Acts 9, 5; 26, 15; Mt 25, 40.—n Acts 9, 7; 26, 13-14.—o Acts 9, 6; 26, 16.—p Acts 9, 8.—q 12-16: Acts 9, 10-19.

21, 28: The charges against Paul by the diaspora Jews are identical to the charges brought against Stephen by diaspora Jews in Acts 6, 13. *Brought Greeks into the temple:* non-Jews were forbidden, under penalty of death, to go beyond the Court of the Gentiles. Inscriptions in Greek and Latin on a stone balustrade marked off the prohibited area.

21, 31: *Cohort commander:* literally, "the leader of a thousand in a cohort." At this period the Roman cohort commander usually led six hundred soldiers, a tenth of a legion; but the number in a cohort varied.

21, 36: *Away with him:* at the trial of Jesus before Pilate in Lk 23, 18, the people similarly shout, "Away with this man."

21, 38: *The Egyptian:* according to the Jewish historian Josephus, an Egyptian gathered a large crowd on the Mount of Olives to witness the destruction of the walls of Jerusalem that would fall at the Egyptian "prophet's" word. The commotion was put down by the Roman authorities and the Egyptian escaped, but only after thousands had been killed. *Four thousand assassins:* literally, *sicarii.* According to Josephus, these were political nationalists who removed their opponents by assassination with a short dagger, called in Latin a *sica.*

21, 40: *In Hebrew:* meaning, perhaps, in Aramaic, which at this time was the Semitic tongue in common use.

22, 1-21: Paul's first defense speech is presented to the Jerusalem crowds. Luke here presents Paul as a devout Jew (3) and zealous persecutor of the Christian community (4-5), and then recounts the conversion of Paul for the second time in Acts (see the note on Acts 9, 1-19).

all the Jews who lived there, [13] came to me and stood there and said, 'Saul, my brother, regain your sight.' And at that very moment I regained my sight and saw him. [14] Then he said, 'The God of our ancestors designated you to know his will, to see the Righteous One, and to hear the sound of his voice; [15] for you will be his witness* before all to what you have seen and heard. [16] Now, why delay? Get up and have yourself baptized and your sins washed away, calling upon his name.'

[17] "After I had returned to Jerusalem and while I was praying in the temple, I fell into a trance [18] and saw the Lord saying to me, 'Hurry, leave Jerusalem at once, because they will not accept your testimony about me.' [19] But I replied, 'Lord, they themselves know that from synagogue to synagogue I used to imprison and beat those who believed in you.[r] [20] And when the blood of your witness Stephen was being shed, I myself stood by giving my approval and keeping guard over the cloaks of his murderers.'[s] [21] Then he said to me,[t] 'Go, I shall send you far away to the Gentiles.' "*

Paul Imprisoned. [22] [u] They listened to him until he said this, but then they raised their voices and shouted, "Take such a one as this away from the earth. It is not right that he should live."* [23] And as they were yelling and throwing off their cloaks and flinging dust into the air, [24] the cohort commander ordered him to be brought into the compound and gave instruction that he be interrogated under the lash to determine the reason why they were making such an outcry against him. [25] [v] But when they had stretched him out for the whips, Paul said to the centurion on duty, "Is it lawful for you to scourge a man who is a Roman citizen and has not been tried?"* [26] When the centurion heard this, he went to the cohort commander and reported it, saying, "What are you going to do? This man is a Roman citizen." [27] Then the commander came and said to him, "Tell me, are you a Roman citizen?" "Yes," he answered. [28] The commander replied, "I acquired this citizenship for a large sum of money." Paul said, "But I was born one." [29] At once those who were going to interrogate him backed away from him, and the commander became alarmed when he realized that he was a Roman citizen and that he had had him bound.

Paul before the Sanhedrin. [30] The next day, wishing to determine the truth about why he was being accused by the Jews, he freed him and ordered the chief priests and the whole Sanhedrin to convene. Then he brought Paul down and made him stand before them.

CHAPTER 23

[1] Paul looked intently at the Sanhedrin and said, "My brothers, I have conducted myself with a perfectly clear conscience before God to this day."[w] [2] The high priest Ananias* ordered his attendants to strike his mouth. [3] Then Paul said to him, "God will strike you,* you whitewashed wall. Do you indeed sit in judgment upon me according to the law and yet in violation of the law order me to be struck?"[x] [4] The attendants said, "Would you revile God's high priest?" [5] Paul answered, "Brothers, I did not realize he was the high priest. For it is written,[y] 'You shall not curse a ruler of your people.' "*

[6] Paul was aware that some were Sadducees and some Pharisees, so he called out before the Sanhedrin, "My brothers, I am a Pharisee, the son of Pharisees; [I] am on trial for hope in the resurrection of the dead."[z] [7] When he said this, a dispute

---

r Acts 8, 3; 9, 1-2; 22, 4-5; 26, 9-11.—s Acts 7, 58; 8, 1.—t Acts 9, 15; Gal 2, 7-9.—u Acts 21, 36; Lk 23, 18; Jn 19, 15.—v Acts 16, 37.—w Acts 24, 16.—x Ez 13, 10-15; Mt 23, 27.—y Ex 22, 27.—z Acts 24, 15.21; 26, 5; Phil 3, 5.

22, 15: *His witness:* like the Galilean followers during the historical ministry of Jesus, Paul too, through his experience of the risen Christ, is to be a witness to the resurrection (compare Acts 1, 8; 10, 39-41; Lk 24, 48).

22, 21: Paul endeavors to explain that his position on the law has not been identical with that of his audience because it has been his prophetic mission to preach to the Gentiles to whom the law was not addressed and who had no faith in it as a way of salvation.

22, 22: Paul's suggestion that his prophetic mission to the Gentiles did not involve his imposing the law on them provokes the same opposition as occurred in Pisidian Antioch (Acts 13, 45).

22, 25: *Is it lawful for you to scourge a man who is a Roman citizen and has not been tried?:* see the note on Acts 16, 37.

23, 2: *The high priest Ananias:* Ananias, son of Nedebaeus, was high priest from A.D. 47 to 59.

23, 3: *God will strike you:* Josephus reports that Ananias was later assassinated in A.D. 66 at the beginning of the First Revolt.

23, 5: Luke portrays Paul as a model of one who is obedient to the Mosaic law. Paul, because of his reverence for the law (Ex 22, 27), withdraws his accusation of hypocrisy, "whitewashed wall" (cf Mt 23, 27), when he is told Ananias is the high priest.

broke out between the Pharisees and Sadducees, and the group became divided. [8] For the Sadducees say that there is no resurrection or angels or spirits, while the Pharisees acknowledge all three. [a] [9] A great uproar occurred, and some scribes belonging to the Pharisee party stood up and sharply argued, "We find nothing wrong with this man. Suppose a spirit or an angel has spoken to him?" [10] The dispute was so serious that the commander, afraid that Paul would be torn to pieces by them, ordered his troops to go down and rescue him from their midst and take him into the compound. [11] [b] The following night the Lord stood by him and said, "Take courage. For just as you have borne witness to my cause in Jerusalem, so you must also bear witness in Rome."*

Transfer to Caesarea. [12] When day came, the Jews made a plot and bound themselves by oath not to eat or drink until they had killed Paul. [13] There were more than forty who formed this conspiracy. [14] They went to the chief priests and elders and said, "We have bound ourselves by a solemn oath to taste nothing until we have killed Paul. [15] You, together with the Sanhedrin, must now make an official request to the commander to have him bring him down to you, as though you meant to investigate his case more thoroughly. We on our part are prepared to kill him before he arrives." [16] The son of Paul's sister, however, heard about the ambush; so he went and entered the compound and reported it to Paul. [17] Paul then called one of the centurions* and requested, "Take this young man to the commander; he has something to report to him." [18] So he took him and brought him to the commander and explained, "The prisoner Paul called me and asked that I bring this young man to you; he has something to say to you." [19] The commander took him by the hand, drew him aside, and asked him privately, "What is it you have to report to me?" [20] He replied, "The Jews have conspired to ask you to bring Paul down to the Sanhedrin tomorrow, as though they meant to inquire about him more thoroughly, [21] but do not believe them. More than forty of them are lying in wait for him; they have bound themselves by oath not to eat or drink until they have killed him. They are now ready and only wait for your consent." [22] As the commander dismissed the young man he directed him, "Tell no one that you gave me this information."

[23] Then he summoned two of the centurions and said, "Get two hundred soldiers ready to go to Caesarea by nine o'clock tonight,* along with seventy horsemen and two hundred auxiliaries. [24] Provide mounts for Paul to ride and give him safe conduct to Felix the governor." [25] Then he wrote a letter with this content: [26] * "Claudius Lysias to his excellency the governor Felix, greetings.* [27] This man, seized by the Jews and about to be murdered by them, I rescued after intervening with my troops when I learned that he was a Roman citizen. [c] [28] I wanted to learn the reason for their accusations against him so I brought him down to their Sanhedrin. [29] I discovered that he was accused in matters of controversial questions of their law and not of any charge deserving death or imprisonment. [d] [30] Since it was brought to my attention that there will be a plot against the man, I am sending him to you at once, and have also notified his accusers to state [their case] against him before you."

[31] So the soldiers, according to their orders, took Paul and escorted him by night to Antipatris. [32] The next day they returned to the compound, leaving the horsemen to complete the journey with him. [33] When they arrived in Caesarea they delivered the letter to the governor and presented Paul to him. [34] When he had read it and asked to what province he belonged, and learned that he was from

a Mt 22, 23; Lk 20, 27.—b Acts 19, 21.—c Acts 21, 30-34; 22, 27.—d Acts 18, 14-15; 25, 18-19.

23, 11: The occurrence of the vision of Christ consoling Paul and assuring him that he will be his witness in Rome prepares the reader for the final section of Acts: the journey of Paul and the word he preaches to Rome under the protection of the Romans.

23, 17: *Centurions:* a centurion was a military officer in charge of one hundred soldiers.

23, 23: *By nine o'clock tonight:* literally, "by the third hour of the night." The night hours began at 6 p.m. *Two hundred auxiliaries:* the meaning of the Greek is not certain. It seems to refer to spearmen from the local police force and not from the cohort of soldiers, which would have numbered only 500-1000 men.

23, 26-30: The letter emphasizes the fact that Paul is a Roman citizen and asserts the lack of evidence that he is guilty of a crime against the empire. The tone of the letter implies that the commander became initially involved in Paul's case because of his Roman citizenship, but this is not an exact description of what really happened (see Acts 21, 31-33; 22, 25-29).

23, 26: M. Antonius Felix was procurator of Judea from A.D. 52 to 60. His procuratorship was marked by cruelty toward and oppression of his Jewish subjects.

Acts

Cilicia, ³⁵he said, "I shall hear your case when your accusers arrive." Then he ordered that he be held in custody in Herod's praetorium.

CHAPTER 24

Trial before Felix. ¹Five days later the high priest Ananias came down with some elders and an advocate, a certain Tertullus, and they presented formal charges against Paul to the governor. ²When he was called, Tertullus began to accuse him, saying, "Since we have attained much peace through you, and reforms have been accomplished in this nation through your provident care, ³we acknowledge this in every way and everywhere, most excellent Felix, with all gratitude. ⁴But in order not to detain you further, I ask you to give us a brief hearing with your customary graciousness. ⁵ ᵉ We found this man to be a pest; he creates dissension among Jews all over the world and is a ringleader of the sect of the Nazoreans.* ⁶He even tried to desecrate our temple, but we arrested him.ᶠ [7]* ⁸If you examine him for yourself about everything of which we are accusing him." ⁹The Jews also joined in the attack and asserted that these things were so.

¹⁰ * Then the governor motioned to him to speak and Paul replied, "I know that you have been a judge over this nation for many years and so I am pleased to make my defense before you. ¹¹As you can verify, not more than twelve days have passed since I went up to Jerusalem to worship. ¹²Neither in the temple, nor in the synagogues, nor anywhere in the city did they find me arguing with anyone or instigating a riot among the people. ¹³Nor can they prove to you the accusations they are now making against me. ¹⁴But this I do admit to you, that according to the Way, which they call a sect, I worship the God of our ancestors and I believe everything that is in accordance with the law and written in the prophets.ᵍ ¹⁵I have the same hope in God as they themselves have that there will be a resurrection of the righteous and the unrighteous.ʰ ¹⁶Because of this, I always strive to keep my conscience clear before God and man.ⁱ ¹⁷After many years, I came to bring alms for my nation and offerings.ʲ ¹⁸While I was so engaged, they found me,

after my purification, in the temple without a crowd or disturbance.ᵏ ¹⁹But some Jews from the province of Asia, who should be here before you to make whatever accusation they might have against me—²⁰or let these men themselves state what crime they discovered when I stood before the Sanhedrin, ²¹unless it was my one outcry as I stood among them, that 'I am on trial before you today for the resurrection of the dead.' "ˡ

²²Then Felix, who was accurately informed about the Way, postponed the trial, saying, "When Lysias the commander comes down, I shall decide your case." ²³He gave orders to the centurion that he should be kept in custody but have some liberty, and that he should not prevent any of his friends from caring for his needs.

Captivity in Caesarea. ²⁴ * Several days later Felix came with his wife Drusilla, who was Jewish. He had Paul summoned and listened to him speak about faith in Christ Jesus. ²⁵But as he spoke about righteousness and self-restraint and the coming judgment, Felix became frightened and said, "You may go for now; when I find an opportunity I shall summon you again." ²⁶At the same time he hoped that a bribe would be offered him by Paul, and so he sent for him very often and conversed with him.

²⁷Two years passed and Felix was succeeded by Porcius Festus. Wishing to ingratiate himself with the Jews, Felix left Paul in prison.*

---

e Acts 24, 14; Lk 23, 2.—f Acts 21, 28.—g Acts 24, 5.—h Dn 12, 2; Jn 5, 28-29.—i Acts 23, 1.—j Rom 15, 25-26; Gal 2, 10.—k 18-19: Acts 21, 26-30.—l Acts 23, 6; 24, 15.

24, 5: *Nazoreans:* that is, followers of Jesus of Nazareth.

24, 7: The Western text has added here a verse (really 6b-8a) that is not found in the best Greek manuscripts. It reads, "and would have judged him according to our own law, but the cohort commander Lysias came and violently took him out of our hands and ordered his accusers to come before you."

24, 10-21: Whereas the advocate Tertullus referred to Paul's activities on his missionary journeys, the apostle narrowed the charges down to the riot connected with the incident in the temple (see Acts 21, 27-30; 24, 17-20). In his defense, Paul stresses the continuity between Christianity and Judaism.

24, 24-25: The way of Christian discipleship greatly disquiets Felix, who has entered into an adulterous marriage with Drusilla, daughter of Herod Agrippa I. This marriage provides the background for the topics Paul speaks about and about which Felix does not want to hear.

24, 27: Very little is known of Porcius Festus who was a procurator of Judea from A.D. 60 to 62.

CHAPTER 25

Appeal to Caesar. [1] Three days after his arrival in the province, Festus went up from Caesarea to Jerusalem [2] where the chief priests and Jewish leaders presented him their formal charges against Paul.* They asked him [3] as a favor to have him sent to Jerusalem, for they were plotting to kill him along the way. [4] Festus replied that Paul was being held in custody in Caesarea and that he himself would be returning there shortly. [5] He said, "Let your authorities come down with me, and if this man has done something improper, let them accuse him."

[6] After spending no more than eight or ten days with them, he went down to Caesarea, and on the following day took his seat on the tribunal and ordered that Paul be brought in. [7] When he appeared, the Jews who had come down from Jerusalem surrounded him and brought many serious charges against him, which they were unable to prove. [8] In defending himself Paul said, "I have committed no crime either against the Jewish law or against the temple or against Caesar." [9] * Then Festus, wishing to ingratiate himself with the Jews, said to Paul in reply, "Are you willing to go up to Jerusalem and there stand trial before me on these charges?" [10] Paul answered, "I am standing before the tribunal of Caesar; this is where I should be tried. I have committed no crime against the Jews, as you very well know. [11] If I have committed a crime or done anything deserving death, I do not seek to escape the death penalty; but if there is no substance to the charges they are bringing against me, then no one has the right to hand me over to them. I appeal to Caesar." [12] Then Festus, after conferring with his council, replied, "You have appealed to Caesar. To Caesar you will go."

Paul before King Agrippa. [13] When a few days had passed, King Agrippa and Bernice* arrived in Caesarea on a visit to Festus. [14] Since they spent several days there, Festus referred Paul's case to the king, saying, "There is a man here left in custody by Felix.[m] [15] When I was in Jerusalem the chief priests and the elders of the Jews brought charges against him and demanded his condemnation. [16] I answered them that it was not Roman practice to hand over an accused person before he has faced his accusers and had the opportunity to defend himself against their charge. [17] So when [they] came together here, I made no delay; the next day I took my seat on the tribunal and ordered the man to be brought in. [18] [n] His accusers stood around him, but did not charge him with any of the crimes I suspected. [19] Instead they had some issues with him about their own religion and about a certain Jesus who had died but who Paul claimed was alive. [20] Since I was at a loss how to investigate this controversy, I asked if he were willing to go to Jerusalem and there stand trial on these charges. [21] And when Paul appealed that he be held in custody for the Emperor's decision, I ordered him held until I could send him to Caesar." [22] Agrippa said to Festus, "I too should like to hear this man." He replied, "Tomorrow you will hear him."

[23] The next day Agrippa and Bernice came with great ceremony and entered the audience hall in the company of cohort commanders and the prominent men of the city and, by command of Festus, Paul was brought in. [24] And Festus said, "King Agrippa and all you here present with us, look at this man about whom the whole Jewish populace petitioned me here and in Jerusalem, clamoring that he should live no longer. [25] I found, however, that he had done nothing deserving death, and so when he appealed to the Emperor, I decided to send him. [26] But I have nothing definite to write about him to our sovereign; therefore I have brought him before all of you, and particularly before you, King Agrippa, so that I may have something to write as a result of this investigation. [27] For it seems senseless to me to send up a prisoner without indicating the charges against him."

---

m Acts 24, 27.—n 18-19: Acts 18, 14-15; 23, 29.

25, 2: Even after two years the animosity toward Paul in Jerusalem had not subsided (see Acts 24, 27).

25, 9-12: Paul refuses to acknowledge that the Sanhedrin in Jerusalem has any jurisdiction over him now (11). Paul uses his right as a Roman citizen to appeal his case to the jurisdiction of the Emperor (Nero, ca. A.D. 60) (12). This move broke the deadlock between Roman protective custody of Paul and the plan of his enemies to kill him (3).

25, 13: *King Agrippa and Bernice:* brother and sister, children of Herod Agrippa I whose activities against the Jerusalem community are mentioned in Acts 12, 1-19. Agrippa II was a petty ruler over small areas in northern Palestine and some villages in Perea. His influence on the Jewish population of Palestine was insignificant.

CHAPTER 26

King Agrippa Hears Paul. [1] Then Agrippa said to Paul, "You may now speak on your own behalf." So Paul stretched out his hand and began his defense. [2] * "I count myself fortunate, King Agrippa, that I am to defend myself before you today against all the charges made against me by the Jews, [3] especially since you are an expert in all the Jewish customs and controversies. And therefore I beg you to listen patiently. [4] My manner of living from my youth, a life spent from the beginning among my people* and in Jerusalem, all [the] Jews know. [5] o They have known about me from the start, if they are willing to testify, that I have lived my life as a Pharisee, the strictest party of our religion. [6] p But now I am standing trial because of my hope in the promise made by God to our ancestors. [7] Our twelve tribes hope to attain to that promise as they fervently worship God day and night; and on account of this hope I am accused by Jews, O king. [8] Why is it thought unbelievable among you that God raises the dead? [9] q I myself once thought that I had to do many things against the name of Jesus the Nazorean, [10] and I did so in Jerusalem. I imprisoned many of the holy ones with the authorization I received from the chief priests, and when they were to be put to death I cast my vote against them. r [11] Many times, in synagogue after synagogue, I punished them in an attempt to force them to blaspheme; I was so enraged against them that I pursued them even to foreign cities.

[12] "On one such occasion I was traveling to Damascus with the authorization and commission of the chief priests. [13] s At midday, along the way, O king, I saw a light from the sky, brighter than the sun, shining around me and my traveling companions. t [14] We all fell to the ground and I heard a voice saying to me in Hebrew, 'Saul, Saul, why are you persecuting me?u It is hard for you to kick against the goad.'* [15] And I said, 'Who are you, sir?' And the Lord replied, 'I am Jesus whom you are persecuting. v [16] Get up now, and stand on your feet. w I have appeared to you for this purpose, to appoint you as a servant and witness of what you have seen [of me] and what you will be shown.* [17] I shall deliver you from this people and from the Gentiles to whom I send you, x [18] to

open their eyes* that they may turn from darkness to light and from the power of Satan to God, so that they may obtain forgiveness of sins and an inheritance among those who have been consecrated by faith in me.' y

[19] "And so, King Agrippa, I was not disobedient to the heavenly vision. [20] On the contrary, first to those in Damascus and in Jerusalem and throughout the whole country of Judea, and then to the Gentiles, I preached the need to repent and turn to God, and to do works giving evidence of repentance. [21] z That is why the Jews seized me [when I was] in the temple and tried to kill me. [22] a But I have enjoyed God's help to this very day, and so I stand here testifying to small and great alike, saying nothing different from what the prophets and Moses foretold,* [23] that the Messiah must suffer* and that, as the first to rise from the dead, he would proclaim light both to our people and to the Gentiles." b

Reactions to Paul's Speech. [24] While Paul was so speaking in his defense, Festus said in a loud voice, "You are mad, Paul; much learning is driving you mad." [25] But Paul replied, "I am not mad, most excellent Festus; I am speaking words of truth and

---

o Phil 3, 5-6; Gal 1, 13-14; 2 Cor 11, 22.—p 6-8: Acts 23, 6; 24, 15.21; 28, 20.—q 9-11: Acts 8, 3; 9, 1-2; 22, 19; Phil 3, 6.—r Acts 9, 14.—s 13-14: Acts 9, 7.—t Acts 9, 3; 22, 6.—u Acts 9, 4; 22, 7.—v Acts 9, 5; 22, 8; Mt 25, 40.—w Acts 9, 6; 22, 10; Ez 2, 1.—x Jer 1, 7.—y Is 42, 7.16; 61, 1 LXX; Col 1, 13.—z Acts 21, 31.—a 22-23: Acts 3, 18; Lk 24, 26-27.44-47.—b Is 42, 6; 49, 6; Lk 2, 32; 1 Cor 15, 20-23.

26, 2-23: Paul's final defense speech in Acts is now made before a king (see Acts 9, 15). In the speech Paul presents himself as a zealous Pharisee and Christianity as the logical development of Pharisaic Judaism. The story of his conversion is recounted for the third time in Acts in this speech (see the note on Acts 9, 1-19).

26, 4: *Among my people:* that is, among the Jews.

26, 14: *In Hebrew:* see the note on Acts 21, 40. *It is hard for you to kick against the goad:* this proverb is commonly found in Greek literature and in this context signifies the senselessness and ineffectiveness of any opposition to the divine influence in his life.

26, 16: The words of Jesus directed to Paul here reflect the dialogues between Christ and Ananias (Acts 9, 15) and between Ananias and Paul (Acts 22, 14-15) in the two previous accounts of Paul's conversion.

26, 18: *To open their eyes:* though no mention is made of Paul's blindness in this account (cf Acts 9, 8-9.12.18; 22, 11-13), the task he is commissioned to perform is the removal of other people's spiritual blindness.

26, 22: *Saying nothing different from what the prophets and Moses foretold:* see the note on Lk 18, 31.

26, 23: *That the Messiah must suffer:* see the note on Lk 24, 26.

reason. [26] The king knows about these matters and to him I speak boldly, for I cannot believe that [any] of this has escaped his notice; this was not done in a corner.* [27] King Agrippa, do you believe the prophets?* I know you believe." [28] Then Agrippa said to Paul, "You will soon persuade me to play the Christian." [29] Paul replied, "I would pray to God that sooner or later not only you but all who listen to me today might become as I am except for these chains."

[30] Then the king rose, and with him the governor and Bernice and the others who sat with them. [31] * And after they had withdrawn they said to one another, "This man is doing nothing [at all] that deserves death or imprisonment." [32] And Agrippa said to Festus, "This man could have been set free if he had not appealed to Caesar." [c]

CHAPTER 27

Departure for Rome. [1] * When it was decided that we should sail to Italy, they handed Paul and some other prisoners over to a centurion named Julius of the Cohort Augusta.* [2] We went on board a ship from Adramyttium bound for ports in the province of Asia and set sail. Aristarchus, a

Macedonian from Thessalonica, was with us. [d] [3] On the following day we put in at Sidon where Julius was kind enough to allow Paul to visit his friends who took care of him. [4] From there we put out to sea and sailed around the sheltered side of Cyprus because of the headwinds, [5] and crossing the open sea off the coast of Cilicia and Pamphylia we came to Myra in Lycia.

Storm and Shipwreck. [6] There the centurion found an Alexandrian ship that was sailing to Italy and put us on board. [7] For many days we made little headway, arriving at Cnidus only with difficulty, and because the wind would not permit us to continue our course we sailed for the sheltered side of Crete off Salmone. [8] We sailed past it with difficulty and reached a place called Fair Havens, near which was the city of Lasea.

[9] Much time had now passed and sailing had become hazardous because the time of the fast* had already gone by, so Paul warned them, [e] [10] "Men, I can see that this voyage will result in severe damage and heavy loss not only to the cargo and the ship, but also to our lives." [11] The centurion, however, paid more attention to the pilot and to the owner of the ship than to what Paul said. [12] Since the harbor was unfavorably situated for spending the winter, the majority planned to put out to sea from there in the hope of reaching Phoenix, a port in Crete facing west-northwest, there to spend the winter.

[13] A south wind blew gently, and thinking they had attained their objective, they weighed anchor and sailed along close to the coast of Crete. [14] Before long an offshore wind of hurricane force called a "Northeaster" struck. [15] Since the ship was caught up in it and could not head into the wind we gave way and let ourselves be driven. [16] We passed along the sheltered side of an island named Cauda and managed only with difficulty to get the dinghy under control. [17] They hoisted it aboard, then used cables to undergird the ship. Because of their fear that they would run aground on the shoal of Syrtis, they lowered the drift anchor and were carried along in this way. [18] We were being pounded by the storm so violently that the next day they jettisoned some cargo, [19] and on the third day with their own hands they threw even the ship's tackle overboard. [20] Neither the

Acts

---

c Acts 25, 11-12.—d Acts 19, 29; 20, 4.—e Lv 16, 29-31.

26, 26: *Not done in a corner:* for Luke, this Greek proverb expresses his belief that he is presenting a story about Jesus and the church that is already well known. As such, the entire history of Christianity is public knowledge and incontestable. Luke presents his story in this way to provide "certainty" to his readers about the instructions they have received (Lk 1, 4).

26, 27-28: If the Christian missionaries proclaim nothing different from what the Old Testament prophets had proclaimed (22-23), then the logical outcome for the believing Jew, according to Luke, is to become a Christian.

26, 31-32: In recording the episode of Paul's appearance before Agrippa, Luke wishes to show that, when Paul's case was judged impartially, no grounds for legal action against him were found (see Acts 23, 29; 25, 25).

27, 1—28, 16: Here Luke has written a stirring account of adventure on the high seas, incidental to his main purpose of showing how well Paul got along with his captors and how his prophetic influence saved the lives of all on board. The recital also establishes the existence of Christian communities in Puteoli and Rome. This account of the voyage and shipwreck also constitutes the final "we-section" in Acts (see the note on Acts 16, 10-17).

27, 1: *Cohort Augusta:* the presence of a Cohort Augusta in Syria during the first century A.D. is attested in inscriptions. Whatever the historical background to this information given by Luke may be, the name Augusta serves to increase the prominence and prestige of the prisoner Paul whose custodians bear so important a Roman name.

27, 9: *The time of the fast:* the fast kept on the occasion of the Day of Atonement (Lv 16, 29-31), which occurred in late September or early October.

sun nor the stars were visible for many days, and no small storm raged. Finally, all hope of our surviving was taken away.

21 When many would no longer eat, Paul stood among them and said, "Men, you should have taken my advice and not have set sail from Crete and you would have avoided this disastrous loss. 22 I urge you now to keep up your courage; not one of you will be lost, only the ship. 23 For last night an angel of the God to whom [I] belong and whom I serve stood by me 24 and said, 'Do not be afraid, Paul. You are destined to stand before Caesar; and behold, for your sake, God has granted safety to all who are sailing with you.'ᶠ 25 Therefore, keep up your courage, men; I trust in God that it will turn out as I have been told. 26 We are destined to run aground on some island."

27 On the fourteenth night, as we were still being driven about on the Adriatic Sea, toward midnight the sailors began to suspect that they were nearing land. 28 They took soundings and found twenty fathoms; a little farther on, they again took soundings and found fifteen fathoms. 29 Fearing that we would run aground on a rocky coast, they dropped four anchors from the stern and prayed for day to come. 30 The sailors then tried to abandon ship; they lowered the dinghy to the sea on the pretext of going to lay out anchors from the bow. 31 But Paul said to the centurion and the soldiers, "Unless these men stay with the ship, you cannot be saved." 32 So the soldiers cut the ropes of the dinghy and set it adrift.

33 Until the day began to dawn, Paul kept urging all to take some food. He said, "Today is the fourteenth day that you have been waiting, going hungry and eating nothing. 34 I urge you, therefore, to take some food; it will help you survive. Not a hair of the head of anyone of you will be lost." 35 When he said this, he took bread,* gave thanks to God in front of them all, broke it, and began to eat.ᵍ 36 They were all encouraged, and took some food themselves. 37 In all, there were two hundred seventy-six of us on the ship. 38 After they had eaten enough, they lightened the ship by throwing the wheat into the sea.

39 When day came they did not recognize the land, but made out a bay with a beach. They planned to run the ship ashore on it,

if they could. 40 So they cast off the anchors and abandoned them to the sea, and at the same time they unfastened the lines of the rudders, and hoisting the foresail into the wind, they made for the beach. 41 But they struck a sandbar and ran the ship aground. The bow was wedged in and could not be moved, but the stern began to break up under the pounding [of the waves]. 42 The soldiers planned to kill the prisoners so that none might swim away and escape, 43 but the centurion wanted to save Paul and so kept them from carrying out their plan. He ordered those who could swim to jump overboard first and get to the shore, 44 and then the rest, some on planks, others on debris from the ship. In this way, all reached shore safely.

CHAPTER 28

Winter in Malta. 1 Once we had reached safety we learned that the island was called Malta. 2 The natives showed us extraordinary hospitality; they lit a fire and welcomed all of us because it had begun to rain and was cold. 3 Paul had gathered a bundle of brushwood and was putting it on the fire when a viper, escaping from the heat, fastened on his hand. 4 When the natives saw the snake hanging from his hand, they said to one another, "This man must certainly be a murderer; though he escaped the sea, Justice* has not let him remain alive." 5 But he shook the snake off into the fire and suffered no harm. 6 They were expecting him to swell up or suddenly to fall down dead but, after waiting a long time and seeing nothing unusual happen to him, they changed their minds and began to say that he was a god.ʰ 7 In the vicinity of that place were lands belonging to a man named Publius, the chief of the island. He welcomed us and received us cordially as his guests for three days. 8 It so happened that the father of Publius was sick with a fever and dysentery. Paul visited him and, after praying, laid his hands on him and healed him. 9 After this had taken place, the rest of the sick on the island came to Paul and were cured. 10 They paid us great honor

---

f Acts 23, 11.—g Mt 15, 36; Mk 6, 41; 8, 6; Lk 22, 19; 1 Cor 11, 23-24.—h Acts 14, 11.

27, 35: *He took bread . . .* : the words recall the traditional language of the celebration of the Eucharist (see Lk 22, 19).

28, 4: *Justice:* in Greek mythology, the pursuing goddess of vengeance and justice.

and when we eventually set sail they brought us the provisions we needed.

Arrival in Rome. [11] Three months later we set sail on a ship that had wintered at the island. It was an Alexandrian ship with the Dioscuri* as its figurehead. [12] We put in at Syracuse and stayed there three days, [13] and from there we sailed round the coast and arrived at Rhegium. After a day, a south wind came up and in two days we reached Puteoli. [14] There we found some brothers and were urged to stay with them for seven days. And thus we came to Rome. [15] The brothers from there heard about us and came as far as the Forum of Appius and Three Taverns to meet us. On seeing them, Paul gave thanks to God and took courage. [16] When he entered Rome,* Paul was allowed to live by himself, with the soldier who was guarding him.

Testimony to Jews in Rome. [17] * Three days later he called together the leaders of the Jews. When they had gathered he said to them, "My brothers, although I had

---

i Acts 24, 12-13; 25, 8.—j Acts 23, 29; 25, 25; 26, 31-32.—k Acts 25, 11.—l Acts 23, 6; 24, 15.21; 26, 6-8.—m Acts 24, 5.14.—n Is 6, 9-10; Mt 13, 14-15; Mk 4, 12; Lk 8, 10; Jn 12, 40; Rom 11, 8.—o Acts 13, 46; 18, 6; Ps 67, 2; Is 40, 5 LXX; Lk 3, 6.

28, 11: *Dioscuri:* that is, the Twin Brothers, Castor and Pollux, the sons of Zeus and the patrons of the sailors.

28, 16: With Paul's arrival in Rome, the programmatic spread of the word of the Lord to "the ends of the earth" (Acts 1, 8) is accomplished. In Rome, Paul is placed under house arrest, and under this mild form of custody he is allowed to proclaim the word in the capital of the civilized world of his day.

28, 17-22: Paul's first act in Rome is to learn from the leaders of the Jewish community whether the Jews of Jerusalem plan to pursue their case against him before the Roman jurisdiction. He is informed that no such plan is afoot, but that the Jews of Rome have heard the Christian teaching denounced. Paul's offer to explain it to them is readily accepted.

28, 20: *The hope of Israel:* in the words of Paul (Acts 23, 6), Luke has identified this hope as hope in the resurrection of the dead.

28, 25-28: Paul's final words in Acts reflect a major concern of Luke's writings: how the salvation promised in the Old Testament, accomplished by Jesus, and offered first to Israel (Acts 13, 26), has now been offered to and accepted by the Gentiles. Quoting Is 6, 9-10, Paul presents the scriptural support for his indictment of his fellow Jews who refuse to accept the message he proclaims. Their rejection leads to its proclamation among the Gentiles.

28, 29: The Western text has added here a verse that is not found in the best Greek manuscripts: "And when he had said this, the Jews left, seriously arguing among themselves."

28, 30-31: Although the ending of Acts may seem to be abrupt, Luke has now completed his story with the establishment of Paul and the proclamation of Christianity in Rome. Paul's confident and unhindered proclamation of the gospel in Rome forms the climax to the story whose outline was provided in Acts 1, 8: "You will be my witnesses in Jerusalem . . . and to the ends of the earth."

---

done nothing against our people or our ancestral customs, I was handed over to the Romans as a prisoner from Jerusalem. [i] [18] After trying my case the Romans wanted to release me, because they found nothing against me deserving the death penalty. [j] [19] But when the Jews objected, I was obliged to appeal to Caesar, even though I had no accusation to make against my own nation. [k] [20] This is the reason, then, I have requested to see you and to speak with you, for it is on account of the hope of Israel* that I wear these chains." [l] [21] They answered him, "We have received no letters from Judea about you, nor has any of the brothers arrived with a damaging report or rumor about you. [22] But we should like to hear you present your views, for we know that this sect is denounced everywhere." [m]

[23] So they arranged a day with him and came to his lodgings in great numbers. From early morning until evening, he expounded his position to them, bearing witness to the kingdom of God and trying to convince them about Jesus from the law of Moses and the prophets. [24] Some were convinced by what he had said, while others did not believe. [25] Without reaching any agreement among themselves they began to leave; then Paul made one final statement.* "Well did the holy Spirit speak to your ancestors through the prophet Isaiah, saying:

[26] 'Go to this people and say: [n]
     You shall indeed hear but not understand.
     You shall indeed look but never see.

[27] Gross is the heart of this people;
        they will not hear with their ears;
        they have closed their eyes,
        so they may not see with their eyes
     and hear with their ears
     and understand with their heart and be converted,
        and I heal them.'

[28] [o] Let it be known to you that this sal᷎ tion of God has been sent to the Gen᷎ they will listen." [29] *

[30] * He remained for two full ye᷎ lodgings. He received all who ca᷎ [31] and with complete assuranc᷎ out hindrance he proclaimed ᷎ of God and taught about t᷎ Christ.

NEW TESTAMENT LETTERS

In the New Testament canon, between the Acts of the Apostles and Revelation, there are twenty-one documents that take the form of letters or epistles. Most of these are actual letters, but some are more like treatises in the guise of letters. In a few cases even some of the more obvious elements of the letter form are absent; see the Introductions to Hebrews and to 1 John.

The virtually standard form found in these documents, though with some variation, is dependent upon the conventions of letter writing common in the ancient world, but these were modified to suit the purposes of Christian writers. The New Testament letters usually begin with a greeting including an identification of the sender or senders and of the recipients. Next comes a prayer, usually in the form of a thanksgiving. The body of the letter provides an exposition of Christian teaching, usually provoked by concrete circumstances, and generally also draws conclusions regarding ethical behavior. There often follows a discussion of practical matters, such as the writer's travel plans, and the letter concludes with further advice and a formula of farewell.

Fourteen of the twenty-one letters have been traditionally attributed to Paul. One of these, the Letter to the Hebrews, does not itself claim to be the work of Paul; when it was accepted into the canon after much discussion, it was attached at the very end of the Pauline corpus. The other thirteen identify Paul as their author, but most scholars believe that some of them were actually written by his disciples; see the Introductions to Ephesians, Colossians, 2 Thessalonians, and 1 Timothy.

Four of the letters in the Pauline corpus (Ephesians, Philippians, Colossians, and Philemon) are called the "Captivity Epistles" because in each of them the author speaks of being in prison at the time of writing. Three others (1-2 Timothy and Titus) are known as the "Pastoral Epistles" because, addressed to individuals rather than communities, they give advice to disciples about caring for the flock. The letters of the Pauline corpus are arranged in roughly descending order of length from Romans to Philemon, with Hebrews added at the end.

The other seven letters of the New Testament that follow the Pauline corpus are collectively referred to as the "Catholic Epistles." This term, which means "universal," refers to the fact that most of them are directed not to a single Christian community, as are most of the Pauline letters, but to a wider audience; see the Introduction to the catholic letters. Three of them (1-2-3 John) are closely related to the fourth gospel and thus belong to the Johannine corpus. The catholic letters, like those of the Pauline corpus, are also arranged in roughly descending order of length, but the three Johannine letters are kept together and Jude is placed at the end.

The genuine letters of Paul are earlier in date than any of our written gospels. The dates of the other New Testament letters are more difficult to determine, but for the most part they belong to the second and third Christian generations rather than to the first.

THE LETTER TO THE ROMANS

INTRODUCTION

Of all the letters of Paul, that to the Christians at Rome has long held pride of place. It is the longest and most systematic unfolding of the apostle's thought, expounding the gospel of God's righteousness that saves all who believe (1, 16-17); it reflects a universal outlook, with special implications for Israel's relation to the church (chs 9-11). Yet, like all Paul's letters, Romans too arose out of a specific situation, when the apostle wrote from Greece, likely Corinth, between A.D. 56 and 58 (cf Acts 20, 2-3).

Paul at that time was about to leave for Jerusalem with a collection of funds for the impoverished Jewish Christian believers there, taken up from his predominantly Gentile congregations (15, 25-27). He planned then to travel on to Rome and to enlist support there for a mission to Spain (15, 24.28). Such a journey had long been on his mind (1, 9-13; 15, 23). Now, with much missionary preaching successfully accomplished in the East (15, 19), he sought new opportunities in the West (15, 20-21), in order to complete the divine plan of evangelization in the Roman world. Yet he recognized that the visit to Jerusalem would be hazardous (15, 30-32), and we know from Acts that Paul was arrested there and came to Rome only in chains, as a prisoner (Acts 21—28, especially 21, 30-33 and 28, 14.30-31).

The existence of a Christian community in Rome antedates Paul's letter there. When it arose, likely within the sizable Jewish population at Rome, and how, we do not know. The Roman historian Suetonius mentions an edict of the Emperor Claudius about A.D. 49 ordering the expulsion of Jews from Rome in connection with a certain "Chrestus," probably involving a dispute in the Jewish community over Jesus as the Messiah ("Christus"). According to Acts 18, 2, Aquila and Priscilla (or Prisca, as in Rom 16, 3) were among those driven out; from them, in Corinth, Paul may have learned about conditions in the church at Rome.

Opinions vary as to whether Jewish or Gentile Christians predominated in the house churches (cf 16, 5) in the capital city of the empire at the time Paul wrote. Perhaps already by then Gentile Christians were in the majority. Paul speaks in Romans of both Jews and Gentiles (3, 9.29; see the note on 1, 14). The letter also refers to those "weak in faith" (14, 1) and those "who are strong" (15, 1); this terminology may reflect not so much differences between believers of Jewish and of Gentile background, respectively, as an ascetic tendency in some converts (14, 2) combined with Jewish laws about clean and unclean foods (14, 14.20). The issues were similar to problems that Paul had faced in Corinth (1 Cor 8). If Romans 16 is part of the letter to Rome (see the note on 16, 1-23), then Paul had considerable information about conditions in Rome through all these people there whom he knew, and our letter does not just reflect a generalized picture of an earlier situation in Corinth.

In any case, Paul writes to introduce himself and his message to the Christians at Rome, seeking to enlist their support for the proposed mission to Spain. He therefore employs formulations likely familiar to the Christians at Rome; see the note on the confessional material at 1, 3-4 and compare 3, 25-26 and 4, 25. He cites the Old Testament frequently (1, 17; 3, 10-18; ch 4; 9, 7.12-13.15.17.25-29.33; 10, 5-13.15-21; 15, 9-12). The gospel Paul presents is meant to be a familiar one to those in Rome, even though they heard it first from other preachers.

As the outline below shows, this gospel of Paul (see 16, 25) finds its center in salvation and justification through faith in Christ (1, 16-17). While God's wrath is revealed against all sin and wickedness of Gentile and Jew alike (1, 18—3, 20). God's power to save by divine righteous or justifying action in Christ is also revealed (1, 16-17; 3, 21—5, 21). The consequences and implications for those who believe are set forth (6, 1—8, 39), as are results for those in Israel (chs 9-11) who, to Paul's great sorrow (9, 1-5), disbelieve. The apostle's hope is that, just as rejection of the gospel by some in Israel has led to a ministry of salvation for non-Jews, so one day, in God's mercy, "all Israel" will be saved (11, 11-15.25-29.30-32). The fuller ethical response of believers is also drawn out, both with reference to life in Christ's body (ch 12) and with regard to the world (13, 1-7), on the basis of the eschatological situation (13, 11-14) and conditions in the community (14, 1—15, 13).

Others have viewed Romans more in the light of Paul's earlier, quite polemical Letter to the Galatians and so see the theme as the relationship between Judaism and Christianity, a topic judged to be much in the minds of the Roman Christians. Each of these religious faiths claimed to be the way of salvation based upon a covenant between God and a people chosen and made the beneficiary of divine gifts. But Christianity regarded itself as the prophetic development and fulfillment of the faith of the Old Testament, declaring that the preparatory Mosaic covenant must now give way to the new and more perfect covenant in Jesus Christ. Paul himself had been the implacable advocate of freedom of Gentiles from the laws of the Mosaic covenant and, especially in Galatia, had refused to allow attempts to impose them on Gentile converts to the gospel. He had witnessed the personal hostilities that developed between the adherents of the two faiths and had written his strongly worded letter to the Galatians against those Jewish Christians who were seeking to persuade Gentile Christians to adopt the religious practices of Judaism. For him, the purity of the religious understanding of Jesus as the source of salvation would be seriously impaired if Gentile Christians were obligated to amalgamate the two religious faiths.

Still others find the theme of Israel and the church as expressed in Romans 9—11 to be the heart of Romans. Then the implication of Paul's exposition of justification by faith rather than by means of law is that the divine plan of salvation works itself out on a broad theological plane to include the whole of humanity, despite the differences in the content of the given religious system to which a human culture is heir. Romans presents a plan of salvation stretching from Adam through Abraham and Moses to Christ (chs 4 and 5) and on to the future revelation at Christ's parousia (8, 18-25). Its outlook is universal.

Paul's Letter to the Romans is a powerful exposition of the doctrine of the supremacy of Christ and of faith in Christ as the source of salvation. It is an implicit plea to the Christians at Rome, and to all Christians, to hold fast to that faith. They are to resist any pressure put on them to accept a doctrine of salvation through works of the law (see the note on 10, 4). At the same time they are not to exaggerate Christian freedom as an abdication of responsibility for others (12, 1-2) or as a repudiation of God's law and will (see the notes on 3, 9-26; 3, 31; 7, 7-12.13-25).

The principal divisions of the Letter to the Romans are the following:

I. Address (1, 1-15)
II. Humanity Lost without the Gospel (1, 16—3, 20)
III. Justification through Faith in Christ (3, 21—5, 21)
IV. Justification and the Christian Life (6, 1—8, 39)
V. Jews and Gentiles in God's Plan (9, 1—11, 36)
VI. The Duties of Christians (12, 1—15, 13)
VII. Conclusion (15, 14—16, 27)

I. ADDRESS

CHAPTER 1

Greeting.* [1]Paul, a slave of Christ Jesus,* called to be an apostle and set apart for the gospel of God,[a] [2]which he promised previously through his prophets in the holy scriptures,[b] [3]* the gospel about his Son, descended from David according to the flesh,[c] [4]but established as Son of God in power according to the spirit of holiness through resurrection from the dead, Jesus Christ our Lord.[d] [5]* Through him we have received the grace of apostleship, to bring about the obedience of faith, for the sake of his name, among all the Gentiles,[e] [6]among whom are you also, who are called to belong to Jesus Christ;[f] [7]to all the beloved of God in Rome, called to be holy.* Grace to you and peace from God our Father and the Lord Jesus Christ.[g]

Thanksgiving. [8]First, I give thanks* to my God through Jesus Christ for all of you, because your faith is heralded throughout the world.[h] [9]God is my witness, whom I serve with my spirit in proclaiming the gospel of his Son, that I remember you constantly,[i] [10]* always asking in my prayers that somehow by God's will I may at last find my way clear to come to you.[j] [11]For I long to see you, that I may share with you some spiritual gift so that you may be strengthened,[k] [12]that is, that you and I may be mutually encouraged by one another's faith, yours and mine. [13]I do not want you to be unaware, brothers,* that I often planned to come to you, though I was prevented until now, that I might harvest some fruit among you, too, as among the rest of the Gentiles.[l] [14]To Greeks and non-Greeks* alike, to the wise and the ignorant, I am under obligation; [15]that is why I am eager to preach the gospel also to you in Rome.[m]

---

a Gal 1, 10; Phil 1, 1; Jas 1, 1 / Acts 9, 15; 13, 2; 1 Cor 1, 1; Gal 1, 15; Ti 1, 1.—b Rom 16, 25-26; Ti 1, 2.—c Rom 9, 5; 2 Sm 7, 12; Mt 1, 1; Mk 12, 35; Jn 7, 42; Acts 13, 22-23; 2 Tm 2, 8; Rv 22, 16.—d Rom 10, 9; Acts 13, 33; Phil 3, 10.—e Rom 15, 15; Gal 2, 7.9 / Rom 15, 18; Acts 9, 15; 26, 16-18; Gal 1, 16; 2, 7.9.—f 1 Cor 1, 9.—g Nm 6, 25-26; 1 Cor 1, 2-3; 2 Cor 1, 1-2.— h Rom 16, 19; 1 Thes 1, 8.—i 2 Cor 1, 23; Eph 1, 16; Phil 1, 8; 1 Thes 1, 2; 2, 5.10; 2 Tm 1, 3.—j Rom 15, 23.32; Acts 18, 21; 1 Cor 4, 19; 1 Thes 2, 17.—k 1 Thes 2, 17; 3, 10.—l Rom 15, 22; Jn 15, 16; Acts 19, 21.—m Acts 28, 30-31.

1, 1-7: In Paul's letters the greeting or *praescriptio* follows a standard form, though with variations. It is based upon the common Greco-Roman epistolary practice, but with the addition of Semitic and specifically Christian elements. The three basic components are: name of sender; name of addressee; greeting. In identifying himself, Paul often adds phrases to describe his apostolic mission; this element is more developed in Rom than in any other letter. Elsewhere he associates co-workers with himself in the greeting: Sosthenes (1 Cor), Timothy (2 Cor; Phil; Phlm), Silvanus (1-2 Thes). The standard secular greeting was the infinitive *chairein,* "greetings." Paul uses instead the similar-sounding *charis,* "grace," together with the Semitic greeting *šālôm* (Greek *eirēnē*), "peace." These gifts, foreshadowed in God's dealings with Israel (see Nm 6, 24-26), have been poured out abundantly in Christ, and Paul wishes them to his readers. In Rom the Pauline *praescriptio* is expanded and expressed in a formal tone; it emphasizes Paul's office as apostle to the Gentiles. Verses 3-4 stress the gospel or kerygma, v 2 the fulfillment of God's promise, and vv 1 and 5 Paul's office. On his call, see Gal 1, 15-16; 1 Cor 9, 1; 15, 8-10; Acts 1, 22; 22, 3-16; 26, 4-18.

1, 1: *Slave of Christ Jesus:* Paul applies the term slave to himself in order to express his undivided allegiance to the Lord of the church, the Master of all, including slaves and masters. "No one can serve (i.e., be a slave to) two masters," said Jesus (Mt 6, 24). It is this aspect of the slave-master relationship rather than its degrading implications that Paul emphasizes when he discusses Christian commitment.

1, 3-4: Paul here cites an early confession that proclaims Jesus' sonship as messianic descendant of David (cf Mt 22, 42; 2 Tm 2, 8; Rv 22, 16) and as Son of God by the resurrection. As "life-giving spirit" (1 Cor 15, 45), Jesus Christ is able to communicate the Spirit to those who believe in him.

1, 5: Paul recalls his apostolic office, implying that the Romans know something of his history. *The obedience of faith:* as Paul will show at length in chs 6-8 and 12-15, faith in God's justifying action in Jesus Christ relates one to God's gift of the new life that is made possible through the death and resurrection of Jesus Christ and the activity of the holy Spirit (see especially Rom 8, 1-11).

1, 7: *Called to be holy:* Paul often refers to Christians as "the holy ones" or "the saints." The Israelite community was called a "holy assembly" because they had been separated for the worship and service of the Lord (see Lv 11, 44; 23, 1-44). The Christian community regarded its members as sanctified by baptism (Rom 6, 22; 15, 16; 1 Cor 6, 11; Eph 5, 26-27). Christians are called to holiness (1 Cor 1, 2; 1 Thes 4, 7), that is, they are called to make their lives conform to the gift they have already received.

1, 8: In Greco-Roman letters, the greeting was customarily followed by a prayer. The Pauline letters usually include this element (except Gal and Ti), expressed in Christian thanksgiving formulas and usually stating the principal theme of the letter. In 2 Cor the thanksgiving becomes a blessing, and in Eph it is preceded by a lengthy blessing. Sometimes the thanksgiving is blended into the body of the letter, especially in 1 Thes. In Rom it is stated briefly.

1, 10-12: Paul lays the groundwork for his more detailed statement in Rom 15, 22-24 about his projected visit to Rome.

1, 13: *Brothers* is idiomatic for all Paul's "kin in Christ," all those who believe in the gospel; it includes women as well as men (cf Rom 4, 3).

1, 14: *Greeks and non-Greeks:* literally, "Greeks and barbarians." As a result of Alexander's conquests, Greek became the standard international language of the Mediterranean world. *Greeks* in Paul's statement therefore means people who know Greek or who have been influenced by Greek culture. *Non-Greeks* were people whose cultures remained substantially unaffected by Greek influences. Greeks called such people "barbarians" (cf Acts 28, 2), meaning people whose speech was foreign. Roman citizens would scarcely classify themselves as such, and Nero, who was reigning when Paul wrote this letter, prided himself on his admiration for Greek culture. *Under obligation:* Paul will expand on the theme of obligation in Rom 13, 8; 15, 1.27.

II. HUMANITY LOST WITHOUT THE GOSPEL

God's Power for Salvation. * [16]For I am not ashamed of the gospel. It is the power of God for the salvation of everyone who believes: for Jew first, and then Greek.[n] [17]For in it is revealed the righteousness of God from faith to faith;* as it is written, "The one who is righteous by faith will live."[o]

Punishment of Idolaters. [18] * The wrath* of God* is indeed being revealed from heaven against every impiety and wickedness[p] of those who suppress the truth by their wickedness. [19]For what can be known about God is evident to them, because God made it evident to them.[q] [20]Ever since the creation of the world, his invisible attributes of eternal power and divinity have been able to be understood and perceived in what he has made.[r] As a result, they have no excuse; [21]for although they knew God they did not accord him glory as God or give him thanks. Instead, they became vain in their reasoning, and their senseless minds were darkened.[s] [22]While claiming to be wise,[t] they became fools [23]and exchanged the glory of the immortal God for the likeness of an image of mortal man or of birds or of four-legged animals or of snakes.[u]

[24]Therefore, God handed them over to impurity through the lusts of their hearts* for the mutual degradation of their bodies.[v] [25]They exchanged the truth of God for a lie and revered and worshiped the creature rather than the creator, who is blessed forever. Amen.[w] [26]Therefore, God handed them over to degrading passions. Their females exchanged natural relations for unnatural, [27]and the males likewise gave up natural relations with females and burned with lust for one another. Males did shameful things with males and thus received in their own persons the due penalty for their perversity.[x] [28]And since they did not see fit to acknowledge God, God handed them over to their undiscerning mind to do what is improper. [29] [y] They are filled with every form of wickedness, evil, greed, and malice; full of envy, murder, rivalry, treachery, and spite. They are gossips [30]and scandalmongers and they hate God. They are insolent, haughty, boastful, ingenious in their wickedness, and rebellious toward their parents. [31]They are senseless, faithless, heartless, ruthless. [32]Although they know the just decree of God that all who practice such things deserve death, they not only do them but give approval to those who practice them.[z]

---

n Ps 119, 46; 1 Cor 1, 18.24 / Rom 2, 9; Acts 3, 26; 13, 46.—o Rom 3, 21-22; Hb 2, 4; Gal 3, 11; Heb 10, 38.—p Rom 2, 5.8-9; Is 66, 15; Eph 5, 6; Col 3, 6.—q 19-32: Wis 13, 1-9; Acts 14, 15-17; 17, 23-29.—r Jb 12, 7-9; Pss 8, 4; 19, 2; Sir 17, 7-9; Is 40, 26; Acts 14, 17; 17, 25-28.—s Eph 4, 17-18.—t Wis 13, 1-9; Is 5, 21; Jer 10, 14; Acts 17, 29-30; 1 Cor 1, 19-21.—u Dt 4, 15-19; Ps 106, 20; Wis 11, 15; 12, 24; 13, 10-19; Jer 2, 11.—v Wis 12, 25; 14, 22-31; Acts 7, 41-42; Eph 4, 19.—w Rom 9, 5; Jer 13, 25-27.—x Lv 18, 22; 20, 13; Wis 14, 26; 1 Cor 6, 9; 1 Tm 1, 10.—y 29-31: Rom 13, 13; Mt 15, 19; Mk 7, 21-22; Gal 5, 19-21; 2 Tm 3, 2-4.—z Acts 8, 1; 2 Thes 2, 12.

1, 16-17: The principal theme of the letter is salvation through faith. *I am not ashamed of the gospel:* Paul is not ashamed to proclaim the gospel, despite the criticism that both Jews and Gentiles leveled against the proclamation of the crucified savior; cf 1 Cor 1, 23-24. Paul affirms, however, that it is precisely through the crucifixion and resurrection of Jesus that God's saving will and power become manifest. *Jew first* (cf Rom 2, 9-10) means that Jews especially, in view of the example of Abraham (ch 4), ought to be the leaders in the response of faith.

1, 17: *In it is revealed the righteousness of God from faith to faith:* the gospel centers in Jesus Christ, in whom God's saving presence and righteousness in history have been made known. Faith is affirmation of the basic purpose and meaning of the Old Testament as proclamation of divine promise (Rom 1, 2; 4, 13) and exposure of the inability of humanity to effect its salvation even through covenant law. Faith is the gift of the holy Spirit and denotes acceptance of salvation as God's righteousness, that is, God's gift of a renewed relationship in forgiveness and power for a new life. Faith is response to God's total claim on people and their destiny. *The one who is righteous by faith will live:* see the note on Hb 2, 4.

1, 18—3, 20: Paul aims to show that all humanity is in a desperate plight and requires God's special intervention if it is to be saved.

1, 18-32: In this passage Paul uses themes and rhetoric common in Jewish-Hellenistic mission proclamation (cf Wis 13, 1—14, 31) to indict especially the non-Jewish world. The close association of idolatry and immorality is basic, but the generalization needs in all fairness to be balanced against the fact that non-Jewish Christian society on many levels displayed moral attitudes and performance whose quality would challenge much of contemporary Christian culture. Romans themselves expressed abhorrence over devotion accorded to animals in Egypt. Paul's main point is that the wrath of God does not await the end of the world but goes into action at each present moment in humanity's history when misdirected piety serves as a facade for self-interest.

1, 18: *The wrath of God:* God's reaction to human sinfulness, an Old Testament phrase that expresses the irreconcilable opposition between God and evil (see Is 9, 11.16.18.20; 10, 4; 30, 27). It is not contrary to God's universal love for his creatures, but condemns Israel's turning aside from the covenant obligations. Hosea depicts Yahweh as suffering intensely at the thought of having to punish Israel (Hos 11, 8-9). God's wrath was to be poured forth especially on the "Day of Yahweh" and thus took on an eschatological connotation (see Zep 1, 15).

1, 24: In order to expose the depth of humanity's rebellion against the Creator, *God handed them over to impurity through the lusts of their hearts.* Instead of curbing people's evil interests, God abandoned them to self-indulgence, thereby removing the facade of apparent conformity to the divine will. Subsequently Paul will show that the Mosaic law produces the same effect; cf Rom 5, 20; 7, 13-24. The divine judgment expressed here is related to the theme of hardness of heart described in Rom 9, 17-18.

CHAPTER 2

God's Just Judgment. 1 * Therefore, you are without excuse,*ᵃ* every one of you who passes judgment.* For by the standard by which you judge another you condemn yourself, since you, the judge, do the very same things. 2 We know that the judgment of God on those who do such things is true. 3 Do you suppose, then, you who judge those who engage in such things and yet do them yourself, that you will escape the judgment of God?*ᵇ* 4 Or do you hold his priceless kindness, forbearance, and patience in low esteem, unaware that the kindness of God would lead you to repentance?*ᶜ* 5 By your stubbornness and impenitent heart,*ᵈ* you are storing up wrath for yourself for the day of wrath and revelation of the just judgment of God, 6 *ᵉ* who will repay everyone according to his works:* 7 eternal life to those who seek glory, honor, and immortality through perseverance in good works, 8 but wrath and fury to those who selfishly disobey the truth and obey wickedness.*ᶠ* 9 Yes, affliction and distress will come upon every human being who does evil, Jew first and then Greek. 10 *ᵍ* But there will be glory, honor, and peace for everyone who does good, Jew first and then Greek. 11 *ʰ* There is no partiality with God.*

Judgment by the Interior Law. * 12 All who sin outside the law will also perish without reference to it, and all who sin under the law will be judged in accordance with it.*ⁱ* 13 For it is not those who hear the law who are just in the sight of God; rather, those who observe the law will be justified.*ʲ* 14 For when the Gentiles who do not have the law by nature observe the prescriptions of the law, they are a law for themselves even though they do not have the law.*ᵏ* 15 They show that the demands of the law are written in their hearts,* while their conscience also bears witness and their conflicting thoughts accuse or even defend them 16 on the day when, according to my gospel, God will judge people's hidden works through Christ Jesus.*ˡ*

Judgment by the Mosaic Law. * 17 Now if you call yourself a Jew and rely on the law and boast of God*ᵐ* 18 and know his will and are able to discern what is important since you are instructed from the law,*ⁿ* 19 and if you are confident that you are a guide for the blind and a light for those in darkness,*ᵒ* 20 that you are a trainer of the foolish and teacher of the simple,*ᵖ* because in the law you have the formulation of knowledge and truth—21 then you who teach another, are you failing to teach yourself? You who preach against stealing, do you steal?*�q* 22 You who forbid adultery, do you commit adultery? You who detest idols, do you rob temples? 23 You who boast of the law, do you dishonor God by breaking the law? 24 *ʳ* For, as it is written, "Because of you the name of God is reviled among the Gentiles."*

25 *ˢ* Circumcision, to be sure, has value if you observe the law; but if you break the law, your circumcision has become uncir-

a Mt 7, 1-2.—b Wis 16, 15-16.—c Rom 3, 25-26; 9, 22; Wis 11, 23; 15, 1; 2 Pt 3, 9.15.—d Ex 33, 3; Acts 7, 51; Rv 6, 17; 11, 18.—e Ps 62, 12; Prv 24, 12; Sir 16, 14; Mt 16, 27; Jn 5, 29; 2 Cor 5, 10.—f 2 Thes 1, 8.—g Rom 1, 16; 3, 9.—h Dt 10, 17; 2 Chr 19, 7; Sir 35, 12-13; Acts 10, 34; Gal 2, 6; Eph 6, 9; Col 3, 25; 1 Pt 1, 17.—i Rom 3, 19.—j Mt 7, 21; Lk 6, 46-49; 8, 21; Jas 1, 22-25; 1 Jn 3, 7.—k Acts 10, 35.—l Acts 10, 42; 17, 31.—m Is 48, 1-2; Mi 3, 11; Phil 3, 4-6.—n Phil 1, 10.—o Mt 15, 14; Lk 6, 39.—p 2 Tm 3, 15.—q Ps 50, 16-21; Mt 23, 3-4.—r Is 52, 5; Ez 36, 20; 2 Pt 2, 2.—s 25-29: Jer 4, 4; 9, 24-25.

2, 1—3, 20: After his general indictment of the Gentile, Paul shows that in spite of special revelation Jews enjoy no advantage in moral status before God (Rom 3, 1-8). With the entire human race now declared guilty before God (Rom 3, 9-20), Paul will then be able to display the solution for the total problem: salvation through God's redemptive work that is revealed in Christ Jesus for all who believe (Rom 3, 21-31).

2, 1-11: As a first step in his demonstration that Jews enjoy no real moral supremacy over Gentiles, Paul explains that the final judgment will be a review of performance, not of privilege. From this perspective Gentiles stand on an equal footing with Jews, and Jews cannot condemn the sins of Gentiles without condemning themselves.

2, 6: *Will repay everyone according to his works:* Paul reproduces the Septuagint text of Ps 62, 12 and Prv 24, 12.

2, 11: *No partiality with God:* this sentence is not at variance with the statements in vv 9-10. Since Jews are the first to go under indictment, it is only fair that they be given first consideration in the distribution of blessings. Basic, of course, is the understanding that God accepts no bribes (Dt 10, 17).

2, 12-16: Jews cannot reasonably demand from Gentiles the standard of conduct inculcated in the Old Testament since God did not address its revelation to them. Rather, God made it possible for Gentiles to know instinctively the difference between right and wrong. But, as Paul explained in Rom 1, 18-32, humanity misread the evidence of God's existence, power, and divinity, and "while claiming to be wise, they became fools" (Rom 1, 22).

2, 15: Paul expands on the thought of Jer 31, 33; Wis 17, 11.

2, 17-29: Mere possession of laws is no evidence of virtue. By eliminating circumcision as an elitist moral sign, Paul clears away the last obstacle to his presentation of justification through faith without claims based on the receipt of circumcision and its attendant legal obligations.

2, 24: According to Is 52, 5 the suffering of Israel prompts her enemies to revile God. Paul uses the passage in support of his point that the present immorality of Israelites is the cause of such defamation.

cumcision.[t] [26]Again, if an uncircumcised man keeps the precepts of the law, will he not be considered circumcised?[u] [27]Indeed, those who are physically uncircumcised but carry out the law will pass judgment on you, with your written law and circumcision, who break the law. [28]One is not a Jew outwardly. True circumcision is not outward, in the flesh.[v] [29]Rather, one is a Jew inwardly, and circumcision is of the heart, in the spirit, not the letter; his praise is not from human beings but from God.[w]

CHAPTER 3

Answers to Objections. [1] * What advantage is there then in being a Jew? Or what is the value of circumcision? [2]Much, in every respect. [For] in the first place, they were entrusted with the utterances of God.[x] [3]What if some were unfaithful? Will their infidelity nullify the fidelity of God?[y] [4]Of course not! God must be true, though every human being is a liar,* as it is written:

"That you may be justified in your words,
and conquer when you are judged."[z]

[5]But if our wickedness provides proof of God's righteousness, what can we say? Is God unjust, humanly speaking, to inflict his wrath?[a] [6]Of course not! For how else is God to judge the world? [7]But if God's truth redounds to his glory through my falsehood, why am I still being condemned as a sinner? [8]And why not say—as we are

accused and as some claim we say—that we should do evil that good may come of it? Their penalty is what they deserve.[b]

Universal Bondage to Sin.* [9]Well, then, are we better off? Not entirely, for we have already brought the charge against Jews and Greeks alike that they are all under the domination of sin,[c] [10]as it is written:[d]

[11] "There is no one just, not one,
there is no one who understands,
there is no one who seeks God.
[12] All have gone astray; all alike are worthless;
there is not one who does good,
[there is not] even one.
[13] Their throats are open graves;
they deceive with their tongues;
the venom of asps is on their lips;[e]
[14] their mouths are full of bitter cursing.[f]
[15] Their feet are quick to shed blood;[g]
[16] ruin and misery are in their ways,
[17] and the way of peace they know not.
[18] There is no fear of God before their eyes."[h]

[19]Now we know that what the law* says is addressed to those under the law, so that every mouth may be silenced and the whole world stand accountable to God,[i] [20]since no human being will be justified in his sight* by observing the law; for through the law comes consciousness of sin.[j]

III. JUSTIFICATION THROUGH FAITH IN CHRIST

Justification apart from the Law.* [21]But now* the righteousness of God has been manifested apart from the law, though tes-

3, 1-4: In keeping with the popular style of diatribe, Paul responds to the objection that his teaching on the sinfulness of all humanity detracts from the religious prerogatives of Israel. He stresses that Jews have remained the vehicle of God's revelation despite their sins, though this depends on the fidelity of God.

3, 4: *Though every human being is a liar:* these words reproduce the Greek text of Ps 116, 11. The rest of the verse is from Ps 51, 6.

3, 9-20: *Well, then, are we better off?:* this phrase can also be translated "Are we at a disadvantage?" but the latter version does not substantially change the overall meaning of the passage. Having explained that Israel's privileged status is guaranteed by God's fidelity, Paul now demonstrates the infidelity of the Jews by a catena of citations from scripture, possibly derived from an existing collection of *testimonia*. These texts show that all human beings share the common burden of sin. They are linked together by mention of organs of the body: throat, tongue, lips, mouth, feet, eyes.

3, 19: *The law:* Paul here uses the term in its broadest sense to mean all of the scriptures; none of the preceding texts is from the Torah or Pentateuch.

3, 20: *No human being will be justified in his sight:* these words are freely cited from Ps 143, 2. In place of the psalmist's "no living person," Paul substitutes "no human being" (literally "no flesh," a Hebraism), and he adds "by observing the law."

3, 21-31: These verses provide a clear statement of Paul's "gospel," i.e., the principle of justification by faith in Christ. God has found a means of rescuing humanity from its desperate plight: Paul's general term for this divine initiative is *the righteousness of God* (21). Divine mercy declares the guilty innocent and makes them so. God does this not as a result of the law but apart from it (21), and not because of any merit in human beings but through forgiveness of their sins (24), in virtue of the redemption wrought in Christ Jesus for all who believe (22.24-25). God has manifested his righteousness in the coming of Jesus Christ, whose saving activity inaugurates a new era in human history.

3, 21: *But now:* Paul adopts a common phrase used by Greek authors to describe movement from disaster to prosperity. The expressions indicate that vv 21-26 are the consolatory answer to vv 9-20.

tified to by the law and the prophets,[k] [22] the righteousness of God through faith in Jesus Christ for all who believe.[l] For there is no distinction; [23] all have sinned and are deprived of the glory of God.[m] [24] They are justified freely by his grace through the redemption in Christ Jesus,[n] [25] whom God set forth as an expiation,* through faith, by his blood, to prove his righteousness because of the forgiveness of sins previously committed,[o] [26] through the forbearance of God—to prove his righteousness in the present time, that he might be righteous and justify the one who has faith in Jesus.

[27] [p] What occasion is there then for boasting?* It is ruled out. On what principle, that of works? No, rather on the principle of faith.* [28] For we consider that a person is justified by faith apart from works of the law.[q] [29] Does God belong to Jews alone? Does he not belong to Gentiles, too? Yes, also to Gentiles,[r] [30] for God is one and will justify the circumcised on the basis of faith and the uncircumcised through faith.[s] [31] Are we then annulling the law by this faith? Of course not![t] On the contrary, we are supporting the law.*

CHAPTER 4*

Abraham Justified by Faith. [1] What then can we say that Abraham found, our ancestor according to the flesh?[u] [2] * Indeed, if Abraham was justified on the basis of his works, he has reason to boast; but this was not so in the sight of God. [3] [v] For what does the scripture say? "Abraham believed God, and it was credited to him as righteousness."* [4] A worker's wage is credited not as a gift, but as something due.[w] [5] But when one does not work, yet believes in the one who justifies the ungodly, his faith is credited as righteousness. [6] So also David declares the blessedness of the person to whom God credits righteousness apart from works:

[7] "Blessed are they whose iniquities are forgiven[x]
and whose sins are covered.
[8] Blessed is the man whose sin the Lord does not record."

[9] Does this blessedness* apply only to the circumcised, or to the uncircumcised as well? Now we assert that "faith was credited to Abraham as righteousness."[y] [10] Under what circumstances was it credited? Was he circumcised or not? He was not circumcised, but uncircumcised. [11] And he received the sign of circumcision as a seal on the righteousness received through faith while he was uncircumcised. Thus he was to be the father of all the uncircumcised who believe, so that to them [also] righteousness might be credited,[z] [12] as well as the father of the circumcised who not only are circumcised but also follow the path of faith that our father Abraham walked while still uncircumcised.

k Is 51, 6-8; Acts 10, 43.—l Rom 1, 17; Gal 2, 16; Phil 3, 9.— m Rom 3, 9; 5, 12.—n Eph 2, 8; Ti 3, 7 / Rom 5, 1-2; Eph 1, 7.— o Lv 16, 12-15; Acts 17, 31; 1 Jn 4, 10.—p Rom 8, 2; 1 Cor 1, 29-31.—q Rom 5, 1; Gal 2, 16.—r Rom 10, 12.—s Dt 6, 4; Gal 3, 20; Jas 2, 19 / Rom 4, 11-12.—t Rom 8, 4; Mt 5, 17.—u Gal 3, 6-9.—v Gn 15, 6; Gal 3, 6; Jas 2, 14.20-24.—w Rom 11, 6.— x 7-8: Ps 32, 1-2.—y Rom 4, 3.—z Gn 17, 10-11; Gal 3, 6-8.

3, 25: *Expiation:* this rendering is preferable to "propitiation," which suggests hostility on the part of God toward sinners. As Paul will be at pains to point out (Rom 5, 8-10), it is humanity that is hostile to God.

3, 27-31: People cannot boast of their own holiness, since it is God's free gift (27), both to the Jew who practices circumcision out of faith and to the Gentile who accepts faith without the Old Testament religious culture symbolized by circumcision (29-30).

3, 27: *Principle of faith:* literally, "law of faith." Paul is fond of wordplay involving the term "law"; cf Rom 7, 21.23; 8, 2. Since "law" in Greek may also connote "custom" or "principle," his readers and hearers would have sensed no contradiction in the use of the term after the negative statement concerning law in v 20.

3, 31: *We are supporting the law:* giving priority to God's intentions. God is the ultimate source of law, and the essence of law is fairness. On the basis of the Mosaic covenant, God's justice is in question if those who sinned against the law are permitted to go free (see Rom 3, 23-26). In order to rescue all humanity rather than condemn it, God thinks of an alternative: the law or

"principle" of faith (Rom 3, 27). What can be more fair than to admit everyone into the divine presence on the basis of forgiveness grasped by faith? Indeed, this principle of faith antedates the Mosaic law, as Paul will demonstrate in ch 4, and does not therefore mark a change in divine policy.

4, 1-25: This is an expanded treatment of the significance of Abraham's faith, which Paul discusses in Gal 3, 6-18; see the notes there.

4, 2-5: Verse 2 corresponds to v 4, and v 3 to v 5. The Greek term here rendered *credited* means "made an entry." The context determines whether it is credit or debit. Verse 8 speaks of "recording sin" as a debit. Paul's repeated use of accountants' terminology in this and other passages can be traced both to the Old Testament texts he quotes and to his business activity as a tentmaker. The commercial term in Gn 15, 6, "credited it to him," reminds Paul in vv 7-8 of Ps 32, 2, in which the same term is used and applied to forgiveness of sins. Thus Paul is able to argue that Abraham's faith involved receipt of forgiveness of sins and that all believers benefit as he did through faith.

4, 3: Jas 2, 24 appears to conflict with Paul's statement. However, James combats the error of extremists who used the doctrine of justification through faith as a screen for moral self-determination. Paul discusses the subject of holiness in greater detail than does James and beginning with ch 6 shows how justification through faith introduces one to the gift of a new life in Christ through the power of the holy Spirit.

4, 9: *Blessedness:* evidence of divine favor.

Inheritance through Faith. [13] It was not through the law that the promise was made to Abraham and his descendants that he would inherit the world, but through the righteousness that comes from faith. [a] [14] For if those who adhere to the law are the heirs, faith is null and the promise is void. [b] [15] For the law produces wrath; [c] but where there is no law, neither is there violation.* [16] For this reason, it depends on faith, so that it may be a gift, and the promise may be guaranteed to all his descendants, not to those who only adhere to the law but to those who follow the faith of Abraham, who is the father of all of us, [d] [17] as it is written, "I have made you father of many nations." He is our father in the sight of God, in whom he believed, who gives life to the dead and calls into being what does not exist. [e] [18] He believed, hoping against hope, [f] that he would become "the father of many nations," according to what was said, "Thus shall your descendants be." [19] [g] He did not weaken in faith when he considered his own body as [already] dead (for he was almost a hundred years old) and the dead womb of Sarah. [20] He did not doubt God's promise in unbelief;* rather, he was empowered by faith and gave glory to God [21] and was fully convinced that what he had promised he was also able to do. [h] [22] That is why "it was credited to him as righteousness." [i] [23] But it was not for him alone that it was written that "it was credited to him"; [24] it was also for us, to whom it will be credited, who believe in the one who raised Jesus our Lord from the dead, [j] [25] who was handed over for our transgressions and was raised for our justification. [k]

CHAPTER 5

Faith, Hope, and Love.* [1] Therefore, since we have been justified by faith, we have peace* with God through our Lord Jesus Christ, [l] [2] through whom we have gained access [by faith] to this grace in which we stand, and we boast in hope of the glory of God. [m] [3] Not only that, but we even boast of our afflictions, knowing that affliction produces endurance, [4] and endurance, proven character, and proven character, hope, [n] [5] and hope does not disappoint, because the love of God has been poured out into our hearts through the holy Spirit that has been given to us. [o] [6] For Christ, while we were still helpless, yet died at the appointed time for the ungodly. [7] Indeed, only with difficulty does one die for a just person, though perhaps for a good person one might even find courage to die.* [8] But God proves his love for us in that while we were still sinners Christ died for us. [p] [9] How much more then, since we are now justified by his blood, will we be saved through him from the wrath. [q] [10] Indeed, if, while we were enemies, we were reconciled to God through the death of his Son, how much more, once reconciled, will we be saved by his life. [r] [11] Not only that, but we also boast of God through our Lord Jesus Christ, through whom we have now received reconciliation.

a Gn 12, 7; 18, 18; 22, 17-18; Sir 44, 21; Gal 3, 16-18.29.—b Gal 3, 18.—c Rom 3, 20; 5, 13; 7, 8; Gal 3, 19.—d Sir 44, 19; Gal 3, 7-9.—e Gn 17, 5; Heb 11, 19 / Is 48, 13.—f Gn 15, 5.—g 19-20: Gn 17, 17; Heb 11, 11.—h Gn 18, 14; Lk 1, 37.—i Gn 15, 6.—j Rom 10, 9; 1 Pt 1, 21.—k Is 53, 4-5.12; 1 Cor 15, 17; 1 Pt 1, 3 / Rom 8, 11.—l Rom 3, 24-28; Gal 2, 16.—m Eph 2, 18; 3, 12.—n 2 Cor 12, 9-10; Jas 1, 2-4; 1 Pt 1, 5-7; 4, 12-14.—o Rom 8, 14-16; Pss 22, 5-6; 25, 20.—p Jn 3, 16; 1 Jn 4, 10.19.—q Rom 1, 18; 1 Thes 1, 10.—r Rom 8, 7-8; 2 Cor 5, 18; Col 1, 21-22.

4, 15: Law has the negative function of bringing the deep-seated rebellion against God to the surface in specific sins; see the note on Rom 1, 18-32.

4, 20: *He did not doubt God's promise in unbelief:* any doubts Abraham might have had were resolved in commitment to God's promise. Heb 11, 8-12 emphasizes the faith of Abraham and Sarah.

5, 1-11: Popular piety frequently construed reverses and troubles as punishment for sin; cf Jn 9, 2. Paul therefore assures believers that God's justifying action in Jesus Christ is a declaration of peace. The crucifixion of Jesus Christ displays God's initiative in certifying humanity for unimpeded access into the divine presence. Reconciliation is God's gift of pardon to the entire human race. Through faith one benefits personally from this pardon or, in Paul's term, is justified. The ultimate aim of God is to liberate believers from the pre-Christian self as described in chs 1-3. Since this liberation will first find completion in the believer's resurrection, salvation is described as future in Rom 5, 10. Because this fullness of salvation belongs to the future it is called the Christian *hope*. Paul's Greek term for *hope* does not, however, suggest a note of uncertainty, to the effect: "I wonder whether God really means it." Rather, God's promise in the gospel fills believers with expectation and anticipation for the climactic gift of unalloyed commitment in the holy Spirit to the performance of the will of God. The persecutions that attend Christian commitment are to teach believers patience and to strengthen this hope, which will not disappoint them because the holy Spirit dwells in their hearts and imbues them with God's love (5).

5, 1: *We have peace:* a number of manuscripts, versions, and church Fathers read "Let us have peace"; cf Rom 14, 19.

5, 7: In the world of Paul's time the *good person* is especially one who is magnanimous to others.

Humanity's Sin through Adam. [12] * Therefore, just as through one person sin entered the world,[s] and through sin, death, and thus death came to all, inasmuch as all sinned*—[13] for up to the time of the law, sin was in the world, though sin is not accounted when there is no law.[t] [14] But death reigned from Adam to Moses, even over those who did not sin after the pattern of the trespass of Adam, who is the type of the one who was to come.[u]

Grace and Life through Christ. [15] But the gift is not like the transgression. For if by that one person's transgression the many died, how much more did the grace of God and the gracious gift of the one person Jesus Christ overflow for the many. [16] And the gift is not like the result of the one person's sinning. For after one sin there was the judgment that brought condemnation; but the gift, after many transgressions, brought acquittal. [17] For if, by the transgression of one person, death came to reign through that one, how much more will those who receive the abundance of grace and of the gift of justification come to reign in life through the one person Jesus Christ. [18] In conclusion, just as through one transgression condemnation came upon all, so through one righteous act acquittal and life came to all.[v] [19] For just as through the disobedience of one person the many were made sinners, so through the obedience of one the many will be made righteous.[w] [20] The law entered in* so that transgression might increase but, where sin increased, grace overflowed all the more,[x] [21] so that, as sin reigned in death, grace also might

reign through justification for eternal life through Jesus Christ our Lord.[y]

IV. JUSTIFICATION AND THE CHRISTIAN LIFE

CHAPTER 6

Freedom from Sin; Life in God. [1] * What then shall we say? Shall we persist in sin that grace may abound? Of course not![z] [2] How can we who died to sin yet live in it?[a] [3] Or are you unaware that we who were baptized into Christ Jesus were baptized into his death?[b] [4] We were indeed buried with him through baptism into death, so that, just as Christ was raised from the dead by the glory of the Father, we too might live in newness of life.[c]

[5] For if we have grown into union with him through a death like his, we shall also be united with him in the resurrection.[d] [6] We know that our old self was crucified with him, so that our sinful body might be done away with, that we might no longer be in slavery to sin.[e] [7] For a dead person has been absolved from sin. [8] If, then, we have died with Christ, we believe that we shall also live with him.[f] [9] We know that Christ, raised from the dead, dies no more; death no longer has power over him.[g] [10] As to his death, he died to sin once and for all; as to his life, he lives for God.[h] [11] Consequently, you too must think of yourselves as [being] dead to sin and living for God in Christ Jesus.[i]

Rom

s Gn 2, 17; 3, 1-19; Wis 2, 24 / Rom 3, 19.23.—t Rom 4, 15.—
u 1 Cor 15, 21.—v 1 Cor 15, 21-22.—w Is 53, 11; Phil 2, 8-9.—
x Rom 4, 15; 7, 7-8; Gal 3, 19.—y Rom 6, 23.—z Rom 3, 5-8.—a
1 Pt 4, 1.—b Gal 3, 27.—c Col 2, 12; 1 Pt 3, 21-22.—d Phil 3,
10-11; 2 Tm 2, 11.—e Gal 5, 24; 6, 14; Eph 4, 22-23.—f 1 Thes
4, 17.—g Acts 13, 34; 1 Cor 15, 26; 2 Tm 1, 10; Rv 1, 18.—h
Heb 9, 26-28; 1 Pt 3, 18.—i 2 Cor 5, 15; 1 Pt 2, 24.

5, 12-21: Paul reflects on the sin of Adam (Gn 3, 1-13) in the light of the redemptive mystery of Christ. Sin, as used in the singular by Paul, refers to the dreadful power that has gripped humanity, which is now in revolt against the Creator and engaged in the exaltation of its own desires and interests. But no one has a right to say, "Adam made me do it," for all are culpable (12): Gentiles under the demands of the law written in their hearts (Rom 2, 14-15), and Jews under the Mosaic covenant. Through the Old Testament law, the sinfulness of humanity that was operative from the beginning (13) found further stimulation, with the result that sins were generated in even greater abundance. According to vv 15-21, God's act in Christ is in total contrast to the disastrous effects of the virus of sin that invaded humanity through Adam's crime.

5, 12: *Inasmuch as all sinned:* others translate "because all sinned," and understand v 13 as a parenthetical remark. Unlike Wis 2, 24, Paul does not ascribe the entry of death to the devil.

5, 20: *The law entered in:* sin had made its entrance (12); now the law comes in alongside sin. See the notes on Rom 1, 18-32; 5, 12-21. *Where sin increased, grace overflowed all the more:* Paul declares that grace outmatches the productivity of sin.

6, 1-11: To defend the gospel against the charge that it promotes moral laxity (cf Rom 3, 5-8), Paul expresses himself in the typical style of spirited diatribe. God's display of generosity or grace is not evoked by sin but, as stated in Rom 5, 8, is the expression of God's love, and this love pledges eternal life to all believers (Rom 5, 21). Paul views the present conduct of the believers from the perspective of God's completed salvation when the body is resurrected and directed totally by the holy Spirit. Through baptism believers share the death of Christ and thereby escape from the grip of sin. Through the resurrection of Christ the power to live anew becomes reality for them, but the fullness of participation in Christ's resurrection still lies in the future. But life that is lived in dedication to God now is part and parcel of that future. Hence anyone who sincerely claims to be interested in that future will scarcely be able to say, "Let us sin so that grace may prosper" (cf Rom 6, 1).

ROMANS, 7 230 Acquaintance with Sin through the Law

[12] * Therefore, sin must not reign over your mortal bodies so that you obey their desires.[j] [13] And do not present the parts of your bodies to sin as weapons for wickedness, but present yourselves to God as raised from the dead to life and the parts of your bodies to God as weapons for righteousness.[k] [14] For sin is not to have any power over you, since you are not under the law but under grace.[l]

[15] What then? Shall we sin because we are not under the law but under grace? Of course not![m] [16] Do you not know that if you present yourselves to someone as obedient slaves,[n] you are slaves of the one you obey, either of sin, which leads to death, or of obedience, which leads to righteousness?[o] [17] But thanks be to God that, although you were once slaves of sin, you have become obedient from the heart to the pattern of teaching to which you were entrusted.* [18] Freed from sin, you have become slaves of righteousness. [19] I am speaking in human terms because of the weakness of your nature. For just as you presented the parts of your bodies as slaves to impurity and to lawlessness for lawlessness, so now present them as slaves to righteousness for sanctification. [20][p] For when you were slaves of sin, you were free from righteousness.* [21] But what profit did you get from the things of which you are now ashamed? For the end of those things is death.[q] [22] But now that you have been freed from sin and have become slaves of God, the benefit that you have leads to sanctification,* and its end is eternal life.[r] [23] For the wages of sin is death, but the gift of God is eternal life in Christ Jesus our Lord.[s]

CHAPTER 7

Freedom from the Law.* [1] Are you unaware, brothers (for I am speaking to people who know the law), that the law has jurisdiction over one as long as one lives? [2] Thus a married woman is bound by law to her living husband; but if her husband dies, she is released from the law in respect to her husband.[t] [3] Consequently, while her husband is alive she will be called an adulteress if she consorts with another man. But if her husband dies she is free from that law, and she is not an adulteress if she consorts with another man.

[4] In the same way, my brothers, you also were put to death to the law through the body of Christ, so that you might belong to another, to the one who was raised from the dead in order that we might bear fruit for God. [5] For when we were in the flesh, our sinful passions, awakened by the law, worked in our members to bear fruit for death.[u] [6] But now we are released from the law, dead to what held us captive, so that we may serve in the newness of the spirit and not under the obsolete letter.[v]

Acquaintance with Sin through the Law. [7] * What then can we say? That the law is sin? Of course not!* Yet I did not know sin except through the law, and I did not know what it is to covet except that the law said, "You shall not covet."[w] [8] But sin, finding an opportunity in the commandment, produced in me every kind of covetousness. Apart from the law sin is dead.[x] [9] I once lived outside the law, but when the commandment came, sin became alive; [10] then

---

j Gn 4, 7.—k Rom 12, 1; Eph 2, 5; 5, 14 / Col 3, 5.—l Gal 5, 18; 1 Jn 3, 6.—m Rom 5, 17.21.—n Jn 8, 31-34; 2 Pt 2, 19.—o 16-18: Jn 8, 32-36.—p Jn 8, 34.—q Rom 8, 6.13; Prv 12, 28; Ez 16, 61.63.—r 1 Pt 1, 9.—s Gn 2, 17; Gal 6, 7-9; Jas 1, 15.—t 1 Cor 7, 39.—u Rom 6, 21; 8, 6.13.—v Rom 8, 2; 2 Cor 3, 6.—w Rom 3, 20; Ex 20, 17; Dt 5, 21.—x Rom 5, 13.20; 1 Cor 15, 56 / Rom 4, 15.

6, 12-19: Christians have been released from the grip of sin, but sin endeavors to reclaim its victims. The antidote is constant remembrance that divine grace has claimed them and identifies them as people who are alive only for God's interests.

6, 17: In contrast to humanity, which was handed over to self-indulgence (Rom 1, 24-32), believers are *entrusted* ("handed over") to God's *pattern of teaching,* that is, the new life God aims to develop in Christians through the productivity of the holy Spirit. Throughout this passage Paul uses the slave-master model in order to emphasize the fact that one cannot give allegiance to both God and sin.

6, 20: *You were free from righteousness:* expressed ironically, for such freedom is really tyranny. The commercial metaphors in vv 21-23 add up only one way: sin is a bad bargain.

6, 22: *Sanctification:* or holiness.

7, 1-6: Paul reflects on the fact that Christians have a different understanding of the law because of their faith in Christ. Law binds the living, not the dead, as exemplified in marriage, which binds in life but is dissolved through death. Similarly, Christians who through baptism have died with Christ to sin (cf Rom 6, 2-4) are freed from the law that occasioned transgressions, which in turn were productive of death. Now that Christians are joined to Christ, the power of Christ's resurrection makes it possible for them to bear the fruit of newness of life for God.

7, 7-25: In this passage Paul uses the first person singular in the style of diatribe for the sake of argument. He aims to depict the disastrous consequences when a Christian reintroduces the law as a means to attain the objective of holiness pronounced in Rom 6, 22.

7, 7-12: The apostle defends himself against the charge of identifying the law with sin. Sin does not exist in law but in human beings, whose sinful inclinations are not overcome by the proclamation of law.

I died, and the commandment that was for life turned out to be death for me.*y* ¹¹For sin, seizing an opportunity in the commandment, deceived me and through it put me to death.*z* ¹²So then the law is holy, and the commandment is holy and righteous and good.*a*

Sin and Death.* ¹³Did the good, then, become death for me? Of course not! Sin, in order that it might be shown to be sin, worked death in me through the good, so that sin might become sinful beyond measure through the commandment.*b* ¹⁴We know that the law is spiritual; but I am carnal, sold into slavery to sin.*c* ¹⁵What I do, I do not understand. For I do not do what I want, but I do what I hate. ¹⁶Now if I do what I do not want, I concur that the law is good. ¹⁷So now it is no longer I who do it, but sin that dwells in me. ¹⁸For I know that good does not dwell in me, that is, in my flesh. The willing is ready at hand, but doing the good is not.*d* ¹⁹For I do not do the good I want, but I do the evil I do not want. ²⁰Now if [I] do what I do not want, it is no longer I who do it, but sin that dwells in me. ²¹So, then, I discover the principle that when I want to do right, evil is at hand. ²²For I take delight in the law of God, in my inner self, ²³ *e* but I see in my members another principle at war with the law of my mind, taking me captive to the law of sin that dwells in my members.* ²⁴Miserable one that I am! Who will deliver me from this mortal body? ²⁵Thanks be to God through Jesus Christ our Lord. Therefore, I myself, with my mind, serve the law of God but, with my flesh, the law of sin.*f*

CHAPTER 8

The Flesh and the Spirit.* ¹Hence, now there is no condemnation for those who are in Christ Jesus. ²For the law of the spirit of life in Christ Jesus has freed you from the law of sin and death.*g* ³For what the law, weakened by the flesh, was powerless to do, this God has done: by sending his own Son in the likeness of sinful flesh and for the sake of sin, he condemned sin in the flesh,*h* ⁴so that the righteous decree of the law might be fulfilled in us, who live not according to the flesh but according to the spirit.*i* ⁵For those who live according to the flesh are concerned with the things of the flesh, but those who live according to the spirit with the things of the spirit. ⁶The concern of the flesh is death, but the concern of the spirit is life and peace.*j* ⁷For the concern of the flesh is hostility toward God; it does not submit to the law of God, nor can it;*k* ⁸and those who are in the flesh cannot please God.*l* ⁹But you are not in the flesh; on the contrary, you are in the spirit, if only the Spirit of God dwells in you. Whoever does not have the Spirit of Christ does not belong to him.*m* ¹⁰But if Christ is in you, although the body is dead because of sin, the spirit is alive because of righteousness.*n* ¹¹If the Spirit of the one who raised Jesus from the dead dwells in you, the one who raised Christ from the dead will give life to your mortal bodies also, through his Spirit that dwells in you. ¹²Consequently, brothers, we are not debtors to the flesh, to live according to the flesh. ¹³For if you live according to the flesh, you will die, but if by the spirit you put to death the deeds of the body, you will live.*o*

Rom

---

y Lv 18, 5.—z Gn 3, 13; Heb 3, 13.—a 1 Tm 1, 8.—b Rom 4, 15; 5, 20.—c Rom 8, 7-8; Ps 51, 7.—d Gn 6, 5; 8, 21; Phil 2, 13.—e Gal 5, 17; 1 Pt 2, 11.—f 1 Cor 15, 57.—g Rom 7, 23-24; 2 Cor 3, 17.—h Acts 13, 38; 15, 10 / Jn 3, 16-17; 2 Cor 5, 21; Gal 3, 13; 4, 4; Phil 2, 7; Col 1, 22; Heb 2, 17; 4, 15; 1 Jn 4, 9.— i Gal 5, 16-25.—j Rom 6, 21; 7, 5; 8, 13; Gal 6, 8.—k Rom 5, 10; Jas 4, 4.—l 1 Jn 2, 16.—m 1 Cor 3, 16.—n Gal 2, 20; 1 Pt 4, 6.—o Gal 5, 24; 6, 8; Eph 4, 22-24.

7, 13-25: Far from improving the sinner, law encourages sin to expose itself in transgressions or violations of specific commandments (see Rom 1, 24; 5, 20). Thus persons who do not experience the justifying grace of God, and Christians who revert to dependence on law as the criterion for their relationship with God, will recognize a rift between their reasoned desire for the goodness of the law and their actual performance that is contrary to the law. Unable to free themselves from the slavery of sin and the power of death, they can only be rescued from defeat in the conflict by the power of God's grace working through Jesus Christ.

7, 23: As in Rom 3, 27, Paul plays on the term *law*, which in Greek can connote custom, system, or *principle*.

8, 1-13: After his warning in ch 7 against the wrong route to fulfillment of the objective of holiness expressed in Rom 6, 22, Paul points his addressees to the correct way. Through the redemptive work of Christ, Christians have been liberated from the terrible forces of sin and death. Holiness was impossible so long as the *flesh* (or our "old self"), that is, self-interested hostility toward God (7), frustrated the divine objectives expressed in the law. What is worse, sin used the law to break forth into all manner of lawlessness (8). All this is now changed. At the cross God broke the power of sin and pronounced sentence on it (3). Christians still retain the flesh, but it is alien to their new being, which is life in the spirit, namely the new self, governed by the holy Spirit. Under the direction of the holy Spirit Christians are able to fulfill the divine will that formerly found expression in the law (4). The same Spirit who enlivens Christians for holiness will also resurrect their bodies at the last day (11). Christian life is therefore the experience of a constant challenge to put to death the evil deeds of the body through life of the spirit (13).

Children of God through Adoption.* [14] For those who are led by the Spirit of God are children of God.*p* [15] For you did not receive a spirit of slavery to fall back into fear, but you received a spirit of adoption, through which we cry, *Abba*,* "Father!"*q* [16] The Spirit itself bears witness with our spirit that we are children of God,*r* [17] and if children, then heirs, heirs of God and joint heirs with Christ, if only we suffer with him so that we may also be glorified with him.*s*

Destiny of Glory.* [18] I consider that the sufferings of this present time are as nothing compared with the glory to be revealed for us.*t* [19] For creation awaits with eager expectation the revelation of the children of God; [20] for creation was made subject to futility, not of its own accord but because of the one who subjected it,*u* in hope [21] that creation itself would be set free from slavery to corruption and share in the glorious freedom of the children of God.*v* [22] We know that all creation is groaning in labor pains even until now;*w* [23] and not only that, but we ourselves, who have the firstfruits of the Spirit, we also groan within ourselves as we wait for adoption, the redemption of our bodies.*x* [24] For in hope we were saved. Now hope that sees for itself is not hope. For who hopes for what one sees?*y* [25] But if we hope for what we do not see, we wait with endurance.

[26] In the same way, the Spirit too comes to the aid of our weakness; for we do not know how to pray as we ought, but the Spirit itself intercedes with inexpressible groanings. [27] And the one who searches hearts knows what is the intention of the Spirit, because it intercedes for the holy ones according to God's will.*z*

God's Indomitable Love in Christ. [28] * We know that all things work for good for those who love God,* who are called according to his purpose.*a* [29] For those he foreknew he also predestined to be conformed to the image* of his Son, so that he might be the firstborn among many brothers.*b* [30] And those he predestined he also called; and those he called he also justified; and those he justified he also glorified.*c*

[31] * What then shall we say to this? If God is for us, who can be against us?*d* [32] He who did not spare his own Son but handed him over for us all, how will he not also give us everything else along with him?*e* [33] Who will bring a charge against God's chosen ones?*f* It is God who acquits us. [34] Who will condemn? It is Christ [Jesus] who died, rather, was raised, who also is at the right hand of God, who indeed intercedes for us.*g* [35] What will separate us from the love of Christ? Will anguish, or distress, or persecution, or famine, or nakedness, or peril, or the sword? [36] As it is written:*h*

> "For your sake we are being slain all the day;
> we are looked upon as sheep to be slaughtered."

[37] No, in all these things we conquer overwhelmingly through him who loved us.*i*

---

p Gal 5, 18.—q Mk 14, 36; Gal 4, 5-6; 2 Tm 1, 7.—r Jn 1, 12; Gal 3, 26-29.—s Gal 4, 7; 1 Pt 4, 13; 5, 1.—t 2 Cor 4, 17.—u Gn 3, 17-19.—v 2 Pt 3, 12-13; Rv 21, 1.—w 2 Cor 5, 2-5.—x 2 Cor 1, 22; Gal 5, 5.—y 2 Cor 5, 7; Heb 11, 1.—z Ps 139, 1; 1 Cor 4, 5.—a 28-29: Eph 1, 4-14; 3, 11.—b Eph 1, 5; 1 Pt 1, 2.—c Is 45, 25; 2 Thes 2, 13-14.—d Ps 118, 6; Heb 13, 6.—e Jn 3, 16.—f 33-34: Is 50, 8.—g Ps 110, 1; Heb 7, 25; 1 Jn 2, 1.—h Ps 44, 23; 1 Cor 4, 9; 15, 30; 2 Cor 4, 11; 2 Tm 3, 12.—i 1 Jn 5, 4.

8, 14-17: Christians, by reason of the Spirit's presence within them, enjoy not only new life but also a new relationship to God, that of adopted children and heirs through Christ, whose sufferings and glory they share.

8, 15: *Abba:* see the note on Mk 14, 36.

8, 18-27: The glory that believers are destined to share with Christ far exceeds the sufferings of the present life. Paul considers the destiny of the created world to be linked with the future that belongs to the believers. As it shares in the penalty of corruption brought about by sin, so also will it share in the benefits of redemption and future glory that comprise the ultimate liberation of God's people (19-22). After patient endurance in steadfast expectation, the full harvest of the Spirit's presence will be realized. On earth believers enjoy the firstfruits, i.e., the Spirit, as a guarantee of the total liberation of their bodies from the influence of the rebellious old self (23).

8, 28-30: These verses outline the Christian vocation as it was designed by God: *to be conformed to the image of his Son*, who is to *be the firstborn among many brothers* (29). God's redemptive action on behalf of the believers has been in process before the beginning of the world. Those whom God chooses are *those he foreknew* (29) or elected. Those who are *called* (30) are *predestined* or predetermined. These expressions do not mean that God is arbitrary. Rather, Paul uses them to emphasize the thought and care that God has taken for the Christian's salvation.

8, 28: *We know that all things work for good for those who love God:* a few ancient authorities have God as the subject of the verb, and some translators render: "We know that God makes everything work for good for those who love God. . . ."

8, 29: *Image:* while man and woman were originally created in God's image (Gn 1, 26-27), it is through baptism into Christ, the image of God (2 Cor 4, 4; Col 1, 15), that we are renewed according to the image of the Creator (Col 3, 10).

8, 31-39: The all-conquering power of God's love has overcome every obstacle to Christians' salvation and every threat to separate them from God. That power manifested itself fully when God's own Son was delivered up to death for their salvation. Through him Christians can overcome all their afflictions and trials.

[38] For I am convinced that neither death, nor life, nor angels, nor principalities, nor present things,* nor future things, nor powers,[j] [39] nor height, nor depth,* nor any other creature will be able to separate us from the love of God in Christ Jesus our Lord.

V. JEWS AND GENTILES IN GOD'S PLAN*

CHAPTER 9

Paul's Love for Israel.* [1] I speak the truth in Christ, I do not lie; my conscience joins with the holy Spirit in bearing me witness[k] [2] that I have great sorrow and constant anguish in my heart. [3] For I could wish that I myself were accursed and separated from Christ for the sake of my brothers, my kin according to the flesh.[l] [4] They are Israelites; theirs the adoption, the glory, the covenants, the giving of the law, the worship, and the promises;[m] [5] theirs the patriarchs, and from them, according to the flesh, is the Messiah. God who is over all* be blessed forever. Amen.[n]

God's Free Choice. [6] But it is not that the word of God has failed. For not all who are of Israel are Israel,[o] [7] nor are they all children of Abraham because they are his descendants; but "It is through Isaac that descendants shall bear your name."[p] [8] This means that it is not the children of the flesh who are the children of God, but the children of the promise are counted as descendants.[q] [9] For this is the wording of the promise, "About this time I shall return and Sarah will have a son."[r] [10] And not only that,[s] but also when Rebecca had conceived children by one husband, our father Isaac*—[11] before they had yet been born or had done anything, good or bad, in order that God's elective plan might continue, [12] not by works but by his call—she was told, "The older shall serve the younger."[t] [13] As it is written:[u]

> "I loved Jacob
> but hated Esau."*

[14] * What then are we to say? Is there injustice on the part of God? Of course not![v] [15] For he says to Moses:

> "I will show mercy to whom I will,
> I will take pity on whom I will."[w]

[16] So it depends not upon a person's will or exertion, but upon God, who shows mercy.[x] [17] For the scripture says to Pharaoh, "This is why I have raised you up, to show my power through you that my name may be proclaimed throughout

---

j 38-39: 1 Cor 3, 22; Eph 1, 21; 1 Pt 3, 22.—k 2 Cor 11, 31; 1 Tm 2, 7.—l Ex 32, 32.—m 4-5: Rom 3, 2; Ex 4, 22; Dt 7, 6; 14, 1-2.—n Mt 1, 1-16; Lk 3, 23-38 / Rom 1, 25; Ps 41, 14.—o Nm 23, 19 / Mt 3, 9.—p Gn 21, 12; Gal 3, 29.—q Gal 4, 23.28.—r Gn 18, 10.14.—s Gn 25, 21.—t Rom 11, 5-6 / Gn 25, 23-24.—u Mal 1, 3.—v Dt 32, 4. w Ex 33, 19. x Eph 2, 8; Ti 3, 5.

8, 38: *Present things* and *future things* may refer to astrological data. Paul appears to be saying that the gospel liberates believers from dependence on astrologers.

8, 39: *Height, depth* may refer to positions in the zodiac, positions of heavenly bodies relative to the horizon. In astrological documents the term for "height" means "exaltation" or the position of greatest influence exerted by a planet. Since hostile spirits were associated with the planets and stars, Paul includes *powers* (38) in his list of malevolent forces.

9, 1—11, 36: Israel's unbelief and its rejection of Jesus as savior astonished and puzzled Christians. It constituted a serious problem for them in view of God's specific preparation of Israel for the advent of the Messiah. Paul addresses himself here to the essential question of how the divine plan could be frustrated by Israel's unbelief. At the same time, he discourages both complacency and anxiety on the part of Gentiles. To those who might boast of their superior advantage over Jews, he warns that their enjoyment of the blessings assigned to Israel can be terminated. To those who might anxiously ask, "How can we be sure that Israel's fate will not be ours?" he replies that only unbelief can deprive one of salvation.

9, 1-5: The apostle speaks in strong terms of the depth of his grief over the unbelief of his own people. He would willingly undergo a curse himself for the sake of their coming to the knowledge of Christ (3; cf Lv 27, 28-29). His love for them derives from God's continuing choice of them and from the spiritual benefits that God bestows on them and through them on all of humanity (4-5).

9, 5: Some editors punctuate this verse differently and prefer the translation, "Of whom is Christ according to the flesh, who is God over all." However, Paul's point is that *God who is over all* aimed to use Israel, which had been entrusted with every privilege, in outreach to the entire world through the Messiah.

9, 10: *Children by one husband, our father Isaac:* Abraham had two children, Ishmael and Isaac, by two wives, Hagar and Sarah, respectively. In that instance Isaac, although born later than Ishmael, became the bearer of the messianic promise. In the case of twins born to Rebecca, God's elective procedure is seen even more dramatically, and again the younger, contrary to Semitic custom, is given the preference.

9, 13: The literal rendering, *"Jacob I loved, but Esau I hated,"* suggests an attitude of divine hostility that is not implied in Paul's statement. In Semitic usage "hate" means to love less; cf Lk 14, 26 with Mt 10, 37. Israel's unbelief reflects the mystery of the divine election that is always operative within it. Mere natural descent from Abraham does not ensure the full possession of the divine gifts; it is God's sovereign prerogative to bestow this fullness upon, or to withhold it from, whomsoever he wishes; cf Mt 3, 9; Jn 8, 39. The choice of Jacob over Esau is a case in point.

9, 14-18: The principle of divine election does not invite Christians to theoretical inquiry concerning the nonelected, nor does this principle mean that God is unfair in his dealings with humanity. The instruction concerning divine election is a part of the gospel and reveals that the gift of faith is the enactment of God's mercy (16). God raised up Moses to display that mercy, and Pharaoh to display divine severity in punishing those who obstinately oppose their Creator.

the earth."[y] [18] Consequently, he has mercy upon whom he wills,[z] and he hardens whom he wills.*

[19] * You will say to me then, "Why [then] does he still find fault? For who can oppose his will?"[a] [20] But who indeed are you, a human being, to talk back to God?[b] Will what is made say to its maker, "Why have you created me so?" [21] Or does not the potter have a right over the clay, to make out of the same lump one vessel for a noble purpose and another for an ignoble one? [22] What if God, wishing to show his wrath and make known his power, has endured with much patience the vessels of wrath made for destruction?[c] [23] This was to make known the riches of his glory to the vessels of mercy, which he has prepared previously for glory, [24] namely, us whom he has called, not only from the Jews but also from the Gentiles.

Witness of the Prophets. [25] As indeed he says in Hosea:

"Those who were not my people I will
    call 'my people,'
and her who was not beloved* I will
    call 'beloved.'[d]

[26] And in the very place where it was said
    to them, 'You are not my people,'
there they shall be called children of
    the living God."[e]

[27] [f] And Isaiah cries out concerning Israel, "Though the number of the Israelites were

like the sand of the sea, only a remnant will be saved; [28] for decisively and quickly will the Lord execute sentence upon the earth." [29] And as Isaiah predicted:

"Unless the Lord of hosts had left us
    descendants,
we would have become like Sodom
    and have been made like Gomor-
    rah."[g]

Righteousness Based on Faith.* [30] What then shall we say? That Gentiles, who did not pursue righteousness, have achieved it, that is, righteousness that comes from faith;[h] [31] but that Israel, who pursued the law of righteousness, did not attain to that law?[i] [32] Why not? Because they did it not by faith, but as if it could be done by works.[j] They stumbled over the stone that causes stumbling,* [33] as it is written:

"Behold, I am laying a stone in Zion
    that will make people stumble
and a rock that will make them fall,
and whoever believes in him shall not
    be put to shame."[k]

CHAPTER 10

[1] * Brothers, my heart's desire and prayer to God on their behalf is for salvation.[l] [2] I testify with regard to them that they have zeal for God, but it is not discerning.[m] [3] For, in their unawareness of the righteousness that comes from God and their attempt to establish their own [righteousness], they did not submit to the righteousness of God.[n] [4] For Christ is the end* of the law for the justification of everyone who has faith.[o]

---

y Ex 9, 16.—z Rom 11, 30-32; Ex 4, 21; 7, 3.—a Rom 3, 7; Wis 12, 12.—b 20-21: Wis 15, 7; Is 29, 16; 45, 9; Jer 18, 6.—c Rom 2, 4; Wis 12, 20-21; Jer 50, 25.—d Hos 2, 25.—e Hos 2, 1.—f 27-28: Is 10, 22-23; Hos 2, 1 / Rom 11, 5 / Is 28, 22.—g Is 1, 9; Mt 10, 15.—h Rom 10, 4.20.—i Rom 10, 3.—j Is 8, 14.—k Is 28, 16; 1 Pt 2, 6-8.—l Rom 9, 1.3.—m Acts 22, 3.—n Rom 9, 31-32; Phil 3, 9.—o Acts 13, 38-39; 2 Cor 3, 14; Heb 8, 13.

9, 18: The basic biblical principle is: those who will not see or hear *shall* not see or hear. On the other hand, the same God who thus makes stubborn or hardens the heart can reconstruct it through the work of the holy Spirit.

9, 19-29: The apostle responds to the objection that if God rules over faith through the principle of divine election, God cannot then accuse unbelievers of sin (19). For Paul, this objection is in the last analysis a manifestation of human insolence, and his "answer" is less an explanation of God's ways than the rejection of an argument that places humanity on a level with God. At the same time, Paul shows that God is far less arbitrary than appearances suggest, for God endures *with much patience* (22) a person like the Pharaoh of the Exodus.

9, 25: *Beloved:* in Semitic discourse means "preferred" or "favorite" (cf 13). See Hos 2, 1, which is transposed after Hos 3, 5 in the NAB.

9, 30-33: In the conversion of the Gentiles and, by contrast, of relatively few Jews, the Old Testament prophecies are seen to be fulfilled; cf 25-29. Israel feared that the doctrine of justification through faith would jeopardize the validity of the Mosaic law, and so they never reached their goal of righteousness that they had

sought to attain through meticulous observance of the law (31). Since Gentiles, including especially Greeks and Romans, had a great regard for righteousness, Paul's statement concerning Gentiles in v 30 is to be understood from a Jewish perspective: quite evidently they had not been interested in "God's" righteousness, for it had not been revealed to them; but now in response to the proclamation of the gospel they respond in faith.

9, 32: Paul discusses Israel as a whole from the perspective of contemporary Jewish rejection of Jesus as Messiah. The Old Testament and much of Jewish noncanonical literature in fact reflect a fervent faith in divine mercy.

10, 1-13: Despite Israel's lack of faith in God's act in Christ, Paul does not abandon hope for her salvation (1). However, Israel must recognize that the Messiah's arrival in the person of Jesus Christ means the termination of the Mosaic law as the criterion for understanding oneself in a valid relationship to God. Faith in God's saving action in Jesus Christ takes precedence over any such legal claim (6).

10, 4: The Mosaic legislation has been superseded by God's action in Jesus Christ. Others understand *end* here in the sense that Christ is the goal of the law, i.e., the true meaning of the Mosaic law, which cannot be correctly understood apart from him. Still others believe that both meanings are intended.

5 * Moses writes about the righteousness that comes from [the] law, "The one who does these things will live by them."[p] 6 But the righteousness that comes from faith says,[q] "Do not say in your heart, 'Who will go up into heaven?' (that is, to bring Christ down) 7 * or 'Who will go down into the abyss?' (that is, to bring Christ up from the dead)."[r] 8 But what does it say?

"The word is near you,
  in your mouth and in your heart"[s]

(that is, the word of faith that we preach), 9 for, if you confess* with your mouth that Jesus is Lord and believe in your heart that God raised him from the dead, you will be saved.[t] 10 For one believes with the heart and so is justified, and one confesses with the mouth and so is saved. 11 For the scripture says, "No one who believes in him will be put to shame."[u] 12 For there is no distinction between Jew and Greek; the same Lord is Lord of all, enriching all who call upon him.[v] 13 For "everyone who calls on the name of the Lord will be saved."[w]

14 * But how can they call on him in whom they have not believed? And how can they believe in him of whom they have not heard? And how can they hear without someone to preach?[x] 15 And how can people preach unless they are sent? As it is written,[y] "How beautiful are the feet of those who bring [the] good news!"* 16 But not everyone has heeded the good news; for Isaiah says, "Lord, who has believed what was heard from us?"[z] 17 Thus faith comes from what is heard, and what is heard comes through the word of Christ.[a] 18 But I ask, did they not hear? Certainly they did; for

"Their voice has gone forth to all the earth,
  and their words to the ends of the world."[b]

19 But I ask, did not Israel understand?[c] First Moses says:

"I will make you jealous of those who are not a nation;
  with a senseless nation I will make you angry."

20 [d] Then Isaiah speaks boldly and says:

"I was found [by] those who were not seeking me;
  I revealed myself to those who were not asking for me."

21 But regarding Israel he says, "All day long I stretched out my hands to a disobedient and contentious people."

CHAPTER 11

The Remnant of Israel.* 1 I ask, then, has God rejected his people? Of course not![e] For I too am an Israelite, a descendant of Abraham, of the tribe of Benjamin.[f] 2 God has not rejected his people whom he foreknew. Do you not know what the scripture says about Elijah, how he pleads with God against Israel? 3 "Lord, they have killed your prophets, they have torn down your altars, and I alone am left, and they are seeking my life."[g] 4 But what is God's response to him? "I have left for myself seven thousand men who have not knelt to Baal."[h] 5 So also at the present time there is a remnant, chosen by grace.[i] 6 But if by grace, it is no longer because of works; otherwise grace would no longer be grace.[j] 7 What then? What Israel was seeking it did not attain, but the elect attained it; the rest were hardened,[k] 8 as it is written:

"God gave them a spirit of deep sleep,
  eyes that should not see
  and ears that should not hear,
  down to this very day."[l]

---

p Lv 18, 5; Gal 3, 12.—q Dt 9, 4; 30, 12.—r Dt 30, 13; 1 Pt 3, 19.—s Dt 30, 14.—t 1 Cor 12, 3.—u Rom 9, 33; Is 28, 16.—v Rom 1, 16; 3, 22.29; Acts 10, 34; 15, 9.11; Gal 3, 28; Eph 2, 14.—w Jl 3, 5; Acts 2, 21.—x Acts 8, 31.—y Is 52, 7; Na 2, 1; Eph 6, 15.—z Is 53, 1; Jn 12, 38.—a Jn 17, 20.—b Ps 19, 5; Mt 24, 14.—c Rom 11, 11.14; Dt 32, 21.—d 20- 21: Rom 9, 30; Is 65, 1-2.—e 2 Cor 11, 22; Phil 3, 5.—f 1-2: 1 Sm 12, 22; Ps 94, 14.—g 1 Kgs 19, 10.14.—h 1 Kgs 19, 18.—i Rom 9, 27.—j Rom 4, 4; Gal 3, 18.—k Rom 9, 31.—l Dt 29, 3; Is 29, 10; Mt 13, 13-15; Acts 28, 26-27.

10, 5-6: The subject of the verb *says* (6) is *righteousness* personified. Both of the statements in vv 5 and 6 derive from Moses, but Paul wishes to contrast the language of law and the language of faith.

10, 7: Here Paul blends Dt 30, 13 and Ps 107, 26.

10, 9-11: To confess Jesus as Lord was frequently quite hazardous in the first century (cf Mt 10, 18; 1 Thes 2, 2; 1 Pt 2, 18-21; 3, 14). For a Jew it could mean disruption of normal familial and other social relationships, including great economic sacrifice. In the face of penalties imposed by the secular world, Christians are assured that *no one who believes in* Jesus *will be put to shame* (11).

10, 14-21: The gospel has been sufficiently proclaimed to Israel, and Israel has adequately understood God's plan for the messianic age, which would see the gospel brought to the uttermost parts of the earth. As often in the past, Israel has not accepted the prophetic message; cf Acts 7, 51-53.

10, 15: *How beautiful are the feet of those who bring [the] good news:* in Semitic fashion, the parts of the body that bring the messenger with welcome news are praised; cf Lk 11, 27.

11, 1-10: Although Israel has been unfaithful to the prophetic message of the gospel (Rom 10, 14-21), God remains faithful to Israel. Proof of the divine fidelity lies in the existence of Jewish Christians like Paul himself. The unbelieving Jews, says Paul, have been blinded by the Christian teaching concerning the Messiah.

Rom

9 And David says:[m]

"Let their table become a snare and a trap,
a stumbling block and a retribution for them;
10 let their eyes grow dim so that they may not see,
and keep their backs bent forever."

The Gentiles' Salvation. 11 * Hence I ask, did they stumble so as to fall? Of course not! But through their transgression salvation has come to the Gentiles, so as to make them jealous.[n] 12 Now if their transgression is enrichment for the world, and if their diminished number is enrichment for the Gentiles, how much more their full number.

13 Now I am speaking to you Gentiles. Inasmuch then as I am the apostle to the Gentiles, I glory in my ministry[o] 14 in order to make my race jealous and thus save some of them. 15 For if their rejection is the reconciliation of the world, what will their acceptance be but life from the dead? 16 * If the firstfruits are holy, so is the whole batch of dough; and if the root is holy, so are the branches.[p]

17 But if some of the branches were broken off, and you, a wild olive shoot, were grafted in their place and have come to share in the rich root of the olive tree,[q] 18 do not boast against the branches. If you do boast, consider that you do not support the root; the root supports you.[r] 19 Indeed you will say, "Branches were broken off so that I might be grafted in." 20 That is so. They were broken off because of unbelief, but you are there because of faith. So do not become haughty, but stand in awe.[s]

21 For if God did not spare the natural branches, [perhaps] he will not spare you either.[t] 22 See, then, the kindness and severity of God: severity toward those who fell, but God's kindness to you, provided you remain in his kindness; otherwise you too will be cut off.[u] 23 And they also, if they do not remain in unbelief, will be grafted in, for God is able to graft them in again.[v] 24 For if you were cut from what is by nature a wild olive tree, and grafted, contrary to nature, into a cultivated one, how much more will they who belong to it by nature be grafted back into their own olive tree.

God's Irrevocable Call. * 25 I do not want you to be unaware of this mystery, brothers, so that you will not become wise [in] your own estimation: a hardening has come upon Israel in part, until the full number of the Gentiles comes in,[w] 26 and thus all Israel will be saved,[x] as it is written:[y]

"The deliverer will come out of Zion,
he will turn away godlessness from Jacob;
27 and this is my covenant with them
when I take away their sins."[z]

28 In respect to the gospel, they are enemies on your account; but in respect to election, they are beloved because of the patriarchs.[a] 29 For the gifts and the call of God are irrevocable.[b]

Triumph of God's Mercy. 30 * Just as you once disobeyed God but have now received mercy because of their disobedience, 31 so they have now disobeyed in order that, by virtue of the mercy shown to you, they too may [now] receive mercy. 32 For God delivered all to disobedience, that he might have mercy upon all.[c]

---

m 9-10: Pss 69, 23-24; 35, 8.—n Acts 13, 46; 18, 6; 28, 28 / Rom 10, 19; Dt 32, 21.—o Rom 1, 5.—p Nm 15, 17-21; Ez 44, 30; Neh 10, 36-38.—q Eph 2, 11-19.—r 1 Cor 1, 31.—s Rom 12, 16.—t 1 Cor 10, 12.—u Jn 15, 2.4; Heb 3, 14.—v 2 Cor 3, 16.—w Prv 3, 7 / Rom 12, 16; Mk 13, 10; Lk 21, 24; Jn 10, 16.—x Mt 23, 39.—y 26-27: Ps 14, 7; Is 59, 20-21.—z Is 27, 9; Jer 31, 33-34.—a Rom 15, 8; 1 Thes 2, 15-16.—b Rom 9, 6; Nm 23, 19; Is 54, 10.—c Gal 3, 22; 1 Tm 2, 4.

11, 11-15: The unbelief of the Jews has paved the way for the preaching of the gospel to the Gentiles and for their easier acceptance of it outside the context of Jewish culture. Through his mission to the Gentiles Paul also hopes to fill his fellow Jews with jealousy. Hence he hastens to fill the entire Mediterranean world with the gospel. Once all the Gentile nations have heard the gospel, Israel as a whole is expected to resurrection of the dead, that is, the reappearance of Jesus Christ with all the believers at the end of time.

11, 16-24: Israel remains holy in the eyes of God and stands as a witness to the faith described in the Old Testament because of *the firstfruits* (or the first piece baked) (16), that is, the converted remnant, and *the root* that *is holy,* that is, the patriarchs (16). The Jews' failure to believe in Christ is a warning to Gentile Christians to be on guard against any semblance of anti-Jewish arrogance, that is, failure to recognize their total dependence on divine grace.

11, 25-29: In God's design, Israel's unbelief is being used to grant the light of faith to the Gentiles. Meanwhile, Israel remains dear to God (cf Rom 9, 13), still the object of special providence, the mystery of which will one day be revealed.

11, 30-32: Israel, together with the Gentiles who have been handed over to all manner of vices (ch 1), has been *delivered . . . to disobedience.* The conclusion of v 32 repeats the thought of Rom 5, 20, "Where sin increased, grace overflowed all the more."

33 * Oh, the depth of the riches and wisdom and knowledge of God! How inscrutable are his judgments and how unsearchable his ways!ᵈ

34 "For who has known the mind of the Lord*
  or who has been his counselor?"ᵉ

35 "Or who has given him anythingᶠ
  that he may be repaid?"*

36 For from him and through him and for him are all things. To him be glory forever. Amen.ᵍ

VI. THE DUTIES OF CHRISTIANS*

CHAPTER 12

Sacrifice of Body and Mind. 1 *I urge you therefore, brothers, by the mercies of God, to offer your bodies as a living sacrifice, holy and pleasing to God, your spiritual worship.ʰ 2 Do not conform yourself to this age but be transformed by the renewal of your mind, that you may discern what is the will of God, what is good and pleasing and perfect.ⁱ

Many Parts in One Body. 3 ʲ For by the grace given to me I tell everyone among you not to think of himself more highly than one ought to think, but to think soberly, each according to the measure of faith that God has apportioned. 4 ᵏ For as in one body we have many parts, and all the parts do not have the same function, 5 so we, though many, are one body in Christ* and individually parts of one another. 6 ˡ Since we have gifts that differ according to the grace given to us, let us exercise them:* if prophecy, in proportion to the faith; 7 if ministry, in ministering; if one is a teacher, in teaching; 8 if one exhorts, in exhortation; if one contributes, in generosity; if one is over others,* with diligence; if one does acts of mercy, with cheerfulness.

Mutual Love. 9 Let love be sincere; hate what is evil, hold on to what is good;ᵐ 10 love one another with mutual affection; anticipate one another in showing honor.ⁿ 11 Do not grow slack in zeal, be fervent in spirit, serve the Lord.ᵒ 12 Rejoice in hope, endure in affliction, persevere in prayer.ᵖ 13 Contribute to the needs of the holy ones,�q exercise hospitality. 14 * Bless those who persecute [you],ʳ bless and do not curse them.ˢ 15 Rejoice with those who rejoice, weep with those who weep.ᵗ 16 Have the same regard for one another; do not be haughty but associate with the lowly; do not be wise in your own estimation.ᵘ 17 Do not repay anyone evil for evil; be con-

Rom

---

d Jb 11, 7-8; Ps 139, 6.17-18; Wis 17, 1; Is 55, 8-9.—e Jb 15, 8; Wis 9, 13; Is 40, 13; Jer 23, 18; 1 Cor 2, 11-16.—f Jb 41, 3; Is 40, 14.—g 1 Cor 8, 6; Col 1, 16-17.—h 2 Cor 1, 3 / Rom 6, 13; 1 Pt 2, 5.—i Eph 4, 17.22-23; 1 Pt 1, 14 / Eph 5, 10.17; Phil 1, 10.—j Rom 15, 15 / Phil 2, 3 / 1 Cor 12, 11; Eph 4, 7.—k 4-5: 1 Cor 12, 12.27; Eph 4, 25.—l 6-8: 1 Cor 12, 4-11.28-31; Eph 4, 7-12; 1 Pt 4, 10-11 / 2 Cor 9, 7.—m 2 Cor 6, 6; 1 Tm 1, 5; 1 Pt 1, 22 / Am 5, 15.—n Jn 13, 34; 1 Thes 4, 9; 1 Pt 2, 17; 2 Pt 1, 7 / Phil 2, 3.—o Acts 18, 25.—p Rom 5, 2-3; Col 4, 2; 1 Thes 5, 17.—q Heb 13, 2; 1 Pt 4, 9.—r 14-21: Mt 5, 38-48; 1 Cor 4, 12; 1 Pt 3, 9.—s Lk 6, 27-28.—t Ps 35, 13; Sir 7, 34; 1 Cor 12, 26.—u Rom 15, 5; Phil 2, 2-3 / Rom 11, 20; Prv 3, 7; Is 5, 21.

11, 33-36: This final reflection celebrates the wisdom of God's plan of salvation. As Paul has indicated throughout these chapters, both Jew and Gentile, despite the religious recalcitrance of each, have received the gift of faith. The methods used by God in making this outreach to the world stagger human comprehension but are at the same time a dazzling invitation to abiding faith.

11, 34: The citation is from the Greek text of Is 40, 13. Paul does not explicitly mention Isaiah in this verse, nor Job in v 35.

11, 35: Paul quotes from an old Greek version of Jb 41, 3a, which differs from the Hebrew text (Jb 41, 11a).

12, 1—13, 14: Since Christ marks the termination of the Mosaic law as the primary source of guidance for God's people (Rom 10, 4), the apostle explains how Christians can function, in the light of the gift of justification through faith, in their relation to one another and the state.

12, 1-8: The Mosaic code included elaborate directions on sacrifices and other cultic observances. The gospel, however, invites believers to present their *bodies as a living sacrifice* (1). Instead of being limited by specific legal maxims, Christians are lib-

erated for the exercise of good judgment as they are confronted with the many and varied decisions required in the course of daily life. To assist them, God distributes a variety of gifts to the fellowship of believers, including those of prophecy, teaching, and exhortation (6-8). Prophets assist the community to understand the will of God as it applies to the present situation (6). Teachers help people to understand themselves and their responsibilities in relation to others (7). One who *exhorts* offers encouragement to the community to exercise their faith in the performance of all that is pleasing to God (8). Indeed, this very section, beginning with v 1, is a specimen of Paul's own style of exhortation.

12, 5: *One body in Christ:* on the church as the body of Christ, see 1 Cor 12, 12-27.

12, 6: Everyone has some gift that can be used for the benefit of the community. When the instruction on justification through faith is correctly grasped, the possessor of a gift will understand that it is not an instrument of self-aggrandizement. Possession of a gift is not an index to quality of faith. Rather, the gift is a challenge to faithful use.

12, 8: *Over others:* usually taken to mean "rule over" but possibly "serve as a patron." Wealthier members in Greco-Roman communities were frequently asked to assist in public service projects. In view of the references to contributing *in generosity* and to *acts of mercy*, Paul may have in mind people like Phoebe (Rom 16, 1-2), who is called a *benefactor* (or "patron") because of the services she rendered to many Christians, including Paul.

12, 14-21: Since God has justified the believers, it is not necessary for them to take justice into their own hands by taking vengeance. God will ultimately deal justly with all, including those who inflict injury on the believers. This question of personal rights as a matter of justice prepares the way for more detailed consideration of the state as adjudicator.

cerned for what is noble in the sight of all.*v* [18] If possible, on your part, live at peace with all.*w* [19] Beloved, do not look for revenge but leave room for the wrath; for it is written, "Vengeance is mine, I will repay, says the Lord."*x* [20] Rather, "if your enemy is hungry, feed him; if he is thirsty, give him something to drink; for by so doing you will heap burning coals upon his head."*y* [21] Do not be conquered by evil but conquer evil with good.

CHAPTER 13

Obedience to Authority.* [1] Let every person be subordinate to the higher authorities, for there is no authority except from God, and those that exist have been established by God.*z* [2] Therefore, whoever resists authority opposes what God has appointed, and those who oppose it will bring judgment upon themselves. [3] For rulers are not a cause of fear to good conduct, but to evil.*a* Do you wish to have no fear of authority? Then do what is good and you will receive approval from it, [4] for it is a servant of God for your good. But if you do evil, be afraid, for it does not bear the sword without purpose; it is the servant of God to inflict wrath on the evildoer.*b* [5] Therefore, it is necessary to be subject not only because of the wrath but also because of conscience.*c* [6] This is why you also pay taxes, for the authorities are ministers of God, devoting themselves to this very thing. [7] Pay to all their dues, taxes to whom taxes are due, toll to whom toll is due, respect to whom respect is due, honor to whom honor is due.*d*

Love Fulfills the Law.* [8] Owe nothing to anyone, except to love one another; for the one who loves another has fulfilled the law.*e* [9] The commandments, "You shall not commit adultery; you shall not kill; you shall not steal; you shall not covet," and whatever other commandment there may be, are summed up in this saying, [namely] "You shall love your neighbor as yourself."*f* [10] Love does no evil to the neighbor; hence, love is the fulfillment of the law.*g*

Awareness of the End of Time.* [11] And do this because you know the time; it is the hour now for you to awake from sleep. For our salvation is nearer now than when we first believed;*h* [12] the night is advanced, the day is at hand. Let us then throw off the works of darkness [and] put on the armor of light;*i* [13] let us conduct ourselves properly as in the day,* not in orgies and drunkenness, not in promiscuity and licentiousness, not in rivalry and jealousy.*j* [14] But put on the Lord Jesus Christ, and make no provision for the desires of the flesh.*k*

CHAPTER 14

To Live and Die for Christ. [1] * Welcome anyone who is weak in faith,*l* but not for disputes over opinions.*m* [2] One person be-

---

v Prv 3, 4; 1 Thes 5, 15; 1 Pt 3, 9.—w Heb 12, 14.—x Lv 19, 18; Dt 32, 35.41; Mt 5, 39; 1 Cor 6, 6-7; Heb 10, 30.—y Prv 25, 21-22; Mt 5, 44.—z Prv 8, 15-16; Wis 6, 3; Jn 19, 11; 1 Pt 2, 13-17; Ti 3, 1.—a 1 Pt 2, 13-14; 3, 13.—b Rom 12, 19.—c 1 Pt 2, 19.—d Mt 22, 21; Mk 12, 17; Lk 20, 25.—e Jn 13, 34; Gal 5, 14.—f Ex 20, 13-17 / Lv 19, 18; Dt 5, 17-21; Mt 5, 43-44; 19, 18-19; 22, 39; Mk 12, 31; Lk 10, 27; Gal 5, 14; Jas 2, 8.—g Mt 22, 40; 1 Cor 13, 4-7.—h Eph 5, 8-16; 1 Thes 5, 5-7.—i Jn 8, 12; 1 Thes 5, 4-8; 1 Jn 2, 8 / 2 Cor 6, 7; 10, 4; Eph 5, 11; 6, 13-17.—j Lk 21, 34; Eph 5, 18.—k Gal 3, 27; 5, 16; Eph 4, 24; 6, 11.—l 1-23: 1 Cor 8, 1-13.—m Rom 15, 1.7; 1 Cor 9, 22.

13,1-7: Paul must come to grips with the problem raised by a message that declares people free from the law. How are they to relate to Roman authority? The problem was exacerbated by the fact that imperial protocol was interwoven with devotion to various deities. Paul builds on the traditional instruction exhibited in Wis 6, 1-3, according to which kings and magistrates rule by consent of God. From this perspective, then, believers who render obedience to the governing authorities are obeying the one who is highest in command. At the same time, it is recognized that Caesar has the responsibility to make just ordinances and to commend uprightness; cf Wis 6, 4-21. That Caesar is not entitled to obedience when such obedience would nullify God's prior claim to the believers' moral decision becomes clear in the light of the following verses.

13, 8-10: When love directs the Christian's moral decisions, the interest of law in basic concerns, such as familial relationships, sanctity of life, and security of property, is safeguarded (9).

Indeed, says Paul, the same applies to any *other commandment* (9), whether one in the Mosaic code or one drawn up by local magistrates under imperial authority. Love anticipates the purpose of public legislation, namely, to secure the best interests of the citizenry. Since Caesar's obligation is to punish the wrongdoer (4), the Christian who acts in love is free from all legitimate indictment.

13, 11-14: These verses provide the motivation for the love that is encouraged in vv 8-10.

13, 13: *Let us conduct ourselves properly as in the day:* the behavior described in Rom 1, 29-30 is now to be reversed. Secular moralists were fond of making references to people who could not wait for nightfall to do their carousing. Paul says that Christians claim to be people of the new day that will dawn with the return of Christ. Instead of planning for nighttime behavior they should be concentrating on conduct that is consonant with avowed interest in the Lord's return.

14, 1—15, 6: Since Christ spells termination of the law, which included observance of specific days and festivals as well as dietary instruction, the jettisoning of long-practiced customs was traumatic for many Christians brought up under the Mosaic code. Although Paul acknowledges that in principle no food is a source of moral contamination (14), he recommends that the consciences of Christians who are scrupulous in this regard be respected by other Christians (21). On the other hand, those who have scruples are not to sit in judgment on those who know that the gospel has liberated them from such ordinances (10). See 1 Cor 8 and 10.

lieves that one may eat anything, while the weak person eats only vegetables.ⁿ ³The one who eats must not despise the one who abstains, and the one who abstains must not pass judgment on the one who eats; for God has welcomed him.ᵒ ⁴Who are you to pass judgment on someone else's servant? Before his own master he stands or falls. And he will be upheld, for the Lord is able to make him stand.ᵖ ⁵[For] one person considers one day more important than another, while another person considers all days alike.�q Let everyone be fully persuaded in his own mind.* ⁶Whoever observes the day, observes it for the Lord. Also whoever eats, eats for the Lord, since he gives thanks to God; while whoever abstains, abstains for the Lord and gives thanks to God. ⁷None of us lives for oneself, and no one dies for oneself. ⁸For if we live, we live for the Lord,* and if we die, we die for the Lord; so then, whether we live or die, we are the Lord's.ʳ ⁹For this is why Christ died and came to life, that he might be Lord of both the dead and the living.ˢ ¹⁰Why then do you judge your brother? Or you, why do you look down on your brother? For we shall all stand before the judgment seat of God;ᵗ ¹¹for it is written:

---

n Gn 1, 29; 9, 3; 1 Cor 8, 1-13; 10, 14-33.—o Col 2, 16.—p Rom 2, 1; Mt 7, 11; Jas 4, 11-12.—q Gal 4, 10.—r Lk 20, 38; 2 Cor 5, 15; Gal 2, 20; 1 Thes 5, 10.—s Acts 10, 42.—t Acts 17, 31; 2 Cor 5, 10.—u Is 49, 18 / Is 45, 23; Phil 2, 10-11.—v Gal 6, 5.—w 1 Cor 8, 9.13.—x Mk 7, 5.20; Acts 10, 15; 1 Cor 10, 25-27; 1 Tm 4, 4.—y 1 Cor 8, 11-13.—z Rom 2, 24; Ti 2, 5.—a 1 Cor 8, 8.—b Rom 12, 18 / Rom 5, 2.—c 20-21: 1 Cor 8, 11-13; 10, 28-29; Ti 1, 15.—d Ti 1, 15; Jas 4, 17.—e Rom 14, 1-2.—f Rom 14, 1.19; 1 Cor 9, 19; 10, 24.33.—g Ps 69, 10.—h Rom 4, 23-24; 1 Mc 12, 9; 1 Cor 10, 11; 2 Tm 3, 16.—i Rom 12, 16; Phil 2, 2; 4, 2.

14, 5: Since the problem to be overcome was humanity's perverted mind or judgment (Rom 1, 28), Paul indicates that the *mind* of the Christian is now able to function with appropriate discrimination (cf Rom 12, 2).

14, 8: *The Lord:* Jesus, our Master. The same Greek word, *kyrios,* was applied to both rulers and holders of slaves. Throughout the Letter to the Romans Paul emphasizes God's total claim on the believer; see the note on Rom 1, 1.

14, 19: Some manuscripts, versions, and church Fathers read, "We then pursue . . ."; cf Rom 5, 1.

14, 23: *Whatever is not from faith is sin:* Paul does not mean that all the actions of unbelievers are sinful. He addresses himself to the question of intracommunity living. *Sin* in the singular is the dreadful power described in Rom 5, 12-14.

15, 3: Liberation from the law of Moses does not make the scriptures of the old covenant irrelevant. Much consolation and motivation for Christian living can be derived from the Old Testament, as in the citation from Ps 69, 10. Because this psalm is quoted several times in the New Testament, it has been called indirectly messianic.

15, 5: *Think in harmony:* a Greco-Roman ideal. Not rigid uniformity of thought and expression but thoughtful consideration of other people's views finds expression here.

"As I live, says the Lord, every knee
    shall bend before me,
and every tongue shall give praise to
    God."ᵘ

¹²So [then] each of us shall give an account of himself [to God].ᵛ

Consideration for the Weak Conscience. ¹³Then let us no longer judge one another, but rather resolve never to put a stumbling block or hindrance in the way of a brother.ʷ ¹⁴I know and am convinced in the Lord Jesus that nothing is unclean in itself; still, it is unclean for someone who thinks it unclean.ˣ ¹⁵If your brother is being hurt by what you eat, your conduct is no longer in accord with love. Do not because of your food destroy him for whom Christ died.ʸ ¹⁶So do not let your good be reviled.ᶻ ¹⁷For the kingdom of God is not a matter of food and drink, but of righteousness, peace, and joy in the holy Spirit;ᵃ ¹⁸whoever serves Christ in this way is pleasing to God and approved by others. ¹⁹Let us* then pursue what leads to peace and to building up one another.ᵇ ²⁰For the sake of food, do not destroy the work of God.ᶜ Everything is indeed clean, but it is wrong for anyone to become a stumbling block by eating; ²¹it is good not to eat meat or drink wine or do anything that causes your brother to stumble. ²²Keep the faith [that] you have to yourself in the presence of God; blessed is the one who does not condemn himself for what he approves. ²³ ᵈ But whoever has doubts is condemned if he eats, because this is not from faith; for whatever is not from faith is sin.*

CHAPTER 15

Patience and Self-Denial. ¹We who are strong ought to put up with the failings of the weak and not to please ourselves;ᵉ ²let each of us please our neighbor for the good, for building up.ᶠ ³For Christ did not please himself; but, as it is written,ᵍ "The insults of those who insult you fall upon me."* ⁴For whatever was written previously was written for our instruction, that by endurance and by the encouragement of the scriptures we might have hope.ʰ ⁵May the God of endurance and encouragement grant you to think in harmony* with one another, in keeping with Christ Jesus,ⁱ ⁶that with one accord you may with one voice glorify the God and Father of our Lord Jesus Christ.

God's Fidelity and Mercy.* [7]Welcome one another, then, as Christ welcomed you, for the glory of God.[j] [8]For I say that Christ became a minister of the circumcised to show God's truthfulness, to confirm the promises to the patriarchs,[k] [9]but so that the Gentiles might glorify God for his mercy. As it is written:

"Therefore, I will praise you among the Gentiles
and sing praises to your name."[l]

[10]And again it says:[m]

"Rejoice, O Gentiles, with his people."*

[11]And again:

"Praise the Lord, all you Gentiles,
and let all the peoples praise him."[n]

[12]And again Isaiah says:

"The root of Jesse shall come,
raised up to rule the Gentiles;
in him shall the Gentiles hope."[o]

[13]May the God of hope fill you with all joy and peace in believing, so that you may abound in hope by the power of the holy Spirit.[p]

VII. CONCLUSION

Apostle to the Gentiles. [14] * I myself am convinced about you, my brothers, that you yourselves are full of goodness,* filled with all knowledge, and able to admonish one another. [15]But I have written to you rather boldly in some respects to remind you, because of the grace given me by God[q] [16]to be a minister of Christ Jesus to the Gentiles in performing the priestly service of the gospel of God, so that the offering up of the Gentiles may be acceptable, sanctified by the holy Spirit.[r] [17]In Christ Jesus, then, I have reason to boast in what pertains to God. [18]For I will not dare to speak of anything except what Christ has accomplished through me to lead the Gentiles to obedience by word and deed,[s] [19]by the power of signs and wonders, by the power of the Spirit [of God], so that from Jerusalem all the way around to Illyricum* I have finished preaching the gospel of Christ. [20]Thus I aspire* to proclaim the gospel not where Christ has already been named, so that I do not build on another's foundation,[t] [21]but as it is written:[u]

"Those who have never been told of him shall see,
and those who have never heard of him shall understand."*

Paul's Plans; Need for Prayers. [22]That is why I have so often been prevented from coming to you. [23]But now, since I no longer have any opportunity in these regions and since I have desired to come to you for many years,[v] [24]I hope to see you in passing as I go to Spain and to be sent on my way there by you, after I have enjoyed being with you for a time.[w] [25] * Now, however, I am going to Jerusalem to minister to the holy ones.[x] [26]For Macedonia and Achaia* have decided to make some contribution for the poor among the holy ones in Jerusalem;[y] [27]they decided to do it, and in fact they are indebted to them, for if the Gentiles have come to share in their spiritual blessings, they ought also to serve them in material blessings.[z] [28]So when I

j Rom 14, 1.—k Mt 15, 24 / Mi 7, 20; Acts 3, 25.—l Rom 11, 30 / 2 Sm 22, 50; Ps 18, 50.—m Dt 32, 43.—n Ps 117, 1.—o Is 11, 10; Rv 5, 5; 22, 16.—p Rom 5, 1-2.—q Rom 1, 5; 12, 3.—r Rom 11, 13; Phil 2, 17.—s Acts 15, 12; 2 Cor 12, 12.—t 2 Cor 10, 13-18.—u Is 52, 15.—v Rom 1, 10-13; Acts 19, 21-22.—w 1 Cor 16, 6.—x Acts 19, 21; 20, 22.—y 1 Cor 16, 1; 2 Cor 8, 1-4; 9, 2.12.—z Rom 9, 4 / 1 Cor 9, 11.

15, 7-13: True oneness of mind is found in pondering the ultimate mission of the church: to bring it about that God's name be glorified throughout the world and that Jesus Christ be universally recognized as God's gift to all humanity. Paul here prepares his addressees for the climactic appeal he is about to make.

15, 10: Paul's citation of Dt 32, 43 follows the Greek version.

15, 14-33: Paul sees himself as apostle and benefactor in the priestly service of the gospel and so sketches plans for a mission in Spain, supported by those in Rome.

15, 14: *Full of goodness:* the opposite of what humanity was filled with according to Rom 1, 29-30.

15, 19: *Illyricum:* Roman province northwest of Greece on the eastern shore of the Adriatic.

15, 20: *I aspire:* Paul uses terminology customarily applied to philanthropists. Unlike some philanthropists of his time, Paul does not engage in cheap competition for public acclaim. This explanation of his missionary policy is to assure the Christians in Rome that he is also not planning to remain in that city and build on other people's foundations (cf 2 Cor 10, 12-18). However, he does solicit their help in sending him on his way to Spain, which was considered the limit of the western world. Thus Paul's addressees realize that evangelization may be understood in the broader sense of mission or, as in Rom 1, 15, of instruction within the Christian community that derives from the gospel.

15, 21: The citation from Is 52, 15 concerns the Servant of the Lord. According to Isaiah, the Servant is first of all Israel, which was to bring the knowledge of Yahweh to the nations. In chs 9-11 Paul showed how Israel failed in this mission. Therefore, he himself undertakes almost singlehandedly Israel's responsibility as the Servant and moves as quickly as possible with the gospel through the Roman empire.

15, 25-27: Paul may have viewed the contribution he was gathering from Gentile Christians for the poor in Jerusalem (cf 2 Cor 8 and 9) as a fulfillment of the vision of Is 60, 5-6. In confidence that the messianic fulfillment was taking place, Paul stresses in chs 14-16 the importance of harmonious relationships between Jews and Gentiles.

15, 26: *Achaia:* the Roman province of southern Greece.

have completed this and safely handed over this contribution to them, I shall set out by way of you to Spain; [29] and I know that in coming to you I shall come in the fullness of Christ's blessing.

[30] I urge you, [brothers,] by our Lord Jesus Christ and by the love of the Spirit, to join me in the struggle by your prayers to God on my behalf,[a] [31] that I may be delivered from the disobedient in Judea, and that my ministry for Jerusalem may be acceptable to the holy ones, [32] so that I may come to you with joy by the will of God and be refreshed together with you. [33] The God of peace be with all of you. Amen.[b]

CHAPTER 16

Phoebe Commended. [1] * I commend to you Phoebe our sister, who is [also] a minister* of the church at Cenchreae,[c] [2] that you may receive her in the Lord in a manner worthy of the holy ones, and help her in whatever she may need from you, for she has been a benefactor to many and to me as well.

Paul's Greetings. [3] Greet Prisca and Aquila,* my co-workers in Christ Jesus,[d] [4] who risked their necks for my life, to whom not only I am grateful but also all the churches of the Gentiles; [5] greet also the church at their house.* Greet my beloved Epaenetus, who was the firstfruits in Asia for Christ.[e] [6] Greet Mary, who has worked hard for you. [7] Greet Andronicus and Junia,* my relatives and my fellow prisoners; they are prominent among the apostles and they were in Christ before me.

[8] Greet Ampliatus, my beloved in the Lord. [9] Greet Urbanus, our co-worker in Christ, and my beloved Stachys. [10] Greet Apelles, who is approved in Christ. Greet those who belong to the family of Aristobulus. [11] Greet my relative Herodion. Greet those in the Lord who belong to the family of Narcissus. [12] Greet those workers in the Lord, Tryphaena and Tryphosa. Greet the beloved Persis, who has worked hard in the Lord. [13] Greet Rufus,* chosen in the Lord, and his mother and mine.[f] [14] Greet Asyncritus, Phlegon, Hermes, Patrobas, Hermas, and the brothers who are with them. [15] Greet Philologus, Julia, Nereus and his sister, and Olympas, and all the holy ones who are with them. [16] Greet one another with a holy kiss. All the churches of Christ greet you.[g]

Against Factions. [17] * I urge you, brothers, to watch out for those who create dissensions and obstacles, in opposition to the teaching that you learned; avoid them.[h] [18] For such people do not serve our Lord Christ but their own appetites, and by fair and flattering speech they deceive the hearts of the innocent.[i] [19] For while your obedience is known to all, so that I rejoice over you, I want you to be wise as to what is good, and simple as to what is evil;[j] [20] then the God of peace will quickly crush Satan* under your feet. The grace of our Lord Jesus be with you.[k]

Greetings from Corinth. [21] Timothy, my co-worker, greets you; so do Lucius and Jason and Sosipater, my relatives.[l] [22] I, Tertius, the writer of this letter, greet you in the Lord. [23] [m] Gaius, who is host to me

---

a 2 Cor 1, 11; Phil 1, 27; Col 4, 3; 2 Thes 3, 1.—b Rom 16, 20; 2 Cor 13, 11; Phil 4, 9; 1 Thes 5, 23; 2 Thes 3, 16; Heb 13, 20.— c Acts 18, 18.—d Acts 18, 2.18-26; 1 Cor 16, 19; 2 Tm 4, 19.—e 1 Cor 16, 19; Col 4, 15; Phlm 2 / 1 Cor 16, 15.—f Mk 15, 21.—g 1 Cor 16, 20; 2 Cor 13, 12; 1 Thes 5, 26; 1 Pt 5, 14.—h Mt 7, 15; Ti 3, 10.—i Phil 3, 18-19 / Col 2, 4; 2 Pt 2, 3.—j Rom 1, 8; Mt 10, 16; 1 Cor 14, 20.—k Rom 15, 33; Gn 3, 15; Lk 10, 19 / 1 Cor 16, 23; 1 Thes 5, 28; 2 Thes 3, 18.—l Acts 16, 1-2; 19, 22; 20, 4; 1 Cor 4, 17; 16, 10; Phil 2, 19-22; Heb 13, 23.—m Acts 19, 29; 1 Cor 1, 14 / 2 Tm 4, 20.

16, 1-23: Some authorities regard these verses as a later addition to the letter, but in general the evidence favors the view that they were included in the original. Paul endeavors through the long list of greetings (3-16; 21-23) to establish strong personal contact with congregations that he has not personally encountered before. The combination of Jewish and Gentile names dramatically attests the unity in the gospel that transcends previous barriers of nationality, religious ceremony, or racial status.

16, 1: *Minister:* in Greek, *diakonos;* see the note on Phil 1, 1.

16, 3: *Prisca and Aquila:* presumably the couple mentioned at Acts 18, 2; 1 Cor 16, 19; 2 Tm 4, 19.

16, 5: *The church at their house:* i.e., that meets there. Such local assemblies (cf 1 Cor 16, 19; Col 4, 15; Phlm 2) might consist of only one or two dozen Christians each. It is understandable, therefore, that such smaller groups might experience difficulty in relating to one another on certain issues. *Firstfruits:* cf Rom 8, 23; 11, 16; 1 Cor 16, 15.

16, 7: The name Junia is a woman's name. One ancient Greek manuscript and a number of ancient versions read the name "Julia." Most editors have interpreted it as a man's name, Junias.

16, 13: This Rufus cannot be identified to any degree of certainty with the Rufus of Mk 15, 21.

16, 17-18: Paul displays genuine concern for the congregations in Rome by warning them against self-seeking teachers. It would be a great loss, he intimates, if their obedience, which is known to all (cf Rom 1, 8), would be diluted.

16, 20: This verse contains the only mention of Satan in Romans.

and to the whole church, greets you. Erastus,* the city treasurer, and our brother Quartus greet you. [24]*

Doxology.* [25 Now to him who can strengthen you, according to my gospel and the proclamation of Jesus Christ,ⁿ according to the revelation of the mystery

kept secret for long ages* 26 but now manifested through the prophetic writings, according to the command of the eternal God, made known to all nations to bring about the obedience of faith,ᵒ 27 to the only wise God, through Jesus Christ be glory forever and ever. Amen.]ᵖ

n 1 Cor 2, 7; Eph 1, 9; 3, 3-9; Col 1, 26.—o 2 Tm 1, 10 / Rom 1, 5; Eph 3, 4-5.9; 1 Pt 1, 20.—p Rom 11, 36; Gal 1, 5; Eph 3, 20-21; Phil 4, 20; 1 Tm 1, 17; 2 Tm 4, 18; Heb 13, 21; 1 Pt 4, 11; 2 Pt 3, 18; Jude 25; Rv 1, 6.

16, 23: This Erastus is not necessarily to be identified with the Erastus of Acts 19, 22 or of 2 Tm 4, 20.

16, 24: Some manuscripts add, similarly to v 20, "The grace of our Lord Jesus Christ be with you all. Amen."

16, 25-27: This doxology is assigned variously to the end of chs 14, 15, and 16 in the manuscript tradition. Some manuscripts omit it entirely. Whether written by Paul or not, it forms an admirable conclusion to the letter at this point.

16, 25: Paul's gospel reveals *the mystery kept secret for long ages:* justification and salvation through faith, with all the implications for Jews and Gentiles that Paul has developed in the letter.

THE FIRST LETTER TO THE CORINTHIANS

INTRODUCTION

Paul's first letter to the church of Corinth provides us with a fuller insight into the life of an early Christian community of the first generation than any other book of the New Testament. Through it we can glimpse both the strengths and the weaknesses of this small group in a great city of the ancient world, men and women who had accepted the good news of Christ and were now trying to realize in their lives the implications of their baptism. Paul, who had founded the community and continued to look after it as a father, responds both to questions addressed to him and to situations of which he had been informed. In doing so, he reveals much about himself, his teaching, and the way in which he conducted his work of apostleship. Some things are puzzling because we have the correspondence only in one direction. For the person studying this letter, it seems to raise as many questions as it answers, but without it our knowledge of church life in the middle of the first century would be much poorer.

Paul established a Christian community in Corinth about the year 51, on his second missionary journey. The city, a commercial crossroads, was a melting pot full of devotees of various pagan cults and marked by a measure of moral depravity not unusual in a great seaport. The Acts of the Apostles suggests that moderate success attended Paul's efforts among the Jews in Corinth at first, but that they soon turned against him (Acts 18, 1-8). More fruitful was his year and a half spent among the Gentiles (Acts 18, 11), which won to the faith many of the city's poor and underprivileged (1, 26). After his departure the eloquent Apollos, an Alexandrian Jewish Christian, rendered great service to the community, expounding "from the scriptures that the Messiah is Jesus" (Acts 18, 24-28).

While Paul was in Ephesus on his third journey (16, 8; Acts 19, 1-20), he received disquieting news about Corinth. The community there was displaying open factionalism, as certain members were identifying themselves exclusively with individual Christian leaders and interpreting Christian teaching as a superior wisdom for the initiated few (1, 10—4, 21). The community lacked the decisiveness to take appropriate action against one of its members who was living publicly in an incestuous union (5, 1-13). Other members engaged in legal conflicts in pagan courts of law (6, 1-11); still others may have participated in religious prostitution (6, 12-20) or temple sacrifices (10, 14-22).

The community's ills were reflected in its liturgy. In the celebration of the Eucharist certain members discriminated against others, drank too freely at the agape, or fellowship meal, and denied Christian social courtesies to the poor among the membership (11, 17-22). Charisms such as ecstatic prayer, attributed freely to the impulse of the holy Spirit, *were more highly prized than works of charity (13, 1-2.8), and were used at times in a disorderly way (14, 1-40). Women appeared at the assembly without the customary head-covering (11, 3-16), and perhaps were quarreling over their right to address the assembly (14, 34-35).*

 Still other problems with which Paul had to deal concerned matters of conscience discussed among the faithful members of the community: the eating of meat that had been sacrificed to idols (8, 1-13), the use of sex in marriage (7, 1-7), and the attitude to be taken by the unmarried toward marriage in view of the possible proximity of Christ's second coming (7, 25-40). There was also a doctrinal matter that called for Paul's attention, for some members of the community, despite their belief in the resurrection of Christ, were denying the possibility of general bodily resurrection.

 To treat this wide spectrum of questions, Paul wrote this letter from Ephesus about the year 56. The majority of the Corinthian Christians may well have been quite faithful. Paul writes on their behalf to guard against the threats posed to the community by the views and conduct of various minorities. He writes with confidence in the authority of his apostolic mission, and he presumes that the Corinthians, despite their deficiencies, will recognize and accept it. On the other hand, he does not hesitate to exercise his authority as his judgment dictates in each situation, even going so far as to promise a direct confrontation with recalcitrants, should the abuses he scores remain uncorrected (4, 18-21).

 The letter illustrates well the mind and character of Paul. Although he is impelled to insist on his office as founder of the community, he recognizes that he is only one servant of God among many and generously acknowledges the labors of Apollos (3, 5-8). He provides us in this letter with many valuable examples of his method of theological reflection and exposition. He always treats the questions at issue on the level of the purity of Christian teaching and conduct. Certain passages of the letter are of the greatest importance for the understanding of early Christian teaching on the Eucharist (10, 14-22; 11, 17-34) and on the resurrection of the body (15, 1-58).

 Paul's authorship of 1 Corinthians, apart from a few verses that some regard as later interpolations, has never been seriously questioned. Some scholars have proposed, however, that the letter as we have it contains portions of more than one original Pauline letter. We know that Paul wrote at least two other letters to Corinth (see 5, 9; 2 Cor 2, 3-4) in addition to the two that we now have; this theory holds that the additional letters are actually contained within the two canonical ones. Most commentators, however, find 1 Corinthians quite understandable as a single coherent work.

 The principal divisions of the First Letter to the Corinthians are the following:

I. *Address (1, 1-9)*
II. *Disorders in the Corinthian Community (1, 10—6, 20)*
 A. *Divisions in the Church (1, 10—4, 21)*
 B. *Moral Disorders (5, 1—6, 20)*
III. *Answers to the Corinthians' Questions (7, 1—11, 1)*
 A. *Marriage and Virginity (7, 1-40)*
 B. *Offerings to Idols (8, 1—11, 1)*
IV. *Problems in Liturgical Assemblies (11, 2—14, 40)*
 A. *Women's Headdresses (11, 3-16)*
 B. *The Lord's Supper (11, 17-34)*
 C. *Spiritual Gifts (12, 1—14, 40)*
V. *The Resurrection (15, 1-58)*
 A. *The Resurrection of Christ (15, 1-11)*
 B. *The Resurrection of the Dead (15, 12-34)*
 C. *The Manner of the Resurrection (15, 35-58)*
VI. *Conclusion (16, 1-24)*

1Cor

I. ADDRESS*

CHAPTER 1

Greeting. [1] Paul, called to be an apostle of Christ Jesus by the will of God,* and Sosthenes our brother,[a] [2] to the church of God that is in Corinth, to you who have been sanctified in Christ Jesus, called to be holy, with all those everywhere who call upon the name of our Lord Jesus Christ, their Lord and ours.[b] [3] Grace to you and peace from God our Father and the Lord Jesus Christ.

Thanksgiving. [4] I give thanks to my God always on your account for the grace of God bestowed on you in Christ Jesus, [5] that in him you were enriched in every way, with all discourse and all knowledge, [6] as the testimony* to Christ was confirmed among you, [7] so that you are not lacking in any spiritual gift as you wait for the revelation of our Lord Jesus Christ.[c] [8] He will keep you firm to the end, irreproachable on the day of our Lord Jesus [Christ].[d] [9] God is faithful, and by him you were called to fellowship with his Son, Jesus Christ our Lord.[e]

---

a Rom 1, 1.—b Acts 18, 1-11.—c Ti 2, 13.—d Phil 1, 6.—e 1 Jn 1, 3.—f Phil 2, 2.—g 1 Cor 3, 4.22; 16, 12; Acts 18, 24-28.—h Acts 18, 8 / Rom 16, 23.—i 1 Cor 16, 15-17.—j 1 Cor 2, 1.4.—k 1 Cor 2, 14 / Rom 1, 16.—l Is 29, 14.

1, 1-9: Paul follows the conventional form for the opening of a Hellenistic letter (cf Rom 1, 1-7), but expands the opening with details carefully chosen to remind the readers of their situation and to suggest some of the issues the letter will discuss.

1, 1: *Called . . . by the will of God:* Paul's mission and the church's existence are grounded in God's initiative. God's call, grace, and fidelity are central ideas in this introduction, emphasized by repetition and wordplays in the Greek.

1, 6: *The testimony:* this defines the purpose of Paul's mission (see also 1 Cor 15, 15 and the note on 1 Cor 2, 1). The forms of his testimony include oral preaching and instruction, his letters, and the life he leads as an apostle.

1, 10—4, 21: The first problem Paul addresses is that of divisions within the community. Although we are unable to reconstruct the situation in Corinth completely, Paul clearly traces the divisions back to a false self-image on the part of the Corinthians, coupled with a false understanding of the apostles who preached to them (cf 1 Cor 4, 6.9; 9, 1-5) and of the Christian message itself. In these chapters he attempts to deal with those underlying factors and to bring the Corinthians back to a more correct perspective.

1, 12: *I belong to:* the activities of Paul and Apollos in Corinth are described in Acts 18. *Cephas* (i.e., "the Rock," a name by which Paul designates Peter also in 1 Cor 3, 22; 9, 5; 15, 5 and in Gal 1, 18; 2, 9.11.14) may well have passed through Corinth; he could have baptized some members of the community either there or elsewhere. The reference to *Christ* may be intended ironically here.

1, 13-17: The reference to baptism and the contrast with preaching the gospel in v 17a suggest that some Corinthians were paying special allegiance to the individuals who initiated them into the community.

II. DISORDERS IN THE CORINTHIAN COMMUNITY

A. Divisions in the Church*

Groups and Slogans. [10] I urge you, brothers, in the name of our Lord Jesus Christ, that all of you agree in what you say, and that there be no divisions among you, but that you be united in the same mind and in the same purpose.[f] [11] For it has been reported to me about you, my brothers, by Chloe's people, that there are rivalries among you. [12] I mean that each of you is saying, "I belong to* Paul," or "I belong to Apollos," or "I belong to Cephas," or "I belong to Christ."[g] [13] * Is Christ divided? Was Paul crucified for you? Or were you baptized in the name of Paul? [14] I give thanks [to God] that I baptized none of you except Crispus and Gaius,[h] [15] so that no one can say you were baptized in my name. [16] (I baptized the household of Stephanas also; beyond that I do not know whether I baptized anyone else.)[i] [17] For Christ did not send me to baptize but to preach the gospel, and* not with the wisdom of human eloquence,* so that the cross of Christ might not be emptied of its meaning.[j]

Paradox of the Cross. [18] The message of the cross is foolishness to those who are perishing, but to us who are being saved it is the power of God.[k] [19] For it is written:

> "I will destroy the wisdom of the wise,
>   and the learning of the learned I will
>   set aside."[l]

1, 17b-18: The basic theme of chs 1-4 is announced. Adherence to individual leaders has something to do with differences in rhetorical ability and also with certain presuppositions regarding wisdom, eloquence, and effectiveness (power), which Paul judges to be in conflict with the gospel and the cross.

1, 17b: *Not with the wisdom of human eloquence:* both of the nouns employed here involve several levels of meaning, on which Paul deliberately plays as his thought unfolds. *Wisdom (sophia)* may be philosophical and speculative, but in biblical usage the term primarily denotes practical knowledge such as is demonstrated in the choice and effective application of means to achieve an end. The same term can designate the arts of building (cf 1 Cor 3, 10) or of persuasive speaking (cf 1 Cor 2, 4) or effectiveness in achieving salvation. *Eloquence (logos):* this translation emphasizes one possible meaning of the term *logos* (cf the references to rhetorical style and persuasiveness in 1 Cor 2, 1.4). But the term itself may denote an internal reasoning process, plan, or intention, as well as an external word, speech, or message. So by his expression *ouk en sophia logou* in the context of gospel preaching, Paul may intend to exclude both human ways of reasoning or thinking about things and human rhetorical technique. *Human:* this adjective does not stand in the Greek text but is supplied from the context. Paul will begin immediately to distinguish between *sophia* and *logos* from their divine counterparts and play them off against each other.

²⁰Where is the wise one? Where is the scribe? Where is the debater of this age? Has not God made the wisdom of the world foolish?^m ²¹ * For since in the wisdom of God the world did not come to know God through wisdom, it was the will of God through the foolishness of the proclamation to save those who have faith. ²²For Jews demand signs and Greeks look for wisdom,ⁿ ²³but we proclaim Christ crucified, a stumbling block to Jews and foolishness to Gentiles,^o ²⁴but to those who are called, Jews and Greeks alike, Christ the power of God and the wisdom of God. ²⁵For the foolishness of God is wiser than human wisdom, and the weakness of God is stronger than human strength.

The Corinthians and Paul.* ²⁶Consider your own calling, brothers. Not many of you were wise by human standards, not many were powerful, not many were of noble birth. ²⁷Rather, God chose the foolish of the world to shame the wise, and God chose the weak of the world to shame the strong,^p ²⁸and God chose the lowly and despised of the world, those who count for nothing, to reduce to nothing those who are something, ²⁹so that no human being might boast* before God.^q ³⁰It is due to him that you are in Christ Jesus, who became for us wisdom from God, as well as righteousness, sanctification, and redemption,^r ³¹so that, as it is written, "Whoever boasts, should boast in the Lord."^s

---

m Is 19, 12.—n Mt 12, 38; 16, 1 / Acts 17, 18-21.—o 1 Cor 2, 2; Gal 3, 1 / Gal 5, 11.—p Jas 2, 5.—q Eph 2, 9.—r Rom 4, 17 / 1 Cor 6, 11; Rom 3, 24-26; 2 Cor 5, 21 / Eph 1, 7; Col 1, 14; 1 Thes 5, 23.—s Jer 9, 23; 2 Cor 10, 17.—t 1 Cor 1, 17.—u 1 Cor 1, 23; Gal 6, 14.—v 1 Cor 4, 20; Rom 15, 19; 1 Thes 1, 5.—w 2 Cor 4, 7.—x Is 64, 3.—y Mt 11, 25; 13, 11; 16, 17.

1, 21-25: True wisdom and power are to be found paradoxically where one would least expect them, in the place of their apparent negation. To human eyes the crucified Christ symbolizes impotence and absurdity.

1, 26—2, 5: The pattern of God's wisdom and power is exemplified in their own experience, if they interpret it rightly (1 Cor 1, 26-31), and can also be read in their experience of Paul as he first appeared among them preaching the gospel (1 Cor 2, 1-5).

1, 29-31: "Boasting (about oneself)" is a Pauline expression for the radical sin, the claim to autonomy on the part of a creature, the illusion that we live and are saved by our own resources. "Boasting in the Lord" (31), on the other hand, is the acknowledgment that we live only from God and for God.

2, 1: *The mystery of God:* God's secret, known only to himself, is his plan for the salvation of his people; it is clear from 1 Cor 1, 18-25; 2, 2.8-10 that this secret involves Jesus and the cross. In place of *mystery,* other good manuscripts read "testimony" (cf 1 Cor 1, 6).

2, 3: The *weakness* of the crucified Jesus is reflected in Paul's own bearing (cf 2 Cor 10—13). *Fear and much trembling:* reverential fear based on a sense of God's transcendence

CHAPTER 2

¹When I came to you, brothers, proclaiming the mystery of God,* I did not come with sublimity of words or of wisdom.^t ²For I resolved to know nothing while I was with you except Jesus Christ, and him crucified.^u ³I came to you in weakness* and fear and much trembling, ⁴and my message and my proclamation were not with persuasive [words of] wisdom,* but with a demonstration of spirit and power,^v ⁵so that your faith might rest not on human wisdom but on the power of God.^w

The True Wisdom.* ⁶Yet we do speak a wisdom to those who are mature, but not a wisdom of this age, nor of the rulers of this age who are passing away. ⁷Rather, we speak God's wisdom,* mysterious, hidden, which God predetermined before the ages for our glory, ⁸and which none of the rulers of this age* knew for, if they had known it, they would not have crucified the Lord of glory. ⁹But as it is written:

> "What eye has not seen, and ear has not heard,
> and what has not entered the human heart,
> what God has prepared for those who love him,"^x

¹⁰ ^y this God has revealed to us through the Spirit.

permeates Paul's existence and preaching. Compare his advice to the Philippians to work out their salvation with "fear and trembling" (Phil 2, 12), because God is at work in them just as his exalting power was paradoxically at work in the emptying, humiliation, and obedience of Jesus to death on the cross (Phil 2, 6-11).

2, 4: Among many manuscript readings here the best is either "not with the persuasion of wisdom" or "not with persuasive words of wisdom," which differ only by a nuance. Whichever reading is accepted, the inefficacy of human wisdom for salvation is contrasted with the power of the cross.

2, 6—3, 4: Paul now asserts paradoxically what he has previously been denying. To the Greeks who "are looking for wisdom" (1 Cor 1, 22), he does indeed bring a wisdom, but of a higher order and an entirely different quality, the only wisdom really worthy of the name. The Corinthians would be able to grasp Paul's preaching as wisdom and enter into a wisdom-conversation with him if they were more open to the Spirit and receptive to the new insight and language that the Spirit teaches.

2, 7-10a: *God's wisdom:* his plan for our salvation. This was his own eternal secret that no one else could fathom, but in this new age of salvation he has graciously revealed it to us. For the pattern of God's secret, hidden to others and now revealed to the Church, cf also Rom 11, 25-36; 16, 25-27; Eph 1, 3-10; 3, 3-11; Col 1, 25-28.

2, 8: *The rulers of this age:* this suggests not only the political leaders of the Jews and Romans under whom Jesus was crucified (cf Acts 4, 25-28) but also the cosmic powers behind them (cf Eph 1, 20-23; 3, 10). *They would not have crucified the Lord of glory:* they became the unwitting executors of God's plan, which will paradoxically bring about their own conquest and submission (1 Cor 15, 24-28).

1Cor

For the Spirit scrutinizes everything, even the depths of God. [11] Among human beings, who knows what pertains to a person except the spirit of the person that is within? Similarly, no one knows what pertains to God except the Spirit of God. [12] We have not received the spirit of the world but the Spirit that is from God, so that we may understand the things freely given us by God. [13] And we speak about them not with words taught by human wisdom, but with words taught by the Spirit, describing spiritual realities in spiritual terms.*

[14] Now the natural person* does not accept what pertains to the Spirit of God, for to him it is foolishness, and he cannot understand it, because it is judged spiritually. [15] The spiritual person, however, can judge everything but is not subject to judgment* by anyone.

[16] For "who has known the mind of the Lord, so as to counsel him?" But we have the mind of Christ. [z]

CHAPTER 3

[1] * Brothers, I could not talk to you as spiritual people, but as fleshly people,* as infants in Christ. [2] I fed you milk, not solid food, because you were unable to take it. Indeed, you are still not able, even now, [a]

---

[3] for you are still of the flesh. While there is jealousy and rivalry among you,* are you not of the flesh and behaving in an ordinary human way? [b] [4] Whenever someone says, "I belong to Paul," and another, "I belong to Apollos," are you not merely human? [c]

The Role of God's Ministers.* [5] What is Apollos, after all, and what is Paul? Ministers* through whom you became believers, just as the Lord assigned each one. [6] I planted, Apollos watered, but God caused the growth. [d] [7] Therefore, neither the one who plants nor the one who waters is anything, but only God, who causes the growth. [8] The one who plants and the one who waters are equal, and each will receive wages in proportion to his labor. [9] For we are God's co-workers; you are God's field, God's building. [e]

[10] * According to the grace of God given to me, like a wise master builder I laid a foundation, and another is building upon it. But each one must be careful how he builds upon it, [11] for no one can lay a foundation other than the one that is there, namely, Jesus Christ. [12] If anyone builds on this foundation with gold, silver, precious stones, wood, hay, or straw, [13] the work of each will come to light, for the Day* will disclose it. It will be revealed with fire, and the fire [itself] will test the

---

z Wis 9, 13; Is 40, 13; Rom 11, 34.—a Heb 5, 12-14.—b Jas 3, 13-16.—c 1 Cor 1, 12.—d Acts 18, 1-11.24-28.—e Eph 2, 20-22; 1 Pt 2, 5.

2, 13: *In spiritual terms:* the Spirit teaches spiritual people a new mode of perception (12) and an appropriate language by which they can share their self-understanding, their knowledge about what God has done in them. The final phrase in v 13 can also be translated "describing spiritual realities to spiritual people," in which case it prepares for vv 14-16.

2, 14: *The natural person:* see the note on 1 Cor 3, 1.

2, 15: *The spiritual person . . . is not subject to judgment:* since spiritual persons have been given knowledge of what pertains to God (11-12), they share in God's own capacity to judge. One to whom the mind of the Lord (and of Christ) is revealed (16) can be said to share in some sense in God's exemption from counseling and criticism.

3, 1-4: The Corinthians desire a sort of wisdom dialogue or colloquy with Paul; they are looking for solid, adult food, and he appears to disappoint their expectations. Paul counters: if such a dialogue has not yet taken place, the reason is that they are still at an immature stage of development (cf 1 Cor 2, 6).

3, 1: *Spiritual people . . . fleshly people:* Paul employs two clusters of concepts and terms to distinguish what later theology will call the "natural" and the "supernatural." (1) The natural person (1 Cor 2, 14) is one whose existence, perceptions, and behavior are determined by purely natural principles, the *psychē* (1 Cor 2, 14) and the *sarx* (flesh, a biblical term that connotes creatureliness, 1 Cor 3, 1.3). Such persons are only infants (1 Cor 3, 1); they remain on a purely human level *(anthrōpoi,* 1 Cor 3, 4). (2) On the other hand, they are called to be animated by a

higher principle, the *pneuma,* God's spirit. They are to become spiritual *(pneumatikoi,* 1 Cor 3, 1) and mature (1 Cor 2, 6) in their perceptions and behavior (cf Gal 5, 16-26). The culmination of existence in the Spirit is described in 1 Cor 15, 44-49.

3, 3-4: Jealousy, rivalry, and divisions in the community are symptoms of their arrested development; they reveal the immaturity both of their self-understanding (4) and of the judgments about their apostles (21).

3, 5—4, 5: The Corinthians tend to evaluate their leaders by the criteria of human wisdom and to exaggerate their importance. Paul views the role of the apostles in the light of his theology of spiritual gifts (cf chs 12-14, where the charism of the apostle heads the lists). The essential aspects of all spiritual gifts (1 Cor 12, 4-6 presents them as gifts of grace, as services, and as modes of activity) are exemplified by the apostolate, which is a gift of grace (1 Cor 3, 10) through which God works (1 Cor 3, 9) and a form of service (1 Cor 3, 5) for the common good (elsewhere expressed by the verb "build up," suggested here by the image of the building, 1 Cor 3, 9). The apostles serve the church, but their accountability is to God and to Christ (1 Cor 4, 1-5).

3, 5: *Ministers:* for other expressions of Paul's understanding of himself as minister or steward to the church, cf 1 Cor 4, 1; 9, 17.19-27; 2 Cor 3, 6-9; 4, 1; 5, 18; 6, 3-4; and 2 Cor 11, 23 (the climax of Paul's defense).

3, 10-11: There are diverse functions in the service of the community, but each individual's task is serious, and each will stand accountable for the quality of his contribution.

3, 13: *The Day:* the great day of Yahweh, the day of judgment, which can be a time of either gloom or joy. *Fire* both destroys and purifies.

quality of each one's work.^{f} ^{14}If the work stands that someone built upon the foundation, that person will receive a wage. ^{15}But if someone's work is burned up, that one will suffer loss; the person will be saved,* but only as through fire. ^{16}Do you not know that you are the temple of God, and that the Spirit of God dwells in you?^{g} ^{17}If anyone destroys God's temple, God will destroy that person; for the temple of God, which you are, is holy.*

^{18}Let no one deceive himself. If anyone among you considers himself wise in this age, let him become a fool so as to become wise.^{h} ^{19}For the wisdom of this world is foolishness in the eyes of God, for it is written:^{i}

"He catches the wise in their own ruses,"

^{20}and again:

"The Lord knows the thoughts of the wise, that they are vain."^{j}

^{21} * So let no one boast about human beings, for everything belongs to you,^{k} ^{22}Paul or Apollos or Cephas, or the world or life or death, or the present or the future: all belong to you, ^{23}and you to Christ, and Christ to God.

---

f Mt 3, 11-12; 2 Thes 1, 7-10.—g 1 Cor 6, 19; 2 Cor 6, 16; Eph 2, 20-22.—h 1 Cor 8, 2; Is 5, 21; Gal 6, 3.—i 1 Cor 1, 20 / Jb 5, 13.—j Ps 94, 11.—k 1 Cor 4, 6 / Rom 8, 32.—l Ti 1, 7; 1 Pt 4, 10.—m 2 Cor 1, 12 / Rom 2, 16; 2 Cor 5, 10.

3, 15: *Will be saved:* although Paul can envision very harsh divine punishment (cf 1 Cor 3, 17), he appears optimistic about the success of divine corrective means both here and elsewhere (cf 1 Cor 5, 5; 11, 32 [discipline]). The text of v 15 has sometimes been used to support the notion of purgatory, though it does not envisage this.

3, 17: *Holy:* i.e., "belonging to God." The cultic sanctity of the community is a fundamental theological reality to which Paul frequently alludes (cf 1 Cor 1, 2.30; 6, 11; 7, 14).

3, 21-23: These verses pick up the line of thought of 1 Cor 1, 10-13. If the Corinthians were genuinely wise (18-20), their perceptions would be reversed, and they would see everything in the world and all those with whom they exist in the church in their true relations with one another. Paul assigns all the persons involved in the theological universe a position on a scale: God, Christ, church members, church leaders. Read from top to bottom, the scale expresses ownership; read from bottom to top, the obligation to serve. This picture should be complemented by similar statements such as those in 1 Cor 8, 6 and 1 Cor 15, 20-28.

4, 6-21: This is an emotionally charged peroration to the discussion about divisions. It contains several exhortations and statements of Paul's purpose in writing (cf 6.14-17.21) that counterbalance the initial exhortation at 1 Cor 1, 10.

4, 6: *That you may learn from us not to go beyond what is written:* the words "to go" are not in the Greek, but have here been added as the minimum necessary to elicit sense from this difficult passage. It probably means that the Corinthians should avoid the false wisdom of vain speculation, contenting themselves with Paul's proclamation of the cross, which is the fulfillment of

---

CHAPTER 4

^{1}Thus should one regard us: as servants of Christ and stewards of the mysteries of God.^{l} ^{2}Now it is of course required of stewards that they be found trustworthy. ^{3}It does not concern me in the least that I be judged by you or any human tribunal; I do not even pass judgment on myself; ^{4}I am not conscious of anything against me, but I do not thereby stand acquitted; the one who judges me is the Lord.^{m} ^{5}Therefore, do not make any judgment before the appointed time, until the Lord comes, for he will bring to light what is hidden in darkness and will manifest the motives of our hearts, and then everyone will receive praise from God.

Paul's Life as Pattern.* ^{6}I have applied these things to myself and Apollos for your benefit, brothers, so that you may learn from us not to go beyond what is written,* so that none of you will be inflated with pride in favor of one person over against another. ^{7}Who confers distinction upon you? What do you possess that you have not received? But if you have received it, why are you boasting as if you did not receive it? ^{8}You are already satisfied; you have already grown rich; you have become kings* without us! Indeed, I wish that you had become kings, so that we also might become kings with you.

^{9} * For as I see it, God has exhibited us apostles as the last of all, like people sen-

---

God's promises in the Old Testament (what is written). *Inflated with pride:* literally, "puffed up," arrogant, filled with a sense of self-importance. The term is particularly Pauline, found in the New Testament only in 1 Cor 4, 6.18-19; 5, 2; 8, 1; 13, 4; Col 2, 18 (cf the related noun at 2 Cor 12, 20). It sometimes occurs in conjunction with the theme of "boasting," as in vv 6-7 here.

4, 8: *Satisfied . . . rich . . . kings:* these three statements could also be punctuated as questions continuing the series begun in v 7. In any case these expressions reflect a tendency at Corinth toward an overrealized eschatology, a form of self-deception that draws Paul's irony. The underlying attitude has implications for the Corinthians' thinking about other issues, notably morality and the resurrection, that Paul will address later in the letter.

4, 9-13: A rhetorically effective catalogue of the circumstances of apostolic existence, in the course of which Paul ironically contrasts his own sufferings with the Corinthians' illusion that they have passed beyond the folly of the passion and have already reached the condition of glory. His language echoes that of the beatitudes and woes, which assert a future reversal of present conditions. Their present sufferings ("to this very hour," 11) place the apostles in the class of those to whom the beatitudes promise future relief (Mt 5, 3-11; Lk 6, 20-23); whereas the Corinthians' image of themselves as "already" filled, rich, ruling (8), as wise, strong, and honored (10) places them paradoxically in the position of those whom the woes threaten with future undoing (Lk 6, 24-26). They have lost sight of the fact that the reversal is predicted for the future.

1Cor

tenced to death, since we have become a spectacle to the world, to angels and human beings alike.ⁿ ¹⁰We are fools on Christ's account, but you are wise in Christ; we are weak, but you are strong; you are held in honor, but we in disrepute.ᵒ ¹¹To this very hour we go hungry and thirsty, we are poorly clad and roughly treated, we wander about homeless;ᵖ ¹²and we toil, working with our own hands. When ridiculed, we bless; when persecuted, we endure;ᑫ ¹³when slandered, we respond gently. We have become like the world's rubbish, the scum of all, to this very moment.

¹⁴I am writing you this not to shame you, but to admonish you as my beloved children.* ¹⁵Even if you should have countless guides to Christ, yet you do not have many fathers, for I became your father in Christ Jesus through the gospel.ʳ ¹⁶Therefore, I urge you, be imitators of me.ˢ ¹⁷For this reason I am sending you Timothy, who is my beloved and faithful son in the Lord; he will remind you of my ways in Christ [Jesus], just as I teach them everywhere in every church.ᵗ

¹⁸ * Some have become inflated with pride, as if I were not coming to you. ¹⁹But I will come to you soon, if the Lord is willing, and I shall ascertain not the talk of these inflated people but their power.

²⁰For the kingdom of God is not a matter of talk but of power.ᵘ ²¹Which do you prefer? Shall I come to you with a rod, or with love and a gentle spirit?ᵛ

B. Moral Disorders*

CHAPTER 5

A Case of Incest.* ¹It is widely reported that there is immorality among you, and immorality of a kind not found even among pagans—a man living with his father's wife.ʷ ²And you are inflated with pride.* Should you not rather have been sorrowful? The one who did this deed should be expelled from your midst. ³I, for my part, although absent in body but present in spirit, have already, as if present, pronounced judgment on the one who has committed this deed,ˣ ⁴in the name of [our] Lord Jesus: when you have gathered together and I am with you in spirit with the power of the Lord Jesus, ⁵you are to deliver this man to Satan* for the destruction of his flesh, so that his spirit may be saved on the day of the Lord.ʸ

⁶ ᶻ Your boasting is not appropriate. Do you not know that a little yeast* leavens all the dough? ⁷ * Clear out the old yeast, so

n 1 Cor 15, 31; Rom 8, 36; 2 Cor 4, 8-12; 11, 23 / Heb 10, 33.—o 1 Cor 1, 18; 3, 18; 2 Cor 11, 19 / 1 Cor 2, 3; 2 Cor 13, 9.—p Rom 8, 35; 2 Cor 11, 23-27.—q Acts 9, 6-14; 18, 3; 20, 34; 1 Thes 2, 9 / 1 Pt 3, 9.—r Gal 4, 19; Phlm 10.—s 1 Cor 11, 1; Phil 3, 17; 4, 9; 1 Thes 1, 6; 2 Thes 3, 7.9.—t 1 Cor 16, 10; Acts 19, 22.—u 1 Cor 2, 4; 1 Thes 1, 5.—v 2 Cor 1, 23; 10, 2.—w Lv 18, 7-8; 20, 11; Dt 27, 20.—x Col 2, 5.—y 1 Tm 1, 20.—z Gal 5, 9.

4, 14-17: *My beloved children:* the close of the argument is dominated by the tender metaphor of the father who not only gives his children life but also educates them. Once he has begotten them through his preaching, Paul continues to present the gospel to them existentially, by his life as well as by his word, and they are to learn, as children do, by imitating their parents (16). The reference to the *rod* in v 21 belongs to the same image-complex. So does the image of the *ways* in v 17: the ways that Paul teaches everywhere, "his ways in Christ Jesus," mean a behavior pattern quite different from the human ways along which the Corinthians are walking (1 Cor 3, 3).

4, 18-21: Verse 20 picks up the contrast between a certain kind of talk (*logos*) and true power (*dynamis*) from 1 Cor 1, 17-18 and 1 Cor 2, 4-5. The kingdom, which many of them imagine to be fully present in their lives (8), will be rather unexpectedly disclosed in the strength of Paul's encounter with them, if they make a powerful intervention on his part necessary. Compare the similar ending to an argument in 2 Cor 13, 1-4.10.

5, 1—6, 20: Paul now takes up a number of other matters that require regulation. These have come to his attention by hearsay (1 Cor 5, 1), probably in reports brought by "Chloe's people" (1 Cor 1, 11).

5, 1-13: Paul first deals with the incestuous union of a man with his stepmother (1-8) and then attempts to clarify general admonitions he has given about associating with fellow Christians guilty of immorality (9-13). Each of these three brief paragraphs expresses the same idea: the need of separation between the holy and the unholy.

5, 2: *Inflated with pride:* this remark and the reference to *boasting* in v 6 suggest that they are proud of themselves despite the infection in their midst, tolerating and possibly even approving the situation. The attitude expressed in 1 Cor 6, 2.13 may be influencing their thinking in this case.

5, 5: *Deliver this man to Satan:* once the sinner is expelled from the church, the sphere of Jesus' lordship and victory over sin, he will be in the region outside over which Satan is still master. *For the destruction of his flesh:* the purpose of the penalty is medicinal: through affliction, sin's grip over him may be destroyed and the path to repentance and reunion laid open. With Paul's instructions for an excommunication ceremony here, contrast his recommendations for the reconciliation of a sinner in 2 Cor 2, 5-11.

5, 6: *A little yeast:* yeast, which induces fermentation, is a natural symbol for a source of corruption that becomes all-pervasive. The expression is proverbial.

5, 7-8: In the Jewish calendar, Passover was followed immediately by the festival of Unleavened Bread. In preparation for this feast all traces of old bread were removed from the house, and during the festival only unleavened bread was eaten. The sequence of these two feasts provides Paul with an image of Christian existence: Christ's death (the true Passover celebration) is followed by the life of the Christian community, marked by newness, purity, and integrity (a perpetual feast of unleavened bread). Paul may have been writing around Passover time (cf 1 Cor 16, 5); this is a little Easter homily, the earliest in Christian literature.

that you may become a fresh batch of dough, inasmuch as you are unleavened. For our paschal lamb, Christ, has been sacrificed.[a] [8]Therefore, let us celebrate the feast, not with the old yeast, the yeast of malice and wickedness, but with the unleavened bread of sincerity and truth.[b]

[9] * I wrote you in my letter not to associate with immoral people, [10]not at all referring to the immoral of this world or the greedy and robbers or idolaters; for you would then have to leave the world.[c] [11]But I now write to you not to associate with anyone named a brother, if he is immoral, greedy, an idolater, a slanderer, a drunkard, or a robber, not even to eat with such a person.[d] [12]For why should I be judging outsiders? Is it not your business to judge those within? [13]God will judge those outside. "Purge the evil person from your midst."[e]

CHAPTER 6

Lawsuits before Unbelievers. * [1]How can any one of you with a case against another dare to bring it to the unjust for judgment instead of to the holy ones? [2] * Do you not know that the holy ones will judge the world? If the world is to be judged by you, are you unqualified for the lowest law courts?[f] [3]Do you not know that we will judge angels? Then why not everyday matters? [4]If, therefore, you have courts for everyday matters, do you seat as judges

people of no standing in the church? [5]I say this to shame you. Can it be that there is not one among you wise enough to be able to settle a case between brothers? [6]But rather brother goes to court against brother, and that before unbelievers?

[7]Now indeed [then] it is, in any case, a failure on your part that you have lawsuits against one another. Why not rather put up with injustice? Why not rather let yourselves be cheated?[g] [8]Instead, you inflict injustice and cheat, and this to brothers. [9] * Do you not know that the unjust will not inherit the kingdom of God? Do not be deceived; neither fornicators nor idolaters nor adulterers nor boy prostitutes* nor sodomites[h] [10]nor thieves nor the greedy nor drunkards nor slanderers nor robbers will inherit the kingdom of God. [11]That is what some of you used to be; but now you have had yourselves washed, you were sanctified, you were justified in the name of the Lord Jesus Christ and in the Spirit of our God.[i]

Sexual Immorality. * [12]"Everything is lawful for me,"* but not everything is beneficial. "Everything is lawful for me," but I will not let myself be dominated by anything.[j] [13]"Food for the stomach and the stomach for food," but God will do away with both the one and the other. The body, however, is not for immorality, but for the Lord, and the Lord is for the body; [14]God raised the Lord and will also raise us by his power.[k]

1Cor

---

a Ex 12, 1-13; Dt 16, 1-2; 1 Pt 1, 19.—b Ex 12, 15-20; 13, 7; Dt 16, 3.—c 1 Cor 10, 27; Jn 17, 15.—d Mt 18, 17; 2 Thes 3, 6.14; 2 Jn 10.—e Dt 13, 6; 17, 7; 22, 24.—f Wis 3, 8; Mt 19, 28; Rv 20, 4.—g Mt 5, 38-42; Rom 12, 17-21; 1 Thes 5, 15.—h 1 Cor 15, 50; Gal 5, 19-21; Eph 5, 5.—i Ti 3, 3-7.—j 1 Cor 10, 23.—k Rom 8, 11; 2 Cor 4, 14.

5, 9-13: Paul here corrects a misunderstanding of his earlier directives against associating with immoral fellow Christians. He concedes the impossibility of avoiding contact with sinners in society at large but urges the Corinthians to maintain the inner purity of their own community.

6, 1-11: Christians at Corinth are suing one another before pagan courts. A barrage of rhetorical questions (1-9) betrays Paul's indignation over this practice, which he sees as an infringement upon the holiness of the Christian community.

6, 2-3: The principle to which Paul appeals is an eschatological prerogative promised to Christians: they are to share with Christ the judgment of the world (cf Dn 7, 22.27). Hence they ought to be able to settle minor disputes within the community.

6, 9-10: A catalogue of typical vices that exclude from the kingdom of God and that should be excluded from God's church. Such lists (cf 1 Cor 5, 10) reflect the common moral sensibility of the New Testament period.

6, 9: The Greek word translated as *boy prostitutes* may refer to catamites, i.e., boys or young men who were kept for purposes of prostitution, a practice not uncommon in the Greco-Roman world. In Greek mythology this was the function of Ganymede, the "cupbearer of the gods," whose Latin name was Catamitus. The term translated *sodomites* would then refer to adult males who indulged in homosexual practices with such boys. See similar condemnations of such practices in Rom 1, 26-27; 1 Tm 1, 10.

6, 12-20: Paul now turns to the opinion of some Corinthians that sexuality is a morally indifferent area (12-13). This leads him to explain the mutual relation between the Lord Jesus and our bodies (13b) in a densely packed paragraph that contains elements of a profound theology of sexuality (15-20).

6, 12-13: *Everything is lawful for me:* the Corinthians may have derived this slogan from Paul's preaching about Christian freedom, but they mean something different by it: they consider sexual satisfaction a matter as indifferent as food, and they attribute no lasting significance to bodily functions (13a). Paul begins to deal with the slogan by two qualifications, which suggest principles for judging sexual activity. *Not everything is beneficial:* cf 1 Cor 10, 23, and the whole argument of chs 8-10 on the finality of freedom and moral activity. *Not let myself be dominated:* certain apparently free actions may involve in fact a secret servitude in conflict with the lordship of Jesus.

¹⁵ Do you not know that your bodies are members of Christ? Shall I then take Christ's members and make them the members of a prostitute?* Of course not!¹ ¹⁶ [Or] do you not know that anyone who joins himself to a prostitute becomes one body with her? For "the two," it says, "will become one flesh."*ᵐ ¹⁷ But whoever is joined to the Lord becomes one spirit with him.ⁿ ¹⁸ Avoid immorality. Every other sin a person commits is outside the body, but the immoral person sins against his own body.* ¹⁹ Do you not know that your body is a temple* of the holy Spirit within you, whom you have from God, and that you are not your own?ᵒ ²⁰ For you have been purchased at a price. Therefore glorify God in your body.ᵖ

III. ANSWERS TO THE CORINTHIANS' QUESTIONS

A. Marriage and Virginity*

CHAPTER 7

Advice to the Married.* ¹ Now in regard to the matters about which you wrote: "It is a good thing for a man not to touch a woman,"* ² but because of cases of immorality every man should have his own wife, and every woman her own husband. ³ The husband should fulfill his duty toward his wife, and likewise the wife toward her husband. ⁴ A wife does not have authority over her own body, but rather her husband, and similarly a husband does not have authority over his own body, but rather his wife. ⁵ Do not deprive each other, except perhaps by mutual consent for a time, to be free for prayer, but then return to one another, so that Satan may not tempt you through your lack of self-control. ⁶ This I say by way of concession,* however, not as a command. ⁷ Indeed, I wish everyone to be as I am, but each has a particular gift from God,* one of one kind and one of another.�q

⁸ ʳ Now to the unmarried and to widows I say: it is a good thing for them to remain as they are, as I do,* ⁹ but if they cannot exercise self-control they should marry, for it is better to marry than to be on fire. ¹⁰ ˢ To the married, however, I give this instruction (not I, but the Lord):* a wife should not separate from her husband ¹¹ —and if she does separate she must either remain single or become reconciled

---

l 1 Cor 12, 27; Rom 6, 12-13; 12, 5; Eph 5, 30.—m Gn 2, 24; Mt 19, 5; Mk 10, 8; Eph 5, 31.—n Rom 8, 9-10; 2 Cor 3, 17.—o 1 Cor 3, 16-17; Rom 5, 5.—p 1 Cor 3, 23; 7, 23; Acts 20, 28 / Rom 12, 1; Phil 1, 20.—q Mt 19, 11-12.—r 1 Tm 5, 11-16 / 1 Cor 9, 5.—s 10-11: Mt 5, 32; 19, 9.

6, 15b-16: *A prostitute:* the reference may be specifically to religious prostitution, an accepted part of pagan culture at Corinth and elsewhere; but the prostitute also serves as a symbol for any sexual relationship that conflicts with Christ's claim over us individually. *The two . . . will become one flesh:* the text of Gn 2, 24 is applied positively to human marriage in Mt and Mk, and in Eph 5, 29-32: love of husband and wife reflects the love of Christ for his church. The application of the text to union with a prostitute is jarring, for such a union is a parody, an antitype of marriage, which does conflict with Christ's claim over us. This explains the horror expressed in 15b.

6, 18: *Against his own body:* expresses the intimacy and depth of sexual disorder, which violates the very orientation of our bodies.

6, 19-20: Paul's vision becomes trinitarian. *A temple:* sacred by reason of God's gift, his indwelling Spirit. *Not your own:* but "for the Lord," who acquires ownership by the act of redemption. *Glorify God in your body:* the argument concludes with a positive imperative to supplement the negative "avoid immorality" of v 18. Far from being a terrain that is morally indifferent, the area of sexuality is one in which our relationship with God (and his Christ and his Spirit) is very intimately expressed: he is either highly glorified or deeply offended.

7, 1-40: Paul now begins to answer questions addressed to him by the Corinthians (1 Cor 7, 1—11, 1). The first of these concerns marriage. This chapter contains advice both to the married (1-16) and to the unmarried (25-38) or widowed (39-40); these two parts are separated by vv 17-24, which enunciate a principle applicable to both.

7, 1-16: It seems that some Christians in Corinth were advocating asceticism in sexual matters. The pattern *it is a good thing . . . , but* occurs twice (1-2.8-9; cf 1 Cor 7, 26), suggesting that in this matter as in others the Corinthians have seized upon a genuine value but are exaggerating or distorting it in some way. Once again Paul calls them to a more correct perspective and a better sense of their own limitations. The phrase *it is a good thing* (1) may have been the slogan of the ascetic party at Corinth.

7, 1-7: References to Paul's own behavior (7-8) suggest that his celibate way of life and his preaching to the unmarried (cf 1 Cor 7, 25-35) have given some the impression that asceticism within marriage, i.e., suspension of normal sexual relations, would be a laudable ideal. Paul points to their experience of widespread immorality to caution them against overestimating their own strength (2); as individuals they may not have the particular gift that makes such asceticism feasible (7) and hence are to abide by the principle to be explained in vv 17-24.

7, 6: *By way of concession:* this refers most likely to the concession mentioned in v 5a: temporary interruption of relations for a legitimate purpose.

7, 7: *A particular gift from God:* use of the term *charisma* suggests that marriage and celibacy may be viewed in the light of Paul's theology of spiritual gifts (chs 12-14).

7, 8: Paul was obviously unmarried when he wrote this verse. Some interpreters believe that he had previously been married and widowed; there is no clear evidence either for or against this view, which was expressed already at the end of the second century by Clement of Alexandria.

7, 10-11: *(Not I, but the Lord):* Paul reminds the married of Jesus' principle of nonseparation (Mk 10, 9). This is one of his rare specific references to the teaching of Jesus.

to her husband—and a husband should not divorce his wife.

12 To the rest* I say (not the Lord): if any brother has a wife who is an unbeliever, and she is willing to go on living with him, he should not divorce her; 13 and if any woman has a husband who is an unbeliever, and he is willing to go on living with her, she should not divorce her husband. 14 For the unbelieving husband is made holy through his wife, and the unbelieving wife is made holy through the brother. Otherwise your children would be unclean, whereas in fact they are holy.[t]

15 If the unbeliever separates,* however, let him separate. The brother or sister is not bound in such cases; God has called you to peace. 16 For how do you know, wife, whether you will save your husband; or how do you know, husband, whether you will save your wife?

The Life That the Lord Has Assigned.*
17 Only, everyone should live as the Lord has assigned, just as God called each one. I give this order in all the churches. 18 Was someone called after he had been circumcised? He should not try to undo his circumcision. Was an uncircumcised person called? He should not be circumcised.[u]

---

t Rom 11, 16.—u 1 Mc 1, 15 / Acts 15, 1-2.—v Rom 2, 25.29; Gal 5, 6; 6, 15.—w Eph 6, 5-9; Col 3, 11; Phlm 16.—x 1 Cor 6, 20.—y 1 Cor 7, 8.—z Rom 13, 11.—a Lk 14, 20.—b 1 Tm 5, 5.—c Lk 10, 39-42.

7, 12-14: *To the rest:* marriages in which only one partner is a baptized Christian. Jesus' prohibition against divorce is not addressed to them, but Paul extends the principle of nonseparation to such unions, provided they are marked by peacefulness and shared sanctification.

7, 15-16: *If the unbeliever separates:* the basis of the "Pauline privilege" in Catholic marriage legislation.

7, 17-24: On the ground that distinct human conditions are less significant than the whole new existence opened up by God's call, Paul urges them to be less concerned with changing their states of life than with answering God's call where it finds them. The principle applies both to the married state (1 Cor 7, 1-16) and to the unmarried (1 Cor 7, 25-38).

7, 25-28: Paul is careful to explain that the principle of v 17 does not bind under sin but that present earthly conditions make it advantageous for the unmarried to remain as they are (28). These remarks must be complemented by the statement about "particular gifts" from v 7.

7, 29-31: *The world . . . is passing away:* Paul advises Christians to go about the ordinary activities of life in a manner different from those who are totally immersed in them and unaware of their transitoriness.

19 Circumcision means nothing, and uncircumcision means nothing; what matters is keeping God's commandments.[v] 20 Everyone should remain in the state in which he was called.

21 Were you a slave when you were called? Do not be concerned but, even if you can gain your freedom, make the most of it. 22 For the slave called in the Lord is a freed person in the Lord, just as the free person who has been called is a slave of Christ.[w] 23 You have been purchased at a price. Do not become slaves to human beings.[x] 24 Brothers, everyone should continue before God in the state in which he was called.

Advice to Virgins and Widows. 25 Now in regard to virgins I have no commandment from the Lord,* but I give my opinion as one who by the Lord's mercy is trustworthy. 26 So this is what I think best because of the present distress: that it is a good thing for a person to remain as he is.[y] 27 Are you bound to a wife? Do not seek a separation. Are you free of a wife? Then do not look for a wife. 28 If you marry, however, you do not sin, nor does an unmarried woman sin if she marries; but such people will experience affliction in their earthly life, and I would like to spare you that.

29 * I tell you, brothers, the time is running out. From now on, let those having wives act as not having them,[z] 30 those weeping as not weeping, those rejoicing as not rejoicing, those buying as not owning, 31 those using the world as not using it fully. For the world in its present form is passing away.

32 I should like you to be free of anxieties. An unmarried man is anxious about the things of the Lord, how he may please the Lord. 33 But a married man is anxious about the things of the world, how he may please his wife,[a] 34 and he is divided. An unmarried woman or a virgin is anxious about the things of the Lord, so that she may be holy in both body and spirit. A married woman, on the other hand, is anxious about the things of the world, how she may please her husband.[b] 35 I am telling you this for your own benefit, not to impose a restraint upon you, but for the sake of propriety and adherence to the Lord without distraction.[c]

1Cor

³⁶ * If anyone thinks he is behaving improperly toward his virgin, and if a critical moment has come* and so it has to be, let him do as he wishes. He is committing no sin; let them get married. ³⁷ The one who stands firm in his resolve, however, who is not under compulsion but has power over his own will, and has made up his mind to keep his virgin, will be doing well. ³⁸ So then, the one who marries his virgin does well; the one who does not marry her will do better.

³⁹ * A wife is bound to her husband as long as he lives. But if her husband dies, she is free to be married to whomever she wishes, provided that it be in the Lord. *ᵈ* ⁴⁰ She is more blessed, though, in my opinion, if she remains as she is, and I think that I too have the Spirit of God. *ᵉ*

B. Offerings to Idols*

CHAPTER 8

Knowledge Insufficient. ¹ Now in regard to meat sacrificed to idols:* we realize that "all of us have knowledge"; knowledge inflates with pride, but love builds up. *ᶠ* ² If anyone supposes he knows something, he does not yet know as he ought to know. ³ But if one loves God, one is known by him. *ᵍ*

⁴ So about the eating of meat sacrificed to idols: we know that "there is no idol in the world," and that "there is no God but one." *ʰ* ⁵ Indeed, even though there are so-called gods in heaven and on earth (there are, to be sure, many "gods" and many "lords"), ⁶ * yet for us there is

one God, the Father,
    from whom all things are and for
      whom we exist,
and one Lord, Jesus Christ,
    through whom all things are and
      through whom we exist. *ⁱ*

Practical Rules. ⁷ But not all have this knowledge. There are some who have been so used to idolatry up until now that, when they eat meat sacrificed to idols, their conscience, which is weak, is defiled. *ʲ*

⁸ * Now food will not bring us closer to God. We are no worse off if we do not eat, nor are we better off if we do. *ᵏ* ⁹ But make sure that this liberty of yours in no way becomes a stumbling block to the weak. *ˡ* ¹⁰ If someone sees you, with your knowledge, reclining at table in the temple of an idol, may not his conscience too, weak as it is, be "built up" to eat the meat sacrificed to idols? ¹¹ Thus through your knowledge, the weak person is brought to destruction, the brother for whom Christ died. *ᵐ*

---

d Rom 7, 2.—e 1 Cor 7, 25.—f Rom 15, 14 / 1 Cor 13, 1-13; Rom 14, 15.19.—g Rom 8, 29; Gal 4, 9.—h 1 Cor 10, 19; Dt 6, 4.—i Mal 2, 10 / Rom 11, 36; Eph 4, 5-6 / 1 Cor 1, 2-3 / Jn 1, 3; Col 1, 16.—j 1 Cor 10, 28; Rom 14, 23 / Rom 14, 1; 15, 1.—k Rom 14, 17.—l Rom 14, 13.20-21.—m Rom 14, 15.20.

7, 36-38: The passage is difficult to interpret, because it is unclear whether Paul is thinking of a father and his unmarried daughter (or slave), or of a couple engaged in a betrothal or spiritual marriage. The general principles already enunciated apply: there is no question of sin, even if they should marry, but staying as they are is "better" (for the reasons mentioned in 1 Cor 7, 28-35). Once again the *charisma* of v 7, which applies also to the unmarried (1 Cor 7, 8-9), is to be presupposed.

7, 36: *A critical moment has come:* either because the woman will soon be beyond marriageable age, or because their passions are becoming uncontrollable (cf 1 Cor 7, 9).

7, 39-40: Application of the principles to the case of widows. If they do choose to remarry, they ought to prefer Christian husbands.

8, 1—11, 1: The Corinthians' second question concerns meat that has been sacrificed to idols; in this area they were exhibiting a disordered sense of liberation that Paul here tries to rectify. These chapters contain a sustained and unified argument that illustrates Paul's method of theological reflection on a moral dilemma. Although the problem with which he is dealing is dated, the guidelines for moral decisions that he offers are of lasting validity.

Essentially Paul urges them to take a communitarian rather than an individualistic view of their Christian freedom. Many decisions that they consider pertinent only to their private relationship with God have, in fact, social consequences. Nor can moral decisions be determined by merely theoretical considerations; they must be based on concrete circumstances, specifically on the value and needs of other individuals and on mutual responsibility within the community. Paul here introduces the theme of "building up" *(oikodomē),* i.e., of contributing by individual action to the welfare and growth of the community. This theme will be further developed in ch 14; see the note on 1 Cor 14, 3b-5. Several years later Paul would again deal with the problem of meat sacrificed to idols in Rom 14, 1—15, 6.

8, 1a: *Meat sacrificed to idols:* much of the food consumed in the city could have passed through pagan religious ceremonies before finding its way into markets and homes. *"All of us have knowledge":* a slogan, similar to 1 Cor 6, 12, which reveals the self-image of the Corinthians. Verse 4 will specify the content of this knowledge.

8, 6: This verse rephrases the monotheistic confession of v 4 in such a way as to contrast it with polytheism (5) and to express our relationship with the one God in concrete, i.e., in personal and Christian terms. *And for whom we exist:* since the Greek contains no verb here and the action intended must be inferred from the preposition *eis,* another translation is equally possible: "toward whom we return." *Through whom all things:* the earliest reference in the New Testament to Jesus' role in creation.

8, 8-9: Although the food in itself is morally neutral, extrinsic circumstances may make the eating of it harmful. *A stumbling block:* the image is that of tripping or causing someone to fall (cf 1 Cor 8, 13; 9, 12; 10, 12.32; 2 Cor 6, 3; Rom 14, 13.20-21). This is a basic moral imperative for Paul, a counterpart to the positive imperative to "build one another up"; compare the expression "giving offense" as opposed to "pleasing" in 1 Cor 10, 32-33.

[12] When you sin in this way against your brothers and wound their consciences, weak as they are, you are sinning against Christ. [13] *n* Therefore, if food causes my brother to sin, I will never eat meat again, so that I may not cause my brother to sin.*

CHAPTER 9*

Paul's Rights as an Apostle. [1] Am I not free? Am I not an apostle? Have I not seen Jesus our Lord? Are you not my work in the Lord?*o* [2] Although I may not be an apostle for others, certainly I am for you, for you are the seal of my apostleship in the Lord. [3] My defense against those who would pass judgment on me* is this. [4] * Do we not have the right to eat and drink? [5] Do we not have the right to take along a Christian wife, as do the rest of the apostles, and the brothers of the Lord, and Cephas? [6] Or is it only myself and Barnabas who do not have the right not to work?*p* [7] Who ever serves as a soldier at his own expense? Who plants a vineyard without eating its produce? Or who shepherds a flock without using some of the milk from the flock?*q* [8] Am I saying this on human authority, or does not the law also speak of these things? [9] It is written in the law of Moses, "You shall not muzzle an ox while it is treading out the grain."*r* Is God concerned about oxen, [10] or is he not really speaking for our sake? It was written for our sake, because the plowman should plow in hope, and the thresher in hope of receiving a share.*s* [11] If we have sown spiritual seed for you, is it a great thing that we reap a material harvest from you?*t* [12] If others share this rightful claim on you, do not we still more?*u*

Reason for Not Using His Rights. Yet we have not used this right.* On the contrary, we endure everything so as not to place an obstacle to the gospel of Christ. [13] * Do you not know that those who perform the temple services eat [what] belongs to the temple, and those who minister at the altar share in the sacrificial offerings?*v* [14] In the same way, the Lord ordered that those who preach the gospel should live by the gospel.*w*

[15] * I have not used any of these rights, however, nor do I write this that it be done so in my case. I would rather die. Certainly no one is going to nullify my boast.*x* [16] If I preach the gospel, this is no reason for me to boast, for an obligation has been imposed on me, and woe to me if I do not preach it!*y* [17] If I do so willingly, I have a recompense, but if unwillingly, then I have been entrusted with a stewardship.*z* [18] What then is my recompense? That, when I preach, I offer the gospel free of charge so as not to make full use of my right in the gospel.*a*

---

n Mt 18, 6; Rom 14, 20-21.—o 1 Cor 9, 19 / 2 Cor 12, 12 / 1 Cor 15, 8-9; Acts 9, 17; 26, 16.—p Acts 4, 36-37; 13, 1-2; Gal 2, 1.9.13; Col 4, 10.—q 2 Tm 2, 3-4.—r Dt 25, 4; 1 Tm 5, 18.—s 2 Tm 2, 6.—t Rom 15, 27.—u 2 Cor 11, 7-12; 12, 13-18; 2 Thes 3, 6-12.—v Nm 18, 8.31; Dt 18, 1-5.—w Mt 10, 10; Lk 10, 7-8.—x 2 Cor 11, 9-10.—y Acts 26, 14-18.—z 1 Cor 4, 1; Gal 2, 7.—a 2 Cor 11, 7-12.

8, 13: His own course is clear: he will avoid any action that might harm another Christian. This statement prepares for the paradigmatic development in ch 9.

9, 1-27: This chapter is an emotionally charged expansion of Paul's appeal to his own example in 1 Cor 8, 13; its purpose is to reinforce the exhortation of 1 Cor 8, 9. The two opening questions introduce the themes of Paul's freedom and his apostleship (1), themes that the chapter will develop in reverse order, vv 1-18 treating the question of his apostleship and the rights that flow from it, and vv 19-27 exploring dialectically the nature of Paul's freedom. The language is highly rhetorical, abounding in questions, wordplays, paradoxes, images, and appeals to authority and experience. The argument is unified by repetitions; its articulations are highlighted by inclusions and transitional verses.

9, 3: *My defense against those who would pass judgment on me:* the reference to a defense *(apologia)* is surprising, and suggests that Paul is incorporating some material here that he has previously used in another context. The defense will touch on two points: the fact of Paul's rights as an apostle (4-12a and 13-14) and his nonuse of those rights (12b and 15-18).

9, 4-12a: Apparently some believe that Paul is not equal to the other apostles and therefore does not enjoy equal privileges. His defense on this point (here and in 13-14) reinforces the assertion of his apostolic character in v 2. It consists of a series of analogies from natural equity (7) and religious custom (13) designed to establish his equal right to support from the churches (4-6.11-12a); these analogies are confirmed by the authority of the law (8-10) and of Jesus himself (14).

9, 12b: It appears, too, that suspicion or misunderstanding has been created by Paul's practice of not living from his preaching. The first reason he asserts in defense of this practice is an entirely apostolic one; it anticipates the developments to follow in vv 19-22. He will give a second reason in vv 15-18.

9, 13-14: The position of these verses produces an interlocking of the two points of Paul's defense. These arguments by analogy (13) and from authority (14) belong with those of vv 7-10 and ground the first point. But Paul defers them until he has had a chance to mention "the gospel of Christ" (12b), after which it is more appropriate to mention Jesus' injunction to his preachers and to argue by analogy from the sacred temple service to his own liturgical service, the preaching of the gospel (cf Rom 1, 9; 15, 16).

9, 15-18: Paul now assigns a more personal motive to his nonuse of his right to support. His preaching is not a service spontaneously undertaken on his part but a stewardship imposed by a sort of divine compulsion. Yet to merit any reward he must bring some spontaneous quality to his service, and this he does by freely renouncing his right to support. The material here is quite similar to that contained in Paul's "defense" at 2 Cor 11, 5-12; 12, 11-18.

All Things to All. [19] * Although I am free in regard to all, I have made myself a slave to all so as to win over as many as possible.[b] [20] To the Jews I became like a Jew to win over Jews; to those under the law I became like one under the law—though I myself am not under the law—to win over those under the law. [21] To those outside the law I became like one outside the law—though I am not outside God's law but within the law of Christ—to win over those outside the law. [22] To the weak I became weak, to win over the weak. I have become all things to all, to save at least some.[c] [23] All this I do for the sake of the gospel, so that I too may have a share in it.

[24] * Do you not know that the runners in the stadium all run in the race, but only one wins the prize? Run so as to win.[d] [25] Every athlete exercises discipline in every way. They do it to win a perishable crown, but we an imperishable one.[e] [26] Thus I do not run aimlessly; I do not fight as if I were shadowboxing. [27] No, I drive my body and train it, for fear that, after having preached to others, I myself should be disqualified.*

CHAPTER 10

Warning against Overconfidence. [1] * I do not want you to be unaware, brothers, that our ancestors were all under the cloud and all passed through the sea,[f] [2] and all of them were baptized into Moses in the cloud and in the sea.[g] [3] All ate the same spiritual food, [4] and all drank the same spiritual drink, for they drank from a spiritual rock that followed them,* and the rock was the Christ.[h] [5] Yet God was not pleased with most of them, for they were struck down in the desert.[i]

[6] * These things happened as examples for us, so that we might not desire evil things, as they did.[j] [7] And do not become idolaters, as some of them did, as it is written, "The people sat down to eat and drink, and rose up to revel."[k] [8] Let us not indulge in immorality as some of them did, and twenty-three thousand fell within a single day.[l] [9] Let us not test Christ* as some of them did, and suffered death by serpents.[m] [10] Do not grumble as some of them did, and suffered death by the destroyer.[n] [11] These things happened to them as an example, and they have been written down as a warning to us, upon whom the end of the ages has come.* [12] Therefore, whoever thinks he is standing secure should take care not to fall.* [13] No trial has come to you but what is human. God is faithful and will not let you be tried beyond your strength; but with the trial he will also provide a way out, so that you may be able to bear it.[o]

---

b Mt 20, 26-27.—c 1 Cor 10, 33; Rom 15, 1; 2 Cor 11, 29.—d Heb 12, 1.—e 2 Tm 2, 5 / 2 Tm 4, 7-8; Jas 1, 12; 1 Pt 5, 4.—f Ex 13, 21-22; 14, 19-20 / Ex 14, 21-22.26-30.—g Rom 6, 3; Gal 3, 27 / Ex 16, 4-35.—h Ex 17, 1-7; Nm 20, 7-11; Dt 8, 15.—i Nm 14, 28-38; Jude 5.—j Nm 11, 4.34.—k Ex 32, 6.—l Nm 25, 1-9.—m Nm 21, 5-9.—n Nm 14, 2-37; 16, 1-35.—o Mt 6, 13; Jas 1, 13-14 / 1 Cor 1, 9.

9, 19-23: In a rhetorically balanced series of statements Paul expands and generalizes the picture of his behavior and explores the paradox of apostolic freedom. It is not essentially freedom *from* restraint but freedom *for* service—a possibility of constructive activity.

9, 24-27: A series of miniparables from sports, appealing to readers familiar with Greek gymnasia and the nearby Isthmian games.

9, 27: *For fear that . . . I myself should be disqualified:* a final paradoxical turn to the argument: what appears at first a free, spontaneous renunciation of rights (12-18) seems subsequently to be required for fulfillment of Paul's stewardship (to preach effectively he must reach his hearers wherever they are, 19-22), and finally is seen to be necessary for his own salvation (23-27). Mention of the possibility of disqualification provides a transition to ch 10.

10, 1-5: Paul embarks unexpectedly upon a panoramic survey of the events of the Exodus period. The privileges of Israel in the wilderness are described in terms that apply strictly only to the realities of the new covenant ("baptism," "spiritual food and drink"); interpreted in this way they point forward to the Christian experience (1-4). But those privileges did not guarantee God's permanent pleasure (5).

10, 4: *A spiritual rock that followed them:* the Torah speaks only about a rock from which water issued, but rabbinic legend amplified this into a spring that followed the Israelites throughout their migration. Paul uses this legend as a literary type: he makes the rock itself accompany the Israelites, and he gives it a spiritual sense. *The rock was the Christ:* in the Old Testament, Yahweh is the Rock of his people (cf Dt 32, Moses' song to Yahweh the Rock). Paul now applies this image to the Christ, the source of the living water, the true Rock that accompanied Israel, guiding their experiences in the desert.

10, 6-13: This section explicitates the typological value of these Old Testament events: the desert experiences of the Israelites are examples, meant as warnings, to deter us from similar sins (idolatry, immorality, etc.) and from a similar fate.

10, 9: *Christ:* to avoid Paul's concept of Christ present in the wilderness events, some manuscripts read "the Lord."

10, 11: *Upon whom the end of the ages has come:* it is our period in time toward which past ages have been moving and in which they arrive at their goal.

10, 12-13: *Take care not to fall:* the point of the whole comparison with Israel is to caution against overconfidence, a sense of complete security (12). This warning is immediately balanced by a reassurance, based, however, on God (13).

Warning against Idolatry.* [14] Therefore, my beloved, avoid idolatry.[p] [15] I am speaking as to sensible people; judge for yourselves what I am saying. [16] The cup of blessing that we bless, is it not a participation in the blood of Christ? The bread that we break, is it not a participation in the body of Christ?[q] [17] Because the loaf of bread is one, we, though many, are one body, for we all partake of the one loaf.[r]

[18] Look at Israel according to the flesh; are not those who eat the sacrifices participants in the altar?[s] [19] So what am I saying? That meat sacrificed to idols is anything? Or that an idol is anything? [20] No, I mean that what they sacrifice, [they sacrifice] to demons,* not to God, and I do not want you to become participants with demons.[t] [21] You cannot drink the cup of the Lord and also the cup of demons. You cannot partake of the table of the Lord and of the table of demons.[u] [22] Or are we provoking the Lord to jealous anger? Are we stronger than he?[v]

Seek the Good of Others.* [23] "Everything is lawful," but not everything is beneficial.* "Everything is lawful," but not everything builds up.[w] [24] No one should seek his own advantage, but that of his neighbor.[x] [25] * Eat anything sold in the market, without raising questions on grounds of conscience, [26] for "the earth and its fullness are the Lord's."[y] [27] If an unbeliever invites you and you want to go, eat whatever is placed before you, without raising questions on grounds of conscience. [28] But if someone says to you, "This was offered in sacrifice," do not eat it on account of the one who called attention to it and on account of conscience; [29] I mean not your own conscience, but the other's. For why should my freedom be determined by someone else's conscience? [30] If I partake thankfully, why am I reviled for that over which I give thanks?[z]

[31] So whether you eat or drink, or whatever you do, do everything for the glory of God. [32] * Avoid giving offense, whether to Jews or Greeks or the church of God, [33] just as I try to please everyone in every way, not seeking my own benefit but that of the many, that they may be saved.[a]

CHAPTER 11 1Cor

[1] Be imitators of me, as I am of Christ.[b]

IV. PROBLEMS IN LITURGICAL ASSEMBLIES*

[2] I praise you because you remember me in everything and hold fast to the traditions, just as I handed them on to you.[c]

---

p 1 Jn 5, 21.—q Mt 26, 26-29; Acts 2, 42.—r Rom 12, 5; Eph 4, 4.—s Lv 7, 6.—t Dt 32, 17.—u 2 Cor 6, 14-18.—v Dt 32, 21 / Eccl 6, 10.—w 1 Cor 6, 12.—x Rom 15, 2; Phil 2, 4.21.—y Pss 24, 1; 50, 12.—z Rom 14, 6; 1 Tm 4, 3-4.—a 1 Cor 9, 22; Rom 15, 2.—b 1 Cor 4, 16; Phil 3, 17.—c 1 Cor 15, 3; 2 Thes 2, 15.

10, 14-22: The warning against idolatry from v 7 is now repeated (14) and explained in terms of the effect of sacrifices: all sacrifices, Christian (16-17), Jewish (18), or pagan (20), establish communion. But communion with Christ is exclusive, incompatible with any other such communion (21). Compare the line of reasoning at 1 Cor 6, 15.

10, 20: *To demons:* although Jews denied divinity to pagan gods, they often believed that there was some nondivine reality behind the idols, such as the dead, or angels, or demons. The explanation Paul offers in v 20 is drawn from Dt 32, 7: the power behind the idols, with which the pagans commune, consists of demonic powers hostile to God.

10, 23—11, 1: By way of peroration Paul returns to the opening situation (ch 8) and draws conclusions based on the intervening considerations (chs 9-10).

10, 23-24: He repeats in the context of this new problem the slogans of liberty from 1 Cor 6, 12, with similar qualifications. Liberty is not merely an individual perfection, nor an end in itself, but is to be used for the common good. The language of v 24 recalls the description of Jesus' self-emptying in Phil 2.

10, 25-30: A summary of specific situations in which the eating of meat sacrificed to idols could present problems of conscience. Three cases are considered. In the first (the marketplace, 25-26) and the second (at table, 27), there is no need to be concerned with whether food has passed through a pagan sacrifice or not, for the principle of 1 Cor 8, 4-6 still stands, and the whole creation belongs to the one God. But in the third case (28), the situation changes if someone present explicitly raises the question of the sacrificial origin of the food; eating in such circumstances may be subject to various interpretations, some of which could be harmful to individuals. Paul is at pains to insist that the enlightened Christian conscience need not change its judgment about the neutrality, even the goodness, of the food in itself (29-30); yet the total situation is altered to the extent that others are potentially endangered, and this calls for a different response, for the sake of others.

10, 32—11, 1: In summary, the general rule of mutually responsible use of their Christian freedom is enjoined first negatively (32), then positively, as exemplified in Paul (33), and finally grounded in Christ, the pattern for Paul's behavior and theirs (1 Cor 11, 1; cf Rom 15, 1-3).

11, 2—14, 40: This section of the letter is devoted to regulation of conduct at the liturgy. The problems Paul handles have to do with the dress of women in the assembly (1 Cor 11, 3-16), improprieties in the celebration of community meals (1 Cor 11, 17-34), and the use of charisms or spiritual gifts (1 Cor 12, 1—14, 40). The statement in 1 Cor 11, 2 introduces all of these discussions, but applies more appropriately to the second (cf the mention of praise in 1 Cor 11, 17 and of tradition in 1 Cor 11, 23).

A. Women's Headdresses*

Man and Woman. [3] But I want you to know that Christ is the head of every man, and a husband the head of his wife,* and God the head of Christ. [d] [4] * Any man who prays or prophesies with his head covered brings shame upon his head. [5] But any woman who prays or prophesies with her head unveiled brings shame upon her head, for it is one and the same thing as if she had had her head shaved. [6] For if a woman does not have her head veiled, she may as well have her hair cut off. But if it is shameful for a woman to have her hair cut off or her head shaved, then she should wear a veil.

[7] * A man, on the other hand, should not cover his head, because he is the image and glory of God, but woman is the glory of man. [e] [8] For man did not come from woman, but woman from man; [f] [9] nor was man created for woman, but woman for man; [g] [10] for this reason a woman should have a sign of authority* on her head, because of the angels. [11] * Woman is not independent of man or man of woman in the Lord. [h] [12] For just as woman came from man, so man is born of woman; but all things are from God. [i]

---

d Eph 5, 23.—e Gn 1, 26-27; 5, 1.—f Gn 2, 21-23.—g Gn 2, 18.—h Gal 3, 27-28.—i 1 Cor 8, 6; Rom 11, 36.—j 1 Cor 1, 10-12; Gal 5, 20.

11, 3-16: Women have been participating in worship at Corinth without the head-covering normal in Greek society of the period. Paul's stated goal is to bring them back into conformity with contemporary practice and propriety. In his desire to convince, he reaches for arguments from a variety of sources, though he has space to develop them only sketchily and is perhaps aware that they differ greatly in persuasiveness.

11, 3: *A husband the head of his wife:* the specific problem suggests to Paul the model of the head as a device for clarifying relations within a hierarchical structure. The model is similar to that developed later in greater detail and nuance in Eph 5, 21-33. It is a hybrid model, for it grafts onto a strictly theological scale of existence (cf 1 Cor 3, 21-23) the hierarchy of sociosexual relations prevalent in the ancient world: men, dominant, reflect the active function of Christ in relation to his church; women, submissive, reflect the passive role of the church with respect to its savior. This gives us the functional scale: God, Christ, man, woman.

11, 4-6: From man's direct relation to Christ, Paul infers that his head should not be covered. But woman, related not directly to Christ on the scale but to her husband, requires a covering as a sign of that relationship. *Shameful . . . to have her hair cut off:* certain less honored classes in society, such as lesbians and prostitutes, are thought to have worn their hair close-cropped.

11, 7-9: The hierarchy of v 3 is now expressed in other metaphors: the image *(eikōn)* and the reflected glory *(doxa)*. Paul is alluding basically to the text of Gn 1, 27, in which mankind as a whole, the male-female couple, is created in God's image and given the command to multiply and together dominate the lower creation. But Gn 1, 24 is interpreted here in the light of the sec-

---

[13] * Judge for yourselves: is it proper for a woman to pray to God with her head unveiled? [14] Does not nature itself teach you that if a man wears his hair long it is a disgrace to him, [15] whereas if a woman has long hair it is her glory, because long hair has been given [her] for a covering? [16] But if anyone is inclined to be argumentative, we do not have such a custom, nor do the churches of God.

B. The Lord's Supper*

An Abuse at Corinth. [17] In giving this instruction, I do not praise the fact that your meetings are doing more harm than good. [18] First of all, I hear that when you meet as a church there are divisions among you, and to a degree I believe it; [j] [19] there have to be factions among you in order that [also] those who are approved among you may become known.* [20] When you meet in one place, then, it is not to eat the Lord's supper, [21] for in eating, each one goes ahead with his own supper, and one goes hungry while another gets drunk. [22] Do you not have houses in which you can eat and drink? Or do you show contempt for the church of God and make those who have nothing feel ashamed? What can I say to

---

ond creation narrative in Gn 2, in which each of the sexes is created separately (first the man and then the woman *from* man and *for* him, to be his helpmate, Gn 2, 20-23), and under the influence of the story of the fall, as a result of which the husband rules over the woman (Gn 3, 16). This interpretation splits the single image of God into two, at different degrees of closeness.

11, 10: *A sign of authority:* "authority" *(exousia)* may possibly be due to mistranslation of an Aramaic word for "veil"; in any case, the connection with v 9 indicates that the covering is a sign of woman's subordination. *Because of the angels:* a surprising additional reason, which the context does not clarify. Presumably the reference is to cosmic powers who might inflict harm on women or whose function is to watch over women or the cult.

11, 11-12: These parenthetical remarks relativize the argument from Gn 2—3. *In the Lord:* in the Christian economy the relation between the sexes is characterized by a mutual dependence, which is not further specified. And even in the natural order conditions have changed: the mode of origin described in Gn 2 has been reversed (12a). But the ultimately significant fact is the origin that all things have in common (12b).

11, 13-16: The argument for conformity to common church practice is summed up and pressed home. Verses 14-15 contain a final appeal to the sense of propriety that contemporary Greek society would consider "natural" (cf 1 Cor 11, 5-6).

11, 17-34: Paul turns to another abuse connected with the liturgy, and a more serious one, for it involves neglect of basic Christian tradition concerning the meaning of the Lord's Supper. Paul recalls that tradition for them and reminds them of its implications.

11, 19: *That . . . those who are approved among you may become known:* Paul situates their divisions within the context of the eschatological separation of the authentic from the inauthentic and the final revelation of the difference. The notion of authenticity-testing recurs in the injunction to self-examination in view of present and future judgment (28-32).

you? Shall I praise you? In this matter I do not praise you. [k]

Tradition of the Institution. [23] * For I received from the Lord what I also handed on to you, [l] that the Lord Jesus, on the night he was handed over, took bread, [24] and, after he had given thanks, broke it and said, "This is my body that is for you. Do this in remembrance of me." [25] In the same way also the cup, after supper, saying, "This cup is the new covenant in my blood. Do this, as often as you drink it, in remembrance of me." [m] [26] For as often as you eat this bread and drink the cup, you proclaim the death of the Lord until he comes.

[27] Therefore whoever eats the bread or drinks the cup of the Lord unworthily will have to answer for the body and blood of the Lord.* [28] A person should examine himself,* and so eat the bread and drink the cup. [29] For anyone who eats and drinks without discerning the body, eats and drinks judgment* on himself. [30] That is why many among you are ill and infirm, and a considerable number are dying. [31] If we discerned ourselves, we would not be under judgment; [32] but since we are judged by [the] Lord, we are being disciplined so that we may not be condemned along with the world. [n]

[33] Therefore, my brothers, when you come together to eat, wait for one another. [34] If anyone is hungry, he should eat at home, so that your meetings may not result in judgment. The other matters I shall set in order when I come.

C. Spiritual Gifts*

CHAPTER 12

Unity and Variety. [1] Now in regard to spiritual gifts, brothers, I do not want you to be unaware. [2] * You know how, when you were pagans, you were constantly attracted and led away to mute idols. [o] [3] Therefore, I tell you that nobody speaking by the spirit of God says, "Jesus be accursed." And no one can say, "Jesus is Lord," except by the holy Spirit. [p]

[4] * There are different kinds of spiritual gifts but the same Spirit; [q] [5] there are different forms of service but the same Lord; [6] there are different workings but the same God who produces all of them in everyone. [7] To each individual the manifestation of the Spirit is given for some benefit. [8] To one is given through the Spirit the expression of wisdom; to another the expression of knowledge according to the same Spirit; [r] [9] to another faith by the same Spirit; to another gifts of healing by the one Spirit; [10] to another mighty deeds; to another prophecy; to another discernment of spirits; to another varieties of tongues; to another interpretation of tongues. [s] [11] But one and the same Spirit produces all

k Jas 2, 1-7.—l 1 Cor 11, 2; 15, 3 / 1 Cor 10, 16-17; Mt 26, 26-29; Mk 14, 22-25; Lk 22, 14-20.—m Ex 24, 8; 2 Cor 3, 6; Heb 8, 6-13.—n Dt 8, 5; Heb 12, 5-11.—o Eph 2, 11-18.—p Rom 10, 9; 1 Jn 4, 2-3.—q Rom 12, 6; Eph 4, 7.11.—r 1 Cor 2, 6-13.—s 1 Cor 14, 5.26.39; Acts 2, 4.

11, 23-25: This is the earliest written account of the institution of the Lord's Supper in the New Testament. The narrative emphasizes Jesus' action of self-giving (expressed in the words over the bread and the cup) and his double command to repeat his own action.

11, 27: It follows that the only proper way to celebrate the Eucharist is one that corresponds to Jesus' intention, which fits with the meaning of his command to reproduce his action in the proper spirit. If the Corinthians eat and drink unworthily, i.e., without having grasped and internalized the meaning of his death for them, they *will have to answer for the body and blood,* i.e., will be guilty of a sin against the Lord himself (cf 1 Cor 8, 12).

11, 28: *Examine himself:* the Greek word is similar to that for "approved" in v 19, which means "having been tested and found true." The self-testing required for proper eating involves *discerning the body* (29), which, from the context, must mean understanding the sense of Jesus' death (26), perceiving the imperative to unity that follows from the fact that Jesus gives himself to all and requires us to repeat his sacrifice in the same spirit (18-25).

11, 29-32: *Judgment:* there is a series of wordplays in these verses that would be awkward to translate literally into English;

it includes all the references to judgment *(krima,* 29.34; *krino,* 31.32), discernment *(diakrino,* 29.31), and condemnation *(katakrino,* 32). The judgment is concretely described as the illness, infirmity, and death that have visited the community. These are signs that the power of Jesus' death is not yet completely recognized and experienced. Yet even the judgment incurred is an expression of God's concern; it is a medicinal measure meant to rescue us from condemnation with God's enemies.

12, 1—14, 40: Ecstatic activity and charismatic activity were common in early Christian experience, as they were in other ancient religions. But the Corinthians seem to have developed a disproportionate esteem for certain phenomena, especially tongues, to the detriment of order in the liturgy. Paul's response to this development provides us with the fullest exposition we have of his theology of the charisms.

12, 2-3: There is an experience of the Spirit and an understanding of ecstatic phenomena that are specifically Christian and that differ, despite apparent similarities, from those of the pagans. It is necessary to discern which spirit is leading one; ecstatic phenomena must be judged by their effect (2). Verse 3 illustrates this by an example: power to confess Jesus as Lord can come only from the Spirit, and it is inconceivable that the Spirit would move anyone to curse the Lord.

12, 4-6: There are some features common to all charisms, despite their diversity: all are *gifts (charismata),* grace from outside ourselves; all are *forms of service (diakoniai),* an expression of their purpose and effect; and all are *workings (energemata),* in which God is at work. Paul associates each of these aspects with what later theology will call one of the persons of the Trinity, an early example of "appropriation."

of these, distributing them individually to each person as he wishes.[t]

One Body, Many Parts.* [12] As a body is one though it has many parts, and all the parts of the body, though many, are one body, so also Christ.[u] [13] For in one Spirit we were all baptized into one body, whether Jews or Greeks, slaves or free persons, and we were all given to drink of one Spirit.[v]

[14] Now the body is not a single part, but many. [15] If a foot should say, "Because I am not a hand I do not belong to the body," it does not for this reason belong any less to the body. [16] Or if an ear should say, "Because I am not an eye I do not belong to the body," it does not for this reason belong any less to the body. [17] If the whole body were an eye, where would the hearing be? If the whole body were hearing, where would the sense of smell be? [18] But as it is, God placed the parts, each one of them, in the body as he intended. [19] If they were all one part, where would the body be? [20] But as it is, there are many parts, yet one body. [21] The eye cannot say to the hand, "I do not need you," nor again the head to the feet, "I do not need you." [22] Indeed, the parts of the body that seem to be weaker are all the more necessary, [23] and those parts of the body that we consider less honorable we surround with greater honor, and our less presentable parts are treated with greater propriety, [24] whereas our more presentable parts do not need this. But God has so constructed the body as to give greater honor to a part

that is without it, [25] so that there may be no division in the body, but that the parts may have the same concern for one another. [26] If [one] part suffers, all the parts suffer with it; if one part is honored, all the parts share its joy.

Application to Christ.* [27] Now you are Christ's body, and individually parts of it.[w] [28] Some people God has designated in the church to be, first, apostles;* second, prophets; third, teachers; then, mighty deeds; then gifts of healing, assistance, administration, and varieties of tongues.[x] [29] Are all apostles? Are all prophets? Are all teachers? Do all work mighty deeds? [30] Do all have gifts of healing? Do all speak in tongues? Do all interpret? [31] Strive eagerly for the greatest spiritual gifts.

The Way of Love. But I shall show you a still more excellent way.

CHAPTER 13*

[1] If I speak in human and angelic tongues* but do not have love, I am a resounding gong or a clashing cymbal.[y] [2] And if I have the gift of prophecy and comprehend all mysteries and all knowledge; if I have all faith so as to move mountains but do not have love, I am nothing.[z] [3] If I give away everything I own, and if I hand my body over so that I may boast but do not have love, I gain nothing.[a]

[4] * Love is patient, love is kind. It is not jealous, [love] is not pompous, it is not inflated,[b] [5] it is not rude, it does not seek its own interests, it is not quick-tempered, it does not brood over injury,[c] [6] it does not rejoice over wrongdoing but rejoices with the truth. [7] It bears all things, believes all

---

t 1 Cor 7, 7; Eph 4, 7.—u 1 Cor 10, 17; Rom 12, 4-5; Eph 2, 16; Col 3, 15.—v Gal 3, 28; Eph 2, 13-18; Col 3, 11 / Jn 7, 37-39.—w Rom 12, 5-8; Eph 1, 23; 4, 12; 5, 30; Col 1, 18.24.—x Eph 2, 20; 3, 5; 4, 11.—y 1 Cor 8, 1; 16, 14; Rom 12, 9-10; 13, 8-10.—z 1 Cor 4, 1; 14, 2 / 1 Cor 5, 8, 1-3; 12, 8 / Mt 17, 20; 21, 21; Col 2, 3.—a Mt 6, 2.—b Eph 4, 2 / 1 Cor 4, 6.18; 5, 2; 8, 1.—c 1 Cor 10, 24.33; Phil 2, 4.21; 1 Thes 5, 15.

12, 12-26: The image of *a body* is introduced to explain Christ's relationship with believers (12). Verse 13 applies this model to the church: by baptism all, despite diversity of ethnic or social origins, are integrated into one organism. Verses 14-26 then develop the need for diversity of function among the parts of a body without threat to its unity.

12, 27-30: Paul now applies the image again to the church as a whole and its members (27). The lists in vv 28-30 spell out the parallelism by specifying the diversity of functions found in the church (cf Rom 12, 6-8; Eph 4, 11).

12, 28: *First, apostles:* apostleship was not mentioned in vv 8-10, nor is it at issue in these chapters, but Paul gives it pride of place in his listing. It is not just one gift among others but a prior and fuller gift that includes the others. They are all demonstrated in Paul's apostolate, but he may have developed his theology of charisms by reflecting first of all on his own grace of apostleship

(cf 1 Cor 3, 5—4, 14; 9, 1-27; 2 Cor 2, 14—6, 13; 10, 1—13, 30, esp. 11, 23 and 12, 12).

13, 1-13: This chapter involves a shift of perspective and a new point. All or part of the material may once have been an independent piece in the style of Hellenistic eulogies of virtues, but it is now integrated, by editing, into the context of chs 12-14 (cf the reference to tongues and prophecy) and into the letter as a whole (cf the references to knowledge and to behavior). The function of ch 13 within the discussion of spiritual gifts is to relativize all the charisms by contrasting them with the more basic, pervasive, and enduring value that gives them their purpose and their effectiveness. The rhetoric of this chapter is striking.

13, 1-3: An inventory of gifts, arranged in careful gradation: neither tongues (on the lowest rung), nor prophecy, knowledge, or faith, nor even self-sacrifice has value unless informed by love.

13, 4-7: This paragraph is developed by personification and enumeration, defining love by what it does or does not do. The Greek contains fifteen verbs; it is natural to translate many of them by adjectives in English.

things, hopes all things, endures all things.[d]

8 * Love never fails. If there are prophecies, they will be brought to nothing; if tongues, they will cease; if knowledge, it will be brought to nothing. [9]For we know partially and we prophesy partially, [10]but when the perfect comes, the partial will pass away. [11]When I was a child, I used to talk as a child, think as a child, reason as a child; when I became a man, I put aside childish things. [12]At present we see indistinctly, as in a mirror, but then face to face. At present I know partially; then I shall know fully, as I am fully known.[e] [13]So faith, hope, love remain, these three;[f] but the greatest of these is love.*

CHAPTER 14

Prophecy Greater than Tongues. [1] * Pursue love, but strive eagerly for the spiritual gifts, above all that you may prophesy.[g] [2] * For one who speaks in a tongue does not speak to human beings but to God, for no one listens; he utters mysteries in spirit. [3]On the other hand, one who prophesies does speak to human beings, for their building up,* encouragement, and solace.[h] [4]Whoever speaks in a tongue builds himself up, but whoever prophesies builds up the church. [5]Now I should like all of you to speak in tongues, but even more to prophesy. One who prophesies is greater

than one who speaks in tongues, unless he interprets, so that the church may be built up.

[6] * Now, brothers, if I should come to you speaking in tongues, what good will I do you if I do not speak to you by way of revelation, or knowledge, or prophecy, or instruction? [7]Likewise, if inanimate things that produce sound, such as flute or harp, do not give out the tones distinctly, how will what is being played on flute or harp be recognized? [8]And if the bugle gives an indistinct sound, who will get ready for battle? [9]Similarly, if you, because of speaking in tongues, do not utter intelligible speech, how will anyone know what is being said? For you will be talking to the air. [10]It happens that there are many different languages in the world, and none is meaningless; [11]but if I do not know the meaning of a language, I shall be a foreigner to one who speaks it, and one who speaks it a foreigner to me. [12]So with yourselves: since you strive eagerly for spirits, seek to have an abundance of them for building up the church.

Need for Interpretation.* [13]Therefore, one who speaks in a tongue should pray to be able to interpret. [14][For] if I pray in a tongue, my spirit* is at prayer but my mind is unproductive. [15]So what is to be done? I will pray with the spirit, but I will also pray with the mind. I will sing praise

1Cor

---

d Prv 10, 12; 1 Pt 4, 8.—e 2 Cor 5, 7; Heb 11, 1 / 2 Tm 2, 19; 1 Jn 3, 2.—f Col 1, 4; 1 Thes 1, 3; 5, 8.—g 1 Cor 14, 5.12.39.—h 1 Cor 14, 4-5.12.17.26; 3, 9; 8, 1.10; 10, 23.

13, 8-13: The final paragraph announces its topic, *Love never fails* (8), then develops the permanence of love in contrast to the charisms (9-12), and finally asserts love's superiority even over the other "theological virtues" (13).

13, 13: In speaking of love, Paul is led by spontaneous association to mention faith and hope as well. They are already a well-known triad (cf 1 Thes 1, 3), three interrelated (cf 1 Cor 13, 7) features of Christian life, more fundamental than any particular charism. *The greatest . . . is love:* love is operative even within the other members of the triad (7), so that it has a certain primacy among them. Or, if the perspective is temporal, love will remain (cf "never fails," 8) even when faith has yielded to sight and hope to possession.

14, 1-5: Verse 1b returns to the thought of 1 Cor 12, 31a and reveals Paul's primary concern. The series of contrasts in vv 2-5 discloses the problem at Corinth: a disproportionate interest in tongues, with a corresponding failure to appreciate the worth of prophecy. Paul attempts to clarify the relative values of those gifts by indicating the kind of communication achieved in each and the kind of effect each produces.

14, 2-3a: They involve two kinds of communication: tongues, private speech toward God in inarticulate terms that need interpretation to be intelligible to others (see 1 Cor 14, 27-28); prophecy, communication with others in the community.

14, 3b-5: They produce two kinds of effect. One who speaks in tongues *builds himself up;* it is a matter of individual experience and personal perfection, which inevitably recalls Paul's previous remarks about being inflated, seeking one's own good, pleasing oneself. But a prophet *builds up the church:* the theme of "building up" or "edifying" others, the main theme of the letter, comes to clearest expression in this chapter (3.4.5.12.17). It has been anticipated at 1 Cor 8, 1 and 1 Cor 10, 23, and by the related concept of "the beneficial" in 1 Cor 6, 12; 10, 23; 12, 7; etc.

14, 6-12: Sound, in order to be useful, must be intelligible. This principle is illustrated by a series of analogies from music (7-8) and from ordinary human speech (10-11); it is applied to the case at hand in v 9 and v 12.

14, 13-19: The charism of interpretation lifts tongues to the level of intelligibility, enabling them to produce the same effect as prophecy (cf 1 Cor 14, 5.26-28).

14, 14-15: *My spirit:* Paul emphasizes the exclusively ecstatic, nonrational quality of tongues. The tongues at Pentecost are also described as an ecstatic experience (Acts 2, 4.12-13), though Luke superimposes further interpretations of his own. *My mind:* the ecstatic element, dominant in earliest Old Testament prophecy as depicted in 1 Sam 5-13; 19, 20-24, seems entirely absent from Paul's notion of prophecy and completely relegated to tongues. He emphasizes the role of reason when he specifies instruction as a function of prophecy (6.19.31). But he does not exclude intuition and emotion; cf references to encouragement and consolation (3.31) and the scene describing the ideal exercise of prophecy (24-25).

with the spirit, but I will also sing praise with the mind.[i] [16]Otherwise, if you pronounce a blessing [with] the spirit, how shall one who holds the place of the uninstructed say the "Amen" to your thanksgiving, since he does not know what you are saying? [17]For you may be giving thanks very well, but the other is not built up. [18]I give thanks to God that I speak in tongues more than any of you, [19]but in the church I would rather speak five words with my mind, so as to instruct others also, than ten thousand words in a tongue.

Functions of These Gifts. [20] * Brothers, stop being childish in your thinking. In respect to evil be like infants, but in your thinking be mature.[j] [21]It is written in the law:

> "By people speaking strange tongues
>   and by the lips of foreigners
> I will speak to this people,
>   and even so they will not listen to
>   me,[k]

says the Lord." [22]Thus, tongues are a sign not for those who believe but for unbelievers, whereas prophecy is not for unbelievers but for those who believe.

[23] * So if the whole church meets in one place and everyone speaks in tongues, and then uninstructed people or unbelievers should come in, will they not say that you are out of your minds?[l] [24]But if everyone is prophesying, and an unbeliever or uninstructed person should come in, he will be convinced by everyone and judged by everyone, [25]and the secrets of his heart will be disclosed, and so he will fall down and worship God, declaring, "God is really in your midst."[m]

Rules of Order. [26] * So what is to be done, brothers? When you assemble, one has a psalm, another an instruction, a revelation, a tongue, or an interpretation. Everything should be done for building up.[n] [27]If anyone speaks in a tongue, let it be two or at most three, and each in turn, and one should interpret. [28]But if there is no interpreter, the person should keep silent in the church and speak to himself and to God.

[29]Two or three prophets should speak, and the others discern. [30]But if a revelation is given to another person sitting there, the first one should be silent. [31]For you can all prophesy one by one, so that all may learn and all be encouraged. [32]Indeed, the spirits of prophets are under the prophets' control, [33]since he is not the God of disorder but of peace.

As in all the churches of the holy ones,* [34]women should keep silent in the churches, for they are not allowed to speak, but should be subordinate, as even the law says.[o] [35]But if they want to learn anything, they should ask their husbands at home. For it is improper for a woman to speak in the church. [36]Did the word of God go forth from you? Or has it come to you alone?

[37]If anyone thinks that he is a prophet or a spiritual person, he should recognize that what I am writing to you is a commandment of the Lord. [38]If anyone does not acknowledge this, he is not acknowledged.

---

i Eph 5, 19; Col 3, 16.—j Mt 10, 16; Rom 16, 19; Eph 4, 14.— k Is 28, 11-12; Dt 28, 49.—l Acts 2, 6.13.—m 1 Cor 4, 5 / Is 45, 14; Zec 8, 23.—n Eph 4, 12.—o 1 Tm 2, 11-15; 1 Pt 3, 1.

14, 20-22: The Corinthians pride themselves on tongues as a sign of God's favor, a means of direct communication with him (2.28). To challenge them to a more mature appraisal, Paul draws from scripture a less flattering explanation of what speaking in tongues may signify. Isaiah threatened the people that if they failed to listen to their prophets, the Lord would speak to them (in punishment) through the lips of Assyrian conquerors (Is 28, 11-12). Paul compresses Isaiah's text and makes God address his people directly. Equating tongues with foreign languages (cf 1 Cor 14, 10-11), Paul concludes from Isaiah that *tongues are a sign not for those who believe,* i.e., not a mark of God's pleasure for those who listen to him but a mark of his displeasure with those in the community who are faithless, who have not heeded the message that he has sent through the prophets.

14, 23-25: Paul projects the possible missionary effect of two hypothetical liturgical experiences, one consisting wholly of tongues, the other entirely of prophecy. *Uninstructed (idiōtai):* the term may simply mean people who do not speak or understand tongues, as in v 16, where it seems to designate Christians. But coupled with the term "unbelievers" it may be another way of designating those who have not been initiated into the community of faith; some believe it denotes a special class of non-Christians who are close to the community, such as catechumens. *Unbelievers (apistoi):* he has shifted from the inner-community perspective of v 22; the term here designates non-Christians (cf 1 Cor 6, 6; 7, 15; 10, 27).

14, 26-33a: Paul concludes with specific directives regarding exercise of the gifts in their assemblies. Verse 26 enunciates the basic criterion in the use of any gift: it must contribute to "building up."

14, 33b-36: Verse 33b may belong with what precedes, so that the new paragraph would begin only with v 34. Verses 34-35 change the subject. These two verses have the theme of submission in common with ch 11, despite differences in vocabulary, and a concern with what is or is not becoming; but it is difficult to harmonize the injunction to silence here with ch 11, which appears to take it for granted that women do pray and prophesy aloud in the assembly (cf 1 Cor 11, 5.13). Hence the verses are often considered an interpolation, reflecting the discipline of later churches; such an interpolation would have to have antedated our manuscripts, all of which contain them, though some transpose them to the very end of the chapter.

[39] So, [my] brothers, strive eagerly to prophesy, and do not forbid speaking in tongues, [40] but everything must be done properly and in order.

V. THE RESURRECTION

A. The Resurrection of Christ

CHAPTER 15*

The Gospel Teaching.* [1] Now I am reminding you, brothers, of the gospel I preached to you, which you indeed received and in which you also stand. [2] Through it you are also being saved, if you hold fast to the word I preached to you, unless you believed in vain. [3] * For I handed on to you as of first importance what I also received: that Christ died for our sins in accordance with the scriptures;[p] [4] that he was buried; that he was raised on the third day in accordance with the scriptures;[q] [5] that he appeared to Cephas, then to the Twelve.[r] [6] After that, he appeared to more than five hundred brothers at once, most of whom are still living, though some have fallen asleep. [7] After that he appeared to James, then to all the apostles. [8] Last of all, as to one born abnormally, he appeared to me.[s] [9] For I am the least* of the apostles, not fit to be called an apostle, because I persecuted the church of God.[t] [10] But by the grace of God I am what I am, and his grace to me has not been ineffective. Indeed, I have toiled harder than all of them; not I, however, but the grace of God [that is] with me. [11] Therefore, whether it be I or they, so we preach and so you believed.

B. The Resurrection of the Dead

Results of Denial.* [12] But if Christ is preached as raised from the dead, how can some among you say there is no resurrection of the dead? [13] If there is no resurrection of the dead, then neither has Christ been raised.[u] [14] And if Christ has not been raised, then empty [too] is our preaching; empty, too, your faith. [15] Then we are also false witnesses to God, because we testified against God that he raised Christ, whom he did not raise if in fact the dead are not raised.[v] [16] For if the dead are not raised, neither has Christ been raised, [17] and if Christ has not been raised,* your faith is vain; you are still in your sins. [18] Then those who have fallen asleep in Christ have perished. [19] If for this life only we have hoped in Christ, we are the most pitiable people of all.

Christ the Firstfruits.* [20] *w* But now Christ has been raised from the dead, the firstfruits* of those who have fallen asleep.

1Cor

---

p 1 Cor 11, 23 / 1 Pt 2, 24; 3, 18 / Is 53, 4-12.—q Acts 2, 23-24 / Ps 16, 8-11; Hos 6, 1-2; Jon 2, 1 —r Mk 16, 14; Mt 28, 16-17; Lk 24, 36; Jn 20, 19.—s 1 Cor 9, 1; Acts 9, 3-6; Gal 1, 16.—t Acts 8, 3; 9, 1-2; Gal 1, 23; Eph 3, 8; 1 Tm 1, 15.—u 1 Thes 4, 14.—v Acts 5, 32.—w Rom 8, 11; Col 1, 18; 1 Thes 4, 14.

15, 1-58: Some consider this chapter an earlier Pauline composition inserted into the present letter. The problem that Paul treats is clear to a degree: some of the Corinthians are denying the resurrection of the dead (12), apparently because of their inability to imagine how any kind of bodily existence could be possible after death (35). It is plausibly supposed that their attitude stems from Greek anthropology, which looks with contempt upon matter and would be content with the survival of the soul, and perhaps also from an overrealized eschatology of gnostic coloration, such as that reflected in 2 Tm 2, 18, which considers the resurrection a purely spiritual experience already achieved in baptism and in the forgiveness of sins. Paul, on the other hand, will affirm both the essential corporeity of the resurrection and its futurity.

His response moves through three steps: a recall of the basic kerygma about Jesus' resurrection (1-11), an assertion of the logical inconsistencies involved in denial of the resurrection (12-34), and an attempt to perceive theologically what the properties of the resurrected body must be (35-58).

15, 1-11: Paul recalls the tradition (3-7), which he can presuppose as common ground and which provides a starting point for his argument. This is the fundamental content of all Christian preaching and belief (1-2.11).

15, 3-7: The language by which Paul expresses the essence of the "gospel" (1) is not his own but is drawn from older credal formulas. This credo highlights Jesus' death for our sins (confirmed by his burial) and Jesus' resurrection (confirmed by his

appearances) and presents both of them as fulfillment of prophecy. *In accordance with the scriptures:* conformity of Jesus' passion with the scriptures is asserted in Mt 16, 1; Lk 24, 25-27.32.44-46. Application of some Old Testament texts (Pss 2, 7; 16, 8-11) to his resurrection is illustrated by Acts 2, 27-31; 13, 29-39; and Is 52, 13—53, 12 and Hos 6, 2 may also have been envisaged.

15, 9-11: A persecutor may have appeared disqualified *(ouk . . . hikanos)* from apostleship, but in fact God's grace has qualified him. Cf the remarks in 2 Cor about his qualifications (2 Cor 2, 16; 3, 5) and his greater labors (2 Cor 11, 23). These verses are parenthetical, but a nerve has been touched (the references to his abnormal birth and his activity as a persecutor may echo taunts from Paul's opponents), and he is instinctively moved to self-defense.

15, 12-19: Denial of the resurrection (12) involves logical inconsistencies. The basic one, stated twice (13.16), is that if there is no such thing as (bodily) resurrection, then it has not taken place even in Christ's case.

15, 17-18: The consequences for the Corinthians are grave: both forgiveness of sins and salvation are an illusion, despite their strong convictions about both. Unless Christ is risen, their faith does not save.

15, 20-28: After a triumphant assertion of the reality of Christ's resurrection (20a), Paul explains its positive implications and consequences. As a soteriological event of both human (20-23) and cosmic (24-28) dimensions, Jesus' resurrection logically and necessarily involves ours as well.

15, 20: *The firstfruits:* the portion of the harvest offered in thanksgiving to God implies the consecration of the entire harvest to come. Christ's resurrection is not an end in itself; its finality lies in the whole harvest, ourselves.

21 * For since death came through a human being, the resurrection of the dead came also through a human being. 22 For just as in Adam all die, so too in Christ shall all be brought to life,ˣ 23 but each one in proper order: Christ the firstfruits; then, at his coming, those who belong to Christ;ʸ 24 then comes the end,* when he hands over the kingdom to his God and Father, when he has destroyed every sovereignty and every authority and power.ᶻ 25 For he must reign until he has put all his enemies under his feet.ᵃ 26 The last enemyᵇ to be destroyed is death,* 27 for "he subjected everything under his feet."ᶜ But when it says that everything has been subjected, it is clear that it excludes the one who subjected everything to him.* 28 When everything is subjected to him, then the Son himself will [also] be subjected to the one who subjected everything to him, so that God may be all in all.ᵈ

Practical Arguments.* 29 Otherwise, what will people accomplish by having themselves baptized for the dead?* If the dead are not raised at all, then why are they having themselves baptized for them?

30 * Moreover, why are we endangering ourselves all the time?ᵉ 31 Every day I face death; I swear it by the pride in you [brothers] that I have in Christ Jesus our Lord.ᶠ 32 If at Ephesus I fought with beasts, so to speak, what benefit was it to me? If the dead are not raised:

"Let us eat and drink,
   for tomorrow we die."ᵍ

33 Do not be led astray:

"Bad company corrupts good morals."

34 Become sober as you ought and stop sinning. For some have no knowledge of God; I say this to your shame.ʰ

C. The Manner of the Resurrection*

35 * But someone may say, "How are the dead raised? With what kind of body will they come back?"

The Resurrection Body. 36 * You fool! What you sow is not brought to life unless it dies.ⁱ 37 And what you sow is not the body that is to be but a bare kernel of wheat, perhaps, or of some other kind; 38 ʲ but God gives it a body as he chooses, and to each of the seeds its own body. 39 * Not all flesh is the same, but there is one kind

---

x Gn 3, 17-19; Rom 5, 12-19.—y 1 Thes 4, 15-17.—z Eph 1, 22.—a Ps 110, 1.—b Rom 6, 9; 2 Tm 1, 10; Rv 20, 14; 21, 4.—c Ps 8, 7; Eph 1, 22; Phil 3, 21.—d Eph 4, 6; Col 3, 11.—e 2 Cor 4, 8-12; 11, 23-27.—f Ps 44, 23; Rom 8, 36.—g 1 Cor 4, 9; 2 Cor 4, 10-11 / Wis 2, 5-7; Is 22, 13.—h Mt 22, 29; Mk 12, 24.—i Jn 12, 24.—j Gn 1, 11.

15, 21-22: Our human existence, both natural and supernatural, is corporate, involves solidarity. *In Adam . . . in Christ:* the Hebrew word *'ādām* in Genesis is both a common noun for mankind and a proper noun for the first man. Paul here presents Adam as at least a literary type of Christ; the parallelism and contrast between them will be developed further in vv 45-49 and in Rom 5, 12-21.

15, 24-28: Paul's perspective expands to cosmic dimensions, as he describes the climax of history, *the end.* His viewpoint is still christological, as in vv 20-23. Verses 24 and 28 describe Christ's final relations to his enemies and his Father in language that is both royal and military; vv 25-28 insert a proof from scripture (Pss 110, 1; 8, 7) into this description. But the viewpoint is also theological, for God is the ultimate agent and end, and likewise soteriological, for we are the beneficiaries of all the action.

15, 26: *The last enemy . . . is death:* a parenthesis that specifies the final fulfillment of the two Old Testament texts just referred to, Ps 110, 1 and Ps 8, 7. Death is not just one cosmic power among many, but the ultimate effect of sin in the universe (cf 1 Cor 15, 56; Rom 5, 12). Christ defeats death where it prevails, in our bodies. The destruction of the last enemy is concretely the "coming to life" (22) of "those who belong to Christ" (23).

15, 27b-28: *The one who subjected everything to him:* the Father is the ultimate agent in the drama, and the final end of the process, to whom the Son and everything else is ordered (24.28). *That God may be all in all:* his reign is a dynamic exercise of creative power, an outpouring of life and energy through the uni-universe, with no further resistance. This is the supremely positive meaning of "subjection": that God may fully be God.

15, 29-34: Paul concludes his treatment of logical inconsistencies with a listing of miscellaneous Christian practices that would be meaningless if the resurrection were not a fact.

15, 29: *Baptized for the dead:* this practice is not further explained here, nor is it necessarily mentioned with approval, but Paul cites it as something in their experience that attests in one more way to belief in the resurrection.

15, 30-34: A life of sacrifice, such as Paul describes in 1 Cor 4, 9-13 and 2 Cor, would be pointless without the prospect of resurrection; a life of pleasure, such as that expressed in the Epicurean slogan of v 32, would be far more consistent. *I fought with beasts:* since Paul does not elsewhere mention a combat with beasts at Ephesus, he may be speaking figuratively about struggles with adversaries.

15, 35-58: Paul imagines two objections that the Corinthians could raise: one concerning the manner of the resurrection *(how?),* the other pertaining to the qualities of the risen body *(what kind?).* These questions probably lie behind their denial of the resurrection (12), and seem to reflect the presumption that no kind of body other than the one we now possess would be possible. Paul deals with these objections in inverse order, in vv 36-49 and vv 50-58. His argument is fundamentally theological and its appeal is to the understanding.

15, 35-49: Paul approaches the question of the nature of the risen body *(what kind of body?)* by means of two analogies: the seed (36-44) and the first man, Adam (45-49).

15, 36-38: The analogy of the seed: there is a change of attributes from seed to plant; the old life-form must be lost for the new to emerge. By speaking about the seed as a *body* that dies and comes to life, Paul keeps the point of the analogy before the reader's mind.

15, 39-41: The expression "its own body" (38) leads to a development on the marvelous diversity evident in bodily life.

for human beings, another kind of flesh for animals, another kind of flesh for birds, and another for fish. [40] There are both heavenly bodies and earthly bodies, but the brightness of the heavenly is one kind and that of the earthly another. [41] The brightness of the sun is one kind, the brightness of the moon another, and the brightness of the stars another. For star differs from star in brightness.

[42] * So also is the resurrection of the dead. It is sown corruptible; it is raised incorruptible. [43] It is sown dishonorable; it is raised glorious. It is sown weak; it is raised powerful.[k] [44] It is sown a natural body; it is raised a spiritual body. If there is a natural body, there is also a spiritual one.

[45] So, too, it is written, "The first man, Adam,* became a living being," the last Adam a life-giving spirit.[l] [46] But the spiritual was not first; rather the natural and then the spiritual. [47] The first man was from the earth, earthly; the second man, from heaven. [48] As was the earthly one, so also are the earthly, and as is the heavenly one, so also are the heavenly. [49] Just as we have borne the image of the earthly one, we shall also bear the image* of the heavenly one.[m]

The Resurrection Event. [50] * This I declare, brothers: flesh and blood cannot inherit the kingdom of God, nor does corruption* inherit incorruption.[n] [51] * Behold, I tell you a mystery. We shall not all fall asleep, but we will all be changed,[o] [52] in an instant, in the blink of an eye, at the last trumpet. For the trumpet will sound, the dead will be raised incorruptible, and we shall be changed.[p] [53] For that which is corruptible must clothe itself with incorruptibility, and that which is mortal must clothe itself with immortality.[q] [54] And when this which is corruptible clothes itself with incorruptibility and this which is mortal clothes itself with immortality, then the word that is written shall come about:[r]

"Death is swallowed up in victory.*
[55] Where, O death, is your victory?
Where, O death, is your sting?"[s]

[56] The sting of death is sin,* and the power of sin is the law.[t] [57] But thanks be to God who gives us the victory through our Lord Jesus Christ.[u]

[58] Therefore, my beloved brothers, be firm, steadfast, always fully devoted to the work of the Lord, knowing that in the Lord your labor is not in vain.

1Cor

---

k Phil 3, 20-21; Col 3, 4.—l Gn 2, 7 / Jn 5, 21-29; 2 Cor 3, 6.17.—m Gn 5, 3 / Rom 8, 29; Phil 3, 21.—n Jn 3, 3-6.—o 1 Thes 4, 14-17.—p Jl 2, 1; Zec 9, 14; Mt 24, 31; Rv 11, 15-18.—q 2 Cor 5, 2-4.—r Is 25, 8; 2 Cor 5, 4; 2 Tm 1, 10; Heb 2, 14-15.—s Hos 13, 14.—t Rom 4, 15; 7, 7.13.—u Jn 16, 33; 1 Jn 5, 4.

15, 42-44: The principles of qualitative difference before and after death (36-38) and of diversity on different levels of creation (39-41) are now applied to the human body. Before: a body animated by a lower, natural life-principle *(psychē)* and endowed with the properties of natural existence (corruptibility, lack of glory, weakness). After: a body animated by a higher life-principle *(pneuma;* cf 45) and endowed with other qualities (incorruptibility, glory, power, spirituality), which are properties of God himself.

15, 45: The analogy of *the first man, Adam,* is introduced by a citation from Gn 2, 7. Paul alters the text slightly, adding the adjective *first,* and translating the Hebrew *'ādām* twice, so as to give it its value both as a common noun (*man*) and as a proper name (*Adam*). Verse 45b then specifies similarities and differences between the two Adams. *The last Adam,* Christ (cf 1 Cor 15, 21-22) has become *a . . . spirit (pneuma),* a life-principle transcendent with respect to the natural soul *(psychē)* of the first Adam (on the terminology here, cf the note on 1 Cor 3, 1). Further, he is not just alive, but *life-giving,* a source of life for others.

15, 49: *We shall also bear the image:* although it has less manuscript support, this reading better fits the context's emphasis on futurity and the transforming action of God; on future transformation as conformity to the image of the Son, cf Rom

8, 29; Phil 3, 21. The majority reading, "let us bear the image," suggests that the image of the heavenly man is already present and exhorts us to conform to it.

15, 50-57: These verses, an answer to the first question of v 35, explain theologically how the change of properties from one image to another will take place: God has the power to transform, and he will exercise it.

15, 50-53: *Flesh and blood . . . corruption:* living persons and the corpses of the dead, respectively. In both cases, the gulf between creatures and God is too wide to be bridged unless God himself transforms us.

15, 51-52: *A mystery:* the last moment in God's plan is disclosed; cf the notes on 1 Cor 2, 1.7-10a. The final trumpet and the awakening of the dead are stock details of the apocalyptic scenario. *We shall not all fall asleep:* some of his contemporaries might still be alive at Christ's return; after the death of Paul and his whole generation, copyists altered this statement in various ways. *We will all be changed:* the statement extends to all Christians, for Paul is not directly speaking about anyone else. Whether they have died before the end or happen still to be alive, all must be transformed.

15, 54-55: *Death is swallowed up in victory:* scripture itself predicts death's overthrow. *O death:* in his prophetic vision Paul may be making Hosea's words his own, or imagining this cry of triumph on the lips of the risen church.

15, 56: *The sting of death is sin:* an explanation of Hosea's metaphor. Death, scorpion-like, is equipped with a sting, sin, by which it injects its poison. Christ defeats sin, the cause of death (Gn 3, 19; Rom 5, 12).

VI. CONCLUSION

CHAPTER 16

The Collection.* [1] Now in regard to the collection* for the holy ones, you also should do as I ordered the churches of Galatia. [v] [2] On the first day of the week each of you should set aside and save whatever he can afford, so that collections will not be going on when I come. [3] And when I arrive, I shall send those whom you have approved with letters of recommendation to take your gracious gift to Jerusalem. [4] If it seems fitting that I should go also,* they will go with me.

Paul's Travel Plans.* [5] I shall come to you after I pass through Macedonia (for I am going to pass through Macedonia), [w] [6] and perhaps I shall stay or even spend the winter with you, so that you may send me on my way wherever I may go. [7] For I do not wish to see you now just in passing, but I hope to spend some time with you, if the Lord permits. [x] [8] I shall stay in Ephesus [y] until Pentecost,* [9] because a door has opened for me wide and productive for work, but there are many opponents. [z]

[10] If Timothy comes, see that he is without fear in your company, for he is doing the work of the Lord just as I am. [a] [11] Therefore, no one should disdain him.

Rather, send him on his way in peace that he may come to me, for I am expecting him with the brothers. [12] Now in regard to our brother Apollos, I urged him strongly to go to you with the brothers, but it was not at all his will that he go now. He will go when he has an opportunity. [b]

Exhortation and Greetings. [13] Be on your guard, stand firm in the faith, be courageous, be strong. [14] Your every act should be done with love.

[15] I urge you, brothers—you know that the household of Stephanas [c] is the firstfruits of Achaia and that they have devoted themselves to the service of the holy ones—[16] be subordinate to such people and to everyone who works and toils with them. [17] I rejoice in the arrival of Stephanas, Fortunatus, and Achaicus, because they made up for your absence, [18] for they refreshed my spirit as well as yours. So give recognition to such people. [d]

[19] * The churches of Asia send you greetings. Aquila and Prisca together with the church at their house send you many greetings in the Lord. [e] [20] All the brothers greet you. Greet one another with a holy kiss. [f]

[21] I, Paul, write you this greeting in my own hand. [g] [22] If anyone does not love the Lord, let him be accursed.* *Marana tha.* [h] [23] The grace of the Lord Jesus be with you. [24] My love to all of you in Christ Jesus. [i]

---

v Acts 24, 17; Rom 15, 25-32; 2 Cor 8-9; Gal 2, 10.—w Acts 19, 21; Rom 15, 26; 2 Cor 1, 15-16.—x Acts 18, 21.—y 1 Cor 15, 32; Acts 18, 19; 19, 1-10.—z Acts 14, 27; 2 Cor 2, 12.—a 1 Cor 4, 17; Acts 16, 1; 19, 22; Phil 2, 19-23.—b 1 Cor 1, 12; 3, 4-6.22; Acts 18, 24-28.—c 1 Cor 1, 16.—d 1 Thes 5, 12-13.—e Acts 18, 2.18.26; Rom 16, 3-5.—f Rom 16, 16; 2 Cor 13, 12; 1 Thes 5, 26; 1 Pt 5, 14.—g Gal 6, 11; Col 4, 18; 2 Thes 3, 17.—h 1 Cor 12, 3; Rom 9, 3; Gal 1, 8-9; Rv 22, 20.—i Rom 16, 20.

16, 1-4: This paragraph contains our earliest evidence for a project that became a major undertaking of Paul's ministry. The collection for the church at Jerusalem was a symbol in his mind for the unity of Jewish and Gentile Christianity. Cf Gal 2, 10; Rom 15, 25-29; 2 Cor 8—9 and the notes to this last passage.

16, 1: *In regard to the collection:* it has already begun in Galatia and Macedonia (cf 2 Cor 8), and presumably he has already instructed the Corinthians about its purpose.

16, 4: *That I should go also:* presumably Paul delivered the collection on his final visit to Jerusalem; cf Rom 15, 25-32; Acts 24, 14.

16, 5-12: The travel plans outlined here may not have materialized precisely as Paul intended; cf 2 Cor 1, 8—2, 13; 7, 4-16.

16, 8: *In Ephesus until Pentecost:* this tells us the place from which he wrote the letter and suggests he may have composed it about Easter time (cf 1 Cor 5, 7-8).

16, 19-24: These paragraphs conform to the normal epistolary conclusion, but their language is overlaid with liturgical coloration as well. The *greetings* of the Asian churches are probably to be read, along with the letter, in the liturgy at Corinth, and the union of the church is to be expressed by *a holy kiss* (19-20). Paul adds to this his own greeting (21) and blessings (23-24).

16, 22: *Accursed:* literally, "anathema." This expression (cf 1 Cor 12, 3) is a formula for exclusion from the community; it may imply here a call to self-examination before celebration of the Eucharist, in preparation for the Lord's coming and judgment (cf 1 Cor 11, 17-34). *Marana tha:* an Aramaic expression, probably used in the early Christian liturgy. As understood here ("O Lord, come!"), it is a prayer for the early return of Christ. If the Aramaic words are divided differently *(Maran atha,* "Our Lord has come"), it becomes a credal declaration. The former interpretation is supported by what appears to be a Greek equivalent of this acclamation in Rv 22, 20: "Amen. Come, Lord Jesus!"

THE SECOND LETTER TO THE CORINTHIANS

INTRODUCTION

The Second Letter to the Corinthians is the most personal of all of Paul's extant writings, and it reveals much about his character. In it he deals with one or more crises that have arisen in the Corinthian church. The confrontation with these problems caused him to reflect deeply on his relationship with the community and to speak about it frankly. One moment he is venting his feelings of frustration and uncertainty, the next he is pouring out his relief and affection. The importance of the issues at stake between them calls forth from him an enormous effort of personal persuasion, as well as doctrinal considerations that are of great value for us. Paul's ability to produce profound theological foundations for what may at first sight appear to be rather commonplace circumstances is perhaps nowhere better exemplified than in Second Corinthians. The emotional tone of the letter, its lack of order, and our ignorance of some of its background do not make it easy to follow, but it amply repays the effort required of the reader.

Second Corinthians is rich and varied in content. The interpretation of Exodus in chapter 3, for instance, offers a striking example of early apologetic use of the Old Testament. Paul's discussion of the collection in chs 8-9 contains a theology of sharing of possessions, of community of goods among Christian churches, which is both balanced and sensitive. Furthermore, the closing chapters provide an illustration of early Christian invective and polemic, because the conflict with intruders forces Paul to assert his authority. But in those same chapters Paul articulates the vision and sense of values that animate his own apostolate, revealing his faith that Jesus' passion and resurrection are the pattern for all Christian life and expressing a spirituality of ministry unsurpassed in the New Testament.

The letter is remarkable for its rhetoric. Paul falls naturally into the style and argumentation of contemporary philosophic preachers, employing with ease the stock devices of the "diatribe." By a barrage of questions, by challenges both serious and ironic, by paradox heaped upon paradox, even by insults hurled at his opponents, he strives to awaken in his hearers a true sense of values and an appropriate response. All his argument centers on the destiny of Jesus, in which a paradoxical reversal of values is revealed. But Paul appeals to his own personal experience as well. In passages of great rhetorical power (4, 7-15; 6, 3-10; 11, 21-29; 12, 5-10; 13, 3-4) he enumerates the circumstances of his ministry and the tribulations he has had to endure for Jesus and the gospel, in the hope of illustrating the pattern of Jesus' existence in his own and of drawing the Corinthians into a reappraisal of the values they cherish. Similar passages in the same style in his other letters (cf especially Rom 8, 31-39; 1 Cor 1, 26-31; 4, 6-21; 9, 1-27; 13, 1-13; Phil 4, 10-19) confirm Paul's familiarity with contemporary rhetoric and demonstrate how effectively it served to express his vision of Christian life and ministry.

Second Corinthians was occasioned by events and problems that developed after Paul's first letter reached Corinth. We have no information about these circumstances except what is contained in the letter itself, which of course supposes that they are known to the readers. Consequently the reconstruction of the letter's background is an uncertain enterprise about which there is not complete agreement.

The letter deals principally with these three topics: (1) a crisis between Paul and the Corinthians, occasioned at least partially by changes in his travel plans (1, 12—2, 13), and the successful resolution of that crisis (7, 5-16); (2) further directives and encouragement in regard to the collection for the church in Jerusalem (8, 1—9, 15); (3) the definition and defense of Paul's ministry as an apostle. Paul's reflections on this matter are oc-

casioned by visitors from other churches who passed through Corinth, missionaries who differed from Paul in a variety of ways, both in theory and in practice. Those differences led to comparisons. Either the visitors themselves or some of the local church members appear to have sown confusion among the Corinthians with regard to Paul's authority or his style, or both. Paul deals at length with aspects of this situation in 2, 14—7, 4 and again in 10, 1—13, 10, though the manner of treatment and the thrust of the argument differ in each of these sections.

Scholars have noticed a lack of continuity in this document. For example, the long section of 2, 14—7, 4 seems abruptly spliced into the narrative of a crisis and its resolution. Identical or similar topics, moreover, seem to be treated several times during the letter (compare 2, 14—7, 4 with 10, 1—13, 10, and 8, 1-24 with 9, 1-15). Many judge, therefore, that this letter as it stands incorporates several briefer letters sent to Corinth over a certain span of time. If this is so, then Paul himself or, more likely, some other editor clearly took care to gather those letters together and impose some literary unity upon the collection, thus producing the document that has come down to us as the Second Letter to the Corinthians. Others continue to regard it as a single letter, attributing its inconsistencies to changes of perspective in Paul that may have been occasioned by the arrival of fresh news from Corinth during its composition. The letter, or at least some sections of it, appears to have been composed in Macedonia (2, 12-13; 7, 5-6; 8, 1-4; 9, 2-4). It is generally dated about the autumn of A.D. 57; if it is a compilation, of course, the various parts may have been separated by intervals of at least some months.

The principal divisions of the Second Letter to the Corinthians are the following:

I.   *Address (1, 1-11)*
II. *The Crisis between Paul and the Corinthians (1, 12—7, 16)*
    A. Past Relationships (1, 12—2, 13)
    B. Paul's Ministry (2, 14—7, 4)
    C. Resolution of the Crisis (7, 5-16)
III. *The Collection for Jerusalem (8, 1—9, 15)*
IV. *Paul's Defense of His Ministry (10, 1—13, 10)*
V. *Conclusion (13, 11-13)*

I. ADDRESS

CHAPTER 1

Greeting. [1] * Paul, an apostle of Christ Jesus by the will of God, and Timothy our brother, to the church of God that is in Corinth, with all the holy ones throughout Achaia:[a] [2] grace to you and peace from God our Father and the Lord Jesus Christ.

Thanksgiving. [3] [b] Blessed be the God and Father of our Lord Jesus Christ, the Father of compassion and God of all encouragement,* [4] who encourages us in our every affliction, so that we may be able to encourage those who are in any affliction with the encouragement with which we ourselves are encouraged by God.[c] [5] For as Christ's sufferings overflow to us, so

through Christ* does our encouragement also overflow. [6] If we are afflicted, it is for your encouragement and salvation; if we are encouraged, it is for your encouragement, which enables you to endure the

---

a Eph 1, 1; Col 1, 1 / 2 Cor 1, 19; Acts 16 / Rom 1, 7; 1 Cor 1, 2.—b 1 Cor 15, 24; Eph 1, 3; 1 Pt 1, 3 / Rom 15, 5.—c 2 Cor 7, 6-7.13; 1 Thes 3, 6-8; 2 Thes 2, 16.

1, 1-11: The opening follows the usual Pauline form, except that the thanksgiving takes the form of a doxology or glorification of God (3). This introduces a meditation on the experience of suffering and encouragement shared by Paul and the Corinthians (4-7), drawn, at least in part, from Paul's reflections on a recent affliction (8-10). The section ends with a modified and delayed allusion to thanksgiving (11).

1, 3: *God of all encouragement:* Paul expands a standard Jewish blessing so as to state the theme of the paragraph. The theme of "encouragement" or "consolation" *(paraklēsis)* occurs ten times in this opening, against a background formed by multiple references to "affliction" and "suffering."

1, 5: *Through Christ:* the Father of compassion is the Father of our Lord Jesus (3); Paul's sufferings and encouragement (or "consolation") are experienced in union with Christ. Cf Lk 2, 25: the "consolation of Israel" is Jesus himself.

same sufferings that we suffer. [7] Our hope for you is firm, for we know that as you share in the sufferings, you also share in the encouragement.*

[8] We do not want you to be unaware, brothers, of the affliction that came to us in the province of Asia;* we were utterly weighed down beyond our strength, so that we despaired even of life.[d] [9] Indeed, we had accepted within ourselves the sentence of death,* that we might trust not in ourselves but in God who raises the dead.[e] [10] He rescued us from such great danger of death, and he will continue to rescue us; in him we have put our hope [that] he will also rescue us again,[f] [11] as you help us with prayer, so that thanks may be given by many on our behalf for the gift granted us through the prayers of many.[g]

II. THE CRISIS BETWEEN PAUL AND THE CORINTHIANS

A. Past Relationships*

Paul's Sincerity and Constancy. [12] * For our boast is this, the testimony of our conscience that we have conducted ourselves in the world, and especially toward you, with the simplicity and sincerity of God, [and] not by human wisdom but by the grace of God. [13] For we write you nothing but what you can read and understand, and I hope that you will understand completely, [14] as you have come to understand us partially, that we are your boast as you also are ours, on the day of [our] Lord Jesus.[h]

[15] With this confidence I formerly intended to come* to you so that you might receive a double favor, [16] namely, to go by way of you to Macedonia, and then to come to you again on my return from Macedonia, and have you send me on my way to Judea.[i] [17] So when I intended this, did I act lightly?* Or do I make my plans according to human considerations, so that with me it is "yes, yes" and "no, no"?[j] [18] As God is faithful,* our word to you is not "yes" and "no." [19] For the Son of God, Jesus Christ, who was proclaimed to you by us, Silvanus and Timothy and me, was not "yes" and "no," but "yes" has been in him.[k] [20] For however many are the promises of God, their Yes is in him;[l] therefore, the Amen from us also goes through him to God for glory. [21] * But the one who gives us security with you in Christ and who anointed us is God;[m] [22] he has also put his seal upon us and given the Spirit in our hearts as a first installment.[n]

2Cor

---

d Acts 20, 18-19; 1 Cor 15, 32.—e 2 Cor 4, 7-11; Rom 4, 17.—f 2 Tm 4, 18.—g 2 Cor 4, 15; 9, 12.—h Phil 2, 16; 1 Thes 2, 19-20.—i 1 Cor 16, 5-9, Acts 19, 21.—j Mt 5, 37, Jas 5, 12.—k Acts 16, 1-3; 1 Thes 1, 1; 2 Thes 1, 1.—l 1 Cor 14, 16; Rv 3, 14.—m 1 Jn 2, 20.27.—n Eph 1, 13-14; 4, 30 / 2 Cor 5, 5; Rom 5, 5; 8, 16.23.

1, 7: *You also share in the encouragement:* the eschatological reversal of affliction and encouragement that Christians expect (cf Mt 5, 4; Lk 6, 24) permits some present experience of reversal in the Corinthians' case, as in Paul's.

1, 8: *Asia:* a Roman province in western Asia Minor, the capital of which was Ephesus.

1, 9-10: *The sentence of death:* it is unclear whether Paul is alluding to a physical illness or to an external threat to life. The result of the situation was to produce an attitude of faith in God alone. *God who raises the dead:* rescue is the constant pattern of God's activity; his final act of encouragement is the resurrection.

1, 12—2, 13: The autobiographical remarks about the crisis in Asia Minor lead into consideration of a crisis that has arisen between Paul and the Corinthians. Paul will return to this question, after a long digression, in 2 Cor 7, 5-16. Both of these sections deal with travel plans Paul had made, changes in the plans, alternative measures adopted, a breach that opened between him and the community, and finally a reconciliation between them.

1, 12-14: Since Paul's own conduct will be under discussion here, he prefaces the section with a statement about his habitual behavior and attitude toward the community. He protests his openness, single-mindedness, and conformity to God's grace; he hopes that his relationship with them will be marked by mutual understanding and pride, which will constantly increase until it reaches its climax at the judgment. Two references to boasting

frame this paragraph (12.14), the first appearances of a theme that will be important in the letter, especially in chs 10-13; the term is used in a positive sense here (cf the note on 1 Cor 1, 29 31).

1, 15: *I formerly intended to come:* this plan reads like a revision of the one mentioned in 1 Cor 16, 5. Not until 2 Cor 1, 23—2, 1 will Paul tell us something his original readers already knew, that he has canceled one or the other of these projected visits.

1, 17: *Did I act lightly?:* the subsequent change of plans casts suspicion on the original intention, creating the impression that Paul is vacillating and inconsistent or that *human considerations* keep dictating shifts in his goals and projects (cf the counterclaim of 12). *"Yes, yes" and "no, no":* stating something and denying it in the same or the next breath; being of two minds at once, or from one moment to the next.

1, 18-22: *As God is faithful:* unable to deny the change in plans, Paul nonetheless asserts the firmness of the original plan and claims a profound constancy in his life and work. He grounds his defense in God himself, who is firm and reliable; this quality can also be predicated in various ways of those who are associated with him. Christ, Paul, and the Corinthians all participate in analogous ways in the constancy of God. A number of the terms here, which appear related only conceptually in Greek or English, would be variations of the same root, *'mn,* in a Semitic language, and thus naturally associated in a Semitic mind, such as Paul's. These include the words *yes* (17-20), *faithful* (18), *Amen* (20), *gives us security* (21), *faith, stand firm* (24).

1, 21-22: The commercial terms *gives us security, seal, first installment* are here used analogously to refer to the process of initiation into the Christian life, perhaps specifically to baptism. The passage is clearly trinitarian. The Spirit is the *first installment* or "down payment" of the full messianic benefits that God guarantees to Christians. Cf Eph 1, 13-14.

Paul's Change of Plan. ²³ ᵒ But I call upon God as witness, on my life, that it is to spare you that I have not yet gone to Corinth.* ²⁴ Not that we lord it over your faith; rather, we work together for your joy, for you stand firm in the faith.

CHAPTER 2

¹ For I decided not to come to you again in painful circumstances. ² For if I inflict pain upon you, then who is there to cheer me except the one pained by me? ³ And I wrote as I did* so that when I came I might not be pained by those in whom I should have rejoiced, confident about all of you that my joy is that of all of you. ⁴ For out of much affliction and anguish of heart I wrote to you with many tears, not that you might be pained but that you might know the abundant love I have for you.

The Offender.* ⁵ If anyone has caused pain, he has caused it not to me, but in some measure (not to exaggerate) to all of you. ⁶ This punishment by the majority is enough for such a person, ⁷ so that on the contrary you should forgive and encourage him instead, or else the person may be overwhelmed by excessive pain.ᵖ ⁸ Therefore, I urge you to reaffirm your love for him. ⁹ For this is why I wrote, to know your proven character, whether you were obedient in everything.�q ¹⁰ Whomever you forgive anything, so do I. For indeed what I have forgiven, if I have forgiven anything, has been for you in the presence of Christ, ¹¹ so that we might not be taken advantage of by Satan, for we are not unaware of his purposes.ʳ

Paul's Anxiety.* ¹² When I went to Troas for the gospel of Christ, although a door was opened for me in the Lord,ˢ ¹³ I had no relief in my spirit because I did not find my brother Titus.ᵗ So I took leave of them and went on to Macedonia.*

B. Paul's Ministry*

Ministers of a New Covenant. ¹⁴ * But thanks be to God,* who always leads us in triumph in Christ* and manifests through

---

o 2 Cor 13, 2.—p Col 3, 13.—q 2 Cor 7, 15.—r Eph 4, 27.—s Acts 16, 8.—t 2 Cor 7, 6; 1 Tm 1, 3.

1, 23-24: *I have not yet gone to Corinth:* some suppose that Paul received word of some affair in Corinth, which he decided to regulate by letter even before the first of his projected visits (cf 2 Cor 1, 16). Others conjecture that he did pay the first visit, was offended there (cf 2 Cor 2, 5), returned to Ephesus, and sent a letter (2 Cor 2, 3-9) in place of the second visit. The expressions *to spare you* (23) and *work together for your joy* (24) introduce the major themes of the next two paragraphs, which are remarkable for insistent repetition of key words and ideas. These form two clusters of terms in the English translation: (1) cheer, rejoice, encourage, joy; (2) pain, affliction, anguish. These clusters reappear when Paul resumes treatment of this subject in 2 Cor 7, 5-16.

2, 3-4: *I wrote as I did:* we learn for the first time about the sending of a letter in place of the proposed visit. Paul mentions the letter in passing, but emphasizes his motivation in sending it: to avoid being saddened by them (cf 2 Cor 2, 1), and to help them realize the depth of his love. Another motive will be added in 2 Cor 7, 12: to bring to light their own concern for him. *With many tears:* it has been suggested that we may have all or part of this "tearful letter" somewhere in the Corinthian correspondence, either in 1 Cor 5 (the case of the incestuous man), or in 1 Cor as a whole, or in 2 Cor 10—13. None of these hypotheses is entirely convincing. See the note on 2 Cor 13, 1.

2, 5-11: The nature of the *pain* (5) is unclear, though some believe an individual at Corinth rejected Paul's authority, thereby scandalizing many in the community. In any case, action has been taken, and Paul judges the measures adequate to right the situation (6). The follow-up directives he now gives are entirely positive: forgive, encourage, love. *Overwhelmed* (7): a vivid metaphor (literally "swallowed") that Paul employs positively at 2 Cor 5, 4 and in 1 Cor 15, 54 (7). It is often used to describe satanic activity (cf 1 Pt 5, 8); note the reference to Satan here in v 11.

2, 12-13: *I had no relief:* Paul does not explain the reason for his anxiety until he resumes the thread of his narrative at 2 Cor 7, 5: he was waiting to hear how the Corinthians would respond to his letter. Since 2 Cor 7, 5-16 describes their response in entirely positive terms, we never learn in detail why he found it necessary to defend and justify his change of plans, as in 2 Cor 1, 15-24. Was this portion of the letter written before the arrival of Titus with his good news (2 Cor 7, 6-7)?

2, 13: *Macedonia:* a Roman province in northern Greece.

2, 14—7, 4: This section constitutes a digression within the narrative of the crisis and its resolution (2 Cor 1, 12—2, 13 and 2 Cor 7, 5-16). The main component (2 Cor 2, 14—6, 10) treats the nature of Paul's ministry and his qualifications for it; this material bears some similarity to the defense of his ministry in chs 10-13, but it may well come from a period close to the crisis. This is followed by a supplementary block of material quite different in character and tone (2 Cor 6, 14—7, 1). These materials may have been brought together into their present position during final editing of the letter; appeals to the Corinthians link them to one another (2 Cor 6, 11-13) and lead back to the interrupted narrative (2 Cor 7, 2-4).

2, 14—6, 10: The question of Paul's adequacy (2 Cor 2, 16; cf 2 Cor 3, 5) and his credentials (2 Cor 3, 1-2) has been raised. Paul responds by an extended treatment of the nature of his ministry. It is a ministry of glory (2 Cor 3, 7—4, 6), of life (2 Cor 4, 7—5, 10), of reconciliation (2 Cor 5, 11—6, 10).

2, 14-16a: The initial statement plunges us abruptly into another train of thought. Paul describes his personal existence and his function as a preacher in two powerful images (14) that constitute a prelude to the development to follow.

2, 14a: *Leads us in triumph in Christ:* this metaphor of a festive parade in honor of a conquering military hero can suggest either a positive sharing in Christ's triumph or an experience of defeat, being led in captivity and submission (cf 2 Cor 4, 8-11; 1 Cor 4, 9). Paul is probably aware of the ambiguity, as he is in the case of the next metaphor.

us the odor of the knowledge of him* in every place. ¹⁵ For we are the aroma of Christ for God among those who are being saved and among those who are perishing,ᵘ ¹⁶ to the latter an odor of death that leads to death, to the former an odor of life that leads to life. Who is qualified* for this? ¹⁷ For we are not like the many who trade on the word of God; but as out of sincerity, indeed as from God and in the presence of God, we speak in Christ.ᵛ

CHAPTER 3

¹ ʷ Are we beginning to commend ourselves again? Or do we need, as some do, letters of recommendation to you or from you?* ² You are our letter,* written on our hearts, known and read by all, ³ ˣ shown to be a letter of Christ administered by us, written not in ink but by the Spirit of the living God, not on tablets of stone but on tablets that are hearts of flesh.*

u 2 Cor 4, 3; 1 Cor 1, 18.—v 2 Cor 4, 2; 1 Cor 5, 8.—w Acts 18, 27; Rom 16, 1; 1 Cor 16, 3.—x Ex 24, 12; 31, 18; 32, 15-19 / Jer 31, 33; Ez 11, 19; 36, 26-27.—y Jn 3, 27.—z Eph 3, 7 / Jer 31, 31-34.—a Ex 34, 29-35.

2, 14b-16a: *The odor of the knowledge of him:* incense was commonly used in triumphal processions. The metaphor suggests the gradual diffusion of the knowledge of God through the apostolic preaching. *The aroma of Christ:* the image shifts from the fragrance Paul diffuses to the aroma that he is. Paul is probably thinking of the "sweet odor" of the sacrifices in the Old Testament (e.g., Gn 8, 21; Ex 29, 18) and perhaps of the metaphor of wisdom as a sweet odor (Sir 24, 15). *Death . . . life:* the aroma of Christ that comes to them through Paul is perceived differently by various classes of people. To some his preaching and his life (cf 1 Cor 1, 17—2, 6) are perceived as *death,* and the effect is death for them; others perceive him, despite appearances, as *life,* and the effect is life for them. This fragrance thus produces a separation and a judgment (cf the function of the "light" in John's gospel).

2, 16b-17: *Qualified:* Paul may be echoing either the self-satisfied claims of other preachers or their charges about Paul's deficiencies. No one is really qualified, but the apostle contrasts himself with those who dilute or falsify the preaching for personal advantage and insists on his totally good conscience: his ministry is from God, and he has exercised it with fidelity and integrity (cf 2 Cor 3, 5-6).

3, 1: Paul seems to allude to certain preachers who pride themselves on their written credentials. Presumably they reproach him for not possessing similar credentials and compel him to spell out his own qualifications (2 Cor 4, 2; 5, 12; 6, 4). The Corinthians themselves should have performed this function for Paul (2 Cor 5, 12; cf 2 Cor 12, 11). Since he is forced to find something that can recommend him, he points to them: their very existence constitutes his *letter* of recommendation (1-2). Others who engage in self-commendation will also be mentioned in 2 Cor 10, 12-18.

3, 2-3: Mention of "letters of recommendation" generates a series of metaphors in which Paul plays on the word "letter": (1) the community is Paul's letter of recommendation (2a); (2) they are a letter engraved on his affections for all to see and read (2b); (3) they are a letter from Christ that Paul merely delivers (3a); (4) they are a letter written by the Spirit on the tablets of human hearts (3b). One image dissolves into another.

⁴ * Such confidence we have through Christ toward God. ⁵ Not that of ourselves we are qualified to take credit for anything as coming from us; rather, our qualification comes from God,ʸ ⁶ who has indeed qualified us as ministers of a new covenant, not of letter but of spirit;ᶻ for the letter brings death, but the Spirit gives life.*

Contrast with the Old Covenant. ⁷ * Now if the ministry of death,* carved in letters on stone, was so glorious that the Israelites could not look intently at the face of Moses because of its glory that was going to fade,ᵃ ⁸ how much more* will the ministry of the Spirit be glorious? ⁹ For if the ministry of condemnation was glorious, the ministry of righteousness will abound much more in glory. ¹⁰ Indeed, what was endowed with glory has come to have no glory in this respect because of the glory that surpasses it.

3, 3b: This verse contrasts Paul's letter with those *written . . . in ink* (like the credentials of other preachers) and those *written . . . on tablets of stone* (like the law of Moses). These contrasts suggest that the other preachers may have claimed special relationship with Moses. If they were Judaizers zealous for the Mosaic law, that would explain the detailed contrast between the old and the new covenants (2 Cor 3, 6; 4, 7—6, 10). If they were charismatics who claimed Moses as their model, that would explain the extended treatment of Moses himself and his glory (2 Cor 3, 7—4, 6). *Hearts of flesh:* cf Ezekiel's contrast between the heart of flesh that the Spirit gives and the heart of stone that it replaces (Ez 36, 26); the context is covenant renewal and purification that makes observance of the law possible.

3, 4-6: These verses resume 2 Cor 2, 1—3, 3. Paul's confidence (4) is grounded in his sense of God-given mission (2 Cor 2, 17), the specifics of which are described in vv 1-3. Verses 5-6 return to the question of his qualifications (2 Cor 2, 16), attributing them entirely to God. Verse 6 further spells out the situation described in v 3b and "names" it: Paul is living within *a new covenant,* characterized by the Spirit, which *gives life.* The usage of a *new covenant* is derived from Jer 31, 31-33, a passage that also speaks of writing on the heart; cf 2 Cor 3, 2.

3, 6b: This verse serves as a topic sentence for 2 Cor 3, 7—6, 10. For the contrast between *letter* and *spirit,* cf Rom 2, 29; 7, 5-6.

3, 7—4, 6: Paul now develops the contrast enunciated in 2 Cor 3, 6b in terms of the relative glory of the two covenants, insisting on the greater glory of the new. His polemic seems directed against individuals who appeal to the glorious Moses and fail to perceive any comparable glory either in Paul's life as an apostle or in the gospel he preaches. He asserts in response that Christians have a glory of their own that far surpasses that of Moses.

3, 7: *The ministry of death:* from his very first words, Paul describes the Mosaic covenant and ministry from the viewpoint of their limitations. They lead to *death* rather than life (6-7; cf 2 Cor 4, 7—5, 10), to *condemnation* rather than reconciliation (9; cf 2 Cor 5, 11—6, 10). *Was so glorious:* the basic text to which Paul alludes is Ex 34, 29-35, to which his opponents have undoubtedly laid claim. *Going to fade:* Paul concedes the glory of Moses' covenant and ministry, but grants them only temporary significance.

3, 8-11: *How much more:* the argument "from the less to the greater" is repeated three times (8.9.11). Verse 10 expresses another point of view: the difference in glory is so great that only the new covenant and ministry can properly be called "glorious" at all.

[11] For if what was going to fade was glorious, how much more will what endures be glorious.

[12] Therefore, since we have such hope,* we act very boldly [13] and not like Moses,* who put a veil over his face so that the Israelites could not look intently at the cessation of what was fading. [14] Rather, their thoughts were rendered dull, for to this present day* the same veil remains unlifted when they read the old covenant, because through Christ it is taken away. [15] To this day, in fact, whenever Moses is read, a veil lies over their hearts,[b] [16] but whenever a person turns to the Lord the veil is removed.[c] [17] Now the Lord is the Spirit,* and where the Spirit of the Lord is, there is freedom. [18] * All of us, gazing with unveiled face on the glory of the Lord, are being transformed into the same image from glory to glory, as from the Lord who is the Spirit.[d]

CHAPTER 4

Integrity in the Ministry. [1] * Therefore, since we have this ministry through the mercy shown us, we are not discouraged. [2] Rather, we have renounced shameful, hidden things; not acting deceitfully or falsifying the word of God, but by the open declaration of the truth we commend ourselves to everyone's conscience in the sight of God.[e] [3] And even though our gospel is veiled,* it is veiled for those who are perishing,[f] [4] in whose case the god of this age has blinded the minds of the unbelievers, so that they may not see the light of the gospel of the glory of Christ, who is the image of God.[g] [5] For we do not preach ourselves* but Jesus Christ as Lord, and ourselves as your slaves for the sake of Jesus. [6] * For God who said, "Let light shine out of darkness," has shone in our hearts to bring to light the knowledge of the glory of God on the face of [Jesus] Christ.[h]

b Rom 11, 7-10.—c Ex 34, 34.—d Rom 8, 29-30; 12, 2; Gal 4, 19; Phil 3, 10.20-21 / 2 Cor 4, 4-6; 1 Cor 15, 49; Col 1, 15; 3, 9-11; 1 Jn 3, 2.—e 2 Cor 2, 17; 1 Thes 2, 4-7.—f 2 Cor 2, 15-16; 2 Thes 2, 10.—g Jn 12, 31-36 / 1 Tm 1, 11.—h Gn 1, 3; Is 9, 1; Acts 26, 13-23; Gal 1, 15-16 / Jn 8, 12; Heb 1, 3.

3, 12: *Such hope:* the glory is not yet an object of experience, but that does not lessen Paul's confidence. *Boldly:* the term *parrēsia* expresses outspoken declaration of Christian conviction (cf 2 Cor 4, 1-2). Paul has nothing to hide and no reason for timidity.

3, 13-14a: *Not like Moses:* in Exodus Moses veiled his face to protect the Israelites from God's reflected glory. Without impugning Moses' sincerity, Paul attributes another effect to the veil. Since it lies between God's glory and the Israelites, it explains how they could fail to notice the glory disappearing. *Their thoughts were rendered dull:* the problem lay with their understanding. This will be expressed in vv 14b-16 by a shift in the place of the veil: it is no longer over Moses' face but over their perception.

3, 14b-16: The parallelism in these verses makes it necessary to interpret corresponding parts in relation to one another. *To this present day:* this signals the shift of Paul's attention to his contemporaries; his argument is typological, as in 1 Cor 10. The Israelites of Moses' time typify the Jews of Paul's time, and perhaps also Christians of Jewish origin or mentality who may not recognize the temporary character of Moses' glory. *When they read the old covenant:* the lasting dullness prevents proper appraisal of Moses' person and covenant. When his writings are read in the synagogue, a veil still impedes their understanding. *Through Christ:* i.e., in the new covenant. *Whenever a person turns to the Lord:* Moses in Exodus appeared before God without the veil and gazed on his face unprotected. Paul applies that passage to converts to Christianity: when they turn to the Lord fully and authentically, the impediment to their understanding is removed.

3, 17: *The Lord is the Spirit:* the "Lord" to whom the Christian turns (16) is the Spirit of whom Paul has been speaking, the life-giving Spirit of the living God (6.8), the inaugurator of the new covenant and ministry, who is also the Spirit of Christ. *The Spirit of the Lord:* the Lord here is the living God (3), but there may also be an allusion to Christ as Lord (14.16). *Freedom:* i.e., from the ministry of death (7) and the covenant that condemned (9).

3, 18: Another application of the veil image. *All of us . . . with unveiled face:* Christians (Israelites from whom the veil has been removed) are like Moses, standing in God's presence, beholding and reflecting his glory. *Gazing:* the verb may also be translated "contemplating as in a mirror"; 2 Cor 4, 6 would suggest that the mirror is Christ himself. *Are being transformed:* elsewhere Paul speaks of transformation, conformity to Jesus, God's image, as a reality of the end time, and even v 12 speaks of the glory as an object of hope. But the life-giving Spirit, the distinctive gift of the new covenant, is already present in the community (cf 2 Cor 1, 22, the "first installment"), and the process of transformation has already begun. *Into the same image:* into the image of God, which is Christ (2 Cor 4, 4).

4, 1-2: A ministry of this sort generates confidence and forthrightness; cf 2 Cor 1, 12-14; 2, 17.

4, 3-4: *Though our gospel is veiled:* the final application of the image. Paul has been reproached either for obscurity in his preaching or for his manner of presenting the gospel. But he confidently asserts that there is no veil over his gospel. If some fail to perceive its light, that is because of unbelief. The veil lies over their eyes (2 Cor 3, 14), a blindness induced by Satan, and a sign that they are headed for destruction (cf 2 Cor 2, 15).

4, 5: *We do not preach ourselves:* the light seen in his gospel is the glory of Christ (4). Far from preaching himself, the preacher should be a transparent medium through whom Jesus is perceived (cf 2 Cor 4, 10-11). *Your slaves:* Paul draws attention away from individuals as such and toward their role in relation to God, Christ, and the community; cf 1 Cor 3, 5; 4, 1.

4, 6: Autobiographical allusion to the episode at Damascus clarifies the origin and nature of Paul's service; cf Acts 9, 1-19; 22, 3-16; 26, 2-18. *"Let light shine out of darkness":* Paul seems to be thinking of Gn 1, 3 and presenting his apostolic ministry as a new creation. There may also be an allusion to Is 9, 1, suggesting his prophetic calling as servant of the Lord and light to the nations; cf Is 42, 6.16; 49, 6; 60, 1-2, and the use of light imagery in Acts 26, 13-23. *To bring to light the knowledge:* Paul's role in the process of revelation, expressed at the beginning under the image of the odor and aroma (2 Cor 2, 14-15), is restated now, at the end of this first moment of the development, in the imagery of light and glory (3-6).

The Paradox of the Ministry. 7 * But we hold this treasure* in earthen vessels, that the surpassing power may be of God and not from us. 8 * We are afflicted in every way, but not constrained; perplexed, but not driven to despair;[i] 9 persecuted, but not abandoned; struck down, but not destroyed; 10 * always carrying about in the body the dying of Jesus, so that the life of Jesus may also be manifested in our body.[j] 11 For we who live are constantly being given up to death for the sake of Jesus, so that the life of Jesus may be manifested in our mortal flesh.[k]

12 * So death is at work in us, but life in you. 13 * Since, then, we have the same spirit of faith, according to what is written, "I believed, therefore I spoke," we too believe and therefore speak,[l] 14 knowing that the one who raised the Lord Jesus will raise us also with Jesus and place us with you in his presence.[m] 15 Everything indeed is for you, so that the grace bestowed in abundance on more and more people may cause the thanksgiving to overflow for the glory of God.[n]

16 * Therefore, we are not discouraged;* rather, although our outer self is wasting away, our inner self is being renewed day by day.[o] 17 For this momentary light affliction is producing for us an eternal weight of glory beyond all comparison,[p] 18 as we look not to what is seen but to what is unseen; for what is seen is transitory, but what is unseen is eternal.[q]

CHAPTER 5

Our Future Destiny. 1 [r] For we know that if our earthly dwelling,* a tent, should be destroyed, we have a building from God, a dwelling not made with hands, eternal in heaven. 2 * For in this tent we groan, longing to be further clothed with our heavenly habitation[s] 3 if indeed, when we have taken it off,* we shall not be found naked. 4 For while we are in this tent we groan and are

2Cor

i 2 Cor 6, 4-10; 1 Cor 4, 9-13.—j Col 1, 24.—k Rom 8, 36; 1 Cor 15, 31.—l Ps 116, 10.—m Rom 4, 24-25; 8, 11; 1 Cor 6, 14; 1 Thes 4, 14.—n 2 Cor 1, 11.—o 2 Cor 4, 11.—p Mt 5, 11-12; Rom 8, 18.—q Rom 8, 24-25; Heb 11, 1.—r Is 38, 12 / Col 3, 1-4 / Mk 14, 58; Col 2, 11; Heb 9, 11.24.—s Rom 8, 23 / 1 Cor 15, 51-54.

4, 7—5, 10: Paul now confronts the difficulty that his present existence does not appear glorious at all; it is marked instead by suffering and death. He deals with this by developing the topic already announced in 2 Cor 3, 3.6, asserting his faith in the presence and ultimate triumph of life, in his own and every Christian existence, despite the experience of death.

4, 7: *This treasure:* the glory that he preaches and into which they are being transformed. *In earthen vessels:* the instruments God uses are human and fragile; some imagine small terracotta lamps in which light is carried.

4, 8-9: A catalogue of his apostolic trials and afflictions. Yet in these the negative never completely prevails; there is always some experience of rescue, of salvation.

4, 10-11: Both the negative and the positive sides of the experience are grounded christologically. The logic is similar to that of 2 Cor 1, 3-11. His sufferings are connected with Christ's, and his deliverance is a sign that he is to share in Jesus' resurrection.

4, 12-15: His experience does not terminate in himself, but in others (12.15; cf 2 Cor 1, 4-5). Ultimately, everything is ordered even beyond the community, toward God (15; cf 2 Cor 1, 11).

4, 13-14: Like the Psalmist, Paul clearly proclaims his faith, affirming life within himself despite death (10-11) and the life-giving effect of his experience upon the church (12.14-15). *And place us with you in his presence:* Paul imagines God presenting him and them to Jesus at the parousia and the judgment; cf 2 Cor 11, 2; Rom 14, 10.

4, 16-18: In a series of contrasts Paul explains the extent of his faith in life. Life is not only already present and revealing itself (8-11.16) but will outlast his experience of affliction and dying: it is eternal (17-18).

4, 16: *Not discouraged:* i.e., despite the experience of death. Paul is still speaking of himself personally, but he assumes his faith and attitude will be shared by all Christians. *Our outer self:* the individual subject of ordinary perception and observation, in contrast to the interior and hidden self, which undergoes renewal. *Is being renewed day by day:* this suggests a process that has already begun; cf 2 Cor 3, 18. The renewal already taking place even in Paul's dying is a share in the life of Jesus, but this is recognized only by faith (13.18; 2 Cor 5, 7).

5, 1: *Our earthly dwelling:* the same contrast is restated in the imagery of a dwelling. The language recalls Jesus' saying about the destruction of the temple and the construction of another building *not made with hands* (Mk 14, 58), a prediction later applied to Jesus' own body (Jn 2, 20).

5, 2-5: Verses 2-3 and 4 are largely parallel in structure. *We groan, longing:* see the note on 2 Cor 5, 5. *Clothed with our heavenly habitation:* Paul mixes his metaphors, adding the image of the garment to that of the building. *Further clothed:* the verb means strictly "to put one garment on over another." Paul may desire to put the resurrection body on over his mortal body, without dying; vv 2 and 4 permit this meaning but do not impose it. Or perhaps he imagines the resurrection body as a garment put on over the Christ-garment first received in baptism (Gal 3, 27) and preserved by moral behavior (Rom 13, 12-14; Col 3, 12; cf Mt 22, 11-13). Some support for this interpretation may be found in the context; cf the references to baptism (5), to judgment according to works (10), and to present renewal (2 Cor 4, 16), an idea elsewhere combined with the image of "putting on" a new nature (Eph 4, 22-24; Col 3, 1-5.9-10).

5, 3: *When we have taken it off:* the majority of witnesses read "when we have put it on," i.e., when we have been clothed (in the resurrection body), then we shall not be without a body (naked). This seems mere tautology, though some understand it to mean: whether we are "found" (by God at the judgment) clothed or naked depends upon whether we have preserved or lost our original investiture in Christ (cf the previous note). In this case to "put it on" does not refer to the resurrection body, but to keeping intact the Christ-garment of baptism. The translation follows the western reading (Codex Bezae, Tertullian), the sense of which is clear: to "take it off" is to shed our mortal body in death, after which we shall be clothed in the resurrection body and hence not "naked" (cf 1 Cor 15, 51-53).

weighed down, because we do not wish to be unclothed* but to be further clothed, so that what is mortal may be swallowed up by life.[t] [5] Now the one who has prepared us for this very thing is God,[u] who has given us the Spirit as a first installment.*

[6] * So we are always courageous, although we know that while we are at home in the body we are away from the Lord, [7] for we walk by faith, not by sight. [8] Yet we are courageous, and we would rather leave the body and go home to the Lord.[v] [9] Therefore, we aspire to please him, whether we are at home or away. [10] For we must all appear* before the judgment seat of Christ, so that each one may receive recompense, according to what he did in the body, whether good or evil.[w]

The Ministry of Reconciliation. [11] * Therefore, since we know the fear of the Lord, we try to persuade others; but we are clearly apparent to God, and I hope we are also apparent to your consciousness.[x] [12] We are not commending ourselves to you again but giving you an opportunity to boast of us, so that you may have something to say to those who boast of external appearance rather than of the heart.[y] [13] For

if we are out of our minds,* it is for God; if we are rational, it is for you. [14] * For the love of Christ impels us, once we have come to the conviction that one died for all; therefore, all have died.[z] [15] He indeed died for all, so that those who live might no longer live for themselves but for him who for their sake died and was raised.[a]

[16] Consequently,* from now on we regard no one according to the flesh; even if we once knew Christ according to the flesh, yet now we know him so no longer. [17] [b] So whoever is in Christ is a new creation: the old things have passed away; behold, new things have come. [18] * And all this is from God, who has reconciled us to himself through Christ and given us the ministry of reconciliation, [19] namely, God was reconciling the world to himself in Christ, not counting their trespasses against them and entrusting to us the message of reconciliation.[c] [20] So we are ambassadors for Christ, as if God were appealing through us. We implore you on behalf of Christ, be reconciled to God.[d] [21] For our sake he made him to be sin who did not know sin,[e] so that we might become the righteousness of God in him.*

---

t Is 25, 8; 1 Cor 15, 54.—u 2 Cor 1, 22.—v Phil 1, 21-23.—w Mt 16, 27; 25, 31-46; Rom 2, 16; 14, 10-11.—x 2 Cor 1, 12-14.—y 2 Cor 3, 1 / 2 Cor 1, 14; Phil 1, 26.—z Rom 6, 1-6.—a Rom 4, 25; 6, 4-11; 14, 9; Col 3, 3-4.—b Gal 6, 15; Eph 2, 15 / Is 43, 18-21; Rv 21, 5.—c Rom 5, 10-11; Col 1, 20.—d Eph 6, 20; Phlm 9.—e Is 53, 6-9; Gal 3, 13 / Rom 3, 24-26; 1 Cor 1, 30; 1 Pt 2, 24; 1 Jn 3, 5-8.

5, 4: *We do not wish to be unclothed:* a clear allusion to physical death (2 Cor 4, 16; 5, 1). Unlike the Greeks, who found dissolution of the body desirable (cf Socrates), Paul has a Jewish horror of it. He seems to be thinking of the "intermediate period," an interval between death and resurrection. *Swallowed up by life:* cf 1 Cor 15, 54.

5, 5: God has created us for resurrected bodily life and already prepares us for it by the gift of the Spirit in baptism. *The Spirit as a first installment:* the striking parallel to 2 Cor 5, 1-5 in Rom 8, 17-30 describes Christians who have received the "firstfruits" (cf "first installment" here) of the Spirit as "groaning" (cf 2.4 here) for the resurrection, the complete redemption of their bodies. In place of clothing and building, Rom 8 uses other images for the resurrection: adoption and conformity to the image of the Son.

5, 6-9: Tension between present and future is expressed by another spatial image, the metaphor of the country and its citizens. At present we are like citizens in exile or far away from home. The Lord is the distant homeland, believed in but unseen (7).

5, 10: *We must all appear:* the verb is ambiguous: we are scheduled to "appear" for judgment, at which we will be "revealed" as we are (cf 2 Cor 5, 11; 2, 14; 4, 10-11).

5, 11-15: This paragraph is transitional. Paul sums up much that has gone before. Still playing on the term "appearance," he reasserts his transparency before God and the Corinthians, in contrast to the self-commendation, boasting, and preoccupation with externals that characterize some others (cf 2 Cor 1, 12-14; 2, 14; 3, 1; 3, 7—4, 6). Verse 14 recalls 2 Cor 3, 7—4, 6, and sums up 2 Cor 4, 7—5, 10.

5, 13: *Out of our minds:* this verse confirms that a concern for ecstasy and charismatic experience may lie behind the discussion about "glory" in 2 Cor 3, 7—4, 6. Paul also enjoys such experiences but, unlike others, does not make a public display of them or consider them ends in themselves. *Rational:* the Greek virtue *sōphrosynē,* to which Paul alludes, implies reasonableness, moderation, good judgment, self-control.

5, 14-15: These verses echo 2 Cor 4, 14 and resume the treatment of "life despite death" from 2 Cor 4, 7—5, 10.

5, 16-17: *Consequently:* the death of Christ described in vv 14-15 produces a whole new order (17) and a new mode of perception (16). *According to the flesh:* the natural mode of perception, characterized as "fleshly," is replaced by a mode of perception proper to the Spirit. Elsewhere Paul contrasts what Christ looks like according to the old criteria (weakness, powerlessness, folly, death) and according to the new (wisdom, power, life); cf 2 Cor 5, 15.21; 1 Cor 1, 17—3, 3. Similarly, he describes the paradoxical nature of Christian existence, e.g., in 2 Cor 4, 10-11.14. *A new creation:* rabbis used this expression to describe the effect of the entrance of a proselyte or convert into Judaism or of the remission of sins on the Day of Atonement. The new order created *in Christ* is the new covenant (2 Cor 3, 6).

5, 18-21: Paul attempts to explain the meaning of God's action by a variety of different categories; his attention keeps moving rapidly back and forth from God's act to his own ministry as well. *Who has reconciled us to himself:* i.e., he has brought all into oneness. *Not counting their trespasses:* the reconciliation is described as an act of justification (cf "righteousness," 21); this contrasts with the covenant that condemned (2 Cor 3, 8). *The ministry of reconciliation:* Paul's role in the wider picture is described: entrusted with the message of reconciliation (19), he is Christ's ambassador, through whom God appeals (20a). In v 20b Paul acts in the capacity just described.

5, 21: This is a statement of God's purpose, expressed paradoxically in terms of sharing and exchange of attributes. As Christ became our righteousness (1 Cor 1, 30), we become God's righteousness (cf 2 Cor 5, 14-15).

CHAPTER 6

The Experience of the Ministry. [1] * Working together,[f] then, we appeal to you not to receive the grace of God in vain.* [2] For he says:

"In an acceptable time* I heard you,
and on the day of salvation I helped you."[g]

Behold, now is a very acceptable time; behold, now is the day of salvation. [3] [h] We cause no one to stumble* in anything, in order that no fault may be found with our ministry; [4] * on the contrary, in everything we commend ourselves as ministers of God, through much endurance,* in afflictions, hardships, constraints,[i] [5] beatings, imprisonments, riots, labors, vigils, fasts;[j] [6] * by purity, knowledge, patience, kindness, in a holy spirit, in unfeigned love,[k] [7] in truthful speech, in the power of God; with weapons of righteousness at the right and at the left;[l] [8] through glory and dishonor, insult and praise. We are treated as deceivers and yet are truthful;* [9] as unrecognized and yet acknowledged; as dying and behold we live; as chastised and yet not put to death;[m] [10] as sorrowful yet always rejoicing; as poor yet enriching many; as having nothing and yet possessing all things.[n]

[11] * We have spoken frankly to you, Corinthians; our heart is open wide. [12] You are not constrained by us; you are constrained by your own affections.[o] [13] As recompense in kind (I speak as to my children), be open yourselves.[p]

Call to Holiness. [14] * Do not be yoked with those who are different, with unbelievers.* For what partnership do righteousness and lawlessness have? Or what fellowship does light have with darkness? [15] What accord has Christ with Beliar? Or what has a believer in common with an unbeliever? [16] [q] What agreement has the temple of God with idols? For we are the temple of the living God; as God said:

"I will live with them and move among them,*
and I will be their God
and they shall be my people.

2Cor

f 1 Cor 3, 9; 1 Thes 3, 2.—g Is 49, 8.—h 1 Cor 9, 12; 10, 32 / 2 Cor 8, 20-21.—i 2 Cor 4, 8-11; 11, 23-27; 1 Cor 4, 9-13.—j Acts 16, 23.—k Gal 5, 22-23.—l 2 Cor 10, 4; Rom 13, 12; Eph 6, 11-17.—m 2 Cor 4, 10-11; Rom 8, 36.—n Rom 8, 32; 1 Cor 3, 21.—o 2 Cor 7, 3.—p Gal 4, 19.—q 1 Cor 10, 20-21 / 1 Cor 3, 16-17; 6, 19 / Ex 25, 8; 29, 45; Lv 26, 12; Jer 31, 1; 32, 38; Ez 37, 27.

6, 1-10: This paragraph is a single long sentence in the Greek, interrupted by the parenthesis of v 2. The one main verb is "we appeal." In this paragraph Paul both exercises his ministry of reconciliation (cf 2 Cor 5, 20) and describes how his ministry is exercised: the "message of reconciliation" (2 Cor 5, 19) is lived existentially in his apostolic experience.

6, 1: *Not to receive . . . in vain:* i.e., conform to the gift of justification and new creation. The context indicates how this can be done concretely: become God's righteousness (2 Cor 5, 21), not live for oneself (2 Cor 5, 15), be reconciled with Paul (2 Cor 6, 11-13; 7, 2-3).

6, 2: *In an acceptable time:* Paul cites the Septuagint text of Is 49, 8; the Hebrew reads "in a time of favor"; it is parallel to "on the day of salvation." *Now:* God is bestowing favor and salvation at this very moment, as Paul is addressing his letter to them.

6, 3: *Cause no one to stumble:* the language echoes that of 1 Cor 8—10, as does the expression "no longer live for themselves" in 2 Cor 5, 15. *That no fault may be found:* i.e., at the eschatological judgment (cf 1 Cor 4, 2-5).

6, 4a: This is the central assertion, the topic statement for the catalogue that follows. *We commend ourselves:* Paul's self-commendation is ironical (with an eye on the charges mentioned in 2 Cor 3, 1-3) and paradoxical (pointing mostly to experiences that would not normally be considered points of pride but are perceived as such by faith). Cf also the self-commendation in 2 Cor 11, 23-29. *As ministers of God:* the same Greek word, *diakonos*, means "minister" and "servant"; cf 2 Cor 11, 23, the central assertion in a similar context, and 1 Cor 3, 5.

6, 4b-5: *Through much endurance:* this phrase functions as a subtitle; it is followed by an enumeration of nine specific types of trials endured.

6, 6-7a: A list of virtuous qualities in two groups of four, the second fuller than the first.

6, 8b-10: A series of seven rhetorically effective antitheses, contrasting negative external impressions with positive inner reality. Paul perceives his existence as a reflection of Jesus' own and affirms an inner reversal that escapes outward observation. The final two members illustrate two distinct kinds of paradox or apparent contradiction that are characteristic of apostolic experience.

6, 11-13: Paul's tone becomes quieter, but his appeal for acceptance and affection is emotionally charged. References to the heart and their mutual relations bring the development begun in 2 Cor 2, 14—3, 3 to an effective conclusion.

6, 14—7, 1: Language and thought shift noticeably here. Suddenly we are in a different atmosphere, dealing with a quite different problem. Both the vocabulary and the thought, with their contrast between good and evil, are more characteristic of Qumran documents or the Book of Revelation than they are of Paul. Hence, critics suspect that this section was inserted by another hand.

6, 14-16a: The opening injunction to separate from unbelievers is reinforced by five rhetorical questions to make the point that Christianity is not compatible with paganism. Their opposition is emphasized also by the accumulation of five distinct designations for each group. These verses are a powerful statement of God's holiness and the exclusiveness of his claims.

6, 16c-18: This is a chain of scriptural citations carefully woven together. God's covenant relation to his people and his presence among them (16) is seen as conditioned on cultic separation from the profane and cultically impure (17); that relation is translated into the personal language of the parent-child relationship, an extension to the community of the language of 2 Sm 7, 14 (18). Some remarkable parallels to this chain are found in the final chapters of Revelation. God's presence among his people (Rv 21, 22) is expressed there, too, by applying 2 Sm 7, 14 to the community (Rv 21, 7). There is a call to separation (Rv 18, 4) and exclusion of the unclean from the community and its liturgy (Rv 21, 27). The title "Lord Almighty" (*Pantokratōr*) occurs in the New Testament only here in 18 and nine times in Rv.

17 Therefore, come forth from them
    and be separate," says the Lord,
    "and touch nothing unclean;
    then I will receive you[r]
18 and I will be a father to you,
    and you shall be sons and daughters
      to me,
says the Lord Almighty."[s]

CHAPTER 7

1 Since we have these promises, beloved, let us cleanse ourselves from every defilement of flesh and spirit, making holiness perfect in the fear of God.

2 * Make room for us; we have not wronged anyone, or ruined anyone, or taken advantage of anyone. 3 I do not say this in condemnation, for I have already said that you are in our hearts, that we may die together and live together.[t] 4 I have great confidence in you, I have great pride in you; I am filled with encouragement, I am overflowing with joy all the more because of all our affliction.

C. Resolution of the Crisis*

Paul's Joy in Macedonia. 5 * For even when we came into Macedonia,* our flesh had no rest, but we were afflicted in every way—external conflicts, internal fears.[u] 6 But God, who encourages the downcast, encouraged us by the arrival of Titus,[v] 7 and not only by his arrival but also by the encouragement with which he was encouraged in regard to you, as he told us of your yearning, your lament, your zeal for me, so that I rejoiced even more. 8 * For even if I saddened you by my letter, I do not regret it; and if I did regret it ([for] I see that that letter saddened you, if only for a while),[w] 9 I rejoice now, not because you were saddened, but because you were saddened into repentance; for you were saddened in a godly way, so that you did not suffer loss in anything because of us. 10 For godly sorrow produces a salutary repentance without regret, but worldly sorrow produces death. 11 For behold what earnestness this godly sorrow has produced for you, as well as readiness for a defense, and indignation, and fear, and yearning, and zeal, and punishment. In every way you have shown yourselves to be innocent in the matter. 12 So then even though I wrote to you, it was not on account of the one who did the wrong, or on account of the one who suffered the wrong, but in order that your concern for us might be made plain to you in the sight of God.[x] 13 For this reason we are encouraged.

And besides our encouragement,* we rejoice even more because of the joy of Titus, since his spirit has been refreshed by all of you. 14 For if I have boasted to him about you, I was not put to shame. No, just as everything we said to you was true, so our boasting before Titus proved to be the truth. 15 And his heart goes out to you all the more, as he remembers the obedience of all of you, when you received him with fear and trembling.[y] 16 I rejoice, because I have confidence in you in every respect.

---

r Is 52, 11; Ez 20, 34.41; Rv 18, 4; 21, 27.—s 2 Sm 7, 14; Ps 2, 7; Is 43, 6; Jer 31, 9; Rv 21, 7 / Rv 4, 8; 11, 17; 15, 3; 21, 22.—t 2 Cor 6, 11-13.—u 2 Cor 2, 13.—v 2 Cor 7, 13-14; 1 Thes 3, 6-8.—w 2 Cor 2, 2-4; Heb 12, 11.—x 2 Cor 2, 3.9; 7, 8.—y 2 Cor 2, 9.

7, 2-4: These verses continue the thought of 2 Cor 6, 11-13, before the interruption of 2 Cor 6, 14—7, 1. Verse 4 serves as a transition to the next section: the four themes it introduces (confidence; pride or "boasting"; encouragement; joy in affliction) are developed in vv 5-16. All have appeared previously in the letter.

7, 5-16: This section functions as a peroration or formal summing up of the whole first part of the letter, chs 1-7. It deals with the restoration of right relations between Paul and the Corinthians, and it is marked by fullness and intensity of emotion.

7, 5-7: Paul picks up the thread of the narrative interrupted at 2 Cor 2, 13 (5) and describes the resolution of the tense situation there depicted (6-7). Finally Titus arrives and his coming puts an end to Paul's restlessness (2 Cor 2, 13; 7, 5), casts out his fears, and reverses his mood. The theme of encouragement and affliction is reintroduced (cf 2 Cor 1, 3-11); here, too, encouragement is traced back to God and is described as contagious (6). The language of joy and sorrow also reappears in v 7 (cf 2 Cor 1, 23—2, 1 and the note on 2 Cor 1, 23-24).

7, 5: *Macedonia:* see the note on 2 Cor 2, 13.

7, 8-12: Paul looks back on the episode from the viewpoint of its ending. The goal of their common activity, promotion of their joy (2 Cor 1, 24), has been achieved, despite and because of the sorrow they felt. That sorrow was God-given. Its salutary effects are enumerated fully and impressively in vv 10-11; not the least important of these is that it has revealed to them the attachment they have to Paul.

7, 13-16: Paul summarizes the effect of the experience on Titus: encouragement, joy, love, relief. Finally, he describes its effects on himself: encouragement, joy, confidence, pride or "boasting" (i.e., the satisfaction resulting from a boast that proves well-founded; cf 2 Cor 7, 4; 1, 12.14).

III. THE COLLECTION FOR JERUSALEM*

CHAPTER 8

Generosity in Giving. 1 * We want you to know, brothers,* of the grace of God* that has been given to the churches of Macedonia,^{z} 2 * for in a severe test of affliction, the abundance of their joy and their profound poverty overflowed in a wealth of generosity on their part. 3 * For according to their means, I can testify, and beyond their means, spontaneously, 4 they begged us insistently for the favor of taking part in the service to the holy ones,^{a} 5 and this, not as we expected, but they gave themselves first to the Lord and to us* through the will of God, 6 so that we urged Titus* that, as he had already begun, he should also complete for you this gracious act also.^{b} 7 Now as you excel in every re-

spect, in faith, discourse, knowledge, all earnestness, and in the love we have for you,^{c} may you excel in this gracious act also.*

8 I say this not by way of command, but to test the genuineness of your love by your concern for others. 9 ^{d} For you know the gracious act of our Lord Jesus Christ, that for your sake he became poor although he was rich, so that by his poverty you might become rich.* 10 And I am giving counsel in this matter, for it is appropriate for you who began not only to act but to act willingly last year:^{e} 11 complete it now, so that your eager* willingness may be matched by your completion of it out of what you have. 12 * For if the eagerness is there, it is acceptable according to what one has, not according to what one does not have; 13 not that others should have re-

---

^{z} 2 Cor 11, 9; Rom 15, 26.—a Acts 24, 17; Rom 15, 31.—b 2 Cor 2, 13; 7, 6-7.13-14; 8, 16.23; 12, 18.—c 1 Cor 1, 5.—d 2 Cor 6, 10; Phil 2, 6-8.—e 2 Cor 9, 2; 1 Cor 16, 1-4.

8, 1—9, 15: Paul turns to a new topic, the collection for the church in Jerusalem. There is an early precedent for this project in the agreement mentioned in Gal 2, 6-10. According to Acts, the church at Antioch had sent Saul and Barnabas to Jerusalem with relief (Acts 11, 27-30). Subsequently Paul organized a project of relief for Jerusalem among his own churches. Our earliest evidence for it comes in 1 Cor 16, 1-4, after it had already begun (see the notes there); by the time Paul wrote Rom 15, 25-28 the collection was completed and ready for delivery. Chapters 8 and 9 contain what appear to be two letters on the subject. In them Paul gives us his fullest exposition of the meaning he sees in the enterprise, presenting it as an act of Christian charity and as an expression of the unity of the church, both present and eschatological. These chapters are especially rich in the recurrence of key words, on which Paul plays; it is usually impossible to do justice to these wordplays in the translation.

8, 1-24: This is a letter of recommendation for Titus and two unnamed companions, written from Macedonia probably at least a year later than 1 Cor 16. The recommendation proper is prefaced by remarks about the ideals of sharing and equality within the Christian community (1-15). Phil 4, 10-20 shows that Paul has reflected on his personal experience of need and relief in his relations with the community at Philippi; he now develops his reflections on the larger scale of relations between his Gentile churches and the mother church in Jerusalem.

8, 1-5: The example of the Macedonians, a model of what ought to be happening at Corinth, provides Paul with the occasion for expounding his theology of "giving."

8, 1: *The grace of God:* the fundamental theme is expressed by the Greek noun *charis,* which will be variously translated throughout these chapters as "grace" (2 Cor 8, 1; 9, 8.14), "favor" (2 Cor 8, 4), "gracious act" (2 Cor 8, 6.7.9) or "gracious work" (2 Cor 8, 19), to be compared to "gracious gift" (1 Cor 16, 3). The related term, *eucharistia,* "thanksgiving," also occurs at 2 Cor 9, 11.12. The wordplay is not superficial; various mutations of the same root signal inner connection between aspects of a single reality, and Paul consciously exploits the similarities in vocabulary to highlight that connection.

8, 2: Three more terms are now introduced. *Test (dokimē):* the same root is translated as "to test" (8) and "evidence" (2 Cor 9, 13); it means to be tried and found genuine. *Abundance:* variations on the same root lie behind "overflow" (2 Cor 8, 2; 9, 12),

"excel" (2 Cor 8, 7), "surplus" (2 Cor 8, 14), "superfluous" (2 Cor 9, 1), "make abundant" and "have an abundance" (2 Cor 9, 8). These expressions of fullness contrast with references to need (2 Cor 8, 14; 9, 12). *Generosity:* the word *haplotēs* has nuances of both simplicity and sincerity; here and in 2 Cor 9, 11.13 it designates the singleness of purpose that manifests itself in generous giving.

8, 3-4: Paul emphasizes the spontaneity of the Macedonians and the nature of their action. *They begged us insistently:* the same root is translated as "urge," "appeal," "encourage" (2 Cor 8, 6.17; 9, 5). *Taking part:* the same word is translated "contribution" in 2 Cor 9, 13 and a related term as "partner" in 2 Cor 8, 23. *Service (diakonia):* this word occurs also in 2 Cor 9, 1.13 as "service"; in 2 Cor 9, 12 it is translated "administration," and in 2 Cor 8, 19.20 the corresponding verb is rendered "administer."

8, 5: *They gave themselves . . . to the Lord and to us:* on its deepest level their attitude is one of self-giving.

8, 6: *Titus:* 1 Cor 16 seemed to leave the organization up to the Corinthians, but apparently Paul has sent Titus to initiate the collection as well; 2 Cor 8, 16-17 will describe Titus' attitude as one of shared concern and cooperation.

8, 7: The charitable service Paul is promoting is seen briefly and in passing within the perspective of Paul's theology of the charisms. *Earnestness (spoudē):* this or related terms occur also in v 22 ("earnest") and 2 Cor 8, 8.16.17 ("concern").

8, 9: The dialectic of Jesus' experience, expressed earlier in terms of life and death (2 Cor 5, 15), sin and righteousness (2 Cor 5, 21), is now rephrased in terms of poverty and wealth. Many scholars think this is a reference to Jesus' preexistence with God (his "wealth") and to his incarnation and death (his "poverty"), and they point to the similarity between this verse and Phil 2, 6-8. Others interpret the wealth and poverty as succeeding phases of Jesus' earthly existence, e.g., his sense of intimacy with God and then the desolation and the feeling of abandonment by God in his death (cf Mk 15, 34).

8, 11: *Eager:* the word *prothymia* also occurs in 2 Cor 8, 12.19; 9, 2.

8, 12-15: Paul introduces the principle of *equality* into the discussion. The goal is not impoverishment but sharing of resources; balance is achieved at least over the course of time. In v 15 Paul grounds his argument unexpectedly in the experience of Israel gathering manna in the desert: equality was achieved, independently of personal exertion, by God, who gave with an even hand according to need. Paul touches briefly here on the theme of "living from God."

2Cor

lief while you are burdened, but that as a matter of equality [14]your surplus at the present time should supply their needs, so that their surplus may also supply your needs, that there may be equality. [15]As it is written:

"Whoever had much did not have more,
and whoever had little did not have less."[f]

Titus and His Collaborators.* [16]But thanks be to God who put the same concern for you into the heart of Titus, [17]for he not only welcomed our appeal but, since he is very concerned, he has gone to you of his own accord. [18]With him we have sent the brother* who is praised in all the churches for his preaching of the gospel.[g] [19]And not only that, but he has also been appointed our traveling companion by the churches in this gracious work administered by us for the glory of the Lord [himself] and for the expression of our eagerness.[h] [20]This we desire to avoid, that anyone blame us* about this lavish gift administered by us, [21]for we are concerned for what is honorable not only in the sight of the Lord but also in the sight of others.[i] [22]And with them we have sent our brother whom we often tested in many ways and found earnest, but who is now much more earnest because of his great confidence in you. [23]As for Titus, he is my partner and co-worker for you; as for our brothers, they are apostles of the churches, the glory of Christ. [24]So give proof before the churches of your love and of our boasting about you to them.*

CHAPTER 9

God's Indescribable Gift.* [1]Now about the service to the holy ones, it is superfluous for me to write to you, [2]for I know your eagerness, about which I boast of you to the Macedonians, that Achaia* has been ready since last year; and your zeal has stirred up most of them.[j] [3]Nonetheless, I sent the brothers* so that our boast about you might not prove empty in this case, so that you might be ready, as I said, [4]for fear that if any Macedonians come with me and find you not ready we might be put to shame (to say nothing of you) in this conviction. [5]So I thought it necessary to encourage the brothers to go on ahead to you and arrange in advance for your promised gift, so that in this way it might be ready as a bountiful gift and not as an exaction.

[6]Consider this: whoever sows sparingly will also reap sparingly, and whoever sows bountifully will also reap bountifully.[k] [7]Each must do as already determined, without sadness or compulsion, for God loves a cheerful giver.[l] [8]Moreover, God is able to make every grace abundant for you, so that in all things, always having all you need, you may have an abundance for every good work. [9]As it is written:

"He scatters abroad, he gives to the poor;
his righteousness endures forever."[m]

[10]The one who supplies seed to the sower and bread for food will supply and multiply your seed and increase the harvest of your righteousness.[n]

---

f Ex 16, 18.—g 2 Cor 12, 18.—h 1 Cor 16, 3-4.—i Rom 12, 17.—j 2 Cor 8, 10; Rom 15, 26.—k Prv 11, 24-25.—l Prv 22, 8 LXX.—m Ps 112, 9.—n Is 55, 10.

8, 16-24: In recommending Titus and his companions, Paul stresses their personal and apostolic qualities, their good dispositions toward the Corinthians, and their authority as messengers of the churches and representatives of Christ.

8, 18: *The brother:* we do not know the identity of this co-worker of Paul, nor of the third companion mentioned below in v 22.

8, 20-22: *That anyone blame us:* 2 Cor 12, 16-18 suggests that misunderstandings may indeed have arisen concerning Paul's management of the collection through the messengers mentioned here, but those same verses seem to imply that the Corinthians by and large would recognize the honesty of Paul's conduct in this area as in others (cf 2 Cor 6, 3).

8, 24: As Paul began by holding up the Macedonians as examples to be imitated, he closes by exhorting the Corinthians to show their love (by accepting the envoys and by cooperating as the Macedonians do), thus justifying the pride Paul demonstrates because of them before other churches.

9, 1-15: Quite possibly this was originally an independent letter, though it deals with the same subject and continues many of the same themes. In that case, it may have been written a few weeks later than ch 8, while the delegation there mentioned was still on its way.

9, 2: *Achaia:* see the note on Rom 15, 26.

9, 3: *I sent the brothers:* the Greek aorist tense here could be epistolary, referring to the present; in that case Paul would be sending them now, and ch 9 would merely conclude the letter of recommendation begun in ch 8. But the aorist may also refer to a sending that is past as Paul writes; then ch 9, with its apparently fresh beginning, is a follow-up message entrusted to another carrier.

9, 8-10: The behavior to which he exhorts them is grounded in God's own pattern of behavior. God is capable of overwhelming generosity, as scripture itself attests (9), so that they need not fear being short. He will provide in abundance, both supplying their natural needs and increasing their righteousness. Paul challenges them to godlike generosity and reminds them of the fundamental motive for encouragement: God himself cannot be outdone.

11 * You are being enriched in every wa͵ for all generosity, which through us produces thanksgiving to God, 12 for the administration of this public service is not only supplying the needs of the holy ones but is also overflowing in many acts of thanksgiving to God. 13 Through the evidence of this service, you are glorifying God for your obedient confession of the gospel of Christ and the generosity of your contribution to them and to all others,ᵒ 14 while in prayer on your behalf they long for you, because of the surpassing grace of God upon you. 15 Thanks be to God for his indescribable gift!ᵖ

IV. PAUL'S DEFENSE OF HIS MINISTRY*

CHAPTER 10

Accusation of Weakness. * 1 Now I myself, Paul, urge you through the gentleness and clemency of Christ,* I who am humble when face to face with you, but brave toward you when absent, 2 �q I beg you that, when present, I may not have to be brave with that confidence with which I intend to act boldly against some who consider us as acting according to the flesh.* 3 For, although we are in the flesh, we do not battle according to the flesh,* 4 for the weapons of our battle* are not of flesh but are enormously powerful, capable of destroying fortresses.ʳ We destroy arguments 5 and every pretension raising itself against the knowledge of God, and take every thought captive in obedience to Christ, 6 and we are ready to punish every disobedience, once your obedience is complete.ˢ

7 ᵗ Look at what confronts you. Whoever is confident of belonging to Christ should consider that as he belongs to Christ, so do we.* 8 ᵘ And even if I should boast a little too much of our authority, which the Lord gave for building you up and not for tearing you down, I shall not be put to shame. 9 * May I not seem as one frightening you through letters. 10 For someone will say, "His letters are severe and forceful, but his bodily presence is weak, and his speech contemptible."ᵛ 11 Such a person must understand that what we are in word through letters when

2Cor

ᵒ 2 Cor 8, 4; Rom 15, 31.—ᵖ Rom 5, 15-16.—�q 2 Cor 13, 2.10; 1 Cor 4, 21.—ʳ 2 Cor 6, 7; 13, 2-3; 1 Cor 1, 25; Eph 6, 10-14.—ˢ 2 Cor 2, 9.—ᵗ 1 Cor 1, 12.—ᵘ 2 Cor 13, 10.—ᵛ 1 Cor 2, 3.

9, 11-15: Paul's vision broadens to take in all the interested parties in one dynamic picture. His language becomes liturgically colored and conveys a sense of fullness. With a final play on the words *charis* and *eucharistia* (see the note on 2 Cor 8, 1), he describes a circle that closes on itself: the movement of grace overflowing from God to them and handed on from them through Paul to others is completed by the prayer of praise and thanksgiving raised on their behalf to God.

10, 1—13, 10: These final chapters have their own unity of structure and theme and could well have formed the body of a separate letter. They constitute an *apologia* on Paul's part, i.e., a legal defense of his behavior and his ministry; the writing is emotionally charged and highly rhetorical. In the central section (2 Cor 11, 16—12, 10), the *apologia* takes the form of a boast. This section is prepared for by a prologue (2 Cor 11, 1-15) and followed by an epilogue (2 Cor 12, 11-18), which are similar in content and structure. These sections, in turn, are framed by an introduction (2 Cor 10, 1-18) and a conclusion (2 Cor 12, 19—13, 10), both of which assert Paul's apostolic authority and confidence and define the purpose of the letter. The structure that results from this disposition of the material is chiastic, i.e., the first element corresponds to the last, the second to the second last, etc., following the pattern *a b c b¹ a¹*.

10, 1-18: Paul asserts his apostolic authority and expresses the confidence this generates in him. He writes in response to certain opinions that have arisen in the community and certain charges raised against him and in preparation for a forthcoming visit in which he intends to set things in order. This section gives us an initial glimpse of the situation in Corinth that Paul must address; much of its thematic material will be taken up again in the finale (2 Cor 12, 19—13, 10).

10, 1-2: A strong opening plunges us straight into the conflict. Contrasts dominate here: presence versus absence, gentleness-clemency-humility versus boldness-confidence-bravery. *Through the gentleness and clemency of Christ:* the figure of the gentle Christ, presented in a significant position before any specifics of the situation are suggested, forms a striking contrast to the picture of the bold and militant Paul (2-6); this tension is finally resolved in 2 Cor 13, 3-4. *Absent . . . present:* this same contrast, with a restatement of the purpose of the letter, recurs in 2 Cor 13, 10, which forms an inclusion with 2 Cor 10, 1-2.

10, 2b-4a: *Flesh:* the Greek word *sarx* can express both the physical life of the body without any pejorative overtones (as in "we are in the flesh," 3) and our natural life insofar as it is marked by limitation and weakness (as in the other expressions) in contrast to the higher life and power conferred by the Spirit; cf the note on 1 Cor 3, 1. The wordplay is intended to express the paradoxical situation of a life already taken over by the Spirit but not yet seen as such except by faith. Lack of empirical evidence of the Spirit permits misunderstanding and misjudgment, but Paul resolutely denies that his behavior and effectiveness are as limited as some suppose.

10, 3b-6: Paul is involved in combat. The strong military language and imagery are both an assertion of his confidence in the divine power at his disposal and a declaration of war against those who underestimate his resources. The threat is echoed in 2 Cor 13, 2-3.

10, 7-8: *Belonging to Christ . . . so do we:* these phrases already announce the pattern of Paul's boast in 2 Cor 11, 21b-29, especially 2 Cor 11, 22-23. *For building you up and not for tearing you down:* Paul draws on the language by which Jeremiah described the purpose of the prophetic power the Lord gave to him (Jer 1, 9-10; 12, 16-17; 24, 6). Though Paul's power may have destructive effects on others (2-6), its intended effect on the community is entirely constructive (cf 2 Cor 13, 10). *I shall not be put to shame:* his assertions will not be refuted; they will be revealed as true at the judgment.

10, 9-10: Paul cites the complaints of some who find him lacking in personal forcefulness and holds out the threat of a personal *parousia* (both "return" and "presence") that will be forceful, indeed will be a demonstration of Christ's own power (cf 2 Cor 13, 2-4).

absent, that we also are in action when present.[w]

12 * Not that we dare to class or compare ourselves with some of those who recommend themselves. But when they measure themselves by one another and compare themselves with one another, they are without understanding.[x] 13 But we will not boast beyond measure but will keep to the limits* God has apportioned us, namely, to reach even to you. 14 For we are not overreaching ourselves, as though we did not reach you; we indeed first came to you with the gospel of Christ. 15 We are not boasting beyond measure, in other people's labors; yet our hope is that, as your faith increases, our influence among you may be greatly enlarged, within our proper limits, 16 so that we may preach the gospel even beyond you, not boasting of work already done in another's sphere.[y] 17 [z] "Whoever boasts, should boast in the Lord."* 18 For it is not the one who recommends himself who is approved,* but the one whom the Lord recommends.[a]

---

w 2 Cor 13, 1-2.—x 2 Cor 3, 1-2; 4, 2; 5, 12; 6, 4; 10, 18; 12, 11.—y Rom 15, 20-21.—z Jer 9, 22-23; 1 Cor 1, 31.—a 2 Cor 13, 3-9.—b 2 Cor 11, 21; 12, 11.—c Hos 2, 21-22; Eph 5, 26-27.—d Gn 3, 1-6.—e Gal 1, 6-9.—f 2 Cor 12, 11.—g 1 Cor 1, 5.17; 2, 1-5.

10, 12-18: Paul now qualifies his claim to boldness, indicating its limits. He distinguishes his own behavior from that of others, revealing those "others" as they appear to him: as self-recommending, immoderately boastful, encroaching on territory not assigned to them, and claiming credit not due to them.

10, 13: *Will keep to the limits:* the notion of proper limits is expressed here by two terms with overlapping meanings, *metron* and *kanōn,* which are played off against several expressions denoting overreaching or expansion beyond a legitimate sphere.

10, 17: *Boast in the Lord:* there is a legitimate boasting, in contrast to the immoderate boasting to which vv 13 and 15 allude. God's work through Paul in the community is the object of his boast (13-16; 2 Cor 1, 12-14) and constitutes his recommendation (2 Cor 3, 1-3). Cf the notes on 2 Cor 1, 12-14 and 1 Cor 1, 29-31.

10, 18: *Approved:* to be approved is to come successfully through the process of testing for authenticity (cf 2 Cor 13, 3-7 and the note on 2 Cor 8, 2). *Whom the Lord recommends:* self-commendation is a premature and unwarranted anticipation of the final judgment, which the Lord alone will pass (cf 1 Cor 4, 3-5). Paul alludes to this judgment throughout chs 10-13, frequently in final or transitional positions; cf 2 Cor 11, 15; 12, 19a; 13, 3-7.

11, 1-15: Although these verses continue to reveal information about Paul's opponents and the differences he perceives between them and himself, 2 Cor 11, 1 signals a turn in Paul's thought. This section constitutes a prologue to the boasting that he will undertake in 2 Cor 11, 16—12, 10, and it bears remarkable similarities to the section that follows the central boast, 2 Cor 12, 11-18.

11, 1: *Put up with a little foolishness from me:* this verse indicates more clearly than the general statement of intent in 2 Cor 10, 13 the nature of the project Paul is about to undertake. He alludes ironically to the Corinthians' toleration for others.

CHAPTER 11

Preaching without Charge.* 1 If only you would put up with a little foolishness from me!* Please put up with me.[b] 2 * For I am jealous of you with the jealousy of God, since I betrothed you to one husband to present you as a chaste virgin to Christ.[c] 3 But I am afraid that, as the serpent deceived Eve* by his cunning, your thoughts may be corrupted from a sincere [and pure] commitment to Christ.[d] 4 For if someone comes and preaches another Jesus* than the one we preached,[e] or if you receive a different spirit from the one you received or a different gospel from the one you accepted, you put up with it well enough. 5 [f] For I think that I am not in any way inferior to these "superapostles."* 6 Even if I am untrained in speaking, I am not so in knowledge;[g] in every way we have made this plain to you in all things.*

Foolishness: Paul qualifies his project as folly from beginning to end; see the note on 2 Cor 11, 16—12, 10.

11, 2: Paul gives us a sudden glimpse of the theological values that are at stake. *The jealousy of God:* the perspective is that of the covenant, described in imagery of love and marriage, as in the prophets; cf 1 Cor 10, 22. *I betrothed you:* Paul, like a father (cf 2 Cor 12, 14), betroths the community to Christ as his bride (cf Eph 5, 21-33) and will present her to him at his second coming. Cf Mt 25, 1-13 and the nuptial imagery in Rv 21.

11, 3: *As the serpent deceived Eve:* before Christ can return for the community Paul fears a repetition of the primal drama of seduction. Corruption of minds is satanic activity (see 2 Cor 2, 11; 4, 4). Satanic imagery recurs in 2 Cor 11, 13-15.20; 12, 7b.16-17; see the notes on these passages.

11, 4: *Preaches another Jesus:* the danger is specified, and Paul's opponents are identified with the cunning serpent. The battle for minds has to do with the understanding of Jesus, the Spirit, the gospel; the Corinthians have flirted with another understanding than the one that Paul handed on to them as traditional and normative.

11, 5: *These "superapostles":* this term, employed again in 2 Cor 12, 11b, designates the opponents of whom Paul has spoken in 2 Cor 10 and again in 2 Cor 11, 4. They appear to be intruders at Corinth. Their preaching is marked at least by a different emphasis and style, and they do not hesitate to accept support from the community. Perhaps these itinerants appeal to the authority of church leaders in Jerusalem and even carry letters of recommendation from them. But it is not those distant leaders whom Paul is attacking here. The intruders are "superapostles" not in the sense of the "pillars" at Jerusalem (Gal 2), but in their own estimation. They consider themselves superior to Paul as apostles and ministers of Christ, and they are obviously enjoying some success among the Corinthians. Paul rejects their claim to be apostles in any superlative sense *(hyperlian),* judging them bluntly as "false apostles," ministers of Satan masquerading as apostles of Christ (13-15). On the contrary, he himself will claim to be a superminister of Christ *(hyper egō,* 23).

11, 6: Apparently found deficient in both rhetorical ability (cf 2 Cor 10, 10) and knowledge (cf 2 Cor 10, 5), Paul concedes the former charge but not the latter. *In every way:* in all their contacts with him revelation has been taking place. Paul, through whom God reveals the knowledge of himself (2 Cor 2, 14), and in whom the death and life of Jesus are revealed (2 Cor 4, 10-11; cf 2 Cor 6, 4), also demonstrates his own role as the bearer of true knowledge. Cf 1 Cor 1, 18—2, 16.

7 * Did I make a mistake when I humbled myself so that you might be exalted, because I preached the gospel of God to you without charge?*h* 8 I plundered other churches by accepting from them in order to minister to you. 9 And when I was with you and in need, I did not burden anyone, for the brothers who came from Macedonia supplied my needs. So I refrained and will refrain from burdening you in any way.*i* 10 By the truth of Christ in me, this boast of mine shall not be silenced in the regions of Achaia.*j* 11 * And why? Because I do not love you? God knows I do!*k*

12 And what I do I will continue to do, in order to end this pretext of those who seek a pretext for being regarded as we are in the mission of which they boast. 13 * For such people are false apostles, deceitful workers, who masquerade as apostles of Christ. 14 And no wonder, for even Satan masquerades as an angel of light. 15 So it is not strange that his ministers also masquerade as ministers of righteousness. Their end will correspond to their deeds.

Paul's Boast: His Labors. 16 * I repeat, no one should consider me foolish;* but if you do, accept me as a fool, so that I too may boast a little.* 17 What I am saying I am not saying according to the Lord but as in foolishness, in this boastful state. 18 Since many boast according to the flesh, I too will boast. 19 For you gladly put up with fools, since you are wise yourselves. 20 * For you put up with it if someone enslaves you, or devours you, or gets the better of you, or puts on airs, or slaps you in the face. 21 To my shame I say that we were too weak!*

But what anyone dares to boast of (I am speaking in foolishness) I also dare. 22 * Are they Hebrews? So am I. Are they Israelites? So am I. Are they descendants of Abraham? So am I.*l* 23 Are they ministers of Christ? (I am talking like an insane person.)*m* I am still more,* with far greater labors, far more imprisonments, far worse beatings, and numerous brushes with death.* 24 Five times at the hands of the Jews I received forty lashes minus one.*n* 25 Three times I was beaten with rods, once I was stoned, three times I was shipwrecked, I passed a night and a day on the deep;*o* 26 on frequent journeys, in dangers from rivers, dangers from robbers, dangers from my own race, dangers from Gentiles, dangers in the city, dangers in the wilder-

---

h 2 Cor 12, 13-18; Acts 18, 3; 1 Cor 9, 6-18.—i Phil 4, 15.18.—j 1 Cor 9, 15.—k 2 Cor 12, 15.—l Acts 22, 3 / Rom 11, 1; Phil 3, 5-6.—m 2 Cor 6, 5; Acts 16, 22-24; 1 Cor 15, 31-32.—n Dt 25, 2-3.—o Acts 14, 19; 27, 43-44.

11, 7-10: Abruptly Paul passes to another reason for complaints: his practice of preaching without remuneration (cf 1 Cor 9, 3-18). He deftly defends his practice by situating it from the start within the pattern of Christ's own self-humiliation (cf 2 Cor 10, 1) and reduces objections to absurdity by rhetorical questions (cf 2 Cor 12, 13).

11, 11-12: Paul rejects lack of affection as his motive (possibly imputed to him by his opponents) and states his real motive, a desire to emphasize the disparity between himself and the others (cf 2 Cor 11, 19-21). The topic of his gratuitous service will be taken up once more in 2 Cor 12, 13-18. 1 Cor 9, 15-18 gives a different but complementary explanation of his motivation.

11, 13-15: Paul picks up again the imagery of v 3 and applies it to the opponents: they are false apostles of Christ, really serving another master. *Deceitful . . . masquerade:* deception and simulation, like cunning (3), are marks of the satanic. *Angel of light:* recalls the contrast between light and darkness, Christ and Beliar at 2 Cor 6, 14-15. *Ministers of righteousness:* recalls the earlier contrast between the ministry of condemnation and that of righteousness (2 Cor 3, 9). *Their end:* the section closes with another allusion to the judgment, when all participants in the final conflict will be revealed or unmasked and dealt with as they deserve.

11, 16—12, 10: Paul now accepts the challenge of his opponents and indulges in boasting similar to theirs, but with differences that he has already signaled in 2 Cor 10, 12-18 and that become clearer as he proceeds. He defines the nature of his project and unmistakably labels it as folly at the beginning and the end (2 Cor 11, 16-23; 12, 11). Yet his boast does not spring from ignorance (2 Cor 11, 21; 12, 6) nor is it concerned merely with human distinctions (2 Cor 11, 18). Paul boasts "in moderation" (2 Cor 10, 13.15) and "in the Lord" (2 Cor 10, 17).

11,16-29: The first part of Paul's boast focuses on labors and afflictions, in which authentic service of Christ consists.

11, 16-21: These verses recapitulate remarks already made about the foolishness of boasting and the excessive toleration of the Corinthians. They form a prelude to the boast proper.

11, 20: Paul describes the activities of the "others" in terms that fill out the picture drawn in vv 3-4.13-15. Much of the vocabulary suggests fleshly or even satanic activity. *Enslaves:* cf Gal 2, 4. *Devours:* cf 1 Pt 5, 8. *Gets the better:* the verb *lambanō* means "to take," but is used in a variety of senses; here it may imply financial advantage, as in the English colloquialism "to take someone." It is similarly used at 2 Cor 12, 16 and is there connected with cunning and deceit. *Puts on airs:* the same verb is rendered "raise oneself" (2 Cor 10, 5) and "be too elated" (2 Cor 12, 7).

11, 21: Paul ironically concedes the charge of personal weakness from 2 Cor 10, 1-18 but will refute the other charge there mentioned, that of lack of boldness, accepting the challenge to demonstrate it by his boast.

11, 22: The opponents apparently pride themselves on their "Jewishness." Paul, too, can claim to be a Jew by race, religion, and promise. *Descendants of Abraham:* elsewhere Paul distinguishes authentic from inauthentic heirs of Abraham and the promise (Rom 4, 13-18; 9, 7-13; 11, 1; Gal 3, 9.27-29; cf Jn 8, 33-47). Here he grants his opponents this title in order to concentrate on the principal claim that follows.

11, 23a: *Ministers of Christ . . . I am still more:* the central point of the boast (cf the note on 2 Cor 11, 5). *Like an insane person:* the climax of his folly.

11, 23b-29: Service of the humiliated and crucified Christ is demonstrated by trials endured for him. This rhetorically impressive catalogue enumerates many of the labors and perils Paul encountered on his missionary journeys.

2Cor

ness, dangers at sea, dangers among false brothers; [27] in toil and hardship, through many sleepless nights, through hunger and thirst, through frequent fastings, through cold and exposure.[p] [28] And apart from these things, there is the daily pressure upon me of my anxiety for all the churches. [29] Who is weak, and I am not weak? Who is led to sin, and I am not indignant?[q]

Paul's Boast: His Weakness.* [30] If I must boast, I will boast of the things that show my weakness. [31] * The God and Father of the Lord Jesus knows, he who is blessed forever, that I do not lie. [32] At Damascus, the governor under King Aretas guarded the city of Damascus, in order to seize me, [33] but I was lowered in a basket through a window in the wall and escaped his hands.[r]

CHAPTER 12

[1] I * must boast; not that it is profitable, but I will go on to visions and revelations of the Lord. [2] I know someone in Christ who, fourteen years ago (whether in the body or out of the body I do not know,

God knows), was caught up to the third heaven. [3] And I know that this person (whether in the body or out of the body I do not know, God knows) [4] was caught up into Paradise and heard ineffable things, which no one may utter.[s] [5] About this person* I will boast, but about myself I will not boast, except about my weaknesses. [6] Although if I should wish to boast, I would not be foolish, for I would be telling the truth. But I refrain, so that no one may think more of me than what he sees in me or hears from me [7] because of the abundance of the revelations. Therefore, that I might not become too elated,* a thorn in the flesh was given to me, an angel of Satan, to beat me, to keep me from being too elated.[t] [8] Three times* I begged the Lord about this, that it might leave me,[u] [9] but he said to me,* "My grace is sufficient for you, for power is made perfect in weakness." I will rather boast most gladly of my weaknesses,* in order that the power of Christ may dwell with me.[v] [10] Therefore, I am content with weaknesses, insults, hardships, persecutions, and constraints,

---

p 1 Cor 4, 11.—q 1 Cor 9, 22.—r Acts 9, 23-25.—s Lk 23, 43; Rv 2, 7.—t Nm 33, 55; Jos 23, 13; Ez 28, 24.—u Mt 26, 39-44.—v 2 Cor 4, 7.

11, 30—12, 10: The second part of Paul's boast, marked by a change of style and a shift in focus. After recalling the project in which he is engaged, he states a new topic: his weaknesses as matter for boasting. Everything in this section, even the discussion of privileges and distinctions, will be integrated into this perspective.

11, 31-32: The episode at Damascus is symbolic. It aptly illustrates Paul's weakness but ends in deliverance (cf 2 Cor 4, 7-11).

12, 1-4: *In the body or out of the body:* he seemed no longer confined to bodily conditions, but he does not claim to understand the mechanics of the experience. *Caught up:* i.e., in ecstasy. *The third heaven . . . Paradise:* ancient cosmologies depicted a multitiered universe. Jewish intertestamental literature contains much speculation about the number of heavens. Seven is the number usually mentioned, but the Testament of Levi (2, 7-10; 3, 1-4) speaks of three; God himself dwelt in the third of these. Without giving us any clear picture of the cosmos, Paul indicates a mental journey to a nonearthly space, set apart by God, in which secrets were revealed to him. *Ineffable things:* i.e., privileged knowledge, which it was not possible or permitted to divulge.

12, 5-7: *This person:* the indirect way of referring to himself has the effect of emphasizing the distance between that experience and his everyday life, just as the indirect *someone in Christ* (2) and all the passive verbs emphasize his passivity and recep-

tivity in the experience. The revelations were not a personal achievement, nor were they meant to draw attention to any quality of his own.

12, 7b: *That I might not become too elated:* God assures that there is a negative component to his experience, so that he cannot lose proper perspective; cf 2 Cor 1, 9; 4, 7-11. *A thorn in the flesh:* variously interpreted as a sickness or physical disability, a temptation, or a handicap connected with his apostolic activity. But since Hebrew "thorn in the flesh," like English "thorn in my side," refers to persons (cf Nm 33, 55; Ez 28, 24), Paul may be referring to some especially persistent and obnoxious opponent. The language of vv 7-8 permits this interpretation. If this is correct, the frequent appearance of singular pronouns in depicting the opposition may not be merely a stylistic variation; the singular may be provoked and accompanied by the image of one individual in whom criticism of Paul's preaching, way of life, and apostolic consciousness is concentrated, and who embodies all the qualities Paul attributes to the group. *An angel of Satan:* a personal messenger from Satan; cf the satanic language already applied to the opponents in 2 Cor 11, 3.13-15.20.

12, 8: *Three times:* his prayer was insistent, like that of Jesus in Gethsemane, a sign of how intolerable he felt the thorn to be.

12, 9: *But he said to me:* Paul's petition is denied; release and healing are withheld for a higher purpose. The Greek perfect tense indicates that Jesus' earlier response still holds at the time of writing. *My grace is sufficient for you:* this is not a statement about the sufficiency of grace in general. Jesus speaks directly to Paul's situation. *Is made perfect:* i.e., is given most fully and manifests itself fully.

12, 9b-10a: Paul draws the conclusion from the autobiographical anecdote and integrates it into the subject of this part of the boast. *Weaknesses:* the apostolic hardships he must endure, including active personal hostility, as specified in a final catalogue (10a). *That the power of Christ may dwell with me:* Paul pinpoints the ground for the paradoxical strategy he has adopted in his self-defense.

for the sake of Christ;^w for when I am weak, then I am strong.*

Selfless Concern for the Church.* [11] I have been foolish. You compelled me, for I ought to have been commended by you. For I am in no way inferior to these "superapostles,"^x even though I am nothing. [12] * The signs of an apostle were performed among you with all endurance, signs and wonders, and mighty deeds.^y [13] * In what way were you less privileged than the rest of the churches, except that on my part I did not burden you? Forgive me this wrong!^z

[14] Now I am ready to come to you this third time. And I will not be a burden, for I want not what is yours, but you. Children ought not to save for their parents, but parents for their children. [15] I will most gladly spend and be utterly spent for your sakes. If I love you more, am I to be loved less? [16] But granted that I myself did not burden you, yet I was crafty and got the better of you by deceit.^a [17] Did I take advantage of you through any of those I sent to you? [18] I urged Titus to go and sent the brother with

him. Did Titus take advantage of you? Did we not walk in the same spirit? And in the same steps?^b

Final Warnings and Appeals.* [19] Have you been thinking all along that we are defending* ourselves before you? In the sight of God we are speaking in Christ, and all for building you up, beloved. [20] For I fear that* when I come I may find you not such as I wish, and that you may find me not as you wish; that there may be rivalry, jealousy, fury, selfishness, slander, gossip, conceit, and disorder.^c [21] I fear that when I come again* my God may humiliate me before you, and I may have to mourn over many of those who sinned earlier and have not repented of the impurity, immorality, and licentiousness they practiced.

CHAPTER 13

[1] This third time I am coming* to you. "On the testimony of two or three witnesses a

2Cor

---

w 2 Cor 6, 4-5; Rom 5, 3 / Phil 4, 13.—x 2 Cor 11, 5.—y 2 Cor 15, 19; 1 Thes 1, 5.—z 2 Cor 11, 9-12.—a 2 Cor 11, 3.13.—b 2 Cor 2, 13; 8, 16.23.—c 1 Cor 1, 11; 3, 3.

12, 10b: *When I am weak, then I am strong:* Paul recognizes a twofold pattern in the resolution of the weakness-power (and death-life) dialectic, each of which looks to Jesus as the model and is experienced in him. The first is personal, involving a reversal in oneself (Jesus, 2 Cor 13, 4a; Paul, 2 Cor 1, 9-10; 4, 10-11; 6, 9). The second is apostolic, involving an effect on others (Jesus, 2 Cor 5, 14-15; Paul, 2 Cor 1, 6; 4, 12; 13, 9). The specific kind of "effectiveness in ministry" that Paul promises to demonstrate on his arrival (2 Cor 13, 4b; cf 2 Cor 10, 1-11) involves elements of both; this, too, will be modeled on Jesus' experience and a participation in that experience (2 Cor 12, 9; 13, 3b).

12, 11-18: This brief section forms an epilogue or concluding observation to Paul's boast, corresponding to the prologue in 2 Cor 11, 1-15. A four-step sequence of ideas is common to these two sections: Paul qualifies his boast as folly (2 Cor 11, 1; 12, 11a), asserts his noninferiority to the "superapostles" (2 Cor 11, 5; 12, 11b), exemplifies this by allusion to charismatic endowments (2 Cor 11, 6; 12, 12), and finally denies that he has been a financial burden to the community (2 Cor 11, 7-12; 12, 13-18).

12, 12: Despite weakness and affliction (suggested by the mention of *endurance*), his ministry has been accompanied by demonstrations of power (cf 1 Cor 2, 3-4). *Signs of an apostle:* visible proof of belonging to Christ and of mediating Christ's power, which the opponents require as touchstones of apostleship (2 Cor 12, 11; cf 2 Cor 13, 3).

12, 13-18: Paul insists on his intention to continue refusing support from the community (cf 2 Cor 11, 8-12). In defending his practice and his motivation, he once more protests his love (cf 2 Cor 11, 11) and rejects the suggestion of secret self-enrichment. He has recourse here again to language applied to his opponents earlier: "cunning" (2 Cor 11, 3), "deceit" (2 Cor 11, 13), "got the better of you" (see the note on 2 Cor 11, 20), "take advantage" (2 Cor 2, 11).

12, 19—13, 10: This concludes the development begun in ch 10. In the chiastic arrangement of the material (see the note on 2 Cor 10, 1—13, 10), this final part corresponds to the opening; there are important similarities of content between the two sections as well.

12, 19: This verse looks back at the previous chapters and calls them by their proper name, a defense, an *apologia* (cf 1 Cor 9, 3). Yet Paul insists on an important distinction: he has indeed been speaking for their benefit, but the ultimate judgment to which he submits is God's (cf 1 Cor 4, 3-5). This verse also leads into the final section, announcing two of its themes: judgment and building up.

12, 20: *I fear that . . . . :* earlier Paul expressed fear that the Corinthians were being victimized, exploited, seduced from right thinking by his opponents (2 Cor 11, 3-4.19-21). Here he alludes unexpectedly to moral disorders among the Corinthians themselves. The catalogue suggests the effects of factions that have grown up around rival apostles.

12, 21: *Again:* one can also translate, "I fear that when I come my God may again humiliate me." Paul's allusion to the humiliation and mourning that may await him recall the mood he described in 2 Cor 2, 1-4, but there is no reference here to any individual such as there is in 2 Cor 2, 5-11. The crisis of ch 2 has happily been resolved by integration of the offender and repentance (2 Cor 7, 4-16), whereas 2 Cor 12, 21 is preoccupied with still unrepentant sinners. The sexual sins recall 1 Cor 5—7.

13, 1: *This third time I am coming:* designation of the forthcoming visit as the "third" (cf 2 Cor 12, 14) may indicate that, in addition to his founding sojourn in Corinth, Paul had already made the first of two visits mentioned as planned in 2 Cor 1, 15, and the next visit will be the long-postponed second of these. If so, the materials in 2 Cor 1, 12—2, 13 plus 2 Cor 7, 4-16 and chs 10-13 may date from the same period of time, presumably of some duration, between Paul's second and third visit, though it is not clear that they are addressing the same crisis. The chronology is too unsure and the relations between sections of 2 Cor too unclear to yield any certainty. The hypothesis that chs 10-13 are themselves the "tearful letter" mentioned at 2 Cor 2, 3-4 creates more problems than it solves.

fact shall be established."*d* ²I warned those who sinned earlier* and all the others, and I warn them now while absent, as I did when present on my second visit, that if I come again I will not be lenient, ³ * since you are looking for proof of Christ speaking in me. He is not weak toward you but powerful in you. ⁴For indeed he was crucified out of weakness, but he lives by the power of God. So also we are weak in him, but toward you we shall live with him by the power of God.

⁵ * Examine yourselves to see whether you are living in faith. Test yourselves. Do you not realize that Jesus Christ is in you?—unless, of course, you fail the test. ⁶I hope you will discover that we have not failed. ⁷But we pray to God that you may not do evil, not that we may appear to have passed the test but that you may do what is right, even though we may seem to have failed. ⁸For we cannot do anything against the truth, but only for the truth. ⁹For we rejoice when we are weak but you are strong. What we pray for is your improvement.

¹⁰ *e* I am writing this while I am away, so that when I come I may not have to be severe in virtue of the authority that the Lord has given me to build up and not to tear down.*

V. CONCLUSION*

¹¹Finally, brothers, rejoice. Mend your ways, encourage one another, agree with one another, live in peace, and the God of love and peace will be with you. ¹²Greet one another with a holy kiss. All the holy ones greet you.*f*

¹³The grace of the Lord Jesus Christ and the love of God and the fellowship of the holy Spirit be with all of you.*g*

---

d Dt 19, 15; Mt 18, 16; Jn 8, 17; Heb 10, 28.—e 2 Cor 10, 8.—f Rom 16, 16; 1 Cor 16, 20 / Phil 4, 22; 1 Thes 5, 26; 1 Pt 5, 14.—g Rom 16, 20; 1 Cor 16, 23.

13, 2: *I warned those who sinned earlier:* mention of unrepentant sinners (2 Cor 12, 21 and here) and of an oral admonition given them on an earlier visit complicates the picture at the very end of Paul's development. It provides, in fact, a second explanation for the show of power that has been threatened from the beginning (2 Cor 10, 1-6), but a different reason for it, quite unsuspected until now. It is not clear whether Paul is merely alluding to a dimension of the situation that he has not previously had occasion to mention, or whether some other community crisis, not directly connected with that behind chs 10-13, has influenced the final editing. *I will not be lenient:* contrast Paul's hesitation and reluctance to inflict pain in 2 Cor 1, 23 and 2 Cor 2, 1-4. The next visit will bring the showdown.

13, 3-4: Paul now gives another motive for severity when he comes, the charge of weakness leveled against him as an apostle. The motive echoes more closely the opening section (2 Cor 10, 1-18) and the intervening development (especially 2 Cor 11, 30—12, 10). *Proof of Christ speaking in me:* the threat of 2 Cor 10, 1-2 is reworded to recall Paul's conformity with the pattern of Christ, his insertion into the interplay of death and life, weakness and power (cf the note on 2 Cor 12, 10b).

13, 5-9: Paul turns the challenge mentioned in v 3 on them: they are to put themselves to the test to demonstrate whether Christ is in them. These verses involve a complicated series of plays on the theme of *dokimē* (testing, proof, passing and failing a test). Behind this stands the familiar distinction between present human judgment and final divine judgment. This is the final appearance of the theme (cf 2 Cor 10, 18; 11, 15; 12, 19).

13, 10: *Authority . . . to build up and not to tear down:* Paul restates the purpose of his letter in language that echoes 2 Cor 10, 2.8, emphasizing the positive purpose of his authority in their regard. This verse forms an inclusion with the topic sentence of the section (2 Cor 12, 19), as well as with the opening of this entire portion of the letter (2 Cor 10, 1-2).

13, 11-13: These verses may have originally concluded chs 10-13, but they have nothing specifically to do with the material of that section. It is also possible to consider them a conclusion to the whole of 2 Cor in its present edited form. The exhortations are general, including a final appeal for peace in the community. The letter ends calmly, after its many storms, with the prospect of ecclesial unity and divine blessing. The final verse is one of the clearest trinitarian passages in the New Testament.

THE LETTER TO THE GALATIANS

INTRODUCTION

The Galatians to whom the letter is addressed were Paul's converts, most likely among the descendants of Celts who had invaded western and central Asia Minor in the third century B.C. and had settled in the territory around Ancyra (modern Ankara, Turkey). Paul had passed through this area on his second missionary journey (Acts 16, 6) and again on his third (Acts 18, 23). It is less likely that the recipients of this letter were Paul's churches in the southern regions of Pisidia, Lycaonia, and Pamphylia where he had preached earlier in the Hellenized cities of Perge, Iconium, Pisidian Antioch, Lystra, and Derbe (Acts 13, 13—14, 27); this area was part of the Roman province of Galatia, and some scholars think that South Galatia was the destination of this letter.

If it is addressed to the Galatians in the north, the letter was probably written around A.D. 54 or 55, most likely from Ephesus after Paul's arrival there for a stay of several years on his third missionary journey (Acts 19; 20, 31). On the South Galatian theory, the date would be earlier, perhaps A.D. 48-50. Involved is the question of how one relates the events of 2, 1-10 to the "Council of Jerusalem" described in Acts 15 (see the notes on each passage).

In any case, the new Christians whom Paul is addressing were converts from paganism (4; 8-9) who were now being enticed by other missionaries to add the observances of the Jewish law, including the rite of circumcision, to the cross of Christ as a means of salvation. For, since Paul's visit, some other interpretation of Christianity had been brought to these neophytes, probably by converts from Judaism (the name "Judaizers" is sometimes applied to them); it has specifically been suggested that they were Jewish Christians who had come from the austere Essene sect.

These interlopers insisted on the necessity of following certain precepts of the Mosaic law along with faith in Christ. They were undermining Paul's authority also, asserting that he had not been trained by Jesus himself, that his gospel did not agree with that of the original and true apostles in Jerusalem, that he had kept from his converts in Galatia the necessity of accepting circumcision and other key obligations of the Jewish law, in order more easily to win them to Christ, and that his gospel was thus not the full and authentic one held by "those of repute" in Jerusalem (2, 2). Some scholars also see in chapters 5 and 6 another set of opponents against whom Paul writes, people who in their emphasis on the Spirit set aside all norms for conduct and became libertines in practice.

When Paul learned of the situation, he wrote this defense of his apostolic authority and of the correct understanding of the faith. He set forth the unique importance of Christ and his redemptive sacrifice on the cross, the freedom that Christians enjoy from the old burdens of the law, the total sufficiency of Christ and of faith in Christ as the way to God and to eternal life, and the beauty of the new life of the Spirit. Galatians is thus a summary of basic Pauline theology. Its themes were more fully and less polemically developed in the Letter to the Romans.

Autobiographically, the letter gives us Paul's own accounts of how he came to faith (1, 15-24), the agreement in "the truth of the gospel" (2, 5.14) that he shared with the Jewish Christian leaders in Jerusalem, James, Cephas, and John (2, 1-10), and the rebuke he had to deliver to Cephas in Antioch for inconsistency, contrary to the gospel, on the issue of table fellowship in the racially mixed church of Jewish and Gentile Christians *in Antioch (2, 11-14; cf 15-21). At the conclusion of the letter (6, 11-18), Paul wrote in his own hand (cf 2 Thes 3, 17-18) a vivid summary of the message to the Galatians.*

In his vigorous emphasis on the absolute preeminence of Christ and his cross as God's way to salvation and holiness, Paul stresses Christian freedom and the ineffectiveness of the Mosaic law for gaining divine favor and blessings (3, 19-29). The pious Jew saw in the law a way established by God to win divine approval by a life of meticulous observance of ritual, social, and moral regulations. But Paul's profound insight into the higher designs of God in Christ led him to understand and welcome the priority of promise and faith (shown in the experience of Abraham, 3, 6-18) and the supernatural gifts of the Spirit (3, 2-5; 5, 16—6, 10). His enthusiasm for this new vision of the life of grace in Christ and of the uniquely salvific role of Christ's redemptive death on the cross shines through this whole letter.

The principal divisions of the Letter to the Galatians are the following:

I.   *Address (1, 1-5)*
II.   *Loyalty to the Gospel (1, 6-10)*
III. *Paul's Defense of His Gospel and His Authority (1, 11— 2, 21)*
IV. *Faith and Liberty (3, 1—4, 31)*
V.   *Exhortation to Christian Living (5, 1—6, 10)*
VI. *Conclusion (6, 11-18)*

I. ADDRESS

CHAPTER 1

Greeting.* [1] *a* Paul, an apostle* not from human beings nor through a human being but through Jesus Christ and God the Father who raised him from the dead,*b* [2] and all the brothers* who are with me, to the churches of Galatia: [3] grace to you and peace from God our Father and the Lord Jesus Christ, [4] * who gave himself for our sins that he might rescue us from the present evil age in accord with the will of our God and Father,*c* [5] to whom be glory forever and ever. Amen.*d*

---

a 1-3: Rom 1, 1-7; 1 Cor 1, 1-3.—b Gal 1, 11-12.—c Gal 2, 20; Eph 5, 2; 1 Tm 2, 6 / 1 Jn 5, 19 / Rom 12, 2; Eph 5, 16; Heb 10, 10.—d Rom 16, 27; 2 Tm 4, 18.—e 6-7: Gal 5, 8.10; Acts 15, 1.24; 2 Cor 11, 4.—f 8-9: 1 Cor 16, 22 / Gal 5, 3.21; 2 Cor 13, 2.—g 2 Cor 5, 11 / 1 Thes 2, 4.

1, 1-5: See the note on Rom 1, 1-7, concerning the greeting.

1, 1: *Apostle:* because of attacks on his authority in Galatia, Paul defends his apostleship. He is not an apostle commissioned by a congregation (Phil 2, 25; 2 Cor 8, 23) or even by prophets (1 Tm 1, 18 and 1 Tm 4, 14) but *through Jesus Christ and God the Father.*

1, 2: *All the brothers:* fellow believers in Christ, male and female; cf Gal 3, 27-28. Paul usually mentions the co-sender(s) at the start of a letter, but the use of *all* is unique, adding weight to the letter. *Galatia:* central Turkey more likely than the Roman province of Galatia; see Introduction.

1, 4: The greeting in v 3 is expanded by a christological formula that stresses deliverance through the Lord Jesus from a world dominated by Satan; cf 2 Cor 4, 4; Eph 2, 2; 6, 12.

II. LOYALTY TO THE GOSPEL*

[6] *e* I am amazed that you are so quickly forsaking the one who called you* by [the] grace [of Christ] for a different gospel [7] (not that there is another). But there are some who are disturbing you and wish to pervert the gospel of Christ. [8] *f* But even if we or an angel from heaven should preach [to you] a gospel other than the one that we preached to you, let that one be accursed!* [9] As we have said before, and now I say again, if anyone preaches to you a gospel other than the one that you received, let that one be accursed!

[10] *g* Am I now currying favor with human beings or God? Or am I seeking to please people? If I were still trying to please people, I would not be a slave of Christ.*

1, 6-10: In place of the usual thanksgiving (see the note on Rom 1, 8), Paul, with little to be thankful for in the Galatian situation, expresses amazement at the way his converts are deserting the gospel of Christ for a perverted message. He reasserts the one gospel he has preached (7-9) and begins to defend himself (10).

1, 6: *The one who called you:* God or Christ, though in actuality Paul was the divine instrument to call the Galatians.

1, 8: *Accursed:* in Greek, *anathema;* cf Rom 9, 3; 1 Cor 12, 3; 16, 22.

1, 10: This charge by Paul's opponents, that he sought to conciliate people with flattery and to curry favor with God, might refer to his mission practices (cf 1 Cor 9, 19-23) but the word *still* suggests it refers to his pre-Christian days (cf Gal 1, 14; Phil 3, 6). The self-description *slave of Christ* is one Paul often uses in a greeting (Rom 1, 1).

III. PAUL'S DEFENSE OF HIS GOSPEL AND HIS AUTHORITY*

His Call by Christ. [11] *h* Now I want you to know, brothers, that the gospel preached by me is not of human origin. [12] For I did not receive it from a human being, nor was I taught it, but it came through a revelation of Jesus Christ.*

[13] * For you heard of my former way of life in Judaism, how I persecuted the church of God beyond measure and tried to destroy it,*i* [14] and progressed in Judaism beyond many of my contemporaries among my race, since I was even more a zealot for my ancestral traditions.*j* [15] But when [God], who from my mother's womb had set me apart and called me through his grace, was pleased*k* [16] to reveal his Son to me,*l* so that I might proclaim him to the Gentiles, I did not immediately consult flesh and blood,* [17] nor did I go up to Jerusalem to those who were apostles be-fore me; rather, I went into Arabia* and then returned to Damascus.

[18] * Then after three years* I went up to Jerusalem to confer with Cephas and re-mained with him for fifteen days.*m* [19] But I did not see any other of the apostles,*n* only James the brother of the Lord.* [20] (As to what I am writing to you, behold, before God, I am not lying.)*o* [21] Then I went into the regions of Syria and Cilicia.*p* [22] And I was unknown personally to the churches of Judea that are in Christ; [23] they only kept hearing that "the one who once was persecuting us is now preaching the faith he once tried to destroy."*q* [24] So they glorified God because of me.

CHAPTER 2

The Council of Jerusalem. * [1] Then after fourteen years* I again went up to Jerusalem with Barnabas, taking Titus along also.*r* [2] I went up in accord with a revelation,* and I presented to them the

---

h 11-12: 1 Cor 15, 1 / Gal 1, 1; Eph 3, 3.—i Acts 8, 1-3; 9, 1-2; 1 Cor 15, 9.—j Acts 26, 4-5.—k Is 49, 1; Jer 1, 4.—l Gal 1, 11-12; Rom 1, 5; 1 Cor 15, 10; Acts 9, 3-9 / Gal 2, 2.7 / Mt 16, 17.—m Acts 9, 26-30 / Jn 1, 42.—n Gal 2, 9; Mt 13, 55; Acts 12, 17.—o Rom 9, 1; 2 Cor 11, 31.—p Acts 9, 30.—q Gal 1, 13.—r Acts 15, 2.

1, 11—2, 21: Paul's presentation on behalf of his message and of his apostleship reflects rhetorical forms of his day: he first narrates the facts about certain past events (Gal 1, 12—2, 14) and then states his contention regarding justification by faith as the gospel message (Gal 2, 15-21). Further arguments follow from both experience and scripture in chs 3 and 4, before he draws out the ethical consequences (Gal 5, 1—6, 10). The specific facts that he takes up here to show that his gospel is not a human invention (Gal 1, 11) but *came through a revelation of Jesus Christ* (Gal 1, 12) deal with his own calling as a Christian missionary (Gal 1, 13-17), his initial relations with the apostles in Jerusalem (Gal 1, 18-24), a later journey to Jerusalem (Gal 2, 1-10), and an incident in Antioch involving Cephas and persons from James (Gal 2, 11-14). The content of Paul's revealed gospel is then set forth in the heart of the letter (Gal 2, 15-21).

1, 12: Although Paul received his gospel *through a revelation* from Christ, this did not exclude his use of early Christian confessional formulations. See the note on Gal 1, 4.

1, 13-17: Along with Phil 3, 4-11, which also moves from autobiography to its climax in a discussion on justification by faith (cf Gal 2, 15-21), this passage is Paul's chief account of the change from his *former way of life* (13) to service as a Christian missionary (16); cf Acts 9, 1-22; 22, 4-16; 26, 9-18. Paul himself does not use the term "conversion" but stresses revelation (12.16). In v 15 his language echoes the Old Testament prophetic call of Jeremiah. Unlike the account in Acts (cf Acts 22, 4-16), the calling of Paul here includes the mission to proclaim Christ *to the Gentiles* (16).

1, 16: *Flesh and blood:* human authorities (cf Mt 16, 17; 1 Cor 15, 50). Paul's apostleship comes from God (1).

1, 17: *Arabia:* probably the region of the Nabataean Arabs, east and south of Damascus.

1, 18-24: Paul's first journey to Jerusalem as a Christian, according to Galatians (cf Acts 9, 23-31 and the note on Acts 12, 25). He is quite explicit about contacts there, testifying under oath (20). On returning to *Syria* (perhaps specifically Damascus,

cf Gal 1, 17) *and Cilicia* (including his home town Tarsus, cf Acts 9, 30; 22, 3), Paul most likely engaged in missionary work. He underscores the fact that Christians in Judea knew of him only by reputation.

1, 18: *After three years:* two years and more, since Paul's call. To *confer with* Cephas may mean simply "pay a visit" or more specifically "get information from" him about Jesus, over a two-week period. *Cephas:* Aramaic name of Simon (Peter); cf Mt 16, 16-18 and the notes there.

1, 19: *James the brother of the Lord:* not one of the twelve, but a brother of Jesus (see the note on Mk 6, 3). He played an important role in the Jerusalem church (see the note on Gal 2, 9), the leadership of which he took over from Peter (Acts 12, 17). Paul may have regarded James as an apostle.

2, 1-10: Paul's second journey to Jerusalem, according to Galatians, involved a private meeting with *those of repute* (2). At issue was a Gentile, Titus, and the question of circumcision, which *false brothers* (4) evidently demanded for him. Paul insists that the gospel he preaches (2; cf Gal 1, 9.11) remained intact with no addition by those of repute (6); that *Titus* was not *compelled* to accept circumcision (3); and that he and the reputed *pillars* in Jerusalem agreed on how each would advance the missionary task (7-10). Usually, 1-10 is equated with the "Council of Jerusalem," as it is called, described in Acts 15. See the notes on Acts 15, 6-12 and Acts 15, 13-35, the latter concerning the "decree" that Paul does not mention.

2, 1: *After fourteen years:* thirteen or more years, probably reckoned from the return to Syria and Cilicia (Gal 1, 21), though possibly from Paul's calling as a Christian (Gal 1, 15). *Barnabas:* cf Gal 2, 9.13; 1 Cor 9, 6. A Jewish Christian missionary, with whom Paul worked (Acts 4, 36-37; 11, 22.25.30; 12, 25; 13, 1-3; 15, 2). *Titus:* a missionary companion of Paul (2 Cor 2, 13; 7, 6.13-15; 8, 6.16.23; 12, 18), non-Jewish (Gal 2, 3), never mentioned in Acts.

2, 2: *A revelation:* cf Gal 1, 1.12. Paul emphasizes it was God's will, not Jerusalem authority, that led to the journey. Acts 15, 2 states that the church in Antioch appointed Paul and Barnabas for the task. *Those of repute:* leaders of the Jerusalem church; the term, while positive, may be slightly ironic (cf Gal 2, 6.9). *Run, in vain:* while Paul presents a positive picture in what follows, his missionary work in Galatia would have been to no purpose if his opponents were correct that circumcision is needed for complete faith in Christ.

Gal

gospel that I preach to the Gentiles—but privately to those of repute—so that I might not be running, or have run, in vain.*s* *3*Moreover, not even* Titus, who was with me, although he was a Greek, was compelled to be circumcised,*t* *4*but because of the false brothers* secretly brought in, who slipped in to spy on our freedom that we have in Christ Jesus,*u* that they might enslave us—*5*to them we did not submit even for a moment, so that the truth of the gospel* might remain intact for you.*v* *6*But from those who were reputed to be important (what they once were makes no difference to me; God shows no partiality)—those of repute made me add nothing.*w* *7* * On the contrary, when they saw that I had been entrusted with the gospel to the uncircumcised, just as Peter to the circumcised,*x* *8*for the one who worked in Peter for an apostolate to the circumcised worked also in me for the Gentiles, *9*and when they recognized the grace bestowed upon me, James and Cephas and John,* who were reputed to be pillars, gave me and Barnabas their right hands in partnership, that we should go to the Gentiles and they

to the circumcised.*y* *10*Only, we were to be mindful of the poor,* which is the very thing I was eager to do.*z*

Peter's Inconsistency at Antioch. * *11* *a* And when Cephas came to Antioch, I opposed him to his face because he clearly was wrong.* *12*For, until some people came from James,* he used to eat with the Gentiles; but when they came, he began to draw back and separated himself, because he was afraid of the circumcised.*b* *13*And the rest of the Jews* [also] acted hypocritically along with him, with the result that even Barnabas was carried away by their hypocrisy.*c* *14*But when I saw that they were not on the right road in line with the truth of the gospel, I said to Cephas in front of all,*d* "If you, though a Jew, are living like a Gentile and not like a Jew, how can you compel the Gentiles to live like Jews?"*

Faith and Works. * *15*We, who are Jews by nature and not sinners from among the Gentiles, *16* *e* [yet] who know that a person is not justified by works of the law but through faith in Jesus Christ, even we have believed in Christ Jesus that we may be justified by faith in Christ and not by works of the law, because by works of the

s Gal 1, 11-12.16 / Gal 1, 16 / Phil 2, 16.—t 2 Cor 2, 13; 7, 6-7; 8, 16-17; 12, 18; Ti 1, 4 / Gal 2, 14; 6, 12.—u Gal 5, 1; Acts 15, 1.24.—v Gal 2, 14; 4, 16.—w Dt 10, 17; Rom 2, 11.—x Gal 1, 15-16; Acts 9, 15; 15, 12; 22, 21; Rom 1, 5.—y Rom 15, 15 / Gal 1, 18-19; Jn 1, 42; Acts 12, 17 / Gal 2, 1.—z Acts 11, 29-30; Rom 15, 25-28; 1 Cor 16, 1-4; 2 Cor 8, 9.—a Gal 1, 18 / Acts 11, 19-30; 15, 1-2.—b Acts 10, 15.28; 11, 3.—c Gal 2, 1.9.—d Gal 2, 5 / Gal 1, 18; Gal 2, 9 / Gal 2, 3.—e Gal 3, 2.11; Ps 143, 1-2; Rom 3, 20.28; 4, 5; 11, 6; Eph 2, 8-9; Phil 3, 9.

2, 3: *Not even* a Gentile Christian like Titus was compelled to receive the rite of circumcision. The Greek text could be interpreted that he voluntarily accepted circumcision, but this is unlikely in the overall argument.

2, 4: *False brothers:* Jewish Christians who took the position that Gentile Christians must first become Jews through circumcision and observance of the Mosaic law in order to become Christians; cf Acts 15, 1.

2, 5: *The truth of the gospel:* the true gospel, in contrast to the false one of the opponents (Gal 1, 6-9); the gospel of grace, used as a norm (14).

2, 7-9: Some think that actual "minutes" of the meeting are here quoted. Paul's apostleship to the Gentiles (Gal 1, 16) is recognized alongside that of Peter to the Jews. Moreover, the right to proclaim the gospel without requiring circumcision and the Jewish law is sealed by a handshake. That Paul and colleagues *should go to the Gentiles* did not exclude his preaching to the Jews as well (Rom 1, 13-16) or Cephas to Gentile areas.

2, 9: *James and Cephas and John:* see the notes on Gal 1, 18 and 19; on Peter and John as leaders in the Jerusalem church, cf Acts 3, 1 and Acts 8, 14. The order here, with James first, may reflect his prominence in Jerusalem after Peter (Cephas) departed (Acts 12, 17).

2, 10: *The poor:* Jerusalem Christians or a group within the church there (cf Rom 15, 26). The collection for them was extremely important in Paul's thought and labor (cf Rom 15, 25-28; 1 Cor 16, 1-4; 2 Cor 8 and 9).

2, 11-14: The decision reached in Jerusalem (3-7) recognized the freedom of Gentile Christians from the Jewish law. But the problem of table fellowship between Jewish Christians, who possibly still kept kosher food regulations, and Gentile believers was not yet settled. When Cephas first came to the racially mixed community of Jewish and Gentile Christians in Antioch (12), he ate with non-Jews. Pressure from persons arriving later from Jerusalem caused him and Barnabas to draw back. Paul therefore publicly rebuked Peter's inconsistency toward the gospel (14). Some think that what Paul said on that occasion extends through v 16 or v 21.

2, 11: *Clearly was wrong:* literally, "stood condemned," by himself and also by Paul. His action in breaking table fellowship was especially grievous if the eating involved the meal at the Lord's supper (cf 1 Cor 11, 17-25).

2, 12: *Some people came from James:* strict Jewish Christians (cf Acts 15, 1.5; 21, 20-21), either sent by James (Gal 1, 19; 2, 9) or claiming to be from the leader of the Jerusalem church. *The circumcised:* presumably Jewish Christians, not Jews.

2, 13: *The Jews:* Jewish Christians, like Barnabas. *Hypocrisy:* literally, "pretense," "play-acting"; moral insincerity.

2, 14: *Compel the Gentiles to live like Jews:* that is, conform to Jewish practices, such as circumcision (3-5) or regulations about food (12).

2, 15-21: Following on the series of incidents cited above, Paul's argument, whether spoken to Cephas at Antioch or only now articulated, is pertinent to the Galatian situation, where believers were having themselves circumcised (Gal 6, 12-13) and obeying other aspects of Jewish law (Gal 4, 9-10; 5, 1-4). He insists that salvation is by faith in Christ, not by works of the law. His teaching on the gospel concerns justification by faith (16) in relation to sin (17), law (19), life in Christ (19-20), and grace (21).

law no one will be justified.* [17]But if, in seeking to be justified in Christ, we ourselves are found to be sinners, is Christ then a minister of sin?* Of course not! [18]But if I am building up again those things that I tore down, then I show myself to be a transgressor.* [19]For through the law I died to the law,* that I might live for God. I have been crucified with Christ;[f] [20]yet I live, no longer I, but Christ lives in me; insofar as I now live in the flesh, I live by faith in the Son of God who has loved me and given himself up for me.[g] [21]I do not nullify the grace of God; for if justification comes through the law, then Christ died for nothing.[h]

IV. FAITH AND LIBERTY

CHAPTER 3

Justification by Faith.* [1]O stupid* Galatians! Who has bewitched you, before whose eyes Jesus Christ was publicly portrayed as crucified?[i] [2]I want to learn only this from you:[j] did you receive the Spirit from works of the law, or from faith in what you heard?* [3]Are you so stupid?[k] After beginning with the Spirit, are you now ending with the flesh?* [4]Did you ex-

---

f Gal 6, 14; Rom 6, 6.8.10; 7, 6.—g Gal 1, 4; Rom 8, 10-11; Col 3, 3-4.—h Gal 5, 2.—i Gal 5, 7; 1 Cor 1, 23.—j Gal 2, 16 / Gal 3, 14; Rom 10, 17.—k Gal 5, 16-18.—l Gal 2, 16.—m Gn 15, 6; Rom 4, 3; Jas 2, 23.—n Gal 3, 29; Rom 4, 11-12 / Sir 44, 19-21.—o Gn 12, 3; 18, 17-19; Acts 3, 25.—p Rom 4, 16.—q Dt 27, 26; Jas 2, 10.—r Gal 2, 16; Hb 2, 4; Rom 1, 17.—s Lv 18, 5; Rom 10, 5.

2, 16: *No one will be justified:* Ps 143, 2 is reflected.

2, 17: *A minister of sin:* literally, "a servant of sin" (cf Rom 15, 8), an agent of sin, one who promotes it: This is possibly a claim by opponents that justification on the basis of faith in Christ makes Christ an abettor of sin when Christians *are found to be sinners.* Paul denies the conclusion (cf Rom 6, 1-4).

2, 18: To return to observance of the law as the means to salvation would entangle one not only in inevitable transgressions of it but also in the admission that it was wrong to have abandoned the law in the first place.

2, 19: *Through the law I died to the law:* this is variously explained: the law revealed sin (Rom 7, 7-9) and led to death and then to belief in Christ; or, the law itself brought the insight that law cannot justify (Gal 2, 16; Ps 143, 2); or, the "law of Christ" (Gal 6, 2) led to abandoning the Mosaic law; or, the law put Christ to death (cf Gal 3, 13) and so provided a way to our salvation, through baptism into Christ, through which we die (*crucified with Christ;* see Rom 6, 6). Cf also Gal 3, 19-25 on the role of the law in reference to salvation.

3, 1-14: Paul's contention that justification comes not through the law or the works of the law but by faith in Christ and in his death (Gal 2, 16.21) is supported by appeals to Christian experience (1-5) and to scripture (6-14). The gift of God's Spirit to the Galatians came from the gospel received in faith, not from doing

perience so many things* in vain?—if indeed it was in vain. [5]Does, then, the one who supplies the Spirit to you and works mighty deeds among you do so from works of the law or from faith in what you heard?[l] [6]Thus Abraham "believed God,[m] and it was credited to him as righteousness."*

[7] * Realize then that it is those who have faith who are children of Abraham.[n] [8]Scripture, which saw in advance that God would justify the Gentiles by faith, foretold the good news to Abraham, saying, "Through you shall all the nations be blessed."[o] [9]Consequently, all those who have faith are blessed along with Abraham who had faith.[p] [10] * For all who depend on works of the law are under a curse; for it is written, "Cursed be everyone who does not persevere in doing all the things written in the book of the law."[q] [11]And that no one is justified before God by the law is clear, for "the one who is righteous by faith will live."[r] [12]But the law does not depend on faith; rather, "the one who does these things will live by them."[s] [13]Christ ransomed us from the curse of the law by becoming a curse for us, for it is written, "Cursed be everyone who hangs on a

Gal

---

what the law enjoins. The story of Abraham shows that faith in God brings *righteousness* (6; Gn 15, 6). The promise to Abraham (8; Gn 12, 3) extends to the Gentiles (14).

3, 1: *Stupid:* not just senseless, for they were in danger of deserting their salvation.

3, 2: *Faith in what you heard:* Paul's message received with faith. The Greek can also mean "the proclamation of the faith" or "a hearing that comes from faith."

3, 3: On the contrast of *Spirit* and *flesh,* cf Rom 8, 1-11. Having received the Spirit, they need not be circumcised now.

3, 4: *Experience so many things:* probably the *mighty deeds* of v 5 but possibly the experience of sufferings.

3, 6: *Abraham . . . righteousness:* see Gn 15, 6; Rom 4, 3. The Galatians like Abraham heard with faith and experienced justification. This first argument forms the basis for the further scriptural evidence that follows.

3, 7-9: *Faith* is what matters, for *Abraham* and the *children of Abraham,* in contrast to the claims of the opponents that circumcision and observance of the law are needed to bring the promised blessing of Gn 12, 3; cf Gn 18, 18; Sir 44, 21; Acts 3, 25.

3, 10-14: Those *who depend* not on promise and faith but *on works of the law are under a curse* because they do *not persevere in doing all the things written in the book of the law* (10; Dt 27, 26) about executed criminals hanged in public view), to free us from *the curse of the law* (13). That the Gentile Galatians have received the promised Spirit (14) by faith and in no other way returns the argument to the experience cited in vv 1-5.

tree,"[t] [14]that the blessing of Abraham might be extended to the Gentiles through Christ Jesus, so that we might receive the promise of the Spirit through faith.[u]

The Law Did Not Nullify the Promise. [15] * Brothers, in human terms I say that no one can annul or amend even a human will once ratified.[v] [16]Now the promises were made to Abraham and to his descendant.* It does not say, "And to descendants," as referring to many, but as referring to one, "And to your descendant," who is Christ.[w] [17]This is what I mean: the law, which came four hundred and thirty years afterward,* does not annul a covenant previously ratified by God, so as to cancel the promise.[x] [18]For if the inheritance comes from the law,[y] it is no longer from a promise; but God bestowed it on Abraham through a promise.*

[19] * Why, then, the law? It was added for transgressions, until the descendant* came to whom the promise had been made; it was promulgated by angels at the hand of a mediator.[z] [20]Now there is no mediator when only one party is involved, and God is one.[q] [21]Is the law then opposed to the promises [of God]? Of course not! For if a law had been given that could bring life,

then righteousness would in reality come from the law.[b] [22]But scripture confined all things under the power of sin, that through faith in Jesus Christ the promise might be given to those who believe.[c]

What Faith Has Brought Us.* [23]Before faith came, we were held in custody under law, confined for the faith that was to be revealed.[d] [24]Consequently, the law was our disciplinarian* for Christ, that we might be justified by faith.[e] [25]But now that faith has come, we are no longer under a disciplinarian.[f] [26]For through faith you are all children of God* in Christ Jesus.[g] [27] * For all of you who were baptized into Christ[h] have clothed yourselves with Christ.* [28]There is neither Jew nor Greek, there is neither slave nor free person, there is not male and female; for you are all one in Christ Jesus.[i] [29]And if you belong to Christ, then you are Abraham's descendant, heirs according to the promise.[j]

CHAPTER 4

God's Free Children in Christ.* [1]I mean that as long as the heir is not of age,* he is no different from a slave, although he is

---

t Dt 21, 23; Rom 8, 3; 2 Cor 5, 21.—u Gal 3, 2-3.5; Is 44, 3; Jl 3, 1-2; Acts 2, 33.—v Rom 3, 5 / Heb 9, 16-17.—w Gn 12, 7; 13, 15; 17, 8; 22, 17; 24, 7; Mt 1, 1.—x Ex 12, 40.—y Rom 4, 16; 11, 6.—z Rom 4, 15; 5, 20; 7, 7.13 / Acts 7, 38.53.—a Dt 6, 4.—b Rom 7, 7.10; 8, 2-4.—c Rom 3, 9-20.23; 11, 32.—d Gal 4, 3-5; 5, 18.—e Gal 2, 16.—f Rom 10, 4.—g Gal 4, 5-7; Jn 1, 12; Rom 8, 14-17.—h Rom 6, 3; 13, 14; Eph 4, 24.—i Rom 10, 12; 1 Cor 12, 13; Col 3, 11.—j Gal 3, 7.14.16.18; Rom 4, 16-17; 9, 7 / Gal 4, 1.7; Rom 4, 13-14; 8, 17; Heb 6, 12; Jas 2, 5.

3, 15-18: A third argument to support Paul's position that salvation is not through the law but by promise (1-14) comes from legal practice and scriptural history. A legal agreement or *human will*, duly *ratified*, is unalterable (15). God's *covenant* with *Abraham* and its repeated promises (Gn 12, 2-3.7; 13, 15; 17, 7-8; 22, 16-18; 24, 7) is not superseded by *the law*, which came much later, in the time of Moses. *The inheritance* (of the Spirit and the blessings) is by promise, not by law (18). Paul's argument hinges on the fact that the same Greek word, *diathēkē*, can be rendered as *will* or testament (15) and as *covenant* (17).

3, 16: *Descendant:* literally, "and to his seed." The Hebrew, as in Gn 12, 7; 15, 18; 22, 17-18, is a collective singular, traditionally rendered as a plural, *descendants*, but taken by Paul in its literal number to refer to *Christ* as descendant of Abraham.

3, 17: *Four hundred and thirty years afterward:* follows Ex 12, 40 in the Greek (Septuagint) version, in contrast to Gn 15, 13 and Acts 7, 6, for chronology.

3, 18: This refutes the opponents' contention that the promises of God are fulfilled only as a reward for human observance of the law.

3, 19-22: A digression: if the Mosaic law, then, does not save or *bring life*, why was it given? Elsewhere, Paul says the law served to show what sin is (Rom 3, 20; 7, 7-8). Here the further implication is that the law in effect served to produce transgressions. Moreover, it was received at second hand *by angels*, through a *mediator*, not directly from God (19). The law does

not, however, oppose God's purposes, for it carries out its function (22), so that *righteousness* comes by *faith* and *promise*, not by human works of the law.

3, 19: *The descendant:* Christ (16). *By angels:* Dt 33, 2-4 stressed their presence as enhancing the importance of the law; Paul uses their role to diminish its significance (cf Acts 7, 38.53). *A mediator:* Moses. But in a covenant of promise, where all depends on the one God, no mediator is needed (20).

3, 23-29: Paul adds a further argument in support of righteousness or justification by faith and through God's promise rather than by works of the law (Gal 2, 16; 3, 22): as *children of God, baptized into Christ*, the Galatians are all *Abraham's descendant* and *heirs of the promise* to Abraham (8.14.16-18.29). The teaching in 23-25, that since *faith* (Christianity) *has come, we are no longer under* the law, could be taken with the previous paragraph on the role of the Mosaic law, but it also fits here as a contrast between the situation *before faith* (23) and the results after faith has come (25-29).

3, 24-25: *Disciplinarian:* the Greek *paidagōgos* referred to a slave who escorted a child to school but did not teach or tutor; hence, a guardian or monitor. Applying this to the law fits the role of the law described in vv 19-25.

3, 26: *Children of God:* literally "sons," in contrast to the young child under the disciplinarian in vv 24-25. The term includes males and females (28).

3, 27-28: Likely a formula used at baptism that expresses racial, social-economic, and sexual equality in Christ (cf Col 3, 11).

3, 27: *Clothed yourselves with Christ:* literally, "have put on Christ"; cf Rom 13, 14; Eph 4, 24; Col 3, 10. Baptismal imagery, traceable to the Old Testament (Jb 29, 14; Is 59, 17) but also found in pagan mystery cults.

4, 1-7: What Paul has argued in Gal 3, 26-29 is now elaborated in terms of the Christian as *the heir* (1.7; cf Gal 3, 18.29) freed from control by others. Again, as in Gal 3, 2-5, the proof that Christians are children of God is the gift of the Spirit of Christ relating them intimately to God.

4, 1.3: *Not of age:* an infant or minor.

the owner of everything, [2] but he is under the supervision of guardians and administrators until the date set by his father. [3] *k* In the same way we also, when we were not of age, were enslaved to the elemental powers of the world.* [4] But when the fullness of time had come, God sent his Son, born of a woman, born under the law, *l* [5] to ransom those under the law, so that we might receive adoption. *m* [6] As proof that you are children,* God sent the spirit of his Son into our hearts, crying out, "Abba, Father!" *n* [7] So you are no longer a slave but a child, and if a child then also an heir, through God. *o*

Do Not Throw This Freedom Away.* [8] *p* At a time when you did not know God, you became slaves to things that by nature are not gods;* [9] but now that you have come to know God, or rather to be known by God, how can you turn back again to the weak and destitute elemental powers? Do you want to be slaves to them all over again? *q* [10] You are observing days, *r* months, seasons, and years.* [11] I am afraid on your account that perhaps I have labored for you in vain.*

Appeal to Former Loyalty.* [12] I implore you, brothers, be as I am, because I have also become as you are.* You did me no wrong; *s* [13] you know that it was because of a physical illness* that I originally preached the gospel to you, [14] and you did not show disdain or contempt because of the trial caused you by my physical condition, but rather you received me as an angel of God, as Christ Jesus. [15] Where now is that blessedness of yours?* Indeed, I can testify to you that, if it had been possible, you would have torn out your eyes and given them to me. [16] So now have I become your enemy by telling you the truth? [17] They show interest in you, but not in a good way; they want to isolate you,* so that you may show interest in them. *t* [18] Now it is good to be shown interest for good reason at all times, and not only when I am with you. *u* [19] My children, for whom I am again in labor until Christ be formed in you! [20] I would like to be with you now and to change my tone, for I am perplexed because of you.

An Allegory on Christian Freedom.* [21] Tell me, you who want to be under the law, do you not listen to the law? [22] For it is written that Abraham had two sons, one by the slave woman and the other by the freeborn woman. *v* [23] The son of the slave woman was born naturally, the son of the freeborn through a promise. *w* [24] Now this is an al-

Gal

---

k Gal 3, 23 / Gal 4, 9; Col 2, 20.—l Mk 1, 15.—m Gal 3, 13.26.—n Gal 3, 26; Rom 8, 15.—o Gal 3, 29; Rom 8, 16-17.—p 1 Cor 12, 2.—q Gal 4, 3; Col 2, 20.—r Col 2, 16-20.—s 1 Cor 11, 1.—t Gal 1, 7; 6, 12; Acts 20, 30.—u 1 Cor 4, 14-15; 2 Cor 6, 13; 1 Thes 2, 7-8.—v Gn 16, 15; 21, 2-3.—w Gn 17, 16; Rom 4, 19-20; 9, 7-9.

4, 3: *The elemental powers of the world:* while the term can refer to the "elements" like earth, air, fire, and water or to elementary forms of religion, the sense here is more likely that of celestial beings that were thought in pagan circles to control the world; cf Gal 4, 8; Col 2, 8.20.

4, 6: *Children:* see the note on Gal 3, 26; here in contrast to the infant or young person *not of age* (1.3). *Abba:* cf Mk 14, 36 and the note; Rom 8, 15.

4, 8-11: On the basis of the arguments advanced from Gal 3, 1 through Gal 4, 7, Paul now launches his appeal to the Galatians with the question, *how can you turn back* to the slavery of the law (9)? The question is posed with reference to bondage to the *elemental powers* (see the note on Gal 4, 3) because the Galatians had originally been converted to Christianity from paganism, not Judaism (8). The use of the direct question is like Gal 3, 3-5.

4, 8: *Things that by nature are not gods:* or "gods that by nature do not exist."

4, 10: This is likely a reference to ritual observances from the Old Testament, promoted by opponents: sabbaths or Yom Kippur, new moon, Passover or Pentecost, sabbatical years.

4, 11: Cf Gal 2, 2. If the Galatians become *slaves . . . all over again* to the law (9), Paul will have worked in vain among them.

4, 12-20: A strongly personal section. Paul appeals to past ties between the Galatians and himself. He speaks sharply of the opponents (17-18) and pastorally to the Galatians (19-20).

4, 12: *Because I have also become as you are:* a terse phrase in Greek, meaning "Be as I, Paul, am," i.e., living by faith, independent of the law, for, in spite of my background in Judaism (Gal 1, 13), I have become as you Galatians are now, a brother in Christ.

4, 13: *Physical illness:* because its nature is not described, some assume an eye disease (15); others, epilepsy; some relate it to 2 Cor 12, 7-9. *Originally:* this may also be translated "formerly" or "on the first (of two) visit(s)"; cf Acts 16, 6; 18, 23.

4, 15: *That blessedness of yours:* possibly a reference to the Galatians' initial happy reception of Paul (14) and of his gospel (Gal 1, 6; 3, 1-4) and their felicitation at such blessedness, but the phrase could also refer ironically to earlier praise by Paul of the Galatians, no longer possible when they turn from the gospel to the claims of the opponents (Gal 4, 17-18; 1, 7). If the word is a more literal reference to a beatitude, Gal 3, 26-28 may be in view.

4, 17: *Isolate you:* that is, from the blessings of the gospel and/or from Paul.

4, 21-31: Paul supports his appeal for the gospel (Gal 4, 9; 1, 6-9; 2, 16; 3, 1-4) by a further argument from scripture (cf Gal 3, 6-18). It involves the relationship of *Abraham* (Gal 3, 6-16) to his wife, Sarah, the *freeborn woman*, and to Hagar, *the slave woman*, and the contrast between the sons born to each, *Isaac*, child of promise, and Ishmael, son of Hagar (Gn 16 and 21). Only through Isaac is the promise of God preserved. This *allegory* (24), with its equation of the Sinai covenant and Mosaic law with slavery and of the promise of God with freedom, Paul uses only in light of previous arguments. His quotation of Gn 21, 10 at v 30 suggests on a scriptural basis that the Galatians should expel those who are troubling them (Gal 1, 7).

legory. These women represent two covenants. One was from Mount Sinai, bearing children for slavery; this is Hagar.[x] [25]Hagar represents Sinai,* a mountain in Arabia; it corresponds to the present Jerusalem, for she is in slavery along with her children. [26]But the Jerusalem above is freeborn, and she is our mother.[y] [27]For it is written:

"Rejoice, you barren one who bore no children;[z]

break forth and shout, you who were not in labor;

for more numerous are the children of the deserted one

than of her who has a husband."*

[28]Now you, brothers, like Isaac, are children of the promise.[a] [29]But just as then the child of the flesh persecuted the child of the spirit, it is the same now. [30]But what does the scripture say?

"Drive out the slave woman and her son!

For the son of the slave woman shall not share the inheritance with the son"[b]

of the freeborn. [31]Therefore, brothers, we are children not of the slave woman but of the freeborn woman.[c]

V. EXHORTATION TO CHRISTIAN LIVING

CHAPTER 5

The Importance of Faith.* [1]For freedom* Christ set us free; so stand firm and do not submit again to the yoke of slavery.[d]

[2]It is I, Paul, who am telling you that if you have yourselves circumcised, Christ will be of no benefit to you.[e] [3]Once again I declare to every man who has himself circumcised[f] that he is bound to observe the entire law.* [4]You are separated from Christ, you who are trying to be justified by law; you have fallen from grace. [5][g] For through the Spirit, by faith, we await the hope of righteousness. [6][h] For in Christ Jesus, neither circumcision nor uncircumcision counts for anything, but only faith working through love.*

Be Not Misled.* [7]You were running well;* who hindered you from following [the] truth? [8][i] That enticement does not come from the one who called you.* [9]A little yeast leavens the whole batch of dough.[j] [10]I am confident of you in the Lord that you will not take a different view, and that the one who is troubling you will bear the condemnation, whoever he may be.[k] [11]As for me, brothers, if I am still preaching circumcision,* why am I still being persecuted? In that case, the stumbling block of the cross has been abolished.[l] [12]Would that those who are upsetting you might also castrate themselves!*

Freedom for Service.* [13]For you were called for freedom, brothers.[m] But do not use this freedom as an opportunity for the flesh; rather, serve* one another through

x Gal 3, 17 / Ex 19, 20 / Gn 16, 1.—y Heb 12, 22; Rv 21, 2.—z Is 54, 1.—a Rom 9, 8.—b Gn 21, 10.—c Gal 3, 29; Jn 8, 35.—d Gal 2, 4; 4, 5.9; Jn 8, 32.36.—e Gal 2, 21; Acts 15, 1-29.—f Gal 3, 10; Rom 2, 25; Jas 2, 10.—g Rom 8, 23.25.—h Gal 3, 28; 6, 15; 1 Cor 7, 19.—i Gal 1, 6.—j 1 Cor 5, 6.—k Gal 1, 7.—l Gal 6, 12.14; 1 Cor 1, 23.—m Gal 5, 1 / Rom 6, 18; 1 Cor 8, 9; 1 Pt 2, 16.

4, 25: *Hagar represents Sinai . . . :* some manuscripts have what seems a geographical note, "For Sinai is a mountain in Arabia."

4, 27: Is 54, 1 in the Septuagint translation is applied to Sarah as the *barren one* (in Gn 15) who ultimately becomes the mother not only of Isaac but now of numerous children, i.e., of all those who believe, the *children of the promise* (28).

5, 1-6: Paul begins the exhortations, continuing through Gal 6, 10, with an appeal to the Galatians to side with freedom instead of slavery (1). He reiterates his message of justification or righteousness by faith instead of law and circumcision (2-5); cf Gal 2, 16; 3, 3. Faith, not circumcision, is what counts (6).

5, 1: *Freedom:* Paul stresses as the conclusion from the allegory in Gal 4, 21-31 this result of Christ's work for us. It is a principle previously mentioned (Gal 2, 4), the responsible use of which v 13 will emphasize.

5, 3: Cf Gal 3, 10-12. Just as those who seek to live by the law must carry out all its contents, so those who have faith and live by promise must stand firm in their freedom (1.13).

5, 6: Cf Rom 2, 25-26; 1 Cor 7, 19; Gal 6, 15. The Greek for *faith working through love* or "faith expressing itself through love" can also be rendered as "faith energized by (God's) love."

5, 7-12: Paul addresses the Galatians directly: with questions (7.11), a proverb (9), a statement (8), and biting sarcasm (12), seeking to persuade the Galatians to break with those trying to add law and circumcision to Christ as a basis for salvation.

5, 7: *Running well:* as in an athletic contest; cf Gal 2, 2; 1 Cor 9, 24-26; Phil 2, 16; 3, 14.

5, 8: *The one who called you:* see the note on Gal 1, 6.

5, 11: *Preaching circumcision:* this could refer to Paul's pre-Christian period (possibly as a missionary for Judaism); more probably it arose as a charge from opponents, based perhaps on the story in Acts 16, 1-3 that Paul had circumcised Timothy "on account of the Jews." Unlike the Gentile Titus in Gal 2, 3, Timothy was the son of a Jewish mother. *The stumbling block of the cross:* cf 1 Cor 1, 23.

5, 12: A sarcastic half-wish that their knife would go beyond mere circumcision; cf Phil 3, 2 and the note there.

5, 13-26: In light of another reminder of the freedom of the gospel (13; cf Gal 5, 1), Paul elaborates on what believers are called to do and be; they fulfill the law by love of neighbor (14-15), walking in the Spirit (16-26), as is illustrated by concrete *fruit of the Spirit* in their lives.

5, 13: *Serve . . . through love:* cf Gal 5, 6.

love. ¹⁴For the whole law*ⁿ* is fulfilled in one statement, namely, "You shall love your neighbor as yourself."* ¹⁵But if you go on biting and devouring one another, beware that you are not consumed by one another.

¹⁶ *o* I say, then: live by the Spirit and you will certainly not gratify the desire of the flesh.* ¹⁷For the flesh has desires against the Spirit, and the Spirit against the flesh; these are opposed to each other, so that you may not do what you want.*ᵖ* ¹⁸But if you are guided by the Spirit, you are not under the law.*q* ¹⁹ * Now the works of the flesh are obvious: immorality, impurity, licentiousness,*ʳ* ²⁰idolatry, sorcery, hatreds, rivalry, jealousy, outbursts of fury, acts of selfishness, dissensions, factions,*ˢ* ²¹occasions of envy,* drinking bouts, orgies, and the like. I warn you, as I warned you before, that those who do such things will not inherit the kingdom of God. ²²In contrast, the fruit of the Spirit is love, joy, peace, patience, kindness, generosity, faithfulness,*ᵗ* ²³gentleness, self-control. Against such there is no law.*ᵘ* ²⁴Now those who belong to Christ [Jesus] have crucified their flesh with its passions and desires.*ᵛ* ²⁵If we live in the Spirit, let us also follow the Spirit.*ʷ* ²⁶Let us not be conceited, provoking one another, envious of one another.*ˣ*

CHAPTER 6

Life in the Community of Christ.* ¹Brothers, even if a person is caught in some transgression, you who are spiritual should correct that one in a gentle spirit, looking to yourself, so that you also may not be tempted.*ʸ* ²Bear one another's burdens,*ᶻ* and so you will fulfill the law of Christ.* ³ *a* For if anyone thinks he is something when he is nothing, he is deluding himself. ⁴ * Each one must examine his own work, and then he will have reason to boast with regard to himself alone, and not with regard to someone else; ⁵for each will bear his own load.*ᵇ*

⁶ *c* One who is being instructed in the word should share all good things with his instructor.* ⁷Make no mistake: God is not mocked, for a person will reap only what he sows, ⁸because the one who sows for his flesh will reap corruption from the flesh, but the one who sows for the spirit will reap eternal life from the spirit.*d* ⁹Let us not grow tired of doing good, for in due time we shall reap our harvest, if we do not give up.*e* ¹⁰So then, while we have the opportunity, let us do good to all,*f* but especially to those who belong to the family of the faith.*

VI. CONCLUSION

Final Appeal.* ¹¹See with what large letters* I am writing to you in my own hand!*g*

Gal

---

n Lv 19, 18; Mt 22, 39; Rom 13, 8-10.—o Gal 5, 24-25; Rom 8, 5.—p Rom 7, 15.23; 8, 6.—q Rom 6, 14; 8, 14.—r 19-21: Rom 1, 29-31; 1 Cor 6, 9-10; Col 3, 5-6.8.—s Rv 22, 15.—t Eph 5, 9 / 1 Cor 13, 4-7; 2 Cor 6, 6; 1 Tm 4, 12; 2 Pt 1, 6.—u 1 Tm 1, 9.—v Gal 2, 19; Rom 6, 6; 8, 13.—w Gal 5, 16.—x Phil 2, 3.—y Mt 18, 15; Jas 5, 19 / 1 Cor 10, 12-13.—z Col 3, 13 / 1 Cor 9, 21.—a 3-4: 1 Cor 3, 18; 8, 2; 2 Cor 12, 11.—b Rom 14, 12.— c 1 Cor 9, 14.—d Prv 11, 18; Rom 8, 6.13.—e 2 Thes 3, 13; Heb 12, 1-3.—f 1 Thes 5, 15.—g 1 Cor 16, 21.

5, 14: Lv 19, 18, emphasized by Jesus (Mt 22, 39; Lk 10, 27); cf Rom 13, 8-10.

5, 16-25: *Spirit . . . flesh:* cf Gal 3, 3 and the note on Rom 8, 1-13.

5, 19-23: Such lists of vices and virtues (cf Rom 1, 29-31; 1 Cor 6, 9-10) were common in the ancient world. Paul contrasts *works of the flesh* (19) with *fruit* (not "works") *of the Spirit* (22). Not law, but the Spirit, leads to such traits.

5, 21: *Occasions of envy:* after the Greek word *phthonoi,* "envies," some manuscripts add a similar sounding one, *phonoi,* "murders."

6, 1-10: The ethical exhortations begun at Gal 5, 1 continue with a variety of admonitions to the community (*brothers:* see the note on Gal 1, 2). Nearly every sentence contains a separate item of practical advice; the faith and freedom of the gospel underlie each maxim. Tensions and temptation within communal life have previously been addressed in Gal 5, 15.26, and v 1 continues with a case in which *a person is caught in some transgression* such as those in Gal 5, 19-21; cf Gal 2, 17.

6, 2: *The law of Christ:* cf Rom 8, 2; 1 Cor 9, 21; Gal 5, 14. The principle of love for others is meant. To *bear one another's burdens* is to "serve one another through love" (Gal 5, 13).

6, 4-5: Self-examination is the cure for self-deception. Compare what you are with what you were before, and give the glory to God; cf Rom 6, 19-22. *Load:* used elsewhere of a soldier's pack. Correcting one's own conduct avoids burdening others with it.

6, 6: Implies oral instruction in the faith by catechists; these are to be remunerated for their service; cf Rom 15, 27.

6, 10: *The family of the faith:* the Christian household or church. Doing good has a universal object (*to all*), but the local community makes specific the reality of those to be served.

6, 11-18: A postscript in Paul's own hand, as was his practice (see 1 Cor 16, 21; 2 Thes 3, 17). Paul summarizes his appeal against his opponents (12-13), then returns to his message of glorying in the cross, not in circumcision, as the means of salvation (14-15); cf Gal 5, 11). A benediction follows at v, 16. In the polemical spirit that the attack on his apostleship called forth (Gal 1, 11—2, 21), Paul reasserts his missionary credentials (17) before giving a final benediction (18).

6, 11: *Large letters:* in contrast to the finer hand of the scribe who wrote the letter up to this point. The larger Greek letters make Paul's message even more emphatic. Some find a hint of poor eyesight on Paul's part. See the note on Gal 4, 13.

12 * It is those who want to make a good appearance in the flesh who are trying to compel you to have yourselves circumcised, only that they may not be persecuted for the cross of Christ.ʰ ¹³Not even those having themselves circumcised* observe the law themselves; they only want you to be circumcised so that they may boast of your flesh. ¹⁴But may I never boast except in the cross of our Lord Jesus Christ, through which* the world has been crucified to me, and I to the world.ⁱ ¹⁵For neither does circumcision mean anything, nor does uncircumcision,ʲ but only a new creation.* ¹⁶Peace and mercy be to all who follow this rule* and to the Israel of God.ᵏ

¹⁷From now on, let no one make troubles for me; for I bear the marks of Jesus* on my body.ˡ

¹⁸The grace of our Lord Jesus Christ be with your spirit, brothers. Amen.ᵐ

---

h Gal 5, 2.11.—i Gal 2, 20; 1 Cor 2, 2.—j Gal 5, 6; 1 Cor 7, 19 / 2 Cor 5, 17.—k Pss 125, 5; 128, 6.—l 2 Cor 4, 10.—m Phil 4, 23; 2 Tm 4, 22; Phlm 25.

6, 12-15: The Jewish Christian opponents wished *not to be persecuted,* possibly by Jews. But since Judaism seems to have had a privileged status as a religion in the Roman empire, circumcised Christians might, if taken as Jews, thereby avoid persecution from the Romans. In any case, Paul instead stresses conformity with *the cross of our Lord Jesus Christ;* cf Gal 2, 19-21; 5, 11.

6, 13: *Those having themselves circumcised:* other manuscripts read, "those who have had themselves circumcised."

6, 14: *Through which:* or "through whom."

6, 15: *New creation:* or "new creature"; cf 2 Cor 5, 17.

6, 16: *This rule:* the principle in vv 14 and 15. *The Israel of God:* while the church may be meant (the phrase can be translated "to all who follow this rule, even the Israel of God"; cf Gal 6, 10; 1 Cor 10, 18), the reference may also be to God's ancient people, Israel; cf Pss 125, 5; 128, 6.

6, 17: *The marks of Jesus:* slaves were often branded by marks (*stigmata*) burned into their flesh to show to whom they belonged; so also were devotees of pagan gods. Paul implies that instead of outdated circumcision, his body bears the scars of his apostolic labors (2 Cor 11, 22-31), such as floggings (Acts 16, 22; 2 Cor 11, 25) and stonings (Acts 14, 19), that mark him as belonging to the Christ who suffered (cf Rom 6, 3; 2 Cor 4, 10; Col 1, 24) and will protect his own.

THE LETTER TO THE EPHESIANS

INTRODUCTION

Ephesians is the great Pauline letter about the church. It deals, however, not so much with a congregation in the city of Ephesus in Asia Minor as with the worldwide church, the head of which is Christ (4, 15), the purpose of which is to be the instrument for making God's plan of salvation known throughout the universe (3, 9-10). Yet this ecclesiology is anchored in God's saving love, shown in Jesus Christ (2, 4-10), and the whole of redemption is rooted in the plan and accomplishment of the triune God (1, 3-14). The language is often that of doxology (1, 3-14) and prayer (cf 1, 15-23; 3, 14-19), indeed of liturgy and hymns (3, 20-21; 5, 14).

The majestic chapters of Ephesians emphasize the unity in the church of Christ that has come about for both Jews and Gentiles within God's household (1, 15—2, 22, especially 2, 11-22) and indeed the "seven unities" of church, Spirit, hope; one Lord, faith, and baptism; and the one God (4, 4-6). Yet the concern is not with the church for its own sake but rather as the means for mission in the world (3, 1—4, 24). The gifts Christ gives its members are to lead to growth and renewal (4, 7-24). Ethical admonition is not lacking either; all aspects of human life and relationships are illumined by the light of Christ (4, 25—6, 20).

The letter is seemingly addressed by Paul to Christians in Ephesus (1, 1), a place where the apostle labored for well over two years (Acts 19, 10). Yet there is a curiously impersonal tone to the writing for a community with which Paul was so intimately acquainted (cf 3, 2 and 4, 21). There are no personal greetings (cf 6, 23). More significantly, important early manuscripts omit the words "in Ephesus" (see the note on 1, 1). Many therefore regard the letter as an encyclical or "circular letter" sent to a number of churches in Asia Minor, the addressees to be designated in each place by its bearer,

Tychicus (6, 21-22). Others think that Ephesians is the letter referred to in Colossians 4, 16 as "to the Laodiceans."

Paul, who is designated as the sole author at 1, 1, is described in almost unparalleled terms with regard to the significant role he has in God's plan for bringing the Gentiles to faith in Christ (3, 1-12). Yet at the time of writing he is clearly in prison (3, 1; 4, 1; 6, 20), suffering afflictions (3, 13). Traditionally this "Captivity Epistle" has, along with Colossians, Philippians, and Philemon, been dated to an imprisonment in Rome, likely in A.D. 61-63. Others appeal to an earlier imprisonment, perhaps in Caesarea (Acts 23, 27—27, 2). Since the early nineteenth century, however, much of critical scholarship has considered the letter's style and use of words (especially when compared with Colossians), its concept of the church, and other points of doctrine put forward by the writer as grounds for serious doubt about authorship by Paul. The letter may then be the work of a secretary writing at the apostle's direction or of a later disciple who sought to develop Paul's ideas for a new situation around A.D. 80-100.

The principal divisions of the Letter to the Ephesians are the following:

I. *Address (1, 1-14)*
II. *Unity of the Church in Christ (1, 15—2, 22)*
III. *World Mission of the Church (3, 1—4, 24)*
IV. *Daily Conduct, an Expression of Unity (4, 25—6, 20)*
V. *Conclusion (6, 21-24)*

I. ADDRESS

CHAPTER 1

Greeting.* [1]Paul, an apostle of Christ Jesus by the will of God, to the holy ones who are [in Ephesus]* faithful in Christ Jesus:[a] [2]grace to you and peace from God our Father and the Lord Jesus Christ.[b]

The Father's Plan of Salvation. [3] * Blessed be the God and Father of our Lord Jesus Christ,[c] who has blessed us in Christ with every spiritual blessing in the heavens,* [4]as he chose us in him, before the founda-

tion of the world, to be holy and without blemish before him.[d] In love [5]he destined us for adoption to himself through Jesus Christ, in accord with the favor of his will,[e] [6]for the praise of the glory of his grace that he granted us in the beloved.[f]

Fulfillment through Christ. [7]In him we have redemption by his blood, the forgiveness of transgressions, in accord with the riches of his grace[g] [8]that he lavished upon us. In all wisdom and insight,[h] [9]he has made known to us the mystery* of his will in accord with his favor that he set forth in

Eph

---

a Rom 1, 7; 1 Cor 1, 1-2; Col 1, 1.—b Col 1, 2.—c Eph 2, 6; 2 Cor 1, 3.—d Eph 5, 27; Jn 15, 16; 17, 24; Rom 8, 29; 2 Thes 2, 13.—e Jn 1, 12; 1 Jn 3, 1.—f Mt 3, 17; Col 1, 13.—g Eph 2, 7-13; Rom 3, 24; Col 1, 14.20.—h Col 1, 9.

1, 1-2: For the epistolary form used at the beginning of letters, see the note on Rom 1, 1-7. Twenty-two of the thirty Greek words in vv 1-2 also occur in Col 1, 1-2.

1, 1: *[In Ephesus]:* the phrase is lacking in important early witnesses such as P[46] (3rd cent.), and Sinaiticus and Vaticanus (4th cent.), appearing in the latter two as a fifth-century addition. Basil and Origen mention its absence from manuscripts. See Introduction. Without the phrase, the Greek can be rendered, as in Col 1, 2, "to the holy ones and faithful brothers in Christ."

1, 3-14: While a Pauline letter usually continues after the greeting with a prayer of thanksgiving, as in 15-23 below, Ephesians first inserts a blessing of God for the blessings Christians have experienced, as in 2 Cor 1, 3-4 and 1 Pt 1, 3-12. The blessing here, akin to a Jewish *berakah*, is rich in images almost certainly drawn from hymns and liturgy. Many ideas here are also found in Col 1, 3-23. Certain phrases are frequently repeated, such as *in Christ* (3.10.12) or *in him* (4.7.9.11.13) or *in the Beloved* (6) and *(for) the praise of (his) glory* (6.12.14). Some

terms like *chose* (4) and *destined* (5) reflect Old Testament theology (Dt 7, 7; 9, 4-6; 23, 5) or Pauline themes (*redemption,* 7.14; *grace,* 6.7) or specific emphases in Col (*forgiveness,* Col 1, 14).

A triadic structure is discernible in vv 3-14: *God the Father* (3-6.8.11), *Christ* (3.5.7-10.12), and the *Spirit* (13-14). The spiritual blessings Christians have received through Christ (3) are gratefully enumerated: the call to holiness (4; cf Col 1, 22); the gift of divine *adoption* establishing a unique spiritual relationship with God the Father through Christ (5; cf Gal 4, 5); liberation from sin through Christ's sacrificial death (7); revelation of God's plan of salvation in Christ (9; cf Eph 3, 3-4; Rom 16, 25); the gift of election and faith in Christ bestowed upon Jewish Christians (see the note on 12, *we who first hoped in Christ*); and finally, the same gift granted to Gentiles (13, *you also*). In the Christ-centered faith and existence of the Christian communities the apostle sees the predetermined *plan* of God to bring all creation under the final rule of Christ (4-5.9-10) being *made known* (9) and carried through, to God's *glory* (6.12.14).

1, 3: *In the heavens:* literally, "in the heavenlies" or "in the heavenly places," a term in Eph for the divine realm.

1, 9: *Mystery:* as in Rom 16, 25; Col 1, 26.27 and elsewhere, a secret of God now revealed in the *plan* to save and *sum up all things in Christ* (10); cf Eph 3, 3-6.

him[i] [10]as a plan for the fullness of times, to sum up all things in Christ, in heaven and on earth.[j]

Inheritance through the Spirit. [11]In him we were also chosen, destined in accord with the purpose of the One who accomplishes all things according to the intention of his will,[k] [12]so that we might exist for the praise of his glory, we who first hoped* in Christ. [13]In him you also, who have heard the word of truth, the gospel of your salvation, and have believed in him, were sealed* with the promised holy Spirit,[l] [14]which is the first installment* of our inheritance toward redemption as God's possession, to the praise of his glory.[m]

II. UNITY OF THE CHURCH IN CHRIST

The Church as Christ's Body.* [15]Therefore, I, too, hearing of your faith in the Lord Jesus and of your love* for all the holy ones,[n] [16]do not cease giving thanks for you, remembering you in my prayers,[o] [17]that the God of our Lord Jesus Christ, the Father of glory, may give you a spirit of

wisdom and revelation resulting in knowledge of him.[p] [18]May the eyes of [your] hearts be enlightened, that you may know what is the hope that belongs to his call, what are the riches of glory in his inheritance among the holy ones,[q] [19]and what is the surpassing greatness of his power for us who believe, in accord with the exercise of his great might,[r] [20]which he worked in Christ, raising him from the dead and seating him at his right hand in the heavens,[s] [21]far above every principality, authority, power, and dominion, and every name that is named not only in this age but also in the one to come.[t] [22]And he put all things beneath his feet and gave him as head over all things to the church,[u] [23]which is his body,* the fullness of the one who fills all things in every way.[v]

CHAPTER 2*

Generosity of God's Plan.* [1] [w] You were dead in your transgressions and sins* [2]in which you once lived following the age of this world,* following the ruler of the power of the air, the spirit that is now at

---

i Eph 3, 3.9; Rom 16, 25.—j Gal 4, 4; Col 1, 16.20.—k Is 46, 10; Rom 8, 28; Col 1, 12; Rv 4, 11.—l Eph 4, 30; Acts 2, 33; Col 1, 5-6.—m 2 Cor 1, 22; 5, 5.—n Col 1, 3-4; Phlm 4-5.—o Col 1, 3.9.—p Eph 3, 14.16; Col 1, 9-10; 1 Jn 5, 20.—q Eph 4, 4; Col 1, 12.27.—r 2 Cor 13, 4; Col 1, 11; 2, 12.—s Ps 110, 1; Heb 1, 3.—t Phil 2, 9; Col 1, 16; 1 Pt 3, 22.—u Eph 4, 15; Ps 8, 7; Mt 28, 18; Col 1, 18.—v Eph 4, 10.12; Rom 12, 5; 1 Cor 12, 27; Col 1, 19.—w Col 1, 21; 2, 13.

1, 12: *We who first hoped:* probably Jewish Christians (contrast 13, *you,* the Gentiles); possibly the people of Israel, "we who already enjoyed the hope of Christ," or perhaps present hope in contrast to future redemption (cf Eph 1, 14).

1, 13: *Sealed:* by God, in baptism; cf Eph 4, 30; 2 Cor 1, 22.

1, 14: *First installment:* down payment by God on full salvation, as at 2 Cor 1, 22.

1, 15-23: See the note on Rom 1, 8 for the thanksgiving form in a letter. Much of the content parallels thoughts in Col 1, 3-20. The prayer moves from God and Christ (17.20-21) to the Ephesians (17-19) and the church (22-23). Paul asks that the blessing imparted by God the Father (3) to the Ephesians will be strengthened in them through the message of the gospel (13.17-19). Those blessings are seen in the context of God's *might* in establishing the sovereignty of Christ over all other creatures (19-21) and in appointing him *head* of the church (22-23). For the allusion to angelic spirits in v 21, see Rom 8, 38 and Col 1, 16. Here, as in 1 Cor 15, 24-25 and Col 2, 15, every such *principality* and *power* is made subject to Christ.

1, 15: *Your faith . . . your love:* some manuscripts omit the latter phrase, but cf Col 1, 4.

1, 23: *His body:* the church (22); cf the note on Col 1, 18. Only in Eph and Col is Christ the *head* of the body, in contrast to the view in 1 Cor 12 and Rom 12, 4-8 where Christ is equated with the entire body or community. *Fullness:* see the note on Col 1, 19. Some take *the one who fills* as God, others as Christ (cf Eph 4, 10). If in Christ "dwells the fullness of the deity bodily" (Col 2, 9), then, as God "fills" Christ, Christ in turn fills the church and the believer (Eph 3, 19; 5, 18). But the difficult

phrases here may also allow the church to be viewed as the "complement" of Christ who is "being filled" as God's plan for the universe is carried out through the church (cf Eph 3, 9-10).

2, 1-22: The gospel of *salvation* (Eph 1, 13) that God *worked in Christ* (Eph 1, 20) is reiterated in terms of what God's *great love* (4), expressed in Christ, means for us. The passage sometimes addresses *you,* Gentiles (1-2.8.11-13.19.22), but other times speaks of *all of us* who believe (3-7.10.14.18). In urging people to *remember* their grim past when they were *dead* in sins (1-3.11-12) and what they are *now in Christ* (4-10.13), the author sees both Jew and Gentile reconciled with God, now *one new person,* a new humanity, *one body, the household of God, a temple* and *dwelling place* of God's Spirit (15-16.19-22). The presentation falls into two parts, the second stressing more the meaning for the church.

2, 1-10: The recipients of Paul's letter have experienced, in their redemption from *transgressions and sins,* the effect of Christ's supremacy over the power of the devil (1-2; cf Eph 6, 11-12), who rules not from the netherworld but from the *air* between God in heaven and human beings on earth. Both Jew and Gentile have experienced, through Christ, God's free gift of salvation that already marks them for a future heavenly destiny (3-7). The language *dead, raised us up,* and *seated us . . . in the heavens* closely parallels Jesus' own passion and Easter experience. The terms in vv 8-9 describe salvation in the way Paul elsewhere speaks of justification: *by grace, through faith, the gift of God, not from works;* cf Gal 2, 16-21; Rom 3, 24-28. Christians are a newly created people in Christ, fashioned by God for a life of goodness (10).

2, 1-7: These verses comprise one long sentence in Greek, the main verb coming in v 5, God *brought us to life,* the object you/us *dead in . . . transgressions* being repeated in 1 and 5; cf Col 2, 13.

2, 2: *Age of this world:* or "aeon," a term found in gnostic thought, possibly synonymous with *the rulers of this world,* but also reflecting the Jewish idea of "two ages," this present evil age and "the age to come"; cf 1 Cor 3, 19; 5, 10; 7, 31; Gal 1, 4; Ti 2, 12. *The disobedient:* literally, "the sons of disobedience," a Semitism as at Is 30, 9.

work in the disobedient.ˣ ³All of us once lived among them in the desires of our flesh, following the wishes of the flesh and the impulses, and we were by nature children of wrath, like the rest.ʸ ⁴But God, who is rich in mercy, because of the great love he had for us, ⁵ ᶻ even when we were dead in our transgressions, brought us to life with Christ* (by grace you have been saved), ⁶raised us up with him, and seated us with him in the heavens in Christ Jesus,ᵃ ⁷that in the ages to come he might show the immeasurable riches of his grace in his kindness to us in Christ Jesus.ᵇ ⁸For by grace you have been saved through faith, and this is not from you; it is the gift of God;ᶜ ⁹it is not from works, so no one may boast.ᵈ ¹⁰For we are his handiwork, created in Christ Jesus for the good works that God has prepared in advance, that we should live in them.ᵉ

One in Christ.* ¹¹Therefore, remember that at one time you, Gentiles in the flesh, called the uncircumcision by those called the circumcision, which is done in the flesh by human hands, ¹²were at that time without Christ, alienated from the community of Israel* and strangers to the covenants of promise, without hope and without God in the world.ᶠ ¹³But now in Christ Jesus you who once were far off have become near by the blood of Christ.ᵍ

¹⁴ * For he is our peace, he who made both one and broke down the dividing wall of enmity, through his flesh,ʰ ¹⁵abolishing the law with its commandments and legal claims, that he might create in himself one new person* in place of the two, thus establishing peace,ⁱ ¹⁶and might reconcile both with God, in one body, through the cross, putting that enmity to death by it.ʲ ¹⁷He came and preached peace to you who were far off and peace to those who were near,ᵏ ¹⁸for through him we both have access in one Spirit to the Father.ˡ

¹⁹So then you are no longer strangers and sojourners, but you are fellow citizens with the holy ones and members of the household of God,ᵐ ²⁰built upon the foundation of the apostles and prophets,ⁿ with Christ Jesus himself as the capstone.* ²¹Through him the whole structure is held together and grows into a temple sacred in the Lord;ᵒ ²²in him you also are being built together into a dwelling place of God in the Spirit.ᵖ

III. WORLD MISSION OF THE CHURCH

CHAPTER 3

Commission to Preach God's Plan.* ¹Because of this,�q I, Paul, a prisoner of Christ* [Jesus] for you Gentiles— ²if, as I suppose, you have heard of the stewardship* of God's grace that was given to me

Eph

---

x Eph 6, 12; Jn 12, 31; Col 1, 13.—y Col 3, 6-7.—z Rom 5, 8; 6, 13; Col 2, 13.—a Rom 8, 10-11; Phil 3, 20; Col 2, 12.—b Eph 1, 7.—c Rom 3, 24; Gal 2, 16.—d 1 Cor 1, 29.—e Eph 4, 24; Ti 2, 14.—f Rom 9, 4; Col 1, 21.27.—g Eph 2, 17; Is 57, 19; Col 1, 20.—h Gal 3, 28.—i 2 Cor 5, 17; Col 2, 14.—j Col 1, 20.22.—k Is 57, 19; Zec 9, 10.—l Eph 3, 12.—m Heb 12, 22-23.—n Is 28, 16; Rv 21, 14.—o 1 Cor 3, 16; Col 2, 19.—p 1 Pt 2, 5.—q Phil 1, 7.13; Col 1, 24-29; 4, 18; Phlm 1, 9; 2 Tm 2, 9.

2, 5: Our relation through baptism *with Christ*, the risen Lord, is depicted in terms of realized eschatology, as already exaltation, though v 7 brings in the future aspect too.

2, 11-22: The Gentiles lacked Israel's messianic expectation, lacked the various *covenants* God made with *Israel*, lacked *hope* of salvation and knowledge of the true *God* (11-12); but through Christ all these religious barriers between Jew and Gentile have been transcended (13-14) by the abolition of the Mosaic covenant-law (15) for the sake of uniting Jew and Gentile into a single religious community (15-16), imbued with the same holy *Spirit* and worshiping the same *Father* (18). The Gentiles are now included in God's *household* (19) as it arises upon the *foundation* of *apostles* assisted by those endowed with the prophetic gift (Eph 3, 5), the preachers of Christ (20; cf 1 Cor 12, 28). With Christ as the *capstone* (20; cf Is 28, 16; Mt 21, 42), they are being built into the holy *temple* of God's people where the divine presence dwells (21-22).

2, 12: *The community of Israel:* or "commonwealth"; cf Eph 4, 18. *The covenants:* cf Rom 9, 4: with Abraham, with Moses, with David.

2, 14-16: The elaborate imagery here combines pictures of Christ as *our peace* (Is 9, 5), his crucifixion, the ending of the Mosaic law (cf Col 2, 14), reconciliation (2 Cor 5, 18-21), and

the destruction of *the dividing wall* such as kept people from God in the temple or a barrier in the heavens.

2, 15: *One new person:* a corporate body, the Christian community, made up of Jews and Gentiles, replacing ancient divisions; cf Rom 1, 16.

2, 20: *Capstone:* the Greek can also mean cornerstone or keystone.

3, 1-13: Paul reflects on his mission to the Gentiles. He alludes to his call and appointment to the apostolic office (2-3) and how his *insight* through revelation, as well as that of the other apostles and charismatic prophets in the church (4-5), has deepened understanding of God's plan of salvation in Christ. Paul is the special herald (7) of a new *promise* to the *Gentiles* (6): that the divine plan includes them in the spiritual benefits promised to Israel. Not only is this unique apostolic role his; Paul also has been given the task of explaining to all the divine *plan* of salvation (8-9), once *hidden*. Through *the church*, God's plan to save through Christ is becoming manifest to angelic beings (10; cf Eph 1, 21), in accord with God's *purpose* (11). The fulfillment of the plan in Christ gives the whole church more *confidence* through *faith* in God (12). The readers of this letter are also thereby encouraged to greater confidence despite Paul's imprisonment (13).

3, 1: *A prisoner of Christ:* see Introduction. Paul abruptly departs from his train of thought at the end of v 1, leaving an incomplete sentence.

3, 2: *Stewardship:* the Greek is the same term employed at Eph 1, 10 for the *plan* that God administers (Col 1, 25) and in which Paul plays a key role.

for your benefit,[r] [3][namely, that] the mystery* was made known to me by revelation, as I have written briefly earlier.[s] [4]When you read this you can understand my insight into the mystery of Christ, [5]which was not made known to human beings in other generations as it has now been revealed to his holy apostles and prophets by the Spirit,[t] [6]that the Gentiles are coheirs, members of the same body, and copartners in the promise in Christ Jesus through the gospel.[u]

[7]Of this I became a minister by the gift of God's grace that was granted me in accord with the exercise of his power.[v] [8]To me, the very least of all the holy ones, this grace was given, to preach to the Gentiles the inscrutable riches of Christ,[w] [9]and to bring to light [for all]* what is the plan of the mystery hidden from ages past in God who created all things,[x] [10]so that the manifold wisdom of God might now be made known through the church to the principalities and authorities* in the heavens.[y] [11]This was according to the eternal purpose that he accomplished in Christ Jesus our Lord, [12]in whom we have boldness of speech and confidence of access through faith in him.[z] [13]So I ask you not to lose heart over my afflictions for you; this is your glory.[a]

Prayer for the Readers.* [14]For this reason I kneel before the Father, [15]from whom every family* in heaven and on earth is

named, [16]that he may grant you in accord with the riches of his glory to be strengthened with power through his Spirit in the inner self,[b] [17]and that Christ may dwell in your hearts through faith; that you, rooted and grounded in love,[c] [18]may have strength to comprehend with all the holy ones what is the breadth and length and height and depth,[d] [19]and to know the love of Christ that surpasses knowledge, so that you may be filled with all the fullness of God.[e]

[20]Now to him who is able to accomplish far more than all we ask or imagine, by the power at work within us,[f] [21]to him be glory in the church and in Christ Jesus to all generations, forever and ever. Amen.

CHAPTER 4

Unity in the Body. [1]* I, then, a prisoner for the Lord, urge you to live in a manner worthy of the call you have received,[g] [2]with all humility and gentleness, with patience, bearing with one another through love,[h] [3]striving to preserve the unity of the spirit through the bond of peace: [4] * one body and one Spirit, as you were also called to the one hope of your call;[j] [5]one Lord, one faith, one baptism;[k] [6]one God and Father of all, who is over all and through all and in all.[l]

Diversity of Gifts. [7]But grace was given to each of us according to the measure of Christ's gift.[m] [8]Therefore, it says:

---

r Col 1, 25.—s Eph 1, 9-10; Col 1, 26.—t Col 1, 26.—u Eph 2, 13.18-19.—v Rom 15, 15; Col 1, 25.29.—w 1 Cor 15, 8-10; Gal 1, 16; 2, 7-9.—x Rom 16, 25; Col 1, 26-27.—y 1 Pt 1, 12.—z Rom 5, 1-2; Heb 4, 16.—a Col 1, 22.24; 2 Tm 2, 10.—b Eph 6, 10; Rom 7, 22; 2 Cor 4, 16; Col 1, 11.—c Jn 14, 23; Col 1, 23; 2, 7.—d Col 2, 2.—e Col 2, 3.9.—f Rom 16, 25-27; Col 1, 29.—g Eph 3, 1; Col 1, 10.—h Col 3, 12-13.—i Col 3, 14-15.—j Rom 12, 5; 1 Cor 10, 17; 12, 12-13.—k 1 Cor 8, 6.—l 1 Cor 12, 6.—m Rom 12, 3.6; 1 Cor 12, 28.

3, 3-4: *The mystery:* God's resolve to deliver Gentiles along with Israel through Christ; cf the notes on Eph 1, 10; 3, 9.

3, 9: *[For all]:* while some think this phrase was added so as to yield the sense "to enlighten all about the plan . . . ," it is more likely that some manuscripts and Fathers omitted it accidentally or to avoid the idea that *all* conflicted with Paul's assignment to preach to *the Gentiles* (8) specifically.

3, 10: *Principalities and authorities:* see the note on Eph 1, 15-23 regarding v 21.

3, 14-21: The apostle prays that those he is addressing may, like the rest of the church, deepen their understanding of God's plan of salvation in Christ. It is a plan that affects the whole universe (15) with *the breadth and length and height and depth* of God's love in Christ (18) or possibly the universe in all its dimensions. The apostle prays that they may perceive the redemptive love of Christ for them and be completely immersed in the fullness of God (19). The prayer concludes with a doxology to God (20-21).

3, 14-15: *Every family:* in the Greek there is wordplay on the word for *the Father (patria, patēr).* The phrase could also mean "God's whole family" (cf Eph 2, 21).

4, 1-16: A general plea for unity in the church. Christians have been fashioned through the *Spirit* into a single harmonious religious community *(one body,* 4.12; cf Eph 4, 16), belonging to a single *Lord* (in contrast to the many gods of the pagan world), and by one way of salvation through *faith,* brought out especially by the significance of *baptism* (1-6; cf Rom 6, 1-11). But Christian unity is more than adherence to a common belief. It is manifested in the exalted Christ's gifts to individuals to serve so as to make the community more Christlike (11-16). This teaching on Christ as the source of the gifts is introduced in v 8 by a citation of Ps 68, 18, which depicts Yahweh triumphantly leading Israel to salvation in Jerusalem. It is here understood of Christ, ascending *above all the heavens,* the *head* of the church; through his redemptive death, resurrection, and ascension he has become the source of the church's spiritual gifts. The "descent" of Christ (9-10) refers more probably to the incarnation (cf Phil 2, 6-8) than to Christ's presence after his death in the world of the dead (cf 1 Pt 3, 19).

4, 4-6: The "seven unities" (church, *Spirit,* hope; *Lord, faith* in Christ [Eph 1, 13], *baptism; one God*) reflect the triune structure of later creeds in reverse.

"He ascended* on high and took prisoners captive;
he gave gifts to men."[n]

9 What does "he ascended" mean except that he also descended into the lower [regions] of the earth? 10 The one who descended is also the one who ascended far above all the heavens, that he might fill all things.

11 * And he gave some as apostles, others as prophets, others as evangelists, others as pastors and teachers,[o] 12 to equip the holy ones for the work of ministry,* for building up the body of Christ, 13 until we all attain to the unity of faith and knowledge of the Son of God, to mature manhood,* to the extent of the full stature of Christ,[p] 14 so that we may no longer be infants, tossed by waves and swept along by every wind of teaching arising from human trickery, from their cunning in the interests of deceitful scheming.[q] 15 Rather, living the truth in love, we should grow in every way into him who is the head,[r] Christ,* 16 from whom the whole body, joined and held together by every supporting ligament, with the proper functioning of each part, brings about the body's growth and builds itself up in love.[s]

Renewal in Christ.* 17 So I declare and testify in the Lord that you must no longer live as the Gentiles do, in the futility of their minds;[t] 18 darkened in understanding, alienated from the life of God because of their ignorance, because of their hardness of heart,[u] 19 they have become callous and have handed themselves over to licentiousness for the practice of every kind of impurity to excess.[v] 20 That is not how you learned Christ, 21 assuming that you have heard of him and were taught in him, as truth is in Jesus, 22 that you should put away the old self of your former way of life, corrupted through deceitful desires,[w] 23 and be renewed in the spirit of your minds,[x] 24 and put on* the new self, created in God's way in righteousness and holiness of truth.[y]

IV. DAILY CONDUCT, AN EXPRESSION OF UNITY*

Rules for the New Life. 25 Therefore, putting away falsehood, speak the truth, each one to his neighbor, for we are members one of another.[z] 26 Be angry but do not sin;[a] do not let the sun set on your anger,* 27 and do not leave room for the devil.[b] 28 The thief must no longer steal, but rather labor, doing honest work* with his [own] hands, so that he may have something to share with one in need.[c] 29 No foul language should come out of your mouths, but only such as is good for needed edification, that it may impart grace to those who hear.[d] 30 And do not grieve the holy Spirit of God, with which you were sealed for the day of redemption.* 31 All bitterness, fury, anger, shouting, and reviling must be removed from you, along with all malice.[e] 32 [And] be kind to one another, compassionate, forgiving one another as God has forgiven you in Christ.[f]

Eph

---

n Ps 68, 19; Col 2, 15.—o 1 Cor 12, 28.—p Col 1, 28.—q 1 Cor 14, 20; Col 2, 4.8; Heb 13, 9; Jas 1, 6.—r 1 Cor 11, 3; Col 1, 18; 2, 19.—s Col 2, 19.—t Rom 1, 21.—u Col 1, 21; 1 Pt 1, 14.—v Col 3, 5.—w Rom 8, 13; Gal 6, 8; Col 3, 9.—x Rom 12, 2.—y Gn 1, 26-27; Col 3, 10.—z Zec 8, 16.—a Ps 4, 5 LXX; Mt 5, 22.—b 2 Cor 2, 11.—c 1 Thes 4, 11.—d Eph 5, 4; Col 3, 16; 4, 6.—e Col 3, 8.—f Mt 6, 14; Col 3, 12-13.

4, 8-10: While the emphasis is on an ascension and gift-giving by Christ, there is also a reference in taking *prisoners captive* to the aeons and powers mentioned at Eph 1, 21; 2, 2; 3, 10; and 6, 12.

4, 11: Concerning this list of ministers, cf 1 Cor 12, 28 and Rom 12, 6-8. *Evangelists:* missionary preachers (cf Acts 21, 8 and 2 Tm 4, 5), not those who wrote gospels. *Pastors and teachers:* a single group in the Greek, shepherding congregations.

4, 12: The ministerial leaders in v 11 are to equip the whole people of God for their *work of ministry.*

4, 13: *Mature manhood:* literally, "a perfect man" (cf Col 1, 28), possibly the "one new person" of Eph 2, 15, though there *anthrōpos* suggests humanity, while here *anēr* is the term for male. This personage becomes visible in the church's growing to its fullness in the unity of those who believe in Christ.

4, 15-16: *The head, Christ:* cf Col 1, 18 and contrast 1 Cor 12, 12-27 and Rom 12, 4-5 where Christ is identified with the whole body, including the head. The imagery may derive from ancient views in medicine, the *head* coordinating and caring for the body, each *ligament* (perhaps the ministers of v 11) supporting the whole. But as at Eph 2, 19-22, where the temple is depicted as a growing organism, there may also be the idea here of growing toward the capstone, Christ.

4, 17-24: Paul begins to indicate how the new life in Christ contrasts with the Gentiles' old way of existence. Literally, *the old self* (22) and *the new self* (24) are "the old man" and "the new man" (*anthrōpos,* person), as at Eph 2, 15; cf the note on Eph 4, 13.

4, 24: *Put on:* in baptism. See the note on Gal 3, 27.

4, 25—6, 20: For similar exhortations to a morally good life in response to God's gift of faith, see the notes on Rom 12, 1—13, 14 and Gal 5, 13-26.

4, 26: If angry, seek reconciliation that day, not giving the devil (Eph 6, 11) opportunity to lead into sin.

4, 28: *Honest work:* literally, "the good." *His [own] hands:* some manuscripts have the full phrase as in 1 Cor 4, 12.

4, 30: See the note on Eph 1, 13.

CHAPTER 5

[1] So be imitators of God,* as beloved children,[g] [2] and live in love, as Christ loved us and handed himself over for us as a sacrificial offering to God for a fragrant aroma.[h] [3] Immorality or any impurity or greed must not even be mentioned among you, as is fitting among holy ones,[i] [4] no obscenity or silly or suggestive talk, which is out of place, but instead, thanksgiving.[j] [5] Be sure of this, that no immoral or impure or greedy person, that is, an idolater, has any inheritance in the kingdom of Christ and of God.[k]

Duty to Live in the Light. [6] [l] Let no one deceive you with empty arguments, for because of these things the wrath of God is coming upon the disobedient.* [7] So do not be associated with them. [8] For you were once darkness, but now you are light in the Lord. Live as children of light,[m] [9] for light produces every kind of goodness and righteousness and truth.[n] [10] Try to learn what is pleasing to the Lord.[o] [11] Take no part in the fruitless works of darkness; rather expose them,[p] [12] for it is shameful even to mention the things done by them in secret; [13] but everything exposed by the light becomes visible,[q] [14] for everything that becomes visible is light. Therefore, it says:[r]

"Awake, O sleeper,
    and arise from the dead,
and Christ will give you light."*

[15] * Watch carefully then how you live, not as foolish persons but as wise,[s] [16] making the most of the opportunity, because the days are evil. [17] Therefore, do not continue in ignorance, but try to understand what is the will of the Lord. [18] And do not get drunk on wine, in which lies debauchery, but be filled with the Spirit,[t] [19] addressing one another [in] psalms and hymns and spiritual songs, singing and playing to the Lord in your hearts,[u] [20] giving thanks always and for everything in the name of our Lord Jesus Christ to God the Father.[v]

Wives and Husbands. [21] * Be subordinate to one another[w] out of reverence for Christ.* [22] Wives should be subordinate to their husbands as to the Lord.[x] [23] For the husband is head of his wife just as Christ is head of the church, he himself the savior of the body.[y] [24] As the church is subordinate to Christ, so wives should be subordinate to their husbands in everything. [25] Husbands, love your wives, even as Christ loved the church and handed himself over for her[z] [26] to sanctify her, cleansing her by the bath of water with the word,[a] [27] that he might present to himself the church in splendor, without spot or wrinkle or any such thing, that she might be holy and without blemish.[b] [28] So [also] husbands should love their wives as their own bodies. He who loves his wife loves himself. [29] For no one hates his own flesh but rather nourishes and cherishes it, even as Christ does the church, [30] because we are members of his body.[c]

[31] "For this reason a man shall leave [his]
    father and [his] mother
    and be joined to his wife,
and the two shall become one flesh."[d]

[32] This is a great mystery, but I speak in reference to Christ and the church.[e] [33] In any case, each one of you should love his wife as himself, and the wife should respect her husband.

g Mt 5, 45.48.—h Ex 29, 18; Ps 40, 7; Gal 2, 20; 1 Jn 3, 16.—i Gal 5, 19; Col 3, 5.—j Eph 4, 29; Col 3, 8.—k 1 Cor 6, 9-10; Gal 5, 21; Col 3, 5.—l Rom 1, 18; Col 2, 4.8.—m Eph 2, 11-13; Jn 12, 36; Col 1, 12-13.—n Gal 5, 22.—o Rom 12, 2.—p Rom 13, 12.—q Jn 3, 20-21.—r Is 26, 19; 60, 1.—s 15-16: Col 4, 5.—t Prv 23, 31 LXX; Lk 21, 34.—u Ps 33, 2-3; Col 3, 16.—v Col 3, 17.—w 1 Pt 5, 5.—x Col 3, 18—4, 1; 1 Pt 3, 1-7.—y 1 Cor 11, 3; Col 1, 18.—z Col 3, 19; 1 Tm 2, 6.—a Rom 6, 4; Ti 3, 5-7.—b 2 Cor 11, 2; Col 1, 22.—c Rom 12, 5; 1 Cor 6, 15.—d Gn 2, 24; Mt 19, 5; Mk 10, 7-8.—e Rv 19, 7.

5, 1: *Imitators of God:* in forgiving (Eph 4, 32) and in loving (as exhibited in how *Christ loved us*).

5, 6: See the note on Eph 2, 2.

5, 14: An early Christian hymn, possibly from a baptismal liturgy. For the content compare Eph 2, 5-6; 3, 9 and Is 60, 1.

5, 15-16.19-20: The wording is similar to Col 4, 5 and Eph 3, 16-17.

5, 21—6, 9: Cf the notes on Col 3, 18—4, 1 and 1 Pt 2, 18—3, 7 for a similar listing of household duties where the inferior is admonished first *(wives,* Eph 5, 22; *children,* Eph 6, 1; *slaves,* Eph 6, 5), then the superior *(husbands,* Eph 5, 25; *fathers,* Eph

6, 4; *masters,* Eph 6, 9). Paul varies this pattern by an emphasis on mutuality (see Eph 5, 20); use of Old Testament material about *father and mother* in Eph 6, 2; the judgment to come for slave-owners *(you have a Master in heaven,* Eph 6, 9); and above all the initial principle of subordination *to one another* under *Christ,* thus effectively undermining exclusive claims to domination by one party. Into the section on *wives* and *husbands* an elaborate teaching on *Christ* and *the church* has been woven (Eph 5, 22-33).

5, 21-33: The apostle exhorts married Christians to a strong mutual love. Holding with Gn 2, 24 that marriage is a divine institution (31), Paul sees Christian marriage as taking on a new meaning symbolic of the intimate relationship of love between Christ and the church. The wife should serve her husband in the same spirit as that of the church's service to Christ (22.24), and the husband should care for his wife with the devotion of Christ to the church (25-30). Paul gives to the Genesis passage its highest meaning in the light of the union of Christ and the church, of which Christlike loyalty and devotion in Christian marriage are a clear reflection (31-33).

CHAPTER 6

Children and Parents. ¹Children, obey your parents [in the Lord], for this is right.*ᶠ* ²"Honor your father and mother."*ᵍ* This is the first commandment with a promise, ³"that it may go well with you and that you may have a long life on earth." ⁴Fathers, do not provoke your children to anger, but bring them up with the training and instruction of the Lord.*ʰ*

Slaves and Masters. ⁵Slaves, be obedient to your human masters with fear and trembling, in sincerity of heart, as to Christ,*ⁱ* ⁶not only when being watched, as currying favor, but as slaves of Christ, doing the will of God from the heart,*ʲ* ⁷willingly serving the Lord and not human beings, ⁸knowing that each will be requited from the Lord for whatever good he does, whether he is slave or free. ⁹Masters, act in the same way toward them, and stop bullying, knowing that both they and you have a Master in heaven and that with him there is no partiality.*ᵏ*

Battle against Evil. ¹⁰ * Finally, draw your strength from the Lord and from his mighty power. ¹¹Put on the armor of God so that you may be able to stand firm against the tactics of the devil.*ˡ* ¹²For our struggle is not with flesh and blood but with the principalities, with the powers, with the world rulers of this present darkness, with the evil spirits in the heavens.*ᵐ* ¹³Therefore, put on the armor of God, that you may be able to resist on the evil day and, having done everything, to hold your ground.*ⁿ* ¹⁴So stand fast with your loins girded in truth, clothed with righteousness as a breastplate,*ᵒ* ¹⁵and your feet shod in readiness for the gospel of peace.*ᵖ* ¹⁶In all circumstances, hold faith as a shield, to quench all [the] flaming arrows of the evil one.*�q* ¹⁷And take the helmet of salvation and the sword of the Spirit, which is the word of God.*ʳ*

Constant Prayer. ¹⁸With all prayer and supplication, pray at every opportunity in the Spirit. To that end, be watchful with all perseverance and supplication for all the holy ones*ˢ* ¹⁹and also for me, that speech may be given me to open my mouth, to make known with boldness the mystery of the gospel*ᵗ* ²⁰for which I am an ambassador in chains, so that I may have the courage to speak as I must.*ᵘ*

V. CONCLUSION

A Final Message. * ²¹So that you also may have news of me and of what I am doing, Tychicus, my beloved brother and trustworthy minister in the Lord, will tell you everything.*ᵛ* ²²I am sending him to you for this very purpose, so that you may know about us and that he may encourage your hearts.*ʷ*

²³Peace be to the brothers, and love with faith, from God the Father and the Lord Jesus Christ. ²⁴Grace be with all who love our Lord Jesus Christ in immortality.*ˣ*

---

f Prv 6, 20; Sir 3, 1-6; Col 3, 20.—g 2-3: Ex 20, 12; Dt 5, 16.—h Col 3, 21-22.—i Col 3, 22-25; 1 Tm 6, 1-2; Ti 2, 9-10.— j 1 Pt 2, 18.—k Col 4, 1.—l Rom 13, 12; 2 Cor 6, 7; 10, 4; Jas 4, 7.—m Eph 1, 21; 2, 2; Col 1, 13.—n Rom 13, 12.—o Wis 5, 17-20; Is 11, 5; Lk 12, 35; 1 Thes 5, 8.—p Is 52, 7.—q 1 Pt 5, 9.—r Is 59, 17; 1 Thes 5, 8.—s Mt 26, 41; Col 4, 2-3.—t Acts 4, 29; Col 4, 3; 2 Thes 3, 1.—u 2 Cor 5, 20; Col 4, 4.—v Acts 20, 4; Col 4, 7; 2 Tm 4, 12.—w Col 4, 8.—x 1 Pt 1, 8.

6, 10-20: A general exhortation to courage and prayer. Drawing upon the imagery and ideas of Is 11, 5; 59, 16-17; and Wis 5, 17-23, Paul describes the Christian in terms of the dress and equipment of Roman soldiers. He observes, however, that the Christian's readiness for combat is not directed against human beings but against the spiritual powers of evil (10-17; cf Eph 1, 21; 2, 2; 3, 10). Unique importance is placed upon prayer (18-20).

6, 21-24: *Tychicus:* the bearer of the letter; see the note on Col 4, 7. Verses 21-22 parallel Col 4, 7-8, often word for word. If Ephesians is addressed to several Christian communities (see Introduction), it is understandable that no greetings to individual members of these communities should have been included in it.

Eph

THE LETTER TO THE PHILIPPIANS

INTRODUCTION

Philippi, in northeastern Greece, was a city of some importance in the Roman province of Macedonia. Lying on the great road from the Adriatic coast to Byzantium, the Via Egnatia, and in the midst of rich agricultural plains near the gold deposits of Mt. Pangaeus, it was in Paul's day a Roman town (Acts 16, 21), with a Greek-Macedonian population and a small group of Jews (see Acts 16, 13). Originally founded in the sixth century B.C. as Krenides by the Thracians, the town was taken over after 360 B.C. by Philip II of Macedon, the father of Alexander the Great, and was renamed for himself, "Philip's City." The area became Roman in the second century B.C. On the plains near Philippi in October 42 B.C., Antony and Octavian decisively defeated the forces of Brutus and Cassius, the slayers of Julius Caesar. Octavian (Augustus) later made Philippi a Roman colony and settled many veterans of the Roman armies there.

Paul, according to Acts (16, 9-40), established at Philippi the first Christian community in Europe. He came to Philippi, via its harbor town of Neapolis (modern Kavalla), on his second missionary journey, probably in A.D. 49 or 50, accompanied by Silas and Timothy (Acts 15, 40; 16, 3; cf Phil 1, 1) and Luke, if he is to be included in the "we" references of Acts 16, 10-17. The Acts account tells of the conversion of a business woman, Lydia; the exorcism of a slave girl; and, after an earthquake, while Paul and Silas were imprisoned in Philippi, the faith and baptism of a jailer and his family. None of these persons, however, is directly mentioned in Philippians (cf the notes on 4, 2 and 4, 3). Acts 16 concludes its account by describing how Paul (and Silas), asked by the magistrates to leave Philippi, went on to Thessalonica (Acts 17, 1-10), where several times his loyal Philippians continued to support him with financial aid (Phil 4, 16). Later, Paul may have passed through Philippi on his way from Ephesus to Greece (Acts 20, 1-2), and he definitely stopped there on his fateful trip to Jerusalem (Acts 20, 6).

Paul's letter to the Christians at Philippi was written while he was in a prison somewhere (1, 7.13.14.17), indeed in danger of death (1, 20-23). Although under guard for preaching Christ, Paul rejoices at the continuing progress of the gospel (1, 12-26) and expresses gratitude for the Philippians' renewed concern and help in an expression of thanks most clearly found at 4, 10-20. Much of the letter is devoted to instruction about unity and humility within the Christian community at Philippi (1, 27—2, 18) and exhortations to growth, joy, and peace in their life together (4, 1-9). The letter seems to be drawing to a close at the end of what we number as ch 2, as Paul reports the plans of his helper Timothy and of Epaphroditus (whom the Philippians had sent to aid Paul) to come to Philippi (2, 19—3, 1), and even Paul's own expectation that he will go free and come to Philippi (1, 25-26; 2, 24). Yet quite abruptly at 3, 2, Paul erupts into warnings against false teachers who threaten to impose on the Philippians the burdens of the Mosaic law, including circumcision. The section that follows, 3, 2-21, is a vigorous attack on these Judaizers (cf Gal 2, 11—3, 29) or Jewish Christian teachers (cf 2 Cor 11, 12-23), giving us insights into Paul's own life story (3, 4-6) and into the doctrine of justification, the Christian life, and ultimate hope (3, 7-21).

The location of Paul's imprisonment when he wrote to the Philippians, and thus the date of the letter, are uncertain. The traditional view has been that it stems from Paul's confinement in Rome, between A.D. 59 and 63 (cf Acts 28, 14-31). One modern view suggests the period when he was imprisoned at Caesarea, on the coast of Palestine, A.D.

57 or 58 (Acts 23, 23—26, 32); another suggests Corinth (cf 2 Cor 11, 9). Much recent scholarship favors Ephesus, around A.D. 55, a situation referred to in 2 Cor 1, 8 concerning "the affliction that came to us" in Asia Minor (cf also 1 Cor 15, 32). The reference at 1, 13 to the "praetorium" (cf also 4, 22) can be understood to mean the imperial guard or government house at Ephesus (or Caesarea), or the praetorian camp in Rome. Involved in a decision are the several journeys back and forth between Philippi and wherever Paul is imprisoned, mentioned in the letter (2, 25-28; 4, 14); this factor causes many to prefer Ephesus because of its proximity to Philippi. The Ephesian hypothesis dates the composition of Philippians to the mid-50s when most of Paul's major letters were written.

There is also a likelihood, according to some scholars, that the letter as we have it is a composite from parts of three letters by Paul to the Philippians. Seemingly 4, 10-20 is a brief note of appreciation for help sent through Epaphroditus. The long section from 1, 3 to 3, 1 is then another letter, with news of Paul's imprisonment and reports on Timothy and Epaphroditus (who has fallen ill while with Paul), along with exhortations to the Philippians about Christian conduct; and 3, 2-21 a third communication warning about threats to Philippian Christianity. The other verses in ch 4 and 1, 1-2, are variously assigned by critics to these three underlying letters, which an editor presumably put together to produce a picture of Paul writing earnestly from prison (chs 1-2), facing opponents of the faith (ch 3), and with serene joy advising and thanking his Philippians (ch 4). If all four chapters were originally a unity, then one must assume that a break occurred between the writing of 3, 1 and 3, 2, possibly involving the receipt of bad news from Philippi, and that Paul had some reasons for delaying his words of thanks for the aid brought by Epaphroditus till the end of his letter.

This beautiful letter is rich in insights into Paul's theology and his apostolic love and concern for the gospel and his converts. In Philippians, Paul reveals his human sensitivity and tenderness, his enthusiasm for Christ as the key to life and death (1, 21), and his deep feeling for those in Christ who dwell in Philippi. With them he shares his **Phil** *hopes and convictions, his anxieties and fears, revealing the total confidence in Christ that constitutes faith (3, 8-10). The letter incorporates a hymn about the salvation that God has brought about through Christ (2, 6-11), applied by Paul to the relations of Christians with one another (2, 1-5). Philippians has been termed "the letter of joy" (4, 4.10). It is the rejoicing of faith, based on true understanding of Christ's unique role in the salvation of all who profess his lordship (2, 11; 3, 8-12.14.20-21).*

The principal divisions of the Letter to the Philippians are the following:

   I.   Address (1, 1-11)
  II.   Progress of the Gospel (1, 12-26)
 III.   Instructions for the Community (1, 27—2, 18)
 IV.   Travel Plans of Paul and His Assistants (2, 19—3, 1)
  V.   Polemic: Righteousness and the Goal in Christ (3, 2-21)
 VI.   Instructions for the Community (4, 1-9)
VII.   Gratitude for the Philippians' Generosity (4, 10-20)
VIII.   Farewell (4, 21-23)

I. ADDRESS

CHAPTER 1

Greeting.* [1] Paul and Timothy, slaves* of Christ Jesus, to all the holy ones in Christ Jesus who are in Philippi, with the overseers and ministers:[a] [2] [b] grace to you and peace from God our Father and the Lord Jesus Christ.*

Thanksgiving.* [3] I give thanks to my God at every remembrance of you,[c] [4] praying always with joy in my every prayer for all of you, [5] because of your partnership for the gospel from the first day until now. [6] [d] I am confident of this, that the one who began a good work in you will continue to complete it until the day of Christ Jesus.* [7] It is right that I should think this way about all of you, because I hold you in my heart, you who are all partners with me in grace, both in my imprisonment and in the defense and confirmation of the gospel. [8] For God is my witness, how I long for all of you with the affection of Christ Jesus.[e] [9] And this is my prayer: that your love may increase ever more and more in knowledge and every kind of perception,[f] [10] to discern what is of value, so that you may be pure and blameless for the day of Christ, [g] [11] filled with the fruit of righteousness that comes through Jesus Christ for the glory and praise of God.[h]

II. PROGRESS OF THE GOSPEL*

[12] [i] I want you to know, brothers, that my situation has turned out rather to advance the gospel, [13] so that my imprisonment has become well known in Christ throughout the whole praetorium* and to all the rest,[j] [14] * and so that the majority of the brothers, having taken encouragement in the Lord from my imprisonment, dare more than ever to proclaim the word fearlessly.

[15] Of course, some preach Christ from envy and rivalry, others from good will. [16] The latter act out of love, aware that I am here for the defense of the gospel; [17] the former proclaim Christ out of selfish ambition, not from pure motives, thinking that they will cause me trouble in my imprisonment. [18] What difference does it make, as long as in every way, whether in pretense or in truth, Christ is being proclaimed?[k] And in that I rejoice.*

---

a Rom 1, 1; 2 Cor 1, 1; 1 Thes 1, 1; Phlm 1 / 1 Tm 3, 1-13.—b Rom 1, 7; Gal 1, 3; Phlm 3.—c Rom 1, 8; 1 Cor 1, 4; 1 Thes 1, 2.—d Phil 2, 13 / Phil 1, 10; 2, 16; 1 Cor 1, 8.—e Rom 1, 9; 2 Cor 1, 23; 1 Thes 2, 5.—f Eph 3, 14-19; Col 1, 9-10; Phlm 6.—g Rom 2, 18; 12, 2 / Phil 1, 6.—h Jn 15, 8.—i 12-13: Eph 3, 1; 6, 20; 2 Tm 2, 9; Phlm 9.—j Phil 4, 22.—k Phil 4, 10.

1, 1-2: See the note on Rom 1, 1-7, concerning the greeting.

1, 1: *Slaves:* Paul usually refers to himself at the start of a letter as an apostle. Here he substitutes a term suggesting the unconditional obligation of himself and Timothy to the service of Christ, probably because, in view of the good relationship with the Philippians, he wishes to stress his status as a co-servant rather than emphasize his apostolic authority. Reference to Timothy is a courtesy: Paul alone writes the letter, as the singular verb throughout shows (Phil 1, 3-26), and the reference (Phil 2, 19-24) to Timothy in the third person. *Overseers:* the Greek term *episkopos* literally means "one who oversees" or "one who supervises," but since the second century it has come to designate the "bishop," the official who heads a local church. In New Testament times this office had not yet developed into the form that it later assumed, though it seems to be well on the way to such development in the Pastorals; see 1 Tm 3, 2 and Ti 1, 7, where it is translated *bishop.* At Philippi, however (and at Ephesus, according to Acts 20, 28), there was more than one *episkopos,* and the precise function of these officials is uncertain. In order to distinguish this office from the later stages into which it developed, the term is here translated as *overseers. Ministers:* the Greek term *diakonoi* is used frequently in the New Testament to designate "servants," "attendants," or "ministers." Paul refers to himself and to other apostles as "ministers of God" (2 Cor 6, 4) or "ministers of Christ" (2 Cor 11, 23). In the Pastorals (1 Tm 3, 8.12) the *diakonos* has become an established official in the local church; hence the term is there translated as *deacon.* The *diakonoi* at Philippi seem to represent an earlier stage of development of the office; we are uncertain about their precise functions. Hence the term is here translated as *ministers.* See Rom 16, 1, where Phoebe is described as a *diakonos (minister)* of the church of Cenchreae.

1, 2: The gifts come *from* Christ the Lord, not simply through him from the Father; compare the christology in Phil 2, 6-11.

1, 3-11: As in Rom 1, 8-15 and all the Pauline letters except Galatians, a thanksgiving follows, including a direct prayer for the Philippians (9-11); see the note on Rom 1, 8. On their *partnership for the gospel* (5), cf Phil 1, 29-30; 4, 10-20. Their devotion to the faith and to Paul made them his pride and joy (Phil 4, 1). The characteristics thus manifested are evidence of the community's continuing preparation for the Lord's parousia (6.10). Paul's especially warm relationship with the Philippians is suggested here (7.8) as elsewhere in the letter. The eschatology serves to underscore a concern for ethical growth (9-11), which appears throughout the letter.

1, 6: *The day of Christ Jesus:* the parousia or triumphant return of Christ, when those loyal to him will be with him and share in his eternal glory; cf Phil 1, 10; 2, 16; 3, 20-21; 1 Thes 4, 17; 5, 10; 2 Thes 1, 10; 1 Cor 1, 8.

1, 12-26: The body of the letter begins with an account of Paul's present *situation,* i.e., his *imprisonment* (12-13; see Introduction), and then goes on with advice for the Philippians (Phil 1, 27—2, 18). The *advance of the gospel* (12) and the *progress* of the Philippians *in the faith* (25) frame what is said.

1, 13: *Praetorium:* either the praetorian guard in the city where Paul was imprisoned or the governor's official residence in a Roman province (cf Mk 15, 16; Acts 23, 35). See Introduction on possible sites.

1, 14-18: Although Paul is imprisoned, Christians there nonetheless go on preaching Christ. But they do so with varied motives, *some* with personal hostility toward Paul, others out of personal ambition.

1, 18: *Rejoice:* a major theme in the letter; see Introduction.

Indeed I shall continue to rejoice, [19] * for I know that this will result in deliverance for me* through your prayers and support from the Spirit of Jesus Christ.[l] [20] My eager expectation and hope is that I shall not be put to shame in any way, but that with all boldness, now as always, Christ will be magnified in my body, whether by life or by death.[m] [21] For to me life is Christ, and death is gain.[n] [22] If I go on living in the flesh, that means fruitful labor for me. And I do not know which I shall choose.[o] [23] I am caught between the two. I long to depart this life and be with Christ, [for] that is far better.[p] [24] Yet that I remain [in] the flesh is more necessary for your benefit. [25] And this I know with confidence, that I shall remain and continue in the service of all of you for your progress and joy in the faith, [26] so that your boasting in Christ Jesus may abound on account of me when I come to you again.

III. INSTRUCTIONS FOR THE COMMUNITY

Steadfastness in Faith.* [27] Only, conduct yourselves in a way worthy of the gospel of Christ, so that, whether I come and see you or am absent, I may hear news of you, that you are standing firm in one spirit, with one mind struggling together for the faith of the gospel,[q] [28] not intimidated in any way by your opponents. This is proof to them of destruction, but of your salvation. And this is God's doing. [29] For to you has been granted, for the sake of Christ, not only to believe in him but also to suffer for him.[r] [30] Yours is the same struggle[s] as you saw in me and now hear about me.*

CHAPTER 2

Plea for Unity and Humility.* [1] If there is any encouragement in Christ, any solace in love, any participation in the Spirit, any compassion and mercy, [2] complete my joy by being of the same mind, with the same love, united in heart, thinking one thing.[t] [3] Do nothing out of selfishness or out of vainglory; rather, humbly regard others as more important than yourselves,[u] [4] each looking out not for his own interests, but [also] everyone for those of others.[v]

[5] Have among yourselves the same attitude that is also yours in Christ Jesus,*

[6] Who,* though he was in the form of God,[w]

did not regard equality with God something to be grasped.*

l Jb 13, 16 / 2 Cor 1, 11 —m 1 Cor 6, 20; 1 Pt 4, 16.—n Gal 2, 20.—o Rom 1, 13.—p 2 Cor 5, 8.—q Eph 4, 1; Col 1, 10; 1 Thes 2, 12 / Phil 4, 3.—r Mt 5, 10; 10, 38; Mk 8, 34; Acts 5, 41.—s Phil 1, 13; Acts 16, 22-24.—t Rom 15, 5; 1 Cor 1, 10.— u Rom 12, 3.10; Gal 5, 26.—v 1 Cor 10, 24.33; 13, 5.—w Jn 1, 1-2; 17, 5; Col 2, 9; Heb 1, 3.

1, 19-25: Paul earnestly debates his prospects of martyrdom or continued missionary labor. While he may *long to depart this life* and thus *be with Christ* (23), his overall and final expectation is that he will be delivered from his imprisonment and *continue in the service* of the Philippians and of others (19.25; Phil 2, 24). In either case, Christ is central (20.21); if to live means Christ for Paul, death means to be united with Christ in a deeper sense.

1, 19: *Result in deliverance for me:* an echo of Jb 13, 16, hoping that God will turn suffering to ultimate good and deliverance from evil.

1, 27-30: Ethical admonition begins at this early point in the letter, emphasizing steadfastness and congregational unity in the face of possible suffering. The *opponents* (28) are those in Philippi, probably pagans, who oppose the gospel cause. *This is proof . . .* (28) may refer to the whole outlook and conduct of the Philippians, turning out for their salvation but to the judgment of the opponents (cf 2 Cor 2, 15-16), or possibly the sentence refers to the opinion of the opponents, who hold that the obstinacy of the Christians points to the destruction of such people as defy Roman authority (though in reality, Paul holds, such faithfulness leads to salvation).

1, 30: A reference to Paul's earlier imprisonment in Philippi (Acts 16, 19-24; 1 Thes 2, 2) and to his present confinement.

2, 1-11: The admonition to likemindedness and unity (2-5) is based on the believers' threefold experience with Christ, God's love, and the Spirit. The appeal to humility (3) and to obedience (12) is rooted in christology, specifically in a statement about Christ Jesus (6-11) and his humbling of self and obedience to the point of death (8).

2, 5: *Have . . . the same attitude that is also yours in Christ Jesus:* or, "that also Christ Jesus had." While it is often held that Christ here functions as a model for moral imitation, it is not the historical Jesus but the entire Christ event that vv 6-11 depict. Therefore, the appeal is to have in relations among yourselves that same relationship you have in Jesus Christ, i.e., serving one another as you serve Christ (4).

2, 6-11: Perhaps an early Christian hymn quoted here by Paul. The short rhythmic lines fall into two parts, vv 6-8 where the subject of every verb is Christ, and vv 9-11 where the subject is God. The general pattern is thus of Christ's humiliation and then exaltation. More precise analyses propose a division into six three-line stanzas (6; 7abc; 7d-8; 9; 10; 11) or into three stanzas (6-7ab; 7cd-8; 9-11). Phrases such as *even death on a cross* (8c) are considered by some to be additions (by Paul) to the hymn, as are vv 10c and 11c.

2, 6: Either a reference to Christ's preexistence and those aspects of divinity that he was willing to give up in order to serve in human form, or to what the man Jesus refused to grasp at to attain divinity. Many see an allusion to the Genesis story: unlike Adam, Jesus, *though . . . in the form of God* (Gn 1, 26-27), did not reach out for *equality with God,* in contrast with the first Adam in Gn 3, 5-6.

7 Rather, he emptied himself,
   taking the form of a slave,
   coming in human likeness;*
   and found human in appearance,[x]
8 he humbled himself,[y]
   becoming obedient to death,
   even death on a cross.*
9 Because of this, God greatly exalted
   him
   and bestowed on him the name*
   that is above every name,[z]
10 that at the name of Jesus
   every knee should bend,*
   of those in heaven and on earth and
   under the earth,[a]
11 and every tongue confess that
   Jesus Christ is Lord,*
   to the glory of God the Father.[b]

Obedience and Service in the World.* [12] [c]
So then, my beloved, obedient as you have always been, not only when I am present but all the more now when I am absent, work out your salvation with fear and trembling.* [13] For God is the one who, for his good purpose, works in you both to desire and to work.[d] [14] Do everything without grumbling or questioning,[e] [15] that you may be blameless and innocent, children of God without blemish in the midst of a crooked and perverse generation,* among whom you shine like lights in the world,[f] [16] as you hold on to the word of life, so that

my boast for the day of Christ may be that I did not run in vain or labor in vain.[g] [17] But, even if I am poured out as a libation* upon the sacrificial service of your faith, I rejoice and share my joy with all of you.[h] [18] In the same way you also should rejoice and share your joy with me.[i]

IV. TRAVEL PLANS OF PAUL AND HIS ASSISTANTS*

Timothy and Paul. [19] I hope, in the Lord Jesus, to send Timothy* to you soon, so that I too may be heartened by hearing news of you.[j] [20] For I have no one comparable to him for genuine interest in whatever concerns you. [21] For they all seek their own interests, not those of Jesus Christ.[k] [22] But you know his worth, how as a child with a father he served along with me in the cause of the gospel. [23] He it is, then, whom I hope to send as soon as I see how things go with me, [24] but I am confident in the Lord that I myself will also come soon.*

Epaphroditus. [25] With regard to Epaphroditus,* my brother and co-worker and fellow soldier, your messenger and minister in my need, I consider it necessary to send him to you.[l] [26] For he has been longing for all of you and was distressed because you heard that he was ill. [27] He was indeed ill, close to death; but God had mercy on him, not just on him but also on me, so that I might not have sorrow upon

---

x Is 53, 3.11; Jn 1, 14; Rom 8, 3; 2 Cor 8, 9; Gal 4, 4; Heb 2, 14.17.—y Mt 26, 39; Jn 10, 17; Heb 5, 8; 12, 2.—z Acts 2, 33; Mt 23, 12; Eph 1, 20-21; Heb 1, 3-4.—a Is 45, 23; Jn 5, 23; Rom 14, 11; Rv 5, 13.—b Acts 2, 36; Rom 10, 9; 1 Cor 12, 3.—c Ps 2, 11; 1 Cor 2, 3; 2 Cor 7, 15.—d Phil 1, 6; 1 Cor 12, 6; 15, 10; 2 Cor 3, 5.—e 1 Cor 10, 10; 1 Pt 4, 9.—f 1 Thes 3, 13 / Dt 32, 5; Mt 10, 16; Acts 2, 40 / Dn 12, 3; Mt 5, 14.16; Eph 5, 8.—g 1 Thes 2, 19 / Is 49, 4; 65, 23; Gal 2, 2.—h Rom 15, 16; 2 Tm 4, 6.—i Phil 3, 1; 4, 4.—j Acts 16, 1-3; 17, 14-15; 1 Cor 4, 17; 16, 10.—k 1 Cor 13, 5; 2 Tm 4, 10.—l Phil 4, 10-11.15-16.18.

2, 7: *Taking the form of a slave, coming in human likeness:* or "... taking the form of a slave. // Coming in human likeness, and found human in appearance." While it is common to take vv 6 and 7 as dealing with Christ's preexistence and v 8 with his incarnate life, so that lines 7b and c are parallel, it is also possible to interpret so as to exclude any reference to preexistence (see the note on Phil 2, 6) and to take vv 6-8 as presenting two parallel stanzas about Jesus' human state (6-7b; 7cd-8); in the latter alternative, *coming in human likeness* begins the second stanza and parallels 6a to some extent.

2, 8: There may be reflected here language about the servant of the Lord, Is 52, 13—53, 12, especially Is 53, 12.

2, 9: *The name:* "Lord" (11), revealing the true nature of the one who is named.

2, 10-11: *Every knee should bend . . . every tongue confess:* into this language of Is 45, 23 there has been inserted a reference to the three levels in the universe, according to ancient thought, *heaven, earth, under the earth.*

2, 11: *Jesus Christ is Lord:* a common early Christian acclamation; cf 1 Cor 12, 3; Rom 10, 9. But doxology to God the Father is not overlooked here (11c) in the final version of the hymn.

2, 12-18: Paul goes on to draw out further ethical implications for daily life (14-18) from the salvation God works in Christ.

2, 12: *Fear and trembling:* a common Old Testament expression indicating awe and seriousness in the service of God (cf Ex 15, 16; Jdt 2, 28; Ps 2, 11; Is 19, 16).

2, 15-16: *Generation . . . as you hold on to . . . :* or "... generation. Among them shine like lights in the world because you hold the word of life. . . ."

2, 17: *Libation:* in ancient religious ritual, the pouring out on the ground of a liquid offering as a sacrifice. Paul means that he may be facing death.

2, 19—3, 1: The plans of Paul and his assistants for future travel are regularly a part of a Pauline letter near its conclusion; cf Rom 15, 22-29; 1 Cor 16, 5-12.

2, 19: *Timothy:* already known to the Philippians (Acts 16, 1-15; cf 1 Cor 4, 17; 16, 10).

2, 24: *I myself will also come soon:* cf Phil 1, 19-25 for the significance of this statement.

2, 25: *Epaphroditus:* sent by the Philippians as their *messenger* (literally, "apostle") to aid Paul in his imprisonment, he had fallen seriously ill; Paul commends him as he sends him back to Philippi.

sorrow. [28] I send him therefore with the greater eagerness, so that, on seeing him, you may rejoice again, and I may have less anxiety. [29] Welcome him then in the Lord with all joy and hold such people in esteem,[m] [30] because for the sake of the work of Christ he came close to death, risking his life to make up for those services to me that you could not perform.

CHAPTER 3

Concluding Admonitions. [1] Finally, my brothers, rejoice* in the Lord. Writing the same things to you is no burden for me but is a safeguard for you.[n]

V. POLEMIC: RIGHTEOUSNESS AND THE GOAL IN CHRIST*

Against Legalistic Teachers. [2] * Beware of the dogs! Beware of the evil-workers![o] Beware of the mutilation!* [3] For we are the circumcision,* we who worship through the Spirit of God, who boast in Christ Jesus and do not put our confidence in flesh,[p] [4] although I myself have grounds for confidence even in the flesh.[q]

Paul's Autobiography. If anyone else thinks he can be confident in flesh, all the more can I. [5] Circumcised on the eighth day,* of the race of Israel, of the tribe of Benjamin, a Hebrew of Hebrew parentage, in observance of the law a Pharisee,[r] [6] in zeal I persecuted the church, in righteousness based on the law I was blameless.[s]

Righteousness from God. [7] [But] whatever gains I had, these I have come to consider a loss* because of Christ.[t] [8] More than that, I even consider everything as a loss because of the supreme good of knowing Christ Jesus my Lord. For his sake I have accepted the loss of all things and I consider them so much rubbish, that I may gain Christ [9] and be found in him, not having any righteousness of my own based on the law but that which comes through faith in Christ,[u] the righteousness from God, depending on faith [10] to know him and the power of his resurrection and [the] sharing of his sufferings by being conformed to his death,[v] [11] if somehow I may attain the resurrection from the dead.[w]

Forward in Christ.* [12] x It is not that I have already taken hold of it or have already attained perfect maturity,* but I continue my pursuit in hope that I may possess it, since I have indeed been taken possession of by Christ [Jesus]. [13] Brothers, I for my part do not consider myself to have taken possession. Just one thing: forgetting what lies behind but straining forward to what lies ahead, [14] I continue my pursuit toward the goal, the prize of

Phil

m 1 Cor 16, 18.—n Phil 2, 18; 4, 4.—o Ps 22, 17.21; Rv 22, 15 / 2 Cor 11, 13 / Gal 5, 6.12.—p Rom 2, 28-29; Col 2, 11.—q 2 Cor 11, 18.21-23.—r Lk 1, 59; 2, 21 / Acts 22, 3; 23, 6; 26, 5.—s Acts 8, 3; 22, 4; 26, 9-11.—t Mt 13, 44.46; Lk 14, 33.—u Rom 3, 21-22.—v Rom 6, 3-5; 8, 17; Gal 6, 17.—w Jn 11, 23-26; Acts 4, 2; Rv 20, 5-6.—x 1 Tm 6, 12.19.

3, 1: *Finally . . . rejoice:* the adverb often signals the close of a letter; cf Phil 4, 8; 2 Cor 13, 11. While the verb could also be translated "good-bye" or "farewell," although it is never so used in Greek epistolography, the theme of joy has been frequent in the letter (Phil 1, 18; 2, 2.18); note also Phil 4, 4 and the addition of "always" there as evidence for the meaning "rejoice." To write *the same things* may refer to what Paul has previously taught in Philippi or to what he has just written or to what follows.

3, 2-21: An abrupt change in content and tone, either because Paul at this point responds to disturbing news he has just heard about a threat to the faith of the Philippians in the form of false teachers, or because part of another Pauline letter was inserted here; see Introduction. The chapter describes these teachers in strong terms as *dogs.* The persons meant are evidently different from the rival preachers of Phil 1, 14-18 and the opponents of Phil 1, 28. Since vv 2-4 emphasize Jewish terms like *circumcision* (2-3.5), some relate them to the "Judaizers" of the Letter to the Galatians. Other phrases make them appear more like the false teachers of 2 Cor 11, 12-15, the *evil-workers.* The latter part of the chapter depicts the *many* who are *enemies* of

Christ's cross in terms that may sound more Gentile or even "gnostic" than Jewish (18-19). Accordingly, some see two groups of false teachers in ch 3, others one group characterized by a claim of having attained "perfect maturity" (12-15).

3, 2-11: Paul sets forth the Christian claim, especially using personal, autobiographical terms that are appropriate to the situation. He presents his own experience in coming to know Christ Jesus in terms of *righteousness* or justification (cf Rom 1, 16-17; 3, 21—5, 11; Gal 2, 5-11), contrasting *the righteousness from God* through faith and that of one's own *based on the law* as two exclusive ways of pleasing God.

3, 2: *Beware of the mutilation:* literally, "incision," an ironic wordplay on "circumcision"; cf Gal 5, 12. There may be an association with the self-inflicted mutilations of the prophets of Baal (1 Kgs 18, 28) and of devotees of Cybele who slashed themselves in religious frenzy.

3, 3: *We are the circumcision:* the true people of God, seed and offspring of Abraham (Gal 3, 7.29; 6, 15). *Spirit of God:* some manuscripts read "worship God by the Spirit."

3, 5: *Circumcised on the eighth day:* as the law required (Gn 17, 12; Lv 12, 3).

3, 7: *Loss:* his knowledge of Christ led Paul to reassess the ways of truly pleasing and serving God. His reevaluation indicates the profound and lasting effect of his experience of the meaning of Christ on the way to Damascus some twenty years before (Gal 1, 15-16; Acts 9, 1-22).

3, 12-16: To be *taken possession of by Christ* does not mean that one has already arrived at perfect spiritual maturity. Paul and the Philippians instead press on, trusting in God.

3, 12: *Attained perfect maturity:* possibly an echo of the concept in the mystery religions of being an initiate, admitted to divine secrets.

God's upward calling, in Christ Jesus.[y] [15]Let us, then, who are "perfectly mature" adopt this attitude. And if you have a different attitude, this too God will reveal to you. [16]Only, with regard to what we have attained, continue on the same course.*

Wrong Conduct and Our Goal.* [17]Join with others in being imitators of me,* brothers, and observe those who thus conduct themselves according to the model you have in us.[z] [18]For many, as I have often told you and now tell you even in tears, conduct themselves as enemies of the cross of Christ.[a] [19]Their end is destruction. Their God is their stomach; their glory is in their "shame." Their minds are occupied with earthly things.[b] [20]But our citizenship* is in heaven, and from it we also await a savior, the Lord Jesus Christ.[c] [21]He will change our lowly body to conform with his glorified body by the power that enables him also to bring all things into subjection to himself.[d]

VI. INSTRUCTIONS FOR THE COMMUNITY*

CHAPTER 4

Live in Concord. [1]Therefore, my brothers, whom I love and long for, my joy and crown, in this way stand firm in the Lord, beloved.[e]

[2]I urge Euodia and I urge Syntyche* to come to a mutual understanding in the Lord. [3]Yes, and I ask you also, my true yokemate,* to help them, for they have struggled at my side in promoting the gospel, along with Clement and my other co-workers, whose names are in the book of life.[f]

Joy and Peace. [4]Rejoice* in the Lord always. I shall say it again: rejoice![g] [5]Your kindness* should be known to all. The Lord is near.[h] [6]Have no anxiety at all, but in everything, by prayer and petition, with thanksgiving, make your requests known to God.[i] [7]Then the peace of God that surpasses all understanding will guard your hearts and minds in Christ Jesus.[j]

[8] [k] Finally, brothers, whatever is true, whatever is honorable, whatever is just, whatever is pure, whatever is lovely, whatever is gracious, if there is any excellence and if there is anything worthy of praise, think about these things.* [9]Keep on doing what you have learned and received and heard and seen in me.[l] Then the God of peace will be with you.*

VII. GRATITUDE FOR THE PHILIPPIANS' GENEROSITY*

[10]I rejoice greatly in the Lord that now at last you revived your concern for me. You were, of course, concerned about me but lacked an opportunity.[m] [11]Not that I say this because of need, for I have

---

y 1 Cor 9, 24-25; 2 Tm 4, 7.—z 1 Cor 4, 16; 11, 1; 1 Thes 1, 7; 1 Pt 5, 3.—a 1 Cor 1, 17.23; Gal 6, 12.—b Rom 8, 5-6; 16, 18.—c Eph 2, 6.19; Col 3, 1-3; Heb 12, 22.—d Rom 8, 23.29; 1 Cor 15, 42-57; 2 Cor 3, 18; 5, 1-5 / 1 Cor 15, 27-28.—e 1 Thes 2, 19-20.—f Ex 32, 32-33; Ps 69, 29; Dn 12, 1; Lk 10, 20; Rv 3, 5; 13, 8; 17, 8; 20, 12.15; 21, 27.—g Phil 2, 18; 3, 1.—h Ti 3, 2 / Ps 145, 18; Heb 10, 37; Jas 5, 8-9.—i Mt 6, 25-34; 1 Pt 5, 7 / Col 4, 2.—j Jn 14, 27; Col 3, 15.—k Rom 12, 17.—l 1 Thes 4, 1 / Rom 15, 33; 16, 20; 1 Cor 14, 33; 1 Thes 5, 23.—m Phil 1, 18; 2, 25; 1 Cor 9, 11; 2 Cor 11, 9.

3, 16: Some manuscripts add, probably to explain Paul's cryptic phrase, "thinking alike."

3, 17-21: Paul and those who live a life centered in Christ, envisaging both his suffering and his resurrection, provide a model that is the opposite of opponents who reject Christ's cross (cf 1 Cor 1, 23).

3, 17: *Being imitators of me:* not arrogance, but humble simplicity, since all his converts know that Paul is wholly dedicated to imitating Christ (1 Cor 11, 1; cf also Phil 4, 9; 1 Thes 1, 6; 2 Thes 3, 7.9; 1 Cor 4, 6).

3, 20: *Citizenship:* Christians constitute a colony of heaven, as Philippi was a *colonia* of Rome (Acts 16, 12). The hope Paul expresses involves the final coming of Christ, not a status already attained, such as the opponents claim.

4, 1-9: This series of ethical admonitions rests especially on the view of Christ and his coming (cf 5) in Phil 3, 20-21. Paul's instructions touch on unity within the congregation, joy, prayer, and the Christian outlook on life.

4, 2: *Euodia . . . Syntyche:* two otherwise unknown women in the Philippian congregation; on the advice to them, cf Phil 2, 2-4.

4, 3: *Yokemate:* or "comrade," although the Greek *syzygos* could also be a proper name. *Clement:* otherwise unknown, although later writers sought to identify him with Clement, bishop of Rome (Eusebius, *Ecclesiastical History* 3.15.1).

4, 4: *Rejoice:* see the note on Phil 3, 1.

4, 5: *Kindness:* considerateness, forbearance, fairness. *The Lord is near:* most likely a reference to Christ's parousia (Phil 1, 6.10; 3, 20-21; 1 Cor 16, 22), although some sense an echo of Ps 119, 151 and the perpetual presence of the Lord.

4, 8: The language employs terms from Roman Stoic thought.

4, 9: Cf the note on Phil 3, 17.

4, 10-20: Paul, more directly than anywhere else in the letter (cf Phil 1, 3-5), here thanks the Philippians for their gift of money sent through Epaphroditus (Phil 2, 25). Paul's own policy was *to be self-sufficient* as a missionary, supporting himself by his own labor (1 Thes 2, 5-9; 1 Cor 9, 15-18; cf Acts 18, 2-3). In spite of this reliance on self and on God to provide (11-13), Paul accepted gifts from the Philippians *not only once but more than once* (16) when he was in Thessalonica (Acts 17, 1-9), as he does now, in prison (*my distress,* 14). While commercial terms appear in the passage, like an *account of giving and receiving* (15) and *received full payment* (18), Paul is most concerned about the spiritual growth of the Philippians (10.17.19); he emphasizes that God will care for their needs, through Christ.

learned, in whatever situation I find myself, to be self-sufficient.[n] [12] I know indeed how to live in humble circumstances; I know also how to live with abundance. In every circumstance and in all things I have learned the secret of being well fed and of going hungry, of living in abundance and of being in need. [13] I have the strength for everything through him who empowers me.[o] [14] Still, it was kind of you to share in my distress.

[15] You Philippians indeed know that at the beginning of the gospel,* when I left Macedonia, not a single church shared with me in an account of giving and receiving, except you alone. [16] For even when I was at Thessalonica you sent me something for my needs, not only once but more than once. [17] It is not that I am eager for the gift;

rather, I am eager for the profit that accrues to your account. [18] I have received full payment and I abound. I am very well supplied because of what I received from you through Epaphroditus, "a fragrant aroma," an acceptable sacrifice,* pleasing to God.[p] [19] My God will fully supply whatever you need, in accord with his glorious riches in Christ Jesus.[q] [20] To our God and Father, glory for ever and ever. Amen.[r]

VIII. FAREWELL*

[21] Give my greetings to every holy one in Christ Jesus. The brothers who are with me send you their greetings; [22] [s] all the holy ones send you their greetings, especially those of Caesar's household.* [23] The grace of the Lord Jesus Christ be with your spirit.

---

n 11-12: 1 Cor 4, 11; 2 Cor 6, 10; 11, 27 / 2 Cor 12, 9-10.—o Col 1, 29; 2 Tm 4, 17.—p Gn 8, 21; Ex 29, 18; Eph 5, 2; Heb 13, 16.—q 1 Thes 3, 11.13.—r Rom 16, 27; Eph 5, 20.—s Phil 1, 13.

4, 15: *The beginning of the gospel:* it was at Philippi that Paul first preached Christ in Europe, going on from there to Thessalonica and Beroea (Acts 16, 9—17, 14).

4, 18: *Aroma . . . sacrifice:* Old Testament cultic language (cf Gn 8, 21; Ex 29, 18.25.41; Lv 1, 9.13; Ez 20, 41) applied to the Philippians' gift; cf Eph 5, 2; 2 Cor 2, 14-16.

4, 21-23: On the usual greetings at the conclusion of a letter, see the note on 1 Cor 16, 19-24. Inclusion of greetings from *all the holy ones* in the place from which Paul writes would involve even the Christians of Phil 1, 14-18 who had their differences with Paul.

4, 22: *Those of Caesar's household:* minor officials or even slaves and freedmen, found in Ephesus or Rome, among other places.

THE LETTER TO THE COLOSSIANS

INTRODUCTION

This letter is addressed to a congregation at Colossae in the Lycus Valley in Asia Minor, east of Ephesus. At the time of writing, Paul had not visited there, the letter says (1, 4; 2, 1). The community had apparently been established by Epaphras of Colossae (1, 7; 4, 12; Phlm 23). Problems, however, had arisen, brought on by teachers who emphasized Christ's relation to the universe (cosmos). Their teachings stressed angels (2, 18; "principalities and powers," 2, 15), which were connected with astral powers and cultic practices (see the note on 2, 16) and rules about food and drink and ascetical disciplines (2, 16.18). These teachings, Paul insists, detract from the person and work of Christ for salvation as set forth magnificently in a hymnic passage at 1, 15-20 and reiterated throughout the letter. Such teachings are but "shadows"; Christ is "reality" (2, 17).

For help in dealing with these problems that the new teachers posed at Colossae, Epaphras sought out Paul, who was then imprisoned (4, 10.18) at a place that the letter does not mention. Paul, without entering into debate over the existence of angelic spirits or their function, simply affirms that Christ possesses the sum total of redemptive power (1, 19) and that the spiritual renewal of the human person occurs through contact in baptism with the person of Christ, who died and rose again (2, 9-14). It is unnecessary for the Christian to be concerned about placating spirits (2, 15) or avoiding imagined defilement through ascetical practices in regard to food and drink (2, 20-23). True Christian asceticism consists in the conquering of personal sins (3, 5-10) and the practice of love of neighbor in accordance with the standard set by Christ (3, 12-16).

Paul commends the community as a whole (1, 3-8); this seems to indicate that, though the Colossians have been under pressure to adopt the false doctrines, they have not yet succumbed. The apostle expresses his prayerful concern for them (1, 9-14). His preaching has cost him persecution, suffering, and imprisonment, but he regards these as reflective of the sufferings of Christ, a required discipline for the sake of the gospel (see the note on 1, 24; cf 1, 29; 2, 1). His instructions to the Christian family and to slaves and masters require a new spirit of reflection and action. Love, obedience, and service are to be rendered "in the Lord" (3, 18—4, 1).

Colossians follows the outline of a typical Pauline letter. It is distinguished by the poetic lines in 1, 15-20 concerning who Christ is and what Christ means in creation and redemption. This hymn may be compared with similar passages in Philippians 2, 6-11; 1 Timothy 3, 16; and John 1, 1-18. It was apparently familiar liturgical material to the author, the audience, and the false teachers. In 1, 21—2, 7, however, Paul interprets the relation between the body of Christ, which he insists is the church (1, 18), and the world or cosmos to be one not simply of Christ's preexistence and rule but one of missionary advance into the world by the spreading of the word (1, 25.28). In this labor of the missionary body of Christ, Paul as a minister plays a prime part in bringing Christ and the gospel as hope to the Gentiles (1, 23.25.27). To "every creature under heaven" the word is to be proclaimed, so that everyone receives Christ, is established in faith, and walks in Christ (1, 28; 2, 6.7).

Paul wrote the Letter to the Colossians while in prison, but his several imprisonments leave the specific place and date of composition uncertain. On this point the same problem exists as with Ephesians and Philippians (see the Introductions to these letters). Traditionally the house arrest at Rome, in which Paul enjoyed a certain restricted freedom in preaching (see Acts 28, 16-28), or a second Roman imprisonment has been claimed as the setting. Others suggest a still earlier imprisonment at Caesarea (see Acts 23, 12—27, 1) or in Ephesus (see Acts 19). Still others regard the letter as the work of some pupil or follower of Paul, writing in his name. In any case, the contents are often closely paralleled by thoughts in Ephesians.

The principal divisions of the Letter to the Colossians are the following:

I.   Address (1, 1-14)
II.   The Preeminence of Christ (1, 15—2, 3)
III. Warnings against False Teachers (2, 4-23)
IV.   The Ideal Christian Life in the World (3, 1—4, 6)
V.   Conclusion (4, 7-18)

I. ADDRESS

CHAPTER 1

Greeting.* [1] Paul, an apostle of Christ Jesus by the will of God, and Timothy our brother,[a] [2] to the holy ones and faithful brothers in Christ in Colossae: grace to you and peace from God our Father.

Thanksgiving.* [3] We always give thanks to God, the Father of our Lord Jesus Christ, when we pray for you,[b] [4] for we have heard of your faith in Christ Jesus and the love that you have for all the holy ones [5] because of the hope reserved for you in heaven. Of this you have already heard through the word of truth, the gospel,[c]

a Eph 1, 1.—b Eph 1, 15-16; Phlm 4-5.—c Eph 1, 13.18; 1 Pt 1, 4.

1, 1-2: For the epistolary form used by Paul at the beginning of his letters, see the note on Rom 1, 1-7. On *holy ones* or "God's people," see the note on Rom 1, 7. Awareness of their calling helps this group to be *faithful brothers* and sisters *in Christ*, i.e., dedicated to the tasks implied in their calling.

1, 3-8: On thanksgiving at the start of a letter, see the note on Rom 1, 8. The apostle, recalling his own prayers for them and the

good report about them he has received (3-4), congratulates the Colossians upon their acceptance of Christ and their faithful efforts to live the gospel (Col 3, 6-8). To encourage them he mentions the success of the gospel elsewhere (6) and assures them that his knowledge of their community is accurate, since he has been in personal contact with Epaphras (7-8), who likely had evangelized Colossae and other cities in the Lycus Valley of Asia Minor (cf Col 4, 12.13; Phlm 23). On *faith, love,* and *hope* (4.5.8), see the note on 1 Cor 13, 13; cf 1 Thes 1, 3; 5, 8.

[6] that has come to you. Just as in the whole world it is bearing fruit and growing, so also among you, from the day you heard it and came to know the grace of God in truth, [7] [d] as you learned it from Epaphras* our beloved fellow slave, who is a trustworthy minister of Christ on your behalf [8] and who also told us of your love in the Spirit.

Prayer for Continued Progress.* [9] Therefore, from the day we heard this, we do not cease praying for you and asking that you may be filled with the knowledge of his will through all spiritual wisdom and understanding[e] [10] to live in a manner worthy of the Lord, so as to be fully pleasing, in every good work bearing fruit and growing in the knowledge of God, [11] strengthened with every power, in accord with his glorious might, for all endurance and patience, with joy [12] * giving thanks to the Father, who has made you fit to share in the inheritance of the holy ones in light.[f] [13] He delivered us from the power of darkness and transferred us to the kingdom of his beloved Son, [14] in whom we have redemption, the forgiveness of sins.[g]

---

d Phlm 23.—e Eph 1, 15-17; 5, 17; Phil 1, 9.—f Col 3, 17; Jn 8, 12; Acts 26, 18; 1 Tm 6, 16; 1 Pt 2, 9.—g Eph 1, 7.—h Ps 89, 28; Jn 1, 3.18; 2 Cor 4, 4.—i 1 Cor 8, 6; Eph 1, 10.21.—j 1 Cor 11, 3; 12, 12.27; 15, 20; Eph 1, 22-23; Rv 1, 5.—k 2 Cor 5, 18-19; Eph 1, 10.—l Eph 2, 14-16.

1, 7: *Epaphras:* now with Paul but a Colossian, founder of the church there.

1, 9-14: Moved by Epaphras' account, the apostle has prayed and continues to pray fervently for the Colossians that, in their response to the gospel, they *may be filled with the knowledge of* God's *will* (9; cf Col 3, 10). Paul expects a mutual interaction between their life according to the gospel and this knowledge (10), yielding results (*fruit,* 10; cf Col 1, 6) *in every good work:* growth, strength, *endurance, patience, with joy* (11), and the further giving of thanks (12).

1, 12-14: A summary about *redemption* by *the Father* precedes the statement in vv 15-20 about the *beloved Son* who is God's love in person (13). Christians share *the inheritance . . . in light* with *the holy ones,* here probably the angels (12). The imagery reflects the Exodus (*delivered . . . transferred*) and Jesus' theme of *the kingdom.* Redemption is explained as *forgiveness of sins* (cf Acts 2, 38; Rom 3, 24-25; Eph 1, 7).

1, 15-20: As the poetic arrangement indicates, these lines are probably an early Christian hymn, known to the Colossians and taken up into the letter from liturgical use (cf Phil 2, 6-11; 1 Tm 3, 16). They present Christ as the mediator of creation (15-18a) and of redemption (18b-20). There is a parallelism between *firstborn of all creation* (15) and *firstborn from the dead* (18). While many of the phrases were at home in Greek philosophical use and even in gnosticism, the basic ideas also reflect Old Testament themes about Wisdom found in Prv 8, 22-31; Wis 7, 22—8, 1; and Sir 1, 4. See also the notes on what is possibly a hymn in Jn 1, 1-18.

1, 15: *Image:* cf Gn 1, 27. Whereas the man and the woman were originally created in the image and likeness of God (see also Gn 1, 26), Christ as image (2 Cor 4, 4) of *the invisible God* (Jn 1, 18) now shares this new nature in baptism with those redeemed (cf Col 3, 10-11).

II. THE PREEMINENCE OF CHRIST
His Person and Work

[15] * He is the image* of the invisible God,
    the firstborn of all creation.[h]
[16] For in him* were created all things in heaven and on earth,
    the visible and the invisible,
    whether thrones or dominions or principalities or powers;
    all things were created through him and for him.[i]
[17] He is before all things,
    and in him all things hold together.
[18] He is the head of the body, the church.*
He is the beginning, the firstborn from the dead,
    that in all things he himself might be preeminent.[j]
[19] For in him all the fullness* was pleased to dwell,
[20]   and through him to reconcile all things for him,
    making peace by the blood of his cross*
    [through him], whether those on earth or those in heaven.[k]
[21] * And you who once were alienated and hostile in mind because of evil deeds[l] [22] he

1, 16-17: Christ (though not mentioned by name) is preeminent and supreme as God's agent in the creation of *all things* (cf Jn 1, 3), as prior to *all things* (17; cf Heb 1, 3).

1, 18: *Church:* such a reference seemingly belongs under "redemption" in the following lines, not under the "creation" section of the hymn. Stoic thought sometimes referred to the world as "the body of Zeus." Pauline usage is to speak of the church as the body of Christ (1 Cor 12, 12-27; Rom 12, 4-5). Some think that the author of Colossians has inserted the reference to the church here so as to define "head of the body" in Paul's customary way. See v 24. *Preeminent:* when Christ was raised by God as *firstborn from the dead* (cf Acts 26, 23; Rv 1, 5), he was placed over the community, the church, that he had brought into being, but he is also indicated as crown of the whole new creation, over *all things.* His further role is to *reconcile all things* (20) for God or possibly "to himself."

1, 19: *Fullness:* in gnostic usage this term referred to a spiritual world of beings above, between God and the world; many later interpreters take it to refer to *the fullness of the deity* (Col 2, 9); the reference could also be to the fullness of grace (cf Jn 1, 16).

1, 20: *The blood of his cross:* the most specific reference in the hymn to redemption through Christ's death, a central theme in Paul; cf Col 2, 14-15; 1 Cor 1, 17.18.23. *[Through him]:* the phrase, lacking in some manuscripts, seems superfluous but parallels the reference to reconciliation through Christ earlier in the verse.

1, 21-23: Paul, in applying this hymn to the Colossians, reminds them that they have experienced the reconciling effect of Christ's death. He sees the effects of the cross in the redemption of human beings, not of cosmic powers such as those referred to in vv 16 and 20 (*all things*). Paul also urges adherence to Christ in faith and begins to point to his own role as minister (23), sufferer (24), and proclaimer (27-28) of this gospel.

Col

has now reconciled in his fleshly body through his death, to present you holy, without blemish, and irreproachable before him, 23 provided that you persevere in the faith, firmly grounded, stable, and not shifting from the hope of the gospel that you heard, which has been preached to every creature under heaven, of which I, Paul, am a minister.

Christ in Us. * 24 Now I rejoice in my sufferings for your sake, and in my flesh I am filling up what is lacking* in the afflictions of Christ on behalf of his body, which is the church, 25 of which I am a minister in accordance with God's stewardship given to me to bring to completion for you the word of God, 26 the mystery hidden from ages and from generations past. But now it has been manifested to his holy ones,*m* 27 to whom God chose to make known the riches of the glory of this mystery among the Gentiles; it is Christ in you, the hope for glory.*n* 28 It is he whom we proclaim, admonishing everyone and teaching everyone with all wisdom, that we may present everyone perfect in Christ.*o* 29 For this I labor and struggle, in accord with the exercise of his power working within me.*p*

CHAPTER 2

1 For I want you to know how great a struggle I am having for you and for those in

m Rom 16, 25-26; 1 Cor 2, 7; Eph 3, 3.9.—n Col 3, 4; Rom 8, 10.—o Eph 4, 13.—p Col 2, 1; 4, 12; Phil 4, 13.—q Col 1, 26-27; Eph 3, 18-19.—r Prv 2, 4-5; Is 45, 3; Rom 11, 33; 1 Cor 1, 30.—s Eph 4, 14.—t 1 Cor 5, 3; Phil 1, 27.—u Eph 2, 20-22; 3, 17.—v Gal 4, 3; Eph 5, 6.—w Col 1, 19; Eph 3, 19.—x Col 1, 22; Jer 4, 4; Rom 2, 25-29; Phil 3, 3.

1, 24—2, 3: As the community at Colossae was not personally known to Paul (see Introduction), he here invests his teaching with greater authority by presenting a brief sketch of his apostolic ministry and sufferings as they reflect those of Christ on behalf of the church (24). The preaching of God's word (25) carries out the divine plan (*the mystery*, 26) to make Christ known to the Gentiles (27). It teaches the God-given wisdom about Christ (28), whose power works mightily in the apostle (29). Even in those communities that do not know him personally (Col 2, 1), he can increase the perception of God in Christ, unite the faithful more firmly in love, and so bring encouragement to them (Col 2, 2). He hopes that his apostolic authority will make the Colossians perceive more readily the defects in the teaching of others who have sought to delude them, the next concern in the letter.

1, 24: *What is lacking:* although variously interpreted, this phrase does not imply that Christ's atoning death on the cross was defective. It may refer to the apocalyptic concept of a quota of "messianic woes" to be endured before the end comes; cf Mk 13, 8.19-20.24 and the note on Mt 23, 29-32. Others suggest that Paul's mystical unity with Christ allowed him to call his own *sufferings the afflictions of Christ.*

2, 1: *Laodicea:* chief city in Phrygia, northwest of Colossae; cf Col 4, 13.16; Rv 3, 14-22.

Laodicea* and all who have not seen me face to face, 2 that their hearts may be encouraged as they are brought together in love, to have all the richness of fully assured understanding, for the knowledge of the mystery of God, Christ,*q* 3 in whom are hidden all the treasures of wisdom and knowledge.*r*

III. WARNINGS AGAINST FALSE TEACHERS*

A General Admonition. 4 I say this so that no one may deceive you by specious arguments.*s* 5 For even if I am absent in the flesh, yet I am with you in spirit, rejoicing as I observe your good order and the firmness of your faith in Christ.*t* 6 So, as you received Christ Jesus the Lord, walk in him, 7 rooted in him and built upon him and established in the faith as you were taught, abounding in thanksgiving.*u* 8 See to it that no one captivate you with an empty, seductive philosophy according to human tradition, according to the elemental powers of the world* and not according to Christ.*v*

Sovereign Role of Christ. 9 *w* For in him dwells the whole fullness of the deity* bodily, 10 and you share in this fullness in him, who is the head of every principality and power. 11 *x* In him* you were also circumcised with a circumcision not adminis-

2, 4-23: In face of the threat posed by false teachers (4), the Colossians are admonished to adhere to the gospel as it was first preached to them (6), steeping themselves in it with grateful hearts (7). They must reject religious teachings originating in any source except the gospel (8) because in Christ alone will they have access to God, *the deity* (9). So fully has Christ enlightened them that they need no other source of religious knowledge or virtue (10). They do not require *circumcision* (11), for *in baptism* their whole being has been affected by Christ (12) through forgiveness of sin and resurrection to a new life (13; cf Col 3, 1 and Rom 6, 1-11).

On the cross Christ canceled the record of the debt that stood against us with all its claims (14), i.e., he eliminated the law (cf Eph 2, 15) that human beings could not observe—and that could not save them. He forgave sins against the law (14) and exposed as false and misleading (15) all other powers (cf Col 1, 16) that purport to offer salvation. Therefore, the Colossians are not to accept judgments from such teachers on *food and drink* or to keep certain religious festivals or engage in certain cultic practices (16), for the Colossians would thereby risk severing themselves from Christ (19). If, when they accepted the gospel, they believed in Christ as their savior, they must be convinced that their salvation cannot be achieved by appeasing ruling spirits through dietary practices or through a wisdom gained simply by means of harsh asceticism (20-23).

2, 8: *Elemental powers of the world:* see the note on Gal 4, 3.

2, 9: *Fullness of the deity:* the divine nature, not just attributes; see the note on Col 1, 19.

2, 11: A description of baptism (12) in symbolic terms of the Old Testament rite for entry into the community. The false teachers may have demanded physical circumcision of the Colossians.

tered by hand, by stripping off the carnal body, with the circumcision of Christ. [12] You were buried with him in baptism, in which you were also raised with him through faith in the power of God, who raised him from the dead.[y] [13] [z] And even when you were dead [in] transgressions and the uncircumcision of your flesh, he brought you to life along with him, having forgiven us all our transgressions; [14] * obliterating the bond against us, with its legal claims, which was opposed to us, he also removed it from our midst, nailing it to the cross;[a] [15] despoiling the principalities and the powers, he made a public spectacle of them,[b] leading them away in triumph by it.*

Practices Contrary to Faith. [16] [c] Let no one, then, pass judgment on you in matters of food and drink or with regard to a festival or new moon or sabbath.* [17] These are shadows of things to come; the reality belongs to Christ.[d] [18] Let no one disqualify you, delighting in self-abasement and worship of angels, taking his stand on visions,* inflated without reason by his fleshly mind,[e] [19] and not holding closely to the head, from whom the whole body, supported and held together by its ligaments and bonds, achieves the growth that comes from God.[f]

[20] If you died with Christ to the elemental powers of the world, why do you submit to regulations as if you were still living in the world? [21] "Do not handle! Do not taste! Do not touch!" [22] These are all things

destined to perish with use; they accord with human precepts and teachings.[g] [23] While they have a semblance of wisdom in rigor of devotion and self-abasement [and] severity to the body, they are of no value against gratification of the flesh.

IV. THE IDEAL CHRISTIAN LIFE IN THE WORLD

CHAPTER 3

Mystical Death and Resurrection. * [1] If then you were raised with Christ, seek what is above, where Christ is seated at the right hand of God.[h] [2] Think of what is above, not of what is on earth. [3] For you have died, and your life is hidden with Christ in God.[i] [4] When Christ your life appears, then you too will appear with him in glory.

Renunciation of Vice. * [5] Put to death, then, the parts of you that are earthly:[j] immorality, impurity, passion, evil desire, and the greed that is idolatry.* [6] Because of these the wrath of God* is coming [upon the disobedient].[k] [7] By these you too once conducted yourselves, when you lived in that way. [8] But now you must put them all away:* anger, fury, malice, slander, and obscene language out of your mouths.[l] [9] Stop lying to one another, since you have taken off the old self with its practices[m] [10] and have put on the new self, which is being renewed, for knowledge, in the image* of its creator.[n] [11] Here there is not Greek and Jew, circumcision and uncircumcision, barbarian, Scythian,* slave, free; but Christ is all and in all.[o]

y Rom 6, 3-4.—z Eph 2, 1.5.—a Eph 2, 14-15.—b Col 1, 16.20; 2 Cor 2, 14; Eph 1, 21.—c Rom 14, 3-4; 1 Tm 4, 3.—d Heb 8, 5; 10, 1.—e Col 2, 23; Mt 24, 4.—f Eph 2, 21-22; 4, 16.—g Is 29, 13.—h Col 2, 12; Ps 110, 1; Phil 3, 20; Eph 2, 6.—i Rom 6, 2-5.—j Mt 15, 19; Rom 1, 29-30; Gal 5, 19-21; Eph 5, 3.5.—k Rom 1, 18.—l Eph 4, 22.25.31.—m Rom 6, 4.6; Eph 4, 22-25; Heb 12, 1; 1 Pt 2, 1; 4, 2.—n Gn 1, 26-27.—o 1 Cor 12, 13; Gal 3, 27-28.

2, 14: The elaborate metaphor here about how God canceled the legal claims against us through Christ's cross depicts not Christ being nailed to the cross by men but *the bond . . . with its legal claims* being nailed to the cross by God.

2, 15: The picture derives from the *public spectacle* and *triumph* of a Roman emperor's victory parade, where captives marched in subjection. *The principalities and the powers* are here conquered, not reconciled (cf Col 1, 16.20). An alternate rendering for *by it* (the cross) is "by him" (Christ).

2, 16: *Festival or new moon or sabbath:* yearly, monthly, and weekly observances determined by religious powers associated with a calendar set by the heavenly bodies, sun, moon, and stars (cf Col 2, 8).

2, 18: Ascetic practices encouraged by the false teachers included subjection of self humbly to their rules, worship of angels, and cultivation of visions, though exact details are unclear.

3, 1-4: By retaining the message of the gospel that the risen, living Christ is the source of their salvation, the Colossians will be free from false religious evaluations of the things of the world (1-2). They have died to these; but one day *when Christ . . . appears,* they will live with Christ in the presence of God (3-4).

3, 5-17: In lieu of false asceticism and superstitious festivals, the apostle reminds the Colossians of the moral life that is to characterize their response to God through Christ. He urges their participation in the liturgical hymns and prayers that center upon God's plan of salvation in Christ (16).

3, 5.8: The two lists of five vices each are similar to enumerations at Rom 1, 29-31 and Gal 5, 19-21.

3, 6: *The wrath of God:* see the note on Rom 1, 18. Many manuscripts add, as at Eph 5, 6, "upon the disobedient."

3, 8-10: *Put . . . away; have taken off; have put on:* the terms may reflect baptismal practice, taking off garments and putting on new ones after being united with Christ, here translated into ethical terms.

3, 10: *Image:* see the note on Col 1, 15.

3, 11: *Scythian:* a barbarous people from north of the Black Sea.

¹²Put on then, as God's chosen ones, holy and beloved, heartfelt compassion, kindness, humility, gentleness, and patience,ᵖ ¹³bearing with one another and forgiving one another, if one has a grievance against another; as the Lord has forgiven you, so must you also do.�q ¹⁴And over all these put on love, that is, the bond of perfection.ʳ ¹⁵And let the peace of Christ control your hearts, the peace into which you were also called in one body. And be thankful.ˢ ¹⁶Let the word of Christ dwell in you richly, as in all wisdom you teach and admonish one another, singing psalms, hymns, and spiritual songs with gratitude in your hearts to God.ᵗ ¹⁷And whatever you do, in word or in deed, do everything in the name of the Lord Jesus, giving thanks to God the Father through him.ᵘ

The Christian Family. ¹⁸ * Wives, be subordinate to your husbands, as is proper in the Lord.ᵛ ¹⁹Husbands, love your wives, and avoid any bitterness toward them. ²⁰Children, obey your parents in everything, for this is pleasing to the Lord.ʷ ²¹Fathers, do not provoke your children, so they may not become discouraged.ˣ

Slaves and Masters. ²²Slaves,* obey your human masters in everything, not only when being watched, as currying favor, but in simplicity of heart, fearing the Lord.ʸ ²³Whatever you do, do from the heart, as for the Lord and not for others, ²⁴knowing that you will receive from the Lord the due payment of the inheritance; be slaves of the Lord Christ. ²⁵For the wrongdoer will receive recompense for the wrong he committed, and there is no partiality.ᶻ

CHAPTER 4

¹Masters, treat your slaves justly and fairly, realizing that you too have a Master in heaven.

Prayer and Apostolic Spirit. ²Persevere in prayer, being watchful in it with thanksgiving;ᵃ ³at the same time, pray for us, too, that God may open a door to us for the word, to speak of the mystery of Christ, for which I am in prison,ᵇ ⁴that I may make it clear, as I must speak. ⁵Conduct yourselves wisely toward outsiders, making the most of the opportunity.ᶜ ⁶Let your speech always be gracious, seasoned with salt, so that you know how you should respond to each one.

V. CONCLUSION*

Tychicus and Onesimus. ⁷Tychicus,* my beloved brother, trustworthy minister, and fellow slave in the Lord, will tell you all the news of me.ᵈ ⁸I am sending him to you for this very purpose, so that you may know about us and that he may encourage your hearts, ⁹together with Onesimus, a trustworthy and beloved brother, who is one of you. They will tell you about everything here.ᵉ

From Paul's Co-Workers. ¹⁰Aristarchus,* my fellow prisoner, sends you greetings, as does Mark the cousin of Barnabas (concerning whom you have received instructions; if he comes to you, receive him),ᶠ ¹¹and Jesus,* who is called Justus, who are of the circumcision; these alone are my co-workers for the kingdom of God, and they have been a comfort to me. ¹²Epaphras* sends you greetings; he is one of you, a slave of Christ [Jesus], always striving for you in his prayers so that you may be perfect and fully assured in all the will of

---

p Eph 4, 1-2.32; 1 Thes 5, 15.—q Mt 6, 14; 18, 21-35; Eph 4, 32.—r Rom 13, 8-10.—s Rom 12, 5; 1 Cor 12, 12; Eph 2, 16; 4, 3-4; Phil 4, 7.—t Eph 5, 19-20.—u 1 Cor 10, 31.—v Eph 5, 22; Ti 2, 5; 1 Pt 3, 1.—w Eph 6, 1.—x Eph 6, 4.—y Eph 6, 5; 1 Tm 6, 1; Ti 2, 9-10; 1 Pt 2, 18.—z Rom 2, 11.—a Lk 18, 1; Rom 12, 12; Eph 6, 18-20; 1 Thes 5, 17.—b Rom 15, 30; 1 Cor 16, 9; Eph 6, 19; 2 Thes 3, 1.—c Eph 5, 15-16.—d Acts 20, 4; Eph 6, 21-22; Phil 1, 12.—e Phlm 10-11.—f Acts 19, 29; 20, 4; 27, 2 / Acts 12, 12.25; 13, 13; 15, 37.40; 2 Tm 4, 11; Phlm 24; 1 Pt 5, 13.

3, 18—4, 6: After general recommendations that connect family life and the social condition of slavery with the service of Christ (Col 3, 18—4, 1), Paul requests prayers for himself, especially in view of his imprisonment (2-3), and recommends friendly relations and meaningful discussions of Christian teaching with *outsiders*, i.e., non-Christians (5-6). See the note on Eph 5, 21—6, 9.

3, 22-25: *Slaves:* within this table of duties in family and societal relations, involving wives and husbands, children and parents (18-21), such as also appears in Eph 5, 22—6, 9, slaves here

receive special attention because of the case of Onesimus the slave returning to his master (Col 4, 9; Phlm 10-12).

4, 7-18: Paul concludes with greetings and information concerning various Christians known to the Colossians.

4, 7: *Tychicus:* Acts 20, 4 mentions his role in the collection for Jerusalem; Eph 6, 21 repeats what is said here; see also 2 Tm 4, 12; Ti 3, 12.

4, 10: *Aristarchus:* a Thessalonian who was with Paul at Ephesus and Caesarea and on the voyage to Rome (Acts 19, 29; 20, 4; 27, 2). *Mark:* also referred to at Phlm 24 and 2 Tm 4, 11 and, as "John Mark," in Acts (Acts 12, 12.25; 13, 13; 15, 37-40). See also 1 Pt 5, 13 and the note there. Traditionally the author of the second gospel.

4, 11: *Jesus:* a then common Jewish name, the Greek form of Joshua.

4, 12: *Epaphras:* see the notes on Col 1, 3-8 and Col 1, 7.

God.[g] [13] For I can testify that he works very hard for you and for those in Laodicea* and those in Hierapolis. [14] Luke* the beloved physician sends greetings, as does Demas.[h]

A Message for the Laodiceans. [15] Give greetings to the brothers in Laodicea and to Nympha and to the church in her house.* [16] And when this letter is read before you, have it read also in the church of the Laodiceans, and you yourselves read the one from Laodicea.* [17] And tell Archippus, "See that you fulfill the ministry* that you received in the Lord."[i]

[18] The greeting is in my own hand,* Paul's. Remember my chains. Grace be with you.[j]

---

g Col 1, 7; Rom 15, 30.—h Phlm 24; 2 Tm 4, 10-11.—i Phlm 2.—j 1 Cor 16, 21; Gal 6, 11; Eph 3, 1; 2 Thes 3, 17.

4, 13: *Laodicea:* see the note on Col 2, 1. *Hierapolis:* a city northeast of Laodicea and northwest of Colossae.

4, 14: *Luke:* only here described as a medical doctor; cf Phlm 24 and 2 Tm 4, 11. Traditionally the author of the third gospel. *Demas:* cf Phlm 24; he later deserted Paul (2 Tm 4, 10).

4, 15: *Nympha and . . . her house:* some manuscripts read a masculine for the house-church leader, "Nymphas and . . . his house."

4, 16: *The one from Laodicea:* either a letter by Paul that has been lost or the Letter to the Ephesians (cf the note on Eph 1, 1, *in Ephesus*).

4, 17: *Fulfill the ministry:* usually taken to mean that *Archippus,* the son of Philemon and Apphia (Phlm 1-2), is "pastor" at Colossae. An alternate interpretation is that Archippus, not Philemon, is the owner of the slave Onesimus and that Paul is asking Archippus to complete the service he has received in the Lord by sending Onesimus back to minister to Paul in his captivity (cf Phlm 20).

4, 18: *My own hand:* a postscript in Paul's own hand was his custom; cf Gal 6, 11-18 and 2 Thes 3, 17-18.

THE FIRST LETTER TO THE THESSALONIANS

INTRODUCTION

When Paul parted from Barnabas (Acts 15, 36-41) at the beginning of what is called his second missionary journey, he chose Silvanus (Silas) as his traveling companion. Soon afterwards he took Timothy along with him (Acts 16, 1-3). Paul was now clearly at the head of his own missionary band. About A.D. 50, he arrived in Greece for the first time. In making converts in Philippi and, soon afterwards, in Thessalonica, he was beset by persecution from Jews and Gentiles alike. Moving on to Beroea, he was again harassed by enemies from Thessalonica and hurriedly left for Athens (Acts 16, 11—17, 15). Silvanus and Timothy remained behind for a while. Paul soon sent Timothy back to Thessalonica to strengthen that community in its trials (3, 1-5). Timothy and Silvanus finally returned to Paul when he reached Corinth (Acts 18, 1-18), probably in the early summer of A.D. 51. Timothy's return with a report on conditions at Thessalonica served as the occasion for Paul's first letter (3, 6-8).

The letter begins with a brief address (1, 1) and concludes with a greeting (5, 26-28). The body of the letter consists of two major parts. The first (1, 2—3, 13) is a set of three sections of thanksgiving connected by two apologiae (defenses) dealing, respectively, with the missionaries' previous conduct and their current concerns. Paul's thankful optimism regarding the Thessalonians' spiritual welfare is tempered by his insistence on their recognition of the selfless love shown by the missionaries. In an age of itinerant peddlers of new religions, Paul found it necessary to emphasize not only the content of his gospel but also his manner of presenting it, for both attested to God's grace as freely bestowed and powerfully effected.

The second part of the letter (4, 1—5, 25) is specifically hortatory or parenetic. The superabundant love for which Paul has just prayed (3, 12-13) is to be shown practically by living out the norms of conduct that he has communicated to them. Specific "imperatives" of Christian life, principles for acting morally, stem from the "indicative" of one's relationship to God through Christ by the sending of the holy Spirit. Thus, moral conduct is the practical, personal expression of one's Christian faith, love, and hope.

The principal divisions of the First Letter to the Thessalonians are the following:

I.   *Address (1, 1-10)*
II. *Previous Relations with the Thessalonians (2, 1—3, 13)*
III. *Specific Exhortations (4, 1—5, 25)*
IV. *Final Greeting (5, 26-28)*

I. ADDRESS

CHAPTER 1

Greeting. [1] *a* Paul, Silvanus, and Timothy to the church of the Thessalonians in God the Father and the Lord Jesus Christ: grace to you and peace.*

Thanksgiving for Their Faith. [2] We give thanks to God always for all of you, remembering you in our prayers, unceasingly[b] [3] calling to mind your work of faith and labor of love and endurance in hope* of our Lord Jesus Christ, before our God and Father, [4] knowing, brothers loved by God, how you were chosen. [c] [5] For our gospel did not come to you in word alone, but also in power and in the holy Spirit and [with] much conviction. You know what sort of people we were [among] you for your sake.[d] [6] And you became imitators* of us and of the Lord, receiving the word in great affliction, with joy from the holy Spirit, [7] so that you became a model for all the believers in Macedonia and in Achaia.[e] [8] For from you the word of the Lord has sounded forth not only in Macedonia and [in] Achaia, but in every place your faith in God has gone forth, so that we have no need to say anything.[f] [9] For they themselves openly declare about us what sort of reception we had among you, and how you turned to God from idols to serve the living and true God[g] [10] and to await his Son from heaven, whom he raised from [the] dead, Jesus, who delivers us from the coming wrath.[h]

II. PREVIOUS RELATIONS WITH THE THESSALONIANS

CHAPTER 2

Paul's Ministry Among Them. [1] For you yourselves know, brothers, that our reception among you was not without effect. [2] Rather, after we had suffered and been insolently treated, as you know, in Philippi, we drew courage through our God to speak to you the gospel of God with much struggle.[i] [3] Our exhortation was not from delusion or impure motives, nor did it work through deception. [4] But as we were judged worthy* by God to be entrusted with the gospel, that is how we speak, not as trying to please human beings, but rather God, who judges our hearts.[j] [5] Nor, indeed, did we ever appear with flattering speech, as you know, or with a pretext for greed— God is witness—[6] nor did we seek praise from human beings, either from you or from others,[k] [7] although we were able to impose our weight as apostles of Christ. Rather, we were gentle* among you, as a nursing mother cares for her children. [8] With such affection for you, we were determined to share with you not only the gospel of God, but our very selves as well, so dearly beloved had you become to us. [9] You recall, brothers, our toil and drudgery. Working night and day in order not to burden any of you, we proclaimed to you the gospel of God.[l] [10] You are witnesses, and so is God, how devoutly and justly and blamelessly we behaved toward you

---

a Acts 15, 40; 16, 1-3.19; 17, 14-15; 2 Thes 1, 1-2.—b 2 Thes 1, 3.—c 2 Thes 2, 13.—d Acts 13, 52; 17, 1-9.—e 2 Thes 1, 4; 1 Cor 4, 16; 11, 1 / 1 Thes 2, 14; Phil 3, 17.—f Rom 1, 8.—g Acts 14, 15; Gal 4, 8 / 1 Thes 4, 5.—h Rom 2, 1-16; 5, 9; 13, 4 / 1 Thes 5, 9.—i Acts 16, 19—17, 10.—j Gal 1, 10.—k Jn 5, 41.44; 1 Cor 10, 31; 2 Cor 4, 17.—l Acts 20, 34; 1 Cor 4, 12; 9, 3-18; 2 Thes 3, 7-9.

1, 1: On the address, see the note on Rom 1, 1-7.

1, 3: *Faith . . . love . . . hope:* this, along with 1 Thes 5, 8, is the earliest mention in Christian literature of the three "theological virtues" (see 1 Cor 13, 13). The order here stresses eschatological hope, in line with the letter's emphasis on the Lord's

second, triumphal coming, or parousia (1 Thes 1, 10; 2, 12.19; 3, 13; 4, 13—5, 11; 5, 23).

1, 6: *Imitators:* the Pauline theme of "imitation" (see 1 Thes 2, 14; 1 Cor 4, 16; 11, 1; 2 Thes 3, 9) is rooted in Paul's view of solidarity in Christ through sharing in Jesus' cross and in the Spirit of the risen Lord.

2, 4: *Judged worthy:* Paul regards "worthiness" not as grounded in one's own talent or moral self-righteousness but in God's discernment of genuinely selfless attitudes and actions (see 2 Cor 10, 17-18).

2, 7: *Gentle:* many excellent manuscripts read "infants" *(nēpioi),* but "gentle" *(ēpioi)* better suits the context here.

believers. [11] As you know, we treated each one of you as a father treats his children,[m] [12] exhorting and encouraging you and insisting that you conduct yourselves as worthy of the God who calls you into his kingdom and glory.[n]

Further Thanksgiving. [13] And for this reason we too give thanks to God unceasingly, that, in receiving the word of God from hearing us, you received not a human word but, as it truly is, the word of God, which is now at work in you who believe. [14] * For you, brothers, have become imitators of the churches of God that are in Judea in Christ Jesus. For you suffer the same things from your compatriots as they did from the Jews, [15] * who killed both the Lord Jesus and the prophets and persecuted us; they do not please God, and are opposed to everyone,[o] [16] trying to prevent us from speaking to the Gentiles that they may be saved, thus constantly filling up the measure of their sins. But the wrath of God has finally begun to come upon them.[p]

Paul's Recent Travel Plans. [17] Brothers, when we were bereft of you for a short time, in person, not in heart, we were all the more eager in our great desire to see you in person.[q] [18] We decided to go to you—I, Paul, not only once but more than once—yet Satan thwarted us.[r] [19] For what is our hope or joy or crown to boast of in the presence of our Lord Jesus at his coming if not you yourselves?[s] [20] For you are our glory and joy.

CHAPTER 3

[1] That is why, when we could bear it no longer, we decided to remain alone in Athens[t] [2] and sent Timothy, our brother and co-worker for God in the gospel of Christ, to strengthen and encourage you in your faith,[u] [3] so that no one be disturbed in these afflictions. For you yourselves know that we are destined* for this. [4] For even when we were among you, we used to warn you in advance that we would undergo affliction, just as has happened, as you know.[v] [5] For this reason, when I too could bear it no longer, I sent to learn about your faith, for fear that somehow the tempter had put you to the test and our toil might come to nothing.

[6] But just now Timothy has returned to us from you, bringing us the good news of your faith and love, and that you always think kindly of us and long to see us as we long to see you. [7] Because of this, we have been reassured about you, brothers, in our every distress and affliction, through your faith. [8] For we now live, if you stand firm in the Lord.

Concluding Thanksgiving and Prayer. [9] * What thanksgiving, then, can we render to God for you, for all the joy we feel on your account before our God? [10] Night and day we pray beyond measure to see you in person and to remedy the deficiencies of your faith. [11] Now may God himself, our Father, and our Lord Jesus direct our way to you, [12] and may the Lord make you increase and abound in love for one another and for all, just as we have for you,[w] [13] so as to strengthen your hearts, to be blameless in holiness before our God and Father at the coming of our Lord Jesus with all his holy ones. [Amen.][x]

III. SPECIFIC EXHORTATIONS

CHAPTER 4

General Exhortations. [1] Finally, brothers, we earnestly ask and exhort you in the Lord Jesus that, as you received from us

m Acts 20, 31.—n 1 Pt 5, 10 / 1 Thes 4, 7; 2 Thes 2, 14.—o Acts 2, 23; 7, 52.—p Gn 15, 16; 2 Mc 6, 14 / Rom 1, 18; 2, 5-6.—q 1 Thes 3, 10; Rom 1, 10-11.—r Rom 15, 22.—s 2 Cor 1, 14; Phil 2, 16; 4, 1.—t Acts 17, 14.—u Acts 16, l-2; 1 Cor 3, 5-9.—v Acts 14, 22; 2 Thes 2, 5-7; 2 Tm 3, 12.—w 1 Thes 4, 9-10; 2 Thes 1, 3.—x 1 Thes 5, 23; 1 Cor 1, 8.

2, 14: Luke's picture of the persecutions at Philippi (by Gentiles) and in Thessalonica and Beroea (by Jews) seems to be considerably schematized (Acts 16, 11-40; 17, 1-15). Paul pictures the Thessalonian community as composed of converts from paganism (1 Thes 1, 9) and speaks here of persecution by their (pagan) compatriots rather than by Jews.

2, 15-16: Paul is speaking of historical opposition on the part of Palestinian Jews in particular and does so only some twenty years after Jesus' crucifixion. Even so, he quickly proceeds to depict the persecutors typologically, in apocalyptic terms. His remarks give no grounds for anti-Semitism to those willing to understand him, especially in view of Paul's pride in his own ethnic and religious background (Rom 9, 1-5; 10, 1; 11, 1-3; Phil

3, 4-6). Sinful conduct (16) is itself an anticipation of the ultimate wrath or judgment of God (Rom 1, 18—2, 5), whether or not it is perceived as such.

3, 3: *We are destined:* the Greek phraseology and the context suggest Paul's concern to alert his readers to difficulties he knew they would necessarily face and to enable them to see their present experience in the light of what he warned them would happen in the future. This line of thought is followed in 2 Thes 2, 1-15.

3, 9-10: The tension between Paul's optimism concerning the Thessalonians' faith and his worries about their perseverance remains unresolved. Perhaps this is accounted for not only by the continuing harassment but also by the shortness of his own stay in Thessalonica (even if that were over twice as long as the conventional three weeks that Luke assigns to it, Acts 17, 2).

how you should conduct yourselves to please God—and as you are conducting yourselves—you do so even more. ²For you know what instructions* we gave you through the Lord Jesus.

Holiness in Sexual Conduct.* ³This is the will of God, your holiness: that you refrain from immorality, ⁴that each of you know how to acquire a wife for himself in holiness and honor, ⁵not in lustful passion as do the Gentiles who do not know God;*ʸ* ⁶not to take advantage of or exploit a brother in this matter, for the Lord is an avenger in all these things, as we told you before and solemnly affirmed. ⁷For God did not call us to impurity but to holiness. ⁸Therefore, whoever disregards this, disregards not a human being but God, who [also] gives his holy Spirit to you.*ᶻ*

Mutual Charity. ⁹On the subject of mutual charity you have no need for anyone to write you, for you yourselves have been taught by God to love one another.*ᵃ* ¹⁰Indeed, you do this for all the brothers throughout Macedonia. Nevertheless we urge you, brothers, to progress even more,*ᵇ* ¹¹and to aspire to live a tranquil life, to mind your own affairs, and to work with your [own] hands, as we instructed you, ¹²that you may conduct yourselves properly toward outsiders and not depend on anyone.

Hope for the Christian Dead. ¹³We do not want you to be unaware, brothers, about those who have fallen asleep, so that you may not grieve like the rest, who have no hope. ¹⁴For if we believe that Jesus died and rose, so too will God, through Jesus, bring with him those who have fallen asleep.*ᶜ* ¹⁵Indeed, we tell you this, on the word of the Lord, that we who are alive,

who are left until the coming of the Lord,* will surely not precede those who have fallen asleep.*ᵈ* ¹⁶For the Lord himself, with a word of command, with the voice of an archangel and with the trumpet of God, will come down from heaven, and the dead in Christ will rise first.*ᵉ* ¹⁷Then we who are alive, who are left, will be caught up together* with them in the clouds to meet the Lord in the air. Thus we shall always be with the Lord. ¹⁸Therefore, console one another with these words.

CHAPTER 5

Vigilance. ¹Concerning times and seasons, brothers, you have no need for anything to be written to you.*ᶠ* ²For you yourselves know very well that the day of the Lord will come like a thief at night.*ᵍ* ³When people are saying, "Peace and security," then sudden disaster comes upon them, like labor pains upon a pregnant woman, and they will not escape.

⁴But you, brothers, are not in darkness, for that day to overtake you like a thief.*ʰ* ⁵For all of you are children of the light* and children of the day. We are not of the night or of darkness. ⁶Therefore, let us not sleep as the rest do, but let us stay alert and sober.*ⁱ* ⁷Those who sleep go to sleep at night, and those who are drunk get drunk at night. ⁸But since we are of the day, let us be sober, putting on the breastplate of faith and love and the helmet that is hope for salvation.*ʲ* ⁹For God did not destine us for wrath, but to gain salvation through

---

y Ps 79, 6; Jer 10, 25; 2 Thes 1, 8; 1 Pt 3, 7.—z Lk 10, 16.—a Jn 6, 45; 13, 34; 1 Jn 2, 20-21.27; 4, 7.—b 2 Thes 3, 6-12.—c 1 Cor 15, 3-4.12.20.—d 1 Cor 15, 51; Rv 14, 13; 20, 4-6.—e Mt 24, 31; 1 Cor 15, 23.52.—f Mt 24, 36-45.—g 2 Pt 3, 10.—h Eph 5, 8-9.—i Mt 24, 42; Rom 13, 12-13; 1 Pt 5, 8.—j Is 59, 17; Rom 13, 11-14; Eph 6, 11.14-17.

4, 2: *Instructions:* these include specific guidelines on the basis of the Lord's authority, not necessarily sayings Jesus actually uttered. More profoundly, as v 8 implies, the instructions are practical principles that Paul worked out in accordance with his understanding of the role of the Spirit.

4, 3-8: Many think that this passage deals with a variety of moral regulations (fornication, adultery, sharp business practices). It can be more specifically interpreted as bringing general norms to bear on a specific problem, namely, marriage within degrees of consanguinity (as between uncle and niece) forbidden in Jewish law but allowed according to a Greek heiress law, which would insure retention of an inheritance within the family and

perhaps thereby occasion divorce. In that case, "immorality" (3) should be rendered as "unlawful marriage" and "this matter" (6) as "a lawsuit." The phrase in v 4, "acquire a wife for himself," has often been interpreted to mean "control one's body."

4, 15: *Coming of the Lord:* Paul here assumes that the second coming, or parousia, will occur within his own lifetime but insists that the time or season is unknown (1 Thes 5, 1-2). Nevertheless, the most important aspect of the parousia for him was the fulfillment of union with Christ. His pastoral exhortation focuses first on hope for the departed faithful, then (5, 1-3) on the need of preparedness for those who have to achieve their goal.

4, 17: *Will be caught up together:* literally, snatched up, carried off; cf 2 Cor 12, 2; Rv 12, 5. From the Latin verb here used, *rapiemur.* has come the idea of "the rapture," when believers will be transported away from the woes of the world; this construction combines this verse with Mt 24, 40-41 (see the note there) // Lk 17, 34-35 and passages from Rv in a scheme of millennial dispensationalism.

5, 5: *Children of the light:* that is, belonging to the daylight of God's personal revelation and expected to achieve it (an analogous development of imagery that appears in Jn 12, 36).

our Lord Jesus Christ, [10]who died for us, so that whether we are awake or asleep we may live together with him.* [11]Therefore, encourage one another and build one another up, as indeed you do.[k]

Church Order. [12]We ask you, brothers, to respect those who are laboring among you and who are over you in the Lord and who admonish you, [13]and to show esteem for them with special love on account of their work. Be at peace among yourselves.

[14]We urge you, brothers, admonish the idle, cheer the fainthearted, support the weak, be patient with all. [15]See that no one returns evil for evil; rather, always seek what is good [both] for each other and for all.[l] [16]Rejoice always. [17]Pray without ceasing. [18]In all circumstances give thanks, for this is the will of God for you in Christ Jesus.[m] [19] * Do not quench the Spirit. [20]Do not despise prophetic utterances. [21]Test everything; retain what is good. [22]Refrain from every kind of evil.

Concluding Prayer. [23] * May the God of peace himself make you perfectly holy and may you entirely, spirit, soul, and body, be preserved blameless for the coming of our Lord Jesus Christ.[n] [24]The one who calls you is faithful, and he will also accomplish it. [25]Brothers, pray for us [too].

IV. FINAL GREETING

[26]Greet all the brothers with a holy kiss.* [27]I adjure you by the Lord that this letter be read to the brothers. [28]The grace of our Lord Jesus Christ be with you.

---

k Rom 15, 2; 1 Cor 8, 1; 14, 12.26; Eph 4, 29.—l Prv 20, 22; Mt 5, 38-42; Rom 12, 17.—m Eph 5, 20.—n 2 Thes 3, 16.

5, 10: Characteristically, Paul plays on words suggesting ultimate and anticipated death and life. Union with the crucified and risen Lord at his parousia is anticipated in some measure in contrasted states of our temporal life. The essential element he urges is our indestructible personal union in Christ's own life (see Rom 5, 1-10).

5, 19-21: Paul's buoyant encouragement of charismatic freedom sometimes occasioned excesses that he or others had to remedy (see 1 Cor 14; 2 Thes 2, 1-15; 2 Pt 3, 1-16).

5, 23: Another possible translation is, "May the God of peace himself make you perfectly holy and sanctify your spirit fully, and may both soul and body be preserved blameless for the coming of our Lord Jesus Christ." In either case, Paul is not offering an anthropological or philosophical analysis of human nature. Rather, he looks to the wholeness of what may be called the supernatural and natural aspects of a person's service of God.

5, 26: *Kiss:* the holy embrace (see Rom 16, 16; 1 Cor 16, 20; 2 Cor 13, 12; 1 Pt 5, 14) was a greeting of respect and affection, perhaps given during a liturgy at which Paul's letter would have been read.

THE SECOND LETTER TO THE THESSALONIANS   `2Thes`

INTRODUCTION

    This letter is addressed to the same church as the letter that precedes it in the canon and contains many expressions parallel to those in the First Letter to the Thessalonians, indeed verbatim with them. Yet other aspects of the contents of the Second Letter to the Thessalonians suggest a more impersonal tone and changed circumstances in the situation at Thessalonica.

    The letter begins with an address (1, 1-2) that expands only slightly on that of 1 Thes 1, 1. It ends with a greeting insisting on its Pauline authority in the face of false claims made in Paul's name (see the note on 2, 2). The body of the letter falls into three short parts, of which the second is notoriously difficult (ch 2).

    The opening thanksgiving and prayer (1, 3-12) speak of the Thessalonians' increasing faith and love in the face of outside persecution. God's eventual judgment against persecutors and his salvation for the faithful are already evidenced by the very fact of persecution. The second part (2, 1-17), the heart of the letter, deals with a problem threatening the faith of the community. A message involving a prophetic oracle and apparently a forged letter, possibly presented at a liturgical gathering (cf 2, 2 and 1 Cor 14, 26-33), to the effect that the day of the Lord and all that it means have already come, has upset the life of the Thessalonian church.

The writer counters their preoccupation with the date of the parousia (or coming again of the Lord Jesus from heaven, 2, 1) by recalling Paul's teaching concerning what must happen first and by going on to describe what will happen at the Lord's coming (2, 8); he indicates the twofold process by which the "activity of Satan" and God's actions (2, 9-11) are working out, namely, a growing division between believers and those who succumb to false prophecy and "the lie." He concludes by insisting on Pauline traditions and by praying for divine strength (2, 13-17). The closing part of the letter (3, 1-16) deals in particular with the apostle's directives and model style of life and with correction of disorderly elements within the community.

Traditional opinion holds that this letter was written shortly after 1 Thessalonians. Occasionally it has been argued that 2 Thessalonians was written first or that the two letters are addressed to different segments within the church at Thessalonica (2 Thessalonians being directed to the Jewish Christians there) or even that 2 Thessalonians was originally written to some other nearby place where Paul carried out mission work, such as Philippi or Beroea. Increasingly in recent times, however, the opinion has been advanced that 2 Thessalonians is a pseudepigraph, that is, a letter written authoritatively in Paul's name, to maintain apostolic traditions in a later period, perhaps during the last two decades of the first century.

In any case, the presumed audience of Second Thessalonians and certain features of its style and content require that it be read and studied in a Pauline context, particularly that provided by 1 Thessalonians. At the same time, and especially if the letter is regarded as not by Paul himself, its apocalyptic presentation of preconditions for the parousia (2, 1-12) may profit from and require recourse to a wider biblical basis for interpretation, namely Old Testament books such as Daniel and Isaiah and especially, in the New Testament, the synoptic apocalyptic discourse (Mk 13; Mt 24—25; Lk 21, 5-36) and the Book of Revelation.

The principal divisions of the Second Letter to the Thessalonians are the following:

   I.   *Address (1, 1-12)*
   II.   *Warning against Deception Concerning the Parousia (2, 1-17)*
   III. *Concluding Exhortations (3, 1-16)*
   IV. *Final Greetings (3, 17-18)*

I. ADDRESS

CHAPTER 1

Greeting.* [1] Paul, Silvanus, and Timothy to the church of the Thessalonians in God our Father and the Lord Jesus Christ:[a] [2] grace to you and peace from God [our] Father and the Lord Jesus Christ.

Thanksgiving. [3] * We ought to thank God always for you, brothers, as is fitting, because your faith flourishes ever more, and the love of every one of you for one another grows ever greater.[b] [4] Accordingly, we

ourselves boast of you in the churches of God regarding your endurance and faith in all your persecutions and the afflictions you endure.

[5] This is evidence of the just judgment of God, so that you may be considered worthy of the kingdom of God for which you are suffering.[c] [6] For it is surely just on God's part to repay with afflictions those who are afflicting you, [7] and to grant rest along with us to you who are undergoing afflictions, at the revelation of the Lord Jesus from heaven with his mighty angels, [8] in blazing fire, inflicting punishment on those who do not acknowledge God and on those who do not obey the gospel of our

---

a 1 Thes 1, 1.—b 1 Cor 1, 4; 1 Thes 1, 2; 3, 12.—c Phil 1, 28; 1 Thes 2, 12.

1, 1-2: On the address, see the note on Rom 1, 1-7 and cf 1 Thes 1, 1.

1, 3-12: On the thanksgiving, see the note on Rom 1, 8 and cf 1 Thes 1, 2-10. Paul's gratitude to God for the faith and love of the Thessalonians (3) and his Christian pride in their faithful en-

durance (4-5) contrast with the condemnation announced for those who afflict them, a judgment to be carried out at the parousia (6-10), which is described in vivid language drawn from Old Testament apocalyptic. A prayer for the fulfillment of God's purpose in the Thessalonians (11-12) completes the section, as is customary in a Pauline letter (cf 1 Thes 1, 2-3).

Lord Jesus.[d] [9]These will pay the penalty of eternal ruin, separated from the presence of the Lord and from the glory of his power,[e] [10]when he comes to be glorified among his holy ones* and to be marveled at on that day among all who have believed, for our testimony to you was believed.[f]

Prayer. [11]To this end, we always pray for you, that our God may make you worthy of his calling and powerfully bring to fulfillment every good purpose and every effort of faith,[g] [12]that the name of our Lord Jesus may be glorified in you, and you in him,[h] in accord with the grace of our God and Lord Jesus Christ.*

II. WARNING AGAINST DECEPTION CONCERNING THE PAROUSIA

CHAPTER 2

Christ and the Lawless One.* [1]We ask you, brothers, with regard to the coming of our Lord Jesus Christ and our assembling with him,[i] [2]not to be shaken out of your minds suddenly, or to be alarmed either by a "spirit,"* or by an oral statement, or by a letter allegedly from us to the effect that the day of the Lord is at hand.[j] [3]Let no one deceive you in any way. For unless the apostasy comes first and the lawless one is revealed,* the one doomed to perdition, [4][k] who opposes and exalts himself above every so-called god and object of worship, so as to seat himself in the temple of God,* claiming that he is a god—[5]do you not recall that while I was still with you I told you these things? [6]And now you know what is restraining,* that he may be re-

---

d Ps 79, 5-6; Is 66, 15; Jer 10, 25.—e Is 2, 10.19.21.—f Ps 89, 8; Dn 7, 18-22.27; 1 Thes 3, 13.—g 1 Thes 1, 2-3.—h Is 66, 5.—i 1 Thes 4, 13-17.—j Mt 24, 6; 1 Cor 14, 26.32-33; 1 Thes 5, 1-2.—k Dn 11, 36-37; Ez 28, 2.

1, 10: *Among his holy ones:* in the Old Testament, this term can refer to an angelic throng (cf also Jude 14), but here, in parallel with *among all who have believed,* it can refer to the triumphant people of God.

1, 12: *The grace of our God and Lord Jesus Christ:* the Greek can also be translated, "the grace of our God and of the Lord Jesus Christ."

2, 1-17: The Thessalonians have been *shaken* by a message purporting to come from Paul himself that *the day of the Lord* is already present. He warns against this deception in eschatology by citing a scenario of events that must first occur (3-12) before the end will come. The overall point Paul makes is the need to reject such lies as Satan sends; he also reaffirms the Thessalonians in their calling (13-14). They are to uphold what Paul himself has taught (15). There is a concluding prayer for their strengthening (16-17). As in 2 Thes 1, 8-10, the Old Testament provides a good deal of coloring; cf especially Is 14, 13-14; 66, 15.18-21; Ez 28, 2-9; Dn 11, 36-37. The contents of 2 Thes 2, 3b-8 may come from a previously existing apocalypse. The details have been variously interpreted.

An alternative to the possibilities noted below understands that an oracular utterance, supposedly coming from a prophetic spirit (2-3a), has so disrupted the community's thinking that its effects may be compared to those of the mania connected with the worship of the Greek god Dionysus. On this view, the writer seems to allude in vv 6-8 to Dionysiac "seizure," although, of course, ironically, somewhat as Paul alludes to witchcraft ("an evil eye") in Gal 3, 1 in speaking of the threat to faith posed by those disturbing the Galatians (Gal 1, 6-7; 5, 10b). On this view of 2 Thes 2, the Greek participles *katechon* (rendered above as *what is restraining*) and *katechōn* (*the one who restrains*) are to be translated "the seizing power" in v 6 and "the seizer" in v 7. They then allude to a pseudocharismatic force or spirit of Dionysiac character that has suddenly taken hold of the Thessalonian community (see 2). The addressees *know* (6) this force or

spirit because of the problem it is causing. This pseudocharismatic force or spirit is a kind of anticipation and advance proof of the ultimate, climactic figure (*the lawless one* or the rebel, 3), of which the community has been warned (see the note on 1 Thes 3, 3). It is, however, only the beginning of the end that the latter's manifestation entails; the end is not yet. For in the course of the *mystery of lawlessness* (7), false prophetism, after it ceases in the Thessalonian community, will be manifested in the world at large (8-12), where it will also be eliminated in turn by the Lord Jesus.

2, 2: *"Spirit":* a Spirit-inspired utterance or ecstatic revelation. *An oral statement:* literally, a "word" or pronouncement, not necessarily of ecstatic origin. *A letter allegedly sent by us:* possibly a forged letter, so that Paul calls attention in 2 Thes 3, 17 to his practice of concluding a genuine letter with a summary note or greeting in his own hand, as at Gal 6, 11-18 and elsewhere.

2, 3b-5: This incomplete sentence (anacoluthon, 4) recalls what the Thessalonians had already been taught, an apocalyptic scenario depicting, in terms borrowed especially from Dn 11, 36-37 and related verses, human self-assertiveness against God in *the temple of God* itself. *The lawless one* represents the climax of such activity in this account.

2, 4: *Seat himself in the temple of God:* a reflection of the language in Dn 7, 23-25; 8, 9-12; 9, 27; 11, 36-37; and 12, 11 about the attempt of Antiochus IV Epiphanes to set up a statue of Zeus in the Jerusalem temple and possibly of the Roman emperor Caligula to do a similar thing (Mk 13, 14). Here the imagery suggests an attempt to install someone in the place of God, *claiming that he is a god* (cf Ez 28, 2). Usually, it is the Jerusalem temple that is assumed to be meant; on the alternative view sketched above (see the note on 2 Thes 2, 1-17), *the temple* refers to the Christian community.

2, 6-7: *What is restraining . . . the one who restrains:* neuter and masculine, respectively, of a force and person holding back the lawless one. The Thessalonians know what is meant (6), but the terms, seemingly found only in this passage and in writings dependent on it, have been variously interpreted. Traditionally, v 6 has been applied to the Roman empire and v 7 to the Roman emperor (in Paul's day, Nero) as bulwarks holding back chaos (cf Rom 13, 1-7). A second interpretation suggests that cosmic or angelic powers are binding Satan (9) and so restraining him; some relate this to an anti-Christ figure (1 Jn 2, 18) or to Michael the archangel (Rv 12, 7-9; 20, 1-3). A more recent view suggests that it is the preaching of the Christian gospel that restrains the end, for in God's plan the end cannot come until the gospel is preached to all nations (Mk 13, 10); in that case, Paul as missionary preacher par excellence is "the one who restrains," whose removal (death) will bring the end (7). On the alternative view (see the note on 2 Thes 2, 1-17), the phrases should be referred to that which and to him who seizes (a prophet) in ecstasy so as to have him speak pseudo-oracles.

2Thes

vealed in his time. [7] * For the mystery of lawlessness is already at work. But the one who restrains is to do so only for the present, until he is removed from the scene.[l] [8] And then the lawless one will be revealed, whom the Lord [Jesus] will kill with the breath of his mouth and render powerless by the manifestation of his coming,[m] [9] the one whose coming springs from the power of Satan in every mighty deed and in signs and wonders that lie,[n] [10] and in every wicked deceit for those who are perishing because they have not accepted the love of truth so that they may be saved. [11] Therefore, God is sending them a deceiving power so that they may believe the lie, [12] that all who have not believed the truth but have approved wrongdoing may be condemned.

[13] But we ought to give thanks to God for you always, brothers loved by the Lord, because God chose you as the firstfruits* for salvation through sanctification by the Spirit and belief in truth.[o] [14] To this end he has [also] called you through our gospel to possess the glory of our Lord Jesus Christ.[p] [15] Therefore, brothers, stand firm and hold fast to the traditions that you were taught, either by an oral statement or by a letter of ours.*

[16] May our Lord Jesus Christ himself and God our Father, who has loved us and given us everlasting encouragement and good hope through his grace, [17] encourage your hearts and strengthen them in every good deed and word.

---

l Mt 13, 36-43; Acts 20, 29; Gal 5, 10; 2 Pt 2, 1; Rv 22, 11.—m Is 11, 4; Rv 19, 15.—n Mt 24, 24; Rv 13, 13.—o 1 Thes 2, 13; 5, 9.—p Rom 5, 1-10; 8, 29-30; 1 Thes 4, 7; 5, 9.—q Eph 6, 19; Col 4, 3.—r 1 Thes 5, 24 / 1 Cor 16, 13 / Mt 6, 13.—s 2 Cor 7, 16; 1 Thes 4, 1-2.—t 1 Thes 2, 9.—u Mt 10, 10; Phil 3, 17.—v 1 Thes 4, 11.—w 1 Thes 5, 14.

2, 7-12: *The lawless one* and *the one who restrains* are involved in an activity or process, *the mystery of lawlessness,* behind which *Satan* stands (9). The action of *the Lord [Jesus]* in overcoming the lawless one is described in Old Testament language (*with the breath of his mouth;* cf Is 11, 4; Jb 4, 9; Rv 19, 15). His *coming* is literally the Lord's "parousia." The biblical concept of the "holy war," eschatologically conceived, may underlie the imagery.

2, 13: As *the firstfruits:* there is also strong manuscript evidence for the reading, "God chose you from the beginning," thus providing a focus on God's activity from beginning to end; *firstfruits* is a Pauline term, however; cf Rom 8, 23; 11, 16; 16, 5, among other references.

2, 15: Reference to *an oral statement* and *a letter* (2) and the content here, including a formula of conclusion (cf 1 Cor 16, 13; Gal 5, 1), suggest that vv 1-15 or even 1-17 are to be taken

III. CONCLUDING EXHORTATIONS

CHAPTER 3*

Request for Prayers. [1] Finally, brothers, pray for us, so that the word of the Lord may speed forward and be glorified, as it did among you,[q] [2] and that we may be delivered from perverse and wicked people, for not all have faith. [3] But the Lord is faithful; he will strengthen you and guard you from the evil one.[r] [4] We are confident of you in the Lord that what we instruct you, you [both] are doing and will continue to do.[s] [5] May the Lord direct your hearts to the love of God and to the endurance of Christ.

Neglect of Work. [6] We instruct you, brothers, in the name of [our] Lord Jesus Christ, to shun any brother who conducts himself in a disorderly way and not according to the tradition they received from us.* [7] For you know how one must imitate us. For we did not act in a disorderly way among you, [8] nor did we eat food received free from anyone. On the contrary, in toil and drudgery, night and day we worked, so as not to burden any of you.[t] [9] Not that we do not have the right. Rather, we wanted to present ourselves as a model for you, so that you might imitate us.[u] [10] In fact, when we were with you, we instructed you that if anyone was unwilling to work, neither should that one eat.[v] [11] We hear that some are conducting themselves among you in a disorderly way, by not keeping busy but minding the business of others.[w] [12] Such people we instruct and urge in the Lord Jesus Christ to work quietly and to eat their own food. [13] But

---

as a literary unit, notwithstanding the incidental thanksgiving formula in v 13.

3, 1-18: The final chapter urges the Thessalonians to pray for Paul and his colleagues (1-2) and reiterates confidence in the Thessalonians (3-5), while admonishing them about a specific problem in their community that has grown out of the intense eschatological speculation, namely, not to work but to become instead disorderly busybodies (6-15). A benediction (16) and postscript in Paul's own hand round out the letter. On vv 17-18, cf the note on 2 Thes 2, 2.

3, 6: Some members of the community, probably because they regarded the parousia as imminent or the new age of the Lord to be already here (2 Thes 2, 2), had apparently ceased to work for a living. The disciplinary problem they posed could be rooted in distorted thinking about Paul's own teaching (cf 1 Thes 2, 16; 3, 3-4; 5, 4-5) or, more likely, in a forged letter (2 Thes 2, 2) and the type of teaching dealt with in 2 Thes 2, 2-15. The apostle's own moral teaching, reflected in his selfless labors for others, was rooted in a deep doctrinal concern for the gospel message (cf 1 Thes 2, 3-10).

you, brothers, do not be remiss in doing good. ¹⁴ If anyone does not obey our word as expressed in this letter, take note of this person not to associate with him, that he may be put to shame. ¹⁵ Do not regard him as an enemy but admonish him as a brother.^x ¹⁶ May the Lord of peace himself give you peace at all times and in every way. The Lord be with all of you.^y

IV. FINAL GREETINGS

¹⁷ This greeting is in my own hand, Paul's. This is the sign in every letter; this is how I write.^z ¹⁸ The grace of our Lord Jesus Christ be with all of you.

x 2 Cor 2, 7; Gal 6, 1.—y Jn 14, 27; Rom 15, 33.—z 1 Cor 16, 21; Gal 6, 11.

THE FIRST LETTER TO TIMOTHY

INTRODUCTION

The three letters, First and Second Timothy and Titus, form a distinct group within the Pauline corpus. In the collection of letters by the Apostle to the Gentiles, they differ from the others in form and contents. All three suggest they were written late in Paul's career. The opponents are not "Judaizers" as in Galatians but false teachers stressing "knowledge" (gnōsis; see the note on 1 Tm 6, 20-21). Attention is given especially to correct doctrine and church organization. Jesus' second coming recedes into the background compared to references in Paul's earlier letters (though not Colossians and Ephesians). The three letters are addressed not to congregations but to those who shepherd congregations (Latin, pastores). These letters were first named "Pastoral Epistles" in the eighteenth century because they all are concerned with the work of a pastor in caring for the community or communities under his charge.

The first of the Pastorals, 1 Timothy, is presented as having been written from Macedonia. Timothy, whom Paul converted, was of mixed Jewish and Gentile parentage (Acts 16, 1-3). He was the apostle's companion on both the second and the third missionary journeys (Acts 16, 3; 19, 22) and was often sent by him on special missions (Acts 19, 22; 1 Cor 4, 17; 1 Thes 3, 2). In 1 Timothy (1, 3), he is described as the administrator of the entire Ephesian community.

1Tm

The letter instructs Timothy on his duty to restrain false and useless teaching (1, 3-11; 4, 1-5; 6, 3-16) and proposes principles pertaining to his relationship with the older members of the community (5, 1-2) and with the presbyters (5, 17-22). It gives rules for aid to widows (5, 3-8) and their selection for charitable ministrations (5, 9-16) and also deals with liturgical celebrations (2, 1-15), selections for the offices of bishop and deacon (3, 1-13), relation of slaves with their masters (6, 1-2), and obligations of the wealthier members of the community (6, 17-19). This letter also reminds Timothy of the prophetic character of his office (1, 12-20) and encourages him in his exercise of it (4, 6-16). The central passage of the letter (3, 14-16) expresses the principal motive that should guide the conduct of Timothy—preservation of the purity of the church's doctrine against false teaching. On this same note the letter concludes (6, 20-21).

From the late second century to the nineteenth, Pauline authorship of the three Pastoral Epistles went unchallenged. Since then, the attribution of these letters to Paul has been questioned. Most scholars are convinced that Paul could not have been responsible for the vocabulary and style, the concept of church organization, or the theological expressions found in these letters. A second group believes, on the basis of statistical evidence, that the vocabulary and style are Pauline, even if at first sight the contrary seems to be the case. They state that the concept of church organization in the letters is not as advanced as the questioners of Pauline authorship hold since the notion of hierarchical order in a religious community existed in Israel before the time of Christ, as evidenced in the Dead Sea Scrolls. Finally, this group sees affinities between the theological thought of the Pastorals and that of the unquestionably genuine letters of Paul. Other scholars, while conceding a degree of validity to the positions mentioned above, suggest that the apostle made use of a secretary who was responsible for the composition of the letters. A fourth group of scholars believes that these letters are the work of a compiler, that they are based on traditions about Paul in his later years, and that they include, in varying amounts, actual fragments of genuine Pauline correspondence.

If Paul is considered the more immediate author, the Pastorals are to be dated between the end of his first Roman imprisonment (Acts 28, 16) and his execution under Nero (A.D. 63-67); if they are regarded as only more remotely Pauline, their date may be as late as the early second century. In spite of these problems of authorship and dating, the Pastorals are illustrative of early Christian life and remain an important element of canonical scripture.

The principal divisions of the First Letter to Timothy are the following:

    I.   *Address (1, 1-2)*
   II.   *Sound Teaching (1, 3-20)*
  III.   *Problems of Discipline (2, 1—4, 16)*
  IV.   *Duties toward Others (5, 1—6, 2a)*
   V.   *False Teaching and True Wealth (6, 2b-19)*
  VI.   *Final Recommendation and Warning (6, 20-21)*

I. ADDRESS

CHAPTER 1

Greeting.* [1]Paul, an apostle of Christ Jesus by command of God our savior and of Christ Jesus our hope,[a] [2]to Timothy, my true child in faith: grace, mercy, and peace from God the Father and Christ Jesus our Lord.[b]

II. SOUND TEACHING

Warning against False Doctrine. [3] * I repeat the request I made of you when I was on my way to Macedonia,[c] that you stay in Ephesus to instruct certain people not to teach false doctrines [4] [d] or to concern themselves with myths and endless genealogies, which promote speculations rather than the plan of God that is to be re-

ceived by faith.* [5]The aim of this instruction is love from a pure heart, a good conscience, and a sincere faith.[e] [6]Some people have deviated from these and turned to meaningless talk,[f] [7]wanting to be teachers of the law, but without understanding either what they are saying or what they assert with such assurance.

[8] * We know that the law is good, provided that one uses it as law,[g] [9]with the understanding that law is meant not for a righteous person but for the lawless and unruly, the godless and sinful, the unholy and profane, those who kill their fathers or mothers, murderers, [10]the unchaste, sodomites,* kidnapers, liars, perjurers, and whatever else is opposed to sound teaching,[h] [11]according to the glorious gospel of the blessed God, with which I have been entrusted.[i]

---

a 1 Tm 2, 3; Lk 1, 47; Ti 1, 3; 2, 10 / Col 1, 27.—b 2 Tm 1, 2; Ti 1, 4.—c Acts 20, 1.—d 1 Tm 4, 7; Ti 1, 14; 3, 9; 2 Pt 1, 16.—e Rom 13, 10.—f 1 Tm 6, 4.20; Ti 1, 10.—g Rom 7, 12.16.—h 1 Tm 4, 6; 6, 3; 2 Tm 4, 3; Ti 1, 9; 2, 1.—i Ti 1, 3.

1, 1-2: For the Pauline use of the conventional epistolary form, see the note on Rom 1, 1-7.

1, 3-7: Here Timothy's initial task *in Ephesus* (cf Acts 20, 17-35) is outlined: to suppress the idle religious speculations, probably about Old Testament figures (3-4, but see the note on 1 Tm 6, 20-21), which do not contribute to the development of love within the community (5) but rather encourage similar useless conjectures (6-7).

1, 4: *The plan of God that is to be received by faith:* the Greek may also possibly mean "God's trustworthy plan" or "the training in faith that God requires."

1, 8-11: Those responsible for the speculations that are to be suppressed by Timothy do not present the Old Testament from the Christian viewpoint. The Christian values the Old Testament not as a system of law but as the first stage in God's revelation of his saving plan, which is brought to fulfillment in the good news of salvation through faith in Jesus Christ.

1, 10: *Sodomites:* see 1 Cor 6, 9 and the note there.

Gratitude for God's Mercy.* [12]I am grateful to him who has strengthened me, Christ Jesus our Lord, because he considered me trustworthy in appointing me to the ministry.[j] [13]I was once a blasphemer and a persecutor and an arrogant man, but I have been mercifully treated because I acted out of ignorance in my unbelief.[k] [14]Indeed, the grace of our Lord has been abundant, along with the faith and love that are in Christ Jesus.[l] [15]This saying is trustworthy* and deserves full acceptance: Christ Jesus came into the world to save sinners. Of these I am the foremost.[m] [16]But for that reason I was mercifully treated, so that in me, as the foremost, Christ Jesus might display all his patience as an example for those who would come to believe in him for everlasting life. [17]To the king of ages,* incorruptible, invisible, the only God, honor and glory forever and ever. Amen.[n]

Responsibility of Timothy.* [18]I entrust this charge to you, Timothy, my child, in accordance with the prophetic words once spoken about you.* Through them may you fight a good fight[o] [19]by having faith

and a good conscience. Some, by rejecting conscience, have made a shipwreck of their faith,[p] [20]among them Hymenaeus* and Alexander, whom I have handed over to Satan to be taught not to blaspheme.[q]

III. PROBLEMS OF DISCIPLINE

CHAPTER 2

Prayer and Conduct. [1] * First of all, then, I ask that supplications, prayers, petitions, and thanksgivings be offered for everyone,[r] [2]for kings and for all in authority, that we may lead a quiet and tranquil life in all devotion and dignity. [3]This is good and pleasing to God our savior,[s] [4]who wills everyone to be saved and to come to knowledge of the truth.[t]

[5] For there is one God.
    There is also one mediator between God
        and the human race,
        Christ Jesus, himself human,[u]
[6] who gave himself as ransom for all.

This was the testimony* at the proper time.[v] [7]For this I was appointed preacher and apostle (I am speaking the truth, I am not lying), teacher of the Gentiles in faith and truth.[w]

---

j Phil 4, 13 / Acts 9, 15; Gal 1, 15-16.—k Acts 8, 3; 9, 1-2; 1 Cor 15, 9; Gal 1, 13.—l Rom 5, 20; 2 Tm 1, 13.—m Lk 15, 2; 19, 10.—n Rom 16, 27.—o 1 Tm 4, 14 / 1 Tm 6, 12; 2 Tm 4, 7; Jude 3.—p 1 Tm 3, 9.—q 2 Tm 2, 17; 4, 14 / 1 Cor 5, 5.—r Eph 6, 18; Phil 4, 6.—s 1 Tm 1, 1; 4, 10.—t 2 Tm 3, 7; 2 Pt 3, 9.—u 1 Cor 8, 6; Heb 8, 6; 9, 15; 12, 24 / Rom 5, 15.—v Mk 10, 45; Gal 1, 4; 2, 20; Eph 5, 25; Ti 2, 14.—w Acts 9, 15; 1 Cor 9, 1; Gal 2, 7-8.

1, 12-17: Present gratitude for the Christian apostleship leads Paul to recall an earlier time when he had been a fierce persecutor of the Christian communities (cf Acts 26, 9-11) until his conversion by intervention of divine mercy through the appearance of Jesus. This and his subsequent apostolic experience testify to the saving purpose of Jesus' incarnation. The fact of his former ignorance of the truth has not kept the apostle from regarding himself as having been the worst of sinners (15). Yet he was chosen to be an apostle, that God might manifest his firm will to save sinful humanity through Jesus Christ (16). The recounting of so great a mystery leads to a spontaneous outpouring of adoration (17).

1, 15: *This saying is trustworthy:* this phrase regularly introduces in the Pastorals a basic truth of early Christian faith; cf 1 Tm 3, 1; 4, 9; 2 Tm 2, 11; Ti 3, 8.

1, 17: *King of ages:* through Semitic influence, the Greek expression could mean "everlasting king"; it could also mean "king of the universe."

1, 18-20: Timothy is to be mindful of his calling, which is here compared to the way Barnabas and Saul were designated by Christ as prophets for missionary service; cf Acts 13, 1-3. Such is probably the sense of the allusion to the prophetic words (18). His task is not to yield, whether in doctrine or in conduct, to erroneous opinions, taking warning from what has already happened at Ephesus in the case of Hymenaeus and Alexander (19-20).

1, 18: *The prophetic words once spoken about you:* the Greek may also be translated, "the prophecies that led (me) to you." It probably refers to testimonies given by charismatic figures in the Christian communities. *Fight a good fight:* this translation preserves the play on words in Greek. The Greek terms imply a lengthy engagement in battle and might well be translated "wage a good campaign."

1, 20: *Hymenaeus:* mentioned in 2 Tm 2, 17 as saying that the resurrection has already taken place (in baptism). *Alexander:* probably the Alexander mentioned in 2 Tm 4, 14 as the coppersmith who "did me a great deal of harm." *Whom I have handed over to Satan:* the same terms are used in the condemnation of the incestuous man in 1 Cor 5, 5.

2, 1-7: This marked insistence that the liturgical prayer of the community concern itself with the needs of all, whether Christian or not, and especially of those in authority, may imply that a disposition existed at Ephesus to refuse prayer for pagans. In actuality, such prayer aids the community to achieve peaceful relationships with non-Christians (2) and contributes to salvation, since it derives its value from the presence within the community of Christ, who is the one and only savior of all (3-6). The vital apostolic mission to the Gentiles (7) reflects Christ's purpose of universal salvation.
Verse 5 contains what may well have been a very primitive creed. Some interpreters have called it a Christian version of the Jewish *shema:* "Hear, O Israel, the LORD is our God, the LORD alone . . ." (Dt 6, 4-5). The assertion in v 7, "I am speaking the truth, I am not lying," reminds one of similar affirmations in Rom 9, 1; 2 Cor 11, 31; and Gal 1, 20.

2, 6: *The testimony:* to make sense of this overly concise phrase, many manuscripts supply "to which" (or "to whom"); two others add "was given." The translation has supplied "this was."

[8] * It is my wish, then, that in every place the men should pray, lifting up holy hands, without anger or argument. [9] Similarly, [too,] women should adorn themselves with proper conduct, with modesty and self-control, not with braided hairstyles and gold ornaments, or pearls, or expensive clothes,[x] [10] but rather, as befits women who profess reverence for God, with good deeds.[y] [11] A woman must receive instruction silently and under complete control.[z] [12] I do not permit a woman to teach or to have authority over a man.* She must be quiet. [13] For Adam was formed first, then Eve.[a] [14] Further, Adam was not deceived, but the woman was deceived and transgressed.[b] [15] But she will be saved through motherhood, provided women persevere in faith and love and holiness, with self-control.[c]

CHAPTER 3

Qualifications of Various Ministers. [1] *
This saying is trustworthy:* whoever aspires to the office of bishop desires a noble task.[d] [2] Therefore, a bishop must be irreproachable, married only once, temperate, self-controlled, decent, hospitable, able to teach, [3] not a drunkard, not aggressive, but gentle, not contentious, not a lover of money.[e] [4] He must manage his own house-

hold well, keeping his children under control with perfect dignity; [5] for if a man does not know how to manage his own household, how can he take care of the church of God? [6] He should not be a recent convert, so that he may not become conceited and thus incur the devil's punishment.* [7] He must also have a good reputation among outsiders, so that he may not fall into disgrace, the devil's trap.[f]

[8] * Similarly, deacons must be dignified, not deceitful, not addicted to drink, not greedy for sordid gain, [9] holding fast to the mystery of the faith with a clear conscience. [10] Moreover, they should be tested first; then, if there is nothing against them, let them serve as deacons. [11] Women,* similarly, should be dignified, not slanderers, but temperate and faithful in everything.[g] [12] Deacons may be married only once and must manage their children and their households well. [13] Thus those who serve well as deacons gain good standing and much confidence in their faith in Christ Jesus.

The Mystery of Our Religion.* [14] I am writing you about these matters, although I hope to visit you soon. [15] But if I should be delayed, you should know how to behave in the household of God, which is the

---

x 1 Pt 3, 3-5.—y 1 Tm 5, 10; 1 Pt 3, 1.—z 11-12: 1 Cor 14, 34-35.—a Gn 1, 27; 2, 7.22; 1 Cor 11, 8-9.—b Gn 3, 6.13; 2 Cor 11, 3.—c 1 Tm 5, 14.—d 1-7: Ti 1, 6-9.—e Heb 13, 5.—f 2 Cor 8, 21; 2 Tm 2, 26.—g Ti 2, 3.

2, 8-15: The prayer of the community should be unmarred by internal dissension (8); cf Mt 5, 21-26; 6, 14; Mk 11, 25. At the liturgical assembly the dress of women should be appropriate to the occasion (9); their chief adornment is to be reputation for good works (10). Women are not to take part in the charismatic activity of the assembly (11-12; cf 1 Cor 14, 34) or exercise authority; their conduct there should reflect the role of man's helpmate (13; cf Gn 2, 18) and not the later relationship of Eve to Adam (14; cf Gn 3, 6-7). As long as women perform their role as wives and mothers in faith and love, their salvation is assured (15).

2, 12: *A man:* this could also mean "her husband."

3, 1-7: The passage begins by commending those who aspire to the office of bishop *(episkopos;* see the note on Phil 1, 1) within the community, but this first sentence (1) may also imply a warning about the great responsibilities involved. The writer proceeds to list the qualifications required: personal stability and graciousness; talent for teaching (2); moderation in habits and temperament (3); managerial ability (4); and experience in Christian living (5-6). Moreover, the candidate's previous life should provide no grounds for the charge that he did not previously practice what he now preaches. No list of qualifications for presbyters appears in 1 Tm. The presbyter-bishops here and in Ti (see the note on Ti 1, 5-9) lack certain functions reserved here for Paul and Timothy.

3, 1: *This saying is trustworthy:* the saying introduced is so unlike others after this phrase that some later Western manuscripts read, "This saying is popular." It is understood by some in-

interpreters as concluding the preceding section (1 Tm 2, 8-15). *Bishop:* literally, "overseer"; see the note on Phil 1, 1.

3, 6: *The devil's punishment:* this phrase could mean the punishment once incurred by the devil (objective genitive) or a punishment brought about by the devil (subjective genitive).

3, 8-13: Deacons, besides possessing the virtue of moderation (8), are to be outstanding for their faith (9) and well respected within the community (10). Women in the same role, although some interpreters take them to mean wives of deacons, must be dignified, temperate, dedicated, and not given to malicious talebearing (11). Deacons must have shown stability in marriage and have a good record with their families (12), for such experience prepares them well for the exercise of their ministry on behalf of the community (13). See further the note on Phil 1, 1.

3, 11: *Women:* this seems to refer to women deacons but may possibly mean wives of deacons. The former is preferred because the word is used absolutely; if deacons' wives were meant, a possessive "their" would be expected. Moreover, they are also introduced by the word "similarly," as in v 8; this parallel suggests that they too exercised ecclesiastical functions.

3, 14-16: In case there is some delay in the visit to Timothy at Ephesus planned for the near future, the present letter is being sent on ahead to arm and enlighten him in his task of preserving sound Christian conduct in the Ephesian church. The care he must exercise over this community is required by the profound nature of Christianity. It centers in Christ, appearing in human flesh, vindicated by the holy Spirit; the mystery of his person was revealed to the angels, announced to the Gentiles, and accepted by them in faith. He himself was taken up (through his resurrection and ascension) to the divine glory (16). This passage apparently includes part of a liturgical hymn used among the Christian communities in and around Ephesus. It consists of three couplets in typical Hebrew balance: flesh-spirit (contrast), seen-proclaimed (complementary), world-glory (contrast).

church of the living God, the pillar and foundation of truth.[h] [16]Undeniably great is the mystery of devotion,

> Who* was manifested in the flesh,
> vindicated in the spirit,
> seen by angels,
> proclaimed to the Gentiles,
> believed in throughout the world,
> taken up in glory.[i]

CHAPTER 4

False Asceticism.* [1]Now the Spirit explicitly says that in the last times some will turn away from the faith by paying attention to deceitful spirits and demonic instructions[j] [2]through the hypocrisy of liars with branded consciences. [3]They forbid marriage and require abstinence from foods that God created to be received with thanksgiving by those who believe and know the truth.[k] [4]For everything created by God is good, and nothing is to be rejected when received with thanksgiving,[l] [5]for it is made holy by the invocation of God in prayer.*

Counsel to Timothy. [6] * If you will give these instructions to the brothers, you will be a good minister of Christ Jesus, nourished on the words of the faith and of the sound teaching you have followed. [7]Avoid profane and silly myths. Train

yourself for devotion,[m] [8]for, while physical training is of limited value, devotion is valuable in every respect, since it holds a promise of life both for the present and for the future.[n] [9]This saying is trustworthy and deserves full acceptance.[o] [10]For this we toil and struggle,* because we have set our hope on the living God, who is the savior of all, especially of those who believe.[p]

[11] * Command and teach these things. [12]Let no one have contempt for your youth,* but set an example for those who believe, in speech, conduct, love, faith, and purity.[q] [13]Until I arrive, attend to the reading,* exhortation, and teaching. [14]Do not neglect the gift you have, which was conferred on you through the prophetic word* with the imposition of hands of the presbyterate.[r] [15]Be diligent in these matters, be absorbed in them, so that your progress may be evident to everyone. [16]Attend to yourself and to your teaching; persevere in both tasks, for by doing so you will save both yourself and those who listen to you.

IV. DUTIES TOWARD OTHERS
CHAPTER 5

[1] * Do not rebuke an older man, but appeal to him as a father. Treat younger men

---

h Eph 2, 19-22.—i Jn 1, 14; Rom 1, 3-4.—j 2 Tm 3, 1; 4, 3; 2 Pt 3, 3; Jude 18.—k Gn 9, 3; Rom 14, 6; 1 Cor 10, 30-31.—l Gn 1, 31; Acts 10, 15.—m 1 Tm 1, 4; 2 Tm 2, 16; Ti 1, 14.—n 1 Tm 6, 6.—o 1 Tm 1, 15; 2 Tm 2, 11; Ti 3, 8.—p 1 Tm 2, 4; Ti 2, 11.—q 1 Cor 16, 11; Ti 2, 15 / Phil 3, 17.—r 1 Tm 5, 22; Acts 6, 6; 8, 17; 2 Tm 1, 6.

3, 16: *Who:* the reference is to Christ, who is himself "the mystery of our devotion." Some predominantly Western manuscripts read "which," harmonizing the gender of the pronoun with that of the Greek word for mystery; many later (eighth/ninth century on), predominantly Byzantine manuscripts read "God," possibly for theological reasons.

4, 1-5: Doctrinal deviations from the true Christian message within the church have been prophesied, though the origin of the prophecy is not specified (1-2); cf Acts 20, 29-30. The letter warns against a false asceticism that prohibits marriage and regards certain foods as forbidden, though they are part of God's good creation (3).

4, 5: *The invocation of God in prayer:* literally, "the word of God and petition." The use of "word of God" without an article in Greek suggests that it refers to the name of God being invoked in blessing rather than to the "word of God" proclaimed to the community.

4, 6-10: Timothy is urged to be faithful, both in his teaching and in his own life, as he looks only to God for salvation.

4, 10: *Struggle:* other manuscripts and patristic witnesses read "suffer reproach."

4, 11-16: Timothy is urged to preach and teach with confidence, relying on the gifts and the mission that God has bestowed on him.

4, 12: *Youth:* some commentators find this reference a sign of pseudepigraphy. Timothy had joined Paul as a missionary already in A.D. 49, some fifteen years before the earliest supposed date of composition.

4, 13: *Reading:* the Greek word refers to private or public reading. Here, it probably designates the public reading of scripture in the Christian assembly.

4, 14: *Prophetic word:* this may mean the utterance of a Christian prophet designating the candidate or a prayer of blessing accompanying the rite. *Imposition of hands:* this gesture was used in the Old Testament to signify the transmission of authority from Moses to Joshua (Nm 27, 18-23; Dt 34, 9). The early Christian community used it as a symbol of installation into an office: the Seven (Acts 6, 6) and Paul and Barnabas (Acts 13, 3). *Of the presbyterate:* this would mean that each member of the college of presbyters imposed hands and appears to contradict 2 Tm 1, 6, in which Paul says that he imposed hands on Timothy. This latter text, however, does not exclude participation by others in the rite. Some prefer to translate "for the presbyterate," and thus understand it to designate the office into which Timothy was installed rather than the agents who installed him.

5, 1-16: After a few words of general advice based on common sense (1-2), the letter takes up, in its several aspects, the subject of widows. The first responsibility for their care belongs to the family circle, not to the Christian community as such (3-4.16). The widow left without the aid of relatives may benefit the community by her prayer, and the community should consider her material sustenance its responsibility (5-8). Widows who wish to work directly for the Christian community should not be accepted unless they are well beyond the probability of marriage, i.e., sixty years of age, married only once, and with a reputation for good works (9-10). Younger widows are apt to be troublesome and should be encouraged to remarry (11-15).

as brothers,[s] [2] older women as mothers, and younger women as sisters with complete purity.

Rules for Widows. [3] Honor widows who are truly widows. [4] But if a widow has children or grandchildren, let these first learn to perform their religious duty to their own family and to make recompense to their parents, for this is pleasing to God. [5] The real widow, who is all alone, has set her hope on God and continues in supplications and prayers night and day.[t] [6] But the one who is self-indulgent is dead while she lives. [7] Command this, so that they may be irreproachable. [8] And whoever does not provide for relatives and especially family members has denied the faith and is worse than an unbeliever.

[9] Let a widow be enrolled if she is not less than sixty years old, married only once, [10] with a reputation for good works, namely, that she has raised children, practiced hospitality, washed the feet of the holy ones, helped those in distress, involved herself in every good work.[u] [11] But exclude younger widows, for when their sensuality estranges them from Christ, they want to marry [12] and will incur condemnation for breaking their first pledge. [13] And furthermore, they learn to be idlers, going about from house to house, and not only idlers but gossips and busybodies as well, talking about things that ought not to be mentioned.[v] [14] So I would like younger widows to marry, have children, and manage a home, so as to give the adversary no pretext for maligning us.[w] [15] For some have already turned away to follow Satan. [16] If any woman believer* has widowed rel-

atives, she must assist them; the church is not to be burdened, so that it will be able to help those who are truly widows.

Rules for Presbyters.* [17] Presbyters who preside well deserve double honor, especially those who toil in preaching and teaching.[x] [18] For the scripture says, "You shall not muzzle an ox when it is threshing," and, "A worker deserves his pay."[y] [19] Do not accept an accusation against a presbyter unless it is supported by two or three witnesses.[z] [20] Reprimand publicly those who do sin, so that the rest also will be afraid.[a] [21] I charge you before God and Christ Jesus and the elect angels to keep these rules without prejudice, doing nothing out of favoritism. [22] Do not lay hands too readily on anyone, and do not share in another's sins. Keep yourself pure.[b] [23] Stop drinking only water, but have a little wine for the sake of your stomach and your frequent illnesses.

[24] Some people's sins are public, preceding them to judgment; but other people are followed by their sins. [25] Similarly, good works are also public; and even those that are not cannot remain hidden.

CHAPTER 6

Rules for Slaves. [1] * Those who are under the yoke of slavery must regard their masters as worthy of full respect, so that the name of God and our teaching* may not suffer abuse.[c] [2] Those whose masters are believers must not take advantage of them because they are brothers but must give better service because those who will profit from their work are believers and are beloved.[d]

s Lv 19, 32; Ti 2, 2.—t Jer 49, 11; Lk 2, 37; 18, 7.—u Jn 13, 14; Heb 13, 2.—v 2 Thes 3, 11.—w 1 Cor 7, 9.—x 1 Cor 16, 18; Phil 2, 29.—y Dt 25, 4; 1 Cor 9, 8 / Mt 10, 10; Lk 10, 7.—z Dt 17, 6; 19, 15; Mt 18, 16; 2 Cor 13, 1.—a Gal 2, 14; Eph 5, 11; 2 Tm 4, 2; Ti 1, 9.13.—b 1 Tm 4, 14; 2 Tm 1, 6.—c Eph 6, 5; Ti 2, 9-10.—d Phlm 16.

5, 16: *Woman believer:* some early Latin manuscripts and Fathers have a masculine here, while most later manuscripts and patristic quotations conflate the two readings, perhaps to avoid unfair restriction to women.

5, 17-25: The function of presbyters is not exactly the same as that of the *episkopos,* "bishop" (1 Tm 3, 1); in fact, the relation of the two at the time of this letter is obscure (but cf the note on Ti 1, 5-9). The Pastorals seem to reflect a transitional stage that developed in many regions of the church into the monarchical episcopate of the second and third centuries. The presbyters possess the responsibility of preaching and teaching, for which functions they are supported by the community (17-18). The realization that their position subjects them to adverse criticism

is implied in the direction to Timothy (19-20) to make sure of the truth of any accusation against them before public reproof is given. He must be as objective as possible in weighing charges against presbyters (21), learning from his experience to take care in selecting them (22). Some scholars take v 22 as a reference not to ordination of presbyters but to reconciliation of public sinners. The letter now sounds an informal note of personal concern in its advice to Timothy not to be so ascetic that he even avoids wine (23). Judgment concerning the fitness of candidates to serve as presbyters is easy with persons of open conduct, more difficult and prolonged with those of greater reserve (24-25).

6, 1-2: Compare the tables for household duties, such as that of Col 3, 18—4, 1. Domestic relationships derive new meaning from the Christian faith.

6, 1: *Our teaching:* this refers to the teaching of the Christian community.

V. FALSE TEACHING AND TRUE WEALTH

Teach and urge these things.* [3] Whoever teaches something different and does not agree with the sound words of our Lord Jesus Christ and the religious teaching[e] [4] is conceited, understanding nothing, and has a morbid disposition for arguments and verbal disputes. From these come envy, rivalry, insults, evil suspicions, [5] and mutual friction among people with corrupted minds, who are deprived of the truth, supposing religion to be a means of gain.[f] [6] Indeed, religion with contentment* is a great gain.[g] [7] For we brought nothing into the world, just as we shall not be able to take anything out of it.[h] [8] If we have food and clothing, we shall be content with that.[i] [9] Those who want to be rich are falling into temptation and into a trap and into many foolish and harmful desires, which plunge them into ruin and destruction.[j] [10] For the love of money is the root of all evils, and some people in their desire for it have strayed from the faith and have pierced themselves with many pains.

Exhortations to Timothy.* [11] But you, man of God,* avoid all this. Instead, pursue righteousness, devotion, faith, love, patience, and gentleness.[k] [12] Compete well for the faith. Lay hold of eternal life, to which you were called when you made the noble confession in the presence of many witnesses.[l] [13] I charge [you] before God, who gives life to all things, and before Christ Jesus, who gave testimony under Pontius Pilate for the noble confession,[m] [14] to keep the commandment without stain or reproach until the appearance of our Lord Jesus Christ [15] that the blessed and only ruler will make manifest at the proper time, the King of kings and Lord of lords,[n] [16] who alone has immortality, who dwells in unapproachable light, and whom no human being has seen or can see. To him be honor and eternal power. Amen.[o]

Right Use of Wealth.* [17] Tell the rich in the present age not to be proud and not to rely on so uncertain a thing as wealth but rather on God, who richly provides us with all things for our enjoyment.[p] [18] Tell them to do good, to be rich in good works, to be generous, ready to share, [19] thus accumulating as treasure a good foundation for the future, so as to win the life that is true life.[q]

VI. FINAL RECOMMENDATION AND WARNING*

[20] O Timothy, guard what has been entrusted to you. Avoid profane babbling and the absurdities of so-called knowledge.[r] [21] By professing it, some people have deviated from the faith.

Grace be with all of you.[s]

---

e Gal 1, 6-9; 2 Tm 1, 13; Ti 1, 1.—f 2 Tm 3, 8; 4, 4; Ti 1, 14.—g 1 Tm 4, 8; Phil 4, 11-12; Heb 13, 5.—h Jb 1, 21; Eccl 5, 14.—i Prv 30, 8.—j Prv 23, 4; 28, 22.—k 2 Tm 2, 22.—l 1 Cor 9, 26; 2 Tm 4, 7.—m Jn 18, 36-37; 19, 11.—n 2 Mc 13, 4; Rv 17, 14.—o Ex 33, 20; Ps 104, 2.—p Ps 62, 11; Lk 12, 20.—q Mt 6, 20.—r 2 Tm 1, 14 / 1 Tm 4, 7.—s 1 Tm 1, 6; 2 Tm 2, 18.

6, 2b-10: Timothy is exhorted to maintain steadfastly the position outlined in this letter, not allowing himself to be pressured into any other course. He must realize that false teachers can be discerned by their pride, envy, quarrelsomeness, and greed for material gain. Verse 6 is rather obscure and is interpreted, and therefore translated, variously. The suggestion seems to be that the important gain that religion brings is spiritual, but that there is material gain, too, up to the point of what is needed for physical sustenance (cf 1 Tm 6, 17-19).

6, 6: *Contentment:* the word *autarkeia* is a technical Greek philosophical term for the virtue of independence from material goods (Aristotle, Cynics, Stoics).

6, 11-16: Timothy's position demands total dedication to God and faultless witness to Christ (11-14) operating from an awareness, through faith, of the coming revelation in Jesus of the invisible God (15-16).

6, 11: *Man of God:* a title applied to Moses and the prophets (Dt 33,1; 1 Sm 2, 27; 1 Kgs 12, 22; 13, 1; etc.).

6, 17-19: Timothy is directed to instruct the rich, advising them to make good use of their wealth by aiding the poor.

6, 20-21: A final solemn warning against the heretical teachers, with what seems to be a specific reference to gnosticism, the great rival and enemy of the church for two centuries and more (the Greek word for "knowledge" is *gnōsis*). If gnosticism is being referred to here, it is probable that the warnings against "speculations" and "myths and genealogies" (cf especially 1 Tm 1, 4; Ti 3, 9) involve allusions to that same kind of heresy. Characteristic of the various gnostic systems of speculation was an elaborate mythology of innumerable superhuman intermediaries, on a descending scale ("genealogies"), between God and the world. This would be explained the emphasis upon Christ's being the *one* mediator (as in 1 Tm 2, 5). Although fully developed gnosticism belonged to the second and later centuries, there are signs that incipient forms of it belonged to Paul's own period.

1Tm

THE SECOND LETTER TO TIMOTHY

INTRODUCTION

The authorship and date of this letter, as one of the Pastoral Epistles, are discussed in the Introduction to the First Letter to Timothy.

The tone here is more personal than in First Timothy, for this letter addresses Timothy in vivid terms (1, 6-14; 2, 1-13) and depicts Paul's courage and hope in the face of discouragements late in the course of his apostolic ministry (1, 15-18; 3, 10-17; 4, 9-18). Indeed, the letter takes on the character of a final exhortation and testament from Paul to the younger Timothy (4, 1-8). Paul is portrayed as a prisoner (1, 8.16; 2, 9) in Rome (1, 17), and there is a hint that Timothy may be in Ephesus (2, 17). The letter reveals that, with rare exceptions, Christians have not rallied to Paul's support (1, 15-18) and takes a pessimistic view of the outcome of his case (4, 6). It describes Paul as fully aware of what impends, looking to God, not to human beings, for his deliverance (4, 3-8.18). It recalls his mission days with Timothy (1, 3-5; cf Acts 16, 1-4). It points to his preaching of the gospel as the reason for his imprisonment and offers Timothy, as a motive for steadfastness, his own example of firmness in faith despite adverse circumstances (1, 6-14). The letter suggests that Timothy should prepare others to replace himself as Paul has prepared Timothy to replace him (2, 1-2). Paul urges him not to desist out of fear from preserving and spreading the Christian message (2, 3-7). It presents the resurrection of Jesus and his messianic role as the heart of the gospel for which Paul has been ready to lay down his life (2, 8-9) and thus not only to express his own conviction fully but to support the conviction of others (2, 10-13).

This letter, like the preceding one, urges Timothy to protect the community from the inevitable impact of false teaching (2, 14—3, 9), without fear of the personal attacks that may result (3, 10-13). It recommends that he rely on the power of the scriptures, on proclamation of the word, and on sound doctrine (3, 14—4, 2), without being troubled by those who do not accept him (4, 3-5). The letter poignantly observes in passing that Paul has need of his reading materials and his cloak (4, 13) and, what will be best of all, a visit from Timothy.

On the theory of authorship by Paul himself, Second Timothy appears to be the last of the three Pastoral Epistles. The many scholars who argue that the Pastorals are products of the Pauline school often incline toward Second Timothy as the earliest of the three and the one most likely to have actual fragments of material from Paul himself.

The principal divisions of the Second Letter to Timothy are the following:

I. Address (1, 1-5)
II. Exhortations to Timothy (1, 6—2, 13)
III. Instructions Concerning False Teaching (2, 14—4, 8)
IV. Personal Requests and Final Greetings (4, 9-22)

I. ADDRESS

CHAPTER 1

Greeting.* [1] Paul, an apostle of Christ Jesus by the will of God[a] for the promise of life in Christ Jesus,* [2] to Timothy, my dear child: grace, mercy, and peace from God the Father and Christ Jesus our Lord.

Thanksgiving. [3] [b] I am grateful to God, whom I worship with a clear conscience as my ancestors did,* as I remember you con-

---

a 1 Tm 4, 8.—b 1 Tm 3, 9 / Phil 3, 5.

1, 1-2: For the formula of address and greeting, see the note on Rom 1, 1-7.

1, 1: The promise of life in Christ Jesus: that God grants through union with Christ in faith and love; cf Col 3, 4; 1 Tm 4, 8.

1, 3: As my ancestors did: this emphasizes the continuity of Judaism and Christianity; for a similar view, see Rom 9, 3-5; Phil 3, 4-6.

stantly in my prayers, night and day. 4 * I yearn to see you again, recalling your tears, so that I may be filled with joy, 5 as I recall your sincere faith that first lived in your grandmother Lois and in your mother Eunice and that I am confident lives also in you.*c*

II. EXHORTATIONS TO TIMOTHY

The Gifts Timothy Has Received.
6 For this reason, I remind you to stir into flame the gift of God* that you have through the imposition of my hands.*d* 7 For God did not give us a spirit of cowardice but rather of power and love and self-control.*e* 8 So do not be ashamed of your testimony to our Lord,* nor of me, a prisoner for his sake; but bear your share of hardship for the gospel with the strength that comes from God.*f*

9 * He saved us and called us to a holy life, not according to our works but according to his own design and the grace bestowed on us in Christ Jesus before time began,*g* 10 but now made manifest through the appearance of our savior Christ Jesus, who destroyed death and brought life and immortality to light through the gospel,*h* 11 for which I was appointed preacher and apostle*i* and teacher.* 12 On this account I am suffering these things; but I am not ashamed,*j* for I know him in whom I have believed and am confident that he is able to guard what has been entrusted to me until

that day.* 13 Take as your norm the sound words that you heard from me, in the faith and love that are in Christ Jesus.*k* 14 Guard this rich trust with the help of the holy Spirit that dwells within us.*l*

Paul's Suffering.
15 *m* You know that everyone in Asia deserted me, including Phygelus and Hermogenes.* 16 May the Lord grant mercy to the family of Onesiphorus*n* because he often gave me new heart and was not ashamed of my chains.* 17 But when he came to Rome, he promptly searched for me and found me. 18 May the Lord grant him to find mercy from the Lord* on that day. And you know very well the services he rendered in Ephesus.*o*

CHAPTER 2

Timothy's Conduct.
1 * So you, my child, be strong in the grace that is in Christ Jesus. 2 And what you heard from me through many witnesses entrust to faithful people who will have the ability to teach others as well. 3 Bear your share of hardship along with me like a good soldier of Christ Jesus.*p* 4 To satisfy the one who recruited him, a soldier does not become entangled in the business affairs of life.*q* 5 Similarly, an athlete cannot receive the winner's crown except by competing according to the rules.*r* 6 The hardworking farmer ought to have the first share of the crop.*s* 7 Reflect on what I am saying, for

c 1 Tm 1, 5 / Acts 16, 1.—d 1 Tm 4, 14; 5, 22 / Acts 6, 6; 8, 17.—e Rom 5, 5; 8, 15; 1 Cor 2, 4.—f 2 Tm 2, 3.15; Rom 1, 16.—g Eph 2, 8-9; Ti 3, 5 / Eph 1, 4; Ti 1, 2.—h Rom 16, 26; 1 Pt 1, 20 / 1 Tm 6, 14 / Phil 3, 20; Ti 1, 4; 2, 13; 2 Pt 1, 11 / 1 Cor 15, 54-55; Heb 2, 14 / 1 Cor 15, 53-54.—i 1 Tm 2, 7.—j 1 Pt 4, 16 / 1 Tm 1, 10-11.—k 1 Tm 1, 14.—l 1 Tm 6, 20 / Rom 8, 11.—m 2 Tm 4, 16.—n 2 Tm 4, 19.—o Jude 21.—p 2 Tm 1, 8; 4, 5; Phlm 2.—q 1 Cor 9, 6.—r 1 Cor 9, 25.—s 1 Cor 9, 7-10.

1, 4-5: Purportedly written from prison in Rome (2 Tm 1, 8.17; 4, 6-8) shortly before the writer's death, the letter recalls the earlier sorrowful parting from Timothy, commending him for his faith and expressing the longing to see him again.

1, 6: *The gift of God:* the grace resulting from the conferral of an ecclesiastical office. *The imposition of my hands:* see the note on 1 Tm 4, 14.

1, 8: *Do not be ashamed of your testimony to our Lord:* i.e., of preaching and suffering for the sake of the gospel.

1, 9-10: Redemption from sin and the call to holiness of life are not won by personal deeds but are freely and graciously bestowed according to God's eternal plan; cf Eph 1, 4.

1, 11: *Teacher:* the overwhelming majority of manuscripts and Fathers read "teacher of the nations," undoubtedly a harmonization with 1 Tm 2, 7.

1, 12: *He is able to guard . . . until that day:* the intervening words can also be translated "what I have entrusted to him" (i.e., the fruit of his ministry) as well as "what has been entrusted

to me" (i.e., the faith). The same difficult term occurs in v 14, where it is modified by the adjective "rich" and used without a possessive.

1, 15: Keen disappointment is expressed, here and later (2 Tm 4, 16), that the Christians of the province of Asia, especially Phygelus and Hermogenes, should have abandoned the writer and done nothing to defend his case in court.

1, 16-18: *The family of Onesiphorus because he . . . of my chains:* Onesiphorus seems to have died before this letter was written. His family is mentioned twice (here and in 2 Tm 4, 19), though it was Onesiphorus himself who was helpful to Paul in prison and rendered much service to the community of Ephesus. Because the apostle complains of abandonment by all in Asia during his second imprisonment and trial, the assistance of Onesiphorus seems to have been given to Paul during his first Roman imprisonment (A.D. 61-63).

1, 18: *Lord . . . Lord:* the first "Lord" here seems to refer to Christ, the second "Lord" to the Father.

2, 1-7: This passage manifests a characteristic deep concern for safeguarding the faith and faithfully transmitting it through trustworthy people (1-2; cf 2 Tm 1, 14; 1 Tm 6, 20; Ti 1, 9). Comparisons to the soldier's detachment, the athlete's sportsmanship, and the farmer's arduous work as the price of recompense (4-6) emphasize the need of singleness of purpose in preaching the word, even at the cost of hardship, for the sake of Christ (3).

the Lord will give you understanding in everything.[t]

8 * Remember Jesus Christ, raised from the dead, a descendant of David: such is my gospel,[u] 9 for which I am suffering, even to the point of chains, like a criminal. But the word of God is not chained.[v] 10 Therefore, I bear with everything for the sake of those who are chosen, so that they too may obtain the salvation that is in Christ Jesus, together with eternal glory.[w] 11 This saying is trustworthy:

If we have died with him
    we shall also live with him;[x]
12 if we persevere
    we shall also reign with him.
But if we deny him
    he will deny us.[y]
13 If we are unfaithful
    he remains faithful,
    for he cannot deny himself.[z]

III. INSTRUCTIONS CONCERNING FALSE TEACHING

Warning against Useless Disputes. 14 * Remind people of these things and charge them before God* to stop disputing about words. This serves no useful purpose since it harms those who listen.[a] 15 Be eager to present yourself as acceptable to God, a workman who causes no disgrace, imparting the word of truth without deviation.[b] 16 Avoid profane, idle talk, for such people will become more and more godless,[c] 17 and their teaching will spread like gangrene. Among them are Hymenaeus and Philetus,[d] 18 who have deviated from the truth by saying that [the] resurrection has already taken place and are upsetting the faith of some.[e] 19 Nevertheless, God's solid foundation stands, bearing this inscription, "The Lord knows those who are his"; and, "Let everyone who calls upon the name of the Lord avoid evil."[f]

20 In a large household there are vessels not only of gold and silver but also of wood and clay, some for lofty and others for humble use. 21 If anyone cleanses himself of these things, he will be a vessel for lofty use, dedicated, beneficial to the master of the house, ready for every good work.[g] 22 So turn from youthful desires and pursue righteousness, faith, love, and peace, along with those who call on the Lord* with purity of heart.[h] 23 Avoid foolish and ignorant debates, for you know that they breed quarrels.[i] 24 A slave of the Lord should not quarrel, but should be gentle with everyone, able to teach, tolerant,[j] 25 correcting opponents with kindness. It may be that God will grant them repentance that leads to knowledge of the truth,[k] 26 and that they may return to their senses out of the devil's snare,[l] where they are entrapped by him, for his will.*

CHAPTER 3

The Dangers of the Last Days.* 1 But understand this: there will be terrifying times in the last days.[m] 2 People will be self-centered and lovers of money, proud, haughty, abusive, disobedient to their parents, ungrateful, irreligious,[n] 3 callous, im-

t Prv 2, 6.—u Rom 1, 3; 1 Cor 15, 4.20 / Rom 2, 16; Gal 1, 11; 2, 2.—v Phil 1, 12-14.—w Col 1, 24; 1 Tm 1, 15.—x Rom 6, 8.—y Mt 10, 22.33; Lk 12, 9.—z Nm 23, 19; Rom 3, 3-4; 1 Cor 10, 13; Ti 1, 2.—a 1 Tm 6, 4.—b 2 Tm 1, 8; 2 Cor 6, 7; Eph 1, 13; Col 1, 5.—c 1 Tm 4, 7.—d 1 Tm 1, 20.—e 2 Thes 2, 2.—f Is 28, 16; 1 Cor 3, 10-15 / Nm 16, 5; Jn 10, 14. —g 2 Tm 3, 17.—h Gal 5, 22; 1 Tm 6, 11 / Rom 10, 13; 1 Cor 1, 2.—i 1 Tm 1, 4; 4, 7; 6, 4; Ti 3, 9.—j 1 Tm 3, 2-3.—k 2 Tm 3, 7; 1 Tm 2, 4.—l 1 Tm 3, 7.—m 1 Tm 4, 1; 2 Pt 3, 3; Jude 18.—n 2-4: Rom 1, 29-31.

2, 8-13: The section begins with a sloganlike summary of Paul's gospel about Christ (8) and concludes with what may be part of an early Christian hymn (11b-12a; most exegetes include the rest of v 12 and all of v 13 as part of the quotation). The poetic lines suggest that through baptism Christians die spiritually with Christ and hope to live with him and reign with him forever, but the Christian life includes endurance, witness, and even suffering, as the final judgment will show and as Paul's own case makes clear; while he is imprisoned for preaching the gospel (9), his sufferings are helpful to the elect for obtaining the salvation and glory available in Christ (10), who will be true to those who are faithful and will disown those who deny him (12-13).

2, 14-19: For those who dispute about mere words (cf 2 Tm 2, 23-24) and indulge in irreligious talk to the detriment of their listeners (16-19), see the notes on 1 Tm 1, 3-7; 6, 20-21.

Hymenaeus and Philetus (17), while accepting the Christian's mystical death and resurrection in Christ through baptism, claimed that baptized Christians are already risen with Christ in this life and thus that there is no future bodily resurrection or eternal glory to come. The first quotation in v 19 is from Nm 16, 5; the other quotation is from some unidentified Jewish or Christian writing.

2, 14: *Before God:* many ancient manuscripts read "before the Lord."

2, 22: *Those who call on the Lord:* those who believe in Christ and worship him as Lord, i.e., Christians (Acts 9, 14-16.20-21; Rom 10, 12-13; cf 2 Tm 2, 19, literally, "Everyone who names the name of the Lord").

2, 26: Some interpreters would render this passage, "Thus they may come to their senses and, forced to do his (i.e., God's) will, may escape the devil's trap." This interpretation of the Greek is possible, but the one accepted in the text seems more likely.

3, 1-9: The moral depravity and false teaching that will be rampant in the last days are already at work (1-5). The frivolous and superficial, too, devoid of the true spirit of religion, will be easy victims of those who pervert them by falsifying the truth (6-8), just as Jannes and Jambres, Pharaoh's magicians of Egypt (Ex 7, 11-12.22), discredited the truth in Moses' time. Exodus does not name the magicians, but the two names are widely found in much later Jewish, Christian, and even pagan writings. Their origins are legendary.

placable, slanderous, licentious, brutal, hating what is good, [4] traitors, reckless, conceited, lovers of pleasure rather than lovers of God, [5] as they make a pretense of religion but deny its power. Reject them.[o] [6] For some of these slip into homes and make captives of women weighed down by sins, led by various desires,[p] [7] always trying to learn but never able to reach a knowledge of the truth.[q] [8] Just as Jannes and Jambres opposed Moses, so they also oppose the truth—people of depraved mind, unqualified in the faith.[r] [9] But they will not make further progress, for their foolishness will be plain to all, as it was with those two.

Paul's Example and Teaching.* [10] You have followed my teaching, way of life, purpose, faith, patience, love, endurance, [11] persecutions, and sufferings, such as happened to me in Antioch, Iconium, and Lystra, persecutions that I endured. Yet from all these things the Lord delivered me.[s] [12] In fact, all who want to live religiously in Christ Jesus will be persecuted.[t] [13] But wicked people and charlatans will go from bad to worse, deceivers and deceived. [14] But you, remain faithful to what you have learned and believed, because you know from whom you learned it,[u] [15] and that from infancy you have known [the] sacred scriptures, which are capable of giving you wisdom for salvation through faith in Christ Jesus.[v] [16] All scripture[w] is inspired by God* and is useful for teaching, for refutation, for correction, and for training in righteousness,* [17] so that one who belongs to God may be competent, equipped for every good work.[x]

CHAPTER 4

Solemn Charge.* [1] I charge you in the presence of God and of Christ Jesus, who will judge the living and the dead, and by his appearing and his kingly power:[y] [2] proclaim the word; be persistent whether it is convenient or inconvenient; convince, reprimand, encourage through all patience and teaching.[z] [3] For the time will come when people will not tolerate sound doctrine but, following their own desires and insatiable curiosity,* will accumulate teachers[a] [4] and will stop listening to the truth and will be diverted to myths.[b] [5] But you, be self-possessed in all circumstances; put up with hardship; perform the work of an evangelist; fulfill your ministry.

Reward for Fidelity. [6] [c] For I am already being poured out like a libation, and the time of my departure is at hand.* [7] I have competed well; I have finished the race;[d] I have kept the faith.* [8] From now on the crown of righteousness awaits me, which the Lord, the just judge, will award to me on that day,[e] and not only to me, but to all who have longed for his appearance.*

IV. PERSONAL REQUESTS AND FINAL GREETINGS

Paul's Loneliness. [9] * Try to join me soon, [10] for Demas, enamored of the pres-

o Rom 2, 20-22; Ti 1, 16.—p Ti 1, 11.—q 2 Tm 2, 25.—r Ex 7, 11.22; 1 Tm 6, 5.—s Acts 13, 50; 14, 5.19 / Ps 34, 20.—t Jn 15, 20; Acts 14, 22.—u 2 Tm 2, 2.—v Jn 5, 39.—w Rom 15, 4; 2 Pt 1, 19-21.—x 2 Tm 2, 21.—y 1 Tm 5, 21; 6, 14 / Acts 10, 42; Rom 14, 9-10; 1 Pt 4, 5.—z Acts 20, 20.31; 1 Tm 5, 20.—a 1 Tm 4, 1.—b 1 Tm 1, 4; 4, 7; Ti 1, 14.—c Phil 2, 17.—d 1 Tm 1, 18; 6, 12; Jude 3 / Acts 20, 24; 1 Cor 9, 24; Heb 12, 1.—e 2 Tm 2, 5; Wis 5, 16; 1 Cor 9, 25; Phil 3, 14; Jas 1, 12; 1 Pt 5, 4; Rv 2, 10.

3, 10-17: Paul's example for Timothy includes persecution, a frequent emphasis in the Pastorals. Timothy is to be steadfast to what he has been taught and to scripture. The scriptures are the source of wisdom, i.e., of belief in and loving fulfillment of God's word revealed in Christ, through whom salvation is given.

3, 16: *All scripture is inspired by God:* this could possibly also be translated, "All scripture inspired by God is useful for. . . ." In this classic reference to inspiration, God is its principal author, with the writer as the human collaborator. Thus the scriptures are the word of God in human language. See also 2 Pt 1, 20-21.

3, 16-17: *Useful for teaching . . . every good work:* because as God's word the scriptures share his divine authority. It is exercised through those who are ministers of the word.

4, 1-5: The gravity of the obligation incumbent on Timothy to preach the word can be gauged from the solemn adjuration: in the presence of God, and of Christ coming as universal judge, and by

his appearance and his kingly power (1). Patience, courage, constancy, and endurance are required despite the opposition, hostility, indifference, and defection of many to whom the truth has been preached (2-5).

4, 3: *Insatiable curiosity:* literally, "with itching ears."

4, 6: The apostle recognizes his death through martyrdom to be imminent. He regards it as an act of worship in which his blood will be poured out in sacrifice; cf Ex 29, 38-40; Phil 2, 17.

4, 7: At the close of his life Paul could testify to the accomplishment of what Christ himself foretold concerning him at the time of his conversion, "I will show him what he will have to suffer for my name" (Acts 9, 16).

4, 8: When the world is judged at the parousia, all who have eagerly looked for the Lord's appearing and have sought to live according to his teachings will be rewarded. The crown is a reference to the laurel wreath placed on the heads of victorious athletes and conquerors in war; cf 2 Tm 2, 5; 1 Cor 9, 25.

4, 9-13: Demas either abandoned the work of the ministry for worldly affairs or, perhaps, gave up the faith itself (10). Luke (11) may have accompanied Paul on parts of his second and third missionary journeys (Acts 16, 10-12; 20, 5-7). Notice the presence of the first personal pronoun "we" in these Acts passages, suggesting to some that Luke (or at least some traveling companion of Paul's) was the author of Acts. Mark, once rejected by Paul (Acts 13, 13; 15, 39), is now to render him a great service (11); cf Col 4, 10; Phlm 24. For Tychicus, see Eph 6, 21; cf also Acts 20, 4; Col 4, 7.

ent world, deserted me and went to Thessalonica, Crescens to Galatia,* and Titus to Dalmatia.*f* [11] Luke is the only one with me. Get Mark and bring him with you, for he is helpful to me in the ministry.*g* [12] I have sent Tychicus to Ephesus.*h* [13] When you come, bring the cloak I left with Carpus in Troas, the papyrus rolls, and especially the parchments.*i*

[14] Alexander* the coppersmith did me a great deal of harm; the Lord will repay him according to his deeds.*j* [15] You too be on guard against him, for he has strongly resisted our preaching.

[16] At my first defense no one appeared on my behalf, but everyone deserted me. May it not be held against them!*k* [17] But the Lord stood by me and gave me strength, so that through me the proclamation might be completed and all the Gentiles might hear it. And I was rescued from the lion's mouth.*l* [18] The Lord will rescue me from every evil threat and will bring me safe to his heavenly kingdom. To him be glory forever and ever. Amen.*m*

Final Greeting. [19] Greet Prisca and Aquila* and the family of Onesiphorus.*n* [20] Erastus* remained in Corinth, while I left Trophimus sick at Miletus.*o* [21] Try to get here before winter. Eubulus, Pudens, Linus,* Claudia, and all the brothers send greetings.

[22] The Lord be with your spirit. Grace be with all of you.*p*

---

f Col 4, 14; Phlm 24 / 2 Cor 2, 13; 7, 6-7; 8, 23; Gal 2, 3; Ti 1, 4.—g Col 4, 14; Phlm 24 / Col 4, 10; Phlm 24.—h Acts 20, 4; Eph 6, 21; Col 4, 7.—i Acts 16, 8; 20, 6.—j 1 Tm 1, 20 / 2 Sm 3, 39; Pss 28, 4; 62, 12; Prv 24, 12; Rom 2, 6.—k 2 Tm 1, 15.— l Acts 23, 11; 27, 23; Phil 4, 13 / 1 Mc 2, 60; Ps 22, 22; Dn 6, 23.—m 2 Cor 1, 10 / Rom 16, 27.—n Acts 18, 2; Rom 16, 3; 1 Cor 16, 19 / 2 Tm 1, 16.—o Acts 19, 22; Rom 16, 24 / Acts 20, 4; 21, 29.—p Gal 6, 18; Phil 4, 23; Col 4, 18; 1 Tm 6, 21; Ti 3, 15.

4, 10: *Galatia:* some manuscripts read "Gaul" or "Gallia."

4, 14-18: *Alexander:* an opponent of Paul's preaching (14-15), perhaps the one who is mentioned in 1 Tm 1, 20. Despite Paul's abandonment by his friends in the province of Asia (cf 2 Tm 1, 15-16), the divine assistance brought this first trial to a

successful issue, even to the point of making the gospel message known to those who participated in or witnessed the trial (16-17).

4, 19: *Prisca and Aquila:* they assisted Paul in his ministry in Corinth (Acts 18, 2-3) and Ephesus (Acts 18, 19.26; 1 Cor 16, 19). They risked death to save his life, and all the Gentile communities are indebted to them (Rom 16, 3-5).

4, 20: *Erastus:* he was the treasurer of the city of Corinth (Rom 16, 24); cf also Acts 19, 22. *Trophimus:* from the province of Asia, he accompanied Paul from Greece to Troas (Acts 20, 4-5).

4, 21: *Linus:* Western tradition sometimes identified this Linus with the supposed successor of Peter as bishop of Rome, and Claudia as the mother of Linus (*Apostolic Constitutions,* fourth century).

THE LETTER TO TITUS

INTRODUCTION

The third of the Pastoral Epistles in the New Testament is addressed to a different coworker of Paul than are First and Second Timothy. The situation is different, too, for Titus is addressed as the person in charge of developing the church on the large Mediterranean island of Crete (1, 5), a place Paul had never, according to the New Testament, visited. The tone is closer to that of First Timothy as three topics of church life and structure are discussed: presbyter-bishops (see the note on 1, 5-9), groups with which one must work in the church (2, 1-10), and admonitions for conduct based on the grace and love of God that appeared in Jesus Christ (2, 11—3, 10). The warmer personal tone of Second Timothy is replaced by emphasis on church office and on living in the society of the day, in which deceivers and heretics abound (1, 10-16; 3, 9-10).

The Pauline assistant who is addressed, Titus, was a Gentile Christian, but we are nowhere informed of his place of birth or residence. He went from Antioch with Paul and Barnabas to Jerusalem (Gal 2, 1; cf Acts 15, 2). According to 2 Corinthians (2, 13; 7, 6.13-14), he was with Paul on his third missionary journey; his name, however, does not appear in Acts. Besides being the bearer of Paul's severe letter to the Corinthians (2 Cor 7, 6-8), he had the responsibility of taking up the collection in Corinth for the Christian community of Jerusalem (2 Cor 8, 6.16-19.23). In the present letter (1, 5), he is mentioned as the administrator of the Christian community in Crete, charged with the task of organizing it through the appointment of presbyters and bishops (1, 5-9; here the two terms refer to the same personages).

The letter instructs Titus about the character of the assistants he is to choose in view of the pastoral difficulties peculiar to Crete (1, 5-16). It suggests the special individual and social virtues that the various age groups and classes in the Christian community should be encouraged to acquire (2, 1-10). The motivation for transformation of their lives comes from christology, especially the redemptive sacrifice of Christ and his future coming, as applied through baptism and justification (2, 11-14; 3, 4-8). The community is to serve as a leaven for Christianizing the social world about it (3, 1-3). Good works are to be the evidence of their faith in God (3, 8); those who engage in religious controversy are, after suitable warning, to be ignored (3, 9-11).

The authorship and date of the Letter to Titus are discussed in the Introduction to 1 Timothy. Those who assume authorship by Paul himself usually place Titus after 1 Timothy and before 2 Timothy. Others see it as closely related to 1 Timothy, in a growing emphasis on church structure and opposition to heresy, later than the letters of Paul himself and 2 Timothy. It has also been suggested that, if the three Pastorals once circulated as a literary unit, Titus was meant to be read ahead of 1 and 2 Timothy.

The principal divisions of the Letter to Titus are the following:

    I.   Address (1, 1-4)
    II. Pastoral Charge (1, 5-16)
   III. Teaching the Christian Life (2, 1—3, 15)

I. ADDRESS

CHAPTER 1

Greeting.* [1] Paul, a slave of God and apostle of Jesus Christ for the sake of the faith of God's chosen ones and the recognition of religious truth,[a] [2] in the hope of eternal life that God, who does not lie, promised before time began,[b] [3] who indeed at the proper time revealed his word in the proclamation with which I was entrusted by the command of God our savior,[c] [4] to Titus, my true child in our common faith: grace and peace from God the Father and Christ Jesus our savior.[d]

II. PASTORAL CHARGE

Titus in Crete. [5] * For this reason I left you in Crete so that you might set right what remains to be done and appoint pres-

byters in every town, as I directed you, [6] [e] on condition that a man be blameless, married only once, with believing children who are not accused of licentiousness or rebellious. [7] For a bishop as God's steward must be blameless, not arrogant, not irritable, not a drunkard, not aggressive, not greedy for sordid gain, [8] but hospitable, a lover of goodness, temperate, just, holy, and self-controlled, [9] holding fast to the true message as taught so that he will be able both to exhort with sound doctrine and to refute opponents.[f] [10] * For there are also many rebels, idle talkers and deceivers, especially the Jewish Christians.* [11] It is imperative to silence them, as they are upsetting whole families by teaching for sordid gain what they should not. [12] One of them, a prophet of their own, once said, "Cretans have always been liars, vicious beasts, and lazy gluttons."* [13] That

a 1 Tm 2, 4; 4, 3; 2 Tm 2, 25; 3, 7; Heb 10, 26.—b Ti 3, 7; 2 Tm 1, 1; 1 Jn 2, 25.—c Ti 2, 10; 3, 4; Ps 24, 5; 1 Tm 1, 1; 2, 3; 4, 10; Jude 25.—d Ti 2, 13; 3, 6; Phil 3, 20; 2 Tm 1, 10; 2 Pt 1, 1.11; 2, 20; 3, 2.18.—e 6-7: 1 Tm 3, 2-7; 2 Tm 2, 24-26.—f Ti 1, 13; 2, 1-2.8; 1 Tm 1, 10; 6, 3; 2 Tm 1, 13; 4, 3.

1, 1-4: On the epistolary form, see the note on Rom 1, 1-7. The apostolate is the divinely appointed mission to lead others to the true faith and through it to eternal salvation (1-3).

1, 5-9: This instruction on the selection and appointment of presbyters, substantially identical with that in 1 Tm 3, 1-7 on a bishop (see the note there), was aimed at strengthening the authority of Titus by apostolic mandate; cf Ti 2, 15. In vv 5.7 and

Acts 20, 17.28, the terms *episkopos* and *presbyteros* ("bishop" and "presbyter") refer to the same persons. Deacons are not mentioned in Titus. See also the note on Phil 1, 1.

1, 10-16: This adverse criticism of the defects within the community is directed especially against certain Jewish Christians, who busy themselves with useless speculations over persons mentioned in the Old Testament, insist on the observance of Jewish ritual purity regulations, and thus upset whole families by teaching things they have no right to teach; cf Ti 3, 9; 1 Tm 1, 3-10.

1, 10: *Jewish Christians:* literally, "those of the circumcision."

1, 12: *Cretans . . . gluttons:* quoted from Epimenides, a Cretan poet of the sixth century B.C.

testimony is true. Therefore, admonish them sharply, so that they may be sound in the faith,[g] [14] instead of paying attention to Jewish myths and regulations of people who have repudiated the truth.[h] [15] To the clean all things are clean, but to those who are defiled and unbelieving nothing is clean; in fact, both their minds and their consciences are tainted.[i] [16] They claim to know God, but by their deeds they deny him. They are vile and disobedient and unqualified for any good deed.

III. TEACHING THE CHRISTIAN LIFE

CHAPTER 2

Christian Behavior.* [1] As for yourself, you must say what is consistent with sound doctrine, namely,[j] [2] that older men should be temperate, dignified, self-controlled, sound in faith, love, and endurance. [3] Similarly, older women should be reverent in their behavior, not slanderers, not addicted to drink, teaching what is good, [4] so that they may train younger women to love their husbands and children, [5] to be self-controlled, chaste, good homemakers, under the control of their husbands, so that the word of God may not be discredited.[k]

[6] Urge the younger men, similarly, to control themselves, [7] showing yourself as a model of good deeds in every respect, with integrity in your teaching, dignity, [8] and sound speech that cannot be criticized, so that the opponent will be put to shame without anything bad to say about us.

[9] Slaves are to be under the control of their masters in all respects, giving them satisfaction, not talking back to them[l] [10] or

stealing from them, but exhibiting complete good faith, so as to adorn the doctrine of God our savior in every way.[m]

Transformation of Life. [11] * For the grace of God has appeared, saving all[n] [12] and training us to reject godless ways and worldly desires and to live temperately, justly, and devoutly in this age, [13] as we await the blessed hope, the appearance* of the glory of the great God and of our savior Jesus Christ,[o] [14] who gave himself for us to deliver us from all lawlessness and to cleanse for himself a people as his own, eager to do what is good.[p]

[15] Say these things. Exhort and correct with all authority. Let no one look down on you.[q]

CHAPTER 3

[1] * Remind them to be under the control of magistrates and authorities,* to be obedient, to be open to every good enterprise.[r] [2] They are to slander no one, to be peaceable, considerate, exercising all graciousness toward everyone. [3] For we ourselves were once foolish, disobedient, deluded, slaves to various desires and pleasures, living in malice and envy, hateful ourselves and hating one another.[s]

[4] But when the kindness and generous love
    of God our savior appeared,[t]
[5] not because of any righteous deeds we had done
    but because of his mercy,
    he saved us through the bath of rebirth and renewal by the holy Spirit,[u]
[6] whom he richly poured out on us
    through Jesus Christ our savior,[v]

---

g Ti 1, 9.—h Ti 3, 9; 1 Tm 1, 4; 4, 7; 2 Tm 4, 4; 2 Pt 1, 16.—i Mk 7, 18-23; Acts 10, 15; Rom 14, 14-23.—j Ti 1, 9.13; 2, 8; 1 Tm 1, 10; 6, 3; 2 Tm 1, 13; 4, 3.—k 1 Cor 11, 3; 14, 34; Eph 5, 22-24; Col 3, 18; 1 Tm 2, 11-15; 1 Pt 3, 1-6.—l 1 Cor 7, 21-22; Eph 6, 5-8; Col 3, 22-25; 1 Tm 6, 1-2; 1 Pt 2, 18.—m Ti 1, 3; 3, 4; Ps 24, 5; 1 Tm 1, 1; 2, 3; 4, 10; Jude 25.—n 1 Tm 2, 4; 4, 10.—o 1 Cor 1, 7; Phil 3, 20; 1 Thes 1, 10 / 2 Tm 1, 10 / Ti 1, 4; 3, 6; 2 Pt 1, 1.11; 2, 20; 3, 2.18.—p Gal 1, 4; 2, 20; Eph 5, 2.25; 1 Tm 2, 6; 1 Pt 1, 18-19 / Ps 130, 8.—q 1 Tm 4, 12.—r Rom 13, 1-7; 1 Tm 2, 1-2; 1 Pt 2, 13-14.—s 1 Cor 6, 9-11; Eph 2, 1-3; 5, 8; Col 3, 5-7; 1 Pt 4, 3.—t Ti 1, 3; 2, 10; Ps 24, 5; 1 Tm 1, 1; 2, 3; 4, 10; Jude 25.—u Dt 9, 5; Eph 2, 4-5.8-9; 2 Tm 1, 9.—v Ti 1, 4; 2, 13; Phil 3, 20; 2 Tm 1, 10; 2 Pt 1, 1.11; 2, 20; 3, 2.18.

2, 1-10: One of Titus' main tasks in Crete is to become acquainted with the character of the Cretans and thereby learn to cope with its deficiencies (see Ti 1, 12). The counsel is not only for Titus himself but for various classes of people with whom he must deal: older men and women (2-4), younger women and men (4-7), and slaves (9-10); cf Eph 6, 1-9; Col 3, 18—4, 1.

2, 11-15: Underlying the admonitions for moral improvement in Ti 2, 1-10 as the moving force is the constant appeal to God's revelation of salvation in Christ, with its demand for transformation of life.

2, 13: *The blessed hope, the appearance:* literally, "the blessed hope and appearance," but the use of a single article in Greek strongly suggests an epexegetical, i.e., explanatory sense. *Of the great God and of our savior Jesus Christ:* another possible translation is "of our great God and savior Jesus Christ."

3, 1-8: The list of Christian duties continues from Ti 2, 9-10, undergirded again as in Ti 2, 11-13 by appeal to what God in Christ has done (4-7; cf Ti 2, 11-14). The spiritual renewal of the Cretans, signified in God's merciful gift of baptism (4-7), should be reflected in their improved attitude toward civil authority and in their Christian relationship with all (1-3).

3, 1: *Magistrates and authorities:* some interpreters understand these terms as referring to the principalities and powers of the heavenly hierarchy. *To be open to every good enterprise:* this implies being good citizens. It could also be translated "ready to do every sort of good work" (as Christians); cf Ti 3, 14.

[7] so that we might be justified by his grace and become heirs in hope of eternal life. [w]

[8] This saying is trustworthy.

Advice to Titus.* I want you to insist on these points, that those who have believed in God be careful to devote themselves to good works; these are excellent and benefi-

cial to others. [x] [9] Avoid foolish arguments, genealogies, rivalries, and quarrels about the law, [y] for they are useless and futile.* [10] After a first and second warning, break off contact with a heretic, [z] [11] realizing that such a person is perverted and sinful and stands self-condemned.

Directives, Greetings, and Blessing.* [12] When I send Artemas to you, or Tychicus, try to join me at Nicopolis, where I have decided to spend the winter. [a] [13] Send Zenas the lawyer and Apollos on their journey soon, and see to it that they have everything they need. [b] [14] But let our people, too, learn to devote themselves to good works to supply urgent needs, so that they may not be unproductive. [c]

[15] All who are with me send you greetings. Greet those who love us in the faith.

Grace be with all of you. [d]

---

w Ti 1, 2; 2 Tm 1, 1; 1 Jn 2, 25.—x 1 Tm 1, 15; 3, 1; 4, 9; 2 Tm 2, 11.—y 1 Tm 1, 4; 4, 7; 2 Tm 2, 23.—z Mt 18, 15-18; Rom 16, 17; 1 Cor 5, 11; 2 Thes 3, 6.14-15.—a Acts 20, 4; Eph 6, 21; Col 4, 7; 2 Tm 4, 12.—b Acts 18, 24-26; 1 Cor 1, 12; 3, 4-6.22; 4, 6; 16, 12.—c Ti 2, 14; 3, 8; Heb 10, 24; 1 Pt 3, 13.—d Heb 13, 25.

3, 8-11: In matters of good conduct and religious doctrine, Titus is to stand firm.

3, 9: See the note on 1 Tm 6, 20-21.

3, 12-15: *Artemas* or *Tychicus* (2 Tm 4, 12) is to replace Titus, who will join Paul in his winter sojourn at Nicopolis in Epirus, on the western coast of Greece.

THE LETTER TO PHILEMON

INTRODUCTION

This short letter addressed to three specific individuals was written by Paul during an imprisonment, perhaps in Rome between A.D. 61 and 63 (see the Introduction to Colossians for other possible sites). It concerns Onesimus, a slave from Colossae (Col 4, 9), who had run away from his master, perhaps guilty of theft in the process (18). Onesimus was converted to Christ by Paul (10). Paul sends him back to his master (12) with this letter asking that he be welcomed willingly by his old master (8-10.14.17) not just as a slave but as a brother in Christ (16). Paul uses very strong arguments (especially 19) in his touching appeal on behalf of Onesimus. It is unlikely that Paul is subtly hinting that he would like to retain Onesimus as his own slave, lent to Paul by his master. Rather, he suggests he would like to have Onesimus work with him for the gospel (13.20-21). There is, however, little evidence connecting this Onesimus with a bishop of Ephesus of the same name mentioned by Ignatius of Antioch (ca. A.D. 110).

Paul's letter deals with an accepted institution of antiquity, human slavery. But Paul breathes into this letter the spirit of Christ and of equality within the Christian community. He does not attack slavery directly, for this is something the Christian communities of the first century were in no position to do, and the expectation that Christ would soon come again militated against social reforms. Yet Paul, by presenting Onesimus as "brother, beloved . . . to me, but even more so to you" (16), voiced an idea revolutionary in that day and destined to break down worldly barriers of division "in the Lord."

Phil

Address and Greeting. [1] Paul, a prisoner* for Christ Jesus, and Timothy our brother, to Philemon, our beloved and our co-

worker, [a] [2] to Apphia our sister,* to Archippus our fellow soldier, and to the

---

a Phlm 9; Eph 3, 1; 4, 1; Phil 1, 7.13.

1: *Prisoner:* as often elsewhere (cf Rom, 1 Cor, Gal especially), the second word in Greek enunciates the theme and sets the tone of the letter. Here it is the prisoner appealing rather than the apostle commanding.

2: *Apphia our sister:* sister is here used (like brother) to indicate a fellow Christian. *The church at your house:* here is singular. It more likely refers to Philemon than to the last one named, Archippus; Philemon is then the owner of the slave Onesimus (10). An alternate view is that the actual master of the slave is Archippus and that the one to whom the letter is addressed, Philemon, is the most prominent Christian there; see the note on Col 4, 17.

church at your house.[b] [3]Grace to you and peace* from God our Father and the Lord Jesus Christ.[c]

Thanksgiving. [4] [d] I give thanks to my God always, remembering you in my prayers,* [5]as I hear of the love and the faith you have in the Lord Jesus and for all the holy ones,* [6]so that your partnership in the faith may become effective in recognizing every good there is in us* that leads to Christ.[e]

Plea for Onesimus. [7]For I have experienced much joy and encouragement* from your love, because the hearts of the holy ones have been refreshed by you, brother.[f] [8]Therefore, although I have the full right* in Christ to order you to do what is proper, [9]I rather urge you out of love, being as I am, Paul, an old man,* and now also a prisoner for Christ Jesus.[g] [10]I urge you on behalf of my child Onesimus, whose father I have become in my imprisonment,[h] [11]who was once useless to you but is now useful* to [both] you and me. [12]I am sending him, that is, my own heart, back to you. [13]I should have liked to retain him for myself, so that he might serve* me on your behalf in my imprisonment for the gospel,[i] [14]but I did not want to do anything with-

out your consent, so that the good you do might not be forced but voluntary.[j] [15]Perhaps this is why he was away from* you for a while, that you might have him back forever, [16]no longer as a slave but more than a slave, a brother, beloved especially to me, but even more so to you, as a man* and in the Lord.[k] [17]So if you regard me as a partner, welcome him as you would me. [18] * And if he has done you any injustice or owes you anything, charge it to me. [19]I, Paul, write this in my own hand: I will pay. May I not tell you that you owe me your very self.[l] [20]Yes, brother, may I profit from you in the Lord. Refresh my heart in Christ.

[21]With trust in your compliance I write to you, knowing that you will do even more than I say. [22]At the same time prepare a guest room for me, for I hope to be granted to you through your prayers.[m]

Final Greetings. [23]Epaphras,* my fellow prisoner in Christ Jesus, greets you,[n] [24]as well as Mark, Aristarchus, Demas, and Luke, my co-workers. [25]The grace of the Lord Jesus Christ be with your spirit.[o]

---

b Col 4, 17.—c Rom 1, 7; Gal 1, 3; Phil 1, 2.—d 4-5: Rom 1, 8-9; Eph 1, 15-16.—e Phil 1, 9; Col 1, 9.—f 2 Cor 7, 4.—g Phlm 1; Eph 3, 1; 4, 1; Phil 1, 7.13.—h 1 Cor 4, 14-15; Gal 4, 19; Col 4, 9.—i Phil 2, 30.—j 2 Cor 9, 7; 1 Pt 5, 2.—k 1 Tm 6, 2.—l Gal 6, 11; 2 Thes 3, 17.—m Heb 13, 19.—n Col 1, 7; 4, 12-13.—o Acts 12, 12.15; 13, 13; 15, 37-39; 19, 29; 20, 4; 27, 2; Col 4, 10.14; 2 Tm 4, 10-13.

3: *Grace . . . and peace:* for this greeting, which may be a combination of Greek and Aramaic epistolary formulae, see the note on Rom 1, 1-7.

4: *In my prayers:* literally, "at the time of my prayers."

5: *Holy ones:* a common term for members of the Christian community (so also 7).

6: *In us:* some good ancient manuscripts have *in you* (plural). *That leads to Christ: leads to* translates the Greek preposition *eis,* indicating direction or purpose.

7: *Encouragement:* the Greek word *paraklēsis* is cognate with the verb translated "urge" in vv 9.10, and serves as an introduction to Paul's plea. *Hearts:* literally, "bowels," expressing in Semitic fashion the seat of the emotions, one's "inmost self." The same Greek word is used in v 12 and again in v 20, where it forms a literary inclusion marking off the body of the letter.

8: *Full right:* often translated "boldness," the Greek word *parrēsia* connotes the full franchise of speech, as the right of a citizen to speak before the body politic, claimed by the Athenians as their privilege (Euripides).

9: *Old man:* some editors conjecture that Paul here used a similar Greek word meaning "ambassador" (cf Eph 6, 20). This conjecture heightens the contrast with "prisoner" but is totally without manuscript support.

11: *Useless . . . useful:* here Paul plays on the name Onesimus, which means "useful" or "beneficial." The verb translated "profit" in v 20 is cognate.

13: *Serve:* the Greek *diakoneō* could connote a ministry.

15: *Was away from:* literally, "was separated from," but the same verb means simply "left" in Acts 18, 1. It is a euphemism for his running away.

16: *As a man:* literally, "in the flesh." With this and the following phrase, Paul describes the natural and spiritual orders.

18-19: *Charge it to me . . . I will pay:* technical legal and commercial terms in account keeping and acknowledgment of indebtedness.

23-24: *Epaphras:* a Colossian who founded the church there (Col 1, 7) and perhaps also in Laodicea and Hierapolis (Col 2, 1; 4, 12-13). *Aristarchus:* a native of Thessalonica and fellow worker of Paul (Acts 19, 29; 20, 4; 27, 2). For Mark, Demas, and Luke, see 2 Tm 4, 9-13 and the note there.

THE LETTER TO THE HEBREWS

INTRODUCTION

As early as the second century, this treatise, which is of great rhetorical power and force in its admonition to faithful pilgrimage under Christ's leadership, bore the title "To the Hebrews." It was assumed to be directed to Jewish Christians. Usually Hebrews was attached in Greek manuscripts to the collection of letters by Paul. Although no author is mentioned (for there is no address), a reference to Timothy (13, 23) suggested connections to the circle of Paul and his assistants. Yet the exact audience, the author, and even whether Hebrews is a letter have long been disputed.

The author saw the addressees in danger of apostasy from their Christian faith. This danger was due not to any persecution from outsiders but to a weariness with the demands of Christian life and a growing indifference to their calling (2, 1; 4, 14; 6, 1-12; 10, 23-32). The author's main theme, the priesthood and sacrifice of Jesus (chs 3-10), is not developed for its own sake but as a means of restoring their lost fervor and strengthening them in their faith. Another important theme of the letter is that of the pilgrimage of the people of God to the heavenly Jerusalem (11, 10; 12, 1-3.18-29; 13, 14). This theme is intimately connected with that of Jesus' ministry in the heavenly sanctuary (9, 11—10, 22).

The author calls this work a "message of encouragement" (13, 22), a designation that is given to a synagogue sermon in Acts 13, 15. Hebrews is probably therefore a written homily, to which the author gave an epistolary ending (13, 22-25).

The author begins with a reminder of the preexistence, incarnation, and exaltation of Jesus (1, 3) that proclaimed him the climax of God's word to humanity (1, 1-3). He dwells upon the dignity of the person of Christ, superior to the angels (1, 4—2, 2). Christ is God's final word of salvation communicated (in association with accredited witnesses to his teaching: cf 2, 3-4) not merely by word but through his suffering in the humanity common to him and to all others (2, 5-16). This enactment of salvation went beyond the pattern known to Moses, faithful prophet of God's word though he was, for Jesus as high priest expiated sin and was faithful to God with the faithfulness of God's own Son (2, 17—3, 6).

Just as the infidelity of the people thwarted Moses' efforts to save them, so the infidelity of any Christian may thwart God's plan in Christ (3, 6—4, 13). Christians are to reflect that it is their humanity that Jesus took upon himself, with all its defects save sinfulness, and that he bore the burden of it until death out of obedience to God. God declared this work of his Son to be the cause of salvation for all (4, 14—5, 10). Although Christians recognize this fundamental teaching, they may grow weary of it and of its implications, and therefore require other reflections to stimulate their faith (5, 11—6, 20).

Therefore, the author presents to the readers for their reflection the everlasting priesthood of Christ (7, 1-28), a priesthood that fulfills the promise of the Old Testament (8, 1-13). It also provides the meaning God ultimately intended in the sacrifices of the Old Testament (9, 1-28): these pointed to the unique sacrifice of Christ, which alone obtains forgiveness of sins (10, 1-18). The trial of faith experienced by the readers should resolve itself through their consideration of Christ's ministry in the heavenly sanctuary and his perpetual intercession there on their behalf (7, 25; 8, 1-13). They should also be *strengthened by the assurance of his foreordained parousia, and by the fruits of faith that they have already enjoyed (10, 19-39).*

It is in the nature of faith to recognize the reality of what is not yet seen and is the object of hope, and the saints of the Old Testament give striking example of that faith (11, 1-40). The perseverance to which the author exhorts the readers is shown forth in the early life of Jesus. Despite the afflictions of his ministry and the supreme trial of his suffering and death, he remained confident of the triumph that God would bring him (12, 1-3). The difficulties of human life have meaning when they are accepted as God's discipline (12, 4-13), and if Christians persevere in fidelity to the word in which they have believed, they are assured of possessing forever the unshakable kingdom of God (12, 14-29).

The letter concludes with specific moral commandments (13, 1-17), in the course of which the author recalls again his central theme of the sacrifice of Jesus and the courage needed to associate oneself with it in faith (13, 9-16).

As early as the end of the second century, the church of Alexandria in Egypt accepted Hebrews as a letter of Paul, and that became the view commonly held in the East. Pauline authorship was contested in the West into the fourth century, but then accepted. In the sixteenth century, doubts about that position were again raised, and the modern consensus is that the letter was not written by Paul. There is, however, no widespread agreement on any of the other suggested authors, e.g., Barnabas, Apollos, or Prisc(ill)a and Aquila. The document itself has no statement about its author.

Among the reasons why Pauline authorship has been abandoned are the great difference of vocabulary and style between Hebrews and Paul's letters, the alternation of doctrinal teaching with moral exhortation, the different manner of citing the Old Testament, and the resemblance between the thought of Hebrews and that of Alexandrian Judaism. The Greek of the letter is in many ways the best in the New Testament.

Since the letter of Clement of Rome to the Corinthians, written about A.D. 96, most probably cites Hebrews, the upper limit for the date of composition is reasonably certain. While the letter's references in the present tense to the Old Testament sacrificial worship do not necessarily show that temple worship was still going on, many older commentators and a growing number of recent ones favor the view that it was and that the author wrote before the destruction of the temple of Jerusalem in A.D. 70. In that case, the argument of the letter is more easily explained as directed toward Jewish Christians rather than those of Gentile origin, and the persecutions they have suffered in the past (cf 10, 32-34) may have been connected with the disturbances that preceded the expulsion of the Jews from Rome in A.D. 49 under the emperor Claudius. These were probably caused by disputes between Jews who accepted Jesus as the Messiah and those who did not.

The principal divisions of the Letter to the Hebrews are the following:

   I.   *Introduction (1, 1-4)*
  II.   *The Son Higher than the Angels (1, 5—2, 18)*
 III.   *Jesus, Faithful and Compassionate High Priest (3, 1—5, 10)*
 IV.   *Jesus' Eternal Priesthood and Eternal Sacrifice (5, 11—10, 39)*
  V.   *Examples, Discipline, Disobedience (11, 1—12, 29)*
 VI.   *Final Exhortation, Blessing, Greetings (13, 1-25)*

I. INTRODUCTION*

CHAPTER 1

[1] In times past, God spoke in partial and various ways to our ancestors through the prophets; [2] in these last days, he spoke to us through a son, whom he made heir of all things and through whom he created the universe,[a]

[3] who is the refulgence of his glory,
   the very imprint of his being,
and who sustains all things by his
   mighty word.
When he had accomplished purification
   from sins,
he took his seat at the right hand of the
   Majesty on high,[b]
[4] as far superior to the angels
as the name he has inherited is more excellent than theirs.[c]

II. THE SON HIGHER THAN THE ANGELS

Messianic Enthronement.* [5] For to which of the angels did God ever say:
   "You are my son; this day I have begot-
      ten you"?[d]
Or again:
   "I will be a father to him, and he shall
      be a son to me"?

[6] And again, when he leads* the first-born into the world, he says:

   "Let all the angels of God worship
      him."[e]
[7] Of the angels he says:
   "He makes his angels winds
      and his ministers a fiery flame";[f]
[8] but of the Son:
   "Your throne, O God,* stands forever
      and ever;
   and a righteous scepter is the scepter
      of your kingdom.[g]
[9] You loved justice and hated wicked-
      ness;
   therefore God, your God, anointed
      you
   with the oil of gladness above your
      companions";
[10] and:
   "At the beginning, O Lord, you estab-
      lished the earth,[h]
   and the heavens are the works of your
      hands.
[11] They will perish, but you remain;
   and they will all grow old like a gar-
      ment.
[12] You will roll them up like a cloak,
   and like a garment they will be
      changed.
   But you are the same, and your years
      will have no end."

---

a Is 2, 2; Jer 23, 20; Ez 38, 16; Dn 10, 14 / Jn 3, 17; Rom 8, 3; Gal 4, 4 / Prv 8, 30; Wis 7, 22; Jn 1, 3; 1 Cor 8, 6; Col 1, 16.— b Wis 7, 26; 2 Cor 4, 4; Col 1, 15 / Heb 8, 1; 10, 12; 12, 2; Mk 16, 19; Acts 2, 33; 7, 55-56; Rom 8, 34; Eph 1, 20; Col 3, 1; 1 Pt 3, 22.—c Eph 1, 21; Phil 2, 9-11.—d Ps 2, 7 / 2 Sm 7, 14.—e Dt 32, 43 LXX; Ps 97, 7.—f Ps 104, 4 LXX.—g Ps 45, 7-8.—h 10-12: Ps 102, 26-28.

1, 1-4: The letter opens with an introduction consisting of a reflection on the climax of God's revelation to the human race in his Son. The divine communication was initiated and maintained during Old Testament times in fragmentary and varied ways through *the prophets* (1), including Abraham, Moses, and all through whom God spoke. But now *in these last days* (2), the final age, God's revelation of his saving purpose is achieved *through a son,* i.e., one who is Son, whose role is redeemer and mediator of creation. He was made *heir of all things* through his death and exaltation to glory, yet he existed before he appeared as man; through him God *created the universe.* Verses 3-4, which may be based upon a liturgical hymn, assimilate the Son to the personified Wisdom of the Old Testament as *refulgence of* God's *glory* and *imprint of his being* (3; cf Wis 7, 26). These same terms are used of the Logos in Philo. The author now turns from the cosmological role of the preexistent Son to the redemptive work of Jesus: he brought about purification from sins and has been exalted to the right hand of God (see Ps 110, 1). The once-humiliated and crucified Jesus has been declared God's Son, and

this name shows his superiority to the angels. The reason for the author's insistence on that superiority is, among other things, that in some Jewish traditions angels were mediators of the old covenant (see Acts 7, 53; Gal 3, 19). Finally, Jesus' superiority to the angels emphasizes the superiority of the new covenant to the old because of the heavenly priesthood of Jesus.

1, 5-14: Jesus' superiority to the angels is now demonstrated by a series of seven Old Testament texts. Some scholars see in the stages of Jesus' exaltation an order corresponding to that of enthronement ceremonies in the ancient Near East, especially in Egypt, namely, elevation to divine status (5-6); presentation to the angels and proclamation of everlasting lordship (7-12); enthronement and conferral of royal power (13). The citations from the Psalms in vv 5 and 13 were traditionally used of Jesus' messianic sonship (cf Acts 13, 33) through his resurrection and exaltation (cf Acts 2, 33-35); those in vv 8 and 10-12 are concerned with his divine kingship and his creative function. The central quotation in v 7 serves to contrast the angels with the Son. The author quotes it according to the Septuagint translation, which is quite different in meaning from that of the Hebrew ("You make the winds your messengers, and flaming fire your ministers"). The angels are only *sent to serve . . . those who are to inherit salvation* (14).

1, 6: *And again, when he leads:* the Greek could also be translated "And when he again leads" in reference to the parousia.

1, 8-12: *O God:* the application of the name "God" to the Son derives from the preexistence mentioned in vv 2-3; the psalmist had already used it of the Hebrew king in the court style of the original. See the note on Ps 45, 7. It is also important for the author's christology that in vv 10-12 an Old Testament passage addressed to God is redirected to Jesus.

Heb

13 But to which of the angels has he ever said:

"Sit at my right hand
    until I make your enemies your footstool"?[i]

14 Are they not all ministering spirits sent to serve, for the sake of those who are to inherit salvation?[j]

CHAPTER 2

Exhortation to Faithfulness.* 1 Therefore, we must attend all the more to what we have heard, so that we may not be carried away. 2 For if the word announced through angels proved firm, and every transgression and disobedience received its just recompense,[k] 3 how shall we escape if we ignore so great a salvation? Announced originally through the Lord, it was confirmed for us by those who had heard.[l] 4 God added his testimony by signs, wonders, various acts of power, and distribution of the gifts of the holy Spirit according to his will.[m]

Exaltation through Abasement.* 5 For it was not to angels that he subjected the world to come, of which we are speaking. 6 Instead, someone has testified somewhere:

"What is man that you are mindful of him,
    or the son of man that you care for him?[n]

7 You made him for a little while lower than the angels;
    you crowned him with glory and honor,
8   subjecting all things under his feet."

In "subjecting" all things [to him], he left nothing not "subject to him." Yet at present we do not see "all things subject to him,"[o] 9 but we do see Jesus "crowned with glory and honor" because he suffered death, he who "for a little while" was made "lower than the angels," that by the grace of God he might taste death for everyone.[p]

10 For it was fitting that he, for whom and through whom all things exist, in bringing many children to glory, should make the leader to their salvation perfect through suffering.[q] 11 He who consecrates and those who are being consecrated all have one origin. Therefore, he is not ashamed to call them "brothers,"[12] saying:

"I will proclaim your name to my brothers,
    in the midst of the assembly I will praise you";[r]

13 and again:

"I will put my trust in him";

and again:

"Behold, I and the children God has given me."[s]

14 Now since the children share in blood and flesh, he likewise shared in them, that through death he might destroy the one

i Ps 110, 1.—j Ps 91, 11; Dn 7, 10.—k Acts 7, 38.53; Gal 3, 19.—l Heb 10, 29; 12, 25.—m Mk 16, 20; Acts 14, 3; 19, 11.— n Ps 8, 5-7.—o Mt 28, 18; 1 Cor 15, 25-28; Eph 1, 20-23; Phil 3, 21; 1 Pt 3, 22.—p Phil 2, 6-11.—q Heb 12, 2; Is 53, 4 / Rom 11, 36; 1 Cor 8, 6.—r Ps 22, 23.—s Is 8, 17.18.

2, 1-4: The author now makes a transition into exhortation, using an a fortiori argument (as at Heb 7, 21-22; 9, 13-14; 10, 28-29; 12, 25). The *word announced through angels* (2), the Mosaic law, is contrasted with the more powerful word that Christians have received (3-4). Christ's supremacy strengthens Christians against being *carried away* from their faith.

2, 5-18: The humanity and the suffering of Jesus do not constitute a valid reason for relinquishing the Christian faith. Ps 8 (6-7) is also applied to Jesus in 1 Cor 15, 27; Eph 1, 22; and probably 1 Pt 3, 22. This christological interpretation, therefore, probably reflects a common early Christian tradition, which may have originated in the expression *the son of man* (6). The psalm contrasts God's greatness with man's relative insignificance but also stresses the superiority of man to the rest of creation, of which he is lord. Heb applies this christologically: Jesus lived a truly human existence, *lower than the angels*, in the days of his earthly life, particularly in his suffering and death; now, *crowned with glory and honor*, he is raised above all creation. The author considers all things as already *subject to him* because of his exaltation (8-9), though *we do not see* this yet. The reference to Jesus as

leader (10) sounds the first note of an important leitmotif in Heb: the journey of the people of God to the sabbath rest (Heb 4, 9), the heavenly sanctuary, following Jesus, their "forerunner" (Heb 6, 20). It was fitting that God should make him *perfect through suffering*, consecrated by obedient suffering. Because he is perfected as high priest, Jesus is then able to consecrate his people (11); access to God is made possible by each of these two consecrations. If Jesus is able to help human beings, it is because he has become one of us; we are his "brothers." The author then cites three Old Testament texts as proofs of this unity between ourselves and the Son. Psalm 22, 23 is interpreted so as to make Jesus the singer of this lament, which ends with joyful praise of the Lord in the assembly of "brothers." The other two texts are from Is 8, 17.18. The first of these seems intended to display in Jesus an example of the trust in God that his followers should emulate. The second curiously calls these followers "children"; probably this is to be understood to mean children of Adam, but the point is our solidarity with Jesus. By sharing human nature, including the ban of death, Jesus broke the power of the devil over death (14); the author shares the view of Hellenistic Judaism that death was not intended by God and that it had been introduced into the world by the devil. The *fear of death* (15) is a religious fear based on the false conception that death marks the end of a person's relations with God (cf Ps 115, 17-18; Is 38, 18). Jesus deliberately allied himself with *the descendants of Abraham* (16) in order to be *a merciful and faithful high priest*. This is the first appearance of the central theme of Heb, Jesus the great high priest expiating *the sins of the people* (17), as one who experienced the same tests as they (18).

who has the power of death, that is, the devil,[t] [15]and free those who through fear of death had been subject to slavery all their life. [16]Surely he did not help angels but rather the descendants of Abraham; [17]therefore, he had to become like his brothers in every way, that he might be a merciful and faithful high priest before God to expiate the sins of the people.[u] [18]Because he himself was tested through what he suffered, he is able to help those who are being tested.

III. JESUS, FAITHFUL AND COMPASSIONATE HIGH PRIEST

CHAPTER 3

Jesus, Superior to Moses.[*] [1]Therefore, holy "brothers," sharing in a heavenly calling, reflect on Jesus, the apostle and high priest of our confession, [2]who was faithful to the one who appointed him, just as Moses was "faithful in [all] his house."[v] [3]But he is worthy of more "glory" than Moses, as the founder of a house has more "honor" than the house itself.[w] [4]Every house is founded by someone, but the founder of all is God. [5]Moses was "faithful in all his house" as a "servant" to testify to what would be spoken, [6] [x] but Christ was faithful as a son placed over his house. We are his house, if [only] we hold fast to our confidence and pride in our hope.[*]

[t] Is 25, 8; Hos 13, 14; Jn 12, 31; Rom 6, 9; 1 Cor 15, 54-55; 2 Tm 1, 10; Rv 12, 10.—u Heb 4, 15; 5, 1-3.—v Nm 12, 7.—w 2 Cor 3, 7-8.—x Heb 10, 21; Eph 2, 19; 1 Tm 3, 15; 1 Pt 4, 17.—y 7-11 Ps 95, 7-11.—z Ex 17, 7; Nm 20, 2-5.—a Rom 8, 17.—b Ps 95, 7-8.—c 16-19: Nm 14, 1-38; Dt 1, 19-40.

3, 1-6: The author now takes up the two qualities of Jesus mentioned in Heb 2, 17, but in inverse order: faithfulness (Heb 3, 1—4, 13) and mercy (Heb 4, 14—5, 10). Christians are called holy "brothers" because of their common relation to him (Heb 2, 11), the *apostle*, a designation for Jesus used only here in the New Testament (cf Jn 13, 16; 17, 3), meaning one sent as God's final word to us (Heb 1, 2). He is compared with Moses probably because he is seen as mediator of the new covenant (Heb 9, 15) just as Moses was of the old (Heb 9, 19-22, including his sacrifice). But when the author of Heb speaks of Jesus' sacrifice, he does not consider Moses as the Old Testament antitype, but rather the high priest on the Day of Atonement (Heb 9, 6-15). Moses' faithfulness "in [all] his house" refers back to Nm 12, 7, on which this section is a midrashic commentary. In vv 3-6, the author does not indicate that he thinks of either Moses or Christ as the founder of the household. *His house* (2.5.6) means God's house, not that of Moses or Christ; in the case of Christ, compare v 6 with Heb 10, 21. The *house* of v 6 is the Christian community; the author suggests its continuity with Israel by speaking not of two houses but of only one. Verse 6 brings out the reason why Jesus is superior to Moses: the latter was the faithful *servant* laboring *in* the house founded by God, but Jesus is God's *son*, placed *over* the house.

3, 6: The majority of manuscripts add "firm to the end," but these words are not found in the three earliest and best witnesses and are probably an interpolation derived from v 14.

Israel's Infidelity a Warning. [7] [*] Therefore, as the holy Spirit says:

"Oh, that today you would hear his voice,[y]

[8]   'Harden not your hearts as at the rebellion
        in the day of testing in the desert,
[9]   where your ancestors tested and tried me
        and saw my works[z] [10]for forty years.
     Because of this I was provoked with that generation
        and I said, "They have always been of erring heart,
        and they do not know my ways."
[11]   As I swore in my wrath,
        "They shall not enter into my rest."' "

[12]Take care, brothers, that none of you may have an evil and unfaithful heart, so as to forsake the living God. [13]Encourage yourselves daily while it is still "today," so that none of you may grow hardened by the deceit of sin. [14]We have become partners of Christ if only we hold the beginning of the reality firm until the end,[a] [15]for it is said:

"Oh, that today you would hear his voice:
'Harden not your hearts as at the rebellion.' "[b]

[16] [c] Who were those who rebelled when they heard? Was it not all those who came

3, 7—4, 13: The author appeals for steadfastness of faith in Jesus, basing his warning on the experience of Israel during the Exodus. In the Old Testament the Exodus had been invoked as a symbol of the return of Israel from the Babylonian exile (Is 42, 9; 43, 16-21; 51, 9-11). In the New Testament the redemption was similarly understood as a new exodus, both in the experience of Jesus himself (Lk 9, 31) and in that of his followers (1 Cor 10, 1-4). The author cites Ps 95, 7-11, a salutary example of hardness of heart, as a warning against the danger of growing weary and giving up the journey. To call God *living* (12) means that he reveals himself in his works (cf Jos 3, 10; Jer 10, 10). The *rest* (11) into which Israel was to enter was only a foreshadowing of that rest to which Christians are called. They are to remember the example of Israel's revolt in the desert that cost a whole generation the loss of the promised land (15-19; cf Nm 14, 20-29). In Heb 4, 1-11, the symbol of *rest* is seen in deeper dimension: because the promise to the ancient Hebrews foreshadowed that given to Christians, it is *good news;* and because the promised land was the place of rest that God provided for his people, it was a share in his own rest, which he enjoyed after he had finished his creative work (3-4; cf Gn 2, 2). The author attempts to read this meaning of God's rest into Ps 95, 7-11 (6-9). The Greek form of the name of Joshua, who led Israel into the promised land, is Jesus (8). The author plays upon the name but stresses the superiority of Jesus, who leads his followers into heavenly rest. Verses 12 and 13 are meant as a continuation of the warning, for the word of God brings judgment as well as salvation. Some would capitalize *the word of God* and see it as a personal title of Jesus, comparable to that of Jn 1, 1-18.

Heb

out of Egypt under Moses? [17] With whom was he "provoked for forty years"? Was it not those who had sinned, whose corpses fell in the desert?[d] [18] And to whom did he "swear that they should not enter into his rest," if not to those who were disobedient?[e] [19] And we see that they could not enter for lack of faith.

CHAPTER 4

The Sabbath Rest. [1] Therefore, let us be on our guard while the promise of entering into his rest remains, that none of you seem to have failed. [2] For in fact we have received the good news just as they did. But the word that they heard did not profit them, for they were not united in faith with those who listened. [3] For we who believed enter into [that] rest, just as he has said:[f]

"As I swore in my wrath,
   'They shall not enter into my rest,' "

and yet his works were accomplished at the foundation of the world. [4] For he has spoken somewhere about the seventh day in this manner, "And God rested on the seventh day from all his works";[g] [5] and again, in the previously mentioned place, "They shall not enter into my rest."[h] [6] Therefore, since it remains that some will enter into it, and those who formerly received the good news did not enter because of disobedience, [7] he once more set a day, "today," when long afterwards he spoke through David, as already quoted:[i]

"Oh, that today you would hear his voice:
   'Harden not your hearts.' "

[8] Now if Joshua had given them rest, he would not have spoken afterwards of another day.[j] [9] Therefore, a sabbath rest still remains for the people of God. [10] And whoever enters into God's rest, rests from his own works as God did from his. [11] Therefore, let us strive to enter into that rest, so that no one may fall after the same example of disobedience.

[12] Indeed, the word of God is living and effective, sharper than any two-edged sword, penetrating even between soul and spirit, joints and marrow, and able to discern reflections and thoughts of the heart.[k] [13] No creature is concealed from him, but everything is naked and exposed to the eyes of him to whom we must render an account.[l]

Jesus, Compassionate High Priest. [14] * Therefore, since we have a great high priest who has passed through the heavens, Jesus, the Son of God, let us hold fast to our confession.[m] [15] For we do not have a high priest who is unable to sympathize with our weaknesses, but one who has similarly been tested in every way, yet without sin.[n] [16] So let us confidently approach the throne of grace to receive mercy and to find grace for timely help.[o]

CHAPTER 5

[1] * Every high priest is taken from among men and made their representative before God, to offer gifts and sacrifices for sins.* [2] He is able to deal patiently* with the ignorant and erring, for he himself is beset by weakness [3] and so, for this reason, must make sin offerings for himself as well as for the people.[p] [4] No one takes this honor

---

d Nm 14, 29.—e Nm 14, 22-23; Dt 1, 35.—f Heb 3, 11; Ps 95, 11.—g Gn 2, 2.—h Ps 95, 11.—i Heb 3, 7-8.15; Ps 95, 7-8.—j Dt 31, 7; Jos 22, 4.—k Wis 18, 15-16; Is 49, 2; Eph 6, 17; Rv 1, 16; 2, 12.—l Jb 34, 21-22; Pss 90, 8; 139, 2-4.—m Heb 9, 11.24.—n Heb 2, 17-18; 5, 2.—o Heb 8, 1; 10, 19.22.35; 12, 2; Eph 3, 12.—p Lv 9, 7; 16, 15-17.30.34.

4, 14-16: These verses, which return to the theme first sounded in Heb 2, 16—3, 1, serve as an introduction to the section that follows. The author here alone calls Jesus *a great high priest* (14), a designation used by Philo for the Logos; perhaps he does so in order to emphasize Jesus' superiority over the Jewish high priest. He has *been tested in every way, yet without sin* (15); this indicates an acquaintance with the tradition of Jesus' temptations, not only at the beginning (as in Mk 1, 13) but throughout his public life (cf Lk 22, 28). Although the reign of the exalted Jesus is a theme that occurs elsewhere in Heb, and Jesus' throne is mentioned in Heb 1, 8, *the throne of grace* (16) refers to the throne of God. The similarity of v 16 to Heb 10, 19-22 indicates that the author is thinking of our confident access to God, made possible by the priestly work of Jesus.

5, 1-10: The true humanity of Jesus (see the note on Heb 2, 5-18) makes him a more rather than a less effective high priest to the Christian community. In Old Testament tradition, the high priest was identified with the people, guilty of personal sin just as they were (1-3). Even so, the office was of divine appointment (4), as was also the case with the sinless Christ (5). For v 6, see the note on Ps 110, 4. Although Jesus was Son of God, he was destined as a human being to learn obedience by accepting the suffering he had to endure (8). Because of his perfection through this experience of human suffering, he is the cause of salvation for all (9), a *high priest according to the order of Melchizedek* (10; cf Heb 5, 6 and Heb 7, 3).

5, 1: *To offer gifts and sacrifices for sins:* the author is thinking principally of the Day of Atonement rite, as is clear from Heb 9, 7. This ritual was celebrated to atone for "all the sins of the Israelites" (Lv 16, 34).

5, 2: *Deal patiently:* the Greek word *metriopathein* occurs only here in the Bible; this term was used by the Stoics to designate the golden mean between excess and defect of passion. Here it means rather the ability to sympathize.

upon himself but only when called by God, just as Aaron was.[q] [5]In the same way, it was not Christ who glorified himself in becoming high priest, but rather the one who said to him:

"You are my son;
this day I have begotten you";[r]

[6]just as he says in another place:*

"You are a priest forever
according to the order of Melchizedek."[s]

[7]In the days when he was in the flesh, he offered prayers and supplications with loud cries and tears to the one who was able to save him from death,* and he was heard because of his reverence.[t] [8]Son though he was,* he learned obedience from what he suffered;[u] [9]and when he was made perfect, he became the source of eternal salvation for all who obey him,[v] [10]declared by God high priest according to the order of Melchizedek.[w]

IV. JESUS' ETERNAL PRIESTHOOD AND ETERNAL SACRIFICE

Exhortation to Spiritual Renewal. [11] * About this we have much to say, and it is difficult to explain, for you have become sluggish in hearing. [12]Although you should be teachers by this time, you need to have someone teach you again the basic elements of the utterances of God. You need milk, [and] not solid food.[x] [13]Everyone who lives on milk lacks experience of the word of righteousness, for he is a child. [14]But solid food is for the mature, for those whose faculties are trained by practice to discern good and evil.

CHAPTER 6

[1]Therefore, let us leave behind the basic teaching about Christ and advance to maturity, without laying the foundation all over again: repentance from dead works and faith in God,[y] [2]instruction about baptisms* and laying on of hands, resurrection of the dead and eternal judgment.[z] [3]And we shall do this, if only God permits. [4]For it is impossible in the case of those who have once been enlightened and tasted the heavenly gift* and shared in the holy Spirit[a] [5]and tasted the good word of God and the powers of the age to come,* [6]and then have fallen away, to bring them to repentance again, since they are recrucifying the Son of God for themselves* and holding him up to contempt.[b] [7]Ground that has absorbed the rain falling upon it repeatedly and brings forth crops useful to those for whom it is cultivated receives a blessing from God.[c] [8]But if it produces thorns and thistles, it is rejected; it will soon be cursed and finally burned.[d]

---

q Ex 28, 1.—r Ps 2, 7.—s Ps 110, 4.—t Mt 26, 38-44; Mk 14, 34-40; Lk 22, 41-46; Jn 12, 27.—u Rom 5, 19; Phil 2, 8.—v Heb 7, 24-25.28.—w Heb 6, 20; Ps 110, 4.—x 1 Cor 3, 1-3.—y Heb 9, 14.—z Heb 9, 10; Mk 7, 4 / Acts 6, 6; 8, 17; 13, 3; 19, 6; 1 Tm 4, 14; 5, 22; 2 Tm 1, 6.—a Heb 10, 26.32; Ps 34, 6; 2 Cor 4, 6.—b 2 Pt 2, 21.—c Gn 1, 11-12; Dt 11, 11.—d Gn 3, 17-18; Mt 7, 16; 13, 7; Mk 4, 7; Lk 8, 7.

5, 6-8: The author of Heb is the only New Testament writer to cite v 4 of Ps 110, here and in Heb 7, 17.21, to show that Jesus has been called by God to his role as priest. Verses 7-8 deal with his ability to sympathize with sinners, because of his own experience of the trials and weakness of human nature, especially fear of death. In his present exalted state, weakness is foreign to him, but he understands what we suffer because of his previous earthly experience.

5, 7: *He offered prayers . . . to the one who was able to save him from death:* at Gethsemane (cf Mk 14, 35), though some see a broader reference (see the note on Jn 12, 27).

5, 8: *Son though he was:* two different though not incompatible views of Jesus' sonship coexist in Heb, one associating it with his exaltation, the other with his preexistence. The former view is the older one (cf Rom 1, 4).

5, 11—6, 20: The central section of Heb (5, 11—10, 39) opens with a reprimand and an appeal. Those to whom the author directs his teaching about Jesus' priesthood, which is *difficult to explain,* have become *sluggish in hearing* and forgetful of even *the basic elements* (Heb 5, 12). But rather than treating of basic teachings, the author apparently believes that the challenge of more advanced ones may shake them out of their inertia (*therefore,* Heb 6, 1). The six examples of *basic teaching* in Heb 6, 1-3 are probably derived from a traditional catechetical list. No effort is made to address apostates, for their very hostility to the Christian message cuts them off completely from Christ (Heb 6, 4-8). This harsh statement seems to rule out repentance after apostasy, but perhaps the author deliberately uses hyperbole in order to stress the seriousness of abandoning Christ. With Heb 6, 9 a milder tone is introduced, and the criticism of the community (Heb 6, 1-3.9) is now balanced by an expression of confidence that its members are living truly Christian lives, and that God will justly reward their efforts (10). The author is concerned especially about their persevering (11-12), citing in this regard the achievement of Abraham, who relied on God's promise and on God's oath (13-18; cf Gn 22, 16), and proposes to them as a firm anchor of Christian hope the high priesthood of Christ, who is now living with God (19-20).

6, 2: *Instruction about baptisms:* not simply about Christian baptism but about the difference between it and similar Jewish rites, such as proselyte baptism, John's baptism, and the washings of the Qumran sectaries. *Laying on of hands:* in Acts 8, 17; 19, 6 this rite effects the infusion of the holy Spirit; in Acts 6, 6; 13, 3; 1 Tm 4, 14; 5, 22; 2 Tm 1, 6 it is a means of conferring some ministry or mission in the early Christian community.

6, 4: *Enlightened and tasted the heavenly gift:* this may refer to baptism and the Eucharist, respectively, but more probably means the neophytes' enlightenment by faith and their experience of salvation.

6, 5: *Tasted the good word of God and the powers of the age to come:* the proclamation of the *word of God* was accompanied by signs of the Spirit's power (1 Thes 1, 5; 1 Cor 2, 4).

6, 6: *They are recrucifying the Son of God for themselves:* a colorful description of the malice of apostasy, which is portrayed as again crucifying and deriding the Son of God.

Heb

[9] But we are sure in your regard, beloved, of better things related to salvation, even though we speak in this way. [10] For God is not unjust so as to overlook your work and the love you have demonstrated for his name by having served and continuing to serve the holy ones. [11] We earnestly desire each of you to demonstrate the same eagerness for the fulfillment of hope until the end,[e] [12] so that you may not become sluggish, but imitators of those who, through faith and patience,[f] are inheriting the promises.*

God's Promise Immutable. [13] [g] When God made the promise to Abraham, since he had no one greater by whom to swear, "he swore by himself,"* [14] and said, "I will indeed bless you and multiply" you.[h] [15] And so, after patient waiting,[i] he obtained the promise.* [16] Human beings swear by someone greater than themselves; for them an oath serves as a guarantee and puts an end to all argument. [17] So when God wanted to give the heirs of his promise an even clearer demonstration of the immutability of his purpose, he intervened with an oath,[j] [18] so that by two immutable things,* in which it was impossible for God to lie, we who have taken refuge might be strongly encouraged to hold fast to the hope that lies before us.[k] [19] This we have as an anchor of the soul,[l] sure and firm, which reaches into the interior behind the veil.* [20] where Jesus has entered on our behalf as forerunner, becoming high priest forever according to the order of Melchizedek.[m]

CHAPTER 7

Melchizedek, a Type of Christ. [1] * This "Melchizedek, king of Salem and priest of God Most High,"* "met Abraham as he returned from his defeat of the kings" and "blessed him."[n] [2] And Abraham apportioned to him "a tenth of everything." His name first means righteous king, and he was also "king of Salem," that is, king of peace.* [3] Without father, mother, or ancestry, without beginning of days or end of life,* thus made to resemble the Son of God, he remains a priest forever.[o]

[4] * See how great he is to whom the patriarch "Abraham [indeed] gave a tenth" of his spoils.[p] [5] The descendants of Levi who receive the office of priesthood have a commandment according to the law to exact tithes from the people, that is, from their brothers, although they also have come from the loins of Abraham.[q] [6] But he who was not of their ancestry received tithes from Abraham and blessed him who had received the promises. [7] Unquestionably, a lesser person is blessed by a greater.* [8] In

---

e Heb 3, 14.—f Heb 5, 11; Gal 3, 14; Eph 1, 13-14.—g Gn 22, 16.—h Gn 22, 17.—i Heb 6, 12; Rom 4, 20.—j Heb 6, 12.—k Nm 23, 19; 1 Sm 15, 29; Jn 8, 17; 2 Tm 2, 13.—l Heb 10, 20; Ex 26, 31-33; Lv 16, 2.—m Heb 5, 10; Ps 110, 4.—n Gn 14, 17-20.—o Heb 4, 14; 6, 6; 10, 29.—p Gn 14, 20.—q Nm 18, 21 / Gn 35, 11.

6, 12: *Imitators of those . . . inheriting the promises:* the author urges the addressees to imitate the faith of the holy people of the Old Testament, who now possess the promised goods of which they lived in hope. This theme will be treated fully in ch 11.

6, 13: *He swore by himself:* God's promise to Abraham, which he confirmed by an oath ("I swear by myself," Gn 22, 16), was the basis for the hope of all Abraham's descendants.

6, 15: *He obtained the promise:* this probably refers not to Abraham's temporary possession of the land but to the eschatological blessings that Abraham and the other patriarchs have now come to possess.

6, 18: *Two immutable things:* the promise and the oath, both made by God.

6, 19: *Anchor . . . into the interior behind the veil:* a mixed metaphor. The Holy of Holies, beyond the veil that separates it from the Holy Place (Ex 26, 31-33), is seen as the earthly counterpart of the heavenly abode of God. This theme will be developed in ch 9.

7, 1-3: Recalling the meeting between Melchizedek and Abraham described in Gn 14, 17-20, the author enhances the significance of this priest by providing the popular etymological meaning of his name and that of the city over which he ruled (2). Since Genesis gives no information on the parentage or the death of Melchizedek, he is seen here as a type of Christ, representing a priesthood that is unique and eternal (3).

7, 1: The author here assumes that Melchizedek was a priest of the God of Israel (cf Gn 14, 22 and the note there).

7, 2: In Gn 14, the Hebrew text does not state explicitly who gave tithes to whom. The author of Heb supplies Abraham as the subject, according to a contemporary interpretation of the passage. This supports the argument of the midrash and makes it possible to see in Melchizedek a type of Jesus. The messianic blessings of righteousness and peace are foreshadowed in the names "Melchizedek" and "Salem."

7, 3: *Without father, mother, or ancestry, without beginning of days or end of life:* this is perhaps a quotation from a hymn about Melchizedek. The rabbis maintained that anything not mentioned in the Torah does not exist. Consequently, since the Old Testament nowhere mentions Melchizedek's ancestry, birth, or death, the conclusion can be drawn that he *remains . . . forever.*

7, 4-10: The tithe that Abraham gave to Melchizedek (4), a practice later followed by the levitical priesthood (5), was a gift (6) acknowledging a certain superiority in Melchizedek, the foreign priest (7). This is further indicated by the fact that the institution of the levitical priesthood was sustained by hereditary succession in the tribe of Levi, whereas the absence of any mention of Melchizedek's death in Gn implies that his personal priesthood is permanent (8). The levitical priesthood itself, through Abraham, its ancestor, paid tithes to Melchizedek, thus acknowledging the superiority of his priesthood over its own (9-10).

7, 7: *A lesser person is blessed by a greater:* though this sounds like a principle, there are some examples in the Old Testament that do not support it (cf 2 Sm 14, 22; Jb 31, 20). The author may intend it as a statement of a liturgical rule.

the one case, mortal men receive tithes; in the other, a man of whom it is testified that he lives on. [9] One might even say that Levi* himself, who receives tithes, was tithed through Abraham, [10] for he was still in his father's loins when Melchizedek met him.

[11] * If, then, perfection came through the levitical priesthood, on the basis of which the people received the law, what need would there still have been for another priest to arise according to the order of Melchizedek, and not reckoned according to the order of Aaron?[r] [12] When there is a change of priesthood, there is necessarily a change of law as well. [13] Now he of whom these things are said* belonged to a different tribe, of which no member ever officiated at the altar. [14] It is clear that our Lord arose from Judah,* and in regard to that tribe Moses said nothing about priests.[s] [15] * It is even more obvious if another priest is raised up after the likeness of Melchizedek, [16] who has become so, not by a law expressed in a commandment concerning physical descent but by the power of a life that cannot be destroyed.* [17] For it is testified:

"You are a priest forever
  according to the order of Melchizedek."[t]

r Heb 5, 6; Ps 110, 4.—s Gn 49, 10; Is 11, 1; Mt 1, 1-2.16.20; 2, 6; Lk 1, 27; 2, 4; Rom 1, 3; Rv 5, 5.—t Heb 5, 6; Ps 110, 4.—u Heb 10, 1.—v Ps 110, 4.—w Heb 8, 6-10; 9, 15-20; 10, 29; 12, 24; 13, 20.—x Heb 5, 6; 13, 8.—y Rom 8, 34; 1 Jn 2, 1; Rv 1, 18.—z Heb 4, 14.15.

7, 9: *Levi:* for the author this name designates not only the son of Jacob mentioned in Genesis but the priestly tribe that was thought to be descended from him.

7, 11-14: The levitical priesthood was not typified by the priesthood of Melchizedek, for Ps 110, 4 speaks of a priesthood of a new order, the order of Melchizedek, to arise in messianic times (11). Since the levitical priesthood served the Mosaic law, a new priesthood (12) would not come into being without a change in the law itself. Thus Jesus was not associated with the Old Testament priesthood, for he was a descendant of the tribe of Judah, which had never exercised the priesthood (13-14).

7, 13: *He of whom these things are said:* Jesus, the priest "according to the order of Melchizedek." According to the author's interpretation, Ps 110 spoke prophetically of Jesus.

7, 14: *Judah:* the author accepts the early Christian tradition that Jesus was descended from the family of David (cf Mt 1, 1-2.16.20; Lk 1, 27; 2, 4; Rom 1, 3). The Qumran community expected two Messiahs, one descended from Aaron and one from David; Heb shows no awareness of this view or at least does not accept it. Our author's view is not attested in contemporaneous Judaism.

7, 15-19: Jesus does not exercise a priesthood through family lineage but through his immortal existence (15-16), fulfilling Ps 110, 4 (17; cf Heb 7, 3). Thus he abolishes forever both the levitical priesthood and the law it serves, because neither could effectively sanctify people (18) by leading them into direct communication with God (19).

[18] On the one hand, a former commandment is annulled because of its weakness and uselessness,[u] [19] for the law brought nothing to perfection; on the other hand, a better hope* is introduced, through which we draw near to God. [20] * And to the degree that this happened not without the taking of an oath*—for others became priests without an oath, [21] but he with an oath, through the one who said to him:

"The Lord has sworn, and he will not
  repent:[v]
  'You are a priest forever' "—

[22] w to that same degree has Jesus [also] become the guarantee of an [even] better covenant.* [23] Those priests were many because they were prevented by death from remaining in office, [24] but he, because he remains forever, has a priesthood that does not pass away.[x] [25] Therefore, he is always able to save those who approach God through him, since he lives forever to make intercession* for them.[y]

[26] z It was fitting that we should have such a high priest:* holy, innocent, undefiled, separated from sinners, higher than the heavens.* [27] He has no need, as did the

7, 16: *A life that cannot be destroyed:* the life to which Jesus has attained by virtue of his resurrection; it is his exaltation rather than his divine nature that makes him priest. The Old Testament speaks of the Aaronic priesthood as eternal (see Ex 40, 15); our author does not explicitly consider this possible objection to his argument but implicitly refutes it in vv 23-24.

7, 19: *A better hope:* this hope depends upon the sacrifice of the Son of God; through it we "approach the throne of grace" (Heb 4, 16); cf Heb 6, 19.20.

7, 20-25: As was the case with the promise to Abraham (Heb 6, 13), though not with the levitical priesthood, the eternal priesthood of the order of Melchizedek was confirmed by God's oath (20-21); cf Ps 110, 4: Thus Jesus becomes the guarantee of a permanent covenant (22) that does not require a succession of priests as did the levitical priesthood (23) because his high priesthood is eternal and unchangeable (24). Consequently, Jesus is able to save all who draw near to God through him since he is their ever-living intercessor (25).

7, 20: *An oath:* God's oath in Ps 110, 4.

7, 22: *An [even] better covenant:* better than the Mosaic covenant because it will be eternal, like the priesthood of Jesus upon which it is based. Verse 12 argued that a change of priesthood involves a change of law; since "law" and "covenant" are used correlatively, a new covenant is likewise instituted.

7, 25: *To make intercession:* the intercession of the exalted Jesus, not the sequel to his completed sacrifice but its eternal presence in heaven; cf Rom 8, 34.

7, 26-28: Jesus is precisely the high priest whom the human race requires, holy and sinless, installed far above humanity (26); one having no need to offer sacrifice daily for sins but making a single offering of himself (27) once for all. The law could only appoint high priests with human limitations, but the fulfillment of God's oath regarding the priesthood of Melchizedek (Ps 110, 4) makes the Son of God the perfect priest forever (28).

7, 26: This verse with its list of attributes is reminiscent of v 3 and is perhaps a hymnic counterpart to it, contrasting the exalted Jesus with Melchizedek.

Heb

high priests, to offer sacrifice day after day,[a] first for his own sins and then for those of the people; he did that once for all when he offered himself.* [28] For the law appoints men subject to weakness to be high priests, but the word of the oath, which was taken after the law, appoints a son, who has been made perfect forever.[b]

CHAPTER 8

Heavenly Priesthood of Jesus.* [1] The main point of what has been said is this: we have such a high priest, who has taken his seat at the right hand of the throne of the Majesty in heaven,[c] [2] a minister of the sanctuary* and of the true tabernacle that the Lord, not man, set up.[d] [3] Now every high priest is appointed to offer gifts and sacrifices; thus the necessity for this one also to have something to offer.[e] [4] If then he were on earth, he would not be a priest, since there are those who offer gifts according to the law.[f] [5] They worship in a copy and shadow of the heavenly sanctuary, as Moses was warned when he was about to erect the tabernacle. For he says, "See that you make everything according to the pattern shown you on the mountain."[g] [6] Now he has obtained so much more excellent a ministry as he is mediator of a better covenant, enacted on better promises.[h]

Old and New Covenants.* [7] For if that first covenant had been faultless, no place would have been sought for a second one.

[8] But he finds fault with them and says:*

"Behold, the days are coming, says the Lord,[i]

when I will conclude a new covenant with the house of Israel and the house of Judah.

[9] It will not be like the covenant I made with their fathers

the day I took them by the hand to lead them forth from the land of Egypt;

for they did not stand by my covenant and I ignored them, says the Lord.

[10] But this is the covenant I will establish with the house of Israel

after those days, says the Lord:

I will put my laws in their minds and I will write them upon their hearts.

I will be their God, and they shall be my people.[j]

[11] And they shall not teach, each one his fellow citizen

and kinsman, saying, 'Know the Lord,'

for all shall know me, from least to greatest.

[12] For I will forgive their evildoing and remember their sins no more."

[13] [k] When he speaks of a "new" covenant, he declares the first one obsolete. And what has become obsolete and has grown old is close to disappearing.*

---

a Heb 5, 3; 9, 12.25-28; 10, 11-14; Ex 29, 38-39; Lv 16, 6.11.15-17; Nm 28, 3-4; Is 53, 10; Rom 6, 10.—b Heb 5, 1.2.9.—c Heb 1, 3; 4, 14; 7, 26-28.—d Heb 9, 11; Ex 33, 7; Nm 24, 6 LXX.—e Heb 5, 1.—f Heb 7, 13.—g Heb 9, 23; Ex 25, 40; Acts 7, 44; Col 2, 17.—h Heb 7, 22; 9, 15.—i Jer 31, 31-34.—j Heb 10, 16-17.—k Rom 10, 4.

7, 27: Such daily sacrifice is nowhere mentioned in the Mosaic law; only on the Day of Atonement is it prescribed that the high priest must *offer sacrifice . . . for his own sins and then for those of the people* (Lv 16, 11-19). *Once for all:* this translates the Greek words *ephapax/hapax* that occur eleven times in Heb.

8, 1-6: The Christian community has in Jesus the kind of high priest described in Heb 7, 26-28. In virtue of his ascension Jesus has taken his place at God's right hand in accordance with Ps 110, 1 (1), where he presides over the heavenly sanctuary established by God himself (2). Like every high priest, he has his offering to make (3; cf Heb 9, 12.14), but it differs from that of the levitical priesthood in which he had no share (4) and which was in any case but a shadowy reflection of the true offering in the heavenly sanctuary (5). But Jesus' ministry in the heavenly sanctuary is that of mediator of a superior covenant that accomplishes what it signifies (6).

8, 2: *The sanctuary:* the Greek term could also mean "holy things" but bears the meaning "sanctuary" elsewhere in Heb (Heb 9, 8.12.24.25; 10, 19; 13, 11). *The true tabernacle:* the heavenly tabernacle *that the Lord . . . set up* is contrasted with the earthly tabernacle that Moses set up in the desert. *True* means "real" in contradistinction to a mere "copy and shadow" (5); compare the Johannine usage (e.g., Jn 1, 9; 6, 32; 15, 1). The idea that the earthly sanctuary is a reflection of a heavenly model may be based upon Ex 25, 9, but probably also derives from the Platonic concept of a real world of which our observable world is merely a shadow.

8, 7-13: Since the first covenant was deficient in accomplishing what it signified, it had to be replaced (7), as Jeremiah (Jer 31, 31-34) had prophesied (8-12). Even in the time of Jeremiah, the first covenant was antiquated (13). In Heb 7, 22-24, the superiority of the new covenant was seen in the permanence of its priesthood; here the superiority is based on better promises, made explicit in the citation of Jer 31 (LXX: 38), 31-34, namely, in the immediacy of the people's knowledge of God (11) and in the forgiveness of sin (12).

8, 8-12: In citing Jer the author follows the Septuagint; some apparent departures from it may be the result of a different Septuagintal text rather than changes deliberately introduced.

8, 13: *Close to disappearing:* from the prophet's perspective, not that of the author of Heb.

CHAPTER 9

The Worship of the First Covenant.* [1] Now [even] the first covenant had regulations for worship and an earthly sanctuary. [2] For a tabernacle was constructed, the outer one,* in which were the lampstand, the table, and the bread of offering; this is called the Holy Place.*l* [3] Behind the second veil* was the tabernacle called the Holy of Holies,*m* [4] in which were the gold altar of incense* and the ark of the covenant entirely covered with gold. In it were the gold jar containing the manna, the staff of Aaron that had sprouted, and the tablets of the covenant.*n* [5] Above it were the cherubim of glory overshadowing the place of expiation.* Now is not the time to speak of these in detail.*o*

[6] With these arrangements for worship, the priests, in performing their service,* go into the outer tabernacle repeatedly,*p* [7] but the high priest alone goes into the inner one once a year, not without blood* that he offers for himself and for the sins of the people.*q* [8] In this way the holy Spirit shows that the way into the sanctuary had not yet been revealed while the outer tabernacle still had its place. [9] This is a symbol of the present time,* in which gifts and sacrifices are offered that cannot perfect the worshiper in conscience [10] but only in matters of food and drink and various ritual washings: regulations concerning the flesh, imposed until the time of the new order.*r*

Sacrifice of Jesus. [11] * But when Christ came as high priest of the good things that have come to be,* passing through the greater and more perfect tabernacle not made by hands, that is, not belonging to this creation,*s* [12] he entered once for all into the sanctuary, not with the blood of goats and calves but with his own blood, thus obtaining eternal redemption.*t* [13] For if the blood of goats and bulls and the sprinkling of a heifer's ashes* can sanctify those who are defiled so that their flesh is cleansed,*u* [14] how much more will the blood of Christ, who through the eternal spirit* offered himself unblemished to God, cleanse our consciences from dead works to worship the living God.*v*

---

l Ex 25, 23-30.—m Ex 26, 31-34.—n Ex 16, 32-34; 25, 10.16.21; 30, 1-10; Lv 16, 12-13; Nm 17, 2-7.16-26.—o Ex 25, 16-22; 26, 34; Lv 16, 14-15.—p Ex 27, 21; 30, 7; Lv 24, 8.—q Ex 30, 10; Lv 16, 1-14.—r Heb 13, 9; Lv 11; 14, 8; Nm 19, 11-21; Col 2, 16.—s Heb 4, 14; 10, 1.20.—t Heb 7, 27; Mt 26, 28.—u Heb 10, 4; Lv 16, 6-16; Nm, 19, 9.14-21.—v Heb 10, 10; Rom 5, 9; 1 Tm 3, 9; Ti 2, 14; 1 Pt 1, 18-19; 1 Jn 1, 7; Rv 1, 5.

9, 1-10: The regulations for worship under the old covenant permitted all the priests to enter the Holy Place (Heb 2, 6), but only the high priest to enter the Holy of Holies and then only once a year (3-5.7). The description of the sanctuary and its furnishings is taken essentially from Ex 25—26. This exclusion of the people from the Holy of Holies signified that they were not allowed to stand in God's presence (8) because their offerings and sacrifices, which were merely symbols of their need of spiritual renewal (10), could not obtain forgiveness of sins (9).

9, 2: *The outer one:* the author speaks of *the outer tabernacle* (6) and *the inner one* (7) rather than of one Mosaic tabernacle divided into two parts or sections.

9, 3: *The second veil:* what is meant is the veil that divided the Holy Place from the Holy of Holies. It is here called *the second,* because there was another veil at the entrance to the Holy Place, or "outer tabernacle" (Ex 26, 36).

9, 4: *The gold altar of incense:* Ex 30, 6 locates this altar in the Holy Place, i.e., the first tabernacle, rather than in the Holy of Holies. Neither is there any Old Testament support for the assertion that the jar of manna and the staff of Aaron were in the ark of the covenant. For the tablets of the covenant, see Ex 25, 16.

9, 5: *The place of expiation:* the gold "mercy seat" (Greek *hilastērion,* as in Rom 3, 25), where the blood of the sacrificial animals was sprinkled on the Day of Atonement (Lv 16, 14-15). This rite achieved "expiation" or atonement for the sins of the preceding year.

9, 6: *In performing their service:* the priestly services that had to be performed regularly in the Holy Place or *outer tabernacle* included burning incense on the incense altar twice each day (Ex 30, 7), replacing the loaves on the table of the bread of offering once each week (Lv 24, 8), and constantly caring for the lamps on the lampstand (Ex 27, 21).

9, 7: *Not without blood:* blood was essential to Old Testament sacrifice because it was believed that life was located in the blood. Hence blood was especially sacred, and its outpouring functioned as a meaningful symbol of cleansing from sin and reconciliation with God. Unlike Heb, the Old Testament never says that the blood is "offered." The author is perhaps retrojecting into his description of Mosaic ritual a concept that belongs to the New Testament antitype, as Paul does when he speaks of the Israelites' passage through the sea as a "baptism" (1 Cor 10, 2).

9, 9: *The present time:* this expression is equivalent to the "present age," used in contradistinction to the "age to come."

9, 11-14: Christ, the high priest of the spiritual blessings foreshadowed in the Old Testament sanctuary, has actually entered the true sanctuary of heaven that is not of human making (11). His place there is permanent, and his offering is his own blood that won eternal redemption (12). If the sacrifice of animals could bestow legal purification (13), how much more effective is the blood of the sinless, divine Christ who spontaneously offered himself to purge the human race of sin and render it fit for the service of God (14).

9, 11: *The good things that have come to be:* the majority of later manuscripts here read "the good things to come"; cf Heb 10, 1.

9, 13: *A heifer's ashes:* ashes from a red heifer that had been burned were mixed with water and used for the cleansing of those who had become ritually defiled by touching a corpse; see Nm 19, 9.14-21.

9, 14: *Through the eternal spirit:* this expression does not refer either to the holy Spirit or to the divine nature of Jesus but to the life of the risen Christ, "a life that cannot be destroyed" (Heb 7, 16).

Heb

¹⁵ * For this reason he is mediator of a new covenant: since a death has taken place for deliverance from transgressions under the first covenant, those who are called may receive the promised eternal inheritance.^w ¹⁶ * Now where there is a will, the death of the testator must be established. ¹⁷ For a will takes effect only at death; it has no force while the testator is alive. ¹⁸ Thus not even the first covenant was inaugurated without blood. ¹⁹ * When every commandment had been proclaimed by Moses to all the people according to the law, he took the blood of calves [and goats], together with water and crimson wool and hyssop, and sprinkled both the book itself and all the people,^x ²⁰ saying, "This is 'the blood of the covenant which God has enjoined upon you.' "^y ²¹ In the same way, he sprinkled also the tabernacle* and all the vessels of worship with blood.^z ²² According to the law almost everything is purified by blood,^a and without the shedding of blood there is no forgiveness.*

²³ * Therefore, it was necessary for the copies of the heavenly things to be purified by these rites, but the heavenly things themselves by better sacrifices than these.^b ²⁴ For Christ did not enter into a sanctuary made by hands, a copy of the true one, but heaven itself, that he might now appear before God on our behalf.^c ²⁵ Not that he might offer himself repeatedly, as the high priest enters each year into the sanctuary with blood that is not his own; ²⁶ if that were so, he would have had to suffer repeatedly from the foundation of the world. But now once for all he has appeared at the end of the ages* to take away sin by his sacrifice.^d ²⁷ Just as it is appointed that human beings die once, and after this the judgment,^e ²⁸ so also Christ, offered once to take away the sins of many,* will appear a second time, not to take away sin but to bring salvation to those who eagerly await him.^f

---

w 1 Tm 2, 5.—x Heb 9, 12-13.—y Ex 24, 3-8; Mt 26, 28; Mk 14, 24.—z Ex 40, 9; Lv 8, 15.19.—a Lv 17, 11.—b Jb 15, 15.—c Heb 7, 25; Rom 8, 34; 1 Jn 2, 1-2.—d Heb 7, 27; Jn 1, 29; Gal 4, 4.—e Gn 3, 19.—f Heb 10, 10; Is 53, 12.

9, 15-22: Jesus' role as *mediator of the new covenant* is based upon his sacrificial *death* (cf Heb 8, 6). His death has effected *deliverance from transgressions,* i.e., deliverance from sins committed under the old covenant, which the Mosaic sacrifices were incapable of effacing. Until this happened, the *eternal inheritance* promised by God could not be obtained (15). This effect of his work follows the human pattern by which a last will and testament becomes effective only with the death of the testator (16-17). The Mosaic covenant was also associated with death, for Moses made use of blood to seal the pact between God and the people (18-21). In Old Testament tradition, guilt could normally not be remitted without the use of blood (22; cf Lv 17, 11).

9, 16-17: *A will . . . death of the testator:* the same Greek word *diathēkē,* meaning "covenant" in vv 15 and 18, is used here with the meaning *will.* The new covenant, unlike the old, is at the same time a will that requires *the death of the testator.* Jesus as eternal Son is the one who established the new covenant together with his Father, author of both covenants; at the same time he is the testator whose death puts his *will* into effect.

9, 19-20: A number of details here are different from the description of this covenant rite in Ex 24, 5-8. Exodus mentions only calves ("young bulls," NAB), not goats (but this addition in Heb is of doubtful authenticity), says nothing of the use of *water and crimson wool and hyssop* (these features probably came from a different rite; cf Lv 14, 3-7; Nm 19, 6-18), and describes Moses as splashing blood on the altar, whereas Heb says he sprinkled it on the book (but both book and altar are meant to symbolize the agreement of God). The words of Moses are also slightly different from those in Exodus and are closer to the words of Jesus at the Last Supper in Mk 14, 24 // Mt 26, 28.

9, 21: According to Ex, the tabernacle did not yet exist at the time of the covenant rite. Moreover, nothing is said of sprinkling it with blood at its subsequent dedication (Ex 40, 9-11).

9, 22: *Without the shedding of blood there is no forgiveness:* in fact, ancient Israel did envisage other means of obtaining forgiveness; the Old Testament mentions contrition of heart (Ps 51, 19), fasting (Jl 2, 12), and almsgiving (Sir 3, 29). The author is limiting his horizon to the sacrificial cult, which did always involve the shedding of blood for its expiatory and unitive value.

9, 23-28: Since the blood of animals became a cleansing symbol among Old Testament prefigurations, it was necessary that the realities foreshadowed be brought into being by a shedding of blood that was infinitely more effective by reason of its worth (23). Christ did not simply prefigure the heavenly realities (24) by performing an annual sacrifice with a blood not his own (25); he offered the single sacrifice of himself as the final annulment of sin (26). Just as death is the unrepeatable act that ends a person's life, so Christ's offering of himself for all is the unrepeatable sacrifice that has once for all achieved redemption (27-28).

9, 26: *At the end of the ages:* the use of expressions such as this shows that the author of Heb, despite his interest in the Platonic concept of an eternal world above superior to temporal reality here below, nevertheless still clings to the Jewish Christian eschatology with its sequence of "the present age" and "the age to come."

9, 28: *To take away the sins of many:* the reference is to Is 53, 12. Since the Greek verb *anapherō* can mean both "to take away" and "to bear," the author no doubt intended to play upon both senses: Jesus took away sin by bearing it himself. See the similar wordplay in Jn 1, 29. *Many* is used in the Semitic meaning of "all" in the inclusive sense, as in Mk 14, 24. *To those who eagerly await him:* Jesus will appear *a second time* at the parousia, as the high priest reappeared on the Day of Atonement, emerging from the Holy of Holies, which he had entered *to take away sin.* This dramatic scene is described in Sir 50, 5-11.

CHAPTER 10

One Sacrifice instead of Many. [1] * Since the law has only a shadow of the good things to come,* and not the very image of them, it can never make perfect those who come to worship by the same sacrifices that they offer continually each year.[g] [2]Otherwise, would not the sacrifices have ceased to be offered, since the worshipers, once cleansed, would no longer have had any consciousness of sins? [3]But in those sacrifices there is only a yearly remembrance of sins,[h] [4]for it is impossible that the blood of bulls and goats take away sins.[i] [5]For this reason, when he came into the world, he said:*

"Sacrifice and offering you did not desire,[j]
    but a body you prepared for me;
[6] holocausts and sin offerings you took no delight in.
[7] Then I said, 'As is written of me in the scroll,
    Behold, I come to do your will, O God.' "

[8]First he says, "Sacrifices and offerings, holocausts and sin offerings,* you neither desired nor delighted in." These are offered according to the law.[k] [9]Then he says, "Behold, I come to do your will." He takes away the first to establish the second.[l] [10]By this "will," we have been consecrated through the offering of the body of Jesus Christ once for all.[m]

[11] * Every priest stands daily at his ministry, offering frequently those same sacrifices that can never take away sins.[n] [12]But this one offered one sacrifice for sins, and took his seat forever at the right hand of God;[o] [13]now he waits until his enemies are made his footstool.* [14]For by one offering he has made perfect forever those who are being consecrated.[p] [15]The holy Spirit also testifies to us, for after saying:*

[16] "This is the covenant I will establish with them after those days, says the Lord:
'I will put my laws in their hearts, and I will write them upon their minds,' "[q]

[17]he also says:*

"Their sins and their evildoing I will remember no more."[r]

[18]Where there is forgiveness of these, there is no longer offering for sin.

---

g Heb 8, 5; Col 2, 17.—h Lv 16, 21; Nm 5, 15 LXX.—i Is 1, 11; Mi 6, 6-8.— j 5-7: Ps 40, 7-9.—k Heb 10, 5-6; Ps 40, 7.—l Heb 10, 7; Ps 40, 8; Mt 26, 39; Mk 14, 36; Lk 22, 42; Jn 6, 38.—m Heb 9, 12.14.—n Heb 7, 27; Dt 10, 8; 18, 7.—o 12-13: Ps 110, 1.—p Heb 9, 28.—q Heb 8, 10; Jer 31, 33.—r Heb 8, 12; Jer 31, 34.

10, 1-10: Christian faith now realizes that the Old Testament sacrifices did not effect the spiritual benefits to come but only prefigured them (1). For if the sacrifices had actually effected the forgiveness of sin, there would have been no reason for their constant repetition (2). They were rather a continual reminder of the people's sins (3). It is not reasonable to suppose that human sins could be removed by the blood of animal sacrifices (4). Christ, therefore, is here shown to understand his mission in terms of Ps 40, 6-8, cited according to the Septuagint (5-7). Jesus acknowledged that the Old Testament sacrifices did not remit the sins of the people and so, perceiving the will of God, offered his own body for this purpose (8-10).

10, 1: *A shadow of the good things to come:* the term *shadow* was used in Heb 8, 5 to signify the earthly counterpart of the Platonic heavenly reality. But here it means a prefiguration of what is to come in Christ, as it is used in the Pauline literature; cf Col 2, 17.

10, 5-7: A passage from Ps 40, 7-9a is placed in the mouth of the Son at his incarnation. As usual, the author follows the Septuagint text. There is a notable difference in v 5 (= Ps 40, 7b), where the Masoretic text reads "ears you have dug for me" ("ears open to obedience you gave me," NAB), but most Septuagint manuscripts have "a body you prepared for me," a reading obviously more suited to the interpretation of Heb.

10, 8: *Sacrifices and offerings, holocausts and sin offerings:* these four terms taken from the preceding passage of Ps 40 (with the first two changed to plural forms) are probably intended as equivalents to the four principal types of Old Testament sacrifices: peace offerings (Lv 3, here called *sacrifices*); cereal offerings (Lv 2, here called *offerings*); holocausts (Lv 1); and *sin offerings* (Lv 4—5). This last category includes the guilt offerings of Lv 5, 14-26.

10, 11-18: Whereas the levitical priesthood offered daily sacrifices that were ineffectual in remitting sin (11), Jesus offered a single sacrifice that won him a permanent place at God's right hand. There he has only to await the final outcome of his work (12-13; cf Ps 110, 1). Thus he has brought into being in his own person the new covenant prophesied by Jeremiah (Jer 31, 33-34) that has rendered meaningless all other offerings for sin (14-18).

10, 13: *Until his enemies are made his footstool:* Ps 110, 1 is again used; the reference here is to the period of time between the enthronement of Jesus and his second coming. The identity of the *enemies* is not specified; cf 1 Cor 15, 25-27.

10, 15-17: The testimony of the scriptures is now invoked to support what has just preceded. The passage cited is a portion of the new covenant prophecy of Jer 31, 31-34, which the author previously used in Heb 8, 8-12.

10, 17: *He also says:* these words are not in the Greek text, which has only *kai*, "also," but the expression *after saying* in v 15 seems to require such a phrase to divide the Jeremiah text into two sayings. Others understand "the Lord says" of v 16 (here rendered *says the Lord*) as outside the quotation and consider v 16b as part of the second saying. Two ancient versions and a number of minuscules introduce the words "then he said" or a similar expression at the beginning of v 17.

Heb

Recalling the Past.* [19] Therefore, brothers, since through the blood of Jesus we have confidence of entrance into the sanctuary[s] [20] by the new and living way he opened for us through the veil,[t] that is, his flesh,* [21] [u] and since we have "a great priest over the house of God,"* [22] let us approach with a sincere heart and in absolute trust, with our hearts sprinkled clean from an evil conscience* and our bodies washed in pure water.[v] [23] Let us hold unwaveringly to our confession that gives us hope, for he who made the promise is trustworthy.[w] [24] We must consider how to rouse one another to love and good works. [25] We should not stay away from our assembly,* as is the custom of some, but encourage one another, and this all the more as you see the day drawing near.[x]

[26] [y] If we sin deliberately* after receiving knowledge of the truth, there no longer remains sacrifice for sins [27] but a fearful prospect of judgment and a flaming fire that is going to consume the adversaries.[z] [28] Anyone who rejects the law of Moses* is put to death without pity on the testimony of two or three witnesses.[a] [29] Do you not think that a much worse punishment is due the one who has contempt for the Son of God, considers unclean the covenant-blood by which he was consecrated, and insults the spirit of grace?[b] [30] We know the one who said:

"Vengeance is mine; I will repay,"

and again:

"The Lord will judge his people."[c]

[31] It is a fearful thing to fall into the hands of the living God.[d]

[32] Remember the days past when, after you had been enlightened,* you endured a great contest of suffering.[e] [33] At times you were publicly exposed to abuse and affliction; at other times you associated yourselves with those so treated.[f] [34] You even joined in the sufferings of those in prison and joyfully accepted the confiscation of your property, knowing that you had a better and lasting possession.[g] [35] Therefore, do not throw away your confidence; it will have great recompense.[h] [36] You need endurance to do the will of God and receive what he has promised.[i]

[37] "For, after just a brief moment,*
    he who is to come shall come;
    he shall not delay.[j]
[38] But my just one shall live by faith,
    and if he draws back I take no pleasure in him."[k]

[39] We are not among those who draw back and perish, but among those who have faith and will possess life.

s Heb 3, 6; 4, 16; 6, 19-20; Eph 1, 7; 3, 12.—t Jn 14, 6 / Heb 6, 19-20; 9, 8.11-12; Mt 27, 51; Mk 15, 38; Lk 23, 45.—u Heb 3, 6.—v Heb 9, 13-14; Ez 36, 25; 1 Cor 6, 11; Ti 3, 5; 1 Pt 3, 21.—w Heb 3, 1.6; 4, 14; 1 Cor 10, 13.—x Rom 13, 12; 1 Cor 3, 13.—y Heb 3, 12; 6, 4-8.—z Heb 10, 31; 9, 27; Is 26, 11 LXX; Zep 1, 18.—a Dt 17, 6.—b Heb 6, 6.—c Dt 32, 35.36; Rom 12, 19.—d Heb 10, 27; Mt 10, 28; Lk 12, 4-5.—e Heb 6, 4.—f 1 Cor 4, 9.—g Heb 13, 3; Mt 6, 19-20; Lk 12, 33-34.—h Heb 4, 16.—i Lk 21, 19.—j Is 26, 20; Hb 2, 3.—k Hb 2, 4; Rom 1, 17; Gal 3, 11.

10, 19-39: Practical consequences from these reflections on the priesthood and the sacrifice of Christ should make it clear that Christians may now have direct and confident access to God through the person of Jesus (19-20), who rules God's house as high priest (21). They should approach God with sincerity and faith, in the knowledge that through baptism their sins have been remitted (22), reminding themselves of the hope they expressed in Christ at that event (23). They are to encourage one another to Christian love and activity (24), not refusing, no matter what the reason, to participate in the community's assembly, especially in view of the parousia (25; cf 1 Thes 4, 13-18). If refusal to participate in the assembly indicates rejection of Christ, no sacrifice exists to obtain forgiveness for so great a sin (26); only the dreadful judgment of God remains (27). For if violation of the Mosaic law could be punished by death, how much worse will be the punishment of those who have turned their backs on Christ by despising his sacrifice and disregarding the gifts of the holy Spirit (28-29). Judgment belongs to the Lord, and he enacts it by his living presence (30-31). There was a time when the spirit of their community caused them to welcome and share their sufferings (32-34). To revitalize that spirit is to share in the courage of the Old Testament prophets (cf Is 26, 20; Hb 2, 3-4), the kind of courage that must distinguish the faith of the Christian (35-39).

10, 20: *Through the veil, that is, his flesh:* the term *flesh* is used pejoratively. As the temple veil kept people from entering the Holy of Holies (it was rent at Christ's death, Mk 15, 38), so the flesh of Jesus constituted an obstacle to approaching God.

10, 21: *The house of God:* this refers back to Heb 3, 6, "we are his house."

10, 22: *With our hearts sprinkled clean from an evil conscience:* as in Heb 9, 13 (see the note there), the sprinkling motif refers to the Mosaic rite of cleansing from ritual impurity. This could produce only an external purification, whereas sprinkling with the blood of Christ (Heb 9, 14) cleanses the *conscience. Washed in pure water:* baptism is elsewhere referred to as a washing; cf 1 Cor 6, 11; Eph 5, 26.

10, 25: *Our assembly:* the liturgical *assembly* of the Christian community, probably for the celebration of the Eucharist. *The day:* this designation for the parousia also occurs in the Pauline letters, e.g., Rom 2, 16; 1 Cor 3, 13; 1 Thes 5, 2.

10, 26: *If we sin deliberately:* verse 29 indicates that the author is here thinking of apostasy; cf Heb 3, 12; 6, 4-8.

10, 28: *Rejects the law of Moses:* evidently not any sin against the law, but idolatry. Dt 17, 2-7 prescribed capital punishment for idolaters who were convicted on the testimony of two or three witnesses.

10, 32: *After you had been enlightened:* "enlightenment" is an ancient metaphor for baptism (cf Eph 5, 14; Jn 9, 11), but see Heb 6, 4 and the note there.

10, 37-38: In support of his argument, the author uses Hb 2, 3-4 in a wording almost identical with the text of the Codex Alexandrinus of the Septuagint but with the first and second lines of v 4 inverted. He introduces it with a few words from Is 26, 20: *after just a brief moment.* Note the Pauline usage of Hb 2, 4 in Rom 1, 17; Gal 3, 11.

V. EXAMPLES, DISCIPLINE, DISOBEDIENCE

CHAPTER 11*

Faith of the Ancients. [1] Faith is the realization of what is hoped for and evidence* of things not seen.[l] [2] Because of it the ancients were well attested. [3] [m] By faith we understand that the universe was ordered by the word of God,* so that what is visible came into being through the invisible. [4] * By faith Abel offered to God a sacrifice greater than Cain's. Through this he was attested to be righteous, God bearing witness to his gifts, and through this, though dead, he still speaks.[n] [5] By faith Enoch was taken up so that he should not see death, and "he was found no more because God had taken him." Before he was taken up, he was attested to have pleased God.[o] [6] But without faith it is impossible to please him,[p] for anyone who approaches God must believe that he exists and that he rewards those who seek him.* [7] By faith Noah, warned about what was not yet seen, with reverence built an ark for the salvation of his household. Through this he condemned the world and inherited the righteousness that comes through faith.[q]

[8] By faith Abraham obeyed when he was called to go out to a place that he was to re-ceive as an inheritance; he went out, not knowing where he was to go.[r] [9] By faith he sojourned in the promised land as in a foreign country, dwelling in tents with Isaac and Jacob, heirs of the same promise;[s] [10] for he was looking forward to the city with foundations, whose architect and maker is God.[t] [11] By faith he received power to generate, even though he was past the normal age—and Sarah herself was sterile—for he thought that the one who had made the promise was trustworthy.[u] [12] So it was that there came forth from one man, himself as good as dead, descendants as numerous as the stars in the sky and as countless as the sands on the seashore.[v]

[13] All these died in faith. They did not receive what had been promised but saw it and greeted it from afar and acknowledged themselves to be strangers and aliens on earth,[w] [14] for those who speak thus show that they are seeking a homeland. [15] If they had been thinking of the land from which they had come, they would have had opportunity to return. [16] But now they desire a better homeland, a heavenly one. Therefore, God is not ashamed to be called their God, for he has prepared a city for them.[x]

[17] By faith Abraham, when put to the test, offered up Isaac, and he who had received the promises was ready to offer his only son,[y] [18] of whom it was said, "Through Isaac descendants shall bear

---

l Heb 1, 3; 3, 14; Rom 8, 24; 2 Cor 4, 18.—m Gn 1, 3; Ps 33, 6; Wis 9, 1; Jn 1, 3.—n Heb 12, 24; Gn 4, 4.10.—o Gn 5, 24; Sir 44, 16.—p Wis 4, 10.—q Gn 6, 8-22; Sir 44, 17-18; Mt 24, 37-39; Lk 17, 26-27; 1 Pt 3, 20; 2, Pt 2, 5.—r Gn 12, 1-4; 15, 7-21; Sir 44, 19-22; Acts 7, 2-8; Rom 4, 16-22.—s Gn 12, 8; 13, 12; 23, 4; 26, 3; 35, 27.—t Heb 12, 22; 13, 14; Rv 21, 10-22.—u Gn 17, 19; 21, 2; Rom 4, 19-21 / 1 Cor 10, 13.—v Gn 15, 5; 22, 17; 32, 13; Ex 32, 13; Dt 10, 22; Dn 3, 36 LXX.—w Gn 23, 4; Ps 39, 13.—x Heb 13, 14; Ex 3, 6.—y Gn 22, 1-10; Sir 44, 20; 1 Mc 2, 52; Jas 2, 21.

11, 1-40: This chapter draws upon the people and events of the Old Testament to paint an inspiring portrait of religious faith, firm and unyielding in the face of any obstacles that confront it. These pages rank among the most eloquent and lofty to be found in the Bible. They expand the theme announced in Heb 6, 12, to which the author now returns (Heb 10, 39). The material of this chapter is developed chronologically. Verses 3-7 draw upon the first nine chapters of Gn; vv 8-22, upon the period of the patriarchs; vv 23-31, upon the time of Moses; vv 32-38, upon the history of the judges, the prophets, and the Maccabean martyrs. The author gives the most extensive description of faith provided in the New Testament, though his interest does not lie in a technical, theological definition. In view of the needs of his audience he describes what authentic faith does, not what it is in itself. Through faith God guarantees the blessings to be hoped for from him, providing evidence in the gift of faith that what he promises will eventually come to pass (1). Because they accepted in faith God's guarantee of the future, the biblical personages discussed in vv 3-38 were themselves commended by God (2). Christians have even greater reason to remain firm in faith since they, unlike the Old Testament men and women of faith, have perceived the beginning of God's fulfillment of his messianic promises (39-40).

11, 1: *Faith is the realization . . . evidence:* the author is not attempting a precise definition. There is dispute about the meaning of the Greek words *hypostasis* and *elenchos,* here translated *realization* and *evidence,* respectively. *Hypostasis* usually means "substance," "being" (as translated in Heb 1, 3), or "reality" (as translated in Heb 3, 14); here it connotes something more subjective, and so *realization* has been chosen rather than "assurance" (RSV). *Elenchos,* usually "proof," is used here in an objective sense and so translated *evidence* rather than the transferred sense of "(inner) conviction" (RSV).

11, 3: *By faith . . . God:* this verse does not speak of the faith of the Old Testament men and women but is in the first person plural. Hence it seems out of place in the sequence of thought.

11, 4: The "Praise of the Ancestors" in Sir 44, 1—50, 21 gives a similar list of heroes. The Cain and Abel narrative in Gn 4, 1-16 does not mention Abel's faith. It says, however, that God "looked with favor on Abel and his offering" (Gn 4, 4); in view of v 6 the author probably understood God's favor to have been activated by Abel's faith. *Though dead, he still speaks:* possibly because his blood "cries out to me from the soil" (Gn 4, 10), but more probably a way of saying that the repeated story of Abel provides ongoing witness to faith.

11, 6: One must believe not only that God *exists* but that he is concerned about human conduct; the Old Testament defines folly as the denial of this truth; cf Ps 52, 2.

your name."[z] [19]He reasoned that God was able to raise even from the dead,[a] and he received Isaac back as a symbol.* [20]By faith regarding things still to come Isaac* blessed Jacob and Esau.[b] [21]By faith Jacob, when dying, blessed each of the sons of Joseph and "bowed in worship, leaning on the top of his staff."[c] [22]By faith Joseph, near the end of his life, spoke of the Exodus of the Israelites and gave instructions about his bones.[d]

[23] [e] By faith Moses was hidden by his parents for three months after his birth, because they saw that he was a beautiful child, and they were not afraid of the king's edict. [24] * By faith Moses, when he had grown up, refused to be known as the son of Pharaoh's daughter;[f] [25]he chose to be ill-treated along with the people of God rather than enjoy the fleeting pleasure of sin. [26]He considered the reproach of the Anointed greater wealth than the treasures of Egypt, for he was looking to the recompense. [27]By faith he left Egypt, not fearing the king's fury, for he persevered as if seeing the one who is invisible.[g] [28]By faith he kept the Passover and sprinkled the blood, that the Destroyer of the firstborn might not touch them.[h] [29]By faith they crossed the Red Sea as if it were dry land, but when the Egyptians attempted it they were drowned.[i] [30]By faith the walls of Jericho fell after being encircled for seven days.[j] [31]By faith Rahab the harlot did not perish with the disobedient, for she had received the spies in peace.[k]

[32]What more shall I say? I have not time to tell of Gideon, Barak, Samson, Jephthah, of David and Samuel and the prophets,[l] [33]who by faith conquered kingdoms, did what was righteous, obtained the promises; they closed the mouths of lions,[m] [34]put out raging fires, escaped the devouring sword; out of weakness they were made powerful, became strong in battle, and turned back foreign invaders.[n] [35]Women received back their dead through resurrection. Some were tortured and would not accept deliverance, in order to obtain a better resurrection.[o] [36]Others endured mockery, scourging, even chains and imprisonment.[p] [37]They were stoned, sawed in two, put to death at sword's point; they went about in skins of sheep or goats, needy, afflicted, tormented.[q] [38]The world was not worthy of them. They wandered about in deserts and on mountains, in caves and in crevices in the earth.[r]

[39]Yet all these, though approved because of their faith, did not receive what had been promised. [40]God had foreseen something better for us, so that without us they should not be made perfect.*

CHAPTER 12

God our Father.* [1]Therefore, since we are surrounded by so great a cloud of witnesses, let us rid ourselves of every burden and sin that clings to us* and persevere in running the race that lies before us [2]while keeping our eyes fixed on Jesus, the leader and perfecter of faith. For the sake of the joy that lay before him he endured the cross, despising its shame, and has taken his seat at the right of the throne of God.[s] [3]Consider how he endured such opposition from sinners, in order that you may not grow weary and lose heart. [4]In your struggle against sin you have not yet resisted to

z Gn 21, 12 LXX; Rom 9, 7.—a Rom 4, 16-22.—b Gn 27, 27-40.—c Gn 27, 38-40; 47, 31 LXX; 48, 15-16.—d Gn 50, 24-25.—e Ex 2, 2; Acts 7, 20.—f 24-25: Ex 2, 10-15; Acts 7, 23-29.—g Ex 2, 15; Acts 7, 29.—h Ex 12, 21-23; Wis 18, 25; 1 Cor 10, 10.—i Ex 14, 22-28.—j Jos 6, 12-21.—k Jos 2, 1-21; 6, 22-25; Jas 2, 25.—l Jgs 4, 6-22; 6, 11—8, 32; 11, 1—12, 7.—m Dn 6, 23.—n Dn 3, 22-25.49-50.—o 1 Kgs 17, 17-24; 2 Kgs 4, 18-37; 2 Mc 6, 18—7, 42.—p 2 Chr 36, 16; Jer 20, 2; 37, 15.—q Chr 24, 21.—r 1 Mc 2, 28-30.—s Heb 2, 10; Ps 110, 1; Phil 2, 6-8.

11, 19: *As a symbol:* Isaac's "return from death" is seen as a *symbol* of Christ's resurrection. Others understand the words *en parabolē* to mean "in figure," i.e., the word *dead* is used figuratively of Isaac, since he did not really die. But in the one other place that *parabolē* occurs in Heb, it means symbol (Heb 9, 9).

11, 20-22: Each of these three patriarchs, Isaac, Jacob, and Joseph, had faith in the future fulfillment of God's promise and renewed this faith when near death.

11, 24-27: The reason given for Moses' departure from Egypt differs from the account in Ex 2, 11-15. The author also gives a christological interpretation of his decision to share the trials of his people.

11, 40: *So that without us they should not be made perfect:* the heroes of the Old Testament obtained their recompense only after the saving work of Christ had been accomplished. Thus they already enjoy what Christians who are still struggling do not yet possess in its fullness.

12, 1-13: Christian life is to be inspired not only by the Old Testament men and women of faith (1) but above all by Jesus. As the architect of Christian faith, he had himself to endure the cross before receiving the glory of his triumph (2). Reflection on his sufferings should give his followers courage to continue the struggle, if necessary even to the shedding of blood (3-4). Christians should regard their own sufferings as the affectionate correction of the Lord, who loves them as a father loves his children.

12, 1: *That clings to us:* the meaning is uncertain, since the Greek word *euperistatos,* translated *cling,* occurs only here. The papyrus P46 and one minuscule read *euperispastos,* "easily distracting," which also makes good sense.

the point of shedding blood. ⁵You have
also forgotten the exhortation addressed to
you as sons:

"My son, do not disdain the discipline
of the Lord[t]
or lose heart when reproved by him;
⁶ for whom the Lord loves, he disciplines;
he scourges every son he acknowledges."

⁷Endure your trials as "discipline"; God
treats you as sons. For what "son" is there
whom his father does not discipline?[u] ⁸If
you are without discipline, in which all
have shared, you are not sons but bastards.
⁹Besides this, we have had our earthly
fathers to discipline us, and we respected
them. Should we not [then] submit all the
more to the Father of spirits and live?[v]
¹⁰They disciplined us for a short time as
seemed right to them, but he does so for
our benefit, in order that we may share his
holiness. ¹¹At the time, all discipline seems
a cause not for joy but for pain, yet later it
brings the peaceful fruit of righteousness
to those who are trained by it.[w]

¹²So strengthen your drooping hands
and your weak knees.[x] ¹³Make straight
paths for your feet, that what is lame may
not be dislocated but healed.[y]

Penalties of Disobedience. ¹⁴ [z] Strive for
peace with everyone, and for that holiness
without which no one will see the Lord. ¹⁵
* See to it that no one be deprived of the
grace of God, that no bitter root spring up
and cause trouble, through which many
may become defiled,[a] ¹⁶that no one be an
immoral or profane person like Esau, who
sold his birthright for a single meal.[b] ¹⁷For

you know that later, when he wanted to inherit his father's blessing, he was rejected
because he found no opportunity to change
his mind, even though he sought the blessing with tears.[c]

¹⁸ * You have not approached that
which could be touched[d] and a blazing fire
and gloomy darkness and storm* ¹⁹and a
trumpet blast and a voice speaking words
such that those who heard begged that no
message be further addressed to them,[e]
²⁰for they could not bear to hear the command: "If even an animal touches the
mountain, it shall be stoned."[f] ²¹Indeed,
so fearful was the spectacle that Moses
said, "I am terrified and trembling."[g]
²²No, you have approached Mount Zion
and the city of the living God, the heavenly
Jerusalem, and countless angels in festal
gathering,[h] ²³and the assembly of the
firstborn enrolled in heaven,* and God the
judge of all, and the spirits of the just made
perfect,[i] ²⁴and Jesus, the mediator of a
new covenant, and the sprinkled blood
that speaks more eloquently* than that of
Abel.[j]

²⁵See that you do not reject the one who
speaks. For if they did not escape when
they refused the one who warned them on
earth, how much more in our case if we
turn away from the one who warns from
heaven.[k] ²⁶His voice shook the earth at
that time, but now he has promised, "I will
once more shake not only earth but
heaven."[l] ²⁷That phrase, "once more,"
points to [the] removal of shaken, created
things, so that what is unshaken may remain.[m] ²⁸Therefore, we who are receiving
the unshakable kingdom should have

---

t 5-6: Prv 3, 11-12 / Dt 8, 5; 1 Cor 11, 32.—u Prv 13, 24; Sir
30, 1.—v Nm 16, 22; 27, 16 LXX.—w 2 Cor 4, 17; Phil 1, 11;
Jas 3, 18.—x Is 35, 3; Sir 25, 23; Jb 4, 3-4.—y Prv 4, 26
LXX.—z Rom 12, 18; 14, 19.—a Dt 29, 18 (17 LXX).—b Gn 25,
33.—c Gn 27, 34-38.—d Ex 19, 12-14; Dt 4, 11; 5, 22-23.—e
Ex 19, 16.19; 20, 18-19.—f Ex 19, 12-13.—g Dt 9, 19.—h Gal
4, 26; Rv 21, 2.—i Lk 10, 20; Rv 5, 11.—j Heb 7, 22; 8, 6; 9,
15 / Heb 11, 4; Gn 4, 10.—k Ex 20, 19.—l Ex 19, 18; Jgs 5, 4-5;
Ps 68, 9; Hg 2, 6.—m Is 66, 22; Mt 24, 35; Mk 13, 31; Lk 21,
33.

12, 15-17: Esau serves as an example in two ways: his *profane* attitude illustrates the danger of apostasy, and his inability
to secure a blessing afterward illustrates the impossibility of repenting after falling away (see Heb 6, 4-6).

12, 18-29: As a final appeal for adherence to Christian teaching, the two covenants, of Moses and of Christ, are compared. The
Mosaic covenant, the author argues, is shown to have originated
in fear of God and threats of divine punishment (18-21). The covenant in Christ gives us direct access to God (22), makes us members of the Christian community, God's children, a sanctified

people (23), who have Jesus as mediator to speak for us (24). Not
to heed the voice of the risen Christ is a graver sin than the rejection of the word of Moses (25-26). Though Christians fall away,
God's kingdom in Christ will remain and his justice will punish
those guilty of deserting it (28-29).

12, 18-24: This remarkably beautiful passage contrasts two
great assemblies of people: that of the Israelites gathered at
Mount Sinai for the sealing of the old covenant and the promulgation of the Mosaic law, and that of the followers of Jesus gathered
at *Mount Zion, the heavenly Jerusalem,* the assembly of the
new covenant. This latter scene, marked by the presence of
countless angels and of *Jesus* with his redeeming *blood,* is
reminiscent of the celestial liturgies of the Book of Revelation.

12, 23: *The assembly of the firstborn enrolled in heaven:*
this expression may refer to the angels of v 22, or to the heroes
of the Old Testament (see ch 11), or to the entire assembly of the
new covenant.

12, 24: *Speaks more eloquently:* the blood of Abel, the first
human blood to be shed, is contrasted with that of Jesus. Abel's
blood cried out from the earth for vengeance, but the blood of
Jesus has opened the way for everyone, providing cleansing and
access to God (Heb 10, 19).

Heb

gratitude, with which we should offer worship pleasing to God in reverence and awe.[n] [29] For our God is a consuming fire.[o]

VI. FINAL EXHORTATION, BLESSING, GREETINGS

CHAPTER 13

[1] * Let mutual love continue. [2] Do not neglect hospitality, for through it some have unknowingly entertained angels.[p] [3] Be mindful of prisoners as if sharing their imprisonment, and of the ill-treated as of yourselves, for you also are in the body.[q] [4] Let marriage be honored among all and the marriage bed be kept undefiled, for God will judge the immoral and adulterers.[r] [5] Let your life be free from love of money but be content with what you have, for he has said, "I will never forsake you or abandon you."[s] [6] Thus we may say with confidence:

"The Lord is my helper,
[and] I will not be afraid.
What can anyone do to me?"[t]

[7] Remember your leaders who spoke the word of God to you. Consider the outcome of their way of life and imitate their faith. [8] Jesus Christ is the same yesterday, today, and forever.[u]

[9] Do not be carried away by all kinds of strange teaching.* It is good to have our hearts strengthened by grace and not by foods, which do not benefit those who live by them.[v] [10] We have an altar* from which those who serve the tabernacle have no right to eat. [11] The bodies of the animals whose blood the high priest brings into the sanctuary as a sin offering are burned outside the camp.[w] [12] Therefore, Jesus also suffered outside the gate, to consecrate the people by his own blood.[x] [13] Let us then go to him outside the camp, bearing the reproach that he bore. [14] For here we have no lasting city, but we seek the one that is to come.[y] [15] Through him [then] let us continually offer God a sacrifice of praise, that is, the fruit of lips that confess his name.[z] [16] Do not neglect to do good and to share what you have; God is pleased by sacrifices of that kind.[a]

[17] * Obey your leaders and defer to them, for they keep watch over you and will have to give an account, that they may fulfill their task with joy and not with sorrow, for that would be of no advantage to you.

[18] Pray for us, for we are confident that we have a clear conscience, wishing to act rightly in every respect. [19] I especially ask for your prayers that I may be restored to you very soon.

[20] * May the God of peace, who brought up from the dead the great shepherd of the sheep by the blood of the eternal covenant, Jesus our Lord,[b] [21] furnish you with all that is good, that you may do his will. May he carry out in you what is pleasing to him through Jesus Christ, to whom be glory forever [and ever]. Amen.

[22] Brothers, I ask you to bear with this message of encouragement, for I have written to you rather briefly. [23] I must let you know that our brother Timothy has been set free. If he comes soon, I shall see you together with him.[c] [24] Greetings to all your leaders and to all the holy ones. Those from Italy send you greetings. [25] Grace be with all of you.[d]

---

n Dn 7, 14.18 / Rom 1, 9.—o Dt 4, 24; Is 33, 14.—p Gn 18, 3; 19, 2-3; Jgs 6, 11-22; Tb 5, 4.—q Mt 25, 36.—r 1 Cor 5, 13; Eph 5, 5.—s Dt 31, 6.8; Jos 1, 5.—t Pss 27, 1-3; 118, 6.—u Heb 1, 12; 7, 24; Rv 1, 17.—v Rom 14, 17; 1 Cor 8, 8; Eph 4, 14; Col 2, 16.—w Ex 29, 14; Lv 16, 27.—x Mt 21, 39; Mk 12, 8; Lk 20, 15; Jn 19, 17.—y Heb 11, 10.14.—z Hos 14, 3.—a Phil 4, 18.—b Is 63, 11; Zec 9, 11; Jn 10, 11; Acts 2, 24; Rom 15, 33.—c Acts 16, 1.—d Ti 3, 15.

13, 1-16: After recommendations on social and moral matters (1-6), the letter turns to doctrinal issues. The fact that the original leaders are dead should not cause the recipients of this letter to lose their faith (7), for Christ still lives and he remains always the same (8). They must not rely for their personal sanctification on regulations concerning foods (9), nor should they entertain the notion that Judaism and Christianity can be intermingled (10; cf the notes on Gal 2, 11-14 and Gal 2, 15-21). As Jesus died separated from his own people, so must the Christian community remain apart from the religious doctrines of Judaism (11-14). Christ must be the heart and center of the community (15-16).

13, 9: *Strange teaching:* this doctrine about *foods* probably refers to the Jewish food laws; in view of v 10, however, the author may be thinking of the Mosaic sacrificial banquets.

13, 10: *We have an altar:* this does not refer to the Eucharist, which is never clearly mentioned in Heb, but to the sacrifice of Christ.

13, 17-25: Recommending obedience to the leaders of the community, the author asks for prayers (17-19). The letter concludes with a blessing (20-21), a final request for the acceptance of its message (22), information regarding Timothy (23), and general greetings (24-25).

13, 20-21: These verses constitute one of the most beautiful blessings in the New Testament. The resurrection of Jesus is presupposed throughout Heb, since it is included in the author's frequently expressed idea of his exaltation, but this is the only place where it is explicitly mentioned.

THE CATHOLIC LETTERS

In addition to the thirteen letters attributed to Paul and the Letter to the Hebrews, the New Testament contains seven other letters. Three of these are attributed to John, two to Peter, and one each to James and Jude, all personages of the apostolic age. The term "catholic letter" first appears, with reference only to 1 John, in the writings of Apollonius of Ephesus, a second-century apologist, known only from a citation in Eusebius' *Ecclesiastical History*. Eusebius himself (A.D. 260-340) used the term to refer to all seven letters.

The reason for the term "catholic," which means "universal," was the perception that these letters, unlike those of Paul, which were directed to a particular local church, were apparently addressed more generally to the universal church. This designation is not entirely accurate, however. On the one hand, Hebrews has no specifically identified addressees, and originally this was probably true of Ephesians as well. On the other hand, 3 John is addressed to a named individual, 2 John to a specific, though unnamed, community, and 1 Peter to a number of churches that are specified as being located in Asia Minor.

While all seven of these writings begin with an epistolary formula, several of them do not appear to be real letters in the modern sense of the term. In the ancient world it was not unusual to cast an exhortation in the form of a letter for literary effect, a phenomenon comparable to the "open letter" that is sometimes used today.

With the exception of 1 Peter and 1 John, the ancient church showed reluctance to include the catholic letters in the New Testament canon. The reason for this was widespread doubt whether they had actually been written by the apostolic figures to whom they are attributed. The early Christians saw the New Testament as the depository of apostolic faith; therefore, they wished to include only the testimony of apostles. Today we distinguish more clearly between the authorship of a work and its canonicity: even though written by other, later witnesses than those whose names they bear, these writings nevertheless testify to the apostolic faith and constitute canonical scripture. By the late fourth or early fifth centuries, most objections had been overcome in both the Greek and the Latin churches (though not in the Syriac), and all seven of the catholic letters have since been acknowledged as canonical.

THE LETTER OF JAMES
INTRODUCTION

The person to whom this letter is ascribed can scarcely be one of the two members of the Twelve who bore the name James (see Mt 10, 2-3; Mk 3, 17-18; Lk 6, 14-15), for he is not identified as an apostle but only as "slave of God and of the Lord Jesus Christ" (1, 1). This designation most probably refers to the third New Testament personage named James, a relative of Jesus who is usually called "brother of the Lord" (see Mt 13, 55; Mk 6, 3). He was the leader of the Jewish Christian community in Jerusalem whom Paul acknowledged as one of the "pillars" (Gal 2, 9). In Acts he appears as the authorized spokesman for the Jewish Christian position in the early Church (Acts 12, 17; 15, 13-21). According to the Jewish historian Josephus (Antiquities 20, 9, 1 §§200-203), he was stoned to death by the Jews under the high priest Ananus II in A.D. 62.

The letter is addressed to "the twelve tribes in the dispersion." In Old Testament terminology the term "twelve tribes" designates the people of Israel; the "dispersion" or "diaspora" refers to the non-Palestinian Jews who had settled throughout the Greco-Roman world (see Jn 7, 35). Since in Christian thought the church is the new Israel, the address probably designates the Jewish Christian churches located in Palestine, Syria, and elsewhere. Or perhaps the letter is meant more generally for all Christian communities, and the "dispersion" has the symbolic meaning of exile from our true home, as it has in the address of 1 Peter (1, 1). The letter is so markedly Jewish in character that some scholars have regarded it as a Jewish document subsequently "baptized" by a few Christian insertions, but such an origin is scarcely tenable in view of the numerous contacts discernible between the Letter of James and other New Testament literature.

From the viewpoint of its literary form, James is a letter only in the most conventional sense; it has none of the characteristic features of a real letter except the address. It belongs rather to the genre of parenesis or exhortation and is concerned almost exclusively with ethical conduct. It therefore falls within the tradition of Jewish wisdom literature, such as can be found in the Old Testament (Proverbs, Sirach) and in the extracanonical Jewish literature (Testaments of the Twelve Patriarchs, the Books of Enoch, the Manual of Discipline found at Qumran). More specifically, it consists of sequences of didactic proverbs, comparable to Tb 4, 5-19, to many passages in Sirach, and to sequences of sayings in the synoptic gospels. Numerous passages in James treat of subjects that also appear in the synoptic sayings of Jesus, especially in Matthew's Sermon on the Mount, but the correspondences are too general to establish any literary dependence. James represents a type of early Christianity that emphasized sound teaching and responsible moral behavior. Ethical norms are derived not primarily from christology, as in Paul, but from a concept of salvation that involves conversion, baptism, forgiveness of sin, and expectation of judgment (1, 17; 4, 12).

Paradoxically, this very Jewish work is written in an excellent Greek style, which ranks among the best in the New Testament and appears to be the work of a trained Hellenistic writer. Those who continue to regard James of Jerusalem as its author are therefore obliged to suppose that a secretary must have put the letter into its present literary form. This assumption is not implausible in the light of ancient practice. Some regard the letter as one of the earliest writings in the New Testament and feel that its content accurately reflects what we would expect of the leader of Jewish Christianity. Moreover, they argue that the type of Jewish Christianity reflected in the letter cannot be situated historically after the fall of Jerusalem in A.D. 70.

Others, however, believe it more likely that James is a pseudonymous work of a later period. In addition to its Greek style, they observe further that (a) the prestige that the writer is assumed to enjoy points to the later legendary reputation of James; (b) the discussion of the importance of good works seems to presuppose a debate subsequent to that in Paul's own day; (c) the author does not rely upon prescriptions of the Mosaic law, as we would expect from the historical James; (d) the letter contains no allusions to James's own history and to his relationship with Jesus or to the early Christian community of Jerusalem. For these reasons, many recent interpreters assign James to the period A.D. 90-100.

The principal divisions of the Letter of James are the following:

    I.   Address (1, 1)
    II. The Value of Trials and Temptation (1, 2-18)
    III. Exhortations and Warnings (1, 19—5, 12)
    IV. The Power of Prayer (5, 13-20)

I. ADDRESS

CHAPTER 1

 ¹ James, a slave of God and of the Lord Jesus Christ,* to the twelve tribes in the dispersion, greetings.ᵃ

II. THE VALUE OF TRIALS AND TEMPTATION

Perseverance in Trial. ² ᵇ Consider it all joy, my brothers, when you encounter various trials,* ³ for you know that the testing* of your faith produces perseverance. ⁴ And let perseverance be perfect, so that you may be perfect and complete, lacking in nothing. ⁵ But if any of you lacks wisdom,* he should ask God who gives to all generously and ungrudgingly, and he will be given it.ᶜ ⁶ But he should ask in faith, not doubting, for the one who doubts is like a wave of the sea that is driven and tossed about by the wind.ᵈ ⁷ For that person must not suppose that he will receive anything from the Lord, ⁸ since he is a man of two minds, unstable in all his ways.

⁹ The brother in lowly circumstances* should take pride in his high standing,ᵉ ¹⁰ and the rich one in his lowliness, for he will pass away "like the flower of the field."ᶠ ¹¹ For the sun comes up with its scorching heat and dries up the grass, its flower droops, and the beauty of its appearance vanishes. So will the rich person fade away in the midst of his pursuits.

Temptation. ¹² ᵍ Blessed is the man who perseveres in temptation,* for when he has been proved he will receive the crown of life that he promised to those who love him. ¹³ * No one experiencing temptation should say, "I am being tempted by God"; for God is not subject to temptation to evil, and he himself tempts no one.ʰ ¹⁴ Rather, each person is tempted when he is lured and enticed by his own desire. ¹⁵ Then desire conceives and brings forth sin, and when sin reaches maturity it gives birth to death.

---

a Jn 7, 35; 1 Pt 1, 1.—b Rom 5, 3-5; 1 Pt 1, 6; 4, 13-16.—c Prv 2, 2-6; Wis 9, 4.9-12.—d Mt 7, 7; Mk 11, 24.—e Jas 2, 5.— f Is 40, 6-7.—g 1 Cor 9, 25; 2 Tm 4, 8; 1 Pt 5, 4; Rv 2, 10.—h Sir 15, 11-20; 1 Cor 10, 13.

1, 1: *James, a slave of God and of the Lord Jesus Christ:* a declaration of the writer's authority for instructing the Christian communities; cf Rom 1, 1. Regarding the identity of the author, see Introduction. *Dispersion:* see Introduction.

1, 2: *Consider it all joy . . . various trials:* a frequent teaching of the New Testament derived from the words and sufferings of Jesus (Mt 5, 10-12; Jn 10, 11; Acts 5, 41).

1, 3-8: The sequence of testing, perseverance, and being perfect and complete indicates the manner of attaining spiritual maturity and full preparedness for the coming of Christ (Jas 5, 7-12; cf 1 Pt 1, 6-7; Rom 5, 3-5). These steps require wisdom (5).

1, 5: *Wisdom:* a gift that God readily grants to all who ask in faith and that sustains the Christian in times of trial. It is a kind of knowledge or understanding not accessible to the unbeliever or those who doubt, which gives the recipient an understanding of the real importance of events. In this way a Christian can deal with adversity with great calm and hope (cf 1 Cor 2, 6-12).

1, 9-11: Throughout his letter (see Jas 2, 5; 4, 10.13-16; 5, 1-6), the author reaffirms the teaching of Jesus that worldly prosperity is not necessarily a sign of God's favor but can even be a hindrance to proper humility before God (cf Lk 6, 20-25; 12, 16-21; 16, 19-31).

1, 12: *Temptation:* the Greek word used here is the same one used for "trials" in v 2. *The crown of life:* in ancient Palestine, crowns or wreaths of flowers were worn at festive occasions as signs of joy and honor. In the Hellenistic world, wreaths were given as a reward to great statesmen, soldiers, athletes. *Life:* here means eternal life. *He promised:* some manuscripts read "God" or "the Lord," while the best witnesses do not specify the subject of "promised."

1, 13-15: It is contrary to what we know of God for God to be the author of human temptation (13). In the commission of a sinful act, one is first beguiled by passion (14), then consent is given, which in turn causes the sinful act. When sin permeates the entire person, it incurs the ultimate penalty of death (15).

Jas

16 * Do not be deceived, my beloved brothers: 17 all good giving and every perfect gift* is from above, coming down from the Father of lights, with whom there is no alteration or shadow caused by change. 18 *i* He willed to give us birth by the word of truth that we may be a kind of firstfruits of his creatures.*

III. EXHORTATIONS AND WARNINGS

Doers of the Word. 19 Know this, my dear brothers: everyone should be quick to hear,* slow to speak, slow to wrath,*j* 20 for the wrath of a man does not accomplish the righteousness of God.*k* 21 Therefore, put away all filth and evil excess and humbly welcome the word that has been planted in you and is able to save your souls.*l*

22 Be doers of the word and not hearers only, deluding yourselves.*m* 23 For if anyone is a hearer of the word and not a doer, he is like a man who looks at his own face in a mirror. 24 He sees himself, then goes off and promptly forgets what he looked like. 25 But the one who peers into the perfect law* of freedom and perseveres, and is not a hearer who forgets but a doer who acts, such a one shall be blessed in what he does.*n*

26 * If anyone thinks he is religious and does not bridle his tongue* but deceives his heart, his religion is vain.*o* 27 Religion that is pure and undefiled before God and

the Father is this: to care for orphans and widows* in their affliction and to keep oneself unstained by the world.*p*

CHAPTER 2

Sin of Partiality. * 1 My brothers, show no partiality as you adhere to the faith in our glorious Lord Jesus Christ. 2 For if a man with gold rings on his fingers and in fine clothes comes into your assembly, and a poor person in shabby clothes also comes in, 3 and you pay attention to the one wearing the fine clothes and say, "Sit here, please," while you say to the poor one, "Stand there," or "Sit at my feet," 4 have you not made distinctions among yourselves and become judges with evil designs?*

5 Listen, my beloved brothers. Did not God choose those who are poor* in the world to be rich in faith and heirs of the kingdom that he promised to those who love him?*q* 6 But you dishonored the poor person. Are not the rich oppressing you? And do they themselves not haul you off to court? 7 Is it not they who blaspheme the noble name that was invoked over you?*r* 8 However, if you fulfill the royal* law according to the scripture, "You shall love your neighbor as yourself," you are doing well.*s* 9 But if you show partiality, you commit sin, and are convicted by the law as transgressors.*t* 10 For whoever keeps the whole law, but falls short in one particular, has become guilty in respect to all of it.*u* 11 For he who said, "You shall not commit

---

i Jn 1, 12-13; 1 Pt 1, 23.—j Prv 14, 17; Sir 5, 11.—k Eph 4, 26.—l Col 3, 8.—m Mt 7, 26; Rom 2, 13.—n Jas 2, 12; Ps 19, 8; Rom 8, 2.—o Jas 3, 2; Ps 34, 14.—p Ex 22, 21.—q 1 Cor 1, 26-28; Rv 2, 9.—r 1 Pt 4, 4.—s Lv 19, 18; Mt 22, 39; Rom 13, 9.—t Dt 1, 17.—u Gal 3, 10.

1, 16-18: The author here stresses that God is the source of all good and of good alone, and the evil of temptation does not come from him.

1, 17: *All good giving and every perfect gift* may be a proverb written in hexameter. *Father of lights:* God is here called the Father of the heavenly luminaries, i.e., the stars, sun, and moon that he created (Gn 1, 14-18). Unlike orbs moving from nadir to zenith, he never changes or diminishes in brightness.

1, 18: Acceptance of the gospel message, *the word of truth,* constitutes new birth (Jn 3, 5-6) and makes the recipient the *firstfruits* (i.e., the cultic offering of the earliest grains, symbolizing the beginning of an abundant harvest) of a new creation; cf 1 Cor 15, 20; Rom 8, 23.

1, 19-25: To *be quick to hear* the gospel is to accept it readily and to act in conformity with it, removing from one's soul whatever is opposed to it, so that it may take root and effect salvation (19-21). To listen to the gospel message but not practice it is failure to improve oneself (22-24). Only conformity of life to the perfect law of true freedom brings happiness (25).

1, 25: *Peers into the perfect law:* the image of a person doing this is paralleled to that of hearing God's word. The *perfect law* applies the Old Testament description of the Mosaic law to the gospel of Jesus Christ that brings freedom.

1, 26-27: A practical application of v 22 is now made.

1, 26: For control of the tongue, see the note on Jas 3, 1-12.

1, 27: In the Old Testament, orphans and widows are classical examples of the defenseless and oppressed.

2, 1-13: In the Christian community there must be no discrimination or favoritism based on status or wealth (2-4; cf Mt 5, 3; 11, 5; 23, 6; 1 Cor 1, 27-29). Divine favor rather consists in God's election and promises (5). The rich who oppress the poor blaspheme the name of Christ (6-7). By violating one law of love of neighbor, they offend against the whole law (8-11). On the other hand, conscious awareness of the final judgment helps the faithful to fulfill the whole law (12).

2, 4: When Christians show favoritism to the rich they are guilty of the worst kind of prejudice and discrimination. The author says that such Christians set themselves up as judges who judge not by divine law but by the basest, self-serving motives.

2, 5: The poor, "God's poor" of the Old Testament, were seen by Jesus as particularly open to God for belief in and reliance on him alone (Lk 6, 20). God's law cannot tolerate their oppression in any way (9).

2, 8: *Royal:* literally, "kingly"; because the Mosaic law came from God, the universal king. There may be an allusion to Jesus' uses of this commandment in his preaching of the kingdom of God (Mt 22, 39; Mk 12, 31; Lk 10, 27).

adultery," also said, "You shall not kill."*v* Even if you do not commit adultery but kill, you have become a transgressor of the law. 12 *w* So speak and so act as people who will be judged by the law of freedom.* 13 For the judgment is merciless to one who has not shown mercy; mercy triumphs over judgment.*x*

Faith and Works.* 14 What good is it, my brothers, if someone says he has faith but does not have works? Can that faith save him?*y* 15 If a brother or sister has nothing to wear and has no food for the day, 16 and one of you says to them, "Go in peace, keep warm, and eat well," but you do not give them the necessities of the body, what good is it?*z* 17 So also faith of itself, if it does not have works, is dead.

18 Indeed someone might say, "You have faith and I have works." Demonstrate your faith to me without works, and I will demonstrate my faith to you from my works. 19 You believe that God is one. You do well. Even the demons believe that and tremble. 20 Do you want proof, you ignoramus, that faith without works is useless? 21 Was not Abraham our father justified by works when he offered his son Isaac upon the altar?*a* 22 You see that faith was active along with his works, and faith was completed by the works. 23 Thus the scripture was fulfilled that says, "Abraham believed God, and it was credited to him as righteousness," and he was called "the friend of God."*b* 24 See how a person is justified by works and not by faith alone. 25 And in the same way, was not Rahab the harlot also justified by works when she welcomed the messengers and sent them out by a different route?*c* 26 For just as a body without a spirit is dead, so also faith without works is dead.

CHAPTER 3

Power of the Tongue.* 1 Not many of you should become teachers, my brothers, for you realize that we will be judged more strictly, 2 for we all fall short in many respects. If anyone does not fall short in speech, he is a perfect man, able to bridle his whole body also.*d* 3 If we put bits into the mouths of horses to make them obey us, we also guide their whole bodies. 4 It is the same with ships: even though they are so large and driven by fierce winds, they are steered by a very small rudder wherever the pilot's inclination wishes. 5 In the same way the tongue is a small member and yet has great pretensions.

Consider how small a fire can set a huge forest ablaze. 6 The tongue is also a fire. It exists among our members as a world of malice, defiling the whole body and setting the entire course of our lives on fire, itself set on fire by Gehenna. 7 For every kind of beast and bird, of reptile and sea creature, can be tamed and has been tamed by the human species, 8 but no human being can tame the tongue. It is a restless evil, full of deadly poison.*e* 9 With it we bless the Lord and Father, and with it we curse human beings who are made in the likeness of God. 10 From the same mouth come blessing and cursing. This need not be so, my brothers. 11 Does a spring gush forth from the same opening both pure and brackish water? 12 Can a fig tree, my brothers, produce olives, or a grapevine figs? Neither can salt water yield fresh.*f*

True Wisdom.* 13 Who among you is wise and understanding? Let him show his works by a good life in the humility that comes from wisdom.*g* 14 But if you have bitter jealousy and selfish ambition in your hearts, do not boast and be false to the truth. 15 Wisdom of this kind does not come down from above but is earthly, un-

Jas

---

v Ex 20, 13-14; Dt 5, 17-18.—w Jas 1, 25; Rom 8, 2.—x Mt 5, 7; 6, 14-15; 18, 32-33.—y Mt 25, 31-46; Gal 5, 6.—z 1 Jn 3, 17.—a Gn 22, 9-12; Heb 11, 17.—b Gn 15, 6; Rom 4, 3; Gal 3, 6 / 2 Chr 20, 7; Is 41, 8.—c Jos 2, 1-21.—d Jas 1, 26; Prv 13, 3; Sir 28, 12-26.—e Ps 140, 4.—f Mt 7, 16-17.—g Eph 4, 1-2.

2, 12-13: The law upon which the last judgment will be based is the law of freedom. As Jesus taught, mercy (which participates in God's own loving mercy) includes forgiveness of those who wrong us (see Mt 6, 12.14-15).

2, 14-26: The theme of these verses is the relationship of faith and works (deeds). It has been argued that the teaching here contradicts that of Paul (see especially Rom 4, 5-6). The problem can only be understood if the different viewpoints of the two authors are seen. Paul argues against those who claim to participate in God's salvation because of their good deeds as well as because they have committed themselves to trust in God through Jesus Christ (Paul's concept of faith). Paul certainly understands, however, the implications of true faith for a life of love and generosity (see Gal 5, 6.13-15). The author of James is well aware that proper conduct can only come about with an authentic commitment to God in faith (18.26). Many think he was seeking to correct a misunderstanding of Paul's view.

3, 1-12: The use and abuse of the important role of teaching in the church (1) are here related to the good and bad use of the tongue (9-12), the instrument through which teaching was chiefly conveyed (see Sir 5, 11—6, 1; 28, 12-26).

3, 13-18: This discussion of true wisdom is related to the previous reflection on the role of the teacher as one who is in control of his speech. The qualities of the wise man endowed from above are detailed (17-18; cf Gal 5, 22-23), in contrast to the qualities of earthbound wisdom (14-16; cf 2 Cor 12, 20).

spiritual, demonic. [16]For where jealousy and selfish ambition exist, there is disorder and every foul practice. [17]But the wisdom from above is first of all pure, then peaceable, gentle, compliant, full of mercy and good fruits, without inconstancy or insincerity. [h] [18]And the fruit of righteousness is sown in peace for those who cultivate peace. [i]

CHAPTER 4

Causes of Division.* [1]Where do the wars and where do the conflicts among you come from? Is it not from your passions* that make war within your members?[j] [2]You covet but do not possess. You kill and envy but you cannot obtain; you fight and wage war. You do not possess because you do not ask. [3]You ask but do not receive, because you ask wrongly, to spend it on your passions. [4]Adulterers!* Do you not know that to be a lover of the world means enmity with God? Therefore, whoever wants to be a lover of the world makes himself an enemy of God. [k] [5]Or do you suppose that the scripture speaks without meaning when it says, "The spirit that he has made to dwell in us tends toward jealousy"?* [6]But he bestows a greater grace; therefore, it says: [l]

"God resists the proud,
   but gives grace to the humble."*

[7]So submit yourselves to God. Resist the devil, and he will flee from you. [m] [8]Draw near to God, and he will draw near to you. Cleanse your hands, you sinners, and purify your hearts, you of two minds. [n] [9]Begin to lament, to mourn, to weep. Let your laughter be turned into mourning and your joy into dejection. [10]Humble yourselves before the Lord and he will exalt you. [o]

[11]Do not speak evil of one another, brothers. Whoever speaks evil of a brother or judges his brother speaks evil of the law and judges the law.* If you judge the law, you are not a doer of the law but a judge. [12]There is one lawgiver and judge who is able to save or to destroy. Who then are you to judge your neighbor?[p]

Warning against Presumption.* [13]Come now, you who say, "Today or tomorrow we shall go into such and such a town, spend a year there doing business, and make a profit"—[14]you have no idea what your life will be like tomorrow.* You are a puff of smoke that appears briefly and then disappears. [q] [15]Instead you should say, "If the Lord wills it,* we shall live to do this or that." [16]But now you are boasting in your arrogance. All such boasting is evil. [17] [r] So for one who knows the right thing to do and does not do it, it is a sin.*

---

h Jas 1, 17; Wis 7, 22-23.—i Mt 5, 9.—j Rom 7, 23; 1 Pt 2, 11.—k Mt 6, 24; Lk 16, 13; Rom 8, 7; 1 Jn 2, 15-16.—l Jb 22, 29; Prv 3, 34; Mt 23, 12; 1 Pt 5, 5.—m 1 Pt 5, 8-9.—n Zec 1, 3; Mal 3, 7.—o Jb 5, 11; Mt 23, 12; Lk 14, 11; 18, 14; 1 Pt 5, 6.—p Mt 7, 1; Rom 2, 1; 14, 4.—q Prv 27, 1 / Ps 39, 6-7.—r Lk 12, 47.

4, 1-12: The concern here is with the origin of conflicts in the Christian community. These are occasioned by love *of the world,* which *means enmity with God* (4). Further, the conflicts are bound up with failure to pray properly (cf Mt 7, 7-11; Jn 14, 13; 15, 7; 16, 23), that is, not asking God at all or using God's kindness only for one's pleasure (2-3). In contrast, the proper dispositions are submission to God, repentance, humility, and resistance to evil (7-10).

4,1: *Passions:* the Greek word here (literally, "pleasures") does not indicate that pleasure is evil. Rather, as the text points out (2-3), it is the manner in which one deals with needs and desires that determines good or bad. The motivation for any action can be wrong, especially if one does not pray properly but seeks only selfish enjoyment (3).

4, 4: *Adulterers:* a common biblical image for the covenant between God and his people is the marriage bond. In this image, breaking the covenant with God is likened to the unfaithfulness of adultery.

4, 5: The meaning of this saying is difficult because the author of Jas cites, probably from memory, a passage that is not in any extant manuscript of the Bible. Other translations of the text with

---

a completely different meaning are possible: "The Spirit that he (God) made to dwell in us yearns (for us) jealously," or, "He (God) yearns jealously for the spirit that he has made to dwell in us." If this last translation is correct, the author perhaps had in mind an apocryphal religious text that echoes the idea that God is zealous for his creatures; cf Ex 20, 5; Dt 4, 24; Zec 8, 2.

4, 6: The point of this whole argument is that God wants the happiness of all, but that selfishness and pride can make that impossible. We must work with him in humility (10).

4, 11: Slander of a fellow Christian does not break just one commandment but makes mockery of the authority of law in general and therefore of God.

4, 13-17: The uncertainty of life (14), its complete dependence on God, and the necessity of submitting to God's will (15) all help one know and do what is right (17). To disregard this is to live in pride and arrogance (16); failure to do what is right is a sin (17).

4, 14: Some important Greek manuscripts here have, "You who have no idea what tomorrow will bring. Why, what is your life?"

4, 15: *If the Lord wills it:* often in piety referred to as the "conditio Jacobaea," the condition James says we should employ to qualify all our plans.

4, 17: *It is a sin:* those who live arrogantly, forgetting the contingency of life and our dependence on God (13-16), are guilty of sin.

CHAPTER 5

Warning to the Rich.* ¹Come now, you rich, weep and wail over your impending miseries.ˢ ²Your wealth has rotted away, your clothes have become moth-eaten,ᵗ ³your gold and silver have corroded, and that corrosion will be a testimony against you; it will devour your flesh like a fire. You have stored up treasure for the last days.ᵘ ⁴Behold, the wages you withheld from the workers who harvested your fields are crying aloud, and the cries of the harvesters have reached the ears of the Lord of hosts.ᵛ ⁵You have lived on earth in luxury and pleasure; you have fattened your hearts for the day of slaughter.ʷ ⁶You have condemned; you have murdered the righteous one;ˣ he offers you no resistance.*

Patience and Oaths. ⁷ * Be patient, therefore, brothers, until the coming of the Lord. See how the farmer waits for the precious fruit of the earth, being patient with it until it receives the early and the late rains.* ⁸You too must be patient. Make your hearts firm, because the coming of the Lord is at hand.ʸ ⁹Do not complain, brothers, about one another, that you may not be judged. Behold, the Judge is standing before the gates. ¹⁰Take as an example of hardship and patience, brothers, the prophets who spoke in the name of the Lord. ¹¹Indeed we call blessed those who have persevered. You have heard of the perseverance of Job, and you have seen the purpose of the Lord, because "the Lord is compassionate and merciful."ᶻ

¹² ᵃ But above all, my brothers, do not swear, either by heaven or by earth or with any other oath, but let your "Yes" mean "Yes" and your "No" mean "No," that you may not incur condemnation.*

IV. THE POWER OF PRAYER

Anointing of the Sick. ¹³Is anyone among you suffering? He should pray. Is anyone in good spirits? He should sing praise. ¹⁴Is anyone among you sick?* He should summon the presbyters of the church, and they should pray over him and anoint [him] with oil in the name of the Lord,ᵇ ¹⁵and the prayer of faith will save the sick person, and the Lord will raise him up. If he has committed any sins, he will be forgiven.*

Confession and Intercession. ¹⁶Therefore, confess your sins to one another and pray for one another, that you may be healed. The fervent prayer of a righteous person is very powerful. ¹⁷Elijah was a human being like us; yet he prayed earnestly that it might not rain, and for three years and six months it did not rain upon the land.ᶜ ¹⁸Then he prayed again, and the sky gave rain and the earth produced its fruit.ᵈ

Conversion of Sinners. ¹⁹ ᵉ My brothers, if anyone among you should stray from the truth and someone bring him back, ²⁰ ᶠ he should know that whoever brings back a sinner from the error of his way will save his soul from death and will cover a multitude of sins.*

---

s Lk 6, 24.—t Mt 6, 19.—u Ps 21, 10; Prv 11, 4; Jdt 16, 17.—v Lv 19, 13; Dt 24, 14-15; Mal 3, 5.—w Jer 12, 3; Lk 16, 19-25.—x Wis 2, 10-20.—y Lk 21, 19; Heb 10, 36 / Heb 10, 25; 1 Pt 4, 7.—z Ex 34, 6; Ps 103, 8.—a Mt 5, 34-37.—b Mk 6, 13.—c 1 Kgs 17, 1; Lk 4, 25.—d 1 Kgs 18, 45.—e Mt 18, 15; Gal 6, 1.—f Prv 10, 12; 1 Pt 4, 8.

5, 1-6: Continuing with the theme of the transitory character of life on earth, the author points out the impending ruin of the godless. He denounces the unjust rich, whose victims cry to heaven for judgment on their exploiters (4-6). The decay and corrosion of the costly garments and metals, which symbolize wealth, prove them worthless and portend the destruction of their possessors (2-3).

5, 6: The author does not have in mind any specific crime in his readers' communities but rather echoes the Old Testament theme of the harsh oppression of the righteous poor (see Prv 1, 11; Wis 2, 10.12.20).

5, 7-11: Those oppressed by the unjust rich are reminded of the need for patience, both in bearing the sufferings of human life (9) and in their expectation of the coming of the Lord. It is then that they will receive their reward (7-8.10-11; cf Heb 10, 25; 1 Jn 2, 18).

5, 7: *The early and the late rains:* an expression related to the agricultural season in ancient Palestine (see Dt 11, 14; Jer 5, 24; Jl 2, 23).

5, 12: This is the threat of condemnation for the abuse of swearing oaths (cf Mt 5, 33-37). *By heaven or by earth:* these words were substitutes for the original form of an oath, to circumvent its binding force and to avoid pronouncing the holy name of God (see Ex 22, 10).

5, 14: In case of sickness a Christian should ask for the presbyters of the church, i.e., those who have authority in the church (cf Acts 15, 2.22-23; 1 Tm 5, 17; Ti 1, 5). They are to pray over the person and anoint with oil; oil was used for medicinal purposes in the ancient world (see Is 1, 6; Lk 10, 34). In Mk 6, 13, the Twelve anoint the sick with oil on their missionary journey. *In the name of the Lord:* by the power of Jesus Christ.

5, 15: The results of the prayer and anointing are physical health and forgiveness of sins. The Roman Catholic Church (Council of Trent, Session 14) declared that this anointing of the sick is a sacrament "instituted by Christ and promulgated by blessed James the apostle."

5, 20: When a Christian is instrumental in the conversion of a sinner, the result is forgiveness of sins and a reinstatement of the sinner to the life of grace.

Jas

THE FIRST LETTER OF PETER

INTRODUCTION

This letter begins with an address by Peter to Christian communities located in five provinces of Asia Minor (1, 1), including areas evangelized by Paul (Acts 16, 6-7; 18, 23). Christians there are encouraged to remain faithful to their standards of belief and conduct in spite of threats of persecution. Numerous allusions in the letter suggest that the churches addressed were largely of Gentile composition (1, 14.18; 2, 9-10; 4, 3-4), though considerable use is made of the Old Testament (1, 24; 2, 6-7.9-10.22; 3, 10-12).

The contents following the address both inspire and admonish these "chosen sojourners" (1, 1) who, in seeking to live as God's people, feel an alienation from their previous religious roots and the society around them. Appeal is made to Christ's resurrection and the future hope it provides (1, 3-5) and to the experience of baptism as new birth (1, 3.23-25; 3, 21). The suffering and death of Christ serve as both source of salvation and example (1, 19; 2, 21-25; 3, 18). What Christians are in Christ, as a people who have received mercy and are to proclaim and live according to God's call (2, 9-10), is repeatedly spelled out for all sorts of situations in society (2, 11-17), work (even as slaves, 2, 18-20), the home (3, 1-7), and general conduct (3, 8-12; 4, 1-11). But over all hangs the possibility of suffering as a Christian (3, 13-17). In 4, 12-19 persecution is described as already occurring, so that some have supposed the letter was addressed both to places where such a "trial by fire" was already present and to places where it might break out.

The letter constantly mingles moral exhortation (paraklēsis) with its catechetical summaries of mercies in Christ. Encouragement to fidelity in spite of suffering is based upon a vision of the meaning of Christian existence. The emphasis on baptism and allusions to various features of the baptismal liturgy suggest that the author has incorporated into his exposition numerous homiletic, credal, hymnic, and sacramental elements of the baptismal rite that had become traditional at an early date.

From Irenaeus in the late second century until modern times, Christian tradition regarded Peter the apostle as author of this document. Since he was martyred at Rome during the persecution of Nero between A.D. 64 and 67, it was supposed that the letter was written from Rome shortly before his death. This is supported by its reference to "Babylon" (5, 13), a code name for Rome in the early church.

Some modern scholars, however, on the basis of a number of features that they consider incompatible with Petrine authenticity, regard the letter as the work of a later Christian writer. Such features include the cultivated Greek in which it is written, difficult to attribute to a Galilean fisherman, together with its use of the Greek Septuagint translation when citing the Old Testament; the similarity in both thought and expression to the Pauline literature; and the allusions to widespread persecution of Christians, which did not occur until at least the reign of Domitian (A.D. 81-96). In this view the letter would date from the end of the first century or even the beginning of the second, when there is evidence for persecution of Christians in Asia Minor (the letter of Pliny the Younger to Trajan, A.D. 111-12).

Other scholars believe, however, that these objections can be met by appeal to use of a secretary, Silvanus, mentioned in 5, 12. Such secretaries often gave literary expression to the author's thoughts in their own style and language. The persecutions may refer to local harassment rather than to systematic repression by the state. Hence there is nothing in the document incompatible with Petrine authorship in the 60s.

Still other scholars take a middle position. The many literary contacts with the Pauline literature, James, and 1 John suggest a common fund of traditional formulations *rather than direct dependence upon Paul. Such liturgical and catechetical traditions must have been very ancient and in some cases of Palestinian origin.*

Yet it is unlikely that Peter addressed a letter to the Gentile churches of Asia Minor while Paul was still alive. This suggests a period after the death of the two apostles, perhaps A.D. 70-90. The author would be a disciple of Peter in Rome, representing a Petrine group that served as a bridge between the Palestinian origins of Christianity and its flowering in the Gentile world. The problem addressed would not be official persecution but the difficulty of living the Christian life in a hostile, secular environment that espoused different values and subjected the Christian minority to ridicule and oppression.

The principal divisions of the First Letter of Peter are the following:

I. *Address (1, 1-2)*
II. *The Gift and Call of God in Baptism (1, 3—2, 10)*
III. *The Christian in a Hostile World (2, 11—4, 11)*
IV. *Advice to the Persecuted (4, 12—5, 11)*
V. *Conclusion (5, 12-14)*

I. ADDRESS

CHAPTER 1

Greeting.* [1] Peter, an apostle of Jesus Christ, to the chosen sojourners of the dispersion* in Pontus, Galatia, Cappadocia, Asia, and Bithynia,[a] [2] in the foreknowledge of God the Father, through sanctification by the Spirit, for obedience and sprinkling with the blood of Jesus Christ: may grace and peace be yours in abundance.[b]

II. THE GIFT AND CALL OF GOD IN BAPTISM

Blessing. [3] * Blessed be the God and Father of our Lord Jesus Christ, who in his great mercy gave us a new birth to a living hope through the resurrection of Jesus Christ from the dead,[c] [4] to an inheritance that is imperishable, undefiled, and unfading, kept in heaven for you[d] [5] who by the power of God are safeguarded through faith, to a salvation that is ready to be re-

vealed in the final time. [6] * In this you rejoice, although now for a little while you may have to suffer through various trials,[e] [7] so that the genuineness of your faith, more precious than gold that is perishable even though tested by fire, may prove to be for praise, glory, and honor at the revelation of Jesus Christ.[f] [8] Although you have not seen him you love him; even though you do not see him now yet believe in him, you rejoice with an indescribable and glorious joy,[g] [9] as you attain the goal of [your] faith, the salvation of your souls.

[10] * Concerning this salvation, prophets who prophesied about the grace that was to be yours searched and investigated it, [11] investigating the time and circumstances that the Spirit of Christ within them indicated when it testified in advance to the sufferings destined for Christ and the glories to follow them.[h] [12] It was revealed to them that they were serving not themselves but you with regard to the things that have now been announced to you by those who preached the good news to you [through] the holy Spirit sent from heaven, things into which angels longed to look.

---

a Jas 1, 1.—b Rom 8, 29.—c Ti 3, 5.—d Mt 6, 19-20.—e Jas 1, 2-3.—f 1 Cor 3, 13.—g 2 Cor 5, 6-7.—h Is 52, 13—53, 12; Dn 9, 24.

1, 1-2: The introductory formula names *Peter* as the writer (but see Introduction). In his comments to the presbyters (1 Pt 5, 1), the author calls himself a "fellow presbyter." He addresses himself to the Gentile converts of Asia Minor. Their privileged status as a *chosen* and sanctified people makes them worthy of God's *grace* and *peace*. In contrast is their actual existence as aliens and *sojourners*, scattered among pagans, far from their true country.

1, 1: *Dispersion:* literally, diaspora; see Jas 1, 1 and Introduction to that letter. *Pontus . . . Bithynia:* five provinces in Asia Minor, listed in clockwise order from the north, perhaps in the sequence in which a messenger might deliver the letter.

1, 3-5: A prayer of praise and thanksgiving to God who bestows the gift of new life and hope in baptism *(new birth,* 3) *through the resurrection of Jesus Christ from the dead.* The new birth is a sign of an *imperishable inheritance* (4), of *salvation* that is still in the future *(to be revealed in the final time,* 5).

1, 6-9: As the glory of Christ's resurrection was preceded by his sufferings and death, the new life of faith that it bestows is to be subjected to many *trials* (6) while achieving its goal: the glory of the fullness of *salvation* (9) at the coming of Christ (7).

1, 10-12: The *Spirit of Christ* (11) is here shown to have been present in the prophets, moving them to search, investigate, and prophesy about the *grace* of *salvation* that was to come (10), and in the apostles impelling them to preach the fulfillment of salvation in the message of Christ's sufferings and glory (12).

1Pt

Obedience. [13] * Therefore, gird up the loins of your mind,* live soberly, and set your hopes completely on the grace to be brought to you at the revelation of Jesus Christ. [14] Like obedient children, do not act in compliance with the desires of your former ignorance* [15] but, as he who called you is holy, be holy yourselves in every aspect of your conduct,[i] [16] for it is written, "Be holy because I [am] holy."[j]

Reverence. [17] Now if you invoke as Father him who judges impartially according to each one's works, conduct yourselves with reverence during the time of your sojourning,[k] [18] realizing that you were ransomed from your futile conduct, handed on by your ancestors, not with perishable things like silver or gold[l] [19] but with the precious blood of Christ[m] as of a spotless unblemished lamb.* [20] He was known before the foundation of the world but revealed in the final time for you, [21] who through him believe in God who raised him from the dead and gave him glory, so that your faith and hope are in God.

Mutual Love. * [22] Since you have purified yourselves by obedience to the truth for sincere mutual love, love one another intensely from a [pure] heart.[n] [23] You have been born anew,[o] not from perishable but from imperishable seed, through the living and abiding word of God,* [24] for:

"All flesh is like grass,
    and all its glory like the flower of the field;

the grass withers,
    and the flower wilts;[p]
[25] but the word of the Lord remains forever."

This is the word that has been proclaimed to you.

CHAPTER 2

God's House and People. [1] * Rid yourselves of all malice and all deceit, insincerity, envy, and all slander;[q] [2] like newborn infants, long for pure spiritual milk so that through it you may grow into salvation, [3] [r] for you have tasted that the Lord is good.* [4] Come to him, a living stone,* rejected by human beings but chosen and precious in the sight of God,[s] [5] and, like living stones, let yourselves be built* into a spiritual house to be a holy priesthood to offer spiritual sacrifices acceptable to God through Jesus Christ.[t] [6] For it says in scripture:

"Behold, I am laying a stone in Zion,
    a cornerstone, chosen and precious,
and whoever believes in it shall not be
    put to shame."[u]

[7] Therefore, its value is for you who have faith, but for those without faith:

"The stone which the builders rejected
    has become the cornerstone,"[v]
[8] and

"A stone that will make people stumble,
    and a rock that will make them fall."

They stumble by disobeying the word, as is their destiny.[w]

---

i Mt 5, 48; 1 Jn 3, 3.—j Lv 11, 44; 19, 2.—k 1 Pt 2, 11.—l Is 52, 3; 1 Cor 6, 20.—m Ex 12, 5; Jn 1, 29; Heb 9, 14.—n Rom 12, 10.—o 1 Jn 3, 9.—p Is 40, 6-8.—q 1-2: Jas 1, 21.—r Ps 34, 9.—s Ps 118, 22; Mt 21, 42; Acts 4, 11.—t Eph 2, 21-22.—u Is 28, 16.—v Ps 118, 22; Mt 21, 42; Lk 20, 17; Acts 4, 11.—w Is 8, 14; Rom 9, 33.

1, 13-25: These verses are concerned with the call of God's people to holiness and to mutual love by reason of their redemption through the blood of Christ (18-21).

1, 13: *Gird up the loins of your mind:* a figure reminiscent of the rite of Passover when the Israelites were in flight from their oppressors (Ex 12, 11), and also suggesting the vigilance of the Christian people in expectation of the parousia of Christ (Lk 12, 35).

1, 14-16: The *ignorance* here referred to (14) was their former lack of knowledge of God, leading inevitably to godless conduct. Holiness (15-16), on the contrary, is the result of their call to the knowledge and love of God.

1, 19: Christians have received the redemption prophesied by Isaiah (Is 52, 3), through the blood (Jewish symbol of life) of the spotless lamb (Is 53, 7.10; Jn 1, 29; Rom 3, 24-25; cf 1 Cor 6, 20).

1, 22-25: The new birth of Christians (23) derives from Christ, the *imperishable seed* or sowing that produces a new and lasting existence in those who accept the gospel (24-25), with the consequent duty of loving *one another* (22).

1, 23: *The living and abiding word of God:* or, "the word of the living and abiding God."

2, 1-3: Growth toward salvation is seen here as two steps: first, stripping away all that is contrary to the new life in Christ; second, the nourishment (*pure spiritual milk*) that the newly baptized have received.

2, 3: *Tasted that the Lord is good:* cf Ps 34, 9.

2, 4-8: Christ is the cornerstone (cf Is 28, 16) that is the foundation of the spiritual edifice of the Christian community (5). To unbelievers, Christ is an obstacle and a stumbling block on which they are destined to fall (8); cf Rom 11, 11.

2, 5: *Let yourselves be built:* the form of the Greek word could also be indicative passive, "you are being built" (cf 9).

9 * But you are "a chosen race, a royal priesthood, a holy nation, a people of his own, so that you may announce the praises" of him who called you out of darkness into his wonderful light.ˣ 10 Once you were "no people"
but now you are God's people;
you "had not received mercy"
but now you have received mercy.ʸ

III. THE CHRISTIAN IN A HOSTILE WORLD

Christian Examples. 11 * Beloved, I urge you as aliens and sojourners* to keep away from worldly desires that wage war against the soul.ᶻ 12 Maintain good conduct among the Gentiles, so that if they speak of you as evildoers, they may observe your good works and glorify God on the day of visitation.

Christian Citizens.* 13 Be subject to every human institution for the Lord's sake, whether it be to the king as supremeᵃ 14 or to governors as sent by him for the punishment of evildoers and the approval of those who do good. 15 For it is the will of God that by doing good you may silence the ignorance of foolish people. 16 Be free, yet without using freedom as a pretext for evil, but as slaves of God.ᵇ 17 Give honor to all,

love the community, fear God, honor the king.ᶜ

Christian Slaves. 18 * Slaves, be subject to your masters with all reverence, not only to those who are good and equitable but also to those who are perverse.ᵈ 19 For whenever anyone bears the pain of unjust suffering because of consciousness of God, that is a grace. 20 But what credit is there if you are patient when beaten for doing wrong? But if you are patient when you suffer for doing what is good, this is a grace before God. 21 For to this you have been called, because Christ also suffered* for you, leaving you an example that you should follow in his footsteps.ᵉ 22 "He committed no sin,ᶠ
and no deceit was found in his mouth."*
23 When he was insulted, he returned no insult; when he suffered, he did not threaten; instead, he handed himself over to the one who judges justly.ᵍ 24 He himself bore our sins in his body upon the cross, so that, free from sin, we might live for righteousness. By his wounds you have been healed.ʰ 25 For you had gone astray like sheep,ⁱ but you have now returned to the shepherd and guardian of your souls.*

---

x Ex 19, 6; Is 61, 6; Rv 1, 6; 20, 6. — y Hos 1, 9; 2, 25 / Hos 1, 6.—z Gal 5, 24.—a Rom 13, 1-7.—b Gal 5, 13.—c Prv 24, 21; Mt 22, 21.—d Eph 6, 5.—e Mt 16, 24.—f Is 53, 9.—g Mt 5, 39.—h Is 53, 4.12 / Is 53, 5.—i Is 53, 6.

2, 9-10: The prerogatives of ancient Israel mentioned here are now more fully and fittingly applied to the Christian people: "a chosen race" (cf Is 43, 20-21) indicates their divine election (Eph 1, 4-6); "a royal priesthood" (cf Ex 19, 6) to serve and worship God in Christ, thus continuing the priestly functions of his life, passion, and resurrection; "a holy nation" (Ex 19, 6) reserved for God, a people he claims for his own (cf Mal 3, 17) in virtue of their baptism into his death and resurrection. This transcends all natural and national divisions and unites the people into one community to glorify the one who led them from the darkness of paganism to the light of faith in Christ. From being "no people" deprived of all mercy, they have become the very people of God, the chosen recipients of his mercy (cf Hos 1, 9; 2, 25).

2, 11—3, 12: After explaining the doctrinal basis for the Christian community, the author makes practical applications in terms of the virtues that should prevail in all the social relationships of the members of the community: good example to Gentile neighbors (1 Pt 2, 11-12); respect for human authority (1 Pt 2, 13-17); obedience, patience, and endurance of hardship in domestic relations (1 Pt 2, 18-25); Christian behavior of husbands and wives (1 Pt 3, 1-7); mutual charity (1 Pt 3, 8-12).

2, 11: *Aliens and sojourners:* no longer signifying absence from one's native land (Gn 23, 4), this image denotes rather their estrangement from the world during their earthly pilgrimage (see also 1 Pt 1, 1.17).

2, 13-17: True Christian freedom is the result of being servants of God (16; see the note on 1 Pt 2, 18-23). It includes reverence for God, esteem for every individual, and committed love for fellow Christians (17). Although persecution may threaten, subjection to human government is urged (13.17) and concern for the impact of Christians' conduct on those who are not Christians (12.15).

2, 18-21: Most of the labor in the commercial cities of first-century Asia Minor was performed by a working class of slaves. The sense of freedom contained in the gospel undoubtedly caused great tension among Christian slaves: witness the special advice given concerning them here and in 1 Cor 7, 21-24; Eph 6, 5-8; Col 3, 22-25; Phlm. The point made here does not have so much to do with the institution of slavery, which the author does not challenge, but with the nonviolent reaction (20) of slaves to unjust treatment. Their patient suffering is compared to that of Jesus (21), which won righteousness for all humanity.

2, 21: *Suffered:* some ancient manuscripts and versions read "died" (cf 1 Pt 3, 18).

2, 22-25: After the quotation of Is 53, 9b, the passage describes Jesus' passion with phrases concerning the Suffering Servant from Is 53, 4-12, perhaps as employed in an early Christian confession of faith; cf 1 Pt 1, 18-21 and 1 Pt 3, 18-22.

2, 25: *The shepherd and guardian of your souls:* the familiar shepherd and flock figures express the care, vigilance, and love of God for his people in the Old Testament (Ps 23; Is 40, 11; Jer 23, 4-5; Ez 34, 11-16) and of Jesus for all humanity in the New Testament (Mt 18, 10-14; Lk 15, 4-7; Jn 10, 1-16; Heb 13, 20).

1Pt

CHAPTER 3

Christian Spouses. [1] * Likewise, you wives should be subordinate to your husbands so that, even if some disobey the word, they may be won over without a word by their wives' conduct [2] when they observe your reverent and chaste behavior.[j] [3] Your adornment should not be an external one: braiding the hair, wearing gold jewelry, or dressing in fine clothes,[k] [4] but rather the hidden character of the heart, expressed in the imperishable beauty of a gentle and calm disposition, which is precious in the sight of God. [5] For this is also how the holy women who hoped in God once used to adorn themselves and were subordinate to their husbands; [6] thus Sarah obeyed Abraham, calling him "lord." You are her children when you do what is good and fear no intimidation.

[7] [l] Likewise, you husbands should live with your wives in understanding, showing honor to the weaker female sex, since we are joint heirs of the gift of life, so that your prayers may not be hindered.*

Christian Conduct. * [8] Finally, all of you, be of one mind, sympathetic, loving toward one another, compassionate, humble. [9] Do not return evil for evil, or insult for insult; but, on the contrary, a blessing, because to this you were called, that you might inherit a blessing.[m] [10] For:

"Whoever would love life[n]
   and see good days
must keep the tongue from evil
   and the lips from speaking deceit,

[11] must turn from evil and do good,
   seek peace and follow after it
[12] For the eyes of the Lord are on the righteous
   and his ears turned to their prayer,
but the face of the Lord is against evildoers."

Christian Suffering. * [13] Now who is going to harm you if you are enthusiastic for what is good? [14] But even if you should suffer because of righteousness, blessed are you. Do not be afraid or terrified with fear of them, [15] but sanctify Christ as Lord in your hearts. Always be ready to give an explanation to anyone who asks you for a reason for your hope,[o] [16] but do it with gentleness and reverence, keeping your conscience clear, so that, when you are maligned, those who defame your good conduct in Christ may themselves be put to shame. [17] For it is better to suffer for doing good, if that be the will of God, than for doing evil.

[18] For Christ also suffered* for sins once, the righteous for the sake of the unrighteous, that he might lead you to God. Put to death in the flesh, he was brought to life in the spirit.[p] [19] In it he also went to preach to the spirits in prison,* [20] who had once been disobedient while God patiently waited in the days of Noah during the building of the ark, in which a few persons, eight in all, were saved through water.[q] [21] This prefigured baptism, which saves you now. It is not a removal of dirt from the body but an appeal to God* for a clear conscience, through the resurrection

---

j 1 Cor 7, 12-16; Eph 5, 22-24; Col 3, 18; 1 Tm 2, 9-15.—k 1 Tm 2, 9-10.—l Eph 5, 25-33; Col 3, 19.—m Mt 5, 44; Lk 6, 28; Rom 12, 14.—n 10-12: Ps 34, 13-17.—o Is 8, 12.—p 1 Cor 15, 45.—q Gn 7, 7.17; 2 Pt 2, 5.

3, 1-6: The typical marital virtues of women of the ancient world, obedience, reverence, and chastity (1-2), are outlined here by the author, who gives them an entirely new motivation: Christian wives are to be virtuous so that they may be instrumental in the conversion of their husbands. In imitation of *holy women* in the past (5) they are to cultivate the interior life (4) instead of excessive concern with their appearance (3).

3, 7: Husbands who do not respect their wives will have as little success in prayer as those who, according to Paul, have no love: their prayers will be "a resounding gong or a clashing cymbal" (1 Cor 13, 1). Consideration for others is shown as a prerequisite for effective prayer also in Mt 5, 23-24; 1 Cor 11, 20-22; Jas 4, 3. After all, whatever the social position of women in the world and in the family, they are equal recipients of the gift of God's salvation. Paul is very clear on this point, too (see 1 Cor 11, 11-12; Gal 3, 28).

3, 8-12: For the proper ordering of Christian life in its various aspects as described in 1 Pt 2, 11—3, 9, there is promised the blessing expressed in Ps 34, 13-17. In the Old Testament this refers to longevity and prosperity; here, it also refers to eternal life.

3, 13-22: This exposition, centering on v 17, runs as follows: by his suffering and death Christ the righteous one saved the unrighteous (18); by his resurrection he received new life in the spirit, which he communicates to believers through the baptismal bath that cleanses their consciences from sin. As Noah's family was saved *through water*, so Christians are saved through the waters of baptism (19-22). Hence they need not share the fear of sinners; they should rather rejoice in suffering because of their hope in Christ. Thus their innocence disappoints their accusers (13-16; cf Mt 10, 28; Rom 8, 35-39).

3, 18: *Suffered:* very many ancient manuscripts and versions read "died." *Put to death in the flesh:* affirms that Jesus truly died as a human being. *Brought to life in the spirit:* that is, in the new and transformed existence freed from the limitations and weaknesses of natural human life (cf 1 Cor 15, 45).

3, 19: *The spirits in prison:* it is not clear just who these spirits are. They may be the spirits of the sinners who died in the flood, or angelic powers, hostile to God, who have been overcome by Christ (cf 1 Pt 3, 22; Gn 6, 4; Enoch 6-36, especially 21, 6; 2 Enoch 7, 1-5).

3, 21: *Appeal to God:* this could also be translated "pledge," that is, a promise on the part of Christians to live with a good conscience before God, or a pledge from God of forgiveness and therefore a good conscience for us.

of Jesus Christ,[r] [22] who has gone into heaven and is at the right hand of God, with angels, authorities, and powers subject to him.[s]

CHAPTER 4

Christian Restraint.* [1] Therefore, since Christ suffered in the flesh, arm yourselves also with the same attitude (for whoever suffers in the flesh has broken with sin), [2] so as not to spend what remains of one's life in the flesh on human desires, but on the will of God. [3] For the time that has passed is sufficient for doing what the Gentiles like to do: living in debauchery, evil desires, drunkenness, orgies, carousing, and wanton idolatry.[t] [4] They are surprised that you do not plunge into the same swamp of profligacy, and they vilify you; [5] but they will give an account to him who stands ready to judge the living and the dead.[u] [6] For this is why the gospel was preached even to the dead* that, though condemned in the flesh in human estimation, they might live in the spirit in the estimation of God.

Christian Charity.* [7] The end of all things is at hand. Therefore, be serious and sober for prayers. [8] [v] Above all, let your love for one another be intense, because love covers a multitude of sins.* [9] Be hospitable to one another without complaining.[w] [10] As each one has received a gift, use it to serve one another as good stewards of God's varied grace.[x] [11] Whoever preaches, let it be with the words of God; whoever serves, let it be with the strength that God supplies, so that in all things God may be glorified through Jesus Christ,[y] to whom belong glory and dominion forever and ever. Amen.*

---

r Eph 5, 26; Heb 10, 22.—s Eph 1, 20-21.—t Eph 2, 2-3; 4, 17-19; Col 3, 7; Ti 3, 3.—u Acts 10, 42; 2 Tm 4, 1.—v Prv 10, 12; Jas 5, 20.—w Heb 13, 2.—x Rom 12, 6-8; 1 Cor 12, 4-11.—y 1 Cor 10, 31.—z 1 Pt 1, 6-7; 3, 14.17.—a Rom 5, 3-5; 8, 17; 2 Tm 2, 12.—b Acts 5, 41 / Is 11, 2.—c Lk 23, 31; 2 Thes 1, 8.—d Prv 11, 31 LXX.

4, 1-6: Willingness to suffer with Christ equips the Christian with the power to conquer sin (1). Christ is here portrayed as the judge to whom those guilty of pagan vices must render an account (5; cf Jn 5, 22-27; Acts 10, 42; 2 Tm 4, 1).

4, 6: *The dead:* these may be the sinners of the flood generation who are possibly referred to in 1 Pt 3, 19. But many scholars think that there is no connection between these two verses, and that *the dead* here are Christians who have died since hearing the preaching of the gospel.

4, 7-11: The inner life of the eschatological community is outlined as *the end* (the parousia of Christ) draws near in terms of seriousness, sobriety, prayer, and love expressed through hospitality and the use of one's gifts for the glory of God and of Christ.

IV. ADVICE TO THE PERSECUTED

Trial of Persecution.* [12] Beloved, do not be surprised that a trial by fire is occurring among you, as if something strange were happening to you.[z] [13] But rejoice to the extent that you share in the sufferings of Christ, so that when his glory is revealed you may also rejoice exultantly.[a] [14] If you are insulted for the name of Christ, blessed are you, for the Spirit of glory and of God rests upon you.[b] [15] But let no one among you be made to suffer as a murderer, a thief, an evildoer, or as an intriguer. [16] But whoever is made to suffer as a Christian should not be ashamed but glorify God because of the name. [17] For it is time for the judgment to begin with the household of God; if it begins with us, how will it end for those who fail to obey the gospel of God?[c]

[18] "And if the righteous one is barely saved,
where will the godless and the sinner appear?"[d]

[19] As a result, those who suffer in accord with God's will hand their souls over to a faithful creator as they do good.

CHAPTER 5

Advice to Presbyters.* [1] So I exhort the presbyters* among you, as a fellow presbyter and witness to the sufferings of Christ and one who has a share in the glory to be revealed. [2] Tend the flock of God in your midst, [overseeing] not by constraint but willingly, as God would have it, not for

---

4, 8: *Love covers a multitude of sins:* a maxim based on Prv 10, 12; see also Ps 32, 1; Jas 5, 20.

4, 11: Some scholars feel that this doxology concludes the part of the homily addressed specifically to the newly baptized, begun in 1 Pt 1, 3; others that it concludes a baptismal liturgy. Such doxologies do occur within a New Testament letter, e.g., Rom 9, 5. Some propose that v 11 was an alternate ending, with 1 Pt 4, 12—5, 14 being read in places where persecution was more pressing. But such doxologies usually do not occur at the end of letters (the only examples are 2 Pt 3, 18, Jude 25, and Rom 16, 27, the last probably a liturgical insertion).

4, 12-19: The suffering to which the author has already frequently referred is presented in more severe terms. This has led some scholars to see these verses as referring to an actual persecution. Others see the heightening of the language as only a rhetorical device used at the end of the letter to emphasize the suffering motif.

5, 1-4: In imitation of Christ, the chief shepherd, those entrusted with a pastoral office are to tend the flock by their care and example.

5, 1: *Presbyters:* the officially appointed leaders and teachers of the Christian community (cf 1 Tm 5, 17-18; Ti 1, 5-8; Jas 5, 14).

1Pt

shameful profit but eagerly.ᵉ ³Do not lord it over those assigned to you, but be examples to the flock. ⁴ ᶠ And when the chief Shepherd is revealed, you will receive the unfading crown of glory.*

Advice to the Community.* ⁵Likewise, you younger members,* be subject to the presbyters. And all of you, clothe yourselves with humility in your dealings with one another, for:

"God opposes the proud
but bestows favor on the humble."ᵍ

⁶So humble yourselves under the mighty hand of God, that he may exalt you in due time.ʰ ⁷Cast all your worries upon him because he cares for you.ⁱ

---

e Acts 20, 28; Ti 1, 7.—f Wis 5, 15-16; 1 Cor 9, 25; 2 Tm 4, 8; Jas 1, 12.—g Prv 3, 34.—h Jb 22, 29; Jas 4, 10.—i Ps 55, 23; Mt 6, 25-33; Lk 12, 22-31; Phil 4, 6.—j 1 Thes 5, 6.—k Rom 8, 18; 2 Cor 4, 17.—l Rom 16, 16; 1 Cor 16, 20; 2 Cor 13, 12.

5, 4: See the note on 1 Pt 2, 25.

5, 5-11: The community is to be subject to the presbyters and to show humility toward one another and trust in God's love and care (5-7). With sobriety, alertness, and steadfast faith they must resist the evil one; their sufferings are shared with Christians everywhere (8-9). They will be strengthened and called to eternal glory (10-11).

5, 5: *Younger members:* this may be a designation for office-holders of lesser rank.

5, 12: *Silvanus:* the companion of Paul (see 2 Cor 1, 19; 1 Thes 1, 1; 2 Thes 1, 1). Jews and Jewish Christians, like Paul,

⁸Be sober and vigilant. Your opponent the devil is prowling around like a roaring lion looking for [someone] to devour.ʲ ⁹Resist him, steadfast in faith, knowing that your fellow believers throughout the world undergo the same sufferings. ¹⁰The God of all grace who called you to his eternal glory through Christ [Jesus] will himself restore, confirm, strengthen, and establish you after you have suffered a little.ᵏ ¹¹To him be dominion forever. Amen.

V. CONCLUSION

¹²I write you this briefly through Silvanus,* whom I consider a faithful brother, exhorting you and testifying that this is the true grace of God. Remain firm in it. ¹³The chosen one* at Babylon sends you greeting, as does Mark, my son. ¹⁴Greet one another with a loving kiss. Peace to all of you who are in Christ.ˡ

---

often had a Hebrew name (Saoul, Silas) and a Greek or Latin name (Paul, Silvanus). On Silvanus's possible role as amanuensis, see Introduction.

5, 13: *The chosen one:* feminine, referring to the Christian community (*ekklēsia*) at Babylon, the code name for Rome in Rv 14, 8; 17, 5; 18, 2. *Mark, my son:* traditionally a prominent disciple of Peter and co-worker at the church in Rome, perhaps the John Mark referred to in Acts 12, 12.25; 13, 5.13; and in Acts 15, 37-39, a companion of Barnabas. Perhaps this is the same Mark mentioned as Barnabas's cousin in Col 4, 10, a co-worker with Paul in Phlm 24 (see also 2 Tm 4, 11).

THE SECOND LETTER OF PETER

INTRODUCTION

This letter can be appreciated both for its positive teachings and for its earnest warnings. It seeks to strengthen readers in faith (1, 1), hope for the future (3, 1-10), knowledge (1, 2.6.8), love (1, 7), and other virtues (1, 5-6). This aim is carried out especially by warning against false teachers, the condemnation of whom occupies the long central section of the letter (2, 1-22). A particular crisis is the claim by "scoffers" that there will be no second coming of Jesus, a doctrine that the author vigorously affirms (3, 1-10). The concept of God's "promises" is particularly precious in the theology of 2 Peter (1, 4; 3, 4.9.13). Closing comments at 3, 17-18 well sum up the twin concerns: that you not "be led into" error and "fall" but instead "grow in grace" and "knowledge" of Jesus Christ.

Second Peter is clearly structured in its presentation of these points. It reminds its readers of the divine authenticity of Christ's teaching (1, 3-4), continues with reflections on Christian conduct (1, 5-15), then returns to the exalted dignity of Jesus by incorporating into the text the apostolic witness to his transfiguration (1, 16-18). It takes up the question of the interpretation of scripture by pointing out that it is possible to misunderstand the sacred writings (1, 19-21) and that divine punishment will overtake false teachers (2, 1-22). It proclaims that the parousia is the teaching of the Lord and of the apostles and is therefore an eventual certainty (3, 1-13). At the same time, it warns that the meaning of Paul's writings on this question should not be distorted (3, 14-18).

In both content and style this letter is very different from 1 Peter, which immediately precedes it in the canon. The opening verse attributes it to "Symeon Peter, a slave and apostle of Jesus Christ." Moreover, the author in 3, 1 calls his work a "second letter," referring probably to 1 Peter as his first, and in 1, 18 counts himself among those present at the transfiguration of Jesus.

Nevertheless, acceptance of 2 Peter into the New Testament canon met with great resistance in the early church. The oldest certain reference to it comes from Origen in the early third century. While he himself accepted both Petrine letters as canonical, he testifies that others rejected 2 Peter. As late as the fifth century some local churches still excluded it from the canon, but eventually it was universally adopted. The principal reason for the long delay was the persistent doubt that the letter stemmed from the apostle Peter.

Among modern scholars there is wide agreement that 2 Peter is a pseudonymous work, i.e., one written by a later author who attributed it to Peter according to a literary convention popular at the time. It gives the impression of being more remote in time from the apostolic period than 1 Peter; indeed, many think it is the latest work in the New Testament and assign it to the first or even the second quarter of the second century.

The principal reasons for this view are the following. The author refers to the apostles and "our ancestors" as belonging to a previous generation, now dead (3, 2-4). A collection of Paul's letters exists and appears to be well known, but disputes have arisen about the interpretation of them (3, 14-16). The passage about false teachers (2, 1-18) contains a number of literary contacts with Jude 4-16, and it is generally agreed that 2 Peter depends upon Jude, not vice versa. Finally, the principal problem exercising the author is the false teaching of "scoffers" who have concluded from the delay of the parousia that the Lord is not going to return. This could scarcely have been an issue during the lifetime of Simon Peter.

The Christians to whom the letter is addressed are not identified, though it may be the intent of 3, 1 to identify them with the churches of Asia Minor to which 1 Peter was sent. Except for the epistolary greeting in 1, 1-2, 2 Peter does not have the features of a genuine letter at all, but is rather a general exhortation cast in the form of a letter. The author must have been a Jewish Christian of the dispersion for, while his Jewish heritage is evident in various features of his thought and style, he writes in the rather stilted literary Greek of the Hellenistic period. He appeals to tradition against the twin threat of doctrinal error and moral laxity, which appear to reflect an early stage of what later developed into full-blown gnosticism. Thus he forms a link between the apostolic period and the church of subsequent ages.

The principal divisions of the Second Letter of Peter are the following:

I. Address (1, 1-2)
II. Exhortation to Christian Virtue (1, 3-21)
III. Condemnation of the False Teachers (2, 1-22)
IV. The Delay of the Second Coming (3, 1-16)
V. Final Exhortation and Doxology (3, 17-18)

2Pt

I. ADDRESS

CHAPTER 1

Greeting. [1] Symeon Peter,* a slave and apostle of Jesus Christ, to those who have received a faith of equal value to ours through the righteousness of our God and savior Jesus Christ: [2] may grace and peace be yours in abundance through knowledge* of God and of Jesus our Lord.

II. EXHORTATION TO CHRISTIAN VIRTUE

The Power of God's Promise. [3] * His divine power has bestowed on us everything that makes for life and devotion, through the knowledge of him[a] who called us by his own glory and power.* [4] Through these, he has bestowed on us the precious and very great promises, so that through them you may come to share in the divine nature, after escaping from the corruption that is in the world because of evil desire.[b] [5] * For this very reason, make every effort to supplement your faith with virtue, virtue with knowledge,[c] [6] knowledge with self-control, self-control with endurance, endurance with devotion, [7] devotion with mutual affection, mutual affection with love. [8] If these are yours and increase in abundance, they will keep you from being idle or unfruitful in the knowledge of our Lord Jesus Christ. [9] [d] Anyone who lacks

them is blind and shortsighted, forgetful of the cleansing of his past sins. [10] * Therefore, brothers, be all the more eager to make your call and election firm, for, in doing so, you will never stumble. [11] For, in this way, entry into the eternal kingdom of our Lord and savior Jesus Christ will be richly provided for you.

Apostolic Witness. [12] * Therefore, I will always remind you of these things, even though you already know them and are established in the truth you have. [13] I think it right, as long as I am in this "tent,"* to stir you up by a reminder, [14] since I know that I will soon have to put it aside, as indeed our Lord Jesus Christ has shown me.[e] [15] I shall also make every effort to enable you always to remember these things after my departure.

[16] We did not follow cleverly devised myths when we made known to you the power and coming* of our Lord Jesus Christ, but we had been eyewitnesses of his majesty.[f] [17] For he received honor and glory from God the Father* when that unique declaration came to him from the majestic glory, "This is my Son, my beloved, with whom I am well pleased."[g] [18] We* ourselves heard this voice come from heaven while we were with him on the holy mountain. [19] [h] Moreover, we pos-

---

a 2 Cor 4, 6; 1 Pt 2, 9.—b 2 Cor 7, 1; 1 Jn 2, 15.—c 5-7: Gal 5, 22-23.—d 1 Jn 2, 9.11.—e Is 38, 12; Jn 21, 18-19.—f Lk 9, 28-36; Jn 1, 14.—g Ps 2, 7; Mt 17, 4-6.—h Lk 1, 78-79; Rv 2, 28.

1, 1: *Symeon Peter:* on the authorship of 2 Peter, see Introduction; on the spelling here of the Hebrew name *Šim'ōn,* cf Acts 15, 14. The greeting is especially similar to those in 1 Peter and Jude. The words translated *our God and savior Jesus Christ* could also be rendered "our God and the savior Jesus Christ"; cf 2 Pt 1, 11; 2, 20; 3, 2.18.

1, 2: *Knowledge:* a key term in the letter (2 Pt 1, 3.8; 2, 20; 3, 18), perhaps used as a Christian emphasis against gnostic claims.

1, 3-4: Christian life in its fullness is a gift of divine power effecting a knowledge of Christ and the bestowal of divine promises (2 Pt 3, 4.9). *To share in the divine nature,* escaping from a corrupt world, is a thought found elsewhere in the Bible but expressed only here in such Hellenistic terms, since it is said to be accomplished through *knowledge* (3); cf 2 Pt 1, 2; 2, 20; but see also Jn 15, 4; 17, 22-23; Rom 8, 14-17; Heb 3, 14; 1 Jn 1, 3; 3, 2.

1, 3: *By his own glory and power:* the most ancient papyrus and the best codex read "through glory and power."

1, 5-9: Note the climactic gradation of qualities (5-7), beginning with faith and leading to the fullness of Christian life, which is love; cf Rom 5, 3-4; Gal 5, 6.22 for a similar series of "virtues," though the program and sense here are different than in Paul. The fruit of these is knowledge of Christ (8) referred to in v 3; their absence is spiritual blindness (9).

1, 10-11: Perseverance in the Christian vocation is the best preventative against losing it and the safest provision for attaining its goal, the kingdom. *Kingdom of . . . Christ,* instead of "God," is unusual; cf Col 1, 13 and Mt 13, 41, as well as the *righteousness of . . . Christ* (1).

1, 12-19: The purpose in writing is to call to mind the apostle's witness to the truth, even as he faces the end of his life (12-15), his eyewitness testimony to Christ (16-18), and the true prophetic message (19) through the Spirit in scripture (20-21), in contrast to what false teachers are setting forth (ch 2).

1, 13: *Tent:* a biblical image for transitory human life (Is 38, 12), here combined with a verb that suggests not folding or packing up a tent but its being discarded in death (cf 2 Cor 5, 1-4).

1, 16: *Coming:* in Greek *parousia,* used at 2 Pt 3, 4.12 of the second coming of Christ. The word was used in the extrabiblical writings for the visitation of someone in authority; in Greek cult and Hellenistic Judaism it was used for the manifestation of the divine presence. What the apostles *made known* has been interpreted to refer to Jesus' transfiguration (17) or to his entire first coming or to his future coming in power (ch 3).

1, 17: The author assures the readers of the reliability of the apostolic message (including Jesus' power, glory, and coming; cf the note on 2 Pt 1, 16) by appeal to the transfiguration of Jesus in glory (cf Mt 17, 1-8 and parallels) and by appeal to the prophetic message (2 Pt 1, 19; perhaps Nm 24, 17). Here, as elsewhere, the New Testament insists on continued reminders as necessary to preserve the historical facts about Jesus and the truths of the faith; cf 2 Pt 3, 1-2; 1 Cor 11, 2; 15, 1-3. *My Son, my beloved:* or, "my beloved Son."

1, 18: *We:* at Jesus' transfiguration, referring to Peter, James, and John (Mt 17, 1).

sess the prophetic message that is altogether reliable. You will do well to be attentive to it, as to a lamp shining in a dark place, until day dawns and the morning star rises in your hearts. 20 * Know this first of all, that there is no prophecy of scripture that is a matter of personal interpretation, 21 for no prophecy ever came through human will; but rather human beings moved by the holy Spirit spoke under the influence of God.

III. CONDEMNATION OF THE FALSE TEACHERS

CHAPTER 2

False Teachers. * 1 There were also false prophets among the people, just as there will be false teachers among you, who will introduce destructive heresies and even deny the Master who ransomed them, bringing swift destruction on themselves. *i* 2 Many will follow their licentious ways, and because of them the way of truth will be reviled. *j* 3 In their greed they will exploit you with fabrications, but from of old their condemnation has not been idle and their destruction does not sleep. *k*

Lessons from the Past. 4 * For if God did not spare the angels when they sinned, but condemned them to the chains of Tartarus* and handed them over to be kept for judgment; *l* 5 * and if he did not spare the ancient world, even though he preserved

---

i Mt 24, 11.24; 1 Tm 4, 1; Jude 4.—j Is 52, 5.—k Rom 16, 18.—l Jude 6.—m Gn 8, 15-19; Heb 11, 7.—n Gn 19, 24-25; Jude 7.—o 1 Cor 10, 13; Rv 3, 10.—p Jude 8.—q Jude 9.—r Ps 49, 13-15; Jude 10.—s Jude 12.

1, 20-21: Often cited, along with 2 Tm 3, 16, on the "inspiration" of scripture or against private interpretation, these verses in context are directed against the false teachers of ch 2 and clever tales (16). The prophetic word in scripture comes admittedly through *human beings* (21), but *moved by the holy Spirit*, not from their own interpretation, and is a matter of what the author and Spirit intended, not the *personal interpretation* of false teachers. Instead of *under the influence of God*, some manuscripts read "holy ones of God."

2, 1-3: The pattern of *false prophets* among the Old Testament people of God will recur through *false teachers* in the church. Such destructive opinions of heretical sects bring loss of faith in Christ, contempt for the way of salvation (cf 2 Pt 2, 21), and immorality.

2, 4-6: The false teachers will be punished just as surely and as severely as were the fallen *angels* (4; cf Jude 6; Gn 6, 1-4), the sinners of Noah's day (5; Gn 7, 21-23), and the inhabitants of the cities of the Plain (6; Jude 7; Gn 19, 25). Whereas there are three examples in Jude 5-7 (Exodus and wilderness; rebellious angels; Sodom and Gomorrah), 2 Peter omitted the first of these, has inserted a new illustration about Noah (5) between Jude's second and third examples, and listed the resulting three examples in their Old Testament order (Gn 6; 7; 19).

Noah, a herald of righteousness, together with seven others, when he brought a flood upon the godless world; *m* 6 and if he condemned the cities of Sodom and Gomorrah [to destruction], reducing them to ashes, making them an example for the godless [people] of what is coming; *n* 7 and if he rescued Lot, a righteous man oppressed by the licentious conduct of unprincipled people 8 (for day after day that righteous man living among them was tormented in his righteous soul at the lawless deeds that he saw and heard), 9 then the Lord knows how to rescue the devout from trial and to keep the unrighteous under punishment for the day of judgment, *o* 10 and especially those who follow the flesh with its depraved desire and show contempt for lordship. *p*

False Teachers Denounced. * Bold and arrogant, they are not afraid to revile glorious beings,* 11 whereas angels, *q* despite their superior strength and power, do not bring a reviling judgment against them from the Lord.* 12 But these people, like irrational animals born by nature for capture and destruction, revile things that they do not understand, and in their destruction they will also be destroyed, *r* 13 suffering wrong* as payment for wrongdoing. Thinking daytime revelry a delight, they are stains and defilements as they revel in their deceits while carousing with you. *s* 14 Their eyes are full of adultery and insatiable for sin. They seduce unstable people, and their hearts are trained in

---

2, 4: *Chains of Tartarus:* cf Jude 6; other manuscripts in 2 Peter read "pits of Tartarus." *Tartarus:* a term borrowed from Greek mythology to indicate the infernal regions.

2, 5-10a: Although God did not spare the sinful, he kept and saved the righteous, such as *Noah* (5) and *Lot* (7), and he *knows how to rescue the devout* (9), who are contrasted with the false teachers of the author's day. On Noah, cf Gn 5, 32—9, 29, especially 7, 1. On Lot, cf Gn 13 and 19.

2, 10b-22: Some take 10b and 11 with the preceding paragraph. Others begin the new paragraph with 10a, supplying from v 9 *The Lord knows how . . . to keep . . . under punishment,* with reference to God and probably specifically Christ (1). The conduct of the false teachers is described and condemned in language similar to that of Jude 8-16. This arrogance knows no bounds; animal-like, they are due to be caught and destroyed. They seduce even those who have knowledge of Christ (20).

2, 10b: *Glorious beings:* literally, "glories"; cf Jude 8. While some think that illustrious personages are meant or even political officials behind whom (fallen) angels stand, it is more likely that the reference is to glorious angelic beings (cf Jude 9).

2, 11: *From the Lord:* some manuscripts read "before the Lord"; cf Jude 9.

2, 13: *Suffering wrong:* some manuscripts read "receiving a reward." *In their deceits:* some manuscripts read "in their love feasts" (Jude 12).

2Pt

greed. Accursed children! [15] Abandoning the straight road, they have gone astray, following the road of Balaam, the son of Bosor,* who loved payment for wrongdoing,[t] [16] but he received a rebuke for his own crime: a mute beast spoke with a human voice and restrained the prophet's madness.[u]

[17] These people are waterless springs and mists driven by a gale; for them the gloom of darkness has been reserved.[v] [18] For, talking empty bombast, they seduce with licentious desires of the flesh those who have barely escaped* from people who live in error.[w] [19] They promise them freedom, though they themselves are slaves of corruption, for a person is a slave of whatever overcomes him.[x] [20] For if they, having escaped the defilements of the world through the knowledge of [our] Lord and savior Jesus Christ, again become entangled and overcome by them, their last condition is worse than their first.[y] [21] For it would have been better for them not to have known the way of righteousness than after knowing it to turn back from the holy commandment handed down* to them.[z] [22] What is expressed in the true proverb has happened to them,[a] "The dog returns to its own vomit," and "A bathed sow returns to wallowing in the mire."*

---

t Nm 31, 16; Jude 11.—u Nm 22, 28-33.—v Jude 12-13.—w Jude 16.—x Jn 8, 34; Rom 6, 16-17.—y Mt 12, 45.—z Ez 3, 20.—a Prv 26, 11.—b Jude 17.—c 1 Tm 4, 1; 2 Tm 3, 1; Jude 18.—d Is 5, 19.—e Gn 1, 2.6.8; Ps 24, 2.—f Gn 7, 21.—g Is 51, 6; Mt 3, 12.—h Ps 90, 4.

2, 15: *Balaam, the son of Bosor:* in Nm 22, 5, Balaam is said to be the son of Beor, and it is this name that turns up in a few ancient Greek manuscripts by way of "correction" of the text. Balaam is not portrayed in such a bad light in Nm 22. His evil reputation and his *madness* (16), and possibly his surname *Bosor,* may have come from a Jewish tradition about him in the first/second century, of which we no longer have any knowledge.

2, 18: *Barely escaped:* some manuscripts read "really escaped."

2, 21: *Commandment handed down:* cf 2 Pt 3, 2 and Jude 3.

2, 22: The second proverb is of unknown origin, while the first appears in Prv 26, 11.

3, 1-4: The false teachers not only flout Christian morality (cf Jude 8-19); they also deny the second coming of Christ and the judgment (4; cf 2 Pt 3, 7). They seek to justify their licentiousness by arguing that the promised return of Christ has not been realized and the world is the same, no better than it was before (3-4). The author wishes to strengthen the faithful against such errors by reminding them in this *second letter* of the instruction in 1 Pt and of the teaching of the *prophets* and of Christ, conveyed through the *apostles* (1-2; cf Jude 17); cf 1 Pt 1, 10-12.16-21, especially 16-21; Eph 2, 20.

3, 3: *Scoffers:* cf Jude 18, where, however, only the passions of the scoffers are mentioned, not a denial on their part of Jesus' parousia.

IV. THE DELAY OF THE SECOND COMING

CHAPTER 3

Denial of the Parousia. [1] * This is now, beloved, the second letter I am writing to you; through them by way of reminder I am trying to stir up your sincere disposition, [2] to recall the words previously spoken by the holy prophets and the commandment of the Lord and savior through your apostles.[b] [3] Know this first of all, that in the last days scoffers* will come [to] scoff, living according to their own desires[c] [4] and saying, "Where is the promise of his coming?* From the time when our ancestors fell asleep, everything has remained as it was from the beginning of creation."[d] [5] They deliberately ignore the fact that the heavens existed of old and earth was formed out of water and through water* by the word of God;[e] [6] through these the world that then existed was destroyed,[f] deluged with water.* [7] The present heavens and earth have been reserved by the same word for fire, kept for the day of judgment and of destruction of the godless.[g]

[8] * But do not ignore this one fact, beloved, that with the Lord one day is like a thousand years* and a thousand years like one day.[h] [9] The Lord does not delay his promise, as some regard "delay," but he is patient with you, not wishing that any should perish but that all should come to

---

3, 4-7: The false teachers tried to justify their immorality by pointing out that the promised *coming (parousia)* of the Lord has not yet occurred, even though early Christians expected it in their day. They thus insinuate that God is not guiding the world's history anymore, since nothing has changed and the first generation of Christians, *our ancestors* (4), has all died by this time. The author replies that, just as God destroyed the earth by water in the flood (5-6, cf 2 Pt 2, 5), so he will destroy it along with the false teachers on judgment day (7). *The word of God,* which called the world into being (Gn 1; Ps 33, 6) and *destroyed* it by the waters of a flood, will destroy it again by fire on *the day of judgment* (5-7).

3, 5: *Formed out of water and through water:* Gn 1, 2.6-8 is reflected as well as Greek views that water was the basic element from which all is derived.

3, 6: *Destroyed, deluged with water:* cf 2 Pt 2, 5; Gn 7, 11—8, 2.

3, 8-10: The scoffers' objection (4) is refuted also by showing that *delay* of the Lord's second coming is not a failure to fulfill his word but rather a sign of his patience: God is giving time for repentance before the final judgment (cf Wis 11, 23-26; Ez 18, 23; 33, 11).

3, 8: Cf Ps 90, 4

repentance.[i] [10]But the day of the Lord will come like a thief,* and then the heavens will pass away with a mighty roar and the elements will be dissolved by fire, and the earth and everything done on it will be found out.[j]

Exhortation to Preparedness.* [11]Since everything is to be dissolved in this way, what sort of persons ought [you] to be, conducting yourselves in holiness and devotion,[k] [12]waiting for and hastening the coming of the day of God,[l] because of which the heavens will be dissolved in flames and the elements melted by fire.* [13]But according to his promise we await new heavens and a new earth* in which righteousness dwells.[m]

[14]Therefore, beloved, since you await these things, be eager to be found without

spot or blemish before him, at peace. [15]And consider the patience of our Lord as salvation, as our beloved brother Paul, according to the wisdom given to him, also wrote to you,[n] [16]speaking of these things* as he does in all his letters. In them there are some things hard to understand that the ignorant and unstable distort to their own destruction, just as they do the other scriptures.

V. FINAL EXHORTATION AND DOXOLOGY*

[17]Therefore, beloved, since you are forewarned, be on your guard not to be led into the error of the unprincipled and to fall from your own stability.[o] [18]But grow in grace and in the knowledge of our Lord and savior Jesus Christ. To him be glory now and to the day of eternity. [Amen.][p]

---

i Ez 18, 23; 1 Tm 2, 4.—j Is 66, 15-16; Mt 24, 29.—k Acts 3, 19-21.—l Is 34, 4; Heb 10, 27.—m Is 65, 17; 66, 22; Rom 8, 21; Rv 21, 1.27.—n Rom 8, 19; Jude 24.—o Mk 13, 5; Heb 2, 1.—p Rom 16, 27.

3, 10: *Like a thief:* Mt 24, 43; 1 Thes 5, 2; Rv 3, 3. *Will be found out:* cf 1 Cor 3, 13-15. Some few versions read, as the sense may demand, "will not be found out"; many manuscripts read "will be burned up"; there are further variants in other manuscripts, versions, and Fathers. Total destruction is assumed (11).

3, 11-16: The second coming of Christ and the judgment of the world are the doctrinal bases for the moral exhortation to readiness through vigilance and a virtuous life; cf Mt 24, 42.50-51; Lk 12, 40; 1 Thes 5, 1-11; Jude 20-21.

3, 12: *Flames . . . fire:* although this is the only New Testament passage about a final conflagration, the idea was common in apocalyptic and Greco-Roman thought. *Hastening:* eschatology is here used to motivate ethics (11), as elsewhere in the New Testament. Jewish sources and Acts 3, 19-20 assume that proper

ethical conduct can help bring the promised day of the Lord; cf 2 Pt 3, 9. Some render the phrase, however, "desiring it earnestly."

3, 13: *New heavens and a new earth:* cf Is 65, 17; 66, 22. The divine promises will be fulfilled after the day of judgment will have passed. The universe will be transformed by the reign of God's *righteousness* or justice; cf Is 65, 17-18; Acts 3, 21; Rom 8, 18-25; Rv 21, 1.

3, 16: *These things:* the teachings of this letter find parallels in Paul, e.g., God's will to save (Rom 2, 4; 9, 22-23; 1 Cor 1, 7-8), the coming of Christ (1 Thes 4, 16-17; 1 Cor 15, 23-52), and preparedness for the judgment (Col 1, 22-23; Eph 1, 4-14; 4, 30; 5, 5-14). *Other scriptures:* used to guide the faith and life of the Christian community. The letters of Paul are thus here placed on the same level as books of the Old Testament. Possibly other New Testament writings could also be included.

3, 17-18: To avoid the dangers of *error* and loss of *stability,* Christians are *forewarned* to be *on guard* and to *grow* in *grace and knowledge* (2 Pt 1, 2) of Christ. The doxology (18) recalls 1 Pt 4, 11. Some manuscripts add *Amen.*

THE FIRST LETTER OF JOHN

INTRODUCTION

Early Christian tradition identified this work as a letter of John the apostle. Because of its resemblance to the fourth gospel in style, vocabulary, and ideas, it is generally agreed that both works are the product of the same school of Johannine Christianity. The terminology and the presence or absence of certain theological ideas in 1 John suggest that it was written after the gospel; it may have been composed as a short treatise on ideas that were developed more fully in the fourth gospel. To others, the evidence suggests that 1 John was written after the fourth gospel as part of a debate on the proper interpretation of that gospel. Whatever its relation to the gospel, 1 John may be dated toward the end of the first century. Unlike 2 and 3 John, it lacks in form the salutation and epistolary conclusion of a letter. These features, its prologue, and its emphasis on doctrinal teaching make it more akin to a theological treatise than to most other New Testament letters.

The purpose of the letter is to combat certain false ideas, especially about Jesus, and to deepen the spiritual and social awareness of the Christian community (3, 17). Some former members (2, 19) of the community refused to acknowledge Jesus as the Christ (2,

1Jn

22) and denied that he was a true man (4, 2) The specific heresy described in this letter cannot be identified exactly, but it is a form of docetism or gnosticism; the former doctrine denied the humanity of Christ to insure that his divinity was untainted, and the latter viewed the appearance of Christ as a mere stepping-stone to higher knowledge of God. These theological errors are rejected by an appeal to the reality and continuity of the apostolic witness to Jesus. The author affirms that authentic Christian love, ethics, and faith take place only within the historical revelation and sacrifice of Jesus Christ. The fullness of Christian life as fellowship with the Father must be based on true belief and result in charitable living; knowledge of God and love for one another are inseparable, and error in one area inevitably affects the other. Although the author recognizes that Christian doctrine presents intangible mysteries of faith about Christ, he insists that the concrete Christian life brings to light the deeper realities of the gospel.

The structure and language of the letter are straightforward yet repetitious. The author sets forth the striking contrasts between light and darkness, Christians and the world, and truth and error to illustrate the threats and responsibilities of Christian life. The result is not one of theological argument but one of intense religious conviction expressed in simple truths. The letter is of particular value for its declaration of the humanity and divinity of Christ as an apostolic teaching and for its development of the intrinsic connection between Christian moral conduct and Christian doctrine.

The principal divisions of the First Letter of John are the following:

I.   Prologue (1, 1-4)
II. God as Light (1, 5—3, 10)
III. Love for One Another (3, 11—5, 12)
IV. Epilogue (5, 13-21)

I. PROLOGUE

CHAPTER 1

The Word of Life*

1 What was from the beginning,
  what we have heard,
  what we have seen with our eyes,
  what we looked upon
  and touched with our hands
  concerns the Word of life—[a]
2 for the life was made visible;
  we have seen it and testify to it
  and proclaim to you the eternal life
  that was with the Father and was made
      visible to us—[b]
3 what we have seen and heard
  we proclaim now to you,

so that you too may have fellowship
  with us;
for our fellowship is with the Father
  and with his Son, Jesus Christ.[c]
4 We are writing this so that our joy may
    be complete.[d]

II. GOD AS LIGHT

God is Light. [5] Now this is the message that we have heard from him and proclaim to you: God is light,* and in him there is no darkness at all. [6] If we say, "We have fellowship with him," while we continue to walk in darkness, we lie and do not act in truth.[e] [7] But if we walk in the light as he is in the light, then we have fellowship with one another, and the blood of his Son Jesus cleanses us from all sin.[f] [8] If we say, "We are without sin," we deceive ourselves,*

---

a 1 Jn 2, 13; Jn 1, 1.14; 20, 20.25.27.—b Jn 15, 27; 17, 5.—c Jn 17, 21; Acts 4, 20.—d Jn 15, 11; 2 Jn 12.—e Jn 12, 35.—f Mt 26, 28; Rom 3, 24-25; Heb 9, 14; 1 Pt 1, 19; Rv 1, 5.

1, 1-4: There is a striking parallel to the prologue of the gospel of John (Jn 1, 1-18), but the emphasis here is not on the preexistent Word but rather on the apostles' witness to the incarnation of *life* by their experience of the historical Jesus. He is *the Word of life* (1; cf Jn 1, 4), *the eternal life that was with the Father and was made visible* (2; cf Jn 1, 14), and was *heard, seen, looked upon,* and *touched* by the apostles. The purpose of their teaching is to share that *life,* called *fellowship . . . with the Father and with his Son, Jesus Christ,* with those who receive their witness (3; Jn 1, 14.16).

1, 5-7: *Light* is to be understood here as truth and goodness; *darkness* here is error and depravity (cf Jn 3, 19-21; 17, 17; Eph 5, 8). To *walk* in light or darkness is to live according to truth or error, not merely intellectual but moral as well. Fellowship with God and with one another consists in a life according to the truth as found in God and in Christ.

1, 8-10: Denial of the condition of sin is self-deception and even contradictory of divine revelation; there is also the continual possibility of sin's recurrence. Forgiveness and deliverance from sin through Christ are assured through acknowledgment of them and repentance.

and the truth is not in us.[g] [9]If we acknowledge our sins, he is faithful and just and will forgive our sins and cleanse us from every wrongdoing.[h] [10]If we say, "We have not sinned," we make him a liar, and his word is not in us.[i]

CHAPTER 2

Christ and His Commandments. [1]My children,* I am writing this to you so that you may not commit sin. But if anyone does sin, we have an Advocate with the Father, Jesus Christ the righteous one.[j] [2]He is expiation for our sins, and not for our sins only but for those of the whole world.[k] [3]The way we may be sure* that we know him is to keep his commandments.[l] [4]Whoever says, "I know him," but does not keep his commandments is a liar, and the truth is not in him.[m] [5]But whoever keeps his word, the love of God is truly perfected in him. This is the way we may know that we are in union with him:[n] [6]whoever claims to abide in him ought to live [just] as he lived.

The New Commandment.* [7]Beloved, I am writing no new commandment to you but an old commandment that you had from the beginning. The old commandment is the word that you have heard.[o] [8]And yet I do write a new commandment to you, which holds true in him and among you,* for the darkness is passing away, and the true light is already shining.[p] [9]Whoever says he is in the light, yet hates his brother, is still in the darkness.[q] [10]Whoever loves his brother remains in the light, and there

is nothing in him to cause a fall.[r] [11]Whoever hates his brother is in darkness; he walks in darkness and does not know where he is going because the darkness has blinded his eyes.

Members of the Community.* [12]I am writing to you, children, because your sins have been forgiven[s] for his name's sake.*

[13]I am writing to you, fathers, because you know him who is from the beginning.

I am writing to you, young men, because you have conquered the evil one.[i]

[14]I write to you, children, because you know the Father.

I write to you, fathers, because you know him who is from the beginning.

I write to you, young men, because you are strong and the word of God remains in you, and you have conquered the evil one.

[15]Do not love the world or the things of the world.* If anyone loves the world, the love of the Father is not in him.[u] [16]For all that is in the world, sensual lust,* enticement for the eyes, and a pretentious life, is not from the Father but is from the world. [17]Yet the world and its enticement are passing away. But whoever does the will of God remains forever.[v]

Antichrists. [18]Children, it is the last hour;* and just as you heard that the antichrist was coming, so now many antichrists have appeared. Thus we know this is the last hour.[w] [19]They went out from us, but they were not really of our number;* if

g 2 Chr 6, 36; Prv 20, 9.—h Prv 28, 13; Jas 5, 16.—i 1 Jn 5, 10.—j Jn 14, 16; Heb 7, 25.—k 1 Jn 4, 10.—l Jn 14, 15; 15, 10.—m 1 Jn 4, 20.—n Jn 14, 23.—o 1 Jn 3, 11; Dt 6, 5; Mt 22, 37-40.—p Jn 13, 34 / Jn 1, 5; Rom 13, 12.—q Jn 8, 12.—r Eccl 2, 14; Jn 11, 10.—s 1 Cor 6, 11.—t 1 Jn 1, 1; Jn 1, 1.—u Rom 8, 7-8; Jas 4, 4; 2 Pt 1, 4.—v Is 40, 8; Mt 7, 21; 1 Cor 7, 31; 1 Pt 4, 2.—w 1 Tim 4, 1.

2, 1: *Children:* like the term "beloved," this is an expression of pastoral love (cf Jn 13, 33; 21, 5; 1 Cor 4, 14). *Advocate:* for the use of the term, see Jn 14, 16. Forgiveness of sin is assured through Christ's intercession and expiation or "offering"; the death of Christ effected the removal of sin.

2, 3-6: *The way we may be sure:* to those who claim, "I have known Christ and therefore I know him," our author insists on not mere intellectual knowledge but obedience to God's commandments in a life conformed to the example of Christ; this confirms our knowledge of him and is *the love of God . . . perfected.* Disparity between moral life and the commandments proves improper belief.

2, 7-11: The author expresses the continuity and freshness of mutual charity in Christian experience. Through Christ the commandment of love has become the *light* defeating the *darkness* of evil in a new age. All hatred as darkness is incompatible with the light and Christian life. Note also the characteristic Johannine polemic in which a positive assertion is emphasized by the negative statement of its opposite.

2, 8: *Which holds true in him and among you:* literally, "a thing that holds true in him and in you."

2, 12-17: The Christian community that has experienced the grace of God through forgiveness of sin and knowledge of Christ is armed against the evil one.

2, 12: *For his name's sake:* because of Christ our sins are forgiven.

2, 15: *The world:* all that is hostile toward God and alienated from him. Love of the *world* and love of God are thus mutually exclusive; cf Jas 4, 4.

2, 16: *Sensual lust:* literally, "the lust of the flesh," inordinate desire for physical gratification. *Enticement for the eyes:* literally, "the lust of the eyes," avarice or covetousness; the eyes are regarded as the windows of the soul. *Pretentious life:* literally, "pride of life," arrogance or ostentation in one's earthly style of life that reflects a willful independence from God and others.

2, 18: *It is the last hour:* literally, "a last hour," the period between the death and resurrection of Christ and his second coming. *The antichrist:* opponent or adversary of Christ; the term appears only in 1-2 John, but "pseudochrists" (translated "false messiahs") in Mt 24, 24 and Mk 13, 22, and Paul's "lawless one" in 2 Thes 2, 3, are similar figures. *Many antichrists:* Mt, Mk, and Rv seem to indicate a collectivity of persons, here related to the false teachers.

2, 19: *Not really of our number:* the apostate teachers only proved their lack of faith by leaving the community.

1Jn

they had been, they would have remained with us. Their desertion shows that none of them was of our number. [20] But you have the anointing that comes from the holy one,* and you all have knowledge.[x] [21] I write to you not because you do not know the truth but because you do, and because every lie is alien to the truth.[y] [22] * Who is the liar? Whoever denies that Jesus is the Christ. Whoever denies the Father and the Son, this is the antichrist.[z] [23] No one who denies the Son has the Father, but whoever confesses the Son has the Father as well.[a]

Life from God's Anointing. [24] [b] Let what you heard from the beginning remain in you. If what you heard from the beginning remains in you, then you will remain in the Son and in the Father.* [25] And this is the promise that he made us: eternal life.[c] [26] I write you these things about those who would deceive you. [27] As for you, the anointing that you received from him remains in you, so that you do not need anyone to teach you. But his anointing teaches you about everything and is true and not false; just as it taught you, remain in him.

Children of God. [28] * And now, children, remain in him, so that when he appears we may have confidence and not be put to shame by him at his coming. [29] If you consider that he is righteous, you also know that everyone who acts in righteousness is begotten by him.

CHAPTER 3

[1] * See what love the Father has bestowed on us that we may be called the children of God. Yet so we are. The reason the world does not know us is that it did not know him.[d] [2] Beloved, we are God's children now; what we shall be has not yet been revealed. We do know that when it is revealed* we shall be like him, for we shall see him as he is.[e] [3] Everyone who has this hope based on him makes himself pure, as he is pure.[f]

Avoiding Sin. [4] Everyone who commits sin commits lawlessness, for sin is lawlessness.* [5] You know that he was revealed to take away sins, and in him there is no sin.[g] [6] No one who remains in him sins; no one who sins has seen him or known him. [7] Children, let no one deceive you. The person who acts in righteousness is righteous, just as he is righteous. [8] Whoever sins belongs to the devil, because the devil has sinned from the beginning. Indeed, the Son of God was revealed to destroy the works of the devil.[h] [9] No one who is begotten by God commits sin, because God's seed remains in him; he cannot sin because he is begotten by God.* [10] In this way, the children of God and the children of the devil are made plain; no one who fails to act in righteousness belongs to God, nor anyone who does not love his brother.

III. LOVE FOR ONE ANOTHER

[11] * For this is the message you have heard from the beginning: we should love one another,[i] [12] unlike Cain who belonged to the evil one and slaughtered his brother. Why did he slaughter him? Because his own works were evil, and those of his

---

x Jn 14, 26.—y 1 Jn 3, 19; 2 Pt 1, 12.—z 2 Thes 2, 4.—a Jn 14, 7-9.—b Jn 14, 23.—c Jn 5, 24; 10, 28; 17, 2.—d Jn 1, 12; Eph 1, 5 / Jn 15, 21; 17, 25.—e Phil 3, 21.—f 1 Jn 2, 6.—g Is 53, 9; Jn 1, 29; 8, 46; 1 Pt 2, 22.—h Jn 8, 44; 12, 31-32.—i 1 Jn 2, 7; Jn 13, 34; 15, 12.17.

2, 20: *The anointing that comes from the holy one:* this anointing is in the Old Testament sense of receiving the Spirit of God. The *Holy One* probably refers to Christ. True knowledge is the gift of the Spirit (cf Is 11, 2), and the function of the Spirit is to lead Christians to the truth (Jn 14, 17.26; 16, 13).

2, 22-23: Certain gnostics denied that the earthly Jesus was the Christ; to deny knowledge of the Son is to deny the Father, since only through the Son has God been fully revealed (Jn 1, 18; 14, 8-9).

2, 24: Continuity with the apostolic witness as proclaimed in the prologue is the safeguard of right belief.

2, 28-29: Our confidence at his judgment is based on the daily assurance of salvation. Our actions reflect our true relation to him.

3, 1-3: The greatest sign of God's love is the gift of his Son (Jn 3, 16) that has made Christians true children of God. This relationship is a present reality and also part of the life to come; true knowledge of God will ultimately be gained, and Christians prepare themselves now by virtuous lives in imitation of the Son.

3, 2: *When it is revealed:* or "when he is revealed" (the subject of the verb could be Christ).

3, 4: *Lawlessness:* a reference to the activity of the antichrist, so it is expressed as hostility toward God and a rejection of Christ. The author goes on to contrast the states of sin and righteousness. Christians do not escape sin but realize that when they sin they cease to have fellowship with God. Virtue and sin distinguish the children of God from the children of the devil.

3, 9: A habitual sinner is a child of the devil, while a child of God, who by definition is in fellowship with God, cannot sin. *Seed:* Christ or the Spirit who shares the nature of God with the Christian.

3, 11-18: Love, even to the point of self-sacrifice, is the point of the commandment. The story of Cain and Abel (12-15; Gn 4, 1-16) presents the rivalry of two brothers, in a contrast of evil and righteousness, where envy led to murder. For Christians, proof of deliverance is love toward others, after the example of Christ. This includes concrete acts of charity, out of our material abundance.

brother righteous.[j] [13]Do not be amazed, [then,] brothers, if the world hates you.[k] [14]We know that we have passed from death to life because we love our brothers. Whoever does not love remains in death.[l] [15]Everyone who hates his brother is a murderer, and you know that no murderer has eternal life remaining in him.[m] [16]The way we came to know love was that he laid down his life for us; so we ought to lay down our lives for our brothers.[n] [17]If someone who has worldly means sees a brother in need and refuses him compassion, how can the love of God remain in him?[o] [18]Children, let us love not in word or speech but in deed and truth.[p]

Confidence before God.* [19][Now] this is how we shall know that we* belong to the truth and reassure our hearts before him [20]in whatever our hearts condemn, for God is greater than our hearts and knows everything. [21]Beloved, if [our] hearts do not condemn us, we have confidence in God [22]and receive from him whatever we ask, because we keep his commandments and do what pleases him.[q] [23]And his commandment is this: we should believe in the name of his Son, Jesus Christ, and love one another just as he commanded us.[r] [24]Those who keep his commandments remain in him, and he in them, and the way we know that he remains in us is from the Spirit that he gave us.[s]

CHAPTER 4

Testing the Spirits.* [1]Beloved, do not trust every spirit but test the spirits to see whether they belong to God, because many false prophets have gone out into the world.[t] [2]This is how you can know the Spirit of God: every spirit that acknowledges Jesus Christ come in the flesh belongs to God,[u] [3]and every spirit that does not acknowledge Jesus* does not belong to God. This is the spirit of the antichrist that, as you heard, is to come, but in fact is already in the world.[v] [4]You belong to God, children, and you have conquered them, for the one who is in you is greater than the one who is in the world. [5]They belong to the world; accordingly, their teaching belongs to the world, and the world listens to them.[w] [6]We belong to God, and anyone who knows God listens to us, while anyone who does not belong to God refuses to hear us. This is how we know the spirit of truth and the spirit of deceit.[x]

God's Love and Christian Life. [7] * Beloved, let us love one another, because love is of God; everyone who loves is begotten by God and knows God. [8]Whoever is without love does not know God, for God is love. [9]In this way the love of God was revealed to us: God sent his only Son into the world so that we might have life through him.[y] [10]In this is love: not that we have loved God, but that he loved us and sent his Son as expiation for our sins.[z] [11]Beloved, if God so loved us, we also must love one another. [12]No one has ever seen God. Yet, if we love one another, God remains in us, and his love is brought to perfection in us.[a]

[13] * This is how we know that we remain in him and he in us, that he has given us of his Spirit. [14]Moreover, we have seen and

---

j Gn 4, 8; Jude 11.—k Mt 24, 9; Jn 15, 18; 17, 14.—l Lv 19, 17; Jn 5, 24.—m Jn 8, 44.—n Mt 20, 28; Jn 10, 11; 15, 13.—o Dt 15, 7.11; Jas 2, 15-16.—p Jas 1, 22.—q 1 Jn 5, 15; Mt 7, 7-11; 21, 22; Jn 14, 13-14.—r Jn 13, 34; 15, 17.—s 1 Jn 4, 13; Jn 14, 21-23.—t 1 Jn 2, 18; Mt 24, 24.—u 1 Cor 12, 3; 1 Thes 5, 21.—v 1 Jn 1, 22.—w Jn 15, 19.—x Jn 8, 47; 10, 16.—y Jn 3, 16.—z Rom 5, 8.—a Jn 1, 18; 1 Tm 6, 16.

3, 19-24: Living a life of faith in Jesus and of Christian love assures us of abiding in God no matter what our feelings may at times tell us. Our obedience gives us confidence in prayer and trust in God's judgment. This obedience includes our belief in Christ and love for one another.

3, 19b-20: This difficult passage may also be translated "we shall be at peace before him in whatever our hearts condemn, for . . ." or "and before God we shall convince our hearts, if our hearts condemn us, that God is greater than our hearts."

4, 1-6: Deception is possible in spiritual phenomena and may be tested by its relation to Christian doctrine (cf 1 Cor 12, 3): those who fail to acknowledge Jesus Christ in the flesh are false prophets and belong to the antichrist. Even though these false prophets are well received in the world, the Christian who belongs to God has a greater power in the truth.

4, 3: *Does not acknowledge Jesus:* some ancient manuscripts add "Christ" and/or "to have come in the flesh" (cf 1 Jn 4, 2), and others read "every spirit that annuls (or severs) Jesus."

4, 7-12: Love as we share in it testifies to the nature of God and to his presence in our lives. One who loves shows that one is a child of God and knows God, for God's very being is love; one without love is without God. The revelation of the nature of God's love is found in the free gift of his Son to us, so that we may share life with God and be delivered from our sins. The love we have for one another must be of the same sort: authentic, merciful; this unique Christian love is our proof that we know God and can "see" the invisible God.

4, 13-21: The testimony of the Spirit and that of faith join the testimony of love to confirm our knowledge of God. Our love is grounded in the confession of Jesus as the Son of God and the example of God's love for us. Christian life is founded on the knowledge of God as love and on his continuing presence that relieves us from fear of judgment (16-18). What Christ is gives us confidence, even as we live and love in this world. Yet Christian love is not abstract but lived in the concrete manner of love for one another.

1Jn

testify that the Father sent his Son as savior of the world. [15] Whoever acknowledges that Jesus is the Son of God, God remains in him and he in God. [16] We have come to know and to believe in the love God has for us.

God is love, and whoever remains in love remains in God and God in him. [17] In this is love brought to perfection among us, that we have confidence on the day of judgment because as he is, so are we in this world.[b] [18] There is no fear in love, but perfect love drives out fear because fear has to do with punishment, and so one who fears is not yet perfect in love. [19] We love because he first loved us. [20] If anyone says, "I love God," but hates his brother, he is a liar; for whoever does not love a brother whom he has seen cannot love God* whom he has not seen.[c] [21] This is the commandment we have from him: whoever loves God must also love his brother.[d]

CHAPTER 5

Faith is Victory over the World. [1] * Everyone who believes that Jesus is the Christ is begotten by God, and everyone who loves the father loves [also] the one begotten by him.[e] [2] In this way we know that we love the children of God when we love God and obey his commandments. [3] For the love of God is this, that we keep his commandments. And his commandments are not burdensome,[f] [4] for whoever is begotten by God conquers the world. And the victory that conquers the world is our faith.[g] [5] Who [indeed] is the victor over the world but the one who believes that Jesus is the Son of God?[h]

[6] This is the one who came through water and blood,* Jesus Christ, not by water alone, but by water and blood. The Spirit is the one that testifies, and the Spirit is truth.[i] [7] So there are three that testify, [8] the Spirit, the water, and the blood, and the three are of one accord.[j] [9] If we accept human testimony, the testimony of God is surely greater. Now the testimony of God is this, that he has testified on behalf of his Son.[k] [10] Whoever believes in the Son of God has this testimony within himself. Whoever does not believe God has made him a liar by not believing the testimony God has given about his Son.[l] [11] And this is the testimony: God gave us eternal life, and this life is in his Son.[m] [12] Whoever possesses the Son has life; whoever does not possess the Son of God does not have life.

IV. EPILOGUE*

Prayer for Sinners. [13] I write these things to you so that you may know that you have eternal life, you who believe in the name of the Son of God.[n] [14] And we have this confidence in him, that if we ask anything according to his will, he hears us.[o] [15] And if we know that he hears us in regard to whatever we ask, we know that what we have asked him for is ours. [16] If anyone sees his brother sinning, if the sin is not deadly, he should pray to God and he will give him life. This is only for those whose sin is not deadly. There is such a thing as deadly sin, about which I do not say that you should pray.[p] [17] All wrongdoing is sin, but there is sin that is not deadly.

[18] We know that no one begotten by God sins; but the one begotten by God he protects, and the evil one cannot touch him.

---

b 1 Jn 2, 28.—c 1 Jn 2, 4.—d Jn 13, 34; 14, 15.21; 15, 17.—e Jn 8, 42; 1 Pt 1, 23.—f Jn 14, 15.—g Jn 16, 33.—h 1 Cor 15, 57.—i Jn 15, 26; 19, 34.—j Jn 5, 32.36; 15, 26.—k Jn 5, 32.37.—l 1 Jn 3, 33.—m 1 Jn 1, 2; Jn 1, 4; 5, 21.26; 17, 3.—n Jn 1, 12; 20, 31.—o 1 Jn 3, 21-22; Mt 7, 7; Jn 14, 13-14.—p Mt 12, 31.

4, 20: *Cannot love God:* some ancient manuscripts read "how can he love . . . ?"

5, 1-5: Children of God are identified not only by their love for others (1 Jn 4, 7-9) and for God (1 Jn 5, 1-2) but by their belief in the divine sonship of Jesus Christ. Faith, the acceptance of Jesus in his true character and the obedience in love to God's commands (3), is the source of the Christian's power in the world and conquers the world of evil (4-5), even as Christ overcame the world (Jn 16, 33).

5, 6-12: *Water and blood* (6) refers to Christ's baptism (Mt 3, 16-17) and to the shedding of his blood on the cross (Jn 19, 34). *The Spirit* was present at the baptism (Mt 3, 16; Mk 1, 10; Lk 3, 22; Jn 1, 32.34). *The testimony* to Christ as the Son of

God is confirmed by divine witness (7-9), greater by far than the two legally required human witnesses (Dt 17, 6). To deny this is to deny God's truth; cf Jn 8, 17-18. The gist of the divine witness or *testimony* is that *eternal life* (11-12) is given in Christ and nowhere else. To *possess the Son* is not acceptance of a doctrine but of a person who lives now and provides life.

5, 13-21: As children of God we have confidence in prayer because of our intimate relationship with him (14-15). In love, we pray (16-17) for those who are in *sin*, but not in *deadly sin* (literally, "sin unto death"), probably referring to apostasy or activities brought on under the antichrist; cf Mk 3, 29; Heb 6, 4-6; 10, 26-31. Even in the latter case, however, prayer, while not enjoined, is not forbidden. The letter concludes with a summary of the themes of the letter (18-20). There is a sharp antithesis between the children of God and those belonging to the world and to the evil one. The Son reveals the God of truth; Christians dwell in the true God, *in his Son,* and have eternal life. The final verse (21) voices a perennial warning about *idols,* any type of rival to God.

¹⁹We know that we belong to God, and the whole world is under the power of the evil one. ²⁰We also know that the Son of God

q Jer 24, 7; Jn 17, 3; Eph 1, 17.

has come and has given us discernment to know the one who is true. And we are in the one who is true, in his Son Jesus Christ. He is the true God and eternal life. *q* ²¹Children, be on your guard against idols.

THE SECOND LETTER OF JOHN

INTRODUCTION

Written in response to similar problems, the Second and Third Letters of John are of the same length, perhaps determined by the practical consideration of the writing space on one piece of papyrus. In each letter the writer calls himself "the Presbyter," and their common authorship is further evidenced by internal similarities in style and wording, especially in the introductions and conclusions. The literary considerations that link 2 and 3 John also link them with the First Letter and the Gospel of John. The concern with "truth," christology, mutual love, the new commandment, antichrist, and the integrity of witness to the earthly Jesus mark these works as products of the Johannine school. The identity of the Presbyter is problematic. The use of the title implies more than age, and refers to his position of leadership in the early church. The absence of a proper name indicates that he was well known and acknowledged in authority by the communities to which he writes. Although traditionally attributed to John the apostle, these letters were probably written by a disciple or scribe of an apostle. The traditional place and date of composition, Ephesus at the end of the first century, are plausible for both letters.

The Second Letter is addressed to "the chosen Lady" and "to her children." This literary image of a particular Christian community reflects the specific destination and purpose of the letter. Unlike 1 John, this brief letter is not a theological treatise but a reply to problems within the church. The Johannine themes of love and truth are used to support practical advice on Christian living. The Presbyter encourages community members to show their Christianity by adhering to the great commandment of mutual love and to the historical truth about Jesus. The false teaching present among them is a spiritualizing christology that may tempt some members to discount teachings about the incarnation and death of Jesus the Christ; cf 1 Jn 4, 2. For their protection the Presbyter forbids hospitality toward unknown or "progressive" Christians to prevent their infiltration of the community. The Second Letter preserves the Johannine concerns of doctrinal purity and active love in the form of pastoral advice to a threatened community.

---

¹ *a* The Presbyter to the chosen Lady* and to her children whom I love in truth— and not only I but also all who know the truth—²because of the truth that dwells in

a Jn 8, 32; 3 Jn 1.

us and will be with us forever. ³Grace, mercy, and peace* will be with us from God the Father and from Jesus Christ the Father's Son in truth and love.

1: *The chosen Lady:* literally "elected"; this could also be translated "Kyria (a woman's name) chosen (by God)" or "the lady Electa" or "Electa Kyria." The adjective "chosen" is applied to all Christians at the beginning of other New Testament letters (1 Pt 1, 1; Ti 1, 1). The description is of a specific community with "children" who are its members. *The truth:* the affirmation of Jesus in the flesh and in contrast to false teaching (7).

3: *Grace, mercy, and peace:* like 1 and 2 Tm this letter adds *mercy* to the terms used frequently in a salutation to describe Christian blessing; it appears only here in the Johannine writings. The author also puts the blessing in relation to *truth* and *love,* the watchwords of the Johannine teaching. *The Father's Son:* the title that affirms the close relationship of Christ to God; similar variations of this title occur elsewhere (Jn 1, 14; 3, 35), but the precise wording is not found elsewhere in the New Testament.

2Jn

⁴I rejoiced greatly to find some of your children* walking in the truth just as we were commanded by the Father.*b* ⁵But now, Lady, I ask you, not as though I were writing a new commandment but the one we have had from the beginning: let us love one another.*c* ⁶For this is love, that we walk according to his commandments;* this is the commandment, as you heard from the beginning, in which you should walk.*d*

⁷ *e* Many deceivers have gone out into the world, those who do not acknowledge Jesus Christ as coming in the flesh; such is the deceitful one and the antichrist.* ⁸Look to yourselves that you* do not lose what we worked for but may receive a full recompense. ⁹ *f* Anyone who is so "progressive"* as not to remain in the teaching of the Christ does not have God; whoever remains in the teaching has the Father and the Son. ¹⁰ * If anyone comes to you and does not bring this doctrine, do not receive him in your house or even greet him;*g* ¹¹for whoever greets him shares in his evil works.

¹²Although I have much to write to you, I do not intend to use paper and ink. Instead, I hope to visit you and to speak face to face so that our joy* may be complete.*h* ¹³The children of your chosen sister* send you greetings.

b 3 Jn 3.—c Jn 13, 34; 15, 12; 1 Jn 4, 7.—d Jn 13, 34; 14, 15; 1 Jn 5, 3.—e 1 Jn 2, 22; 4, 2.—f Jn 8, 31; 1 Jn 2, 23; 4, 15.—g Rom 16, 17; 2 Thes 3, 6.—h Jn 15, 11; 1 Jn 1, 4; 3 Jn 13.

4: *Some of your children:* this refers to those whom the Presbyter has recently encountered, but it may also indicate the presence of false doctrine in the community: the Presbyter encourages those who have remained faithful. *Walking in the truth:* an expression used in the Johannine writings to describe a way of living in which the Christian faith is visibly expressed; cf 1 Jn 1, 6-7; 2, 6.11; 3 Jn 3.

6: *His commandments:* cf 1 Jn 3, 23; 2, 7-8; 4, 21; obedience to the commandment of faith and love includes all others.

7: *The antichrist:* see 1 Jn 2, 18-19.22; 4, 3.

8: *You* (plural): it is not certain whether this means the Christians addressed or includes the Presbyter, since some of the ancient Greek manuscripts and Greek Fathers have "we."

9: *Anyone who is so "progressive":* literally, "Anyone who goes ahead." Some gnostic groups held the doctrine of the Christ come in the flesh to be a first step in belief, which the more advanced and spiritual believer surpassed and abandoned in his knowledge of the spiritual Christ. The author affirms that fellowship with God may be gained only by holding to the complete doctrine of Jesus Christ (1 Jn 2, 22-23; 4, 2; 5, 5-6).

10-11: At this time false teachers were considered so dangerous and divisive as to be shunned completely. From this description they seem to be wandering preachers. We see here a natural suspicion of early Christians concerning such itinerants and can envisage the problems faced by missionaries such as those mentioned in 3 Jn 10.

12: *Our joy:* a number of other Greek manuscripts read "your joy."

13: *Chosen sister:* the community of which the Presbyter is now a part greets you (singular), the community of the Lady addressed.

THE THIRD LETTER OF JOHN

INTRODUCTION

The Third Letter of John preserves a brief glimpse into the problems of missionary activity and local autonomy in the early church. In contrast to the other two letters of John, this work was addressed to a specific individual, Gaius. This letter is less theological in content and purpose. The author's goal was to secure hospitality and material support for his missionaries, and the Presbyter is writing to another member of the church who has welcomed missionaries in the past. The Presbyter commends Gaius for his hospitality and encourages his future help. He indicates he may come to challenge the policy of Diotrephes that is based on evil gossip.

The problems of the Presbyter in this short letter provide us with valuable evidence of the flexible and personal nature of authority in the early church. The Presbyter writes to Gaius, whom perhaps he had converted or instructed, on the basis of their personal links. The brothers have also confirmed him as a loyal Christian in action and belief. Gaius accepted the missionaries from the Presbyter and presumably will accept Demetrius on the Presbyter's recommendation. In contrast, Diotrephes refuses to receive either letters or friends of the Presbyter. Although he is portrayed as ambitious and hostile, he perhaps exemplifies the cautious and sectarian nature of early Christianity; for its own protection the local community mistrusted missionaries as false teachers. Most interestingly, Diotrephes seems comfortable in ignoring the requests of the Presbyter. The Presbyter seems to acknowledge that only a personal confrontation with Diotrephes will remedy the situation (10). *The division, however, may also rest on doctrinal disagreement in which Gaius and the other "friends" accept the teaching of the Presbyter, and Diotrephes does not; the missionaries are not received for suspicion of theological error. Diotrephes has thus been viewed by some as an overly ambitious local upstart trying to thwart the advance of orthodox Christianity, by others as an orthodox church official suspicious of the teachings of the Presbyter and those in the Johannine school who think as he does, or by still others as a local leader anxious to keep the debates in the Johannine community out of his own congregation.*

This brief letter and the situation that it mirrors show us how little we know about some details of early development in the church: schools of opinion existed around which questions of faith and life were discussed, and personal ties as well as doctrine and authority played a role in what happened amid divisions and unity.

¹The Presbyter to the beloved Gaius* whom I love in truth. *ᵃ*

²Beloved, I hope you are prospering in every respect and are in good health, just as your soul is prospering. ³I rejoiced greatly when some of the brothers* came and testified to how truly you walk in the truth.*ᵇ* ⁴Nothing gives me greater joy than to hear that my children are walking in the truth.*ᶜ*

⁵Beloved, you are faithful in all you do* for the brothers, especially for strangers;*ᵈ* ⁶they have testified to your love before the church.*ᵉ* Please help them in a way worthy of God to continue their journey.* ⁷For they have set out for the sake of the Name* and are accepting nothing from the pagans. ⁸Therefore, we ought to support such persons, so that we may be co-workers in the truth.

⁹I wrote to the church, but Diotrephes, who loves to dominate,* does not acknowledge us. ¹⁰Therefore, if I come,* I will draw attention to what he is doing, spreading evil nonsense about us. And not content with that, he will not receive the brothers, hindering those who wish to do so and expelling them from the church.

¹¹Beloved, do not imitate evil* but imitate good. Whoever does what is good is of God; whoever does what is evil has never seen God.*ᶠ* ¹²Demetrius* receives a good report from all, even from the truth itself. We give our testimonial as well, and you know our testimony is true.*ᵍ*

¹³I have much to write to you, but I do not wish to write with pen and ink.*ʰ* ¹⁴Instead, I hope to see you soon, when we can talk face to face. ¹⁵Peace be with you. The friends greet you; greet the friends* there each by name.*ⁱ*

---

a 2 Jn 1.—b 3 Jn 5; Gal 6, 10; 2 Jn 4.—c 1 Thes 2, 11-12; 1 Tm 1, 2; 2 Tm 1, 2; 1 Jn 2, 1; 2 Jn 4.—d Rom 12, 13; Gal 6, 10; Heb 13, 2.—e Acts 15, 3; Col 1, 10; 1 Thes 2, 12.—f 1 Jn 2, 29; 3, 6.10.—g Jn 19, 35; 21, 24; 1 Tm 3, 7.—h 2 Jn 12.—i Jn 20, 19.21.26; Eph 6, 23; 1 Pt 5, 14.

1: *Beloved Gaius:* a frequent form of address for fellow Christians in New Testament epistolary literature.

3: *The brothers:* in this letter, the term may refer to Christians who have been missionaries and received hospitality from Gaius (5-6). *Walk in the truth:* the common Johannine term to describe Christian living; this description presents Gaius as following the teachings of the Presbyter in contrast to Diotrephes.

5: *You are faithful in all you do:* Gaius's aid to the missionaries is a manifestation of his true Christian faith.

6: *Help them . . . to continue their journey:* the Presbyter asks Gaius not only to continue to welcome the missionaries to his community but also to equip them for further travels.

7: *The Name:* of Jesus Christ (cf Acts 5, 41; 1 Jn 2, 12; 3, 23; 5, 13). *Accepting nothing:* not expecting support from the pagans to whom they preach the gospel, so that they will not be con-

considered as beggars; they required support from other Christians; cf Paul's complaints to the Corinthians (1 Cor 9, 3-12).

9: *Who loves to dominate:* the Presbyter does not deny Diotrephes' place as leader but indicates that his ambition may have caused him to disregard his letter and his influence.

10: *If I come:* the Presbyter may visit the community to challenge the actions of Diotrephes toward himself and the missionaries. *Will not receive the brothers:* Diotrephes may have been critical of the teachings of the Presbyter and sought to maintain doctrinal purity; cf 1 Jn 2, 19 and 2 Jn 10-11.

11: *Do not imitate evil:* Gaius should not be influenced by the behavior of Diotrephes.

12: *Demetrius:* because of the fear of false teachers, Demetrius, perhaps the bearer of the letter, is provided with a recommendation from the Presbyter; cf 2 Cor 3, 1; Rom 16, 1. *Even from the truth itself:* this refers probably to the manner of Demetrius's life that testifies to his true belief; cf Gaius above (v 3).

15: *Friends:* although a Johannine term for Christians (Jn 15, 15), the word here may refer to those in the community loyal to the Presbyter and to Gaius.

3Jn

THE LETTER OF JUDE

INTRODUCTION

This letter is by its address attributed to "Jude, a slave of Jesus Christ and brother of James" (1). Since he is not identified as an apostle, this designation can hardly be meant to refer to the Jude or Judas who is listed as one of the Twelve (Lk 6, 16; Acts 1, 13; cf Jn 14, 22). The person intended is almost certainly the other Jude, named in the gospels among the relatives of Jesus (Mt 13, 55; Mk 6, 3), and the James who is listed there as his brother is the one to whom the Letter of James is attributed (see the Introduction to James). Nothing else is known of this Jude, and the apparent need to identify him by reference to his better-known brother indicates that he was a rather obscure personage in the early church.

The letter is addressed in the most general terms to "those who are called, beloved in God the Father and kept safe for Jesus Christ" (1), hence apparently to all Christians. But since its purpose is to warn the addressees against false teachers, the author must have had in mind one or more specific Christian communities located in the unidentified region where the errors in question constituted a danger. While the letter contains some Semitic features, there is nothing to identify the addressees specifically as Jewish Christians; indeed, the errors envisaged seem to reflect an early form of gnosticism, opposed to law, that points rather to the cultural context of the Gentile world. Like James and 2 Peter, the Letter of Jude manifests none of the typical features of the letter form except the address.

There is so much similarity between Jude and 2 Peter, especially Jude 4-16 and 2 Peter 2, 1-18, that there must be a literary relationship between them. Since there is no evidence for the view that both authors borrowed from the same source, it is usually supposed that one of them borrowed from the other. Most scholars believe that Jude is the earlier of the two, principally because he quotes two apocryphal Jewish works, the Assumption of Moses (9) and the Book of Enoch (14-15), as part of his structured argument, whereas 2 Peter omits both references. Since there was controversy in the early church about the propriety of citing noncanonical literature that included legendary material, it is more probable that a later writer would omit such references than that he would add them.

Many interpreters today consider Jude a pseudonymous work dating from the end of the first century or even later. In support of this view they adduce the following arguments: (a) the apostles are referred to as belonging to an age that has receded into the past (17-18); (b) faith is understood as a body of doctrine handed down by a process of tradition (3); (c) the author's competent Greek style shows that he must have had a Hellenistic cultural formation; (d) the gnostic character of the errors envisaged fits better into the early second century than into a period several decades earlier. While impressive, these arguments are not entirely compelling and do not completely rule out the possibility of composition around the year A.D. 80, when the historical Jude may still have been alive.

This little letter is an urgent note by an author who intended to write more fully about salvation to an unknown group of readers, but who was forced by dangers from false teachers worming their way into the community (3-4) to dash off a warning against them (5-16) and to deliver some pressing Christian admonitions (17-23). The letter is justly famous for its majestic closing doxology (24-25).

Address and Greeting. [1] Jude, a slave of Jesus Christ and brother of James,* to those who are called, beloved in God the Father and kept safe for Jesus Christ:[a] [2] may mercy, peace, and love be yours in abundance.[b]

Occasion for Writing. [3] Beloved, although I was making every effort to write to you about our common salvation,* I now feel a need to write to encourage you to contend for the faith that was once for all handed down to the holy ones.[c] [4] For there have been some intruders, who long ago were designated for this condemnation, godless persons, who pervert the grace of our God into licentiousness and who deny our only Master and Lord, Jesus Christ.[d]

The False Teachers. [5] [e] I wish to remind you, although you know all things, that [the] Lord who once saved a people from the land of Egypt later destroyed those who did not believe.* [6] [f] The angels too, who did not keep to their own domain but deserted their proper dwelling, he has kept in eternal chains, in gloom, for the judgment of the great day.* [7] Likewise, Sodom, Gomorrah, and the surrounding towns, which, in the same manner as they, indulged in sexual promiscuity and practiced unnatural vice,* serve as an example by undergoing a punishment of eternal fire.[g]

[8] Similarly, these dreamers* nevertheless also defile the flesh, scorn lordship, and revile glorious beings. [9] Yet the archangel Michael, when he argued with the devil in a dispute over the body of Moses, did not venture to pronounce a reviling judgment* upon him but said, "May the Lord rebuke you!"[h] [10] But these people revile what they do not understand and are destroyed by what they know by nature like irrational animals.[i] [11] Woe to them![j] They followed the way of Cain, abandoned themselves to Balaam's error for the sake of gain, and perished in the rebellion of Korah.* [12] These are blemishes on your love feasts,* as they carouse fearlessly and look after themselves. They are waterless clouds blown about by winds, fruitless trees in late autumn, twice dead and uprooted.[k] [13] They are like wild waves of the sea, foaming up their shameless deeds, wandering stars for whom the gloom of darkness has been reserved forever.

[14] * Enoch, of the seventh generation from Adam, prophesied also about them when he said,[l] "Behold, the Lord has come with his countless holy ones [15] to execute judgment on all and to convict everyone for all the godless deeds that they committed and for all the harsh words godless sinners have uttered against him." [16] These

---

a Mt 13, 55; Mk 6, 3; Acts 12, 17; Rom 1, 7.—b Gal 6, 16; 1 Tm 1, 2; 2 Pt 1, 2.—c Jude 17.20; 1 Tm 6, 12.—d Gal 2, 4; 2 Tm 3, 6; 2 Pt 2, 1.—e Nm 14, 35; 1 Cor 10, 5; Heb 3, 16.17.—f 2 Pt 2, 4.9.—g Dt 29, 22-24; Mt 25, 41; 2 Thes 1, 8-9; 2 Pt 2, 6; 3, 7.—h Dn 10, 21; 12, 1.—i 2 Pt 2, 12.—j Gn 4, 8-16; 1 Jn 3, 12 / Nm 31, 15-16; 2 Pt 2, 15; Rv 2, 14 / Nm 16, 19-35.—k 2 Pt 2, 13.17.—l 14-15: Mt 16, 27; Heb 12, 22-23.

1: *Jude . . . brother of James:* for the identity of the author of this letter, see Introduction. *To those who are called:* the vocation to the Christian faith is God's free gift to those whom he loves and whom he safely protects in Christ until the Lord's second coming.

3-4: *Our common salvation:* the teachings of the Christian faith derived from the apostolic preaching and to be kept by the Christian community.

5: For this first example of divine punishment on those who had been saved but did not then keep faith, see Nm 14, 28-29 and the note there. Some manuscripts have the word "once" (*hapax* as at Jude 3) after "you know"; some commentators have suggested that it means "knowing one thing" or "you know all things once for all." Instead of "[the] Lord" manuscripts vary, having "Jesus," "God," or no subject stated.

6: This second example draws on Gn 6, 1-4 as elaborated in the apocryphal Book of Enoch (cf Jude 14): heavenly beings came to earth and had sexual intercourse with women. God punished them by casting them out of heaven into darkness and bondage.

7: *Practiced unnatural vice:* literally, "went after alien flesh." This example derives from Gn 19, 1-25, especially 4-11, when the townsmen of Sodom violated both hospitality and morality by demanding that Lot's two visitors (really messengers of Yahweh) be handed over to them so that they could abuse them

sexually. *Unnatural vice:* this refers to the desire for intimacies by human beings with angels (the reverse of the example in Jude 6). Sodom (whence "sodomy") and Gomorrah became proverbial as object lessons for God's punishment on sin (Is 1, 9; Jer 50, 40; Am 4, 11; Mt 10, 15; 2 Pt 2, 6).

8: *Dreamers:* the writer returns to the false teachers of v 4, applying charges from the three examples in vv 5, 6, 7. This may apply to claims they make for revelations they have received by night (to the author, hallucinations). *Defile the flesh:* this may mean bodily pollutions from the erotic dreams of sexual license (7). *Lordship . . . glorious beings:* these may reflect the Lord (5; Jesus, 4) whom they spurn and the angels (6; cf the note on 2 Pt 2, 10, here, as there, literally, "glories").

9: *The archangel Michael . . . judgment:* a reference to an incident in the apocryphal Assumption of Moses. Dt 34, 6 had said of Moses, literally in Greek, "they buried him" or "he (God?) buried him" (taken to mean "he was buried"). The later account tells how Michael, who was sent to bury him, was challenged by the devil's interest in the body. Our author draws out the point that if an archangel refrained from reviling even the devil, how wrong it is for mere human beings to revile glorious beings (angels).

11: *Cain . . . Balaam . . . Korah:* examples of rebellious men and of the punishment their conduct incurred; cf Gn 4, 8-16; Nm 16, 1-35; 31, 16. See the note on 2 Pt 2, 15.

12: *Blemishes on your love feasts:* or "hidden rocks" or "submerged reefs" (cf Jude 13). The opponents engaged in scandalous conduct in connection with community gatherings called *love feasts* (agape meals), which were associated with eucharistic celebrations at certain stages of early Christian practice; cf 1 Cor 11, 18-34 and the note on 2 Pt 2, 13.

14-15: Cited from the apocryphal Book of Enoch 1, 9.

Jude

people are complainers, disgruntled ones who live by their desires; their mouths utter bombast as they fawn over people to gain advantage.*m*

Exhortations. [17] But you, beloved, remember the words spoken beforehand by the apostles of our Lord Jesus Christ,*n* [18] for they told you,*o* "In [the] last time there will be scoffers who will live according to their own godless desires."* [19] These are the ones who cause divisions; they live on the natural plane, devoid of the Spirit.*p* [20] But you, beloved, build yourselves up in your most holy faith; pray in the holy Spirit.*q* [21] Keep yourselves in the love of God and wait for the mercy of our Lord Jesus Christ that leads to eternal life.*r* [22] On those who waver, have mercy;* [23] save others by snatching them out of the fire; on others have mercy with fear,* abhorring even the outer garment stained by the flesh.

Doxology.* [24] To the one who is able to keep you from stumbling and to present you unblemished and exultant, in the presence of his glory,*s* [25] to the only God, our savior, through Jesus Christ our Lord be glory, majesty, power, and authority from ages past, now, and for ages to come. Amen.*t*

---

m Jude 18; 1 Cor 10, 10; 2 Pt 2, 10.18.—n Heb 2, 3; 2 Pt 3, 2.—o 1 Tm 4, 1; 2 Tm 3, 1-5; 2 Pt 3, 3.—p 1 Cor 2, 14; Jas 3, 15.—q Jude 2; Eph 6, 18; Col 2, 7.—r Ti 2, 13.—s 2 Cor 4, 14; 1 Pt 4, 13.—t Rom 11, 36; 1 Tm 1, 17.

18: This is the substance of much early Christian preaching rather than a direct quotation of any of the various New Testament passages on this theme (see Mk 13, 22; Acts 20, 30; 1 Tm 4, 1-3; 2 Pt 3, 3).

22: *Have mercy:* some manuscripts read "convince," "confute," or reprove." Others have "even though you waver" or "doubt" instead of *who waver.*

23: *With fear:* some manuscripts connect the phrase "with fear" with the imperative "save" or with the participle "snatching." Other manuscripts omit the phrase "on others have mercy," so that only two groups are envisioned. Rescue of those led astray and caution in the endeavor are both enjoined. *Outer garment stained by the flesh:* the imagery may come from Zec 3, 3-5, just as that of *snatching. . . out of the fire* comes from Zec 3, 2; the very garments of the godless are to be abhorred because of their contagion.

24-25: With this liturgical statement about the power of God to keep the faithful from stumbling, and praise to him through Jesus Christ, the letter reaches its conclusion by returning to the themes with which it began (1-2).

THE BOOK OF REVELATION

INTRODUCTION

The Apocalypse, or Revelation to John, the last book of the Bible, is one of the most difficult to understand because it abounds in unfamiliar and extravagant symbolism, which at best appears unusual to the modern reader. Symbolic language, however, is one of the chief characteristics of apocalyptic literature, of which this book is an outstanding example. Such literature enjoyed wide popularity in both Jewish and Christian circles from ca. 200 B.C. to A.D. 200.

This book contains an account of visions in symbolic and allegorical language borrowed extensively from the Old Testament, especially Ezekiel, Zechariah, and Daniel. Whether or not these visions were real experiences of the author or simply literary conventions employed by him is an open question.

This much, however, is certain: symbolic descriptions are not to be taken as literal descriptions, nor is the symbolism meant to be pictured realistically. One would find it difficult and repulsive to visualize a lamb with seven horns and seven eyes; yet Jesus Christ is described in precisely such words (5, 6). The author used these images to suggest Christ's universal (seven) power (horns) and knowledge (eyes). A significant feature of apocalyptic writing is the use of symbolic colors, metals, garments (1, 13-16; 3, 18; 4, 4; 6, 1-8; 17, 4; 19, 8), and numbers (four signifies the world, six imperfection, seven totality of perfection, twelve Israel's tribes or the apostles, one thousand immensity). Finally the vindictive language in the book (6, 9-10; 18, 1—19, 4) is also to be understood symbolically and not literally. The cries for vengeance on the lips of Christian martyrs that sound so harsh are in fact literary devices the author employed to evoke in the reader and hearer a feeling of horror for apostasy and rebellion that will be severely punished by God.

The lurid descriptions of the punishment of Jezebel (2, 22) and of the destruction of the great harlot, Babylon (16, 9—19, 2), are likewise literary devices. The metaphor of Babylon as harlot would be wrongly construed if interpreted literally. On the other hand, the stylized figure of the woman clothed with the sun (12, 1-6), depicting the New Israel, may seem to be a negative stereotype. It is necessary to look beyond the literal meaning to see that these images mean to convey a sense of God's wrath at sin in the former case and trust in God's providential care over the church in the latter.

The Book of Revelation cannot be adequately understood except against the historical background that occasioned its writing. Like Daniel and other apocalypses, it was composed as resistance literature to meet a crisis. The book itself suggests that the crisis was ruthless persecution of the early church by the Roman authorities; the harlot Babylon symbolizes pagan Rome, the city on seven hills (17, 9). The book is, then, an exhortation and admonition to Christians of the first century to stand firm in the faith and to avoid compromise with paganism, despite the threat of adversity and martyrdom; they are to await patiently the fulfillment of God's mighty promises. The triumph of God in the world of men and women remains a mystery, to be accepted in faith and longed for in hope. It is a triumph that unfolded in the history of Jesus of Nazareth and continues to unfold in the history of the individual Christian who follows the way of the cross, even, if necessary, to a martyr's death.

Though the perspective is eschatological—ultimate salvation and victory are said to take place at the end of the present age when Christ will come in glory at the parousia— the book presents the decisive struggle of Christ and his followers against Satan and his cohorts as already over. Christ's overwhelming defeat of the kingdom of Satan ushered in the everlasting reign of God (11, 15; 12, 10). Even the forces of evil unwittingly carry out the divine plan (17, 17), for God is the sovereign Lord of history.

The Book of Revelation had its origin in a time of crisis, but it remains valid and meaningful for Christians of all time. In the face of apparently insuperable evil, either from within or from without, all Christians are called to trust in Jesus' promise, "Behold, I am with you always, until the end of the age" (Mt 28, 20). Those who remain steadfast in their faith and confidence in the risen Lord need have no fear. Suffering, persecution, even death by martyrdom, though remaining impenetrable mysteries of evil, do not comprise an absurd dead end. No matter what adversity or sacrifice Christians may endure, they will in the end triumph over Satan and his forces because of their fidelity to Christ the victor. This is the enduring message of the book; it is a message of hope and consolation and challenge for all who dare to believe.

The author of the book calls himself John (1, 1.4.9; 22, 8), who because of his Christian faith has been exiled to the rocky island of Patmos, a Roman penal colony. Although he never claims to be John the apostle, whose name is attached to the fourth gospel, he was so identified by several of the early church Fathers, including Justin, Irenaeus, Clement of Alexandria, Tertullian, Cyprian, and Hippolytus. This identification, however, was denied by other Fathers, including Denis of Alexandria, Eusebius of Caesarea, Cyril of Jerusalem, Gregory Nazianzen, and John Chrysostom. Indeed, vocabulary, grammar, and style make it doubtful that the book could have been put into its present form by the same person(s) responsible for the fourth gospel. Nevertheless, there are definite linguistic and theological affinities between the two books. The tone of the letters to the seven churches (1, 4—3, 22) is indicative of the great authority the author enjoyed over the Christian communities in Asia. It is possible, therefore, that he was a disciple of John the apostle, who is traditionally associated with that part of the world. The date of the book in its present form is probably near the end of the reign of Domitian (A.D. 81-96), a fierce persecutor of the Christians.

The principal divisions of the Book of Revelation are the following:

   I.   *Prologue (1, 1-3)*
  II. *Letters to the Churches of Asia (1, 4—3, 22)*
 III. *God and the Lamb in Heaven (4, 1—5, 14)*
 IV. *The Seven Seals, Trumpets, and Plagues, with Interludes (6, 1—16, 21)*
  V. *The Punishment of Babylon and the Destruction of Pagan Nations (17, 1—20, 15)*
 VI. *The New Creation (21, 1—22, 5)*
VII. *Epilogue (22, 6-21)*

I. PROLOGUE*

CHAPTER 1

[1] The revelation of Jesus Christ, which God gave to him, to show his servants what must happen soon. He made it known by sending his angel to his servant John,[a] [2] who gives witness to the word of God and to the testimony of Jesus Christ by reporting what he saw. [3] Blessed is the one* who reads aloud and blessed are those who listen to this prophetic message and heed what is written in it, for the appointed time is near.[b]

---

a Rv 22, 6-8.20; Dn 2, 28 / Rv 19, 10.—b Rv 22, 7 / Lk 11, 28.

1, 1-3: This prologue describes the source, contents, and audience of the book and forms an inclusion with the epilogue (Rv 22, 6-21), with its similar themes and expressions.

1, 3: *Blessed is the one:* this is the first of seven beatitudes in this book; the others are in Rv 14, 13; 16, 15; 19, 9; 20, 6; 22, 7.14. *This prophetic message:* literally "the words of the prophecy"; so Rv 22, 7.10.18.19 by inclusion. *The appointed time:* when Jesus will return in glory; cf Rv 1, 7; 3, 11; 22, 7.10.12.20.

II. LETTERS TO THE CHURCHES OF ASIA

Greeting.* [4]John, to the seven churches in Asia:* grace to you and peace from him who is and who was and who is to come, and from the seven spirits before his throne,[c] [5]and from Jesus Christ, the faithful witness, the firstborn of the dead and ruler of the kings of the earth. To him who loves us and has freed us* from our sins by his blood,[d] [6]who has made us into a kingdom, priests for his God and Father, to him be glory and power forever [and ever]. Amen.[e]

[7] Behold, he is coming amid the clouds,
　　and every eye will see him,
　　even those who pierced him.
All the peoples of the earth will lament him.
　　Yes. Amen.[f]

[8]"I am the Alpha and the Omega,"* says the Lord God, "the one who is and who was and who is to come, the almighty."[g]

The First Vision.* [9]I, John, your brother, who share with you the distress, the kingdom, and the endurance we have in Jesus, found myself on the island called Patmos* because I proclaimed God's word and gave testimony to Jesus. [10]I was caught up in spirit on the Lord's day* and heard behind me a voice as loud as a trumpet, [11]which said, "Write on a scroll* what you see and send it to the seven churches: to Ephesus, Smyrna, Pergamum, Thyatira, Sardis, Philadelphia, and Laodicea." [12] * Then I turned to see whose voice it was that spoke to me, and when I turned, I saw seven gold lampstands [13]and in the midst of the lampstands one like a son of man,* wearing an ankle-length robe, with a gold sash around his chest.[h] [14]The hair of his head was as white as white wool or as snow,* and his eyes were like a fiery flame. [15]His feet were like polished brass refined in a furnace,* and his voice was like the sound of rushing water. [16]In his right hand he held seven stars.* A sharp two-edged sword came out of his mouth, and his face shone like the sun at its brightest.[i]

[17]When I caught sight of him, I fell down at his feet as though dead.* He touched me with his right hand and said, "Do not be afraid. I am the first and the last,[j] [18]the one who lives. Once I was dead, but now I am alive forever and ever. I hold the keys to death and the netherworld.* [19]Write down, therefore, what

---

c Rv 1, 8; 4, 8; 11, 17; 16, 5; Ex 3, 14.—d Rv 3, 14; 1 Cor 15, 20; Col 1, 18 / Heb 9, 14; 1 Pt 1, 19; 1 Jn 1, 7.—e Ex 19, 6; 1 Pt 2, 9.—f Dn 7, 13 / Zec 12, 10; Mt 24, 30; Jn 19, 37.—g Rv 1, 17; 21, 6; 22, 13; Is 41, 4; 44, 6; 48, 12.— h Dn 7, 13; 10, 5.—i Heb 4, 12.—j Dn 8, 18 / Rv 1, 8.

1, 4-8: Although Revelation begins and ends (Rv 22, 21) with Christian epistolary formulae, there is nothing between chs 4 and 22 resembling a letter. The author here employs the standard word order for greetings in Greek letter writing: "N. to N., greetings . . ."; see the note on Rom 1, 1.

1, 4: *Seven churches in Asia:* Asia refers to the Roman province of that name in western Asia Minor (modern Turkey); these representative churches are mentioned by name in v 11, and each is the recipient of a message (Rv 2, 1—3, 22). *Seven* is the biblical number suggesting fullness and completeness; thus the seer is writing for the whole church.

1, 5: *Freed us:* the majority of Greek manuscripts and several early versions read "washed us"; but "freed us" is supported by the best manuscripts and fits well with Old Testament imagery, e.g., Is 40, 2.

1, 8: *The Alpha and the Omega:* the first and last letters of the Greek alphabet. In Rv 22, 13 the same words occur together with the expressions "the First and the Last, the Beginning and the End"; cf Rv 1, 17; 2, 8; 21, 6; Is 41, 4; 44, 6.

1, 9-20: In this first vision, the seer is commanded to write what he sees to the seven churches (9-11). He sees Christ in glory, whom he depicts in stock apocalyptic imagery (12-16), and hears him describe himself in terms meant to encourage Christians by emphasizing his victory over death (17-20).

1, 9: *Island called Patmos:* one of the Sporades islands in the Aegean Sea, some fifty miles south of Ephesus, used by the Romans as a penal colony. *Because I proclaimed God's word:* literally, "on account of God's word."

1, 10: *The Lord's day:* Sunday. *As loud as a trumpet:* the imagery is derived from the theophany at Sinai (Ex 19, 16.19; cf Heb 12, 19 and the trumpet in other eschatological settings in Is 27, 13; Jl 2, 1; Mt 24, 31; 1 Cor 15, 52; 1 Thes 4, 16).

1, 11: *Scroll:* a papyrus roll.

1, 12-16: A symbolic description of Christ in glory. The metaphorical language is not to be understood literally; cf Introduction.

1, 13: *Son of man:* see the note on Mk 8, 31. *Ankle-length robe:* Christ is priest; cf Ex 28, 4; 29, 5; Wis 18, 24; Zec 3, 4. *Gold sash:* Christ is king; cf Ex 28, 4; 1 Mc 10, 89; 11, 58; Dn 10, 5.

1, 14: *Hair . . . as white as white wool or as snow:* Christ is eternal, clothed with the dignity that belonged to the "Ancient of Days"; cf Rv 1, 18; Dn 7, 9. *His eyes were like a fiery flame:* Christ is portrayed as all-knowing; cf Rv 2, 23; Ps 7, 10; Jer 17, 10; and similar expressions in Rv 2, 18; 19, 12; cf Dn 10, 6.

1, 15: *His feet . . . furnace:* Christ is depicted as unchangeable; cf Ez 1, 27; Dn 10, 6. The Greek word translated "refined" is unconnected grammatically with any other word in the sentence. *His voice . . . water:* Christ speaks with divine authority; cf Ez 1, 24.

1, 16: *Seven stars:* in the pagan world, Mithras and the Caesars were represented with seven stars in their right hand, symbolizing their universal dominion. *A sharp two-edged sword:* this refers to the word of God (cf Eph 6, 17; Heb 4, 12) that will destroy unrepentant sinners; cf Rv 2, 16; 19, 15; Wis 18, 15; Is 11, 4; 49, 2. *His face . . . brightest:* this symbolizes the divine majesty of Christ; cf Rv 10, 1; 21, 23; Jgs 5, 31; Is 60, 19; Mt 17, 2.

1, 17: It was an Old Testament belief that for sinful human beings to see God was to die; cf Ex 19, 21; 33, 20; Jgs 6, 22-23; Is 6, 5.

1, 18: *Netherworld:* Greek Hades, Hebrew Sheol, the abode of the dead; cf Rv 20, 13-14; Nm 16, 33.

Rv

you have seen, and what is happening, and what will happen afterwards.* [20]This is the secret meaning* of the seven stars you saw in my right hand, and of the seven gold lampstands: the seven stars are the angels of the seven churches, and the seven lampstands are the seven churches.

CHAPTER 2

To Ephesus. [1] * "To the angel of the church* in Ephesus,* write this:

" 'The one who holds the seven stars in his right hand and walks in the midst of the seven gold lampstands says this: [2]"I know your works, your labor, and your endurance, and that you cannot tolerate the wicked; you have tested those who call themselves apostles but are not, and discovered that they are impostors.* [3]Moreover, you have endurance and have suffered for my name, and you have not grown weary. [4]Yet I hold this against you: you have lost the love you had at first. [5]Realize how far you have fallen. Repent, and do the works you did at first. Otherwise, I will come to you and remove your lampstand from its place, unless you repent. [6]But you have this in your favor: you hate the works of the Nicolaitans,* which I also hate.

[7]" ' "Whoever has ears ought to hear what the Spirit says to the churches. To the victor* I will give the right to eat from the tree of life that is in the garden of God." '[k]

To Smyrna.* [8]"To the angel of the church in Smyrna,* write this:

" 'The first and the last, who once died but came to life, says this: [9]"I know your tribulation and poverty, but you are rich.* I know the slander of those who claim to be Jews and are not, but rather are members of the assembly of Satan.[l] [10]Do not be afraid of anything that you are going to suffer. Indeed, the devil will throw some of you into prison, that you may be tested, and you will face an ordeal for ten days. Remain faithful until death, and I will give you the crown of life.

[11]" ' "Whoever has ears ought to hear what the Spirit says to the churches.[m] The victor shall not be harmed by the second death." '*

To Pergamum.* [12]"To the angel of the church in Pergamum,* write this:

---

k Rv 2, 11.17.29; 3, 6.13.22; 13, 9; Mt 11, 15.—l Jas 2, 5.—m Rv 20, 6.14; 21, 8.

1, 19: *What you have seen, and what is happening, and what will happen afterwards:* the three parts of the Book of Revelation, the vision (10-20), the situation in the seven churches (chs 2-3), and the events of chs 6-22.

1, 20: *Secret meaning:* literally, "mystery." *Angels:* these are the presiding spirits of the seven churches. Angels were thought to be in charge of the physical world (cf Rv 7, 1; 14, 18; 16, 5) and of nations (Dn 10, 13; 12, 1), communities (the seven churches), and individuals (Mt 18, 10; Acts 12, 15). Some have seen in the "angel" of each of the seven churches its pastor or a personification of the spirit of the congregation.

2, 1—3, 22: Each of the seven letters follows the same pattern: address; description of the exalted Christ; blame and/or praise for the church addressed; threat and/or admonition; final exhortation and promise to all Christians.

2, 1-7: The letter to Ephesus praises the members of the church there for their works and virtues, including discerning false teachers (2-3), but admonishes them to repent and return to their former devotion (4-5). It concludes with a reference to the Nicolaitans (see the note on 6) and a promise that the victor will have access to eternal life (7).

2, 1: *Ephesus:* this great ancient city had a population of ca. 250,000; it was the capital of the Roman province of Asia and the commercial, cultural, and religious center of Asia. The other six churches were located in the same province, situated roughly in a circle; they were selected for geographical reasons rather than for the size of their Christian communities. *Walks in the midst of the seven gold lampstands:* this signifies that Christ is always present in the church; see the note on Rv 1, 4.

2, 2: *Who call themselves . . . impostors:* this refers to unauthorized and perverse missionaries; cf Acts 20, 29-30.

2, 6: *Nicolaitans:* these are perhaps the impostors of v 2; see the note on vv 14-15. There is little evidence for connecting this group with Nicolaus, the proselyte from Antioch, mentioned in Acts 6, 5.

2, 7: *Victor:* referring to any Christian individual who holds fast to the faith and does God's will in the face of persecution. *The tree of life that is in the garden of God:* this is a reference to the tree in the primeval paradise (Gn 2, 9); cf Rv 22, 2.14.19. The decree excluding humanity from the tree of life has been revoked by Christ.

2, 8-11: The letter to Smyrna encourages the Christians in this important commercial center by telling them that although they are impoverished, they are nevertheless rich, and calls those Jews who are slandering them members of the assembly of Satan (9). There is no admonition; rather, the Christians are told that they will suffer much, even death, but the time of tribulation will be short compared to their eternal reward (10), and they will thus escape final damnation (11).

2, 8: *Smyrna:* modern Izmir, ca. thirty miles north of Ephesus, and the chief city of Lydia, with a temple to the goddess Roma. It was renowned for its loyalty to Rome, and it also had a large Jewish community very hostile toward Christians.

2, 9-10: The church in Smyrna was materially poor but spiritually rich. Accusations made by Jewish brethren there occasioned the persecution of Christians; cf Acts 14, 2.19; 17, 5.13.

2, 11: *The second death:* this refers to the eternal death, when sinners will receive their final punishment; cf Rv 20, 6.14-15; 21, 8.

2, 12-17: The letter to Pergamum praises the members of the church for persevering in their faith in Christ even in the midst of a pagan setting and in face of persecution and martyrdom (13). But it admonishes them about members who advocate an unprincipled morality (14; cf 2 Pt 2, 15; Jude 11) and others who follow the teaching of the Nicolaitans (15; see the note there). It urges them to repent (16) and promises them the hidden manna and Christ's amulet (17).

2, 12: *Pergamum:* modern Bergama, ca. forty-five miles northeast of Smyrna, a center for various kinds of pagan worship. It also had an outstanding library (the word *parchment* is derived from its name).

" 'The one with the sharp two-edged sword says this: [13]"I know that you live where Satan's throne* is, and yet you hold fast to my name and have not denied your faith in me, not even in the days of Antipas, my faithful witness, who was martyred among you, where Satan lives. [14] * Yet I have a few things against you. You have some people there who hold to the teaching of Balaam, who instructed Balak to put a stumbling block before the Israelites: to eat food sacrificed to idols and to play the harlot.[n] [15] Likewise, you also have some people who hold to the teaching of [the] Nicolaitans. [16] Therefore, repent. Otherwise, I will come to you quickly and wage war against them with the sword of my mouth.

[17]" ' "Whoever has ears ought to hear what the Spirit says to the churches. To the victor I shall give some of the hidden manna;* I shall also give a white amulet upon which is inscribed a new name, which no one knows except the one who receives it." '[o]

To Thyatira.* [18]"To the angel of the church in Thyatira,* write this:

" 'The Son of God, whose eyes are like a fiery flame and whose feet are like polished brass, says this: [19]"I know your works, your love, faith, service, and endurance, and that your last works are greater than the first. [20] Yet I hold this against you, that you tolerate the woman Jezebel, who calls herself a prophetess, who teaches and mis-

leads my servants to play the harlot and to eat food sacrificed to idols.* [21] I have given her time to repent, but she refuses to repent of her harlotry. [22] So I will cast her on a sickbed and plunge those who commit adultery with her into intense suffering unless they repent of her works. [23] I will also put her children* to death. Thus shall all the churches come to know that I am the searcher of hearts and minds and that I will give each of you what your works deserve.[p] [24] But I say to the rest of you in Thyatira, who do not uphold this teaching and know nothing of the so-called deep secrets of Satan:* on you I will place no further burden, [25] except that you must hold fast to what you have until I come.

[26] " ' "To the victor,* who keeps to my ways* until the end,
I will give authority over the nations.[q]
[27] He will rule them with an iron rod.
Like clay vessels will they be smashed,
[28] just as I received authority from my Father. And to him I will give the morning star.

[29]" ' "Whoever has ears ought to hear what the Spirit says to the churches." '

CHAPTER 3

To Sardis.* [1]"To the angel of the church in Sardis,* write this:

---

n Nm 22—24; 25, 1-3; 31, 16; 2 Pt 2, 15; Jude 11.—o Is 62, 2; 65, 15.—p 1 Sm 16, 7; Jer 11, 20; 17, 10.—q Rv 12, 5; Ps 2, 8-9.

2, 13: *Satan's throne:* the reference is to emperor worship and other pagan practices that flourished in Pergamum, perhaps specifically to the white marble altar erected and dedicated to Zeus by Eumenes II (197-160 B.C.).

2, 14-15: Like Balaam, the biblical prototype of the religious compromiser (cf Nm 25, 1-3; 31, 16; 2 Pt 2, 15; Jude 11), the Nicolaitans in Pergamum and Ephesus (6) accommodated their Christian faith to paganism. They abused the principle of liberty enunciated by Paul (1 Cor 9, 19-23).

2, 17: *The hidden manna:* this is the food of life; cf Ps 78, 24-25. *White amulet:* literally, "white stone," on which was written a magical name, whose power could be tapped by one who knew the secret name. It is used here as a symbol of victory and joy; cf Rv 3, 4-5. *New name:* this is a reference to the Christian's rebirth in Christ; cf Rv 3, 12; 19, 12; Is 62, 2; 65, 15.

2, 18-29: The letter to Thyatira praises the progress in virtue of this small Christian community (19) but admonishes them for tolerating a false prophet who leads them astray (20). Her fate is sealed, but there is hope of repentance for her followers (21-22). Otherwise, they too shall die (23). They are warned against Satanic power or knowledge (24-25). Those who remain faithful will share in the messianic reign, having authority over nations (26-27), and will in fact possess Christ himself (28).

2, 18: *Thyatira:* modern Akhisar, ca. forty miles southeast of Pergamum, a frontier town famous for its workers' guilds (cf Acts 16, 14), membership in which may have involved festal meals in pagan temples.

2, 20: The scheming and treacherous Jezebel of old (cf 1 Kgs 19, 1-2; 21, 1-14; 2 Kgs 9, 22.30-34) introduced pagan customs into the religion of Israel; this new Jezebel was doing the same to Christianity.

2, 23: *Children:* spiritual descendants.

2, 24: *The so-called deep secrets of Satan:* literally, "the deep things of Satan," a scathing reference to the perverse teaching of the Nicolaitans (15).

2, 26-28: The Christian who perseveres in faith will share in Christ's messianic authority (cf Ps 2, 8-9) and resurrection victory over death, symbolized by the morning star; cf Rv 22, 16.

2, 26: *Who keeps to my ways:* literally, "who keeps my works."

3, 1-6: The letter to Sardis does not praise the community but admonishes its members to watchfulness, mutual support, and repentance (2-3). The few who have remained pure and faithful will share Christ's victory and will be inscribed in the book of life (4-5).

3, 1: *Sardis:* this city, located ca. thirty miles southeast of Thyatira, was once the capital of Lydia, known for its wealth at the time of Croesus (6th century B.C.). Its citadel, reputed to be unassailable, was captured by surprise, first by Cyrus and later by Antiochus. The church is therefore warned to be on guard.

Rv

" 'The one who has the seven spirits of God and the seven stars says this: "I know your works, that you have the reputation of being alive, but you are dead. [2] Be watchful and strengthen what is left, which is going to die, for I have not found your works complete in the sight of my God. [3] Remember then how you accepted and heard; keep it, and repent. If you are not watchful, I will come like a thief, and you will never know at what hour I will come upon you.ʳ [4] However, you have a few people in Sardis who have not soiled their garments; they will walk with me dressed in white, because they are worthy.ˢ

[5] " ' "The victor will thus be dressed in white,* and I will never erase his name from the book of life but will acknowledge his name in the presence of my Father and of his angels.ᵗ

[6] " ' "Whoever has ears ought to hear what the Spirit says to the churches." '

To Philadelphia.* [7] "To the angel of the church in Philadelphia,* write this:

" 'The holy one, the true,
    who holds the key of David,
    who opens and no one shall close,
    who closes and no one shall open,ᵘ
says this:

[8] " ' "I know your works (behold, I have left an open door* before you, which no one can close). You have limited strength, and yet you have kept my word and have not denied my name. [9] Behold, I will make those of the assembly of Satan who claim to be Jews and are not, but are lying, behold I will make them come and fall prostrate at your feet, and they will realize that I love you.ᵛ [10] Because you have kept my message of endurance,* I will keep you safe in the time of trial that is going to come to the whole world to test the inhabitants of the earth. [11] I am coming quickly. Hold fast to what you have, so that no one may take your crown.ʷ

[12] " ' "The victor I will make into a pillar* in the temple of my God, and he will never leave it again. On him I will inscribe the name of my God and the name of the city of my God, the new Jerusalem, which comes down out of heaven from my God, as well as my new name.ˣ

[13] " ' "Whoever has ears ought to hear what the Spirit says to the churches." '

To Laodicea.* [14] "To the angel of the church in Laodicea,* write this:

" 'The Amen, the faithful and true witness, the source of God's creation, says this:ʸ [15] "I know your works; I know that you are neither cold nor hot.* I wish you were either cold or hot. [16] * So, because you are lukewarm, neither hot nor cold, I

---

r Mt 24, 42-44; Mk 13, 33; 1 Thes 5, 2; 2 Pt 3, 10.—s Rv 7, 13-14.—t Ps 69, 29; Dn 12, 1 / Mt 10, 32.—u Is 22, 22; Mt 16, 19.—v Rv 2, 9 / Is 45, 14; 60, 14.—w Rv 2, 25; 22, 7.20.—x Rv 21, 2-3; Ez 48, 35 / Rv 19, 13.—y Rv 1, 5.

3, 5: *In white:* white is a sign of victory and joy as well as resurrection; see the note on Rv 2, 17. *The book of life:* the roll in which the names of the redeemed are kept; cf Rv 13, 8; 17, 8; 20, 12.15; 21, 27; Phil 4, 3; Dn 12, 1. They will be acknowledged by Christ in heaven; cf Mt 10, 32.

3, 7-13: The letter to Philadelphia praises the Christians there for remaining faithful even with their limited strength (8). Members of the assembly of Satan are again singled out (9; see Rv 2, 9 above). There is no admonition; rather, the letter promises that they will be kept safe at the great trial (10-11) and that the victors will become pillars of the heavenly temple, upon which three names will be inscribed: God, Jerusalem, and Christ (12).

3, 7: *Philadelphia:* modern Alasehir, ca. thirty miles southeast of Sardis, founded by Attalus II Philadelphus of Pergamum to be an "open door" (8) for Greek culture; it was destroyed by an earthquake in A.D. 17. Rebuilt by money from the Emperor Tiberius, the city was renamed Neo-Caesarea; this may explain the allusions to "name" in v 12. *Key of David:* to the heavenly city of David (cf Is 22, 22), "the new Jerusalem" (12), over which Christ has supreme authority.

3, 8: *An open door:* opportunities for sharing and proclaiming the faith; cf Acts 14, 27; 1 Cor 16, 9; 2 Cor 2, 12.

3, 10: *My message of endurance:* this does not refer to a saying of Jesus about patience but to the example of Christ's patient endurance. *The inhabitants of the earth:* literally, "those who live on the earth." This expression, which also occurs in Rv 6, 10; 8, 13; 11, 10; 13, 8.12.14; 17, 2.8, always refers to the pagan world.

3, 12: *Pillar:* this may be an allusion to the rebuilding of the city; see the note on v 7. *New Jerusalem:* it is described in Rv 21, 10—22, 5.

3, 14-22: The letter to Laodicea reprimands the community for being lukewarm (15-16), but no particular faults are singled out. Their material prosperity is contrasted with their spiritual poverty, their violet tunics that were the source of their wealth with the white robe of baptism, and their famous eye ointment with true spiritual perception (17-18). But Christ's chastisement is inspired by love and a desire to be allowed to share the messianic banquet with his followers in the heavenly kingdom (19-21).

3, 14: *Laodicea:* ca. forty miles southeast of Philadelphia and ca. eighty miles east of Ephesus, a wealthy industrial and commercial center, with a renowned medical school. It exported fine woolen garments and was famous for its eye salves. It was so wealthy that it was proudly rebuilt without outside aid after the devastating earthquake of A.D. 60/61. *The Amen:* this is a divine title (cf Hebrew text of Is 65, 16) applied to Christ; cf 2 Cor 1, 20. *Source of God's creation:* literally, "the beginning of God's creation," a concept found also in Jn 1, 3; Col 1, 16-17, Heb 1, 2; cf Prv 8, 22-31; Wis 9, 1-2.

3, 15-16: Halfhearted commitment to the faith is nauseating to Christ; cf Rom 12, 11.

3, 16: *Spit:* literally, "vomit." The image is that of a beverage that should be either hot or cold. Perhaps there is an allusion to the hot springs of Hierapolis across the Lycus river from Laodicea, which would have been lukewarm by the time they reached Laodicea.

will spit you out of my mouth. ¹⁷ ᶻ For you say, 'I am rich and affluent and have no need of anything,' and yet do not realize that you are wretched, pitiable, poor, blind, and naked.* ¹⁸ I advise you to buy from me gold refined by fire* so that you may be rich, and white garments to put on so that your shameful nakedness may not be exposed, and buy ointment to smear on your eyes so that you may see. ¹⁹ Those whom I love, I reprove and chastise. Be earnest, therefore, and repent. ᵃ

²⁰ " "Behold, I stand at the door and knock. If anyone hears my voice and opens the door, [then] I will enter his house and dine with him, and he with me.* ²¹ I will give the victor the right to sit with me on my throne, as I myself first won the victory and sit with my Father on his throne. ᵇ

²²" " "Whoever has ears ought to hear what the Spirit says to the churches." ' "

III. GOD AND THE LAMB IN HEAVEN

CHAPTER 4

Vision of Heavenly Worship.* ¹ After this I had a vision of an open door* to heaven, and I heard the trumpetlike voice that had spoken to me before, saying, "Come up here and I will show you what must happen afterwards." ² * At once I was caught up in spirit. ᶜ A throne was there in heaven, and on the throne sat ³ one whose appearance sparkled like jasper and carnelian. Around the throne was a halo as brilliant as an emerald. ⁴ Surrounding the throne I saw

twenty-four other thrones on which twenty-four elders* sat, dressed in white garments and with gold crowns on their heads. ᵈ ⁵ From the throne came flashes of lightning, rumblings, and peals of thunder.* Seven flaming torches burned in front of the throne, which are the seven spirits of God. ⁶ ᵉ In front of the throne was something that resembled a sea of glass like crystal.*

In the center and around the throne, there were four living creatures covered with eyes in front and in back. ⁷ The first creature resembled a lion, the second was like a calf, the third had a face like that of a human being, and the fourth looked like an eagle* in flight. ⁸ The four living creatures, each of them with six wings,* were covered with eyes inside and out. Day and night they do not stop exclaiming:

"Holy, holy, holy is the Lord God almighty,
who was, and who is, and who is to come." ᶠ

⁹ Whenever the living creatures give glory and honor and thanks to the one who sits on the throne, who lives forever and ever, ¹⁰ the twenty-four elders fall down before the one who sits on the throne and worship him, who lives forever and ever. They throw down their crowns before the throne, exclaiming:

¹¹ "Worthy are you, Lord our God,
to receive glory and honor and power,
for you created all things;
because of your will they came to be and were created." ᵍ

z Prv 13, 7; Lk 12, 21.—a Prv 3, 11-12; 1 Cor 11, 32; Heb 12, 5-11.—b Lk 22, 28-30; Mt 19, 28.—c 2-3: Is 6, 1 / Ez 1, 26-28.—d Is 24, 23.—e Ex 24, 10.—f Is 6, 2-3 / Rv 1, 4.8; 11, 17; 16, 5.—g Rom 4, 17; 16, 27.

3, 17: Economic prosperity occasioned spiritual bankruptcy.

3, 18: *Gold . . . fire:* God's grace. *White garments:* symbol of an upright life; the city was noted for its violet/purple cloth. *Ointment . . . eyes:* to remove spiritual blindness; one of the city's exports was eye ointment (see the note on Rv 3, 14).

3, 20: Christ invites all to the messianic banquet in heaven; cf Is 25, 6; Lk 14, 15; 22, 30.

4, 1-11: The seer now describes a vision of the heavenly court in worship of God enthroned. He reverently avoids naming or describing God but pictures twenty-four elders in priestly and regal attire (4) and God's throne and its surroundings made of precious gems and other symbols that traditionally express the majesty of God (5-6). Universal creation is represented by the four living creatures (6-7). Along with the twenty-four elders, they praise God unceasingly in humble adoration (8-11).

4, 1: The ancients viewed heaven as a solid vault, entered by way of actual doors.

4, 2-8: Much of the imagery here is taken from Ez 1 and 10.

4, 4: *Twenty-four elders:* these represent the twelve tribes of Israel and the twelve apostles; cf Rv 21, 12-14.

4, 5: *Flashes of lightning, rumblings, and peals of thunder:* as in other descriptions of God's appearance or activity; cf Rv 8, 5; 11, 19; 16, 18; Ex 19, 16; Ez 1, 4.13. *The seven spirits of God:* the seven "angels of the presence" as in Rv 8, 2 and Tb 12, 15.

4, 6: *A sea of glass like crystal:* an image adapted from Ez 1, 22-26. *Four living creatures:* these are symbols taken from Ez 1, 5-21; they are identified as cherubim in Ez 10, 20. *Covered with eyes:* these suggest God's knowledge and concern.

4, 7: *Lion . . . calf . . . human being . . . eagle:* these symbolize, respectively, what is noblest, strongest, wisest, and swiftest in creation. *Calf:* traditionally translated "ox," the Greek word refers to a heifer or young bull. Since the second century, these four creatures have been used as symbols of the evangelists Mark, Luke, Matthew, and John, respectively.

4, 8: *Six wings:* like the seraphim of Is 6, 2.

Rv

CHAPTER 5

The Scroll and the Lamb.* [1] I saw a scroll* in the right hand of the one who sat on the throne. It had writing on both sides and was sealed with seven seals. [h] [2] Then I saw a mighty angel who proclaimed in a loud voice, "Who is worthy to open the scroll and break its seals?" [3] But no one in heaven or on earth or under the earth was able to open the scroll or to examine it. [4] I shed many tears because no one was found worthy to open the scroll or to examine it. [5] One of the elders said to me, "Do not weep. The lion of the tribe of Judah, the root of David,* has triumphed, enabling him to open the scroll with its seven seals." [i]

[6] Then I saw standing in the midst of the throne and the four living creatures and the elders a Lamb* that seemed to have been slain. He had seven horns and seven eyes; these are the [seven] spirits of God sent out into the whole world. [j] [7] He came and received the scroll from the right hand of the one who sat on the throne. [8] When he took it, the four living creatures and the twenty-four elders fell down before the Lamb. Each of the elders held a harp and gold bowls filled with incense, which are the prayers of the holy ones. [9] They sang a new hymn:

"Worthy are you to receive the scroll
     and to break open its seals,
for you were slain and with your
     blood you purchased for God
those from every tribe and tongue,
     people and nation.
[10] You made them a kingdom and priests
     for our God,
and they will reign on earth." [k]

[11] I looked again and heard the voices of many angels who surrounded the throne and the living creatures and the elders. They were countless* in number, [l] [12] and they cried out in a loud voice:

"Worthy is the Lamb that was slain
     to receive power and riches, wisdom
         and strength,
honor and glory and blessing."

[13] Then I heard every creature in heaven and on earth and under the earth and in the sea, everything in the universe, cry out:

"To the one who sits on the throne and
     to the Lamb
be blessing and honor, glory and
     might,
forever and ever."

[14] The four living creatures answered, "Amen," and the elders fell down and worshiped.

IV. THE SEVEN SEALS, TRUMPETS, AND PLAGUES, WITH INTERLUDES*

CHAPTER 6*

The First Six Seals. [1] * Then I watched while the Lamb broke open the first of the seven seals, and I heard one of the four living creatures cry out in a voice like thunder, "Come forward." [2] I looked, and there was a white horse, and its rider had a

---

h Is 29, 11.—i Is 11, 1.10; Rom 15, 12.—j Jn 1, 29.—k Rv 1, 6; Ex 19, 6; Is 61, 6.—l Dn 7, 10; Jude 14-15.

5, 1-14: The seer now describes a papyrus roll in God's right hand (1) with seven seals indicating the importance of the message. A mighty angel asks who is worthy to open the scroll, i.e., who can accomplish God's salvific plan (2). There is despair at first when no one in creation can do it (3-4). But the seer is comforted by an elder who tells him that Christ, called the lion of the tribe of Judah, has won the right to open it (5). Christ then appears as a Lamb, coming to receive the scroll from God (6-7), for which he is acclaimed as at a coronation (8-10). This is followed by a doxology of the angels (11-12) and then finally by the heavenly church united with all of creation (13-14).

5, 1: *A scroll:* a papyrus roll possibly containing a list of afflictions for sinners (cf Ez 2, 9-10) or God's plan for the world. *Sealed with seven seals:* it is totally hidden from all but God. Only the Lamb (7-9) has the right to carry out the divine plan.

5, 5: *The lion of the tribe of Judah, the root of David:* these are the messianic titles applied to Christ to symbolize his victory; cf Rv 22, 16; Gn 49, 9; Is 11, 1.10; Mt 1, 1.

5, 6: Christ is the Paschal Lamb without blemish, whose blood saved the new Israel from sin and death; cf Ex 12; Is 53, 7; Jn 1, 29.36; Acts 8, 32; 1 Pt 1, 18-19. This is the main title for Christ in Rv, used twenty-eight times. *Seven horns and seven eyes:* Christ has the fullness (see the note on Rv 1, 4) of power (horns) and knowledge (eyes); cf Zec 4, 10. *[Seven] spirits:* as in Rv 1, 4; 3, 1; and 4, 5.

5, 11: *Countless:* literally, "100,000,000 plus 1,000,000," used by the author to express infinity.

6, 1—16, 21: A series of seven disasters now begins as each seal is broken (Rv 6, 1—8, 1), followed by a similar series as seven trumpets sound (Rv 8, 2—11, 19) and as seven angels pour

bowls on the earth causing plagues (Rv 15, 1—16, 21). These gloomy sequences are interrupted by longer or shorter scenes suggesting the triumph of God and his witnesses (e.g., chs 7, 10, 11, 12, 13, 14).

6, 1-17: This chapter provides a symbolic description of the contents of the sealed scroll. The breaking of the first four seals reveals four riders. The first rider (of a white horse) is a conquering power (1-2), the second (red horse) a symbol of bloody war (3-4), the third (black horse) a symbol of famine (5-6), the fourth (pale green horse) a symbol of Death himself, accompanied by Hades (the netherworld) as his page (7-8). Verse 8b summarizes the role of all four riders. The breaking of the fifth seal reveals Christian martyrs in an attitude of sacrifice as blood poured out at the foot of an altar begging God for vindication, which will come only when their quota is filled; but they are given a white robe symbolic of victory (9-11). The breaking of the sixth seal reveals typical apocalyptic signs in the sky and the sheer terror of all people at the imminent divine judgment (12-17).

6, 1-8: The imagery is adapted from Zec 1, 8-10; 6, 1-8.

bow.* He was given a crown, and he rode forth victorious to further his victories. *m*

³ When he broke open the second seal, I heard the second living creature cry out, "Come forward." ⁴ *n* Another horse came out, a red one. Its rider was given power to take peace away from the earth, so that people would slaughter one another. And he was given a huge sword.*

⁵ When he broke open the third seal, I heard the third living creature cry out, "Come forward." I looked, and there was a black horse,* and its rider held a scale in his hand. ⁶ I heard what seemed to be a voice in the midst of the four living creatures. It said, "A ration of wheat costs a day's pay,* and three rations of barley cost a day's pay. But do not damage the olive oil or the wine." *o*

⁷ When he broke open the fourth seal, I heard the voice of the fourth living creature cry out, "Come forward." ⁸ I looked, and there was a pale green* horse. Its rider was named Death, and Hades accompanied him. They were given authority over a quarter of the earth, to kill with sword, famine, and plague, and by means of the beasts of the earth. *p*

⁹ When he broke open the fifth seal, I saw underneath the altar* the souls of those who had been slaughtered because of the witness they bore to the word of God. ¹⁰ They cried out in a loud voice, "How long will it be, holy and true master,* before you sit in judgment and avenge our blood on the inhabitants of the earth?" ¹¹ Each of them was given a white robe, and they were told to be patient a little while longer until the number was filled of their fellow servants and brothers who were going to be killed as they had been.

¹² * Then I watched while he broke open the sixth seal, and there was a great earthquake; the sun turned as black as dark sackcloth* and the whole moon became like blood. *q* ¹³ The stars in the sky fell to the earth like unripe figs* shaken loose from the tree in a strong wind. ¹⁴ Then the sky was divided* like a torn scroll curling up, and every mountain and island was moved from its place. *r* ¹⁵ The kings of the earth, the nobles,* the military officers, the rich, the powerful, and every slave and free person hid themselves in caves and among mountain crags. ¹⁶ They cried out to the mountains and the rocks, "Fall on us and hide us from the face of the one who sits on the throne and from the wrath of the Lamb, *s* ¹⁷ because the great day of their* wrath has come and who can withstand it?"

CHAPTER 7*

The 144,000 Sealed. ¹ After this I saw four angels standing at the four corners of the earth,* holding back the four winds of

---

m Zec 1, 8-10; 6, 1-3.—n Ez 21, 14-16.—o Lv 26, 26; Ez 4, 16-17.—p Ez 14, 21. —q Jl 3, 4; Mt 24, 29.—r Is 34, 4 / Rv 16, 20.—s Is 2, 19; Hos 10, 8; Lk 23, 30.

6, 2: *White horse . . . bow:* this may perhaps allude specifically to the Parthians on the eastern border of the Roman empire. Expert in the use of the bow, they constantly harassed the Romans and won a major victory in A.D. 62; see the note on Rv 9, 13-21. But the Old Testament imagery typifies the history of oppression of God's people at all times.

6, 4: *Huge sword:* this is a symbol of war and violence; cf Ez 21, 14-17.

6, 5: *Black horse:* this is a symbol of famine, the usual accompaniment of war in antiquity; cf Lv 26, 26; Ez 4, 16-17. The *scale* is a symbol of shortage of food with a corresponding rise in price.

6, 6: *A day's pay:* literally, "a denarius," a Roman silver coin that constitutes a day's wage in Mt 20, 2. Because of the famine, food was rationed and sold at an exorbitant price. A liter of flour was considered a day's ration in the Greek historians Herodotus and Diogenes Laertius. *Barley:* food of the poor (Jn 6, 9.13; cf 2 Kgs 7, 1.16.18); it was also used to feed animals; cf 1 Kgs 5, 8. *Do not damage:* the olive and the vine are to be used more sparingly in time of famine.

6, 8: *Pale green:* symbol of death and decay; cf Ez 14, 21.

6, 9: *The altar:* this altar corresponds to the altar of holocausts in the temple in Jerusalem; see also Rv 11, 1. *Because of the witness . . . word of God:* literally, "because of the word of God and the witness they bore."

6, 10: *Holy and true master:* Old Testament usage as well as the context indicates that this is addressed to God rather than to Christ.

6, 12-14: Symbolic rather than literal description of the cosmic upheavals attending the day of the Lord when the martyrs' prayer for vindication (10) would be answered; cf Am 8, 8-9; Is 34, 4; 50, 3; Jl 2, 10; 3, 3-4; Mt 24, 4-36; Mk 13, 5-37; Lk 21, 8-36.

6, 12: *Dark sackcloth:* for mourning, sackcloth was made from the skin of a black goat.

6, 13: *Unripe figs:* literally, "summer (or winter) fruit."

6, 14: *Was divided:* literally, "was split," like a broken papyrus roll torn in two, each half then curling up to form a roll on either side.

6, 15: *Nobles:* literally, "courtiers," "grandees." *Military officers:* literally, "commanders of 1,000 men," used in Josephus and other Greek authors as the equivalent of the Roman *tribunus militum.* The listing of various ranks of society represents the universality of terror at the impending doom.

6, 17: *Their:* this reading is attested in the best manuscripts, but the vast majority read "his" in reference to the wrath of the Lamb in the preceding verse.

7, 1-17: An interlude of two visions precedes the breaking of the seventh seal, just as two more will separate the sixth and seventh trumpets (ch 10). In the first vision (1-8), the elect receive the seal of the living God as protection against the coming cataclysm; cf Rv 14, 1; Ez 9, 4-6; 2 Cor 1, 22; Eph 1, 13; 4, 30. The second vision (9-17) portrays the faithful Christians before God's throne to encourage those on earth to persevere to the end, even to death.

7, 1: *The four corners of the earth:* the earth is seen as a table or rectangular surface.

Rv

the earth so that no wind could blow on land or sea or against any tree *t* ²Then I saw another angel come up from the East,* holding the seal of the living God. He cried out in a loud voice to the four angels who were given power to damage the land and the sea, ³"Do not damage the land or the sea or the trees until we put the seal on the foreheads of the servants of our God."*u* ⁴I heard the number of those who had been marked with the seal, one hundred and forty-four thousand marked* from every tribe of the Israelites:*v* ⁵twelve thousand were marked from the tribe of Judah,* twelve thousand from the tribe of Reuben, twelve thousand from the tribe of Gad, ⁶twelve thousand from the tribe of Asher, twelve thousand from the tribe of Naphtali, twelve thousand from the tribe of Manasseh, ⁷twelve thousand from the tribe of Simeon, twelve thousand from the tribe of Levi, twelve thousand from the tribe of Issachar, ⁸twelve thousand from the tribe of Zebulun, twelve thousand from the tribe of Joseph, and twelve thousand were marked from the tribe of Benjamin.

Triumph of the Elect. ⁹After this I had a vision of a great multitude, which no one could count, from every nation, race, people, and tongue. They stood before the throne and before the Lamb, wearing white robes and holding palm branches* in their hands. ¹⁰They cried out in a loud voice:

"Salvation comes from* our God, who
　is seated on the throne,
　and from the Lamb."

¹¹All the angels stood around the throne and around the elders and the four living creatures. They prostrated themselves before the throne, worshiped God, ¹²and exclaimed:

"Amen. Blessing and glory, wisdom
　and thanksgiving,
honor, power, and might
be to our God forever and ever.
　Amen."

¹³Then one of the elders spoke up and said to me, "Who are these wearing white robes, and where did they come from?" ¹⁴I said to him, "My lord, you are the one who knows." He said to me, "These are the ones who have survived the time of great distress;* they have washed their robes and made them white in the blood of the Lamb.*w*

¹⁵ "For this reason they stand before
　God's throne
　and worship him day and night in his
　　temple.
　The one who sits on the throne will
　　shelter them.
¹⁶ They will not hunger or thirst anymore,
　nor will the sun or any heat strike
　　them.*x*
¹⁷ For the Lamb who is in the center of
　the throne will shepherd them
　and lead them to springs of life-giv-
　　ing water,*
　and God will wipe away every tear
　from their eyes."*y*

CHAPTER 8*

The Seven Trumpets. ¹When he broke open the seventh seal, there was silence in heaven* for about half an hour.*z* ²And I saw that the seven angels who stood before God were given seven trumpets.*a*

---

t Jer 49, 36; Zec 6, 5.—u Ex 12, 7-14; Ez 9, 4; 2 Cor 1, 22; Eph 1, 13; 4, 30.—v Rv 14, 1.—w Mt 24, 21.—x Is 49, 10.—y Rv 21, 4; Is 25, 8.—z Hb 2, 20; Zep 1, 7; Zec 2, 17.—a Rv 4, 5; Tb 12, 15.

7, 2: *East:* literally, "rising of the sun." The east was considered the source of light and the place of paradise (Gn 2, 8). *Seal:* whatever was marked by the impression of one's signet ring belonged to that person and was under his protection.

7, 4-9: *One hundred and forty-four thousand:* the square of twelve (the number of Israel's tribes) multiplied by a thousand, symbolic of the new Israel (cf Rv 14, 1-5; Gal 6, 16; Jas 1, 1) that embraces people *from every nation, race, people, and tongue* (9).

7, 5-8: Judah is placed first because of Christ; cf "the Lion of the tribe of Judah" (Rv 5, 5). Dan is omitted because of a later tradition that the antichrist would arise from it.

7, 9: *White robes . . . palm branches:* symbols of joy and victory; see the note on Rv 3, 5.

7, 10: *Salvation comes from:* literally, "(let) salvation (be ascribed) to." A similar hymn of praise is found at the fall of the dragon (Rv 12, 10) and of Babylon (Rv 19, 1).

7, 14: *Time of great distress:* fierce persecution by the Romans; cf Introduction.

7, 17: *Life-giving water:* literally, "the water of life," God's grace, which flows from Christ; cf Rv 21, 6; 22, 1.17; Jn 4, 10.14.

8, 1-13: The breaking of the seventh seal produces at first silence and then seven symbolic disasters, each announced by a trumpet blast, of which the first four form a unit as did the first four seals. A minor liturgy (3-5) is enclosed by a vision of seven angels (2.6). Then follow the first four trumpet blasts, each heralding catastrophes modeled on the plagues of Egypt affecting the traditional prophetic third (cf Ez 5, 12) of the earth, sea, fresh water, and stars (7-12). Finally, there is a vision of an eagle warning of the last three trumpet blasts (13).

8, 1: *Silence in heaven:* as in Zep 1, 7, a prelude to the eschatological woes that are to follow; cf Introduction.

The Gold Censer. ³Another angel came and stood at the altar,* holding a gold censer. He was given a great quantity of incense to offer, along with the prayers of all the holy ones, on the gold altar that was before the throne.ᵇ ⁴The smoke of the incense along with the prayers of the holy ones went up before God from the hand of the angel. ⁵Then the angel took the censer, filled it with burning coals from the altar, and hurled it down to the earth. There were peals of thunder, rumblings, flashes of lightning, and an earthquake.ᶜ

The First Four Trumpets. ⁶The seven angels who were holding the seven trumpets prepared to blow them.ᵈ

⁷When the first one blew his trumpet, there came hail and fire mixed with blood, which was hurled down to the earth. A third of the land was burned up, along with a third of the trees and all green grass.*

⁸ * When the second angel blew his trumpet, something like a large burning mountain was hurled into the sea. A third of the sea turned to blood,ᵉ ⁹a third of the creatures living in the sea* died, and a third of the ships were wrecked.

¹⁰When the third angel blew his trumpet, a large star burning like a torch fell from the sky. It fell on a third of the rivers and on the springs of water.ᶠ ¹¹The star was called "Wormwood,"* and a third of all the water turned to wormwood. Many people died from this water, because it was made bitter.ᵍ

¹²When the fourth angel blew his trumpet, a third of the sun, a third of the moon, and a third of the stars were struck, so that a third of them became dark. The day lost its light for a third of the time, as did the night.ʰ

¹³Then I looked again and heard an eagle flying high overhead cry out in a loud voice, "Woe! Woe! Woe* to the inhabitants of the earth from the rest of the trumpet blasts that the three angels are about to blow!"

CHAPTER 9

The Fifth Trumpet. * ¹Then the fifth angel blew his trumpet, and I saw a star* that had fallen from the sky to the earth. It was given the key for the passage to the abyss. ²It opened the passage to the abyss,ⁱ and smoke came up out of the passage like smoke from a huge furnace. The sun and the air were darkened by the smoke from the passage.ʲ ³Locusts came out of the smoke onto the land, and they were given the same power as scorpions* of the earth.ᵏ ⁴They were told not to harm the grass of the earth or any plant or any tree, but only those people who did not have the seal of God on their foreheads. ⁵They were not allowed to kill them but only to torment them for five months;* the torment they inflicted was like that of a scorpion when it stings a person. ⁶During that time these people will seek death but will not find it, and they will long to die but death will escape them.ˡ

⁷ * The appearance of the locusts was like that of horses ready for battle. On their heads they wore what looked like crowns of gold; their faces were like human faces,ᵐ ⁸and they had hair like women's hair. Their teeth were like lions' teeth,ⁿ ⁹and they had chests like iron breastplates. The

---

b Ps 141, 2; Tb 12, 12.—c Ez 10, 2; Ps 11, 6 / Rv 4, 5; 11, 19; 16, 18.—d Rv 16, 1-21.—e Ex 7, 20.—f Is 14, 12.—g Jer 9, 14.—h Ex 10, 21-23.—i Rv 20, 1.—j Gn 19, 28.—k Ex 10, 12-15; Wis 16, 9.—l Jb 3, 21.—m Jl 2, 4.—n Jl 1, 6.

8, 3: *Altar:* there seems to be only one altar in the heavenly temple, corresponding to the altar of holocausts in Rv 6, 9, and here to the altar of incense in Jerusalem; cf also Rv 9, 13; 11, 1; 14, 18; 16, 7.

8, 7: This woe resembles the seventh plague of Egypt (Ex 9, 23-24); cf Jl 3, 3.

8, 8-11: The background of these two woes is the first plague of Egypt (Ex 7, 20-21).

8, 9: *Creatures living in the sea:* literally, "creatures in the sea that had souls."

8, 11: *Wormwood:* an extremely bitter and malignant plant symbolizing the punishment God inflicts on the ungodly; cf Jer 9, 12-14; 23, 15.

8, 13: *Woe! Woe! Woe:* each of the three woes pronounced by the angel represents a separate disaster; cf Rv 9, 12; 11, 14. The final woe, released by the seventh trumpet blast, includes the plagues of ch 16.

9, 1-12: The fifth trumpet heralds a woe containing elements from the eighth and ninth plagues of Egypt (Ex 10, 12-15.21-23) but specifically reminiscent of the invasion of locusts in Jl 1, 4—2, 10.

9, 1: *A star:* late Judaism represented fallen powers as stars (Is 14, 12-15; Lk 10, 18; Jude 13), but a comparison with Rv 1, 20 and Rv 20, 1 suggests that here it means an angel. *The passage to the abyss:* referring to Sheol, the netherworld, where Satan and the fallen angels are kept for a thousand years, to be cast afterwards into the pool of fire; cf Rv 20, 7-10. The abyss was conceived of as a vast subterranean cavern full of fire. Its only link with the earth was a kind of passage or mine shaft, which was kept locked.

9, 3: *Scorpions:* their poisonous sting was proverbial; Ez 2, 6; Lk 11, 12.

9, 5: *For five months:* more or less corresponding to the life-span of locusts.

9, 7-10: Eight characteristics are listed to show the eschatological and diabolical nature of these locusts.

Rv

sound of their wings was like the sound of many horse-drawn chariots racing into battle. [10] They had tails like scorpions; with their tails they had power to harm people for five months. [11] They had as their king the angel of the abyss, whose name in Hebrew is Abaddon* and in Greek Apollyon.

[12] The first woe has passed, but there are two more to come.

The Sixth Trumpet.* [13] Then the sixth angel blew his trumpet, and I heard a voice coming from the [four]* horns of the gold altar before God,[o] [14] telling the sixth angel who held the trumpet, "Release the four angels* who are bound at the banks of the great river Euphrates." [15] So the four angels were released, who were prepared for this hour, day, month, and year to kill a third of the human race. [16] The number of cavalry troops was two hundred million; I heard their number. [17] Now in my vision this is how I saw the horses and their riders. They wore red, blue,* and yellow breastplates, and the horses' heads were like heads of lions, and out of their mouths came fire, smoke, and sulfur.[p] [18] By these three plagues of fire, smoke, and sulfur that came out of their mouths a third of the human race was killed. [19] For the power of the horses is in their mouths and in their tails; for their tails are like snakes, with heads that inflict harm.

[20] The rest of the human race, who were not killed by these plagues, did not repent of the works of their hands,* to give up the worship of demons and idols made from gold, silver, bronze, stone, and wood, which cannot see or hear or walk.[q] [21] Nor did they repent of their murders, their magic potions, their unchastity, or their robberies.

CHAPTER 10

The Angel with the Small Scroll. [1] * Then I saw another mighty angel come down from heaven wrapped in a cloud, with a halo around his head; his face was like the sun and his feet were like pillars of fire. [2] In his hand he held a small scroll that had been opened. He placed his right foot on the sea and his left foot on the land,* [3] and then he cried out in a loud voice as a lion roars. When he cried out, the seven thunders* raised their voices, too.[r] [4] When the seven thunders had spoken, I was about to write it down; but I heard a voice from heaven say, "Seal up what the seven thunders have spoken, but do not write it down." [5] Then the angel I saw standing on the sea and on the land raised his right hand to heaven [6] and swore by the one who lives forever and ever, who created heaven and earth and sea* and all that is in them, "There shall be no more delay.[s] [7] At the time when you hear the seventh angel blow his trumpet, the mysterious plan of God* shall be fulfilled, as he promised to his servants the prophets."[t]

[8] Then the voice that I had heard from heaven spoke to me again and said, "Go, take the scroll that lies open in the hand of the angel who is standing on the sea and on the land." [9] So I went up to the angel and told him to give me the small scroll. He

---

o Ex 30, 1-3.—p Jb 41, 10-13.—q Ps 135, 15-17; Is 17, 8; Dn 5, 4.—r Ps 29, 3-9; Jer 25, 30; Am 3, 8.—s Dt 32, 40; Dn 12, 7 / Ez 12, 28.—t Am 3, 7.

9, 11: *Abaddon:* Hebrew (more precisely, Aramaic) for destruction or ruin. *Apollyon:* Greek for the "Destroyer."

9, 13-21: The sixth trumpet heralds a woe representing another diabolical attack symbolized by an invasion by the Parthians living east of the Euphrates; see the note on Rv 6, 2. At the appointed time (15), the frightful horses act as God's agents of judgment. The imaginative details are not to be taken literally; see Introduction and the note on Rv 6, 12-14.

9, 13: *[Four]:* many Greek manuscripts and versions omit the word. The horns were situated at the four corners of the altar (Ex 27, 2; 30, 2-3); see the note on Rv 8, 3.

9, 14-15: *The four angels:* they are symbolic of the destructive activity that will be extended throughout the universe.

9, 17: *Blue:* literally, "hyacinth-colored." *Yellow:* literally, "sulfurous."

9, 20: *The works of their hands:* i.e., the gods their hands had made.

10, 1—11, 14: An interlude in two scenes (Rv 10, 1-11 and Rv 11, 1-14) precedes the sounding of the seventh trumpet; cf Rv 7, 1-17. The first vision describes an angel astride sea and land like a colossus, with a small scroll open, the contents of which indicate that the end is imminent (ch 10). The second vision is of the measuring of the temple and of two witnesses, whose martyrdom means that the kingdom of God is about to be inaugurated.

10, 1-4: *The seven thunders:* God's voice announcing judgment and doom; cf Ps 29, 3-9, where thunder, as the voice of Yahweh, is praised seven times.

10, 2: *He placed . . . on the land:* this symbolizes the universality of the angel's message, as does the figure of the small scroll open to be read.

10, 6: *Heaven and earth and sea:* the three parts of the universe. *No more delay:* cf Dn 12, 7; Hb 2, 3.

10, 7: *The mysterious plan of God:* literally, "the mystery of God," the end of the present age when the forces of evil will be put down (Rv 17, 1—19, 4.11-21; 20, 7-10; cf 2 Thes 2, 6-12; Rom 16, 25-26), and the establishment of the reign of God when all creation will be made new (Rv 21, 1—22, 5).

10, 9-10: The small scroll was sweet because it predicted the final victory of God's people; it was sour because it also announced their sufferings. Cf Ez 3, 1-3.

said to me, "Take and swallow it. It will turn your stomach sour, but in your mouth it will taste as sweet* as honey." [10] I took the small scroll from the angel's hand and swallowed it. In my mouth it was like sweet honey, but when I had eaten it, my stomach turned sour.ᵘ [11] Then someone said to me, "You must prophesy again about many peoples, nations, tongues, and kings."*

CHAPTER 11

The Two Witnesses. [1] ᵛ Then I was given a measuring rod like a staff and I was told, "Come and measure the temple of God and the altar, and count those who are worshiping in it.* [2] But exclude the outer court* of the temple; do not measure it, for it has been handed over to the Gentiles, who will trample the holy city for forty-two months. [3] I will commission my two witnesses* to prophesy for those twelve hundred and sixty days, wearing sackcloth." [4] ʷ These are the two olive trees and the two lampstands* that stand before the Lord of the earth. [5] * If anyone wants to harm them, fire comes out of their mouths and devours their enemies. In this way, anyone wanting to harm them is sure to be slain. [6] They have the power to close up the sky so that no rain can fall during the time of their prophesying. They also have power to turn water into blood and to afflict the earth with any plague as often as they wish.ˣ

[7] When they have finished their testimony, the beast that comes up from the abyss* will wage war against them and conquer them and kill them.ʸ [8] Their corpses will lie in the main street of the great city,* which has the symbolic names "Sodom" and "Egypt," where indeed their Lord was crucified. [9] * Those from every people, tribe, tongue, and nation will gaze on their corpses for three and a half days, and they will not allow their corpses to be buried. [10] The inhabitants of the earth will gloat over them and be glad and exchange gifts because these two prophets tormented the inhabitants of the earth. [11] But after the three and a half days, a breath of life from God entered them. When they stood on their feet, great fear fell on those who saw them.ᶻ [12] Then they heard a loud voice from heaven say to them, "Come up here." So they went up to heaven in a cloud as their enemies looked on.ᵃ [13] At that moment there was a great earthquake, and a tenth of the city fell in ruins. Seven thousand people* were killed during the earthquake; the rest were terrified and gave glory to the God of heaven.

[14] The second woe has passed, but the third is coming soon.

The Seventh Trumpet. * [15] Then the seventh angel blew his trumpet. There were loud voices in heaven, saying, "The kingdom of the world now belongs to our Lord and to his Anointed, and he will reign forever and ever." [16] The twenty-four elders who sat on their thrones before God

---

u Ez 3, 1-3.—v Ez 40, 3-5 / Zec 2, 5-9.—w Zec 4, 3.14.—x Ex 7, 17.—y Dn 7, 21.—z Ez 37, 5.10.—a 2 Kgs 2, 11.

10, 11: This further prophecy is contained in chs 12-22.

11, 1: The temple and altar symbolize the new Israel; see the note on Rv 7, 4-9. The worshipers represent Christians. The measuring of the temple (cf Ez 40, 3—42, 20; 47, 1-12; Zec 2, 5-6) suggests that God will preserve the faithful remnant (cf Is 4, 2-3) who remain true to Christ (Rv 14, 1-5).

11, 2: *The outer court:* the Court of the Gentiles. *Trample . . . forty-two months:* the duration of the vicious persecution of the Jews by Antiochus IV Epiphanes (Dn 7, 25; 12, 7); this persecution of three and a half years (half of seven, counted as 1260 days in Rv 11, 3; 12, 6) became the prototype of periods of trial for God's people; cf Lk 4, 25; Jas 5, 17. The reference here is to the persecution by the Romans; cf Introduction.

11, 3: The two witnesses, wearing sackcloth symbolizing lamentation and repentance, cannot readily be identified. Do they represent Moses and Elijah, or the Law and the Prophets, or Peter and Paul? Most probably they refer to the universal church, especially the Christian martyrs, fulfilling the office of witness (two because of Dt 19, 15; cf Mk 6, 7; Jn 8, 17).

11, 4: *The two olive trees and the two lampstands:* the martyrs who stand in the presence of the Lord; the imagery is taken from Zec 4, 1-3.11-14, where the olive trees refer to Zerubbabel and Joshua.

11, 5-6: These details are derived from stories of Moses, who turned *water into blood* (Ex 7, 17-20), and of Elijah, who called down fire from heaven (1 Kgs 18, 36-40; 2 Kgs 1, 10) and closed up the sky for three years (1 Kgs 17, 1; cf 18, 1).

11, 7: *The beast . . . from the abyss:* the Roman emperor Nero, who symbolizes the forces of evil, or the antichrist (Rv 13, 1.8; 17, 8); cf Dn 7, 2-8.11-12.19-22 and Introduction.

11, 8: *The great city:* this expression is used constantly in Rv for Babylon, i.e., Rome; cf Rv 14, 8; 16, 19; 17, 18; 18, 2.10.21. *"Sodom" and "Egypt":* symbols of immorality (cf Is 1, 10) and oppression of God's people (cf Ex 1, 11-14). *Where indeed their Lord was crucified:* not the geographical but the symbolic Jerusalem that rejects God and his witnesses, i.e., Rome, called Babylon in chs 16-18; see the note on Rv 17, 9 and Introduction.

11, 9-12: Over the martyrdom (7) of the two witnesses, now called prophets, the ungodly rejoice *for three and a half days,* a symbolic period of time; see the note on v 2. Afterwards they go in triumph to heaven, as did Elijah (2 Kgs 2, 11).

11, 13: *Seven thousand people:* a symbolic sum to represent all social classes (seven) and large numbers (thousands); cf Introduction.

11, 15-19: The seventh trumpet proclaims the coming of God's reign after the victory over diabolical powers; see the note on Rv 10, 7.

prostrated themselves and worshiped God [17] and said:

"We give thanks to you, Lord God almighty,
who are and who were.
For you have assumed your great power
and have established your reign.
[18] The nations raged,
but your wrath has come,
and the time for the dead to be judged,
and to recompense your servants, the prophets,
and the holy ones and those who fear your name,
the small and the great alike,
and to destroy those who destroy the earth."[b]

[19] Then God's temple in heaven was opened, and the ark of his covenant could be seen in the temple. There were flashes of lightning, rumblings, and peals of thunder, an earthquake, and a violent hailstorm.

CHAPTER 12

The Woman and the Dragon. [1] * A great sign appeared in the sky, a woman* clothed with the sun, with the moon under her feet, and on her head a crown of twelve stars.[c] [2] She was with child and wailed aloud in pain as she labored to give birth.* [3] Then another sign appeared in the sky; it was a huge red dragon,* with seven heads and ten horns, and on its heads were seven diadems.[d] [4] Its tail swept away a third of the stars in the sky and hurled them down to the earth. Then the dragon stood before the woman about to give birth, to devour her child when she gave birth.[e] [5] She gave birth to a son, a male child, destined to rule all the nations with an iron rod.* Her child was caught up to God and his throne.[f] [6] The woman herself fled into the desert where she had a place prepared by God, that there she might be taken care of for twelve hundred and sixty days.*

[7] * Then war broke out in heaven; Michael* and his angels battled against the dragon. The dragon and its angels fought back, [8] but they did not prevail and there was no longer any place for them in heaven. [9] The huge dragon, the ancient serpent,* who is called the Devil and Satan, who deceived the whole world, was thrown down to earth, and its angels were thrown down with it.[g]

[10] Then I heard a loud voice in heaven say:

"Now have salvation and power come,
and the kingdom of our God
and the authority of his Anointed.
For the accuser* of our brothers is cast out,
who accuses them before our God day and night.
[11] They conquered him by the blood of the Lamb
and by the word of their testimony;

---

b Ps 2, 1.5 / Am 3, 7.—c Gn 37, 9.—d Dn 7, 7.—e Dn 8, 10.—f Is 66, 7 / Ps 2, 9.—g Gn 3, 1-4 / Lk 10, 18.

12, 1—14, 20: This central section of Rv portrays the power of evil, represented by a dragon, in opposition to God and his people. First, the dragon pursues the woman about to give birth, but her son is saved and "caught up to God and his throne" (Rv 12, 5). Then Michael and his angels cast the dragon and his angels out of heaven (Rv 12, 7-9). After this, the dragon tries to attack the boy indirectly by attacking members of his church (Rv 12, 13-18). A beast, symbolizing the Roman empire, then becomes the dragon's agent, mortally wounded but restored to life and worshiped by all the world (Rv 13, 1-10). A second beast arises from the land, symbolizing the antichrist, which leads people astray by its prodigies to idolize the first beast (Rv 13, 11-18). This is followed by a vision of the Lamb and his faithful ones, and the proclamation of imminent judgment upon the world in terms of the wine of God's wrath (Rv 14, 1-20).

12, 1-6: The woman adorned with the sun, the moon, and the stars (images taken from Gn 37, 9-10) symbolizes God's people in the Old and the New Testament. The Israel of old gave birth to the Messiah (5) and then became the new Israel, the church, which suffers persecution by the dragon (6.13-17); cf Is 50, 1; 66, 7; Jer 50, 12. This corresponds to a widespread myth throughout the ancient world that a goddess pregnant with a savior was pursued by a horrible monster; by miraculous intervention, she bore a son who then killed the monster.

12, 2: Because of Eve's sin, the woman gives birth in distress and pain (Gn 3, 16; cf Is 66, 7-14).

12, 3: *Huge red dragon:* the Devil or Satan (cf Rv 12, 9; 20, 2), symbol of the forces of evil, a mythical monster known also as Leviathan (Ps 74, 13-14) or Rahab (Jb 26, 12-13; Ps 89, 11). *Seven diadems:* these are symbolic of the fullness of the dragon's sovereignty over the kingdoms of this world; cf Christ with many diadems (Rv 19, 12).

12, 5: *Rule . . . iron rod:* fulfilled in Rv 19, 15; cf Ps 2, 9. *Was caught up to God:* reference to Christ's ascension.

12, 6: God protects the persecuted church in the desert, the traditional Old Testament place of refuge for the afflicted, according to the typology of the Exodus; see the note on Rv 11, 2.

12, 7-12: Michael, mentioned only here in Rv, wins a victory over the dragon. A hymn of praise follows.

12, 7: *Michael:* the archangel, guardian and champion of Israel; cf Dn 10, 13.21; 12, 1; Jude 9. In Hebrew, the name Michael means "Who can compare with God?"; cf Rv 13, 4.

12, 9: *The ancient serpent:* who seduced Eve (Gn 3, 1-6), mother of the human race; cf Rv 20, 2; Eph 6, 11-12. *Was thrown down:* allusion to the expulsion of Satan from heaven; cf Lk 10, 18.

12, 10: *The accuser:* the meaning of the Hebrew word "Satan," found in v 9; Jb 1—2; Zec 3, 1; 1 Chr 21, 1; he continues to accuse Christ's disciples.

love for life did not deter them from death.

12 Therefore, rejoice, you heavens,
and you who dwell in them.
But woe to you, earth and sea,
for the Devil has come down to you
in great fury,
for he knows he has but a short
time."

13 When the dragon saw that it had been thrown down to the earth, it pursued the woman who had given birth to the male child. *h* 14 But the woman was given the two wings of the great eagle,* so that she could fly to her place in the desert, where, far from the serpent, she was taken care of for a year, two years, and a half-year.*i* 15 The serpent,* however, spewed a torrent of water out of his mouth after the woman to sweep her away with the current. 16 But the earth helped the woman and opened its mouth and swallowed the flood that the dragon spewed out of its mouth. 17 Then the dragon became angry with the woman and went off to wage war against the rest of her offspring, those who keep God's commandments and bear witness to Jesus.* 18 It took its position* on the sand of the sea.*j*

CHAPTER 13

The First Beast.* 1 Then I saw a beast come out of the sea with ten horns and seven heads; on its horns were ten diadems, and on its heads blasphemous name[s].*k* 2 The beast I saw was like a leopard, but it had feet like a bear's, and its mouth was like the mouth of a lion.*l* To it the dragon gave its own power and throne,

along with great authority.* 3 I saw that one of its heads seemed to have been mortally wounded, but this mortal wound was healed.* Fascinated, the whole world followed after the beast. 4 They worshiped the dragon because it gave its authority to the beast; they also worshiped the beast* and said, "Who can compare with the beast or who can fight against it?"

5 * The beast was given a mouth uttering proud boasts and blasphemies,*m* and it was given authority to act for forty-two months.* 6 It opened its mouth to utter blasphemies against God, blaspheming his name and his dwelling and those who dwell in heaven. 7 It was also allowed to wage war against the holy ones and conquer them, and it was granted authority over every tribe, people, tongue, and nation.*n* 8 All the inhabitants of the earth will worship it, all whose names were not written from the foundation of the world in the book of life, which belongs to the Lamb who was slain.*o*

9 Whoever has ears ought to hear these words.*p*
10 Anyone destined for captivity goes into captivity.
Anyone destined to be slain by the sword shall be slain by the sword.*q*
Such is the faithful endurance of the holy ones.

The Second Beast.* 11 Then I saw another beast come up out of the earth; it had two horns like a lamb's but spoke like a dragon. 12 It wielded all the authority of the first beast in its sight and made the earth and its inhabitants worship the first beast, whose mortal wound had been healed. 13 It

---

h Gn 3, 15.—i Ex 19, 4; Dn 7, 25; 12, 7.—j Gn 3, 15.—k 2 Thes 2, 3-12.—l Dn 7, 3-6.—m Dn 7, 8.11.25; 8, 14; 9, 27; 11, 36; 12, 7.—n Dn 7, 21.—o Rv 3, 5; 17, 8; 20, 12.—p Mt 13, 9.—q Jer 15, 2.

12, 14: *Great eagle:* symbol of the power and swiftness of divine help; cf Ex 19, 4; Dt 32, 11; Is 40, 31.

12, 15: The serpent is depicted as the sea monster; cf Rv 13, 1; Is 27, 1; Ez 32, 2; Ps 74, 13-14.

12, 17: Although the church is protected by God's special providence (16), the individual Christian is to expect persecution and suffering.

12, 18: *It took its position:* many later manuscripts and versions read "I took my position," thus connecting the sentence to the following paragraph.

13, 1-10: This wild beast, combining features of the four beasts in Dn 7, 2-28, symbolizes the Roman empire; the seven heads represent the emperors; see the notes on Rv 17, 10 and Rv 17, 12-14. The blasphemous names are the divine titles assumed by the emperors.

13, 2: Satan (Rv 12, 9), the prince of this world (Jn 12, 31), commissioned the beast to persecute the church (5-7).

13, 3: This may be a reference to the popular legend that Nero would come back to life and rule again after his death (which occurred in A.D. 68 from a self-inflicted stab wound in the throat); cf Rv 13, 14; 17, 8. Domitian (A.D. 81-96) embodied all the cruelty and impiety of Nero. Cf Introduction.

13, 4: *Worshiped the beast:* allusion to emperor worship, which Domitian insisted upon and ruthlessly enforced. *Who can compare with the beast:* perhaps a deliberate parody of the name Michael; see the note on Rv 12, 7.

13, 5-6: Domitian, like Antiochus IV Epiphanes (Dn 7, 8.11.25), demanded that he be called by divine titles such as "our lord and god" and "Jupiter." See the note on Rv 11, 2.

13, 5: *Forty-two months:* this is the same duration as the profanation of the holy city (Rv 11, 2), the prophetic mission of the two witnesses (Rv 11, 3), and the retreat of the woman into the desert (Rv 12, 6.14).

13, 11-18: The second beast is described in terms of the false prophets (cf Rv 16, 13; 19, 20; 20, 10) who accompany the false messiahs (the first beast); cf Mt 24, 24; Mk 13, 22; 2 Thes 2, 9; cf also Dt 13, 2-4. Christians had either to worship the emperor and his image or to suffer martyrdom.

performed great signs, even making fire come down from heaven to earth in the sight of everyone.[r] [14] It deceived the inhabitants of the earth with the signs it was allowed to perform in the sight of the first beast, telling them to make an image for the beast who had been wounded by the sword and revived. [15] It was then permitted to breathe life into the beast's image, so that the beast's image could speak and [could] have anyone who did not worship it put to death.[s] [16] It forced all the people, small and great, rich and poor, free and slave, to be given a stamped image on their right hands or their foreheads,[t] [17] so that no one could buy or sell except one who had the stamped image of the beast's name or the number that stood for its name.

[18] [u] Wisdom is needed here; one who understands can calculate the number of the beast, for it is a number that stands for a person. His number is six hundred and sixty-six.*

CHAPTER 14

The Lamb's Companions.* [1] Then I looked and there was the Lamb standing on Mount Zion,* and with him a hundred and forty-four thousand who had his name and his Father's name written on their foreheads.[v] [2] I heard a sound from heaven like the sound of rushing water or a loud peal of thunder. The sound I heard was like that of harpists playing their harps. [3] They were singing [what seemed to be] a new hymn before the throne, before the four living creatures and the elders. No one could learn this hymn except the hundred and forty-four thousand who had been ransomed from the earth.[w] [4] These are they who were not defiled with women; they are virgins* and these are the ones who follow the Lamb wherever he goes. They have been ransomed as the firstfruits of the human race for God and the Lamb.[x] [5] On their lips no deceit* has been found; they are unblemished.[y]

The Three Angels.* [6] Then I saw another angel flying high overhead, with everlasting good news* to announce to those who dwell on earth, to every nation, tribe, tongue, and people. [7] He said in a loud voice, "Fear God and give him glory, for his time has come to sit in judgment. Worship him who made heaven and earth and sea and springs of water."[z]

[8] A second angel followed, saying:

"Fallen, fallen is Babylon the great,[a]
    that made all the nations drink
    the wine of her licentious passion."*

[9] A third angel followed them and said in a loud voice, "Anyone who worships the beast or its image, or accepts its mark on forehead or hand, [10] will also drink the wine of God's fury,* poured full strength into the cup of his wrath, and will be tormented in burning sulfur before the holy angels and before the Lamb. [11] The smoke of the fire that torments them will rise forever and ever, and there will be no relief day or night for those who worship the

---

r Dt 13, 2-4; Mt 24, 24; 2 Thes 2, 9-10.—s Dn 3, 5-7.15.—t Rv 14, 9; 16, 2; 19, 20; 20, 4.—u Rv 17, 9.—v Jl 3, 5; 0b 17; Acts 2, 21.—w Pss 33, 3; 96, 1; 98, 1; Is 42, 10.—x Jer 2, 2; Jas 1, 18.—y Zep 3, 13.—z Rv 2, 10; Mt 10, 28.—a Rv 18, 2-3; Is 21, 9; Jer 51, 8 / Is 51, 17; Jer 25, 15-17.

13, 18: Each of the letters of the alphabet in Hebrew as well as in Greek has a numerical value. Many possible combinations of letters will add up to 666, and many candidates have been nominated for this infamous number. The most likely is the emperor Caesar Nero (see the note on Rv 13, 3), the Greek form of whose name in Hebrew letters gives the required sum. (The Latin form of this name equals 616, which is the reading of a few manuscripts.) Nero personifies the emperors who viciously persecuted the church. It has also been observed that "6" represents imperfection, falling short of the perfect number "7," and is represented here in a triple or superlative form.

14, 1-5: Now follows a tender and consoling vision of the Lamb and his companions.

14, 1: *Mount Zion:* in Jerusalem, the traditional place where the true remnant, the Israel of faith, is to be gathered in the messianic reign; cf 2 Kgs 19, 30-31; Jl 3, 5; 0b 17; Mi 4, 6-8; Zep 3, 12-20. *A hundred and forty-four thousand:* see the note on Rv 7, 4-9. *His Father's name . . . foreheads:* in contrast to the pagans who were marked with the name or number of the beast (Rv 13, 16-17).

14, 4: *Virgins:* metaphorically, because they never indulged in any idolatrous practices, which are considered in the Old Testament to be adultery and fornication (Rv 2, 14-15.20-22; 17, 1-6; cf Ez 16, 1-58; 23, 1-49). The parallel passages (Rv 7, 3; 22, 4) indicate that the 144,000 whose foreheads are sealed represent all Christian people.

14, 5: *No deceit:* because they did not deny Christ or do homage to the beast. Lying is characteristic of the opponents of Christ (Jn 8, 44), but the Suffering Servant spoke no falsehood (Is 53, 9; 1 Pt 2, 22). *Unblemished:* a cultic term taken from the vocabulary of sacrificial ritual.

14, 6-13: Three angels proclaim imminent judgment on the pagan world, calling all peoples to worship God the creator. Babylon (Rome) will fall, and its supporters will be tormented forever.

14, 6: *Everlasting good news:* that God's eternal reign is about to begin; see the note on Rv 10, 7.

14, 8: This verse anticipates the lengthy dirge over Babylon (Rome) in Rv 18, 1—19, 4. The oracle of Is 21, 9 to Babylon is applied here.

14, 10-11: *The wine of God's fury:* image taken from Is 51, 17; Jer 25, 15-16; 49, 12; 51, 7; Ez 23, 31-34. Eternal punishment in the fiery pool of burning sulfur (or "fire and brimstone"; cf Gn 19, 24) is also reserved for the Devil, the beast, and the false prophet (Rv 19, 20; 20, 10; 21, 8).

beast or its image or accept the mark of its name."[b] [12] Here is what sustains the holy ones who keep God's commandments[c] and their faith in Jesus.*

[13] [d] I heard a voice from heaven say, "Write this: Blessed are the dead who die in the Lord from now on." "Yes," said the Spirit, "let them find rest from their labors, for their works accompany them."*

The Harvest of the Earth. * [14] Then I looked and there was a white cloud, and sitting on the cloud one who looked like a son of man, with a gold crown on his head and a sharp sickle in his hand.[e] [15] Another angel came out of the temple, crying out in a loud voice to the one sitting on the cloud, "Use your sickle and reap the harvest, for the time to reap has come, because the earth's harvest is fully ripe."[f] [16] So the one who was sitting on the cloud swung his sickle over the earth, and the earth was harvested.

[17] Then another angel came out of the temple in heaven who also had a sharp sickle. [18] Then another angel [came] from the altar,* [who] was in charge of the fire, and cried out in a loud voice to the one who had the sharp sickle, "Use your sharp sickle and cut the clusters from the earth's vines, for its grapes are ripe." [19] So the angel swung his sickle over the earth and cut the earth's vintage. He threw it into the great wine press of God's fury.[g] [20] The wine press was trodden outside the city and blood poured out of the wine press to the height of a horse's bridle for two hundred miles.*

CHAPTER 15

The Seven Last Plagues. [1] * Then I saw in heaven another sign,* great and awe-inspiring: seven angels with the seven last plagues, for through them God's fury is accomplished.

[2] Then I saw something like a sea of glass mingled with fire.* On the sea of glass were standing those who had won the victory over the beast and its image and the number that signified its name. They were holding God's harps,[h] [3] and they sang the song of Moses,* the servant of God, and the song of the Lamb:

"Great and wonderful are your works,
    Lord God almighty.
Just and true are your ways,
    O king of the nations.[i]
[4] Who will not fear you, Lord,
    or glorify your name?
For you alone are holy.
    All the nations will come
    and worship before you,
    for your righteous acts have been revealed."[j]

[5] * After this I had another vision. The temple that is the heavenly tent of testimony* opened, [6] and the seven angels with the seven plagues came out of the temple. They were dressed in clean white linen, with a gold sash around their chests.[k] [7] One of the four living creatures gave the seven angels seven gold bowls filled with the fury of God, who lives forever and ever. [8] Then the temple became so filled with the smoke from God's glory and might that no one could enter it until the seven plagues of the seven angels had been accomplished.[l]

---

b Rv 19, 3.—c Rv 12, 17.—d Mt 11, 28-29; 2 Thes 1, 7; Heb 4, 10.—e Rv 1, 7; Dn 7, 13.—f Jl 4, 13; Mt 13, 36-43.—g Rv 19, 15; Is 63, 1-6.—h Rv 7, 9.14; 13, 15-18.—i Pss 92, 6; 98, 1 / Dt 32, 4; Ps 145, 17.—j Ps 86, 9-10; Jer 10, 7.—k Rv 19, 8.—l 1 Kgs 8, 10; Is 6, 4.

14, 12: In addition to *faith in Jesus*, the seer insists upon the necessity and value of works, as in Rv 2, 23; 20, 12-13; 22, 12; cf Mt 16, 27; Rom 2, 6.

14, 13: See the note on Rv 1, 3. According to Jewish thought, people's actions followed them as witnesses before the court of God.

14, 14-20: The reaping of the harvest symbolizes the gathering of the elect in the final judgment, while the reaping and treading of the grapes symbolizes the doom of the ungodly (cf Jl 4, 12-13; Is 63, 1-6) that will come in Rv 19, 11-21.

14, 18: *Altar:* there was only one altar in the heavenly temple; see the notes above on Rv 6, 9; 8, 3; 11, 1.

14, 20: *Two hundred miles:* literally sixteen hundred stades. The *stadion*, a Greek unit of measurement, was about 607 feet in length, approximately the length of a furlong.

15, 1—16, 21: The seven bowls, the third and last group of seven after the seven seals and the seven trumpets, foreshadow the final cataclysm. Again, the series is introduced by a heavenly prelude, in which the victors over the beast sing the canticle of Moses (15, 2-4).

15, 1-4: A vision of the victorious martyrs precedes the vision of woe in Rv 15, 5—16, 21; cf Rv 7, 9-12.

15, 2: *Mingled with fire:* fire symbolizes the sanctity involved in facing God, reflected in the trials that have prepared the victorious Christians or in God's wrath.

15, 3: *The song of Moses:* the song that Moses and the Israelites sang after their escape from the oppression of Egypt (Ex 15, 1-18). The martyrs have escaped from the oppression of the Devil. *Nations:* many other Greek manuscripts and versions read "ages."

15, 5-8: Seven angels receive the bowls of God's wrath.

15, 5: *Tent of testimony:* the name of the meeting tent in the Greek text of Ex 40. Cf 2 Mc 2, 4-7.

CHAPTER 16

The Seven Bowls.* [1] I heard a loud voice speaking from the temple to the seven angels, "Go and pour out the seven bowls of God's fury upon the earth."

[2] The first angel went and poured out his bowl on the earth. Festering and ugly sores broke out on those who had the mark of the beast or worshiped its image.*

[3] * The second angel poured out his bowl on the sea. The sea turned to blood like that from a corpse; every creature living in the sea died.

[4] The third angel poured out his bowl on the rivers and springs of water. These also turned to blood. [m] [5] Then I heard the angel in charge of the waters say:

"You are just, O Holy One,
     who are and who were,
in passing this sentence. [n]
[6] For they have shed the blood of the
     holy ones and the prophets,
and you [have] given them blood to
     drink;
it is what they deserve." [o]

[7] Then I heard the altar cry out,

"Yes, Lord God almighty,
     your judgments are true and
     just." [p]

[8] The fourth angel poured out his bowl on the sun. It was given the power to burn people with fire. [9] People were burned by the scorching heat and blasphemed the name of God who had power over these plagues, but they did not repent or give him glory. [q]

[10] [r] The fifth angel poured out his bowl on the throne of the beast.* Its kingdom was plunged into darkness, and people bit their tongues in pain [11] and blasphemed the God of heaven because of their pains and sores. But they did not repent of their works. [s]

[12] The sixth angel emptied his bowl on the great river Euphrates. Its water was dried up to prepare the way for the kings of the East.* [13] I saw three unclean spirits like frogs* come from the mouth of the dragon, from the mouth of the beast, and from the mouth of the false prophet. [t] [14] These were demonic spirits who performed signs. They went out to the kings of the whole world to assemble them for the battle on the great day of God the almighty. [u] [15] ("Behold, I am coming like a thief."* Blessed is the one who watches and keeps his clothes ready, so that he may not go naked and people see him exposed.) [v] [16] They then assembled the kings in the place that is named Armageddon* in Hebrew.

[17] The seventh angel poured out his bowl into the air. A loud voice came out of the temple from the throne, saying, "It is done." [w] [18] Then there were lightning flashes, rumblings, and peals of thunder, and a great earthquake. It was such a violent earthquake that there has never been one like it since the human race began on earth. [x] [19] The great city* was split into three parts, and the gentile cities fell. But God remembered great Babylon, giving it the cup filled with the wine of his fury and wrath. [20] * Every island fled, and mountains disappeared. [21] Large hailstones like huge weights came down from the sky on people, and they blasphemed God for the plague of hail because this plague was so severe. [y]

---

m Ex 7, 14-24.—n Rv 1, 4.—o Ez 35, 6; Mt 23, 34-35.—p Dn 3, 27; Tb 3, 2.—q Am 4, 6.—r Ex 10, 21-23.—s Ex 9, 8-11 / Jer 5, 3.—t Ex 8, 2-3.—u 1 Cor 1, 8.—v Mt 24, 42-44 / Rv 3, 17.— w Is 66, 6.—x Mk 13, 19.—y Ex 9, 22-26.

16, 1-21: These seven bowls, like the seven seals (Rv 6, 1-17; 8, 1) and the seven trumpets (Rv 8, 2—9, 21; 11, 15-19), bring on a succession of disasters modeled in part on the plagues of Egypt (Ex 7—12). See the note on Rv 6, 12-14.

16, 2: Like the sixth Egyptian plague (Ex 9, 8-11).

16, 3-4: Like the first Egyptian plague (Ex 7, 20-21). The same woe followed the blowing of the second trumpet (Rv 8, 8-9).

16, 10: *The throne of the beast:* symbol of the forces of evil. *Darkness:* like the ninth Egyptian plague (Ex 10, 21-23); cf Rv 9, 2.

16, 12: *The kings of the East:* Parthians; see the notes on Rv 6, 2 and Rv 17, 12-13. *East:* literally, "rising of the sun," as in Rv 7, 2.

16, 13: *Frogs:* possibly an allusion to the second Egyptian plague (Ex 7, 26—8, 11). *The false prophet:* identified with the two-horned second beast (Rv 13, 11-18 and the note there).

16, 15: *Like a thief:* as in Rv 3, 3 (cf Mt 24, 42-44; 1 Thes 5, 2). *Blessed:* see the note on Rv 1, 3.

16, 16: *Armageddon:* in Hebrew, this means "Mountain of Megiddo." Since Megiddo was the scene of many decisive battles in antiquity (Jgs 5, 19-20; 2 Kgs 9, 27; 2 Chr 35, 20-24), the town became the symbol of the final disastrous rout of the forces of evil.

16, 19: *The great city:* Rome and the empire.

16, 20-21: See the note on Rv 6, 12-14. *Hailstones:* as in the seventh Egyptian plague (Ex 9, 23-24); cf Rv 8, 7. *Like huge weights:* literally, "weighing a talent," about one hundred pounds.

V. THE PUNISHMENT OF BABYLON AND THE DESTRUCTION OF PAGAN NATIONS

CHAPTER 17

Babylon the Great. 1 * Then one of the seven angels who were holding the seven bowls came and said to me, "Come here. I will show you the judgment on the great harlot* who lives near the many waters.ᶻ 2 The kings of the earth have had intercourse with her,ᵃ and the inhabitants of the earth became drunk on the wine of her harlotry."* 3 Then he carried me away in spirit to a deserted place where I saw a woman seated on a scarlet beast* that was covered with blasphemous names, with seven heads and ten horns.ᵇ 4 The woman was wearing purple and scarlet and adorned with gold, precious stones, and pearls.ᶜ She held in her hand a gold cup that was filled with the abominable and sordid deeds of her harlotry.* 5 On her forehead was written a name, which is a mystery, "Babylon the great, the mother of harlots and of the abominations of the earth." 6 I saw that the woman was drunk on the blood of the holy ones and on the blood of the witnesses to Jesus.

Meaning of the Beast and Harlot.* When I saw her I was greatly amazed. 7 The angel said to me, "Why are you amazed? I will explain to you the mystery of the woman and of the beast that carries her, the beast with the seven heads and the ten horns. 8 ᵈ The beast that you saw existed once but now exists no longer. It will come up from the abyss and is headed for destruction. The inhabitants of the earth whose names have not been written in the book of life from the foundation of the world shall be amazed when they see the beast, because it existed once but exists no longer, and yet it will come again.* 9 Here is a clue* for one who has wisdom. The seven heads represent seven hills upon which the woman sits. They also represent seven kings:ᵉ 10 five have already fallen, one still lives, and the last has not yet come,* and when he comes he must remain only a short while. 11 The beast* that existed once but exists no longer is an eighth king, but really belongs to the seven and is headed for destruction. 12 The ten horns that you saw represent ten kings who have not yet been crowned;* they will receive royal authority along with the beast for one hour.ᶠ 13 They are of one mind and will give their power and authority to the beast. 14 They will fight with the Lamb, but the Lamb will conquer them, for he is Lord of lords and king of kings, and those with him are called, chosen, and faithful."ᵍ

15 Then he said to me, "The waters that you saw where the harlot lives represent large numbers of peoples, nations, and tongues. 16 The ten horns* that you saw and the beast will hate the harlot; they will leave her desolate and naked; they will eat her flesh and consume her with fire.ʰ 17 For God has put it into their minds to carry out his purpose and to make them come to an agreement to give their kingdom to the beast until the words of God are accomplished. 18 The woman whom you saw represents the great city that has sovereignty over the kings of the earth."

ᶻ Jer 50, 38; 51, 13.—ᵃ Jer 51, 7.—ᵇ Rv 13, 1.—ᶜ Rv 18, 16.—ᵈ Rv 13, 3-4 / Rv 3, 5; 13, 8; 20, 12.—ᵉ Rv 13, 18.—ᶠ Dn 7, 24.—ᵍ Rv 19, 11-21; 2 Mc 13, 4; 1 Tm 6, 15 / Rom 1, 6; 1 Pt 2, 9; Jude 1.—ʰ Ez 16, 37-41; 23, 25-29.

17, 1—19, 10: The punishment of Babylon is now described as a past event and, metaphorically, under the image of the great harlot who leads people astray into idolatry.

17, 1-6: Babylon, the symbolic name (5) of Rome, is graphically described as "the great harlot."

17, 2: *Intercourse . . . harlotry:* see the note on Rv 14, 4. The pagan kings subject to Rome adopted the cult of the emperor.

17, 3: *Scarlet beast:* see the note on Rv 13, 1-10. *Blasphemous names:* divine titles assumed by the Roman emperors; see the note on Rv 13, 5-6.

17, 4: Reference to the great wealth and idolatrous cults of Rome.

17, 6b-18: An interpretation of the vision is here given.

17, 8: Allusion to the belief that the dead Nero would return to power (11); see the note on Rv 13, 3.

17, 9: *Here is a clue:* literally, "Here a mind that has wisdom." *Seven hills:* of Rome.

17, 10: There is little agreement as to the identity of the Roman emperors alluded to here. The number seven (9) suggests that all the emperors are meant; see the note on Rv 1, 4.

17, 11: *The beast:* Nero; see the note on Rv 17, 8.

17, 12-13: *Ten kings who have not yet been crowned:* perhaps Parthian satraps who are to accompany the revived Nero (the beast) in his march on Rome to regain power; see the note on Rv 13, 3. In Rv 19, 11-21, the Lamb and his companions will conquer them.

17, 16-18: *The ten horns:* the ten pagan kings (12) who unwittingly fulfill God's will against harlot Rome, the great city; cf Ez 16, 37.

Rv

CHAPTER 18

The Fall of Babylon.* ¹ After this I saw another angel coming down from heaven, having great authority, and the earth became illumined by his splendor.ⁱ ² He cried out in a mighty voice:

"Fallen, fallen is Babylon the great.ʲ
    She has become a haunt for demons.
She is a cage for every unclean spirit,
    a cage for every unclean bird,
    [a cage for every unclean] and disgusting [beast].*
³ For all the nations have drunk*
    the wine of her licentious passion.
The kings of the earth had intercourse with her,
    and the merchants of the earth grew rich from her drive for luxury."ᵏ

⁴ Then I heard another voice from heaven say:

"Depart from her,* my people,
    so as not to take part in her sins
    and receive a share in her plagues,ˡ
⁵ for her sins are piled up to the sky,
    and God remembers her crimes.ᵐ
⁶ Pay her back as she has paid others.
    Pay her back double for her deeds.
    Into her cup pour double what she poured.ⁿ
⁷ To the measure of her boasting and wantonness
    repay her in torment and grief;
for she said to herself,
    'I sit enthroned as queen;
    I am no widow,
    and I will never know grief.'ᵒ
⁸ Therefore, her plagues will come in one day,
    pestilence, grief, and famine;
    she will be consumed by fire.
For mighty is the Lord God who judges her."

⁹ The kings of the earth who had intercourse with her in their wantonness will weep and mourn over her when they see the smoke of her pyre. ¹⁰ They will keep their distance for fear of the torment inflicted on her, and they will say:

"Alas, alas, great city,
    Babylon, mighty city.
In one hour your judgment has come."

¹¹ The merchants of the earth will weep and mourn for her, because there will be no more markets* for their cargo: ¹² their cargo of gold, silver, precious stones, and pearls; fine linen, purple silk, and scarlet cloth; fragrant wood of every kind, all articles of ivory and all articles of the most expensive wood, bronze, iron, and marble; ¹³ cinnamon, spice,* incense, myrrh, and frankincense; wine, olive oil, fine flour, and wheat; cattle and sheep, horses and chariots, and slaves, that is, human beings.

¹⁴ "The fruit you craved
    has left you.
All your luxury and splendor are gone,
    never again will one find them."ᵖ

¹⁵ The merchants who deal in these goods, who grew rich from her, will keep their distance for fear of the torment inflicted on her. Weeping and mourning, ¹⁶ they cry out:

"Alas, alas, great city,
    wearing fine linen, purple and scarlet,
    adorned [in] gold, precious stones, and pearls.�q
¹⁷ In one hour this great wealth has been ruined."

Every captain of a ship, every traveler at sea, sailors, and seafaring merchants stood at a distance ¹⁸ and cried out when they saw the smoke of her pyre, "What city could compare with the great city?" ¹⁹ ʳ They threw dust on their heads and cried out, weeping and mourning:

ⁱ Ez 43, 2.—j Rv 14, 8; Is 21, 9; Jer 50, 2-3; 51, 8.—k Rv 17, 2; Jer 51, 7.—l Is 48, 20; Jer 50, 8.—m Jer 51, 9.—n Jer 50, 15 / Jer 16, 18.—o Is 47, 8-9.—p Hos 10, 5 / Am 6, 7.—q Rv 17, 4.—r Ez 27, 27-32.

18, 1—19, 4: A stirring dirge over the fall of Babylon-Rome. The perspective is prophetic, as if the fall of Rome had already taken place. The imagery here, as elsewhere in this book, is not to be taken literally. The vindictiveness of some of the language, borrowed from the scathing Old Testament prophecies against Babylon, Tyre, and Nineveh (Is 23; 24; 27; Jer 50—51; Ez 26—27), is meant to portray symbolically the inexorable demands of God's holiness and justice; cf Introduction. The section concludes with a joyous canticle on the future glory of heaven.

18, 2: Many Greek manuscripts and versions omit *a cage for every unclean . . . beast.*

18, 3-24: Rome is condemned for her immorality, symbol of idolatry (see the note on Rv 14, 4), and for persecuting the church; cf Rv 19, 2.

18, 4: *Depart from her:* not evacuation of the city but separation from sinners, as always in apocalyptic literature.

18, 11: Ironically, the merchants weep not so much for Babylon-Rome, but for their lost markets; cf Ez 27, 36.

18, 13: *Spice:* an unidentified spice plant called in Greek *amōmon.*

"Alas, alas, great city,
in which all who had ships at sea
grew rich from her wealth.
In one hour she has been ruined.
20 Rejoice over her, heaven,
you holy ones, apostles, and prophets.
For God has judged your case against
her." *s*

21 A mighty angel picked up a stone like a
huge millstone and threw it into the sea
and said:
"With such force will Babylon the great
city be thrown down,
and will never be found again. *t*
22 No melodies of harpists and musicians,
flutists and trumpeters,
will ever be heard in you again.
No craftsmen in any trade
will ever be found in you again.
No sound of the millstone
will ever be heard in you again. *u*
23 No light from a lamp
will ever be seen in you again.
No voices of bride and groom
will ever be heard in you again.
Because your merchants were the great
ones of the world,
all nations were led astray by your
magic potion. *v*
24 In her was found the blood of prophets
and holy ones
and all who have been slain on the
earth." *w*

---

s Rv 19, 1-2; Dt 32, 43.—t Jer 51, 63-64; Ez 26, 21.—u Is 24,
8; Ez 26, 13.—v Jer 7, 34; 16, 9; 25, 10.—w Rv 16, 6.—x Dn
3, 27 / Jer 51, 48-49.—y Rv 14, 11; Is 34, 10.—z Rv 11, 18; Ps
115, 13.—a Mt 22, 9; Eph 5, 27.—b Rv 15, 6; Is 61, 10; Mt 22,
11-12.—c Mt 8, 11; Lk 14, 15.—d Rv 22, 8-9.

19, 1.3.4.6: *Alleluia:* found only here in the New Testament,
this frequent exclamation of praise in the Hebrew psalms was important in Jewish liturgy.

19, 5-10: A victory song follows, sung by the entire church,
celebrating the marriage of the Lamb, the union of the Messiah
with the community of the elect.

19, 7: *The wedding day of the Lamb:* symbol of God's reign
about to begin (Rv 21, 1—22, 5); see the note on Rv 10, 7. *His*
bride: the church; cf 2 Cor 11, 2; Eph 5, 22-27. Marriage is one
of the biblical metaphors used to describe the covenant relationship between God and his people; cf Hos 2, 16-22; Is 54, 5-6; 62,
5; Ez 16, 6-14. Hence, idolatry and apostasy are viewed as adultery and harlotry (Hos 2, 4-15; Ez 16, 15-63); see the note on Rv
14, 4.

19, 8: See the note on Rv 14, 12.

19, 9: *Blessed:* see the note on Rv 1, 3.

19, 10: *The spirit of prophecy:* as the prophets were inspired to proclaim God's word, so the Christian is called to give
witness to the Word of God (13) made flesh; cf Rv 1, 2; 6, 9; 12,
17.

19, 11-16: Symbolic description of the exalted Christ (cf Rv 1,
13-16) who together with the armies of heaven overcomes the
beast and its followers; cf Rv 17, 14.

CHAPTER 19

1 After this I heard what sounded like the
loud voice of a great multitude in heaven,
saying:
"Alleluia!*
Salvation, glory, and might belong to
our God,
2 for true and just are his judgments.
He has condemned the great harlot
who corrupted the earth with her
harlotry.
He has avenged on her the blood of his
servants." *x*
3 They said a second time:
"Alleluia! Smoke will rise from her
forever and ever." *y*
4 The twenty-four elders and the four living
creatures fell down and worshiped God
who sat on the throne, saying, "Amen. Alleluia."

The Victory Song.* 5 A voice coming from
the throne said:
"Praise our God, all you his servants,
[and] you who revere him, small and
great." *z*
6 Then I heard something like the sound of
a great multitude or the sound of rushing
water or mighty peals of thunder, as they
said:
"Alleluia!
The Lord has established his reign,
[our] God, the almighty.
7 Let us rejoice and be glad
and give him glory.
For the wedding day of the Lamb* has
come,
his bride has made herself ready. *a*
8 She was allowed to wear
a bright, clean linen garment." *b*
(The linen represents the righteous deeds
of the holy ones.)*
9 Then the angel said to me, "Write this:
Blessed* are those who have been called to
the wedding feast of the Lamb." And he
said to me, "These words are true; they
come from God." *c* 10 I fell at his feet to
worship him. But he said to me, "Don't! I
am a fellow servant of yours and of your
brothers who bear witness to Jesus. Worship God. *d* Witness to Jesus is the spirit of
prophecy."*

The King of Kings. 11 * Then I saw the
heavens opened, and there was a white
horse; its rider was [called] "Faithful and

Rv

True." He judges and wages war in righteousness.[a] [12]His eyes were [like] a fiery flame, and on his head were many diadems. He had a name* inscribed that no one knows except himself.[f] [13]He wore a cloak that had been dipped in* blood, and his name was called the Word of God.[g] [14]The armies of heaven followed him, mounted on white horses and wearing clean white linen.[h] [15]Out of his mouth came a sharp sword to strike the nations. He will rule them with an iron rod, and he himself will tread out in the wine press* the wine of the fury and wrath of God the almighty.[i] [16]He has a name written on his cloak and on his thigh, "King of kings and Lord of lords."[j]

[17] * Then I saw an angel standing on the sun. He cried out [in] a loud voice to all the birds flying high overhead, "Come here. Gather for God's great feast, [18]to eat the flesh of kings, the flesh of military officers, and the flesh of warriors, the flesh of horses and of their riders, and the flesh of all, free and slave, small and great."[k] [19]Then I saw the beast and the kings of the earth and their armies gathered to fight against the one riding the horse and against his army. [20]The beast was caught and with it the false prophet* who had performed in its sight the signs by which he led astray those who had accepted the mark of the beast and those who had worshiped its image. The two were thrown alive into the fiery pool burning with sulfur.[l] [21]The rest were killed by the sword that came out of the mouth of the one riding the horse, and all the birds gorged themselves on their flesh.

---

e Is 11, 4.—f Rv 1, 14-16; 2, 18 / Lk 10, 22.—g Is 63, 1 / Jn 1, 1.—h Rv 15, 6; 19, 8.—i Rv 14, 20; Is 63, 3.—j Rv 17, 14; 2 Mc 13, 4.—k Ez 39, 17-20.—l Rv 14, 10.—m Rv 9, 1.—n Gn 3, 1.—o Mt 19, 28.—p Ez 38, 2.9.16.

19, 12: *A name:* in Semitic thought, the name conveyed the reality of the person; cf Mt 11, 27; Lk 10, 22.

19, 13: *Had been dipped in:* other Greek manuscripts and versions read "had been sprinkled with"; cf Rv 19, 15. *The Word of God:* Christ is the revelation of the Father; cf Jn 1, 1.14; 1 Jn 2, 14.

19, 15: The treading of the wine press is a prophetic symbol used to describe the destruction of God's enemies; cf Is 63, 1-6; Jl 4, 13.

19, 17-21: The certainty of Christ's victory is proclaimed by an angel, followed by a reference to the mustering of enemy forces and a fearsome description of their annihilation. The gruesome imagery is borrowed from Ez 39, 4.17-20.

19, 20: *Beast . . . false prophet:* see the notes on ch 13. *The fiery pool . . . sulfur:* symbol of God's punishment (Rv 14, 10; 20, 10.14-15), different from the abyss; see the note on Rv 9, 1.

CHAPTER 20

The Thousand-year Reign. [1] * Then I saw an angel come down from heaven, holding in his hand the key to the abyss* and a heavy chain.[m] [2]He seized the dragon, the ancient serpent, which is the Devil or Satan,* and tied it up for a thousand years[n] [3]and threw it into the abyss, which he locked over it and sealed, so that it could no longer lead the nations astray until the thousand years are completed. After this, it is to be released for a short time.

[4]Then I saw thrones; those who sat on them were entrusted with judgment. I also saw the souls of those who had been beheaded for their witness to Jesus and for the word of God, and who had not worshiped the beast or its image nor had accepted its mark* on their foreheads or hands. They came to life and they reigned with Christ for a thousand years.[o] [5]The rest of the dead did not come to life until the thousand years were over. This is the first resurrection. [6]Blessed* and holy is the one who shares in the first resurrection. The second death has no power over these; they will be priests of God and of Christ, and they will reign with him for [the] thousand years.

[7] * When the thousand years are completed, Satan will be released from his prison. [8]He will go out to deceive the nations at the four corners of the earth, Gog and Magog,* to gather them for battle; their number is like the sand of the sea.[p] [9]They invaded the breadth of the earth* and surrounded the camp of the holy ones

---

20, 1-6: Like the other numerical values in this book, the thousand years are not to be taken literally; they symbolize the long period of time between the chaining up of Satan (a symbol for Christ's resurrection-victory over death and the forces of evil) and the end of the world. During this time God's people share in the glorious reign of God that is present to them by virtue of their baptismal victory over death and sin; cf Rom 6, 1-8; Jn 5, 24-25; 16, 33; 1 Jn 3, 14; Eph 2, 1.

20, 1: *Abyss:* see the note on Rv 9, 1.

20, 2: *Dragon . . . serpent . . . Satan:* see the notes on Rv 12, 3.9.10.15.

20, 4: *Beast . . . mark:* see ch 13 and its notes.

20, 6: *Blessed:* see the note on Rv 1, 3. *Second death:* see the note on Rv 2, 11. *Priests:* as in Rv 1, 6; 5, 10; cf 1 Pt 2, 9.

20, 7-10: A description of the symbolic battle to take place when Satan is released at the end of time, when the thousand years are over; see the note on Rv 20, 1-6.

20, 8: *Gog and Magog:* symbols of all pagan nations; the names are taken from Ez 38, 1—39, 20.

20, 9: *The breadth of the earth:* Palestine. *The beloved city:* Jerusalem; see the note on Rv 14, 1.

and the beloved city. But fire came down from heaven and consumed them.*q* ¹⁰The Devil who had led them astray was thrown into the pool of fire and sulfur, where the beast and the false prophet were. There they will be tormented day and night forever and ever.

The Large White Throne.* ¹¹Next I saw a large white throne and the one who was sitting on it. The earth and the sky fled from his presence and there was no place for them.*r* ¹²I saw the dead, the great and the lowly, standing before the throne, and scrolls were opened. Then another scroll was opened, the book of life.* The dead were judged according to their deeds, by what was written in the scrolls.*s* ¹³The sea gave up its dead; then Death and Hades* gave up their dead. All the dead were judged according to their deeds. ¹⁴ *t* Then Death and Hades were thrown into the pool of fire. (This pool of fire is the second death.*) ¹⁵Anyone whose name was not found written in the book of life was thrown into the pool of fire.

VI. THE NEW CREATION*

CHAPTER 21

The New Heaven and the New Earth. ¹ *u*Then I saw a new heaven and a new earth. The former heaven and the former earth had passed away, and the sea was no more.* ²I also saw the holy city, a new Jerusalem,* coming down out of heaven from God, prepared as a bride adorned for her husband.*v* ³I heard a loud voice from

---

q Ez 38, 22.—r 2 Pt 3, 7.10.12.—s Rom 2, 6.—t 1 Cor 15, 26.54-55.—u Is 65, 17; 66, 22; Rom 8, 19-23; 2 Pt 3, 13.—v Rv 19, 7-9.—w Ez 37, 27.—x Rv 7, 17; Is 25, 8; 35, 10.—y Is 43, 19; 2 Cor 5, 17.—z Rv 22, 17; Ps 36, 8-9; Is 55, 1.—a 2 Sm 7, 14.—b Rv 22, 15; Rom 1, 29-32.—c Ez 40, 2.—d Heb 11, 10.— e Ez 48, 31-35.

20, 11-15: A description of the final judgment. After the intermediate reign of Christ, all the dead are raised and judged, thus inaugurating the new age.

20, 12: *The book of life:* see the note on Rv 3, 5. *Judged . . . scrolls:* see the note on Rv 14, 12.

20, 13: *Hades:* the netherworld; see the note on Rv 1, 18.

20, 14: *Second death:* see the note on Rv 2, 11.

21, 1—22, 5: A description of God's eternal kingdom in heaven under the symbols of a new heaven and a new earth; cf Is 65, 17-25; 66, 22; Mt 19, 28.

21, 1: *Sea . . . no more:* because as home of the dragon it was doomed to disappear; cf Jb 7, 12.

21, 2: *New Jerusalem . . . bride:* symbol of the church (Gal 4, 26); see the note on Rv 19, 7.

21, 3: *People:* other ancient manuscripts read a plural, "peoples."

the throne saying, "Behold, God's dwelling is with the human race.*w* He will dwell with them and they will be his people* and God himself will always be with them [as their God].* ⁴He will wipe every tear from their eyes, and there shall be no more death or mourning, wailing or pain, [for] the old order has passed away."*x*

⁵The one who sat on the throne* said, "Behold, I make all things new." Then he said, "Write these words down, for they are trustworthy and true."*y* ⁶He said to me, "They are accomplished.* I [am] the Alpha and the Omega, the beginning and the end. To the thirsty I will give a gift from the spring of life-giving water.*z* ⁷The victor* will inherit these gifts, and I shall be his God, and he will be my son.*a* ⁸But as for cowards,* the unfaithful, the depraved, murderers, the unchaste, sorcerers, idol-worshipers, and deceivers of every sort, their lot is in the burning pool of fire and sulfur, which is the second death."*b*

The New Jerusalem.* ⁹One of the seven angels who held the seven bowls filled with the seven last plagues came and said to me, "Come here. I will show you the bride, the wife of the Lamb."* ¹⁰He took me in spirit to a great, high mountain and showed me the holy city Jerusalem coming down out of heaven from God.*c* ¹¹It gleamed with the splendor of God. Its radiance was like that of a precious stone, like jasper, clear as crystal.*d* ¹²It had a massive, high wall, with twelve gates where twelve angels were stationed and on which names were inscribed, [the names] of the twelve tribes of the Israelites. ¹³There were three gates facing east, three north, three south, and three west.*e* ¹⁴The wall of the city had

---

21, 3-4: Language taken from Ez 37, 27; Is 25, 8; 35, 10; cf Rv 7, 17.

21, 5: *The one . . . on the throne:* God himself; cf Rv 4, 1-11.

21, 6: *They are accomplished:* God's reign has already begun; see the note on Rv 20, 1-6. *Alpha . . . Omega:* see the note on Rv 1, 8. *Life-giving water:* see the note on Rv 7, 17.

21, 7: *The victor:* over the forces of evil; see the conclusions of the seven letters (Rv 2, 7.11.17.26; 3, 5.12.21). *He will be my son:* the victorious Christian enjoys divine affiliation by adoption (Gal 4, 4-7; Rom 8, 14-17); see the note on Rv 2, 26-28.

21, 8: *Cowards:* their conviction is so weak that they deny Christ in time of trial and become traitors. *Second death:* see the note on Rv 2, 11.

21, 9—22, 5: Symbolic descriptions of the new Jerusalem, the church. Most of the images are borrowed from Ez 40—48.

21, 9: *The bride, the wife of the Lamb:* the church (2), the new Jerusalem (10); cf 2 Cor 11, 2.

Rv

twelve courses of stones as its foundation, on which were inscribed the twelve names of the twelve apostles* of the Lamb.*ᶠ*

15 * The one who spoke to me held a gold measuring rod to measure the city, its gates, and its wall. ¹⁶The city was square, its length the same as [also] its width. He measured the city with the rod and found it fifteen hundred miles* in length and width and height. ¹⁷He also measured its wall: one hundred and forty-four cubits* according to the standard unit of measurement the angel used. ¹⁸ * The wall was constructed of jasper, while the city was pure gold, clear as glass. ¹⁹The foundations of the city wall were decorated with every precious stone; the first course of stones was jasper, the second sapphire, the third chalcedony, the fourth emerald,*ᵍ* ²⁰the fifth sardonyx, the sixth carnelian, the seventh chrysolite, the eighth beryl, the ninth topaz, the tenth chrysoprase, the eleventh hyacinth, and the twelfth amethyst. ²¹The twelve gates were twelve pearls, each of the gates made from a single pearl; and the street of the city was of pure gold, transparent as glass.

22 *ʰ* I saw no temple in the city, for its temple is the Lord God almighty and the Lamb.* ²³The city had no need of sun or moon to shine on it,*ⁱ* for the glory of God gave it light, and its lamp was the Lamb.* ²⁴The nations will walk by its light,* and to it the kings of the earth will bring their treasure.*ʲ* ²⁵During the day its gates will never be shut, and there will be no night there. ²⁶The treasure and wealth of the nations will be brought there, ²⁷but nothing unclean will enter it, nor any[one] who

does abominable things or tells lies. Only those will enter whose names are written in the Lamb's book of life.*ᵏ*

CHAPTER 22

¹Then the angel showed me the river of life-giving water,* sparkling like crystal, flowing from the throne of God and of the Lamb*ˡ* ²down the middle of its street. On either side of the river grew the tree of life* that produces fruit twelve times a year, once each month; the leaves of the trees serve as medicine for the nations. ³Nothing accursed will be found there anymore. The throne of God and of the Lamb will be in it, and his servants will worship him. ⁴They will look upon his face,* and his name will be on their foreheads. ⁵Night will be no more, nor will they need light from lamp or sun, for the Lord God shall give them light, and they shall reign forever and ever.*ᵐ*

VII. EPILOGUE*

⁶And he said to me, "These words are trustworthy and true, and the Lord, the God of prophetic spirits, sent his angel to show his servants what must happen soon."*ⁿ* ⁷"Behold, I am coming soon."* Blessed* is the one who keeps the prophetic message of this book.*ᵒ*

⁸It is I, John, who heard and saw these things, and when I heard and saw them I fell down to worship at the feet of the angel who showed them to me. ⁹But he said to me, "Don't! I am a fellow servant of yours and of your brothers the prophets and of

---

f Eph 2, 20.—g Is 54, 11-12.—h Jn 2, 19-20.—i Is 60, 1-2.19-20.—j Is 60, 11.—k Is 35, 8; 52, 1; Zec 13, 2 / Rv 3, 5; 20, 12.—l Ez 47, 1-12.—m Is 60, 20.—n Rv 1, 1.—o Rv 22, 12.20 / Rv 1, 3.

21, 14: *Courses of stones . . . apostles:* literally, "twelve foundations"; cf Eph 2, 19-20.

21, 15-17: The city is shaped like a gigantic cube, a symbol of perfection (cf 1 Kgs 6, 19-20). The measurements of the city and its wall are multiples of the symbolic number twelve; see the note on Rv 7, 4-9.

21, 16: *Fifteen hundred miles:* literally, twelve thousand stades, about 12,000 furlongs (see the note on Rv 14, 20); the number is symbolic: twelve (the apostles as leaders of the new Israel) multiplied by 1,000 (the immensity of Christians); cf Introduction. *In length and width and height:* literally, "its length and width and height are the same."

21, 17: *One hundred and forty-four cubits:* the cubit was about eighteen inches in length. *Standard unit of measurement the angel used:* literally, "by a human measure, i.e., an angel's."

21, 18-21: The gold and precious gems symbolize the beauty and excellence of the church; cf Ex 28, 15-21; Tb 13, 16-17; Is 54, 11-12.

21, 22: Christ is present throughout the church; hence, no temple is needed as an earthly dwelling for God; cf Mt 18, 20; 28, 20; Jn 4, 21.

21, 23: *Lamp . . . Lamb:* cf Jn 8, 12.

21, 24-27: All men and women of good will are welcome in the church; cf Is 60, 1.3.5.11. *The . . . book of life:* see the note on Rv 3, 5.

22, 1.17: *Life-giving water:* see the note on Rv 7, 17.

22, 2: *The tree of life:* cf Rv 22, 14; see the note on Rv 2, 7. *Fruit . . . medicine:* cf Ez 47, 12.

22, 4: *Look upon his face:* cf Mt 5, 8; 1 Cor 13, 12; 1 Jn 3, 2.

22, 6-21: The book ends with an epilogue consisting of a series of warnings and exhortations and forming an inclusion with the prologue by resuming its themes and expressions; see the note on Rv 1, 1-3.

22, 7.12.20: *I am coming soon:* Christ is the speaker; see the note on Rv 1, 3.

22, 7.14: *Blessed:* see the note on Rv 1, 3.

those who keep the message of this book. Worship God."*p*

¹⁰ Then he said to me, "Do not seal up the prophetic words of this book, for the appointed time* is near. ¹¹ Let the wicked still act wickedly, and the filthy still be filthy. The righteous must still do right, and the holy still be holy."

¹² "Behold, I am coming soon. I bring with me the recompense I will give to each according to his deeds.*q* ¹³ I am the Alpha and the Omega,*r* the first and the last, the beginning and the end."*

¹⁴ Blessed are they who wash their robes so as to have the right to the tree of life and enter the city* through its gates.*s* ¹⁵ Outside are the dogs, the sorcerers, the unchaste, the murderers, the idol-worshipers, and all who love and practice deceit.*t*

---

p Rv 19, 10.—q Rv 22, 7.20 / Ps 62, 12; 2 Tm 4, 14.—r Rv 1, 8; 21, 6; Is 41, 4; 44, 6.—s Rv 7, 14-15; 22, 2.—t Rv 21, 8; Rom 1, 29-32.—u Rv 1, 1.11-12; 22, 6 / Rv 2, 28.—v Rv 21, 6; Is 55, 1.—w Dt 4, 2.—x Rv 22, 7.12 / Acts 3, 20-21; 1 Cor 15, 23; 16, 22.

22, 10: *The appointed time:* see the note on Rv 1, 3.

22, 13: Christ applies to himself words used by God in Rv 1, 8.

22, 14: *The city:* heavenly Jerusalem; see the note on Rv 21, 2.

¹⁶ "I, Jesus, sent my angel to give you this testimony for the churches. I am the root and offspring of David,* the bright morning star."*u*

¹⁷ The Spirit and the bride* say, "Come." Let the hearer say, "Come." Let the one who thirsts come forward, and the one who wants it receive the gift of life-giving water.*v*

¹⁸ I warn everyone who hears the prophetic words in this book: if anyone adds to them, God will add to him the plagues described in this book, ¹⁹ and if anyone takes away from the words in this prophetic book, God will take away his share in the tree of life and in the holy city described in this book.*w*

²⁰ *x* The one who gives this testimony says, "Yes, I am coming soon." Amen! Come, Lord Jesus!*

²¹ The grace of the Lord Jesus be with all.

22, 16: *The root . . . of David:* see the note on Rv 5, 5. *Morning star:* see the note on Rv 2, 26-28.

22, 17: *Bride:* the church; see the note on Rv 21, 2.

22, 20: *Come, Lord Jesus:* a liturgical refrain, similar to the Aramaic expression *Marana tha*—"Our Lord, come!"—in 1 Cor 16, 22; cf the note there. It was a prayer for the coming of Christ in glory at the parousia; see the note on Rv 1, 3.

COLLABORATORS ON THE OLD TESTAMENT OF THE NEW AMERICAN BIBLE

BISHOPS' COMMITTEE OF THE CONFRATERNITY OF CHRISTIAN DOCTRINE

Most Rev. Charles P. Greco, D.D., *Chairman*
Most Rev. Joseph T. McGucken, S.T.D.
Most Rev. Vincent S. Waters, D.D.
Most Rev. Romeo Blanchette, D.D.
Most Rev. Christopher J. Weldon, D.D.

EDITORS IN CHIEF

Rev. Louis F. Hartman, C.SS.R., S.S.L., Ling. Or. L., *Chairman*
Rev. Msgr. Patrick W. Skehan, S.T.D., LL.D., *Vice-Chairman*
Rev. Stephen J. Hartdegen, O.F.M., S.S.L., *Secretary*

ASSOCIATE EDITORS AND TRANSLATORS

Rev. Edward P. Arbez, S.S., S.T.D.
Rev. Msgr. Edward J. Byrne, Ph.D., S.T.D.
Rev. Edward A. Cerny, S.S., S.T.D.
Rev. James E. Coleran, S.J., S.T.L., S.S.L.
Rev. John J. Collins, S.J., M.A., S.S.L.
Sr. M. Emmanuel Collins, O.S.F., Ph.D.
Prof. Frank M. Cross, Jr., Ph.D.
Rev. Patrick Cummins, O.S.B., S.T.D.
Rev. Antonine A. De Guglielmo, O.F.M., S.T.D., S.S.L., S.S. Lect. Gen.
Rev. Alexander A. DiLella, O.F.M., S.T.L., S.S.L., Ph.D.
Most Rev. John J. Dougherty, S.T.L., S.S.D.
William A. Dowd, S.J., S.T.D., S.S.L.
Prof. David Noel Freedman, Ph.D.
Rev. Michael J. Gruenthaner, S.J., S.T.D., S.S.D.
Rev. Msgr. Maurice A. Hofer, S.S.L.
Rev. Justin Krellner, O.S.B., S.T.D.
Rev. Joseph L. Lilly, C.M., S.T.D., S.S.L.
Rev. Roderick F. MacKenzie, S.J., M.A., S.S.D.
Rev. Edward A. Mangan, C.SS.R., S.S.L.
Rev. Daniel W. Martin, C.M., S.T.L., S.S.L.

Rev. William H. McClellan, S.J.
Rev. James McGlinchey, C.M., S.T.D.
Rev. Frederick Moriarty, S.J., S.S.L., S.T.D.
Rev. Richard T. Murphy, O.P., S.T.D., S.S.D.
Rev. Roland E. Murphy, O. Carm., M.A., S.T.D., S.S.L.
Rev. Msgr. William R. Newton, M.S., S.S.D.
Rev. Eberhard Olinger, O.S.B.
Rev. Charles H. Pickar, O.S.A., S.T.L., S.S.L.
Rev. Christopher Rehwinkel, O.F.M., S.T.D., S.S. Lect. Gen.
Rev. Msgr. John R. Rowan, S.T.D., S.S.L.
Prof. J. A. Sanders, Ph.D.
Rev. Edward F. Siegman, C.PP.S., S.T.D., S.S.L.
Rev. Msgr. Matthew P. Stapleton, S.T.D., S.S.L.
Rev. Msgr. John E. Steinmueller, S.T.D., S.S.L.
Rev. John Ujlaki, O.S.B., Litt.D.
Rev. Bruce Vawter, C.M., S.T.L., S.S.D.
Rev. John B. Weisengoff, S.T.D., S.S.L.

COLLABORATORS ON THE REVISED PSALMS
OF THE NEW AMERICAN BIBLE

BISHOPS' AD HOC COMMITTEE
Most Rev. Enrique San Pedro, S.J.
Most Rev. Richard Sklba, D.D.
Most Rev. Donald W. Troutman, S.T.D., S.S.L.
Most Rev. Emil A. Wcela
Most Rev. John F. Whealon, S.S.L., *Chairman*

BOARD OF EDITORS
Rev. Richard Clifford, S.J.
Brother Aloysius Fitzgerald, F.S.C.
Rev. Joseph Jensen, O.S.B. *(Chair)*
Rev. Roland Murphy, O. CARM.
Sr. Irene Nowell, O.S.B.
Dr. Judith Sanderson

REVISERS
Prof. Gary Anderson
Rev. Michael L. Barré
Rev. Christopher T. Begg
Dr. Joseph Blenkinsopp
Rev. Anthony R. Ceresko, O.S.F.S.
Rev. Richard J. Clifford, S.J.
Rev. Aelred Cody, O.S.B.
Prof. Michael D. Coogan
Rev. Alexander A. Di Lella, O.F.M.
Dr. Robert A. Di Vito
Br. Aloysius Fitzgerald, F.S.C.
Rev. Michael D. Guinan, O.F.M.
Rev. William L. Holladay
Rev. William Irwin, C.S.B.
Rev. Joseph Jensen, O.S.B.
Rev. John S. Kselman
Dr. Conrad E. L'Heureux
Rev. Leo Laberge, O.M.I.
Dr. Paul G. Mosca
Rev. Dr. Roland E. Murphy, O. CARM.
Dr. Michael Patrick O'Connor
Rev. Brian J. Peckham, S.J.
Prof. Jimmy J. Roberts
Sr. Eileen M. Schuller, O.S.U.
Dr. Byron E. Shafer
Prof. Mark S. Smith
Prof. Matitiahu Tsevat
Dr. Eugene C. Ulrich
Prof. James C. VanderKam
Rev. Jerome T. Walsh

ENGLISH CONSULTANTS
Dr. Catherine Dunn
Brother Daniel Burke, F.S.C.

BUSINESS MANAGER
Charles A. Buggé

COLLABORATORS ON THE
REVISED NEW TESTAMENT OF
THE NEW AMERICAN BIBLE

BISHOPS' AD HOC COMMITTEE
Most Rev. Theodore E. McCarrick, D.D.
Most Rev. Richard J. Sklba, D.D.
Most Rev. J. Francis Stafford, D.D.
Most Rev. John F. Whealon, D.D., *Chairman*

BOARD OF EDITORS
Rev. Msgr. Myles M. Bourke
Rev. Francis T. Gignac, S.J., *Chairman*
Rev. Stephen J. Hartdegen, O.F.M., *Secretary*
Rev. Claude J. Peifer, O.S.B.
Rev. John H. Reumann

REVISERS
Rev. Msgr. Myles M. Bourke
Rev. Frederick W. Danker
Rev. Alexander A. Di Lella, O.F.M.
Rev. Charles H. Giblin, S.J.
Rev. Francis T. Gignac, S.J.
Rev. Stephen J. Hartdegen, O.F.M.
Dr. Maurya P. Horgan
Rev. John R. Keating, S.J.
Rev. John Knox
Dr. Paul J. Kobelski
Dr. J. Rebecca Lyman
Bro. Elliott C. Maloney, O.S.B.
Dr. Janet A. Timbie

CONSULTANTS
Rev. Joseph Jensen, O.S.B.
Rev. Aidan Kavanagh, O.S.B.
Dr. Marianne Sawicki

BUSINESS MANAGER
Charles A. Buggé

WORD PROCESSOR
Suzanna Jordan

411

BIBLE DICTIONARY

ABEL. The religious and just son of Adam and Eve whose sacrifice pleased God, yet aroused the murderous envy of his brother Cain. He was a shepherd and offered the firstlings of his flock to the Lord (Gn 4, 2-8).

ABRAHAM. "Father of believers." At God's command he left his home in Ur of the Chaldees about 2000 B.C. and settled in Palestine. God made a covenant with him and promised him a great posterity. In his old age his wife Sarah bore him a son (Isaac) in fulfillment of God's promise (Gn 11—25).

ABYSS. In the Old Testament this word refers to the primordial ocean of the ancient Semitic cosmogony. After God's creative activity this vast body forms the salt-water seas (Gn 1, 9f); part of it is the fresh water under the earth as springs and fountains (Gn 7, 11). Part of it, "the upper water" (Ps 148, 4), is held up by the dome of the sky (Gn 1, 6f), from which rain descends on the earth (Gn 7, 11). In the New Testament this word is used to describe the depths of the earth, variously considered the abode of the dead (Rom 10, 7) or of the demons (Lk 8, 3; Rv 9, 1ff; 11, 7; 17, 8; 20, 1.3). Sheol, Pool of Fire, Gehenna and the nether world are similar conceptions.

ADONAI. One of the names of God. It is a plural of majesty and signifies "my lord." In Jewish tradition, it is the word which designates God and replaces the "ineffable Name" (YHWH), which no one was permitted to pronounce. *See* **LORD. NAME. YAHWEH.**

ALLELUIA. Triumphal acclamation signifying: "Praise God," which is often found at the beginning or the end of certain psalms (105-107; 135; Rv 19, 1). It has passed over, untranslated, into the Catholic liturgy.

ALPHA AND OMEGA. The first and last letters of the Greek alphabet. The Hebrews used these two letters to symbolize the fulness, the eternity of God. The Christians inherited this tradition and used alpha and omega to express their belief that in Jesus, the Son of God, is to be found all grace and truth (Rv 1, 8; 21, 6; 22, 13).

ALTAR. A stone or pile of stones, or any structure or place on which sacrifices were burned or incense was offered to God. In the temple at Jerusalem there was an altar of bronze. Solomon had a special altar constructed for burning incense (2 Chr 4, 1).

AMEN. A Hebrew word meaning, "certainly, truly," used to give assent to a statement, a curse, a blessing, a prayer, or the like; in this sense of "so be it," the term came to be employed in Jewish worship and as such the Christian liturgy also uses it after prayers and blessings. In the Gospels, Jesus uses it to give force to his statements (Mt 5, 18. 26). However, the present translation does not reproduce "Amen" but translates it according to the sense of the context.

ANANIAS. Three persons bear this name in the New Testament: (1) the husband of Sapphira (Acts 5); (2) a Christian who received Paul after his conversion (Acts 9 and 22); (3) a high priest who ordered St. Paul to be slapped (Acts 23) and was later assassinated (66 A.D.).

ANATHEMA (DOOMED). In Hebrew: *herem*, which originally signified some thing (or person) set aside from profane use and made sacred to the Lord (Dt 12, 12ff; Jos 11, 11. 14). Hence, it could not be appropriated by anyone; in a good number of cases, the obligation existed to destroy it. This often barbaric custom expressed God's absolute rights over every creature. In the course of time, the term was softened and came to refer to nothing more than objects offered to God (Lv 27, 28; Ez 44, 27; Mk 7, 11). The Greek term *anathema* in the New Testament is used in the sense of "cursed," "separated from God." Later Christianity used this word in the sense of "excommunication" (1 Cor 12, 3: "let a curse be upon him").

ANCIENTS. The forebears of Israel, whose traditions were supposed to be the authority for the unwritten law (Mt 5, 27-33; 15, 2). *See* **ELDERS.**

ANGEL OF THE LORD. Someone who has received a divine delegation, through whom God reveals himself, says, or does something (Jgs 6, 11ff). In numerous biblical texts, the word designates the visible manifestation of God (Gn 16, 7-13; Zec 3, 1ff). In the New Testament, *angels* are heavenly spirits (Heb 1, 7).

ANGER (WRATH) OF GOD. This expression is to be compared with other similar expressions: repentance, jealousy, hand and arm of God. It is an "anthropomorphism," a figure of speech, an image. Seeking to explain the external phenomena supposedly produced by God (storms, floods, earthquakes, catastrophes), we attribute to him sentiments or attitudes which would be found in similar circumstances among men (Ps 78; Dt 32, 15ff; Is 1, 18-20; Lk 13, 3-5).

ANTICHRIST. This word, which is found only in the Epistles of St. John (1 Jn 2, 18-22; 4, 3; 2 Jn 7), designates a personage who is at once both an enemy of Christ and his evildoing imitator. The idea stems from the Jewish writers of the age preceding Christianity. These described the Messiah as having to appear at the end of times to renew all things, but as having to take part in a very violent struggle against a mysterious Adversary. This idea is found throughout the New Testament. Paul calls him "the man of lawlessness," "the son of perdition and adversity" (2 Thes 2, 3. 8; 2 Cor 6, 15). Matthew, Mark and Revelation seem to refer to a collectivity of persons (Mt 24, 23f; Mk 13, 14-20; Rv 13, 17; 17, 7-14).

ANTIOCH. Capital of the Roman province of Syria, it was the most active center of early Christianity (Acts 11, 26).

APOCRYPHA. Religious books used by both Jews and Christians which were not included in the collection of inspired writings. In the Protestant Church, this term designates the books of Tobit, Judith, Maccabees, Wisdom, Baruch, and Ecclesiasticus, which were introduced rather late into the collection of the Bible. Catholics call them "deuterocanonical" books.

APOSTLES. Twelve men chosen by Christ to enjoy special jurisdiction and to teach. They are: Peter, Andrew, James, John, Philip, Bartholomew, Thomas, Matthew, James the Less, Jude, Simon the Zealot and Judas, who was replaced by Matthias. Within the circle of Jesus' disciples, the Twelve were given a privileged position. They alone were present with him at the Last Supper (Mk 14, 17). Later they exercised leadership over the primitive community in Jerusalem (Acts 1, 26; 2, 14; 5, 20f), and were responsible for the information about Jesus that developed into the gospel tradition (Acts 6, 2. 4). Paul and Barnabas are also called Apostles (Gal 2, 7ff), which means literally "one who is sent" (Lk 24, 35. 48; Mt 28, 19-20).

ARK OF THE COVENANT. Wooden chest, overlaid with gold, fashioned by Moses, which contained the two tablets of the law (Ex 25, 10-16; 37, 1-5). It was the symbol of the covenant and God's presence among his people. God was pictured as resting his feet on its golden lid (called "propitiatory"). The ark was placed in the sanctuary of the temple (1 Kgs 8, 1-9) in Jerusalem and disappeared in its ruin at the destruction of the city by the Chaldeans in 586 B.C. (2 Kgs 25, 1-21).

ARMOR. Leather or metal covering which was worn by warriors. It included a helmet, breastplate and shield (Eph 6, 13-17).

ASIA. In the New Testament, used of the Roman Province of Asia, which included only the western third of what is now Asia Minor. Ephesus was its capital, and of its other important cities and districts many are mentioned in the New Testament. The evangelization of the province was accomplished by St. Paul on his third missionary journey (Acts 18—21), St. Peter addressed the churches of Asia (1 Pt 1, 7), and the Book of Revelation conveys messages to each of its most important cities, the "seven churches" (Rv 1, 4ff).

ASSYRIA. A country occupying the northern and middle part of Mesopotamia, including Babylonia and Chaldea. The Assyrians were probably of Semitic origin, descendants of Asshur, one of the sons of Shem (Gn 10, 22). An independent kingdom began about the seventeenth century B.C. In 605 B.C. Nineveh was destroyed by the Medes and Babylonians, and Assyria became a province of these countries.

ASTARTE. Phoenician goddess of fertility, often associated with Baal. Her cult experienced great success in Palestine and her attraction frequently led the Hebrews into idolatry (Jgs 2, 13; 10, 6; 2 Kgs 17, 16).

AZYMES. Unleavened bread which was the only kind permitted during the week of the Jewish Passover. They recalled at the same time the agricultural feast of the barley harvest and the exodus from Egypt, when the Hebrews in their haste were unable to have their dough leavened (Ex 34, 25; 23, 18).

BAAL. This Hebrew word is translated as master, lord. It designates the chief god of the Canaanites and the Phoenicians. His cult was preserved by the Hebrews in Palestine, in spite of the efforts of the prophets (1 Kgs 16, 31-33). The word Baal also designates small local gods (Jgs 2, 11).

BABYLON. Capital of Babylonia, to which many Jewish captives were deported after the fall of Jerusalem in 586 B.C.; this is known as the Babylonian Captivity (2 Kgs 25, 7ff). The name was then applied to any nation hostile to God (Rv 14; 17; etc.).

BALANCES. Scales for weighing money and other items. The moral necessity of a just balance and true weights and the iniquity of false ones are frequently emphasized by the prophets (Am 8, 5; Mi 6, 11).

BAPTISM. The baptism of John the Baptist (Mt 3, 1) is thought to stem from the rabbinical custom of baptizing proselytes who had converted to the faith of Israel (Mt 21, 25). This seems to be a remembrance of the baptism the Jewish people received in crossing the sea (1 Cor 10, 1-2) to acquire the law at Sinai and to attain the promised land. The events of the Exodus foreshadowed the imminent coming of the Lord. Jesus himself underwent baptism to inaugurate his mission (Mt 3, 13ff; Jn 1, 32). He thus became one with the Jewish people and took personal charge of them (Is 53). In this sense, baptism was a preparation for the cross (Mk 10, 38; Lk 12, 50). After the Redemption, baptism became a sacrament for entering a new state of grace (Mt 28, 19; Acts 2, 38-41), the way of regeneration to the divine life.

BEELZEBUL (BAALZEBUB). Name of the god of the nation of Canaan. In the Old Testament it appears under the form *Baalzebub*, "Baal (Lord) of Flies." Later association with the Aramaic *beeldebaba*, "enemy," gave the ancient name its connotation of "devil," and the New Testament uses Beelzebul to refer to the prince of demons (Mt 10, 25; 12, 24; Lk 11, 15).

BETHEL. In Hebrew: house of God. This town was originally called Luz. It is there that Abraham established one of the first sanctuaries and that Jacob had the famous vision of the ladder (Gn 12, 8; 13, 3 and 28, 10). King Jeroboam established the idol of the golden calf here after the schism of the northern tribes (1 Kgs 12, 26-30). The prophets saw therein the symbol of idolatry and gave it the surname of *Bethaven*, house of iniquity (Hos 4, 15).

BISHOP. Greek word signifying "overseer." From the beginning, it has designated the heads of the Christian communities, also called "presbyters" or "elders" (1 Tm 3, 1-7).

BLESSING. The word *bless* changes its meaning according to whether its subject is God or man. Man blesses God by his acts of adoration and thanksgiving (Ps 103, 1. 2); men bless other men by wishing them well or happiness (Mt 5, 44). The ancient Hebrews believed that such wishes were always efficacious (belief in magic) just as they did in the case of maledictions which are the opposite of blessings.

God blesses men by giving them material or spiritual benefits (Gn 24, 1).

Finally, man pronounces blessings on objects, on nourishment, to consecrate them to God (1 Cor 10, 16) or on persons, to sanctify them (Gn 49).

BLOOD. According to the ancients, blood is the seat and sign of life over which only God has power and so must be respected (Gn 9, 4). It is forbidden to consume it in the various offerings (Lv 1-7). This abstention was extended to the consummation of all fleshly nourishment. In the solemn sacrifice of the Day of Atonement, the blood of the victim was spilled over the ark of the convenant. Hence, the blood of Christ, who died for men, has in the eyes of Christians taken on an expiatory value (Heb 9, 28).

BREAD. In an extended sense, this often designates all that is necessary for subsistence. In the Gospels, we find the expression "bread of life," and "living bread" (Jn 6, 31-35), an image by which Jesus affirms that he is the principle of eternal life; at the same time it suggests the use of the Eucharist. Bread of heaven refers first of all to manna and secondly to the sacrament of the Eucharist.

In the Acts of the Apostles, the rite of breaking bread designates the Eucharist (Acts 2, 42).

BREAK BREAD. Among the Jews, the person who presided at the repast would break bread and distribute it to those at table. This is what Jesus did at the multiplication of the loaves (Mt 14, 19) and the Last Supper (Mt 26, 26).

BROTHERS OF THE LORD. Persons who formed part of Jesus' entourage. Among them are James, Joseph, Jude, and Simon. They are "relatives" of Jesus. For Greek-speaking Semites used the terms *adelphos* and *adelphe* not only in the ordinary sense of blood brother and sister but also for nephew, niece, half-brother, half-sister and cousin. Since, according to tradition, Jesus was Mary's only child, this expression is understood in the sense of "cousin," as belonging to the same blood (Mk 6, 1-6).

CAIAPHAS. High priest functioning at Jerusalem from the year 18 to 36 A.D. He was the son-in-law of the former high priest Annas and involved in the conspiracy to destroy Jesus (Jn 11, 49; Mt 26, 57). He was deposed by the legate of Syria, Vitellius, after the recall of Pontius Pilate in 36 A.D.

CALENDAR. (1) The civil *day* was reckoned from sunset to sunset, and hence Jewish Sabbaths and feasts began with the setting of the sun. (2) The *hours* of the day were twelve, beginning at about our 6:00 A.M. and ending at 6:00 P.M. The third, sixth, ninth and twelfth hours were specially sacred to prayer. The night was divided into four watches, the evening watch beginning at 6:00 P.M., the midnight watch at 9:00, "cockcrow" at 12:00, the morning watch at 3:00 A.M. (3) The *week* contained seven days ending in the sabbath, or "Rest." The "first day of the week" became sacred for Christians because of Christ's Resurrection (Jn 20, 19; Acts 20, 7). (4) The *year* consisted of twelve lunar months of twenty-nine or thirty days — i.e., 354 days. The month began with the new moon, and this first day was observed as a holy day. To preserve the proper relation between the lunar and solar calendars, an extra lunar month was intercalated every two or three years. The first month, Nisan, always began on the new moon nearest to and preceding the vernal equinox, March 21.

CANAANITE. Inhabitant of the country of Canaan situated east of the Jordan River (Mt 15, 22). At the time of Jesus, a variant of this word ("Canaanean," translated from the Greek as "Zealot") signified a political party which laid claim to national independence. The apostle Simon was a member of this movement (Mt 10, 4).

CAPTIVITY. This word denotes the exile and deportation of the northern kingdom into Babylonia in 721 (2 Kgs 17—18) and more especially of the southern kingdom in 586 (2 Kgs 25). After the latter date, Israel continually asks God for deliverance from her slavery, the return of the exiles, and the restoration of the chosen people. In 539 Cyrus the Great conquered Babylonia and allowed the Israelites to return home (Ezr 1, 1-4). From then on the Babylonian captivity became a symbol of man's state after Adam's sin from which Jesus has delivered him (Heb 2, 14-15).

CENTURION. Officer in charge of a century (originally 100 men), sixtieth part of the Roman legion. Legionnaires in Palestine were recruited locally, but officers were Roman (Mt 8, 5-13).

CHALICE-CUP. These words are often taken in a figurative sense. For a cup contains either a bitter beverage, symbol of trial (the cup of the divine wrath, for example) (Rv 15, 7) or a sweet beverage, symbol of divine blessing (Rv 5, 8). Since the Last Supper, in which it contained Christ's blood, it has become the expression for the eucharistic mystery (1 Cor 10, 21). In another sense, the word signifies man's destiny, fixed by God. Indeed, in an apportionment the lots to be drawn were in a cup (Ps 16, 5-6).

CHARISM. Word copied from the Greek. It designates, in the Epistles of St. Paul, certain extraordinary spiritual gifts, enabling Christians to collaborate fruitfully in the building up of the mystical body of Christ. For example, the gifts of healing, preaching, and teaching (1 Cor 13).

CHARITY. Word taken from the Latin *caritas* but translating the Greek term *agape*. It designates a very elevated and pure love similar to the love of God for men and the love of Christians for God and their brothers. This word is not to be confused with the sense of almsgiving, or charitable work. The fraternal meals of the first Christians often followed by the Eucharist received the name *agape* (Jude 12; 2 Pt 2, 13) translated by "feast" in this Bible.

CHRIST. This word, derived from the Greek, signifies "anointed" and translates the Hebrew word for *Messiah*. The Hebrew king was anointed with holy oil: so was the high priest (2 Sm 12, 7; Ex 29, 21). In the Bible, it is the title given to the one who, in the future, will come to restore Israel (Dn 9, 25-26). Jesus presents himself as the expected Messiah (Mk 14, 62). St. Paul and the first Christians gave him the name *Christos* (past participle of the verb) which quickly became a proper name: Jesus Christ, Christ Jesus, or simply Christ (Acts 17, 3). *See* JESUS.

CHRISTIAN. This word is derived from *Christ*. It was used for the first time at Antioch around 35 A.D. to designate the disciples of Jesus Christ who until then had been called *Nazoreans* (Acts 11, 26).

CHURCH. (1) Among the Hebrews, this word designates the sacred assembly of the Israelites (cf Jgs 21, 8 where it is translated "assembly"). (2) In the New Testament, it refers first to the assembly of the Christians of Jerusalem (Acts 5, 11). Later, the word was applied to each of the communities founded by St. Paul (1 Cor 1, 2). Finally, it designates the totality of Christians and that ideal church which will be fully realized only at the end of times. In this sense, the church is the body of Christ (Mt 16, 18).

CIRCUMCISION. Removal of the prepuce. It is a very ancient ethical practice which the Hebrews converted into a religious rite. Abraham received it as a sign of the covenant (Gn 17, 10ff). Later, the prophets stressed the fact that this bodily mark has no value unless it is accompanied by an "internal circumcision" signifying moral purity (Jer 9, 25f).

COMING. Translation of the Greek word *parousia*. This word designates the second coming of Christ for the last judgment (Mt 24, 3; 1 Thes 4, 15). The belief in a twofold messianic coming distinguishes the Christian mentality from Jewish messianism.

COMMUNION. State in which the faithful is united to God, is close to God, and enjoys his intimacy. Christianity has as its object to place us in communion with the Father and the Son through the action of the Holy Spirit, that is, to give us a share in the divine life (Jn 15). In the Bible, the word never signifies sacramental communion in the Eucharist.

CONSECRATE. Withdrawal of an object or person from secular use so as to transfer it into the domain of God and keep it there (Ex 13, 1; 30, 29).

CONVERSION. This word is frequently associated with other terms of repentance and penitence. It signifies changing one's life. In their preaching, the apostles ask that their hearers be converted (repent) and be baptized (Acts 2, 38). In the Bible, the word conversion is never used in the sense of "changing one's religion."

COVENANT. Man has always sought to place himself in contact with the divinity. In sacred history, this contact has taken the form of a kind of contract between God and the people of Israel. But there had already been a personal covenant between God and Noah (Gn 6, 18-22), and between God and Abraham (with the sign of circumcision: Gn 17, 10-14). This covenant is made by God without the opinion of the other party being asked. It is therefore gratuitous. But it is bilateral by reason of the promises of the contracting parties: the people promise to observe the law, and God promises to reward fidelity (Ex 19, 4-8; Dt 5, 1-21).

Unfortunately, the people were often unfaithful. It is then that the prophets promise (for the messianic times) a new covenant in which the union between God and man will no longer be solely in a national religion but in an interior and spiritual piety (Jer 31, 31-34; 11, 1-17).

This hope is realized by the Gospel in Jesus Christ, in whom Christians receive the grace promised (Mt 26, 28; Heb 10, 9-18).

Hence, the two parts of the Bible were designated by the first Christians with the terms Old Covenant, New Covenant. However, since the Greek word *diatheke* (covenant) also signifies testament, the custom arose (we do not know why) in Latin and the modern languages of using this latter word, even though the meaning is almost incomprehensible.

CREATION. This notion is at the basis of the faith of Israel. It is presented not only as an abstract notion (2 Mc 7, 28), but also as the corollary to the existence of an active Creator, present in the world (Ps 104; Jb 38). It expresses itself in popular cosmological descriptions of the time (Gn 1—3) and establishes the fundamental relation between man and God in the Judaeo-Christian religion. The revelation and redemption of the Messiah sometimes appears as a re-creation: "new world," "new heaven" (Is 45, 8), reestablishing the order and first destiny of things and of men, lost through sin.

CROSS. This instrument of Roman torture reserved for slaves was particularly infamous. It was known to Jesus who preached a type of detachment to his disciples which would go as far as this humiliation of the cross (Mt 10, 38). He himself followed this way of self-denial out of love and obedience (Phil 2, 8). The death on the cross of the Messiah, Son of God, is a scandal, the paradox which will become the most incontestable historical and spiritual center of the work of salvation accomplished by Jesus (1 Cor 1, 18-23). By his abasement on the cross which paid men's debt to sin and crushed the devil (1 Cor 2, 8; Col 2, 14) Jesus is elevated (2 Cor 13, 4) and the wood of infamy has become a tree of life (Rv 2, 7). Crucified with Christ through baptism and the life of faith (Gal 2, 19; Rom 6, 6), the Christian must glory only in the cross of Jesus (Gal 6, 12-15).

DAGON. Word derived from the root *dag*: fish. It is the name originally of a Mesopotamian deity who became the principal god of the Philistines. His body was half-man and half-fish (Jgs 16, 23).

DAMASCUS. Capital of Syria, destroyed in 732 B.C. (2 Kgs 16, 9), which had a large Jewish population. It was the scene of Paul's conversion (Acts 9, 1-27).

DARKNESS. Absence of light. In the Bible God, who is eternal truth, is considered the true light and the source of all light (Is 10, 17); therefore darkness becomes a symbol of estrangement from God. Jesus said that those who followed him would not walk in darkness (John 8, 12), i.e., he would show them clearly the truth.

DAY OF THE LORD (JUDGMENT). This is the day on which God will judge. The judgment is often conceived of as a punishment. The "day of the Lord" was announced by the prophets as affecting chiefly the pagan nations, who were guilty of attacking and enslaving the people of God (Is 2, 12-22). Later, the same prophets will affirm that the judgment will also touch Israel (Zep 1, 7. 14-18) and, at the end of times, all mankind (Zec 14, 1-7). In the New Testament, this idea persists, and it is toward this glorious manifestation of Christ that the whole of Christian hope tends (1 Cor 1, 8; 1 Thes 5, 2. 4).

DEACON. This word signifies server, assistant. It has taken on a particular meaning with the institution of the deacons in the early church to serve the poor and assist the apostles (Acts 6, 1-6).

DEMON. The Jews recognized the existence of destructive evil spirits, wicked powers dedicated to doing harm. These are the demons, enslaved by Satan, who dwell within and stir up those who are possessed (Mt 8, 28-32).

DESERT. This word holds a major place in biblical thought: it is in the desert that the people has experienced divine intimacy (Ex 19). The desert symbolizes the desolate sojourn of the times of trial. Jesus withdraws to the desert before beginning his ministry (Mt 4, 1).

DIASPORA (DISPERSION). This word designates the Jews scattered throughout the pagan regions of the Roman Empire (Jn 7, 35).

DIVORCE. The Bible presents marriage as a union of the natural order, indissoluble and allowable once for each couple, in order to assure the mutual complement of man and woman (Gn 2, 24). Moses, for reasons of "hardness of heart" and in order to limit the abuses of polygamy, codified the custom of repudiation then in use, exacting a tribute, that is, a written piece of paper which the married man had to give his wife signifying that her freedom was restored. He was not allowed to take her back again (Dt 24, 1-4). Our Lord, in bringing the law of charity and a higher moral order, renewed the natural precept of Gn 2, 24, and gave marriage its original unity and indissolubility (Mt 19, 3; 5, 32; Mk 10, 2; Lk 16, 18).

ELDER. In the Old Testament the word refers to an official class having both civil and religious jurisdiction (Ex 3, 16; 24, 1). In the New Testament it refers to an official of the early Christian church, such as a bishop or priest (Acts 20, 17. 28; Jas 5, 14).

ELECT, ELECTION. This refers to the divine choice. (1) Abraham is chosen and taken from his family and country. This election culminates in the election of Israel (Gn 12, 1-7; Ex 19, 1-9). (2) Certain persons are said to be chosen (David, the Messiah) (2 Sm 7, 14ff). (3) Jesus is called the elect ("chosen one") of God (Lk 23, 35). (4) Christ chooses his apostles (Mt 10, 2-4). (5) All Christians are the object of a divine election (Rom 1, 6).

ELOHIM. Ordinary Hebrew word for God. It is the plural of majesty. Elohim ordinarily designates God in his action on the world in contrast to Yahweh which is used of the God of the covenant (Ex 3, 14).

ESSENES. The Dead Sea Scrolls have indicated that the Essenes ranked in importance with the Pharisees and Sadducees. There were about 4000 Essenes although only 200 lived in Qumran, their most important center. A member had to undergo a one-year "postulancy" and a three-year "novitiate." He then vowed to be reverent, just, hate sinners, help the just, obey his superiors, tell the truth, share his property, and keep Essene teaching secret. Meals and ritual baths were of great importance. Some think that John the Baptist was a member of this sect (Lk 1, 80; 3, 1-21).

ETERNAL. This corresponds to the Hebrew word *olam*, signifying a long period of time; these terms indicate primarily something that perdures throughout the centuries (Gn 17, 8); then something that has neither beginning nor end, like God (Gn 21, 33); and, finally, something outside of time (1 Jn 5, 11-12).

EXPIATION-PROPITIATION. Translation of the Hebrew *Kippur* signifying pardon or suppression of sin. Jesus is called "expiation" because he assures pardon of all sins (Rom 3, 25).

FAITH. In the Old Testament, faith is rarely mentioned. Its essential component is trust in God. Thus, Abraham's trust becomes the type of true faith (Gal 3, 6). In the New Testament, faith holds a predominant place: Jesus requires faith in himself which presupposes the acceptance of his message and trust in the person of the Master (Jn 6, 29-40) In St. Paul, faith is the chief element of his teaching and the key to salvation (Rom 1, 16).

FASTS. The chief Jewish fast was that of the Day of Atonement known as "the (autumn) fast" (Acts 27, 9). The especially devout customarily fasted on the second and fifth days of the week (Mt 9, 14; Lk 18, 12). Our Lord's great fast (Mt 4, 2) was foreshadowed by those of Moses (Ex 24, 18) and Elijah (1 Kgs 19, 8).

FEAR OF GOD. (1) Feeling experienced before any kind of divine manifestation: dread, fear, dismay (Ex 20, 18ff). (2) The same word also serves to denote the service of God, religion (Dt 4, 10). (3) The term "God-fearer" was used of a pagan who had adopted Jewish religious practices, without however belonging completely to the religion of Israel (Acts 10, 1).

FEASTS. In memory of the rest of God after the work of creation, the Jews kept as sacred the seventh day, or sabbath, the seventh month, the seventh or sabbatical year, and the fiftieth or jubilee year (Gn 2, 1-3; Lv 25, 1-22).

The weekly sabbath was observed by special sacrifices, by rest from servile work, and by attendance at religious instruction (Ex 20, 8-11; Lv 23, 2f).

The first day of the month, the New Moon, was a holy day on which special offerings were made (Nm 28, 11-15; Col 2, 16).

The three major feasts of the year, on which male Israelites were required to go to the temple, were Passover, in March or April, Pentecost, fifty days later, and Tabernacles, toward the end of September.

Passover began on the evening of the fourteenth Nisan with the eating of the lamb. On the fourteenth, after all leaven had been removed from the house, the lamb was sacrificed at the temple, and then brought home for cooking. It was eaten with herbs and unleavened bread in memory of the going out of Israel from Egypt (Lv 23, 5f; Heb 11, 27-29). The following week was known as the days of the Unleavened Bread (Lv 23, 6-8). The eve of the sabbath within this week was the Preparation Day (Mt 27, 62). During this week the first-fruits of the barley harvest were presented as the opening of the seven weeks of harvest.

Pentecost recalled the giving of the law, and it offered in thanks the first-fruits of the wheat harvest (Lv 23, 15-11). At Pentecost the Holy Spirit came upon the apostles and the others gathered in the Upper Room (Acts 2, 1ff).

Tabernacles was celebrated in the month of Tishri. The first day of that month was the feast of Trumpets, the civil New Year. On the tenth fell the Day of Atonement, a day of fast and of expiatory sacrifices, when the high priest entered the holy of holies to sprinkle blood (Lv 16; 23, 23-36; Nm 29, 7-11). From the fifteenth to the twenty-first of the month the feast of Tabernacles (Booths) was celebrated. It recalled the wanderings of the Israelites in the desert. This week marked the end of the harvest of fruit, wine and oil (Lv 23, 39-43). The last day of the feast was a day of rest on which were observed the ceremonies of water libation and the lighting of the four great golden candelabra (Jn 7, 37; 8, 12).

Two minor feasts were kept during the winter, Dedication and Purim (Lots). The former was held in our December, and was a joyous commemoration of the rededication of the temple by Judas Maccabeus (1 Mc 4, 56-59). It was also known as the feast of Lights, since during it the temple was illuminated (Jn 10, 22). Purim, held at the close of winter, recalled the rescue of the Jews by Esther when Haman cast lots to determine the day on which they should be destroyed (Est 9, 20-32; 2 Mc 15, 36).

FIGURE (TYPE). A person, event, or object which in God's intention signifies or foreshadows something else. Many realities of the Old Testament foreshadowed those of the New (Heb 7, 1-22).

FIRE. This is used as a symbol to express the divinity which radiates and consumes at the same time, with a joyous or terrifying aspect: God present in the fire on Mt. Sinai, in a storm (Ex 19, 18). On the altar of the temple, there was a perpetual fire (Lv 6, 5; 2 Chr 4, 1). God, a devouring fire, consumes Sodom and Gomorrah (Gn 19, 24-25). Jesus is said to baptize "with fire," that is, with the Holy Spirit (Mt 3, 11).

FIRST-BORN. By right, every first-born male must be reserved for God. He must be either immolated or (since infant-sacrifice was abolished by the Hebrews) redeemed (Ex 13, 2; Nm 3, 11-13). The title "first-born" could be given to the boy even if he had no brother or sister. And it entailed the privilege of "birthright," entitling him to a position of honor in the family and to a double share in the possessions inherited from the father (Ex 25, 31). Jesus is called the first-born of creation because of his position as the head of mankind (Heb 1, 6).

FIRST-FRUITS. The first fruits of the season which out of obligation were offered to God (Ex 23, 19). Paul calls Jesus "the first fruits" of the dead, showing that his resurrection will be followed by theirs (1 Cor 15, 20. 23).

FLESH. (1) First meaning: the flesh of an animal in contrast to the blood and bones (Gn 9, 3ff). (2) Everything that has life (Gn 6, 13). (3) Man in contrast to God by reason of his weakness; hence, the person, human nature (Mt 26, 41). (4) Especially in St. Paul's Epistles, natural man, without grace, with his weaknesses and tendencies toward sin, in contrast to the "spirit" which designates the faculty that enables man to share in the Holy Spirit through the new birth of baptism (Rom 7, 14).

FOREIGNERS. Term reserved for those who were not of Hebrew stock, the Gentiles (Ex 12, 44).

GALILEE. The most northerly region of Palestine and the most favored by nature. Among its flourishing towns were Cana, Chorazin, Nazareth, Capernaum, Bethsaida, Tiberias. The population was predominantly Jewish, but there was a noticeable Galilean dialect (Mt 26, 73). The Galileans were very loyal to their religion and nation, though regarded by the Judeans as ignorant and lawless (Jn 7, 41; Mk 14, 70). Our Lord was reared in Galilee, he spent most of his time preaching there, and all but one of his apostles were from Galilee.

GALILEE, SEA OF. A lake which formed the eastern boundary of Galilee. It was also called the Lake of Gennesaret, from the plain on its northwest corner (Lk 5, 1), and the Sea of Tiberias, from the city of this name, the residence of Herod Antipas (Jn 6, 1). The lake is about thirteen miles long and six broad.

GEHENNA. This comes from the Hebrew "Valley of Hinnom," a place near Jerusalem where ritual infant-sacrifices had been practiced (2 Chr 28, 3). This place was later used as a depot for refuse. The word became synonymous with place of malediction (Jer 7, 31) and then in the New Testament with the abode of the damned, a place of torment, unquenchable fire and the consuming worm (Mt 5, 29; 10, 28; 18, 8f; Mk 9, 44ff). See **SHEOL.**

GETHSEMANI. This word, which signifies "oil press," became the name for a plantation of olive trees located opposite the temple of Jerusalem, east of the torrent of Kidron. This is the "mount of Olives," scene of Christ's agony and betrayal (Mt 26, 36-56).

GLORY. A very important notion in biblical theology. In Hebrew (*kabod*), the word designates "to be heavy," "to be illustrious." It often denotes the radiant manifestation of God in his grandeur (Ez 1, 28). This divine glory is possessed by Jesus (Jn 1, 14). According to St. Paul, every Christian shares in this divine glory already here below (Phil 3, 21).

GOEL. See **KIN, NEXT OF.**

GOLGOTHA. Aramaic word signifying "skull place." It was the name of a little hill located northwest of the city of Jerusalem. Those condemned were executed there, and it was here that Jesus suffered crucifixion (Mt 27, 33). The Latin rendering of this word is *Calvaria* which is the origin of our "Calvary."

GOOD NEWS. See **GOSPEL.**

GOSPEL. In Greek, this word signifies good news, and specifically the good news of the Kingdom of God (Heb 4, 2; Mt 4, 23). St. Paul uses the word to indicate his preaching; later, the same word will be applied to the accounts of Christ's life (1 Cor 9, 16; Rom 1, 3).

GRACE. This word (in Greek: *doxa*) has a great variety of meanings: favor, benevolence, benefit. Hence, it signifies God's gratuitous love which makes the creature its acceptable beneficiary (Rom 11, 5. 6). The grace par excellence is salvation, justification (Eph 2, 5). In the plural—graces—it signifies the supernatural gifts and helps given to each one by the Holy Spirit.

HASIDEANS. This word is derived from the Hebrew word *hasidim*, "pious ones," and designates the faithful servants of God. They are mentioned in the book of Proverbs (2, 8) and in the Psalms (40, 5; 50, 5; 148, 14). They played a leading part during the resistance directed by Judas Maccabeus (1 Mc 2, 42 and 7, 6; 2 Mc 14, 6). They are undoubtedly at the origin of the Essenes, the brotherhood established in the monastery of Qumran which left us the famous Dead Sea Scrolls.

HEART. The Hebrews regarded the heart as the seat not only of emotions but also of thoughts and voluntary acts. Thus, the heart represents the whole man (Jl, 2, 13; 1 Pt 3, 4).

HEAVEN. This word has several meanings: (1) the firmament in which the stars are perceived (Gn 1, 14-17); (2) the region of the atmosphere where the birds fly (Dt 4, 17); (3) the place of God's residence, the throne-room where the Everlasting One is seated surrounded by the angels (Mt 5, 12; 24, 36). Jewish tradition had imagined several heavens or firmaments superimposed on one another, populated with various kinds of angels. It is in this sense that they spoke of the "heavenly host" and that St. Paul spoke of having been caught up in ecstasy "to the third heaven" (2 Cor 12, 2).

HELL. The place of eternal punishment, also called Gehenna. *See* **GEHENNA. SHEOL.**

HELLENIST. A Jew, or a Jew turned Christian, living in a foreign land and speaking Greek (Acts 6, 1).

HERITAGE. *See* **INHERITANCE.**

HEROD. The Herodian family, though Jewish in religion, was Idumean in origin. Herod "the Great" (B.C. 62 to 4) was appointed by Rome as king of Judea in B.C. 40, to the exclusion of the native Hasmonean line. He rebuilt the temple, and was in general an efficient ruler, but his cruelties made him odious. He slaughtered the infants at Bethlehem (Mt 2, 16-18). Four of his children are mentioned in the New Testament: Archelaus, Antipas and two named Philip.

Archelaus, ethnarch of Judea (4 B.C.-6 A.D.), was deposed on account of his cruelty and exiled to Vienne in Gaul.

Antipas, tetrarch of Galilee and Perea, was deposed in 39 A.D. He divorced his wife, the daughter of King Aretas, and married Herodias, the wife of his brother Philip, who resided in Rome. He imprisoned and later beheaded John the Baptizer (Mt 14, 1ff). He was present in Jerusalem at the time of our Lord's trial (Lk 23, 7-12).

Philip, tetrarch of Trachonitis (4 B.C.—34 A.D.) unlike his brothers, was a moderate and peaceful ruler.

Two other descendants of Herod are also mentioned in the New Testament. Herod Agrippa I, grandson of Herod the Great, was king of all Palestine from 41 to 44 A.D. He was a strict observer of Judaism, and a persecutor of Christianity (Acts 12, 1ff). His death is mentioned in Acts 12, 23. His son, Agrippa II, ruled in Trachonitis until his death in 100 A.D. This Agrippa and his sister Bernice heard St. Paul's defense (Acts 25—26). Another sister, Drusilla, was married to the procurator Felix (Acts 24, 24).

HERODIANS. These were partisans and courtiers of the reigning dynasty of the Herods. Though they were Jews in religion, their spirit was Gentile. They conspired with their enemies the Pharisees against Christ (Mt 22, 16).

HERODIAS. Daughter of Aristobulus and granddaughter of Herod the Great and Mariamme. She was the wife of Philip but left him to marry Antipas. Her daughter Salome (who has unfortunately achieved some notoriety) resulted from the first marriage (Mt 14, 6-10).

HIGH PLACES. In Hebrew *bamoth* designates the sanctuaries ordinarily built on the heights by the inhabitants of Canaan (Nm 33, 52) as well as the Hebrews before the temple was built (1 Kgs 3, 2). However, later they became the symbol of idolatry for Israel, a symbol to which the ancient Jewish people constantly returned, in spite of the prohibition of Deuteronomy (12, 4ff), and the constant condemnations of the prophets (Ez 6, 3-6).

HIGH PRIEST. The chief of the sacred ministers among the Jews. He was supreme in religious matters, and to him was reserved the exclusive right of offering the great sacrifice of expiation and of entering the holy of holies (Heb 9, 7). Through him at times God announced things to come (Jn 11, 51). He was a member of the Sanhedrin and ordinarily presided over its deliberations (Mt 26, 57; Acts 4, 5f; 5, 27; etc.). Induction into this high priesthood was by anointing or by investiture in the precious robes of the office. The dignity descended at first by primogeniture from Aaron and the elder branch of Aaron's family and was held for life. But in the days of Christ the high priests were appointed and removed at will by the Herods and the Roman procurators. During the lifetime of our Lord some fifteen different individuals held the office, the most noted of whom were Annas (6-5 A.D.) and his son-in-law Caiaphas (18-36 A.D.). Annas and Caiaphas, often named together, judged Christ (Jn 18, 13. 24), Peter and John (Acts 4, 6), then all the Apostles (Acts 5, 17ff) and St. Stephen (Acts 6, 12ff), while Ananias acted against Paul (Acts 23, 2; 24, 1).

HOLOCAUST. In the ancient sacrifices only the blood and certain parts of the victim were offered to God; the rest was divided among the priest and faithful who had offered it (Lv 7, 11-21). A holocaust (from the Greek "wholly burned") was a sacrifice in which an entire animal except its hide was consumed in the fire on the altar, with the primary purpose of rendering glory to God (Lv 1, 1ff).

HOLY (SANCTIFY). The term "holy" is applied to anything that is consecrated to God, and hence withdrawn from all (secular) human use. In this sense, holy or sacred implies that no one can touch the object, for such contact would entail an "impurity" (1 Kgs 8, 4). God is "holy," because he is completely apart from any contact with the universe; but also because he possesses moral perfection. The people of Israel was to be "holy" in order to resemble God (Lv 20, 7. 26). Christians are "holy" because they have been consecrated to God by baptism. They are thus called to achieve moral perfection (Rom 6, 3ff). To *sanctify* means to consecrate something or someone to the service of God (Heb 13, 12). God shows himself to be holy by manifesting his justice (Is 5, 16).

HOPE. The messianic hope is at the center of the life of Israel, the source of all its unity, its action, and influence on others. The Hebrew terms which designate it express the tension of a bow ready to shoot its arrow to infinity (Zec 9, 13-14); this hope thus represents a search, an absolute confidence and a concentration of all one's energy flowing from God's covenant with Israel. It does not rest on human resources and initiative, but on the all-powerful Presence of God (Ps 18; 7). It is unshakable in spite of all the vicissitudes of the history of Israel (Mi 7, 7-9; Ps 22, 5-6; Jer 30, 7). It is the constant on which many of the words of the prophets are predicated (Mi 4—5; Is 40ff; Jer 30—33; Ez 40ff). This hope was confirmed and reinforced by the coming of the Messiah, the incarnation and redemption of Christ. Christian hope takes its character from this absolute witness of love and God's fidelity to his promises. It brings the gospel to the far corners of the world as well as souls to a more complete assurance of salvation (Rom 5, 1-11; Heb 6, 18-20) until the end of time (1 Pt 1, 3-5).

HORNS. These are the symbol of power and strength (1 Sm 2, 1). The Bible often speaks of the horns of the altar, ornaments jutting out over the four corners of the altar of the temple of Jerusalem (1 Kgs 1, 50).

HOSANNA Hebrew expression signifying: "may God save," used in the course of Jewish feasts (Ps 118, 25f). It served as an acclamation during Christ's entrance into Jerusalem, in the sense of "Long live," and it is always chanted during the course of the Catholic liturgy (Mt 21, 9).

HOSTS. Translation of the Hebrew word *sabaoth* which signifies armies. These armies are either a warrior grouping (material sense) (Ex 14, 17) or the multitude (such as an army) of stars (Ps 33, 6) or angelic beings that express God's glory (Jb 25, 3).

IMPOSITION OF HANDS. The customary Jewish way of designating a person for a task and invoking upon him the divine blessing and power to perform it (Nm 8, 10-11). Jesus used it when healing (Mk 6, 5). By the imposition of hands, the apostles conferred the Holy Spirit (Acts 8, 17), the diaconate (Acts 6, 6), and the priesthood (1 Tm 4, 14).

INHERITANCE. The corresponding Greek indicates a portion (of a share) as the result of drawing lots. This word designates the various parts of the promised land chosen for each Israelite tribe (Jos 15, 1). The word is retained in the New Testament in reference to Jesus who has been constituted by God as the heir of all things (Heb 1, 2); and in reference to Christians, sons and heirs of God, through Jesus Christ (Rom 4, 13-16; 8, 17).

ISRAEL. Proper name signifying "one who struggles with God." The popular explanation of this glorious surname recalling Jacob's struggle (Gn 32, 29) then passes on to his posterity and designates the People of the Promise (Ex 3, 16).

JEALOUS (GOD). This is the translation used for a Hebrew verb which contains the concept of ardor; it can characterize the divine justice as ardent, zealous, and prompt to chastise sinners (Ex 20, 5). God is also termed jealous because since he is unique he cannot allow man not to render single-minded worship to him (Ex 34, 14).

JERUSALEM. In Hebrew, *Yerushalaim*, vision of peace. But the origin of the name seems to be *Ursalim* which signifies "foundation of Salem," a Canaanite divinity. The city was a citadel of the Jebusites (Jgs 1, 8). It was conquered by David who made it his capital (2 Sm 5; 6). Destroyed in 586 B.C., it was rebuilt by the Jews who returned from the exile, in the fifth century before the Christian era (2 Kgs 25, 1-21; Ezr 3—6). It was besieged and destroyed for the second time by the emperor Titus in 70 A.D. At the time of Christ, Jerusalem was the chief city of Palestine and the religious center of Judaism. Situated on a plateau, its walls looked down into deep ravines, the Kidron on the east and the Valley of Hinnom on the south and west. Within the walls the city was divided by the Valley of the Tyropoean, and sloped gradually toward the southeast.

The northeastern part of the city rested on Mount Moriah and was occupied chiefly by the temple and the fortress Antonia. North of the temple were the Sheep Gate and the Pool of Bethesda (Jn 5, 2). The Golden Gate, in the eastern wall of the city, opened on the road to Gethsemani, Mount Olivet, Bethany and Jericho. On its western side the temple had a bridge that led over the Tyropoean to the Upper City. The southeastern section of the city was the ancient city of David, whose walls contained the tower of Siloam (Lk 13, 4) and the various gates that led to the fountains outside the walls. This part of the city was inhabited largely by priests. The southwestern section of the city contained the business districts, the palaces of Annas and Caiaphas, of Herod and of the Hasmoneans. To the east of it was the Pool of Siloam (Jn 9, 7), and to the south the Valley of Hinnom (a place for refuse) and Akeldama ("Blood Field") (Mt 27, 8; Acts 1, 19).

Another section of the city lay to the northwest, across from the temple. Beyond its walls were fields, gardens and places of burial. The Ephraim Gate which opened here on the highway to Jaffa was not far from the place of the Crucifixion, which lay just outside the city (Jn 19, 17-20; Heb 13, 12).

JESUS. This name, which was common in Israel, signifies "God saves." It was bestowed by God (Lk 1, 31) on the son of the Virgin Mary—who was truly man (Acts 2, 22. 32) and later recognized as Lord (Phil 2, 11) and Savior (2 Tm 1, 10)—in consequence of his mission (Mt 1, 21).

But before being recognized as the Messiah and Son of God, Jesus of Nazareth is taken for the son of Joseph and Mary, and he appears in history at the moment when John the Baptizer is preaching repentance in Judea (Lk 3, 1ff). Jesus wins the admiration of the crowds by his preaching and healing, proclaiming the good news of the kingdom of God and doing good. He is soon followed by numerous disciples and like John his precursor becomes a sign of contradiction for the Judaism of his time (Mt 10, 34; Lk 4, 15; 11, 27). He speaks with authority in the synagogues and is called Teacher and Rabbi. He criticizes the formalism of certain religious practices

(the sabbath, ablutions), questions the worship tied down to the perdurance of the temple, and overturns social barriers (publicans and sinners draw near to him). He allows himself to be called Messiah and Son of David by the enthusiastic crowds. However, Jesus knows that this is an ambiguous messianism and so he reveals his true identity to a few of those chosen for their faith (Mt 16, 16; Jn 6, 67-70).

Jesus is condemned as a blasphemer by those who hand him over to the Roman authority to be crucified (Mt 26, 65). Under the Roman procurator Pontius Pilate (26-36 A.D.) he is put to death for the crime of having made himself "King of the Jews."

All the direct testimonies about Jesus and his work (the New Testament) concern firstly his resurrection and the divine character of his person. Foretold by the prophets and all the Scriptures (Lk 18, 31; 24, 25-27; Heb 1, 1ff), Jesus can be known only in the light of the Spirit of God. He will be understood only after his resurrection when he has sent forth this Spirit to the witnesses of his work, chosen by him. They will then recognize him as the Suffering Servant (Mt 3, 17; Phil 2, 7), the Son of David (Jn 7, 41-42), the High Priest and Mediator of the new Covenant (Jn 16, 26; Heb 3, 1; 8, 6), the Son of Man manifested as the savior at the time willed by God (1 Tm 1, 1-5), the Lord, image and Son of God, and God himself (Acts 2, 36; 11, 20; Rom 8, 29; 9, 5; Phil 2, 11; Heb 1, 3); the one who has come from God in the humility of the flesh (Jn 1; 7, 15-16. 27; 8, 14; Phil 2, 6-7) and, after his death, has been exalted by the Father whom he has revealed (Jn 3, 14; 12, 32).

All these titles—Word, Elect or Holy One of God, Lamb of God, Rabbi, Messiah, Son of God, Son of Man, King of Israel—are gathered together by John in the introduction accorded Jesus in the first chapter of his Gospel. But his name Jesus is henceforth above every name (Phil 2, 9). Lord of the universe and head of the church, he is the salvation which he brings to us (Lk 1, 71); thus the one who believes in him will desire to be worthy to die for his name (Acts 15, 26; 21, 13).

JORDAN. The foremost river of Palestine. From the Lebanons to the Dead Sea it covers a distance of 125 miles, though with its meanderings the stream itself is more than double that. The width varies from 80 to 150 feet, and the depth in summer from 4 to 12 feet. The river is generally hidden by a thick growth of willow. There are many fords which allow passage from the one bank to the other (Jos 2, 7; Mt 3, 13).

JUBILEE. Year of joy and amnesty, celebrated at the end of each 49 year period, in the course of which one's debts must be remitted and slaves set free (Lv 25, 8-55).

JUDGMENT. In the Old Testament, judgment is related to the covenant. Judges and kings were established to maintain or reestablish the faithfulness to the covenant in the midst of national difficulties and in matters concerning the observation of the law (1 Kgs 3, 6). They represented the supreme Judge (Is 11, 3-5). Referring to God, judgment designates divine intervention, sometimes to assure his people victory or deliverance and at other times to condemn and punish them after an infidelity (Dt 32, 36; Jer 30, 11ff).

In the Psalms Yahweh appears as the supreme Judge above all in the great deeds of the "Day of the Lord" *(see this term)* and his power extends over all the earth. Among the prophets this perspective becomes more and more connected with the eschatological plane (Zec 14; Dn 7, 12).

In the New Testament, judgment is connected with the work of Christ, accepted by the faithful or rejected by the unbelievers. It is already present and marks a difference between groups of people (Jn 3, 17-21; 8, 15; 12, 31). Hence, it is necessary to be on one's guard, because judgment is coming. It will be made evident at the last day, which will be marked by the definitive triumph of Christ (Mt 25, 31; 1 Thes 4, 16; 2 Thes 2, 3-10).

JUST (JUSTICE). The just man is one who is virtuous, faithful to God and to the law of Moses (Mt 19, 17-20). In the New Testament the "just" man is one who does the will of God (Mt 7, 21). In the teachings of St. Paul, the terms justice and justification appear often: God makes man "just," free from sin and pleasing to God through grace (grace attested by faith) (Rom 3, 20-30).

KINGDOM (REIGN) OF GOD. The Kingdom will be established by the Messiah, over Israel first (Zep 3, 14-15), and then over all the nations of the earth (Zec 14, 9). "Kingdom" signifies a state of things in which God is recognized as King to whom everything must be submitted: Kingdom of God and Kingdom of heaven are equivalent. The Kingdom is proclaimed by John the Baptizer (Mt 3, 2), inaugurated by Jesus (Mt 12, 25-28), continued in the church (Mt 10, 7; 16, 19), and will be definitively accomplished in the glory of Christ's return (Mt 24, 26-31). The members of the Kingdom are children of God and even in this life enjoy that eternal life which will be completely expanded in the future world (Jn 3, 15-16; Rv 22, 2).

KIN (NEXT OF), AVENGER OF BLOOD, GOEL. *See* **LEVIRATE.**

KISHON. Name of a brook flowing at the foot of Mt. Tabor. It witnessed several violent scenes and battles (Jgs 4, 13; 1 Kgs 18, 40).

KITTIM. This name referred originally to inhabitants of Kiti, capital of the isle of Cyprus, then to any Cypriots (Gn 10, 4; Is 23, 1; Jer 2, 10), later to Greeks in general (Nm 24, 24), and finally even to Romans (Dn 11, 30).

KNOW. God knows everything, since he is the Creator (Jb 37, 16). He knows his people, since he has chosen it (Gn 18, 19). On his part, man seeks to know God in faith (Dt 29, 3; Jer 31, 31-34). The word "know" has a third meaning in the Bible: man "knows" his wife; he has carnal relations with her (Gn 4, 1).

LAW OF MOSES. The law, respected by all Jews as from God, consisted of the five books of Moses. These formed the basis of the Scripture reading and instruction in the synagogue services. In addition the Pharisees observed a traditional law, the *Mishna*, which they taught also had its author in Moses. Our Lord observed the Mosaic law and promulgated for his followers its essential element, the Ten Commandments (Mt 5, 17). He criticized the Pharisees for their neglect of it in favor of their traditions (Mt 15, 2-9).

LEBANON. Mountainous chain north of Palestine. Its name, derived from *laban* which signifies "to be white," alludes to its tops covered with permanent snows (Jer 18, 14).

LEVIATHAN. A mythological sea monster symbolizing the chaos that existed in the beginning of creation. Also used for a crocodile or a whale (Ps 74, 14).

LEVIRATE. This word, derived from the Latin *levir* (brother-in-law) designates an ancient Israelite custom (Gn 38, 8ff), codified in the Bible: when a man dies without leaving a male child, the closest relative of the deceased—generally, his brother—must marry the widow who is his sister-in-law and thus perpetuate the line. The first son born of this union would be considered the son and heir of the dead man (Dt 25, 5-10).

LEVITES. Sacred ministers of lowest rank among the Jews. Unlike the priests, they were members of the tribe of Levi who did not belong to the house of Aaron. While on duty they wore a distinctive linen dress, but they entered only the inner court and not the holy place of the temple. The higher levites assisted the officiating priests, others had charge of the music during the services, and still others acted as doorkeepers and overseers of the temple (1 Chr 23, 4-6).

LIGHT. Has various meanings in Scripture: (1) material sense of outward light or daybreak (Gn 1, 3); (2) symbol of God (showing his incorporeal, pure and holy nature) (1 Jn 1, 5); (3) symbol of Christ (Jn 8, 12); (4) Christians are children of light because they have received the spiritual light of truth and grace, and are to radiate it in the world by their good example (Mt 5, 14; Eph 5, 8).

LORD. Originally, this title signified nothing more than "sir." From the 3rd century B.C. onward, the Jews replaced the ineffable name *Yahweh* with *Adonai* (Lord) in reading the Bible. Applied to Jesus by the first Christians, the name "Lord" was thus equivalent to an affirmation of his divinity (Acts 2, 36). *See* **ADONAI. NAME. YAHWEH.**

LOVE. In the Old Testament, the love of God expresses itself in his many interventions of creation (Gn 1, 3; Jb 38ff) and the history of Israel (Dt 4, 37; Ps 41, 12). It is a freely-given elective love (Dt 7, 7) working for the salvation of mankind, ever merciful in the face of human infidelity (Hos 11, 1-4).
The New Testament explores these first glimmerings more fully. The love of God is historical because God has not spared his own Son and has delivered him to death in order to save us (Jn 3, 16). It is also freely-given and elective by the work of Christ, which was in perfect correspondence with the will of the Father and which made the faithful the beloved ones of God (Jn 5, 20-25; Col 3, 12). Finally, this love in action is merciful, as shown above all by the cross and explained in the parables (Jn 15, 13; Lk 15, 11-32).
The love of man for God is thus a love which is returned. It must be sealed by a total obedience to the Commandments, a fidelity to the covenant. In the New Testament it must respond without limit to the prior love of God and Christ (1 Jn 3, 1-16; 4, 10-19).

MAGI. In the texts of the Old Testament, they are often associated with sorcerers and diviners. They seem to have been a Persian religious caste of royal advisers (Jer 39, 2: "princes"), and were regarded as wise men, astrologers. In the Gospel of Matthew, many think it refers to learned men from Babylon who had contact with Jewish Messianism (cf Dn 2, 2). In the Acts of the Apostles, the word is taken in the pejorative sense in the case of a magician who sets himself up as an adversary of Paul the Apostle (Acts 8, 9).

MEDIATOR. In its primary sense, the word signifies an intermediary, a third person who intervenes between other parties to bring them together or reconcile them. Moses was thus a mediator between God and the people (Nm 14, 13-20). Applied to Jesus, the term takes on an even more profound meaning, for Jesus is at the same time God and man; he belongs, at once, to the two parties. Through Christ we have access to the Father, and through Christ the Father gives himself to mankind (Heb 9, 11-25; 12, 24).

MERCY. This word is found in both Testaments, but retains all the primitive value of the Hebrew word *hesed*, which suggests love more than pity (Jas 2, 1-13).

MESSIAH. Hebrew word signifying "one who has been anointed." The kings of Israel were anointed in the name of God (1 Sm 9, 16). The term Messiah later was used to designate a "future king" who would make all things new (Dn 9, 25-26). This son of David, expected by the Jewish nation, was the Messiah par excellence (Mk 10, 47-48), a term that has been rendered in Greek by *Christos*. This was a common name that ultimately became a title for Jesus the Savior (Rom 1, 1). *See* **CHRIST. JESUS.**

MIRACLES. This word corresponds to two biblical words: sign and wonder. In the sense of "sign," a miracle is an unaccustomed and unexpected event which serves as a motive for credibility by manifesting the power of Christ, and leads the spectator to believe in his person (Jn 2, 11).

MISSION. Out of love the Father sends his only Son into the world. Jesus speaks in this way of his "mission" which is to save men by giving them Life (Jn 16, 27-28). Then, just as the Father has sent the Son into the world, so Jesus sends the apostles into the world (Jn 20, 21). This second mission is a prolongation of the former one.

MONEY. In the time of our Lord the coins current in Palestine were Roman, Greek, Syrian and Jewish. The Jews might issue coins only in bronze.

1) Large sums were expressed in *talents* and *mnas*. The talent equalled about $1920.00 in United States currency. The mna was one-sixtieth of a talent, or about $32.00. The units of Luke 19, 13ff were mnas.

2) Silver coins mentioned in the New Testament are: the Syrian *stater*(51 cents), the Roman *denarius* (about 17 cents), the Greek *drachme*, equivalent to the denarius. The stater was accepted as equal to the Jewish *shekel*, one-fiftieth of a mna

(about 64 cents), the temple tax for two persons (Mt 17, 26). The denarius was the usual day's wage for a laborer in the field, and it was the coin of the tax to the Emperor (Mt 20, 2; 22, 19).

3) Bronze coins referred to are the Roman *assarion* (one cent) and *quadrans* (one-fourth of a cent), the Jewish *perutah* or *lepton* (one-eighth of a cent), the coin of the "widow's mite" (Mt 10, 29; 5, 26; Mk 12, 42).

It should be remembered that the coin values here given are only approximate, and that the purchasing power of money was much greater in ancient times than today.

MOUNTAIN (MOUNT). A mountain is regarded as the dwelling place of divinity. Sanctuaries were set up on a good many mounts. It was on mountains that God chose to give his revelations (Sinai, Tabor) (Dt 33, 2; Mt 17, 1ff). Zion is called the "mountain God has chosen" (Ps 68, 17).

MUSICAL INSTRUMENTS. The Hebrews were devoted to music and used it for both secular and religious purposes. Various types of instruments are mentioned in the Bible — stringed, wind and percussive instruments (Ps 150, 3-5).

MYSTERY. The origin of this word is Greek. It signified first of all the place where religious ceremonies took place which were reserved only to those who had been "initiated." In the plural, it signified the rites themselves. In a derived sense, the word is synonymous with divine secret. St. Paul uses it in the sense of divine plan (inaccessible to man, secret, but revealed by Jesus Christ), having the salvation of men as its object (Rom 16, 25-26). In Scripture it must never be taken in the sense (to which the catechism has accustomed us) of revealed truth incomprehensible to the human intelligence (for example, the mystery of the Blessed Trinity).

NAME. According to the conception of the ancients, the *Name* designates more than the external person; it tends to express his basic character, his personality (Gn 21, 3ff). We might say it is an emanation of the person himself. Change of vocation entailed changing one's name (Mt 16, 16-19). In the ancient texts of the Bible, to name or give a name can signify "to have power over" (Gn 2, 19-21). The "name of God" thus signifies God himself. Hence, we find the expressions: God acting for his name's sake — to glorify and sanctify his name (Ez 20, 14; Is 29, 23). In the same way sin profanes the name of God (Lv 18, 21). Among the Israelites, the veneration which came to be accorded to the name of God approached superstition. The Israelites did not dare pronounce this name and forbade even the use of the name *Yahweh*. In place of this word whose consonants were written out, the reader had to read *Adonai* (Lord). This custom continues to exist in present-day Judaism. Hence, the first Christians surrounded the name of Jesus with great veneration and the expressions: "in the name of Jesus" and "for the name of Jesus" occur frequently in the sense of: "acting in such an intention in dependence on Jesus" and "by authority of Jesus" (Col 3, 17). In John's Gospel, we are urged to pray "in the name of Jesus" (Jn 14, 13). Moreover, this manner of speaking has been retained until our own day; for example, we say: "In the name of the Father, and of the Son, and of the Holy Spirit." In the Our Father, the expression: "Hallowed be thy name," signifies that we pray for God's holiness to be acknowledged and adored by all men.

NATIONS. The Israelites distinguished themselves from foreign peoples. They designated the latter by the Hebrew term *goïm*; this word, which includes a certain nuance of scorn, is often translated in our modern languages as "nations" or "Gentiles" (Is 49, 6). *See* **FOREIGNERS.**

NAZIRITE. This term stems from the Hebrew word *nazir*, meaning "set apart as sacred, dedicated, vowed." The nazirite vow could be either for a limited period or for life. Those bound by this vow had to abstain from all the products of the grapevine, from cutting or shaving their hair, and from contact with a corpse. They were regarded as men of God like the prophets; cf Am 2, 11f. Examples of lifelong nazirites were Samson (Jgs 13, 4f. 7; 16, 17), Samuel (1 Sm 1, 11), and John the Baptizer (Lk 1, 15). At the time of Christ the practice of taking the nazirite vow for a limited period seems to have been quite common, even among the early Christians; cf Acts 18, 18; 21, 23f. 26.

NAZOREAN. A title of Jesus which the Gospel derives from the name of the' town of Nazareth (Mt 2, 23). The Christians were called Nazoreans for a long time (Acts 24, 5). In Hebrew this word has a certain resemblance with the word *nezer* which signifies "shoot." Primitive Christian tradition thus saw in this an allusion to a passage of Isaiah (11, 11) in which the Messiah is presented as the shoot par excellence of David, son of Jesse.

NUMBERS. In the Bible, numbers often have a symbolic value. For example 7 (seven days, seven angels, seven lights ..); 12 (tribes, apostles); 40 (days of rain, days of prayer on Sinai, days of fast, period before the Ascension); 144,000 (the elect, in the Book of Revelation). It must also be noted that in the ancient accounts numbers must be regarded in accord with Oriental custom and they are subject to poetic approximation: *thousand* can signify a group or family. In the military accounts, most numbers are considerably exaggerated (Dt 32, 30).

PARACLETE (COUNSELLOR). Word derived from the Greek. It is used only in John's Gospel and signifies "advocate or defender." This word is applied either to Christ, who fulfilled this role toward his disciples, or to the Holy Spirit, who continues to exercise it with Christ himself (Jn 14, 16).

PARADISE. Word of Persian origin, which passed over into Hebrew and then Greek, used to designate a garden; in particular, the garden of Eden (Gn 2, 15). Later, it signified the eternal abode of the just (Lk 23, 43).

PASSOVER. *See* **FEASTS.**

PASTOR. *See* **SHEPHERD.**

PEACE. This word is used in the Bible to express two ideas: (1) peace with God,

reestablished by the covenant, often a synonym for reconciliation, and (2) peace between individuals and peoples.

The promises of the messianic covenant are often accompanied by the announcement of peace. Thus the Messiah will be called the "Prince of Peace" (Is 9, 5). The word "peace" is contained in the literal translation of the word Jerusalem (Salem) (Heb 7, 2). Peace demands faithfulness to the covenant and justice among men (Ps 72, 3-7) so often invoked by the prophets. Christ came to bring peace (Lk 2, 14) and to render it effective by a reconciliation of mankind to God (Jn 14, 27; Eph 2, 14-17). The extension of the peaceful reign of Christ is thus for the true Christian the condition and source of true peace and true justice between individuals and between nations.

PEOPLE OF GOD. This is how Israel is designated throughout the Bible. God has gratuitously chosen her and she is his own possession (Dt 7, 6). God dwells in her midst (Ex 25, 8). The people is thus holy and set apart from other peoples (Lv 20, 24). In its turn, Christianity is also called the People "[God] claims for his own," but it rejects any kind of national particularism (1 Pt 2, 9).

PERFECT. In the ancient text, this word indicates someone who avoids sin' and practices the law. The passage in which Jesus says: "Be perfected as your heavenly Father is perfect" (Mt 5, 48) signifies — according to its context — that one must imitate the divine mercy and impartiality. In a single passage (Mt 19, 21) Jesus speaks of the perfection of the disciple who goes beyond his ordinary duties. St. Paul uses the term perfect of the "spiritually mature" Christians who know true wisdom and want all men to be perfect in Christ (1 Cor 2, 6ff).

PHARISEES. A religious sect of the Jews that numbered about 6000 in the time of Christ. Originating in the days of the Greek conquest of Palestine, they sought above all to preserve the Jews from the contamination of foreign religion, and to this end insisted upon strict separation from the Gentiles. They insisted also on strict loyalty to the Scriptures and to the traditions of the rabbis. Among many Pharisaic hedges about the law, ceremonial purity and payment of religious dues were emphasized. In doctrine the Pharisees were inclined to fatalism, but on the other hand they strongly upheld the resurrection and the future life. By the time of Christ their primitive zeal had degenerated into fanaticism and hypocrisy. They took a leading part in the opposition to Christ, and he scathingly rebuked their insincerity (Mt 23, 25; Lk 11, 39; 18, 9-14). That they were not all bad is evidenced by such men as Gamaliel (Acts 5, 34).

PHILADELPHIA. A city of Lydia in Asia Minor, founded by Attalus II Philadelphus, king of Pergamum. The book of Revelation alludes to it twice (1, 11 and 3, 7).

PHILISTINES. Non-Semitic invaders who gave their name to all of Palestine although they occupied only its southwestern plains. They were subdued by David (2 Sm 5, 17-25), but became practically independent under the separated kingdom and disappeared as a people after the time of the Maccabees.

PIETY. In Hebrew as in English, account must be taken of the relationship between this word *piety* and *pity* (in the sense of goodness). God is called pious, that is, good (Is 1, 4). Men are termed pious, that is, faithful, just and devoted to God (Acts 10, 7).

POOR. Originally, this word had merely an economic and social meaning. Gradually, it took on the meaning of humble, modest, small, the little people often oppressed by the rich and powerful but who remained faithful to God (Am 2, 6-7). It was in this sense that Jesus said: "Blest are the poor in spirit" (Mt 5, 3).

PRESBYTER. *See* **ELDER.**

PRIESTS, JEWISH. Sacred ministers, whose duty it was to offer sacrifice at the altar of holocausts, and to enter morning and evening into the holy place to burn incense at the golden altar (Heb 7, 27; 10, 11). They also had care of the loaves of proposition (Mt 12, 4) and certified the cure of lepers (Lk 17, 13f). They were divided into twenty-four classes, each of which in turn officiated for a week at the temple (Lk 1, 5). During the three great feasts all the classes ministered together. Their dress comprised a long linen tunic, ornamented sash and turban. The priesthood was hereditary, by descent from the tribe of Levi through the younger branch of Aaron's family (Heb 7, 5). For their support the priests received tithes and other offerings.

PROMISE. This term of Greek origin is employed only in the New Testament. It designates and interprets the meaning of all the previous prophetic history of the chosen people in their messianic mission. The Old Testament gave promise of Christ. But it is in Christ that all this preparatory and figurative history finds its perfect fulfillment (Mt 5, 17; Acts 13, 32-33; Rom 15, 8; 2 Cor 1, 20; Gal 3, 14). An analogous relationship exists between Christ's work of the Redemption and his second coming which, at the end of time, will asssure the glorious consummation of all things (Acts 1, 4-5; 2, 16-21) and fulfill the promise of Christ's work.

PROPHET. One who speaks to another on the part of God (Dt 18, 18). Prophets are also called "seers" by reason of their gift of reading thoughts. Prophet does not necessarily signify that one foretells the future and there were prophets in the first Christian communities (1 Cor 12, 28ff).

PUBLICANS. Management of imperial taxation was farmed by the Roman government to the highest bidders, who in turn entrusted the collection in the provinces to native agents by whom the privilege had been purchased with advance payments. These agents are the "publicans." They were often guilty of merciless extortion, and were universally hated as plunderers of their own people. Among the Jews they were also considered as disloyal to their religion, since they cooperated with Gentiles and exacted tribute from the race that God had made free (Jn 8, 33; Mt 22, 17). Like the Baptizer, our Lord condemned the injustice of the publicans, but did not reject those who were sincerely repentant (Mt 5, 46; 21, 31f). Two publicans are distinguished in the Gospels, Zacchaeus (Lk 19, 2) and Matthew (Mt 10, 3), who became an apostle and evangelist.

PURITY (RITUAL). State of the man who fulfills the conditions imposed by the Mosaic law on every one of the faithful who appeared for worship (Lv 7, 19-21). Certain bodily functions, contact with forbidden animals, and with corpses forbade participation in worship; anyone who was guilty of such things was "impure" or "unclean" (Nm 19, 1-10). "Purity" could be recovered by various rites: sacrifices, washings, aspersions, etc. (Nm 19, 19). There is no relation between this term and what we call "purity" in the sense of chastity.

REDEMPTION. This word comes from the Latin *redimere* which signifies to buy back or redeem. The corresponding Hebrew term was used in the Bible for the first time with reference to the exodus from Egypt (Ex 15, 13). God has redeemed his people from the bondage of Egypt, gratuitously, just as a master sets free his slave (Lv 19, 20). In the New Testament, it signifies that God, through Jesus Christ (gratuitously), redeems his people in order to establish his kingdom (Rom 3, 24).

REMNANT. An expression often used by the prophets. It designates the survivors of great catastrophes: the flood, the exile (Gn 7, 1f; Is 6, 13). God reserves this remnant for himself to help in the restoration (Is 37, 31). It is they who are and will remain the depositaries of the promise (Mi 4, 6-7). In the New Testament, the church is presented as fulfilling the function of the faithful Remnant and the "Israel after the flesh" is contrasted with the "Israel of God" which is the church (Rom 9, 27; 1 Cor 10, 18; Gal 6, 16); and this interpretation follows the teaching of the Old Testament.

RESURRECTION. The Bible does not have this unique and specific term. It uses the verbs to awake, to raise up, to cure, or the intransitive verbs, to get up, to appear, to show (one's self) sometimes as an act showing the power of God, sometimes as a manifestation of the victory of life over death. In the Old Testament, the idea is made known little by little at first in the perspective of the entire people (Ez 37, 1, 14), then for the Servant of Yahweh (Is 53) but always in a very limited fashion (Pss 16, 10ff; 49, 16; 73, 26; 17, 15). In the New Testament, this idea takes on an elemental importance through the resurrection of Jesus, which became the fundamental historical fact, the principal witness of his divinity (1 Cor 15, 4. 12). The Resurrection is also the divine judgment which has ordered the defeat of death and pledges salvation and resurrection to all the faithful (Rom 4, 25; Col 2, 12ff; Eph 2, 1-7). This resurrection in grace is the prelude to the final and glorious resurrection (1 Cor 15, 2ff; 1 Thes 4, 14ff).

SACRED. The same Hebrew word has both the active meaning of "holy," that is, keeping oneself free from profane impurities, and the passive meaning of "sacred," that is, set apart from what is profane and therefore treated with religious reverence (Lv 21, 6).

SACRIFICE. The supreme form of divine worship, by which some creature is offered to God and used in adoration as an acknowledgment of his majesty and the creature's subjection. True sacrifices were offered in the Old Law (Heb 9, 1ff), but they were only preparations for the perfect sacrifice of Christ on the cross (Heb 9, 11).

SADDUCEES. A religious sect of the Jews, less numerous than their rivals the Pharisees, but very influential on account of the many noble and wealthy persons who belonged to their ranks (Acts 4, 1; 5, 17). They set aside traditions and even rejected truths taught in the Sacred Books themselves. They insisted upon human free will, but denied immortality, the resurrection and the existence of angels (Mt 22, 23; Mk 12, 18; Lk 20, 27; Acts 23, 8). They were denounced by John the Baptizer (Mt 3, 7) and by our Lord (Mt 16, 6). Though less prominent in their opposition to Christ than the Pharisees, they nevertheless sought to entrap him (Mt 16, 1; 22, 23), and through their representatives joined in his condemnation by the Sanhedrin. They also strongly opposed the early church because the apostles proclaimed our Lord's Resurrection (Acts 4, 1f; etc.).

SALVATION, SAVIOR. Inasmuch as the terms express redemption (cf. **REDEMPTION**) and appear as a cause of salvation, the Hebrew uses one word: *Yacha*, which means to be generous, to deliver from slavery or from distress. This term in the Old Testament expresses the Work of God, assuring the deliverance of his people as a whole (Hos 5, 13; Is 31, 1; Ps 33, 16-17) and their personal salvation (Ps 51, 14) — the whole bound up in the messianic and eschatological perspective. This term provides the substantive "machia," translated as Savior (Is 45, 21). In the New Testament, the term is employed very frequently for a cure, the health of the body, but often, in connection with faith, of the soul (Mk 5, 34; Lk 8, 48; 18, 42). Thus, the work of the New Testament even in its temporal action is entirely oriented toward the work of spiritual salvation, of remission of sins (Lk 17, 19) and the liberation from the servitude that sin brings to man (Mt 1, 21; Lk 1, 77; Acts 5, 31, etc.) and leading the Christian to his highest destiny (Rom 1, 16; 5, 9-10; 1 Cor 15, 2; Jas 1, 21). This work will be definitively manifested at the last judgment (Rom 8, 22-25).

SAMARITANS. The inhabitants of Samaria were a mixed race, descended from intermarriage of Israelites and Assyrian colonists. The enmity between the Jews and the Samaritans was so great that travelers between Galilee and Judea often had to cross the Jordan into Perea for safety. In various uprisings this race was almost exterminated, and only a small remnant survives today.

In religion the Samaritans acknowledged the Pentateuch, Joshua and Judges, but not the additional revelation or Jewish traditional doctrine. They looked for the Messiah who would teach all truth (Jn 4, 25f). In practice they worshiped the same God as the Jews, and in such matters as sabbaths and feasts, circumcision and worship, they did not dissent. But through vying with the Jews in the strict observance of Mosaic regulations, they disowned the Jerusalem temple and priesthood. The rival sanctuary of Gerizim they revered as their holy place (Jn 4, 20). Our Lord passed through their country more than once, and preached and worked miracles among the people. He also spoke well of them (Lk 10, 30-37), defended them (Lk 9, 51-56), and commanded that the gospel be preached to them. This was done with success, and a Christian community was early formed among the Samaritans (Acts 8, 4-17; 9, 31; 15, 3).

SANHEDRIN. Literally *session*, a council, national or local, endowed with authority to pass on cases ecclesiastical or civil.

1) The national Sanhedrin, or Great Council, of the Jews met at Jerusalem. The high priest himself seems to have presided as a rule. The full membership was seventy-two, representing equally the three groups of priests, scribes and elders. This council took cognizance of grave matters of a doctrinal, judicial or administrative character affecting the Jewish religion and nation. The Romans acknowledged the decrees of the Sanhedrin, and guards attended the meetings to fulfill the orders of the judges (Mt 26, 58). Sentence of death, however, was reserved to the Roman authority (Jn 18, 31).

2) Local tribunals, subordinate to the supreme Sanhedrin, were found in the towns of Palestine. Their membership varied from three to twenty-three, according to the size of the male population of the place. The "Sanhedrin" of Mt 5, 22 probably refers to one of these lower tribunals.

SAVIOR. Exact translation of the word *Yehoshua* which has become "Jesus" (Lk 1, 31ff). See **SALVATION**.

SCRIBES. Literally this title means a writer, but in the New Testament the reference is to the learned class among the Jews, the official authorities on the written law and oral traditions. One who had made successful studies became a scribe at the age of thirty by receiving imposition of hands with the delivery of a tablet and key.

As the function of the priests was ritualistic, that of the scribes was doctrinal. These latter were interpreters of the Scriptures (Mt 2, 4; 17, 10; Mk 12, 35), but our Lord condemned them for their burdensome additions to the divine law (Mt 23). They taught by quoting the celebrated doctors of the past (Mk 1, 22). In our Lord's day the chief rival schools among the scribes were those of the liberal Hillel and the severe Shammai. Generally the scribes opposed the Sadducees (Lk 20, 39) and upheld the Pharisees. Like the Pharisees, the scribes were noted for hypocrisy, pride, and contradiction of Christ (Mt 23, 2ff; Mk 12, 28-30; Lk 20, 46; Mt 9, 3). But there were noble and sincere characters among them (Mt 8, 19), especially Nicodemus and Gamaliel (Jn 3; Acts 5, 34).

SCRIPTURES. (1) The inspired books, the work of the Holy Spirit. They were customarily divided into three series: the Law, the Prophets, and the Writings. (2) Christianity added its own writings: the Gospels and the Letters of the Apostles.

SEPTUAGINT. Translation into Greek of the Hebrew and Aramaic Old Testament (including the deuterocanonical books) made in Egypt by various authors during the period between 250 B.C. and 100 B.C. Its name comes from the fact that legend ascribes the work to a group of seventy-two scholars and it is designated by the Roman numerals LXX. It is by far the most important ancient version of the Old Testament and until recently was our sole witness for the state of the original text of the Hebrew Old Testament before the Christian era. The Septuagint was the version used by the Hebrews in Christ's time, by the apostles and New Testament writers, and by the Greek Fathers of the Church; it is still the official text of the Greek Church.

SHEOL. The ancient concept of the abode of the dead (*the nether world*, in Hebrew, *Sheol*) supposed no activity or lofty emotion among the deceased, who were pictured as surrounded by the darkness of oblivion (Nm 16, 30ff; Ps 6, 6). The Hebrews shared in this common idea almost to the time of Christ, when God revealed a clearer notion of the hearafter (Wis 3). It is at this time that belief in the resurrection of the dead was introduced (Dn 12, 2). Some (for example, the Sadducees) refused to believe it; but the people embraced it like some great revelation. In the New Testament, the whole concept is transfigured in the light of Christ's resurrection. His body did not see corruption in Hades; he has the keys of death and the nether world (Rv 1, 18). The word "Gehenna" (hell) is used of the nether world when punishment is involved (Mt 5, 29; 10, 28). *See* **GEHENNA.**

SIN. In the Old Testament sin is not so much a wrong action in one's conscience as something which disrupts the order of the world wished by God, and particularly the covenant fixed by the law. Thus the Israelite did not search himself for deep causes or establish its relationship with original sin; it is necessary to wait for the book of Wisdom to find such an allusion (2, 24). The New Testament describes sin as relating to original sin and tells of the universal sorrow because of sin (Rom 1—5) erased by the Redemption (Rom 5—8). It describes responsibility for it. This conception of sin thus became linked with the ideas of faith and love which gave life to Christians (Rom 13, 8ff; 1 Cor 5, 9; 13, 4ff).

SON. In Hebrew, this word is used to designate diverse relations or dependencies: (1) relations of direct descendence (Ex 1, 1-5); (2) relations of disciples to their master (Prv 1, 8); (3) relations of origin or analogy (Jb 1, 3; 42, 13); (4) moral relations (Jos 7, 19).

SON OF MAN. An enigmatic title. Jewish apocryphal tradition (1 Henoch, 2 Esdras, 2 Baruch) uses it to describe a unique religious personage, a messiah with extraordinary spiritual endowments. Jesus' use of it seems to derive from Ez 2, where it is a title of humility, and Dn 7, 13f, where it indicates a clearly messianic figure. It expresses for him his twofold destiny, of suffering (Mk 8, 31; 9, 11. 30; 10, 33; 12, 31; 14, 21) and of glory (Mk 8, 38; 12, 36; 14, 62). Peter, along with the other disciples, fails (despite his confession) to grasp the association of suffering and death with the office of Messiah. Only after the resurrection does the Christian community endow it with its messianic meaning (Acts 7, 56; Rv 1, 3).

SOUL. In its first sense, the Hebrew word *nephesh* signifies breath, life, the principle of animal life (Gn 1, 20). It was only much later (toward the beginning of the Christian era) that the Hebrews adopted the distinction (of Greek philosophy) of soul and body (Rv 6, 9; 20, 4).

SPIRIT. Literally, breath. It is an element with as little materiality as possible; it is the innermost part of man, more subtle than his soul. The Old Testament attributes to the Spirit of God both external and internal actions that surpass human powers (Nm 11, 24-29). The Spirit is a person distinct from the Father and the Son

(Jn 14, 26). Each Christian possesses the Spirit. He is the principle of life and a pledge of resurrection (Rom 8, 2. 11).

SYNAGOGUES. Minor places of religious assembly among the Jews, used also as schools, libraries and halls of judgment. The central place of worship was the temple, the one national sanctuary and the only place of sacrifice. The synagogue served local communities or separate congregations for less solemn religious functions. Every considerable Jewish community, whether in or out of Palestine, had at least one synagogue. The building, commonly rectangular, was erected on the plan of the temple. There was a gallery reserved for women, another space for men, and the worshipers faced toward Jerusalem and the holy of holies. In front was a platform on which stood the holy ark containing the Scriptures and an eight-branch candlestick burning before it. Nearest the platform were the chief seats, where sat the leading men facing the congregation (Mt 23, 6; Mk 12, 39; Lk 11, 43; 20, 46). Among these leading men were the ruler of the synagogue and the elders, and various functionaries whom they appointed.

TEMPLE. The sacred place of worship on Mount Moriah, including all buildings and courts. The first temple was built by Solomon, in 967 to 964 B.C., but was destroyed by the Chaldeans in 586 B.C. The second was erected by Zerubbabel in 515 B.C., but was profaned in 167 B.C. by the Syrians. Herod the Great began a magnificent restoration of this temple. It is his structure that is the temple referred to in the time of our Lord. In a more restricted sense, the term applies only to the "House" in which were the holy place and the holy of holies, or to the immediate precincts of this "House." The space covered by the temple and its courts was about 585 by 600 feet.

The temple proper (Naos) measured 30 feet north to south, and 90 feet east to west. The innermost part of this building was the holy of holies, set apart from the outer room, the holy place, by a double curtain (Mt 27, 51). The holy of holies contained the stone on which once rested the ark of the covenant. It was entered once a year by the high priest (Heb 9, 3-5). The holy place had within it the golden altar of incense (Lk 1, 11), and the table of loaves (Mt 12, 4). About the Naos ran an uncovered court reserved to the priests. In front of the entrance to the holy place stood the altar of holocausts (Ex 27, 1-8). The lay Israelite might approach this altar only to bring his sacrifice to the priests (Mt 5, 23).

Outside this court of the priests, toward the east, was the court of the Israelites, where the laity could assist at the services. Beyond this was an outer court known as the court of the women, since to it women were admitted. This court was surrounded by rooms, one of which was the treasury with thirteen boxes for contributions (Lk 21, 1ff). To these courts only Jews were admitted, inscriptions warning non-Jews not to enter under pain of death (Acts 21, 28). By a staircase of fifteen steps one descended to the outer court which was known as that of the Gentiles. This outside court was surrounded by walls with high towers. The court of the Gentiles was open to all, and it was used for buying and selling (Mk 11, 15). Against the walls of this court on the

interior were porches or colonnades where the people listened to religious teachers (Lk 2, 46; Mt 26, 55). The porch attached to the eastern wall was known as Solomon's (Jn 10, 23; Acts 3, 11; 5, 12). At its northwestern corner this court was adjacent to the fortress Antonia, whose garrison was ready to keep order among the crowds (Acts 21, 30ff). But the Jews had also their own temple police, with captains and officers, who patrolled the whole area day and night (Lk 22, 52; Acts 4, 1).

TIME. In Hebrew, *olam* designates a very long and indefinite period. In Greek, this word has been translated by two terms: "world" and "age" which are often taken for one another. Hence, one says: this world, the next world or the ages to come. In the plural, ages is practically equivalent to eternity (Mt 12, 32; Eph 2, 7).

TONGUES (SPEAK IN). Two passages of the New Testament speak of the *gift of tongues* (Acts 2 and 1 Cor 14). In the first, we find the mention of the miracle by which the apostles suddenly began to speak in tongues foreign to them — or by which their auditors each understand in their own language what the apostles said to them in the apostles' tongue. In the second, it is a case of a phenomenon that is difficult to describe and analyze: this was a manner of expressing oneself in inarticulate sounds or cries, proper to certain states of mystical exaltation.

TRUTH. This word, in Hebrew *emeth*, designates something firm and solid, hence something faithful. The adjective "true" signifies not only what is true and authentic but also what is the principle of this truth and this authenticity (Gn 32, 10; Ps 12, 1-2).

VULGATE. The official Latin translation of the Bible which was prepared almost entirely by St. Jerome from 382 to 405 A.D. Jerome borrowed heavily from Origen in translating the Psalter and took Ecclesiasticus, Baruch and both books of Maccabees from Old Latin texts. He translated everything else from the existing Hebrew, Aramaic or Greek manuscripts. The Council of Trent declared the Vulgate to be "authentic in public readings, disputations, preachings and exposition" because it conforms to the original texts and contains no errors in faith or morals. Since 1907 the Benedictine Order has, at the request of St. Pius X, been working on a revised edition of the modern Vulgate text to make it conform as closely as possible to the text of St. Jerome, and several parts have already been published.

YAHWEH. The proper personal name of the God of Israel, signifying, "I am who am" (Ex 3, 14-15). It is commonly explained in reference to God as the absolute and necessary Being. It may be understood of God as the Source of all created beings. Out of reverence for this name, the term *Adonai*, "my Lord," was later used as a substitute. The word Lord in the present version represents this traditional usage. The word "Jehovah" arose from a false reading of this name as it is written in the current Hebrew text. *See* **ADONAI. NAME.**

THE NEW 3 - YEAR CYCLE OF READINGS
FOR SUNDAY MASS

Year A

1987	1993	1999	2005	2011
1990	1996	2002	2008	2014

GUIDE —
1- refers to Reading I
2- refers to Reading II
3- refers to Gospel

	Old Test.	New Test.
ADVENT SEASON		
1st Sunday of Advent		
1- Is 2, 1-5	826	
2- Rom 13, 11-14		238
3- Mt 24, 37-44		56
2nd Sunday of Advent		
1- Is 11, 1-10	836	
2- Rom 15, 4-9		239
3- Mt 3, 1-12		13
3rd Sunday of Advent		
1- Is 35, 1-6a. 10	858	
2- Jas 5, 7-10		361
3- Mt 11, 2-11		29
4th Sunday of Advent		
1- Is 7, 10-14	831	
2- Rom 1, 1-7		233
3- Mt 1, 18-24		11
CHRISTMAS SEASON		
Christmas Vigil		
1- Is 62, 1-5	887	
2- Acts 13, 16-17. 22-25		198
3- Mt 1, 1-25		11
Christmas (At Midnight)		
1- Is 9, 1-6	833	
2- Ti 2, 11-14		334
3- Lk 2, 1-14		100
Christmas (At Dawn)		
1- Is 62, 11-12	888	
2- Ti 3, 4-7		334
3- Lk 2, 15-20		101
Christmas (During the Day)		
1- Is 52, 7-10	878	
2- Heb 1, 1-6		339
3- Jn 1, 1-18		145
Sunday After Christmas		
(Holy Family)		
1- Sir 3, 2-6. 12-14	773	
2- Col 3, 12-21		312
3- Mt 13-15. 19-23		13
January 1		
(Solemnity of Mary, Mother of God)		
1- Nm 6, 22-27	139	
2- Gal 4, 4-7		289
3- Lk 2, 16-21		101

	Old Test.	New Test.
2nd Sunday After Christmas		
1- Sir 24, 1-2. 8-12	793	
2- Eph 1, 3-6. 15-18		293
3- Jn 1, 1-18		145
Epiphany		
1- Is 60, 1-6	885	
2- Eph 3, 2-3a. 5-6		195
3- Mt 2, 1-12		14
Sunday After Epiphany		
(Baptism of the Lord)		
1- Is 42, 1-4. 6-7	886	
2- Acts 10, 34-38		195
3- Mt 3, 13-17		14
LENTEN SEASON		
Ash Wednesday		
1- Jl 2, 12-18	1055	
2- 2 Cor 5, 20—6, 2		272
3- Mt 6, 1-6. 16-18		18
1st Sunday of Lent		
1- Gn 2, 7-9; 3, 1-7	5	
2- Rom 5, 12-19		229
3- Mt 4, 1-11		14
2nd Sunday of Lent		
1- Gn 12, 1-4a	14	
2- 2 Tm 1, 8b-10		329
3- Mt 17, 1-9		39
3rd Sunday of Lent		
1- Ex 17, 3-7	75	
2- Rom 5, 1-2. 5-8		228
3- Jn 4, 5-42		150
4th Sunday of Lent		
1- 1 Sm 16, 1b. 6-7 10-13a	280	
2- Eph 5, 8-14		298
3- Jn 9, 1-41		160
5th Sunday of Lent		
1- Ez 37, 12-14	1008	
2- Rom 8, 8-11		231
3- Jn 11, 1-45		162
Passion Sunday (Palm Sunday)		
Procession: Mt 21, 1-11		46
1- Is 50, 4-7	876	
2- Phil 2, 6-11		303
3- Mt 26, 14—27, 66		59
EASTER TRIDUUM		
AND EASTER SEASON		
Holy Thursday		
Chrism Mass		
1- Is 61, 1-3a. 6a, 8b-9	886	
2- Rv 1, 5-8		387
3- Lk 4, 16-21		105

	Old Test.	New Test.
Mass of Lord's Supper		
1- Ex 12, 1-8. 11-14	69	
2- 1 Cor 11, 23-26		257
3- Jn 13, 1-15		166
Good Friday		
1- Is 52, 13—53, 12	879	
2- Heb 4, 14-16; 5, 7-9		342
3- Jn 18, 1—19, 42		172
Easter Vigil		
1- Gn 1, 1—2, 2	4	
Gn 22, 1-18	24	
Ex 14, 15—15, 1	72	
Is 54, 5-14	880	
Is 55, 1-11	880	
Bar 3, 9-15. 32—4, 4	966	
Ez 36, 16-28	1007	
2- Rom 6, 3-11		229
3- Mt 28, 1-10		65
Easter Sunday		
1- Acts 10, 34a. 37-43		195
2- Col 3, 1-4		311
or 1 Cor 5, 6b-8		248
3- Jn 20, 1-9		176
or Mt 28, 1-10		65
Evening: 3- Lk 24,		
13-35		141
2nd Sunday of Easter		
1- Acts 2, 42-47		183
2- 1 Pt 1, 3-9		363
3- Jn 20, 19-31		177
3rd Sunday of Easter		
1- Acts 2, 14. 22-28		182
2- 1 Pt 1, 17-21		364
3- Lk 24, 13-35		124
4th Sunday of Easter		
1- Acts 2, 14a. 36-41		182
2- 1 Pt 2, 20b-25		365
3- Jn 10, 1-10		161
5th Sunday of Easter		
1- Acts 6, 1-7		188
2- 1 Pt 2, 4-9		364
3- Jn 14, 1-12		168
6th Sunday of Easter		
1- Acts 8, 5-8, 14-17		191
2- 1 Pt 3, 15-18		366
3- Jn 14, 15-21		168
Ascension of Our Lord		
1- Acts 1, 1-11		180
2- Eph 1, 17-23		294
3- Mt 28, 16-20		66

	Old Test.	New Test.
7th Sunday of Easter		
1- Acts 1, 12-14		181
2- 1 Pt 4, 13-16		367
3- Jn 17, 1-11a		171
Pentecost		
Vigil		
1- Gn 11, 1-9	13	
or Ex 19, 3-8a. 16-20b	77	
or Ex 37, 1-14	1007	
or Jl 3, 1-5	1056	
2- Rom 8, 22-27		232
3- Jn 7, 37-39		157
Mass of the Day		
1- Acts 2, 1-11		181
2- 1 Cor 12, 3b-7. 12-13		257
3- Jn 20, 19-23		177
SOLEMNITIES OF THE LORD DURING ORDINARY TIME		
Trinity Sunday		
(Sunday after Pentecost)		
1- Ex 34, 4b-6. 8-9	93	
2- 2 Cor 13, 11-13		282
3- Jn 3, 16-18		149
Corpus Christi		
1- Dt 8, 2-3. 14b-16a	183	
2- 1 Cor 10, 16-17		255
3- Jn 6, 51-58		155
Sacred Heart of Jesus		
1- Dt 7, 6-11	182	
2- 1 Jn 4, 7-16		377
3- Mt 11, 25-30		28
ORDINARY TIME		
1st Sunday		
(See Baptism of the Lord, above)		
2nd Sunday		
1- Is 49, 3. 5-6	874	
2- 1 Cor 1, 1-3		244
3- Jn 1, 29-34		146
3rd Sunday		
1- Is 8, 23b—9, 3	833	
2- 1 Cor 1, 10-13. 17		244
3- Mt 4, 12-23		15
4th Sunday		
1- Zep 2, 3; 3, 12-13	1085	
2- 1 Cor 1, 26-31		245
3- Mt 5, 1-12a		16
5th Sunday		
1- Is 58, 7-10	883	
2- 1 Cor 2, 1-5		245
3- Mt 5, 13-16		16
6th Sunday		
1- Sir 15, 15-20	784	
2- 1 Cor 2, 6-10		245
3- Mt 5, 17-37		17
7th Sunday		
1- Lv 19, 1-2. 17-18	119	
2- 1 Cor 3, 16-23		247
3- Mt 5, 38-48		18

	Old Test.	New Test.
8th Sunday		
1- Is 49, 14-15	875	
2- 1 Cor 4, 1-5		247
3- Mt 6, 24-34		20
9th Sunday		
1- Dt 11, 18. 26-28	186	
2- Rom 3, 21-25a. 28		226
3- Mt 7, 21-27		24
10th Sunday		
1- Hos 6, 3-6	1047	
2- Rom 4, 18-25		228
3- Mt 9, 9-13		24
11th Sunday		
1- Ex 19, 2-6a	77	
2- Rom 5, 6-11		228
3- Mt 9, 36—10, 8		25
12th Sunday		
1- Jer 20, 10-13	917	
2- Rom 5, 12-15		229
3- Mt 10, 26-33		26
13th Sunday		
1- 2 Kgs 4, 8-11. 14-16a	354	
2- Rom 6, 3-4. 8-11		229
3- Mt 10, 37-42		27
14th Sunday		
1- Zec 9, 9-10	1095	
2- Rom 8, 9. 11-13		231
3- Mt 11, 25-30		28
15th Sunday		
1- Is 55, 10-11	881	
2- Rom 8, 18-23		231
3- Mt 13, 1-23		31
16th Sunday		
1- Wis 12, 13. 16-19	761	
2- Rom 8, 26-27		232
3- Mt 13, 24-43		32
17th Sunday		
1- 1 Kgs 3, 5. 7-12	326	
2- Rom 8, 28-30		232
3- Mt 13, 44-52		33
18th Sunday		
1- Is 55, 1-3	880	
2- Rom 8, 35. 37-39		232
3- Mt 14, 13-21		34
19th Sunday		
1- 1 Kgs 19, 9a. 11-13a	345	
2- Rom 9, 1-5		233
3- Mt 14, 22-33		35
20th Sunday		
1- Is 56, 1. 6-7	881	
2- Rom 11, 13-14. 29-32		236
3- Mt 15, 21-28		36
21st Sunday		
1- Is 22, 19-23	845	
2- Rom 11, 33-36		237
3- Mt 16, 13-20		37

	Old Test.	New Test.
22nd Sunday		
1- Jer 20, 7-9	916	
2- Rom 12, 1-2		237
3- Mt 16, 21-27		38
23rd Sunday		
1- Ez 33, 7-9	1003	
2- Rom 13, 8-10		238
3- Mt 18, 15-20		42
24th Sunday		
1- Sir 27, 30—28, 7	797	
2- Rom 14, 7-8		239
3- Mt 18, 21-35		42
25th Sunday		
1- Is 55, 6-9	881	
2- Phil 1, 20c-24. 27a		303
3- Mt 20, 1-16a		45
26th Sunday		
1- Ez 18, 25-28	987	
2- Phil 2, 1-11		303
3- Mt 21, 28-32		48
27th Sunday		
1- Is 5, 1-7	829	
2- Phil 4, 6-9		306
3- Mt 21, 33-43		49
28th Sunday		
1- Is 25, 6-10a	848	
2- Phil 4, 12-14. 19-20		307
3- Mt 22, 1-14		49
29th Sunday		
1- Is 45, 1. 4-6	870	
2- 1 Thes 1, 1-5b		314
3- Mt 22, 15-21		50
30th Sunday		
1- Ex 22, 20-26	81	
2- 1 Thes 1, 5c-10		314
3- Mt 22, 34-40		51
31st Sunday		
1- Mal 1, 14b—2, 2b. 8-10	1100	
2- 1 Thes 2, 7b-9, 13		314
3- Mt 23; 1-12		52
32nd Sunday		
1- Wis 6, 12-16	754	
2- 1 Thes 4, 13-18		316
3- Mt 25, 1-13		57
33rd Sunday		
1- Prv 31, 10-13. 19-20. 30-31	733	
2- 1 Thes 5, 1-6		316
3- Mt 25, 14-30		57
34th Sunday		
(Christ the King)		
1- Ez 34, 11-12. 15-17	1005	
2- 1 Cor 15, 20-26. 28		261
3- Mt 25, 31-46		58

	1988	1994	2000	2006	2012
	1991	1997	2003	2009	2015

GUIDE —
1- refers to Reading I
2- refers to Reading II
3- refers to Gospel

	Old Test.	New Test.
ADVENT SEASON		
1st Sunday of Advent		
1- Is 63, 16b-17. 19b;		
64, 2b-7	889	
2- 1 Cor 1, 3-9		244
3- Mk 13, 33-37		89
2nd Sunday of Advent		
1- Is 40, 1-5. 9-11	863	
2- 2 Pt 3, 8-14		372
3- Mk 1, 1-8		69
3rd Sunday of Advent		
1- Is 61, 1-2a. 10-11	886	
2- 1 Thes 5, 16-24		317
3- Jn 1, 6-8. 19-28		145
4th Sunday of Advent		
1- 2 Sm 7, 1-5. 8b-11. 16	301	
2- Rom 16, 25-27		242
3- Lk 1, 26-38		98
CHRISTMAS SEASON		
Christmas Vigil		
1- Is 62, 1-5	887	
2- Acts 13, 16-17. 22-25		198
3- Mt 1, 1-25		11
Christmas (At Midnight)		
1- Is 9, 1-6	833	
2- Ti 2, 11-14		334
3- Lk 2, 1-14		100
Christmas (At Dawn)		
1- Is 62, 11-12	888	
2- Ti 3, 4-7		334
3- Lk 2, 15-20		101
Christmas (During the Day)		
1- Is 52, 7-10	878	
2- Heb 1, 1-6		339
3- Jn 1, 1-18		145
Sunday After Christmas		
(Holy Family)		
1- Sir 3, 2-6. 12-14	773	
2- Col 3, 12-21		312
3- Lk 2, 22-40		101
January 1		
(Solemnity of Mary, Mother of God)		
1- Nm 6, 22-27	139	
2- Gal 4, 4-7		289
3- Lk 2, 16-21		101
2nd Sunday After Christmas		
1- Sir 24, 1-2. 8-12	793	
2- Eph 1, 3-6. 15-18		293
3- Jn 1, 1-18		145

	Old Test.	New Test.
Epiphany		
1- Is 60, 1-6	885	
2- Eph 3, 2-3a. 5-6		295
3- Mt 2, 1-12		12
Sunday After Epiphany		
(Baptism of the Lord)		
1- Is 42, 1-4. 6-7	866	
2- Acts 10, 34-38		195
3- Mk 1, 6b-11		69
LENTEN SEASON		
Ash Wednesday		
1- Jl 2, 12-18	1055	
2- 2 Cor 5, 20—6, 2		272
3- Mt 6, 1-6. 16-18		18
1st Sunday of Lent		
1- Gn 9, 8-15	11	
2- 1 Pt 3, 18-22		366
3- Mk 1, 12-15		70
2nd Sunday of Lent		
1- Gn 22, 1-2. 9a. 10-13.		
15-18	24	
2- Rom 8, 31b-34		232
3- Mk 9, 2-10		82
3rd Sunday of Lent		
1- Ex 20, 1-17	78	
2- 1 Cor 1, 22-25		245
3- Jn 2, 13-25		148
4th Sunday of Lent		
1- 2 Chr 36, 14-16. 19-23	443	
2- Eph 2, 4-10		295
3- Jn 3, 14-21		149
5th Sunday of Lent		
1- Jer 31, 31-34	930	
2- Heb 5, 7-9		343
3- Jn 12, 20-33		165
Passion Sunday (Palm Sunday)		
Procession: Mk 11, 1-10 ...		85
or Jn 12, 12-16		165
1- Is 50, 4-7	876	
2- Phil 2, 6-11		303
3- Mk 14, 1—15, 47		89
EASTER TRIDUUM		
AND EASTER SEASON		
Holy Thursday		
Chrism Mass		
1- Is 61, 1-3a. 6a. 8b-9	886	
2- Rv 1, 5-8		387
3- Lk 4, 16-21		105
Mass of Lord's Supper		
1- Ex 12, 1-8. 11-14	69	
2- 1 Cor 11, 23-26		257
3- Jn 13, 1-15		166

	Old Test.	New Test.
Good Friday		
1- Is 52, 13—53, 12	879	
2- Heb 4, 14-16. 5, 7-9		342
3- Jn 18, 1—19, 42		172
Easter Vigil		
1- Gn 1, 1—2, 2	4	
Gn 22, 1-18	24	
Ex 14, 15—15, 1	72	
Is 54, 5-14	880	
Is 55, 1-11	880	
Bar 3, 9-15. 32—4, 4	966	
Ez 36, 16-28	1007	
2- Rom 6, 3-11		229
3- Mk 16, 1-8		64
Easter Sunday		
1- Acts 10, 34a. 37-43		195
2- Cor 3, 1-4		311
or 1 Cor 5, 6b-8		248
3- Jn 20, 1-9		176
or Mk 16, 1-8		93
Evening: 3- Lk 24, 13-35		141
2nd Sunday of Easter		
1- Acts 4, 32-35		186
2- 1 Jn 5, 1-6		378
3- Jn 20, 19-31		177
3rd Sunday of Easter		
1- Acts 3, 13-15. 17-19		184
2- 1 Jn 2, 1-5a		375
3- Lk 24, 35-48		142
4th Sunday of Easter		
1- Acts 4, 8-12		185
2- 1 Jn 3, 1-2		376
3- Jn 10, 11-18		161
5th Sunday of Easter		
1- Acts 9, 26-31		193
2- 1 Jn 3, 18-24		377
3- Jn 15, 1-8		169
6th Sunday of Easter		
1- Acts 10, 25-26. 34-35.		
44-48		195
2- 1 Jn 4, 7-10		377
3- Jn 15, 9-17		169
Ascension of Our Lord		
1- Acts 1, 1-11		180
2- Eph 1, 17-23		294
3- Mk 16, 15-20		94
7th Sunday of Easter		
1- Acts 1, 15-17. 20a.		
20c-26		181
2- 1 Jn 4, 11-16		377
3- Jn 17, 11b-19		172

	Old Test.	New Test.
Pentecost		
Vigil		
1- Gn 11, 1-9	13	
or Ex 19, 3-a. 16-20b	77	
or Ez 37, 1-14	1007	
or Jl 3, 1-5	1056	
2- Rom 8, 22-27		232
3- Jn 7, 37-39		157
Mass of the Day		
1- Acts 2, 1-11		181
2- 1 Cor 12, 3b-7. 12-13		257
3- Jn 20, 19-23		177

SOLEMNITIES OF THE LORD DURING ORDINARY TIME

	Old Test.	New Test.
Trinity Sunday		
(Sunday after Pentecost)		
1- Dt 4, 32-34. 39-40	179	
2- Rom 8, 14-17		232
3- Mt 28, 16-20		66
Corpus Christi		
1- Ex 24, 3-8	82	
2- Heb 9, 11-15		347
3- Mk 14, 12-16. 22-26		90
Sacred Heart of Jesus		
1- Hos 11, 1. 3-4. 8c-9	1051	
2- Eph 3, 8-12. 14-19		296
3- Jn 19, 31-37		175

ORDINARY TIME

	Old Test.	New Test.
1st Sunday		
(See Baptism of the Lord, above)		
2nd Sunday		
1- 1 Sm 3, 3b-10. 19	267	
2- 1 Cor 6, 13c-15a. 17-20		249
3- Jn 1, 35-42		146
3rd Sunday		
1- Jon 3, 1-5. 10	1070	
2- 1 Cor 7, 29-31		251
3- Mk 1, 14-20		70
4th Sunday		
1- Dt 18, 15-20	193	
2- 1 Cor 7, 32-35		251
3- Mk 1, 21-28		70
5th Sunday		
1- Jb 7, 1-4. 6-7	575	
2- 1 Cor 9, 16-19. 22-23		253
3- Mk 1, 29-39		70
6th Sunday		
1- Lv 13, 1-2. 45-46	111	
2- 1 Cor 10, 31—11, 1		255
3- Mk 1, 40-45		71
7th Sunday		
1- Is 43, 18-19. 21-22. 24b-25	868	
2- 2 Cor 1, 18-22		267
3- Mk 2, 1-12		71

	Old Test.	New Test.
8th Sunday		
1- Hos 2, 16b. 17b. 21-22	1043	
2- 2 Cor 3, 1b-6		267
3- Mk 2, 18-22		72
9th Sunday		
1- Dt 5, 12-15	180	
2- 2 Cor 4, 6-11		270
3- Mk 2, 23—3, 6		72
10th Sunday		
1- Gn 3, 9-15	6	
2- 2 Cor 4, 13—5, 1		271
3- Mk 3, 20-35		73
11th Sunday		
1- Ez 17, 22-24	986	
2- 2 Cor 5, 6-10		272
3- Mk 4, 26-34		74
12th Sunday		
1- Jb 38, 1. 8-11	598	
2- 2 Cor 5, 14-17		272
3- Mk 4, 35-41		75
13th Sunday		
1- Wis 1, 13-15; 2, 23-24	751	
2- 2 Cor 8, 7. 9. 13-15		275
3- Mk 5, 21-43		76
14th Sunday		
1- Ez 2, 2-5	973	
2- 2 Cor 12, 7-10		280
3- Mk 6, 1-6		76
15th Sunday		
1- Am 7, 12-15	1064	
2- Eph 1, 3-14		293
3- Mk 6, 7-13		77
16th Sunday		
1- Jer 23, 1-6	919	
2- Eph 2, 13-18		295
3- Mk 6, 30-34		78
17th Sunday		
1- 2 Kgs 4, 42-44	355	
2- Eph 4, 1-6		296
3- Jn 6, 1-15		153
18th Sunday		
1- Ex 16, 2-4. 12-15	74	
2- Eph 4, 17. 20-24		297
3- Jn 6, 24-35		154
19th Sunday		
1- 1 Kgs 19, 4-8	345	
2- Eph 4, 30—5, 2		297
3- Jn 6, 41-45		155
20th Sunday		
1- Prv 9, 1-6	709	
2- Eph 5, 15-20		298
3- Jn 6, 51-58		155
21st Sunday		
1- Jos 24, 1-2a. 15-17. 18b	234	
2- Eph 5, 21-32		298
3- Jn 6, 60-69		155

	Old Test.	New Test.
22nd Sunday		
1- Dt 4, 1-2. 6-8	178	
2- Jas 1, 17-18. 21b-22. 27		358
3- Mk 7, 1-8. 14-15. 21-23		79
23rd Sunday		
1- Is 35, 4-7a	857	
2- Jas 2, 1-5		358
3- Mk 7, 31-37		80
24th Sunday		
1- Is 50, 5-9a	876	
2- Jas 2, 14-18		359
3- Mk 8, 27-35		81
25th Sunday		
1- Wis 2, 12. 17-20	751	
2- Jas 3, 16—4, 3		360
3- Mk 9, 30-37		83
26th Sunday		
1- Nm 11, 25-29	145	
2- Jas 5, 1-6		361
3- Mk 9, 38-43. 45. 47-48		83
27th Sunday		
1- Gn 2, 18-24	5	
2- Heb 2, 9-11		340
3- Mk 10, 2-16		84
28th Sunday		
1- Wis 7, 7-11	756	
2- Heb 4, 12-13		342
3- Mk 10, 17-30		84
29th Sunday		
1- Is 53, 10-11	879	
2- Heb 4, 14-16		342
3- Mk 10, 35-43		85
30th Sunday		
1- Jer 31, 7-9	929	
2- Heb 5, 1-6		342
3- Mk 10, 46-53		85
31st Sunday		
1- Dt 6, 2-6	181	
2- Heb 7, 23-28		345
3- Mk 12, 28b-34		87
32nd Sunday		
1- 1 Kgs 17, 10-16	343	
2- Heb 9, 24-28		348
3- Mk 12, 38-44		88
33rd Sunday		
1- Dn 12, 1-3	1038	
2- Heb 10, 11-14. 18		349
3- Mk 13, 24-32		89
34th Sunday		
(Christ the King)		
1- Dn 7, 13-14	1032	
2- Rv 1, 5-8		387
3- Jn 18, 33b-37		173

Year C

| 1989 | 1995 | 2001 | 2007 | 2013 |
| 1992 | 1998 | 2004 | 2010 | 2016 |

GUIDE —
1- refers to Reading I
2- refers to Reading II
3- refers to Gospel

	Old Test.	New Test.

ADVENT SEASON

1st Sunday of Advent
1- Jer 33, 14-16 933
2- 1 Thes 3, 12—4, 2   315
3- Lk 21, 25-28. 34-36   136

2nd Sunday of Advent
1- Bar 5, 1-9 969
2- Phil 1, 4-6. 8-11   302
3- Lk 3, 1-6   102

3rd Sunday of Advent
1- Zep 3, 14-18a 1087
2- Phil 4, 4-7   306
3- Lk 3, 10-18   103

4th Sunday of Advent
1- Mi 5, 1-4a 1074
2- Heb 10, 5-10   349
3- Lk 1, 39-45   98

CHRISTMAS SEASON

Christmas Vigil
1- Is 62, 1-6 887
2- Acts 13, 16-17. 22-25 .   198
3- Mt 1, 1-25   11

Christmas (At Midnight)
1- Is 9, 1-6 833
2- Ti 2, 11-14   334
3- Lk 2, 1-14   100

Christmas (At Dawn)
1- Is 62, 11-12 888
2- Ti 3, 4-7   334
3- Lk 2, 15-20   101

Christmas (During the Day)
1- Is 57, 7-10 878
2- Heb 1, 1-6   339
3- Jn 1, 1-18   145

Sunday After Christmas (Holy Family)
1- Sir 3, 2-6. 12-14 773
2- Col 3, 12-21   312
3- Lk 2, 41-52   102

January 1 (Solemnity of Mary, Mother of God)
1- Nm 6, 22-27 139
2- Gal 4, 4-7   289
3- Lk 2, 16-21   101

2nd Sunday After Christmas
1- Sir 24, 1-2. 8-12 793
2- Eph 1, 3-6. 15-18   293
3- Jn 1, 1-18   145

Epiphany
1- Is 60, 1-6 885
2- Eph 3, 2-3a. 5-6   295
3- Mt 2, 1-12   12

	Old Test.	New Test.

Sunday After Epiphany (Baptism of the Lord)
1- Is 42, 1-4. 6-7 866
2- Acts 10, 34-38   195
3- Lk 3, 15-16. 21-22   103

LENTEN SEASON

Ash Wednesday
1- Jl 2, 12-18 1055
2- 2 Cor 5, 20—6, 2   272
3- Mt 6, 1-6. 16-18   18

1st Sunday of Lent
1- Dt 26, 4-10 200
2- Rom 10, 8-13   235
3- Lk 4, 1-13   104

2nd Sunday of Lent
1- Gn 15, 5-12. 17-18   17
2- Phil 3, 17—4, 1   306
3- Lk 9, 28b-36   116

3rd Sunday of Lent
1- Ex 3, 1-8a. 13-15   60
2- 1 Cor 10, 1-6. 10-12 ...   254
3- Lk 13, 1-9   123

4th Sunday of Lent
1- Jos 5, 9a. 10-12 216
2- 2 Cor 5, 17-21   272
3- Lk 15, 1-3. 11-32   126

5th Sunday of Lent
1- Is 43, 16-21 868
2- Phil 3, 8-14   305
3- Jn 8, 1-11   157

Passion Sunday (Palm Sunday)
Procession: Lk 19, 28-40 ..   132
1- Is 50, 4-7 876
2- Phil 2, 6-11   303
3- Lk 22, 14—23, 56   137

EASTER TRIDUUM AND EASTER SEASON

Holy Thursday
Chrism Mass
1- Is 61, 1-3a. 6a. 8b-9 ... 886
2- Rv 1, 5-8   387
3- Lk 4, 16-21   105

Mass of Lord's Supper
1- Ex 12, 1-8. 11-14   69
2- 1 Cor 11, 23-26   257
3- Jn 13, 1-15   166

Good Friday
1- Is 52, 13—53, 12 879
2- Heb 4, 14-16; 5, 7-9 ...   342
3- Jn 18, 1—19, 42   172

Easter Vigil
1- Gn 1, 1—2, 2   4
Gn 22, 1-18   24
Ex 14, 15—15, 1   72

	Old Test.	New Test.

Is 54, 5-14 880
Is 55, 1-11 880
Bar 3, 9-15. 32—4, 4 .   966
Ez 36, 16-28 1007
2- Rom 6, 3-11   229
3- Lk 24, 1-12   140

Easter Sunday
1- Acts 10, 34a. 37-43   195
2- Col 3, 1-4   311
or 1 Cor 5, 6b-8   248
3- Jn 20, 1-9   176
or Lk 24, 1-12   140
Evening: 3- Lk 24, 13-35 .   141

2nd Sunday of Easter
1- Acts 5, 12-16   186
2- Rv 1, 9-11a. 12-13. 17-19   387
3- Jn 20, 19-31   177

3rd Sunday of Easter
1- Acts 5, 27b-32. 40b-41   187
2- Rv 5, 11-14   392
3- Jn 21, 1-19   177

4th Sunday of Easter
1- Acts 13, 14. 43-52   198
2- Rv 7, 9. 14b-17   394
3- Jn 10, 27-30   162

5th Sunday of Easter
1- Acts 14, 21-27   198
2- Rv 21, 1-5a   407
3- Jn 13, 31-33a. 34-35 ..   167

6th Sunday of Easter
1- Acts 15, 1-2. 22-29   201
2- Rv 21, 10-14. 22-23 ...   407
3- Jn 14, 23-29   169

Ascension of the Lord
1- Acts 1, 1-11   180
2- Eph 1, 17-23   294
3- Lk 24, 46-53   142

7th Sunday of Easter
1- Acts 7, 55-60   190
2- Rv 22, 12-14. 16-17. 20   409
3- Jn 17, 20-26   172

Pentecost
Vigil
1- Gn 11, 1-9   13
or Ex 19, 3-8a. 16-20b .   77
or Ez 37, 1-14 1007
or Jl 3, 1-5 1056
2- Rom 8, 22-27   232
3- Jn 7, 37-39   157

Mass of the Day
1- Acts 2, 1-11   181
2- 1 Cor 12, 3b-7. 12-13 .   257
3- Jn 20, 19-23   177

	Old Test.	New Test.

SOLEMNITIES OF THE LORD DURING ORDINARY TIME

Trinity Sunday
(Sunday After Pentecost)
1- Prv 8, 22-31 709
2- Rom 5, 1-5 228
3- Jn 16, 12-15 170

Corpus Christi
1- Gn 14, 18-20 17
2- 1 Cor 11, 23-26 257
3- Lk 9, 11b-17 115

Sacred Heart of Jesus
1- Ez 34, 11-16 1005
2- Rom 5, 5-11 228
3- Lk 15, 3-7 126

ORDINARY TIME

1st Sunday
(See Baptism of the Lord, above)

2nd Sunday
1- Is 62, 1-5 887
2- 1 Cor 12, 4-11 257
3- Jn 2, 1-12 147

3rd Sunday
1- Neh 8, 1-4a. 5-6. 8-10 . 462
2- 1 Cor 12, 12-30 258
3- Lk 1, 1-4; 4, 14-21 97

4th Sunday
1- Jer 1, 4-5. 17-19 893
2- 1 Cor 12. 31—13, 13 . 258
3- Lk 4, 21-30 105

5th Sunday
1- Is 6, 1-2a. 3-8 830
2- 1 Cor 15, 1-11 261
3- Lk 5, 1-11 106

6th Sunday
1- Jer 17, 5-8 913
2- 1 Cor 15, 12. 16-20 ... 261
3- Lk 6, 17. 20-26 109

7th Sunday
1- 1 Sm 26, 2. 7-9. 12-13.
22-23 291
2- 1 Cor 15, 45-49 263
3- Lk 6, 27-38 109

8th Sunday
1- Sir 27, 4-7 796
2- 1 Cor 15, 54-58 263
3- Lk 6, 39-45 110

9th Sunday
1- 1 Kgs 8, 41-43 333
2- Gal 1, 1-2. 6-10 284
3- Lk 7, 1-10 110

10th Sunday
1- 1 Kgs 17, 17-24 344
2- Gal 1, 11-19 285
3- Lk 7, 11-17 110

11th Sunday
1- 2 Sm 12, 7-10. 13 305
2- Gal 2, 16. 19-21 286
3- Lk 7, 36—8, 3 111

12th Sunday
1- Zec 12, 10-11 1097
2- Gal 3, 26-29 288
3- Lk 9, 18-24 115

13th Sunday
1- 1 Kgs 19, 16b. 19-21 .. 346
2- Gal 5, 1. 13-18 290
3- Lk 9, 51-62 117

14th Sunday
1- Is 66, 10-14c 891
2- Gal 6, 14-18 292
3- Lk 10, 1-12. 17-20 117

15th Sunday
1- Dt 30, 10-14 205
2- Col 1, 15-20 309
3- Lk 10, 25-37 118

16th Sunday
1- Gn 18, 1-10a. 19
2- Col 1, 24-28 310
3- Lk 10, 38-42 119

17th Sunday
1- Gn 18, 20-32 20
2- Col 2, 12-14 311
3- Lk 11, 1-13 119

18th Sunday
1- Eccl 1, 2; 2, 21-23 734
2- Col 3, 1-5. 9-11 311
3- Lk 12, 13-31 122

19th Sunday
1- Wis 18, 6-9 768
2- Heb 11, 1-2. 8-19 351
3- Lk 12, 32-48 122

20th Sunday
1- Jer 38, 4-6. 8-10 938
2- Heb 12, 1-4 352
3- Lk 12, 49-53 123

21st Sunday
1- Is 66, 18-21 892
2- Heb 12, 5-7. 11-13 353
3- Lk 13, 22-30 124

22nd Sunday
1- Sir 3, 17-18. 20. 28-29 . 794
2- Heb 12, 18-19. 22-24a . 353
3- Lk 14, 1. 7-14 125

23rd Sunday
1- Wis 9, 13-18b 758
2- Phlm 9b-10. 12-17 336
3- Lk 14, 25-33 126

24th Sunday
1- Ex 32, 7-11. 13-14 91
2- 1 Tm 1, 12-17 323
3- Lk 15, 1-32 126

25th Sunday
1- Am 8, 4-7 1065
2- 1 Tm 2, 1-8 323
3- Lk 16, 1-13 127

26th Sunday
1- Am 6, 1a. 4-7 1063
2- 1 Tm 6, 11-16 327
3- Lk 16, 19-31 128

27th Sunday
1- Hb 1, 2-3; 2, 2-4 1081
2- 2 Tm 1, 6-8. 13-14 329
3- Lk 17, 5-10 129

28th Sunday
1- 2 Kgs 5, 14-17 356
2- 2 Tm 2, 8-13 330
3- Lk 17, 11-19 129

29th Sunday
1- Ex 17, 8-13 76
2- 2 Tm 3, 14—4, 2 331
3- Lk 18, 1-8 130

30th Sunday
1- Sir 35, 12-14. 16-18 ... 805
2- 2 Tm 4, 6-8. 16-18 331
3- Lk 18, 9-14 130

31st Sunday
1- Wis 11, 23—12, 2 761
2- 2 Thes 1, 11—2, 2 319
3- Lk 19, 1-10 131

32nd Sunday
1- 2 Mc 7, 1-2. 9-14 555
2- 2 Thes 2, 16—3, 5 320
3- Lk 20, 27-38 134

33rd Sunday
1- Mal 3, 19-20a 1103
2- 2 Thes 3, 7-12 320
3- Lk 21, 5-19 135

34th Sunday
(Christ the King)
1- 2 Sm 5, 1-3 300
2- Col 1, 12-20 309
3- Lk 23, 35-43 140

DOCTRINAL BIBLE INDEX

Other subjects will be found in the Bible Dictionary, pp. 412ff. The cross references to the passages cited below should also be consulted.

— A —

Absolution, the power promised and given to the pastors of the church, Mt 16, 19; 18, 18; Jn 20, 22f.

Abstinence, from food: God forbids Adam to eat the fruit of a certain tree, Gn 2, 17; 3, 11;
—from flesh with its blood, forbidden, Gn 9, 4; Dt 12, 16; Acts 15, 29;
—paschal lamb not to be eaten raw, or boiled, Ex 12, 9;
—leaven forbidden, Ex 13, 7;
—ox that has killed a man not to be eaten, Ex 21, 28;
—observed by St. John the Baptizer, Lk 1, 15;
—even permitted food to be abstained from, so as not to scandalize others, 2 Mc 6, 24; 7, 1f; Rom 4, 20f; 1 Cor 8, 13.

Adoption, of Israel by God, Ex 4, 22; Nm 6, 27; Jer 3, 19; Hos 11, 1; Rom 9, 4;
—adoption of children of God described, Rom 8, 14-17; Gal 3, 26-29; 4, 1-7; Eph 1, 5; Heb 2, 10;
—effects, 2 Cor 6, 17. 18; 7, 1; Heb 12, 5-11; 1 Jn 3, 2-5;
—of Gentiles, Rom 9, 24-26; Acts 15, 17.

Affliction, lot of the children of God, Prv 3, 11f; Wis 11, 10; Isa 1, 26;
—not a mark of sin, Eccl 8, 14;
—to be borne patiently, Sir 2, 2;
—comes from God, Is 45, 7; Hos 6, 2; Am 3, 6; Jdt 8, 21-27;
—days of affliction shortened on account of the elect, Mt 24, 22; Mk 13, 20;
—no proportion between the affliction of this life and the glory to come, Rom 8, 18.

Agriculture, practiced by Adam, Gn 3, 23;
—practiced by Cain, Gn 4, 2;
—practiced by Noah, Gn 9, 20;
—practiced by the Egyptians, Gn 47, 24;
—Mosaic laws as to, Ex 22, 5; 23; Dt 14; 15; 16;
—serves as an example for spiritual lessons, Jer 12, 13; Jl 1, 8-14; Mt 13, 3-43; 2 Cor 9, 6; Gal 6, 7-9.

Almsgiving, Ex 22, 24; 23, 11; Lv 19, 10; 23, 22; 25, 34; Dt 15, 7. 10; 24, 19; 1 Kgs 17, 10; Neh 8, 10; Mt 6, 3; 10, 42; 19, 21; 25, 35. 42; Lk 3, 11; 6, 35; 11, 41; 12, 33; 14, 13.

Altar, erected by God's command, Ex 20, 24-26;
—of holocausts, Ex 27, 1;
—dedicated, Nm 7;

—of incense, Ex 30, 1-7; 38, 25; 40, 10;
—of rough stones after passage of Jordan, Dt 27, 2;
—erected by David, 2 Sm 24, 21; 1 Chr 21, 18;
—Solomon at, 2 Chr 1, 6; 6, 12;
—the horn of the, 1 Kgs 1, 50;
—Solomon's, 2 Chr 4;
—dedicated, 2, Chr 7;
—Asa restores, 2 Chr 15, 8;
—Elijah erects, 1 Kgs 18, 32;
—Ahaz profanes, 2 Kgs 16, 14;
—restored by Zerubbabel, Ezr 3, 2; 6, 16;
—restored by Judas Maccabeus, 1 Mc 4, 47. 53.

Angels, they have a charge over us, Mt 18, 10; Heb 1, 14. **See** also Ex 23, 20f; Ps 91, 11f;
—pray for us, Rv 8, 4; Zec 1, 12;
—communion with, Heb 12, 22;
—fall of, Jb 4, 18; Is 14, 12; Lk 10, 18; Jude 6; Rv 12, 4; 20, 9.

Anger, Ps. 4, 5; 37, 8; Prv 15, 18; 26, 21; 27, 3f; 29, 22; Sir 8, 16; 25, 13; 27, 30; 28, 3-11; Mt 5, 22; Eph 4, 26. 31; Jas 1, 19f.

Animals, created, Gn 1, 24f;
—receive their names, Gn 2, 20;
—first offered in sacrifice, Gn 4, 4;
—Mosaic law as to, Nm 15; 18, 17; 19, 2;
—clean and unclean, Gn 7, 2; Dt 14; 15, 19; 21, 4; Lv 11;
—which to be offered in sacrifice and when, Lv 12;
—seen in a dream by Ezekiel, Ez 1, 4;
—seen in a vision by St. Peter, Acts 10, 12;
—not to be cruelly treated, Gn 23; Ex 23, 12; Nm 32, 26; Dt 5, 14; 22, 10; Prv 12, 10; Sir 7, 22.

Apostles, chosen from the disciples, Lk 6, 13;
—sent to announce the kingdom of God in Judea, Mt 10;
—sent to evangelize the whole world, Mt 18, 19; Mk 16, 15; Lk 24, 46; Jn 15, 16. 27; 20, 21; Acts 1, 8; 10, 42.

Apostolical Traditions, 1 Cor 11, 2; 2 Thes 2, 15; 3, 6; 2 Tm 1, 13; 2, 2; 3, 14. **See** also Dt 32, 7; Ps 44, 2; 78, 3.

Ark of the Covenant, Ex 25, 10-22;
—not to be approached, Jos 3, 4;
—in the middle of the Jordan, Jos 3, 8;
—captured, 1 Sm 4;
—overthrows idol of Dagon, 1 Sm 5;
—sent back, 1 Sm 6;
—at Kiriath-jearim, 1 Sm 7;
—David removes it, 2 Sm 6;
—Uzzah killed for touching it, 2 Sm

6, 7;
—at Obed-edom's house, 2 Sm 6, 11;
—God's footstool, 1 Chr 28, 2; Pss 99, 5; 132, 7; Lam 2, 1;
—manna placed in, Ex 16, 34;
—also the tables of the law placed in, Dt 10, 2; 1 Kgs 8, 6;
—Book of the law placed in, Dt 31, 26.

Avarice, Ps 39, 7; 119, 36; Prv 15, 27; 28, 16; 29, 4; Eccl 5, 9. 14; Sir 10, 9f; 14, 3; Is 5, 8; 57, 17; Hb 2, 9; Lk 12, 15-21; 1 Cor 5, 11; 6, 9f; Eph 5, 3. 5; Col 3, 5; 1 Tm 6, 9; Heb 13, 5.

— B —

Beasts, Daniel's vision of four, Dn 7, 3;
—of the Apocalypse, Rv 17, 3.

Beatitudes, Mt 5, 3-11; Lk 6, 20-23.

Birds, created, Gn 1, 22; 7, 14;
—offered in holocaust, Lv 1, 14;
—law as to nests of, Dt 22, 6.

Bishop, at Ephesus, Acts 20, 28;
—at Philippi, Phil 1, 1;
—qualities required of, 1 Tm 3, 1-7; Ti 1, 6-9.

Blasphemy, punished, Lv 24, 10; Neh 9, 18; Tb 13, 16; Is 1, 4; 5, 24; 48, 11; 53, 5; Jer 23, 17; Ez 20, 28; 1 Mc 7, 38; 2 Mc 8, 4; 12, 14; 15, 24; Rom 2, 24; 1 Tm 1, 20; Jude 8;
—against Jesus Christ; Mt 27, 39; Lk 23, 39;
—against the Holy Spirit, not forgiven, Mt 12, 31.

Blessings, by which creatures are consecrated and sanctified, Ex 28, 2; 29, 6. 27; Lv 21, 10; 22, 2; 27, 28-30; Nm 5, 17; 31, 6; Jos 6, 24; Jgs 17, 3; 2 Sm 21, 5; 1 Chr 18, 11; 1 Tm 4, 5; Heb 19, 2f;
—temporal, promised to Israel, Ex 15, 26; Lv 26, 4-12; Dt 4, 1; 5, 29;
—conditions for these blessings, Dt 15, 5;
—spiritual blessings: salvation, Ps 91, 16; Acts 4, 12; presence of God, Ex 33, 14-17; Mt 28, 20; strength, Col 1, 11; help, Heb 2, 18; joy, Ps 40, 4; Acts 13, 52; peace, Jn 14, 27; Phil 4, 7;
—of praise, Gn 24, 48; Ps 68, 27; 1 Cor 1, 9.

Blindness, cured by Christ, Mt 9, 27-30; 12, 22; 20, 30-34; Jn 9;
—inflicted as a punishment, Jn 12, 40; Acts 28, 26; Rom 11, 8. 10; Gn 19, 11; 2 Kgs 6, 18; Acts 13, 11;
—inflicted by Satan, 2 Cor 4, 4
—prayers to be delivered from, Ps 13, 4; 119, 18.

Body, of Christian is temple of Holy Spirit, 1 Cor 3, 16. 17; 2 Cor 6, 16, and member of Christ, 1 Cor 6, 15; 12, 27;

—Church is body of Christ, Eph 1, 22. 23; Col 3, 15; 1 Cor 10, 17;

—of man will be raised up, Jb 19, 26. 27; Mt 22, 23-32; 1 Cor 15, 12-57;

—Word of God received a human body, Mt 1, 18-23; Jn 1, 14; Heb 10, 5;

—which was crucified, Jn 19, 17-18. 33; and raised again, 1 Cor 15, 3-8.

Bread, given from heaven to the Israelites in the desert, Ex 16, 2-4. 35; Jos 5, 12; Ps 78, 24;

—Jesus, the bread which came down from heaven, Jn 4, 31; 1 Cor 10, 16; 11, 27; **see** Eucharist.

—unleavened, Ex 7, 18;

—brought to Elijah miraculously, 1 Kgs 17, 4;

—multiplied by Christ, Mt 16, 19; Mk 6, 41; 8, 20; Lk 9, 13; Jn 6, 11.

— C —

Ceremonies, of exterior worship, Gn 8, 20;

—of Melchizedek, Gn 14, 18;

—circumcision, Gn 17, 10;

—paschal lamb, Ex 2, 19; Lv 8, 34;

—sanctification of priests, Lv 9, 12-14; 23; Nm 1, 50; 4-9; 15;

—for the singers, 1 Chr 23;

—dedication of the temple, Ezr 6;

—at prayer, 1 Kgs 8, 22; 17; 1 Cor 11, 4;

—signs of things to come, Ex 13, 9; Nm 15, 39; Ez 20, 12; 1 Cor 10, 11; 2 Cor 3, 13; Heb 7; 8, 5; 9, 1; 10, 1.

Charity, a virtue more excellent than faith, Prv 10, 12; Mt 22, 38; 1 Cor 13, 13;

—fraternal, Gn 13, 8; Lv 19, 18; Dt 22, 1; 1 Sm 18, 1; Sir 25, 2; Ps 133, 1; Prv 10, 12; Mt 7, 3; 19, 19; 22, 38; Jn 13, 14. 34; 15, 12; Rom 12, 10; 13, 9; 1 Cor 13; Gal 5, 14; Eph 4, 15; 5, 2; Phil 2, 2; Col 3, 13f; 1 Thes 4, 9; 1 Tm 1, 5; Heb 13; 1 Pt 4, 8; 1 Jn 3, 23; 4, 7;

—toward our enemies, Ex 23, 4; 1 Sm 24, 5. 7; 26, 5; 30, 11; 2 Sm 19, 19; 2 Kgs 6, 21; Jb 31, 29; Prv 25, 21; Mt 5, 44; Lk 6, 27. 35; 23, 33; Acts 7, 60; Rom 12, 20;

—produced by the Holy Spirit, Col 1, 8;

—exemplified by Jesus, Jn 13, 1—16, 34; 15, 12; Eph 5, 2. 25; Rv 1, 5.

Chastity, praised, Tb 6, 16; Jgs 15, 11; 16, 26; Prv 22, 11; Wis 3, 13; 4, 1; 6, 20; Sir 6, 28; 26, 20; Is 5, 14; Zec 9, 17;

—virginity preferable to marriage, Ps 45, 15; Wis 6, 20; Mt 22, 30;

—evangelical perfection, Mt 19, 12; 1 Cor 7, 25;

—recommended to ministers of the church, 1 Tm 3, 2. 8;

—recommended to women, Ti 2, 5.

Children, of Hebrews, drowned by Pharaoh, Ex 1, 22;

—first-born of Egyptians struck dead, Ex 11, 5;

—devoured by bears, 2 Kgs 2, 24;

—massacred by Herod, Mt 2, 16;

—blessed by our Lord, Mt 10, 16; Lk 18, 17;

—duty to parents, Gn 9, 23; 28, 7; 37, 14; Ex 20, 12; 21, 17; Lv 19, 3; Dt 21, 18; 27, 16; Jgs 14, 1; 1 Sm 2, 22; 18, 5; 1 Kgs 2, 19; 2 Kgs 2, 23; Sir 3, 2; 6, 18; 7, 27; 8, 9; 22, 3; 23, 14; 25, 7; Tb 14, 5; Jb 8, 4; Prv 1, 8; 4, 1; 6, 20; 10, 1; 13, 1; 15, 20; 19, 26; 23, 19; 28, 24; 30, 17; Jer 35, 16; Mt 10, 35; 19, 19; Mk 10, 19; Lk 2, 51; Acts 7, 14; Col 3, 20; 1 Pt 5, 5.

Christ, Jesus, foretold in Old Testament, Gn 3, 15; 49, 10; Nm 24, 17; Dt 18, 15; 2 Sm 7, 12-16; Ps 2, 1-9; Is 7, 14; 9, 6; 11, 1; 49, 1; 50, 4; 52, 13; Jer 23, 5; Ez 34, 23-24; Dn 7, 13; Mi 5, 2; Zec 6, 12; 9, 9; Mal 3, 1;

—Son of Man, Mt 9, 6; 26, 64; Mk 8, 31; Lk 19, 10; Jn 3, 13-14; 5, 27; Acts 7, 55;

—Son of David, Mt 1, 1; 9, 27; Jn 7, 42;

—Son of Mary, Mt 1, 21; Lk 2, 7; Jn 19, 25; Acts 1, 14;

—Son of God, Mt 3, 17; 4, 3; 14, 33; 16, 16; Mk 1, 1; Lk 1, 32; Jn 1, 34; 10, 36; Rom 1, 3;

—the same God with his Father, and equal to him, Jn 5, 18. 19. 23; 10, 30; 14, 1. 9; 16, 14f; 17, 10; Phil 2, 5f;

—true God, Jn 1, 1; 20, 28f; Acts 20, 25; Rom 9, 5; Ti 2, 13; 1 Jn 5, 20; Is 9, 6; 35, 4f; Mt 1, 23; Lk 1, 16f; Heb 1, 8;

—Creator of all things, Jn 1, 3. 10f; Col 1, 16f; Heb 1, 2. 10-12; 3, 4;

—the Lord of glory, 1 Cor 2, 8;

—the King of kings and Lord of lords, Rv 17, 14; 19, 16;

—the Alpha and Omega, the beginning and the end, Rv 1, 7f. 17f; 2, 8; 22, 12f;

—circumcised, Lk 2, 21;

—baptized in the Jordan, Mt 3, 16; Mk 1, 9; Lk 3, 21;

—preached the kingdom, Mt 3, 2; Mk 1, 15; Acts 2, 38;

—performed many signs, Mt 4, 23f; Lk 7, 21f;

—obedient to the Father, Mt 11, 25; Mk 14, 36; Lk 2, 49; Jn 4, 34; Phil 2, 8;

—immune from sin, Jn 8, 46; 2 Cor 5, 21; Heb 4, 15; 1 Pt 2, 22;

—he died for all, Jn 3, 16f; Rom 5, 18; 2 Cor 5, 14f; 1 Tm 2, 3-6; 4, 10; Heb 2, 9; 1 Jn 2, 1f;

—even for the reprobate, Rom 14, 15; 1 Cor 8, 11; 2 Pt 2, 1;

—rose from the dead and appeared to many, Mt 12, 39f; 28, 6; Acts 1, 22; 2, 24; Rom 4, 24; 1 Cor 15, 4. 14;

—is seated at the right hand of the Father, Mk 14, 62; 16, 19; Acts 7, 55; Rom 8, 34; Eph 1, 20; Col 3, 6; Heb 1, 3; 1 Pt 3, 22;

—will come to judge all men, Mt 19, 28; 24, 30-51; 25, 31-46; Jn 5, 22; Acts 10, 42; Rom 14, 10; 2 Cor 5, 10;

—designated by various titles: Lamb of God, Jn 1, 29; good shepherd, Jn 10, 11; light of the world, Jn 8, 12; image of God, 2 Cor 4, 4; eternal priest, Heb 7, 24; mediator of the new covenant, Heb 9, 15; head of the Church, Col 1, 18.

Church, of God, 1 Cor 1, 2. 10. 32; 11, 22; 1 Thes 1, 4; 1 Tm 3, 5. 15;

—and of Christ, Mt 16, 18; Acts 20, 28;

—body of Christ, 1 Cor 12, 12f. 27; Rom 12, 5; Eph 1, 22f;

—God's building and temple, 1 Cor 3, 9. 10. 16;

—royal priesthood, 1 Tm 2, 1; 1 Pt 2, 5. 9;

—bride, 2 Cor 11, 2; Eph 5, 25. 27. 29; Rv 19, 7;

—flock, Lk 12, 32; Jn 10, 3-5. 11;

—founded on Christ, 1 Cor 3, 11;

—will last forever, Mt 16, 18;

—possesses the means of salvation, Eph 4, 11. 12;

—organization and government, Acts 6, 2-6; 14, 23; 1 Tm 3, 8-13; 1 Cor 12, 4-11; Eph 4, 11-13;

—infallible in matters of faith or morals; this follows from the promises, Mt 16, 18; 28, 19f; Lk 22, 32; Jn 14, 16f. 26; 16, 13; 17, 11. 20; 1 Tm 3, 14f; 1 Jn 2, 27; Is 35, 8; 54, 9f; 59, 19-21.

Church Guides, and their authority, Dt 17, 18f; Mt 18, 17f; 28, 18-20; Lk 10, 16; Jn 14, 16f. 26; 16, 13; 20, 21; Eph 4, 11f; Heb 13, 7. 17; 1 Jn 4, 6.

Circumcision, Law of, Gn 17, 10-14; Lv 12, 3;

—ceased under the New Testament, Rom 2, 26-29; 3, 30; Col 2, 11;

—of the heart, Dt 10, 16; Jer 4, 4; Rom 2, 29; Col 2, 11.

Commandments, of God, twice written on stone on Mount Sinai, Ex 20; 31, 18; 34, 28.

Communion in one kind, sufficient for salvation, Jn 6, 51 57 58;
—body and blood of Christ now inseparable, Rom 6, 9;
—mention of one kind alone, Lk 24, 30f; Acts 2, 42. 46; 20, 7; 1 Cor 10, 17.

Concupiscence, forbidden and punished, Ex 20, 17; Nm 11, 33; 21, 5; Jos 7; Sir 18, 30; 19, 1; 41, 21; 42, 11; Jb 31, 1; Prv 6, 25; Mt 5, 28; Mk 4, 19; Gal 5, 16; Col 3, 5; 1 Thes 4, 3; 1 Tm 5, 6. 11; 2 Tm 2, 22; 1 Cor 10, 6; 2 Pt 1, 4; 1 Jn 2, 16; Jas 1, 14; 4, 1.

Confession of sins, Nm 5, 6f; Mt 3, 6; Acts 19, 18; Jas 5, 16;
—obligation of confession is gathered from the judiciary power of binding and loosing, forgiving and retaining sins, given to the pastors of Christ's Church, Mt 18, 18; Jn 20, 22f.

Confidence in God, Pss 27, 1; 46, 2f; 118, 6. 8; 125, 1; Prv 3, 5; Wis 3, 9; Sir 11, 21; Jer 17, 5-8; Dn 3, 40; Lk 12, 32; Jn 14, 1; 16, 33.

Conscience, the happiness of a good, Prv 15, 15; Sir 13, 23; 1 Jn 3, 21; 2 Cor 1, 12;
—confusion of a bad, Wis 17, 11f;
—of others must be respected, Rom 14, 1-4. 10. 13. 15. 16. 21.

Conscientious Objection, Ex 23, 2; Dt 32, 35; Mt 5, 39. 44; Lk 6, 27-29. 31-33. 35; Acts 4, 19; 5, 29; Rom 12, 17-21; 1 Thes 5, 15; Heb 10, 30; 12, 14; 1 Pt 3, 9.

Consulting, the Lord and his ministers when in doubt, Gn 25, 22; Ex 19, 17; Lv 24, 12; Nm 9, 8; 15, 34f; 27, 4f; Dt 1, 17; 17, 8; Jos 9, 14; Jgs 1, 1; 18, 5; 20, 18; 21, 2; 1 Sm 10, 22; 23, 4; 30, 8; 2 Sm 2, 1; 5, 19; 21, 1; 1 Kgs 14, 2; 22, 5; 2 Kgs 3, 11; 8, 8; 22, 13; 2 Chr 18, 4; 33, 18; Ps 119, 24; Is 8, 11; 30, 1; 45, 11; Jer 37, 5; 43, 2; Ez 14, 2; Zec 7, 2; Tb 4, 19; Sir 37, 15; Lk 16, 29;
—diviners and soothsayers not to be consulted, Lv 19, 31; 20, 6; Dt 18, 10f; 1 Kgs 22, 6; 2 Kgs 1, 2; 3, 13; 2 Chr 18, 5; Dn 4, 4f.

Continency, possible, Mt 19, 11f;
—vow of, binding, Dt 23, 22;
—breach of vow of, 1 Tm 5, 12;
—practice commended, 1 Cor 7, 7f. 27. 37. 38. 40;
—for the clergy, 1 Cor 7, 32. 33. 35.

Contrition, commended and preached, Jer 3, 1. 11; 4, 1; Mt 3, 2; 4, 17; Lk 13, 3; 24, 47; Acts 2, 38; 3, 19; 8, 22; 17, 30; 20, 21; 26, 20;
—remission of sins promised to true contrition, Ex 4, 29-31; 30, 2f; 1 Sm 7, 3; 2 Chr 7, 14; 30, 6; 34, 27f; Jb 22, 23-25; Prv 28, 13; Is 1, 16-18; 30, 18; 55, 7; 59, 20;

Jer 3, 17; 18, 8; 29, 12f; 31, 18; Ez 18, 21; Jon 3, 9; Zec 1, 3; Sir 18, 19f; Acts 3, 19; 26, 18. 20.

Conversion, comes from God, 1 Kgs 18, 37; Jer 3, 18; Rom 15, 18;
—prayer for, Ps 51, 12; Lk 18, 13; of Jews, Acts 2, 41-47; 3, 25-26; 4, 4. 32;
—of Paul, Acts 9, 1-22;
—of Gentiles predicted, Is 49, 6; Jl 2, 28-32; accomplished, Acts 8, 26-39; 10, 11-13; Eph 2, 11-17.

Correction, fraternal, Gn 37, 21; Prv 10, 17; 12, 1; 13, 1; 15, 31; 17, 10; 24, 25; 25, 12; 27, 5; 28, 23; 29, 1; Eccl 7, 5; Sir 20, 1; 21, 6; Hos 4, 4; Mt 18, 15; Gal 2, 11; 1 Tm 5, 20; Heb 3, 13; Jas 5, 19;
—qualities for correcting, Mt 7, 3; Jn 8, 7; Ti 1, 6-9.

Councils of the Church, gathered in Christ's name are assisted by Christ, Mt 18, 20;
—assisted by the Holy Spirit, Acts 15, 28;
—decrees diligently to be observed by the faithful, Acts 15, 41; 16, 4. See Church Guides.

Creation, of heaven and earth, Gn 1, 1;
—of man, Gn 1, 26f;
—of woman, Gn 2, 21f.

Cross and Tribulation, lot of all who wish to live piously, Ps 34, 20; Sir 2, 1; Mt 16, 24; 1 Thes 3, 3; 2 Tm 3, 12;
—folly of the cross, 1 Cor 1, 18;
—crosses sent us by God for our good, 2 Cor 11, 30; 1 Pt 3, 14. 17; 4, 12-18;
—cross to be borne patiently and joyfully, Mt 5, 12; 10, 38; 16, 24; Jas 1, 2.

— D —

Damnation, eternal, prepared for the devil and the reprobate, Wis 5; Jb 10, 22; Is 24, 5f. 17. 22; 30, 33; Dn 7, 11; Mt 3, 12; 5, 29; 13, 50; 22, 13; Lk 3, 17; 16, 22ff; Heb 10, 27; 2 Pt 2, 4; Rv 19, 20; 20, 10f; 21, 8.

Dance, effects of, Ex 32, 6. 19; Jgs 11, 34; 21, 21; 2 Sm 6, 14; Ps 149, 3; Eccl 3, 4; Jer 31, 13; Mt 14, 6.

Day, of light, Gn 1, 5. 16; Jn 9, 4; 11, 9;
—period of time, Gn 1, 5. 8. 14; 2, 2;
—epoch, Ps 50, 15; Is 2, 11f. 17; Lk 19, 42;
—day of rest, the sabbath, Ex 16, 23; 20, 8-11; Lk 6, 6-10;
—day of the Lord (Yahweh), Is 2, 6-21; Jl 2, 1ff; Am 5, 18ff; Zeph 1, 14ff;
—day of the Lord (Jesus), 1 Cor 1, 8; 1 Thes 5, 2. 4;
—day of judgment, Mt 10, 15; 12, 36. 41f; Lk 10, 14; Acts 17, 31; 2 Pt 2, 9; 1 Jn 4, 17; Jude 6;

—last day, Jn 6, 39; 11, 24; 12, 48;
—last days, Acts 2, 17; 2 Tm 3, 1; 2 Pt 3, 3.

Dead, mourning for the, Sir 22, 11; 38, 16. 23; Jn 11, 35;
—praying for the, 2 Mc 12, 43-46;
—resurrection of, Jb 19, 26f; Is 26, 19; Dn 12, 2; Jn 5, 25. 28f; 1 Cor 15, 12. 42.

Death, Gn 3, 17-19; Nm 23, 10; 2 Sm 14, 14; 1 Kgs 2, 1f; Jb 30, 23; 34, 15; Ps 89, 49; Eccl 2, 16; 3, 19f; 8, 8; 9, 10. 12; 12, 1-7; Wis 1, 13; 2, 23f; 3, 1; 4, 7; 7, 6; Sir 7, 36; 10, 11; 14, 17-19; 38, 23; 41, 1-4. 11. 13; Jn 9, 4; Rom 5, 12; 1 Cor 15, 21f. 26.

Despair, causes of, Lv 26, 36-39; Dt 28, 15. 34. 67; Jer 2, 26-28; Rom 7, 23f; Rv 6, 16; 16, 10;
—remedy for, Dt 20, 3f; Pss 31, 24f; 27, 14; 42, 12; Lk 18, 1; 2 Cor 4, 8f; Gal 6, 9; Heb 12, 2f.

Detraction, forbidden and punished, Ps 15, 3; Prv 10, 18; 11, 13; 16, 28; 20, 19; 26, 20; Eccl 10, 20; Rom 1, 30; 2 Cor 12, 20; 1 Pt 2, 1; Jas 4, 11.

Devil, always seeks to injure men, Gn 3, 1; 1 Chr 21, 1; Jb 1, 11; Zec 3, 1; Lk 8, 12; Acts 13, 8; Eph 6, 11; Rv 2, 10; 12, 9;
—tempts our Lord, Mt 4, 1-11;
—transforms himself into an angel of light, 2 Cor 11, 14;
—his empire destroyed by Christ, Mt 12, 25-29; Lk 10, 18; 11, 20-22; Jn 12, 31; Col 1, 13; 2 Tm 1, 10; Heb 2, 14; 1 Jn 3, 8; Rv 20, 9.

Divorce, allowed in the Old Law, Dt 24, 1-4;
—forbidden in the New, Mt 5, 31f; 19, 3-9; Mk 10, 2-12; Lk 16, 18; 1 Cor 7, 10-13.

Drunkenness, calls forth the ire of God, Is 5, 11. 22; 28, 1; Dn 5, 2; Jl 1, 4f; 1 Cor 6, 10;
—causes one to lose his reason, Prv 20, 1; Hos 7, 5; Eph 5, 18;
—reveals secrets, Hb 2, 15;
—excites one to quarrels and disputes, Prv 20, 1; 23, 29f; Sir 31, 29f; Hos 7, 5.

— E —

Ecumenism, Jn 17, 9-11. 20-23; Eph 4, 3-16; 1 Cor 10, 17; 12, 12-27; Rom 12, 5; 9, 6-8; Mt 7, 21-23.

Elect, Christ, Lk 23, 35; 1 Pt 2, 4. 6 (Is 42, 1);
—Israel, Dt 14, 2; Is 14, 1; Ps 105, 6. 43;
—the Church, Mt 24, 22. 24. 31; Lk 18, 7; Rom 8, 33; 2 Tm 2, 10; 1 Pt 1, 2; 2, 9.

Enemies, attitude toward, Ex 23, 4f; Dt 23, 35; 1 Kgs 3, 11; Jb 31, 29; Mt 5, 24. 38f; Lk 6, 29; Rom 12, 17ff;

—God saves from enemies, 1 Sm 12, 11; Ezr 8, 31; Pss 18, 47-49, 59, 1-5; Acts 16, 19-40;

—punishment for enemies of God, Ex 15, 6f; Dt 32, 41; Ps 68, 2f; 2 Thes 1, 6-9; Rv 21, 8.

Envy, Ps 37, 1; Prv 3, 31; 14, 30; Wis 2, 24; 6, 23; Sir 30, 24; 40, 5; Mt 27, 18; Acts 5, 17; Phil 1, 15.

Eternity of Hell's torments, Mt 3, 12; 25, 41. 46; Mk 9, 43-46. 48; Lk 3, 17; 2 Thes 1, 7-9; Jude 6-7; Rv 14, 10f; 20, 10. **See** also Is 33, 14.

Eucharist, real presence of the body and blood of Christ, Mt 26, 26-28; Mk 14, 22-24; Lk 22, 19f; Jn 6, 51f; 1 Cor 10, 16; 11, 24f. 27. 29.

Excommunication, used by the Apostles, 1 Cor 5, 3-5. 9-13; 2 Thes 3, 6. 14; 1 Tm 1, 20; Ti 3, 10f;

—of the Pharisees, Jn 9, 22. 34; 12, 42; 16, 2.

Expiation, effected under the old law, Lv 1; 4; 5; 16; Heb 9, 7. 13;

—effected by Christ, Lk 19, 22; Jn 1, 29. 36; Rom 5, 6-10; 1 Cor 1, 30; Gal 4, 5; Eph 2, 13-18; Heb 9, 12. 14. 28; 1 Pt 3, 8.

— F —

Faith, necessary to salvation, Mk 16, 16; Acts 2, 44-47; 4, 12; Heb 11, 6;

—without good works is dead, Jas 2, 14. 17. 20;

—alone, does not justify, Jas 2, 24;

—working with charity, Gal 5, 6;

—does not imply an absolute assurance of our being in grace; much less of our eternal salvation, Rom 11, 20-22; 1 Cor 9, 27; 10, 12; Phil 2, 12; Rv 3, 11.

Fasting, commended in Scripture, Jl 2, 12;

—practiced by God's servants, Ezr 8, 23; Neh 1, 4; Dn 10, 3;

—moves God to mercy, Jon 3, 5. 10;

—of great efficacy against the devil, Mt 9, 15; Mk 2, 20; Lk 5, 35; **See** also Acts 13, 3; 14, 22; 2 Cor 6, 5; 11, 27;

—the obligation of, Jl 2, 12; Tb 12, 8; Mt 6, 16; Mk 2, 20; Lk 2, 36f; 5, 35; Acts 13, 2f; 14, 22; Rom 13, 13f; 2 Cor 6, 5; 11, 27; Eph 5, 18; 1 Thes 5, 6; 1 Pt 1, 13; 5, 8;

—merits of, Jer 35, 14. 19; Jon 3, 7. 9f; Jdt 4, 8; 8, 6; Mt 6, 17; Lk 2, 37; 1 Sm 31, 13; 2 Sm 1, 12;

—Christ fasting for forty days, Mt 4, 2;

Fear of God, and keep him always before our eyes, Ex 20, 20; Dt 4, 10; 6, 2. 13; 10, 12; 13, 5; Jos 24, 14; 2 Kgs 17, 36; 2 Chr 19, 7; Ps 27, 1; 33, 8; Mt 10, 28; Lk 12, 5; 1 Pt 2, 17; Rv 14, 7;

—is the beginning of wisdom, Prv 9, 10;

—is the source of life, Prv 14, 27;

—surpasses all else, Sir 25, 11;

—fruit of the fear of God and his praise, Gn 20, 11; Dt 6, 24; Jb 28, 28; Ps 103, 17; 111, 5; 112, 1; Prv 8, 13; 10, 27; 14, 26; 16, 6; Sir 1, 9-18; 40, 26; Acts 9, 31;

—not opposed to faith, Eccl 9, 1; Sir 2, 8; Rom 11, 20; Heb 3, 14; 4, 1.

Fidelity, demanded by God of his servants, Mt 24, 45f; 25, 21. 23; Lk 12, 42-46; 1 Cor 4, 2;

—toward men, Dt 1, 16f; Ps 141, 5; Prv 11, 13; Lk 16, 10; 1 Tm 3, 11; Ti 2, 10;

—God's fidelity, Pss 36, 5; 40, 11f; 100, 5; Rom 3, 3.

Fornication, provokes God's anger, Dt 22, 21; Jer 5, 7; Hos 4, 14; 1 Cor 6, 9; Heb 13, 4;

—occasions of, to be avoided, Sir 9, 4; 42, 12;

—desire of, forbidden, Ex 20, 17; Mt 5, 28;

—idolatry so called, Dt 31, 16.

Fraud, condemned, Jer 9, 6; Ps 35, 20-23; Prv 12, 17; Mk 7, 21f; Acts 5, 2; Rom 1, 29.

Free-will, Gn 4, 7; Dt 30, 19; Sir 15, 14;

—often resists the grace of God, Prv 1, 24; Is 5, 4; Ez 18, 23. 31f; 33, 11; Mt 23, 37; Lk 13, 34; Acts 7, 51; Heb 12, 15; 2 Pt 3, 9; Rv 20, 4.

Friend, not to be listened to against God, Dt 13, 6; 33, 9;

—pretended, Ps 41, 10; Jn 13, 18;

—Jonathan's friendship for David, 1 Sm 19, 1; 20, 2. 30;

—the rich have many friends, Prv 14, 20;

—a friend loves at all times, Prv 17, 17;

—tells the truth, Prv 24, 26;

—better than a brother, Prv 18, 24; 27, 10;

—some not to be taken as, Prv 20, 19; 22, 24;

—a giver has many friends, Prv 19, 6;

—marks of a true friend, Prv 6, 11. 17; 17, 17; 24, 26; Eccl 4, 9f.

Friendship, Lv 19, 18; Jb 6, 14; Prv 3, 28f; 6, 1f; 11, 12; 17, 17; 19, 4; 25, 9f; 27, 6. 10. 17; Sir 6, 1-17; 9, 14f; 12, 8f; 14, 13; 19, 12-16; 20, 15f; 22, 19-26; 25, 9; 37, 1-6.

— G —

Gentiles, conversion of, Gn 49, 10; Nm 24, 17; Pss 2, 8; 68, 33; 82, 8; 87, 4; Is 2, 2; 11, 10; Jer 9, 24; Hos 2, 1; Mi 4, 2; Zep 3, 8f; Zec 2, 11; Mt 8, 11; Jn 10, 16; Acts 8, 26f; 1 Cor 12, 12f.

Gifts of God, Jesus, Jn 3, 16; 2 Cor 9, 15;

—the Holy Spirit, Lk 11, 13; Acts 2, 38;

—salvation, Eph 2, 8;

—eternal life, Jn 10, 28; Rom 6, 23; 1 Jn 5, 11;

—grace and glory, Ps 84, 12; Jas 4, 6;

—various spiritual gifts, 1 Cor 1, 7; 12, 1-11; Jas 1, 17.

Glory, of God, to be sought in all things, Jos 7, 19; Ps 115, 1; Mt 6, 9; Jn 17, 4; Acts 3, 13; 12, 23; 1 Cor 6, 20; 10, 31; Phil 1, 20; Col 3, 17; Ti 2, 10.

Gluttony, Gn 25, 29. 34; Prv 21, 17; 23, 20f; Sir 37, 26-30; Heb 12, 16f.

God, a pure spirit and self-existent, Ex 3, 14. 16; 6, 2; Jn 4, 24;

—He is one, Dt 6, 4; 32, 39; Wis 12, 13; Is 43, 10; 44, 6; 45, 6; Eph 4, 5f;

—there are three persons in one God, the Creator — Elohim (plural), Gn 1, 1. 2. 26; the Son, Heb 1, 8-10; the Spirit of God, Jb 33, 4; revealed at the baptism of Jesus, Mt 3, 16f; at the transfiguration, Lk 9, 28-35; by Jesus, Mt 28, 19; Jn 3, 16; 5, 21-23; 14, 16f;

—he is infinite, Jb 36, 26; Ps 145, 3; Wis 11, 23;

—eternal, Jb 36, 26; Ps 90, 2; 102, 25; Is 57, 15; Dn 7, 14;

—unchangeable, Nm 23, 19; Ps 102, 26; Mal 3, 6; Jas 1, 17;

—omniscient, 2 Chr 16, 9; Est 14, 14; Jb 21, 22; 28, 24; 34, 21; Ps 139, 1-6. 16; Prv 16, 2; Sir 39, 20; Dn 13, 42; 1 Cor 2, 10; Heb 4, 13; 1 Jn 3, 20;

—almighty, Gn 17, 1; Jb 9, 13; 11, 10; 23, 13; Prv 21, 30f; Wis 11, 22f; 16, 13. 15; Sir 43; Is 44, 24;

—Creator of all things, Gn 1, 1. 31; 2, 4; Pss 33, 6f; 74, 16f; 148, 4-6; Is 37, 16; 45, 18; Jn 1, 3; Acts 17, 24; Col 1, 16; Heb 3, 4; 11, 3; Rv 4, 11;

—his fidelity, Dt 7, 9. 12; 32, 4; Ps 100, 5; Is 49, 7; 1 Cor 1, 9; 2 Thes 3, 3; Heb 10, 23; 1 Jn 1, 9;

—his justice, Dt 32, 4; 1 Sm 26, 23; Jb 34, 10. 12. 19; Pss 11, 7; 119, 75. 137. 142; Eccl 7, 14; 12, 14; Sir 35, 12. 16; Acts 10, 34f; Rom 11, 22. 33;

—his mercy, Ex 20, 6; 34, 6; Nm 14, 18; Pss 25, 10; 33, 5; 103, 8. 11. 17; 118, 1; 136; 145, 9; Sir 18, 11f; Is 30, 18; Lam 3, 32; Hb 3, 2; Lk 1, 50; Jas 2, 13;

—his grace, Ps 33, 22; Lk 2, 40; Acts 13, 43; 20, 24; Rom 9, 15; 2 Cor 12, 9; 1 Pt 5, 10;

—loves all men, Wis 11, 23f. 26; 12, 2; Jer 31, 3; Hos 11, 4; Jn 3, 16; 16, 27; Rom 5, 8f; 8, 32; 1 Tm 2, 4;

—wills all to be saved, Wis 1, 13; Ez 18, 32; Mt 23, 37; Jn 6, 39f; 1 Tm 2, 4.

Good Works, meritorious, Gn 4, 7; 22, 16. 18; Pss 18, 21. 23-25; 19, 8.

11; Mt 5, 11f; 10, 42; 16, 27; 1 Cor 3, 8; 2 Tm 4, 8.

Gospel, the preaching of, Gn 3, 15; Is 53, 1; 55, 5; 61, 1; Mt 1, 21; 11, 28; 28, 19f; Mk 16, 15; Lk 2, 10; 24; 46f; Jn 3, 16; 6, 35; 8, 12; 10, 9; 12, 46; Rom 1, 16; 3, 21. 24f; 8, 3; 1 Cor 1, 17. 23; 4, 15; 15, 1; 2 Cor 5, 18; Gal 1, 6. 11; Eph 1, 13; 1 Tm 1, 15; 2 Tm 1, 8; 2, 8; 1 Pt 4, 17.

Grace, spoken of in Scripture as a favor, Gn 6, 8; 18, 3; 19, 19; 39, 21; Ex 12, 36; Ru 2, 20; 2 Sm 2, 6; 15, 20; Tb 3, 13; Est 2, 17; Prv 13, 15; Dn 1, 9; Acts 2, 47; 25, 9;
—as a reward expected from God, Prv 1, 9; 12, 2; 2 Mc 12, 46; Lk 6, 33; 1 Pt 2, 19;
—as a supernatural gift, Ps 84, 12; Lk 1, 28; 2, 40; Jn 1, 16; Rom 1, 7; 1 Cor 16, 23; 2 Cor 1, 12; Gal 5, 4f; Heb 13, 9; Jas 4, 6;
—before and after meals, Dt 8, 10; 1 Sm 9, 13; Is 62, 9; Mt 14, 19; 15, 36; 26, 26; Mk 6, 41; 8, 6; 14, 22; Lk 9, 16; Jn 6, 11. 23; Acts 27, 35; Rom 14, 6; 1 Cor 10, 30; 1 Tm 4, 3.

Gratitude, recommended, Nm 15, 18-20; Dt 4, 9; 2 Chr 15, 11; Sir 7, 21; Acts 4, 21; Eph 5, 19f; Phil 4, 6; Col 2, 7; 3, 15.

— H —

Happiness, condition for, Dt 4, 40; 5, 29. 33; Pss 32, 1f; 40, 5; 84, 6. 13; 128, 1; Prv 3, 13; 29, 18; Is 56, 1f; Mt 5, 1-12; Lk 11, 28; Jn 13, 17; Rom 4, 7f.

Hardness, of heart, insensibility punished, Jb 20, 19; Prv 21, 10; Mt 18, 30. 34; 25, 42; Jas 2, 13;
—hard-heartedness of the Egyptians to the Hebrews, Ex 1, 13;
—of the rich man (Dives), Lk 16, 21.

Hatred, forbidden, Lv 19, 17;
—of God's enemies, Ps 139, 21;
—reconciliation enjoined, Mt 5, 23f;
—of the world for the disciples of Christ, Mk 13, 13;
—of evil, Ps 97, 10; Am 6, 8.

Heart, purified and sanctified by our Lord, Ps 1, 12; Jn 13, 10; 15, 3; Acts 15, 9; 1 Cor 6, 11; Heb 1, 3; 9, 14; 10, 14; 13, 12;
—God accepts a man's heart or good will as an action, Gn 4, 4; 22, 12; Ex 25, 2; 35, 5; Dt 19, 5f; Mt 15, 8; Mk 12, 41-44; Lk 21, 1-4; 2 Cor 8, 12.

Heaven, joys of, Ps 16, 11; Dn 12, 3; Mt 5, 12; 13, 43; Jn 12, 26; 14, 3; 17, 24; 1 Cor 13, 12; Rv 7, 16;
—those who will attain it, Pss 15, 2; 24, 3f; Mt 5, 8; 25, 33-40; Rom 8, 17; Phil 4, 3; Heb 12, 23; Rv 3, 5;

—new heaven, Is 65, 17; 66, 22; 2 Pt 3, 13; Rv 21, 1.

Hell, pains of, Dt 32, 22; Jb 24, 19; Pss 21, 10; 112, 10; Sir 21, 10; Is 33, 14; 34, 9; Jer 9, 15; Mal 4, 1; Mt 8, 12; Lk 13, 28; Rv 14, 10;
—proportioned to sins, Wis 11, 16; Lk 16, 25; Rv 18, 7;
—endless, Is 66, 24; Mt 25, 41; 2 Thes 1, 9.

Holy Scripture, divinely inspired, 2 Tm 3, 16f; 2 Pt 1, 21;
—purpose of, to instruct, Dt 6, 6-9; Ps 19, 8. 12; Rom 15, 4; give spiritual nourishment, Dt 8, 3; Mt 4, 4; 1 Pt 2, 2; lead to faith, Jn 20, 31; sanctify, Jn 17, 17; Eph 5, 26; edify, Acts 20, 32; 2 Tm 3, 16f;
—fulfilled by Christ, Mt 5, 17; Lk 24, 25-27; Jn 19, 30;
—explained by the apostles, Acts 2, 16-21. 25-36; Rom 3, 10-18;
—danger of rejecting them, Jn 12, 48; Heb 2, 2-4; 10, 28-31.

Holy Spirit, his divinity, Acts 5, 3f; 28, 25f; 1 Cor 2, 10f; 6, 11. 19f. **See** also Mt 12, 31f; Acts 13, 2; 20, 28; 2 Cor 13, 13 and the solemn form of baptism, Mt 28, 19f;
—proceeds from the Father and the Son, Jn 15, 26;
—his works, Gn 1, 2; Jb 33, 14; Ps 104, 30; Jn 3, 3-8; 6, 63; 14, 16f. 26; 16, 12-14; Rom 5, 5; 8, 14. 26; Gal 5, 18; Eph 6, 18; Phil 3, 3; governs the work of the Church, Acts 13, 2. 4; 20, 22. 28;
—dwells within the followers of Christ, Jn 14, 16f.

Hope, in God, Pss 31, 25; 71, 5; Is 8, 17; Jer 14, 22; Rom 15, 13; Acts 24, 15; 1 Tm 4, 10;
—in Christ, Acts 28, 20; 1 Cor 15, 19; 1 Tm 1, 1;
—effects of, Rom 5, 5; 12, 12; 2 Cor 3, 12; Heb 3, 6; 1 Jn 3, 3.

Hospitality, commended, Tb 4, 7; Lk 14, 13; Rom 12, 13; 1 Tm 3, 2; 3 Jn 5;
—examples of, Gn 18; 19; 24; Jgs 13, 15; 1 Kgs 17, 10-16;
—want of, punished, Jgs 8, 5-9; 19, 18; 1 Sm 25; Wis 19, 13.

Humility, agreeable to God, Gn 18, 27; 29, 31; Jgs 6, 15; 1 Sm 1; 2, 18; 7, 9f; 2 Sm 6, 16. 21; 2 Chr 12, 6-8. 12; 32, 26; 33, 12; 34, 26f; Jdt 4, 7. 11; Sir 3, 17-27; Is 37, 1; Jer 1, 6; Mt 3, 11; Mk 9, 34; Jn 13, 4f; Acts 10, 25; Rom 11, 20; 12, 16; 1 Cor 4, 6; Phil 2, 3; Col 3, 12; Heb 11, 24-26; 1 Pt 5, 5; Jas 1, 9; 4, 10; Rv 4, 10f; 19, 10.

Hypocrisy, described. Prv 26, 23-26; Ez 33, 30-33; Mt 23, 14; Col 2, 18; 2 Tm 3, 5;
—condemned, Is 29, 15; 32, 5; Mt 23, 13-36;
—exhortations to avoid, Mt 6, 2; Jas 3, 17; 1 Pt 2, 1.

— I —

Idolatry, folly and sin of, Wis 13-15; Jer 10, 1-16; Is 46, 1;
—forbidden, Ex 20, 4;
—punished, Ex 32, 27f. 35; Wis 14, 30.

Ignorance, dangers of, Acts 3, 17; 17, 29-31; Eph 4, 18f; 1 Pt 1, 14;
—mercy of God for the ignorant, Acts 17, 30; 1 Tm 1, 13; Heb 5, 2; Ps 19, 13.

Image, man created in God's, Gn 1, 26f; 1 Cor 11, 7;
—Christ is image of God, 2 Cor 4, 4; Phil 2, 6; Col 1, 15; Heb 1, 3.

Immortality, of God, 1 Tm 1, 17; 6, 16; 2 Tm 1, 10;
—of men, Rom 2, 7; 1 Cor 15, 53.

Imposition, of hands, Gn 48, 14; Ex 29, 10; Lv 1, 4; Nm 27, 23; Dn 13, 34; Mk 10, 16;
—in confirmation, Acts 8, 17; 19, 6;
—in holy orders, Acts 6, 6; 13, 3; 1 Tm 4, 14; 5, 22; 2 Tm 1, 6.

Infidelity, punished, Gn 19, 11. 17. 26; Nm 11, 21-23; 14, 2. 11; 20, 12; Dt 9, 20; 2 Kgs 7, 2. 17; Sir 2, 12-15 Mt 8, 28ff; 14, 30; 17, 17-19; 24, 25; Jn 3, 18. 36; 8, 24; 12, 48; 20, 27; Rom 11, 20; Heb 3, 18; 4, 2; 11, 6; Rv 21, 8.

Ingratitude, punishment for, Gn 31, 1ff; Ex 1, 8; Jgs 2, 1-3; 1 Sm 10, 18f; 2 Sm 14, 30; 2 Chr 24, 20-22; Prv 17, 13; Wis 16, 29; Is 1, 2; Jer 2, 5f; Ez 16; Hos 10, 1-4; Mi 6, 3f; 1 Mc 16. 16f. 19; Mt 11, 20; Lk 17, 18; Jn 11, 46; Rom 1, 21; 2 Tm 3, 2.

Injustice, not to be attributed to God, Jb 1, 22; 34, 10; Jn 7, 18; Rom 3, 5f;
—not to be committed, Ex 22, 21; Ps 82, 2f; Prv 22, 16; Jer 22, 3; Lk 16, 10;
—retribution, Jb 4, 8; Prv 28, 8; Is 10, 1-4; Am 8, 5-9; 2 Thes 2, 12; 2 Pt 2, 9.

— J —

Jews, their reprobation announced by St. Paul, Rom 10, 1:
—persecute the apostles, Acts 5, 18;
—three thousand converted, Acts 2, 41;
—five thousand converted, Acts 4, 4;
—Greek Jews murmur as to alms, Acts 6, 1;
—rise against St. Stephen, Acts 7;
—gospel preached to, Acts 11, 19;
—resist St. Paul, Acts 13, 45;
—abandoned for the Gentiles, Acts 13, 46;
—persecute St. Paul, Acts 13, 50;
—do themselves what they condemn,

Rom 2, 1;
—their privileges over the Gentiles, Rom 3, 1;
—their salvation excites St. Paul's zeal, Rom 9, 1. 3;
—their fall does not make void God's promises, Rom 9, 6;
—zeal of the ignorant Jews, Rom 10, 2;
—their incredulity opposed, Rom 10, 21;
—their future recall, Rom 11, 26;
—Christ promised to them, Rom 15, 5;
—the cross a scandal to them, 1 Cor 1, 23;
—Jews in tutelage under the law, Gal 4, 2;
—their union with the Gentiles, Eph 2, 19;
—true Jews, Rom 2, 28f.

Joy, of the People of God, 1 Kgs 1, 40; Ezr 6, 16; Ps 149, 2; Is 35, 1f; Hb 3, 18; Mt 2, 10; Jn 15, 11; Acts 2, 46; Rom 14, 17; 2 Cor 8, 2;
—follows afflictions, Pss 30, 5f; 126, 5f; Is 35, 10; 66, 10-14; Jn 16, 20-22; Jas 1, 2-4;
—sources of, 2 Chr 20, 27; Ps 89, 16f; Is 61, 10; Lk 10, 20f; Acts 2, 28; Rom 15, 13;
—in heaven over repentant sinners, Lk 15, 7. 10;
—vanity of human joys, Eccl 2; 12, 1f; Is 16, 10.

Judgment, men should examine before judging, after the example of God, Gn 3, 9-19; 11, 5; 18, 21; Ex 3, 7f; 23, 2; Dt 13, 4; 17, 9; 19, 18; Jos 7, 19; 23, 12f; Jgs 20, 3. 12; Prv 18, 13; Sir 11, 7-9; 1 Mc 7, 7;
—we must not judge rashly, Mt 7, 1; 12, 7; Lk 7, 33f; Jn 7, 24; 9, 16; Acts 28, 3-6; Rom 14, 4. 13; 1 Cor 4, 5; 1 Tm 5, 21;
—last judgment announced by our Lord, and reserved to him alone, Jn 5, 22;
—last judgment described, Mt 25, 31-46; Rv 6, 14-17; 7; 8, 9;
—particular judgment, Wis 3, 1f; Eccl 8, 6-8; 11, 9; 12, 14; Sir 11, 28f; 16, 13-22; 2 Mc 12, 43-46; Lk 16, 19-31; Heb 9, 27; 10, 31.

Justification, through faith, Rom 1, 17; 3, 20-30; 4; 5; Gal 3, 11; Acts 13, 39.

— K —

Kingdom, of God, 1 Chr 29, 11; Is 24, 23; Dn 2, 44; Mt 6, 10; Lk 11, 2; Acts 1, 3;
—of Christ, Is 2, 1-5; 29, 17-24; 61, 4-9; Mt 26, 29; Jn 18, 36f;
—of heaven, Mt 3, 2; 5, 19; 7, 21; 23, 13;
—parables of, Mt 13, 1-52; 20, 1-16; 22, 2-14; 25.

— L —

Law, the first, given, Gn 2, 16;
—the first, violated, Gn 3, 4-6;
—of the ten commandments given to Moses, Ex 20; Dt 5;
—tablets, of the, given, Ex 31, 18; Dt 5, 22;
tablets, of the, broken, Ex 32, 19; Dt 9, 17;
—other tablets, of the, given, Ex 34, 27; Dt 10, 1;
—the Old and the New, Rom 3, 20; 4, 15; 5, 20; 7, 1-7; Gal 3, 19; 1 Tm 1, 8; Heb 7, 18-27;
—the natural, Rom 1, 18-23; 2, 12-16;
—ceremonies of the, abrogated by Christ, Mt 15, 1-20; Mk 15, 38; Acts 13, 38; 15, 11; Rom 6, 14; 7, 4; 8, 3; Gal 3, 13; 4, 5; Eph 2, 13; Col 2, 14; 1 Pt 1, 11-19.

Lepers, healed, Kgs 5, 14; Mt 8, 2f; Mk 1, 40-42; Lk 17, 12-14.

Leprosy, different kinds of, and their marks; law as to, Lv 13;
—sacrifices for the purification of; leprosy in houses, Lv 14;
—God strikes sinners with leprosy, Nm 12; Dt 24, 9; 2 Kgs 15, 5.

Liberty, evangelical, Jn 8, 32; Rom 6, 18; 8, 2. 21; Gal 5, 13; 1 Pt 1, 18; 2, 16; 2 Pt 2, 19;
—evil and condemned liberty, Jer 34, 14ff.

Light, Jesus Christ is the light of the world, Is 9, 2; 49, 6; 60, 1. 19; 62, 1; Jn 1, 5; 8, 12; 9, 5; 12, 36. 46; 1 Jn 1, 5; 2, 8
—how Christians are, Prv 4, 19; Mt 5, 14; Rom 2, 19; Phil 2, 15.

— M —

Magic, its ineffectiveness, Is 44, 25; 47, 9;
—condemned, Is 57, 3; Mal 3, 5; Acts 13, 6-11; 19, 19; Gal 5, 20; Rv 21, 8; 22, 15.

Man, creation and dignity, Gn 1, 26f; 2, 7; Dt 4, 32; Eccl 7, 29; Is 43, 7; 45, 12; 1 Cor 11, 7;
—his fall, Gn 3, 2 Cor 11, 3;
—his sinful state, Ps 51, 1-6. 9-12; Rom 3, 13-18; 7, 18; 1 Jn 1, 8;
—his weakness, Jb 14, 1-12; Pss 39, 5-14; 103, 14-16; Eccl 12, 4-10; Mt 6, 27; 1 Cor 3, 7;
—his redemption, Rom 5; 1 Cor 1, 30; Gal 3, 14; Eph 3; Col 1, 12-29; Heb 2, 9-18; 1 Pt 1, 18f;
—lot of wicked man, Jb 18, 5-21; 8, 11-15; of the child of God, Ps 31, 16; Acts 13, 48; 22, 14; 1 Thes 3, 5; 1 Pt 1, 3-5.

Mary, mother of God, foretold and prefigured, Gn 3, 15; Pss 45, 10; 46, 5; 85, 2; 87, 3; 132, 8; Prv 31, 10-31; Song; Sir 24; Is 7, 14; 11, 1; 19, 1; 45, 8; Jer 31, 22;

—called mother of our Lord, Lk 1, 43;
—mother of Jesus, Mt 2, 13;
—the angel Gabriel sent to, Lk 1, 26;
—visits St. Elizabeth, Lk 1, 39f;
—composes her canticle, the Magnificat, Lk 1, 46;
—gives birth to our Savior, Mt 1, 16; Lk 2, 7;
—presents Jesus in the temple, Lk 2, 22;
—sorrows prophesied to her, Lk 2, 34f;
—flees into Egypt, Mt 2, 13f;
—returns to Nazareth, Mt 2, 20-23;
—loses him in the temple, Lk 2, 42-51;
—at the foot of the cross, Jn 19, 25;
—St. John given to her as a son, Jn 19, 26f;
—remains with the apostles, Acts 1, 14.

Mass, sacrifice of, prefigured, Gn 14, 18; 22, 13;
—foretold, Mal 1, 10f;
—instituted by Christ, Lk 22, 19f;
—attested, 1 Cor 10, 16. 18-21; Heb 13, 10. **See** Eucharist.

Meekness, commended, Mt 5, 4; Gal 6, 1; Eph 4, 2; Col 3, 12; Ti 3, 2;
—especially to ministers of the Lord, 2 Tm 2, 24f;
—one of the fruits of the Holy Spirit, Gal 5, 23;
—example of Joshua, Jos 7, 19;
—example of David, 1 Sm 25, 32; 2 Sm 16, 10;
—example of Christ, Mt 11, 29;
—a mild answer calms wrath, Prv 15, 1.

Mercy, to our neighbor, 1 Sm 15, 6; 2 Chr 28, 9-15; Pss 112, 4. 8; Prv 14, 21f. 31; Hos 12, 6; Mi 6, 8; Zec 7, 9; Mt 5, 7; 9, 13; 10, 42; 18, 33. 35; 25, 40; Rom 12, 13; Eph 4, 32; Col 3, 12; 1 Tm 5, 10. **See** Almsgiving.

Messiah, he is promised to Adam, Gn 3, 15;
—promised to Abraham, Gn 12, 3; 21, 12; 22, 18;
—he will have a precursor, Mal 3, 1; 4, 5f;
—his birth miraculously announced, Is 7, 14; Jer 23, 5f;
—time of his coming revealed to Daniel, Dn 9, 24ff;
place of his birth designated, Mi 5, 2. 5;
—his reign described, Jer 23, 5;
—his presence in the second temple, Hg 2, 8;
—his abode among men, Is 12, 6;
—he will be rejected by his people, Ps 22, 7; Is 49, 7;
—called the Christ, Jn 1, 41; 4, 25; 7, 41; 11, 27; Mt 26, 63f; Acts 17, 3; 18, 28;
—he is the Lamb of God, Jn 1, 29. 36;
—his passion prefigured and foretold; his birth, life, works and death. **See** Christ.

Moses, the birth of, Ex 2, 1ff; Acts 7, 20;
—the flight to Midian, Ex 2, 11-15;
—takes Zipporah to wife, Ex 2, 21;
—returns to Egypt with his children, Ex 4, 20;
—is sent to Pharaoh in Egypt, Ex 3, 10; 5, 1; 6, 10f; 7; 8; 9; 10;
—prays for the Pharaoh, Ex 8, 21-27; 9, 28-33; 10, 18;
—prays for his people, Ex 14, 15; 17, 4-11; 32, 11. 13. 31; Nm 11, 2; 14, 13-17; 21, 7; Dt 9, 18-26;
—receives the first tablets of the law, Ex 31, 18;
—breaks the tablets of the law, Ex 32, 19;
—accepts the new tablets of the law, Ex 34, 28;
—appears in the transfiguration of Christ, Mt 17, 3; Lk 9, 30f.

— N —

Name, of God, to be venerated, Dt 5, 11; Lv 18, 21; Ps 111, 9; Mi 4, 5; 1 Tm 6, 1; Ez 36, 20f; Lk 1, 49;
—of Christ, to be confessed, Acts 9, 15. 28; 19, 17; 2 Thes 1, 12; 2 Tm 2, 19;
—actions done in Christ's name, Mt 28, 19; Mk 9, 41; Jn 14, 13; 16, 23f; Acts 3, 6; 4, 10; 1 Cor 5, 4f; Eph 5, 20; Col 3, 17; Heb 13, 15;
—salvation in Christ's name, Acts 2, 21; Rom 10, 13; 1 Cor 6, 11; 1 Jn 3, 23; 5, 13.
Neighbor, duties toward, Ex 2, 13; 20, 16; 22, 26; Lv 19, 18; Dt 15, 2; 27, 17; Prv 3, 28; 24, 28; 25, 8. 17; Lk 10, 25-37; Rom 3, 9; Gal 5, 14; Jas 2, 8.

— O —

Obedience, Prv 25, 12; Rom 6, 16; 13, 5; 1 Pt 1, 22;
—to God, Dt 11, 27f; 30, 19f; 1 Sm 15, 22f; Eccl 4, 17; Jer 43, 7; Acts 4, 19;
—to parents, Ex 20, 12; 21, 15. 17; Lv 19, 3; Dt 5, 16; Tb 4, 3f; Prv 19, 26; 30, 17; Sir 3, 1-16; 23, 14; Mt 15, 4; 19, 19; Mk 7, 10; Eph 6, 1-4; 2 Tm 3, 2; Heb 12, 7;
—to masters and those in authority, Eph 6, 5-9; Heb 13, 17;
—of Christ, Lk 2, 51; Phil 2, 8; Heb 5, 8f.
Original Sin, Jb 14, 4; 15, 14; Ps 51, 7; Sir 8, 5; Rom 3, 9. 23; 5, 12;
—its effects, Gn 8, 21; Rom 5, 12. 17; 6, 23; 8, 6-8. 11. 13. 17; Gal 5, 17; Eph 2, 3.

— P —

Pardon, granted by God alone, Mk 2, 7; Lk 5, 21; Ps 51, 6;

—granted in virtue of Christ's blood, Mt 26, 28, Eph 1, 7; Heb 9, 12. 22, 1 Pt 1, 18f; as a result of faith in Jesus, Acts 10, 43; 26, 18; in Christ, Eph 4, 32; Col 1, 14; after repentance, Mk 1, 4; Lk 3, 3; 24, 47; Acts 5, 31; through baptism, Acts 2, 38;
—power to pardon granted by Jesus to disciples, Jn 20, 23;
—happiness of those pardoned, Ps 32, 1; Rom 4, 7;
—pardon, one another, Mt 6, 14f; 18, 23-35; Mk 11, 25f; Lk 6, 37; 2 Cor 2, 7; Eph 4, 32; Col 3, 13; Jas 2, 13.
Parents, their duties, Gn 18, 19; 21, 19; 24, 2; 25, 6; 34, 4ff; 49; Ex 10, 2; 12, 26; 13, 14; 21, 9f; Lv 19, 29; Nm 30, 6; Dt 4, 9; 6, 7; 11, 19; 21, 19; 22, 15; 32, 46, Jos 4, 21; 1 Sm 2, 23; 3, 13; 1 Kgs 2, 1; Tb 1, 10; 4; 10, 12f; 14, 5. 12; Jb 1, 5; Ps 78, 5; Prv 1, 8; 4, 1; 5, 7; 11, 29; 13, 24; 19, 18; 20, 7; 22, 6. 15; 23, 13; 29, 17; Sir 4, 23; 7, 23; 8, 9; 25, 7; 30, 1-13; 42, 5. 9-14; Dn 13, 3; 1 Mc 2, 49ff; 2 Mc 6, 24. 28; 7, 20-29; Mt 10, 37; Eph 6, 4; Col 3, 21; 2 Tm 3, 15; Ti 2, 4.
Peace, of God, Lv 26, 6; Prv 16, 7; Jb 11, 18f; Rom 1, 7; 2 Cor 1, 2; Phil 4, 7;
—of Christ, Lk 7, 50; 8, 48; Jn 14, 27; Rom 5, 1; 1 Cor 1, 3; Gal 1, 3; 2 Thes 3, 16;
—fruit of the Spirit, Rom 8, 6; Gal 5, 22; Eph 2, 17;
—peace with God, Is 27, 5; Acts 10, 34-36; Rom 5, 1; 2 Cor 5, 18-20; Eph 2, 12-18;
—no peace for the wicked, Is 48, 22; 57, 21; 59, 8; Jer 12, 12; 16, 5; Rom 3, 17; Rv 6, 4.
Penance, satisfaction for sins, Ps 6, 7; Mt 3, 8; Lk 3, 8; Acts 2, 38; 8, 22; 2 Cor 7-10;
—is preached, Jer 7, 3; Mt 3, 2. 4. 8; Lk 3, 3. 8; 13, 3; 24, 47; Acts 2, 38; 3, 19; 8, 21; 17, 30; 20, 21; 26, 20;
—examples of true, Jgs 10, 15; 2 Sm 12, 13; 24, 10-17; 2 Chr 12, 6f; 33, 12; Jdt 4, 7-9; Jon 3; Mt 26, 75; Lk 7, 37-44; 15, 18; 18, 13; 19, 8; 22, 62; 23, 41; Acts 2, 37-41;
—examples of false, Gn 4, 13; 27, 38; Ex 8, 4-11; 9, 27; 10, 16; Jos 7, 20; Jgs 1, 7; 1 Sm 15, 24. 30; 24, 19; 1 Kgs 13, 6; 21, 27; Wis 5, 3; 1 Mc 6, 12; 2 Mc 9, 12; Mt 27, 4; Acts 8, 13-23; Heb 12, 17.
People of God, privileges and blessings, Dt 32, 9; 33; 2 Sm 7, 23f; Pss 3, 9; 149, 4; Lk 1, 17; Rom 11, 1 Pt 2, 9; Rv 21, 3-7;
—belongs to God, Ps 103, 3; Ti 2, 14; Heb 8, 10;
—saved, Mt 1, 21; Rv 5, 9;

—happiness of, Ps 144, 15;
—will never be abandoned, 1 Sm 12, 22; Ps 94, 14;
—the rest of God, Heb 4, 9-11.
Persecution, foretold, Gn 15, 13; Dt 30, 7; Mt 5, 11; 13, 21; 23, 34; Mk 10, 30; Lk 10, 49; 21, 12; Jn 15, 20; 2 Tm 3, 12;
—how to be endured, Mt 5, 12. 44; 10, 23; Acts 5, 41; Rom 12, 14; Heb 10, 34; 1 Pt 4, 12-19;
—blessings of, Mt 5, 11f; 1 Thes 1, 4-7; Rv 6, 9-11.
Perseverance, exhortations to, Mt 10, 22; 24, 13; Lk 9, 62; Acts 13, 43; 1 Cor 15, 58; Eph 6, 18; Heb 3, 6. 13; 10, 23. 28; 2 Pt 3, 17;
—rewarded, Is 56, 4-7; Lk 8, 15; Rom 2, 7; 15, 4; Heb 6, 15; Jas 1, 25;
—examples of, Acts 1, 14; 2, 42; 1 Cor 15, 1; Rv 1, 9.
Poor, not to be oppressed, Ex 22, 25; Dt 24, 10-17; Is 3, 14f; Prv 14, 31; 28, 3; Eccl 5, 7; Am 2, 6f; 4, 1f; 5, 11f; Zec 7, 10; Jas 2, 2-6;
—duties toward, Ex 23, 11; Lv 19, 10; Dt 1, 17; 15, 7-10; Pss 82, 3f; 112, 9; Prv 21, 13; 24, 23; 29, 7; Is 58, 7; Jer 22, 3; Mt 5, 42; Lk 3, 11; Gal 2, 10; Eph 4, 28; 1 Tm 6, 18; 1 Jn 3, 17;
—equal to the rich before God, Ex 30, 15; Jb 31, 15; 34, 19; Ps 49, 2f; Prv 22, 2;
—promises of God for, Jb 5, 15; Pss 9, 19; 72, 7; 132, 15; Zep 3, 12; 2 Cor 8, 9;
—to be consoled by the Church, Acts 6, 1; 11, 29f; 1 Cor 16, 1; 2 Cor 8, 1-3; 9, 11-13; Gal 2, 10; Heb 13, 16;
—blest are the poor in spirit, Mt 5, 3; Lk 6, 20; Is 66, 2.
Pope, or chief bishop, St. Peter, by Christ's ordinance, was raised to this dignity, Mt 16, 18f; Lk 22, 31f; Jn 21, 15; 17. See also Mt 10, 2; Acts 5, 29; Gal 2, 7f.
Prayer, Gn 18, 27; Ex 17, 11; Tob 4, 20; 12, 8; Jdt 4, 12; Ps 141, 2; Prv 28, 9; Wis 16, 28; Sir 2, 10; 7, 10. 14; 35, 12-18; Is 29, 13f; Mt €, 5-13; 7, 7-11; 18, 19f; Mk 14, 24-26; Lk 11, 2-13; 18, 1; Jn 14, 13f; 15, 7; 16, 23f; Rom 8, 26f; Eph 6, 18; Phil 4, 6; Col 4, 2; 1 Thes 5, 17; 1 Tm 2, 1-3; Jas 4, 3; 5, 16-18; 1 Jn 3, 22; 5, 14f;
—the Lord's, Mt 6, 9-13; Lk 11, 2-4;
—of Christ for his disciples, Jn 17;
—of the apostles, Acts 4, 24-30.
Prayers for the Dead, 2 Mc 12, 43.
Preaching, of repentance, Jon 3; Mt 3, 1-12; 4, 17; 12, 41; Mk 1, 4-8. 14; Lk 3, 3-20;
—of the gospel, by Jesus, Mt 4, 23; 5; 6; 7; Mk 1, 14; Lk 4, 18-27; by the apostles, Mt 28, 19f; Mk 16, 15; Lk 24, 47; Acts 2, 14-40; 3,

12-26; 4, 8-12; 10, 34-48; 13, 16-41; 17, 22-31; 26, 1-29.

Presumption, chastised, Nm 14, 44f; Dt 1, 42-46;
—condemned among the prophets, Dt 18, 20; Jer 14, 14f;
—is a sin, Nm 15, 30f; Dt 17, 12; Jas 4, 13-16.

Pride, Nm 15, 30; Ps 36, 12; Prv 6, 17; Wis 5, 8; Sir 3, 27; 10, 6-18; Is 2, 11f; Dn 5, 20; Mt 23, 12; Lk 1, 51f; 18, 9-14; Gal 6, 3; Jas 4, 6. 16; 1 Pt 5, 5.

Promises, of God, inviolable, Nm 23, 19; Dt 7, 8f; Jos 23, 14; Ps 89, 3; 1 Kgs 8, 56; 2 Cor 1, 20; Heb 6, 17f; obtained by faith and perseverance, Heb 6, 12; 10, 36; Rom 4, 13; Lk 1, 45; of a celestial inheritance, 1 Pt 1, 3f; of the reestablishment of Israel, Is 43, 5f; Jer 31, 4; Hos 14, 4-8; Zec 10, 6-12; made to the poor and orphans, Dt 10, 18; Ps 9, 19; Prv 15, 25; Jer 49, 11; Hos 14, 3; made to Abraham, Gn 12, 2. 3. 7; 13, 14-17; 15; 17; 18. 10. 14; 22, 15-18; made to David and Solomon, 2 Sm 7, 11-16; 1 Kgs 3, 12-14; 9, 2-9;
—of Christ, to his disciples, Mt 6, 4. 6. 18; 7, 7-10; 16, 8. 19, 25. 28; Lk 11, 9f; 12, 31f; Jn 14, 15; 16; 20, 21-23; about his return, Mt 24, 30. 44; Mk 13, 26; Lk 12, 40; 21; 27; Jn 14, 3; Acts 1, 11.

Prophecy, gift of God, Is 44, 7; 45, 21; Lk 1, 70; of the Spirit, 1 Cor 12, 9f; 1 Pt 1, 21; of Jesus, Eph 4, 11; Rv 1, 1; 11, 3;
—how to receive it, Lk 24, 25; 1 Thes 5, 20; 2 Pt 1, 19; Rv 1, 3; 22, 7;
—prophecies concerning Jesus the Messiah and their fulfillment:
Gn 12, 3; 18, 18 — Acts 3, 25f
Dt 18, 15. 18 — Acts 3, 22f
Ps 2, 1f — Acts 4, 25-28
Ps 2, 7 — Acts 13, 33; Heb 1, 5
Ps 22, 2 — Mt 27, 46
                 Mk 15, 34
Ps 22, 19 — Mt 27, 35
                 Jn 19, 23
Ps 69, 22 — Mt 27, 34. 48
Is 7, 14 — Mt 1, 18-23
Is 8, 23—9, 1 — Mt 4, 15f
Is 53, 12 — Mk 15, 27f
             Lk 23, 33f
Mi 5, 1 — Mt 2, 1. 5f
Zec 9, 9 — Mt 21, 1-9
Zec 11, 13 — Mt 27, 3-10
Zec 13, 7 — Mt 26, 31. 56
Mal 3, 1 — Mt 11, 7-10
Mal 3, 23 — Mt 11, 13f; 17, 10

Prophecies pronounced by Jesus, about his death and resurrection, Mt 12, 40; 17, 22f; 20, 18f; Jn 2, 19-22; 12, 32f; about Judas' betrayal, Mt 26, 21-25; Jn 6, 70f; 13, 18f; about Peter's denial, Mt 26,

34; Jn 13, 38; about the sending of the Holy Spirit, Jn 14, 16; Lk 24, 49; Acts 1, 5. 8; about the preaching of the gospel, Mt 24, 14; 26, 13; Mk 13, 10; about persecutions, Mt 10, 17-25; Jn 16, 2. 32f; about destruction of Jerusalem, Mt 24; Mk 13; Lk 19, 43f; 21.

Prudence, described, Prv 12, 16. 23; 13, 16; 14, 8; 15, 5. 18; 16, 21-23; 22, 3; Am 5, 13;
—exhortations to, Mt 24, 45: 25, 13; 26, 41; Lk 12, 35; 21, 36; 1 Cor 10, 12; 1 Thes 5, 6; 2 Tm 4, 5; 1 Pt 4, 7; 5, 8.

Purgatory, or a middle state of souls, suffering for a time on account of their sins, is shown by those many texts of Scripture which affirm that God will **render to every man according to his works**, so that such as die in lesser sins shall not escape without punishment, 2 Mc 12, 43-46; Mt 5, 25f; 12, 32; Lk 12, 58f; 1 Cor 3, 15; 1 Pt 3, 18-20; 1 Jn 5, 16; Rv 5, 3. 13.

Purifications, law relative to, Lv 12, 4f; 14, 23. 49; 15, 28; 1 Chr 23, 28;
—of the temple, 2 Mc 1, 18. 36; 2, 20; 10, 3. 5. 6;
—water jars for purifying, Jn 2, 6;
—dispute between Jn's disciples and the Jews concerning purifications, Jn 3, 25.

— Q —

Quarrels, to be avoided, Sir 8, 1. 3. 16; 1 Cor 6, 6f; Phil 2, 14f; 2 Tm 2, 23f.

Questions, useless questions to be avoided, Gn 3, 1. 6; Prv 25, 27; Eccl 7, 10; Sir 3, 20f; Jn 21, 21; Acts 1, 16f; 1 Tm 1, 4; 6, 3f; 2 Tm 2, 16; Ti 3, 9.

— R —

Redemption, Jb 19, 25; Ps 31, 6; 49, 16; 71, 23; 111, 9; 130, 7f; Is 63, 16; Hos 13, 14; Lk 21, 28; Rom 3, 24; 1 Cor 6, 20; 7, 23; 15, 55; 2 Cor 5, 15; 1 Tm 2, 5f; 2 Tm 1, 9; Ti 2, 14; Heb 9, 11f; 1 Pt 1, 18f; Rv 1, 5; 5, 9.

Relics, miraculous, 2 Kgs 13, 21; Mt 9, 20f; Acts 19, 11f.

Repentance, preached by John the Baptizer, Mt 3, 2; 8, 11; Mk 1, 4; Lk 3, 3. 8. 19;
—preached by Jesus, Mt 4, 17; Mk 1, 15; Lk 15; 24, 27;
—preached by the disciples, Mk 6, 12; Acts 2, 38; 3, 19; 17, 30;
—exhortations to, Hos 14; Zep 2, 1-3; Zec 1, 3f; Mal 3, 7; Mt 3, 3; 4, 17; Rv 2, 5. 16. 21; 3, 3. 19.

Revelation, communications to man of hidden things, Dt 29, 29; Is 21, 2; Jer 33, 3; Dn 2, 19; Am 3, 7; Mt 11; 25; Rom 8, 18; 1 Cor 2, 9f; 1 Pt 1, 5. 12; Rom 16, 25; Col 1, 26;
—God the author of, Is 22, 14; 53, 1; Jer 33, 3; Dn 2, 22f. 28; Mt 16, 17;
—through the Spirit, 1 Cor 2, 10; Eph 3, 5;
—depositaries of, chosen by God and Christ, Mt 11, 25-27; Lk 10, 22; Jn 11, 38-40; Gal 1, 15f;
—Jesus reveals God, Jn 1, 18; Col 1, 15; Mt 11, 27; Lk 10, 22; his justice, Rom 8, 19; his love, 1 Jn 4, 9; Jn 3, 16.

Reward, promised to the just, Pss 19, 10. 12; 58, 12; Prv 11, 18; 25, 22; Is 61, 8; Mt 10, 41f; Lk 6, 35;
—promised to those unjustly persecuted, Mt 5, 11f;
—promised to each according to his works, 1 Cor 3, 8; Col 3, 23f; 2 Jn 8; Rv 22, 12.

Riches, dangers of, Dt 8, 13ff; 32, 15; Jb 31, 24f; Ps 62, 11; Prv 11, 28; 18, 23; 30, 8f; Eccl 5, 12; Jer 9, 23; Hos 12, 9; Mi 6, 12; Mt 6, 19; Lk 12, 15; 1 Tm 6, 9. 17; Jas 2, 6;
—evils brought on by, Neh 9, 25f; Mt 10, 22f; 13, 22; 19, 23f; Mk 10, 22; 1 Tm 6, 10;
—true riches, Mt 6, 20; Lk 12, 33; Col 3, 1f; 1 Tm 6, 19; Rv 2, 9; 3, 18; Rom 11, 33; Is 45, 3;
—duties imposed by, Dt 8, 18; 1 Chr 29, 3-5. 12f; Jb 31, 16-20; Mt 19, 21; 1 Tm 6, 18f; 1 Jn 3, 17.

— S —

Sacraments, they produce Grace, Jn 6, 57ff; Acts 2, 37f; 19, 5; 8, 17; 1 Pt 3, 20f;

BAPTISM, commanded by Christ, Mt 28, 19; Mk 16, 16; Jn 3, 5;
—taught and administered by the apostles, Acts 2, 38. 41; Acts 8, 12. 38; 9, 18; 10, 48; 16, 15, etc;
—the laver of regeneration, 1 Pt 2, 21; Ti 3, 5;
—takes away all sin, Mk 1, 4; 16, 16; Jn 3, 5; 1, 33; Acts 2, 38; 8, 12f; 16, 33; Rom 6, 3-6; Gal 3, 27; 1 Cor 6, 11; Eph 5, 26; Col 2, 12-14; Lk 3, 3; Heb 10, 22;
—not to be repeated, Eph 4, 5; Heb 6, 4-6; 10, 26;
—signifies passion or suffering, Mk 10, 38; Lk 12, 50;
—to be administered to children, Mt 18, 14; 19, 13f; Mk 10, 13-16; Lk 18, 15. 17; Jn 3, 5; Acts 2, 39; 16, 15. 33; 1 Cor 1, 16; 15, 22;
—persons baptized receive the Holy Spirit, Acts 2, 38; 19, 5f;

—the baptized put on Christ, Gal 3, 27;

—Christians are baptized in Christ's death, Rom 6, 3;

—are baptized in one body, 1 Cor 12, 13. 27;

CONFIRMATION, Acts 19, 6. 20; 8, 17; Heb 6, 2; 2 Cor 1, 21f; Eph 1, 13;

HOLY EUCHARIST, prophesied, Mal 1, 11;

—prefigured, Ex 16, 15;

—promised, Jn 6, 32-60;

—instituted, Mt 26, 26-28; Mk 14, 22-24; Lk 22, 19f; 1 Cor 11, 23-27; 10, 16; 11, 27. 29;

—should be frequently received, Acts 2, 42; 20, 7; Ps 78, 24f; Prv 9, 2f; Wis 16, 20;

—Eucharist under one kind, Lk 24, 30f; Jn 6, 59. **See** also verses 33, 38, 51, 52, 58; Acts 2, 42; 20, 7; 1 Cor 11, 27;

PENANCE, Mt 18, 18; 16, 19; Jn 20, 22f; 2 Cor 5, 20. **See** verses 18, 19;

ANOINTING OF THE SICK, Jas 5, 14f; Mk 6, 12f;

HOLY ORDERS, instituted by Christ, Lk 22, 19; Jn 20, 22f.

—conferred by imposition of hands, Acts 6, 6; 13, 3; 14, 22;

—give grace, 1 Tm 4, 14; 2 Tm 1, 6.

MATRIMONY, Eph 5, 25. 31f; Mt 19, 5, Mk 10, 7; 1 Thes 4, 4; 1 Tm 2, 15.

Saints, departed, assist us by their prayers, Lk 16, 9; 1 Cor 12, 12. 20f; Rv 5, 8;

—we have a communion with them, 1 Cor 12, 26; Heb 12, 22f;

—they have power over nations, Rv 2, 26f; 5, 10;

—they are with Christ in heaven, before the general resurrection, 2 Cor 5, 1. 6-8; Phil 1, 23f; Rv 4, 4; 6, 9; 7, 9. 14. 15; 14, 1. 3f; 19, 1. 4-6; 20, 4;

—their invocation, consult the texts quoted above with relation to angels, and such as testify to the great power which the prayers of God's servants have with him, and which authorize us to call for their prayers. For which **see** Ex 32, 11. 14; 1 Sm 7, 8-10; Jb 42, 7f; Rom 15, 30; Eph 6, 18f; 1 Thes 5, 25; Heb 13, 18; Jas 5, 16.

Sin, against the Holy Spirit, Mt 12, 31; Mk 3, 29; Lk 11, 15; 12, 10; Heb 6, 4-6; 10, 26; 1 Jn 5, 16;

—crying for vengeance, Gn 4, 10; 18, 20; Ex 22, 21-23. 25f; Sir 35, 15-19; Jas 5, 4.

Sinner, prayer of, for pardon, 2 Sm 19, 18-20; 24, 10. 17; Ezr 9, 6-15; Neh 1, 5-11; 9, 7-37; Jdt 9, 16f; Pss 6; 32; 38; 51; 102; 130; 143; Is 59, 12f; 64, 8f; Jer 17, 14; Mt 8, 2; Lk 15, 17-19; 18, 13.

Spirit (Divining), girl with a, delivered from the devil, Acts 16, 16-18.

Spouses, relations with each other, Gn 2, 23f; Mt 19, 4-6; Mk 10, 6-9; 1 Cor 7, 3-5; Eph 5, 22-24; Col 3, 18; 1 Pt 3, 7;

—fidelity owed each other, Ex 20, 14; Dt 5, 18; Mk 10, 12; Lk 18, 20; Rom 7, 2f;

—love one another, Eph 5, 25-33; Col 3, 19;

—figure of Christ and the Church, Mt 9, 15; 25, 1-13; 2 Cor 11, 2; Eph 5, 23. 24; Rv 19, 7.

— T —

Temptation, of Jesus by the devil, Mt 4, 1-11; Mk 1, 12f; Lk 4, 1-13;

—of the People of God, Dn 12, 10; Zec 13, 9; Ps 66, 10-12; Lk 22, 31f. 40; 1 Cor 7, 5; Jas 1, 12; 1 Pt 1, 7; 4, 12;

—God's help in, Mt 6, 13; Lk 11, 4; 1 Cor 10, 13; Heb 2, 18; Rv 3, 10;

—need for watchfulness and prayer, Mt 26, 41; Mk 14, 38; Lk 22, 46; Gal 6, 1.

Trinity, prefigured and declared, Gn 1, 26; 18, 2; Ex 3, 6. 15f; 4, 5; Ps 33, 6; Is 6, 3; 34, 16; 48, 16; 61, 1; Mt 3, 16; 10, 20; 17, 5; 28, 19; Lk 4, 18; Jn 3, 34f; 14, 16. 26; 1 Jn 5, 7.

— U —

Unbelief, sin of, Mk 16, 14; Jn 16, 9; Ti 1, 15; 1 Jn 5, 10;

—whence it comes, Lk 8, 12; 24, 25; Jn 10, 26; 12, 38-40; Acts 19, 9; 2 Cor 4, 4; 2 Thes 2, 11f; Heb 3, 12;

—effects of, 2 Kgs 7, 2. 19f; Ps 78, 19-22; Is 53, 1; Jn 5, 38; 12, 37; 16, 9; Acts 14, 2; Heb 4, 2.

— W —

War, is punishment for sin, Lv 26, 23-25; Dt 28, 36. 49; Jgs 2, 13f; 3, 1. 8; 4, 1f; 6, 1; 10, 6f; 13, 1; Is 5, 25-30; Jer 5, 15-17.

Wicked, lot of, Jb 8, 13; 11, 20; 15, 34; 20, 5; 27, 8. 13-23; Is 33, 14; 2 Pt 3, 7;

—Christ died for the, Rom 4, 5; 5, 6.

Will, accommodated to the divine will, 1 Sm 3, 18; 2 Sm 10, 12; 15, 20; 1 Mc 3, 60; Mt 6, 10; 26, 39; Mk 14, 35; Lk 22, 42; Acts 21, 14; 1 Cor 4, 19; Heb 6, 3; Jas 4, 15.

Will of God, Mt 7, 21; 12, 50; Mk 3, 36; Jn 6, 39; Rom 12, 2; Eph 5, 17; Col 1, 9; 1 Thes 4, 3; 1 Tm 2, 4; 1 Jn 2, 17.

Women, must not preach or teach, 1 Cor 14, 34f. 37; 1 Tm 2, 11f.

Women, beauty of, Gn 12, 4; Song 1, 8; 4, 1-7; 5, 9; Sir 36, 22;

—celebrated in salvation history, Gn 11, 29; 24, 15-67; 35, 19f; Nm 20, 1; Jgs 4, 1—5, 32; 1 Sm 25, 3-39; 2 Sm 11, 21; Jdt 15, 13; Mt 1, 1-17; Lk 2, 36f; 1 Pt 3, 5;

—complement man, Gn 1, 27; 2, 23; 3, 12; 5, 2; Mt 19, 4; 1 Cor 11, 7;

—condition of, 1 Cor 14, 34; Eph 5, 22; Col 3, 18; 1 Tm 2, 12;

—emancipation of, Lk 10, 38; 24, 22; Acts 1, 14; 16, 13; 3, 28;

—gift of God, Gn 2, 22; Prv 19, 14; Sir 26, 14f;

—helpmate for man, Sir 36, 24; 40, 19ff;

—ideal wife, Prv 31, 10-31;

—love for, Sir 7, 19. 26; Mk 10, 7f;

—strength of, Jgs 5, 29; 9, 10f; 11, 21; 13, 18; Song 4, 1-5; 7, 2-10.

Word of God, one of names given to Jesus, Jn 1, 1. 14; 1 Jn 1, 1; Rv 19, 16; **see** also Holy Spirit.

Works, of God, Jb 9, 1-20; 37—41; Pss 8; 19; 89, 6-15; 104; 111; 145; Eccl 8, 17; Jer 10, 12-16;

—inadequacy of works of law, Rom 3, 20; Gal 2, 16; Eph 2, 9;

—demonstrate faith, Acts 26, 20; Jas 2, 14-26;

—exhortations to good works, Mt 5, 16; Acts 9, 36; 2 Cor 8, 9; Eph 2, 10; Phil 2, 12; 1 Thes 4, 11f; 2 Thes 2, 17; 3, 7-13; Heb 10, 24; 1 Pt 2, 12.

World, creation of, 1 Sm 2, 8; 1 Chr 16, 30; Pss 19, 5; 24, 1; 50, 12; 93, 1; Prv 8, 26; Jer 10, 12; Mt 13, 35; Jn 1, 10; Acts 17, 24; Rom 1, 20; Heb 1, 2; 11, 3.

Worship, to be offered to God alone, Ex 20, 3-5; Dt 5, 7-9; Mt 4, 10; Lk 4, 8; Acts 10, 26;

—manner of offering, Lv 10, 3; Eccl 5, 1-6; Ps 100; Jn 4, 23f; Eph 5, 19; Col 3, 16.